14:00	15:00	16:00	17:00						23:00	MIDNIGHT	1:00	2:00	3:00	4:00
+2	+3	+4	+5	+6	+7	+8	+9	+10	+11	PM	AM	−11	−10	−9	−8

Moscow
16:00
16:00
16:00

18:00

18:00

Anchorage

Monday
Sunday

Ankara
16:00

Tehran
15:30   16:30

Beijing

20:00

Tokyo

Cairo

Riyadh

Delhi
18:00

Hong Kong

17:30   18:30

INTERNATIONAL DATE LINE

18:00

Nairobi

20:00
Singapore

EQUATOR

Jakarta

18:30

21:30

23:30

22:30

Perth

Sydney

Auckland

0:45

30°	45°	60°	75°	90°	105°	120°	135°	150°	165°	180°	165°

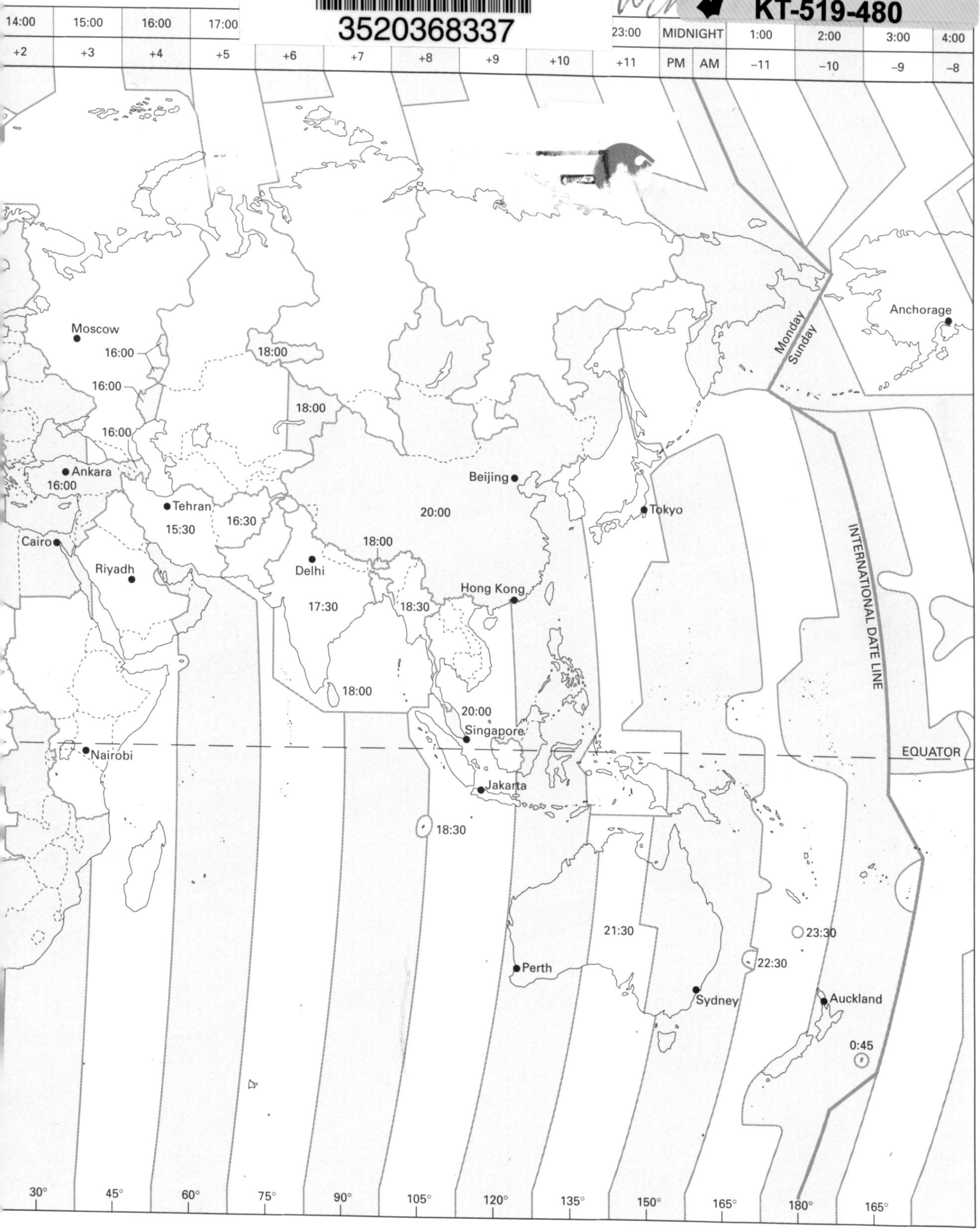

THE
STATESMAN'S
YEARBOOK
2007

'In a theatre, it happened that a fire started offstage. The clown came out to tell the audience. They thought it was a joke and applauded. He told them again, and they become still more hilarious. This is the way, I suppose, that the world will be destroyed—amid the universal hilarity of wits and wags who think it is all a joke.'

Søren Kierkegaard, 1843.

Editors

Frederick Martin	1864–1883
Sir John Scott-Keltie	1883–1926
Mortimer Epstein	1927–1946
S. H. Steinberg	1946–1969
John Paxton	1969–1990
Brian Hunter	1990–1997
Barry Turner	1997–

Credits

Publisher	Alison Jones (London)
	Garrett Kiely (New York)
Editor	Barry Turner
Editorial Assistant	Jill Fenner
Senior Research Editor	Nicholas Heath-Brown
Research	James Matthews
	Daniel Smith
	Emma Watts
	Naomi Colvin
	Richard German
	Robert McGowan
	Aaron Gatti
	Reena Badiani
	Andrew Clarke
	Liane Jones
	Nicola Varns
	Martha Nyman
Index	Richard German
Production (print and online)	Phillipa Davidson-Blake
	Melissa Kucharczyk
	Michael Card
	Shirley Card
Design	Jim Weaver
Marketing	Sanphy Thomas (London)
	Erin Igoe (New York)

email: sybcomments@palgrave.com

THE STATESMAN'S YEARBOOK

THE POLITICS, CULTURES AND ECONOMIES OF THE WORLD

2007

Edited by
BARRY TURNER

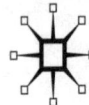
Published annually since 1864

This edition published 2006 by
PALGRAVE MACMILLAN
Houndmills, Basingstoke, Hampshire RG21 6XS and
175 Fifth Avenue, New York, N. Y. 10010
Companies and representatives throughout the world

PALGRAVE MACMILLAN is the global academic imprint of the Palgrave Macmillan division of St. Martin's Press, LLC and of Palgrave Macmillan Ltd. Macmillan® is a registered trademark in the United States, United Kingdom and other countries. Palgrave is a registered trademark in the European Union and other countries.

ISBN-10 1-4039-9276-2
ISBN-13 978-1-40390-9276-5
ISSN 0081-4601

This book is printed on paper suitable for recycling and made from fully managed and sustained forest sources.

A catalogue record for this book is available from the British Library.

A catalogue record for this book is available from the Library of Congress.

10 9 8 7 6 5 4 3 2 1
15 14 13 12 11 10 09 08 07 06

Printed in Malaysia

PREFACE

There are only a handful of reference books that enjoy the same level of recognition and respect as *The Statesman's Yearbook*. For nearly a century and a half not only statesmen but scholars, students, journalists, business people and the general public have trusted it for accurate, objective information on political, economic and social affairs in every country of the world.

Anyone familiar with SYB will see at a glance that this edition is substantially different to those that have preceded it over the last 142 years. For one thing it is physically larger, and this has allowed us to add over 20% more content than previous editions: biographical profiles of current leaders for every country, government histories, expanded economic overviews, historical economic statistics, and new essays on issues of particular importance: in this edition we focus on the economic consequences of globalization, the changing nature of democracy, and the use and misuse of military expenditure. We've also added detailed line maps for each country, and redesigned the page to make the text more readable.

Another innovation is that the full text is now available online. A single-concurrency local area network licence to access the online site is included in the price of the print edition, and an institution can purchase a site licence for an additional fee to allow unlimited access. Reading the text online offers several additional benefits: there are sophisticated search and browse functions to help readers find answers to questions even more rapidly, and to identify related information that might be of interest to them. There is a built-in citation tool, particularly useful for students using the text in essays. Equally important, the online text will be regularly updated: it's been a perennial frustration for us that countries continue to elect new leaders and new statistics continue to be released after we've gone to press each year, but now customers can have access to our database as it's updated so that they can be confident of having the most current information.

For too many people, research into current affairs now means keying a country name into a search engine. We believe passionately that the need for carefully researched and verified information from an objective source with no political agenda has never been greater, and the changes we've made to *The Statesman's Yearbook 2007*, in consultation with librarians worldwide, are designed to make that quality information even more accessible, accurate and comprehensive.

Alison Jones
Publisher, *The Statesman's Yearbook*

CONTENTS

KEY WORLD FACTS

- World population in 2006 — 6,540 million (3,286 million males and 3,254 million females)

- World population under 30 in 2006 — 3,503 million
- World population over 60 in 2006 — 691 million
- World population over 100 in 2006 — 290,000
- World economic growth rate in 2005 — 4·8%
- Number of illiterate people — 960 million
- Number of unemployed people — 185 million
- Average world life expectancy — 69·1 years for females; 64·9 years for males
- Annual world population increase — 75·53 million people
- Number of people living outside country of birth — 185 million, or nearly 3% of the world's population

- Fertility rate — 2·7 births per woman
- Urban population — 48·3% of total population
- World defence expenditure — US$997·2 billion
- Number of TV sets — 1·36 billion
- Number of radio receivers — 2·18 billion
- Number of cigarettes smoked — 5,600 billion a year
- Number of Internet users — 1·02 billion
- Number of mobile phone users — 1·76 billion
- Number of motor vehicles on the road — 647 million
- Number of people who cross international borders every day — 2 million
- Number of people living in extreme poverty — 1·1 billion
- Number of people living in urban slums — 924 million
- Number of malnourished people — 852 million
- Number of overweight people — 1·1 billion
- Number of obese adults — 300 million
- Number of people dying of starvation — 24,000 every day
- Number of people lacking clean drinking water — 1 billion
- Number of people lacking adequate sanitation — 3 billion
- Number of reported executions in 2005 — 2,148
- Number of people worldwide exposed to indoor air pollution that exceeds WHO guidelines — 1 billion
- Annual carbon dioxide emissions — 6·9 billion tonnes of carbon equivalent

ISO COUNTRY CODES

Below is a list of the codes of sovereign states produced by the International Organization for Standardization (ISO). There has been widespread use of these ISO codes as TLDs ('top level domains') in Internet applications (used in lower case), managed by the Internet Assigned Numbers Association (IANA), to denote 'national' domains in addition to the common TLDs such as '.com' and '.org'. There are some IANA codes used in preference to the above on the Internet (eg. '.uk' rather than '.gb').

AD	ANDORRA	ET	ETHIOPIA
AE	UNITED ARAB EMIRATES	FI	FINLAND
AF	AFGHANISTAN	FJ	FIJI ISLANDS
AG	ANTIGUA AND BARBUDA	FM	MICRONESIA
AL	ALBANIA	FR	FRANCE
AM	ARMENIA	GA	GABON
AO	ANGOLA	GB	UNITED KINGDOM OF GREAT BRITAIN AND NORTHERN IRELAND
AR	ARGENTINA		
AT	AUSTRIA	GD	GRENADA
AU	AUSTRALIA	GE	GEORGIA
AZ	AZERBAIJAN	GH	GHANA
BA	BOSNIA-HERZEGOVINA	GM	THE GAMBIA
BB	BARBADOS	GN	GUINEA
BD	BANGLADESH	GQ	EQUATORIAL GUINEA
BE	BELGIUM	GR	GREECE
BF	BURKINA FASO	GT	GUATEMALA
BG	BULGARIA	GW	GUINEA-BISSAU
BH	BAHRAIN	GY	GUYANA
BI	BURUNDI	HN	HONDURAS
BJ	BENIN	HR	CROATIA
BN	BRUNEI	HT	HAITI
BO	BOLIVIA	HU	HUNGARY
BR	BRAZIL	ID	INDONESIA
BS	BAHAMAS	IE	IRELAND
BT	BHUTAN	IL	ISRAEL
BW	BOTSWANA	IN	INDIA
BY	BELARUS	IQ	IRAQ
BZ	BELIZE	IR	IRAN
CA	CANADA	IS	ICELAND
CD	CONGO (DEMOCRATIC REPUBLIC OF)	IT	ITALY
CF	CENTRAL AFRICAN REPUBLIC	JM	JAMAICA
CG	CONGO (REPUBLIC OF)	JO	JORDAN
CH	SWITZERLAND	JP	JAPAN
CI	CÔTE D'IVOIRE	KE	KENYA
CL	CHILE	KG	KYRGYZSTAN
CM	CAMEROON	KH	CAMBODIA
CN	CHINA	KI	KIRIBATI
CO	COLOMBIA	KM	COMOROS
CR	COSTA RICA	KN	ST KITTS AND NEVIS
CS	SERBIA AND MONTENEGRO	KP	NORTH KOREA
CU	CUBA	KR	KOREA
CV	CAPE VERDE	KW	KUWAIT
CY	CYPRUS	KZ	KAZAKHSTAN
CZ	CZECH REPUBLIC	LA	LAOS
DE	GERMANY	LB	LEBANON
DJ	DJIBOUTI	LC	ST LUCIA
DK	DENMARK	LI	LIECHTENSTEIN
DM	DOMINICA	LK	SRI LANKA
DO	DOMINICAN REPUBLIC	LR	LIBERIA
DZ	ALGERIA	LS	LESOTHO
EC	ECUADOR	LT	LITHUANIA
EE	ESTONIA	LU	LUXEMBOURG
EG	EGYPT	LV	LATVIA
ER	ERITREA	LY	LIBYA
ES	SPAIN	MA	MOROCCO

MC	MONACO		SD	SUDAN
MD	MOLDOVA		SE	SWEDEN
MG	MADAGASCAR		SG	SINGAPORE
MH	MARSHALL ISLANDS		SI	SLOVENIA
MK	MACEDONIA		SK	SLOVAKIA
ML	MALI		SL	SIERRA LEONE
MM	MYANMAR		SM	SAN MARINO
MN	MONGOLIA		SN	SENEGAL
MR	MAURITANIA		SO	SOMALIA
MT	MALTA		SR	SURINAME
MU	MAURITIUS		ST	SÃO TOMÉ E PRÍNCIPE
MV	MALDIVES		SV	EL SALVADOR
MW	MALAŴI		SY	SYRIA
MX	MEXICO		SZ	SWAZILAND
MY	MALAYSIA		TD	CHAD
MZ	MOZAMBIQUE		TG	TOGO
NA	NAMIBIA		TH	THAILAND
NE	NIGER		TJ	TAJIKISTAN
NG	NIGERIA		TL	EAST TIMOR
NI	NICARAGUA		TM	TURKMENISTAN
NL	THE NETHERLANDS		TN	TUNISIA
NO	NORWAY		TO	TONGA
NP	NEPAL		TR	TURKEY
NR	NAURU		TT	TRINIDAD AND TOBAGO
NZ	NEW ZEALAND		TV	TUVALU
OM	OMAN		TZ	TANZANIA
PA	PANAMA		UA	UKRAINE
PE	PERU		UG	UGANDA
PG	PAPUA NEW GUINEA		US	UNITED STATES OF AMERICA
PH	PHILIPPINES		UY	URUGUAY
PK	PAKISTAN		UZ	UZBEKISTAN
PL	POLAND		VA	VATICAN CITY STATE
PT	PORTUGAL		VC	ST VINCENT AND THE GRENADINES
PW	PALAU		VE	VENEZUELA
PY	PARAGUAY		VN	VIETNAM
QA	QATAR		VU	VANUATU
RO	ROMANIA		WS	SAMOA
RU	RUSSIA		YE	YEMEN
RW	RWANDA		ZA	SOUTH AFRICA
SA	SAUDI ARABIA		ZM	ZAMBIA
SB	SOLOMON ISLANDS		ZW	ZIMBABWE
SC	SEYCHELLES			

CHRONOLOGY

CHRONOLOGY

April 2005–March 2006

Week beginning 3 April 2005

In presidential elections in Moldova, Vladimir Voronin was re-elected with 75 votes. His opponent Gheorghe Duca received one vote. Voronin re-appointed Vasile Tarlev prime minister.

In Austria, Wolfgang Schüssel's government survived a vote of no-confidence by 94 votes to 84.

In Jordan, the government of prime minister Faisal al-Fayez resigned and Adnan Badran was appointed prime minister. A new government was later sworn in with Badran doubling as defence minister, Farouq Al Qasrawi as minister of foreign affairs, Awni Yerfas as interior minister and Basem Awadallah as finance minister.

In Iraq, Jalal Talabani was elected president by the National Assembly with Sheikh Ghazi al-Yawer and Adil Abdel-Mahdi becoming vice-presidents. Ibrahim al-Jaafari was appointed prime minister.

Prince Rainier III of Monaco died and was succeeded by his son Albert II.

In Djibouti, president Ismail Omar Guelleh was re-elected with 100% of votes after opposition parties boycotted the elections.

Week beginning 10 April 2005

The Estonian parliament approved Andrus Ansip's cabinet which included Urmas Paet as minister of foreign affairs, Jaak Jõerüüt as defence minister and Aivar Sõerd as finance minister.

After failing to form a new government Omar Karami resigned as prime minister of Lebanon and was replaced by Najib Mikati. The new cabinet included Elias Murr as deputy prime minister and defence minister.

In a cabinet reshuffle in Zimbabwe, Simbarashe Mumbengegwi replaced Stanislaus Mudenge as foreign minister.

Martinho Dafa Cabi replaced Daniel Gomes as defence minister in a cabinet reshuffle in Guinea-Bissau.

In Tonga, the defence minister 'Aloua Fetu'utolu Tupou died and was replaced by the foreign minister, Sonatane Tu'a Taumoepeau Tupou, in an acting capacity.

Week beginning 17 April 2005

In Ecuador, the congress voted unanimously to dismiss President Lucio Gutiérrez. He was replaced by Vice-President Alfredo Palacio whose new cabinet included Antonio Parra as minister of foreign relations, Aníbal Solón as defence minister and Rafael Correa as economy and finance minister.

Italian prime minister Silvio Berlusconi formed a new government but kept the key ministers unchanged. His government later survived a confidence vote in the Chamber of Deputies by 334 votes to 240 and in the Senate by 170 votes to 117.

In Liechtenstein, a new government was sworn retaining Otmar Hasler as its head but introducing Rita Kieber-Beck as foreign minister and Martin Meyer as interior minister.

Week beginning 24 April 2005

In parliamentary elections in Andorra the Liberal Party of Andorra won 14 seats (41·2% of the vote), the Social Democratic Party 12 and the Andorran Democratic Centre 2.

In presidential elections in Togo, Faure Gnassingbé of the Togolese People's Assembly won with 60·2% of the vote. Emmanuel Bob Akitani of the Union des Forces de Changement took 38·2%. Nicolas Lawson won 1·0% and Harry Olympio won 0·6%. Akitani disputed the results but the Constitutional Court later confirmed Gnassingbé as president.

Week beginning 1 May 2005

In a cabinet reshuffle in Algeria, Mohammed Bedjaoui became foreign affairs minister and Mourad Medelci finance minister.

José Miguel Insulza was elected Secretary-General of the Organization of American States after winning 31 of 34 votes.

The new Iraqi government of Ibrahim al-Jaafari included Hoshyar Zebari as foreign affairs minister and Saadoun al-Duleimi as defence minister.

In Bosnia-Herzegovina, the House of Representatives appointed Ivo Miro Jović as the Croat member of the presidency.

In parliamentary elections in Dominica the ruling Dominica Labour Party won 12 of the 21 available seats with 52·1% of the votes cast, the United Workers Party won 8 and independents 1. In the subsequent cabinet reshuffle Charles Savarin became minister of foreign affairs.

In parliamentary elections in the UK the Labour Party won 356 seats with 35·2% of votes cast; the Conservative Party 197 with 32·3%; the Liberal Democratic Party 62 with 22·1%; others 3. In Prime Minister Tony Blair's new cabinet John Reid was appointed defence secretary but the other leading posts remained unchanged.

Week beginning 8 May 2005

In the presidential run-off in the Central African Republic, incumbent Gen. François Bozizé won 64·7% of the vote against Martin Ziguélé who won 35·3%. Following the second round of National Assembly elections the National Convergence coalition had 42 seats (including the National Unity Party with 3 seats and the Movement for Democracy and Development with 2), ahead of the Liberation Movement of the Central African People with 11 and the Central African Democratic Rally with 8.

In Belgium, Guy Verhofstadt's government won a vote of confidence by 97 votes to 50.

Jiří Paroubek's coalition government won a confidence vote in the Czech Republic by 101 votes to 99.

Week beginning 15 May 2005

In Canada, Paul Martin's government won a vote of confidence in the House of Commons by 153 votes to 152.

In a cabinet reshuffle in St Vincent and the Grenadines, Mike Browne replaced Louis Straker as minister of foreign affairs.

Week beginning 22 May 2005

In a cabinet reshuffle in Djibouti, Mahamoud Ali Youssouf became foreign minister and Ali Farah Assoweh finance minister. Ougoureh Kifleh Ahmed was reappointed defence minister.

In presidential elections in Mongolia, Nambaryn Enkhbayar won 53·4% of the vote against Mendsaikhany Enkhsaikhan with 19·7%.

Hong Kong's acting chief executive Donald Tsang resigned. Financial Secretary Henry Tang became the acting chief executive.

In parliamentary elections in Suriname, the ruling New Front for Democracy coalition won 23 of the 51 available seats with 41·5% of the vote, ahead of the National Democratic Party, which won 15 seats with 22·8%.

Week beginning 29 May 2005

At referendums in France and the Netherlands voters rejected the proposed EU constitution.

In the first round of parliamentary elections in Lebanon, Saad El Hariri's Martyr Rarik Hariri List won all 19 seats in Beirut.

In France, the prime minister Jean-Pierre Raffarin resigned and Dominique de Villepin, the interior minister, was appointed his successor. De Villepin's new cabinet included Philippe Douste-Blazy as foreign minister and Nicolas Sarkozy interior minister. Michèle Alliot-Marie was reappointed defence minister. The new government survived a vote of confidence in the National Assembly by 363 votes to 178 (with four abstentions) and in the Senate by 174 votes to 126.

In Mexico, Carlos Abascal became interior minister after Santiago Creel Miranda resigned.

In São Tomé and Príncipe, the prime minister Damião Vaz de Almeida resigned and was replaced by Carmo Silveira, who also became finance minister in the new cabinet.

In Andorra, Albert Pintat's new government included Juli Minoves Triquell as foreign minister and Ferran Mirapeix Lucas as finance minister.

Week beginning 5 June 2005

In the second round of parliamentary elections in Lebanon the Amal Movement won 6 of the 23 available seats in southern Lebanon and its allies the Resistance and Development Bloc 7. Hizbollah won 5 seats and its allies 1.

Bolivian president Carlos Mesa Gilbert resigned and was replaced by Eduardo Rodríguez. The new cabinet included Armando Loaiza as foreign minister and Gonzalo Méndez as defence minister.

In Hungary, László Sólyom was elected president by parliament in a third round of voting. Sólyom won with 185 votes against Katalin Szili with 182.

Edem Kodjo was named as prime minister of Togo. His new cabinet included Zarifou Ayéva as foreign minister, Kpatcha Gnassingbé as defence minister and Payadowa Boukpessi as finance minister.

Week beginning 12 June 2005

In Greece, the prime minister, Kostas Karamanlis, won a parliamentary vote of confidence by 165 votes to 120.

In the third round of parliamentary elections in Lebanon, Michel Aoun's Free Patriotic Movement won 15 of 58 seats in Mount Lebanon and the Bekaa Valley. The Progressive Socialist Party won 14 seats, the Zahleh Dignity and Bekaa Accord Bloc 6 and the Future Tide Movement 5. Hizbollah won 4 seats and its allies 3.

Célestin Gaombalet resigned and was replaced as prime minister of the Central African Republic by Élie Doté. The new cabinet included Jean-Paul Ngoupandé as foreign minister and Théodore Dabanga as finance minister. President Gen. François Bozizé remained defence minister and interior minister Michel Sallé was reappointed.

Dismissed by president Thabo Mbeki, South Africa's deputy prime minister, Jacob Zuma, was replaced by Phumzile Mlambo-Ngcuka.

In presidential elections in Iran, the former president Ali Akbar Hashemi Rafsanjani won 21·0% of the votes followed by Mahmoud Ahmadinejad with 19·5%, Mehdi Karroubi 17·3% and Mohammed Baqer Qalibaf 13·9%. A subsequent run-off resulted in Ahmadinejad being elected with 61·7% of the votes against Rafsanjani with 35·9%.

Week beginning 19 June 2005

In presidential elections in Guinea-Bissau, former acting president Malam Bacai Sanhá won 35·5% of the votes ahead of former president João Bernardo Vieira with 28·9% and Kumba Ialá with 25·0%.

In the fourth and final round of parliamentary elections in Lebanon, independent candidates won 12 of the 28 seats available in Northern Lebanon. The Future Tide Movement won 7 seats, the Lebanese Forces 4 and the Qornet Shehwan Grouping 3. Overall the Opposition Bloc won 72 of 128 seats, Hizbollah, Amal and their allies won 35, and the Free Patriotic Movement and their allies 21. President Emile Lahoud subsequently appointed Fouad Siniora prime minister.

In Mongolia, Nambaryn Enkhbayar was inaugurated as president.

In parliamentary elections in Bulgaria, the Coalition for Bulgaria won 82 of the 240 available seats with 31·1% of the votes cast, ahead of the National Movement Simeon II with 53 and 19·9%, and the Movement for Rights and Freedoms with 34 and 12·7%.

Week beginning 26 June 2005

In Bosnia-Herzegovina, Ivo Miro Jović took over as presidency chairman.

The finance minister of the former Soviet republic of Georgia, Valery Chachelashvili, resigned and was replaced by Aleksi Aleksishvili. Irakli Chogovadze subsequently succeeded Alexishvili as economic development minister.

In Germany, chancellor Gerhard Schröder lost a vote of confidence by 296 votes to 151 with 148 abstentions.

Week beginning 3 July 2005

In parliamentary elections in Albania, the Democratic Party won 56 of the 140 available seats, the Socialist Party of Albania 42, the Republican Party 11 and the Social Democratic Party 7.

In parliamentary elections in Mauritius, the Social Alliance won 42 of 70 seats with 48·8% of the votes cast, ahead of the coalition of the Mauritian Socialist Movement and the Mauritian Militant Movement with 24 and 42·6%. In the new cabinet Navin Ramgoolam became prime minister as well as defence and interior minister, with Madan Dulloo as foreign minister and Rama Sithanen finance minister.

In Burundi, the National Council for the Defence of Democracy-Forces for the Defence of Democracy (CNDD-FDD) won 64 of the 118 available seats with 58·6% of the votes cast, ahead of the ruling Front for Democracy in Burundi (Frodebu) party with 30 and 21·7%, and the Party of Unity for National Progress (UPRONA) with 15 and 7·2%.

In a cabinet reshuffle in Comoros, Adou Mari Madi replaced M'Saidie Houmed as defence minister, Aboudou Soefou replaced Souef Mohamed Elamine as foreign minister and Oubeidi Mze Chei succeeded Ahamadi Abdoulbastoi as finance minister.

Mark Vaile succeeded John Anderson as deputy prime minister of Australia.

In Slovakia, prime minister Mikuláš Dzurinda survived a vote of no-confidence which was supported by only sixty votes from the 122 Members of Parliament present in the 150-seat legislature.

In co-ordinated attacks, four suicide bombers struck central London and detonated three bombs on underground trains and a fourth an hour later on a bus. 52 people were killed and a further 700 injured.

The leaders of the Group of Eight (G-8) countries met at a summit in Gleneagles, Scotland to discuss aid for developing countries. The leaders agreed to cancel the debt of the 18 poorest African countries and to increase aid by US$50bn. by 2010.

Week beginning 10 July 2005

In presidential elections in Kyrgyzstan, acting president Kurmanbek Bakiyev won 88·9% of the votes, followed by Bakir Tursunbai with only 3·8%.

In Croatia, the parliament approved the appointment of Ivica Kirin as interior minister.

In a cabinet reshuffle in the Maldives, Ahmed Shaheed replaced Fathullah Jameel as minister of foreign affairs and Ahmed Thasmeen Ali became minister of home affairs.

Week beginning 17 July 2005

A new cabinet was named in Lebanon, including Fouad Siniora as prime minister, with Elias Murr as defence minister, Fawzi Salloukh as foreign minister and Jihad Azour as finance minister. The new government subsequently won a confidence vote by 92 to 14.

In Portugal, finance minister Luís Campos e Cunha resigned and was replaced by Fernando Teixeira dos Santos.

In Jordan, the cabinet of prime minister Adnan Badran won a confidence vote by 66 votes to 37.

Week beginning 24 July 2005

In Guinea-Bissau's second round run-off for the presidency, João Bernado Vieira was elected president with 52·4% of the vote against 47·6% for Malam Bacai Sanhá.

In Bulgaria, the parliament approved Sergey Stanishev as chairman of the council of ministers (prime minister) by 120 votes to 119.

Week beginning 31 July 2005

King Fahd of Saudi Arabia died. He was succeeded by his brother-in-law, Abdullah.

Mahmoud Ahmadinejad was sworn in as president of Iran. His new cabinet included Manouchehr Mottaki as foreign minister, Mostafa Mohammad-Najjar as defence minister and Davoud Danesh-Jaafari as finance minister.

In Mauritania, a coup resulted in the overthrow of president Maaouya Ould Sid'Ahmed Taya while he was attending the funeral of King Fahd. A Military Council for Justice and Democracy was formed, led by Col. Ely Ould Mohamed Vall, after which the incumbent prime minister Sghaïr Ould M'Bareck and his government resigned. Subsequently Sidi Mohamed Ould Boubacar was appointed prime minister. His cabinet included Ahmed Ould Sid Hamed as foreign minister and Abdallahi Ould Souleymane Ould Cheikh Sidiya as finance minister.

In Suriname, the United People's Assembly re-elected Ronald Venetiaan president with 560 of the 879 available votes against Rabin Parmessar with 315.

Week beginning 7 August 2005

In a cabinet reshuffle in Chad, Ahmad Allam-mi was appointed foreign minister, Bichara Issa Djadallah defence minister and Abbas Mahamat Tolli finance minister.

Binyamin Netanyahu resigned as Israel's finance minister and was replaced by Ehud Olmert.

In Bulgaria, Sergey Stanishev's new cabinet included Ivailo Kalfin as foreign minister, Vesselin Bliznakov as defence minister and Plamen Oresharski as finance minister.

Pedro Pablo Kuczynski became prime minister of Peru with Óscar Maúrtua de Romaña as foreign minister, Marciano Rengifo Ruiz as defence minister and Fernando Zavala as economy and finance minister. Kuczynski subsequently won a vote of confidence by 60 votes to six with 29 abstentions.

In Sri Lanka, foreign minister Lakshman Kadirgamar was assassinated and was replaced by Anura Bandaranaike.

Week beginning 14 August 2005

Kurmanbek Bakiyev was sworn in as president of Kyrgyzstan and named Feliks Kulov acting prime minister.

In Singapore, incumbent president S. R. Nathan was re-elected as the only eligible candidate.

A cabinet reshuffle in Tunisia saw Abdelwahab Abdallah appointed foreign minister and Kamel Morjane defence minister.

In presidential elections in Burundi, the legislature elected Pierre Nkurunziza by 151 votes to 9. His new cabinet included Martin Nduwimana and Alice Nzomukunda as first and second vice-presidents, Antoinette Batumubwira as foreign minister, Gen. Germain Niyoyankana as defence minister and Dieudonné Ngowembona as finance minister.

Solón Espinosa resigned as defence minister of Ecuador and was replaced by Oswaldo Jarrín.

Week beginning 21 August 2005

Manasseh Nshuti was named Rwanda's new finance minister.

In a cabinet reshuffle in Romania, finance minister Ionut Popescu was replaced by Sebastian Vlădescu.

Week beginning 28 August 2005

In Cyprus, the finance minister, Makis Keravnos, resigned and was replaced by Michalakis Sarris.

Oil prices reached a record high of US$70·85 per barrel.

In Kyrgyzstan, the premiership of Feliks Kulov was confirmed in parliament by 55 votes to eight.

In Suriname, a new cabinet took office which included Lygia Kraag-Keteldijk as foreign minister, Ivan Fernald as defence minister and Humphrey Hildenberg reappointed as finance minister.

Albanian president Alfred Moisiu asked Sali Berisha to form a government. The cabinet included Besnik Mustafaj as foreign minister, Fatmir Mediu as defence minister and Ridvan Bode as finance minister. The administration was confirmed in parliament by 84 votes to 53.

Week beginning 4 September 2005

Bhutan's prime minister, Yeshey Zimba, was replaced by Sangay Ngedup.

In presidential elections in Egypt, incumbent Hosni Mubarak was re-elected with 88·6% of the votes, followed by Ayman Nour with 7·3% and Noaman Gomaa with 2·8%.

President Viktor Yushchenko of Ukraine dismissed prime minister Yuliya Tymoshenko, appointing her predecessor Yuriy Yekhanurov in her place. Yekhanurov was subsequently approved by parliament in a second vote.

In Serbia and Montenegro, defence minister Prvoslav Davinić resigned.

Week beginning 11 September 2005

In parliamentary elections in Japan, prime minister Junichiro Koizumi's Liberal Democratic Party won 296 of 480 seats with 38·2% of the votes cast, ahead of the Democratic Party with 113 and 31·0%, and the New Komeito Party with 31 and 13·3%.

In Norway's parliamentary elections the Labour Party won 61 of 169 seats with 32·7% of the votes cast, followed by the Progress Party with 38 and 22·1%, and the Conservative Party with 23 and 14·1%.

The Labour Party won 50 of 121 seats with 41·1% of the votes cast in New Zealand's parliamentary elections, ahead of the National Party with 48 and 39·1%, and the New Zealand First Party with 7 and 5·7%.

Week beginning 18 September 2005

In parliamentary elections in Germany, the Christian Democratic Union/Christian Social Union won 226 of 614 seats with 35·2% of the votes cast, followed by the Social Democratic Party with 222 and 34·2%, and the Free Democratic Party with 61 and 9·8%.

In Sudan, a national unity government was formed with Dr Lam Akol as foreign minister and Lieut.-Gen. Abdel Rahim Mohamed Hussein as defence minister. Al-Zobeir Ahmed Hassan remained finance minister.

Domenico Siniscalco, Italian economy and finance minister, resigned and was replaced by Giulio Tremonti.

Week beginning 25 September 2005

In parliamentary elections in Poland, the Law and Justice Party won 155 of 460 seats with 27·0% of the votes cast, followed by the Citizen's Platform with 133 and 24·1%, and the Self-Defence of the Polish Republic with 56 and 11·4%.

Sheikh Khalid bin Ahmed Al-Khalifa was named foreign minister of Bahrain.

Estonian defence minister Jaak Jõerüüt resigned.

In Iceland, Davíð Oddsson resigned as foreign minister and was succeeded by Geir H. Haarde. Árni Mathiesen replaced Haarde as finance minister.

Week beginning 2 October 2005

In Estonia, Jürgen Ligi was appointed defence minister.

President Svetozar Marović nominated Zoran Stanković as Serbia and Montenegro's new defence minister.

Week beginning 9 October 2005

In the first round of presidential elections in Poland, Donald Tusk won 36·3% of the votes, followed by Lech Kaczyński with 33·1% and Andrzej Lepper 15·1%. In the subsequent second round run-off Kaczyński won 54·0% and Tusk 46·0%.

In Nicaragua, the National Assembly elected Alfredo Gómez vice-president by 83 votes to 0.

A new cabinet was appointed in Ethiopia with Kuma Demeksa becoming defence minister.

In presidential elections in Liberia, George Weah of the Congress for Democratic Change won 28·3% of the vote, followed by Ellen Johnson-Sirleaf of the Unity Party with 19·8% and Charles Brumskine of the Liberal Party 13·9%.

Week beginning 16 October 2005

The new government of prime minister Jens Stoltenberg was formed in Norway. It included Jonas Gahr Støre as foreign minister, Anne-Grete Strøm-Erichsen as defence minister and Kristin Halvorsen as finance minister.

In the former Soviet republic of Georgia, prime minister Zurab Noghaideli replaced foreign minister Salome Zurabishvili with Gela Bezhuashvili.

Prime minister Helen Clark's new government in New Zealand included Winston Peters as foreign minister and Phil Goff as defence minister. Michael Cullen remained finance minister.

In Poland, prime minister Marek Belka resigned and Kazimierz Marcinkiewicz was asked to form a new government by president Aleksander Kwasniewski. Marcinkiewicz was subsequently sworn in with a cabinet that included Stefan Meller as foreign minister, Radosław Sikorski as defence minister and Teresa Lubińska as finance minister.

Week beginning 23 October 2005

In parliamentary elections to the Chamber of Deputies in Argentina, the Front for Victory won 50 of 127 seats with 29·9% of the votes cast, followed by the Radical Civic Union with ten seats and 8·9%. The Front for Victory plus its allies took 69 seats and the Radical Civic Union plus its allies 19.

Lamin Kaba Bajo was appointed foreign minister in a cabinet reshuffle in The Gambia.

In Guinea-Bissau, president João Bernardo Vieira dismissed the government of prime minister Carlos Gomes Júnior. Aristides Gomes was subsequently sworn in as prime minister and appointed acting interior minister. A government was formed that included António Isaac Monteiro as foreign minister, Hélder Proença as defence minister and Vítor Mandinga as finance minister.

Week beginning 30 October 2005

In a cabinet reshuffle in Japan, Taro Aso was appointed foreign minister, Fukushiro Nukaga defence minister, Heizo Takenaka internal affairs minister and Sadakazu Tanigaki was retained as finance minister.

Week beginning 6 November 2005

In parliamentary elections in Azerbaijan, the ruling New Azerbaijan Party won 58 of 125 available seats, independents won 40 and the Azadlig opposition bloc 8.

Indian foreign minister K. Natwar Singh resigned and his portfolio was taken over by prime minister Manmohan Singh.

In the presidential run-off in Liberia, Ellen Johnson-Sirleaf won 59·6% of the votes cast with George Weah receiving 40·4%.

In Poland, the government of prime minister Kazimierz Marcinkiewicz won a vote of confidence in the lower house by 272 votes to 187.

Week beginning 13 November 2005

In presidential elections in Burkina Faso, incumbent Blaise Compaoré was re-elected with 80·3% of the votes cast, ahead of Bénéwendé Stanislas Sankara with 4·9%.

In presidential elections in Sri Lanka, prime minister Mahinda Rajapaksa was elected with 50·3% of the votes cast against Ranil Wickremesinghe with 48·4%. Rajapaksa was subsequently sworn in and Ratnasiri Wickremanayake became prime minister. The new government included Rajapaksa as defence and finance minister, and Mangala Samaraweera as foreign minister.

Kadyr Gulyamov was replaced as Uzbekistan's defence minister by Ruslan Mirzayev.

Week beginning 20 November 2005

In Germany, the Bundestag elected Angela Merkel chancellor by 397 votes to 202 with 12 abstentions. Her new cabinet included Frank-Walter Steinmeier as foreign minister, Franz Josef Jung as defence minister, Peer Steinbrück as finance minister and Wolfgang Schäuble as interior minister.

Jordanian prime minister Adnan Badran resigned and was replaced by Marouf al-Bakhit who also took on the role of defence minister. Bakhit's new cabinet included Abdul Ilah Khatib as foreign minister, Ziad Fariz as finance minister and Eid al-Fayez as interior minister.

Week beginning 27 November 2005

In presidential elections in Gabon, incumbent Omar Bongo Ondimba won 79·2% of the votes cast followed by Pierre Mamboundou with 13·6% and Zacharie Myboto with 6·6%.

In presidential elections in Honduras, Manuel Zelaya won 49·9% of the votes cast ahead of Porfirio Lobo Salsa with 46·2%. In

parliamentary elections, the Liberal Party won 62 of 128 available seats, the National Party won 55, the Democratic Unification Party 5, the Christian Democratic Party 4, and the Innovation and Unity Party-Social Democracy 2.

In a cabinet reshuffle in Argentina, Jorge Taiana became foreign minister, Nilda Garré defence minister and Felisa Miceli economy minister.

A motion of no-confidence in Canadian prime minister Paul Martin's government was passed in the House of Commons by 171 votes to 133.

Week beginning 4 December 2005

In Côte d'Ivoire, presidents Thabo Mbeki of South Africa and Olusegun Obasanjo of Nigeria, acting as mediators, announced the nomination of Charles Konan Banny as prime minister for a transitional period. A new cabinet was subsequently announced which included Banny as finance minister, Youssouf Bakayoko as foreign minister, René Aphing Kouassi as defence minister and Joseph Dja Blé as interior minister.

In presidential elections in Kazakhstan, incumbent Nursultan Nazarbaev was re-elected with 91·2% of the votes cast ahead of Zharmakhan Tuyakbai with 6·6%.

In parliamentary elections Venezuelan president Hugo Chávez's Fifth Republic Movement won 114 of 167 available seats, with the remaining seats being won by his allies.

The National Democratic Party won 388 of 432 allocated seats in Egypt's parliamentary elections, followed by independents with 112 seats (including 88 affiliated to the Muslim Brotherhood) and the New Wafd Party 6.

In parliamentary elections in St Vincent and the Grenadines, prime minister Ralph Gonsalves' Unity Labour Party won 12 of 15 seats with 55·3% of the votes cast, ahead of the New Democratic Party with 3 seats and 44·7%. Gonsalves subsequently took over the national security ministry.

The Swiss parliament elected Moritz Leuenberger as president for 2006 in parliament with 159 votes of 225. Micheline Calmy-Rey was elected vice-president with 167 of 218 votes.

Week beginning 11 December 2005

In presidential elections in Chile, Michelle Bachelet of the Concertación coalition won 45·9% of the votes cast followed by Sebastián Piñera with 25·4% and Joaquín Lavín with 23·2%. In elections to the chamber of deputies, the Concertación coalition won 65 of 120 available seats with 51·8% of the votes cast ahead of the Alliance for Chile coalition with 54 seats and 38·6%.

Foreign minister Jakaya Kikwete won 80·3% of the votes cast in Tanzania's presidential elections, ahead of Ibrahim Lipumba with 11·7% and Freeman Mbowe with 5·9%. In parliamentary elections, the CCM won 206 of 232 available seats, the Civic United Front 19 and the Party for Democracy and Progress 5. Edward Lowassa was subsequently named prime minister and sworn in.

Palestinian president Mahmoud Abbas appointed Nabil Shaath acting prime minister after the resignation of Ahmed Qureia.

Two weeks beginning 18 December 2005

In presidential elections in Bolivia, Evo Morales of the Movement Towards Socialism won 53·7% of the votes cast, ahead of former president Jorge Quiroga with 28·6% and Samuel Doria Medina with 7·8%. In parliamentary elections the Movement Towards Socialism won 72 of 130 available seats in the Chamber of Deputies, followed by Democratic and Social Power with 43 seats, the National Unity Front 8 and the Revolutionary Nationalist Movement 7.

In Uzbekistan, interior minister Zokirjon Almatov resigned and was replaced by Anvar Salikhbayev.

Justice minister Solvita Aboltina became acting defence minister for Latvia after the resignation of Einars Repše.

Week beginning 1 January 2006

Moritz Leuenberger took office as president of Switzerland.

In Israel, deputy prime minister Ehud Olmert became acting prime minister after Ariel Sharon suffered a second stroke and brain haemorrhaging.

Tanzanian president Jakaya Kikwete announced his cabinet which included Asha-Rose Migiro as foreign minister, Juma Kapuya as defence minister and Zakia Meghji as finance minister.

In the United Arab Emirates, vice-president and prime minister Sheikh Rashid bin Said al-Maktoum died and was replaced by his brother Sheikh Muhammad bin Rashid al-Maktoum.

Week beginning 8 January 2006

Benin's defence minister, Pierre Osho, resigned.

In Mongolia, ministers from the Mongolian People's Revolutionary Party, including foreign minister Tsendiin Munkh-Orgil, defence minister Tserenhuugiin Sharavdorj, and justice and internal affairs minister Batbold Sundui, resigned and ended the government of prime minister Tsakhiagiyn Elbegdorj. The parliament subsequently elected Miyeegombo Enkhbold as prime minister; his cabinet included Nyamaa Enkhbold as foreign minister, Mishigiin Sonompil as defence minister and Nadmidiin Bayartsaikhan as finance minister.

Tzipi Livni was appointed Israeli foreign minister following the resignation of Silvan Shalom.

Week beginning 15 January 2006

In the presidential election run-off in Chile, Michelle Bachelet won 53·5% of the votes cast against Sebastián Piñera with 46·5%. Bachelet's new cabinet included Alejandro Foxley as foreign minister, Vivianne Blanlot as defence minister and Andrés Zaldívar as interior minister.

Finland's incumbent president Tarja Halonen won 46·3% of votes cast in the presidential election, ahead of Sauli Niinistö with 24·1%, prime minister Matti Vanhanen with 18·6% and Heidi Hautala with 3·5%. In the subsequent run-off, Halonen won 51·8% and Niinistö 48·2%.

Shaikh Jaber al-Ahmed al-Jaber al-Sabah, the 13th Amir of Kuwait, died. Although initially replaced by the crown prince, prime minister Shaikh Sabah al-Ahmed al-Jaber al-Sabah subsequently took over as amir.

In Liberia, Ellen Johnson-Sirleaf was sworn in as president and announced a cabinet that included Brownie J. Samukai as defence minister, Antoinette M. Sayeh as finance minister and George Wallace as foreign minister.

Brendan Nelson was appointed Australian defence minister after Robert Hill resigned.

President Omar Bongo Ondimba of Gabon named Jean Eyeghe Ndong as prime minister. The new cabinet included Jean Ping as foreign minister, Paul Toungui as finance minister and Ali Bongo Ondimba as defence minister.

Week beginning 22 January 2006

Evo Morales became Bolivian president and Álvaro García vice-president. The new cabinet included David Choquehuanca as foreign minister, Walker San Miguel as defence minister, Alicia Muñoz as interior minister and Luis Alberto Arce as finance minister.

In parliamentary elections in Cape Verde, the African Party for the Independence of Cape Verde won 41 of 72 available seats with 52·2% of the votes cast, followed by the Movement for Democracy with 29 and 44·0% and the Christian, Independent and Democratic Union with 2 and 2·6%.

Former prime minister Aníbal Cavaco Silva won 50·5% of the votes cast in the Portuguese presidential elections, ahead of Manuel Alegre with 20·7% and former president Mário Soares with 14·3%.

In parliamentary elections in Canada, the Conservative Party won 124 of 308 available seats with 36·3% of the vote, followed by the Liberal Party with 103 and 30·2%, the Bloc Québécois 51 with 10·5% and the New Democratic Party with 29 and 17·5%.

Change and Reform (Hamas) won 74 of 132 seats ahead of Fatah with 45 in parliamentary elections in the Palestinian-administered Territory.

In Honduras, Manuel Zelaya was sworn in as president, with Milton Jiménez as foreign minister, Arístides Mejía defence minister, Jorge Arturo Reina interior minister and Hugo Noé Pino finance minister.

Week beginning 29 January 2006

In the USA, Ben Bernanke became the 14th chairman of the Federal Reserve Board.

David Mwiraria resigned as Kenya's finance minister and was subsequently replaced by Amos Kimunya.

Martin Fedor was appointed defence minister in Slovakia.

In Angola, interior minister Osvaldo Serra Van-Dúnem died.

Violence escalated around the world in the wake of the publication in a Danish newspaper of cartoons satirizing the Prophet Mohammed.

Week beginning 5 February 2006

In presidential elections in Costa Rica, former president Óscar Arias Sánchez of the National Liberation Party won 40·5% of the votes cast followed by Ottón Solís of the Citizens' Action Party with 40·3% and Otto Guevara of the Libertarian Movement with 8·4%. In parliamentary elections the National Liberation Party won 25 of 57 seats, the Citizens' Action Party 18, the Libertarian Movement 6 and the Social Christian Unity Party 4.

Stephen Harper was sworn in as prime minister of Canada. His cabinet included Peter MacKay as foreign minister, Gordon O'Connor as defence minister and James Flaherty as finance minister.

In presidential elections in Haiti, former president René Préval won 51·2% of the votes cast followed by former president Leslie Manigat with 12·4% and Charles Henry Baker with 8·2%.

In Kuwait, the Amir HH Sheikh Sabah nominated his half-brother Sheikh Nawaf, the interior minister, as crown prince and appointed his half-nephew Sheikh Nasser as prime minister. Defence minister Sheikh Jabir was subsequently given the interior portfolio and the parliament unanimously approved Nawaf as crown prince.

Week beginning 12 February 2006

In presidential elections in Cape Verde, incumbent president Pedro Pires won 51·0% of the votes cast against former prime minister Carlos Veiga with 49·0%.

Fred Sevele was appointed acting prime minister in Tonga following the resignation of Prince Lavaka ata Ulukalala.

In a cabinet reshuffle in Greece, Dora Bakoyannis became foreign minister and Evangelos Meimarkis defence minister.

Week beginning 19 February 2006

Jean-Louis Schiltz became Luxembourg's defence minister in a cabinet reshuffle.

In a cabinet reshuffle in Swaziland, Moses Mathendele Dlamini became foreign minister.

In presidential elections in Uganda, incumbent Yoweri Museveni won 59·3% of the votes cast ahead of Kizza Besigye with 37·4%.

Week beginning 26 February 2006

Sulejman Tihić became chairman of the Presidency in Bosnia-Herzegovina.

In a cabinet reshuffle in South Korea, Lee Yong-sup became the minister for government administration and home affairs.

Week beginning 5 March 2006

In presidential elections in Benin, Yayi Boni won 35·6% of the votes cast followed by Adrien Houngbédji with 24·1%, Bruno Amoussou with 16·2% and Léhadi Vinagnon with 8·4%. In the subsequent run-off Boni won 74·5% against Houngbédji with 25·5%.

Al-Baghdadi Al-Mahmoudi became general secretary of the General People's Committee in Libya and Ahmad Mounsi finance minister.

Ratu Josefa Iloilo was reappointed president of the Fiji Islands by the Council of Chiefs and vice-president Ratu Joni Madraiwiwi was also reappointed.

In Portugal, Aníbal Cavaco Silva was sworn in as president.

US interior secretary Gale Norton resigned.

In Chile, Michelle Bachelet took office as president and appointed Alejandro Foxley foreign minister, Vivianne Blanlot defence minister, Andrés Zaldívar interior minister and Andrés Velasco finance minister.

Week beginning 12 March 2006

In parliamentary elections in Colombia, the Colombian Liberal Party won 38 of 166 seats ahead of the Social National Unity Party with 30 and the Colombian Conservative Party with 29. In the elections to the Senate the Social National Unity Party won 20 seats, the Colombian Conservative Party 18 and the Colombian Liberal Party 17.

Han Duck-soo became acting prime minister of South Korea after Lee Hae-chan resigned. Han Myung-sook was subsequently nominated as prime minister.

Week beginning 19 March 2006

In presidential elections in Belarus, incumbent Alyaksandr Lukashenka won 87·5% of the votes cast followed by Alyaksandr Milinkevich with 6·5% and Sergei Gaidukevich with 3·7%.

The Palestinian prime minister, Ismail Haniya, proposed a new cabinet with Mahmoud Zahar as foreign minister, Omar Abdel-Razeq finance minister and Said Siam interior minister. The cabinet was subsequently approved by parliament with 21 votes in favour and 4 against.

In Sweden, foreign minister Laila Freivalds resigned and was replaced temporarily by deputy prime minister Bosse Ringholm. Jan Eliasson was later appointed foreign minister.

In a cabinet reshuffle in Afghanistan, Rangin Dadfar Spanta became foreign minister while acting interior minister Zarar Ahmad Moqbel was confirmed in his job.

Najah al-Attar was appointed second vice-president in Syria.

Week beginning 26 March 2006

In parliamentary elections in São Tomé e Príncipe, the Force for Change Democratic Movement won 23 seats with 36·8% of votes cast, ahead of the Liberation Movement of São Tomé e Príncipe 20 (29·5%) and Independent Democratic Action 11 (20·0%).

In Ukraine's parliamentary elections, the Party of Regions of Ukraine won 186 of 450 seats with 32·1% of votes cast, the Yuliya Tymoshenko Election Bloc 129 (22·3%), the Our Ukraine Party 81 (13·9%), the Socialist Party 33 (5·7%) and the Communist Party 21 (3·7%).

Kadima won 29 of 120 seats with 21·8% of votes cast in parliamentary elections in Israel, followed by Labour with 19 and 15·1%, Shas with 12 and 9·6% and Likud with 12 and 8·9%.

Jamaican prime minister Percival J. Patterson, who had earlier announced his retirement, was replaced by Portia Simpson-Miller.

Parliamentary elections in Samoa were won by the Human Rights Protection Party with 29 of 49 seats, followed by the Samoa Democratic United Party with 12.

ADDENDA

ADDENDA

All dates are 2006

AZERBAIJAN. On 18 April *President* Ilham Aliyev dismissed the *Finance Minister*, Avaz Alekperov, and named Samir Sharifov as his replacement.

A partial re-run of parliamentary elections took place on 13 May in the ten constituencies where electoral fraud was officially recognized to have changed the outcome of the elections on 6 Nov. 2005.

BELIZE. In a cabinet reshuffle on 12 April Eamon Courtenay became *Foreign Minister*.

CYPRUS. In parliamentary elections on 21 May the Communist Progressive Party of the Working People won 18 of 59 available seats with 31·2% of votes cast, followed by the Democratic Rally with 18 and 30·3%, the Democratic Party 11 and 17·9%, the Socialist Party 5 and 8·9% and the European Party 3 and 5·7%.

ESTONIA. On 9 May Estonia ratified the new EU constitution. The parliament approved the treaty by 73 votes to 1.

FIJI ISLANDS. In parliamentary elections held 6–13 May, incumbent *Prime Minister* Laisenia Qarase's Fiji United Party won 36 of 71 available seats followed by the Fiji Labour Party with 31, the United People's Party 2 and ind. 2.

GHANA. A cabinet reshuffle on 27 April included Albert Kan-Dapaah being appointed *Interior Minister*.

INDIA. In Kerala's legislative elections held on 22 and 29 April and 3 May, the Communist Party of India (Marxist) won 61 seats followed by the Indian National Congress 24, the Communist Party of India 17, the Muslim League Kerala State Committee 7 and the Kerala Congress 7. *Chief Minister* Oommen Chandy subsequently resigned and was replaced by V. S. Achuthanandan.

In legislative elections in Tamil Nadu held on 8 May, the Dravida Munnetra Kazhagam won 96 seats, the Indian National Congress 34 and the Pattali Makkal Katchi 18. *Chief Minister* Jayaram Jayalalitha subsequently resigned and was replaced by Kalaignar Muthuvel Karunanidhi.

In West Bengal's legislative elections held on 17, 22, 27 April and 3 and 8 May, the Communist Party of India (Marxist) won 175 seats, the All India Trinamool Congress 29, the All India Forward Bloc 23, the Indian National Congress 21 and the Revolutionary Socialist Party 20.

In Pondicherry's legislative elections held on 3 and 8 May, the Indian National Congress won 10 seats followed by the Dravida Munnetra Kazhagam 7, the All India Anna Dravida Munnetra Kazhagam 3 and the Pudhucherry Munnetra Congress 3.

IRAQ. On 20 May Nouri al-Maliki was sworn in as *Prime Minister*. His cabinet included himself as acting *Interior Minister*, Salam al-Zobaie acting *Defence Minister*, Babyar Jabr *Finance Minister* and Hoshyar Zebari, who retained his position as *Foreign Minister*.

ITALY. Romano Prodi was sworn in as Italian *Prime Minister* on 8 May. His new cabinet included Massimo D'Alema as *Foreign Minister*, Arturo Parisi as *Defence Minister*, Giuliano Amato as *Interior Minister* and Tommaso Padoa Schioppa as *Economy and Finance Minister*.

KYRGYZSTAN. *Prime Minister* Feliks Kulov submitted the resignation of his cabinet on 2 May but was refused by *President* Kurmanbek Bakiyev.

POLAND. The *Foreign Minister*, Stefan Meller, announced his resignation on 5 May and was subsequently replaced by Anna Fotyga.

SERBIA AND MONTENEGRO. Montenegro voted for independence from Serbia in a referendum held on 21 May. 55·4% voted for secession, just above the 55% required for victory.

UNITED KINGDOM—NORTHERN IRELAND. On 15 May the Northern Ireland Assembly met for the first time since its suspension in Oct. 2002. On 22 May Democratic Unionist Party leader Ian Paisley turned down his nomination by Sinn Féin for the post of *First Minister*.

ZIMBABWE. On 12 May it was announced that the inflation rate had passed the 1,000% mark. The annual rate of price growth had been 1,042·9% in April.

International Relations

LIBYA/USA. On 15 May the USA renewed full diplomatic ties with Tripoli and removed Libya from its list of state sponsors of terrorism.

WORLD HEALTH ORGANIZATION. Dr Lee Jong-wook, *Director-General* of the World Health Organization, died on 22 May two days after emergency surgery for a blood clot on his brain.

PART I

INTERNATIONAL ORGANIZATIONS

LOOKING BACK

As China and India make their impact on the world economy,
William Keegan fears a return to protectionism

If last year our theme was that 'nationalism is back in fashion', the most marked development since then on the economic front has been something traditionally associated with nationalism: the rise of protectionist sentiment in some of the major economies, and with it a feeling of insecurity which leads nations to move away from the 'multilateralist' ideals of the post-Second World War period towards nationalist strategies, bilateral trade deals and economic decisions based on strategic considerations.

This is a far cry from the perhaps naive triumphalism that followed the fall of the Berlin Wall in 1989 and the collapse of the Soviet Union in 1991. Notwithstanding the 'irrational exuberance' (in former Federal Reserve chairman Alan Greenspan's famous phrase) that led to the Dot.Com boom, and its subsequent collapse, the 1990s and early years of the new millennium were characterized by a widely shared sense (on the part of both proponents and opponents) that neo-liberal economies had swept the board; that 'globalization' was the name of the game; and that economic interdependence and multilateral trading links were contributing to a more peaceful world.

In some ways the more extreme apostles for globalization were as optimistic as those, in an earlier phase of this phenomenon during the second half of the nineteenth century and early years of the twentieth, who convinced themselves that such global economic links would somehow provide nations with an economic incentive to eschew war. How wrong they were then, and how tempting of fate were those who took similar views during this more recent phase of globalization.

'Globalization' means many things to many people: essentially it has involved a proliferation of the links between different national economies formed by a growth in world trade at a far faster rate than the expansion of gross domestic product; and, in particular, a veritable boom in the size of overseas investment—foreign direct investment, or FDI as it is known by economists.

The importance of FDI is graphically illustrated by the official calculation that some 60 percent of China's exports and imports are accounted for by foreign-owned or foreign-controlled companies. Having turned inward for several centuries, China, under its Communist rulers, began to cultivate foreign capital and the expertise of foreign management during the closing decades of the twentieth century, in an attempt to 'catch up' with the 'capitalist' West, while persisting with one-party rule. After 1991 the Chinese rulers saw the chaos of 'Wild East' capitalism in the former Soviet Union, and were determined to exercise, when it came to encouraging the country's re-engagement with the rest of the world, a very Chinese form of 'economic liberalism'.

It is important to see China, and the much more democratic India, as re-engaging with the world economy after a long period of relative quiescence. Thus in 1820 China's share of world GDP had been some 33 percent, and India's 16 per cent, compared with 24 percent for Western Europe and less than two percent for the United States. The nineteenth and the twentieth centuries saw the economic dominance first of Europe and then the United States. By 1973 China's share of world GDP was 4·5 percent and India's 3 percent, against 26 percent for Western Europe and 22 percent for the United States.[1]

Between 1973 and 1998 China's share almost trebled (to 11·5 percent). India was slower off the mark—rising from a 3 percent share to a 5 percent share during that period; but by the time of the January 2006 meeting of the World Economic Forum in Davos, the surge in economic growth in both countries was one of the principal focuses of interest. By 2004 China had overtaken France and Italy in size of GDP, and in 2005, according to one reckoning, it was the turn of the UK to be overhauled. This meant that, although not a member of the Group of Eight countries (the US, Japan, Germany, France, the UK, Italy, Canada and Russia that attend the annual economic summits), China was now ranked fourth largest in the world economy, although in terms of GDP per capita it was still way down the list, with average income of US$1,500 per capita, compared with $40,000 for the US.

Economic analysts have been vying with one another in the production of forecasts of when China might eventually overtake the US in sheer size of the economy; and, of course, there has been much discussion of whether the entire Chinese growth phenomenon is sustainable, or whether there will be some kind of social implosion.

Whatever the outcome, the importance for the world economy has been that the 'outsourcing' of so much industrial production and assembly to Chinese 'cheap labour' has led to a revival of protectionist pressures in the West, most notably in the United States. One may also see the negative results of the referendums on the European Constitutional Treaty in France and the Netherlands in 2005 as in part reflecting 'fears for jobs' associated with the 'outsourcing' that has become a feature of globalization.

There is a paradox here, because when they go to the shops or buy (as happens increasingly) 'on line', members of the public benefit from the low prices resulting from intense competition in what economists like to call 'product markets', and in particular from the competition that comes from 'low wage' countries such as China. But the problem is that often this is perceived to be at the price of jobs at home. Economists can preach until the cows come home about the virtues of 'comparative advantage' (each country specializing in producing what it is especially good at, and at the most economic prices) but the victims who lose their jobs (and therefore have less to spend at Wal-Mart) are understandably less enthusiastic. In theory international trade is not a 'zero sum game'; in practice economic policymakers do not conduct policy in such an enlightened fashion that the 'losers' can easily find alternative jobs elsewhere, for all the politicians' talk of 're-skilling' and improving 'competitiveness'.

A closely related paradox has been the coincidence in recent years of a remarkable period of sustained economic expansion in the US and a marked rise in protectionist feeling in Congress. In France, during the 2005 referendum, unease about globalization and neo-liberal economics was manifested less in complaints about the Chinese threat than in fears of competition from the Polish plumber.

It is interesting, but perhaps not reassuring, that protectionist sentiment has been manifested both on a side of the Atlantic where unemployment was relatively high (Western Europe) and a side where, until the Federal Reserve embarked on a deliberate policy of monetary 'tightening', unemployment was relatively low.

The importance politicians, officials and economists attach to China was graphically illustrated when, in discussing the impact of the sharp rise in energy prices between 2002 and 2005, Mervyn King, the Governor of the Bank of England, preferred to couch the impact on the rest of the world in terms of a 'China shock' rather than, as economists have traditionally done, an 'energy shock'.

Thus a spectacular increase in demand for energy on the part of the Chinese and Indian economies had contributed

3

to a doubling of the price of oil within four years. By past standards, notably the two 'oil shocks' of the 1970s, this could have been both 'inflationary', in prompting trade unions to press for higher wages in compensation for lost purchasing power, and 'deflationary', in that the diversion of purchasing power from domestically-produced goods to imported oil can have an adverse effect on demand and employment.

But the 'China shock' seemed to alter the equation: while the price of energy rose, there was little sign of inflation in the price of internationally traded goods; and the reduced power of the trade unions diminished their ability to secure compensatory increases in wages, and thus produce what economists call 'second round effects' (on inflation).

Here one can point to a significant difference between the experience of 'globalization' in the nineteenth and early twentieth centuries, and the more recent phenomenon. In the hey-day of the British Empire, Britain was 'the workshop of the world', and the Empire provided it with both a source of raw materials for its products and a market for those products. The modern phase of globalization, however, involves the production or assembly of those goods themselves in cheap locations all over the world, not least China.

Before the Thatcher Revolution and the revival of neo-liberal economics, with their emphasis on the importance of 'markets' and 'the consumer', there was a widespread feeling that governments in Europe tended to be cowed by 'producer groups'. When a factory was threatened with closure, it would be bailed out by government funds in order to preserve jobs. The neo-liberal counter-revolution was against such practices, and in favour of letting ailing firms take their punishment in the market place. If consumers' preference had shifted, or if they wished to buy similar goods from cheaper sources, then the market was said to be 'working'. In the 1980s and the 1990s the bias of economic policy shifted away from interventionism and towards the interests of the consumer as opposed to the producer.

But, as regards the labour force, the consumer and the producer may be the same person. As noted above, 'losers' cannot always find employment elsewhere, as the economics textbooks glibly suggest.

One can see the dilemma in the 'China shock'. Multinational firms, the 'capitalists' of old, seek higher profits (or to restore falling profit margins in a more competitive world) by 'outsourcing' to, or producing in, 'cheap labour' locations such as China. The Western consumer takes advantage of what seem amazingly cheap prices. But he or she or their cousin may lose their job. It is this phenomenon that lies behind the growing protectionist pressure in the US Congress, and the reaction against 'neo-liberal economics' in the French referendum in May 2005.

But there is another aspect to the 'China shock', and that is the impact on the global energy balance. For, although the price of oil and gas had been rising for several years, it was in 2005–06 that the world became conscious once again of the possibility of a serious energy crisis.

During the golden years of economic prosperity that followed the reconstruction efforts after the Second World War, energy, in the words of one OECD economist 'was something we took for granted'. The quintupling of oil prices in the mid-1970s by the newly aggressive OPEC group was most certainly a shock, as was the second oil crisis in 1979. There were sporadic efforts at conservation and there was a search for new sources of supply. And despite a protracted false dawn, when the real price of

oil seemed to have stabilized in the late 1980s and 1990s at a lower level than the crisis points of the 1970s, there was some conservation. As a result, the initial reaction to the rise in the price in recent years was that there was no need to panic, because energy consumption per unit of GDP was virtually half what it had been in the 1970s.

On the other hand, there was a lot more GDP, not least in China and India. By 2005–06 it had become clear that there was also a shortage of refining capacity. Despite President Carter's dictum in the late 1970s that the battle to cope with the energy crisis had become 'the moral equivalent of war', the US, for all its natural endowments of energy, was still dependent on supplies from the troubled Middle East. Indeed, somewhat ironically in view of the way things turned out, the desire to secure supplies of energy was undoubtedly one of the factors that prompted the joint US/UK invasion of Iraq in 2003.

By 2005 Britain, which had enjoyed the remarkable windfall of North Sea oil and gas from the 1970s, had once again become a net importer of oil. During the intervening period, with 'globalization' and privatization all the rage, the prevailing philosophy was that it did not really matter who owned the ultimate sources of energy supply, and Mrs Thatcher had insouciantly made a virtue out of fighting the miners and running down indigenous sources of coal in favour of imports.

But with the revival of nationalism, and the doubling in the price of oil between 2002 and 2005, came a revival of concerns about security of energy supplies. These concerns were epitomized in the shocked reaction around the world to the brief period in January 2006 when the Russian energy company Gazprom cut off supplies of gas to Ukraine, with consequential effects on a number of Western European countries during what happened to be a particularly cold spell.

Although brief, and followed by protestations from President Putin and his colleagues that this was a special case to do with a prolonged political dispute between Russia and Ukraine, the episode concentrated minds on the issue of the security and reliability of energy supplies. In the UK, for instance, the controversial subject of nuclear power came back onto the agenda. Moreover, such were the alarmist forecasts about future pressures on resources of energy that the government appeared to be seeing nuclear energy not as an alternative to other sources, but as part of an approach in which no possible source of supply could be dismissed from the equation of future needs.

Meanwhile nineteenth century geo-politics seemed to have returned with a vengeance as China and India in their turn sought to establish secure sources of energy from regimes that met varying degrees of approval or disapproval from Washington, and complicated the US government's attempts to formulate an agreed United Nations policy towards Iran and its nuclear ambitions. In one particularly interesting episode, Congressional opposition prevented China from making a bid for a prominent US energy corporation.

On top of all these worries about security of energy supply and protectionist pressures associated with 'globalization' there was increasing concern about the medium to long-term implications of demand for energy for the future of the world as we know it. This promised to make the 'sustainability' of economic growth a key concern of governments and economics in the next few years.

[1] *The World Economy*, Angus Maddison, OECD, 2004

IN SEARCH OF THE PEACE DIVIDEND

The sense of relief that greeted the end of the cold war was soon joined by an eager anticipation of the peace dividend, an economic rebate after years of massive military spending. In the event the relief was palpable but the economic impact was short-lived. While world military expenditure in 2004 was still six per cent below the 1988 cold war peak, this has to be balanced against an average annual rate of increase over the past six years of 4·2 per cent in real terms. In the three years to 2004, this figure bounced up to six per cent.

The major contributor to the escalation is the US budget for the 'global war on terrorism', primarily for operations in Afghanistan and Iraq, although the latter had no demonstrable link to terrorism. The money has come largely from supplementary appropriations on top of the regular defence budget. In 2003–05, these amounted to $238 billion, more than the combined military spending in 2004 of the entire developing world, including China and the Middle East.

But developing countries have also increased their military spending, even more than official figures suggest, often to finance internecine warfare. Low national income and violent conflict seem to go together since eight out of ten of the world's poorest countries are suffering or have recently suffered from large-scale armed conflict.[1]

The costs are hard to pin down. Governments engaged in civil war tend to play down military expenditure, which, in any case, does not take account of spending by non-government forces, often financed from the sale of natural resources. Moreover, the cost of fighting is only part of the total cost of war. Also to be taken into account, though difficult to quantify, is the impact on economic growth both on the country at war and on neighbouring countries that have nothing to do with the conflict.

Put like this it might seem that a sustainable peace dividend will remain beyond our grasp. But though not immediately apparent, there are grounds for optimism. Knowledge is increasingly emerging about the root causes of civil conflict starting with political, economic and social inequalities, extreme poverty, economic stagnation, poor government services, high unemployment and environmental degradation.[2] While some strategists call for the adoption of 'co-operative imperialism' which implies active military intervention in the affairs of developing countries by major powers, others argue that a long-term remedy requires an integrated policy on security and development, including new types of economic aid programmes, debt cancellation, the removal of barriers to trade in goods and services from low income countries and the sharing of technological know-how, some of which could be financed through a reallocation of resources from military to civil means of promoting peace and security.

This debate overlaps with the war on terrorism. The first official US reaction to the events of September 11, 2001 was to boost military spending and to spend more on internal security with increases in police manpower, more sophisticated intelligence services and tighter border controls. While these moves addressed the symptoms of terrorism, governments are aware of the need to address also the causes of terrorism. The National Strategy for Combating Terrorism, adopted by the USA in February 2003, specifies long-term measures against the 'underlying conditions that promote the despair and the destructive visions of political change that lead people to embrace, rather than shun, terrorism'.

Yet the USA still gives priority to military expenditure of a sort that could only be justified if a continental war was in prospect. Furthermore, the war on terrorism has also had a strong domestic impact in the USA. The Patriot Act, introduced after the attacks of September 11, 2001, sliced into civil liberties with powers for law enforcement agencies to use wire taps, search warrants and other surveillance techniques, often under the cloak of secrecy. That these radical changes to the US legal system were introduced with little in the way of public debate or protest is a measure of the widespread fear in the USA of what terrorists might achieve if they get their hands on high-tech weapons. But little has been done to help towards eradicating the breeding grounds of violence.

European countries spend less on the military but also give emphasis to internal security with wider powers to the police to hold suspects without trial, seemingly unaware that they risk the erosion of civil liberties and the alienation of minority groups whose co-operation is crucial to the success of counterterrorism.

All the evidence suggests that there will be little progress towards lifting the threat of terrorism until resources are reallocated from military build-up and ever more onerous domestic security in the richer nations to helping poorer countries achieve social cohesion, political stability and economic development. Policies to these ends might even produce the elusive peace dividend.

This is the thinking behind the concept of 'global public goods', embraced by the United Nations Development Programme.[3] At the national level, public goods, such as health, education and defence, are paid for, not by the individual citizen but by community-wide taxes. Similarly, global public goods—measures to promote peace and security—should be raised above individual countries to become world concerns. This may seem an obvious point but it has failed to make the required impact on developed countries. In fact, net resource flows from member countries of the OECD to countries in need of aid fell from $264 billion in 1995 to $151 billion in 2002. A World Bank study estimates that another $40–60 billion a year in foreign aid is required to reach the UN's Millennium Development Goals by 2015.[4] Broader policies to provide for poor countries and fragile states would require substantially more resources.

How is the necessary money to be raised? Various forms of global taxes have been suggested. In the 1980s, the Brandt Commission put forward the idea of imposing taxes on international trade, notably the arms trade, for development purposes. Grants from private foundations and other non-government organizations have increased in recent years. At the time of writing, Bill Gates has backed a health foundation for the developing world to the tune of $29 billion. However, national governments are notoriously slow to get the point. The best laid plans are liable to be disrupted by short-sighted politicians in pursuit of votes. Yet in an increasingly interdependent world the international financing of peace and security on an unprededented scale is a matter of urgency. We should not wait for another terrorist outrage to spur action.

Elisabeth Sköns (Stockholm International Peace Research Institute)

---

[1] F. Stewart. Root causes of violent conflict in developing countries. *British Medical Journal*, vol. 324, 9 Feb. 2002; p. 342

[2] F. Stewart and V. FitzGerald (eds.) *War and Underdevelopment, vol. 1, The Economic and Social Consequences of Conflict*, OUP, 2001. (See also the UN's High Level Panel Report: http://www.un.org/secureworld/)

[3] I. Kaul et al, *Providing Global Public Goods: Managing Globalization*. UN Development Programme, OUP, 2003

[4] World Bank. The costs of attaining the Millennium Development Goals

TWO CHEERS FOR DEMOCRACY

Barry Turner charts the uneven course for a political ideal

It is one of the great ironies of contemporary politics that while the western powers proclaim the virtues of democracy to the rest of the world, they themselves seem to be losing faith in the legitimacy of popular governments.

Judged by election figures, political participation has never been lower. In the OECD countries levels of voting in national and local elections is down by about 70 per cent on 30 years ago. Political parties as mass organizations are a distant memory. Long gone are the days when party membership was the strength of grass roots organization. Even those voters who do turn out on election days are reluctant to involve themselves in the mechanics of democracy. Young people in particular find no virtue in championing political heroes; too many have turned out to have had feet of clay. Of all social groups politicians command least respect. Derided in the media for apparent or real ineptitude they are like the dreamer of the recurring nightmare entering a public stage, floundering with lines that have no relationship to the rest of the action. Few now look to politicians for examples of altruistic service to the community. The assumption is that they are in the job for all they can get.

The questions then arise: does all this amount to democracy in crisis? Should we not look to our own faults before counselling developing countries on how to manage their affairs? Even if it is pitching it too strong to talk of crisis to describe the state we are in, there are good reasons for reassessing the western practice of democracy, the better to avoid a crisis while giving constructive support to those countries that aspire to accountable government.

The starting point is to decide what democracy really means to us. Whatever this is, it is certainly not the same as the meaning attached to democracy by earlier generations. For the ancient Athenians, who were the first to put a form of democracy into practice, it suggested a process by which citizens could debate and decide collectively on matters of general concern. This sounds close to a perfect democracy until it is realized that the citizens of Athens were a small, highly select group. Nobody thought to consult the slaves who did most of the hard work, or those who were resident but unable to claim citizenship by birth or that half of the population who happened to be women.

When, two thousand years later, democracy re-entered the European imagination, elitism was still the guiding principle. Those with property were alone regarded as qualified to have a share in government. A rising mercantile and professional class sought not an ideal of common consent so much as the right for themselves to determine how their taxes should be spent. The few communities where democracy had real substance were small and self-sufficient such as in Iceland where the sturdy and often aggressive individualism of the early Vikings was contained by the sure knowledge that to survive in a part of the world where nature gave little away, there was a need to stick together. Assemblies of freemen to resolve disputes were topped up by the Althing which served as a legislator, a fair, a marriage mart and the focus for a summer festival. It was by a majority vote in the Althing that Christianity was adopted as Iceland's official religion.

More mainstream were the Puritan congregations that devolved from the Reformation. Denying the authority of the priesthood and proclaiming equality in the sight of God, their experience of self government in religious and social matters gave them a taste for democracy as we might begin to understand it. Rejecting force as a means of implementing decisions, the Puritans sought collective agreement by the 'fellowship of discussion', or what the Quakers called 'the sense of the meeting'. It was a short step from the theological stance to a belief that politics could be managed in the same way.

The issue was put to the test in the Putney Debates (1647–49) which took place during the English Civil War that overthrew the monarchy and led to the trial and execution of Charles I. It was here that the practicalities of government, of getting things done, came up against the idealism of denominational egalitarianism which looked to rule by consent. That everyone should agree to every law before it could be implemented was clearly a non-starter. No matter, the radical voices at the Putney Debates made a powerful case for the universal right to be heard. As Colonel Rainboro famously asserted, 'the poorest he that is in England hath a life to live as the richest he'. It followed that 'every man that is to live under a government ought first by his own consent put himself under that government'. And in a later passage from the Debates, 'Every man born in England cannot, ought not, neither by the law of God nor the law of nature, to be exempted from the choice of those who are to make laws for him to live under and, for ought I know, to lose his life under'.

Rainboro's strict logic came up against the fear that the uneducated and property-less rabble would act irresponsibly to destroy the social fabric. At the same time there was a firm rejection of the creed professed by Charles I on the scaffold, that a distinction had to be drawn between those born to rule and the rest who were born to obey. The argument would be familiar today in countries groping towards some form of democracy.

A century on from the English Civil War, civil upheavals on both sides of the Atlantic restored democracy to the forefront of political discourse. The starting point was the independence of the American colonies. The newly created states began with a clear political slate on which to draw the framework for government at regional and at national level. Borrowing from the philosopher John Locke, the constitution makers stressed individual rights to life, liberty and the pursuit of happiness as the essential safeguard against government abuse of power. What emerged was a hands-off type of administration that suited the vigorous, self reliant society that was pioneering the new America.

The contrast with France in the wake of its own revolution could not have been greater. An established and independent nation sought to turn the political structure on its head by promoting the power of the people over the claims of aristocracy and monarchy to rule on their own terms. In February 1794, Maximilien Robespierre, the dominant figure of the Revolution who had a distinctly undemocratic way of dealing with those who disagreed with him, defined democracy as 'a state in which the sovereign people, guided by laws which are its own work, does by itself all it can do well, and by delegates all that it could not'. Since, for the most part, Athenian-style democracy was impractical for a country the size and social complexity of France, it was to representative government that Robespierre looked to express the general will. But having chosen their representatives, the people had to accept what was enacted in their name. In this way, the sovereignty of the nation took on an almost mystical power, a contrast indeed from the American model which supported a self-regulating society with little need of government.

The two ideals, though much adapted over two hundred years, remain distinct and thus a source of confusion in any discussion of the function and organization of democracy. Following to varying degrees the example of France, other European countries tend to favour the state over the individual. In the US, the reverse holds good. European citizens expect their governments to do ever more to enhance their welfare and economic well being. Hence the social model that is derided in the US for its failure to acknowledge the virtue of rugged individualism. It is no coincidence that socialism thrived in Europe but failed even to establish a toe hold in the US.

On the face of it, there is no reason why the two styles of democracy should not continue to coexist, offering a choice to those nations that still have some way to catch up. The problem is that neither model is setting an example of unqualified success. As we saw earlier there are signs of disillusionment with democracy as a force for good government.

The reasons are not far to seek. Start with Europe. The distance between politicians and their electorates is widening. Those in power profess their enthusiasm for communicating with the populace but they do so in a hectoring, propagandist manner aimed more at manipulation than enlightenment. Sound bites have supplanted constructive debate. Rarely does a politician admit to error or even to lack of knowledge. Opposition, as defined by those under attack, is ill informed and counter proposals are seen as counter productive. Taking its cue, the media treats politics as a knockabout contest, a branch of the entertainment industry with not quite the pulling power of sport.

The gulf between government and people is nowhere better demonstrated than in the evolution of the European Union, a noble ideal that is foundering on the refusal of the administrative elite to accept the need for public accountability. Power is concentrated on an unelected Commission backed by a Council of Ministers who speak for their governments but who cannot be said to have any direct relationship with those for whom they legislate. Such accountability as there is centres on the European Parliament, a sad excuse for a popular forum which serves chiefly as a gravy train for politicians who have been unable to make the grade on their home ground.

Predictably, when there is a reluctant acknowledgement of the obligation to carry public opinion, the process can go horribly wrong. So it was with the referenda in France and the Netherlands on the proposed European constitution. That it was rejected decisively in both countries should not have come as a surprise. Next to no attempt was made to explain to voters what the constitution entailed or why it was thought to be necessary. The patronizing assumption that they had no need to worry their heads about such complicated matters produced the inevitable angry response. But even then, the European establishment was unwilling to accept the lesson. The first reaction from on high was that the referenda would have to be repeated because, first time, they had failed to produce the 'correct' result. The same tendency can be seen in national politics where each state is citing the complexity of modern life as the excuse to take more power to itself in the day-to-day management of public affairs. This has happened most obviously with the counter action against terrorism, now regarded as a self evident justification for lightly discarding civil rights.

Here the spotlight switches to the US, the country that traditionally governs with a light touch. For those of us who admire American democracy and the dynamic society it has created, it comes as a shock to find that the president can assume the power to imprison without trial anyone he decides is an 'enemy combatant' and wiretap ordinary Americans without a warrant. His defenders argue that the war on terrorism justifies extreme measures but it is precisely at times of national emergency that politicians, if they are to be effective, need to be sensitive to views of ordinary people. To ignore governmental checks and balances is to suggest a contempt for the electorate that must surely undermine the democratic process.

The irony is that President Bush has put great store by promoting democracy in those countries where terrorism thrives. Not surprisingly, many are confused by the messages coming from Washington. To the impartial observer it would seem that the American democracy is moving closer to the European concept of the state, with its attendant bureaucracy, demanding a loyalty that overrides minority or even majority concerns. This impression is strengthened by the role that money now plays in America in electing anyone to high office. The starting point for a Congressional seat is a fighting fund of up to $5 million. To aspire to the presidency increases the stakes a hundred-fold. The advantages this gives to the wealthy and well connected hardly needs to be spelt out.

There are those who look to the IT revolution to restore power to the people. In a world in which everyone can talk to everyone else, opinion can surely be mobilized as never before. An example was provided in the run-up to the last presidential election. When Howard Dean announced his bid for the Democratic nomination, he was a long odds outsider with just 432 signed up supporters and $1,100,000 in the bank. Within weeks he was a serious contender thanks to a campaign manager who used the Internet and mobile phones to win over 700,000 converts and raise $50 million, mostly from donations. Though Dean fell well short of his ultimate objective, it is a safe assumption that presidential campaigns will never be quite the same again.

There is comfort too in knowing that while the authority of elected assemblies is increasingly called into question, citizens of the old-established democracies are finding other ways of making their opinions count. The power of lobbies in the democratic system is still imperfectly understood. While, by clever manipulation of the media, pressure groups representing dubious causes can exercise an influence out of all proportion to their popular appeal, there is a profusion of voluntary organizations, including leading charities, which engage the interest and energy of those who might otherwise belong to political parties. In the UK, over 50 per cent of the population is regularly engaged in clubs and other social groups, all of which have the potential for exercising political influence.

There is one other source of comfort for true democrats. This is in knowing that even if politicians are inclined to ignore basic liberties when they think they can get away with it, there are two safeguards built into the system—multiple political parties and open and free elections. Politicians who take too much upon themselves while ignoring those who put them in power, are liable, eventually, to meet their comeuppance. Electoral apathy can reverse dramatically if, as A. D. Lindsay argued in his classic study of *The Modern Democratic State*, the average voter 'feels his shoes pinching'. 'Only he, the ordinary man, can tell whether the shoes pinch and where; and without that knowledge the wisest statesman cannot make good laws.' The low turnout at recent elections in the US and in Europe suggests that for the moment the shoes are not pinching too hard.

But this can change. Meanwhile, it ill becomes those countries that are used to democracy in one form or another to assume that they are beyond improvement. Equally, we must acknowledge that democracy comes in all shapes and sizes and what may fit one country at any particular time may not necessarily suit all. Countries like Russia and China that are only now beginning the slow progression towards responsible government deserve understanding and support.

It is a truism to say that democracy is most valued where it is absent. Wherever there is dictatorship, aspirations to democracy are growing ever more vocal. The appeal lies not so much in what democracy can do as in its hope of ending the corruption and cruelty associated with unaccountable authority. Those of us who are lucky enough to live in relatively free societies must recognize the need to protect and nourish what we have, the better to support those who are trying to join the club.

Further Reading

John Dunn, *Setting the People Free. The Story of Democracy*. Atlantic, 2005
Robert Fatton and R. K. Famazani (eds.), *The Future of Liberal Democracy. Thomas Jefferson and the Contemporary World*. Palgrave, 2004
A. D. Lindsay, *The Modern Democratic State*, OUP, 1943
A. S. P. Woodhouse (ed.), *Puritanism and Liberty*, Dent, 1951

United Nations (UN)

Origin and Aims. The United Nations is an association of states, or intergovernmental organizations, pledged to maintain international peace and security and to co-operate in solving international political, economic, social, cultural and humanitarian problems. The name 'United Nations' was devised by US President Franklin D. Roosevelt and was first used in the Declaration by United Nations of 1 Jan. 1942, during the Second World War, when 26 nations pledged to continue fighting the Axis Powers.

The United Nations Charter was drawn up by the representatives of 50 countries at the United Nations Conference on International Organization, which met in San Francisco from 25 April to 26 June 1945. Delegates started with proposals worked out by the representatives of China, the Soviet Union, the United Kingdom and the United States at Dumbarton Oaks (Washington, D.C.) from 21 Aug. to 28 Sept. 1944. The Charter was signed on 26 June 1945 by the representatives of the 50 countries. Poland, which was not represented at the Conference, signed later and became one of the original 51 member states. The United Nations came into existence officially on 24 Oct. 1945, with the deposit of the requisite number of ratifications of the Charter with the US Department of State. United Nations Day is celebrated on 24 Oct.

In recent years, most of the UN's work has been devoted to helping developing countries. Major goals include the protection of human rights; saving children from starvation and disease; providing relief assistance to refugees and disaster victims; countering global crime, drugs and disease; and assisting countries devastated by war and the long-term threat of landmines.

Members. New member states are admitted by the General Assembly on the recommendation of the Security Council. The Charter provides for the suspension or expulsion of a member for violation of its principles, but no such action has ever been taken. The UN has 191 member states, comprising every internationally recognized sovereign state, with the exception of the Holy See. (For a list of these, see below.)

Finance. Contributions from member states constitute the main source of funds. These are in accordance with a scale specified by the Assembly, and determined primarily by the country's share of the world economy and ability to pay, in the range 22%–0·001%. The Organization is prohibited by law from borrowing from commercial institutions.

A Working Group on the Financial Situation of the United Nations was established in 1994 to address the long-standing financial crisis caused by non-payment of assessed dues by many member states. As of 31 Dec. 2005 member states owed the UN a total of US$3,287m., of which the USA owed US$1,111m. (34%). Total debts outstanding as of 31 Dec. 2005 were US$333m., of which the USA's share was US$252m. (76%).

Official languages: Arabic, Chinese, English, French, Russian and Spanish.

Structure. The UN has six principal organs established by the founding Charter. All have their headquarters in New York except the International Court of Justice, which has its seat in The Hague. These core bodies work through dozens of related agencies, operational programmes and funds, and through special agreements with separate, autonomous, intergovernmental agencies, known as Specialized Agencies, to provide a programme of action in the fields of peace and security, justice and human rights, humanitarian assistance, and social and economic development. The six principal UN organs are:

1. **The General Assembly**, composed of all members, with each member having one vote. Meeting once a year, proceedings begin on the Tuesday of the third week of Sept. The 60th Session opened on 13 Sept. 2005. Following a three-day High-level·Plenary Meeting (World Summit) of heads of state and government, the general debate ran for ten days, beginning on 17 Sept.

At least three months before the start of each session, the Assembly elects a new President, 21 vice-presidents and the chairs of its six main committees, listed below. To ensure equitable geographical representation, the presidency of the Assembly rotates each year among the five geographical groups of states: Africa, Asia, Eastern Europe, Latin America and the Caribbean, and Western Europe and other States. Special sessions may be convoked by the Secretary-General if requested by the Security Council, by a majority of members, or by one member if the majority of the members concur. Emergency sessions may be called within 24 hours at the request of the Security Council on the vote of any nine Council members, or a majority of United Nations members, or one member if the majority of members concur. Decisions on important questions, such as peace and security, new membership and budgetary matters, require a two-thirds majority; other questions require a simple majority of members present and voting.

The work of the General Assembly is divided between six Main Committees, on which every member state is represented: the Disarmament and International Security Committee (First Committee); the Economic and Financial Committee (Second Committee); the Social, Humanitarian and Cultural Committee (Third Committee); the Special Political and Decolonization Committee (Fourth Committee); the Administrative and Budgetary Committee (Fifth Committee); and the Legal Committee (Sixth Committee).

There is also a General Committee charged with the task of co-ordinating the proceedings of the Assembly and its Committees, and a Credentials Committee, which examines the credentials of representatives of Member States. The General Committee consists of 28 members: the president and 21 vice-presidents of the General Assembly and the chairs of the six main committees. The Credentials Committee consists of nine members appointed by the Assembly on the proposal of the President at each session. In addition, the Assembly has two standing committees—an Advisory Committee on Administrative and Budgetary Questions and a Committee on Contributions—and may establish subsidiary and *ad hoc* bodies when necessary to deal with specific matters. These include the Special Committee on Peacekeeping Operations (100 members), the Human Rights Committee (18 individual expert members), the Committee on the Peaceful Uses of Outer Space (67 members), the Conciliation Commission for Palestine (3 members), the Conference on Disarmament (66 members), the International Law Commission (34 independent members), the Scientific Committee on the Effects of Atomic Radiation (21 members), the Special Committee on the Situation with Regard to the Implementation of the Declaration on the Granting of Independence to Colonial Countries and Peoples (known as the Special Committee of 24 on Decolonization; 24 members), and the Commission on International Trade Law (60 members).

The General Assembly has the right to discuss any matters within the scope of the Charter and, with the exception of any situation or dispute on the agenda of the Security Council, may make recommendations accordingly. Occupying a central position in the UN, the Assembly receives reports from other organs, admits new members, directs activities for development, sets policies and determines programmes for the Secretariat and approves the UN budget. The Assembly appoints the Secretary-General, who reports annually to it on the work of the Organization.

Under the 'Uniting For Peace' resolution (377) adopted by the General Assembly in Nov. 1950, the Assembly is also empowered to take action if the Security Council, because of a lack of unanimity of its permanent members, fails to exercise its primary responsibility for the maintenance of international peace and security in any case where there appears to be a threat to the peace, breach of the peace or act of aggression. In this event, the General Assembly may consider the matter immediately with a view to making appropriate recommendations to members for collective measures, including, in the case of a breach of the peace or act of aggression, the use of armed force to maintain or restore international peace and security.

The first Emergency Special Session of the Assembly was called in 1956 during the Suez Crisis by Yugoslavia, which cited Resolution 377; demands were made for the withdrawal of British, French and Israeli troops from Egypt. On the Assembly's recommendations, the United Nations Emergency Force (UNEF1) was formed as the UN's first peacekeeping force.

Website: http://www.un.org/ga
President: Jan Eliasson (Sweden), took office for the Sixtieth Session on 13 Sept. 2005.

2. **The Security Council** has primary responsibility for the maintenance of international peace and security. Under the Charter, the Security Council alone has the power to take decisions that member states are obligated to carry out. A representative of each of its members must be present at all times at UN Headquarters, but it may meet elsewhere as best facilitates its work.

The Presidency of the Council rotates monthly, according to the English alphabetical order of members' names. The Council consists of 15 members: five permanent and ten non-permanent elected for a two-year term by a two-thirds majority of the General Assembly. Each member has one vote. Retiring members are not eligible for immediate re-election. Any other member of the United Nations may participate without a vote in the discussion of questions specially affecting its interests.

Decisions on procedural questions are made by an affirmative vote of at least nine members. On all other matters, the affirmative vote of nine members must include the concurring votes of all permanent members (subject to the provision that when the Council is considering methods for the peaceful settlement of a dispute, parties to the dispute abstain from voting). Consequently, a negative vote from a permanent member has the power of veto. If a permanent member does not support a decision but does not wish to veto it, it may abstain. From 1945–91 the USSR employed its veto 119 times, the USA 69 times, the UK 32 times, France 18 times and China three times. From 1992–2004 the USA vetoed 11 resolutions, Russian Federation three and China two; France and the UK did not veto any resolutions.

The Council has two standing committees—the Committee of Experts on Rules of Procedure and the Committee on the Admission of New Members. It may establish *ad hoc* committees and commissions, which include all Council members. Currently they include: the Committee on Council Meetings Away from Headquarters; the Governing Council of the United Nations Compensation Commission, established in 1991 by Security Council Resolution 692 to compensate for losses related to the Iraqi invasion of Kuwait; and the Counter-Terrorism Committee, established pursuant of Resolution 1373 (2001).

When a threat to peace is brought before the Council, it may undertake mediation, setting out principles for a settlement, and may take measures to enforce its decisions by ceasefire directives, economic sanctions, peacekeeping missions or, in some cases, by collective military action. For the maintenance of international peace and security, the Council can, subject to special agreements, call on the armed forces, assistance and facilities of the member states. It is assisted by a Military Staff Committee consisting of the Chiefs of Staff of the permanent members of the Council or their representatives.

The Council also makes recommendations to the Assembly on the appointment of the Secretary-General and, with the Assembly, elects the judges of the International Court of Justice.

Peacekeeping. The Charter contains no explicit provisions for peacekeeping operations (PKOs), yet they have the highest profile of all the UN's operations. PKOs are associated with humanitarian intervention though their emergence was primarily a result of the failure of the Charter's collective security system during the Cold War and the absence of a UN Force. The end of the Cold War and the rise of intra-state conflict led to a proliferation of PKOs from the late 1980s and a greater proportion of armed missions. However, notable failures in the early and mid-1990s, such as the missions to Somalia in 1993 and to Rwanda in 1994, account for a drop in PKOs and shorter mandates. In 1992 Secretary-General Boutros Boutros-Ghali presented the 'Agenda for Peace', which laid out four phases to prevent or end conflict: preventative diplomacy; peacemaking with civilian and military means; peacekeeping, in its traditional sense of operations in the field; and post-conflict peace-building, an area seen as comparatively neglected in previous missions. Secretary-General Kofi Annan presented a report aimed at conflict prevention in July 2001 emphasizing inter-agency co-operation and long-term strategies to prevent regional instability.

Recent History. In Nov. 2002 the Security Council adopted Resolution 1441, holding Iraq in 'material breach' of disarmament obligations. Weapons inspectors, led by Hans Blix (Sweden), returned to Iraq four years after their last inspections but US and British suspicion that the Iraq regime was failing to comply led to increasing tension. The USA, the UK and Spain reserved the right to disarm Iraq without the need for a further Security Council resolution. Other Council members, notably China, France, Germany and Russia, opposed such action. On 20 March 2003 US forces, supported by the UK, launched attacks on Iraq, bringing an end to Saddam Hussein's rule. In May 2003 the Council adopted Resolution 1483, empowering the occupying coalition as an interim authority and peacekeeping force. The Resolution recognized a transitional Iraqi governing council and withdrew all previous sanctions against Iraq. Resolution 1483 did not address the legality of the invasion, treating the USA and the UK as *de facto* occupying powers. Resolution 1546, approved in June 2004, recognized the transfer of sovereignty to the interim government of Iraq.

Reform. The composition of the Security Council, with its five permanent members having qualified as the principal Second World War victors, has been subject to intense debate in recent years. The lack of permanent representation from Latin America and the Caribbean or from Africa and the Islamic World is frequently cited to demonstrate that the Council is unrepresentative. However, reform is in the hands of the permanent members and a unanimous agreement has proved elusive. In Sept. 2004 Brazil, Germany, India and Japan (the G4) launched a joint bid for permanent membership, along with a seat for an African state. In March 2005 Secretary-General Annan proposed either six new permanent members and three new non-permanent members or the election of a new type of member, eight of which would be elected for a four-year period. The World Summit in Sept. 2005 failed to agree on Security Council reform but pledged to continue negotiations.

Permanent Members. China, France, Russian Federation, UK, USA (Russian Federation took over the seat of the former USSR in Dec. 1991).

Non-Permanent Members. Argentina, Denmark, Greece, Japan, Tanzania (until 31 Dec. 2006); Republic of the Congo, Ghana, Peru, Qatar and Slovakia (until 31 Dec. 2007).

Finance. The budget for UN peacekeeping operations in 2005–06 was US$5·0bn. The estimated total cost of operations between 1948 and mid-2004 was US$31·5bn. In Nov. 2005 outstanding contributions to peacekeeping totalled US$2·0bn.

3. The Economic and Social Council (ECOSOC) is responsible under the General Assembly for co-ordinating international economic, social, cultural, educational, health and related matters.

The Council consists of 54 member states elected by a two-thirds majority of the General Assembly for a three-year term. Members are elected according to the following geographic distribution: Africa, 14 members; Asia, 11; Eastern Europe, 6; Latin America and Caribbean, 10; Western Europe and other States, 13. A third of the members retire each year. Retiring members are eligible for immediate re-election. Each member has one vote. Decisions are made by a majority of the members present and voting.

The Council holds one five-week substantive session a year, alternating between New York and Geneva, and one organizational session in New York. The substantive session includes a high-level meeting attended by Ministers, to discuss economic and social issues. Special sessions may be held if required. The President is elected for one year and is eligible for immediate re-election.

The subsidiary machinery of ECOSOC is as follows:

Nine Functional Commissions. Statistical Commission; Commission on Population and Development; Commission for Social Development; Commission on Human Rights (and Subcommission on Prevention of Discrimination and Protection of Minorities); Commission on the Status of Women; Commission on Narcotic Drugs (and Subcommission on Illicit Drug Traffic and Related Matters in the Near and Middle East); Commission on Science and Technology for Development; Commission on Crime Prevention and Criminal Justice; Commission on Sustainable Development.

Five Regional Economic Commissions. ECA (Economic Commission for Africa, Addis Ababa, Ethiopia); ESCAP (Economic and Social Commission for Asia and the Pacific, Bangkok, Thailand); ECE (Economic Commission for Europe, Geneva, Switzerland); ECLAC (Economic Commission for Latin America and the Caribbean, Santiago, Chile); ESCWA (Economic Commission for Western Asia, Beirut, Lebanon).

Nine Standing Committees and Subsidiary Expert Bodies. Committee for Programme and Co-ordination; Commission on Human Settlements; Committee on Non-Governmental Organizations; Committee on Natural Resources; Committee for Development Planning; Committee on Economic, Social and Cultural Rights; Committee on New and Renewable Sources of Energy and on Energy for Development; Ad Hoc Group of Experts on International Co-operation in Tax Matters; Committee of Experts on the Transport of Dangerous Goods.

Other related operational programmes, funds and special bodies reporting to ECOSOC (and/or the General Assembly) include: the United Nations Children's Fund (UNICEF); Office of the United Nations High Commissioner for Refugees (UNHCR); United Nations Conference on Trade and Development (UNCTAD); United Nations Development Programme (UNDP) and Population Fund (UNFPA); United Nations Environment Programme (UNEP); World Food Programme (WFP); International Research and Training Institute for the Advancement of Women (INSTRAW); United Nations Office on Drugs and Crime (UNODC).

In addition, the Council may consult international non-governmental organizations (NGOs) and, after consultation with the member concerned, with national organizations. Over 2,700 NGOs have consultative status. NGOs may send observers to ECOSOC's public meetings and those of its subsidiary bodies, and may submit written statements relevant to its work. They may also consult with the UN Secretariat on matters of mutual concern. The term of office of the members listed below expires on 31 Dec. of each year.

Members. Albania (2007), Angola (2008), Armenia (2006), Austria (2008), Australia (2007), Bangladesh (2006), Belgium (2006), Belize (2006), Benin (2008), Brazil (2007), Canada (2006), Chad (2007), China (2007), Colombia (2006), Congo, Democratic Republic of the (2007), Costa Rica (2007), Cuba (2008), Czech Republic (2008), Denmark (2007), France (2008), Germany (2008), Guinea (2007), Guinea-Bissau (2008), Guyana (2008), Haiti (2008), Iceland (2007), India (2007), Indonesia (2006), Italy (2006), Japan (2008), South Korea (2006), Lithuania (2007), Madagascar (2008), Mauritania (2008), Mauritius (2006), Mexico (2007), Namibia (2006), Nigeria (2006), Pakistan (2007), Panama (2006), Paraguay (2008), Poland (2006), Russia (2007), Saudi Arabia (2008), South Africa (2007), Spain (2008), Sri Lanka (2008), Tanzania (2006), Thailand (2007), Tunisia (2006), Turkey (2008), United Arab Emirates (2006), United Kingdom (2007), USA (2006).

Finance. In 2003, US$9,678m. in socio-economic development assistance grants was provided through the organizations of the UN system.

4. The Trusteeship Council was established to ensure that Governments responsible for administering Trust Territories take adequate steps to prepare them for self-government or independence. It consists of five permanent members of the Security Council. The task of decolonization was completed in 1994, when the Security Council terminated the Trusteeship Agreement for the last of the original UN Trusteeships (Palau), administered by the USA. All Trust Territories attained self-government or independence either as separate States or by joining neighbouring independent countries. The Council formally suspended operations on 1 Nov. 1994 following Palau's independence. By a resolution adopted on 25 May 1994 the Council amended its rules of procedure to drop the obligation to meet annually and agreed to meet as occasion required.

The proposal from UN Secretary-General Kofi Annan, in the second part of his reform programme, in July 1997, is that it should be used as a forum to exercise their 'trusteeship' for the global commons, environment and resource systems. However, in his 2005 report, *In Larger Freedom*, Annan called for the deletion of the Council from the UN Charter.

Members. China, France, Russia, UK, USA.

5. The International Court of Justice is the principal judicial organ of the UN. It has a dual role: to settle in accordance with international law the legal disputes submitted to it by States; and to give opinions on legal questions referred to it by authorized international organs and agencies.

The Court operates under a Statute of the United Nations Charter. Only States may apply to and appear before the court. The Court is composed of 15 judges, each of a different nationality, elected by an absolute majority by the General Assembly and the Security Council to nine-year terms of office. The composition of the Court must reflect the main forms of civilization and principal legal systems of the world. Elections are held every three years for one-third of the seats; retiring judges may be re-elected. Judges do not represent their respective governments but sit as independent magistrates. They must have the qualifications required in their respective countries for appointment to the highest judicial offices, or be jurists of recognized competence in international law. Candidates are nominated by the national panels of jurists in the Permanent Court of Arbitration established by The Hague Conventions of 1899 and 1907. The Court elects its own President and Vice-President for a three-year term, and is permanently in session.

Decisions are taken by a majority of judges present, subject to a quorum of nine members, with the President having a casting vote. Judgment is final and without appeal, but a revision may be applied for within ten years from the date of the judgment on the ground of new decisive evidence. When the Court does not include a judge of the nationality of a State party to a case, that State has the right to appoint a judge *ad hoc* for that case. While the Court normally sits in plenary session, it can form chambers of three or more judges to deal with specific matters. Judgments by chambers are considered as rendered by the full Court. In 1993, in view of the global expansion of environmental law and protection, the Court formed a seven-member Chamber for Environmental Matters.

Judges. The nine-year terms of office of the judges currently serving end on 5 Feb. of each year indicated: Rosalyn Higgins, President (UK) (2009), Awn Shawkat Al-Khasawneh, Vice-President (Jordan) (2009), Ronny Abraham (France) (2009), Gonzalo Parra-Aranguren (Venezuela) (2009), Raymond Ranjeva (Madagascar) (2009), Shi Jiuyong (China) (2012), Abdul G. Koroma (Sierra Leone) (2012), Hishashi Owada (Japan) (2012), Bruno Simma (Germany) (2012), Peter Tomka (Slovakia) (2012), Mohamed Bennouna (Morocco) (2015), Thomas Buergenthal (USA) (2015), Kenneth Keith (New Zealand) (2015), Bernardo Sepúlveda Amor (Mexico) (2015), Leonid Skotnikov (Russian Federation) (2015).

Competence and Jurisdiction. In contentious cases, only States may apply to or appear before the Court. The conditions under which the Court will be open to non-member states are laid down by the Security Council. The jurisdiction of the Court covers all matters that parties refer to it and all matters provided for in the Charter or in treaties and conventions in force. Disputes concerning the jurisdiction of the Court are settled by the Court's own decision. The Court may apply in its decision:

(a) international conventions;

(b) international custom;

(c) the general principles of law recognized by civilized nations;

(d) as subsidiary means for the determination of the rules of law, judicial decisions and the teachings of highly qualified publicists. If the parties agree, the Court may decide a case *ex aequo et bono*.

Since 1946 the Court has delivered 92 judgments on disputes concerning *inter alia* land frontiers and maritime boundaries, territorial sovereignty, the use of force, interference in the internal affairs of States, diplomatic relations, hostage-taking, the right of asylum, nationality, guardianship, rights of passage and economic rights.

The Court may also give advisory opinions on legal questions to the General Assembly, the Security Council, certain other organs of the UN and 16 specialized agencies of the UN family.

Since 1946 the Court has given 25 advisory opinions, concerning *inter alia* admission to United Nations membership, reparation for injuries suffered in the service of the United Nations, the territorial status of South-West Africa (Namibia) and Western Sahara, expenses of certain United Nations operations, the status of human rights informers, the threat or use of nuclear weapons and legal consequences of the construction of a wall in the Occupied Palestinian Territory.

Finance. The expenses of the Court are borne by the UN. No court fees are paid by parties to the Statute.

Official languages: English, French.
Headquarters: The Peace Palace, 2517 KJ The Hague, Netherlands.
Website: http://www.icj-cij.org
Registrar: Philippe Couvreur (Belgium).

6. **The Secretariat** services the other five organs of the UN, carrying out their programmes, providing administrative support and information. It has a staff of 8,900 at the UN Headquarters in New York and around the world. At its head is the Secretary-General, appointed by the General Assembly on the recommendation of the Security Council for a five-year, renewable term. The Secretary-General acts as chief administrative officer in all meetings of the General Assembly, Security Council, Economic and Social Council and Trusteeship Council. An Office of Internal Oversight, established in 1994 under the tenure of former Secretary-General Boutros Boutros-Ghali (Egypt), pursues a cost-saving mandate to investigate and eliminate waste, fraud and mismanagement within the system. The Secretary-General is assisted by Under-Secretaries-General and Assistant Secretaries-General. A new position of Deputy Secretary-General was agreed by the General Assembly in Dec. 1997 to assist in the running of the Secretariat and to raise the economic, social and development profile of the UN. Peacekeeping operations (PKOs) are chiefly run by Secretariat officials, who present a report to, and are authorized by, the Security Council.

Finance. The financial year coincides with the calendar year. The budget for the two-year period 2006–07 is US$3,798,912,500, compared to US$3,160,860,300 in 2004–05.

Headquarters: United Nations Plaza, New York, NY 10017, USA.
Website: http://www.un.org
Secretary-General: Kofi Annan (appointed 1 Jan. 1997 and re-elected 29 June 2001, Ghana). *Deputy Secretary-General:* Louise Fréchette (appointed 12 Jan. 1998, Canada).

Current Leaders

Kofi Annan

Position
Secretary-General

Introduction
After over thirty years working in various UN bodies, including the Peacekeeping Department, the Ghanaian Kofi Annan was elected the seventh UN Secretary-General in 1997. He was joint recipient with the UN of the Nobel Peace Prize in 2001 and re-appointed that year to serve until the end of 2006. As Secretary-General he has attempted to diffuse conflicts in Indonesia, Iraq, Israel and Morocco. He has highlighted poverty and the HIV/AIDS epidemic as part of the human security agenda that promotes the protection of individuals regardless of sovereign interests. However, Annan refused to support the US-led invasion of Iraq, putting relations between the USA and the UN under further pressure.

Early Life
The son of a Fante tribal leader and governor of the Asante province, Annan was born on 8 April 1938 in Kumasi, Ghana. After attending the University of Science and Technology in his hometown, he studied economics in St Paul, Minnesota. Graduate studies in Geneva were followed by his appointment in 1962 to the WHO administration. Thereafter, he worked continuously for the UN except in 1974–76, which he spent as the Ghana Tourist Development Company's director. During his career he worked within several UN bodies including the Economic Commission for Africa, the UN Emergency Force and the UN High Commission for Refugees.

Annan came to prominence in 1990 during the Gulf War when he negotiated the safe exit of 900 UN members from Iraq. His leadership of the Peacekeeping Department (1993–96) coincided with the peak of UN peacekeeping efforts spanning several major conflicts. These included Bosnia-Herzegovina, for which Annan oversaw the transition from UN Protection Force to NATO-led forces, and Rwanda and Somalia.

Career in Office

In 1997 Annan succeeded Boutros Boutros-Ghali as UN Secretary-General, the first to emerge from a career in the UN. Annan's main challenge was to balance the secretariat budget by reducing administrative costs, mending relations with the US and seeking closer ties with the business world. These last two initiatives raised concerns about the UN's impartiality.

Annan has championed the causes of Africa and the developing nations and attempted to raise global awareness of HIV and AIDS by forging an international policy of action. He has pursued a series of high-profile political arbitrations, with particular attention to Africa and the Middle East. The long-running war between Morocco and the Polisario Front in Western Sahara has received special attention from the Secretary-General, who has shown increasing frustration with the intransigence of both sides. In 1998 Annan embarked on a mission to encourage Nigeria's return to civil rule.

He has aimed to ease tensions in the Middle East, specifically those concerning Israel. In Nov. 2003 he declared 'deeply counter-productive' the security wall built by the Israeli government against international opposition. Annan has worked to improve relations between Libya and the international community and supported the independence of East Timor. Following an appeal from Annan, the leader of the East Timorese independence movement and current president, Xanana Gusmão, was released from imprisonment by the Indonesian government. In 2001 Annan was joint recipient with the UN of the Nobel Peace Prize. In the same year he was re-appointed by the general council for a second term.

In 1998 as tensions with Iraq and the international community mounted, he negotiated an agreement in Baghdad allowing for 'immediate, unconditional and unrestricted access' to all suspected weapons sites (although UN inspectors were withdrawn soon after). Four years later he warned US President George W. Bush against unilateral action in Iraq and urged diplomatic resolution. Bush called for the UN to prove its relevance, listing the resolutions the Iraqi government had defied. Annan appeared to agree to the unconditional return of UN inspectors in Sept. 2002, an offer the USA treated with scepticism.

Several members of the Security Council refused to sanction an invasion of Iraq in early 2003. Annan failed to convince the USA and UK not to act without an explicit resolution and accordingly the invasion of Iraq in March 2003 excluded UN involvement. After the fall of Saddam Hussein's government, Annan tried to negotiate a working relationship with the occupying powers. American reluctance to relinquish overall military leadership and anger at the opposition to the war in the Security Council prevented a deal. The UN presence in Iraq was diminished by an attack on the UN's Baghdad headquarters in Aug. 2003 that killed the special representative, Sérgio Vieira de Mello.

Member States of the UN

The 191 member states, with percentage scale of contributions to the Regular Budget in 2005 and year of admission:

	% contribution	Year of admission		% contribution	Year of admission		% contribution	Year of admission
Afghanistan	0·002	1946	Costa Rica[1]	0·030	1945	Ireland, Rep. of	0·350	1955
Albania	0·005	1955	Côte d'Ivoire	0·010	1960	Israel	0·467	1949
Algeria	0·076	1962	Croatia	0·037	1992	Italy	4·885	1955
Andorra	0·005	1993	Cuba[1]	0·043	1945	Jamaica	0·008	1962
Angola	0·001	1976	Cyprus	0·039	1960	Japan	19·468	1956
Antigua and Barbuda	0·003	1981	Czech Republic[2]	0·183	1993	Jordan	0·011	1955
Argentina[1]	0·956	1945	Denmark[1]	0·718	1945	Kazakhstan	0·025	1992
Armenia	0·002	1992	Djibouti	0·001	1977	Kenya	0·009	1963
Australia[1]	1·592	1945	Dominica	0·001	1978	Kiribati	0·001	1999
Austria	0·859	1955	Dominican Republic[1]	0·035	1945	Korea (North)	0·010	1991
Azerbaijan	0·005	1992	East Timor	0·001	2002	Korea (South)	1·796	1991
Bahamas	0·013	1973	Ecuador[1]	0·019	1945	Kuwait	0·162	1963
Bahrain	0·030	1971	Egypt[1, 3]	0·120	1945	Kyrgyzstan	0·001	1992
Bangladesh	0·010	1974	El Salvador[1]	0·022	1945	Laos	0·001	1955
Barbados	0·010	1966	Equatorial Guinea	0·002	1968	Latvia	0·015	1991
Belarus[1, 4]	0·018	1945	Eritrea	0·001	1993	Lebanon[1]	0·024	1945
Belgium[1]	1·069	1945	Estonia	0·012	1991	Lesotho	0·001	1966
Belize	0·001	1981	Ethiopia[1]	0·004	1945	Liberia[1]	0·001	1945
Benin	0·002	1960	Fiji Islands	0·004	1970	Libya	0·132	1955
Bhutan	0·001	1971	Finland	0·533	1955	Liechtenstein	0·005	1990
Bolivia[1]	0·009	1945	France[1]	6·030	1945	Lithuania	0·024	1991
Bosnia-Herzegovina	0·003	1992	Gabon	0·009	1960	Luxembourg[1]	0·077	1945
Botswana	0·012	1966	Gambia	0·001	1965	Macedonia[5]	0·006	1993
Brazil[1]	1·523	1945	Georgia	0·003	1992	Madagascar	0·003	1960
Brunei	0·034	1984	Germany[6]	8·662	1973	Malawi	0·001	1964
Bulgaria	0·017	1955	Ghana	0·004	1957	Malaysia[7]	0·203	1957
Burkina Faso	0·002	1960	Greece[1]	0·530	1945	Maldives	0·001	1965
Burundi	0·001	1962	Grenada	0·001	1974	Mali	0·002	1960
Cambodia	0·002	1955	Guatemala[1]	0·030	1945	Malta	0·014	1964
Cameroon	0·008	1960	Guinea	0·003	1958	Marshall Islands	0·001	1991
Canada[1]	2·813	1945	Guinea-Bissau	0·001	1974	Mauritania	0·001	1961
Cape Verde	0·001	1975	Guyana	0·001	1966	Mauritius	0·011	1968
Central African Rep.	0·001	1960	Haiti[1]	0·003	1945	Mexico[1]	1·883	1945
Chad	0·001	1960	Honduras[1]	0·005	1945	Micronesia	0·001	1991
Chile[1]	0·223	1945	Hungary	0·126	1955	Moldova	0·001	1992
China[1]	2·053	1945	Iceland	0·034	1946	Monaco	0·003	1993
Colombia[1]	0·155	1945	India[1]	0·421	1945	Mongolia	0·001	1961
Comoros	0·001	1975	Indonesia[8]	0·142	1950	Morocco	0·047	1956
Congo,			Iran[1]	0·157	1945	Mozambique	0·001	1975
Dem. Rep. of the[9]	0·003	1960	Iraq[1]	0·016	1945	Myanmar[10]	0·010	1948
Congo, Rep. of the	0·001	1960						

	% contribution	Year of admission		% contribution	Year of admission		% contribution	Year of admission
Namibia	0·006	1990	St Vincent			Tajikistan	0·001	1992
Nauru	0·001	1999	and the Grenadines	0·001	1980	Tanzania[11]	0·006	1961
Nepal	0·004	1955	Samoa	0·001	1976	Thailand	0·209	1946
Netherlands[1]	1·690	1945	San Marino	0·003	1992	Togo	0·001	1960
New Zealand[1]	0·221	1945	São Tomé e Príncipe	0·001	1975	Tonga	0·001	1999
Nicaragua[1]	0·001	1945	Saudi Arabia[1]	0·713	1945	Trinidad and Tobago	0·022	1962
Niger	0·001	1960	Senegal	0·005	1960	Tunisia	0·032	1956
Nigeria	0·042	1960	Serbia and			Turkey[1]	0·372	1945
Norway[1]	0·679	1945	Montenegro[1,12,13]	0·019	1945	Turkmenistan	0·005	1992
Oman	0·070	1971	Seychelles	0·002	1976	Tuvalu	0·001	2000
Pakistan	0·055	1947	Sierra Leone	0·001	1961	Uganda	0·006	1962
Palau	0·001	1994	Singapore[14]	0·388	1965	Ukraine[1]	0·039	1945
Panama[1]	0·019	1945	Slovakia[2]	0·051	1993	United Arab		
Papua New Guinea	0·003	1975	Slovenia	0·082	1992	Emirates	0·235	1971
Paraguay[1]	0·012	1945	Solomon Islands	0·001	1978	UK[1]	6·127	1945
Peru[2]	0·092	1945	Somalia	0·001	1960	USA[1]	22·000	1945
Philippines[1]	0·095	1945	South Africa[1]	0·292	1945	Uruguay[1]	0·048	1945
Poland[1]	0·461	1945	Spain	2·520	1955	Uzbekistan	0·014	1992
Portugal	0·470	1955	Sri Lanka	0·017	1955	Vanuatu	0·001	1981
Qatar	0·064	1971	Sudan	0·008	1956	Venezuela[1]	0·171	1945
Romania	0·060	1955	Suriname	0·001	1975	Vietnam	0·021	1977
Russia[1,15]	1·100	1945	Swaziland	0·002	1968	Yemen[16]	0·006	1947
Rwanda	0·001	1962	Sweden	0·998	1946	Zambia	0·002	1964
St Kitts and Nevis	0·001	1983	Switzerland	1·197	2002	Zimbabwe	0·007	1980
St Lucia	0·002	1979	Syria[1,17]	0·038	1945			

[1]Original member. [2]Pre-partition Czechoslovakia (1945–92) was an original member. [3]As United Arab Republic, 1958–71, following union with Syria (1958–61). [4]As Byelorussia, 1945–91. [5]Pre-independence (1992), as part of Yugoslavia, which was an original member. [6]Pre-unification (1990) as two states: the Federal Republic of Germany and the German Democratic Republic. [7]As the Federation of Malaya till 1963, when the new federation of Malaysia (including Singapore, Sarawak and Sabah) was formed. [8]Withdrew temporarily, 1965–66. [9]As Zaïre, 1960–97. [10]As Burma, 1948–89. [11]As two states: Tanganyika, 1961–64, and Zanzibar, 1963–64, prior to union as one republic under new name. [12]As Yugoslavia, 1945–2003. [13]Excluded from the General Assembly in 1992; re-admitted in Nov. 2000. [14]As part of Malaysia, 1963–65. [15]As USSR, 1945–91. [16]As Yemen, 1947–90, and Democratic Yemen, 1967–90, prior to merger of the two. [17]As United Arab Republic, by union with Egypt, 1958–61.

The USA is the leading contributor to the Peacekeeping Operations Budget, with 26·4838% of the total at July 2005, followed by Japan (19·4680%), Germany (8·6620%), UK (7·3757%), France (7·2590%), Italy (4·8850%), Canada (2·8130%), Spain (2·5200%) and China (2·4714%). All other countries contribute less than 2%.

Publications. Yearbook of the United Nations. New York, 1947 ff.—*United Nations Chronicle. Quarterly.—Monthly Bulletin of Statistics.—General Assembly: Official Records: Resolutions.—Reports of the Secretary-General of the United Nations on the Work of the Organization.* 1946 ff.—*Charter of the United Nations and Statute of the International Court of Justice.—Official Records of the Security Council, the Economic and Social Council, Trusteeship Council and the Disarmament Commission.—Demographic Yearbook.* New York.—*Basic Facts About the United Nations.* New York, 2002.—*Statistical Yearbook.* New York, 1947 ff.—*Yearbook of International Statistics.* New York, 1950 ff.—*World Economic Survey.* New York, 1947 ff.—*Economic Survey of Asia and the Far East.* New York, 1946 ff.—*Economic Survey of Latin America.* New York, 1948 ff.—*Economic Survey of Europe.* New York, 1948 ff.—*Economic Survey of Africa.* New York, 1960 ff.—*United Nations Reference Guide in the Field of Human Rights.* UN Centre for Human Rights, 1993.

Further Reading

Arnold, G., *World Government by Stealth: The Future of the United Nations.* Macmillan, 1998
Bailey, S. D. and Daws, S., *The United Nations: a Concise Political Guide.* 3rd ed. London, 1994
Baratta, J. P., *United Nations System* [Bibliography]. Oxford and New Brunswick (NJ), 1995
Beigbeder, Y., *The Internal Management of United Nations Organizations: the Long Quest for Reform.* London, 1996
Butler, R., *The Greatest Threat: Iraq, Weapons of Mass Destruction and the Crisis of Global Security.* Public Affairs, New York, 2000
Carnegie Commission on Preventing Deadly Conflict, Preventing Deadly Conflict: Final Report. New York, 1997
Cortright, D. and Lopez, G. A., *The Sanctions Decade: Assessing UN Strategies in the 1990s.* Lynne Rienner Publishers, Boulder, 2000
Durch, W. J., *The Evolution of UN Peacekeeping: Case Studies and Comparative Analysis.* New York, 1993

Gareis, S. B. and Varwick, J., *The United Nations: An Introduction.* Basingstoke and New York, 2005
Ginifer, J. (ed.) *Development Within UN Peace Missions.* London, 1997
Hoopes, T., and Brinkley, D., *FDR and the Creation of the UN.* Yale Univ. Press, 1998
Luard, E., *The United Nations: How It Works and What It Does.* 2nd ed. London, 1994
Meisler, S., *United Nations: The First Fifty Years.* Atlantic Monthly Press, 1998
New Zealand Ministry of Foreign Affairs, *UN Handbook.* 1997
Osmanczyk, E., *Encyclopaedia of the United Nations.* London, 1985
Parsons, A., *From Cold War to Hot Peace: UN Interventions, 1947–94.* London, 1995
Pugh, M., *The UN, Peace and Force.* London, 1997
Ratner, S. R., *The New UN Peacekeeping: Building Peace in Lands of Conflict after the Cold War.* London, 1995
Righter, R., *Utopia Lost: the United Nations and World Order.* New York, 1995
Roberts, A. and Kingsbury, B. (eds.) *United Nations, Divided World: the UN's Roles in International Relations.* 2nd ed. Oxford, 1993
Simma, B. (ed.) *The Charter of the United Nations: a Commentary.* OUP, 1995
Williams, D., *The Specialized Agencies of the United Nations.* London, 1987

Universal Declaration of Human Rights

On 10 Dec. 1948 the General Assembly of the United Nations adopted and proclaimed the Universal Declaration of Human Rights.

Preamble

Whereas recognition of the inherent dignity and of the equal and inalienable rights of all members of the human family is the foundation of freedom, justice and peace in the world,

Whereas disregard and contempt for human rights have resulted in barbarous acts which have outraged the conscience of mankind, and the advent of a world in which human beings shall enjoy freedom of speech and belief and freedom from fear and want has been proclaimed as the highest aspiration of the common people,

Whereas it is essential, if man is not to be compelled to have recourse, as a last resort, to rebellion against tyranny and oppression, that human rights should be protected by the rule of law,

Whereas it is essential to promote the development of friendly relations between nations,

Whereas the peoples of the United Nations have in the Charter reaffirmed their faith in fundamental human rights, in the dignity and worth of the human person and in the equal rights of men and women and have determined to promote social progress and better standards of life in larger freedom,

Whereas Member States have pledged themselves to achieve, in co-operation with the United Nations, the promotion of universal respect for and observance of human rights and fundamental freedoms,

Whereas a common understanding of these rights and freedoms is of the greatest importance for the full realization of this pledge,

Now, Therefore THE GENERAL ASSEMBLY proclaims THIS UNIVERSAL DECLARATION OF HUMAN RIGHTS as a common standard of achievement for all peoples and all nations, to the end that every individual and every organ of society, keeping this Declaration constantly in mind, shall strive by teaching and education to promote respect for these rights and freedoms and by progressive measures, national and international, to secure their universal and effective recognition and observance, both among the peoples of Member States themselves and among the peoples of territories under their jurisdiction.

Article 1. All human beings are born free and equal in dignity and rights. They are endowed with reason and conscience and should act towards one another in a spirit of brotherhood.

Article 2. Everyone is entitled to all the rights and freedoms set forth in this Declaration, without distinction of any kind, such as race, colour, sex, language, religion, political or other opinion, national or social origin, property, birth or other status. Furthermore, no distinction shall be made on the basis of the political, jurisdictional or international status of the country or territory to which a person belongs, whether it be independent, trust, non-self governing or under any other limitation of sovereignty.

Article 3. Everyone has the right to life, liberty and security of person.

Article 4. No one shall be held in slavery or servitude; slavery and the slave trade shall be prohibited in all their forms.

Article 5. No one shall be subjected to torture or to cruel, inhuman or degrading treatment or punishment.

Article 6. Everyone has the right to recognition everywhere as a person before the law.

Article 7. All are equal before the law and are entitled without any discrimination to equal protection of the law. All are entitled to equal protection against any discrimination in violation of this Declaration and against any incitement to such discrimination.

Article 8. Everyone has the right to an effective remedy by the competent national tribunals for acts violating the fundamental rights granted him by the constitution or by law.

Article 9. No one shall be subjected to arbitrary arrest, detention or exile.

Article 10. Everyone is entitled in full equality to a fair and public hearing by an independent and impartial tribunal, in the determination of his rights and obligations and of any criminal charge against him.

Article 11. (1) Everyone charged with a penal offence has the right to be presumed innocent until proved guilty according to law in a public trial at which he has had all the guarantees necessary for his defence.

(2) No one shall be held guilty of any penal offence on account of any act or omission which did not constitute a penal offence, under national or international law, at the time when it was committed. Nor shall a heavier penalty be imposed than the one that was applicable at the time the penal offence was committed.

Article 12. No one shall be subjected to arbitrary interference with his privacy, family, home or correspondence, nor to attacks upon his honour and reputation. Everyone has the right to the protection of the law against such interference or attacks.

Article 13. (1) Everyone has the right to freedom of movement and residence within the borders of each state.

(2) Everyone has the right to leave any country, including his own, and to return to his country.

Article 14. (1) Everyone has the right to seek and enjoy in other countries asylum from persecution.

(2) This right may not be invoked in the case of prosecutions genuinely arising from non-political crimes or from acts contrary to the purposes and principles of the United Nations.

Article 15. (1) Everyone has the right to a nationality.

(2) No one shall be arbitrarily deprived of his nationality nor denied the right to change his nationality.

Article 16. (1) Men and women of full age, without any limitation due to race, nationality or religion, have the right to marry and to found a family. They are entitled to equal rights as to marriage, during marriage and at its dissolution.

(2) Marriage shall be entered into only with the free and full consent of the intending spouses.

(3) The family is the natural and fundamental group unit of society and is entitled to protection by society and the State.

Article 17. (1) Everyone has the right to own property alone as well as in association with others.

(2) No one shall be arbitrarily deprived of his property.

Article 18. Everyone has the right to freedom of thought, conscience and religion; this right includes freedom to change his religion or belief, and freedom, either alone or in community with others and in public or private, to manifest his religion or belief in teaching, practice, worship and observance.

Article 19. Everyone has the right to freedom of opinion and expression; this right includes freedom to hold opinions without interference and to seek, receive and impart information and ideas through any media and regardless of frontiers.

Article 20. (1) Everyone has the right to freedom of peaceful assembly and association.

(2) No one may be compelled to belong to an association.

Article 21. (1) Everyone has the right to take part in the government of his country, directly or through freely chosen representatives.

(2) Everyone has the right of equal access to public service in his country.

(3) The will of the people shall be the basis of the authority of government; this will shall be expressed in periodic and genuine elections which shall be by universal and equal suffrage and shall be held by secret vote or by equivalent free voting procedures.

Article 22. Everyone, as a member of society, has the right to social security and is entitled to realization, through national effort and international co-operation and in accordance with the organization and resources of the State, of the economic, social and cultural rights indispensable for his dignity and the free development of his personality.

Article 23. (1) Everyone has the right to work, to free choice of employment, to just and favourable conditions of and to protection against unemployment.

(2) Everyone, without any discrimination, has the right to equal pay for equal work.

(3) Everyone who works has the right to just and favourable remuneration ensuring for himself and his family an existence worthy of human dignity, and supplemented, if necessary, by other means of social protection.

(4) Everyone has the right to form and to join trade unions for the protection of his interests.

Article 24. Everyone has the right to rest and leisure, including reasonable limitation of working hours and periodic holidays with pay.

Article 25. (1) Everyone has the right to a standard of living adequate for the health and well-being of himself and his family, including food, clothing, housing and medical care and necessary social services, and the right to security in the event of unemployment, sickness, disability, widowhood, old age or other lack of livelihood in circumstances beyond his control.

(2) Motherhood and childhood are entitled to special care and assistance. All children, whether born in or out of wedlock, shall enjoy the same social protection.

Article 26. (1) Everyone has the right to education. Education shall be free, at least in the elementary and fundamental stages. Elementary education shall be compulsory. Technical and professional education shall be made generally available and higher education shall be equally accessible to all on the basis of merit.

(2) Education shall be directed to the full development of the human personality and to the strengthening of respect for human rights and fundamental freedoms. It shall promote understanding, tolerance and friendship among all nations, racial or religious groups, and shall further the activities of the United Nations for the maintenance of peace.

(3) Parents have a prior right to choose the kind of education that shall be given to their children.

Article 27. (1) Everyone has the right freely to participate in the cultural life of the community, to enjoy the arts and to share in scientific advancement and its benefits.

(2) Everyone has the right to the protection of the moral and material interests resulting from any scientific, literary or artistic production of which he is the author.

Article 28. Everyone is entitled to a social and international order in which the rights and freedoms set forth in this Declaration can be fully realized.

Article 29. (1) Everyone has duties to the community in which alone the free and full development of his personality is possible.

(2) In the exercise of his rights and freedoms, everyone shall be subject only to such limitations as are determined by law solely for the purpose of securing due recognition and respect for the rights and freedoms of others and of meeting the just requirements of morality, public order and the general welfare in a democratic society.

(3) These rights and freedoms may in no case be exercised contrary to the purposes and principles of the United Nations.

Article 30. Nothing in this Declaration may be interpreted as implying for any State, group or person any right to engage in any activity or to perform any act aimed at the destruction of any of the rights and freedoms set forth herein.

Nobel Peace Prize Winners: 1981–2005

When the scientist, industrialist and inventor Alfred Nobel died in 1896, he made provision in his will for his fortune to be used for prizes in Physics, Chemistry, Physiology or Medicine, Literature and Peace. A prize for Economics was added later.

The Norwegian Nobel Committee awards the Nobel Peace Prize, and the Nobel Foundation in Stockholm (founded 1900; Mailing address: Box 5232, SE-10245, Stockholm, Sweden) awards the other five prizes. The Prize Awarding Ceremony takes place on 10 Dec., the anniversary of Nobel's death. The last 25 recipients of the Nobel Peace Prize, worth 10m. Sw. kr. in 2005, are:

2005 – Mohamed ElBaradei and the IAEA for their efforts to prevent nuclear energy from being used for military purposes and to ensure that nuclear energy for peaceful purposes is used in the safest possible way.

2004 – Wangari Maathai (Kenya) for her contribution to sustainable development, democracy and peace.

2003 – Shirin Ebadi (Iran) for her work fighting for democracy and the rights of women and children.

2002 – Jimmy Carter (USA) for his decades of untiring effort to find peaceful solutions to international conflicts, to advance democracy and human rights, and to promote economic and social development.

2001 – the United Nations and Kofi Annan for a better organized and more peaceful world.

2000 – Kim Dae-jung for his work for democracy and human rights in South Korea and in East Asia in general, and for peace and reconciliation with North Korea in particular.

1999 – *Médecins Sans Frontières* (Doctors Without Borders) in recognition of the organization's pioneering humanitarian work on several continents.

1998 – John Hume and David Trimble for their efforts to find a peaceful solution to the conflict in Northern Ireland.

1997 – ICBL (*International Campaign to Ban Landmines*) and Jody Williams for their work for the banning and clearing of anti-personnel mines.

1996 – Carlos Felipe Ximenes Belo and José Ramos-Horta for their work towards a just and peaceful solution to the conflict in East Timor.

1995 – Joseph Rotblat and the *Pugwash Conferences on Science and World Affairs* for their efforts to diminish the part played by nuclear arms in international politics and eventually to eliminate such arms.

1994 – Yasser Arafat (Chairman of the Executive Committee of the PLO, President of the Palestinian National Authority), Shimon Peres (Foreign Minister of Israel) and Yitzhak Rabin (Prime Minister of Israel) for their efforts to create peace in the Middle East.

1993 – Nelson Mandela (Leader of the ANC) and Fredrik Willem De Klerk (President of the Republic of South Africa).

1992 – Rigoberta Menchú Tum (Guatemala) for his campaign work for human rights, especially for indigenous peoples.

1991 – Aung San Suu Kyi (Myanmar), opposition leader and human rights advocate.

1990 – Mikhail Sergeyevich Gorbachev (president of the USSR) for helping bring the Cold War to an end.

1989 – The 14th Dalai Lama (Tenzin Gyatso) for his religious and political leadership of the Tibetan people.

1988 – *The United Nations Peace-Keeping Forces.*

1987 – Oscar Arias Sánchez (President of Costa Rica) for initiating peace negotiations in Central America.

1986 – Elie Wiesel (USA), author and humanitarian.

1985 – *International Physicians for the Prevention of Nuclear War*, Boston, USA.

1984 – Desmond Mpilo Tutu (South Africa, Bishop of Johannesburg) for his work against apartheid.

1983 – Lech Wałęsa (Poland), founder of Solidarity and human rights campaigner.

1982 – Alva Myrdal (Sweden) and Alfonso García Robles (Mexico) for their work as delegates to the United Nations General Assembly on Disarmament.

1981 – *Office of the United Nations High Commissioner for Refugees*, Geneva, Switzerland.

Norwegian Nobel Committee Headquarters: Det Norske Nobelinstitutt, Drammensveien 19, N-0255 Oslo, Norway. *Website:* http://www.nobel.no/

United Nations System

Operational Programmes and Funds. The total operating expenses for the entire UN system, including the World Bank, IMF and all the UN funds, programmes and specialized agencies, came to US$12,379m. in 2001.

Social and economic development, aimed at achieving a better life for people everywhere, is a major part of the UN system of organizations. In the forefront of efforts to bring about such progress is the United Nations Development Programme (UNDP), the world's largest agency for multilateral technical and pre-investment co-operation. It is the funding source for most of the technical assistance provided for sustainable human development by the UN system, and in 2000 helped people in 174 countries and territories, supporting some 5,000 projects, which focus on poverty elimination, environmental regeneration, job creation and the advancement of women.

UNDP assistance is provided only at the request of governments and in response to their priority needs, integrated into overall national and regional plans. Its activities are funded mainly by voluntary contributions outside the regular UN budget. 87% of the UNDP's core programme funds go to countries with an annual per capita GNP of US$750 or less, which are home to 90% of the world's poorest peoples. Headquartered in New York, the UNDP is governed by a 36-member Executive Board, representing both developing and developed countries.

Administrator: Kemal Derviş (Turkey).

United Nations development agencies include the *United Nations Children's Fund (UNICEF)*. It was established in 1946 by the United Nations General Assembly as the United Nations International Children's Emergency Fund, to meet the emergency needs of children of post-war Europe. In 1953 the organization became a permanent part of the UN and its mandate was expanded to carry out long-term programmes to benefit children worldwide. Guided by the Convention on the Rights of the Child and its Optional Protocols, UNICEF supports low-cost community-based programmes in immunization, nutrition, education, HIV/AIDS, water supply, environmental sanitation, gender issues and development, and child protection in more than 158 countries and territories. In 2001, with the assistance of UNICEF, WHO and other key partners, a record 575m. children were vaccinated against polio. UNICEF is the largest supplier of vaccines to developing countries, providing 40% of the world's doses of vaccine for children. UNICEF also provides relief and rehabilitation assistance in emergencies.

UNICEF served as the substantive secretariat for the UN General Assembly Special Session on Children held in New York from 8–10 May 2002, and supported a wide range of consultations and events around the world to ensure that children and young people had a voice in the process and in the Session itself. The Special Session adopted the outcome document, 'A World Fit For Children', setting 21 concrete time-bound goals for children on four key priorities: promoting healthy lives; providing quality education for all; protecting children against abuse, exploitation and violence; and combating HIV/AIDS.

In 2003 UNICEF intensified its '25 by 2005' campaign to accelerate progress in 25 countries where girls fall behind boys in enrolment, and where intensified actions would make the greatest impact.

UNICEF works towards eliminating the worst forms of child labour, protecting children affected by armed conflict and, in 2003, also supported programmes for children orphaned by HIV/AIDS in 38 countries in sub-Saharan Africa.

Executive Director: Ann Veneman (USA).

The United Nations Population Fund (UNFPA) was established in 1969 and is the world's largest multilateral source of population assistance. About a quarter of all population assistance from donor nations to developing countries is channeled through UNFPA. The fund extends assistance to developing countries at their request to help them address reproductive health and population issues, and raises awareness of these issues in all countries.

In 2005 UNFPA provided assistance to some 146 developing nations, with special emphasis on increasing the quality of reproductive health services, ending gender discrimination and violence, formulating effective population policies and reducing the spread of HIV/AIDS.

UNFPA's main objectives are to expand access to comprehensive reproductive health care, including family planning and sexual health, skilled birth attendance, and emergency obstetric care, to all couples and individuals in or before the year 2015. It also supports population and development strategies that enable capacity-building in population programming. UNFPA's strategy focuses on helping to meet the needs of individual women and men. Key to this approach is providing women with more choices through expanded access to education, health services and employment opportunities, and promoting the equal rights of women all over the world. UNFPA's *The State of World Population* report is published annually.

Executive Director: Thoraya Obaid (Saudi Arabia).

The UN Environment Programme (UNEP), established in 1972, works to encourage sustainable development through sound environmental practices everywhere. UNEP has its headquarters in Nairobi, Kenya and other offices in Paris, Geneva, Bangkok, Washington, D.C., New York, Osaka, Manama and Mexico City. Its activities cover a wide range of issues, from atmosphere and terrestrial ecosystems, to the promotion of environmental science and information, to an early warning and emergency response capacity to deal with environmental disasters and emergencies. UNEP's present priorities include: environmental information, assessment and research; enhanced co-ordination of environmental conventions and development of policy instruments; fresh water; technology transfer and industry; and support to Africa. Information networks and monitoring systems established by the UNEP include: the Global Environment Information Exchange Network (INFOTERRA); Global Resource Information Database (GRID); the International Register of Potentially Toxic Chemicals (IRPTC); and the recent UNEP.net, a web-based interactive catalogue and multifaceted portal that offers access to environmentally relevant geographic, textual and pictoral information. In June 2000 the World Conservation and Monitoring Centre (WCMC) based in Cambridge, UK became UNEP's key biodiversity assessment centre. UNEP's latest state-of-the-environment report is the *GEO Year Book, 2006*.

Executive Director: Klaus Töpfer (Germany).

Other UN programmes working for development include: the *UN Conference on Trade and Development (UNCTAD)*, which promotes international trade, particularly by developing countries, in an attempt to increase their participation in the global economy; and the *World Food Programme (WFP)*, the world's largest international food aid organization, which is dedicated to both emergency relief and development programmes.

The *UN Centre for Human Settlements (Habitat)*, which assists over 600m. people living in health-threatening housing conditions, was established in 1978. The 58-member *UN Commission on Human Settlements (UNCHS)*, Habitat's governing body, meets every two years. The Centre serves as the focal point for human settlements action and the co-ordination of activities within the UN system.

In addition to its regular programmes, the UNDP administers various special-purpose funds, such as the *UN Capital Development Fund (UNCDP)*, a multilateral donor agency working to develop new solutions for poverty reduction in the least developed countries, the *United Nations Volunteers (UNV)* and the *UN Development Fund for Women (UNIFEM)*, whose mission is the empowerment of women and gender equality in all levels of development planning and practice. Its three areas of immediate concern are: strengthening women's economic capacity; engendering governance and leadership; and promoting women's rights. Together with the World Bank and UNEP, the UNDP is one of the managing partners of the Global Environment Facility (GEF), a US$2,000m. fund to help countries translate global concerns into national action so as to help fight ozone depletion, global warming, loss of biodiversity and pollution of international waters.

The United Nations Development Programme is active in 166 countries. At country level, it is responsible for all UN development activity. The head of each country office acts as Resident Co-ordinator for UNDP.

The United Nations Office on Drugs and Crime (UNODC) educates the world about the dangers of drug abuse; strengthens international action against drug production, trafficking and drug related crime; promotes efforts to reduce drug abuse, particularly among the young and vulnerable; builds local, national and international partnerships to address drug issues; provides information, analysis and expertise on the drug issue; promotes international co-operation in crime prevention and control; supports the development of criminal justice systems; and assists member states in addressing the challenges and threats posed by the changing nature of transnational organized crime.

Executive Director: Antonio Maria Costa (Italy).

The UN work in crime prevention and criminal justice aims to lessen the human and material costs of crime and its impact on socio-economic development. The UN Congress on the Prevention of Crime and Treatment of Offenders has convened every five years since 1955 and provides a forum for the presentation of policies and progress. The Tenth Crime Congress (Vienna, 2000) discussed how to promote the rule of law and to strengthen the criminal justice system and also international co-operation in combating transnational organized crime. The *Commission on Crime Prevention and Criminal Justice*, a functional body of ECOSOC, established in 1992, seeks to strengthen UN activities in the field, and meets annually in Vienna. The interregional research and training arm of the UN crime and criminal justice programme is the *United Nations Interregional Crime and Justice Research Institute (UNICRI)* in Rome. An autonomous body, it seeks through action-oriented research to contribute to the formulation of improved policies in crime prevention and control.

Humanitarian assistance to refugees and victims of natural and man-made disasters is also an important function of the UN system. The main refugee organizations within the system are the *Office of the United Nations High Commissioner for Refugees (UNHCR)* and the *United Nations Relief and Works Agency for Palestine Refugees in the Near East (UNRWA)*.

UNHCR was created in 1951 to resettle 1·2m. European refugees left homeless in the aftermath of the Second World War. It was initially envisioned as a temporary office with a projected lifespan of three years. However, in 2003, in a move to strengthen UNHCR's capacity to carry out its work more effectively, the General Assembly removed the time limitation on the organization's mandate and extended it indefinitely, until 'the refugee problem is solved'. Today, with some 17m. persons of concern across the globe, UNHCR has become one of the world's principal humanitarian agencies. Its Executive Committee currently comprises 66 member states. With its Headquarters in Geneva, UNHCR has some 6,300 staff, 83% of whom work in field locations in 115 countries across the globe, and has twice been awarded the Nobel Peace Prize. UNHCR is a subsidiary organ of the United Nations General Assembly.

The work of UNHCR is humanitarian and non-political. International protection is its primary function. Its main objective is to promote and safeguard the rights and interests of refugees. In so doing UNHCR devotes special attention to promoting access to asylum and seeks to improve the legal, material and physical safety of refugees in their country of residence. Crucial to this status is the principle of *non-refoulement*, which prohibits the expulsion from or forcible return of refugees to a country where they may have reason to fear persecution. UNHCR pursues its objectives in the field of protection by encouraging the conclusion of intergovernmental legal instruments in favour of refugees, by supervising the implementation of their provisions and by encouraging Governments to adopt legislation and administrative procedures for the benefit of refugees. UNHCR is often called upon to provide material assistance (e.g. the provision of food, shelter, medical care and essential supplies) while durable solutions are being sought. Durable solutions generally take one of three forms: voluntary repatriation, local integration or resettlement in another country.

UNHCR works in tandem with governmental and non-governmental organizations, and within the UN framework one of its closest partnerships is with the World Food Programme (WFP). Other bodies with which significant collaborative work is undertaken include UNICEF, WHO, UNDP, ILO, the UN Centre for Human Settlements (UN-Habitat), the Joint UN Programme on HIV/AIDS (UNAIDS), the UN Department of Peacekeeping Operations (DPKO), the Office for the Coordination of Humanitarian Affairs (OCHA), the Office of the High Commissioner for Human Rights (OHCHR), the International Organization for Migration (IOM), the Red Cross/Red Crescent Movement Institutions (ICRC and IFRC) and many non-governmental organizations (NGOs). The Office also liaises closely with the World Bank and affiliated institutions, particularly in helping refugees to rebuild their lives and communities once they have returned home. At present, UNHCR is funded almost entirely by voluntary contributions. In 2004 UNHCR's expenditure amounted to approximately US$1bn.

High Commissioner: António Guterres (Portugal).

UNRWA was created by the General Assembly in 1949 as a temporary, non-political agency to provide relief to the nearly 750,000 people who became refugees as a result of the disturbances during and after the creation of the State of Israel in the former British Mandate territory of Palestine. 'Palestine refugees', as defined by UNRWA's mandate, are persons or descendants of persons whose normal residence was Palestine for at least two years prior to the 1948 conflict and who, as a result of the conflict, lost their homes and means of livelihood. UNRWA has also been called upon to help persons displaced by renewed hostilities in the Middle East in 1967. The situation of Palestine refugees in south Lebanon, affected in the aftermath of the 1982 Israeli invasion of Lebanon, was of special concern to the Agency in 1984. UNRWA provides education, health, relief and social services to eligible refugees among the 3·7m. registered Palestine refugees in its five fields of operation: Jordan, Lebanon, Syria, the West Bank and the Gaza Strip. Its mandate is renewed at intervals by the UN

General Assembly, and has most recently been extended until 30 June 2008. The budget for 2005 amounted to US$367·6m.

Commissioner-General: Peter Hansen (Denmark).

The UN's activities in the field of human rights are the primary responsibility of the *High Commissioner for Human Rights*, a post established in 1993 under the direction and authority of the Secretary-General. The High Commissioner is nominated by the Secretary-General for a four-year term, renewable once. The principal co-ordinating human rights organ of the UN was until mid-2006 the 53-member *Commission on Human Rights*, set up by ECOSOC in 1946. On 15 March 2006 the UN General Assembly voted overwhelmingly to abolish the Commission after it was criticized for having member countries with poor human rights records. A new 47-member *Human Rights Council* was established as its successor and was scheduled to hold its first meeting on 19 June 2006.

Training and Research Institutes. There are six training and research institutes within the UN, all of them autonomous.

United Nations Institute for Training and Research (UNITAR). The Institute was established in 1965 with a mandate to enhance the effectiveness of the UN in achieving its major objectives. Recently, its focus has shifted to training, with basic research being conducted only if extra-budgetary funds can be made available. Training is provided at various levels for agencies and institutions of UN member states, diplomatic personnel, universities, public interest groups and the private sector. By the end of 2003 some 65,000 participants from 200 countries had attended UNITAR courses, seminars or workshops.

Address: Palais des Nations, 1211 Geneva 10, Switzerland.
Website: http://www.unitar.org

United Nations Institute for Disarmament Research (UNIDIR). Established in 1980 to undertake research on disarmament and security with the aim of assisting the international community in their disarmament thinking, decisions and efforts. Through its research projects, publications, small meetings and expert networks, UNIDIR promotes creative thinking and dialogue on both current and future security issues, through examination of topics as varied as tactical nuclear weapons, refugee security, computer warfare, regional confidence-building measures and small arms.

Address: Palais des Nations, 1211 Geneva 10, Switzerland.
Website: http://www.unidir.org

United Nations Research Institute for Social Development (UNRISD). Established in 1963 to conduct multidisciplinary research into the social dimensions of contemporary problems affecting development, it aims to provide governments, development agencies, grassroots organizations and scholars with a better understanding of how development policies and processes of economic, social and environmental change affect different social groups.

Address: Palais des Nations, 1211 Geneva 10, Switzerland.
Website: http://www.unrisd.org

United Nations International Research and Training Institute for the Advancement of Women (INSTRAW). Established by ECOSOC and endorsed by the General Assembly in 1976, INSTRAW provides training, conducts research, and collects and disseminates information to promote gender equality and stimulate and assist women's advancement. Its 11-member Board of Trustees, which reports to ECOSOC, meets annually to review its programme and to formulate the principles and guidelines for INSTRAW's activities.

Address: POB 21747, Santo Domingo, Dominican Republic.
Website: http://www.un-instraw.org

United Nations University (UNU). Sponsored jointly by the UN and UNESCO, UNU is guaranteed academic freedom by a charter approved by the General Assembly in 1973. It is governed by a 28-member Council of scholars and scientists, of whom 24 are appointed by the Secretary-General of the UN and the Director-General of UNESCO. Unlike a traditional university with a campus, students and faculty, it works through networks of collaborating institutions and individuals to undertake multidisciplinary research on problems of human survival, development and welfare; and to strengthen research and training capabilities in developing countries. It also provides postgraduate fellowships and PhD internships to scholars and scientists from developing countries. The University focuses its work within two programme areas: peace and governance, and environment and development.

Address: 53–70 Jingumae 5-chome, Shibuya-ku, Tokyo 150-8925, Japan.
Website: http://www.unu.edu

University for Peace. Founded in 1980 to conduct research on, *inter alia*, disarmament, mediation, the resolution of conflicts, preservation of the environment, international relations, peace education and human rights. It organizes graduate degree programmes, undergraduate certificate programmes, and seminars and training for mid-career professionals.

Address: POB 138, Ciudad Colon, Costa Rica.
Website: http://www.upeace.org/

Information. The *UN Statistics Division* in New York provides a wide range of statistical outputs and services for producers and users of statistics worldwide, facilitating national and international policy formulation, implementation and monitoring. It produces printed publications of statistics and statistical methods in the fields of international merchandise trade, national accounts, demography and population, gender, industry, energy, environment, human settlements and disability, as well as general statistics compendiums including the *Statistical Yearbook* and *World Statistics Pocketbook*. Many of its databases are available on CD-ROM, diskette, magnetic tape and the Internet.

Website: http://unstats.un.org

UN Information Centre. Public Inquiries Unit, Department of Public Information, Room GA-57, United Nations Plaza, New York, NY 10017. There are also 33 UN Information Centres in other parts of the world.

Website: http://www.un.org

Specialized Agencies of the UN

The intergovernmental agencies related to the UN by special agreements are separate autonomous organizations which work with the UN and each other through the co-ordinating machinery of the Economic and Social Council. Of these, 19 are 'Specialized Agencies' within the terms of the UN Charter, and report annually to ECOSOC.

Food and Agriculture Organization of the United Nations (FAO)

Origin. In 1943 the International Conference on Food and Agriculture, at Hot Springs, Virginia, set up an Interim Commission, based in Washington, with a remit to establish an organization. Its Constitution was signed on 16 Oct. 1945 in Quebec City. Today, membership totals 187 countries. The European Union was made a member as a 'regional economic integration organization' in 1991.

Aims and Activities. The aims of FAO are to raise levels of nutrition and standards of living; to improve the production and distribution of all food and agricultural products from farms, forests and fisheries; to improve the living conditions of rural populations; and, by these means, to eliminate hunger. Its priority objectives are to encourage sustainable agriculture and rural development as part of a long-term strategy for the conservation and management of natural resources; and to ensure the availability of adequate food supplies, by maximizing stability in the flow of supplies and securing access to food by the poor.

In carrying out these aims, FAO promotes investment in agriculture, better soil and water management, improved yields of crops and livestock, agricultural research and the transfer of technology to developing countries; and encourages the conservation of natural resources and rational use of fertilizers and pesticides; the development and sustainable utilization of marine and inland fisheries; the sustainable management of forest resources and the combating of animal disease. Technical assistance is provided in all of these fields, and in nutrition, agricultural engineering, agrarian reform, development communications, remote sensing for climate and vegetation, and the prevention of post-harvest food losses. In addition, FAO works to maintain global biodiversity with the emphasis on the genetic diversity of crop plants and domesticated animals; and plays a major role in the collection, analysis and dissemination of information on agricultural production and commodities. Finally, FAO acts as a neutral forum for the discussion of issues, and advises governments on policy, through international conferences like the 1996 World Food Summit in Rome and the World Food Summit: five years later, held in Rome in 2002.

Special FAO programmes help countries prepare for, and provide relief in the event of, emergency food situations, in particular through the rehabilitation of agriculture after disasters. The *Special Programme for Food Security*, launched in 1994, is designed to assist target countries to increase food production and productivity as rapidly as possible, primarily through the widespread adoption by farmers of available improved production technologies, with the emphasis on high-potential areas. FAO provides support for the global co-ordination of the programme and helps attract funds. The *Emergency Prevention System for Transboundary Animal and Plant Pests and Diseases (EMPRES)*, established in 1994, strengthens FAO's existing contribution to the prevention, control and eradication of diseases and pests before they compromise food security, with locusts and rinderpest among its priorities. The *Global Information and Early Warning System (GIEWS)* provides current information on the world food situation and identifies countries threatened by shortages to guide potential donors. The interagency Food Insecurity and Vulnerability Information and Mapping System initiative (FIVIMS) was established in 1997, with FAO as its secretariat. More than 60 countries have nominated national focal points to co-ordinate efforts to collect and use statistics related to food insecurity more efficiently. Together with the UN, FAO sponsors the *World Food Programme (WFP)*.

Finance. The budget for the 2004–05 biennium was US$749·1m. FAO's Regular Programme budget, financed by contributions from member governments, covers the cost of its secretariat and Technical Co-operation Programme (TCP), and part of the costs of several special programmes.

FAO continues to provide technical advice and support through its field programmes in all areas of food and agriculture, fisheries, forestry and rural development. In 2003 expenditures in the field totalled US$405m., which paid for 1,600 field programme projects, about 380 of which were emergency operations. The programme was funded from FAO's regular budget, trust funds and the UN Development Programme. In addition, since 1964, over 1,470 projects prepared with the FAO Investment Centre's assistance have been approved for financing for total investments of US$76bn., including support loans from financing institutions of US$44bn.

Organization. The FAO Conference, composed of all members, meets every other year to determine policy and approve the FAO's budget and programme. The 49-member Council, elected by the Conference, serves as FAO's governing body between conference sessions. Much of its work is carried out by dozens of regional or specialist commissions, such as the Asia-Pacific Fishery Commission, the European Commission on Agriculture and the Commission on Plant Genetic Resources. The Director-General is elected for a renewable six-year term.

Headquarters: Viale delle Terme di Caracalla, 00100 Rome, Italy.
Website: http://www.fao.org
Director-General: Jacques Diouf (Senegal).

Publications. Unasylva (quarterly), 1947 ff.; *The State of Food and Agriculture* (annual), 1947 ff.; *Animal Health Yearbook* (annual), 1957 ff.; *Statistical Yearbook* (annual), 2004 ff.; *FAO Commodity Review* (annual), 1961 ff.; *Yearbook of Forest Products* (annual), 1947 ff.; *Yearbook of Fishery Statistics* (in two volumes); *FAO Plant Protection Bulletin* (quarterly); *Environment and Energy Bulletin; Food Outlook* (monthly); *The State of World Fisheries and Aquaculture* (annual); *The State of the World's Forests; World Watch List for Domestic Animal Diversity; The State of Food Insecurity in the World.*

International Bank for Reconstruction and Development (IBRD) — The World Bank

Origin. Conceived at the UN Monetary and Financial Conference at Bretton Woods (New Hampshire, USA) in July 1944, the IBRD, frequently called the World Bank, began operations in June 1946, its purpose being to provide funds, policy guidance and technical assistance to facilitate economic development in its poorer member countries. The Group comprises four other organizations (see below).

Activities. The Bank obtains its funds from the following sources: capital paid in by member countries; sales of its own securities; sales of parts of its loans; repayments; and net earnings. A resolution of the Board of Governors of 27 April 1988 provides that the paid-in portion of the shares authorized to be subscribed under it will be 3%. The Bank is self-supporting, raising most of its money on the world's financial markets. In the fiscal year ending 30 June 2002 it achieved a net income of US$2,778m. Income totalled US$7,876m. and expenditure US$5,952m.

In the fiscal year 2002 the Bank lent US$11·5bn. for 96 new operations in 40 countries. Cumulative lending had totalled US$371bn. by March 2003. 89% of borrowers took advantage of the new single-currency loans which became available in June 1996 to provide borrowers with the flexibility to select IBRD loan terms that are consistent with their debt-managing strategy and suited to their debt-servicing capacity. In order to eliminate wasteful overlapping of development assistance and to ensure that the funds available are used to the best possible effect, the Bank has organized consortia or consultative groups of aid-giving nations for many countries. These include Bangladesh, Belarus, Bolivia, Bulgaria, Egypt, Ethiopia, Jordan, Kazakhstan, Kenya, Kyrgyzstan, Macedonia, Malawi, Mauritania, Moldova, Mozambique, Nicaragua, Pakistan, Peru, Romania, Sierra Leone, Tanzania, the [Palestinian] West Bank and Gaza Strip, Zambia, Zimbabwe and the Caribbean Group for Co-operation in Economic Development.

For the purposes of its analytical and operational work, in 2003 the IBRD characterized economies as follows: low income (average annual *per capita* gross national income of $765 or less); lower middle income (between $766 and $3,035); upper middle income (between $3,036 and $9,385); and high income ($9,386 or more).

A wide variety of technical assistance is at the core of IBRD's activities. It acts as executing agency for a number of pre-investment surveys financed by the UN Development Programme. Resident missions have been established in 64 developing member countries and there are regional offices for East and West Africa, the Baltic States and South-East Asia which assist in the preparation and implementation of projects. The Bank maintains a staff college, the *Economic Development Institute* in Washington, D.C., for senior officials of member countries.

The Strategic Compact. Unanimously approved by the Executive Board in March 1997, the Strategic Compact set out a plan for fundamental reform to make the Bank more effective in delivering its regional programme and in achieving its basic mission of reducing poverty. Decentralizing the Bank's relationships with borrower countries is central to the reforms. The effectiveness of devolved country management and the bank's promotion of good governance and anti-corruption measures to developing countries are likely to be key policies of the new strategy.

Organization. As of Jan. 2006 the Bank had 184 members, each with voting power in the institution, based on shareholding which in turn is based on a country's economic growth. The president is selected by the Bank's Board of Executive Directors. The Articles of Agreement do not specify the nationality of the president but by custom the US Executive Director makes a nomination, and by a long-standing, informal agreement, the president is a US national (while the managing director of the IMF is European). The initial term is five years, with a second of five years or less.

European office: 66 avenue d'Iéna, 75116 Paris, France. *London office:* New Zealand House, Haymarket, London SW1Y 4TE, England. *Tokyo office:* Kokusai Building, 1–1, Marunouchi 3-chome, Chiyoda-ku, Tokyo 100, Japan.

Headquarters: 1818 H St., NW, Washington, D.C., 20433, USA.
Website: http://www.worldbank.org
President: Paul Wolfowitz (USA).

Publications. World Bank Annual Report; Summary Proceedings of Annual Meetings; The World Bank and International Finance Company, 1986; The World Bank Atlas (annual); Catalog of Publications, 1986 ff.; World Development Report (annual); World Bank Economic Review (thrice yearly); World Bank and the Environment (annual); World Bank News (weekly); World Bank Research Observer; World Tables (annual); Social Indicators of Development (annual); ICSID Annual Report; ICSID Review: Foreign Investment Law Journal (twice yearly); Research News (quarterly).

Current Leaders

Paul Wolfowitz

Position
President

Introduction
An American political scientist and military strategist in successive US administrations, Paul Wolfowitz was responsible for shaping the country's foreign policy in the aftermath of the Cold War. He is a 'neoconservative' and is considered to be one of the intellectual driving forces behind America's 'War on Terror' and an architect of the invasion of Iraq in 2003. He took over as president of the World Bank on 1 June 2005.

Early Life
Paul Dundes Wolfowitz was born on 22 Dec. 1943 in Brooklyn, New York, the son of a Polish mathematician of Jewish descent. The family moved to Ithaca, New York, and he attended school there. In 1957, aged 14, Wolfowitz spent a year in Israel while his father taught at Haifa University. Graduating from Ithaca High School in 1961, he went to Cornell University to study mathematics and chemistry. He was influenced by the conservative views of Allan Bloom, a professor of philosophy at the university, and embarked on postgraduate study in political science under Bloom's mentor, Leo Strauss, and Albert Wohlstetter at the University of Chicago. He wrote his doctorate on the dangers of a nuclearized Middle East, combining his research with lecturing in political science at Yale University from 1970.

In 1972 Wolfowitz joined the US Arms Control and Disarmament Agency (ACDA), providing research and strategy documents on defence policy for President Nixon's administration at the height of the Cold War. ACDA often made the case for US military intervention abroad as a means of preventing future arms proliferation and conflict, a view that contrasted sharply with the policy of détente and containment adopted by President Jimmy Carter from 1976. Wolfowitz joined the Pentagon in 1977, where he was employed as deputy assistant secretary of defense for regional programs. While exploring potential threats to US interests, his team produced a report warning of possible Soviet attempts to gain control over oil supplies in the Persian Gulf.

Having resigned from the Pentagon in early 1980, Wolfowitz became visiting professor at the Paul H. Nitze School of Advanced International Studies (SAIS) at Johns Hopkins University. His return to academe was short-lived, however. In 1981, following Ronald Reagan's inauguration as president, he was offered the position of head of foreign policy planning at the US State Department. Wolfowitz's team, which included his protégés Lewis Libby and Francis Fukuyama, opposed attempts to begin dialogue with the Palestine Liberation Organization (PLO) and criticized the US government's support of Saddam Hussein in the Iran–Iraq war. In 1982 Wolfowitz shifted his focus eastwards; he was appointed assistant secretary for East Asian and Pacific affairs by the new US Secretary of State, George Shultz, and was involved in the diplomacy of shoring-up American interests in the Philippines against a backdrop of revolution and the ousting of the country's pro-US dictator, Ferdinand Marcos.

In 1986 Wolfowitz was appointed the US ambassador to Indonesia, a position he held for three years. He learnt the language and was reportedly a popular and able diplomat but also attracted criticism for failing to promote democracy or challenge corrupt practices under the country's authoritarian leader, General Suharto. Returning to Washington, D.C. in 1989, Wolfowitz served as US under-secretary for defense policy in the government of George H. Bush. He was given the task of reshaping American military policy in the aftermath of the Cold War. Following the victory of the Democrat Bill Clinton in the presidential election of Nov. 1992, Wolfowitz left politics and returned to academic life, as dean of the School of Advanced International Studies at Johns Hopkins University. He also worked as a consultant to the aerospace and defence firm Northrop Grumman.

In 1997 Wolfowitz joined the Project for a New American Century (PNAC), a 'neoconservative' organization advocating 'American Global Leadership'. Although the PNAC's calls for military intervention in Iraq were ignored by the Clinton administration, they gained an audience after George W. Bush's victory in the 2000 presidential election. Wolfowitz, having been sworn in as deputy secretary of defense on 2 March 2001, advocated military strikes in Afghanistan (in the aftermath of the attacks on New York on 11 Sept. 2001) and the invasion of Iraq in March 2003. He spoke optimistically about the USA being welcomed as 'liberators' and suggested that costs would be met by revenues from Iraq's oilfields. On 16 March 2005 Wolfowitz was nominated by President Bush to be the next head of the World Bank, replacing James Wolfensohn. Despite some opposition, the directors of the World Bank, representing 184 countries, unanimously approved Wolfowitz as the organization's new president.

Career in Office

Wolfowitz's appointment as president of the World Bank was deemed controversial. There was criticism of his hawkish stance in successive US administrations, but also praise from some East Asian governments, who pointed to Wolfowitz's experience of working in the region. At a press conference in late June 2005, Wolfowitz said he wanted the World Bank to do 'as much as it possibly can' to support development in Africa. He added that other priorities include supporting equal rights for women to help foster economic growth, and harmonizing the way the bank works with other aid agencies to reduce the administrative burden on countries that receive assistance.

International Development Association (IDA)

A lending agency established in 1960 and administered by the IBRD to provide assistance on concessional terms to the poorest developing countries. Its resources consist of subscriptions and general replenishments from its more industrialized and developed members, special contributions, and transfers from the net earnings of IBRD. Officers and staff of the IBRD serve concurrently as officers and staff of the IDA at the World Bank headquarters.

In fiscal year 2002 disbursements totalled US$6,603m. for 813 operations. Pakistan was the single largest recipient of disbursements from adjustment lending.

International Finance Corporation (IFC)

Established in 1956 to help strengthen the private sector in developing countries, through the provision of long-term loans, equity investments, quasi-equity instruments, standby financing, and structured finance and risk management products. It helps to finance new ventures and assist established enterprises as they expand, upgrade or diversify. In partnership with other donors, it provides a variety of technical assistance and advisory services to public and private sector clients. To be eligible for financing, projects must be profitable for investors, must benefit the economy of the country concerned, and must comply with IFC's environmental and social guidelines.

The majority of its funds are borrowed from the international financial markets through public bond issues or private placements. Its authorized capital is US$2,361m.; total capital at 30 June 2004 was US$7,782m. IFC committed US$5,633m. in total financing in fiscal year 2004 and committed 217 projects in 65 developing countries. It has 178 members.

Headquarters: 2121 Pennsylvania Ave., NW, Washington, D.C., 20433, USA.
Website: http://www.ifc.org
President: Paul Wolfowitz (USA).

Publications. Annual Reports; Lessons of Experience (series); *Paths Out of Poverty.*

Multilateral Investment Guarantee Agency (MIGA)

Established in 1988 to encourage the flow of foreign direct investment to, and among, developing member countries, MIGA is the insurance arm of the World Bank. It provides investors with investment guarantees against non-commercial risk, such as expropriation and war, and gives advice to governments on improving climate for foreign investment. It may insure up to 90% of an investment, with a current limit of US$50m. per project. In March 1999 the Council of Governors adopted a resolution for a capital increase for the Agency of approximately US$850m. In addition US$150m. was transferred to MIGA by the World Bank as operating capital. In Jan. 2006 it had 167 member countries. It is located at the World Bank headquarters (see above).

Headquarters: 1818 H Street, NW, Washington, D.C., 20433, USA.
Website: http://www.miga.org

International Centre for Settlement of Investment Disputes (ICSID)

Founded in 1966 to promote increased flows of international investment by providing facilities for the conciliation and arbitration of disputes between governments and foreign investors. The Centre does not engage in such conciliation or arbitration. This is the task of conciliators and arbitrators appointed by the contracting parties, or as otherwise provided for in the Convention. Recourse to conciliation and arbitration by members is entirely voluntary.

In Jan. 2006 its Convention had been signed by 155 countries. 84 cases had been concluded by it and 72 were pending. Disputes involved a variety of investment sectors: agriculture, banking, construction, energy, health, industrial, mining and tourism.

ICSID also undertakes research, publishing and advisory activities in the field of foreign investment law. Like IDA, IFC and MIGA, it is located at the World Bank headquarters in Washington (see above).

Website: http://www.worldbank.org/icsid
Secretary-General: Roberto Dañino (Peru).

Publications. ICSID Annual Report; News from ICSID; ICSID Review: Foreign Investment Law Journal; Investment Laws of the World; Investment Treaties.

Further Reading

Caufield, C., *Masters of Illusion: The World Bank and the Poverty of Nations.* London, 1997
Nelson, P. J., *The World Bank and Non-Government Organizations: The Limits of Apolitical Development.* London, 1995
Salda, A. C. M., *World Bank* [Bibliography]. Oxford and New Brunswick (NJ), 1994
Wilson, C. R., *The World Bank Group: A Guide to Information Sources.* New York, 1991

International Civil Aviation Organization (ICAO)

Origin. The Convention providing for the establishment of the ICAO was drawn up by the International Civil Aviation Conference held in Chicago in 1944. A Provisional International Civil Aviation Organization (PICAO) operated for 20 months until the formal establishment of ICAO on 4 April 1947. The Convention on International Civil Aviation superseded the provisions of the Paris Convention of 1919 and the Pan American Convention on Air Navigation of 1928.

Functions. It assists international civil aviation by establishing technical standards for safety and efficiency of air navigation and promoting simpler procedures at borders; develops regional plans for ground facilities and services needed for international flying; disseminates air-transport statistics and prepares studies on aviation economics; fosters the development of air law conventions and provides technical assistance to states in developing civil aviation programmes.

Organization. The principal organs of ICAO are an Assembly, consisting of all members of the Organization, and a Council, which is composed of 36 states elected by the Assembly for three years, which meets in virtually continuous session. In electing these states, the Assembly must give adequate representation to: (1) states of major importance in air transport; (2) states which make the largest contribution to the provision of facilities for the international civil air navigation; and (3) those states not otherwise included whose election would ensure that all major geographical areas of the world were represented. The budget approved for 2006 was US$65·8m.

Headquarters: 999 University St., Montreal, PQ, Canada H3C 5H7.
Website: http://www.icao.int
President of the Council: Dr Assad Kotaite (Lebanon).
Secretary-General: Taïeb Chérif (Algeria).

Publications. Annual Report of the Council; ICAO Journal (six yearly; quarterly in Russian); ICAO Training Manual; Aircraft Accident Digest; Procedures for Air Navigation Services.

International Fund for Agricultural Development (IFAD)

The idea for an International Fund for Agricultural Development arose at the 1974 World Food Conference. An agreement to establish IFAD entered into force on 30 Nov. 1977, and the agency began its operations the following month. IFAD's purpose is to mobilize additional funds for improved food production and better nutrition among low-income groups in developing countries through projects and programmes directly benefiting the poorest rural populations while preserving their natural resource base. In line with the Fund's focus on the rural poor, its resources are made available in highly concessional loans and grants. By March 2003 the Fund had invested US$7·7bn. in loans and US$35·4m. in grants financing 628 projects in 115 developing countries.

Organization. The highest body is the Governing Council, on which all 164 member countries are represented. Operations are overseen by an 18-member Executive Board (with 17 alternate members), which is responsible to the Governing Council. The Fund works with many co-operating institutions, including the World Bank, regional development banks and financial agencies, and other UN agencies; many of these co-finance IFAD projects.

Headquarters: 107 Via del Serafico, Rome 00142, Italy.
Website: http://www.ifad.org
President: Lennart Båge (Sweden).

Publications. Annual Report; IFAD Update (thrice yearly); Staff Working Papers (series); The State of World Rural Poverty.

International Labour Organization (ILO)

Origin. The ILO was established in 1919 under the Treaty of Versailles as an autonomous institution associated with the League of Nations. An agreement establishing its relationship with the UN was approved in 1946, making the ILO the first Specialized Agency to be associated with the UN. An intergovernmental agency with a tripartite structure, in which representatives of governments, employers and workers participate, it seeks through international action to improve labour and living conditions, to promote productive employment and social justice for working people everywhere. On its fiftieth anniversary in 1969 it was awarded the Nobel Peace Prize. In Jan. 2006 it numbered 178 members.

Functions. One of the ILO's principal functions is the formulation of international standards in the form of International Labour Conventions and Recommendations. Member countries are required to submit Conventions to their competent national authorities with a view to ratification. If a country ratifies a Convention it agrees to bring its laws into line with its terms and to report periodically how these regulations are being applied. More than 7,000 ratifications of 185 Conventions had been deposited by 30 Sept. 2004. Procedures are in place to ascertain whether Conventions thus ratified are effectively applied. Recommendations do not require ratification, but member states are obliged to consider them with a view to giving effect to their provisions by legislation or other action. By 30 Sept. 2005 the International Labour Conference had adopted 195 Recommendations.

The ILO's programme and budget set out four strategic objectives for the Organization at the turn of the century: i) to promote and realize fundamental principles and rights at work; ii) to create greater opportunities for women and men to secure decent employment and income; iii) to enhance the coverage and effectiveness of social protection for all; iv) to strengthen tripartism and social dialogue.

Activities. In addition to its research and advisory activities, the ILO extends technical co-operation to governments under its regular budget and under the UN Development Programme and Funds-in-Trust in the fields of employment promotion, human resources development (including vocational and management training), development of social institutions, small-scale industries, rural development, social security, industrial safety and hygiene, productivity, etc. Technical co-operation also includes expert missions and a fellowship programme.

In 1994 the technical services offered by the ILO to its tripartite constituents came under scrutiny leading to a re-affirmation of technical co-operation as one of the principal means of ILO action. Since 1994 the process of implementing the new Active Partnership Policy made significant progress and today 16 multidisciplinary advisory teams are engaged in a dialogue with ILO constituents centred on the identification of Country Objectives to form the basis of the ILO's contribution.

In June 1998 delegates to the 86th International Labour Conference adopted a solemn ILO Declaration in Fundamental Principles and Rights at Work, committing the Organization's member states to respect the principles inherent in a number of core labour standards: the right of workers and employers to freedom of association and the effective right to collective bargaining, and to work toward the elimination of all forms of forced or compulsory labour, the effective abolition of child labour and the elimination of discrimination in respect of employment and occupation.

In June 1999 delegates to the 87th International Labour Conference adopted a new Convention banning the worst forms of child labour. The International Labour Conference 2005 adopted a budget of US$594·3m. for the 2006–07 biennium.

Field Activities. The ILO's *International Institute for Labour Studies* promotes the study and discussion of policy issues. The core theme of its activities is the interaction between labour institutions, development and civil society in a global economy. It identifies emerging social and labour issues by opening up new areas for research and action; and encourages systematic dialogue on social policy between the tripartite constituency of the ILO and the international academic community, and other public opinion-makers.

The *International Training Centre* of the ILO, in Turin, was set up in 1965 to lead the training programmes implemented by the ILO as part of its technical co-operation activities. Member states and the UN system also call on its resources and experience, and a UN Staff College was established on the Turin Campus in 1996.

Organization. The International Labour Conference is the supreme deliberative organ of the ILO; it meets annually in Geneva. National delegations are composed of two government delegates, one employers' delegate and one workers' delegate. The Governing Body, elected by the Conference, is the Executive Council. It is composed of 28 government members, 14 workers' members and 14 employers' members. Ten governments of countries of industrial importance hold permanent seats on the Governing Body. These are: Brazil, China, Germany, France, India, Italy, Japan, Russia, UK and USA. The remaining 18 government members are elected every three years. Workers' and employers' representatives are elected as individuals, not as national candidates. The ILO has a branch office in London (for UK and Republic of Ireland), and regional offices in Addis Ababa (for Africa), Bangkok (for Asia and the Pacific), Lima (for Latin America and the Caribbean) and Beirut (for Arab States).

> *Headquarters:* International Labour Office, CH-1211 Geneva 22, Switzerland.
> *London Office:* Vincent House, Vincent Square, London SW1P 2NB, UK.
> *Website:* http://www.ilo.org
> *Director-General:* Juan Somavia (Chile).
> *Governing Body Chairman:* Carlos A. Tomada (Argentina).

Publications (available in English, French and Spanish) include: *International Labour Review; Bulletin of Labour Statistics; Official Bulletin and Labour Education; Yearbook of Labour Statistics* (annual); *World Labour Report* (annual); *World Employment Report* (annual); *Encyclopaedia of Occupational Health and Safety; Key Indicators of the Labour Market (KILM); World of Work* (three a year).

International Maritime Organization (IMO)

Origin. The International Maritime Organization (formerly the InterGovernmental Maritime Consultative Organization) was established as a specialized agency of the UN by a convention drafted in 1948 at a UN maritime conference in Geneva. The Convention became effective on 17 March 1958 when it had been ratified by 21 countries, including seven with at least 1m. gross tons of shipping each. The IMCO started operations in 1959 and changed its name to the IMO in 1982.

Functions. To facilitate co-operation among governments on technical matters affecting merchant shipping, especially concerning safety and security at sea; to prevent and control marine pollution caused by ships; to facilitate international maritime traffic. The IMO is responsible for convening international maritime conferences and for drafting international maritime conventions. It also provides technical assistance to countries wishing to develop their maritime activities, and acts as a depositary authority for international conventions regulating maritime affairs. *The World Maritime University (WMU),* at Malmö, Sweden, was established in 1983; the *IMO International Maritime Law Institute (IMLI),* at Valletta, Malta and the *IMO International Maritime Academy,* at Trieste, Italy, both in 1989.

Organization. The IMO has 166 members and three associate members. The Assembly, composed of all member states, normally meets every two years. The 40-member Council acts as governing body between sessions. There are four principal committees (on maritime safety, legal matters, marine environment protection and technical co-operation), which submit reports or

recommendations to the Assembly through the Council, and a Secretariat. The budget for 2004–05 amounted to £46,194,900.

> *Headquarters:* 4 Albert Embankment, London SE1 7SR, UK.
> *Website:* http://www.imo.org
> *e-mail:* info@imo.org
> *Secretary-General:* Efthimios Mitropoulos (Greece).

Publication. IMO News.

International Monetary Fund (IMF)

The International Monetary Fund was established on 27 Dec. 1945 as an independent international organization and began financial operations on 1 March 1947; its relationship with the UN is defined in an agreement of mutual co-operation which came into force on 15 Nov. 1947. The first amendment to the IMF's Articles creating the special drawing right (SDR) took effect on 28 July 1969. The second amendment took effect on 1 April 1978. The third amendment came into force on 11 Nov. 1992; it allows for the suspension of voting and related rights of a member which persists in its failure to settle its outstanding obligations to the IMF.

Aims. To promote international monetary co-operation, the expansion of international trade and exchange rate stability; to assist in the removal of exchange restrictions and the establishment of a multilateral system of payments; and to alleviate any serious disequilibrium in members' international balance of payments by making the financial resources of the IMF available to them, usually subject to economic policy conditions to ensure the revolving nature of IMF resources.

Activities. Each member of the IMF undertakes a broad obligation to collaborate with the IMF and other members to ensure orderly exchange arrangements and to promote a system of stable exchange rates. In addition, members are subject to certain obligations relating to domestic and external policies that can affect the balance of payments and the exchange rate. The IMF makes its resources available, under proper safeguards, to its members to meet short-term or medium-term payment difficulties. The first allocation of SDRs was made on 1 Jan. 1970. A total of SDR 21·4bn. has been allocated to members in two allocations, completed in 1981.

To enhance its balance of payments assistance to its members, the IMF established a Compensatory Financing Facility on 27 Feb. 1963; temporary oil facilities in 1974 and 1975; a Trust Fund in 1976; and an Extended Fund Facility (EFF) for medium-term assistance to members with special balance of payments problems on 13 Sept. 1974. In March 1986 it established the Structural Adjustment Facility (SAF) to provide assistance to low-income countries. In Dec. 1987 it established the Enhanced Structural Adjustment Facility (ESAF) to provide further assistance to low-income countries facing high levels of indebtedness. In Oct. 1999 the ESAF was renamed as the Poverty Reduction and Growth Facility (PRGF) to reflect the increased focus on poverty reduction. In Dec. 1997 the Supplemental Reserve Facility (SRF) was established to provide short-term assistance to countries experiencing exceptional balance of payments problems owing to a large short-term financing need resulting from a sudden disruptive loss of market confidence, reflected in pressure on the capital account and the member's reserves.

Capital Resources. The capital resources of the IMF comprise SDRs and currencies that the members pay under quotas calculated for them when they join the IMF. A member's quota is largely determined by its economic position relative to other members; it is also linked to their drawing rights on the IMF under both regular and special facilities, their voting power and their share of SDR allocations. Every IMF member is required to subscribe to the IMF an amount equal to its quota. An amount not exceeding 25% of the quota has to be paid in reserve assets, the balance in the member's own currency. The members with the largest quotas are: 1st, the USA; joint 2nd, Germany and Japan; joint 4th, France and the UK.

An increase of almost 60% in IMF quotas became effective in Nov. 1992 as a result of the 9th General Review of Quotas. Quotas were not increased under the 10th General Review. In the 11th General Review, the IMF's Executive Board adopted a resolution at its 1997 annual meeting, approving a one-time equity allocation of SDRs of SDR 21,400m., which would equalize all members' ratio of SDRs to quota at 29·3%. The Board also agreed to recommend a 45% increase in IMF quotas, which would raise total quotas from SDR 145,300m., in Sept. 1997, to SDR 209,500m.; an 85% majority of member countries is required for the quota increase to take effect. In Jan. 1999 the 85% majority had been met. As of Feb. 2003, on the conclusion of the 12th General Review, total quotas were SDR 213,000m.

Borrowing Resources. The IMF is authorized under its Articles of Agreement to supplement its resources by borrowing. In Jan. 1962 a four-year agreement was concluded with ten industrial members (Belgium, Canada, France, Germany, Italy, Japan, Netherlands, Sweden, UK, USA) who undertook to lend the IMF up to US$6,000m. in their own currencies, if this should be needed to forestall or cope with an impairment of the international monetary system. Switzerland subsequently joined the group. These arrangements, known as the General Arrangements to Borrow (GAB), have been extended several times. In early 1983 agreement was reached to increase the credit arrangements under the GAB to SDR 17,000m.; to permit use of GAB resources in transactions with IMF members that are not GAB participants; to authorize Swiss participation; and to permit borrowing arrangements with non-participating members to be associated with the GAB. Saudi Arabia and the IMF have entered into such an arrangement under which the IMF will be able to borrow up to SDR 1,500m. to assist in financing purchases by any member for the same purpose and under the same circumstances as in the GAB. The changes became effective by 26 Dec. 1983.

Surveillance. In order to oversee the compliance of members with their obligations under the Articles of Agreement, the IMF is required to exercise firm surveillance over members' exchange rate policies. In April 1996 the IMF established the Special Data Dissemination Standard (SDDS) to improve access to reliable economic statistical information for member countries that have, or are seeking, access to international capital markets. In Dec. 1997 it established the General Data Dissemination Standard (GDDS), which applies to all member countries and focuses on improved production and dissemination of core economic data. Information on both are available on the IMF's website.

The IMF works with the IBRD (World Bank) to address the problems of the most heavily indebted poor countries (most in Sub-Saharan Africa) through their Initiative for the Heavily Indebted Poor Countries (HIPCs). The HIPC Initiative is designed to ensure that HIPCs with a sound track record of economic adjustment receive debt relief sufficient to help them attain a sustainable debt situation over the medium term. The HIPC Initiative was enhanced in late 1999 to provide deeper and more rapid debt relief to a larger number of countries. The Poverty Reduction and Growth Facility (PRGF) is a concessional facility that helps low-income member countries with loans at a 0·5% annual interest rate with biannual repayments over five and a half to ten years. Members qualifying for PRGF funding may borrow up to 140% (under exceptional circumstances, 185%) of their quota under a three-year arrangement.

Organization. The highest authority is the Board of Governors, on which each member government is represented. Normally the Governors meet once a year, and may take votes by mail or other means between meetings. The Board of Governors has delegated many of its powers to the 24 executive directors in Washington, who are appointed or elected by individual member countries or groups of countries. The managing director is selected by the executive directors and serves as chairman of the Executive Board, but may not vote except in case of a tie. The term of office is for five years, but may be extended or terminated at the discretion of the executive directors. The managing director is responsible for the ordinary business of the IMF, under the direction of the executive directors, and supervises a staff of about 2,600. Under a long-standing, informal agreement, the managing director is European (while the President of the World Bank is a US national). There are three deputy managing directors. As of Jan. 2006 the IMF had 184 members.

The *IMF Institute* is a specialized department of the IMF providing training in macroeconomic analysis and policy, and related subjects, for officials of member countries, at the Fund's headquarters in Washington, the Joint Vienna Institute, the Joint Africa Institute, the Singapore Regional Training Institute, the IMF-Arab Monetary Fund Regional Training Program, the Joint China-IMF Training Program and the Joint Regional Training Center for Latin America. In addition, the IMF operates regional training centres: the Pacific Financial Technical Assistance Center (PFTAC), the Caribbean Regional Technical Assistance Center (CARTAC) and two Regional Technical Assistance Centers in Africa (AFRITAC). Since its establishment in 1964 the Institute has trained more than 10,900 officials from 181 countries.

Headquarters: 700 19th St. NW, Washington, D.C., 20431, USA.
Offices in Paris and Geneva and a regional office for Asia and the Pacific in Tokyo.
Website: http://www.imf.org
Managing Director: Rodrigo Rato (Spain).

Publications. Annual Report; Annual Report on Exchange Arrangements and Exchange Restrictions; International Financial Statistics (monthly); *IMF Survey* (2 a month); *Balance of Payments Statistics Yearbook; Staff Papers* (4 a year); *IMF Economic Issues pamphlets; IMF Occasional Paper series; Direction of Trade Statistics* (quarterly); *Government Finance Statistics Yearbook; World Economic Outlook* (2 a year); *The International Monetary Fund, 1945–65: Twenty Years of International Monetary Co-operation,* 3 vols. Washington, 1969; de Vries, M. G., *The International Monetary Fund, 1966–1971: The System Under Stress,* 2 vols. Washington, 1976; *The International Monetary Fund 1972–1978: Co-operation on Trial.* 3 vols. Washington, 1985; *Silent Witness, International Monetary Fund 1979–89.* Washington, 2001.

Further Reading

Humphreys, N. K., *Historical Dictionary of the International Monetary Fund.* Metuchen (NJ), 1994
James, H., *International Monetary Cooperation since Bretton Woods.* OUP, 1996
Salda, A. C. M., *The International Monetary Fund.* [Bibliography] Oxford and New Brunswick (NJ), 1993

International Telecommunication Union (ITU)

Origin. Founded in Paris in 1865 as the International Telegraph Union, the International Telecommunication Union took its present name in 1934 and became a specialized agency of the United Nations in 1947. Therefore, the ITU is the world's oldest intergovernmental body.

Functions. To maintain and extend international co-operation for the improvement and rational use of telecommunications of all kinds, and promote and offer technical assistance to developing countries in the field of telecommunications; to promote the development of technical facilities and their most efficient operation to improve the efficiency of telecommunication services, increasing their usefulness and making them, so far as possible, generally available to the public; to harmonize the actions of nations in the attainment of these ends.

Organization. The supreme organ of the ITU is the Plenipotentiary Conference, which normally meets every four years. A 46-member Council, elected by the Conference, meets annually in Geneva and is responsible for ensuring the co-ordination of the four permanent organs at ITU headquarters: the General Secretariat; Radiocommunication Sector; Telecommunication Standardization Sector; and Telecommunication Development Sector. The Secretary-General is also elected by the Conference. ITU has 189 member countries; a further 576 scientific and technical companies, public and private operators, broadcasters and other organizations are also ITU members.

Headquarters: Place des Nations, CH-1211 Geneva 20, Switzerland.
Website: http://www.itu.int
Secretary-General: Yoshio Utsumi (Japan).

United Nations Educational, Scientific and Cultural Organization (UNESCO)

Origin. UNESCO's Constitution was signed in London on 16 Nov. 1945 by 37 countries and the Organization came into being in Nov. 1946 on the premise that: 'Since wars begin in the minds of men, it is in the minds of men that the defences of peace must be constructed'. In Jan. 2006 UNESCO had 191 members including the UK, which rejoined in 1997 having left in 1985, and the USA, which rejoined in 2003 having left in 1984. They include six associate members which are not members of the UN (Aruba; British Virgin Islands; Cayman Islands; Macao; Netherlands Antilles; Tokelau).

Aims and Activities. UNESCO's primary objective is to contribute to peace and security in the world by promoting collaboration among the nations through education, science, communication, culture, and the social and human sciences in order to further universal respect for justice, democracy, the rule of the law, human rights and fundamental freedoms, affirmed for all peoples by the UN Charter.

Education. Various activities support and foster national projects to renovate education systems and develop alternative educational strategies towards a goal of lifelong education for all. The World Development Forum in Dakar in 2000 set an agenda for progress towards this aim expressed as six goals. Two of these, attaining universal primary education by 2015 and gender parity in schooling by 2005, were also UN Millennium Development Goals. Three elements define the context for pursuing this purpose: promoting education as a fundamental right, improving the quality of education and stimulating experimentation, innovation and policy dialogue. There are regional and sub-regional offices for education in 57 countries.

Science. UNESCO seeks to promote international scientific co-operation and encourages scientific research designed to improve living conditions and to protect ecosystems. Several international programmes to better understand the Earth's resources towards the advancement of sustainable development have been initiated, including the Man and the Biosphere (MAB) programme, the International Hydrological Programme (IHP), the Intergovernmental Oceanographic Commission (IOC) and the International Geoscience Programme (IGCP).

Culture. Promoting cultural diversity and intercultural dialogue is the principal priority of UNESCO's cultural programmes. The World Heritage Centre, with its World Heritage List now covering 812 sites around the world, promotes the preservation of monuments and natural sites.

Communication. Activities are geared to promoting the free flow of information, freedom of expression, press freedom, media independence and pluralism. Another priority is to bridge the digital divide and help disadvantaged groups in North and South participate in the knowledge societies created through the information and communication technologies. To this end, UNESCO promotes access to public domain information and free software, as well as encouraging the creation of local content.

Social and Human Sciences. UNESCO works to advance knowledge and intellectual co-operation in order to facilitate social transformations conducive to justice, freedom, peace and human dignity. It seeks to identify evolving social trends and develops and promotes principles and standards based on universal values and ethics, such as the *Universal Declaration on the Human Genome and Human Rights* (1997) and the *International Declaration on Human Genetic Data* (2003).

Organization. The General Conference, composed of representatives from each member state, meets biennially to decide policy, programme and budget. A 58-member Executive Board elected by the Conference meets twice a year and there is a Secretariat. In addition, national commissions act as liaison groups between UNESCO and the educational, scientific and cultural life of their own countries. The budget for the biennium 2004–05 was US$610m.

There are also twelve separate UNESCO institutes: the International Bureau of Education (IBE), in Geneva; the UNESCO Institute for Education (UIE), in Hamburg; the International Institute for Educational Planning (IIEP), in Paris; the International Institute for Capacity Building in Africa (IICBA), in Addis Ababa; the International Institute for Higher Education in Latin America and the Caribbean (IESALC), in Caracas; the Institute for Information Technologies in Education (IITE), in Moscow; the UNESCO Institute for Statistics (UIS), in Montreal; the Institute for Water Education (UNESCO-IHE), in Delft; the UNESCO International Centre for Technical and Vocational Education and Training (UNEVOC), in Bonn; the International Centre for Theoretical Physics (ICTP) and the Third World Academy of Sciences (TWAS), both in Trieste; and the European Centre for Higher Education (CEPES), in Bucharest.

Headquarters: UNESCO House, 7 Place de Fontenoy, 75352 Paris 07 SP, France.
Website: http://www.unesco.org
Director-General: Koïchiro Matsuura (Japan).

Periodicals (published quarterly). *Museum International; International Social Science Journal; The New Courier; Prospects; Copyright Bulletin; World Heritage Review.*

United Nations Industrial Development Organization (UNIDO)

Origin. UNIDO was established by the UN General Assembly in 1966 and became a UN specialized agency in 1985.

Aims. UNIDO helps developing countries, and countries with economies in transition, in their fight against marginalization and poverty in today's globalized world. It mobilizes knowledge, skills, information and technology to promote productive employment, a competitive economy and a sound environment.

UNIDO focuses its efforts on relieving poverty by fostering productivity growth and economic development.

Activities. As a global forum, UNIDO generates and disseminates knowledge relating to industrial matters and provides a platform for the various actors—decision makers in the public and private sectors, civil society organizations and the policy-making community in general—to enhance co-operation, establish dialogue and develop partnerships in order to address the challenges ahead. As a technical co-operation agency, UNIDO designs and implements programmes to support the industrial development efforts of its clients. It also offers tailor-made specialized support for programme development. The two core functions are both complementary and mutually supportive. On the one hand, experience gained in the technical co-operation work of UNIDO can be shared with policy makers; on the other, the Organization's analytical work shows where technical co-operation will have the greatest impact by helping to define priorities.

Organization. As part of the United Nations common system, UNIDO has the responsibility for promoting industrialization throughout the developing world, in co-operation with its 171 member states. Its headquarters are in Vienna, Austria, and with 28 smaller country and regional offices, 13 investment and technology promotion offices and a number of offices related to specific aspects of its work, UNIDO maintains an active presence in the field. The General Conference meets every two years to determine policy and approve the budget. The 53-member Industrial Development Board (membership according to constitutional lists) is elected by the General Conference. The General Conference also elects a 27-member Programme and Budget Committee for two years and appoints a Director-General for four years.

Finance. UNIDO's financial resources come from the regular and operational budgets, as well as contributions for technical co-operation activities, budgeted at US$133·7m., US$22·0m. and US$193·6m. respectively, totalling US$349·3m. for 2002–03. Administrative costs represent 7·6% of the total budget estimates. The regular budget derives from assessed contributions from member states.

Technical co-operation is funded mainly from voluntary contributions from donor countries and institutions as well as UNDP, the Multilateral Fund for the Implementation of the Montreal Protocol, the Global Environment Facility and the Common Fund for Communities.

> *Headquarters:* Vienna International Centre, POB 300, A-1400 Vienna, Austria.
> *Website:* http://www.unido.org
> *Director-General:* Kandeh Yumkella (Sierra Leone).

Publications. UNIDOScope (weekly Internet newspaper); *UNIDO Annual Report; Industry for Growth into the New Millennium, African Industry 2000: The Challenge of Going Global; Using Statistics for Process Control and Improvement: An Introduction to Basic Concepts and Techniques; Guidelines for Project Evaluation; Practical Appraisal for Industrial Project Applications—Application of Social Cost-Benefit Analysis in Pakistan; Manual for the Evaluation of Industrial Projects; Guide to Practical Project Appraisal—Social Benefit-Cost Analysis in Developing Countries; Manual for Small Industrial Businesses: Project Design and Appraisal; Manual for the Preparation of Industrial Feasibility Studies; Manual on Technology Transfer Negotiations; Guidelines for Infrastructure Development Through Build-Operate-Transfer (BOT) Projects; Gearing up for a New Development Agenda; Reforming the UN System: UNIDO's Need-Driven Model; World Directory of Industrial Information Sources; Woodworking Machinery: A Manual on Selection Options; Competition and the World Economy; The International Yearbook of Industrial Statistics 2005; Industrial Development Report 2005.*

Universal Postal Union (UPU)

Origin. The UPU was established in 1875, when the Universal Postal Convention adopted by the Postal Congress of Berne on 9 Oct. 1874 came into force. It has 190 member countries.

Functions. The UPU provides co-operation between postal services and helps to ensure a universal network of up-to-date products and services. To this end, UPU members are united in a single postal territory for the reciprocal exchange of correspondence. A Specialized Agency of the UN since 1948, the UPU is governed by its Constitution, adopted in 1964 (Vienna), and subsequent protocol amendments (1969, Tokyo; 1974, Lausanne; 1979, Rio de Janeiro; 1984, Hamburg; 1989, Washington; 1994, Seoul; 1999, Beijing; 2004, Bucharest).

Organization. It is composed of a Universal Postal Congress which meets every four years; a 41-member Council of Administration, which meets annually and is responsible for supervising the affairs of the UPU between Congresses; a 40-member Postal Operations Council; and an International Bureau which functions as the permanent secretariat, responsible for strategic planning and programme budgeting. A new UPU body, the Consultative Committee, was created at the Bucharest Congress. This committee represents the external shareholders of the postal sector as well as UPU member countries. The budget for the biennial period 2003–04 was 71·4m. Swiss francs.

> *Headquarters:* Weltpoststrasse 4, 3000 Berne 15, Switzerland.
> *Website:* http://www.upu.int
> *Director-General:* Edouard Dayan (France).

Publications. Bucharest World Postal Strategy (2004), Postal Statistics (annual), *Postal Market 2004: Review and Outlook, Post 2005—Follow-up and Trends* (2000), *Union Postale* (quarterly), *POST*Code* (also in CD-ROM).

World Health Organization (WHO)

Origin. An International Conference convened by the UN Economic and Social Council to consider a single health organization resulted in the adoption on 22 July 1946 of the Constitution of the World Health Organization, which came into force on 7 April 1948.

Functions. WHO's objective, as stated in the first article of the Constitution, is 'the attainment by all peoples of the highest possible level of health'. As the directing and co-ordinating authority on international health, it establishes and maintains collaboration with the UN, specialized agencies, governments, health administrations, professional and other groups concerned with health. The Constitution also directs WHO to assist governments to strengthen their health services; to stimulate and advance work to eradicate diseases; to promote maternal and child health, mental health, medical research and the prevention of accidents; to improve standards of teaching and training in the health professions, and of nutrition, housing, sanitation, working conditions and other aspects of environmental health. The Organization is also empowered to propose conventions, agreements and regulations, and make recommendations about international health matters; to revise the international nomenclature of diseases, causes of death and public health practices; to develop, establish and promote international standards concerning foods, biological, pharmaceutical and similar substances.

Methods of work. Co-operation in country projects is undertaken only on the request of the government concerned, through the six regional offices of the Organization. Worldwide technical services are made available by headquarters. Expert committees, chosen from the 55 advisory panels of experts, meet to advise the Director-General on a given subject. Scientific groups and consultative meetings are called for similar purposes. To further the education of health personnel of all categories, seminars, technical conferences and training courses are organized, and advisors, consultants and lecturers are provided. WHO awards fellowships for study to nationals of member countries.

Activities. The main thrust of WHO's activities in recent years has been towards promoting national, regional and global strategies for the attainment of the main social target of the member states: 'Health for All in the 21st Century', or the attainment by all citizens of the world of a level of health that will permit them to lead a socially and economically productive life. Almost all countries indicated a high level of political commitment to this goal; and guiding principles for formulating corresponding strategies and plans of action were subsequently prepared.

The WHO has organized its responsibilities into four priorities: enhancing global health security, which includes preventing, detecting and containing disease outbreaks, preparing the world for controlling pandemic influenza, combating new diseases such as SARS, preparing for emergencies and responding quickly to minimize death and suffering; accelerating progress on the Millennium Development Goals (MDGs) by reducing maternal and child mortality, tackling the global epidemics of HIV/AIDS, tuberculosis and malaria, promoting safe drinking water and sanitation, promoting gender equality and increasing access to essential medicines; responding to non-communicable disease such as cardiovascular diseases, diabetes and cancers by reducing smoking, promoting a healthy diet and physical activity and reducing violence and road traffic crashes; promoting equity in health through strengthening health systems to reach everyone, particularly the most vulnerable people.

World Health Day is observed on 7 April every year. The 2006 theme for World Health Day was Working Together for Health; the theme for 2005 was Make Every Mother and Child Count. World No-Tobacco Day is held on 31 May each year; International Day Against Drug Abuse on 26 June; World AIDS Day on 1 Dec.

The 50th World Health Assembly which met in 1997 adopted numerous resolutions on public health issues. *The World Health Report, 1997: Conquering suffering, enriching humanity* focused on 'non-communicable diseases'. It warned that the human and social costs of cancer, heart disease and other chronic diseases will rise unless confronted now.

The number of cancer cases was expected to double in most countries by 2020. The incidence of lung cancers in women and prostate cancers in men in the Western world is becoming far more prevalent. The incidence of other cancers is also rising rapidly, especially in developing countries. Heart disease and stroke, the leading causes of death in richer nations, will become more common in poorer countries. Globally, diabetes will more than double by 2025, with the number of people affected rising from about 135m. to 300m., and there is likely to be a huge rise in some mental and neurological disorders, especially dementias and particularly Alzheimer's disease. Already an estimated 23m. people suffer from dementia, and at least 400m. suffer from other mental disorders ranging from mood and personality disorders to neurological conditions like epilepsy, which affects some 40m. worldwide.

These projected increases are reported to be owing to a combination of factors, not least population ageing and the rising prevalence of unhealthy lifestyles. Average life expectancy at birth globally reached 65 years in 1996. It is now well over 70 years in many countries and exceeds 80 years in some. In 1997 there were an estimated 380m. people over 65 years. By 2020 that number is expected to rise to more than 690m.

The ten leading killer diseases in the world are: coronary heart disease, 7·2m. deaths annually; cancer (all sites), 6·2m.;

cerebrovascular disease, 4·6m.; acute lower respiratory infection, 3·7m.; perinatal conditions, 3·6m.; tuberculosis, 2·9m.; chronic obstructive pulmonary disease, 2·9m.; diarrhoea and dysentery, 2·5m.; HIV/AIDS, 2·3m.; malaria, 2·1m. Tobacco-related deaths, primarily from lung cancer and circulatory disease, amount to 4·9m. a year. Smoking accounts for one in seven cancer cases worldwide, and if the trend of increasing consumption in many countries continues, the epidemic has many more decades to run.

In response, WHO has called for an intensified and sustained global campaign to encourage healthy lifestyles and attack the main risk factors responsible for many of these diseases: unhealthy diet, inadequate physical activity, smoking and obesity.

The WHO Framework Convention on Tobacco Control (WHO FCTC) was developed in response to the globalization of the tobacco epidemic, and is the first global health treaty negotiated under the auspices of the World Health Organization. The provisions in the Treaty require countries to ban tobacco advertising, sponsorship and promotion; establish new packaging and labelling of tobacco products with prominent health warnings; establish smoking bans in public places, increase price and tax on tobacco products; and strengthen legislation to clamp down on tobacco smuggling, among other measures.

World Health Report, 2005: Make every mother and child count stated that pregnancy and childbirth and their consequences are still the leading causes of death, disease and disability among women of reproductive age in developing countries. It noted that over 300m. women in the developing world suffer from illness brought about by pregnancy and childbirth and that 529,000 die each year. The report also highlighted that approximately 2·2m. women living with HIV/AIDS give birth each year and that there are 3·3m. stillbirths annually. More than 50% of all child deaths occur in just six countries: China, the Democratic Republic of the Congo, Ethiopia, India, Nigeria and Pakistan.

The report suggests that the death toll could be sharply reduced 'through wider use of key interventions and a "continuum of care" approach for mother and child that begins before pregnancy and extends through childbirth and into the baby's childhood'. This is primarily based on the estimate that two-thirds of women in less developed countries and less than one-third in the least developed countries have their children delivered by a skilled attendant. It was stated that almost 90% of all deaths among children under five years of age are attributable to just six conditions and that many of these deaths are avoidable through existing interventions including the increased availability of drugs and healthcare workers. The report adds that putting in place the health workforce needed for scaling up maternal, newborn and child health services is the most pressing task and that US$3·5bn. is required for human resources alone.

Joint UN Programme on HIV/AIDS (UNAIDS). In 1996 the Assembly reviewed implementation of the global strategy for the prevention and control of AIDS, and progress of the Joint UN Programme on HIV/AIDS (UNAIDS), which became operational in 1996. The impact of the HIV/AIDS epidemic is seen to be expanding and intensifying, particularly in developing countries, and new resource mobilization mechanisms were called for to support countries in combating HIV/AIDS. The Assembly requested WHO to facilitate the incorporation of UNAIDS-specific policies, norms and strategies into the activities of WHO at global, regional and country levels, and to collaborate in all aspects of resource mobilization for HIV/AIDS activities.

Organization. The principal organs of WHO are the World Health Assembly, the Executive Board and the Secretariat. Each of the 192 member states has the right to be represented at the Assembly, which meets annually in Geneva. The 32-member Executive Board is composed of technically qualified health experts designated by as many member states as elected by the Assembly. The Secretariat consists of technical and administrative staff headed by a Director-General, who is appointed for not more than two five-year terms. Health activities in member countries are carried out through regional organizations which have been established in Africa (Brazzaville), South-East Asia (New Delhi), Europe (Copenhagen), Eastern Mediterranean (Cairo) and Western Pacific (Manila). The Pan American Sanitary Bureau in Washington serves as the regional office of WHO for the Americas. It is the oldest international health agency in the world and is the secretariat of the Pan American Health Organization (PAHO). Co-operation in country projects is undertaken only at the request of the government concerned, through the six regional offices.

Finance. The total two-year budget planned for 2006–07 was US$3·3bn.

> *Headquarters*: Avenue Appia, CH-1211 Geneva 27, Switzerland.
> *Website*: http://www.who.int
> *Director-General*: Dr Lee Jong-wook (South Korea).

Publications. Annual Report on World Health; Bulletin of WHO (6 issues a year); International Digest of Health Legislation (quarterly); Health and Safety Guides; International Statistical Classification of Diseases and Related Health Problems; WHO Technical Report Series; WHO AIDS Series; Public Health Papers; World Health Statistics Annual; Weekly Epidemiological Record; WHO Drug Information (quarterly).

Current Leaders

Dr Lee Jong-wook

Position
Director-General

Introduction
Lee Jong-wook became director general of the World Health Organization in July 2003. Best known for his work in fighting tuberculosis and vaccine-preventable childhood diseases, he began working for the WHO in 1984. A respected administrator, he had a low political profile and was a surprise choice for the role.

Early Life
Lee was born on 12 April 1945 in Seoul, South Korea. He graduated in medicine from Seoul National University and took a Masters in public health from the University of Hawaii. Having worked in leper colonies in South Korea, he became a leprosy consultant to the WHO in 1983, based in the South Pacific.

Lee was employed in technical, managerial and policy-making roles and headed high profile programmes including vaccines and immunizations and the Stop Tuberculosis campaign.

When incumbent Dr Gro Harlem Brundtland declined to stand for re-election in 2003 Lee was one of five candidates and the only one already working within the organization. In a run-off against Peter Piot, the head of UNAIDS, Lee won by 17 votes to 15.

Career in Office
Lee was sworn in on 21 July 2003, becoming the first South Korean to hold control of a UN agency. He was widely expected to continue many of the policies championed by his predecessor but will look to restore internal stability following several restructurings during the early years of the 21st century. Lee has named the fight against AIDS, particularly in Africa, as his top priority.

World Intellectual Property Organization (WIPO)

Origin. The roots of the World Intellectual Property Organization go back to the Paris Convention for the Protection of Industrial Property, adopted in 1883, and the Berne Convention for the Protection of Literary and Artistic Works (adopted 1886). The Convention establishing WIPO was signed at Stockholm in 1967 by 51 countries, and entered into force in April 1970. WIPO became a UN specialized agency in 1974.

Aims. To promote the protection of intellectual property throughout the world through co-operation among member states; and to ensure administrative co-operation among the intellectual property unions created by the Paris and Berne Conventions.

Intellectual property comprises two main branches: industrial property (inventions, trademarks and industrial designs) and copyright and neighbouring rights (literary, musical, artistic, photographic and audiovisual works).

Activities. There are three principal areas of activity: the progressive development of international intellectual property law; global protection systems and services; and co-operation for development. WIPO seeks to harmonize national intellectual property legislation and procedures; provide services for international applications for industrial property rights; exchange intellectual property information; provide training and legal and technical assistance to developing and other countries; facilitate the resolution of private intellectual property disputes; and marshal information technology as a tool for storing, accessing and using valuable intellectual property information. World Intellectual Property Day is held annually on 26 April.

New approaches to the progressive development of international intellectual property law. The development and application of international norms and standards is a fundamental part of WIPO's activities. It administers 23 treaties (15 on industrial property, eight on copyright). The Organization plays an increasing role in making national and regional systems for the registration of intellectual property more user-friendly by harmonizing and simplifying procedures.

Global protection systems and services. The most successful and widely used treaty is the Patent Co-operation Treaty (PCT), which implements the concept of a single international patent application that is valid in many countries. Once such application is filed, an applicant has time to decide in which countries to pursue the application, thereby streamlining procedures and reducing costs. In 2004 the PCT system recorded over 120,000 applications.

The treaties dealing with the international registration of marks and industrial designs are, respectively, the Madrid Agreement (and its Protocol) and the Hague Agreement. In 2004 there were 29,482 registrations of marks under the Madrid System. By the end of 2004 WIPO had registered nearly 35,000 international deposits of industrial designs.

Co-operation for development. On 1 Jan. 2000 many developing and other countries, as members of the World Trade Organization, brought their national legislative and administrative structures into conformity with the Agreement on Trade-Related Aspects of Intellectual Property Rights (TRIPS). WIPO and WTO agreed, in the framework of a Co-operation Agreement which entered into force on 1 Jan. 1996, and a Joint Initiative launched in July 1998, on a joint technical co-operation initiative to provide assistance to developing countries to meet their obligations to comply with the TRIPS Agreement. This represented a major step in the international harmonization of the scope, standards and enforcement of Intellectual Property rights.

The newly created WIPO Worldwide Academy co-ordinates training activities, originates new approaches and methods to expand the scope, impact and accessibility of WIPO programmes, and creates more effective training tailored for diverse-user groups. The Academy has also launched an Internet-based distance-learning programme.

Impact of digital technology on intellectual property law. WIPO takes a range of initiatives to tackle the implications of modern digital and communications technology for copyright and industrial property law, and in electronic commerce transcending national jurisdictions. The WIPO Arbitration and Mediation Centre was established in 1994 to provide online dispute-resolution services. The Centre developed an operational and legal framework for the administration of disputes, including those relating to new technologies such as Internet Domain Name Disputes.

Organization. WIPO has three governing bodies: the General Assembly, the Conference and the Co-ordination Committee. Each treaty administered by WIPO has one or more Governing Bodies of its own, composed of representatives of the respective member states. In addition, the Paris and Berne Unions have Assemblies and Executive Committees. The executive head of WIPO is the Director-General, who is elected by the General Assembly. In Jan. 2006 WIPO had 183 member states, with an international staff of around 850 from 86 countries. The approved budget for 2006–07 is 531m. Swiss francs, the majority of which is covered by revenue earned by the Organization's international registration and publication activities.

> *Official languages:* Arabic, Chinese, English, French, Russian and Spanish.
> *Headquarters:* 34 chemin des Colombettes, 1211 Geneva 20, Switzerland.
> *Website:* http://www.wipo.int
> *Director-General:* Dr Kamil Idris (Sudan).

Periodicals. Industrial Property and Copyright (monthly, bi-monthly, in Spanish); *PCT Gazette* (weekly); *PCT Newsletter* (monthly); *International Designs Bulletin* (monthly); *WIPO Gazette of International Marks* (fortnightly); *Intellectual Property in Asia and the Pacific* (quarterly).

World Meteorological Organization (WMO)

Origin. A 1947 (Washington) Conference of Directors of the International Meteorological Organization (est. 1873) adopted a Convention creating the World Meteorological Organization. The WMO Convention became effective on 23 March 1950 and WMO was formally established. It was recognized as a Specialized Agency of the UN in 1951.

Functions. (1) To facilitate worldwide co-operation in the establishment of networks of stations for the making of meteorological observations as well as hydrological or other geophysical observations related to meteorology, and to promote the establishment and maintenance of meteorological centres charged with the provision of meteorological and related services; (2) to promote the establishment and maintenance of systems for the rapid exchange of meteorological and related information; (3) to promote standardization of meteorological and related observations and ensure the uniform publication of observations and statistics; (4) to further the application of meteorology to aviation, shipping, water problems, agriculture and other human activities; (5) to promote activities in operational hydrology and to further close co-operation between meteorological and hydrological services; and (6) to encourage research and training in meteorology and, as appropriate, to assist in co-ordinating the international aspects of such research and training.

Organization. WMO has 181 member states and six member territories responsible for the operation of their own meteorological services. Congress, which is its supreme body, meets every four years to approve policy, programme and budget, and adopt regulations. The Executive Council meets at least once a year to prepare studies and recommendations for Congress, and supervises the implementation of Congress resolutions and regulations. It has 37 members, comprising the President and three Vice-Presidents, as well as the Presidents of the six Regional Associations (Africa, Asia, South America, North America, Central America and the Caribbean, South-West Pacific, Europe), whose task is to co-ordinate meteorological activity within their regions, and 27 members elected in their personal capacity. There are eight Technical Commissions composed of experts nominated by members of WMO, whose remit includes the following areas: basic systems, climatology, instruments and methods of observation, atmospheric sciences, aeronautical meteorology, agricultural meteorology, hydrology, oceanography and marine meteorology. A permanent Secretariat is maintained in Geneva. There are three regional offices for Africa, Asia and the Pacific, and the Americas. The budget for 2004–07 was 253·8m. Swiss francs.

> *Headquarters:* 7 bis, avenue de la Paix, Case Postale 2300, CH-1211 Geneva 2, Switzerland.
> *Website:* http://www.wmo.int
> *e-mail:* wmo@wmo.int
> *Secretary-General:* Michel Jarraud (France).

Publications. WMO Bulletin (quarterly); *WMO Annual Report.*

World Tourism Organization (UNWTO)

Origin. Established in 1925 in The Hague as the International Congress of Official Tourist Traffic Associations. Renamed the International Union for Official Tourism Organizations after the Second World War when it moved to Geneva, it was renamed the World Tourism Organization in 1975 and moved its headquarters to Madrid the following year.

The World Tourism Organization became an executing agency of the United Nations Development Programme in 1976 and in 1977 a formal co-operation agreement was signed with the UN itself. With a UN resolution on 23 Dec. 2003 the World Tourism Organization became a specialized agency of the United Nations.

Aims. The World Tourism Organization exists to help nations throughout the world maximize the positive impacts of tourism, such as job creation, new infrastructure and foreign exchange earnings, while at the same time minimizing negative environmental or social impacts.

Membership. The World Tourism Organization has three categories of membership: full membership which is open to all sovereign states; associate membership which is open to all territories not responsible for their external relations; and affiliate membership which comprises a wide range of organizations and companies working either directly in travel and tourism or in related sectors. In Jan. 2006 the World Tourism Organization had 146 full members, seven associate members and almost 350 affiliate members.

Organization. The General Assembly meets every two years to approve the budget and programme of work and to debate topics of vital importance to the tourism sector. The Executive Council is the governing board, responsible for ensuring that the organization carries out its work and keeps within its budget. The World Tourism Organization has six regional commissions—Africa, the Americas, East Asia and the Pacific, Europe, the Middle East and South Asia—which meet at least once a year. Specialized committees of World Tourism Organization members advise on management and programme content.

> *Headquarters:* Capitán Haya 42, 28020 Madrid, Spain.
> *Website:* http://www.world-tourism.org
> *Secretary-General:* Francesco Frangialli (France).

Publications. Yearbook of Tourism Statistics (annual); *Compendium of Tourism Statistics* (annual); *Travel and Tourism Barometer* (3 per year); *UNWTO News* (4 per year); *various others* (about 100 a year).

Other Organs Related to the UN

International Atomic Energy Agency (IAEA)

Origin. An intergovernmental agency, the IAEA was established in 1957 under the aegis of the UN and reports annually to the General Assembly. Its Statute was approved on 26 Oct. 1956 at a conference at UN Headquarters.

Functions. To accelerate and enlarge the contribution of atomic energy to peace, health and prosperity throughout the world; and to ensure that assistance provided by it or at its request or under its supervision or control is not used in such a way as to further any military purpose. In addition, under the terms of the Non-Proliferation Treaty, the Treaty of Tlatelolco, the Treaty of Rarotonga, the Pelindaba Treaty and the Bangkok Treaty: to verify states' obligation to prevent diversion of nuclear fissionable material from peaceful uses to nuclear weapons or other nuclear explosive devices.

Activities. The IAEA gives advice and technical assistance to developing countries on nuclear power development, nuclear safety and security, radioactive waste management, legal aspects of atomic energy use, and prospecting for and exploiting nuclear raw materials. In addition, it promotes the use of radiation and isotopes in agriculture, industry, medicine and hydrology through expert services, training courses and fellowships, grants of equipment and supplies, research contracts, scientific meetings and publications. During 2003 support for operational projects for technical co-operation involved 3,121 expert and lecturer assignments, 2,848 meeting and workshop participants, 2,107 participants in training courses and 1,411 fellows and visiting scientists.

Safeguards are the technical means applied by the IAEA to verify that nuclear equipment or materials are used exclusively for peaceful purposes. IAEA safeguards cover more than 95% of civilian nuclear installations outside the five nuclear-weapon states (China, France, Russia, UK and USA). These five nuclear-weapon states have concluded agreements with the Agency which permit the application of IAEA safeguards to all their civil nuclear activities. A total of 232 safeguards agreements in force in 148 states involved 2,363 safeguard inspections performed in 2003. Safeguards activities are applied routinely at over 900 facilities in 71 countries. A programme designed to prevent and combat illicit trafficking of nuclear weapons came into force in April 1996.

Organization. The Statute provides for an annual General Conference, a 35-member Board of Governors and a Secretariat headed by a Director-General. The IAEA had 139 member states in Jan. 2006.

There are also research laboratories in Austria and Monaco. *The International Centre for Theoretical Physics* was established in Trieste, in 1964, and is operated jointly by UNESCO and the IAEA.

> *Headquarters:* Vienna International Centre, PO Box 100, A-1400 Vienna, Austria.
> *Website:* http://www.iaea.org
> *Director-General:* Dr Mohamed ElBaradei (Egypt).

Publications. Annual Report; IAEA Bulletin (quarterly); IAEA Yearbook; INIS Reference Series; Legal Series; Nuclear Fusion (monthly); Nuclear Safety Review (annual); INIS Atomindex (CD-Rom); Technical Directories; Technical Reports Series.

World Trade Organization (WTO)

Origin. The WTO is founded on the General Agreement on Tariffs and Trade (GATT), which entered into force on 1 Jan. 1948. Its 23 original signatories were members of a Preparatory Committee appointed by the UN Economic and Social Council to draft the charter for a proposed International Trade Organization. Since this charter was never ratified, the General Agreement remained the only international instrument laying down trade rules. In Dec. 1993 there were 111 contracting parties, and a further 22 countries applying GATT rules on a *de facto* basis. On 15 April 1994 trade ministers of 123 countries signed the Final Act of the GATT Uruguay Round of negotiations at Marrakesh, bringing the WTO into being on 1 Jan. 1995. As of Jan. 2006 the WTO had 150 members.

The object of the Act is the liberalization of world trade. By it, member countries undertake to apply fair trade rules covering commodities, services and intellectual property. It provides for the lowering of tariffs on industrial goods and tropical products; the abolition of import duties on a variety of items; the progressive abolition of quotas on garments and textiles; the gradual reduction of trade-distorting subsidies and import barriers; and agreements on intellectual property and trade in services. Members are required to accept the results of the Uruguay Round talks in their entirety, and subscribe to all the WTO's agreements and disciplines. There are no enforcement procedures, however; decisions are ultimately reached by consensus.

Functions. The WTO is the legal and institutional foundation of the multilateral trading system. Surveillance of national trade policies is an important part of its work. At the centre of this is the *Trade Policy Review Mechanism (TPRM)*, agreed by Ministers in 1994 (Article III of the Marrakesh Agreement). The TPRM was broadened in 1995 when the WTO came into being, to cover services trade and intellectual property. Its principal objective is to facilitate the smooth functioning of the multilateral trading system by enhancing the transparency of members' trade policies. All members are subject to review under the TPRM, which mandates that four members with the largest share of world trade (European Union, USA, Japan, Canada) be reviewed every two years; the next 16, every four years; and others every six, with a longer period able to be fixed for the least-developed members. Also, in 1994, flexibility of up to six months was introduced into the review cycles, and in 1996, it was agreed that every second review of each of the first four trading entities should be an interim review. Reviews are conducted by the Trade Policy Review Body (TPRB) on the basis of a policy statement by the member under review and a report by economists in the Secretariat's Trade Policy Review Division.

The *International Trade Centre* (since 1968 operated jointly with the United Nations through UNCTAD) was established by GATT in 1964 to provide information and training on export markets and marketing techniques, and thereby to assist the trade of developing countries. In 1984 the Centre became an executing agency of the UN Development Programme, responsible for carrying out UNDP-financed projects related to trade promotion.

Organization. A two-yearly ministerial meeting is the ultimate policy-making body. The 148-member General Council has some 30 subordinate councils and committees. The *Dispute Settlement Body* was set up to deal with disputes between countries. Appeals against its verdicts are heard by a seven-member *Appellate Body*. In 2005 it was composed of representatives of Australia, Brazil, Egypt, India, Italy Japan and USA. Dispute panels may be set up *ad hoc*, and objectors to their ruling may appeal to the Appellate Body whose decision is binding. Refusal to comply at this stage can result in the application of trade sanctions. Each appeal is heard by three of the Appellate Body members. Before cases are heard by dispute panels, there is a 60-day consultation period. The previous GATT Secretariat now serves the WTO, which has no resources of its own other than its operating budget. The budget for 2005 was 168,703,400 Swiss francs.

Headquarters: Centre William Rappard, 154 rue de Lausanne,
CH-1211 Geneva 21, Switzerland.
Website: http://www.wto.org
e-mail: enquiries@wto.org
Director-General: Pascal Lamy (France).

Publications. Annual Report; International Trade: Trends and Statistics (annual); *WTO Focus* (ten a year).

Further Reading

Croome, J., *Reshaping the World Trading System.* WTO, 1996
Preeg, E., *Traders in a Brave New World.* Chicago Univ. Press, 1996

Preparatory Commission for the Comprehensive Nuclear-Test-Ban Treaty Organization (CTBTO)

The Preparatory Commission for the Comprehensive Nuclear-Test-Ban Treaty Organization (CTBTO Preparatory Commission) is an international organization established by the States Signatories to the Treaty on 19 Nov. 1996. It carries out the necessary preparations for the effective implementation of the Treaty, and prepares for the first session of the Conference of the States Parties to the Treaty.

The Preparatory Commission consists of a plenary body composed of all the States Signatories, and the Provisional Technical Secretariat (PTS). Upon signing the Treaty a state becomes a member of the Commission. Member states oversee the work of the Preparatory Commission and fund its activities. The Commission's main task is the establishment of the 337 facility International Monitoring System and the International Data Centre, its provisional operation and the development of operational manuals. The Comprehensive Nuclear-Test-Ban Treaty prohibits any nuclear weapon test explosion or any other nuclear explosion anywhere in the world. As of Feb. 2006 the Treaty had 176 States Signatories and 129 ratifications.

Headquarters: Vienna International Centre, PO Box 1200, A-1400 Vienna, Austria.
Website: http://www.ctbto.org
Executive Secretary: Wolfgang Hoffmann (Germany).

Organization for the Prohibition of Chemical Weapons (OPCW)

The OPCW is responsible for the implementation of the Chemical Weapons Convention (CWC), which became effective on 29 April 1997. The principal organ of the OPCW is the Conference of the States Parties, composed of all the members of the Organization.

Given the relative simplicity of producing chemical warfare agents, the verification provisions of the CWC are far-reaching. The routine monitoring regime involves submission by States Parties of initial and annual declarations to the OPCW and initial visits and systematic inspections of declared weapons storage, production and destruction facilities. Verification is also applied to chemical industry facilities which produce, process or consume dual-use chemicals listed in the convention. The OPCW also when requested by any State Party conducts short-notice challenge inspections at any location under its jurisdiction or control of any other State Party.

The OPCW also co-ordinates assistance to any State Party that falls victim of chemical warfare as it fosters international co-operation in the peaceful application of chemistry.

By Feb. 2006 a total of 176 countries and territories were States Parties to the Chemical Weapons Convention.

Headquarters: Johan de Wittlaan 32, 2517 JR The Hague, Netherlands.

Website: http://www.opcw.org
Director General: Rogelio Pfirter (Argentina).

European Union (EU)

Origin. The Union is founded on the existing European communities set up by the Treaties of Paris (1951) and Rome (1957), supplemented by revisions, the Single European Act in 1986, the Maastricht Treaty on European Union in 1992, the Treaty of Amsterdam in 1997 and the Treaty of Nice in 2000.

Members. (25). Austria, Belgium, Cyprus (Greek-Cypriot sector only), the Czech Republic, Denmark, Estonia, Finland, France, Germany, Greece, Hungary, Ireland, Italy, Latvia, Lithuania, Luxembourg, Malta, the Netherlands, Poland, Portugal, Slovakia, Slovenia, Spain, Sweden and the UK.

History. European disillusionment with nationalism after the Second World War fostered a desire to bind key European states—France and (West) Germany—to each other and prevent future conflict. In 1946 Winston Churchill called for a moral union in the form of a 'united states of Europe'. Unsupported by the British Government, Churchill chaired the 1948 European Congress of The Hague, a meeting of 800 Europeanists that resulted in the creation of the *Council of Europe,* a European assembly of nations whose aim (Art. 1 of the Statute) was: 'to achieve a greater unity between its members for the purpose of safeguarding and realizing the ideals and principles which are their common heritage'.

The formation of the *Benelux Economic Union* in 1948 provided a model for a regional customs union; the free movement of goods, people, capital and services was achieved by 1960. Further European integration and the eradication of tariff trade barriers were encouraged by the US-financed European Recovery Program (Marshall Plan) and the *Organisation for European Economic Co-operation* (later the *OECD*). Western European co-operation was also spurred on by distrust of Soviet power in the East, leading to the Brussels Treaty of 1948; the collective defence pact that established the *Western European Union (WEU)*. The North Atlantic Treaty of 1949 cemented Western European (and American) security co-operation.

Jean Monnet, a French economic advisor, suggested joint development to solve Franco-German tensions over the industrial power of the Ruhr and Saarland. Monnet's plan was championed by the French foreign minister, Robert Schuman, whose Declaration of 9 May 1950 (now celebrated as Europe Day) proposed the pooling of coal and steel production. Belgium, France, the Federal Republic of Germany, Italy, Luxembourg and the Netherlands signed the Treaty of Paris establishing the *European Coal and Steel Community (ECSC),* regarded as a first step towards a united Europe. However, the *European Defence Community (EDC)* of 1952 was rejected by the French Parliament, ending hopes for a *European Political Community.* Encouraged by the success of the ECSC, European integrationists pressed for further economic co-operation. The *European Economic Community (EEC)* and the *European Atomic Energy Community (EAEC* or *Euratom)* were subsequently created under separate treaties signed in Rome on 25 March 1957. The treaties provided for the establishment by stages of a common market with a customs union at its core, the development of common transport and agricultural policies, and the promotion of growth and research in the nuclear industries for peaceful purposes. Euratom was awarded monopoly powers of acquisition of fissile materials for civil purposes (it is not concerned with the military uses of nuclear power).

The executives of the three communities (ECSC, Euratom, EEC) were amalgamated by a treaty signed in Brussels in 1965, forming a single Council and single Commission of the European Communities, today the core of the EU. The Commission is advised on matters relating to Euratom by a Scientific and Technical Committee.

Enlargement. On 30 June 1970 membership negotiations began between the European Community and the UK, Denmark, Ireland and Norway. On 22 Jan. 1972 all four countries signed a Treaty of Accession but Norway rejected membership in a referendum in Nov. The UK, Denmark and Ireland became full members on 1 Jan. 1973 (though Greenland exercised its autonomy under the Danish Crown to secede in 1985). Greece joined on 1 Jan. 1981; Spain and Portugal on 1 Jan. 1986. The former German Democratic Republic entered into full membership on reunification with Federal Germany in Oct. 1990, and following referenda in favour, Austria, Finland and Sweden became members on 1 Jan. 1995. In a referendum in Nov. 1994 Norway again rejected membership. On 1 May 2004 a further ten countries became members—Cyprus, the Czech Republic, Estonia, Hungary, Latvia, Lithuania, Malta, Poland, Slovakia and Slovenia.

Single European Act. The enlarging of the Community resulted in renewed efforts to promote European integration, culminating in the signing in 1986 of the Single European Act. The SEA represented the first major revision of the Treaty of Rome. It provided for greater involvement of the European Parliament in the decision-making process and it extended Qualified Majority Voting (QMV). The SEA also removed barriers within the EEC to movement and transnational business.

Maastricht Treaty on European Union. Following German reunification, closer European integration was pursued in the political as well as economic spheres. The Maastricht Summit of Dec. 1991 produced a new framework—a European Union based on three 'pillars': a central pillar of the existing European Communities and two supporting pillars based on formal intergovernmental co-operation. One pillar comprised a Common Foreign and Security Policy (CFSP) and the other focused on justice and home affairs, including policing, immigration and law enforcement. Signed in Feb. 1992, the Treaty on European Union laid down a timetable for the creation of a common currency (subject to specific conditions, including an opt-out clause for the UK). The Community Charter of Fundamental Social Rights for Workers, signed in 1989 by all members except the UK, was strengthened by a protocol, allowing member states to use EC institutions to co-ordinate social policy. The UK agreed to abide to the protocol in 1998. Ratification by member states of the Maastricht Treaty proved controversial. In June 1992 it was rejected in a Danish referendum but approved in a second referendum in May 1993. Ratification was finally completed during 1993, with the UK ratifying on 2 Aug. The European Union (EU) came into being officially on 1 Nov. that year.

Treaty of Amsterdam. The Turin Inter-Governmental Conference (IGC) of 1996 failed to advance the reform programme, in part because of the British Conservative Government's opposition to extending EU powers. The election in 1997 of a more Europeanist Labour Government led to the adoption of most of the IGC's proposals at the Amsterdam summit in 1997. Designed to further political integration, the Treaty did little more than adjust the institutions to prepare for EU enlargement. Strengthened policies included police co-operation, freedom of movement and the promotion of employment. Elements of the justice and home affairs 'pillar' were transferred to the Communities. The treaty also allows for member states to progress with selected areas of policy at different rates.

Treaty of Nice. Many of the problems unanswered at Amsterdam were left until the Dec. 2000 IGC at Nice. However, the tense summit failed to find consensus on key institutional reforms. The Treaty included a re-weighting of votes in the Council of Ministers, adjustments to the composition of the Commission and several extensions to QMV. Ireland rejected the Treaty in a referendum in June 2001; this was reversed in the referendum in Oct. 2002. The Treaty came into effect on 1 Feb. 2003.

Charter of Fundamental Rights. The Charter, based on the Universal Declaration of Human Rights (UDHR), contains several provisions such as workers' rights and the right to good administration that are not included in the political and civil rights of the European Convention on Human Rights (ECHR). The Treaty was proclaimed by the European Parliament, the Commission and the Council—at the Nice IGC in 2000—but was not incorporated in the Treaty of Nice.

European Convention. In Dec. 2001 the Laeken European Conference adopted the Declaration on the Future of the European Union, committing the EU to becoming more democratic, transparent and effective, opening the way to a constitution for the people of Europe. The European Council set up a convention, comprising 105 members—chaired by Valéry Giscard d'Estaing, a former French president—to draft the Treaty establishing a Constitution for Europe (the EU constitution), which must be ratified by all 25 states. The Treaty will confer legal personality on the European Union, giving it the right to represent itself as a single body under international law. The constitution includes provision for a President of the European Council, to replace the current six-month rotating presidency, to be elected by member states for 2½-year terms. The European Parliament will be granted co-legislative powers in all policy areas with the Council. A new position of Union Minister of Foreign Affairs will merge the responsibilities of the external relations Commissioner and the High Representative for the CFSP. The constitution incorporates the Charter of Fundamental Rights. Member states will have reduced powers of veto, although the veto would remain in key areas including taxation, defence and foreign policy. Plans for the new constitution to be ready for EU governments to sign after the ten new members joined on 1 May 2004 were dropped when the Brussels summit of Dec. 2003 ended in stalemate over the weighting of voting rights in the Council of Ministers. On 29 Oct. 2004 the Treaty was approved for ratification by the 25 member countries, either by referendum or parliamentary vote. On 29 May 2005, after nine countries had ratified the Treaty, France became the first to reject it; the Netherlands followed suit three days later. Since then a further four countries have ratified the Treaty. Denmark, Poland, Portugal and the UK have postponed their referenda indefinitely.

Recent and Future Enlargement. On 15 July 1997 the European Commission adopted *Agenda 2000*, which included a detailed strategy for consolidating the Union through enlargement as far eastwards as Ukraine, Belarus and Moldova. It recommended the early start of accession negotiations with the Czech Republic, Estonia, Hungary, Poland and Slovenia under the provision of Article O of the Maastricht Treaty, whereby 'any European State may apply to become a member of the Union' (subject to the Copenhagen Criteria set by the European Council at its summit in 1993).

In 2002 it was announced that ten countries would be ready to join in 2004: Cyprus, the Czech Republic, Estonia, Hungary, Latvia, Lithuania, Malta, Poland, Slovakia and Slovenia. Following a series of referenda held in 2003 they all became members on 1 May 2004. Bulgaria and Romania signed an accession treaty in April 2005; accession, set for 2007, is still subject to the passage of key judicial reforms. Entry talks with Croatia began in Oct. 2005, in response to greater co-operation with the International

Criminal Tribunal for the former Yugoslavia. Turkey is also hoping to join, but talks on membership which also began in Oct. 2005 may take up to 15 years. Switzerland applied for membership in May 1992 but this was rejected by a Swiss referendum later that year. The first Switzerland-EU summit, in 2004, brought Switzerland closer to the EU with a series of bilateral agreements. A referendum in June 2005 approved joining the Schengen Accord (see below). The former Yugoslav Republic of Macedonia (FYROM) applied for membership in March 2004; in Dec. 2005 it was recognized as an official candidate country.

Objectives. The Maastricht Treaty claimed the ultimate goal of the EU is 'an ever closer union among the peoples of Europe, in which decisions are taken as closely as possible to the citizen'. However, there are competing views over what that 'union' should be: political confederation or federation or primarily economic union. Priorities include: economic and monetary union; further expansion of the scope of the Communities; implementation of a common foreign and security policy; and development in the fields of justice and home affairs. The Lisbon Strategy, presented in 2000, strives to turn the EU into 'the most competitive and dynamic knowledge-based economy in the world'. Yet tensions remain over how to balance economic growth measures and social welfare provisions.

Structure. The EU's main institutions are: the European Commission, an independent policy-making executive with powers of proposal; the Council of the European Union (known informally as the Council of Ministers), a decision-making body drawn from the national Governments; the European Parliament, which has joint legislative powers in most policy areas and final say over the EU budget; and the European Court of Justice, the EU's supreme court.

Defence. In Nov. 2000 EU defence ministers agreed to commit personnel and equipment to a rapid reaction force that could be deployed in tackling crises in an area up to 4,000 km from Brussels at short notice. Two 'battle group' rapid reaction forces became operational in May 2005; 13 groups are planned to be operational by 2007. There will ultimately be a pool of approximately 100,000 personnel, 400 combat aircraft and 100 warships, but a maximum of 60,000 personnel will be serving at any one time to allow for the rotation of forces in the event of a lengthy operation. Although final numbers have not yet been agreed, Britain, France and Germany are likely to provide the largest number of troops, at around 12,000 to 13,000 each out of the total of 60,000. Denmark has decided to opt out. The European Union's first ever peacekeeping force (EUFOR) officially started work in Macedonia on 1 April 2003.

The European Union Institute for Security Studies (EUISS) was created by a Council Joint Action in July 2001 with the status of an autonomous agency. It contributes to the development of the Common Foreign and Security Policy (CFSP) through research and debate on major security and defence issues. The European Defence Agency, headed by Javier Solana, the EU's High Representative, was founded by the Council in July 2004 to improve defence co-ordination, especially crisis management.

Major Policy Areas. The major policy areas of the EU were laid down in the 1957 Treaty of Rome, which guaranteed certain rights to the citizens of all member states. Economic discrimination by nationality was outlawed, and member states were bound to apply 'the principle that men and women should receive equal pay for equal work'.

The Single Internal Market. The core of the process of economic integration is characterized by the removal of obstacles to the four fundamental freedoms of movement for persons, goods, capital and services. Under the Treaty, individuals or companies from one member state may establish themselves in another country (for the purposes of economic activity) or sell goods or services there on the same basis as nationals of that country. With a few exceptions, restrictions on the movement of capital have also been ended. Under the Single European Act the member states bound themselves to achieve the suppression of all barriers to free movement of persons, goods and services by 31 Dec. 1992.

The *Schengen Accord* abolished border controls on persons and goods between certain EU states plus Norway and Iceland. It came into effect on 26 March 1995 and was signed by Austria, Belgium, Denmark, Finland, France, Germany, Greece, Iceland, Italy, Luxembourg, the Netherlands, Norway, Portugal, Spain and Sweden. The ten new EU members have signed the treaty and will implement it in Oct. 2007. Switzerland has signed it but has yet to implement it.

Economic and Monetary Union. The establishment of the single market provided for the next phase of integration: economic and monetary union. The *European Monetary System (EMS)* was founded in March 1979 to control inflation, protect European trade from international disturbances and ultimately promote convergence between the European economies. At its heart was the *Exchange Rate Mechanism (ERM)*. The ERM is run by the finance ministries and central banks of the EU countries on a day-to-day basis; monthly reviews are carried out by the EU Monetary Committee (finance ministries) and the EU Committee of Central Bankers. Sweden is not in the ERM; the UK suspended its membership on 17 Sept. 1992. In Jan. 1995 Austria joined the ERM. Finland followed in 1996, and in Nov. that year the Italian lira, which had been temporarily suspended, was re-admitted.

With the introduction of the euro, exchange rates have been fixed for all member countries. The member countries are Austria, Belgium, Finland, France, Germany, Greece, Ireland, Italy, Luxembourg, the Netherlands, Portugal and Spain. The euro became legal tender from 1 Jan. 2002 across the region. National currencies were phased out by the end of Feb. 2002.

European Monetary Union (EMU). The single European currency with 11 member states came into operation in Jan. 1999, although it was not until 2002 that the currency came into general circulation. Greece subsequently joined in Jan. 2001. The euro-zone is the world's second largest economy after the USA in terms of output and the largest in terms of trade. EMU currency consists of the euro of 100 cents. EU member countries not in EMU will select a central rate for their currency in consultation with members of the euro bloc and the European Central Bank. The rate is set according to an assessment of each country's chances of joining the euro zone.

An agreement on the legal status of the euro and currency discipline, the Stability and Growth Pact, was reached by all member states at the Dublin summit on 13 Dec. 1996. Financial penalties are meant to be applied to member states running a GDP deficit (negative growth) of up to 0·75%. If GDP falls between 0·75% and 2%, EU finance ministers have discretion as to whether to apply penalties. France and Germany have exceeded their deficit limits repeatedly, despite the efforts of the Commission to penalise them. However, the Council of Ministers has decided to suspend penalties. Members running an excessive deficit are automatically exempt from penalties in the event of a natural disaster or if the fall in GDP is at least 2% over one year.

Environment. The Single European Act made the protection of the environment an integral part of economic and social policies. Public support for EU environmental activism is strong, as evinced by the success of Green parties in the parliamentary elections. Community policy aims to prevent pollution (the Prevention Principle), rectify pollution at source, impose the costs of prevention or rectification on the polluters themselves (the Polluter Pays Principle), and promote sustainable development.

Water pollution policy covers quality standards for drinking, bathing and aquaculture and binds EU members to international waterway conventions. The European Environment Agency (see page 39) was established to ensure that policy was based on reliable scientific data.

In March 2002 the 15 EU member states agreed to the 1997 Kyoto Protocol to the United Nations Framework on Climate Change, which commits the EU to reduce its emissions of greenhouse gases by 8% of 1990 levels between 2008–12.

The Common Agricultural Policy (CAP). The objectives set out in the Treaty of Rome are to increase agricultural productivity, to ensure a fair standard of living for the agricultural community, to stabilize markets, to assure supplies, and to ensure reasonable consumer prices. In Dec. 1960 the Council laid down the fundamental principles on which the CAP is based: a single market, which calls for common prices, stable currency parities and the harmonizing of health and veterinary legislation; Community preference, which protects the single Community market from imports; common financing, through the European Agricultural Guidance and Guarantee Fund (EAGGF), which seeks to improve agriculture through its Guidance section, and to stabilize markets against world price fluctuations through market intervention, with levies and refunds on exports. The CAP has made the EU virtually self-sufficient in food.

Following the disappearance of stable currency parities, artificial currency levels have been applied in the CAP. This factor, together with over-production owing to high producer prices, meant that the CAP consumed about two-thirds of the Community budget. In May 1992 it was agreed to reform CAP and to control over-production by reducing the price supports to farmers by 29% for cereals, 15% for beef and 5% for dairy products. In June 1995 the guaranteed intervention price for beef was decreased by 5%. In July 1996 agriculture ministers agreed a reduction in the set-aside rate for cereals from 10% to 5%. Fruit and vegetable production subsidies were fixed at no more than 4% of the value of total marketed production, rising to 4·5% in 1999. Compensatory grants are made available to farmers who remove land from production or take early retirement. The CAP reform aims to make the agricultural sector more responsive to supply and demand. The 1999 Berlin summit agreed to stabilize CAP spending, at an average annual expenditure of €42·5bn. from 2000–06. Agriculture and fisheries accounted for 43% of the 2005 EU budget but accounts for only 1·8% of Europe's GDP.

Customs Union and External Trade Relations. Goods or services originating in one member state have free circulation within the EU, which implies common arrangements for trade with the rest of the world. Member states can no longer make bilateral trade agreements with third countries; this power has been ceded to the EU. The Customs Union was achieved in July 1968.

In Oct. 1991 a treaty forming the *European Economic Area (EEA)* was approved by the member states of the then EC and European Free Trade Association (EFTA). The EEA consists of the 25 EU members plus Iceland, Liechtenstein and Norway; a Swiss referendum rejected ratification of the EEA in Dec. 1992. Association agreements, which could lead to customs union, have been made with Israel and Morocco. The customs union with Turkey came into force on 1 Jan. 1996. Commercial, industrial, technical and financial aid agreements have been made with Algeria, Egypt, Jordan, Lebanon, Morocco, Russia, Serbia and Montenegro, Syria and Tunisia. In 1976 Canada signed a framework agreement for co-operation in industrial trade, science and natural resources, and a transatlantic pact was signed with the USA in Dec. 1995. Co-operation agreements also exist with a number of Latin American countries and groupings, and with Arab and Asian countries, and an economic and commercial agreement has been signed with the Association of South East Asian Nations (ASEAN). Partnership and co-operation agreements were signed

with Ukraine in 1994, Kazakhstan and Kyrgyzstan in 1995 and with Uzbekistan in 1996. In the Development Aid sector, the EU has an agreement (the Cotonou Agreement, signed in 2000, the successor of the Lomé Convention, originally signed in 1975 but renewed and enlarged in 1979, 1984 and 1989) with some 60 African, Caribbean and Pacific (ACP) countries that removes customs duties without reciprocal arrangements for most of their imports to the Community.

The application of common duties has been conducted mainly within the framework of the *General Agreement on Tariffs and Trade (GATT),* which was succeeded in 1995 by the establishment of the World Trade Organization.

Fisheries. The Common Fisheries Policy (CFP) came into effect in Jan. 1983. All EU fishermen have equal access to the waters of member countries (a zone extending up to 200 nautical miles from the shore), with the total allowable catch for each species being set and shared out between member countries according to pre-established quotas. In some cases 'historic rights' apply, as well as special rules to preserve marine biodiversity and ensure sustainable fishing. The Financial Instrument for Fisheries Guidance (FIFG) provides financial support to the fishing industry; €5·6bn. was allocated for the 2000–06 period.

A number of agreements are operating with third countries (with 13 African countries, the Faroe Islands, Greenland, Iceland, Kiribati, Norway and the Solomon Islands) allowing reciprocal fishing rights. When Greenland withdrew from the Community in 1985 EU boats retained their fishing rights subject to quotas and limits, which were revised in 1995 owing to concern about the overfishing of Greenland halibut. An agreement was initialled with Argentina in 1992.

Transport. Failure to create a common transport policy, as expected by the Treaty of Rome, led in 1982 to Parliamentary proceedings against the Council at the Court of Justice. Under the Maastricht Treaty, the Community must contribute to the establishment and development of Trans-European Networks (TENs) in the areas of transport, telecommunications and energy infrastructures. The TEN budget for 2000–06 is €4·6bn. Enlargement into Central and Eastern Europe necessitates a much larger budget; the Commission has recommended earmarking €20·7bn. for 2007–13. Common transport policy includes safety agreements, such as lorry weight and driver hours limits, the easing of border crossings for commercial vehicles and progress towards a common transport market. Rail plans include a 35,000 km high-speed train (HST) network, incorporating France's TGV and Germany's ICE networks.

Competition. The Competition (anti-trust) law of the EU is based on two principles: that businesses should not seek to nullify the creation of the common market by the erection of artificial national (or other) barriers to the free movement of goods; and that there should not be any abuse of dominant positions in any market. These two principles have led to the outlawing of prohibitions on exports to other member states, of price-fixing agreements and of refusal to supply; and to the refusal by the Commission to allow mergers or takeovers by dominant undertakings in specific cases. Increasingly heavy fines are imposed on offenders.

A number of structural funds have been established in an attempt to counter specific problems within and across the Community. These include:

European Social Fund. Provides resources with the aim of combating long-term unemployment and facilitating integration into the labour market of young people and the socially disadvantaged. The 2004 budget included an allocation of around €10,605m. for the Fund's commitments.

European Regional Development Fund. Intended to compensate for the unequal rate of development among different regions of the EU by encouraging investment and improving infrastructure in poor and economically depressed regions. Regional policy accounts for 35·5% of the EU budget expenditure for 2005.

Finances. The general budget of the EU covers all EEC and Euratom expenditure, and the administrative expenditure of the ECSC.

EU revenue in €1m.:

	Financial year 2004
Agricultural duties	1,313·4
Customs duties	10,592·1
VAT-based resource	13,912·2
GNI-based resource	68,981·1
Miscellaneous revenue	8,180·9
Total (including others)	103,233·3

Expenditure for the financial year 2004 was €102,603·1m., of which the European Agricultural Guidance and Guarantee Fund Guarantee Section accounted for €43,664·7m.

The resources of the Community (the levies and duties mentioned above, and up to a 1·4% VAT charge) have been agreed by Treaty. The Budget is made by the Council and the Parliament acting jointly as the Budgetary Authority. The Parliament has control, within a certain margin, of non-obligatory expenditure (where the amount to be spent is not set out in the legislation concerned), and can also reject the Budget. Otherwise, the Council decides.

Official languages: Czech, Danish, Dutch, English, Estonian, Finnish, French, German, Greek, Hungarian, Italian, Latvian, Lithuanian, Maltese, Polish, Portuguese, Slovak, Slovenian, Spanish and Swedish.

Website: http://www.europa.eu.int

EU Institutions

European Commission

The European Commission consists of 25 members appointed by the member states to serve for five years. The Commission President is selected by a consensus of member state heads of government and serves a five-year term. The Commission acts as the EU executive body and as guardian of the Treaties. In this it has the right of initiative (putting proposals to the Council of Ministers for action) and of execution (once the Council has decided). It can take the other institutions or individual countries before the European Court of Justice should any of these fail to comply with European Law. Decisions on legislative proposals made by the Commission are taken in the Council of the European Union. Members of the Commission swear an oath of independence, distancing themselves from partisan influence from any source. The Commission operates through 37 Directorates-General and services.

At the European Summit held in Nice in Dec. 2000 it was decided that from 2005 each EU member state would have one commissioner until there are 27 members. A permanent limit of fewer than 27 will then be set, with the seats being rotated among member states.

The current Commission took office in Nov. 2004. Members, their nationality and political affiliation (S-Socialist/Social Democrat; C-Christian Democrat/Conservative; L-Liberal; G-Green; Ind-Independent) in Jan. 2006 were as follows.

President: José Manuel Durão Barroso (Portugal, S).

The commissioners are:

Vice-president: Margot Wallström (Sweden, S); responsible for institutional relations and communication strategy.

Vice-president: Jacques Barrot (France, C); responsible for transport.

Vice-president: Siim Kallas (Estonia, L); responsible for administrative affairs, audit and anti-fraud.

Vice-president: Günter Verheugen (Germany, S); responsible for enterprise and industry.

Vice-president: Franco Frattini (Italy, C); responsible for justice, freedom and security.

Agriculture and Rural Development and Fisheries: Mariann Fischer Boel (Denmark, L).

Competition: Neelie Kroes (Netherlands, L).

Development and Humanitarian Aid: Louis Michel (Belgium, L).

Economic and Monetary Affairs: Joaquín Almunia Amann (Spain, S).

Education, Training, Culture and Multilingualism: Ján Figeľ (Slovakia, C).

Employment, Social Affairs and Equal Opportunities: Vladimír Špidla (Czech Republic, S).

Energy: Andris Piebalgs (Latvia, L).

Enlargement: Olli Rehn (Finland, L).

Environment: Stavros Dimas (Greece, C).

External Relations and European Neighbourhood Policy: Benita Ferrero-Waldner (Austria, C).

Financial Programming and Budget: Dalia Grybauskaitė (Lithuania, Ind).

Fisheries and Maritime Affairs: Joe Borg (Malta, C).

Health and Consumer Protection: Markos Kyprianou (Cyprus, S).

Information Society and Media: Viviane Reding (Luxembourg, C).

Internal Market and Services: Charlie McCreevy (Ireland, C).

Justice, Freedom and Security: Franco Frattini (Italy, C).

Regional Policy: Danuta Hübner (Poland, Ind).

Science and Research: Janez Potočnik (Slovenia, Ind).

Taxation and Customs Union: László Kovács (Hungary, S).

Trade: Peter Mandelson (UK, S).

Headquarters: 200 rue de la Loi/Wetstraat, B-1049 Brussels, Belgium.

Secretary-General: Catherine Day (Ireland).

Current Leaders

José Manuel Durão Barroso

Position
President of the European Commission

Introduction
Former prime minister of Portugal and leader of the right-wing Partido Social Democrata (Social Democrats, PSD), José Manuel Durão Barroso was nominated to succeed Romano Prodi as president of the European Commission in June 2004. His candidacy was approved by a secret ballot of Members of the European Parliament (MEPs). He took up office in Brussels on 23 Nov. 2004.

Early Life
Born on 23 March 1956, Durão Barroso studied law at the Universidade de Lisboa. He gained a masters in political science from the Université de Genève before taking European studies. He lectured at universities in Geneva and the USA, as well as working for the department of international relations at Universidade Lusíada, Lisbon. He wrote for several science journals and founded a political science magazine.

In 1980 Durão Barroso joined the PSD. In 1985, 1995 and 1999 he was elected PSD deputy for Lisbon; in 1987 and 1991 for Viseu.

He was president of the foreign office commission between 1995–96, then the interior ministry's deputy secretary before becoming foreign secretary. Between 1992–95 Durão Barroso was foreign minister under the PSD prime minister, Aníbal Cavaco Silva. He led a delegation to Bosnia-Herzegovina in Sept. 1996, and was a UN peace officer in Tanzania in Oct. 1997. He was vice president of the European People's Party in 1999.

In 1999 he was elected party leader, replacing Marcelo Rebelo de Sousa. In the same year Durão Barroso stood for election against incumbent Socialist prime minister António Guterres. Violent clashes during East Timor's transition to independence from Indonesia in Aug. 1999 took the focus away from domestic politics and the election. Guterres' successful handling of the precarious situation helped his election campaign. The PSD attempted a coalition with the right-wing Partido Popular (PP) but the alliance was shortlived and both parties suffered from the fall-out. Durão Barroso came second with 32·3% of votes to Guterres' 44·1%.

Two years later, with increasing criticism of the government's heavy public spending, the PSD recorded gains in local elections taking the key cities of Lisbon, Oporto and Coimbra. Guterres resigned and elections were brought forward from 2004 to March 2002. The PSD claimed a narrow victory with 40% of votes to 38% and 102 out of 230 seats, and Durão Barroso was appointed prime minister. To gain an assembly majority the party renewed its coalition with the PP, fuelling concerns over the party's influence on government policy. On election Durão Barroso set about reviving the economy. A reduction in public spending affected local authorities' budgets and civil service recruitment, while plans were made to streamline or dissolve numerous state bodies. He also planned to accelerate privatization and introduce labour reforms. In Nov. 2002 public-sector workers held a 24-hour strike, the first in ten years. Durão Barroso reaffirmed his determination to press ahead with his policies. To cut Portugal's deficit to 2·7%, the Durão Barroso government imposed a wage freeze on employees earning more than €1,000, affecting half of Portugal's workforce.

In Jan. 2003 Durão Barroso was one of eight European leaders to issue a combined declaration of support for the United States in its efforts to disarm Iraq, while making it clear that Portugal would not take part in military action.

Following the agreement of the 25 EU ministers in June 2004 on the new EU constitution, Portugal announced that it would hold a referendum on the issue. After dropping earlier reservations concerning the European Commission's next president, Spain and France joined the other members in June 2004 to invite Durão Barroso to succeed the incumbent president, Romano Prodi. Following his appointment, Durão Barroso resigned as prime minister of Portugal and was replaced by Pedro Santana Lopes.

Career in Office
Durão Barroso was quickly embroiled in controversy. A row broke out in the European Parliament over the nomination of Rocco Buttiglione, who had outspoken views on women and homosexuality, as justice commissioner. Durão Barroso opted to withdraw the entire team of his 24 commissioner-designates rather than have it rejected by parliament under their new powers of veto. In the ensuing reshuffle Buttiglione was replaced by outgoing Italian foreign minister Franco Frattini, Hungary's socialist nominee was moved and Latvia replaced its controversial candidate. On 17 Nov. the European Parliament approved the new team of commissioners by 449 votes to 149. The Commission took up office at the Berlaymont building in Brussels on 23 Nov. 2004, three weeks later than planned. Durão Barroso denied that he had been weakened by the debacle: 'We are able to say to the people of Europe that we have come out of this experience with strengthened institutions, in a better position to meet their expectations.' Durão Barroso's priorities for the European

Commission include reviving the EU's sluggish economy, reforming the Eurozone's financial rules and establishing a new seven-year spending plan for the 25-nation bloc.

Council of the European Union
(Council of Ministers)

The Council of Ministers consists of ministers from the 25 national governments and is the only institution which directly represents the member states' national interests. It is the Union's principal decision-making body. Here, members legislate for the Union, set its political objectives, co-ordinate their national policies and resolve differences between themselves and other institutions. The presidency rotates every six months. Austria had the presidency during the first half of 2006 and Finland has the presidency during the second half of 2006, Germany will have it during the first half of 2007 and Portugal during the second half of 2007. There is only one Council, but it meets in different configurations depending on the items on the agenda. The meetings are held in Brussels, except in April, June and Oct. when all meetings are in Luxembourg. Around 100 formal ministerial sessions are held each year.

Decisions are taken either by qualified majority vote or by unanimity. Since the entry into force of the Single European Act in 1987 an increasing number of decisions are by majority vote, although some areas such as taxation and social security, immigration and border controls are reserved to unanimity. At the Nice Summit in Dec. 2000 agreement was reached that a further 39 articles of the EU's treaties would move to qualified majority voting. 26 votes were then needed to veto a decision (blocking minority), and member states were allocated the following number of votes: France, Germany, Italy and the UK, 10; Spain, 8; Belgium, Greece, the Netherlands and Portugal, 5; Austria and Sweden, 4; Denmark, Finland and the Republic of Ireland, 3; Luxembourg, 2. During a six-month transitional period that followed the accession of the ten new member states on 1 May 2004 these vote weightings remained unchanged, while the new members were allocated the following number of votes: Poland, 8; Czech Republic and Hungary, 5; Estonia, Latvia, Lithuania, Slovakia and Slovenia, 3; Cyprus and Malta, 2. As from 1 Nov. 2004 the allocation of vote weightings is: France, Germany, Italy and the UK, 29; Poland and Spain, 27; the Netherlands, 13; Belgium, the Czech Republic, Greece, Hungary and Portugal, 12; Austria and Sweden, 10; Denmark, Finland, the Republic of Ireland, Lithuania and Slovakia, 7; Cyprus, Estonia, Latvia, Luxembourg and Slovenia, 4; Malta 3. A qualified majority will be reached if a majority of member states approve a proposal and a minimum of 232 votes is cast in favour of the proposal. Each member state has a national delegation in Brussels known as the Permanent Representation, headed by Permanent Representatives, senior diplomats whose committee (Coreper) prepares ministerial sessions. Coreper meets weekly and its main task is to ensure that only the most difficult and sensitive issues are dealt with at ministerial level.

The General Secretariat of the Council provides the practical infrastructure of the Council at all levels and prepares the meetings of the Council and the European Council by advising the Presidency and assisting the Coreper and the various committees and working groups of the Council.

Legislation. The Community's legislative process starts with a proposal from the Commission (either at the suggestion of its services or in pursuit of its declared political aims) to the Council, or in the case of co-decision, to both the Council and the European Parliament. The Council generally seeks the views of the European Parliament on the proposal, and the Parliament adopts a formal Opinion after consideration of the matter by its specialist Committees. The Council may also (and in some cases is obliged to) consult the Economic and Social Committee and the Committee of the Regions which similarly deliver an opinion. When these opinions have been received, the Council will decide. Most decisions are taken on a majority basis, but will take account of reservations expressed by individual member states. The text eventually approved may differ substantially from the original Commission proposal.

Provisions of the Treaties and secondary legislation may be either directly applicable in member states or only applicable after member states have enacted their own implementing legislation. Community law, adopted by the Council (or by Parliament and the Council in the framework of the co-decision procedure) may take the following forms: (1) *Regulations*, which are of general application and binding in their entirety and directly applicable in all member states; (2) *Directives*, which are binding upon each member state as to the result to be achieved within a given time, but leave to the national authorities the choice of form and method of achieving this result; and (3) *Decisions*, which are binding in their entirety on their addressees. In addition the Council and Commission can issue recommendations, opinions, resolutions and conclusions which are essentially political acts and not legally binding.

Transparency. In order to make its decision-making process more transparent to the European citizens, the Council has, together with the European Parliament and the Commission, introduced a set of rules concerning public access to the documents of the three institutions. A considerable number of Council documents can be accessed electronically via the Council's public register of documents, whereas other documents which may not be directly accessible can be released to the public upon request. With a view to ensure the widest possible access to its decision-making process, some Council debates and deliberations are open to the public. The Council systematically publishes votes and explanations of votes and minutes of its meetings when it is acting as legislator.

Headquarters: 175 rue de la Loi, B-1048 Brussels, Belgium.
Website: http://www.consilium.eu.int; http://ue.eu.int
e-mail: public.info@consilium.eu.int
Secretary-General and High Representative for the Common Foreign and Security Policy of the European Union: Dr Javier Solana Madariaga (Spain).

The European Council

Since 1974 Heads of State or Government have met at least twice a year (until the end of 2002 in the capital of the member state currently exercising the presidency of the Council of European Union, since 2003 primarily in Brussels) in the form of the European Council or European Summit as it is commonly known. Its membership includes the President of the European Commission, and the President of the European Parliament is invited to make a presentation at the opening session. The European Council has become an increasingly important element of the Union, setting priorities, giving political direction, providing the impetus for its development and resolving contentious issues that prove too difficult for the Council of the European Union. It has a direct role to play in the context of the Common Foreign and Security Policy (CFSP) when deciding upon common strategies, and at a more general level, when deciding upon the establishing of closer co-operation between member states within certain policy areas covered by the EU-treaties. Moreover, during recent years, the European Council has played a preponderant role in defining the general political guidelines within key policy areas with a bearing on growth and employment and in the context of the strengthening of the EU as an area of freedom, security and justice.

European Parliament

The European Parliament consists of 732 members, elected in all 25 EU member states for five-year terms between 10–13 June 2004. For the five-year term from 1999–2004 there had been 626 members elected in what were then the 15 member countries, but in June 2004 voting also took place in the ten countries that had joined the EU on 1 May 2004.

All EU citizens may stand or vote in their adoptive country of residence. Germany returned 99 members in 2004 (99 in 1999), France, Italy and the UK 78 each (87 each in 1999), Poland and Spain 54 each (Spain 64 in 1999), the Netherlands 27 (31 in 1999), Belgium, Czech Republic, Greece, Hungary and Portugal 24 each (Belgium, Greece and Portugal 25 each in 1999), Sweden 19 (22 in 1999), Austria 18 (21 in 1999), Denmark, Finland and Slovakia 14 each (Denmark and Finland 16 each in 1999), Ireland and Lithuania 13 each (Ireland 15 in 1999), Latvia 9, Slovenia 7, Cyprus, Estonia and Luxembourg 6 each (Luxembourg 6 in 1999), and Malta 5.

Political groupings. Following the 2004 elections to the European Parliament the European People's Party–European Democrats (EPP-ED) had 268 seats, Party of European Socialists (PES) 200, Alliance of Liberals and Democrats for Europe (ALDE) 88, Greens/European Free Alliance (Greens/EFA) 42, European Unitary Left/Nordic Green Left (EUL/NGL) 41, Independence and Democracy Group (IND/DEM) 37, Union for a Europe of Nations (UEN) 27, Non-attached members (NI) 29.

The Parliament has a right to be consulted on a wide range of legislative proposals and forms one arm of the Community's Budgetary Authority. Under the Single European Act, it gained greater authority in legislation through the 'concertation' procedure under which it can reject certain Council drafts in a second reading procedure. Under the Maastricht Treaty, it gained the right of 'co-decision' on legislation with the Council of Ministers on a restricted range of domestic matters. The President of the European Council must report to the Parliament on progress in the development of foreign and security policy. It also plays an important role in appointing the President and members of the Commission. It can hold individual commissioners to account and can pass a motion of censure on the entire Commission, a prospect that was realized in March 1999 when the Commission, including the President, Jacques Santer, was forced to resign following an investigation into mismanagement and corruption. Parliament's seat is in Strasbourg where the one-week plenary sessions are held each month. In the Chamber, members sit in political groups, not as national delegations. All the activities of the Parliament and its bodies are the responsibility of the Bureau, consisting of the President and 14 Vice-Presidents elected for a two-and-a-half year period.

Location: Brussels, but meets at least once a month in Strasbourg.
President: Josep Borrell (Spain; PES).

Court of Justice of the European Communities

The Court of Justice of the European Communities is composed of 25 judges and eight advocates general. It is responsible for the adjudication of disputes arising out of the application of the treaties, and its findings are enforceable in all member countries. A Court of First Instance (est. 1989) handles certain categories of cases, including cases arising under the competition rules of the EC and cases brought by Community officials.

Address: Court of Justice of the European Communities, L-2925 Luxembourg.
President of the Court of Justice: Vassilios Skouris (Greece).

President of the Court of First Instance: Bo Vesterdorf (Denmark).

European Court of Auditors

The European Court of Auditors was established by a treaty of 22 July 1975 which took effect on 1 June 1977. It consists of 25 members (one from each member state) and was raised to the status of a full EU institution by the 1993 Maastricht Treaty. It audits the accounts and verifies the implementation of the budget of the EU.

Address: 12, rue Alcide De Gasperi, L-1615 Luxembourg.
Website: http://www.eca.eu.int
e-mail: euraud@eca.eu.int
President: Hubert Weber (Austria).

European Ombudsman

The Ombudsman was inaugurated in 1995 and deals with complaints from citizens, companies and organizations concerning maladministration in the activities of the institutions and bodies of the European Union. The present incumbent is P. Nikiforos Diamandouros (Greece).

Address: 1 avenue du Président Robert Schuman, B.P. 403, F-67001 Strasbourg Cedex, France.
Website: http://www.euro-ombudsman.eu.int
e-mail: euro-ombudsman@europarl.eu.int

European Investment Bank (EIB)

The EIB is the financing institution of the European Union, created by the Treaty of Rome in 1958 as an autonomous body set up to finance capital investment furthering European integration. To this end, the Bank raises its resources on the world's capital markets where it mobilizes significant volumes of funds on favourable terms. It directs these funds towards capital projects promoting EU economic policies. Outside the Union the EIB implements the financial components of agreements concluded under European Union development aid and co-operation policies. The members of the EIB are the member states of the European Union, who have all subscribed to the Bank's capital. Its governing body is its Board of Governors consisting of the ministers designated by each of the member states, usually the finance ministers.

Address: 100 Bd Konrad Adenauer, L-2950 Luxembourg.
Website: http://www.eib.org
President and Chairman of the Board: Philippe Maystadt (Belgium).

European System of Central Banks (ESCB)

The ESCB is composed of the European Central Bank (ECB) and 25 National Central Banks (NCBs). The NCBs of the member states not participating in the euro area are members with special status; while they are allowed to conduct their respective national monetary policies, they do not take part in decision-making regarding the single monetary policy for the euro area and the implementation of these policies. The Governing Council of the ECB makes a distinction between the ESCB and the 'Eurosystem' which is composed of the ECB and the 12 fully participating NCBs.

Members. The 12 fully participating National Central Banks are from: Austria, Belgium, Finland, France, Germany, Greece, Ireland, Italy, Luxembourg, Netherlands, Portugal and Spain. The other 13 EU members (those which do not use the euro as their currency) have special status.

Functions. The primary objective of the ESCB is to maintain price stability. Without prejudice to this, the ESCB supports general economic policies in the Community with a view to contributing to the achievement of the objectives of the Community. Tasks to be carried out include: i) defining and implementing the monetary policy of the Community; ii) conducting foreign exchange operations; iii) holding and managing the official foreign reserves of the participating member states; iv) promoting the smooth operation of payment systems; v) supporting the policies of the competent authorities relating to the prudential supervision of credit institutions and the stability of the financial system.

The ECB has the exclusive right to issue banknotes within the Community.

Organization. The ESCB is governed by the decision-making bodies of the ECB: the Governing Council and the Executive Board. The Governing Council is the supreme decision-making body and comprises all members of the Executive Board plus the governors of the NCBs forming the Eurosystem. The Executive Board comprises the president, vice-president and four other members, appointed by common accord of the heads of state and government of the participating member states. There is also a General Council which will exist while there remain members with special status.

Address: Kaiserstrasse 29, 60311 Frankfurt am Main, Germany.
President: Jean-Claude Trichet (France).

The Consultative Bodies There are two main consultative committees whose members are appointed in a personal capacity and are not bound by any mandatory instruction.

1. *Economic and Social Committee.* The 222-member committee is consulted by the Council of Ministers or by the European Commission, particularly with regard to agriculture, free movement of workers, harmonization of laws and transport. It is served by a permanent and independent General Secretariat, headed by a Secretary-General.

Secretary-General: Patrick Venturini (France).

2. *Committee of the Regions.* A political assembly which provides representatives of local, regional and city authorities with a voice at the heart of the European Union. Established by the Maastricht Treaty, the Committee consists of 317 full members and an equal number of alternates appointed for a four-year term. It must be consulted by the European Commission and Council of Ministers whenever legislative proposals are made in areas which have repercussions at the regional or local level. The Committee can also draw up opinions on its own initiative, which enables it to put issues on the EU agenda.

President: Peter Straub (Germany).

Statistical Office of the European Communities (Eurostat)

Eurostat's mission is to provide the EU with a high-quality statistical service. It receives statistical data collected according to uniform rules from the national statistical institutes of member states, then consolidates and harmonizes the data, before making them available to the public as printed or electronic publications. The data are directly available from the Eurostat website.

Address: Jean Monnet Building, L-2920 Luxembourg.
Website: http://www.europa.eu.int/comm/eurostat

EU general information. The Office for Official Publications of the European Communities is the publishing house of the institutions and other bodies of the European Union. It is responsible for producing and distributing EU publications on all media and by all means.

Address: 2 rue Mercier, L-2985 Luxembourg.
Website: http://publications.eu.int

EU Agencies and Other Bodies

Community Plant Variety Office

Launched in 1995 to administer a system of plant variety rights. The system allows Community Plant Variety Rights (CPVRs), valid throughout the European Union, to be granted for new plant varieties as sole and exclusive form of Community intellectual property rights.

Address: P.O Box 2141-3, Boulevard Maréchal Foch, F-49021 Angers Cédex 02, France.

European Medicines Agency

Founded in 1995 (as European Agency for the Evaluation of Medicinal Products) to evaluate the quality and effectiveness of health products for human and veterinary use.

Address: 7 Westferry Circus, Canary Wharf, London E14 4HB, UK.

European Agency for Reconstruction

Founded in 2000, with responsibility for the management of the main EU assistance programmes in Serbia and Montenegro and the former Yugoslav Republic of Macedonia.

Address: Egnatia 4, Thessaloniki 54626, Greece.

European Agency for Safety and Health at Work

Founded in 1996 in order to serve the information needs of people with an interest in occupational safety and health.

Address: Gran Via 33, E-48009 Bilbao, Spain.

European Centre for the Development of Vocational Training

Generally known as Cedefop (Centre Européen pour le Développement de la Formation Professionnelle), it was set up to help policy-makers and practitioners of the European Commission, the member states and social partner organizations across Europe make informed choices about vocational training policy.

Address: PO Box 22427, Thessaloniki 55102, Greece.

European Environment Agency

Launched by the EU in 1993 with a mandate to orchestrate, cross-check and put to strategic use information of relevance to the protection and improvement of Europe's environment. Based in Copenhagen, it has a mandate to ensure objective, reliable and comprehensive information on the environment at European level to enable its members to take the requisite measures to protect it. The Agency carries out its tasks through the European Information and Observation Network (EIONET). Membership is open to countries outside the EU that share the Agency's concerns. Current membership includes all EU countries, Bulgaria, Iceland, Liechtenstein, Norway, Romania and Turkey.

Address: Kongens Nytorv 6, 1050 Copenhagen K, Denmark.

European Foundation for the Improvement of Living and Working Conditions

Launched in 1975 to contribute to the planning and establishment of better living and working conditions. The Foundation's role is to provide findings, knowledge and advice from comparative research managed in a European perspective, which respond to the needs of the key parties at the EU level.

Address: Wyatville Road, Loughlinstown, Dublin 18, Ireland.

European Investment Fund

Founded in 1994 as a subsidiary of the European Investment Bank and the European Union's specialized financial institution. It has a dual mission that combines the pursuit of objectives such as innovation, the creation of employment and regional development with maintaining a commercial approach to investments. It particularly provides venture capital and guarantee instruments for the growth of small and medium-sized enterprises (SMEs). In 2002 it began advising entities in the setting up of financial enterprise and venture capital and SME guarantee schemes. A team has been created to structure and expand its advisory services.

Address: 43 avenue J. F. Kennedy, L-2968 Luxembourg.

European Monitoring Centre for Drugs and Drug Addiction

Established in 1993 to provide the European Union and its member states with objective, reliable and comparable information on a European level concerning drugs and drug addiction and their consequences.

Address: Rua da Cruz de Santa Apolónia 23–25, PT-1149-045 Lisbon, Portugal.

European Monitoring Centre on Racism and Xenophobia

Established in 1997 as an independent body to contribute towards the combat against racism, xenophobia and anti-semitism throughout Europe. It has the task of reviewing the extent and development of the racist, xenophobic and anti-semitic phenomena in the European Union and promoting 'best practice' among the member states.

Address: Rahlgasse 3, A-1060 Vienna, Austria.

European Training Foundation

Launched in 1995 to contribute to the process of vocational education and training reform that is currently taking place within the EU's partner countries and territories.

Address: Villa Gualino, viale Settimio Severo 65, I-10133 Turin, Italy.

Europol

Founded on 3 Jan. 1994 to exchange criminal intelligence between EU countries. Its precursor was the Europol Drug Unit, which initially dealt with the fight against drugs, progressively adding other areas. Europol took up its full activities on 1 July 1999. Europol's current mandate includes the prevention and combat of illicit drug trafficking, crimes involving illegal immigration networks, illicit vehicle trafficking, trafficking in human beings including child pornography, forgery of money and means of payment, terrorism and associated money laundering activities. There are about 490 staff members from all member states. Of these, 80 are ELOs (Europol Liaison Officers) working for their national police, gendarmerie, customs or immigration services. The 2005 budget was €63·4m. Member countries subscribe in proportion to their GNP.

Address: Raamweg 47, The Hague, Netherlands.
Website: http://www.europol.eu.int
e-mail: info@europol.eu.int
Director: Max-Peter Ratzel (Germany).

Office for Harmonization in the Internal Market

The Office was established in 1994, and is responsible for registering Community trade marks and designs. Both Community trade marks and Community designs confer their proprietors a uniform right, which confers all member states of the EU by means of one single application and one single registration procedure.

Address: Avenida de Europa 4, Apartado de Correos 77, E-03080 Alicante, Spain.

Translation Centre for Bodies of the European Union

Established in 1994, the Translation Centre's mission is to meet the translation needs of the other decentralized Community agencies. It also participates in the Interinstitutional Committee for Translation and Interpretation.

Address: Bâtiment Nouvel Hémicycle 1, rue du Fort Thüngen, L-1499 Luxembourg Kirchberg, Luxembourg.

European Food Safety Agency

Founded in 2002 to provide independent scientific advice on all matters with a direct or indirect impact on food safety.

Address: Rue de Genève 1, B-1140 Brussels, Belgium.

Further Reading

Official Journal of the European Communities.—General Report on the Activities of the European Communities (annual, from 1967).—*The Agricultural Situation in the Community* (annual).—*The Social Situation in the Community* (annual).—*Report on Competition Policy in the European Community* (annual).—*Bulletin of the European Community* (monthly).—*Register of Current Community Legal Instruments* (biannual).
Brittan, L., *The Europe We Need.* London, 1994.— *A Diet of Brussels: The Changing Face of Europe.* London, 2000
Burca, de, Gràinne and Scott, Joanne, *Constitutional Change in the EU: From Uniformity to Flexibility?* Hart, Oxford, 2000
Cowles, M. G. and Dinan, D., *Developments in the European Union 2.* Palgrave Macmillan, Basingstoke and New York, 2004
Davies, N., *Europe: A History.* London, 1997
Dinan, D., *The Encyclopaedia of the European Union.* Boulder (CO) and Basingstoke, 2000.—*Europe Recast: A History of European Union.* Boulder (CO) and Basingstoke, 2004.—*Ever Closer Union? An Introduction to the European Union.* 3rd ed. Boulder (CO) and Basingstoke, 2005
Dod's European Companion. Hurst Green, East Sussex. Occasional
Greenwood, J., *Interest Representation in the European Union.* Palgrave Macmillan, Basingstoke and New York, 2003
Hitiris, T., *European Community Economics: a Modern Introduction.* London, 1991
Judge, D. and Earnshaw, D., *The European Parliament.* Palgrave Macmillan, Basingstoke and New York, 2003
Lea, Ruth, *The Essential Guide to the European Union.* Centre for Policy Studies, London, 2004
Lewis, D. W. P., *The Road to Europe: History, Institutions and Prospects of European Integration, 1945–1993.* Berne, 1994
Mancini, Judge G. F., *Democracy and Constitutionalism in the European Union.* Hart, Oxford, 2000
Mazower, M., *Dark Continent: Europe's 20th Century.* London, 1998
McCormick, J., *Understanding the European Union.* 3rd ed. Palgrave Macmillan, Basingstoke and New York, 2005
Nugent, N., *The European Commission.* Palgrave, Basingstoke and New York, 2000.—*The Government and Politics of the European Union.* 5th ed. Basingstoke and Durham (NC), 2003.—*European Union Enlargement.* Palgrave Macmillan, Basingstoke and New York, 2004
Wallace, Helen, Wallace, William and Pollack, Mark, (eds.) *Policy-Making in the European Union.* 5th ed. OUP, 2005

Council of Europe

Origin and Membership. In 1948 the Congress of Europe, bringing together at The Hague nearly 1,000 influential Europeans from 26 countries, called for the creation of a united Europe, including a European Assembly. This proposal, examined first by the Ministerial Council of the Brussels Treaty Organization, then by a conference of ambassadors, was at the origin of the Council of Europe, which is, with its 46 member States, the widest organization bringing together all European democracies. The Statute of the Council was signed at London on 5 May 1949 and came into force two months later.

The founder members were Belgium, Denmark, France, Ireland, Italy, Luxembourg, the Netherlands, Norway, Sweden and the UK. Turkey and Greece joined in 1949, Iceland in 1950, the Federal Republic of Germany in 1951 (having been an associate since 1950), Austria in 1956, Cyprus in 1961, Switzerland in 1963, Malta in 1965, Portugal in 1976, Spain in 1977, Liechtenstein in 1978, San Marino in 1988, Finland in 1989, Hungary in 1990, Czechoslovakia (after partitioning, the Czech Republic and Slovakia rejoined in 1993) and Poland in 1991, Bulgaria in 1992, Estonia, Lithuania, Romania and Slovenia in 1993, Andorra in 1994, Albania, Latvia, Macedonia, Moldova and Ukraine in 1995, Croatia and Russia in 1996, Georgia in 1999, Armenia and Azerbaijan in 2001, Bosnia-Herzegovina in 2002, Serbia and Montenegro in 2003 and Monaco in 2004.

Membership is limited to European states which 'accept the principles of the rule of law and of the enjoyment by all persons within [their] jurisdiction of human rights and fundamental freedoms'. The Statute provides for both withdrawal (Article 7) and suspension (Articles 8 and 9). Greece withdrew during 1969–74.

Aims and Achievements. Article 1 of the Statute states that the Council's aim is 'to achieve a greater unity between its members for the purpose of safeguarding and realizing the ideals and principles which are their common heritage and facilitating their economic and social progress'; 'this aim shall be pursued ... by discussion of questions of common concern and by agreements and common action'. The only limitation is provided by Article 1 (d), which excludes 'matters relating to national defence'.

The main areas of the Council's activity are: human rights, the media, social and socio-economic questions, education, culture and sport, youth, public health, heritage and environment, local and regional government, and legal co-operation. 198 Conventions and Agreements have been concluded covering such matters as social security, cultural affairs, conservation of European wildlife and natural habitats, protection of archaeological heritage, extradition, medical treatment, equivalence of degrees and diplomas, the protection of television broadcasts, adoption of children and transportation of animals.

Treaties in the legal field include the adoption of the European Convention on the Suppression of Terrorism, the European Convention on the Legal Status of Migrant Workers and the Transfer of Sentenced Persons. The Committee of Ministers adopted a European Convention for the protection of individuals with regard to the automatic processing of personal data (1981), a Convention on the compensation of victims of violent crimes (1983), a Convention on spectator violence and misbehaviour at sports events and in particular at football matches (1985), the European Charter of Local Government (1985), and a Convention for the Prevention of Torture and Inhuman or Degrading Treatment or Punishment (1987). The European Social Charter of 1961 sets out the social and economic rights which all member governments agree to guarantee to their citizens.

European Social Charter. The Charter defines the rights and principles which are the basis of the Council's social policy, and guarantees a number of social and economic rights to the citizen, including the right to work, the right to form workers' organizations, the right to social security and assistance, the right of the family to protection and the right of migrant workers to protection and assistance. Two committees, comprising independent and government experts, supervise the parties' compliance with their obligations under the Charter. A revised charter, incorporating new rights such as protection for those without jobs and opportunities for workers with family responsibilities, was opened for signature on 3 May 1996 and entered into force on 1 July 1999.

Human rights. The promotion and development of human rights is one of the major tasks of the Council of Europe. The European Convention on Human Rights, signed in 1950, set up special machinery to guarantee internationally fundamental rights and freedoms. The European Commission of Human Rights which was set up has now been abolished and has been replaced by the new European Court of Human Rights, which came into operation on 1 Nov. 1998. The European Court of Human Rights in Strasbourg, set up under the European Convention on Human Rights as amended, is composed of a number of judges equal to that of the Contracting States (currently 46). There is no restriction on the number of judges of the same nationality. Judges are elected by the Parliamentary Assembly of the Council of Europe for a term of six years. The terms of office of one half of the judges elected at the first election expired after three years, so as to ensure that the terms of office of one half of the judges are renewed every three years. Any Contracting State (State application) or individual claiming to be a victim of a violation of the Convention (individual application) may lodge directly with the Court in Strasbourg an application alleging a breach by a Contracting State of one of the Convention rights.

President of the European Court of Human Rights: Luzius Wildhaber (Switzerland).

The Development Bank, formerly the Social Development Fund, was created in 1956. The main purpose of the Bank is to give financial aid in the spheres of housing, vocational training, regional planning and development.

The *European Youth Foundation* provides money to subsidize activities by European youth organizations in their own countries.

Structure. Under the Statute, two organs were set up: an intergovernmental *Committee of [Foreign] Ministers* with powers of decision and recommendation to governments, and an interparliamentary deliberative body, the *Parliamentary Assembly* (referred to in the Statute as the Consultative Assembly)—both served by the Secretariat. A Joint Committee acts as an organ of co-ordination and liaison between the two and gives members an opportunity to exchange views on matters of important European interest. In addition, a number of committees of experts have been established. On municipal matters the Committee of Ministers receives recommendations from the Congress of Local and Regional Authorities of Europe. The Committee usually meets twice a year and has a rotatory chair; their deputies meet once a week.

The *Parliamentary Assembly* consists of 315 parliamentarians elected or appointed by their national parliaments (Albania 4, Andorra 2, Armenia 4, Austria 6, Azerbaijan 6, Belgium 7, Bosnia-Herzegovina 5, Bulgaria 6, Croatia 5, Cyprus 3, the Czech Republic 7, Denmark 5, Estonia 3, Finland 5, France 18, Georgia 5, Germany 18, Greece 7, Hungary 7, Iceland 3, Ireland 4, Italy 18, Latvia 3, Liechtenstein 2, Lithuania 4, Luxembourg 3, Macedonia 3, Malta 3, Moldova 5, Monaco 2, Netherlands 7, Norway 5, Poland 12, Portugal 7, Romania 10, Russia 18, San Marino 2, Serbia and Montenegro 7, Slovakia 5, Slovenia 3, Spain 12, Sweden 6, Switzerland 6, Turkey 12, Ukraine 12, UK 18). It meets three times a year for approximately a week. The work of the Assembly is prepared by parliamentary committees. Since June 1989 representatives of a number of central and East European countries have been permitted to attend as non-voting members ('special guests'). Armenia and Azerbaijan have subsequently become full members.

Although without legislative powers, the Assembly acts as the powerhouse of the Council, initiating European action in key areas by making recommendations to the Committee of Ministers. As the widest parliamentary forum in Western Europe, the Assembly also acts as the conscience of the area by voicing its opinions on important current issues. These are embodied in Resolutions. The Ministers' role is to translate the Assembly's recommendations into action, particularly as regards lowering the barriers between the European countries, harmonizing their legislation or introducing, where possible, common European laws, abolishing discrimination on grounds of nationality, and undertaking certain tasks on a joint European basis.

Official languages: English and French.
Headquarters: Council of Europe, F-67075 Strasbourg Cedex, France.
Website: http://www.coe.int
e-mail: infopoint@coe.int
Secretary-General: Terry Davis (UK).

Publications. European Yearbook, The Hague; *Yearbook on the Convention on Human Rights,* Strasbourg; *Catalogue of Publications* (annual); *Activities Report* (annual). Information on other bulletins and documents is available on the Council of Europe's website.

Further Reading

Cook, C. and Paxton, J., *European Political Facts of the Twentieth Century.* Macmillan, London, 2000

Western European Union (WEU)

Origin. In March 1948 the signing of the Brussels Treaty of Economic, Social and Cultural Collaboration and Collective Defence by Belgium, France, Luxembourg, the Netherlands and the UK opened the way for the establishment of Western European Union. Six years later, the Paris Agreements, signed in Oct. 1954, which amended the Brussels Treaty, gave birth to WEU as a new international organization and provided for the Federal Republic of Germany and Italy to join. WEU came into being in 1955. Today, as an international defence and security organization, it brings together 28 nations encompassing four types of status: member state, associate member, observer and associate partner. Only the ten member states are signatories to the modified Brussels Treaty and have full decision making rights in WEU. The other 18 countries have been increasingly associated with WEU's activities. WEU's role and operational capabilities developed considerably after 1991. This development was based on close co-operation with the European Union and NATO. WEU acquired the necessary instruments to undertake any European-led crisis management operations and worked to develop them further as preparation for the establishment within the European Union of a crisis management capability in accordance with the decisions taken at the Cologne European Council in June 1999. Following decisions taken by the European Council since its meeting in Cologne to strengthen the European Security and Defence Policy within the EU, WEU relinquished its crisis management functions to the EU on 1 July 2001.

Member states. Belgium, France, Germany, Greece, Italy, Luxembourg, the Netherlands, Portugal, Spain and the UK. Associate members: Czech Republic, Hungary, Iceland, Norway, Poland and Turkey. Observers: Austria, Denmark, Finland, Ireland and Sweden. Associate partners: Bulgaria, Estonia, Latvia, Lithuania, Romania, Slovakia and Slovenia.

Reform. A joint meeting of the foreign and defence ministers within the WEU framework, held in Rome on 26–27 Oct. 1984, was marked by the adoption of the founding text of WEU's reactivation: the *Rome Declaration*. Work on the definition of a European security identity and the gradual harmonization of its members' defence policies were among the stated objectives. Ministers recognized the 'continuing necessity to strengthen western security, and that better utilization of WEU would not only contribute to the security of Western Europe but also to an improvement in the common defence of all the countries of the Atlantic Alliance'.

In 1987 WEU foreign and defence ministers adopted the *Hague Platform on European Security Interests*, defining the conditions and criteria for European security, and the responsibilities of WEU members to provide an integrated Europe with a security and defence dimension. In 1987 and 1988, following the laying of mines in the Persian Gulf during the Iran–Iraq war, mine-sweepers dispatched by WEU countries helped secure free movement in international waters. Operation Cleansweep helped to complete the clearance of a 480-km sea lane from the Strait of Hormuz, and was the first instance of a concerted action in WEU. During the Gulf Crisis, at the end of 1990 and early 1991, co-ordinated action took place among WEU nations contributing forces and other forms of support to the coalition forces involved in the liberation of Kuwait.

At the Alliance Summit of Jan. 1994 NATO leaders gave their full support to the development of a European Security and Defence Identity (ESDI) and to the strengthening of WEU. They declared their readiness to make collective assets of the Alliance available for WEU operations. The Alliance leaders also endorsed the concept of Combined Joint Task Forces (CJTFs) with the objective not only of adapting Alliance structures to NATO's new missions but also of improving co-operation with WEU, and in order to reflect the emerging ESDI. Work on the CJTF concept came to fruition at the NATO Ministerial meeting in Berlin in June 1996. One of the fundamental objectives of the Alliance adaptation process identified by NATO Ministers in Berlin was the development of the European Security and Defence Identity within the Alliance.

With the agreement on the Treaty of Amsterdam revising the Treaty on European Union, WEU has drawn closer to the EU. In particular, the European Council's guidelines for the Common Foreign Security Policy (CFSP) 'shall obtain in respect of WEU for those matters for which the Union avails itself of the WEU'; and the Petersberg tasks have been incorporated into the EU Treaty. It is stated that WEU is an integral part of the development of the European Union, giving the Union access to an operational capability, notably in the context of the Petersberg tasks. In the WEU Ministerial Declaration of 22 July 1997 responding to the Treaty of Amsterdam, WEU confirmed its readiness to develop WEU's relations with the EU and work out arrangements for enhanced co-operation.

Operations. In the context of the Yugoslav conflict, WEU has undertaken three operations, two of them to help in the enforcement of sanctions imposed by the UN Security Council (the WEU/NATO operation SHARP GUARD in the Adriatic and the WEU Danube operation) and one to assist in the European Union administration of the town of Mostar. From 1997 to 2001 WEU deployed a Multinational Advisory Police Element (MAPE) in Albania to assist in the reorganization of the Albanian Police. A WEU Demining Assistance Mission to Croatia (WEUDAM), operating from May 1999 to Nov. 2001, provided advice, technical expertise and training support to the Croatian Mine Action Centre.

Organization. WEU comprises an intergovernmental policy-making council and an assembly of parliamentary representatives, together with a number of subsidiary bodies set up by the council to facilitate its work. Since the 1984 reforms, the Council, supreme authority of the WEU, meets twice a year at ministerial level (foreign and defence) in the capital of the presiding country. The presidency rotates biannually. The Permanent Council, chaired by the Secretary-General, meets whenever necessary at ambassadorial level, at the WEU headquarters in Brussels. The WEU Assembly, located in Paris, comprises 115 parliamentarians of member states and meets twice a year, in plenary sessions in Paris. There are Permanent Committees on: defence questions and armaments; political affairs; technological and aerospace questions; budgetary affairs and administration; rules of procedure and privileges; and parliamentary and public relations.

Headquarters: WEU, B-1000 Brussels, Belgium.
Websites: http://www.weu.int; http://www.assembly-weu.org
Secretary-General: Dr Javier Solana Madariaga (Spain).

Organization for Security and Co-operation in Europe (OSCE)

The OSCE is a pan-European security organization of 55 participating states. It has been recognized under the UN Charter as a primary instrument in its region for early warning, conflict prevention, crisis management and post-conflict rehabilitation.

Origin. Initiatives from both NATO and the Warsaw Pact culminated in the first summit Conference on Security and Co-operation in Europe (CSCE) attended by heads of state and government in Helsinki on 30 July–1 Aug. 1975. It adopted the *Helsinki Final Act* laying down ten principles governing the behaviour of States towards their citizens and each other, concerning human rights, self-determination and the interrelations of the participant states. The CSCE was to serve as a multilateral forum for dialogue and negotiations between East and West.

The Helsinki Final Act comprised three main sections: 1) politico-military aspects of security: principles guiding relations between and among participating States and military confidence-building measures; 2) co-operation in the fields of economics, science and technology and the environment; 3) co-operation in humanitarian and other fields.

From CSCE to OSCE. The Paris Summit of Nov. 1990 set the CSCE on a new course. In the Charter of Paris for a New Europe, the CSCE was called upon to contribute to managing the historic change in Europe and respond to the new challenges of the post-Cold War period. At the meeting, members of NATO and the Warsaw Pact signed an important Treaty on Conventional Armed Forces in Europe (CFE) and a declaration that they were 'no longer adversaries' and did not intend to 'use force against the territorial integrity or political independence of any state'. All 34 participants adopted the Vienna Document comprising Confidence and Security-Building Measures (CSBMs), which pertain to the exchange of military information, verification of military installations, objection to unusual military activities etc., and signed the Charter of Paris. The Charter sets out principles of human rights, democracy and the rule of law to which all the signatories undertake to adhere, and lays down the basis for East-West co-operation and other future action. The 1994 Budapest Summit recognized that the CSCE was no longer a conference and on 1 Jan. 1995 the CSCE changed its name to the Organization for Security and Co-operation in Europe (OSCE). The 1996 Lisbon Summit elaborated the OSCE's key role in fostering security and stability in all their dimensions. It also stimulated the development of an OSCE Document-Charter on European Security.

Members. Albania, Andorra, Armenia, Austria, Azerbaijan, Belarus, Belgium, Bosnia-Herzegovina, Bulgaria, Canada, Croatia, Cyprus, the Czech Republic, Denmark, Estonia, Finland, France, Georgia, Germany, Greece, Holy See, Hungary, Iceland, Ireland, Italy, Kazakhstan, Kyrgyzstan, Latvia, Liechtenstein, Lithuania, Luxembourg, Macedonia, Malta, Moldova, Monaco, Netherlands, Norway, Poland, Portugal, Romania, Russian Federation, San Marino, Serbia and Montenegro, Slovak Republic, Slovenia, Spain, Sweden, Switzerland, Tajikistan, Turkey, Turkmenistan, Ukraine, UK, USA and Uzbekistan. *Partners for co-operation:* Afghanistan, Japan, Mongolia, South Korea and Thailand. *Mediterranean partners for co-operation:* Algeria, Egypt, Israel, Jordan, Morocco, Tunisia.

Organization. The OSCE's regular body for political consultation and decision-making is the Permanent Council. Its members, the Permanent Representatives of the OSCE participating States, meet weekly in the Hofburg Congress Center in Vienna to discuss and take decisions on all issues pertinent to the OSCE. The Forum for Security Co-operation (FSC), which deals with arms control and confidence- and security-building measures, also meets weekly in Vienna. Summits—periodic meetings of Heads of State or Government of OSCE participating States—set priorities and provide orientation at the highest political level. In the years between these summits, decision-making and governing power lies with the *Ministerial Council*, which is made up of the Foreign Ministers of the OSCE participating States. In addition, a Senior Council also meets once a year in special session as the Economic Forum. The Chairman-in-Office has overall responsibility for executive action and agenda-setting. The Chair rotates annually. The Secretary-General acts as representative of the Chairman-in-Office and manages OSCE structures and operations.

The Secretariat is based in Vienna and includes a *Conflict Prevention Centre* which provides operational support for OSCE field missions. There are some 400 staff employed in OSCE institutions, and about 1,000 professionals, seconded by OSCE-participating states, work at OSCE missions and other field operations, together with another 2,500 local staff.

The *Office for Democratic Institutions and Human Rights* is located in Warsaw. It is active in monitoring elections and developing national electoral and human rights institutions, providing technical assistance to national legal institutions, and promoting the development of the rule of law and civil society.

The *Office of the Representative on Freedom of the Media* is located in Vienna. Its main function is to observe relevant media developments in OSCE participating States with a view to providing an early warning on violations of freedom of expression.

The *Office of the High Commissioner on National Minorities* is located in The Hague. Its function is to identify and seek early resolution of ethnic tensions that might endanger peace, stability or friendly relations between the participating States of the OSCE.

The budget for 2004 was €181m.

Headquarters: Kärntner Ring 5–7, A-1010 Vienna, Austria.
Website: http://www.osce.org
Chairman-in-Office: Karel De Gucht (Belgium).
Secretary-General: Marc Perrin de Brichambaut (France).

Further Reading
Freeman, J., *Security and the CSCE Process: the Stockholm Conference and Beyond.* London, 1991

European Bank for Reconstruction and Development (EBRD)

History. The European Bank for Reconstruction and Development was established in 1991 when communism was collapsing in central and eastern Europe and ex-Soviet countries needed support to nurture a new private sector in a democratic environment.

Activities. The EBRD is the largest single investor in the region and mobilizes significant foreign direct investment beyond its own financing. It is owned by 60 countries and two intergovernmental institutions. But despite its public sector shareholders, it invests mainly in private enterprises, usually together with commercial partners. Today the EBRD uses the tools of investment to help build market economies and democracies in 27 countries from Central Europe to Central Asia.

It provides project financing for banks, industries and businesses, for both new ventures and investments in existing companies. It also works with publicly-owned companies, to support privatization, restructuring of state-owned firms and improvement of municipal services. The EBRD uses its close relationship with governments in the region to promote policies that will bolster the business environment.

The mandate of the EBRD stipulates that it must only work in countries that are committed to democratic principles. Respect for the environment is part of the strong corporate governance attached to all EBRD investments.

Organization. All the powers of the EBRD are vested in a Board of Governors, to which each member appoints a governor, generally the minister of finance or an equivalent. The Board of Governors delegates powers to the Board of Directors, which is responsible for the direction of the EBRD's general operations and policies. The President is elected by the Board of Governors and is the legal representative of the EBRD. The President conducts the current business of the Bank under the guidance of the Board of Directors.

Headquarters: 1 Exchange Square, London EC2A 2JN, UK.
Website: http://www.ebrd.com
President: Jean Lemierre (France).
Secretary-General: Horst Reichenbach (Germany).

European Free Trade Association (EFTA)

History and Membership. The Stockholm Convention establishing the Association entered into force on 3 May 1960. Founder members were Austria, Denmark, Norway, Portugal, Sweden, Switzerland and the UK. With the accession of Austria, Denmark, Finland, Portugal, Sweden and the UK to the EU, EFTA was reduced to four member countries: Iceland, Liechtenstein, Norway and Switzerland. In June 2001 the Vaduz Convention was signed. It liberalizes trade further among the four EFTA States in order to reflect the Swiss–EU bilateral agreements.

Activities. Free trade in industrial goods among EFTA members was achieved by 1966. Co-operation with the EU began in 1972 with the signing of free trade agreements and culminated in the establishment of a *European Economic Area (EEA)*, encompassing the free movement of goods, services, capital and labour throughout EFTA and the EU member countries. The Agreement was signed by all members of the EU and EFTA on 2 May 1992, but was rejected by Switzerland in a referendum on 6 Dec. 1992. The agreement came into force on 1 Jan. 1994.

The main provisions of the EEA Agreement are: free movement of products within the EEA from 1993 (with special arrangements to cover food, energy, coal and steel); EFTA to assume EU rules on company law, consumer protection, education, the environment, research and development, and social policy; EFTA to adopt EU competition rules on anti-trust matters, abuse of a dominant position, public procurement, mergers and state aid; EFTA to create an EFTA Surveillance Authority and an EFTA Court; individuals to be free to live, work and offer services throughout the EEA, with mutual recognition of professional qualifications; capital movements to be free with some restrictions on investments; EFTA countries not to be bound by the Common Agricultural Policy (CAP) or Common Fisheries Policy (CFP).

The EEA-EFTA states have established a Surveillance Authority and a Court to ensure implementation of the Agreement among the EFTA-EEA states. Political direction is given by the EEA Council which meets twice a year at ministerial level, while ongoing operation of the Agreement is overseen by the EEA Joint Committee. Legislative power remains with national governments and parliaments.

EFTA has formal relations with several other states. Declarations on co-operation were signed with Hungary, former Czechoslovakia and Poland (1990), Bulgaria, Estonia, Latvia, Lithuania and Romania (1991), Slovenia and Albania (1992), Egypt, Morocco and Tunisia (1995), the former Yugoslav Republic of Macedonia and the Palestine Liberation Organization (1996), Jordan and Lebanon (1997), Croatia, the Gulf Co-operation Council, Serbia and Montenegro and MERCOSUR (2000) and Algeria (2002). Free trade agreements have been signed with Turkey (1991), Israel and Czechoslovakia (1992, with protocols on succession with the Czech Republic and Slovakia in 1993), Poland and Romania (1992), Bulgaria and Hungary (1993), Estonia, Latvia, Lithuania and Slovenia (1995), Morocco (1997), the Former Yugoslav Republic of Macedonia and Mexico (2000), Jordan and Croatia (2001), Singapore (2002), Chile (2003) and Lebanon and Tunisia (2004). In Dec. 1998 an interim free trade agreement was signed with the Palestinian Authority and talks on an agreement began with Egypt. Negotiations on free trade agreements are ongoing with Canada, Egypt and Cyprus.

Organization. The operation of the free trade area among the EFTA states is the responsibility of the EFTA Council which meets regularly at ambassadorial level in Geneva. The Council is assisted by a Secretariat and standing committees. Each EFTA country holds the chairmanship of the Council for six months. For EEA matters there is a separate committee structure.

Brussels Office (EEA matters, press and information): 12–16 Rue Joseph II, B-1000 Brussels.

Headquarters: 9–11 rue de Varembé, 1211 Geneva 20, Switzerland.
Website: http://www.efta.int
e-mail: efta-mailbox@secrbru.efta.be
Secretary-General: William Rossier (Switzerland).

Publications. Convention Establishing the European Free Trade Association; EFTA Annual Report; EFTA Fact Sheets: Information Papers on Aspects of the EEA; EFTA Bulletin.

European Space Agency (ESA)

History. Established in 1975, replacing the European Space Research Organization (ESRO) and the European Launcher Development Organization (ELDO).

Members. Austria, Belgium, Denmark, Finland, France, Germany, Greece, Ireland, Italy, Luxembourg, the Netherlands, Norway, Portugal, Spain, Sweden, Switzerland, United Kingdom. Canada takes part in some projects under a co-operation agreement.

Activities. ESA is the intergovernmental agency in Europe responsible for the exploitation of space science, research and technology for exclusively peaceful purposes. Its aim is to define and put into effect a long-term European space policy that allows Europe to remain competitive in the field of space technology. It has a policy of co-operation with various partners on the basis that pooling resources and sharing work will boost the effectiveness of its programmes. Its space plan covers the fields of science, Earth observation, telecommunications, navigation, space segment technologies, ground infrastructures, space transport systems and microgravity research.

Headquarters: 8–10 rue Mario Nikis, 75738 Paris Cedex 15, France.
Website: http://www.esa.int
e-mail: contactesa@esa.int
Director-General: Jean-Jacques Dordain (France).

CERN – The European Organization for Nuclear Research

Founded in 1954, CERN is the world's leading particle physics research centre. By studying the behaviour of nature's fundamental particles, CERN aims to find out what our Universe is made of and how it works. CERN's biggest accelerator, the Large Hadron Collider (LHC), is scheduled for completion in 2007. One of the beneficial byproducts of CERN activity is the Worldwide Web, developed at CERN to give particle physicists easy access to shared data. One of Europe's first joint ventures, CERN now has a membership of 20 member states: Austria, Belgium, Bulgaria, Czech Republic, Denmark, Finland, France, Germany, Greece, Hungary, Italy, the Netherlands, Norway, Poland, Portugal, Slovak Republic, Spain, Sweden, Switzerland, United Kingdom. Some 6,500 scientists, half of the world's particle physicists, use CERN's facilities. They represent 500 institutions and 85 nationalities.

Address: CH-1211 Geneva 23, Switzerland.
Website: http://www.cern.ch
Director-General: Dr Robert Aymar (France).

Central European Initiative (CEI)

In Nov. 1989 Austria, Hungary, Italy and Yugoslavia met on Italy's initiative to form an economic and political co-operation group in the region.

Members. Albania, Austria, Belarus, Bosnia-Herzegovina, Bulgaria, Croatia, Czech Republic, Hungary, Italy, Macedonia, Moldova, Poland, Romania, Serbia and Montenegro, Slovakia, Slovenia, Ukraine.

Address: Executive Secretariat, Via Genova 9, 34132 Trieste, Italy.
Website: http://www.ceinet.org
e-mail: cei-es@cei-es.org

Nordic Council

Founded in 1952 as a co-operative link between the parliaments and governments of the Nordic states. The co-operation focuses on Intra-Nordic co-operation, co-operation with Europe/EU/EEA and co-operation with the adjacent areas. The Council consists of 87 elected MPs and the committees meet several times a year, as required. Every year the Nordic Council grants prizes for literature, music, nature and environment.

Members. Denmark (including the Faroe Islands and Greenland), Finland (including Åland), Iceland, Norway, Sweden.

Address: Store Strandstræde 18, DK-1255 Copenhagen K, Denmark.
Website: http://www.norden.org/
e-mail: nordisk-rad@norden.org
President: Ole Stavad (Denmark).

Nordic Development Fund (NDF)

Established in 1989, the NDF is a development aid organization of the five Nordic countries, Denmark, Finland, Iceland, Norway and Sweden. NDF capital totals SDR 515m. and €330m. Credits are offered to developing countries, with poorer African, Asian and Latin American countries taking priority.

Address: Fabianinkatu 34, PO Box 185, FIN-00171 Helsinki, Finland.
Website: http://www.ndf.fi
e-mail: info.ndf@ndf.fi
President: Jens Lund Sørensen (Denmark).

Nordic Investment Bank (NIB)

The Nordic Investment Bank, which commenced operations in Aug. 1976, is a multilateral financial institution owned by Denmark, Estonia, Finland, Iceland, Latvia, Lithuania, Norway and Sweden. It finances public and private projects both within and outside the Nordic area. Priority is given to projects furthering economic co-operation between the member countries or improving the environment. Focal points include the neighbouring areas of the member countries.

Address: Fabianinkatu 34, PO Box 249, FI-00171 Helsinki, Finland.

Website: http://www.nib.int
e-mail: info@nib.int
President: Johnny Åkerholm (Finland).

Council of the Baltic Sea States

Established in 1992 in Copenhagen following a conference of ministers of foreign affairs.

Members. Denmark, Estonia, Finland, Germany, Iceland, Latvia, Lithuania, Norway, Poland, Russia, Sweden and the European Commission.

Aims. To promote co-operation in the Baltic Sea region in the field of trade, investment and economic exchanges, combating organized crime, civil security, culture and education, transport and communication, energy and environment, human rights and assistance to democratic institutions.

The Council meets at ministerial level once a year, chaired by rotating foreign ministers; it is the supreme decision-making body. Between annual sessions the Committee of Senior Officials and three working groups meet at regular intervals. In Oct. 1999 ministers of energy of the CBSS member states agreed to achieve the goal of creating effective, economically and environmentally sound and more integrated energy systems in the Baltic Sea region. Five summits at the level of heads of government of CBSS member states and the President of the European Commission have taken place; in 1996, 1998, 2000, 2002 and 2004. The Baltic Sea Region Energy Cooperation (BASREC) is made up of energy ministers from the region and is chaired by the energy minister from the chair country of the CBSS.

Official language: English.
CBSS Secretariat: Strömsborg, PO Box 2010, S-103 11 Stockholm, Sweden.
Website: http://www.cbss.st
Director of the Secretariat: Dr Gabriele Kötschau (Germany).

European Broadcasting Union (EBU)

Founded in 1950 by western European radio and television broadcasters the EBU is the world's largest professional association of national broadcasters, with 72 active members in 52 countries of Europe, North Africa and the Middle East, and 50 associate members in 30 countries elsewhere in Africa, the Americas and Asia.

The EBU merged with the OIRT, its counterpart in eastern Europe, in 1993. The EBU's Eurovision Operations Department has a permanent network offering 50 digital channels on five satellites. Two satellite channels also relay radio concerts, operas, sports fixtures and major news events for Euroradio.

Headquarters: Ancienne Route 17, CH-1218 Grand-Saconnex, Geneva, Switzerland.
Websites: http://www.ebu.ch; http://www.eurovision.net
e-mail: ebu@ebu.ch

Black Sea Economic Cooperation (BSEC)

Founded in 1992 to promote economic co-operation in the Black Sea region. Priority areas of interest include: trade and economic development; banking and finance; communications; energy; transport; agriculture and agro-industry; healthcare and pharmaceutics; environmental protection; tourism; science and technology; exchange of statistical data and economic information; combating organized crime, illicit trafficking of drugs, weapons and radioactive materials, all acts of terrorism and illegal immigration.

Members. Albania, Armenia, Azerbaijan, Bulgaria, Georgia, Greece, Moldova, Romania, Russia, Serbia and Montenegro, Turkey, Ukraine.

Observers. Austria, Belarus, Black Sea Commission, Croatia, Czech Republic, Energy Charter Secretariat, France, Germany, International Black Sea Club, Israel, Italy, Poland, Slovakia, Tunisia, USA.

The *Parliamentary Assembly of the Black Sea Economic Cooperation* is the BSEC parliamentary dimension. The *BSEC Business Council* is composed of representatives from the business circles of the member states. The *Black Sea Trade and Development Bank* is considered as the financial pillar of the BSEC. There is also an *International Center for Black Sea Studies* and a *Coordination Center for the Exchange of Statistical Data and Economic Information.*

> *Headquarters:* İstinye Cad., Müşir Fuad Paşa Yalısı, Eski Tersane 80860, İstinye, İstanbul, Turkey.
> *Website:* http://www.bsec-organization.org/
> *e-mail:* info@bsec-organization.org
> *Secretary-General:* Tedo Japaridze (Georgia).

Danube Commission

History and Membership. The Danube Commission was constituted in 1949 according to the Convention regarding the regime of navigation on the Danube signed in Belgrade on 18 Aug. 1948. The Belgrade Convention, amended by the Additional Protocol of 26 March 1998, declares that navigation on the Danube from Kelheim to the Black Sea (with access to the sea through the Sulina arm and the Sulina Canal) is equally free and open to the nationals, merchant shipping and merchandise of all states as to harbour and navigation fees as well as conditions of merchant navigation. The Commission holds annual sessions and is composed of one representative from each of its 11 member countries: Austria, Bulgaria, Croatia, Germany, Hungary, Moldova, Romania, Russia, Serbia and Montenegro, Slovakia and Ukraine.

Functions. To ensure that the provisions of the Belgrade Convention are carried out; to establish a uniform buoying system on all navigable waterways; to establish the basic regulations for navigation on the river and ensure facilities for shipping; to co-ordinate the regulations for river, customs and sanitation control as well as the hydrometeorological service; to collect relevant statistical data concerning navigation on the Danube; to propose measures for the prevention of pollution of the Danube caused by navigation; and to update its recommendations regularly with a view to bringing them in line with European Union regulations on inland waterway navigation.

> *Official languages:* German, French, Russian.
> *Headquarters:* Benczúr utca 25, H-1068 Budapest, Hungary.
> *Website:* http://www.danubecom-intern.org
> *e-mail:* secretariat@danubecom-intern.org
> *President:* Dr Stanko Nick (Croatia).
> *Director-General:* Capt. Danail Nedialkov (Bulgaria).

European Trade Union Confederation (ETUC)

Established in 1973, the ETUC is recognized by the EU, the Council of Europe and EFTA as the only representative cross-sectoral trade union organization at a European level. It has grown steadily with a membership of 76 National Trade Union Confederations from 35 countries and 11 European Industry Federations with a total of 60m. members. The Congress meets every four years; the 10th Statutory Congress took place in Prague in May 2003.

> *Address:* 5 Boulevard Roi Albert II, B-1210 Brussels, Belgium.
> *Website:* http://www.etuc.org
> *e-mail:* etuc@etuc.org
> *General Secretary:* John Monks (UK).

Amnesty International (AI)

Origin. Founded in 1961 by British lawyer Peter Benenson as a one-year campaign for the release of prisoners of conscience, Amnesty International has grown to become a worldwide organization, winning the Nobel Peace Prize in 1977.

Activities. AI is a worldwide movement of people who campaign for human rights. It works independently and impartially to promote respect for all the human rights set out in the Universal Declaration of Human Rights.

Historically, the main focus of AI's campaigning has been: to free all prisoners of conscience; to ensure a prompt and fair trial for all political prisoners; to abolish the death penalty, torture and other cruel, inhuman or degrading treatment or punishment; to end extrajudicial executions and 'disappearances'; to fight impunity by working to ensure perpetrators of such abuses are brought to justice in accordance with international standards.

AI has over 1·5m. members, subscribers and regular donors in more than 150 countries. The organization is a democratic, self-governing movement. Major policy decisions are taken by an International Council made up of representatives from all national sections. AI's national sections and local volunteer groups are primarily responsible for funding the movement. During the financial year 1 April 2002–31 March 2003 the international budget adopted by AI was £23,728,000 (including contingency).

Every year AI produces a global report detailing human rights violations in all regions of the world.

> *International Secretariat:* Peter Benenson House, 1 Easton Street, London WC1X 0DW, UK.
> *Website:* http://www.amnesty.org
> *Secretary-General:* Irene Khan (Bangladesh).

Bank for International Settlements (BIS)

Origin. Founded on 17 May 1930, the Bank for International Settlements fosters international monetary and financial co-operation and serves as a bank for central banks.

Aims. The BIS fulfils its mandate by acting as: a forum to promote discussion and facilitate decision-making processes among central banks and within the international financial community; a centre for economic and monetary research; a prime counterparty for central banks in their financial transactions; and an agent or trustee in connection with international financial operations.

Finance. Around 140 central banks and international financial institutions place deposits with the BIS. The total of currency deposits placed with the BIS amounted to SDR 200bn. at the end of March 2004, representing 6·5% of world foreign exchange reserves.

Organization and Membership. There are 55 member central banks. These are the central banks or monetary authorities of Algeria, Argentina, Australia, Austria, Belgium, Bosnia-Herzegovina, Brazil, Bulgaria, Canada, Chile, China, Croatia, the Czech Republic, Denmark, Estonia, Finland, France, Germany, Greece, Hong Kong, Hungary, Iceland, India, Indonesia, Ireland, Israel, Italy, Japan, South Korea, Latvia, Lithuania, Macedonia, Malaysia, Mexico, the Netherlands, New Zealand, Norway, Philippines, Poland, Portugal, Romania, Russia, Saudi Arabia, Singapore, Slovakia, Slovenia, South Africa, Spain, Sweden, Switzerland, Thailand, Turkey, UK and USA, as well as the European Central Bank.

The BIS is administered by a Board of Directors, which is comprised of the governors of the central banks of Belgium, France, Germany, Italy and the UK and the Chairman of the Board of Governors of the US Federal Reserve System as *ex officio* members, each of whom appoints another member of the same nationality. The Statutes also provide for the election to the Board of not more than nine Governors of other member central banks. The Governors of the central banks of Canada, Japan, the Netherlands, Sweden and Switzerland are currently elected members of the Board.

Headquarters: Centralbahnplatz 2 and Aeschenplatz 1, CH-Basle, Switzerland.
Website: http://www.bis.org
e-mail: email@bis.org
Chairman: Nout Wellink (Netherlands).
Representative Office for Asia and the Pacific: 78th Floor, Two International Finance Centre, 8 Finance Street, Central, Hong Kong SAR, People's Republic of China.
Representative Office for the Americas: Torre Chapultepec, Rubén Dario 281, Col. Bosque de Chapultepec, 11580 México, D. F., Mexico.

Further Reading

Deane, M. and Pringle, R., *The Central Banks*. London and New York, 1995
Fleming's Who's Who in Central Banking. London, 1997
Goodhart, C. A. E., *The Central Bank and the Financial System.* London, 1995

Commonwealth

The Commonwealth is a free association of sovereign independent states. It numbered 53 members in 2005. With a membership of 1·7bn. people, it represents over 30% of the world's population. There is no charter, treaty or constitution; the association is expressed in co-operation, consultation and mutual assistance for which the Commonwealth Secretariat is the central co-ordinating body.

Origin. The Commonwealth was first defined by the Imperial Conference of 1926 as a group of 'autonomous Communities within the British Empire, equal in status, in no way subordinate one to another in any aspect of their domestic or external affairs,

though united by a common allegiance to the Crown, and freely associated as members of the British Commonwealth of Nations'. The basis of the association changed from one owing allegiance to a common Crown, and the modern Commonwealth was born in 1949 when the member countries accepted India's intention of becoming a republic at the same time as continuing 'her full membership of the Commonwealth of Nations and her acceptance of the King as the symbol of the free association of its independent member nations and as such the Head of the Commonwealth'. In 2005 the Commonwealth consisted of 32 republics and 21 monarchies, of which 16 are Queen's realms. All acknowledge the Queen symbolically as Head of the Commonwealth. The Queen's legal title rests on the statute of 12 and 13 Will. III, c. 3, by which the succession to the Crown of Great Britain and Ireland was settled on the Princess Sophia of Hanover and the 'heirs of her body being Protestants'.

A number of territories, formerly under British jurisdiction or mandate, did not join the Commonwealth: Egypt, Iraq, Transjordan, Burma (now Myanmar), Palestine, Sudan, British Somaliland and Aden. Five countries, Ireland in 1948, South Africa in 1961, Pakistan in 1972, Fiji (now Fiji Islands) in 1987 and Zimbabwe in 2003 have left the Commonwealth. Pakistan was re-admitted to the Commonwealth in 1989, South Africa in 1994, Fiji Islands in 1997. Nigeria was suspended in 1995 for violation of human rights but was fully reinstated on 29 May 1999. Pakistan was suspended from the Commonwealth's councils following a coup in Oct. 1999 but was readmitted in May 2004. Fiji Islands was suspended from the Commonwealth's councils in June 2000 following a coup there but was re-admitted in Dec. 2001 following the restoration of democracy. Zimbabwe was suspended from the Commonwealth's councils for a year on 19 March 2002 for a 'high level of politically motivated violence' during the vote that saw President Robert Mugabe re-elected. In March 2003 it was suspended for a further nine months. The suspension was extended at the Abuja meeting in Dec. 2003. Mugabe responded by withdrawing Zimbabwe from the Commonwealth. Mozambique, admitted in Nov. 1995, is the first member state not to have been a member of the former British Commonwealth or Empire.

Member States of the Commonwealth

The 53 member states, with year of admission:

	Year of admission		Year of admission
Antigua and Barbuda	1981	Maldives	1982
Australia[1]	1931	Malta	1964
Bahamas	1973	Mauritius	1968
Bangladesh	1972	Mozambique	1995
Barbados	1966	Namibia	1990
Belize	1981	Nauru[2]	1968
Botswana	1966	New Zealand[1]	1931
Brunei[5]	1984	Nigeria[3]	1960
Cameroon	1995	Pakistan[4]	1989
Canada[1]	1931	Papua New Guinea	1975
Cyprus	1961	St Kitts and Nevis	1983
Dominica	1978	St Lucia	1979
Fiji Islands[6]	1997	St Vincent and Grenadines	1979
Gambia	1965	Samoa	1970
Ghana	1957	Seychelles	1976
Grenada	1974	Sierra Leone	1961
Guyana	1966	Singapore	1965
India	1947	Solomon Islands	1978
Jamaica	1962	South Africa[7]	1994
Kenya	1963	Sri Lanka	1948
Kiribati	1979	Swaziland	1968
Lesotho	1966	Tanzania	1961
Malawi	1964	Tonga[5]	1970
Malaysia	1957	Trinidad and Tobago	1962

	Year of admission		Year of admission
Tuvalu	1978	Vanuatu	1980
Uganda	1982	Zambia	1964
United Kingdom	1931		

[1]Independence given legal effect by the Statute of Westminster 1931.
[2]Nauru was first a Mandate, then a Trust territory.
It became a full member in 1999.
[3]Nigeria was suspended in 1995 but readmitted
as a full member in 1999.
[4]Left 1972, rejoined 1989.
[5]Brunei and Tonga had been sovereign states in treaty relationship
with Britain.
[6]Fiji left in 1987 but rejoined in 1997. It changed its name to
Fiji Islands in 1998.
[7]Left 1961, rejoined 1994.

Aims and Conditions of Membership. Membership involves acceptance of certain core principles, as set out in the Harare Declaration of 1991, and is subject to the approval of other member states. The Harare Declaration charted a course to take the Commonwealth into the 21st century affirming members' continued commitment to the Singapore Declaration of 1971, by which members committed themselves to the pursuit of world peace and support of the UN.

The core principles defined by the Harare Declaration are: political democracy, human rights, good governance and the rule of law, and the protection of the environment through sustainable development. Commitment to these principles was made binding as a condition of membership at the 1993 Heads of Government meeting in Cyprus.

The Millbrook Action Programme of 1995 aims to support countries in implementing the Harare Declaration, providing assistance in constitutional and judicial matters, running elections, training and technical advice. Violations of the Harare Declaration will provoke a series of measures by the Commonwealth Secretariat, including: expression of disapproval, encouragement of bilateral actions by member states, appointment of fact-finders and mediators, stipulation of a period for the restoration of democracy, exclusion from ministerial meetings, suspension of all participation and aid and finally punitive measures including trade sanctions. A nine-member *Commonwealth Ministerial Action Group on the Harare Declaration (CMAG)* may be convened by the Secretary-General as and when necessary to deal with violations. The Group held its first meeting in Dec. 1995. Its terms of reference are as set out in the Millbrook Action Programme.

The *Commonwealth Parliamentary Association* was founded in 1911. As defined by its constitution, its objectives are to 'promote knowledge of the constitutional, legislative, economic, social and cultural aspects of parliamentary democracy'. It meets these objectives by organizing conferences, meetings and seminars for members, arranging exchange visits between members, publishing books, newsletters, reports, studies and a quarterly journal and providing an information service. Its principal governing body is the General Assembly, which meets annually during the Commonwealth Parliamentary Conference and is composed of members attending that Conference as delegates. The Association elects an Executive Committee comprising a Chair, President, Vice-President, Treasurer and 27 regional representatives, which meets twice a year. The Chair is elected for three-year terms.

Commonwealth Secretariat. The Commonwealth Secretariat is an international body at the service of all 53 member countries. It provides the central organization for joint consultation and co-operation in many fields. It was established in 1965 by Commonwealth Heads of Government as a 'visible symbol of the spirit of co-operation which animates the Commonwealth', and has observer status at the UN General Assembly.

The Secretariat disseminates information on matters of common concern, organizes and services meetings and conferences, co-ordinates many Commonwealth activities, and provides expert technical assistance for economic and social development through the multilateral Commonwealth Fund for Technical Co-operation. The Secretariat is organized in divisions and sections which correspond to its main areas of operation: political affairs, economic affairs, human rights, gender affairs, youth affairs, education, information, law, health and a range of technical assistance and advisory services. Within this structure the Secretariat organizes the biennial meetings of Commonwealth Heads of Government (CHOGMs), annual meetings of Finance Ministers of member countries, and regular meetings of Ministers of Education, Law, Health, Gender Affairs and others as appropriate. To emphasize the multilateral nature of the association, meetings are held in different cities and regions within the Commonwealth. Heads of Government decided that the Secretariat should work from London as it has the widest range of communications of any Commonwealth city, as well as the largest assembly of diplomatic missions from Commonwealth member countries.

Commonwealth Heads of Government Meetings (CHOGMs). Outside the UN, the CHOGM remains the largest inter-governmental conference in the world. Meetings are held every two years. The 2002 CHOGM in Coolum, Australia, scheduled for Oct. 2001 but postponed following the attacks on the United States of 11 Sept. 2001, was dominated by the Zimbabwe issue, as was the meeting held in Abuja, Nigeria in Dec. 2003. The last meeting was held in Nov. 2005 in Malta. The 2007 CHOGM is scheduled to be held in Uganda. A host of Commonwealth organizations and agencies are dedicated to enhancing inter-Commonwealth relations and the development of the potential of Commonwealth citizens. They are listed in the Commonwealth Yearbook which is published by the Secretariat.

Commonwealth Day is celebrated on the second Monday in March each year. The theme for 2006 was 'Health and Vitality—The Commonwealth Challenge'.

Overseas Territories and Associated States. There are 14 United Kingdom overseas territories (see pages 1317–33), six Australian external territories (see pages 153–5), two New Zealand dependent territories and two New Zealand associated states (see pages 928–31). A dependent territory is a territory belonging by settlement, conquest or annexation to the British, Australian or New Zealand Crown.

United Kingdom Overseas Territories administered through the Foreign and Commonwealth Office comprise, in the Indian Ocean: British Indian Ocean Territory; in the Mediterranean: Gibraltar, the Sovereign Base Areas of Akrotiri and Dhekelia in Cyprus; in the Atlantic Ocean: Bermuda, Falkland Islands, South Georgia and South Sandwich Islands, British Antarctic Territory, St Helena and Dependencies (Ascension and Tristan da Cunha); in the Caribbean: Montserrat, British Virgin Islands, Cayman Islands, Turks and Caicos Islands, Anguilla; in the Western Pacific: Pitcairn Group of Islands.

The Australian external territories are: Ashmore and Cartier Islands, Australian Antarctic Territory, Christmas Island, Cocos (Keeling) Islands, Coral Sea Islands, Heard and McDonald Islands and Norfolk Island. The New Zealand external territories are: Tokelau Islands and the Ross Dependency. The New Zealand associated states are: Cook Islands and Niue.

Headquarters: Marlborough House, Pall Mall, London
SW1Y 5HX, UK.
Websites: http://www.thecommonwealth.org;
http://www.youngcommonwealth.org
Secretary-General: Don McKinnon (New Zealand).

Selected publications. Commonwealth Yearbook; Commonwealth Today (biannual); *The Commonwealth at the Summit: Communiqués of Commonwealth Heads of Government Meetings.*

Further Reading

The Cambridge History of the British Empire. 8 vols. CUP, 1929 ff.

Austin, D., *The Commonwealth and Britain.* London, 1988

Ball, M., *The 'Open' Commonwealth.* Duke University Press, Durham (North Carolina), 1971

Chan, S., *Twelve Years of Commonwealth Diplomatic History: Summit Meetings, 1979–1991.* Lampeter, 1992

Hall, H. D., *Commonwealth: A History of the British Commonwealth.* London and New York, 1971

Judd, D. and Slinn, P., *The Evolution of the Modern Commonwealth.* London, 1982

Keeton, G. W. (ed.) *The British Commonwealth: Its Laws and Constitutions.* 9 vols. London, 1951 ff.

Larby, P. and Hannam, H., *The Commonwealth* [Bibliography]. Oxford and New Brunswick (NJ), 1993

Madden, F. and Fieldhouse, D., (eds.) *Selected Documents on the Constitutional History of the British Empire and Commonwealth.* Greenwood Press, New York, 1994

Mansergh, N., *The Commonwealth Experience.* Macmillan, London, 1982

McIntyre, W. D., *The Significance of the Commonwealth, 1965–90.* Macmillan, London, 1991

Moore, R. J., *Making the New Commonwealth.* Oxford, 1987

Commonwealth of Independent States (CIS)

The Commonwealth of Independent States, founded on 8 Dec. 1991 in Viskuli, a government villa in Belarus, is a community of independent states which proclaimed itself the successor to the Union of Soviet Socialist Republics in some aspects of international law and affairs. The member states are the founders, Russia, Belarus and Ukraine, and eight subsequent adherents: Armenia, Azerbaijan, Georgia, Kazakhstan, Kyrgyzstan, Moldova, Tajikistan and Uzbekistan. Turkmenistan withdrew its permanent member status on 26 Aug. 2005 and became an associate member.

History. Extended negotiations in the Union of Soviet Socialist Republics (USSR) in 1990 and 1991, under the direction of President Gorbachev, sought to establish a 'renewed federation' or, subsequently, to conclude a new union treaty that would embrace all the 15 constituent republics of the USSR at that date. According to a referendum conducted in March 1991, 76% of the population (on an 80% turn-out) wished to maintain the USSR as a 'renewed federation of equal sovereign republics in which the human rights and freedoms of any nationality would be fully guaranteed'. In Sept. 1991 the three Baltic republics—Estonia, Latvia and Lithuania—were nonetheless recognized as independent states by the USSR State Council, and subsequently by the international community. Most of the remaining republics reached agreement on the broad outlines of a new 'union of sovereign states' in Nov. 1991, which would have retained a directly elected President and an all-union legislature, but which would have limited central authority to those powers specifically delegated to it by the members of the union.

A referendum in Ukraine in Dec. 1991, however, showed overwhelming support for full independence, and following this the three Slav republics (Russia, Belarus and Ukraine) concluded the Minsk Agreement on 8 Dec. 1991, establishing a Commonwealth of Independent States (CIS), headquartered in Minsk. The USSR, as a subject of international law and a geopolitical reality, was declared no longer in existence, and each of the three republics individually renounced the 1922 treaty through which the USSR had been established.

The CIS declared itself open to other former Soviet republics, and to states elsewhere that shared its objectives, and on 21 Dec. 1991 in Alma-Ata, a further declaration was signed with eight other republics: Armenia, Azerbaijan, Kazakhstan, Kyrgyzstan, Moldova, Tajikistan, Turkmenistan and Uzbekistan. The declaration committed signatories to recognize the independence and sovereignty of other members, to respect human rights including those of national minorities, and to the observance of existing boundaries. Relations among the members of the CIS were to be conducted on an equal, multilateral, interstate basis, but it was agreed to endorse the principle of unitary control of strategic nuclear arms and the concept of a 'single economic space'. In a separate agreement the heads of member states agreed that Russia should take up the seat at the United Nations formerly occupied by the USSR, and a framework of interstate and intergovernment consultation was established. Following these developments Mikhail Gorbachev resigned as USSR President on 25 Dec. 1991, and on 26 Dec. the USSR Supreme Soviet voted a formal end to the 1922 Treaty of Union, and dissolved itself. Georgia decided to join on 9 Dec. 1993 and on 1 March 1994 the national parliament ratified the act.

The Charter, adopted on 22 Jan. 1993 in Minsk, proclaims that the Commonwealth is based on the principles of the sovereign equality of all members. It is not a state and does not have supranational authority.

Activities and Institutions. The principal organs of the CIS, according to the agreement concluded in Alma-Ata on 21 Dec. 1991, are the *Council of Heads of States*, which meets twice a year, and the *Council of Heads of Government*, which meets every three months. Both councils may convene extraordinary sessions, and may hold joint sittings. There is also a *Council of Defence Ministers*, established in Feb. 1992, and a *Council of Foreign Ministers* (Dec. 1993). The Secretariat is the standing working organ.

At a summit meeting of heads of states (with the exception of Azerbaijan) in July 1992, agreements were reached on a way to divide former USSR assets abroad; on the legal cessionary of state archives of former Soviet states; on the status of an Economic Court; and on collective security. In 1992 an *Inter-Parliamentary Assembly* was established by seven member states (Armenia, Belarus, Kazakhstan, Kyrgyzstan, Russia, Tajikistan and Uzbekistan).

At a subsequent meeting in Jan. 1993 Armenia, Belarus, Kazakhstan, Kyrgyzstan, Russia, Tajikistan and Uzbekistan agreed on a charter to implement co-operation in political, economic, ecological, humanitarian, cultural and other spheres; thorough and balanced economic and social development within the common economic space; interstate co-operation and integration; and to ensure human rights and freedoms. Three participants (Ukraine, Moldova and Turkmenistan) agreed only to a declaration that the decision would be open for signing in the future. For the purpose of the maintenance and development of multilateral industrial, trade and financial relations, Heads of State established an *Inter-State Bank* and adopted a Provision on it. Its charter was signed by ten Heads of State (Armenia, Belarus, Kazakhstan, Kyrgyzstan, Moldova, Russia, Tajikistan, Turkmenistan, Ukraine, Uzbekistan) on 22 Dec. 1993.

The *CIS Inter-State Bank* was set up with a starting capital of 5,000m. roubles, to facilitate multilateral clearing of CIS interstate transactions. Members' contributions (by %), based on their share of foreign trade turnover in 1990, were as follows: Russia, 50%; Ukraine, 20·7%; Belarus, 8·4%; Kazakhstan, 6·1%; Uzbekistan, 5·5%; Moldova, 2·9%; Armenia, 1·8%; Tajikistan, 1·6%; Kyrgyzstan, 1·5%; Turkmenistan, 1·5%. The bank is an international settlement and financial-credit institution, established in accordance with the rules of international public law. The authorized capital on 1 Jan. 1999 was 20,000m. roubles.

In accordance with the Agreement on Armed Forces and Border Troops, concluded on 30 Dec. 1991, it was decided to consider and solve the issue on the transference of the management of the General-Purpose Armed Forces in accordance with the national legislation of member states. On 14 Feb. 1992 the *Council of Defence Ministers* was established. In 1993 the Office of Commander-in-Chief of CIS Joint Armed Forces was reorganized in a Staff for Co-ordinating Military Co-operation. Its Chief of Staff is appointed by the Council of Heads of State.

On 24 Sept. 1993 Armenia, Azerbaijan, Belarus, Kazakhstan, Kyrgyzstan, Moldova, Russia, Tajikistan and Uzbekistan signed an agreement to form an *Economic Union*. Georgia and Turkmenistan signed later (14 and 23 Jan. 1994). Ukraine became an associated member on 15 April 1994. In Oct. 1994 a summit meeting established the *Inter-State Economic Committee (MEK)* to be based in Moscow. Members include all CIS states except Turkmenistan. The Committee's decisions are binding if voted by 80% of the membership. Russia commands 50% of the voting power; Ukraine 14%. The Committee's remit is to co-ordinate energy, transport and communications policies. A *Customs Union* to regulate payments between member states with non-convertible independent currencies and a regulatory *Economic Court* have also been established.

On 29 March 1996 Belarus, Kazakhstan, Kyrgyzstan and Russia signed an agreement increasing their mutual economic and social integration by creating a *Community of Integrated States* (Tajikistan signed in 1998). The agreement established a Supreme Inter-Governmental Council comprising heads of state and government and foreign ministers, with a rotatory Chair, an integration committee of Ministers and an Inter-Parliamentary Committee.

On 2 April 1996 the Presidents of Belarus and Russia signed a treaty providing for political, economic and military integration, creating the nucleus of a *Community of Russia and Belarus*. The agreement establishes a Supreme Council comprising the Presidents, Prime Ministers and Speakers of both countries and the Chairman of the Executive Committee. A further treaty was signed on 22 May 1997, instituting common citizenship, common deployment of military forces and the harmonization of the two economies with a view to the creation of a common currency. The Community was later renamed the *Union of Belarus and Russia* and signed subsequent agreements on equal rights for its citizens and equal conditions for state and private entrepreneurship.

In March 1994 the CIS was accorded observer status in the UN.

Headquarters: 220000 Minsk, Kirava 17, Belarus.
Website: http://www.cis.minsk.by
Executive Secretary: Yurii Yarov (Russia).

Further Reading

Brzezinski, Z. and Sullivan, P. (eds.) *Russia and the Commonwealth of Independent States: Documents, Data and Analysis.* Armonk (NY), 1996

International Air Transport Association (IATA)

Founded in 1945 for inter-airline co-operation in promoting safe, reliable, secure and economical air services, IATA has over 230 members from more than 130 nations worldwide. IATA is the successor to the International Air Traffic Association, founded in The Hague in 1919, the year of the world's first international scheduled services.

Main offices: IATA Centre, Route de l'Aéroport 33, PO Box 416, CH-1215 Geneva, Switzerland. 800 Place Victoria, PO Box 113, Montreal, Quebec, Canada H4Z 1M1. 77 Robinson Road, #05-00 SIA Building, Singapore 068896.
Website: http://www.iata.org
Director-General: Giovanni Bisignani (Italy).

International Committee of the Red Cross (ICRC)

The International Committee of the Red Cross (ICRC) is an impartial, neutral and independent organization whose exclusively humanitarian mission is to protect the lives and dignity of victims of war and internal violence and to provide them with assistance.

Established in 1863, the ICRC is at the origin of the International Red Cross and Red Crescent Movement and of international humanitarian law, notably the Geneva Conventions. As the promoter and guardian of international humanitarian law, the ICRC must encourage respect for the law. It does so by spreading knowledge of the humanitarian rules and by reminding parties to conflicts of their obligations.

The ICRC has a permanent mandate under international law to take impartial action for prisoners, the wounded and sick, and civilians affected by conflict.

With its HQ in Geneva, Switzerland, the ICRC is based in around 80 countries and has a total of more than 12,000 staff.

In situations of conflict the ICRC co-ordinates the response by national Red Cross and Red Crescent societies and their International Federation. It acts in consultation with all other organizations involved in humanitarian work.

The ICRC relies for its financing on voluntary contributions from States signatories to the Geneva Conventions, supranational organizations such as the European Union, and public and private sources. To obtain the necessary funding the ICRC launches annual appeals.

In 2004 ICRC delegates visited more than 570,000 people deprived of their freedom in some 80 countries. ICRC water, sanitation and construction projects catered for the needs of around 20m. people. The ICRC supported hospitals and health care facilities serving some 2·8m. people. It also provided essential household goods to more than 2·2m. people, food aid to 1·3m. people and assistance to another 1·1m. people in the form of sustainable food production and micro-economic initiatives.

Headquarters: 19 Avenue de la Paix, 1202 Geneva, Switzerland.
Website: http://www.icrc.org
President: Jakob Kellenberger (Switzerland).

Further Reading

Moorehead, Caroline, *Dunant's Dream: War, Switzerland and the History of the Red Cross.* HarperCollins, London, 1998

International Confederation of Free Trade Unions (ICFTU)

Origin. The founding congress of the ICFTU was held in London in Dec. 1949 following the withdrawal of some Western trade unions from the World Federation of Trade Unions (WFTU), which had come under Communist control. The constitution, as amended, provides for co-operation with the UN and the ILO, and for regional organizations to promote free trade unionism, especially in developing countries. By Jan. 2005 the ICFTU represented 145m. workers across 233 national trade union centres in 154 countries and territories.

Aims. The ICFTU aims to promote the interests of working people and to secure recognition of workers' organizations as free bargaining agents; to reduce the gap between rich and poor; and to defend fundamental human and trade union rights. In 1996 it campaigned for the adoption by the WTO of a social clause, with legally binding minimum labour standards.

Organization. The Congress meets every four years. The 18th Annual World Congress was held in Miyazaki, Japan in Dec. 2004. It elects the General Secretary and an Executive Board of 53 members nominated on an area basis for a four-year period. Five seats are reserved for women, nominated by the Women's Committee, and one reserved for a representative of young workers. The Board meets at least once a year. Various committees cover economic and social policy, violation of trade union and other human rights, trade union co-operation projects and also the administration of the International Solidarity Fund. There are joint ICFTU–Global Union Federations for co-ordinating activities.

The ICFTU has branch offices in Geneva, New York and Washington, and regional organizations in Latin America (Caracas), Asia (Singapore) and Africa (Nairobi).

Headquarters: Bd. du Roi Albert II, N° 5, bte 1, Brussels 1210, Belgium.
Website: http://www.icftu.org
e-mail: intnetpo@icftu.org
General Secretary: Guy Ryder (UK).
President: Sharan Burrow (Australia).

Publications. Trade Union World (monthly); *Annual Survey of Violations of Trade Union Rights* (annual); *ICFTU On-Line* (daily electronic news bulletin). Other publications available; contact the press department.

International Criminal Court (ICC)

Origin. As far back as 1946 an international congress called for the adoption of an international criminal code prohibiting crimes against humanity and the prompt establishment of an international criminal court, but for more than 40 years little progress was made. In 1989 the end of the Cold War brought a dramatic increase in the number of UN peacekeeping operations and a world where the idea of establishing an International Criminal Court became more viable. The United Nations Conference of Plenipotentiaries on the Establishment of an International Criminal Court took place from 15 June–17 July 1998 in Rome, Italy.

Aims and Activities. The International Criminal Court is a permanent court for trying individuals who have been accused of committing genocide, war crimes and crimes against humanity, and is thus a successor to the *ad hoc* tribunals set up by the UN Security Council to try those responsible for atrocities in the former Yugoslavia and Rwanda. Ratification by 60 countries was required to bring the statute into effect. The court began operations on 1 July 2002 with 139 signatories and after ratification by 76 countries. By Nov. 2005 the number of ratifications had increased to 100.

Judges. The International Criminal Court's first 18 judges were elected in Feb. 2003, with six serving for three years, six for six years and six for nine years. Every three years six new judges will be elected. At present the 18 judges, with the year in which their term of office is scheduled to end, are: René

Blattmann (Bolivia, 2009); Maureen Harding Clark (Ireland, 2012); Fatoumata Dembele Diarra (Mali, 2012); Adrian Fulford (United Kingdom, 2012); Karl Hudson-Phillips (Trinidad and Tobago, 2012); Claude Jorda (France, 2009); Hans-Peter Kaul (Germany, 2015); Philippe Kirsch (Canada, 2009); Erkki Kourula (Finland, 2015); Akua Kuenyehia (Ghana, 2015); Elizabeth Odio Benito (Costa Rica, 2012); Georghios Pikis (Cyprus, 2009); Navanethem Pillay (South Africa, 2009); Mauro Politi (Italy, 2009); Song Sang-hyun (South Korea, 2015); Sylvia Helena de Figueiredo Steiner (Brazil, 2012); Ekaterina Trendafilova (Bulgaria, 2015), Anita Ušacka (Latvia, 2015).

Prosecutor. Luis Moreno-Ocampo (Argentina) was elected the first prosecutor of the Court on 21 April 2003.

Headquarters: Maanweg 174, 2516 AB The Hague, Netherlands.
Website: http://www.icc-cpi.int

Further Reading

Macedo, Stephen (ed.), *Universal Jurisdiction: National Courts and the Prosecution of Serious Crimes Under International Law.* Univ. of Pennsylvania Press, 2003
Reydams, Luc, *Universal Jurisdiction: International and Municipal Perspectives.* OUP, 2003

International Institute for Democracy and Electoral Assistance (IDEA)

Created in 1995, International IDEA is an intergovernmental organization that promotes sustainable democracy worldwide. Global in membership and independent of specific national interests, IDEA works with both new and long-established democracies. IDEA brings together those who analyse and monitor trends in democracy and those who engage in political reform. Its partners include international, regional and national bodies devoted to democratic principles.

Aims and Activities. IDEA aims to: assist countries in developing and strengthening democratic institutions; offer researchers, policymakers, activists and professionals a forum to discuss democratic principles; blend research and field experience, and develop practical tools to improve democratic processes; promote transparency, accountability and efficiency in managing elections; help local citizens evaluate, monitor and promote democracy. The principal areas of activity include: democracy building and conflict management; electoral processes; political parties, including political equality and participation.

Membership. The International IDEA had 24 full member states and one observer state in Jan. 2006.

Organization. IDEA has regional offices in Armenia, Costa Rica, Ghana, Indonesia, Mexico, Peru and South Africa. In 2005 there were 51 international employees.

Headquarters: Strömsborg, 103 34 Stockholm, Sweden.
Website: http://www.idea.int
Secretary-General: Vidar Helgesen (Norway).

International Mobile Satellite Organization (IMSO)

Founded in 1979 as the International Maritime Satellite Organization (Inmarsat) to establish a satellite system to improve maritime communications for distress and safety and commercial applications. Its competence was subsequently expanded to include aeronautical and land mobile communications. Privatization, which was completed in April 1999, transferred the business to a newly created company and the Organization remains as a regulator to ensure that the company fulfils its public services obligations. The company has taken the Inmarsat name and the Organization uses the acronym IMSO. In Jan. 2006 the Organization had 88 member parties.

Organization. The Assembly of all Parties to the Convention meets every two years.

Headquarters: 99 City Road, London EC1Y 1AX, UK.
IMSO Website: http://www.imso.org
e-mail: info@imso.org
Immarsat Website: http://www.inmarsat.com
Director of the Secretariat, IMSO: Jerzy Vonau.
Chief Executive, Inmarsat Ltd: Andrew Sukawaty.

International Olympic Committee (IOC)

Founded in 1894 by French educator Baron Pierre de Coubertin, the International Olympic Committee is an international non-governmental, non-profit organization whose members act as the IOC's representatives in their respective countries, not as delegates of their countries within the IOC. The Committee's main responsibility is to supervise the organization of the summer and winter Olympic Games. It owns all rights to the Olympic symbols, flag, motto, anthem and Olympic Games.

Aims. 'To contribute to building a peaceful and better world by educating youth through sport, practised without discrimination of any kind and in the Olympic Spirit, which requires mutual understanding with a spirit of friendship, solidarity and fair play.'

Finances. The IOC receives no public funding. Its only source of funding is from private sectors, with the substantial part of these revenues coming from television broadcasters and sponsors.

Address: Château de Vidy, Case Postale 356, CH–1007 Lausanne, Switzerland.
Website: http://www.olympic.org
President: Jacques Rogge (Belgium).

International Organization for Migration (IOM)

Established in Brussels in 1951 to help solve European population and refugee problems through migration, and to stimulate the creation of new economic opportunities in countries lacking certain manpower. IOM is committed to the principle that humane and orderly migration benefits migrants and society.

Members (116 as of Dec. 2005). Afghanistan, Albania, Algeria, Angola, Argentina, Armenia, Australia, Austria, Azerbaijan, Bahamas, Bangladesh, Belarus, Belgium, Belize, Benin, Bolivia, Bosnia-Herzegovina, Brazil, Bulgaria, Burkina Faso, Cambodia, Cameroon, Canada, Cape Verde, Chile, Colombia, Congo (Democratic Republic of), Congo (Republic of), Costa Rica, Côte d'Ivoire, Croatia, Cyprus, Czech Republic, Denmark, Dominican Republic, Ecuador, Egypt, El Salvador, Estonia, Finland, France, Gabon, Gambia, Georgia, Germany, Greece, Guatemala, Guinea, Guinea-Bissau, Haiti, Holy See, Honduras, Hungary, Iran, Ireland, Israel, Italy, Jamaica, Japan, Jordan, Kazakhstan, Kenya,

South Korea, Kyrgyzstan, Latvia, Liberia, Libya, Lithuania, Luxembourg, Madagascar, Mali, Malta, Mauritania, Mexico, Moldova, Morocco, Netherlands, New Zealand, Nicaragua, Niger, Nigeria, Norway, Pakistan, Panama, Paraguay, Peru, Philippines, Poland, Portugal, Romania, Rwanda, Senegal, Serbia and Montenegro, Sierra Leone, Slovakia, Slovenia, South Africa, Sri Lanka, Sudan, Sweden, Switzerland, Tajikistan, United Republic of Tanzania, Thailand, Togo, Tunisia, Turkey, Uganda, Ukraine, UK, USA, Uruguay, Venezuela, Yemen, Zambia and Zimbabwe. 24 governments and a large number of government agencies and NGOs have observer status.

Activities. As an intergovernmental body, IOM acts with its partners in the international community to: assist in meeting the operational challenges of migration; advance understanding of migration issues; encourage social and economic development through migration; work towards effective respect of human dignity and the well-being of migrants. Since 1952 the IOM has assisted some 11m. refugees and migrants to settle in over 125 countries. Throughout 2001 the organization assisted in the humanitarian emergency unfolding in Afghanistan by way of shelter programmes and the registration of IDPs (internally displaced persons), and by meeting the needs of the displaced brought on by drought and conflict. In 2001 IOM launched a 'Migration and Development in Africa Programme' and a 'Migration Policy and Research Programme'. IOM's operational budget in 2004 was US$641m.

Official languages: English, French, Spanish.
Headquarters: Route des Morillons 17, POB 71, 1211 Geneva 19, Switzerland.
Website: http://www.iom.int
Director-General: Brunson McKinley (USA).

International Organization for Standardization (ISO)

Established in 1947, the International Organization for Standardization is a non-governmental federation of national standards bodies from some 145 countries worldwide, one from each country. ISO's work results in international agreements which are published as International Standards. The first ISO standard was published in 1951 with the title 'Standard reference temperature for industrial length measurement'.

Some 15,400 ISO International Standards are available on subjects in such diverse fields as information technology, textiles, packaging, distribution of goods, energy production and utilization, building, banking and financial services. ISO standardization activities include the widely recognized ISO 9000 family of quality management system and standards and the ISO 14000 series of environmental management system standards. Standardization programmes are now being developed in completely new fields, such as food safety, security, social responsibility and the service sector.

Mission. To promote the development of standardization and related activities in the world with a view to facilitating the international exchange of goods and services, and to developing co-operation in the spheres of intellectual, scientific, technological and economic activity.

Headquarters: 1 rue de Varembé, Case postale 56, CH-1211 Geneva 20, Switzerland.
Website: http://www.iso.org
e-mail: central@iso.org
Secretary-General: Alan Bryden.

International Organization of the Francophonie

The International Organization of the Francophonie represents 63 countries and provinces/regions (including ten with observer status) using French as an official language. Objectives include the promotion of peace, democracy, and economic and social development, through political and technical co-operation. The Secretary-General is based in Paris.

Members. Albania, Andorra, Belgium, Benin, Bulgaria, Burkina Faso, Burundi, Cambodia, Cameroon, Canada, Canada–New Brunswick, Canada–Quebec, Cape Verde, Central African Republic, Chad, Comoros, Republic of the Congo, Democratic Republic of the Congo, Côte d'Ivoire, Djibouti, Dominica, Egypt, Equatorial Guinea, France, French Community of Belgium, Gabon, Greece, Guinea, Guinea-Bissau, Haiti, Laos, Lebanon, Luxembourg, Macedonia, Madagascar, Mali, Mauritania, Mauritius, Moldova, Monaco, Morocco, Niger, Romania, Rwanda, St Lucia, São Tomé e Príncipe, Senegal, Seychelles, Switzerland, Togo, Tunisia, Vanuatu, Vietnam. *Observers.* Armenia, Austria, Croatia, Czech Republic, Georgia, Hungary, Lithuania, Poland, Slovakia, Slovenia.

Headquarters: 28 rue de Bourgogne, 75007 Paris, France.
Website: http://www.francophonie.org
Secretary-General: Abdou Diouf (Senegal).

International Road Federation (IRF)

The IRF is a non-profit, non-political service organization whose purpose is to encourage better road and transportation systems worldwide and to help apply technology and management practices to give maximum economic and social returns from national road investments.

Founded following the Second World War, over the years the IRF has led major global road infrastructure developments, including achieving 1,000 km of new roads in Mexico in the 1950s, and promoting the Pan-American Highway linking North and South America. It publishes *World Road Statistics*, as well as road research studies, including a 140-country inventory of road and transport research in co-operation with the US Bureau of Public Roads.

Headquarters: 2 chemin de Blandonnet, CH-1214 Vernier/GE, Switzerland.
Website: http://www.irfnet.org
Director-General (Geneva/Brussels): Tony Pearce (UK).
Director-General (Washington, D.C.): C. Patrick Sankey (USA).

International Seabed Authority (ISA)

The ISA is an autonomous international organization established under the UN Convention on the Law of the Sea (UNCLOS) of 1982 and the 1994 Agreement relating to the implementation of Part XI of the above Convention. It came into existence on 16 Nov. 1994 and became fully operational in June 1996.

The administrative expenses are met from assessed contributions from its members. Membership numbered 149 in Jan. 2006; the budget for the biennium 2003–04 was US$10,509,700.

The Convention on the Law of the Sea covers almost all ocean space and its uses: navigation and overflight, resource exploration and exploitation, conservation and pollution, fishing and shipping. It entitles coastal states and inhabited islands to proclaim a 200-mile exclusive economic zone or continental shelf (which may be larger). Its 320 Articles and nine Annexes constitute a guide for behaviour by states in the world's oceans, defining maritime zones, laying down rules for drawing sea boundaries, assigning legal rights, duties and responsibilities to States, and providing machinery for the settlement of disputes.

Organization. The Assembly, consisting of representatives from all member states, is the supreme organ. The 36-member Council, elected by the Assembly, includes the four largest importers or consumers of seabed minerals, four largest investors in seabed minerals, four major exporters of the same, six developing countries representing special interests and 18 members from all the geographical regions. The Council is the executive organ of the Authority. There are also two subsidiary bodies: the Legal and Technical Commission (currently 24 experts) and the Finance Committee (currently 15 experts). The Secretariat serves all the bodies of the Authority and under the 1994 Agreement is performing functions of the Enterprise (until such time as it starts to operate independently of the Secretariat). The Enterprise is the organ through which the ISA carries out deep seabed activities directly or through joint ventures.

Activities. In July 2000 the ISA adopted the Regulations for Prospecting and Exploration for Polymetallic Nodules in the Area. Pursuant thereto, it signed exploration contracts with seven contractors who have submitted plans of work for deep seabed exploration. These are: Institut Français de Recherche pour l'Exploitation de la Mer (IFREMER) and Association Française pour l'Etude de la Recherche des Nodules (AFERNOD), France; Deep Ocean Resources Development Co. Ltd (DORD), Japan; State Enterprise Yuzhmorgeologiya, Russian Federation; China Ocean Minerals Research and Development Association (COMRA); Interoceanmetal Joint Organization (IOM), a consortium sponsored by Bulgaria, Cuba, Czech Republic, Poland, Russian Federation and Slovakia; the government of South Korea; and the government of India.

Between 1998 and 2002 the ISA organized five workshops: the development of guidelines for the assessment of the possible environmental impacts arising from exploration for polymetallic nodules; proposed technologies for deep seabed mining of polymetallic nodules; the available knowledge on mineral resources other than polymetallic nodules in the deep seabed; a standardized system of data interpretation; prospects for international collaboration in marine environmental research. While continuing to develop a database on polymetallic nodules (POLYDAT), the Authority has also made significant progress towards the establishment of a central data repository for all marine minerals in the deep seabed.

Headquarters: 14–20 Port Royal St., Kingston, Jamaica.
Website: http://www.isa.org.jm
Secretary-General: Satya N. Nandan (Fiji Islands).

Publications. Handbook 2005; plus selected decisions and documents from the Authority's sessions; various others.

International Telecommunications Satellite Organization (ITSO)

Founded in 1964 as Intelsat, the organization was the world's first commercial communications satellite operator. Today, with capacity on a fleet of geostationary satellites and expanding terrestrial network assets, Intelsat continues to provide connectivity for telephony, corporate network, broadcast and Internet services.

Organization. In 2001 the member states of the organization implemented restructuring by transferring certain assets to Intelsat Ltd, a new Bermuda-based commercial company under the supervision of the International Telecommunications Satellite Organization, now known as ITSO. The Intelsat Global Service Corporation is located in Washington, D.C., and Intelsat Global Services & Marketing Ltd, the sales arm of the international firm, has its headquarters in London. Intelsat also has offices in Australia, Brazil, China, France, Germany, Hawaii, India, Peru and South Africa. There were 148 member countries in Jan. 2006.

Headquarters: 3400 International Drive, NW, Washington, D.C., 20008–3006, USA.
Website: http://www.itso.int
Director-General: Ahmed Toumi (Morocco).

International Tribunal for the Law of the Sea (ITLOS)

The International Tribunal for the Law of the Sea (ITLOS), founded in Oct. 1996 and based in Hamburg, adjudicates on disputes relating to the interpretation and application of the United Nations Convention on the Law of the Sea. The Convention gives the Tribunal jurisdiction to resolve a variety of international law of the sea disputes such as the delimitation of maritime zones, fisheries, navigation and the protection of the marine environment. Its Seabed Disputes Chamber has compulsory jurisdiction to resolve disputes amongst States, the International Seabed Authority, companies and private individuals, arising out of the exploitation of the deep seabed. The Tribunal also has compulsory jurisdiction in certain instances to protect the rights of parties to a dispute or to prevent serious harm to the marine environment, and over the prompt release of arrested vessels and their crews upon the deposit of a security. The jurisdiction of the Tribunal also extends to all matters specifically provided for in any other agreement which confers jurisdiction on the Tribunal. The Tribunal is composed of 21 judges, elected by signatories from five world regional blocs: five each from Africa and Asia; four from Western Europe and other States; four from Latin America and the Caribbean; and three from Eastern Europe. The judges serve a term of nine years, with one third of the judges' terms expiring every three years.

Headquarters: Am Internationalen Seegerichtshof 1, D-22609 Hamburg, Germany.
Website: http://www.itlos.org
Registrar: Philippe Gautier (Belgium).

International Union Against Cancer (UICC)

Founded in 1933, the UICC is an international non-governmental association of 263 member organizations in 84 countries.

Objectives. The UICC is the only non-governmental organization dedicated exclusively to the global control of cancer. Its objectives are to advance scientific and medical knowledge in research, diagnosis, treatment and prevention of cancer, and to promote all other aspects of the campaign against cancer throughout the world. Particular emphasis is placed on professional and public education.

Membership. The UICC is made up of voluntary cancer leagues, patient organizations, associations and societies as well as cancer research and treatment centres and, in some countries, ministries of health.

Activities. The UICC creates and carries out programmes around the world in collaboration with several hundred volunteer experts, most of whom are professionally active in UICC member organizations. It promotes co-operation between cancer organizations, researchers, scientists, health professionals and cancer experts, with a focus in four key areas: building and enhancing cancer control capacity, tobacco control, population-based cancer prevention and control, and transfer of cancer knowledge and dissemination. The next UICC World Cancer Congress is scheduled to take place in 2008.

Address: 3 rue du Conseil-Général, 1205-Geneva, Switzerland.
Website: http://www.uicc.org
President: Dr John Seffrin (USA).
Executive Director: Isabel Mortara (Switzerland).
Secretary-General: Dr Stener Kvinnsland (Norway).

Inter-Parliamentary Union (IPU)

Founded in 1889 by William Randal Cremer (UK) and Frédéric Passy (France), the Inter-Parliamentary Union was the first permanent forum for political multilateral negotiations. The Union is a centre for dialogue and parliamentary diplomacy among legislators representing every political system and all the main political leanings in the world. It was instrumental in setting up what is now the Permanent Court of Arbitration in The Hague.

Activities. The IPU fosters contacts, co-ordination and the exchange of experience among parliaments and parliamentarians of all countries; considers questions of international interest and concern, and expresses its views on such issues in order to bring about action by parliaments and parliamentarians; contributes to the defence and promotion of human rights—an essential factor of parliamentary democracy and development; contributes to better knowledge of the working and development of representative institutions and to the strengthening of representative democracy.

Membership. The IPU had 143 members and seven associate members in Jan. 2006.

Headquarters: Chemin du Pommier 5, C.P. 330, 1218 Le Grand Saconnex, Geneva 19, Switzerland.
Website: http://www.ipu.org
President: Pier Ferdinando Casini (Italy).
Secretary-General: Anders B. Johnsson (Sweden).

Interpol (International Criminal Police Organization)

Organization. Interpol was founded in 1923, disbanded in 1938 and reconstituted in 1946. The International Criminal Police

Organization—Interpol was founded to ensure and promote the widest possible mutual assistance between all criminal police authorities within the limits of the law existing in the different countries worldwide and the spirit of the Universal Declaration of Human Rights, and to establish and develop all institutions likely to contribute effectively to the prevention and suppression of ordinary law crimes.

Aims. Interpol provides a co-ordination centre (General Secretariat) for its 181 member countries. Its priority areas of activity concern criminal organizations, public safety and terrorism, drug-related crimes, financial crime and high-tech crime, trafficking in human beings and tracking fugitives from justice. Interpol centralizes records and information on international offenders; it operates a worldwide communication network.

Interpol's General Assembly is held annually. The General Assembly is the body of supreme authority in the organization. It is composed of delegates appointed by the members of the organization. Interpol's Executive Committee, which meets four times a year, supervises the execution of the decisions of the General Assembly. The Executive Committee is composed of the president of the organization, the three vice-presidents and nine delegates. Interpol's General Secretariat is the centre for co-ordinating the fight against international crime. Its activities, undertaken in response to requests from the police services and judicial authorities in its member countries, focus on crime prevention and law enforcement.

As of Jan. 2006 Interpol's Sub-Regional Bureaus were located in Abidjan, Buenos Aires, El Salvador, Harare and Nairobi. Interpol's Liaison Office for Asia is located in Bangkok.

Headquarters: 200 Quai Charles de Gaulle, 69006 Lyon, France.
Website: http://www.interpol.int
e-mail: cp@interpol.int
President: Jackie Selebi (South Africa).

Islamic Development Bank

The Agreement establishing the IDB (Banque islamique de développement) was adopted at the Second Islamic Finance Ministers' Conference held in Jeddah, Saudi Arabia in Aug. 1974. The Bank, which is open to all member countries of the Organization of the Islamic Conference, commenced operations in 1975. Its main objective is to foster economic development and social progress of member countries and Muslim communities individually as well as jointly in accordance with the principles of the Sharia. It is active in the promotion of trade and the flow of investments among member countries, and maintains a Special Assistance Fund for member countries suffering natural calamities. The Fund is also used to finance health and educational projects aimed at improving the socio-economic conditions of Muslim communities in non-member countries. A US$1·5bn. IDB Infrastructure Fund was launched in 1998 to invest in projects such as power, telecommunications, transportation, energy, natural resources, petro-chemical and other infrastructure-related sectors in member countries.

Members (56 as of Jan. 2006). Afghanistan, Albania, Algeria, Azerbaijan, Bahrain, Bangladesh, Benin, Brunei, Burkina Faso, Cameroon, Chad, Comoros, Côte d'Ivoire, Djibouti, Egypt, Gabon, The Gambia, Guinea, Guinea-Bissau, Indonesia, Iran, Iraq, Jordan, Kazakhstan, Kuwait, Kyrgyzstan, Lebanon, Libya, Malaysia, Maldives, Mali, Mauritania, Morocco, Mozambique, Niger, Nigeria, Oman, Pakistan, Palestine, Qatar, Saudi Arabia, Senegal, Sierra Leone, Somalia, Sudan, Suriname, Syria, Tajikistan, Togo, Tunisia, Turkey, Turkmenistan, Uganda, United Arab Emirates, Uzbekistan, Yemen.

Official language: Arabic. *Working languages:* English, French.
Headquarters: PO Box 5925, Jeddah 21432, Saudi Arabia.
Website: http://www.isdb.org
President: Ahmed Mohamed Ali (Saudi Arabia).

Médecins Sans Frontières (MSF)

Origin. Médecins sans Frontières was founded in 1971 by a small group of doctors and journalists who believed that all people have a right to emergency relief.

Functions. MSF was one of the first non-governmental organizations to provide both urgently needed medical assistance and to publicly bear witness to the plight of the people it helps. Today MSF is an international medical humanitarian movement with branch offices in 18 countries. In 2003 MSF volunteer doctors, nurses, other medical professionals, logistical experts, water-and-sanitation engineers, and administrators departed on more than 3,400 missions and joined more than 16,000 locally hired staff to provide medical aid in nearly 80 countries. MSF was awarded the 1999 Nobel Peace Prize.

Headquarters: MSF International Office, Rue de Lausanne 78, CH-1211 Geneva 21, Switzerland.
Website: http://www.msf.org
Secretary-General: Marine Buissonnière.
President: Dr Rowan Gillies (Australia).

North Atlantic Treaty Organization (NATO)

Origin. On 4 April 1949 the foreign ministers of Belgium, Canada, Denmark, France, Iceland, Italy, Luxembourg, the Netherlands, Norway, Portugal, the UK and the USA signed the North Atlantic Treaty, establishing the *North Atlantic Alliance.* In 1952 Greece and Turkey acceded to the Treaty; in 1955 the Federal Republic of Germany; in 1982 Spain; in 1999 the Czech Republic, Hungary and Poland; and in 2004 Bulgaria, Estonia, Latvia, Lithuania, Romania, Slovakia and Slovenia, bringing the total to 26 member countries. The Alliance enables these countries to meet and co-operate in the field of security and defence.

Functions. The Alliance was established as a defensive political and military alliance of independent countries in accordance with the terms of the UN Charter. Its fundamental role is to safeguard the freedom and security of its members by political and military means. It also encourages consultation and co-operation with non-NATO countries in a wide range of security-related areas to help prevent conflicts within and beyond the frontiers of its member countries. NATO promotes democratic values and is committed to the peaceful resolution of disputes. If diplomatic efforts fail, it has the military capacity needed to undertake crisis-management operations alone or in co-operation with other countries and international organizations.

Reform and Transformation of the Alliance. Following the demise of the Warsaw Pact in 1991, and the improved relations with Russia, NATO established close security links with the states of

Central and Eastern Europe and those of the former USSR through the North Atlantic Co-operation Council (NACC). Established in Dec. 1991 as an integral part of NATO's new Strategic Concept, which was adopted earlier that year, the NACC was replaced by the Euro-Atlantic Partnership Council (EAPC) in 1997. The EAPC brings together NATO's member countries and its partner countries (the members of Partnership for Peace).

The Partnership for Peace (PfP) programme. The PfP builds on the momentum of co-operation created by the NACC. It was launched in 1994 and has since been adapted to expand and intensify political and military co-operation throughout Europe. Its core objectives are: the facilitation of transparency in national defence planning and budgeting processes; democratic control of defence forces; members' maintenance of capability and readiness to contribute to operations under the authority of the UN; development of co-operative military relations with NATO (joint planning, training and exercises) in order to strengthen participants' ability to undertake missions in the fields of peacekeeping, search and rescue, and humanitarian operations; development, over the longer term, of forces better able to operate with those of NATO member forces. NATO will consult with any active Partner which perceives a direct threat to its territorial integrity, political independence or security; and active participation in the Partnership is to play an important role in the process of NATO's expansion.

One of the most tangible aspects of co-operation between partner countries and NATO has been their individual participation in NATO-led peace-support operations. PfP has done much to facilitate this and has also been a key factor in promoting a spirit of practical co-operation and commitment to the democratic principles that underpin the Alliance. Joint peacekeeping exercises take place on a regular basis in the PfP framework in both NATO and partner countries. A large number of nationally sponsored exercises in the spirit of PfP have also been set up. In March 2004 following the accession of the seven new members NATO had 20 PfP partners: Albania, Armenia, Austria, Azerbaijan, Belarus, Croatia, Finland, Georgia, Ireland, Kazakhstan, Kyrgyzstan, Macedonia, Moldova, Russia, Sweden, Switzerland, Tajikistan, Turkmenistan, Ukraine and Uzbekistan. Many of these countries have accepted the Alliance's invitation to send liaison officers to permanent facilities at NATO Headquarters in Brussels and to the Partnership Co-ordination Cell in Mons, Belgium, where the Supreme Headquarters Allied Powers Europe (SHAPE) is located.

On 27 May 1997, in Paris, NATO and Russia signed the Founding Act on Mutual Relations, Co-operation and Security, committing themselves to build together a lasting peace in the Euro-Atlantic area, and establishing a new forum for consultation and co-operation called the NATO-Russia Permanent Joint Council. In May 2002 the Permanent Joint Council was replaced by a new NATO-Russia Council which brings together the 26 NATO member countries and Russia in a forum in which they work as equal partners, identifying and pursuing opportunities for joint action in areas of common concern.

At the meeting in Sintra, Portugal, in May 1997, a NATO-Ukraine charter was drawn up and signed in Madrid in July. At the same time, foreign ministers agreed to enhance their dialogue, begun in 1995, with six countries of the Mediterranean (Egypt, Israel, Jordan, Mauritania, Morocco and Tunisia). A new committee, the Mediterranean Co-operation Group was established to take the Mediterranean Dialogue forward and Algeria joined in March 2000. Later, in 2004, NATO also launched the İstanbul Co-operation Initiative that aims to develop co-operation with countries in the Middle East.

Changes in NATO's partnerships also include greater co-operation with other international organizations such as the United Nations, the European Union and the Organization for Security and Co-operation in Europe.

In the case of the European Union (EU), NATO has gradually developed a strategic partnership. Efforts to strengthen the security and defence role of NATO's European Allies (the European Security and Defence Identity) were initially organized through the Western European Union (WEU). In 2000 the crisis management responsibilities of the WEU were increasingly assumed by the EU. A number of milestones can be identified in the development of the European Security and Defence Identity (ESDI) between NATO, the WEU and the EU: the signing of the Maastricht Treaty in 1992, which allowed for the development of a common European security and defence policy; the endorsement of the concept of Combined Joint Task Forces in 1994 and of 'separable but not separate forces' that could be made available for European-led crisis response operations other than collective defence; the Berlin decisions in 1996, which included the building up of ESDI within the alliance; the EU Summits in Cologne and Helsinki in 1999, which led to important decisions on strengthening the European Security and Defence Policy and the development of an EU rapid reaction capability, and further developments in NATO-EU co-operation culminating in a joint declaration issued in Dec. 2002, which provided a formal basis for co-operation between the two organizations, outlining the political principles defining co-operation and giving the EU assured access to NATO planning capabilities for its own military operations. These decisions paved the way for the two organizations to work out the modalities for the transfer of responsibilities to the EU for the NATO-led military operations in the former Yugoslav Republic of Macedonia in 2003 and, from Dec. 2004, in Bosnia-Herzegovina.

Operations. One of the most significant aspects of NATO's transformation has been the decision to undertake peace-support and crisis-management operations in the Euro-Atlantic area and further afield. In the wake of the disintegration of the former Yugoslavia, the Alliance has focused much of its attention on the Balkans. NATO first committed itself to Bosnia-Herzegovina in 1995, through the NATO-led Implementation Force (IFOR), which was replaced by the Stabilisation Force (SFOR) in 1996. NATO put an end to its operation in Dec. 2004.

Since 1999 NATO has led a peacekeeping mission in Serbia and Montenegro in the province of Kosovo (KFOR). NATO has also intervened in the former Yugoslav Republic of Macedonia at the request of the government to help avoid a civil war.

Following the attacks on New York and Washington, D.C. on 11 Sept. 2001, NATO invoked article 5 of the Washington Treaty for the first time in its history, declaring it considered the attack on the USA as an attack against all members of the Alliance. It subsequently launched a series of initiatives aimed at curtailing terrorist activity. Operation Active Endeavour is a maritime operation led by NATO's naval forces to detect and deter terrorist activity in the Mediterranean. Operation Eagle Assist was one of the measures requested by the United States in the aftermath of the attacks in Sept. 2001. Aircraft from NATO's Airborne Warning and Control System (AWACS) patrolled American airspace for a period of seven months from mid-Oct. 2001 to mid-May 2002. Approximately 830 crew members from 13 NATO countries flew nearly 4,300 hours and over 360 operational sorties.

NATO has also taken over responsibility for the International Security Assistance Force in Afghanistan, training missions in Iraq and support to the African Union in Sudan. This widened scope of NATO military operations has radically transformed the military requirements of the Alliance. The large defence forces of the past have been replaced by forces geared toward relatively small-scale crisis response operations dependent upon flexibility and mobility and on the ability to deploy at significant distances from their normal operating bases. At the Prague Summit in 2002 the member governments launched a modernization process designed to ensure that NATO could effectively deal with the security challenges of the 21st century. A package of measures to enhance the Alliance's military operational capabilities was agreed. It included a new capabilities initiative called the Prague Capabilities Commitment, the creation of a NATO Response Force and the streamlining of the Alliance's military command structure. In addition, NATO heads of state and government called for increased efforts in the areas of intelligence sharing and crisis response arrangements, as well as greater co-operation with partner countries. Five nuclear, biological and chemical (NBC) weapons defence initiatives were also endorsed, as well as the creation of a multinational chemical, biological, radiological and nuclear battalion. Other initiatives included measures for defence against cyber attacks, and the launch of a new NATO Missile Defence Feasibility Study (MDFS) to examine options for protecting Alliance territory, forces and population centres against missile threats. At their Summit in İstanbul in 2004, heads of state and government pursued the transformation of military capabilities, agreeing to numerous initiatives that would help to protect both civilians and military forces from terrorist attacks and the spread of weapons of mass destruction.

Organization. The North Atlantic Council (NAC) is the highest decision-making body and forum for consultation within the Atlantic Alliance. It is composed of Permanent Representatives of all the member countries meeting together at least once a week. The NAC also meets at higher levels involving foreign ministers or heads of state or government, but it has the same authority and powers of decision-making, and its decisions have the same status and validity at whatever level it meets. All decisions are taken on the basis of consensus, reflecting the collective will of all member governments. The NAC is the only body within the Atlantic Alliance which derives its authority explicitly from the North Atlantic Treaty. The NAC has responsibility under the Treaty for setting up subsidiary bodies. Committees and planning groups have since been created to support the work of the NAC or to assume responsibility in specific fields such as defence planning, nuclear planning and military matters.

The Military Committee is responsible for making recommendations to the Council and the Defence Planning Committee on military matters and for supplying guidance to the Allied Commanders. Composed of the Chiefs-of-Staff of member countries (Iceland, which has no military forces, may be represented by a civilian), the Committee is assisted by an International Military Staff. It meets at Chiefs-of-Staff level at least twice a year but remains in permanent session at the level of national military representatives. The military command structure of the Alliance is divided into two strategic commands, one based in Europe, responsible for operations (Allied Command Operations) and the other based in the USA, responsible for the continuous transformation of allied military capabilities to enable them to undertake new challenges and to respond to changing military requirements (Allied Command Transformation).

Finance. The greater part of each member country's contribution to NATO, in terms of resources, comes indirectly through its expenditure on its own national armed forces and on its efforts to make them interoperable with those of other members so that they can participate in multinational operations. Member countries also incur the deployment costs involved whenever they volunteer forces to participate in NATO-led operations.

Member countries make direct contributions to three budgets managed directly by NATO: namely the Civil Budget, the Military Budget and the Security Investment Programme. Member countries pay contributions to each of these budgets in accordance with agreed cost-sharing formulae broadly calculated in relation to their ability to pay. The contributions represent a small percentage of each member's overall defence budget.

Under the terms of the Partnership for Peace strategy, partner countries undertake to make available the necessary personnel,

assets, facilities and capabilities to participate in the programme, and share the financial cost of any military exercises in which they participate.

Headquarters: NATO, 1110 Brussels, Belgium.
Website: http://www.nato.int
Secretary General: Jaap De Hoop Scheffer (Netherlands).

Publications. NATO publishes a series of printed and/or on-line publications, reference and audio-visual materials including the *NATO Review* (periodical); *NATO Update; NATO Briefings; the NATO Handbook; NATO in the 21st Century;* and *NATO Transformed.* Further details are available on the NATO website.

Current Leaders

Jaap De Hoop Scheffer

Position
Secretary General

Introduction
A career diplomat turned politician, Jaap De Hoop Scheffer became the 11th Secretary General of the North Atlantic Treaty Organization (NATO) on 5 Jan. 2004, taking over from Lord Robertson. He served at the Dutch mission to NATO in the 1980s, before entering the Dutch parliament where he became leader of the centre-right Christian Democrats (CDA). He was foreign minister under Jan Peter Balkenende's from July 2002 to Dec. 2003 and his deft handling of the transatlantic arguments over military intervention in Iraq in 2003 was widely praised. Steered by De Hoop Scheffer, the Dutch government managed to avoid alienating the United States, while remaining on good terms with anti-war France and Germany.

Early Life
Jakob Gijsbert (Jaap) De Hoop Scheffer was born in Amsterdam on 3 April 1948. After completing his secondary education, he studied law at Leiden University, graduating in 1974. Military service took the form of two years in the Royal Netherlands Air Force, giving him the chance to pilot cargo aircraft. De Hoop Scheffer was recruited by the ministry of foreign affairs in 1976 and he served at the Dutch embassy in Accra, Ghana for two years. He then worked at the permanent delegation to NATO in Brussels until 1980, where he was responsible for defence planning. During the next six years, he was in charge of the private offices of four successive ministers of foreign affairs.

In June 1986 De Hoop Scheffer was elected as a Christian Democrat (CDA) member of parliament. He became the party's spokesperson on foreign policy, asylum and refugee policy and European justice matters. In 1990, during the Gulf crisis, he served as EU rapporteur on the consequences of the invasion of Kuwait and continuing operations in the Gulf region. From 1994–97 he was a member of the North Atlantic Assembly. He served as deputy leader of the CDA in the House of Representatives from Dec. 1995 to March 1997, when he was elected leader.

The run-up to the May 2002 general elections witnessed an extraordinary series of events, starting with the resignation of Prime Minister Wim Kok and his Labour party-led coalition over its failure to prevent the massacre of Muslims by Bosnian Serb forces at Srebrenica in 1995. Meanwhile, De Hoop Scheffer's position as leader of the CDA became uncertain. After a power struggle with the party chairman, Marnix van Rij, he resigned and was succeeded by Jan Peter Balkenende. The newly-established List Pim Fortuyn Party was doing well in the polls, with its charismatic leader campaigning on an anti-immigration platform. But days before the 15 May election, Pim Fortuyn was assassinated and a shocked electorate voted in the Christian Democrats, who won 43 seats.

The new prime minister, Jan Peter Balkenende, appointed De Hoop Scheffer as foreign minister in his short-lived first cabinet, a position he retained in his second cabinet after the elections of 22

Jan. 2003. The Netherlands provided political support to the 2003 Iraq War and deployed 1,100 troops after the end of hostilities to help British troops in the Al Muthanna province in southern Iraq. Although the government supported the US-led invasion, De Hoop Scheffer expressed his desire for the Netherlands to play a mediating role between the USA's European supporters and those European states opposed to the war.

Career in Office

Lord Robertson announced his intention to step down as NATO's Secretary General in Feb. 2003. On 5 Jan. 2004 Jaap De Hoop Scheffer was announced as his successor, having secured the endorsement of the ambassadors of the then 19 member nations. He is reportedly keen to reinvigorate and modernize the alliance.

Further Reading

Carr, F. and Infantis, K., *NATO in the New European Order.* London, 1996

Cook, D., *The Forging of an Alliance.* London, 1989

Heller, F. H. and Gillingham, J. R. (eds.) *NATO: the Founding of the Atlantic Alliance and the Integration of Europe.* London, 1992

Smith, J. (ed.) *The Origins of NATO.* Exeter Univ. Press, 1990

Williams, P., *North Atlantic Treaty Organization* [Bibliography]. Oxford and New Brunswick (NJ), 1994

Yost, David S., *NATO Transformed: The Alliance's New Roles in International Security.* United States Institute for Peace, Washington, D.C., 1999

Organisation for Economic Co-operation and Development (OECD)

Origin. Founded in 1961 to replace the Organisation for European Economic Co-operation (OEEC), which was linked to the Marshall Plan and was established in 1948. The change of title marks the Organisation's altered status and functions: with the accession of Canada and USA as full members, it ceased to be a purely European body, and at the same time added development aid to the list of its priorities. The aims of the Organisation are to promote policies designed to achieve the highest sustainable economic growth and employment and a rising standard of living in member countries, while maintaining financial stability, and thus to contribute to the development of the world economy; to contribute to sound economic expansion in member as well as non-member countries in the process of economic development; and to contribute to the expansion of world trade on a multilateral, non-discriminatory basis in accordance with international obligations.

Members. Australia, Austria, Belgium, Canada, Czech Republic, Denmark, Finland, France, Germany, Greece, Hungary, Iceland, Ireland, Italy, Japan, South Korea, Luxembourg, Mexico, Netherlands, New Zealand, Norway, Poland, Portugal, Slovakia, Spain, Sweden, Switzerland, Turkey, UK and USA.

Activities. The OECD's main fields of programming are: economic policy; statistics; energy; development co-operation; sustainable development; public governance and territorial development; international trade; financial and enterprise affairs; tax policy and administration; food, agriculture and fisheries; environment; science, technology and industry; biotechnology and biodiversity; education; employment, labour and social affairs; entrepreneurship, small and middle-sized enterprises, and local development.

Relations with non-members. The OECD maintains co-operative relations with a wide range of economies outside the OECD area covering topics of mutual interest. The Centre for Co-operation with Non-Members develops the overall architecture of co-operation and general liaison with non-members, while the substantive directorates implement the programmes and activities in each policy area. OECD member country officials engage their non-member counterparts in policy dialogue and conduct peer assessments while sharing each other's policy experiences. Activities with non-OECD members are grouped around Global Forums in nine policy areas where the OECD has particular expertise and where global dialogue can have an important impact on policy-making. The Global Forums aim to achieve sustained results and to develop stable active networks of policy-makers in OECD member and non-member economies on: sustainable development, the knowledge economy, governance, trade, agriculture, taxation, international investment, competition and education. The regional approaches provide for more targeted co-operation with non-OECD economies in Europe, Asia, South America, the Middle East and Northern Africa (MENA) and Africa more generally. The OECD also implements specific programmes for three countries: China, Brazil and the Russian Federation. There is also a sub-regional programme for South-Eastern Europe. In Africa, the OECD supports the objectives of the New Partnership for Africa's Development (NEPAD).

Relations with developing countries. The OECD's Development Assistance Committee (DAC) is the principal body through which the Organisation deals with issues related to co-operation with developing countries. OECD member countries are major aid donors, and collectively they account for more than 90% of total official development assistance (ODA), which amounted to US\$79·5bn. in 2004. Much of the Organisation's development work is focused on how to spend and invest this aid in the most effective manner, so as to reduce poverty and ensure sustainable development in developing countries. Major developments in 2005 included work on aid effectiveness, fragile states, scaling up of aid, aid for trade, capacity development and growth and poverty reduction.

The OECD Development Centre is a policy research and dialogue unit with a mandate to explore and optimise the links between OECD members, emerging economies and developing countries. The two-yearly work programme includes projects on financing development, public and corporate governance, social provision in poor countries, trade and civil society. The Centre's mandate is to share its findings with all countries in the hope of stimulating growth with poverty reduction through policy change. In 2005 its *African Economic Outlook,* jointly published with the African Development Bank, concentrated on stimulating the growth of small and medium-sized enterprises in developing countries. The 2006 edition will focus on infrastructure development and how to achieve it. The Sahel and West Africa Club plays a bridging role, an interface between OECD's member countries and West Africa. Its main objectives are to: help identify strategic questions related to medium and long-term development in West Africa; contribute to mobilizing and strengthening African capacities within a network approach; promote constructive debates that lead to innovative decisions within and outside the region. Its four main areas of concentration are: Medium- and Long-term Development Perspectives; Agricultural Transformation; Local Development and Regional Integration; Governance, Peace and Security.

Relations with other international organizations. Under a protocol signed at the same time as the OECD Convention, the European Commission takes part in the work of the OECD. EFTA may also send representatives to attend OECD meetings. Formal relations exist with a number of other international organizations, including the Asian Development Bank, Inter-American Development Bank, World Bank, UNCTAD, WHO and the Parliamentary Assemblies of the Council of Europe and NATO.

Relations with civil society. Consultations with civil society organizations (CSOs) take place across the whole range of the OECD's work. The Business and Industry Advisory Committee to the OECD (BIAC) and the Trade Union Advisory Committee to the OECD (TUAC) have been granted consultative status enabling them to discuss subjects of common interest and be consulted in a particular field by the relevant OECD Committee or its officers. Individual committees are in direct dialogue with CSOs interested in following their areas of work and establish modalities for consultations, and in some exceptional cases CSOs have observer status. Since 2000 the OECD has organized, annually, the OECD Forum, an international public conference, offering business, labour and civil society the opportunity to discuss key issues of the 21st century with government ministers and leaders of international organizations.

Organization. The governing body of OECD is the Council, made up of representatives of each member country and the European Commission. It meets from time to time (usually once a year) at the level of government ministers, with the chairmanship at ministerial level being rotated among member governments. The Council also meets regularly at official level, when it comprises the Secretary-General (chairman) and the Permanent Representatives to OECD (ambassadors who head resident diplomatic missions). It is responsible for all questions of general policy and may establish subsidiary bodies as required to achieve the aims of the Organisation. Decisions and recommendations of the Council are adopted by consensus of all its members.

The Council is assisted by an Executive Committee which prepares its work and is also called upon to carry out specific tasks where necessary. Apart from its regular meetings, the Executive Committee meets occasionally in special sessions attended by senior government officials. The greater part of the work of the OECD is prepared and carried out by about 200 specialized bodies (Committees, Working Parties, etc.). All members are normally represented on these bodies, except a few which have a more restricted membership. Delegates are usually officials coming either from the capitals of member states or from the Permanent Delegations to the OECD. They are serviced by an international secretariat headed by the OECD Secretary-General. Funding is by contributions from member states, based on a formula related to their size and economy.

The International Energy Agency (IEA), and the Nuclear Energy Agency (NEA) are also part of the OECD system.

Headquarters: 2 rue André Pascal, 75775 Paris Cedex 16, France.
Website: http://www.oecd.org
Secretary-General: Ángel Gurría (Mexico).
Deputy Secretaries-General: Herwig Schlögl (Germany), Richard E. Hecklinger (USA), Berglind Ásgeirsdóttir (Iceland), Kiyotaka Akasaka (Japan).

Publications include: Economic, Environmental and Social Statistics (annual); *OECD Policy Briefs* (20 a year); *OECD Economic Surveys* (by country); *Environmental Performance Reviews* (by country); *OECD Economic Outlook* (twice a year); *Economic Policy Reform: Going for Growth* (annual); *OECD Agricultural Outlook* (annual); *Education at a Glance* (annual); *OECD Employment Outlook* (annual); *OECD Science, Technology and Industry Outlook* (biennial); *Trends in International Migration* (annual); *Health at a Glance* (biennial); *Society at a Glance* (biennial); *OECD Health Data* (CD-ROM; annual); *Financial Market Trends* (twice a year); *Statistics of International Trade* (monthly); *International Trade by Commodity Statistics* (annual); *Main Economic Indicators* (monthly); *Energy Balances* (annual); *World Energy Outlook* (annual); *National Accounts* (quarterly and annual); *African Economic Outlook* (annual); *OECD Observer* (six a year); *Quarterly Labour Force Statistics; Model Tax Convention; Development Centre Policy Briefs; OECD Factbook.* For a full list of OECD publications, visit the website: http://www.oecd.org/bookshop.

Further Reading

Blair, D. J., *Trade Negotiations in the OECD: Structures, Institutions and States.* London, 1993

Organization of the Islamic Conference (OIC)

Founded in 1969, the objectives of the OIC are to promote Islamic solidarity among member states; to consolidate co-operation among member states in the economic, social, cultural, scientific and other vital fields of activities, and to carry out consultations among member states in international organizations; to endeavour to eliminate racial segregation, discrimination and to eradicate colonialism in all its forms; to take the necessary measures to support international peace and security founded on justice; to strengthen the struggle of all Muslim peoples with a view to safeguarding their dignity, independence and national rights; to create a suitable atmosphere for the promotion of co-operation and understanding among member states and other countries.

Members (57 as of Jan. 2006). Afghanistan, Albania, Algeria, Azerbaijan, Bahrain, Bangladesh, Benin, Brunei, Burkina Faso, Cameroon, Chad, Comoros, Côte d'Ivoire, Djibouti, Egypt, Gabon, The Gambia, Guinea, Guinea-Bissau, Guyana, Indonesia, Iran, Iraq, Jordan, Kazakhstan, Kuwait, Kyrgyzstan, Lebanon, Libya, Malaysia, Maldives, Mali, Mauritania, Morocco, Mozambique, Niger, Nigeria, Oman, Pakistan, Palestine, Qatar, Saudi Arabia, Senegal, Sierra Leone, Somalia, Sudan, Suriname, Syria, Tajikistan, Togo, Tunisia, Turkey, Turkmenistan, Uganda, United Arab Emirates, Uzbekistan, Yemen. *Observer states:* Bosnia-Herzegovina, Central African Republic, Thailand.

Headquarters: PO Box 5925, Jeddah, Saudi Arabia.
Website: http://www.oic-un.org
Secretary-General: Dr Ekmeleddin İhsanoğlu (Turkey).

Unrepresented Nations and Peoples Organization (UNPO)

UNPO is an international organization created by nations and peoples around the world who are not represented in the world's principal international organizations, such as the UN. Founded in 1991, UNPO now has 53 members representing over 100m. people worldwide.

Membership. Open to all nations and peoples unrepresented, subject to adherence to the five principles which form the basis of UNPO's charter: equal right to self-determination of all nations and peoples; adherence to internationally accepted human rights standards; to the principles of democracy; promotion of non-violence; and protection of the environment. Applicants must show that they constitute a 'nation or people' as defined in the Covenant.

Functions and Activities. UNPO offers an international forum for occupied nations, indigenous peoples, minorities and oppressed majorities, who struggle to regain their lost countries, preserve their cultural identities, protect their basic human and economic rights, and safeguard their environment.

It does not represent those peoples; rather it assists and empowers them to represent themselves more effectively. To this end, it provides professional services and facilities as well as education and training in the fields of diplomacy, human rights law, democratic processes, conflict resolution and environmental protection. Members, private foundations and voluntary contributions fund the Organization.

In total six former members of UNPO (Armenia, Belau, East Timor, Estonia, Georgia and Latvia) subsequently achieved full independence and gained representation in the UN. Belau is now called Palau. Current members Bougainville and Kosovo are progressively achieving self-determination.

> *Headquarters:* 40A Javastraat, NL-2585 AP The Hague, Netherlands.
> *Website:* http://www.unpo.org
> *General Secretary:* Marino Busdachin.

Publication. UNPO News (quarterly).

World Confederation of Labour (WCL)

Founded in 1920 as the International Federation of Christian Trade Unions, it went out of existence in 1940 as a large proportion of its 3·4m. members were in Italy and Germany, where affiliated unions were suppressed by the Fascist and Nazi regimes. Reconstituted in 1945 and declining to merge with the WFTU or ICFTU, its policy was based on the papal encyclicals *Rerum novarum* (1891) and *Quadragesimo anno* (1931), and in 1968 it became the WCL and dropped its openly confessional approach.

Today, it has Christian, Buddhist and Muslim member confederations, as well as organizations without religious reference. The WCL defines itself as pluralist and humanist. In its concern to defend trade union freedoms and assist trade union development, the WCL differs little in policy from the ICFTU (see pages 50–1). A membership of 26m. in 116 countries is claimed. The biggest group is the Confederation of Christian Trade Unions (CSC) of Belgium (1·6m.).

Organization. The WCL is organized on a federative basis which leaves wide discretion to its autonomous constituent unions. Its governing body is the Congress, which meets every four years. The Congress appoints (or re-appoints) the Secretary-General at each four-yearly meeting. The General Council, which meets at least once a year, is composed of the members of the Confederal Board (at least 22 members, elected by the Congress) and representatives of national confederations, international trade federations, and trade union organizations where there is no confederation affiliated to the WCL. The Confederal Board is responsible for the general leadership of the WCL, in accordance with the decisions and directives of the Council and Congress. There are regional organizations in Latin America (Caracas), Africa (Lomé) and Asia (Manila), and three liaison offices (Bucharest, Geneva and Washington).

> *Headquarters:* 33 rue de Trèves, Brussels 1040, Belgium.
> *Website:* http://www.cmt-wcl.org
> *Secretary-General:* Willy Thys (Belgium).
> *President:* Basile Mahan Gahé (Côte d'Ivoire).

Publications. Annual Report on Workers Rights; Teleflash (20 a year); *Labor Magazine* (4 a year).

World Council of Churches

The World Council of Churches was formally constituted on 23 Aug. 1948 in Amsterdam. Today, member churches number over 340 from more than 120 countries.

Origin. The World Council was founded by the coming together of Christian movements, including the overseas mission groups gathered from 1921 in the International Missionary Council, the Faith and Order Movement, and the Life and Work Movement. On 13 May 1938, at Utrecht, a provisional committee was appointed to prepare for the formation of a World Council of Churches.

Membership. The basis of membership (1975) states: 'The World Council of Churches is a fellowship of Churches which confess the Lord Jesus Christ as God and Saviour according to the Scriptures and therefore seek to fulfil together their common calling to the glory of the one God, Father, Son and Holy Spirit.' Membership is open to Churches which express their agreement with this basis and satisfy such criteria as the Assembly or Central Committee may prescribe. Today, more than 340 Churches of Protestant, Anglican, Orthodox, Old Catholic and Pentecostal confessions belong to this fellowship.

Activities. The WCC's Central Committee comprises the Programme Committee and the Finance Committee. Within the Programme Committee there are advisory groups on issues relating to communication, women, justice, peace and creation, youth, ecumenical relations and inter-religious relations. Following the WCC's 8th General Assembly in Harare, Zimbabwe in 1998 the work of the WCC was restructured. Activities were grouped into four 'clusters'—Relationships; Issues and Themes; Communication; and Finance, Services and Administration. The Relationships cluster comprises four teams (Church and Ecumenical Relations, Regional Relations and Ecumenical Sharing, Inter-Religious Relations and International Relations), as well as two programmes (Action by Churches Together and the Ecumenical Church Loan Fund). The Issues and Themes cluster comprises four teams (Faith and Order; Mission and Evangelism; Justice, Peace and Creation; and Education and Ecumenical Formation).

In Aug. 1997 the WCC launched a Peace to the City campaign, as the initial focus of a programme to overcome violence in troubled cities. The Decade to Overcome Violence was launched in Feb. 2001 during the meeting of the WCC Central Committee in Berlin.

Organization. The governing body of the World Council, consisting of delegates specially appointed by the member Churches, is the Assembly, which meets every seven or eight years to frame policy. It has no legislative powers and depends for the implementation of its decisions upon the action of member Churches. The 9th General Assembly, held in Porto Alegre, Brazil in Feb. 2006, had as its theme 'God, in your grace, transform the world'. A 154-member Central Committee meets annually to carry out the Assembly mandate, with a smaller 25-member Executive Committee meeting twice a year.

> *Headquarters:* PO Box 2100, 150 route de Ferney, 1211 Geneva 2, Switzerland.
> *Website:* http://www.wcc-coe.org
> *General Secretary:* Rev. Dr Samuel Kobia (Kenya).

Publications. Annual Reports; Dictionary of the Ecumenical Movement, Geneva, 1991; *Directory of Christian Councils,* 1985; *A History of the Ecumenical Movement,* Geneva, 1993; *Ecumenical Review* (quarterly); *Ecumenical News International* (weekly); *International Review of Mission* (quarterly).

Further Reading

Castro, E., *A Passion for Unity.* Geneva, 1992
Raiser, K., *Ecumenism in Transition.* Geneva, 1994
Van Elderen, M. and Conway, M., *Introducing the World Council of Churches revised and enlarged edition.* Geneva, 1991

World Customs Organization

Established in 1952 as the Customs Co-operation Council, the World Customs Organization is an intergovernmental body with worldwide membership, whose mission it is to enhance the effectiveness and efficiency of customs administrations throughout the world. It has 164 member countries or territories.

Headquarters: Rue de l'Industrie 26–38, B-1040 Brussels, Belgium.
Website: http://www.wcoomd.org
Secretary-General: Michel Danet (France).

World Federation of Trade Unions (WFTU)

Origin and History. The WFTU was founded on a worldwide basis in 1945 at the international trade union conferences held in London and Paris, with the participation of all the trade union centres in the countries of the anti-Hitler coalition. The aim was to reunite the world trade union movement at the end of the Second World War. The acute political differences among affiliates, especially the east–west confrontation in Europe on ideological lines, led to a split. A number of affiliated organizations withdrew in 1949 and established the ICFTU. The WFTU now draws its membership from the industrially developing countries like India, Vietnam and other Asian countries, Brazil, Peru, Cuba and other Latin American countries, Syria, Lebanon, Kuwait and other Arab countries, and it has affiliates and associates in more than 20 European countries. It has close relations with the International Confederation of Arab Trade Unions, the Organization of African Trade Union Unity as well as the All-China Federation of Trade Unions. The 15th Congress was held in Havana, Cuba in Dec. 2005 and used the slogan 'The working people of the world against globalization and exploitation. For social justice, full employment, solidarity and peace'. Its Trade Unions Internationals (TUIs) have affiliates in Russia, the Czech Republic, Poland and other East European countries, Portugal, France, Spain, Japan and other OECD countries.

The headquarters of the TUIs are situated in Helsinki, New Delhi, Budapest, Mexico, Paris and Moscow. The WFTU and its TUIs have 130m. members, organized in 92 affiliated or associated national federations and six Trade Unions Internationals, in 130 countries. It has regional offices in Athens, New Delhi, Havana, Dakar, Damascus and Moscow and Permanent Representatives accredited to the UN in New York, Geneva, Paris and Rome.

Headquarters: POB 80, Posta 411, 14200 Prague 4, Czech Republic.
Website: http://www.wftu.cz
e-mail: wftu@login.cz
President: Mohammad Assouz (Syria).
General Secretary: George Mavrikos (Greece).

Publications. Flashes From the Trade Unions (fortnightly, published in English, French, Spanish and Arabic), reports of Congresses, etc.

World Wide Fund for Nature (WWF)

Origin. WWF was officially formed and registered as a charity on 11 Sept. 1961. The first National Appeal was launched in the United Kingdom on 23 Nov. 1961, shortly followed by the United States and Switzerland.

Organization. WWF is the world's largest and most experienced independent conservation organization with over 4·7m. supporters and a global network of 27 National Organizations, five Associates and 24 Programme Offices.

The National Organizations carry out conservation activities in their own countries and contribute technical expertise and funding to WWF's international conservation programme. The Programme Offices implement WWF's fieldwork, advise national and local governments, and raise public understanding of conservation issues.

Mission. WWF has as its mission preserving genetic, species and ecosystem diversity; ensuring that the use of renewable natural resources is sustainable now and in the longer term, for the benefit of all life on Earth; promoting actions to reduce to a minimum pollution and the wasteful exploitation and consumption of resources and energy. WWF's ultimate goal is to stop, and eventually reverse, the accelerating degradation of our planet's natural environment, and to help build a future in which humans live in harmony with nature.

Address: Avenue du Mont-Blanc, CH–1196 Gland, Switzerland.
Website: http://www.panda.org
Director General: James P. Leape (USA).
President Emeritus: HRH The Prince Philip, Duke of Edinburgh.
President: Chief Emeka Anyaoku (Nigeria).

African Development Bank

Established in 1964 to promote economic and social development in Africa.

Regional Members. (53) Algeria, Angola, Benin, Botswana, Burkina Faso, Burundi, Cameroon, Cape Verde, Central African Republic, Chad, Comoros, Congo (Dem. Rep. of), Congo (Rep. of), Côte d'Ivoire, Djibouti, Egypt, Equatorial Guinea, Eritrea, Ethiopia, Gabon, The Gambia, Ghana, Guinea, Guinea-Bissau, Kenya, Lesotho, Liberia, Libya, Madagascar, Malawi, Mali, Mauritania, Mauritius, Morocco, Mozambique, Namibia, Niger, Nigeria, Rwanda, São Tomé e Príncipe, Senegal, Seychelles, Sierra Leone, Somalia, South Africa (Rep. of), Sudan, Swaziland, Tanzania, Togo, Tunisia, Uganda, Zambia, Zimbabwe.

Non-regional Members. (24) Argentina, Austria, Belgium, Brazil, Canada, China, Denmark, Finland, France, Germany, India, Italy, Japan, South Korea, Kuwait, Netherlands, Norway, Portugal, Saudi Arabia, Spain, Sweden, Switzerland, UK, USA.

Within the ADB Group is the African Development Fund, established in 1972, which provides development finance on concessional terms to low-income Regional Member Countries which are unable to borrow on the non-concessional terms of the African Development Bank. Membership of the Fund is made up of 25 non-African State Participants, the African Development Bank and the Nigerian Trust Fund.

Official languages: English, French.
Headquarters: 01 BP 1387, Abidjan 01, Côte d'Ivoire.
Website: http://www.afdb.org
e-mail: afdb@afdb.org
President: Donald Kaberuka (Rwanda).

African Export–Import Bank (Afreximbank)

Established in 1987 under the auspices of the African Development Bank to facilitate, promote and expand intra-African and extra-African trade. Membership is made up of three categories of shareholders: Class 'A' Shareholders consisting of African governments, African central banks and sub-regional and regional financial institutions and economic organizations; Class 'B' Shareholders consisting of African public and private financial institutions; and Class 'C' Shareholders consisting of international financial institutions, economic organizations and non-African states, banks, financial institutions and public and private investors.

Official languages: English, French, Arabic, Portuguese.
Headquarters: World Trade Center, 1191 Corniche El-Nil, Cairo 11221, Egypt.
Website: http//www.afreximbank.com
President and Chairman of the Board: Jean-Louis Ekra (Côte d'Ivoire).

African Union (AU)

History. The Fourth Extraordinary Session of the Assembly of the Heads of State and Government of the Organization of African Unity (OAU) held in Sirté, Libya on 9 Sept. 1999 decided to establish an African Union. At Lomé, Togo on 11 July 2000 the OAU Assembly of the Heads of State and Government adopted the Constitutive Act of the African Union, which was later ratified by the required two-thirds of the member states of the Organization of African Unity (OAU); it came into force on 26 May 2001. The Lusaka Summit, in July 2001, gave a mandate to translate the transformation of the Organization of African Unity into the African Union, and on 9 July 2002 the Durban Summit, in South Africa, formally launched the African Union.

Aims. The African Union aims to promote unity, solidarity, cohesion and co-operation among the peoples of Africa and African states, and at the same time to co-ordinate efforts by African people to realize their goals of achieving economic, political and social integration.

Activities. The African Union became fully operational in July 2002, and is working towards establishing 17 organs among which are a Pan-African parliament and a Peace and Security Council (both of which have now been inaugurated), the Economic, Social and Cultural Council (ECOSOC), a Central Bank and a Court of Justice.

Official languages: Arabic, English, French, Ki-Swahili, Portuguese and Spanish.
Headquarters: POB 3243, Addis Ababa, Ethiopia.
Website: http://www.africa-union.org
Chairman: Denis Sassou-Nguesso (Republic of the Congo).

Bank of Central African States (BEAC)

The Bank of Central African States (Banque des Etats de l'Afrique Centrale) was established in 1973 when a new Convention of Monetary Co-operation with France was signed. The five original members, Cameroon, Central African Republic, Chad, Republic of the Congo and Gabon, were joined by Equatorial Guinea in 1985. Under its Convention and statutes, the BEAC is declared a 'Multi-national African institution in the management and control of which France participates in return for the guarantee she provides for its currency'.

Official language: French.
Headquarters: Avenue Monseigneur Vogt, Yaoundé, Cameroon.
Website: http://www.beac.int (French only)
Governor: Jean-Félix Mamalepot.

Publications. Etudes et Statistiques (monthly bulletins); *Annual Report; Directory of Banks and Financial Establishments of BEAC Monetary Area* (annual); *Bulletin du Marché Monétaire* (monthly bulletins); *Annual Report of the Banking Commission.*

Central Bank of West African States (BCEAO)

Established in 1962, the Central Bank of West African States (Banque Centrale des Etats de l'Afrique de l'Ouest) is the common central bank of the eight member states which form the West African Monetary Union (WAMU). It has the sole right of currency issue throughout the Union territory and is responsible for the pooling of the Union's foreign exchange reserve; the management of the monetary policy of the member states; the keeping of the accounts of the member states treasury; and the definition of the banking law applicable to banks and financial establishments.

Members. Benin, Burkina Faso, Côte d'Ivoire, Guinea-Bissau, Mali, Niger, Senegal, Togo.

Official language: French.
Headquarters: Avenue Abdoulaye Fadiga, Dakar, Senegal.
Website: http://www.bceao.int
Governor (acting): Justin Baro Damo (Burkina Faso).

Publications. Rapport annuel (annual); *Annuaire des Banques* (annual); *Bilan des Banques U.M.O.A.* (annual); *Notes d'information et statistiques* (monthly bulletin).

Common Market for Eastern and Southern Africa (COMESA)

COMESA is an African economic grouping of 20 member states who are committed to the creation of a Common Market for Eastern and Southern Africa. It was established in 1994 as a building block for the African Economic Community and replaced the Preferential Trade Area for Eastern and Southern Africa, which had been in existence since 1981.

Members. Angola, Burundi, Comoros, Democratic Republic of Congo, Djibouti, Egypt, Eritrea, Ethiopia, Kenya, Libya, Madagascar, Malaŵi, Mauritius, Rwanda, Seychelles, Sudan, Swaziland, Uganda, Zambia and Zimbabwe.

Objectives. To facilitate the removal of the structural and institutional weaknesses of member states so that they are able to attain collective and sustainable development.

Activities. COMESA's Free Trade Area (FTA) was launched on 31 Oct. 2000 at a Summit of Heads of States and Government in Lusaka, Zambia. The FTA participating states have zero tariff on goods and services produced in these countries.

In addition to creating the policy environment for freeing trade, COMESA has also created specialized institutions like the Eastern and Southern African Trade and Development Bank

(PTA Bank), the PTA Reinsurance Company (ZEP-RE), the Clearing House and the COMESA Court of Justice, to provide the required financial infrastructure and service support. COMESA has also promoted a political risk guarantee scheme, the Africa Trade Insurance Agency (ATI), a Leather and Leather Products Institute (LLPI), as well as a cross-border insurance scheme, the COMESA Yellow Card.

Official languages: English, French, Portuguese.
Headquarters: COMESA Secretariat, COMESA Centre, Ben Bella Road, PO Box 30051, 10101 Lusaka, Zambia.
Website: http://www.comesa.int
Secretary General: Erastus Mwencha (Kenya).

East African Community

The East African Community (EAC) was formally established on 30 Nov. 1999 with the signing in Arusha, Tanzania of the Treaty for the Establishment of the East African Community. The Treaty envisages the establishment of a Customs Union, as the entry point of the Community, a Common Market, subsequently a Monetary Union and ultimately a Political Federation of the East African States. In Nov. 2003 the EAC partner states signed a Protocol on the Establishment of the East African Customs Union, which came into force on 1 Jan. 2005.

Members. Kenya, Tanzania, Uganda.

Headquarters: PO Box 1096, Arusha, Tanzania.
Website: http://www.eac.int
Secretary General: Nuwe Amanya-Mushega (Uganda).

East African Development Bank (EADB)

Established originally under the Treaty for East African Co-operation in 1967 with Kenya, Tanzania and Uganda as signatories, a new Charter for the Bank (with the same signatories) came into force in 1980. Under the original Treaty the Bank was confined to the provision of financial and technical assistance for the promotion of industrial development in member states but with the new Charter its remit was broadened to include involvement in agriculture, forestry, tourism, transport and the development of infrastructure, with preference for projects which promote regional co-operation.

Official language: English.
Headquarters: 4 Nile Avenue, Kampala, Uganda.
Website: http://www.eadb.org
Chairman of the Board: Christopher Kassami (Uganda).

Economic Community of Central African States (CEEAC)

The Economic Community of Central African States (Communauté Economique des Etats de l'Afrique Centrale) was established in 1983 to promote regional economic co-operation and to establish a Central African Common Market. Plans were announced in Jan. 2004 for a free trade zone to be set up by the end of 2007.

Members. Angola, Burundi, Cameroon, Central African Republic, Chad, Democratic Republic of the Congo, Republic of the Congo, Equatorial Guinea, Gabon, Rwanda, São Tomé e Príncipe.

Headquarters: BP 2112, Libreville, Gabon.
President: Denis Sassou-Nguesso (Republic of the Congo).
Secretary-General: Louis Sylvain-Goma (Republic of the Congo).

Economic Community of West African States (ECOWAS)

Founded in 1975 as a regional common market, and now aiming to introduce a single currency in 2009, ECOWAS later also became a political forum involved in the promotion of a democratic environment and the pursuit of fundamental human rights. In July 1993 it revised its treaty to assume responsibility for the regulation of regional armed conflicts, acknowledging the inextricable link between development and peace and security. Thus it now has a new role in conflict management and prevention through its Mediation and Security Council, which monitors the moratorium on the export, import and manufacture of light weapons and ammunition. However, it still retains a military arm, ECOMOG. It is also involved in the war against drug abuse and illicit drug trafficking.

Members. Benin, Burkina Faso, Cape Verde, Côte d'Ivoire, The Gambia, Ghana, Guinea, Guinea-Bissau, Liberia, Mali, Niger, Nigeria, Senegal, Sierra Leone, Togo.

Organization. It meets at yearly summits which rotate in the different capitals of member states. The institution is governed by the Council of Ministers, and has a secretariat in Abuja which is run by an Executive Secretary.

Official languages: English, French, Portuguese.
Headquarters: 60 Yakubu Gowon Crescent, Asokoro, Abuja, Nigeria.
Website: http://www.ecowas.int
e-mail: info@ecowasmail.net
Executive Secretary: Dr Mohamed Ibn Chambas (Ghana).

Intergovernmental Authority on Development

The Intergovernmental Authority on Development was created on 21 March 1996 and has its origins in the Intergovernmental Authority on Drought and Development, which had been established in 1986. It has three priority areas of co-operation: conflict prevention, management and humanitarian affairs; infrastructure development; food security and environment protection.

Members. Djibouti, Eritrea, Ethiopia, Kenya, Somalia, Sudan, Uganda.

Headquarters: PO Box 2653, Djibouti, Republic of Djibouti.
Website: http://www.igad.org
Executive Secretary: Dr Attalla Hamad Bashir (Sudan).

Lake Chad Basin Commission

Established by a Convention and Statute signed on 22 May 1964 by Cameroon, Chad, Niger and Nigeria, and later by the Central African Republic, to regulate and control utilization of the water and other natural resources in the Basin (Sudan has also been admitted as an observer); to initiate, promote and co-ordinate natural resources development projects and research within the Basin area; and to examine complaints and promote settlement of disputes, with a view to promoting regional co-operation.

In Dec. 1977, at Enugu in Nigeria, the 3rd summit of heads of state of the commission signed the protocol for the Harmonization of the Regulations Relating to Fauna and Flora in member countries, and adopted plans for the multi-donor approach towards major integrated development for the conventional basin. An international campaign to save Lake Chad following a report on the environmental degradation of the conventional basin was launched by heads of state at the 8th summit of the Commission in Abuja in March 1994. The 10th summit, held in N'Djaména in 2000, saw agreement on a US$1m. inter-basin water transfer project.

The Commission operates an annual budget of 1bn. francs CFA, and receives assistance from various international and donor agencies including the FAO, and UN Development and Environment Programmes.

Official languages: English, French.
Headquarters: BP 727, N'Djaména, Chad.
e-mail: lcbc@intnet.td
Executive Secretary: Engr. Muhammad Sani Adamu.

Niger Basin Authority

As a result of a special meeting of the Niger River Commission (established in 1964), to discuss the revitalizing and restructuring of the organization to improve its efficiency, the Niger Basin Authority was established in 1980. Its responsibilities cover the harmonization and co-ordination of national development policies; the formulation of the general development policy of the Basin; the elaboration and implementation of an integrated development plan of the Basin; the initiation and monitoring of an orderly and rational regional policy for the utilization of the waters of the Niger River; the design and conduct of studies, researches and surveys; the formulation of plans, the construction, exploitation and maintenance of structure, and the elaboration of projects.

Members. Benin, Burkina Faso, Cameroon, Chad, Côte d'Ivoire, Guinea, Mali, Niger, Nigeria.

Official languages: English, French.
Headquarters: BP 729, Niamey, Niger.
Website: http://www.abn.ne
Executive Secretary: Muhammad Bello Tuga (Nigeria).

Southern African Development Community (SADC)

The Southern African Development Co-ordination Conference (SADCC), the precursor of the Southern African Development Community (SADC), was formed in Lusaka, Zambia on 1 April 1980, following the adoption of the Lusaka Declaration—*Southern Africa: Towards Economic Liberation*—by the nine founding member states.

Members. The nine founder member countries were Angola, Botswana, Lesotho, Malaŵi, Mozambique, Swaziland, Tanzania, Zambia and Zimbabwe. The Democratic Republic of the Congo, Madagascar, Mauritius, Namibia, the Seychelles and South Africa have since joined. However, the Seychelles left in July 2004. As a result there are now 14 members.

Aims and Activities. SADC's Common Agenda includes the following: the promotion of sustainable and equitable economic growth and socio-economic development that will ensure poverty alleviation with the ultimate objective of its eradication; the promotion of common political values, systems and other shared values that are transmitted through institutions that are democratic, legitimate and effective; and the consolidation and maintenance of democracy, peace and security.

In contrast to the country-based co-ordination of sectoral activities and programmes, SADC has now adopted a more centralized approach through which the 21 sectoral programmes are grouped into four clusters; namely: Trade, Industry, Finance and Investment; Infrastructure and Services; Food, Agriculture and Natural Resources; Social and Human Development and Special Programmes.

SADC has made significant progress in implementing its integration agenda since the 1992 Treaty came into force. Since then, 23 Protocols to spearhead the sectoral programmes and activities have been signed. The following protocols have entered into force: Immunities and Privileges; Combating Illicit Drug Trafficking; Energy; Transport, Communications and Meteorology; Shared Watercourse Systems; Mining; Trade; Education and Training; Development of Tourism; Health; Wildlife Conservation and Law Enforcement; Tribunal and the Rules of Procedure; Revised Protocol on Shared Watercourses; Amendment Protocol on Trade; Politics, Defense and Security Co-operation; Control of Firearms, Ammunition and Other Related Materials in SADC; Fisheries.

Official languages: English, French, Portuguese.
Headquarters: Private Bag 0095, Gaborone, Botswana.
Website: http://www.sadc.int
e-mail: registry@sadc.int
Executive Secretary: Tomaz Augusto Salomão (Mozambique).

West African Development Bank (BOAD)

The West African Development Bank (Banque Ouest Africaine de Développement) was established in Nov. 1973 by an Agreement signed by the member states of the West African Monetary Union (UMOA), now the West African Economic and Monetary Union (UEMOA).

Aims. To promote balanced development of the States of the Union and to achieve West African economic integration.

Members. Benin, Burkina Faso, Côte d'Ivoire, Guinea-Bissau, Mali, Niger, Senegal, Togo.

Official language: French.
Headquarters: 68 Avenue de la Libération, Lomé, Togo.
Website: http://www.boad.org (French only)
e-mail: boadsiege@boad.org
President (acting): Issa Coulibaly (Mali).

West African Economic and Monetary Union (UEMOA)

Founded in 1994, the UEMOA (Union Economique et Monétaire Ouest Africaine) aims to reinforce the competitiveness of the economic and financial activities of member states in the context of an open and rival market and a rationalized and harmonized juridical environment; to ensure the convergence of the macro-economic performances and policies of member states; to create a common market among member states; to institute a co-ordination for the national sector-based policies; and to harmonize the legislation, especially the fiscal system, of the member states.

Members. Benin, Burkina Faso, Côte d'Ivoire, Guinea-Bissau, Mali, Niger, Senegal, Togo.

> *Headquarters:* 01 B.P. 543, Ouagadougou 01, Burkina Faso.
> *Website:* http://www.uemoa.int
> *President:* Soumaïla Cisse (Mali).

Agency for the Prohibition of Nuclear Weapons in Latin America and the Caribbean (OPANAL)

The Agency (Organismo para la Proscripción de las Armas Nucleares en la América Latina y el Caribe) was established following the Cuban missile crisis to guarantee implementation of the world's first Nuclear-Weapon-Free-Zone (NWFZ) in the region. Created by the Treaty of Tlatelolco (1967), OPANAL is an inter-governmental agency responsible for ensuring that the requirements of the Treaty are enforced. OPANAL has played a major role in establishing other NWFZs throughout the world.

Organization. The Agency consists of three main bodies: the General Conference which meets for biennial sessions and special sessions when deemed necessary; the Council of OPANAL consisting of five member states which meet every two months plus special meetings when necessary; and the Secretariat General.

Members of the Treaty. Antigua and Barbuda, Argentina, Bahamas, Barbados, Belize, Bolivia, Brazil, Chile, Colombia, Costa Rica, Cuba, Dominica, Dominican Republic, Ecuador, El Salvador, Grenada, Guatemala, Guyana, Haiti, Honduras, Jamaica, Mexico, Nicaragua, Panama, Paraguay, Peru, St Kitts and Nevis, St Lucia, St Vincent and the Grenadines, Suriname, Trinidad and Tobago, Uruguay, Venezuela.

> *Headquarters:* Schiller No. 326, 5th Floor, Col. Chapultepec Morales, México, D. F. 11570, Mexico.
> *Website:* http://www.opanal.org
> *e-mail:* info@opanal.org
> *Secretary-General:* Edmundo Vargas Carreño (Chile).

Andean Community

On 26 May 1969 an agreement was signed by Bolivia, Chile, Colombia, Ecuador and Peru establishing the Cartagena Agreement (also referred to as the Andean Pact or the Andean Group). Chile withdrew from the Group in 1976. Venezuela, which was actively involved, did not sign the agreement until 1973. In 1997 Peru announced its withdrawal for five years.

The Andean Free Trade Area came into effect on 1 Feb. 1993 as the first step towards the creation of a common market. Bolivia, Colombia, Ecuador, Peru and Venezuela have fully liberalized their trade. A Common External Tariff for imports from third countries has been in effect since 1 Feb. 1995.

In March 1996 at the Group's 8th summit in Trujillo in Peru, member countries (Bolivia, Colombia, Ecuador, Peru, Venezuela) set up the Andean Community, to promote greater economic, commercial and political integration between member countries under a new Andean Integration System (SAI).

The member countries and bodies of the Andean Integration System are working to establish an Andean Common Market and to implement a Common Foreign Policy, a social agenda, a Community policy on border integration, and policies for achieving joint macroeconomic targets.

Organization. The Andean Presidential Council, composed of the presidents of the member states, is the highest-level body of the Andean Integration System (SAI). The Commission and the Andean Council of Foreign Ministers are legislative bodies. The General Secretariat is the executive body and the Andean Parliament is the deliberative body of the SAI. The Court of Justice, which began operating in 1984, resolves disputes between members and interprets legislation. The SAI has other institutions: Andean Development Corporation (CAF), Latin American Reserve Fund (FLAR), Simon Bolivar Andean University, Andean Business Advisory Council, Andean Labour Advisory Council and various Social Agreements.

Further to the treaty signed by 12 South American countries in Dec. 2004, the Andean Community will gradually be integrated into the new South American Community of Nations.

> *Official language:* Spanish.
> *Headquarters:* Avda Paseo de la República 3895, San Isidro, Lima 17, Peru.
> *Website:* http://www.comunidadandina.org
> *e-mail:* contacto@comunidadandina.org
> *Secretary-General:* Allan Wagner Tizón (Peru).

Association of Caribbean States (ACS)

The Convention establishing the ACS was signed on 24 July 1994 in Cartagena de Indias, Colombia, with the aim of promoting consultation, co-operation and concerted action among all the countries of the Caribbean, comprising 25 full member states and three associate members. A total of eight other non-independent Caribbean countries are eligible for associate membership.

Members. Antigua and Barbuda, Bahamas, Barbados, Belize, Colombia, Costa Rica, Cuba, Dominica, Dominican Republic, El Salvador, Grenada, Guatemala, Guyana, Haiti, Honduras, Jamaica, Mexico, Nicaragua, Panama, St Kitts and Nevis, St Lucia, St Vincent and the Grenadines, Suriname, Trinidad and Tobago, Venezuela.

Associate members. Aruba, France (on behalf of French Guiana, Guadeloupe and Martinique) and the Netherlands Antilles.

The CARICOM Secretariat, the Latin American Economic System (SELA), the Central American Integration System (SICA) and the Permanent Secretariat of the General Agreement on Central American Economic Integration (SIECA) were declared Founding Observers of the ACS in 1996. The United Nations Economic Commission for Latin America and the Caribbean (ECLAC) and the Caribbean Tourism Organization (CTO) were admitted as Founding Observers in 2000 and 2001 respectively.

Functions. The objectives of the ACS are enshrined in the Convention and are based on the following: the strengthening of the regional co-operation and integration process, with a view to creating an enhanced economic space in the region; preserving the environmental integrity of the Caribbean Sea which is regarded as the common patrimony of the peoples of the region; and promoting the sustainable development of the Greater Caribbean. Its current focal areas are trade, transport, sustainable tourism and natural disasters.

Organization. The main organs of the Association are the Ministerial Council and the Secretariat. There are Special Committees on: Trade Development and External Economic Relations; Sustainable Tourism; Transport; Natural Disasters; Budget and Administration. There is also a Council of National Representatives of the Special Fund responsible for overseeing resource mobilization efforts and project development.

Headquarters: ACS Secretariat, 5–7 Sweet Briar Road, St Clair, PO Box 660, Port of Spain, Trinidad and Tobago.
Website: http://www.acs-aec.org
e-mail: mail@acs-aec.org
Secretary-General: Dr Rubén Arturo Silié Valdez (Dominican Republic).

Caribbean Community (Caricom)

Origin. The Treaty of Chaguaramas establishing the Caribbean Community and Common Market was signed by the prime ministers of Barbados, Guyana, Jamaica and Trinidad and Tobago at Chaguaramas, Trinidad, on 4 July 1973.

Six additional countries and territories (Belize, Dominica, Grenada, St Lucia, St Vincent and the Grenadines, Montserrat) signed the Treaty on 17 April 1974, and the Treaty came into effect for those countries on 1 May 1974. Antigua acceded to membership on 4 July that year; St Kitts and Nevis on 26 July; the Bahamas on 4 July 1983 (not Common Market); Suriname on 4 July 1995.

Members. Antigua and Barbuda, Bahamas, Barbados, Belize, Dominica, Grenada, Guyana, Haiti, Jamaica, Montserrat, St Kitts and Nevis, St Lucia, St Vincent and the Grenadines, Suriname, and Trinidad and Tobago. Anguilla, Bermuda, the British Virgin Islands, Cayman Islands and Turks and Caicos Islands are associate members.

Objectives. The Caribbean Community has the following objectives: improved standards of living and work; full employment of labour and other factors of production; accelerated, co-ordinated and sustained economic development and convergence; expansion of trade and economic relations with third States; enhanced levels of international competitiveness; organization for increased production and productivity; the achievement of a greater measure of economic leverage and effectiveness of member states in dealing with third States, groups of States and entities of any description; enhanced co-ordination of member states' foreign and foreign economic policies; enhanced functional co-operation.

At its 20th Meeting in July 1999 the Conference of Heads of Government of the Caribbean Community approved for signature the agreement establishing the Caribbean Court of Justice. They mandated the establishment of a Preparatory Committee comprising the Attorneys General of Barbados, Guyana, Jamaica, St Kitts and Nevis, St Lucia and Trinidad and Tobago assisted by other officials, to develop and implement a programme of public education within the Caribbean Community and to make appropriate arrangements for the inauguration of the Caribbean Court of Justice prior to the establishment of the CARICOM Single Market and Economy. To this end at its 23rd Meeting in July 2002 the Heads of Government agreed on immediate measures to inaugurate the Court by the second half of 2003, although delays meant it was not inaugurated until April 2005. Among the measures adopted was the establishment of a Trust Fund with a one-time settlement of US$100m. to finance the Court. The President of the Caribbean Development Bank was authorized to raise the funds on international capital markets, so that member states could access these funds to meet their assessed contributions towards the financing of the Court. The agreement establishing the Regional Justice Protection Programme was also approved for signature. The agreement establishes a framework for regional co-operation in the protection of witnesses, jurors, judicial and legal officers, law enforcement personnel and their associates.

Structure. The Conference of Heads of Government is the principal organ of the Community, and its primary responsibility is to determine and provide the policy direction for the Community. It is the final authority on behalf of the Community for the conclusion of treaties and for entering into relationships between the Community and international organizations and States. It is responsible for financial arrangements to meet the expenses of the Community.

The Community Council of Ministers is the second highest organ of the Community and consists of Ministers of Government responsible for Community Affairs. The Community Council has primary responsibility for the development of Community strategic planning and co-ordination in the areas of economic integration, functional co-operation and external relations.

The Secretariat is the principal administrative organ of the Community. The Secretary-General is appointed by the Conference (on the recommendation of the Community Council) for a term not exceeding five years, and may be re-appointed. The Secretary-General is the Chief Executive Officer of the Community and acts in that capacity at all meetings of the Community Organs.

Associate Institutions. Caribbean Development Bank (CDB); University of Guyana (UG); University of the West Indies (UWI); Caribbean Law Institute (CLI)/Caribbean Law Institute Centre (CLIC); Secretariat of the Organisation of Eastern Caribbean States.

Official language: English.
Headquarters: Bank of Guyana Building, PO Box 10827, Georgetown, Guyana.
Website: http://www.caricom.org
Secretary-General: Edwin W. Carrington (Trinidad and Tobago).

Publications. CARICOM Perspective (1 a year); *Annual Report; Treaty Establishing the Caribbean Community; Caribbean Trade and Investment Report 2000.*

Further Reading

Parry, J. H., *et al. A Short History of the West Indies.* Rev. ed. London, 1987

Caribbean Development Bank (CDB)

Established in 1969 by 16 regional and two non-regional members. Membership is open to all states and territories of the region and to non-regional states which are members of the UN or its Specialized Agencies or of the International Atomic Energy Agency.

Members—regional countries and territories: Anguilla, Antigua and Barbuda, Bahamas, Barbados, Belize, British Virgin Islands, Cayman Islands, Colombia, Dominica, Grenada, Guyana, Jamaica, Mexico, Montserrat, St Kitts and Nevis, St Lucia, St Vincent and the Grenadines, Trinidad and Tobago, Turks and Caicos Islands, Venezuela. *Non-regional countries:* Canada, China, Germany, Italy, United Kingdom.

Function. To contribute to the economic growth and development of the member countries of the Caribbean and promote economic co-operation and integration among them, with particular regard to the needs of the less developed countries.

Headquarters: PO Box 408, Wildey, St Michael, Barbados.
Website: http://www.caribank.org
e-mail: info@caribank.org
President: Dr Compton Bourne (Guyana).

Publications. Annual Report; Basic Information; Caribbean Development Bank: Its Purpose, Role and Functions; Summary of Proceedings of Annual Meetings of Board of Governors; Statements by the President; Financial Policies; Guidelines for Procurement; Procedures for the Selection and Engagement of Consultants by Recipients of CDB Financing; Special Development Fund Rules; Sector Policy Papers; CDB News (newsletter).

Central American Bank for Economic Integration (CABEI)

Established in 1960, the Bank is the financial institution created by the Central American Economic Integration Treaty and aims to implement the economic integration and balanced economic growth of the member states.

Members. (Regional) Costa Rica, El Salvador, Guatemala, Honduras, Nicaragua. (Non-regional) Argentina, China, Colombia, Mexico, Spain.

Official languages: Spanish, English.
Headquarters: Apartado Postal 772, Tegucigalpa, DC, Honduras.
Website: http://www.bcie.org
President: Dr Harry Brautigam (Nicaragua).

Central American Common Market (CACM)

In Dec. 1960 El Salvador, Guatemala, Honduras and Nicaragua concluded the General Treaty of Central American Economic Integration under the auspices of the Organization of Central American States (ODECA) in Managua. Long-standing political and social conflicts in the area have repeatedly dogged efforts to establish integration towards the establishment of a common market.

Members. Costa Rica, El Salvador, Guatemala, Honduras and Nicaragua.

A protocol to the 1960 General Treaty signed by all five members and Panama in Oct. 1993 reaffirmed an eventual commitment to full economic integration with a common external tariff of 20% to be introduced only voluntarily and gradually.

A Treaty on Democratic Security in Central America was signed by all six members at San Pedro Sula, Honduras in Dec. 1995, with a view to achieving a proper 'balance of forces' in the region, intensifying the fight against trafficking of drugs and arms, and reintegrating refugees and displaced persons.

In addition, the CACM countries signed a new framework co-operation agreement with the EC in Feb. 1993, revising the previous (1985) failing agreement between them, to provide support to CACM's integration plans.

Headquarters: 4a Avenida 10–25, Zona 14, Ciudad de Guatemala, Guatemala.
Secretary-General: Haroldo Rodas Melgar (Guatemala).

Eastern Caribbean Central Bank (ECCB)

The Eastern Caribbean Central Bank was established in 1983, replacing the East Caribbean Currency Authority (ECCA). Its purpose is to regulate the availability of money and credit; to promote and maintain monetary stability; to promote credit and exchange conditions and a sound financial structure conducive to the balanced growth and development of the economies of the territories of the participating Governments; and to actively promote, through means consistent with its other objectives, the economic development of the territories of the participating Governments.

Members. Anguilla, Antigua and Barbuda, Dominica, Grenada, Montserrat, St Kitts and Nevis, St Lucia, St Vincent and the Grenadines.

Official language: English.
Headquarters: PO Box 89, Bird Rock, Basseterre, St Kitts and Nevis.
Website: http://www.eccb-centralbank.org/
e-mail: eccbinfo@caribsurf.com
Governor: Sir Dwight Venner (St Vincent and the Grenadines).

Inter-American Development Bank (IDB)

The IDB, the oldest and largest regional multilateral development institution, was established in 1959 to help accelerate economic and social development in Latin America and the Caribbean. The Bank's original membership included 19 Latin American and Caribbean countries and the USA. Today, membership totals 47 nations, including non-regional members.

Members. Argentina, Austria, Bahamas, Barbados, Belgium, Belize, Bolivia, Brazil, Canada, Chile, Colombia, Costa Rica, Croatia, Denmark, Dominican Republic, Ecuador, El Salvador, Finland, France, Germany, Guatemala, Guyana, Haiti, Honduras, Israel, Italy, Jamaica, Japan, South Korea, Mexico, the Netherlands, Nicaragua, Norway, Panama, Paraguay, Peru, Portugal, Slovenia, Spain, Suriname, Sweden, Switzerland, Trinidad and Tobago, UK, USA, Uruguay, Venezuela.

The Bank's total lending up to 2000 has been US$106bn. for projects with a total cost of over US$263bn. Its lending has increased dramatically from the US$294m. approved in 1961 to US$6,311m. in 2002.

Current lending priorities include poverty reduction and social equity, modernization and integration, and the environment. The Bank has a Fund for Special Operations for lending on concessional terms for projects in countries classified as economically less developed. An additional facility, the Multilateral Investment Fund (MIF), was created in 1992 to help promote and accelerate investment reforms and private-sector development throughout the region.

The Board of Governors is the Bank's highest authority. Governors are usually Ministers of Finance, Presidents of Central Banks or officers of comparable rank. The IDB has country offices in each of its borrowing countries, and in Paris and Tokyo.

Official languages: English, French, Portuguese, Spanish.
Headquarters: 1300 New York Avenue, NW, Washington, D.C., 20577, USA.
Website: http://www.iadb.org
President: Luis Alberto Moreno (Colombia).

Latin American Economic System (SELA)

Established in 1975 by the Panama Convention, SELA (Sistema Económico Latinoamericano) promotes co-ordination on economic issues and social development among the countries of Latin America and the Caribbean.

Members. Argentina, Bahamas, Barbados, Belize, Bolivia, Brazil, Chile, Colombia, Costa Rica, Cuba, Dominican Republic, Ecuador, El Salvador, Grenada, Guatemala, Guyana, Haiti, Honduras, Jamaica, Mexico, Nicaragua, Panama, Paraguay, Peru, Suriname, Trinidad and Tobago, Uruguay, Venezuela.

Official languages: English, French, Portuguese, Spanish.
Headquarters: Apartado 17035, Caracas 1010–4, Venezuela.
Website: http://www.sela.org
e-mail: difusion@sela.org
Permanent Secretary: Roberto Guarnieri (Venezuela).

Publications. Capitulos (in Spanish and English, published thrice yearly); *SELA Antenna in the United States* (quarterly bulletin); *Integration Bulletin on Latin America and the Caribbean* (monthly).

Latin American Integration Association (ALADI/LAIA)

The ALADI was established to promote freer trade among member countries in the region.

Members. (12) Argentina, Bolivia, Brazil, Chile, Colombia, Cuba, Ecuador, Mexico, Paraguay, Peru, Uruguay and Venezuela.

Observers. (26) Andean Development Corporation (CAF), China, Commission of the European Communities, Costa Rica, Dominican Republic, El Salvador, Guatemala, Honduras, Inter-American Development Bank, Inter-American Institute for Cooperation on Agriculture (IICA), Italy, Japan, South Korea, Latin American Economic System (SELA), Nicaragua, Organization of American States (OAS), Pan American Health Organization (PAHO), Panama, Portugal, Romania, Russia, Spain, Switzerland, UN Development Programme, UN Economic Commission for Latin America and the Caribbean (ECLAC), World Health Organization (WHO).

Official languages: Portuguese, Spanish.
Headquarters: Calle Cebollatí 1461, Casilla de Correos 20005, 11200 Montevideo, Uruguay.
Website: http://www.aladi.org
Secretary-General: Dr Didier Opertti Badán (Uruguay).

Latin American Reserve Fund

Established in 1991 as successor to the Andean Reserve Fund, the Latin American Reserve Fund assists in correcting payment imbalances through loans with terms of up to four years and guarantees extended to members, to co-ordinate their monetary, exchange and financial policies and to promote the liberalization of trade and payments in the Andean sub-region.

Members. Bolivia, Colombia, Costa Rica, Ecuador, Peru, Venezuela.

Official language: Spanish.
Headquarters: Edificio Banco de Occidente, Carrera 13, No. 27–47, Piso 10, Santafe de Bogota, DC, Colombia.
Website: http://www.flar.net
Executive President: Julio Velarde (Peru).

Organization of American States (OAS)

Origin. On 14 April 1890 representatives of the American republics, meeting in Washington at the First International Conference of American States, established an International Union of American Republics and, as its central office, a Commercial Bureau of American Republics, which later became the Pan-American Union. This international organization's object was to foster mutual understanding and co-operation among the nations of the western hemisphere. This led to the adoption on 30 April 1948 by the Ninth International Conference of American States, at Bogotá, Colombia, of the Charter of the Organization of American States. This co-ordinated the work of all the former independent official entities in the inter-American system and defined their mutual relationships. The Charter of 1948 was subsequently amended by the Protocol of Buenos Aires (1967) and the Protocol of Cartagena de Indias (1985).

Members. This is on a basis of absolute equality, with each country having one vote and there being no veto power. Members (2006): Antigua and Barbuda, Argentina, Bahamas, Barbados, Belize, Bolivia, Brazil, Canada, Chile, Colombia, Costa Rica, Cuba (suspended 1962), Dominica, Dominican Republic, Ecuador, El Salvador, Grenada, Guatemala, Guyana, Haiti, Honduras, Jamaica, Mexico, Nicaragua, Panama, Paraguay, Peru, St Kitts and Nevis, St Lucia, St Vincent and the Grenadines, Suriname, Trinidad and Tobago, USA, Uruguay, Venezuela.

Permanent Observers. Algeria, Angola, Armenia, Austria, Azerbaijan, Belgium, Bosnia-Herzegovina, Bulgaria, China, Croatia, Cyprus, Czech Republic, Denmark, Egypt, Equatorial Guinea, Estonia, EU, Finland, France, Georgia, Germany, Ghana, Greece, Holy See, Hungary, India, Ireland, Israel, Italy, Japan, Kazakhstan, South Korea, Latvia, Lebanon, Luxembourg, Morocco, the Netherlands, Nigeria, Norway, Pakistan, Philippines, Poland, Portugal, Qatar, Romania, Russia, Saudi Arabia, Serbia and Montenegro, Slovakia, Slovenia, Spain, Sri Lanka, Sweden, Switzerland, Thailand, Tunisia, Turkey, UK, Ukraine, Yemen.

Aims and Activities. To strengthen the peace and security of the continent; promote and consolidate representative democracy, with due respect for the principle of non-intervention; prevent possible causes of difficulties and ensure the peaceful settlement of disputes among member states; provide for common action in the event of aggression; seek the solution of political, juridical and economic problems; promote by co-operative action economic, social and cultural development; and achieve an effective limitation of conventional weapons.

The Santiago Commitment to Democracy and the Renewal of the Inter-American System. With the emergence of democratically elected governments throughout the continent, the OAS has been increasingly concerned with the preservation, protection and promotion of democracy. At its 21st Regular Session (Santiago, Chile, 1991) the OAS General Assembly adopted the Santiago Commitment to Democracy and the Renewal of the Inter-American System as well as the Protocol of Washington (1992) to amend the Charter by provisions of the Resolution 1080 on representative democracy.

Declaration of Belém do Pará. At its 24th Regular Session (June 1994, Belém do Pará), the General Assembly adopted the Declaration of Belém do Pará, in which the ministers of foreign affairs and heads of delegation of member states declared their commitment to strengthening the OAS as the main hemispheric forum of political consensus, so that it may support: the realization of the aspirations of member states in promoting and consolidating peace, democracy, social justice and development; their decision to promote and deepen co-operative relations in the economic, social, educational, cultural, scientific, technological and political fields; their commitment to continue and further the dialogue on hemispheric security; their determination to continue to contribute to the objective of general and complete disarmament; their determination to strengthen regional co-operation to increase the effectiveness of efforts to combat the illicit use of narcotic drugs and traffic therein; their decision to co-operate in a reciprocal effort towards preventing and punishing terrorist acts, methods and practices, and the development of international law in this matter; and their commitment to promote economic and social development for the indigenous populations of their countries.

Organization. Under its Charter the OAS accomplishes its purposes by means of:
  (a) The General Assembly, which meets annually.
  (b) The Meeting of Consultation of Ministers of Foreign Affairs, held to consider problems of an urgent nature and of common interest.
  (c) The Councils: The Permanent Council, which meets on a permanent basis at OAS headquarters and carries out decisions of the General Assembly, assists the member states in the peaceful settlement of disputes, acts as the Preparatory Committee of that Assembly, submits recommendations with regard to the functioning of the Organization, and considers the reports to the Assembly of the other organs. The Inter-American Council for Integral Development (CIDI) directs and monitors OAS technical co-operation programmes.
  (d) The Inter-American Juridical Committee which acts as an advisory body to the OAS on juridical matters and promotes the development and codification of international law. 11 jurists, elected for four-year terms by the General Assembly, represent all the American States.
  (e) The Inter-American Commission on Human Rights which oversees the observance and protection of human rights. Seven members elected for four-year terms by the General Assembly represent all the OAS member states.
  (f) The General Secretariat, which is the central and permanent organ of the OAS.
  (g) The Specialized Conferences, meeting to deal with special technical matters or to develop specific aspects of inter-American co-operation.
  (h) The Specialized Organizations, intergovernmental organizations established by multilateral agreements to discharge specific functions in their respective fields of action, such as women's affairs, agriculture, child welfare, Indian affairs, geography and history, and health.
  In Sept. 2001 an Inter-American Democratic Charter was adopted. It sets out a simple, clear declaration: 'The peoples of the Americas have a right to democracy and their governments have an obligation to promote and defend it.' The Charter compels the OAS to take action against any member state that disrupts its own democratic institutions.

The Secretary-General is elected by the General Assembly for five-year terms. The General Assembly approves the annual budget which is financed by quotas contributed by the member governments. The budget in 2003 amounted to US$83·17m.

Headquarters: 17th Street and Constitution Avenue, NW, Washington, D.C., 20006, USA.
Website: http://www.oas.org
Secretary-General: José Miguel Insulza (Chile).

Publications. Charter of the Organization of American States. 1948.—As Amended by the Protocol of Buenos Aires in 1967 and the Protocol of Cartagena de Indias in 1985; The OAS and the Evolution of the Inter-American System; Annual Report of the Secretary-General; Status of Inter-American Treaties and Conventions (annual).

Further Reading

Sheinin, D., *The Organization of American States* [Bibliography]. Oxford and Metuchen (NJ), 1995

Organization of Eastern Caribbean States (OECS)

Founded in 1981 when seven eastern Caribbean states signed the Treaty of Basseterre agreeing to co-operate with each other to promote unity and solidarity among the members.

Members. Antigua and Barbuda, Dominica, Grenada, Montserrat, St Kitts and Nevis, St Lucia, St Vincent and the Grenadines. The British Virgin Islands and Anguilla have associate membership.

Functions. As set out in the Treaty of Basseterre: to promote co-operation among the member states and to defend their sovereignty and independence; to assist member states in the realization of their obligations and responsibilities to the international community with due regard to the role of international law as a standard of conduct in their relationships; to assist member states in the realization of their obligations and responsibilities to the international community with due regard to the role of international issues; to establish and maintain, where possible, arrangements for joint overseas representation and common services; to pursue these through its respective institutions by discussion of questions of common concern and by agreement on common action.

OECS' work is carried out through the office of the Director General which encompasses: the Legal Unit, Research and Communication Information Services, Functional Co-operation Services, Overseas Diplomatic Mission, Social and Sustainable Development Division, Economic Affairs Division and Corporate Service Division. These oversee the work of a number of specialized institutions, work units and projects in four countries. There is an OECS secretariat in St Lucia, which is comprised of several operating units, responsible for the following functions: Education and Human Resource Development, Export Development Unit, Legal Unit, Environment and Sustainable Development Unit, Pharmaceutical Procurement Service, Social Development Unit and OECS Sports Desk.

Official language: English.
Headquarters: Morne Fortune, PO Box 179, Castries, St Lucia.
Website: http://www.oecs.org
e-mail: oecs@oecs.org
Director-General: Dr Len Ishmael (St Lucia).

Secretariat for Central American Economic Integration (SIECA)

SIECA (Secretaría de Integración Económica Centroamericana) was created by the General Treaty of Central American Economic Integration in Dec. 1960. The General Treaty incorporates the Agreement on the Regime for Central American Integration Industries. In Oct. 1993 the Protocol to the General Treaty on Central Economic Integration, known as the Guatemala Protocol, was signed.

Members. Costa Rica, El Salvador, Guatemala, Honduras, Nicaragua. *Observer:* Panama.

Official language: Spanish.
Headquarters: 4a Avenida 10–25, Zona 14, Ciudad de Guatemala, Guatemala.
Website: http://www.sieca.org.gt
Secretary-General: Haroldo Rodas Melgar (Guatemala).

South American Community of Nations (CSN/SACN)

In Dec. 2004 representatives of 12 South American countries signed the 'Cuzco Declaration' thereby founding a political and economic bloc modelled on the European Union. The aim is to establish a single currency, passport and parliament. The South American Community of Nations (SACN) will be created by the merger of the two existing major South American trade blocs: the Andean Community (Bolivia, Colombia, Ecuador, Peru and Venezuela) and the Southern Common Market or MERCOSUR (Argentina, Brazil, Paraguay and Uruguay), in addition to the market of Chile, and eventually those of Suriname and Guyana. The agreement paves the way for much-needed improvements in transport, energy and other infrastructure, thus facilitating intra-continental trade. The SACN aims to eliminate tariffs on non-sensitive products by 2014 and those on sensitive products by 2019. The bloc will create a single market of 361m. people with a combined GDP of US$973bn. However, insufficiently defined goals and ongoing disputes between members of the already-existing blocs may hamper development, as may future bilateral trade negotiations with the USA.

Southern Common Market (MERCOSUR)

Founded in March 1991 by the Treaty of Asunción between Argentina, Brazil, Paraguay and Uruguay, MERCOSUR committed the signatories to the progressive reduction of tariffs culminating in the formation of a common market on 1 Jan. 1995. This duly came into effect as a free trade zone affecting 90% of commodities. A common external tariff averaging 14% applies to 80% of trade with countries outside MERCOSUR. Details were agreed at foreign minister level by the Protocol of Ouro Preto signed on 17 Dec. 1994.

In 1996 Chile negotiated a free-trade agreement with MERCOSUR which came into effect on 1 Oct. Subsequently Bolivia, Colombia, Ecuador and Peru have all been granted associate member status.

Organization. The member states' foreign ministers form a Council responsible for leading the integration process, the chairmanship of which rotates every six months. The permanent executive body is the Common Market Group of member states, which takes decisions by consensus. There is a Trade Commission and Joint Parliamentary Commission, an arbitration tribunal whose decisions are binding on member countries, and a secretariat in Montevideo.

Further to the treaty signed by 12 South American countries in Dec. 2004, MERCOSUR will gradually be integrated into the new South American Community of Nations.

Headquarters: Rincón 575 P12, 11000 Montevideo, Uruguay.
Website: http://www.mercosur.org.uy (Spanish and Portuguese only)
Administrative Secretary: Reginaldo Braga Arcuri (Brazil).

Asian Development Bank

A multilateral development finance institution established in 1966 to promote economic and social progress in the Asian and Pacific region, the Bank's strategic objectives in the medium term are to foster economic growth, reduce poverty, improve the status of women, support human development (including population planning) and protect the environment.

The bank's capital stock is owned by 64 member countries, 46 regional and 18 non-regional. The bank makes loans and equity investments, and provides technical assistance grants for the preparation and execution of development projects and programmes; promotes investment of public and private capital for development purposes; and assists in co-ordinating development policies and plans in its developing member countries (DMCs).

The bank gives special attention to the needs of smaller or less developed countries, giving priority to regional, sub-regional and national projects which contribute to the economic growth of the region and promote regional co-operation. Loans from ordinary capital resources on non-concessional terms account for about 80% of cumulative lending. Loans from the bank's principal special fund, the Asian Development Fund, are made on highly concessional terms almost exclusively to the poorest borrowing countries.

Regional members. Afghanistan, Armenia, Australia, Azerbaijan, Bangladesh, Bhutan, Cambodia, China, Cook Islands, East Timor, Fiji Islands, Hong Kong, India, Indonesia, Japan, Kazakhstan, Kiribati, South Korea, Kyrgyzstan, Laos, Malaysia, Maldives, Marshall Islands, Micronesia, Mongolia, Myanmar, Nauru, Nepal, New Zealand, Pakistan, Palau, Papua New Guinea, Philippines, Samoa, Singapore, Solomon Islands, Sri Lanka, Taiwan, Tajikistan, Thailand, Tonga, Turkmenistan, Tuvalu, Uzbekistan, Vanuatu and Vietnam.

Non-regional members. Austria, Belgium, Canada, Denmark, Finland, France, Germany, Italy, Luxembourg, Netherlands, Norway, Portugal, Spain, Sweden, Switzerland, Turkey, UK, USA.

Organization. The bank's highest policy-making body is its Board of Governors, which meets annually. Its executive body is the 12-member Board of Directors (each with an alternate), eight from the regional members and four non-regional.

The ADB also has resident missions: in Bangladesh; Cambodia; China; India; Indonesia; Kazakhstan; Kyrgyzstan; Laos; Nepal; Pakistan; the Philippines; Sri Lanka; Uzbekistan; Vietnam; and a regional mission in Port Vila, Vanuatu. There are also three representative offices: in Tokyo, Frankfurt and Washington, D.C.

Official language: English.
Headquarters: 6 ADB Avenue, Mandaluyong, Metro Manila, Philippines.

Website: http://www.adb.org
President: Haruhiko Kuroda (Japan).

Asia-Pacific Economic Co-operation (APEC)

Origin and Aims. APEC was originally established in 1989 to take advantage of the interdependence among Asia-Pacific economies, by facilitating economic growth for all participants and enhancing a sense of community in the region. Begun as an informal dialogue group, APEC is the premier forum for facilitating economic growth, co-operation, trade and investment in the Asia-Pacific region. APEC has a membership of 21 economic jurisdictions, a population of over 2·5bn. and a combined GDP of US\$19trn. accounting for 47% of world trade.

APEC is working to achieve what are referred to as the 'Bogor Goals' of free and open trade and investment in the Asia-Pacific by 2010 for developed economies and 2020 for developing economies.

Members. Australia, Brunei, Canada, Chile, China, Hong Kong, Indonesia, Japan, South Korea, Malaysia, Mexico, New Zealand, Papua New Guinea, Peru, Philippines, Russia, Singapore, Taiwan, Thailand, USA and Vietnam.

Activities. APEC works in three broad areas to meet the Bogor Goals. These three broad work areas, known as APEC's 'Three Pillars', are: Trade and Investment Liberalization—reducing and eliminating tariff and non-tariff barriers to trade and investment, and opening markets; Business Facilitation—reducing the costs of business transactions, improving access to trade information and bringing into line policy and business strategies to facilitate growth, and free and open trade; Economic and Technical Co-operation—assisting member economies build the necessary capacities to take advantage of global trade and the new economy. The 15th APEC Ministerial Meeting, held in Bangkok, Thailand in Oct. 2003, called for increased measures to stop the spread of terrorism and weapons of mass destruction.

Official language: English.
Headquarters: 35 Heng Mui Keng Terrace, Singapore 119616.
Website: http://www.apecsec.org.sg
Executive Director: Tran Trong Toan (Vietnam).

Association of South East Asian Nations (ASEAN)

History and Membership. ASEAN is a regional intergovernmental organization formed by the governments of Indonesia, Malaysia, the Philippines, Singapore and Thailand through the Bangkok Declaration which was signed by their foreign ministers on 8 Aug. 1967. Brunei joined in 1984, Vietnam in 1995, Laos and Myanmar in 1997 and Cambodia in 1999. Papua New Guinea also has observer status.

Objectives. The main objectives are to accelerate economic growth, social progress and cultural development, to promote active collaboration and mutual assistance in matters of common interest, to ensure the political and economic stability of the South East Asian region, and to maintain close co-operation with existing international and regional organizations with similar aims.

Activities. Principal projects concern economic co-operation and development, with the intensification of intra-ASEAN trade, and trade between the region and the rest of the world; joint research and technological programmes; co-operation in transportation and communications; promotion of tourism, South East Asian studies, cultural, scientific, educational and administrative exchanges. The decision to set up an *ASEAN Free Trade Area (AFTA)* was taken at the Fourth Summit meeting, in Singapore in 1992, with the aim of creating a common market in 15 years, subsequently brought forward to 2002. AFTA applies to its first six signatories, namely Brunei, Indonesia, Malaysia, Philippines, Singapore and Thailand. In 2003 ASEAN leaders signed a declaration to establish a free trade area by 2020.

In Dec. 1995 heads of government meeting in Bangkok established a South-East Asia Nuclear-Free Zone, which was extended to cover offshore economic exclusion zones. Individual signatories were to decide whether to allow port visits or transportation of nuclear weapons by foreign powers through territorial waters. The *ASEAN Regional Forum (ARF)* was proposed at a meeting of foreign ministers in July 1993 to discuss security issues in the region. Its first formal meeting took place in July 1994 attended by all seven members and its dialogue partners (Australia, Canada, the EU, Japan, South Korea, New Zealand and the USA) and observers (China, Laos, Papua New Guinea, Russia and Vietnam).

ASEAN is committed to resolving the dispute over sovereignty of the Spratly Islands, a group of more than 100 small islands and reefs in the South China Sea. Some or all of the largely uninhabited islands have been claimed by Brunei, China, Malaysia, the Philippines, Taiwan and Vietnam. The disputed areas have oil and gas resources.

Organization. The highest authority is the meeting of Heads of Government, which takes place annually. The highest policy-making body is the annual Meeting of Foreign Ministers, commonly known as AMM, the ASEAN Ministerial Meeting, which convenes in each of the member countries on a rotational basis in alphabetical order. The AEM (ASEAN Economic Meeting) meets each year to direct ASEAN economic co-operation. The AEM and AMM report jointly to the heads of government at summit meetings. Each capital has its own national secretariat. The central secretariat in Jakarta is headed by the Secretary-General, a post that revolves among the member states in alphabetical order every five years.

Official language: English.
Headquarters: POB 2072, Jakarta 12110, Indonesia.
Website: http://www.aseansec.org
Secretary-General: Ong Keng Yong (Singapore).

ASEAN-Mekong Basin Development Co-operation (Mekong Group)

The ministers and representatives of Brunei, Cambodia, China, Indonesia, Laos, Malaysia, Myanmar, Philippines, Singapore, Thailand and Vietnam met in Kuala Lumpur on 17 June 1996 and agreed the following basic objectives for the Group: to co-operate in the economic and social development of the Mekong Basin area and strengthen the link between it and ASEAN member countries, through a process of dialogue and common project identification.

Priorities include: development of infrastructure capacities in the fields of transport, telecommunications, irrigation and energy; development of trade and investment-generating activities; development of the agricultural sector to enhance production for domestic consumption and export; sustainable development of forestry resources and development of mineral resources; development of the industrial sector, especially small to medium enterprises; development of tourism; human resource development and support for training; co-operation in the fields of science and technology.

Further Reading

Broinowski, A., *Understanding ASEAN*. London, 1982.—(ed.) *ASEAN into the 1990s*. London, 1990

Van Hoa, Tran, (ed.) *Economic Developments and Prospects in the ASEAN*. London, 1997

Wawn, B., *The Economics of the ASEAN Countries*. London, 1982

Colombo Plan

History. Founded in 1950 to promote the development of newly independent Asian member countries, the Colombo Plan has grown from a group of seven Commonwealth nations into an organization of 24 countries. Originally the Plan was conceived for a period of six years. This was renewed from time to time until the Consultative Committee gave the Plan an indefinite life span in 1980.

Members. (Permanent Member Countries) Afghanistan, Australia, Bangladesh, Bhutan, Fiji Islands, India, Indonesia, Islamic Republic of Iran, Japan, South Korea, Lao People's Democratic Republic, Malaysia, Maldives, Myanmar, Nepal, New Zealand, Pakistan, Papua New Guinea, Philippines, Singapore, Sri Lanka, Thailand, USA and Vietnam. *(Provisional member country)* Mongolia.

Aims. The aims of the Colombo Plan are: (1) to provide a forum for discussion, at local level, of development needs; (2) to facilitate development assistance by encouraging members to participate as donors and recipients of technical co-operation; and (3) to execute programmes to advance development within member countries. The Plan currently has the following programmes: Programme for Public Administration (PPA); South-South Technical Co-operation Data Bank Programme (SSTC/DB); Drug Advisory Programme (DAP); Programme for Private Sector Development (PPSD); Colombo Plan Staff College for Technician Education (CPSC).

Structure. The Consultative Committee is the principal policy-making body of the Colombo Plan. Consisting of all member countries, it meets every two years to review the economic and social progress of members, exchange views on technical co-operation programmes and generally review the activities of the Plan. The Colombo Plan Council represents each member government and meets several times a year to identify development issues, recommend measures to be taken and ensure implementation.

Headquarters: 12 Melbourne Avenue, PO Box 596, Colombo 4, Sri Lanka.
Website: http://www.colombo-plan.org
e-mail: cplan@slt.lk
Secretary-General: Kittipan Kanjanapipatkul (Thailand).

Publications. Consultative Committee Meeting—Proceedings and Conclusions (biennial); *Report of the Colombo Plan Council* (annual); *The Colombo Plan Brochure* (annual); *The Colombo Plan Focus* (quarterly newsletter); *South-South Technical Co-operation in Selected Member Countries.*

Economic Co-operation Organization (ECO)

The Economic Co-operation Organization (ECO) is an inter-governmental regional organization established in 1985 by Iran, Pakistan and Turkey. ECO is the successor of the Regional Co-operation for Development (RCD). ECO was later expanded in 1992 to include seven new members: Afghanistan, Azerbaijan, Kazakhstan, Kyrgyzstan, Tajikistan, Turkmenistan and Uzbekistan. The objectives of the organization, stipulated in its Charter, the Treaty of Izmir, include the promotion of conditions for sustained economic growth in the region. While transport and communications, trade and investment, and energy are the high priority areas in ECO's scheme of work, other fields of co-operation such as industry, agriculture, health, science and education, drug control and human development are also on the agenda.

While summit meetings lend reaffirmation of the high level commitment of ECO member states to the goals and objectives of the organization, the Council of Ministers (COM) remains the highest policy and decision-making body of the organization, which meets at least once a year and is chaired by rotation among the member states.

ECO Summits were instituted with the First Summit held in Tehran in 1992; the Second Summit was held in İstanbul in 1993, the Third in Islamabad in 1995, the Fourth in Ashgabat in 1996, the Fifth in Almaty in May 1999, the Sixth in Tehran in 2000, the Seventh in İstanbul in 2002, the Eighth in Dushanbe in 2004 and the Ninth in Baku in 2006.

The long-term perspectives and priorities of ECO are defined in the form of two Action Plans: the Quetta Plan of Action and the İstanbul Declaration and Economic Co-operation Strategy.

ECO enjoys observer status with the United Nations, World Trade Organization and the Organization of Islamic Conference. A number of resolutions have been adopted in the UN General Assembly in the context of expansion of co-operation with ECO in the 1990s, most recently in Dec. 2001.

Headquarters: 1 Goulbou Alley, Kamranieh, PO Box 14155-6176, Tehran, Islamic Republic of Iran.
Website: http://www.ecosecretariat.org
e-mail: registry@ecosecretariat.org
Secretary-General: Askhat Orazbay (Kazakhstan).

Pacific Islands Forum (PIF)

In Oct. 2000 the South Pacific Forum changed its name to the Pacific Islands Forum. As the South Pacific Forum it held its first meeting of Heads of Government in New Zealand in 1971. The Agreement Establishing the Forum Secretariat defines the membership of the Forum and the Secretariat. Decisions are reached by consensus. The administrative arm of the Forum, known officially as the Pacific Islands Forum Secretariat, is based in Suva, Fiji. In Oct. 1994 the Forum was granted observer status to the UN.

Members. (2006) Australia, Cook Islands, Fiji Islands, Kiribati, Marshall Islands, Micronesia, Nauru, New Zealand, Niue, Palau, Papua New Guinea, Samoa, Solomon Islands, Tonga, Tuvalu and Vanuatu.

In 1999 the French territory of New Caledonia was admitted to the Forum as an observer. In 2002 East Timor was admitted to the Forum as a Special Observer.

Functions. The Secretariat's mission is to provide policy options to the Pacific Islands Forum, and to promote Forum decisions and regional and international co-operation. The organization seeks to promote political stability and regional security; enhance the management of economies and the development process; improve trade and investment performance; and efficiently manage the resources of the Secretariat.

Activities. The Secretariat has four core divisions: Trade and Investment; Political and International Affairs; Development and

Economic Policy; Corporate Services. The Secretariat provides policy advice to members on a wide range of social, economic and political issues. Since 1989 the Forum has held Post Forum Dialogues with key dialogue partners at ministerial level. There are currently twelve partners: Canada, China, EU, France, India, Indonesia, Japan, South Korea, Malaysia, the Philippines, the United Kingdom and the United States.

Organization. The South Pacific Bureau for Economic Co-operation (SPEC) began as a trade bureau and was established in 1972, before being re-organized as the South Pacific Forum Secretariat in 1988. It changed its name to the Pacific Islands Forum Secretariat in 2000. The Secretariat is headed by a Secretary-General and Deputy Secretary-General who form the Executive. The governing body is the Forum Officials Committee, which acts as an intermediary between the Secretariat and the Forum. The Secretariat operates four Trade Offices in Auckland, Beijing, Sydney and Tokyo.

The Secretary-General is the permanent Chair of the Council of Regional Organisations in the Pacific (CROP), which brings together ten main regional organizations in the Pacific region: Fiji School of Medicine (FSM); Forum Fisheries Agency (FFA); Pacific Islands Development Programme (PIDP); Pacific Islands Forum Secretariat (PIFS); Secretariat for the Pacific Community (SPC); South Pacific Applied Geoscience Commission (SOPAC); South Pacific Board for Educational Assessment (SPBEA); South Pacific Regional Environment Programme (SPREP); South Pacific Tourism Organisation (SPTO); and the University of the South Pacific (USP).

Official language: English.
Headquarters: Ratu Sukuna Road, Suva, Fiji Islands.
Website: http://www.forumsec.org.fj
Secretary-General: Gregory Urwin (Australia).

Secretariat of the Pacific Community (SPC)

Until Feb. 1998 known as the South Pacific Commission, this is a regional intergovernmental organization founded in 1947 under an Agreement commonly referred to as the Canberra Agreement. It is funded by assessed contributions from its 26 members and by voluntary contributions from member and non-member countries, international organizations and other sources.

Members. American Samoa, Australia, Cook Islands, Fiji Islands, France, French Polynesia, Guam, Kiribati, Marshall Islands, Federated States of Micronesia, Nauru, New Caledonia, New Zealand, Niue, Northern Mariana Islands, Palau, Papua New Guinea, Pitcairn Islands, Samoa, Solomon Islands, Tokelau, Tonga, Tuvalu, USA, Vanuatu, and Wallis and Futuna.

Functions. The SPC has three main areas of work: land resources, marine resources and social resources. It conducts research and provides technical assistance and training in these areas to member Pacific Island countries and territories of the Pacific.

Organization. The Conference of the Pacific Community is the governing body of the Community. Its key focus is to appoint the Director-General, to consider major national or regional policy issues and to note changes to the Financial and Staff Regulations approved by the CRGA, the Committee of Representatives of Governments and Administrations. It meets every two years. The CRGA meets once a year and is the principal decision-making organ of the Community. There is also a regional office in Fiji Islands.

Headquarters: BP D5, 98848 Nouméa Cedex, New Caledonia.
Website: http://www.spc.int
e-mail: spc@spc.int
Director-General: Lourdes Pangelinan (Guam).

South Asian Association for Regional Co-operation (SAARC)

SAARC was established to accelerate the process of economic and social development in member states through joint action in agreed areas of co-operation. The foreign ministers of the seven member countries met for the first time in New Delhi in Aug. 1983 and adopted the Declaration on South Asian Regional Co-operation whereby an Integrated Programme of Action (IPA) was launched. The charter establishing SAARC was adopted at the first summit meeting in Dhaka in Dec. 1985.

Members. Afghanistan, Bangladesh, Bhutan, India, Maldives, Nepal, Pakistan, Sri Lanka. *Observers.* China, Japan.

Objectives. To promote the welfare of the peoples of South Asia; to accelerate economic growth, social progress and cultural development; to promote and strengthen collective self-reliance among members; to promote active collaboration and mutual assistance in the economic, social, cultural, technical and scientific fields; to strengthen co-operation with other developing countries and among themselves. Co-operation within the framework is based on respect for the principles of sovereign equality, territorial integrity, political independence, non-interference in the internal affairs of other states and mutual benefit. Agreed areas of co-operation under the *Integrated Programme of Action (IPA)* include agriculture and rural development; human resource development; environment, meteorology and forestry; science and technology; transport and communications; energy; and social development.

A SAARC Preferential Trading Arrangement (SAPTA) designed to reduce tariffs on trade between SAARC member states was signed in April 1993 and entered into force in Dec. 1995. In 1998 at the Tenth Summit in Colombo, the importance of achieving a South Asian Free Trade Area (SAFTA) as mandated by the Malé Summit in 1997 was reiterated and it was decided to set up a Committee of Experts to work on drafting a comprehensive treaty regime for creating a free trade area. The Colombo Summit agreed that the text of this regulatory framework would be finalized by 2001.

Organization. The highest authority of the Association rests with the heads of state or government, who meet annually at Summit level. The Council of Foreign Ministers, which meets twice a year, is responsible for formulating policy, reviewing progress and deciding on new areas of co-operation and the mechanisms deemed necessary for that. The Council is supported by a Standing Committee of Foreign Secretaries, by the Programming Committee and by 11 Technical Committees which are responsible for individual areas of SAARC's activities. There is a secretariat in Kathmandu, headed by a Secretary-General, who is assisted in his work by seven Directors, appointed by the Secretary-General upon nomination by member states for a period of three years which may in special circumstances be extended.

Official language: English.
Headquarters: PO Box 4222, Kathmandu, Nepal.
Website: http://www.saarc-sec.org
Secretary-General: Lyonpo Chenkyab Dorji (Bhutan).

Arab Fund for Economic and Social Development (AFESD)

Established in 1968, the Fund commenced operations in 1974.

Functions. AFESD is an Arab regional financial institution that assists the economic and social development of Arab countries through: financing development projects, with preference given to overall Arab development and to joint Arab projects; encouraging the investment of private and public funds in Arab projects; and providing technical assistance services for Arab economic and social development.

Members. Algeria, Bahrain, Djibouti, Egypt, Iraq*, Jordan, Kuwait, Lebanon, Libya, Mauritania, Morocco, Oman, Palestine, Qatar, Saudi Arabia, Somalia*, Sudan, Syria, Tunisia, United Arab Emirates, Republic of Yemen. *Membership suspended since 1993.

Headquarters: PO Box 21923, Safat 13080, Kuwait.
Website: http://www.arabfund.org
Director General and Chairman of the Board of Directors: Abdulatif Y. Al Hamad.

Publications. Annual Report; Joint Arab Economic Report.

Arab Maghreb Union

The Arab Maghreb Union was founded in 1989 to promote political co-ordination, co-operation and 'complementarity' across various fields, with integration wherever and whenever possible.

Members. Algeria, Libya, Mauritania, Morocco, Tunisia.

By late 1996 joint policies and projects under way or under consideration included: the establishment of the Maghreb Investment and Foreign Trade Bank to fund joint agricultural and industrial projects; free movement of citizens within the region; joint transport undertakings, including railway improvements and a Maghreb highway; creation of a customs union; and establishment of a common market. Since then activities have been put on ice, largely because of the unsolved issue of Western Sahara.

A Declaration committing members to the establishment of a free trade zone was adopted at the AMU's last summit in Tunis (April 1994). In Nov. 1992 members adopted a charter on protection of the environment.

Official language: Arabic.
Headquarters: 14 Rue Zalagh, Agdal, Rabat, Morocco.
Website: http://www.maghrebarabe.org
Secretary-General: Habib Ben Yahia (Tunisia).

Arab Monetary Fund (AMF)

Origin. The Agreement establishing the Arab Monetary Fund was approved by the Economic Council of the League of Arab States in April 1976 and the first meeting of the Board of Governors was held on 19 April 1977.

Aims. To assist member countries in eliminating payments and trade restrictions, in achieving exchange rate stability, in developing capital markets and in correcting payments imbalances through the extension of short- and medium-term loans; the co-ordination of monetary policies of member countries; and the liberalization and promotion of trade and payments, as well as the encouragement of capital flows among member countries.

Members. Algeria, Bahrain, Comoros, Djibouti, Egypt, Iraq, Jordan, Kuwait, Lebanon, Libya, Mauritania, Morocco, Oman, Palestine, Qatar, Saudi Arabia, Somalia, Sudan, Syria, Tunisia, United Arab Emirates, Republic of Yemen.

Headquarters: PO Box 2818, Abu Dhabi, United Arab Emirates.
Website: http://www.amf.org.ae
Director General and Chairman of the Board of Directors: Jassim A. Al-Mannai (Bahrain).

Publications (in English and Arabic): *Annual Report; The Articles of Agreement of the Arab Monetary Fund; Money and Credit in Arab Countries* (annual); *National Accounts of Arab Countries* (annual); *Foreign Trade of Arab Countries* (annual); *Cross Exchange Rates of Arab Currencies* (annual); *Arab Countries: Economic Indicators* (annual); *Balance of Payments and External Public Debt of Arab Countries* (annual); *AMF Publications Catalogue* (annual); *Arab Monetary Fund: Structure and Activities (1977–83).* (In Arabic only): *The Joint Arabic Economic Report* (annual); *AMF Economic Bulletin; Developments in Arab Capital Markets* (quarterly).

Arab Organization for Agricultural Development (AOAD)

The AOAD was established in 1970 and commenced operations in 1972. Its aims are to develop natural and human resources in the agricultural sector and improve the means and methods of exploiting these resources on scientific bases; to increase agricultural productive efficiency and achieve agricultural integration between the Arab States and countries; to increase agricultural production with a view to achieving a higher degree of self-sufficiency; to facilitate the exchange of agricultural products between the Arab States and countries; to enhance the establishment of agricultural ventures and industries; and to increase the standards of living of the labour force engaged in the agricultural sector.

Organization. The structure comprises a General Assembly consisting of ministers of agriculture of the member states, an Executive Council, a Secretariat General, seven technical departments—Food Security, Human Resources Development, Water Resources, Studies and Research, Projects Execution, Technical Scientific Co-operation, and Financial Administrative Department—and two centres—the Arab Center for Agricultural Information and Documentation, and the Arab Bureau for Consultation and Implementation of Agricultural Projects.

Members. Algeria, Bahrain, Djibouti, Egypt, Iraq, Jordan, Kuwait, Lebanon, Libya, Mauritania, Morocco, Oman, Palestine, Qatar, Saudi Arabia, Somalia, Sudan, Syria, Tunisia, United Arab Emirates, Republic of Yemen.

Official languages: Arabic (English and French used in translated documents and correspondence).
Headquarters: Street No. 7, Al-Amarat, Khartoum, Sudan.
Website: http://www.aoad.org
Director General: Dr Salem Al-Lozi.

Gulf Co-operation Council (GCC)

Origin. Also referred to as the Co-operation Council for the Arab States of the Gulf (CCASG), the Council was established on 25

May 1981 on signature of the Charter by Bahrain, Kuwait, Oman, Qatar, Saudi Arabia and the United Arab Emirates.

Aims. To assure security and stability of the region through economic and political co-operation; promote, expand and enhance economic ties on solid foundations, in the best interests of the people; co-ordinate and unify economic, financial and monetary policies, as well as commercial and industrial legislation and customs regulations; achieve self-sufficiency in basic foodstuffs.

Organization. The Supreme Council is formed by the heads of member states and is the highest authority. Its presidency rotates, based on the alphabetical order of the names of the member states. It holds one regular session every year, in addition to a mid-year consultation session. The Co-operation Council has a commission, called 'Commission for the Settlement of Disputes', which is attached to the Supreme Council. Also attached to the Supreme Council is the Consultative Commission. The Ministerial Council is formed of the Foreign Ministers of the member states or other delegated ministers and meets quarterly. The Secretariat-General is composed of Secretary-General, Assistant Secretaries-General and a number of staff as required. The Secretariat consists of the following sectors: Political Affairs, Military Affairs, Legal Affairs, Human and Environment Affairs, Information Centre, Media Department, Gulf Standardization Organization (GSO), GCC Patent Office, Secretary-General's Office, GCC Delegation in Brussels, Technical Telecommunications Bureau in Bahrain. In Jan. 2003 it launched a customs union, introducing a 5% duty on foreign imports across the trade bloc.

Finance. The annual budget of the GCC Secretariat is shared equally by the six member states.

Headquarters: PO Box 7153, Riyadh-11462, Saudi Arabia.
Website: http://www.GCC-SG.org
Secretary-General: Abdul Rahman bin Hamad Al-Attiyah.

Publications. Attaawun (quarterly, in Arabic); *GCC Economic Bulletin* (annual); *Statistical Bulletin* (annual); *Legal Bulletin* (quarterly, in Arabic).

Further Reading

Twinam, J. W., *The Gulf, Co-operation and the Council: an American Perspective.* Washington, 1992

League of Arab States

Origin. The League of Arab States is a voluntary association of sovereign Arab states, established by a Pact signed in Cairo on 22 March 1945 by the representatives of Egypt, Iraq, Saudi Arabia, Syria, Lebanon, Jordan and Yemen. It seeks to promote closer ties among member states and to co-ordinate their economic, cultural and security policies with a view to developing collective co-operation, protecting national security and maintaining the independence and sovereignty of member states, in order to enhance the potential for joint Arab action across all fields.

Members. Algeria, Bahrain, Comoros, Djibouti, Egypt, Iraq, Jordan, Kuwait, Lebanon, Mauritania, Morocco, Oman, Palestine, Qatar, Saudi Arabia, Somalia, Sudan, Syria, Tunisia, United Arab Emirates and Republic of Yemen. Libya left the League of Arab States in Oct. 2002, citing its 'inefficiency' in dealing with the stand-off between Iraq and the USA and the Israeli–Palestinian conflict.

Joint Action. In the political field, the League is entrusted with defending the supreme interests and national causes of the Arab world through the implementation of joint action plans at regional and international levels, and with examining any disputes that may arise between member states with a view to settling them by peaceful means. The Joint Defence and Economic Co-operation Treaty signed in 1950 provided for the establishment of a Joint Defence Council as well as an Economic Council (renamed the Economic and Social Council in 1977). Economic, social and cultural activities all constitute vital elements of the joint action initiative.

Arab Common Market. An Arab Common Market came into operation on 1 Jan. 1965. The agreement, reached on 13 Aug. 1964, provided for the abolition of customs duties on agricultural products and natural resources within five years, by reducing tariffs at an annual rate of 20%. Customs duties on industrial products were to be reduced by 10% annually. However, it never became reality although it has remained the ambition of many people throughout the Arab world for many years since.

Organization. The machinery of the League consists of a Council, 11 specialized ministerial committees entrusted with drawing up common policies for the regulation and advancement of co-operation in their fields (information, internal affairs, justice, housing, transport, social affairs, youth and sports, health, environment, telecommunications and electricity), and a permanent secretariat.

The League is considered to be a regional organization within the framework of the United Nations at which its Secretary-General is an observer. It has permanent delegations in New York and Geneva for the UN, in Addis Ababa for the African Union (AU), as well as offices in Athens, Beijing, Berlin, Brussels, London, Madrid, Moscow, New Delhi, Paris, Rome, Vienna and Washington, D.C.

Headquarters: Al Tahrir Square, Cairo, Egypt.
Website: http://www.arableagueonline.org
Secretary-General: Amre Moussa (Egypt).

Further Reading

Clements, F. A., *Arab Regional Organizations* [Bibliography]. Oxford and New Brunswick (NJ), 1992
Gomaa, A. M., *The Foundation of the League of Arab States.* London, 1977

Organization of Arab Petroleum Exporting Countries (OAPEC)

Established in 1968 to promote co-operation and close ties between member states in economic activities related to the oil industry; to determine ways of safeguarding their legitimate interests, both individual and collective, in the oil industry; to unite their efforts so as to ensure the flow of oil to consumer markets on equitable and reasonable terms; and to create a favourable climate for the investment of capital and expertise in their petroleum industries.

Members. Algeria, Bahrain, Egypt, Iraq, Kuwait, Libya, Qatar, Saudi Arabia, Syria, Tunisia*, United Arab Emirates. *Tunisia's membership was made inactive in 1986.

Headquarters: PO Box 20501, Safat 13066, Kuwait.
Website: http://www.oapecorg.org
Secretary-General: Abdulaziz A. Al-Turki.

Publications. Secretary General's Annual Report (Arabic and English editions); *Oil and Arab Co-operation* (quarterly; Arabic with English abstracts and bibliography); *OAPEC Monthly Bulletin* (Arabic and

English editions); *Energy Resources Monitor* (Arabic); *OAPEC Annual Statistical Report* (Arabic/English).

Organization of the Petroleum Exporting Countries (OPEC)

Origin and Aims. Founded in Baghdad in 1960 by Iran, Iraq, Kuwait, Saudi Arabia and Venezuela. The principal aims are: to unify the petroleum policies of member countries and determine the best means for safeguarding their interests, individually and collectively; to devise ways and means of ensuring the stabilization of prices in international oil markets with a view to eliminating harmful and unnecessary fluctuations; and to secure a steady income for the producing countries, an efficient, economic and regular supply of petroleum to consuming nations, and a fair return on their capital to those investing in the petroleum industry. It is estimated that OPEC members possess 75% of the world's known reserves of crude petroleum, of which about two-thirds are in the Middle East.

Members. (2005) Algeria, Indonesia, Iran, Iraq, Kuwait, Libya, Nigeria, Qatar, Saudi Arabia, United Arab Emirates and Venezuela. Membership applications may be made by any other country having substantial net exports of crude petroleum, with fundamentally similar interests to those of member countries. Gabon became an associated member in 1973 and a full member in 1975, but in 1996 withdrew owing to difficulty in meeting its percentage contribution. Ecuador joined the Organization in 1973 but left in 1992.

Organization. The main organs are the Conference, the Board of Governors and the Secretariat. The Conference, which is the supreme authority meeting at least twice a year, consists of delegations from each member country, normally headed by the respective minister of oil, mines or energy. All decisions, other than those concerning procedural matters, must be adopted unanimously.

Headquarters: Obere Donaustrasse 93, A-1020 Vienna, Austria.
Website: http://www.opec.org
e-mail: prid@opec.org
Secretary-General (acting): Mohammed Barkindo (Nigeria).

Publications. Annual Statistical Bulletin; Annual Report; OPEC Bulletin (monthly); *OPEC Review* (quarterly); *OPEC General Information; Monthly Oil Market Report;* OPEC Statute.

Further Reading

Al-Chalabi, F., *OPEC at the Crossroads.* Oxford, 1989
Skeet, I., *OPEC: 25 Years of Prices and Policies.* CUP, 1988

OPEC Fund for International Development

The OPEC Fund for International Development was established in 1976 to provide financial aid on advantageous terms to developing countries (other than OPEC members) and international development agencies whose beneficiaries are developing countries. In 1980 the Fund was transformed into a permanent autonomous international agency and renamed the OPEC Fund for International Development. It is administered by a Ministerial Council and a Governing Board. Each member country is represented on the Council by its finance minister.

The initial endowment of the fund amounted to US$800m. At the start of 2004 pledged contributions totalled US$3,435m., and the Fund had extended 1,024 loans totalling US$5,845·7m. including US$4,582·6m. for project financing, US$724·2m.

for balance-of-payments support, US$314·8m. for programme funding and US$174·0m. for debt relief within the context of the Highly Indebted Poor Countries Initiative. In addition, and through its private sector window, the Fund had approved financing worth a total of US$335·4m. in 67 operations in support of private sector entities in Africa, Asia, Latin America, the Caribbean and Europe. Through its grant programme the Fund had also committed a total of US$321·7m. in support of a wide range of initiatives, ranging from technical assistance, research and emergency aid to dedicated operations to combat HIV/AIDS and relief hardship in Palestine.

Headquarters: POB 995, A-1011 Vienna, Austria.
Website: http://www.opecfund.org
e-mail: info@opecfund.org
Director-General: Suleiman Jasir al-Herbish (Saudi Arabia).

Antarctic Treaty

Antarctica is an island continent some 15·5m. sq. km in area which lies almost entirely within the Antarctic Circle. Its surface is composed of an ice sheet over rock, and it is uninhabited except for research and other workers in the course of duty. It is in general ownerless: for countries with territorial claims, *see* ARGENTINA; AUSTRALIA: Australian Antarctic Territory; CHILE; FRANCE: Southern and Antarctic Territories; NEW ZEALAND: Ross Dependency; NORWAY: Queen Maud Land; UNITED KINGDOM: British Antarctic Territory.

12 countries which had maintained research stations in Antarctica during International Geophysical Year, 1957–58 (Argentina, Australia, Belgium, Chile, France, Japan, New Zealand, Norway, South Africa, the USSR, the UK and the USA) signed the Antarctic Treaty (Washington Treaty) on 1 Dec. 1959. Austria, Brazil, Bulgaria, Canada, China, Colombia, Cuba, Czech Republic, Denmark, Ecuador, Estonia, Finland, Germany, Greece, Guatemala, Hungary, India, Italy, South Korea, North Korea, the Netherlands, Papua New Guinea, Peru, Poland, Romania, Slovakia, Spain, Sweden, Switzerland, Turkey, Ukraine, Uruguay and Venezuela subsequently acceded to the Treaty. The Treaty reserves the Antarctic area south of 60° S. lat. for peaceful purposes, provides for international co-operation in scientific investigation and research, and preserves, for the duration of the Treaty, the *status quo* with regard to territorial sovereignty, rights and claims. The Treaty entered into force on 23 June 1961. The 45 nations party to the Treaty (27 full voting signatories and 18 adherents) meet biennially.

An agreement reached in Madrid in April 1991 and signed by all 39 parties in Oct. imposes a ban on mineral exploitation in Antarctica for 50 years, at the end of which any one of the 27 voting parties may request a review conference. After this the ban may be lifted by agreement of three quarters of the nations then voting, which must include the present 27.

Headquarters: Av. Leandro Alem 884–4° Piso, C1001AAQ, Buenos Aires, Argentina.
Website: http://www.nsf.gov/od/opp/antarct/anttrty.jsp
e-mail: secret@ats.org.ar
Executive Secretary: Johannes Huber (Netherlands).

Further Reading

Elliott, L. M., *International Environmental Politics: Protecting the Antarctic.* London, 1994
Jørgensen-Dahl, A. and Østreng, W., *The Antarctic Treaty System in World Politics.* London, 1991
Meadows, J., *et al., The Antarctic* [Bibliography]. Oxford and New Brunswick (NJ), 1994

Kyoto Protocol

The protocol is an international environmental agreement signed by 84 countries under the UN Framework Convention on Climate Change. The agreement, adopted on 11 Dec. 1997, is based on principles set out in a framework convention signed at the Rio Summit in 1992, but did not become a legally binding treaty until 16 Feb. 2005.

Under the Kyoto Protocol governments must gather and share information on greenhouse gas emissions, launch national strategies for reducing greenhouse emissions and co-operate in preparing to adapt to the impacts of climate change.

The developed countries have committed themselves to reducing their collective emissions of six greenhouse gases to at least 5% below 1990 levels. These targets are scheduled to be met by the period 2008–12 with final reductions to be calculated as an average over this five-year period.

Actual emission reductions are expected to exceed substantially the minimum 5%. In particular, the richest industrialized countries will need to reduce their collective output by about 10%. This especially applies to the three most important gases—carbon dioxide, methane and nitrous oxide. The USA, the largest producer of greenhouse gas, has not ratified the protocol.

Headquarters: United Nations Framework Convention on Climate Change, Haus Carstanjen, Martin-Luther-King-Strasse 8, D-53175 Bonn, Germany.
Website: http://unfccc.int
e-mail: secretariat@unfccc.int
Executive Secretary: Vacant.

PART II

COUNTRIES OF THE WORLD
A—Z

AFGHANISTAN

© Research Machines plc 2005

Islamic Republic of Afghanistan

Capital: Kabul
Population projection, 2010: 35·64m.
GDP per capita: not available

KEY HISTORICAL EVENTS

For much of the 19th century Afghanistan was part of the power struggle between Britain, the dominant power in India, and the Russian empire. While the country achieved independence after the First World War, tribal wars and banditry restricted economic and social development. Stability came in the period of Záhir Shah who ruled for 40 years. In 1964 he was able to overcome opposition and established parliamentary democracy. In 1973 there was a military coup led by his cousin and brother-in-law, and a former prime minister, Mohammed Daoud, who abolished the 1964 constitution and declared a republic. Záhir Shah abdicated on 24 Aug. 1973.

In April 1978 President Daoud was killed in a further coup which installed a pro-Soviet government. The new president, Noor Mohammad Taraki, was overthrown in Sept. 1979, whereupon the Soviet Union invaded Afghanistan in Dec., deposed his successor and placed Babrak Karmal at the head of government.

In Dec. 1986 Sayid Mohammed Najibullah became president amid continuing civil war between government and rebel Muslim forces. The USSR provided military support and development aid to the pro-Soviet administration while the USA extended limited support to the rebels. In the mid-1980s the UN began negotiations on the withdrawal of Soviet troops and the establishment of a government of national unity. Soviet troops began withdrawing from Afghanistan in early 1988.

After talks in Nov. 1991 with Afghan opposition movements ('mujahideen'), the Soviet government transferred its support from the Najibullah regime to an 'Islamic Interim Government'. As mujahideen insurgents closed in on Kabul, President Najibullah stepped down in April 1992 but fighting continued.

In 1994 a newly formed militant Islamic movement, 'Taliban' (i.e. 'students of religion'), took Kabul, apparently with Pakistani support. The Taliban, most of whose leaders were Pashtuns, were in turn defeated by the troops of President Rabbani but in Sept. 1996 Taliban forces recaptured Kabul and set up an interim government under Mohamed Rabbani. Afghanistan was declared a complete Islamic state under Sharia law.

Government forces which had retreated to the north of Kabul counter-attacked but a new Taliban offensive, launched on 27 Dec. 1996, gave Taliban control of most of the country. The opposition Northern Alliance controlled the northeast of the country. Under the Taliban, irregular forces were disarmed and roads cleared of bandits. Rebuilding of towns and villages started. But the strict application of Islamic law ran counter to western sensitivities with the result that only three countries—Pakistan, Saudi Arabia and the United Arab Emirates—recognized the Taliban as the legal government.

In March 2001 Afghanistan was widely condemned for the destruction of ancient monuments that the Taliban deemed un-Islamic, including the world's tallest Buddhas. In May 2001 the ruling Taliban refused to extradite Osama bin Laden, a Saudi militant, to the USA to face charges connected to the bombing of American embassies in Kenya and Tanzania in 1998. In Sept. 2001 Ahmed Shah Masood, leader of the Northern Alliance, was killed by two suicide bombers.

Following the attacks on the USA on 11 Sept. 2001 Saudi Arabia and the United Arab Emirates broke off diplomatic relations with Afghanistan. The USA put pressure on the ruling Taliban to hand over Osama bin Laden, but without success. Consequently the USA launched air strikes on Afghanistan on 7 Oct. On 13 Nov. the Northern Alliance took the capital Kabul, effectively bringing an end to Taliban rule, and with the surrender of Kandahar the Taliban lost control of their last stronghold. On 27 Nov. representatives of rival factions, but excluding the Taliban, joined United Nations-sponsored talks in Germany on the future of their country. Hamid Karzai, a Pashtun tribal leader, was chosen to head an interim power-sharing council, which took office in Kabul from 22 Dec. He was subsequently appointed president of the transitional government in June 2002. In Sept. 2002 he survived an assassination attempt.

'Whether or not Afghanistan can survive comes down, in part, to one simple question: are the forces of national integration there greater than the forces of local disintegration? Optimists say yes. They think Afghanistan is more stable than at any time in the past 24 years.' (*The Economist*, 16 Aug. 2003).

TERRITORY AND POPULATION

Afghanistan is bounded in the north by Turkmenistan, Uzbekistan and Tajikistan, east by China, east and south by Pakistan and west by Iran.

The area is 645,807 sq. km (249,346 sq. miles). The estimated population in 2005 was 29·9m. In 2001 an estimated 22·3% of the population lived in urban areas.

The UN gives a projected population for 2010 of 35·64m.

According to humanitarian agencies in Jan. 2002 there were almost 1·2m. internally displaced persons in Afghanistan. An estimated 4m. sought asylum outside Afghanistan including 2m. in Pakistan, 1·5m. in Iran, 26,000 in Turkmenistan, Tajikistan and Uzbekistan, and several hundred thousand in western European countries, Australia and North America. Approximately half of the internally displaced persons in Afghanistan moved prior to the events of Sept. 2001, for reasons such as drought and food scarcity. As a consequence of the US war in Afghanistan, numbers of refugees to Pakistan and Iran increased dramatically. Pakistan took more than 70,000 Afghan refugees in the months following 11 Sept. 2001 while Iran admitted some 60,000. In the meantime more than 1·6m. Afghans have returned to their country since a UN-sponsored programme began in early 2002, and in Dec. 2002 Pakistan and Afghanistan agreed to repatriate the remaining refugees, lodged in various camps in Pakistan, within three years.

The country is divided into 32 regions (*velayat*). Area and estimated population in 2000:

Region	Area (sq. km)	Population (1,000)	Region	Area (sq. km)	Population (1,000)
Badakhshan	44,059	923	Kunar	4,941	494
Badghis	20,591	413	Kunduz	8,040	1,254
Baghlan	21,118	944	Laghman	3,843	627
Balkh	17,248	1,114	Logar	3,880	425
Bamyan	14,175	476	Nangarhar	7,727	1,452
Farah	48,471	484	Nimroz	41,005	200
Faryab	20,293	1,070	Nurestan[1]	9,225	—
Ghazni	22,915	1,246	Paktika	19,482	494
Ghowr	36,479	810	Paktiya	6,432	931
Helmand	58,584	1,035	Parwan	9,584	919
Herat	54,778	1,520	Samangan	11,262	595
Jawzjan	11,798	1,194	Saripul[1]	15,999	—
Kabul	4,462	2,839	Takhar	12,333	845
Kandahar	54,022	1,159	Uruzgan	30,784	737
Kapisa	1,842	530	Vardak	8,938	730
Khost[1]	4,151	—	Zabul	17,343	350

[1]Khost, Nurestan and Saripul did not exist at the time of the 2000 population estimates.

The capital, Kabul, had a population of 2·68m. in 2002. Other towns (with population estimates, 2002): Kandahar (316,000), Herat (249,000), Mazar i Sharif (183,000), Jalalabad (96,000).

Main ethnic groups: Pashtuns, 38%; Tajiks, 25%; Hazaras, 19%; Uzbeks, 6%; others, 12%. The official languages are Pashto and Dari.

SOCIAL STATISTICS

Based on 2001 estimates: birth rate, 41 per 1,000 population; death rate, 18 per 1,000; infant mortality, 147 per 1,000 live births; annual population growth rate, 3·5%. Life expectancy at birth, 47 years for men and 45 for women. Fertility rate, 2001, 6·8 births per woman.

The maternal mortality rate is among the highest in the world with some 16,000 pregnancy-related deaths every year.

CLIMATE

The climate is arid, with a big annual range of temperature and very little rain, apart from the period Jan. to April. Winters are very cold, with considerable snowfall, which may last the year round on mountain summits. Kabul, Jan. 27°F (−2·8°C), July 76°F (24·4°C). Annual rainfall 13" (338 mm).

CONSTITUTION AND GOVERNMENT

Following UN-sponsored talks in Bonn, Germany in Nov. 2001, on 22 Dec. 2001 power was handed over to an Afghan Interim Authority, designed to oversee the restructuring of the country until a second stage of government, the Transitional Authority, could be put into power. This second stage resulted from a *Loya Jirga* (Grand Council), which convened between 10–16 June 2002. The Loya Jirga established the Transitional Islamic State of Afghanistan. A Constitutional Commission was established, with UN assistance, to help the Constitutional Loya Jirga prepare a new constitution. A draft constitution was produced for public scrutiny in Nov. 2003 and was approved by Afghanistan's *Loya Jirga* on 4 Jan. 2004. The new constitution creates a strong presidential system, providing for a *President* and two *Vice-Presidents*, and a bicameral parliament. The lower house is the 249-member House of the People (*Wolesi Jirga*), directly elected for a five-year term, and the upper house the 102-member House of Elders (*Meshrano Jirga*). The upper house is elected in three divisions. The provincial councils elect one third of its members for a four-year term. The district councils elect the second third of the members for a three-year term. The President appoints the remaining third for a five-year term. At least one woman is elected to the *Wolesi Jirga* from each of the country's 32 regions, and half of the president's appointments to the *Meshrano Jirga*

must be women. The president appoints ministers, the attorney general and central bank governor with the approval of the *Wolesi Jirga*. Cabinet ministers must be university graduates. Presidential and parliamentary elections, the first in 25 years, were scheduled for June 2004 but were put back to Oct. 2004. The parliamentary elections were subsequently delayed again and were set to be held in April 2005, but were postponed a further time until Sept. 2005. In Dec. 2005 an elected parliament sat for the first time since 1973.

RECENT ELECTIONS

Elections were held by the *Loya Jirga* on 13 June 2002. Hamid Karzai was elected president with 1,295 out of 1,575 votes cast, against 171 for Masooda Jalal and 89 for Mir Mohammad Mahfoz Nadai.

Afghanistan's first-ever presidential election, held on 9 Oct. 2004, was won by head of the transitional government Hamid Karzai, with 55·4% of votes cast, defeating Yunus Qanooni, with 16·3% of the vote, Haji Mohammad Mohaqiq with 11·6% and Abdul Rashid Dostum with 10·0%. There were 18 candidates in total. Turnout was 70%.

Although not staged on a party political basis, delayed national elections for a new 249-member parliament took place on 18 Sept. 2005. Turnout was about 50%. Of the 249 non-partisans elected, former warlords and their followers gained the majority of seats.

CURRENT ADMINISTRATION

In May 2006 the government was composed as follows:
President: Hamid Karzai; b. 1957 (Pashtun; sworn in 19 June 2002).
Vice Presidents: Ahmad Zia Masood (Tajik); Karim Khalili (Hazara Shia).
Minister of Agriculture: Obaidullah Ramin. *Anti-Narcotics:* Habibollah Qaderi. *Border and Tribal Affairs:* Abdolkarim Brahwi. *Commerce:* Hedayat Amin Arsala. *Communications:* Amirzai Senguin. *Defence:* Abdul Rahim Wardak. *Economy:* Mir-Mohammad Amin Farhang. *Education:* Nour Mohammad Qarqin. *Finance:* Anwar ul-Haq Ahady. *Foreign Affairs:* Rangin Dadfar Spanta. *Hajj (Pilgrimage) and Awqaf:* Nematollah Chahrani. *Higher Education:* Seyyed Amir-Shah Hasanyar. *Information and Culture:* Seyyed Rahin Makhdoom. *Interior:* Zarar Ahmad Moqbel. *Justice:* Sarwar Danesh. *Labour and Social Affairs:* Seyyed Ekramoddin Makroumi. *Martyrs and Disabled:* Sediqa Balkhi. *Mines and Industries:* Mir-Mohammad Sediq. *Public Health:* Seyyed Mohammad-Amin Fatemi. *Public Works:* Sohrab Ali Safari. *Return of Refugees:* Azam Dadfar. *Rural Development:* Mohammad Hanif Atmar. *Transport:* Enayatullah Qasemi. *Urban Development and Housing:* Mohammad Yousof Pashtun. *Water and Power:* Ismail Khan. *Women's Affairs:* Suraya Raheen Subhrang. *Youth:* Amina Afzali.

Government Website: http://www.afghangovernment.com

CURRENT LEADERS

Hamid Karzai

Position
President

Introduction
Hamid Karzai was sworn in as interim president of Afghanistan in Dec. 2001 at a conference in Bonn, Germany before taking the position permanently in June 2002. He was appointed by the United Nations in consultation with the Northern Alliance and the *Loya Jirga*, a group of elected delegates.

Early Life
Karzai was born on 24 Dec. 1957 into the Popolzai tribe, one of Southern Afghanistan's most powerful factions. His father, who

was chief of the Popolzai clan, was assassinated in 1999 in what was widely believed to be a Taliban attack.

Karzai believes in a system of broad-based government called the *Loya Jirga*, with an integrated approach intended to reduce violence between tribal warlords. He first entered politics in the early 1980s during the Soviet invasion and organized the Pashtun Popolzai against Moscow. He spent time in Pakistan, during which time he developed his nationalist philosophy. Karzai returned to Afghanistan in 1992 and linked up with the leader of the Northern Alliance, Burhanuddin Rabbani. When Rabbani formed the first Mujaheddin government, Karzai served as the deputy foreign minister, but left the government because of infighting.

Karzai initially supported the Taliban when it was created in 1994 but in 1995 he rejected a government post, disillusioned by increasing foreign interference. Karzai left the country in 1996 but secretly re-entered in 2001 during America's post-11 Sept. air strikes. He co-ordinated Pashtun resistance to the Taliban and only narrowly evaded capture.

Career in Office
Hamid Karzai was sworn in as chairman of the interim administration in Dec. 2001, taking the title president in June 2002. In his first speech as president, he vowed to resign if he failed to introduce 'forceful Islamic government'. He has since enjoyed the support of a majority of the main tribal leaders. However, his lack of military strength has required him to maintain alliances with armed regional factions and his rule has been tenuous outside the capital. In Sept. 2002 he survived an assassination attempt in Kandahar, two months after his vice president Haji Abdul Qadir had been assassinated by two unidentified gunmen. Despite the precarious security situation throughout Afghanistan, Karzai won outright the country's first-ever democratic presidential election on 9 Oct. 2004 with 55·4% of votes cast. He was inaugurated on 7 Dec.

DEFENCE

In 2001 military expenditure totalled US$245m. (US$11 per capita), representing 12·2% of GDP.

A UN-mandated international force, ISAF, assists the government in the maintenance of security. It has been led by NATO since Aug. 2003 and comprises 8,000 peacekeepers, mostly from Europe.

Army
The decimation of the Taliban's armed forces left Afghanistan without an army. A multi-ethnic Afghan National Army, under the command of President Hamid Karzai, has been established, currently numbering 15,000 but ultimately with a strength of 70,000. Border guards number around 12,000.

Air Force
Afghanistan's air forces have been severely damaged, but there are now plans for a new air force with a strength of 8,000.

INTERNATIONAL RELATIONS

UN sanctions were imposed in 1999 but were withdrawn following the collapse of the Taliban regime.

Afghanistan is a member of the UN, Asian Development Bank, ECO, Colombo Plan, OIC, IOM, Islamic Development Bank and SAARC. In April 2003 the transitional government applied for membership of the WTO although membership negotiations are expected to take several years.

ECONOMY

In 2002 agriculture accounted for 49·1% of GDP, industry 19·8% and services 29·7%.

Overview
Reconstruction in Afghanistan started at the end of 2001, when the economy was in an impoverished state after more than 20

years of conflict, earthquakes and drought. Problems included largely defunct government and financial institutions, weak administrative capacity and a devastated infrastructure. Social indicators were among the worst in the world. Progress has been made in rebuilding institutions and in the implementation of sound economic policies. There has been a strong commitment to fiscal discipline. A new currency was launched in late 2002 and monetary policy has been restrained since then. Economic recovery has been high, real GDP, excluding opium production, is estimated to have grown by almost 30% in 2002–03. GDP growth was largely driven by the end of a prolonged drought and by donor assistance. Following the military campaign in Afghanistan pledges of economic aid came from many countries, totalling more than US$4·5bn, of which the USA pledged US$1·8bn. The informal sector seems to be growing alongside the formal—opium production is estimated by the UN to have reached 3,400 tonnes and the sector accounts for about half of overall GDP.

Currency
A new currency was introduced in Oct. 2002. Called the *afghani* (as was its predecessor), one of the new notes is worth 1,000 of the old ones. The old *afghani* had been trading at around 46,000 to the US$. Inflation was 23·9% in 2003 and 14·3% in 2004.

Budget
The financial year runs from 21 March. Revenues in 2002–03 were US$600m. and expenditures US$150m.

Performance
Real GDP growth was 28·6% in 2002, 15·7% in 2003 and 7·5% in 2004. Total GDP in 2004 was US$5·8bn.

Banking and Finance
Da Afghanistan Bank undertakes the functions of a central bank, holding the exclusive right of note issue. Founded in 1939, its *Governor* is Anwarulhaq Ahadi. The banking sector has undergone major reconstruction since the removal of the Taliban government in 2001.

Weights and Measures
The metric system is in increasingly common use. Local units include: one *khurd* = 0·11 kg; one *pao* = four khurds; one *charak* = four paos; one *sere* = four charaks; one *kharwar* = 580 kg or 16 maunds of 36·25 kg each; one *gaz* = 101·6 cm; one *jarib* = 60 × 60 kabuli yd or 0·202 ha.; one *kulba* = 40 jaribs (area in which 2½ kharwars of seed can be sown); one jarib yd = 73·66 cm.

ENERGY AND NATURAL RESOURCES

Electricity
In 2000 there were six generating plants, four of which were hydro-electric. Installed capacity was 0·5m. kW in 2000. Production was estimated at 480m. kWh in 2000 with consumption an estimated 575m. kWh.

Oil and Gas
Natural gas reserves were 99bn. cu. metres in 2002. Production in 1998 was 137m. cu. metres. A consortium of oil and gas companies ('CentGas') was planning a US$2bn. natural gas pipeline from Turkmenistan through Afghanistan to Pakistan, although the withdrawal from the project of the US oil company Unocal in April 1998 led to doubts over the viability of the project. Since the installation of the Interim Authority, and with the developments of the past few years, both the CentGas project and other major oil and gas ventures within the region from US, Chinese and Iranian companies seem likely to proceed.

Minerals
There are deposits of coal, copper, barite, lapis lazuli, emerald, talc and salt.

Agriculture

The greater part of Afghanistan is mountainous but there are many fertile plains and valleys. In 2001 there were 7·91m. ha. of arable land and 0·14m. ha. of permanent cropland; 2·39m. ha. were irrigated in 2001. 66·3% of the economically active population were engaged in agriculture in 2002. Principal crops include grains, rice, fresh and dried fruits, vegetables, cottonseed and potatoes.

Production, 2000, in 1,000 tonnes: wheat, 1,469; grapes, 330; potatoes, 235; rice, 233; maize, 115. Opium production in 2001 was just 200 tonnes (down from 4,581 tonnes in 1999), but in 2002 it rose again to 3,400 tonnes, and further to 3,600 tonnes in 2003 and 4,2000 tonnes in 2004. In 2003 the harvest was worth an estimated US$1·0bn. The area under cultivation in 2004 was a record high 131,000 ha., up from 80,000 ha. in 2003. It had been just 7,606 ha. in 2001. For several years Afghanistan's annual narcotics production was more than twice that of the second largest producer, Myanmar. In Feb. 2001 the United Nations Drug Control Programme reported that opium production had been almost totally eradicated after the Taliban outlawed the cultivation of poppies. As a result in 2001 Myanmar became the largest producer of opium, but since then Afghanistan has again been the leading producer. Despite a renewed clampdown on opium production and trafficking since the fall of the Taliban, Afghanistan's farmers are being forced by poverty to revive the industry.

Livestock (2000): cattle, 3·5m.; sheep, 18·0m.; goats, 7·4m.; asses, 920,000; camels, 290,000; horses, 104,000; chickens, 7m.

Forestry

In 2000 forests covered 1·35m. ha., or 2·1% of the total land area. Timber production in 2001 was 3·07m. cu. metres.

Fisheries

In 2001 the total catch was estimated to be 800 tonnes, exclusively from inland waters.

INDUSTRY

Major industries include natural gas, fertilizers, cement, coalmining, small vehicle assembly plants, building, carpet weaving, cotton textiles, clothing and footwear, leather tanning and fruit canning.

Labour

The workforce was 8,851,000 in 1996 (65% males). In 1995 the unemployment rate was estimated at 8%.

INTERNATIONAL TRADE

Imports and Exports

Total imports (1999), US$600m.; exports US$150m. Main imports: foodstuffs and live animals, beverages and tobacco, mineral fuels, manufactured goods, chemicals and related products, machinery and transport equipment. Main exported products: opium (illegal trade), non-edible crude materials (excluding fuels), manufactured goods (raw material intensive), machinery and transport equipment, fruits, nuts, hand-woven carpets, wool, hides, precious and semi-precious gems. The illegal trade in opium is the largest source of export earnings and accounts for half of Afghanistan's GDP. Main import sources in 1997 were Singapore (19·2%), Japan (18·5%), China (6·9%) and India (4·8%). Leading export destinations were Pakistan (20·1%), Belgium-Luxembourg (8·7%), France (7·4%) and USA (6·7%).

Imports and exports were largely unaffected by the sanctions imposed during the Taliban regime.

COMMUNICATIONS

Roads

There were 20,720 km of roads in 2001, of which 3,120 km were paved. Approximately half of all road surfaces are in a poor state of repair as a result of military action, but rebuilding is underway. In Jan. 2003 women regained the right to drive after a ten-year ban. Approximately 33,500 passenger cars (1·4 per 1,000 inhabitants) and 26,500 trucks and vans were in use in 2002.

Rail

There are two short stretches of railway in the country, extensions of the Uzbek and Turkmen networks. A Trans-Afghan Railway was proposed in an Afghan-Pakistan-Turkmen agreement of 1994.

Civil Aviation

There is an international airport at Kabul (Khwaja Rawash Airport). The national carrier is Ariana Afghan Airlines, which in 2003 operated direct flights from Kabul to Amritsar, Delhi, Dubai, Frankfurt, Islamabad, İstanbul, Sharjah and Tehran. In 1999 scheduled airline traffic of Afghanistan-based carriers flew 2·7m. km, carrying 140,000 passengers (36,000 on international flights). The UN sanctions imposed on 14 Nov. 1999 included the cutting off of Afghanistan's air links to the outside world. In Jan. 2002 Ariana Afghan Airlines resumed services and Kabul airport was reopened. The airport was heavily bombed during the US campaign and although it is now functioning with some civilian flights it is still being used extensively by the military authorities. Afghanistan's first private airline, Kam Air, was launched in Nov. 2003.

Shipping

There are practically no navigable rivers. A port has been built at Qizil Qala on the Oxus and there are three river ports on the Amu Darya, linked by road to Kabul. The container port at Kheyrabad on the Amu Darya river has rail connections to Uzbekistan.

Telecommunications

In 2002 there were 33,100 telephone main lines, or 1·4 per 1,000 inhabitants—the lowest penetration rate of any country outside Africa. There were 12,000 mobile phone subscribers in 2002 and 1,000 Internet users.

Postal Services

In 2003 there were 313 post offices.

SOCIAL INSTITUTIONS

Justice

A Supreme Court was established in June 1978. It retained its authority under the Taliban regime.

Under the Taliban, a strict form of Sharia law was followed. This law, which was enforced by armed police, included prohibitions on alcohol, television broadcasts, Internet use and photography, yet received its widest condemnation for its treatment of women. Public executions and amputations were widely used as punishment under the regime.

A Judicial Commission will create a civil justice system in accordance with Islamic principles, international standards, the rule of law and Afghan legal traditions. In April 2004 Afghanistan carried out its first execution since the fall of the Taliban.

Education

Adult literacy was 31·5% in 1995 (male, 46·2%; female, 16·1%).

The primary enrolment ratio in 1999 was 38% for boys and 3% for girls. Enrolment at secondary and tertiary levels was even lower. In Jan. 2002 there were an estimated 3,600 primary schools, two-thirds of which were government-supported.

In 1995–96 there were five universities, one university of Islamic studies, one state medical institute and one polytechnic. Kabul University had 9,500 students and 500 academic staff. Formerly one of Asia's finest educational institutes, Kabul University lost many of its staff during the Taliban regime, and following the US bombing attacks it was closed down, although it has since re-opened.

In areas controlled by the Taliban education was forbidden for girls. Boys' schools taught only religious education and military training. Female teachers and pupils have now returned to education after five years of exclusion.

Health

Afghanistan is one of the least successful countries in the battle against undernourishment. Between 1980 and 2000 the proportion of undernourished people rose from 33% of the population to 70%. Half of all Afghan children suffer from chronic malnutrition. One in four children die before reaching the age of five, largely as a result of diarrhoea, pneumonia, measles and other similar illnesses.

The bombing of Afghanistan beginning in Oct. 2001 severely disrupted the supply of aid to the country and left much of the population exposed to starvation.

In 2001 there were 4,104 physicians, 630 dentists (1999), 4,752 nurses and 525 pharmacists (1999) in Afghanistan.

In 2000 only 13% of the population had access to safe drinking water (the lowest percentage of any country).

RELIGION

The predominant religion is Islam. An estimated 86% of the population are Sunni Muslims, and 9% Shias.

The Taliban provoked international censure in May 2001 by forcing the minority population of Afghan Hindus and Sikhs to wear yellow identification badges.

CULTURE

World Heritage Sites

There are two UNESCO sites in Afghanistan: the Minaret and Archaeological Remains of Jam (inscribed in 2002), a 12th century minaret; the Cultural Landscape and archaeological Remains of the Bamiyan Valley (2003), including the monumental Buddha statues destroyed by the Taliban in 2001.

Broadcasting

In 2000 there were 2·95m. radio receivers and 362,000 television receivers (colour by PAL).

Under the Taliban television stations were closed down—only one remained in operation, in a Northern Alliance-controlled area. Television sets were smashed or even publicly hanged. The single radio broadcasting station to remain in operation, Radio Afghanistan, was renamed Voice of Shariah and was used to broadcast official propaganda and religious sermons. It proclaimed itself as the only radio station in the world where music of any kind was banned. Since the collapse of the regime Radio Afghanistan has resumed services, as have Kabul TV and a number of other broadcasters.

Cinema

Cinemas were banned under the Taliban but have since reopened. The Afghan Film Institute is responsible for censorship.

Press

Afghanistan had approximately 300 publications in 2004. The main dailies were *Hewad*, *Anis* and the English language publications *Daily Arman* and *Kabul Times*.

Tourism

In 1998 there were 4,000 foreign tourists bringing in receipts of US$1m.

Calendar

The Afghan Interim Authority replaced the lunar calendar with the traditional Afghan solar calendar. The solar calendar was used in Afghanistan until 1999 when it was changed by the Taliban authorities who wanted the country to adopt the system used in Saudi Arabia. The change means the current year is 1385.

DIPLOMATIC REPRESENTATIVES

Of Afghanistan in the United Kingdom (31 Prince's Gate, London, SW7 1QQ)
Ambassador: Ahmad Wali Masoud.

Of the United Kingdom in Afghanistan (15th St., Roundabout Wazir Akbar Khan, PO Box 334, Kabul)
Ambassador: Dr Rosalind Marsden, CMG.

Of Afghanistan in the USA (2341 Wyoming Ave., NW, Washington, D.C., 20008)
Ambassador: Said Tayeb Jawad.

Of the USA in Afghanistan (Great Masood Rd between Radio Afghanistan and Ministry of Public Health, Kabul)
Ambassador: Ronald E. Neumann.

Of Afghanistan to the United Nations
Ambassador: Ravan Farhadi.

Of Afghanistan to the European Union
Ambassador: Humayun Tandar.

FURTHER READING

Amin, S. H., *Law, Reform and Revolution in Afghanistan.* London, 1991
Arney, G., *Afghanistan.* London, 1990
Edwards, David B., *Before Taliban: Genealogies of the Afghan Jihad.* Univ. of California Press, Berkeley, 2002
Evans, Martin, *Afghanistan, A New History.* Curzon Press, Richmond, 2001
Goodson, Larry, *Afghanistan's Endless War: State Failure, Regional Politics and the Rise of the Taliban.* University of Washington Press, 2001
Griffiths, John, *Afghanistan: A History of Conflict.* Andre Deutsch, London, 2001
Hyman, A., *Afghanistan under Soviet Domination, 1964–1991.* 3rd ed. London, 1992
Jones, Schuyler, *Afghanistan.* [Bibliography] ABC-Clio, Oxford and Santa Barbara (CA), 1992
Magnus, Ralph H. and Naby, Eden, *Afghanistan: Mullah, Marx and Mujahid.* Revised ed. Westview Press, Boulder, 2002
Margolis, Eric, *War at the Top of the World: The Struggle for Afghanistan, Kashmir and Tibet.* Routledge, New York, 2001
Montgomery, John Dickey D. and Rondinelli, Dennis A., (eds.) *Beyond Reconstruction in Afghanistan: Lessons from Development Experience.* Palgrave Macmillan, Basingstoke, 2004
Nojumi, Neamatollah, *The Rise of the Taliban in Afghanistan.* Palgrave Macmillan, Basingstoke, 2001
Roy, O., *Islam and Resistance in Afghanistan.* 2nd ed. CUP, 1990
Rubin, B. R., *The Fragmentation of Afghanistan: State Formation and Collapse in the International System.* Yale Univ. Press, 1995.—*The Search for Peace in Afghanistan: from Buffer State to Failed State.* Yale Univ. Press, 1996
Smith, Mary, *Before the Taliban: Living with War, Hoping for Peace.* Iynx Publishing, Aberdour, 2002
Vogelsang, Willem, *The Afghans.* Blackwell, Oxford, 2002

National Statistical Office: Central Statistics Office, Ansar-i-Watt, Kabul.
Website: http://www.aims.org.af/cso

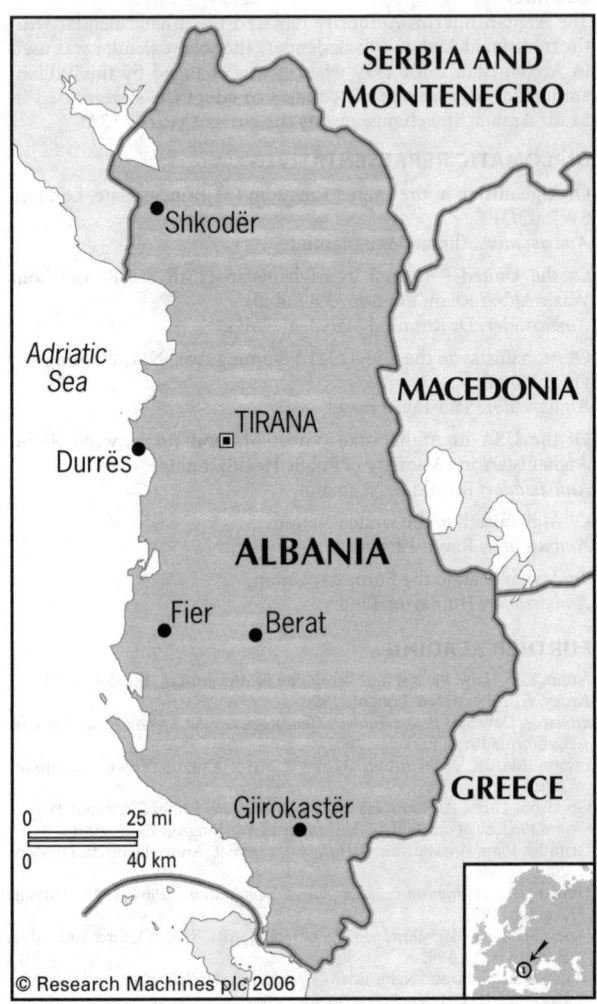

© Research Machines plc 2006

Republika e Shqipërisë

Capital: Tirana
Population projection, 2010: 3·22m.
GDP per capita, 2003: (PPP$) 4,584
HDI/world rank: 0·780/72

KEY HISTORICAL EVENTS

In antiquity Albania was part of Illyria, stretching along the eastern coastal region of the Adriatic. By 168 BC the Romans conquered all of Illyria, administering it as a province (Illyricum) of their empire. From AD 395 Illyria became part of the eastern Byzantine empire, the decline of which over the following centuries encouraged waves of Slavic invasions across the region. During the middle ages the name Albania began to be increasingly applied to the modern day region, possibly deriving from Albanoi, the name of an Illyrian tribe. Ottoman intrusion began in the 14th century and, despite years of resistance under the leadership of national hero Gjergj Kastrioti, Turkish suzerainty was imposed from 1478. During the 15th and 16th centuries, many Albanians fled to southern Italy to escape Ottoman rule and conversion to Islam. After the Russo-Turkish war of 1877–78

there were demands for independence from Turkey. With the defeat of Turkey in the Balkan war of 1912, Albanian nationalists proclaimed independence and set up a provisional government.

During the First World War Albania became a battlefield for warring occupation forces. Albania was admitted to the League of Nations in Dec. 1920. In Nov. 1921 the conference of ambassadors confirmed its 1913 frontiers with minor alterations. Although declared a republic in 1925, Albania then became a monarchy from 1928 until April 1939 when Italy's dictator, Mussolini, invaded and set up a puppet state. During the Second World War Albania suffered first Italian and then German occupation. Resistance was led by royalist, nationalist republican and Communist movements, often at odds with each other. The Communists enjoyed the support of Tito's partisans, who were instrumental in forming the Albanian Communist Party on 8 Nov. 1941. Communists dominated the Anti-Fascist National Liberation Committee which became the Provisional Democratic Government on 22 Oct. 1944 after the German withdrawal, with Enver Hoxha, a French-educated school teacher and member of the Communist Party Central Committee, at its head. Large estates were broken up and the land distributed, although full collectivization was not brought in until 1955–59. Close ties were forged with the USSR. However, following Khrushchev's reconciliation with Tito in 1956, China replaced the Soviet Union as Albania's powerful patron from 1961 until the end of the Maoist phase in 1977. The regime then adopted a policy of 'revolutionary self-sufficiency'.

Following the collapse of the USSR, the People's Assembly legalized opposition parties. The Communists won the first multi-party elections in April 1991, but soon resigned from office following a general strike. They were replaced firstly by a coalition government, which collapsed in Dec. 1991, and then by an interim technocratic administration. A new, non-Communist government was elected in March 1992.

In 1997 Albania was disrupted by financial crises caused by the collapse of fraudulent pyramid finance schemes. A period of violent anarchy led to the fall of the administration and to fresh elections which returned a Socialist-led government. A UN peacekeeping force withdrew in Aug. 1997, but sporadic violence continued.

In April 1999 the Kosovo crisis which led to NATO air attacks on Yugoslavian military targets set off a flood of refugees into Albania.

Having won a decisive victory in the 2001 elections, the ruling Socialist Party lost power to the opposition Democratic Party in the July 2005 polling, the results of which were only confirmed in Sept. following a lengthy appeals process and reruns in three constituencies.

TERRITORY AND POPULATION

Albania is bounded in the north by Serbia and Montenegro, east by Macedonia, south by Greece and west by the Adriatic. The area is 28,748 sq. km (11,100 sq. miles). At the census of April 2001 the population was 3,126,163; density, 109 per sq. km. The United Nations population estimate for 2005 was 3·13m.

The UN gives a projected population for 2010 of 3·22m.

In 2003, 56·2% of the population lived in rural areas. The capital is Tirana (population in 2003, 555,565); other large towns (population in 2003) are Elbasan (226,670), Durrës (209,289), Fier (201,397), Shkodër (184,989), Vlorë (148,821), Lushnjë (145,762), Korçë (144,439), Berat (126,608), Kavajë (81,145) and Gjirokastër (Argyrocastro) (56,664).

The country is administratively divided into 12 prefectures, 36 districts, 306 communes and 65 municipalities.

Districts	Area (sq. km)	Population (2003)	Districts	Area (sq. km)	Population (2003)
Berat	939	126,608	Lezhë	479	72,001
Bulqizë	469	38,105	Librazhd	1,023	70,045
Delvinë	348	11,628	Lushnjë	712	145,762
Devoll	429	34,951	Malësi e Madhe	555	37,232
Dibër	1,088	79,582	Mallakastër	393	38,458
Durrës	433	209,989	Mat	1,029	58,391
Elbasan	1,372	226,670	Mirditë	867	34,202
Fier	785	201,397	Peqin	109	32,777
Gjirokastër	1,137	56,664	Përmet	930	23,777
Gramsh	695	31,852	Pogradec	725	71,738
Has	393	19,360	Pukë	1,034	33,444
Kavajë	414	81,145	Sarandë	749	40,398
Kolonjë	805	16,316	Shkodër	1,973	184,989
Korçë	1,752	144,439	Skrapar	775	25,093
Krujë	333	66,084	Tepelenë	817	30,189
Kuçovë	84	35,557	Tirana	1,238	555,565
Kukës	938	62,778	Tropojë	1,043	24,270
Kurbin	273	54,886	Vlorë	1,609	148,821

In most cases districts are named after their capitals. Exceptions are: Devoll, capital—Bilisht; Dibër—Peshkopi; Has—Krumë; Kolonjë—Ersekë; Kurbin—Laç; Mallakastër—Ballsh; Malësi e Madhe—Koplik; Mat—Burrel; Mirditë—Rrëshen; Skrapar—Çorovodë; Tropojë—Bajram Curri.

Albanians account for 91·7% of the population, Aromanians 3·6%, Greeks 2·3% and others 2·4%.

The official language is Albanian.

SOCIAL STATISTICS

2003: births, 47,012; deaths, 17,967. Rates in 2003 (per 1,000): births, 14·8; deaths, 5·7. Infant mortality, 2001, was 26 per 1,000 live births. Fertility rate (number of births per woman), 2·1 in 2000. Annual population growth rate, 1992–2002, −0·4%. Life expectancy at birth, 2003, 75·4 years for both males and females. Abortion was legalized in 1991.

CLIMATE

Mediterranean-type, with rainfall mainly in winter, but thunderstorms are frequent and severe in the great heat of the plains in summer. Winters in the highlands can be severe, with much snow. Tirana, Jan. 44°F (6·8°C), July 75°F (23·9°C). Annual rainfall 54" (1,353 mm). Shkodër, Jan. 39°F (3·9°C), July 77°F (25°C). Annual rainfall 57" (1,425 mm).

CONSTITUTION AND GOVERNMENT

A new constitution was adopted on 28 Nov. 1998. The supreme legislative body is the single-chamber *People's Assembly* of 140 deputies, 100 directly elected and 40 elected by proportional representation, for four-year terms. Where no candidate wins an absolute majority, a run-off election is held. The *President* is elected by Parliament for a five-year term.

National Anthem

'Rreth Flamurit të përbashkuar' ('The flag that united us in the struggle'); words by A. S. Drenova, tune by C. Porumbescu.

RECENT ELECTIONS

Parliamentary elections took place on 3 July 2005. The opposition Democratic Party of Albania won 56 of the 140 seats with 40·0% of votes cast, the ruling Socialist Party of Albania 42 with 30·0%, the Republican Party 11 with 7·9%, the Social Democrat Party 7 with 5·0%, and the Socialist Movement for Integration 5 with 3·6%. Other parties won four seats or fewer. The Democratic Party of Albania and its allies received a total of 81 seats and the Socialist Party and its allies 59.

Parliament chose Alfred Moisiu (ind.) as president on 24 June 2002.

CURRENT ADMINISTRATION

President: Alfred Moisiu; b. 1929 (in office since 24 July 2002).

In March 2006 the coalition government comprised:

Prime Minister: Sali Berisha; b. 1944 (Democratic Party; sworn in 11 Sept. 2005, having previously been president from April 1992–July 1997).

Deputy Prime Minister: Ilir Rusmaji.

Minister for Agriculture: Jemin Gjana. *Defence:* Fatmir Mediu. *Economy, Trade and Energy:* Genc Ruli. *Education and Science:* Genc Pollo. *Environment, Water Management and Forests:* Lufter Xhuveli. *Finance:* Ridvan Bode. *Foreign Affairs:* Besnik Mustafaj. *Health:* Maksim Cikuli. *Integration:* Arenca Troshani. *Interior:* Sokol Olldashi. *Justice:* Aldo Bumçi. *Labour, Social Affairs and Equal Opportunities:* Koço Barka. *Public Works, Transportation and Telecommunications:* Lulzim Basha. *Tourism, Culture, Youth and Sports:* Bujar Leskaj.

Albanian Parliament: http://www.parlament.al

CURRENT LEADERS

Alfred Moisiu

Position
President

Introduction
Alfred Moisiu was chosen as Albania's president by parliament in June 2002. A non-partisan, military professional, he has won praise for his ability to find common ground among rival factions across the political spectrum. He is pro-Western and a prominent advocate of Albanian accession to NATO.

Early Life
Moisiu was born on 1 Dec. 1929 in Shkodër, northern Albania. He went to school in Tirana and from 1943–45 was active in the war against the occupying German forces. In 1946 he began studying at the Military Engineering School in St Petersburg, Russia, leaving two years later and becoming a platoon commander at the Joint Officers' School in Tirana. Between 1949–51 he was an instructor at the Skanderbeg Military Academy in Tirana.

From 1952–58 he went to the Academy of Military Engineering in Moscow. Returning to Albania, he worked in the engineering directory of the Ministry of Defence until 1966. He then assumed command of the Pontoon Brigade at Kavajë until 1971, meanwhile undertaking a year-long course for senior general staff at Tirana's Defence Academy.

In 1971 he was appointed head of the office of engineering and fortifications at the Ministry of Defence. He held that post until 1981 (acquiring a PhD in military sciences in 1979) and then became vice minister of defence until Oct. 1982. After heading an engineering company in Burrel in the northwest of the country, he retired from 1985 until 1991 when he was appointed defence minister in Vilson Ahmeti's interim 'government of experts' that ruled from the collapse of communism until the democratic elections held in March 1992.

Moisiu worked as a defence adviser from 1992–94 before becoming vice minister of defence again in the government of Prime Minister Aleksander Meksi. In this role he advised on the reconstruction of the armed services and supported preparations for NATO membership. In 1994 he also became chairman of the Albanian Atlantic Association (a post he held until his election as state president). He left government office in 1997 following the electoral victory of the Socialist Party, but maintained a prominent role in international conferences concerned with regional and peace issues.

When Rexhep Meidani left the state presidency in 2002, Moisiu emerged as an acceptable candidate to both the Socialist and Democratic parties. Following a poll in the national assembly (in which he received 97 votes, with 19 against and 14 abstentions), he was sworn into office on 24 July 2002.

Career in Office
On assuming office, Moisiu pledged to keep his distance from party political issues. Nevertheless, he was critical of the then Socialist Prime Minister Fatos Nano for the slow pace of political reform. Following the parliamentary elections in July 2005, he asked Democratic Party leader Sali Berisha to form a government, which was sworn in on 11 Sept. 2005. Moisiu's foreign policy aims include lasting peace in the Balkans and Albania's accession to NATO.

Sali Berisha

Position
Prime Minister

Introduction
Dr Sali Berisha returned as prime minister on 11 Sept. 2005 after eight years in opposition. He was a leading opponent of the communist regime in the late 1980s and served as Albania's first elected post-communist president from 1992–97. Breathing life into Albania's ailing economy, reforming its institutions and tackling corruption and organized crime are the priorities for his administration.

Early Life
Sali Ram Berisha was born in Vuçidol, Tropoja region, northern Albania on 15 Oct. 1944, the year in which the communist leader, Enver Hoxha, seized power and established a hard-line Stalinist regime. Berisha graduated in medicine from the University of Tirana in 1967 and specialized in cardiology, becoming assistant professor of medicine and cardiologist at Tirana General Hospital. He joined the communist Party of Labour in 1971. Having secured a grant from UNESCO, Berisha travelled to Paris in 1978 for advanced studies in cardiology. In 1980 he returned to the University of Tirana as 'Professor Doctor' and went on to publish numerous textbooks and scientific papers.

In the late 1980s Berisha was one of a group of intellectuals who called for democratic reforms. Following student protests at the University of Tirana in early Dec. 1990, he founded the Democratic Party of Albania (PDSH) and was elected a member of parliament in the country's first multi-party elections on 31 March 1991. During the PDSH's first Congress in Sept. 1991 Berisha was voted chairman and led the party to victory in the general election of 22 March 1992. Elected president of Albania on 9 April 1992, he set out to open up the economy, promote foreign investment and reform the country's institutions. However, the administration was marred by corruption and Albania has remained mired in poverty. Tens of thousands emigrated and Berisha faced growing opposition to his increasingly authoritarian rule, particularly in the south of the country.

Support for Berisha was further eroded by the collapse of various pyramid investment schemes in 1997. An uprising in the south threatened to spill over into civil war and tensions remained high when Berisha refused to step down after the electoral victory of a socialist-led coalition in June 1997. He eventually resigned under international pressure on 23 July 1997, to be replaced by the head of the Socialist Party, Rexhep Meidani. Fatos Nano, a fellow socialist and arch-rival of Berisha, became prime minister.

Tensions between the two main parties remained. Berisha accused Fatos Nano's administration of corruption and incompetence and withdrew from parliament between 1998 and early 2002. The arrival of hundreds of thousands of ethnic Albanian refugees from Kosovo in 1999 placed further strain on the faltering economy and infrastructure. Berisha fought the general election on 3 July 2005 on an anti-corruption platform and the PDSH claimed victory, although foreign monitors criticized the vote as falling short of international standards. Having formed a coalition with other centre-right groups to take control of 81 of the 140 seats in the legislature, Berisha was sworn in as prime minister on 11 Sept. 2005.

Career in Office
Berisha promised to build a 'social state' by streamlining the government and purging it of corrupt elements, reducing taxes and enabling private enterprise to flourish. He intends to seek membership of NATO and the EU.

DEFENCE

Conscription is for 12 months. Albania's armed forces are being reconstituted, a process that should be completed by 2010. In 2003 defence expenditure totalled US$76m. (US$24 per capita), representing 1·2% of GDP.

Army
Strength in 2002 was 20,000. There is an internal security force, and frontier guards number 500.

Navy
Navy personnel in 2002 totalled 2,500 officers and ratings. Of the 24 vessels in the navy there were 11 torpedo craft. There are naval bases at Durrës, Sarandë, Shëngjin and Vlorë.

Air Force
The Air Force had (2002) about 4,500 personnel, and operated 98 combat aircraft including MiG-15s, MiG-17s and MiG-19s.

INTERNATIONAL RELATIONS

Albania is a member of the UN, WTO, the Council of Europe, OSCE, the Central European Initiative, BSEC, IOM, OIC, Islamic Development Bank and the NATO Partnership for Peace.

ECONOMY

In 2002 agriculture accounted for 25·3% of GDP, industry 18·9% and services 55·7%.

Overview
The Albanian economy collapsed during the political turmoil of 1990. Unemployment rose to 30% and industrial production fell by nearly half by 1992. The government embarked on a reform programme of privatization and economic liberalization with the help of the World Bank and the IMF. The Tirana Stock Exchange was established in 1996 during a period of strong economic growth; GDP annual growth had averaged 9% between 1993–95. Privatization of land, small businesses and housing was achieved in 1991–93. A privatization programme for large enterprises was initiated in 1995 under the aegis of the National Privatization Agency. However, the lack of banking sector reform led to informal credit arrangements such as pyramid schemes that grew enormously and collapsed in 1997. This sparked widespread social unrest and the downfall of the government.

The agricultural sector has experienced a revival under private ownership and represented 25% of GDP in 2002. The industrial sector shrank from 44% to 19% of GDP between 1990 and 2002. Privatization of the state telecommunications company, Albtelecom, failed in 2002, hindered by a weak international market.

Currency
The monetary unit is the *lek* (ALL), notionally of 100 *qindars*. In Sept. 1991 the lek (plural, *lekë* or leks) was pegged to the ecu at a rate of 30 leks = one ecu. In June 1992 it was devalued from 50 to 110 to US$1. After several years of high inflation (225% in 1992), there was inflation of 2·4% in 2003 and 2·9% in 2004. Foreign exchange reserves were US$319m. in June 2002, total money supply was 156,469m. leks and gold reserves totalled 111,000 troy oz.

Budget
The fiscal year is the calendar year. Government revenues in 2000 totalled 130,642m. leks (tax revenue, 79·7%; non-tax revenue, 20·3%) and expenditures 170,621m. leks (current expenditure, 78·7%; capital expenditure, 21·3%).

Performance
Total GDP in 2004 was US$7·6bn. After the economy contracted by 10·5% in 1997 following the collapse of pyramid finance schemes, real GDP growth averaged 7·5% from 1998 to 2004. The economy grew by 6·0% in 2003 and 5·9% in 2004.

Banking and Finance
The central bank and bank of issue is the Bank of Albania, founded in 1925 with Italian aid as the Albanian State Bank and renamed in 1993. Its *Governor* is Ardian Fullani. The Savings Bank of Albania, which serves around 75% of the Albanian market, was sold by the government to Raiffeisen Zentralbank Österreich AG in Dec. 2003. In 2002 it had total assets of US$1·4bn., approximately 60% of the total assets of the Albanian banking sector. In 2002 there were six other banks: American Bank of Albania; Arab-Albanian Islamic Bank; Fefad Bank; Italian-Albanian Bank; National Commercial Bank of Albania; and Tirana Bank SA.

A stock exchange opened in Tirana in 1996.

ENERGY AND NATURAL RESOURCES

Environment
Albania's carbon dioxide emissions from the consumption and flaring of fossil fuels in 2002 were the equivalent of 1·2 tonnes per capita.

Electricity
Albania is rich in hydro-electric potential. Although virtually all of the electricity is generated by hydro-electric power plants only 30% of potential hydro-electric sources are currently being used. Power cuts are common. Electricity capacity was 1·67m. kW in 2001. Production was 3·69bn. kWh in 2001 and consumption per capita 1,181 kWh.

Oil and Gas
Offshore exploration began in 1991. Oil has been produced onshore since 1920. Oil reserves in 2002 were 206m. bbls. Crude oil production in 2003, 359,253 tonnes. Natural gas is extracted. Reserves in 2002 totalled 4bn. cu. metres; output in 2000 was 17m. cu. metres.

Minerals
Mineral wealth is considerable and includes lignite, chromium, copper and nickel. Production, in 1999 (in 1,000 tonnes): chromium ore, 79; lignite (2000), 42; copper ore, 34. Nickel reserves are 60m. tonnes of iron containing 1m. tonnes of nickel, but extraction had virtually ceased by 1996. A consortium of British and Italian companies is modernizing the chrome industry with the aim of making Albania the leading supplier of ferrochrome to European stainless steel producers.

Agriculture
In 2001 the agricultural population was 1·78m., of whom 748,000 were economically active. The country is mountainous, except for the Adriatic littoral and the Korçë Basin, which are fertile. Only 24% of the land area is suitable for cultivation; 15% of Albania is used for pasture. In 2001 there were 578,000 ha. of arable land and 121,000 ha. of permanent cropland. 129,000 ha. were irrigated in 2000.

A law of Aug. 1991 privatized co-operatives' land. Families received allocations, according to their size, from village committees. In 1998 there were 466,659 private agricultural holdings with a total area of 451,917 ha.; average 0·96 ha. Since 1995 owners have been permitted to buy and sell agricultural land. In 2003 there were 7,774 tractors in use and 875 harvester-threshers.

Production (in 1,000 tonnes), 2003: total grains, 489 (including wheat 260 and maize 207); potatoes, 458; tomatoes, 203; grapes (2000), 79; sugarbeets (2000), 42; wine (2000), 7,413 hectolitres.

Livestock, 2003: sheep, 1,903,000; goats, 1,101,000; cattle, 684,000; asses, 170,000; pigs, 132,000; horses, 48,000; chickens, 4,087,000. Livestock products, 2001 (in 1,000 tonnes): beef, 59; mutton, lamb and goat, 32; pork, 10; poultry, 5; cheese (2000), 12; milk, 831; eggs, 608m. units.

Forestry
Forests covered 1,455,000 ha. in 2003 (36·9% of the total land area), mainly oak, elm, pine and birch. Timber production in 2003 was 573,000 cu. metres.

Fisheries
The total catch in 2003 amounted to 3,703 tonnes (1,921 tonnes from sea fishing).

INDUSTRY
Output is small, and the principal industries are agricultural product processing, textiles, oil products and cement. Closures of loss-making plants in the chemical and engineering industries built up in the Communist era led to a 60% decline in production by 1993. Output in 2000 (in 1,000 tonnes): distillate fuel oil, 72; residual fuel oil, 63; kerosene, 58; cement (2001), 30; petrol, 24; rolled steel (1994), 17; beer (2003), 39·0m. litres; wine (2001), 1·4m. litres; 40m. bricks (1994); 126m. cigarettes (2001).

Labour
In 2003 the workforce was 1,089,000, of which 926,000 were employed (745,000 in the private sector). Unemployment was 15·0% at the end of 2003.

The average monthly wage in 2002 was 16,390 leks; the official minimum wage in 2003 was 10,060 leks. Minimum wages may not fall below one-third of maximum. Retirement age is 60 for men and 55 for women.

Trade Unions
Independent trade unions became legal in Feb. 1991.

INTERNATIONAL TRADE
Foreign investment was legalized in Nov. 1990. Foreign debt was US$1,312m. in 2002.

Imports and Exports
Imports in 2002 totalled US$1,485m.; exports, US$330m. Principal imports in 2001: food and beverages, 19·4%; nonelectrical and electrical machinery, 18·4%; mineral fuels, 13·8%; textiles and clothing, 10·4%; base and fabricated metals, 8·8%. Leading exports in 2001: textiles and clothing, 37·4%; footwear and related products, 28·6%; base and fabricated metals, 8·0%. Main import suppliers, 2001 (% of total trade): Italy, 36·5%; Greece, 31·5%; Turkey, 6·7%. Main export markets: Italy, 71·6%; Greece, 13·1%; Germany, 5·6%.

COMMUNICATIONS

Roads
In 2002 there were 3,220 km of main roads, 4,300 km of secondary roads and 10,480 km of other roads. There were 148,531 passenger cars in 2002, as well as 21,026 buses and coaches and 51,960 lorries and vans. There were 428 road accidents in 2000 (280 fatalities).

Rail
Total length in operation in 2000 was 400 km. Passenger-km travelled in 2003 came to 105m. and freight tonne-km to 18m. In Aug. 2003 the government announced plans to re-establish

rail links with Montenegro and the European network and construct a railway to Macedonia with the financial assistance of the World Bank.

Civil Aviation
The national carrier is Albanian Airlines, a joint venture with a Kuwaiti firm. It began operations in Oct. 1995. In 2002 it flew services to Bologna, Frankfurt, İstanbul, Priština and Rome. Air civil transportation is carried out by 12 airlines, of which ten are foreign airlines and two are joint ventures. In 1999 scheduled airline traffic of Albania-based carriers flew 0·3m. km, carrying 20,000 passengers (all on international flights). The main airport is Mother Teresa International Airport at Rinas, 25 km from Tirana, which handled 356,823 passengers in 1999.

Shipping
In 2002 merchant shipping totalled 49,000 GRT. The main port is Durrës, with secondary ports being Vlorë, Sarandë and Shëngjin.

Telecommunications
In 2003 there were 222,000 telephone main lines. A state-owned mobile telephone network was set up in 1996, initially serving 8,000 subscribers. By 2003 there were 1·15m. mobile subscribers. There were 36,000 PCs in use in 2002 (8·9 for every 1,000 persons). Albania had 12,000 Internet users in 2002.

Postal Services
In 2003 there were 565 post offices. The volume of postal traffic in 2000 was 2,095,000 pieces of ordinary mail and 892,000 pieces of registered post.

SOCIAL INSTITUTIONS

Justice
A new criminal code was introduced in June 1995. The administration of justice (made up of First Instance Courts, The Courts of Appeal and the Supreme Court) is presided over by the *Council of Justice*, chaired by the President of the Republic, which appoints judges to courts. A Ministry of Justice was re-established in 1990 and a Bar Council set up. In Nov. 1993 the number of capital offences was reduced from 13 to six and the death penalty was abolished for women. In 2000 the death penalty was abolished for peacetime offences. The prison population in Nov. 2001 was 3,053 (90 per 100,000 of national population).

Education
Primary education is free and compulsory in eight-year schools from seven to 15 years. Secondary education is also free and lasts four years. Secondary education is divided into three categories: general; technical and professional; vocational. There were, in 2003–04, 1,763 nursery schools with 79,905 pupils and 3,770 teachers; 27,248 primary school teachers with 505,141 pupils; and 142,402 pupils and 6,873 teachers at secondary schools. In 2000–01 there were five universities, one agricultural university, one technological university, one polytechnic, one academy of fine arts and one higher institute of physical education. There were 53,255 university students registered and 1,750 academic staff in 2003–04; Tirana is the largest university, with 12,190 students in 2003–04. Adult literacy in 2003 was 98·7% (99·2% among males and 98·3% among females).

In 2000 total expenditure on education came to 3% of GNP.

Health
Medical services are free, though medicines are charged for. In 2003 there were 50 hospitals, 4,100 doctors and 11,470 nurses or midwives. In 2003 there were 9,514 hospital beds. The expenditure on health in 1999 was 12,077m. leks (7·3% of total government expenditure).

Welfare
The retirement age is 60 (men), or 55 (women); to be eligible for a state pension contributions over 35 years are required. Old-age benefits consist of a basic pension and an earnings-related increment. The basic pension is indexed according to price changes of selected commodities.

Unemployment benefit was 3,960 leks per month as of 2003.

RELIGION

In 2001, 39% of the population were Muslims, mainly Sunni with some Belaktashi, 17% Roman Catholic, 10% Albanian Orthodox and the remainder other religions. The Albanian Orthodox Church is autocephalous; it is headed by an Exarch, Anastasios, Archbishop of Tirana, Durrës and All Albania, and three metropolitans. In 2001 there were 118 priests. The Roman Catholic cathedral in Shkodër has been restored and the cathedral in Tirana has been rebuilt, opening in 2002. In 2000 there were one Roman Catholic archbishop and three bishops.

CULTURE

World Heritage Sites
In 1992 Butrint was added to the UNESCO World Heritage List. Butrint is a settlement in the southwest of the country, near the port of Sarandë, which was inhabited from 800 BC and is now a major site of archaeological investigation. The historic town of Gjirokastër was inscribed in 2005 and is a rare example of a well-preserved Ottoman town built around the 13th century.

Broadcasting
Broadcasting is regulated by the National Council for Radio-Television (NCRT), one member of which is appointed by the president, and the other six by the permanent Commission on the Media, which is composed equally of representatives of government and opposition parties. In Dec. 2000 the NCRT licensed two national television stations, 45 local television stations, 31 local radio stations and one national radio station. There are also a number of privately owned television broadcasting stations. In 2000 there were 756,000 radio receivers and 480,000 TV receivers (colour by SECAM H).

Cinema
In 2002 there were 25 cinemas, compared to 65 in 1991.

Press
In 1996 there were five national dailies (combined circulation of 116,000, at a rate of 37 per 1,000 inhabitants).

Tourism
In 2001, 34,000 foreign tourists visited Albania; tourist spending totalled US$446m. There were 102 hotels in 1999.

Libraries
The National Library in Tirana contains over 1m. items.

Theatre and Opera
The National Albanian Theatre, Tirana, is the most prestigious, with a capacity of 540. The Opera and Ballet Theatre, Tirana, is the home of the Albanian Philharmonic Orchestra.

Museums and Galleries
The largest museum is the National Historical Museum in Tirana.

DIPLOMATIC REPRESENTATIVES

Of Albania in the United Kingdom (2nd Floor, 24 Buckingham Gate, London, SW1E 6LB)
Ambassador: Kastriot Robo.

Of the United Kingdom in Albania (Rruga Skenderbeg 12, Tirana)
Ambassador: Richard Jones.

Of Albania in the USA (2100 S St., NW, Washington, D.C., 20008)
Ambassador: Aleksandër Sallabanda.

Of the USA in Albania (Tirana Rruga Elbasanit 103, Tirana)
Ambassador: Marcie Ries.

Of Albania to the United Nations
Ambassador: Agim Nesho.

Of Albania to the European Union
Ambassador: Artur Kuko.

FURTHER READING

Fischer, Bernd, *Albania at War 1939–45.* C. Hurst, London, 1999
Hutchings, R., *Historical Dictionary of Albania.* Lanham (MD), 1997
Sjoberg, O., *Rural Change and Development in Albania.* Boulder (CO), 1992
Vickers, M., *The Albanians: a Modern History.* London, 1997
Vickers, M. and Pettifer, J., *Albania: from Anarchy to a Balkan Identity.* Farnborough, 1997
Winnifrith, T. (ed.) *Perspectives on Albania.* London, 1992
Young, A., *Albania.* [Bibliography] 2nd ed. ABC-Clio, Oxford and Santa Barbara (CA), 1997

National Statistical Office: Albanian Institute of Statistics, Tirana.
Director General: Gerta Picari.
Website: http://www.instat.gov.al/

ALGERIA

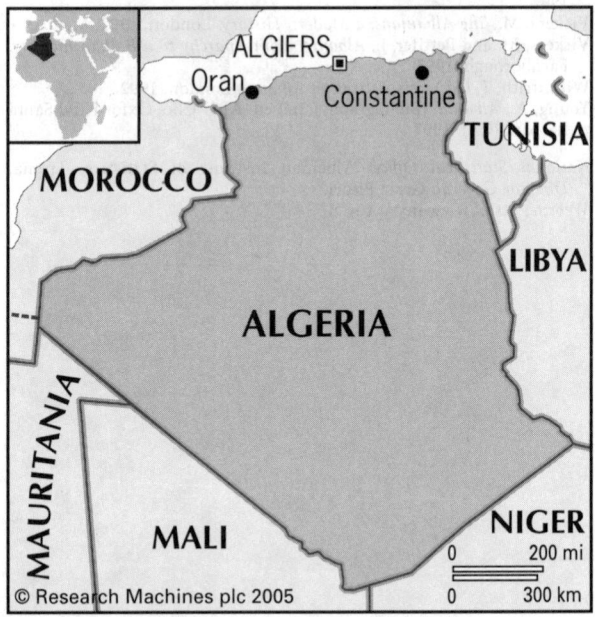

© Research Machines plc 2005

Jumhuriya al-Jazairiya ad-Dimuqratiya ash-Shabiya (People's Democratic Republic of Algeria)

Capital: Algiers
Population projection, 2010: 35·42m.
GDP per capita, 2003: (PPP$) 6,107
HDI/world rank: 0·722/103

KEY HISTORICAL EVENTS

Algeria came under French control in the 1850s. French settlers developed political and economic power at the expense of the indigenous Muslim population. In Nov. 1954 the *Front de Libération Nationale* (FLN), representing the Muslim majority, declared open warfare against the French administration. There was extensive loss of life and property during the fighting which continued unabated until March 1962 when a ceasefire was agreed between the French government and the nationalists. Against the wishes of the French in Algeria, Gen. de Gaulle conceded Algerian independence on 3 July 1962.

The Political Bureau of the FLN took over the functions of government, a National Constituent Assembly was elected and the Republic was declared on 25 Sept. 1962. One of the founders of the FLN, Ahmed Ben Bella, became prime minister, and president the following year. On 15 June 1965 the government was overthrown by a junta of army officers, who established a Revolutionary Council under Col. Houari Boumedienne. After ten years of rule, Boumedienne proposed elections for a president and a National Assembly. A new constitution was accepted in a referendum in Nov. 1976 and Boumedienne was elected president unopposed. With all parties except the FLN banned from participating, a National Assembly was elected in Feb. 1977.

On the death of the president in Dec. 1978 the Revolutionary Council again took over the government. The Islamic Salvation Front (FIS) was banned in March 1992. The head of state, Mohamed Boudiaf, was assassinated on 29 July 1992, and a campaign of terrorism by fundamentalists has continued to the present day. It is estimated that over 100,000 lives have been lost, although Algeria has emerged from the worst of the war, with most of the guerrilla activity now restricted to the countryside. Unrest among Berbers, Algeria's main ethnic community, erupted into violence in May 2001, resulting in 60 people losing their lives in the Berber region of Kabylie. In March 2002 President Bouteflika agreed to grant the Berber language official status alongside Arabic.

TERRITORY AND POPULATION

Algeria is bounded in the west by Morocco and Western Sahara, southwest by Mauritania and Mali, southeast by Niger, east by Libya and Tunisia, and north by the Mediterranean Sea. It has an area of 2,381,741 sq. km (919,595 sq. miles). Population (census 1998) 29,100,867; density, 12·2 per sq. km. 2005 estimate: 32·85m. In 2003, 58·8% of the population lived in urban areas.

The UN gives a projected population for 2010 of 35·42m.

2·5m. Algerians live in France.

86% of the population speak Arabic, 14% Berber; French is widely spoken. A law of Dec. 1996 made Arabic the sole official language, but in March 2002 Tamazight, the Berber language, was given official status and also made a national language.

The 1998 census populations of the 48 *wilayat* (provincial councils) were as follows:

Adrar	311,615	Mila	674,480
Ain Defla	660,342	Mostaganem	631,057
Ain Témouchent	327,331	M'Sila	805,519
Al-Jaza'ir (Algiers)	2,562,428	Naâma	127,314
Annaba	557,818	Ouahran (Oran)	1,213,839
Batna	962,623	Ouargla	445,619
al-Bayadh	168,789	al-Oued	504,401
Béchar	225,546	Oum al-Bouaghi	519,170
Béjaia	856,840	Qacentina (Constantine)	810,914
Biskra	575,858	Relizane	642,205
Blida	784,283	Saida	279,526
Bordj Bou Arreridj	555,402	Sétif	1,311,413
Bouira	629,560	Sidi-bel-Abbès	525,632
Boumerdes	647,389	Skikda	786,154
Chlef	858,695	Souk Ahras	367,455
Djelfa	797,706	Tamanrasset	137,175
Ghardaia	300,516	at-Tarf	352,588
Guelma	430,000	Tébessa	549,066
Illizi	34,108	Tiaret	725,853
Jijel	573,208	Tindouf	27,060[1]
Khenchela	327,917	Tipaza	506,053
Laghouat	317,125	Tissemsilt	264,240
Mascara	676,192	Tizi-Ouzou	1,108,708
Médéa	802,078	Tlemcen	842,053

[1]Excluding Saharawi refugees in camps.

The capital is Algiers (1998 population, 1,519,570). Other major towns (with 1998 census populations): Oran, 655,852; Constantine, 462,187; Batna, 242,514; Annaba, 215,083; Sétif, 211,859; Sidi-bel-Abbès, 180,260; Biskra, 170,956; Djelfa, 154,265; Tébassa, 153,246; Blida, 153,083; Skikda, 152,335; Béjaia, 147,076; Tiaret, 145,332; Chlef, 133,874; al-Buni, 133,471; Béchar, 131,010.

SOCIAL STATISTICS

2001 estimates: births, 618,000; deaths, 129,000; marriages, 194,273. Rates (2001 estimates): births, 20·1 per 1,000; deaths, 4·2 per 1,000. Infant mortality in 2001 was 39 per 1,000 live births. Expectation of life (2003), 72·4 years for females and 69·8 years for males. Annual population growth rate, 1992–2002, 1·8%. Fertility rate, 2001, 2·9 births per woman.

CLIMATE

Coastal areas have a warm temperate climate, with most rain in winter, which is mild, while summers are hot and dry. Inland, conditions become more arid beyond the Atlas Mountains. Algiers, Jan. 54°F (12.2°C), July 76°F (24.4°C). Annual rainfall 30" (762 mm). Biskra, Jan. 52°F (11.1°C), July 93°F (33.9°C). Annual rainfall 6" (158 mm). Oran, Jan. 54°F (12.2°C), July 76°F (24.4°C). Annual rainfall 15" (376 mm).

CONSTITUTION AND GOVERNMENT

A referendum was held on 28 Nov. 1996. The electorate was 16,434,527; turnout was 79·6%. The electorate approved by 85·8% of votes cast a new Constitution which defines the fundamental components of the Algerian people as Islam, Arab identity and Berber identity. It was signed into law on 7 Dec. 1996. Political parties are permitted, but not if based on a separatist feature such as race, religion, sex, language or region. The terms of office of the President are limited to two, but the President's powers of nomination are widened (General-Secretary of the government, governor of the national bank, judges, chiefs of security organs and prefects). Parliament is bicameral: a 389-member *National Assembly* elected by direct universal suffrage using proportional representation, and a 144-member *Council of the Nation*, one-third nominated by the President and two-thirds indirectly elected by the 48 local authorities. The Council of the Nation debates bills passed by the National Assembly which become law if a three-quarters majority is in favour.

In a referendum on 16 Sept. 1999 voters were asked 'Do you agree with the president's approach to restore peace and civilian concord?' Turnout was 85·1% and 98·6% of the votes cast were in favour.

National Anthem

'Qassaman bin nazilat Il-mahiqat' ('We swear by the lightning that destroys'); words by M. Zakaria, tune by Mohamed Fawzi.

GOVERNMENT CHRONOLOGY

(FLN = National Liberation Front; PRS = Revolutionary Socialist Party; RND = National Rally for Democracy; n/p = non-partisan)

Heads of State since 1962.

President of the Provisional Executive

1962	FLN	Abderrahmane Farès

Chairman of the National Constituent Assembly

1962	FLN	Ferhat Abbas

President of the Republic

1962–65	FLN	Ahmed Ben Bella

Chairman of the Revolutionary Council

1965–76	military/FLN	Houari Boumedienne

Presidents of the Republic

1976–78	FLN	Houari Boumedienne
1979–92	FLN	Chadli Bendjedid

Chairman of the Constitutional Council

1992	FLN	Abdelmélik Benhabilès

High Council of State (HCE) (collective presidency)

1992	military	Gen. Khaled Nezzar
	FLN	Ali Hussain Kafi
	FLN	Ali Haroun
	n/p	El-Tidjani Haddam

Chairman of the HCE

1992	PRS	Mohamed Boudiaf

High Council of State (HCE) (collective presidency)

1992	n/p	Redha Malek
	military	Gen. Khaled Nezzar
	FLN	Ali Hussain Kafi
	FLN	Ali Haroun
	n/p	El-Tidjani Haddam

Chairman of the HCE

1992–94	FLN	Ali Hussain Kafi

Presidents of the Republic

1994–99	n/p, RND	Liamine Zéroual
1999–	n/p	Abdelaziz Bouteflika

Prime Ministers since 1962.

1962–63	FLN	Ahmed Ben Bella
1979–84	FLN	Mohammed Abdelghani
1984–88	FLN	Abdelhamid Brahimi
1988–89	FLN	Kasdi Merbah
1989–91	FLN	Mouloud Hamrouche
1991–92	FLN	Sid Ahmed Ghozali
1992–93	FLN	Belaid Abdessalam
1993–94	n/p	Redha Malek
1994–95	n/p	Mokdad Sifi
1995–98	n/p, RND	Ahmed Ouyahia
1998–99	n/p	Smail Hamdani
1999–2000	n/p	Ahmed Benbitour
2000–03	FLN	Ali Benflis
2003–	RND	Ahmed Ouyahia

RECENT ELECTIONS

In presidential elections on 8 April 2004 Abdelaziz Bouteflika won a second term of office, gaining 85·0% of the votes cast; Ali Benflis (Front pour la Libération Nationale; FLN—National Liberation Front) received 6·4% of votes cast; Abdallah Djaballah (el-Islah), 5·0%; Said Sadi, 1·9%; Louiza Hanoune, 1·0%; and Fawzi Rebaine, 0·6%. Turnout was 58·1%.

Parliamentary elections were held on 30 May 2002. Prime Minister Ali Benflis' FLN won 199 out of 389 seats with 34·3% of votes cast; the Rassemblement National Démocratique (RND—National Rally for Democracy), 47 seats with 8·2%; el-Islah, 43 with 9·5%; the Movement of the Society for Peace, 38 with 7·0%; and the Workers' Party, 21 with 3·3%. Turnout was 46·2%.

CURRENT ADMINISTRATION

President and Minister of Defence: Abdelaziz Bouteflika; b. 1937 (ind.; sworn in 27 April 1999; re-elected 8 April 2004). In March 2006 the government comprised:

Prime Minister: Ahmed Ouyahia; b. 1952 (RND; appointed 5 May 2003, having previously held office from Dec. 1995 to Dec. 1998).

Minister of State, Personal Representative of the Head of State: Abdelaziz Belkhadem. *Minister of State, Foreign Affairs:* Mohammed Bejaoui. *Minister of State, Interior and Local Communities:* Noureddine Yazid Zerhouni. *Minister of State without Portfolio:* Bouguerra Soltani.

Minister of Agriculture and Rural Development: Saïd Berkat. *Commerce:* El-Hachemi Djaaboub. *Culture:* Khalida Toumi. *Energy and Mines:* Chakib Khelil. *Environment and Land Development:* Chérif Rahmani. *Finance:* Mourad Medelci. *Fisheries and Marine Resources:* Smaïl Mimoune. *Health, Population and Hospital Reform:* Amar Tou. *Higher Education and Scientific Research:* Rachid Harraoubia. *Housing and Urban Planning:* Mohamed Nadir Hamimid. *Industry:* Mahmoud Khoudri. *Justice and Keeper of the Seals:* Tayeb Belaiz. *Labour and Social Security:* Tayeb Louh. *Moudjahidine (War Veterans):* Mohamed Cherif Abbes. *National Education:* Boubekeur Benbouzid. *National Solidarity and Employment:* Djamel Ould Abbas. *Participation and Promotion of Investments:* Abdelhamid Temmar. *Postal Services, and Information and Communication Technologies:* Boudjemaa Haichour. *Public Works:* Omar Ghoul. *Relations with Parliament:* Abdelaziz Ziari. *Religious Affairs:* Bouabdellah Ghlamallah. *Small and Medium-Sized Businesses, and Handicrafts:* Mustapha Benbada. *Tourism:* Nouredine

Moussa. *Transport:* Mohamed Maghlaoui. *Vocational Training:* El-Hadi Khaldi. *Water Resources:* Abdelmalek Sellal. *Youth and Sports:* Yahia Guidoum.

President's Website (Arabic and French only):
http://www.elmouradia.dz

CURRENT LEADERS

Abdelaziz Bouteflika

Position
President

Introduction
Abdelaziz Bouteflika became president in April 1999 following disputed elections, vowing to improve Algeria's weak economy and end civil discord. Improvements in the economy and state reform have since been slow, hindered by the breakdown of relations with his former ally and prime minister, Ali Benflis. However, the significant reduction in Islamist rebel violence following an amnesty in 1999 was a key factor in Bouteflika's re-election in 2004, making him the first Algerian leader to be returned to power in a democratic vote since the country's independence. His proposed charter for peace and national reconciliation was approved in a national referendum in Sept. 2005.

Early Life
Bouteflika was born on 2 March 1937 in Morocco. In 1956 he joined the Armée de Libération Nationale—a wing of the Front de Libération Nationale (FLN; National Liberation Front). Stationed in southern Algeria in 1960, he was involved in secret talks with the French authorities, which eventually led to Algerian independence two years later.

Bouteflika joined the government of Ahmed Ben Bella as minister of youth, sport and tourism and was appointed foreign minister in 1963. He retained the position in the government of Houari Boumedienne. Having failed to secure military support to succeed Boumedienne, he was pushed out of the political mainstream. In 1981 he was charged with corruption and forced into exile for seven years. With the charges dropped, he re-entered Algeria in Jan. 1987.

In Oct. 1988 he protested against human rights violations by government troops against young demonstrators. He rejoined the FLN congress the following year and was elected to the central committee. In Dec. 1998 he announced his intention to contest the presidency. At the elections, he won almost three quarters of the vote after his six opponents all stood down from the race the day before polling, accusing him of vote rigging.

Career in Office
Having become president and commanding army support, Bouteflika declared that his primary aim was to end Algeria's many years of civil unrest. In July 1999 parliament passed the National Harmony Law, which offered an amnesty to all rebels who had not been directly responsible for loss of life. The Islamic Salvation Army declared a ceasefire, although a radical wing—the Armed Islamic Group—continued its campaign along with elements of other groups. A national referendum in Sept. 1999 approved the amnesty scheme, with nearly 99% in favour. Violence continued, but at a greatly reduced rate.

In order to alleviate Algeria's widespread poverty, Bouteflika has pursued the exploitation of the country's large oil and gas reserves. In foreign policy, he has striven to improve relations with Morocco, declaring a period of public mourning on the death of King Hassan in 1999 and leaving the resolution of the thorny question of Western Sahara to the UN (although he opposed proposals for autonomy for the disputed territory made by UN Special Envoy James Baker in 2001, arguing that the envisaged referendum would deprive the Sahrawis of their right to self-determination).

In 2000 he made the first state visit by an Algerian leader to Europe since the civil war. His visit to Paris, although historic, failed to win concessions, such as the resumption of Air France flights to Algiers. However, large debt repayment reductions and visa concessions were promised by the French government.

Violence in Algeria increased in 2001, including car bombs in major urban areas. Bouteflika meanwhile attempted to negotiate with Berber groups after demonstrations in the Kabylie region; the Berber language was given official status but few other political demands were met. Attempts to wipe out the Islamist rebel insurgency increased in 2003. Particular attention was paid to the Salafist Group for Preaching and Combat (GSPC), which had drawn international media attention following the capture of 32 tourists in the Algerian Sahara. Over 150 GSPC rebels were reported killed after raids in northeastern Algeria in Sept. 2003. The following month the GSPC voiced its support for al-Qaeda in jihad against the USA.

Bouteflika's relations with his prime ministers have been turbulent. Ahmed Benbitour, prime minister from Dec. 1999 to Aug. 2000, resigned over divergent attitudes on economic recovery. His successor, Ali Benflis, was a personal friend and the leader of the largest party, the FLN. However, Benflis' reformist agenda was too radical for Bouteflika, who feared violent insurrection. Since Benflis' resignation in May 2003, the two have been at political loggerheads. Bouteflika appointed Ahmed Ouyahia to succeed Benflis.

Benflis refused to support the president's bid for re-election in 2004, instead announcing his own candidacy, supported by the FLN, in Oct. 2003. However, Bouteflika's bid was supported by a coalition of the Rassemblement National Démocratique (RND; National Rally for Democracy), the Islamic Mouvement de la Société pour la Paix (MSP; Movement of the Society for Peace) and also renegade members of the FLN. The elections on 8 April 2004 gave Bouteflika a resounding victory with 85% of the vote in a 58% turn-out—against just 6% for Benflis. International observers declared the elections free and fair, despite opposition claims of electoral fraud. His dramatic win was ascribed to the much improved security situation and a steadily growing economy, even though unemployment remained around 30%.

Bouteflika has pledged to investigate the disappearance of around 7,000 Algerians, allegedly killed or imprisoned by the security forces during the 1990s. Improving relations with the Berber community remains a priority—election disturbances in 2004 were mainly limited to the Berber Kabylie region. He has also promised reform of Algeria's family law, which he describes as unfair to women. In Sept. 2005 his proposed charter for peace and national reconciliation to end 13 years of civil war, envisaging a limited amnesty and compensation for some victims of violence, was approved in a national referendum.

Ahmed Ouyahia

Position
Prime Minister

Introduction
Ahmed Ouyahia was appointed prime minister on 5 May 2003, having previously served as prime minister from Dec. 1995 to Dec. 1998. He is the head of the second largest party, the Rassemblement National Démocratique (RND; National Rally for Democracy). Widely regarded as Bouteflika's *sale boulot* ('dirty work') aide and a hard-line technocrat, he lacks popular support among Algerians largely because of his austere economic restructuring programme. Born in the Berber Kabylie, he has been critical of the government's approach towards Berber rights.

Early Life
Ouyahia was born at Sidi-Aich in the Petite Kabylie of Eastern Algeria in 1952. In 1974, while studying at the École Nationale

d'Administration (ENA) in Algiers, he was recruited by the Sécurité Militaire (SM), then under the control of Noureddine Zerhouni, the present interior minister. After gaining a political sciences diploma from the University of Algiers, Ouyahia worked as an administrator at the presidency until 1979. His subsequent diplomatic training took him to the Algerian embassy in Abidjan from 1981–84 before he joined the permanent mission to the United Nations.

In 1989 he returned to Algeria to head the African department at the foreign ministry until his appointment as ambassador to Mali in Sept. 1992. A year later he joined Redha Malek's government as secretary of state for Maghrebi Co-operation and Affairs.

Career in Office
President Liamine Zéroual appointed Ouyahia prime minister on 31 Dec. 1995. His first term in office was dominated by the implementation of an IMF-sponsored programme for economic reconstruction. The harsh austerity measures taken to reduce inflation and create a free-market economy made him extremely unpopular. About 500,000 people lost their jobs as hundreds of companies went bankrupt, but inflation was reduced to 5% and foreign currency reserves were replenished.

The ongoing civil unrest was a major problem for Ouyahia's administration. In Jan. 1998 he accused Iran, among others, of providing arms and financial backing for Islamist terrorists. He also criticized European countries for allowing extremist groups to operate in their territories. His government made little progress in ending the violence ignited by the military intervention in the 1992 elections.

Ouyahia resigned on 15 Dec. 1998 after widespread criticism of his economic programme. The drop in oil prices at that time was particularly damaging to the Algerian economy, which remains heavily dependent on the sale of oil and gas. Workers in many key services, such as teaching and the postal system, had come out on strike. The parliamentary opposition had also accused him of vote rigging in the previous year's municipal elections. He was replaced by Smail Hamdani.

Ouyahia concentrated on party politics after leaving office. His party—the RND, which had been created in 1997—was deeply divided, partly as a result of resistance to military influence. In Jan. 1999 he usurped Tahar Benbaibeche as secretary general of the party and supported Abdelaziz Bouteflika (seen as the army's choice) in the presidential elections in April 1999.

Prime Minister Ahmed Benbitour's new government was formed in Dec. 1999, with Ouyahia as minister of justice. President Bouteflika used Ouyahia, the only high-ranking minister of state, as a roving ambassador. He was sent to manage the OAU-sponsored peace talks between Ethiopia and Eritrea during their long-running border war, and also took part in the negotiations over Western Sahara in 2000 as a go-between for the Polisario Front and the UN's special representative, James Baker.

As minister of justice, Ouyahia promoted a penal code amendment to curb the freedom of the press in April 2001, provoking condemnation by Reporters sans Frontières, the international press freedom organization. He also cracked down on prison violence, suppressing numerous riots in overcrowded prisons.

The parliamentary elections of May 2002 were a triumph for Prime Minister Ali Benflis' FLN party, relegating the RND to opposition. President Bouteflika placed Ouyahia in Benflis' new cabinet as his personal representative. However, having refused to support the president for the 2004 presidential elections, Benflis was sacked on 5 May 2003. The appointment of Ouyahia as his successor was a particularly controversial decision because the constitution demands that the prime minister be chosen from the majority party in parliament—the FNL.

Bouteflika was re-elected in April 2004 and Ouyahia was confirmed as prime minister in May, with a reform agenda focusing on the justice and education systems, and on women's rights.

DEFENCE
Conscription is for 18 months (six months basic training and 12 months civilian tasks) at the age of 19.

Military expenditure totalled US$2,206m. in 2003 (US$69 per capita), representing 3·4% of GDP.

Army
There are six military regions. The Army had a strength of 120,000 (75,000 conscripts) in 2002. The Ministry of the Interior maintains National Security Forces of 20,000. The Republican Guard numbers 1,200 personnel and the Gendarmerie 60,000. There were in addition legitimate defence groups (self-defence militia and communal guards) numbering around 100,000.

Navy
Naval personnel in 2002 totalled 6,700. The Navy's 28 vessels included two submarines and three frigates. There are naval bases at Algiers, Annaba, Mers el Kebir and Jijel.

Air Force
The Air Force in 2002 had 10,000 personnel, 222 combat aircraft and 63 armed helicopters.

INTERNATIONAL RELATIONS
Algeria is a member of the UN, the African Union, the League of Arab States, Arab Maghreb Union, OPEC, African Development Bank, IOM, OIC and Islamic Development Bank.

ECONOMY
In 2002 agriculture accounted for 10·0% of GDP, industry 52·7% and services 37·3%.

Overview
The Algerian economy is heavily dependent on the sale of oil and gas. Following the collapse of oil prices in 1986 the government negotiated heavy loans that became unmanageable. In 1994 an IMF-sponsored programme for economic reconstruction was implemented. Austerity measures taken to reduce inflation and create a free-market economy successfully lifted the country's debt burden but also generated large-scale unemployment. Privatization policy got off the ground in 1994, as demanded by the IMF, but failed to make significant strides. The economy has achieved growth in every year since 1995, averaging 3·7% annually in the following decade. However, Algeria's economic performance has been disappointing for a developing country with high foreign investment rates. The economy has grown at a more robust pace since 2003 on the back of rising oil prices. With violence confined to remote rural areas, there are signs that citizens are putting the civil war behind them and making productive investments. Foreign companies have stepped up their investments, especially in the hydrocarbons sector. Yet unemployment remains a problem and the government, flush with oil revenues, has increased spending on labour-intensive infrastructure projects in recent years. However, it is feared that economic reform may lose momentum under President Bouteflika.

Currency
The unit of currency is the *Algerian dinar* (DZD) of 100 *centimes*. Foreign exchange reserves were US$21,133m. in June 2002, with gold reserves 5·58m. troy oz. Total money supply was 1,287bn. dinars in March 2002. Inflation rates (based on IMF statistics):

1995	1996	1997	1998	1999	2000	2001	2002	2003	2004
29·8%	18·7%	5·7%	5·0%	2·6%	0·3%	4·2%	1·4%	2·6%	3·6%

The dinar was devalued by 40% in April 1994.

Budget

The fiscal year starts on 1 Jan. In 2002 budgetary central government revenue totalled 1,603,200m. dinars and expenditure 1,097,700m. dinars.

Performance

Real GDP growth rates (based on IMF statistics):

1995	1996	1997	1998	1999	2000	2001	2002	2003	2004
3·8%	3·8%	1·1%	5·1%	3·2%	2·1%	2·6%	4·7%	6·9%	5·2%

Total GDP was US$84·6bn. in 2004.

Banking and Finance

The central bank and bank of issue is the Banque d'Algérie. The *Governor* is Mohammed Laksaci. In 2002 it had total reserves of US$23·5bn. Private banking recommenced in Sept. 1995. In 2002 there were five state-owned commercial banks, four development banks, nine private banks and two foreign banks.

ENERGY AND NATURAL RESOURCES

Environment

Algeria's carbon dioxide emissions from the consumption and flaring of fossil fuels in 2002 were the equivalent of 2·6 tonnes per capita.

Electricity

Installed capacity was 6·8m. kW in 2002 (4·0% is hydro-electric). Production in 2002 was 27·65bn. kWh, with consumption per capita 881 kWh.

Oil and Gas

A law of Nov. 1991 permits foreign companies to acquire up to 49% of known oil and gas reserves. Oil and gas production accounted for 23·2% of GDP in 1994. Oil production in 2003 was 79·0m. tonnes; oil reserves in 2002 totalled 9·2bn. bbls. Production of natural gas in 2002 was 80·4bn. cu. metres (the fifth highest in the world); proven reserves in 2002 were 4,520bn. cu. metres.

Minerals

Output in 2001 (in 1,000 tonnes): gypsum (2000), 1,341; iron ore, 1,291; phosphate rock, 939; salt, 195; zinc, 13·5; lead (1999), 1·2. There are also deposits of mercury, silver, gold, copper, antimony, kaolin, marble, onyx, salt and coal.

Agriculture

Much of the land is unsuitable for agriculture. The northern mountains provide grazing. There were 7·67m. ha. of arable land in 2001 and 0·59m. ha. of permanent crops. 0·56m. ha. were irrigated in 2001. In 1987 the government sold back to the private sector land which had been nationalized on the declaration of independence in 1962; a further 0·5m. ha., expropriated in 1973, were returned to some 30,000 small landowners in 1990. In 2002 the agricultural population was 13·04m. There were 93,700 tractors and 9,250 harvester-threshers in 2001.

The chief crops in 2000 were (in 1,000 tonnes): potatoes, 950; tomatoes, 800; wheat, 800; melons and watermelons, 540; dates, 430; barley, 400; onions, 380; olives, 350; oranges, 310; grapes, 180; chillies and green peppers, 155; carrots, 135.

Livestock, 2000: sheep, 18·2m.; goats, 3·4m.; cattle, 1·65m.; asses, 202,000; camels, 151,000; mules, 72,000; horses, 55,000; chickens, 110m. Livestock products, 2000 (in 1,000 tonnes): poultry meat, 200; lamb and mutton, 170; beef and veal, 117; eggs, 120; cow's milk, 1,000; sheep's milk, 220; goat's milk, 150.

Forestry

Forests covered 2·15m. ha. in 2000, or 0·9% of the total land area. The greater part of the state forests are brushwood, but there are large areas with cork-oak trees, Aleppo pine, evergreen oak and cedar. The dwarf-palm is grown on the plains, alfalfa on the tableland. Timber is cut for firewood and for industrial purposes, and bark for tanning. Timber production in 2003 was 7·52m. cu. metres.

Fisheries

There are extensive fisheries for sardines, anchovies, sprats, tuna and shellfish. The total catch in 2003 amounted to 141,528 tonnes, exclusively from marine waters.

INDUSTRY

Output (in 1,000 tonnes): cement (2001), 8,710; distillate fuel oil (2002), 6,044; residual fuel oil (2002), 5,833; petrol (2002), 1,939; jet fuels (2002), 1,393; crude steel (2000), 842; pig iron (2000), 767; rolled steel (1997), 439; phosphate fertilizers (2001), 254; ammonitrates (1992), 193; concrete bars (1992), 134; steel tubes (2001), 62; bricks (2001), 1,428,000 cu. metres. Production in units: lorries (2001), 2,811 (assembled); tractors (2001), 2,105; TV sets (2001), 245,000.

Labour

In 2000 there were 5,726,000 employed persons. The main areas of activity were: public administration and defence/compulsory social security, 1,773,000; education and other community, social and personal service activities, 933,000; agriculture, hunting, fishing and forestry, 898,000; mining, quarrying and manufacturing, and electricity, gas and water supply, 721,000. By 2001 unemployment was approaching 30%.

INTERNATIONAL TRADE

Foreign debt was US$22,800m. in 2002. Foreign investors are permitted to hold 100% of the equity of companies, and to repatriate all profits.

Imports and Exports

In 2000 imports (c.i.f.) were valued at US$9,152m. and exports (f.o.b.) at US$22,031m. Main import suppliers in 1999 (in US$1m.): France, 2,086; Italy, 907; USA, 770; Germany, 679; Spain, 508. Main export markets (in US$1m.): Italy, 2,942; USA, 1,755; France, 1,719; Spain, 1,329; Netherlands, 1,021. Main imports in 1999 (in US$1m.): machinery and transport equipment, 3,035; food and live animals, 2,222; manufactured goods, 1,667; chemicals and related products, 1,073. Main exports (in US$1m.): petroleum and products, 6,940; gas, 5,227.

COMMUNICATIONS

Roads

There were, in 2002, an estimated 104,000 km of roads including 640 km of motorways. There were approximately 1,651,000 passenger cars (53·9 cars per 1,000 inhabitants) and 984,700 trucks and vans in 2002.

Rail

In 2000 there were 2,888 km of 1,435 mm route (283 km electrified) and 1,085 km of 1,055 mm gauge. The railways carried 7·8m. tonnes of freight and 28·3m. passengers in 2000.

Civil Aviation

The main international airport is at Algiers (Houari Boumedienne), with some international services also using Annaba, Constantine and Oran. The national carrier is the state-owned Air Algérie which in 2003 operated direct flights to Frankfurt, Geneva and London. There were direct international flights in 2003 with other airlines to Barcelona, Cairo, Casablanca, Damascus, İstanbul, Lille, Lyon, Malaga, Marseille, Milan, Montpellier, Munich, Nantes, Nice, Palma de Mallorca, Paris, Rome, Strasbourg, Toulouse, Tripoli and Tunis. In 2001 Houari Boumedienne International Airport handled 3,397,867 passengers (1,871,052 on domestic flights) and 16,191 tonnes of freight. In 1999 scheduled airline traffic of Algerian-based carriers flew 32·2m. km, carrying 2,937,000 passengers (1,663,000 on international flights).

Shipping

In 2001 vessels totalling 118,994,000 GRT entered ports and vessels totalling 119,074,000 GRT cleared. The state shipping line, Compagnie Nationale Algérienne de Navigation, owned 47 vessels in 2001. The merchant shipping fleet totalled 936,000 GRT in 2002, including oil tankers 19,000 GRT.

Telecommunications

In 2002 there were 2,308,000 telephone subscribers, or 73·8 per 1,000 inhabitants, and 242,000 PCs in use (7·7 per 1,000 persons). Mobile phone subscribers numbered 400,000 in 2002. In 2002 there were approximately 500,000 Internet users and 9,700 fax machines.

Postal Services

There were 3,272 post offices in 2002.

SOCIAL INSTITUTIONS

Justice

The judiciary is constitutionally independent. Judges are appointed by the Supreme Council of Magistrature chaired by the President of the Republic. Criminal justice is organized as in France. The Supreme Court is at the same time Council of State and High Court of Appeal. The death penalty is in force for terrorism.

The population in penal institutions in Dec. 2001 was 34,243 (110 per 100,000 of national population).

Education

Adult literacy in 2003 was 69·8% (79·5% among males and 60·1% among females). In 2000–01 there were 46,670 children in pre-primary education. There were 4,720,950 pupils and 169,559 teachers in primary schools in 2000–01 and 2,991,232 pupils (51% female) with 157,725 teachers in secondary schools.

In 1995–96 there were six universities, two universities of science and technology, five university centres, one agronomic institute, one telecommunications institute, one veterinary institute, one school of architecture and town planning and one *école normale supérieure*. In 1996 there were 160,000 university students and 7,947 academic staff.

In 1996 expenditure on education came to 5·1% of GNP and represented 16·4% of total government expenditure.

Health

In 2002 there were 28,642 physicians, 8,662 dentists and 5,198 pharmacists. There were 185 government hospitals, 1,252 health centres, 497 polyclinics and 3,964 care centres in 2000.

Welfare

Welfare payments to 7·4m. beneficiaries on low incomes were introduced in March 1992.

RELIGION

The 1996 Constitution made Islam the state religion, established a consultative *High Islamic Council*, and forbids practices 'contrary to Islamic morality'. Over 99% of the population are Sunni Muslims. There are also around 180,000 Ibadiyah Muslims and 90,000 others. The Armed Islamic Group (GIA) vowed in 1994 to kill 'Jews, Christians and polytheists' in Algeria. Hundreds of foreign nationals, including priests and nuns, have since been killed. Signalling an increasing tolerance amongst the Muslim community, the Missionaries of Africa's house at Ghardaia Oasis was re-opened in 2000.

CULTURE

World Heritage Sites

There are seven UNESCO sites in Algeria: Al Qal'a of Beni Hammad (inscribed in 1980), the 11th century ruined capital of the Hammadid emirs; Tassili n'Ajjer (1982), a group of over 15,000 prehistoric cave drawings; the M'zab Valley (1982), a tenth century community settlement of the Ibadites; Djémila (1982), or Cuicul, a mountainous Roman town; Tipasa (1982), an ancient Carthaginian port; Timgad (1982), a military colony founded by the Roman emperor Trajan in AD 100; the Kasbah of Algiers (1992), the medina of Algiers.

Broadcasting

The state-controlled Radiodiffusion Algérienne and Entreprise Nationale de Télévision broadcast home services in Arabic, Kabyle (Berber) and French, and an external service. There are 18 TV transmitting stations (colour by PAL). There were 7·4m. radio receivers in 2000 and 3·5m. TV sets in 2001.

Press

Algeria had 24 daily newspapers in 1998, with a combined circulation of 796,440.

Tourism

In 2002 there were 988,000 foreign tourists; spending by tourists totalled US$133m.

DIPLOMATIC REPRESENTATIVES

Of Algeria in the United Kingdom (54 Holland Park, London, W11 3RS)
Ambassador: Mohammed Salah Dembri.

Of the United Kingdom in Algeria (Hilton Hotel, Pins Maritimes, El Mohammadia, Algiers 16000)
Ambassador: Andrew Tesoriere.

Of Algeria in the USA (2118 Kalorama Rd, NW, Washington, D.C., 20008)
Ambassador: Amine Kherbi.

Of the USA in Algeria (4 Chemin Cheich Bachir Ibrahimi, Algiers)
Ambassador: Richard W. Erdman.

Of Algeria to the United Nations
Ambassador: Abdallah Baali.

Of Algeria to the European Union
Ambassador: Halim Benattallah.

FURTHER READING

Ageron, C.-R., *Modern Algeria: a History from 1830 to the Present.* London, 1991

Heggoy, A. A. and Crout, R. R., *Historical Dictionary of Algeria.* Metuchen (NJ), 1995

Roberts, Hugh, *The Battlefield: Algeria 1998–2002, Studies in a Broken Polity.* Verso, London, 2003

Ruedy, J., *Modern Algeria: the Origins and Development of a Nation.* Indiana Univ. Press, 1992

Stone, M., *The Agony of Algeria.* Columbia University Press, 1997

Volpi, Frédéric, *Islam and Democracy: The Failure of Dialogue in Algeria, 1998–2001.* Pluto Press, London, 2003

Willis, M., *The Islamist Challenge in Algeria: A Political History.* New York, 1997

National Statistical Office: Office National des Statistiques, 8–10 rue des Moussebilines, Algiers.
Website: http://www.ons.dz

ANDORRA

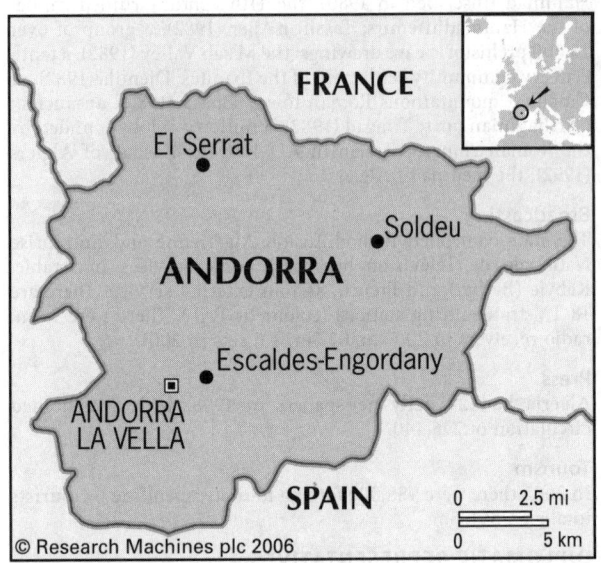

Principat d'Andorra

Capital: Andorra la Vella
Population, 2000: 66,000
GDP per capita: not available

KEY HISTORICAL EVENTS

The Andosini, a tribe subdued by Hannibal in 218 BC, are the first recorded inhabitants of the Pyreneean state of Andorra. In the 9th century the Holy Roman Emperor, Charles II, reputedly made the bishop of Seo de Urgel the overlord of Andorra. The *Paréage* of 1278 placed Andorra under the joint suzerainty of the bishop of Seo de Urgel and the Comte de Foix. The rights vested in the house of Foix passed by marriage to that of Bearn and, on the accession of Henri IV, to the French crown. In the 19th century the *Consell General* (parliament) was strengthened, but the constitution remained traditional and unwritten until 8 Sept. 1993, when political parties and labour unions were legalized and Andorra joined the UN.

TERRITORY AND POPULATION

The co-principality of Andorra is situated in the eastern Pyrenees on the French–Spanish border. The country is mountainous and has an average altitude of 1,996 metres. Area, 464 sq. km. In lieu of a census, a register of population is kept. The estimated population in 2004 was 76,875; density, 166 per sq. km.

In 2003, 93% of the population lived in urban areas.

The chief towns are Andorra la Vella, the capital (estimated population, 22,884 in 2004) and Escaldes-Engordany (16,918). 35·7% of the residential population are Andorran, 37·4% Spanish, 13·0% Portuguese and 6·6% French. Catalan is the official language, but Spanish and French are widely spoken.

SOCIAL STATISTICS

Births in 2001 numbered 777 (rate of 11·6 per 1,000 inhabitants) and deaths 237 (3·6 per 1,000 inhabitants). Life expectancy (2000): male, 89·8 years; female, 91·1 years. Annual population growth rate, 1992–2002, 1·8%. Fertility rate, 2001, 1·3 births per woman.

CLIMATE

Escaldes-Engordany, Jan. 35·8°F (2·1°C), July 65·8°F (18·8°C). Annual rainfall 34·9" (886 mm).

CONSTITUTION AND GOVERNMENT

The joint heads of state are the President of the French Republic and the Bishop of Urgel, the co-princes.

A new democratic constitution was approved by 74·2% of votes cast at a referendum on 14 March 1993. The electorate was 9,123; turnout was 75·7%. The new Constitution, which came into force on 4 May 1993, makes the co-princes a single constitutional monarch and provides for a parliament, the unicameral *General Council of the Valleys*, with 28 members, two from each of the seven parishes and 14 elected by proportional representation from the single national constituency, for four years. In 1982 an *Executive Council* was appointed and legislative and executive powers were separated. The General Council elects the President of the Executive Council, who is the head of the government.

There is a *Constitutional Court* of four members who hold office for eight-year terms, renewable once.

National Anthem

'El Gran Carlemany, mon pare' ('Great Charlemagne, my father'); words by D. J. Benlloch i Vivò, tune by Enric Marfany Bons.

RECENT ELECTIONS

Elections to the General Council were held on 24 April 2005. The Liberal Party of Andorra won 14 seats (41·2% of the vote), the Social Democratic Party 12 (38·1%) and the Andorran Democratic Centre 2 (11·0%). Turnout was 80·4%.

CURRENT ADMINISTRATION

In March 2006 the government comprised:

President, Executive Council: Albert Pintat Santolària; b. 1943 (Liberal Party of Andorra; sworn in 27 May 2005).

Minister for Agriculture: Pere Torres Montellà. *Economy:* Joel Font Coma. *Education:* Roser Bastida Areny. *Finance:* Ferran Mirapeix Lucas. *Foreign Affairs, Culture and Co-operation:* Juli Minoves Triquell. *Health and Social Affairs:* Monserrat Gil Torné. *Housing, Youth, Higher Education and Research:* Meritxell Mateu Pi. *Interior and Justice:* Josep Maria Cabanes Dalmau. *Sports:* Carles Font Rossell. *Territorial Planning:* Manel Pons Pifarré. *Tourism and Environment:* Antoni Puigdellivol Riberaygua.

Government Website (Catalan only): http://www.govern.ad

CURRENT LEADERS

Albert Pintat Santolària

Position
President, Executive Council

Introduction
Albert Pintat became president of the executive council (head of government) following the electoral success of the Liberal Party in April 2005.

Early Life
Albert Pintat Santolària was born in 1943 in Sant Julià de Lòria. He graduated in economics from the Catholic University of Fribourg, Switzerland in 1967.

He was personal secretary to Prime Minister Josep Pintat-Solans from 1984–85. In 1986 he was elected to the country's general council, where he stayed until 1991. He was then ambassador to the Benelux countries and, from 1995, to the European Union. He returned to Andorra in 1997 to take charge of the foreign affairs portfolio in the government of Marc Forné, a post he held until 2001. He was subsequently appointed ambassador to Switzerland and, later, to the UK.

The Liberals won the elections of April 2005, claiming half of the available 28 seats. He was sworn in as president of the executive council on 27 May 2005.

Career in Office
Pintat is expected to pursue a traditional Liberal party centre-right agenda.

INTERNATIONAL RELATIONS

The 1993 Constitution empowers Andorra to conduct its own foreign affairs, with consultation on matters affecting France or Spain.

Andorra is a member of the UN, UNESCO, WIPO, the Council of Europe, the OSCE and the International Organization of the Francophonie.

ECONOMY

Currency
Since 1 Jan. 2002 Andorra has been using the euro. Inflation was 2·8% in 2001, rising to 3·4% in 2002.

Budget
2001: revenue, €234,705,780; expenditure, €250,775,790.

Performance
Real GDP growth was 3·8% in 2000.

Banking and Finance
The banking sector, with its tax-haven status, contributes substantially to the economy. Leading banks include: Andbane-Grup Agricol Reig; Banc Internacional d'Andorra SA; Banca Mora SA; Banca Privada d'Andorra SA; CaixaBank SA; and Crèdit Andorrà.

ENERGY AND NATURAL RESOURCES

Electricity
Installed capacity was 26,500 kW in 2000. Production in 1998 was 116m. kWh. 60% of Andorra's electricity comes from Spain.

Agriculture
In 2001 there were some 1,000 ha. of arable land (2% of total) and 1,000 ha. of permanent crops. Tobacco and potatoes are principal crops. The principal livestock activity is sheep raising.

INDUSTRY

Labour
Only 1% of the workforce is employed in agriculture, the rest in tourism, commerce, services and light industry. Manufacturing consists mainly of cigarettes, cigars and furniture.

INTERNATIONAL TRADE

Imports and Exports
2000 imports, €1,160·0m.; exports, €49·5m. Leading import suppliers (2000): Spain, 48·5%; France, 26·6%. Main export markets (2000): Spain, 60·9%; France, 26·1%. The European Union accounted for 89·2% of imports in 2000 and 92·3% of exports.

COMMUNICATIONS

Roads
In 1994 there were 269 km of roads (198 km paved). Motor vehicles (2000) totalled 60,287, including 46,421 cars and 6,029 trucks and vans.

Civil Aviation
There is an airport at Seo de Urgel.

Telecommunications
In 2000 there were 34,215 telephone main lines, or 519·6 per 1,000 inhabitants. There were 25,099 mobile phone subscribers in Dec.

2000 and 24,500 Internet users in April 2001. In 1998 there were 5,000 fax machines.

SOCIAL INSTITUTIONS

Justice
Justice is administered by the High Council of Justice, comprising five members appointed for single six-year terms. The independence of judges is constitutionally guaranteed. Judicial power is exercised in civil matters in the first instance by Magistrates' Courts and a Judge's Court. Criminal justice is administered by the *Corts*, consisting of the judge of appeal, a general attorney and an attorney nominated for five years alternately by each of the co-princes. There is also a *raonador* (ombudsman) elected by the General Council of the Valleys.

Education
Free education in French- or Spanish-language schools is compulsory: six years primary starting at six years, followed by four years secondary. A Roman Catholic school provides education in Catalan. In 1996–97 there were 18 schools altogether with 8,079 pupils.

Health
In 2004 there was one public hospital; in 2001 there were 175 physicians, 42 dentists, 204 nurses and 64 pharmacists.

RELIGION

The Roman Catholic is the established church, but the 1993 Constitution guarantees religious liberty. In 2001 around 88% of the population were Catholics.

CULTURE

World Heritage Sites
There is one UNESCO site in Andorra: Madriu-Perafita-Claror Valley (entered on the list in 2004).

Broadcasting
Servei de Telecomunicacions d'Andorra relays French and Spanish programmes. Radio Andorra is a commercial public station; Radio Valira is commercial. Number of receivers: radio (2000), 16,000; TV (2001), 36,000. Colour is by PAL.

Press
In 1996 there were three daily newspapers with a combined circulation of 4,000, at a rate of 60 per 1,000 inhabitants.

Tourism
Tourism is the main industry, averaging 11m. visitors a year and accounting for 80% of GDP.

DIPLOMATIC REPRESENTATIVES

Of Andorra in the United Kingdom (63 Westover Rd, London, SW18 2RF)
Ambassador: Vacant.
Chargé d'Affaires a.i.: Maria Rosa Picart de Francis.

Of the United Kingdom in Andorra
Ambassador: Stephen J. L. Wright, CMG (resides in Madrid).

Of Andorra in the USA (2 United Nations Plaza, 25th Floor, N.Y. 10017)
Ambassador: Vacant.
Chargé d'Affaires a.i.: Jelena V. Pia-Comella.

Of USA in Andorra
Ambassador: Eduardo Aguirre, Jr (resides in Madrid).

Of Andorra to the United Nations
Ambassador: Julià Vila Coma.

Of Andorra to the European Union
Ambassador: Meritxell Mateu i Pi.

FURTHER READING

Taylor, Barry, *Andorra*. [Bibliography] ABC-Clio, Oxford and Santa Barbara (CA), 1993.

National Statistical Office: Servie d'Estudis, Ministeri de Finances, c/Doctor Vilanova, núm. 13, Edifici Davi, Esc. c, 5è, Andorra la Vella.

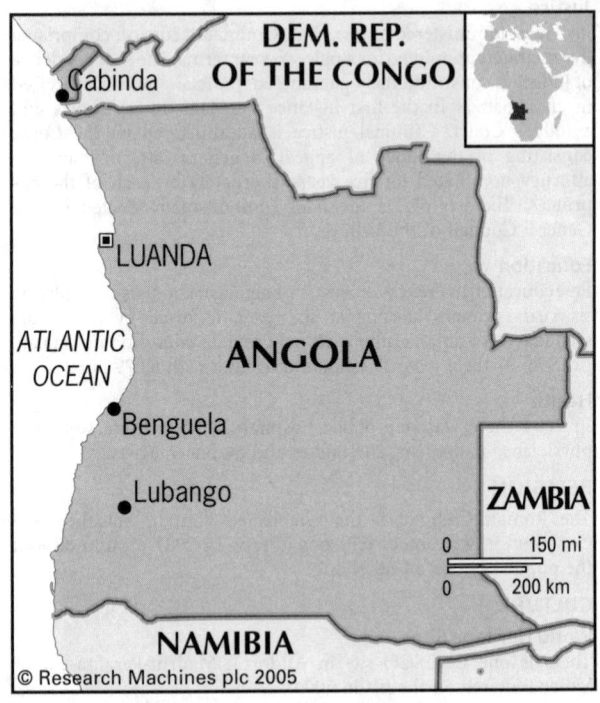

República de Angola

Capital: Luanda
Population projection, 2010: 18·33m.
GDP per capita, 2003: (PPP$) 2,344
HDI/world rank: 0·445/160

KEY HISTORICAL EVENTS

The Portuguese were dominant from the late 19th century. Angola remained a Portuguese colony until 11 June 1951, when it became an Overseas Province of Portugal.

A guerrilla war broke out in 1961 when the People's Movement for the Liberation of Angola launched an offensive to end colonial rule. After the coup d'état in Portugal in April 1974, negotiations with Portugal, the MPLA (Popular Movement for the Liberation of Angola), the FNLA (National Front for the Liberation of Angola) and UNITA (National Union for the Total Liberation of Angola) led to independence on 11 Nov. 1975. The FNLA tried to seize power by force but was driven out of the capital. As independence approached, invasion from the north was combined with a South African invasion in support of UNITA. The MPLA declared independence and subsequently, with the help of Cuban troops, defeated the FNLA in the north and drove the invading South African army out of the country. South African invasions and the occupation of large areas of Angola continued until the signing of the New York Agreement in Dec. 1988, when South Africa agreed to withdraw its forces from Angola and Namibia (and grant independence to Namibia), while Angola and Cuba agreed to the phased withdrawal of Cuban troops.

After abortive attempts to end the conflict with UNITA, a peace agreement was signed on 31 May 1991. A national army was to be formed and multi-party elections held. In Sept. 1992 the MPLA won the elections and José Eduardo dos Santos was re-elected president against UNITA leader Jonas Savimbi. But the latter rejected the election results, withdrew his generals from the unified army and went back to war, seizing an estimated 70% of the country.

On 20 Nov. 1994 a peace agreement was signed in Lusaka, allowing for UNITA to share in government.

In Jan. 1998 Jonas Savimbi, UNITA's leader, met with President dos Santos but talks soon foundered and serious fighting resumed in the north, raising fears of a major new offensive by the Angolan Armed Forces against the UNITA rebels. Meanwhile, Angolan troops fought in the Democratic Republic of the Congo alongside the forces of President Kabila in his efforts to quash a Rwandan-backed rebellion in the east of his country. They remained after the assassination of Kabila in Jan. 2001 but renewed hopes of peace resulted in their withdrawal in Jan. 2002. In Feb. 2002 Jonas Savimbi was killed in fighting with government troops. On 4 April 2002 commanders of the Angolan army and UNITA signed a ceasefire agreement. More than half a million Angolans died in the civil unrest that plagued the country for over a quarter of a century.

TERRITORY AND POPULATION

Angola is bounded in the north by the Republic of the Congo, north and northeast by the Democratic Republic of the Congo, east by Zambia, south by Namibia and west by the Atlantic Ocean. The area is 1,246,600 sq. km (481,324 sq. miles) including the province of Cabinda, an exclave of territory separated by 30 sq. km of the Democratic Republic of the Congo's territory. The population at census, 1970, was 5,646,166, of whom 14% were urban. Estimate, 2005, 15·94m.; density, 12·8 per sq. km. In 2003, 64·3% of the population were living in rural areas. Population figures are rough estimates because the civil war led to huge movements of population. More than 300,000 Angolan refugees have returned to the country since the civil war ended in 2002.

There were 0·3m. Angolan refugees in the Democratic Republic of the Congo, Zambia and the Republic of the Congo in 1995.

The UN gives a projected population for 2010 of 18·33m.

Area, population and chief towns of the provinces:

Province	Area (in sq. km)	Population estimate, 1995 (in 1,000)	Chief town
Bengo	31,371	184	Caxito
Benguela	31,788	702	Benguela
Bié	70,314	1,246	Kuito
Cabinda	7,270	185	Cabinda
Cunene	88,342	245	Ondjiva
Huambo	34,274	1,687	Huambo
Huíla	75,002	948	Lubango
Kuando-Kubango	199,049	137	Menongue
Kwanza Norte	24,110	412	Ndalatando
Kwanza Sul	55,660	688	Sumbe
Luanda	2,418	2,002	Luanda
Lunda Norte	102,783	311	Lucapa
Lunda Sul	56,985	160	Saurimo
Malanje	87,246	975	Malanje
Moxico	223,023	349	Luena
Namibe	58,137	135	Namibe
Uíge	58,698	948	Uíge
Zaire	40,130	247	Mbanza Congo

The most important towns are Luanda, the capital (2000 population, 2·34m.), Huambo, Lobito, Benguela, Kuito, Lubango, Malanje and Namibe.

The main ethnic groups are Umbundo (Ovimbundo), Kimbundo, Bakongo, Chokwe, Ganguela, Luvale and Kwanyama.

Portuguese is the official language. Bantu and other African languages are also spoken.

SOCIAL STATISTICS

Life expectancy at birth, 2003, 39·3 years for males and 42·3 years for females. 2001 births (estimates), 656,000; deaths, 246,000. Estimated birth rate in 2001 was 51·2 per 1,000 population; estimated death rate, 19·2. Annual population growth rate, 1992–2002, 2·9%. Fertility rate, 2001, 7·2 births per woman; infant mortality, 2001, 154 per 1,000 live births. Angola has one of the highest rates of child mortality in the world, at nearly 300 deaths among children under five per 1,000 live births in 1999.

CLIMATE

The climate is tropical, with low rainfall in the west but increasing inland. Temperatures are constant over the year and most rain falls in March and April. Luanda, Jan. 78°F (25·6°C), July 69°F (20·6°C). Annual rainfall 13" (323 mm). Lobito, Jan. 77°F (25°C), July 68°F (20°C). Annual rainfall 14" (353 mm).

CONSTITUTION AND GOVERNMENT

Under the Constitution adopted at independence, the sole legal party was the MPLA. In Dec. 1990, however, the MPLA announced that the Constitution would be revised to permit opposition parties. The supreme organ of state is the 220-member *National Assembly*. There is an executive *President* elected for renewable terms of five years, who appoints a *Council of Ministers*.

In Dec. 2002 Angola's ruling party and the UNITA party of former rebels agreed on a new constitution. The president would keep key powers, including the power to name and to remove the prime minister. The president will also appoint provincial governors, rather than letting voters elect them, but the governor must be from the party that received a majority of votes in that province. A draft constitution was submitted to the constitutional commission of the Angolan parliament for consideration in Jan. 2004 but it has yet to be adopted.

National Anthem

'O Pátria, nunca mais esqueceremos' ('Oh Fatherland, never shall we forget'); words by M. R. Alves Monteiro, tune by R. A. Dias Mingas.

GOVERNMENT CHRONOLOGY

Presidents since 1975. (MPLA = Popular Movement for the Liberation of Angola)

1975–79	MPLA	António Agostinho Neto
1979–	MPLA	José Eduardo dos Santos

RECENT ELECTIONS

At the presidential and parliamentary elections of 29–30 Sept. 1992 the electorate was 4,862,748. Turnout was about 90%. José Eduardo dos Santos (MPLA) was re-elected as president with 49·5% of votes cast against 40·5% for his single opponent, Jonas Savimbi (UNITA). The latter refused to accept the result. The MPLA gained 129 seats in the National Assembly with 53·7% of votes cast, and UNITA 77 with 34·1%. Ten other parties gained six seats or fewer.

On 11 April 1997 a Government of National Unity was installed, with three ministerial posts going to UNITA. Jonas Savimbi, UNITA's leader, received the specially created position of Chief of the Principal Opposition Party.

Presidential and parliamentary elections may take place in late 2006.

CURRENT ADMINISTRATION

President: José Eduardo dos Santos; b. 1943 (MPLA; since 10 Sept. 1979; re-elected 9 Dec. 1985 and 29–30 Sept. 1992).

Prime Minister: Fernando da Piedade Dias dos Santos 'Nando'; b. 1952 (MPLA; since 6 Dec. 2002).

In March 2006 the government comprised:

Minister for Agriculture and Rural Development: Gilberto Lutucuta. *Assistance and Social Reintegration:* João Kussumua. *Commerce:* Joaquim Ekuma Muafumua. *Culture:* Boaventura Cardoso. *Education:* António Burity da Silva Neto. *Energy and Water:* José Maria Botelho de Vasconcelos. *Environment and Urban Development:* Diakunpuna Sita José. *External Relations:* João Bernardo de Miranda. *Family and Women's Affairs:* Cândida Celeste da Silva. *Finance:* José Pedro de Morais. *Fisheries:* Salomão Luheto Xirimbimbi. *Geology and Mines:* Manuel António Africano. *Health:* Sebastião Sapuile Veloso. *Hotels and Tourism:* Eduardo Jonatão Chingungi. *Industry:* Joaquim Duarte da Costa David. *Information:* Pedro Hendrik Vaal Neto. *Interior:* Roberto Leal Monteiro. *Justice:* Manuel da Costa Aragão. *National Defence:* Kundy Paihama. *Oil:* Desidério da Graça Veríssimo e Costa. *Planning:* Ana Dias Lourenço. *Posts and Telecommunications:* Licínio Tavares Ribeiro. *Public Administration, Employment and Social Welfare:* António Domingos Pitra da Costa Neto. *Public Works:* Francisco Higino Carneiro. *Science and Technology:* João Baptista Ngandagina. *Territorial Administration:* Virgílio Fontes Pereira. *Transport:* André Luís Brandão. *War Veterans:* Pedro José Van-Dúnem. *Youth and Sports:* José Marcos Barrica.

Government Website: http://www.angola.org

CURRENT LEADERS

José Eduardo dos Santos

Position
President

Introduction
José Eduardo dos Santos, one of Africa's longest-serving leaders, has been president of Angola since the death of the country's first post-colonial president Agostinho Neto in 1979. He is also head of the ruling Movimento Popular de Libertação de Angola (MPLA; Popular Movement for the Liberation of Angola), and was prime minister from 1999–2002. He has said that he will stand down at the next elections, which can take place when Angola recovers sufficiently from the years of civil war with UNITA rebels led by Jonas Savimbi.

Early Life
Dos Santos was born on 28 Aug. 1942 in Luanda. In 1961 he joined Neto's MPLA rebel movement, fighting for Angolan independence. The movement was forced into exile in neighbouring Zaïre (now the Democratic Republic of the Congo). As his party standing increased, dos Santos founded the MPLA youth movement before being sent to Moscow to study telecommunications and petroleum engineering. He returned to fight for Angolan independence, which finally came in 1975. Under Neto's presidency, dos Santos served first as prime minister (1975–78) and then planning minister (1978–79). After Neto's death in Sept 1979, dos Santos assumed the leadership as Angola's second post-independence president.

Career in Office
During the first ten years dos Santos upheld the MPLA's traditional Marxist doctrine and the government's single party rule while continuing the war against the UNITA rebels begun under his predecessor. The government received Cuban military help in the conflict and the Soviet Union supplied funds. The USA and South Africa meanwhile backed UNITA's leader Jonas Savimbi.

A rapprochement began in 1988 when both Cuba and South Africa withdrew their forces. In 1990, following the collapse of communism, dos Santos moved away from Marxism to adopt 'democratic socialism'. This allowed for the introduction of a free market economy and multi-party elections. The following year, a peace agreement signed in Lisbon culminated in Angola's first nationwide elections in 1992. In a turnout of 91% of registered voters, the MPLA won 54% compared to UNITA's 34%. In the presidential poll dos Santos secured 49·6%, while Savimbi polled 40·7%. Before a second round run-off, Savimbi rejected the election, claiming the first round results had been fraudulent. The civil war resumed and elections scheduled for 1997 were postponed indefinitely.

Attempts to resolve the conflict through amnesties, military action and peace talks all failed. In 1999 dos Santos assumed the role of prime minister and took over control of the armed forces. In Feb. 2002 Savimbi was killed by government soldiers and two months later a ceasefire was signed between the government and the rebels. In 2001 dos Santos announced his intention to step down from the presidency at the next elections, although these will not take place until there is free movement of people and goods in the country and the many Angolans displaced by the conflict have returned home.

DEFENCE
Conscription is for two years. Angola has one of the worst records in terms of child soldier conscription in the world. Defence expenditure totalled US$750m. in 2003 (US$55 per capita), representing 5·7% of GDP.

Army
In 2002 the Army had 35 regiments. Total strength was estimated at 90,000. In addition the paramilitary Rapid Reaction Police numbered 10,000.

Navy
Naval personnel in 2002 totalled about 4,000 with seven operational vessels. There is a naval base at Luanda.

Air Force
The Angolan People's Air Force (FAPA) was formed in 1976 and has about 6,000 personnel. Since the elections in 1992 and the relative calm, the Air Force has been run down and serviceability of combat aircraft is low. In 2002 there were 85 combat aircraft and 40 armed helicopters.

INTERNATIONAL RELATIONS
Angola is a member of the UN, WTO, the African Union, African Development Bank, COMESA, SADC, IOM and is an ACP member state of the ACP-EU relationship.

ECONOMY
In 2002 agriculture accounted for 8·1% of GDP, industry 65·2% and services 26·7%.

Overview
Reforms are under way to introduce a market economy and restore private property. In April 2000 Angola signed a far-reaching agreement with the International Monetary Fund which stipulates economic reforms. In July 2000 the World Bank also signed an agreement approving a series of reforms in return for help with the country's huge foreign debt.

Currency
The unit of currency is the *kwanza* (AOA), introduced in Dec. 1999, replacing the *readjusted kwanza* at a rate of 1 kwanza = 1m. readjusted kwanzas. Foreign exchange reserves were US$902m. in June 2002. Gold reserves were 46,500 troy oz in 1990. Inflation was 4,146% in 1996. It has slowed since then, and in 2004 was 43·6%. However, only Zimbabwe and the Dominican Republic had higher annual inflation rates in 2004.

Budget
Revenues in 2001 were KZr88·9bn. and expenditures KZr96·7bn.

Performance
Total GDP was US$20·1bn. in 2004. The civil war meant GDP growth in 1993 was negative, at –24·0%, but a recovery followed and in 2003 and 2004 it was 3·4% and 11·1% respectively, mainly thanks to booming diamond exports and post-war rebuilding. Angola's 14·4% growth in 2002 was among the highest in the world for the year.

Banking and Finance
The Banco Nacional de Angola is the central bank and bank of issue (*Governor*, Amadeu Mauricio). All banks were state-owned until the sector was re-opened to commercial competition in 1991. In 2002 there were three commercial banks, one development bank, one investment bank and three foreign banks.

Angola received US$1·8bn. in foreign direct investment in 2000, approximately 90% of which was in the oil sector.

ENERGY AND NATURAL RESOURCES
Environment
In 2002 Angola's carbon dioxide emissions from the consumption and flaring of fossil fuels were the equivalent of 1·2 tonnes per capita.

Electricity
Installed capacity was 0·5m. kW in 2000. Production in 2000 was 1·45bn. kWh, with consumption per capita 110 kWh.

Oil and Gas
Oil is produced mainly offshore and in the Cabinda exclave. Oil production and supporting activities contribute some 45% of Angolan GDP and provide the government with approximately US$3·5bn. annually. The oil industry is expected to invest US$3·5bn. a year in offshore Angola in the early part of the 21st century. There are plans for a new US$3·3bn. oil refinery near Lobito which is scheduled to be completed by 2010. Only Nigeria among sub-Saharan African countries produces more oil. It is believed that there are huge oil resources yet to be discovered. Proven crude petroleum reserves in 2002 were 6bn. bbls. Total production (2003) 43·6m. tonnes. Natural gas reserves (2002) 113bn. cu. metres; production, 2000, 565m. cu. metres.

Minerals
Mineral production in Angola is dominated by diamonds and 90% of all workers in the mining sector work in the diamond industry. Production in 2002 totalled 6·0m. carats. Angola has billions of dollars worth of unexploited diamond fields. In 2000 the government regained control of the nation's richest diamond provinces from UNITA rebels. Other minerals produced (2001) include granite, 1·5m. cu. metres; marble, 100,000 cu. metres; salt, 30,000 tonnes. Iron ore, phosphate, manganese and copper deposits exist.

Agriculture
In 2001 there were 3·0m. ha. of arable land and 0·3m. ha. of permanent crops. 75,000 ha. were irrigated in 2001. The agricultural population in 2002 was 8·50m., of whom 4·29m. were economically active. Although more than 70% of the economically active population are engaged in agriculture it only accounts for 8% of GDP. There were 10,300 tractors in 2001. Principal crops (with 2000 production, in 1,000 tonnes): cassava (3,130); maize (428); sugarcane (330); bananas (290); sweet potatoes (182); millet (102); citrus fruits (75); dry beans (68).

Livestock (2000): 4·0m. cattle, 350,000 sheep, 2·15m. goats, 800,000 pigs.

Forestry
In 2000, 69·76m. ha., or 56·0% of the total land area, was covered by forests, including mahogany and other hardwoods. Timber production in 2001 was 4·36m. cu. metres.

Fisheries

Total catch in 2001 came to 252,518 tonnes, mainly from sea fishing.

INDUSTRY

The principal manufacturing branches are foodstuffs, textiles and oil refining. Output, 2000 (in 1,000 tonnes): residual fuel oil, 595; distillate fuel oil, 558; cement (1997), 301; jet fuels, 295; flour (1998), 172; petrol, 111; beer (2003), 160m. litres; 33,000 TV sets (1992); 29,000 radio sets (1992).

Labour

In 1996 the total labour force numbered 5,144,000 (54% males).

INTERNATIONAL TRADE

In 2002 total foreign debt was US$10,134m.

Imports and Exports

Imports and exports for calendar years in US$1m.:

	2000	2001	2002	2003	2004
Imports (f.o.b.)	3,039	3,179	3,760	5,480	5,832
Exports (f.o.b.)	7,921	6,534	8,328	9,508	13,475

Main exports, 2001 (in US$1m.): crude oil, 5,690; diamonds, 689; refined oil products, 93. Chief import suppliers (1999): Portugal (18·8%); USA (14·6%); South Africa (11·9%); France (8·2%). Chief export markets (1999): USA (59·5%); China (8·2%); Taiwan (7·7%); Germany (2·4%).

COMMUNICATIONS

Roads

There were, in 2001, 51,429 km of roads (7,944 km highways; 10·4% of all roads surfaced), and in 2002 approximately 109,800 passenger cars and 44,600 commercial vehicles. Many roads remain mined as a result of the civil war; a programme of de-mining and rehabilitation is under way.

Rail

Prior to the civil war there was in excess of 2,900 km of railway (predominantly 1,067 mm gauge track), but much of the network was damaged during the war. However, restoration and redevelopment of the network is now under way, notably the Benguela Railway, linking the port city of Lobito with Huambo in Angola's rich farmlands and neighbouring Democratic Republic of the Congo and Zambia.

Civil Aviation

There is an international airport at Luanda (Fourth of February). The national carrier is Linhas Aéreas de Angola (TAAG), which operated direct flights in 2003 to Johannesburg, Kinshasa, Paris, Pointe-Noire, Rio de Janeiro, São Tomé and Windhoek. There were direct flights in 2003 with other airlines to Addis Ababa, Brussels, Libreville, Lisbon, London and Moscow. In 1999 scheduled airline traffic of Angola-based carriers flew 6·5m. km, carrying 531,000 passengers (120,000 on international flights).

Shipping

There are ports at Luanda, Lobito and Namibe, and oil terminals at Malongo, Lobito and Soyo. In 2002 the merchant fleet totalled 55,000 GRT, including oil tankers 3,000 GRT.

Telecommunications

There were 215,000 telephone subscribers in 2002, or 15·4 per 1,000 inhabitants. It is intended to privatize Angola Telecom, although no date has been set. In 2002 there were 130,000 mobile phone subscribers and 27,000 PCs were in use. In 2002 there were 41,000 Internet users.

Postal Services

In 2003 there were 55 post offices, or one for every 248,000 persons.

SOCIAL INSTITUTIONS

Justice

The Supreme Court and Court of Appeal are in Luanda. The death penalty was abolished in 1992. In 2002–03 the US government's Agency for International Development assisted in the modernization of the judicial system. Measures including the introduction of a court case numbering system were intended to reduce legal costs and attract foreign investment.

The population in penal institutions in 2002 was 4,975 (36 per 100,000 of national population).

Education

The education system provides three levels of general education totalling eight years, followed by schools for technical training, teacher training or pre-university studies. In 2000–01 there were 1,178,485 pupils and 33,478 teachers at primary schools, 399,712 pupils and 19,798 teachers at secondary schools and (1999–2000) 7,845 students with 796 academic staff in tertiary education institutions. There is one university. Private schools have been permitted since 1991. The University of Luanda has campuses at Luanda, Huambo and Lubango. It had 8,954 students in 1991–92. The adult literacy rate was 66·8% in 2003 (82·1% among males and 53·8% among females).

In 2000–01 expenditure on education came to 3·4% of GNP.

Health

In 1997 there were 736 physicians, 10,942 nurses and 411 midwives. In 1990 there were 266 hospitals and health centres with 11,857 beds. There were 1,339 medical posts.

In 2000 only 38% of the population had access to safe drinking water. In 2000 it was estimated that 60% of the 3·9m. displaced people were suffering from malnutrition.

RELIGION

In 2001 there were 6·44m. Roman Catholics, 1·55m. Protestants and 710,000 African Christians, and most of the remainder follow traditional animist religions. In May 2005 there was one cardinal.

CULTURE

Broadcasting

There were 710,000 TV receivers in Angola in 2001 and 750,000 radio receivers in 2000. The government-controlled Rádio Nacional de Angola broadcasts three programmes and an international service. There are also regional stations. Televisão Popular de Angola transmits from seven stations (colour by PAL).

Press

Angola had five daily newspapers in 1998, with a combined circulation of 133,000. The government daily is the *Jornal de Angola*. The *Diário da República* is the official gazette. There is an independent weekly, *Agora*, and there are around 100 specialized and independent publications.

Tourism

In 2001 there were 67,000 foreign tourists, bringing revenue of US$22m.

DIPLOMATIC REPRESENTATIVES

Of Angola in the United Kingdom (22 Dorset St., London, W1U 6QY)
Ambassador: Ana Maria Teles Carreira.

Of the United Kingdom in Angola (Rua Diogo Cão 4, Luanda)
Ambassador: Ralph Publicover.

Of Angola in the USA (2108 16th St., NW, Washington, D.C., 20009)
Ambassador: Josefina Pitra Diakite.

Of the USA in Angola (32 rua Houari Boumedienne, Miramar, Luanda)
Ambassador: Cynthia G. Efird.

Of Angola to the United Nations
Ambassador: Ismael Gaspar Martins.

Of Angola to the European Union
Ambassador: Vacant.
Chargé d'Affaires a.i.: Maria Eugénia Feijo de Almeida Ferreira dos Santos.

FURTHER READING

Brittain, Victoria, *Death of Dignity: Angola's Civil War.* Pluto, London, 1999
Guimarães, Fernando Andersen, *The Origins of the Angolan Civil War: Foreign Intervention and Domestic Political Conflict.* Palgrave, Basingstoke, 2001
Hodges, Tony, *Angola From Afro-Stalinism to Petro-Diamond Capitalism.* James Currey, Oxford, 2001
James, W. M., *Political History of the War in Angola.* New York, 1991

National Statistical Office: Instituto Nacional de Estatística, Luanda.

ANTIGUA AND BARBUDA

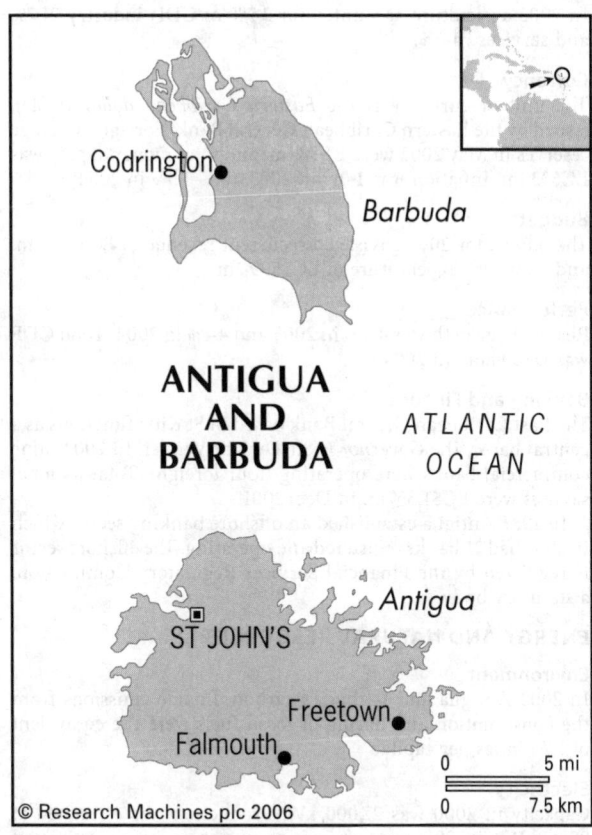

Capital: St John's
Population, 2002: 67,000
GDP per capita, 2003: (PPP$) 10,294
HDI/world rank: 0·797/60

KEY HISTORICAL EVENTS

Antigua and Barbuda were populated by Arawak-speaking people from at least 1000 BC. By 1493, when Colombus passed Antigua, it was occupied by Carib Indians. English settlers arrived in 1632, initially cultivating tobacco for export. Sugar plantations, using African slave labour, appeared during the 1650s. The slave population of Antigua reached a height of about 37,000 in 1774. As British colonies, Antigua and Barbuda formed part of the Leeward Islands Federation from 1871 until 30 June 1956, when they became a separate Crown Colony. This was part of the West Indies Federation from 3 Jan. 1958 until 31 May 1962 and became an Associated State of the UK on 27 Feb. 1967. Antigua and Barbuda gained independence on 1 Nov. 1981.

TERRITORY AND POPULATION

Antigua and Barbuda comprises three islands of the Lesser Antilles situated in the eastern Caribbean with a total land area of 442 sq. km (171 sq. miles); it consists of Antigua (280 sq. km), Barbuda, 40 km to the north (161 sq. km) and uninhabited Redonda, 40 km to the southwest (one sq. km). The population in July 2002 was 67,448 (1,400 on Barbuda); density, 153 per sq. km. In 2003, 62·2% of the population lived in rural areas.

The chief towns are St John's, the capital on Antigua (25,000 inhabitants in 1999) and Codrington (1,400), the only settlement on Barbuda.

English is the official language; local dialects are also spoken.

SOCIAL STATISTICS

Expectation of life, 2003: males, 70·0 years, females, 75·0. Annual population growth rate, 1992–2002, 1·2%. Births, 2000, 1,528; deaths, 2000, 451. Infant mortality in 2001 was 12 per 1,000 live births; fertility rate, 2001, 1·6 births per woman.

CLIMATE

A tropical climate, but drier than most West Indies islands. The hot season is from May to Nov., when rainfall is greater. Mean annual rainfall is 40" (1,000 mm).

CONSTITUTION AND GOVERNMENT

H.M. Queen Elizabeth, as Head of State, is represented by a Governor-General appointed by her on the advice of the Prime Minister. There is a bicameral legislature, comprising a 17-member Senate appointed by the Governor-General and a 17-member House of Representatives elected by universal suffrage for a five-year term. The Governor-General appoints a Prime Minister and, on the latter's advice, other members of the Cabinet.

Barbuda is administered by a nine-member directly-elected council.

National Anthem

'Fair Antigua and Barbuda'; words by N. H. Richards, tune by W. G. Chambers.

RECENT ELECTIONS

At the elections to the House of Representatives of 24 March 2004 the United Progressive Party (UPP) won 12 seats, the Antigua Labour Party (ALP) 4 and the Barbuda People's Movement (BPM) 1.

CURRENT ADMINISTRATION

Governor General: Sir James Beethoven Carlisle, GCMG; b. 1937 (in office since 10 June 1993).

In March 2006 the UPP government comprised:

Prime Minister and Minister of Barbuda Affairs, National Security, Foreign Affairs and International Trade: Baldwin Spencer; b. 1948 (UPP; in office since 24 March 2004).

Minister of Agriculture, Food Production and Marine Affairs: Charlesworth Samuel. Education: Bertrand Joseph. Finance and the Economy: Eroll Cort. Health, Sports and Youth Affairs: John Maginley. Housing, Culture and Social Transformation: Hilson Baptiste. Justice and Legal Affairs: Colin Derrick. Labour, Public Administration and Empowerment: Jacqui Quinn-Leandro. Tourism and Civil Aviation: Harold Lovell. Works and the Environment: Wilmouth Daniel. Attorney General: Justin Simon. Minister without Portfolio: Aziz Hadeed.

Government Website: http://www.ab.gov.ag/gov_v2

CURRENT LEADERS

Baldwin Spencer

Position
Prime Minister

Introduction
Baldwin Spencer is leader of the United Progressive Party (UPP) and took office as prime minister in March 2004, defeating the

Antigua Labour Party (ALP), which had held power continuously since 1976.

Early Life
Baldwin Spencer was born on 8 Oct. 1948 in the ghetto area of Grays Green, Antigua. After attending Greenbay Primary School and Princess Margaret Secondary School, he studied social leadership at St Francis Xavier University's Coady International Institute in Nova Scotia. He also obtained a diploma in labour and economic studies from Ruskin College (based at Oxford in the UK) and in labour and industrial relations from Oslo University.

In the 1970s Spencer worked as a trade unionist, serving as vice-president and, later, assistant general secretary of the Antigua and Barbuda Workers' Union (AWU). He also served as president of the Caribbean Maritime and Aviation Council.

In 1989 Spencer entered parliament as the United Democratic Party (UNDP) representative for St John's Rural West constituency. In 1991 he became leader of the UNDP and, as leader of the opposition in parliament, formed an alliance with the two other main opposition parties, the Antigua Caribbean Liberation Movement and the Progressive Labour Movement. They merged in 1992 to form the UPP.

During the 1990s Spencer regularly accused Prime Minister Vere Bird, Sr and his ALP of corruption. The campaign helped exploit rifts within the government and Bird's own son, Lester Bird, called for his father's resignation. Lester Bird took over as prime minister shortly before the general election of March 2004. Spencer led the UPP into the election promising a more transparent 'Sunshine Government'. The UPP won 12 of 17 seats and Spencer was returned as prime minister.

Career in Office
Spencer has vowed to combat corruption, develop tourism and foster economic co-operation with other countries. In the first year of his tenure he introduced legislation to improve government accountability and transparency and took steps to de-politicize the government-owned media. However, progress in corruption investigations has been hampered by the loss of government files and in 2005 Spencer set up a task-force to combat organized crime and corruption among government officials.

In Oct. 2004 an IMF report concluded that Antigua and Barbuda's economy suffered from high levels of public debt and over-reliance on the government for jobs (accounting for 40% of total employment). Spencer responded in June 2005 by launching a drive to expand the tourism industry. He has pursued closer ties with Brazil, China, India, Russia and neighbouring Caribbean countries. He also warned of a tougher approach to government-employed workers, prompting fears of a run-in with the union movement he helped to build. In 2004 Spencer served as chair of CARICOM.

DEFENCE
The Antigua and Barbuda Defence Force numbers 170. There are some 75 reserves. A coastguard service has been formed.

In 2003 defence expenditure totalled US$4m. (US$56 per capita), representing 0·6% of GDP.

Army
The strength of the Army section of the Defence Force was 125 in 2002.

Navy
There was a naval force of 45 operating three patrol craft in 2002.

INTERNATIONAL RELATIONS
Antigua and Barbuda is a member of the UN, the World Bank, ILO, IMO, IMF, UNESCO, WHO, WIPO, WTO, the Commonwealth, OAS, ACS, CARICOM, OECS and is an ACP member state of the ACP-EU relationship.

ECONOMY
In 2002 agriculture accounted for 3·7% of GDP, industry 21·7% and services 74·6%.

Currency
The unit of currency is the *Eastern Caribbean dollar* (ECD), issued by the Eastern Caribbean Central Bank. Foreign exchange reserves in May 2002 were US$84m. and total money supply was EC$334m. Inflation was 1·0% in 2003 and –1·3% in 2004.

Budget
The budget for 2002 envisaged recurrent revenue of EC$571·1m. and recurrent expenditure of EC$599·2m.

Performance
Real GDP growth was 4·9% in 2003 and 4·1% in 2004. Total GDP was US$0·8bn. in 2004.

Banking and Finance
The East Caribbean Central Bank based in St Kitts functions as a central bank. The *Governor* is Sir Dwight Venner. In 2002, nine commercial banks were operating (four foreign). Total national savings were EC$1,357m. in Dec. 2001.

In 1981 Antigua established an offshore banking sector which in 2002 had 21 banks registered and operating. The offshore sector is regulated by the Financial Services Regulatory Commission, a statutory body.

ENERGY AND NATURAL RESOURCES
Environment
In 2002 Antigua and Barbuda's carbon dioxide emissions from the consumption and flaring of fossil fuels were the equivalent of 7·7 tonnes per capita.

Electricity
Capacity in 2000 was 27,000 kW. Production was estimated at 99m. kWh in 2000 and consumption per capita an estimated 1,523 kWh.

Water
There is a desalination plant with a capacity of 0·6m. gallons per day, sufficient to meet the needs of the country.

Agriculture
In 2001 there were 8,000 ha. of arable land and 2,000 ha. of permanent crops. Cotton and fruits are the main crops. Production (2000) of fruits, 8,000 tonnes (notably melons and mangoes).

Livestock (2000): cattle, 16,000; pigs, 2,000; sheep, 12,000; goats, 12,000.

Forestry
Forests covered 9,000 ha., or 20·5% of the total land area, in 2000.

Fisheries
Total catch in 2001 came to approximately 1,583 tonnes, exclusively from sea fishing.

INDUSTRY
Manufactures include beer, cement, toilet tissue, stoves, refrigerators, blenders, fans, garments and rum (molasses imported from Guyana).

Labour
The unemployment rate in 1998 was the lowest in the Caribbean, at 4·5%. Between 1994 and 1998, 2,543 jobs were created. The average annual salary in 1998 was US$8,345 per head of population.

INTERNATIONAL TRADE

Imports and Exports
Imports in 2002 were estimated at US$336m. and exports US$45m. The main trading partners were CARICOM, the USA, the UK and Canada.

COMMUNICATIONS

Roads
In 1995 there were 384 km of main roads, 164 km of secondary roads, 320 km of rural roads and 293 km of other roads. 23,700 passenger cars and 5,200 commercial vehicles were in use in 2002. More than EC$64m. was spent to rebuild major roads and highways in the three years following damage caused by hurricanes Luis and Marilyn in 1995.

Civil Aviation
V. C. Bird International Airport is near St John's. There were flights in 2003 to Anguilla, Barbados, Dominica, Dominican Republic, Georgetown, Grenada, Kingston, London, Milan, Montego Bay, New York, Paris, Philadelphia, Puerto Rico, St Croix, St Kitts and Nevis, St Lucia, St Vincent, Tampa, Toronto, Trinidad and Tobago and the British and US Virgin Islands. A domestic flight links the airports on Antigua and Barbuda.

Shipping
The main port is St John's Harbour. The merchant shipping fleet of 762 vessels totalled 4,541,940 GRT in Dec. 2001. In 1997 vessels totalling 94,907,000 NRT entered ports and vessels totalling 667,126,000 NRT cleared.

Telecommunications
There were 62,300 main telephone subscribers in 2001, or 804·2 per 1,000 inhabitants. There is a mobile phone system, with 38,200 subscribers in 2002. There were 10,000 Internet users in 2002.

Postal Services
The main post office is located in St John's. In 2003 there were 13 post offices in total.

SOCIAL INSTITUTIONS

Justice
Law is based on UK common law as exercised by the Eastern Caribbean Supreme Court (ECSC) on St Lucia. There are Magistrates' Courts and a Court of Summary Jurisdiction. Appeals lie to the Court of Appeal of ECSC, or ultimately to the UK Privy Council. Antigua and Barbuda was one of ten countries to sign an agreement in Feb. 2001 establishing a Caribbean Court of Justice to replace the British Privy Council as the highest civil and criminal court. In the meantime the number of signatories has risen to twelve. The court was inaugurated at Port-of-Spain, Trinidad on 16 April 2005.

The population in penal institutions in Jan. 2005 was 184 (equivalent to 269 per 100,000 of national population).

Education
Adult literacy was 95% in 1998. In 1999–2000 there were 13,025 pupils and 695 teachers at primary schools, and 5,276 pupils and 394 teachers at secondary schools. In 1992–93 there were 72 government primary and secondary schools. Other schools were run by religious organizations. The Antigua State College offers technical and teacher training. Antigua is a partner in the regional University of the West Indies.

In 1999–2000 expenditure on education came to 3·5% of GNP.

Health
There is one general hospital, a private clinic, seven health centres and 17 associated clinics. A new medical centre at Mount St John's is set to open during 2006. In 1996 there were 75 physicians, 12 dentists, 187 nurses and 13 pharmacists.

Welfare
The state operates a Medical Benefits Scheme providing free medical attention, and a Social Security Scheme, providing age and disability pensions and sickness benefits.

RELIGION
In 2001 there were 30,000 Protestants, 23,000 Anglicans and 8,000 Roman Catholics.

CULTURE

Broadcasting
Radio and television services are provided by the government-owned Antigua and Barbuda Broadcasting Service (ABS). Other radio and/or TV stations are Observer Radio, Caribbean Radio Lighthouse (Baptist Mission), Radio ZDK (commercial), Caribbean Relay (BBC and Deutsche Welle), CTV Entertainment Systems (12 US cable channels). In 2000 there were 36,000 radios and, in 1998, 31,000 TV receivers.

Press
The main newspapers are The Antigua Sun and The Daily Observer. The Outlet Newspaper, the National Informer and the Worker's Voice are published weekly. The Chamber of Commerce has a monthly publication.

Tourism
Tourism is the main industry, contributing about 70% of GDP and 80% of foreign exchange earnings and related activities. In 2001 there were 193,126 staying visitors and 429,406 cruise ship arrivals. Income from tourism amounted to US$272m. in 2001.

Festivals
Of particular interest are the International Sailing Week (April–May); Annual Tennis Championship (May); Mid-Summer Carnival (July–Aug.).

Museums and Galleries
The main attractions are the Museum of Antigua and Barbuda; Coates Cottage; Aiton Place; Harmony Hall; Cedars Pottery; SOFA (Sculpture Objects Functional Art); Pigeon Point Pottery; Harbour Art Gallery; Nelson's Dockyard; Shirley Heights.

DIPLOMATIC REPRESENTATIVES
Of Antigua and Barbuda in the United Kingdom (15 Thayer St., London, W1U 3JT)
High Commissioner: Carl Roberts.

Of the United Kingdom in Antigua and Barbuda (Price Waterhouse Centre, 11 Old Parham Rd, St John's, Antigua)
High Commissioner: Duncan Taylor (resides in Bridgetown, Barbados).

Of Antigua and Barbuda in the USA (3216 New Mexico Ave., NW, Washington, D.C., 20016)
Ambassador: Deborah Mae Lovell.

Of the USA in Antigua and Barbuda
Ambassador: Mary E. Kramer (resides in Bridgetown, Barbados).

Of Antigua and Barbuda to the United Nations
Ambassador: John W. Ashe.

Of Antigua and Barbuda to the European Union
Ambassador: Vacant.

FURTHER READING
Berleant-Schiller, Riva, *et al.*, *Antigua and Barbuda.* [Bibliography] ABC-Clio, Oxford and Santa Barbara (CA), 1995
Nicholson, Desmond, *Antigua, Barbuda and Redonda: A Historical Sketch.* St John's, 1991

ARGENTINA

© Research Machines plc 2006

República Argentina

Capital: Buenos Aires
Population projection, 2010: 40·74m.
GDP per capita, 2003: (PPP$) 12,106
HDI/world rank: 0·863/34

KEY HISTORICAL EVENTS

Before European colonization two main indigenous American groups and numerous nomadic tribes peopled the region that is now Argentina, probably constituting a population of some 300,000. Both groups—the Diaguita people in the northwest, and the Guarani people in the south and east—created the basis for a permanent agricultural civilization. The Diaguita also prevented the powerful Inca from expanding their empire from Bolivia into Argentina.

Europeans first came to Argentina in the early 16th century and a series of expeditions and attempts at colonization followed. The explorer Sebastian Cabot established the first Spanish settlement in 1526, abandoned just three years later following attacks by natives. He reported Argentina's natural silver resources, possibly inspiring the name *Argentina* ('of silver'). Ten years later Pedro de Mendoza founded Buenos Aires; however, it was not until its re-establishment in 1580 that the region's indigenous peoples, weakened by European diseases as much as European military campaigns, were finally defeated and Spanish rule established.

Largely neglected as Spain looked instead to the riches of Peru, the majority of settlers in Argentina hailed from the neighbouring colonies of Chile, Peru and Paraguay. Missions established by the Roman Catholic Church played an important part in the colonizing process.

In 1776 Buenos Aires, known throughout the 18th century as a smuggler's haunt, was made a free port at the centre of a viceroyalty comprising Argentina, Uruguay, Paraguay and Bolivia. As trade with Europe became increasingly important, Buenos Aires adopted the ideas of the European enlightenment and was seen as more cosmopolitan than its rivals.

When Spain came under Napoleonic control the British attacked Buenos Aires, first in 1806 and then again in 1807. On both occasions the city was able to repel the invasions without any help from Spanish forces, and the event in part helped to trigger the independence movement. In 1810 the first locally elected government was formed in Buenos Aires where nationalists took advantage of the weakness of the Spanish crown to implement the libertarian principles of the American and French Revolutions.

Independence
Having separated from Paraguay in 1814, Argentina gained its independence from Spain in 1816. Unable to control its outlying regions, it lost Bolivia in 1825 and Uruguay in 1828. During the early years of independence, the country was embroiled in bitter internal struggles between the Unitarists and the Federalists. Unitarists wanted a strong central government, particularly as Britain agreed to recognize Argentinian independence only if it could devise a government representing the whole country. Federalists, on the other hand, advocated regional control, as each province had formed its own political regime, based on local interests and reinforced by the leadership of military powers dominant since the war. The two sides were also divided on the power to be concentrated on the country's capital, Buenos Aires.

In 1827 Argentinians joined forces with Uruguay to repel a Brazilian invasion, thereby securing independence for Uruguay and encouraging Argentinian unification. From 1835–52, the Federalists held power under Gen. Juan Manuel de Rosas, an important landowner and commander of a rural militia. Governor of Buenos Aires from 1829, Rosas proved a formidable leader, who used a secret police force, the Mazorca, to defeat his opponents. He also consolidated church support, compelling priests to display his portrait at the altar.

Rosas' difficulties in foreign policy saw Britain seize the Falkland Islands (Islas Malvinas) in 1833, while Bolivia,

Paraguay and Uruguay continued to isolate the federation. In 1838, following a trade dispute with Uruguay, Argentinian political exiles gained French support in an attempt to overthrow Rosas. But he remained in power until 1853 when he was ousted by Gen. Justo José de Urquiza. The Unitarists were then able to inaugurate a new constitution and achieve a more stable government, although Urquiza's overthrow by Santiago Derquai led to another civil war. An agreement between Urquiza and Gen. Bartolomé Mitre, governor of Buenos Aires, saw a return of stability, and established the city as the seat of government.

The next 50 years saw a steady period of presidential succession along with impressive economic growth. In the period 1862–80 schools were built, public works started, and liberal reforms instituted. From 1865–70 Argentina was also involved in the War of the Triple Alliance, joining with Uruguay and Brazil in a campaign against Paraguay. This ultimately strengthened the newly centralized Argentina, and was seminal in defining the role of the military.

From 1880–86 Argentina thrived under the leadership of Gen. Julio Roca, as agricultural practice was reformed and commerce expanded. A Federalist, Roca nevertheless retained Buenos Aires as the capital. During his second term of office, Roca restored peace with Chile after years of dispute over territory.

Argentina became a magnet for European immigration, putting pressure on the political system to broaden its representation. The immigrants, mainly Italian and Spanish, established the new Socialist, Anarchist and Union Civica Radical parties. This latter group became the main political force and under the leadership of Hipólito Irigoyen won their first presidential election in 1916, following Roque Sáenz Peña's electoral reforms of 1910–14. The conservatives regained power in 1930, supported by the military, and the activities of Radicals were restricted, until Gen. Augustín Pedro Justin, heading a coalition of conservatives, Radicals and independent socialists, was elected in 1931. A succession of leaders within this regime instigated controversial political and economic reforms, resulting in agreements with Britain over trade and a gradual improvement in the economic climate.

Perón

Although Argentina remained neutral at the outbreak of the Second World War, another coup in 1943 brought Gen. Juan Domingo Perón to power. He chose to side with the allies and before the conflict ended declared war on the axis powers.

An extremely strong leader, Perón led a regime that was autocratic but populist, winning presidential elections in 1946 and 1951 with the support of the urban working class that industrialization had created. His political success was reinforced by his second wife Eva Duarte de Perón, 'Evita'. Acting as *de facto* minister of health and labour, she awarded wage increases that led to inflation. In 1952 her death, caused by cancer, combined with Perón's increasing authoritarianism and his excommunication from the church, led to a fall in his popularity. In 1955 a coup by the armed forces sent him into exile.

In 1957 Argentina reverted to the constitution of 1853, and a year later Dr Arturo Frondizi was elected president. With US-promised financial aid, Frondizi attempted to stabilize the economy, but faced heavy criticism from left-wing parties and from the Peronists, the political party that had established itself around the Peróns. Frondizi also fell out of favour with the military, whose intervention continued to inform Argentinian politics throughout the period, despite the establishment of an officially civilian government. After the Peronists achieved the highest number of votes in elections in 1962, the military took control and banned them, along with the Communist party, before elections in 1963. Dr Arturo Illia, a moderate liberal, was elected and many political prisoners were released. An attempted return by Perón in 1964 drove the military to install Gen. Carlos Onganía as president. Responding to popular resistance, the military eventually allowed the re-election of Perón in 1973.

After Perón's death in 1974 his third wife, María Estela Martínez de Perón, 'Isabelita', succeeded him, becoming the Americas' first woman chief of state. She was deposed by military coup two years later and the army's commander-in-chief, Gen. Jorge Videla, became president. Once in power, Videla dissolved Congress, banned trade unions, and imposed military control. Censorship and military curfews were imposed and the secret police was used extensively. His savagely repressive regime implemented what became known as the 'Dirty War'. Playing on the fears of the Argentinian people, Videla justified the 'disappearance' of 13,000–15,000 countrymen, many believed to have been tortured and executed, claiming that they threatened to undermine the government.

Falklands War

Videla was eventually succeeded by Gen. Leopoldo Galtieri, the army commander-in-chief. In April 1982 Galtieri in an effort to distract attention from internal tension, invaded the Falkland Islands. The subsequent military defeat helped to precipitate Galtieri's fall in July 1982. The war in the Falklands exacerbated the country's problems. Decades of state intervention, regulation, inward looking policies and special interest subsidies had caused economic chaos. Presidential elections were held in Oct. 1983 and civilian rule was restored under Raúl Alfonsín, leader of the middle-class Union Civica Radical. Despite attempting to redress the finances of the bloated public sector, growing unemployment and four-figure inflation led to a Peronist victory in the 1989 elections and Carlos Menem, a Peronist, became Argentina's new president.

In Dec. 1990 an attempted military coup failed, and in Jan. 1991 Menem instigated a major cabinet reshuffle, following allegations of corruption within the country's privatization programme. This new cabinet oversaw Economy Minister Domingo Cavallo's plan to stabilize the economy, allowing Menem to alter the constitution in 1994 to permit his re-election for a second term.

By 1999, with economic recession in South America affecting Argentina's employment levels, Menem's popularity had plummeted and in the election that year Fernando de la Rúa of the centrist Alliance became the first president from outside of the Peronist party in ten years. Menem was later charged with illegal arms deals, but was released by a federal court and announced his intention to return to politics.

A state of emergency was introduced in Dec. 2001 as Argentina verged on bankruptcy in the face of an ever-worsening economic crisis. De la Rúa resigned on 20 Dec. 2001 after days of rioting, protests and looting across the country. Three interim presidents held power over a period of just 11 days before Eduardo Duhalde was elected president by Congress. With the economy still in crisis, Duhalde held office until the election of Peronist Néstor Kirchner in May 2003. The economy subsequently experienced strong recovery as the global climate improved.

TERRITORY AND POPULATION

The second largest country in South America, the Argentine Republic is bounded in the north by Bolivia, in the northeast by Paraguay, in the east by Brazil, Uruguay and the Atlantic Ocean, and the west by Chile. The republic consists of 23 provinces and one federal district with the following areas and estimated populations in 2001 (in 1,000):

Provinces	Area (sq. km)	Population (census 2001)	Capital	Population (census 2001)
Buenos Aires	307,571	13,827	La Plata	564
Catamarca	102,602	335	Catamarca	141
Chaco	99,633	984	Resistencia	274
Chubut	224,686	413	Rawson	22
Córdoba	165,321	3,067	Córdoba	1,268
Corrientes	88,199	931	Corrientes	315
Entre Ríos	78,781	1,158	Paraná	236

Provinces	Area (sq. km)	Population (census 2001)	Capital	Population (census 2001)
Formosa	72,066	487	Formosa	198
Jujuy	53,219	612	San Salvador de Jujuy	231
La Pampa	143,440	299	Santa Rosa	94
La Rioja	89,680	290	La Rioja	144
Mendoza	148,827	1,580	Mendoza	111
Misiones	29,801	966	Posadas	253
Neuquén	94,078	474	Neuquén	202
Río Negro	203,013	553	Viedma	47
Salta	155,488	1,079	Salta	462
San Juan	89,651	620	San Juan	113
San Luis	76,748	368	San Luis	153
Santa Cruz	243,943	197	Río Gallegos	79
Santa Fé	133,007	3,001	Santa Fé	369
Santiago del Estero	136,351	804	Santiago del Estero	231
Tierra del Fuego	21,571	101	Ushuaia	45
Tucumán	22,524	1,339	San Miguel de Tucumán	527
Federal Capital	200	2,776	Buenos Aires	2,776

Argentina also claims territory in Antarctica.

The area is 2,780,400 sq. km excluding the claimed Antarctic territory, and the population at the 2001 census was 36,260,130, giving a density of 13 per sq. km. The estimated population in 2005 was 38·75m.

The UN gives a projected population for 2010 of 40·74m.

In 2003, 90·1% of the population were urban.

In April 1990 the National Congress declared that the Falklands and other British-held islands in the South Atlantic were part of the new province of Tierra del Fuego formed from the former National Territory of the same name. The 1994 Constitution reaffirms Argentine sovereignty over the Falkland Islands.

The population of the main metropolitan areas in 2001 was: Buenos Aires, 12,046,799; Córdoba, 1,368,301; Rosario, 1,161,188; Mendoza, 848,660; Tucumán, 738,479; La Plata, 694,253.

97% speak the national language, Spanish, while 2% speak Italian and 1% other languages. In 2002, 10,395 immigrants were granted permanent residency, down from 19,916 in 2001.

SOCIAL STATISTICS

2001 births, 683,495; deaths, 285,941. Rates, 2001 (per 1,000 population): birth, 18·2; death, 7·6. Infant mortality, 2001, 16 per 1,000 live births. Life expectancy at birth, 2003, 70·7 years for males and 78·2 years for females. Annual population growth rate, 1992–2002, 1·3%; fertility rate, 2001, 2·5 births per woman.

CLIMATE

The climate is warm temperate over the pampas, where rainfall occurs in all seasons, but diminishes towards the west. In the north and west, the climate is more arid, with high summer temperatures, while in the extreme south conditions are also dry, but much cooler. Buenos Aires, Jan. 74°F (23·3°C), July 50°F (10°C). Annual rainfall 37" (950 mm). Bahía Blanca, Jan. 74°F (23·3°C), July 48°F (8·9°C). Annual rainfall 21" (523 mm). Mendoza, Jan. 75°F (23·9°C), July 47°F (8·3°C). Annual rainfall 8" (190 mm). Rosario, Jan. 76°F (24·4°C), July 51°F (10·6°C). Annual rainfall 35" (869 mm). San Juan, Jan. 78°F (25·6°C), July 50°F (10°C). Annual rainfall 4" (89 mm). San Miguel de Tucumán, Jan. 79°F (26·1°C), July 56°F (13·3°C). Annual rainfall 38" (970 mm). Ushuaia, Jan. 50°F (10°C), July 34°F (1·1°C). Annual rainfall 19" (475 mm).

CONSTITUTION AND GOVERNMENT

On 10 April 1994 elections were held for a 230-member constituent assembly to reform the 1853 constitution. The Justicialist National Movement (Peronist) gained 39% of votes cast and the Radical Union 20%. On 22 Aug. 1994 this assembly unanimously adopted a new Constitution. This reduces the presidential term of office from six to four years, but permits the President to stand for two terms. The President is no longer elected by an electoral college, but directly by universal suffrage. A presidential candidate is elected with more than 45% of votes cast, or 40% if at least 10% ahead of an opponent; otherwise there is a second round. The Constitution reduces the President's powers by instituting a *Chief of Cabinet*. The bicameral *National Congress* consists of a Senate and a Chamber of Deputies. The Senate comprises 72 members (previously consisting of three members appointed by each provincial legislature and three from the Federal District for nine years, but in the process of changing to one-third of the members being elected every two years to six-year terms). The Chamber of Deputies comprises 255 members (one-half of the members elected every two years to four-year terms) directly elected by universal suffrage (at age 18).

National Anthem

'Oíd, mortales, el grito sagrado: Libertad' ('Hear, mortals, the sacred cry of Liberty'); words by V. López y Planes, 1813; tune by J. Blas Parera.

GOVERNMENT CHRONOLOGY

Presidents since 1944. (FREJULI = Justicialista Liberation Front; PJ = Justicialist Party; PL = Labor Party; PP = Peronist Party; UCR = Radical Civic Union; UCRI = Radical Intransigent Civic Union; UCRP = People's Radical Civic Union)

1944–46	military	Edelmiro Julián Farrell Plaul
1946–55	military/PL/PP	Juan Domingo Perón Sosa
1955	military	Eduardo A. Lonardi Doucet
1955–58	military	Pedro Eugenio Aramburu Cilveti
1958–62	UCRI	Arturo Frondizi Ercoli
1962–63	UCRI	José María Guido
1963–66	UCRP	Arturo Umberto Illia Francesconi
1966–70	military	Juan Carlos Onganía Carballo
1970–71	military	Roberto Marcelo Levingston Laborda
1971–73	military	Alejandro Agustín Lanusse Gelly
1973	FREJULI	Héctor José Cámpora Demaestre
1973	FREJULI	Raúl Alberto Lastiri
1973–74	PJ	Juan Domingo Perón Sosa
1974–76	PJ	María Estela Martínez de Perón
1976–81	military	Jorge Rafael Videla
1981	military	Roberto Eduardo Viola
1981–82	military	Leopoldo Fortunato Galtieri
1982–83	military	Reynaldo Benito Bignone
1983–89	UCR	Raúl Ricardo Alfonsín
1989–99	PJ	Carlos Saúl Menem
1999–2001	UCR	Fernando de la Rúa
2003–	PJ	Néstor Carlos Kirchner

RECENT ELECTIONS

In the first round of presidential elections held on 27 April 2003, Carlos Menem (Peronist) won 24·4% of the vote, followed by Néstor Kirchner (Peronist) with 22·0%, Ricardo López Murphy (ind.) with 16·3%, Elisa Carrió (ind.) with 14·1% and Adolfo Rodriguez Saá (Peronist) with 14·1%. There were three other candidates. Turnout was 77·6%. On 14 May Menem pulled out of the second round, leaving Kirchner as winner by default.

In the elections to the Chamber of Deputies held on twelve dates between April and Nov. 2003 the Justicialist Party won 65 of 130 seats, the Radical Union 24, Support for an Egalitarian Republic (ARI) 7 and the remaining seats went to local parties. In the elections of 23 Oct. 2005 for the 127 seats not contested at the 2003 elections, the Front for Victory and its allies won 69 seats (of which the Front for Victory Party won 50), the Radical Civic Union and its allies 19 (of which the Radical Civic Union Party won 10), the Justicialist Party and its allies 11 (of which the Justicialist Party won 9) and others 28.

CURRENT ADMINISTRATION

President: Néstor Carlos Kirchner; b. 1950 (Peronist; sworn in 25 May 2003).

Vice-President: Daniel Osvaldo Scioli.

In March 2006 the cabinet comprised:

Chief of the Cabinet: Alberto Fernández. *Minister of Defence:* Nilda Garré. *Economy and Production:* Felisa Miceli. *Education and Culture:* Daniel Filmus. *Federal Planning:* Julio de Vido. *Foreign Affairs:* Jorge Taiana. *Interior:* Dr Anibal Fernández. *Health:* Ginés González García. *Justice:* Alberto Iribarne. *Labour:* Carlos Tomada. *Social Development:* Juan Carlos Nadalich. *Secretary General of the Presidency:* Oscar Parrilli. *Secretary of State Intelligence:* Héctor Icazuriaga.

Office of the President (Spanish only):
http://www.presidencia.gov.ar

CURRENT LEADERS

Néstor Kirchner

Position

President

Introduction

Néstor Kirchner, a Peronist, became president of Argentina in May 2003. Following the withdrawal of his opponent, Carlos Menem, from a run-off, Kirchner took office with only 22% support from a first round of voting. His tenure has been largely focused on trying to restore Argentina's faltering economy.

Early Life

Kirchner was born on 25 Feb. 1950 in Río Gallegos in the Santa Cruz province. In 1976 he graduated in law from La Universidad Nacional de La Plata and became active in the Justicialist Party and the Peronist youth movement.

In 1983 he took a job in the local government of Río Gallegos and in 1987 was elected mayor. He ran an efficient administration and in 1991 was elected governor of Santa Cruz. The province had one of the strongest economies in the country, benefiting from high oil revenues and a low population, and Kirchner won a reputation for his financial skills. However, he was criticized for depositing public money in Swiss and Luxembourgian banks and for unpopular spending cuts. He introduced changes to the regional constitution allowing him to keep the governorship for multiple terms and was re-elected in 1995 and 1999.

At the presidential elections of 2003 Kirchner represented Frente para la Victoria (Front for Victory), the Peronist grouping of incumbent president Eduardo Duhalde, against seven opponents. Kirchner won 22% of the vote in the first round while former president Carlos Menem, representing a rival Peronist group, polled 24%. Menem's opposition rallied behind Kirchner in the build-up to the run-off and, facing heavy defeat, Menem withdrew from the race. The move further splintered the already divided Peronists and left Kirchner without the clear mandate many observers considered essential to the rebuilding of the Argentinian economy. Kirchner was sworn in on 25 May 2003.

Career in Office

Kirchner has sought to repair the economy which fell into crisis in Dec. 2001 and remains fragile. Following his election, in a bid to win support from the commercial sector, he retained Roberto Lavagna, a Duhalde-appointment, as finance minister (Lavagna having been widely praised for restoring some economic stability in the aftermath of the 2001 crash). Once in office Kirchner set about persuading creditors to overlook defaulted debt repayments worth billions of dollars and instead accept repayments on the balance over several decades. He also undertook a purge of the national defence forces and the police.

In Aug. 2003 congress abolished amnesty laws that provided members of the repressive military regime of 1976–83 with immunity from prosecution for alleged human rights abuses. Kirchner, who had himself been briefly imprisoned by the military junta, had vowed to end this immunity, stating that 'a society without justice or memory does not have a destiny.'

Argentina failed to make a US$3bn. debt repayment on 10 Sept. 2003, fuelling fears that Kirchner's government would fail in its attempt to turn the economy around. However, the following day an agreement was struck with the IMF for a three-year aid plan. US$21bn. of debt was refinanced in a bid to put Argentina back on the road to solvency. Kirchner has since taken much of the credit for a recovery that has seen the economy grow by about 25% since the 2001–02 collapse.

In congressional elections on 23 Oct. 2005, Peronist supporters of Kirchner won 69 seats in the Chamber of Deputies.

DEFENCE

Conscription was abolished in 1995. In 2003 defence expenditure totalled US$2,030m. (US$53 per capita), representing 1·5% of GDP (compared to over 8% in 1981).

Army

In 2004 the Army was 41,400 strong. There are no reserves formally established or trained.

There is a paramilitary gendarmerie of 18,000 run by the Ministry of Interior.

Navy

The Argentinian Fleet (2004) included three diesel submarines, five destroyers and eight frigates. Total personnel was 17,500 including 2,000 in Naval Aviation and 2,500 marines. Main bases are at Buenos Aires, Puerto Belgrano, Mar del Plata and Ushuaia.

The Naval Aviation Service had 20 combat aircraft in 2004, including Super-Etendard strike aircraft, and 21 armed helicopters.

Air Force

The Air Force is organized into Air Operations, Air Regions, Logistics and Personnel Commands. There were (2004) 12,500 personnel and 99 combat aircraft including Mirage 5 and Mirage III jet fighters. In addition there were 28 armed helicopters.

INTERNATIONAL RELATIONS

Argentina is a member of the UN, WTO, BIS, OAS, Inter-American Development Bank, LAIA, MERCOSUR, IOM and the Antarctic Treaty, and is set to apply for membership of the OECD. Diplomatic relations with Britain, broken since the 1982 Falklands War, were re-opened in 1990. Praising Argentina's 'call to peace', in Nov. 1997 US President Clinton announced his intention to give the country 'major non-NATO ally' status. The alignment with US foreign policy came after years of anti-American sentiment and a policy of neutrality.

In Jan. 2006 the government repaid the country's entire US$9·57bn. debt to the IMF ahead of schedule.

ECONOMY

Agriculture contributed 10·7% of GDP in 2002, industry 21·3% and services 57·3%.

Overview

By the late 1980s macroeconomic mismanagement in Argentina had caused hyperinflation and the economy shrunk at an average annual rate of 0·7% over the decade. Structural reforms and a 1991 convertibility plan establishing a currency board peg to the US dollar helped the economy achieve stability for most of the 1990s. Between 1991 and 1997 GDP grew at an average rate of 6·2% per year. Argentina's fixed exchange-rate regime survived the Mexican and Asian financial crises but its balance of payments was unable to withstand the pressure cause by subsequent shocks. By the fourth quarter of 1998 the economy was in recession which, combined with insufficient fiscal surplus accumulation during past growth years and weak fiscal restraint in the provinces, threatened the country's ability to continue to pay its foreign debt. The growing strength of the US dollar and the devaluation of the Brazilian *real* in 1999 both put pressure on the pegged peso.

The slowdown of the global economy in 2001 added to Argentina's economic plight. In Dec. 2001 Argentina recorded the largest sovereign debt default in history and in Jan. 2002 abandoned the convertibility law. Recession lasted four years from 1999–2002, during which time the economy contracted by 18·4% and poverty grew dramatically. From 2003–05 the economy experienced strong recovery underpinned by a firm fiscal policy, successful debt restructuring and favourable international market conditions including high commodity prices, low interest rates and strong world growth. The export sector has been aided by exchange rate intervention by the Kirchner government. However, following the departure in late 2005 of economy minister Roberto Lavagna, some observers fear the adoption of populist policies to the detriment of fiscal health. Economic well-being is also threatened by possible energy shortages resulting from underinvestment in utilities after the country's default.

Currency
The monetary unit is the *peso* (ARP), which replaced the austral on 1 Jan. 1992 at a rate of one peso = 10,000 australs. For nearly a decade the peso was pegged at parity with the US dollar, but it was devalued by nearly 30% in Jan. 2002 and floated in Feb. 2002. Inflation rates (based on IMF statistics):

1995	1996	1997	1998	1999	2000	2001	2002	2003	2004
3·4%	0·2%	0·5%	0·9%	−1·2%	−0·9%	−1·1%	25·9%	13·4%	4·4%

Gold reserves were 9,000 troy oz in June 2002 (4·4m. troy oz in 1995); foreign exchange reserves were US$9,621m. (US$20,780m. in June 2001). Total money supply was 15,701m. pesos in Dec. 2001.

Budget
The financial year commences on 1 Jan.
Government revenue and expenditure (in 1m. pesos):

	1998	1999	2000	2001
Revenue	41,188·6	39,765·2	40,346·0	37,093·9
Expenditure	45,930·4	48,056·6	48,224·7	46,013·4

Performance
Real GDP growth rates (based on IMF statistics):

1995	1996	1997	1998	1999	2000	2001	2002	2003	2004
−2·8%	5·5%	8·1%	3·8%	−3·4%	−0·8%	−4·4%	−10·9%	8·8%	9·0%

The economy grew in 1998 by 3·8% but shrank by 3·4% and 0·8% in 1999 and 2000 respectively, mainly as a result of the recession in Brazil, which started in 1998, and the devaluation of the Brazilian *real* in Jan. 1999. Total GDP was US$151·5bn. in 2004. In March 2001 the economy minister, José Luis Machinea, resigned after a turbulent 15 months in which he had failed to revive a stagnant economy. As the economic situation deteriorated Argentina had a further five economy ministers in the space of just over a year. In Nov. 2001 the government tried to persuade creditors to accept a restructuring of the US$132bn. public debt, but on 23 Dec. 2001 interim President Adolfo Rodríguez Saá announced that Argentina would default on the debt payments—the biggest debt default in history. One in five Argentines now lives in extreme poverty and more than half the population lives below the official poverty line.

Banking and Finance
The total assets of the Argentine Central Bank (BCRA) in Feb. 2001 were 41·90bn. pesos. The *President* of the Central Bank is Martín Redrado. In early 2002 banks and financial markets were temporarily closed as an emergency measure in response to the economic crisis that made the country virtually bankrupt. In 2002 there were 16 government banks, 24 private commercial banks, four co-operative banks, one other national bank (Banco Hipotecario Nacional) and 17 foreign banks.

There is a main stock exchange at Buenos Aires and there are others in Córdoba, Rosario, Mendoza and La Plata.

ENERGY AND NATURAL RESOURCES
Environment
Argentina's carbon dioxide emissions from the consumption and flaring of fossil fuels in 2002 were the equivalent of 3·2 tonnes per capita. An *Environmental Sustainability Index* compiled for the World Economic Forum meeting in Jan. 2005 ranked Argentina ninth in the world, with 62·7%. The index measured the ability of countries to maintain favourable environmental conditions and examined various factors including pollution levels and the use or abuse of natural resources.

Electricity
Installed capacity in 2002 was 25·4m. kW. Electric power production (2002) was 82,924m. kWh (5,821m. kWh nuclear); consumption per capita in 2002 was 2,383 kWh. In 2003 there were two nuclear reactors. The electricity market is almost entirely under private ownership, much of it in foreign hands.

Oil and Gas
Crude oil production (2003) was 39·0m. tonnes. Reserves were estimated at some 2·9bn. bbls. in 2002. The oil industry was privatized in 1993. Natural gas extraction in 2002 was 36·1bn. cu. metres. Reserves were about 758bn. cu. metres in 2002. The main area in production is the Neuquen basin in western Argentina, with over 40% of the total oil reserves and nearly half the gas reserves. Natural gas accounts for approximately 45% of all the energy consumed in Argentina. In 2001 Argentina exported 13% of the natural gas produced, mainly to Chile and Uruguay.

Minerals
Minerals (with estimated production in 2002) include clays (1·6m. tonnes), salt (0·8m. tonnes), aluminium (262,000 tonnes in 2000), coal (259,000 tonnes in 2000), copper (204,027 tonnes in 2001), borates (169,000 tonnes), bentonite (88,685 tonnes), zinc (37,325 tonnes of metal), lead (12,011 tonnes of metal), silver (126 tonnes), beryllium (10 tonnes of metal in 2000), gold (32,486 kg), granite, marble and tungsten. Production from the US$1·1bn. Alumbrera copper and gold mine, the country's biggest mining project, in Catamarca province in the northwest, started in late 1997. In 1993 the mining laws were reformed and state regulation was swept away creating a more stable tax regime for investors. In Dec. 1997 Argentina and Chile signed a treaty laying the legal and tax framework for mining operations straddling the 5,000 km border, allowing mining products to be transported out through both countries.

Agriculture
In 2001 there were 33·7m. ha. of arable land and 1·3m. ha. of permanent crops. The agricultural population was 4·37m. in 2001, of whom 1·46m. were economically active. 1·56m. ha. were irrigated in 2001. In 2003 organic crops were grown in an area covering 2·96m. ha. (the second largest area after Australia), representing 1·7% of all farmland.

Livestock (2001): cattle, 48,851,000; sheep, 13,561,000; goats, 3,490,000. There were 2,042,400 pigs in 2002 and 1,994,241 horses in 1998. In 2000 wool production was 38,892 tonnes; milk (in 2002), 8,110m. litres; eggs (in 2002, provisional), 380m. dozen.

Crop production (in 1,000 tonnes) in 2002–03: soybeans, 35,000; sugarcane (1998–99), 18,193; maize, 15,000; wheat, 12,300; sunflower seed, 3,800; potatoes (1997–98), 3,412. Cotton, vine, citrus fruit, olives and *yerba maté* (Paraguayan tea) are also cultivated. Wine is fast becoming a major product. Argentina is the world's leading producer of sunflower seeds, and is now the sixth largest wine producer (1·2m. tonnes in 2002) after France, Italy, Spain, USA and Australia; the value of wine exports has grown from US$19m. in 1995 to an estimated US$200m. in 2000.

Forestry

The woodland area was 34·65m. ha., or 12·7% of the total land area, in 2000. Production in 2001 included 1·44m. cu. metres of sawn wood, 4·96m. tonnes of round logs, 1·15m. tonnes of paper and cardboard and 403,000 cu. metres of chipboard. Timber production totalled 9·31m. cu. metres in 2003.

Fisheries

Fish landings in 2002 amounted to 882,815 tonnes, almost exclusively from sea fishing. Hake and squid are the most common catches.

INDUSTRY

The leading companies by market capitalization in Argentina in Nov. 2005 were: Tenaris (US$13·1bn.), a manufacturer of steel pipes; Petrobras Energía Participaciones (US$2·8bn.), an energy conglomerate; Grupo Financiero Galicia (US$0·7bn.), a holding company and bank.

Production, 2002 (in 1,000 tonnes): distillate fuel oil, 9,462; cement (2001), 6,119; petrol, 4,884; crude steel, 4,400; pig iron, 2,200; sugar (2003), 1,816; residual fuel oil, 1,803; paper (2003), 1,394; jet fuel, 1,305; polyethylene (2003), 547; primary aluminium (2003), 272; synthetic rubber (2000), 54. Motor vehicles produced in 2003 totalled 109,364; tyres, 9,578,000; motorcycles, 11,430.

Labour

In 2001 the economically active population totalled 15·26m., of which 10·92m. were employed; there were 1·46m. unemployed in 2000. The urban unemployment rate, which had been 12·9% in 1998, rose to a record 21·5% by May 2002 at the height of the economic crisis before falling to 15·6% in May 2003.

INTERNATIONAL TRADE

External debt was US$132,314m. in 2002.

Imports and Exports

Foreign trade (in US$1m.):

	1998	1999	2000	2001	2002	2003
Imports	29,531	24,103	23,889	19,158	8,470	13,119
Exports	26,434	23,309	26,341	26,543	25,709	29,566

Principal imports in 2002 (in US$1m., provisional) were nuclear reactors and machinery, and mechanical goods (1,281); organic chemical products (987); vehicles (722); and machines and electrical materials (598).

Principal exports in 2002 (in US$1m., provisional) were fuels, mineral lubricants and related products (4,375); food industry residues (2,783); cereals (2,127); animal and vegetable oils (2,084); and vehicles (1,603).

In 2002 imports (in US$1m.) were mainly from Brazil (2,517); USA (1,804); Germany (554); China, including Hong Kong (342); Japan (314); and Italy (311). Exports went mainly to Brazil (4,828); Chile (2,960); USA (2,957); China, including Hong Kong (1,176); Spain (1,146); and the Netherlands (1,038).

COMMUNICATIONS

Roads

In 2002 there were 216,558 km of roads, including 875 km of motorways. The four main roads constituting Argentina's portion of the Pan-American Highway were opened in 1942. Vehicles in use in 1998 totalled 6,544,197, of which 5,047,630 were passenger cars, 1,453,335 trucks and vans, and 43,232 buses and coaches. In 2002, 3,178 people were killed in road accidents. In 2002, 101,143 new vehicles were registered.

Rail

Much of the 33,000 km state-owned network (on 1,000 mm, 1,435 mm and 1,676 mm gauges; 210 km electrified) was privatized in 1993–94. 30-year concessions were awarded to five freight operators; long-distance passenger services are run by contractors to the requirements of local authorities. Metro, light rail and suburban railway services are also operated by concessionaires.

In 2002 railways carried 17,469,000 tonnes of freight and 355,420,000 passengers. There were 37,856 km of track in 2002.

The metro and light rail network in Buenos Aires extends to 52 km.

Civil Aviation

The main international airport is Buenos Aires Ezeiza, which handled 5,442,640 passengers on international flights out of a total of 5,537,297 passengers in 2001. The second busiest airport is Buenos Aires Aeroparque, which handled 5,051,824 passengers in 2001. It is much more important as a domestic airport, with only 581,953 passengers on international flights in 2001 but 4,469,871 on domestic flights. The national carrier, Aerolíneas Argentinas, is 5% state-owned. In 2003 it operated direct flights to Asunción, Auckland, Caracas, Florianópolis, Lima, London, Madrid, Miami, Montevideo, New York, Paris, Pôrto Alegre, Rio de Janeiro, Rome, Santa Cruz, Santiago, São Paulo and Sydney. There were direct flights in 2003 with other airlines to Barcelona, Bogotá, Cancún, Cape Town, Chicago, Cochabamba, Colonia, Dallas, Fortaleza, Frankfurt, Guayaquil, Havana, Johannesburg, Kuala Lumpur, La Paz, Los Angeles, Mexico City, Milan, the Netherlands Antilles, Panama City, Puerto Montt, Punta Cana, Punta del Este, Quito, Puerto Rico, Salvador, Varadero and Zürich.

In 2000 a total of 13·63m. passengers and 203,606 tonnes of freight were carried on domestic and international airlines. In 1998 Aerolíneas Argentinas flew 83·2m. km, carrying 4,024,600 passengers (2,060,000 on international flights).

Shipping

The merchant shipping fleet totalled 423,000 GRT in 2002, including oil tankers totalling 51,000 GRT.

Telecommunications

The telephone service Entel was privatized in 1990. The sell-off split Argentina into two monopolies, operated by Telefonica Internacional de España, and a holding controlled by France Telecom and Telecom Italia. In Nov. 2000 the industry was opened to unrestricted competition. The number of subscribers in 2002 totalled 14,509,400 (396·4 per 1,000 inhabitants). Mobile phone subscribers numbered 6,500,000 in 2002. There were 3,000,000 PCs in use in 2002 (82·0 per 1,000 persons) and 113,000 fax machines. Argentina had 4·1m. Internet users in 2002.

Postal Services

In 2003 there were 5,724 post offices. In 2002, 5·3m. telegrams were sent.

SOCIAL INSTITUTIONS

Justice

Justice is administered by federal and provincial courts. The former deal only with cases of a national character, or those in which different provinces or inhabitants of different provinces are parties. The chief federal court is the Supreme Court, with five judges whose appointment is approved by the Senate. Other federal courts are the appeal courts, at Buenos Aires, Bahía Blanca, La Plata, Córdoba, Mendoza, Tucumán and Resistencia. Each province has its own judicial system, with a Supreme Court (generally so designated) and several minor chambers. The death penalty was re-introduced in 1976 for the killing of government, military police and judicial officials, and for participation in terrorist activities. The population in penal institutions in Dec. 2002 was 56,313 (148 per 100,000 of national population). In 2002 there were 1,340,529 crimes reported; and 23,538 guilty verdicts were passed.

The police force is centralized under the Federal Security Council.

Education
Adult literacy was 97·2% in 2003 (97·2% for both males and females). In 2001, 1,331,155 children attended pre-school institutions, 6,716,653 were in basic general education, 1,503,920 in 'multimodal' secondary schooling and 494,461 in higher non-universities.

In 2001, in the public sector, there were 33 universities; one technical university; and university institutes of aeronautics, military studies, naval and maritime studies and police studies. In the private sector, there were 42 universities, including seven Roman Catholic universities. In 2001 there were 1,196,581 students attending public universities and (1999) 171,783 at private universities. In 2000 there was a total of 117,596 academic staff in public universities.

In 2000–01 total expenditure on education came to 4·7% of GNP and 13·6% of total government spending.

Health
Free medical attention is obtainable from public hospitals. In 2001 there were 7,833 public health care institutions which had an average of 75,075 available beds. In 1998 there were 108,800 physicians.

Welfare
Until the end of 1996 trade unions had a monopoly in the handling of the compulsory social security contributions of employees, but private insurance agencies are now permitted to function alongside them.

Unique Social Security System Expenditure (in 1m. pesos):

	1999	2000
Retirement and pensions	17,508	17,386
Healthcare assistance and other forms of social insurance	5,249	5,440
Family allowances	1,879	1,920
Unemployment insurance, employment and training programmes	519	484
Work risks insurance	323	367
Other	2,201	2,361
Total	27,679	27,958

RELIGION
The Roman Catholic religion is supported by the State; affiliation numbered 29·92m. in 2001. There were three cardinals in May 2005. There were 2·04m. Protestants of various denominations in 2001, 730,000 Muslims and 500,000 Jews. There were 275,000 Latter-day Saints (Mormons) in 1998.

CULTURE

World Heritage Sites
Argentina's heritage sites as classified by UNESCO (with year entered on list) are: Los Glaciares national park (1981), the Iguazu National Park (1984), and the Ischigualasto and Talampaya Natural Parks (2000). The Cueva de las Manos (Cave of Hands, 1999), in Patagonia, contains cave art that is between 1,000 and 10,000 years old. The Península Valdés (1999) in Patagonia protects several endangered species of marine mammal. The Jesuit Block and Estancias of Córdoba (2000) are the principal buildings of the Jesuit community from the 17th and 18th century. Shared with Brazil, the Jesuit Missions of the Guaranis (1984) encompasses the ruins of five Jesuit missions. The Quebrada de Humahuaca (2003) is a valley on the Camino Inca trade route.

Broadcasting
There are state-owned, provincial, municipal and private radio stations overseen by the Secretaria de Comunicaciones, the Comité Federal de Radiodifusión, the Servicio Oficial de Radiodifusión (which also operates an external service and a station in Antarctica) and the Asociación de Teleradiodifusoras Argentinas. There were 24·3m. radio sets in 2000 and 11·8m. TV receivers (colour by PAL N) in 2001. In 2001 there were 5·0m. cable TV subscribers.

Cinema
In 2002 there were 1,003 cinemas with an audience of approximately 27,178,000.

Press
In 2000 there were 106 daily newspapers with a combined circulation of 1·5m., a rate of 40 per 1,000 inhabitants. In 2002 a total of 15,137 book titles were published.

Tourism
In 2000, 2,949,139 tourists visited Argentina, including 567,967 from Chile, 499,831 from Paraguay, 488,007 from Uruguay and 466,016 from Brazil. Receipts in 2001 totalled US$2·55bn. In 2002 there were 7,433 hotels providing 398,653 beds.

Libraries
In 1995 there were 2,700 public libraries. They held a combined 13,496,000 volumes.

DIPLOMATIC REPRESENTATIVES
Of Argentina in the United Kingdom (65 Brook St., London, W1K 4AH)
Ambassador: Federico Mirré.

Of the United Kingdom in Argentina (Dr Luis Agote 2141/52, 1425 Buenos Aires)
Ambassador: John Hughes.

Of Argentina in the USA (1600 New Hampshire Ave., NW, Washington, D.C., 20009)
Ambassador: José Octavio Bordón.

Of the USA in Argentina (4300 Colombia, 1425 Buenos Aires)
Ambassador: Lino Gutierrez.

Of Argentina to the United Nations
Ambassador: César Mayoral.

Of Argentina to the European Union
Ambassador: D. Jorge Remes Lenicov.

FURTHER READING
Bethell, L. (ed.) *Argentina since Independence.* CUP, 1994
Biggins, Alex, *Argentina.* [Bibliography] ABC-Clio, Oxford and Santa Barbara (CA), 1991
Lewis, P., *The Crisis of Argentine Capitalism.* North Carolina Univ. Press, 1990
Manzetti, L., *Institutions, Parties and Coalitions in Argentine Politics.* Univ. of Pittsburgh Press, 1994
Romero, Luis Alberto, *A History of Argentina in the Twentieth Century;* translated from Spanish. Pennsylvania State Univ. Press, 2002
Shumway, N., *The Invention of Argentina.* California Univ. Press, 1992
Turner, Barry, (ed.) *Latin America Profiled.* Macmillan, London, 2000
Wynia, G. W., *Argentina: Illusions and Realities.* 2nd ed. Hoddesdon, 1993

National Statistical Office: Instituto Nacional de Estadística y Censos (INDEC). Av. Julio A. Roca 615, PB (1067) Buenos Aires. *Director:* Dr Lelio Mármora.
Website: http://www.indec.mecon.ar

ARMENIA

Hayastani Hanrapetoutiun
(Republic of Armenia)

Capital: Yerevan
Population projection, 2010: 2·98m.
GDP per capita, 2003: (PPP$) 3,671
HDI/world rank: 0·759/83

KEY HISTORICAL EVENTS

According to tradition, the kingdom was founded in the region of Lake Van by Haig, or Haik, a descendant of Noah. Historically, the region and former kingdom that was Greater Armenia lay east of the Euphrates River; Little, or Lesser, Armenia was west of the river. In 189 BC the Armenians split from the Syrians to found a native dynasty, the Artashesids. The imperialistic ambitions of King Tigranes led to war with Rome and defeated Armenia became a tributary kingdom. In the 3rd century AD it was overrun by Sassanian Persia. Armenia was the first country to adopt Christianity as its state religion, in the early 4th century. The persecution of Christians under Persian rule kindled nationalism, particularly after the partition in 387 AD of the kingdom between Persia and Rome. However, because of its strategic location, attempts at independence were short-lived, as Armenia was the constant prey of the Persians, Byzantines and Arabs, and later of the Turkish and Russian Empires.

In the early part of the 20th century the Armenians under Turkish rule suffered brutal persecution. An estimated 1·75m. were massacred or deported to present-day Syria from their homeland in Anatolia. Armenia enjoyed a brief period of independence after the First World War but in 1920 the country was proclaimed a Soviet Socialist Republic. After the collapse of Communism, 99% of voters supported a breakaway from the Soviet Union. A declaration of independence in Sept. 1991

was followed by presidential elections after which President Levon Ter-Petrosyan came to an agreement on economic co-operation with the other Soviet republics and joined the CIS. A new constitution adopted in July 1995 led to National Assembly elections. President Ter-Petrosyan was re-elected in Sept. 1996. OSCE observers noted 'very serious irregularities' in the conduct of the election and there were demonstrations of protest in Yerevan, leading to several deaths.

Hostilities with Azerbaijan over the enclave of Nagorno-Karabakh were brought to an end with a 1994 ceasefire. Resigning over Nagorno-Karabakh in Feb. 1998, President Ter-Petrosyan was succeeded by Robert Kocharyan, who was sworn in as president in April 1998. On 27 Oct. 1999, five men burst into the parliamentary chamber, killing the Prime Minister, Vazgen Sarkisian, and seven other officials. Aram Sarkisian, brother of the slain prime minister, was named as his successor. In April 2001 a first round of high-level talks on the settlement of the Nagorno-Karabakh conflict was held in Florida. Armenia and Azerbaijan have agreed, in principle, to continue talks.

TERRITORY AND POPULATION

Armenia covers an area of 29,743 sq. km (11,484 sq. miles). It is bounded in the north by Georgia, in the east by Azerbaijan and in the south and west by Turkey and Iran.

The 2001 census population was 3,213,011 (53·1% females); population density, 108 per sq. km. Armenians account for 97%, Kurds 1·6% and Russians 0·8%—in 1989, 2·6% of the population were Azeris, prior to the Nagorno-Karabakh conflict. 64·5% lived in urban areas in 2003. The United Nations population estimate for 2001 was 3,065,000.

The UN gives a projected population for 2010 of 2·98m.

According to the Second Armenia-Diaspora Conference in May 2002 there are approximately 10m. Armenians worldwide.

The capital is Yerevan (1·1m. population in 2001). Other large towns are Gyumri (formerly Leninakan) (150,900 in 2001) and Vanadzor (formerly Kirovakan) (107,300 in 2001).

The official language is Armenian.

SOCIAL STATISTICS

2001 births, 32,065; deaths, 24,003; marriages, 12,302; divorces, 1,776. Rates, 2001 (per 1,000 population): births, 8·4; deaths, 6·3; marriage, 3·2; divorce, 0·5. Infant mortality, 2001, 31 per 1,000 live births. Annual population growth rate, 1992–2002, –1·3%. Life expectancy at birth, 2003, 68·0 years for men and 74·7 years for women; fertility rate, 2000, 1·1 births per woman.

CLIMATE

Summers are very dry and hot although nights can be cold. Winters are very cold, often with heavy snowfall. Yerevan, Jan. –9°C, July 28°C. Annual rainfall 318 mm.

CONSTITUTION AND GOVERNMENT

The constitution was adopted by a nationwide referendum on 5 July 1995. The head of state is the *President*, directly elected for five-year terms. Parliament is a 131-member *Azgayin Zhoghov* (National Assembly), with 75 deputies elected by party list and 56 chosen by direct election (vice-versa until 2002). The government is nominated by the President.

National Anthem

'Mer Hayrenik, azat ankakh' ('Land of our fathers, free and independent'); words by M. Nalbandyan, tune by B. Kanachyan.

RECENT ELECTIONS

In presidential elections held on 19 Feb. 2003 incumbent president Robert Kocharian received 48·3% of votes cast, ahead of Stepan Demirchyan with 27·4% and Artashes Geghamyan 16·9%. Turnout was 61·2%. The OSCE said that the election process 'fell short of international standards in several key respects'. In the run-off on 5 March 2003 between the two leading candidates Robert Kocharian won 67·5% of the vote against 32·5% for Stepan Demirchyan. Again observers claimed the elections failed to meet international standards.

Elections to the National Assembly were held on 25 May 2003. The Republican Party of Armenia (HHK) won 31 seats with 23·5% of the vote. Rule of Law Country (Orinants Erkir, OE) won 19 seats (12·3%), Ardartyun (Justice) 14 seats (13·6%), Dashnak (Armenian Revolutionary Federation) 11 seats (11·4%), National Unity 9 seats (8·8%) and the United Labour Party 6 seats (5·7%). The All Armenian Labour Party and Hanrapetutiun (Republic) both won one seat. 36 non-partisans were also elected. Turnout was 51·5%.

CURRENT ADMINISTRATION

President: Robert Kocharian, formerly President of Nagorno-Karabakh, the Armenian-inhabited enclave in Azerbaijan; b. 1954 (in office since 4 Feb. 1998).

In March 2006 the government comprised:

Prime Minister: Andranik Markaryan; b. 1951 (HHK; appointed 12 May 2000).

Minister of Foreign Affairs: Vardan Oskanian. *Defence:* Serge Sargsyan. *Justice:* Davit Harutyunyan. *Education and Science:* Sergo Yeritzyan. *Health:* Norayr Davidyan. *Culture and Youth Affairs:* Gevorg Gevorgyan. *Industry and Trade:* Karen Chshmaritian. *Transportation and Telecommunications:* Andranik Manukyan. *Agriculture:* Davit Lokyan. *Environment:* Vardan Ayvazyan. *Finance and Economy:* Vardan Khachatryan. *Energy:* Armen Movsissyan. *Urban Development:* Aram Harutyunyan. *Territorial Administration:* Hovik Abrahamyan. *Labour and Social Affairs:* Aghvan Vardanyan. *Cabinet Chief of Staff:* Manook Topuzyan.

CURRENT LEADERS

Robert Kocharian

Position
President

Introduction
Robert Kocharian became president of Armenia in 1998, a year after being appointed prime minister. He had previously served as premier and president of Nagorno-Karabakh, the Armenian-dominated region at the centre of a dispute between Armenia and Azerbaijan since the collapse of the Soviet Union. Kocharian's past as a leading independence fighter has remained a source of contention with Azerbaijan.

Early Life
Kocharian was born on 31 Aug. 1954 in Stepanakert in Nagorno-Karabakh, then an autonomous region within the Soviet Republic of Azerbaijan. From 1972–74 he served in the Red Army and in 1982 graduated in electrical engineering from the Polytechnic Institute in Armenia's capital, Yerevan. He took a position as a factory engineer in Stepanakert and was active within Komsomol (the Soviet youth wing) and the communist party of Karabakh.

Calls for self-determination in Nagorno-Karabakh by the Armenian majority increased during the 1980s, amid an atmosphere of *glasnost* and *perestroika* engendered by Mikhail Gorbachev's regime in Moscow. Kocharian was involved with the Groong movement, which promoted Armenian history and culture, and later founded Miatsum (Unification), which called for re-unification with Armenia.

He was elected to the Supreme Council of Armenia in 1989 as the representative for Nagorno-Karabakh. In the same year fighting began in the enclave between Armenian nationalists and the Azeri minority, with Kocharian a key figure in organizing armed nationalist forces. With the collapse of the Soviet Union in late 1991, Kocharian was elected to the first Supreme Council of the Republic of Nagorno-Karabakh (RNK) and again took responsibility for military organization. Conflict escalated in Nagorno-Karabakh and the Azeri army occupied large areas of the region in 1992. Kocharian was elected prime minister of the RNK and, as head of the state defence committee, oversaw the expulsion of Azeri forces. In 1994 RNK and Azerbaijan agreed a ceasefire and a peace process began, brokered by the Organization for Security and Co-operation in Europe. Kocharian was elected president of the RNK and set about rebuilding the ravaged economy.

In 1997 Kocharian was made prime minister of Armenia by Armenia's President Levon Ter-Petrosyan, despite having only obtained citizenship a short time before. Ter-Petrosyan resigned over the Nagorno-Karabakh issue in Feb. 1998 and Kocharian was approved by the electoral commission to stand for the presidency. He stood against Karen Demirchyan in a run-off in March 1998 and won with 59·7% of the vote.

Career in Office
Kocharian's victory caused some international unease. The USA announced that it would not support any move by Armenia to annex Nagorno-Karabakh, while Azerbaijan viewed the appointment as a 'provocation'.

Once in office, Kocharian was faced with a severely depressed economy. He authorized tax cuts in a bid to kick-start the industrial sector and reduce unemployment and attempted to bring in foreign investment. Significant funds were directed to repairing infrastructure destroyed during the Spitak earthquake of 1988 which killed 25,000 people, notably in Guyumri.

In Oct. 1999 Armenian Prime Minister Vazgen Sarkisian, the parliamentary speaker and six other officials were shot dead when a gang stormed Yerevan's parliament building. The assassins claimed they wanted to highlight Armenia's economic plight and government mismanagement and corruption. In late 2000 Armenia and Azerbaijan agreed to consolidate their ceasefire agreement and in Jan. 2001 the nations jointly gained membership of the Council of Europe. In Sept. 2001 Armenia received Russia's President Vladimir Putin, the first visit by a Russian leader since the collapse of the USSR.

In presidential elections in Feb. 2003 Kocharian won a further term, defeating Stepan Demirchyan in a run-off. The OSCE said that the election process 'fell short of international standards in several key respects'. In early 2004 there were sporadic opposition demonstrations calling for his resignation. The issue of Nagorno-Karabakh remains a major focus of his tenure.

DEFENCE

There is conscription for 24 months. Total active forces numbered 44,160 in 2002, including 33,100 conscripts.

Defence expenditure in 2003 totalled US$700m. (US$229 per capita), representing 6·4% of GDP.

Army

Current troop levels are 38,900, plus air and defence aviation forces of 3,160 and paramilitary forces of 1,000. There are approximately 210,000 Armenians who have received some kind of military service experience within the last 15 years.

INTERNATIONAL RELATIONS

There is a dispute over the mainly Armenian-populated enclave of Nagorno-Karabakh, which lies within Azerbaijan's borders—Armenia and Azerbaijan are technically still at war.

Armenia is a member of the UN, WTO, NATO Partnership for Peace, Council of Europe, CIS, OSCE, BSE, IOM and the

Asian Development Bank. It is among biggest recipients of US government aid.

ECONOMY

In 2002 agriculture contributed 25·9% of GDP, industry 35·1% and services 39·0%.

Overview

Privatization began after independence in 1991 with the privatization of most agricultural land. In 1998 the Greek telecommunications company OTE bought a 90% stake in ArmenTel, the Armenian state company. By 1998 approximately 60% of enterprises had been privatized, rising to over 80% of medium and large enterprises and 90% of small enterprises by the end of 2000. The IMF and the World Bank have supported Armenia's privatization and economic restructuring.

Currency

In Nov. 1993 a new currency unit, the *dram* (AMD) of 100 *lumma*, was introduced to replace the rouble. Inflation, which had been 5,273% in 1994, was just 4·7% in 2003 and 6·9% in 2004. Foreign exchange reserves were US$323m. in June 2002, gold reserves were 28,000 troy oz and total money supply was 74,904m. drams.

Budget

In 2000 total revenue was 172,132·8m. drams and total expenditure 222,886·4m. drams.

Performance

Real GDP growth was 13·2% in 2002, 13·9% in 2003 and 10·1% in 2004. Total GDP in 2004 was US$3·5bn.

Banking and Finance

The *Chairman* of the Central Bank (founded in 1993) is Tigran Sargsyan. In 2002 there were 28 commercial banks and one savings bank. There are commodity and stock exchanges in Yerevan and Gyumri.

ENERGY AND NATURAL RESOURCES

Environment

Armenia's carbon dioxide emissions from the consumption and flaring of fossil fuels in 2002 were the equivalent of 2·6 tonnes per capita.

Electricity

Output of electricity in 2000 was 5·57bn. kWh. Capacity was 3·0m. kW in 2000. Consumption per capita was 1,445 kWh in 2000. A nuclear plant closed in 1989 was re-opened in 1995 because of the blockade of the electricity supply by Azerbaijan; it was anticipated that domestic supply would be raised from four to 12 hours daily.

Minerals

There are deposits of copper, zinc, aluminium, molybdenum, marble, gold and granite.

Agriculture

The chief agricultural area is the valley of the Arax and the area round Yerevan. Here there are cotton plantations, orchards and vineyards. Almonds, olives and figs are also grown. In the mountainous areas the chief pursuit is livestock raising. In 2001 there were 495,000 ha. of arable land and 65,000 ha. of permanent crops. Major agricultural production (in tonnes in 2000): potatoes, 290,300; wheat, 177,800; tomatoes, 143,700; grapes, 115,800; barley, 32,900. Livestock (2000): cattle, 497,306; sheep, 539,992; pigs, 68,912; horses, 11,400; chickens, 4m.

Forestry

In 2000 forests covered 351,000 ha., or 12·4% of the total land area. Timber production in 2001 was 42,000 cu. metres.

Fisheries

Total catch in 2001 came to 866 tonnes, exclusively from inland waters.

INDUSTRY

Among the chief industries are chemicals, producing mainly synthetic rubber and fertilizers, the extraction and processing of building materials, ginning- and textile-mills, carpet weaving and food processing, including wine-making.

Labour

In 2000 the population of working age was 2·35m., of whom 1·3m. were employed: 44% in agriculture, 14% in industry. The registered unemployment rate was 9·4% of the workforce in 2002. The official average monthly salary in Jan. 2001 was 20,612 drams.

INTERNATIONAL TRADE

External debt was US$1,149m. in 2002.

Imports and Exports

Imports and exports for calendar years in US$1m.:

	1998	1999	2000	2001	2002
Imports	806·3	721·4	773·4	773·3	882·5
Exports	228·9	247·3	309·9	353·1	513·8

The main import suppliers in 2000 were Russia (14·9%), USA (11·6%), Belgium (9·5%) and Iran (9·4%). Principal export markets were Belgium (25·2%), Russia (15·0%), USA (12·7%) and Iran (9·3%). Foodstuffs account for 26% of Armenia's imports, mineral products 19%, and equipment and machinery 15%. Cut diamonds and jewellery from precious metals and stones account for 45% of Armenia's exports, non-precious metals 15% and mineral products 13%.

COMMUNICATIONS

Roads

There were 15,918 km of road network in 2000, including 7,527 km of motorways. In 1996 there were 5,760 passenger cars, buses, coaches, lorries and vans as well as 7,200 motorcycles and mopeds. There were 214 fatalities as a result of road accidents in 2000.

Rail

Total length in 2000 was 711 km of 1,000 mm gauge. Passenger-km travelled in 2000 came to 52m. and freight tonne-km to 354m.

There is a metro and a tramway in Yerevan.

Civil Aviation

There is an international airport at Yerevan (Zvartnots). The main Armenia-based carriers are Armavia and Armenian International Airways. In 2003 there were direct flights to Adler/Sochi, Amsterdam, Anapa, Ashgabat, Astrakhan, Athens, Donetsk, Dubai, Ekaterinburg, Frankfurt, İstanbul, Kharkiv, Krasnodar, Kyiv, Larnaca, London, Mineralnye Vody, Minsk, Moscow, Nizhny Novgorod, Novosibirsk, Odesa, Paris, Rostov, St Petersburg, Samara, Saratov, Simferopol, Stavropol, Tashkent, Tbilisi, Tehran, Vienna and Volgograd. In 1999 scheduled airline traffic of Armenian-based carriers flew 8·2m. km, carrying 343,000 passengers (all on international flights).

Telecommunications

Telephone subscribers numbered 614,800 in 2002 (161·7 per 1,000 inhabitants) and 60,000 PCs were in use (15·8 for every 1,000 persons). There were 71,900 mobile phone subscribers in 2002. Armenia had 60,000 Internet users in 2002.

Postal Services

In 2002 there were 943 post offices.

SOCIAL INSTITUTIONS

Justice
In 2000, 12,048 crimes were reported, including 127 murders or attempted murders. The population in penal institutions in Feb. 2000 was 6,789 (178 per 100,000 of national population).

Education
Armenia's literacy rate was 99·4% in 2003 (99·7% among males and 99·2% among females). At the end of 2000, 46,300 children (17% of those eligible) attended pre-school institutions. In 2000–01 there were 176,302 pupils in primary schools (and 13,620 teachers in 1996–97) and 292,368 pupils in secondary schools. In 2000–01 there were 25 technical colleges with 26,870 students and 19 higher educational institutions with 43,615 students. Yerevan houses the National Academy of Sciences of the Republic of Armenia (NAS RA), 43 scientific institutes, a medical institute and other technical colleges, and a state university. NAS RA is composed of more than 50 institutions and organizations with a staff of 4,500.

In 2000–01 there were seven universities (including the Yerevan State University and the American University), with 22,400 students, out of a total of 19 public higher education establishments.

Total expenditure on education in 2000–01 came to 2·9% of GNP.

Health
In 2000 there were some 12,270 doctors, 22,672 junior medical personnel and 146 hospitals with 20,795 beds.

Welfare
In 2000 there were 501,711 old age, and 58,371 other, pensioners.

RELIGION

Armenia adopted Christianity in AD 301, thus becoming the first Christian nation in the world. The Armenian Apostolic Church is headed by its Catholicos (Karekin II, b. 1951) whose seat is at Etchmiadzin, and who is head of all the Armenian (Gregorian) communities throughout the world. In 1995 it numbered 7m. adherents (4m. in diaspora). The Catholicos are elected by representatives of parishes. The Catholicos of the diaspora is Aram I (b. 1947) of Cilicia, with seat at Antelias. In 2001, 65% of the population belonged to the Armenian Apostolic Church.

CULTURE

World Heritage Sites
There are three UNESCO sites in Armenia: the Monasteries of Haghpat and Sanahin (inscribed in 1996); the Monastery of Geghard and the Upper Azat Valley (2000); the Cathedral and Churches of Echmiatsin and the Archaeological Site of Zvartnots (2000).

Broadcasting
The state-owned Armenian Radio broadcasts two national programmes and relays of Radio Moscow and Voice of America, and a foreign service, Radio Yerevan (Armenian, English, French, Spanish, Arabic, Kurdish, Russian). Television broadcasting is by the state-controlled Armenian Television (colour by SECAM H). In 2001 there were 870,000 TV receivers and in 2000 there were 700,000 radio receivers.

Press
In 2000 there were 91 daily publications.

Tourism
In 2001 there were 123,000 foreign tourists bringing in receipts of US$65m.

Libraries
There were 1,138 libraries in 2000, which lent 5·1m. items.

Theatre and Opera
360,000 people attended 21 theatres in 2000.

Museums and Galleries
In 2000 there were 93 museums with 874,100 visitors.

DIPLOMATIC REPRESENTATIVES

Of Armenia in the United Kingdom (25A Cheniston Gdns, London, W8 6TG)
Ambassador: Vahe Gabrielyan.

Of the United Kingdom in Armenia (34 Baghramyan Ave., Yerevan 375019)
Ambassador: Anthony Cantor.

Of Armenia in the USA (2225 R St, NW, Washington, D.C., 20008)
Ambassador: Tatoul Markarian.

Of the USA in Armenia (1 American Ave., Yerevan 375082)
Ambassador: John Evans.

Of Armenia to the United Nations
Ambassador: Armen Martirosian.

Of Armenia to the European Union
Ambassador: Viguen Tchitetchian.

FURTHER READING

Brook, S., *Claws of the Crab: Georgia and Armenia in Crisis.* London, 1992

Hovannisian, R. G., *The Republic of Armenia.* 4 vols. Univ. of California Press, 1996

Malkasian, M., *Gha-Ra-Bagh: the Emergence of the National Democratic Movement in Armenia.* Wayne State Univ. Press, 1996

Nersessian, V. N., *Armenia.* [Bibliography] ABC-Clio, Oxford and Santa Barbara (CA), 1993

Walker, C. J., *Armenia: The Survival of a Nation.* 2nd ed. London, 1990

National Statistical Office: National Statistical Service of the Republic of Armenia. *President:* Stepan L. Mnatsakanyan.

Website: http://www.armstat.am

AUSTRALIA

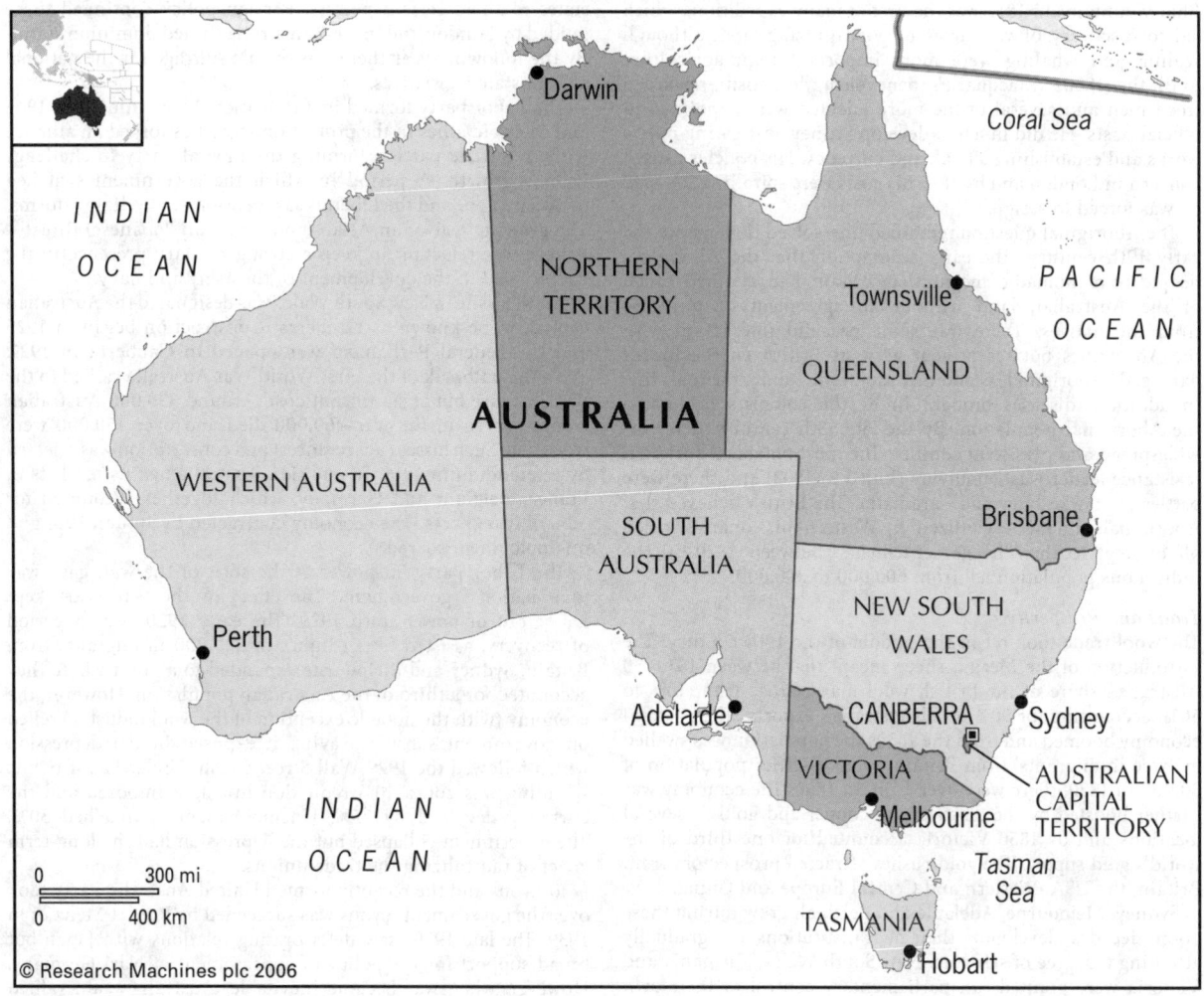

Darwin

INDIAN
OCEAN

NORTHERN
TERRITORY

Coral Sea

Townsville

PACIFIC
OCEAN

QUEENSLAND

AUSTRALIA

WESTERN AUSTRALIA

Brisbane

SOUTH
AUSTRALIA

NEW SOUTH
WALES

Perth

Adelaide

CANBERRA

Sydney

INDIAN
OCEAN

VICTORIA

Melbourne

AUSTRALIAN
CAPITAL
TERRITORY

Tasman
Sea

TASMANIA

Hobart

| 0 | 300 mi |
| 0 | 400 km |

© Research Machines plc 2006

Commonwealth of Australia

Capital: Canberra
Population projection, 2010: 21·20m.
GDP per capita, 2003: (PPS$) 29,632
HDI/world rank: 0·955/3

KEY HISTORICAL EVENTS

The Australian landmass, reaching northwards to Papua New Guinea and including Tasmania in the south, was inhabited in prehistoric times until adverse climatic conditions led to a population exodus between 15,000 and 25,000 years ago. A population using stone tools was in evidence by 2,000–1,000 BC.

The Aboriginal society was composed of extended family groups linked by marriage, common language and shared beliefs. At maximum there were 1m. Aborigines, using 200 different languages. By the early 18th century there was contact with traders from the area of modern Indonesia and Papua New Guinea.

Various dates are given for the European discovery of Australia but the north coast was explored by traders from the South long before any Europeans ventured into the area. Australia was sighted in 1522 by compatriot explorers of the Portuguese Ferdinand Magellan and in 1642 the Dutch explorer Abel Tasman mapped what is now Tasmania and part of New Zealand's east coast. By the middle of the century the Dutch had charted the western part of Australia, calling it New Holland.

But while the Dutch, Portuguese and Spanish made the early running in charting the continent, it was the discovery of the east coast by Capt. James Cook in 1770 that prompted colonization. Over the course of several voyages he charted the Torres Strait and 8,000 kilometres of coastline. Having lost their penal settlements in the American War of Independence, the British decided to send convicts to Australia. Botany Bay was selected as the first settlement.

By 1800 the colony was self-sufficient in food and convicts had established legal rights as crown subjects. Many freed men were able to make a successful living. However, there were several uprisings against penal rule culminating in the Rum Rebellion of 1808, in which John Macarthur led a troop of New South Wales officers against Gov. William Bligh. The response of the

British government was to appoint Lachlan Macquarie, who promoted reform.

His tenure began a period of development in which Australia ceased to be primarily a penal settlement. The crossing of the Blue Mountains in 1813 was the first of many expeditions which led to discovery of vast areas of good grazing land, although sealing and whaling were more important than agriculture until the 1830s. Macquarie's benevolent despotism rewarded freed men and several of the more talented were appointed to official posts. He did much to develop Sydney, instigating public works and establishing a bank and currency. His policies caused concern in London and by 1815 his costs were spiralling. In 1822 he was forced to resign.

The Aboriginal question remained unresolved throughout the early 19th century. The early assumption that the Aboriginal people were nomadic meant that Britain had claimed much of the Australian land without an agreement of purchase from the natives. There was some peaceful interaction with the Aborigines but resentment grew as British encroachment damaged Aboriginal economic, domestic and spiritual life. In addition, diseases brought in by the colonists decimated the Aboriginal population. By the late 18th century there was widespread and persistent conflict. The most notable Aboriginal resistance leader was Pemulwuy (killed in 1802) and there were battles at Hawkesbury and Paramatta. The British believed that Aboriginals should be 'civilized' by Western missionaries, killed off or kept to their fringe settlements. Between 1820–50 the indigenous population fell from 600,000 to 300,000.

Trade and Prosperity

The wool trade took off in the middle of the 19th century. The introduction of the Merino sheep meant that between 1830–50 Australia's share of the British wool market rose from 10% to 50%, accounting for 90% of all Australia's exports. The pastoral economy boomed and from the 1830s the population was swelled by 'free immigrants' from Britain. From a settler population of 30,000 in 1820, there were over 1·1m. in 1860. The economy was further boosted by the discovery of copper and gold in several locations and by 1850 Victoria accounted for one third of the world's gold supply. The gold rushes attracted prospectors from Britain, the USA, Western and Central Europe and China.

Sydney, Melbourne, Adelaide and Perth all grew during these boom decades, developing their own institutions and gradually attaining a degree of self-rule. New South Wales, Tasmania and Victoria were granted full parliamentary control of their own affairs in 1855, with South Australia and the newly formed Queensland following in the next five years. However, the UK government retained control of foreign policy and kept a power of veto.

By the 1860s there was a culture of bushranging as epitomized by Ned Kelly. Bad relations between settlers, immigrant workers and the Aboriginal population persisted. The population passed 3m. in 1888. In the 1890s recession the economy shrank by 30%. Unemployment among skilled workers stood at 30% in 1893 and was higher among unskilled workers, for whom records were not kept. Problems were exacerbated by a severe drought in the east of the country.

Social and Constitutional Reform

Trade unionism grew from the 1870s, gaining strength in the 1890s. Between 1899, when a first Labor government took power in Queensland, and the outbreak of the First World War, Labor was in government in every state. Union membership included a third of all workers. The 1890s witnessed the emergence of the federalist movement, with Sydney hosting conventions in 1891 and 1897–98. On 1 Jan. 1901 the six separately constituted colonies of New South Wales, Victoria, Queensland, South Australia, Western Australia and Tasmania were federated under the name of the Commonwealth of Australia, the designation of

'colonies' being at the same time changed into that of 'states'—except in the case of Northern Territory, which was transferred from South Australia to the Commonwealth as a 'territory' on 1 Jan. 1911. A bicameral parliament was established while the states retained certain powers. Foreign policy continued to be guided by London and in 1907 Australia gained dominion status. By the following year there was female suffrage for the national and all state legislatures.

The Labor party formed its first national government in 1904 and their old allies in the protectionist parties forged an alliance with free trade parties, forming the Liberal party to challenge Labor's growth. A period in which the government switched between Labor and the Liberals saw pension and welfare reforms. The growing fear of an Asian (and especially Japanese) threat—Britain was reluctant to keep a strong military presence in the Pacific—led to the development of the army and navy.

In 1911 a site in New South Wales was designated the Australian capital, to be known as Canberra. Construction began in 1923 and the Federal Parliament was opened in Canberra in 1927. With the outbreak of the First World War Australia rallied to the British cause but at significant cost. Around 330,000 Australian troops served in the war—60,000 died and over 150,000 were wounded. Such losses caused unrest and conscription was rejected by referendum in 1916. In addition Australia lost its markets in France, Belgium and Germany, which together accounted for 30% of its exports. The economy contracted by 10% in 1914 and unemployment soared.

The Labor party, in power at the start of the war, gave way to a national government. The effect of the war years kept Labor out of power until 1929. The early 1920s was a period of recovery, assisted by an influx of 200,000 immigrants from Britain. Sydney and Melbourne expanded to a point where they accounted for a third of the Australian population. However, the economy (with the notable exception of the wool industry) relied on government subsidy, leaving it exposed in the depression which followed the 1929 Wall Street Crash. Under Labor public spending was cut, a 10% reduction in wages imposed and the currency devalued by 25%. Unemployment approached 30%. The government collapsed but the depression had the long-term effect of radicalizing the trade unions.

Jo Lyons and the recently formed United Australia Party took over the government. Lyons was succeeded by Robert Menzies in 1939. The late 1930s saw deteriorating relations with Japan but broad support for the policy of appeasement of Nazi Germany. However, when war became inevitable, Australia again rallied to the imperial cause. 100,000 Australian troops were killed or wounded. Fear of Japan escalated after Pearl Harbor and Darwin was attacked in 1942. These events marked a watershed in foreign relations, with the Labor prime minister, John Curtin, commenting that 'Australia looks to America, free from any pangs about our traditional links of friendship to Britain.'

Post War Recovery

The war encouraged the rapid expansion of Australian industry and the 1950s and 1960s were something of a golden age. Robert Menzies led successive Liberal governments from 1949–66. The population nearly doubled as immigration from Britain and continental Europe was encouraged. Unemployment was consistently low and the economy tripled in size during the two decades. Aware of its 'junior partner' status in the relationship with America, Australia undertook nuclear development with Britain. In 1951 it entered the ANZUS group with New Zealand and the USA and three years later joined the South-East Asian Treaty Organization. Australia's new found confidence was reflected in the success of the 1956 Melbourne Olympics.

The growing number of non-English speaking immigrants accentuated racial problems, with a succession of governments holding to a monocultural policy. The future of the Aboriginal population was one of assimilation. The movement for Aboriginal rights grew after the war, with a strike by Aboriginal workers at Pilbara in 1946 marking a new phase in the conflict. It climaxed in 1966 when an Aboriginal demand for equal pay in Northern Australia turned into demands for land. There was a swathe of moderate reforms favouring the Aboriginal population between 1959–67 but at the same time the assimilation policy allowed for the forced removal of large numbers of children from their families. The last of the Aboriginal reserves was taken over in the 1960s. The policy of forced removal of children did not prompt an apology until the 1980s.

When Menzies retired in 1966 he was followed by a succession of leaders who weakened the standing of the Liberals. Australia's participation in the Vietnam War also drew criticism. Gough Whitlam led the Labor party to power in 1972 and oversaw a radical administration. He withdrew Australian forces from Vietnam, set about modernizing the education and health programmes and funded extensive urban renewal. Government expenditure doubled over his three years in office and Australia was ill-prepared when the global oil crisis struck in 1974.

Whitlam's Liberal opponents, many of whom regarded him as a dangerous maverick, led a parliamentary revolt. A failure to win approval for the national budget led to a constitutional crisis in which the Governor-General John Kerr (himself appointed by Whitlam) dismissed the prime minister and invited Malcolm Fraser to form an administration. Fraser believed that Australian society had become overly dependent on the state. He authorized cuts in public spending but was unable to counter rising unemployment and inflation and was voted out of government in 1983.

Free Market Politics

Bob Hawke took power at the head of a Labor government, assisted by his finance minister (and successor as prime minister), Paul Keating. Their terms of office, spanning 1983–96, saw a shift in Labor's stance on state control and economic planning to allow for an ambitious programme of privatization and financial deregulation. Trade with Asia took on increasing importance and Hawke stood fully behind US foreign policy. In March 1986 the Australia Act abolished the remaining legislative, executive and judicial controls of the British Parliament. By the end of the decade unemployment stood at a respectable 6% but the Australian dollar had suffered a 40% loss of value in 1986 and foreign debt stood at around 30% of GNP. Keating described the recession of the late 1980s as 'necessary'.

Keating took over the premiership in 1991 and mounted a programme of economic reform. He was replaced in 1996 by the Liberal John Howard, who continued the process of economic reform and won re-election two years later. The Aboriginal question continued to test every government. There were some symbolic gestures such as the return of Ayers Rock (with its Aboriginal name Uluru restored) in 1988. The High Court's Mabo ruling of 1992, which overturned a previous ruling that the Aboriginal title to land had not survived British settlement of the continent, raised expectations. Keating officially acknowledged the injustice done to the Aboriginal population when the 'Native Title' legislation was passed in Dec. 1993. Howard's tenure, however, saw disputes over indigenous land rights following a 1996 court ruling against Aboriginal access to sites of cultural tradition owned by non-Aboriginals. Relations were further strained when Howard refused to reiterate apologies for past wrongs.

A referendum to decide if Australia should become a republic was held on 6 Nov. 1999. 54·87% of votes cast were in favour of the monarchy with Queen Elizabeth II as head of state, against 45·13% for a republic with a president chosen by parliament. In foreign policy Howard agreed to military involvement in UN peacekeeping in East Timor and NATO action against Serbia. His government's approach to immigration came under the spotlight in July 2001, when a refugee-laden Norwegian cargo ship was caught in a diplomatic gridlock between Australia,

the UN and Norway. Its passengers were eventually diverted to Papua New Guinea, with Howard assuming a firm and populist stance against asylum seekers. He won a further term of office at the elections of Nov. 2001. The Liberals also won the elections of Oct. 2004. Howard has pursued an interventionist foreign policy in the Pacific region—with notable success in the peacekeeping mission to the Solomon Islands—and committed Australia to the US-led war in Iraq in 2003.

TERRITORY AND POPULATION

Australia, excluding external territories, covers an estimated land area of 7,692,030 sq. km, extending from Cape York (10° 41' S) in the north some 3,680 km to South East Cape, Tasmania (43° 39' S), and from Cape Byron, New South Wales (153° 39' E) in the east some 4,000 km west to Steep Point, Western Australia (113° 9' E). External territories under the administration of Australia comprise the Ashmore and Cartier Islands, Australian Antarctic Territory, Christmas Island, the Cocos (Keeling) Islands, the Coral Sea Islands, the Heard and McDonald Islands and Norfolk Island. For these *see below*.

Growth in census population has been:

1901	3,774,310	1966	11,599,498	1986	15,763,000
1911	4,455,005	1971	12,755,638	1991	16,852,258
1921	5,435,734	1976	13,915,500	1996	17,892,423
1947	7,579,358	1981	15,053,600	2001	18,972,350
1961	10,508,186				

Of the 2001 census population, 9,618,981 were females.

Population (preliminary estimate) at 30 June 2005 was 20,328,600.

The UN gives a projected population for 2010 of 21·20m.

At 30 June 2002 density was 2·6 per sq. km. In 2003, 91·9% of the population lived in urban areas.

Areas and populations of the States and Territories at the 2001 census:

States and Territories	Area (sq. km)	Population	Per sq. km
New South Wales (NSW)	800,640	6,371,745	8·0
Victoria (Vic.)	227,420	4,644,950	20·4
Queensland (Qld.)	1,730,650	3,655,139	2·1
South Australia (SA)	983,480	1,467,261	1·5
Western Australia (WA)	2,529,880	1,851,252	0·7
Tasmania (Tas.)	68,400	456,652	6·7
Northern Territory (NT)	1,349,130	210,664	0·2
Australian Capital Territory (ACT)	2,360	311,947	132·2

Estimated population at 31 March 2005: New South Wales, 6,764,600; Victoria, 5,012,700; Queensland, 3,945,800; South Australia, 1,540,200; Western Australia, 2,003,800; Tasmania, 484,700; Northern Territory, 201,800; Australian Capital Territory, 325,100.

Estimated resident population in capitals and other statistical districts with more than 150,000 population at 30 June 2003:

Capital	State	Population	Capital	State	Population
Canberra	ACT	322,492	Darwin	NT	107,922
Sydney	NSW	4,201,493	*Statistical district*		
Melbourne	Vic.	3,559,654	Newcastle	NSW	501,687
Brisbane	Qld.	1,733,227	Gold Coast[1]	Qld.	456,485
Adelaide	SA	1,119,920	Wollongong	NSW	273,427
Perth	WA	1,433,217	Sunshine Coast[2]	Qld.	200,139
Hobart	Tas.	199,886	Geelong	Vic.	162,835

[1]Includes part of Tweed Shire (in NSW).
[2]Includes Caloundra, Maroochy and Noosa.

The median age of the 2001 census population was 35 years.

Australians born overseas (census 2001), 4,105,444 (21·6%), of whom 1,036,245 (5·5%) were from the UK.

Aboriginals have been included in population statistics only since 1967. At the 2001 census 410,003 people identified themselves as being of indigenous origin (2·2% of the total population). A 1992 High Court ruling that the Meriam people of the Murray Islands had land rights before the European settlement reversed the previous assumption that Australia was *terra nullius* before that settlement. The Native Title Act setting up a system for deciding claims by Aborigines came into effect on 1 Jan. 1994.

Overseas arrivals and departures:

	Settler arrival numbers[1]	Permanent departure numbers	Net permanent migration
1999–2000	92,300	41,100	51,200
2000–01	107,400	46,500	60,800
2001–02	88,900	48,200	40,700
2002–03	93,900	50,500	43,500

[1]Equals the total number of people entitled to permanent residence actually arriving.

The Migration Act of Dec. 1989 sought to curb illegal entry and ensure that annual immigrant intakes were met but not exceeded. Provisions for temporary visitors to become permanent were restricted. According to the 2001 census, 74% of the population born overseas have become Australian citizens.

The national language is English.

SOCIAL STATISTICS

Life expectancy at birth, 2003, 77·7 years for males and 82·8 years for females.

Statistics for years ended 30 June:

	Births	Deaths	Marriages	Divorces
2000	249,600	128,100	113,400	49,900
2001	246,400	128,540	103,130	55,330
2002	251,000	133,700	105,440	54,000
2003	251,200	132,300	106,400	53,100
2004	254,200	132,500	111,000	52,747

In 2004 the median age for marrying was 32 years for males and 29 for females. Infant mortality, 2004, was 4·7 per 1,000 live births. Population growth rate in the year ended 30 June 2005, 1·2%; fertility rate, 2004, 1·77 births per woman.

Suicide rates (per 100,000 population, 2002): 11·8 (men, 19·5; women, 5·2).

CLIMATE

Over most of the continent, four seasons may be recognized. Spring is from Sept. to Nov., summer from Dec. to Feb., autumn from March to May and winter from June to Aug., but because of its great size there are climates that range from tropical monsoon to cool temperate, with large areas of desert as well. In northern Australia there are only two seasons, the wet one lasting from Nov. to March, but rainfall amounts diminish markedly from the coast to the interior. Central and southern Queensland are subtropical, north and central New South Wales are warm temperate, as are parts of Victoria, Western Australia and Tasmania, where most rain falls in winter. Canberra, Jan. 68°F (20°C), July 42°F (5·6°C). Annual rainfall 25" (635 mm). Adelaide, Jan. 73°F (22·8°C), July 52°F (11·1°C). Annual rainfall 21" (528 mm). Brisbane, Jan. 77°F (25°C), July 58°F (14·4°C). Annual rainfall 45" (1,153 mm). Darwin, Jan. 83°F (28·3°C), July 77°F (25°C). Annual rainfall 59" (1,536 mm). Hobart, Jan. 62°F (16·7°C), July 46°F (7·8°C). Annual rainfall 23" (584 mm). Melbourne, Jan. 67°F (19·4°C), July 49°F (9·4°C). Annual rainfall 26" (659 mm). Perth, Jan. 74°F (23·3°C), July 55°F (12·8°C). Annual rainfall 35" (873 mm). Sydney, Jan. 71°F (21·7°C), July 53°F (11·7°C). Annual rainfall 47" (1,215 mm).

CONSTITUTION AND GOVERNMENT

Federal Government
Under the Constitution legislative power is vested in a Federal Parliament, consisting of the Queen, represented by a Governor-

General, a Senate and a House of Representatives. Under the terms of the constitution there must be a session of parliament at least once a year.

The Senate (Upper House) comprises 76 Senators (12 for each State voting as one electorate and, as from Aug. 1974, two Senators respectively for the Australian Capital Territory and the Northern Territory). Senators representing the States are chosen for six years. The terms of Senators representing the Territories expire at the close of the day next preceding the polling day for the general elections of the House of Representatives. In general, the Senate is renewed to the extent of one-half every three years, but in case of disagreement with the House of Representatives, it, together with the House of Representatives, may be dissolved, and an entirely new Senate elected. Elections to the Senate are on the single transferable vote system; voters list candidates in order of preference. A candidate must reach a quota to be elected, otherwise the lowest-placed candidate drops out and his or her votes are transferred to other candidates.

The *House of Representatives* (Lower House) consists, as nearly as practicable, of twice as many Members as there are Senators, the numbers chosen in the several States being in proportion to population as shown by the latest statistics, but not less than five for any original State. The 150 membership is made up as follows: New South Wales, 50; Victoria, 37; Queensland, 27; South Australia, 12; Western Australia, 15; Tasmania, 5; ACT, 2; Northern Territory, 2. Elections to the House of Representatives are on the alternative vote system; voters list candidates in order of preference, and if no one candidate wins an overall majority, the lowest-placed drops out and his or her votes are transferred. The first Member for the Australian Capital Territory was given full voting rights as from the Parliament elected in Nov. 1966. The first Member for the Northern Territory was given full voting rights in 1968. The House of Representatives continues for three years from the date of its first meeting, unless sooner dissolved.

Every Senator or Member of the House of Representatives must be a subject of the Queen, be of full age, possess electoral qualifications and have resided for three years within Australia. The franchise for both Houses is the same and is based on universal (males and females aged 18 years) suffrage. Compulsory voting was introduced in 1925. If a Member of a State Parliament wishes to be a candidate in a federal election, he must first resign his State seat.

Executive power is vested in the *Governor-General*, advised by an Executive Council. The Governor-General presides over the Council, and its members hold office at his pleasure. All Ministers of State, who are members of the party or parties commanding a majority in the lower House, are members of the Executive Council under summons. A record of proceedings of meetings is kept by the Secretary to the Council. At Executive Council meetings the decisions of the Cabinet are (where necessary) given legal form, appointments made, resignations accepted, proclamations, regulations and the like made.

The policy of a ministry is, in practice, determined by the Ministers of State meeting without the Governor-General under the chairmanship of the Prime Minister. This group is known as the *Cabinet*. There are 11 Standing Committees of the Cabinet comprising varying numbers of Cabinet and non-Cabinet Ministers. In Labor governments all Ministers have been members of Cabinet; in Liberal and National Country Party governments, only the senior ministers. Cabinet meetings are private and deliberative, and records of meetings are not made public. The Cabinet does not form part of the legal mechanisms of government; the decisions it takes have, in themselves, no legal effect. The Cabinet substantially controls, in ordinary circumstances, not only the general legislative programme of Parliament but the whole course of Parliamentary proceedings. In effect, though not in form, the Cabinet, by reason of the fact that all Ministers are members of the Executive Council, is also the dominant element in the executive government of the country.

The legislative powers of the Federal Parliament embrace trade and commerce, shipping, etc.; taxation, finance, banking, currency, bills of exchange, bankruptcy, insurance, defence, external affairs, naturalization and aliens, quarantine, immigration and emigration; the people of any race for whom it is deemed necessary to make special laws; postal, telegraph and like services; census and statistics; weights and measures; astronomical and meteorological observations; copyrights; railways; conciliation and arbitration in disputes extending beyond the limits of any one State; social services; marriage, divorce, etc.; service and execution of the civil and criminal process; recognition of the laws, Acts and records, and judicial proceedings of the States. The Senate may not originate or amend money bills. Disagreement with the House of Representatives may result in dissolution and, in the last resort, a joint sitting of the two Houses. The Federal Parliament has limited and enumerated powers, the several State parliaments retaining the residuary power of government over their respective territories. If a State law is inconsistent with a Commonwealth law, the latter prevails.

The Constitution also provides for the admission or creation of new States. Proposed laws for the alteration of the Constitution must be submitted to the electors, and they can be enacted only if approved by a majority of the States and by a majority of all the electors voting.

The Australia Acts 1986 removed residual powers of the British government to intervene in the government of Australia or the individual states.

In Feb. 1998 an Australian Constitutional Convention voted for Australia to become a republic. In a national referendum, held on 6 Nov. 1999, 54·9% voted against Australia becoming a republic.

State Government

In each of the six States (New South Wales, Victoria, Queensland, South Australia, Western Australia, Tasmania) there is a State government whose constitution, powers and laws continue, subject to changes embodied in the Australian Constitution and subsequent alterations and agreements, as they were before federation.

The system of government is basically the same as that described above for the Commonwealth—i.e., the Sovereign, her representative (in this case a Governor), an upper and lower house of Parliament (except in Queensland, where the upper house was abolished in 1922), a cabinet led by the Premier and an Executive Council. Among the more important functions of the State governments are those relating to education, health, hospitals and charities, law, order and public safety, business undertakings such as railways and tramways, and public utilities such as water supply and sewerage. In the domains of education, hospitals, justice, the police, penal establishments, and railway and tramway operation, State government activity predominates. Care of the public health and recreative activities are shared with local government authorities and the Federal government; social services other than those referred to above are now primarily the concern of the Federal government; the operation of public utilities is shared with local and semi-government authorities.

Administration of Territories

Since 1911 responsibility for administration and development of the Australian Capital Territory (ACT) has been vested in Federal Ministers and Departments. The ACT became self-governing on 11 May 1989. The ACT House of Assembly has been accorded the forms of a legislature, but continues to perform an advisory function for the Minister for the Capital Territory.

On 1 July 1978 the Northern Territory of Australia became a self-governing Territory with expenditure responsibilities and revenue-raising powers broadly approximating those of a State.

National Anthem

'Advance Australia Fair' (adopted 19 April 1984; words and tune by P. D. McCormick). The 'Royal Anthem' (i.e. 'God Save the Queen') is used in the presence of the British Royal Family.

GOVERNMENT CHRONOLOGY

Prime Ministers since 1945. (ALP = Australian Labor Party; LP = Liberal Party; CP = Australian Country Party)

1945	ALP	Francis Michael (Frank) Forde
1945–49	ALP	Joseph Benedict (Ben) Chifley
1949–66	LP	Robert Gordon Menzies
1966–67	LP	Harold Edward Holt
1967–68	CP	John (Jack) McEwen (acting)
1968–71	LP	John Grey Gorton
1971–72	LP	William (Bill) McMahon
1972–75	ALP	(Edward) Gough Whitlam
1975–83	LP	(John) Malcolm Fraser
1983–91	ALP	Robert James Lee (Bob) Hawke
1991–96	ALP	Paul John Keating
1996–	LP	John Winston Howard

RECENT ELECTIONS

The 41st Parliament was elected on 9 Oct. 2004.

House of Representatives

Liberal Party (LP), 74 seats and 40·5% of votes cast; Australian Labor Party (ALP), 60 seats and 37·6% of votes cast; National Party of Australia (NP), 12 (5·9%); Northern Territory Country Liberal Party, 1 (0·3%); ind. and others, 3 (2·4%).

Senate

As at March 2006 the make-up of the Senate was Liberal Party, 34; Australian Labor Party, 28; Australian Democratic Party, 4; National Party of Australia, 4; Greens, 4, Northern Territory Country Liberal Party, 1; Family First, 1.

CURRENT ADMINISTRATION

Governor-General: Maj.-Gen. (retd) Michael Jeffery, AC, CVO, MC; b. 1937 (took office on 11 Aug. 2003).

Following the 2004 general election a new LP–NP coalition government was formed on 26 Oct. 2004. In March 2006 the cabinet comprised:

Prime Minister: John Winston Howard; b. 1939 (LP; in office since 11 March 1996).

Deputy Prime Minister and Minister for Trade: Mark Vaile (NP). Treasurer: Peter Costello (LP). Defence: Brendan Nelson (LP). Communications, Information Technology and the Arts: Helen Coonan (LP). Employment and Workplace Relations, and Minister Assisting the Prime Minister for the Public Service: Kevin Andrews (LP). Foreign Affairs: Alexander Downer (LP). Environment and Heritage: Ian Campbell (LP). Industry, Tourism and Resources: Ian Macfarlane (LP). Agriculture, Fisheries and Forestry: Peter McGauran (NP). Transport and Regional Services: Warren Truss (NP). Health and Ageing and Leader of the House of Representatives: Tony Abbott (LP). Education, Science and Training, and Minister Assisting the Prime Minister for Women's Issues: Julie Bishop (LP). Finance and Administration: Nicholas Minchin (LP). Families, Community Services and Indigenous Affairs: Mal Brough (LP). Immigration and Multicultural Affairs: Amanda Vanstone (LP). Attorney General: Philip Ruddock (LP).

The Speaker is David Hawker (LP).

The President of the Senate is Paul Calvert (LP).

Leader of the Opposition: Kim Beazley (ALP).

Government: http://www.gov.au

CURRENT LEADERS

John Howard

Position
Prime Minister

Introduction
Liberal Party member for Bennelong in northwest Sydney since 1974, John Howard became Australia's 25th prime minister in March 1996. Known as an economic rationalist, Howard is also a staunch monarchist who nevertheless organized the 1999 referendum on establishing a republic. His second and third terms were dominated by foreign policy initiatives, in the Asia-Pacific region and in support of the invasion of Iraq in 2003. Successes in East Timor and the Solomon Islands boosted his support domestically but strained relations with several close neighbours, most notably Malaysia and Papua New Guinea. His fourth term of office began in Oct. 2004.

Early Life
John Winston Howard was born on 26 July 1939 in Earlwood, an industrial suburb of Sydney. After attending schools in the city he went on to graduate from Sydney University with a Bachelor of Laws in 1961. Howard joined the Young Liberal Movement at age 18, and in 1963 he became a member of the party's state executive. Practising as a solicitor in a Sydney firm until his election to parliament as member for Bennelong on 18 May 1974, Howard also served as Liberal vice-president for New South Wales during 1972–74. A year after his election, he was appointed minister for business and consumer affairs by Liberal prime minister Malcolm Fraser. In the months leading up to the 1977 election, Howard was made minister for special trade negotiations and minister assisting the prime minister. He was promoted to treasurer just prior to the Dec. election, at which Liberal victory secured Howard's position. He remained treasurer until Fraser lost to Labor in 1983, at which time he became deputy party leader and shadow treasurer. Howard led the party for four years from 5 Sept. 1985, eventually being replaced by his rival, former leader Andrew Peacock. Between 1989–94 he occupied a variety of shadow ministry positions, including industrial relations and industry, technology, and communications. He also served as chair of the Manpower and Labour Market Reform Group, and manager of opposition parliamentary business. Voted back as Liberal leader after Alexander Downer in Jan. 1995, Howard fought the next year's election campaign on the basis of economic reform. He became prime minister on 11 March 1996, ending 13 years of Labor government with a 44 seat Liberal-National coalition majority.

Career in Office
Upon gaining office, Howard pledged to slash government spending by $A8bn. between 1996–99. This motivated the sale of numerous state-owned services, most controversially the telecommunications firm Telstra. Howard's bill for the sale of one third of Telstra was passed by the upper house in June 1999. Within the same week a set of bills was passed allowing a 'consumption' tax on goods and services (GST), the proposal of which had crippled Liberal support at the 1993 election. Howard described the success of the GST and Telstra legislation as personal achievements. Other important issues in his first term in office included a dispute over indigenous land rights following a 1996 court ruling against Aboriginal access to sites of cultural tradition owned by non-Aboriginals, and the contentious introduction of a 'work for the dole' scheme in 1998. The scheme became a new outlet for a longstanding disagreement over compulsory union membership between the trade unions and the Howard government. A bitter union dispute was also sparked in April of the same year when a major stevedoring company, acting with government support, replaced its 1,500 workforce with non-union staff overnight.

Howard survived a considerable swing to Labor, losing 11 seats, at the 3 Oct. 1998 election. In Nov. of the following year, he organized a referendum on the amendment of Australia's constitution to become a republic with a parliament-appointed president. This proposal was rejected. Howard's second term was characterized by criticism over immigration and foreign policy, particularly concerning Australia's military contributions to UN peacekeeping in East Timor and NATO action against Serbia. In response to complaints that he was not providing for those displaced in the Serbian conflict, Howard welcomed Kosovar refugees in person at Sydney airport in May 1999. However, in July 2001 the refugee-laden Norwegian cargo ship Tampa was caught in a diplomatic gridlock between Australia, the UN, and Norway. The 'boat people' were eventually diverted to Papua New Guinea, with Howard taking a stern position against asylum seekers, to popular acclaim. His coalition government was re-elected at the 10 Nov. 2001 election with 82 seats. However, when Ansett, the country's second largest airline, stopped flying in Feb. 2002, Howard came under fire for failing to underwrite a last-minute sale. Owned by Air New Zealand but an Australian icon, the carrier had gone into administration in Sept. of the previous year.

In May 2003 Peter Hollingworth, Australia's governor-general, resigned. Hollingworth had been the subject of allegations of a rape in the 1960s (the charges were later dropped) and was censured for his failure to dismiss a paedophile member of the clergy when he was archbishop of Brisbane. Howard, who had recommended Hollingworth's appointment, accepted the resignation but confirmed his right to make future appointments without consultation.

Australian foreign policy in the Asia-Pacific region has become more aggressive under Howard's leadership. His interventionist approach was first tested in East Timor in Sept. 1999 and deemed a success by the Australian public. The mission was strengthened by the confirmation of East Timor's independence by the Indonesian parliament on 19 Oct. 1999, the same day a mass grave was unearthed. Australian involvement in the region was highlighted by the terrorist attack on a nightclub in Bali, Indonesia, on 16 Nov. 2002 when 88 Australians were killed. Despite the sympathy of Asian neighbours, Howard was criticized for declaring Australia's willingness to act pre-emptively if under threat. Malaysia's prime minister, Dr Mahathir Mohamad, accused Howard of arrogance in his approach to regional security, and the Thai government rejected suggestions that external assistance was necessary in controlling domestic terrorist threats.

In July 2003 Australia led a peacekeeping mission to the Solomon Islands at the request of the prime minister, Sir Allan Kemakeza. Although New Zealand, Papua New Guinea, the Fiji Islands and Tonga also contributed troops, Australia was seen to dominate the mission, causing unease among ex-colonies. Relations with the government of Papua New Guinea, led by Sir Michael Somare since Aug. 2002, became strained in mid-2003 over the issue of Australian involvement in Papua New Guinea's administration. Howard had enjoyed good relations with Somare's predecessor, Sir Mekere Morauta, and had declared him his country's last hope for political and economic revival. Howard insisted that Somare accepted Australian police and professionals for operational rather than observational involvement, threatening the withdrawal of Australia's crucial aid package.

Howard's support for the US-led invasion of Iraq in March 2003 attracted vociferous domestic opposition. The subsequent failure to demonstrate an Iraqi programme for weapons of mass destruction (WMD) provoked accusations of lying to justify the attack. However, opinion polls demonstrated strong support for

Howard and involvement in the war. He was re-elected for a further term when the Liberal Party won the election of 9 Oct. 2004 taking 74 seats and 40·5% of the vote. In Dec. 2004 he became Australia's second longest-serving prime minister after Sir Robert Menzies.

DEFENCE

The Minister for Defence has responsibility under legislation for the control and administration of the Defence Force. The Chief of Defence Force Staff is vested with command of the Defence Force. He is the principal military adviser to the Minister. The Chief of Naval Staff, the Chief of the General Staff and the Chief of the Air Staff command the Navy, Army and Air Force respectively. They have delegated authority from the Chief of Defence Force Staff and the Secretary to administer matters relating to their particular Service.

2004 defence expenditure was US$11,758m., amounting to US$591 per capita and representing 2·3% of GDP.

Army

The strength of the Army was 25,445, including 2,609 women, as at 30 June 2004. The effective strength of the Army Reserve was 16,445.

Women have been eligible for combat duties since 1993.

Navy

The all-volunteer Navy as at 30 June 2004 was 13,133 including 2,301 women. The Fleet Air Arm included six diesel-powered submarines and nine frigates.

The fleet main base is at Sydney, with subsidiary bases at Cockburn Sound (Western Australia), Cairns and Darwin.

Air Force

The Royal Australian Air Force (RAAF) operated 152 combat aircraft including 29 F-111 and 71 F-18 'Hornets' in 2004. As at 30 June 2003 personnel numbered 13,455, including 2,037 women. There is also an Australian Air Force Reserve, 2,800-strong.

INTERNATIONAL RELATIONS

Australia is a member of the UN, WTO, BIS, the Commonwealth, OECD, Asian Development Bank, Colombo Plan, APEC, IOM, the Pacific Islands Forum, the Pacific Community and the Antarctic Treaty.

ECONOMY

In the year ended 30 June 2003 service industries accounted for almost 80% of GDP and manufacturing 10·7%.

According to the anti-corruption organization *Transparency International*, Australia ranked 9th in the world in a 2005 survey of the countries with the least corruption in business and government. It received 8·8 out of 10 in the annual index.

Overview

The Australian economy has experienced robust expansion since 1992. GDP growth averaged 3·7% between 1992 and 2004, exceeding average OECD growth by more than 1%. Australia began implementing deep economic reforms in the 1980s, a process which intensified in the early 1990s. Significant improvement in economic performance in recent years is attributed to the liberalization of what was previously a heavily protected and highly regulated economy. Increased competition and technological advances have helped drive productivity gains. The Economist Intelligence Unit (EIU) estimates that average annual total factor productivity growth over the period 1991–2000 was 1·67%, over five times greater than the 0·27% average of the previous decade. The OECD also stresses the importance of the country's adoption of sound macroeconomic policies backed by a framework emphasizing transparency, accountability and protection from political influence. The combination of deep

structural reform and sound macroeconomic management allowed Australia to grow robustly over the years even when faced with slowdowns in regional and global demand owing to the Asian crisis in 1997–98 and the US downturn in 2001–02.

The impact of a severe drought in 2003 and the global slowdown was withstood by the buoyant domestic economy, fuelled by strong domestic demand growth and heavy spending on private housing. Per capita GDP has improved relative to other developed economies over the last decade and now compares with that of Western European countries. Like most developed countries, services account for most of the country's output but mining and agriculture are the principal foreign exchange earning sectors.

An OECD survey of Feb. 2005 stressed that further reform progress is necessary in order to ensure that average income levels do not decline in the medium-run as a result of population ageing. The main threats posed by population ageing are the increase in public health costs and the decrease in labour supply. While Australia's demographic picture compares favourably with other developed countries, in order to ensure that growth remains robust enough to maintain income levels in the future the OECD recommends that policy efforts focus on strengthening competition and raising labour supply. Despite significant competition policy improvement over the years, restrictions were still found in 'agricultural marketing arrangements, liquor licensing, compulsory insurance schemes, pharmacies, the professions and some occupations'. Regarding labour supply, the OECD recommends encouraging greater unskilled labour participation by lowering the minimum wage and overhauling the excessively legalistic industrial wage award system, and increasing skilled labour activity by raising the upper tax bracket floor and reducing the tax rate. A concern highlighted by the EIU is the country's low level of domestic savings and investment, relative to expenditure. In 2002–03 private consumption spending accounted for 60% of GDP while spending on gross fixed investment equalled roughly 25%.

Currency

On 14 Feb. 1966 Australia adopted a system of decimal currency. The currency unit, the Australian dollar (AUD), is divided into 100 *cents*.

Foreign exchange reserves were US$40,972m. in Dec. 2005 and gold reserves US$1,316m. Total money supply was $A176·1m. in June 2005.

Inflation rates (based on OECD statistics):

1995	1996	1997	1998	1999	2000	2001	2002	2003	2004
4·6%	2·6%	0·3%	0·9%	1·5%	4·5%	4·4%	3·0%	2·8%	2·3%

According to the Reserve Bank of Australia the inflation rate in the year to Dec. 2005 was 2·8%, up from 2·6% in the year to Dec. 2004.

Budget

In Aug. 1998 the Commonwealth government introduced a tax reform package including, from 2000, the introduction of a Goods and Services Tax (GST) at a 10% rate, with all the revenues going to the states in return for the abolition of a range of other indirect taxes; the abolition of Financial Assistance Grants to states; the abolition of wholesale sales tax (which is levied by the Commonwealth government); cuts in personal income tax; and increases in social security benefits, especially for families. In the 2005–06 Mid-Year Economic and Fiscal Outlook an underlying cash surplus of $A11·5bn. (1·2% of GDP) was anticipated in 2005–06, an increase of $A2·5bn. since the 2005–06 budget.

The Australian Government levies income taxes. State expenditure is backed by federal grants. Australian Government General Government Sector expenses and revenue outcomes (in $A1m.):

	2004–05	2005–06[1]
Total expenses (by function)	195,293	207,038
including		
General public services	13,935	12,939
Defence	14,346	15,761
Public order and safety	2,345	2,715
Education	14,362	15,690
Health	35,561	37,986
Social security and welfare	82,962	87,137
Housing and community amenities	2,012	2,235
Recreation and culture	2,246	2,709
Fuel and energy	4,369	4,026
Agriculture, fisheries and forestry	1,813	3,181
Mining and mineral resources (other than		
fuels), manufacturing and construction	1,702	2,022
Transport and communications	2,769	3,033
Other economic affairs	4,895	4,921
Other purposes	11,975	12,685
Total revenue (by source)	206,218	218,622
including		
Income tax		
Individuals and other witholding	98,250	112,140
Companies	43,106	48,740
Superannuation funds	6,410	6,690
Petroleum resource rent tax	1,465	2,130
Indirect tax		
Excise duty—Petroleum products and crude oil	14,350	14,120
Other excise	7,631	7,780
Total excise duty	21,981	21,900
Customs duty	5,548	5,062
Other indirect taxes	1,164	1,190
Fringe benefit tax	3,089	3,470
Other taxes	1,973	2,455
Non-tax revenue	12,965	14,845

[1]Estimate.

Performance

Real GDP growth rates (based on OECD statistics):

1995	1996	1997	1998	1999	2000	2001	2002	2003	2004
3·8%	4·0%	3·7%	5·4%	4·2%	3·3%	2·7%	3·8%	3·5%	3·0%

The current account deficit was expected to narrow to 5·25% of GDP in 2005–06, reflecting an improvement in the country's terms of trade. During much of the 1990s the real GDP growth rate, along with lower inflation, made the Australian economic performance one of the best in the OECD area. In 2004 total GDP was US$631·3bn.

According to the *OECD Economic Survey* of Feb. 2005 'The Australian economy is still benefiting from the programme of … reforms that … resulted in a thirteen year long economic expansion, accompanied by low inflation, high resilience to external and domestic shocks, and very healthy public finances. … The short-term outlook is for continuing strong growth of productivity and output, low inflation and budget surpluses accompanied by tax cuts.'

Banking and Finance

From 1 July 1998 a new financial regulatory framework based on three agencies was introduced by the Australian government, following recommendations by the Financial System Inquiry. The framework included changes in the role of the Reserve Bank of Australia and creation of the Australian Prudential Regulation Authority (APRA) with responsibility for the supervision of deposit-taking institutions (comprising banks, building societies and credit unions), friendly societies, life and general insurance companies and superannuation funds. It further involved replacement of the Australian Securities Commission with the Australian Securities and Investments Commission (ASIC) with responsibility for the regulation of financial services and Australia's 1·2m. companies.

The banking system comprises:

(*a*) The Reserve Bank of Australia is the central bank. It has two broad responsibilities—monetary policy and the maintenance of financial stability, including stability of the payments system. It also issues Australia's currency notes and provides selected banking and registry services to Commonwealth Government customers and some overseas official institutions. Within the Reserve Bank there are two Boards: the Reserve Bank Board and the Payments System Board; the *Governor* (present incumbent, Ian Macfarlane) is the Chairman of each.

At 30 June 2005 total assets of the Reserve Bank of Australia were $A84,959m., including gold and foreign exchange, $A62,422m.; and Australian dollar securities, $A20,900m. At 30 June 2005 capital and reserves were $A9,558m. and main liabilities were Australian notes on issue, $A35,624m.; and deposits, $A29,228m.

A wholly owned subsidiary of the Reserve Bank (Note Printing Australia Limited) manufactures currency notes and other security documents for Australia and for export.

(*b*) Four major banks: (i) The Commonwealth Bank of Australia; (ii) the Australia and New Zealand Banking Group Ltd; (iii) Westpac Banking Corporation; (iv) National Australia Bank.

(*c*) The Commonwealth Bank of Australia has a subsidiary—Commonwealth Development Bank. There are nine other Australian-owned banks—Adelaide Bank Ltd, AMP Bank Ltd, Bank of Queensland Ltd, Bendigo Bank Ltd, Elders Rural Bank (50% owned by Bendigo Bank Ltd), Macquarie Bank Ltd, Members Equity Pty Ltd, St George Bank Ltd and Suncorp-Metway Ltd.

(*d*) There are 11 banks incorporated in Australia which are owned by foreign banks and 28 branches of foreign banks (these figures include five foreign banks which have both a subsidiary and a branch presence in Australia).

(*e*) According to the Australian Prudential Regulation Authority (APRA), as at 30 June 2005 there were 50 authorized banks with Australian banking assets of $A1,264·7bn., with 4,960 branches, 24,173 reported ATMs and 518,532 reported EFTPOS terminals. As at 30 June 2005 there were 14 building societies with assets of $A16·3bn. and 161 credit unions with assets of $A33·1bn.

There is an Australian Stock Exchange (ASX) in Sydney.

ENERGY AND NATURAL RESOURCES

Environment

Australia's carbon dioxide emissions from the consumption and flaring of fossil fuels were the equivalent of 21·0 tonnes per capita in 2002. An *Environmental Sustainability Index* compiled for the World Economic Forum meeting in Jan. 2005 ranked Australia 13th in the world, with 61·0%. The index measured the ability of countries to maintain favourable environmental conditions and examined various factors including pollution levels and the use or abuse of natural resources.

With only 0·003% of the world's population, Australia emits 1·4% of the world's greenhouse gases, making the country the largest generator of greenhouse gases per capita. However, in 2004 the government launched a $A1·8bn. Climate Change Strategy. A centrepiece of the government's Energy White Paper is a $A500m. Low Emissions Technology Demonstration Fund. A mandatory target has been set of 9,500 GWh of electricity generation from renewable sources by 2010.

Electricity

Electricity supply is the responsibility of the State governments. 2002–03 total production was 201,141m. kWh (7·6% hydroelectric). In the year ended 30 June 2002 total consumption stood at 176,279m. kWh, including 51,012m. kWh by residential customers.

Oil and Gas

The main fields are Gippsland (Vic.) and Carnarvon (WA). Crude oil and condensate production was 33,321m. litres in

2002–03, a decrease of 7·7% over the previous year. The value of oil and natural gas production in 2000–01 was estimated to total $A16·4bn. Oil reserves at the end of 2002 totalled 3·1bn. bbls. and natural gas reserves 2,550bn. cu. metres. Australia's most productive oilfield in 2000 was Laminaria in Northern Territory with peak production of around 180,000 bbls. and average production at Nov. 2000 of around 167,000 bbls. per day. Natural gas production (2002) was 34·5bn. cu. metres. Natural gas reserves (2002) totalled 2,265bn. cu. metres.

Minerals
Australia is the world's largest producer of bauxite and alumina. It is also the world's largest producer of diamonds (mostly for industrial use) and the third-largest gold producer. Black coal is Australia's major source of energy. Reserves are large (2002: 39·7bn. economically recoverable tonnes) and easily worked. The main fields are in New South Wales and Queensland. Brown coal (lignite) reserves are mined only in Victoria. In 2004–05 raw coal production was 387m. tonnes; lignite production (estimate), 68m. tonnes; and iron ore and concentrates (estimate), 251·8m. tonnes.

Production of other major minerals in 2004–05 (in tonnes): bauxite, 57·8m.; alumina, 17·2m.; salt (estimate), 12·4m.; manganese (estimate), 3·6m.; zinc, 1·4m.; nickel, 198,000 (content of concentrates); uranium, 11,964; silver (estimate), 2,330; gold (estimate), 265. Diamond production, 2004–05: 32·4m. carats. Australia is the world's largest producer of diamonds, ranking first for industrial-grade diamonds and second for gem-grade diamonds, after Botswana.

Agriculture
At 30 June 2003 there were an estimated 132,983 establishments mainly engaged in agriculture. Agricultural production in 2002–03 was estimated to total $A32·6bn. At 30 June 2003 the estimated total area of land under agricultural use was 439·5m. ha. (about 57·1% of total land area). In 2002–03 there were 24·1m. ha. of crops. 2·37m. ha. of crops and pastures were irrigated in 2002–03. Important crops (2002–03): wheat (10·1m. tonnes from 11·2m. ha.); barley (1·0m. tonnes from 3·9m. ha.); grain sorghum (1·5m. tonnes from 0·67m. ha.); oats (1·4m. tonnes from 0·91m. ha.); canola (1·8m. tonnes from 1·3m. ha.); sugarcane (37·0m. tonnes from 0·45m. ha.). In 2002–03, 1·5m. tonnes of grapes were harvested from 157,492 ha. of vines.

Beef cattle farming represents the largest sector, accounting for 25% of farming establishments. Livestock totals at June 2003: beef cattle and calves, 23·6m.; dairy cattle, 3·0m.; sheep and lambs, 99·3m.; pigs, 2·7m. Gross value of agricultural production in 2002–03, $A32·6bn., including (in $A1bn.) cattle and calves slaughtering, 6·4; sheep and lamb slaughtering, 2·0; wheat, 2·7; wool, 3·3; milk, 2·8. Livestock products (in 1,000 tonnes) at June 2002–03: beef, 2,035; lamb and mutton, 597; pigmeat, 420; veal, 38; chicken meat, 690; wool, 551. Milk in the same year, 10,326m. litres.

Fruit and vegetable production in 2002–03 (in 1,000 tonnes): potatoes, 1,247·3; oranges, 599·5; apples, 326·1; bananas, 264·8; onions, 228·6.

In 2003 organic crops were grown in an area covering 10m. ha. (the largest area of any country in the world), representing 2·2% of all farmland.

Australia is the world's leading wool producer; only China has more sheep.

Forestry
The Federal government is responsible for forestry at the national level. Each State is responsible for the management of publicly owned forests. Estimated total native forest cover was 162·7m. ha. at Feb. 2003 (approximately 21% of Australia's land area), made up of (in 1,000 ha.): public forest, 121·6m.; privately owned, 38·9m. The major part of wood supplies derives from coniferous

plantations, of which there were 988,000 ha. at 30 Dec. 2002. Australia also had 638,000 ha. of hardwood plantation at that date. Production of sawn timber in 2003–04 was 4,037,300 cu. metres.

Fisheries
The Australian Fishing Zone covers an area 16% larger than the Australian land mass and is the third largest fishing zone in the world, but fish production is insignificant by world standards owing to low productivity of the oceans. The major commercially exploited species are prawns, rock lobster, abalone, tuna, other fin fish, scallops, oysters and pearls. Total fisheries production in 2003–04 came to 267,000 tonnes with a gross value of $A2·2bn. In the same year aquaculture production was an estimated 43,475 tonnes with a gross value of $A732·5m., which represented 34% of the total value of fisheries production.

INDUSTRY
The leading companies by market capitalization in Australia, excluding banking and finance, in May 2004 were: The News Corporation Ltd (US$52·2bn.); Telstra Corporation Ltd (US$42·3bn.), a telecommunications company; and BHP Billiton Ltd (US$32·4bn.), a resources company.

Manufacturing industry in 2002–03 contributed around 11% to Australia's GDP. In May 2004 almost 1·1m. people were employed, 11% of Australia's total employed.

Manufacturing by sector, 2002–03 (estimates):

	Labour costs in $A1m.	Total income in $A1m.
Food, beverages and tobacco	8,602	69,312
Textiles, clothing, footwear and leather products	1,985	11,446
Wood and paper products	2,843	18,619
Printing, publishing and reorded media	4,787	21,757
Chemical, petroleum, coal and associated products	5,287	51,171
Non-metallic mineral products	2,057	12,950
Metal products	7,878	57,094
Machinery and equipment	10,727	61,728
Other manufacturing	2,424	12,794

Manufactured products in 2002–03 included: clay bricks, 1,639m.; portland cement, 7·5m. tonnes; ready-mixed concrete, 21·0m. cu. metres; tobacco and cigarettes, 19,561 tonnes; newsprint, 407m. tonnes; pig iron, 6·6m. tonnes; aviation turbine fuel, 5,149m. litres; beer, 1,727m. litres.

Labour
In 2003–04 the total workforce (persons aged 15 and over) numbered 10,145,500 (4,520,600 females). In 2003–04 there were 9,559,500 employed persons (52·3% females) with 2,719,100 in part-time employment (45·6% females). The majority of wage and salary earners have had their minimum wages and conditions of work prescribed in awards by the Industrial Relations Commission. In Oct. 1991 the Commission decided to allow direct employer-employee wage bargaining, provided agreements reached are endorsed by the Commission. In some States, some conditions of work (e.g., weekly hours of work, leave) are set down in State legislation. Average weekly wage, Feb. 2004, $A754·30 (men, $A900·10; women, $A591·70). Average weekly hours worked by full-time employed person, 2003–04: 40·4 hours. Four weeks annual leave is standard. In 2003–04 part-time work accounted for 28% of all employment in Australia and persons born overseas made up 25% of the total labour force.

Employees in all States are covered by workers' compensation legislation and by certain industrial award provisions relating to work injuries.

During 2003 there were 643 industrial disputes recorded which accounted for 439,400 working days lost (70% increase on 2002). In these disputes 275,600 workers were involved.

As at 30 Nov. 2004 retail trade (15·2% of employed persons) and property and business services (11·5%) had overtaken the manufacturing industry (11·1%) as the largest employers. Health and community services employ 10·1%.

In Aug. 2005, 1,612,500 wage and salary earners worked in the public sector and (Feb. 2001) 5,898,900 in the private sector.

The following table shows the percentage distribution of employed persons in 2003–04 according to the *Australian Standard Classification of Occupations*:

	Employed persons (%)
Professionals	19·0
Intermediate clerical, sales and service workers	17·0
Tradespersons and related workers	12·8
Associate professionals	12·2
Elementary clerical, sales and service workers	10·0
Labourers and related workers	9·3
Intermediate production and transport workers	8·3
Managers and administrators	7·4
Advanced clerical and service workers	4·0

In 2003–04, 586,000 persons were unemployed, of whom 21·0% had been unemployed for more than one year. The unemployment rate in Jan. 2006 was 5·3%.

Trade Unions

In Aug. 2003, 1,866,700 employees were members of a trade union representing 23·0% of all full-time employees (22·0% females). Many of the larger trade unions are affiliated with central labour organizations, the oldest and by far the largest being the Australian Council of Trade Unions (ACTU) formed in 1927. In 2002, 46 unions were affiliated to ACTU, representing approximately 1·8m. workers. In July 1992 the Industrial Relations Legislation Amendment Act freed the way for employers and employees to negotiate enterprise-based awards and agreements.

INTERNATIONAL TRADE

In 1990 Australia and New Zealand completed a Closer Economic Relations agreement (initiated in 1983) which establishes free trade in goods. Net foreign debt was $A359·0bn. as at 30 June 2003 (an increase of 9·0% on the previous year). In 1998 the effect of the Asian meltdown on exports resulted increasingly in shipments of commodities and exports of manufactures and some services being redirected to other destinations, notably the USA and Europe. Merchandise exports decreased by 5% in 2002–03 against the previous year while imports rose by 11%.

Imports and Exports

Merchandise imports and exports for years ending 30 June (in $A1m.):

	Imports	Exports
2000–01	118,317	119,539
2001–02	119,681	121,176
2002–03	133,131	115,442
2003–04	131,020	108,906

The Australian customs tariff provides for preferences to goods produced in and shipped from certain countries as a result of reciprocal trade agreements. These include the UK, New Zealand, Canada and Ireland.

Most valuable commodity imports, 2003–04 (in $A1m.): passenger motor vehicles, 11,217; crude petroleum oils, 6,321; computing equipment, 5,127; medicaments, 4,898; telecommunications equipment, 4,359; aircraft, associated equipment and spacecraft, 3,818. Most valuable commodity exports, 2003–04 (in $A1m.): coal, 10,893; non-monetary gold, 5,651; iron ore, 5,216; crude petroleum products, 4,643; bovine meat, 3,917; aluminium, 3,803; aluminium ores and concentrates (including alumina), 3,710.

Australia is the world's largest exporter of black coal, bauxite, lead, diamonds, mineral sands, beef and wool.

Trade by bloc or country in 2003–04 (in $A1m.):

	Imports	Exports
APEC	91,094	77,692
ASEAN	20,555	12,263
EU	31,026	12,722
OECD	81,861	61,263
China	15,339	9,912
Indonesia	3,766	2,983
Japan	16,101	19,798
South Korea	4,878	8,473
Malaysia	4,705	2,225
New Zealand	5,056	8,080
Singapore	5,107	3,056
Taiwan	3,395	3,701
Germany	7,985	1,309
UK	5,430	5,132
USA	19,945	9,453

COMMUNICATIONS

Roads

As at 30 June 2004 there was a total of 741,621 km of roads, of which 57·8% were paved.

At 31 March 2005 registration totals were: 10,896,410 passenger vehicles, 2,030,254 light commercial vehicles, 458,205 trucks, 72,620 buses, 40,693 campervans and 421,923 motorcycles

In 2003, 1,633 persons were killed in road accidents (1,723 in the previous year).

Rail

Privatization of government railways began in Victoria in 1994 with West Coast Railway and Hoys Transport being granted seven-year franchises. Specialised Container Transport (SCT) won the first private rail freight franchise in 1995 followed by TNT (now Toll Holdings). Australian National Railway Commission was sold by the Commonwealth Government in Nov. 1997 and in Feb. 1999 V/Line Freight Corporation, owned by the Victorian Government, was sold to Freight Australia. Rail passenger services in Victoria were franchised in mid-1999. The Australian Railroad Group acquired Western Australia's government rail freight operation, Westrail, in Nov. 2000. In Jan. 2002 Toll Holdings and Lang acquired the rolling stock of the National Rail Corporation (NRC) and New South Wales freight carrier, FreightCorp. These two sales leave QR as the only government-owned rail freight operator in Australia.

At 30 June 2003 the total length of track was 4,150 km (broad gauge, 1,600 mm); 17,720 km (standard, 1,435 mm); 15,160 km (narrow, 1,067 mm); 4,150 km (narrow, 610 mm gauge); and 281 km (dual gauge). In 2002–03 a total of 598·6m. tonnes of freight were carried; passengers carried totalled 586m. urban (including train and tram); 9m. non-urban.

Under various Commonwealth–State standardization agreements, all the State capitals are now linked by standard gauge track. The 'AustralAsia Rail Project', which involved the construction of 1,420 km standard gauge railway between Alice Springs and Darwin, has been completed and passenger services from Adelaide through Alice Springs and on to Darwin commenced on 1 Feb. 2004.

There are also private industrial and tourist railways, and tramways in Adelaide, Melbourne and Sydney. In the latter two cities there are also metro systems.

Civil Aviation

Qantas Airways is Australia's principal international airline. In 1992 Qantas merged with Australian Airlines, and in 1993, 25% of the company was purchased by British Airways. The remainder is government-owned. Qantas relaunched Australian Airlines in Oct. 2002 to connect Asia-Pacific with Cairns and the Gold Coast. A total of 49 international airlines operated scheduled air services to and from Australia in 2004. There are 13 international airports, the main ones being Adelaide, Brisbane, Cairns, Darwin, Melbourne, Perth and Sydney. In 2003–04 international passenger traffic increased by 12·6% to 18·1m.; international freight decreased by 1·3% to 627,002 tonnes; mail increased by 3·0% to 28,444 tonnes.

Sydney (Kingsford Smith) handled the most traffic (29·5%) in Australia in 2003–04 (26,072,647 passengers, of which 15,817,603 on domestic flights), followed by Melbourne International (21·1%) and Brisbane (15·6%).

Internal airlines (domestic and regional) carried 40·6m. passengers in the year ended 31 July 2005. Domestic airlines were deregulated in Oct. 1990.

In 2003–04 there were 256 licensed, registered and certified aerodromes in Australia and its external territories. At 30 June 2004 there were 17,532 registered aircraft.

Shipping
The chief ports are Brisbane, Dampier, Fremantle, Gladstone, Hay Point, Melbourne, Newcastle, Port Hedland, Port Kembla, Port Walcott, Sydney and Weipa. Dampier, Australia's busiest port, handled 101,928,968 tonnes of cargo in 2002–03. As at 30 June 2003 the trading fleet comprised 74 vessels totalling 2,135,982 DWT, 1,628,203 GRT.

Coastal cargo handled at Australian ports in 2002–03 (in gross weight tonnes): loaded, 52·8m.; unloaded, 53·5m. International trade loaded, 529·4m. tonnes; unloaded, 62·2m. tonnes. Calls to ports made by commercial ships in 2002–03 totalled 23,454 with 395 made by passenger vessels.

Telecommunications
Australian telecommunications are in the latter stages of an evolution from a state-owned monopoly. In 1989 the domestic market became a regulated monopoly with Telstra as the government-owned company providing all services and, in 1991, a duopoly (with Optus) in fixed network services. In 1993 Vodafone joined Telstra and Optus in the provision of mobile phone services. A new regulatory regime was created by the introduction of the Telecommunications Act 1997 and both markets were opened to wholesale and retail competition. There is no limit to the number of carriers that can hold licences under the new arrangements and by June 2002 a total of 83 licences had been issued. The Australian Communications Authority (ACA) and the Australian Competition and Consumer Commission (ACCC) are the primary regulators with responsibility for the industry's development. Telstra is set to be fully privatized in late 2006 with the sale of the government's 51·8% stake in the company.

Telephone subscribers numbered 23,169,000 in 2002 (1,178·3 per 1,000 inhabitants), and there were 11,111,000 PCs in use, or 565·1 per 1,000 persons. In Feb. 2002 there were 12·87m. mobile phone subscribers (the largest supplier being Optus, with 4·59m. subscribers). As at 31 March 2005 there were 5·98m. Internet subscribers.

Three telecommunications satellites are in orbit covering the entire continent.

Postal Services
Postal services are operated by Australia Post, operating under the Australian Postal Corporation Act 1989 as a government business enterprise. In the year ended 30 June 2005 revenue was $A4,292m., expenditure $A3,727m. There were 3,853 corporate outlets and licensed post offices and other agencies in 2002–03, and 5,262·0m. postal items were handled.

SOCIAL INSTITUTIONS

Justice
The judicial power of the Commonwealth of Australia is vested in the High Court of Australia (the Federal Supreme Court), in the Federal courts created by the Federal Parliament (the Federal Court of Australia and the Family Court of Australia) and in the State courts invested by Parliament with Federal jurisdiction.

High Court
The High Court consists of a Chief Justice and six other Justices, appointed by the Governor-General in Council. The Constitution confers on the High Court original jurisdiction, *inter alia*, in all matters arising under treaties or affecting consuls or other foreign representatives, matters between the States of the Commonwealth, matters to which the Commonwealth is a party and matters between residents of different States. Federal Parliament may make laws conferring original jurisdiction on the High Court, *inter alia*, in matters arising under the Constitution or under any laws made by the Parliament. It has in fact conferred jurisdiction on the High Court in matters arising under the Constitution and in matters arising under certain laws made by Parliament.

The High Court may hear and determine appeals from its own Justices exercising original jurisdiction, from any other Federal Court, from a Court exercising Federal jurisdiction and from the Supreme Courts of the States. It also has jurisdiction to hear and determine appeals from the Supreme Courts of the Territories. The right of appeal from the High Court to the Privy Council in London was abolished in 1986.

Other Federal Courts
Since 1924, four other Federal courts have been created to exercise special Federal jurisdiction, i.e. the Federal Court of Australia, the Family Court of Australia, the Australian Industrial Court and the Federal Court of Bankruptcy. The Federal Court of Australia was created by the Federal Court of Australia Act 1976 and began to exercise jurisdiction on 1 Feb. 1977. It exercises such original jurisdiction as is invested in it by laws made by the Federal Parliament including jurisdiction formerly exercised by the Australian Industrial Court and the Federal Court of Bankruptcy, and in some matters previously invested in either the High Court or State and Territory Supreme Courts. The Federal Court also acts as a court of appeal from State and Territory courts in relation to Federal matters. Appeal from the Federal Court to the High Court will be by way of special leave only. The State Supreme Courts have also been invested with Federal jurisdiction in bankruptcy.

State Courts
The general Federal jurisdiction of the State courts extends, subject to certain restrictions and exceptions, to all matters in which the High Court has jurisdiction or in which jurisdiction may be conferred upon it.

Industrial Tribunals
The chief federal industrial tribunal is the Australian Conciliation and Arbitration Commission, constituted by presidential members (with the status of judges) and commissioners. The Commission's functions include settling industrial disputes, making awards, determining the standard hours of work and wage fixation. Questions of law, the judicial interpretation of awards and imposition of penalties in relation to industrial matters are dealt with by the Industrial Division of the Federal Court.

At 30 June 2005 the prison population was 25,353, an increase of almost 45% since 1995.

Each State has its own individual police service which operates almost exclusively within its State boundaries. State police investigations include murder, robbery, street-level drug dealing, kidnapping, domestic violence and motor vehicle offences. State police activities are broadly known as community policing.

The role of the Australian Federal Police (AFP) is to enforce Commonwealth criminal law and protect Commonwealth and national interests from crime in Australia and overseas.

Responsibilities include combating organized crime, trans-national crime, money laundering, illicit drug trafficking, e-crime, the investigation of fraud against the Australian Government and handling special references from Government. The AFP also provides a protection service to dignitaries and crucial witnesses as well as community policing services to the people of the Australian Capital Territory, Jervis Bay and Australia's External Territories.

Total Australian Federal Police personnel (excluding ACT policing) as at 30 June 2003 was 3,496, of which 2,297 were sworn employees (police members) and 1,199 unsworn employees. There are approximately 48,000 police officers in Australia.

Education
The governments of the Australian States and Territories have the major responsibility for education, including the administration and substantial funding of primary, secondary, and technical and further education. In most States, a single Education Department is responsible for these three levels but in Queensland, Western Australia and the Northern Territory, separate departments deal with school-based and technical and further education issues.

School attendance is compulsory between the ages of six and 15 years (16 years in Tasmania), at either a government school or a recognized non-government educational institution. Many children attend pre-schools for a year before entering school (usually in sessions of two–three hours, for two–five days per week). Government schools are usually co-educational and comprehensive. Non-government schools have been traditionally single-sex, particularly in secondary schools, but there is a trend towards co-education. Tuition is free at government schools, but fees are normally charged at non-government schools.

In Aug. 2004 there were 6,938 government (and 2,677 non-government) primary and secondary schools with 2,249,076 (1,082,888) full-time pupils and 156,156 (76,910) full-time teachers.

Vocational education and training (VET) is essentially a partnership between the Commonwealth, the States and Territories and industry. The Commonwealth is involved in VET through an agreed set of national arrangements for sharing responsibility with the States and Territories. The current mechanism for giving effect to this is the Australian National Training Authority (ANTA) Agreement, which sets out the roles and responsibilities for VET: they provide two-thirds of the funding and have all of the regulatory responsibility for the sector. They are also the 'owners' of the network of public Technical and Further Education (TAFE) institutes. In 2003 publicly-funded VET programmes were offered by some 79 TAFEs and other government institutions. A further 531 community education providers and 1,339 other providers (mainly private providers) delivering VET were at least partly publicly funded. In 2003 there were over 1·7m. people enrolled in VET courses.

In 2003, 45 higher education institutions received Common-wealth Government funding. Most of these institutions operate under State and Territory legislation although several operate under Commonwealth legislation. There is also a completely privately-funded university and numerous private higher education providers in a range of specialist fields. Institutions established by appropriate legislation are autonomous and have the authority to accredit their own programmes and are primarily responsible for their own quality assurance. There were 929,952 university students in 2003. Fields of university study with the largest number of award course students in 2003 were management and commerce (27·5%); society and culture (21·8%); health (10·8%); and education (9·7%).

The higher education sector contributes a significant proportion of the research and research training undertaken in Australia. The Australian Research Council provides advice on research issues and administers the allocation of some research grants to higher education sector researchers and institutions.

The Commonwealth Government offers a number of programmes which provide financial assistance to students. The Youth Allowance is available for eligible full-time students aged 16 to 24, depending on the circumstances of study. Austudy is available to eligible full-time students aged over 25. Abstudy provides financial assistance for eligible Aboriginal and Torres Strait Islanders who undertake full-time or part-time study. AIC—the Assistance for Isolated Children scheme—provides special support to families whose children are isolated from schooling or who have physical disabilities.

Most students contribute to the cost of their higher education through the Higher Education Contribution Scheme (HECS). They can choose to make an upfront contribution (with a 25% discount) or to defer all or part of their payment until their income reaches a certain level when they must begin repaying their contribution through the taxation system. Overseas students generally pay full tuition fees. Universities are also able to offer full-fee places in postgraduate courses and to a limited number of domestic undergraduate students. In 2000 Australia hosted approximately 150,000 international students, mostly from Asia, who contributed around $A3·7bn. to the local economy in fees and expenditure on goods and services.

Total operating expenses of Australian Government on education in 2002–03 were $A41,004m. Private expenditure on education amounted to $A12,443m. The figures include government grants to the private sector which are also included in the operating expenses of Australian governments.

International education is becoming increasingly important, with 385,000 overseas students attending Australian educational institutions in 2002, compared to just 56,000 in 1988. It is now Australia's third largest service export sector. Nearly 18% of university students are foreign, the highest proportion of any country.

The adult literacy rate is at least 99%.

Health
In 2002–03 there were 729 public hospitals (including 19 psychiatric hospitals) and 536 private hospitals (including acute and psychiatric hospitals); there were an average 2·6 public hospital beds per 1,000 population (down from 3·0 in 1997–98). In 2002–03 there were 164,700 registered nurses, 36,700 general medical practitioners and 10,100 physiotherapists. The Royal Flying Doctor Service serves remote areas. Estimated total government expenditure on health goods and services (public and private sectors) in 2003–04 was $A78·6bn. ($A72·5bn. in the previous year), representing 9·7% of GDP.

At 31 Dec. 2003 there were estimated to be 20,580 HIV cases, 9,380 AIDS diagnoses and 6,385 deaths following AIDS.

In 1999–2000, 21% of the adult population (aged 25 years and over) were considered obese (having a body mass index over 30), compared to 8·7% in 1990 and 7·1% in 1980.

Welfare
All Commonwealth government social security pensions, benefits and allowances are financed from the Commonwealth government's general revenue. In addition, assistance is provided for welfare services.

Age Pensions—age pensions are payable to men 65 years of age or more who have lived in Australia for a specified period and, unless permanently blind, also satisfy an income and assets test. The minimum age for women's eligibility was raised by six months to 62 years on 1 July 2001 and is being lifted in six-month increments every two years until 1 July 2013 when it will be 65 years. The qualifying age at 1 July 2004 was 62 years 6 months. In the year ending 30 June 2004, 1,876,250 age pensioners received a total of $A19,540·4m.

Disability Support Pension (DSP)—payable to persons aged 16 years or over with a physical, intellectual or psychiatric impairment of at least 20%, assessed as being unable to work for at least 30 hours a week. DSP for those of 21 years or over is paid at the same rate as Age Pensions and is subject to the same means test except for those who are permanently blind. In the year ending 30 June 2004, 696,742 disability support pensioners received a total of $A7,492·5m.

Carer Payment—payable to a person unable to support themselves owing to providing constant care and attention at home for a severely disabled person aged 16 or over, or a person who is frail aged, either permanently or for an extended period. Since 1 July 1998 Carer Payment has been extended to carers of children under 16 years of age with profound disabilities. Subject to income and assets tests, the rate of Carer Payment is the same as for other pensions. In the year ending 30 June 2004, 67,260 carers received a total of $A595·8m.

Carer Allowance—supplementary payment to a person providing constant care and attention at home for an adult or child with a disability or severe medical condition. The allowance is not income or assets tested. In the year ending 30 June 2004, 297,607 carers received a total of $A965·4m.

Sickness Allowance—paid to those over school-leaving age but below Age Pension age who are unable to work or continue full-time study temporarily owing to illness or injury. Eligibility rests on the person having a job or study course to which they can return. In the year ending 30 June 2004 a total of $A85·4m. was paid to beneficiaries.

Family Tax Benefit (FTB)—replaced *Family Allowance* and *Family Tax Payment* on 1 July 2000. Family Tax Benefit Part A is paid to assist families with children under 21 years of age or dependent full-time students aged 21–24 years; Family Tax Benefit Part B provides additional assistance to families with only one income earner and children under 16 years of age or dependent full-time students aged 16–18 years. Both benefits are subject to an income and assets test. In the year ending 30 June 2004 FTB Part A and Part B payments were made to a total of 3·0m. families comprising 5·8m. children.

Parenting Payment (Single) and (Partnered)—is paid to assist those who care for children under 16, with income and assets under certain amounts, and have been an Australian resident for at least two years or a refugee or have become a lone parent while an Australian resident. Parenting Payment (Single) is paid to lone parents under pension rates and conditions; Parenting Payment (Partnered) is paid to one of the parents in the couple. [Since 1 July 2000 the basic component of Parenting Payment (Partnered) was incorporated into Family Tax Benefit with 375,233 beneficiaries transferring to Family Tax Benefit Part B.] In the year ending 30 June 2004, 449,312 Parenting Payment (Single) beneficiaries and 177,157 Parenting Payment (Partnered) beneficiaries received a total of $A5,995·1m.

Maternity Payment—was introduced as part of the 'More Help for Families' package in the 2004–05 budget. Recognizing the costs associated with a new baby, all families with a child born or adopted from 1 July 2004 are eligible for the payment with no income or assets test applying. This replaces the Maternity Allowance and Baby Bonus. The Maternity Immunization Allowance is not subject to an income test for children born on or after 1 Jan. 2003. In the year ended 30 June 2004 a total of $A223·3m. was paid.

Newstart Allowance (NSA)—payable to those who are unemployed and are over 21 years of age but less than Age Pension age. Eligibility is subject to income and assets tests and recipients must satisfy the 'activity test' whereby they are actively seeking and willing to undertake suitable paid work, including casual and part-time work. To be eligible for benefit a person must

have resided in Australia for at least 12 months preceding his or her claim or intend to remain in Australia permanently; unemployment must not be as a result of industrial action by that person or by members of a union to which that person is a member. In the year ended 30 June 2004 a total of $A4,754·7m. was paid to NSA beneficiaries.

Youth Allowance—replaced five former schemes for young people, including the Youth Training Allowance. In the year ending 30 June 2004 a total of $A2,257·4m. was paid to YA beneficiaries.

Mature Age Allowance (MAA)—paid to older long-term unemployed, over 60 years of age but less than Age Pension age. MAA is non-activity tested. In the year ended June 2004 a total of $A372·5m. was paid.

Service Pensions—are paid by the Department of Veterans' Affairs. Male veterans who have reached the age of 60 years or are permanently unemployable, and who served in a theatre of war, are eligible subject to an income and assets test. The minimum age for female veterans' eligibility is being lifted from 55 to 60 years in six-month increments every two years over the period 1995–2013. The qualifying age at 1 July 2004 was 57 years. Wives of service pensioners are also eligible, provided that they do not receive a pension from the Department of Social Security. Disability pension is a compensatory payment in respect of incapacity attributable to war service. It is paid at a rate commensurate with the degree of incapacity and is free of any income test. In the year ended 30 June 2004, $A2,830·5m. of service pensions and $A2,743·6m. of disability and war widows' dependants' pensions were paid out; at 30 June 2004 there were 307,514 eligible veterans.

In addition to cash benefits, welfare services are provided, either directly or through State and local government authorities and voluntary agencies, for people with special needs.

Medicare—covers: automatic entitlement under a single public health fund to medical and optometrical benefits of 85% of the Medical Benefits Schedule fee, with a maximum patient payment for any service where the Schedule fee is charged; access without direct charge to public hospital accommodation and to inpatient and outpatient treatment by doctors appointed by the hospital; the restoration of funds for community health to approximately the same real level as 1975; a reduction in charges for private treatment in shared wards of public hospitals, and increases in the daily bed subsidy payable to private hospitals.

The Medicare programme is financed in part by a 1·5% levy on taxable incomes, with low income cut-off points, which were $A15,902 p.a. for a single person in 2004–05 and $A26,834 p.a. for a family with an extra allowance of $A2,464 for each child. A levy surcharge of 1% was introduced from 1 July 1997 for single individuals with taxable incomes in excess of $A50,000 p.a. and couples and families with combined taxable incomes in excess of $A100,000 who do not have private hospital cover through private health insurance.

Medicare benefits are available to all persons ordinarily resident in Australia. Visitors from the UK, New Zealand, Italy, Sweden, the Netherlands and Malta have immediate access to necessary medical treatment, as do all visitors staying more than six months.

RELIGION

Under the Constitution the Commonwealth cannot make any law to establish any religion, to impose any religious observance or to prohibit the free exercise of any religion. The following percentages refer to those religions with the largest number of adherents at the census of 2001. Answering the census question on religious adherence was not obligatory, however.

Christian, 68·0% of population: Catholic, 26·6%; Anglican, 20·7%; Uniting Church, 6·7%; Presbyterian and Reformed, 3·4%;

Orthodox, 2·8%; Baptist, 1·6%; Lutheran, 1·3%; Pentecostal, 1·0%; Jehovah's Witnesses, 0·4%; Salvation Army, 0·4%; Churches of Christ, 0·3%; other Christian, 2·7%. Religions other than Christian 5·0%: Buddhism, 1·9%; Islam, 1·5%; Hinduism, 0·5%; Judaism, 0·4%; other religions, 0·5%; no religion, 15·5%; no statement, 11·7%.

The Anglican Synod voted for the ordination of ten women in Nov. 1992. In May 2005 the Roman Catholic church had three cardinals.

Thompson, R. C., *Religion in Australia, a History*. OUP, 1995

CULTURE

World Heritage Sites
There are 16 sites under Australian jurisdiction that appear on the UNESCO World Heritage List. They are (with year entered on list): Great Barrier Reef (1981), Kakadu National Park (1981), Willandra Lakes Region (1981), Tasmanian Wilderness (1982), Lord Howe Island Group (1982), Uluru-Kata Tjuta National Park (1987), Central Eastern Rainforest Reserves (1987), Wet Tropics of Queensland (1988), Shark Bay (1991), Fraser Island (1992), Australian Fossil Mammal Sites (Riversleigh/Naracoorte) (1994), Heard and McDonald Islands (1997), Macquarie Island (1997), the Greater Blue Mountains Area (2000), Purnululu National Park (2003) and Royal Exhibition Building and Carlton Gardens in Melbourne (2004).

Broadcasting
Broadcasting is regulated by the Australian Broadcasting Authority (ABA), established under the Broadcasting Services Act 1992. Foreign ownership of commercial radio and TV companies is restricted to 20%. The national broadcasting service is provided by the Australian Broadcasting Corporation (ABC) (established 1932), an independent statutory corporation receiving 82% of its funding from the Federal Government and the remainder from independent sources, and the Special Broadcasting Service (established 1978). The latter provides radio and TV services in more than 100 languages. The transmission system is PAL. There are also commercial radio and TV services operated by companies under licence, subscription TV services, community radio services operated on a non-profit basis and a parliamentary radio service to state capitals, Canberra and Newcastle. The international service Radio Australia broadcasts via short-wave to Papua New Guinea and the Pacific and also via satellite to the Asia-Pacific regions in English and other languages. Digital television broadcasting commenced in the five mainland metropolitan areas on 1 Jan. 2001. As at 30 June 2003 the ABA had licensed 53 commercial TV services, 257 commercial radio services and 334 community radio services. The ABA had allocated licences for two new commercial radio and 22 community radio services in 2002–03. In 2000 there were 36·7m. radio receivers.

In 2000 there were estimated to be 7·0m. TV households and 14·13m. TV sets (99% of households had at least one set). In 2002, 21% of households subscribed to pay-TV (17% in 2000).

Cinema
At 30 June 2000 there were 326 cinema sites with a total of 1,514 screens, 374,000 seats and paid admissions of $A79·4m. In 2002, 69·9% of the population aged 18 years and over (10·1m. people) attended a cinema, drive-in or other public screening of a film at least once.

Press
There were 48 daily metropolitan newspapers in 2005 (two national, 11 metropolitan and 35 regional). The papers with the largest circulations are the *Sunday Telegraph* (New South Wales), with an average of 730,000 per issue in 2004; the *Sunday Mail* (Queensland), with an average of 613,000 per issue; and the *Sun-Herald* (New South Wales), with an average of 530,000 per issue.

At least 24 magazines had an average circulation of over 100,000 copies per issue in 2004.

Tourism
In 2002–03 the total number of overseas visitors for the year stood at 4·7m. (a 2·0% decrease on 2001–02). The top source countries for visitors in 2002–03 were New Zealand (839,100); UK (627,800); Japan (627,700); USA (422,100); Singapore (253,400); and South Korea (207,300). Tourism is Australia's largest single earner of foreign exchange.

Festivals
In the year ended 30 June 2003 there were 176 performing arts festivals of more than two days' duration with a total income of $A88·5m. Attendance was estimated to be 7·5m. people.

Libraries
As at 30 June 2004 there were 548 public libraries and archive organizations operating through 1,754 locations. During 2003–04 there were 105m. visits to local government, national and State libraries. Total government funding for libraries in 2003–04 was $A879·2m.

Theatre and Opera
Opera Australia is the largest performing arts organization in the country with almost 250 performances staged annually. In 2002, 26·4% of the population aged 18 years and over (almost 3·8m. people) had attended at least one popular music concert; 18·0% (almost 2·6m.), at least one theatre performance; 18·7% (over 2·7m.), at least one opera or musical.

Museums and Galleries
At 30 June 2000 there were 2,049 museums, including 250 art museums and 400 historic properties, employing 36,919 people (including volunteers) and receiving 27·5m. visitors. Most admissions (60%) were free of charge. Government funding represents 68% of the museums' total income of $A716m.

DIPLOMATIC REPRESENTATIVES

Of Australia in the United Kingdom (Australia House, Strand, London, WC2B 4LA)
High Commissioner: Richard Alston.

Of the United Kingdom in Australia (Commonwealth Ave., Yarralumla, Canberra)
High Commissioner: Helen Liddell.

Of Australia in the USA (1601 Massachusetts Ave., NW, Washington, D.C., 20036)
Ambassador: Dennis Richardson.

Of the USA in Australia (Moonah Pl., Canberra, A.C.T. 2600)
Ambassador: Vacant.
Chargé d'Affaires a.i.: William A. Stanton.

Of Australia to the United Nations
Ambassador: John Dauth, LVO.

Of Australia to the European Union
Ambassador: Peter Charles Grey.

FURTHER READING

Australian Bureau of Statistics (ABS). *Year Book Australia.—Pocket Year Book Australia.—Monthly Summary of Statistics.* ABS also publish numerous specialized statistical digests.
Australian Encyclopædia. 12 vols. Sydney, 1983
Blainey, G., *A Short History of Australia.* Melbourne, 1996
The Cambridge Encyclopedia of Australia. CUP, 1994
Clark, M., *Manning Clark's History of Australia*; abridged by M. Cathcart. London, 1994
Concise Oxford Dictionary of Australian History. 2nd ed. OUP, 1995
Davison, Graeme, *et al.*, (eds.) *The Oxford Companion to Australian History.* 2nd ed. OUP, 2002
Docherty, J. D., *Historical Dictionary of Australia.* Metuchen (NJ), 1993
Foster, S. G., Marsden, S. and Russell, R. (compilers) *Federation. A guide to records.* Australian Archives, Canberra, 2000

Gilbert, A. D. and Inglis, K. S. (eds.) *Australians: a Historical Library*. 5 vols. CUP, 1988

Hirst, John, *The Sentimental Nation: The Making of the Australian Commonwealth*. OUP, 2000.—*Australia's Democracy: A Short History*. Allen and Unwin, Sydney, 2002

Irving, H. (ed.) *The Centenary Companion to Australian Federation*. CUP, 2000

Kepars, I., *Australia*. [Bibliography] 2nd ed. ABC-Clio, Oxford and Santa Barbara (CA), 1994

Knightley, Phillip, *Australia: A biography of a Nation*. Cape, London, 2000

Macintyre, S., *A Concise History of Australia*. CUP, 2000

Oxford History of Australia. vol 2: 1770–1860. OUP, 1992. vol 5: 1942–88. OUP, 1990

The Oxford Illustrated Dictionary of Australian History. OUP, 1993

Turnbull, M., *The Reluctant Republic*. London, 1994

Ward, Stuart, *Australia and the British Embrace: The Demise of the Imperial Ideal*. Melbourne Univ. Press, 2002

A more specialized title is listed under RELIGION, *above*

National library: The National Library, Canberra, ACT.

National Statistical Office: Australian Bureau of Statistics (ABS), Belconnen, ACT. The statistical services of the states are integrated with the Bureau.

ABS Website: http://www.abs.gov.au/

AUSTRALIAN TERRITORIES AND STATES

Australian Capital Territory

KEY HISTORICAL EVENTS

The area that is now the Australian Capital Territory (ACT) was explored in 1820 by Charles Throsby who named it Limestone Plains. Settlement commenced in 1824. In 1901 the Commonwealth constitution stipulated that a land tract of at least 260 sq. km in area and not less than 160 km from Sydney be reserved as a capital district. The Canberra site was adopted by the Seat of Government Act 1908. The present site, together with an area for a port at Jervis Bay, was surrendered by New South Wales and accepted by the Commonwealth in 1909. By subsequential proclamation the Territory became vested in the Commonwealth from 1 Jan. 1911. In 1911 an international competition for the city plan was won by W. Burley Griffin of Chicago but construction was delayed by the First World War. It was not until 1927 that Canberra became the seat of government. Located on the Molonglo River surrounding an artificial lake, it was built as a compromise capital to stop squabbling between Melbourne and Sydney following the 1901 Federation of Australian States.

In Dec. 1988 self-government was proclaimed and in May 1989 the first ACT assembly was elected.

TERRITORY AND POPULATION

The total area is 2,360 sq. km, of which 60% is hilly or mountainous. Timbered mountains are located in the south and west, and plains and hill country in the north. The ACT lies within the upper Murrumbidgee River catchment, in the Murray-Darling Basin. The Murrumbidgee flows throughout the Territory from the south, and its tributary, the Molonglo, from the east. The Molonglo was dammed in 1964 to form Lake Burley Griffin. As at 31 March 2005 the resident population (preliminary estimate) was 325,100 (annual growth rate, 0·4%). Increase in the annual growth rate during 2003–04 was 0·2%. Population at the 2001 census was 311,947 (1996: 299,243).

SOCIAL STATISTICS

2003: births, 4,128; deaths, 1,414; marriages, 1,558; divorces, 1,652. Infant mortality rate (per 1,000 live births), 5·8. Expectation of life, 2003: males, 79·2 years; females, 83·8 years.

CLIMATE

ACT has a continental climate, characterized by a marked variation in temperature between seasons, with warm to hot summers and cold winters.

CONSTITUTION AND GOVERNMENT

The ACT became self-governing on 11 May 1989. It is represented by two members in the Commonwealth House of Representatives and two senators.

The parliament of the ACT, the *Legislative Assembly*, consists of 17 members elected for a three-year term. Its responsibilities are at State and Local government level. The Legislative Assembly elects a Chief Minister and a four-member cabinet.

RECENT ELECTIONS

At the elections of 16 Oct. 2004 the Labor Party won ten seats (46·9% of the vote) with the Liberal Party taking six seats (34·7%) and the Green Party one seat (9·3%).

CURRENT ADMINISTRATION

The ACT Australian Labor Party Ministry was as follows in Feb. 2006:

Chief Minister, Attorney General, Minister for Arts, Heritage, Indigenous Affairs and the Environment: Jon Stanhope.

Deputy Chief Minister, Treasurer, Minister for Economic Development and Business, Tourism, Sport and Recreation, and Racing and Gaming: Ted Quinlan. *Health and Planning:* Simon Corbell. *Disability, Housing and Community Services, Urban Services, Police and Emergency Services:* John Hargreaves. *Education, Youth and Family Services, Women and Industrial Relations:* Katy Gallagher.

Speaker: Wayne Berry.

ACT Government website: http://www.act.gov.au

ECONOMY

Budget

The ACT fully participates in the federal-state model underpinning the Australian Federal System. As a city-State, the ACT Government reflects State and local (municipal) government responsibilities, which is unique within the federal system. However, the ACT is treated equitably with the States and Northern Territory regarding the distribution of federal funding.

In 2003–04 the Territory received revenues of \$A2,936m. (including extraordinaries) and had expenditure of \$A2,827m. (including extraordinaries) achieving a surplus of \$A109m. on an accrual basis.

Banking and Finance

In March 2002 bank deposits totalled, \$A6,597m.; loans, \$A7,962m.; Housing Finance for Owner Occupation (all lenders), total commitments 2002–03, \$A1,762m.

ENERGY AND NATURAL RESOURCES

Electricity
See NEW SOUTH WALES.

Water
ACTEW (Australian Capital Territory, Electricity & Water) provides more than 100m. litres of water each day to Canberra

residents. There were 45 reservoirs in 2001–02 with a capacity of 912m. litres.

Agriculture

Sheep and/or beef cattle farming is the main agricultural activity. In 2002–03 there were 91 farming establishments with a total area of 50,000 ha.

Forestry

There is about 23,838 ha. of plantation forest in the ACT (approximately 10% of the land area). Most of the area is managed for the production of softwood timber. After harvesting, 500–1,000 ha. of land are planted with new pine forest each year. No native forests or woodlands have been cleared for plantation since the mid-1970s.

INDUSTRY

Manufacturing industries at June 2001 employed 4,400 persons and generated $A274m., a fall of 5% on the previous year.

Labour

In Feb. 2003 there were an estimated 171,200 employed persons and 7,600 unemployed persons. The annual average unemployment rate in the ACT has fallen since 1996–97 (7·5%) to an average of 4·2% in Feb. 2003.

In the year ending Feb. 2003, 25% of the ACT labour force was employed in public administration and defence; 14% in property and business services; 12% in retail trade. The average weekly wage in Feb. 2003 was $A1,031·80 (males $A1,122·40, females $A916·10).

Trade Unions

As at Aug. 2003 there were 37,600 people belonging to a trade union (24% of total employees).

INTERNATIONAL TRADE

Imports and Exports

In 2002–03 imports were valued at $A216·5m. ($A5·4m. in 2001–02); exports at $A4·3m. ($A10·6m. in 2001–02). Machinery and transport equipment accounted for 99% of total imports and 54% of total exports.

COMMUNICATIONS

Roads

At March 2004 there were 2,645 km of road. At 31 March 2003 there were 213,396 vehicles registered in the ACT. In the year ended Aug. 2003, 13 fatalities were caused by traffic accidents.

Civil Aviation

In 2002–03 Canberra International Airport handled an estimated 1,916,351 passengers.

Telecommunications

In 2002 there were 96,000 households with home computer access (78% of the population) and 72,000 households with home Internet access (59%).

Postal Services

See NEW SOUTH WALES.

SOCIAL INSTITUTIONS

Justice

In 2002–03 there were 47,375 criminal incidents recorded by police. During the same year there were 594 full-time sworn police officers in the ACT and 205 unsworn police staff.

Education

In Feb. 2004 there were 219 schools comprising 80 pre-schools, 139 primary and secondary schools (including colleges) and five special schools. Of these 176 were government schools. There was a total of 60,165 full-time students. There were four higher education institutions in 2003: the Signadou Campus of the Australian Catholic University (ACU) had 617 students enrolled; the Australian National University, 13,384 students; the University of Canberra, 11,270; and the Australian Defence Force Academy, 2,078.

Health

The ACT is serviced by two public and nine private hospitals (six of the private hospitals are day surgery only). At June 2003 there were 255 dental practitioners.

Welfare

At June 2003 there were 17,060 age pensioners (5·3% of ACT population); 6,648 persons received disability support pension (2·1%).

RELIGION

At the 2001 census, 63% of the population were Christian. Of these, 45% were Roman Catholic and 29% Anglican. Non-Christian religions accounted for 5%, the largest groups being Buddhism, Islam and Hinduism.

CULTURE

In 2000–01 total funding on culture by the ACT Government was $A30·0m., an 8% decrease on the previous year.

Tourism

In the year ended 31 Dec. 2003, 171,500 international visitors came to the ACT. Of these, the largest proportion (19%) was from the UK. At Dec. 2002 there were 266 accommodation establishments employing 4,146 persons.

FURTHER READING

Regional Statistics (Cat. no. 1362.8), Australian Capital Territory.

Australian Capital Territory in Focus (formerly *Statistical Summary*). Australian Bureau of Statistics. Annual

Sources: *ACT in Focus 1307.8, Labour Force, Australia 6203.0* and *Labour Force, New South Wales and Australian Capital Territory 6201.1.*

Northern Territory

KEY HISTORICAL EVENTS

The Northern Territory, after forming part of New South Wales, was annexed on 6 July 1863 to South Australia. After the agreement of 7 Dec. 1907 for the transfer of the Northern Territory to the Commonwealth, it passed to the control of the Commonwealth government on 1 Jan. 1911. On 1 Feb. 1927 the Northern Territory was divided into two territories but in 1931 it was again administered as a single territory. The Legislative Council for the Northern Territory, constituted in 1947, was reconstituted in 1959. In that year, citizenship rights were granted to Aboriginal people of 'full descent'. On 1 July 1978 self-government was granted.

TERRITORY AND POPULATION

The Northern Territory's total area is 1,352,212 sq. km and includes adjacent islands. It has 5,100 km of mainland coastline and 2,100 km of coast around the islands. The greater part of the interior consists of a tableland with excellent pasturage. The southern part is generally sandy and has a small rainfall.

The population (preliminary estimate) at 30 June 2005 was 202,800 (annual growth rate, 1·5%). The 2001 census population was 210,664 (1996: 181,843). The capital, seat of government and principal port is Darwin, on the north coast; estimated population 68,516 at 30 June 2003. Other main centres (estimated totals) include Katherine (8,610); Alice Springs (26,229); Tennant Creek (2,983); Nhulunbuy (3,768); and Jabiru (1,164). There are also a number of large self-contained Aboriginal communities. People identifying themselves as indigenous numbered 57,600 at 30 June 2001.

SOCIAL STATISTICS

2003 totals: births, 3,790; deaths, 875; marriages, 723; divorces, 490. Infant mortality rate per 1,000 live births, 8·4. Life expectancy, 2003: 72·0 years for males, 77·3 for females. The annual rates per 1,000 population in 2003 were: births, 19·1; deaths, 4·4; marriages, 3·6; divorces, 2·5.

CLIMATE

See AUSTRALIA: Climate.

The highest temperature ever recorded in the NT was 118·9°F (48·3°C) at Finke in 1960, while the lowest recorded temperature was 18·5°F (–7·5°C) at Alice Springs in 1976.

CONSTITUTION AND GOVERNMENT

The Northern Territory (Self-Government) Act 1978 established the Northern Territory as a body politic as from 1 July 1978, with Ministers having control over and responsibility for Territory finances and the administration of the functions of government as specified by the Federal government. Regulations have been made conferring executive authority for the bulk of administrative functions.

The Northern Territory has federal representation, electing one member to the House of Representatives and two members to the Senate.

The Legislative Assembly has 25 members, directly elected for a period of four years. The *Administrator* (Ted Egan) appoints Ministers on the advice of the Leader of the majority party.

RECENT ELECTIONS

In parliamentary elections held in June 2005 the Australian Labor Party won 19 seats against 4 for the Country Liberal Party and 2 for ind.

CURRENT ADMINISTRATION

Administrator: Ted Egan, AM.

The NT Territory Labor Party Cabinet was as follows in Feb. 2006:

Chief Minister, Minister for Asian Relations and Trade, AustralAsia Railway, Indigenous Affairs and Tourism: Clare Martin.

Deputy Chief Minister, Treasurer, Minister for Employment, Education and Training, and Racing, Gaming and Licensing: Sydney Stirling. *Attorney General, Minister for Justice, Health and Central Australia:* Peter Toyne. *Business and Economic Development, Regional Development, Police, Fire and Emergency Services, Defence Support, and Essential Services:* Paul Henderson. *Transport and Infrastructure, Lands and Planning, Public Employment, Corporate and Information Services, and Communications:* Chris Burns. *Mines and Energy, Primary Industry and Fisheries, and Multicultural Affairs:* Konstantine Vatskalis. *Natural Resources, the Environment and Heritage, Parks and Wildlife, Arts and Museums, Young Territorians, Senior Territorians and Women's Policy:* Marion Scrymgour. *Local Government, and Housing:* Elliot McAdam. *Family and Community Services, Sport and Recreation:* Delia Lawrie.

NT Government website: http://www.nt.gov.au

ECONOMY

Budget

Revenue and expenditure in $A1m.[1]:

	2001–02	2002–03	2003–04
Revenue	2,289	2,361	2,455
Expenditure	2,307	2,362	2,450

[1]Based on Northern Territory Outcomes reports for 2001–02 and 2002–03. 2003–04 figures based on latest estimates in the Northern Territory's 2003–04 Mid-Year Report.

Using accrual uniform presentation framework standards, total revenue in 2003–04 was expected to be $A2,455m. of which $A1,997m. grants to the Northern Territory from the Commonwealth, and $A458m. Northern Territory Government own-source revenue, which includes $A256m. in state-like taxes.

Expenditure during 2003–04 included $A530m. for education; $A487m. for health; $A243m. for public order and safety; $A205m. for recreation and culture; and $A146m. for general public services.

Banking and Finance

At March 2002 there were 11 banks operating in the Territory with total deposits, $A1,549m.; loans, $A3,452m.

ENERGY AND NATURAL RESOURCES

Environment

There are 93 parks and reserves covering 43,709 sq. km. Twelve of the parks are classified as national parks, including the Kakadu and Uluru-Kata Tjuta National Park which are included on the World Heritage List.

Electricity

The Power and Water Corporation supplies power to 78 indigenous and remote communities as well as the major centres. In the year ended 30 June 2003 total electricity generated was 1,651 GWh; total consumption was 1,549m. kWh, including 1,055m. kWh by business customers.

Oil and Gas

The Timor Sea is a petroleum producing province with five fields and more than 22m. cu. ft of known gas reserves. Gas is currently supplied from the Palm Valley and Mereenie fields in the onshore Amadeus Basin to the Channel Island Power Station in Darwin via one of Australia's longest onshore gas pipelines. The value of energy mineral production in the Territory increased by 77·3% in 2000–01. The total value of oil and gas production in 2000–01 was $A2,622m., an increase of $A1,192m. over 1999–2000. This is largely a result of an increase in crude oil production which rose by 86·3% in 2000–01. The Territory produced 5,316 megalitres of crude oil and 458m. cu. metres of natural gas in 2000–01.

Minerals

Mining is the major contributor to the Territory's economy. Compared to 2001–02 the overall value of production in the mining industry decreased by 13·1% in 2002–03. Value of major mineral commodities production in 2002–03 (in $A1m.): bauxite/alumina, 594; gold, 352; manganese, 199; uranium, 154; lead/zinc concentrate, 106; diamonds, 14.

Agriculture

In the year ended June 2002 there were 406 agricultural establishments with a total area under holding of 65·2m. ha. Gross value of agricultural production in 2001–02 rose by 19% to $A321m. Beef cattle production constitutes the largest farming industry. Total value of livestock slaughter and products in 2001–02 was $A247m., an increase of 23% on the previous year. Fruit production consists mainly of mangoes, bananas and melons. The banana crop decreased significantly from 6,851 tonnes in 2001 to 3,943 tonnes in 2002 while grape production increased by 3% to 698,000 tonnes. There were eight crocodile farms in 2001 producing a total of 16,335·25 kg of meat in the period Jan.–June 2001.

Forestry

In 2001 there were 35m. ha. of native forest, accounting for 26% of the Territory's total land area. Of the total native forest cover, 1% is rainforest, 23% open forest and 76% woodland. Total area of plantation forest is around 5,500 ha., consisting mainly of softwoods. Hardwood plantations of fast growing Acacia Mangium have been established on the Tiwi Islands for the production of woodchip for paper pulp. In addition, a number of operations for the production of sandalwood oil and neem products have been established near Batchelor. Teak plantations are planned for designated farmland in the Katherine/Daly development region.

Fisheries

Estimated total fisheries production in 2003–04 came to 5,796 tonnes with a gross value of $A59·1m. In the same year, aquaculture production was worth an estimated $A28m.

INDUSTRY

At 30 June 2000 the manufacturing industry turnover was $A1,020·2m.; 3,300 persons were employed and salaries totalled $A144·9m. In Nov. 2001, 15,102 persons were employed in the wholesale and retail trade.

Labour

The labour force totalled 102,000 in Jan. 2004, of whom 97,400 were employed. The unemployment rate was 4·5%, down from 5·7% in Jan. 2003. The average weekly wage in Nov. 2003 was $A720·10 (males $A820·20, females $A619·40).

Trade Unions

In June 1996, 26 trade unions had 19,300 members.

INTERNATIONAL TRADE

Imports and Exports

In 2003–04 the value of the Territory's imports totalled $A899m. Major sources of imports for 2003–04 (figures in $A1m.): Singapore, 239; Kuwait, 107; Japan, 100; Italy, 89; USA, 57. 2003–04 exports totalled $A1,878m. Major export destinations (figures in $A1m.): China, 404; Singapore, 298; Canada, 164; Republic of Korea, 146; Hong Kong, 143.

COMMUNICATIONS

Roads

At 30 June 2004 there were 22,097 km of roads. Registered motor vehicles at 31 Dec. 2002 numbered 126,562, including 93,002 passenger vehicles, 3,216 motorcycles and 1,420 buses. There were 48 road accident fatalities in the year ended Aug. 2003.

Rail

In 1980 Alice Springs was linked to the Trans-continental network by a standard (1,435 mm) gauge railway to Tarcoola in South Australia (830 km). A new 1,410 km standard gauge line operates between Darwin and Alice Springs. This $A1·3bn. AustralAsia Railway project links Darwin and Adelaide. The first train to complete the journey of 1,860 miles arrived in Darwin on 3 Feb. 2004.

Civil Aviation

Darwin and most regional centres in the Territory are serviced by daily flights to all State capitals and major cities. In 2003 there were direct international services connecting Darwin to Brunei, East Timor, Hong Kong, Indonesia and Singapore. In 2003 Darwin airport handled 924,000 domestic and an estimated 77,700 international passengers, and Alice Springs (2003–04), 610,000 domestic passengers.

Shipping

In 2002–03, 704 commercial vessels called at Northern Territory ports. General cargo imported in 2002–03 was 117,794 mass tonnes and general cargo exported was 216,573 mass tonnes.

Telecommunications

In 2001 there were 63,480 households with home computer access and 26,801 households with home Internet access.

Postal Services

At 30 June 2004 there were 586 Australia Post retail facilities in South Australia and Northern Territory.

SOCIAL INSTITUTIONS

Justice

Voluntary euthanasia for the terminally ill was legalized in 1995 but the law was overturned by the Federal Senate on 24 March 1997. The first person to have recourse to legalized euthanasia died on 22 Sept. 1996.

Police personnel (sworn and unsworn) at 30 June 2003, 1,178. In addition there were 49 Aboriginal community police officers. At 30 June 2002 the Territory had three prisons with a daily average of 667 prisoners held.

Education

Education is compulsory from the age of six to 15 years. There were (Aug. 2003) 32,556 full-time students enrolled in 151 government schools and 8,773 enrolled in 33 non-government schools with an additional 3,480 in pre-schools. Teaching staff totalled 2,534 in government schools and 754 in non-government schools. The proportion of Indigenous students in the Territory is high, comprising 38% of all primary and secondary students at Aug. 2004. Bilingual programmes operate in some Aboriginal communities where traditional Aboriginal culture prevails.

The Northern Territory University (NTU), founded in 1989 by amalgamating the existing University College of the Northern Territory and the Darwin Institute of Technology, joined with the Alice Springs' Centralian College in 2004 to form the Charles Darwin University. At 31 March 2003, 1,711 students were enrolled in higher education courses of whom 5·2% were identified as Indigenous. The Batchelor Institute of Indigenous Tertiary Education, which provides higher and vocational education and training for Aboriginal and Torres Straits Islanders, had 605 students enrolled in higher education courses in 2001. In 2002 there were 27,096 enrolments in Vocational Education and Training activities.

Health

In 2002 there were five public hospitals with a total of 569 beds and two private hospitals. Community health services are provided from urban and rural Health Centres including mobile units. Remote communities are served by resident nursing staff, aboriginal health workers and in larger communities, resident GPs. Emergency services are supported by the Aerial Medical Services throughout the Territory.

Welfare

The Aged and Disability Program administers NT and Commonwealth funds ($A32m. in 1999–2000) to provide a number of services for senior Territorians and those with a disability. At June 2002 the numbers of pensioners receiving concessions was 16,252. Concessions include allowances on electricity; water, sewerage and property rates; vehicle registrations; spectacles; urban bus travel; and interstate travel. In 2001–02 disability services expenditure was $A14,618m.

CULTURE

Broadcasting

Darwin's radio services include four ABC stations, one SBS station, two commercial stations and a community station. Darwin has two commercial, one ABC and one SBS TV service. Most other Northern Territory centres have one commercial and one national radio service, with one each of ABC, SBS and commercial television.

Tourism

In 2003–04 a total of 1·5m. people visited the Northern Territory, a decrease of 10% over the previous year. In the same year tourist expenditure was $A1·2bn. Tourism is the second largest revenue earner after the mining industry.

FURTHER READING

Profile of Australia's Northern Territory—1997/98. Protocol and Public Affairs Branch, Dept. of the Chief Minister, GPO Box 4396, Darwin

The Northern Territory: Annual Report. Dept. of Territories, Canberra, from 1911. Dept. of the Interior, Canberra, from 1966–67. Dept. of Northern Territory, from 1972

Australian Territories, Dept. of Territories, Canberra, 1960 to 1973. Dept. of Special Minister of State, Canberra, 1973–75. Department of Administrative Services, 1976

Northern Territory in Focus (formerly *Statistical Summary*). Australian Bureau of Statistics, Canberra, from 1960

Donovan, P. F., *A Land Full of Possibilities: A History of South Australia's Northern Territory 1863-1911.* 1981.—*At the Other End of Australia: The Commonwealth and the Northern Territory 1911-1978.* Univ. of Queensland Press, 1984

Heatley, A., *Almost Australians: the Politics of Northern Territory Self-Government.* Australian National Univ. Press, 1990

Powell, A., *Far Country: A Short History of the Northern Territory.* Melbourne Univ. Press, 1996

New South Wales

KEY HISTORICAL EVENTS

The name New South Wales was applied to the entire east coast of Australia when Capt. James Cook claimed the land for the British Crown on 23 Aug. 1770. The separate colonies of Tasmania, South Australia, Victoria and Queensland were proclaimed in the 19th century. In 1911 and 1915 the Australian Capital Territory around Canberra and Jervis Bay was ceded to the Commonwealth. New South Wales was thus gradually reduced to its present area. The first settlement was made at Port Jackson in 1788 as a penal settlement. A partially elective council was established in 1843 and responsible government in 1856.

Gold discoveries from 1851 brought an influx of immigrants, and responsible government was at first unstable, with seven ministries holding office in the five years after 1856. Bitter conflict arose from land laws enacted in 1861. Lack of transport hampered agricultural expansion.

New South Wales federated with the other Australian states to form the Commonwealth of Australia in 1901.

TERRITORY AND POPULATION

New South Wales (NSW) is situated between the 29th and 38th parallels of S. lat. and 141st and 154th meridians of E. long., and comprises 800,640 sq. km, inclusive of Lord Howe Island, 17 sq. km, but exclusive of the Australian Capital Territory (2,360 sq. km) and 70 sq. km at Jervis Bay.

The population at the 2001 census was 6,371,745 (6,038,696 at 1996 census), of which 3,226,300 were female. In 2001 there were eight people per sq. km. At 30 June 2005 the resident population (preliminary estimate) was 6,774,200 (annual growth rate, 0·8%). Although NSW comprises only 10·4% of the total area of Australia, over 33·9% of the Australian population live there. During the year ended June 2003, 36,431 permanent settlers arrived in New South Wales (35,301 June 2002).

The state is divided into 12 *Statistical Divisions.* The estimated population of these (in 1,000) at 30 June 2002 was: Sydney, 4,170·9; Hunter, 595·0; Illawarra, 405·0; Mid-North Coast, 284·5; Richmond-Tweed, 219·0; South Eastern, 195·9; Northern, 180·4;

Central West, 178·6; Murrumbidgee, 153·0; North Western, 119·6; Murray, 114·1; Far West, 24·2. Population of the Statistical Subdivisions Newcastle (within Hunter) and Wollongong (within Illawarra) was 497·5 and 272·1 respectively.

Lord Howe Island — 31° 33' 4" S., 159° 4' 26" E., which is part of New South Wales, is situated about 702 km northeast of Sydney; area, 1,654 ha., of which only about 120 ha. are arable; resident population (2001 census), 401 (205 females). The Island, which was discovered in 1788, is of volcanic origin. Mount Gower, the highest point, reaches a height of 866 metres.

The Lord Howe Island Board manages the affairs of the Island and supervises the Kentia palm-seed industry.

SOCIAL STATISTICS

Statistics for calendar years:

	Live births	Deaths	Marriages	Divorces
2000	86,752	45,409	39,323	14,756
2001	84,578	44,552	36,109	16,057
2002	86,583	46,384	36,321	16,957
2003	86,344	46,111	36,872	16,285

The annual rates per 1,000 of mean estimated resident population in 2003 were: births, 12·9; deaths, 6·9; marriages, 5·5; divorces, 2·4; infant mortality, 4·6 per 1,000 live births. Expectation of life in 2003: males, 77·7 years, females, 82·9.

CLIMATE

See AUSTRALIA: Climate.

CONSTITUTION AND GOVERNMENT

Within the State there are three levels of government: the Commonwealth government, with authority derived from a written constitution; the State government with residual powers; the local government authorities with powers based upon a State Act of Parliament, operating within incorporated areas extending over almost 90% of the State.

The Constitution of New South Wales is drawn from several diverse sources; certain Imperial statutes such as the Commonwealth of Australia Constitution Act (1900); the Australian States Constitution Act (1907); an element of inherited English law; amendments to the Commonwealth of Australia Constitution Act; the (State) Constitution Act; the Australia Acts of 1986; the Constitution (Amendment) Act 1987 and certain other State Statutes; numerous legal decisions; and a large amount of English and local convention.

The Parliament of New South Wales may legislate for the peace, welfare and good government of the State in all matters not specifically reserved to the Commonwealth government. The State Legislature consists of the Sovereign, represented by the Governor, and two Houses of Parliament, the Legislative Council (upper house) and the Legislative Assembly (lower house). Australian citizens aged 18 and over, and other British subjects who were enrolled prior to 26 Jan. 1984, men and women aged 18 years and over, are entitled to the franchise. Enrolment and voting is compulsory. The optional preferential method of voting is used for both houses. The Legislative Council has 42 members elected for a term of office equivalent to two terms of the Legislative Assembly, with 21 members retiring at the same time as the Legislative Assembly elections. The whole State constitutes a single electoral district. The Legislative Assembly has 93 members elected in single-seat electoral districts for a maximum period of four years.

RECENT ELECTIONS

In elections held on 22 March 2003 the Australian Labor Party won 56 of 93 seats, the Liberal Party of Australia 18, the National Party 12 and ind. 7.

CURRENT ADMINISTRATION

In Feb. 2006 the Legislative Council consisted of the following parties: Australian Labor Party, 18; Liberal Party of Australia, 9; National Party, 4; Greens, 3; Christian Democratic Party (Fred Nile Group), 2; ind., 2; Australian Democrats, 1; Outdoor Recreation Party, 1; Shooters Party, 1; Unity, 1.

The Legislative Assembly, which was elected in 2003, consisted of the following parties in Feb. 2006: Australian Labor Party, 55 seats; Liberal Party of Australia, 19; National Party, 12; ind., 7.

Governor: Prof. Marie Bashir, AC.

The New South Wales ALP Ministry was as follows in Feb. 2006:

Premier, Treasurer and Minister for Citizenship: Morris Iemma (b. 1961).

Deputy Premier, Minister for Transport and State Development: John Watkins. *Special Minister of State, Minister for Commerce, Industrial Relations, Ageing and Disability Services:* John Della Bosca. *Attorney General, Minister for the Environment and for the Arts:* Bob Debus. *Police, and Utilities:* Carl Scully. *Education and Training:* Carmel Tebbutt. *Finance, Infrastructure and Minister for the Hunter:* Michael Costa. *Health:* John Hatzistergos. *Planning, and Science and Medical Research:* Frank Sartor. *Community Services, and Youth:* Reba Meagher. *Tourism, Sport and Recreation, and Women:* Sandra Nori. *Natural and Mineral Resources, and Primary Industries:* Ian Macdonald. *Rural Affairs, Justice and Juvenile Justice, Emergency Services, and Lands:* Tony Kelly. *Regional Development, Illawarra, and Small Business:* David Campbell. *Fair Trading:* Diane Beamer. *Roads:* Joseph Tripodi. *Gaming and Racing, and the Central Coast:* Grant McBride. *Local Government:* Kerry Hickey. *Ports and Waterways:* Eric Roozendaal. *Housing:* Cherie Burton. *Aboriginal Affairs:* Milton Orkopoulos.

Speaker of the Legislative Assembly: John Murray.

NSW Government website: http://www.nsw.gov.au

ECONOMY

Budget

Government sector revenue and expenses ($A1m.):

	2003–04	2004–05	2005–06[1]
Revenue	39,328	40,361	42,211
Expenditure	38,037	39,525	41,100
	[1]Forward estimate.		

In 2003–04 State government revenue from taxes amounted to $A14,932m.; grants and subsidies totalled $A16,881m.

Performance

In 2002–03 the gross state product of New South Wales represented 34·95% of Australia's total GDP.

Banking and Finance

Lending activity of financial institutions in New South Wales in 2002–03 comprised (in $A1m.): commercial, 134,274; personal, 23,102; lease financing, 2,682. In March 2002 total deposits held by banks was $A238,488m.; loans, $A245,119m.

ENERGY AND NATURAL RESOURCES

Electricity

In the year ended 30 June 2002 total consumption (including ACT total consumption) stood at 60,383m. kWh, of which 41,215m. kWh was by business customers. In 2001–02, 63,911m. kWh were produced, a decrease of 1·4% on the previous year. Coal is the main fuel source for electricity generation in the state, producing 83% of the total in the year ended 30 June 2002. Total installed capacity at 30 June 2002 was 12,147 MW.

Oil and Gas

No natural gas is produced in NSW. Almost all gas is imported from the Moomba field in South Australia plus, since 2001, a small amount from Bass Strait.

Water

Ground water represents the largest source with at least 130 communities relying on it for drinking water.

Minerals

New South Wales contains extensive mineral deposits. For the year ended 30 June 2000, turnover from 123 mining establishments in the coal and metal ore mining industries, employing 10,461 people, was $A5,660m. The value of metallic minerals produced in 2001–02 was $A1·18bn.; construction materials, $A389·5m.; industrial minerals, $A124·5m. Output of principal products, 2002–03 (in tonnes): coal, 143·1m.; zinc, 238,000; copper, 144,000; lead, 107,000; tin, 919; silver, 88; gold, 27.

Agriculture

NSW accounts for around 26% of the value of Australia's total agricultural production with a gross value of $A10·2bn. in 2001–02. In 2001–02 GDP at factor income for agriculture, forestry, hunting and fishing was $A5,808m. In that year farm income (including Australian Capital Territory) was $A2,682m., 21·3% of the Australian total agricultural income. In the year ended 30 June 2002 there were 41,651 farming establishments with a total area under holding of 63·4m. ha. of which 6·64m. ha. were under crops.

Principal crops in 2001–02 with production in 1,000 tonnes: wheat for grain, 8,257; barley, 1,389; sorghum, 785; canola, 716. Estimated value of crops, 2001–02, came to $A5·7bn. with wheat totalling $A2·0bn. and cotton $A0·9bn. (Data relates to farms whose estimated value of agricultural operations was $A5,000 or more at the census.)

The total area under vines in 2002 was 37,381 ha. (including 3,376 ha. not yet bearing fruit); winegrape production totalled 415,026 tonnes.

In the year ended June 2002 there were 2,600 ha. of banana plantations, with production of 31,600 tonnes; 195,600 tonnes of oranges were produced (43% of the Australian total).

2001–02 gross value of livestock products was $A1·6bn., including wool produced, $A1·0bn.; and milk, $A434m. In 2002–03 production (in tonnes) of beef and veal, 488,000; mutton and lamb, 191,400; pig meat, 140,200.

Forestry

The area of forests managed by State Forests of NSW in 2002–03 totalled 2·9m. ha. of native forest; 212,000 ha. of softwood and 57,000 ha. of hardwood plantation with a total yield (1999–2000) of 2·78m. cu. metres of sawlogs and veneer logs.

Fisheries

Estimated total fisheries production in 2003–04 came to 19,226 tonnes with a gross value of $A139·4m. In the same year aquaculture production was an estimated 986 tonnes with a gross value of $A49·6m.

INDUSTRY

A wide range of manufacturing is undertaken in the Sydney area, and there are large iron and steel works near the coalfields at Newcastle and Port Kembla. Around one-third of Australian manufacturing takes place in NSW.

Manufacturing establishments' operations, 2000–01:

Industry	No. of persons employed	Wages and salaries ($A1m.)	Turnover ($A1m.)	Industry gross product ($A1m.)
Food, beverages and tobacco	52,989	2,269·1	17,177·8	4,681·3
Textiles, clothing, footwear and leather	15,201	476·1	2,525·6	681·1
Wood and paper products	19,813	743·4	4,762·0	1,510·8

Industry	No. of persons employed	Wages and salaries ($A1m.)	Turnover ($A1m.)	Industry gross product ($A1m.)
Printing, publishing and recorded media	35,299	1,633·7	6,863·0	2,688·2
Petroleum, coal, chemical and associated products	34,121	1,573·8	14,878·5	3,104·6
Non-metallic mineral products	10,991	534·5	3,021·3	1,175·5
Metal products	52,033	2,189·5	14,104·8	4,339·8
Machinery and equipment	58,744	2,559·6	13,163·1	4,115·4
Other manufacturing	16,409	525·9	2,162·9	790·7
Total manufacturing	295,600	12,505·7	78,659·1	23,067·4

Labour

In May 2003 the labour force was estimated to number 3,354,200 persons, of whom 3,152,100 were employed: 611,300 as professionals; 564,700 as intermediate clerical, sales and service workers; 390,500 as tradespersons and related workers; 275,900 as labourers and related workers; 262,900 as intermediate production and transport workers; 237,500 as managers and administrators; and 126,000 as advanced clerical and service workers. There were 202,100 unemployed (a rate of 6·0%) in May 2003. The average weekly wage in Feb. 2003 was $A950·90 (males $A1,016·50, females $A842·10).

Industrial tribunals are authorized to fix minimum rates of wages and other conditions of employment. Their awards may be enforced by law, as may be industrial agreements between employers and organizations of employees, when registered.

During 2002, 48,000 workers were directly involved in 234 industrial disputes. A total of 73,400 working days were lost.

Trade Unions

Registration of trade unions is effected under the New South Wales Trade Union Act 1881, which follows substantially the Trade Union Acts of 1871 and 1876 of England. Registration confers a quasi-corporate existence with power to hold property, to sue and be sued, etc., and the various classes of employees covered by the union are required to be prescribed by the constitution of the union. For the purpose of bringing an industry under the review of the State industrial tribunals, or participating in proceedings relating to disputes before Commonwealth tribunals, employees and employers must be registered as industrial unions, under State or Commonwealth industrial legislation respectively. Trade union membership was held by 26% of employees in Aug. 2001.

INTERNATIONAL TRADE

Imports and Exports

External commerce, exclusive of interstate trade, is included in the statement of the commerce of Australia. Overseas commerce of New South Wales in $A1m. for years ending 30 June:

	Imports	Exports		Imports	Exports
1998–99	42,142	17,950	2001–02	51,901	22,920
1999–2000	47,927	18,966	2002–03	55,248	20,235
2000–01	52,503	22,750	2003–04	53,774	19,025

The principal imports in 2003–04 (in $A1m.) were computers, 4,084; passenger motor vehicles, 3,962; medicaments, including veterinary, 3,841; telecommunications equipment, 3,132. Major commodities exported were coal, 2,804; aluminium, 1,401; copper ores, 720; bovine meat, 719; medicaments, including veterinary, 691.

Major sources of supply in 2003–04 (in $A1m.) were USA, 8,241; China, 7,424; Japan, 5,956; Germany, 2,987; UK, 2,851. Principal destinations of exports were Japan, 4,427; USA, 1,954; New Zealand, 1,928; Republic of Korea, 1,207; China, 1,168.

COMMUNICATIONS

Roads

At 30 June 2004 there were 182,167 km of public roads in total. The Roads and Traffic Authority of New South Wales is responsible for the administration and upkeep of major roads. In 2003 there were 20,586 km of roads under its control, comprising 3,105 km of national highways, 14,519 km of state roads and 2,962 km of regional and local roads.

The number of registered motor vehicles (excluding tractors and trailers) at 31 March 2003 was 3,944,900, including 3,163,300 passenger vehicles, 531,800 light commercial vehicles, 130,900 trucks, 18,800 buses and 100,000 motorcycles. There were 535 fatalities in road accidents in the year ended Aug. 2003.

Rail

The Rail Infrastructure Corporation (formerly known as the Rail Access Corporation) owns, operates and maintains the rail tracks and related infrastructure. It leases trackage rights to the State Rail Authority (consisting of CityRail and Countrylink), which operates passenger trains, and to the rail freight operators (state-owned FreightCorp was privatized in 2001). In 2002–03, 273·5m. passengers were carried on CityRail and 2·1m. on Countrylink. In the year ended 31 March 2001, 112m. tonnes of freight were transported. Also open for traffic are 325 km of Victorian government railways which extend over the border, 68 km of private railways (mainly in mining districts) and 53 km of Commonwealth government-owned track.

A tramway opened in Sydney in 1996. There is also a small overhead railway in the city centre.

Civil Aviation

Sydney Airport (Kingsford Smith) is the major airport in New South Wales and Australia's principal international air terminal. In 2002 it was sold to Macquarie Airports. In 2002–03 it handled a total of 23,442,248 passengers (14,158,215 on domestic flights). It is also the leading airport for freight, handling 377,460 tonnes in 2002–03. At 13 Sept. 2003 registered aircraft totalled 3,593.

Shipping

The main ports are at Sydney, Newcastle, Port Kembla and Botany Bay. In 2002–03, 655 commercial vessels called at New South Wales ports. General cargo imported in 2002–03 was 25,992,725 mass tonnes and general cargo exported 7,919,655 mass tonnes.

Telecommunications

At 30 June 2003 there were 14·3m. mobile telephone subscribers (11·2m. in 2001). In 2002 there were 1·53m. households with home computer access (61% of all households) and 1,196,000 households home Internet access (48%).

Postal Services

At 30 June 2003 a total of 1,473 post offices, post office agencies and community mail agencies provided Australia Post services throughout NSW and the ACT.

SOCIAL INSTITUTIONS

Justice

Legal processes may be conducted in Local Courts presided over by magistrates or in higher courts (District Court or Supreme Court) presided over by judges. There is also an appellate jurisdiction. Persons charged with more serious crimes must be tried before a higher court.

Children's Courts remove children as far as possible from the atmosphere of a public court. There are also a number of tribunals exercising special jurisdiction, e.g. the Industrial Commission and the Compensation Court.

As at 30 June 2005 there was a daily average of 9,819 persons held in prison. Police personnel (sworn and unsworn) at 30 June 2003, 18,798.

Education

The State government maintains a system of free primary and secondary education, and attendance at school is compulsory from six to 15 years of age. Non-government schools are subject to government inspection.

In Aug. 2002 there were 2,191 government schools with 753,700 pupils (449,482 primary and 304,218 secondary) and 50,084 teachers, and 904 non-government schools with 351,081 pupils (179,930 primary and 171,151 secondary) and 24,228 teachers. There were 289,886 students in higher education in 2002, with the largest numbers enrolled in management and commerce (27% of total enrolments) and society and culture (24%). Student enrolments in 2002: University of Sydney (founded 1850), 42,305; University of New England at Armidale (incorporated 1954), 18,202; University of New South Wales (founded 1949), 42,333; University of Newcastle (granted autonomy 1965), 23,502; University of Wollongong, 18,764; Macquarie University in Sydney (founded 1964), 27,239; University of Technology, Sydney, 29,290; University of Western Sydney, 35,361; Charles Sturt University, 39,776. Colleges of advanced education were merged with universities in 1990. Post-school technical and further education is provided at State TAFE colleges. Enrolments in 2002 totalled 526,083.

Health

In 2002–03 there were 25,281 medical practitioners, 4,153 dentists and 79,244 registered nurses. In the same year there were 218 public and 180 private hospitals.

Welfare

The number of income support payments in June 2003 included: age, 611,513; disability support, 219,820; single parent, 140,941; child care benefit, 224,820; carer payment, 26,910.

Direct State government social welfare services are limited, for the most part, to the assistance of persons not eligible for Commonwealth government pensions or benefits, and the provision of certain forms of assistance not available from the Commonwealth government. The State also subsidizes many approved services for needy persons.

RELIGION

At the 2001 census of those who stated a religion, 29% were Roman Catholic and 24% Anglican. These two religions combined had over 3·3m. followers.

CULTURE

Broadcasting

In addition to national broadcasting, at Sept. 2001 there were 22 commercial television services (including stations whose licence covers part of NSW as well as remote satellite services) and a total of 36 AM and 48 FM commercial radio services. The first cable-pay television service commenced in Sept. 1995, and satellite-delivered services in Nov. 1995.

Tourism

In 2003–04, 1·43m. overseas visitors arrived for short-term visits, a 7·4% increase on the previous year. At 31 March 2003 there were 1,301 hotels, motels, guest houses and serviced apartments providing 62,691 rooms.

FURTHER READING

Statistical Information: The NSW Government Statistician's Office was established in 1886, and in 1957 was integrated with the Commonwealth Bureau of Census and Statistics (now called the Australian Bureau of Statistics). Its principal publications are:

New South Wales Year Book (1886/87–1900/01 under the title Wealth and Progress of New South Wales). Annual.—Regional Statistics.—New South Wales Pocket Year Book.—Monthly Summary of Statistics.—New South Wales in Brief.

State Library: The State Library of NSW, Macquarie St., Sydney.

Queensland

KEY HISTORICAL EVENTS

Queensland was discovered by Capt. Cook in 1770. From 1778 it was part of New South Wales and was made a separate colony, with the name of Queensland, by letters patent of 8 June 1859, when responsible government was conferred. Although by 1868 gold had been discovered, wool was the colony's principal product. The first railway line was opened in 1865. Queensland federated with the other Australian states to form the Commonwealth of Australia in 1901.

TERRITORY AND POPULATION

Queensland comprises the whole northeastern portion of the Australian continent, including the adjacent islands in the Pacific Ocean and in the Gulf of Carpentaria. Estimated area 1,730,650 sq. km.

At the 2001 census the population was 3,655,139 (3,368,850 at 1996 census), of which 1,847,409 were female. At the 2001 census there were 112,772 Aboriginals and Torres Strait Islanders. Statistics on birthplaces from the 2001 census are as follows: Australia, 77·7% (81·3% in 1991); UK and Ireland, 5·1% (5·9%); New Zealand, 3·6% (2·9%); Germany, 0·6% (0·6%). Resident population (preliminary estimate) at 30 June 2005, 3,964,000 (annual growth rate, 2·0%).

Brisbane, the capital, had at 30 June 2003 (estimate) a resident population of 1,732,978 (Statistical Division). The resident populations of the other major centres (Statistical Districts) at the 2001 Census were: Gold Coast-Tweed (including that part in New South Wales), 396,588; Sunshine Coast, 192,357; Townsville, 135,142; Cairns, 126,364; Mackay, 63,145; Rockhampton, 62,845; Bundaberg, 55,998; Gladstone, 39,003.

SOCIAL STATISTICS

Statistics (including Aboriginals) for calendar years:

	Births	Deaths	Marriages	Divorces
2000	47,278	22,425	22,842	10,092
2001	47,678	22,856	20,314	12,085
2002	46,908	23,584	21,264	10,920
2003	48,298	22,925	22,273	10,681

The annual rates per 1,000 population in 2003 were: births, 12·7; deaths, 6·0; marriages, 5·9; divorces, 2·8. The infant mortality rate in 2003 was 4·8 per 1,000 live births. Life expectancy, 2003: 77·6 years for males, 82·8 for females.

CLIMATE

A typical subtropical to tropical climate. High daytime temperatures during Oct. to March give a short spring and long summer. Centigrade temperatures in the hottest inland areas often exceed the high 30s before the official commencement of summer on 1 Dec. Daytime temperatures in winter are quite mild, in the low- to mid-20s. Average rainfall varies from about 150 mm in the desert in the extreme southwestern corner of the State to about 4,000 mm in parts of the sugar lands of the wet northeastern coast, the latter being the wettest part of Australia.

CONSTITUTION AND GOVERNMENT

Queensland, formerly a portion of New South Wales, was formed into a separate colony in 1859, and responsible government was conferred. The power of making laws and imposing taxes is vested in a parliament of one house—the Legislative Assembly—which comprises 89 members, returned from four electoral zones for three years, elected from single-member constituencies by compulsory ballot.

Queensland elects 26 members to the Commonwealth House of Representatives.

The Elections Act, 1983, provides franchise for all males and females, 18 years of age and over, qualified by six months' residence in Australia and three months in the electoral district.

RECENT ELECTIONS

Legislative Assembly elections on 7 Feb. 2004 gave the ruling Australian Labor Party (ALP) 63 seats, the National Party (NP) 15, the Liberal Party (LP) 5 and One Nation 1. Five independents were elected. The NP/LP coalition forms the opposition.

CURRENT ADMINISTRATION

Governor of Queensland: Quentin Bryce, AC (took office on 29 July 2003).

In Feb. 2006 the ALP administration was as follows:

Premier and Minister for Trade: Peter Beattie (appointed 29 June 1998).

Deputy Premier, Treasurer and Minister for State Development, Trade and Innovation: Anna Bligh. *Attorney General, Justice:* Linda Lavarch. *Employment, Training and Industrial Relations, and Sport:* Tom Barton. *Public Works, Housing and Racing:* Rob Schwarten. *Police and Corrective Services:* Judy Spence. *Education, and the Arts:* Rod Welford. *Transport and Main Roads:* Paul Lucas. *Natural Resources, Mines and Water:* Henry Palaszczuk. *Health:* Stephen Robertson. *Child Safety:* Mike Reynolds. *Communities, Disability Services and Seniors:* Warren Pitt. *Tourism, Fair Trading and Wine Industry Development:* Margaret Keech. *Energy, Aboriginal and Torres Strait Islander Policy:* John Mickel. *Small Business, Information Technology and Multicultural Affairs:* Chris Cummins. *Emergency Services:* Pat Purcell. *Primary Industries and Fisheries:* Tim Mulherin.

QLD Government website: http://www.qld.gov.au

ECONOMY

Budget

In 2004–05 general government expenses by the state were expected to total $A23,363m.; revenue and grants received were expected to be $A24,009m.

Banking and Finance

In March 2002 deposits at all banks in Queensland totalled $A64,443m. Other lending totalled $A88,382m.

ENERGY AND NATURAL RESOURCES

Electricity

The government-owned sector of the state's electricity industry has been restructured, and since Dec. 1998 it has operated as part of the wholesale national electricity market. Part of the restructuring was the formation of a single corporation, Ergon Energy, by the amalgamation of the six former regional distribution corporations. In the year ended 30 June 2002 total consumption stood at 39,544m. kWh by 1,684,488 customers, including 27,900m. kWh by business customers. Coal is the main fuel source for electricity generation in the state, producing 45,967m. kWh in the year ended 30 June 2002; installed generation capacity stood at 10,700 MW.

Minerals

There are large reserves of coal, bauxite, gold, copper, silver, lead, zinc, nickel, phosphate rock and limestone. The state is the largest producer of black coal in Australia. Most of the coal produced comes from the Bowen Basin coalfields in central Queensland. Copper, lead, silver and zinc are mined in the northwest and the State's largest goldmines are in the north. The total value of metallic minerals in 2002–03 was $A3·54bn. In 2002–03 there were 37 coal mines in operation producing 153·6m. tonnes of saleable coal (an increase of 3·5% on the previous year); and at 30 June 2003, 10,713 persons were employed in mining.

Agriculture

Queensland is Australia's leading beef-producing state and its chief producer of fruit and vegetables. In the year ended 30 June 2003 there were 27,503 agricultural establishments farming 139·0m. ha. of which 2·3m. ha. were under crops. Livestock numbered (at 30 June 2003) 10,507,000 beef cattle; 4,815,000 sheep and lambs; and 663,000 pigs. Total value of wool production, 2001–02: $A189m. The gross value of agricultural commodity production in 2002–03 was $A7·3bn. which comprised crops, $A3·5bn.; livestock disposals, $A3·4bn.; and livestock products, $A438m.

Forestry

Of a total of 54m. ha. of forests and woodlands in 1999, 6% was in national parks and World Heritage areas while 7% was in State forests and timber reserves outside World Heritage sites. Queensland's plantation forests supply around 40% of Australia's wood and paper products. The forestry industry is an important part of the state's economy, employing around 17,000 people with a gross output of $A1,700m.

Fisheries

Estimated total fisheries production in 2003–04 came to 33,688 tonnes with a gross value of $A294·7m. In the same year aquaculture production was an estimated 4,668 tonnes with a gross value of $A65·6m.

INDUSTRY

In 2000–01 the manufacturing industry turnover totalled $A40,292m. with a total of 156,500 people employed. The largest manufacturing sector was food, beverages and tobacco (2000–01 turnover: $A12,314m.).

Labour

In 2003–04 the labour force numbered 1,967,800, of whom 1,845,000 (825,600 females) were employed. In 2003–04 unemployment stood at 6·2%, the lowest total for two years. The average weekly wage in Feb. 2003 was $A820·10 (males $A856·60, females $A754·50).

Trade Unions

In Aug. 1999, 332,373 employees were members of a trade union (25·0% of total employment).

INTERNATIONAL TRADE

Imports and Exports

Total value of direct overseas imports and exports f.o.b. port of shipment for both imports and exports in 2003–04: imports, $A18,052m.; exports, $A20,0126m.

Chief sources of imports in 2003–04 (in $A1m.): USA, 3,052; Japan, 2,861; China, 1,614; Papua New Guinea, 920; Germany, 861. Exports went chiefly to (in $A1m.): Japan, 5,301; Republic of Korea, 2,194; USA, 1,421; China, 1,409; India, 1,041.

Principal overseas imports were (in $A1m.): passenger vehicles, 2,446; crude petroleum, 2,074; aircraft and parts, 1,199; motor vehicles for transporting goods, 815; non-monetary gold, 575; civil engineering equipment, 538. The chief exports overseas in 2003–04 (in $A1m.) were: coal, 5,929; bovine meat, 2,375; aluminium, 891; other ores, 807; copper, 490.

COMMUNICATIONS

Roads

At 30 June 2004 there were 181,305 km of roads open to the public. Of these, 70,608 km were surfaced with sealed pavement. At 31 March 2003 motor vehicles registered totalled 2,552,061, comprising 1,999,117 passenger vehicles and motorcycles, 441,358 light commercial vehicles and 111,586 trucks, buses and prime movers. There were 286 fatalities in road accidents in the year ended Aug. 2003.

Rail

Queensland Rail is a State government-owned corporation. Total length of line, 2001–02 was 9,514 km. In 2003–04, 49·1m. passengers and 161·9m. tonnes of freight were carried.

Civil Aviation

Queensland is well served with a network of air services, with overseas and interstate connections. Subsidiary companies provide planes for taxi and charter work, and the Flying Doctor Service operates throughout western Queensland. In 1997–98 all Federal airports were leased to private sector operators—Brisbane, Archerfield, Coolangatta, Mount Isa and Townsville Airports (the latter is operated jointly with the Department of Defence). In 2002–03 Brisbane handled 11,841,196 passengers (8,771,730 on domestic flights); Cairns, 2,900,472 passengers (1,899,991 on domestic flights). The number of aircraft registered at 30 June 1999 was 2,423.

Shipping

Queensland has 14 modern trading ports, two community ports and a number of non-trading ports. In 2002–03 general cargo imported through Queensland ports was 1,588,964 mass tonnes and general cargo exported was 4,138,321 mass tonnes. There were 1,963 commercial ship calls during 2002–03.

Telecommunications

In 2000 there were 668,000 households with home computer access (50% of all households) and 408,000 households with home Internet access (31%).

Postal Services

At 30 June 2004 there were 826 post offices, post office agencies and community mail agencies.

SOCIAL INSTITUTIONS

Justice

Justice is administered by Higher Courts (Supreme and District), Magistrates' Courts and Children's Courts. The Supreme Court comprises the Chief Justice and 21 judges; the District Courts, 34 district court judges. Stipendiary magistrates preside over the Magistrates' and Children's Courts, except in the smaller centres, where justices of the peace officiate. A parole board may recommend prisoners for release.

Total police personnel (sworn and unsworn) at 30 June 2003 was 11,961. As at 30 June 2005 the average daily number of prisoners stood at 5,354.

Education

Education is compulsory between the ages of six and 15 years and is provided free in government schools.

Primary and secondary education comprises 12 years of full-time formal schooling, and is provided by both the government and non-government sectors. In 2002 the State administered 1,291 schools with 284,262 primary students and 155,802 secondary students. In 2002 there were 35,071 teachers in government schools. There were 435 private schools in 2002 with 92,497 primary students and 87,026 secondary students. Educational programmes at private schools were provided by 13,803 teachers in 2002. In 2002 there were 2,061,500 subject enrolments in Vocational Education and Training activities. The seven publicly funded universities had 174,000 full-time students in 2002.

Health

At 30 June 2003 there were 175 public acute hospitals and six public psychiatric hospitals; 44 private free-standing day hospital facilities and 55 other private hospitals (including acute and psychiatric hospitals). In 2001 Queensland had the highest rate of obesity (18·5% of the State's population).

Welfare

Welfare institutions providing shelter and social care for the aged, the handicapped and children are maintained or assisted by the State. A child health service is provided throughout the State. Age, invalid, widows', disability and war service pensions, family allowances, and unemployment and sickness benefits are paid by the Federal government. The number of age and disability pensions (including wives' and carers' pensions) at 30 June 1999 was: age, 284,852; disability support, 105,276; carer, 7,770. There were 5,879 widows' and 80,318 single parent payments current at 30 June 1999, and basic family payment was being paid for 654,363 children under 16 years.

RELIGION

Religious affiliation at the 1996 census: Roman Catholic, 25·2%; Anglican, 23·6%; Uniting Church, 9·5%; Presbyterian, 4·7%; Lutheran, 2·2%; Baptist, 1·9%; other Christian, 6·8%; non-Christian, 1·5%; no religion, 15·3%; not stated, 9·0%.

CULTURE

Broadcasting

In addition to the national networks Queensland is served by 13 public radio stations (non-profit-making), 44 commercial radio stations and three commercial TV channels.

Tourism

Overseas visitors to Queensland in the year ending June 2004 totalled 1·96m., the main source being from Asia, with Japanese tourists totalling 454,157 (23% of the total). Visitors from New Zealand accounted for 17%; UK, 14%; and USA, 7%.

FURTHER READING

Statistical Information: The Statistical Office (now Australian Bureau of Statistics, 313 Adelaide St., Brisbane) was set up in 1859. A *Queensland Official Year Book* was issued in 1901, the annual *ABC of Queensland Statistics* from 1905 to 1936 with exception of 1918 and 1922. Present publications include: *Queensland Year Book*. Annual, from 1937 (omitting 1942, 1943, 1944, 1987, 1991).—*Queensland Pocket Year Book*. Annual from 1950.—*Monthly Summary of Statistics, Queensland*. From Jan. 1961. Selected statistics available at *website:* http://www.abs.gov.au

Australian Sugar Year Book. Brisbane, from 1941

Johnston, W. R., *A Bibliography of Queensland History*. Brisbane, 1981.—*The Call of the Land: A History of Queensland to the Present Day*. Brisbane, 1982

Johnston, W. R. and Zerner, M., *Guide to the History of Queensland*. Brisbane, 1985

State library: The State Library of Queensland, Queensland Cultural Centre, PO Box 3488, South Bank, South Brisbane.

Local Statistical Office: Office of Economic and Statistical Research, PO Box 15037, City East, Qld 4002.

Website: http://www.oesr.qld.gov.au

South Australia

KEY HISTORICAL EVENTS

South Australia was surveyed by Tasman in 1644 and charted by Flinders in 1802. It was made into a British province by letters of patent of Feb. 1836, and a partially elective legislative council was established in 1851. From 6 July 1863 the Northern Territory was placed under the jurisdiction of South Australia until the establishment of the Commonwealth of Australia in 1911.

TERRITORY AND POPULATION

The total area of South Australia is 983,480 sq. km. The settled part is divided into counties and hundreds. There are 49 counties proclaimed, and 536 hundreds, covering 23m. ha., of which 19m. ha. are occupied. Outside this area there are extensive pastoral districts, covering 76m. ha., 49m. of which are under pastoral leases.

The resident population (preliminary estimate) at 30 June 2005 was 1,542,000 (annual growth rate, 0·6%). The 2001 census population was 1,467,261 (23,425 Aboriginal and Torres Strait Islanders). The 1996 census totalled 1,427,936.

At 30 June 2003 the Adelaide Statistical Division had an estimated 1,119,718 persons (73·3% of South Australia's total population) in 25 councils and four municipalities and other districts. Urban centres outside this area (with estimated populations at 30 June 2003) are Mount Gambier (23,571), Whyalla (21,604), Port Pirie (17,490), Port Lincoln (14,273) and Port Augusta (13,795).

SOCIAL STATISTICS

Statistics for calendar years:

	Live Births	Deaths	Marriages	Divorces
2000	17,859	11,843	8,227	—
2001	17,439	11,767	7,434	4,545
2002	17,481	11,578	7,373	4,409
2003	17,443	12,185	7,609	4,151

The rates per 1,000 population in 2003 were: births, 11·4; deaths, 8·0; marriages, 5·0; divorces, 2·7. The infant mortality rate in 2003 was 3·7 per 1,000 live births. Life expectancy for 2003 was 77·7 years for men and 82·7 years for women.

CONSTITUTION AND GOVERNMENT

The present Constitution dates from 24 Oct. 1856. It vests the legislative power in an elected Parliament, consisting of a Legislative Council and a House of Assembly. The former is composed of 22 members. Eleven members are elected at alternate elections for a term of at least six years and are elected on the basis of preferential proportional representation with the State as one multi-member electorate. The House of Assembly consists of 47 members elected by a preferential system of voting for the term of a Parliament (four years). Election of members of both Houses takes place by secret ballot. Voting is compulsory for those on the Electoral Roll. The qualifications of an elector are to be an Australian citizen, or a British subject who was, at some time within the period of three months commencing on 26 Oct. 1983, enrolled under the Repealed Act as an Assembly elector or enrolled on an electoral roll maintained under the Commonwealth or a Commonwealth Territory, must be at least 18 years of age and have lived in the subdivision for which the person is enrolled for at least one month. By the Constitution Act Amendment Act, 1894, the franchise was extended to women, who voted for the first time at the general election of 25 April 1896. Certain persons are ineligible for election to either House.

Electors enrolled (30 Dec. 2002) numbered 1,050,000.

The executive power is vested in a Governor appointed by the Crown and an Executive Council, consisting of the Governor and the Ministers of the Crown. The Governor has the power to dissolve the House of Assembly but not the Legislative Council, unless that Chamber has twice consecutively with an election intervening defeated the same or substantially the same Bill passed in the House of Assembly by an absolute majority.

RECENT ELECTIONS

The House of Assembly, elected on 18 March 2006, consisted of the following members: Australian Labor Party (ALP), 28; Liberal Party (LIB), 15; Independent (ind.), 3; National, 1.

CURRENT ADMINISTRATION

Governor: Marjorie Jackson-Nelson, AC, CVO, MBE.

In Feb. 2006 the Labor Ministry was as follows:

Premier, Minister for Economic Development, Social Inclusion and the Arts: Mike Rann.

Deputy Premier, Treasurer, Minister Assisting the Premier in Economic Development and Police: Kevin Foley. *Industry and Trade:* Paul Holloway. *Infrastructure, Energy and Transport:* Patrick Conlon. *Attorney-General, Justice and Multicultural Affairs:* Michael Atkinson. *Aboriginal Affairs, Reconciliation and Correctional Services:* Terry Roberts. *Health, Environment and Conservation:* John Hill. *Employment, Training and Further Education, Youth and the Status of Women:* Stephanie Key. *Administrative Services, Industrial Relations, Recreation, Sport and Racing and Gambling:* Michael Wright. *Education and Children's Services:* Jane Lomax-Smith. *Families and Communities, Housing, Ageing and Disability:* Jay Weatherill. *Agriculture, Food and Fisheries, State/Local Government Relations and Forests:* Rory McEwen (ind.). *River Murray, Regional Development, Small Business and Consumer Affairs, Science and Information Technology:* Karlene Maywald (National). *Emergency Services, Mental Health and Substance Abuse:* Carmel Zollo.

Speaker: Bob Such (ind.).

President: Ron Roberts (ALP).

SA Government website: http://www.sa.gov.au

ECONOMY

Budget

Estimated government sector revenue and expenses ($A1m.):

	2001–02	2002–03	2003–04
Revenue	9,367	10,172	10,707
Expenditure	9,487	9,696	10,294

In 2003–04 State government revenue from taxes amounted to $A2,783m.; grants and subsidies totalled $A5,081m.

Performance

South Australia's 2002–03 gross state product represented 6·63% of Australia's total GDP.

Banking and Finance

In March 2002 total deposits held by banks was $A22,717m. and loans totalled $A29,739m.

ENERGY AND NATURAL RESOURCES

Electricity

In the year ended 30 June 2002 total consumption stood at 11,213m. kWh, including 6,813m. kWh by business customers. At June 2002 installed generation capacity stood at 3,479 MW.

Minerals

The principal metallic minerals produced are copper, iron ore, uranium oxide, gold and silver. The total value of minerals produced in 2002–03 was $A1,655·2m. including copper, $A514·6m.; natural gas, $A336·1m.; uranium oxide, $A131·3m.; opals (estimate), $A33·0m. In 2002–03 there were 4,000 persons employed in mining.

Agriculture

In the year ended 30 June 2002 there were 14,824 establishments mainly engaged in agriculture with a total area under holding of 53·5m. ha. of which 4·18m. ha. were under crops. The gross value of agricultural production in 2002–03 was $A4·1bn. Total value of wool production, $A403·9m. Value of chief crops in 2001–02: wheat, $A1·3bn.; barley, $A588m.; potatoes, $A135m. Production of grapes (2001–02) was 697,700 tonnes with virtually all being used for winemaking (vineyards' total area, 67,000 ha., including 6,500 ha. not yet bearing). Fruit culture is extensive with citrus and orchard fruits. The most valuable vegetable crops are potatoes, onions and carrots.

Livestock, 30 June 2003: cattle, 1,401,000; sheep and lambs, 13,059,000; pigs, 381,000. Gross value of livestock slaughtered, 2002–03, \$A846·7m.

Forestry
Total area of plantations at 30 June 2003 totalled 81,126 ha.

Fisheries
Estimated total fisheries production in 2003–04 came to 59,872 tonnes with a gross value of \$A460·3m. In the same year aquaculture production was an estimated 15,355 tonnes with a gross value of \$A277·8m.

INDUSTRY

The turnover for manufacturing industries for 2000–01 was \$A23,623m.; wages and salaries totalled \$A3,557m.

Industry sub-division	Persons employed (1,000)	Turnover (\$A1m.)
Food, beverages and tobacco	21·1	4,881·2
Textiles, clothing, footwear and leather manufacturing	4·5	716·1
Wood and paper products manufacturing	5·9	1,374·3
Printing, publishing and recorded media	5·0	833·3
Chemical, petroleum, coal and associated products	7·2	1,614·0
Non-metallic mineral products	2·8	710·1
Metal products manufacturing	12·9	2,827·4
Machinery and equipment	33·9	7,814·0
Other manufacturing	4·6	671·2
Total	97·9	21,442·0

Labour
In Nov. 2004 the labour force stood at 767,400. There were 42,400 unemployed, a rate of 5·5%. The average weekly wage in Aug. 2004 was \$A662·50 (males \$A785·50, females \$A526·70).

INTERNATIONAL TRADE

Imports and Exports
Overseas imports and exports in \$A1m. (year ending 30 June):

	2001–02	2002–03	2003–04
Imports	5,347	5,724	5,163
Exports	9,103	8,365	7,604

Principal imports in 2003–04 were (with values in \$A1m.): refined petroleum, 481; motor vehicles parts, 409; passenger motor vehicles, 384; internal combustion piston engines, 222; measuring and controlling instruments, 138. Principal exports in 2003–04 were (with values in \$A1m.): alcoholic beverages, 1,411; passenger motor vehicles, 1,110; wheat, 693; copper, 398; fish 247; meat, excluding bovine, 217.

In 2003–04 the leading suppliers of imports were (with values in \$A1m.): Japan, 891; USA, 652; Singapore, 547; China, 371; Canada, 311. Main export markets were USA, 1,391; UK, 784; Japan, 695; New Zealand, 557; Saudi Arabia, 444.

COMMUNICATIONS

Roads
At 30 June 2004 there were 28,557 km of sealed and 68,017 km of unsealed roads. Motor vehicles registered as at 31 Dec. 2004: passenger vehicles (cars and station wagons), 877,984; trailers, 230,792; motorcycles, 31,835. In the year ended Aug. 2003 there were 143 road accident fatalities.

Rail
In Aug. 1997 the passenger operations of Australian National Railways were sold to Great Southern Railway and the freight operations to Australian Southern Railroad. Australian National Railways operates 4,415 km of railway in country areas.

TransAdelaide operates 120 km of railway in the metropolitan area of Adelaide. In the year ended 31 March 2001, 19m. tonnes of freight were carried.

There is a tramway in Adelaide that runs from the city centre to the coast. A joint South Australia and Northern Territory project, The AustralAsia Rail Project between Alice Springs and Darwin, carried its first passenger train in Feb. 2004.

Civil Aviation
The main airport is Adelaide International Airport, which handled 4,350,836 passengers (3,841,475 on domestic flights) in 2002–03.

Shipping
There are ten state and five private deep-sea ports. In 2002–03, 1,361 commercial vessels arrived in South Australia. General cargo imported in 2002–03 was 678,338 mass tonnes and general cargo exported was 1,610,919 mass tonnes.

Telecommunications
In 2004 residential telephone penetration was 93·1% (98·0% in 1998). In 2000 there were 295,000 households with home computer access (50% of all households) and 176,000 households with home Internet access (30%).

Source: Roy Morgan Single Source January–March 2005

Postal Services
At 30 June 2004 there were 586 Australia Post retail facilities in South Australia and Northern Territory.

SOCIAL INSTITUTIONS

Justice
There is a Supreme Court, which incorporates admiralty, civil, criminal, land and valuation, and testamentary jurisdiction; district criminal courts, which have jurisdiction in many indictable offences; and magistrates courts, which include the Youth Court. Circuit courts are held at several places. At 30 June 2004 the police force numbered 3,910. The average daily number of prisoners at 30 June 2003 was 1,455.

Education
Education is compulsory for children between the ages of six and 15 years although most children are enrolled at age five or soon after. Primary and secondary education at government schools is secular and free. In Aug. 2001 there were 812 schools operating, of which 611 were government and 201 non-government schools. In that year there were 114,287 children in government and 43,500 in non-government primary schools, and 61,935 children in government and 31,800 in non-government secondary schools. In 2001 there were 167,900 enrolments in Vocational Education and Training activities. There were 30,627 students enrolled at the University of South Australia in 2002; University of Adelaide, 16,188; and Flinders University, 13,644.

Health
In 2003–04 there were 80 public hospitals and 55 private hospitals. Beds available in public and private hospitals totalled 6,553.

Welfare
The number of age and disability pensions (including wives' and carers' pensions) on 30 June 2002 was: age, 170,648; disability support, 62,977. There were 50,692 Newstart and Mature Age allowances and 35,079 single parent payments current at 30 June 2002.

RELIGION

Religious affiliation at the 1996 census: Catholic, 296,048; Anglican, 228,151; Uniting Church, 180,604; Lutheran, 70,970; Orthodox, 42,053; Baptist, 26,251; Presbyterian, 23,994; other Christians, 74,868; non-Christians, 25,236; indefinite, 4,885; no religion, 310,908; not stated, 138,554.

CULTURE

Broadcasting
There are 131 radio stations (24 AM and 107 FM) and four commercial TV stations, one community service TV station and the national ABC service.

Tourism
In the year ended 30 June 2000 international visitors totalled 350,100 (over 50% from Europe), an increase of 12% on the previous year. At 30 June 2002 there were 236 hotels, motels, guest houses and serviced apartments with 10,955 rooms.

FURTHER READING
Statistical Information: The State office of the Australian Bureau of Statistics is at 55 Currie St., Adelaide (GPO Box 2272). Although the first printed statistical publication was the *Statistics of South Australia, 1854*, with the title altered to *Statistical Register* in 1859, there is a manuscript volume for each year back to 1838. These contain simple records of trade, demography, production, etc. and were prepared only for the information of the Colonial Office; one copy was retained in the State.

The publications of the State office include the *South Australian Year Book* (now discontinued), a monthly *South Australian Economic Indicators*, a quarterly bulletin of building activity, and approximately 40 special bulletins issued each year as particulars of various sections of statistics become available.

Gibbs, R. M., *A History of South Australia: from Colonial Days to the Present*. 3rd ed. revised, Adelaide, 1995

Prest, Wilfred, Round, Kerrie and Fort, Carol, (eds.) *The Wakefield Companion to South Australian History*. Wakefield Press, Kent Town, 2002

Whitelock, D., *Adelaide from Colony to Jubilee: a Sense of Difference*. Adelaide, 1985

State Library: The State Library of S.A., North Terrace, Adelaide.

Tasmania

KEY HISTORICAL EVENTS
Abel Janszoon Tasman discovered Van Diemen's Land (Tasmania) on 24 Nov. 1642. The island became a British settlement in 1803 as a dependency of New South Wales. In 1825 its connection with New South Wales was terminated and in 1851 a partially elected Legislative Council was established. In 1856 a fully responsible government was inaugurated. On 1 Jan. 1901 Tasmania was federated with the other Australian states into the Commonwealth of Australia.

TERRITORY AND POPULATION
Tasmania is a group of islands separated from the mainland by Bass Strait with an area (including islands) of 68,400 sq. km, of which 63,447 sq. km form the area of the main island. The population at the 7 Aug. 2001 census was 456,652 (459,659 at 1996 census); 21,910 were born in the UK or Ireland, 11,120 in other European countries and 386,036 in Australia. The resident population (preliminary estimate) at 30 June 2005 was 485,300 (annual growth rate, 0·6%).

The largest cities and towns (with populations at the 2001 census) are: Hobart (191,169), Launceston (95,604), Devonport (23,030) and Burnie (18,145).

SOCIAL STATISTICS
Statistics for calendar years:

	Births	Deaths	Marriages	Divorces
2000	5,692	3,711	2,589	1,329
2001	6,430	3,876	2,182	1,439
2002	6,003	3,979	2,605	1,386
2003	5,752	3,965	2,599	1,336

The annual rates per 1,000 of the mean resident population in 2003 were: births, 12·1; deaths, 8·3; marriages, 5·4; divorces, 2·8. Infant mortality rate, 2003, 7·0 per 1,000 live births. Expectation of life, 2003: males, 76·6 years; females, 81·4 years.

CLIMATE
Mostly a temperate maritime climate. The prevailing westerly airstream leads to a west coast and highlands that are cool, wet and cloudy, and an east coast and lowlands that are milder, drier and sunnier.

CONSTITUTION AND GOVERNMENT
Parliament consists of the Governor, the Legislative Council and the House of Assembly. The Council has 15 members, elected by adults with six months' residence. Members sit for six years, with either two or three retiring annually. There is no power to dissolve the Council. The House of Assembly has 25 members; the maximum term for the House of Assembly is four years. Women received the right to vote in 1903. Proportional representation was adopted in 1907, the method now being the single transferable vote in five member constituencies.

A Minister must have a seat in one of the two Houses.

RECENT ELECTIONS
At the elections of 18 March 2006 the Australian Labor Party won 14 seats in the House of Assembly, the Liberal Party 7 and the Tasmanian Greens 4.

CURRENT ADMINISTRATION
Governor: William Cox; b. 1936 (took office on 15 Dec. 2004, having been acting governor from 9 Aug. 2004–3 Dec. 2004).

The Legislative Council is predominantly independent without formal party allegiance; four members are Labor-endorsed.

In Feb. 2006 the Labor government comprised:

Premier and Treasurer: Paul Lennon (took office on 21 March 2004).

Deputy Premier and Minister for Health and Human Services, and Police and Public Safety: David Llewellyn. *Minister for Economic Development and the Arts:* Lara Giddings. *Justice, Industrial Relations, Environment and Planning, Parks and Heritage and Attorney General:* Judy Jackson. *Education, Tourism and Women Tasmania:* Paula Wriedt. *Finance, Racing, Sport and Recreation:* Jim Cox. *Infrastructure, Energy and Resources:* Bryan Green. *Primary Industries and Water:* Steven Kons. *Leader of the Government in the Legislative Council:* Michael Aird.

Speaker of the House of Assembly: Michael Polley.

TAS Government website: http://www.tas.gov.au

ECONOMY

Budget
Consolidated Revenue Fund receipts and expenditure, in $A1m., for financial years ending 30 June:

	2002–03	2003–04
Revenue	2,551	3,212
Expenditure	2,542	2,916

In 2003–04 State government revenue from taxes amounted to $A631m.; grants and subsidies totalled $A1,997m.

Banking and Finance
In March 2002 total deposits held by banks was $A3,958m. and loans totalled $A5,540m.

ENERGY AND NATURAL RESOURCES

Electricity
Installed capacity is 2,502 MW. In the year ended 30 June 2003 total consumption stood at 9,780m. kWh, including 1,820m. kWh by residential customers.

Minerals

Output of principal metallic minerals in 2002–03 was (in 1,000 tonnes): iron ore pellets, 2,142·3; zinc, 141·9; copper, 108·1; lead, 42·2; tin, 8·5.

Agriculture

There were 4,027 agricultural establishments at 30 June 2002 occupying a total area of 1·8m. ha. Principal crops in 2000–01 (in 1,000 tonnes): potatoes, 331,018; apples, 56,105; barley, 25,992; wheat, 25,554; oats, 12,616. Gross value of recorded production from agriculture in 2000–01 was (in $A1m.): crops, 350·1; livestock products, 244·4; livestock slaughterings and other disposals, 160·4; total gross value, 755·0. Livestock, 2001–02: cattle, 661,000; sheep and lambs, 3,380,200; pigs, 18,000. Wool produced during 2001–02 was 14,268 tonnes.

Forestry

Indigenous forests, which cover a considerable part of the State, support sawmilling and woodchipping industries. Production of sawn timber in 2002–03 was 398,500 cu. metres. Newsprint and paper are produced from native hardwoods.

Fisheries

Estimated total fisheries production in 2003–04 came to 27,214 tonnes with a gross value of $A278·4m. In the same year aquaculture production was an estimated 18,334 tonnes with a gross value of $A132·6m.

INDUSTRY

The most important manufactures for export are refined metals, woodchips, newsprint and other paper manufactures, pigments, woollen goods, fruit pulp, confectionery, butter, cheese, preserved and dried vegetables, sawn timber, and processed fish products. The electrolytic-zinc works at Risdon produce zinc, sulphuric acid, superphosphate, sulphate of ammonia, cadmium and other by-products. At George Town, large-scale plants produce refined aluminium and manganese alloys. In 2000–01 employment in manufacturing establishments was 20,600; wages and salaries totalled $A776·2m.; turnover, $A5,043·6m.

Labour

In 2002–03 the labour force stood at 219,600. There were 18,900 unemployed, a rate of 8·6%. The average weekly wage in Feb. 2003 was $A826·00 (males $A863·00, females $A748·30).

Trade Unions

In 2000 Tasmania had the highest rate of trade union membership of any Australian State, at 31·3%. This compared with 34·6% in Aug. 1998 and 39·3% in Aug. 1996.

INTERNATIONAL TRADE

Imports and Exports

In 2003–04 direct imports into Tasmania totalled $A699m. In that year the principal suppliers of imports were (with values in $A1m.): Indonesia, 115; Germany, 100; USA, 71. In 2003–04 exports totalled $A2,312m. The principal countries of destination in 2003–04 (with values in $A1m.) for overseas exports were: Japan, 589; Hong Kong, 282; USA, 275; Republic of Korea, 207; China, 160. Commodities by value (in $A1m.) imported from overseas countries in 2003–04 included: ships, boats and floating structures, 172; pulp and waste paper, 68; rotating electric plant, 68. Commodities by value (in $A1m.) exported to overseas countries in 2003–04 included: zinc, 345; aluminium, 333; crustaceans, 90; bovine meat, 89.

COMMUNICATIONS

Roads

At 30 June 2004 there were 24,644 km of roads open to general traffic. Motor vehicles registered at 31 Oct. 2001 comprised 246,367 passenger vehicles, 76,432 commercial vehicles and 8,469 motorcycles. In the year ended Aug. 2003 there were 33 road accident fatalities.

Rail

Tasmania's rail network, incorporating 867 km of railways, is primarily a freight system with no regular passenger services. There are some small tourist railways, notably the newly rebuilt 34 km Abt Wilderness Railway on the west coast.

Civil Aviation

Regular passenger and freight services connect the south, north and northwest of the State with the mainland. During 2000–01 the six main airports handled 1,825,828 passengers and 5,593·9 tonnes of freight.

Shipping

There are four major commercial ports: Burnie, Devonport, Launceston and Hobart. In 2002–03, 1,443 commercial vessels called at Tasmanian ports. General cargo imported in 2002–03 was 1,846,595 mass tonnes and general cargo exported was 2,852,972 mass tonnes. Passenger ferry services connect Tasmania with the mainland and offshore islands.

Telecommunications

In 2000 there were 84,000 households with home computer access (45% of all households) and 48,000 households with home Internet access. In 2000, 49% of all households had access to a mobile phone.

Postal Services

In April 1999 there were 34 post offices and 152 licensees.

SOCIAL INSTITUTIONS

Justice

The Supreme Court of Tasmania is a superior court of record, with both original and appellate jurisdiction, and consists of a Chief Justice and five puisne judges. There are also inferior civil courts with limited jurisdiction.

In 2000–01 there were 58,295 recorded offences, including 51,339 against property; 3,660 against the person; and 2,879 fraud and similar offences. Total police personnel (sworn and unsworn) at 30 June 2003 was 1,548. There are three prisons and one detention centre which received a combined total of 427 prisoners at 30 June 2002.

Education

Education is controlled by the State and is free, secular and compulsory between the ages of six and 16. In 2003, 214 government schools had a total enrolment of 61,157 pupils; 67 private schools had a total enrolment of 21,219 pupils.

In 2003 there were 54,814 enrolments in Vocational Education and Training activities.

Tertiary education is offered at the University of Tasmania and the Australian Maritime College. In 2003 the University (established 1890) had 14,506 students and the Australian Maritime College 2,724 students.

Health

In 2002–03 there were 25 public hospitals with 1,136 beds and 11 private hospitals with 1,098 beds, a total of 4·7 beds per 1,000 population.

Welfare

The number of age and disability pensions (including wives' and carers' pensions) on 30 June 2001 was: age, 48,499; disability support, 21,655; carer, 2,005. There were 976 widows' and 20,217 single parent payments current at 30 June 2001, and basic family payment was being paid for 83,433 children under 16 years.

RELIGION

At the census of 2001 the following numbers of adherents of the principal religions were recorded:

Anglican Church	147,413	Other Christian	10,526
Roman Catholic	87,691	Indefinite and not stated	47,430
Uniting Church	30,376	No religion	78,672
Presbyterian	12,508	Non-Christian	2,975
Baptist	8,984		
		Total	456,652

CULTURE

Broadcasting
In 2002 there were four TV broadcasters and 21 radio stations.

Press
There were three daily papers with a combined circulation of 120,710 in March 2001. The largest circulation for a Tasmanian daily is for the Saturday edition of *The Mercury*, with a circulation of 65,097.

Tourism
In 2002–03 an estimated 652,200 adult visitors arrived in Tasmania, a 25·5% increase on 2001–02.

FURTHER READING

Statistical Information: The State Government Statistical Office (200 Collins St., Hobart), established in 1877, became in 1924 the Tasmanian Office of the Australian Bureau of Statistics, but continues to serve State statistical needs as required.

Main publications: Annual Statistical Bulletins (e.g., *Demography, Agriculture, Government Finance, Manufacturing Industry* etc.).—*Tasmanian Pocket Year Book*. Annual (from 1913).—*Tasmanian Year Book*. Annual (from 1967; biennial from 1986).—Monthly *Tasmanian Statistical Indicators* (from July 1945).

E-mail address: Sales and Inquiries: *client.services@abs.gov.au*
Website: http://www.abs.gov.au

Kepars, I., *Tasmania*. [Bibliography] ABC-Clio, Oxford and Santa Barbara (CA), 1997

Robson, L., *A History of Tasmania. Vol. 1: Van Diemen's Land from the Earliest Times to 1855*. Melbourne, 1983.—*A History of Tasmania. Vol. 2: Colony and State from 1856 to the 1980s*. Melbourne, 1990

State library: The State Library of Tasmania, 91 Murray St., Hobart, TAS 7000.
Website: http://statelibrary.tas.gov.au

Victoria

KEY HISTORICAL EVENTS

The first permanent settlement was formed at Portland Bay in 1834. A government was established in 1839. Victoria, formerly a portion of New South Wales, was proclaimed a separate colony in 1851 at much the same time as gold was discovered. A new constitution giving responsible government to the colony was proclaimed on 23 Nov. 1855. This event had far-reaching effects, as the population increased from 76,162 in 1850 to 589,160 in 1864. By this time the impetus for the search for gold had waned and new arrivals made a living from pastoral and agricultural holdings and from the development of manufacturing industries. Victoria federated with the other Australian states to form the Commonwealth of Australia in 1901.

TERRITORY AND POPULATION

The State has an area of 227,420 sq. km, and, at 30 June 2005, a resident population (preliminary estimate) of 5,022,300 (annual growth rate, 1·2%). The 2001 census population was 4,644,950 (4,373,520 at 1996 census). Victoria has the greatest proportion of people from non-English-speaking countries of any State or Territory, with (1996 census) 2·3% from Italy, 1·4% from Greece and 1·3% from Vietnam.

Estimated population at 30 June 2002, within 11 'Statistical Divisions': Melbourne, 3,524,103; Barwon, 259,549; Goulburn,

196,545; Loddon, 169,088; Gippsland, 161,204; Central Highlands, 143,179; Western District, 100,894; Ovens-Murray, 94,264; Mallee, 91,170; East Gippsland, 81,178; Wimmera, 51,364.

SOCIAL STATISTICS

Statistics for calendar years:

	Births	Deaths	Marriages	Divorces
2000	59,171	32,018	26,852	12,401
2001	58,626	32,295	24,953	13,722
2002	61,478	33,772	25,058	12,987
2003	61,058	32,925	25,211	12,865

The annual rates per 1,000 of the mean resident population in 2003 were: births, 12·4; deaths, 6·7; marriages, 5·1; divorces, 2·6. Infant mortality rate, 2003, 5·1 per 1,000 live births. Expectation of life, 2003: males, 78·2 years; females, 83·1 years.

CLIMATE

See AUSTRALIA: Climate.

CONSTITUTION AND GOVERNMENT

Victoria, formerly a portion of New South Wales, was, in 1851, proclaimed a separate colony, with a partially elective Legislative Council. In 1856 responsible government was conferred, the legislative power being vested in a parliament consisting of a Legislative Council (Upper House) and a Legislative Assembly (Lower House). At present the Council consists of 44 members who are elected for two terms of the Assembly, with half of the seats up for renewal at each election. The Assembly consists of 88 members, elected for four years from the date of its first meeting unless sooner dissolved by the Governor. Members and electors of both Houses must be aged 18 years and Australian citizens or those British subjects previously enrolled as electors, according to the Constitution Act 1975. Single voting (one elector one vote) and compulsory preferential voting apply to Council and Assembly elections. Enrolment for Council and Assembly electors is compulsory. The Council may not initiate or amend money bills, but may suggest amendments in such bills other than amendments which would increase any charge. A bill shall not become law unless passed by both Houses.

In the exercise of the executive power the Governor is advised by a Cabinet of responsible Ministers. Section 50 of the Constitution Act 1975 provides that the number of Ministers shall not at any one time exceed 22, of whom not more than six may sit in the Legislative Council and not more than 17 may sit in the Legislative Assembly.

RECENT ELECTIONS

In elections to the Legislative Assembly on 30 Nov. 2002 the Labor Party (ALP) won 62 seats with 47·9% of votes cast; the Liberal Party (LP), 17 (33·9%); the National Party (NP), 7 (4·3%). Two independents were elected. The Greens took 9·7% of the vote but no seats. Turnout was 76·3%.

In the simultaneous elections to the Legislative Council the ALP won 17 seats, the LP 3, and the NP 2. Total seats in March 2004: ALP 25, LP 15, and NP 4.

CURRENT ADMINISTRATION

Governor: David de Kretser.
The Labor Cabinet was as follows in Feb. 2006:
Premier, Minister for Multicultural Affairs: Stephen Bracks.
Deputy Premier, Minister for the Environment, Water and Victorian Communities: John Thwaites. *Transport:* Peter Batchelor. *Local Government and Housing:* Candy Broad. *State and Regional Development, Innovation and Treasurer:* John Brumby. *Agriculture:* Bob Cameron. *Health:* Bronwyn Pike. *Education and Training:* Lynne Kosky. *Community Services and Children:* Sherryl Garbutt. *Finance, Major Projects and*

Workcover: John Lenders. *Manufacturing and Export, Small Business and Financial Services:* Andre Haermeyer. *Arts and Women's Affairs:* Mary Delahunty. *Education Services, Youth Affairs and Employment:* Jacinta Allan. *Consumer Affairs, Information and Communication Technology:* Marsha Thomson. *Attorney General, Minister for Industrial Relations and Planning:* Rob Hulls. *Sport and Recreation, Commonwealth Games:* Justin Madden. *Gaming and Racing, and Tourism:* John Pandazopoulos. *Aged Care, Aboriginal Affairs:* Gavin Jennings. *Police, Emergency Services and Corrections:* Tim Holding. *Energy Industries and Resources:* Theo Theophanous.

Speaker of the Legislative Assembly: Judy Maddigan.

VIC Government website: http://www.vic.gov.au

ECONOMY

Budget
In 2004–05 general government expenses by the state were expected to total $A28,439.9m.; revenue and grants received were expected to increase by 4.5% to $A28,984.9m. ($A27,731.2m. in 2003–04).

Performance
In 2002–03 Victoria's gross state product represented 25.59% of Australia's total GDP.

Banking and Finance
The State Bank of Victoria, the largest bank in the State, provides domestic and international services for business and personal customers and is the largest supplier of housing finance in Victoria. In 1990 it ran into debt and was acquired by the Commonwealth from the Victorian government in Sept. 1990.

The 11 major trading banks in Victoria are the Commonwealth Bank of Australia, the Australia and New Zealand Banking Group, the Westpac Banking Corporation, the National Australia Bank, the Bank of Melbourne, the St George Bank, the Challenge Bank, the Metway Bank, the State Bank of New South Wales, Bendigo Bank and Citibank. Banks had a total of 1,217 branches and 1,262 agencies between them at 30 June 2000.

As at March 2002 bank deposits repayable totalled $A112,233m. and loans $A141,664m.

ENERGY AND NATURAL RESOURCES

Electricity
In the year to 30 June 2002 total production was 49,438m. kWh; total consumption stood at 39,007m. kWh, including 28,156m. kWh by business customers.

In 1993 the State government began a major restructure of the government-owned electricity industry along competitive lines. The distribution sector was privatized in 1995, and four generator companies in 1997.

About 90% of power generated is supplied by four brown-coal fired generating stations. There are two other thermal stations and three hydro-electric stations in northeast Victoria. Victoria is also entitled to approximately 30% of the output of the Snowy Mountains hydro-electric scheme and half the output of the Hume hydro-electric station, both of which are in New South Wales.

Oil and Gas
Crude oil in commercially recoverable quantities was first discovered in 1967 in two large fields offshore, in East Gippsland in Bass Strait, between 65 and 80 km from land. These fields, with 20 other fields since discovered, have been assessed as containing initial recoverable oil reserves of 4,063.4m. bbls. Estimated remaining oil reserves as at 30 June 2001 is 432.0m. bbls. Production of crude oil in the fiscal year 2002–03 was valued at about $A3.2bn. with output at 133,000 bbls. per day (15% less than the previous year).

Natural gas was discovered offshore in East Gippsland in 1965. The initial recoverable gas reserves were 272.0m. cu. metres. Estimated remaining gas reserves (30 June 2001), 117.68m. cu. metres. Production of natural gas (2000–01), 6.43m. cu. metres.

Liquefied petroleum gas is produced after extraction of the propane and butane fractions from the untreated oil and gas.

Brown Coal
Major deposits of brown coal are located in the Central Gippsland region and comprise approximately 94% of the total resources in Victoria. In 1993 the resource was estimated to be 0.2m. megatonnes, of which about 52,000 megatonnes was economically recoverable. It is young and soft with a water content of 60% to 70%. In the Latrobe Valley section of the region, the thick brown coal seams underlie an area from 10 to 30 km wide extending over approximately 70 km from Yallourn in the west to the south of Sale in the east. It can be won continuously in large quantities and at low cost by specialized mechanical plant.

The primary use of these reserves is to fuel electricity generating stations. Production of brown coal in 2000–01 was 66.0m. tonnes.

Minerals
Production, 1999–2000: basalt, 13,074,000 tonnes; sand for concrete, 4,977,000 tonnes. In 2002–03, 3,048 kg of gold were produced (around 32% of Australian gold production).

Agriculture
In the year ended 30 June 2002 there were 33,581 agricultural establishments (excluding those with an estimated value of agricultural operations less than $A5,000) with a total area of 12.8m. ha. of which 2.96m. ha. were under crops. Gross value of agricultural production, 2001–02, $A9.3bn. Preliminary estimates of principal crops produced in 2001–02 (in 1,000 tonnes): wheat, 2,812; barley, 1,692; canola, 355; oats, 352.

Gross value of livestock production in 2001–02 totalled $A3.1bn., including wool production $A569m.

Grape growing, particularly for winemaking, is an important crop. In 2002, 338,536 tonnes of winegrapes were produced from 38,653 ha. of vineyards (including 3,618 ha. not yet bearing).

Forestry
Commercial timber production is an increasingly important source of income. As at Dec. 2002 there were 360,000 ha. of plantation. Of Victoria's 7.9m. ha. of native forest (Dec. 2002), 6.6m. ha. (83.4%) were publicly owned (3.1m. ha. in conservation reserves).

Fisheries
Estimated total fisheries production in 2003–04 came to 8,073 tonnes with a gross value of $A95.4m. In the same year aquaculture production was an estimated 2,945 tonnes with a gross value of $A21.4m.

INDUSTRY
Total turnover in the manufacturing industry in 2000–01 was $A74,311.9m. At 30 June 2000 there were 292,100 persons employed in the manufacturing sector.

Labour
At Aug. 2001 there were 2,455,100 persons in the labour force (63.2% of the civilian population aged 15 years and over), of whom 2,303,100 were employed: wholesale and retail trade, 463,300; finance, insurance, property and business services, 349,800; manufacturing, 361,100; health and community services, 221,200; education, 165,700; construction, 158,100; culture, recreation, personal and other services, 143,600; transport and storage, 103,900; agriculture, forestry and fishing, 91,300; accommodation, cafes and restaurants, 91,000; government administration and defence, 80,600; communication services,

49,200; electricity, gas and water supply, 20,500; mining, 3,800. There were 152,000 unemployed persons in Aug. 2001 (6·2% of the labour force). The average weekly wage in Feb. 2003 was $A902·00 (males $A954·20, females $A807·30).

Trade Unions
There were 57 trade unions with a total membership of 680,000 at 30 June 1996.

INTERNATIONAL TRADE

Imports and Exports
The total value of the overseas imports and exports of Victoria, including bullion and specie, was as follows (in $A1m.):

	2001–02	2002–03	2003–04
Imports	37,558	42,129	40,739
Exports[1]	22,237	18,904	17,997

[1]Includes re-exports.

The chief imports in 2003–04 (in $A1m.) were: passenger motor vehicles, 3,40; crude petroleum, 1,618; aircraft and parts, 1,571; medicaments (including veterinary), 1,012; telecommunications equipment, 945. Imports in 2003–04 (in $A1m.) came mainly from the USA, 6,530; China, 5,274; Japan, 4,963; Germany, 3,280; France, 1,926.

The chief exports in 2003–04 (in $A1m.) were: passenger motor vehicles, 1,467; aluminium, 1,081; milk and cream, 1,060; wool, 970; cheese and curd, 567. Exports in 2003–04 (in $A1m.) went mainly to New Zealand, 2,095; USA, 1,949; China, 1,889; Japan, 1,626; Saudi Arabia, 945.

COMMUNICATIONS

Roads
At 30 June 2004 there were 162,700 km of roads open to general traffic. The number of registered motor vehicles (other than tractors and motorcycles) at 31 March 2001 was 3,222,941. There were 321 road accident fatalities in the year ended Aug. 2003.

Rail
The railways are the property of the State and the land is owned and managed by the Victorian Rail Track Corporation (VicTrack). The railway land and infrastructure was transferred from the Public Transport Corporation (PTC) to VicTrack during privatization in 1996–99. In 1999 the non-electrified intra-State railway was leased (for a total of 45 years) to Freight Victoria (trading as Freight Australia), a private company which in May 1999 purchased the business of V/Line Freight Corporation from the State. The passenger rail businesses were franchised to the following private operators in Aug. 1999: National Express, Melbourne Transport Enterprises Pty Ltd, and Metrolink Victoria Pty Ltd.

Victoria's rail network consists of over 5,000 km of track, comprising 1,274 km of standard gauge (1,435 mm). There are 3,745 km of broad gauge (1,600 mm) of which 336 km are electrified. 849 km of standard gauge lines form part of the interstate rail network from Brisbane to Perth and are under the control of the Australian Rail Track Corporation. In the year ended 31 March 2001, 10m. tonnes of freight were carried by Freight Australia and there were a total of 139·4m. passenger boardings (11·5m. non-urban). Melbourne's tramway and light rail network extends to 241 km and is the tenth longest in the world. There were 131·4m. boardings in 2000–01.

Civil Aviation
There were 13,245,878 domestic and regional passenger movements and 3,136,420 international passenger movements in 2002–03 at Melbourne (Tullamarine) airport (Australia's second busiest airport after Sydney). Total freight handled in 2000 was 271,605 tonnes (international, 199,437; domestic, 72,168).

Shipping
The four major commercial ports are at Melbourne, Geelong, Portland and Hastings. In 2002–03, 3,687 commercial vessels called at Victorian ports. General cargo imported in 2002–03 was 9,573,802 mass tonnes and general cargo exported was 9,908,314 mass tonnes.

Telecommunications
In 2004, 94·2% of households had a fixed telephone connected; 74·0% had mobile phones in 2002. In 2000 there were 973,000 households with home computer access (56% of all households) and 598,000 households with home Internet access (34%).

Source: Roy Morgan Single Source January–March 2005

Postal Services
At June 2001 there were 1,055 retail outlets including 842 licensed post offices. Postal items handled by Australia Post in Victoria (1999–2000) totalled 1,637·2m.

SOCIAL INSTITUTIONS

Justice
There is a Supreme Court with a Chief Justice and 21 puisne judges. There are a county court, magistrates' courts, a court of licensing and a bankruptcy court.

During 1996–97 the State's prisons were replaced with new facilities developed, owned and operated by the private sector. During 1999–2000 approximately 45% of Victoria's prison population was accommodated in the three private prisons. There are ten public prisons remaining. At 30 June 2005 the daily average of prisoners held stood at 3,692. Police personnel (sworn and unsworn) at 30 June 2003, 12,924.

Education
In 2002 there were 1,623 government schools with 533,417 pupils and 37,520 full-time teaching staff plus full-time equivalents of part-time teaching staff: 316,843 pupils were in primary schools and 216,574 in secondary schools. As from 1990 students attending special schools have not been identified separately and have been allocated to either primary or secondary level of education. They are integrated where possible into mainstream education. There were, in 2002, 697 non-government schools, excluding commercial colleges, with 18,830 (2000) teaching staff and 281,076 pupils; 139,821 pupils at primary schools; and 141,255 pupils at secondary schools.

All higher education institutions, excluding continuing education and technical and further education (TAFE), now fall under the Unified National System, and can no longer be split into universities and colleges of advanced education. In addition, a number of institutional amalgamations and name changes occurred in the 12 months prior to the commencement of the 1992 academic year. In 2001 there were 479,900 enrolments in Vocational Education and Training activities.

There are ten publicly funded higher education institutions including eight State universities, Marcus Oldham College and the Australian Catholic University (partly privately funded), and the Melbourne University Private, established in 1998. In 2002 there were 228,561 students in higher education.

Health
In 2002–03 there were 144 public hospitals with 11,938 beds, and 140 private hospitals with 6,628 beds. Total government outlay on health in 2002–03 was $A6,376m.

Welfare
Victoria was the first State of Australia to make a statutory provision for the payment of Age Pensions. The Act came into operation on 18 Jan. 1901, and continued until 1 July 1909, when the Australian Invalid and Old Age Pension Act came into force. The Social Services Consolidation Act, which came into operation

on 1 July 1947, repealed the various legislative enactments relating to age and invalid pensions, maternity allowances, child endowment, unemployment and sickness benefits and, while following in general the Acts repealed, considerably liberalized many of their provisions.

The number of age and disability pensions (including wives' and carers' pensions) on 30 June 1999 was: age, 439,595; disability support, 136,218; carer, 10,266. There were 7,680 widows' and 84,368 single parent payments current at 30 June 1999, and basic family payment was being paid for 789,899 children under 16 years.

RELIGION

There is no State Church, and no State assistance has been given to religion since 1875. At the 1991 census the following were the enumerated numbers of the principal religions: Catholic, 1,237,399; Anglican, 772,632; Uniting, 342,493 (including Methodist); Orthodox, 199,063; Presbyterian, 193,300; other Christian, 255,375; Muslim, 49,617; Buddhist, 42,350; Jewish, 33,882; no religion, 612,074; not stated, 474,921.

CULTURE

Tourism

In 1999–2000 the number of short-term overseas visitors to Australia who specified Victoria as their main destination was 685,950 (14·7% of total overseas visitors to Australia), with 466,480 nominating 'holiday' or 'visiting friends/relatives' as purpose of their visit. New Zealand represented the major source of international visitors with 19·9%; followed by the UK and Ireland (11·7%), USA (11·3%), Singapore (7·5%) and Japan (6·8%).

FURTHER READING

Australian Bureau of Statistics Victorian Office. *Victorian Year Book.— Summary of Statistics* (annual).

State library: The State Library of Victoria, 328 Swanston St., Melbourne 3000.

State Statistical Office: Victorian Office, 5th Floor, Commercial Union Tower, 485 LaTrobe Street, Melbourne 3000.

Western Australia

KEY HISTORICAL EVENTS

In 1791 the British navigator George Vancouver took possession of the country around King George Sound. In 1826 the government of New South Wales sent 20 convicts and a detachment of soldiers to form a settlement then called Frederickstown. The following year, Capt. James Stirling surveyed the coast from King George Sound to the Swan River, and in May 1829 Capt. Charles Fremantle took possession of the territory. In June 1829 Capt. Stirling founded the Swan River Settlement (now the Commonwealth State of Western Australia) and the towns of Perth and Fremantle. He was appointed Lieut.-Governor.

Grants of land were made to the early settlers until, in 1850, with the colony languishing, they petitioned for the colony to be made a penal settlement. Between 1850 and 1868 (in which year transportation ceased), 9,668 convicts were sent out. In 1870 partially representative government was instituted. Western Australia federated with the other Australian states to form the Commonwealth of Australia in 1901.

In the 1914–18 war Western Australia provided more volunteers for overseas military service in proportion to population than any other State. The worldwide depression of 1929 brought unemployment (30% of trade union membership), and in 1933 over two-thirds voted to leave the Federation. While there were modest improvements in the standard of living through the 1930s, it was the 1939–45 war which brought full employment. Japanese aircraft attacked the Western Australia coast in 1942. Talk of a 'Brisbane line', which would abandon the West to invasion, only served to reinforce Western Australia's sense of isolation from the rest of the nation. The post-war years saw increasing demand for wheat and wool but the 1954–55 decline in farm incomes led to diversification. Work began in the early 1950s on steel production and oil processing. Oil was discovered in 1953 but it was not until 1966 that it was commercially exploited. The discovery of deposits of iron ore in the Pilbara, bauxite in the Darling scarp, nickel in Kambalda and ilmenite from mineral sands led to the State becoming a major world supplier of mineral exports by 1965.

TERRITORY AND POPULATION

Western Australia has an area of 2,529,880 sq. km and 12,500 km of coastline.

The population at the 2001 census was 1,851,252 (1,726,095 at 1996 census). Of the total, 1,241,786 (67·8%) were born in Australia and 928,984 were females. The resident population (preliminary estimate) at 30 June 2005 was 2,010,100 (annual growth rate, 1·6%). Perth, the capital, had an estimated resident population (June 2002) of 1,413,700.

Principal local government areas outside the metropolitan area, with population at the 2001 census: Mandurah, 45,020; Albany, 29,571; Kalgoorlie-Boulder, 28,818; Bunbury, 28,682; Busselton, 22,060; Geraldton, 19,275; Roebourne, 15,974; Port Hedland, 13,099.

SOCIAL STATISTICS

Statistics for calendar years[1]:

	Births	Deaths	Marriages	Divorces
2000	25,093	10,668	11,000	5,276
2001	24,002	10,779	10,484	5,351
2002	23.601	11,326	10,484	5,252
2003	24,273	11,311	9,549	5,685

[1]Figures are on state of usual residence basis.

The annual rates per 1,000 of the mean resident population in 2003 were: births, 12·4; deaths, 5·8; marriages, 4·9; divorces, 2·9. Infant mortality rate, 2003, 4·1 per 1,000 live births. Expectation of life, 2003: males, 78·1 years; females, 83·0 years.

CLIMATE

Western Australia is a region of several climate zones, ranging from the tropical north to the semi-arid interior and Mediterranean-style climate of the southwest. Most of the State is a plateau between 300 and 600 metres above sea level. Except in the far southwest coast, maximum temperatures in excess of 40°C have been recorded throughout the State. The normal average number of sunshine hours per day is 8·0.

CONSTITUTION AND GOVERNMENT

The *Legislative Council* consists of 34 members elected for a term of four years. There are six electoral regions for Legislative Council elections. Four electoral regions return five members and the other two electoral regions seven members. Each member represents the entire region.

There are 57 members of the *Legislative Assembly*, each member representing one of the 57 electoral districts of the State. Members are elected for a period of up to four years. A system of proportional representation is used to elect members.

RECENT ELECTIONS

In elections to the Legislative Assembly on 26 Feb. 2005 the Labor Party (ALP) won 32 seats with 41·9% of votes cast; the

Liberal Party (LP), 18 (35·6%); the National Party (NP), 5 (3·7%); ind., 2 (4·6%).

CURRENT ADMINISTRATION

Governor: Dr Ken Michael.

Lieut.-Governor and Chief Justice: David Kingsley Malcolm, AC.

In Feb. 2006 the Cabinet comprised:

Premier, Minister for Public Sector Management, Federal Affairs, and State Development: Alan Carpenter.

Deputy Premier, Treasurer, Minister for Government Enterprises: Eric Ripper. *Agriculture and Food, Forestry, the Midwest and Wheatbelt:* Kim Chance. *Education and Training:* Ljiljanna Ravlich. *Water Resources, Sport and Recreation:* John Kobelke. *Attorney General, Minister for Health and Electoral Affairs:* Jim McGinty. *Housing and Works, Consumer Protection, Heritage and Land Information:* Michelle Roberts. *Planning and Infrastructure:* Alannah MacTiernan. *Indigenous Affairs, Tourism, Culture and the Arts:* Sheila McHale. *Environment, Racing and Gaming:* Mark McGowan. *Energy, Science and Innovation:* Francis Logan. *Resources and Employment Protection:* John Bowler. *Police and Emergency Services, Justice and Community Safety:* John D'Orazio. *Local Government and Regional Development, and Fisheries:* Jon Ford. *Disability Services, Citizenship, Multicultural and Women's Interests:* Margaret Quirk. *Small Business:* Norm Marlborough. *Community Development, Youth, Seniors and Volunteering:* David Templeman.

Speaker of the Legislative Assembly: Fred Riebeling.

WA Government website:
http://www.onlinewa.com.au/enhanced

ECONOMY

Budget

Revenue and expenditure (in $A1m.) in years ending 30 June:

	2000–01	2001–02	2002–03	2003–04[1]
Revenue	10,597	11,035	11,771	12,049
Expenditure	10,429	10,838	11,517	11,908

[1]Projected.

A general government net operating surplus of $A142m. was projected for 2003–04. This is the fourth consecutive general government surplus since 2000–01, reinforcing the turnaround in the State's finances from the deficits recorded in the mid- to late-1990s.

Banking and Finance

In March 2002 bank deposits totalled $A32,539m., and loans $A55,412m.

ENERGY AND NATURAL RESOURCES

Electricity

Deregulation of the energy industry was passed by the Office of Energy during 1996–97. Electricity users can obtain power from Western Power or private sector operators. In the year ended 30 June 2002 Western Power customer consumption stood at 12,081m. kWh, including 8,251m. kWh by business customers.

Oil and Gas

Petroleum continued to be the State's largest resource sector with a sales increase of $A2·9bn. to $A10·6bn. in 2000–01. During the same year crude oil was the most valuable product with a 16% increase in the quantity of sales to 14bn. litres and value of sales at 52% to $A4·8bn. The State accounts for around 48% of Australia's oil and condensate production.

Western Australia has significant natural gas resources and, with a $A2·4bn. expansion of the North West Shelf liquefied natural gas (LNG) project, exports are forecast to rise by around $A1bn. Total natural gas production, 2002–03: 20,179 gigalitres.

Source: Western Australian Department of Mineral and Petroleum Resources

Minerals

Mining is a significant contributor to the Western Australia economy. The State is the world's third largest producer of iron ore and accounts for almost 88% of Australia's iron ore production.

Principal minerals produced in 2003–04 were: gold, 173 tonnes; iron ore, 193·3m. tonnes; diamonds, 24·3m. carats; crude oil (2002–03), 19,428 megalitres. Most of the State's coal production (an estimated 6·6m. tonnes in 2003–04) is used by Western Power's electricity generation.

Agriculture

In the year ended 30 June 2002 there were 12,688 establishments mainly engaged in agriculture with a total area of 109·0m. ha. of which 7·53m. ha. were under crops. Gross value of agricultural production in 2001–02 totalled $A5·5bn., an increase of 26% on the previous year.

Preliminary estimates of crops produced in 2001–02 (in 1,000 tonnes): wheat, 7,931; barley, 2,243; lupins for grain, 896; oats, 567; canola, 439; sugarcane, 308.

Value of livestock products in 2001–02 totalled $A656m. Total value of wool produced in 2001–02 was $A514m.

Forestry

The area of State forests and timber reserves at 30 June 2003 was 1,169,300 ha. Jarrah and Karri hardwoods supply about 0·5m. cu. metres of sawn wood and pine plantations, 1m. cu. metres of logs for panel manufacture, sawmilling and export.

Fisheries

Estimated total fisheries production in 2003–04 came to 40,444 tonnes with a gross value of $A553·2m. In the same year aquaculture production was an estimated 1,188 tonnes with a gross value of $A156·8m. Pearling is the most valuable form of aquaculture in the State with the Pearl Oyster Fishery producing an estimated $A150m. worth of pearls from wild captured and hatchery produced oysters in 2003–04.

INDUSTRY

Heavy industry is concentrated in the southwest, and is largely tied to export-orientated mineral processing, especially alumina and nickel.

The following table shows manufacturing industry statistics for 1999–2000:

Industry sub-division	Persons employed 1,000	Wages and salaries $A1m.	Turnover $A1m.
Food, beverages and tobacco	13·6	447·0	3,508·5
Textiles, clothing and leather products	3·2	86·2	386·6
Wood and paper products	4·3	144·0	834·9
Printing and publishing and recorded media	7·0	232·0	958·0
Petroleum, coal, chemical products	6·7	301·1	3,847·3
Non-metallic mineral products	4·6	199·4	1,250·9
Metal products	15·7	634·8	4,960·3
Machinery and equipment	12·9	468·3	2,202·1
Other manufacturing	6·3	142·6	703·0

Labour

The labour force comprised 970,900 employed and 61,300 unemployed persons in 2002–03 (an unemployment rate of 5·9%). The average weekly wage in Feb. 2003 was $A889·30 (males $A960·70, females $A752·20).

Trade Unions

In 1996 there were 54 trade unions with a total of 135,200 male members and 86,500 female members.

INTERNATIONAL TRADE

Imports and Exports

Value of foreign imports and exports (i.e. excluding inter-state trade) for years ending 30 June (in $A1m.):

	2001–02	2002–03	2003–04
Imports	9,320	11,755	11,690
Exports	30,224	32,439	32,220

The chief imports in 2003–04 (in $A1m.) were: non-monetary gold, 1,956; crude petroleum, 1,086; passenger motor vehicles, 954; refined petroleum, 572; motor vehicles for transporting goods, 420. Imports in 2003–04 (in $A1m.) came mainly from the USA, 1,340; Japan, 1,315; Indonesia, 1,246; Singapore, 870; China, 613.

The chief exports in 2003–04 (in $A1m.) were: non-monetary gold, 5,554; iron ore, 5,159; crude petroleum, 3,641; natural gas, 2,174; wheat, 1,785; nickel ores, 598. Exports in 2003–04 (in $A1m.) went mainly to Japan, 6,931; China, 4,400; Republic of Korea, 3,207; India, 2,809; UK, 1,916.

COMMUNICATIONS

Roads

At 30 June 2004 there were 148,456 km of roads open to general traffic. New motor vehicles registered during the year ended 30 June 2001 were 77,642.

In the year ended Aug. 2003 there were 152 fatalities in road accidents.

Rail

In 1999–2000, 29·5m. passenger journeys were made on urban services. In the year ended 31 March 2001, 196m. tonnes of freight were carried.

Civil Aviation

An extensive system of regular air services operates for passengers, freight and mail. In 2002–03 Perth International Airport handled 5,189,365 passengers (3,402,600 on domestic flights).

Shipping

In 2002–03, 2,781 commercial vessels called at Western Australian ports (1,569 at Fremantle). General cargo imported in 2002–03 was 2,686,346 mass tonnes and general cargo exported was 3,033,257 mass tonnes.

Telecommunications

In 2000 there were 390,000 households with home computer access (56% of all households) and 241,000 households with home Internet access.

Postal Services

At 30 June 2004 the Australia Post Corporation had 479 outlets and 945,159 delivery points in Western Australia.

SOCIAL INSTITUTIONS

Justice

Justice is administered by a Supreme Court, consisting of a Chief Justice, 16 other judges and two masters; a District Court comprising a chief judge and 20 other judges; a Magistrates Court, a Chief Stipendiary Magistrate, 37 Stipendiary Magistrates and Justices of the Peace. All courts exercise both civil and criminal jurisdiction except Justices of the Peace who deal with summary criminal matters only. Juvenile offenders are dealt with by the

Children's Court. The Family Court also forms part of the justice system.

At 30 June 2005 there was a daily average of 3,482 prisoners held. At 30 June 2003 police personnel (sworn and unsworn) stood at 6,347.

Education

School attendance is compulsory from the age of six until the end of the year in which the child attains 15 years. In Aug. 2002 there were 775 government primary and secondary schools (with 15,136 full-time equivalent teaching staff, excluding pre-primary teaching staff) providing free education to 250,096 primary and secondary students; in Aug. 2002 there were 308 non-government schools for 108,629 kindergarten, pre-primary, primary and secondary students (with 7,745 full-time equivalent teaching staff in Aug. 2000, excluding pre-primary teaching staff).

Higher education is available through four state universities and one private (Notre Dame). In 2001 there were 170,700 enrolments in Vocational Education and Training activities. In 2002 there was a total of 70,932 students in tertiary education at the University of Western Australia, Murdoch University, the University of Notre Dame Australia, Curtin University of Technology and the Edith Cowan University.

Health

In 2002–03 there were 93 acute public hospitals and one public psychiatric hospital, 27 acute private hospitals and 14 day hospitals.

Welfare

The Department for Community Development is responsible for the provision of welfare and community services throughout the State.

The number of age and disability pensions (including wives' and carers' pensions) on 30 June 1999 was: age, 140,033; disability support, 47,768; carer, 2,602. There were 2,473 widows' and 38,694 single parent payments current at 30 June 1999, and basic family payment was being paid for 326,692 children under 16 years.

RELIGION

At the census of 6 Aug. 1996 the principal denominations were: Catholic, 427,848; Anglican, 410,233; Uniting, 87,549; Presbyterian and Reformed, 45,761; Baptist, 27,618; other Christian, 126,041. There were 48,294 persons practising non-Christian religions and 367,491 persons had no religion.

CULTURE

Tourism

In 2002–03 there were 460,534 short-term overseas visitors. Of these, 24·3% were from the UK and Ireland, 18·5% from Singapore and 12·5% from Japan.

FURTHER READING

Statistical Information: The State Government Statistician's Office was established in 1897 and now functions as the Western Australian Office of the Australian Bureau of Statistics (Level 15, Exchange Plaza, Sherwood Court, Perth 6001). Its principal publications are: *Western Australia: Facts and Figures* (from 1989). *Monthly Summary of Statistics* (from 1958)

Broeze, F. J. A. (ed.) *Private Enterprise, Government and Society.* Univ. of Western Australia, 1993

Crowley, F. K., *Australia's Western Third: A History of Western Australia from the First Settlements to Modern Times.* (Rev. ed.) Melbourne, 1970

Stannage, C. T. (ed.) *A New History of Western Australia.* Perth, 1980

State library: Alexander Library Building, Perth.

AUSTRALIAN EXTERNAL TERRITORIES

Australian Antarctic Territory

An Imperial Order in Council of 7 Feb. 1933 placed under Australian authority all the islands and territories other than Adélie Land situated south of 60° S. lat. and lying between 160° E. long. and 45° E. long. The Order came into force with a Proclamation issued by the Governor-General on 24 Aug. 1936 after the passage of the Australian Antarctic Territory Acceptance Act 1933. The boundaries of Adélie Land were definitively fixed by a French Decree of 1 April 1938 as the islands and territories south of 60° S. lat. lying between 136° E. long. and 142° E. long. The Australian Antarctic Territory Act 1954 declared that the laws in force in the Australian Capital Territory are, so far as they are applicable and are not inconsistent with any ordinance made under the Act, in force in the Australian Antarctic Territory.

The area of the territory is estimated at 6,119,818 sq. km (2,362,875 sq. miles).

There is a research station on MacRobertson Land at lat. 67° 37' S. and long. 62° 52' E. (Mawson), one on the coast of Princess Elizabeth Land at lat. 68° 34' S. and long. 77° 58' E. (Davis), and one at lat. 66° 17' S. and long. 110° 32' E. (Casey). The Antarctic Division also operates a station on Macquarie Island.

Cocos (Keeling) Islands

The Cocos (Keeling) Islands are two separate atolls comprising some 27 small coral islands with a total area of about 14·2 sq. km, and are situated in the Indian Ocean at 12° 05' S. lat. and 96° 53' E. long. They lie 2,768 km northwest of Perth. The islands are low-lying, flat and thickly covered by coconut palms, and surround a lagoon in which ships drawing up to seven metres may be anchored. There is an equable and pleasant climate, affected for much of the year by the southeast trade winds. Temperatures range over the year from 68° F (20° C) to 88° F (31·1° C) and rainfall averages 80" (2,000 mm) a year.

The main islands are: West Island (the largest, about 10 km long), home to most of the European community; Home Island, occupied by the Cocos Malay community; Direction, South and Horsburgh Islands, and North Keeling Island, 24 km to the north of the group. The population of the Territory (2001 Census) was 621, distributed between Home Island (75%) and West Island (25%). About 85% are Muslim and 15% Christian.

The islands were discovered in 1609 by Capt. William Keeling but remained uninhabited until 1826. In 1857 the islands were annexed to the Crown; the governments of Ceylon and Singapore held jurisdiction over the islands at different periods until they were placed under the authority of the Australian government as the Territory of Cocos (Keeling) Islands on 23 Nov. 1955. An *Administrator* (Evan Williams; took office in Nov. 2003), appointed by the Governor-General, is the government's representative in the Territory and is responsible to the Minister for Territories and Local Government. The Cocos (Keeling) Islands Council, established as the elected body of the Cocos Malay community in July 1979, advises the Administrator on all issues affecting the Territory.

In 1978 and 1993 the Australian government purchased the interests of the Clunies-Ross family, who had been granted the land in its entirety by Queen Victoria. A Cocos Malay co-operative was established to take over the running of the Clunies-Ross copra plantation and to engage in other business with the Commonwealth in the Territory, including construction projects.

The Islands are served by 15 km of roads and an airport on West Island, with flights operated by National Jet to Christmas Island and Perth (2003). In 1992 there was one primary school on each island, with a combined enrolment of 98 pupils and seven teachers. There were two secondary schools with 70 pupils and nine teachers and a technical school with 29 students. In 1992 there was one doctor and seven nursing personnel.

Christmas Island

GENERAL DETAILS

Christmas Island is an isolated peak in the Indian Ocean, lat. 10° 25' 22" S., long. 105° 39' 59" E. It lies 360 km S. 8° E. of Java Head, and 417 km N. 79° E. from Cocos Islands, 1,310 km from Singapore and 2,623 km from Fremantle. Area: 136·7 sq. km. The climate is tropical with temperatures varying little over the year at 27° C. The wet season lasts from Nov. to April with an annual total of about 2,673 mm. The island was formally annexed by the UK on 6 June 1888, placed under the administration of the Governor of the Straits Settlements in 1889, and incorporated with the Settlement of Singapore in 1900. Sovereignty was transferred to the Australian government on 1 Oct. 1958. The population at the 2001 census was 1,508.

The legislative, judicial and administrative systems are regulated by the Christmas Island Act, 1958–73. They are the responsibility of the Commonwealth government and are operated by an Administrator. The Territory underwent major changes to its legal system when the Federal Parliament passed the Territories Law Reform Bill of 1992; Commonwealth and State laws applying in the state of Western Australia now apply in the Territory as a result, although some laws have been repealed to take into account the unique status of the Territory. The first Island Assembly was elected in Sept. 1985, and is now replaced by the elected members of the Christmas Island Shire Council.

Extraction and export of rock phosphate dust is the main industry. The government is also encouraging the private sector development of tourism.

CONSTITUTION AND GOVERNMENT

The Christmas Island Assembly has nine annually-elected members. The last elections were on 3 May 2003. All non-partisan candidates were elected unopposed.

CURRENT ADMINISTRATION

Administrator: Evan Williams (appointed Nov. 2003).

ECONOMY

Currency
The Australian dollar is legal tender.

COMMUNICATIONS

Roads
The Shire of Christmas Island has responsibility for approximately 140 km of roads with the remaining 100 km of haul roads and tracks maintained by Christmas Island Phosphates and Park Australia North. In 1999 there were 1,398 registered vehicles.

Civil Aviation
In 2003 National Jet operated scheduled flights to Perth and Cocos Island.

Postal Services

There was one post office in 1999, operated by Australia Post licensees.

SOCIAL INSTITUTIONS

Education

In 1999 there were 530 students at the Christmas Island District High School; 15% were pre-primary, 60% primary and 25% secondary level pupils.

Health

There is a nine-bed hospital, the island's only one, which was completed in 1994. There are two doctors, one dentist, a director of nursing and 20 locally engaged staff. Specialists visit about every three months.

RELIGION

About 50% of the population are Buddhists or Taoists, 16% Muslims and 30% Christians.

CULTURE

Broadcasting

A local radio and television station operate 24 hours per day. Local Radio VLU2 broadcasts in English, Malay and Chinese.

Norfolk Island

KEY HISTORICAL EVENTS

The island was formerly part of the colony of New South Wales and then of Van Diemen's Land (now known as Tasmania). A penal colony between 1788–1814 and 1825–55, it was separated from the state of Tasmania in 1856 and placed under the jurisdiction of the Australian State of New South Wales. Following the Norfolk Island Act 1913 (Cth), the Island was accepted as a Territory of Australia with the Australian Federal Government having jurisdiction for the Island.

TERRITORY AND POPULATION

Situated 29° 02' S. lat. 167° 57' E. long.; area 3,455 ha.; permanent population (Aug. 2001), 2,601.

Descendants of the *Bounty* mutineer families constitute the 'original' settlers and are known locally as 'Islanders', while later settlers, mostly from Australia and New Zealand, are identified as 'mainlanders'. 80% of the Island's permanent population are Australian citizens with 16% being New Zealand citizens. Descendants of the Pitcairn Islanders make up about 46% of the permanent resident population. Over the years the Islanders have preserved their own lifestyle and customs, and their language remains a mixture of West Country English, Gaelic and Tahitian.

SOCIAL STATISTICS

Births in 2000–01 totalled 17 and deaths 28.

CLIMATE

Sub-tropical. Summer temperatures (Dec.–March) average about 75°F (25°C), and 65°F (18°C) in winter (June–Sept.). Annual rainfall is approximately 50" (1,200 mm), most of which falls in winter.

CONSTITUTION AND GOVERNMENT

An Administrator, appointed by the Governor-General and responsible to the Minister for Territories and Local Government, is the senior government representative in the Territory. The seat of administration is Kingston.

The Norfolk Island Act 1979 gives Norfolk Island responsible legislative and executive government to enable it to run its own affairs. Wide powers are exercised by the Norfolk Island Legislative Assembly of nine members, elected for a period of three years, and by an Executive Council. The Norfolk Island Act also provides for consultation with the Federal Government in respect of certain types of laws proposed by Norfolk Island's Legislative Assembly.

RECENT ELECTIONS

At the last elections, on 20 Oct. 2004, only non-partisans were elected.

CURRENT ADMINISTRATION

Administrator: Grant Tambling (since 2003).
    Chief Minister: Geoffrey Robert Gardner (since 2001).

ECONOMY

The office of the Administrator is financed from Commonwealth expenditure which in 2004–05 was $A1,195,000; local revenue for 2002–03 totalled $A23,251,000; expenditure, $A21,531,000.

Currency

Australian notes and coins are the legal currency.

Banking and Finance

There are two banks, Westpac and the Commonwealth Bank of Australia.

COMMUNICATIONS

Roads

There are 100 km of roads (53 km paved), some 2,800 passenger cars and 200 commercial vehicles.

Civil Aviation

In 2003 there were scheduled flights to Auckland, Brisbane, Melbourne and Sydney.

Postal Services

There is one post office located in Burnt Pine.

SOCIAL INSTITUTIONS

Justice

The Island's Supreme Court sits as required and a Court of Petty Sessions exercises both civil and criminal jurisdiction. Appeals from decisions of the Norfolk Island Supreme Court are heard by the Federal Court of Australia and by the High Court of Australia.

Education

A school is run by the New South Wales Department of Education covering pre-school to Year 12. It had 320 pupils at 30 June 1999.

Health

In 1999 there were two doctors, one dentist, a pharmacist and a hospital with 24 beds.

RELIGION

40% of the population are Anglicans.

CULTURE

Broadcasting

In 1999 there were 1,500 television receivers and 1,600 radio receivers.

Tourism

In 2000–01, 40,221 tourists visited Norfolk Island.

Heard and McDonald Islands

These islands, about 2,500 miles southwest of Fremantle, were transferred from British to Australian control from 26 Dec. 1947. Heard Island is about 43 km long and 21 km wide; Shag Island is about 8 km north of Heard. The total area is 412 sq. km (159 sq. miles). The McDonald Islands are 42 km to the west of Heard. Heard is an active stratovolcano that has erupted eight times since 1910, most recently in 1993. In 1985–88 a major research programme was set up by the Australian National Antarctic Research Expeditions to investigate the wildlife as part of international studies of the Southern Ocean ecosystem. Subsequent expeditions followed from June 1990 through to 1992.

Territory of Ashmore and Cartier Islands

By Imperial Order in Council of 23 July 1931, Ashmore Islands (known as Middle, East and West Islands) and Cartier Island, situated in the Indian Ocean, some 320 km off the northwest coast of Australia (area, 5 sq. km), were placed under the authority of the Commonwealth. Under the Ashmore and Cartier Islands Acceptance Act, 1933, the islands were accepted by the Commonwealth as the Territory of Ashmore and Cartier Islands. It was the intention that the Territory should be administered by the State of Western Australia but owing to administrative difficulties the Territory was deemed to form part of the Northern Territory of Australia (by amendment to the Act in 1938). On 16 Aug. 1983 Ashmore Reef was declared a National Nature Reserve. The islands are uninhabited but Indonesian fishing boats fish within the Territory and land to collect water in accordance with an agreement between the governments of Australia and Indonesia. It is believed that the islands and their waters may house considerable oil reserves.

Territory of Coral Sea Islands

The Coral Sea Islands, which became a Territory of the Commonwealth of Australia under the Coral Sea Islands Act 1969, comprises scattered reefs and islands over a sea area of about 1m. sq. km. The Territory is uninhabited apart from a meteorological station on Willis Island.

FURTHER READING

Australian Department of Arts, Sport, the Environment, Tourism and Territories. *Christmas Island: Annual Report.—Cocos (Keeling) Islands: Annual Report.—Norfolk Island: Annual Report.*

AUSTRIA

Republik Österreich

Capital: Vienna
Population projection, 2010: 8·25m.
GDP per capita, 2003: (PPP$) 30,094
HDI/world rank: 0·936/17

KEY HISTORICAL EVENTS

The oldest historical site in Austria is at the Gudenus caves in the Kremstal valley, where hunters' stone implements and bones dating from the Paleolothic Age have been found. The Early Iron Age Hallstatt culture prevailed from around 750–400 BC, covering the area north of the Alps, large parts of Slovakia, the north Balkans and Hungary. This area became renowned for its ceramics, ornamental Hallstatt burial grounds and the industrial development of salt mining.

In the 5th century BC Celtic tribes stormed the eastern Alps, their culture named after the site in Switzerland (La-Tène) where tools, weapons and other artefacts were found. La-Tène culture showed Greek and Etruscan influences. Around the middle of the second century BC some of these tribes united to found Noricum, the first recognizable state on Austrian territory. In 113 BC a treaty of friendship was signed between Rome and Noricum. Around 15 BC Noricum was incorporated into the Roman Empire. Present day Austria (with parts of Germany, Switzerland, Slovenia and Hungary) was eventually divided into the three Roman provinces of Raetia, Noricum and Pannonia.

Germanic tribes, in particular the Marcomanni and Quadi, later known as Bavarians, invaded in AD 166–80. Emperor Marcus Aurelius campaigned against them from Vindobona (Vienna), where he died in battle in AD 180. His successors fought unsuccessfully against the Alemanni and other invading tribes. Brigantium (Bregenz) became a border town of the Roman Empire after a peace agreement was signed with the Alemanni.

Charlemagne conquered the Bavarian duke Tassilo III and the Avars at the end of the 8th century and established a territory in the Danube Valley known as the Ostmark in 803. The church of Salzburg (Roman Juvavum) was founded at the end of the 8th century and consequently became the Bavarian-Frankish spiritual centre and archbishopric. Christianity spread throughout the region, led by the Slav apostles Cyril and Methodius.

The Magyar invasions culminated in the battle for Vienna in 881 and the loss of Lower Austrian territories. The Babenbergs took over the margravate of Bavaria in 976 under Leopold I. The name 'Ostarichi', originating from Old High German, first appeared in a document of Emperor Otto III in 996. In 1156 the margravate of Austria became a separate duchy.

From 1160–1200 Vienna, the most important trading town on the Danube, became the residence of the art-loving Babenberger dukes, receiving its town charter in 1198. In 1246 the last Babenberger, Friedrich II, fell in the battle of Leitha against King Bela IV of Hungary. Count Rudolf IV of Habsburg was elected German King Rudolf I in 1273 and set about conquering the former Babenberg lands, naming his son Duke Albert I the sole ruler in 1283. From the rule of Albert's son and successor Frederick I onwards, the territory of the Habsburgs was known as the *dominium Austriae*.

Holy Roman Empire

In 1452 Frederick III became Holy Roman Emperor. In one of the first of a series of dynastic marriages to expand the Habsburg realm, his son Maximilian I was married to Mary, the heiress of Burgundy. The marriage of their son, Philip the Handsome, to Juana, the heiress of the Spanish crowns, forged a massive and disparate Habsburg inheritance, encompassing Spain and its empire, Hungary, Bohemia, the Burgundian Netherlands and territory in Italy. Austria was harried by the Ottoman Turks, whose armies had advanced remorselessly across southeast Europe as far as Hungary under Sultan Süleyman the Magnificent. A truce was agreed after the Ottoman defeat at Vienna in 1529.

The Reformation brought Protestantism to Austria but was resisted by Rudolf II. Brought up a strict Catholic, he embraced the Counter-Reformation in 1576. Tensions between Protestants and Catholics came to a head with the Defenestration of Prague in 1618, which led to the Thirty Years War. Peace was restored by the Treaty of Westphalia in 1648.

Philip, a grandson of Louis XIV of France, was designated heir to the last of the Spanish Habsburgs, Charles II. During the subsequent War of the Spanish Succession, Holland and England joined the coalition forces. Peace Negotiations at Rastatt awarded Austria Spanish territory in Italy and the Netherlands. Austrian boundaries reached their furthest limit in 1720.

In 1740 Emperor Charles VI died without a male heir. By pragmatic sanction, his daughter Maria Theresa was allowed to succeed him as the first female Habsburg ruler, though she was denied the Imperial crown. Challenged by Prussia, the War of the Austrian Succession divided the two alliances of Bavaria, France, Spain and Prussia against Austria, Holland and Great Britain. Maria Theresa introduced a number of reforms aimed at strengthening the Habsburg monarchy. The army was almost doubled in size, a public education system was introduced and administrative and financial structures were overhauled, centralizing government and laying the foundations of a modern state. During the Seven Year's War (1756–63) Maria Theresa aimed to re-conquer Silesia, lost in the War of the Austrian Succession. However, the Austrians, bereft of allies, were defeated at Burkersdorf in July 1762. Silesia was settled on Prussia by the Peace of Hubertusburg.

Enlightened Despotism

In 1772 Austria, Prussia and Russia carried out the first partition of Poland, with Austria gaining Galicia. Maria Theresa's youngest daughter of 16 children, Marie-Antoinette, married Louis XVI, thus achieving a closer political alliance with France. Maria Theresa was succeeded by Joseph, her eldest son. Also a reformist, and heavily influenced by the Enlightenment, Joseph II proclaimed the Edict of Toleration in 1781, giving more rights to faiths other than Catholicism. He also abolished serfdom and homogenized land tax laws. Not all of these reforms were popular. He introduced German as the official language in the Hungarian government. His heavy-handed reforms provoked resistance, leading to a revolt in the Austrian Netherlands opposing absolutist rule. In the face of widespread opposition to his reforms, Joseph revoked a number of them in 1790.

From 1792–1815 the Habsburgs were involved in almost continuous warfare. The Habsburgs saw the ideals of the French Revolution as a major threat; Austria and Prussia jointly voiced their disapproval in the Declaration of Pillnitz. Ill-received by the French government, this led to a declaration of war followed by 23 years of hostilities and five separate wars. During the first, second and third coalition wars Vienna was occupied twice by French troops. Napoleon defeated Austria in the Battle of Austerlitz in 1805, forcing Francis to surrender his title of Holy Roman Emperor and to hand over one of his daughters, Archduchess Marie Louise, in marriage. After Napoleon was vanquished and exiled to Elba in 1814, the Congress of Vienna met to re-establish Europe's internal borders. In charge of Austria's foreign policy, Prince von Metternich created the German confederation of 35 states and four free cities to succeed the Holy Roman Empire. A staunch conservative, Metternich suppressed opposition.

The first half of the 19th century saw an industrial burgeoning. With the growth of the cities came an expansion of the markets for agricultural goods. The first Austrian railway line, the Kaiser-Ferdinand Nordbahn, was built between Linz and Budweis and steam navigation started on the Danube. An uprising in Vienna in 1848 forced the Habsburgs to flee the city and Metternich to resign. Ferdinand I abdicated in Dec. and was succeeded by his 18-year-old nephew, Francis Joseph I. The pan-European wave of revolution spread to Hungary, where the fight for emancipation was led by Lajos Kossuth. The Habsburgs refused to accept Hungary's independence and enlisted Russian aid to quell the uprising. Italian and Slavic revolts followed. In 1859, during the Austro-Italian war, the Habsburgs were defeated and Italy was unified.

The German unification campaign was headed by Otto von Bismarck, who expanded Prussian influence by isolating Austria from her allies. This led to the Austro-Prussian war of 1866. Austria's defeat at the battle of Königgrätz stripped it of all presiding powers over Germany. The loss of Venetia in 1867 added a further blow to the shrinking Habsburg empire. Emperor Francis Joseph I was forced to compromise with Hungary and engaged in negotiating the 'Ausgleich' in 1867, giving Hungary its own constitution and quasi-independent status. Francis Joseph was henceforth recognized as the Apostolic king of Hungary and emperor of Austria within the Austro-Hungarian monarchy, also referred to as the Dual Monarchy. Foreign policy, the army and finances were administered jointly.

German Alliance
In 1879 Austria entered the Dual Alliance with the German Reich and the two states pledged mutual support in the eventuality of Russian aggression. Italy joined in 1882, making a Triple Alliance. Tensions between Austria and Russia heightened over territory in the Balkans, with an uprising in Macedonia in 1903. King Alexander of Serbia was assassinated while the Serbs were fighting for the unification of the Southern Slavs. The Habsburg empire responded with a livestock embargo, known as the Pig War. Austria-Hungary then annexed the two provinces of Bosnia and Herzegovina in 1908, prompting a Serb revolt and protests by the pan-Slav movement. Austria tried to gain control over Serbia during the Balkan wars of 1912–13. In June 1914 the heir to the Habsburg throne, Archduke Franz Ferdinand, and his wife were assassinated in Sarajevo by a Bosnian nationalist. The refusal of Serbia to accept the blame led to an Austrian declaration of war on Serbia in July. German backing for Austria encompassed a settling of its own scores with France and Russia. Austria was obliged to support Germany against France and Russia. Germany

declared war on Russia and France in early Aug., beginning the First World War. The Austro-Hungarian army suffered major setbacks and the monarchy began to crumble after Francis Joseph I's death in 1916. His great-nephew, Charles I of Austria, succeeded him, trying but failing to achieve a secret truce with the Allies. A series of strikes, mutiny in the army and navy and food shortages were among the factors that defeated Austro-Hungarian forces in the spring and summer of 1918. About 1·2m. soldiers from Austria-Hungary died during the war.

Emperor Charles I issued a manifesto on 17 Oct. 1918 guaranteeing the independence of the non-German speaking states. Each province established a national council which then developed into a government. The Poles declared themselves an independent unified state in Warsaw on 7 Oct. 1918; the Czechs founded an independent republic in Prague and the Southern Slavs merged with Serbia. An armistice was agreed on 3 Nov. and the Hungarian government announced its complete separation from Austria. Within days Austria and Hungary declared republics. The Habsburg monarchy was formally dissolved on 11 Nov. with the abdication of Charles I. The Treaty of Saint Germain in 1919 stipulated that the German–Austrian lands were not permitted to unite (Anschluss) with Germany without the consent of the League of Nations. Austria was declared a federal state on 1 Oct. 1920.

Nazism
The economic crises of the 1920s led to the rise of a nationalist movement much influenced by Germany's adoption of National Socialism. When Engelbert Dollfuss of the conservative Christian Socialists became chancellor in 1932 he faced Nazi and Marxist opposition. He dissolved parliament and governed by emergency decree, founding the conservative Fatherland Front in 1933. The anti-Marxist Heimwehr (home defence forces) supported him. When the Social Democrats fought back they were defeated by Dollfuss with the backing of the Heimwehr. All political parties except the Fatherland Front were subsequently banned. On 25 July 1934 a Nazis gang murdered Dollfuss but was forced to surrender and the coup leaders were executed. Dollfuss' successor, Kurt Schuschnigg, signed the Austrian–German agreement whereby Germany recognized Austria's sovereignty in return for Austria calling itself a German state. German Nazis pressurized Schuschnigg to allow them more influence, Hitler demanding that leading Nazis take on top positions in the Austrian cabinet. Schuschnigg planned a plebiscite to decide upon Anschluss but on 12 March 1938 German forces marched into Austria, establishing a Nazi government led by Arthur Seyss-Inquart. Renamed 'Ostmark', Austria was put under the central authority of the German Third Reich. A plebiscite held on 10 April 1938 showed over 99% support for Hitler.

The Allied Moscow conference of 1943 agreed Austrian independence along the demarcation lines of 1937. The borders were finally set at the Yalta conference of Feb. 1945. On 13 April 1945 Vienna was liberated by Soviet troops. Two weeks later, Dr Karl Renner proclaimed a provisional government and Austria a republic, recognized officially by western powers at the Potsdam conference. The first elections were held in Nov., with former Nazis excluded from voting. Leopold Figl of the Austrian People's Party (Christian Socialists) became the first chancellor of the Second Republic, with Karl Renner as its first president. The Paris treaty of Sept. 1946 granted autonomy for South Tyrol within Italy, the Allies refusing to return it to Austria. Financial support from the United Nations and the Marshall Plan enabled Austria to begin rebuilding its economy.

The forces of the Soviet Union, Britain, France and the USA occupied Austria until 1955, when the country reaffirmed its neutrality. Full sovereignty was restored by the State Treaty in Vienna. Anschluss between Austria and Germany or restoration of the Habsburgs were expressly prohibited. The rights of ethnic minorities were guaranteed and former German assets confiscated by the Western allies were returned. The Soviet Union, however, demanded reparations including US$150m. for former German businesses. Austria joined the United Nations. In 1959 Austria joined EFTA and, in 1960, the OECD.

The first all-socialist cabinet was formed in 1970 under Chancellor Bruno Kreisky, who carried out a number of reforms and established economic stability and prosperity throughout the 1970s. The late 1970s saw the emergence of the Green party, with the planned construction of a nuclear power station becoming a central political issue. Kreisky's achievements were followed by political scandals which led to his resignation in 1983.

Kurt Waldheim (elected as secretary general of the UN in 1971) became Austrian president in 1986 despite allegations of a Nazi past. Although this was never proved, his undisguised sympathies and political leanings caused him to be placed on the USA's list of undesirable aliens. In 1995 Austria became a member of the EU. In Jan. 2000 the Freedom Party, headed by the far-right leader Jörg Haider, joined the government. Although Haider, described as a 'dangerous extremist' by EU leaders, did not take a post in the government, he continued to exercise political influence and remained popular with the Austrian electorate. Sanctions against Austria were imposed by the European Union in Feb. 2000 but were lifted in Sept. 2000. In the parliamentary elections of Oct. 2002 the Freedom Party, with a new leader, saw its support fall by half. Nevertheless the Freedom Party was again invited to join a coalition government.

TERRITORY AND POPULATION

Austria is bounded in the north by Germany and the Czech Republic, east by Slovakia and Hungary, south by Slovenia and Italy, and west by Switzerland and Liechtenstein. It has an area of 83,858 sq. km (32,378 sq. miles). Population (2001 census) 8,032,926; density, 95·8 per sq. km. Previous population censuses: (1923) 6·53m., (1934) 6·76m., (1951) 6·93m., (1971) 7·49m., (1981) 7·56m., (1991) 7·96m. In 2003, 65·8% of the population lived in urban areas. The estimated population in 2005 was 8·19m.

In 2001, 91·1% of residents were of Austrian nationality and, in 2003, 92% were German-speaking. Principal minorities in 2003: former Yugoslavians, 175,000; Turks, 122,000; Hungarians, 34,000; Slovenes, 30,000; Czechs, 19,000. Since the mid-1980s the number of foreigners living in Austria has more than doubled, from just over 4% to nearly 9%.

The UN gives a projected population for 2010 of 8·25m.

The areas, populations and capitals of the nine federal states:

Federal States	Area (sq. km)	Population at censuses (1991)	(2001)	State capitals
Vienna (Wien)	415	1,539,848	1,550,123	Vienna
Lower Austria (Niederösterreich)	19,174	1,473,813	1,545,804	St Pölten
Burgenland	3,965	270,880	277,569	Eisenstadt
Upper Austria (Oberösterreich)	11,980	1,333,480	1,376,797	Linz
Salzburg	7,154	482,365	515,327	Salzburg
Styria (Steiermark)	16,388	1,184,720	1,183,303	Graz
Carinthia (Kärnten)	9,533	547,798	559,404	Klagenfurt
Tyrol	12,648	631,410	673,504	Innsbruck
Vorarlberg	2,601	331,472	351,095	Bregenz

The populations of the principal towns at the census of 2001 (and 1991): Vienna, 1,550,123 (1,539,848); Graz, 226,244 (237,810); Linz, 183,504 (203,044); Salzburg, 142,662 (143,978); Innsbruck, 113,392 (118,112); Klagenfurt, 90,141 (89,415); Villach, 57,497 (54,640); Wels, 56,478 (52,594); St Pölten, 49,121 (50,026).

The official language is German. For orthographical changes agreed in 1996 *see* GERMANY: Territory and Population.

SOCIAL STATISTICS

Statistics, 2003: live births, 76,944 (rate of 9·5 per 1,000 population); deaths, 77,209 (rate of 9·5 per 1,000 population);

infant deaths, 343; stillborn, 492; marriages, 37,195; divorces, 18,727. In 2003 there were 1,456 suicides (rate of 17·9 per 100,000 population), of which 1,068 males and 388 females. Average annual population growth rate, 1992–2002, 0·3%. Life expectancy at birth, 2003, 81·8 years for women and 76·0 years for men. In 2003 the most popular age range for marrying was 30–34 for males and 25–29 for females. Infant mortality, 2001, was 4·8 per 1,000 live births; fertility rate, 2001, 1·3 children per woman. In 2000 some 370,700 Austrians resided permanently abroad: 186,000 lived in Germany, 28,000 in Switzerland, 17,000 in South Africa, and 16,000 in both Australia and the USA. In 2002 Austria received 37,074 asylum applications, equivalent to 4·6 per 1,000 inhabitants (the highest ratio in Europe).

CLIMATE

The climate is temperate and from west to east in transition from marine to more continental. Depending on the elevation, the climate is also predominated by alpine influence. Winters are cold with snowfall. In the eastern parts summers are warm and dry.

Vienna, Jan. 0·0°C, July 20·2°C. Annual rainfall 624 mm. Graz, Jan. -1·0°C, July 19·4°C. Annual rainfall 825 mm. Innsbruck, Jan. -1·7°C, July 18·1°C. Annual rainfall 885 mm. Salzburg, Jan. -0·9°C, July 18·6°C. Annual rainfall 1,174 mm.

CONSTITUTION AND GOVERNMENT

The Constitution of 1 Oct. 1920 was revised in 1929 and restored on 1 May 1945. Austria is a democratic federal republic comprising nine states *(Länder)*, with a federal *President (Bundespräsident)* directly elected for not more than two successive six-year terms, and a bicameral National Assembly which comprises a National Council and a Federal Council.

The National Council *(Nationalrat)* comprises 183 members directly elected for a four-year term by proportional representation in a three-tier system by which seats are allocated at the level of 43 regional and nine state constituencies, and one federal constituency. Any party gaining 4% of votes cast nationally is represented in the National Council.

The Federal Council *(Bundesrat)* has 62 members appointed by the nine states for the duration of the individual State Assemblies' terms; the number of deputies for each state is proportional to that state's population. In Feb. 2006 the SPÖ held 29 of the 62 seats, the ÖVP 26, the Greens 4 and non-attached 3.

The head of government is a *Federal Chancellor*, who is appointed by the President (usually the head of the party winning the most seats in National Council elections). The *Vice-Chancellor*, the *Federal Ministers* and the *State Secretaries* are appointed by the President at the Chancellor's recommendation.

National Anthem

'Land der Berge, Land am Strome' ('Land of mountains, land on the river'); words by Paula Preradovic; tune attributed to Mozart.

GOVERNMENT CHRONOLOGY

Presidents since 1945. (ÖVP = Austrian People's Party; SPÖ = Social Democratic Party)

1945–50	SPÖ	Karl Renner
1951–57	SPÖ	Theodor Körner
1957–65	SPÖ	Adolf Schärf
1965–74	SPÖ	Franz Joseph Jonas
1974–86	SPÖ	Rudolf Kirchschläger
1986–92	ÖVP	Kurt Josef Waldheim
1992–2004	ÖVP	Thomas Klestil
2004–	SPÖ	Heinz Fischer

Federal Chancellors since 1945.

1945	SPÖ	Karl Renner
1945–53	ÖVP	Leopold Figl
1953–61	ÖVP	Julius Raab
1961–64	ÖVP	Alfons Gorbach

1964–70	ÖVP	Josef Klaus
1970–83	SPÖ	Bruno Kreisky
1983–86	SPÖ	Alfred (Fred) Sinowatz
1986–97	SPÖ	Franz Vranitzky
1997–2000	SPÖ	Viktor Klima
2000–	ÖVP	Wolfgang Schüssel

RECENT ELECTIONS

Elections were held on 24 Nov. 2002. The Austrian People's Party (ÖVP) won 79 seats with 42·3% of votes cast (52 with 26·9% in 1999); the Social Democratic Party (SPÖ), 69 with 36·9% (65 with 33·2%); the Freedom Party (FPÖ), 18 with 10·2% (52 with 26·9%); and the Greens, 17 with 9·0% (14 with 7·4%). Turnout was 80·5%.

In the presidential election held on 25 April 2004 Heinz Fischer (SPÖ) won 52·4% of the vote against 47·6% for Minister for Foreign Affairs Benita Ferrero-Waldner (ÖVP). Turnout was 70·8%.

European Parliament
Austria has 18 (21 in 1999) representatives. At the June 2004 elections turnout was 41·8% (49·0% in 1999). The SPÖ won 7 seats with 33·5% of votes cast (political affiliation in European Parliament: Party of European Socialists); the ÖVP, 6 with 32·7% (European People's Party–European Democrats); Liste Martin, 2 with 14·0% (non-attached); the Greens, 2 with 12·8% (Greens/European Free Alliance); the FPÖ, 1 with 6·3% (non-attached).

CURRENT ADMINISTRATION

President: Dr Heinz Fischer; b. 1938 (SPÖ; took office on 8 July 2004).

Following the elections of Nov. 1999 the ÖVP and the right-wing FPÖ agreed in Feb. 2000 to form a coalition government, with Dr Wolfgang Schüssel (ÖVP) as chancellor. In Sept. 2002 the coalition collapsed in the wake of a bitter power struggle within the FPÖ. Chancellor Schüssel called for new elections, held on 24 Nov 2002 and won by the ÖVP, which revived the coalition with the FPÖ. In March 2006 the government comprised:

Chancellor: Dr Wolfgang Schüssel; b. 1945 (ÖVP; sworn in 4 Feb. 2000).

Deputy-Chancellor and Minister for Transport, Innovation and Technology: Hubert Gorbach (FPÖ).

Minister for Foreign Affairs: Ursula Plassnik (ÖVP). *Economic Affairs and Labour:* Martin Bartenstein (ÖVP). *Finance:* Karl-Heinz Grasser (ind.). *Justice:* Karin Gastinger (FPÖ). *Defence:* Günther Platter (ÖVP). *Agriculture, Forestry and Environment:* Josef Pröll (ÖVP). *Health Affairs and Women's Issues:* Maria Rauch-Kallat (ÖVP). *Interior:* Liese Prokop (ÖVP). *Education, Science and Culture:* Elisabeth Gehrer (ÖVP). *Social Security, Generations and Consumer Protection:* Ursula Haubner (FPÖ). *State Secretary in the Ministry for Finance:* Alfred Finz (ÖVP). *State Secretaries in the Federal Chancellery:* Franz Morak (ÖVP); Karl Schweitzer (FPÖ). *State Secretary in the Ministry for Social Security and Generations:* Sigisbert Dolinschek (FPÖ). *State Secretaries in the Ministry for Transport, Innovation and Technology:* Helmut Kukacka (ÖVP); Eduard Mainoni (FPÖ).

Government Website: http://www.austria.gv.at

CURRENT LEADERS

Dr Heinz Fischer

Position
President

Introduction
Following his electoral victory on 25 April 2004 at the age of 65, Dr Heinz Fischer took office as Austria's first socialist federal president for 18 years on 8 July 2004. He is committed to maintaining the country's neutral foreign policy and the welfare state. Critics have labelled him a *Berufspolitiker* ('professional politician') who has tended to avoid controversy and conflict.

Early Life
Heinz Fischer was born into a political family in Graz on 9 Oct. 1938. His father, Rudolf Fischer, was State Secretary in the Ministry of Trade from 1954–56 under the government led by Julius Raab. Fischer attended the Humanistisches Gymnasium in Vienna and went on to study law and political science at the University of Vienna, graduating with a PhD in 1961. He entered politics two years later, becoming secretary to the Social Democratic Party (SPÖ) in the Austrian Parliament, a position he held until 1975. Despite being elected as a member of parliament in 1971, Fischer continued his academic career. He was appointed associate professor of political science at the University of Innsbruck in 1978 and was made a full professor in 1994.

Fischer served as Federal Minister of Science and Research from 1983–86, under a coalition government headed by Fred Sinowatz of the SPÖ. In 1986 the SPÖ joined the Austrian People's Party (ÖVP) in a 'grand coalition' that retained control of the government through the 1990s. Fischer was elected President of the National Council in Nov. 1990, holding the office for twelve years until Dec. 2002. He also served as a member of the National Security Council and the Foreign Affairs Council.

In Jan. 2004 he declared his candidacy to succeed Thomas Klestil as federal president. He was elected on 25 April 2004 as the SPÖ candidate, polling 52·4% of the vote to defeat Benita Ferrero-Waldner, foreign minister in the ruling ÖVP-led conservative coalition.

Career in Office
On 8 July 2004 Fischer was sworn in for a six-year term as the eighth Austrian federal president in a ceremony overshadowed by Klestil's death from a heart attack just two days before the handover. Although the post is largely ceremonial, the president is commander-in-chief of the country's military forces and has the constitutional power to reject nominations for cabinet ministers and to remove them from office.

In his opening address as president, Fischer recalled how many Austrians had grown up 'sensitive to war and peace' and aware that 'peace and the politics to promote peace... must have a central role in our political efforts'. The consolidation of the basic values of democracy is another of his priorities: '...Consensus is very important to me. But consensus means to build bridges. Bridges between solid shores'.

Fischer is the author of numerous books and publications on law and political science, including *Das politische System Österreich* (*The Austrian Political System*) and *Wende Zeiten. Ein österreichischer Zwischenbefund* (*Times of Change. An Austrian Interim Diagnosis*). He is also co-editor of the Austrian *Zeitschrift für Politikwissenschaft* (*Journal of Political Science*) and *Journal für Rechtspolitik* (*Journal of Law Policy*).

Wolfgang Schüssel

Position
Chancellor

Introduction
A former lawyer, Schüssel came through the ranks of the Austrian People's Party (ÖVP) to become, on 4 Feb. 2000, Austria's first centre-right chancellor in 30 years. He achieved this in a controversial alliance with Jörg Haider's far-right Freedom Party (FPÖ). A pro-European moderate, his resistance to EU diplomatic sanctions (imposed in response to the FPÖ presence in government) in his first few months of office transformed him into a dominant political figure. His coalition collapsed in Sept. 2002 when the FPÖ succumbed to internal wranglings. In new elections in Nov. 2002 he led the ÖVP to sweeping gains but revived the coalition with the FPÖ.

Early Life
Schüssel was born 7 June 1945 in Vienna and educated at Schottengymnasium until 1963. Having gained a PhD in law

from Vienna University in 1968, he was secretary to the ÖVP parliamentary group until 1975 and then secretary-general of the Austrian Economic Federation (a post he retained until 1991). He was elected a member of the National Council in 1979, serving as leader of the Group of Economic Federation parliamentary delegates, deputy chairman of the parliamentary ÖVP and deputy chairman of the parliamentary finance committee before his appointment as minister of economic affairs in April 1989. In April 1995 he was elected party leader (following the slide in his party's popularity in the 1994 elections) and assumed the federal posts of vice chancellor and foreign minister in the SPÖ-ÖVP coalition government.

Career in Office

Schüssel first announced that he would take the ÖVP into opposition after it was beaten into third place (albeit by a few hundred votes) by the right-wing FPÖ in the Oct. 1999 elections. However, in Feb. 2000 he made a controversial strategic move to include the FPÖ in a coalition government, although it was emphasized that the ÖVP did not embrace that party's more extreme policies. As a result Austria was boycotted diplomatically by its European Union partners. Schüssel did not relent and in Sept. 2000 the EU lifted its sanctions, by which time Haider had resigned as official FPÖ leader and Schüssel's political standing in Europe had been strengthened.

Schüssel's government initiated tough policy measures to reform the public sector (notably the *proporz* system under which public-sector appointments were shared between party supporters), to reduce the budget deficit and to accelerate privatization. However, he was vulnerable to tensions with his coalition partners on issues such as EU enlargement and immigration.

In Sept. 2002 two FPÖ ministers resigned their government posts and the coalition government collapsed. Schüssel declared his readiness to form a new administration with any of the three main opposition parties, but the Social Democrats (the second biggest party) ruled out an agreement. He therefore called new elections, which were held on 24 Nov. 2002 and won by the ÖVP, and revived the ruling alliance with the FPÖ. However, the coalition's stability was again undermined in April 2005 as Jörg Haider and his supporters left the FPÖ to form a new political party.

DEFENCE

The Federal President is C.-in-C. of the armed forces. Conscription is for a seven-month period, with liability for at least another 30 days' reservist refresher training spread over eight to ten years. Since 1992 the total 'on mobilization strength' of the forces has been reduced from approximately 200,000 to 110,000 troops. In 2002 approximately 1,000 personnel from so-called 'prepared units' were deployed in peace support operations in places such as Afghanistan, Bosnia, Cyprus, the Golan Heights and Syria.

Defence expenditure in 2003 totalled US$2,488m. (US$309 per capita), representing 1·0% of GDP.

Army

The Army is structured in five brigades and nine provincial military commands. Two brigades are mechanized, the rest infantry brigades. The mechanized brigades are equipped with Leopard 2/A4 main battle tanks. One of three infantry brigades is earmarked for airborne operations, the second is equipped with Pandur wheeled armoured personnel carriers and the third infantry brigade is specialized in mountain operations. The artillery units are brigade-directed. M-109 armoured self-propelled guns equip the artillery battalions. In addition to these standing units, some 20 infantry battalions under the direction of the provincial military commands are available on mobilization. Active personnel, 2002, 34,600 (to be 26,100)

including 17,200 conscripts. Women started to serve in the armed forces on 1 April 1998.

Air Force

The Air Force Command comprises three aviation and three air-defence regiments with about 6,500 personnel, more than 150 aircraft and a number of fixed- and mobile radar stations. Some 23 Draken interceptors equip a surveillance wing responsible for the defence of the Austrian air space and a fighter-bomber wing operates SAAB 105s. Helicopters including the S-70 Black Hawk equip six squadrons for transport/support, communication, observation, and search and rescue duties. Fixed-wing aircraft including PC-6s, PC-7s, Skyvans and C-130 Hercules are operated as trainers and for transport. The procurement of a fourth generation fighter is also planned for the near future.

INTERNATIONAL RELATIONS

Austria is a member of the UN, WTO, BIS, NATO Partnership for Peace, OECD, EU, Council of Europe, OSCE, CERN, CEI, Danube Commission, Inter-American Development Bank, Asian Development Bank, IOM and the Antarctic Treaty. Austria is a signatory to the Schengen accord abolishing border controls between Austria, Belgium, Denmark, Finland, France, Germany, Greece, Iceland, Italy, Luxembourg, Netherlands, Norway, Portugal, Spain and Sweden. In May 2005 Austria became the eighth country to ratify the proposed EU constitution when the *Nationalrat* voted in favour by 182 votes to 1 on 11 May and the *Bundesrat* ratified the constitution by 59 votes to 3 on 25 May.

ECONOMY

Trade and services account for about two-thirds of value added, and the industrial sector about one-third.

According to the anti-corruption organization *Transparency International*, Austria ranked 10th in the world in a 2005 survey of the countries with the least corruption in business and government. It received 8·7 out of 10 in the annual index.

Overview

Austria has experienced one of the strongest manufacturing productivity growth rates in the OECD during the last decade while maintaining an unemployment rate that is below the OECD average. Austrian market share in Central and Eastern European countries has expanded significantly, while membership of the EU and the EMU have added momentum. EU membership has led to a more liberal market and many companies have been taken over by foreign (particularly German) companies. Since 2004 high oil prices have had a notable impact on inflation, which reached 2·3% in 2005. Social partnership in the labour market has ensured wage moderation and low unemployment (5·2% in 2005). Though there are few manufacturers and service providers in the high-tech sector, it has benefited from a skilled labour force and good industrial relations. Tourism is also important and benefits from Austria's central location and alpine appeal.

Accession of the former Eastern Bloc nations to the EU has provided a further stimulus to exports. Exports to CEECs (Central and Eastern European Countries) are estimated to have created 40,000 jobs in manufacturing. Links with the CEECs have helped to diversify the economy and to cushion it from less favourable developments in Germany and the rest of Europe. Closer ties have seen high and rising levels of foreign direct investment into the CEECs and increased immigration into Austria. Continued export to these markets requires diversification into new markets; Austria's net comparative advantage in manufacturing with respect to the CEECs has declined, particularly in machinery, as the CEECs increase their own exports of machinery to Austria.

The advancement of research and development (R&D)-intensive industries has been slow in Austria, a net importer of R&D-intensive products. Austrian exports to dynamic Asian markets remain relatively low. The share of Austrian exports to China is 1·1% of total exports, compared to 2·7% in Germany, and Austria's share of OECD exports to China has declined.

Government spending accounts for 50% of GDP, placing it in the highest group of spenders in the OECD. The state controls many key industrial companies and utilities while local authorities control several savings banks. The general government deficit, having met target levels at the beginning of the 2000s, overshot the government's objective, specified in the Stability Programme, in 2004. This was attributed primarily to structural reasons, including increases in social and health care spending and reductions in corporate and personal income tax. A major goal of the government is to reduce the tax burden to 40% of GDP by 2010. The public pension system, absorbing around 14·5% of GDP, is one of the most expensive in Europe; pension reform, which commenced in 2003, aims to reduce the total cost of the system to the benefit of long-term financial sustainability.

Currency

On 1 Jan. 1999 the euro (EUR) became the legal currency in Austria; irrevocable conversion rate 13·7603 schillings to one euro. The euro, which consists of 100 cents, has been in circulation since 1 Jan. 2002. There are seven euro notes in different colours and sizes denominated in 500, 200, 100, 50, 20, 10 and 5 euros, and eight coins denominated in 2 and 1 euros, then 50, 20, 10, 5, 2 and 1 cents. On the introduction of the euro there was a 'dual circulation' period before the schilling ceased to be legal tender on 28 Feb. 2002.

Inflation rates (based on OECD statistics):

1995	1996	1997	1998	1999	2000	2001	2002	2003	2004
1·6%	1·8%	1·2%	0·8%	0·5%	2·0%	2·3%	1·7%	1·3%	2·0%

The inflation rate in 2005 according to the Oesterreichische Nationalbank was 2·3%.

Foreign exchange reserves were US$12,020m. in June 2002 and gold reserves were 10·21m. troy oz. Total money supply was €9,258m. in June 2002.

Budget

The federal budget for calendar years provided revenue and expenditure as follows (in €1m.):

	2000	2001	2002	2003[1]
Revenue	58,247	60,403	61,803	61,459
Expenditure	55,393	58,988	59,413	57,518

[1]Provisional.

VAT is 20% (reduced rate, 10%).

Performance

Real GDP growth rates (based on OECD statistics):

1995	1996	1997	1998	1999	2000	2001	2002	2003	2004
2·2%	2·4%	2·0%	3·5%	3·4%	3·5%	0·9%	1·0%	1·4%	2·4%

Total GDP was US$290·1bn. in 2004.

Banking and Finance

The Oesterreichische Nationalbank, central bank of Austria, opened on 1 Jan. 1923 but was taken over by the German Reichsbank on 17 March 1938. It was re-established on 3 July 1945. Its *Governor* is Klaus Liebscher. At 31 Dec. 2002 it had total reserves of US$13·2bn.

In the first two quarters of 2003, banking and insurance accounted for 5·8% of gross domestic product at current prices. In 2002 an average of 110,356 individuals were engaged in banking and insurance (76,475 in banking, 28,164 in insurance and 5,717 in banking and insurance), representing 3·5% of Austria's wage and salary earners.

By June 2003, 906 credit institutions and branch offices from banks located in the European Union were active in Austria. 40 credit institutions from countries outside the EU have established representative offices. The leading banks with total assets in 2002 (in €1bn) were: Bank Austria Group of Companies, 147,969; Erste Bank, 95,564; Bank für Arbeit und Wirtschaft AG–PSK, 48,842; and Raiffeisenzentralbank Österreich AG, 46,405.

There is a stock exchange in Vienna (VEX). It is one of the oldest in Europe and one of the smallest.

ENERGY AND NATURAL RESOURCES

Environment

Austria's carbon dioxide emissions from the consumption and flaring of fossil fuels were the equivalent of 8·7 tonnes per capita in 2002. An *Environmental Sustainability Index* compiled for the World Economic Forum meeting in Jan. 2005 ranked Austria tenth in the world, with 62·7%. The index measured the ability of countries to maintain favourable environmental conditions and examined various factors including pollution levels and the use or abuse of natural resources.

Austria is one of the world leaders in recycling. In 2000, 50% of all municipal waste was recycled.

Electricity

The Austrian electricity market was fully liberalized on 1 Oct. 2001. Installed capacity was 18·3m. kW in 2002. Production in 2002 was 62·48bn. kWh. Consumption per capita, 2002: 7,845 kWh.

Oil and Gas

The commercial production of petroleum began in the early 1930s. Production of crude oil, 2003: 922,173 tonnes. Crude oil reserves, 2002, were some 86m. bbls.

The Austrian gas market was fully liberalized on 1 Oct. 2002. Production of natural gas, 2003: 2,091m. cu. metres. Natural gas reserves in 2002 amounted to 24bn. cu. metres.

Minerals

The most important minerals are limestone and marble (2003 production, 24,476,840 tonnes), quartz and arenaceous quartz (2003 production, 7,305,244 tonnes), dolomite (2003 production, 5,468,300 tonnes), lignite (2002 production, 1,412,000 tonnes), basalt, clay and kaolin.

Agriculture

In 1998, 149,600 persons were employed in agriculture as their main occupation. In 1998 the total cultivated area amounted to 3,422,449 ha. There were 1·40m. ha. of arable land in 2001 and 71,000 ha. of permanent crops. There were 252,110 farms in 1999. In 2003 Austria set aside 297,000 ha. (11·6% of its agricultural land—the second highest proportion in the world after Liechtenstein) for the growth of organic crops. Agriculture accounted for 1·4% of GDP, 4·9% of exports and 7·0% of imports in 1999.

The chief products in 2003 (area in 1,000 ha.; yield in tonnes) were as follows: barley (212·3; 882,322); oats (34·4; 128,533); potatoes (21·1; 560,340); rye (40·0; 132,839); sugarbeets (43·2; 2,485,386); wheat (272·0; 1,191,380). Other important agricultural products include apples (423,000 tonnes in 2003) and pears (175,000 tonnes in 2003). Wine production in 2002–03 totalled 2,599,483 hectolitres.

Livestock in 2003: cattle, 2,052,033; pigs, 3,244,866; sheep, 325,495; goats, 54,607; horses (1999), 81,600; poultry, 13,027,145.

Forestry

Forested area in 2000, 3·9m. ha. (47% of the land area), around three-quarters of which was coniferous. Felled timber, in 1,000 cu. metres: 2000, 13,276·3; 2001, 13,466·5; 2002, 14,845·4; 2003, 17,055·2.

Fisheries

Total catch in 2003 came to 372 tonnes, exclusively from inland waters.

INDUSTRY

The leading companies by market capitalization in Austria in May 2004 were: Erste Bank (US$9·3bn.), Bank Austria Creditanstalt (US$8·4bn.) and Telekom Austria (US$7·0bn.).

Production, 2002 (in 1,000 tonnes): pig iron, 4,600; paper and paperboard (2000), 4,386; distillate fuel oil, 3,984; cement (2001), 3,863; petrol, 2,002; residual fuel oil, 1,012; sugar (2000), 447; sawnwood (2000), 10·39m. cu. metres; soft drinks (2001), 1,524·3m. litres; beer (2001), 852·8m. litres.

Labour

Austria has the second highest per capita income among the euro-12 countries and one of the lowest unemployment rates (5·2% in Dec. 2005). During 2000 Austria experienced its biggest fall in joblessness since the mid 1950s. Youth unemployment, at 6·0% in 2001, was also one of the lowest in the world.

In 2003 there were an average of 3,184,117 employed persons, with an average of 588,946 persons working in manufacturing; 493,288 in wholesale and retail trade, and repair of motor vehicles, motorcycles and personal and household goods; 471,062 in public administration and defence; 285,883 in real estate, renting and business activities; 237,677 in construction; and 215,243 in transport, storage and communication. In 2003 there were an average of 21,716 job vacancies.

The number of foreigners who may be employed in Austria is limited to 9% of the potential workforce. There were four strikes in 2002, with 6,305 participants (none in 2001). There were no strikes in 1996, 1998 or 1999. Between 1994 and 2003 strikes cost Austria an average of 42 days per 1,000 employees a year.

Austria has one of the lowest average retirement ages but reforms passed in 1997 now make it less attractive to retire before 60. Only 15% of men and 6% of women in the 60–65 age range work, although the legal retirement ages are 60 for women and 65 for men.

Trade Unions

The 13 unions in the Austrian Trade Union Confederation (Österreichischer Gewerkschaftsbund, ÖGB) had 1,385,000 members in Dec. 2003.

INTERNATIONAL TRADE

Imports and Exports

Imports and exports for calendar years, in €1m.:

	1999	2000	2001	2002	2003
Imports	65,316	74,935	78,692	77,104	80,993
Exports	60,266	69,692	74,251	77,400	78,903

Main import suppliers in 2003 (% of total imports): Germany, 41·0%; Italy, 7·0%; Switzerland, 4·1%; France, 3·9%; USA, 3·9%. Main export markets: Germany, 31·8%; Italy, 9·0%; Switzerland, 5·2%; USA, 5·2%; France, 4·4%. Other EU-member countries accounted for 65·9% of imports and 59·5% of exports.

In 2003 chemicals, manufactured goods classified chiefly by material and miscellaneous manufactured articles accounted for 43·0% of Austria's imports and 46·4% of exports; machinery and transport equipment 39·3% of imports and 41·9% of exports; food, live animals, beverages and tobacco 5·9% of imports and 5·8% of exports; mineral fuels, lubricants and related materials 8·0% of imports and 2·5% of exports; and crude materials, inedible, animal and vegetable oil and fats 3·8% of imports and 3·4% of exports.

Trade Fairs

Vienna ranked as the fourth most popular convention city behind Paris, London and Brussels in 2002 according to the Union des Associations Internationales (UAI).

COMMUNICATIONS

Roads

In 2002 the road network totalled 200,000 km (Autobahn, 1,645 km; highways, 10,334 km; secondary roads, 23,657 km). On 31 Dec. 2003 motor vehicles registered numbered 5,505,927, including 4,054,308 passenger cars, 326,087 trucks, 9,231 buses and 606,868 motorcycles. There were 931 fatalities in road accidents in 2003.

Rail

The Austrian Federal Railways (ÖBB) has been restructured and was split up into ten new companies, which became operational on 1 Jan. 2005. Length of route in 2003, 5,656 km, of which 3,526 km were electrified. There are also a number of private railways with a total length of 589 km. In 2003, 183·73m. passengers and 87·0m. tonnes of freight were carried by Federal Railways. There is a metro and tramway in Vienna, and tramways in Gmunden, Graz, Innsbruck and Linz.

Civil Aviation

The national airline is Austrian Airlines, which is 39·7% state-owned. There are international airports at Vienna (Schwechat), Linz, Salzburg, Graz, Klagenfurt and Innsbruck. In 2003 services were provided by 62 other airlines. In 2003, 273,064 commercial aircraft and 16,344,253 passengers arrived and departed; 118,081 tonnes of freight and 11,554 tonnes of mail were handled. In 2003 Vienna handled 12,709,432 passengers and 115,686 tonnes of freight. Austrian Airlines carried 7,070,344 passengers in 2002.

Shipping

The Danube is an important waterway. Goods traffic (in 1,000 tonnes): 10,980 in 2000; 11,634 in 2001; 12,316 in 2002; 10,737 in 2003 (including the Rhine-Main-Danube Canal). The merchant shipping fleet totalled 30,000 GRT in 2002.

Telecommunications

Österreichische Industrie Holding AG, the Austrian investment and privatization agency, holds a 29·99% stake in Telekom Austria. There were 10,588,000 telephone subscribers in 2002 (1,297·7 per 1,000 inhabitants). Mobile phone subscribers numbered 6,415,000 in 2002 and there were 3,013,000 PCs in use (369·3 per 1,000 persons). The number of Internet users in June 2002 was approximately 3·7m.

Postal Services

The Postal Savings Bank was privatized in 2000. In 2002 there were 1,669 post offices and 120 post-agencies, the so-called 'Post-Partner'. A total of 4,541m. postal items were handled in 2000.

SOCIAL INSTITUTIONS

Justice

The Supreme Court of Justice (Oberster Gerichtshof) in Vienna is the highest court in civil and criminal cases. In addition, in 2003 there were four Courts of Appeal (Oberlandesgerichte), 20 High Courts (Landesgerichte) and 148 District Courts (Bezirksgerichte). There is also a Supreme Constitutional Court (Verfassungsgerichtshof) and a Supreme Administrative Court (Verwaltungsgerichtshof), both seated in Vienna. In 2003 a total of 634,286 criminal offences were reported to the police and 41,749 people were convicted of offences. The population in penal institutions in Nov. 2003 was 8,114 (100 per 100,000 of national population).

Education

In 2002–03 there were 4,900 general compulsory schools (including special education) with 74,957 teachers and 683,290 pupils. Secondary schools totalled 1,687 in 2002–03 with 531,828 pupils.

In 2002–03 there were also 121 commercial academies with 42,813 pupils and 5,616 teachers, 82 higher schools of economic professions (secondary level) with 24,361 pupils, 112 schools of technical and industrial training with 11,907 pupils and 108 agricultural technical schools with 10,686 pupils. 114 professional schools had 13,472 pupils in 2002–03.

The dominant institutions of higher education are the 13 universities and six colleges of arts, which are publicly financed. In 1994 Higher Technical Study Centres (*Fachhochschul-Studiengänge*, FHS) were established, which are private, but government-dependent, institutions. In the winter term 2002–03 there were 19,728 students enrolled at the universities, 9,113 at the colleges of arts and 17,409 at 124 FHS.

In 2001–02 public expenditure on education came to 5·9% of GNP and 11·1% of total government spending. The adult literacy rate is at least 99%.

Health

In 2003 there were 37,447 doctors, 4,037 dentists, 40,113 nurses (2002) and 1,671 midwives. In 2002 there were 278 hospitals and 70,376 hospital beds. In 2002 Austria spent 7·6% of its GDP on health.

Welfare

Maternity/paternity leave is until the child's second birthday. A new parenting allowance was introduced on 1 Jan. 2002, replacing the maternity/paternity allowance. The new system is based on family benefit financed from the Family Fund instead of the insurance principle. The basic allowance is €436 per month for a maximum of three years. In June 2003 a reform of the pensions system was approved involving the reduction of pension benefits by 10%, the raising of the retirement age to 65 by increasing the workers' contribution period from 40 to 45 years and the abolition of early retirement by 2017. There were 2,496,140 pensioners in Dec. 2003.

RELIGION

In 2001 there were 5,915,000 Roman Catholics (73·6%), 376,000 Evangelical Lutherans (4·7%), 339,000 Muslims (4·2%), 963,000 without religious allegiance (12·0%) and 439,000 others (5·5%). The Roman Catholic Church has two archbishoprics and seven bishoprics. In May 2005 there were two cardinals.

CULTURE

World Heritage Sites

There are seven sites under Austrian jurisdiction. They are (with year entered on list): the historic centre of the city of Salzburg (1996); the Palace and gardens of Schönbrunn (1996); Hallstatt-Dachstein Salzkammergut cultural landscape (1997); Semmering Railway (1998); the historic centre of the city of Graz (1999); the Wachau cultural landscape (2000); and the historic centre of the city of Vienna (2001).

Austria also shares the Cultural Landscape of Fertö/Neusiedlersee site (2001) with Hungary.

Broadcasting

The 'Österreichische Rundfunk' (Austrian Broadcasting Corporation) is state-controlled. It transmits four national and nine regional radio programmes. An additional programme in English and French can be received all over the country; there is also a 24-hour foreign service (short wave). There were 2·97m. radio licenses and 2·94m. television licenses (colour by PAL) issued in 2003. There were also 1,087,791 cable TV subscribers in 2003.

Cinema

In 2003 there were 176 cinemas (553 screens) with a seating capacity of 100,725. Audience numbers totalled 17,719,500.

Press

There were 16 daily newspapers (seven of them in Vienna), 224 non-daily newspapers and 2,772 other periodicals in 2003.

The most popular newspaper is the mass-market tabloid *Neue Kronen-Zeitung*, which is read on a daily basis by 42% of the population. In 2003 a total of 21,581 books were published, including 8,733 new titles.

Tourism

Tourism is an important industry. In 2003, 17,384 hotels and boarding houses had a total of 608,953 beds available. In 2002, 18,611,000 foreigners visited Austria and tourist receipts were US$11·24bn. Tyrol is the most popular province for visits, recording more than a third of all overnight stays in 2003. Of 117,966,984 overnight stays in tourist accommodation in 2003, 31,618,992 were by Austrians and 52,804,677 by Germans.

Festivals

The main festivals are Salzburger Festspiele, held every July–Aug. (219,944 visitors in 2003), and Bregenzer Festspiele, also held in July–Aug. (204,482 visitors in 2003). The Haydn Days in Eisenstadt, held every Sept., is also considered to be one of the leading annual festivals.

Libraries

In 1997 there were 5,642,000 library users and 26,123,000 volumes in scientific and special libraries, and 1,149,300 users and 11,252,800 volumes in public libraries.

Theatre and Opera

The attendance at federal theatres was 1,280,300 in 2002–03.

Museums and Galleries

In 2002 there were 21,716,900 visitors to museums, exhibitions and similar attractions (10,461,700 in Vienna).

DIPLOMATIC REPRESENTATIVES

Of Austria in the United Kingdom (18 Belgrave Mews West, London, SW1X 8HU)
Ambassador: Gabriele Matzner-Holzer.

Of the United Kingdom in Austria (Jaurèsgasse 12, 1030 Vienna)
Ambassador: John M. Macgregor, CVO.

Of Austria in the USA (3524 International Court, NW, Washington, D.C., 20008)
Ambassador: Eva Nowotny.

Of the USA in Austria (Boltzmanngasse 16, A-1091 Vienna)
Ambassador: Susan McCaw.

Of Austria to the United Nations
Ambassador: Dr Gerhard Pfanzelter.

FURTHER READING

Austrian Central Statistical Office. *Main publications: Statistisches Jahrbuch für die Republik Österreich.* New Series from 1950. Annual.—*Statistische Nachrichten.* Monthly.—*Beiträge zur österreichischen Statistik.*—*Statistik in Österreich 1918–1938.* [Bibliography] 1985.—*Veröffentlichungen des Österreichischen Statistischen Zentralamtes 1945–1985.* [Bibliography], 1990.—*Republik Österreich, 1945–1995.*

Brook-Shepherd, G., *The Austrians: a Thousand-Year Odyssey.* London, 1997

Peniston-Bird, C. M., *Vienna.* [Bibliography] ABC-Clio, Oxford and Santa Barbara (CA), 1997

Pick, Hella, *Guilty Victim: Austria from the Holocaust to Haider.* I. B. Tauris, London, 2000

Sully, M. A., *A Contemporary History of Austria.* London, 1990

Wolfram, H. (ed.) *Österreichische Geschichte.* 10 vols. Vienna, 1994

National library: Österreichische Nationalbibliothek, Josefsplatz, 1015 Vienna.

National Statistical Office: Austrian Central Statistical Office, POB 9000, A-1033 Vienna.

Website: http://www.statistik.at

AZERBAIJAN

RUSSIA
GEORGIA
Caspian Sea
Gandja
Sumgait
BAKU
ARMENIA
AZERBAIJAN
Salyan
IRAN
© Research Machines plc 2005
0   50 mi
0   75 km

Azarbaijchan Respublikasy

Capital: Baku
Population projection, 2010: 8·74m.
GDP per capita, 2003: (PPP$) 3,617
HDI/world rank: 0·729/101

KEY HISTORICAL EVENTS

In 1920 Azerbaijan was proclaimed a Soviet Socialist Republic. From 1922, with Georgia and Armenia, it formed the Transcaucasian Soviet Federal Socialist Republic. Conflict with Armenia over the enclave of Nagorno-Karabakh escalated in 1988, leading to violent expulsions of Armenians in Azerbaijan and Azeris in Armenia. In 'Black January' 1990 Soviet tanks moved in to react to rioting in Baku, and over 100 civilians were killed. War broke out between the two countries in 1992, with a ceasefire agreed in 1994. The dispute over territory remains unsettled, although negotiations in Florida in 2001 promised a peaceful solution. In 1990 it adopted a declaration of republican sovereignty and on 18 Aug. 1991 the Supreme Soviet of Azerbaijan declared independence. Under the presidency of Heydar Aliyev, elected in Oct. 1993, parliament ratified association with the CIS on 20 Sept. 1993. A treaty of friendship and co-operation was signed with Russia on 3 July 1997 and Aliyev was re-elected in Oct. 1998, although the administration of the election was criticized by international observers.

TERRITORY AND POPULATION

Azerbaijan is bounded in the west by Armenia, in the north by Georgia and the Russian Federation (Dagestan), in the east by the Caspian sea and in the south by Turkey and Iran. Its area is 86,600 sq. km (33,430 sq. miles), and it includes the Nakhichevan Autonomous Republic and the largely Armenian-inhabited Nagorno-Karabakh.

The population at the 1999 census was 7,953,000 (4,119,000 females); density, approximately 92 per sq. km. Estimate, 1 Jan. 2004, 8,265,700. At 1 Jan. 2004, 51·5% of the population lived in urban areas. There are 69 towns, nine of which have over 50,000 people. The population breaks down into 82·7% Azerbaijanis, 5·6% Armenians, 5·6% Russians and 2·4% Lezgis (1999 census).

The UN gives a projected population for 2010 of 8·74m.

Chief cities: Baku (at 1 Jan. 2004, 1,839,800), Gandja (303,100) and Sumgait (290,700).

The official language is Azeri. On 1 Aug. 2001 Azerbaijan abolished the use of the Cyrillic alphabet and switched to using Latin script.

SOCIAL STATISTICS

In 2003: births, 113,467; deaths, 49,001; marriages, 56,091; divorces, 6,671. Rates, 2003 (per 1,000 population): births, 14·0; deaths, 6·0; infant mortality (2001, per 1,000 live births), 74. Life expectancy in 2003: 70·5 years for females and 63·2 years for males. Annual population growth rate, 1990–2003, 0·8%; fertility rate, 2003, 2·0 children per woman.

CLIMATE

The climate is almost tropical in summer and the winters slightly warmer than in regions north of the Caucasus. Cold spells do occur, however, both on the high mountains and in the enclosed valleys. There are nine climatic zones. Baku, Jan. –6°C, July 25°C. Annual rainfall 318 mm.

CONSTITUTION AND GOVERNMENT

Parliament is the 125-member *Melli-Majlis.* 100 seats are elected from single-member districts, and 25 distributed proportionally among political parties. For the majority seats there is a minimum 50% turnout requirement. There is an 8% threshold. A constitutional referendum and parliamentary elections were held on 12 Nov. 1995. Turnout for the referendum was 86%. The new Constitution was approved by 91·9% of votes cast. As a result of a referendum held on 24 Aug. 2002 on a number of changes to the constitution, all 125 members were elected from single-member districts in the parliamentary elections of Nov. 2005. The validity of the outcome of the referendum was questioned by international observers.

National Anthem

'Azerbaijan! Azerbaijan!'; words by A. Javad, tune by U. Hajibeyov.

RECENT ELECTIONS

At elections on 15 Oct. 2003 Ilham Aliyev of the New Azerbaijan Party (YAP) was elected president with 76·8% of votes cast. Isa Qambar of the Equality Party won 14·0%, Lala-Sovkat Haciyeva of National Unity won 3·6% and Ehtibar Mammadov of the Azerbaijan National Independence Party (AMIP) won 2·9%. There were four other candidates who all received less than 1% of the vote.

At the parliamentary elections held on 6 Nov. 2005 the YAP gained 56 seats; ind. 40 and the Azadlig (Freedom) opposition bloc 6 (the Musavat Party 5 and the Azerbaijan Popular Front Party 1). A number of smaller parties took either one or two seats. Turnout was 42·2%. International observers declared that the poll failed to meet international standards.

CURRENT ADMINISTRATION

President: Ilham Aliyev; b. 1961 (YAP; sworn in 31 Oct. 2003).

In March 2006 the government comprised:

Prime Minister: Artur Rasizade; b. 1935 (YAP; in office since 6 Aug. 2003, until 4 Nov. as acting prime minister, having previously been prime minister from 20 July 1996 to 4 Aug. 2003).

First Deputy Prime Ministers: Abbas Abbasov, Yagub Eyyubov.
Deputy Prime Ministers: Elchin Efendiyev, Ali Hasanov, Abid Sharifov.

Minister of Foreign Affairs: Elmar Mamedyarov. *Interior:* Ramil Usubov. *Culture and Tourism:* Abulfaz Garayev. *Education:* Misir Mardanov. *Emergency Situations:* Kamaladdin Heydarov. *National Security:* Eldar Mahmudov. *Defence:* Lieut.-Gen. Safar Abiyev. *Communications and Information Technologies:* Ali Abbasov. *Agriculture and Food:* Ismat Abbasov. *Justice:* Fikret Mamedov. *Health:* Ogtay Shiraliyev. *Finance:* Avaz Alekperov. *Labour and Social Protection:* Fizuli Alakbarov. *Youth and Sport:* Azad Rahimov. *Economic Development:* Heydar Babayev. *Ecology and Natural Resources:* Huseyngulu Bagirov. *Industry and Energy:* Natig Aliyev. *Taxation:* Fazil Mamedov. *Transport:* Ziya Mammadov.

Chairman of the National Assembly (Melli-Majlis): Oktai Asadov.

Office of the President: http://www.president.az

CURRENT LEADERS

Ilham Aliyev

Position
President

Introduction
Ilham Aliyev succeeded his father, Heidar Aliyev, as president in Oct. 2003. The Moscow-educated politician has presided over a rapidly growing economy but heightened political tension followed the parliamentary elections of 6 Nov. 2005.

Early Life
Ilham Heidar oğlu Aliyev was born in Baku, capital of the Soviet Socialist Republic of Azerbaijan, on 24 Dec. 1961. His father was Heidar Aliyev, who became deputy prime minister of the Soviet Union under Mikhail Gorbachev and, in Oct. 1993, president of Azerbaijan. Ilham graduated in history from the Moscow State Institute for International Relations in 1982. He subsequently gained a PhD in history and began teaching at the Institute. Plans to enter the diplomatic service were curtailed by the collapse of the Soviet Union in 1991 and Ilham established 'business interests' in Moscow and İstanbul. Between 1991 and 1994 his flamboyant lifestyle attracted media attention and he was accused of accumulating large gambling debts.

Ilham was appointed vice-president of Azerbaijan's state oil company in May 1994. Four months later President Aliyev signed a 30-year deal valued at more than US$7bn. with eight foreign companies to develop the country's substantial oil reserves. In 1995 Ilham was elected to parliament and was subsequently appointed president of the national Olympic committee and head of the Azerbaijan delegation to the Council of Europe. In Dec. 1999 he became a deputy of the ruling New Azerbaijan Party (YAP) and, in 2001, was appointed party vice president.

Following the surprise resignation of Prime Minister Artur Rasizade in Aug. 2003, Heidar Aliyev appointed Ilham as prime minister. The move was approved by a 101–1 vote in the National Assembly but opposition parties boycotted the election. Critics took the move as proof that the increasingly frail Heidar planned to hand over power to his son (an amendment to the constitution in Aug. 2002 providing for the prime minister to become interim president in the event that the president dies in office or is incapacitated). A few weeks before the presidential elections of Oct. 2003 Heidar pulled out of the running, leaving Ilham as YAP's candidate.

Official results gave Ilham victory with 76·8% of the vote but opposition parties staged mass protests over alleged intimidation and fraud, charges backed by international observers. Aliyev was sworn in as the president on 31 Oct. 2003. His father died on 12 Dec. 2003.

Career in Office
Ilham has presided over a rapidly expanding economy, a consequence of the discovery of offshore gas fields, high international oil prices and the completion of pipelines crossing from the Caucasus to Turkey. Unemployment and poverty levels nonetheless remain high, especially in rural areas.

Ilham released a number of opposition figures from prison in March 2005 following international pressure, particularly from the Council of Europe. However, his administration was criticized for intimidating opposition activists in the run-up to parliamentary elections in Nov. 2005. The YAP, led by Ilham since March 2005, won 56 of 125 parliamentary seats but the OSCE's international election observer mission reported harassment and vote buying. The opposition Azadlig party refused to accept the election results and organized mass protests in Nov. and Dec. 2005.

Artur Rasizade

Position
Prime Minister

Introduction
Artur Rasizade, an oil engineer-turned-politician, has been prime minister since 1996. He was appointed by President Heidar Aliyev and has served under his son, Ilham Aliyev, since Oct. 2003.

Early Life
Artur Tahir oğlu Rasizade was born on 26 Feb. 1935 in Ganja in the Transcaucasian Soviet Federated Socialist Republic. Educated at the Azerbaijan Institute of Industry in Baku, Azerbaijan Soviet Socialist Republic, Rasizade began work as an engineer at the Institute of Oil Machine Construction in 1957. He served as chief engineer at Trust Soyuzneftemash from 1973–77, before taking the post of deputy head of the Azerbaijan state planning committee.

In 1986, after five years as bureau chief of the central committee of the Communist Party of Azerbaijan, Rasizade became first deputy prime minister under Kamran Baghirov, who has been widely blamed for the Republic's economic stagnation and the escalating tension with Armenia over Nagorno-Karabakh.

Following the break-up of the Soviet Union and Azerbaijan's declaration of independence in Aug. 1991, Rasizade became an advisor to the foundation for economic reforms. He served as an assistant to President Heidar Aliyev in early 1996 and was then appointed first deputy prime minister. He was appointed prime minister when Fuad Kuliev resigned following accusations by Aliyev of economic mismanagement. The national assembly endorsed Rasizade's appointment and he took office on 26 Dec. 1996.

Career in Office
Heidar Aliyev won the presidential election in Oct. 1998 and retained Rasizade (a fellow member of the New Azerbaijan party) as prime minister until 4 Aug. 2003, when the premier unexpectedly resigned. Rasizade's departure, ostensibly for health reasons, paved the way for Ilham Aliyev to assume office. Ilham Aliyev contested the presidential election of 15 Oct. 2003 and emerged victorious, although the opposition staged mass protests, alleging intimidation and fraud. On 4 Nov. 2003 Rasizade was formally reinstated as prime minister.

DEFENCE

Conscription is for 17 months. Defence expenditure in 2003 totalled US$950m. (US$115 per capita), representing 3·2% of GDP.

Army

Personnel, 2002, 62,000. In addition there is a reserve force of 300,000 Azerbaijanis who have received some kind of military service experience within the last 15 years. There is also a paramilitary Ministry of the Interior militia of about 10,000 and a border guard of approximately 5,000.

Navy
The flotilla is based at Baku on the Caspian Sea and numbered about 2,200 in 2002 including six patrol craft.

Air Force
How many ex-Soviet aircraft are usable is not known but there are 48 combat aircraft and 15 armed helicopters. Personnel, 7,900 in 2002.

INTERNATIONAL RELATIONS
Azerbaijan is a member of the UN, the NATO Partnership for Peace, Council of Europe, OSCE, CIS, IMO, the World Bank, IMF, EBRD, BSEC, ECO, IOM, OIC, Islamic Development Bank and OEC. There is a dispute with Armenia over the status of the chiefly Armenian-populated Azerbaijani enclave of Nagorno-Karabakh. A ceasefire was negotiated from 1994 with 20% of Azerbaijan's land in Armenian hands and with 1m. Azeri refugees and displaced persons.

ECONOMY
In 2003 agriculture accounted for 13·1% of GDP, industry 37·8% and services 49·1%.

Currency
The *manta* (AZM) of 100 *gyapiks* replaced the rouble in Jan. 1994. Inflation was 2·2% in 2003 and 6·7% in 2004. Foreign exchange reserves were US$763m. in June 2002 and total money supply was 1,729·57bn. manats.

Budget
Government revenue and expenditure (in 1m. manats):

	2000	2001	2002	2003
Revenue	3,573,200	3,924,000	4,551,200	6,131,900
Expenditure	3,819,800	4,037,500	4,658,800	6,173,000

VAT accounted for 2,048,600m. manats of the 2003 budget revenue and profits tax accounted for 891,500m. manats. Of the 2003 expenditure, education accounted for 1,170,000m. manats, social security and welfare 1,070,000m. manats, law enforcement 603,400m. manats, state administration bodies 289,500m. manats and health 276,600m. manats.

Performance
Total GDP was US$8·5bn. in 2004. Azerbaijan has one of the fastest growing economies in the world. Real GDP growth was 9·2% in 2000, 6·5% in 2001, 8·1% in 2002, 11·5% in 2003 and 10·2% in 2004. This was largely thanks to foreign investment into the country and the oil boom.

Banking and Finance
The central bank and bank of issue is the National Bank (*Chairman*, Dr Elman Rustamov). In 2003 there were two state-owned banks (International Bank of Azerbaijan and the United Joint Stock Bank). In 2003 there were 46 privately-owned commercial banks of varying size.

ENERGY AND NATURAL RESOURCES

Environment
Azerbaijan's carbon dioxide emissions from the consumption and flaring of fossil fuels were the equivalent of 4·2 tonnes per capita in 2002.

Electricity
Output was 21·1bn. kWh in 2003; consumption per capita in 2000 was 2,404 kWh. Capacity in 2000 was 5·2m. kW.

Oil and Gas
The most important industry is crude oil extraction. Baku is at the centre of oil exploration in the Caspian. Partnerships with Turkish, western European and US companies have been forged.

In 2003 oil reserves totalled 7·0bn. bbls. A century ago Azerbaijan produced half of the world's oil, but production today is less than 1% of the total. An average of 15·0m. tonnes of oil are produced annually. Oil production in 2003 was 113m. bbls. In July 1999 BP Amoco announced a major natural gas discovery in the Shakh Deniz offshore field, with reserves of at least 700bn. cu. metres and perhaps as much as 1,000bn. cu. metres. There were proven reserves of 850bn. cu. metres in 2002. Natural gas production in 2003 amounted to 5·1bn. cu. metres.

Accords for the construction of an oil pipeline from Baku, the Azerbaijani capital, on the Caspian Sea through Georgia to Ceyhan in southern Turkey were signed in Nov. 1999. Work on the pipeline began in Sept. 2002 and it was officially opened in May 2005.

Minerals
The republic is rich in natural resources: iron, bauxite, manganese, aluminium, copper ores, lead, zinc, precious metals, sulphur pyrites, nepheline syenites, limestone and salt. Cobalt ore reserves have been discovered in Dashkasan, and Azerbaijan has the largest iodine-bromine ore reserves of the former Soviet Union (the Neftchala region has an iodine-bromine mill).

Agriculture
In 2003 the total area devoted to agriculture was 4·8m. ha., of which 1·8m. ha. was under crop and 223,774 ha. were orchards and vineyards. In 2003 there were 1·80m. ha. of arable land and 0·23m. ha. of permanent crops. 1·42m. ha. were irrigated in 2003. In 2003, 40% of the economically active population was engaged in agriculture. Principal crops include grain, cotton, rice, grapes, citrus fruit, vegetables, tobacco and silk.

Output of main agricultural products (in 1,000 tonnes) in 2003: wheat, 1,547; potatoes, 769; tomatoes, 421; melons and watermelons, 357; barley, 334; apples, 154.

Livestock (2003): cattle, 2·24m.; sheep, 6·68m.; goats, 604,000; chickens, 18m. Livestock products (2003, in 1,000 tonnes): beef and veal, 67; lamb and mutton, 39; cow's milk, 1,147; eggs, 38.

Forestry
In 2003 forests covered 1,037,000 ha., or 12·0% of the total land area. Timber production in 2001 was 14,000 cu. metres.

Fisheries
About ten tonnes of caviar from the Caspian sturgeon are produced annually. Total fish catch in 2003 came to approximately 23,300 tonnes, exclusively from inland waters.

INDUSTRY
There are oil extraction and refining, oil-related machinery, iron and steel, aluminium, copper, chemical, cement, building materials, timber, synthetic rubber, salt, textiles, food and fishing industries. Production (2003) in 1,000 tonnes: residual fuel oil, 2,470; distillate fuel oil, 1,641; cement, 1,012; petrol, 720; bread and bakery products, 686; jet fuel, 631. Output of other products: footwear (2003), 455,900 pairs; 17,000 drilling and boring machines (1997).

Labour
In 2003 the economically active workforce numbered 3,747,000. The main areas of activity were: agriculture, hunting and forestry, 1,497,000; wholesale and retail trade/repair of motor vehicles, motorcycles and personal and household goods, 618,300; education, 330,000; public administration and defence/compulsory social security, 265,000. The unemployment rate in 2003 was 10·9%. The average monthly salary in 2003 was 368,974 manats.

INTERNATIONAL TRADE
Total external debt was US$1,598m. in 2003.

Imports and Exports

In 2003 imports (f.o.b.) were valued at US$2,626·4m. and exports (f.o.b.) at US$2,591·7m.

Principal imports in 2003 were machinery, power, cereals, steel tubes, sugar and sweets. Petroleum and related products accounted for approximately 85% of exports. Cotton, chemicals, tobacco, beverages, air conditioners, wool and refrigerators are also important exports.

Leading import suppliers in 2003 were Russia (21·3%), UK (10·9%), Turkey (7·4%), Turkmenistan (7·2%), Germany (6·5%). The main export markets were Italy (51·7%), France (8·1%), Israel (5·3%), Russia (5·3%), Georgia (4·3%), Turkey (4·1%).

COMMUNICATIONS

Roads

There were 25,021 km of roads (6,897 km highways and main roads) in 2003. Passenger cars in use in 2003 totalled 370,439 (45 per 1,000 inhabitants). In addition, there were 77,019 trucks and vans and 18,781 buses and coaches. There were 837 fatalities as a result of road accidents in 2003.

Rail

Total length in 2003 was 2,112 km of 1,520 mm gauge (1,270 km electrified). Passenger-km travelled in 2003 came to 654m. and freight tonne-km to 7·70bn.

There is a metro and tramway in Baku and a tramway in Sumgait.

Civil Aviation

There is an international airport at Baku. Azerbaijan Airlines had international flights in 2003 to Aktau, Aleppo, Ankara, Dubai, İstanbul, Kabul, Kyiv, London, Paris, Tbilisi, Tehran, Tel Aviv, Trabzon and Urumqi. There were direct flights in 2003 with other airlines to Almaty, Ashgabat, Bishkek, Donetsk, Ekaterinburg, Frankfurt, Kazan, Mineralnye Vody, Minsk, Moscow, Nizhnevartovsk, Novosibirsk, Omsk, St Petersburg, Samara, Surgut, Tashkent, Tyumen and Volgograd. In 1999 Azerbaijan Airlines flew 10·4m. km, carrying 571,700 passengers (187,500 on international flights).

Shipping

In 2002 merchant shipping totalled 633,000 GRT (including oil tankers 175,000 GRT). In 2000 vessels totalling 5,118,000 NRT entered ports and vessels totalling 703,000 NRT cleared.

Telecommunications

Telephone subscribers numbered 1,793,800 in 2002 (220·3 per 1,000 inhabitants) including 870,000 mobile phone subscribers. In 2003 there were 2,170 fax machines. Internet users numbered 300,000 in 2002.

Postal Services

There were 1,377 post offices in 2003.

SOCIAL INSTITUTIONS

Justice

The number of reported crimes in 2003 was 15,206, including 285 murders or attempted murders (449 in 1997). There were 187 crimes per 1,000 inhabitants and 94% of crimes were solved (80% in 1997).

The population in penal institutions in Jan. 2003 was 17,795 (217 per 100,000 of national population).

The death penalty was abolished in 1998.

Education

In 2003–04 there were 603,894 pupils and 40,876 teachers at 4,533 primary schools, and 1,070,636 pupils at secondary schools. There were 110,891 children enrolled at pre-school institutions. In 2003 there were 175,229 students at 42 institutes of higher education and 60 specialized secondary schools. There were 33 institutes of higher education in Baku, with 95,068 students in 2003–04 (including correspondence students). The Azerbaijan Academy of Sciences, founded in 1945, has 31 research institutes. Adult literacy was estimated to be 99% in 2003.

In 2003 total expenditure on education came to 3·3% of GNP and represented 18·8% of total government expenditure.

Health

In 2003 there were 734 hospitals with 68,000 beds. In 2003 there were 29,687 physicians, 2,275 dentists, 59,531 nurses, 1,842 pharmacists and 9,803 midwives.

Welfare

In Jan. 2004 there were 751,000 age pensioners and 576,000 other pensioners.

RELIGION

In 2003 the population was 92% Muslim (mostly Shia), the balance being mainly Russian Orthodox, Armenian Apostolic and Judaism.

CULTURE

World Heritage Sites

There is one UNESCO site in Azerbaijan: the Walled City of Baku with the Shirvanshah's Palace and Maiden Tower (2000). The site was damaged by an earthquake in 2000.

Broadcasting

The government-controlled Azerbaijan Radio broadcasts two national and one regional programme, a relay of Radio Moscow and a foreign service, Radio Baku (Azeri, Arabic, Iranian and Turkish). There are a number of private TV and radio stations. There were 2·5m. TV receivers in 2001 and 177,000 radio receivers in 2000.

Press

In 2002 Azerbaijan published 285 different newspapers, of which 25 were national daily newspapers with a combined circulation of 158,000. There is one daily, published by parliament, with a circulation of 5,000, and two independent thrice-weeklies with a combined circulation of 30,000. In 2002 a total of 478 book titles were published.

Tourism

In 2003 there were 1,066,000 foreign tourists; spending by tourists totalled US$63m. in 2000.

Museums and Galleries

There were 159 museums including a National Museum of History in 2003.

DIPLOMATIC REPRESENTATIVES

Of Azerbaijan in the United Kingdom (4 Kensington Court, London, W8 5DL)
Ambassador: Rafael Ibrahimov.

Of the United Kingdom in Azerbaijan (45 Khagani St., AZ1000 Baku)
Ambassador: Dr Laurie Bristow.

Of Azerbaijan in the USA (2741 34th St., NW, Washington, D.C., 20008)
Ambassador: Hafiz Mir Jalal Pashayev.

Of the USA in Azerbaijan (83 Azadliq Prospect, Baku 37007)
Ambassador: Reno L. Harnish, III.

Of Azerbaijan to the United Nations
Ambassador: Yashar Aliyev.

Of Azerbaijan to the European Union
Ambassador: Arif Mamedov.

FURTHER READING
Swietochowski, T., *Russia and a Divided Azerbaijan*. Columbia University Press, 1995
Van Der Leeuw, C., *Azerbaijan*. Saint Martin's Press, New York, 1999

Nakhichevan

This territory, on the borders of Turkey and Iran, forms part of Azerbaijan although separated from it by the territory of Armenia. Its population in 1989 was 95·9% Azerbaijani. It was annexed by Russia in 1828. In June 1923 it was constituted as an Autonomous Region within Azerbaijan. On 9 Feb. 1924 it was elevated to the status of Autonomous Republic. The 1996 Azerbaijani Constitution defines it as an Autonomous State within Azerbaijan.

Area, 5,500 sq. km (2,120 sq. miles); population (Dec. 2003), 369,800. Capital, Nakhichevan (Jan. 2003, 64,400).

There were 46,644 ha. of crops in 2003. Approximately 70% of the economically active population are engaged in agriculture of which the main branches are cotton and tobacco growing. Fruit and grapes are also produced.

In 2003–04 there were 232 primary and secondary schools with 72,179 pupils, and (1989–90) 2,200 students in higher educational institutions. There were 292 public libraries in Nakhichevan in 2003.

Nakhichevan had 52 hospitals and 3,540 hospital beds in 2003; there were 647 doctors and 2,765 paramedic staff.

Nagorno-Karabakh

Established on 7 July 1923 as an Autonomous Region within Azerbaijan, in 1989 the area was placed under a 'special form of administration' subordinate to the USSR government. In Sept. 1991 the regional Soviet and the Shaumyan district Soviet jointly declared a Nagorno-Karabakh republic, which declared itself independent with a 99·9% popular vote (only the Armenian community took part in this vote as the Azeri population had already been expelled from Nagorno-Karabakh) in Dec. 1991. The autonomous status of the region was meanwhile abolished by the Azerbaijan Supreme Soviet in Nov. 1991, and the capital renamed Khankendi. A presidential decree of Jan. 1992 placed the region under direct rule. Azeri-Armenian fighting for possession of the region culminated in its occupation by Armenia in 1993 (and the occupation of seven other Azerbaijani regions outside it), despite attempts at international mediation. Since May 1994 there has been a ceasefire. Negotiations on settlements are conducted within the OSCE Minsk Group. International pressure on Azerbaijan and Armenia to find a resolution to the conflict increased in 2005, following an OSCE fact-finding mission in the occupied provinces, but bilateral talks held in Aug. of that year proved to be inconclusive.

Area, 4,400 sq. km (1,700 sq. miles); population (Jan. 2003 est.), 146,000. Capital, Khankendi (Jan. 2003 est., 54,600). It is populated by Armenians (76·9% at the 1989 census) and Azerbaijanis (21·5%).

In presidential elections held on 11 Aug. 1997 the hard-line independence candidate Arkady Gukasyan received more than 89% of votes cast, and was sworn in on 8 Sept. He was re-elected on 11 Aug. 2002 with 88·4% of votes cast. Legislative elections were held on 19 June 2005. The Democratic Artsakh Party, which supports President Gukasyan, won 12 seats; the Free Motherland Party 10; ARF Dashnaktsutyun–Movement 88 Bloc 3; and ind. 8. The *Prime Minister* is Anushavan Danielyan.

Main industries are silk, wine, dairying and building materials. Crop area is 67,200 ha.; cotton, grapes and winter wheat are grown. There are 33 collective and 38 state farms.

In 1989–90, 34,200 pupils were studying in primary and secondary schools, 2,400 in colleges and 2,100 in higher educational institutions.

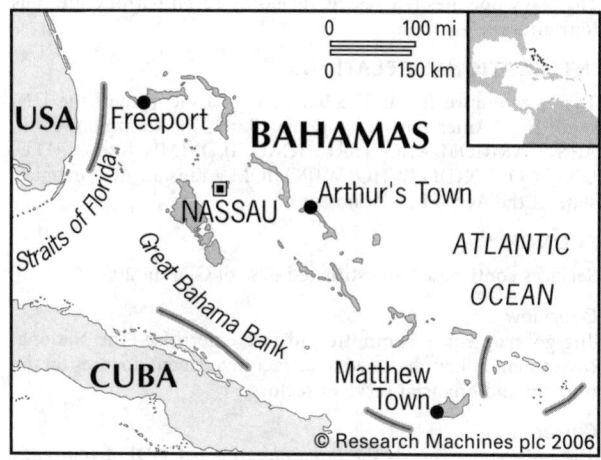

	Area (in sq. km)	Population
Harbour Island	8	1,639
Spanish Wells	26	1,527
San Salvador	163	970
Inagua	1,551	969
Berry Islands	31	709
Acklins	497	428
Crooked Island	241	350
Mayaguana	285	259
Rum Cay	78	80
Ragged Island	36	72

Total census population for 2000 was 303,611 (155,833 females). The estimated population in 2005 was 323,000.

The UN gives a projected population for 2010 of 344,000.

In 2003, 89·4% of the population were urban. The capital is Nassau on New Providence Island (210,832 in 2000); the other large town is Freeport (46,994 in 2000) on Grand Bahama.

English is the official language. Creole is spoken among Haitian immigrants.

SOCIAL STATISTICS

2003: births, 5,054; deaths, 1,649. Rates, 2003 (per 1,000 population): birth, 16·0; death, 5·2; infant mortality (per 1,000 live births), 2003, 17·2. Expectation of life was 66·5 years for males and 73·0 years for females in 2003. Annual population growth rate, 1992–2003, 1·9%; fertility rate, 2003, 1·9 children per woman.

CLIMATE

Winters are mild and summers pleasantly warm. Most rain falls in May, June, Sept. and Oct., and thunderstorms are frequent in summer. Rainfall amounts vary over the islands from 30" (750 mm) to 60" (1,500 mm). Nassau, Jan. 71°F (21·7°C), July 81°F (27·2°C). Annual rainfall 47" (1,179 mm).

CONSTITUTION AND GOVERNMENT

The Commonwealth of The Bahamas is a free and democratic sovereign state. Executive power rests with Her Majesty the Queen, who appoints a Governor-General to represent her, advised by a Cabinet whom he appoints. There is a bicameral legislature. The *Senate* comprises 16 members all appointed by the Governor-General for five-year terms, nine on the advice of the Prime Minister, four on the advice of the Leader of the Opposition, and three after consultation with both of them. The *House of Assembly* consists of 40 members elected from single-member constituencies for a maximum term of five years.

National Anthem

'Lift up your head to the rising sun, Bahamaland'; words and tune by T. Gibson.

RECENT ELECTIONS

In parliamentary elections held on 2 May 2002 the Progressive Liberal Party (PLP) won 50·8% of votes cast and 29 out of 40 seats, the Free National Movement (FNM) 41·1% (7) and ind. 5·2% (4). Turnout was 82·4%.

CURRENT ADMINISTRATION

Governor-General: Arthur Dion Hanna; b. 1928 (sworn in 1 Feb. 2006).

In March 2006 the cabinet was composed as follows:

Prime Minister and Minister of Finance: Perry Gladstone Christie; b. 1943 (PLP; sworn in 3 May 2002).

Commonwealth of The Bahamas

Capital: Nassau
Population projection, 2010: 344,000
GDP per capita, 2000: (PPP$) 17,012
HDI/world rank: 0·832/50

KEY HISTORICAL EVENTS

First inhabited in the 9th century by the Lucayans, a branch of the Arawaks, the Bahamas received their name 'Baja Mar' (low sea) from Christopher Columbus who landed on San Salvador in 1492. Colonized by English puritans from Bermuda during the 17th century, the Bahamas were later plagued by notorious pirates such as Blackbeard, until they were driven out by Governor Woodes Rogers in 1718. The Bahamas played an important part in the American Civil War—blockaded by the Union navy in 1861, the islanders traded Confederate cotton with Britain and supplied military equipment to the Confederacy. During Prohibition the Bahamas prospered as a rum-smuggling base but experienced a severe economic downturn when the Prohibition law was repealed in 1933. An important Atlantic base during WWII, the tourist industry benefited greatly from Cuba's closure to western visitors in the 1950s. Internal self-government with cabinet responsibility was introduced on 7 Jan. 1964 and full independence achieved on 10 July 1973.

TERRITORY AND POPULATION

The Commonwealth of The Bahamas consists of over 700 islands and inhabited cays off the southeast coast of Florida extending for about 260,000 sq. miles. Only 22 islands are inhabited. Land area, 5,382 sq. miles (13,939 sq. km).

The areas and populations of the 19 divisions used for the most recent census in 2000 were as follows:

	Area (in sq. km)	Population
New Providence	207	210,832
Grand Bahama	1,373	46,994
Abaco	1,681	13,170
Eleuthera	484	7,999
Andros	5,954	7,686
Exuma and Cays	290	3,571
Long Island	596	2,992
Biminis	23	1,717
Cat Island	388	1,647

Deputy Prime Minister and Minister of National Security: Cynthia Pratt. *Agriculture and Marine Resources:* Leslie Miller. *Local Government and Consumer Affairs:* Alfred Gray. *Transportation and Aviation:* Glenys Hanna-Martin. *Foreign Affairs and Public Service:* Fred Mitchell. *Education, Science and Technology:* Alfred Sears. *Financial Services and Investments:* Vincent Peet. *Energy and Environment:* Marcus Bethel. *Works and Utilities:* Bradley Roberts. *Immigration, Labour and Training:* Shane Gibson. *Social Services and Community Development:* Melanie Griffin. *Trade and Industry:* Leslie Miller. *Youth, Sports and Housing:* Neville Wisdom. *Tourism:* Obie Wilchcombe. *Health and National Insurance:* Bernard Nottage. *Legal Affairs and Attorney General:* Allyson Maynard-Gibson.

Office of the Prime Minister: http://www.bahamas.gov.bs

CURRENT LEADERS

Perry Christie

Position
Prime Minister

Introduction
The Bahamas' third prime minister since independence, Perry Gladstone Christie took office in 2002, ending a decade of political dominance by the Free National Movement. His principal aims are to improve the nation's economy and to fight crime and corruption.

Early Life
Perry Gladstone Christie was born in Nassau on 21 Aug. 1943. He was schooled in New Providence before moving to the UK, graduating from Birmingham University in 1969 before being called to the Bar in London at Inner Temple. A talented athlete, he represented the Bahamas in the triple jump at the 1962 Central American and Caribbean Games.

Christie was appointed a senator in Nov. 1974 by Prime Minister Lynden Pindling. He served until June 1977 and in Jan. 1977 was made head of the national gaming board.

Christie stood successfully as the Progressive Liberal Party (PLP) candidate for the Centreville constituency at the general elections of 1977 and was subsequently named minister of health and national insurance. Following the 1982 election he took over the tourism portfolio but left the government two years later amid allegations that several of his party colleagues had taken bribes. He reclaimed his seat in 1987 as an independent but returned to the PLP in March 1990 as minister for agriculture, trade and industry.

At the general election of 1992 the PLP lost power for the first time since independence, giving way to the Free National Movement. In Jan. 1993 Christie was elected PLP deputy leader. He was selected as leader of the PLP in April 1997, succeeding Pindling, and led the party to a landslide victory at the polls in May 2002.

Career in Office
Christie has promised to encourage foreign investment and to introduce a public integrity bill in an on-going fight against corruption in public life. Illegal immigration and drug trafficking remain serious problems for his government.

In Sept. 2004 Hurricanes Frances and Jeanne wreaked damage on the country. In May 2005 it was announced that Christie had suffered a minor stroke.

DEFENCE

The Royal Bahamian Defence Force is a primarily maritime force tasked with naval patrols and protection duties in the extensive waters of the archipelago. Personnel in 2004 numbered 1,022 (including 166 women), and the base is at Coral Harbour on New Providence Island.

In 2004 defence expenditure totalled US$34·3m. (US$108 per capita), representing 0·8% of GDP.

Navy
The Navy operates ten vessels including seven patrol craft, plus four aircraft.

INTERNATIONAL RELATIONS

The Commonwealth of The Bahamas is a member of the UN, OAS, Inter-American Development Bank, the Commonwealth, ACS, CARICOM, FAO, IBRD, ICAO, ILO, IMF, Intelsat, ITU, UNESCO, UNIDO, WHO, WIPO, IOM and is an ACP member state of the ACP-EU relationship.

ECONOMY

Services contributed an estimated 92% of GDP in 2003.

Overview
The government is committed to free enterprise. The National Investment Policy, designed to attract investment, focuses on the tourism and financial services sectors.

Currency
The unit of currency is the *Bahamian dollar* (BSD) of 100 *cents*. American currency is generally accepted. Inflation was 3·0% in 2003 and 0·9% in 2004. Foreign exchange reserves were US$461m. in June 2002 and total money supply was B$812m.

Budget
Government revenue and expenditure (in B$1m.):

	2000	2001	2002	2003	2004
Revenue	958·0	857·0	902·0	944·0	1,052·0
Expenditure	933·0	1,000·3	1,047·0	1,075·0	1,185·0

The main sources of revenue are import duties, stamp duty from land sales, work permits and residence fees, and accommodation tax. There is no direct taxation.

Performance
The Bahamas experienced a recession during the period 1988–94; this was mainly owing to the recession in the USA leading to a fall in the number of American tourists. The economy has been growing since, and there are continuing efforts to diversify. Freeport's tax-free status was extended by 25 years in 1995, and import duties were reduced in the 1996–97 budget.

Real GDP growth was 1·9% in 2003 and 3·0% in 2004. Total GDP in 2004 was US$4·3bn.

Banking and Finance
The Central Bank of The Bahamas was established in 1974. Its *Governor* is Wendy Craigg. The Bahamas is an important centre for offshore banking. Financial business produced 11·3% of GDP in 2004. In 2004, 259 banks and trust companies were licensed, about half being branches of foreign companies. Leading Bahamian-based banks include The Bank of Bahamas Ltd, The Commonwealth Bank Ltd and Private Investment Bank Ltd. There is also a Development Bank.

A stock exchange, the Bahamas International Securities Exchange (BISX) based in Nassau, was inaugurated in May 2000.

Weights and Measures
The Bahamas follows the USA in using linear, dry and liquid measures.

ENERGY AND NATURAL RESOURCES

Environment
The carbon dioxide emissions of the Bahamas from the consumption and flaring of fossil fuels were the equivalent of 10·9 tonnes per capita in 2002.

Electricity

In 2000 installed capacity was 0·4m. kW, all thermal. Output in 2000 was approximately 1·66bn. kWh; consumption per capita in 2000 was an estimated 5,479 kWh.

Oil and Gas

The Bahamas does not have reserves of either oil or gas, but oil is refined in the Bahamas. The Bahamas Oil Refining Company (BORCO), in Grand Bahama, operates as a terminal which trans-ships, stores and blends oil.

Minerals

Aragonite is extracted from the seabed.

Agriculture

In 2001 there were some 8,000 ha. of arable land and 4,000 ha. of permanent crops. Production (in 1,000 tonnes), 2000: sugarcane, 45; fruit, 22 (notably grapefruit, lemons and limes); vegetables, 21.

Livestock (2000): cattle, 1,000; sheep, 6,000; goats, 15,000; pigs, 6,000; chickens, 5m.

Forestry

In 2000 forests covered 842,000 ha. or 84·1% of the total land area. Timber production in 2001 was 17,000 cu. metres.

Fisheries

The estimated total catch in 2004 amounted to 5,128 tonnes, mainly lobsters, and exclusively from sea fishing. Total value in 2004 of fish landings was B$84·7m

INDUSTRY

Tourism and offshore banking are the main industries. Two industrial sites, one in New Providence and the other in Grand Bahama, have been developed as part of an industrialization programme. The main products are pharmaceutical chemicals, salt and rum.

Labour

A total of 176,330 persons were in employment in April 2004 (excluding armed forces). The main areas of activity were: wholesale and retail trade, restaurants and hotels, 32%; community, social and personal services, 30%; construction, 11%; financing, insurance, real estate and business services, 11%. Unemployment was 10·2% in 2004.

Trade Unions

In 2004 there were 34 unions, the largest being The Bahamas Hotel, Catering and Allied Workers' Union (6,000 members).

INTERNATIONAL TRADE

Public-sector foreign debt was US$289,837 in Dec. 2004. There is a free trade zone on Grand Bahama. Although a member of CARICOM, the Bahamas is not a signatory to its trade protocol.

Imports and Exports

Imports and exports for calendar years in US$1m.:

	2000	2001	2002	2003	2004
Imports f.o.b.	2,133	2,040	1,838	1,874	1,977
Exports f.o.b.	444	370	389	365	401

In 2004 the principal imports were (in US$1m.): machinery and transport equipment, 422; food and live animals, 310; and manufactured goods, 299. The principal exports were (in US$1m.): chemicals, 109; food and live animals, 90; and crude materials except fuels, 64. In 2004 the USA was the source of 86% of imports; the main export markets were USA (76%) and France (9%).

COMMUNICATIONS

Roads

There were about 2,717 km of roads in 2002 (57·4% paved). In 2002 there were around 112,900 passenger cars and 19,200 lorries and vans.

Civil Aviation

There are international airports at Nassau and Freeport (Grand Bahama Island). The national carrier is the state-owned Bahamasair, which in 2003 flew to Fort Lauderdale, Miami, Orlando and the Turks and Caicos Islands, as well as providing services between different parts of the Bahamas. There were direct flights in 2003 with other airlines to Atlanta, Baltimore, Boston, Charlotte, Cincinnati, Cleveland, Daytona Beach, Detroit, Hartford, Havana, Houston, Key West, Kingston, London, Manchester, Melbourne, Milwaukee, Montreal, New York, Philadelphia, Pittsburgh, Raleigh, Richmond, Rochester, Salt Lake City, San Diego, Tampa, Trinidad, Toronto, Washington, D.C. and West Palm Beach. In 1999 scheduled airline traffic of Bahamas-based carriers flew 6·8m. km, carrying 1,719,000 passengers (944,000 on international flights).

Shipping

The Bahamas' shipping registry consisted of a fleet of 35·6m. GRT in 2004, a figure exceeded only by the fleets of Panama and Liberia. There were 1,400 vessels in 2004, including 258 tankers.

Telecommunications

New Providence and most of the other major islands have automatic telephone systems in operation, interconnected by a radio network, while local distribution within the islands is by overhead and underground cables. In 2004 there were 134,000 telephone subscribers, or 441·3 per 1,000 inhabitants. International telecommunications service is provided by a submarine cable system to Florida, USA, and an INTELSAT Standard 'A' Earth Station and a Standard 'F2' Earth Station. International operator-assisted and direct dialling telephone services are available to all major countries. There is a packet switching system for data transmission, and land mobile and marine telephone services. There were 110,000 mobile phone subscribers and approximately 90,000 GSM cellular subscribers in 2004 and 500 fax machines in 1995. There were 60,000 Internet users in 2002.

Postal Services

In 2004 there were 158 post offices.

SOCIAL INSTITUTIONS

Justice

English Common Law is the basis of the Bahamian judicial system, although there is a large volume of Bahamian Statute Law. The highest tribunal in the country is the Court of Appeal. New Providence has 14 Magistrates' Courts, Grand Bahama has three and Abaco one.

The strength of the police force (2004) was 3,352 officers.

There were 44 murders in 2004 (a rate of 14·5 per 100,000 population). The death penalty is in force, the most recent execution being carried out in Jan. 2000. The population in penal institutions in Oct. 2004 was 1,515 (470 per 100,000 of national population).

Education

Education is compulsory between five and 16 years of age. The adult literacy rate in 2001 was 95·5% (94·6% among males and 96·3% among females). In 2004 there were 188 schools (30 independent). In 2004–05 there were 62,110 pupils with 1,365 teachers in primary schools and 26,185 pupils with 1,792 teachers in secondary education. Courses lead to The

Bahamas General Certificate of Secondary Education (BGCSE). Independent schools provide education at primary, secondary and high school levels.

The four institutions offering higher education are: the government-sponsored College of The Bahamas, established in 1974; the University of the West Indies (regional), affiliated with the Bahamas since 1960; The Bahamas Hotel Training College, sponsored by the Ministry of Education and the hotel industry; and The Bahamas Technical and Vocational Institute, established to provide basic skills. Several schools of continuing education offer secretarial and academic courses.

Health

In 2003 there was a government general hospital (423 beds) and a psychiatric/geriatric care centre (515 beds) in Nassau, and a hospital in Freeport (88 beds). The Family Islands, comprising 33 health districts, had 21 health centres and 66 main clinics in 2003. There were two private hospitals (495 beds) in New Providence in 2003. In 2004 there were 720 physicians, 76 dentists and 1,323 nurses.

Welfare

Social Services are provided by the Department of Social Services, a government agency which grants assistance to restore, reinforce and enhance the capacity of the individual to perform life tasks, and to provide for the protection of children in the Bahamas.

The Department's divisions include: community support services, child welfare, family services, senior citizens, disability affairs, Family Island and research planning, training and community relations.

RELIGION

In 2001, 44% of the population were Protestant, 16% Roman Catholic, 10% Anglican and the remainder other religions.

CULTURE

Broadcasting

The Broadcasting Corporation of the Bahamas is a government-owned company which operates five radio broadcasting stations and a TV service with one channel, ZNS TV 13. In 2004, five independent radio stations were operating. There were 303,000 television receivers in 2004 and 215,000 radio receivers in 2000. TV colour is by NTSC. There is cable TV on Grand Bahama, New Providence and the majority of the Family Islands.

Press

There were three national dailies and one weekly in 2004.

Tourism

Tourism is the most important industry, accounting for about 70% of GDP. In 2003 there were 1,510,169 non-resident air arrivals and in 2004 there were 3,360,012 cruise ship visitors. Tourist expenditure was US$1,884m. in 2004.

Festivals

Junkanoo is the quintessential Bahamian celebration, a parade or 'rush-out', characterized by colourful costumes, goatskin drums, cowbells, horns and a brass section. It is staged in the early hours of 26 Dec. and the early hours of 1 Jan.

Libraries

There were 32 libraries in the Bahamas in 2004.

Theatre and Opera

The Bahamas had one National Theatre in 2004, the Dundas Centre for the Performing Arts.

Museums and Galleries

In 2004 there were four museums and 13 art galleries.

DIPLOMATIC REPRESENTATIVES

Of the Bahamas in the United Kingdom (10 Chesterfield St., London, W1J 5JL)
High Commissioner: Basil G. O'Brien, CMG.

Of the United Kingdom in the Bahamas
High Commissioner: Jeremy Cresswell (resides in Kingston, Jamaica).

Of the Bahamas in the USA (2220 Massachusetts Ave., NW, Washington, D.C., 20008)
Ambassador: Joshua Sears.

Of the USA in the Bahamas (Mosmar Bldg, Queen St., Nassau)
Ambassador: John Rood.

Of the Bahamas to the United Nations
Ambassador: Paulette Bethel.

Of the Bahamas to the European Union
Ambassador: Basil G. O'Brien, CMG.

FURTHER READING

Cash, P., *et al.*, *Making of Bahamian History.* London, 1991
Craton, M. and Saunders, G., *Islanders in the Stream: a History of the Bahamian People.* 2 vols. Univ. of Georgia Press, 1998

National Statistical Office: Department of Statistics, PO Box N-3904, Nassau.
Website: http://www.bahamas.gov.bs/statistics

BAHRAIN

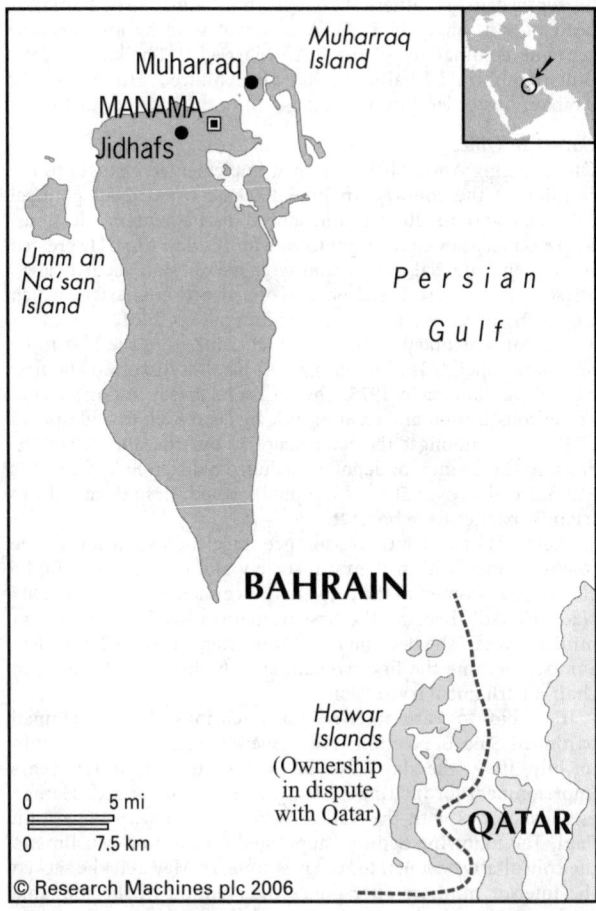

Al-Mamlaka Al-Bahrayn
(Kingdom of Bahrain)

Capital: Manama
Population projection, 2010: 791,000
GDP per capita, 2002: (PPP$) 17,170
HDI/world rank: 0·846/43

KEY HISTORICAL EVENTS

Bahrain was controlled by the Portuguese from 1521 until 1602. The Khalifa family gained control in 1783 and has ruled since that date. British assistance was sought to retain independence and from 1861 until 1971 Bahrain was in all but name a British protectorate. Bahrain declared its independence in 1971. Sheikh Isa bin Salman Al-Khalifa became the Amir. A constitution was ratified in June 1973 providing for a National Assembly of 30 members, popularly elected for a four-year term, together with all members of the cabinet (appointed by the Amir). However, in 1975 the National Assembly was dissolved and the Amir began ruling by decree. In 1987 the main island was joined to the Saudi mainland by a causeway. In Feb. 2002 Bahrain became a kingdom, with the Amir proclaiming himself king.

TERRITORY AND POPULATION

The Kingdom of Bahrain forms an archipelago of 36 low-lying islands in the Persian Gulf, between the Qatar peninsula and the mainland of Saudi Arabia. The total area is 720 sq. km.

The island of Bahrain (578 sq. km) is connected by a 2·4 km causeway to the second largest island, Muharraq to the northeast, and by a causeway with the island of Sitra to the east. A causeway links Bahrain with Saudi Arabia. From Sitra, oil pipelines and a causeway carrying a road extend out to sea for 4·8 km to a deep-water anchorage.

Total census population in 2001 was 650,604. Population (2003 est.) 689,418 (males, 396,278; females, 293,140), of which 427,955 were Bahraini and 261,463 non-Bahraini. The population density was 957 per sq. km in 2003. In 2003, 90·0% of the population were urban.

The UN gives a projected population for 2010 of 791,000.

There are 12 regions: Central, Eastern, Hamad Town, Hidd Town, Isa Town, Jidhafs, Manama, Muharraq, Northern, Rifa'a, Sitra, Western. Manama, the capital and commercial centre, had a 2001 census population of 143,035. Other towns (2001 census population) are Muharraq (91,307), Rifa'a (79,550), Hamad Town (52,718), Al-Ali (47,529) and Isa Town (36,833).

Arabic is the official language. English is widely used in business.

SOCIAL STATISTICS

Statistics 2002: births, 13,576 (Bahraini, 10,539); deaths, 2,035 (Bahraini, 1,672). Rates (per 1,000 population) in 2002: birth, 20·2; death, 3·0. Infant mortality (per 1,000 live births), 13 (2001). Life expectancy at birth, 2003, was 73·1 years for men and 75·9 years for women. Annual population growth rate, 1992–2002, 3·0%; fertility rate, 2001, 2·4 children per woman. In 2002 there were 4,909 marriages and 838 divorces.

The Shia make up 65% of the national population, half of whom are under 15.

CLIMATE

The climate is pleasantly warm between Dec. and March but from June to Sept. the conditions are very hot and humid. The period June to Nov. is virtually rainless. Bahrain, Jan. 66°F (19°C), July 97°F (36°C). Annual rainfall 5·2" (130 mm).

CONSTITUTION AND GOVERNMENT

The ruling family is the Al-Khalifa who have been in power since 1783.

The constitution changing Bahrain from an Emirate to a Kingdom dates from 14 Feb. 2002. The new constitutional hereditary monarchy has a bicameral legislature, inaugurated on 14 Dec. 2002. National elections for a legislative body took place on 24 and 31 Oct. 2002 (the first since the National Assembly was adjourned 27 years earlier). One chamber (*House of Deputies*) is a directly elected assembly while the second (upper) chamber, a *Shura* consultative council of experts, is appointed by the government. Both chambers have 40 members. All Bahraini citizens over the age of 21—men and women—are able to vote for the elected assembly. In the Oct. 2002 national elections women stood for office for the first time.

National Anthem

'Bahrain ona, baladolaman' ('Our Bahrain, secure as a country'); words by M. S. Ayyash, tune anonymous.

GOVERNMENT CHRONOLOGY

Heads of State since 1942.
Hakims
1942–61   Sheikh Salman bin Hamad Al-Khalifa
1961–71   Sheikh Isa bin Salman Al-Khalifa

Amirs
1971–99   Sheikh Isa bin Salman Al-Khalifa
1999–2002   Sheikh Hamad bin Isa Al-Khalifa

King
2002–   Sheikh Hamad bin Isa Al-Khalifa

RECENT ELECTIONS

On 24 and 31 Oct. 2002 the first national elections since Dec. 1973 were held. Despite a call from opposition parties for the election to be boycotted, turnout was over 50%. 21 out of 40 seats were won by secular candidates, with the remaining seats going to Sunni and Shia representatives. There were eight women among a total of 177 candidates running for the legislature, although males won all of the seats.

CURRENT ADMINISTRATION

The present king (formerly Amir), HH Sheikh Hamad bin Isa Al-Khalifa, KCMG (b. 1950), succeeded on 6 March 1999 and became king on 14 Feb. 2002.

In March 2006 the cabinet was composed as follows:

Prime Minister: Sheikh Khalifa bin Salman Al-Khalifa; b. 1936. He is currently the longest-serving prime minister of any sovereign country, having been Bahrain's prime minister since it became independent in Aug. 1971.

Deputy Prime Minister and Minister of Islamic Affairs: Sheikh Abdullah bin Khalid Al-Khalifa. *Deputy Prime Minister and Minister of Transportation and Communication:* Sheikh Ali bin Khalifa Al-Khalifa. *Deputy Prime Minister for Ministry Committees' Affairs:* Sheikh Mohammed bin Mubarak Al-Khalifa.

Minister of Defence: Sheikh Khalifa bin Ahmed Al-Khalifa. *Education:* Majid Ali Al-Nuaymi. *Electricity and Water:* Sheikh Abdulla bin Salman Al-Khalifa. *Finance:* Sheikh Ahmad bin Muhammad Al-Khalifa. *Foreign Affairs:* Sheikh Khalid bin Ahmed bin Mohammed Al-Khalifa. *Health:* Nada Abbas Haffadh. *Industry and Commerce:* Dr Hassan bin Abdullah Fakhro. *Information:* Dr Mohammed Abd Al-Ghaffar. *Interior:* Gen. Rashed bin Abdullah bin Ahmed Al-Khalifa. *Justice:* Dr Mohammed Ali bin Al-Shaikh Mansoor Al-Sitri. *Labour:* Dr Majeed bin Mohsin Al-Alawi. *Municipalities and Agriculture:* Ali Saleh Al-Saleh. *Prime Minister's Court:* Sheikh Khalid bin Abdulla Al-Khalifa. *Social Affairs:* Dr Fatima Ahmed Al-Beloushi. *Works and Housing:* Fahmi bin Ali Al-Jowdar.

Government Website (Arabic only): http://www.bahrain.gov.bh

CURRENT LEADERS

HH Sheikh Hamad bin Isa Al-Khalifa

Position
King

Introduction
HH Sheikh Hamad bin Isa Al-Khalifa became Amir in March 1999. In Feb. 2001 his 'national action charter', encompassing a broad range of reforms, was approved by popular referendum. The state became a kingdom and Sheikh Hamad's title was changed to King. The king is the supreme authority in Bahrain, with members of the ruling family holding the majority of senior political and military positions.

Early Life
Sheikh Hamad bin Isa Al-Khalifa was born on 28 Jan. 1950 in Ar-Rifa', Bahrain. He was educated at Cambridge University in the UK before pursuing a military career. He attended Mons Officer Cadet School in Aldershot, UK, and continued his military training at the US Army Command and Staff College in Fort Leavenworth, Kansas. In 1968 Sheikh Hamad founded the Bahrain Defence Force (BDF) and served as the minister of defence from 1971–88. In Feb. 1979 he was awarded the British Knight of the Order of St Michael and St George.

Bahrain has been headed by the Al-Khalifa family since 1783 and Sheikh Hamad was crown prince from 1964 until he succeeded his father, Sheikh Isa bin Salman Al-Khalifa, as head of state in early 1999. As head of state he also became supreme commander of the BDF. Married to Sheikha Sabeeka Bint Ebrahim Al-Khalifa, he has four children. His interest in Arabian horses led him to establish the Amiri Stables in 1977.

Career in Office
On becoming Amir, Sheikh Hamad implemented changes to the running of the country. In June 1999 he released all political prisoners and in 2002 re-introduced parliamentary elections, with women granted the right to vote for the first time. He created the supreme judicial council and scrapped old state security laws. These reforms were based on a 'national action charter', which won 98% favour in a public referendum in Feb. 2001.

The parliamentary elections of Oct. 2002 were the first to be held since Sheikh Isa bin Salman Al-Khalifa dissolved the first elected parliament in 1975. Sheikh Isa's subsequent suspension of the constitution and ensuing rule by decree led to widespread civil unrest amongst the Shia majority but the 2002 elections ensured the council of deputies included a dozen Shia MPs. It is estimated that over 50% of the public voted, despite calls from Islamist parties for a boycott.

Sheikh Hamad continues to encourage the expansion of the role of women within Bahraini society and politics. In 2000 he elected four women to the consultative council and in April 2004 Nada Haffadh became the first woman to head a government ministry when she became health minister. In April 2005 Alees Samoan became the first woman, and the first non-Muslim, to chair a parliamentary session.

In a bid to ease inter-religious tensions, Sheikh Hamad pardoned Shia opposition leader Sheikh Abdel Amir al-Jamin in July 1999, the day after he was sentenced to ten years imprisonment for inciting hostility. In Jan. 2000 Sheikh Hamad established ties with the Vatican when he met with Pope John Paul. The following Sept. he appointed several non-Muslims to the consultative council for the first time. In May 2004 he sacked the interior minister after police intervention in the Manama rioting of Shias against the Iraqi war led to violence and injuries to at least 20 civilians.

In March 2001 the international court of justice settled Bahrain's territorial dispute with Qatar over the Hawar Islands, declaring them the property of Bahrain. Sheikh Hamad subsequently invited international companies to drill for oil there. In Sept. 2004 Bahrain signed a free trade pact with the USA.

Despite widespread public support for the King and his government reforms, thousands attended marches in 2005 to demand a fully elected government.

DEFENCE

The Crown Prince is C.-in-C. of the armed forces. An agreement with the USA in Oct. 1991 gave port facilities to the US Navy and provided for mutual manoeuvres.

Military expenditure totalled US$314m. in 2002 (US$435 per capita), representing 4·0% of GDP.

Army

The Army consists of one armoured brigade, one infantry brigade, one artillery brigade, one special forces battalion and one air defence battalion. Personnel, 2002, 8,500. In addition there is a National Guard of approximately 900 and a paramilitary police force of 9,000.

Navy

The Naval force based at Mina Sulman numbered 1,000 in 2002.

Air Force

Personnel (2002), 1,200. Equipment includes 30 combat aircraft and 40 armed helicopters.

INTERNATIONAL RELATIONS

Bahrain is a member of the UN, WTO, the League of Arab States, the Gulf Co-operation Council, OAPEC (Organization of Arab Petroleum Exporting Countries), OIC and Islamic Development Bank.

In March 2001 the International Court of Justice ruled on a long-standing dispute between Bahrain and Qatar over the boundary between the two countries and ownership of certain islands. Both countries accepted the decision.

ECONOMY

In 2002 industry accounted for 42·8% of GDP and services 56·6%.

Currency

The unit of currency is the *Bahraini dinar* (BHD), divided into 1,000 *fils*. In June 2002 foreign exchange reserves were US$1,675m., total money supply was BD602m. and gold reserves were 150,000 troy oz. Inflation was 1·6% in 2003 and 4·9% in 2004, following five years of deflation.

In 2001 the six Gulf Arab states—Bahrain, along with Kuwait, Oman, Qatar, Saudi Arabia and the United Arab Emirates—signed an agreement to establish a single currency by 2010.

Budget

Budgetary central government revenue and expenditure (in BD1m.):

	2001	2002	2003
Revenue	929·9	972·9	1,089·8
Expenditure	703·4	836·2	868·9

Performance

Total GDP in 2001 was US$7·9bn. Real GDP growth was 7·2% in 2003 and 5·4% in 2004.

Banking and Finance

The Bahrain Monetary Agency (*Governor*, Rasheed Mohammed Al Maraj) has central banking powers. In 2001 Bahrain had 51 offshore banking units. Offshore banking units may not engage in local business; their assets totalled US$62,503m. in March 1996. In 2001 there were six locally incorporated commercial banks, ten foreign commercial banks and two specialized financial institutions. There were also several investment banks.

There is a stock exchange in Manama linked with those of Kuwait and Oman.

ENERGY AND NATURAL RESOURCES

Environment

Bahrain's carbon dioxide emissions from the consumption and flaring of fossil fuels in 2002 were the equivalent of 33·1 tonnes per capita, among the highest in the world.

Electricity

In 2000 installed capacity was 1·4m. kW; about 6·30bn. kWh were produced in 2000. Electricity consumption per capita was an estimated 9,113 kWh in 2000.

Oil and Gas

In 1931 oil was discovered. Operations were at first conducted by the Bahrain Petroleum Co. (BAPCO) under concession. In 1975 the government assumed a 60% interest in the oilfield and related crude oil facilities of BAPCO. Oil reserves in 2002 were 125m. bbls. Production (2000) was 1·9m. tonnes. Refinery distillation output amounted to 12·7m. tonnes in 2000.

There were known natural gas reserves of 91bn. cu. metres in 2002. Production in 2002 was 9·2bn. cu. metres. Gas reserves are government-owned.

Water

Water is obtained from artesian wells and desalination plants and there is a piped supply to Manama, Muharraq, Isa Town, Rifa'a and most villages.

Minerals

Aluminium is Bahrain's oldest major industry after oil and gas; production in 2001 was 522,000 tonnes.

Agriculture

In 2001 there were 2,000 ha. of arable land and 4,000 ha. of permanent crops. There are about 900 farms and smallholdings (average 2·5 ha.) operated by about 2,500 farmers who produce a wide variety of fruits (22,000 tonnes in 2000) including dates (17,000 tonnes). In 2000 an estimated 12,000 tonnes of vegetables were produced. The major crop is alfalfa for animal fodder.

Livestock (2000): cattle, 11,000; camels, 1,000; sheep, 18,000; goats, 16,000.

In 2000 an estimated 5,000 tonnes of lamb and mutton, 5,000 tonnes of poultry meat, 3,000 tonnes of eggs and 14,000 tonnes of fresh milk were produced. Agriculture contributed 0·6% of GDP in 2003.

Fisheries

The total catch in 2001 was 11,230 tonnes, exclusively from sea fishing.

INDUSTRY

Industry is being developed with foreign participation: aluminium smelting (and ancillary industries), shipbuilding and repair, petrochemicals, electronics assembly and light industry.

Traditional crafts include boatbuilding, weaving and pottery.

Labour

The workforce (estimate 2003) was 328,865 of which 136,215 were Bahraini. There were 16,965 unemployed persons in 2001.

Trade Unions

Trade unions have been permitted since 2002; all unions belong to the General Federation of Workers Trade Unions in Bahrain (GFWTUB).

INTERNATIONAL TRADE

Totally foreign-owned companies have been permitted to register since 1991.

Bahrain, along with Kuwait, Oman, Qatar, Saudi Arabia and the United Arab Emirates began the implementation of a customs union in Jan. 2003.

Imports and Exports

In 2002 imports (f.o.b.) totalled US$4,672·9m. and exports (f.o.b.) US$5,785·6m. In 1999 mineral fuels and related materials made up 35% of imports and 62% of exports. In 1999 the main import sources were Australia, Saudi Arabia, USA and UK; the main export markets were Saudi Arabia, USA and India.

COMMUNICATIONS

Roads

A 25-km causeway links Bahrain with Saudi Arabia. In 2002 there were 3,459 km of roads (76·7% paved), including 428 km of main roads and 474 km of secondary roads. Bahrain has one of the densest road networks in the world. In 2002 there were 249,121 vehicles in use, including 206,544 passenger cars (307·3 per 1,000 inhabitants). In 2000 there were 1,656 road accidents resulting in 53 deaths.

Civil Aviation

Bahrain has a 25% share (with Oman, Qatar and UAE) in Gulf Air. In 2001 Bahrain International Airport handled 3·44m. passengers (all on international flights) and 152,100 tonnes of freight. In 1999 scheduled airline traffic of Bahrain-based carriers flew 20·8m. km, carrying 1,307,000 passengers (all on international flights).

Shipping

In 2002 the merchant fleet totalled 288,000 GRT, including oil tankers 81,000 GRT. The port of Mina Sulman is a free transit and industrial area; about 800 vessels are handled annually.

Telecommunications

The telecommunications industry was fully liberalized on 1 July 2004. In 2002 there were 564,400 telephone subscribers (846·4 per 1,000 inhabitants) and 107,000 PCs were in use (160·4 for every 1,000 persons). There were 389,000 mobile phone subscribers in 2002 and 4,400 fax machines. Bahrain had 165,000 Internet users in 2002.

Postal Services

There were 13 post offices in 2003.

SOCIAL INSTITUTIONS

Justice

The new constitution which came into force in Feb. 2002 includes the creation of an independent judiciary. The State Security Law and the State Security Court were both abolished in the lead-up to the change to a constitutional monarchy.

The population in penal institutions in Dec. 1997 was 911 (155 per 100,000 of national population).

Education

Adult literacy was 87·7% in 2003 (male, 92·5%; female, 83·0%). Government schools provide free education from primary to technical college level. Schooling is in three stages: primary (six years), intermediate (three years) and secondary (three years). Secondary education may be general or specialized. In 2000–01 there were 62,917 primary school pupils, 28,972 intermediate school pupils and 23,366 secondary school pupils; there were a total of 192 schools and 7,128 teachers in 2000–01. There was also one religious institute with 460 male students and 44 teachers.

In the private sector there were 42 schools with 25,128 pupils and 1,789 teachers in 2000–01.

There were seven universities (2002–03) with 38,364 students in attendance; and 3,047 persons attending adult education centres.

In 2000–01 total expenditure on education came to 3·1% of GNP and 11·4% of total government spending.

Health

There is a free medical service for all residents. In 2003 there were 1,295 physicians, 186 dentists, 3,156 nurses and 158 pharmacists. In 2003 there were ten general hospitals (four government; six private), 21 health centres and five maternity hospitals.

Welfare

In 1976 a pensions, sickness benefits and unemployment, maternity and family allowances scheme was established. Employers contribute 7% of salaries and Bahraini employees 11%. In 1994, 36,612 persons received state benefit payments totalling BD3,715,158. A total of BD5,975,700 was paid out to pensioners, and BD306,600 to recipients of social insurance.

RELIGION

Islam is the state religion. In 2001, 87% of the population were Muslim (65% Shia and 22% Sunni). There are also Christian, Jewish, Bahai, Hindu and Parsee minorities.

CULTURE

World Heritage Sites

In 2005 Qal'at al-Bahrain archaelogical site was added to the UNESCO World Heritage List. The site is an area of human occupation from about 2,300 BC to the 16th century. It is now a site of major excavation.

Broadcasting

Radio Bahrain is government-controlled, Bahrain Television part-commercial. In 1997 there were 338,000 radio receivers and in 2001 there were 280,000 TV receivers (colour by PAL).

In 1998 there were six television channels—two in English and four in Arabic—as well as a satellite channel.

Cinema

There were six cinemas in 2002; the total attendance was 1,207,520.

Press

There were five daily newspapers in 2003. In 1996 the daily newspapers had a combined circulation of 67,000, at a rate of 117 per 1,000 inhabitants.

Tourism

In 2002 there were 3,167,000 foreign tourists, spending US$741m. In 2003 there were 90 hotels with 6,788 rooms.

Libraries

In 2003 there were ten public libraries; a total of 190,756 books were borrowed in that year.

DIPLOMATIC REPRESENTATIVES

Of Bahrain in the United Kingdom (30 Belgrave Square, London, SW1X 8QB)
Ambassador: Vacant.
Chargé d'Affaires a.i.: Yusuf Jameel.

Of the United Kingdom in Bahrain (21 Government Ave., Manama 306, PO Box 114, Bahrain)
Ambassador: Robin Lamb.

Of Bahrain in the USA (3502 International Dr., NW, Washington, D.C., 20008)
Ambassador: Naser Al Belooshi.

Of the USA in Bahrain (Building No. 979, Road No. 3119, Block 331, Zinj District, Manama)
Ambassador: William T. Monroe.

Of Bahrain to the United Nations
Ambassador: Tawfeeq Ahmed Khalil Almansoor.

Of Bahrain to the European Union
Ambassador: Haya bint Rashid Al-Khalifa.

FURTHER READING

Bahrain Monetary Authority. *Quarterly Statistical Bulletin.*
Central Statistics Organization. *Statistical Abstract.* Annual

Al-Khalifa, A. and Rice, M. (eds.) *Bahrain through the Ages.* London, 1993
Al-Khalifa, H. bin I., *First Light: Modern Bahrain and its Heritage.* London, 1995

National Statistical Office: Central Statistics Organization, Council of Ministers, Manama.

BANGLADESH

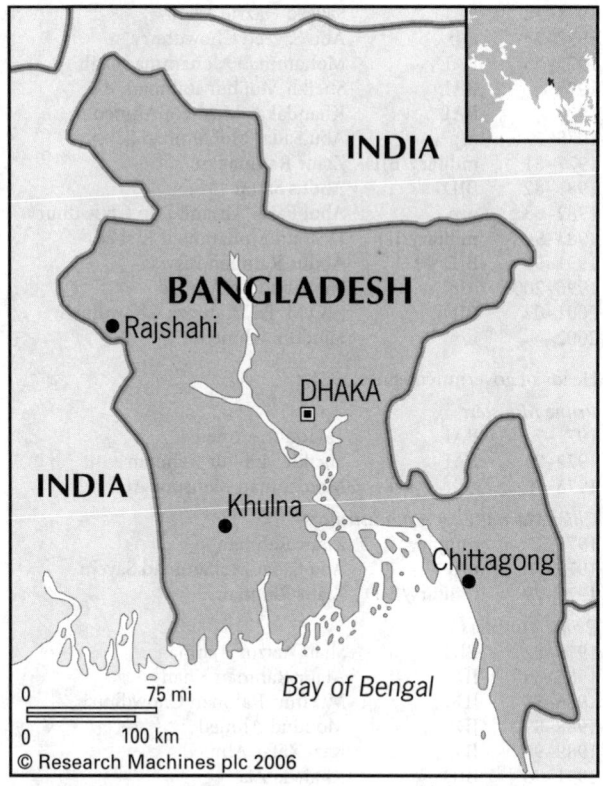

0   75 mi
0   100 km
© Research Machines plc 2006

Gana Prajatantri Bangladesh
(People's Republic of Bangladesh)

Capital: Dhaka
Population projection, 2010: 154·96m.
GDP per capita, 2003: (PPP$) 1,770
HDI/world rank: 0·520/139

KEY HISTORICAL EVENTS

India's Maurya Empire established Buddhism in Bengal (*Bangla*) in the 3rd century BC. The Buddhist Pala Dynasty ruled Bengal and Bihar independently from 750 AD, exporting Buddhism to Tibet. Hinduism regained dominance under the Sena Dynasty in the 11th century until the Muslim invasions in 1203–04. Rule from Delhi was broken in the 14th century by local Bengali kings. The Afghan adventurer Sher Shah conquered Bengal in 1539 and defeated the Mughal Emperor Humayun, creating an extensive administrative empire in North India. However, Mughal power was re-established by Akbar in 1576.

The Portuguese arrived in the 15th century, drawn to the rich Bengali cotton trade. They were followed by the Dutch and the British, whose East India Company was centred at Calcutta. The Nawab of Bengal was defeated by Robert Clive's army at the Battle of Plassey in 1757. British rule was maintained through the mainly Hindu *zamindar* land-owners and the Company was replaced by the Crown in 1858.

The partition of Bengal in 1905 was an attempt to undermine the nationalist influence of the *bhadralok*, the Hindu middle-classes, by forming a Muslim-dominated eastern province. Religious violence increased and political interests were represented by newly formed parties, including the All-India Muslim League. The partition was reversed in 1912. Tensions between the Muslim and Hindu communities escalated in the 1930s. The League suffered electoral defeat in 1936 but calls for a Muslim state were strengthened by the Pakistan Resolution of 1940. An agreement between Hindu and Muslim leaders to create an independent, secular Bengal was resisted by Mahatma Gandhi. Further violence, such as the Great Calcutta Killing in 1946, put pressure on the administration and India was hastily partitioned—East Bengal was united with the northwestern Muslim provinces as Pakistan. East Pakistan (as East Bengal became under the 1956 constitution) received 0·7m. Muslims, mainly from Bihar and West Bengal, while over 2·5m. Hindus left for India.

Relations with West Pakistan were strained from the outset. Bengali demands for recognition of their language and resentment of preferential investment in their western partner led to the formation of the Awami League in 1949 to represent Bengali interests. Led by Sheikh Mujibur Rahman (Mujib), the Awami League triumphed as part of the 'United Front' in elections in 1954 but its government was dismissed by Governor-General Ghulam Mohammad after two months. A military government was installed from 1958–62 and in 1966 Mujib was arrested. Civilian government was again suspended in 1969 and in elections in 1970–71 the Awami League won all East Pakistani seats. While talks to form a government foundered, President Yahya Khan sent troops to the East and suspended the assembly, provoking a civil disobedience campaign. On 25 March 1971 the army began a crackdown. Members of the Awami League were arrested or fled to Calcutta, where they declared a provisional Bengali government. 10m. Bengalis fled to India to escape the bloody repression. India, with Soviet support, invaded on 3 Dec. 1971, forcing the surrender of the Pakistani army on 16 Dec. Mujib was released to become prime minister of independent Bangladesh.

Bangladesh suffered famine in 1974 and disorder led to Mujib assuming the presidency with dictatorial powers. Assassinated in Aug. 1975, a coup brought to power Maj.-Gen. Ziaur Rahman, who turned against the former ally, India. Rahman was assassinated in 1981. Hussain Mohammad Ershad became martial law administrator in 1982 and president in 1983. Ershad's National Party triumphed in parliamentary elections in May 1986 but presidential elections in Oct. were boycotted by opposition parties. A campaign of demonstrations and national strikes forced Ershad's resignation in 1990. Rahman's widow, Khaleda, became prime minister after her Bangladesh Nationalist Party (BJD) won nearly half the seats. The Awami League's victory in 1996 brought Mujib's daughter, Sheikh Hasina Wajed, to the premiership but Khaleda Zia returned to power in 2001.

TERRITORY AND POPULATION

Bangladesh is bounded in the west and north by India, east by India and Myanmar and south by the Bay of Bengal. The area is 147,570 sq. km (56,977 sq. miles). In 1992 India granted a 999-year lease of the Tin Bigha corridor linking Bangladesh with its enclaves of Angarpota and Dahagram. At the 1991 census the population was 111,455,000 (54,141,000 females). The most recent census took place in Jan. 2001; population, 129,247,233 (65,841,419 males), giving a density of 876 persons per sq. km. The United Nations population estimate for 2001 was 131,461,000.

The UN gives a projected population for 2010 of 154·96m.

In 2003, 75·7% of the population lived in rural areas. The country is administratively divided into six divisions, subdivided into 21 *anchal* and 64 *zila*. Area (in sq. km) and population (in 1,000) in 2001 of the six divisions:

	Area	Population
Barisal division	13,297	8,514
Chittagong division	33,771	25,187
Dhaka division	31,119	40,592
Khulna division	22,274	15,185
Rajshahi division	34,513	31,478
Sylhet division	12,596	8,291

The populations of the chief cities (2001 census) were as follows:

Dhaka[1]	5,644,235	Mymensingh	236,989
Chittagong[2]	2,199,590	Barisal	212,253
Khulna[3]	811,490	Jessore	187,098
Rajshahi[4]	402,646	Comilla	176,713
Sylhet	299,431	Dinajpur	165,131
Tongi	295,883	Nawabganj	160,838
Rangpur	264,158	Bogra	157,570
Narayanganj	241,694		

[1]Metropolitan area, 10,403,597. [2]Metropolitan area, 3,361,244.
[3]Metropolitan area, 1,287,987. [4]Metropolitan area, 678,728.

The official language is Bengali. English is also in use for official, legal and commercial purposes.

SOCIAL STATISTICS

2002 births, 4,027,000; deaths, 1,150,000. In 2002 the birth rate was 28·0 per 1,000 population; death rate, 8·0; infant mortality, 2001, 51 per 1,000 live births. Life expectancy at birth, 2003, 63·7 years for females and 62·1 years for males. Annual population growth rate, 1992–2002, 2·3%. The fertility rate dropped from 4·5 births per woman in 1991 to 3·6 births per woman in 2001. Bangladesh has made some of the best progress in recent years in reducing child mortality. The number of deaths per 1,000 live births among children under five was reduced from nearly 150 in 1990 to 77 in 2001.

CLIMATE

A tropical monsoon climate with heat, extreme humidity and heavy rainfall in the monsoon season, from June to Oct. The short winter season (Nov.–Feb.) is mild and dry. Rainfall varies between 50" (1,250 mm) in the west to 100" (2,500 mm) in the southeast and up to 200" (5,000 mm) in the northeast. Dhaka, Jan. 66°F (19°C), July 84°F (28·9°C). Annual rainfall 81" (2,025 mm). Chittagong, Jan. 66°F (19°C), July 81°F (27·2°C). Annual rainfall 108" (2,831 mm). In mid-1998 the Ganges and other rivers flowing into Bangladesh burst their banks causing a deluge that covered two-thirds of the country. More than 22m. were made homeless and 700 died in the floods.

CONSTITUTION AND GOVERNMENT

Bangladesh is a unitary republic. The Constitution came into force on 16 Dec. 1972 and provides for a parliamentary democracy. The head of state is the *President*, elected by parliament every five years, who appoints a *Vice-President*. A referendum of Sept. 1991 was in favour of abandoning the executive presidential system and opted for a parliamentary system. Turnout was low. An amendment to the constitution in 1996 allowed for a caretaker government, which the president may instal to supervise elections should the parliament be dissolved. There is a *Council of Ministers* to assist and advise the President. The President appoints the government ministers.

Following a constitutional amendment made in May 2004 parliament has one chamber of 345 members, 300 directly elected every five years by citizens over 18 and 45 reserved for women, elected by the 300 MPs based on proportional representation in parliament. Prior to the amendment the parliament had just contained 300 directly elected members.

National Anthem

'Amar Sonar Bangla, ami tomay bhalobashi' ('My Bengal of gold, I love you'); words and tune by Rabindranath Tagore.

GOVERNMENT CHRONOLOGY

Presidents since 1971. (BAL = Bangladesh Awami League; BJD = Bangladesh Jatiyatabadi Dal; JD = National Party; n/p = non-partisan)

1971–72	BAL	Sayeed Nazrul Islam
1972–73	n/p	Abu Sayeed Chowdhury
1973–75	BAL	Mohammad Mohammadullah
1975	BAL	Sheikh Mujibur Rahman
1975	BAL	Khandakar Mushtaq Ahmed
1975–77	n/p	Abu Sadat Mohammad Sayem
1977–81	military/BJD	Ziaur Rahman
1981–82	BJD	Abdus Sattar
1982–83	n/p	Abul Fazal Ahsanuddin Chowdhury
1983–90	military/JD	Hossain Mohammad Ershad
1991–96	BJD	Abdur Rahman Biswas
1996–2001	n/p	Shahabuddin Ahmed
2001–02	BJD	A.Q.M. Badruddoza Chowdhury
2002–	n/p	Iajuddin Ahmed

Heads of government since 1971.

Prime Ministers

1971–72	BAL	Tajuddin Ahmed
1972–75	BAL	Sheikh Mujibur Rahman
1975		Mohammad Mansoor Ali

Chief Martial Law Administrators

1975	military	Ziaur Rahman
1975–76	n/p	Abu Sadat Mohammad Sayem
1976–79	military/BJD	Ziaur Rahman

Prime Ministers

1979–82	BJD	Shah Azizur Rahman
1984–86	JD	Ataur Rahman Khan
1986–88	JD	Mizanur Rahman Chowdhury
1988–89	JD	Moudud Ahmed
1989–90	JD	Kazi Zafar Ahmed
1991–96	BJD	Khaleda Zia
1996	n/p	Mohammad Habibur Rahman
1996–2001	BAL	Sheikh Hasina Wajed
2001	n/p	Latifur Rahman
2001–	BJD	Khaleda Zia

RECENT ELECTIONS

Iajuddin Ahmed was declared president-elect on 5 Sept. 2002 after the opposition Bangladesh Awami League failed to put forward a rival candidate.

In parliamentary elections of 1 Oct. 2001 the Bangladesh Jatiyatabadi Dal (BJD) and its coalition partners gained 47% of votes cast. The BJD itself gained 191 seats, with allies the Jamaat-e-Islami Bangladesh (JIB) gaining 18, the Jatiya Dal-Naziur (JD-N) 4 and the Islami Oikya Jote (IOJ) 2. The Bangladesh Awami League (BAL) gained 62 seats (40%), the Jatiya Dal-Ershad (JD-E) 14 (7·5%) with remaining seats going to other parties. Turnout was 74·9%.

CURRENT ADMINISTRATION

President: Iajuddin Ahmed; b. 1931 (since 6 Sept. 2002).

In March 2006 the government comprised:

Prime Minister and Minister of Defence, Chittagong Hill Tracts Affairs, Cabinet Affairs, Energy and Mineral Resources, Primary and Mass Education, and Establishment: Khaleda Zia; b. 1945 (BJD; sworn in 10 Oct. 2001).

Minister of Agriculture: M. K. Anwar. *Commerce:* Altaf Hossain Chowdhury. *Communications:* Nazmul Huda. *Education:* Osman Faruq. *Environment and Forestry:* Tariqul Islam. *Finance and Planning:* Saifur Rahman. *Fisheries and Livestock:* Abdullah Al-Noman. *Food and Disaster Management:* Chowdhury Kamal Ibne Yusuf. *Foreign Affairs:* Morshed Khan. *Health and Family Welfare:* Dr Khandaker Mosharraf Hossain. *Housing and Public Works:*

Mirza Abbas. *Industries:* Matiur Rahman Nizami. *Information:* Shamsul Islam. *Law, Justice and Parliamentary Affairs:* Moudud Ahmed. *Local Government, Rural Development and Co-operatives:* Abdul Mannan Bhuiyan. *Post and Telecommunications:* Aminul Haque. *Science and Information and Communication Technology:* Dr Abdul Moyeen Khan. *Shipping:* Akbar Hossain. *Social Welfare:* Ali Ahsan Mohammed Mujahid. *Textiles and Jute:* Shahjahan Siraj. *Water Resources:* Hafizuddin Ahmad Bir Bakram. *Women and Children's Affairs:* Khurshid Jahan Haque. *Minister without Portfolio:* Abdul Matin Chowdhury.

Government Website: http://www.bangladesh.gov.bd

CURRENT LEADERS

Begum Khaleda Zia

Position
Prime Minister

Introduction
Bangladesh's first female prime minister (1991–96) and widow of Ziaur Rahman, the country's president between 1977–81, Khaleda Zia returned to office in Oct. 2001 at the head of the Bangladesh Jatiyatabadi Dal (Bangladesh Nationalist Party; BJD). Her re-election took place amidst social and political unrest over the treatment of Bangladesh's Hindu, Buddhist and Christian minorities, with both her and her main political rival, former premier and leader of the Awami League, Sheikh Hasina Wahed, accused of fomenting communal violence.

Early Life
Khaleda Zia was born on 15 Aug. 1945 in the Dinajpur district of what was then East Bengal to a businessman father, Iskander Majumder.

In 1960 she married Ziaur Rahman. A hero of the 1971 secessionist war against Pakistan, Rahman became president of Bangladesh in 1977, forming the centre-right BJD. Following his assassination in 1981 as part of a failed military coup, leadership went to Rahman's vice-president, Abdus Sattar, who ruled until a second coup, a year later, which put the country under the dictatorial sway of Gen. H. M. Ershad. Ershad proclaimed martial law on 24 March 1982, abolishing all political parties and suspending the constitution. Having remained in the shadows during her husband's presidency, after his death Zia joined the BJD. In 1983 she was made a vice-chairman, going on to be elected leader of the party the following year. In 1983 the BJD formed a seven-party alliance. By 1990 the growing popularity of Zia's alliance and the eight-party alliance formed by Sheikh Hasina Wajed, the daughter of Bangladesh's first prime minister, Sheikh Mujibur Rahman, forced the resignation of Gen. Ershad. During the eight years of Ershad's rule, Zia had been imprisoned seven times. Although Zia's BJD failed to win an overall majority in parliament, it received sufficient support from several smaller parties to gain power. On 20 March 1991 Zia was sworn in as prime minister.

Career in Office
Zia's first months in office were beset with catastrophe as Bangladesh experienced one of its worst cyclones in recent years, causing 131,000 deaths and damage at US$2bn. Although Zia appealed for international assistance, relief efforts were hindered by flooding and storms. Her leadership subsequently came under fire for her failure to deal effectively with the crisis.

In Aug. 1991 she was successful in reinstating a parliamentary system of government and in Sept. she became head of government after new elections. She tried to revitalize the agricultural industry and undertook reforms in education including the introduction of compulsory free primary education and measures to increase female enrolment.

In 1992 the destruction of the Babri Masjid Mosque in neighbouring India and the ensuing violence provoked fundamentalist sentiment and attacks against Hindus which Zia failed to quash. At this time, Zia's government intelligence unit shared links with Pakistan's Inter-Services Intelligence (ISI), an agency which has since been denounced for its involvement with militant Islamic fundamentalism and terrorist activities.

Although Zia won the election held on 15 Feb. 1996 giving her a second consecutive term in power, the election was boycotted by all major opposition parties. Handing over power to a caretaker administration, Zia was then forced into opposition by the Awami League, headed by Sheikh Hasina Wajed.

In 1999 she formed a four-party alliance with the Jatiya Party, the Jamaat-e-Islami and the Islami Oikya Jote, both linked to violence against Bangladesh's Hindu minority. In the 2001 election she accused the Awami League of failing to protect Hindus, though the Awami League, traditionally seen as tolerant towards minorities, put the blame for the violence on the BJD. In the 2001 election, held on 1 Oct., the BJD achieved a two-thirds majority and Zia was returned as prime minister. Balloting was chaotic and the next month saw a spate of violence against Hindus by supporters of the BJD alliance.

Among the dominant issues which Zia's government faces is the export of natural gas to India. A liberalization of trade in this area has long been pushed by the Indian government, the USA and the World Bank, yet Zia has held back, citing doubts as to the extent of natural gas reserves and future domestic demands. Successful handling of the issue could, however, bear fruit both for Bangladesh's economy and for its relations with India. Illegal emigration to India has long been a source of contention. Talks between the two countries in April 2003 aimed to alleviate tensions over their joint border.

The poor state of the economy has played second place to political rivalry and the issue of communal violence. A third of the country's clothing factories closed following the attacks on New York and Washington of 11 Sept. 2001 and the subsequent war in Afghanistan. Roughly 74% of the country's export revenue comes from this industry. Coupled with fallen foreign exchange reserves, the onus rests on Zia to revitalize the economy.

In Dec. 2002 Zia held break-through talks with Senior Gen. Than Shwe, leader of neighbouring Myanmar, on closer economic co-operation and improved road and shipping links. Ties between the two governments had been strained since the early 1990s, when up to 250,000 Muslim Rohingya refugees entered Bangladesh from Myanmar. The situation had been aggravated by Myanmar's plans for a controversial dam on the shared Naf River, until Than Shwe abandoned the project in 2001. The first authorized sea route between the two countries was opened in Feb. 2003. In March 2003 Zia made the first official visit to Myanmar by a Bangladeshi prime minister.

In May 2004 Zia's government approved a constitutional amendment providing for 45 seats to be reserved for female MPs. The opposition orchestrated a series of general strikes throughout 2004 aimed at destabilizing the government. Zia has responded to international criticism over her government's treatment of opposition groups, the country's weak human rights record and the growth in influence of radical Islamic groups by warning that foreign countries and international aid organizations had no business interfering in the nation's domestic politics. Over several months in 2004 serious flooding killed several hundred and left several million homeless and in need of food. In Aug. 2005 a banned Islamic militant group claimed responsibility for a series of minor explosions throughout the country.

DEFENCE

The supreme command of defence services is vested in the president. Defence expenditure in 2003 totalled US$645m. (US$5 per capita), representing 1·2% of GDP.

Army

Strength (2002) 120,000. There is also an armed police reserve, 5,000 strong, 20,000 security guards (Ansars) and the Bangladesh Rifles (border guard) numbering 38,000. There is a further potential reserve Ansar force of 180,000.

Navy

Naval bases are at Chittagong, Dhaka, Kaptai, Khulna and Mongla. The fleet comprises five frigates, ten missile craft, four torpedo craft and 19 patrol craft. Personnel, 2002, 10,500.

Air Force

There are four fighter squadrons and three helicopter squadrons. Personnel strength (2002) 6,500. There were 83 combat aircraft in 2002.

INTERNATIONAL RELATIONS

Bangladesh is a member of the UN, WTO, the Commonwealth, Asian Development Bank, Colombo Plan, IOM, Organization of the Islamic Conference, SAARC, Islamic Development Bank and the Non-Aligned Movement.

ECONOMY

In 2002 agriculture accounted for 22·7% of GDP, industry 26·4% and services 50·9%.

Overview

In 2003 the economy grew at 5·8%. In 2004 the country suffered from severe flooding but the economy proved resilient and again grew at 5·8%. Agriculture generates employment for the majority of the population (62·1% in 2000) but labour productivity has been increasing over the years.

Unlike many other Asian countries, Bangladesh has been running dual trade and current-account deficits in recent years and has attracted relatively little foreign direct investment. However, this is expected to pick up, with investment from the UAE's Abu Dhabi Group and, potentially, from India's Tata Group. Coal discoveries could help balance the country's trade deficit in the future but Bangladesh's ability to supply its own energy needs is hindered by poor infrastructure. It is hoped the elimination of international textile and apparel quotas in 2005 will benefit Bangladesh, which has a competitive advantage in labour-intensive production. With lower wages than China and other competitors, an increasing focus on textile production has boosted Bangladesh's export and employment prospects. The IMF says that reform progress was made in 2004–05 but endemic corruption and potential political instability in the lead up to the 2007 elections pose a threat to productivity and further reform.

Currency

The unit of currency is the *taka* (BDT) of 100 *poisha*, which was floated in 1976. Foreign exchange reserves in June 2002 were US$1,543m. and gold reserves 112,000 troy oz. Inflation was 5·4% in 2003 and 6·1% in 2004. Total money supply was Tk.231,658m. in May 2002.

Budget

The fiscal year ends on 30 June. Budget, 2002–03: revenue, Tk.326bn.; expenditure, Tk.448bn.

Performance

Real GDP growth was 5·8% in both 2003 and 2004. Total GDP was US$56·8bn. in 2004.

Banking and Finance

Bangladesh Bank is the central bank (*Governor*, Dr Salehuddin Ahmed). There are four nationalized commercial banks, 16 private commercial banks, nine foreign commercial banks and ten development finance organizations. In 1999 the Bangladesh Bank had Tk.9,118m. deposits. In 1999 Sonali Bank was the largest of the nationalized commercial banks with deposits of Tk.170,961m.

There are stock exchanges in Dhaka and Chittagong.

Weights and Measures

The metric system was introduced from July 1982, but some imperial and traditional measures are still in use. One *tola* = 11·66 g; one *maund* = 37·32 kg = 40 *seers*; one *seer* = 0·93 kg.

ENERGY AND NATURAL RESOURCES

Environment

Bangladesh's carbon dioxide emissions from the consumption and flaring of fossil fuels in 2002 were the equivalent of 0·2 tonnes per capita.

Electricity

Installed capacity, 2000, 3·5m. kW. Electricity generated, 2000, about 15·55bn. kWh; consumption per capita in 2000 was an estimated 113 kWh.

Oil and Gas

In 2002 Bangladesh had proven natural gas reserves of 300,000m. cu. metres in about 20 mainly onshore fields. Some international companies believe the actual figure to be very much higher. Total natural gas production in 2002 amounted to 11·2bn. cu. metres.

Water

A Ganges water-sharing accord was signed with India in 1997, ending a 25-year dispute which had hindered and dominated relations between the two countries.

By 2000 it was estimated that 85m. people out of the total population of 128m. had been accidentally poisoned over the previous 30 years through arsenic-contaminated drinking water. A World Health Organization report has described it as 'the largest mass poisoning of a population in history'.

Minerals

The principal minerals are lignite, limestone, china clay and glass sand. There are reserves of good-quality coal of 300m. tonnes. Production, 2001–02: limestone, 32,000 tonnes; kaolin, 8,100 tonnes.

Agriculture

In 2002 the agricultural population was 106·18m., of whom 39·18m. were economically active. There were 8·09m. ha. of arable land in 2001 and 0·4m. ha. of permanent crops. 4·42m. ha. were irrigated in 2001. Bangladesh is a major producer of jute: production, 2000, 1·53m. tonnes. Rice is the most important food crop; production in 2000 (in 1m. metric tonnes), 35·82. Other major crops (1m. tonnes): sugarcane, 6·95; wheat, 1·90; potatoes, 1·70; bananas, 0·56.

Livestock in 2000: cattle, 23,652,000; goats, 33,800,000; sheep, 1,121,000; buffalo, 828,000; chickens, 139,000,000. Livestock products in 2000 (tonnes): beef and veal, 170,000; goat meat, 127,000; poultry meat, 112,000; goat milk, 1,296,000; cow's milk, 755,000; buffalo milk, 22,000; sheep milk, 22,000; eggs, 132,000. Bangladesh is the second largest producer of goat milk, after India.

Forestry

In 2000 the area under forests was 1·33m. ha., or 10·2% of the total land area. Timber production in 2001 was 28·42m. cu. metres.

Fisheries

Bangladesh is a major producer of fish and fish products. There are 500,000 sea- and 800,000 inland-fishermen, with 1,249 mechanized boats, including 52 trawlers, and 3,317 motor boats. The total catch in 2001 amounted to approximately 1,000,000 tonnes, of which 670,000 tonnes came from inland waters. Only China and India have larger annual catches of freshwater fish.

INDUSTRY

Manufacturing contributes around 11% of GDP. The principal industries are jute and cotton textiles, tea, paper, newsprint, cement, chemical fertilizers and light engineering. Production, in 1,000 tonnes: cement (2000–01), 2,340; nitrogenous fertilizer (2001), 1,875; jute goods (2001–02), 536; sugar (2002), 229. Output of other products: cotton woven fabrics (2000–01), 63m. sq. metres; cigarettes (2000–01), 20·1bn. units; television sets (2001), 133,000 units; bicycles (2000–01), 13,000 units.

Labour

In 2000 the economically active workforce totalled 51,764,000 over the age of 15 years (32,369,000 males). The main areas of activity (in 1,000) were as follows: agriculture, hunting, forestry and fishing, 32,171; wholesale and retail trade, restaurants and hotels, 6,275; manufacturing, 3,783; community, social and personal services, 2,969; transport, storage and communication, 2,509; construction, 1,099. On average, wage rates (US$0·23 an hour, 1997) are among the lowest of developing countries. In 1999–2000, 3·3% of the workforce aged 15 or over were unemployed.

INTERNATIONAL TRADE

Foreign companies are permitted wholly to own local subsidiaries. Tax concessions are available to foreign firms in the export zones of Dhaka and Chittagong. Foreign debt was US$17,037m. in 2002.

Imports and Exports

The main imports are machinery, transport equipment, manufactured goods, minerals, fuels and lubricants, and the main exports are jute and jute goods, tea, hides and skins, newsprint, fish and garments.

Imports and exports for calendar years in US$1m.:

	1998	1999	2000	2001	2002
Imports f.o.b.	6,715·7	7,535·5	8,052·9	8,133·4	7,714·0
Exports f.o.b.	5,141·4	5,458·3	6,399·2	6,084·7	6,078·4

In 1998, 15% of imports came from India, 10% from China, 7% from Japan and 6% from Singapore. 39% of exports in 1998 went to the USA, 9% to France, 9% to Germany and 7% to the UK.

Since the early 1980s the garment industry has developed from virtually nothing to earn some 70% of the country's hard currency. Garment exports in 1997 earned US$3·5bn.

COMMUNICATIONS

Roads

In 2002 the total road network covered 216,614 km, including 20,585 km of national roads and 17,986 km of secondary roads. Some 10,000 km of roads were destroyed in the floods of 1998. In 1998 there were 30,361 buses and coaches, 42,425 trucks and lorries, 2,235 taxis (1995), 46,561 motorized rickshaws (1995) and 57,068 passenger cars. In 1995 there were also 411,000 rickshaws and 727,000 bullock carts. There were 5,820 road accidents in 1998, resulting in 3,375 fatalities.

Rail

In 1999 there were 2,706 km of railways, comprising 884 km of 1,676 mm gauge and 1,822 km of metre gauge. Passenger-km travelled in 1999 came to 3·68bn. and freight tonne-km to 896m.

Civil Aviation

There are international airports at Dhaka (Zia) and Chittagong, and eight domestic airports. Biman Bangladesh Airlines is state-owned. In addition to domestic routes, in 2003 it operated international services to Abu Dhabi, Bahrain, Bangkok, Bombay, Brussels, Calcutta, Dammam, Delhi, Doha, Dubai, Frankfurt, Hong Kong, Jeddah, Karachi, Kathmandu, Kuala Lumpur, Kuwait, London, Muscat, New York, Paris, Rangoon (Yangon), Riyadh, Rome, Singapore and Tokyo. There were direct flights in 2003 with other airlines to Madinah, Paro, Tashkent and Tehran. In 2001 Dhaka's Zia International Airport handled 2,863,575 passengers (2,322,743 on international flights) and 106,291 tonnes of freight. In 1999 Biman Bangladesh Airlines flew 21·0m. km, carrying 1,215,400 passengers (891,600 on international flights).

Shipping

There are sea ports at Chittagong and Mongla, and inland ports at Dhaka, Chandpur, Barisal, Khulna and five other towns. There are 8,000 km of navigable inland waterways. The Bangladesh Shipping Corporation owned 18 ships in 1994. Total tonnage registered, 2002, 432,000 GRT (including oil tankers 63,000 GRT). In 1993–94 the two sea ports handled 8·20m. tonnes of imports and 1·66m. tonnes of exports. In 1999–2000 vessels totalling 6,509,000 NRT entered ports and vessels totalling 2,949,000 NRT cleared. The Bangladesh Inland Water Transport Corporation had 288 vessels in 1994. 70·29m. passengers were carried in 1992–93.

Telecommunications

Telephone subscribers numbered 1,757,000 in 2002 (13·2 per 1,000 inhabitants), of which 1,075,000 were mobile phone subscribers. International communications are by the Indian Ocean Intelsat IV satellite. There were 450,000 PCs in use in 2002 (3·4 for every 1,000 persons) and 6,200 fax machines. Bangladesh had 204,000 Internet users in 2002.

Postal Services

There were 9,859 post offices in 2003.

SOCIAL INSTITUTIONS

Justice

The Supreme Court comprises an Appellate and a High Court Division, the latter having control over all subordinate courts. Judges are appointed by the President and retire at 65. There are benches at Comilla, Rangpur, Jessore, Barisal, Chittagong and Sylhet, and courts at District level.

The population in penal institutions in 2002 was 64,866 (45 per 100,000 of national population).

The death penalty is still in force. In 2005 there were five executions (down from 12 in 2004).

Education

In 2000–01 there were 17·7m. pupils and 309,341 teachers at primary schools; 10·3m. pupils and 269,237 teachers in secondary schools; 878,537 students and 47,137 academic staff in tertiary education. In 1993–94 there were 80 professional colleges with 43,503 students and 2,752 teachers.

In 1995–96 there were five universities, an Islamic university, an open university and universities of agriculture, engineering and technology, and science and technology; there were five teacher training colleges, five medical, three law and two fine arts colleges, an institute of ophthalmology and a rehabilitation institute. In 1997 there were 67,282 university students and 4,015 academic staff. Adult literacy was 41·1% in 2002 (50·3% among males and 31·4% among females).

In 2000–01 total expenditure on education came to 2·5% of GNP and 15·7% of total government spending.

Health

In 1997 there were 976 hospitals, with the equivalent of four beds per 10,000 persons. There were 32,498 physicians, 938 dentists (1997), 18,135 nurses and 15,794 midwives in 2001.

RELIGION

Islam is the state religion. In 2001 the population was 87% Muslim and 12% Hindu.

CULTURE

World Heritage Sites

There are three UNESCO sites in Bangladesh: the Historic Mosque City of Bagerhat (inscribed on the list in 1985); the Ruins of the Buddhist Vihara at Paharpur (1985); the Sundarbans (1997), 140,000 ha. of mangrove forest.

Broadcasting

The government-controlled Bangladesh Betam and part-commercial Bangladesh Television transmit a home service and an external service radio programme, and a TV programme (colour by PAL). In 2000 there were 6·4m. radio receivers and in 2001 there were 2·2m. TV receivers.

Press

In 1996 there were 37 daily newspapers with a combined circulation of 1·1m., at a rate of 9·3 per 1,000 inhabitants. In 1994, 1,258 book titles were published (122 in English).

Tourism

In 2002 there were 207,000 foreign tourists. Receipts totalled US$57m.

Museums and Galleries

The main museums are: The National Museum; Muktijuddha Judughar (War of Liberation Museum); and The Bangabandhu Memorial Museum.

DIPLOMATIC REPRESENTATIVES

Of Bangladesh in the United Kingdom (28 Queen's Gate, London, SW7 5JA)
High Commissioner: Sabihuddin Ahmed.
(There are also Assistant High Commissioners in Birmingham and Manchester)

Of the United Kingdom in Bangladesh (United Nations Rd, Baridhara, Dhaka 12)
High Commissioner: Anwar Choudhury.

Of Bangladesh in the USA (3510 International Drive, NW, Washington, D.C., 20008)
Ambassador: Shamsher Mobin Chowdhury.

Of the USA in Bangladesh (Madani Ave., Baridhara, Dhaka 1212)
Ambassador: Vacant.
Chargé d'Affaires a.i.: Judith A. Chammas.

Of Bangladesh to the United Nations
Ambassador: Iftekhar Ahmed Chowdhury.

Of Bangladesh to the European Union
Ambassador: Syed Maudud Ali.

FURTHER READING

Bangladesh Bureau of Statistics. *Statistical Yearbook of Bangladesh.— Statistical Pocket Book of Bangladesh.*
Ahmed, A. F. S., *Bangladesh: Tradition and Transformation.* Dhaka, 1987
Hajnoczy, R., *Fire of Bengal.* Bangladesh Univ. Press, 1993
Muhith, A. M. A., *Issues of Governance in Bangladesh.* Mowla Brothers, Dhaka, 2000
Rashid, H. U., *Foreign Relations of Bangladesh.* Rishi Publications, Varanasi, 2001
Tajuddin, M., *Foreign Policy of Bangladesh: Liberation War to Sheikh Hasina.* National Book Organisation, New Delhi, 2001
Ziring, L., *Bangladesh from Mujib to Ershad: an Interpretive Study.* OUP, 1993

National Statistical Office: Bangladesh Bureau of Statistics, Ministry of Planning, Dhaka.
Website: http://www.bbsgov.org/

BARBADOS

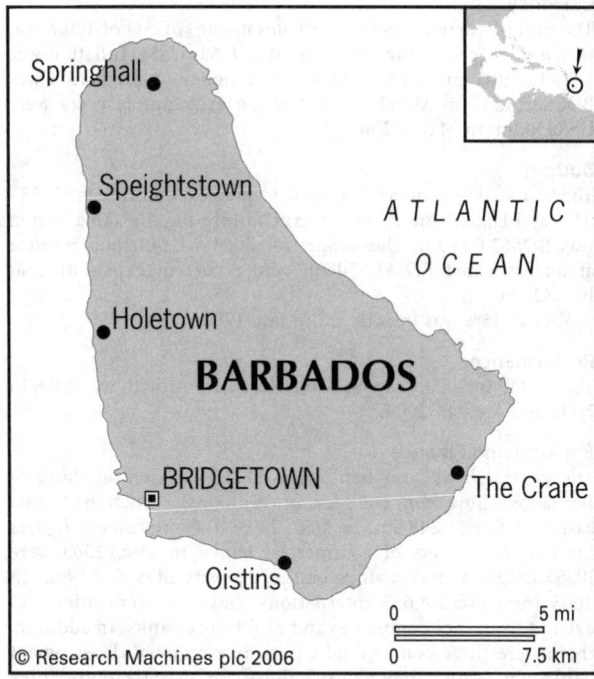

Capital: Bridgetown
Population projection, 2010: 273,000
GDP per capita, 2003: (PPP$) 15,720
HDI/world rank: 0·878/30

KEY HISTORICAL EVENTS

Archaeological evidence suggests that Barbados was inhabited by Barrancoid Indians from at least 1000 BC, and by Arawak people for about 400 years from around 1000 AD. Portuguese mariners who landed on the island in 1536 reported that it was uninhabited. An Englishman, William Courteen, established Jamestown in 1627. Sugar plantations were developed in the 1640s, using imported slave labour from Africa until the practice was abolished in 1834. In 1951 universal suffrage was introduced, followed in 1954 by cabinet government. Full internal self-government was attained in Oct. 1961. On 30 Nov. 1966 Barbados became an independent sovereign state within the British Commonwealth.

TERRITORY AND POPULATION

Barbados lies to the east of the Windward Islands. Area 430 sq. km (166 sq. miles). In 2000 the census population was 268,792. 2005 estimate: 270,000; density 627·9 per sq. km.

The UN gives a projected population for 2010 of 273,000.

In 2003, 51·7% of the population were urban. Bridgetown is the principal city: population (including suburbs), 133,000 in 1999.

The official language is English.

SOCIAL STATISTICS

In 2003: births, 3,748; deaths, 2,274; birth rate, 13·0 per 1,000 population; death rate, 8·4; infant mortality, 9·9 per 1,000 live births. Expectation of life, 2003, males 71·4 years and females 78·5. Population growth rate, 2003, 0·3%; fertility rate, 2001, 1·5 children per woman.

CLIMATE

An equable climate in winter, but the wet season, from June to Nov., is more humid. Rainfall varies from 50" (1,250 mm) on the coast to 75" (1,875 mm) in the higher interior. Bridgetown, Jan. 76°F (24·4°C), July 80°F (26·7°C). Annual rainfall 51" (1,275 mm).

CONSTITUTION AND GOVERNMENT

The head of state is the British sovereign, represented by an appointed Governor-General. The bicameral Parliament consists of a Senate and a House of Assembly. The *Senate* comprises 21 members appointed by the Governor-General, 12 being appointed on the advice of the Prime Minister, two on the advice of the Leader of the Opposition and seven at the Governor-General's discretion. The *House of Assembly* comprises 30 members elected every five years. In 1963 the voting age was reduced to 18.

The *Privy Council* is appointed by the Governor-General after consultation with the Prime Minister. It consists of 12 members and the Governor-General as chairman. It advises the Governor-General in the exercise of the royal prerogative of mercy and in the exercise of his disciplinary powers over members of the public and police services.

National Anthem

'In plenty and in time of need'; words by Irvine Burgie, tune by V. R. Edwards.

RECENT ELECTIONS

In the general election of 21 May 2003 the Barbados Labour Party (BLP) gained 23 seats (55·8% of the total vote) and the Democratic Labour Party (DLP) 7 seats (44·1%).

CURRENT ADMINISTRATION

Governor-General: Sir Clifford Husbands, GCMG, KA; b. 1926.

In March 2006 the government comprised:

Prime Minister and Minister of Finance: Owen S. Arthur; b. 1950 (BLP; appointed 7 Sept. 1994).

Deputy Prime Minister and Minister of Economic Affairs and Development: Mia Amor Mottley. *Attorney General and Minister of Home Affairs:* Dale Marshall. *Minister of Agriculture and Rural Development:* Erskine Griffith. *Commerce, Consumer Affairs and Business Development:* Lynette Eastmond. *Education, Youth Affairs and Sports:* Anthony Wood. *Energy and the Environment:* Elizabeth Thompson. *Foreign Affairs and Foreign Trade:* Billie A. Miller. *Health and Water:* Dr Jerome Walcott. *Housing and Lands:* Reginald Farley. *Labour and Civil Service:* Rawle C. Eastmond. *Public Works and Transportation:* Gline Arley Clarke. *Social Transformation:* Trevor Prescod. *Tourism and International Transport:* Noel Anderson Lynch.

Government of Barbados Information Network:
  http://www.barbados.gov.bb

CURRENT LEADERS

Owen Arthur

Position
Prime Minister

Introduction
Owen Arthur is Barbados' fifth prime minister and leader of the Barbados Labour Party (BLP). He took office in 1994 and was re-elected in 1999 and 2003. He favours Barbados becoming a republic.

Early Life

Owen Seymour Arthur was born on 17 Oct. 1949 in Barbados. He studied in Jamaica at the University of the West Indies, graduating with a masters in economics. He worked in Jamaica for much of the 1970s, firstly as a researcher at the university's department of management, then at the national planning agency and later as director of economic research at the Jamaican bauxite institute.

In 1981 he joined the Barbados ministry of finance and planning as chief project analyst. He then became a research fellow at the University of the West Indies' institute of social and economic research. He also held positions on the boards of the Jamaican council for scientific research, the Barbados industrial development corporation and the central bank of Barbados. Between 1982–84 he was chairman of the Barbados agricultural development corporation.

Arthur began his political career in 1983 when he was appointed to the Barbados senate and the following year he was elected to the house of assembly. From 1993–94 he served as leader of the opposition. He led the BLP into the 1994 general election promising to develop a 'modern, technologically-dynamic economy'. The BLP won 19 of 28 available seats and Arthur was returned as prime minister.

Career in Office

Arthur has made economic development a main priority with emphasis on promotion of international trade and investment, incorporating an expansion of the tourism sector.

In the build-up to the 1999 election he vowed to make Barbados a republic, proposing that a ceremonial president replace the queen as head of state. There are plans for a referendum on the subject. Arthur's BLP won a landslide victory at the 1999 polls, claiming 26 of the 28 seats. In 2000 the OECD placed Barbados on a list of nations designated as uncooperative tax havens but was removed from the list two years later. Arthur's majority was slightly reduced at the election of 2003 when the BLP won 23 seats on a platform of reduced taxation and increased prosperity.

Arthur has been active in regional politics, taking a leading role in developing the Caribbean single market and economy. Additionally he was the chair of the Commonwealth ministerial group on small states, chair of the global conference on small states and a consultant to the OAS and CARICOM.

In 2004 relations with Trinidad and Tobago declined following a sea border disagreement when several Barbadian fishermen were arrested. The dispute was referred to the UN for adjudication. Ties between Barbados and Trinidad took a further knock in 2005 when Arthur suggested Tobago would be better off in a union with Barbados.

Arthur is minister of finance in addition to being prime minister.

DEFENCE

The Barbados Defence Force has a strength of about 610. In 2003 defence expenditure totalled US$13m. (US$48 per capita), representing 0·5% of GDP.

Army

Army strength was 500 with reserves numbering 430 in 2002.

Navy

A small maritime unit numbering 110 (2002) operates five patrol vessels. The unit is based at St Ann's Fort Garrison, Bridgetown.

INTERNATIONAL RELATIONS

Barbados is a member of the UN, WTO, OAS, Inter-American Development Bank, ACS, CARICOM, the Commonwealth and is an ACP member state of the ACP-EU relationship.

ECONOMY

In 2003 agriculture accounted for 4% of GDP, industry 16% and services 80%.

Currency

The unit of currency is the *Barbados dollar* (BDS$) of 100 *cents*, which is pegged to the US dollar at BDS$2=US$1. Inflation was 1·6% in 2003 and 1·4% in 2004. Total money in circulation was BDS$2,242m. in March 2003. Foreign exchange reserves were USS$506m. in March 2003.

Budget

The financial year runs from April. Capital expenditure for 2003–04 was BDS$253·7m.; current expenditure for the same period was BDS$2,048·3m. The budget for 2003–04 put total revenue at an estimated BDS$1,850·5m. and recurrent expenditure at BDS$2,080·5m.

VAT at 15% was introduced in Jan. 1997.

Performance

Total GDP in 2003 was US$2·7bn. Real GDP growth was 2·0% in 2003 and 4·4% in 2004.

Banking and Finance

The central bank and bank of issue is the Central Bank of Barbados (*Governor,* Dr Marion Williams), which had total assets of BDS$1,248·5m. in Dec. 2003. The provisional figures for the total assets of commercial banks in Dec. 2003 were BDS$6,812·6m. and savings banks' deposits BDS$5,493·8m. In 2003 there were 4,635 international business companies, 413 exempt insurance companies and 51 offshore banks. In addition, there were three commercial banks, one regional development bank, one National Bank (scheduled for privatization), three foreign banks and seven trust companies.

There is a stock exchange which participates in the regional Caribbean exchange.

Weights and Measures

Both Imperial and metric systems are in use.

ENERGY AND NATURAL RESOURCES

Environment

Carbon dioxide emissions from the consumption and flaring of fossil fuels in Barbados in 2002 were the equivalent of 6·0 tonnes per capita.

Electricity

Production in 2003, 900·5m. kWh. Capacity in 2000 was 0·2m kW. Consumption per capita was an estimated 2,961 kWh in 2003.

Oil and Gas

Crude oil production in 2003 was 370,909 bbls. and reserves in 2002 were 2·5m. bbls. Output of gas (2003) 22·4m. cu. metres, and reserves (2003) 130m. cu. metres. Production of Liquid Petroleum Gas (LPG) was 3,691 bbls. in 2003.

Agriculture

The agricultural sector accounted for 4·4% of GDP in 2003 (24% in 1967). Of the total labour force in 2003, 4·6% were employed in agriculture. Of the total area of Barbados (42,995 ha.), about 16,000 ha. are arable land, which is intensively cultivated. In 2003, 7,515 ha. were under sugarcane cultivation. Production, 2003 (in tonnes): sugarcane, 48,500; sweet potatoes, 2,610; cucumbers, 2,018; okra, 1,446; tomatoes, 1,234; yams, 1,234; carrots, 1,012; cabbages, 640.

Meat and dairy products, 2003 (in tonnes): poultry, 11,458; cow's milk, 7,017; pork, 1,756; eggs, 1,620; beef, 346.

Livestock (2000): cattle, 23,000; sheep, 41,000; pigs, 33,000; chickens, 4m.

Forestry

Timber production in 2001 was 5,000 cu. metres.

Fisheries

In 2003 there were 954 fishing vessels employed during the flying-fish season. The catch in 2003 was 2,400 tonnes, exclusively from sea fishing.

INDUSTRY

Industry has traditionally been centred on sugar, but there is also light manufacturing and component assembly for export. In 2003, 36,300 tonnes of raw sugar were produced.

Labour

In 2003 the workforce was 145,500, of whom 129,500 were employed. Unemployment stood at 11·0%, down from 24·5% in 1993.

Trade Unions

About one-third of employees are unionized. The Barbados Workers' Union was founded in 1938 and has the majority of members. There are also a National Union of Public Workers and two teachers' unions.

INTERNATIONAL TRADE

External debt was BDS$2,224m. in 2004 (provisional).

Imports and Exports

In 2004 imports were valued at BDS$2,752m. and exports (excluding petroleum products) at BDS$498m. The main import suppliers in 2004 were the USA (37·0%), Trinidad and Tobago (18·9%), UK (6·0%) and Canada (3·9%). Principal export markets in 2004 were the USA (15·4%), Trinidad and Tobago (11·0%), UK (10·5%) and Jamaica (5·2%).

The main imports are foodstuffs, cars, chemicals, mineral fuels, and machinery and equipment. Main exports are electrical components, sugar, rum, cement, chemicals and petroleum (re-export) products.

COMMUNICATIONS

Roads

There were 1,793 km of roads in 2000. In 2004 there were 86,240 cars; 10,748 lorries, vans and pickups; 5,896 buses, coaches and taxis; 1,156 other commercial vehicles. There were 29 deaths as a result of road accidents in 2000.

Civil Aviation

The Grantley Adams International Airport is 16 km from Bridgetown. In 2001 it handled 1,763,500 passengers (all on international flights) and 14,094 tonnes of freight.

Shipping

There is a deep-water harbour at Bridgetown. 665,595 tonnes of cargo were handled in 1994. Shipping registered in 2002 totalled 328,000 GRT, including oil tankers 8,000 GRT. The number of merchant vessels entering in 2001 was 2,087 of 18·6m. net tonnes.

Telecommunications

In Dec. 2001 there were 127,632 telephone main lines (474·8 per 1,000 inhabitants), 39,789 of which were business lines. There were 28,000 PCs in use in 2002 (104·1 per 1,000 inhabitants). Barbados had 53,100 mobile phone subscribers in 2001 and 30,000 Internet users in 2002. In 2002 there were 2,800 fax machines.

Postal Services

There is a general post office in Bridgetown and 17 branches on the island.

SOCIAL INSTITUTIONS

Justice

Justice is administered by the Supreme Court and Justices' Appeal Court, and by magistrates' courts. All have both civil and criminal jurisdiction. There is a Chief Justice, three judges of appeal, five puisne judges of the Supreme Court and nine magistrates. The death penalty is authorized. Final appeal lies to the Privy Council in London. Barbados was one of ten countries to sign an agreement in Feb. 2001 establishing a Caribbean Court of Justice to replace the British Privy Council as the highest civil and criminal court. In the meantime the number of signatories has risen to twelve. The court was inaugurated at Port-of-Spain, Trinidad on 16 April 2005.

In 1996 the police force numbered 1,221. The population in penal institutions in Nov. 2003 was 992 (367 per 100,000 of national population).

Education

The adult literacy rate was 99·7% in 2002 (males, 99·7%; females, 99·7%). In 2002–03 there were 25,265 primary and 20,375 secondary school pupils in government schools and 3,730 primary and 1,139 secondary pupils in private schools. There were 23 public and eight private secondary schools in 2003. Education is free in all government-owned and government-maintained institutions from primary to university level.

In 2000–01 total expenditure on education came to 7·3% of GNP and 18·5% of total government spending.

In 2002–03 the University of the West Indies in Barbados (founded 1963) had 4,363 students, the Community College had 3,697, the Samuel Jackman Prescod Polytechnic had 2,972 and Erdiston Teachers' College had 223 students.

Health

In 2001 there was one general hospital, one psychiatric hospital, five district hospitals, eight health centres and two private hospitals with 35 beds. There were 2,049 hospital beds and 420 doctors in the same year.

Welfare

The National Insurance and Social Security Scheme provides contributory sickness, age, maternity, disability and survivors benefits. Sugar workers have their own scheme.

RELIGION

In 2001, 63% of the population were Protestants, 5% Roman Catholics and the remainder other religions.

CULTURE

Broadcasting

The Caribbean Broadcasting Corporation is a government-owned commercial TV and radio service. There are two other commercial services. In 2001 there were 202,000 radios and 88,000 television sets (colour by NTSC).

Cinema

In 2001 there were two cinemas and one drive-in cinema for 600 cars.

Press

In 2003 there were two daily newspapers, the *Barbados Advocate* (est. 1895) and the *Daily Nation* (est. 1973), and a weekly business publication, the *Broad Street Journal*. The *Daily Nation* has an average daily circulation of 25,000; the *Barbados Advocate*, 15,000.

Tourism

There were 531,211 foreign tourists in 2003, plus 559,119 cruise ship arrivals, bringing revenue of BDS$1,493·8m. and contributing 11·8% of the country's GDP.

Festivals

The National Cultural Foundation organizes three annual national festivals: the nine-day Congaline Carnival which begins in the last week of April; Crop Over, a three-week festival held from mid-July until Aug.; the National Independence Festival of Creative Arts (NIFCA) which runs throughout Nov.

Libraries

The National Library Service operates seven branch libraries around the island and the Adult and Children's libraries in Bridgetown.

Museums and Galleries

There are four museums: the Barbados Museum at Bridgetown, which is housed in the former British military prison; Sunbury Plantation House; Hutson Sugar Museum; Tyrol Cot Heritage Village.

DIPLOMATIC REPRESENTATIVES

Of Barbados in the United Kingdom (1 Great Russell St., London, WC1B 3ND)
High Commissioner: L. Edwin Pollard.

Of the United Kingdom in Barbados (Lower Collymore Rock, Bridgetown)
High Commissioner: Duncan Taylor.

Of Barbados in the USA (2144 Wyoming Ave., NW, Washington, D.C. 20008)
Ambassador: Michael I. King.

Of the USA in Barbados (PO Box 302, Bridgetown)
Ambassador: Mary E. Kramer.

Of Barbados to the United Nations
Ambassador: Christopher Hackett.

Of Barbados to the European Union
Ambassador: Errol L. Humphrey.

FURTHER READING

Beckles, H., *A History of Barbados: from Amerindian Settlement to Nation-State.* Cambridge Univ. Press, 1990

Hoyos, F. A., *Tom Adams: a Biography.* London, 1988.—*Barbados: A History from the Amerindians to Independence.* 2nd ed. London, 1992

National Statistical Office: Barbados Statistical Service, Fairchild Street, Bridgetown.

BELARUS

Province	Area sq. km	Population 2004	Capital	Population 2004
Brest	32,300	1,462,900	Brest	298,300
Homel	40,400	1,505,400	Homel	481,100
Hrodno	25,000	1,146,100	Hrodno	314,800
Mahilyou	29,000	1,169,200	Mahilyou	365,100
Minsk	40,800	3,244,400	Minsk	1,741,300
Vitebsk	40,100	1,321,100	Vitebsk	342,300

Belarusian is the national language. Russian is also spoken.

SOCIAL STATISTICS

2001 births, 91,677 (rate of 9·2 per 1,000 population); deaths, 139,904 (rate of 14·0 per 1,000 population); marriages, 68,697; divorces, 40,850. In 1999 abortions totalled 1,451 per 1,000 live births—one of the highest rates in the world. In 2001 there were 4·1 divorces per 1,000 population, also one of the highest rates in the world. Annual population growth rate, 1992–2002, –0·4%. Life expectancy at birth, 2003, was 62·4 years for men and 74·0 years for women. Infant mortality, 2001, 9·1 per 1,000 live births; fertility rate, 2001, 1·3 children per woman.

CLIMATE

Moderately continental and humid with temperatures averaging 20°F (–6°C) in Jan. and 64°F (18°C) in July. Annual precipitation is 22–28" (550–700 mm).

CONSTITUTION AND GOVERNMENT

A new Constitution was adopted on 15 March 1994. It provides for a *President* who must be a citizen of at least 35 years of age, have resided for ten years in Belarus and whose candidacy must be supported by the signatures of 70 deputies or 100,000 electors. At a referendum held on 17 Oct. 2004, 86·2% of votes cast were in favour of the abolition of the two-term limit on the presidency. The vote was widely regarded as fraudulent.

There is an 11-member *Constitutional Court*. The chief justice and five other judges are appointed by the president.

Four referendums held on 14 May 1995 gave the president powers to dissolve parliament; work for closer economic integration with Russia; establish Russian as an official language of equal status with Belarusian; and introduce a new flag.

At a further referendum of 24 Nov. 1996 turnout was 84%. 79% of votes cast were in favour of the creation of an upper house of parliament nominated by provincial governors and 70% in favour of extending the presidential term of office by two years to five years. The Supreme Soviet was dissolved and a 110-member lower *House of Representatives* established, whose members are directly elected by universal adult suffrage every four years. The upper chamber is the *Council of the Republic* (64 seats; 56 members elected by regional councils and eight members appointed by the president, all for four-year terms). In practice, since 1996 the Belarusian parliament has only had a ceremonial function.

National Anthem

'My Bielarusy' ('We, the Belarusians'); words by M. Klimkovich and U. Karyzna, tune by Nester Sakalouski.

GOVERNMENT CHRONOLOGY

Heads of State since 1991.

Chairmen of the Supreme Council
1991–94   Stanislau Stanislavavich Shushkevich
1994   Myechyslau Ivanavich Hryb

President
1994–   Alyaksandr Rygoravich Lukashenka

Respublika Belarus

Capital: Minsk
Population projection, 2010: 9·48m.
GDP per capita, 2003: (PPP$) 6,052
HDI/world rank: 0·786/67

KEY HISTORICAL EVENTS

Belarus was fully integrated with Russia until the Gorbachev reforms of the mid-1980s encouraged demands for greater freedom. On 25 Aug. 1991 Belarus declared its independence and in Dec. it became a founder member of the CIS. The Communists retained power in Belarus despite formidable opposition and it was not until a new constitution was adopted in March 1994 that the economic reformers began to influence events. Alyaksandr Lukashenka was elected president in July 1994. By 1996, only 11% of state enterprises had been privatized and the government remains pro-Russian, striving for eventual unification with Russia within the Russia–Belarus Union. A referendum held over 9–24 Nov. 1996 extended the President's term of office from three to five years and increased his powers to rule by decree. The last two parliamentary elections have been criticized by the OSCE for a lack of transparency.

TERRITORY AND POPULATION

Belarus is situated along the western Dvina and Dnieper. It is bounded in the west by Poland, north by Latvia and Lithuania, east by Russia and south by Ukraine. The area is 207,600 sq. km (80,155 sq. miles). The capital is Minsk. Other important towns are Homel, Vitebsk, Mahilyou, Bobruisk, Hrodno and Brest. On 2 Nov. 1939 western Belorussia was incorporated with an area of over 108,000 sq. km and a population of 4·8m. Census population, 1999, 10,045,237. Estimated population, 2005, 9,755,000; density, 47·0 per sq. km.

The UN gives a projected population for 2010 of 9·48m.

In 2003, 70·9% of the population lived in urban areas. Major ethnic groups: 81·2% Belarusians, 11·4% Russians, 3·9% Poles, 2·4% Ukrainians, 1·1% others.

Belarus comprises six provinces. Areas and estimated populations:

RECENT ELECTIONS

Parliamentary elections were held on 17 and 31 Oct. 2004. In the first round, 107 of 110 deputies were elected, all supporters of the government, with 12 of them representing political parties. The remaining three seats were to be decided in a second round which has yet to take place. The results of the first round have been widely disputed.

Presidential elections were held on 19 March 2006. Alyaksandr Lukashenka was re-elected with 87·5% of votes cast against 6·5% for Alyaksandr Milinkevich and 3·7% for Sergei Gaidukevich. The election took place amid accusations of vote rigging. No independent observers were allowed to watch the count. Turnout was 92·7%.

CURRENT ADMINISTRATION

President: Alyaksandr Lukashenka; b. 1954 (sworn in 20 July 1994 and re-elected in Sept. 2001 and March 2006).

Prime Minister: Sergei Sidorsky; b. 1954 (took office on 19 Dec. 2003).

In March 2006 the government comprised:

First Deputy Prime Minister: Vladimir Semashko. *Deputy Prime Ministers:* Andrei Kobyakov; Aleksandr Kosinets; Vassili Gapeev; Vassili Dologolev; Ivan Bambiza.

Minister for Agriculture and Food: Leonid Rusak. *Architecture and Construction:* Gennady Kurochkin. *Communication:* Vladimir Goncharenko. *Culture:* Vladimir Matveichuk. *Defence:* Leonid Maltsev. *Economy:* Nikolai Zaychenko. *Education:* Alexander Radkov. *Emergencies:* Enver Bariyev. *Energy:* Alexander Ageyev. *Finance:* Nikolai Korbut. *Foreign Affairs:* Sergei Martynov. *Forestry:* Pyotr Semashko. *Health:* Viktor Rudenko. *Housing and Communal Services:* Vladimir Belokhvostov. *Industry:* Anatoly Rusetsky. *Information:* Vladimir Rusakevich. *Internal Affairs:* Vladimir Naumov. *Justice:* Viktor Golovanov. *Labour and Social Protection:* Antonina Morova. *Natural Resources and Environmental Protection:* Leonty Khoruzhik. *Sports and Tourism:* Yuri Sivakov. *Statistics and Analysis:* Vladimir Zinovsky. *Taxes and Duties:* Anna Deiko. *Trade:* Alexander Ivankov. *Transport and Communications:* Vladimir Sosnovsky.

Government Website (Russian only): http://www.government.by

CURRENT LEADERS

Alyaksandr Rygorovich Lukashenka

Position
President

Introduction
Alyaksandr Lukashenka has been president of Belarus since 1994. A member of the communist party from an early age, Lukashenka sought closer ties with Russia and rejected his predecessor's plans to implement free market policies. He has strengthened his powers within the constitution, but drawn international condemnation for his autocratic leadership and human rights abuses against opposition politicians and journalists.

Early Life
Lukashenka was born on 30 Aug. 1954 in Kepys. After studying history and agricultural economics, he taught at the Mohilyou Teaching Institute and the Belarusian SSR Agro-economics Academy. He was a member of Komsomol, a young communists' group, before working on collective farms while gaining political experience. After working in local politics, he became a deputy on the Belarusian Supreme Council in 1990. When Belarus gained independence the following year, he opposed the formation of the CIS, set up by Russia, Belarus and the Ukraine, as well as Stanislau Shushkevich's nationalist tendencies and his plans for privatization. By the time of the 1994 presidential elections, Shushkevich (the first post-independence leader) had been forced to stand down. Campaigning on a pro-Russian manifesto,

Lukashenka stood against Shushkevich and took 45% of votes to 10%. In a second round run-off with former prime minister (1990–94) Vyachaslau Kebich, he received 80·1% of votes.

Career in Office
Following his election, Lukashenka set about increasing presidential powers and strengthening state control. Countering Shushkevich's efforts to promote Belarusian culture, he reinstated Russian as the official language and sought closer ties, not always successfully, with the Russian Federation. Trade agreements were made with Russia and several other former Soviet states. Establishing what he called a 'vertical' presidency, in 1996 he pressed through constitutional changes to give himself more power and to extend his term of office by two years to 2001. He reversed reforms made by his predecessor after the collapse of the Soviet Union and secured his control over the state-owned media and security services. This caused conflicts with the constitutional court as well as the Supreme Council. He also rejected Shushkevich's previous moves towards privatization. In 1999 a mere 20% of economic output was being produced by the private sector.

Lukashenka used his presidential decree to impose restrictions on opponents, and journalists in particular have been subject to harassment and censorship for criticizing his regime. He has been condemned by the international community for human rights abuses and disregard for democracy.

In the 2000 parliamentary elections, Lukashenka's supporters won 81 of 110 seats. The following year Lukashenka won a second presidential term, taking 75·6% of the vote against 15·4% for Uladzimir Hancharyk. No independent observers were allowed to watch the count. However, experts estimated that the opposition actually gained between 30% and 40% of the vote. Both elections were criticized by international observers as undemocratic, with many opposition politicians either boycotting them or remaining in exile. International organizations continued to criticize Lukashenka's repressive regime during 2002 (when the authorities expelled an OSCE delegation) and 2003. The USA meanwhile passed legislation allowing the provision of financial support to the democratic opposition in Belarus.

Further parliamentary elections and a referendum were held on 17 Oct. 2004. No opposition candidates won a parliamentary seat in the poll, while Lukashenka claimed overwhelming support in the referendum for his intention to change the constitution and run for another presidential term. The results were dismissed as fraudulent by most international observers, raising fears among human rights activists and opposition politicians that his already authoritarian rule would progress to dictatorship.

Lukashenka was re-elected for a further term in March 2006, again amid accusations of vote rigging.

DEFENCE

Conscription is for 9–12 months. A treaty with Russia of April 1993 co-ordinates their military activities. All nuclear weapons had been transferred to Russia by Dec. 1996. Total active armed forces in 2002 numbered 79,800, including 30,000 conscripts and 4,000 women.

Defence expenditure in 2003 totalled US$2,400m. (US$243 per capita), representing 4·0% of GDP.

Army

There is a motor rifle division, three independent mobile brigades, one artillery division and one artillery regiment. In 2002 Army personnel numbered 29,300. In addition there were 289,500 reserves.

Air Force

In 2002 the Air Force operated 212 combat aircraft, including MiG-23s, MiG-29s, Su-24s, Su-25s and Su-27s, and 58 attack helicopters. Personnel, 2002, 22,000 including 10,200 in Air Defence.

INTERNATIONAL RELATIONS

A treaty of friendship with Russia was signed on 21 Feb. 1995. A further treaty signed by the respective presidents on 2 April 1997 provided for even closer integration.

Belarus is a member of the UN, CIS, IMF, the World Bank, European Bank, OSCE, CEI, IOM and the NATO Partnership for Peace.

ECONOMY

In 2002 agriculture contributed 11·8% of GDP, industry 37·0% and services 51·2%. In 1999 an estimated 20% of economic output was being produced by the private sector.

Currency

The rouble was retained under an agreement of Sept. 1993 and a treaty with Russia on monetary union of April 1994. Foreign currencies ceased to be legal tender in Oct. 1994. In Nov. 2000 President Lukashenka and President Putin of Russia agreed the introduction of a single currency. There are plans to introduce the Russian rouble in Jan. 2008. The inflation rate in 1994 was 2,434%. It has since been declining and in 2004 was 18·1%. Foreign exchange reserves in June 2002 were US$392m. and total money supply was 1,047·53bn. roubles.

Budget

Government revenue and expenditure (in 1bn. roubles):

	1996	1997	1998	1999	2000	2001
Revenue	58·99	117·87	206·59	876·23	2,646·11	4,938·20
Expenditure	62·51	121·79	213·23	933·88	2,639·80	5,080·21

In 2000 tax revenue totalled 2,447·22bn. roubles (including domestic taxes on goods and services, 1,016·56bn. roubles) and non-tax revenue 172·47bn. roubles. Main items of expenditure were: social security and welfare, 1,018·17bn. roubles; agriculture, forestry, fisheries and hunting, 219·53bn. roubles; general public services, 121·25bn. roubles; defence, 113·06bn. roubles.

Performance

Real GDP growth was 7·0% in 2003 and 11·0% in 2004. Total GDP in 2004 was US$22·8bn.

Banking and Finance

The central bank is the National Bank (*Chairman*, Petr P. Prokopovich). In 2003 there were 28 commercial banks. There is a stock exchange in Minsk.

ENERGY AND NATURAL RESOURCES

Environment

Carbon dioxide emissions from the consumption and flaring of fossil fuels in Belarus were the equivalent of 6·0 tonnes per capita in 2002.

Electricity

Installed capacity was 7·8m. kW in 2000. Production was 26·10bn. kWh in 2000. Consumption per capita in 2000 was 3,330 kWh.

Oil and Gas

In 2000 output of crude petroleum totalled 1·9m. tonnes; reserves in 2002 were 198m. bbls. Natural gas production in 2000 was 261m. cu. metres; in 2002 reserves were 2·8bn. cu. metres.

Minerals

Particular attention has been paid to the development of the peat industry with a view to making Belarus as far as possible self-supporting in fuel. There are over 6,500 peat deposits. There are rich deposits of rock salt and of iron ore.

Agriculture

Belarus is hilly, with a general slope towards the south. It contains large tracts of marshland, particularly to the southwest.

Agriculturally, it may be divided into three main sections—Northern: growing flax, fodder, grasses and breeding cattle for meat and dairy produce; Central: potato growing and pig breeding; Southern: good natural pasture land, hemp cultivation and cattle breeding for meat and dairy produce. In 2002 agriculture employed 12·1% of the workforce.

Output of main agricultural products (in 1m. tonnes) in 2000: potatoes, 8·50; barley, 1·70; rye, 1·45; sugarbeets, 1·50; wheat, 0·95; cabbage, 0·52; oats, 0·52; milk, 4·32; eggs, 0·19. In 2000 there were 4·33m. cattle; 3·57m. pigs; 221,000 horses; and 30m. chickens.

Since 1991 individuals may own land and pass it to their heirs, but not sell it. In 2003 there were 5·56m. ha. of arable land and 124,000 ha. of permanent crops. There were 4,723 farms in 2003. The private and commercial sectors accounted for 49% of the value of agricultural output in 2003, but only 20% of the total agricultural land. Agricultural output grew by 12·9% in 2004, the fifth successive year of growth. In 2004 state support for the agricultural sector accounted for 4% of GDP.

Forestry

Forests occupied 9·40m. ha., or 45·3% of the land area, in 2000. There are valuable reserves of oak, elm, maple and white beech. Timber production in 2001 was 6·27m. cu. metres.

Fisheries

Fish landings in 2001 amounted to 943 tonnes, exclusively from inland waters.

INDUSTRY

There are food-processing, chemical, textile, artificial silk, flax-spinning, motor vehicle, leather, machine-tool and agricultural machinery industries. Output in 1,000 tonnes: fertilizers (2004), 5,403; residual fuel oil (2000), 4,629; distillate fuel oil (2000), 3,847; cement (2004), 2,731; petrol (2000), 1,964; crude steel (2002), 1,607; wheat flour (1995), 1,417. Output of other products: 10,356m. cigarettes (2000); refrigerators (2000), 812,000; TV sets (2000), 532,000; tractors (2004), 34,000; lorries (2004), 21,500; beer (2003), 200m. litres; footwear (2002), 12·7m. pairs; woven cotton (1997), 48m. sq. metres; linen fabrics (1995), 41·5m. sq. metres. Machine-building equipment and chemical products are also important. Most industry is still state-controlled.

Labour

In 2001 the labour force totalled 4,519,000. In 2001, out of 4,417,000 economically active people, 1,300,000 were in industry; 660,000 in agriculture; 500,000 in education; 420,000 in trade and public catering, material and technical supply and sale. In 2002 there were 130,500 unemployed persons, or 3·0% of the workforce.

Trade Unions

Trade unions are grouped in the Federation of Trade Unions of Belarus.

INTERNATIONAL TRADE

Foreign debt was US$908m. in 2002.

Imports and Exports

In 2002 imports were valued at US$9,092m. and exports at US$8,021m. The main import suppliers in 2002 were Russia (65·1%), Germany (7·6%), Ukraine (3·2%), Italy (2·4%) and Poland (2·4%). Principal export markets were Russia (49·6%), Latvia (6·5%), United Kingdom (6·2%), Germany (4·3%) and the Netherlands (3·5%). Main import commodities are petroleum, natural gas, rolled metal and coal. Export commodities include machinery and transport equipment, diesel fuel, synthetic fibres and consumer goods.

COMMUNICATIONS

Roads

In 2002 there were 79,990 km of motor roads (86·7% paved), including 15,371 km of national roads. There were 1,548,472 passenger cars in use in 2002 (156 per 1,000 inhabitants). In

2000 public transport totalled 9,235m. passenger-km and freight 8,982m. tonne-km. There were 1,594 fatalities as a result of road accidents in 2000.

Rail

In 2000 there were 5,512 km of 1,520 mm gauge railways (874 km electrified). Passenger-km travelled in 2000 came to 17·7bn. and freight tonne-km to 31·4bn. There is a metro in Minsk.

Civil Aviation

The main airport is Minsk International 2, which handled 421,000 passengers (all international) and 2,700 tonnes of freight in 2001. The national carrier is Belavia. In 2003 Belavia flew on domestic routes and operated international services to Adler/Sochi, Baku, Berlin, Frankfurt, Hurghada, İstanbul, Kaliningrad, Kyiv, Larnaca, London, Moscow, Paris, Prague, Rome, Shannon, Stockholm, Tashkent, Tbilisi, Tel Aviv, Vienna, Warsaw and Yerevan. In 1999 scheduled airline traffic of Belarus-based carriers flew 8·0m. km, carrying 212,000 passengers (all on international flights).

Shipping

In 2002 inland waterways carried 2m. passenger-km and 59m. tonne-km of freight.

Telecommunications

In 2002 there were 3,432,400 telephone subscribers (346·3 per 1,000 inhabitants). There are plans to privatize Beltelecom, the state monopoly, in 2007. There were 462,600 mobile phone subscribers in 2002 and 32,000 fax machines. Belarus had 808,700 Internet users in 2002.

Postal Services

In 2003 there were 3,752 post offices.

SOCIAL INSTITUTIONS

Justice

The death penalty is retained following the constitutional referendum of Nov. 1996 and was used in 2000.

135,540 crimes were reported in 2000. In Dec. 2001 there were 55,156 prisoners, giving Belarus one of the highest rates of imprisonment in the world, with 554 prisoners per 100,000 population.

Education

Adult literacy rate in 2001 was 99·7% (male, 99·8%; female, 99·6%). There were 254,595 children and 52,459 teachers at pre-school institutions in 2000–01, 551,486 pupils and 32,166 teachers at primary schools, 980,603 pupils and 105,312 teachers in secondary schools, and 437,995 students and 40,470 academic staff at institutions of tertiary education.

In 2001 there were 58 state higher educational establishments including: four universities; specialized universities of agriculture, culture, economics, information technology and radio-electronics, linguistics, teacher training and transport; academies of agriculture, arts, music, physical culture and sport, and a polytechnical academy; four medical, three polytechnical and three teacher training institutes, and institutes of agriculture, co-operation, light industry technology, machine-building and veterinary science. In 2001–02 there were 301,800 people enrolled at state higher education establishments.

In 1999–2000 total expenditure on education came to 6·0% of GNP.

Health

In 2002 there were 44,800 doctors (45·3 per 10,000 population); and, in 1999, 4,522 dentists, 47,343 nurses and 5,826 midwives. In 2001 there were 126 hospital beds per 10,000 persons.

Welfare

To qualify for an old-age pension men must be age 60 with 25 years of insurance coverage and women must be 55 with 20 years of insurance coverage. Minimum old-age pension is 25% of the average per capita subsistence budget. The maximum pension is 75% of wage base. The minimum unemployment benefit is the minimum wage and the maximum benefit is twice the minimum wage. The minimum wage in 2001 was 3,600 roubles a month. Benefits are adjusted periodically according to changes in the minimum wage.

RELIGION

The Orthodox is the largest church. There is a Roman Catholic archdiocese of Minsk and Mahilyou, and five dioceses embracing 455 parishes. In 2001, 32% of the population were Belarusian Orthodox and 18% Roman Catholics. In May 2005 there was one cardinal.

CULTURE

World Heritage Sites

There are four UNESCO sites in Belarus: the Mir Castle Complex, begun in the 15th century (inscribed on the list in 2000); the Belovezhskaya Pushcha/Bialowieza Forest site (1979 and 1992), shared with Poland; the Radziwill Family complex at Nesvizh (2005); and the Struve Geodetic Arc (2005). The Arc is a chain of survey triangulations spanning from Norway to the Black Sea that helped establish the exact shape and size of the earth and is shared with nine other countries.

Broadcasting

The government-controlled Belarus Radio broadcasts two national programmes and various regional programmes, a foreign service (Belarusian, German) and a shared relay with Radio Moscow. Belarus Television broadcasts on one channel (colour by SECAM H). In 2001 there were 3·5m. TV receivers and in 2000 there were 3·0m. radio receivers.

Press

There were two state-owned daily newspapers in Jan. 2006. The only independent daily newspaper, *Narodnaya Volya*, has been published in Russia since Oct. 2005. There is also a Belarusian edition of the Russian daily *Komsomolskaya Pravda*. In 1998 a total of 6,073 book titles were published.

Tourism

In 2001 there were 61,000 foreign tourists. Receipts totalled US$171m.

DIPLOMATIC REPRESENTATIVES

Of Belarus in the United Kingdom (6 Kensington Court, London, W8 5DL)
Ambassador: Dr Alyaksei Mazhukhou.

Of the United Kingdom in Belarus (37 Karl Marx St., Minsk 220030)
Ambassador: Brian M. Bennett.

Of Belarus in the USA (1619 New Hampshire Ave., NW, Washington, D.C., 20009)
Ambassador: Mikhail Khvostov.

Of the USA in Belarus (46 Starovilenskaya, Minsk 220002)
Ambassador: George Krol.

Of Belarus to the United Nations
Ambassador: Andrei Dapkiunas.

Of Belarus to the European Union
Ambassador: Vacant.
Deputy Head of Mission: Aleksandr Baichorov.

FURTHER READING

Marples, D. R., *Belarus: from Soviet Rule to Nuclear Catastrophe.* London, 1996
Zaprudnik, J., *Belarus at the Crossroads in History.* Boulder (CO), 1993

National Statistical Office: Ministry of Statistics and Analysis of the Republic of Belarus, Minsk.
Website: http://www.belstat.gov.by

BELGIUM

Royaume de Belgique — Koninkrijk België
(Kingdom of Belgium)

Capital: Brussels
Population projection, 2010: 10·49m.
GDP per capita, 2003: (PPP$) 28,335
HDI/world rank: 0·945/9

KEY HISTORICAL EVENTS

The prehistory of Belgium begins around 20,000 years ago with flint objects excavated in Limburg. The Neanderthal Mousterian culture of the Ardennes region produced flint tools between 80–35,000 years ago. Omalien tribes of the early Neolithic period (5–4,000 BC) developed settled agricultural practices, sophisticated tools and decorated black pottery. The Bronze Age Hilversum culture left evidence of contact overseas in Wessex, southern England. During the pre-Roman period Celtic and Germanic tribes moved across the region. Much of northern Gaul and southern Britain was settled by a Celtic group known as the Belgae, forming numerous tribes including the seafaring Morini and Menapii in what is now Flanders and the bellicose Nervii in Artois. In alliance with Germanic and other Belgic tribes, the Nervii led resistance to the invasion of Julius Caesar in 59 BC, succumbing five years later. Roman control was extended as far north as the Rhine and the area divided into the provinces of Gallia Belgica and Germania Inferior. Several tribes survived as Roman administrative *civitates*.

The network of Roman power, based around wealthy *villae* (country estates), declined from the mid-3rd century AD, despite the bolstering effect of the campaigns of Julian, who became emperor in 361 AD. The massive influx of Germanic tribes (known commonly as the Barbarian invasions) over the Rhine in 406/7 effectively brought Roman rule in Belgium to an end. Chief among the German tribes were the Franks, who settled in Toxandria (modern Brabant). The Frankish Merovingian Empire, established by Childeric I, was based at Tournai and extended by Childeric's son, Clovis. The successors to the Merovingians, the Pippins (or Carolingians), ruled all but in name from Austrasia in the Ardennes. A partnership between the nobility and the church allowed the expansion of Frankish power north and east across the Rhine, bringing Christianity to the Low Countries by the 7th century, under the sees of Arras, Tournai, Cambrai and, from 720, Liège.

The death of Louis the Pious in 840 precipitated the fragmentation of Charlemagne's huge empire. Viking attacks on the Low Countries came at the end of the 8th century, intensifying in the period 841–75. Resistance began under Charlemagne; provincial princes capitalized on the fortification process and land reclamation to increase their own power. Baldwin 'Iron Arm', count of Flanders, fortified Ghent around 867, cementing his authority over the Flemish towns. His successors extended control into Artois (and to Hainault by personal union) in defiance of the French kings. Philippe IV of France was defeated in 1302 at the Battle of the Golden Spurs at Kortrijk, Flanders and formally recognized Flemish independence. Flanders' alliance with England during the Hundred Years War created an advantageous trading relationship, especially the importation of English wool for the textile industry. Brugge (Bruges), Ypres and Ghent flourished and in the 14th century had to be forcibly restrained from becoming city-states by Philip of Burgundy.

Other principalities emerged in the wake of the Carolingian empire, most notably the duchies of Brabant and Limburg and the prince-bishopric of Liège. Their union was forged under the dukes of Burgundy. The marriage of Philip the Bold, duke of Burgundy, to Margaret of Flanders in 1369 was the first step towards what became the Burgundian *Kreis* (lands) under Emperor Charles V. The addition of Hainault-Holland, Namur and Luxembourg encouraged Burgundian ambitions of centralization and even a unitary empire, vainly attempted by Duke Charles the Bold in the 1470s. The provinces and towns jealously guarded their imperial and local privileges and resisted the high taxation imposed by their Burgundian lord. Burgundian authority was reinforced by the 1477 marriage of Charles' daughter (and heir), Mary, to the Habsburg Maximilian of Austria, later Holy Roman Emperor, beginning over three centuries of Habsburg rule in the Low Countries.

Trade Centres

Brugge became the principal market of northwest Europe in the 14th century, ceding its role in the 1490s (on account of silting of its waterways) to Antwerp. The volume of Portuguese and English traders and Italian financiers testified to the importance of Antwerp as a mercantile and financial centre; the *Antwerpen beurs* (stock exchange) was established in 1531. Antwerp's population reached 100,000 in the mid-16th century. The artistic achievements of the 15th century were reliant on the patronage of the court and nobility. Artists such as Rogier van der Weyden in Brussels and Jan van Eyck in Ghent formed part of a Flemish school that greatly influenced northern European art. The University of Louvain (Leuven), founded in 1425, was a centre of Dutch Humanism made famous by scholars such as Erasmus.

Dynastic pressures increased with the marriage of Archduke Philip the Handsome to the heiress of the Spanish crowns, Juana the Mad, leaving the Netherlands (the Burgundian Low Countries, including Belgium) under the supervision of governors-general in Brussels. Centralization continued under Philip's son, Charles of Ghent (Holy Roman Emperor Charles V), who regulated the succession to his Burgundian territories by pragmatic sanction. However, it was the imposition of a new ecclesiastical hierarchy by Charles' son, Philip II of Spain, that unified opposition in the Netherlands.

The Netherlands was highly receptive to religious reformist ideas, most notably those of Jean Calvin, whose influence had extended to Antwerp by 1545. Appealing to the urban middle

191

classes and the lower nobility, Calvinism became the target of government repression, especially after the radical iconoclasm of 1566. The following year Philip sent the duke of Alba to stamp out the religious and political uprisings, sparking full revolt in Holland and other northern provinces. The execution of the counts of Hoorne and Egmond in Brussels in 1568 encouraged explicit rejection of 'Spanish rule'.

The secession of the northern Netherlands was partly the result of the inability of the Spanish armies to penetrate the marshes and dendritic waterways of Holland and Zeeland. Although Alba managed to reassert Philip's authority in the south, his armies never retook the provinces north of the Rhine after 1574. Separation was also caused by the extreme demands of the northern Calvinists, who alienated the more Catholic southern provinces. However, a measure of unity was achieved at the Pacification of Ghent after the atrocities of the 'Spanish Fury'—Spanish troops massacred 7,000 people in Antwerp in 1576.

In 1578 Philip appointed as governor-general Alessandro Farnese, duke of Parma, who ejected Protestants from the governments of the southern provinces and waged successful campaigns against the revolutionaries. The Union of Arras (1579), led by Flanders and Hainault, accepted the sovereignty of the Spanish king, supported Catholicism and ended the revolt of the southern provinces. In reaction the northern provinces drew up the Union of Utrecht, thus marking the birth of the 'Dutch Republic', though Philip was not rejected as sovereign in the north until 1581. Farnese took Antwerp in 1585, effectively creating the boundaries of the renegade Dutch state. Although fighting resumed after the Twelve Year Truce (1609–21), the Habsburg government accepted the independence of the Dutch Netherlands at the Peace of Westphalia in 1648.

The Spanish Netherlands was governed autonomously for much of the 17th century—Liège remained neutral in the revolt and separate until 1795. Antwerp was at first eclipsed as the principal trading centre of the region by Dutch Amsterdam, which attracted many of the south's skilled artisans and merchants. Economic recovery was helped by new industries such as linen production and diamond processing in Antwerp. Art was dominated by the Baroque style, patronized by the Catholic Church and employed by Rubens, Van Dyck and Jordaens.

War of Succession

The death of Charles II of Spain without issue in 1700 caused a constitutional crisis and the War of the Spanish Succession. Philip of Anjou, the heir-designate and a grandson of Louis XIV of France, was urged to hand over the Spanish Netherlands to France. The intervention of England and the Dutch was motivated by the fear of either Franco-Spanish union or the reuniting of the Austrian and Spanish Habsburgs. The Spanish Netherlands were finally settled on Emperor Charles VI after the Treaty of Utrecht in 1713, thus bringing the Netherlands under the sway of the Austrian Habsburgs.

Dynastic succession was again the cause of war after the death of Charles VI in 1740. By pragmatic sanction, his daughter, Archduchess Maria Theresa, succeeded to the Habsburg territories but was barred from the Imperial crown (it was secured for her husband, Francis Stephen of Lorraine). Supported by Great Britain, the Dutch and the Hungarian diet, Maria Theresa's armies repelled the French from the Austrian Netherlands, establishing her authority by the Treaty of Aix-la-Chapelle in 1748 (though she lost Silesia to Prussia). Her popular reign saw great economic gains in the Netherlands and the beginning of industrial capitalism thanks to good trading relations with Great Britain.

The Austrian regime lost popular support under Maria Theresa's successor, Emperor Joseph II, whose abolition of local privileges and his attempts to swap the Austrian Netherlands for Bavaria made him highly unpopular. Coupled with his attacks on the power of the Catholic Church, his 'Belgian' subjects—conservatives and progressives alike—revolted in 1789. The bulk of Joseph's forces being engaged on the Ottoman frontier, the Austrian army was easily routed at Turnhout. Conservative elements were victorious in the 'Brabant Revolution' and proclaimed the United States of Belgium in 1790.

Although Joseph's brother, Leopold II, reasserted Austrian authority, the seeds of revolution had been sown, encouraged by events in France. Republican France invaded Belgium in 1795, ending the independence and religious rule of Liège. Discontent with French rule was immediate, partly in reaction to the denial of autonomy, military conscription and persecution of the Church. After peasant uprisings in 1798 the Napoleonic consulate agreed a compromise with the papacy and the Belgian church, ending persecution.

Towards Independence

Napoleon's defeat in 1814 left Belgium in the hands of the Great Powers. Belgium was reunified with the Dutch Netherlands as the Kingdom of the Netherlands at the Congress of Vienna. Despite cultural and linguistic affinities, the relationship between the two Netherlands was uneasy. Belgium, ruled by the Dutch William of Orange, was underrepresented in the States General and its French-speaking elite alienated by the declaration of Dutch as the sole legal language. The two economies were in contrast, the Dutch being primarily mercantile while the Belgian was geared towards mechanized industry. Belgium was one of the first areas of continental Europe to adopt the innovations of the Industrial Revolution, most notably in the Ghent textile industry and coal mining in Hainaut. The loss of the French market in 1814 and William's refusal to increase tariffs to protect Belgian industry impacted heavily on the Belgian economy.

Dissent took the form of unionism in the late 1820s, fomenting opposition to the union with the Dutch and paving the way for the Belgian Revolution of 1830. The secession of Belgium was secured by the intervention of France and Britain, which recognized Belgian independence in 1831. Repelled by the French, William accepted the loss of Belgium in 1838. Limburg and Luxembourg were partitioned and a liberal constitution implemented. The great powers insisted on a Belgian monarch and Prince Leopold of Saxe-Coburg was duly installed.

A Liberal government was brought to power in 1847 after three devastating harvests. The Liberal prime minister, Walthère Frère-Orban, championed the removal of church control of the schools. The Schools War dominated the political agenda and saw a conservative counter-offensive with the establishment of a network of independent Catholic schools. A conservative Catholic victory in 1884 brought Auguste Beernaert to the premiership. Closely associated with the Flemish revivalists, Beernaert managed the Flemish Equality Law, giving the Flemish language the same rights as French. Changes in the electoral system brought in full male suffrage (over 25 years of age) in 1893.

The Congo

Belgian foreign policy was bound by recognition (and imposition) of neutrality. King Leopold II, set on expanding his kingdom, looked to Africa. The Belgian Congo, acquired as his personal possession in 1885, was soon infamous for colonial abuse and exploitation. After widespread international condemnation, the 'Congo Free State' was formally annexed by Belgium in 1908, thus curbing Leopold's inhuman regime. In Europe, threats were perceived to the west and east. Attempts by Albert I (reigned 1909–34) to arm Belgium against French and German aggression were frustrated by the domestic pacifist movement led by Beernaert. Belgian neutrality was violated by Germany in 1914 after Albert's refusal to allow German free passage. Albert remained with his army on the Yser River throughout the First World War, supported by Allied troops. Neutrality, seen by many Belgians as a hindrance, was abolished under the Treaty of Versailles in 1919; Belgium was awarded the provinces of Eupen and Malmédy and jurisdiction over Ruanda-Urundi from the defeated Germany.

Belgium underwent massive change after the First World War. Its economy wrecked by German occupation—heavy industry in the south was particularly affected—the government followed an international economic policy. Economic union with Luxembourg was achieved in 1921 and the gold standard re-established to assist the export industry. The exploitative potential of the Belgian Congo was resolutely pursued once its wealth of minerals was discovered. Constitutional changes were made including the equal suffrage of all men over 21 (women were denied the vote until 1948) and the formal linguistic separation of Flanders and Wallonia (excluding Brussels).

The 1930s was a time of rising unemployment—exports were seriously affected by the relinquishment of the British gold standard in 1931—and concern over German ambitions. Defences were built between Antwerp and Namur despite protestations of neutrality. Germany invaded Belgium on 10 May 1940. Capitulation after just 18 days made King Leopold III unpopular, despite his refusal to flee to France (and later to London) with the government. Collaboration with the German government of occupation was resisted by most and an underground army was active for much of the Second World War. Insurgents managed to protect the port of Antwerp, crucial for Allied support, during the liberation of Belgium in Sept. 1944.

The infrastructure of the economy was much less affected by the Second World War than the preceding occupation, allowing for a speedy recovery. Collaborators were treated harshly with many detentions. Political unity was disturbed by the royal question; a referendum on the return of the king from imprisonment in Austria caused violent protest in Wallonia and in 1951 Leopold was persuaded to abdicate in favour of his son, Baudouin.

European Union

Belgium embarked on international co-operation with marked enthusiasm under the leadership of Prime Minister Paul-Henri Spaak. Economic union with Luxembourg was re-established and extended to include the Netherlands, forming the Benelux Economic Union. In 1949 Belgium joined the North Atlantic Treaty Organization (NATO) and in 1951 the European Coal and Steel Community (ECSC). Encouraged by the success of the ECSC, plans were laid for the establishment of two more communities. The European Economic Community (EEC) and the European Atomic Energy Community (Euratom) were subsequently created under separate treaties signed in Rome on 25 March 1957.

The administration of the Belgian Congo resisted reform or demands for greater participation until the 1950s. After violent protest and agitation, moderate local government reform was passed in 1957 but was too late to quell the independence movement, led by Patrice Lumumba. The government accepted these demands in 1959 and allowed a hurried decolonization programme, leaving Congo abruptly in 1960. Rwanda and Burundi became independent in 1962.

A milestone in domestic politics was reached in 1958 with the School Pact, ending a century of conflict between secularists and conservative Catholics. Prime Minister Gaston Eyskens negotiated a guarantee of funding for state secondary schools and private religious schools. Relations between Walloon and Flemish society became difficult as a result of the decline of Walloon industry. Strikes and discontent with government subsidies set Belgium on the course of federalization. After the division of Brabant along linguistic lines Belgium officially became a federal state in 1993. King Baudouin, who died in 1993, was respected for his even-handed approach to Belgium's divided society and seen as an important symbol of unity. He was succeeded by his brother, Albert II.

TERRITORY AND POPULATION

Belgium is bounded in the north by the Netherlands, northwest by the North Sea, west and south by France, and east by Germany and Luxembourg. Its area is 30,528 sq. km. Population (2001 census), 10,296,350. Population (at 1 Jan. 2004), 10,396,421 (5,309,245 females); density, 340·6 per sq. km. The Belgian exclave of Baarle-Hertog in the Netherlands has an area of seven sq. km and a population (2003) of 2,247. There were 850,077 resident foreign nationals as at 1 Jan. 2003. In 2003, 97·2% of the population lived in urban areas.

The UN gives a projected population for 2010 of 10·49m.

Dutch (Flemish) is spoken by the Flemish section of the population in the north, French by the Walloon south. The linguistic frontier passes south of the capital, Brussels, which is bilingual. Some German is spoken in the east. Each language has official status in its own community. (Bracketed names below signify French/Dutch and where relevant English alternatives.)

Area, population and chief towns of the ten provinces on 1 Jan. 2004:

Province	Area (sq. km)	Population	Chief Town
Flemish Region			
Antwerp	2,867	1,668,812	Antwerpen (Anvers/ Antwerp)
East Flanders	2,982	1,373,720	Gent (Gand/Ghent)
West Flanders	3,144	1,135,802	Brugge (Bruges)
Flemish Brabant	2,106	1,031,904	Leuven (Louvain)
Limburg	2,422	805,786	Hasselt
Walloon Region			
Hainaut (Henegouwen)	3,786	1,283,200	Mons (Bergen)
Liège (Luik)	3,862	1,029,605	Liège (Luik)
Namur (Namen)	3,666	452,856	Namur (Namen)
Walloon Brabant	1,091	360,717	Wavre (Waver)
Luxembourg	4,440	254,120	Arlon (Aarlen)

Population of the regions on 1 Jan. 2004: Brussels-Capital Region, 999,899; Flemish Region, 6,016,024; Walloon Region, 3,380,498 (including the German-speaking Region, 71,571 in 2003).

The most populous towns, with population on 1 Jan. 2004:

Brussel (Bruxelles/Brussels)[1]	999,899	Kortrijk (Courtrai)	73,984
Antwerpen (Anvers/Antwerp)	455,148	Hasselt	69,127
Gent (Gand/Ghent)	229,344	St Niklaas (St Nicolas)	68,820
Charleroi	200,608	Oostende (Ostende/ Ostend)	68,273
Liège (Luik)	185,488		
Brugge (Bruges)	117,025	Tournai (Doornik)	67,341
Namur (Namen)	106,213	Genk	63,550
Mons (Bergen)	91,185	Seraing	60,579
Leuven (Louvain)	89,777	Roeselare (Roulers)	55,273
Mechelen (Malines)	76,981	Verviers	52,804
Aalst (Alost)	76,852	Mouscron (Moeskroen)	52,290
La Louvière	76,784		

[1]19 communes.

SOCIAL STATISTICS

Statistics for calendar years:

	Births	Deaths	Marriages	Divorces	Immigration[1]	Emigration[1]
1999	113,469	104,904	44,171	26,423	521,684	509,432
2000	114,883	104,903	45,123	27,002	511,180	486,051
2001	114,172	103,447	42,110	29,314	524,626	489,263
2002	111,225	105,642	40,434	30,628	542,191	500,885
2003	112,149	107,039	41,805	31,373	552,608	512,592

[1]Including internal.

In 2002 Belgium received 18,805 asylum applications, equivalent to 1·8 per 1,000 inhabitants. Annual population growth rate, 1992–2002, 0·3%. Life expectancy at birth, 2003, was 75·7 years for men and 82·0 years for women. 2003 birth rate (per 1,000 population): 10·8; death rate: 10·3. Infant mortality,

2001, 5 per 1,000 live births; fertility rate, 2001, 1·5 children per woman.

CLIMATE

Cool temperate climate influenced by the sea, giving mild winters and cool summers. Brussels, Jan. 36°F (2·2°C), July 64°F (17·8°C). Annual rainfall 33" (825 mm). Ostend, Jan. 38°F (3·3°C), July 62°F (16·7°C). Annual rainfall 31" (775 mm).

CONSTITUTION AND GOVERNMENT

According to the constitution of 1831, Belgium is a constitutional, representative and hereditary monarchy. The legislative power is vested in the King, the federal parliament and the community and regional councils. The King convokes parliament after an election or the resignation of a government, and has the power to dissolve it in accordance with Article 46 of the Constitution.

The reigning King is **Albert II**, born 6 June 1934, who succeeded his brother, Baudouin, on 9 Aug. 1993. Married on 2 July 1959 to Paola Ruffo di Calabria, daughter of Don Fuleo and Donna Luisa Gazelli de Rossena. *Offspring:* Prince Philippe, Duke of Brabant, b. 15 April 1960; Princess Astrid, b. 5 June 1962; Prince Laurent, b. 19 Oct. 1963. Prince Philippe married Mathilde d'Udekem d'Acoz, 4 Dec. 1999. *Offspring:* Princess Elizabeth, b. 25 Oct. 2001; Prince Gabriel, b. 20 Aug. 2003; Prince Emmanuel, b. 4 Oct. 2005. Princess Astrid married Archduke Lorenz of Austria, 22 Sept. 1984. *Offspring:* Prince Amedeo, b. 21 Feb. 1986; Princess Maria Laura, b. 26 Aug. 1988; Prince Joachim, b. 9 Dec. 1991; Princess Luisa Maria, b. 11 Oct. 1995; Princess Laetitia Maria, b. 23 April 2003. Prince Laurent married Claire Coombs, 12 April 2003. *Offspring:* Princess Louise, b. 6 Feb. 2004; Prince Nicolas, b. 13 Dec. 2005; Prince Aymeric, b. 13 Dec. 2005.

The Dowager Queen — Queen Fabiola de Mora y Aragón, daughter of the Conde de Mora y Aragón and Marqués de Casa Riera; married to King Baudouin on 15 Dec. 1960. *Sister of the King.* Josephine Charlotte, Princess of Belgium, b. 11 Oct. 1927; married to Prince Jean of Luxembourg, 9 April 1953. *Half-brother and half-sisters of the King.* Prince Alexandre, b. 18 July 1942; Princess Marie Christine, b. 6 Feb. 1951; Princess Maria-Esmeralda, b. 30 Sept. 1956.

A constitutional amendment of June 1991 permits women to accede to the throne.

The King receives a basic annual tax-free sum from the civil list of €6,049,000 for the duration of his reign; Queen Fabiola receives €1,116,000; Prince Philippe, €788,400; Princess Astrid and Prince Laurent, €273,000 each. These figures are adapted annually in accordance with the general price index.

Constitutional reforms begun in Dec. 1970 culminated in May 1993 in the transformation of Belgium from a unitary into a 'federal state, composed of communities and regions'. The communities are three in number and based on language: Flemish, French and German. The regions also number three, and are based territorially: Flemish, Walloon and the Brussels-Capital Region.

Since 1995 the federal parliament has consisted of a 150-member *Chamber of Representatives*, directly elected by obligatory universal suffrage from 20 constituencies on a proportional representation system for four-year terms; and a *Senate* of 71 members (excluding senators by right, i.e. certain members of the Royal Family). 25 senators are elected by a Dutch-speaking, and 15 by a French-speaking, electoral college; 21 are designated by community councils (ten Flemish, ten French and one German). These senators co-opt a further ten senators (six Dutch-speaking and four French-speaking).

The federal parliament's powers relate to constitutional reform, federal finance, foreign affairs, defence, justice, internal security, social security and some areas of public health. The Senate is essentially a revising chamber, though it may initiate certain legislation, and is equally competent with the Chamber of Representatives in matters concerning constitutional reform and the assent to international treaties.

The number of ministers in the federal government is limited to 15. The Council of Ministers, apart from the Prime Minister, must comprise an equal number of Dutch- and French-speakers. Members of parliament, if appointed ministers, are replaced in parliament by the runner-up on the electoral list for the minister's period of office. Community and regional councillors may not be members of the Chamber of Representatives or Senate.

National Anthem

'La Brabançonne'; words by A. Dechet, tune by F. van Campenhout. The Flemish version is 'O dierbaar België, O heilig land der vaad'ren' ('Noble Belgium, for ever a dear land').

GOVERNMENT CHRONOLOGY

Prime Ministers since 1939. (BSP/PSB = Belgian Socialist Party; CVP = Christian People's Party; CVP/PSC = Christian People's/Social Christian Party; VLD = Flemish Liberals and Democrats)

1939–45	CVP/PSC	Hubert Pierlot
1945–46	BSP/PSB	Achille Van Acker
1946	BSP/PSB	Paul-Henri Spaak
1946	BSP/PSB	Achille Van Acker
1946–47	BSP/PSB	Camille Huysmans
1947–49	BSP/PSB	Paul-Henri Spaak
1949–50	CVP/PSC	Gaston Eyskens
1950	CVP/PSC	Jean Pierre Duvieusart
1950–52	CVP/PSC	Louis Marie Joseph Pholien
1952–54	CVP/PSC	Jean Marie Van Houtte
1954–58	BSP/PSB	Achille Van Acker
1958–61	CVP/PSC	Gaston Eyskens
1961–65	CVP/PSC	Théodore Lefèvre
1965–66	CVP/PSC	Pierre Charles Harmel
1966–68	CVP/PSC	Paul Vanden Boeynants
1968–73	CVP	Gaston Eyskens
1973–74	BSP/PSB	Edmond Jules Leburton
1974–78	CVP	Léo Tindemans
1978–79	CVP	Paul Vanden Boeynants
1979–81	CVP	Wilfried Martens
1981	CVP	Mark Eyskens
1981–92	CVP	Wilfried Martens
1992–99	CVP	Jean-Luc Dehaene
1999–	VLD	Guy Verhofstadt

RECENT ELECTIONS

Elections to the 150-member Chamber of Representatives were held on 18 May 2003. The Flemish Liberals and Democrats (VLD) won 25 seats with 15·4% of votes cast; The Socialist Party (PS) won 25 seats (13·0%); the Reformist Movement (MR) won 24 seats (11·4%); SPA (Socialist Party Different)-Spirit coalition won 23 seats (14·9% of the vote); the Christian Democratic and Flemish Party (CD&V) won 21 seats (13·3%); the Vlaams Blok (Flemish Block, VB) won 18 seats (11·6%); the Humanist Democratic Centre (CDH) won 8 seats (5·5%); Ecolo won 4 seats (3·1%); the New Flemish Alliance (N-VA) won 1 seat (3·1%); and the National Front (FN) won 1 seat (2·0%). Agalev (2·5%) and Vivant (1·2%) won no seats. Prime Minister Guy Verhofstadt's VLD won two more seats than in the 1999 elections.

Voting for the 40 electable seats in the Senate took place on the same day. SPA-Spirit and VLD both won 7 seats; CD&V and PS won 6; MR and VB, 5; CDH, 2; and Ecolo and FN 1. There are also 31 indirectly elected senators.

European Parliament

Belgium has 24 (25 in 1999) representatives. At the June 2004 elections turnout was 90·8% (95·0% in 1999). The CD&V/N-VA won 4 seats with 17·4% of the vote (political affiliation in European Parliament: European People's Party–European Democrats); the PS, 4 with 13·5% (Party of European Socialists); the VB, 3 with

14·3% (non-attached); the VLD-Vivant, 3 with 13·6% (Alliance of Liberals and Democrats for Europe); SPA-Spirit, 3 with 11·0% (Party of European Socialists); the MR, 3 with 10·4% (Alliance of Liberals and Democrats for Europe); the CDH, 1 with 5·7% (European People's Party–European Democrats); Groen!, 1 with 4·9% (Greens/European Free Alliance); Ecolo, 1 with 3·7% (Greens/European Free Alliance); the Christian-Social Party, 1 with 0·2% (European People's Party–European Democrats).

CURRENT ADMINISTRATION

In March 2006 the coalition government comprised:

Prime Minister: Guy Verhofstadt; b. 1953 (VLD; in office since 12 July 1999 and re-elected on 18 May 2003).

Deputy Prime Ministers: Laurette Onkelinx (PS; also *Minister of Justice*); Didier Reynders (MR; also *Minister of Finance*); Freya Van den Bossche (SPA; also *Minister of Budget and Consumer Protection*); Patrick Dewael (VLD: also *Minister of Interior*).

Minister for the Civil Service, Social Integration, Urban Policy and Equal Opportunities: Christian Dupont (PS). *Defence:* André Flahaut (PS). *Development Co-operation:* Armand De Decker (MR). *Economy, Energy, Foreign Trade and Science:* Marc Verwilghen (VLD). *Employment:* Peter Vanvelthoven (SPA). *Environment and Pensions:* Bruno Tobback (SPA). *Foreign Affairs:* Karel De Gucht (VLD). *Self-Employed and Agriculture:* Sabine Laruelle (MR). *Social Affairs and Public Health:* Rudy Demotte (PS). *Transport:* Renaat Landuyt (SPA).

Government Website: http://www.belgium.fgov.be

CURRENT LEADERS

Guy Verhofstadt

Position
Prime Minister

Introduction
Guy Verhofstadt is the leader of the Flemish Liberals and Democrats (VLD; Vlaamse Liberalen en Demokraten) and the current prime minister of Belgium. He began his first term of office following the June 1999 general election, which not only ousted the centre-left coalition government headed by Jean-Luc Dehaene but also ended decades of dominance by Christian Democrat parties.

Early Life
Verhofstadt was born on 11 April 1953 in Dendermonde, one of three children of a trade union lawyer. He attended secondary school in Ghent and went on to study law at the city's university. Having graduated in 1975, he became involved in local politics the following year. His first major step in national politics came four years later when he was elected chairman of the Young Liberals, introducing a new radical manifesto to attract younger voters. In 1982 he was appointed chairman of the Flemish Liberal Party (PVV) and in 1985 was elected to the Belgian parliament, subsequently holding senior ministerial portfolios in the coalition government. Forced into opposition in 1988, Verhofstadt planned a radical overhaul of the party, which in November 1992 adopted the new name of the Flemish Liberals and Democrats (VLD). In the 1995 general election the VLD failed to oust the Christian Democrats from power and in the summer of that year Verhofstadt resigned as party chairman. He returned to the political arena in May the following year with a revised citizen's manifesto appealing to the middle ground. In 1997 he resumed the VLD leadership. The party made significant gains in the June 1999 parliamentary elections and Verhofstadt became the country's first Liberal prime minister for more than 50 years.

Career in Office
In the immediate aftermath of the 1999 election Verhofstadt was successful in resolving the dioxin crisis that had hit Belgian agriculture and resulted in the downfall of his predecessor. Then, presiding over a 'rainbow coalition' of Liberals, Socialists and Greens (representing Belgium's two main linguistic communities), he pledged in his first term to achieve a balanced budget, reduce taxation and promulgate an amnesty for asylum seekers. This latter policy led to conflict with an increasingly vocal far-right anti-immigration lobby. Verhofstadt meanwhile maintained his strong support for European integration.

In parliamentary elections on 18 May 2003 the VLD won the largest vote share with 15·4% and 25 seats in the 150-member Chamber of Representatives (two more seats than in 1999). Verhofstadt reconstituted his coalition government (but without environmentalist representation) and he was inaugurated for his second term as prime minister on 12 July 2003. The previous month he announced plans to reform war crimes legislation which, under existing terms, allowed for charges to be brought against foreign nationals accused of abuses committed outside Belgian jurisdiction. This issue had attracted US hostility, particularly in the light of Belgium's opposition to the 2003 invasion of Iraq.

Following an earlier reshuffle in July 2004, Verhofstadt's government by March 2005 comprised the VLD, the Socialist Party (PS), the (francophone socialist) Reformist Movement (MR) and the SPA (Socialist Party Different)-Spirit coalition.

DEFENCE

Conscription was abolished in 1995 and the Armed Forces were restructured, with the aim of progressively reducing the size and making more use of civilian personnel. The Interforces Territorial Command is responsible for assignments to assure the safety of the National Territory and for logistic support in those fields which are mutual for the different forces.

In 2003 defence expenditure totalled US$3,923m. (US$379 per capita), representing 1·3% of GDP.

Army

The Army has a joint service territorial command and an operations command HQ. There is a mechanized infantry division, a combat support division, a parachute commando brigade and a light aviation group. Total strength (2002) 26,400 including 1,500 women. In addition there are 71,500 army reserves.

Navy

The naval forces, based at Ostend and Zeebrugge, include three frigates. Naval personnel (2002) totalled 2,400.

The naval air arm comprises three general utility helicopters.

Air Force

The Belgian Royal Air Force has a strength of (2002) 8,600 personnel. There are three fighter-ground attack squadrons, one fighter-ground attack reconnaissance squadron, two fighter squadrons, two transport squadrons, three training squadrons and one search and rescue squadron. Equipment includes 90 combat aircraft, including F-16s, plus 45 in store.

INTERNATIONAL RELATIONS

Belgium is a member of the UN, WTO, NATO, BIS, OECD, EU, Council of Europe, WEU, OSCE, CERN, Inter-American Development Bank, Asian Development Bank, IOM, Antarctic Treaty and the International Organization of the Francophonie. Belgium is a signatory to the Schengen accord abolishing border controls between Austria, Belgium, Denmark, Finland, France, Germany, Greece, Iceland, Italy, Luxembourg, the Netherlands, Norway, Portugal, Spain and Sweden.

ECONOMY

Services contributed 71·8% of GDP in 2002, with industry accounting for 26·9% and agriculture 1·3%.

According to the anti-corruption organization *Transparency International*, Belgium ranked equal 19th in the world in a 2005 survey of the countries with the least corruption in business and government. It received 7·4 out of 10 in the annual index.

Overview

Belgium's economy is one of the most open in the world and is closely interlinked with those of Germany, France and the Netherlands. In 2003–04 growth exceeded the euro area average, fuelled by strong household spending and residential investment. In 2001 the share of external trade in goods and services in GDP was 88%. However, Belgium has lost export market share at approximately 1% per year over recent years. This loss can be explained by the dominance of intermediate products exports such as chemicals and steel, which have lower structural growth than other products.

Inflexibilities in the labour market, including low labour mobility and wage inflexibility, have contributed to high unemployment. Labour utilization is low by OECD standards; at 60·3% in 2004, the employment rate was the sixth lowest in the OECD. Employment is especially low for older workers (28% of the population is aged between 55 and 64), younger workers (27% of the population is aged between 15 and 24) and minorities. Employment for the rest of the prime-age population is close to international rates. Low employment rates among the young is predominantly found in the French community and reflects poor education and high school drop-out rates in this segment of the population. The unemployment rate of ethnic minorities is three times that of native Belgians, partly because of poorer education, language barriers and an inability to enforce anti-discrimination legislation. More than 60% of unemployed have been so for over two years and over 80% for at least one year.

The government and its social partners have formulated the 'Generation Pact', a reform aimed at increasing employment rates. Passed at the end of 2005 it limits the number of people taking early retirement in a bid to stimulate employers to retain or hire older workers. In addition, cuts in social security contributions for the young and increased on-the-job training aim to increase employment uptake for those entering the job market.

Population ageing has become a major policy focus, with the OECD projecting that the old-age ratio will double by 2050, reducing economic growth and putting pressure on public finances. Belgium's low employment rate can be viewed as an advantage compared to other OECD countries, as it provides scope to offset the effects of population ageing. Since 2000 fiscal discipline has enabled a steady reduction in the public debt ratio, helping to prepare for the impact of population ageing. Public debt fell below 100% of GDP at the end of 2004 for the first time in 30 years.

Currency

On 1 Jan. 1999 the euro (EUR) became the legal currency in Belgium; irrevocable conversion rate BEF40·3399 to EUR1. The euro, which consists of 100 cents, has been in circulation since 1 Jan. 2002. There are seven euro notes in different colours and sizes denominated in 500, 200, 100, 50, 20, 10 and 5 euros, and eight coins denominated in 2 and 1 euros, then 50, 20, 10, 5, 2 and 1 cents. On the introduction of the euro there was a 'dual circulation' period before the Belgian franc ceased to be legal tender on 28 Feb. 2002. Euro banknotes in circulation on 1 Jan. 2002 had a total value of €24·0bn.

Inflation rates (based on OECD statistics):

1995	1996	1997	1998	1999	2000	2001	2002	2003	2004
1·3%	1·8%	1·5%	0·9%	1·1%	2·7%	2·4%	1·6%	1·5%	1·9%

In June 2002 gold reserves were 8·29m. troy oz (20·54m. troy oz in 1995) and foreign exchange reserves US$8,517m. Total money supply was €10,626m. in June 2002.

Budget

Federal government receipts and expenditure in €1m.:

	1999	2000	2001	2002
Revenue	67,754	72,628	74,500	73,592
Expenditure	71,468	73,753	76,750	74,306

Tax revenue in 2002 was €67,513m.; non-tax revenue, €6,079m. VAT is 21% (reduced rates, 12% and 6%).

Performance

Real GDP growth rates (based on OECD statistics):

1995	1996	1997	1998	1999	2000	2001	2002	2003	2004
2·3%	0·8%	3·7%	1·9%	3·1%	3·7%	1·2%	1·5%	0·9%	2·4%

The real GDP growth rate in 2005 according to the National Bank of Belgium was estimated to be 1·5%. Total GDP in 2004 was US$349·8bn.

Banking and Finance

The National Bank of Belgium was established in 1850. The *Governor*—in 2005, Guy Quaden—is appointed for a five-year period. Its shares are listed on Euronext (Brussels); half of them are nominative held by the state.

The law of 22 Feb. 1998 has adapted the status of the National Bank of Belgium in view of the realization of the Economic and Monetary Union.

The National Bank of Belgium is within the ESCB-framework in charge of the issue of banknotes, the execution of exchange rate policy and monetary policy. Furthermore, it is the Bank of banks and the cashier of the federal state.

The law of 4 Dec. 1990 on financial transactions and financial markets defines the legal framework for collective investment institutions, the sole object of which is the collective investment of capital raised from the public. It transposes into Belgian legislation the European Directive of 20 Dec. 1985 on the co-ordination of laws, regulations and administrative provisions relating to undertakings for collective investment in transferable securities.

The law of 6 April 1995 relating to secondary markets, status and supervision of investment firms, intermediaries and investment consultants, provides the credit institutions with direct access to securities' stock exchanges. Stock exchange legislation was also subject to an important reform. The law fundamentally modifies the competitive environment and strengthens exercise conditions for securities' dealers.

On 31 Dec. 2003, 109 credit institutions with a balance sheet totalling €891bn. were established in Belgium: 61 governed by Belgian law and 48 by foreign law. 399 collective investment institutions (132 Belgian and 267 foreign) were marketed in Belgium and supervised by the Banking, Finance and Insurance Commission; and 82 investment firms were operating in Belgium with the approval of the Banking, Finance and Insurance Commission.

There is a stock exchange (a component of Euronext) in Brussels. Euronext was created in Sept. 2000 through the merger of the Amsterdam, Brussels and Paris bourses.

ENERGY AND NATURAL RESOURCES

Environment

Belgium's carbon dioxide emissions from the consumption and flaring of fossil fuels were the equivalent of 14·2 tonnes per capita in 2002.

Electricity

The production of electricity amounted to 82·6bn. kWh in 2002; consumption per capita (2002) was 8,749 kWh. 37% of production in 2002 was nuclear-produced. Belgium had seven nuclear reactors in 2003. Installed capacity (2002) was 15·7m. kW.

Minerals

Belgium's mineral resources are very limited; the most abundantly occurring mineral is calcite.

Agriculture

There were, in 2001, 1,390,191 ha. under cultivation, of which 845,779 ha. were arable land. There were 55,000 farms in 2003. The agricultural sector employs 2·7% of the workforce.

Chief crops	Area in ha.		Produce in tonnes		
	2000	2001	1998	1999	2000
Wheat	204,022	173,270	1,733,046	1,490,247	1,633,854
Barley	48,570	51,504	374,500	387,564	333,381
Oats	5,341	—	28,468	42,552	28,887
Rye	1,098	—	7,130	3,971	4,781
Potatoes	65,845	62,157	2,455,777	3,059,162	2,921,871
Beet (sugar)	90,858	95,553	5,364,649	7,112,021	6,151,978
Beet (fodder)	6,713	5,970	676,396	738,315	670,224
Tobacco	388	380	1,308	1,314	1,166

In 2003 there were 32,093 horses, 2,778,077 cattle, 146,030 sheep, 26,237 goats and 6,538,609 pigs.

Forestry

In 2000 forest covered 671,890 ha. (22·2% of the total land area). Timber production in 2003 was 4·77m. cu. metres.

Fisheries

In 2002 the fishing fleet had a total tonnage of 24,276 GRT. Total catch, 2003, 26,831 tonnes, almost entirely from marine waters.

INDUSTRY

The leading companies by market capitalization in Belgium in Nov. 2005 were: Fortis (US$38·7bn.), Belgium's leading banking institution; KBC (US$26·6bn.), a banking conglomerate; and InBev (US$24·4bn.), a beverage company.

Output, 2002, in 1,000 tonnes: distillate fuel oil, 12,464; crude steel, 11,300; cement (2000), 8,000; residual fuel oil, 7,603; petrol, 5,775; beer (2003), 1,565·0m. litres; mineral water (1998), 809·7m. litres; cigarettes (2001), 14·7bn. units. Output of sugar factories and refineries (1998), 995,053 tonnes.

Labour

Retirement age is flexible for men and 60–65 years for women. In 2002 (Labour Force Survey), 69,278 persons worked in the primary sector (agriculture, fishing and mining), 1,034,693 in the secondary sector (industry and construction) and 2,965,861 in the tertiary sector (services). The unemployment rate was 8·5% in Dec. 2005. In French-speaking Wallonia the rate is more than double that in Flemish-speaking Flanders. In 2004 the participation rate of the active population in the labour market was one of the lowest in the EU, at 60·3%.

Trade Unions

The main trade union organizations are the Confederation of Christian Trade Unions (CSC/ACV), the Belgian Socialist Confederation of Labour (FGTB/ABVV) and the Federation of Liberal Trade Unions of Belgium (CGSLB/ACLVB).

INTERNATIONAL TRADE

In 1922 the customs frontier between Belgium and Luxembourg was abolished; their foreign trade figures are amalgamated.

Imports and Exports

Imports and exports statistics (in €1m.):

	Imports	Exports
2002	168,392·1	178,760·6
2003	170,975·2	180,934·8
2004	188,874·8	197,062·5

Leading imports and exports (in €1m.):

	Imports		Exports	
	2003	2004	2003	2004
Machinery and appliances	29,893·4	31,372·5	25,906·4	27,395·3
Chemicals and pharmaceutical products	23,842·4	26,691·2	28,412·1	30,647·8
Transport equipment	22,554·4	25,435·8	26,913·9	29,047·0
Mineral products	19,515·0	24,042·2	12,555·1	14,731·2
Base metals	12,476·6	15,377·3	14,793·4	18,361·0
Plastics and rubber	10,114·4	11,100·5	15,408·6	17,270·1
Precious stones and precious metals	10,694·3	11,608·8	10,898·3	11,974·2
Food industry	7,328·6	7,466·9	9,150·5	9,562·5
Textile and textile articles	6,997·0	6,967·0	8,573·4	8,335·4
Paper and applications	4,911·3	4,882·1	4,852·9	5,009·3

Trade by selected countries (in €1m.):

	Imports from		Exports to	
	2003	2004	2003	2004
China	3,403·5	4,303·8	2,140·0	2,135·2
France	24,889·7	25,954·5	31,197·2	33,996·9
Germany	28,340·3	31,154·2	31,353·6	34,204·9
India	1,534·0	1,866·9	3,804·7	4,224·5
Ireland	2,275·4	3,217·3	1,077·6	1,358·9
Israel	1,554·3	1,822·2	2,264·3	2,819·2
Italy	5,945·7	6,330·6	10,079·0	10,844·8
Japan	5,228·8	5,690·5	1,589·8	1,713·1
Luxembourg	1,304·9	1,628·5	3,980·3	4,555·0
Netherlands	33,096·0	37,380·5	23,232·2	25,549·9
Russia	2,093·6	2,912·1	1,217·3	1,514·5
Spain	3,848·1	4,146·4	7,454·5	8,017·9
Sweden	4,249·9	4,670·9	2,731·8	2,949·9
UK	14,883·5	14,973·3	16,232·2	17,125·0
USA	9,982·8	10,792·6	8,548·8	8,751·4

In 2004 other EU-member countries accounted for 77·2% of imports and 74·0% of exports.

Trade Fairs

Brussels ranks as the second most popular convention city in the world behind Paris according to the Union des Associations Internationales (UAI), hosting 2·1% of all international meetings held in 2002.

COMMUNICATIONS

Roads

Length of roads, 2002: motorways, 1,729 km; other state roads, 12,610 km; provincial roads, 1,349 km; local roads, about 133,340 km. Belgium has one of the densest road networks in the world. The number of motor vehicles registered on 1 Aug. 2003 was 5,816,339, including 4,820,868 passenger cars, 15,060 buses, 556,397 trucks, 47,102 non-agricultural tractors, 319,480 motorcycles and 57,432 special vehicles. Road accidents caused 1,486 fatalities in 2001.

Rail

The main Belgian lines were a State enterprise from their inception in 1834. In 1926 the *Société Nationale des Chemins de Fer Belges (SNCB)* was formed to take over the railways. The State is sole holder of the ordinary shares of SNCB, which carry the majority vote at General Meetings. The length of railway operated in 2000 was 3,471 km (electrified, 2,705 km). Total operating income in 2000 was BEF125,816m.; total operating expenses, BEF120,664m. In 2003, 55·73m. tonnes of freight were carried; and, in 2000, 153·3m. passengers.

The regional transport undertakings *Société Régionale Wallonne de Transport* and *Vlaamse Vervoermaatschappij* operate tramways around Charleroi (20 km) and from De Panne to Knokke (55 km). There is also a metro and tramway in Brussels (175 km), and tramways in Antwerp (57 km) and Ghent (30 km).

Civil Aviation

The former national airline SABENA (*Société anonyme belge d'exploitation de la navigation aérienne*) was set up in 1923. In 1997 its fleet comprised 33 aircraft. In 1999 SABENA flew 179·1m. km, carrying 9,965,200 passengers. However, in Nov. 2001 it filed for bankruptcy after failing to secure financial assistance from its part-owner Swissair, which itself was on the verge of collapse. Its successor, Delta Air Transport (DAT), a former SABENA subsidiary, was given a new identity in Feb. 2002 as SN Brussels Airlines. Some 60 other airlines also operate services, including Ryanair and Virgin Express, which flies more people out of Brussels National Airport than any other airline. The busiest airport is Brussels National Airport (Zaventem), which handled 15,194,097 passengers in 2003 and 560,000 tonnes of freight in 2001. Charleroi is the second busiest airport in terms of passenger numbers and Liège the third busiest.

Shipping

On 1 Jan. 1999 the merchant fleet was composed of 19 vessels of 345,058 tonnes. There were eight shipping companies in 1997. In 2001 vessels totalling 436,927,000 NRT entered ports and vessels totalling 422,703,000 NRT cleared. In 2002, 131,619,000 tonnes of cargo were handled at the port of Antwerp, with total container throughput 4,777,000 TEUs (twenty-foot equivalent units). Antwerp is Europe's second busiest port in terms of cargo handled after Rotterdam.

The length of navigable inland waterways was 1,493·3 km in 1995. 104m. tonnes of freight were carried on inland waterways in 1998.

Telecommunications

In 2002 telephone subscribers numbered 13,267,900 (1,282·4 per 1,000 inhabitants) and there were 2·5m. PCs in use (241·6 for every 1,000 persons). Belgium had 8,135,500 mobile phone subscribers in 2002. In Aug. 2002 there were 3·76m. Internet users. There were 269,800 fax machines in 2002.

Postal Services

In 2003 there were 1,301 post offices. In 1999 a total of 3,533m. pieces of mail were processed.

SOCIAL INSTITUTIONS

Justice

Judges are appointed for life. There is a court of cassation, five courts of appeal and assize courts for political and criminal cases. There are 27 judicial districts, each with a court of first instance. In each of the 222 cantons is a justice and judge of the peace. There are also various special tribunals. There is trial by jury in assize courts. The death penalty, which had been in abeyance for 45 years, was formally abolished in 1991.

The Gendarmerie ceased to be part of the Army in Jan. 1992.

The population in penal institutions in 2004 was 9,249 (89 per 100,000 of national population).

In Aug. 2003 a new act reformed war crimes legislation introduced in 1993 which allowed for charges to be brought against foreign nationals accused of abuses committed outside Belgian jurisdiction. The amendment requires that either accuser or defendant be a citizen of or resident in Belgium.

Education

Following the constitutional reform of 1988, education is the responsibility of the Flemish and Walloon communities. There were (2000–01) 400,805 pupils and 27,118 teachers in pre-primary schools; 771,889 pupils and 63,626 teachers in primary schools; 1,125,256 pupils and 115,262 teachers (1996–97) in secondary schools; and 359,265 students and 23,041 academic staff in tertiary education. There were 17 universities and 134 non-university colleges and institutes in 1996–97. There are five royal academies of fine arts and five royal conservatoires at Brussels, Liège, Ghent, Antwerp and Mons.

Total expenditure on education in 1999–2000 amounted to 5·8% of GNP and represented 11·6% of total government expenditure.

The adult literacy rate is at least 99%.

Health

On 31 Dec. 2004 there were 41,730 physicians, 8,660 dentists and 11,620 pharmacists. There were 219 hospitals with 72,000 beds in 2001. Total health spending accounted for 9·6% of GDP in 2003. In Jan. 2000 the Belgian government agreed to decriminalize the use of cannabis. Euthanasia became legal on 24 Sept. 2002. The Belgian Chamber of Representatives had given its approval on 16 May 2002 to a measure adopted by the Senate on 26 Oct. 2001. Belgium was the second country to legalize euthanasia, after the Netherlands.

Welfare

Expenditure in 2000: social security (wage earners) €39,114·47m., (self employed) €3,315·46m.; pensions €5,712·17m.

RELIGION

There is full religious liberty, and part of the income of the ministers of all denominations is paid by the State. In 2001 there were 8·31m. Roman Catholics. Numbers of clergy, 1996: Roman Catholic, 3,899; Protestant, 84; Anglican, 9; Jews, 26; Greek Orthodox, 39. There are eight Roman Catholic dioceses subdivided into 260 deaneries. In May 2005 there was one cardinal. The Protestant (Evangelical) Church is under a synod. There is also a Central Jewish Consistory, a Central Committee of the Anglican Church and a Free Protestant Church.

CULTURE

World Heritage Sites

Belgium has nine sites which have been included on the UNESCO world heritage list. They are: the Flemish Beguinages (1998); the four lifts on the Canal du Centre and their environs (1998); La Grand Place in Brussels (1998); the belfries of Belgium and France (1998), shared with France; the historic centre of Bruges (2000); the major town houses of the architect Victor Horta in Brussels (2000); the Neolithic flint mines at Spiennes (2000); Notre Dame cathedral in Tournai (2000); and the Plantin-Moretus Museum, a Renaissance printing and publishing house (2005).

Broadcasting

Broadcasting is organized according to the language communities. VRT, RTBF and BRF fulfil the public service of broadcasting in Dutch, French and German respectively. TV colour is by PAL.

VRT (*Vlaamse Radio- en Televisieomroep*) is organized by decree as a public-sector public-limited company. It has seven radio and three TV services: Radio 1, Radio 2, Klara, Studio Brussel, Radio Donna, DAB klassiek and RVi; TV1, Canvas and Ketnet. In July 2000 VRT started a new branch, e-VRT, which is responsible for the organization and development of a truly multimedia e-service platform and e-service network in Flanders.

RTBF has five radio and three TV services: La Première, FW, Musique 3, Bruxelles Capitale, Radio 21; RTBF International, La Une, La Deux.

BRF transmits a radio programme from three stations.

There are also four commercial networks: VTM (Dutch, cable only), VT4 (under British licence; Dutch, cable only), RTL-TVI (French, one station), Canal Plus (pay TV; French, three channels; Dutch, two channels).

Number of receivers: radios, 8·1m. (2000); TVs, 5·6m. (2001).

Cinema

In 2002 there were 505 cinemas, with an annual attendance of 24·4m.; gross box office receipts came to €128·3m.

Press

In 2002 there were 28 daily newspapers with a combined circulation of 1,479,000, at a rate of 143 per 1,000 inhabitants.

Tourism

Internal Tourism

In 2003, 29,019,000 tourist nights were spent in 3,490 establishments in accommodation for 619,841 persons. In 2001 the number of overnight stays accounted for by leisure, holiday and recreation was 22,033,903, with 2,932,483 for congresses and conferences, and 3,408,532 for other business purposes. Total number of tourists reached 10,641,144 (7,520,461 leisure, 1,465,996 conference, 1,654,687 for other business purposes).

National Tourism

In 1998, 10,972,140 Belgians went on holiday. They spent 6,799,990 nights abroad and 4,172,150 in Belgium. 6,883,752 Belgians went on holiday for four nights or more spending 5,262,232 nights abroad and 1,626,884 in Belgium.

Libraries

In 1997 there were 1,490 public libraries, one National library and 117 Higher Education libraries. They held a combined 53,832,000 volumes for 2,464,000 registered users.

DIPLOMATIC REPRESENTATIVES

Of Belgium in the United Kingdom (103 Eaton Sq., London, SW1W 9AB)
Ambassador: Baron Thierry de Gruben.

Of the United Kingdom in Belgium (Rue d'Arlon 85, 1040 Brussels)
Ambassador: Richard Kinchen, MVO.

Of Belgium in the USA (3330 Garfield St., NW, Washington, D.C., 20008)
Ambassador: Franciskus Van Daele.

Of the USA in Belgium (Blvd du Régent 27, 1000 Brussels)
Ambassador: Tom C. Korologos.

Of Belgium to the United Nations
Ambassador: Johan Verbeke.

FURTHER READING

The Institut National de Statistique. *Statistiques du commerce extérieur* (monthly). *Bulletin de Statistique.* Bi-monthly. *Annuaire Statistique de la Belgique* (from 1870).—*Annuaire statistique de poche* (from 1965).
Service Fédéral d'Information. *Guide de l'Administration Fédérale.* Occasional

Deprez, K., and Vos, L., *Nationalism in Belgium—Shifting Identities, 1780–1995.* London 1998
Fitzmaurice, J., *The Politics of Belgium: a Unique Federalism.* Farnborough, 1996
Hermans, T. J., *et al.*, (eds.) *The Flemish Movement: a Documentary History.* London, 1992

National Statistical Office: Institut National de Statistique, Rue de Louvain 44, 1000 Brussels.
Service Fédérale d'Information: POB 3000, 1040 Brussels 4.
Website: http://statbel.fgov.be

BELIZE

© Research Machines plc 2006

Capital: Belmopan
Population projection, 2010: 296,000
GDP per capita, 2003: (PPP$) 6,950
HDI/world rank: 0·753/91

KEY HISTORICAL EVENTS

From the 17th century, British settlers, later joined by British soldiers and sailors disbanded after the capture of Jamaica from Spain in 1655, governed themselves under a form of democracy by public meeting. A constitution was granted in 1765 and, with some modification, continued until 1840 when an executive council was created. In 1862 what was then known as British Honduras was declared a British colony with a legislative assembly and a Lieut.-Governor under the Governor of Jamaica. The administrative connection with Jamaica was severed in 1884. Universal suffrage was introduced in 1964 and thereafter the majority of the legislature were elected rather than appointed. In June 1974 British Honduras became Belize. Independence was achieved on 21 Sept. 1981 and a new constitution introduced.

TERRITORY AND POPULATION

Belize is bounded in the north by Mexico, west and south by Guatemala and east by the Caribbean. Fringing the coast there are three atolls and some 400 islets (cays) in the world's second longest barrier reef (140 miles), which was declared a world heritage site in 1996. Area, 22,964 sq. km.

There are six districts as follows, with area, population and chief city:

District	Area (in sq. km)	Population 2000	Chief City	Population 2000
Belize	4,204	68,197	Belize City	49,050
Cayo	5,338	52,564	San Ignacio	13,260
Corozal	1,860	32,708	Corozal	7,888
Orange Walk	4,737	38,890	Orange Walk	13,483
Stann Creek	2,176	24,548	Dangriga	8,814
Toledo	4,649	23,297	Punta Gorda	4,329

Population (2000 census), 240,204 (121,278 males); density, 10·5 per sq. km. The estimated population in 2005 was 270,000. The UN gives a projected population for 2010 of 296,000.

In 2003, 51·6% of the population were rural. In 1995 some 45,000 Belizeans were working abroad.

The capital is Belmopan (2000 population, 8,130).

English is the official language. Spanish is widely spoken. In 2000 the main ethnic groups were Mestizo (Spanish-Maya), 48·1%; Creole (African descent), 25·1%; Mayans, 10·2%; and Garifuna (Caribs), 6·7%.

SOCIAL STATISTICS

2004 births (est.), 8,100; deaths (est.), 1,300. In 2004 (est.) the birth rate per 1,000 was 27·7 and the death rate 4·6; infant mortality in 2001 was 34 per 1,000 live births; there were 2,020 marriages in 2004. Life expectancy in 2003 was 69·5 years for males and 74·5 for females. Annual population growth rate, 1992–2002, 2·5%; fertility rate, 2004, 3·6 children per woman.

CLIMATE

A tropical climate with high rainfall and small annual range of temperature. The driest months are Feb. and March. Belize City, Jan. 74°F (23·3°C), July 81°F (27·2°C). Annual rainfall 76" (1,890 mm).

CONSTITUTION AND GOVERNMENT

The head of state is the British sovereign, represented by an appointed Governor-General. The Constitution, which came into force on 21 Sept. 1981, provided for a National Assembly, with a five-year term, comprising a 29-member *House of Representatives* elected by universal suffrage, and a *Senate* consisting of eight members, five appointed by the Governor-General on the advice of the Prime Minister, two on the advice of the Leader of the Opposition and one on the advice of the Belize Advisory Council.

National Anthem

'O, Land of the Free'; words by S. A. Haynes, tune by S. W. Young.

RECENT ELECTIONS

In parliamentary elections held on 5 March 2003 the People's United Party (PUP) of Prime Minister Said Musa won 22 of the 29 seats in the National Assembly with 53·2% of votes cast against 7 and 45·6% for the United Democratic Party. Turnout was 78·9%.

CURRENT ADMINISTRATION

Governor-General: Sir Colville Young, GCMG; b. 1932 (sworn in 17 Nov. 1993).

In March 2006 the cabinet comprised as follows:

Prime Minister and Minister for Finance and Public Service: Said Musa; b. 1944 (PUP; sworn in 28 Aug. 1998 and re-elected for a second term in March 2003).

Deputy Prime Minister and Minister of Natural Resources, Local Government and the Environment: John Briceño. *Home Affairs and Public Utilities:* Ralph Fonseca. *Foreign Affairs, Foreign Trade, National Emergency Management, Tourism and Information:* Godfrey Smith. *National Development, Investment and Culture:* Mark Espat. *Defence, Housing, Sports and Youth:* Cordel Hyde. *Health, and Labour:* Vildo Marin. *Agriculture and Fisheries:* Michael Espat. *Human Development:* Sylvia Flores. *Education and Attorney General:* Francis Fonseca. *Works, Transport and Communications:* Jose Coye.

Government Website: http://www.belize.gov.bz

CURRENT LEADERS

Said Musa

Position
Prime Minister

Introduction
Said Musa, leader of the People's United Party (PUP), became prime minister in 1998 and won a second term in March 2003. A leading figure in Belize's fight for independence, his tenure has been dominated by ongoing attempts to resolve territorial disputes with Guatemala.

Early Life
Said Wilbert Musa was born on 19 March 1944 in San Ignacio in the Cayo District of what was then British Honduras. In 1966 he graduated in law from the University of Manchester in the UK and the following year was called to the Bar at Gray's Inn. Musa returned to Belize and served as a circuit magistrate and a crown counsel for the office of public prosecutions. He was elected to the presidency of the public service union but in 1970 went into private legal practice. During this period he became involved with the United Black Association for Development and also co-founded the People's Action Committee and the Society for the Promotion of Education and Research.

He joined the PUP in 1974 but was defeated that year in his first bid for a parliamentary seat. Nonetheless, PUP Prime Minister George Price appointed him as a senator for a five-year term of office. In 1979 Musa entered parliament as the representative for Fort George. In the new PUP government he served as Attorney General and education and sports minister, later adding the economic development portfolio.

Musa was a key figure in the negotiations with Britain and Guatemala which preceded full independence in 1981. He represented Belize at the UN, the Commonwealth and CARICOM, and played a leading role in the drafting of a national constitution. After independence Musa was named foreign minister and oversaw entry into the Organization of American States (OAS). He was in regular contact with the government of Guatemala, which claimed a large part of Belize's territory as its own, and helped smooth relations sufficiently that Guatemala recognized Belize's independent sovereignty in 1991.

In 1996 George Price, leader of Belize's independence movement since the 1950s, retired as leader of the PUP and was replaced by Musa. Musa led the PUP to a landslide victory at the elections of 1998 and was sworn in as prime minister.

Career in Office
Musa has had to contend with Guatemala's continuing claim on half of Belize's territory. In early 2000 the Guatemalan government announced its intention to work through the international courts. Following OAS-brokered talks the two sides reached a draft agreement in Sept. 2002 establishing a transition process, to be voted on in referenda in both countries. Musa's first term of office also saw Belize hit by two devastating hurricanes, Keith and Iris, in Oct. 2000 and Oct. 2001.

In parliamentary elections on 5 March 2003 the PUP retained power with a slightly reduced majority. Musa's new government was sworn in two days later.

DEFENCE

The Belize Defence Force numbers 1,050 (2002) with a reserve militia of 700. There is an Air Wing and a Maritime Wing.

In 2003 defence expenditure totalled US$19m. (US$73 per capita), representing 2·4% of GDP.

INTERNATIONAL RELATIONS

Belize is a member of the UN, WTO, the Commonwealth, OAS, Inter-American Development Bank, ACS, CARICOM, IOM and is an ACP member state of the ACP-EU relationship.

ECONOMY

In 2002 agriculture accounted for 15·1% of GDP, industry 19·7% and services 65·2%.

Currency

The unit of currency is the *Belize dollar* (BZD) of 100 *cents*. Since 1976 $B2 has been fixed at US$1. Total money supply was $B352m. in June 2002 and foreign exchange reserves were US$91m. There was inflation of 2·6% in 2003 and 3·1% in 2004.

Budget

Revenues in 2001 were $B450·9m. and expenditures $B581·1m. Tax revenues accounted for 71·5% of total revenues; current expenditure accounted for 57·4% of total expenditures.

Performance

Real GDP growth was 9·2% in 2003 and 4·6% in 2004. Total GDP in 2004 was US$1·1bn.

Banking and Finance

A Central Bank was established in 1981 (*Governor*, Sydney Campbell) and in 2001 had deposits of $B148m. There were (2001) one development bank and six other banks.

ENERGY AND NATURAL RESOURCES

Environment

Carbon dioxide emissions from the consumption and flaring of fossil fuels in Belize were the equivalent of 3·6 tonnes per capita in 2002.

Electricity

Installed capacity in 2000 was 43,000 kW. Production was 137m. kWh in 2000 and consumption per capita in 2000 was 648 kWh. Supply, 110 and 220 volts; 60 Hz.

Oil and Gas

Oil was discovered in 2005 after several years of exploration, although additional testing will be required to determine the commercial viability of the site.

Agriculture

In 2001 there were 65,000 ha. of arable land and 39,000 ha. of permanent crops. Production, 2000 (in 1,000 tonnes): sugarcane, 1,103; oranges, 201; bananas, 65. Livestock (2001): cattle, 56,000; pigs, 28,000; horses, 5,000; mules, 4,000; chickens, 1m.

Forestry

In 2000, 1,348,000 ha. (59·1% of the total land area) were under forests. Timber production in 2001 was 188,000 cu. metres.

Fisheries

There were (1995) 13 registered fishing co-operatives. The total catch in 2001 amounted to 14,370 tonnes, exclusively from sea fishing.

INDUSTRY

Manufacturing is mainly confined to processing agricultural products and timber. There is also a clothing industry. Sugar production was 111,492 tonnes in 2002; molasses, 48,621 in 1995.

Labour

In 2004 the economically active labour force totalled 180,030; the unemployment rate in 2004 was 11·6%.

Trade Unions

There were 14 accredited unions in 1997.

INTERNATIONAL TRADE

External debt was US$835m. in 2002.

Imports and Exports

Imports (f.o.b.) in 2002 totalled US$496·9m. (US$481·9m. in 2001); exports (f.o.b.) in 2002 amounted to US$309·7m. (US$269·1m. in

2001). Main imports in 1999 were: machinery and transport equipment (27%), manufactured goods (16%), food and live animals (15%) and petroleum and related products (14%); main exports were sugar (26%), bananas (17%), orange juice (16%), shellfish (16%) and clothes (12%). Main import suppliers in 1999 were USA (52%), Mexico (12%), Cuba (10%) and UK (4%). Main export markets: USA (52%), UK (25%), Denmark (7%) and Mexico (4%).

COMMUNICATIONS

Roads

In 2002 there were 545 km of main roads and 2,484 km of other roads. In 2002 there were 15,500 passenger cars in use and 12,800 trucks and vans. There were 49 deaths as a result of road accidents in 1998.

Civil Aviation

There is an international airport (Philip S. W. Goldson) in Belize City. The national carrier is Maya Island Air, which in 2003 operated domestic services and international flights to Flores (Guatemala). There were direct flights in 2003 with other airlines to Boston, Charlotte, Dallas, Houston, Indianapolis, Las Vegas, McAllen, Miami, Montego Bay, New York, Raleigh, San Pedreo Sula, San Salvador and Washington, D.C. In 2001 Philip S. W. Goldson International handled 497,464 passengers (364,711 on international flights).

Shipping

The main port is Belize City, with a modern deep-water port able to handle containerized shipping. There are also ports at Commerce Bight and Big Creek. In 2002 the merchant marine totalled 1,473,000 GRT, including oil tankers 236,000 GRT. Nine cargo shipping lines serve Belize, and there are coastal passenger services to the offshore islands and Guatemala.

Telecommunications

Telephone subscribers numbered 83,800 in 2002, or 331·2 per 1,000 inhabitants. In 2002 there were 51,700 mobile telephone subscribers and 35,000 PCs in use (138·3 per 1,000 inhabitants). In 1995 there were 500 fax machines. In 2002 Belize had 30,000 Internet users.

Postal Services

In 2003 there were 136 post offices.

SOCIAL INSTITUTIONS

Justice

Each of the six judicial districts has summary jurisdiction courts (criminal) and district courts (civil), both of which are presided over by magistrates. There is a Supreme Court, a Court of Appeal and a Family Court. There is a Director of Public Prosecutions, a Chief Justice and two Puisne Judges. Belize was one of ten countries to sign an agreement in Feb. 2001 establishing a Caribbean Court of Justice to replace the British Privy Council as the highest civil and criminal court. In the meantime the number of signatories has risen to twelve. The court was inaugurated at Port-of-Spain, Trinidad on 16 April 2005.

In 1995 the police force was 450 strong. The population in penal institutions in 2003 was 1,074 (420 per 100,000 of national population).

Education

The adult literacy rate was 76·9% in 2003 (76·7% among males and 77·1% among females). Education is in English. State education is managed jointly by the government and the Roman Catholic and Anglican Churches. It is compulsory for children between six and 14 years and primary education is free. In 2003–04 there were 63,282 pupils at primary schools and 16,150 at secondary schools.

There are two government-maintained special schools for disabled children. There is a teachers' training college. The University College of Belize opened in 1986. The University of the West Indies maintains an extramural department in Belize City.

In 2000–01 total expenditure on education came to 6·8% of GNP and 20·9% of total government spending.

Health

In 2004 there were 11 hospitals with 23 beds per 10,000 persons. There were 221 physicians, 21 dentists, 449 nurses, 49 pharmacists and (2000) 230 midwives. Medical services in rural areas are provided by health care centres and mobile clinics.

RELIGION

In 2001, 58% of the population was Roman Catholic and 34% Protestant.

CULTURE

World Heritage Sites

The Belize Barrier Reef Reserve System was inscribed on the UNESCO World Heritage List in 1996.

Broadcasting

The Broadcasting Corporation of Belize operates a national broadcasting service. 60% of programmes are in English, the remainder in Spanish and the Amerindian languages. There is also a commercial radio station. There are two commercial TV channels (colour by NTSC). There are satellite links with Bermuda, the USA and the UK, and radio links with Central America. There were 133,000 radio sets in 2000 and 45,000 TV sets in 2001.

Press

There were four weekly newspapers and several monthly magazines in 1995.

Tourism

In 2001 there were 195,955 tourist visitors, of which 106,296 were US citizens and 48,100 arrived on cruise ships. Tourism receipts totalled US$133m. in 2002, representing 16·6% of GDP.

DIPLOMATIC REPRESENTATIVES

Of Belize in the United Kingdom (3rd Floor, 45 Crawford Place, London, W1H 4LP)
High Commissioner: Alexis Rosado.

Of the United Kingdom in Belize (PO Box 91, Belmopan, Belize)
High Commissioner: Alan Jones.

Of Belize in the USA (2535 Massachusetts Ave., NW, Washington, D.C., 20008)
Ambassador: Lisa M. Shoman.

Of the USA in Belize (Gabourel Lane, Belize City)
Ambassador: Robert J. Dieter.

Of Belize to the United Nations
Ambassador: Stuart M. Leslie.

Of Belize to the European Union
Ambassador: Yvonne Hyde.

FURTHER READING

Leslie, Robert, (ed.) *A History of Belize: Nation in the Making.* 2nd ed. Cubola Productions, Benque Viejo, 1995
Shoman, Assad, *Thirteen Chapters of a History of Belize.* Angelus Press, Belize City, 1994
Sutherland, Anne, *The Making of Belize: Globalization in the Margins.* Bergin & Garvey, London, 1998
Wright, Peggy and Coutts, Brian E., *Belize.* [Bibliography] 2nd ed. ABC-Clio, Oxford and Santa Barbara (CA), 1993

National Statistical Office: Central Statistical Office, Belmopan.
Website: http://www.cso.gov.bz

BENIN

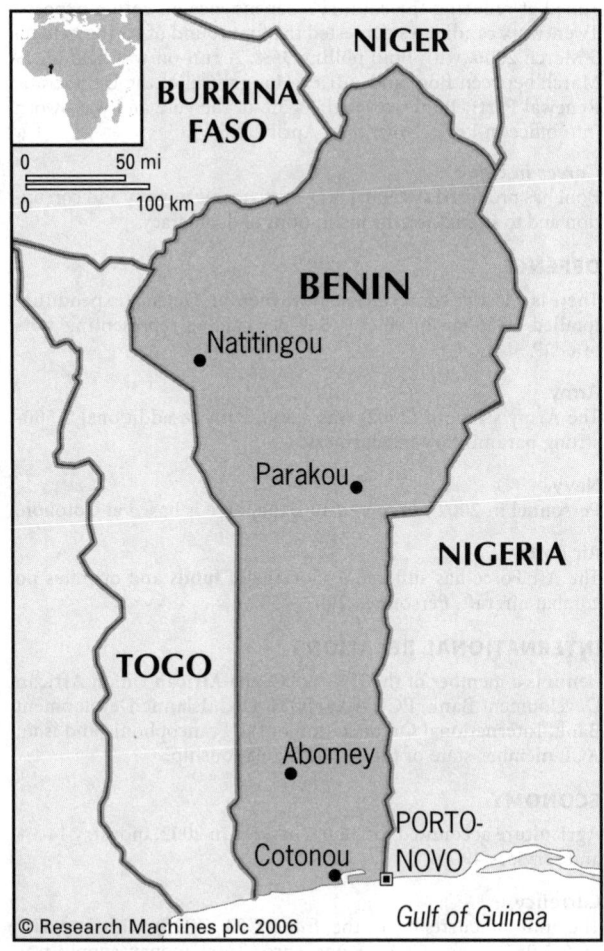

© Research Machines plc 2006

République du Bénin

Capital: Porto-Novo
Population projection, 2010: 9·79m.
GDP per capita, 2003: (PPP$) 1,115
HDI/world rank: 0·431/162

KEY HISTORICAL EVENTS

The People's Republic of Benin is the former Republic of Dahomey. Dahomey was a powerful, well-organized state from the 17th century, trading extensively in slaves through the port of Whydah with the Portuguese, British and French. On the coast an educated African elite grew up in the 19th century.

After the defeat of Dahomey, and the abolition of the monarchy, the French occupied territory inland up to the River Niger and created the colony of Dahomey as part of French West Africa. The African elite protested at French rule as African nationalism grew after the Second World War.

After Dahomey became independent on 1 Aug. 1960 civilian government was interrupted by long periods of military rule. In Oct. 1972 Gen. Mathieu Kérékou seized power and installed a new left-wing regime committed to socialist policies. A constitution was adopted in 1977, based on a single Marxist-Leninist party,

the *Parti de la Révolution Populaire du Bénin* (PRPB). Benin is beset with economic problems, factional fighting and frequent plots to overthrow the regime.

TERRITORY AND POPULATION

Benin is bounded in the east by Nigeria, north by Niger and Burkina Faso, west by Togo and south by the Gulf of Guinea. The area is 112,622 sq. km, and the population (census 2002) 6,769,914; density, 60·1 per sq. km.

The UN gives a projected population for 2010 of 9·79m.

In 2003, 55·4% of the population were rural.

The areas and populations of the 12 departments are as follows:

Province	Sq. km	Census 2002	Province	Sq. km	Census 2002
Alibori	25,683	521,093	Donga	10,691	350,062
Atacora	20,459	549,417	Littoral	79	665,100
Atlantique	3,233	801,683	Mono	1,396	360,037
Borgou	25,310	724,171	Ouémé	2,835	730,772
Collines	13,561	535,923	Plateau	1,865	407,116
Couffo	2,404	524,586	Zou	5,106	599,954

Major towns, with 2002 census population: Cotonou, 665,100; Porto-Novo, 223,552; Parakou, 149,819; Bohicon, 65,974; Abomey, 59,672.

In 1992 the main ethnic groups numbered (in 1,000): Fon, 1,930; Yoruba, 590; Adja, 540; Aizo, 420; Bariba, 420; Somba, 320; Fulani, 270. The official language is French. Over half the people speak Fon.

SOCIAL STATISTICS

2001 (estimates) births, 264,000; deaths, 83,000. Rates, 2001 estimates (per 1,000 population): births, 41·3; deaths, 13·0. Infant mortality, 2001 (per 1,000 live births), 94. Expectation of life in 2003 was 53·2 years for males and 54·7 for females. Annual population growth rate, 1992–2002, 2·8%. Fertility rate, 2001, 5·8 children per woman.

CLIMATE

In coastal parts there is an equatorial climate, with a long rainy season from March to July and a short rainy season in Oct. and Nov. The dry season increases in length from the coast, with inland areas having rain only between May and Sept. Porto-Novo, Jan. 82°F (27·8°C), July 78°F (25·6°C). Annual rainfall 52" (1,300 mm). Cotonou, Jan. 81°F (27·2°C), July 77°F (25°C). Annual rainfall 53" (1,325 mm).

CONSTITUTION AND GOVERNMENT

The Benin Party of Popular Revolution (PRPB) held a monopoly of power from 1977 to 1989.

In Feb. 1990 a 'National Conference of the Active Forces of the Nation' proclaimed its sovereignty and appointed Nicéphore Soglo Prime Minister of a provisional government. At a referendum in Dec. 1990, 93·2% of votes cast were in favour of the new constitution, which has introduced a presidential regime. The *President* is directly elected for renewable five-year terms. Parliament is the unicameral *National Assembly* of 83 members elected by proportional representation for four-year terms.

A 30-member advisory *Social and Economic Council* was set up in 1994. There is a *Constitutional Court*.

National Anthem

'L'Aube Nouvelle' ('The Dawn of a New Day'); words and tune by Gilbert Dagnon.

RECENT ELECTIONS

Presidential elections were held in two rounds on 5 and 19 March 2006. In the first round Yayi Boni (ind.) won 35·6% of the vote, former prime minister Adrien Houngbédji (Democratic Renewal Party) 24·1%, Bruno Amoussou (Social Democratic Party) 16·2% and Léhadi Vinagnon Soglo (Renaissance Party of Benin) 8·4%. There were a further 22 candidates. In the second round Boni won 74·5% of the vote against Houngbédji with 25·5%. Turnout in the first round was 76·9% and in the second round 69·5%.

Parliamentary elections were held on 30 March 2003. The Presidential Movement won 52 of 83 seats (of which the Union for the Benin of the Future 31, the African Movement for Development and Progress 9, the Key Force 5 and smaller parties 7), the Rebirth of Benin 15, the Party of Democratic Renewal 11, the Star Alliance 3, and the New Alliance 2.

CURRENT ADMINISTRATION

President: Yayi Boni; b. 1953 (ind.; sworn in 6 April 2006).

In April 2006 the government comprised:

Minister of Justice and Relations with Institutions: Abraham Zinzindohoue. *Foreign Affairs and African Integration:* Miriam Aladji Boni. *Higher Education and Professional Training:* Mathurin Nago. *Primary and Secondary Education:* Colette Houeto. *Labour and Civil Service:* Emmanuel Tiando. *Mines, Energy and Water Resources:* Jocelyn Degbey. *Environment and Natural Protection:* Jean-Pierre Babatunde. *Development, Finance and Economy:* Pascal Koukpaki. *Public Health:* Flore Gangbo. *Family, Women's and Children's Affairs:* Guecadou Bawa Yorou. *Local Government and Security:* Edgar Alia. *Commerce and Industry:* Issifou Moudjaidou Soumanou. *Public Works and Transport:* Alexandre Dossou Kpeditin. *Agriculture, Husbandry and Fisheries:* Cossi Gaston Dossouhoui. *Culture, Sports and Leisure:* Théophile Montcho. *Handicrafts and Tourism:* Soumanou Toleba. *National Defence:* Issifou Kogui N'Douro. *Administrative and Institutional Reform:* Bio Gonou Idrissou Sina.

Government Website: http://www.gouv.bj

CURRENT LEADERS

Yayi Boni

Position
President

Introduction
Yayi Boni, a former banker with little political experience and no party backing, won a run-off for the presidency by a landslide and was sworn in on 6 April 2006. He succeeded Gen. Mathieu Kérékou, who led the country for 30 of the 34 years following independence.

Early Life
Yayi Boni was born in 1952 in Tchaourou, northern Dahomey, then part of French West Africa. He attended schools in Tchaourou and Parakou, before studying economics at the National University of Benin and then banking and finance at the University of Dakar, Senegal. Boni later read politics and economics at the University of Orléans, France, and received a PhD in economics from Université Paris Dauphine in 1991.

Having worked at the Commercial Bank of Benin for two years, Boni joined the Central Bank of the States of West Africa in 1977. By the time he left in 1989, he was the organization's deputy director. Following a three-year spell as deputy director for professional development at the West African Centre for Banking Studies in Dakar, Boni returned to Benin as an advisor to President Nicéphore Soglo on banking and monetary policy.

Boni was appointed president of the Togo-based West African Development Bank in 1994 and oversaw a programme of modernization. Resigning in 2005 to contest Benin's presidential election, Boni campaigned on a platform of economic reforms aimed at reducing the country's dependence on cotton exports. Twenty-six candidates contested the first round of voting held on 5 March 2006, with Boni polling 36%. A run-off was held on 19 March between Boni and Adrien Houngbédji of the Democratic Renewal Party. Boni won with 74·5% of the vote and was sworn into office in Porto Novo on 6 April 2006.

Career in Office
Boni has promised sweeping reforms to tackle poverty and corruption and to strengthen the institutions of democracy.

DEFENCE

There is selective conscription for 18 months. Defence expenditure totalled US$60m. in 2003 (US$9 per capita), representing 1·6% of GDP.

Army
The Army strength (2002) was 4,300, with an additional 2,500-strong paramilitary gendarmerie.

Navy
Personnel in 2002 numbered 100; the force is based at Cotonou.

Air Force
The Air Force has suffered a shortage of funds and operates no combat aircraft. Personnel, 2002, 150.

INTERNATIONAL RELATIONS

Benin is a member of the UN, WTO, the African Union African Development Bank, ECOWAS, IOM, OIC, Islamic Development Bank, International Organization of the Francophonie and is an ACP member state of the ACP-EU relationship.

ECONOMY

Agriculture accounted for 36·0% of GDP in 2002, industry 14·3% and services 49·7%.

Currency
The unit of currency is the *franc CFA* (XOF) with a parity of 655·957 francs CFA to one euro. Total money supply was 351,786m. francs CFA in May 2002 and foreign exchange reserves were US$563m. Gold reserves in June 2000 were 11,000 troy oz. Inflation was 1·5% in 2003 and 0·9% in 2004.

Budget
The fiscal year is the calendar year. In 2001 revenue was 281bn. francs CFA and expenditure 353bn. francs CFA.

Performance
Real GDP growth was 3·9% in 2003 and 3·1% in 2004. Total GDP was US$4·1bn. in 2004.

Banking and Finance
The bank of issue and the central bank is the regional Central Bank of West African States (BCEAO). The *Acting Governor* is Justin Baro Damo. In Dec. 2001 it had total assets of 5,517,700m. francs CFA. There are five private commercial banks, one savings bank (total deposits 15,758m. francs CFA in 1997) and three credit institutions. The Caisse Autonome d'Amortissement du Bénin manages state funds.

ENERGY AND NATURAL RESOURCES

Environment
Benin's carbon dioxide emissions from the consumption and flaring of fossil fuels in 2002 were the equivalent of 0·3 tonnes per capita.

Electricity

Installed capacity in 2000 was 55,000 kW. In 2000 production was 56m. kWh; Benin also imported 375m. kWh. A solar energy programme was initiated in 1993. Consumption per capita in 2000 was 70 kWh.

Oil and Gas

The Semé oilfield, located 15 km offshore, was discovered in 1968. Production commenced in 1982 and was 44,000 tonnes in 1999. Crude petroleum reserves in 2002 were 8m. bbls.

Agriculture

Benin's economy is underdeveloped, and is dependent on subsistence agriculture. In 2002, 3·69m. persons depended on agriculture, of whom 1·55m. were economically active. Small independent farms produce about 90% of output. In 2001, 2·0m. ha. were arable and 0·27m. ha. permanent crops; 12,000 ha. were irrigated in 2001. There were 185 tractors in 2001. The chief agricultural products, 2000 (in 1,000 tonnes) were: cassava, 2,026; yams, 1,773; maize, 663; seed cotton, 435; cottonseed, 240; sorghum, 136; groundnuts, 81.

Livestock, 2000: cattle, 1,438,000; sheep, 645,000; goats, 1,183,000; pigs, 470,000; poultry, 23m.

Forestry

In 2000 there were 2·65m. ha. of forest (24·0% of the total land area), mainly in the north. Timber production in 2001 was 6·27m. cu. metres.

Fisheries

Total catch, 2001, 38,415 tonnes, of which freshwater fish approximately 78% and marine fish 22%.

INDUSTRY

Only about 2% of the workforce is employed in industry. The main activities include palm-oil processing, brewing and the manufacture of cement, sugar and textiles. Also important are cigarettes, food, construction materials and petroleum. Production (in 1,000 tonnes): cement (2000), 759; palm oil (2000), 15; wheat flour (1999), 9; beer (2002), 57m. litres.

Labour

The labour force numbered 2,490,000 in 1996 (52% males). Approximately half of the economically active population is engaged in agriculture, fishing and forestry.

Trade Unions

In 1973 all trade unions were amalgamated to form a single body, the *Union Nationale des Syndicats des Travailleurs du Bénin*. In 1990 some unions declared their independence from this Union, which itself broke its links with the PRPB. In 1992 there were three trade union federations.

INTERNATIONAL TRADE

Commercial and transport activities, which make up 36% of GDP, are extremely vulnerable to developments in neighbouring Nigeria, with which there is a significant amount of illegal trade. Foreign debt was US$1,843m. in 2002.

Imports and Exports

Imports (f.o.b.) in 2003 totalled US$818·7m.; exports (f.o.b.), US$540·8m.

Principal import suppliers, 1999: France, 22·0%; Côte d'Ivoire, 10·5%; Togo, 5·6%; China, 5·1%; USA, 5·1%. Principal export markets: Brazil, 19·8%; India, 15·5%; Indonesia, 10·0%; Thailand, 5·3%; Bangladesh, 4·7%.

Main imports in 1998 were: manufactured goods (19%); refined oil (19%); food and live animals (18%); machinery and transport equipment (17%). The main exports were: cotton (47%); uranium ores (30%); cigarettes (6%).

COMMUNICATIONS

Roads

There were 6,787 km of roads in 2002 (including 10 km of motorways), of which 20% were surfaced. Passenger cars in use in 2002 totalled 18,300, and there were also 25,000 commercial vehicles; in 1996 there were 7,554 buses and coaches plus approximately 250,000 motorcycles and mopeds. In 1996, 412 people died in road accidents.

Rail

There are 458 km of metre-gauge railway. In 2000, 0·7m. passengers were carried and 0·3m. tonnes of freight.

Civil Aviation

The international airport is at Cotonou (Cadjehoun), which in 2001 handled 227,000 passengers (all on international flights) and 3,200 tonnes of freight. In 1999 scheduled airline traffic of Benin-based carriers flew 3·0m. km, carrying 84,000 passengers (all on international flights). In 2003 Trans African Airlines flew to Abidjan, Bamako, Brazzaville, Dakar, Lomé and Pointe-Noire; Trans Air Benin operated services to Abidjan, Brazzaville and Lomé and Aero Benin flew to Bamako, Brazzaville, Johannesburg, Libreville and Ouagadougou.

Shipping

There is a port at Cotonou. In 2002 the merchant fleet totalled 1,000 GRT. In 2000 vessels entering totalled 1,184,000 NRT.

Telecommunications

In 2002 there were 281,400 telephone subscribers (28·6 per 1,000 persons), of which 218,800 were mobile phone subscribers. There were 12,000 PCs in use in 2002 and 2,000 fax machines. Benin had 50,000 Internet users in 2002.

Postal Services

In 2003 there were 174 post offices.

SOCIAL INSTITUTIONS

Justice

The Supreme Court is at Cotonou. There are Magistrates Courts and a *tribunal de conciliation* in each district. The legal system is based on French civil law and customary law.

The population in penal institutions in Sept. 2000 was 4,961 (81 per 100,000 of national population).

Education

Adult literacy rate was 33·6% in 2003 (46·4% among males and 22·6% among females). In 2000–01 there were 1,054,936 pupils in primary schools with 19,710 teachers and (1999–2000) 229,228 pupils in secondary schools with 9,803 teachers. The University of Benin (Cotonou) had 9,000 students and 240 academic staff in 1994–95.

In 2000–01 total expenditure on education came to 3·2% of GNP.

Health

In 1995 there were 312 physicians, 16 dentists, 1,116 nurses, 85 pharmacists and 432 midwives. Hospital bed provision was just two for every 10,000 persons in 1993.

RELIGION

Some 51% of the population follow traditional animist beliefs. Voodoo became an official religion in 1996. In 2001 there were 1·37m. Roman Catholics and 1·32m. Muslims. In May 2005 there was one cardinal.

CULTURE

World Heritage Sites

The Royal Palaces of Abomey joined the World Heritage List in 1985. They preserve the remains of the palaces of 12 kings who ruled between 1625 and 1900.

Broadcasting

The media are overseen by the nine-member Haute Autorité de l'Audiovisuel et de la Communication. The government-controlled Office de Radiodiffusion et Télévision du Bénin broadcasts a radio programme from Cotonou and a regional programme from Parakou, and a TV service (colour by SECAM V) from Cotonou. In 2000 there were 2,820,000 radio receivers and 289,000 TV receivers.

Press

In 1999 there were 13 daily newspapers with a circulation of 32,500, at a rate of 5·3 per 1,000 inhabitants.

Tourism

In 2002 there were 72,000 foreign tourists. Receipts totalled US$60m.

DIPLOMATIC REPRESENTATIVES

Of Benin in the United Kingdom
Ambassador: Edgar-Yves Monnou (resides in Paris).
Honorary Consul: Lawrence Landau (Dolphin House, 16 The Broadway, Stanmore, Middlesex HA7 4DW).

Of the United Kingdom in Benin
Ambassador: Richard Gozney, CMG (resides in Abuja, Nigeria).

Of Benin in the USA (2124 Kalorama Rd, NW, Washington, D.C., 20008)
Ambassador: Segbe Cyrille Oguin.

Of the USA in Benin (Rue Caporal Bernard Anani, Cotonou)
Ambassador: Wayne E. Neill.

Of Benin to the United Nations
Ambassador: Bodéhoussè Simon Idohou.

Of Benin to the European Union
Ambassador: Euloge Hinvi.

FURTHER READING

Bay, E., *Wives of the Leopard: Gender, Politics, and Culture in the Kingdom of Dahomey.* University Press of Virginia, 1998
Eades, Jerry S. and Allen, Christopher, *Benin.* [Bibliography] ABC-Clio, Oxford and Santa Barbara (CA), 1996

National Statistical Office: Institut National de la Statistique et de l'Analyse Economique, 01 BP 323, Cotonou.

BHUTAN

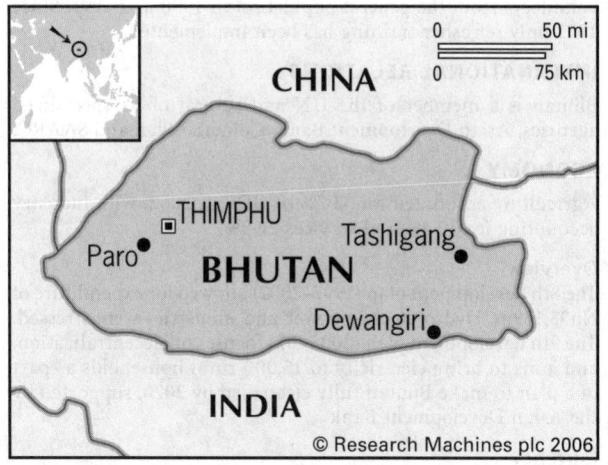

Druk-yul
(Kingdom of Bhutan)

Capital: Thimphu
Population projection, 2010: 2·41m.
GDP per capita, 2002: (PPP$) 1,969
HDI/world rank: 0·536/134

KEY HISTORICAL EVENTS

A sovereign kingdom in the Himalayas, Bhutan was governed by a spiritual ruler and a temporal ruler—the Dharma and Deb Raja—from the 17th century. The interior was organized into districts controlled by governors and fort commanders. These officials formed the electoral council appointing the Deb Raja. During the 19th century civil wars were fought between district governors for the office of the Deb Raja. The election became a formality and the governors of Tongsa and Paro were the most frequently chosen because they were the strongest. In 1863 a British attempt to bring stability to Bhutan led to war on the frontier with India.

In 1907 the office of Dharma Raja came to an end. The governor of Tongsa, Ugyen Wangchuk, was then chosen Maharajah of Bhutan, the throne becoming hereditary in his family (the title is now King of Bhutan). He concluded a treaty with the British in 1910 allowing internal autonomy but British control of foreign policy. The treaty was renewed with the Government of India in 1949. In the early 1990s, tens of thousands of 'illegal immigrants', mostly Nepali-speaking Hindus, were forcibly expelled. More than ten years on, there are still nearly 90,000 people claiming to be Bhutanese refugees in camps set up by the UNHCR in eastern Nepal.

TERRITORY AND POPULATION

Bhutan is situated in the eastern Himalayas, bounded in the north by Tibet and on all other sides by India. In 1949 India retroceded 83 sq. km of Dewangiri, annexed in 1865. Area about 47,000 sq. km (18,000 sq. miles); population estimate, 2005, 2·16m., giving a density of 46 per sq. km.

The UN gives a projected population for 2010 of 2·41m.

In 2003, 91·5% of the population lived in rural areas. Only East Timor has a larger proportion of its population living in rural areas. A Nepalese minority makes up 30–35% of the population, mainly in the south. The capital is Thimphu (1999, 28,000 population).

The official language is Dzongkha.

SOCIAL STATISTICS

2002 (estimates) births, 77,000 (rate of 34·9 per 1,000 population); deaths, 19,000 (rate of 8·7 per 1,000 population). Life expectancy at birth, 2003, was 61·7 years for men and 64·2 years for women. Infant mortality, 2001, 74 per 1,000 live births. Annual population growth rate, 1992–2002, 2·8%; fertility rate, 2001, 5·2 children per woman.

CLIMATE

The climate is largely controlled by altitude. The mountainous north is cold, with perpetual snow on the summits, but the centre has a more moderate climate, though winters are cold, with rainfall under 40" (1,000 mm). In the south, the climate is humid sub-tropical and rainfall approaches 200" (5,000 mm).

CONSTITUTION AND GOVERNMENT

There is as yet no formal constitution, although a draft constitution was unveiled in March 2005 that is set to transform Bhutan into a two-party democratic system. The monarchy acts in consultation with a National Assembly (*Tshogdu*), which was reinstituted in 1953. But King Wangchuck is leaning towards democracy. In July 1998 the National Assembly was given the right to dismiss him. This has 150 members and meets at least once a year. 105 members are elected from village constituencies, 10 are nominated by the Buddhist clergy and 35 are appointed by the King from among the bureaucracy and the government to represent him. All serve for a three-year term. All Bhutanese over 30 years may be candidates.

The reigning King is **Jigme Singye Wangchuck** (b. 1955), who succeeded his father Jigme Dorji Wangchuck (died 21 July 1972). In Dec. 2005 King Wangchuk announced that he would step down as ruler in 2008.

In 1907 the Tongsa Penlop (the governor of the province of Tongsa in central Bhutan), Sir Ugyen Wangchuk, GCIE, KCSI, was elected as the first hereditary Maharaja of Bhutan. The Bhutanese title is *Druk Gyalpo*, and his successor is now addressed as King of Bhutan. Educated in Britain, King Wangchuk is opposed to certain western influences such as jeans. The stated goal is to increase Gross National Happiness.

12 monastic representatives are elected by the central and regional ecclesiastical bodies, while the remaining members are nominated by the King, and include members of the Council of Ministers (the Cabinet) and the Royal Advisory Council.

National Anthem

'Druk tsendhen koipi gyelknap na' ('In the Thunder Dragon Kingdom'); words by Gyaldun Dasho Thinley Dorji, tune by A. Tongmi.

CURRENT ADMINISTRATION

In March 2006 the government comprised:

Prime Minister and Minister for Agriculture: Sangay Ngedup; b. 1953 (in office since 5 Sept. 2005, having previously been prime minister from July 1999–July 2000).

Chairman of the Royal Advisory Council: Rinzin Gyaltshen. *Chief Justice:* Sonam Tobgye. *Education:* Thinley Gyamtso. *Finance:* Wangdi Norbu. *Foreign Affairs:* Khandu Wangchuck. *Health:* Jigmi Singay. *Home and Cultural Affairs:* Jigme Thinley. *Information and Communication:* Leki Dorji. *Labour and Human*

Resources: Ugyen Tshering. *Trade and Industry:* Yeshey Zimba. *Works and Human Settlements:* Kinzang Dorji.

Government Website: http://www.bhutan.gov.bt/

CURRENT LEADERS

Jigme Singye Wangchuk

Position
King

Introduction
Jigme Singye Wangchuk became king of Bhutan in 1972, ruling as an absolute monarch. He has partially opened up the country to foreign influence, but striven at the same time to preserve traditional Bhutanese ways of life. In 1998 he devolved some of his powers to the National Assembly and a ministerial cabinet. A draft constitution, published in March 2005, proposes to make the country a parliamentary democracy with a constitutional monarchy, subject to a referendum. Practical power will nonetheless remain with the throne. There has been international unease about the treatment of the nation's ethnic Nepalese minority.

Early Life
Jigme Singye was born on 11 Nov. 1955, the son of King Jigme Dorji Wangchuck. He was educated in the UK and India before attending the Ugyen Wangchuck Academy in Paro. Jigme Dorji died in July 1972 and Jigme Singye succeeded him, although his formal coronation did not take place until 2 June 1974.

Career in Office
Taking the title of Druk Gyalpo (Dragon King), Jigme Singye continued the cautious modernization of Bhutan begun by his father. This included the admission of foreign tourists for the first time in 1974, although tourist numbers remain restricted. This gradual opening-up was accompanied by a determination to maintain Bhutanese customs, as epitomized by the legal requirement that citizens wear traditional dress. In 1979, the year in which Jigme Singye married four sisters as queens, the government declared that refugees must take Bhutanese citizenship or face repatriation. The move marked the beginning of a steady decline in relations between the government and ethnic minorities.

In 1986 new legislation laid down terms for citizenship on the basis of length of residency. A national census in 1988 declared thousands of people, mostly ethnic Nepalese who had been resident for up to twenty years, to be illegal immigrants. The following year Nepali ceased to be a standard language of tuition in schools. Ethnic tensions spilled into violence in the south of the country in the early 1990s, and thousands of ethnic Nepalese crossed the border into eastern Nepal where they remain in refugee camps, their fate still unresolved. Bhutan has demanded the repatriation of anyone proven to be a Bhutanese national but denies that to be the case for most of those in the camps. Refugee leaders, however, claim that Jigme Singye's regime forcibly removed the majority of the displaced people.

In 1998 the King ceded some of his power, theoretically allowing the National Assembly to dethrone him with a two-thirds majority. The following year he permitted television and Internet access for the first time. The proposed adoption of parliamentary democracy with a constitutional monarchy, details of which were unveiled in early 2005, is subject to ratification in a referendum.

Jigme Singye has overseen Bhutan's entry into numerous international organizations including the IMF, FAO, WHO, UNESCO, UNIDO and ECOSOC.

DEFENCE

In 2003 defence spending totalled US$22m. (US$25 per capita), representing 3·3% of GDP.

Army

In 1996 there was an army of 6,000 men. Three to five weeks militia training was introduced in 1989 for senior students and government officials, and three months training for some 10,000 volunteers from the general population in 1990 and 1991. Since 1992 only refresher training has been implemented.

INTERNATIONAL RELATIONS

Bhutan is a member of the UN and several of its specialized agencies, Asian Development Bank, Colombo Plan and SAARC.

ECONOMY

Agriculture accounted for 33·7% of GDP in 2002, with industry accounting for 39·4% and services 26·9%.

Overview

The 8th development plan (1997–2002) allowed for expenditure of Nu35,169m. Hydro-electric power and industries were stressed. The 9th development plan (2003–07) focuses on decentralization, and aims to bring electricity to 15,000 rural households as part of a plan to make Bhutan fully electrified by 2020, supported by the Asian Development Bank.

Currency

The unit of currency is the *ngultrum* (BTN) of 100 *chetrum*, at parity with the Indian rupee. Indian currency is also legal tender. Foreign exchange reserves were US$273m. in May 2002. Total money supply in May 2002 was Nu4,922m. Inflation was 1·8% in 2003 and 4·5% in 2004.

Budget

Current provincial revenue and expenditure in Nu1m. for fiscal years ending 30 June:

	1997–98	1998–99	1999–2000	2000–01	2001–02[1]
Revenue	3,133·0	3,656·9	4,585·4	4,975·7	5,140·6
Expenditure	4,588·4	7,284·0	8,334·2	10,716·5	9,813·7

[1]Provisional.

Performance

Real GDP growth was 6·8% in 2003 and 7·9% in 2004. Total GDP in 2004 was US$0·7bn.

Banking and Finance

The Royal Monetary Authority (founded 1982; *Managing Director,* Sonam Wangchuk) acts as the central bank. Deposits (Dec. 1995) Nu2,816·3m. Foreign exchange reserves in 1997: US$120m. The Bank of Bhutan, a commercial bank, was established in 1968. The headquarters are at Phuentsholing with 26 branches throughout the country. It is 80%-owned by the government of Bhutan and 20%-owned by the Indian government. There is another commercial bank (the Bhutan National Bank), a development bank (the Bhutan Development Finance Corporation) and a stock exchange in Thimphu.

ENERGY AND NATURAL RESOURCES

Environment

Bhutan's carbon dioxide emissions from the consumption and flaring of fossil fuels in 2002 were the equivalent of 0·1 tonnes per capita.

Electricity

Installed capacity in 2000 was 362,000 kW (of which 350,000 kW hydro-electric). Production (2000) was approximately 1·8bn. kWh. In 1995, 38 towns and 297 villages had electricity. Consumption per capita in 2000 was an estimated 201 kWh. Bhutan exports electricity to India.

Minerals

Large deposits of limestone, marble, dolomite, slate, graphite, lead, copper, coal, talc, gypsum, beryl, mica, pyrites and tufa have been found. Most mining activity (principally limestone, coal, slate and dolomite) is on a small-scale. Output, 1998 estimates: limestone, 272,000 tonnes; dolomite, 255,000 tonnes; coal (2000 estimate), 50,000 tonnes.

Agriculture

The area under cultivation in 1996 was 0·36m. ha. In 2001 there were 145,000 ha. of arable land and 20,000 ha. of permanent crops. The chief products (2000 production in 1,000 tonnes) are maize (70), oranges (58), rice (50), potatoes (34), wheat (20) and sugarcane (13).

Livestock (2000): cattle, 435,000; pigs, 75,000; sheep, 59,000; goats, 42,000; horses, 30,000.

Forestry

In 2000, 3·02m. ha. (64·2% of the land area) were forested. Timber production in 2001 was 4·42m. cu. metres.

Fisheries

The total catch in 2001 amounted to an estimated 300 tonnes, exclusively from inland waters.

INDUSTRY

Industries in Bhutan include cement, wood products, processed fruits, alcoholic beverages and calcium carbide. 2001 production: cement, 160,000 tonnes; veneer sheets, 16,000 cu. metres; particle board, 12,000 cu. metres; plywood, 4,000 cu. metres. In 2001 there were 12,878 licensed industrial establishments, of which 8,536 were construction, 3,773 service and 569 manufacturing industries. The latter included 317 forest-based companies, 116 agriculture-based and 46 mineral-based.

Labour

In 1996 the labour force totalled 888,000 (60% males).

INTERNATIONAL TRADE

External debt in 2002 amounted to US$377m. and cumulative debt service payments in 1999 totalled US$7m.

Financial support is received from India, the UN and other international aid organizations.

Imports and Exports

Trade with India dominates but oranges and apples, timber, cardamom and liquor are also exported to the Middle East, Singapore and Europe. Imports in 1999 amounted to US$182·1m. and exports to US$116·0m. In 1997–98 India accounted for 70·5% of imports and 94·5% of exports.

COMMUNICATIONS

Roads

In 2000 there were about 3,691 km of roads, of which 1,591 km were highways and main roads. In 2002 there were 10,071 cars; 770 buses and coaches; 2,747 trucks and vans plus 8,371 motorcycles and mopeds. A number of sets of traffic lights were installed during the late 1990s but all have subsequently been removed as they were considered to be eyesores. There had previously been just one set.

Civil Aviation

In 2003 Druk-Air flew from Paro to Bangkok, Delhi, Dhaka, Kathmandu, Calcutta and Rangoon (Yangon). In 1999 scheduled airline traffic of Bhutan-based carriers flew 1·0m. km, carrying 31,000 passengers (all on international flights).

Telecommunications

In 2002 there were 19,600 telephone subscribers (28·4 per 1,000 inhabitants). There were 10,000 PCs (14·5 for every 1,000 persons) in use in 2002 and 2,000 fax machines. The country's first Internet cafe was opened in March 2000 in the capital Thimphu. There were 10,000 Internet users in 2002.

Postal Services

In 2003 there were 110 post offices. Prior to the opening of the country to tourism in 1974 the main source of foreign exchange was the sale of commemorative postage stamps.

SOCIAL INSTITUTIONS

Justice

The High Court consists of eight judges appointed by the King. There is a Magistrate's Court in each district, under a *Thrimpon*, from which appeal is to the High Court at Thimphu. The death penalty, not used for 40 years, was abolished in 2004.

Education

In 2004 there were 24,533 pupils and 707 teachers in community primary schools, 26,508 pupils and 752 teachers in primary schools and 79,729 pupils with 2,630 teachers in secondary schools. In 1996 there were 1,795 pupils and 203 teachers in technical, vocational and tertiary-level schools. There were 1,248 students and 61 teachers in seven private schools. Adult literacy was 42% in 1998.

In 2000–01 total expenditure on education came to 5·1% of GNP and 12·9% of total government spending.

Health

In 2000 there were 29 hospitals, 160 basic health units, 447 outreach clinics and 18 indigenous hospital units. There were 140 doctors, 493 nurses and 144 health assistants in 2003. Free health facilities are available to 90% of the population.

RELIGION

The state religion of Bhutan is the Drukpa Kagyupa, a branch of Mahayana Buddhism. There are also Hindu and Muslim minorities.

CULTURE

Broadcasting

In 1994 there were 52 radio stations for internal administrative communications and 13 hydro-met stations. Bhutan Broadcasting Service (autonomous since 1992) broadcasts a daily programme in English, Sharchopkha, Dzongkha and Nepali. The first television station was launched in 1999.

There were 18,000 TV receivers in 2001 and 37,000 radio receivers in 2000.

Cinema

There are two cinemas in Thimphu and four others.

Press

There is one weekly newspaper, published in English, Dzongkha and Nepali. Total circulation (1996) about 12,000.

Tourism

Bhutan was not formally opened to foreign tourists until 1974, but tourism is now the largest source of foreign exchange. In 2000, 8,000 tourists visited Bhutan; revenue totalled US$10m.

DIPLOMATIC REPRESENTATIVES

Of Bhutan to the United Nations
Ambassador: Daw Penjo.

Of Bhutan to the European Union
Ambassador: Bap Kesang.

FURTHER READING

Crossette, B., *So Close to Heaven: The Vanishing Buddhist Kingdoms of the Himalayas.* New York, 1995
Das, B. N., *Mission to Bhutan: a Nation in Transition.* New Delhi, 1995
Hutt, M., *Bhutan: Perspectives on Conflict and Dissent.* London, 1994
Savada, A. M. (ed.) *Nepal and Bhutan: Country Studies.* Washington, D.C., 1993
Sinha, A. C., *Bhutan: Ethnic Identity and National Dilemma.* New Delhi, 1998

National Statistical Office: Central Statistical Organization, Thimphu.

BOLIVIA

República de Bolivia

Capital: Sucre
Seat of government: La Paz
Population projection, 2010: 10·03m.
GDP per capita, 2003: (PPP$) 2,587
HDI/world rank: 0·687/113

KEY HISTORICAL EVENTS

Bolivia was part of the Inca Empire until conquered by the Spanish in the 16th century. Independence was won and the Republic of Bolivia was proclaimed on 6 Aug. 1825. During the first 154 years of its independence, Bolivia had 189 governments, many of them installed by coups. In the 1960s the Argentinian revolutionary and former minister of the Cuban government, Ernesto 'Che' Guevara, was killed in Bolivia while fighting with a left-wing guerrilla group. In 1971 Bolivian instability reached a peak with the brief establishment of a revolutionary Popular Assembly during the regime of Gen. Torres. Later repression under Gen. Hugo Banzer took a heavy toll on the left-wing parties. Banzer was followed by a succession of military-led governments until civilian rule was restored in Oct. 1982 when Dr Siles Zuazo became president. He introduced a period of economic reform embracing free markets and open trade, which succeeded in restoring stability but also widened the gap between rich and poor. Amid growing discontent, in Dec. 2005 Evo Morales was elected to be the country's first indigenous president. Bolivian foreign policy is likely to be influenced by his strong anti-USA stance, particularly over the issue of coca production.

TERRITORY AND POPULATION

Bolivia is a landlocked state bounded in the north and east by Brazil, south by Paraguay and Argentina, and west by Chile and Peru, with an area of some 1,098,581 sq. km (424,165 sq. miles). A coastal strip of land on the Pacific passed to Chile after a war in 1884. In 1953 Chile declared Arica a free port and Bolivia has certain privileges there.

Population (2001 census): 8,274,325; density, 7·5 per sq. km. In 2003 the population was 63·4% urban. The estimated population in 2005 was 9·18m.

The UN gives a projected population for 2010 of 10·03m.

Area and population of the departments (capitals in brackets) at the 1992 and 2001 censuses:

Departments	Area (sq. km)	Census 1992	Census 2001
Beni (Trinidad)	213,564	276,174	362,521
Chuquisaca (Sucre)	51,524	453,756	531,522
Cochabamba (Cochabamba)	55,631	1,110,205	1,455,711
La Paz (La Paz)	133,985	1,900,786	2,350,466
Oruro (Oruro)	53,588	340,114	391,870
Pando (Cobija)	63,827	38,072	52,525
Potosí (Potosí)	118,218	645,889	709,013
Santa Cruz (Santa Cruz)	370,621	1,364,389	2,029,471
Tarija (Tarija)	37,623	291,407	391,226
Total	1,098,581	6,420,792	8,274,325

Population (2001, in 1,000) of the principal towns: Santa Cruz, 1,116; La Paz, 790; El Alto, 647; Cochabamba, 517; Oruro, 201; Sucre, 194; Tarija, 136; Potosí, 133.

Spanish is the official and commercial language. The Amerindian languages Quechua and Aymará are spoken exclusively by 8·1% and 3·2% of the population respectively; Tupi Guaraní is also spoken. Indigenous peoples account for 65% of the population.

SOCIAL STATISTICS

In 2000 births totalled an estimated 265,000 (birth rate of 32·4 per 1,000 population); deaths totalled an estimated 72,000 (rate, 8·8 per 1,000); infant mortality (2001), 60 per 1,000 live births, the highest in South America. Expectation of life (2003) was 62·0 years for men and 66·2 years for women. Annual population growth rate, 1992–2002, 2·2%. Fertility rate, 2001, 4·1 children per woman, also the highest in South America.

CLIMATE

The varied geography produces different climates. The low-lying areas in the Amazon Basin are warm and damp throughout the year, with heavy rainfall from Nov. to March; the Altiplano is generally dry between May and Nov. with sunshine but cold nights in June and July, while the months from Dec. to March are the wettest. La Paz, Jan. 55·9°F (13·3°C), July 50·5°F (10·3°C). Annual rainfall 20·8" (529 mm). Sucre, Jan. 58·5°F (14·7°C), July 52·7°F (11·5°C). Annual rainfall 20·1" (510 mm).

CONSTITUTION AND GOVERNMENT

Bolivia's first constitution was adopted on 19 Nov. 1826. The present constitution, the fourteenth, was adopted on 2 Feb. 1967 and was revised in Aug. 1994. The *President* is elected by universal suffrage for a five-year term. If 50% of the vote is not obtained, the result is determined by a secret ballot in Congress amongst the leading two candidates. The President appoints the members of his Cabinet. There is a bicameral legislature; the *Senate* comprises 27 members, three from each department, and the *Chamber of Deputies* 130 members, all serving terms of five years. The *Vice-President* is also the president of the National Congress. A constitutional amendment of 1996 introduced direct elections for 65 deputies; the remainder are nominated by party leaders. Voting is compulsory.

National Anthem

'Bolivianos, el hado propicio' ('Bolivians, a favourable destiny'); words by I. de Sanjinés, tune by B. Vincenti.

GOVERNMENT CHRONOLOGY

Heads of State since 1943. (ADN = Nationalist Democratic Action; FRB = Front of the Bolivian Revolution; MAS = Movement Towards Socialism; MIR = Movement of Revolutionary Left; MNR = Nationalist Revolutionary Movement; MNRI = Nationalist Revolutionary Movement of the Left; PSD = Social Democratic Party; PURS = Party of the Republican Socialist Union; n/p = non-partisan)

President of the Republic

1943–	military	Gualberto Villarroel López

Presidents of the Provisional Junta of Government

1946	n/p	Néstor Guillén Olmos
1946–47	n/p	Tomás Monje Gutiérrez

Presidents of the Republic

1947–49	PURS	José Enrique Hertzog Garaizábal
1949–51	PURS	Mamerto Urriolagoitia Harriague

President of the Military Junta of Government

1951–52	military	Hugo Ballivián Rojas

Presidents of the Republic

1952	MNR	Hernán Siles Zuazo
1952–56	MNR	Ángel Víctor Paz Estenssoro
1956–60	MNR	Hernán Siles Zuazo
1960–64	MNR	Ángel Víctor Paz Estenssoro

Presidents of the Military Junta of Government

1964	military	Alfredo Ovando Candía
1964–65	military	René Barrientos Ortuño
1965–66	military	René Barrientos Ortuño + Alfredo Ovando Candía
1966	military	Alfredo Ovando Candía

Presidents of the Republic

1966–69	FRB	René Barrientos Ortuño
1969	PSD-FRB	Luis Adolfo Siles Salinas
1969–70	military	Alfredo Ovando Candía
1970–71	military	Juan José Torres González
1971–78	military	Hugo Banzer Suárez
1978	military	Juan Pereda Asbún

President of the Military Junta of Government

1978–79	military	David Padilla Arancibia

Presidents of the Republic

1979	military	Alberto Natusch Busch
1980–81	military	Luis García Meza Tejada
1981–82	military	Celso Torrelio Villa
1982	military	Guido Vildoso Calderón
1982–85	MNRI	Hernán Siles Zuazo
1985–89	MNR	Ángel Víctor Paz Estenssoro
1989–93	MIR	Jaime Paz Zamora
1993–97	MNR	Gonzalo Sánchez de Lozada
1997–2001	ADN	Hugo Banzer Suárez
2001–02	ADN	Jorge Fernando Quiroga Ramírez
2002–03	MNR	Gonzalo Sánchez de Lozada
2003–05	MNR	Carlos Diego Mesa Gisbert
2005–06	n/p	Eduardo Rodríguez Veltzé
2006	MAS	Evo Morales Aima

RECENT ELECTIONS

Presidential elections were held on 18 Dec. 2005. Evo Morales Aima (Movement Towards Socialism) won 53·7% of votes cast against 28·6% for Jorge Quiroga (Democratic and Social Power), 7·8% for Samuel Doria Medina (National Unity Front) and 6·5% for Michiaki Nagatani (Nationalist Revolutionary Movement). There were four other candidates. Turnout was 84·5%.

In elections to the Chamber of Deputies, also held on 18 Dec. 2005, the Movement Towards Socialism won 72 seats with 53·7% of the vote, Democratic and Social Power 43 with 28·6%, the National Unity Front 8 with 7·8% and the Revolutionary Nationalist Movement 7 with 6·5%. In Senate elections of the same day Democratic and Social Power won 13 seats, Movement Towards Socialism 12, National Unity Front 1 and the Nationalist Revolutionary Movement 1.

CURRENT ADMINISTRATION

President: Evo Morales Aima; b. 1959 (Movement Towards Socialism; sworn in 22 Jan. 2006).

Vice-President: Álvaro García Linera.

In March 2006 the cabinet was composed as follows:

Minister of Economic Development and Production: Celinda Sosa. *Education:* Félix Patzi. *Finance:* Luis Alberto Arce Catacora. *Foreign Relations and Worship:* David Choquehuanca Cespedes. *Health and Sports:* Nila Heredia. *Hydrocarbons:* Andrés Soliz Rada. *Interior:* Alicia Muñoz Ala. *Labour:* Santiago Alex Gálvez Mamani. *Mining and Minerals:* Walter Villarroel. *National Defence:* Walker San Miguel Rodriguez. *Presidency:* Juan Ramón Quintana Taborga. *Rural Affairs and Agriculture:* Hugo Salvatierrea. *Services and Public Works:* Salvador Ric Riera. *Sustainable Development and Planning:* Carlos Villegas Quiroga. *Minister without Portfolio for Justice:* Casimira Rodríguez. *Minister without Portfolio for Water:* Abel Mamani Marca.

Government Website (Spanish only): http://www.bolivia.gov.bo

CURRENT LEADERS

Evo Morales Aima

Position

President

Introduction

Evo Morales became Bolivia's first indigenous president in Jan. 2006, having promised to transform the fortunes of South America's poorest country. The former coca farmer and left-wing activist has been a leading critic of US intervention in Bolivia, particularly its 'war on drugs' in the 1990s.

Early Life

Evo Morales Aima was born in the mining town of Orinoca, Oruro in the Bolivian *Altiplano* on 26 Oct. 1959. When the mines began to close in the early 1980s, the Morales family moved to lowland southeastern Bolivia to become farmers. Settling in Chapare, Evo Morales worked as a coca farmer. He became a leader of the *cocaleros* and during the 1990s came into conflict with successive governments, particularly that of the former right-wing military dictator, Hugo Banzer Suárez. Banzer joined the US 'war on drugs' and introduced a five-year 'Dignity Plan' which aimed to eradicate coca cultivation and pressurize the *cocaleros* into growing alternative crops. In 1997 Morales, by then a member of the Movement Towards Socialism (MAS), was elected to congress as a representative of the Chapare and Carrasco de Cochabamba provinces.

Morales continued to fight the government's coca eradication policy, arguing that coca leaf and tea consumption was an accepted part of daily life for workers and that the West had a responsibility to suppress cocaine demand. In April 2000 Morales helped organize mass demonstrations against a multinational corporation that critics claimed would raise water prices in the Cochabamba region beyond the means of the poorest residents.

In Jan. 2002 Morales was removed from his seat in Congress on a terrorism charge related to riots in Sacaba over coca-eradication policies, though many claimed his dismissal followed pressure from the American embassy. Morales nevertheless declared his candidacy for the congressional and presidential elections, held in June 2002, on a platform of nationalizing strategic industries, providing basic services for all, land reform and tackling corruption. The MAS came second with 20·9% of the vote, with Morales crediting much of his success to support from the American ambassador to Bolivia, Manuel Rocha. Refusing to join a coalition with the Nationalist Revolutionary Movement (MNR), led by President Gonzalo Sánchez de Lozada, the MAS became the leading opposition party.

Following a general strike on 29 Sept. 2003, Morales was involved in an uprising that led to the ousting of de Lozada the following month. He was also a key figure in the mass protests that gripped La Paz in April 2005, when demonstrators called for an end to poverty and a greater share of profits from the country's gas reserves. A blockade led to food and fuel shortages in La Paz and when clashes erupted between the police and protesters, Carlos Mesa, the new president, fled the city under armed escort.

Interim president Eduardo Rodríguez Veltzé announced fresh elections for 18 Dec. 2005. Morales edged ahead of the conservative former president, Jorge Quiroga, in the polls and emerged victorious with 53·7% of the vote. He was sworn in as president on 22 Jan. 2006.

Career in Office

In his inaugural address Morales promised to deliver 'equality and justice' for the poor and marginalized. He pledged to secure a new constitution providing greater legal representation and more rights for indigenous people. His choice of inexperienced left-wing activists to fill most of the cabinet led to comparisons with Venezuela's president, Hugo Chávez. Morales swiftly signed a co-operation accord with Chávez under which Venezuela's state-owned oil company will help Bolivia develop its energy reserves. Alliances have also been forged with Cuba's President Fidel Castro and Brazil's President Luiz Inácio Lula da Silva but relations with the USA are strained.

DEFENCE

There is selective conscription for 12 months at the age of 18 years. There has been optional pre-military training for high school pupils since 1998.

In 2003 defence expenditure totalled US$131m. (US$15 per capita), representing 1·7% of GDP.

Army

There are six military regions. Strength (2002): 25,000 (18,000 conscripts), including a Presidential Guard infantry regiment under direct headquarters command.

Navy

A small force exists for river and lake patrol duties. Personnel in 2002 totalled 3,500, including 1,700 marines. There were six Naval Districts in 2002, covering Lake Titicaca and the rivers, each with one flotilla.

Air Force

The Air Force, established in 1923, has 37 combat aircraft and 16 armed helicopters. Personnel strength (2002) about 3,000 (2,000 conscripts).

INTERNATIONAL RELATIONS

Bolivia is a member of the UN, WTO, OAS, Inter-American Development Bank, LAIA, the Andean Group, IOM and the Amazon Pact, and is an associate member of MERCOSUR.

ECONOMY

In 2002 agriculture accounted for 14·6% of GDP, industry 33·3% and services 52·1%.

Overview

The New Economic Policy includes a 'capitalization' programme (partial privatization and 50% distribution of shares to pension funds for adult citizens). State enterprises in oil and gas, telecommunications, electricity, railways, airlines and tin were capitalized between 1995–98. Water privatization in Cochabamba in 2000 was revoked after riots over tariffs.

Currency

The unit of currency is the *boliviano* (BOB) of 100 *centavos*, which replaced the *peso* on 1 Jan. 1987 at a rate of one boliviano = 1m. pesos. Inflation was 3·3% in 2003 and 4·4% in 2004. In June 2002 foreign exchange reserves were US$557m., total money supply was 4,163m. bolivianos and gold reserves totalled 911,000 troy oz.

Budget

Budgetary central government revenue was 14,123m. bolivianos in 2003 (12,516m. bolivianos in 2002) and expenditure 17,462m. bolivianos (16,316m. bolivianos in 2002).

Performance

Real GDP growth was 2·8% in 2003 and 3·6% in 2004. Total GDP was US$8·8bn. in 2004.

Banking and Finance

The Central Bank (*President*, Juan Antonio Morales Anaya) is the bank of issue. In 2000 there were eight commercial banks and five foreign banks.

There are stock exchanges in La Paz and Santa Cruz.

ENERGY AND NATURAL RESOURCES

Environment

In 2002 Bolivia's carbon dioxide emissions from the consumption and flaring of fossil fuels were the equivalent of 1·0 tonnes per capita.

Electricity

Installed capacity was 1·3m. kW in 2000. Production from all sources (2000), 3·95bn. kWh; consumption per capita was 475 kWh in 2000.

Oil and Gas

There are petroleum and natural gas deposits in the Santa Cruz–Camiri areas. Production of oil in 2000 was 11,424,058 bbls. Reserves in 2002 were 441m. bbls. Work has begun on a US$1·9bn. pipeline from eastern Bolivia to São Paulo in Brazil. Natural gas output was 5·4bn. cu. metres in 2002 with proven reserves of 680bn. cu. metres in 2002.

Minerals

Mining accounts for 5·76% of GDP (1996 estimate). Tin-mining had been the mainstay of the economy until the collapse of the international tin market in 1985. Estimated production (in tonnes): zinc (2001), 141,226; tin (2000), 12,039; lead (2000), 9,090; antimony (2000), 2,072; wolfram (2000), 671; silver (2001), 408; gold (2001), 12,395 kg.

Agriculture

The agricultural population was 3·17m. in 2002, of whom 1·56m. were economically active. There were 2·90m. ha. of arable land in 2001 and 0·20m. ha. of permanent crops. Output in 1,000 tonnes in 2000 was: sugarcane, 3,602; soybeans, 1,232; potatoes, 927; bananas, 695; maize, 653; cassava, 515; rice, 310; plantains, 187. In 1992, 77,000 tonnes of coca (the source of cocaine) were grown. Since 1987 Bolivia has received international (mainly US) aid to reduce the amount of coca grown, with compensation for farmers who co-operate.

Livestock, 2000: cattle, 6,725,000; sheep, 8,752,000; pigs, 2,793,000; goats, 1,500,000; asses and mules, 712,000; horses, 322,000; chickens, 74m.

Forestry

Forests covered 53·07m. ha. (48·9% of the land area) in 2000. Tropical forests with woods ranging from the 'iron tree' to the light balsa are exploited. Timber production in 2001 was 2·72m. cu. metres.

Fisheries
In 2001 the total catch was 5,940 tonnes, exclusively from inland waters.

INDUSTRY
In 1998 it was estimated that the industrial sector employed a total of 51,214 persons. The principal manufactures are mining, petroleum, smelting, foodstuffs, tobacco and textiles.

Labour
Out of 3,884,251 people (54·8% male) in employment in 2001, 44·1% were in agriculture, ranching and hunting, 14·0% in retail and repair, 9·2% in industrial manufacturing, 4·9% in construction and 4·6% in transport, storage and communications. The unemployment rate in 2000 was 11·5%. In 2002 the minimum wage was 420 bolivianos a month.

Trade Unions
Unions are grouped in the Confederación de Obreros Bolivianos.

INTERNATIONAL TRADE
An agreement of Jan. 1992 with Peru gives Bolivia duty-free transit for imports and exports through a corridor leading to the Peruvian Pacific port of Ilo from the Bolivian frontier town of Desaguadero, in return for Peruvian access to the Atlantic via Bolivia's roads and railways. The mining code of 1991 gives tax incentives to foreign investors. Foreign debt was US$4,867m. in 2002.

Imports and Exports
In 2002 imports (f.o.b.) amounted to US$1,532·1m. (US$1,477·4m. in 2001); exports (f.o.b.) US$1,298·7m. (US$1,284·8m. in 2001). Main import commodities are road vehicles and parts, machinery for specific industries, cereals and cereal preparations, general industrial machinery, chemicals, petroleum, food, and iron and steel. Main exports (2001 provisional, in US$1m.): soybeans and products, 272·9; natural gas, 237·4; zinc, 120·7; gold, 89·9; food products, 58·1; tin, 51·1; silver ore, 48·9; other fuels, 47·4; wood and products, 41·1.

Main import suppliers, 2001 (provisional, in US$1m.): Argentina, 289·1; USA, 281·7; Brazil, 277·3; Chile, 142·6; Peru, 107·1; China, 69·7. Main export markets, 2001 (provisional, in US$1m.): Brazil, 286·7; Colombia, 186·0; Switzerland, 175·4; USA, 156·8; Venezuela, 96·1; UK, 72·3.

Imports and exports pass chiefly through the ports of Arica and Antofagasta in Chile, Mollendo-Matarani in Peru, through La Quiaca on the Bolivian–Argentine border and through river-ports on the rivers flowing into the Amazon.

COMMUNICATIONS

Roads
The total length of the road system was about 60,282 km in 2002, of which 12,431 km were national roads. Total vehicles in use in 2002 was 85,119, including 26,229 passenger cars and 30,539 trucks and vans.

Rail
In 2002 the railway network totalled 3,815 km of metre gauge track. Passenger-km travelled in 2002 came to 356m. and freight tonne-km to 1,044m.

Civil Aviation
The two international airports are La Paz (El Alto) and Santa Cruz (Viru Viru). The national airlines are the state-owned Aerosur (domestic services only) and Lloyd Aéreo Boliviano (97·5% state-owned), which in 2003 ran scheduled services to Buenos Aires, Bogotá, Cancún, Córdoba, Cuzco, Havana, Lima, Manaus, Mexico City, Miami, Panama City, Rio de Janeiro, Salta, Santiago, São Paulo and Trinidad, as well as internal services. There were direct flights in 2003 with other airlines to Arica, Caracas, Iquique and Montevideo. In 1999 Lloyd Aéreo Boliviano flew 18·8m. km, carrying 1,525,900 passengers (658,800 on international flights).

Shipping
Lake Titicaca and about 19,000 km of rivers are open to navigation. In 2002 the merchant marine totalled 358,000 GRT, including oil tankers 242,000 GRT.

Telecommunications
In 2002 there were 1,436,600 telephone subscribers (172·2 per 1,000 persons), including 872,700 mobile phone subscribers (104·6 per 1,000 persons). There were 190,000 PCs in use (22·8 per 1,000 persons). There were five Internet Service Providers in 1999; Internet users numbered 270,000 in 2002.

Postal Services
In 2001 there were 142 post offices, or one for every 59,500 persons.

SOCIAL INSTITUTIONS

Justice
Justice is administered by the Supreme Court, superior depart-ment courts (of five or seven judges) and courts of local justice. The Supreme Court, with headquarters at Sucre, is divided into two sections, civil and criminal, of five justices each, with the Chief Justice presiding over both. Members of the Supreme Court are chosen on a two-thirds vote of Congress. The death penalty was abolished for ordinary crimes in 1997.

The population in penal institutions in Dec. 2003 was 6,768 (76 per 100,000 of national population).

Education
Adult literacy was 86·5% in 2003 (male, 92·9%; female, 80·4%). Primary instruction is free and obligatory between the ages of six and 14 years. In 1999 there were 13,365 schooling facilities. In 2000–01 there were 1,492,023 pupils and 61,546 teachers in primary schools, 874,669 pupils and 39,192 teachers in secondary schools, and 278,763 students and 12,809 academic staff in tertiary education. The national rate of school attendance (6–19-year-olds) reached 74·3% in 1998.

In 1994–95 there were seven universities, two technical universities, one Roman Catholic university, one musical conservatory, and colleges in the following fields: business, six; teacher training, four; industry, one; nursing, one; technical teacher training, one; fine arts, one; rural education, one; physical education, one. In 1997 state universities had 162,538 students and 7,490 teaching staff. In 1998 there were 35 private universities with 32,253 students and 3,538 teaching staff.

In 2000–01 total expenditure on education came to 5·7% of GNP and 23·1% of total government expenditure.

Health
In 2001 there were 1,999 doctors and 4,025 nurses; and 161 hospitals with 8,638 hospital beds (one per 998 persons).

Welfare
The pensions and social security systems in Bolivia were reformed in 1996. Instead of a defined-benefit publicly managed pension system, a defined-contribution system based on privately managed individual capitalization accounts was introduced. There are now two funds: the Collective Capitalization Fund, made up of 50% of the shares of capitalized companies formerly owned by the state, and the Individual Capitalization Fund, made up of contributions of those associated to the new system with a monthly income of above US$50. A solidarity bonus,

BONOSOL—worth approximately US$250 a year—is paid to all Bolivians over the age of 65.

RELIGION

The Roman Catholic church was disestablished in 1961. It is under a cardinal (in Sucre), an archbishop (in La Paz), six bishops and vicars apostolic. It had 7·54m. adherents in 2001. In 2001, 89% of the population were Roman Catholics and 9% Protestants. In May 2005 there was one cardinal.

CULTURE

World Heritage Sites

There are six UNESCO World Heritage sites in Bolivia: the City of Potosí (inscribed on the list in 1987), the largest industrial mining complex of the 16th century; the Jesuit Missions of the Chiquitos (1990), six settlements for converted Indians built between 1696 and 1760; the Historic City of Sucre (1991), containing 16th century colonial architecture; El Fuerte de Samaipata (1998), a pre-Hispanic sculptured rock and political and religious centre; Noel Kempff Mercado National Park (2000), a 1,523,000 ha. park in the Amazon Basin; and Tiwanaku: Spiritual and Political Centre of the Tiwanaku Culture (2000), monumental remains from AD 500 to 900.

Broadcasting

The broadcasting authority is the Dirección General de Telecomunicaciones. In 1999 there were 321 radio stations. Broadcasts are in Spanish, Aymará and Quechua. There were 5·51m. radios in 2000. There were 48 television stations in 1997 and 990,000 televisions (colour by NTSC) in 2000.

Cinema

In 1999 there were 27 cinemas, with a total attendance for the year of 1·4m.

Press

There were 29 daily newspapers in 1998 with a combined circulation of 788,000, at a rate of 99 per 1,000 inhabitants.

Tourism

In 2001 there were 308,000 foreign tourists, bringing revenue totalling US$156m.

DIPLOMATIC REPRESENTATIVES

Of Bolivia in the United Kingdom (106 Eaton Sq., London, SW1W 9AD)
Ambassador: Gonzalo Montenegro.

Of the United Kingdom in Bolivia (Avenida Arce 2732, La Paz)
Ambassador: Peter Bateman.

Of Bolivia in the USA (3014 Massachusetts Ave., NW, Washington, D.C., 20008)
Ambassador: Jaime Aparicio Otero.

Of the USA in Bolivia (Avenida Arce 2780, La Paz)
Ambassador: David N. Greenlee.

Of Bolivia to the United Nations
Ambassador: Ernesto Araníbar Quiroga.

Of Bolivia to the European Union
Ambassador: Fernando Laredo Aguayo.

FURTHER READING

Fifer, J. V., *Bolivia.* [Bibliography] ABC-Clio, Oxford and Santa Barbara (CA), 2000
Klein, H., *Bolivia: The Evolution of a Multi-Ethnic Society.* OUP, 1982

National Statistical Office: Instituto Nacional de Estadistica, Av. José Carrasco 1391, CP 6129, La Paz.
Website (Spanish only): http://www.ine.gov.bo/

Republika Bosna i Hercegovina

Capital: Sarajevo
Population projection, 2010: 3·93m.
GDP per capita, 2003: (PPP$) 5,967
HDI/world rank: 0·786/68

KEY HISTORICAL EVENTS

Settled by Slavs in the 7th century, Bosnia was conquered by the Turks in 1463 when much of the population was gradually converted to Islam. At the Congress of Berlin (1878) the territory was assigned to Austro-Hungarian administration under nominal Turkish suzerainty. Austria-Hungary's outright annexation in 1908 generated international tensions which contributed to the outbreak of the First World War. After 1918 Bosnia and Herzegovina became part of a new kingdom of Serbs, Croats and Slovenes under the Serbian monarchy. Its name was changed to Yugoslavia in 1929. (*See* SERBIA AND MONTENEGRO for developments up to and beyond the Second World War.)

On 15 Oct. 1991 the National Assembly adopted a 'Memorandum on Sovereignty', the Serbian deputies abstaining. This envisaged Bosnian autonomy within a Yugoslav federation. Though boycotted by Serbs, a referendum in March 1992 supported independence. In March 1992 an agreement was reached by Muslims, Serbs and Croats to set up three autonomous ethnic communities under a central Bosnian authority.

Bosnia-Herzegovina declared independence on 5 April 1992. Fighting broke out between the Serb, Croat and Muslim communities, with particularly heavy casualties and destruction in Sarajevo, leading to extensive Muslim territorial losses and an exodus of refugees. UN-sponsored ceasefires were repeatedly violated.

On 13 Aug. 1992 the UN Security Council voted to authorize the use of force to ensure the delivery of humanitarian aid to besieged civilians. Internationally sponsored peace talks were held in Geneva in 1993, but Serb-Muslim-Croat fighting continued. In April 1993 the UN established havens for Muslim civilians in Sarajevo, Srebrenica and Goražde.

In Dec. 1994 Bosnian Serbs and Muslims signed a countrywide interim ceasefire. Bosnian Croats also signed in Jan. 1995. However, Croatian Serbs and the Muslim secessionist forces under Fikret Abdić did not sign the agreement, and fighting continued. On 16 June 1995 Bosnian government forces launched an attack to break the Bosnian Serb siege of Sarajevo. On 11 July Bosnian Serb forces began to occupy UN security zones despite retaliatory NATO air strikes, and on 28 Aug. shelled Sarajevo. In July Srebrenica was the scene of the worst massacre of the war, when Bosnian Serb troops killed over 7,000 Muslim boys and men after Dutch peacekeeping forces were withdrawn from the city.

To stop the shelling of UN safe areas, more than 60 NATO aircraft attacked Bosnian Serb military installations on 30–31 Aug. On 26 Sept. in Washington the foreign ministers of Bosnia, Croatia and Yugoslavia (the latter negotiating for the Bosnian Serbs) agreed a draft Bosnian constitution under which a central government would handle foreign affairs and commerce and a Serb Zone, and a Muslim-Croat Federation would run their internal affairs. A ceasefire came into force on 12 Oct. 1995.

In Dayton (Ohio) on 21 Nov. 1995 the prime ministers of Bosnia, Croatia and Yugoslavia initialled a US-brokered agreement to end hostilities. The Bosnian state was divided into a Croat-Muslim Federation containing 51% of Bosnian territory and a Serb Republic containing 49%. A central government authority representing all ethnic groups with responsibility for foreign and monetary policy and citizenship issues was established and free elections held. On 20 Dec. 1995 a NATO contingent (IFOR) took over from UN peacekeeping forces to enforce the Paris peace agreements and set up a 4-km separation zone between the Serb and Muslim-Croat territories. After a year IFOR was replaced by SFOR, a 'Stabilization Force'. On 2 Dec. 2004 a 7,000-strong European Union force 'EUFOR' took over from SFOR.

TERRITORY AND POPULATION

The republic is bounded in the north and west by Croatia and in the east and southeast by Serbia and Montenegro. It has a coastline of only 20 km with no harbours. Its area is 51,129 sq. km. The capital is Sarajevo (estimated population, 2003: 380,000).

Population at the 1991 census: 4,377,033, of which the predominating ethnic groups were Muslims (1,905,829), Serbs (1,369,258) and Croats (755,892). Population of the principal cities in 1991: Sarajevo, 415,631 (est. 1999, 522,000); Banja Luka, 142,644; Zenica, 96,238. By 1996, following the civil war, 1,319,250 Bosnians had taken refuge abroad, including 0·45m. in Serbia and Montenegro, 0·32m. in Germany, 0·17m. in Croatia and 0·12m. in Sweden. Population estimate, 2005: 3·91m.

The UN gives a projected population for 2010 of 3·93m.

In 2003, 55·6%% of the population lived in rural areas.

The official languages are Bosnian, Croatian and Serbian.

SOCIAL STATISTICS

2004 births, 35,151; deaths, 32,616. Rates per 1,000, 2004: birth, 9·1; death, 8·5. Annual population growth rate, 1992–2002, 0·4%. Life expectancy at birth, 2003, was 71·4 years for men and 76·8 years for women. Infant mortality, 2004, 7·2 per 1,000 live births; fertility rate, 2004, 1·2 children per woman.

CLIMATE

The climate is generally continental with steady rainfall throughout the year, although in areas nearer the coast it is more Mediterranean.

CONSTITUTION AND GOVERNMENT

On 18 March 1994, in Washington, Bosnian Muslims and Croats reached an agreement for the creation of a federation of cantons with a central government responsible for foreign affairs, defence and commerce. It was envisaged that there would be a president elected by a two-house legislature alternating annually between the nationalities.

On 31 May 1994 the National Assembly approved the creation of the Muslim Croat federation. Alija Izetbegović remained the unitary states' President. An interim government with Hasan Muratović as Prime Minister was formed on 30 Jan. 1996.

The Dayton Agreement including the new constitution was signed and came into force on 14 Dec. 1995. The government structure was established in 1996 as follows:

Heading the state is a three-member *Presidency* (one Croat, one Muslim, one Serb) with a rotating president. The Presidency is elected by direct universal suffrage, and is responsible for foreign affairs and the nomination of the prime minister. There is a two-chamber parliament: the *House of Representatives* (which meets in Sarajevo) comprises 42 directly elected deputies, two-thirds Croat and Muslim and one-third Serb; and the *House of Peoples* (which meets in Lukavica) comprises five Croat, five Muslim and five Serb delegates.

Below the national level the country is divided into two self-governing entities along ethnic lines.

The Bosniak-Croat Federation of Bosnia and Herzegovina (Federacija Bosna i Hercegovina) is headed by a President and Vice-President, alternately Croat and Muslim, a 98-member Chamber of Representatives and a 74-member Chamber of Peoples. The Serb Republic (Republika Srpska) is also headed by an elected President and Vice-President, and there is a National Assembly of 83 members, elected by proportional representation.

Central government is conducted by a *Council of Ministers*, which comprises Muslim and Serb Co-Prime Ministers and a Croat Deputy Prime Minister. The Co-Prime Ministers alternate in office every week.

In Nov. 2005 leaders of the three main ethnic groups agreed on a series of constitutional reforms aimed at enhancing the authority of the central government, reducing the powers of the Federation of Bosnia and Herzegovina and the Serb Republic, and streamlining the parliament and the office of the presidency.

National Anthem

'Intermezzo'; tune by Dusan Sestić; no words.

RECENT ELECTIONS

Elections were held on 5 Oct. 2002 for the Presidium and the federal parliament. Seats for the three-member rotating presidency went to Serb, Croat and Muslim nationalist parties. The elected members were as follows: Sulejman Tihić (Muslim; Party of Democratic Action—SDA); Dragan Čović (Croat; Croatian Democratic Community—HDZ); and Mirko Šarović (Serb; Social Democratic Party—SDS). In the parliamentary elections, the Party for Democratic Action won ten seats with 32·5% of the vote, against five seats for both the Croat Democratic Union and the Serb Democratic Party.

CURRENT ADMINISTRATION

Presidency Chairman: Sulejman Tihić (Muslim; SDA; took rotating presidency on 28 Feb. 2006). *Presidency Members:* Borislav Paravac (Serb; SDS); Ivo Miro Jović (Croat, HDZ).

In March 2006 the cabinet comprised:

Prime Minister: Adnan Terzić (Muslim; SDA); b. 1960 (sworn in 23 Dec. 2002).

Minister of Civil Affairs: Safet Halilović. *Defence:* Nikola Radovanović. *Finance and Treasury:* Ljerka Marić. *Foreign Affairs:* Mladen Ivanić. *Foreign Trade and Economic Relations:*

Dragan Doko. *Human Rights and Refugees:* Mirsad Kebo. *Justice:* Slobodan Kovač. *Security:* Bariša Čolak. *Transportation and Communications:* Branko Dokić.

UN High Representative: Christian Schwarz-Schilling (Germany); b. 1930 (sworn in 31 Jan. 2006).

Office of the High Representative: http://www.ohr.int

CURRENT LEADERS

Sulejman Tihić

Position
President

Introduction
Sulejman Tihić took over the eight-month chairmanship of the tripartite presidency of Bosnia-Herzegovina for the second time in Feb. 2006. During the Yugoslav civil war in the early 1990s, Tihić was captured by Bosnian-Serb paramilitary forces and interned in concentration camps. He testified against Slobodan Milošević before the international criminal tribunal at The Hague.

Early Life
Sulejman Tihić was born on 26 Nov. 1951 in Bosanski Šamac, northern Bosnia, in the Federal People's Republic of Yugoslavia. He graduated in law from the University of Sarajevo in 1975 and worked as a judge and public prosecutor in Bosanski Šamac. From 1983 until 1992 he practised as a lawyer in his hometown. In 1990, amid the collapse of communism in Eastern Europe and economic chaos in Yugoslavia, Tihić co-founded the Party of Democratic Action (SDA). Led by Alija Izetbegović (also born in Bosanski Šamac) from May 1990, the SDA aimed to represent Islamic culture in Yugoslavia.

At Bosnia-Herzegovina's first multi-party elections in Nov. 1990 the SDA emerged as the state's most popular party, winning 35·8% of the vote. Izetbegović became president of a nine-member multi-ethnic collective presidency in Sarajevo. Tihić was subsequently elected president of the municipal board of the SDA in Bosanski Šamac.

In 1991 the initially pro-federation Muslim leadership in Sarajevo were caught up between Serbian centralism and drives for independence in Slovenia and Croatia. After Bosnia-Herzegovina declared independence on 5 April 1992, Serbian forces began seizing territory and embarked on a systematic campaign of 'ethnic cleansing'. Tihić was captured and interned in concentration camps run by Bosnian-Serb forces at Bosanski Šamac, Brčko, Bijeljina, Batajnica and Sremska Mitrovica between May and Aug. 1992. Testifying before the international criminal tribunal in The Hague in Dec. 2003, Tihić claimed that the decision to attack Bosanski Šamac came from Belgrade.

Following his release in Croatia, Tihić served from 1994–96 as head of the consular department of the Bosnian embassy in Bonn, Germany. Returning to Bosnia-Herzegovina, he was appointed advisor on consular affairs to the foreign minister. From 1996–2002 he was also a member of the parliament of Republika Srpska (the territory comprising 49% of Bosnia-Herzegovina legitimized by the Dayton Peace Accord of Nov. 1995), serving as its deputy speaker for the final two years. In 2001 Paddy Ashdown, the UN High Representative in Bosnia-Herzegovina, nominated Tihić as a member of the parliamentary committee on constitutional issues. At the SDA's third congress in Oct. 2001 Tihić succeeded Izetbegović, who was suffering ill health, as party president.

Tihić became a member of Bosnia-Herzegovina's tripartite presidency on 28 Oct. 2002, following general elections earlier in the month at which the SDA won 21·9% of the vote and ten seats in the house of representatives. Tihić and the other two presidency members, Dragan Čović (Bosnian Croat) and Mirko Šarović (Bosnian Serb), were elected to four-year terms. Tihić chaired the presidency from March–Oct. 2004 and took up another eight-month chairmanship on 28 Feb. 2006, succeeding the Bosnian-Croat representative, Ivo Miro Jović.

Career in Office
Tihić hopes to be the last chairman of a collective presidency before constitutional reforms establish a single president. Having identified the government's priorities as economic growth and the fight against crime and corruption, he has promised to work with the international community to achieve these goals. Following the death of the former Yugoslav and Serbian president, Slobodan Milošević, in his cell in The Hague on 11 March 2006, Tihić expressed regret that Milošević had not lived long enough to be punished for his crimes.

DEFENCE

Defence expenditure in 2003 totalled US$152m. (US$37 per capita), representing 2·2% of GDP.

An EU-led peacekeeping contingent 'EUFOR' took over military operations from the NATO-led 'SFOR' on 2 Dec. 2004. Its mission is to focus on the apprehension of indicted war criminals and counter-terrorism, and provide advice on defence reform.

Army
The forces of the Federation of Bosnia and Herzegovina (composed of the Army of Bosnia and Herzegovina and the Croatian Defence Council) numbered 13,200 in 2002, with the personnel of the Serb Republic's armed forces totalling 6,600. In 2002 the forces of the Federation of Bosnia and Herzegovina had 203 main battle tanks and those of the Serb Republic had 137 main battle tanks. There are no armed forces at the state level except for border guards and the Brcko-district police. Under the supervision of the Defence Reform Commission, military change has been rapid. In early 2004 a state-level civilian-led command and control structure was set up, including a Defence Ministry, incorporating the forces of both the Federation of Bosnia and Herzegovina and the Serb Republic.

INTERNATIONAL RELATIONS

Bosnia-Herzegovina is a member of the UN, BIS, OSCE, Central European Initiative and the IOM.

The Serb Republic and Yugoslavia (now Serbia and Montenegro) signed an agreement on 28 Feb. 1997 establishing 'special parallel relations' between them. The agreement envisages co-operation in cultural, commercial, security and foreign policy matters, allows visa-free transit of borders and includes a non-aggression pact. A customs agreement followed on 31 March.

ECONOMY

In 2004 agriculture accounted for 11·9% of GDP, industry 27·5% and services 60·6%.

Currency
A new currency, the *konvertibilna marka* (BAM) consisting of 100 *pfennig*, was introduced in June 1998. Initially trading at a strict 1-to-1 against the Deutsche Mark, it is now pegged to the euro at a rate of 1·95583 convertible marks to the euro. Inflation was 0·4% in 2004 (0·6% in 2003). Total money supply was 3,117m. convertible marks in June 2002.

Budget
Revenue in 2004 was 3,725m. convertible marks; expenditure was 3,489m. convertible marks. VAT of 17% was introduced on 1 Jan. 2006.

Performance
Bosnia-Herzegovina had one of the fastest growing economies in the world during the second half of the 1990s. Real GDP growth was 61·9% in 1996 and 30·0% in 1997, although it has slowed

since then and was 4·0% in 2003 and 5·7% in 2004. Total GDP was US$8·1bn. in 2004.

Banking and Finance
There is a Central Bank (*Governor:* Kemal Kozarić). In 2005 there were 28 commercial banks (19 in the Federation and 9 in the Serb Republic). There are stock exchanges in Banja Luka and Sarajevo.

ENERGY AND NATURAL RESOURCES

Environment
Bosnia-Herzegovina's carbon dioxide emissions from the consumption and flaring of fossil fuels in 2002 were the equivalent of 4·7 tonnes per capita.

Electricity
Installed capacity was 2·7m. kW in 2000. Production in 2000 was 10·43bn. kWh. In 2000 consumption per capita was 2,355 kWh.

Minerals
Output: lignite (2000), 5·3m. tonnes; hard coal (2000), 3·5m. tonnes; aluminium (2001), 175,000 tonnes; iron ore (2001), 100,000 tonnes; bauxite (2001), 75,000 tonnes.

Agriculture
In 2001 there were 690,000 ha. of arable land and 150,000 ha. of permanent crops. 2000 yields (in 1,000 tonnes): maize, 900; potatoes, 397; wheat, 255; plums, 90; cabbages, 74; barley, 55. Livestock in 2000: cattle, 462,000; sheep, 672,000; pigs, 150,000; poultry, 3m.

Forestry
In 2000 forests covered 2·27m. ha., or 44·6% of the total land area. Timber production in 2001 was 3·82m. cu. metres.

Fisheries
Estimated total fish catch in 2001: 2,500 tonnes (exclusively freshwater).

INDUSTRY

Output (in 1,000 tonnes): cement (2000), 300; crude steel (2001), 80. Other products (1990): cars, 38,000 units; tractors, 34,000 units; lorries, 16,000 units; televisions, 21,000 sets.

Labour
The labour force totalled 1,719,000 in 1996 (62% males). Unemployment in 2004 was nearly 40%.

INTERNATIONAL TRADE

External debt was US$2,515m. in 2002.

Imports and Exports
2002 external trade (in US$1m.): imports (f.o.b.), 4,518·7; exports (f.o.b.), 1,115·0. Principal import sources in 2000 were Slovenia, 15·1%; Germany, 12·2%; Italy, 10·6%. Main export markets were Italy, 22·7%; Germany, 11·5%; Slovenia, 6·6%. In 2000 the EU accounted for 43·8% of Bosnia-Herzegovina's imports and 65·4% of exports.

COMMUNICATIONS

Roads
In 2005 there were an estimated 22,419 km of roads (4,104 km main roads). There were 96,182 passenger cars in use in 1996 (23 per 1,000 inhabitants) and 9,783 vans and trucks. There were 199 road accident fatalities in 1996.

Rail
There were 1,032 km of railways in 2000 (779 km electrified); they carried 47m. passenger-km and 214m. tonne-km of freight. It is estimated that up to 80% of the rail network was destroyed in the civil war, and it was not until July 2001 that the first

international services were resumed. There are two state-owned rail companies—the Railways of the Federation of Bosnia and Herzegovina (ZFBH) and the Railway of the Serb Republic (ZRS).

Civil Aviation
There are airports at Sarajevo (Butmir), Tuzla, Banja Luka and Mostar. In 2005 there were direct flights to Belgrade, Cologne/Bonn, Düsseldorf, Frankfurt, İstanbul, Izmir, Ljubljana, Milan, Prague, Stockholm, Stuttgart, Vienna, Zagreb and Zürich. In 2001 Sarajevo handled 313,000 passengers (all international) and 1,300 tonnes of freight.

Telecommunications
Telephone subscribers numbered 1,239,000 in 2002, equivalent to 302·2 per 1,000 inhabitants. There were 748,800 mobile phone subscribers in 2002 and 100,000 Internet users. Three state-owned companies run the telephone networks in different parts of the country, the largest of which is the Sarajevo-based PTT Bih.

Postal Services
In 2003 there were 243 post offices.

SOCIAL INSTITUTIONS

Justice
The population in penal institutions in April 2003 was 2,283.

Police
The European Union Police Mission (EUPM) in Bosnia and Herzegovina, the EU's first civilian crisis management operation, took over from the UN's International Police Task Force on 1 Jan. 2003. It aims to help the authorities develop their police forces to the highest European and international standards.

Education
The adult literacy rate was 94·6% in 2003 (91·1% among females and 98·4% among males). In 2003–04 there were 375,213 pupils in 1,993 primary schools (21,763 teachers), 168,592 in 303 secondary schools (10,892 teachers) and 76,979 students in seven universities.

Health
In 2001 there were 5,443 physicians, 679 dentists, 16,708 nurses and 350 pharmacists. In 1996 there were 48 hospital beds per 10,000 inhabitants.

Welfare
There were 380,000 pensions in 1990 (including 140,000 old age).

RELIGION

In 2001 there were estimated to be 1,690,000 Sunni Muslims, 1,180,000 Serbian Orthodox, 710,000 Roman Catholics and 350,000 followers of other religions. In May 2005 the Roman Catholic church had one cardinal.

CULTURE

World Heritage Sites
There is one UNESCO site in Bosnia-Herzegovina: the Old Bridge area of the Old City of Mostar, an important Ottoman frontier town. It was entered on the list in 2005.

Broadcasting
In 2000 there were 900,000 radio receivers and 411,000 TV receivers.

Press
There were two daily newspapers in 1995 with a combined circulation of 520,000, at a rate of 146 per 1,000 inhabitants.

Tourism
In 2002 there were 160,000 foreign tourists, bringing revenue of US$112m.

DIPLOMATIC REPRESENTATIVES

Of Bosnia-Herzegovina in the United Kingdom (5–7 Lexham Gdns, London, W8 5JJ)
Ambassador: Tanja Milašinović.

Of the United Kingdom in Bosnia-Herzegovina (8 Tina Ujevića, Sarajevo)
Ambassador: Matthew Rycroft.

Of Bosnia-Herzegovina in the USA (2109 E St., NW, Washington, D.C., 20037)
Ambassador: Bisera Turković.

Of the USA in Bosnia-Herzegovina (Alipasina 43, 71000, Sarajevo)
Ambassador: Douglas L. McElhaney.

Of Bosnia-Herzegovina to the United Nations
Ambassador: Miloš Prica.

Of Bosnia-Herzegovina to the European Union
Ambassador: Lidija Topić.

FURTHER READING

Bert, W., *The Reluctant Superpower: United States Policy in Bosnia, 1991–1995.* New York, 1997
Burg, Steven L. and Shoup, Paul S., *The War in Bosnia-Herzegovina.* New York, 1999
Cigar, N., *Genocide in Bosnia: the Policy of Ethnic Cleansing.* Texas Univ. Press, 1995
Fine, J. V. A. and Donia, R. J., *Bosnia-Hercegovina: a Tradition Betrayed.* Farnborough, 1994
Friedman, F., *The Bosnian Muslims: Denial of a Nation.* Boulder (CO), 1996
Garde, P., *Journal de Voyage en Bosnie-Herzégovine.* Paris, 1995
Holbrooke, R., *To End a War.* Random House, London, 1998
Malcolm, N., *Bosnia: a Short History.* 2nd ed. London, 1996
O'Ballance, E., *Civil War in Bosnia, 1992–94.* London, 1995
Rieff, D., *Slaughterhouse: Bosnia and the Failure of the West.* New York, 1997
Sells, M. A., *The Bridge Betrayed: Religion and Genocide in Bosnia.* California Univ. Press, 1996

National Statistical Office: Agency for Statistics of Bosnia and Herzegovina, Zelenih beretki 26, 71000 Sarajevo. *Director:* Zdenko Milinović.

BOTSWANA

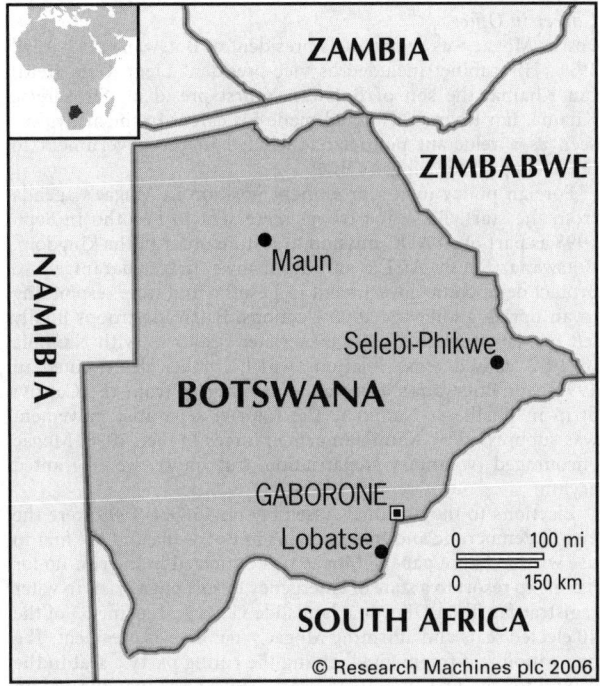

Republic of Botswana

Capital: Gaborone
Population projection, 2010: 1·73m.
GDP per capita, 2003: (PPP$) 8,714
HDI/world rank: 0·565/131

KEY HISTORICAL EVENTS

The Tswana or Batswana people are the principal inhabitants of the country formerly known as Bechuanaland. The territory was declared a British protectorate in 1895. Britain ruled through her High Commissioner in South Africa until the post was abolished in 1964. Frequent suggestions for the addition of Bechuanaland and the other two High Commission Territories to South Africa were rejected, the Africans being strongly against the idea. Economically, however, the country was very closely tied to that of South Africa and has remained so. In Dec. 1960 Bechuanaland received its first constitution. Further constitutional change brought full self-government in 1965 and full independence on 30 Sept. 1966. For years Botswana had great difficulties with the neighbouring settler regime in Rhodesia, until that country became Zimbabwe in 1980. Relations with South Africa were also strained until the ending of apartheid. Today the country enjoys stability and a fast-growing economy.

TERRITORY AND POPULATION

Botswana is bounded in the west and north by Namibia, northeast by Zambia and Zimbabwe, and east and south by South Africa. The area is 581,730 sq. km. Population (2001 census), 1,680,863; density, 2·9 per sq. km. In 2001, 49·4% of the population was urban. The estimated population in 2005 was 1·77m.

The UN gives a projected population for 2010 of 1·73m.

In 2003, 51·6% of the population were urban.

The country is divided into ten districts (Central, Chobe, Ghanzi, Kgalagadi, Kgatleng, Kweneng, Ngamiland, Ngwaketse, North East and South East).

The main towns (with population, 2001) are Gaborone (186,007), Francistown (83,023), Molepolole (54,561), Selebi-Phikwe (49,849), Maun (43,776), Serowe (42,444), Kanye (40,628), Mahalapye (39,719), Mochudi (36,962), Mogoditshane (32,843) and Lobatse (29,689).

The official languages are Setswana and English. Setswana is spoken by over 90% of the population and English by approximately 40%. More than ten other languages, including Herero, Hottentot, Kalanga, Mbukushu, San, and Sekgalagadi are spoken in various tribal areas.

SOCIAL STATISTICS

2001 (estimates) births, 49,000; deaths, 21,000. Rates, 2001 estimates (per 1,000 population): births, 28·9; deaths, 12·4. Infant mortality, 2001 (per 1,000 live births), 56. Expectation of life in 2003 was 35·9 years for males and 36·7 for females. Life expectancy has declined dramatically over the last ten years as a result of the impact of AIDS. In 2001, 35·3% of all adults were infected with HIV, with well over half of those aged between 25 and 29 being HIV positive. Annual population growth rate, 1992–2002, 2·1%. Fertility rate, 2001, 3·3 children per woman.

CLIMATE

In winter, days are warm and nights cold, with occasional frosts. Summer heat is tempered by prevailing northeast winds. Rainfall comes mainly in summer, from Oct. to April, while the rest of the year is almost completely dry with very high sunshine amounts. Gaborone, Jan. 79°F (26·1°C), July 55°F (12·8°C). Annual rainfall varies from 650 mm in the north to 250 mm in the southeast. The country is prone to droughts.

CONSTITUTION AND GOVERNMENT

The Constitution was adopted in March 1965 and became effective on 30 Sept. 1966. It provides for a republican form of government headed by the President with three main organs: the Legislature, the Executive and the Judiciary. The executive rests with the President who is responsible to the National Assembly. The President is elected for five-year terms by the National Assembly.

The *National Assembly* consists of 63 members, of which 57 are elected by universal suffrage, four are specially elected members and two, the President and the Speaker, are *ex officio*.

Elections are held every five years. Voting is on the first-past-the-post system.

There is also a *House of Chiefs* to advise the government. It consists of the Chiefs of the eight tribes who were autonomous during the days of the British protectorate, plus four members elected by and from among the sub-chiefs in four districts; these 12 members elect a further three politically independent members.

National Anthem

'Fatshe leno la rona' ('Blessed be this noble land'); words and tune by K. T. Motsete.

GOVERNMENT CHRONOLOGY

Presidents since 1966. (BDP = Botswana Democratic Party)

1966–80	BDP	Seretse Khama
1980–98	BDP	Quett Ketumile Joni Masire
1998–	BDP	Festus Gontebanye Mogae

RECENT ELECTIONS

In National Assembly elections held on 30 Oct. 2004 the Botswana Democratic Party (BDP) gained 44 seats with 51·7% of the vote, the Botswana National Front 12 with 26·1% and the Botswana Congress Party 1 with 16·6%. Turnout was 77·1%.

CURRENT ADMINISTRATION

President: Festus Mogae; b. 1939 (BDP; sworn in on 1 April 1998).

Vice-President: Lieut.-Gen. Seretse Ian Khama.

In March 2006 the cabinet was as follows:

Minister of Finance and Development Planning: Baledzi Gaolathe. *Foreign Affairs:* Lieut.-Gen. Mompati Merafhe. *Communications, Science and Technology:* Pelonomi Venson. *Health:* Prof. Sheila Tlou. *Works and Transport:* Lesego Motsumi. *Environment, Wildlife and Tourism:* Capt. Kitso Mokaila. *Mineral Resources, Energy and Water Affairs:* Charles Tibone. *Education:* Jacob Nkate. *Labour and Home Affairs:* Major-Gen. Moeng Pheto. *Agriculture:* Johnny Swartz. *Lands and Housing:* Ramadeluka Seretse. *Local Government:* Dr Margaret Nasha. *Trade and Industry:* Neo Moroka. *Presidential Affairs and Public Administration:* Phandu Skelemani.

Government Website: http://www.gov.bw

CURRENT LEADERS

Festus Mogae

Position
President

Introduction
Festus Mogae succeeded Sir Ketumile Masire as president in 1998. An economist and civil servant, Mogae is popular and well-respected in Botswana and abroad. His high-profile campaigning against the spread of HIV/AIDS has been frequently contrasted with the attitude of South African President Thabo Mbeki, who has questioned the exclusivity of HIV as the cause of AIDS. Mogae also stands out for his criticism of Zimbabwe's President Robert Mugabe, with whom few leaders in Southern Africa have broken ranks.

Early Life
Festus Gontebanye Mogae was born at Serowe, Central District, on 21 Aug. 1939. He was educated at Moeng College in Botswana. Mogae then studied economics at Northwest London Polytechnic and the University of Oxford and in 1970 gained an MA in development economics from the University of Sussex. In 1968 he returned to Botswana and joined the Ministry of Finance and Development Planning, becoming permanent secretary in 1975. During this period he was also involved with the IMF, African Development Bank and World Bank.

As permanent secretary to the president, he served on various parastatal boards, including the Housing Corporation and the Meat Commission. Mogae also held the position of director and later chairman of the Botswana Development Corporation and director of the De Beers Botswana Mining Company (diamond mining company). From 1978–80 he was executive director of the IMF for Anglophone Africa in Washington, D.C.

Mogae returned to Botswana in 1980 as governor of the Bank of Botswana before taking up the combined roles of permanent secretary to the president, secretary to the cabinet and supervisor of elections, which he held for most of the following decade. In 1989 he took up his first political position in government as minister of finance and development planning. President Ketumile Masire appointed him vice-president in 1992. From 1992–96 he held the chair of the Council of Ministers of the Southern African Development Community (SADC). In 1994 he was elected to the National Assembly for Palapye constituency.

In Nov. 1997 Masire announced his retirement and designated Mogae as his successor until elections scheduled for 1999. Pressure had been mounting within the Botswana Democratic Party (BDP) for a change of leadership.

Career in Office
Festus Mogae was sworn in as president of Botswana on 1 April 1998. His cabinet included as vice-president Lieut.-Gen. (retd) Ian Khama, the son of Botswana's first president, Sir Seretse Khama. Ian Khama, who had made his career in the army, was seen as a reluctant politician, included in the government to boost support for Mogae's BDP.

Foreign policy took a prominent position in Mogae's agenda from the start. Batswana troops were sent to Lesotho in Sept. 1998 as part of a SADC mission to restore order in the kingdom. Botswana, South Africa and Zimbabwe have guaranteed to protect democratic government in Lesotho and were responding to an uprising after the 1998 elections. Batswana troops finally left in May 1999. A dispute over water resources with Namibia in 1998 caused tense relations which further deteriorated in 1999 over Botswana's acceptance of refugees from the Caprivi Strip in northeast Namibia. The Caprivi separatist movement was suppressed by Namibian armed forces in Oct. 1998. Mogae encouraged voluntary repatriation but most were granted asylum.

Elections to the National Assembly on 16 Oct. 1999 were the eighth democratic and free elections in Botswana and the first to use written ballot papers. Mogae was criticized in the run-up for having to resort to a state of emergency to sort out a crisis in voter registration. The BDP won a landslide victory, securing 33 of the 40 elected seats and affirming Mogae's mandate as president. The opposition had fragmented, giving the ruling party a seat in the capital for the first time in 15 years. Mogae was inaugurated on 20 Oct. 1999. In Dec. he announced that his deputy, Khama, was to take a year-long sabbatical. No explanation was given.

The dominant theme of Mogae's presidency has been the threat of HIV/AIDS. By 2002 Botswana had a prevalence rate of 36%, the highest in the world, according to the UN. This has had a dramatic effect on life expectancy, which fell from 65 years in 1993 to 36 in 2003. Mogae has led a vocal campaign for openness, discussion and education—uncommon among Southern African leaders—devoting approximately 13% of government expenditure in 2000 to the AIDS programme. While the president's efforts have been praised by AIDS organizations, human rights groups have criticized what they see as potential infringements of privacy. His suggestion that AIDS represents a 'threat of annihilation' of the Batswana nation has also received a mixed response.

Mogae's government, like that of his predecessor, has been praised by international organizations for its transparency and moderation. In 2002 Transparency International, a Berlin-based anti-corruption organization of which Mogae is member, placed Botswana as the 24th least corrupt nation in the world and the leader in transparency in Africa. However, in May 2001 the news director at Botswana's national television station resigned having accused the government of trying to control the content of broadcasting, after banning a documentary on the case of Mariette Bosch, a white South African executed in Botswana for murder.

Botswana's economy is heavily dependent on the export of diamonds. Mogae has promoted Batswana diamonds as 'diamonds for development', as opposed to 'conflict diamonds' used to finance civil wars in many parts of Africa. He has also encouraged economic diversification, especially in manufacturing, tourism and services, and encouraged increased productivity in the agricultural sector (which accounts for less than 5% of GDP but involves 80% of the population).

Mogae has viewed the land seizures in Zimbabwe more critically than most African leaders. In 2001 he stated that:

'the region cannot afford to have its second largest economy [Zimbabwe] sinking because of this situation. While we support land reform in Zimbabwe completely, we feel the implementation of the strategy is incorrect.' However, in 2002 he admitted that there was little he could do to arrest developments in Botswana's much more populous neighbour.

Social unrest within Botswana during Mogae's presidency has been focused on the rights of 'Bushmen', or San. These indigenous inhabitants of the Kalahari Desert have resisted efforts to evict them from the Central Kalahari Game Reserve and took the government to court in March 2002. Although as few as 60 Bushmen still live in the area, the international media has followed the progress of their legal battle closely and some have accused the government of being motivated by diamond mining potential.

The BDP won another landslide victory in parliamentary elections on 30 Oct. 2004, taking 44 of the 57 seats in the National Assembly. Limited by the constitution to ten years in office, Mogae has said that he will step down as president in 2008.

DEFENCE

In 2003 defence expenditure totalled US$304m. (US$177 per capita), representing 3·8% of GDP.

Army

The Army personnel (2002) numbered 8,500. There is also a 1,000-strong paramilitary force.

Air Force

The Air Wing operated 30 combat aircraft in 2002 and numbered 500.

INTERNATIONAL RELATIONS

Botswana is a member of the UN, WTO, the Commonwealth, the African Union, African Development Bank, SADC and is an ACP member state of the ACP-EU relationship.

ECONOMY

Services accounted for 51·9% of GDP in 2002, industry 45·6% and agriculture 2·5%.

Overview

The theme of the Ninth National Development Plan (2003–09) is 'Towards Realisation of Vision 2016: Sustainable and Diversified Development through Competitiveness in Global Markets'. Real GDP growth is projected to average 5·5% annually over the six-year duration of the Plan.

Currency

The unit of currency is the *pula* (BWP) of 100 *thebe*. The pula was devalued by 7·5% in Feb. 2004 and 12·5% in May 2005. Inflation was 6·7% in July 2004. Foreign exchange reserves were US$5,163m. in Aug. 2004. Total money supply was P2,409m. in May 2002.

Budget

The fiscal year begins in April. Government finance for recent years (in P1m.):

	2001–02	2002–03	2003–04
Revenue	7,907·5	8,829·1	9,746·7
Expenditure	8,143·3	9,469·9	10,082·2

2003–04 revenue (in P1m.) comprised: mineral taxes, 4,930·0; customs pool, 1,394·1; other revenue, 3,422·6. Expenditure included: recurrent, 7,327·6; development, 2,462·6.

Performance

Real GDP grew by 6·6% in 2003 and 4·9% in 2004. In 2004 total GDP was US$8·7bn.

Banking and Finance

There were five commercial banks in 2004. Total assets were P24,718·2m. at July 2004. The Bank of Botswana (*Governor*, Linah Mohohlo), established in 1976, is the central bank. The National Development Bank, founded in 1964, has six regional offices, and agricultural, industrial and commercial development divisions. The Botswana Co-operative Bank is banker to co-operatives and to thrift and loan societies. The government-owned Post Office Savings Bank (Botswana Post) operates throughout the country.

There is a stock exchange in Gaborone.

ENERGY AND NATURAL RESOURCES

Environment

Botswana's carbon dioxide emissions from the consumption and flaring of fossil fuels in 2002 were the equivalent of 2·2 tonnes per capita.

Electricity

Installed capacity was 132,000 kW in 2003. Production in 2000 was approximately 1·1bn. kWh. The coal-fired power station at Morupule supplies cities and major towns.

Water

Surface water resources are about 18,000m. cu. metres a year. 80% of the land has no surface water, and must be served by some 6,000 boreholes.

Minerals

Botswana is the world's biggest diamond producer in terms of value; in 2003 the total value was estimated to be US$2·5bn. Debswana, a partnership between the government and De Beers, runs three mines producing around 30m. carats a year, with plans to double the capacity of the largest mine from 6m. to 12m. carats a year. Coal reserves are estimated at 17bn. tonnes. There is also copper, salt and soda ash. Mineral production, 2003: diamonds, 30m. carats (the second largest quantity after Australia); coal, 823,000 tonnes; salt, 30,000 tonnes; copper, 8,000 tonnes; gold, 8 kg.

Agriculture

70% of the total land area is desert. 80% of the population is rural, 71% of all land is 'tribal', protected and allocated to prevent over-grazing, maintain small farmers and foster commercial ranching. Agriculture provides a livelihood for over 70% of the population, but accounts for only 2·4% of GDP (2003). In 2003, 360,000 ha. were arable and 3,000 ha. permanent crops. There were 7,000 tractors in 2004 and 102 harvester-threshers. Cattle-rearing is the chief industry after diamond-mining, and the country is more a pastoral than an agricultural one, crops depending entirely upon the rainfall. In 2001, 300,000 persons were economically active in agriculture. In 2002 there were: cattle, 3·1m.; goats, 1·1m.; asses, 330,000; sheep, 273,000; chickens, 866,000. In 1995, 80% of cattle were owned by traditional farmers, about half owning fewer than 20 head. A serious outbreak of cattle lung disease in 1995–96 led to the slaughter of around 300,000 animals.

Production (2002, in tonnes): maize, 16,447; sorghum, 15,807; sunflower seeds, 2,250; pulses, 1,907; other crops (including vegetables), 7,694.

17% of the land is set aside for wildlife conservation and 20% for wildlife management areas, with four national parks and game reserves.

Forestry

Forests covered 139,000 sq. km, or 25·2% of the total land area, in 2003. There are forest nurseries and plantations. Concessions have been granted to harvest 7,500 cu. metres in Kasane and Chobe Forestry Reserves, and up to 2,500 cu. metres in the Masame area. In 2001, 745,000 cu. metres of roundwood were cut.

Fisheries

In 2003 the total catch was 121 tonnes, exclusively from inland waters.

INDUSTRY

The most important sector is the diamond industry. Meat is processed, and beer, soft drinks, textiles and foodstuffs manufactured. Rural technology is being developed and traditional crafts encouraged. In June 2003 there were 16,773 enterprises operating in Botswana, of which a third were in the wholesale and retail trade.

Labour

In 2001, 266,607 persons were in formal employment. At the 2001 census there were 270,679 paid employees (including informal employment) and 28,764 self-employed. A further 76,101 persons worked on a non-cash basis, for example as family helpers. 60,757 were seeking work. In March 1994 there were 12,342 Botswana nationals employed in the mines of South Africa. In 1991 there were 57,001 building workers, 34,322 in trade and 29,325 in domestic service. Botswana's biggest individual employer is the Debswana Diamond Company, with a workforce (1997) of nearly 6,000. In 2003 the unemployment rate was 23·8%.

INTERNATIONAL TRADE

Botswana is a member of the Southern African Customs Union (SACU) with Lesotho, Namibia, South Africa and Swaziland. There are no foreign exchange restrictions. External debt in 2003 totalled US$422m. (P2,058m.).

Imports and Exports

In 2003 imports (f.o.b.) totalled US$2,107·5m. More than three-quarters of all imports are from the SACU countries, the main commodities being machinery and electrical equipment, foodstuffs, vehicles and transport equipment, textiles and petroleum products.

In 2003 exports (f.o.b.) totalled US$2,975·5m., including diamonds, vehicles, copper, nickel and beef.

Principal import sources in 1998 were Southern African Customs Union (SACU), 74·9%; South Korea, 4·8%; Zimbabwe, 3·9%; UK, 3·4%. Main export markets were UK, 55·5%; SACU 17·2%; Zimbabwe 2·9%; USA, 1·0%.

COMMUNICATIONS

Roads

In 2004 the total road network was estimated to be 21,133 km (8,916 km national roads). In Nov. 2004 there were 220,663 motor vehicles registered. As of 15 Nov. 2004 there were 455 deaths in road accidents during 2004.

Rail

The main line from Mafeking in South Africa to Bulawayo in Zimbabwe traverses Botswana. With three branches the total length was 888 km in 2000. Passenger-km travelled in 2000 came to 89m. and freight tonne-km to 1,282m.

Civil Aviation

There are international airports at Gaborone (Sir Seretse Khama) and at Maun and six domestic airports. The national carrier is the state-owned Air Botswana. In 2003 direct flights were operated to Harare and Johannesburg. In 1998 Air Botswana flew 2·6m. km, carrying 123,700 passengers (92,500 on international flights). In Oct. 1999 an Air Botswana pilot who had been suspended two months earlier crashed an empty passenger plane into the airline's two serviceable aeroplanes at Gaborone Airport, killing himself and destroying the airline's complete fleet in the process. In 2001 Gaborone handled 224,385 passengers (174,725 on international flights).

Telecommunications

Botswana had 778,000 telephone subscribers in 2002 (400 per 1,000 inhabitants), including 765,000 mobile phone subscribers. Botswana has the second highest mobile phone penetration rate in Africa, after South Africa. There were 112,000 PCs in use in 2003 and 5,200 fax machines. In 2001 Internet users numbered 80,000.

Postal Services

There were 113 post offices and 70 postal agencies in Nov. 2004. The Botswana Post offers many services including Western Union Money Transfers.

SOCIAL INSTITUTIONS

Justice

Law is based on the Roman-Dutch law of the former Cape Colony, but judges and magistrates are also qualified in English common law. The Court of Appeal has jurisdiction in respect of criminal and civil appeals emanating from the High Court, and in all criminal and civil cases and proceedings. Magistrates' courts and traditional courts are in each administrative district. As well as a national police force there are local customary law enforcement officers. The death penalty is still in force. In 2003 there were four executions. The population in penal institutions in Nov. 2003 was 5,890 (327 per 100,000 of national population).

Education

Adult literacy rate in 2002 was 78·9% (male, 76·1%; female, 81·5%). Basic free education, introduced in 1986, consists of seven years of primary and three years of junior secondary schooling. In 2001 enrolment in 780 primary schools was 326,481 with 13,128 teachers, and 151,847 pupils at secondary level with 9,261 teachers. In 2001 there were 1,404 students in teacher training colleges. 'Brigades' (community-managed private bodies) provide lower-level vocational training. The Department of Non-Formal Education offers secondary-level correspondence courses and is the executing agency for the National Literacy Programme. There is one university (12,286 students in 2001–02).

In 2003–04 expenditure on education came to US$797·4m.

Health

In 2004 there were 16 primary hospitals, one mental hospital, three referral hospitals, 15 health centres, 257 clinics and 366 health posts. There were also 761 stops for mobile health teams. In 2004 there were 89 doctors and 2,129 nurses in government health facilities. There are other private health facilities with more personnel.

RELIGION

Freedom of worship is guaranteed under the Constitution. About 43% of the population is Christian. Non-Christian religions include Bahais, Muslims and Hindus.

CULTURE

World Heritage Sites

Tsodilo was created a UNESCO World Heritage Site in 2001. It is the site of over 4,500 prehistoric rock paintings in the Kalahari Desert.

Broadcasting

The government-controlled Radio Botswana broadcasts daily on two channels in both English and Setswana. There is also the government-run Botswana Television (BTV) which covers almost the whole country and a commercial television company that transmits on a 50 km-radius from Gaborone (colour by PAL).

Most broadcasts are in English.

There were 254,000 radio sets in 2000 and 74,000 TV sets in 2001.

Press

The government owned *Daily News* is distributed free. There are also six weekly independent newspapers. *The Gazette, The Botswana Guardian, The Voice, Mokgosi, Sunday Standard* and *The Mid-Week Sun* are middle-of-the-road politically. For a more distinctive political slant there is a daily independent paper *Mmegi* (The Reporter). The press in Botswana is free from censorship.

Tourism

There were 1·1m. foreign visitors in 2003 with tourism receipts totalling US$356m.

DIPLOMATIC REPRESENTATIVES

Of Botswana in the United Kingdom (6 Stratford Pl., London, W1C 1AY)
High Commissioner: Roy Warren Blackbeard.

Of the United Kingdom in Botswana (Private Bag 0023, Gaborone)
High Commissioner: Frank Martin.

Of Botswana in the USA (1531–1533 New Hampshire Ave., NW, Washington, D.C., 20036)
Ambassador: Lapologang Caesar Lekoa.

Of the USA in Botswana (PO Box 90, Gaborone)
Ambassador: Katherine Canavan.

Of Botswana to the United Nations
Ambassador: Samuel Outlule.

Of Botswana to the European Union
Ambassador: Sasara George.

FURTHER READING

Central Statistics Office. *Statistical Bulletin* (Quarterly).
Ministry of Information and Broadcasting. *Botswana Handbook.—Kutlwano* (Monthly).
Molomo, M. G. and Mokopakgosi, B. (eds.) *Multi-Party Democracy in Botswana.* Harare, 1991
Perrings, C., *Sustainable Development and Poverty Alleviation in Sub-Saharan Africa: the Case of Botswana.* London, 1995
Wiseman, John, *Botswana.* [Bibliography] ABC-Clio, Oxford and Santa Barbara (CA), 1992

National Statistical Office: Central Statistics Office, Private Bag 0024, Gaborone.
Website: http://www.cso.gov.bw

BRASIL

República Federativa do Brasil

Capital: Brasília (Federal District)
Population projection, 2010: 198·50m.
GDP per capita, 2003: (PPP$) 7,790
HDI/world rank: 0·792/63

KEY HISTORICAL EVENTS

There is evidence of human habitation in Brazil dating back to 9000 BC. Before the Portuguese discovery and occupation of Brazil there was a large indigenous population. This population was fragmented into a number of smaller tribes, the largest of which was the Tupi-Guarani, who survived the sub-tropical environment by clearing just enough land for their crops.

The first Europeans to come into contact with the indigenous peoples were exiled criminals, or *degredados*, who learned their language and skills in farming and hunting. Jesuit missionaries later attempted to convert the native people with limited success.

The first Portuguese contact with Brazil was Pedro Alvares Cabral who left Lisbon in 1500 with orders to travel along the Cape of Good Hope route discovered by the Portuguese navigator Vasco da Gama in 1497–98. In an attempt to avoid storms he set a course more westerly than da Gama's and was carried still farther westward by currents, landing in a place he named Terra da Vera Cruz (Land of the True Cross) and later renamed *Terra do Brasil* (Land of Brazil).

Although the official motive for Portuguese exploration was religious—the conversion of the natives to the Catholic faith—the greater incentive was to find a direct all-water trade route with Asia and thereby break Italy's commercial domination. Early Portuguese economic activity in Brazil revolved around the exploitation of the huge timber (Brazilwood) resources. This was soon superseded by sugarcane and, to a lesser extent, tobacco, harvested on plantations that sprang up in the interior in the 16th and 17th centuries. As these industries came to dominate the economy, the need for large-scale labour became more pressing. Where the indigenous people proved unsuitable or unavailable, largely owing to ill health from newly introduced European diseases, millions of Africans were enslaved and shipped to the region.

The first attempt to establish a working government came in 1533 when the Portuguese divided the land into 15 captaincies, subdivided into leagues and ruled by selected governors (*donatários*). In 1549 John III sought to establish a more centralized power structure and appointed Tomé de Sousa as governor general, ruling from the newly founded capital, Salvador (Bahia). In 1567 Governor-General Mem da Sá founded Rio de Janeiro to protect its harbour from French incursions. During the Union of Portugal and Spain (1580–1640), Brazil became subject to attacks from Spanish enemies, notably the Netherlands, whose forces were not expelled until 1654.

The Portuguese settlers had set about conquering the vast Brazilian interior by the late 17th century. Early excursions were made by bandeirantes, men pursuing private enterprise and dreams of vast personal wealth. It was these men who, in forging waterways and paths into the interior, discovered the first gold in the region at Minas Gerais in 1695. This opened up a whole new resource for exploitation by the Portuguese crown. Rio de Janeiro benefited greatly from mining wealth and in 1763 became the colonial capital in place of Salvador. Recife and Ouro Preto were the only other major colonial urban centres.

The third quarter of the 18th century saw Spain accept many of Portugal's claims in the region. Portuguese Prime Minister Sebastião José de Carvalho e Mello ended the rule of the *donatários,* expelled the Jesuits, gave new freedoms to the native population and established two companies to regulate Brazilian trade. As Brazilian government became increasingly centralized a burgeoning nationalism emerged, most famously in the failed rebellion against the Portuguese led by Joaquim José da Silva Xavier (Tiradentes) in 1789.

In 1807 an invasion of Portugal by the French forces of Napoleon Bonaparte forced the royal family to flee Portugal and take refuge in Rio, declaring it the temporary capital of the Portuguese Empire. In 1816 King João VI ascended to the Portuguese throne but refused to return to Lisbon until revolts demanded his presence there five years later. While in Brazil he initiated reforms which ended Portugal's commercial monopoly and in 1815 granted Brazil equal status with Portugal when he established the United Kingdom of Portugal, Brazil and the Algarves. On his return to Portugal João's son, Pedro, became Brazil's regent.

Independence

Pedro's regency ran into trouble when he battled the demands of the Cortes (the Portuguese parliamentary body) for him to return to Portugal. The Cortes repealed many of João's reforms for the former colony and sought to reduce it to its earlier colonial status. When in Sept. 1822 the Cortes decided to reduce Pedro's powers he called for Brazilian independence. On 1 Dec. 1822 he was crowned Constitutional Emperor and Perpetual Defender of Brazil. The United States recognized Brazil's independence in May 1824 followed by Portugal itself in 1825.

Pedro was forced to abdicate in 1831 following a disastrous war with Argentina and a money crisis deepened by his promise to free the slaves. He left his five-year old son Pedro II as the ruler in waiting. In 1840 Pedro II ascended the throne after nine years of weak rule and civil strife. Pedro proceeded to establish himself as leader, free of all political influences, by 1847. He ruled for nearly 50 years and despite a series of uprisings Brazil remained relatively stable and its economy strong.

Pedro was instrumental in the overthrow of Juan Manuel de Rosas in Argentina in the 1850s and became involved in Uruguay's civil war in the 1860s. In the 1870s the three nations united to repel the advances of the Paraguayan forces of Francisco Solano López. Pedro initiated the gradual abolition of slavery by outlawing the slave trade in 1854. Emancipation was achieved in 1888 when three quarters of a million slaves were freed without compensation to their owners. In 1889 General Manuel Deodoro da Fonseca led a military revolt which forced Pedro's abdication. A republic was proclaimed, headed by Fonseca, which instigated the separation of church and state. In Feb.

1891 Brazil officially became a Federal Republic with Fonseca elected as its first president. Forced to resign when he attempted to bypass congress, he was succeeded by Floriano Peixoto who used the military to restore order. In 1894 he was replaced by Brazil's first civilian head of state, Prudente de Morais, the first of a succession of leaders who enjoyed relative peace as Brazil grew rich on coffee exports.

Brazil underwent significant territorial expansion in the early years of the 20th century during the Baron of Rio Branco's tenure as foreign minister. As well as winning 900,000 sq. km of land from other South American nations, he pursued close relations with the USA and UK, which led to a declaration of war against Germany in 1917. However, by the 1920s there was growing internal resentment at the wealth of the coffee barons and in 1922 a failed military coup initiated eight years of civil strife. Amid economic crisis in 1930 Getúlio Vargas lost the presidential election but was swept to power by a military junta which dismissed the legitimately elected government.

The constitution of 1934 provided for universal suffrage and three years later a new constitution, drafted in the aftermath of a failed coup, gave Vargas greatly extended power. During his period of rule some areas, including São Paulo, saw considerable industrial development, helping Brazil to create a modern economy. In the 1940s the first steel plant was built in the state of Rio de Janeiro at Volta Redonda with US financing. In 1942 Brazil followed the lead of the USA and declared war against the Axis powers. In Oct. 1945 the military staged a coup and Vargas was forced to step down.

Economic Problems

The subsequent election was won by Eurico Gaspar Dutra, a favourite of Vargas, whose government promulgated a constitution which set presidential terms at five years and reduced the power of central government. Vargas was returned to power in 1950 but failed to dominate as he had previously. Brazil's economic problems spiralled and in 1954 Vargas was implicated in the attempted murder of a journalist critical of him. When the High Command demanded his resignation Vargas committed suicide by shooting himself.

Juscelino Kubitschek, popularly known as JK, was elected president in 1956. He instigated massive public expenditure including road and hydroelectric schemes and the creation of a new capital, Brasília. It was hoped these programmes would be the catalyst for the development of Brazil's huge interior but instead brought uncontrollable inflation. Jânio Quadros became president in 1961 on a wave of public euphoria but his decoration of Che Guevara in a public ceremony antagonized the right wing military and he resigned after six months in office. Vice-president João Goulart took over but his leftist policies led to his overthrow by the military in 1964.

There followed 20 years of single party rule and censored press. Castelo Branco was installed as president in April 1964. Chosen by the military to enforce fundamental political and economic reforms, Branco instead sought to introduce change through democratic channels. He narrowly survived a coup in 1965 but was forced by the military powerbrokers to take a radical line. Laws passed in Oct. 1965 suspended political parties and gave the president emergency powers. An ostensibly two-party state was created, consisting of the government-backed National Renewal Alliance (ARENA) and the Brazilian Democratic Movement (MDB). The MDB declined to field a candidate at the presidential elections of 1966 and ARENA's Costa e Silva took the presidency.

Brazil's military regime was not as brutal as those of Chile or Argentina, but at its height, around 1968 and 1969 when Costa e Silva awarded himself emergency powers, the use of torture was widespread. Costa e Silva had a stroke in Aug. 1970 and was replaced by Gen. Emílio Garrastazú Médici in Oct. He was succeeded in early 1974 by Gen. Ernesto Geisel. Geisel promoted measures to reduce censorship and increase political freedom but reverted to political oppression when electoral victory seemed doubtful. In April 1977 he dismissed congress when it failed to pass judicial reforms and governed using emergency powers. He resigned in 1979 to be replaced by his favoured successor, Gen. João Baptista de Oliveira Figueiredo. The generals benefited from the Brazilian economic miracle in the late 1960s and '70s, when the economy was growing by more than 10% per year. However, uncoordinated growth led to rampant bureaucracy, corruption and inflation.

Return to Democracy

Confronted with hyperinflation, Figueiredo introduced reforms but conditions for the majority of the population failed to improve. In 1979 the government authorized the restitution of political rights which had been eroded since Quadros came to power. In 1980 a militant working-class movement sprang up under the charismatic leadership of a worker, Luiz Inácio Lula da Silva (better known as Lula). Popular opposition, together with economic problems, forced Figueiredo to adopt the 'abertura' (opening)—a slow process of returning to democratic government.

Tancredo Neves, leader of the Partido do Movimento Democratico Brasiliero (PMDB), the main opposition party, surprised his military opponents by winning the 1985 elections, but died shortly before assuming power. José Sarney, his vice-president, took over and successfully guided the country through the difficult transition from military to civilian rule as well as overseeing the drafting and implementation of a new democratic constitution. Despite this political success the country drifted into the economic chaos which afflicted the whole continent, with finance ministers changing frequently and foreign debt reaching CR$115,000m. Price and wage freezes set out in Sarney's Cruzado Plan succeeded briefly in bringing down inflation but ultimately failed. In the presidential run-off of Dec. 1989 voters backed two of Sarney's most vociferous critics, with Fernando Collor de Mello narrowly defeating Labour Party candidate, Lula.

Collor, of the National Reconstruction party, promised reductions in inflation and corruption. In March 1990 he confiscated 80% of every bank account worth more than US$1,200, promising to release them 18 months later with interest. He also announced the privatization of state-owned companies and the opening of Brazilian markets to foreign competition and capital. By 1992 Collor's government had failed to reach many of its targets and was embroiled in scandals and corruption, some of which were linked directly to his family. Inflation was again spiralling. Parliament, under public pressure, forced an impeachment and Itamar Franco, Collor's vice-president, took office until elections were held in Oct. 1994. Under Franco inflation leapt towards 3,000% but his fourth finance minister, Fernando Henrique Cardoso, was responsible for the introduction of successful economic reforms.

In 1994 Cardoso was elected president for the Partido da Social Democracia Brasiliera, formed in 1990 by PMDB dissidents. He oversaw an economic revolution that included a radical privatization programme, the lowering of trade barriers and the introduction of a new currency, the *real*. He won a second term in 1998 but Brazil began to feel the economic turbulence in the Far East and was reliant on IMF loans. In Jan. 1999 the *real* was devalued, losing 35% of its value against the dollar in two months. A constitutional amendment in 1997 provided for consecutive presidential terms and the following year Cardoso won re-election. In Cardoso's second term the public debt reached US$260bn. and the government was forced to reduce spending on health and welfare while increasing taxes. His government failed to address the problems of social inequality and official corruption and at the 2002 presidential elections

Cardoso's successor, José Serra, was defeated by the left-wing leader, Luiz Inácio Lula da Silva.

Lula, the country's first elected socialist president, pledged to combat Brazil's widespread poverty while co-operating with the business sector and international community. In May 2003 he invited the Democratic Movement into government to ensure the passage of key economic reforms.

TERRITORY AND POPULATION

Brazil is bounded in the east by the Atlantic and on its northern, western and southern borders by all the South American countries except Chile and Ecuador. The total area (including inland water) is 8,514,877 sq. km. Population as at censuses of 1996 and 2000:

Federal Unit and Capital	Area (sq. km)	Census 1996	Census 2000
North	3,853,327		
Rondônia (Porto Velho)	237,576	1,229,306	1,379,787
Acre (Rio Branco)	152,581	483,593	557,526
Amazonas (Manaus)	1,570,746	2,389,279	2,812,557
Roraima (Boa Vista)	224,299	247,131	324,397
Pará (Belém)	1,247,690	5,510,849	6,192,307
Amapá (Macapá)	142,815	379,459	477,032
Tocantins (Palmas)	277,621	1,048,642	1,157,098
North-East	1,554,257[1]		
Maranhão (São Luís)	331,983	5,222,183	5,651,475
Piauí (Teresina)	251,529	2,673,085	2,843,278
Ceará (Fortaleza)	148,826	6,809,290	7,430,661
Rio Grande do Norte (Natal)	52,797	2,558,660	2,776,782
Paraíba (João Pessoa)	56,440	3,305,616	3,443,825
Pernambuco (Recife)	98,312	7,399,071	7,918,344
Alagoas (Maceió)	27,768	2,633,251	2,822,621
Sergipe (Aracajú)	21,910	1,624,020	1,784,475
Bahia (Salvador)	564,693	12,541,675	13,070,250
South-East	924,511		
Minas Gerais (Belo Horizonte)	586,528	16,672,613	17,891,494
Espírito Santo (Vitória)	46,078	2,802,707	3,097,232
Rio de Janeiro (Rio de Janeiro)	43,696	13,406,308	14,391,282
São Paulo (São Paulo)	248,209	34,119,110	37,032,403
South	576,410		
Paraná (Curitiba)	199,315	9,003,804	9,563,458
Santa Catarina (Florianópolis)	95,346	4,875,244	5,356,360
Rio Grande do Sul (Porto Alegre)	281,749	9,634,688	10,187,798
Central West	1,606,372		
Mato Grosso (Cuiabá)	903,358	2,235,832	2,504,353
Mato Grosso do Sul (Campo Grande)	357,125	1,927,834	2,078,001
Goiás (Goiânia)	340,087	4,514,967	5,003,228
Distrito Federal (Brasília)	5,802	1,821,946	2,051,146
Total	8,514,877	157,070,163	169,799,170

[1]Including disputed areas between states of Piauí and Ceará.

Population density, 19·9 per sq. km. The 2000 census showed 83,576,015 males and 86,233,155 females. The urban population comprised 83·0% of the population in 2003. The estimated population in 2005 was 186·40m.

The UN gives a projected population for 2010 of 198·50m.

The official language is Portuguese.

Population of principal cities (2000 census):

São Paulo	10,434,252	Porto Alegre	1,360,590
Rio de Janeiro	5,857,904	Belém	1,280,614
Salvador	2,443,107	Goiânia	1,093,007
Belo Horizonte	2,238,526	Guarulhos	1,072,717
Fortaleza	2,141,402	Campinas	969,396
Brasília	2,051,146	Nova Iguaçu	920,599
Curitiba	1,587,315	São Gonçalo	891,119
Recife	1,422,905	São Luís	870,028
Manaus	1,405,835	Maceió	797,759

Duque de Caxias	775,456	Ribeirão Preto	504,923
Teresina	715,360	Uberlândia	501,214
Natal	712,317	Sorocaba	493,468
São Bernardo do		Cuiabá	483,346
Campo	703,177	Feira de Santana	480,949
Campo Grande	663,216	Aracajú	461,949
Osasco	652,593	Niterói	459,451
Santo André	649,331	Juiz de Fora	456,796
João Pessoa	597,934	São João de Meriti	449,476
Joboatão dos		Londrina	447,065
Guararapes	581,556	Joinville	429,604
São José dos		Santos	417,983
Campos	539,313	Campos dos	
Contagem	538,017	Goytacazes	406,279

The principal metropolitan areas (census, 2000) were São Paulo (17,834,664), Rio de Janeiro (10,872,768), Belo Horizonte (4,811,760), Porto Alegre (3,655,834), Recife (3,335,704), Salvador (3,018,285), Fortaleza (2,975,703), Curitiba (2,725,629) and Belém (1,794,981).

Approximately 54% of the population of Brazil is White, 40% mixed White and Black, and 5% Black. There are some 260,000 native Indians.

SOCIAL STATISTICS

2002: births, 2,581,055 (rate of 19·7 per 1,000 population); deaths, 958,475 (6·7 per 1,000 population). Life expectancy in 2003 was 66·6 years for males and 74·6 for females. Annual population growth rate, 1992–2002, 1·4%; infant mortality, 2002, 28 per 1,000 live births; fertility rate, 2002, 2·2 children per woman.

CLIMATE

Because of its latitude, the climate is predominantly tropical, but factors such as altitude, prevailing winds and distance from the sea cause certain variations, though temperatures are not notably extreme. In tropical parts, winters are dry and summers wet, while in Amazonia conditions are constantly warm and humid. The northeast *sertão* is hot and arid, with frequent droughts. In the south and east, spring and autumn are sunny and warm, summers are hot, but winters can be cold when polar air-masses impinge. Brasília, Jan. 72°F (22·3°C), July 68°F (19·8°C). Annual rainfall 60" (1,512 mm). Belém, Jan. 78°F (25·8°C), July 80°F (26·4°C). Annual rainfall 105" (2,664 mm). Manaus, Jan. 79°F (26·1°C), July 80°F (26·7°C). Annual rainfall 92" (2,329 mm). Recife, Jan. 80°F (26·6°C), July 77°F (24·8°C). Annual rainfall 75" (1,907 mm). Rio de Janeiro, Jan. 83°F (28·5°C), July 67°F (19·6°C). Annual rainfall 67" (1,758 mm). São Paulo, Jan. 75°F (24°C), July 57°F (13·7°C). Annual rainfall 62" (1,584 mm). Salvador, Jan. 80°F (26·5°C), July 74°F (23·5°C). Annual rainfall 105" (2,669 mm). Porto Alegre, Jan. 75°F (23·9°C), July 62°F (16·7°C). Annual rainfall 59" (1,502 mm).

CONSTITUTION AND GOVERNMENT

The present Constitution came into force on 5 Oct. 1988, the eighth since independence. The *President* and *Vice-President* are elected for a four-year term. To be elected candidates must secure 50% plus one vote of all the valid votes, otherwise a second round of voting is held to elect the President between the two most voted candidates. Voting is compulsory for men and women between the ages of 18 and 70 apart from illiterates (for whom it is optional); it is also optional for persons from 16 to 18 years old and persons over 70. A referendum on constitutional change was held on 21 April 1993. Turnout was 80%. 66·1% of votes cast were in favour of retaining a republican form of government, and 10·2% for re-establishing a monarchy. 56·4% favoured an executive presidency, 24·7% parliamentary supremacy.

A constitutional amendment of June 1997 authorizes the re-election of the President for one extra term of four years.

Congress consists of an 81-member *Senate* (three Senators per federal unit) and a 513-member *Chamber of Deputies*. The Senate

is two-thirds directly elected (50% of these elected for eight years in rotation) and one-third indirectly elected. The Chamber of Deputies is elected by universal franchise for four years. There is a *Council of the Republic* which is convened only in national emergencies.

Baaklini, A. I., *The Brazilian Legislature and Political System*. London, 1992

Martinez-Lara, J., *Building Democracy in Brazil: the Politics of Constitutional Change*. London, 1996

National Anthem
'Ouviram do Ipiranga às margens plácidas de um povo heróico o brado retumbante' ('The peaceful banks of the Ipiranga heard the resounding cry of an heroic people'); words by J. O. Duque Estrada, tune by F. M. da Silva.

GOVERNMENT CHRONOLOGY

Presidents since 1930. (ARENA = National Renewal Alliance; PMDB = Brazilian Democratic Movement Party; PRN = Party for National Reconstruction; PSD = Social Democratic Party; PSDB = Party of the Brazilian Social Democracy; PT = Workers' Party; PTB = Brazilian Labour Party; n/p = non-partisan)

1930–45	n/p	Getúlio Dornelles Vargas
1945–46	n/p	José Linhares
1946–51	military/PSD	Eurico Gaspar Dutra
1951–54	PTB	Getúlio Dornelles Vargas
1954–56	PTB	João Fernandes de Campos Café (Filho)
1956–61	PSD	Juscelino Kubitschek de Oliveira
1961	n/p	Jânio da Silva Quadros
1961–64	PTB	João Belchior Marques Goulart
1964–67	military	Humberto de Alencar Castelo Branco
1967–69	military	Artur da Costa e Silva
1969	Triumvirate (military)	Augusto Hamann Rademaker Grünewald, Aurélio de Lyra Tavares, Márcio de Souza e Mello
1969–74	military/ARENA	Emílio Garrastazú Médici
1974–79	military/ARENA	Ernesto (Beckmann) Geisel
1979–85	military/ARENA/PDS	João Baptista de Oliveira Figueiredo
1985–90	PMDB	José Sarney Costa
1990–92	PRN	Fernando Affonso Collor de Mello
1992–95	n/p	Itamar Augusto Cautiero Franco
1995–2003	PSDB	Fernando Henrique Silva Cardoso
2003–	PT	Luiz Inácio Lula da Silva

RECENT ELECTIONS

In the first round of presidential elections held on 6 Oct. 2002, Luiz Inácio Lula da Silva (Workers' Party) won 46·4% of votes cast, twice as many votes as his nearest opponent, José Serra (Brazilian Social Democracy Party), who won 23·2%. The two other candidates, Anthony Garotinho and Ciro Gomes, won 17·9% and 12% respectively. In the run-off held on 27 Oct. 2002 Luiz Inácio Lula da Silva won 61·3% against 38·7% for José Serra, the biggest ever winning margin in a Brazilian presidential election.

Parliamentary elections were also held on 6 Oct. 2002 for both the Chamber of Deputies and the Senate.

In the elections to the 513-seat Chamber of Deputies, the Workers' Party (PT) won 91 seats; the Liberal Front Party (PFL), 84; the Brazilian Democratic Movement Party (PMDB), 74; the Brazilian Social Democracy Party (PSDB), 71; the Brazilian Progressive Party (PPB), 49; the Liberal Party (PL), 26; the

Brazilian Labour Party (PTB), 26; the Brazilian Socialist Party (PSB), 22; the Democratic Labour Party (PDT), 21; the Socialist People's Party (PPS), 15; the Communist Party of Brazil (PCdoB), 12; others, 22. Following the election a ten-party coalition government was formed, but in Dec. 2004 the Brazilian Democratic Movement Party left it.

Following the Senate elections the Brazilian Democratic Movement Party had 19 seats; the Liberal Front Party, 19; the Worker's Party, 14; the Brazilian Social Democracy Party, 11; the Democratic Labour Party, 5; the Brazilian Socialist Party, 4; the Liberal Party, 3; the Brazilian Labour Party, 3; the Socialist People's Party, 1; the Democratic Socialist Party, 1; and the Brazilian Progressive Party, 1.

Presidential and parliamentary elections are scheduled to take place on 1 Oct. 2006.

CURRENT ADMINISTRATION

President: Luiz Inácio Lula da Silva 'Lula'; b. 1945 (Workers' Party; sworn in on 1 Jan. 2003).

Vice-President: José Alencar.

In March 2006 the coalition government was composed as follows:

Minister of Agrarian Development: Miguel Rossetto. *Agriculture:* João Roberto Rodrigues. *Communications:* Hélio Costa. *Culture:* Gilberto Gil. *Defence:* Waldir Pires. *Development, Industry and Foreign Trade:* Luiz Fernando Furlan. *Education:* Fernando Haddad. *Environment:* Marina Silva. *Finance:* Guido Mantega. *Foreign Relations:* Celso Amorim. *Health:* José Saraiva Felipe. *Justice:* Márcio Tomaz Bastos. *Labour:* Luiz Marinho. *Mines and Energy:* Silas Rondeau. *National Integration:* Ciro Gomes. *Planning and Administration:* Paulo Bernardo Silva. *Science and Technology:* Sérgio Rezende. *Social Development and Hunger Alleviation:* Patrus Ananias. *Social Welfare:* Nelson Machado. *Sport:* Agnelo Queiroz. *Tourism:* Walfrido Mares Guia. *Transport:* Alfredo Pereira do Nascimento. *Urban Affairs:* Márcio Fortes.

Government Website: http://www.brasil.gov.br

CURRENT LEADERS

Luiz Inácio Lula da Silva

Position
President

Introduction
A former factory worker and trade union activist, Luiz Inácio Lula da Silva, better known as Lula, was elected president of Brazil in 2002 at his fourth attempt, representing the Workers' Party (PT; Partido dos Trabalhadores). He is the country's first elected socialist leader, and has pledged to combat Brazil's widespread poverty while co-operating with the business sector and international community.

Early Life
Lula was born on 27 Oct. 1945 in Garanhans in the northeastern state of Pernambuco, the seventh of eight surviving siblings. In 1952 his family moved to São Paulo state where his father worked as a docker. Living in Guarujá and Santos, Lula initially worked as a street vendor and shoe-shine boy and had little formal education. When his parents separated in 1956, he moved with his mother to the state capital. Following two years of odd jobs in the city's factories, he was employed from the age of 14 as a lathe operator in a São Paulo metalworks. He continued to work in the industry for the next 20 years.

In the late 1960s, when Brazil was under military rule, Lula became politically active in the metalworkers' trade union. Progressing through the union hierarchy, he was elected leader in 1975 with 92% support. He was re-elected just as emphatically three years later. In 1980 he founded the radical PT

as a combination of trade unionists, left-wing groups and church activists. The party worked closely with the United Workers' Centre (Central Única dos Trabalhadores) from its formation in 1983. Contesting its first elections in 1982, the PT took only six seats, but increased its representation to 19 four years later.

Lula first stood for the presidency in 1989 coming second to the National Reconstruction candidate Fernando Collor. Through the 1990s the party's rhetoric softened, although it continued its commitment to aiding the poor. Nonetheless, in the 1994 and 1998 presidential elections, Lula came second to the Social Democrat candidate Fernando Cardoso.

At the time of the Oct. 2002 elections, Brazil was suffering from the economic fall-out of a growing trade deficit, tax increases and reduced government spending. In the first round, Lula came first with 46·4% of votes. In the second round run-off with the Social Democrat candidate, José Serra, he took 61·3%. The PT also won the most seats in the Chamber of Deputies, taking 91 out of 513.

Career in Office
Lula took office in Jan. 2003, having pledged to reduce poverty and hunger by redistributing wealth, improving education and health, and implementing agrarian reform, with the creation of a new 'social emergency' ministry. Brazil's financial markets were nervous, and the *real* faltered at the prospect of a socialist revolution. However, Lula also promised to co-operate with the business and banking communities, to adhere to IMF guidelines, to repay foreign debt and to continue his predecessor's attempts to control inflation. His government has since pursued sound macroeconomic policies, taking credit for low inflation, significant job creation and strong annual growth in GDP. However, from May 2005 the PT was undermined politically by financial corruption scandals, leading to the resignations of several senior party officials and Lula allies, which have tarnished the government's claim to probity and may jeopardize the president's hopes of re-election for a second term in late 2006. In foreign affairs, Lula has sought increasing engagement with other emerging powers on the world stage, particularly India and China, and expanded Brazil's diplomatic representation in Africa.

DEFENCE

Conscription is for 12 months, extendable by six months.

In 2003 defence expenditure totalled US$9,274m. (US$53 per capita), representing 1·8% of GDP.

Army

There are seven military commands and 12 military regions. Strength, 2004, 189,000 (40,000 conscripts). There is an additional potential first-line 1,115,000 of whom 400,000 are subject to immediate recall. There is a second-line reserve of 225,000 and a paramilitary Public Police Force of some 385,600.

Navy

The principal ship of the Navy and Brazil's only aircraft carrier is the 32,700-tonne *São Paulo* (formerly the French *Foch*), commissioned in 1963 and purchased in 2000. There are also four diesel submarines and 14 frigates including four bought from the UK in 1995 and 1996.

Naval bases are at Rio de Janeiro, Salvador, Natal, Belém, Rio Grande and São Paulo, with river bases at Brasília, Ladário and Manaus.

Active personnel, 2004, totalled 48,600 (3,200 conscripts), including 14,600 Marines and 1,150 in Naval Aviation.

Air Force

The Air Force has four commands: COMGAR (operations), COMDABRA (aerospace defence), COMGAP (logistics) and COMGEP (personnel). There are seven air regions. Personnel strength, 2004, 65,300 (2,500 conscripts). There were 254 combat aircraft in 2004, including Mirage F-103s and F-5Es.

INTERNATIONAL RELATIONS

Brazil is a member of the UN, WTO, BIS, OAS, Inter-American Development Bank, LAIA, MERCOSUR, IOM and the Antarctic Treaty.

In Dec. 2005 the government repaid the country's entire US$15·5bn. debt to the IMF two years ahead of schedule.

ECONOMY

Agriculture accounted for 5·8% of GDP in 2003, industry 19·1% and services 75·1%.

Overview

Brazil, rich in natural resources, is South America's largest economy. Core agricultural products include cocoa, coffee, oranges, soybeans, sugar and tobacco. The country also has a comparative advantage in livestock, mineral, metal and wood products. Following the Second World War, Brazil pursued a strategy of import substituting industrialization (ISI) and a diversified industrial sector was developed behind the protection of tariff barriers. However, by the 1980s the ISI policy was no longer sustaining high growth. From 1981–90 annual growth averaged only 1·7%, compared to an average of 8·5% from 1971–80. In the 1990s Brazil undertook market reforms and moved towards an outward-orientated development strategy. Though still a modest growth performance for a developing country, average annual growth from 1991–2000 improved to 2·7%. In the mid-1990s Brazil managed to break out of a period of hyperinflation and since 1999 prices have been kept under 10% (except in 2003) by the central bank's inflation targeting monetary policy.

Foreign direct investment in the country took off in 1996, growing from less than 1% of GDP in 1995 to over 5% in 1999, before falling to roughly 2% in 2005. Despite the move towards outward orientation in the 1990s the overvaluation of Brazil's pegged currency kept the export sector from making a significant contribution to GDP. At the end of the 1990s Brazil experienced a currency and debt crisis and in 1999 the crawling-peg exchange rate regime was abandoned for a free-floating one. Since then exports have grown in importance and Brazil's comparative advantage in agriculture has made a strong impact on international markets. However, import penetration is still low in comparison to other countries in the region, signalling a still relatively closed economy, at least to countries outside of the Southern Common Market (MERCOSUR), to which Brazil belongs.

In 2002–03, at a time of unfavourable global economic conditions, Brazil's currency again came under downwards pressure, threatening possible debt default. Sound macro-economic management in collaboration with the IMF helped steer Brazil clear of serious trouble. Tight fiscal and monetary policies protected the economy but also stymied growth in 2003. In 2004 the economy rebounded, growing at its greatest rate in over a decade. Public debt was reduced from close to 60% of GDP in 2003 to near 50% in 2005. Brazil is no longer an IMF borrower and the finance ministry announced in Dec. 2005 that all IMF debt would be paid off two years ahead of schedule. Monetary policy has, however, meant that Brazil's real interest rates have remained among the highest in the world. Tight fiscal policy has been necessary to reduce the still high debt-to-GDP ratio and cement investor confidence, making essential spending on social programmes and infrastructure upgrades difficult. According to the World Bank, 'Brazil has made big strides in reducing social and economic inequality' to date, yet Brazil still has the second highest level of income inequality in the world after South Africa. Brazil's growth performance will have to improve significantly in order for the country to live up to its economic potential and to significantly reduce poverty.

Currency

The unit of currency is the *real* (equal to 100 *centavos*), which was introduced on 1 July 1994 to replace the former *cruzeiro real* at a rate of 1 real (R$1) = 2,750 cruzeiros reais (CR$2,750). The *real* was devalued in Sept. 1994, March 1995, June 1995 and Jan. 1999. Inflation rates (based on IMF statistics):

1995	1996	1997	1998	1999	2000	2001	2002	2003	2004
66·0%	16·0%	6·9%	3·2%	4·9%	7·1%	6·8%	8·4%	14·8%	6·6%

In 1994 inflation had been nearly 2,076%. In June 2002 foreign exchange reserves were US$41,838m.; gold reserves totalled 0·46m. troy oz (4·57m. troy oz in 1995). Total money supply in May 2002 was R$74,988m.

Budget

2000 (in R$1m.): revenue was 235,062 (158,781 in 1999) and expenditure 247,253 (163,709 in 1999). Internal federal debt, July 1996, was R$176,478m. Internal states and municipalities (main securities outstanding), R$49,672m.

Performance

Real GDP growth rates (based on IMF statistics):

1995	1996	1997	1998	1999	2000	2001	2002	2003	2004
4·2%	2·7%	3·3%	0·1%	0·8%	4·4%	1·3%	1·9%	0·5%	4·9%

In March 1999 an IMF agreement introduced a tight monetary policy with an emphasis on reducing the ratio of debt to GDP. Total GDP in 2004 was US$604·9bn.

In Feb. 2005 the OECD commented: 'Brazil is reaping the benefits of macroeconomic consolidation…with strong export performance…coupled with improved confidence and resilient, equitable growth.'

Banking and Finance

On 31 Dec. 1964 the Banco Central do Brasil (*President*, Henrique Meirelles) was founded as the national bank of issue and at Dec. 2002 had total reserves of US$37·84bn.

The Bank of Brazil (founded in 1853 and reorganized in 1906) is a state-owned commercial bank; it had 2,927 branches in 2000 throughout the country. The largest private banks are Banco Bradesco, Banco Itaú and Unibanco. On 31 Dec. 1996 deposits were R$33,604m. In 2000 there were 190 banking establishments with 14,892 branches (26 commercial banks with 3,352 branches and 164 multiple banks with 11,540 branches), plus 19 investment banks with 45 branches.

In Nov. 1998 the IMF announced a US$41·5bn. financing package to help shore up the Brazilian economy. In Aug. 2001 it gave approval for a new US$15bn. stand-by credit, and in Aug. 2002 granted an additional US$30bn. loan to try to prevent a financial meltdown that was threatening to devastate the region.

Brazil received US$22·5bn. worth of foreign direct investment in 2001, down from a record US$33·5bn. in 2000. Spain was the leading investor in 2000, providing 21·3% of foreign capital, ahead of the USA.

There is a stock exchange in São Paulo.

ENERGY AND NATURAL RESOURCES

Environment

Brazil's carbon dioxide emissions from the consumption and flaring of fossil fuels in 2002 were the equivalent of 2·0 tonnes per capita. An *Environmental Sustainability Index* compiled for the World Economic Forum meeting in Jan. 2005 ranked Brazil 11th in the world, with 62·2%. The index measured the ability of countries to maintain favourable environmental conditions and examined various factors including pollution levels and the use or abuse of natural resources.

Brazil has the world's biggest river system and about a quarter of the world's primary rainforest. Current environmental issues are deforestation in the Amazon Basin, air and water pollution in Rio de Janeiro and São Paulo (the world's fourth largest city), and land degradation and water pollution caused by improper mining activities. Contaminated drinking water causes 70% of child deaths.

Electricity

Hydro-electric power accounts for nearly 90% of Brazil's total electricity output. Although Brazil was only the tenth largest electricity producer overall in the world in 2002, it was the third largest producer of hydro-electric power. Installed electric capacity (2002) was 82·5m. kW, of which 65·3m. kW hydro-electric. In July 2001 the government announced that supply would be increased by 20,000 MW by the end of 2003 to help solve the country's worst energy crisis in modern times. There were two nuclear power plants in 2003, supplying some 1·5% of total output. Production (2002) 344,644 GWh. Consumption per capita in 2002 was 2,183 kWh.

Oil and Gas

There are 13 oil refineries, of which 11 are state-owned. Crude oil production (2003), 76·8m. tonnes. Crude oil reserves were estimated at 8·3bn. bbls. in 2002. Brazil began to open its markets in 1999 by inviting foreign companies to drill for oil, and in 2000 the monopoly of the state-owned Petrobrás on importing oil products was removed.

Gas production (2002), 9·1bn. cu. metres with reserves of 230bn. cu. metres. One of the most significant developments has been the construction of the 3,150-km Bolivia–Brazil gas pipeline, one of Latin America's biggest infrastructure projects, costing around US$2bn. (£1·2bn.). The pipeline runs from the Bolivian interior across the Brazilian border at Puerto Suárez-Corumbá to the far southern port city of Porto Alegre. Gas from Bolivia began to be pumped to São Paulo in 1999.

Minerals

The chief minerals are bauxite, gold, iron, manganese, nickel, phosphates, platinum, tin and uranium. Output figures, 1999 (in 1,000 tonnes): phosphate rock, 27,000; bauxite (2000), 13,224; salt (2002), 7,000; hard coal (2000), 6,712; asbestos (crude ore), 3,950; manganese ore, 1,674; aluminium (2001), 1,131; magnesite, 869; graphite, 650; chrome (crude ore), 420; zinc (2001), 111; barytes, 49; nickel ore (2002), 45; copper (2000), 32; zirconium, 29; tin (tin content), 13; lead (lead content in concentrate), 10. Deposits of coal exist in Rio Grande do Sul, Santa Catarina and Paraná. Total reserves were estimated at 11,950m. tonnes in 2000.

Iron is found chiefly in Minas Gerais, notably the Cauê Peak at Itabira. The government is opening up iron-ore deposits in Carajás, in the northern state of Pará, with estimated reserves of 35,000m. tonnes, representing a 66% concentration of high-grade iron ore. Total output of iron ore, 2001, mainly from the Vale do Rio Doce mine at Itabira, was 208·7m. tonnes. Brazil is the second largest producer of iron ore after China.

Gold is chiefly from Pará, Mato Grosso and Minas Gerais; total production (2001), 53·2 tonnes. Silver output (2001), 46 tonnes. Diamond output in 2002 was 700,000 carats, mainly from Minas Gerais and Mato Grosso.

Agriculture

In 2002 the agricultural population was 31·22m. There were 4·86m. farms in 1995. There were 58·87m. ha. of arable land in 2001 and 7·6m. ha. of permanent crops. 2·91m. ha. were irrigated in 2001.

Production (in tonnes):

	2002	2003		2002	2003
Apples	875,388	841,821	Beans	3,064,288	3,302,038
Bananas	6,422,855	6,800,981	Cassava	23,065,577	22,961,082

	2002	2003		2002	2003
Coconut (1,000 fruits)	1,928,236	1,985,661	Pineapples (1,000 fruits)	1,433,234	1,440,013
Coffee	2,649,609	1,987,079	Potatoes	3,126,411	3,089,016
Cotton	2,166,014	2,199,268	Rice	10,457,093	10,334,603
Grapes	1,148,648	1,067,422	Soya	42,124,898	51,919,440
Maize	35,932,962	48,327,323	Sugarcane	364,391,016	396,012,158
Onions	1,222,124	1,229,848	Tomatoes	3,251,046	3,708,602
Oranges	18,530,625	16,917,558	Wheat	3,105,658	6,153,500

Brazil is the world's leading producer of sugarcane, oranges and coffee (and the second largest consumer of coffee after the USA). Harvested coffee area, 2003, 2,408,023 ha., principally in the states of Minas Gerais, Espírito Santo, São Paulo and Paraná. Harvested cocoa area, 2003, 605,930 ha. Bahia furnished 84% of the output in 1998. Two crops a year are grown. Brazil accounts for more than a quarter of annual coffee production worldwide. Harvested castor-bean area, 2003, 134,485 ha. Tobacco is grown chiefly in Rio Grande do Sul and Santa Catarina.

Rubber is produced chiefly in the states of São Paulo, Mato Grosso, Bahia, Espírito Santo and Minas Gerais. Output, 2003, 156,318 tonnes.

Livestock, 2003: cattle, 195·6m.; pigs, 32·3m.; sheep, 14·6m.; goats, 9·6m.; horses, 5·8m.; mules, 1·3m.; asses, 1·2m.; chickens and other poultry, 921·3m. Livestock products, 2002 (in 1,000 tonnes): beef and veal, 7,136; pork, bacon and ham, 2,100; poultry meat, 7,229; cow's milk, 22,635; hen's eggs, 1,550; wool (2003), 11; honey (2003), 30.

Forestry

With forest lands covering 543,905,000 ha. in 2000, only Russia had a larger area of forests. In 2000, 64·3% of the total land area of Brazil was under forests. The annual loss of 2,309,000 ha. of forests between 1990 and 2000 was the biggest in any country in the world over the same period. Nevertheless, an independent study commissioned by NASA has found that the rate of deforestation was on the decline and stated that the government had been extremely active since 1990 in reducing the rate of illegal deforestation. In 1996 the government ruled that Amazonian landowners could log only 20% of their holdings, instead of 50%, as had previously been permitted. Timber production in 2003 totalled 238·54m. cu. metres, a figure exceeded only in the USA, India and China. In 1997 the government's environmental agency, Ibama, levied fines of nearly US$11m. on illicit loggers. In 2001 Ibama seized 25,600 cu. metres (US$40m. worth) of illegally-cut mahogany.

Fisheries

In 2003 the fishing industry had a catch of 808,864 tonnes (72% sea fishing and 28% inland).

INDUSTRY

The leading companies by market capitalization in Brazil in Nov. 2005 were: Petróleo Brasileiro SA (Petrobras), US$72·3bn.; Companhia Vale do Rio Doce, the world's largest iron ore producer (US$48·0bn.); and Banco Bradesco (US$28·7bn.).

The main industries are textiles, shoes, chemicals, cement, lumber, iron ore, tin, steel, aircraft, motor vehicles and parts, and other machinery and equipment. The National Iron and Steel Co. at Volta Redonda, State of Rio de Janeiro, furnishes a substantial part of Brazil's steel. Production (in 1,000 tonnes), 2002: cement (2001), 38,735; crude steel, 29,600; pig iron, 29,600; distillate fuel oil, 27,994; cast iron (2000), 27,854; sugar, 23,567; rolled steel (2000), 18,201; residual fuel oil, 16,925; petrol, 13,894; paper (2000), 7,100. Output of other products in 2001: 5·46m. TV sets; 3·37m. refrigerators; 34·4m. rubber tyres for motor vehicles; 1·72m. motor vehicles (2002); beer, 6,790·5m. litres; soft drinks, 6,226·1m. litres.

Labour

In 2003 a total of 79,251,000 persons were in employment (46,401,000 males), including: 16,409,000 engaged in agriculture, hunting, forestry and fishing; 14,047,000 in wholesale and retail trade; 11,387,000 in manufacturing; 5,158,000 in construction. A constitutional amendment of Oct. 1996 prohibits the employment of children under 14 years. However, in 2000 more than 14% of children between 10 and 14 were working. At May 2004 there was a minimum monthly wage of R$260. In 2000, 7·1% of the workforce was unemployed (7·5% in 1999).

Trade Unions

The main union is the United Workers' Centre (CUT).

INTERNATIONAL TRADE

In 1990 Brazil repealed most of its protectionist legislation. Import tariffs on some 13,000 items were reduced in 1995. In 1991 the government permitted an annual US$100m. of foreign debt to be converted into funds for environmental protection. Total foreign debt in 2002 was US$227,932m. (the highest of any developing country).

Imports and Exports

Imports and exports for calendar years (in US$1m.):

	2001	2002	2003	2004
Imports	55,572	47,240	48,290	62,809
Exports	58,223	60,362	73,084	96,475

Principal imports in 1999 were: machinery and transport equipment, 42·9%; chemicals, 18·4%; manufactured goods, 10·0%; petroleum and related products, 9·0%; and food and live animals, 6·9%.

Principal exports in 1999 were: machinery and transport equipment, 23·7%; food and live animals, 21·6%, including coffee (5·1%), oilcake (3·1%), orange juice (2·6%) and sugar (2·4%); iron ore, 5·7%; footwear, 2·7%; and aluminium, 2·5%. Brazil is the world's leading exporter of beef, coffee, orange juice and sugar.

Main import suppliers, 2000: USA, 23·1%; Argentina, 12·3%; Germany, 7·9%; Japan, 5·3%; Italy, 3·9%; France, 3·4%. Main export markets: USA, 23·9%; Argentina, 11·3%; Netherlands, 5·1%; Germany, 4·6%; Japan, 4·5%; Italy, 3·9%.

COMMUNICATIONS

Roads

In 2000 there were 1,724,929 km of roads, of which 94,871 km were paved. In 2000 there were 33,707,640 vehicles registered. Some 56% of freight is carried by truck. In 1998 there were 120,442 road accidents resulting in 5,305 deaths.

Rail

The Brazilian railways have largely been privatized: all six branches of the large RFFSA network are now under private management. In 2000 RFFSA (Rede Ferroviária Federal S.A.) had a route-length of 21,316 km and FERROBAN (Ferrovias Bandeirantes S.A.) a route-length of 4,235 km. Total route-length nationwide was 29,283 km in 2000. Two-thirds is narrow (1·0 metre) gauge, the rest either broad (1·60) or a mix of the two. Passenger-km travelled in 2000 came to 5·85bn. and freight tonne-km to 154·87bn.

There are several important independent freight railways, including the Vitoria à Minas (898 km in 1993), the Ferroeste (238 km), the Carajas (1,076 km in 1991) and the Amapa (194 km). There are metros in São Paulo (44 km), Rio de Janeiro (26 km), Belo Horizonte (29 km), Porto Alegre (27 km), Brasília (39 km) and Recife (53 km).

Civil Aviation

There are major international airports at Rio de Janeiro-Galeão (Antonio Carlos Jobim International) and São Paulo (Guarulhos) and some international flights from Brasília, Porto Alegre, Recife and Salvador. The three main airlines are TAM (with 36% of the market in 2004) Viação Aérea Rio Grande do Sul (Varig) and Gol (a low-cost airline only launched in 2001). In 1999 Varig carried 10,064,000 passengers and TAM 4,775,000 passengers but TAM's market share has since increased while Varig's has decreased.

Brazil's busiest airport is Guarulhos (São Paulo), which handled 13,091,000 passengers in 2001 (up from 6·45m. in 1992) and 352,600 tonnes of freight, followed by Brasília International with 6,194,000 passengers and 4,000 tonnes of freight, and Rio de Janeiro with 5,968,000 passengers and 109,100 tonnes of freight in 2001.

Shipping

Inland waterways, mostly rivers, are open to navigation over some 43,000 km. Tubarão and Itaqui are the leading ports. In 2002 Santos, the leading container port, handled 1·22m. TEUs (twenty-foot equivalent units). During 1997, 28,973 vessels entered and cleared the Brazilian ports; vessels totalling 88,562,000 NRT entered ports in 2001 and vessels totalling 258,962,000 NRT cleared. In 2000 the merchant fleet comprised 505 vessels (77 oil tankers). In 2002 total tonnage registered was 3·45m. GRT, including oil tankers 1·40m. GRT.

Telecommunications

The state-owned telephone system was privatized in 1998. There were 73,691,000 telephone subscribers in 2002 (423·8 per 1,000 inhabitants). Mobile phone services were opened to the private sector in 1996. By 2002 there were 34,881,000 mobile phone subscribers. There were 13·98m. Internet users in Sept. 2002, up from 3·1m. in July 1999. In 2002 PCs numbered 13·0m. (74·8 per 1,000 persons) and there were 647,000 fax machines.

Postal Services

In 2000 there were 25,957 post offices. A total of 8,857m. pieces of mail were handled in 2000.

SOCIAL INSTITUTIONS

Justice

There is a Supreme Federal Court of Justice at Brasília composed of 11 judges, and a Supreme Court of Justice; all judges are appointed by the President with the approval of the Senate. There are also Regional Federal Courts, Labour Courts, Electoral Courts and Military Courts. Each state organizes its own courts and judicial system in accordance with the federal Constitution.

In Dec. 1999 President Cardoso created the country's first intelligence agency (the Brazilian Intelligence Agency) under civilian rule. It replaced informal networks which were a legacy of the military dictatorship, and will help authorities crack down on organized drug gangs.

The prison population was 285,000 in June 2003 (160 per 100,000 of national population). Brazil's annual murder rate, in excess of 25 per 100,000 population, is on the increase and is more than four times that of the USA.

Education

Elementary education is compulsory from seven to 14. Adult literacy in 2003 was 88·4 % (male, 88·3%; female, 88·6%). There were 50,646 literacy classes in 1993 with 1,584,147 students and 75,413 teachers. In 2003 there were 94,741 pre-primary schools, with 5,155,676 pupils and 270,576 teachers; 169,075 primary schools, with 34,438,749 pupils and 1,603,851 teachers; 21,980 secondary schools, with 9,072,942 pupils and 488,376 teachers; and 1,637 higher education institutions, with 3,479,913 students and 227,844 teachers. In 2003, 97·2% of children between the ages of seven and 14 were enrolled at schools. However, only a third of Brazilian teenagers attend school. In Jan. 2001 President Cardoso announced a National Education Plan that involves teaching 10m. young people and adults to read and write within five years and eradicating illiteracy within a decade.

There were 1,859 universities in Brazil in 2003, of which 207 were public and 1,652 were private. Of the 207 public universities, 83 were federal, 65 were state and 59 were municipal institutions.

In 2000–01 total expenditure on education came to 4·0% of GNP and 10·4% of total government expenditure.

Health

In 1999 there were 48,815 hospitals and clinics (26,209 private), of which 7,806 were for in-patients (5,193 private). There were a total of 484,945 hospital beds in 1999 (341,871 private). In 2001 there were 357,888 doctors, 165,599 dentists, 89,710 nurses and 66,727 pharmacists.

Brazil has been one of the most successful countries in the developing world in the campaign against AIDS. It is reported to have reduced AIDS-related deaths by 40% between 1996 and 2000.

Welfare

Old-age pensions begin at 65 years (men) or 60 years (women) for employees and the urban self-employed, and ages 60 (men) or 55 (women) for the rural self-employed. To qualify there must be at least 35 years contributions for men or 30 years contributions for women. The maximum monthly pension was R$1,869·34 in June 2003.

Unemployment benefits vary depending on insurance but, as a general rule, cover 50% of average earnings in the last three months of employment, up to three times the minimum wage. The minimum benefit is 100% of the minimum monthly wage (R$260 in May 2004).

Family allowances are granted to low-income families with one or more children under the age of 14 or with disabled children attending school. In 2003, R$13·48 a month was provided for each child.

RELIGION

In 2000 there were 124,977,000 Roman Catholics (including syncretic Afro-Catholic cults having spiritualist beliefs and rituals) and 26,167,000 Evangelical Protestants, with 2,684,000 followers of other religions. Roman Catholic estimates in 1991 suggest that 90% were baptized Roman Catholic but only 35% were regular attenders. In 1991 there were 338 bishops and some 14,000 priests. In May 2005 there were eight cardinals. There are numerous sects, some evangelical, some African-derived (e.g. *Candomble*).

CULTURE

World Heritage Sites

The sites under Brazilian jurisdiction entered on the UNESCO world heritage list (with year entered) are: the Historic Town of Ouro Preto (1980), the centre of the gold rush founded at the end of the 17th century; the Historic Centre of Olinda (1982), founded by the Portuguese in the 16th century; the Jesuit Missions of the Guaranis (1984), the ruins of five Jesuit missions; the centre of Salvador de Bahia, Brazil's first capital (1549–1763); and the Sanctuary of Bom Jesus do Congonhas, an ornate church dating to the late 18th century (both 1985); the Iguaçu National Park (1986); Brasília (1987), Brazil's purpose built capital city; Serra da Capivara National Park (1991) including cave paintings over 25,000 years old; the Historic Centre of São Luís (1997), which has examples of late 17th-century architecture; the Historic Centre of Diamantina, a colonial village inhabited by diamond prospectors in the 18th century; the Discovery Coast Atlantic Forest Reserves; and Atlantic Forest Southeast Reserves, covering 470,000 ha. over 25 protected areas (all 1999); the Pantanal Conservation Area; and Jaú National Park, covering over 2,250,000 ha. of Amazon basin (both 2000); the Cerrado Protected Areas, comprising Chapada dos Veadeiros and Emas National Parks; Brazilian Atlantic Islands, comprising Fernando de Noronha and Atol das Rocas Reserves; and the Historic Centre of Goiás, established by colonizing powers in the 18th and 19th centuries (all 2001).

Broadcasting

In 1995 there were 2,033 radio and 119 television stations (colour by PAL M). In 2000 there were 74m. radio receivers and in 2001 there were 60m. television receivers.

Cinema

In 2002 there were 1,635 cinema screens. Total admissions were 102·9m. in 2003; 30 Brazilian films were released during 2003.

Press

In 2002 there were 523 daily newspapers with a combined circulation of 6,972,000, at a rate of 40 per 1,000 inhabitants. In 2002 a total of 43,028 book titles were published.

Tourism

In 2002, 3,783,000 tourists visited Brazil. Argentina is the country of origin of the largest number of visitors, ahead of the USA, Uruguay and Paraguay. Receipts in 2002 totalled US$3·12bn.

Festivals

New Year's Eve in Rio de Janeiro is always marked with special celebrations, with a major fireworks display over the bay at Copacabana Beach. Immediately afterwards, preparations start for Carnival, which in 2007 will be held from 17–20 Feb.

Libraries

In 1993 Brazil had a National Library with 5·28m. volumes, and in 1994 a total of 2,739 public libraries.

DIPLOMATIC REPRESENTATIVES

Of Brazil in the United Kingdom (32 Green St., London, W1K 7AT)
Ambassador: José Maurício Bustani.

Of the United Kingdom in Brazil (Setor De Embaixadas Sul, Quadro 801, Conjunto K, CP70.408-900, Brasília, DF *or* Av. das Nações, CP07-0586, 70.359, Brasília, DF)
Ambassador: Peter Collecott, CMG.

Of Brazil in the USA (3006 Massachusetts Ave., NW, Washington, D.C. 20008)
Ambassador: Roberto Abdenur.

Of the USA in Brazil (Av. das Nações, Lote 03, Quadra 801, CEP: 70403-900, Brasília, D.F.)
Ambassador: Vacant.
Chargé d'Affaires a.i.: Philip Chicola.

Of Brazil to the United Nations
Ambassador: Ronaldo Mota Sardenberg.

Of Brazil to the European Union
Ambassador: José Alfredo Graca Lima.

FURTHER READING

Instituto Brasileiro de Geografia e Estatística. *Anuário Estatístico do Brasil.—Censo Demográfico de 1991.—Indicadores IBGE.* Monthly
Boletim do Banco Central do Brasil. Banco Central do Brasil. Brasília. Monthly
Baer, W., *The Brazilian Economy: Growth and Development.* 4th ed. New York, 1995
Eakin, Marshall C., *Brazil: The Once and Future Country.* New York, 1997
Fausto, Boris, *A Concise History of Brazil.* CUP, 1999
Guirmaraes, R. P., *Politics and Environment in Brazil: Ecopolitics of Development in the Third World.* New York, 1991
Stepan, A. (ed.) *Democratizing Brazil: Problems of Transition and Consolidation.* OUP, 1993
Turner, Barry, (ed.) *Latin America Profiled.* Macmillan, London, 2000

For other more specialized titles see under CONSTITUTION AND GOVERNMENT *above.*

National library: Biblioteca Nacional, Avenida Rio Branco 21939, Rio de Janeiro, RJ.

National Statistical Office: Instituto Brasileiro de Geografia e Estatística (IBGE), Rua General Canabarro 666, 20.271-201 Maracanã, Rio de Janeiro, RJ.
Website: http://www.ibge.gov.br

BRUNEI

South China Sea

BANDAR SERI BEGAWAN

Kuala Belait

BRUNEI

Bangar

Sukang

MALAYSIA

0   10 mi
0   15 km

© Research Machines plc 2006

Negara Brunei Darussalam
(State of Brunei Darussalam)

Capital: Bandar Seri Begawan
Population projection, 2010: 414,000
GDP per capita: not available
GNI per capita: $24,100
HDI/world rank: 0·866/33

KEY HISTORICAL EVENTS

Brunei became an independent Sultanate in the 15th century, controlling most of Borneo, its neighbouring islands and the Suhi Archipelago. By the end of the 16th century, however, the power of Brunei was on the wane. By the middle of the 19th century the State had been reduced to its present limits. Brunei became a British protectorate in 1888. The discovery of major oilfields in the western end of the State in the 1920s brought economic stability to Brunei. Brunei was occupied by the Japanese in 1941 and liberated by the Australians in 1945. Self-government was introduced in 1959 but Britain retained responsibility for foreign affairs. In 1965 constitutional changes were made which led to direct elections for a new Legislative Council. Full independence and sovereignty were gained in Jan. 1984.

TERRITORY AND POPULATION

Brunei, on the coast of Borneo, is bounded in the northwest by the South China Sea and on all other sides by Sarawak (Malaysia), which splits it into two parts, the smaller portion forming the Temburong district. Area, 5,765 sq. km (2,226 sq. miles). Population (2001 census) 332,844 (168,925 males), giving a density of 57·8 per sq. km. The estimated population in 2005 was 374,000.

The UN gives a projected population for 2010 of 414,000.

In 2003, 76·1% of the population lived in urban areas. The four districts are Brunei/Muara (1995: 195,000), Belait (60,000),

Tutong (32,500) and Temburong (8,500). The capital is Bandar Seri Begawan (estimate 1999: 85,000); other large towns are Kuala Belait (1991: 21,163) and Seria (1991: 21,082). Ethnic groups include Malays 67% and Chinese 11%.

The official language is Malay but English is in use.

SOCIAL STATISTICS

2000 births, 7,481; deaths, 965. Rates, 2000: birth per 1,000 population, 22·1; death, 2·9. There were 2,184 marriages in 2000. Life expectancy in 2003: males, 74·3 years; females, 79·0. Annual population growth rate, 1992–2002, 2·6%. Infant mortality, 2001, 6 per 1,000 live births; fertility rate, 2001, 2·6 children per woman.

CLIMATE

The climate is tropical marine, hot and moist, but nights are cool. Humidity is high and rainfall heavy, varying from 100" (2,500 mm) on the coast to 200" (5,000 mm) inland. There is no dry season. Bandar Seri Begawan, Jan. 80°F (26·7°C), July 82°F (27·8°C). Annual rainfall 131" (3,275 mm).

CONSTITUTION AND GOVERNMENT

The Sultan and Yang Di Pertuan of Brunei Darussalam is HM Paduka Seri Baginda Sultan Haji Hassanal Bolkiah Mu'izzadin Waddaulah. He succeeded on 5 Oct. 1967 at his father's abdication and was crowned on 1 Aug. 1968. On 10 Aug. 1998 his son, Oxford-graduate Prince Al-Muhtadee Billah, was inaugurated as Crown Prince and heir apparent.

On 29 Sept. 1959 the Sultan promulgated a Constitution, but parts of it have been in abeyance since Dec. 1962. In Sept. 2004 the Constitution was amended and the Legislative Council (*Majlis Masyuarat Megeri*), whose 21 members are at present all appointed by the Sultan, reconvened for the first time since 1984. The amendment allows for the first elections since 1962. A third of the members of a new 45-member parliament will be directly elected. The Sultan is both the head of state and head of government.

A Council of Cabinet Ministers, appointed and presided over by the Sultan, exercises executive powers.

National Anthem

'Ya Allah, lanjutkan lah usia' ('God bless His Majesty'); words by P. Rahim, tune by I. Sagap.

CURRENT ADMINISTRATION

In March 2006 the Council of Ministers was composed as follows:

Prime Minister, Minister of Defence and of Finance: The Sultan.

Minister of Communications: Pehin Dato Seri Haji Awang Abu Bakar bin Haji Apong. *Culture, Youth and Sports:* Pehin Dato Seri Pahlawan Awang Haji Mohammad Haji Daud. *Development:* Pehin Dato Paduka Awang Haji Abdullah. *Education:* Pehin Dato Haji Awang Abdul Rahman. *Energy:* Pehin Dato Awang Haji Yahya bin Dato Haji Bakar. *Finance (No. 2):* Pehin Dato Haji Abdul Rahman bin Haji Ibrahim. *Foreign Affairs and Trade:* Prince Haji Mohammad Bolkiah. *Foreign Affairs and Trade (No. 2):* Pehin Dato Seri Paduka Lim Jock Seng. *Health:* Pehin Dato Paduka Haji Suyoi bin Haji Osman. *Home Affairs:* Pehin Dato Paduka Haji Adanan. *Industry and Primary Resources:* Pehin Dato Dr Haji Ahmad Jumat. *Religious Affairs:* Pehin Dato Dr Haji Mohammad Zain bin Serudin.

Government Website: http://www.brunei.gov.bn

CURRENT LEADERS

Sultan Sir Hassanal Bolkiah (Sultan of Brunei)

Position
Head of State

Introduction
The Sultan was crowned Brunei's 29th head of state on 1 Aug. 1968 following the abdication of his father. He is among the world's richest men with an estimated fortune of US$20bn.

Early Life
The Sultan was born on the 15 July 1946 in Bandar Seri Begawan. He was educated in Darussalam, Brunei and Malaysia. He became the Crown Prince of Brunei in 1961 and in 1966–67 he enlisted as an officer cadet at the Royal Military Academy in Sandhurst in the UK.

In 1978 he led the mission to London which paved the way for Brunei to become a sovereign state. On 1 Jan. 1984 a treaty of friendship ended British control over Brunei's foreign affairs and defence.

Career in Office
The Sultan is head of government as well as head of state. He is prime minister, minister of defence and minister of finance. Under the 1959 constitution and the Malay Muslim Monarchy tradition, he is assisted by a Council of Cabinet Ministers, a Privy Council, Council of Succession and a Religious Council. A Legislative Council (a third of whose 45 members will, following a constitutional amendment in Sept. 2004, be directly elected) is being revived.

Brunei's wealth originates from the country's large oil and gas reserves, although earnings from overseas investments have exceeded those from exports. The people of Brunei enjoy high subsidies and pay no taxes.

DEFENCE

In 2003 military expenditure totalled US$259m. (US$726 per capita), representing 5·1% of GDP.

Army

The armed forces are known as the Task Force and contain the naval and air elements. Only Malays are eligible for service. Strength (2002) 4,900, including 250 women.

There is a 2,000-strong paramilitary Gurkha reserve unit.

Navy

The Royal Brunei Armed Forces Flotilla includes three fast missile-armed attack craft. Personnel in 2002 numbered 1,000 (80 women). The Flotilla is based at Muara.

Air Wing

The Air Wing of the Royal Brunei Armed Forces was formed in 1965. Personnel (2002), 1,100 (75 women). There are no combat aircraft.

INTERNATIONAL RELATIONS

Brunei is a member of the UN, WTO, the Commonwealth, APEC, Mekong Group, ASEAN, OIC and Islamic Development Bank.

ECONOMY

In 1998 agriculture accounted for 2·8% of GDP, industry 44·5% and services 52·7%. The fall in oil prices in 1997–98 led to the setting up of an Economic Council to advise the Sultan on reforms. An investigation was mounted into the affairs of the Amedeo Corporation, Brunei's largest private company run by Prince Jefri, the Sultan's brother.

Currency

The unit of currency is the *Brunei dollar* (BND) of 100 cents, which is at parity with the Singapore dollar (also legal tender). Inflation was 0·3% in 2003 and 0·9% in 2004.

Budget

Revenues in 2000 were B$5·1bn.; expenditure in 2000 was B$4·2bn. Tax revenues accounted for 47·6% of revenues in 2000. Current expenditure accounted for 83·5% of total expenditures in 2000.

Performance

Real GDP growth was 3·8% in 2003 and 1·7% in 2004. Total GDP in 1998 was US$4·9bn.

Banking and Finance

The Brunei Currency Board is the note-issuing monetary authority. In 2002 there were three commercial banks, six foreign banks and one off-shore bank. Total bank assets in 1993 were B$6,567·7m.

The International Brunei Exchange Ltd (IBX) established an international securities exchange in May 2002.

ENERGY AND NATURAL RESOURCES

Environment

Brunei's carbon dioxide emissions from the consumption and flaring of fossil fuels were the equivalent of 14·8 tonnes per capita in 2002.

Electricity

Installed capacity was 0·5m. kW in 2000. Production in 2000 was approximately 2·43bn. kWh and consumption per capita in 2000 an estimated 7,201 kWh.

Oil and Gas

The Seria oilfield, discovered in 1929, has passed its peak production. The high level of crude oil production is maintained through the increase of offshore oilfields production. Output was 10·5m. tonnes in 2003. The crude oil is exported directly, and only a small amount is refined at Seria for domestic uses. There were proven oil reserves of 1·4bn. bbls. in 2002.

Natural gas is produced (11·5bn. cu. metres in 2002) at one of the largest liquefied natural gas plants in the world and is exported to Japan. There were proven reserves of 390bn. cu. metres in 2002.

Agriculture

In 2001 there were 3,000 ha. of arable land and 4,000 ha. of permanent crops. The main crops produced in 2000 were (estimates, in 1,000 tonnes): vegetables, 9; fruit, 6 (notably bananas and pineapples); cassava, 2.

Livestock in 2000: cattle, 2,000; buffaloes, 6,000; pigs, 6,000; goats, 4,000; chickens, 6m.

Forestry

Forests covered 442,000 ha., or 83·9% of the total land area, in 2000. Most of the interior is under forest, containing large potential supplies of serviceable timber. Timber production in 2001 was 229,000 cu. metres.

Fisheries

The 2001 catch totalled 1,492 tonnes, almost exclusively from marine waters.

INDUSTRY

Brunei depends primarily on its oil industry. Other minor products are rubber, pepper, sawn timber, gravel and animal hides. Local industries include boatbuilding, cloth weaving and the manufacture of brass- and silverware.

Labour

The labour force totalled 131,000 in 1996 (66% males).

INTERNATIONAL TRADE

Imports and Exports

In 2001 imports totalled B$2,076m.; exports, B$6,522m. In 2001 basic manufactures constituted 30·7% of imports, with machinery and transport equipment accounting for 30·3%; crude petroleum and partly refined petroleum made up 43·4% of exports in 1999 and natural gas 37·7%. In 2001 Singapore supplied 23% of imports, Malaysia 22% and the USA 9%. Japan took 46% of all exports, South Korea 12% and Thailand 12%.

COMMUNICATIONS

Roads
There were an estimated 3,218 km of roads in 2002. The main road connects Bandar Seri Begawan with Kuala Belait and Seria. In 2000 there were 115,476 private cars and 13,740 vans and trucks. There were 45 fatalities in road accidents in 1999.

Civil Aviation
Brunei International Airport (Bandar Seri Begawan) handled 1,055,000 passengers (all international) in 2001. The national carrier is the state-owned Royal Brunei Airlines (RBA). In 2003 RBA operated services to Abu Dhabi, Bangkok, Brisbane, Calcutta, Darwin, Denpasar Bali, Dubai, Frankfurt, Hong Kong, Jakarta, Jeddah, Kota Kinabalu, Kuala Lumpur, Kuching, London, Manila, Perth, Shanghai, Singapore, Surabaya and Taipei. In 1997 RBA flew 35·3m. km, carrying 876,800 passengers (all on international flights).

Shipping
Regular shipping services operate from Singapore, Hong Kong, Sarawak and Sabah to Bandar Seri Begawan, and there is a daily passenger ferry between Bandar Seri Begawan and Labuan. In 2002 merchant shipping totalled 483,000 GRT. In 2002 vessels totalling 1,735,000 NRT entered ports and vessels totalling 1,732,000 NRT cleared.

Telecommunications
There is a telephone network linking the main centres. In 2001 there were 225,400 telephone subscribers (or 659·2 per 1,000 inhabitants), including 137,000 mobile phone subscribers. In 2002 there were 27,000 PCs (76·7 for every 1,000 persons). There were 35,000 Internet users in 2001 and 3,400 fax machines in 2002.

Postal Services
There were 31 post offices in 2003.

SOCIAL INSTITUTIONS

Justice
The Supreme Court comprises a High Court and a Court of Appeal and the Magistrates' Courts. The High Court receives appeals from subordinate courts in the districts and is itself a court of first instance for criminal and civil cases. The Judicial Committee of the Privy Council in London is the final court of appeal. Shariah Courts deal with Islamic law. 25,310 crimes were reported in 1993.

The Royal Brunei Police numbers 1,750 officers and men (1997). In addition, there are 500 additional police officers mostly employed on static guard duties. The population in penal institutions in 2002 was 454 (133 per 100,000 of national population).

Education
The government provides free education to all citizens from pre-school up to the highest level at local and overseas universities and institutions. In 2000–01 there were 9,837 children in pre-primary education; 44,981 pupils and 3,753 teachers in primary education; 35,945 pupils in secondary education; 3,984 students and 483 academic staff in tertiary education. The University of Brunei Darussalam was founded in 1985; in 1996 there were also six technical and vocational colleges (one teacher training college) and an institute of advanced education.

Adult literacy rate, 2003, 92·7% (male, 95·2%; female, 90·2%). Total expenditure on education came to 3·0% of GNP (1998–99) and 9·1% of total government spending (2000–01).

Health
Medical and health services are free to citizens and those in government service and their dependants. Citizens are sent overseas, at government expense, for medical care not available in Brunei. Flying medical services are provided to remote areas. In 1999 there were four government hospitals and the Panaga private hospital; in 2000 there were 336 physicians, 48 dentists and 892 nurses.

RELIGION
The official religion is Islam. In 2001, 67% of the population were Muslim (mostly Malays). There are Buddhist and Christian minorities.

CULTURE

Broadcasting
Radio Television Brunei operates on medium- and shortwaves in Malay, English, Chinese and Nepali. Number of receivers: radio (2000), 363,000; television (2001), 215,000 (colour by PAL).

Press
In 1996 there was one local newspaper with a circulation of 21,000.

Tourism
In 2000 there were 984,000 foreign tourists. In 1998 receipts totalled US$37m.

DIPLOMATIC REPRESENTATIVES
Of Brunei in the United Kingdom (19/20 Belgrave Sq., London, SW1X 8PG)
High Commissioner: Penigran Haji Yunus.

Of the United Kingdom in Brunei (PO Box 2197, Bandar Seri Begawan 8674)
High Commissioner: John Saville.

Of Brunei in the USA (3520 International Court, NW, Washington, D.C., 20008)
Ambassador: Pengiran Anak Dato Haji Puteh.

Of the USA in Brunei (3rd Floor, Teck Guan Plaza, Jalan Sultan, Bandar Seri Begawan 2085)
Ambassador: Emil Skodon.

Of Brunei to the United Nations
Ambassador: Shofry bin Abdul Ghafor.

Of Brunei to the European Union
Ambassador: Vacant.
Chargé d'Affaires a.i.: Amalina Murad.

FURTHER READING
Ministry of Finance Statistics Department. *Brunei Darussalam Statistical Yearbook.*

Cleary, M. and Wong, S. Y., *Oil, Economic Development and Diversification in Brunei.* London, 1994
Horton, A. V. M., *A Critical Guide to Source Material Relating to Brunei with Special Reference to the British Residential Era, 1906–1959.* Bordesley, 1995
Saunders, G., *History of Brunei.* OUP, 1996

National Statistical Office: Ministry of Finance Statistics Department.

BULGARIA

© Research Machines plc 2006

Republika Bulgaria

Capital: Sofia
Population projection, 2010: 7·45m.
GDP per capita, 2003: (PPP$) 7,731
HDI/world rank: 0·808/55

KEY HISTORICAL EVENTS

The Bulgarians take their name from an invading Asiatic horde (Bulgars) and their language from the Slav population, with whom they merged after 680. The Bulgarians carved out empires against a background of conflict with Byzantium and Serbia but after the Serb-Bulgarian defeat at Kosovo in 1389 Bulgaria finally succumbed to Ottoman encroachment. The Ottoman empire's decline, however, engendered rebellion which met with brutal repression, provoking great power intervention. By the Treaty of Berlin (1878), Macedonia and Thrace reverted to Turkey, Eastern Rumelia became semi-autonomous and Bulgaria proper became a principality under Turkish suzerainty.

After Austria annexed Bosnia in 1908, Bulgaria declared itself independent. To block Austrian expansion into the Balkans, Russia encouraged Greece, Serbia, Montenegro and Bulgaria to attack Turkey (First Balkan War, 1912), but in the dispute which followed over the territorial spoils Bulgaria failed to secure her claims against her formal allies by force (Second Balkan War, 1913). Territorial aspirations led Bulgaria to join the First World War on the German side.

Economic decline caused by the war produced social unrest. Ferdinand was forced to abdicate in favour of his son, Boris III, in Oct. 1918. Bedevilled by Macedonian terrorism and the effects of the world economic depression, parliamentary government was ended by a military coup in May 1934. In 1935 Boris established a royal dictatorship under which political parties were banned. Boris died in 1943 and was succeeded by a regency.

Increasingly drawn into the German economic orbit, Bulgaria joined the Nazis against Britain in March 1941. In Sept. 1944 the Soviet Union declared war and sent its troops across the frontiers. The Communist-dominated Fatherland Front formed a government and a referendum in 1946 abolished the monarchy. Demonstrations in Sofia in Nov. 1989, occasioned by the Helsinki Agreement ecological conference, broadened into demands for political reform. In Dec. the National Assembly approved 21 measures of constitutional reform, including the abolition of the Communist Party's sole right to govern. But attempts at economic reform led to strikes and unrest. In 1996 Petar Stoyanov was elected as an anti-Communist pro-reform President. In the election the following April the anti-Communist Union of Democratic Forces coalition, led by Ivan Kostov and Alexander Bozhkov, swept back to power.

Bulgaria was one of seven countries to join NATO in 2004. It has an EU membership target date of 2007.

TERRITORY AND POPULATION

The area of Bulgaria is 110,994 sq. km (42,855 sq. miles). It is bounded in the north by Romania, east by the Black Sea, south by Turkey and Greece, and west by Serbia and Montenegro and the Republic of Macedonia. The country is divided into 28 districts.

Area and population in 2001 (census):

District	Area (sq. km)	Population	District	Area (sq. km)	Population
Blagoevgrad	6,452	341,245	Shumen	3,380	204,395
Bourgas	7,753	423,608	Silistra	2,844	142,003
Dobrich	4,711	215,232	Sliven	3,544	218,474
Gabrovo	2,046	144,150	Smolyan	3,194	140,067
Haskovo	5,543	277,483	Sofia (city)	1,311	1,173,988
Kardzhali	3,410	164,019	Sofia (district)	7,020	273,252
Kyustendil	3,048	162,622	Stara Zagora	5,147	370,665
Lovech	4,132	169,951	Targovishte	2,732	137,689
Montana	3,618	182,267	Varna	3,820	462,218
Pazardzhik	4,458	310,741	Veliko Turnovo	4,666	293,294
Pernik	2,027	149,856	Vidin	3,022	130,094
Pleven	4,656	312,018	Vratsa	4,006	243,039
Plovdiv	5,928	715,904	Yambol	3,336	156,080
Razgrad	2,415	152,417	Total	110,994	7,932,984
Rousse	2,775	266,213			

The capital, Sofia, has district status.

The population of Bulgaria at the census of 2001 was 7,932,984 (females, 4,066,436); population density 71·5 per sq. km. Bulgaria's population has been declining since the mid-1980s. It has been falling at such a rate that by 2005 it was the same as it had been in the late 1950s. The estimated population in 2005 was 7·73m. In 2003, 69·8% of the population were urban.

The UN gives a projected population for 2010 of 7·45m.

Population of principal towns (2001 census): Sofia, 1,173,988; Plovdiv, 338,302; Varna, 320,668; Bourgas, 209,479; Rousse, 178,435; Stara Zagora, 167,708; Pleven, 149,174; Sliven, 136,148; Pazardzhik, 127,918.

Ethnic groups at the 2001 census: Bulgarians, 6,655,210; Turks, 746,664; Roma (Gypsies), 370,908.

Bulgarian is the official language.

SOCIAL STATISTICS

2002: live births, 66,499; deaths, 112,617; marriages, 29,218; divorces, 10,203. Rates per 1,000 population, 2002: birth, 8·5; death, 14·3; marriage, 3·7; divorce, 1·3; infant mortality, 14 per 1,000 live births (2001). Legal abortions totalled 50,824 in 2002. In 2001 the most popular age range for marrying was 25–29 for males and 20–24 for females. Expectation of life in 2003 was 68·9 years among males and 75·6 years among females. Annual

236

population growth rate, 1992–2002, –0·8%; fertility rate, 2001, 1·1 children per woman (one of the lowest rates in the world).

CLIMATE

The southern parts have a Mediterranean climate, with winters mild and moist and summers hot and dry, but further north the conditions become more Continental, with a larger range of temperature and greater amounts of rainfall in summer and early autumn. Sofia, Jan. 28°F (–2·2°C), July 69°F (20·6°C). Annual rainfall 25·4" (635 mm).

CONSTITUTION AND GOVERNMENT

A new constitution was adopted at Turnovo on 12 July 1991. The *President* is directly elected for not more than two five-year terms. Candidates for the presidency must be at least 40 years old and have lived for the last five years in Bulgaria. American-style primary elections were introduced in 1996; voting is open to all the electorate.

The 240-member *National Assembly* is directly elected by proportional representation. The President nominates a candidate from the largest parliamentary party as Prime Minister.

National Anthem

'Gorda stara planina' ('Proud and ancient mountains'); words and tune by T. Radoslavov.

GOVERNMENT CHRONOLOGY

(BKP = Bulgarian Communist Party; BSP = Bulgarian Socialist Party; NMS = National Movement Simeon II; SDS = Union of Democratic Forces; Zveno = People's League Zveno; n/p = non-party)

Heads of State since 1943.

King

1943–46		Simeon II (Simeon Sakskoburggotski)

Chairman of Provisional Presidency

1946–47	BKP	Vasil Petrov Kolarov

Chairmen of the Presidium of the National Assembly

1947–50	BKP	Mincho Kolev Neychev
1950–58	BKP	Georgi Parvanov Damyanov
1958–64	BKP	Dimitar Ganev Varbanov
1964–71	BKP	Georgi Traykov Girovski

Chairmen of the Council of State

1971–89	BKP	Todor Khristov Zhivkov
1989–90	BKP	Petar Toshev Mladenov

Presidents of the Republic

1990	n/p	Petar Toshev Mladenov
1990–97	SDS	Zhelyu Mitev Zhelev
1997–2002	SDS	Petar Stefanov Stoyanov
2002–	BSP	Georgi Sedefchov Parvanov

Prime Ministers since 1944.

1944–46	Zveno	Kimon Gheorgiev Stoyanov
1946–49	BKP	Georgi Mihaylov Dimitrov
1949–50	BKP	Vasil Petrov Kolarov
1950–56	BKP	Vůlko Velov Chervenkov
1956–62	BKP	Anton Tanev Yugov
1962–71	BKP	Todor Khristov Zhivkov
1971–81	BKP	Stanko Todorov Georgiev
1981–86	BKP	Grisha Stanchev Filipov
1986–90	BKP	Georgi Ivanov Atanasov
1990	BSP	Andrey Karlov Lukanov
1990–91	n/p	Dimitar Popov
1991–92	SDS	Filip Dimitrov Dimitrov
1992–94	n/p	Lyuben Borisov Berov
1995–97	BSP	Zhan Vasilev Videnov
1997–01	SDS	Ivan Yordanov Kostov
2001–05	NMS	Simeon Borisov Sakskoburggotski
2005–	BSP	Sergey Dimitrievich Stanishev

RECENT ELECTIONS

Presidential elections were held in two rounds on 11 and 18 Nov. 2001. Georgi Parvanov won the first round against five opponents with 36·4% of votes cast; turnout was 39·2%. He also won the run-off round against the incumbent president Petar Stoyanov, with 54·1% of votes cast; turnout was 54·4%.

At the elections of 25 June 2005 the Coalition for Bulgaria (headed by the Bulgarian Socialist Party) won 82 of 240 seats with 31·1% of the vote; the National Movement Simeon II, the party of former King Simeon II, won 53 seats with 19·9% of the vote; the Movement for Rights and Freedoms (consisting of the Movement for Rights and Freedoms, the Liberal Union and Euroroma) won 34 seats with 12·8%; the Attack coalition 21 with 8·1%; the Union of Democratic Forces 20 with 7·7%; Democrats for a Strong Bulgaria 17 with 6·5%; and the Bulgarian People's Union 13 with 5·2%. Turnout was 55·8%.

CURRENT ADMINISTRATION

President: Georgi Parvanov; b. 1957 (Bulgarian Socialist Party; in office since 22 Jan. 2002).

Vice-President: Angel Marin.

In March 2006 the coalition government consisting of the Bulgarian Socialist Party-dominated Coalition for Bulgaria, the National Movement Simeon II and the Movement for Rights and Freedoms comprised:

Chairman of the Council of Ministers: Sergey Stanishev; b. 1966 (Bulgarian Socialist Party; sworn in 16 Aug. 2005).

Deputy Prime Ministers: Ivailo Kalfin (also *Minister of Foreign Affairs*), Daniel Valtchev (also *Minister of Education*), Emel Etem (also *Minister of Natural Disasters and Catastrophes*).

Minister of Agriculture and Forestry: Nihat Kabil. *Culture:* Stefan Danailov. *Defence:* Vesselin Bliznakov. *Economy and Energy:* Roumen Ovcharov. *Environment and Water:* Djevdet Chakurov. *European Affairs:* Meglena Kuneva. *Finance:* Plamen Oresharski. *Health:* Radoslav Gaidarski. *Interior:* Roumen Petkov. *Justice:* Georgi Petkanov. *Labour and Social Policy:* Emilia Maslarova. *Public Administration:* Nikolai Vassilev. *Regional Development and Public Works:* Assen Gagaouzov. *Transport:* Petar Moutafchiev.

Government Website: http://www.government.bg

CURRENT LEADERS

Georgi Parvanov

Position
President

Introduction
Georgi Parvanov, leader of the Socialist party, was elected president of Bulgaria in Nov. 2001, defeating his predecessor, Petar Stoyanov. He was sworn into office in Jan. 2002. The 2001 election had the lowest turnout of voters since the fall of communism. The presidency is largely ceremonial and comes with limited political power.

Early Life
Georgi Sedefchov Parvanov was born in Sirishtchnik, Bulgaria on 28 June 1957. He graduated from Mathematics High School in Pernik in 1975 then studied for an MA and a PhD in history at Sofia University St Kliment Ohridski.

Parvanov joined the Bulgarian Communist Party (BCP) in 1981 as a researcher in its institute of history. By 1989 he held the post of senior research associate. In 1990 the BCP changed its name to the Bulgarian Socialist Party (BSP), a year after dethroning their chairman Todor Zhivkov, and in 1991 Parvanov was elected to a party post for the first time. He began a steady climb up the party ladder, becoming deputy chairman in 1994 and in 1996 replacing Zhan Videnov as the elected chairman of the BSP supreme council. He won the post again in 2000.

As an MP from 1994–2001, Parvanov held several posts, including chairman of the parliamentary group for friendship with Greece (1994–97), chairman of the parliamentary group of the Democratic Left (1997–2001) and chairman of the parliamentary group of Coalition for Bulgaria (1997–2001). In 1999, during NATO's air bombing campaign of Yugoslavia, Parvanov led his parliamentary group in a vote against granting NATO access to Bulgarian air space. However, a year later he announced his party's support for Bulgaria's admission to NATO and the European Union.

Career in Office
Georgi Parvanov became the first former communist to win a presidential election in post-communist Bulgaria. Parvanov's priorities include stabilizing the country's economy, modernizing the Bulgarian army and fighting crime and corruption. He wants a stronger role for the state in national life and supports closer ties with former allies such as Russia and Ukraine. In Dec. 2001 parliament agreed to the destruction of Soviet-made missiles.

In Nov. 2002 Bulgaria was invited to join NATO and in March 2004 was granted admission. In 2002, at the urging of the European Union, Bulgaria began closing its nuclear reactors. In April 2005 it signed the EU accession treaty and, provided reforms are implemented in time, EU entry is scheduled for 2007.

Sergey Stanishev

Position
Prime Minister

Introduction
Sergey Stanishev, leader of the Bulgarian Socialist Party (BSP), emerged as prime minister of Bulgaria in Aug. 2005 after a closely-fought general election and weeks of negotiations. The Soviet-educated son of a high-ranking official from the communist era, Stanishev spearheaded sweeping reforms to the BSP. He is committed to liberalizing the economy and steering the country into the EU in 2007. His chief challenges are to hold together the three-party 'grand coalition' while creating jobs and tackling poverty and crime.

Early Life
Sergey Dmitrievich Stanishev was born on 5 May 1966 in Kherson in the Soviet Republic of Ukraine to a Russian mother and a Bulgarian father, a high-ranking official in the Bulgarian Communist Party (BCP). While studying history at Moscow State University (MGU) in the mid- to late-1980s, he was the Moscow correspondent of *Krugozor*, then Bulgaria's main dissident newspaper. Stanishev remained at MGU after his graduation in 1989 to study for a PhD in Russian politics in the late-19th century. On his return to Bulgaria in 1994 he worked as a freelance journalist specializing in foreign-policy issues. A year later, under the BSP-led government of Zhan Videnov, he was appointed senior analyst at the department of foreign policy and international affairs within the BSP's supreme council. In 1996, against a backdrop of economic crisis and severe food shortages which culminated in the resignation of Videnov's cabinet, Stanishev was promoted to director of the BSP's department for foreign policy and international affairs, a position he held for four years. He continued his studies at the School of Political Studies in Moscow in 1998 and later specialized in international relations at the London School of Economics (1999–2000).

Under the guidance of his mentor, the reformist leader of the BSP Georgi Parvanov, Stanishev became more closely involved in the party's organization. Elected to its supreme council in May 2000, he stood in the legislative elections of June 2001 and, despite a generally poor showing by the BSP, went on to represent the town of Rousse in parliament. Following the election of Parvanov as president in Nov. 2001, Stanishev was voted chairman of the BSP and chairman of the parliamentary group of the BSP-led Coalition of Bulgaria. Although inexperienced, he is credited with reforming the structure of the party and updating its image, attracting younger members. Having been re-elected chairman at the 45th BSP Congress in June 2002, he forged alliances with other socialist parties across Europe, and the BSP became a member of Socialist International in Oct. 2003.

In the run-up to the general election of 25 June 2005, Stanishev criticized Simeon II's ruling National Movement (NMS) for failing to improve living standards. Parvanov promised to boost wages and pensions by 20%, spend more on health and social services and create more than 200,000 new jobs. He won the seat of the port city of Bourgas but the BSP-led coalition claimed an insufficient cut of the overall vote to rule alone and political deadlock ensued. On 27 July parliament chose Stanishev as prime minister in a coalition with the NMS but voted against his proposed cabinet, leading to further wrangling. Under pressure from the EU, a grand coalition of the BSP, the NMS and the mostly ethnic-Turkish Movement for Rights and Freedoms (MRF) was formed. On 16 Aug. Stanishev received 168 parliamentary votes (against 67) and was sworn in as prime minister the same day.

Career in Office
Stanishev's priorities are to ensure Bulgaria's accession to the EU in Jan. 2007, sustain economic growth of 6–8% a year, reform the judiciary and introduce measures against crime and corruption. He established a disaster management ministry in the wake of the summer 2005 floods that devastated large areas of the country.

DEFENCE
Conscription is nine months (six months for university graduates).

Defence expenditure in 2003 totalled US$471m. (US$60 per capita), representing 2·4% of GDP. In 1985 the total had been US$1,424m.

Army
There are three military districts based around Sofia, Plovdiv and Sliven. In 2002 the Army had a strength of 31,050 including conscripts. In addition there are reserves of 303,000, 12,000 border guards and 18,000 railway and construction troops.

Navy
The Navy, all ex-Soviet or Soviet-built, includes one old diesel submarine and one small frigate. The Naval Aviation Wing operates nine armed helicopters. The naval headquarters are at Varna (Northern Command) and Bourgas (Southern Command), and there are further bases at Atiya, Vidin, Balchik and Sozopol. Personnel in 2002 totalled 4,370 (2,000 conscripts).

Air Force
The Air Force had (2002) 17,780 personnel. There are 232 combat aircraft, including MiG-21s, MiG-23s and Su-25s, and 43 attack helicopters.

INTERNATIONAL RELATIONS
Bulgaria is a member of the UN, WTO, BIS, NATO, Council of Europe, OSCE, CEI, BSEC, Danube Commission, IOM, Antarctic Treaty and the International Organization of the Francophonie, and is an Associate Member of the EU and an Associate Partner of the WEU. At the European Union's Helsinki Summit in Dec. 1999 Bulgaria, along with five other countries, was invited to begin full negotiations for membership in Feb. 2000. Entry into the EU is likely to be in 2007 at the earliest. It became a member of NATO on 29 March 2004.

ECONOMY
Agriculture accounted for 10·7% of GDP in 2002, industry 25·6% and services 63·7%.

Overview

Bulgaria is classified by the World Bank as a lower-middle income country. Its key sectors are agriculture, tourism, light industry and services. After economic and political crises in 1996–97 the country embarked on a reform programme aimed at ensuring long-term macroeconomic stability. Since the implementation of these reforms inflation has remained low, the country has experienced growth of 4·5% per year and foreign direct investment has been raised to 7% of GDP. In 2003 Bulgaria further tightened fiscal policy, saving half the revenue over-performance and reducing the deficit to 0·4% of GDP. Macroeconomic policies and structural reforms are aimed at entering the European Union. The EU has offered a favourable assessment of the Bulgarian economy and in 2003 it was declared to be a fully functioning market economy. Bulgaria has recently reached two important landmarks in its development path: it joined NATO in March 2004, and in June 2004 it successfully completed EU negotiations. Bulgaria is considered by the European Commission to be on track for EU accession in 2007, provided that the reform momentum is maintained.

Currency

The unit of currency is the *lev* (BGN) of 100 *stotinki*. In May 1996 the lev was devalued by 68%. A new *lev* was introduced on 5 July 1999, at 1 new *lev* = 1,000 old *leva*. Runaway inflation (123·0% in 1996 rising to 1,061% in 1997) forced the closure of 14 banks in 1996. However, by 2004 the rate was down to 6·1%. In June 1997 the new government introduced a currency board financial system which stabilized the lev and renewed economic growth. Under it, the lev is pegged to the euro at one euro = 1·95583 new leva. Foreign exchange reserves were estimated to be US$3,835m. in June 2002; gold reserves were 513,000 troy oz. Total money supply was 4,603m. leva in April 2002.

Budget

The fiscal year is the calendar year.

Government revenue and expenditure (in 1m. new leva):

	1997	1998	1999	2000	2001
Revenue	5,558·0	7,380·4	8,005·7	9,124·5	9,874·3
Expenditure	5,733·2	7,227·6	8,122·7	9,444·8	10,212·6

VAT was first introduced in 1995. In 1996 it was increased from 18% to 22%, but then lowered from 1 Jan. 1999 to 20%.

Performance

Total GDP in 2004 was US$24·1bn. Real GDP growth was 4·3% in 2003 and 5·6% in 2004. In 1997–98 the country pulled itself back from economic and financial disaster. Its success in stabilizing the economy, in the wake of the collapse of the banking system and the lurch into hyperinflation in early 1997, has exceeded expectations.

Banking and Finance

The National Bank (*Governor*, Ivan Iskrov) is the central bank and bank of issue. There is also a Currency Board, established in 1997. The DSK Bank became the last state bank to be privatized in 2003. There were 34 commercial banks in 2003. Foreign direct investment totalled US$1,419m. in 2003 (26% from privatization revenues).

There is a stock exchange in Sofia.

ENERGY AND NATURAL RESOURCES

Environment

Bulgaria's carbon dioxide emissions from the consumption and flaring of fossil fuels were the equivalent of 5·8 tonnes per capita in 2002.

Electricity

Bulgaria has little oil, gas or high-grade coal, and energy policy is based on the exploitation of its low-grade coal and hydro-electric resources. But the country is a major distribution centre for energy in the Black Sea region, a fact underlined by the 1997 deal with Russia which guarantees gas supplies to Bulgaria, while clearing the way for the construction of a transit gas pipeline between Russia and western Turkey. In 2003 there were four nuclear reactors in use, at the country's sole nuclear power plant in Kozloduy (dating from the 1970s). In Dec. 2002 it was announced that the two oldest of six reactors would close in 2003. A further two are scheduled to close by the end of 2006. The closure of the oldest reactor was a condition for the country's EU membership, proposed for 2007. To compensate, the government plans to complete a nuclear plant in Belene, started in the 1980s but suspended in 1990 because of lack of funds and environmental protests. Installed electrical capacity was 11·0m. kW in 2000. Output, 2000, 40·92bn. kWh (48% thermal, 44% nuclear and 8% hydro-electric). Consumption per capita: 4,567 kWh (2000).

Oil and Gas

Oil is extracted in the Balchik district on the Black Sea coast, in an area 100 km north of Varna, and at Dolni Dubnik near Pleven. There are refineries at Bourgas (annual capacity 5m. tonnes) and Dolni Dubnik (7m. tonnes). Crude oil production (2000) was 42,000 tonnes; natural gas (2000), 15m. cu. metres.

Minerals

Production in 2000: lignite, 26·31m. tonnes; iron ore (1999), 466,000 tonnes; coal, 118,000 tonnes. There are also deposits of gold, silver and copper.

Agriculture

In 2002 the total area of land in agricultural use was 5,796,208 ha. (52·2% of the overall territory of the country); there were 3,080,829 ha. under crops (including 2,217,560 ha. for cereals), 2,502,723 ha. of permanent grassland (including meadows and orchards), and 212,656 ha. of perennial plantations. By 1999, 60% of Bulgarian households worked a plot of land, often on a part-time basis. In 2000 around 25% of the labour force was employed in agriculture. There were 25,000 tractors in use in 2001 and 5,500 harvester-threshers.

Legislation of 1991 and 1992 provided for the redistribution of collectivized land to its former owners up to 30 ha. In 2002 there were 37,836 registered agricultural producers, including 33,633 individual farmers.

Production in 2000 (in 1,000 tonnes): wheat, 2,800; maize, 937; barley, 684; potatoes, 566; grapes, 450; tomatoes, 446; sunflower seeds, 438; melons and watermelons, 384; chillies and green peppers, 207; cucumbers and gherkins, 170; cabbages, 140. Bulgaria is a leading producer of attar of roses (rose oil). Bulgaria produced 139,000 tonnes of wine in 2000. Other products (in 1,000 tonnes) in 2000: meat, 445; cow's milk, 1,200; goat milk, 200; sheep milk, 106; eggs, 90.

Livestock (2000, in 1,000): cattle, 682; sheep, 2,549; pigs, 1,512; goats, 1,046; poultry, 14,000.

Forestry

In 2000 forests covered 3·69m. ha., or 33·4% of the total land area; natural forest covered 2·72m. ha. and forest plantations 0·97m. ha. Timber production in 2001 totalled 3·99m. cu. metres.

Fisheries

In 2001 total catch was 6,530 tonnes, mainly from sea fishing. As recently as 1988 the catch amounted to 106,000 tonnes.

INDUSTRY

In 1996 there were 342,261 registered economic units. Units by ownership: state, 9,682; municipal, 9,820; joint-stock companies, 3,588; co-operatives, 5,410; social organizations, 6,306; associations, 2,483; foreign ventures, 9,005; resident, 307,448. Industrial gross output rose by 0·7% in real terms in 2001 and 2·6% in 2002.

Output in 1,000 tonnes: cement (2001), 2,088; crude steel (2000), 2,023; distillate fuel oil (2000), 1,934; nitrogenous fertilizers (1997), 1,846; rolled steel (2000), 1,455; residual fuel oil (2000), 1,127; pig iron (2002), 1,100; petrol (2000), 1,017; sulphuric acid (2001), 620; paper (2002), 171. Production of other products: cotton (1997), 98m. sq. metres; woven wool (1997), 17m. sq. metres; 26·7bn. cigarettes (2001); 145,000 refrigerators (2001).

Labour
There is a 42½-hour five-day working week. The average wage in 2000 was 225 new leva per month. In 2001 the labour force numbered 3,412,600. A total of 2,940,300 persons were in employment in 2001 (excluding the armed forces), with the leading areas of activity as follows: agriculture, fishing, forestry and hunting, 774,100; manufacturing, 591,800; wholesale and retail trade/repair of motor vehicles, motorcycles and personal and household goods, 355,200; transport, storage and communications, 214,200; and health and social work, 138,300. Unemployment was 11·7% in Sept. 2004, the lowest rate in five years.

Trade Unions
The former official Central Council of Trade Unions reconstituted itself in 1990 as the Confederation of Independent Trade Unions; in 2003 it had 390,000 members. An independent white-collar trade union movement, Podkrepa, was formed in 1989; there were an estimated 109,000 members in 2003.

INTERNATIONAL TRADE
Legislation in force as of Feb. 1992 abolished restrictions imposed in 1990 on the repatriation of profits and allows foreign nationals to own and set up companies in Bulgaria. Western share participation in joint ventures may exceed 50%. Total foreign debt was US$10,462m. in 2002.

Imports and Exports
Imports and exports (f.o.b.) for calendar years in US$1m.:

	1998	1999	2000	2001	2002
Imports	4,574·2	5,087·4	6,000·1	6,693·3	7,286·6
Exports	4,193·5	4,006·4	4,824·6	5,113·0	5,692·1

Leading import commodities are mineral products, machinery and apparatus, electrical equipment and parts, textile materials and articles, and transportation facilities. Leading export commodities are non-precious metals and articles, textile materials and articles, mineral products and chemical industry produce.

Leading import suppliers in 2001: Russia, 19·9%; Germany, 15·3%; Italy, 9·6%; Turkey, 3·8%; Ukraine, 3·2%; USA, 2·6%. Main export markets: Italy, 15·0%; Germany, 9·6%; Greece, 8·8%; Turkey, 8·1%; Belgium, 5·6%; France, 5·6%. Trade with the EU has been steadily growing, with imports from the EU rising from 35% of the total in 1996 to 51% in 2000, and exports to the EU increasing from 39% of all exports in 1996 to 56% in 2000.

COMMUNICATIONS

Roads
In 2002 Bulgaria had 37,077 km of roads, including 328 km of motorways and 2,991 km of main roads. In 2002 there were 2,254,222 passenger cars (287·0 per 1,000 inhabitants), 262,641 trucks and vans, 44,255 buses and coaches, and 220,296 motorcycles and mopeds. In 2000 public transport totalled 8·60bn. passenger-km. There were 6,886 road accidents in 2000 with 1,012 fatalities.

Rail
In 2000 there were 4,320 km of 1,435 mm gauge railway (2,744 km electrified). Passenger-km travelled in 2000 came to 3·47bn. and freight tonne-km to 5·54bn.

There is a tramway and a metro in Sofia.

Civil Aviation
There is an international airport at Sofia (Vrazhdebna), which handled 1,101,734 passengers (1,049,738 on international flights) and 7,395 tonnes of freight in 2001. The bankrupt former state-owned Balkan Bulgarian Airlines was replaced by Balkan Air Tour in 2002 as the new national flag carrier. In 2003 Balkan Air Tour operated direct services to Berlin, Brussels, Budapest, Copenhagen, Frankfurt, Lisbon, London, Madrid, Moscow, Paris, Prague, Rome, Stockholm, Tel Aviv, Vienna, Warsaw and Zürich. Balkan Air Tour has in the meantime been renamed Bulgaria Air. The independent Hemus Air operated services in 2003 to Athens, Beirut, Bucharest, Damascus, Dubai, Larnaca, Tirana and Tripoli. In 1999 Balkan Bulgarian Airlines flew 18·5m. km, carrying 695,400 passengers (627,400 on international flights).

Shipping
In 2002 the merchant fleet totalled 889,000 GRT, including oil tankers 114,000 GRT. Bourgas is a fishing and oil-port. Varna is the other important port. There is a rail ferry between Varna and Ilitchovsk (Ukraine). In 2002, 15·5m. tonnes of cargo were carried on international and coastal sea traffic; 60,000 passengers and 1·6m tonnes of freight were carried on inland waterways.

Telecommunications
The Bulgarian Telecommunications Company was privatized in Jan. 2004. About 26% of main lines had been digitalized by 2003. There were 4,463,900 telephone subscribers in 2001 (550·6 per 1,000 inhabitants) and 405,000 PCs in use in 2002 (51·9 per 1,000 persons). Bulgaria had 630,000 Internet users in 2002. There were 2,597,500 mobile phone subscribers in 2002 and 34,500 fax machines.

Postal Services
In 2002 there were 3,021 post offices.

SOCIAL INSTITUTIONS

Justice
A law of Nov. 1982 provides for the election (and recall) of all judges by the National Assembly. There are a Supreme Court, 28 provincial courts (including Sofia) and regional courts. Jurors are elected at the local government elections. The Prosecutor General and judges are elected by the Supreme Judicial Council established in 1992.

The population in penal institutions in Sept. 2003 was 10,500 (134 per 100,000 of national population). The maximum term of imprisonment is 20 years. The death penalty was abolished for all crimes in 1998.

Education
Adult literacy rate in 2003 was 98·2% (male, 98·7%; female, 97·7%). Education is free, and compulsory for children between the ages of 7 and 16.

In 2003–04 there were 6,648 educational establishments: 3,278 kindergartens, 2,823 general and special schools, 496 vocational schools and 51 higher education institutions. There were 122,986 teaching staff (22,532 in higher education) and 1,451,284 pupils and students (228,468 in higher education); 114 schools (with 8,721 pupils) and 14 higher institutions (with 32,802 students) were private. There are eight state universities, four private universities and several specialized higher education institutions, some of which have university status. The Academy of Sciences was founded in 1869.

In 2001–02 total expenditure on education came to 3·6% of GNP.

Health
All medical services are free. Private medical services were authorized in Jan. 1991. In 2003 there were 249 hospitals with 58 beds per 10,000 inhabitants. There were 28,128 physicians, 6,475

dentists, 29,650 nurses, 381 pharmacists and 3,456 midwives in 2003. In 2000 health spending represented 4·3% of GDP.

Welfare

In 2002 the official retirement age was 61 years 6 months (men) and 56 years 6 months (women). However, the age level is to be increased gradually until 2009 when the retirement ages will be 63 (men) and 60 (women). The minimum old-age pension is 115% of the social pension (44 leva a month).

The family allowance is 8·54 leva a month for each child below age 16 (or age 18 if the child attends secondary school).

Unemployment benefits are calculated as 60% of average earnings for the previous nine months.

RELIGION

'The traditional church of the Bulgarian people' (as it is officially described) is that of the Eastern Orthodox Church. It was disestablished under the 1947 Constitution. In 1953 the Bulgarian Patriarchate was revived. The Patriarch is Maksim (enthroned 1971). The seat of the Patriarch is at Sofia. There are 11 dioceses (each under a Metropolitan), ten bishops, 2,600 parishes, 1,500 priests, 120 monasteries (with about 400 monks and nuns), 3,700 churches and chapels, one seminary and one theological college.

In 2002 there were some 80,000 Roman Catholics with 51 priests and 54 parishes in three bishoprics. At the 2001 census, 6,638,870 Christians were recorded and 966,978 Muslims (Pomaks). There is a Chief Mufti elected by regional muftis.

CULTURE

World Heritage Sites

There are nine Bulgarian sites that appear on the UNESCO World Heritage List. They are (with year entered on list): Boyana Church (1979); Madara Rider (1979), an 8th century sculpture carved into a rockface; Rock-hewn Churches of Ivanovo (1979); Thracian Tomb of Kazanlak (1979); Ancient City of Nessebar (1983); Srebarna Nature Reserve (1983); Pirin National Park (1983); Rila Monastery (1983); Thracian tomb of Sveshtari (1985).

Broadcasting

Broadcasting is under the aegis of the state-controlled Bulgarian National Radio and Bulgarian Television. There are four national and six regional radio programmes. There are two TV programmes; Bulgaria also receives transmissions from the French satellite channel TV5. There are two independent TV channels—Nova TV (New Television) and 7 Dni (7 Days). Colour programmes are by the SECAM V system. Radio receivers in 2000, 4·4m.; televisions in 2000, 3·7m.

Cinema

There were 149 cinemas with 52,865 seats in 2003 (attendance, 3·53m.). Six full-length films were made in 1999.

Press

In 2002 there were 48 daily newspapers with a combined daily circulation of 1·40m., giving a rate of 173 per 1,000 persons. A total of 6,432 book titles were published in 2004, including 2,047 in sociology and politics and 1,756 literary texts for adults.

Tourism

There were 3,531,567 foreign tourists in 2003. Most arrived from Serbia and Montenegro, Macedonia, Greece and Germany. In 2003, 903,133 Bulgarians made visits abroad as tourists. Earnings from tourism were US$963m. in 2000.

Libraries

In 1999 there were 4,044 public libraries, one National library and 90 Higher Education libraries. They held a combined 64,011,000 volumes for 1,186,000 registered users.

DIPLOMATIC REPRESENTATIVES

Of Bulgaria in the United Kingdom (186–188 Queen's Gate, London, SW7 5HL)
Ambassador: Lachezar Nikolov Matev.

Of the United Kingdom in Bulgaria (9 Moskovska St., Sofia 1000)
Ambassador: Jeremy Hill.

Of Bulgaria in the USA (1621 22nd St., NW, Washington, D.C., 20008)
Ambassador: Elena Borislavova Poptodorova.

Of the USA in Bulgaria (16 Kozyak St., 1407 Sofia)
Ambassador: John R. Beyrle.

Of Bulgaria to the United Nations
Ambassador: Stefan Tafrov.

Of Bulgaria to the European Union
Ambassador: Stanislav Daskalov.

FURTHER READING

Central Statistical Office. *Statisticheski Godishnik.—Statisticheski Spravochnik* (annual).—*Statistical Reference Book of Republic of Bulgaria* (annual).

Crampton, Richard J., *A Concise History of Bulgaria*. CUP, 1997

Melone, A., *Creating Parliamentary Government: The Transition to Democracy in Bulgaria*. Ohio State Univ. Press, 1998

National Statistical Office: Natsionalen Statisticheski Institut, Sofia.
President: Alexander Hadjiiski.
Website: http://www.nsi.bg/

BURKINA FASO

Province	Sq. km	Population 1998	Province	Sq. km	Population 1998
Balé	4,595	149,925	Mouhoun	6,668	239,063
Bam	4,084	216,098	Nahouri	3,754	131,557
Banwa	5,882	204,386	Namentenga	6,464	275,226
Bazéga	3,963	214,367	Nayala	3,919	143,454
Bougouriba	2,812	73,538	Noumbiel	2,736	51,424
Boulgou	6,692	411,418	Oubritenga	2,778	204,935
Boulkiemdé	4,269	423,779	Oudalan	9,797	110,185
Comoé	15,277	243,082	Passoré	3,867	281,317
Ganzourgou	4,178	289,464	Poni	7,365	201,371
Gnagna	8,468	357,097	Sanguié	5,178	236,740
Gourma	11,117	298,801	Sanmatenga	9,281	497,188
Houet	11,568	354,417	Séno	6,863	214,436
Ioba	3,289	163,874	Sissili	7,136	147,842
Kadiogo	2,805	189,813	Soum	12,222	263,028
Kénédougou	8,137	196,236	Sourou	5,765	195,724
Komondjari	5,048	54,487	Tapoa	14,594	250,798
Kompienga	7,029	44,190	Tuy	5,639	165,072
Kossi	7,324	233,129	Yagha	6,468	127,156
Koulpélogo	2,497	192,861	Yatenga	6,990	421,975
Kouritenga	2,622	256,957	Ziro	5,139	11,680
Kourwéogo	1,588	118,239	Zondoma	1,758	134,590
Léraba	3,129	94,377	Zoundwéogo	3,604	190,686
Loroum	3,592	113,153			

République Démocratique du Burkina Faso

Capital: Ouagadougou
Population projection, 2010: 15·31m.
GDP per capita, 2003: (PPP$) 1,174
HDI/world rank: 0·317/175

KEY HISTORICAL EVENTS

Formerly known as Upper Volta, the country's name was changed in 1984 to Burkina Faso, meaning 'the land of honest men'. The area it covers was settled by farming communities until their invasion by the Mossi people in the 11th century, who successfully resisted Islamic crusades and attacks by neighbouring empires for seven centuries until conquered by the French between 1895 and 1903.

France made Upper Volta a separate colony in 1919, only to abolish it as such in 1932, dividing its territory between the Ivory Coast (now Côte d'Ivoire), French Sudan (now Mali) and Niger. In 1947 the territory of Upper Volta was reconstituted. Upper Volta remained a desperately poor country often hit by drought, particularly in 1972–74 and again in 1982–84. The military has held power for most of the period after independence. In Aug. 1983 a coup brought to power Capt. Thomas Sankara, a leading radical, who headed a left-wing regime. Sankara was overthrown and killed in a coup on 15 Oct. 1987, the fifth since 1960, led by his friend Capt. Blaise Compaoré.

TERRITORY AND POPULATION

Burkina Faso is bounded in the north and west by Mali, east by Niger and south by Benin, Togo, Ghana and Côte d'Ivoire. Area: 267,950 sq. km; 1996 census population, 10,312,609, giving a density of 38·4 per sq. km. In 2003 the population was 82·2% rural. 2005 estimate: 13,228,000.

The UN gives a projected population for 2010 of 15·31m.

The largest cities in 1996 were Ouagadougou, the capital (709,736), Bobo-Dioulasso (309,711), Koudougou (72,490), Ouahigouya (52,193), Banfora (49,724), Pouytenga (35,720) and Kaya (33,958).

Areas and populations of the 45 provinces:

The principal ethnic groups are the Mossi (48%), Fulani (10%), Bobo (7%), Lobi (7%), Mandé (7%), Grosi (5%), Gurma (5%), Sénoufo (5%) and Bissa (4%).

French is the official language.

SOCIAL STATISTICS

2000 births (estimates), 557,000; deaths, 189,000. Estimated birth rate in 2000 was 46·8 per 1,000 population; estimated death rate, 15·9. Annual population growth rate, 1992–2002, 2·9%. Expectation of life at birth, 2003, 48·2 years for females and 46·8 for males. Infant mortality, 2001 (per 1,000 live births), 104. Fertility rate, 2001, 6·8 children per woman.

CLIMATE

A tropical climate with a wet season from May to Nov. and a dry season from Dec. to April. Rainfall decreases from south to north. Ouagadougou, Jan. 76°F (24·4°C), July 83°F (28·3°C). Annual rainfall 36" (894 mm).

CONSTITUTION AND GOVERNMENT

At a referendum in June 1991 a new constitution was approved; there is an executive presidency. Parliament consists of the 111-member *National Assembly*, elected by universal suffrage. The *Chamber of Representatives*, a consultative body representing social, religious, professional and political organizations, was abolished in 2002. There is also an *Economic and Social Council*. In April 2000 parliament passed a law reducing presidential terms from seven to five years, with a maximum of two terms. The new law did not affect President Blaise Compaoré's seven-year term which was to expire in Nov. 2005, and he has now been elected for a further term.

National Anthem

'Contre la férule humiliante' ('Against the shameful fetters'); words by T. Sankara, tune anonymous.

RECENT ELECTIONS

At the presidential elections of 13 Nov. 2005 Blaise Compaoré was re-elected by 80·3% of votes cast against 12 other candidates. Turnout was 57·7%.

Parliamentary elections were held on 5 May 2002. The Congress for Democracy and Progress (CDP) won 57 out of 111 seats, the Alliance for Democracy and the Federation-African Democratic Rally (ADF-RDA) 17, and the Party for Democracy and Progress (PDP) 10. Turnout was 64·1%.

CURRENT ADMINISTRATION

President: Capt. Blaise Compaoré; b. 1951 (CDP; in office since 1987, most recently re-elected on 13 Nov. 2005).

In March 2006 the government comprised:

Prime Minister: Paramanga Ernest Yonli; b. 1956 (CDP; sworn in 7 Nov. 2000).

Minister of State and Minister of Agriculture, Water and Water Resources: Salif Diallo. *Minister of State and Minister for Foreign Affairs and Regional Co-operation:* Youssouf Ouédraogo. *Minister of Animal Resources:* Tiémoko Konaté. *Arts, Tourism and Culture:* Aline Koala. *Basic Education and Mass Literacy:* Odile Bonkoungou. *Civil Service and State Reform:* Lassané Sawadogo. *Defence:* Yéro Boli. *Economy and Development:* Seydou Bouda. *Energy and Mines:* Abdoulaye Abdoulkader Cissé. *Environment and Quality of Life:* Laurent Sédogo. *Finance and Budget:* Jean-Baptiste Compaoré. *Health:* Bédouma Alain Yoda. *Housing and Town Planning:* Sékou Ba. *Human Rights Promotion:* Monique Ilboudo. *Information:* Joseph Kahoun. *Infrastructure and Urban Planning:* Hippolyte Lingani. *Justice and Keeper of the Seals:* Boureima Badini. *Labour and Social Security:* Gérome Boudma. *Post, Information Technologies and Communications:* Joachim Tankouano. *Promotion of Women:* Marie Gisèle Guigma. *Relations with Parliament:* Adama Fofana. *Secondary and Higher Education and Scientific Research:* Joseph Paré. *Security:* Djibrill Yipéné Bassolé. *Social Affairs and National Solidarity:* Pascaline Tamini. *Sports and Leisure:* Maurice Ardiouma Jean Marie Palm. *Territorial Administration and Decentralization:* Clément Sawadogo. *Trade, Industry and Crafts:* Bénoît Ouattara. *Transport:* Gilbert Noel Ouédraogo. *Youth and Employment:* Justin Koutaba.

CURRENT LEADERS

Blaise Compaoré

Position
President

Introduction
Blaise Compaoré came to power in 1987 after the assassination of Thomas Sankara, the president of the Conseil National de la Révolution (CNR; National Revolutionary Council). Compaoré has attempted to deregulate the economy and improve relations with the West. He has said that he wants to democratize the country, but his tenure has been marked by strikes, unrest and political murders. His human rights record has also attracted international condemnation.

Early Life
Born on 3 Feb. 1951 in Ouagadougou, Compaoré received his early education in Burkina Faso and became a secondary school teacher. In 1971 he joined the army and in 1975 went to Cameroon and France for military training. His friendship with Sankara began in Morocco in 1978 while he was serving as a parachute instructor. By 1981 Compaoré had achieved the rank of captain.

Although involved in the establishment in 1982 of the Conseil de Salut du Peuple (CSP; People's Salvation Council, led by Jean-Baptiste Ouedraogo), Compaoré and Sankara broke with the CSP in 1983 to form the more left-wing CNR. When Sankara was later arrested, Compaoré led an anti-government revolt that overthrew Ouedraogo and brought Sankara and the CNR to power. Compaoré was appointed vice-premier. However, growing dissatisfaction with Sankara's increasingly autocratic leadership led in 1987 to his assassination by soldiers loyal to Compaoré, who replaced his former ally as head of state.

Career in Office
Compaoré took office promising a continuation of the CNR's guiding principles, but with 'rectification'. He restored links with the business community, traditional chiefs and the army, and sought to pacify the West on whom he relied for aid. A new party—the Organization for Popular Democracy/Labour Movement (ODP/MT; Organisation pour la Démocratie Populaire/Mouvement du Travail)—was created in 1989 and provision made for the return of multi-party elections. However, political dissent was still treated heavy-handedly and the government virtually controlled the media. That year, two stalwarts of the Sankara era still holding senior office (Boukari Lingani and Henri Zongo) were accused of plotting a coup and executed. In 1991 an amnesty was called on all those guilty of 'political crimes' since 1960 and exiles were offered safe return.

Despite Compaoré's ostensible democratization of the election process and more moderate regime, the 1991 elections were boycotted by opposition groups. Compaoré, the sole candidate, won 90·4% of votes but less than 25% of the population participated. He was sworn in as president on 24 Dec. 1991. Amid high political tension, the assassination of opposition leader Clement Oumarou Ouedraogo and the postponement of legislative elections, Compaoré called a development forum of diverse political and social leaders. In the same year he agreed to a World Bank structural adjustment programme, although the resultant austerity measures led to strikes and protests by students.

The 1991 constitution was amended in 1997, allowing the president to stand for re-election more than once, and also restructuring parliament and provincial government. In addition the national anthem and the flag were modified to break with the revolutionary past. Compaoré was re-elected president in Nov. 1998 with more than 87% of votes (in a 56·1% turnout), although doubt was cast on the legitimacy of the electoral process. On 13 Dec. 1998 a journalist critical of Compaoré, Norbert Zongo, and three of his colleagues were murdered. There followed public protests and the arrest of opposition leaders.

A report of May 1999 suggested that the presidential bodyguard was behind the murders of Zongo and his colleagues. The conclusions led to student protests in the capital. Compaoré's human rights record fell under further scrutiny as more opposition leaders and independent journalists were arrested. Despite the offer of compensation to the victims' families and the release of several political prisoners, tensions remained high, and strikes and other protests persisted.

In parliamentary elections in May 2002, despite a stronger opposition performance, the pro-Compaoré Congress for Democracy and Progress (CDP) won 57 of the 111 National Assembly seats.

Compaoré was re-elected for a further term in Nov. 2005, winning over 80% of the vote.

In foreign policy, Compaoré has forged close links with both Libya and France. However, his regime has been accused more recently of destabilizing interference in war-torn Liberia and Sierra Leone.

DEFENCE

There are six military regions. All forces form part of the Army. Defence expenditure totalled US$55m. in 2003 (US$5 per capita), representing 1·3% of GDP.

Army

Strength (2002), 5,800 with a paramilitary Gendarmerie of 4,200. In addition there is a People's Militia of 45,000.

Air Force

Personnel total (2002), 200 with five combat aircraft.

INTERNATIONAL RELATIONS

Burkina Faso is a member of the UN, WTO, the African Union, African Development Bank, ECOWAS, IOM, OIC, Islamic Development Bank, International Organization of the Francophonie and is an ACP member state of the ACP-EU relationship.

ECONOMY

In 2002 agriculture accounted for 31·0% of GDP, industry 18·0% and services 50·9%.

Currency

The unit of currency is the *franc CFA* (XOF) with a parity of 655·957 francs CFA to one euro. Foreign exchange reserves were US$260m. in May 2002 and total money supply was 256,913m. francs CFA. Gold reserves were 11,000 troy oz in June 2000. There was inflation in 2003 of 2·0%, but then deflation in 2004 of 0·4%.

Budget

Total revenues in 2001 were 376·3bn. francs CFA and expenditures 457·5bn. francs CFA.

Performance

Real GDP growth was 7·9% in 2003 and 4·6% in 2004. Total GDP was US$4·8bn. in 2004.

Banking and Finance

The bank of issue which functions as the central bank is the regional Central Bank of West African States (BCEAO; *Acting Governor*, Justin Baro Damo). There are seven other banks and three credit institutions. There is a stock exchange in Ouagadougou.

ENERGY AND NATURAL RESOURCES

Environment

Burkina Faso's carbon dioxide emissions from the consumption and flaring of fossil fuels in 2002 were the equivalent of 0·1 tonnes per capita.

Electricity

Production of electricity (2000) was about 284m. kWh. There are five thermal power stations with a total capacity in 2000 of 48,000 kW. Hydro-electric capacity in 2000 was 30,000 kW, giving a total installed capacity of 78,000 kW in 2000. Consumption per capita was an estimated 25 kWh in 2000.

Minerals

There are deposits of manganese, zinc, limestone, phosphate and diamonds. Gold production was 886 kg in 1999.

Agriculture

In 2001 there were 3·95m. ha. of arable land and 52,000 ha. of permanent crops. 25,000 ha. were irrigated in 2001. There were 1,995 tractors in 2001. The agricultural population in 2002 totalled 10·45m., of whom 5·47m. were economically active. Production (2000, in 1,000 tonnes): sorghum, 1,100; millet, 900; sugarcane, 400; maize, 350; seed cotton, 300; groundnuts, 205; cottonseed, 175; cotton lint, 125; rice, 88.

Livestock (2000): cattle, 4·70m.; sheep, 6·59m.; goats, 8·40m.; pigs, 610,000; asses, 491,000; chickens, 22m. Livestock products, 2000 (in 1,000 tonnes): beef and veal, 52; goat meat, 22; poultry meat, 26; cow's milk, 163; eggs, 18.

Forestry

In 2000 forests covered 7,089,000 ha., or 25·9% of the total land area. Timber production in 2001 was 11·84m. cu. metres.

Fisheries

In 2001 total catch was approximately 8,500 tonnes, exclusively from inland waters. There is some fish farming.

INDUSTRY

In 2002 manufacturing contributed 14·5% of GDP, primarily food-processing and textiles. Industry is underdeveloped and employs only 1% of the workforce. The country's manufactures are mainly restricted to basic consumer goods and processed foods. Output of major products, in 1,000 tonnes: vegetable oil (2000), 31; sugar (1999), 30; soap (1999), 13; flour (2002), 10; beer (2003), 55·0m. litres; printed fabric (2000), 275,000 sq. metres.

Labour

In 1996 the labour force was 5,419,000 (53% males). Over 90% of the economically active population are engaged in agriculture, fishing and forestry.

Trade Unions

There were six federations in 1999: Confédération Générale de Travailleurs de Burkina (CGTB), Union syndicale des travailleurs du Burkina (USTB), Union générale des travailleurs du Burkina (UGTB), Confédération syndicale Burkinabe (CSB), Confédération nationale des travailleurs Burkinabe (CNTB) and Organisation nationale des syndicats libres (ONSL).

INTERNATIONAL TRADE

Foreign debt was US$1,580m. in 2002.

Imports and Exports

In 2001 imports totalled US$504·2m. and exports US$228·0m. Principal import suppliers, 2000: Côte d'Ivoire, 22·7%; France, 22·4%; Japan, 5·6%; China, 4·1%; USA, 3·7%. Principal export markets: France, 21·6%; Côte d'Ivoire, 11·5%; Belgium-Luxembourg, 8·4%; Italy, 7·7%; Singapore, 5·6%. Cotton is the main export, accounting for about 40% of the country's export income.

COMMUNICATIONS

Roads

The road system comprised 12,264 km in 2002, of which 16% were paved. There were 29,400 passenger cars (2·2 per 1,000 inhabitants) and 24,000 commercial vehicles in use in 2002.

Rail

The railway from Abidjan in Côte d'Ivoire to Kaya (622 km of metre gauge within Burkina Faso) is operated by the mixed public-private company Sitarail, a concessionaire to both governments. The railways carried 0·6m. passengers and 0·2m. tonnes of freight in 1993.

Civil Aviation

The international airports are Ouagadougou (which handled 175,000 passengers in 2001) and Bobo-Dioulasso. The national carrier is Air Burkina, which in 2003 flew to Abidjan, Bamako, Cotonou, Dakar, Lomé and Niamey in addition to operating on domestic routes. In 1999 scheduled airline traffic of Burkina Faso-based carriers flew 3·9m. km, carrying 147,000 passengers (132,000 on international flights).

Telecommunications

There were 154,200 telephone subscribers in 2002, equivalent to 12·9 per 1,000 inhabitants, of which mobile phone subscribers numbered 89,900. In 2002, 19,000 PCs were in use (1·6 per 1,000 persons). There were 25,000 Internet users in 2002.

Postal Services

There were 73 post offices in 2003.

SOCIAL INSTITUTIONS

Justice

Civilian courts replaced revolutionary tribunals in 1993. A law passed in April 2000 split the supreme court into four separate entities—a constitutional court, an appeal court, a council of state and a government audit office.

The population in penal institutions in Sept. 2002 was 2,800 (23 per 100,000 of national population).

Education

In 2001 adult literacy was 24·8% (male, 34·9%; female, 14·9%), among the lowest in the world. In 2000–01 there were 19,007 teachers and 901,321 pupils in primary schools. During the period 1990–95 only 24% of females of primary school age were enrolled in school. In 2000–01 there were 199,278 pupils and 6,432 teachers in secondary schools, and in 2001–02 there were 15,535 students in higher education. There is a university at Ouagadougou, with over 8,000 students.

Health

In 2000 there were two national hospitals, nine regional hospitals and 102 medical centres. There were 490 physicians, 36 dentists, 3,190 nurses, 476 midwives and 60 pharmacists in 2001.

RELIGION

In 2001 there were 5·96m. Muslims and 2·04m. Christians (mainly Roman Catholic). Many of the remaining population follow traditional animist religions.

CULTURE

Broadcasting

Radio and television services (colour by NTSC) are provided by the state-controlled *Radiodiffusion-Télévision Burkina*. Radio Bobo is a regional service and there is a commercial radio station. There were 428,000 radio receivers in 2000 and 150,000 television receivers in 2001.

Press

There were four dailies (one government-owned) with a combined circulation of 14,500 in 1998. There were nine non-dailies and periodicals in 1995.

Tourism

In 2001 there were 128,000 foreign tourists. Receipts totalled US$34m.

DIPLOMATIC REPRESENTATIVES

Of Burkina Faso in the United Kingdom
Ambassador: Kadré Désiré Ouedraogo (resides in Brussels).
Honorary Consul: Stuart Singer (5 Cinnamon Row, Plantation Wharf, London, SW11 3TW).

Of the United Kingdom in Burkina Faso
Ambassador: Gordon Wetherell (resides in Accra, Ghana).

Of Burkina Faso in the USA (2340 Massachusetts Ave., NW, Washington, D.C., 20008)
Ambassador: Tertius Zongo.

Of the USA in Burkina Faso (602 avenue Raoul Follereau, 01 BP 35, Ouagadougou 01)
Ambassador: Vacant.
Chargé d'Affaires a.i.: Cynthia Akuetteh.

Of Burkina Faso to the United Nations
Ambassador: Michel Kafando.

Of Burkina Faso to the European Union
Ambassador: Kadré Désiré Ouedraogo.

FURTHER READING

Decalo, Samuel, *Burkina Faso.* [Bibliography] ABC-Clio, Oxford and Santa Barbara (CA), 1994
Nnaji, B. O., *Blaise Compaoré: Architect of the Burkina Faso Revolution.* Lagos, 1991

National Statistical Office: Institut National de la Statistique et de la Démographie (INSD), 555 Boulevard de l'Indépendance, 01 BP 374, Ouagadougou.
Website (French only): http://www.insd.bf

BURUNDI

Republika y'Uburundi

Capital: Bujumbura
Population projection, 2010: 9·10m.
GDP per capita, 2003: (PPP$) 648
HDI/world rank: 0·378/169

KEY HISTORICAL EVENTS

From 1890 Burundi was part of German East Africa and from 1919 part of Ruanda-Urundi administered by Belgium as a League of Nations mandate. Internal self-government was granted on 1 Jan. 1962, followed by independence on 1 July 1962. In April 1972 fighting broke out between rebels from both Burundi and neighbouring countries and the ruling Tutsi, apparently with the intention of destroying the Tutsi hegemony. Up to 120,000 died. On 1 Nov. 1976 President Micombero was deposed by the Army, as was President Bagaza on 3 Sept. 1987. Pierre Buyoya assumed the presidency on 1 Oct. 1987.

On 1 June 1993 President Buyoya was defeated in elections by Melchior Ndadaye, who thus became the country's first elected president and the first Hutu president, but on 21 Oct. President Ndadaye and six ministers were killed in an attempted military coup. A wave of Tutsi-Hutu massacres broke out, costing thousands of lives. On 6 April 1994 the new president, Cyprien Ntaryamira, was also killed, possibly assassinated, together with the president of Rwanda.

On 25 July 1996 the army seized power, installing Maj. Pierre Buyoya, a Tutsi, as president for the second time. In June 1998 Maj. Buyoya drew up a settlement for a power-sharing transitional government and the replacement of the prime minister by two vice-presidents, one Hutu and one Tutsi. Extremists on both sides denounced the agreement. An attempted coup in April 2001 failed. In July 2001 it was agreed that a three-year transitional government should be installed with Pierre Buyoya as president and Domitien Ndayizeye, a Hutu, as vice-president for the first 18 months, after which the roles would be reversed. A further attempted coup shortly after the announcement of the agreement also failed, although fighting continued. A ceasefire accord was eventually signed in Dec. 2002 by the government and the Forces for the Defense of Democracy (FDD), the country's principal rebel movement. In Oct. 2003 the FDD and the government sealed a peace deal to end the civil war and put into practice the ceasefire agreed in 2002. More than 200,000 people have been killed in civil conflict since 1993. However, developments in the past couple of years, including the holding of a referendum on the post-transition constitution, suggest a more peaceful future.

TERRITORY AND POPULATION

Burundi is bounded in the north by Rwanda, east and south by Tanzania and west by the Democratic Republic of the Congo, and has an area (including inland water) of 27,834 sq. km (10,759 sq. miles). The population at the 1990 census was 5,292,793; estimate (2005) 7,548,000, giving a population density of 271 per sq. km. Only 10·0% of the population was urban in 2003 (90·0% rural), but urbanization is increasing rapidly.

The UN gives a projected population for 2010 of 9·10m.

There are 17 regions, all named after their chief towns. Area and population:

Region	Area (in sq. km.)	Population (1999)
Bubanza	1,089	289,060
Bujumbura Mairie	87	319,098
Bujumbura Rural	1,089	436,896
Bururi	2,465	437,931
Cankuzo	1,965	172,477
Cibitoke	1,636	385,438
Gitega	1,979	628,872
Karusi	1,457	384,187
Kayanza	1,233	458,815
Kirundo	1,703	502,171
Makamba	1,960	357,492
Muramvya	696	252,833
Muyinga	1,836	485,347
Mwaro	840	229,013
Ngozi	1,474	601,382
Rutana	1,959	244,939
Ruyigi	2,339	304,567

The capital, Bujumbura, had an estimated population of 321,000 in 1999. The second largest town, Gitega, had a population in 1990 of 102,000.

There are four ethnic groups—Hutu (Bantu, forming 81% of the total); Tutsi (Nilotic, 16%); Lingala (2%); Twa (pygmoids, 1%). The local language is Kirundi. French is also an official language. Kiswahili is spoken in the commercial centres.

SOCIAL STATISTICS

2000 estimates: births, 288,000; deaths, 130,000. Rates, 2000 estimates (per 1,000 population): birth, 43·5; death, 20·8. Life expectancy at birth, 2003, was 42·6 years for men and 44·5 years for women. Infant mortality, 2001, 114 per 1,000 live births. Annual population growth rate, 1992–2002, 1·3%; fertility rate, 2001, 6·8 children per woman.

CLIMATE

An equatorial climate, modified by altitude. The eastern plateau is generally cool, the easternmost savanna several degrees hotter. The wet seasons are from March to May and Sept. to Dec. Bujumbura, Jan. 73°F (22·8°C), July 73°F (22·8°C). Annual rainfall 33" (825 mm).

CONSTITUTION AND GOVERNMENT

The Constitution of 1981 provided for a one-party state. In Jan. 1991 the government of President Buyoya, leader of the sole party, the Union for National Progress (UPRONA), proposed a new constitution which was approved by a referendum in March 1992 (with 89% of votes cast in favour), legalizing parties not based on ethnic group, region or religion and providing for presidential elections by direct universal suffrage. On 28 Feb. 2005 citizens voted overwhelmingly to adopt a new constitution laying the foundations for the end of a 12-year civil war, with 92% of votes cast in favour of the constitution. The constitution gives Tutsis (who have traditionally held power in Burundi but only make up 15% of the population) 40% of seats in the National Assembly, while the Hutus, who constitute 83% of the population, are given 60% of the seats.

Burundi has a bicameral legislature, consisting of the *National Assembly* of 118 members, with 100 members elected to serve five-year terms and 18 appointed to ensure that ethnic and gender quotas are met, and the *Senate* of 49 members (34 elected and 15 appointed, including four former presidents).

In July 2001 agreement was reached on President Pierre Buyoya's presidency for the first 18 months of a three-year transition period of multi-ethnic broad-based government. In accordance with the terms of the Arusha peace accord, initially he was being assisted by Hutu Vice-President Domitien Ndayizeye, after which the roles were to be reversed for the second 18 months. The transitional government was established on 1 Nov. 2001. On 30 April 2003 Domitien Ndayizeye became president but Alphonse Marie Kadege, like Pierre Buyoya a Tutsi from the Party of Unity and National Progress, became the vice-president. In Oct. 2004 the transitional government was extended for a further six months, with elections scheduled for 22 April 2005. In April 2005 the transitional period was extended for a further four months and a new deadline of 19 Aug. 2005 set for elections. The success of the referendum in Feb. 2005 held under 1993 electoral laws was seen as proof that presidential elections need not be postponed further. Parliamentary elections that were generally deemed free and fair were held in July 2005, with presidential elections following in Aug.

National Anthem

'Burundi Bwacu' ('Dear Burundi'); words by a committee, tune by M. Barengayabo.

RECENT ELECTIONS

Burundi's parliament elected Pierre Nkurunziza, the only candidate, president on 19 Aug. 2005 by 151 votes to nine with one abstention and one null vote. A former Hutu rebel, he thus became the country's first president chosen through democratic means since the assassination of President Melchior Ndadaye in 1993.

At the parliamentary elections of 4 July 2005 the National Council for the Defense of Democracy–Forces for the Defense of Democracy (CNDD–FDD) won 64 of 118 seats with 58·6% of the vote, President Domitien Ndayizeye's ruling Front for Democracy in Burundi (FRODEBU) 30 with 21·7%, the Union for National Progress (UPRONA) 15 with 7·2%, National Council for the Defense of Democracy (CNDD) 4 with 4·1% and Movement for the Rehabilitation of Citizens–Rurenzangemero (MRC–Rurenzangemero) 2 with 2·1%. In addition, three ethnic Twa members were appointed to the National Assembly. In indirect Senate elections held on 29 July 2005 the National Council for the Defense of Democracy–Forces for the Defense of Democracy won 32 of 49 seats, the Front for Democracy in Burundi 7, the Union for National Progress 3, the National Council for the Defense of Democracy 3, ethnic Twa members 3 and the Party for National Recovery (PARENA) 1.

CURRENT ADMINISTRATION

President: Pierre Nkurunziza; b. 1963 (CNDD–FDD; sworn in on 26 Aug. 2005).

First Vice-President: Martin Nduwimana. *Second Vice-President:* Alice Nzomukunda.

In March 2006 the government also comprised:

Minister of Agriculture and Livestock: Elie Buzoya. *Commerce and Industry:* Denise Sinankwa. *Energy and Mining:* Herman Tuyaga. *External Relations and Co-operation:* Antoinette Batumubwira. *Finance:* Dieudonné Ngowembona. *Good Governance, General Inspection of the State and Local Administration:* Venant Ka Mana. *Health:* Barnabé Mbonimpa. *Information, Communication, Parliamentary Relations and Government Spokesperson:* Ramadhani Karenga. *Interior and Public Security:* Evariste Ndayisshimiye. *Justice and Keeper of the Seals:* Clotilde Niragira. *Land Management, Environment and Tourism:* Odette Kayitesi. *National Defence and Former Combatants:* Maj.-Gen. Germain Niyoyankana. *National Education and Culture:* Saidi Kebeya. *National Solidarity, Human Rights and Gender:* Françoise Ngendahayo. *Planning and National Reconstruction:* Marie-Goreth Nizigama. *Public Service, Labour and Social Security:* Juvénal Ngowenubusa. *Public Works and Equipment:* Potame Nizigire. *Transport, Posts and Telecommunications:* Jean Bigirimana. *Youth and Sports:* Jean-Jacques Nyenimigabo. *Presidency, in Charge of AIDS:* Dr Triphonie Nkurunziza.

CURRENT LEADERS

Pierre Nkurunziza

Position
President

Introduction
Pierre Nkurunziza became president in Aug. 2005 in the country's first democratic elections since the start of the civil war in 1993. The former sports teacher and leader of Burundi's largest ethnic Hutu rebel group hopes to lead the country to peace and stability. His key challenges are to rebuild the economy, oversee the repatriation of tens of thousands of refugees and maintain relations with the Tutsi minority.

Early Life
Pierre Nkurunziza was born in Burundi's capital, Bujumbura, on 18 Dec. 1963, the son of Eustache Ngabisha, who was the governor of Ngozi and Kayansi provinces and a member of parliament from 1965. He attended primary school in the northern town of Ngozi and was there in 1972 when his father was killed in a wave of ethnic violence that claimed over 100,000 lives. The family moved to Gitega, where Nkurunziza attended secondary school. He studied physical education at the University of Burundi in Bujumbura and became closely involved with the New Sporting football club as both player and coach. Having graduated in 1990, he combined teaching at Muramvya High School with further studies in psychology and pedagogy. A year later he began lecturing in physical education both at the country's leading military academy and at the University of Burundi.

Civil war was ignited in Oct. 1993 by the assassination of Burundi's first ethnic Hutu president, Melchior Ndadaye, and spilled on to the University of Burundi campus in 1995 when 200 Hutu students were killed by Tutsi militia. Nkurunziza was reportedly shot at but managed to escape and left the capital to join the National Council for the Defense of Democracy–Forces for the Defense of Democracy (CNDD–FDD) as a soldier. The group was one of several rebel Hutu groups that fought the Tutsi-dominated army, a conflict which killed thousands and had created an estimated 700,000 refugees by the late 1990s. In 1998 Nkurunziza was promoted to deputy secretary-general and co-ordinated the activities of the armed and political wings of the CNDD–FDD. In the same year he was sentenced to death by a Burundian court for alleged involvement in a series of ambushes but was granted immunity during peace talks that culminated in the Arusha Peace Accord of Aug. 2000.

Elected chairman of the CNDD–FDD at its first congress in 2001, Nkurunziza began negotiations with Burundi's transitional government. In Nov. 2003 he signed a ceasefire accord, winning official recognition of the CNDD–FDD as a political party. Nkurunziza became state minister of good governance in the transitional government led by Domitien Ndayizeye. As such, he was a key figure in forging a power-sharing agreement and setting a timetable for democratic elections, ratified by heads of state from the Great Lakes region in Aug. 2004.

Following a series of CNDD–FDD victories in elections held in June and July 2005, Nkurunziza was nominated as the party's presidential candidate. He won an overwhelming victory in a vote by members of parliament (acting as an electoral college) on 19 Aug. and was sworn in as president on 26 Aug. 2005.

Career in Office
President Nkurunziza called for the Palipehutu–FNL opposition to lay down arms and rejoin negotiations. He appointed a cabinet of 20 ministers comprising 11 Hutus and nine Tutsis in accordance with the fixed quotas stipulated in the constitution. He announced that free primary education would be available to all children with immediate effect. He also promised to facilitate the return of Burundian refugees from Tanzania and Rwanda.

DEFENCE

Armed forces personnel, including the Gendarmerie, totalled 45,500 in 2002.

Defence expenditure totalled US$42m. in 2003 (US$6 per capita), representing 7·2% of GDP.

Army
The Army had a strength (2002) of 40,000 including an air wing.

Air Force
There were 200 air wing personnel in 2002 with four combat aircraft and one combat helicopter.

INTERNATIONAL RELATIONS

Burundi is a member of the UN, WTO, the African Union, African Development Bank, COMESA, International Organization of the Francophonie, and is an ACP member state of the ACP-EU relationship.

ECONOMY

Agriculture accounted for 49·3% of GDP in 2002, industry 19·4% and services 31·3%.

Currency
The unit of currency is the *Burundi franc* (BIF) of 100 *centimes*. Inflation was 10·7% in 2003 and 8·0% in 2004. In June 2002 gold reserves were 1,000 troy oz and foreign exchange reserves US$26m. Total money supply was 481,193m. Burundi francs in April 2002.

Budget
Government revenue and expenditure (in 1m. Burundi francs):

	1995	1996	1997	1998	1999
Revenue	48,397	46,401	46,253	66,333	72,047
Expenditure	76,403	75,405	80,800	98,061	105,18

Performance
In 2004 real GDP growth was 4·8%, following negative growth of 1·2% in 2003. Total GDP in 2004 was US$0·7bn.

Banking and Finance
The Bank of the Republic of Burundi is the central bank and bank of issue. Its *Governor* is Salvator Toyi. In 1999 it had deposits of 11·23bn. Burundi francs. There are seven commercial banks, a development bank and a co-operative bank.

ENERGY AND NATURAL RESOURCES

Environment
Burundi's carbon dioxide emissions from the consumption and flaring of fossil fuels in 2002 were the equivalent of 0·1 tonnes per capita.

Electricity
Installed capacity was 44,000 kW in 2000. Production was about 128m. kWh in 2000. Consumption per capita in 2000 was 75 kWh.

Minerals
Gold is mined on a small scale. Deposits of nickel (280m. tonnes) and vanadium remain to be exploited. There are proven reserves of phosphates of 17·6m. tonnes.

Agriculture
The main economic activity is agriculture, which contributed 49% of GDP in 2002. In 2001, 0·90m. ha. were arable and 0·36m. ha. permanent crops. 74,000 ha. were irrigated in 2001. There were 170 tractors in 2001. Beans, cassava, maize, sweet potatoes, groundnuts, peas, sorghum and bananas are grown according to the climate and the region.

The main cash crop is coffee, of which about 95% is arabica. It accounts for 90% of exports, and taxes and levies on coffee constitute a major source of revenue. A coffee board (OCIBU) manages the grading and export of the crop. Production (2000) 19,000 tonnes. The main agricultural crops (2000 production, in 1,000 tonnes) are bananas (1,514), sweet potatoes (687), cassava (657), dry beans (187), sugarcane (174), maize (118), taro (81), sorghum (61), rice (52), peas (30) and potatoes (24).

Livestock (2000): 550,000 goats, 390,000 cattle, 120,000 sheep, 50,000 pigs and 4m. chickens.

Forestry
Forests covered 94,000 ha., or 3·7% of the total land area, in 2000. Timber production in 2001 was 8·29m. cu. metres, the majority of it for fuel.

Fisheries
There is a small commercial fishing industry on Lake Tanganyika. In 2001 the total catch was 8,964 tonnes, exclusively from inland waters.

INDUSTRY

The industrial sector is underdeveloped, although a few firms manufacture consumer products, and some process cotton and coffee. In 2001 production of sugar totalled 26,000 tonnes. Other major products are beer (87·5m. litres in 2003), cigarettes (286m. units in 2000) and blankets (141,854 units in 2000).

Labour
In 1996 the labour force was 3,337,000 (51% males).

INTERNATIONAL TRADE

With Rwanda and the Democratic Republic of the Congo, Burundi forms part of the Economic Community of the Great Lakes. Foreign debt was US$1,204m. in 2002.

Imports and Exports
Imports and exports for calendar years in US$1m.:

	1998	1999	2000	2001	2002
Imports f.o.b.	123·5	97·3	107·9	108·3	104·0
Exports f.o.b.	64·0	55·0	49·1	39·2	31·0

Main exports are coffee, manufactures and tea. Main import suppliers, 1999: Belgium, 15%; Saudi Arabia, 13%; Italy, 12%. Main export markets, 1999: Belgium, 31%; Switzerland, 18%; UK, 14%.

COMMUNICATIONS

Roads
In 2002 there were 14,480 km of roads of which 7·1% were paved. There were 19,800 passenger cars (2·8 per 1,000 inhabitants) and 14,400 commercial vehicles in use in 2002.

Civil Aviation
There were direct flights to Addis Ababa, Douala, Entebbe/Kampala, Kigali and Nairobi in 2003. In 1998 scheduled airline traffic of Burundi-based carriers flew 800,000 km, carrying 12,000 passengers (all on international flights). Bujumbura International airport handled 51,936 passengers and 3,319 tonnes of freight in 2001.

Shipping
There are lake services from Bujumbura to Kigoma (Tanzania) and Kalémie (Democratic Republic of the Congo). The main route for exports and imports is via Kigoma, and thence by rail to Dar es Salaam.

Telecommunications
In 2002 there were 74,100 telephone subscribers (10·6 per 1,000 inhabitants), including 52,000 mobile phone subscribers. 5,000 PCs were in use in 2002 (0·7 per 1,000 persons) and there were 5,900 fax machines. The number of Internet users in 2002 was 8,400.

Postal Services
In 2003 there were 29 post offices, equivalent to one for every 235,000 persons.

SOCIAL INSTITUTIONS

Justice
There is a Supreme Court, an appeal court and a court of first instance at Bujumbura, and provincial courts in each provincial capital.

The population in penal institutions in 2002 was 8,647 (129 per 100,000 of national population). The death penalty is in force.

Education
Adult literacy rate was 58·9% in 2003 (66·8% among males and 51·9% among females). In 2000–01 there were 750,589 pupils in primary schools with 14,955 teachers and 113,427 pupils in secondary schools. In 2000–01 there were 6,289 students in higher education institutes with 507 teachers. In 1995–96 there were 3,750 students and 170 academic staff at the university.

In 2000–01 total expenditure on education came to 3·5% of GNP.

Health
In 2000 there were 323 doctors and 1,783 nurses. In 1996 there was less than one hospital bed per 10,000 inhabitants.

RELIGION
In 2001 there were 4·05m. Roman Catholics with an archbishop and three bishops. About 3% of the population are Pentecostal, 1% Anglican and 1% Muslim, while the balance follow traditional tribal beliefs.

CULTURE

Broadcasting
Broadcasting is provided by the state-controlled *Radiodiffusion et Télévision du Burundi*. There were 1·26m. radio receivers in 2000 and 200,000 TV in 2001 (colour by SECAM V) receivers.

Press
There was (1998) one daily newspaper (*Le Renouveau*) with a circulation of 15,000.

Tourism
There were 36,000 foreign tourists in 2001. Receipts totalled US$1m.

DIPLOMATIC REPRESENTATIVES
Of Burundi in the United Kingdom (26 Armitage Rd, London, NW11 8RD)
Ambassador: Vacant (resides at Brussels).
Chargé d'Affaires a.i.: Salvator Siboniyo.

Of the United Kingdom in Burundi
Ambassador: Jeremy Macadie (resides in Kigali, Rwanda).

Of Burundi in the USA (2233 Wisconsin Ave., NW, Suite 212, Washington, D.C., 20007)
Ambassador: Antoine Ntamobwa.

Of the USA in Burundi (PO Box 1720, Ave. des Etats-Unis, Bujumbura)
Ambassador: Patricia Moller.

Of Burundi to the United Nations
Ambassador: Marc Nteturuye.

Of Burundi to the European Union
Ambassador: Ferdinand Nyabenda.

FURTHER READING
Daniels, Morna, *Burundi.* [Bibliography] ABC-Clio, Oxford and Santa Barbara (CA), 1992
Lemarchand, R., *Burundi: Ethnic Conflict and Genocide.* CUP, 1996

National Statistical Office: Service des Etudes et Statistiques, Ministère du Plan, Bujumbura.

CAMBODIA

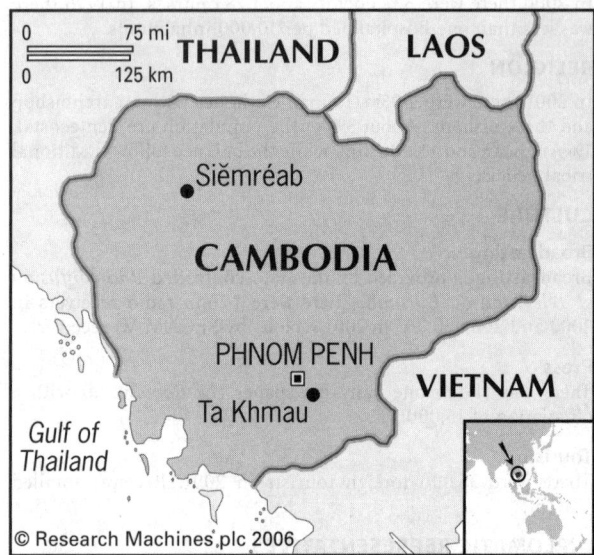

Preah Reach Ana Pak Kampuchea
(Kingdom of Cambodia)

Capital: Phnom Penh
Population projection, 2010: 15·53m.
GDP per capita, 2003: (PPP$) 2,078
HDI/world rank: 0·571/130

KEY HISTORICAL EVENTS

Cambodia was made a French protectorate in 1863. A nationalist movement began in the 1930s, and anti-French feeling strengthened in 1940–41 when the French submitted to Japanese demands for bases in Cambodia. Anti-French guerrillas, active from 1945, gave the impetus to a communist-led revolution. A fragile peace was established before Cambodia gained independence in 1953 but in 1967 the Khmer Rouge took up arms to support peasants against a rice tax. Their aim was to establish a communist rice-growing dynasty, a combination of Maoism and ancient xenophobic nationalism. From 1970 hostilities extended throughout most of the country involving US and North Vietnamese forces. During 1973 direct US and North Vietnamese participation came to an end, leaving a civil war which continued with large-scale fighting between the Khmer Republic, supported by US arms, and the United National Cambodian Front including 'Khmer Rouge' communists, supported by North Vietnam and China. After unsuccessful attempts to capture Phnom Penh in 1973 and 1974, the Khmer Rouge defeated the American backed leader Lon Nol in April 1975, when the remnants of the republican forces surrendered the city.

From 1975 the Khmer Rouge instituted a harsh and highly centralized regime. All cities and towns were forcibly evacuated and the citizens set to work in the fields. In 1978, in response to repeated border attacks, Vietnam invaded Cambodia. On 7 Jan. 1979 Phnom Penh was captured by the Vietnamese, and the Prime Minister, Pol Pot, fled. Over 2m. Cambodian lives were lost from 1975 to 1979. On 23 Oct. 1991 the warring factions and 19 countries signed an agreement in Paris instituting a ceasefire in Cambodia to be monitored by UN troops. Following the election of a constituent assembly in May 1993, a new constitution was promulgated on 23 Sept. 1993 restoring parliamentary monarchy. The Khmer Rouge continued hostilities, refusing to take part in the 1993 elections. By 1996 the Khmer Rouge had split into two warring factions. The leader of one, Ieng Sary, who had been sentenced to death in his absence for genocide, was pardoned by the King in Sept. 1996. In early Nov. 1996 Ieng Sary and some 4,000 of his forces threw in their lot with government forces.

In July 1997 Hun Sen, the second prime minister, engineered a coup which led to the exiling of first prime minister, Prince Norodom Ranariddh. However, on 30 March 1998 he returned with a Japanese-brokered plan to ensure 'fair and free' elections. These took place on 26 July 1998 against a background of violence and general intimidation. Hun Sen's Cambodian People's Party declared victory.

King Norodom Sihanouk abdicated in Oct. 2004 for health reasons and was succeeded by one of his sons, Norodom Sihamoni.

TERRITORY AND POPULATION

Cambodia is bounded in the north by Laos and Thailand, west by Thailand, east by Vietnam and south by the Gulf of Thailand. It has an area of about 181,035 sq. km (69,898 sq. miles).

Population, 11,437,656 (1998 census), of whom 5,926,248 were females. In 2003, 81·4% of the population lived in rural areas. 2005 population estimate: 14,071,000.

The UN gives a projected population for 2010 of 15·53m.

The capital, Phnom Penh, had an estimated population of 938,000 in 1999. Other cities are Kompong Cham and Battambang. Ethnic composition, 2000: Khmer, 85%; Chinese, 6%; Vietnamese, 3%; Cham, 2%; Lao-Thai, 1%.

Khmer is the official language.

SOCIAL STATISTICS

2002 estimated births, 467,000; deaths, 138,000. Rates, 2002 estimates (per 1,000 population): births, 33·8; deaths, 10·0. Infant mortality, 2001 (per 1,000 live births), 97. Expectation of life in 2003 was 52·4 years for males and 59·8 for females. Annual population growth rate, 1992–2002, 2·8%. Fertility rate, 2001, 4·9 children per woman.

CLIMATE

A tropical climate, with high temperatures all the year. Phnom Penh, Jan. 78°F (25·6°C), July 84°F (28·9°C). Annual rainfall 52" (1,308 mm).

CONSTITUTION AND GOVERNMENT

A parliamentary monarchy was re-established by the 1993 constitution. King Norodom Sihamoni (b. 14 May 1953; appointed 14 Oct. 2004 and sworn in 29 Oct. 2004) was chosen in the first ever meeting of the nine-member Throne Council following the abdication of his father King Norodom Sihanouk (b. 31 Oct. 1922) on health grounds. As the Cambodian constitution allowed for a succession only in the event of the monarch's death, a new law had to be approved after King Norodom Sihanouk announced his abdication.

Cambodia has a bicameral legislature. There is a 123-member *National Assembly,* which on 14 June 1993 elected Prince Sihanouk head of state. On 21 Sept. it adopted a constitution (promulgated on 24 Sept.) by 113 votes to five with two abstentions making him monarch of a parliamentary democracy. Its members are elected by popular vote to serve five-year terms. There is also a 61-member *Senate,* established in 1999.

National Anthem

'Nokoreach' ('Royal kingdom'); words by Chuon Nat, tune adapted from a Cambodian folk song.

RECENT ELECTIONS

Parliamentary elections were held on 27 July 2003. Under the UN-brokered constitution, a party had to win two-thirds of seats in the 122-member Parliament in order to form a government. With an 81% turnout, the Cambodian People's Party (KPK) won 68 seats with 47·5% of the vote, the royalist FUNCINPEC party of Prince Norodom Ranariddh won 24 seats with 20·5% and the party of the government critic Sam Rainsy won 31 seats with 22·1%.

CURRENT ADMINISTRATION

In June 2004, nearly a year after elections, the KPK and FUNCINPEC agreed to form a coalition government, including the Sam Rainsy Party.

In March 2006 the government comprised:

Prime Minister: Hun Sen; b. 1951 (KPK; sworn in on 30 Nov. 1998 and reappointed 14 July 2004 having first become prime minister in 1985).

Deputy Prime Ministers: Sar Kheng (also *Minister for Internal Affairs*), Sok An (also *Minister in Charge of the Office of the Council of Ministers*), Lu Lay Sreng (also *Minister of Rural Development*), Gen. Tea Banh (also *Minister for Defence*), Hor Nam Hong (also *Minister of Foreign Affairs and International Co-operation*).

Minister of State for Economy and Finance: Keat Chhon. *Commerce:* Cham Prasidh. *Land Management, Urban Affairs and Construction:* Im Chhun Lim. *Parliamentary Affairs and Inspection:* Mem Som An. *Planning:* Chhay Than. *Environment:* Dr Mok Mareth. *Religious Affairs:* Khun Haing. *Education, Youth and Sports:* Kol Pheng. *Without Portfolio:* You Hockry, Hong Sun Huot, Khy Taing Lim, Veng Sereyvuth, Nhim Vanda, Tav Senghuor, Serey Kosal.

Minister of Agriculture, Forestry and Fisheries: Chan Sarun. *Industry, Mines and Energy:* Suy Sem. *Social Affairs, War Veterans and Youth Rehabilitation:* Ith Sam Heng. *Water Resources:* Lim Kean Hor. *Information:* Khieu Kanharith. *Justice:* Ang Vong Vathana. *Post and Telecommunications:* So Khun. *Health:* Nuth Sokhom. *Public Works and Transport:* Sun Chanthol. *Culture:* Prince Sisowath Panara Sirivudh. *Tourism:* Lay Prohas. *Women's Affairs:* Ing Kantha Phavi. *Labour and Vocational Training:* Nhep Bun Chin.

Government Website: http://www.cambodia.gov.kh

CURRENT LEADERS

Hun Sen

Position
Prime Minister

Introduction
Hun Sen has been the dominant figure in Cambodian politics since becoming prime minister in 1985. His tenure has coincided with national recovery from the rule of the Khmer Rouge in the 1970s and the subsequent occupation by Vietnamese forces. He has been criticized for the tactics he has used to retain power. The economy has suffered from endemic corruption and a failure to attract foreign investment. However, Hun Sen has moved the economy away from state socialism towards one based on free market principles. A tribunal to investigate charges of genocide against prominent Khmer Rouge figures may conclude that turbulent period in the nation's history.

Early Life
Hun Sen was born into a peasant family in Kompang in 1952 and was educated in Phnom Penh by Buddhist monks. In 1970

he joined the Khmer Rouge, losing an eye in battle in 1975, but in 1977 he joined anti-Khmer Rouge forces operating out of Vietnam. After Vietnamese troops invaded Kampuchea in 1979, Hun Sen was appointed foreign minister in the newly-established People's Republic of Kampuchea. He became prime minister in 1985.

Career in Office
On assuming office, Hun Sen was confronted with a country in turmoil as pro- and anti-Vietnamese forces waged guerrilla war. In 1989 Vietnamese forces withdrew from the country, which was renamed the State of Cambodia. Buddhism was re-established as the state religion and Hun Sen announced the end of state socialism. In 1991 the UN brokered a peace treaty and a transitional government was installed, with Prince Sihanouk as head of state.

FUNCINPEC, the royalist party of Prince Norodom Ranariddh, was victorious at the 1993 elections but Hun Sen refused to relinquish power. A compromise government was formed with Ranariddh as first prime minister and Hun Sen as his deputy. In 1997 Hun Sen received international condemnation and saw Cambodia expelled from ASEAN for deposing Ranariddh while he was absent from the country. The Cambodian People's Party (KPK) won the 1998 elections but did not gain enough seats to form a government. Hun Sen agreed to head a coalition that included FUNCINPEC. Ranariddh was found guilty in absentia of arms smuggling but received a royal pardon and was named president of the national assembly. Pol Pot died that year, having been sentenced to life imprisonment for his crimes the previous year.

In 2001 Prince Norodom Sirivudh became leader of the opposition FUNCINPEC Party, having received a royal pardon in 1999 for the ten-year prison sentence he received in absentia for his alleged involvement in an assassination plot against Hun Sen. In the same year the east and west of the country were connected for the first time by a bridge across the Mekong River.

In 2002 Thailand agreed to extradite Sok Yoeun, a leading figure in the Cambodian Sam Rainsy Party, for alleged involvement in an assassination plot against Hun Sen. Sok Yoeun declared that the charges were part of a political attack and Amnesty International classified him as a prisoner of conscience.

In 2002 the KPK was the dominant party at the country's first multi-party local elections, although opposition groups claimed ballots were rigged. At the general elections of 2003 the KPK emerged as the single biggest party but fell short of the two thirds majority required to form the government. Coalition talks were frosty and relations were not improved when Hun Sen removed 17 FUNCINPEC politicians from senior posts, claiming neglect of duty. The opposition FUNCINPEC and Sam Rainsy parties agreed to join a ruling coalition but not under Hun Sen. The king finally confirmed Hun Sen as head of government in July 2004, after almost a year without a properly functioning administration.

After winning senate approval, Cambodia began talks with the UN on a tribunal to try former Khmer Rouge leaders for genocide. Negotiations were protracted and in 2003 the UN concluded that the tribunal was unlikely to function alongside Cambodia's existing judicial system, which claimed precedence over international law. The issue was further complicated by Khmer Rouge leaders transferring allegiance to the government in the years following Pol Pot's fall from power. Hun Sen himself was a soldier in the Khmer Rouge, though he denied claims that he ever held a senior position. In April 2005 the UN approved funding for the war crimes tribunal but in Aug. 2005 Hun Sen suggested it would be at risk if the international community failed to meet the difference between the US$13m. that Cambodia was expected to provide towards tribunal costs against the US$1·5m. it was offering.

In 2003 a Thai celebrity suggested that the religious complex of Angkor Wat had been stolen by Cambodia from Thailand. The comments caused outrage in Cambodia and led to a siege of the Thai embassy in Phnom Penh. Observers accused Hun Sen of aggravating the situation. In 2004 Hun Sen threatened to boycott a joint Asian-European summit if, as the EU was requesting, Myanmar was banned from attending. In the same year, with economic growth and foreign investment falling, Hun Sen outlined proposals to cut business costs, reduce red tape and counter corruption. He also promised to increase civil service salaries. However, he did not offer a timeframe for these developments. Entry into the WTO was ratified in Aug. 2004 after long delays.

Other significant problems confronting Hun Sen's government include deforestation and the spread of AIDS.

DEFENCE

The King is C.-in-C. of the armed forces. Defence expenditure in 2003 totalled US$68m. (US$5 per capita), representing 1·7% of GDP.

Army

Strength in 2002 was 75,000. There are also provincial forces numbering some 45,000 and paramilitary local forces organized at village level.

Navy

Naval personnel in 2002 totalled about 3,000 including a naval infantry of 1,500.

Air Force

Aviation operations were resumed in 1988 under the aegis of the Army. Personnel (2002), 2,000. There are 24 combat aircraft but serviceability is in doubt.

INTERNATIONAL RELATIONS

Cambodia is a member of the UN, WTO, Asian Development Bank, ASEAN, Mekong Group, IOM and the International Organization of the Francophonie.

ECONOMY

Agriculture accounted for 35·6% of GDP in 2002, industry 28·0% and services 36·4%.

Overview

Cambodia is one of the poorest countries in the world with a per capita income of US$290 in 2004. Efforts to reduce poverty have been thwarted by low agricultural productivity, high vulnerability to income shocks, inadequate and expensive infrastructure and a stifling regulatory environment.

The economy was devastated by the Khmer Rouge regime of 1975–79 when trade collapsed back to an agrarian barter system, the industrial base was destroyed and the banking system and domestic currency abolished. Economic progress remained slow until the Paris Peace Accord of 1991 brought about a downturn in the civil war. At the time of signing Cambodia faced rapid inflation, significant exchange rate depreciation, monetary instability, negative real interest rates and high fiscal deficits. Since the accord, and with the aid of the World Bank and the IMF, Cambodia has undertaken reforms to restore monetary stability and improve fiscal performance. Privatization of state-owned enterprises was completed by 1996 and the trade regime was liberalized as Cambodia joined ASEAN and prepared for WTO accession.

The average growth rate has been 6–7% since 1999. However, the percentage of people living in poverty is thought to have increased from 37% in 1996 to 42% by the mid-2000s. Government instability and endemic corruption continue to hamper private sector development, limiting foreign direct investment and eroding the tax base.

Currency

The unit of currency is the *riel* (KHR) of 100 *sen*. Foreign exchange reserves were US$782m. in Aug. 2004. Total money supply in May 2002 was 713,831m. riels. Inflation was 0·5% in 2003 and 5·6% in 2004.

Budget

In 2001 revenues were 1,520bn. riels and expenditures 2,329bn. riels.

Performance

Real GDP growth was 7·1% in 2003 and 7·7% in 2004. Total GDP in 2004 was US$4·6bn.

Banking and Finance

The National Bank of Cambodia (*Governor,* Chea Chanto) is the bank of issue. In 2001 there were operating: one state-owned bank; three specialized banks; 12 locally-incorporated private banks; and five foreign banks. In 2001, 11 banks were closed for failing to comply with new banking legislation.

ENERGY AND NATURAL RESOURCES

Electricity

Installed capacity was 35,000 kW in 2000. Production (2000) was around 229m. kWh. Consumption per capita in 2000 was an estimated 17 kWh. A long-term plan for hydro-electricity has been issued by the government.

Minerals

There are phosphates and high-grade iron-ore deposits. Some small-scale gold panning and gem (mainly zircon) mining is carried out.

Agriculture

The majority of the population is engaged in agriculture, fishing or forestry. Before the spread of war in the 1970s the high productivity provided for a low but well-fed standard of living for the peasant farmers, the majority of whom owned the land they worked before agriculture was collectivized. A relatively small proportion of the food production entered the cash economy. The war and unwise pricing policies led to a disastrous reduction in production, so much so that the country became a net importer of rice. Private ownership of land was restored by the 1989 Constitution. In 2001 there were 3·70m. ha. of arable land and 107,000 ha. of permanent crops.

A crop of 3·76m. tonnes of rice was produced in 2000. Production of other crops, 2000 (in 1,000 tonnes): bananas, 147; sugarcane, 140; maize, 95; cassava, 68; oranges, 63; coconuts, 56.

Livestock (2000): cattle, 3·0m.; pigs, 2·60m.; buffaloes, 710,000; poultry, 13m.

Forestry

Some 9·34m. ha., or 52·9% of the land area, were covered by forests in 2000. Nearly half of the forested area in 1995 was reserved by the government to be awarded to concessionaires. Such areas are not at present worked to any extent. The remainder is available for exploitation by the local residents, and as a result some areas are over-exploited and conservation is not practised. Timber exports have been banned since Dec. 1996. In 1990 the area under forests was 10·65m. ha. There are substantial reserves of pitch pine. Rubber plantations are a valuable asset with production at around 40,000 tonnes per year. There are plans to expand the area under rubber cultivation from 50,000 ha. to 800,000 ha. Timber production in 2001 was 10·04m. cu. metres. In 1997 forestry represented 43% of foreign trade.

Fisheries

2001 catch was approximately 397,200 tonnes (360,000 tonnes from inland waters).

INDUSTRY

Some development of industry had taken place before the spread of open warfare in 1970, but little was in operation by the 1990s except for rubber processing, sea-food processing, jute sack making and cigarette manufacture. Garment manufacture, rice milling, wood and wood products, rubber, cement and textiles production are the main industries. In the private sector small family concerns produce a wide range of goods. Light industry is generally better developed than heavy industry.

Labour

In 1996 the labour force was 5,322,000. Females constituted 52% of the labour force in 1999—the highest proportion of women in the workforce anywhere in the world. More than 60% of the economically active population are engaged in agriculture, fishing and forestry.

INTERNATIONAL TRADE

Foreign investment has been encouraged since 1989. Legislation of 1994 exempts profits from taxation for eight years, removes duties from various raw and semi-finished materials and offers tax incentives to investors in tourism, energy, the infrastructure and labour-intensive industries. External debt was US$2,907m. in 2002.

Imports and Exports

Imports and exports for calendar years in US$1m.:

	1998	1999	2000	2001	2002
Imports f.o.b.	1,165·8	1,591·0	1,939·3	2,094·0	2,313·5
Exports f.o.b.	800·5	1,129·3	1,401·1	1,571·2	1,750·1

The main imports include cigarettes, construction materials, petroleum products, machinery and motor vehicles. Main exports are timber, rubber, soybeans and sesame. Major import sources, 1998: Thailand (16%), Hong Kong (12%), Singapore (9%) and Mainland China (9%). Principal export destinations, 1998: USA (37%), Singapore (17%), Thailand (10%) and Germany (9%).

COMMUNICATIONS

Roads

There were about 12,323 km of roads in 2000, of which 16·2% were paved. 312,303 passenger cars were in use in 2000, 18,918 buses and coaches, and 49,036 trucks and vans. There were 196 fatalities in road accidents in 1999.

Rail

Main lines link Phnom Penh with Sisophon near the Thai border and the port of Kompong Som (total 601 km, metre gauge). After a long period of disruption owing to political unrest, limited services were restored on both lines in 1992. Passenger-km travelled in 2000 came to 15m. and freight tonne-km to 91m.

Civil Aviation

Pochentong airport is 8 km from Phnom Penh and handled 895,000 passengers (670,000 on international flights) in 2001. There are regular domestic services, and in 2003 Mekong Airlines flew to Hong Kong, Kuala Lumpur and Singapore, President Airlines flew to Hong Kong and Taipei, and Royal Phnom Penh Airways and Siem Riep Airways International operated services to Bangkok.

Shipping

There is an ocean port at Kompong Som; the port of Phnom Penh can be reached by the Mekong (through Vietnam) by ships of between 3,000 and 4,000 tonnes. In 2002 merchant shipping totalled 2,426,000 GRT, including oil tankers 141,000 GRT.

Telecommunications

There are telephone exchanges in all the main towns. In 2002 Cambodia had 415,400 telephone subscribers (30·1 per 1,000 persons), of which mobile phone subscribers numbered 380,000. In 2002, 91·5% of all telephone subscribers were mobile phone subscribers—among the highest ratios of mobile to fixed-line subscribers in the world. There were 27,000 PCs in use in 2002 (2·0 for every 1,000 persons) and 5,600 fax machines. In 2002 there were 30,000 Internet users.

Postal Services

In 2003 there were 79 post offices, or one for every 179,000 persons.

SOCIAL INSTITUTIONS

Justice

The population in penal institutions in 2002 was 6,128. In March 2003 the government announced plans to establish a special court in partnership with the UN to try leaders of the former Khmer Rouge regime.

Education

In 2001–02 there were 2,705,453 pupils and 54,519 teachers in 5,741 primary schools, and in general secondary education 24,884 teachers for 465,039 pupils. In 1994–95 there were 16,350 students in vocational establishments. There is a university (with 8,400 students and 350 academic staff in 1995–96) and a fine arts university. Adult literacy in 2003 was 73·6% (male, 84·7%; female, 64·1%).

In 2000–01 total expenditure on education came to 1·9% of GNP and 10·1% of total government spending.

Health

In 2000 there were 2,047 physicians, 209 dentists, 8,085 nurses and 3,040 midwives. Only 30% of the population had access to safe drinking water in 2000.

RELIGION

The Constitution of 1989 reinstated Buddhism as the state religion; it had 10·8m. adherents in 2001. About 2,800 monasteries were active in 1994. There are small Roman Catholic and Muslim minorities.

CULTURE

World Heritage Sites

Angkor was inscribed on the UNESCO World Heritage List in 1992. The Archeological Park contains the Temple of Angkor Wat and the Bayon Temple at Angkor Thom.

Broadcasting

Broadcasting is provided by the state-owned Voice of the People of Cambodia and Cambodian Television (colour by PAL). There were 1·48m. radio sets in 2000 and 102,000 TV sets in 2001.

Press

There are 21 newspapers, two of which are in English.

Tourism

In 2002 there were 787,000 foreign visitors, up from 25,000 in 1991. Tourist numbers in the 1990s increased at a faster rate in Cambodia than in any other country. Receipts in 2002 totalled US$379m.

DIPLOMATIC REPRESENTATIVES

Of Cambodia in the United Kingdom (Wellington Building, 28–32 Wellington Rd, London, NW8 9SP)
Ambassador: Hor Nambora.

Of the United Kingdom in Cambodia (29 St. 75, Phnom Penh)
Ambassador: David Reader.

Of Cambodia in the USA (4530 16th St., NW, Washington, D.C., 20011)
Ambassador: Ek Sereywath.

Of the USA in Cambodia (1 St. 96, Phnom Penh)
Ambassador: Joseph A. Mussomeli.

Of Cambodia to the United Nations
Ambassador: Chem Widhya.

Of Cambodia to the European Union
Ambassador: Vacant.
Roving Ambassador (Francophonie): Yao Chant Rith.

FURTHER READING

Chandler, D. P., *A History of Cambodia*. 2nd ed. Boulder (CO), 1996

Jarvis, Helen, *Cambodia*. [Bibliography] ABC-Clio, Oxford and Santa Barbara (CA), 1997

Martin, M. A, *Cambodia: A Shattered Society*. California Univ. Press, 1994

Peschoux, C., *Le Cambodge dans la Tourmente: le Troisième Conflit Indochinois, 1978–1991*. Paris, 1992.—*Les 'Nouveaux' Khmers Rouges*. Paris, 1992

Short, Philip, *Pol Pot: The History of a Nightmare*. John Murray, London, 2004

National Statistical Office: National Institute of Statistics, Ministry of Planning, 386 Monivong Boulevard, Phnom Penh.
Website: http://www.nis.gov.kh/

CAMEROON

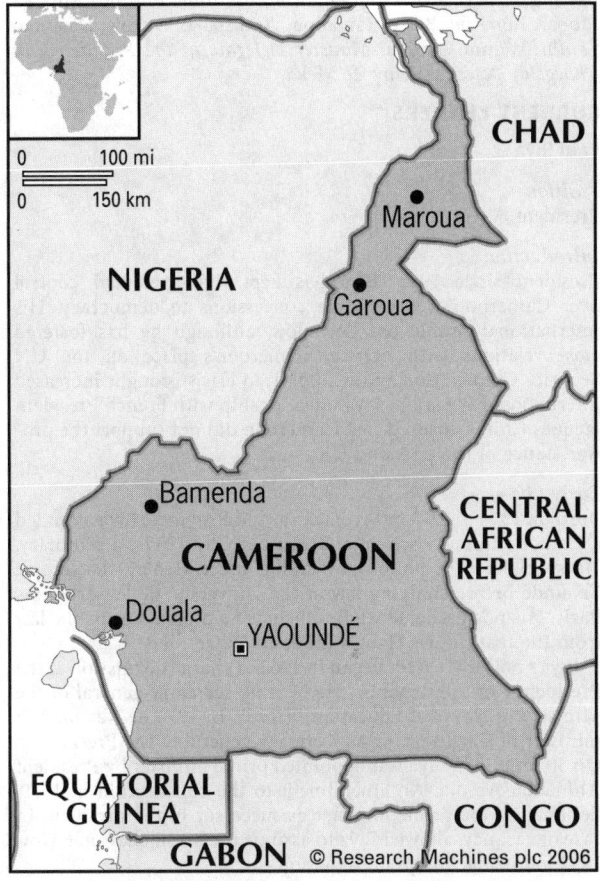

Populations du Cameroun (UPC), founded in 1948, became the major nationalist party, calling for independence and 'reunification' with British Cameroons. In Dec. 1956, when elections were held prior to self-government, the UPC began a guerrilla war against the French and the new Cameroonian government. On 1 Jan. 1960 French Cameroun gained independence. The UPC guerrillas were largely defeated by 1963. On 11 Feb. 1961 British Southern Cameroons voted in a referendum to join ex-French Cameroun, while British Northern Cameroons chose to join Nigeria. The country's name was changed to the Republic of Cameroon in 1984.

TERRITORY AND POPULATION

Cameroon is bounded in the west by the Gulf of Guinea, northwest by Nigeria, east by Chad and the Central African Republic, and south by the Republic of the Congo, Gabon and Equatorial Guinea. The total area (including inland water) is 475,440 sq. km. On 29 March 1994 Cameroon asked the International Court of Justice to confirm its sovereignty over the oil-rich Bakassi Peninsula, occupied by Nigerian troops. The dispute continued for eight years, with Equatorial Guinea also subsequently becoming involved. In Oct. 2002 the International Court of Justice rejected Nigeria's claims and awarded the peninsula to Cameroon. All parties agreed to accept the Court's judgment. At the last census, in 1987, the population was 10,494,000. Estimate (2005) 16·32m.; density, 34·3 per sq. km.

The UN gives a projected population for 2010 of 17·68m.

In 2003, 51·4% of the population were urban.

The areas, estimated populations and chief towns of the ten provinces are:

Province	Sq. km	Estimate 2001	Chief town	Estimate 2001
Adamaoua	63,691	723,600	Ngaoundéré	189,800
Centre	68,926	2,501,200	Yaoundé	1,248,200
Est	109,011	755,100	Bertoua	173,000
Extrême-Nord	34,246	2,721,500	Maroua	271,700
Littoral	20,239	2,202,300	Douala	1,494,700
Nord (Bénoué)	65,576	1,227,000	Garoua	356,900
Nord-Ouest	17,810	1,840,500	Bamenda	316,100
Ouest	13,872	1,982,100	Bafoussam	242,000
Sud	47,110	534,900	Ebolowa	79,500
Sud-Ouest	24,471	1,242,700	Buéa	47,300

The population is composed of Sudanic-speaking people in the north (Fulani, Sao and others) and Bantu-speaking groups, mainly Bamileke, Beti, Bulu, Tikar, Bassa and Duala, in the rest of the country. The official languages are French and English.

SOCIAL STATISTICS

2000 estimates: births, 549,000; deaths, 221,000. Rates, 2000 estimates (per 1,000 population): birth, 36·3; death, 14·6. Annual population growth rate, 1992–2002, 2·4%. Infant mortality, 2001, 96 per 1,000 live births. Life expectancy in 2003: males, 45·1 years; females, 46·5. Fertility rate, 2001, 4·8 children per woman.

CLIMATE

An equatorial climate, with high temperatures and plentiful rain, especially from March to June and Sept. to Nov. Further inland, rain occurs at all seasons. Yaoundé, Jan. 76°F (24·4°C), July 73°F (22·8°C). Annual rainfall 62" (1,555 mm). Douala, Jan. 79°F (26·1°C), July 75°F (23·9°C). Annual rainfall 160" (4,026 mm).

CONSTITUTION AND GOVERNMENT

The constitution was approved by referendum on 20 May 1972 and became effective on 2 June; it was amended in Jan. 1996. It

République du Cameroun
(Republic of Cameroon)

Capital: Yaoundé
Population projection, 2010: 17·68m.
GDP per capita, 2003: (PPP$) 2,118
HDI/world rank: 0·497/148

KEY HISTORICAL EVENTS

The name Cameroon derives from *camaráes* (prawns), introduced by Portuguese navigators. Called Kamerun in German and Cameroun in French, the estuary was later called the Cameroons River by British navigators. The Duala people living there were traders, selling slaves and later palm oil to Europeans. On 12 July 1884 they signed a treaty establishing German rule over Kamerun. Originally covering the Duala's territory on the Wouri, this German colony later expanded to cover a large area inland, home to a number of African peoples. In the First World War Allied forces occupied the territory which was partitioned between France and Britain. British Cameroons consisted of British Southern Cameroons and British Northern Cameroons, adjoining Nigeria. France's mandated territory of Cameroun occupied most of the former German colony. The Dualas continued to take the lead in anti-colonial protest.

In 1946 the French and British territories became Trust Territories of the UN. In French Cameroun the *Union des* provides for a *President* as head of state and government. The President is directly elected for a five-year term, and there is a *Council of Ministers* whose members must not be members of parliament.

The *National Assembly*, elected by universal adult suffrage for five years, consists of 180 representatives. After 1966 the sole legal party was the Cameroon People's Democratic Movement (RDPC), but in Dec. 1990 the National Assembly legalized opposition parties.

National Anthem
'O Cameroon, Thou Cradle of our Fathers'/'O Cameroun, Berceau de nos Ancêtres'; words by R. Afame, tune by R. Afame, S. Bamba and M. Nko'o.

GOVERNMENT CHRONOLOGY
Presidents since 1960. (UC = Cameroonian Union; UNC = Cameroonian National Union; RDPC = Cameroonian People's Democratic Rally)

1960–82	UC, UNC	Ahmadou Babatoura Ahidjo
1982–	UNC, RDPC	Paul Biya

RECENT ELECTIONS
Presidential elections were held on 11 Oct. 2004. Incumbent Paul Biya was re-elected with 70·9% of the votes ahead of John Fru Ndi with 17·4%, Adamou Ndam Njoya with 4·5% and Garga Haman Adji with 3·7%. The opposition denounced the election as fraudulent. Turnout was 82·8%.

The most recent National Assembly elections were held on 30 June and 15 Sept. 2002. The conservative Cameroon People's Democratic Movement (Rassemblement Démocratique du Peuple Camerounais; RDPC) won 149 seats, Social-Democratic Front (Front Social-Démocratique; SDF) 22, Democratic Union of Cameroon (Union Démocratique du Cameroun; UDC) 5, Union of the Peoples of Cameroon (Union des Populations du Cameroun; UPC) 3 and National Union for Democracy and Progress (Union Nationale pour la Démocratie et le Progrès; UNDP) 1.

CURRENT ADMINISTRATION
President: Paul Biya; b. 1933 (RDPC; assumed office 6 Nov. 1982, elected 14 Jan. 1984, re-elected 24 April 1988, also 10 Oct. 1992, 12 Oct. 1997 and once again re-elected 11 Oct. 2004).

In March 2006 the cabinet comprised:

Prime Minister: Ephraïm Inoni; b. 1947 (RDPC; in office since 8 Dec. 2004).

Deputy Prime Minister for Justice, Guardian of the Seals: Amadou Ali.

Minister of State for Culture: Ferdinand Léopold Oyono. *Planning, Programming and Regional Development:* Augustin Frederick Kodock. *Posts and Telecommunications:* Bello Bouba Maigari. *Territorial Administration and Decentralization:* Marafa Hamidou Yaya. *Town Planning and Housing:* Lekene Donfack. *Secretary General at the Presidency:* Jean Marie Atangana Mebara.

Minister for Agriculture: Clobaire Tchatat. *Basic Education:* Adama Haman. *Commerce:* Luc Magoire Mbarga Atangana. *Communication:* Pierre Moukoko Mbonjo. *Economy and Finance:* Polycarpe Abah Abah. *Employment and Professional Training:* Zacharie Perevet. *Energy and Water Resources:* Alphonse Siyam Siwé. *Environment and Nature Protection:* Pierre Hélé. *External Relations:* Laurent Esso. *Forests and Wildlife:* Egbe Achu Hilman. *Health:* Urbain Olanguena Awono. *Higher Education:* Jacques Fame Ndongo. *Industry, Mines and Technological Development:* Charles Salé. *Labour and Social Insurance:* Robert Nkili *Lands and Land Titles:* Louis Marie Abogo Nkono. *Livestock, Fisheries and Animal Industries:* Aboubakari Sarki. *Promotion of Women and Family Affairs:* Suzanne Bombak. *Public Service and Administrative Reforms:* Benjamin Amama Amama. *Public*

Works: Martin Okouda. *Scientific Research and Innovation:* Madeleine Tchuenté. *Secondary Education:* Louis Bapes Bapes. *Small and Medium-Sized Enterprises, Social Economy and Handicrafts:* Bernard Messengue Avom. *Social Affairs:* Cathérine Bakang Mbock. *Sports and Physical Education:* Philippe Mbarga Mboa. *Tourism:* Baba Hamadou. *Transport:* Dakole Daissala. *Youth:* Adoum Garoua. *Minister Delegate at the Presidency in Charge of Defence:* Remy Ze Meka.

CURRENT LEADERS
Paul Biya

Position
President

Introduction
President since 1982, Biya has kept tight personal control over Cameroon, despite some concessions to democracy. His international profile has been low, although he has fostered close relations with France. Cameroon's place on the UN Security Council during the 2003 Iraq crisis brought increased international attention. Biya's relationship with French President Jacques Chirac ensured that Cameroon did not support the pro-war stance of the USA and UK.

Early Life
Born on 13 Feb. 1933 in Mvomeka'a, Sud Province, Biya attended a Catholic mission school and, in the early 1950s, a seminary. He specialized in philosophy at the Lycée Général Leclerc in Yaoundé before studying law at the Université de la Sorbonne, Paris. His postgraduate studies included a diploma in public law from the Institut des Hautes Etudes d'Outre-Mer.

Biya's political career began in 1962 as chargé de mission at the Presidency of the Republic. He became secretary-general of the Ministry of National Education in 1965. In 1970 he was made a minister of state, serving as secretary-general to the Presidency. On 30 June 1975 Biya was appointed prime minister by President Ahmadou Ahidjo. An amendment to the constitution in 1979, designating the prime minister as successor to the president in case of vacancy, allowed Biya to assume the presidency on 6 Nov. 1982 following Ahidjo's resignation.

Career in Office
The succession, although constitutional, was not peaceful. In Aug. 1983 Biya forced Ahidjo into exile, and then consolidated his position by replacing Ahidjo's northern supporters with fellow southerners. Direct presidential elections by universal suffrage were instituted in Jan. 1984, which Biya won. Despite his initial democratic and modernizing aspirations, freedom of speech and the press were soon curtailed, largely as a result of problems with the old regime. The Republican Guard revolt of April 1984 provoked Biya to reform the sole political party, the Cameroon National Union (UNC), which was seen as Ahidjo's personal support base. Transformed into the Cameroon People's Democratic Movement (RDPC; Rassemblement Démocratique du Peuple Camerounais), it elected Biya as party president in March 1985.

In the early 1980s Cameroon's economy suffered from a downturn in the commodity export trade. Biya only admitted the severity of the economic crisis in 1987, submitting the national economy to scrutiny and assistance from the World Bank. Despite popular dissatisfaction, he was re-elected in April 1988.

Opposition political parties were legalized in Dec. 1990, although the delay in organizing multi-party elections and a ban on opposition party meetings caused rioting and a general strike in 1991. Biya relented in Oct. promising elections, which took place in March 1992. The RDPC was forced into coalition with the Movement for the Defence of the Republic (MDR; Mouvement pour la Défense de la République) to attain a majority in the National Assembly. Biya himself was re-elected in Oct. by a narrow majority.

Conflict over the Bakassi Peninsula, on the Nigerian border, and its oil and fishing rights began when the Nigerian leader Gen. Abacha sent troops to claim the area. Biya responded with military force and appealed to the International Court of Justice, which eventually ruled in Cameroon's favour in 2002.

The presidential elections of Oct. 1997 were boycotted by the three main opposition parties after a year of popular unrest. The removal of elected mayors after the 1996 municipal elections and the Supreme Court's controversial rulings concerning the May 1997 National Assembly elections were two of the more prominent causes of the boycott. Biya was re-elected with a large majority of the vote.

Anglophone separatist unrest has marked the latter years of Biya's presidency. The secessionist Southern Cameroon National Council (SCNC), which claims to represent the country's 5m. English speakers, has been repeatedly targeted by the government and its leaders charged with treason. Biya's government has been heavily criticized by the international community for corruption and human rights abuses. In 1998 Transparency International, the Berlin-based anti-corruption organization, classed Cameroon as the most corrupt country of the 85 covered by their survey. Amnesty International claims that extrajudicial executions and politically-motivated detentions continue despite international pressure.

In parliamentary elections in 2002 the RDPC won 149 of the 180 seats in National Assembly. On 11 Oct. 2004 Biya was re-elected for a further presidential term with over 70% of the vote, although opposition parties alleged widespread fraud and international observers said the poll lacked credibility in key areas.

DEFENCE

The President of the Republic is C.-in-C. of the armed forces. Defence expenditure totalled US$172m. in 2003 (US$11 per capita), representing 1·4% of GDP.

Army

Total strength (2002) is 12,500 and includes a Presidential Guard; there is a Gendarmerie 9,000 strong.

Navy

Personnel in 2002 numbered 1,300. There are bases at Douala (HQ), Limbe and Kribi.

Air Force

Aircraft availability is low because of funding problems. Personnel (2002), 300. There are 15 combat aircraft.

INTERNATIONAL RELATIONS

Cameroon is a member of the UN, WTO, the Commonwealth, the African Union, African Development Bank, IOM, OIC, Islamic Development Bank, International Organization of the Francophonie, the Lake Chad Basin Commission and is an ACP member state of the ACP-EU relationship.

ECONOMY

In 2002 agriculture accounted for 44·2% of GDP, industry 19·1% and services 36·7%.

Overview

Agriculture is the economy's key sector, employing two-thirds of the working population. Cameroon's primary export is oil, contributing nearly half of GDP in 2002. Export crops have suffered from low world prices, ageing plantations and disruption in the coffee and cocoa sector. Since the devaluation of the currency in 1994, annual inflation has decreased from 32·5% to 4·5% in 2003. Cameroon's external debt was significantly reduced by the devaluation, though remained high at 80% of

GDP in 2001. Privatization commenced fairly late, in 1995. In the first two waves of reform, privatization has been undertaken and completed in the major export, infrastructure, banking and insurance sectors. Despite structural reforms to the economy, Cameroon's major weaknesses, corruption and poor resource management, remain severe. Cameroon signed a new agreement with the IMF in 2000 giving it access to US$139m. Cameroon's exchange rate is pegged to the euro.

Currency

The unit of currency is the *franc CFA* (XAF) with a parity of 655·957 francs CFA to one euro. In April 2002 foreign exchange reserves were US$508m. (negligible in 1997) and total money supply was 644,230m. francs CFA. Gold reserves were 30,000 troy oz in June 2002. Inflation in 2004 was 0·3%.

Budget

The financial year used to end on 30 June but since 2003 has been the calendar year. In 2000–01 revenues totalled 1,326bn. francs CFA and expenditures 1,175bn. francs CFA.

VAT, introduced in 1999, is 19·2%.

Performance

Real GDP growth was 3·5% in 2004 (4·1% in 2003). Total GDP in 2004 was US$14·7bn.

Banking and Finance

The *Banque des Etats de l'Afrique Centrale* (*Governor*, Jean-Félix Mamalepot) is the sole bank of issue. There are in addition nine commercial banks, three development banks and five other financial institutions.

The Douala Stock Exchange was opened in April 2003.

ENERGY AND NATURAL RESOURCES

Environment

Cameroon's carbon dioxide emissions from the consumption and flaring of fossil fuels in 2002 were the equivalent of 0·4 tonnes per capita.

Electricity

Installed capacity in 2000 was 0·9m. kW. Total production in 2000 was 3·44bn. kWh (97% hydro-electric), with consumption per capita (2000) 231 kWh.

Oil and Gas

Oil production (2003), mainly from Kole oilfield, was 3·5m. tonnes. In 2002 there were proven reserves of 400m. bbls. In June 2000 the World Bank approved funding for a 1,000-km US$4bn. pipeline to run from 300 new oil wells in Chad through Cameroon to the Atlantic Ocean. Oil started pumping in July 2003. Revenues are projected to reach US$20m. per annum.

Minerals

Tin ore and limestone are extracted. There are deposits of aluminium, bauxite, uranium, nickel, gold, cassiterite and kyanite. Aluminium production in 2001 was 81,000 tonnes.

Agriculture

In 2001 there were 5·96m. ha. of arable land and 1·20m. ha. of permanent crops. 33,000 ha. were irrigated in 2001. There were 500 tractors in 2001. Main agricultural crops (with 2000 production in 1,000 tonnes): cassava, 2,067; plantains, 1,403; sugarcane, 1,350; bananas, 850; maize, 850; sorghum, 500; yams, 260; seed cotton, 220; sweet potatoes, 180; dry beans, 170; groundnuts, 160; palm oil, 140; cocoa beans, 120; pumpkins and squash, 120.

Livestock (2000): 5·9m. cattle; 3·88m. sheep; 3·85m. goats; 1·43m. pigs; 30m. chickens.

Livestock products (in 1,000 tonnes), 2000: beef and veal, 90; pork, bacon and ham, 18; lamb and mutton, 17; goat meat, 15; poultry meat, 24; cow's milk, 125; goat's milk, 42; eggs, 14.

Forestry

Forests covered 23·86m. ha. in 2000 (51·3% of the total land area), ranging from tropical rain forests in the south (producing hardwoods such as mahogany, ebony and sapele) to semi-deciduous forests in the centre and wooded savannah in the north. Timber production in 2001 was 10·99m. cu. metres.

Fisheries

In 2001 the total catch was 111,031 tonnes (58,531 tonnes from sea fishing).

INDUSTRY

Manufacturing is largely small-scale, with only some 30 firms employing more than ten workers. Output in 1,000 tonnes: cement (2001), 980; distillate fuel oil (2000), 459; residual fuel oil (2000), 397; petrol (2000), 323; kerosene (2000), 250; sugar (2002), 104. In 2001, 374m. litres of beer and 2·8bn. cigarettes were produced. There are also factories producing shoes, soap, oil and food products.

Labour

In 1996 the workforce numbered 5,500,000 (62% males), of whom over 50% were occupied in agriculture.

Trade Unions

The principal trade union federation is the *Organisation des syndicats des travailleurs camerounais* (OSTC), established on 7 Dec. 1985 to replace the former body, the UNTC.

INTERNATIONAL TRADE

Foreign debt was US$8,502m. in 2002.

Imports and Exports

In 1999 total imports amounted to US$1,315·8m. and exports to US$1,587·7m. Principal exports (in US$1m.), 1999: crude oil, 552·1; sawn wood, 191·1; cocoa, 162·5; coffee, 121·0; aluminium, 94·5.

Main import suppliers, 1999: France, 28%; Nigeria, 12%; Germany, 6%. Main export markets: Italy, 22%; France, 18%; Spain, 13%.

COMMUNICATIONS

Roads

There were about 34,300 km of classified roads in 2002, of which 4,300 km were paved. In 2002 there were 97,500 passenger cars and 82,200 commercial vehicles.

Rail

Cameroon Railways (*Regifercam*), 1,016 km in 2000, link Douala with Nkongsamba and Ngaoundéré, with branches from M'Banga to Kumba and Makak to M'Balmayo. In 2000 railways carried 1·4m. passengers and 1·8m. tonnes of freight.

Civil Aviation

There are 45 airports including three international airports at Douala, Garoua and Yaoundé (Nsimalen). In 2001 Douala handled 485,000 passengers (386,000 on international flights). In 2003 Cameroon Airlines (Camair), the national carrier, operated on domestic routes and provided international services to Abidjan, Bamako, Bangui, Brazzaville, Bujumbura, Cotonou, Dakar, Johannesburg, Kigali, Kinshasa, Lagos, Libreville, Malabo, N'Djaména, Paris and Pointe-Noire. In 1999 scheduled airline traffic of Cameroon-based carriers flew 6·0m. km, carrying 293,000 passengers (204,000 on international flights).

Shipping

In 2002 the merchant marine totalled 17,000 GRT. In 2001 vessels totalling 1,243,000 NRT entered ports. The main port is Douala; other ports are Bota, Campo, Garoua (only navigable in the rainy season), Kribi and Limbo-Tiko.

Telecommunications

In 2002 there were 785,500 telephone subscribers, or 49·7 per 1,000 inhabitants. There were 675,700 mobile phone subscribers in 2002 and 72,000 PCs were in use (4·6 per 1,000 persons). Cameroon had 60,000 Internet users in 2002.

Postal Services

There were 259 post offices in 2003.

SOCIAL INSTITUTIONS

Justice

The Supreme Court sits at Yaoundé, as does the High Court of Justice (consisting of nine titular judges and six surrogates all appointed by the National Assembly). There are magistrates' courts situated in the provinces.

The population in penal institutions in 2002 was 20,000 (129 per 100,000 of national population).

Education

In 2000–01 there were 5,310 teachers for 125,674 children in pre-primary schools and (1999–2000) 32,246 teachers for 2,237,083 pupils in primary schools. In 2000–01 there were 554,830 secondary level pupils in general programmes.

In 2000–01, 68,495 students were in tertiary education. In 1991 there were 33 teacher training colleges and five new institutions of higher education. Total staff: 1,086. In 1994–95 there were six universities and one Roman Catholic university, four specialized *Ecoles Nationales*, an *Ecole Supérieure* for posts and telecommunications, six specialized institutes, a national school of administration and magistracy and a faculty of Protestant theology. In 1995–96 there were 15,220 university students and 830 academic staff. The adult literacy rate in 2003 was 67·9% (77·0% among males and 59·8% among females).

In 2000–01 total expenditure on education came to 3·4% of GNP and 12·5% of total government spending.

Health

In 1988 there were 629 hospitals with 27 beds per 10,000 inhabitants. In 1996 there were 1,031 physicians, 56 dentists, 5,112 nurses and 70 midwives.

RELIGION

In 2001 there were 4·18m. Roman Catholics, 3·35m. Muslims and 3·27m. Protestants. Some of the population follow traditional animist religions. In May 2005 there was one cardinal.

CULTURE

World Heritage Sites

The Dja Faunal Reserve was inscribed on the UNESCO World Heritage List in 1987. Surrounded by the Dja River, it is one of Africa's largest rainforests.

Broadcasting

The state-controlled Cameroon Radio Television provides home, national, provincial and urban radio programmes and a TV service (colour by PAL). There were 2·4m. radio receivers in 2000 and 1·1m. TV receivers in 2001.

Press

In 1997 there was one national government-owned daily newspaper with a circulation of 66,000 and about 100 other periodicals, including 20 weeklies.

Tourism

In 2000 there were 277,000 foreign tourists, bringing revenue of US$39m.

DIPLOMATIC REPRESENTATIVES

Of Cameroon in the United Kingdom (84 Holland Park, London, W11 3SB)
High Commissioner: Dr Samuel Libock Mbei.

Of the United Kingdom in Cameroon (Ave. Winston Churchill, BP 547, Yaoundé)
High Commissioner: Richard Wildash, LVO.

Of Cameroon in the USA (2349 Massachusetts Ave., NW, Washington, D.C., 20008)
Ambassador: Jérôme Mendouga.

Of the USA in Cameroon (Ave. Rosa Parks, BP 817, Yaoundé)
Ambassador: Niels Marquardt.

Of Cameroon to the United Nations
Ambassador: Martin Belinga-Eboutou.

Of Cameroon to the European Union
Ambassador: Isabelle Bassong.

FURTHER READING

National Statistical Office: Direction de la Statistique et de la Comptabilité Nationale, Ministère du Plan et de l'Aménagement du Territoire, Yaoundé.

Ardener, E., *Kingdom on Mount Cameroon: Studies in the History of the Cameroon Coast 1500–1970.* Berghahn Books, Oxford, 1996

DeLancey, M. W., *Cameroon: Dependence and Independence.* London, 1989

CANADA

Capital: Ottawa
Population projection, 2010: 33·68m.
GDP per capita, 2003: (PPP$) 30,677
HDI/world rank: 0·949/5

KEY HISTORICAL EVENTS

The first human habitation in Canada dates from the last stages of the Pleistocene Ice Age up to 30,000 years ago. Mongoloid tribes from Asia crossed the Bering Strait by a land bridge in search of mammoth, bison and elk. These hunter-gatherers were the forefathers of some of Canada's native people referred to today as the First Nations. There are currently two other Aboriginal groups; the Inuit (Arctic people, formerly known as Eskimos) and the Métis. The Inuit were one of the last groups to arrive, around 1000 BC, whereas the Métis evolved from the union of natives and Europeans (mostly French).

The numerous tribes that made up the First Nations consisted of 12 major language groups with a number of sub groups with diverse spiritual beliefs, laws and customs. Around 6000 BC, during the Boreal Archaic age, the glaciers of the Canadian Shield melted and lakes were formed. The Iroquois speaking tribes, including the Mohawks and the Huron, settled along the St Lawrence River and the Great Lakes. Excellent farmers, they lived in large communities. Trade flourished but tribal wars were common. By 1000 BC the Early Woodland Culture had developed in the east. Among the eight tribes were the Algonquin, one of the largest language groups, who spread west to the Plains to hunt buffalo along with the Blackfoot, Sioux and Cree. The tribes of the Pacific Coast, such as the Tlingit and Salish, derived a living from whaling and salmon fishing and enjoyed a more elaborate social structure. The peoples in the north around Yukon and Mackenzie River basins and the Inuit around the Arctic were nomadic hunters foraging for limited food in small family groups. However, one factor common to all was that they were self-governing and politically independent.

In 1963 remains of a Viking settlement were found at L'Anse-aux-Meadows in Newfoundland dating from 1000 AD. Trade had been established between the Norse men and the Inuit but settlements were abandoned when the Norse withdrew from Greenland. John Cabot, an Italian navigator, commissioned by King Henry VII of England in 1497, charted the coasts around Labrador and Newfoundland and found them to have large resources of fish. The Frenchman, Jacques Cartier, discovered the Gulf of St Lawrence in 1534 and claimed it for the French crown. In the following years fisheries were set up by the English and French with Indians bringing valuable furs, mostly beaver, to trade for iron and other goods. Realising the potential, the French sent Samuel de Champlain in 1604 to establish a fur trade and organize a settlement. This he achieved in 1605 in an area called Acadia (now New Brunswick, Nova Scotia and Prince Edward Island). The French traded with the Algonquin and Huron and supported them during fierce raids by the Iroquois. In retaliation the Iroquois later became the fur trading allies of the Dutch and then the English. Champlain, having founded Quebec City, went on to explore Huron territory, now central Ontario, and is considered by many to be the father of New France.

English–French Rivalry
In opposition to French expansion, England sent numerous explorers such as Martin Frobisher, William Baffin and Henry Hudson to claim new territory. Colonies sprang up along the English coast and the Hudson Bay Company was formed in 1670 to gain a fur-trading monopoly over the area. Rivalry between the English and French for trade at Hudson Bay persisted throughout the 17th century. In 1713 the Treaty of Utrecht, signed by Queen Anne of England and Louis XIV, gave England complete control of the Hudson Bay territory, Acadia and Newfoundland. France, however, retained Cape Breton Island, the St Lawrence Islands and fishing rights in Newfoundland. Led by Gen. Wolfe, Britain's victory over France at the Battle of the Plains of Abraham in 1759 gained Quebec, and in 1760 Montreal too was taken. This brought an end to the Seven Years' War (1756–63) confirmed in 1763 by the Treaty of Paris in which all French Canadian territory was ceded to the British.

Relations with Indian tribes formerly allied to the French were strained and there was much resentment at the invasion of their lands by white settlers. The Royal Proclamation of 1763, administered by the Indian Department, ruled that aboriginal peoples could only sell land to crown representatives. Numerous treaties were signed over the following decades, redistributing thousands of acres of land. To soothe the British rule of a French speaking colony, the British government passed the Quebec Act in 1774 allowing French Canadians religious and linguistic freedom, the right to collect tithes and recognition of French civil law.

The attack on Montreal in 1775, during the American War of Independence, failed and Americans, loyal to Britain, sought refuge in Canada. Around 50,000 emigrated to Nova Scotia, from which New Brunswick was created in 1784. In an attempt to keep the peace the Constitutional Act of 1791 divided Quebec into Lower Canada (mostly French) and Upper Canada (mostly British from America).

Exploration continued on the Pacific Coast and into the Plains and the Northwest. Capt. James Cook charted the Pacific Coast from Vancouver to Alaska in 1778. From trading posts set up by the Hudson Bay Company (HBC) expeditions were made by traders including Samuel Hearne who, in 1771, was the first man to reach the Arctic Ocean by land. A rival company, the North West Company (NWC), was set up in Montreal in 1783. In 1793 Alexander Mackenzie, from the NWC, crossed the Rocky Mountains and reached the coast making him the first man to cross the continent. Competition between the two companies erupted into violence between new settlers and established traders, including the Métis who were hired, mainly by NWC, to transport furs and supply food. To resolve the conflict the British government pressed for the merger of the two companies. This was achieved in 1821.

After the American war against Britain in Canada in 1812 (which ended in stalemate), large numbers of English, Scottish and Irish settlers swelled the English-speaking population. By 1837 radical reformers were seeking accountable government with a broader electorate. Rebellions led by William Lyon Mackenzie in Upper Canada and by Louis-Joseph Papineau in Lower Canada were quashed by government troops. Following a report by Lord Durham, who was sent from England as governor-general to conduct an enquiry, the two colonies were united under one central government in 1841 with both enjoying equal representation. Vancouver Island was acknowledged to be British by the Oregon Boundary Treaty of 1846. The 1850s saw a significant period of growth. Railways were built and industry and commerce thrived, enhanced by the Reciprocity Treaty of 1854 with the USA.

Dominion Status
However, by the 1860s ethnic clashes had made Canada almost ungovernable. The American Civil War also posed a threat. Three political leaders, George Étienne Cartier (Conservative–Canada East), George Brown (Reform Movement–Canada West) and John A. Macdonald (Conservative–Canada West) formed a coalition government in 1864. Nova Scotia, New Brunswick and the Canadas (now Ontario and Quebec) were united in 1867 as the Dominion of Canada. What became known as the Constitution Act, confirmed the language and legal rights of the French and provided for the division of power between the federal government and the provinces. John Macdonald was elected prime minister.

One of the first actions of the new federal government was to purchase the Northwest Territories from the HBC, a move that led to rebellion by white settlers and the Métis, under Louis Riel. The result was the creation of Manitoba in 1870 with political power divided between the French and English. British Columbia joined the federation in 1871 and Prince Edward Island in 1873. The former agreed to join on the promise of a federally financed railway. To make way for new settlers from 1868–77 treaties were negotiated with Indians from Ontario to the Rocky Mountains. In return for moving to reserves the Indians were to receive financial support and other concessions. They were also to be assimilated into Christian society. In the years following the government failed in its obligations and many Plains Indians suffered poverty, starvation and disease. Later legislation even outlawed traditional practices such as the Sun Dance and the potlatch (exchange of gifts). Many Métis had moved out of Manitoba and settled further west but were not awarded the same rights as those of the Aboriginal Indians. Resistance grew, and Riel, who had emigrated to Montana, was urged to lead a revolt. In response, troops were rushed in by rail and the rebellion was crushed. The importance of the railway became evident and money was found for its completion across the Rockies. The railway was opened in 1885, the same year in which Riel was executed.

Prosperity and Reform
Following the death of Macdonald in 1891, the Liberal leader Wilfrid Laurier came to power in 1896 and there followed a period of growth and stability. Mineral resources of metal were found in British Columbia and Ontario as well as gold which precipitated the Klondike gold rush of 1897. The Yukon territory was established in 1898 to ensure Canadian jurisdiction over the exploitation of gold. The provinces of Saskatchewan and Alberta were created in 1905 each with its own premier and elected assembly. By 1911 the population in the provinces had doubled and there was a powerful business sector. When reformers called for action to alleviate conditions in overcrowded cities, health and welfare programmes were introduced. A new women's movement campaigned for equal rights and women's suffrage. Anti-monopoly legislation was passed in 1910. However, much industrial investment was backed by American money and many French Canadians began to agitate for autonomy. In 1910 Laurier founded the Canadian Navy with the provision that in time of

war it would be placed under British command. This further angered the French Canadians. Laurier's decision to negotiate a new trade agreement with the USA, coupled with the navy issue, lost him the 1911 election to the Conservatives. Robert Laird Borden became prime minister.

When the First World War broke out in 1914 thousands of British-born Canadians volunteered to fight. At first troops were under British command, but by the time conscription had been introduced in 1917 they were under Canadian leadership. Around 60,000 men lost their lives in the battles of Ypres, Vimy Ridge and Passendaele, and another 173,000 were wounded. Having won recognition for its contribution to the war effort, Canada participated as an independent state at the Paris Peace Conference and joined the League of Nations. At home the French Canadians had been bitterly opposed to Borden's implementation of conscription and to counteract this he formed a joint government of Liberals and Conservatives. This was split into the English speaking Unionists and the French speaking Liberals. At the election in 1917 the Unionists won every province but Quebec.

Women's suffrage was granted in 1918. 1921 saw the Liberals back in power under William Lyon Mackenzie King who strove to unify the nation and gain autonomy. This was achieved in 1931 by the Statute of Westminster in which Canada was granted complete independence. In the same year Norway formally recognized the Canadian title to the Sverdrup group of Arctic islands. Canada thus holds sovereignty in the whole Arctic sector north of the Canadian mainland.

Following the Wall Street Crash of 1929, the country chose the Conservatives under the leadership of Richard Bedford Bennett in the election of 1930. Despite measures to alleviate the effects of the depression and the severe drought in the prairies, Bennett was unsuccessful and in 1935 King was re-elected. King introduced a new Reciprocity Treaty (1936) with the USA, nationalized the Bank of Canada, created the Canadian Broadcasting Corporation and made available federal money to provide social services.

Post War Politics

Canada's contribution in the Second World War was even more extensive than that in the First World War although casualties were lower. A post-war plan introduced unemployment insurance, family allowances, veterans' benefits, subsidized housing, health plans and improved pensions. After the war industrial controls were lifted and trade was encouraged. Canada became a founder member of the United Nations in 1945 and has been active in a peacekeeping role ever since. King retired in 1948 to be succeeded by Louis St Laurent, a Quebec lawyer, who won an overwhelming victory in 1949. In the same year, Newfoundland—including Labrador—became a Canadian province thus completing the Confederation. Also in that year, Canada joined NATO.

An amendment to the Indian Act in 1959 increased opportunities for Indians to influence decisions affecting them, and in 1960 the federal government granted the franchise to all Indians, with several provinces following suit.

For 20 years after 1950 Canada enjoyed growth, prosperity and a 'baby boom'. The face of industrial Canada changed with the discovery of radium, petroleum and natural gas. Canada took a more active part in foreign affairs, especially in the Suez Canal crisis for which Lester B. Pearson, external affairs minister, won the Noble Peace Prize. The North American Air Defense Command (NORAD) was formed with the USA in 1957. In the same year, after 22 years of Liberal rule, the Conservatives won the election with John Diefenbaker as leader. However, internal struggles and an economic recession saw the return of the Liberals in 1963 under Pearson. During his five years as prime minister Canada gained a national flag, a social security system and medical care for all its citizens. Expo '67 was held in Montreal as part of the celebrations of the Centennial of

Canadian Confederation and the Order of Canada was instituted to award outstanding merit and service.

Having chosen Pierre Trudeau to succeed Pearson, the Liberals won the 1968 election. At the same time there was a revival of French nationalism, especially in Quebec, with the formation of the Parti Québécois (PQ) led by René Levasque. Keen to preserve national unity, Trudeau passed the Official Languages Act in 1969 which affirmed the equality of French and English in all governmental activities. However, in 1970 he had to send troops into Quebec following the murder of the Labour minister, Pierre Laporte, by the separatist Front de Libération du Québec. In 1976 the Olympic Games were hosted in Montreal. Also in that year a pledge on separatism won the PQ the provincial election and French became the official language of Quebec. Despite these milestones, a referendum to make the province an independent country was rejected by Quebec voters in 1980.

Indian Rights

In the sixties and seventies Indians sought special rights and settlement of their outstanding treaty claims. The National Indian Brotherhood was formed in 1968 to represent the interest of Indians at federal level. By 1973 the Department of Indian Affairs and Northern Development was instructed to resolve these claims. In 1982, with the exception of Quebec, the country agreed to a new constitution giving Canada, as opposed to the British Parliament, prerogative over all future constitutional changes. At the same time a charter of Rights and Freedoms was introduced recognizing the nation's multi-cultural heritage, affirming the existing rights of native peoples and the principle of equality of benefits to the provinces.

Retiring in 1984, Trudeau was succeeded by John Turner who was ousted the same year by the Conservative leader Brian Mulroney. In 1987 at a meeting in Meech Lake, a series of constitutional amendments were drawn up to win Quebec's acceptance of the new constitution. English Canadians objected to the Meech Lake Accord and it was rejected by Newfoundland and Manitoba. This failure sparked another separatist revival in Quebec leading to the drafting of the Charlottetown Accord incorporating extensive amendments, including recognition of Quebec as a 'distinct society', offering better representation in parliament, and self-government for indigenous peoples. This was defeated in a national referendum in 1992.

Mulroney negotiated a free trade agreement with the United States which went into effect in 1989. This was followed in 1994 by North American Free Trade Agreement (NAFTA) with the USA and Mexico. Voter opposition coupled with a recession in the early nineties forced Mulroney to resign in 1993. He was replaced by Kim Campbell, Canada's first female prime minister. In the Oct. election of that year, Campbell and the Conservatives suffered a major defeat retaining only two of their 154 seats. Led by Jean Chrétien, the Liberals won 177 seats and the Reform Party 52 seats. The PQ became the major opposition party with 54 seats.

Another referendum on Quebec's independence from Canada failed narrowly in 1995. Again in 1997 leaders of all provinces and territories (apart from Quebec) met in Calgary and signed a declaration recognizing the 'unique character' of Quebec's society. The following year the Supreme Court ruled that Quebec was prohibited from declaring itself independent without first negotiating an agreement with the federal government and other provinces.

In the 1990s further protests were made by native peoples anxious to claim their territory. In 1997 the Supreme Court ruled that two aboriginal groups had title to 22,000 square miles of ancestral lands in British Columbia. The following year a formal apology was issued by the government for the treatment Indian and Inuit peoples had received since the arrival of the Europeans. After decades of complex negotiations, the Inuit were granted their own territory of Nunavut in 1999, an area once part of the Northwest Territories. In the same year the government agreed that Indians and the Inuit should have the right of self-government.

Following a period of economic growth Chrétien's government made major tax cuts in 2000. In an attempt to form a more effective opposition, the Reform Party accepted the 'united alternative' proposed by party leader Preston Manning which resulted in the Canadian Alliance (Canadian Reform Conservative Alliance), a broad-based conservative party with Stockwell Day as its first leader. However, with the Progressive Conservative Party declining to join forces, Chrétien was returned for a third term in Nov. 2000 with an increased majority.

Chrétien stood down from the premiership in late 2003 and was replaced by his Liberal colleague, Paul Martin. Martin and his party soon became embroiled in a financial scandal over misuse of government money for advertising. In the Jan. 2006 general elections the Conservative Party, led by Stephen Harper, defeated the Liberals, taking power for the first time in 12 years.

TERRITORY AND POPULATION

Canada is bounded in the northwest by the Beaufort Sea, north by the Arctic Ocean, northeast by Baffin Bay, east by the Davis Strait, Labrador Sea and Atlantic Ocean, south by the USA and west by the Pacific Ocean and USA (Alaska). The area is 9,984,670 sq. km, of which 891,163 sq. km are fresh water. 2001 census population, 30,007,094 (15,693,393 females), giving a density of 3·0 per sq. km. In 2003, 80·4% of the population were urban. Population estimate, 1 July 2005, 32,270,500.

The UN gives a projected population for 2010 of 33·68m.

Population at previous censuses:

1851	2,436,297	1911	7,206,643	1971	21,568,311
1861	3,229,633	1921	8,787,949	1976[1]	22,992,604
1871	3,689,257	1931	10,376,786	1981	24,343,181
1881	4,324,810	1941	11,506,655	1986[1]	25,309,331
1891	4,833,239	1951	14,009,429	1991	27,296,859[2]
1901	5,371,315	1961	18,238,247	1996[1]	28,848,761[2]

[1]It became a statutory requirement to conduct a census every five years in 1971. [2]Excludes data from incompletely enumerated Indian reserves and Indian settlements.

Of the total population in 2001, 80·9% were Canadian-born. Alberta had the biggest population increase between 1996 and 2001 with 10·3%, whilst Newfoundland had the biggest population reduction with –7·0%, more than double the 2·9% rate of decline recorded between 1991 and 1996.

The population (2001) born outside Canada in the provinces was in the following ratio (%): Alberta, 14·9; British Columbia, 26·1; Manitoba, 12·1; New Brunswick, 3·1; Newfoundland, 1·6; Northwest Territories, 6·4; Nova Scotia, 4·6; Nunavut, 1·7; Ontario, 26·8; Prince Edward Island, 3·1; Quebec, 9·9; Saskatchewan, 5·0; Yukon, 10·6.

Figures for the 2001 census population according to ethnic origin (leading categories), were[1]:

Canadian	11,682,680	Chinese	1,094,700
English	5,978,875	Ukrainian	1,071,060
French	4,668,410	North American Indian	1,000,890
Scottish	4,157,210	Dutch	923,310
Irish	3,822,660	Polish	817,085
German	2,742,765	East Indian	713,330
Italian	1,270,370		

[1]Census respondents who reported multiple ethnic origins are counted for each origin they reported.

The aboriginal population (those persons identifying with at least one aboriginal group, and including North American Indian, Métis or Inuit) numbered 976,305 in 2001. In 2001, 59·1% of the population gave their mother tongue as English and 22·9% as French (English and French are both official languages); Chinese was reported as the third most common language, accounting for 2·9% of the total population. In 2001, 1·8m. residents were immigrants who arrived between 1991 and 2001, accounting for 6·2% of the total population; 58% came from Asia (including the Middle East), 20% from Europe, 11% from the Caribbean, Central and South America, 8% from Africa, and 3% from the USA.

Populations of Census Metropolitan Areas (CMA) and Cities (proper), 2001 census:

	CMA	City proper		CMA	City proper
Toronto	4,682,897	2,481,494	Halifax	359,183	119,292
Montreal	3,426,350	1,039,534	Victoria	311,902	74,125
Vancouver	1,986,965	545,671	Windsor	307,877	208,402
Ottawa-Hull	1,063,664	—	Oshawa	296,298	139,051
Ottawa	—	774,072	Saskatoon	225,927	196,811
Hull	—	66,246	Regina	192,800	178,225
Calgary	951,395	878,866	St John's	172,918	99,182
Edmonton	937,845	616,014	Sudbury	155,601	85,354
Quebec	682,757	169,076	Chicoutimi-		
Winnipeg	671,274	619,544	Jonquière	154,938	—
Hamilton	662,401	490,268	Chicoutimi	—	60,008
London	432,451	336,539	Jonquière	—	54,842
Kitchener	414,284	190,399	Sherbrooke	153,811	75,916
St Catharines-			Abbotsford	147,370	115,463
Niagara	377,009	—	Kingston	146,838	114,195
St Catharines	—	129,170	Trois Rivières	137,507	46,295
Niagara Falls	—	78,815	Saint John	122,678	69,661

SOCIAL STATISTICS

Statistics for period from July–June:

	Live births	Deaths
2000–01	327,107	219,114
2001–02	328,155	220,494
2002–03	330,523	224,702
2003–04	335,701	231,260

Average annual population growth rate, 1992–2002, 1·0%. Birth rate, 2003–04 (per 1,000 population), 10·5; death rate, 7·3. Marriages, 2002, numbered 146,738; divorces, 70,155. In 2002 the average age for marrying was 34·0 for males and 31·5 for females. Suicides, 2000, 3,605 (11·7 per 100,000 population). Life expectancy at birth, 2003, was 77·4 years for men and 82·4 years for women. Infant mortality, 2001, 5 per 1,000 live births; fertility rate, 2001, 1·6 children per woman.

CLIMATE

The climate ranges from polar conditions in the north to cool temperate in the south, but with considerable differences between east coast, west coast and the interior, affecting temperatures, rainfall amounts and seasonal distribution. Winters are very severe over much of the country, but summers can be very hot inland.

See individual provinces for climatic details.

CONSTITUTION AND GOVERNMENT

In Nov. 1981 the Canadian government agreed on the provisions of an amended constitution, to the end that it should replace the British North America Act and that its future amendment should be the prerogative of Canada. These proposals were adopted by the Parliament of Canada and were enacted by the UK Parliament as the Canada Act of 1982. This was the final act of the UK Parliament in Canadian constitutional development. The Act gave to Canada the power to amend the Constitution according to procedures determined by the Constitutional Act 1982. The latter added to the Canadian Constitution a charter of Rights and Freedoms, and provisions which recognize the nation's multi-cultural heritage, affirm the existing rights of native peoples, confirm the principle of equalization of benefits among the provinces, and strengthen provincial ownership of natural resources.

Under the Constitution legislative power is vested in Parliament, consisting of the Queen, represented by a Governor-General, a Senate and a House of Commons. The members of the *Senate* are appointed until age 75 by summons of the Governor-General under the Great Seal of Canada. Members appointed before 2 June 1965 may remain in office for life. The Senate consists of 105 senators: 24 from Ontario, 24 from Quebec, 10 from Nova Scotia, 10 from New Brunswick, 6 from Manitoba, 6 from British Columbia, 6 from Alberta, 6 from Saskatchewan, 6 from Newfoundland, 4 from Prince Edward Island, 1 from the Yukon Territory, 1 from the Northwest Territories, and 1 from Nunavut. Each senator must be at least 30 years of age and reside in the province for which he or she is appointed. The *House of Commons*, currently of 308 members, is elected by universal secret suffrage, by a first-past-the-post system, for five-year terms. Representation is based on the population of all the provinces taken as a whole with readjustments made after each census. State of the parties in the Senate (Feb. 2006): Liberals, 66; Conservatives, 23; Progressive Conservatives, 4; New Democratic Party (unofficial), 1; independents, 5; vacant, 6.

The First Nations have representation in the *Assembly of First Nations* (National Chief: Phil Fontaine, elected July 2003).

The office and appointment of the Governor-General are regulated by letters patent of 1947. In 1977 the Queen approved the transfer to the Governor-General of functions discharged by the Sovereign. The Governor-General is assisted by a *Privy Council* composed of Cabinet Ministers.

Canadian Parliamentary Guide. Annual. Ottawa

Bejermi, J., *Canadian Parliamentary Handbook.* Ottawa, 1993

Cairns, A. C., *Charter versus Federalism: the Dilemmas of Constitutional Reform.* Montreal, 1992

Canada: The State of the Federation. Queen's Univ., annual

Forsey, E. A., *How Canadians Govern Themselves.* Ottawa, 1991

Fox, P. W. and White, G., *Politics Canada.* 7th ed. Toronto, 1991

Hogg, P. W., *Constitutional Law of Canada.* 3rd ed. Toronto, 1992

Kaplan, W. (ed.) *Belonging: the Meaning and Future of Canadian Citizenship.* McGill-Queen's Univ. Press, 1993

Kernaghan, K., *Public Administration in Canada: a Text.* Scarborough, 1991

Mahler, G., *Contemporary Canadian Politics, 1970–1994: an Annotated Bibliography.* 2 vols. Westport (CT), 1995

Osbaldston, G. F., *Organizing to Govern.* Toronto, 1992

Reesor, B., *The Canadian Constitution in Historical Perspective.* Scarborough, 1992

Tardi, G., *The Legal Framework of Government: a Canadian Guide.* Aurora, 1992

National Anthem

'O Canada, our home and native land'/'O Canada, terre de nos aïeux'; words by A. Routhier, tune by C. Lavallée.

GOVERNMENT CHRONOLOGY

Prime Ministers since 1935. (CPC = Conservative Party of Canada; LP = Liberal Party; PC = Progressive Conservative Party)

1935–48	LP	William Lyon Mackenzie King
1948–57	LP	Louis Stephen Saint Laurent
1957–63	PC	John George Diefenbaker
1963–68	LP	Lester Bowles Pearson
1968–79	LP	Pierre Elliott Trudeau
1979–80	PC	Charles Joseph (Joe) Clark
1980–84	LP	Pierre Elliott Trudeau
1984	LP	John Napier Turner
1984–93	PC	Martin Brian Mulroney
1993	PC	Avril Phaedra (Kim) Campbell
1993–2003	LP	Joseph Jacques Jean Chrétien
2003–06	LP	Paul Joseph Martin (Jr)
2006–	CPC	Stephen Joseph Harper

RECENT ELECTIONS

At the elections of 23 Jan. 2006 the opposition Conservative Party won 124 seats (99 in 2004) with 36·3% (29·6% in 2004) of votes cast; the Liberal Party 103 with 30·2% (135 in 2004 with 36·7%); the Bloc Québécois 51 with 10·5% (54 in 2004 with 12·4%); the New Democratic Party 29 with 17·5% (19 in 2004 with 15·7%). The Green Party polled 4·5% and took no seats. One independent was elected. Turnout was 64·9% (60·5% in 2004).

CURRENT ADMINISTRATION

Governor-General: Michaëlle Jean (b. 1957; sworn in on 27 Sept. 2005).

In March 2006 the Conservative cabinet comprised:

Prime Minister: Stephen Harper; b. 1959 (Conservative Party; took office on 6 Feb. 2006).

Minister of Agriculture and Agri-Food: Chuck Strahl. *Canadian Heritage:* Beverley Oda. *Citizenship and Immigration:* Monte Solberg. *Environment:* Rona Ambrose. *Finance:* James Flaherty. *Fisheries and Oceans:* Loyola Hearn. *Foreign Affairs:* Peter MacKay. *Health:* Tony Clement. *Human Resources and Social Development:* Diane Finley. *Indian Affairs and Northern Development and Federal Interlocutor for Métis and Non-Status Indians:* Jim Prentice. *Industry:* Maxime Bernier. *International Co-operation:* Josée Verner. *International Trade:* David Emerson. *Justice and Attorney General:* Vic Toews. *Labour:* Jean-Pierre Blackburn. *National Defence:* Gordon O'Connor. *National Revenue and Western Economic Diversification:* Carol Skelton. *Natural Resources:* Gary Lunn. *Public Safety:* Stockwell Day. *Public Works and Government Services:* Michael Fortier. *Transport, Infrastructures and Communities:* Lawrence Cannon. *Veterans Affairs:* Gregory Thompson. *Leader of the Government in the House of Commons and Minister for Democratic Reform:* Robert Nicholson. *Leader of the Government in the Senate:* Marjory LeBreton. *President of the Queen's Privy Council for Canada, Minister of Intergovernmental Affairs and for Sport:* Michael Chong. *President of the Treasury Board:* John Baird.

The *Leader of the Opposition* is Bill Graham.

Office of the Prime Minister: http://www.pm.gc.ca

CURRENT LEADERS

Stephen Harper

Position
Prime Minister

Introduction
Stephen Harper's victory in federal elections in Jan. 2006 represented a shift to the right after 12 years of Liberal government overshadowed by allegations of corruption. The free-market economist and leader of the Conservative Party cast himself as a moderate, progressive, centre-right politician and promised to tackle corruption, reduce taxes and lead a more efficient government.

Early Life
Stephen Harper was born on 30 April 1959 in Toronto, Canada. He graduated from Richview Collegiate Institute in 1978 and moved to Edmonton, Alberta, where he worked as a computer programmer in the oil and gas industry. While studying economics at the University of Calgary in the early 1980s, Harper was influenced by the right-wing monetarist ideas espoused by Ronald Reagan in the USA and Margaret Thatcher in the UK. He graduated with a BA in economics in 1985 and began working for a Conservative member of parliament, Jim Hawkes.

Disillusioned with the Progressive Conservatives (PC) and the government of Brian Mulroney, Harper joined the newly established Reform Party of Canada in 1987, led by the economist Preston Manning. As chief policy officer, Harper helped draft the party's manifesto for the elections of 1988. He became legislative assistant to the Reform Party MP, Deborah Gray, after she won a by-election to represent Beaver River, Alberta in March 1989.

At the elections of Oct. 1993 Harper beat Jim Hawkes to win Calgary West for the Reform Party and became the party's spokesman on finance and national unity. In a run-up to a referendum in Oct. 1995 on the status of Quebec, Harper argued to maintain but decentralize the federation. Disagreements with Manning led to Harper's decision in late 1996 not to stand in the next election. He resigned his seat in Jan. 1997 and was appointed vice president of the conservative lobby group, the National Citizens Coalition. He also worked as a regular political commentator for the Canadian Broadcasting Corporation.

Harper rejected invitations to run for the PC leadership but returned to politics in March 2002 when he was elected to succeed Stockwell Day as leader of the Canadian Alliance party. He successfully contested a by-election for Calgary Southwest two months later and returned to the House of Commons as leader of the opposition. Following protracted negotiations, Harper reached agreement with the PC leader, Peter MacKay, on a merger between the two parties to form the Conservative Party of Canada in Dec. 2003.

Harper won the new party's leadership election in March 2004 and fought the Liberal prime minister, Paul Martin, in the 2004 election. After taking an early lead in the polls, the Conservatives lost ground. Harper was criticized for his support of the US-led war on Iraq in March 2003. The election, on 28 June 2004, saw a victory for the Liberals, who took 135 seats against 99 for the Conservatives.

When the Liberals became mired in a corruption scandal in April 2005, Harper argued that the government had 'lost the moral authority to govern'. He introduced a motion of no confidence in Paul Martin's administration on 24 Nov. 2005, which was passed by 171–133. Parliament was dissolved and elections were scheduled for 23 Jan. 2006. Harper's campaign presented him as head of a modernizing centre-right party that would stimulate economic growth by lowering taxes. Having held a comfortable lead in the opinion polls, the Conservatives won the elections with 36% of the vote, though short of a parliamentary majority. Harper was sworn in as prime minister on 6 Feb. 2006.

Career in Office
Harper has promised a smaller 'more focused and effective' government and his first cabinet had 27 posts, 12 fewer than Paul Martin's. He is expected to pursue closer relations with the USA, including a resolution to the dispute over softwood timber exports to its neighbour that has been running for two decades.

DEFENCE

The armed forces are unified and organized in functional commands: Land Forces (army), Air Command (air forces) and Maritime Command (naval and naval air forces). In 2004 the armed forces numbered 52,300 (6,100 women in 2002); reserves, 36,900.

Military expenditure totalled US$10,118m. in 2003 (US$320 per capita), representing just 1·2% of GDP, the lowest share of GDP since before the Second World War. However, in Feb. 2005 Finance Minister Ralph Goodale announced the biggest increase in defence spending in the past 20 years.

Army
The Land Forces numbered 19,300 in 2004 including 1,600 women; reserves include a Militia of 15,500 and 4,000 Canadian Rangers.

Navy
The naval combatant force, which forms part of the Maritime Command of the unified armed forces, is headquartered at Halifax (Nova Scotia), and includes two diesel submarines (commissioned but not yet operational), four destroyers and 12 helicopter-carrying frigates. Naval personnel in 2004 numbered about 9,000, with 4,000 reserves. The main bases are Halifax, where about two-thirds of the fleet is based, and Esquimalt (British Columbia).

Air Force
The air forces numbered 13,500 in 2004 (1,700 women in 2002) with 140 combat aircraft.

INTERNATIONAL RELATIONS

Canada is a member of the UN, WTO, NATO, the Commonwealth, OAS, OECD, OSCE, APEC, BIS, Inter-American Development Bank, Asian Development Bank, IOM, Antarctic Treaty and the International Organization of the Francophonie.

ECONOMY

Services accounted for 71% of GDP in 2001, industry 27% and agriculture 2%.

According to the anti-corruption organization *Transparency International*, Canada ranked 14th in the world in a 2005 survey of the countries with the least corruption in business and government. It received 8·4 out of 10 in the annual index.

Overview
Canada's industrialization began in the late-19th century. After the Second World War the growth of manufacturing, mining and the service sectors transformed Canada into a primarily industrial and urban nation. While Canada's development record is impressive, its GDP per capita has not kept up with that of the USA over the last three decades. However, it does have a greater degree of income equality than its neighbour and scores slightly higher in the UN Human Development Report.

Canada has vast natural resources, a skilled labour force, modern technological capabilities and a diversified economy. Services account for most of GDP. Of all services, business service providers made the highest contribution to GDP and employment in the 1990s. In 2000 the service sector accounted for roughly two-thirds of total output and employed three-quarters of the population. Industry contributes over a quarter of GDP. The primary sector accounted for less than 6% of GDP and provided employment for only 4% of the workforce in 2000 but remains important to the economy as it accounts for roughly a quarter of total export earnings and is the primary source of income for several provinces.

Structural reforms implemented in the 1980s helped pave the way for productivity gains in the next decade. Fiscal consolidation and the establishment of a credible monetary policy agenda improved the country's macroeconomic framework, helping to lower sustainable real interest rates and increase the effectiveness of counter-cyclical monetary policy. From 1992–2000 labour productivity and total factor productivity measures showed their strongest growth of any period in recent history. The 1989 US–Canada Free Trade Agreement and the 1994 North American Free Trade Agreement, which includes Mexico, touched off a dramatic increase in trade and economic integration. By 1994 the US already accounted for 80% of Canada's exports. By 2001 this figure had grown to 88%. Exports represented 43·5% of Canada's GDP in 2001. This figure shrunk to 38·2% in 2004 but a risk of over reliance on exports to the US market remains. The impact of weaker US demand growth beginning in late 2000 was felt in the Canadian economy. Growth fell from the highs of 1999 to 1·8% in 2001. A recovery in 2002 was reversed in 2003 when the Canadian dollar appreciated sharply, certain industries suffered from transitory shocks and US demand continued to be weak. Economic growth was robust in 2004 and 2005.

Canada has run a budget surplus since 1997 and a current account surplus since 1999. Annual inflation rates were brought down from double-digit growth in the early 1980s to less than 2% in 1992, with prices fairly stable since then. According to the OECD, 'Canada is better prepared than most OECD countries to cope with an ageing population. However, problems remain with healthcare spending—further growth in healthcare costs could make the fiscal position unsustainable.'

Currency

The unit of currency is the *Canadian dollar* (CAD) of 100 *cents*. In June 2002 gold reserves were 0·86m. troy oz and foreign exchange reserves totalled US$32,831m. Total money supply was $258,252m. CDN in June 2002.

Inflation rates (based on OECD statistics):

1995	1996	1997	1998	1999	2000	2001	2002	2003	2004
2·2%	1·6%	1·6%	1·0%	1·7%	2·7%	2·5%	2·2%	2·8%	1·8%

Budget

Consolidated federal, provincial, territorial and local government revenue and expenditure for fiscal years ending 31 March (in $1m. CDN):

	1999–2000	2000–01	2001–02	2002–03
Revenue	414,170	445,311	435,520	440,746
Expenditure	401,520	422,656	435,885	440,006

In 2002–03 revenue included (in $1m. CDN): income taxes, 179,631; consumption taxes, 96,845; property and related taxes, 43,291; sales of goods and services, 35,071; contributions to social security plans, 30,027. Expenditure included: social services, 117,109; health, 81,720; education, 65,002; debt charges, 51,642.

On 1 Jan. 1991 a 7% Goods and Services Tax (GST) was introduced, superseding a 13·5% Manufacturers' Sales Tax.

Performance

Real GDP growth rates (based on OECD statistics):

1995	1996	1997	1998	1999	2000	2001	2002	2003	2004
2·8%	1·6%	4·2%	4·1%	5·5%	5·2%	1·8%	3·1%	2·0%	2·9%

Total GDP was US$979·8bn. in 2004.

The Dec. 2004 *OECD Economic Survey* observed: 'The Canadian economy has delivered solid performance for nearly a decade...demonstrating the benefits of a well-designed macroeconomic framework and the pay-off from a range of structural reforms implemented since the late 1980s. A relatively weak outturn in 2003 was mainly attributed to the impact of the sharp appreciation of the Canadian dollar, lacklustre foreign demand and a series of other unfavourable, but transitory, shocks affecting specific industries....Given recent developments, the economy is expected to expand by around 3 per cent in 2004 and 3½ percent in 2005.'

Banking and Finance

The Bank of Canada (established 1935) is the central bank and bank of issue. The *Governor* (David Dodge) is appointed by the Bank's directors for seven-year terms. The Minister of Finance owns the capital stock of the Bank on behalf of Canada. Banks in Canada are chartered under the terms of the Bank Act, which imposes strict conditions on capital reserves, returns to the federal government, types of lending operations, ownership and other matters. As of July 2002 there were 14 domestic banks, 33 foreign bank subsidiaries and 20 foreign bank branches operating in Canada through over 8,000 branches and managing over $1·7trn. CDN in assets. Chartered banks accounted collectively for over 70% of the total assets of the Canadian financial services sector, with the six largest domestic banks (Canadian Imperial Bank of Commerce, Bank of Nova Scotia, Bank of Montreal, National Bank of Canada, TD Canada Trust and Royal Bank of Canada) accounting for over 90% of the total assets held by the banking industry. In 2002

Canada had the highest number of automated bank machines per capita in the world (with nearly 18,000 ABMs) and the highest penetration levels of electronic banking channels (such as debit cards, Internet banking and telephone banking). In 2000 chartered banks employed over 235,000 people in Canada and had a payroll of approximately $16·1bn. CDN. The First Nations Bank was founded in Dec. 1996 to provide finance to Inuit and Indian entrepreneurs.

The activities of banks are monitored by the federal Office of the Superintendent of Financial Institutions, which reports to the Minister of Finance. Canada's federal financial institutions legislation is reviewed at least every five years. Significant legislative changes were made in 1992, updating the regulatory framework and removing barriers separating the activities of various types of financial institutions. In 1999 legislation was passed allowing foreign banks to establish operations in Canada without having to set up Canadian-incorporated subsidiaries. In 2001 Bill C-8, establishing the Financial Consumer Agency of Canada (the FCAC), was implemented. It aimed to foster competition in the financial sector and provide a holding company option allowing additional organizational flexibility to banks and insurance companies. The FCAC is responsible for enforcing consumer-related provisions of laws governing federal financial institutions.

There are stock exchanges at Calgary (Alberta Stock Exchange), Montreal, Toronto, Vancouver and Winnipeg.

ENERGY AND NATURAL RESOURCES

Environment

Canada's carbon dioxide emissions from the consumption and flaring of fossil fuels in 2002 were the equivalent of 18·9 tonnes per capita. An *Environmental Sustainability Index* compiled for the World Economic Forum meeting in Jan. 2005 ranked Canada sixth in the world, with 64·4%. The index measured the ability of countries to maintain favourable environmental conditions and examined various factors including pollution levels and the use or abuse of natural resources.

Electricity

Generating capacity, 2002, 113·1m. kW. Production, 2002, 601·52bn. kWh (351·39bn. kWh hydro-electric, 173·87bn. kWh thermal and 75·53bn. kWh nuclear); consumption per capita was 18,541 kWh in 2002. In 2003 there were 17 nuclear reactors in use.

Oil and Gas

Oil reserves in 2002 were 6·9bn. bbls.; gas (2002), 1,700,000m. cu. metres. Production of crude petroleum, 2002, 135·6m. tonnes; natural gas (2002), 183·5bn. cu. metres. Canada is the third largest producer of natural gas, after Russia and the USA. Canada's first off-shore field, 250 km off Nova Scotia, began producing in June 1992.

Water

Annual average water usage in Canada is 1,600 cu. metres per person—less than in the USA but nearly twice the average for an industrialized nation.

Minerals

Mineral production in 1,000 tonnes: sand and gravel (2001), 238,795; lignite (2002), 36,952; coal (2000), 33,804; iron ore (2001), 27,900; salt (2002), 13,000; gypsum and anhydrite (2000), 9,232; aluminium (2001), 2,583; lime (2001), 2,235; peat (2001), 1,280; zinc (2001), 1,012; copper (2001), 633; asbestos (2001), 262; nickel (2002), 178 (content of concentrate); lead (2001), 154; uranium (2002), 11·6 (the highest of any country in the world); cobalt (2001), 5·3; silver (2001), 1·27; gold (2001), 159 tonnes; diamonds (2002), 5·0m. carats.

Agriculture

Grain growing, dairy farming, fruit farming, ranching and fur farming are all practised. In 2002, 2·2% of the economically active population was engaged in agriculture.

According to 2001 census the total land area was 9,012,112 sq. km, of which 675,039 sq. km were on farms. There were 264,925 farms in 2001; average size, 273·6 ha. Average farm receipts in 2001 totalled $155,104 CDN. Total farm cash receipts (2003), $34,122,273,000 CDN. There were 732,521 tractors in 2001 and 115,803 harvester-threshers.

The following table shows the value of receipts for selected agricultural commodities in 2003 (in $1m. CDN):

Crops		Livestock and products	
Crops	13,055	Livestock and products	16,213
Barley	387	Beef	5,194
Canola	1,755	Dairy	4,496
Corn for grain	784	Hogs	3,390
Soybeans	715	Poultry	1,785
Wheat	2,441		
Other crops	6,966		

Output (in 1,000 tonnes) and harvested area (in 1,000 ha.) of crops:

	Output		Harvested Area	
	1999	2000	1999	2000
Wheat	26,900	26,804	10,367	10,963
Barley	13,196	13,468	4,069	4,551
Rapeseeds	8,798	7,119	5,564	4,816
Maize	9,161	6,827	1,141	1,088
Potatoes	4,268	4,569	157	158
Oats	3,641	3,389	1,398	1,299
Peas	2,252	2,864	835	1,220
Soybeans	2,781	2,703	1,004	1,061
Lentils	724	914	497	688
Sugarbeets	744	821	17	15
Linseeds	1,022	693	777	591
Tomatoes	683	670	9	8
Chick-peas	197	387	139	283
Carrots	294	279	9	8
Beans	294	261	150	158
Rye	387	260	169	115
Onions	181	189	5	5
Cabbages	180	167	9	8
Sunflower seeds	122	119	79	69

Canada is the world's leading barley and rapeseed producer and the second largest producer of oats.

Livestock

In parts of Saskatchewan and Alberta, stockraising is still carried on as a primary industry, but the livestock industry of the country at large is mainly a subsidiary of mixed farming. The following table shows the numbers of livestock (in 1,000) by provinces in 2001:

Provinces	Milch cows	Total cattle and calves	Sheep and lambs	Pigs
Newfoundland and Labrador	4·7	9·5	7·9	2·7
Prince Edward Island	14·6	84·8	3·6	126·1
Nova Scotia	23·9	108·4	24·9	124·9
New Brunswick	19·0	91·2	9·6	137·0
Quebec	407·2	1,362·8	254·1	4,267·4
Ontario	363·5	2,140·7	337·6	3,457·3
Manitoba	42·4	1,424·4	84·8	2,540·2
Saskatchewan	30·1	2,899·5	149·4	1,109·8
Alberta	84·0	6,615·2	307·3	2,027·5
British Columbia	71·4	814·9	83·3	165·8
Total	1,061·0	15,551·4	1,262·4	13,958·8

Other livestock totals (2000): horses, 385,000; chickens, 158m.; turkeys, 5m.

Livestock products

Slaughterings in 2000: pigs, 19·96m.; cattle, 3·77m.; sheep, 0·53m. Production, 2000 (in 1,000 tonnes): pork, bacon and ham, 1,675; beef and veal, 1,260; poultry meat, 1,065; horsemeat, 18; lamb and mutton, 11; cow's milk, 8,090; hens' eggs, 357; cheese, 351; honey, 32; hides, 94.

Fruit production in 2002, in 1,000 tonnes: apples, 382; grapes, 67; blueberries, 65; cranberries, 52; peaches and nectarines, 29; strawberries, 25; pears, 15; raspberries, 15.

Forestry

Forests make up nearly half of Canada's landmass and 10% of the world's forest cover. Forestry is of great economic importance, and forestry products (pulp, newsprint, building timber) constitute Canada's most valuable exports. In 2002 Canada had 417·6m. ha. of forest land, about 56% (234·5m. ha.) of which was classed as commercial forest. 2·8m. ha. were burned by forest fires in 2002. In 2003, 194·73m. cu. metres of roundwood was produced.

Fur Trade

In 2001, 1,019,400 wildlife pelts (valued at $23,496,600 CDN) and 1,147,100 ranch-raised pelts (valued at $49,971,300 CDN) were produced.

Fisheries

In 2002 landings of commercial fisheries totalled 1,101,376 tonnes; primary fisheries production was valued at $2·8bn. CDN (of which commercial marine $2·1bn. CDN). In 2001 the total catch was 1,063,915 tonnes (more than 96% from sea fishing); Atlantic landings totalled 879,636 tonnes and Pacific landings 184,279 tonnes. Value of sea fisheries landed in 2001 totalled $2,098m. CDN.

INDUSTRY

The leading companies by market capitalization in Canada in Nov. 2005 were: Royal Bank of Canada (US$48·7bn.); Manulife Financial (US$46·4bn.); and EnCana (US$39·9bn.), an oil and gas company.

Value of manufacturing shipments for all industries in 2003 was $545,765·2m. CDN. Principal manufactures in 1,000 tonnes: petrol (2002), 33,737; distillate fuel oil (2002), 29,253; paper and paperboard (2001), 19,828; crude steel (2002), 16,000; cement (producers' shipments, 2001), 12,986; mechanical wood pulp (2001), 11,409; pig iron (2002), 8,700; newsprint (2001), 8,376; residual fuel oil (2002), 6,879; sulphuric acid (2001), 3,846; jet fuel (2002), 3,735; kerosene (2002), 1,527; synthetic rubber (2002), 150; sugar (2002), 64. Output of other products: 2·6m. motor vehicles (2003); 44·4bn. cigarettes (2001); sawn timber (2001), 47·70m. cu. metres; chipboard (2001), 10·73m. cu. metres; plywood (2001), 2·33m. cu. metres.

Labour

In 2001 there were (in 1,000), 15,076·8 (6,967·1 females) in employment, with principal areas of activity as follows: wholesale and retail trade/repair of motor vehicles, motorcycles and personal and household goods, 2,649·6; manufacturing, 2,274·5; real estate, renting and business activities, 1,776·7; health and social work, 1,542·1; transport, storage and communications, 1,162·4; hotels and restaurants, 976·0; education, 966·2; construction, 839·6; public administration and defence/compulsory social security, 764·0. In Dec. 2005 the unemployment rate stood at 6·5%.

In 2002, 3,028,423 working days were lost in industrial disputes.

According to the World Bank's *Doing Business in 2006: Creating Jobs* Canada is the easiest country in the world in which to set up a business.

Trade Unions

Union membership in Jan. 2002 was 4,178,000, of whom 72·8% belonged to the Canadian Labour Congress. Individual unions with the largest memberships in Jan. 2002 were the Canadian Union of Public Employees (521,600), National Union of Public and General Employees (325,000), National Automobile,

Aerospace, Transportation and General Workers Union of Canada (238,000) and United Food and Commercial Workers International Union (220,800).

A trade union to which the majority of employees in a unit suitable for collective bargaining belong generally has certain rights and duties. An employer is required to negotiate with that union to determine wage rates and other working conditions of employees. The employer, trade union and employees affected are bound by the resulting agreement. Generally, work stoppages do not take place until an established conciliation or mediation procedure has been carried out, and are prohibited while an agreement is in effect.

INTERNATIONAL TRADE

A North American Free Trade Agreement (NAFTA) between Canada, Mexico and the USA was signed on 7 Oct. 1992 and came into force on 1 Jan. 1994.

Imports and Exports

Trade in US$1m.:

	1998	1999	2000	2001	2002
Imports f.o.b.	204,617	220,203	243,889	226,495	227,240
Exports f.o.b.	220,539	248,494	289,468	272,359	264,078

Canada is heavily dependent on foreign trade. In 2002 imports of goods and services were equivalent to 37% of GDP and exports equivalent to 41%; merchandise exports to the USA accounted for over 33·5% of GDP. Main import suppliers, 2002 (in $1m. CDN): USA, 254,929·0; Japan, 11,732·2; United Kingdom, 10,312·4; other EU countries, 25,863·3; other OECD countries, 19,670·3; other countries, 33,952·1. Main export markets, 2002 (in $1m. CDN): USA, 346,990·6; Japan, 10,291·6; United Kingdom, 6,239·4; other EU countries, 16,496·4; other OECD countries, 12,341·9; other countries, 21,945·3.

Main categories of imports, 2002 (in $1m. CDN): machinery and equipment, 105,866·7 (industrial and agricultural machinery, 27,553·0; office machines and equipment, 15,699·6); automotive products, 81,449·6 (motor vehicle parts, 43,454·6); industrial goods and materials, 68,873·1 (chemicals and plastics, 25,724·1; metals and metal ores, 16,475·1). Exports, 2002 (in $1m. CDN): machinery and equipment, 97,303·8 (aircraft and other transport equipment, 22,784·1; industrial and agricultural machinery, 20,281·0); automotive products, 97,030·3 (passenger cars and chassis, 49,815·4; motor vehicle parts, 29,357·8); industrial goods and materials, 70,232·5 (chemicals, plastics and fertilizers, 24,302·7; metals and alloys, 22,214·3); energy products, 49,542·0 (crude petroleum, 18,795·3; natural gas, 18,359·4); forestry products, 37,197·9 (lumber and sawmill products, 17,761·1; newsprint and other paper and paperboard products, 12,986·4).

COMMUNICATIONS

Roads

In 2002 there were 1,408,800 km of roads, including 85,800 km of highways, national or main roads, 114,600 km of secondary or regional roads and 16,900 km of motorways.

The National Highway System, spanning almost 25,000 km, includes the Trans-Canada Highway and other major east–west and north–south highways. While representing only 3% of total road infrastructure, the system carries about 30% of all vehicle travel in Canada.

Registered road motor vehicles totalled 18,868,756 in 2003; they comprised 17,755,082 passenger cars and light vehicles, 660,437 trucks and truck tractors (weighing at least 4,500 kg), 79,875 buses and 373,362 motorcycles and mopeds.

In 2001 freight transport totalled 87,522m. tonne-km.

There were 2,778 fatalities (a rate of 8·9% deaths per 100,000 population) in road accidents in 2001.

Rail

Canada has two great trans-continental systems: the Canadian National Railway system (CN), a body privatized in 1995 which operated 31,764 km of routes in 2000, and the Canadian Pacific Railway (CP), operating 22,590 km. A government-funded organization, VIA Rail, operates passenger services in all regions of Canada; 3·8m. passengers were carried in 2003. There are several provincial and private railways operating 17,528 km (2000).

There are metros in Montreal and Toronto, and tram/light rail systems in Calgary, Edmonton, Ottawa, Toronto and Vancouver.

Civil Aviation

Civil aviation is under the jurisdiction of the federal government. The technical and administrative aspects are supervised by Transport Canada, while the economic functions are assigned to the National Transportation Agency.

The busiest Canadian airport is Toronto (Lester B. Pearson International), which in 2001 handled 28,043,000 passengers (15,739,000 on international flights), ahead of Vancouver International, with 15,477,000 passengers (7,869,000 on domestic flights) and Montreal (Dorval International), with 8,169,000 passengers (4,133,000 on international flights). Toronto is also the busiest airport for freight, handling 323,000 tonnes in 2001.

Air Canada (privatized in July 1989) took over its main competitor, Canadian Airlines, in April 2000. In 1999 Air Canada flew 356·6m. km and carried 16,520,600 passengers, and Canadian Airlines International flew 211·9m. km and carried 7,496,900 passengers (3,667,300 on international flights).

Shipping

In 2000 the merchant marine comprised 861 vessels over 100 GRT including 25 oil tankers. Total tonnage, 2002, 2·80m. GRT, including oil tankers 0·40m. GRT. In 2001 vessels totalling 92,790,000 NRT entered ports and vessels totalling 121,712,000 NRT cleared.

Canada's leading port in terms of cargo handled is Vancouver. Other major ports are Saint John, Fraser River, Montreal and Quebec.

The major canals are those of the St Lawrence Seaway. Main commodities moved along the seaway are grain, iron ore, coal, other bulk and steel. The St Lawrence Seaway Management Corporation was established in 1998 as a non-profit making corporation to operate the Canadian assets of the seaway for the federal government under a long-term agreement with Transport Canada.

In 2003 total traffic on the Montreal-Lake Ontario (MLO) section of the seaway was 28,900,440 tonnes; on the Welland Canal section it was 31,870,466 tonnes. There were 3,886 vessel transits in 2003, generating $62,257,197 CDN in toll revenue.

Telecommunications

In 2002 there were 31,811,100 telephone subscribers (1,012·6 per 1,000 persons). Canada had 16·84m. Internet users in March 2002. There were 15·3m. PCs in use in 2002 (487·0 for every 1,000 persons) and 11,849,000 mobile phone subscribers (377·2 for every 1,000 persons). There were 1·3m. fax machines in 2002.

Postal Services

The Canada Post Corporation processed 10·7bn. pieces of mail in 2003. Revenue from operations reached $6·3bn. CDN, an increase of $190m. CDN over 2002. Consolidated net income for 2003 was $253m. CDN, an increase of $182m. CDN over 2002. The Corporation had 23,765 retail points of access at the end of 2003.

SOCIAL INSTITUTIONS

Justice

The courts in Canada are organized in a four-tier structure. The Supreme Court of Canada, based in Ottawa, is the highest court, having general appellate jurisdiction in civil and criminal cases throughout the country. It is comprised of a Chief Justice and eight puisne judges appointed by the Governor-in-Council, with a minimum of three judges coming from Quebec. The second tier consists of the Federal Court of Appeal and the various provincial courts of appeal. The third tier consists of the Federal Court (which replaced the Exchequer Court in 1971), the Tax Court of Canada and the provincial and territorial superior courts (which include both a court of general trial jurisdiction and a provincial court of appeal). The majority of cases are heard by the provincial courts, the fourth tier in the hierarchy. They are generally divided within each province into various divisions defined by the subject matter of their respective jurisdictions (for example a Traffic Division, a Small Claims Division, a Family Division and a Criminal Division).

There were 2,353,926 Criminal Code Offences (excluding traffic) reported in 2000. There were 963 violent crimes per 100,000 population in 2003. In 2003 there were 548 homicides in Canada, giving a rate of 1·7 homicides per 100,000 population (the lowest rate since 1967). The population in penal institutions in 2001 was 31,624 (102 per 100,000 of national population). The death penalty was abolished for all crimes in 1998.

Police
Total police personnel in Canada in June 2003 numbered 59,494. There were 9,352 female police officers, up from 3,573 in June 1990. Policing costs in 2002 totalled $7·8bn. CDN.

Royal Canadian Mounted Police (RCMP)
The RCMP is Canada's national police force maintained by the federal government. Established in 1873 as the North-West Mounted Police, it became the Royal Northwest Mounted Police in 1904. Its sphere of operations was expanded in 1918 to include all of Canada west of Thunder Bay, Ontario. In 1920 the force absorbed the Dominion Police and its headquarters was transferred from Regina, Saskatchewan to Ottawa, Ontario. Its title also changed to Royal Canadian Mounted Police. The RCMP is responsible to the Minister of Public Safety and Emergency Preparedness Canada and is controlled by a Commissioner who is empowered to appoint peace officers in all the provinces and territories of Canada.

The responsibilities of the RCMP are national in scope. The administration of justice within the provinces, including the enforcement of the Criminal Code of Canada, is the responsibility of provincial governments, but all the provinces except Ontario and Quebec have entered into contracts with the RCMP to enforce criminal and provincial laws under the direction of the respective Attorneys-General. In these eight provinces the RCMP is under agreement to provide police services to municipalities as well. The RCMP is also responsible for all police work in the three territories—Yukon, Northwest Territories and Nunavut—enforcing federal law and territorial ordinances. The 16 Divisions, alphabetically designated, make up the strength of the RCMP across Canada; they comprise 740 detachments containing varying numbers of police officers. Headquarters Division, as well as the Office of the Commissioner, is located in Ottawa.

Supporting Canada's law enforcement agencies, the RCMP's National Police Services includes seven diverse service lines providing a broad range of programmes and services throughout Canada. It is comprised of Information and Identification Services, Forensic Laboratory Services, Canadian Police College, Criminal Intelligence Service Canada, Technical Operations, National Child Exploitation Coordination Centre and Chief Information Officer.

In 2005 the Force had a total strength of over 22,000 including regular members, special constables, civilian members and public service employees. It maintained 10,385 motor vehicles, 112 police dog teams across Canada and 195 horses.

The Force has 16 divisions actively engaged in law enforcement, one Headquarters Division and one training division. Marine services are divisional responsibilities and the Force currently has 308 boats at various points across Canada. The Air Services Branch has offices throughout the country and maintains a fleet of 34 operational aircraft.

Education
Under the Constitution the provincial legislatures have powers over education. These are subject to certain qualifications respecting the rights of denominational and minority language schools. School board revenues derive from local taxation on real property, and government grants from general provincial revenue.

In 1999–2000 there were 15,595 elementary and secondary public and private schools with 5,397,068 pupils and 301,757 teachers; there were also 199 community colleges with 408,781 students.

Enrolment for Indian and Inuit children in elementary/secondary schools for 1999–2000: federal schools, 1,708; band-operated schools, 71,823; provincial/private schools, 45,839; giving a total of 119,370 students funded by the Department of Indian and Northern Affairs (DIAND). However, this total represents only a portion of Indian and Inuit students attending elementary/secondary schools.

There were 75 universities in 1999–2000 with 590,663 students and 33,801 teachers. According to 2001 census data, between 1991 and 2001 the proportion of adults aged 25 or over with university credentials grew from 15% to 20%; another 16% had a college diploma in 2001 (up from 12% in 1991) and 12% had a trade certificate. In all, the number of Canadians aged 25 and over with university, college or trade credentials grew by 2·7m. (a 39% increase) between 1991 and 2001.

The adult literacy rate is at least 99%.

In 2000–01 public education expenditure represented 5·5% of GDP.

Health
Constitutional responsibility for health care services rests with the provinces and territories. Accordingly, Canada's national health insurance system consists of an interlocking set of provincial and territorial hospital and medical insurance plans conforming to certain national standards rather than a single national programme. The Canada Health Act (which took effect from April 1984 and consolidated the original federal health insurance legislation) sets out the national standards that provinces and territories are required to meet in order to qualify for full federal health contributions, including: provision of a comprehensive range of hospital and medical benefits; universal population coverage; access to necessary services on uniform terms and conditions; portability of benefits; and public administration of provincial and territorial insurance plans. Starting in the fiscal year 1996–97 the federal government's contribution to provincial health and social programmes was consolidated into a single block transfer—the Canada Health and Social Transfer (CHST). Funding is transferred to provinces as a combination of cash contributions and tax transfers, the latter being the federal government's largest transfer. In 2002–03 the provinces and territories received a total of $35·7bn. CDN in CHST, of which $16·6bn. CDN was in tax transfers. Over and above these health transfers, the federal government also provides financial support for such provincial and territorial extended health care service programmes as nursing-home care, certain home care services, ambulatory health care services and adult residential care services.

The approach taken by Canada is one of state-sponsored health insurance. The advent of insurance programmes produced little change in the ownership of hospitals, almost all of which are owned by non-government non-profit corporations, or in the rights and privileges of private medical practice. Patients are free to choose their own general practitioner. Except for a small percentage of the population whose care is provided for under other legislation (such as serving members of the Canadian Armed Forces and inmates of federal penitentiaries), all residents are eligible, regardless of whether they are in the workforce. Benefits are available without upper limit so long as they are medically necessary, provided any registration obligations are met.

In addition to the benefits qualifying for federal contributions, provinces and territories provide additional benefits at their own discretion. Most fund their portion of health costs out of general provincial and territorial revenues. Most have charges for long-term chronic hospital care geared, approximately, to the room and board portion of the OAS–GIS payment mentioned under Welfare *below*. Health spending accounted for 9·9% of GDP in 2003.

In 2001 there were 58,546 physicians, giving a rate of 187 per 100,000 population; there were 57 dentists per 100,000 population. In 2002 the regulated nursing workforce numbered 296,200.

Welfare

The social security system provides financial benefits and social services to individuals and their families through programmes administered by federal, provincial and municipal governments and voluntary organizations. Federally, Human Resources and Skills Development is responsible for research into the areas of social issues, provision of grants and contributions for various social services and the administration of income security programmes, including the Old Age Security (OAS) programme, the Guaranteed Income Supplement, the Spouse's Allowance and the Canada Pension Plan (CPP).

The Old Age Security pension is payable to persons 65 years of age and over who satisfy the residence requirements stipulated in the Old Age Security Act. The amount payable, whether full or partial, is also governed by stipulated conditions, as is the payment of an OAS pension to a recipient who absents himself from Canada. OAS pensioners with little or no income apart from OAS may, upon application, receive a full or partial supplement known as the Guaranteed Income Supplement (GIS). Entitlement is normally based on the pensioner's income in the preceding year, calculated in accordance with the Income Tax Act. The spouse of an OAS pensioner, aged 60 to 64, meeting the same residence requirements as those stipulated for OAS, may be eligible for a full or partial Spouse's Allowance (SPA). SPA is payable, on application, depending on the annual combined income of the couple (not including the pensioner spouse's basic OAS pension or GIS). In 1979 the SPA programme was expanded to include a spouse, who is eligible for SPA in the month the pensioner spouse dies, until the age of 65 or until remarriage (Extended Spouse's Allowance). Since Sept. 1985 SPA has also been available to low income widow(er)s aged 60–64 regardless of the age of their spouse at death.

As of 1 July 2004 the basic OAS pension was $466·63 CDN monthly; the maximum Guaranteed Income Supplement was $554·59 CDN monthly for a single pensioner or a married pensioner whose spouse was not receiving a pension or a Spouse's Allowance, and $361·24 CDN monthly for each spouse of a married couple where both were pensioners.

The Canada Pension Plan is designed to provide workers with a basic level of income protection in the event of retirement, disability or death. Benefits may be payable to a contributor, a surviving spouse or an eligible child. Actuarially adjusted retirement benefits may begin as early as age 60 or as late as age 70. Benefits are determined by the contributor's earnings and contributions made to the Plan. Contribution is compulsory for most employed and self-employed Canadians aged 18 to 65. The CPP does not operate in Quebec, which has exercised its constitutional prerogative to establish a similar plan. In 2004 the maximum retirement pension payable under CPP was $814·17

CDN; the maximum disability pension was $992·80 CDN; and the maximum surviving spouse's pension was $488·50 CDN (for survivors 65 years of age and over) or 60% of the retirement pension which the deceased contributor would have received at age 65. The survivor pension payable to a surviving spouse under 65 (maximum of $454·42 CDN in 2004) is composed of two parts: a flat-rate component and an earnings-related portion.

As projections indicated that the CPP was lacking sufficient assets to meet long-term obligations, contribution rates were increased from 6% in 1997 to 9·9% of maximum pensionable earnings by 2003. The Canada Pension Plan Investment Board, an independent investment organization separate from the CPP, was established to invest excess CPP funds in a diversified portfolio of securities, beginning operations in April 1998. In 2004 the range of yearly pensionable earnings was from $3,500 CDN to $40,500 CDN. In June 1999 over 5m. Canadians received Canada or Quebec Pension Plan benefits. Social security agreements co-ordinate the operation of the Old Age Security and the CPP with the comparable social security programmes of certain other countries.

Canada Child Tax Benefit (CCTB) is a tax-free monthly payment made to eligible families to help them with the cost of raising children under 18. Included with the CCTB is the National Child Benefit Supplement (NCBS), a monthly benefit for low-income families with children.

RELIGION

Membership of religious denominations (according to census analysis):

	1991	2001	% change 1991–2001
Anglican Church of Canada	2,188,110	2,035,500	−7·0
Canadian Baptist Ministries	663,360	729,470	10·0
Christian Orthodox	387,395	479,620	23·8
Lutheran Church	636,205	606,590	−4·7
Pentecostal Assemblies of Canada	436,435	369,475	−15·3
Presbyterian Church	636,295	409,830	−35·6
Roman Catholic Church	12,203,625	12,793,125	4·8
United Church of Canada	3,093,120	2,839,125	−8·2

Membership of other denominations in 2001 (census figures): Jehovah's Witnesses, 154,745; Jews, 329,995; Latter-day Saints (Mormons), 104,750; Mennonites, 191,465; Muslims, 579,640; Salvation Army, 87,785. In May 2005 the Roman Catholic church had five cardinals.

CULTURE

World Heritage Sites

Sites under Canadian jurisdiction which appear on UNESCO's world heritage list are (with year entered on list): L'Anse aux Meadows National Historic Site (1978), the remains of an 11th-century Viking settlement in Newfoundland; Nahanni National Park (1978); Dinosaur Provincial Park (1979), in Alberta, a major area for fossil discoveries; SGaang Gwaii (Anthony Island) (1981), illustrating the Haida people's art and way of life; Head-Smashed-In Buffalo Jump (1981), in southwest Alberta, incorporating an aboriginal camp—the name relates to the aboriginal custom of killing buffalo by chasing them over a precipice; Wood Buffalo National Park (1983); Canadian Rocky Mountain Parks (1984), incorporating the neighbouring parks of Banff, Jasper, Kootenay and Yoho, as well as the Mount Robson, Mount Assiniboine and Hamber provincial parks, and the Burgess Shale fossil site; Historic District of Québec (1985), retaining aspects of its French colonial past; Gros Morne National Park (1987), in Newfoundland; Old Town Lunenburg (1995), a well-preserved British colonial settlement; Miguasha Park (1999), among the world's most important fossil sites.

Two UNESCO World Heritage Sites fall under joint Canadian and US jurisdiction: Kluane/Wrangell-St Elias/Glacier Bay/

Tatshenshini-Alsek (1979), parks in the Yukon Territory, British Columbia and Alaska; Waterton Glacier International Peace Park (1995), in Alberta and Montana.

Broadcasting

The Canadian Radio-Television and Telecommunications Commission is an independent authority established by parliament in 1968 to regulate the broadcasting and telecommunications systems. The Canadian Broadcasting Corporation operates two national TV networks, one in English and one in French, and there are three private TV networks (colour by NTSC). In 2002 there were 785 cable TV licences (the number having decreased following the CRTC's decision not to regulate cable systems that serve small and rural communities and have fewer than 2,000 subscribers) and there were 7,623,000 subscribers to cable television.

There were 21·5m. TV receivers in 2001 and 32·2m. radio receivers in 2000.

There were 1,959 originating radio stations operating in 2003, of which 432 were AM and 1,527 FM.

Cinema

In 2000–01 there were 3,265 cinema screens (including 106 drive-ins); total admissions in 2000–01 were 116·9m. In 2001–02, 64 feature films were produced in Canada (44 Canadian content).

Press

In 2003 there were 101 daily papers with a total average circulation of 4·93m.; *The Toronto Star* had the largest circulation at 460,000, then *The Globe and Mail* with 315,000.

There were 1,071 non-daily papers in 2003, with a circulation of 21,235,000.

In 2002 a total of 26,810 book titles were published.

Tourism

In 2002 there were 20,057,000 foreign tourists, around 90% of whom were from the USA. The next biggest tourist markets are the UK, Japan, France and Germany. Revenue from visitors was US$9·7bn.

Festivals

The Quebec Winter Festival is held each Feb. The Montreal Jazz Festival is in June while the Calgary Stampede (the world's largest rodeo, incorporating a series of concerts and a carnival) is in July. Also in July are the Ottawa International Jazz Festival, the Québec Festival d'Été/Summer Festival (featuring music and art performances) and the Montréal Juste Pour Rire/Just for Laughs comedy festival. The Toronto international film festival takes place in Sept. and the Vancouver international film festival is the following month. Canada Day, held each July, is marked nationwide with firework displays, parades and parties.

Libraries

In 2002 the National Library and the National Archives of Canada amalgamated to create the Library and Archives of Canada. In 1999 the National Library held 6,955,000 volumes and public libraries had a total of 75,033,000 volumes.

Museums and Galleries

In 1999 there were 2,600 heritage institutions (including museums, historic sites, archives, exhibition centres, planetariums and observatories, aquariums and zoos, and botanical gardens); attendance totalled 118·3m. visits (including 26·5m. visits to museums) and operating revenues were $1·5bn. CDN.

DIPLOMATIC REPRESENTATIVES

Of Canada in the United Kingdom (Macdonald House, 1 Grosvenor Sq., London, W1K 4AB)
High Commissioner: Mel Cappe.

Of the United Kingdom in Canada (80 Elgin St., Ottawa, K1P 5K7)
High Commissioner: David Reddaway, CMG, MBE.

Of Canada in the USA (501 Pennsylvania Ave., NW, Washington, D.C., 20001)
Ambassador: Frank McKenna.

Of the USA in Canada (490 Sussex Drive, Ottawa, K1N 1G8)
Ambassador: David Wilkins.

Of Canada to the United Nations
Ambassador: Allan Rock.

Of Canada to the European Union
Ambassador: Jeremy K. B. Kinsman.

FURTHER READING

Canadian Annual Review. From 1960
Canadian Encyclopedia. 2nd ed. 4 vols. Edmonton, 1988

Brown, R. C., *An Illustrated History of Canada.* Toronto, 1991
Cook, C., *Canada after the Referendum of 1992.* McGill-Queens Univ. Press, 1994
Dawson, R. M. and Dawson, W. F., *Democratic Government in Canada.* 5th ed. Toronto Univ. Press, 1989
Ingles, E., *Canada.* [Bibliography] ABC-Clio, Oxford and Santa Barbara (CA), 1990
Jackson, R. J., *Politics in Canada: Culture, Institutions, Behaviour and Public Policy.* 2nd ed. Scarborough (Ont.), 1990
Longille, P., *Changing the Guard: Canada's Defence in a World in Transition.* Toronto Univ. Press, 1991
Silver, A. I. (ed.) *Introduction to Canadian History.* London, 1994

Other more specialized titles are listed under CONSTITUTION AND GOVERNMENT *above.*

National library: Library and Archives Canada, Ottawa, Ontario. *Librarian and Archivist of Canada:* Ian E. Wilson.
National Statistical Office: Statistics Canada, Ottawa, K1A 0T6.
Website: http://www.statcan.ca/

CANADIAN PROVINCES

GENERAL DETAILS

The ten provinces each have a separate parliament and administration, with a Lieut.-Governor, appointed by the Governor-General in Council at the head of the executive. They have full powers to regulate their own local affairs and dispose of their revenues, provided only that they do not interfere with the action and policy of the central administration. Among the subjects assigned exclusively to the provincial legislatures are: the amendment of the provincial constitution, except as regards the office of the Lieut.-Governor; property and civil rights; direct taxation for revenue purposes; borrowing; management and sale of Crown lands; provincial hospitals, reformatories, etc.; shop, saloon, tavern, auctioneer and other licences for local or provincial purposes; local works and undertakings, except lines of ships, railways, canals, telegraphs, etc., extending beyond the province or connecting with other provinces, and excepting also such works as the Canadian Parliament declares are for the general good; marriages, administration of justice within the province; education. On 18 July 1994 the federal and provincial governments signed an agreement easing inter-provincial barriers on government procurement, labour mobility, transport licences and product standards. Federal legislation of Dec. 1995 grants provinces a right of constitutional veto.

For the administration of the three territories *see* Northwest Territories, Nunavut, Yukon Territory *below*.

Areas of the ten provinces and three territories (Northwest Territories, Nunavut and Yukon) (in sq. km) and population at recent censuses:

Province	Land area	Total land and fresh water area	Population, 1991[1,2]	Population, 1996	Population, 2001[1]
Newfoundland (Nfld.)	373,872	405,212	568,474	551,792	512,930
Prince Edward Island (PEI)	5,660	5,660	129,765	134,557	135,294
Nova Scotia (NS)	53,338	55,284	899,942	909,282	908,007
New Brunswick (NB)	71,450	72,908	723,900	738,133	729,498
Quebec (Que.)	1,365,128	1,542,056	6,895,963	7,138,795	7,237,479
Ontario (Ont.)	917,741	1,076,395	10,084,885	10,753,573	11,410,046
Manitoba (Man.)	553,556	647,797	1,091,942	1,113,898	1,119,583
Saskatchewan (Sask.)	591,670	651,036	988,928	990,237	978,933
Alberta (Alta.)	642,317	661,848	2,545,553	2,696,826	2,974,807
British Columbia (BC)	925,186	944,735	3,282,061	3,724,500	3,907,738
Nunavut (Nvt.)	1,936,113	2,093,190			26,745[3]
Northwest Territories (NWT)	1,183,085	1,346,106	57,649	64,402	37,360[4]
Yukon Territory (YT)	474,391	482,443	27,797	30,766	28,674

[1]Excludes data from incompletely enumerated Indian reserves and Indian settlements.
[2]Comparison of the 1991 census data with data from earlier censuses is affected by a change in the definition of the 1991 census population. Persons in Canada on student authorizations, Minister's permits, and as refugee claimants were enumerated in the 1991 census but not in previous censuses. These persons are referred to as non-permanent residents.
[3]Nunavut only came into existence in 1999.
[4]The population of the Northwest Territories declined so steeply between 1996 and 2001 because of the formation of Nunavut, previously part of the Northwest Territories, in 1999.

Local Government
Under the terms of the British North America Act the provinces are given full powers over local government. All local government institutions are, therefore, supervised by the provinces, and are incorporated and function under provincial acts.

The acts under which municipalities operate vary from province to province. A municipal corporation is usually administered by an elected council headed by a mayor or reeve, whose powers to administer affairs and to raise funds by taxation and other methods are set forth in provincial laws, as is the scope of its obligations to, and on behalf of, the citizens. Similarly, the types of municipal corporations, their official designations and the requirements for their incorporation vary between provinces. The following table sets out the classifications as at the 2001 census:

	Federal electoral districts	Economic regions	Census divisions
Nfld.	7	4	10[1]
PEI	4	1	3[1]
NS	11	5	18[1]
NB	10	5	15[1]
Que.	75	17	99[2]
Ont.	106	11	49[3]
Man.	14	8	23
Sask.	14	6	18
Alta.	28	8	19
BC	36	8	28[4]
Nvt.	1	1	3[5]
NWT	1	1	2[5]
YT	1	1	1[6]

[1]Counties. [2]3 census divisions, 3 communautés urbaines, 93 municipalités régionales de comté. [3]21 counties, 10 districts, 7 census divisions, 1 district municipality, 7 regional municipalities, 3 united counties. [4]1 region, 27 regional districts. [5]Regions. [6]Territory.

SOCIAL INSTITUTIONS

Justice

The administration of justice within the provinces, including the enforcement of the Criminal Code of Canada, is the responsibility of provincial governments, but all the provinces except Ontario and Quebec have entered into contracts with the Royal Canadian Mounted Police (RCMP) to enforce criminal and provincial law. In addition, in these eight provinces the RCMP is under agreement to provide police services to municipalities.

Alberta

KEY HISTORICAL EVENTS

The southern half of Alberta was administered from 1670 as part of Rupert's land by the Hudson's Bay Company. Trading posts were set up after 1783 when the North West Company took a share in the fur trade. In 1869 Rupert's land was transferred from the Hudson's Bay Company (which had absorbed its rival in 1821) to the new Dominion and in the following year this land was combined with the former Crown land of the North Western Territories to form the Northwest Territories. In 1882 'Alberta' first appeared as a provisional 'district', consisting of the southern half of the present province. In 1905 the Athabasca district to the north was added when provincial status was granted to Alberta.

TERRITORY AND POPULATION

The area of the province is 661,185 sq. km, 644,389 sq. km being land area and 16,796 sq. km water area. The population at the 2001 census was 2,974,807. Population estimate, 1 July 2005, was 3,256,816. Alberta has the fastest growing population of any Canadian province, with a 20·8% increase since the 1996 census. The urban population (2001), centres of 1,000 or over, was 80·9% and the rural 19·1%. Population (15 May 2001) of the 16 cities, as well as the two specialized municipalities: Calgary, 878,866; Edmonton, 616,104; Red Deer, 67,707; Lethbridge, 67,374; St Albert, 53,081; Medicine Hat, 51,249; Grande Prairie, 36,983; Airdrie, 20,382; Spruce Grove, 15,983; Leduc, 15,032; Camrose, 14,854; Lloydminster (Alberta portion), 13,148; Fort Saskatchewan, 13,121; Brooks, 11,604; Cold Lake, 11,520; Wetaskiwin, 11,154; Specialized Municipality of Strathcona County (Sherwood Park), 71,986; Specialized Municipality of Wood Buffalo (Fort McMurray), 41,466.

SOCIAL STATISTICS

Births in 2004–05 numbered 38,729 (a rate of 11·9 per 1,000 population) and deaths 16,415 (rate of 5·0 per 1,000 population). There were 17,968 marriages in 2004 and 7,960 divorces in 2003.

CLIMATE

Alberta has a continental climate of warm summers and cold winters—extremes of temperature. For the capital city, Edmonton, the hottest month is usually July (mean 17·5°C), while the coldest are Dec. and Jan. (–12°C). Rainfall amounts are greatest between May and Sept. In a year, the average precipitation is 461 mm (19·6") with about 129·6 cm of snowfall.

CONSTITUTION AND GOVERNMENT

The constitution of Alberta is contained in the British North America Act of 1867, and amending Acts; also in the Alberta Act of 1905, passed by the Parliament of the Dominion of Canada, which created the province out of the then Northwest Territories. The province is represented by five members in the Senate and 26 in the House of Commons of Canada.

The executive is vested nominally in the Lieut.-Governor, who is appointed by the federal government, but actually in the Executive Council or the Cabinet of the legislature. Legislative power is vested in the Assembly in the name of the Queen.

Members of the 83-member Legislative Assembly are elected by the universal vote of adults, 18 years of age and older.

RECENT ELECTIONS

In elections on 22 Nov. 2004 Premier Ralph Klein's Progressive Conservative Party won 47% of the vote (taking 61 of 83 seats), the Liberal Party 29% (17), the New Democrats 10% (4) and the Alberta Alliance 9% (1). As of Dec. 2005 there were 62 Progressive Conservative, 16 Liberal, 4 New Democrat and one Alberta Alliance members in the legislature.

CURRENT ADMINISTRATION

Lieut.-Governor: Normie Kwong (sworn in on 20 Jan. 2005).

As of Feb. 2006 the members of the Executive Council were as follows:

Premier, President of Executive Council: Ralph Klein (b. 1942; Progressive Conservative).

Deputy Premier and Minister of Finance: Shirley McClellan. *Advanced Education:* Dave Hancock. *Justice and Attorney General:* Ron Stevens. *Heath and Wellness:* Iris Evans. *International and Intergovernmental Relations:* Ed Stelmach. *Education:* Gene Zwozdesky. *Energy:* Greg Melchin. *Community Development:* Gary Mar. *Infrastructure and Transportation:* Lyle Oberg. *Human Resources and Employment:* Mike Cardinal. *Environment:* Guy Boutilier. *Children's Services:* Heather Forsyth. *Innovation and Science:* Victor Doerksen. *Sustainable Resource Development:* David Coutts. *Aboriginal Affairs and Northern Development:* Pearl Calahasen. *Government Services:* Ty Lund. *Economic Development:* Clint Dunford. *Gaming:* Gordon Graydon. *Municipal Affairs:* Rob Renner. *Restructuring and Government Efficiency:* Luke Ouellette. *Solicitor General and Public Security:* Harvey Cenaiko. *Seniors and Community Support:* Yvonne Fritz. *Agriculture, Food and Rural Development:* Doug Horner.

Office of the Premier: http://www.gov.ab.ca/premier

ECONOMY

GDP per person in 2004 was $58,398 CDN.

Budget

The budgetary revenue and expenditure (in $1m. CDN) for years ending 31 March were as follows:

	2000–01	2001–02	2002–03	2003–04	2004–05
Revenue	25,527	21,926	22,662	25,887	29,328
Expenditure	18,956	20,845	20,529	21,751	24,153

Performance

Real GDP growth was 1·4% in 2004 (2·7% in 2003).

Banking and Finance

Personal income *per capita* (2004), $34,713 CDN.

ENERGY AND NATURAL RESOURCES

Environment

There are five national parks in Alberta totalling 63,045 sq. km, the largest area of any province in Canada. There are also 519 parks and protected areas in Alberta covering 2,755,634 ha.

Oil and Gas

Oil sands underlie some 60,000 sq. km of Alberta, the four major deposits being: the Athabasca, Cold Lake, Peace River and Buffalo Head Hills deposits. Some 7% (3,250 sq. km) of the Athabasca deposit can be recovered by open-pit mining techniques. The rest of the Athabasca, and all the deposits in the other areas, are deeper reserves which must be developed through *in situ* techniques. These reserves reach depths of 760

metres. In 2004 Alberta produced 773,300 bbls. per day of crude oil and 962,300 bbls. per day of synthetic crude oil and bitumen. The 2004 value of Albertan producers' sales of crude oil, condensate and pentanes was $40·94bn. CDN. Sales of oilsands were worth $14·94bn. CDN. Alberta produced 67% of Canada's crude petroleum output in 2004.

Natural gas is found in abundance in numerous localities. In 2004, 4,923bn. cu. ft valued at $31·1bn. CDN were produced in Alberta.

Minerals

Coal production in 2004 was 27·2m. tonnes with 1·7m. tonnes of coal being exported.

The preliminary value of mineral production in 2004 (excluding oil and gas) was $1,200·0m. CDN.

Agriculture

There were 53,652 farms in Alberta in 2001 with a total area of 21,067,486 ha. About 9,728,181 ha. are land in crop (2001 census). The majority of farms are made up of cattle, followed by grains and oilseed, and wheat. For particulars of livestock *see* CANADA: Agriculture.

Farm cash receipts in 2004 totalled $8,043·4m. CDN of which crops contributed $2,616·8m. CDN, livestock and products $3,993·3m. CDN and direct payments $1,433·3m. CDN.

Forestry

Forest and other wooded land in 2001 covered some 36,388,000 ha. In 2003–04 Alberta had a regulated harvest of 24,819,100 cu. metres of net merchantable forest.

Fisheries

The largest catch in commercial fishing is whitefish. Perch, tullibee, walley, pike and lake trout are also caught in smaller quantities. Commercial fish production in 2003–04 was 2,127 tonnes, value $3·46m. CDN.

INDUSTRY

The leading manufacturing industries are food and beverages, petroleum refining, metal fabricating, wood industries, primary metal, chemical and chemical products and non-metallic mineral products.

Manufacturing shipments had a total value of $52,965·8m. CDN in 2004. Greatest among these shipments were (in $1m. CDN): refined petroleum and coal products, 10,018; chemicals and chemical products, 9,645; food, 9,087; fabricated metal products, 4,135; machinery, 4,062; wood products, 3,753; primary metal, 2,137; paper and allied products, 1,784; non-metal mineral products, 1,695; and computer and electronic products, 1,471.

Total retail sales in 2004 were $43,703m. CDN, as compared to 2003 with $38,925m. CDN in sales. Main sales in 2004 were (in $1m. CDN): automobiles, 10,007·8; food, 7,650·9; general merchandise, 5,032·2; fuel 4,072·8; and pharmacies and personal care, 2,111·8.

Labour

In 2004 the labour force was 1,843,400 (837,200 females), of whom approximately 1,757,900 (797,700) were employed. In 2001 a total of 44,100 new jobs were created. Alberta's unemployment rate dropped to 4·6% in 2004, compared to the national average of 7·2%.

INTERNATIONAL TRADE

Imports and Exports

Alberta's domestic commodity exports were valued at $66·4bn. CDN in 2004, an increase of 17% on 2003. The largest export markets were the USA, China, Japan, Mexico and South Korea, which together accounted for over 90% of Alberta's international exports. Mining and energy accounted for 71% of exports in 2001.

COMMUNICATIONS

Roads
In 2005 there were 30,800 km of provincial highways and 153,500 km of local roads.

On 31 March 2005 there were 2,459,926 motor vehicles registered.

Rail
In 2003 the length of main railway lines was 7,136 km. There are light rail networks in Edmonton (12·3 km) and Calgary (35·7 km).

Civil Aviation
Calgary International is a major international airport. It handled 7,793,000 passengers (5,537,000 on domestic flights) in 2001.

Telecommunications
The primary telephone system is owned and operated by the Telus Corporation. Telus Corporation had 1,998,366 telephone subscriber lines (including residential and business lines) in service in 2002; in all, 98·2% of Alberta's households had fixed telephone lines. In 2002, 60·9% of households had mobile phones. Alberta also had the second highest percentage of households with computers in Canada at 70·6%.

SOCIAL INSTITUTIONS

Justice
The Supreme Judicial authority of the province is the Court of Appeal. Judges of the Court of Appeal and Court of Queen's Bench are appointed by the Federal government and hold office until retirement at the age of 75. There are courts of lesser jurisdiction in both civil and criminal matters. The Court of Queen's Bench has full jurisdiction over civil proceedings. A Provincial Court which has jurisdiction in civil matters up to $2,000 CDN is presided over by provincially appointed judges. Youth Courts have power to try boys and girls 12–17 years old inclusive for offences against the Young Offenders Act.

The jurisdiction of all criminal courts in Alberta is enacted in the provisions of the Criminal Code. The system of procedure in civil and criminal cases conforms as nearly as possible to the English system. In 2003, 325,894 Criminal Code offences were reported, including 63 homicides.

Education
Schools of all grades are included under the term of public school (including those in the separate school system, which are publicly supported). The same board of trustees controls the schools from kindergarten to university entrance. In 2001–02 there were approximately 546,961 pupils enrolled in grades 1–12, including private schools and special education programmes. The University of Alberta (in Edmonton), founded in 1907, had, in 2004–05, 35,666 students; the University of Calgary had 28,306 students; Athabasca University had 29,542 students; the University of Lethbridge had 7,086 students. Alberta has 34 post-secondary institutions including four universities and two technical colleges.

CULTURE

Tourism
Alberta attracted more than 4,661,000 visitors from outside the province in 2003. It is known for its mountains, museums, parks and festivals. Total tourism receipts in 2003 were $4·3bn. CDN.

FURTHER READING
Savage, H., Kroetsch, R., Wiebe, R., *Alberta*. NeWest Press, 1993
Economic Development Edmonton, *Edmonton Info: Edmonton's Official Fact Book 1999*. Edmonton, 1999

Statistical office: Alberta Finance, Statistics, Room 259, Terrace Bldg, 9515–107 St., Edmonton, AB T5K 2C3.
Websites: http://www.alberta-canada.com; http://www.discoveralberta.com

British Columbia

KEY HISTORICAL EVENTS
British Columbia, formerly known as New Caledonia, was first administered by the Hudson's Bay Company. In 1849 Vancouver Island was given crown colony status and in 1853 the Queen Charlotte Islands became a dependency. The discovery of gold on the Fraser river and the following influx of population resulted in the creation in 1858 of the mainland crown colony of British Columbia, to which the Strikine Territory (established 1862) was later added. In 1866 the two colonies were united.

TERRITORY AND POPULATION
British Columbia has an area of 944,735 sq. km of which land area is 926,492 sq. km. The capital is Victoria. The province is bordered westerly by the Pacific Ocean and Alaska Panhandle, northerly by the Yukon and Northwest Territories, easterly by the Province of Alberta and southerly by the USA along the 49th parallel. A chain of islands, the largest of which are Vancouver Island and the Queen Charlotte Islands, affords protection to the mainland coast.

The population at the 2001 census was 3,907,738; July 2005 estimate, 4,254,500.

The principal metropolitan areas and cities and their population census for 2001 are as follows: Metropolitan Vancouver, 1,986,965; Metropolitan Victoria, 325,754; Abbotsford (amalgamated with Matsqui), 115,463; Kelowna, 96,298; Kamloops, 77,281; Nanaimo, 73,000; Prince George, 72,406; Chilliwack, 62,927; Vernon, 33,494; Mission, 31,272; Penticton, 30,985; Campbell River, 29,465; North Cowichan, 26,148; Cranbrook, 18,476; Port Alberni, 17,743.

SOCIAL STATISTICS
Births in 2003–04 numbered 40,099 (a rate of 9·6 per 1,000 population) and deaths 29,657 (rate of 7·1 per 1,000 population). There were 21,247 marriages and 10,125 divorces in 2002.

CLIMATE
The climate is cool temperate, but mountain influences affect temperatures and rainfall considerably. Driest months occur in summer. Vancouver, Jan. 36°F (2·2°C), July 64°F (17·8°C). Annual rainfall 58" (1,458 mm).

CONSTITUTION AND GOVERNMENT
The British North America Act of 1867 provided for eventual admission into Canadian Confederation, and on 20 July 1871 British Columbia became the sixth province of the Dominion.

British Columbia has a unicameral legislature of 79 elected members. Government policy is determined by the Executive Council responsible to the Legislature. The Lieut.-Governor is appointed by the Governor-General of Canada, usually for a term of five years, and is the head of the executive government of the province.

The Legislative Assembly is elected for a maximum term of five years. There are 79 electoral districts. Every Canadian citizen 18 years and over, having resided a minimum of six months in the province, duly registered, is entitled to vote. The province is represented in the Federal Parliament by 36 members in the House of Commons and six Senators.

RECENT ELECTIONS
At the Legislative Assembly elections of 17 May 2005 the Liberal Party won 45·8% of the vote and 46 of the 79 available seats, the New Democratic Party won 41·5% and 33 seats, and the Green Party 9·2%. Turnout was 57·8%.

CURRENT ADMINISTRATION
Lieut.-Governor: Iona Campagnolo, PC, OM, OBC (sworn in on 25 Sept. 2001).

The Liberal Executive Council comprised in Feb. 2006:

Premier, President of the Executive Council: Gordon Campbell.

Deputy Premier, Minister for Education and Minister Responsible for Early Learning and Literacy: Shirley Bond. *Minister of Children and Family Development:* Stan Hagen. *Aboriginal Affairs and Reconciliation:* Tom Christensen. *Attorney General and Minister Responsible for Multiculturalism:* Wally Oppal. *Solicitor General and Minister for Public Safety:* John Les. *Intergovernmental Relations:* John van Dongen. *Finance:* Carole Taylor. *Childcare:* Linda Reid. *Community Services, Women's and Seniors' Issues:* Ida Chong. *Advanced Education, Research and Technology:* Murray Coell. *Labour and Citizens' Services:* Michael de Jong. *Agriculture and Lands:* Pat Bell. *Energy, Mines and Petroleum Resources:* Richard Neufeld. *Environment:* Barry Penner. *Forests, Range and Housing:* Rich Coleman. *Health:* George Abbott. *Mining:* Bill Bennett. *Transportation:* Kevin Falcon. *Small Business, Revenue and Deregulation:* Rick Thorpe. *Economic Development, Asia-Pacific Initiative and the Olympics:* Colin Hansen. *Employment and Income Assistance:* Claude Richmond. *Tourism, Sport and the Arts:* Olga Ilich.

Office of the Premier: http://www.gov.bc.ca/prem

ECONOMY

GDP per person in 2003 was $35,041 CDN.

Budget

Total revenue in 2003–04 was $28,175m. CDN (own source revenue, $24,248m. CDN; general purpose transfers, $3,151m. CDN; special purpose transfers, $776m. CDN). Total expenditures in 2003–04 amounted to $30,896m. CDN (including: health, $11,181m. CDN; education, $6,797m. CDN; social services, $4,445m. CDN; debt charges, $2,538m. CDN; resource conservation and industrial development, $1,761m. CDN; transport and communication, $1,727m. CDN; protection of persons and property, $1,143m. CDN).

Banking and Finance

At Oct. 1997 Canadian chartered banks maintained 925 branches and had total assets of $146·3bn. CDN in British Columbia. In 1997 credit unions at 96 locations had total assets of $20·4bn. CDN. Several foreign banks have Canadian head offices in Vancouver and several others have branches.

ENERGY AND NATURAL RESOURCES

Electricity

Generation in 2003 totalled 63,051 GWh (56,689 GWh from hydro-electric sources), of which 14,717 GWh were delivered outside the province. Available within the province were 60,176 GWh (with imports of 11,842 GWh).

Oil and Gas

In 2001 natural gas production, from the northeastern part of the province, was valued at $5·18bn. CDN.

Water

Canada accounts for a quarter of the world's fresh water supply, a third of which is located in British Columbia. An extensive hydro-electric generation system has been developed in the province.

Minerals

Coal, copper, gold, zinc, silver and molybdenum are the most important minerals produced but natural gas amounts to approximately half of the value of mineral and fuel extraction. The value of mineral and petroleum products production in 2002 was estimated at $7·23bn. CDN. Coal production (from the northeastern and southeastern regions) was valued at $1·0bn. CDN. Copper was the most valuable metal with production

totalling $599m. CDN in 2002; gold production amounted to $336m. CDN.

Agriculture

Only 3% of the total land area is arable or potentially arable. Farm holdings (20,290 in 2001) cover 2·6m. ha. with an average size of 127 ha. Farm cash receipts in 2003 were estimated at $2·2bn. CDN, led by floriculture and nursery products valued at $439m. CDN, dairy products valued at $393m. CDN and vegetables valued at $329m. CDN. For particulars of livestock *see* CANADA: Agriculture.

Forestry

Around 49·9m. ha. are considered productive forest land of which 48·0m. ha. are provincial crown lands managed by the Ministry of Forests. Approximately 96% of the forested land is coniferous. The total timber harvest in 2002 was 69·8m. cu. metres. Output of forest-based products, 2002: lumber, 33·56m. cu. metres; plywood, 1·68m. cu. metres; pulp, 4·49m. tonnes; newsprint, paper and paperboard, 2·90m. tonnes.

Fisheries

In 2003 the total landed value of the catch was $630m. CDN; wholesale value $1bn. CDN. Salmon (wild and farmed) generated 44% of the wholesale value of seafood products, followed by shellfish, groundfish and herring. The seafood sector supported 11,200 jobs in 2001.

INDUSTRY

The value of shipments from all manufacturing industries reached $37·2bn. CDN in 2003 and accounted for around 10% of the province's GDP.

Labour

In 2003 the labour force averaged 2,202,000 persons with 2,023,000 employed (47% female) and 179,000 unemployed (8·1%). Of the employed workforce 1·60m. were in service industries and 422,000 in goods production. There were 321,000 employed in trade, 212,000 in healthcare and social assistance, 206,000 in manufacturing, 165,000 in accommodation and food industries, 127,000 in finance and related business, 122,000 in construction, 114,000 in transportation and warehousing, 92,000 in public administration, 34,000 in agriculture, 29,000 in forestry, 13,000 in mining and 5,000 in fishing and trapping.

Trade Unions

In 2003, 34% of the province's paid workers were unionized. The largest unions are: Canadian Union of Public Employees (63,999 members in early 2003); B.C. Government and Service Employees' Union and affiliates (approximately 60,000); and B.C. Teachers' Federation (43,876 in 1997).

INTERNATIONAL TRADE

Imports and Exports

Imports in 2003 totalled $31,258m. CDN in value, while exports amounted to $28,550m. CDN. The USA is the largest market for products exported through British Columbia customs ports ($18,928m. CDN in 2003), followed by Japan ($3,621m. CDN) and People's Republic of China, including Hong Kong ($1,278m. CDN).

The leading exports in 2001 were: wood products, $10,327m. CDN; paper and allied products, $5,421m. CDN; food, $4,149m. CDN; fabricated metal products, $1,577m. CDN; machinery, $1,467m. CDN.

COMMUNICATIONS

Roads

In 2001 there were 42,440 km of provincial highway, of which 23,710 km were paved. In 2003, 1,829,000 passenger cars and 589,000 commercial vehicles were registered.

Rail

The province is served by two transcontinental railways, the Canadian Pacific Railway and the Canadian National Railway. Passenger service is provided by VIA Rail, a Crown Corporation, and the publicly owned British Columbia Railway. In 1995 the American company Amtrak began operating a service between Seattle and Vancouver after a 14-year hiatus. British Columbia is also served by the freight trains of the B.C. Hydro and Power Authority, the Northern Alberta Railways Company and the Burlington Northern and Southern Railways Inc. The combined route-mileage of mainline track operated by the CPR, CNR and BCR totals 6,800 km. The system also includes CPR and CNR wagon ferry connections to Vancouver Island, between Prince Rupert and Alaska, and interchanges with American railways at southern border points. There is a light rail system in Vancouver, opened in 1985 (50 km). A commuter rail service linking Vancouver and the Fraser Valley was established in 1995 (69 km).

Civil Aviation

International airports are located at Vancouver and Victoria. Total passenger arrivals and departures on scheduled services made by 33 foreign and domestic airlines were 14·3m. in 2003 at Vancouver and 1·1m. in 1997 at Victoria. Daily interprovincial and intraprovincial flights serve all main population centres. Small public and private airstrips are located throughout the province.

Shipping

The major ports are Vancouver (the largest dry cargo port on the North American Pacific coast), Prince Rupert and ports on the Fraser River. Other deep-sea ports include Nanaimo, Port Alberni, Campbell River, Powell River, Kitimat, Stewart and Squamish. Total cargo shipped through the port of Vancouver during 2003 was 66·7m. tonnes. 953,000 cruise passengers visited Vancouver in 2003.

British Columbia Ferries—one of the largest ferry systems in the world—connect Vancouver Island with the mainland and also provide service to other coastal points; in 2003, 21·3m. passengers and 8·3m. vehicles were carried. Service by other ferry systems is also provided between Vancouver Island and the USA. The Alaska State Ferries connect Prince Rupert with centres in Alaska.

Telecommunications

In 2003, 1,544,000 households (95·1%) had telephones. In 2000 there were 800,000 cellular phone subscribers in the province.

SOCIAL INSTITUTIONS

Justice

The judicial system is composed of the Court of Appeal, the Supreme Court, County Courts and various Provincial Courts, including Magistrates' Courts and Small Claims Courts. The federal courts include the Supreme Court of Canada and the Federal Court of Canada.

In 2002, 478,635 Criminal Code offences were reported, including 126 homicides.

Education

Education, free up to Grade XII level, is financed jointly from municipal and provincial government revenues. Attendance is compulsory from the age of five to 16. There were approximately 656,150 pupils enrolled in 1,707 public schools from kindergarten to Grade 12 in Sept. 2003.

The universities had a full-time enrolment of approximately 85,497 for 2002–03. Non-vocational enrolment at leading institutions (2002–03): the University of British Columbia, 39,224; Simon Fraser University, 21,684; University of Victoria, 17,975; University of Northern British Columbia, 3,630; Royal Roads University, 2,984. The regional colleges in 1996 were: Camosun College, Victoria; Capilano College, North Vancouver; Cariboo College, Kamloops; College of New Caledonia, Prince George; Douglas College, New Westminister; East Kootenay Community College, Cranbrook; Fraser Valley College, Chilliwack/Abbotsford; Kwantlen College, Surrey; Malaspina College, Nanaimo; North Island College, Comox; Northern Lights College, Dawson Creek/Fort St John; Northwest Community College, Terrace/Prince Rupert; Okanagan College, Kelowna with branches at Salmon Arm and Vernon; Selkirk College, Castlegar; Vancouver Community College, Vancouver; Langara College, Vancouver.

There are also the British Columbia Institute of Technology, Burnaby; Emily Carr College of Art and Design, Vancouver; Open Learning Institute, Richmond. A televised distance education and special programmes through KNOW, the Knowledge Network of the West, is provided.

Health

The government operates a hospital insurance scheme giving universal coverage after a qualifying period of three months' residence in the province. The province has come under a national medicare scheme which is partially subsidized by the provincial government and partially by the federal government. In March 2003 there were approximately 8,400 acute care and rehabilitation hospital beds. The provincial government spent an estimated \$11·8bn. CDN on health programmes during 2004–05. 39% of the government's total expenditure was for health care.

CULTURE

Broadcasting

In 2001 there were ten television broadcasting stations in operation, with 84% of households subscribing to cable television. In July 1997 there were 130 radio stations originating in British Columbia.

Tourism

British Columbia's greatest attractions are Vancouver, and the provincial parks and ecological reserves that make up the Protected Areas System. The entire Tatshenshini-Alsek region, almost 1m. ha. in northwestern B.C., has been protected as a Class A provincial park and nominated as a World Heritage Site. In 2002 there were 13,302 campsites and 3,000 km of hiking trails. In 2003, 21·87m. tourists spent \$8·95n. CDN in the province.

FURTHER READING

Barman, J., *The West beyond the West: a History of British Columbia.* Toronto Univ. Press, 1991

Statistical office: BC STATS, Ministry of Finance and Corporate Relations, P.O. Box 9410, Stn. Prov. Govt., Victoria V8W 9V1.

Manitoba

KEY HISTORICAL EVENTS

Manitoba was known as the Red River Settlement before it entered the dominion in 1870. During the 18th century its only inhabitants were fur-trappers, but a more settled colonization began in the 19th century. The area was administered by the Hudson's Bay Company until 1869 when it was purchased by the new dominion. In 1870 it was given provincial status. It was enlarged in 1881 and again in 1912 by the addition of part of the Northwest Territories.

TERRITORY AND POPULATION

The area of the province is 647,797 sq. km (250,114 sq. miles), of which 553,557 sq. km are land and 94,240 sq. km water. From north to south it is 1,225 km, and at the widest point it is 793 km.

Population estimate, 1 July 2005, was 1,177,600. The 2001 census showed the following figures for areas of population of over 10,000 people: Winnipeg, the province's capital and largest city, 671,274; City of Brandon, 39,716; City of Thompson, 13,256; City of Portage la Prairie, 12,978; Rural Municipality of Springfield, 12,602; Rural Municipality of Hanover, 10,789; Rural Municipality of St Andrews, 10,695.

SOCIAL STATISTICS

Births in 2003–04 numbered 13,985 (a rate of 12·0 per 1,000 population) and deaths 10,127 (rate of 8·7 per 1,000 population). There were 5,905 marriages and 2,396 divorces in 2002.

CLIMATE

The climate is cold continental, with very severe winters but pleasantly warm summers. Rainfall amounts are greatest in the months May to Sept. Winnipeg, Jan. –3°F (–19·3°C), July 67°F (19·6°C). Annual rainfall 21" (539 mm).

CONSTITUTION AND GOVERNMENT

The provincial government is administered by a *Lieut.-Governor* assisted by an *Executive Council* (Cabinet), which is appointed from and responsible to a *Legislative Assembly* of 57 members elected for five years. Women were enfranchised in 1916. The Electoral Division Act, 1955, created 57 single-member constituencies and abolished the transferable vote. There are 26 rural electoral divisions and 31 urban electoral divisions. The province is represented by six members in the Senate and 14 in the House of Commons of Canada.

RECENT ELECTIONS

In elections to the Legislative Assembly held on 3 June 2003 the New Democratic Party won 35 out of 57 seats (49·2% of the vote), the Progressive Conservative Party 20 seats (36·9%) and the Liberal Party 2 seats (12·8%).

CURRENT ADMINISTRATION

Lieut.-Governor: John Harvard, PC, OM; b. 1938 (took office on 30 June 2004).

The members of the New Democratic Party Ministry in Feb. 2006 were:

Premier, President of the Executive Council, Minister of Federal-Provincial Relations: Gary A. Doer; b. 1948.

Deputy Premier, Minister of Agriculture, Food and Rural Initiatives: Rosann Wowchuk. *Water Stewardship:* Steve Ashton. *Energy, Science and Technology:* David Walter Chomiak. *Aboriginal and Northern Affairs:* Oscar Lathlin. *Justice and Attorney General, Keeper of the Great Seal:* Gord Mackintosh. *Culture, Heritage and Tourism:* Eric Robinson. *Advanced Education and Training:* Diane McGifford. *Health:* Tim Sale. *Transportation and Government Services:* Ron Lemieux. *Finance:* Gregory F. Selinger. *Intergovernmental Affairs and Trade:* Scott Smith. *Conservation:* Stan Struthers. *Labour and Immigration:* Nancy Allan. *Industry, Economic Development and Mines:* Jim Rondeau. *Education, Citizenship and Youth:* Peter Bjornson. *Family Services and Housing:* Christine Melnick. *Healthy Living:* Theresa Oswald.

Manitoba Government Website: http://www.gov.mb.ca

ECONOMY

Nominal GDP in Manitoba grew 3·5% in 2002 to $35·9bn. CDN.

Budget

Provincial revenue and expenditure (current account, excluding capital expenditures, debt/pension repayment and transfers from/to the Fiscal Stabilization Fund) for fiscal years ending 31 March (in $1m. CDN):

	2000–01	2001–02	2002–03[1]	2003–04[2]
Revenue	6,752	6,747	6,990	7,314
Expenditure	6,615	6,738	6,967	7,256

[1]Forecast. [2]Budgeted figure.

Performance

Manitoba's economy grew 3·1% in real terms in 2002, up from 1·5% growth in 2001.

ENERGY AND NATURAL RESOURCES

Electricity

The province's electrical utility, Manitoba Hydro, has a total net generating capacity of 5,466,000 kW. In the year ending 31 March 2003 the provincial Crown corporation produced 29,178m. kWh of electricity. In 2002–03 scheduled power purchases from elsewhere in Canada and the USA totalled 3,043m. kWh. Manitoba provided 18,953m. kWh to its domestic customers. Energy sold outside Manitoba was 9,735m. kWh. This represented a decline in extraprovincial sales for the first time in six years. Revenue declined to $463m. CDN, $125m. CDN less than revenues reported in 2001–02. Of total extraprovincial revenue, $379m. CDN or 82% was derived from the US market while $84m. CDN or 18% was from sales to other Canadian provinces.

Oil and Gas

The value of oil production in 2002 was $152·6m. CDN, up 10·5% from 2001.

Minerals

Principal minerals mined are nickel, zinc, copper, gold and small quantities of silver. The value of mineral production declined 4% in 2002 to $982m. CDN. At $398m. CDN, nickel is Manitoba's most important mineral product, accounting for 40·5% of the province's total value of mineral production. Zinc accounted for 11% of the value of mineral production in 2002. Copper, which accounts for 9% of Manitoba's mineral production, saw moderate declines in both price and volume of production in 2002.

Agriculture

Rich farmland is the main primary resource, although the area in farms is only about 14% of the total land area. In 2002 total farm cash receipts increased by 2·9% to $3·76bn. CDN. Crop receipts surged 24·4% to $1·85bn. CDN while livestock receipts fell 5·2% to $1·7bn. CDN. Crop receipts accounted for 52% of total market receipts while livestock accounted for 48%. The growth of a number of non-traditional crops, such as dry beans and potatoes, underscores the continuing diversification of Manitoba's agricultural base. Manitoba's share of Canada's dry bean production has increased from 7% in 1993 to 57% in 2002. For particulars of livestock *see* CANADA: Agriculture.

Fisheries

From about 57,000 sq. km of rivers and lakes, the value of fisheries production to fishers was about $32·2m. CDN in 2001–02 representing about 14,800 tonnes of fish. Whitefish, sauger, pickerel and pike are the principal varieties of fish caught.

INDUSTRY

Manitoba's diverse manufacturing sector is the province's largest industry, accounting for approximately 12·5% of total GDP. The value of manufacturing shipments grew 0·6% in 2002 to $11·5bn. CDN.

Labour

Manitoba's total employment rose by 9,100 in 2002 (3,500 full-time and 5,600 part-time jobs), a 1·6% increase, bringing employment to a record-high level of 567,000. Manitoba had the lowest unemployment rate among the Canadian provinces at 5·2%. It also had the lowest youth unemployment rate in the country at 10·2%.

INTERNATIONAL TRADE

Products grown and manufactured in Manitoba find ready markets in other parts of Canada, in the USA, particularly the upper Midwest region, and in other countries.

Imports and Exports

In 2002 Manitoba merchandise exports to the US rose 1% to $7·6bn. CDN. Manitoba is the only province in Canada to record higher exports to the USA in 2001 and 2002. Merchandise exports to the USA comprise 82% of Manitoba's total foreign merchandise exports. In 2002 merchandise exports to Japan (Manitoba's second-most important foreign market) increased 3·2% while exports declined to Mexico, Hong Kong, Belgium and China. Manufacturing industries' exports, which account for about two-thirds of Manitoba's total foreign exports, increased by 1%. Gains were posted by four of the five largest manufacturing industry categories. Leading growth export industries include machinery, printing and wood products.

COMMUNICATIONS

Roads

Highways and provincial roads total 18,500 km, with 2,800 bridges and other structures. In 2003 there were 498,880 passenger vehicles (including taxis), 118,823 trucks, 51,122 farm trucks, 27,978 off-road vehicles and 9,138 motorcycles registered in the province.

Rail

The province has about 5,650 km of commercial track, not including industrial track, yards and sidings. Most of the track belongs to the country's two national railways. Canadian Pacific owns about 1,950 km and Canadian National about 2,400 km. The Hudson Bay Railway, operated by Denver-based Omnitrax, has about 1,300 km of track. Fort Worth-based Burlington Northern's railcars are moved in Manitoba on CN and CP tracks and trains.

Civil Aviation

In 2003 there were 61 domestic commercial aviation operators flying from bases in Manitoba. Three were designated private. Fifty-four air taxi companies were licensed to carry fewer than ten passengers; and six commuter operations were licensed to carry up to 19 passengers. Twelve national airlines were licensed to carry more than 19 passengers. Five foreign airlines were landing in the province. In addition, 36 aerial services were licensed (largely for agricultural chemical spraying).

Telecommunications

In 2002 Manitoba Telecom Services provided over 700,000 access services on its wireline network, more than 230,000 cellular subscribers and more than 115,000 Internet access customers.

SOCIAL INSTITUTIONS

Justice

In 2002, 129,935 Criminal Code offences (excluding traffic offences) were reported in Manitoba (a ratio of 11,290 per 100,000 people), including 36 homicides (a ratio of three per 100,000 people).

Education

Education is controlled through locally elected school divisions. There were 179,287 students enrolled in the province's public schools in the 2003–04 school year. Student teacher ratios (including all instructors but excluding school-based administrators) averaged one teacher for every 18·1 students.

Manitoba has four universities with a total full- and part-time undergraduate and graduate enrolment for the 2003–04 academic year of 39,500. They are the University of Manitoba, founded in 1877; the University of Winnipeg; Brandon University; and the Collège universitaire de Saint Boniface.

Community colleges in Brandon, The Pas and Winnipeg offer two-year diploma courses in a number of fields, as well as specialized training in many trades. They also give a large number and variety of shorter courses, both at their campuses and in many communities throughout the province. Provincial government expenditure on education and training for the 2003–04 fiscal year is budgeted at $1·59bn. CDN.

CULTURE

Tourism

Between 2000 and 2002 Manitoba's tourism sector grew 28% and now brings in $1·3bn. CDN a year. Tourism and related industries have created 60,000 jobs in the province, employing one in ten people.

For the period ending 30 Nov. 2002 the total number of overseas tourists entering Manitoba for one or more nights increased by 1·4%. Manitoba was the only Canadian jurisdiction to record positive growth of overseas tourists in the period in question.

FURTHER READING

General Information: Inquiries may be addressed to Manitoba Government Inquiry. *e-mail:* mgi@gov.mb.ca

---

New Brunswick

KEY HISTORICAL EVENTS

Visited by Jacques Cartier in 1534, New Brunswick was first explored by Samuel de Champlain in 1604. With Nova Scotia, it originally formed one French colony called Acadia. It was ceded by the French in the Treaty of Utrecht in 1713 and became a permanent British possession in 1759. It was first settled by British colonists in 1764 but was separated from Nova Scotia, and became a province in June 1784 as a result of the great influx of United Empire Loyalists. Responsible government came into being in 1848 and consisted of an executive council, a legislative council (later abolished) and a House of Assembly. In 1867 New Brunswick entered the Confederation.

TERRITORY AND POPULATION

The area of the province is 72,908 sq. km (28,150 sq. miles), of which 71,450 sq. km (27,587 sq. miles) is land area. The Census counted 729,498 people in New Brunswick on 15 May 2001. At this time, the most frequently reported ethnic origin, whether reported alone or in combination with other origins, was Canadian (58%). French was the second most frequently reported ancestry (27%), followed by English (23%), Irish (19%) and Scottish (18%). A total of 16,990 persons in New Brunswick identified themselves as Aboriginal (that is, as a North American Indian, Métis or Inuit) in 2001.

Population estimate, 1 July 2005, was 752,000.

The six urban centres of the province and their respective populations based on 2001 census figures are: Saint John, 122,678; Moncton, 117,727; Fredericton (capital), 81,346; Bathurst, 23,935; Edmundston, 22,173; Campbellton (part only), 13,310. The official languages are English and French.

SOCIAL STATISTICS

Births in 2003–04 numbered 7,086 (a rate of 9·4 per 1,000 population) and deaths 6,318 (rate of 8·4 per 1,000 population). There were 3,818 marriages and 1,461 divorces in 2002.

CLIMATE

A cool temperate climate, with rain in all seasons but temperatures modified by the influence of the Gulf Stream. Annual average total precipitation in Fredericton: 1,131 mm. Warmest month, July (average high) 25·6°C.

CONSTITUTION AND GOVERNMENT

The government is vested in a Lieut.-Governor, appointed by the Queen's representative in New Brunswick, and a Legislative Assembly of 55 members, each of whom is individually elected to represent the voters in one constituency or riding. The political party with the largest number of elected representatives, after a Provincial election, forms the government.

The province has ten appointed members in the Canadian Senate and elects ten members in the House of Commons.

RECENT ELECTIONS

Elections to the provincial assembly were held on 9 June 2003. The Progressive Conservative Party (PC) won 28 seats (with 45·5% of the vote), the Liberal Party (LIB) 26 seats (44·3%) and the New Democratic Party (NDP) one seat (9·7%). The governing PCs lost 19 seats, including four ministers.

CURRENT ADMINISTRATION

Lieut.-Governor: Herménégilde Chiasson; b. 1946 (took office on 26 Aug. 2003).

The members of the PC cabinet were as follows in Feb. 2006:

Premier, President of Executive Council Office, and Minister for Regional Development Corporation: Bernard Lord; b. 1965.

Deputy Premier, Minister of Supply and Services: Dale Graham. *Justice, Attorney General:* Bradley Green, QC. *Business New Brunswick:* Peter Mesheau. *Intergovernmental and International Relations:* Percy Mockler. *Finance:* Jeannot Volpé. *Agriculture, Fisheries and Aquaculture:* David Alward. *Health and Wellness:* Elvy Robichaud. *Training and Employment Development:* Margaret-Ann Blaney. *Environment and Local Government:* Trevor Holder. *Transportation:* Paul Robichaud. *Public Safety:* Wayne Steeves. *Natural Resources:* Keith Ashfield. *Energy:* Bruce Fitch. *Office of Human Resources:* Rose-May Poirier. *Family and Community Services, Tourism and Parks:* L. Joan MacAlpine-Stiles. *Education:* Madeleine Dubé.

Government of New Brunswick Website: http://www.gnb.ca

ECONOMY

GDP per capita in 2001 was $27,217 CDN. Personal income was $18,115m. CDN; personal income per capita was $24,153 CDN.

Budget

The ordinary budget (in $1m. CDN) is shown as follows (financial years ended 31 March):

	1998	1999	2000	2001	2002
Gross revenue	4,474·1	4,486·4	4,366·6	4,707·2	4,707·2
Gross expenditure	4,439·2	4,650·7	4,297·6	4,488·0	4,725·2

Funded debt and capital loans outstanding (exclusive of Treasury Bills) as of 31 March 1998 was $6,685·1m. CDN.

ENERGY AND NATURAL RESOURCES

Electricity

Hydro-electric, thermal and nuclear generating stations of NB Power had an installed capacity of 3,769 MW at 31 March 2002, consisting of 15 generating stations. The sale of out-of-province power accounted for 17·8% of revenue in 2002–03. Total revenue amounted to $1,273m. CDN.

Oil and Gas

In 2002 Enbridge Gas New Brunswick continued developing the natural gas distribution system in the province, which is now available in Fredericton, Moncton, St John, St George and Oromocto.

Minerals

The total value of minerals produced in 2002 reached $652·3m. CDN. The top four contributors to mineral production are zinc, lead, copper and peat, accounting for 72·9% of total value in 2002. In 2000 New Brunswick ranked first in Canada for the production of zinc, bismuth and lead, third for silver and sixth for copper.

Agriculture

The total area under crops is estimated at 135,008 ha. Farms numbered 3,034 and averaged 149 ha. (census 2001). Potatoes account for 33% of total farm cash receipts and dairy products 11%. New Brunswick is self-sufficient in fluid milk and supplies a processing industry. For particulars of livestock *see* CANADA: Agriculture. Farm cash receipts in 2002 were $421·2m. CDN.

Forestry

New Brunswick contains some 6m. ha. of productive forest lands. The value of manufacturing shipments for the wood-related industries in 2002 was just over $3·8bn. CDN. The paper and allied industry group is the largest component of the industry, contributing 55·2% of forestry output. In 2002 nearly 15,750 people were employed in all aspects of the forest industry.

Fisheries

Commercial fishing is one of the most important primary industries of the province, employing 7,123 in 1999. Landings in 2002 (122,225 tonnes) amounted to $194m. CDN. In 2001 molluscs and crustaceans ranked first with a value of $153m. CDN, 87·6% of the total landed value. Exports in 2001, totalling $644·8m. CDN, went mainly to the USA and Japan.

INDUSTRY

Important industries include food and beverages, paper and allied industries, and timber products.

Labour

New Brunswick's labour force increased by 2·4% in 2002 to 385,700 while employment increased to 345,000. Goods producing industries employed 79,700 and the service-producing industries employed 253,700. Nearly 20% of the industrial labour force work in Saint John. In 2002 unemployment was 10·4%.

INTERNATIONAL TRADE

Imports and Exports

New Brunswick's location, with deepwater harbours open throughout the year and container facilities at Saint John, makes it ideal for exporting. The main exports include lumber, woodpulp, newsprint, refined petroleum products and electricity. In 2002 the major trading partners of the province were the USA with 89·2% of total exports, followed by Japan with 2·4% and the UK with 1·4% of total exports. Imports totalled $5,720m. CDN while exports reached $8,160·8m. CDN in 2002.

COMMUNICATIONS

Roads

There are 21,423 km of roads in the Provincial Highway system, of which 8,333 km consists of arterial, collector and local roads that provide access to most areas. The main highway system, including approximately 964 km of the Trans-Canada Highway, links the province with the principal roads in Quebec, Nova Scotia and Prince Edward Island, as well as the Interstate Highway System in the eastern seaboard states of the USA. At 31 March 2002 total road motor vehicle registrations numbered 549,061 of which 370,990 were passenger automobiles, 147,149 were truck and truck tractors, 13,406 motorcycles and mopeds, and 4,387 other vehicles.

Rail

New Brunswick is served by the Canadian National Railways, Springfield Terminal Railway, New Brunswick Southern Railway,

New Brunswick East Coast Railway, Le Chemin de fer de la Matapédia et du Golfe and VIA Rail. The Salem-Hillsborough rail is popular with tourists.

Civil Aviation
There are three major airports at Fredericton, Moncton and Saint John. There are also a number of small regional airports.

Shipping
New Brunswick has five major ports. The Port of Saint John handles approximately 20m. tonnes of cargo each year including forest products, steel, potash and petroleum. The Port of Belledune is a deep-water port and open all year round. Other ports are Dalhousie, Bayside/St Andrews and Miramichi.

Telecommunications
In 2003, 282,000 households (96·8%) had telephones.

SOCIAL INSTITUTIONS

Justice
In 2002, 56,856 Criminal Code offences were reported, including nine homicides.

Education
Public education is free and non-sectarian.

There were, in Sept. 2002, 120,600 students (including kindergarten) and 7,469 full-time equivalent/professional educational staff in the province's 342 schools.

There are four universities. The University of New Brunswick at Fredericton (founded 13 Dec. 1785 by the Loyalists, elevated to university status in 1823, and reorganized as the University of New Brunswick in 1859) had 9,007 full-time students at the Fredericton campus and 3,017 full-time students at the Saint John campus (2002–03); the Université de Moncton at Moncton, 5,089 full-time students; St Thomas University at Fredericton, 2,897 full-time students; Mount Allison University at Sackville had 2,199 full-time students.

CULTURE

Broadcasting
The province is served by 57 radio stations and a number of television stations, the majority of which broadcast exclusively in English; the remainder broadcast in French (some radio stations are bilingual).

Press
In 2002 New Brunswick had five daily newspapers (one in French), and 23 weekly newspapers, five in French and two bilingual.

Tourism
New Brunswick has a number of historic buildings as well as libraries, museums and other cultural sites. Tourism is one of the leading contributors to the economy. In 2002 tourism revenues reached $1·2bn. CDN.

FURTHER READING

Industrial Information: Dept. of Business New Brunswick, Fredericton. *Economic Information:* Dept. of Finance, New Brunswick Statistics Agency, Fredericton. *General Information:* Communications New Brunswick, Fredericton.

Newfoundland and Labrador

KEY HISTORICAL EVENTS

Archaeological finds at L'Anse-au-Meadow in northern Newfoundland show that the Vikings established a colony here in about AD 1000. This site is the only known Viking colony in North America. Newfoundland was discovered by John Cabot on 24 June 1497, and was soon frequented in the summer months by the Portuguese, Spanish and French for its fisheries. It was formally occupied in Aug. 1583 by Sir Humphrey Gilbert on behalf of the English Crown but various attempts to colonize the island remained unsuccessful. Although British sovereignty was recognized in 1713 by the Treaty of Utrecht, disputes over fishing rights with the French were not finally settled until 1904. By the Anglo-French Convention of 1904, France renounced her exclusive fishing rights along part of the coast, granted under the Treaty of Utrecht, but retained sovereignty of the offshore islands of St Pierre and Miquelon. Self-governing from 1855, the colony remained outside of the Canadian confederation in 1867 and continued to govern itself until 1934, when a commission of government appointed by the British Crown assumed responsibility for governing the colony and Labrador. This body controlled the country until union with Canada in 1949.

TERRITORY AND POPULATION

Area, 405,212 sq. km (156,452 sq. miles), of which freshwater, 31,340 sq. km (12,100 sq. miles). In March 1927 the Privy Council decided the boundary between Canada and Newfoundland in Labrador. This area, now part of the Province of Newfoundland and Labrador, is 294,330 sq. km (113,641 sq. miles) of land area.

Newfoundland island's coastline is punctuated with numerous bays, fjords and inlets, providing many good deep water harbours. Approximately one-third of the area is covered by water. Grand Lake, the largest body of water, has an area of about 530 sq. km. Good agricultural land is generally found in the valleys of the Terra Nova River, the Gander River, the Exploits River and the Humber River, which are also heavily timbered. The Strait of Belle Isle separates the island from Labrador to the north. Bordering on the Canadian province of Quebec, Labrador is a vast, pristine wilderness and extremely sparsely populated (approximately 10 sq. km per person). Labrador's Lake Melville is 2,934 sq. km and its highest peak, Mount Caubvick, is 1,700 metres.

The population at the 2001 census was 516,930. The population is declining at a faster rate than any other Canadian province, with a drop of 7·0% between the censuses of 1996 and 2001. Population estimate, 1 July 2005, was 516,000.

The capital of the province is the City of St. John's (2001 census population, 99,182). The other cities are Mt Pearl (24,964 in 2001) and Corner Brook (20,103); important towns are Conception Bay South (19,772), Grand Falls-Windsor (13,340), Gander (9,651), Paradise (9,598), Happy Valley-Goose Bay (7,969), Labrador City (7,744), Stephenville (7,101), Marystown (5,908), Portugal Cove-St Philip's (5,866), Bay Roberts (5,237), Clarenville (5,104) and Channel-Port aux Basques (4,637).

SOCIAL STATISTICS

Births in 2003–04 numbered 4,595 (a rate of 8·9 per 1,000 population) and deaths 4,349 (rate of 8·4 per 1,000 population). There were 2,959 marriages in 2002 and 842 divorces.

CLIMATE

The cool temperate climate is marked by heavy precipitation, distributed evenly over the year, a cool summer and frequent fogs in spring. St. John's, Jan. –4°C, July 15·8°C. Annual rainfall 1,240 mm.

CONSTITUTION AND GOVERNMENT

Until 1832 Newfoundland was ruled by a British Governor. In that year a Legislature was brought into existence, but the Governor and his Executive Council were not responsible to it. Under the constitution of 1855, the government was administered by the

Governor appointed by the Crown with an Executive Council responsible to the House of Assembly.

Parliamentary government was suspended in 1933 on financial grounds and Government by Commission was inaugurated on 16 Feb. 1934. Confederation with Canada was approved by a referendum in July 1948. In the Canadian Senate on 18 Feb. 1949 Royal Assent was given to the terms of union of Newfoundland and Labrador with Canada, and on 23 March 1949, in the House of Lords, London, Royal Assent was given to an amendment to the British North America Act, made necessary by the inclusion of Newfoundland and Labrador as the tenth Province of Canada.

The province is represented by six members in the Senate and by seven members in the House of Commons of Canada.

RECENT ELECTIONS

Elections were held on 21 Oct. 2003. The Progressive Conservative Party (PC) won 34 of the 48 seats in the House of Assembly (with 58·7% of the vote), defeating the ruling Liberal Party (Lib.) of Premier Roger Grimes, which won 12 seats (33·2%). The New Democratic Party (NDP) won 2 seats (6·9%).

CURRENT ADMINISTRATION

Lieut.-Governor: Edward M. Roberts; b. 1940 (assumed office 1 Nov. 2002).

In Feb. 2006 the Progressive Conservative Cabinet was composed as follows:

Premier and Minister of Business: Danny Williams; b. 1950 (sworn in on 6 Nov. 2003).

Deputy Premier, Minister of Fisheries and Aquaculture and Responsible for Aboriginal Affairs: Tom Rideout. *Education, and Responsible for the Status of Women:* Joan Burke. *Environment and Conservation:* Tom Osborne. *Finance and President of the Treasury Board:* Loyola Sullivan. *Government Services:* Dianne Whalen. *Health and Community Services:* John Ottenheimer. *Human Resources, Labour and Employment and Responsible for Labrador Affairs and Newfoundland and Labrador Housing:* Paul Shelley. *Innovation, Trade and Rural Development:* Kathy Dunderdale. *Justice and Intergovernmental Affairs:* Tom Marshall. *Natural Resources and Government House Leader:* Ed Byrne. *Municipal Affairs:* Jack Byrne. *Tourism, Culture and Recreation:* Tom Hedderson. *Transportation and Works:* Trevor Taylor.

Speaker of the House of Assembly: Harvey Hodder.

Office of the Premier: http://www.premier.gov.nl.ca/premier

ECONOMY

GDP growth for 2003 was expected to be 4·3%. Inflation was estimated to be 2·2% in 2003.

Budget

Government budget in $1,000 CDN in fiscal years ending 31 March:

	2001–02	2002–03	2003–04[1]
Gross Revenue	3,800,799	3,896,047	3,916,285
Gross Expenditure	3,684,975	3,831,485	4,017,878

[1]Estimate.

ENERGY AND NATURAL RESOURCES

Electricity

Newfoundland and Labrador is served by two physically independent electrical systems with a total of 7,401 MW of operational electrical generating capacity. In 2002 total provincial electricity generation equalled 43·9bn. kWh, of which about 94% was from hydro-electric sources. Electricity service for a total of 254,000 retail customers is provided by two utilities and regulated by the Board of Commissioners of Public Utilities.

Oil and Gas

Since 1965, 140 wells have been drilled on the Continental Margin of the Province. Only the Hibernia discovery had commercial capability with production starting in the early 1990s. In 2002 oil production from Hibernia reached 65·9m. bbls. 2003 production was expected to increase to around 78m. bbls. The Terra Nova development produced oil in Jan. 2002 and is permitted to produce almost 59m. bbls. annually.

Minerals

The mineral resources are vast but only partially documented. Large deposits of iron ore, with an ore reserve of over 5,000m. tonnes at Labrador City, Wabush City and in the Knob Lake area, are supplying approximately half of Canada's production. Other large deposits of iron ore are known to exist in the Julienne Lake area. The Central Mineral Belt, which extends from the Smallwood Reservoir to the Atlantic coast near Makkovik, holds uranium, copper, beryllium and molybdenite potential.

The percentage share of mineral shipment value in 2002 stood at 91% for iron ore. Other major mineral products were gold, silver, pyrophyllite, limestone and gypsum. The value of mineral shipments in 2002 totalled $792m. CDN.

Agriculture

The value of farm production in 2002 was $82·7m. CDN, an increase of 1·7% on 2001. Dairy products accounted for 34% of total receipts, hens and chickens 20%, eggs 13% and floriculture and nursery 13%. For particulars of livestock *see* CANADA: Agriculture.

Forestry

The forestry economy in the province is mainly dependent on the operation of three newsprint mills—Corner Brook Pulp and Paper and Abitibi-Consolidated (which operates two mills). In 2002 the estimated value of newsprint exported totalled $541m. CDN, a decrease of 20% over 2001. Lumber mills and saw-log operations produced 144m. flat bd ft in 2001–02.

Fisheries

Closure of the northern cod and other groundfish fisheries has switched attention to secondary seafood production and aquaculture. The total catch in 2002 increased by 2·5% to 267,500 tonnes valued at $515m. CDN. Crab, shrimp and cod together accounted for 59·4% of total landings and 80% of landed value. 16,200 people were employed in the fishing industry in 2002.

INDUSTRY

The total value of manufacturing shipments in 2002 was $2·24bn. CDN, an increase of 1·7% on 2001. This consisted largely of fish products, refined petroleum and newsprint.

Labour

In 2002 those in employment numbered 213,900 with 12,400 workers employed in manufacturing. The unemployment rate was 16·9% in 2002 (16·1% in 2001).

Trade Unions

In 2002 union membership was 39% of the employed workforce. The Newfoundland and Labrador Federation of Labour (NLFL) has 50,000 members; the Newfoundland and Labrador Association of Public and Private Employees (NAPE) has 19,000.

COMMUNICATIONS

Roads

In 2001 there were 8,938 km of roads, of which 6,990 were paved. In 2002 there were 261,842 motor vehicles registered.

Rail

In 1997 the Quebec North Shore and Labrador Railway operated both freight and passenger services on its 588 km main line from Sept-Iles, Quebec, to Shefferville, Quebec and its 58 km spur line from Ross Bay Junction to Labrador City, Newfoundland. In 1996 freight totalled 20·8m. tonnes (iron ore, 20·0m. tonnes).

Civil Aviation
The province is linked to the rest of Canada by regular air services provided by Air Canada and a number of smaller air carriers.

Shipping
At Jan. 2004 there were 1,822 ships on register in Newfoundland. Marine Atlantic, a federal crown corporation, provides a freight and passenger service all year round from Channel-Port aux Basques to North Sydney, Nova Scotia; and seasonal ferries connect Argentia with North Sydney, and Lewisporte with Goose Bay, Labrador.

Telecommunications
In 2003, 192,000 households (97·0%) had telephones.

Postal Services
There were 442 full service post office outlets in 2005.

SOCIAL INSTITUTIONS

Justice
In 2002, 33,939 Criminal Code offences were reported, including two homicides.

Education
In 2002–03 total enrolment for elementary and secondary education was 84,268; full time teachers numbered 6,065; total number of schools was 317. The Memorial University, offering courses in arts, science, engineering, education, nursing and medicine, had 14,000 full-time students in 1999–2000.

CULTURE

Tourism
In 2002, 439,444 non-resident tourists (427,706 in 2001) spent approximately $302·5m. CDN in the province.

FURTHER READING
Statistical office: Newfoundland Labrador Statistics Agency, POB 8700, St. John's, NL A1B 4J6.
Website: http://www.nfstats.gov.nf.ca/

Nova Scotia

KEY HISTORICAL EVENTS
Nova Scotia was visited by John and Sebastian Cabot in 1497–98. In 1605 a number of French colonists settled at Port Royal. The old name of the colony, Acadia, was changed in 1621 to Nova Scotia. The French were granted possession of the colony by the Treaty of St-Germain-en-Laye (1632). In 1654 Oliver Cromwell sent a force to occupy the settlement. Charles II, by the Treaty of Breda (1667), restored Nova Scotia to the French. It was finally ceded to the British by the Treaty of Utrecht in 1713. In the Treaty of Paris (1763) France resigned all claims and in 1820 Cape Breton Island united with Nova Scotia. Representative government was granted as early as 1758 and a fully responsible legislative assembly was established in 1848. In 1867 the province entered the dominion of Canada.

TERRITORY AND POPULATION
The area of the province is 55,284 sq. km (21,345 sq. miles), of which 53,339 sq. km are land area and 1,945 sq. km water area. The population at the 2001 census was 908,007. Population estimate, 1 July 2005, was 937,900.

Population of the major urban areas (2001 census): Halifax Regional Municipality, 359,110; Cape Breton Regional Municipality, 105,965. Principal towns (2001 estimates): Truro, 12,264; New Glasgow, 10,060; Amherst, 9,718; Bridgewater, 7,778; Yarmouth, 7,565; Kentville, 5,536.

SOCIAL STATISTICS
Births in 2003–04 numbered 8,628 (a rate of 9·2 per 1,000 population) and deaths 8,271 (rate of 8·8 per 1,000 population). There were 4,899 marriages in 2002 and 1,990 divorces.

CLIMATE
A cool temperate climate, with rainfall occurring evenly over the year. The Gulf Stream moderates the temperatures in winter so that ports remain ice-free. Halifax, Jan. 23·7°F (–4·6°C), July 63·5°F (17·5°C). Annual rainfall 54" (1,371 mm).

CONSTITUTION AND GOVERNMENT
Under the British North America Act of 1867 the legislature of Nova Scotia may exclusively make laws in relation to local matters, including direct taxation within the province, education and the administration of justice. The legislature of Nova Scotia consists of a Lieut.-Governor, appointed and paid by the federal government, and holding office for five years, and a House of Assembly of 52 members, chosen by popular vote at least every five years. The province is represented in the Canadian Senate by ten members, and in the House of Commons by 11.

RECENT ELECTIONS
At the provincial elections of 5 Aug. 2003 the Progressive Conservatives won 25 seats (36·3% of the vote), the New Democratic Party 15 seats (31·0%) and the Liberals 12 (31·4%). Turnout was 63%.

CURRENT ADMINISTRATION
Lieut.-Governor: Myra Freeman, ONS.
    The members of the Progressive Conservative Ministry in Feb. 2006 were:
    Premier, President of the Executive Council and Minister of Intergovernmental Affairs: Rodney MacDonald.
    Deputy Premier, Deputy President of the Executive Council, Minister of Immigration and Human Resources: Ronald Russell. *Minister of Agriculture, Fisheries and Aquaculture:* Ron Chisholm. *Community Services:* David Morse. *Economic Development:* Kerry Morash. *Education:* Jamie Muir. *Energy:* Bill Dooks. *Environment and Labour:* Carolyn Bolivar-Getson. *Finance and Aboriginal Affairs:* Michael G. Baker QC. *Health Promotion and Protection, African Nova Scotian Affairs and Communications:* Barry Barnet. *Health, Acadian Affairs and Chair of the Senior Citizens' Secretariat:* Chris d'Entremont. *Justice:* Murray Scott. *Natural Resources:* Brooke Taylor. *Service Nova Scotia and Municipal Relations:* Richard Hurlburt. *Tourism, Culture and Heritage:* Judy Streatch. *Transportation and Public Works, Chair of Treasury and Policy Board:* Angus MacIsaac.
    Speaker of the House of Assembly: Cecil Clarke.

Government of Nova Scotia Website: http://www.gov.ns.ca

ECONOMY

Budget
Summary of operations and net funding requirements for the consolidated entity (in $1m. CDN) for fiscal years ending 31 March:

	2001[1]	2002[2]	2003[3]
Revenues	5,240·1	5,423·4	5,628·6
Net Programme Expenditures/Expenses	4,472·1	4,570·1	4,756·5
Net Debt Servicing Costs	940·2	883·1	892·8
Pension Valuation Adjustment	(66·8)	(23·0)	(13·6)

	2001[1]	2002[2]	2003[3]
Total Net Expenditures/Expenses	5,354·6	5,430·2	5,635·7
Consolidation Adjustment	(279·7)	(1·2)	—
Net Income from Government Business Enterprises	308·9	22·5	10·0
Unusual Item	30·9	—	—
Surplus (Deficit)	(54·2)	14·5	2·8

[1]Actual. [2]Forecast. [3]Estimate.

Performance
GDP (market prices) was $27,102m. CDN in 2002, an increase of just over 3·9% on 2001. GDP per person in 2002 was $29,017 CDN.

Banking and Finance
Revenue is derived from provincial sources, payments from the federal government under the equalization agreements and the Canada Health and Social Transfer (CHST).

In the fourth quarter of 2002 deposits with chartered banks totalled $7,893m. CDN.

ENERGY AND NATURAL RESOURCES

Electricity
In 2002 production was 12,117,399 kWh, of which 96% came from thermal sources and the rest from hydro-electric, wind and tidal sources.

Oil and Gas
Significant finds of offshore natural gas are currently under development. Gas is flowing to markets in Canada and the USA (the pipeline was completed in 1999). Total marketable gas receipts for 2002 was 5·2bn. cu. metres.

Minerals
Principal minerals in 2002 were: gypsum, 7·4m. tonnes, valued at $86·9m. CDN; stone, 8·2m. tonnes, valued at $55·6m. CDN. Total value of mineral production in 2002 was $1·3bn. CDN.

Agriculture
In 2001 there were 3,923 farms in the province with 119,221 ha. of land under crops. Dairying, poultry and egg production, livestock and fruit growing are the most important branches. Farm cash receipts for 2002 were $408·2m. CDN. Cash receipts from sale of dairy products were $93·4m. CDN, with total milk and cream sales of 172·9m. litres. The production of poultry meat in 2002 was 36,413 tonnes, of which 32,713 tonnes were chicken and 3,700 tonnes were turkey. Egg production in 2002 was 17·6m. dozen. For particulars of livestock *see* CANADA: Agriculture.

The main fruit crops in 2002 were apples, 37,758 tonnes; blueberries, 18,053 tonnes; strawberries, 2,109 tonnes.

Forestry
The estimated forest area of Nova Scotia is 15,830 sq. miles (40,990 sq. km), of which about 28% is owned by the province. Softwood species represented 85·4% of the 6,066,392 cu. metres of the forest round products produced in 2002. Employment in the forest sector was 3,900 persons in 2002.

Fisheries
The fisheries of the province in 2002 had a landed value of $731m. CDN of sea fish; including lobster fishery, $334m. CDN; and scallop fishery, $120m. CDN. Aquaculture production in 2001 was 8,067 tonnes with a value of $29·7m. CDN; finfish accounted for 81% of total value while shellfish made up the remainder.

INDUSTRY
The number of manufacturing establishments was 1,097 in 2001; the number of employees was 38,621; wages and salaries, $1,324m. CDN. The value of shipments in 2001 was $8,706m. CDN, and the leading industries were food, paper production, and plastic and rubber products.

Labour
In 2002 the labour force was 474,200 (225,700 females), of whom 428,400 (206,800) were employed. The provincial unemployment rate stood at 9·7% while the participation rate was 62·8%.

Trade Unions
Total union membership in 2002 was 103,100 or 28·1% of employees. The largest union membership was in the service sector, followed by public administration and defence.

INTERNATIONAL TRADE

Imports and Exports
Total of imports and exports to and from Nova Scotia (in $1m. CDN):

	1999	2000	2001	2002
Imports	4,523	5,429	5,594	5,138
Exports	4,082	5,219	5,807	5,352

The main exports in 2002 included fish and fish products, natural gas and paper. Major trading partners were the USA with 81·6% of total exports, followed by Japan and the United Kingdom.

COMMUNICATIONS

Roads
In 2002 there were 26,000 km of highways, of which 13,600 km were paved. The Trans Canada and 100 series highways are limited access, all-weather, rapid transit routes. The province's first toll road opened in Dec. 1997. In the fiscal year 2001–02 total road vehicle registrations numbered 546,260 and over 600,000 persons had road motor vehicle operators licences.

Rail
The province has a 805 km network of mainline track operated predominantly by Canadian National Railways. The Cape Breton and Central Nova Scotia Railway operates between Truro and Cape Breton Island. The Windsor and Hantsport Railway operates in the Annapolis Valley region. VIA Rail operates the Ocean for six days a week, a transcontinental service between Halifax and Montreal.

Civil Aviation
There is direct air service to all major Canadian points, and international scheduled services in 2003 to Bermuda, Boston, Frankfurt, Kansas City, London, New York and Omaha. Halifax International Airport is the largest airport, and there are also major airports at Yarmouth and Sydney.

Shipping
Ferry services connect Nova Scotia to the provinces of Newfoundland, Prince Edward Island and New Brunswick as well as to the USA. The deep-water, ice-free Port of Halifax handles about 14m. tonnes of cargo annually.

Telecommunications
In 2003, 357,000 households (96·6%) had telephones. Household Internet use was 57·4% in 2001.

Postal Services
The postal service is provided by the Federal Crown Corporation Canada Post.

SOCIAL INSTITUTIONS

Justice
The Supreme Court (Trial Division and Appeal Division) is the superior court of Nova Scotia and has original and appellate jurisdiction in all civil and criminal matters unless they have been specifically assigned to another court by Statute. An appeal from the Supreme Court, Appeal Division, is to the Supreme Court of Canada.

For the year ending 31 March 2002 there were 1,507 admissions to provincial sentenced custody. In 2002, 71,890 Criminal Code offences were reported, including nine homicides.

Education
Public education in Nova Scotia is free, compulsory and undenominational through elementary and high school. Attendance is compulsory to the age of 16. There were 460 elementary-secondary public schools, with 9,304 full-time teachers and 153,450 pupils, in 2001–02. The province has eleven degree-granting institutions. The Nova Scotia Agricultural College is located at Truro. The Technical University of Nova Scotia, which grants degrees in engineering and architecture, amalgamated with Dalhousie University and is now known as DalTech.

Health
A provincial retail sales tax of 8% provides funds for free hospital in-patient care up to ward level and free medically required services of physicians. The Queen Elizabeth II Hospital in Halifax is the overall referral hospital for the province and, in many instances, for the Atlantic region. The Izaak Walton Killam Hospital provides similar regional specialization for children.

Welfare
General and specialized welfare services in the province are under the jurisdiction of the Department of Community Services. The provincial government funds all of the costs.

RELIGION
The population is predominantly Christian. In 2001, 36·6% were Roman Catholic, 15·9% were United Church, 13·4% Anglicans, 10·6% Baptist and 2·5% Presbyterian.

CULTURE

Broadcasting
Nova Scotia has 22 radio stations and nine television stations. In 1996 there were 85 operating cable television systems with 243,683 subscribers.

Press
Nova Scotia has approximately 50 newspapers, including eight dailies. Daily newspapers with the largest circulations are *The Chronicle Herald* and *Mail Star* of Halifax, *The Daily News* of Dartmouth and *The Cape Breton Post* of Sydney.

Tourism
Tourism revenues were $1·3bn. CDN in 2002. Total number of visitors in 2002 was 2,180,400.

FURTHER READING
Nova Scotia Statistical Review. N. S. Department of Finance, Halifax, 2005
Nova Scotia at a Glance. N. S. Department of Finance, Halifax, 2005

Statistical office: Statistics Division, Department of Finance, POB 187, Halifax, Nova Scotia B3J 2N3.
Website: http://www.gov.ns.ca/finance/statisti/

Ontario

KEY HISTORICAL EVENTS
The French explorer Samuel de Champlain explored the Ottawa River from 1613. The area was governed by the French, first under a joint stock company and then as a royal province, from 1627 and was ceded to Great Britain in 1763. A constitutional act of 1791 created there the province of Upper Canada, largely to accommodate loyalists of English descent who had immigrated after the United States war of independence. Upper Canada entered the Confederation as Ontario in 1867.

TERRITORY AND POPULATION
The area is 1,076,395 sq. km (415,596 sq. miles), of which some 917,741 sq. km (354,340 sq. miles) are land area and some 158,654 sq. km (61,256 sq. miles) are lakes and fresh water rivers. The province extends 1,690 km (1,050 miles) from east to west and 1,730 km (1,075 miles) from north to south. It is bounded in the north by the Hudson and James Bays, in the east by Quebec, in the west by Manitoba, and in the south by the USA, the Great Lakes and the St Lawrence Seaway.

The census population in 2001 was 11,410,046. Population estimate, 1 July 2005, was 12,541,400. Population of the principal cities (2001 census):

Toronto[1]	2,481,494	Markham	208,615	Richmond Hill	132,030
Ottawa	774,072	Windsor	208,402	St Catharines	129,170
Mississauga	612,925	Kitchener	190,399	East York[1]	115,185
North York[1]	608,288	Thunder Bay	190,016	Cambridge	110,372
Scarborough[1]	593,297	Vaughan	182,022	Gloucester	110,264
Hamilton	490,286	Burlington	150,836	Guelph	106,170
Etobicoke[1]	338,117	York[1]	150,255	Barrie	103,710
London	336,539	Oakville	144,738	Brantford	86,417
Brampton	325,428	Oshawa	139,051	Sudbury	85,354

[1]The new City of Toronto was created on 1 Jan. 1998 through the amalgamation of seven municipalities: Metropolitan Toronto and six local area municipalities of Toronto, North York, Scarborough, Etobicoke, East York and York.

There are over 1m. French-speaking people and 0·25m. native Indians. An agreement with the Ontario government of Aug. 1991 recognized Indians' right to self-government.

SOCIAL STATISTICS
Births in 2003–04 numbered 131,121 (a rate of 10·6 per 1,000 population) and deaths 86,371 (a rate of 7·0 per 1,000 population). In 2002 there were 61,615 marriages and 26,170 divorces; in 2002 life expectancy was 77·7 years for males and 82·2 years for females.

CLIMATE
A temperate continental climate, but conditions can be quite severe in winter, though proximity to the Great Lakes has a moderating influence on temperatures. Ottawa, average temperature, Jan. –10·8°C, July 20·8°C. Annual rainfall (including snow) 911 mm. Toronto, average temperature, Jan. –4·5°C, July 22·1°C. Annual rainfall (including snow) 818 mm.

CONSTITUTION AND GOVERNMENT
The provincial government is administered by a *Lieut.-Governor*, a cabinet and a single-chamber 103-member *Legislative Assembly* elected by a general franchise for a period of no longer than five years. The minimum voting age is 18 years.

RECENT ELECTIONS
At the elections on 2 Oct. 2003 to the Legislative Assembly, the Liberal Party won 72 of a possible 103 seats (with 46·4% of the vote), defeating the governing Progressive Conservative Party of Premier Ernie Eves, which took 24 seats (34·6%). The New Democratic Party (NDP) took 7 seats (14·7%).

CURRENT ADMINISTRATION
Lieut.-Governor: James K. Bartleman, O.Ont.; b. 1939 (in office since March 2002).

In Feb. 2006 the Executive Council comprised:
Premier, President of the Council and Minister of Research and Innovation: Dalton McGuinty; b. 1955 (sworn in 23 Oct. 2003).
Minister of Community Safety and Correctional Services: Monte Kwinter. *Finance, Chairman of the Management Board of*

Cabinet: Dwight Duncan. Economic Development and Trade: Joe Cordiano. Children and Youth Services: Mary Anne Chambers. Municipal Affairs and Housing: John Gerretsen. Community and Social Services, Women's Issues and Ontarians with Disabilities: Sandra Pupatello. Attorney General: Michael Bryant. Agriculture, Food and Rural Affairs: Leona Dombrowsky. Labour: Steve Peters. Culture and Francophone Affairs: Madeleine Meilleur. Tourism, Seniors and Government House Leader: Jim Bradley. Natural Resources and Aboriginal Affairs: David Ramsay. Northern Development and Mines: Rick Bartolucci. Energy: Donna Cansfield. Education: Gerard Kennedy. Public Infrastructure Renewal and Deputy Government House Leader: David Caplan. Environment: Laurel Broten. Health and Long-Term Care: George Smitherman. Training, Colleges and Universities: Chris Bentley. Transportation: Harinder Takhar. Citizenship and Immigration: Mike Colle. Health Promotion: Jim Watson. Government Services: Gerry Phillips.

Office of the Premier: http://www.premier.gov.on.ca

ECONOMY

GDP per person in 2002 was $37,049 CDN.

Budget

Provincial revenue and expenditure (in $1m. CDN) for years ending 31 March:

	1998–99	1999–2000	2000–01	2001–02	2002–03[1]
Gross revenue	55,786	62,931	63,824	63,886	66,391
Gross expenditure	57,788	61,909	61,940	63,442	65,907

[1]Estimate.

Gross revenue and expenditure figures reflect accrual and consolidation accounting as recommended by the Public Sector Accounting and Auditing Board of the Canadian Institute of Chartered Accountants. Transactions on behalf of Ontario Hydro are excluded.

Performance

In 2003 real GDP grew at a rate of 1·6% (3·4% in 2002).

ENERGY AND NATURAL RESOURCES

Electricity

Ontario Power Generation recorded for the calendar year 2003 an installed generating capacity of 24,300 MW. Primary energy made available (2003), 109bn. kWh. In 2001 there were 68 hydro-electric, six fossil fuel and five nuclear stations operating. The industry has since been deregulated and Ontario Power Generation now has the province's 80 generating stations. In 1999 Ontario Hydro served 108 direct industrial customers, almost 1m. retail customers (homes, farms and small businesses) and 90 municipal utilities, who in turn serve over 3m. customers.

Oil and Gas

Ontario is Canada's leading petroleum refining region. The province's five refineries have an annual capacity of 170m. bbls. (27m. cu. metres).

Minerals

The total value of mineral production in 2002 was $5·7bn. CDN. In 2003 the most valuable commodities (production in $1m. CDN) were: gold, 1,253; nickel, 1,192; cement, 614; stone, 506; sand and gravel, 410; copper, 393. Total direct employment in the mining industry was 14,000 (9,000, metals) in 2002.

Agriculture

In 2001, 59,728 census farms operated on 5,466,256 ha., with total farm receipts of $8·49bn. CDN. Net farm income in 2003 totalled $138m. CDN. For particulars of livestock *see* CANADA: Agriculture.

Forestry

The forested area totals 69·1m. ha., approximately 65% of Ontario's total area. Composition of Ontario forests: conifer, 56%; mixed, 26%; deciduous, 18%. The total growing stock (62% conifer, 38% hardwood) equals 5·3bn. cu. metres with an annual harvest level of 23m. cu. metres.

INDUSTRY

Ontario is Canada's most industrialized province, with GDP in 2003 of $494,501m. CDN, or 40·6% of the Canadian total. Manufacturing accounts for 21·1% of Ontario's GDP.

Leading manufacturing industries include: motor vehicles and parts; office and industrial electrical equipment; food processing; chemicals; and steel.

In 1998 Ontario was responsible for about 54% ($171,870m. CDN) of Canada's merchandise exports; motor vehicles and parts accounted for about 45%.

Labour

In 2003 the labour force was 6,694,000, of whom 6,229,000 were employed. The major employers (2001 in thousands) were: manufacturing, 984; trade, 951 (wholesale, 279; retail, 672); health care and social assistance, 532; professional, scientific and technical services, 429; accommodation and food services, 380. The unemployment rate in 2003 was 7·0%. In 1999 total labour income was $185,099m. CDN.

INTERNATIONAL TRADE

Imports and Exports

Ontario's imports were $209·9bn. CDN in 2003, down from $224·7bn. CDN in 2003. Exports were $189·1bn. CDN in 2003, down from $206·5bn. CDN.

COMMUNICATIONS

Roads

Almost 40% of the population of North America is within one day's drive of Ontario. There were, in 1998, 159,456 km of roads (municipal, 143,000). Motor licences (on the road) numbered (1999) 8,961,741, of which 5,521,803 were passenger cars, 1,189,414 commercial vehicles, 27,938 buses, 1,616,152 trailers, 103,469 motorcycles and 361,292 snow vehicles.

Rail

In 1999 there were 14 provincial short lines plus the provincially-owned Ontario Northland Railway and 12 federal railways. The Canadian National and Canadian Pacific Railways operate in Ontario. Total track length, approximately 12,500 km. There is a metro and tramway network in Toronto.

Civil Aviation

Toronto's Lester B. Pearson International Airport is Canada's busiest, serving approximately 28m. passengers annually.

Shipping

The Great Lakes/St Lawrence Seaway, a 3,747 km system of locks, canal and natural water connecting Ontario to the Atlantic Ocean, has 95,000 sq. miles of navigable waters and serves the water-borne cargo needs of four Canadian provinces and 17 American States.

Telecommunications

In 2003, 4,431,000 households (97·2%) had telephones.

SOCIAL INSTITUTIONS

Justice

In 2003 there were 6,097 criminal code offences per 100,000 population, compared to a national average of 8,132 per 100,000 population.

Education

There is a provincial system of publicly financed elementary and secondary schools as well as private schools. In 1998–99 publicly financed elementary and secondary schools had a total enrolment of 2,128,642 pupils and 117,098 teachers. In 2001–02, of the $64,270m. CDN total expenditure, 18·5% was on education.

There are 18 universities (Brock, Carleton, Dominicain, Guelph, Lakehead, Laurentian, McMaster, Nipissing, Ottawa, Queen's, Ryerson, Toronto, Trent, Waterloo, Western Ontario, Wilfred Laurier, Windsor and York), the Royal Military College of Canada and the University of Ontario Institute of Technology as well as one institute of equivalent status (Ontario College of Art and Design) with full-time enrolment for 2000–01 of 242,411. All receive operating grants from the Ontario government. There are also 25 publicly financed Colleges of Applied Arts and Technology (CAAT), with a full-time enrolment of 136,170 in 1998–99.

Operating expense (including capital expense) by the Ontario government on education for 1997–98 was $9,470m. CDN.

Health

Ontario Health Insurance Plan health care services are available to eligible Ontario residents at no cost. The Ontario Health Insurance Plan (OHIP) is funded, in part, by an Employer Health Tax.

FURTHER READING

Statistical Information: Annual publications of the Ontario Ministry of Finance include: *Ontario Statistics; Ontario Budget; Public Accounts; Financial Report.*

Prince Edward Island

KEY HISTORICAL EVENTS

The first recorded European visit was by Jacques Cartier in 1534, who named it Isle St-Jean. In 1719 it was settled by the French, but was taken from them by the English in 1758, annexed to Nova Scotia in 1763, and constituted a separate colony in 1769. Named Prince Edward Island in honour of Prince Edward, Duke of Kent, in 1799, it joined the Canadian Confederation on 1 July 1873.

TERRITORY AND POPULATION

The province lies in the Gulf of St Lawrence, and is separated from the mainland of New Brunswick and Nova Scotia by Northumberland Strait. The area of the island is 5,660 sq. km (2,185 sq. miles). Population estimate, 1 July 2005, was 138,100. Population of the principal cities (2001): Charlottetown (capital), 32,245; Summerside, 14,654.

SOCIAL STATISTICS

Births in 2003–04 numbered 1,416 (a rate of 10·3 per 1,000 population) and deaths 1,260 (rate of 9·2 per 1,000 population). There were 901 marriages and 258 divorces in 2002.

CLIMATE

The cool temperate climate is affected in winter by the freezing of the St Lawrence, which reduces winter temperatures. Charlottetown, Jan. –3°C to –11°C, July 14°C to 23°C. Annual rainfall 853·5 mm.

CONSTITUTION AND GOVERNMENT

The provincial government is administered by a Lieut.-Governor-in-Council (Cabinet) and a Legislative Assembly of 27 members who are elected for up to five years.

RECENT ELECTIONS

At provincial elections on 29 Sept. 2003 the Progressive Conservatives won 23 of the available 27 seats (with 54·29% of the vote) and the Liberals took four seats (42·66%). The New Democratic Party won no seats (3·06%).

CURRENT ADMINISTRATION

Lieut.-Governor: J. Léonce Bernard, OPEI; b. 1943 (sworn in on 28 May 2001).

The PC Executive Council was composed as follows in Feb. 2006:

Premier, President of the Executive Council and Minister Responsible for Intergovernmental Affairs: Patrick G. Binns; b. 1948.

Provincial Treasurer: Mitchell Murphy. *Minister for Development and Technology:* Michael Currie. *Agriculture, Fisheries and Aquaculture:* Kevin MacAdam. *Education and Attorney General:* Mildred Dover. *Health and Social Services:* Chester Gillan. *Environment, Energy and Forestry:* James Ballem. *Transportation and Public Works:* Gail Shea. *Community and Cultural Affairs:* Elmer MacFadyen. *Tourism:* Philip Brown.

Office of the Premier: http://www.gov.pe.ca/premier

ECONOMY

Budget

Total revenue in 2002–03 was $1,045m. CDN (own source revenue, $662m. CDN; general purpose transfers, $334m. CDN; special purpose transfers, $49m.). Total expenditures in 2002–03 amounted to $1,074m. CDN (including: health, $310m. CDN; education, $229m. CDN; debt charges, $111m. CDN; social services, $103m. CDN).

ENERGY AND NATURAL RESOURCES

Electricity

Prince Edward Island's electricity supply in 2003 was 1,138,554 MWh, an increase of 5·7% over the preceding year. All but 4% was accessed from other provinces, via an underwater cable which spans the Northumberland Strait. Wind generated power accounted for 11% of the total capacity within the province in 2003.

Oil and Gas

In 1999 Prince Edward Island had more than 400,000 ha. under permit for oil and natural gas exploration.

Agriculture

Total area of farmland occupies approximately half of the total land area of 566,177 ha. Farm cash receipts in 2003 were $353m. CDN, with cash receipts from potatoes accounting for about 50% of the total. Cash receipts from dairy products, hogs and cattle followed in importance. For particulars of livestock, see CANADA: Agriculture.

Forestry

Total forested area is 280,000 ha. Of this 87% is owned by 12,000 woodlot owners. Most of the harvest takes place on private woodlots. The forest cover is 23% softwood, 29% hardwood and 48% mixed wood. In 2003 the volume of wood harvested reached 677,031 cu. metres, an increase of 5·2% on the previous year. The total value of wood industry shipments was $50·6m. CDN in 2003.

Fisheries

The total catch of 147m. lb in 2003 had a landed value of $169·6m. CDN. Lobsters accounted for $108·3m. CDN, around two-thirds of the total value; other shellfish, $47·1m. CDN; pelagic and estuarial, $10·7m. CDN; groundfish, $0·6m. CDN; seaplants, $2·7m. CDN.

INDUSTRY

Value of manufacturing shipments for all industries in 2003 was $1,356·1m. CDN. In 2003 (provisional) provincial GDP in constant prices for manufacturing was $394·9m. CDN; construction, $160·7m. CDN. In 2003 the total value of retail trade was $1,318·0m. CDN.

Labour

The average weekly wage (industrial aggregate) rose from $540·77 CDN in 2002 to $547·04 CDN in 2003. The labour force averaged 78,500 in 2004, with employment averaging 69,600. The unemployment rate was 11·1% in 2003.

COMMUNICATIONS

Roads

In 1999 there were 3,500 km of paved highway and 1,900 km of unpaved road as well as 1,200 bridge structures. The Confederation Bridge, a 12·9 km two-lane bridge that joins Borden-Carleton with Cape Jourimain in New Brunswick, was opened in June 1997. A bus service operates twice daily to the mainland.

Civil Aviation

In 2003 Air Canada provided daily services from Charlottetown to Halifax and Toronto. Canadian Airlines International operated daily services to Boston and Halifax, and there were also services to Moncton, Montreal and St John.

Shipping

Car ferries link the Island to New Brunswick year-round, with ice-breaking ferries during the winter months. Ferry services are operated to Nova Scotia from late April to mid-Dec. A service to the Magdalen Islands (Quebec) operates from 1 April to 31 Jan. The main ports are Summerside and Charlottetown, with additional capacity provided at Souris and Georgetown.

Telecommunications

In 2003, 53,000 households (98·7%) had telephones.

SOCIAL INSTITUTIONS

Justice

In 2003 there were 8,619 Criminal Code offences per 100,000 population, including one homicide.

Education

In 2003–04 there were 10,731 elementary students and 12,352 secondary students in both private and public schools. There is one undergraduate university (3,294 full-time and 599 part-time students), a veterinary college (237 students), and a Master of Science programme (33 students), all in Charlottetown. Holland College provides training for employment in business, applied arts and technology, with approximately 2,500 full-time students in post-secondary and vocational career programmes. The college offers extensive academic and career preparation programmes for adults.

Estimated government expenditure on education, 2000–01, $183·4m. CDN.

CULTURE

Tourism

The value of the tourist industry was estimated at $350m. CDN in 2003, with 1·1m. visitors in that year.

FURTHER READING

Baldwin, D. O., *Abegweit: Land of the Red Soil*. Charlottetown, 1985

Quebec—Québec

KEY HISTORICAL EVENTS

Quebec was known as New France from 1534 to 1763; as the province of Quebec from 1763 to 1790; as Lower Canada from 1791 to 1846; as Canada East from 1846 to 1867, and when, by the union of the four original provinces, the Confederation of the Dominion of Canada was formed, it again became known as the province of Quebec (Québec).

The Quebec Act, passed by the British Parliament in 1774, guaranteed to the people of the newly conquered French territory in North America security in their religion and language, their customs and tenures, under their own civil laws. In a referendum on 20 May 1980, 59·5% voted against 'separatism'. At a further referendum on 30 Oct. 1995, 50·6% of votes cast were against Quebec becoming 'sovereign in a new economic and political partnership' with Canada. The electorate was 5m.; turn-out was 93%. On 20 Aug. 1998 Canada's supreme court ruled that Quebec was prohibited by both the constitution and international law from seceding unilaterally from the rest of the country, but that a clear majority in a referendum would impose a duty on the Canadian government to negotiate. Both sides claimed victory.

TERRITORY AND POPULATION

The area of Quebec (as amended by the Labrador Boundary Award) is 1,542,056 sq. km (595,388 sq. miles), of which 1,365,128 sq. km is land area (including the Territory of Ungava, annexed in 1912 under the Quebec Boundaries Extension Act). The population at the 2001 census was 7,237,479. Population estimate, 1 July 2005, was 7,598,100.

Principal cities (2001 census populations): Montreal, 1,039,534; Laval, 343,005; Quebec (capital), 169,076; Longueuil, 128,016; Gatineau, 103,207; Montreal North, 82,408 (1999 estimate); Saint-Laurent, 77,391; Sherbrooke, 75,916; Saint-Hubert, 75,912; LaSalle, 73,983; Beauport, 72,813; Sainte-Foy, 72,547; Charlesbourg, 70,310; Saint-Léonard, 69,604; Hull, 66,246; Brossard, 65,026; Verdun, 60,564; Chicoutimi, 60,008; Jonquière, 54,842.

SOCIAL STATISTICS

Births in 2003–04 numbered 74,378 (a rate of 9·9 per 1,000 population) and deaths 56,134 (rate of 7·5 per 1,000 population). There were 21,986 marriages and 16,499 divorces in 2002.

CLIMATE

Cool temperate in the south, but conditions are more extreme towards the north. Winters are severe and snowfall considerable, but summer temperatures are quite warm. Quebec, Jan. −12·5°C, July 19·1°C. Annual rainfall 1,123 mm. Montreal, Jan. −10·7°C, July 20·2°C. Annual rainfall 936 mm.

CONSTITUTION AND GOVERNMENT

There is a Legislative Assembly consisting of 125 members, elected in 125 electoral districts for four years.

RECENT ELECTIONS

At the elections of 14 April 2003 the Liberal Party won 76 seats with 45·9% of votes cast, the Parti Québécois won 45 seats with 33·2% and the Action Démocratique won four seats with 18·3%.

CURRENT ADMINISTRATION

Lieut.-Governor: Lise Thibault (took office on 30 Jan. 1997).

Members of the Quebec Liberal Party Cabinet in Feb. 2006:

Premier and President of Executive Council: Jean Charest; b. 1958.

Deputy Premier and Minister of Public Security: Jacques Dupuis. *Government Administration and Chair of the Conseil du trésor:* Monique Jérôme-Forget. *Finance:* Michel Audet. *International Relations:* Monique Gagnon-Tremblay. *Health and Social Services:*

Philippe Couillard. *Education, Recreation and Sports:* Jean-Marc Fournier. *Justice:* Yvon Marcoux. *Economic Development, Innovation and Export Trade:* Claude Béchard. *Agriculture, Fisheries and Food:* Yvon Vallières. *Sustainable Development and Parks:* Thomas Mulcair. *Natural Resources and Wildlife:* Pierre Corbeil. *Transport:* Michel Després. *Municipal Affairs and Regions:* Nathalie Normandeau. *Culture and Communications:* Line Beauchamp. *Government Services:* Pierre Reid. *Revenue:* Lawrence Bergman. *Employment and Social Solidarity:* Michelle Courchesne. *Tourism:* Françoise Gauthier. *Families, Seniors and the Status of Women:* Carole Théberge. *Labour:* Laurent Lessard. *Immigration and Cultural Communities:* Lise Thériault.

In addition to the above, the Cabinet also includes 'Ministers for' (full ministers who assist senior ministers).

Government of Quebec Website: http://www.gouv.qc.ca

ECONOMY

GDP per person in 2003 was $33,856 CDN.

Budget
Revenue and expenditure (in $1,000 CDN) for fiscal years ending 31 March:

	1999–2000	2000–01	2001–02	2002–03
Revenue	47,410,000	51,049,000	50,309,000	50,129,000
Expenditure	47,403,000	49,672,000	51,237,000	50,582,000

The total net debt at 31 March 2003 was $95,457m. CDN.

ENERGY AND NATURAL RESOURCES

Electricity
Water power is one of the most important natural resources of Quebec. Its turbine installation represents about 40% of the aggregate of Canada. At the end of 1997 the installed generating capacity was 34,972 MW. Production, 1997, was 166,255 MWh.

Water
There are 4,500 rivers and 500,000 lakes in Quebec, which possesses 3% of the world's freshwater resources.

Minerals
For 1999 the value of mineral production (metal only) was $2,224m. CDN. Chief minerals: iron ore (confidential); gold, $495·5m. CDN; copper, $314·0m. CDN; zinc, $294·7m. CDN. Non-metallic minerals produced include: asbestos ($160·8m. CDN), titanium-dioxide (confidential), industrial lime, dolomite and brucite, quartz and pyrite. Among the building materials produced were: sand and gravel, $834·0m. CDN; cement, $246·6m. CDN; stone, $218·4m. CDN; lime (confidential).

Agriculture
In 1995 the agricultural area was 3,445,000 ha. The yield of the principal crops was (1998 in 1,000 tonnes):

Crops	Yield	Crops	Yield
Tame hay	4,300	Barley	425
Corn for grain	2,690	Soya	390
Fodder corn	1,520	Oats for grain	197
Potatoes	475	Mixed grains	111

About 38,000 farms were operating in 1995. Cash receipts, 1998, $4,882m. CDN (dairy products, 30·8%; crops, 24·6%; livestock, 21·9%; poultry and eggs, 10·7%). In 1996, 33,906 census farms reported total gross farm receipts of $2,500 CDN or more. For particulars of livestock *see* CANADA: Agriculture.

Forestry
Forests cover an area of 757,900 sq. km. 518,164 sq. km are classified as productive forests, of which 448,929 sq. km are provincial forest land and 66,198 sq. km are privately owned.

Quebec leads the Canadian provinces in pulp and paper production, having nearly half of the Canadian estimated total.

In 1999 production of lumber was: softwood and hardwood, 17,897,000 cu. metres; pulp and paper, 10,092,000 tonnes.

Fisheries
The principal fish are cod, herring, red fish, lobster and salmon. Total catch of sea fish, 1999, 55,257 tonnes, valued at $134m. CDN.

INDUSTRY

In 2001 there were 15,191 industrial establishments in the province; employees, 567,999; salaries and wages, $20,691m. CDN; value of shipments, $141,537m. CDN. Among the leading industries are petroleum refining, pulp and paper mills, smelting and refining, dairy products, slaughtering and meat processing, motor vehicle manufacturing, women's clothing, sawmills and planing mills, iron and steel mills, and commercial printing.

Labour
In 2003 there were 3,650,000 persons (1,689,400 female) in employment.

INTERNATIONAL TRADE

Imports and Exports
In 2003 the value of Canadian imports through Quebec custom ports was $64,228m. CDN; value of exports, $63,635m. CDN.

COMMUNICATIONS

Roads
In 1998 there were 29,140 km of roads and (2004) 6,353,220 registered motor vehicles.

Rail
There were (2003) 8,977 km of railway. There is a metro system in Montreal (65 km).

Civil Aviation
There are two international airports, Dorval (Montreal) and Mirabel (Laurentides).

Telecommunications
In 2003, 2,994,000 households (96·1%) had telephones.

SOCIAL INSTITUTIONS

Justice
In 2002, 476,543 Criminal Code offences were reported; there were 121 homicides.

Education
Education is compulsory for children aged 6–16. Pre-school education and elementary and secondary training are free in some 2,527 public schools. In July 1998 the number of school boards was reduced to 72. These were organized along linguistic lines, 60 French, nine English and three special school boards that served native students in the Cote-Nord and Nord-du-Quebec regions. Just under 10% of the student population attends private schools: in 1999–2000, 272 establishments were authorized to provide pre-school, elementary and secondary education. After six years of elementary and five years of secondary school education, students enter Cegeps, a post-secondary educational institution. In 1999–2000 college, pre-university and technical training for young and adult students was provided by 48 Cegeps, 11 government schools and 77 private establishments.

In 1999–2000 in pre-kindergartens there were 15,174 pupils; in kindergartens, 89,223; in primary schools, 573,102; in secondary schools, 674,964; in colleges (post-secondary, non-university), 219,144; and in classes for children with special needs, 135,838. In 1998–99 the school boards had a total of 92,746 teachers (57,456 full-time and 32,290 part-time).

Expenditure of the Departments of Education for 1999–2000, $9,521·1m. CDN net. This included $1,511·2m. CDN for universities, $5,450·1m. CDN for public primary and secondary schools, $272·1m. CDN for private primary and secondary schools and $1,255·6m. CDN for colleges.

In 1999–2000 the province had nine universities: six French-language universities: Laval (Quebec, founded 1852), Montreal University (opened 1876 as a branch of Laval, independent 1920), Sherbrooke University (founded 1954), University of Quebec (founded 1968) and two others; and three English-language universities, McGill (Montreal, founded 1821), Bishop (Lennoxville, founded 1845) and the Concordia University (Montreal, granted a charter 1975). In 1999 there were 137,183 full-time university students and 94,691 part-time.

Health

Quebec's socio-health network consisted of 478 public and private establishments in 2001, of which 348 were public.

CULTURE

Broadcasting

In 1998 there were 50 television and 171 radio stations.

Press

In 2000 there were 11 French- and three English-language daily newspapers.

FURTHER READING

Dickinson, J. A. and Young, B., *A Short History of Quebec*. 2nd ed. Harlow, 1994

Gagnon, A.- G., *Québec*. [Bibliography] ABC-Clio, Oxford and Santa Barbara (CA), 1998

Young, R. A., *The Secession of Quebec and the Future of Canada*. McGill-Queen's Univ. Press, 1995

Statistical office: Institut de la statistique du Québec, 200 chemin Sainte-Foy, Québec, G1R 5T4.

Website: http://www.stat.gouv.qc.ca

Saskatchewan

KEY HISTORICAL EVENTS

Saskatchewan derives its name from its major river system, which the Cree Indians called 'Kis-is-ska-tche-wan', meaning 'swift flowing'. It officially became a province when it joined the Confederation on 1 Sept. 1905.

In 1670 King Charles II granted to Prince Rupert and his friends a charter covering exclusive trading rights in 'all the land drained by streams finding their outlet in the Hudson Bay'. This included what is now Saskatchewan. The trading company was first known as The Governor and Company of Adventurers of England; later as the Hudson's Bay Company. In 1869 the Northwest Territories was formed, and this included Saskatchewan. In 1882 the District of Saskatchewan was formed. By 1885 the North-West Mounted Police had been inaugurated, with headquarters in Regina (now the capital), and the Canadian Pacific Railway's transcontinental line had been completed, bringing a stream of immigrants to southern Saskatchewan. The Hudson's Bay Company surrendered its claim to territory in return for cash and land around the existing trading posts.

TERRITORY AND POPULATION

Saskatchewan is bounded in the west by Alberta, in the east by Manitoba, in the north by the Northwest Territories and in the south by the USA. The area of the province is 651,036 sq. km (251,365 sq. miles), of which 591,670 sq. km is land area and

59,366 sq. km is water. The population at the 2001 census was 978,933; it was estimated at 994,100 in July 2005. Population of cities, 2001 census: Saskatoon, 196,811; Regina (capital), 178,225; Prince Albert, 34,291; Moose Jaw, 32,131; Yorkton, 15,105; Swift Current, 14,821; North Battleford, 13,692; Estevan, 10,242; Weyburn, 9,534; Lloydminster, 7,840; Melfort, 5,559; Humboldt, 5,161.

SOCIAL STATISTICS

Births in 2003–04 numbered 12,063 (a rate of 12·1 per 1,000 population) and deaths 9,102 (rate of 9·2 per 1,000 population). There were 5,067 marriages and 1,959 divorces in 2002.

CLIMATE

A cold continental climate, with severe winters and warm summers. Rainfall amounts are greatest from May to Aug. Regina, Jan. 0°F (–17·8°C), July 65°F (18·3°C). Annual rainfall 15" (373 mm).

CONSTITUTION AND GOVERNMENT

The provincial government is vested in a Lieut.-Governor, an Executive Council and a Legislative Assembly, elected for five years. Women were given the franchise in 1916.

RECENT ELECTIONS

In elections on 5 Nov. 2003 the New Democrats (NDP) won 30 of 58 seats (44·62% of the vote); the Saskatchewan Party (SP), 28 (39·35%). The Liberal Party received 14·17% of the vote but did not win any seats.

CURRENT ADMINISTRATION

Lieut.-Governor: Dr Lynda M. Haverstock, SOM (took office 21 Feb. 2000).

The New Democratic Party ministry comprised as follows in Feb. 2006:

Premier, President of the Executive Council: Lorne Calvert.

Deputy Premier and Minister of Regional Economic and Co-operative Development: Clay Serby. *Environment:* John Nilson. *Finance:* Andrew Thomson. *Northern Affairs:* Joan Beatty. *First Nations and Métis Relations, and Crown Investments Corporation of Saskatchewan:* Maynard Sonntag. *Community Resources:* Buckley Belanger. *Government Relations:* Harry Van Mulligen. *Corrections and Public Safety:* Kevin Yates. *Labour:* David Forbes. *Health:* Len Taylor. *Industry and Resources:* Eric Cline. *Learning:* Debra Higgins. *Justice and Attorney General:* Frank Quennell. *Agriculture and Food:* Mark Wartman. *Culture, Youth and Recreation:* Glenn Hagel. *Healthy Living Services:* Graham Addley.

Office of the Premier: http://www.gov.sk.ca/govinfo/premier

ECONOMY

GDP per capita in 2002 was $34,298 CDN.

Budget

Budget and net assets (years ending 31 March) in $1,000 CDN:

	1999–2000	2000–01	2001–02	2002–03
Budgetary revenue	6,629,490	6,382,400	6,041,700	6,094,300
Budgetary expenditure	6,785,466	5,967,986	6,302,624	6,319,255

ENERGY AND NATURAL RESOURCES

Agriculture used to dominate the history and economics of Saskatchewan, but the 'prairie province' is now a rapidly developing mining and manufacturing area. It is a major supplier of oil, has the world's largest deposits of potash and the net value of its non-agricultural production accounted for (2002 estimate) 93·8% of the provincial economy.

Electricity

The Saskatchewan Power Corporation generated 16,755m. kWh in 2002.

Minerals

In 2002 mineral sales were valued at $8,266m. CDN, including (in $1m. CDN): petroleum, 4,705·7; potash, 1,717·2; natural gas, 913·7; coal and others, 885·5; sodium sulphate, 23·0; salt, 21·4. Other major minerals included copper, zinc, potassium sulphate, ammonium sulphate, bentonite, coal, uranium, gold and base metals.

Agriculture

Saskatchewan normally produces about two-thirds of Canada's wheat. Wheat production in 2002 (in 1,000 tonnes) was 7,484 (9,851 in 2001) from 15·1m. acres; barley, 2,526 from 5·2m. acres; canola, 1,656 from 4·4m. acres; oats, 1,049 from 2·6m. acres; flax, 445 from 1·2m. acres; rye, 28 from 85,000 acres. Livestock (1 July 2003): cattle and calves, 3·3m.; swine, 1·3m.; sheep and lambs, 145,000. Poultry in 2002: chickens, 21·5m.; turkeys, 758,000. Cash income from the sale of farm products in 2002 was $6,356m. CDN. At the June 2001 census there were 50,598 farms in the province, each being a holding of one acre or more with sales of $250 CDN or more during the previous year.

The South Saskatchewan River irrigation project, the main feature of which is the Gardiner Dam, was completed in 1967. It will ultimately provide for an area of 0·2m. to 0·5m. acres of irrigated cultivation in Central Saskatchewan. As of 2002, 243,077 acres were intensively irrigated. Total irrigated land in the province, 337,284 acres.

Forestry

Half of Saskatchewan's area is forested, but only 115,000 sq. km are of commercial value at present. Forest products valued at $356m. CDN were produced in 2001–02.

Fur Production

In 2000–01 wild fur production was estimated at $1,910,908 CDN. Ranch-raised fur production amounted to $31,226 CDN in 2000 and $11,426 CDN in 2001.

Fisheries

The lakeside value of the 2002–03 commercial fish catch of 3·5m. kg was $4·6m. CDN.

INDUSTRY

In 2001 there were 1,004 manufacturing establishments, employing 20,376 persons. In 2002 manufacturing contributed $2,054·2m. CDN and construction $1,238·9m. CDN to total GDP at basic prices of $28,114·2m. CDN.

Labour

In 2002 the labour force was 511,100 (232,000 females), of whom 482,000 (220,500) were employed.

COMMUNICATIONS

Roads

In 2002 there were 26,249 km of provincial highways and 198,348 km of municipal roads (including prairie trails). Motor vehicles registered totalled 721,999 (2002). Bus services are provided by two major lines.

Rail

In 2002 there were approximately 9,908 km of railway track.

Civil Aviation

There were two major airports and 148 airports and landing strips in 2002.

Telecommunications

There were 613,695 telephone network access services to the Saskatchewan Telecommunications system in 2002.

Postal Services

In 2002 there were 475 post offices (excluding sub-post offices).

SOCIAL INSTITUTIONS

Justice

In 2002, 135,262 Criminal Code offences were reported, including 27 homicides.

Education

The Saskatchewan education system in 2002–03 consisted of 99 school divisions and three comprehensive school boards, of which one is Protestant and 19 are Roman Catholic Separate School Divisions, serving 116,271 elementary pupils, 59,715 high-school students and 1,589 students enrolled in special classes. In addition, the Saskatchewan Institute of Applied Science and Technology (SIAST) had approximately 12,000 full-time and 29,000 part-time and extension course registration students in 2002–03. There are also eight regional colleges with an enrolment of approximately 30,126 students in 2001–02.

The University of Saskatchewan was established at Saskatoon in 1907. In 2001–02 it had 15,368 full-time students, 4,101 part-time students and 961 full-time academic staff. The University of Regina, established in 1974, had 8,975 full-time and 3,205 part-time students and 388 full-time academic staff in 2001–02.

CULTURE

Broadcasting

In 2002 there were 50 TV and re-broadcasting stations, and 28 AM and FM radio stations.

Tourism

An estimated 1·6m. out-of-province tourists spent $480m. CDN in 2002.

FURTHER READING

Archer, J. H., *Saskatchewan: A History*. Saskatoon, 1980
Arora, V., *The Saskatchewan Bibliography*. Regina, 1980

Statistical office: Bureau of Statistics, 5th Floor, 2350 Albert St., Regina, SK, S4P 4A6.

The Northwest Territories

KEY HISTORICAL EVENTS

The Territory was developed by the Hudson's Bay Company and the North West Company (of Montreal) from the 17th century. The Canadian government bought out the Hudson's Bay Company in 1869 and the Territory was annexed to Canada in 1870. The Arctic Islands lying north of the Canadian mainland were annexed to Canada in 1880.

A plebiscite held in March 1992 approved the division of the Northwest Territories into two separate territories. (For the new territory of Nunavut *see* CONSTITUTION AND GOVERNMENT, *below*, and NUNAVUT on page 292).

TERRITORY AND POPULATION

The Northwest Territories comprises all that portion of Canada lying north of the 60th parallel of N. lat. except those portions within Nunavut, the Yukon Territory and the provinces of Quebec and Newfoundland. The total area of the Territories was 3,426,320 sq. km, but since the formation of Nunavut is now 1,346,106 km. Of its five former administrative regions—Fort Smith, Inuvik, Kitikmeot, Keewatin and Baffin—only Fort Smith and Inuvik remain in the Northwest Territories.

The population at the 1991 census was 57,649, 37% of whom were Inuit (Eskimo), 16% Dene (Indian) and 7% Metis. The formation of Nunavut in 1999 out of the Northwest Territories resulted in a large decline in the population. The population at the 2001 census was 37,360. Population estimate, 1 July 2005, was 43,000. The capital is Yellowknife, population (2001); 16,541. Other main centres (with population in 2001): Hay River (3,510), Inuvik (2,894), Fort Smith (2,185), Rae-Edzo (1,552). Iqaluit and Rankin Inlet, formerly in the Northwest Territories, are now in Nunavut. In Aug. 2003 an agreement was reached for the Tlicho First Nation to assume control over 39,000 sq. km of land in the Northwest Territories (including Canada's two diamond mines), creating the largest single block of First Nation-owned land in Canada.

SOCIAL STATISTICS

Births in 2003–04 numbered 706 (a rate of 16·6 per 1,000 population) and deaths 170 (rate of 4·0 per 1,000 population). There were 144 marriages and 68 divorces in 2002.

CLIMATE

Conditions range from cold continental to polar, with long hard winters and short cool summers. Precipitation is low. Yellowknife, Jan. mean high –24·7°C, low –33°C; July mean high 20·7°C, low 11·8°C. Annual rainfall 26·7 cm.

CONSTITUTION AND GOVERNMENT

The Northwest Territories is governed by a Premier, with a cabinet (the Executive Council) of eight members including the Speaker, and a Legislative Assembly, who choose the premier and ministers by consensus. There are no political parties. The Assembly is composed of 19 members elected for a four-year term of office. A Commissioner of the Northwest Territories is the federal government's senior representative in the Territorial government. The seat of government was transferred from Ottawa to Yellowknife when it was named Territorial Capital on 18 Jan. 1967. On 10 Nov. 1997 the governments of Canada and the Northwest Territories signed an agreement so that the territorial government could assume full responsibility to manage its elections.

The Territorial government has assumed most of the responsibility for the administration of the Northwest Territories but political control of Crown lands. In a Territory-wide plebiscite in April 1982, a majority of residents voted in favour of dividing the Northwest Territories into two jurisdictions, east and west. Constitutions for an eastern and western government have been under discussion since 1992. A referendum was held in Nov. 1992 among the Inuit on the formation of a third territory, **Nunavut** ('Our Land'), in the eastern Arctic. Nunavut became Canada's third territory on 1 April 1999.

RECENT ELECTIONS

On 24 Nov. 2003, 19 non-partisan members (MLAs) were returned to the 15th Legislative Assembly. There were 58 candidates, five of whom were unopposed.

CURRENT ADMINISTRATION

Commissioner: Tony Whitford, b. 1941 (took office in April 2005).

Members of the Executive Council of Ministers in Feb. 2006:

Premier, Chairman of the Executive Council, Minister for Aboriginal Affairs: Joseph Handley; b. 1943.

Deputy Premier and Minister of Finance, Public Works and Services: Floyd Roland. *Government House Leader and Minister of Education, Culture and Employment:* Charles Dent. *Justice, and Industry, Tourism and Development:* Brendan Bell. *Transportation, Municipal and Community Affairs, and Youth:* Michael McLeod. *Health and Social Services:* J. Michael Miltenberger.

Speaker: Paul Delorey.

Government of the Northwest Territories Website:
   http://www.gov.nt.ca

ECONOMY

GDP per person in 2003 was $85,983 CDN, the highest of any Canadian province or territory.

Budget

Total revenue in 2002–03 was $976m. CDN (own source revenue, $449m. CDN; general purpose transfers, $411m. CDN; special purpose transfers, $116m. CDN). Total expenditures in 2002–03 amounted to $1,021m. CDN (including: health, $203m. CDN; education, $187m. CDN; social services, $104m. CDN).

Performance

In 2003 real GDP grew at a rate of 20·8%, mainly as a result of the growing mineral sector and in particular diamond exports.

ENERGY AND NATURAL RESOURCES

Oil and Gas

Oil production was 1,535,000 cu. metres in 2000, down from 1,640,000 cu. metres in 1999. Natural gas production in 2000 was 541m. cu. metres, up from 110m. cu. metres in 1999.

Minerals

Mineral production in 2000: gold, 4,372 kg (valued at $58,148,000 CDN); silver, 1 tonne ($248,000 CDN); diamonds, 2,558 carats ($638,161,000 CDN); sand and gravel, 539,000 tonnes ($4,805,000 CDN); stone, 184,000 tonnes ($2,848,000 CDN). Total mineral production in 2000 was valued at $1·14bn. CDN.

Forestry

Forest land area in the Northwest Territories consists of 61·4m. ha., about 18% of the total land area. The principal trees are white and black spruce, jack-pine, tamarack, balsam poplar, aspen and birch. In 2000, 22,000 cu. metres of timber were produced.

Trapping and Game

Wildlife harvesting is the largest economic activity undertaken by aboriginal residents in the Northwest Territories. The value of the subsistence food harvest is estimated at $28m. CDN annually in terms of imports replaced. Fur-trapping (the most valuable pelts being white fox, wolverine, beaver, mink, lynx, and red fox) was once a major industry, but has been hit by anti-fur campaigns. In 1999–2000, 37,124 pelts worth $842,049 CDN were sold.

Fisheries

Fish marketed through the Freshwater Fish Marketing Corporation in 1996–97 totalled 1,742,700 kg at a value of $1,725,000 CDN, principally whitefish, northern pike and trout.

INDUSTRY

Co-operatives

There are 37 active co-operatives, including two housing co-operatives and two central organizations to service local co-operatives, in the Northwest Territories. They are active in handicrafts, furs, fisheries, retail stores, hotels, cable TV, post offices, petroleum delivery and print shops. Total revenue in 2000 was about $97m. CDN.

COMMUNICATIONS

Roads

The Mackenzie Route connects Grimshaw, Alberta, with Hay River, Pine Point, Fort Smith, Fort Providence, Rae-Edzo and Yellowknife. The Mackenzie Highway extension to Fort Simpson and a road between Pine Point and Fort Resolution have both been opened.

Highway service to Inuvik in the Mackenzie Delta was opened in spring 1980, extending north from Dawson, Yukon as the Dempster Highway. The Liard Highway connecting the communities of the Liard River valley to British Columbia opened in 1984.

In 2000 there were 27,703 vehicle registrations, including 21,630 passenger cars and 1,881 trucks and 2,841 trailers.

Rail

There is one small railway system in the north which runs from Hay River, on the south shore of Great Slave Lake, 435 miles south to Grimshaw, Alberta, where it connects with the Canadian National Railways, but it is not in use.

Civil Aviation

In 2000 there were 132,775 take-offs and landings in the Northwest Territories.

Shipping

A direct inland-water transportation route for about 1,700 miles is provided by the Mackenzie River and its tributaries, the Athabasca and Slave rivers. Subsidiary routes on Lake Athabasca, Great Slave Lake and Great Bear Lake total more than 800 miles. Communities in the eastern Arctic are resupplied by ship each summer via the Atlantic and Arctic Oceans or Hudson Bay.

Telecommunications

In 2003, 13,000 households (95·5%) had telephones. Those few communities without a telephone service have high frequency or very high frequency radios for emergency use.

Postal Services

There is a postal service in all communities.

SOCIAL INSTITUTIONS

Education

The Education System in the Northwest Territories is comprised of eight regional bodies (boards) that have responsibilities for the K-12 education programme. Three of these jurisdictions are located in Yellowknife; a public school authority, a catholic school authority and a Commission scolaire francophone that oversees a school operating in Yellowknife, and one in Hay River.

For the 2000–01 school year there were 49 public plus two (small) private schools operating in the NWT. Within this system there were 667 teachers, including Aboriginal Language Specialists, for 9,855 students. 98% of students have access to high school programmes in their home communities. There is a full range of courses available in the school system, including academic, French immersion, Aboriginal language, cultural programmes, technical and occupational programmes.

A range of post secondary programmes are available through the Northwest Territories' Aurora College. The majority of these programmes are offered at the three main campus locations: Inuvik, Yellowknife and Fort Smith.

Health

In 2004 there were eight separate regional boards. Expenditure on health totalled $159·4m. CDN in 1999–2000.

Welfare

Welfare services are provided by professional social workers. Facilities included (1993) for children: seven group homes and two residential treatment centres.

CULTURE

Broadcasting

In 2000 CBC operated radio stations at Yellowknife and Inuvik. There is an English language CBC-owned television station at Yellowknife. There are also two other television broadcasting stations based in Yellowknife.

FURTHER READING

Northwest Territories—2004: By the Numbers. Yellowknife, 2004

Zaslow, M., *The Opening of the Canadian North 1870–1914.* Toronto, 1971

Nunavut

KEY HISTORICAL EVENTS

Inuit communities started entering and moving around what is now the Canadian Arctic between 4500 BC and AD 1000. By the 19th century these communities were under the jurisdiction of the Northwest Territories. In 1963 the Canadian government first introduced legislation to divide the territory, a proposal that failed at the order paper stage. In 1973 the Comprehensive Land Claims Policy was established which sought to define the rights and benefits of the Aboriginal population in a land claim settlement agreement. The Northwest Territories Legislative Assembly voted in favour of dividing the territory in 1980, and in a public referendum of 1982, 56% of votes cast were also for the division. In 1992 the proposed boundary was ratified in a public vote and the Inuit population approved their land claim settlement. A year later, the Nunavut Act (creating the territory) and the Nunavut Land Claim Agreement Act were passed by parliament. Iqaluit was selected as the capital in 1995.

On 15 Feb. 1999 Nunavut held elections for its Legislative Assembly and on 1 April 1999 the territory was officially designated and the government inaugurated.

TERRITORY AND POPULATION

The total area of the region is 2,093,190 sq. km or about 21% of Canada's total mass, making Nunavut Canada's largest territory. It contains seven of Canada's 12 largest islands and two thirds of the country's coastline. The territory is divided into three regions: Qikiqtaaluk (Baffin), Kivalliq (Keewatin) and Kitikmeot. The total population at the 1996 census was 24,720 (12,910 males, 11,810 females) or 97 persons per 10,000 sq. km; at the 2001 census the population was 26,745. Population estimate, 1 July 2005, was 30,000. 85% of the population are Inuit. The population is divided up into 28 communities of which the largest is in the capital Iqaluit, numbering 4,500.

The native Inuit language is Inuktitut.

SOCIAL STATISTICS

Births in 2003–04 numbered 765 (a rate of 26·0 per 1,000 population) and deaths 133 (rate of 4·5 per 1,000 population). Nunavut's birth rate is the highest in Canada and is more than twice the national average of 10·5 per 1,000 births. 56% of the population are under 25 years of age. Life expectancy, 1996: males, 67 years; females, 72 years.

CLIMATE

Conditions range from cold continental to polar, with long hard winters and short cool summers. In Iqaluit there can be as little as four hours sunshine per day in winter and up to 21 hours per day at the summer solstice. Iqaluit, Jan. mean high –22°C; July mean high, 15°C.

CONSTITUTION AND GOVERNMENT

Government is by a Legislative Assembly of 19 elected members, who then choose a leader and ministers by consensus. There are no political parties. The government is being established in evolutionary stages, a process which began in 1993 and is scheduled for completion in 2009. It is intended that government be highly decentralized, consisting of ten departments spread over 11 different communities.

Inuktitut will be the working language of government but government agencies will also offer services in English and French. Although the Inuits will be the dominant force in public government, non-Inuit citizens have the same voting rights.

RECENT ELECTIONS

Legislative Assembly elections were held on 16 Feb. 2004. There were 82 non-partisan candidates; 17 men and two women were elected.

CURRENT ADMINISTRATION

Commissioner: Ann Meekitjuk Hanson (took office in April 2005).

In Feb. 2006 the cabinet was as follows:

Premier and Minister of Executive and Intergovernmental Affairs and of Justice: Paul Okalik; b. 1964 (took office on 1 April 1999 and re-elected in 2004).

Deputy Premier, Minister of Community and Government Services: Levinia Brown. *Health and Social Services, and Responsible for the Status of Women:* Leona Aglukkaq. *Environment, Economic Development and Transportation:* Olayuk Akesuk. *Government House Leader, Education, Energy and Responsible for Homelessness and Immigration:* Ed Picco. *Finance and Administration:* David Simailak. *Culture, Language, Elders and Youth, and Human Resources:* Louis Tapardjuk.

Government of Nunavut Website: http://www.gov.nu.ca

ECONOMY

While the cost of living in Nunavut is around 160–200% that of southern Canadians, the average household income is $31,471 CDN compared to $45,251 CDN for Canada as a whole. With unemployment running high, transport costs expensive and education limited, self-sufficiency is unlikely to be achieved soon.

Currency
The Canadian dollar is the standard currency.

Budget
Total revenue in 2002–03 was $959m. CDN (own source revenue, $115m. CDN; general purpose transfers, $649m. CDN; special purpose transfers, $195m.). Total expenditures in 2002–03 amounted to $1,035m. CDN (including: education, $199m. CDN; health, $168m. CDN; housing, $134m. CDN).

Banking and Finance
Few banks have branches in the province. Iqaluit has two automated cash machines and stores are increasingly installing debit card facilities.

ENERGY AND NATURAL RESOURCES

Minerals
There are two lead and zinc mines operating in the High Arctic region. There are also known deposits of copper, gold, silver and diamonds.

Hunting and Trapping
Most communities still rely on traditional foodstuffs such as caribou and seal. The Canadian government now provides meat inspections so that caribou and musk ox meat can be sold across the country.

Fisheries
Fishing is still very important in Inuit life. The principal catches are shrimp, scallop and arctic char.

INDUSTRY
The main industries are mining, tourism, fishing, hunting and trapping and arts and crafts production.

Labour
Unemployment was running at 20·7% in 1999.

COMMUNICATIONS

Roads
There is one 21-km government-maintained road between Arctic Bay and Nanisivik. There are a few paved roads in Iqaluit and Rankin Inlet, but most are unpaved. Some communities have local roads and tracks but Kivalliq has no direct land connections with southern Canada.

Civil Aviation
There are air connections between communities and a daily air connection between Iqaluit and Montreal/Ottawa.

Shipping
There is an annual summer sea-lift by ship and barge for transport of construction materials, dry goods, non-perishable food, trucks and cars.

Telecommunications
In 2003, 6,000 households (84·9%) had telephones. Because of the wide distances between communities, there is a very high rate of Internet use in Nunavut. However, line speeds are slow and there is a problem with satellite bounce.

Postal Services
There is no door-to-door delivery service, so correspondence has to be retrieved from post offices.

SOCIAL INSTITUTIONS

Justice
A territorial court has been put in place. Policing is by the Royal Canadian Mounted Police (RCMP).

Education
Approximately one third of Nunavut's population aged over 15 have less than Grade 9 schooling. Training and development is seen as central to securing a firm economic foundation for the province. The Canadian government has pledged $40m. CDN for recruiting and training Inuit employees into Nunavut public service.

Courses in computer science, business management and public administration may be undertaken at Arctic College. In 1997–98 there were 39 schools with 7,770 students.

Health
There is one hospital in Iqaluit. 26 health centres provide nursing care for communities. For more specialized treatment, patients of Qikiqtaaluk may be flown to Montreal, patients in Kivalliq to Churchill or Winnipeg and patients in Kitikmeot to Yellowknife's Stanton Regional Hospital.

CULTURE
Broadcasting
The Canadian Broadcasting Corporation (CBC) North transmits television to Iqaluit and other communities. The Inuit Broadcasting Corporation (IBC) transmits in Inuktitut and Television Northern Canada (TVNC) is devoted to programming by and for northerners and native citizens. There are 5½ hours of Inuktitut television programming per week. Cable satellite television is also widely available. CBC is the only local radio station accessible in all Nunavut communities.

Tourism
Auyuittuq National Park is one of the principal tourist attractions, along with the opportunity of seeing Inuit life first-hand. Under the terms of the land claim settlement, three more national parks are planned. It is also hoped that the publicity surrounding the new territory will encourage visitors.

FURTHER READING
The Nunavut Handbook, Ayaya, Iqaluit, 2004

Yukon Territory

KEY HISTORICAL EVENTS
The territory owes its fame to the discovery of gold in the Klondike at the end of the 19th century. Formerly part of the

Northwest Territories, the Yukon was joined to the Dominion as a separate territory on 13 June 1898.

Yukon First Nations People lived a semi-nomadic subsistence lifestyle in the region long before it was established as a territory. The earliest evidence of human activity was found in caves containing stone tools and animal bones estimated to be 20,000 years old. The Athapaskan cultural linguistic tradition to which most Yukon First Nations belong is more than 1,000 years old. The territory's name comes from the native 'Yu-kun-ah' for the great river that drains most of this area.

The Yukon was created as a district of the Northwest Territories in 1895. The Klondike Gold Rush in the late 1890s saw the invasion of thousands of stampeders pouring into the gold fields of the Canadian northwest. Population at the peak of the rush reached 40,000. This event spurred the federal government to set up basic administrative structures in the Yukon. The territory was given the status of a separate geographical and political entity with an appointed legislative council in 1898. In 1953 the capital was moved south from Dawson City to Whitehorse, where most of the economic activity was centred. The federal government granted the Yukon responsible government in 1979.

TERRITORY AND POPULATION

The territory consists of one city, three towns, four villages, two hamlets, 13 unincorporated communities and eight rural communities. It is situated in the northwestern region of Canada and comprises 482,443 sq. km of which 8,052 sq. km is fresh water.

The population at the 2001 census was 28,674. Population estimate, 1 July 2005, was 31,000.

Principal centres in 2001 were Whitehorse, the capital, 19,058; Dawson City, 1,251; Watson Lake, 912; Haines Junction, 531; Faro, 313.

The Yukon represents 4·8% of Canada's total land area.

SOCIAL STATISTICS

Births in 2003–04 numbered 339 (a rate of 11·0 per 1,000 population) and deaths 158 (rate of 5·1 per 1,000 population). There were 143 marriages and 90 divorces in 2002.

CLIMATE

Temperatures in the Yukon are usually more extreme than those experienced in the southern provinces of Canada. A cold climate in winter with moderate temperatures in summer provide a considerable annual range of temperature and moderate rainfall.

Whitehorse, Jan. –18·7°C (–2·0°F), July 14°C (57·2°F). Annual precipitation 268·8 mm. Dawson City, Jan. –30·7°C (–23·3°F), July 15·6°C (60·1°F). Annual precipitation 182·7 mm.

CONSTITUTION AND GOVERNMENT

The Yukon was constituted a separate territory on 13 June 1898. The Yukon Legislative Assembly consists of 17 elected members and functions in much the same way as a provincial legislature. The seat of government is at Whitehorse. It consists of an executive council with parliamentary powers similar to those of a provincial cabinet. The Yukon government consists of 12 departments, as well as a Women's Directorate and four Crown corporations.

RECENT ELECTIONS

At elections held on 4 Nov. 2002 the Yukon Party took 12 of the available 18 seats; the New Democratic Party 5; and the Liberals 1.

CURRENT ADMINISTRATION

Commissioner: Geraldine Van Bibber (took office on 1 Dec. 2005).

In Feb. 2006 the Yukon Party Ministry comprised:

Premier, Minister Responsible for Executive Council Office, including Devolution, Land Claims and Youth Directorate, and Minister of Finance and the Environment: Dennis Fentie.

Deputy Premier, Minister for Tourism and Culture: Elaine Taylor. *Health and Social Services:* Brad Cathers. *Education and Justice:* John Edzerza. *Energy, Mines and Resources:* Archie Lang. *Highways and Public Works, and Community Services:* Glenn Hart. *Economic Development:* Jim Kenyon.

Government of Yukon Website: http://www.gov.yk.ca

ECONOMY

The key sectors of the economy are government, tourism, finance, insurance and real estate.

Budget

Total revenue in 2003–04 was $660m. CDN (own source revenue, $126m. CDN; general purpose transfers, $468m. CDN; special purpose transfers, $65m. CDN). Total expenditures in 2003–04 amounted to $679m. CDN (including: education, $118m. CDN; health, $96m. CDN; social services, $92m. CDN).

Performance

GDP at market prices in 2000 was $1,124m. CDN. Mining, oil and gas production was estimated at $72·8m. CDN in 1998 and revenue from agriculture, forestry, hunting and fishing was estimated at $4m. CDN. In the manufacturing sector, shipments were valued at $2·3m. CDN in 2000. GDP per person in 2000 was $36,258 CDN.

ENERGY AND NATURAL RESOURCES

Environment

The Yukon is recognized as a critical habitat for many species of rare and endangered flowers, big game animals, birds of prey and migratory birds. There are 278 species of birds and 38 species of fish. The vegetation is classified as sub-arctic and alpine.

Three national parks (total area 36,572 sq. km), five territorial parks (7,861 sq. km), two ecological reserves (181 sq. km), eight wildlife management areas (10,651 sq. km) and one wildlife sanctuary (6,450 sq. km) have been established to protect fragile and significant areas for the future.

Electricity

The Yukon currently depends on imported refined petroleum products for about 16% of the energy it uses. At the same time, 94·6% (2000 figure) of the territory's electrical supply comes from four utility-owned hydro-electrical facilities.

Hydro-generated power is supplemented with diesel power plants which are located in most communities. Current capacity is 130·2 MW combined hydrodiesel-generated power. Total generation for 2000 was 268 GWh.

Oil and Gas

In 1997 the Yukon Oil and Gas Act was passed, replacing the federal legislation. This Act provides for the transfer of responsibility for oil and gas resources to Yukon jurisdiction. Five unexplored oil and gas basins with rich potential exist. Current net production is about 1·7m. cu. metres of natural gas per day.

Minerals

Gold and silver are the chief minerals. There are also deposits of lead, zinc, copper, tungsten and iron ore. Gold deposits, both hard rock and placer, are being mined.

Estimates for 2000 mineral production: gold, $51·6m. CDN; and silver, $0·3m. CDN. Total: $51·9m. CDN.

Agriculture

Many areas have suitable soils and climate for the production of forages, cereal grains and vegetables, domestic livestock and game farming. The greenhouse industry is the Yukon's largest horticulture sector.

In 1996 there were 160 farms operating full- and part-time. The total area of farms was 9,890 ha. of which 2,248 ha. are in field crop.

Farm receipts in 1996 were estimated at $3·5m. CDN. Total farm capital, 1996, was $45m. CDN.

Forestry

The forests, covering 275,000 sq. km of the territory, are part of the great Boreal forest region of Canada, which covers 57% of the Yukon. Forestry products include posts and beams for the construction industry, roof trusses, niche products and timber.

Production from forestry was 145·0m. cu. metres in 1999–2000. Fuel wood represents approximately $4m. CDN to $5m. CDN in direct employment and petroleum substitution in the Yukon annually.

Fur Trade

The fur-trapping industry is considered vital to rural and remote residents and especially First Nations people wishing to maintain a traditional lifestyle. Preliminary fur production in 2000 (mostly marten, muskrat, beaver, lynx and wolverine) was valued at $296,896 CDN.

Fisheries

Commercial fishing concentrates on chinook salmon, chum salmon, lake trout and whitefish.

INDUSTRY

The key sectors of the economy are tourism and government.

Labour

The 2000 labour force was 15,242, of whom 13,475 were employed.

INTERNATIONAL TRADE

Imports and Exports

In 2000 exports made up 35·2% of Yukon goods and services produced. In 2000 exports were valued at $396m. CDN.

COMMUNICATIONS

Roads

The Alaska Highway and branch highway systems connect Yukon's main communities with Alaska, the Northwest Territories, southern Canada and the United States. The 735-km Dempster Highway north of Dawson City connects with Inuvik, on the Arctic coast.

In 2000 there were 4,712·5 km of roads maintained by the Yukon Territorial government: 3,178·1 km, Alaska Highway; 1,534·4 km is secondary. Vehicles registered in 2000 totalled 23,915 (excluding buses, motorcycles and trailers), including 21,149 passenger vehicles.

Rail

The 176-km White Pass and Yukon Railway connected Whitehorse with year-round ocean shipping at Skagway, Alaska, but was closed in 1982. A modified passenger service was restarted in 1988 to take cruise ship tourists from Skagway to Carcross, Yukon, over the White Pass summit.

Civil Aviation

Whitehorse has an international airport with direct daily flights from Vancouver, Alaska and the Northwest Territories. In the summer there are regular scheduled flights from Europe. There are ten airports throughout the territory, with many smaller airstrips and aerodromes in remote areas. Commercial airlines offering charter services are located throughout the territory.

Shipping

The majority of goods are shipped into the territory by truck over the Alaska and Stewart-Cassiar Highways. Some goods are shipped through the ports of Skagway and Haines, Alaska, and then trucked to Whitehorse for distribution throughout the territory.

Telecommunications

All telephone and telecommunications, including Internet access in most communities, are provided by Northwestel, a subsidiary of Bell Canada Enterprises. In 2003, 10,000 households (93·4%) had telephones.

SOCIAL INSTITUTIONS

Education

The Yukon Department of Education operates (with the assistance of elected school boards) the territory's 28 schools, both public and private, from kindergarten to grade 12. In 2001 there were 5,579 pupils. There are also one French First Language school and one Roman Catholic school. The total enrolment figure for 1999–2000 was 5,332. The Whitehorse campus is the administrative and programme centre for 13 other campuses located throughout the territory. In 1999–2000 a total of 664 full-time and 4,668 part-time students enrolled in programmes and courses.

Health

In 2000 there were two hospitals with 61 staffed beds, four nursing stations, nine health treatment centres, 55 resident doctors and 15 dentists.

CULTURE

Broadcasting

There are three radio stations in Whitehorse and 15 low-power relay radio transmitters operated by CBC, and six operated by the Yukon government. CHON-FM, operated by Northern Native Broadcasting, is broadcast to virtually all Yukon communities by satellite. There are also 27 basic and 36 extended pay-cable TV channels in Whitehorse, and private cable operations in some communities. Live CBC national television and TVNC is provided by satellite and relayed to all communities.

Press

In 2000 there were one daily and one semi-weekly newspaper in Whitehorse, and a semi-weekly (summer only) and a monthly newspaper in Dawson City. In total, the territory publishes ten newspapers which range in publication from daily to annual.

Tourism

In 1999 there were about 280,500 visitors, generating revenues of $160m. CDN.

Tourism is the largest private sector employer. In 1999, 66% of employed Yukon people were working for businesses that reported some level of tourism revenue. 20% of businesses generate more than 33% of gross revenues from tourism.

FURTHER READING

Annual Report of the Government of the Yukon.
Yukon Executive Council, *Annual Statistical Review.*

Berton, P., *Klondike.* (Rev. ed.) Toronto, 1987
Coates, K. and Morrison, W., *Land of the Midnight Sun: A History of the Yukon.* Edmonton, 1988

There is a Yukon Archive at Yukon College, Whitehorse.

CAPE VERDE

República de Cabo Verde

Capital: Praia
Population projection, 2010: 567,000
GDP per capita, 2003: (PPP$) 5,214
HDI/world rank: 0·721/105

KEY HISTORICAL EVENTS

During centuries of Portuguese rule the islands were gradually peopled with Portuguese, slaves from Africa and people of mixed African-European descent who became the majority. While retaining some African culture, the Cape Verdians spoke Portuguese or the Portuguese-derived Crioulo (Creole) language and became Catholics. In 1956 nationalists from Cape Verde and Portuguese Guinea formed the *Partido Africano da Independência da Guiné e Cabo Verde* (PAIGC). In the 1960s the PAIGC waged a successful guerrilla war. On 5 July 1975 Cape Verde became independent, ruled by the PAIGC, which was already the ruling party in the former Portuguese colony of Guinea-Bissau. But resentment at Cape Verdians' privileged position in Guinea-Bissau led to the end of the ties between the two countries' ruling parties. Although the PAIGC retained its name in Guinea-Bissau, in Jan. 1981 it was renamed the *Partido Africano da Independência do Cabo Verde* (PAICV) in Cape Verde. The Constitution of 1981 made the PAICV the sole legal party but in Sept. 1990 the National Assembly abolished its monopoly and free elections were permitted.

TERRITORY AND POPULATION

Cape Verde is situated in the Atlantic Ocean 620 km off west Africa and consists of ten islands (Boa Vista, Brava, Fogo, Maio, Sal, Santa Luzia, Santo Antão, São Nicolau, São Tiago and São Vicente) and five islets. The islands are divided into two groups, named Barlavento (windward) and Sotavento (leeward). The total area is 4,033 sq. km (1,557 sq. miles). The 2000 census population was 434,625, giving a density of 107·8 per sq. km. The estimated population in 2005 was 507,000. In 2003, 55·9% of population lived in urban areas.

The UN gives a projected population for 2010 of 567,000. About 600,000 Cape Verdeans live abroad. Areas and populations of the islands:

Island	Area (sq. km)	Population Census 1990	Population Census 2000
Santo Antão	779	43,845	47,170
São Vicente[1]	227	51,277	67,163
São Nicolau	388	13,665	13,661
Sal	216	7,715	14,816
Boa Vista	620	3,452	4,209
Barlavento	*2,230*	*119,954*	*147,019*
Maio	269	4,969	6,754
São Tiago	991	175,691	236,627
Fogo	476	33,902	37,421
Brava	67	6,975	6,804
Sotavento	*1,803*	*221,537*	*287,606*

[1]Including Santa Luzia island, which is uninhabited.

The main towns are Praia, the capital, on São Tiago (76,000, 1999 estimate) and Mindelo on São Vicente (47,109, 1990 census). Ethnic groups in 2000 included: Mixed, 70%; Fulani, 12%; Balanta, 10%; Mandyako, 5%. The official language is Portuguese; a creole (Crioulo) is in ordinary use.

SOCIAL STATISTICS

2000 estimates: births, 12,600; deaths, 2,400. Rates, 2000 estimates (per 1,000 population): birth, 29·1; death, 5·6. Annual population growth rate, 1992–2002, 2·2%. Annual emigration varies between 2,000 and 10,000. Life expectancy at birth, 2003, was 67·0 years for men and 73·2 years for women. Infant mortality, 2001, 29 per 1,000 live births; fertility rate, 2001, 3·3 children per woman.

CLIMATE

The climate is arid, with a cool dry season from Dec. to June and warm dry conditions for the rest of the year. Rainfall is sparse, rarely exceeding 5" (127 mm) in the northern islands or 12" (304 mm) in the southern ones. There are periodic severe droughts. Praia, Jan. 72°F (22·2°C), July 77°F (25°C). Annual rainfall 10" (250 mm).

CONSTITUTION AND GOVERNMENT

The Constitution was adopted in Sept. 1992 and was revised in 1995 and 1999.

A constitutional referendum was held on 28 Dec. 1994; turnout was 45%. 82·06% of votes cast favoured a reform extending the powers of the presidency and strengthening the autonomy of local authorities. The *President* is elected for five-year terms by universal suffrage.

The 72-member *National Assembly* (*Assembleia Nacional*) is elected for five-year terms.

National Anthem

'Cântico da Liberdade' ('Song of Freedom'); words by A. S. Lopes, tune by A. H. T. Silva.

RECENT ELECTIONS

Elections for the *National Assembly* of 72 members were held on 22 Jan. 2006. Turnout was 52·2%. The PAICV won 41 seats with 52·2% of votes cast, the Movement for Democracy (MPD) won 29 seats with 44·0% and the Christian, Independent and Democratic Union won 2 with 2·6%. Two smaller parties failed to win any seats.

Presidential elections took place on 12 Feb. 2006. Incumbent Pedro Pires was re-elected with 51·0% of the vote against Carlos Veiga with 49·0%. Turnout was 53·1%.

CURRENT ADMINISTRATION

President: Pedro Pires; b. 1934 (PAICV; sworn in 22 March 2001 and re-elected in Feb. 2006).

In March 2006 the government comprised:

Prime Minister: José Maria Neves; b. 1959 (PAICV; sworn in 1 Feb. 2001).

Senior Minister for Health: Dr Basílio Mosso Ramos. *Senior Minister for Infrastructure and Transport, the Sea and Fisheries:* Manuel Inocêncio Sousa. *Minister for Foreign Affairs, Co-operation and Communities:* Dr Víctor Borges. *Internal Administration:* Dr Júlio Lopes Correira. *Defence, State Reform and President of the Council of Ministers:* Maria Cristina Fontes Lima. *Education and Higher Education:* Dr Filomena Martins. *Environment and Agriculture:* Dr Maria Brito Neves. *Justice:* José Manuel Andrade. *Economy, Growth and Competitiveness:* João Pereira Silva. *Finance and Public Administration:* Dr João Pinto Serra. *Labour, the Family and Solidarity:* Dr Sidónio Monteiro. *Decentralization, Housing and Regional Development:* Ramiro Azevedo. *Culture:* Manuel Veiga. *Communication and Government Spokesperson:* João Batista Pereira.

Government Website (Portuguese only): http://www.governo.cv

CURRENT LEADERS

Pedro Pires

Position
President

Introduction
A veteran politician, Pedro Pires was sworn in as the third president of Cape Verde in March 2001, having previously served three terms as prime minister. As a founder member of the African Party for the Independence of Cape Verde (PAICV), he played a prominent role in Cape Verde's independence movement, taking part in the negotiations with the colonial power, Portugal. He won a further term as president in Feb. 2006.

Early Life
Pedro Verona Rodrigues Pires was born on 29 April 1934 on Fogo Island, where he attended comprehensive school in São Filipe before going on to high school in the capital, Praia. He studied at the Science Faculty of the University of Lisbon in the 1950s and stayed in Portugal to carry out his compulsory military service in the Portuguese Air Force. Contact with nationalists from other Portuguese colonies led to his involvement with Amilcar Cabral's African Party for the Independence of Guinea and Cape Verde (PAIGC). Following the death of the Portuguese dictator, Salazar, in 1975 Portugal relinquished its sovereignty over Cape Verde.

Career in Office
Pires was the first prime minister of the independent Cape Verde, taking office in July 1975. The first multi-party elections were held peacefully in 1991. Pires' PAICV lost to the Movement for Democracy (MPD), the first instance of a West African country seeing a single-party government accept defeat at the polls. The 1992 constitution reduced the powers of the president and increased those of parliament.

The perceived sluggishness of economic reform and factionalism within the MPD allowed the return of the PAICV to power after the parliamentary elections of Jan. 2001. José Maria Neves took office as prime minister. After the presidential elections of Feb. 2001, the MPD candidate Carlos Veiga refused to accept a narrow win for Pires by 17 votes, appealing to the Supreme Court on the basis of electoral irregularities. However, Pires' win was confirmed and he took office on 22 March.

After reversing his decision not to stand in the presidential election of Feb. 2006, Pires again defeated Veiga, winning 51% of the vote, to claim a new five-year term.

DEFENCE

There is selective conscription. Defence expenditure totalled US$5m. in 2003 (US$11 per capita), representing 1·5% of GDP.

Army

The Army is composed of two battalions and had a strength of 1,000 in 2002.

Navy

There is a coast guard of 100 (2002).

Air Force

The Air Force had under 100 personnel and no combat aircraft in 2002.

INTERNATIONAL RELATIONS

Cape Verde is a member of the UN, the African Union, African Development Bank, ECOWAS, IOM, the International Organization of the Francophonie and is an ACP member state of the ACP-EU relationship.

ECONOMY

Agriculture accounted for 10·7% of GDP in 2002, industry 16·4% and services 72·8%.

Currency

The unit of currency is the *Cape Verde escudo* (CVE) of 100 *centavos.* Foreign exchange reserves were US$63m. in June 2002 and total money supply was 20,893m. escudos. There was inflation of 1·2% in 2003 but deflation of 1·9% in 2004.

Budget

In 2001 revenue totalled 14,900m. escudos and expenditure 21,200m. escudos.

Performance

Real GDP growth was 6·2% in 2003 and 4·4% in 2004. Total GDP in 2004 was US$0·9bn.

Banking and Finance

The Banco de Cabo Verde is the central bank (*Governor*, Carlos Burgo) and bank of issue, and was also previously a commercial bank. Its latter functions have been taken over by the Banco Comercial do Atlântico, mainly financed by public funds. The Caixa Econômica de Cabo Verde (CECV) has been upgraded into a commercial and development bank. Two foreign banks have also been established there. In addition, the Fundo de Solidariedade Nacional acts as the country's leading savings institution while the Fundo de Desenvoluimento Nacional administers public investment resources and the Instituto Caboverdiano channels international aid.

ENERGY AND NATURAL RESOURCES

Environment

Cape Verde's carbon dioxide emissions from the consumption and flaring of fossil fuels in 2002 were the equivalent of 0·4 tonnes per capita.

Electricity

Installed capacity was 7,000 kW in 2000. Production was around 43m. kWh in 2000. Consumption per capita in 2000 was an estimated 101 kWh.

Minerals

Salt is obtained on the islands of Sal, Boa Vista and Maio. Volcanic rock (pozzolana) is mined for export. There are also deposits of kaolin, clay, gypsum and basalt.

Agriculture

Some 10–15% of the land area is suitable for farming. In 2001, 39,000 ha. were arable and 2,000 ha. permanent crops, mainly confined to inland valleys. 3,000 ha. were irrigated in 2001. The chief crops (production, 2000, in 1,000 tonnes) are: sugarcane, 13; maize, 11; bananas, 6; cabbages, 6; coconuts, 6; mangoes, 5; sweet potatoes, 4; tomatoes, 4.

Livestock (2000): 640,000 pigs, 110,000 goats, 22,000 cattle, 14,000 asses.

Forestry

In 2000 the woodland area was 85,000 ha., or 21·1% of the total land area.

Fisheries

In 2001 the total catch was 9,653 tonnes (mainly tuna), exclusively from marine waters. About 200 tonnes of lobsters are caught annually.

INDUSTRY

The main industries are the manufacture of paint, beer, soft drinks, rum, flour, cigarettes, canned tuna and shoes.

Labour

In 1996 the workforce was 157,000 (62% males).

INTERNATIONAL TRADE

Foreign debt was US$414m. in 2002.

Imports and Exports

Imports and exports (f.o.b.) for calendar years in US$1m.:

	1998	1999	2000	2001	2002
Imports	218·8	239·0	225·7	231·5	278·0
Exports	32·7	26·0	38·3	37·2	41·8

In 2000 food constituted 32·8% of imports, with machinery and apparatus accounting for 16·1% and transport equipment 9·5%; shoes and shoe parts made up 51·8% of exports in 2000, clothing 35·1% and fish 4·8%.

Main import suppliers, 2000: Portugal, 52·4%; Netherlands, 13·0%; France, 4·4%. Leading export markets, 2000: Portugal, 80·1%; USA, 11·4%; Spain, 3·5%. Approximately 90% of food is imported.

COMMUNICATIONS

Roads

In 2002 there were an estimated 1,100 km of roads (78% paved); and in 1996 there were 3,280 private cars and 820 commercial vehicles.

Civil Aviation

Amilcar Cabral International Airport, at Espargos on Sal, is a major refuelling point on flights to Africa and Latin America. A new airport, Francisco Mendes Airport, has been built at Praia, and was opened in 2003. Transportes Aéreos de Cabo Verde (TACV), the national carrier, provided services to most of the other islands in 2003, and internationally to Abidjan, Amsterdam, Bamako, Bissau, Conakry, Dakar, Fortaleza, Las Palmas, Lisbon, Madrid, Milan, Munich, Paris and Zürich. In 2001 Amilcar Cabral International Airport handled 547,000 passengers (290,000 on international flights) and 4,000 tonnes of freight. In 1999 scheduled airline traffic of Cape Verde-based carriers flew 5·5m. km, carrying 252,000 passengers (114,000 on international flights).

Shipping

The main ports are Mindelo and Praia. In 2002 the merchant marine totalled 16,000 GRT. There is a state-owned ferry service between the islands.

Telecommunications

There were 113,100 telephone subscribers in 2002 (257·7 per 1,000 persons), including 42,900 mobile phone subscribers, and 35,000 PCs were in use. In 2002 there were 2,000 fax machines and 16,000 Internet users.

Postal Services

In 2003 there were 53 post offices.

SOCIAL INSTITUTIONS

Justice

There is a network of People's Tribunals, with a Supreme Court in Praia. The Supreme Court is composed of a minimum of five Judges, of whom one is appointed by the President, one elected by the National Assembly and the other by the Supreme Council of Magistrates.

The population in penal institutions in Dec. 1999 was 755 (178 per 100,000 of national population).

Education

Adult literacy in 2002 was 75·7% (male, 85·4%; female, 68·0%). Primary schooling is followed by lower (13–15 years) and upper (16–18 years) secondary education options. In 2000–01 there were 3,214 primary school teachers for 90,640 pupils; and 1,372 teachers (1997–98) for 45,545 pupils at secondary schools. In 1990 there were 531 students and 52 teachers at a technical school, 211 students and 53 teachers in three teacher-training colleges and about 500 students at foreign universities.

In 1998–99 total expenditure on education came to 4·4% of GNP.

Health

In 1996 there were two central and three regional hospitals, 15 health centres, 22 dispensaries and 60 community health clinics. There were 66 physicians, 213 nurses and six pharmacists in 1996.

RELIGION

In 2001, 83% of the population were Roman Catholic and 8% were followers of other religions.

CULTURE

Broadcasting

There are two national radio stations and a national TV service. Portuguese and French international radio and TV services also broadcast to Cape Verde. There were 71,000 radio receivers in 1997 and 44,000 television receivers in 2001.

Press

In 1996 there were three national newspapers—a state-owned bi-weekly, and a weekly and a fortnightly, owned by political parties. Total circulation approximates 12,000, but publication is suspended from time to time owing to shortage of paper.

Tourism

Tourism is in the initial stages of development. In 2002 there were 126,000 foreign tourists; spending by tourists totalled US$66m. Some 50% of tourists originate from Portugal, 15% from Germany and 7% from France.

DIPLOMATIC REPRESENTATIVES

Of Cape Verde in the United Kingdom
Ambassador: Vacant (resides in Brussels).
2nd Secretary: Clara Manuela da Luz Delgado.

Of the United Kingdom in Cape Verde
Ambassador: Peter Newall (resides in Dakar, Senegal).

Of Cape Verde in the USA (3415 Massachusetts Ave., NW, Washington, D.C., 20007)
Ambassador: José Brito.

Of the USA in Cape Verde (Rua Abilio Macedo 81, Praia)
Ambassador: Donald C. Johnson.

Of Cape Verde to the United Nations
Ambassador: Fátima Veiga.

Of Cape Verde to the European Union
Ambassador: Fernando Jorge Wahnon Ferreira.

FURTHER READING

Carreira, A., *The People of the Cape Verde Islands.* London, 1982
Foy, C., *Cape Verde: Politics, Economics and Society.* London, 1988
Lobban, R., *Cape Verde: Crioulo Colony to Independent Nation.* Westview Press, Boulder (CO), 1998
Meintel, D., *Race, Culture, and Portuguese Colonialism in Cabo Verde.* Syracuse Univ. Press, 1984
Shaw, Caroline E., *Cape Verde Islands.* [Bibliography] ABC-Clio, Oxford and Santa Barbara (CA), 1991

National Statistical Office: Instituto Nacional de Estatística, Praia.
Website (Portuguese only): http://www.ine.cv/

CENTRAL AFRICAN REPUBLIC

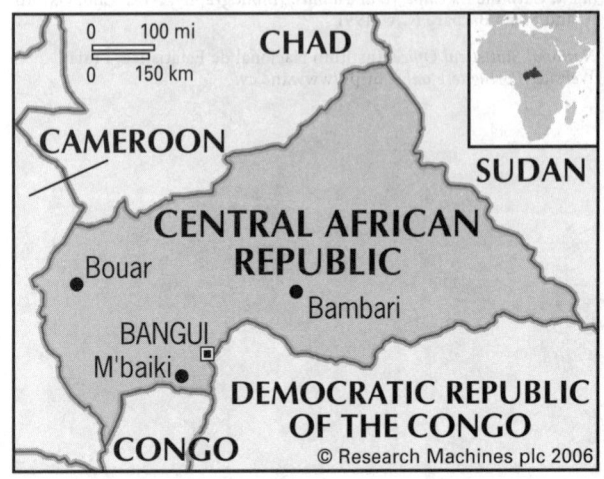

République Centrafricaine

Capital: Bangui
Population projection, 2010: 4·33m.
GDP per capita, 2003: (PPP$) 1,089
HDI/world rank: 0·355/171

KEY HISTORICAL EVENTS

Central African Republic became independent on 13 Aug. 1960, after having been one of the four territories of French Equatorial Africa. A Constitution of 1976 provided for the country to be a parliamentary democracy to be known as the Central African Empire. President Bokassa became Emperor Bokassa I. He was overthrown in 1979. In 1981 Gen. André Kolingba took power, initiating a gradual return to constitutional rule.

On 5 June 1996, following an army mutiny, President Patassé accepted an agreement brokered by France which led to the formation of a government of national unity. But mutineers demanded the replacement of President Patassé. France chaired a mediation committee of various neighbouring French-speaking states. An agreement to end the mutiny was signed in 1997 and a peacekeeping force from neighbouring states, MISAB, was set up. Conflicts between the mutineers and MISAB continued until a ceasefire was concluded on 2 July 1997. There was an attempted coup on 28 May 2001, allegedly led by Gen. Kolingba, who had been the country's military ruler from 1981 to 1993. However, it failed following several days of fighting in and around the capital, Bangui. Fighting erupted once more in Oct. 2002 after another coup attempt. In March 2003 a further coup saw Gen. François Bozizé, a former army chief, seize power.

TERRITORY AND POPULATION

The republic is bounded in the north by Chad, east by Sudan, south by the Democratic Republic of the Congo and the Republic of the Congo, and west by Cameroon. The area (including inland water) covers 622,984 sq. km (240,534 sq. miles). The population at the 2003 census (provisional) was 3,151,072, giving a density of 5 per sq. km. In 2003, 57·3% of the population were rural. The United Nations population estimate for 2003 was 3,937,000.

The UN gives a projected population for 2010 of 4·33m.

The areas, populations and capitals of the prefectures are as follows:

Prefecture	Sq. km	2003 census (provisional)	Capital
Bamingui-Bangoran	58,200	38,437	Ndele
Bangui[1]	67	531,763	Bangui
Basse-Kotto	17,604	203,887	Mobaye
Haute-Kotto	86,650	69,514	Bria
Haut-M'bomou	55,530	38,184	Obo
Kemo	17,204	98,881	Sibut
Lobaye	19,235	214,137	M'baiki
Mambere Kadéi	30,203	289,688	Berbérati
M'bomou	61,150	132,740	Bangassou
Nana Grebizi	19,996	87,341	Kaga-Bandoro
Nana-Mambere	26,600	184,594	Bouar
Ombella-M'poko	31,835	304,025	Bimbo
Ouaka	49,900	224,076	Bambari
Ouham	50,250	280,772	Bossangoa
Ouham-Pendé	32,100	325,567	Bozoum
Sangha M'baéré	19,412	89,871	Nola
Vakaga	46,500	37,595	Birao

[1]Autonomous commune.

The capital, Bangui, had a census population (provisional) in 2003 of 531,763. Other main towns, with 2003 census populations (provisional), are Bimbo (114,086), Bebérati (59,414), Carnot (37,339), Bambari (33,273) and Bouar (29,753).

There are a number of ethnic groups, the largest being Gbaya (34%), Banda (27%) and Mandja (21%).

Sango and French are the official languages.

SOCIAL STATISTICS

2000 births (estimates), 139,000; deaths, 69,000. Estimated birth rate in 2000 was 37·5 per 1,000 population; estimated death rate, 18·6. Infant mortality, 2001 (per 1,000 live births), 115. Expectation of life in 2003 was 38·4 years for males and 40·1 for females. Annual population growth rate, 1992–2002, 2·1%. Fertility rate, 2001, 5·0 children per woman.

CLIMATE

A tropical climate with little variation in temperature. The wet months are May, June, Oct. and Nov. Bangui, Jan. 31·9°C, July 20·7°C. Annual rainfall 1,289·3 mm. Ndele, Jan. 36·3°C, July 30·5°C. Annual rainfall 203·6 mm.

CONSTITUTION AND GOVERNMENT

Under the Constitution adopted by a referendum on 21 Nov. 1986, the sole legal political party was the *Rassemblement Démocratique Centrafricain*. In Aug. 1992 the Constitution was revised to permit multi-party democracy. Further constitutional reforms followed a referendum in Dec. 1994, including the establishment of a *Constitutional Court*. The President is elected by popular vote for not more than two terms of six years, and appoints and leads a Council of Ministers. There is a 109-member *National Assembly*. Following the coup of March 2003 Gen. François Bozizé suspended the constitution and dissolved parliament. However, at a referendum on 5 Dec. 2004, 90·4% of voters approved the adoption of a new constitution; voter participation was 77·4%. The new constitution resembles the previous one but permits the president to serve not more than two terms of five years. It also provides for the appointment of the prime minister from the political party with a parliamentary majority.

National Anthem

'La Renaissance' ('Rebirth'); words by B. Boganda, tune by H. Pepper.

RECENT ELECTIONS

At the presidential elections held on 13 March 2005 there were 11 presidential candidates. Incumbent president Gen. François

Bozizé received 42·9% of the vote, ahead of former prime minister Martin Ziguélé (Liberation Movement of the Central African People) with 23·5% and former president André Kolingba (Central African Democratic Rally) 16·4%. In the second round on 8 May 2005 Gen. François Bozizé won 64·7% of the vote against Martin Ziguélé who won 35·3%. Turnout was 64·6%.

In National Assembly elections on 13 March and 8 May 2005 the National Convergence coalition gained 42 seats (including the National Unity Party with 3 seats and the Movement for Democracy and Development with 2), the Liberation Movement of the Central African People 11, the Central African Democratic Rally 8, Social Democratic Party 4, Patriotic Front for Progress 2, Alliance for Democracy and Progress 2, the Londo Association 1 and ind. 34.

CURRENT ADMINISTRATION

Former army chief Gen. François Bozizé seized power on 15 March 2003 in a coup and the following day declared himself president, saying that he had dissolved the National Assembly and government. A transitional government was formed comprising representatives of civil society and all political parties. Gen. Bozizé said that a transition period would last between one and three years, after which elections would be held to decide on a new government. Bozizé reshuffled the transitional government in Dec. 2003 and in Sept. 2004. The period of transitional government ended with the 2005 elections, following which Gen. François Bozizé again reshuffled the government. In March 2006 it comprised the following:

President and Minister of Defence, Veterans, War Victims, Disarmament and Army Restructuring: Gen. François Bozizé; b. 1946 (since 16 March 2003).

Prime Minister: Élie Doté; b. 1947 (took office on 13 June 2005).

Minister of State for Equipment, Transport and Civil Aviation: Charles Massi. *Foreign Affairs, Regional Integration and Francophonie:* Jean-Paul Ngoupandé. *Communication, National Reconciliation, Democratic Culture and the Promotion of Human Rights:* Jean-Eudes Teya.

Minister of Civil Service: Jacques Bothy. *Commerce, Industry and Small- and Medium-Sized Enterprises:* Emilie Béatrice Epaye. *Water, Forests, Hunting and Fisheries and Responsible for the Environment:* Emmanuel Bizot. *Economy, Planning and International Co-operation:* Sylvain Maliko. *Mines and Energy:* Sylvain Ndoutingaï. *Social Affairs:* Solange Pagonéndji Ndackala. *Finance:* Théodore Dabanga. *Interior and Public Security:* Michel Sallé. *Justice:* Paul Otto. *National Education:* Charles Armel Doubane. *Post and Telecommunications, in Charge of New Technologies:* Fidèle Ngouandjika. *Public Health:* Lalha Konamna. *Reconstruction of Public Buildings, Town Planning and Housing:* Timoléon Mbaikoua. *Agriculture and Rural Development:* Parfait-Anicet Mbay. *Secretary General of the Government, in Charge of Relations with Parliament:* Laurent Ngon Baba. *Tourism Development and Handicrafts:* Col. Mohamed Mahdi Marboua. *Youth, Sports, Arts and Culture:* Guy Désiré Kolingba.

CURRENT LEADERS

François Bozizé

Position
President

Introduction
Gen. François Bozizé declared himself president of the Central African Republic following a military coup in March 2003, having been a prominent figure on the CAR's political scene during the regimes of Andre Kolingba and Ange-Félix Patassé. He was suspected of involvement in coup attempts in 1983, 2001 and 2002 before seizing control.

Early Life
Bozizé was born in 1946. He came to political prominence as a leading critic of Kolingba's military rule which began in 1981. Having led an unsuccessful coup in 1983, he was arrested and tortured by government forces before going into exile in Togo. There he met Patassé with whom he established strong ties. The two stood against each other at the free elections of 1993 and Bozizé lost. Nonetheless, he remained a Patassé ally, defending him against several uprisings during 1996 and 1997.

However, the relationship became increasingly strained. Bozizé accused Patassé's regime of mismanagement as popular discontent grew at government corruption and failure to pay salaries. In May 2001 Patassé used Libyan forces to put down a coup headed by former president Kolingba, who had been assisted by Bozizé. Bozizé was sacked as head of the army. In Nov. 2001 government troops attempted to arrest Bozizé, but fighting broke out with forces loyal to him. Bozizé held the north of Bangui for a period before taking around 300 troops into exile in Chad. In Oct. 2002 pro-Bozizé factions attempted to depose Patassé, but were defeated amid allegations that Bozizé had instigated the coup with support from Chad.

Career in Office
While Patassé was away in Niger in March 2003 Bozizé led around 1,000 troops into Bangui. They faced little opposition and secured vital strategic locations within a day. Patassé attempted to fly back into the city but was diverted to Cameroon. The Congolese rebels, on whose support Patassé had relied, meanwhile fled over the country.

Having seized power, Bozizé imposed a curfew, dissolved parliament, suspended the constitution and was named president amid promises of free elections. He announced plans to negotiate aid from the IMF and World Bank and promised to address government inefficiency and corruption, disunity in the armed forces and the growing AIDS threat.

Reaction to the coup was mixed. Opposition groups within CAR welcomed the removal of Patassé, as did many central African nations. However, France, the former colonial power, described the coup as 'unacceptable' and the African Union threatened CAR's expulsion. There was widespread looting and rioting in Bangui in the days following Bozizé's assumption of power and he appealed to the Economic Community of Central African States to restore order. He was also accused of using backing from Chad in the coup, a charge which provoked widespread unease throughout the country.

Bozizé appointed Abel Goumba, a longstanding opposition figure, as prime minister and in April 2003 Goumba named a 28-man cabinet which included two former Patassé supporters. Bozizé took the defence portfolio. Later in the month he suspended all timber felling and diamond mining licence agreements ahead of an audit of relevant companies to confirm payment of taxes. The two sectors represent the country's biggest foreign currency earners but have been beset by corruption and tax avoidance. In Dec. 2003 Bozizé dismissed Goumba and appointed Célestin Gaombalet as prime minister.

Presidential elections were held over two rounds in March and May 2005, in which Bozizé retained office.

DEFENCE

Selective national service for a two-year period is in force.

Defence expenditure totalled US$29m. in 2003 (US$8 per capita), representing 2·3% of GDP.

Army

The Army consisted (2002) of about 1,400 personnel. There is a territorial defence regiment, a combined arms regiment and a support/HQ regiment. In addition there are some 1,000 personnel in the paramilitary Gendarmerie.

Navy

The Army includes a small naval wing operating a handful of patrol craft.

Air Force

Personnel strength (2002) about 150. There are no combat aircraft.

INTERNATIONAL RELATIONS

The Central African Republic is a member of the UN, WTO, the African Union, African Development Bank, Lake Chad Basin Commission, the International Organization of the Francophonie and is an ACP member state of the ACP-EU relationship.

ECONOMY

Agriculture accounted for 56·5% of GDP in 2002, industry 22·3% and services 21·2%.

Currency

The unit of currency is the *franc CFA* (XAF) with a parity of 655·957 francs CFA to one euro. Total money supply in April 2002 was 103,991m. francs CFA and foreign exchange reserves were US$123m. Gold reserves were 11,000 troy oz in June 2002. In 2004 there was deflation of 2·2%.

Budget

In 2001 expenditure totalled 97,200m. francs CFA and revenue 63,200m. francs CFA.

Performance

Total GDP in 2004 was US$1·3bn. Real GDP growth was 1·3% in 2004 (–7·6% in 2003).

Banking and Finance

The *Banque des Etats de l'Afrique Centrale* (*BEAC*) acts as the central bank and bank of issue. The *Governor* is Jean-Félix Mamalepot. There are three commercial banks, a development bank and an investment bank.

ENERGY AND NATURAL RESOURCES

Environment

The Central African Republic's carbon dioxide emissions from the consumption and flaring of fossil fuels in 2002 were the equivalent of 0·1 tonnes per capita.

Electricity

Installed capacity was 36,890 kW in 2000. Production in 2000 totalled 127·7m. kWh (approximately 98% hydro-electric). Consumption per capita in 2000 was 31 kWh.

Minerals

In 2001, 360,000 carats of gem diamonds and 120,000 carats of industrial diamonds were mined; and, in 2000, 12·3 kg of gold. In 2000, 633,000 kg of sheet aluminium were produced. There are also oil, uranium and other mineral deposits which are for the most part unexploited.

Agriculture

In 2002 the agricultural population numbered 2·21m. persons, of whom 1·27m. were economically active. In 2001, 1·93m. ha. were arable and 90,000 ha. permanent crops. The main crops (production 2000, in 1,000 tonnes) are cassava, 500; yams, 360; bananas, 115; groundnuts, 105; maize, 101; taro, 100; plantains, 82; seed cotton, 35.

Livestock, 2000: cattle, 2·95m.; goats, 2·60m.; sheep, 210,000; pigs, 650,000; chickens, 4m.

Forestry

There were 22·91m. ha. of forest in 2000, or 36·8% of the total land area. The extensive hardwood forests, particularly in the southwest, provide mahogany, obeche and limba. Timber production in 2001 was 3·06m. cu. metres.

Fisheries

The catch in 2001 was approximately 15,000 tonnes, exclusively from inland waters.

INDUSTRY

The small industrial sector includes factories producing wood products, cotton fabrics, footwear, beer and radios. Output: sugar (2001), 13,000 tonnes; oils and fats (2000), 7,000 tonnes; beer (2003), 12·2m. litres; cotton fabrics (1992), 5·32m. metres; sawnwood (2001), 150,000 cu. metres.

Labour

In 1996 the labour force was 1,623,000 (53% males).

INTERNATIONAL TRADE

External debt was US$1,066m. in 2002.

Imports and Exports

Imports in 2000 totalled US$247m. (US$253m. in 1999); exports in 2000 totalled US$181m. (US$178m. in 1999).

Main import suppliers, 1999: France, 33·8%; Cameroon, 12·2%; Belgium-Luxembourg, 7·4%; UK, 4·1%. Main export markets, 2000: Belgium-Luxembourg, 64·7%; Spain, 6·3%; France, 3·2%; Taiwan, 3·2%. Main imports include food, textiles, petroleum products, machinery, electrical equipment and motor vehicles. Main exports are diamonds, coffee, timber and cotton.

COMMUNICATIONS

Roads

There were 23,417 km of roads in 2002, including 5,200 km of highways or main roads. In 1997 there were 966 passenger cars and 662 commercial vehicles. There were 77 road accident deaths in 2000.

Civil Aviation

There is an international airport at M'Poko, near Bangui, which handled 44,000 passengers (41,000 on international flights) in 2001. In 2003 there were direct services operating to Douala, Khartoum, Nyala, Paris and Yaoundé. In 1999 scheduled airline traffic of Central African Republic-based carriers flew 3·0m. km, carrying 84,000 passengers (all on international flights).

Shipping

Timber and barges are taken to Brazzaville (Republic of the Congo).

Telecommunications

There were 21,600 telephone subscribers in 2002 (equivalent to 5·5 per 1,000 persons), including 12,600 mobile phone subscribers, and 8,000 PCs were in use (2·0 per 1,000 persons). In 2002 there were 300 fax machines and 5,000 Internet users.

Postal Services

In 2003 there were 32 post offices.

SOCIAL INSTITUTIONS

Justice

The Criminal Court and Supreme Court are situated in Bangui. There are 16 high courts throughout the country. The population in penal institutions in 2001 was 4,168 (110 per 100,000 of national population).

Education

Adult literacy rate was 48·6% in 2003 (64·8% among males and 33·5% among females). In 2000–01 there were an estimated 457,000 pupils at the *fondamental 1* (lower primary) level being taught in 2,147 schools by 4,555 teachers; and 47,267 pupils at 143 *fondamental 2* and secondary schools with 913 teachers. The University of Bangui, founded in 1969, had 3,590 students and 140 academic staff in 1995–96. In 2000–01 there were 5,523 students in higher education. In 1998–99 total expenditure on education came to 1·9% of GNP.

Health

In 1990 there were 255 hospitals and health centres with 4,120 beds (4,126 beds in 2000). In 2000 there were 114 doctors, 179 midwives and 217 state qualified nurses.

RELIGION

In 2001 there were 660,000 Roman Catholics, 560,000 Muslims and 520,000 Protestants. Traditional animist beliefs are still widespread.

CULTURE

World Heritage Sites

The Manovo-Gounda St Floris National Park was inscribed on the UNESCO World Heritage List in 1988. Poaching and violence closed the park to tourism in 1997.

Broadcasting

Broadcasting is provided by the state-controlled *Radiodiffusion-Télévision Centrafricaine*. There were 280,000 radio receivers in 2000 and 22,000 TV sets in 2001 (colour by SECAM V).

Press

In 1998 there were three daily newspapers with a circulation of 6,200, giving a rate of 1·8 per 1,000 inhabitants.

Tourism

In 2002 there were 13,000 foreign tourists; spending by tourists totalled US$3m.

DIPLOMATIC REPRESENTATIVES

Of Central African Republic in the United Kingdom
Ambassador: Vacant.
First Counsellor: Germain Gresenguet (resides in Paris).

Of the United Kingdom in Central African Republic
Ambassador: Richard Wildash, LVO (resides in Yaoundé, Cameroon).

Of Central African Republic in the USA (1618 22nd St., NW, Washington, D.C., 20008)
Ambassador: Emmanuel Touaboy.

Of the USA in Central African Republic (Ave. David Dacko, Bangui)
Ambassador: Vacant.
Chargé d'Affaires a.i.: James Panos.

Of Central African Republic to the United Nations
Ambassador: Vacant.

Of Central African Republic to the European Union
Ambassador: Armand-Guy Zounguere-Sokambi.

FURTHER READING

Kalck, P., *Historical Dictionary of the Central African Republic.* Scarecrow Press, Metuchen, (NJ), 1992.—*Central African Republic.* [Bibliography] ABC-Clio, Oxford and Santa Barbara (CA), 1993
Titley, B., *Dark Age: The Political Odyssey of Emperor Bokassa.* McGill-University Press, Montreal, 1997

National Statistical Office: Division des Statistiques, des Etudes Economiques et Sociales, BP 696, Bangui.
Website (French only): http://www.stat-centrafrique.com

CHAD

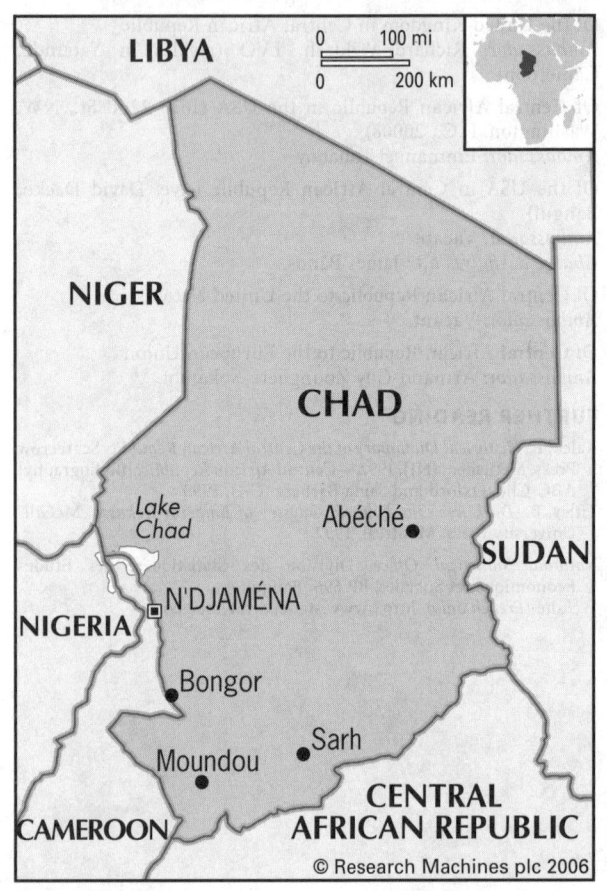

© Research Machines plc 2006

République du Tchad

Capital: N'Djaména
Population projection, 2010: 11·13m.
GDP per capita, 2003: (PPP$) 1,210
HDI/world rank: 0·341/173

KEY HISTORICAL EVENTS

France proclaimed a protectorate over Chad in 1900 and in July 1908 the territory was incorporated into French Equatorial Africa. It became a separate colony in 1920, and in 1946 one of the four constituent territories of French Equatorial Africa. It achieved full independence on 11 Aug. 1960. Conflicts between the government and secessionist groups, particularly in the Muslim north and centre, began in 1965 and developed into civil war. In 1982 forces led by Hissène Habré gained control of the country. In June 1983 Libyan-backed forces re-occupied some territory but a ceasefire took effect in Sept. 1987. Rebel forces of the Popular Salvation Movement led by Idriss Déby entered Chad from Sudan in Nov. 1990. On 4 Dec. 1990 Déby declared himself President. In Feb. 2000 Hissène Habré was charged with torture and barbarity and put under house arrest in Senegal, where he had lived since being toppled in 1990.

TERRITORY AND POPULATION

Chad is bounded in the west by Cameroon, Nigeria and Niger, north by Libya, east by Sudan and south by the Central African

Republic. In Feb. 1994 the International Court of Justice ruled that the Aozou Strip along the Libyan border, occupied by Libya since 1973, was part of Chad. Area, 1,284,000 sq. km. At the 1993 census the population was 6,279,931 (5,929,192 settled, of whom 1,327,570 were urban and 359,069 nomadic). 2005 population estimate, 9,749,000; density, 8 per sq. km.

The UN gives a projected population for 2010 of 11·13m.

In 2003, 75·0% of the population were rural. The capital is N'Djaména with 998,000 inhabitants (1999 estimate), other large towns being (1993 census figures) Moundou (282,103), Sarh (193,753), Bongor (196,713), Abéché (187,936) and Doba (185,461).

The areas, populations and chief towns of the 14 prefectures were:

Prefecture	Area sq. km	Population (1993 census)	Capital
Batha	88,800	288,458	Ati
Biltine	46,850	184,807	Biltine
Borkou-Ennedi-Tibesti	600,350	73,185	Faya (Largeau)
Chari-Baguirmi	82,910	1,251,906	N'Djaména
Guéra	58,950	306,253	Mongo
Kanem	114,520	279,927	Mao
Lac	22,320	252,932	Bol
Logone Occidental	8,695	455,489	Moundou
Logone Oriental	28,035	441,064	Doba
Mayo-Kebbi	30,105	825,158	Bongor
Moyen-Chari	45,180	738,595	Sarh
Ouaddaï	76,240	543,900	Abéché
Salamat	63,000	184,403	Amtiman
Tandjilé	18,045	453,854	Laï

The official languages are French and Arabic, but more than 100 different languages and dialects are spoken. The largest ethnic group is the Sara of southern Chad (27·7% of the total population), followed by the Sudanic Arabs (11·5%).

SOCIAL STATISTICS

2001 estimates: births, 398,000; deaths, 138,000. Rates, 2001 estimates (per 1,000 population): births, 49·1; deaths, 17·0. Annual rate of growth, 1992–2002, 3·1%. Expectation of life in 2003 was 42·5 years among males and 44·7 among females. Infant mortality, 2001 (per 1,000 live births), 117. Fertility rate, 2001, 6·7 children per woman.

CLIMATE

A tropical climate, with adequate rainfall in the south, though Nov. to April are virtually rainless months. Further north, desert conditions prevail. N'Djaména, Jan. 75°F (23·9°C), July 82°F (27·8°C). Annual rainfall 30" (744 mm).

CONSTITUTION AND GOVERNMENT

After overthrowing the regime of Hissène Habré, Idriss Déby proclaimed himself *President* and was sworn in on 4 March 1991.

A law of Oct. 1991 permits the formation of political parties provided they are not based on regionalism, tribalism or intolerance. There were 59 parties in 1996.

At a referendum on 31 March 1996 a new Constitution was approved by 63·5% of votes cast. It defines Chad as a unitary state. The head of state is the *President*, elected by universal suffrage. On 26 May 2004 the *National Assembly* passed an amendment scrapping the two-term limit on the presidency, replacing it with an age limit of 70. The amendment was approved by referendum in June 2005.

The *National Assembly* has 155 members, elected for a four-year term. A *Senate* was stipulated in the 1996 constitution, but has yet to be created.

National Anthem

'Peuple tchadien, debout et à l'ouvrage' ('People of Chad, arise and take up the task'); words by L. Gidrol, tune by P. Villard.

RECENT ELECTIONS

Presidential elections were held on 3 May 2006. Turnout was 61·5%. Incumbent Idriss Déby won re-election, with 77·5% of the vote, against 8·8% for Delwa Kassire Koumakoye, 5·4% for Albert Pahimi Padacké and 4·6% for Mahamat Abdoulaye.

In parliamentary elections held on 21 April 2002 the Patriotic Salvation Movement (MPS) of President Idriss Déby won 102 seats, the Rally for Democracy and Progress (RDP) 12, the Federation Action for the Republic 11, the National Rally for Development and Progress 5, the National Union for Democracy and Renewal 5 and the Union for Renewal and Democracy 3. Turnout was 52·8%.

CURRENT ADMINISTRATION

President: Lieut.-Gen. Idriss Déby; b. 1954 (MPS; in office since Dec. 1990 and re-elected in July 1996, May 2001 and May 2006).

In March 2006 the government comprised:

Prime Minister: Pascal Yoadimnadji; b. 1950 (appointed on 3 Feb. 2005).

Minister of State, Minister of Infrastructure: Adoum Younoussmi. *Minister of State, Minister of National Education, Youth and Sport:* Prof. Avocksouma Djoma.

Minister of Agriculture: Albert Pahimi Padacket. *Civil Service, Labour and Employment:* Fatimé Kimto. *Commerce and Handicrafts:* Ngarmbatina Carmel Sou. *Communications, Culture and Government Spokesman:* Hourmadji Moussa Doumngor. *Defence:* Bichara Issa Djadallah. *Environment and Water Resources:* Hissene Ahmat Senoussi. *Finance:* Abbas Mahamat Tolli. *Foreign Affairs and African Co-operation:* Ahmad Allam-mi. *Justice, Keeper of the Seals:* Edouard Ngarta Mbaihoroum. *Land Management, Town Planning and Housing:* Adoum Chene. *Livestock:* Mahamat Allamine Bourma. *Mines and Energy:* Youssouf Abassallah. *Oil Resources:* Mahamat Hassan Nasser. *Planning, Development and Co-operation:* Mahamat Ali Hassan. *Posts, New Technology and Communications:* Mahamat Garfa. *Public Health:* Moussa Kadam. *Public Security and Immigration:* Routouang Yoma Golom. *Social Action and Family Affairs:* Hassan Terab. *Territorial Administration:* Mahamat Ali Abdallah. *Tourism Development:* Oumar Kadjallami Boukar. *Minister in Charge of State Control and Morals:* Mahamat Bechir Okoromi.

CURRENT LEADERS

Idriss Déby

Position
President

Introduction
Lieut.-Gen. Idris Déby became president in Feb. 1991 after participating in a coup to overthrow Hissène Habré. He oversaw multi-party elections but opponents have cited electoral irregularities after Déby's victories at the 1996 and 2001 polls. His tenure has been marked by civil war and an overspill of fighting from Darfur in neighbouring Sudan, hindering attempts at reducing Chad's extreme poverty. The country's recently acquired status as an oil exporter may boost the economy.

Early Life
Déby was born in 1952 into the Bidyate clan of the Zaghawa peoples. While serving in the army he helped Hissène Habré take power in 1982, overthrowing Goukouki Queddei in a coup. His relationship with Habré declined and in 1989 Déby was accused of involvement in an alleged coup and went into exile in Sudan. In Dec. 1990, as head of the Patriotic Salvation Movement (MPS) and with the support of Libya, he removed Habré from power. Déby was proclaimed president in Feb. 1991 and in 1993 was appointed interim head of a transitional government charged with preparing democratic elections to be held within a year.

Career in Office
Déby went on to establish a multi-party constitution and triumphed at presidential elections held in 1996. The MPS won elections to the legislative assembly the following year.

Déby has had to cope with tensions between the largely Arab-Muslim north and the mainly Christian and animist south. In 1998 there was a surge in rebel activity in the north, spearheaded by the Movement for Democracy and Justice in Chad (MDJT), led by Déby's former defence minister Youssouf Togoimi. In early 2002 Libyan leader Col. Qadhafi, formerly a supporter of Chadian rebel movements, brokered a peace agreement which included provision for an amnesty for MDJT members. It soon failed but in Jan. 2003 the government reached a peace agreement with the rebel National Resistance Army in the east and in Dec. that year a new accord was signed with the MDJT.

Déby was re-elected in 2001 although the electoral commission discounted results from 25% of polling stations for electoral irregularities. Six of Déby's defeated rivals were subsequently arrested for 'inciting violence and civil disobedience' but later released as human rights organizations and trades unions pressed for a general strike. Déby was sworn in to office in Aug. 2001. In 2001 the Senegalese judicial system concluded that it lacked the authority to try Habré, the deposed former president in exile in Senegal, on charges of authorizing torture.

Chad has high levels of poverty and poor social infrastructure. However, an economic upturn is expected following the 2003 opening of a pipeline, costing US$3·7bn., connecting Chad's oil fields with Cameroon. 80% of oil revenues is to be spent on development projects.

Since 2003 fighting has spilled over the border from Darfur in neighbouring Sudan. There has been a large influx of refugees from Darfur into the Chadian interior, many under the supervision of the UNHCR. In 2005 Chad accused Sudan of supporting Chadian rebels.

A constitutional amendment in June 2005 permitted Déby to stand for a third term of office, which he did successfully in May 2006. When parliament approved the amendment in 2004, Déby's opponents called for a national strike. Déby's tenure has seen a steady worsening in relations with France, the former colonial power.

DEFENCE

There are seven military regions. Total armed forces personnel numbered 30,350 in 2002, including republican guards. Defence expenditure totalled US$34m. in 2003 (US$4 per capita), representing 1·3% of GDP.

Army

In 2002 the strength was 25,000. In addition there was a paramilitary Gendarmerie of 4,500 and a Republican Guard of 5,000.

Air Force

Personnel (2002) about 350 including two combat aircraft and two combat helicopters.

INTERNATIONAL RELATIONS

Chad is a member of the UN, WTO, the African Union, African Development Bank, Lake Chad Basin Commission, OIC, Islamic Development Bank, the International Organization of the Francophonie and is an ACP member state of the ACP-EU relationship.

ECONOMY

Agriculture accounted for 38·7% of GDP in 2002, industry 15·4% and services 45·8%.

Overview

After 30 years of civil war, Chad has one of the ten lowest human development index scores in the world. It is dependent on external aid (chiefly from the IMF, the World Bank and the EU) and the agrarian sector supports 80% of the population although it accounts for less than 40% of GDP. Per capita income is less than US$250 per annum, more than half the adult population is illiterate and only 1% of the population has access to electricity. Economic development is hindered by political instability, droughts and primitive infrastructure.

However, there has been substantial recent economic growth resulting from oil-related investments and spillover linked to the completion of the Chad–Cameroon oil pipeline in July 2003. The majority of Chad's oil revenues have been earmarked for priority sectors such as education, health care, infrastructure and rural development. Since the mid-1990s real GDP growth has averaged 5·2% with growth of 10% since 2001 reflecting the oil pipeline construction. Growth in the non-oil sector is more volatile, reflecting the vulnerability of the cotton sector to declines in world prices, weather and disease-based shocks. Reform of the cotton, domestic energy and financial sectors has been encouraged by the IMF and World Bank to reduce dependency on oil revenues and to enable rural poverty to be addressed more directly.

Chad became a member of CAEMU (the Central African Economic and Monetary Union) in 2004 when it met all accession criteria. Monetary policy is conducted on a regional level, since the currency is pegged to the euro and managed by La Banque des Etats de l'Afrique Centrale.

Currency

The unit of currency is the *franc CFA* (XAF) with a parity of 655·957 francs CFA to one euro. There was deflation in 2003 of 1·8% and in 2004 of 5·3%. Foreign exchange reserves were US$154m. in April 2002 and total money supply was 161,104m. francs CFA. Gold reserves were 11,000 troy oz in June 2002.

Budget

Revenues in 2000 were 128·2bn. francs CFA and expenditures 203·2bn. francs CFA.

Performance

Real GDP growth was 11·3% in 2003 and 29·7% in 2004, thanks mainly to the acceleration of the construction of an oil pipeline from Chad to Cameroon. The pipeline will allow Chad to export its oil riches to the world market. Chad became the world's newest oil producer in 2003, and as a result in 2004 recorded economic growth second only to that of Equatorial Guinea. In 2004 total GDP was US$4·3bn.

Banking and Finance

The *Banque des Etats de l'Afrique Centrale* (Governor, Jean-Félix Mamalepot) is the bank of issue. Other leading banks include: Banque Agricole du Soudan au Tchad; Banque Commerciale du Chari; Banque Internationale de l'Afrique au Tchad; Commercial Bank Tchad; Financial Bank Tchad; and Société Générale Tchadienne de Banque.

ENERGY AND NATURAL RESOURCES

Electricity

Installed capacity was 29,000 kW in 2000. Production in 2000 amounted to an estimated 92m. kWh. Consumption per capita was an estimated 12 kWh—the lowest in the world—in 2000.

Oil and Gas

The oilfield in Kanem prefecture has been linked by pipeline to a new refinery at N'Djaména but production has remained minimal. There is a larger oilfield in the Doba Basin. In June 2000 the World Bank approved funding for a 1,070-km US$4bn. pipeline to run from 300 new oil wells in Chad through Cameroon to the Atlantic Ocean. Oil started pumping in July 2003 making Chad the world's newest oil producer. Crude oil production in 2003 was 2·1m. tonnes. Revenues are expected to reach US$80m. per annum.

Minerals

Salt (about 4,000 tonnes per annum) is mined around Lake Chad, and there are deposits of uranium, gold, iron ore and bauxite. There are small-scale workings for gold and iron.

Agriculture

Some 80% of the workforce is involved in subsistence agriculture and fisheries. In 2001, 3·60m. ha. were arable and 30,000 ha. permanent crops. There were 175 tractors in 2001. Cotton growing (in the south) and animal husbandry (in the central zone) are the most important branches. Production, 2000 (in 1,000 tonnes): sorghum, 567; groundnuts, 372; millet, 321; sugarcane, 315; cassava, 255; seed cotton, 235; yams, 230; rice, 131; cottonseed, 125; cotton lint, 90; maize, 87.

Livestock, 2000: cattle, 5,595,000; goats, 5,050,000; sheep, 2,500,000; camels, 715,000; chickens, 5m.

Forestry

In 2000 the area under forests was 12·69m. ha., or 10·1% of the total land area. Timber production in 2001 was 6·76m. cu. metres.

Fisheries

Total catches, from Lake Chad and the Chari and Logone rivers, were approximately 84,000 tonnes in 2001.

INDUSTRY

Output: cotton fibre (1998), 86,260 tonnes; sugar (2002), 32,000 tonnes; soap (1996), 2,958 tonnes; edible oil (1996), 12·55m. litres; beer (2003), 21·6m. litres; cigarettes (2000), 30m. packets; bicycles (1996), 3,444 units.

Labour

In 1996 the labour force was 3,145,000 (56% males). In 1994 approximately 70% of the economically active population were engaged in agriculture, fishing and forestry.

INTERNATIONAL TRADE

External debt was US$1,281m. in 2002.

Imports and Exports

Imports in 2000 totalled US$450m. (US$474m. in 1999); exports in 2000 totalled US$233m. (US$242m. in 1999).

Main import suppliers in 1997 were France, 41·3%; Nigeria, 10·1%; Cameroon, 7·2%; India, 5·8%; Belgium-Luxembourg, 5·1%; Italy, 4·3%. Main export markets were Portugal, 29·9%; Germany, 14·2%; Thailand, 7·5%; Costa Rica, 6·0%; Hong Kong, 4·8%; Taiwan, 4·8%. The principal imports are machinery and transportation equipment, industrial goods, petroleum products and foodstuffs. Cotton exports in 1994, 28,857m. francs CFA; cattle, 15,401 francs CFA. Apart from cotton and cattle, other important exports are textiles and fish.

COMMUNICATIONS

Roads

In 2002 there were estimated to be 33,360 km of roads, of which only 0·8% were surfaced. Approximately 8,900 passenger cars were in use in 2002, plus 12,400 trucks and vans (2000), and 3,640 motorcycles and mopeds (1996).

Civil Aviation

There is an international airport at N'Djaména, from which there were direct flights in 2003 to Addis Ababa, Bamako, Bangui, Douala, Garoua, Kano, Paris, Tripoli and Yaoundé. In 1999 scheduled airline traffic of Chad-based carriers flew 2·9m. km, carrying 84,000 passengers (all on international flights). In 2000 N'Djaména handled 17,000 passengers and 2,300 tonnes of freight.

Telecommunications

In 2002 telephone subscribers numbered 46,000 (5·8 per 1,000 persons) and there were 13,000 PCs in use (1·7 per 1,000 persons). There were 200 fax machines in 2002. Mobile phone subscribers numbered 34,200 in 2002 and Internet users 15,000.

Postal Services

In 2003 there were 42 post offices, or one for every 204,700 persons.

SOCIAL INSTITUTIONS

Justice

There are criminal courts and magistrates courts in N'Djaména, Moundou, Sarh and Abéché, with a Court of Appeal situated in N'Djaména.

The population in penal institutions in 2002 was 3,883 (46 per 100,000 of national population).

The death penalty is still in force. In 2003 there were nine executions (the first since 1991).

Education

In 1999–2000 there were 913,547 pupils in primary schools with 13,313 teachers and 137,269 pupils in secondary schools with 4,260 teachers. In 1999–2000 there were 5,901 students with 409 academic staff at institutes of tertiary education. Adult literacy rate was 25·5% in 2003 (male, 40·6%; female, 12·7%).

In 1999–2000 total expenditure on education came to 2·0% of GNP.

Health

In 1998 there were 4,105 hospital beds. There were 205 doctors, 1,220 nurses, 161 midwives and 38 pharmacists in 2001.

Chad has made significant progress in the reduction of undernourishment in the past 15 years. Between the period 1990–92 and 2000–02 the proportion of undernourished people declined from 58% of the population to 34%.

RELIGION

The northern and central parts of the country are predominantly Muslim. In 2001 there were estimated to be 4,690,000 Muslims, 1,770,000 Roman Catholics and 1,250,000 Protestants. Traditional beliefs are still widespread.

CULTURE

Broadcasting

The state-controlled Radiodiffusion Nationale Tchadienne broadcasts a national and three regional services in French, Arabic and Sara. There were 1·99m. radio sets in 2000. Television is being developed (colour by SECAM V) by the state-controlled Télé-Tchad, and there were 13,500 TV receivers in 2001.

Press

In 1998 there were two daily newspapers with a circulation of 1,560, giving a rate of one per 4,760 inhabitants.

Tourism

There were 55,000 foreign tourists in 2002.

DIPLOMATIC REPRESENTATIVES

Of Chad in the United Kingdom
Ambassador: Vacant (resides in Brussels).
Chargé d'Affaires a.i.: Mayoroum Y. Miayan.

Of the United Kingdom in Chad
Ambassador: Richard Wildash, LVO (resides in Yaoundé, Cameroon).

Of Chad in the USA (2002 R. St., NW, Washington, D.C., 20009)
Ambassador: Mahamoud Adam Bechir.

Of the USA in Chad (Ave. Felix Eboue, N'Djaména)
Ambassador: Mark M. Wall.

Of Chad to the United Nations
Ambassador: Mahamat Ali Adoum.

Of Chad to the European Union
Ambassador: Abderahim Yacoub N'diaye.

FURTHER READING

Joffe, Emille and Day-Viaud, Valerie (eds.) *Chad.* [Bibliography] ABC-Clio, Oxford and Santa Barbara (CA), 1995

National Statistical Office: Direction de la Statistique des Etudes Economiques et Démographiques, Ministère du Plan et de la Cooperation, N'Djaména.

BOLIVIA

Arica

Iquique

Antofagasta

PACIFIC

OCEAN

CHILE

Viña del Mar

Valparaíso □ SANTIAGO

ARGENTINA

Concepción

Temuco

ATLANTIC

OCEAN

0   200 mi

0   300 km

© Research Machines plc 2006

República de Chile

Capital: Santiago (Administrative), Valparaíso (Legislative)
Population projection, 2010: 17·13m.
GDP per capita, 2003: (PPP$) 10,274
HDI/world rank: 0·854/37

KEY HISTORICAL EVENTS

Archaeological evidence suggests the earliest settlements in Chile date from around 10,500 BC. A discovery at Monte Verde, near Puerto Montt in southern Chile, indicates that its inhabitants were hunter-gatherers in a temperate rainforest. They were probably the descendents of Paleo-Indians who crossed from Siberia by way of the Bering Strait (at various times a land bridge). Prior to the arrival of Europeans, the indigenous peoples included the Atacameno (living in small settlements in the northern deserts and influenced by the cultures of the central Andes, such as the Inca empires of Chincha and Quechua), the Araucanians (farmers in the more temperate valleys of central Chile) and the Chono (Alacaluf and Yahgan nomads from the mountainous southern areas).

Ferdinand Magellan was the first European to glimpse what is now Chile in 1520, when he sailed through the bleak archipelago at the tip of South America en route for the Pacific Ocean. Fifteen years later a Spanish expeditionary force, led by Diego de Almagro, set off from the newly-captured Inca city of Cuzco to explore land to the south. Almagro travelled as far as the Itata river but came under repeated attacks from hostile Araucanians and was unable to establish a foothold. He returned to Peru in 1536, with news only of 'a cursed land without gold, inhabited by savages of the worst kind.' Five years passed before the next Spanish expedition to Chile left Cuzco, headed by Pedro de Valdivia. After months of hardship, battles with Araucanians and internal divisions, Valdivia's forces established the settlement of Santiago in early 1541. In the next ten years the Spanish built fortified towns at Concepción, La Serena, Valdivia and Villarrica. North of Concepción, they began to convert the Araucanians to Christianity and established mines run on forced labour. Subjugating the indigenous people south of Concepción, however, proved difficult. In that region, Araucanians known as Mapuche fought hard and quickly adapted their weapons and tactics to become effective guerrilla fighters. 50 years after Valdivia's forces arrived in Chile, the colony remained a frontier, dependent on the Viceroyalty of Peru and governed by military officers based in dispersed fort towns. Gold was discovered but the wealth it generated was minimal compared with the riches that poured out of Mexico and Peru.

Opposition to Spain

Following further military defeats at the hands of the Mapuche and the destruction of Concepción in an earthquake in 1570, King Felipe II of Spain named a veteran conquistador, Rodrigo de Quiroga, as governor of Chile. After 1575 Quiroga attempted to quell rebellion with a brutal campaign against the Araucanians, capturing them for forced labour and mutilating their feet to prevent escape. A subsequent governor, Garcia Onez de Loyola, attempted to moderate these abuses, but was eventually killed at the battle of Curalaba in 1598. Subsequently, all major Spanish settlements south of the Bíobío river were destroyed or abandoned. In 1600 the king of Spain granted a permanent military subsidy to fund the war in Chile and in 1608 he signed a royal decree legalizing the enslavement of 'rebellious' Indians. At around this time, coastal settlements such as Valparaíso came under attack from English and Dutch adventurers and pirates, in search of wealth and as part of a prolonged effort to force Spain to allow other nations to trade with its colonies. The relative lack of mineral wealth in Chile led the 5,000 or so Spanish settlers to develop a pastoral and agricultural society; they grew a wide range of cereals and raised livestock. North of the Bíobío river, there was considerable intermarriage and the rapid growth of a mestizo (mixed Amerindian and European) group. The social status of mestizos was determined by the extent to which they were Hispanicized and by their kinship ties with the landed class.

In 1664 the governorship of Chile passed to Francisco de Meneses, an opportunist who took advantage of the warfare economy, taxing ships unless they carried his merchandise. He demanded bribes and accumulated vast wealth from the slave trade. An earthquake that shook Lima in 1687 severely disrupted the supply of food to the Peruvian city for some years. Chilean merchants cashed in by shipping wheat from the country's central belt and there was a rapid expansion in wheat production. The wheat 'boom' continued until 1700 and the trade was controlled by a clique of merchants who colluded with corrupt officials. Attempts by successive governors to make peace with the Mapuche (the Pact of Quillin) ended in failure, and sporadic fighting continued throughout the 17th and 18th centuries. Many thousands of Mapuche migrated eastwards across the Andes to Argentina.

Bourbon Rule

The Habsburg dynasty's rule over Spain ended in 1700. They were succeeded by the Bourbons who tried to improve the empire's productivity and defence. The Bourbon rulers gave the *audiencia* of Chile (based in Santiago) greater independence from the Viceroyalty of Peru. One of the most charismatic governors of the Bourbon era was the Irish-born Ambrosio O'Higgins, who presided over increased economic production and strengthened the military. In 1791 he also outlawed forced labour. Economic links with Argentina increased after it became the Viceroyalty of the Río de la Plata in 1776 and by the end of the 18th century Chile was engaging in direct trade with Europe. Freer trade brought with it knowledge of politics abroad, particularly the spread of liberalism in Europe and American independence. The Royal University of San Felipe was established at Santiago in 1758 but most educated Chileans followed the traditional ideology of the Spanish crown and the Roman Catholic Church, while the majority of mestizos and Araucanians remained illiterate and subordinate.

The French Revolution and Napoleon Bonaparte's subsequent invasion of Spain in 1807 sent shockwaves through the Spanish colonies, eventually leading to greater autonomy and independence. On 18 Sept. 1810 the Santiago elite, employing the town council as a junta, announced their intention to govern the colony until Fernando VII was reinstated. They remained loyal to the ousted Spanish king but insisted they had the right to rule and immediately relaxed trade restrictions. Chile's first government was led by José Miguel Carrera Verdugo. Carrera and his brothers, as well as Bernardo O'Higgins (son of former governor Ambrosio O'Higgins) soon saw the opportunity to replace temporary self-rule with permanent independence, although others remained loyal to Spain and civil conflict ensued. 1814 saw the start of the Reconquest (La Reconquista), and the Spanish authorities managed to reassert control of Chile by winning the Battle of Rancagua. O'Higgins and many of the Chilean rebels escaped to Argentina, from where they plotted to liberate their country. O'Higgins won the support of the revolutionary government in Buenos Aires under José de San Martín, and their joint forces freed Chile in 1817, defeating the Spaniards and their supporters at the Battle of Chacabuco.

Independence

From 1817–23 Bernardo O'Higgins ruled Chile as supreme director, formally proclaiming independence on 12 Feb. 1818 at Talca. He founded schools and expelled the remaining Spaniards but his authoritarian style and attempted reforms of the land tenure system aroused resistance. The combination of unrest among the powerful landowners and a succession of poor harvests forced him to abdicate in 1823. Civil conflict continued throughout the 1820s, owing largely to a split between the Chilean oligarchs and the army. The civil struggle's harmful effects on the economy, particularly exports, prompted conservatives to seize control in 1830. Diego Portales reached a compromise between the oligarchs and promulgated a constitution in 1833, beginning a prolonged period of political stability and economic revival.

A free port was created at Valparaíso to encourage trade with foreign, especially British, merchants. By the mid-1830s the port had a population of over 20,000. Chilean landowners and merchants profited from new export markets in California and Australia in the 1850s. Economic improvement was underpinned by discoveries of silver and copper in northern Chile and significant coal deposits around Concepción. The period after 1860, known as the 'Liberal Republic', saw the emergence of many rival political groups, most of which were influenced by new economic, scientific and literary ideas brought from Europe. Great Britain became the main trading partner and British entrepreneurs invested in the railways and the modernization of the ports.

A weakening currency and the threat of economic decline attracted Chile to valuable saltpetre (nitrate) deposits in the far north, bordering Peru and Bolivia. Arguments over the ill-defined borders led to the War of the Pacific (1879–83), in which the Chilean army and navy prevailed. During the presidency of José Manuel de Balmaceda (1886–91) the government attempted to use revenue from mineral extraction to strengthen its administration, a policy that was opposed by the oligarchs and led to a brief civil war, forcing Balmaceda's abdication. Thereafter Chile's presidential republic was transformed into a parliamentary republic; the following 20 years saw the emergence of new political parties that tried to represent the emerging working and middle classes. The Democratic Party was formed in 1887 to represent artisans and urban workers, while the Radical Party was backed by the middle class. Marxist ideology spread among workers in the late 1890s and the Socialist Party was established in 1901. By the start of the 20th century Chile was becoming increasingly urbanized; workers poured into the cities from rural areas. Society was polarized, with parts of Santiago and Valparaíso mirroring prosperous and elegant European cities, while the masses remained largely poverty stricken and illiterate. Infant mortality rates were triple those of the United States and higher than in Argentina and Mexico.

The outbreak of the First World War brought disaster to the Chilean economy, as Britain and Germany were leading trading partners. Demand for saltpetre fell away and thousands of workers lost their jobs. Dissatisfied Chileans elected the reformist president Arturo Alessandri Palma in 1920 but his initiatives were blocked by the legislature and he resigned. The army intervened and returned Alessandri to power in 1925, after which the constitution was amended to strengthen the executive at the expense of the legislature. It established a presidential republic, separated church and state, and enshrined new labour and welfare legislation. Various economic reforms attempted to reduce the power of the oligarchs, but failed. Alessandri resigned for a second time and was replaced by Carlos Ibáñez del Campo in 1927. His military dictatorship led to improvements in education and public services but also failed to address the economic power of the oligarchs. The world depression of the 1930s was hard on Chile as it was heavily dependent on mineral exports, the demand for which plummeted. A democratic-leftist coalition, the Popular Front, took power following the elections of 1938. Chile remained neutral in the Second World War until 1942, when President Juan Antonio Ríos declared war on Germany, Italy and Japan.

Conflict with the USA

The Radical Party joined with the Communists to field a left-wing Radical, Gabriel González Videla, for president in the 1946 election. Once in office, González Videla (president, 1946–52) turned against his Communist allies, expelling them from his cabinet and banning them completely in 1948. He also severed relations with the Soviet Union, prompting accusations of a Cold War agreement with the United States. The early 1950s were characterized by slow economic growth, spiralling inflation and increasing social demands, and the political arena became increasingly crowded and heated. By 1952 Chileans were alienated by multiparty politics and reacted by turning to two symbols of the past, firstly the 1920s dictator Ibáñez and, following the 1958 elections, the son of former president Alessandri. The Christian Democrat party, under the leadership of Eduardo Frei Montalva, undertook a 'Chileanization programme', wresting back control from the US-owned copper mines and making progress in land reform (by establishing peasant co-operatives). There were also advances in education and housing. The agrarian reforms led to an increased politicization of the working classes, who tended to join the various Socialist and Communist parties. In 1969 they formed the Popular Unity coalition, headed by the Marxist Salvador Allende Gossens, who was elected president in 1970. Allende nationalized many private companies, attempted to improve conditions for the working classes and established ties with other socialist states. The first year was heralded a success, but in 1971–72 Chile was afflicted by a series of economic woes including rapid inflation and shortages of foods and consumer goods. The United States, which had become by far the largest foreign investor in the decades that followed the Second World War, withdrew much of its backing.

In Sept. 1973, with covert American support, the armed forces staged a coup and Allende died during an assault on the presidential palace in Santiago. Gen. Augusto Pinochet Ugarte was installed as president and he argued that a dictatorship was a necessary transitory stage to restore the economy. The military closed Congress, censored the media, purged the universities and banned Marxist parties and union activities. It is estimated that over 3,000 of Allende's supporters lost their lives, over 30,000 were forced into exile and more than 130,000 were arrested over a three-year period. The return to market capitalism led to steady economic improvement from 1976 but falling copper prices and mounting foreign debt led to spiralling inflation and growing unemployment in the early 1980s. In 1981 a new constitution was approved, guaranteeing an eight-year extension to Pinochet's rule but also allowing a transition to civilian government by the end of the decade. The first free elections since the 1973 coup took place in Dec. 1989 and Patricio Aylwin Azócar emerged victorious, heading a coalition of left and centrist parties. The 1990s saw a rapid strengthening of the economy, underpinned by large inflows of foreign investment.

Pinochet remained head of the military until 1998, after which he claimed his constitutional right to become a senator for life (and hence immune from prosecution). While visiting Britain for medical treatment in 1998, Pinochet was arrested and held on human rights charges instigated by Spain. In early 2000 he returned to Chile after the British government ruled he was too ill to be extradited to Spain to face charges. On his election in Jan. 2000, Ricardo Lagos Escobar, leader of the Coalition of Parties for Democracy (CPD) pledged to reform the labour code, increase the minimum wage, introduce unemployment insurance and provide better health care, education and housing. In March 2003 Lagos' government faced allegations of financial corruption, which damaged investor confidence. Pinochet was stripped of his immunity by a Chilean court in May 2004.

In Jan. 2006 Michelle Bachelet, of the centre-left Concertación coalition, became Chile's first female president.

TERRITORY AND POPULATION

Chile is bounded in the north by Peru, east by Bolivia and Argentina, and south and west by the Pacific Ocean. The area is 756,096 sq. km (291,928 sq. miles) excluding the claimed Antarctic territory. Many islands to the west and south belong to Chile: the Islas Juan Fernández (147 sq. km with 633 inhabitants in 2002) lie about 600 km west of Valparaíso, and the volcanic Isla de Pascua (Easter Island or Rapa Nui, 164 sq. km with 3,791 inhabitants in 2002), lies about 3,000 km west-northwest of Valparaíso. Small uninhabited dependencies include Sala y

Gómez (400 km east of Easter Is.), San Félix and San Ambrosio (1,000 km northwest of Valparaíso, and 20 km apart) and Islas Diego Ramírez (100 km southwest of Cape Horn).

In 1940 Chile declared, and in each subsequent year has reaffirmed, its ownership of the sector of the Antarctic lying between 53° and 90° W. long., and asserted that the British claim to the sector between the meridians 20° and 80° W. long. overlapped the Chilean by 27°. Seven Chilean bases exist in Antarctica. A law of 1955 put the governor of Magallanes in charge of the 'Chilean Antarctic Territory' which has an area of 1,250,000 sq. km and a population (2002) of 2,392.

The population at the census of April 2002 was 15,116,435 (7,668,740 females and 7,447,695 males); density, 20·0 per sq. km. 87·0% of the population lived in urban areas in 2003.

The UN gives a projected population for 2010 of 17·13m.

Area, population and capitals of the 13 regions:

Region	Sq. km	Population (2002 census)	Capital	Population (2002 census)
Aisén del Gral. Carlos				
Ibáñez del Campo	108,494	91,492	Coihaique	50,041
De Antofagasta	126,049	493,984	Antofagasta	296,905
De La Araucanía	31,842	869,535	Temuco	245,347
De Atacama	75,176	254,336	Copiapó	129,091
Del Bíobío	37,063	1,861,562	Concepción	216,061
De Coquimbo	40,580	603,210	La Serena	160,148
Del Libertador				
Gral. B. O'Higgins	16,387	780,627	Rancagua	214,344
De Los Lagos	67,013	1,073,135	Puerto Montt	175,938
De Magallanes y de la				
Antártica Chilena	132,297	150,826	Punta Arenas	119,496
Del Maule	30,296	908,097	Talca	201,797
Metropolitana				
de Santiago	15,403	6,061,185	Santiago	4,668,473
De Tarapacá	59,099	428,594	Iquique	216,419
De Valparaíso	16,396	1,539,852	Valparaíso	275,982

Other large towns (June 2002 populations) are: Puente Alto (458,906), Viña del Mar (350,221), Talcahuano (288,666), San Bernardo (262,623), Arica (189,743), Chillán (176,863), Coquimbo (141,796), Calama (135,526) and Osorno (135,204). 69·7% of the population is mixed or mestizo, 20% are of European descent and 10·3% declared themselves to be indigenous Amerindians of the Mapuche, Aymara, Atacameño and Quechua groups. Language and culture remain of European origin, with 604,349 Mapudungun-speaking (mainly Mapuche) Indians the only sizeable minority.

The official language is Spanish.

SOCIAL STATISTICS

2003 births, 246,827; deaths, 83,672; marriages, 56,659. Rates, 2003 (per 1,000 population): birth, 15·5; death, 5·3; marriage, 3·6. Divorce was only made legal in 2004; abortion remains illegal. Annual population growth rate, 1992–2002, 1·2%. Infant mortality, 2003 (per 1,000 live births), 7·9. In 2003 the most popular age range for marrying was 25–29 for males and 20–24 for females. Expectation of life at birth (2003): males 74·8 years, females 80·9 years. Chile has the highest life expectancy in South America. Fertility rate, 2003, 1·9 children per woman.

CLIMATE

With its enormous range of latitude and the influence of the Andean Cordillera, the climate of Chile is very complex, ranging from extreme aridity in the north, through a Mediterranean climate in Central Chile, where winters are wet and summers dry, to a cool temperate zone in the south, with rain at all seasons. In the extreme south, conditions are very wet and stormy. Santiago, Jan. 67°F (19·5°C), July 46°F (8°C). Annual rainfall 15" (375 mm). Antofagasta, Jan. 69°F (20·6°C), July 57°F (14°C). Annual rainfall 0·5" (12·7 mm). Valparaíso, Jan. 64°F (17·8°C), July 53°F (11·7°C). Annual rainfall 20" (505 mm).

CONSTITUTION AND GOVERNMENT

A new Constitution was approved by 67·5% of the voters on 11 Sept. 1980 and came into force on 11 March 1981. It provided for a return to democracy after a minimum period of eight years. Gen. Pinochet would remain in office during this period after which the government would nominate a single candidate for President. At a plebiscite on 5 Oct. 1988 President Pinochet was rejected as a presidential candidate by 54·6% of votes cast. The Constitution has been amended on a number of occasions since then.

The *President* is directly elected for a non-renewable four-year term. Parliament consists of a 120-member *Chamber of Deputies* and a *Senate* of 48 members (38 by popular vote, nine appointed or 'institutional' members and one former president). In Oct. 2004 Senate voted to make the Senate fully elected, by abolishing the non-elected senators with effect from March 2006 and similarly eliminating life seats for former presidents.

Santiago is the administrative capital of Chile, but since 11 March 1990 Valparaíso has been the legislative capital.

National Anthem

'Dulce patria, recibe los votos' ('Sweet Fatherland, receive the vows'); words by E. Lillo, tune by Ramón Carnicer.

GOVERNMENT CHRONOLOGY

Heads of State since 1942. (APL = Popular Liberating Alliance; FP = Popular Front; PC = Conservative Party; PDC = Christian Democratic Party; PS = Socialist Party)

Presidents of the Republic

1942–46	FP	Juan Antonio Ríos Morales
1946–52	FP	Gabriel González Videla
1952–58	APL	Carlos Ibáñez del Campo
1958–64	PC	Jorge Alessandri Rodríguez
1964–70	PDC	Eduardo Nicanor Frei Montalva
1970–73	PS	Salvador Allende Gossens

Military Junta

1973–74	Gen. Augusto J. R. Pinochet (chair); Gen. César Raúl Benavides Escobar; Admr. José Toribio Merino Castro; Gen. Gustavo Leigh Guzmán; Gen. Fernando Matthei Aubel; Gen. César Mendoza Durán; Gen. Rodolfo Stange Oelckers.

Presidents of the Republic

1974–90	military	Augusto J. R. Pinochet
1990–94	PDC	Patricio Aylwin
1994–2000	PDC	Eduardo Frei Ruiz-Tagle
2000–06	PS	Ricardo Froilán Lagos
2006–	PS	Michelle Bachelet

RECENT ELECTIONS

In the presidential run-off held on 15 Jan. 2006 the leftist 'Concertación' candidate Michelle Bachelet (Socialist Party) polled 53·5%, defeating the centre-right candidate Sebastián Piñera (National Renewal), with 46·5%. Two other candidates had participated in the first round of voting on 11 Dec. 2005.

In elections to the Chamber of Deputies on 11 Dec. 2005 the Coalition of Parties for Democracy/Concertación won 65 seats with 51·8% of the vote (Party for Democracy, 21 seats and 15·5%; Christian Democratic Party, 20 and 20·8%; Socialist Party, 15 and 10·0%; Radical Social Democratic Party, 7 and 3·5%; ind., 2 and 2·0%) against 54 seats (38·7%) for the Alliance for Chile (Independent Democratic Union, 33 and 22·3%; National Renewal, 19 and 14·1%; ind. 2 and 2·2%) and 1 for the Independent Regional Force (1·2%). After partial elections to the Senate on the same day the composition in the Senate was: Coalition of Parties for Democracy, 20 seats, Alliance for Chile, 17; ind. 1.

CURRENT ADMINISTRATION

President: Michelle Bachelet; b. 1951 (Socialist Party; sworn in 11 March 2006).

In March 2006 the government comprised:

Minister of Agriculture: Alvaro Rojas. *Culture and the Arts:* Paulina Urrutia. *Economy:* Ingrid Antonijevic. *Education:* Martín Zilic. *Finance:* Andrés Velasco. *Foreign Affairs:* Alejandro Foxley. *Health:* María Soledad Barría. *Housing and Urban Development:* Patricia Poblete. *Interior:* Andrés Zaldívar. *Justice:* Isidro Solís. *Labour and Social Security:* Osvaldo Andrade. *Mining and Energy:* Karen Poniachik. *National Defence:* Vivianne Blanlot. *National Property:* Romy Schmidt. *National Women's Service:* Laura Albornoz. *Planning and Co-operation:* Clarisa Hardy. *Public Works:* Eduardo Bitrán. *Transport and Telecommunications:* Sergio Espejo. *General Secretary of the Government:* Ricardo Lagos Weber. *General Secretary of the Presidency:* Paulina Veloso.

Government Website (Spanish only):
  http://www.gobiernodechile.cl

CURRENT LEADERS

Michelle Bachelet

Position
President

Introduction
Michelle Bachelet became Chile's first woman president in 2006, having beaten her conservative rival, Sebastián Piñera, in an election run-off. The former doctor had been forced into exile in Australia and East Germany during the early years of the Pinochet dictatorship, but returned in 1979 to become increasingly active in the Socialist Party (PS).

Early Life
Verónica Michelle Bachelet Jeria was born on 29 Sept. 1951 in Santiago, Chile, the daughter of an air force general and an anthropologist. As a consequence of her father's military postings she spent her childhood in various Chilean cities. In 1962 the family moved to Washington, D.C., where her father was assigned to the Chilean embassy. Returning to Chile in 1964, Bachelet attended the Javiera Carrera Lyceum girls' school in Santiago. She then studied medicine at the University of Chile, where she joined the Socialist Youth Movement.

On 11 Sept. 1973 Gen. Augusto Pinochet led a military coup against Salvador Allende's socialist government. The next day Gen. Bachelet was arrested for treason. He was tortured and died in prison six months later. Bachelet and her mother were arrested in Jan. 1975 and held at the notorious Villa Grimalidi in Santiago. Released later that month, they fled to Australia and then to East Germany. Bachelet learned German at the Herder Institute in Leipzig, before continuing her medical studies at the Humboldt University of Berlin.

A member of the PS central committee from 1995, Bachelet joined the party's political committee in 1998 and worked as campaign manager in northwest Santiago for Ricardo Lagos' run for the presidency in 1999. After Lagos took office Bachelet, who was appointed health minister in March 2000, pledged to reform the public health care system. Following a cabinet reshuffle in Jan. 2002 Bachelet was given the defence portfolio and initiated a major modernization programme. Chilean troops were employed in various peacekeeping duties and links were forged with defence ministries throughout Latin America.

In late 2004 Bachelet was proposed as the socialist candidate for the presidency and so resigned as defence minister. She campaigned on a platform of increased economic stability, more jobs, greater equality of opportunity, better education, and more support for small and mid-sized businesses. She received 46% support at the polls of 11 Dec. 2005, insufficient to obtain an absolute majority of seats. In a run-off against Sebastián Piñera on 15 Jan. 2006 she took 53·5% of the vote and was sworn in on 11 March 2006.

Career in Office

Bachelet has promised to build on the ruling centre-left 'Concertación' coalition's record of strong economic growth and has vowed to bridge the gap between rich and poor. She wants more open government, giving voice to women and indigenous groups. Of the members of her first cabinet, half are women.

DEFENCE

Military service is currently for one year in the Army and Air Force and one year to 18 months in the Navy.

In 2003 defence expenditure totalled US$2,537m. (US$161 per capita), representing 3·9% of GDP. In 1985 defence spending had accounted for 10·0% of GDP.

Army

A modernization plan of 1995 provided for the transformation of the seven Army divisions into three garrisons—North, Centre-South and Austral—independent and adapted to the terrains in which they operate. Strength (2005): 41,000 (18,366 conscripts) with 50,000 reserves. There is a 36,800-strong force of Carabineros.

Navy

The principal ships of the Navy are three ex-British destroyers, three diesel submarines and three frigates. There is a Naval Air Service numbering 600 personnel with 13 combat aircraft.

Naval personnel in 2005 totalled 20,092 (1,030 conscripts) including 3,800 marines and 1,300 Coast Guard. There are HQs at Iquique, Valparaíso, Talcahuano and Punta Arenas.

Air Force

Strength (2005) was 9,971 personnel (950 conscripts). There are 76 combat aircraft made up largely of Mirage jets.

INTERNATIONAL RELATIONS

Chile is a member of the UN, WTO, OAS, Inter-American Development Bank, LAIA, APEC, IOM and the Antarctic Treaty, and has a free trade agreement with MERCOSUR.

ECONOMY

Agriculture accounted for 8·9% of GDP in 2004, industry 34·5% and services 56·6%.

Overview

Chile's economy was liberalized ahead of the rest of Latin America under General Pinochet (1973–90) and economic reform continued under the democratic government in the 1990s. The country had the highest foreign direct investment to GDP ratio in Latin America and strong growth for most of the 1990s. In 1998 growth was curtailed by monetary tightening aimed at reversing current account deficits caused by low export earnings in a period of global financial crisis. In 1999 the economy shrank by 0·8%. Growth resumed at an average rate of 4% from 2000–04.

Strong in mining, Chile is the world's leading copper and iodine producer and increasingly a source of gold and non-metallic minerals. Manufacturing's share of GDP has gradually declined while sectors including wood products, fruit, salmon, wines and methanol production have grown. Increasingly diversified export production has been a key engine of growth. In 2005 domestic demand was strong with the construction, retail, catering and financial services sectors seeing particularly high growth. Solid economic performance has been buttressed over the years by sound macroeconomic management. In the

early 1990s the central bank adopted inflation targeting and by the end of the decade inflation was brought within a 2–4% target band. In 1999–2000 a floating exchange rate regime was introduced and a counter cyclical fiscal policy was implemented. The country has signed many foreign trade agreements over the years, notably with the USA and EU, and an FTA cargo agreement with China. Poverty has declined significantly over the years but the income gap is high and at least one sixth of the population lives in poverty.

Currency

The unit of currency is the *Chilean peso* (CLP) of 100 *centavos*. The peso was revalued 3·5% against the US dollar in Nov. 1994. In Sept. 1999 the managed exchange-rate system was abandoned and the peso allowed to float. Inflation rates (based on IMF statistics):

1995	1996	1997	1998	1999	2000	2001	2002	2003	2004
8·2%	7·4%	6·1%	5·1%	3·3%	3·8%	3·6%	2·5%	2·8%	1·1%

In June 2002 gold reserves were 12,000 troy oz (1·22m. troy oz in Jan. 2000). Foreign exchange reserves were US$15,495m. in Dec. 2004 and total money supply 5,238·93bn. pesos.

Budget

The fiscal year is the calendar year.

Central government revenue and expenditure (in 1bn. pesos):

	1998	1999	2000	2001	2002
Revenue	7,907·0	7,910·1	9,114·5	9,795·6	10,128·5
Expenditure	7,775·2	8,412·4	9,058·1	9,908·2	10,493·1

VAT is 19%.

Performance

Real GDP growth rates (based on IMF statistics):

1995	1996	1997	1998	1999	2000	2001	2002	2003	2004
10·8%	7·4%	6·6%	3·2%	−0·8%	4·5%	3·4%	2·2%	3·7%	6·1%

Real GDP growth averaged 7·7% between 1991 and 1997, leading to Chile being labelled the 'tiger of South America'. Total GDP in 2004 was US$94·1bn.

Banking and Finance

Banking is regulated by legislation of 1995. The Superintendencia de Bancos e Instituciones Financieras, affiliated to the finance ministry, is the banking supervisory authority. There is a Central Bank and a State Bank. The Central Bank was made independent of government control in March 1990. The *President* is Vittorio Corbo. There were 21 domestic and six foreign banks in 2005. In Jan. 2005 deposits in domestic banks totalled 25,779,053m. pesos; in foreign banks, 2,163,183m. pesos, and in other finance companies, 4,829,090m. pesos.

There are stock exchanges in Santiago and Valparaíso.

ENERGY AND NATURAL RESOURCES

Environment

Chile's carbon dioxide emissions from the consumption and flaring of fossil fuels in 2002 were the equivalent of 3·5 tonnes per capita.

Electricity

Installed capacity was 11·1m. kW in 2002. Production of electricity was 45·5bn. kWh in 2002, of which just under 60% was hydro-electric. Consumption per capita in 2002 was 2,591 kWh.

Oil and Gas

Production of crude oil, 2003, was 173,000 tonnes. Gas production, 2003, was 85 petajoules. Chile imports much of the natural gas it consumes from neighbouring Argentina.

Minerals

The wealth of the country consists chiefly in its minerals. Chile is the world's largest copper producer; copper is the most important source of foreign exchange and government revenues. Production, 2004, 5,418,800 fine tonnes. Coal is low-grade and difficult to mine, made possible by state subsidies. Production, 2004, 238,307 tonnes.

Output of other minerals, 2004 (in tonnes): limestone, 6,653,343; salt, 4,938,928; iron, 4,849,878; iron pellets (2000), 4,502,456; molybdenum, 41,883; zinc, 27,635; manganese, 7,188; silver, 1,360. Gold (39,986 kg in 2004), lithium, nitrate, iodine and sodium sulphate are also produced.

Agriculture

In 2001, 1·98m. ha. were arable land and 0·32m. ha. permanent crops. 1·9m. ha. were irrigated in 2001. Some 54,000 tractors were in use in 2001 and 8,900 harvester-threshers.

Principal crops were as follows:

Crop	Area harvested, 1,000 ha 2004	Production, 1,000 tonnes 2004	Crop	Area harvested, 1,000 ha 2004	Production, 1,000 tonnes 2004
Sugarbeets	31	2,598	Oats	77	357
Wheat	420	1,852	Onions	6	282[1]
Maize	134	1,508	Rice	25	117
Potatoes	56	1,116	Pumpkins	4	100[1]
Tomatoes	7	470	Carrots	4	97

[1]2000.

Fruit production, 2004 (in 1,000 tonnes): apples, 1,300; grapes, 1,150; peaches and nectarines, 311; plums, 250; pears, 210; lemons and limes, 165; oranges, 140. Wine production in 2003 totalled 5,687,395 hectolitres.

Livestock, 2000: cattle, 3,900,000; sheep, 3,800,000; pigs, 2,300,000; goats, 760,000; horses, 400,000; poultry, 27m.

Livestock products, 2000 (in 1,000 tonnes): pork, bacon and ham, 265; beef and veal, 226; poultry meat, 378; milk, 1,990; eggs, 95.

Since 1985 agricultural trade has been consistently in surplus. Wine exports rose from US$52m. in 1990 to US$844m. in 2004.

Forestry

In 2004, 15·64m. ha., or 20·7% of the total land area, was under forests. There were 13·4m. ha. of natural forest and woodland (larch, araucaria, lenga, coihue, oak are important species), representing 85·9% of the total forested area, and 2·1m. ha. of planted forest. Timber production in 2003 was 27·5m. cu. metres.

Fisheries

Chile has 4,200 km of coastline and exclusive fishing rights to 1·6m. sq. km. There are 220 species of edible fish. The catch in 2004 was 6,013,643 tonnes and came entirely from sea fishing. Exports of fishery commodities in 2004 were valued at US$2·58bn., against imports of US$38·9m. Fish farms produced 486,850 tonnes of salmon in 2003.

INDUSTRY

The leading companies by market capitalization in Chile in Nov. 2005 were: Compañía de Petróleos de Chile SA (COPEC), US$11·6bn.; Endesa Chile (Empresa Nacional de Electricida), US$8·2bn.; and Banco Santander Santiago, US$7·9bn.

Output of major products in 2003 (in 1,000 tonnes): distillate fuel oil (2002), 3,793; cement, 2,870; sulphuric acid, 2,866; petrol (2002), 2,110; cellulose, 1,430; residual fuel oil (2002), 1,368; fishmeal, 580; iron or steel plates, 403; sugar (2004), 401; newsprint, 177; paper and cardboard, 113. Output of other products: soft drinks, 796m. litres; beer, 192m. litres; 20,136 motor vehicles (2001); 4·74m. motor tyres.

Labour

In 2005 there were 5,779,660 people in employment (1,997,690 women). In Sept. 2005, 1,678,880 persons were employed in social or personal services, 1,117,900 in trade, 765,580 in manufacturing, 683,100 in agriculture, forestry and fisheries, 470,110 in transport and communications and 447,480 in building. In 2005 there was a monthly minimum wage of 127,500 pesos. In Sept. 2005, 8·5% of the workforce was unemployed, up from 6·1% in 1997 although down from a peak of 11·4% in Aug. 1999.

Trade Unions

Trade unions were established in the mid-1880s.

INTERNATIONAL TRADE

In Sept. 1991 Chile and Mexico signed the free trade Treaty of Santiago envisaging annual tariff reductions of 10% from Jan. 1992. On 1 Oct. 1996 Chile joined the MERCOSUR free trade zone, but continues to act unilaterally in trade with third countries. Foreign debt was US$4,800m. in 2005.

Imports and Exports

Trade in US$1m.:

	2000	2001	2002	2003	2004
Imports f.o.b.	17,091	16,411	15,827	18,001	23,006
Exports f.o.b.	19,210	18,466	18,340	21,524	32,025

In 2004 the principal exports were (in US$1m.): minerals, 16,633·6 (of which copper, 14,358·4, equivalent to 87·2% of all exports); manufactures, 11,928·7; and agricultural products, 2,339·3. Principal imports in 2004 were (in US$1m.): manufactures, 17,928·7; minerals, 3,919·6; and agricultural products, 416·9. Major import suppliers (in US$1m.), 2001: Argentina, 3,063·8; USA, 2,888·7; Brazil, 1,498·6; China, 1,052·9; Germany, 699·2. Major export markets (in US$1m.), 2004: USA, 4,854·5; China, 3,667·8; Japan, 3,603·7; South Korea, 1,764·2; Brazil, 1,403·4; Mexico, 1,342·4; Italy, 1,322·8.

COMMUNICATIONS

Roads

In 2004 there were 80,505 km of roads, but only 20·8% were hard-surfaced. There were 2,414 km of motorways and 16,785 km of main roads. In 2004 there were 1,303,554 private cars, 633,853 trucks and vans, 61,152 buses and coaches and 22,870 motorcycles and mopeds. In 2003 there were 44,450 road accidents resulting in 1,703 deaths.

Rail

The total length of railway lines was (2004) 5,775 km, including 1,051 km electrified, of broad- and metre-gauge. The state railway (EFE) is now mainly a passenger carrier, and transported 13·3m. passengers in 2004. Freight operations are in the hands of the semi-private companies Ferronor, Pacifico and the Antofagasta (Chili) and Bolivia Railway (973 km, metre-gauge) which links the port of Antofagasta with Bolivia and Argentina. Freight carried totalled 25·3m. tonnes in 2004. Passenger-km travelled in 2004 came to 820m. and freight tonne-km to 3,897m.

There are metro systems in Santiago (46·2 km) and Valparaíso (42·5 km).

Civil Aviation

There are 389 airports, with nine international airports at Antofagasta, Arica, Coihaique, Concepción, Easter Island (Isla de Pascua), Iquique, Puerto Montt, Punta Arenas and Santiago (Comodoro Arturo Merino Benítez). The largest airline is LAN Airlines, formerly Línea Aérea Nacional Chile (LAN-Chile); in 2001 LAN-Chile flew 70·3m. km and carried 5,046,600 passengers. In 2004 Santiago handled 6,057,279 passengers (3,603,267 on international flights) and 269,660 tonnes of freight.

Shipping

The mercantile marine in 2001 totalled 647,820 GRT, including oil tankers 160,179 GRT. The five major ports, Valparaíso, San Antonio, Antofagasta, Arica and Iquique, are state-owned; there are 11 smaller private ports. Valparaíso, the largest port, handled 4,469,302 tonnes of freight in 2001.

Telecommunications

In 2004 there were 3,250,000 telephone main lines, equivalent to 201·9 for every 1,000 persons, and there were 2,137,934 PCs in use (132·8 for every 1,000 persons). There were 4,300,000 Internet users in 2004. Mobile phone subscribers numbered 8,472,000 in 2004 and there were 64,100 fax machines in 2002.

Postal Services

In 2002 there were 752 post offices.

SOCIAL INSTITUTIONS

Justice

There are a High Court of Justice in the capital, 17 courts of appeal distributed over the republic, courts of first instance in the departmental capitals and second-class judges in the sub-delegations. There were 642 public prosecutors, 782 judges and 417 defence lawyers in 2002. In 2000 an amendment to the Chilean Penal Code replaced the inquisitorial trial system with an adversarial model.

The population in penal institutions in Dec. 2004 was 65,262 (417 per 100,000 of national population).

The death penalty for ordinary crimes was abolished in 2001.

Education

In 2004 there were 287,454 children at pre-primary schools, 2·27m. primary school pupils and 989,039 pupils at secondary level. Adult literacy rate in 2003 was 95·7% (male, 95·8%; female, 95·6%).

In 2004 there were 567,114 students in higher education. There were 162 universities with 403,370 students, 140 professional institutes with 101,674 students and 211 technical education centres with 62,070 students. The number of students at higher education institutions has doubled since 1990.

In 2002 total expenditure on education came to 4·3% of GNP and represented 18·7% of total government expenditure.

Health

There were 846 hospitals in 2002. In 2003 there were 15,006 doctors, 2,846 dentists and 6,900 university nurses in the public sector. In 2004 there were 20,776 junior doctors.

Welfare

In 1981 Chile abolished its state-sponsored pension plan and became the first country to establish private mandatory retirement savings. The system is managed by competitive private companies called AFPs (Pension Fund Administrators). Employees are required to save 13% of their pay. In April 2005 it had 7,132,983 members and assets of 35,051,470m. pesos. In 2005 about 65% of the population over the age of 14 had private health insurance.

RELIGION

At the 2002 census Chile had 7,853,428 Roman Catholics. In Jan. 2002 there were five archbishops, 25 bishops and two vicars apostolic. There were two cardinals in May 2005. In 2002 there were 1,699,725 Evangelical Christians, 119,455 Jehovah's Witnesses, 103,735 Latter-day Saints, 14,976 Jews, 6,959 Orthodox Christians and 2,894 Muslims.

CULTURE

World Heritage Sites

Chile's four UNESCO protected sites are the Rapa Nui National Park, the Churches of Chiloé, the Historic Quarter of the Seaport of Valparaíso and the Humberstone and Santa Laura Saltpeter Works. Entered on the list in 1995, the Rapa Nui National Park encompasses much of the coastline of Easter Island and protects the shrines and statues (Moai) carved between the 10th–16th centuries. On the island of Chiloé off the Región de Los Lagos coastline, wooden churches were built by Jesuit missionaries at the turn of the 17th century. The churches were entered on the list in 2000. The Valparaíso site was inscribed on the list in 2003 as a model of urban and architectural development in 19th-century Latin America. The Humberstone and Santa Laura Saltpeter Works were inscribed in 2005 and are where workers from Peru, Chile and Bolivia formed a distinctive communal pampinos culture.

Broadcasting

In 2004 there were 1,128 radio broadcasting stations (including repeaters), 1,005 FM and 123 AM. In 2005 there were seven television channels operating in UHF frequencies on the national territory. 18 other channels were operating on VHF through 400 frequencies. Both data included four university channels (three VHF and one UHF frequency). In 2005 the Televisión Nacional de Chile covered the whole of the country through 200 transmitters. There were 5·2m. radio sets in 2000 and 4·4m. TV sets in 2001.

Cinema

In 2002 there were 238 cinema screens; total admissions in 2002 were 11·4m.

Press

In 2005 there were 93 national daily newspapers; Chile's daily newspapers had total annual sales of 354m. copies. In 2004 a total of 3,151 book titles were published.

Tourism

There were 1,785,024 foreign visitors in 2004. Tourist receipts were US$1,396m. in 2004.

DIPLOMATIC REPRESENTATIVES

Of Chile in the United Kingdom (12 Devonshire St., London, W1G 7DS)
Ambassador: Mariano Fernández Amunátegui.

Of the United Kingdom in Chile (Av. El Bosque Norte 0125, Piso 2, Las Condes, Santiago)
Ambassador: Howard Drake.

Of Chile in the USA (1732 Massachusetts Ave., NW, Washington, D.C., 20036)
Ambassador: Andrés Bianchi Larre.

Of the USA in Chile (Av. Andrés Bello 2800, Las Condes, Santiago)
Ambassador: Craig A. Kelly.

Of Chile to the United Nations
Ambassador: Heraldo Muñoz Valenzuela.

Of Chile to the European Union
Ambassador: Alberto Van Klaveren Stork.

FURTHER READING

Banco Central de Chile. *Boletín Mensual.*
Bethell, L. (ed.) *Chile since Independence.* CUP, 1993
Collier, S. and Sater, W. F., *A History of Chile, 1808–1994.* CUP, 1996
Hickman, J., *News From the End of the Earth: A Portrait of Chile.* C. Hurst, London, 1998
Hojman, D. E., *Chile: the Political Economy of Development and Democracy in the 1990s.* London, 1993.—(ed.) *Change in the Chilean Countryside: from Pinochet to Aylwin and Beyond.* London, 1993
Oppenheim, L. H., *Politics in Chile: Democracy, Authoritarianism and the Search for Development.* Boulder (CO), 1993

National Statistical Office: Instituto Nacional de Estadísticas (INE), Santiago.
Website (Spanish only): http://www.ine.cl/

CHINA

Zhonghua Renmin Gonghe Guo
(People's Republic of China)

Capital: Beijing (Peking)
Population projection, 2010: 1,354·53m.
GDP per capita, 2003: (PPP$) 5,003
HDI/world rank: 0·755/85

KEY HISTORICAL EVENTS

An embryonic Chinese state emerged in the fertile Huang He (Yellow River) basin before 4000 BC. Chinese culture reached the Chang Jiang (Yangtze) basin by 2500 BC and within 500 years the far south was also within the Chinese orbit. Four thousand years ago the Xia dynasty ruled in the Huang He basin. About 1500 BC it was supplanted by the Shang dynasty, under which writing developed using recognizable Chinese characters. The remains of the Shang period show that their state was the cultural ancestor of modern China.

Shang civilization spread out from the Huang He region. In the west, the Shang state came into conflict with the Zhou state, whose rulers replaced the Shang dynasty around 1000 BC. Under the Zhou, a centralized administration developed. In about 500 BC one court official, Kongfuzi (Confucius), outlined his vision of society. Confucianism, which introduced a system of civil service recruitment through examination, remained the principal Chinese belief system until the mid–20th century.

The Zhou expanded the Chinese state south beyond the Chang Jiang. There, dependent territories emerged which, by the 5th century, had become independent Warring States. These insubordinate kingdoms periodically rebelled against the central authority and fought one another. In 221 BC the ruler of the Warring State of Qin became the first emperor of China. He built an empire extending from the South China Sea to the edge of Central Asia, where work was begun on the Great Wall of China, a massive fortification to keep threatening nomads at bay. The Qin dynasty standardized laws, money and administration throughout the empire but it was short-lived. By 206 BC the state had divided into three.

Reunification came gradually under the Han dynasty (202 BC–AD 200). Han emperors ruled through an efficient, centralized bureaucracy. They established a state whose boundaries were similar to those of modern China. Some of the peripheral possessions proved too distant to hold and the Han empire collapsed through rebellion and invasion. It was followed by the Jin (265–316) and Sui (589–612) dynasties, interspersed by a period of inter-state war and anarchy. Reunification was achieved by the Tang dynasty, whose efficient reforming rule

315

brought new prosperity to China from 618–917. Eventually the Tang empire too collapsed as separatism grew.

Under the next dynasty, the Song (960–1127), the balance of power within China shifted south. Song China expanded trade with the rest of Asia. In 1126 nomads from Manchuria invaded the north. The Song state lost control of the area north of the Chang Jiang. A declining Song empire persisted in the south until 1279.

Genghis Khan

The northern invaders were overthrown by the Mongols, led by Genghis Khan (c. 1162–1227), who went on to claim the rest of China. In 1280 their ruler Kublai Khan (1251–94), who had founded the Yuan dynasty in 1271, swept into southern China. The Mongol Yuan dynasty adopted Chinese ways but was overthrown by a nationalist uprising in 1368, led by Hongwu (1328–98), a former beggar who established the Ming dynasty. Hongwu, and several later Ming emperors, made important reforms, resulting in increased levels of prosperity and extended borders.

The Ming empire collapsed in a peasants' revolt in 1644. The capital, Beijing, was only 64 km from the Great Wall and vulnerable to attack from nomads to the north. Within months the peasants' leader was swept aside by the invasion of the Manchus, whose Qing dynasty ruled China until 1911. Preoccupied with threats from the north, China neglected its southern coastal frontier where European traders were attempting to open up the country. The Portuguese, who landed on the Chinese coast in 1516, were followed by the Dutch in 1622 and the English in 1637.

Qing emperors initially ruled fairly and adopted Chinese ways and customs. The empire expanded into Mongolia, Tibet, Vietnam and Kazakhstan. By the 19th century imperial China was suffering from corruption. Under pressure from rural revolts, ignited by crippling taxation and poverty, the Qing empire started to collapse. Through the two Opium Wars (1838–42; 1856–58), Britain forced China to allow the import of opium from India into China, while Britain, France, Germany and other European states gained concessions in 'treaty ports' that virtually came under foreign rule.

The Taiping Rebellion (1851–64) set up a revolutionary egalitarian state in southern China. The European powers intervened to crush the rebellion, but in 1860 British and French forces invaded Beijing and burnt the imperial palace. The Europeans extracted further trading concessions from China. A weakened China was defeated in war by Japan in 1895 and lost both Taiwan and Korea.

The xenophobic Boxer Rebellion, led by members of a secret society called the Fists of Righteous Harmony, broke out in 1900. The Guangxu emperor (1875–1908) attempted modernization in the Hundred Days Reform, but was taken captive by the conservative dowager empress who harnessed the Boxer Rebellion to her own ends. The rebellion was put down by European troops in 1901. China was then divided into zones of influence between the major European states and Japan.

With imperial authority so weakened, much of the country was ungovernable and ripe for rebellion. The turning point came in 1911 when a revolution led by the Kuomintang (Guomintang or Nationalist movement) of Sun Yet-sen (Sun Zhong Shan; 1866–1925) overthrew the emperor and the imperial system. The revolution was followed by a period of anarchy, which included an attempted imperial restoration. The authoritarian Yuan Shih-kai ruled as president from 1913 to 1916. Following the overthrow of Yuan, China disintegrated at the hands of local warlords.

In 1916 Sun founded a republic in southern China. The north remained beyond his control. Sun reorganized the Nationalist party on Soviet lines. At this stage the Nationalists co-operated with the Communists to re-establish national unity, but rivalry between the two parties increased, particularly after the death of Sun in 1925.

Nationalism and Communism

After Sun's death the nationalist movement was taken over by his ally Chiang Kai-shek (Jiang Jie Shi; 1887–1976). As commander in chief of the Nationalist army from 1925, Chiang's power grew. In April 1927 he tried to suppress the Chinese Communist Party in a bloody campaign in which thousands of Communists were slaughtered. The remains of the party fled to the far western province of Jiangxi, beyond the reach of the Nationalists. In 1928 Chiang's army entered Beijing. With the greater part of the country reunited under Chiang's rule, he formed a government in Nanjing, which became the capital of China.

In 1934 the Communists were forced to retreat from Jiangxi province. Led by Mao Zedong (Mao Tse-tung; 1893–1976) they trekked for more than a year on the 5,600-mile Long March. Harried during their journey, they were besieged by the Nationalists when they eventually took refuge in Shaanxi province.

In 1931, against this backdrop of civil unrest, the Japanese had invaded Manchuria and set up the last emperor of China as puppet emperor of Manchukuo. By 1937 the Japanese had seized Beijing and most of coastal China. The Nationalists and Communists finally co-operated against the invader, although the Chinese were unable to achieve much against the superior Japanese forces.

During the Second World War (1939–45), a Nationalist government provided largely ineffectual rule of unoccupied China from a temporary capital in Chongqing. At the end of the war, Nationalist-Communist co-operation was short-lived. The Soviet Union sponsored the Communist Party, which marched into Manchuria in 1946. This action began the civil war which lasted until 1949. Although the Nationalist forces of Chiang Kai-shek received support from some western countries, particularly the United States, the Communists were victorious. On 1 Oct. 1949 Mao declared the People's Republic of China in Beijing.

Chiang fled with the remains of his Nationalist forces to the island of Taiwan, where he established a government that claimed to be a continuation of the Republic of China. At first, that administration was recognized as the government of China by most Western countries and Taiwan kept China's Security Council seat at the United Nations until 1971. Chiang's authoritarian regime was periodically challenged by Red China, which bombed Taiwan's small offshore islands near the mainland. But, supported by the United States, Taiwan endured. In the 1960s and 1970s, Taiwan gradually lost recognition as the legitimate government of China and in 1978 the USA recognized the People's Republic of China.

Expansionism

In 1950 China invaded Tibet, which had been independent in practice since 1916. Repressive Chinese rule quickly alienated the Tibetans, who rose in rebellion in 1959. The Tibetan religious leader, the Dalai Lama, was forced to flee to India. Since then, the settlement of large numbers of ethnic Chinese in the main cities of Tibet has threatened to swamp Tibetan culture.

During the 1950s and 1960s China was involved in a number of border disputes and wars in neighbouring states. The Communists posted 'volunteers' to fight alongside Communist North Korea during the Korean War (1950–53). There were clashes on the Soviet border in the 1950s and the Indian border in the 1960s, when China occupied some Indian territory.

From the establishment of the Peoples' Republic of China, Communist China and the Soviet Union were allies. Communist China initially depended upon Soviet assistance for economic development. A Soviet-style five-year plan was put into action in 1953, but the relationship with Moscow was already showing signs of strain. The two Communist powers fell out regarding their different interpretations of Marxist orthodoxy. By the end of the 1950s the Soviet Union and China were rivals, spurring the Chinese arms race. Chinese research into atomic weapons culminated in the testing of the first Chinese atomic bomb in 1964.

Mao introduced rapid collectivization of farms in 1955. The countryside was to take the lead in implementing Communist economics. Mao's idea was not met with universal approval in the Communist Party but its implementation demonstrated his complete authority over the fortunes of the nation. In 1956 he launched the doctrine of letting a 'hundred flowers bloom', encouraging intellectual debate. However, the new freedoms took a turn Mao did not expect and led to the questioning of the role of the party. Strict controls were reimposed and free-thinkers were sent to work in the countryside to be 're-educated'.

In May 1958 Mao launched another ill-fated policy, the Great Leap Forward. To promote rapid industrialization and socialism, the collectives were reorganized into larger units. Neither the resources nor trained personnel were available for this huge task. Backyard blast furnaces were set up to increase production of iron and steel. The results were disappointing. It is believed that 30m. died in the famine that resulted from the Great Leap Forward. By the early 1960s the Great Leap Forward was in trouble. Soviet advice against the project was ignored and a complete rift in relations with Moscow came in 1963, when Soviet assistance was withdrawn. As relations between the former friends cooled, a rapprochement with the United States was achieved in the early 1970s.

Cultural Revolution
Having published his 'Thoughts' in the 'Little Red Book' in 1964 Mao set the Cultural Revolution in motion. Militant students were organized into groups of Red Guards to attack the party hierarchy. Anyone perceived to lack enthusiasm for Mao Zedong Thought was denounced. Thousands died as the students went out of control and the army was eventually called in to restore order. Once again, Mao's enthusiasm for continuing revolution had ended in disaster.

After Mao's death in 1976 the radical Gang of Four, led by Mao's widow Chang Ch'ing, attempted to seize power. These hard-liners were denounced and arrested. China effectively came under the control of Deng Xiaoping, despite the fact that he held none of the great offices of state. Deng placed an emphasis on economic reform. The country was opened to Western investment. Special Economic Zones and 'open cities' were designated and private enterprise gradually returned, on a small scale at first.

Greatly improved standards of living and a thriving economy increased expectations for civil liberties. The demand for political change climaxed in demonstrations by workers and students in April 1989, following the funeral of Communist Party leader Hu Yaobang. Protests were held in several major cities. In Beijing where demonstrators peacefully occupied Tiananmen Square, they were evicted by the military who opened fire, killing more than 1,500. Hard-liners took control of the government, and martial law was imposed from May 1989 to Jan. 1990.

Since 1989 the leadership has concentrated on economic development. Hong Kong was returned to China from British rule in 1997 and Macao from Portuguese rule in 1999. The late 1990s saw a cautious extension of civil liberties, but the leadership still denies Chinese citizens most basic political rights.

For the background to the handover of Hong Kong in 1997, see page 329.

TERRITORY AND POPULATION

China is bounded in the north by Russia and Mongolia; east by North Korea, the Yellow Sea and the East China Sea, with Hong Kong and Macao as enclaves on the southeast coast; south by Vietnam, Laos, Myanmar, India, Bhutan and Nepal; west by India, Pakistan, Afghanistan, Tajikistan, Kyrgyzstan and Kazakhstan. The total area (including Taiwan, Hong Kong and Macao) is estimated at 9,572,900 sq. km (3,696,100 sq. miles). A law of Feb. 1992 claimed the Spratly, Paracel and Diaoyutasi Islands. An agreement of 7 Sept. 1993 at prime ministerial level settled Sino-Indian border disputes which had first emerged in the war of 1962.

China's fifth national census was held on 1 Nov. 2000. According to preliminary results, the total population of the 31 provinces, autonomous regions and municipalities on the mainland was 1,265,830,000 (612,280,000 females, representing 48·37%); density, 132 per sq. km. The population rose by 132,150,000 (or 11·66%) since the census in 1990. There were 455,940,000 urban residents, accounting for 36·1% of the population. The proportion of the population living in urban areas has more than doubled since 1975. An estimated 300m. people have migrated from the countryside to cities since the economy was opened up in the late 1970s, and a further 300m. are expected to move to towns and cities by 2020. The estimated population in 2005 was 1,315·84m.

The UN gives a projected population for 2010 of 1,354·53m.

China is set to lose its status as the world's most populous country to India in about 2030, and according to UN projections its population will begin to decline around the same time.

1979 regulations restricting married couples to a single child, a policy enforced by compulsory abortions and economic sanctions, have been widely ignored, and it was admitted in 1988 that the population target of 1,200m. by 2000 would have to be revised to 1,270m. Since 1988 peasant couples have been permitted a second child after four years if the first born is a girl, a measure to combat infanticide. In 1999 China started to implement a more widespread gradual relaxation of the one-child policy.

An estimated 34m. persons of Chinese origin lived abroad in 2000.

A number of widely divergent varieties of Chinese are spoken. The official 'Modern Standard Chinese' is based on the dialect of North China. Mandarin in one form or another is spoken by 885m. people in China, or around 70% of the population of mainland China. The Wu language and its dialects has some 77m. native speakers and Cantonese 66m. The ideographic writing system of 'characters' is uniform throughout the country, and has undergone systematic simplification. In 1958 a phonetic alphabet (*Pinyin*) was devised to transcribe the characters, and in 1979 this was officially adopted for use in all texts in the Roman alphabet. The previous transcription scheme (Wade) is still used in Taiwan and Hong Kong.

Mainland China is administratively divided into 22 provinces, five autonomous regions (originally entirely or largely inhabited by ethnic minorities, though in some regions now outnumbered by Han immigrants) and four government-controlled municipalities. These are in turn divided into 332 prefectures, 658 cities (of which 265 are at prefecture level and 393 at county level), 2,053 counties and 808 urban districts.

Government-controlled municipalities	Area (in 1,000 sq. km)	Population (2000 census, in 1,000)	Density per sq. km (in 2000)	Capital
Beijing	16·8	13,820	823	—
Chongqing	82·0	30,090	367	—
Shanghai	6·2	16,740	2,700	—
Tianjin	11·3	10,010	886	—
Provinces				
Anhui	139·9	59,860	428	Hefei
Fujian	123·1	34,710	282	Fuzhou
Gansu[1]	366·5	25,620	70	Lanzhou
Guangdong[1]	197·1	86,420	438	Guangzhou
Guizhou[1]	174·0	35,250	203	Guiyang
Hainan[1]	34·3	7,870	229	Haikou
Hebei[1]	202·7	67,440	333	Shijiazhuang

Provinces	Area (in 1,000 sq. km)	Population (2000 census, in 1,000)	Density per sq. km (in 2000)	Capital
Heilongjiang[1]	463·6	36,890	80	Haerbin
Henan	167·0	92,560	554	Zhengzhou
Hubei[1]	187·5	60,280	321	Wuhan
Hunan[1]	210·5	64,400	306	Changsha
Jiangsu	102·6	74,380	723	Nanjing
Jiangxi	164·8	41,400	251	Nanchang
Jilin[1]	187·0	27,280	146	Changchun
Liaoning[1]	151·0	42,380	281	Shenyang
Qinghai[1]	721·0	5,180	7	Xining
Shaanxi	195·8	36,050	184	Xian
Shandong	153·3	90,790	592	Jinan
Shanxi	157·1	32,970	210	Taiyuan
Sichuan[1]	487·0	83,290	171	Chengdu
Yunnan[1]	436·2	42,880	98	Kunming
Zhejiang[1]	101·8	46,770	459	Hangzhou
Autonomous regions				
Guangxi Zhuang	220·4	44,890	204	Nanning
Inner Mongolia	1,177·5	23,760	20	Hohhot
Ningxia Hui	66·4	5,620	85	Yinchuan
Tibet[2]	1,221·6	2,620	2	Lhasa
Xinjiang Uighur	1,646·9	19,250	12	Urumqi

[1]Also designated minority nationality autonomous area.
[2]See also Tibet below.

Population of largest cities in 2000: Shanghai, 14·35m.; Beijing (Peking), 11·51m.; Chongqing, 9·69m.; Guangzhou (Canton), 8·52m.; Wuhan, 8·31m.; Tianjin, 7·50m.; Shenzhen, 7·01m.; Dongguan, 6·45m.; Shenyang, 5·30m.; Xian, 4·48m.; Chengdu, 4·33m.; Nanjing, 3·62m.; Haerbin, 3·48m.; Dalian, 3·25m.; Changchun, 3·23m.; Kunming, 3·04m.; Jinan, 3·00m.; Guiyang, 2·99m.; Zibo, 2·82m.; Qingdao, 2·72m.; Zhengzhou, 2·59m.; Taiyuan, 2·56m.; Chaoyang, 2·47m.; Hangzhou, 2·45m.; Zhongshan, 2·36m.; Nanhai, 2·13m.; Changsha, 2·12m.; Fuzhou, 2·12m.; Lanzhou, 2·09m.; Xiamen, 2·05m.; Zaozhuang, 2·00m.; Shijiazhuang, 1·97m.; Jilin, 1·95m.; Linyi, 1·94m.; Wenzhou, 1·92m.; Puning, 1·86m.; Nanchang, 1·84m.; Nanchong, 1·77m.; Nanning, 1·77m.; Urumqi (Wulumuqi), 1·75m.; Fuyang, 1·72m.; Yantai, 1·72m.; Tangshan, 1·71m.; Shunde, 1·69m.; Xuzhou, 1·68m.; Baotou, 1·67m.; Hefei, 1·66m.; Tianmen, 1·61m.; Liuan, 1·60m.; Suizhou, 1·60m.; Suzhou, 1·60m.; Nanyang, 1·58m.; Ningbo, 1·57m.; Anshan, 1·56m.; Tengzhou, 1·55m.; Pizhou, 1·54m.; Qiqihaer, 1·54m.; Taian, 1·54m.; Datong, 1·53m.

China has 56 ethnic groups. According to the 2000 census 1,159,400,000 people (91·6%) were of Han nationality and 106,430,000 (8·4%) were from national minorities (including Zhuang, Manchu, Hui, Miao, Uighur, Yi, Tujia, Mongolian and Tibetan). Compared with the 1990 census, the Han population increased by almost 116,920,000 (11·2%), while the ethnic minorities increased by 15,230,000 (16·7%). Non-Han populations predominate in the autonomous regions, most notably in Tibet where national minorities accounted for 97·2% of the population in 1994.

Li Chengrui, *The Population of China*. Beijing, 1992

Tibet

After the 1959 revolt was suppressed, the Preparatory Committee for the Autonomous Region of Tibet (set up in 1955) took over the functions of local government, led by its Vice-Chairman, the Panchen Lama, in the absence of its Chairman, the Dalai Lama, who had fled to India in 1959. In Dec. 1964 both the Dalai and Panchen Lamas were removed from their posts and on 9 Sept. 1965 Tibet became an Autonomous Region. 301 delegates were elected to the first People's Congress, of whom 226 were Tibetans. The senior spiritual leader, the Dalai Lama, is in exile. He was awarded the Nobel Peace Prize in 1989. Following the death of the 10th Panchen Lama (Tibet's second most important spiritual leader) in Jan. 1989, the Dalai Lama announced Gendu Choekyi Nyima (b. 1989) as the 11th Panchen Lama in May 1995. Beijing rejected the choice and

appointed Gyaltsen Norbu (b. 1989) in his place. Gendu Choekyi Nyima has been missing since 1995. The borders were opened for trade with neighbouring countries in 1980. In July 1988 Tibetan was reinstated as a 'major official language', competence in which is required of all administrative officials. Monasteries and shrines have been renovated and reopened. There were some 46,000 monks and nuns in 2004. In 1984 a Buddhist seminary in Lhasa opened with 200 students. A further softening of Beijing's attitude towards Tibet was shown during President Bill Clinton's visit to China in June 1998. Jiang Zemin, China's president, said he was prepared to meet the Dalai Lama provided he acknowledged Chinese sovereignty over Tibet and Taiwan. In Sept. 2002 direct contact between the exiled government and China was re-established after a nine-year gap.

At the 2000 census Tibet had a population of 2·62m., of which 2·42m. were Tibetans and the remainder from other ethnic groups. The average population density was 2·02 persons per sq. km, although the majority of residents live in the southern and eastern parts of the region. Birth rate (per 1,000), 2000, 17·6; death rate, 6·6. Population of the Lhasa (capital) region in 2000 was 403,700. Expectation of life was 67 years in 2000.

In 2000, 1·24m. people were in employment: 909,800 worked in agriculture, forestry, animal husbandry and fisheries; 73,300 in wholesale and retail services; 57,300 in government and party institutions and social organizations; 35,600 in construction; 33,100 in transport and communications; 32,400 in education, culture and media; 28,700 in manufacturing; and 12,400 in health and social welfare. Output in 2000 included 120,000 cu. metres of timber, 493,200 tonnes of cement, 196,628 tonnes of chromium ore, 441,900 garments and 591 tonnes of traditional Chinese medicines. Electricity output in 2000 was 66m. kWh.

In 2000 the total sown area was 230,850 ha. (dry fields, 229,760 ha.; paddy fields, 1,080 ha.). Output (in 1,000 tonnes), 2000: total major crops, 962; including qingke barley, 597; wheat, 307; rice, 5. Livestock numbered 22·6m. in 2000: including 5·3m. cattle; 10·4m. sheep; 5·9m. goats; and 0·2m. pigs.

In 2000 there were 22,503 km of roads (21,842 km in 1990). There are airports at Lhasa and Bangda providing external links. 148,877 tourists visited Tibet in 2000. In 2000 plans were announced to build a railway of some 900 km to link Lhasa with the town of Golmud, which already has a link with the city of Xining. It would be the highest railway in the world. The Chinese government approved the plan on 8 Feb. 2001 with the aim of completing the link by 2008.

By 2000 Tibet had about 4,250 primary schools (including those run by villages); 106 secondary schools (90 middle schools, 16 vocational and polytechnic schools); and 4 higher education institutes (Tibet University, Tibet Ethnic College, Tibet Institute of Agriculture and Animal Husbandry, and Tibetan Medical College). There were more than 300,000 pupils and students.

In 2000 there were 11,027 medical personnel (including 5,262 doctors) and 1,237 medical institutions, with a total of 6,348 beds.

Barnett, R. and Akiner, S. (eds.) *Resistance and Reform in Tibet*. Farnborough, 1994
Margolis, Eric, *War at the Top of the World: The Struggle for Afghanistan, Kashmir and Tibet*. Routledge, New York, 2001
Pinfold, John, *Tibet* [Bibliography]. Oxford and Santa Barbara (CA), 1991
Schwartz, R. D., *Circle of Protest: Political Ritual in the Tibetan Uprising*. Farnborough, 1994
Smith, W. W., *A History of Tibet: Nationalism and Self-Determination*. Oxford, 1996

SOCIAL STATISTICS

Births, 2001, 17,020,000; deaths, 8,180,000. 2001 birth rate (per 1,000 population), 13·38; death rate, 6·43. The birth rate has declined each year since 1987. There were 8,420,044 marriages and 1,212,863 divorces in 2000. In April 2001 parliament passed revisions to the marriage law prohibiting bigamy and cohabitation outside marriage. The Ministry of Health estimated in 2001 that the suicide rate in China was about 22 per 100,000 population. China is the only major country in which the suicide rate is higher among females—over half the world's women suicides occur in China. In 1996 the most popular age for marrying was 25–29 for both men and women. Life expectancy at birth, 2003, was 69·9 years for men and 73·5 years for women. Infant mortality, 2001, 31 per 1,000 live births. Fertility rate, 2001, 1·8 births per woman. Annual population growth rate, 1992–2002, 0·9%. The number of people living on less than US$1 a day at purchasing power parity declined from 470m. in 1990 to 261m. in 2000.

CLIMATE

Most of China has a temperate climate but, with such a large country, extending far inland and embracing a wide range of latitude as well as containing large areas at high altitude, many parts experience extremes of climate, especially in winter. Most rain falls during the summer, from May to Sept., though amounts decrease inland. Monthly average temperatures and annual rainfall (2000): Beijing (Peking), Jan. 20·5°F (−6·4°C), July 85·3°F (29·6°C). Annual rainfall 14·6" (371·1 mm). Chongqing, Jan. 45·8°F (7·7°C), July 83·3°F (28·5°C). Annual rainfall 39·8" (1,010 mm). Shanghai, Jan. 41·2°F (5·1°C), July 84·5°F (29·1°C). Annual rainfall 52·4" (1,332 mm). Tianjin, Jan. 20·3°F (−6·5°C), July 83·8°F (28·8°C). Annual rainfall 18·0" (459 mm).

CONSTITUTION AND GOVERNMENT

On 21 Sept. 1949 the *Chinese People's Political Consultative Conference* met in Beijing, convened by the Chinese Communist Party. The Conference adopted a 'Common Programme' of 60 articles and the 'Organic Law of the Central People's Government' (31 articles). Both became the basis of the Constitution adopted on 20 Sept. 1954 by the 1st National People's Congress, the supreme legislative body. The Consultative Conference continued to exist after 1954 as an advisory body. Three further constitutions have been promulgated under Communist rule—in 1975, 1978 and 1982 (currently in force). The latter was partially amended in 1988, 1993 and 1999, endorsing the principles of a socialist market economy and of private ownership.

The unicameral *National People's Congress* is the highest organ of state power. Usually meeting for one session a year, it can amend the constitution and nominally elects and has power to remove from office the highest officers of state. There are 2,985 members of the Congress, who are elected to serve five-year terms by municipal, regional and provincial people's congresses. The Congress elects a *Standing Committee* (which supervises the *State Council*) and the *President* and *Vice-President* for a five-year term. When not in session, Congress business is carried on by the *Standing Committee*.

The *State Council* is the supreme executive organ and comprises the Prime Minister, Deputy Prime Ministers and State Councillors.

The *Central Military Commission* is the highest state military organ.

National Anthem

'March of the Volunteers'; words by Tien Han, tune by Nie Er.

GOVERNMENT CHRONOLOGY

Leaders of the Communist Party of China since 1935.

Chairmen
1935–76	Mao Zedong
1976–81	Hua Guofeng
1981–82	Hu Yaobang

General Secretaries
1956–57	Deng Xiaoping
1980–87	Hu Yaobang
1987–89	Zhao Ziyang
1989–2002	Jiang Zemin
2002–	Hu Jintao

De facto ruler
1978–97	Deng Xiaoping

Heads of State since 1949.

Chairman of the Central People's Government
1949–54	Mao Zedong

Chairmen (Presidents)
1954–59	Mao Zedong
1959–68	Liu Shaoqi
1968–75	Dong Biwu

Chairmen of the Standing Committee of the National People's Congress
1975–76	Zhu De
1978–83	Ye Jianying

Presidents of the Republic
1983–88	Li Xiannian
1988–93	Yang Shangkun
1993–2003	Jiang Zemin
2003–	Hu Jintao

Prime Ministers since 1949.
1949–76	Zhou Enlai
1976–80	Hua Guofeng
1980–87	Zhao Ziyang
1987–1998	Li Peng
1998–2003	Zhu Rongji
2003–	Wen Jiabao

RECENT ELECTIONS

Elections of delegates to the 10th *National People's Congress* were held between Dec. 2002 and Feb. 2003 by municipal, regional and provincial people's congresses. At its annual session in March 2003 the Congress elected Hu Jintao as *President* and Zeng Qinghong as *Vice-President*.

CURRENT ADMINISTRATION

President and Chairman of Central Military Commission: Hu Jintao; b. 1942 (Chinese Communist Party; elected 15 March 2003).

Deputy President: Zeng Qinghong.

In March 2006 the government comprised:

Prime Minister: Wen Jiabao; b. 1942 (Chinese Communist Party; appointed 16 March 2003).

Deputy Prime Ministers: Huang Ju, Wu Yi, Zeng Peiyan, Hui Liangyu.

Minister of Agriculture: Du Qinglin. *Civil Administration:* Li Xueju. *Commerce:* Bo Xilai. *Construction:* Wang Guangtao. *Culture:* Sun Jiazheng. *Education:* Zhou Ji. *Finance:* Jin Renqing. *Foreign Affairs:* Li Zhaoxing. *Health:* Gao Qiang. *Information Industry:* Wang Xudong. *Justice:* Wu Aiying. *Labour and Social Security:* Tian Chengping. *National Defence:* Cao Gangchuan. *National Land Resources:* Sun Wensheng. *National Security:* Xu Yongyue. *Personnel:* Zhang Bolin. *Public Security:* Zhou Yongkang. *Railways:* Liu Zhijun. *Science and Technology:* Xu Guanhua. *Supervision:* Li Zhilun. *Transportation:* Zhang Chunxian. *Water Resources:* Wang Shucheng.

Ministers heading State Commissions: *Family Planning,* Zhang Weiqing. *Nationalities Affairs,* Li Dezhu. *Development and Reform,* Ma Kai. *Science, Technology and Industry for National Defence,* Zhang Yunchuan.

De facto power is in the hands of the Communist Party of China, which had 66m. members in 2002. There are eight other parties, all members of the Chinese People's Political Consultative Conference.

The members of the Standing Committee of the Politburo in March 2005 were Hu Jintao (*General Secretary*), Wen Jiabao, Luo Gan, Wu Bangguo, Zeng Qinghong, Huang Ju, Jia Qinglin, Li Changchun, Wu Guanzheng.

Government Website (Chinese only): http://www.govonline.cn

CURRENT LEADERS

Hu Jintao

Position
President

Introduction
Hu Jintao was nominated general secretary of the Chinese Communist Party (CCP) in Nov. 2002, formally succeeding Jiang Zemin as head of state in March 2003 and as chairman of the Central Military Commission in Sept. 2004. Although widely perceived as a conservative—having imposed martial law in Tibet and supported the Tiananmen Square massacres in the late 1980s—he has continued Jiang's cautious reformist policies. He has maintained the drive for rapid industrial growth and also further developed China's international contacts, having by late 2005 undertaken visits as state president to Latin America, Africa, Australia, Canada, Central Asia and the UK.

Early Life
Much of Hu's early history is disputed. He is believed to have been born in Dec. 1942 in Jixi, Anhui Province. His mother died when he was six and he was subsequently raised by an aunt. In 1959 he began engineering studies at Qinghua University and graduated in 1964, the same year in which he joined the CCP. He then held a variety of posts at the University and the Ministry of Water Conservancy.

He is reported to have distanced himself from Mao's Cultural Revolution of the mid-1960s and was sentenced to two months of 'reform through labour', during which time he worked on a farm. Over the next few years he worked on several large-scale engineering projects in Gansu province. By the late 1970s Hu was a favourite of Deng Xiaoping, who became China's effective leader. He settled in Beijing in 1980, and within two years he was the youngest member of the party's central committee. Having risen through the ranks of the Communist Youth League, in 1985 he was appointed provincial party secretary for Guizhou. In 1988 he became party secretary in charge of Tibet and authorized the killing of several independence protesters in March 1989. Shortly afterwards he declared martial law and oversaw the introduction of 100,000 troops into the region. Later in the year he was among the first of the provincial party secretaries to express his support for those who took part in the Tiananmen Square massacres.

In 1992 Hu was responsible for organizing Jiang's first party congress as leader. Shortly afterwards he was designated a member of the Politburo Standing Committee. In 1998 he was named vice-president, from which point on he was Jiang's acknowledged successor. The following year he was a key figure in the protests staged at the US and British embassies in Beijing over the accidental bombing of the Chinese embassy in Belgrade during NATO military action against Serbia. He was also named deputy chairman of the Central Military Commission at that time.

Career in Office
At the CCP congress of Nov. 2002, Hu replaced Jiang as party general secretary, ushering in the 'Fourth Generation' of the party leadership; he then succeeded Jiang as state president on 15 March 2003. Hu expressed his commitment to Jiang's *Theory of Three Representations* (treatise on Chinese political thought), while the presence on the Politburo of several Jiang allies also suggested that a radically different style of government was unlikely.

Hu has pursued an active foreign policy, breaking from the Deng model which proscribed taking the lead in diplomatic negotiations. He has sought to resolve the issue of North Korea's nuclear ambitions through the ongoing six-nations talks between North and South Korea, China, Japan, Russia and the USA. He has also developed relations with neighbouring India and Pakistan, establishing military links with both countries in Nov. 2003. Earlier, in June 2003, Hu received the visiting Indian Prime Minister Atal Bihari Vajpayee. India conceded recognition of Tibet as an autonomous region of the People's Republic of China and promised to prevent 'anti-China political activities in India' by Tibetans. The announcement left the future of the Dalai Lama's government-in-exile in Dharmsala unclear. As president, Hu has also visited Australia, Africa, Latin America, Canada and Central Asia, in pursuit of closer economic and commercial links to supply the resources for China's industrial machine.

Human rights and Taiwan remain the most difficult issues in Sino-US relations. Perennial US accusations of 'backsliding' in human rights have been vigorously denied, and Hu's government has pointed to US foreign policy as aggressive and harmful to the rights of civilians. President George W. Bush's less conciliatory attitude towards China over Taiwan has led to a more turbulent relationship between the two countries. Hu visited the USA in May 2002 prior to becoming president. He has since warned the USA not to support Taiwan militarily and to oppose any steps towards independence.

Hu's domestic agenda has centred on alleviating the poverty of China's peasant population, in contrast to Jiang's close links with the business sector. His anti-corruption drive has included the banning of courtesy cars for CCP officials and the sacking of several officials over the handling of the SARS (severe acute respiratory syndrome) epidemic, which hit China in late 2002. His government has pledged increases in agricultural subsidies and the eventual termination of agricultural taxes—a programme interpreted as an attempt to create a larger middle class, committed to the CCP hegemony.

Wen Jiabao

Position
Prime Minister

Introduction
Wen Jiabao was confirmed as China's prime minister in March 2003. Although relatively low-profile, he has established a reputation for reliability and durability. A leading figure in the liberalization of China's economic and environmental policies in the 1990s, he has promoted the development of the traditionally poorer and less urban west of the country.

Early Life
Wen Jiabao was born in Tianjin in the east of China in Sept. 1942. In 1965 he obtained a degree from the Beijing Institute of Geology and joined the Chinese Communist Party (CCP). In 1968 he received his master's degree and began working with the geomechanics survey team at the Gansu provincial geological bureau. He remained at the bureau until 1982, serving as its deputy director-general in his final year.

Having won the patronage of Song Ping, an influential figure within the CCP at the time, Wen moved to Beijing to take a job at the Ministry of Geology and Mineral Resources. After heading the policy and research section he was appointed vice-minister. In 1985 he was made deputy director of the general office of the CCP central committee, working closely with the party chairman, Hu Yaobang. Wen emerged unscathed after Hu's 1987 purging and took over as director of the general office as well as becoming an alternate member of the Politburo of the CCP central committee and secretary of the central committee's work committee of departments.

In 1989 Wen was in attendance when General Secretary Zhao Ziyang visited Tiananmen Square during the student protests. Zhao was subsequently purged, but again Wen's position remained secure. In 1992 he took on additional roles within the CCP central committee. Having led the team responsible for drafting the national five-year plan in 1995, Wen won full membership of the Politburo of the central committee two years later.

Throughout the 1990s Wen was a prominent figure in the formation of the party's economic policy. He was involved in banking reform and the restructuring of the Finance Ministry. By the late 1990s he was increasingly involved in environmental and rural affairs. At the 16th party congress in late 2002 General Secretary Jiang Zemin and Prime Minister Zhu Rhongji were among several high profile figures to retire. On 16 March 2003 Wen was confirmed as Zhu's successor to the premiership with 99·3% support from the National People's Congress.

Career in Office

Wen is perceived as less personally charismatic than Zhu, but has won respect within the Chinese political establishment for his longevity and experience. His management style has traditionally been based on seeking consensus.

When he was in Gansu, Wen became one of the few leading Chinese politicians to work for an extended period in the economically less prosperous west of the country. He has stated that his aim is to narrow the prosperity gap between the east and west of China. In addition, many observers hope that he can confront the problems of China's economically weak agricultural sector. Under Jiang, Wen did much to promote the land rights of the rural peasant population. In addition, he pushed for a reduction in the tax burden on rural communities and promoted freedom for farmers to sell their holdings. He has urged the financial sector to support improvements in the region's infrastructures, education system and use of natural resources.

Despite his key contribution to banking reform in the 1990s, Wen was not expected to champion radical reforms to counter the crippling problem of bad debts. In Oct. 2002 he called for a 'gradual approach' to further deregulation and in Oct. 2003 he stated that China would not be pressured by the international community into a revaluation of the yuan (renminbi). Nevertheless, in July 2005 China did revalue the currency, abandoning its 11-year peg to the US dollar and linking it to a basket of currencies.

Wen's programme for assisting the rural poor took shape at the opening of the National People's Congress in March 2004. Described as *yiren weiben* ('administration for the sake of the people'), the programme stressed the importance of social development in poorer regions and the need to avoid an overheated economy. He highlighted the damaging disparity in wealth between the rich, industrial coastal provinces and the poorer rural provinces of the interior. He promised 30bn. yuan investment in agriculture and announced that taxes on farmers would be cut to zero by 2009. His programme also included the recognition of private property, requiring an amendment to the constitution, designed to prevent the unlawful requisition of property by officials.

The government's slow reaction to SARS, originating in Guangdong in 2002 and 2003, was criticized by the international community. Nearly 350 people died from the virus, despite quarantines and travel bans. About 600 people were quarantined in Beijing in April 2004 in response to fears of another outbreak. The government has also been criticized for ignoring the plight of HIV/AIDS sufferers. In April 2004 Wu Yi, the health minister, announced plans to combat the AIDS epidemic, promising to act against officials and politicians who attempted to hide the facts.

DEFENCE

The Chinese president is chairman of the State and Party's Military Commissions. China is divided into seven military regions. The military commander also commands the air, naval and civilian militia forces assigned to each region.

China's armed forces, totalling more than 2·2m. in 2004, are the largest of any country.

Conscription is compulsory but for organizational reasons selective: only some 10% of potential recruits are called up. Service is for two years. A military academy to train senior officers in modern warfare was established in 1985.

Defence expenditure in 2003 totalled US$55,948m. (US$43 per capita) and represented 3·9% of GDP. Only the USA and Russia spent more on defence in 2003. In the period 1999–2003 China's spending on major conventional weapons was the highest in the world at US$11·8bn., although in 2003 India overtook China as the leading recipient.

Nuclear Weapons

Having carried out its first test in 1964, there have been 45 tests in all at Lop Nur, in Xinjiang (the last in 1996). The nuclear arsenal consisted of approximately 400 warheads in Jan. 2005 according to the Stockholm International Peace Research Institute. China has been helping Pakistan with its nuclear efforts. Despite China's official position, *Deadly Arsenals*, published by the Carnegie Endowment for International Peace, alleges that the Chinese government is secretly pursuing chemical and biological weapons programmes.

Army

The Army (PLA: 'People's Liberation Army') is divided into main and local forces. Main forces, administered by the seven military regions in which they are stationed, but commanded by the Ministry of Defence, are available for operation anywhere and are better equipped. Local forces concentrate on the defence of their own regions. There are 18 Integrated Group Armies comprising 44 infantry divisions, nine armoured divisions, 12 armoured brigades, one mechanized infantry, 22 motorized infantry brigades, seven artillery divisions, 14 artillery brigades, one anti-tank brigade, nine surface-to-air missile brigades and 12 anti-aircraft artillery brigades. Total strength in 2004 was 1·60m. including some 800,000 conscripts. Reserve forces are undergoing major reorganization on a provincial basis but are estimated to number some 800,000.

In Sept. 2003 it was announced that the strength of the PLA was to be reduced by 200,000 as part of a move to modernize the military.

There is a paramilitary People's Armed Police force estimated at 1·5m. under PLA command.

Navy

The naval arm of the PLA comprises one nuclear-powered ballistic missile armed submarine, five nuclear-propelled fleet submarines, one diesel-powered cruise missile submarine and some 61 patrol submarines. Surface combatant forces include 21 missile-armed destroyers, 42 frigates and some 96 missile craft.

There is a land-based naval air force of about 700 combat aircraft, primarily for defensive and anti-submarine service. The force includes H-5 torpedo bombers, Q-5 fighter/ground attack aircraft J-6 (MiG-19) and J-7 (MiG-21) fighters.

The naval arm is split into a North Sea Fleet, an East Sea Fleet and a South Sea Fleet.

In 2004 naval personnel were estimated at 255,000, including 26,000 in the naval air force and 40,000 conscripts.

Air Force

There are five air corps and 32 air divisions. Up to four squadrons make up an air regiment and three air regiments form an air division. The Air Force has an estimated 1,900 combat aircraft.

Equipment includes J-7 (MiG-21) interceptors and fighter-bombers, H-5 (Il-28) jet bombers, H-6 Chinese-built copies of Tu-16 strategic bombers, Q-5 fighter-bombers (evolved from the MiG-19) and Su-27 fighters supplied by Russia. About 180 of a locally-developed fighter designated J-8 (known in the West as 'Finback') are in service.

Total strength (2004) was 400,000 (150,000 conscripts), including 210,000 in air defence organization. The Air Force headquarters are in Beijing.

INTERNATIONAL RELATIONS

The People's Republic of China is a member of UN (and its Security Council), WTO, BIS, the Asian Development Bank, APEC, Mekong Group and the Antarctic Treaty,

China is heavily dependent on foreign aid. In 2000 it received US$1·7bn., more than any other country.

ECONOMY

In 2002 agriculture accounted for 15·4% of GDP, industry 51·1% and services 33·5%.

It has been estimated that corruption cost China US$150bn. in the 1990s, or between 13% and 16% of the country's GDP.

Overview

China's economic performance over the last two and a half decades has been impressive, with annual growth averaging over 9%. China ranks among the world's leading half dozen economies, with some analysts suggesting 2005 figures placed it fourth. On a purchasing power parity (PPP) basis it has been the world's second largest for years. On a PPP basis the economy is estimated to be approximately twice the size of Japan's. China increasingly impacts the global economy, driving down prices of many consumer products, raising prices of raw materials, running significant trade surpluses with western developed countries and trade deficits with other Asian countries. The growth of the Chinese economy is forecast to decelerate over the coming years but its performance has confounded expectations before.

In 1978 China's leadership began moving the economy away from central planning to a more market-oriented system. The economy was increasingly opened up to foreign trade and investment, and decentralized industrial management was allowed to flourish. Though market forces began to play a much greater role in the economy, the system was not converted into the property-rights based system of Western capitalist nations. Much of China's recent dynamism has come from 'collective' enterprises, particularly township and village enterprises (TVEs) run by managers under the auspices of local government. Local governments have had the incentive to see enterprises run efficiently because the central government has allowed officials to keep revenues in surplus of a fixed amount. Much of the productivity enhancing competition that China experienced was therefore competition between local or regional governments with direct interests in productive enterprise.

Private entrepreneurs and foreign investors, often working in partnership with Chinese interests, also came to play an increasingly productive role in the economy and led to a boom in manufacturing output. Even before 1978 China's economy was heavily skewed towards manufacturing but, thereafter, output increased further and there was a significant structural shift away from large state-owned enterprises (SOEs). Over the years the number of state firms has steeply declined, down from 300,000 to 150,000 in the past decade alone. From 1999–2003 SOEs shed 22m. workers while private companies created 18m. jobs. New enterprises have absorbed so much labour because they have focused on labour-intensive industries not dominated by the capital-intensive SOEs. SOEs continue to account for a significant part in the economy. Estimates of the private sector's share of total economic activity differ significantly, with the

Chinese government and some foreign banks estimating that it is only a quarter and the OECD and other organizations estimating that it has reached two-thirds. Economic growth has largely been fuelled by low added value, labour-intensive manufactured good exports but the country has moved up the added value curve and Chinese firms are likely to come into competition with higher added value producers in countries like South Korea.

In light of China's recent development success, the World Bank estimates that the number of people living on less than a dollar a day declined by 170m. between 1990 and 2000. Yet the benefits of China's explosive development have not been felt equally. Over 160m. people still live on consumption levels of below a dollar a day, mostly in rural areas and especially in remote and resource-poor regions in the west and the interior. The Hu government has made development of the agricultural sector a top priority.

There are several threats to China's continued economic growth. The combination of surging growth and inefficient production techniques and equipment has led to a significant deterioration of the environment, especially in the north. Air pollution, soil erosion and a declining water table are particular problems. The fragile and inefficient financial sector is also encumbered with a high proportion of loans that could turn non-performing if the economic environment were to weaken. Although it survived the previous downturn, the economy is thought to be vulnerable to a slump in the USA and Europe. The Chinese authorities seem to be taking a cautious yet progressive approach to the financial sector. Regarded as too weak to be fully liberalized, a few Western banks have recently been allowed to gain a foothold in China's financial sector in exchange for taking responsibility for the liabilities of banks and brokerage houses with weak balance sheets. The authorities are also aware of the need to rely less on investment and trade surpluses and rebalance growth towards domestic demand.

Further structural reform is thought to be necessary in order to redirect China's export-oriented economy, including reforms to increase worker mobility and improve public sector efficiency. The economy's dynamism is also thought to be significantly handicapped by heavy capitalization requirements for start-ups, bias against small private companies by the state-controlled banking system and a deficient stock market that makes family and friends a key source of financing. The OECD highlights the need for reform of bankruptcy law, property rights and corporate law (to eliminate market entry barriers and foster the growth of new firms). SOEs continue to dominate 'strategic' industries and remain burdened by excess labour while China will soon face the growing burden of an ageing population.

Currency

The currency is called Renminbi (*i.e.*, People's Currency). The unit of currency is the *yuan* (CNY) which is divided into ten *jiao*, the *jiao* being divided into ten *fen*. The yuan was floated to reflect market forces on 1 Jan. 1994 while remaining state-controlled. For eleven years the People's Bank of China maintained the yuan at about 8·28 to the US dollar, allowing it to fluctuate but only by a fraction of 1% in closely supervised trading. However, on 21 July 2005 it was revalued and is now pegged against a 'market basket' of currencies the central parities of which are determined every night. The exchange rate was changed from 8·28 yuan to the dollar to 8·11 yuan to the dollar. The yuan became convertible for current transactions from 1 Dec. 1996. Total money supply in June 2002 was 6,565·77bn. yuan and gold reserves were 16·08m. troy oz. Foreign exchange reserves were US$609·9bn. in Dec. 2004 (US$73·6bn. in 1995). Only Japan, with US$844·5bn., had more.

Inflation rates (based on IMF statistics):

1995	1996	1997	1998	1999	2000	2001	2002	2003	2004
17·1%	8·3%	2·8%	−0·8%	−1·4%	0·4%	0·7%	−0·8%	1·2%	3·9%

Budget

Total revenue and expenditure (in 1bn. yuan):

	1997	1998	1999	2000	2001	2002
Revenue	865·1	987·6	1,144·4	1,339·5	1,637·1	1,891·4
Expenditure	923·3	1,079·8	1,318·8	1,588·7	1,884·4	2,201·2

Total revenue in the central budget for 2001 was 917·1bn. yuan, comprising 857·8bn. yuan in revenue collected by central government and 59·3bn. yuan transferred to central government from local authorities. Total expenditure in the central budget amounted to 1,176·9bn. yuan, of which 575·4bn. yuan of expenditure for the central government and 601·5bn. yuan in the form of subsidies for local authorities. Local government revenue in 2001 came to 1,380·8bn. yuan (779·3bn. yuan in revenue collected by local authorities and 601·5bn. yuan in central government subsidies) and expenditure amounted to 1,368·3bn. yuan (1,309·0bn. yuan of expenditure in local budgets and 59·3bn. yuan transferred to central government). The 247·3bn. yuan deficit in 2001 increased to 309·8bn. in 2002.

Performance

GDP totalled US$1,649·3bn. in 2004. It is forecast that by 2050 China will have overtaken the USA to become the world's largest economy. Real GDP growth rates (based on IMF statistics):

1995	1996	1997	1998	1999	2000	2001	2002	2003	2004
10·5%	9·6%	8·8%	7·8%	7·1%	8·0%	7·5%	8·3%	9·5%	9·5%

In spite of high growth in recent years, China's GDP per capita at purchasing power parity was $5,003 in 2003 compared to the high human development average of $25,665.

Banking and Finance

The People's Bank of China is the central bank and bank of issue (*Governor:* Zhou Xiaochuan). There are three state policy banks—the State Development Bank, Export and Import Bank of China and Agricultural Development Bank of China—and four national specialized banks (the Bank of China, Industrial and Commercial Bank of China, Agricultural Bank of China and China Construction Bank). The Bank of China, Industrial and Commercial Bank of China and China Construction Bank have all sold minority stakes to foreign investors. The Bank of China is responsible for foreign banking operations. In April 2003 the China Banking Regulatory Commission was launched, taking over the role of regulating and supervising the country's banks and other deposit-taking financial institutions from the central bank. Legislation of 1995 permitted the establishment of commercial banks; credit co-operatives may be transformed into banks, mainly to provide credit to small businesses. In 2001 there were over 44,000 rural credit co-operatives and 3,200 urban credit co-operatives. In mid-2002 deposits in rural co-operatives amounted to 1,870bn. yuan and loans reached 1,360bn. yuan. Insurance is handled by the People's Insurance Company.

Savings deposits in various forms in all banking institutions totalled 14,363bn. yuan at the end of 2001. Loans amounted to 11,230bn. yuan.

There are stock exchanges in the Shenzhen Special Economic Zone and in Shanghai. A securities trading system linking six cities (Securities Automated Quotations System) was inaugurated in 1990 for trading in government bonds.

China received US$53·5bn. worth of foreign direct investment in 2003 and a record US$60·6bn. in 2004.

Weights and Measures

The metric system is in general use alongside traditional units of measurement.

ENERGY AND NATURAL RESOURCES

Environment

China's carbon dioxide emissions from the consumption and flaring of fossil fuels in 2002 accounted for 13·5% of the world total (the second highest after the USA) and were equivalent to 2·6 tonnes per capita. An *Environmental Sustainability Index* compiled for the World Economic Forum meeting in Jan. 2005 ranked China 133rd in the world out of 146 countries analysed, with 38·6%. The index measured the ability of countries to maintain favourable environmental conditions and examined various factors including pollution levels and the use or abuse of natural resources.

Electricity

Installed generating capacity in 2002 was 353m. kW, compared with 254m. kW in 1997. In 2002 electricity output was 1,654,000 GWh, an 11·7% increase over 2001. Consumption per capita was 1,484 kWh in 2002. Rapidly increasing demand has meant that more than half of China's provinces have had to ration power. Sources of energy in 2001 as percentage of total energy production: coal, 67·7%; crude oil, 20·6%; hydro-electric power, 8·3%; natural gas, 3·4%. In 2003 there were eight nuclear reactors in use with a further three under construction. Generating electricity is not centralized; local units range between 30 and 60 MW of output. In Dec. 2002 China formally broke up its state power monopoly, creating instead five generating and two transmission firms. The Three Gorges dam project on the Yangtze river, launched in 1993 and scheduled for completion in 2009, is intended to produce abundant hydro-electricity (as well as helping flood control); the first three 700,000-kW generators in service at the project's hydro-power station began commercial operation in July 2003. When the project is completed in 2009, its 26 generators will have a combined capacity of 18·2 GW.

Oil and Gas

On-shore oil reserves are found mainly in the northeast (particularly the Daqing and Liaohe fields) and northwest. There are off-shore fields in the continental shelves of east China. Crude oil production was 169m. tonnes in 2002. Proven reserves in 2002 were 18·3bn. bbls.

The largest natural gas reserves are located in the western and north-central regions. Production was 32·6bn. cu. metres in 2002, with proven reserves of 1,510bn. cu. metres.

Minerals

At the end of 2001 there were 156 varieties of proven mineral deposits in China, making it the third richest in the world in total reserves. Recoverable deposits of coal totalled 1,003·3bn. tonnes, mainly distributed in north China (particularly Shanxi province and the Inner Mongolia Autonomous Region). Coal production was 1,380m. tonnes in 2002, an 18·9% increase over 2001.

Iron ore reserves were 45·7bn. tonnes in 2001. Deposits are abundant in the anthracite field of Shanxi, in Hebei and in Shandong, and are found in conjunction with coal and worked in the northeast. Production in 2001 was 217m. tonnes, making China the world's leading iron ore producer.

Tin ore is plentiful in Yunnan, where the tin-mining industry has long existed. Tin production was 62,000 tonnes in 2002.

China is a major producer of wolfram (tungsten ore). Mining of wolfram is carried on in Hunan, Guangdong and Yunnan.

Salt production was 35·0m. tonnes in 2002; gold production was 162 tonnes in 2000. Output of other minerals (in 1,000 tonnes) in 2001: bauxite, 9,500; aluminium (2002), 4,300; zinc, 1,700; lead (2002), 641; copper, 588; diamonds, 1,185,000 carats. Other minerals produced: nickel, barite, bismuth, graphite, gypsum, mercury, molybdenum, silver. Reserves (in tonnes) of salt, 402,400m.; phosphate ore, 15,766m.; sylvite, 458m.

Agriculture

Agriculture accounted for approximately 15·4% of GDP in 2002, compared to over 50% in 1949 at the time of the birth of the People's Republic of China and over 30% in 1980. In 2000 areas harvested for major crops were (in 1m. ha.): rice, 30·50; wheat, 26·65; maize, 22·54; soybeans, 9·03; rapeseed, 7·80; sweet potatoes, 6·21. Intensive agriculture and horticulture have been practised for millennia. Present-day policy aims to avert the traditional threats from floods and droughts by soil conservancy, afforestation, irrigation and drainage projects, and to increase the 'high stable yields' areas by introducing fertilizers, pesticides and improved crops. In spite of this, 18·1m. ha. of land were flooded in 1996 and 20·1m. ha. were covered by drought. In Aug. 1998 more than 21m. ha., notably in the Yangtze valley, were under water as China experienced some of its worst flooding in recent times. The 2002 flood season claimed over 1,500 lives.

'Township and village enterprises' in agriculture comprise enterprises previously run by the communes of the Maoist era, co-operatives run by rural labourers and individual firms of a certain size. Such enterprises employed 130·8m. people in 2001. There were 2,026 state farms in 2000 with 3·92m. employees. In 2001 there were 244·32m. rural households. The rural workforce in 2001 was 490·85m., of whom 324·5m. were employed in agriculture, fishing or land management. Net per capita annual peasant income, 2001: 2,366 yuan. Around 44% of the total workforce is engaged in agriculture, down from 68% in 1980. According to the 2000 census, rural residents accounted for 63·9% of the population.

In 2001 there were 143,625,000 ha. of arable land and 11,650,000 ha. of permanent cropland; 54·8m. ha. were irrigated. There were 1,112,617 tractors in 2001 and 200,000 harvester-threshers.

Agricultural production of main crops (in 1m. tonnes), 2000: rice, 190·17; sweet potatoes, 121·02; maize, 105·23; wheat, 99·37; sugarcane, 70·20; potatoes, 62·04; watermelons, 38·38; cabbages, 20·21; tomatoes, 19·31; cucumbers and gherkins, 17·18; soybeans, 15·40; groundnuts, 15·07; seed cotton, 13·05; onions, 12·18; aubergines, 11·91; rapeseeds, 11·35; cottonseed, 8·70; pears, 8·62; chillies and green peppers, 8·14; sugarbeets, 7·70; tangerines and mandarins, 7·61; garlic, 6·47. Tea production in 2000 was just 721,000 tonnes. China is the world's leading producer of a number of agricultural crops, including rice, sweet potatoes, wheat, potatoes, watermelons, groundnuts and honey. The gross value of agricultural output in 2001 was 2,617,960m. yuan. Agricultural production during the period 1990–97 grew on average by 4·4% every year. Only Vietnam among Asian countries achieved higher annual agricultural growth over the same period.

Livestock, 2000: pigs, 437,551,000; goats, 148,401,000; sheep, 131,095,000; cattle, 104,582,000; buffaloes, 22,599,000; horses, 8,916,000; chickens, 3·62bn.; ducks, 612m. China has more sheep, goats, pigs, horses and chickens than any other country. China also has more than two-thirds of the world's ducks. Meat production in 2000 was 64·44m. tonnes; milk, 7·84m. tonnes; eggs, 19·24m. tonnes; honey, 256,000 tonnes. China is the world's leading producer of meat and eggs.

Powell, S. G., *Agricultural Reform in China: from Communes to Commodity Economy, 1978–1990*. Manchester Univ. Press, 1992

Forestry

In 2000 the area under forests was 163·48m. ha., or 17·5% of the total land area. The average annual increase in forest cover of 1,806,000 ha. between 1990 and 2000 was the highest of any country in the world. Total roundwood production in 2003 was 286·11m. cu. metres, making China the world's third largest timber producer (8·6% of the world total in 2003). It is the world's leading importer of roundwood, accounting for 22·1% of world timber imports in 2003.

Fisheries

Total catch, 2003: 16,755,653 tonnes, of which 14,293,783 tonnes were from marine waters. China's annual catch is the largest in the world, and currently accounts for approximately 19% of the world total. In 1989 the annual catch had been just 5·3m. tonnes.

INDUSTRY

The leading companies by market capitalization in China in Nov. 2005 were: China Mobile (Hong Kong), a mobile telecommunications company (US$96·8bn.); Hutchison Whampoa, a diversified industrial conglomerate (US$40·4bn.); and CNOOC, an oil and natural gas company (US$27·3bn.).

Industry accounted for 52·9% of GDP in 2004, up from 21% in 1949 when the People's Republic of China came into existence. Cottage industries persist into the 21st century. Industrial output grew by 11·1% in 2004. Modern industrial development began with the manufacture of cotton textiles and the establishment of silk filatures, steel plants, flour mills and match factories. In 1999 there were 7,929,900 industrial enterprises. 61,300 were state-owned, 1,659,800 were collectives and 6,126,800 were individually owned. A law of 1988 ended direct state control of firms and provided for the possibility of bankruptcy.

Output of major products, 2003 (in tonnes): cement, 862·1m. (more than a third of the world total); rolled steel, 241·1m.; crude steel, 222·3m.; pig iron, 213·7m.; distillate fuel oil (2002), 76·8m.; petrol (2002), 42·9m.; chemical fertilizers (2002), 37·9m.; paper and paperboard (2001), 37·9m.; sulphuric acid (2002), 30·5m.; residual fuel oil (2002), 18·5m.; sugar, 9·26m. (2002); cotton yarn (2002), 8·50m. Also produced in 2002: cloth, 3,220m. metres; woollen fabrics, 326·9m. metres; beer (2003), 25,404·8m. litres; 184m. watches (2001); 119·6m. mobile telephones; 81·8m. clocks (1997); 56·50m. radios (1996); 51·55m. TV sets; 59·62m. cameras (2001); 31·55m. air conditioners; 29m. bicycles (2000); 15·99m. refrigerators; 14·64m. micro-computers; 13·42m. washing machines (2001); 10·41m. motorcycles and scooters (2001); 3·25m. motor vehicles; 2,207 ships. China is the world's leading steel producer; output has tripled since 2000.

The gross value of industrial output in 1999 was 12,611,100m. yuan.

Labour

The employed population at the 1990 census was 647·2m. (291·1m. female). By the end of 2002 it had risen to 737·4m. (7·15m. more than in 2001), of whom 489·6m. worked in rural areas (1·25m. fewer than in 2001) and 247·8m. in urban areas (8·4m. more than in 2001). By 2015 China's working age population will begin to decline as a consequence of the country's one-child policy. In June 2003 China's registered jobless was 4·2%, with 7·95m. registered unemployed in the country's cities. Between 1995 and 2002, 15m. jobs were lost owing to the closure of state-owned factories. The number of state-controlled companies has halved since 1995. In 2000 there were 333·55m. people working in agriculture, hunting, forestry and fisheries; 80·43m. in manufacturing; 46·86m. in wholesale and retail trade, restaurants and hotels; 35·52m. in construction; and 20·29m. in transport, storage and communication.

By 2001 China had more than 2m. private companies employing 22m. people. It was not until the late 1970s that the private sector even came into existence in China.

The average non-agricultural annual wage in 2001 was 10,870 yuan: 6,867 yuan, urban collectives; 11,178 yuan, state-owned enterprises; 12,140 yuan, other enterprises. There is a 6-day 48-hour working week. Minimum working age was fixed at 16 in 1991. There were 120,000 labour disputes in 1999, up from 8,000 in 1989.

Trade Unions

The All-China Federation of Trade Unions, founded in 1925, is headed by Wang Zhaoguo. In 2003 there were 103m. members. It consists of 31 federations of trade unions. Its National Congress convenes every five years.

INTERNATIONAL TRADE

Foreign debt was US$168,255m. in 2002.

There are five Special Economic Zones at Shenzhen, Xiamen, Zhuhai, Shantou and Hainan in which concessions are made to foreign businessmen. The Pudong New Area in Shanghai is also designated a special development area. Since 1979 joint ventures with foreign firms have been permitted. A law of April 1991 reduced taxation on joint ventures to 33%. There is no maximum limit on the foreign share of the holdings; the minimum limit is 25%.

In May 2000 the USA granted normal trade relations to China, a progression after a number of years when China was accorded 'most favoured nation' status. China subsequently joined the World Trade Organization on 11 Dec. 2001.

Pearson, M. M., *Joint Ventures in the People's Republic of China: the Control of Foreign Direct Investment under Socialism.* Princeton Univ. Press, 1991

Imports and Exports

Trade in US$1m.:

	1999	2000	2001	2002	2003	2004
Imports f.o.b.	158,734	214,657	232,058	281,484	393,618	534,410
Exports f.o.b.	194,716	249,131	266,075	325,651	438,270	593,393

Main imports in 1999 (in US$1bn.): electrical machinery and equipment, 35·2; power generation equipment, 27·8; plastics and articles thereof, 11·6; mineral fuels and oil, 8·9; iron and steel, 8·8; inorganic and organic chemicals, 6·5. Major exports: electrical machinery and equipment, 32·9; textiles and clothing, 27·3; power generation equipment, 19·1; footwear and parts thereof, 8·7; toys and games, 7·7; iron and steel, 6·4. China is now the world's largest importer of steel, having overtaken the USA in 2002. Chinese exports have doubled in just over five years, largely thanks to foreign investment. The value of its exports is exceeded only by Germany and the USA.

Main import suppliers, 2000; Hong Kong, 21·8%; Japan, 18·6%; South Korea, 10·3%; USA, 9·6%. Main export markets in 2000: USA, 33·2%; Hong Kong, 26·7%; Japan, 17·9%; Germany, 5·0%. Customs duties with Taiwan were abolished in 1980. Trade with the European Union is fast expanding, having doubled since 1999.

COMMUNICATIONS

Roads

The total road length in 2002 was 1,765,000 km, including 25,000 km of motorways (there had not been any motorways as recently as the mid-1980s). 10,563m. tonnes of freight and 14,027m. persons were transported by road in 2001. The number of civil motor vehicles reached 18·02m., including 9·93m. buses and cars and 7·65m. trucks in 2001. There were 773,137 traffic accidents in 2002, with 109,381 fatalities.

Rail

In 2001 there were 70,100 km of railway including 22,600 km multiple-tracked and 17,000 km electrified. Gauge is standard except for some 600 mm track in Yunnan. Passenger-km travelled in 2001 came to 476·7bn. and freight tonne-km to 1,457·5bn. There are metro systems in Beijing, Guangzhou, Shanghai and Tianjin.

Civil Aviation

There are major international airports at Beijing, Guangzhou (Baiyun), Hong Kong (Chek Lap Kok) and Shanghai (Hongqiao and Pu Dong). At the end of 2001 there were 139 airports for regular flights. The national and major airlines are state-owned, except Shanghai Airlines (75% municipality-owned, 25% private) and Shenzhen Airlines (private). The leading Chinese airlines operating scheduled services in 1999 were China Southern Airlines (13,266,700 passengers), China Eastern Airlines (8,253,100), Air China (6,521,200), China Southwest Airlines (4,507,600), China Northern Airlines (4,034,000), China Yunnan Airlines (3,018,500), China Northwest Airlines (2,882,500) and Xinjiang Airlines (1,361,400). Other Chinese airlines include Changan Airlines, China National Aviation, Fujian Airlines, Hainan Airlines, Shandong Airlines, Shanghai Airlines, Shanxi Airlines, Shenzhen Airlines, Sichuan Airlines and Xiamen Airlines.

In 2001 the busiest airport was Hong Kong (Chek Lap Kok), with 32,026,944 passengers (31,846,744 on international flights), followed by Beijing, with 24,176,495 passengers (17,000,891 on domestic flights), Guangzhou (Baiyun), with 13,829,250 passengers (12,409,719 on domestic flights) and Shanghai (Hongqiao), with 13,761,410 passengers (8,886,672 on domestic flights). By the end of 2001 China had a total of 1,143 scheduled flight routes, of which 1,009 were domestic air routes, reaching 130 cities, and 134 were international air routes, reaching 62 cities in 33 countries.

Shipping

In 2000 the merchant fleet consisted of 3,322 vessels (561 oil tankers), totalling 16·50m. GRT (oil tankers, 2·25m. GRT).

In 2003, 2,011m. tonnes of freight were handled in major coastal ports, including: Shanghai, 316·2m tonnes; Ningbo, 185·4m.; Guangzhou (Canton), 171·9m.; Tianjin, 161·8m.; Qingdao, 140·9m.; Qinhuangdao, 125·6m.; Dalian, 126·0m. Cargo traffic at Tianjin grew at an average annual rate of 17·3% between 1998 and 2002, the highest rate of growth of any port in the world over the same period. Shanghai handled 6·33m. 20-ft equivalent units (TEUs) in 2001, making it the world's fifth busiest container port in terms of number of containers handled. Construction began in 2002 on the 14·31bn. yuan Yangshan deep-water port that should make Shanghai the world's third busiest port. On completion in 2020 it is estimated that it will have a capacity of 13m. TEUs.

In Jan. 2001 the first legal direct shipping links between the Chinese mainland and Taiwanese islands in more than 50 years were inaugurated.

Inland waterways totalled 121,500 km in 2001. 1,326·7m. tonnes of freight and 186·45m. passengers were carried. In June 2003 the Three Gorges Reservoir on the Chang Jiang River, the largest water control project in the world, reached sufficient depth to support the resumption of passenger and cargo shipping.

Telecommunications

In 2003 there were 263·0m. main telephone lines (209·2 per 1,000 persons) and 269·0m. mobile phone subscribers (214·0 per 1,000 persons), making China the biggest market for both fixed-line users and mobile phones in the world. The two main mobile operators are China Mobile and China Unicom. The main landline operators are China Telecom and China Netcom. There were 59·1m. Internet users in 2002. At the beginning of 1998 there had only been around 500,000 users. By 2007 Chinese is expected to have overtaken English as the most-used language on the Internet. In 2002, 35·5m. PCs were in use (27·6 per 1,000 inhabitants). There were 2·8m. fax machines in 2002.

Postal Services

There were 63,555 post offices in 2003. The use of *Pinyin* transcription of place names has been requested for mail to addresses in China (*e.g.*, 'Beijing' not 'Peking').

SOCIAL INSTITUTIONS

Justice

Six new codes of law (including criminal and electoral) came into force in 1980, to regularize the legal unorthodoxy of previous years. There is no provision for *habeas corpus*. The death penalty has been extended from treason and murder to include rape, embezzlement, smuggling, fraud, theft, drug-dealing, bribery and robbery with violence. There were 78 confirmed executions in 2005 (although there are believed to have been many more). Amnesty International reported at least 1,770 executions in 2005. China carries out more executions every year than any other country. 'People's courts' are divided into some 30 higher, 200 intermediate and 2,000 basic-level courts, and headed by the Supreme People's Court. The latter, the highest state judicial organ, tries cases, hears appeals and supervises the people's courts. It is responsible to the National People's Congress and its Standing Committee. People's courts are composed of a president, vice-presidents, judges and 'people's assessors' who are the equivalent of jurors. 'People's conciliation committees' are charged with settling minor disputes. There are also special military courts. Procuratorial powers and functions are exercised by the Supreme People's Procuracy and local procuracies.

The population in penal institutions in 2002 was 1,512,000 (117 per 100,000 of national population).

Education

An educational reform of 1985 planned to phase in compulsory nine-year education consisting of six years of primary schooling and three years of secondary schooling, to replace a previous five-year system.

In mainland China the 2000 population census revealed the following levels of educational attainment: 45·71m. people had finished university education; 141·09m. had received senior secondary education; 429·89m. had received junior secondary education; and 451·91m. had had primary education. 85·07m. people over 15 years of age or 6·72% of the population were illiterate, although this compared favourably with a 15·88% rate of illiteracy recorded in the 1990 census. In 2000 there were 175,836 kindergartens with 22·44m. children and 856,000 teachers; 553,662 primary schools with 130·13m. pupils and 5·86m. teachers; 89,763 secondary schools (of which: 14,564 senior secondary; 62,704 junior secondary; 3,646 specialized; and 8,849 vocational) with 83·61m. pupils and 4·48m. teachers. There were also 378,000 children at 1,539 special education schools. Institutes of higher education, including universities, numbered 1,225 in 2001, with 7·19m. students (a substantial increase from 5·56m. in 2000) and 532,000 teachers. In 2003, 17% of school-leavers went to university, compared to fewer than 3% in the 1980s. A national system of student loans was established in 1999. Every year 25,000 Chinese go abroad to study, making it the largest exporter of students in the world.

There are more than 1,300 non-governmental private higher education institutions (including 12 private universities) with 1·5m. students, or 39% of the total college and university students nationwide.

There is an Academy of Sciences with provincial branches. An Academy of Social Sciences was established in 1977.

In 1999 total expenditure on education came to 334,904m. yuan; government appropriation was 228,717m. yuan.

Health

Medical treatment is free only for certain groups of employees, but where costs are incurred they are partly borne by the patient's employing organization.

At the end of 2001 there were 330,000 health institutions throughout China, with a total of 3·19m. beds. The 4·49m. health workers included 2·09m. doctors and 1·28m. senior and junior nurses. There were also 6,025 anti-epidemic and disease prevention stations with 220,000 health workers, and 2,539 maternal and child health care institutions with 80,000 health workers. Rural townships had 50,000 commune hospitals with 740,000 beds and 1·03m. health workers. 89·7% of villages across China had medical stations, employing 1·28m. rural doctors and health workers.

Approximately 1m. Chinese were HIV-infected in 2002. Some suggestions indicate that there may be as many as 10m. HIV-positive people by 2010.

In the first half of 2003 China was struck by an epidemic of a pneumonia-type virus identified as SARS (severe acute respiratory syndrome). The virus was first detected in southern China and was subsequently reported in over 30 other countries. According to the Ministry of Health, by the time the outbreak had been contained a total of 5,327 cases had been reported on the Chinese mainland; 4,959 patients were cured and discharged from hospital, and 349 died.

In 1996 some 62% of males smoked, but fewer than 4% of females. The rate among males has been gradually rising over the past 15 years whilst that among females has gradually gone down.

In 2001 approximately 142m. people, then representing 11% of the population, were undernourished. In 1979, 22% of the population had been undernourished.

Welfare

In 2000 there were 42,103 social welfare institutions with 843,000 inmates. Numbers (in 1,000) of beneficiaries of relief funds: persons in poor rural households, 16,676; in poor urban households, 1,556; persons in rural households entitled to 'the five guarantees' (food, clothing, medical care, housing, education for children or funeral expenses), 2,706; retired, laid-off or disabled workers, 497. The major relief funds (in 1,000 yuan) in 2000 were: families of deceased or disabled servicemen, 10,766,050; poor households, 1,648,260; orphaned, disabled, old and young persons, 1,957,370; urban and rural welfare homes (1999), 2,866,620.

RELIGION

Non-religious persons account for 52% of the population. The government accords legality to five religions only: Buddhism, Islam, Protestantism, Roman Catholicism and Taoism. Confucianism, Buddhism and Taoism have long been practised. Confucianism has no ecclesiastical organization and appears rather as a philosophy of ethics and government. Taoism—of Chinese origin—copied Buddhist ceremonial soon after the arrival of Buddhism two millennia ago. Buddhism in return adopted many Taoist beliefs and practices. A more tolerant attitude towards religion had emerged by 1979, and the government's Bureau of Religious Affairs was reactivated.

Ceremonies of reverence to ancestors have been observed by the whole population regardless of philosophical or religious beliefs.

A new quasi-religious movement, Falun Gong, was founded in 1992, but has since been banned by the authorities. The movement claims it has some 100m. adherents, although the Chinese government has maintained the real number is closer to 2m.

Muslims are found in every province of China, being most numerous in the Ningxia-Hui Autonomous Region, Yunnan, Shaanxi, Gansu, Hebei, Henan, Shandong, Sichuan, Xinjiang and Shanxi. They totalled 18,360,000 in 2001.

Roman Catholicism has had a footing in China for more than three centuries. In 2002 there were an estimated 4m. Catholic believers, 4,000 clergy and 4,600 churches and meeting places. Catholics are members of the Patriotic Catholic Association, which declared its independence from Rome in 1958. Protestants are members of the All-China Conference of Protestant Churches. In 2002 they numbered 10m. There were an estimated 76,540,000 Christians in total in 2001.

In 2001 there were also estimated to be 256,260,000 Chinese folk-religionists, 152,990,000 atheists, 108,110,000 Buddhists and 1,280,000 advocates of traditional beliefs.

Legislation of 1994 prohibits foreign nationals from setting up religious organizations.

CULTURE

Beijing will host the Olympic Games in 2008, from 8 to 24 Aug. Shanghai will be hosting Expo 2010.

World Heritage Sites

There are 31 sites in the People's Republic of China that appear on the UNESCO World Heritage List. They are (with year entered on list): the Great Wall of China (1987), Zhoukoudian, the Peking Man site (1987), Beijing imperial palaces (1987), mausoleum of first Qing dynasty emperor, Beijing (1987), Taishan mountain (1987), Mogao Caves (1987), Huangshan mountain (1990), Huanglong Scenic Reserve (1992), Jiuzhaigou National Reserve (1992), Wulingyuan Scenic Reserve (1992), Chengde summer palace and temples (1994), Potala palace, Lhasa (1994), Wudang mountain (1994), Qufu temple, cemetery and mansion of Confucius (1994), the Leshan Buddha (1996), Mount Emei Scenic Reserve (1996), Lijiang old town (1997), Ping Yao old town (1997), Suzhou classical gardens (1997), Summer Palace, Beijing (1998), Temple of Heaven, Beijing (1998), Mount Wuyi (1999), Dazu rock carvings (1999), Mount Qincheng and Dujiangyan irrigation system (2000), Xidi and Hongcun ancient villages, Anhui (2000), Longmen grottoes (2000), Ming and Qing dynasty tombs (2000), the Yungang Grottoes (2001), the Three Parallel Rivers of Yunnan Protected Areas (2003), the Capital Cities and Tombs of the Ancient Koguryo Kingdom (2004) and the historic centre of Macao (2005).

Broadcasting

In 2000 there were 370m. television receivers in China (the greatest number in any country in the world). In 1980 there had been just 9m., representing an increase of 361m. between 1980 and 2000, or more TV sets than were in use in the USA (the country with the second highest number of sets) in 2000. At the end of 2001 there were 358 TV stations, offering programmes to 94·1% of the total population. China Central Television, the largest national station, features 11 channels with a daily air time of more than 200 hours. Cable TV subscribers numbered 88·03m. by the end of 2001 (compared to 50m. in 1997). There were 311 radio broadcasting stations and 770 medium- and short-wave transmitting and relaying stations throughout China at the end of 2001, reaching 92·9% of the population. The Central People's Broadcasting Station, the official radio broadcasting station, has seven channels (including services to Taiwan) and broadcasts for over 100 hours a day. In 2000 there were 428m. radio receivers (only the USA has more).

Cinema

There were an estimated 2,000 regularly-used cinema screens in 2002. A total of 88 feature films and 66 scientific, documentary and cartoon films were produced in 2001.

Press

China has two news agencies: Xinhua (New China) News Agency (the nation's official agency) and China News Service. In 2002 there were 2,137 newspapers and about 8,700 magazines; 21,600m. copies of newspapers and 2,900m. copies of magazines were published in 2001. In 1980 there were fewer than 400 newspapers. The Communist Party newspaper is *Renmin Ribao* (People's Daily), which had a daily circulation of 2·1m. in 1999. The most widely read newspaper is *Sichuan Ribao* (Sichuan Daily), with a daily circulation of 8·0m. in 1999. In July 2003 the State Administration of Press and Publication abolished compulsory

subscription to state newspapers and magazines and funding for subscription-dependent publications, which amount to 40% of the press. By Nov. 2003, 673 newspapers had ceased publication.

There are over 560 publishing houses, producing 6,300m. volumes of books in 2001.

Tourism

36,803,000 tourists visited in 2002. The World Tourism Organization predicts that China will overtake France as the world's most visited destination by 2020 and become the world's fourth most important source of tourists to other countries. More than 16·5m. Chinese travelled abroad in 2002, nearly double the 1998 figure. Income from tourists in 2002 was US$20,385m.

Festivals

The lunar New Year, also known as the 'Spring Festival', is a time of great excitement for the Chinese people. The festivities get under way 22 days prior to the New Year date and continue for 15 days afterwards. Dates of the lunar New Year: Year of the Dog, 29 Jan. 2006; Year of the Pig, 18 Feb. 2007. Lantern Festival, or Yuanxiao Jie, is an important, traditional Chinese festival, which is on the 15th of the first month of the Chinese New Year. Guanyin's Birthday is on the 19th day of the second month of the Chinese lunar calendar. Guanyin is the Chinese goddess of mercy. Tomb Sweeping Day, as the name implies, is a day for visiting and cleaning the ancestral tomb and usually falls on 5 April. Dragon Boat Festival is called Duan Wu Jie in Chinese. The festival is celebrated on the 5th of the 5th month of the Chinese lunar calendar. The Moon Festival is on the 15th of the 8th lunar month. It is sometimes called Mid-Autumn Festival. The Moon Festival is an occasion for family reunion.

Libraries

At the end of 2001 there were 2,689 public libraries. The National Library of China, with 22m. items, is the largest library in Asia. Shanghai library is China's biggest provincial-level library.

Museums and Galleries

There were 1,394 museums in 2001, of which 118 were in Beijing.

DIPLOMATIC REPRESENTATIVES

Of China in the United Kingdom (49–51 Portland Pl., London, W1B 1JL)
Ambassador: Zha Peixin.

Of the United Kingdom in China (11 Guang Hua Lu, Jian Guo Men Wai, Beijing 100600)
Ambassador: Sir Christopher Hum, KCMG.

Of China in the USA (2300 Connecticut Ave., NW, Washington, D.C. 20008)
Ambassador: Zhou Wenzhong.

Of the USA in China (Xiu Shui Bei Jie 3, 100600 Beijing)
Ambassador: Clark T. Randt, Jr.

Of China to the United Nations
Ambassador: Wang Guangya.

Of China to the European Union
Ambassador: Guan Chengyuan.

FURTHER READING

State Statistical Bureau. *China Statistical Yearbook*
China Directory [in Pinyin and Chinese]. Tokyo, annual
Adshead, S. A. M., *China in World History*. Macmillan, London, 1999
Baum, R., *Burying Mao: Chinese Politics in the Age of Deng Xiaoping.* Princeton Univ. Press, 1994
Becker, Jasper, *The Chinese*. John Murray, London, 2000
Brown, Raj, *Overseas Chinese Merchants*. Macmillan, London, 1999
The Cambridge Encyclopaedia of China. 2nd ed. CUP, 1991
The Cambridge History of China. 14 vols. CUP, 1978 ff.

Chang, David Wen-Wei and Chuang, Richard Y., *The Politics of Hong Kong's Reversion to China*. Macmillan, London, 1999

Cook, Sarah, Yao, Shujie and Zhuang, Juzhong, (eds.) *The Chinese Economy Under Transition*. Macmillan, London, 1999

De Crespigny, R., *China This Century*. 2nd ed. OUP, 1993

Dixin, Xu and Chengming, Wu, (eds.) *Chinese Capitalism, 1522–1840*. Macmillan, London, 1999

Dreyer, J. T., *China's Political System: Modernization and Tradition*. 2nd ed. London, 1996

Evans, R., *Deng Xiaoping and the Making of Modern China*. London, 1993

Fairbank, J. K., *The Great Chinese Revolution 1800–1985*. London, 1987.—*China: a New History*. Harvard Univ. Press, 1992

Glassman, R. M., *China in Transition: Communism, Capitalism and Democracy*. New York, 1991

Goldman, M., *Sowing the Seeds of Democracy in China: Political Reform in the Deng Xiaoping Era*. Harvard Univ. Press, 1994

Hayford, C. W., *China*. [Bibliography] ABC-Clio, Oxford and Santa Barbara (CA), 1997

Ho, Samuel P. S. and Kueh, Y. Y. (eds.) *Sustainable Economic Development in South China*. Macmillan, London, 1999

Huang, R., *China: a Macro History*. 2nd ed. Armonk (NY), 1997

Hunter, A. and Sexton, J., *Contemporary China*. Macmillan, London, 1999

Kruger, Rayne, *All Under Heaven: A Complete History of China*. John Wiley, Chichester, 2004

Lieberthal, K. G., *From Revolution through Reform*. New York, 1995.—and Lampton, D. M. (eds.) *Bureaucracy, Politics and Decision-Making in Post-Mao China*. California Univ. Press, 1992

Lu, Aiguo, *China and the Global Economy Since 1840*. Macmillan, London, 1999

Ma, Jun, *Chinese Economy in the 1990s*. Macmillan, London, 1999

MacFarquhar, R. (ed.) *The Politics of China: the Eras of Mao and Deng*. 2nd ed. CUP, 1997.—*The Origins of the Cultural Revolution*. 3 vols. Columbia Univ. Press, 1998

Mackerras, C. and Yorke, A., *The Cambridge Handbook of Contemporary China*. CUP, 1991

Mok, Ka-Ho, *Social and Political Development in Post-Reform China*. Macmillan, London, 1999

Nolan, Peter, *China and the Global Economy*. Palgrave, Basingstoke, 2001

Phillips, R. T., *China Since 1911*. London, 1996

Roberts, J. A. G., *A History of China*. Palgrave, Basingstoke, 2001

Saich, Tony, *Governance and Politics of China*. 2nd ed. Palgrave Macmillan, Basingstoke, 2004

Schram, S. (ed.) *Mao's Road to Power: Revolutionary Writings 1912–1949*. 4 vols. Harvard, 1998

Shen, Xiobai, *The Chinese Road to High Technology*. Macmillan, London, 1999

Sheng Hua, *et al.*, *China: from Revolution to Reform*. London, 1992

Shenkar, Oded, *The Rising Chinese Economy and Its Impact on the Global Economy, the Balance of Power, and Your Job*. Wharton School Publishing, Philadelphia, 2004

Shirk, S. L., *The Political Logic of Economic Reform in China*. Univ. of California Press, 1993

Short, Philip, *Mao: A Life*. Henry Holt, New York and Hodder and Stoughton, London, 2000

Spence, Jonathan, D., *The Chan's Great Continent: China in Western Minds*. W. W. Norton, New York, 1998.—*Mao Zedong*. Viking, New York and Weidenfeld & Nicolson, London, 2000

Suyin, H., *Eldest Son, Zhou Enlai and The Making of Modern China*. Kodansha Globe, 1995

Turner, Barry, (ed.) *China Profiled*. Macmillan, London, 1999

Womack, B. (ed.) *Contemporary Chinese Politics in Historical Perspective*. CUP, 1992

Yan, Yanni, *International Joint Ventures in China*. Macmillan, London, 1999

Yeung, Henry Wai-Cheung and Olds, Kristopher, (eds.) *The Globalisation of Chinese Business Firms*. Macmillan, London, 1999

Zhang, Xiao-Guang, *China's Trade Patterns and International Comparative Advantage*. Macmillan, London, 1999

Other more specialized titles are listed under TERRITORY AND POPULATION; TIBET; AGRICULTURE; INTERNATIONAL TRADE.

National Statistical Office: National Bureau of Statistics, 75 Yuetan Nanjie, Beijing 100826.
Website: http://www.stats.gov.cn/

Hong Kong

Xianggang

Population projection, 2010: 7·42m.
GDP per capita, 2003: (PPP$) 27,179
HDI/world rank: 0·916/22

KEY HISTORICAL EVENTS

Hong Kong island and the southern tip of the Kowloon peninsula were ceded in perpetuity to the British Crown in 1841 and 1860 respectively. The area lying immediately to the north of Kowloon known as the New Territories was leased to Britain for 99 years in 1898. Talks began in Sept. 1982 between Britain and China over the future of Hong Kong after the lease expiry in 1997. On 19 Dec. 1984 the two countries signed a Joint Declaration by which Hong Kong became, with effect from 1 July 1997, a Special Administrative Region of the People's Republic of China, enjoying a high degree of autonomy and vested with executive, legislative and independent judicial power, including that of final adjudication. The existing social and economic systems were to remain unchanged for another 50 years. This 'one country, two systems' principle, embodied in the Basic Law, became the constitution for the Hong Kong Special Administrative Region of the People's Republic of China.

TERRITORY AND POPULATION

Hong Kong ('Xianggang' in Mandarin *Pinyin*) island is situated off the southern coast of the Chinese mainland 32 km east of the mouth of the Pearl River. The area of the island is 79·99 sq. km. It is separated from the mainland by a fine natural harbour. On the opposite side is the peninsula of Kowloon (46·27 sq. km). Total area of the Territory is 1,091 sq. km, a large part of it being steep and unproductive hillside. Country parks and special areas cover over 40% of the land area. Since 1945 the government has reclaimed over 5,400 ha. from the sea, principally from the seafronts of Hong Kong and Kowloon, facing the harbour. The 'New Territories' are on the mainland, north of Kowloon.

Based on the results of the 2001 population census Hong Kong's resident population in March 2001 was 6,708,389 and the population density 6,237 per sq. km. 59·7% of the population was born in Hong Kong, 33·7% in other parts of China and 6·6% in the rest of the world. The estimated population in 2005 was 7·04m.

In 2003, 100% of the population lived in urban areas. Some 10,600 persons emigrated in 2001. The British Nationality Scheme enables persons to acquire citizenship without leaving Hong Kong. There were 53,655 legal entrants (one-way permit holders) from the mainland of China in 2001.

The UN gives a projected population for 2010 of 7·42m.

The official languages are Chinese and English.

SOCIAL STATISTICS

Annual population growth rate, 2001, 0·9%. Vital statistics, 2001: known births, 48,200; known deaths, 33,400; registered marriages, 32,800. Rates (per 1,000): birth, 7·2; death, 5·0; marriage, 4·8; infant mortality, 2001, 2·6 per 1,000 live births (one of the lowest rates in the world). Expectation of life at birth, 2003: males, 78·7 years; females, 84·6. The median age for marrying in 2001 was 31·3 years for males and 28·1 for females. Total fertility rate, 2001, 0·9 child per woman.

CLIMATE

The climate is sub-tropical, tending towards temperate for nearly half the year, the winter being cool and dry and the summer hot and humid, May to Sept. being the wettest months. Normal temperatures are Jan. 60°F (15·8°C), July 84°F (28·8°C). Annual rainfall 87" (2,214·3 mm).

THE BRITISH ADMINISTRATION

Hong Kong used to be administered by the Hong Kong government. The Governor was the head of government and presided over the *Executive Council*, which advised the Governor on all important matters. The last British Governor was Chris Patten. In Oct. 1996 the Executive Council consisted of three *ex officio* members and ten appointed members, of whom one was an official member. The chief functions of the *Legislative Council* were to enact laws, control public expenditure and put questions to the administration on matters of public interest. The Legislative Council elected in Sept. 1995 was, for the first time, constituted solely by election. It comprised 60 members, of whom 20 were elected from geographical constituencies, 30 from functional constituencies encompassing all eligible persons in a workforce of 2·9m., and ten from an election committee formed by members of 18 district boards. A president was elected from and by the members.

At the elections on 17 Sept. 1995 turn-out for the geographical seats was 35·79%, and for the functional seats (21 of which were contested), 40·42%. The Democratic Party and its allies gained 29 seats, the Liberal Party 10 and the pro-Beijing Democratic Alliance 6. The remaining seats went to independents.

CONSTITUTION AND GOVERNMENT

In Dec. 1995 the Standing Committee of China's National People's Congress set up a Preparatory Committee of 150 members (including 94 from Hong Kong) to oversee the retrocession of Hong Kong to China on 1 July 1997. In Nov. 1996 the Preparatory Committee nominated a 400-member Selection Committee to select the Chief Executive of Hong Kong and a provisional legislature to replace the Legislative Council. The Selection Committee was composed of Hong Kong residents, with 60 seats reserved for delegates to the National People's Congress and appointees of the People's Political Consultative Conference. On 11 Dec. 1996 Tung Chee Hwa was elected Chief Executive by 80% of the Selection Committee's votes.

On 21 Dec. 1996 the Selection Committee selected a provisional legislature which began its activities in Jan. 1997 while the Legislative Council was still functioning. In Jan. 1997 the provisional legislature started its work by enacting legislation which would be applicable to the Hong Kong Special Administrative Region and compatible with the Basic Law.

Constitutionally Hong Kong is a Special Administrative Region of the People's Republic of China. The Basic Law enables Hong Kong to retain a high degree of autonomy. It provides that the legislative, judicial and administrative systems which were previously in operation are to remain in place. The Special Administrative Region Government is also empowered to decide on Hong Kong's monetary and economic policies independent of China.

In July 1997 the first-past-the-post system of returning members from geographical constituencies to the Legislative Council was replaced by proportional representation. There were 20 directly elected seats out of 60 for the first elections to the Legislative Council following Hong Kong's return to Chinese sovereignty, increasing in accordance with the Basic Law to 24 for the 2000 election with 36 indirectly elected. In the Sept. 2004 Legislative Council election 30 of the 60 seats were directly elected.

In July 2002 a new accountability or 'ministerial' system was introduced, under which the Chief Executive nominates for appointment 14 policy secretaries, who report directly to the Chief Executive. The Chief Executive is aided by the Executive Council, consisting of the three senior Secretaries of Department (the Chief Secretary, the Financial Secretary and the Secretary for Justice) and eleven other secretaries plus five non-officials.

RECENT ELECTIONS

In the Legislative Council election held on 12 Sept. 2004 turnout was 55·6%, up from 43·6% at the 2000 vote. 30 of the 60 seats were directly elected, the other 30 being returned by committees and professional associations. Pro-Beijing parties won 34 of the 60 seats (34 in 2000) including 12 of the 30 that were directly elected; pro-democracy parties won 25 (22 in 2000), including 18 of the 30 that were directly elected. An independent won the remaining seat (independents won four seats in 2000).

CURRENT ADMINISTRATION

In Feb. 2006 the government of the Hong Kong Special Administrative Region comprised:

Chief Executive: Donald Tsang, OBE, JP; b. 1944 (since 24 June 2005, having previously been acting Chief Executive from 12 March 2005–1 June 2005).

Chief Secretary for Administration: Rafael Hui Si-yan. *Financial Secretary:* Henry Tang, JP. *Secretary for Justice:* Wong Yan-lung. *Commerce, Industry and Technology:* Joseph Wong. *Housing, Planning and Lands:* Michael Suen. *Education and Manpower:* Arthur Li. *Health, Welfare and Food:* York Chow. *Civil Service:* Denise Yue. *Home Affairs:* Dr Patrick Ho. *Security:* Ambrose Lee. *Economic Development and Labour:* Stephen Ip Shu-kwan. *Environment, Transport and Works:* Dr Sarah Liao. *Financial Services and the Treasury:* Frederick Ma Si-hang. *Constitutional Affairs:* Stephen Lam, JP.

Government Website: http://www.info.gov.hk

ECONOMY

Industry accounted for 12·4% of GDP in 2002 and services 87·5%.

According to the anti-corruption organization *Transparency International*, Hong Kong ranked 15th in the world in a 2005 survey of the countries and regions with the least corruption in business and government. It received 8·3 out of 10 in the annual index.

Income tax is a flat 15% and only 25% of the population pay any tax at all. 6% of the population pays 80% of the total income tax bill. Hong Kong represents 20% of China's total worth.

Overview

Hong Kong has a per capita GDP that compares favourably with other OECD countries. Its economic rise was founded on its position as an international trade emporium. After developing as a successful low-cost, labour-intensive manufacturing centre, the structure of the economy has now shifted towards services. The island is dependant on trade for food and other resources. In 1998 and the first quarter of 1999 Hong Kong sank into recession as a result of the Asian financial crisis. Later in 1999 the economy bounced back and in 2000 grew by 10·2%, the highest rate since 1987. In the second quarter of 2001 the economy sank back into recession for three consecutive quarters as a result of the slowdown in the US and global economy. After briefly rebounding, the economy shrank again for one quarter in 2003 as a result of the SARS outbreak. However, the economy again proved resilient and in 2004 and 2005 grew strongly on the back of a rise in Chinese tourism, strong global demand for its exports and growing domestic consumer confidence.

Hong Kong's main engine of growth is its re-export business to and from China. Despite the overwhelming importance of China to Hong Kong's economy, the USA also plays an important role as the second most important export destination. Hong Kong also has significant economic relations with the rest of East Asia and Western Europe.

Currency

The unit of currency is the *Hong Kong dollar* (HKD) of 100 *cents*. Banknotes are issued by the Hongkong and Shanghai Banking

Corporation and the Standard Chartered Bank, and, from May 1994, the Bank of China. Total money supply was HK$216,760m. in May 2002 and gold reserves 67,000 troy oz in June 2002. In 2004 foreign exchange reserves were US$123,540m., up from US$55,398m. in 1995. Hong Kong has been experiencing deflation every year since 1999. There was deflation of 2·6% in 2003 and 0·4% in 2004.

Budget

The total government revenue and expenditure for financial years ending 31 March were as follows (in HK$1m.):

	1998	1999	2000	2001	2002
Revenue[1]	281,226	216,115	232,995	225,060	175,559
Expenditure[2]	194,241	218,811	214,533	224,791	238,585

[1]Including the change in the net worth of investments up to 31 Oct. 1998.
[2]Excluding Capital Investment Fund.

Public expenditure in 2002 (based on revised estimates 2001–02) was divided as follows (HK$1bn.): education, 52·6; support, 35·7; health, 34·0; housing, 33·2; social welfare, 30·7; security, 28·1; infrastructure, 24·7; economic, 14·1; environment and food, 11·3; community and external affairs, 8·5.

The final reserve balance as at 31 March 2002 was HK$372·5bn.

Performance

Total GDP was US$163·0bn. in 2004. Real GDP growth rates (based on IMF statistics):

1995	1996	1997	1998	1999	2000	2001	2002	2003	2004
3·9%	4·3%	5·1%	–5·0%	3·4%	10·2%	0·5%	1·9%	3·2%	8·1%

With the economic contracting by 5·0%, 1998 saw Hong Kong's most severe recession since the 1970s.

Banking and Finance

The Hong Kong Monetary Authority acts as a central bank. The *Chief Executive* is Joseph Yam. As at Dec. 2003 there were 133 banks licensed under the Banking Ordinance, of which 26 were locally incorporated, 46 restricted licence banks, 45 deposit-taking companies and 94 representative offices of foreign banks. Licensed bank deposits were HK$2,601,971m. in June 1997; restricted licence bank deposits were HK$62,033m. There are three banks of issue: Bank of China (Hong Kong); The Hong Kong and Shanghai Banking Corporation; and Standard Chartered Bank.

In March 2000 the stock exchange, the futures exchange and the clearing settlement merged into Hong Kong Exchanges and Clearing (HKEx).

Weights and Measures

The metric system is standard but British Imperial and traditional Chinese measurements are still in use.

ENERGY AND NATURAL RESOURCES

Environment

Hong Kong's carbon dioxide emissions from the consumption and flaring of fossil fuels in 2002 were the equivalent of 8·8 tonnes per capita.

Electricity

Installed capacity was 11·8m. kW in 2002. Production in 2002 was 34·31bn. kWh. Consumption in 2002 was 42·33bn. kWh.

Water

There are 17 impounding reservoirs with a total capacity of 586m. cu. metres. Raw water is also purchased from the Guangdong Province of China (729m. cu. metres in 2001). Consumption in 2001 was 940m. cu. metres.

Agriculture

The local agricultural industry is directed towards the production of high quality fresh food through intensive land use and modern farming techniques. Out of the territory's total land area of 1,097 sq. km, only 27 sq. km is currently farmed. In 1999 local production accounted for 11·7% of fresh vegetables, 18·2% of live poultry and 22·2% of live pigs consumed. Pig production increased by about 17% compared with the previous year. Crop production continued to fall as vegetable prices fell and land was redeveloped for other uses. The common crops cultivated are leafy vegetables, high value cut flowers and ornamental plants. In 1999, 48,000 tonnes of vegetables were produced. Poultry production was 12,650 tonnes. There were 415,400 pigs in 1999.

Forestry

Timber production in 1995 was 200,000 cu. metres.

Fisheries

In 1999 the capture and mariculture fisheries supplied about 36% of seafood consumed in Hong Kong and pond fish farms produced about 10% of the freshwater fish consumed. The capture fishing industry employs some 5,170 fishing vessels and some 12,900 local fishermen. In 2003 the industry produced 157,444 tonnes of fisheries produce. Some 75,000 tonnes were supplied for local consumption and the remainder landed or exported outside Hong Kong. On the other hand, there are 26 fish culture zones occupying a total sea area of 209 ha. with some 1,450 licensed operators. The estimated production in 1999 was 1,250 tonnes, or 7% of local consumption of live marine fish. The inland fish ponds, covering a total of 1,094 ha., produced 4,500 of freshwater fish in 1999. The first phase of the artificial reefs programme was successfully completed in 1999 with more than 110 species of fish recorded on the reefs.

INDUSTRY

The leading companies by market capitalization in Hong Kong in Nov. 2005 were: China Mobile (Hong Kong), a mobile telecommunications company (US$96·8bn.); Hutchison Whampoa, a diversified industrial conglomerate (US$40·4bn.); and CNOOC, an oil and natural gas company (US$27·3bn.).

An economic policy based on free enterprise and free trade, a skilled workforce, an efficient commercial infrastructure, the modern and efficient sea-port (including container shipping terminals) and airport facilities, a geographical position relative to markets in North America and traditional trading links with the UK all contribute to Hong Kong's success as a modern industrial territory. Links with China have been growing increasingly strong in recent years and will remain so.

In Sept. 2001 there were 19,801 manufacturing establishments employing 209,329 persons. Other establishment statistics by product type (and persons engaged) were: printing, publishing and allied industries, 4,778 (42,963); textiles and clothing, 3,696 (58,821); plastics, 973 (5,938); electronics, 748 (20,939); watches and clocks, 347 (2,945); shipbuilding, 325 (3,173); electrical appliances, 49 (390).

Labour

In 2001 the size of the labour force (synonymous with the economically active population) was 3,427,100 (1,461,900 females). The persons engaged in Sept. 2001 included 1,027,000 people in wholesale, retail and import/export trades, restaurants and hotels, 437,000 in finance, insurance, real estate and business services, 209,000 in manufacturing, 177,000 in the civil service and 77,000 in construction sites (manual workers only).

The seasonally-adjusted unemployment rate for July–Sept. 2002 was 7·4%, compared to the equivalent rate for July–Sept. 1997 of 2·1%.

EXTERNAL ECONOMIC RELATIONS

Imports and Exports

Industry is mainly export-oriented. In 2003 the total value of imports (c.i.f.) was HK$1,805·8bn. and total exports (f.o.b.) HK$1,742·4bn. The main suppliers of imports in 2003 were the mainland of China (43·5%), Japan (11·9%), Taiwan (6·9%), USA (5·5%) and Singapore (5·0%). In 2003, 42·6% of total exports went to the mainland of China, 18·6% to the USA, 5·2% to Japan, 3·3% to the United Kingdom and 3·2% to Germany.

The chief import items in 2001 (in HK$1m.) were consumer goods (537,967), raw materials and semi-manufactures (511,367), capital goods (428,147) and foodstuffs (60,353). Domestic exports included: clothing and accessories, 72,240; electrical machinery and parts, 20,322; textiles and fabrics, 8,193; parts and accessories suitable for use solely with office machines and automatic data processing machines, 4,705.

Visible trade normally carries an adverse balance which is offset by a favourable balance of invisible trade, in particular transactions in connection with air transportation, shipping, tourism and banking services.

Hong Kong has a free exchange market. Foreign merchants may remit profits or repatriate capital. Import and export controls are kept to the minimum, consistent with strategic requirements.

COMMUNICATIONS

Roads

In 1998 there were 1,865 km of roads, more than 900 km of which were in the New Territories. There are eight major road tunnels, including two under Victoria Harbour. In 1999 there were 390,000 passenger cars, 116,000 trucks and vans, 19,000 buses and coaches, and 33,000 motorcycles and mopeds. There were 14,714 road accidents in 1999, 217 fatal. A total of 14·8m. tonnes of cargo were transported by road in 1996.

Rail

The railway network covers around 143 km. The electrified Kowloon-Canton Railway runs for 34 km from the terminus at Hung Hom in Kowloon to the border point at Lo Wu. It carried 255m. passengers in 1998. In 1996, 939,000 tonnes of cargo were transported by rail. A light rail system (32 km and 57 stops) is operated by the Kowloon-Canton Railway Corporation in Tuen Mun, Yuen Long and Tin Shui Wai; it carried 105m. passengers in 1998.

The electric tramway on the northern shore of Hong Kong Island commenced operating in 1904 and has a total track length of 16 km. The Peak Tram, a funicular railway connecting the Peak district with the lower levels in Victoria, has a track length of 1,365 metres and a capacity of 120 passengers per trip.

A metro, the Mass Transit Railway system, comprises 74 km with 43 stations and carried 2·3m. passengers per weekday in 1998.

The Airport Express Line (35 km) opened in 1998 and carried a total of 3·9m. passengers in that year.

In 1996 a total of 3·9m. passenger journeys were made on public transport (including local railways, buses, etc.).

Civil Aviation

The new Chek Lap Kok airport, built on reclaimed land off Lantau Island to the west of Hong Kong, opened on 6 July 1998, replacing Hong Kong International Airport (Kai Tak), which was situated on the north shore of Kowloon Bay. More than 70 airlines now operate scheduled services to and from Hong Kong. Cathay Pacific Airways, one of the three Hong Kong-based airlines, operates more than 530 passenger and cargo services weekly to Europe (including 18 passenger and 10 cargo services per week to the UK), the Far and Middle East, South Africa, Australasia and North America. Cathay Pacific flew 197·6m. km in 1999 and carried 12,321,256 passengers in 2002. Hong Kong Dragon Airlines provides scheduled services to 19 cities in Mainland China and nine other destinations in Asia plus 14 cargo services per week to seven destinations (including six weekly services to the UK). AHK Air Hong Kong Ltd., an all-cargo operator, provides seven weekly scheduled services to and from Hong Kong with Incheon, Tokyo and Osaka as destinations. In 2002 (provisional figures), 206,640 aircraft arrived and departed and 33m. passengers and 2·48m. tonnes of freight were carried on aircraft. Hong Kong International Airport handled more international freight in 2001 than any other airport.

Hong Kong–Taipei and vice-versa is the most flown airline route in the world, with 5·43m. passengers flying between the two cities in 2001.

Shipping

The port of Hong Kong handled 22·0m. 20-ft equivalent units in 2004, making it the world's busiest container port. The Kwai Chung Container Port has 24 berths with 7,694 metres of quay backed by 275 ha. of cargo handling area. Merchant shipping in 2004 totalled 25,562,000 GRT, including oil tankers 5,416,000 GRT. In 2004, 35,900 ocean-going vessels, 117,540 river cargo vessels and 71,980 river passenger vessels called at Hong Kong. In 2004, 221m. tonnes of freight were handled. In 2004 vessels totalling 399,031,000 NRT entered ports and vessels totalling 399,025,000 NRT cleared.

Telecommunications

In Dec. 2001 there were 4,940,525 telephones (731 per 1,000 population), of which 1,764,623 were for business use and 2,161,151 were residential lines. There were also 409,000 fax machines in 2002.

The local fixed telecommunications network services (FTNS) market in Hong Kong was liberalized in 1995. Apart from the incumbent FTNS operator at that time, three new local FTNS operators were licensed. In July 1999 the Government invited the industry to apply for licences to operate local wireless fixed networks. On 18 Jan. 2000 the Government announced that five licences for the local fixed wireless FTNS services would be provided. This would further increase the choice of consumers in the local fixed market.

In Dec. 2000 there were six mobile phone operators providing 11 networks in Hong Kong. There were only 687,600 mobile phone subscribers in 1995, since when the sector has expanded substantially. In 2002 there were 6,395,700 mobile phone subscribers (94% of Hong Kong's population). In addition there were 29 radio paging operators in Nov. 2000 serving 333,990 users. The Internet market has also seen considerable growth. In April 2002 there were 4·35m. Internet users, up from 1·85m. in June 2000.

The external telecommunications services market has been fully liberalized since 1 Jan. 1999, and the external telecommunications facilities market was also liberalized starting from 1 Jan. 2000.

In 2002 there were 2·86m. PCs in use (422·9 per 1,000 persons).

Postal Services

In Dec. 2002 there were 131 post offices. In 2001 Hongkong Post handled 1,360m. letters and 923,000 parcels.

SOCIAL INSTITUTIONS

Justice

The Hong Kong Act of 1985 provided for Hong Kong ordinances to replace English laws in specified fields.

The courts of justice comprise the Court of Final Appeal (inaugurated 1 July 1997) which hears appeals on civil and criminal matters from the High Court; the High Court (consisting of the Court of Appeal and the Court of First Instance); the Lands Tribunal which determines on statutory claims for compensation over land and certain landlord and tenant matters; the District

Court (which includes the Family Court); the Magistracies (including the Juvenile Court); the Coroner's Court; the Labour Tribunal, which provides a quick and inexpensive method of settling disputes between employers and employees; the Small Claims Tribunal deals with monetary claims involving amounts not exceeding HK$50,000; and the Obscene Articles Tribunal.

While the High Court has unlimited jurisdiction in both civil and criminal matters, the District Court has limited jurisdiction. The maximum term of imprisonment it may impose is seven years. Magistracies exercise criminal jurisdiction over a wide range of offences, and the powers of punishment are generally restricted to a maximum of two years' imprisonment or a fine of HK$100,000.

After being in abeyance for 25 years, the death penalty was abolished in 1992.

71,962 crimes were reported in 1998, of which 14,682 were violent crimes. 40,422 people were arrested in 1998, of whom 9,207 were for violent crimes. The prison population was 12,900 in Sept. 2003 (184 per 100,000 of national population).

Education
Adult literacy was 93·5% in 2001 (96·9% among males and 89·6% among females). Universal basic education is available to all children aged from six to 15 years. In around three-quarters of the ordinary secondary day schools teaching has been in Cantonese since 1998–99, with about a quarter of ordinary secondary day schools still using English. In 1998 there were 175,073 pupils in 744 kindergartens (all private), 476,802 full-time students in 832 ordinary primary day schools (some 10·7% in private schools) and 455,872 in 37 government, 352 aided and 82 private ordinary secondary day schools.

There were 15,204 full-time and 32,543 part-time students enrolled in the seven Technical Institutes in the academic year 1998–99, and 5,220 full-time and 9,454 part-time students enrolled in the two Technical Colleges. The Hong Kong Technical Institutes and the Hong Kong Technical Colleges were renamed the Hong Kong Institute of Vocational Education in 1999.

The University of Hong Kong (founded 1911) had 10,687 full-time and 2,985 part-time students in the academic year of 1998–99, the Chinese University of Hong Kong (founded 1963), 10,271 full-time and 2,224 part-time students, the Hong Kong University of Science and Technology (founded 1991), 6,446 full-time and 710 part-time students, the Hong Kong Polytechnic University (founded 1972 as the Hong Kong Polytechnic), 11,646 full-time and 6,778 part-time students, the City University of Hong Kong (founded 1984 as the City Polytechnic of Hong Kong), 11,123 full-time and 5,241 part-time students, the Hong Kong Baptist University (founded 1956 as the Hong Kong Baptist College), 4,185 full-time and 517 part-time students, the Lingnan University (founded 1967 as the Lingnan College), 2,133 full-time and three part-time students, and the Hong Kong Institute of Education (founded 1997), 3,037 full-time and 5,954 part-time students.

Estimated total government expenditure on education in 1999–2000 was HK$55·2bn. In 2000–01 total expenditure on education came to 4·0% of GNP and 22·9% of total government spending.

Health
The Department of Health (DH) is the Government's health adviser and regulatory authority. The Hospital Authority (HA) is an independent body responsible for the management of all public hospitals. In 2002 there were 9,021 doctors on the local list, equivalent to 1·5 doctors per 1,000 population. In 2001 there were 1,900 dentists, 42,000 nurses and 136 midwives. In 2002 the total number of hospital beds was 35,100, including 29,432 beds in 41 public hospitals under the HA and 2,928 beds in 12 private hospitals. The bed-population ratio was 5·2 beds per thousand population.

The Chinese Medicine Ordinance was passed by the Legislative Council in July 1999 to establish a statutory framework to control the practice, use, manufacture and trading of Chinese medicine.

Recurrent spending on health amounts to US$4·15bn. (HK$324bn.), an increase of 4% in real terms over the latest estimated spending for 2001–02.

Welfare
Social welfare programmes include social security, family services, child care, services for the elderly, medical social services, youth and community work, probation, and corrections and rehabilitation. 181 non-governmental organizations are subsidized by public funds.

The government gives non-contributory cash assistance to needy families, unemployed able-bodied adults, the severely disabled and the elderly. Caseload as at 31 Dec. 2004 totalled 295,694. Victims of natural disasters, crimes of violence and traffic accidents are financially assisted. Estimated total government expenditure on social welfare for 2004–05 was HK$33·7bn.

RELIGION

In 2001 there were 4,970,000 Buddhists and Taoists, 290,000 Protestants and 280,000 Roman Catholics. The remainder of the population are followers of other religions.

CULTURE

Broadcasting
Broadcasting is regulated by the Broadcasting Authority, a statutory body comprising three government officers and nine non-official members.

There is a public broadcasting station, Radio Television Hong Kong (colour by PAL), which broadcasts seven channels (three Chinese, one English, one bilingual and one Putonhua service, and one for the relay of the BBC World Service), six of which provide a 24-hour service. Hong Kong Commercial Broadcasting Co. Ltd and Metro Broadcast Co. Ltd transmit commercial sound programmes on six channels. Television Broadcasts Ltd and Asia Television Ltd transmit domestic free television programme services in English and Chinese on four channels. Hong Kong Cable Television Ltd offers over 30 TV channels on a subscription basis. The PCCW VOD Ltd launched the world's first commercial scale video-on-demand programme service in March 1998. Four new domestic pay television service licences have been granted respectively to Hong Kong Network TV Ltd, Galaxy Satellite Broadcasting Ltd, Yes Television (Hong Kong) Ltd and Pacific Digital Media (HK) Corp. Ltd. These new services are expected to bring in over 100 television channels. There are four non-domestic television programme services in Hong Kong. Hutchvision Hong Kong broadcasts by satellite to the entire Asian region on 30 TV channels. Galaxy Satellite Broadcasting Ltd offers by satellite two channels covering Asia, Australia, Middle East, South Africa and part of Europe. The third and fourth non-domestic television programme service licensees are APT Satellite Glory Ltd and Starbucks (HK) Ltd.

In 2001 there were 3·39m. TV receivers and in 2000 there were 4·56m. radio receivers.

Press
In 1999 there were 45 newspapers including 22 Chinese-language dailies, three English dailies, six other Chinese and eight other English papers, one bilingual paper and five other language papers. The newspapers with the highest circulation figures are all Chinese-language papers—*Apple Daily*, *Oriental Daily* and *The Sun*. In 1999 there were 722 periodicals of which 452 were Chinese, 152 English, 106 bilingual and 12 in other languages. Circulation of dailies (excluding free papers) in 2000 was 1·5m. At 800 newspapers per 1,000 inhabitants, Hong Kong has one of

the highest rates of circulation in the world. A number of news agency bulletins are registered as newspapers.

Tourism

There were a record 21,811,000 visitor arrivals in 2004. Tourism receipts totalled HK$91,850·0m. in 2004.

FURTHER READING

Statistical Information: The Census and Statistics Department is responsible for the preparation and collation of government statistics. These statistics are published mainly in the *Hong Kong Monthly Digest of Statistics.* The Department also publishes monthly trade statistics, economic indicators and an annual review of overseas trade, etc. Website: http://www.info.gov.hk/censtatd/

Hong Kong [various years] Hong Kong Government Press
Brown, J. M. (ed.) *Hong Kong's Transitions, 1842–1997.* London, 1997
Buckley, R., *Hong Kong: the Road to 1997.* CUP, 1997
Cameron, N., *An Illustrated History of Hong Kong.* OUP, 1991
Cottrell, R., *The End of Hong Kong: the Secret Diplomacy of Imperial Retreat.* London, 1993
Courtauld, C. and Holdsworth, M., *The Hong Kong Story.* OUP, 1997
Flowerdew, J., *The Final Years of British Hong Kong: the Discourse of Colonial Withdrawal.* Hong Kong, 1997
Keay, J., *Last Post: the End of Empire in the Far East.* London, 1997
Lo, C. P., *Hong Kong.* London, 1992
Lo, S.-H., *The Politics of Democratization in Hong Kong.* London, 1997
Morris, J., *Hong Kong: Epilogue to an Empire.* 2nd ed. [of *Hong Kong: Xianggang*]. London, 1993
Roberti, M., *The Fall of Hong Kong: China's Triumph and Britain's Betrayal.* 2nd ed. Chichester, 1997
Roberts, E. V., *et al., Historical Dictionary of Hong Kong and Macau.* Metuchen (NJ), 1993
Scott, Ian, *Hong Kong.* [Bibliography] ABC-Clio, Oxford and Santa Barbara (CA), 1990
Shipp, S., *Hong Kong, China: a Political History of the British Crown Colony's Transfer to Chinese Rule.* Jefferson (NC), 1995
Tsang, S. Y., *Hong Kong: an Appointment with China.* London, 1997
Wang, G. and Wong, S. L. (eds.) *Hong Kong's Transition: a Decade after the Deal.* OUP, 1996
Welsh, F., *A History of Hong Kong.* 3rd ed. London, 1997
Yahuda, M., *Hong Kong: China's Challenge.* London, 1996

Macao

Population projection, 2010: 476,000
GDP per capita: not available
GNP per capita: $14,200

KEY HISTORICAL EVENTS

Macao was visited by Portuguese traders from 1513 and became a Portuguese colony in 1557. Initially sovereignty remained vested in China, with the Portuguese paying an annual rent. In 1848–49 the Portuguese declared Macao a free port and established jurisdiction over the territory. On 6 Jan. 1987 Portugal agreed to return Macao to China on 20 Dec. 1999 under a plan in which it would become a special administrative zone of China, with considerable autonomy.

TERRITORY AND POPULATION

The Macao Special Administrative Region, which lies at the mouth of the Pearl River, comprises a peninsula (8·7 sq. km) connected by a narrow isthmus to the People's Republic of China, on which is built the city of Santa Nome de Deus de Macao, and the islands of Taipa (6·3 sq. km), linked to Macao by a 2-km bridge, and Colôane (7·6 sq. km) linked to Taipa by a 2-km causeway. The total area of Macao is 27·3 sq. km. Land is being reclaimed from the sea. The population (2001 census) was 435,235 (266,370 females). Population on 31 Dec. 2003, 448,495 (232,879 females); density, 16,428 people per sq. km. The

population increased by 1·5% in 2003. An estimated 99·5% of the population lived in urban areas in 2004. The official languages are Chinese and Portuguese, with the majority speaking the Cantonese dialect.

The UN gives a projected population for 2010 of 476,000.

In Dec. 2003, 32,167 foreigners were legally registered for residency in Macao. There were 2,451 legal immigrants from mainland China.

SOCIAL STATISTICS

2003: births, 3,212 (7·2 per 1,000 population); deaths, 1,474 (3·3); marriages, 1,309 (2·9); divorces, 440 (1·0). Infant mortality, 2001, 4·3 per 1,000 live births. Life expectancy at birth (1998–2001), 78·9 years.

CLIMATE

Sub-tropical tending towards temperate, with an average temperature of 23·0°C. The number of rainy days is around a third of the year. Average annual rainfall varies from 47–87" (1,200–2,200 mm). It is very humid from May to Sept.

CONSTITUTION AND GOVERNMENT

Macao's constitution is the 'Basic Law', promulgated by China's National People's Congress on 31 March 1993 and in effect since 20 Dec. 1999. It is a Special Administrative Region (SAR) of the People's Republic of China, and is directly under the Central People's Government while enjoying a high degree of autonomy.

RECENT ELECTIONS

At the elections held on 25 Sept. 2005 the New Democratic Macau Association won two of 12 elected seats with 18·8% of votes cast, the Macau United Citizens Association two with 16·6%, the Union for Development two with 13·3% and the Union Promoting Progress two with 9·6%. Four other parties won a single seat each. Turnout was 58·4%.

Edmund Ho was re-elected chief executive for a second term on 29 Aug. 2004, receiving 296 out of 300 votes in the Election Committee.

CURRENT ADMINISTRATION

Chief Executive: Hau-wah (Edmund) Ho; b. 1955 (appointed 20 Dec. 1999 and re-elected 29 Aug. 2004).

Government Website: http://www.macau.gov.mo

ECONOMY

Gaming is of major importance to the economy of Macao, accounting for around one third of total GDP (2002) and providing billions of dollars in taxes. In 2003, 7·5% of the workforce was directly employed by the casinos.

Currency

The unit of currency is the *pataca* (MOP) of 100 *avos* which is tied to the Hong Kong dollar at parity. Inflation was –2·6% in 2002 and –1·6% in 2003. Foreign exchange reserves were US$4,343m. in 2003. Total money supply was 8,790m. patacas in 2003.

Budget

Final budget figures for 2003 were: revenue, 15,578·0m. patacas; expenditure, 15,578·0m. patacas. Actual figures were: revenue, 18,370·6m. patacas; expenditure, 15,713·0m. patacas.

Performance

Real GDP growth was an estimated 10·0% in 2002 and 15·6% in 2003. Total GDP in 2003 was US$7·9bn.

Banking and Finance

There are two note-issuing banks in Macao—the Macao branch of the Bank of China and the Macao branch of the Banco Nacional

Ultramarino. The Monetary Authority of Macao functions as a central bank (*Director,* Teng Lin Seng). Commercial business is handled (2003) by 23 banks, ten of which are local and 13 foreign. Total deposits, 2003 (including non-resident deposits), 124,977·4m. patacas. There are no foreign-exchange controls within Macao.

ENERGY AND NATURAL RESOURCES

Environment
Macao's carbon dioxide emissions from the consumption and flaring of fossil fuels in 2002 were the equivalent of 3·8 tonnes per capita.

Electricity
Installed capacity was 0·49m. kW in 2003; production, 1·72bn. kWh; net import, 179·8m. kWh.

Oil and Gas
311,324,000 litres of fuel oil were imported in 2003.

Fisheries
The catch in 2001 was approximately 1,500 tonnes.

INDUSTRY

Although the economy is based on gaming and tourism there is a light industrial base of textiles and garments. In 2002 the number of manufacturing establishments was 1,162 (textiles and clothing, 500; metal products, 138; foods, 119; publishing and printing, 117).

Labour
In 2003 a total of 202,588 people were in employment, including 37,077 (18·3%) in manufacturing; 32,824 (16·2%), wholesale and retail trade, repair of motor vehicles, motorcycles and personal and household goods; 23,469 (11·6%), community, social and other personal services; 22,114 (10·9%), hotels, restaurants and similar activities; 17,812 (8·8%), public administration, defence and compulsory social security; 16,283 (8·0%), construction. Employment in 2003 was 60·9% of the labour force (62·3% in 2002); unemployment rate stood at 6·0% (6·3% in 2002).

INTERNATIONAL TRADE

Imports and Exports
In 2003 imports were valued at 22,097m. patacas, of which the main products were consumer goods, raw materials and semi-manufactured goods, capital goods, fuels and lubricants. Main markets for imports (in 1m. patacas): mainland China, 9,489·9; Hong Kong, 2,794·4; European Union, 2,643·3.

2003 exports were valued at 20,700m. patacas, of which the main products were textiles and garments, machinery and apparatus, footwear, cement and toys. Main markets for exports (in 1m. patacas): 10,320·2, USA; 4,724·6, European Union.

COMMUNICATIONS

Roads
In 2003 there were 345·2 km of roads. In 2003 there were 58,667 passenger cars in use (131 cars per 1,000 inhabitants), 1,317 buses and coaches (excluding school buses), 3,863 trucks and vans, and 66,399 motorcycles and mopeds. In 2003 there were 17 fatalities in 11,764 traffic accidents.

Civil Aviation
An international airport opened in Dec. 1995. In 2003 Macau International Airport handled 2,904,118 passengers and 141,223 tonnes of freight (including transit cargo). In 2003 Air Macau flew to Bangkok, Beijing, Chengdu, Guilin, Haikou, Kaohsiung, Kota Kinabalu, Kuala Lumpur, Kunming, Manila, Nanjing, Ningbo, Shanghai, Singapore, Taipei and Xiamen. It flew a total of 11·5m. km in 1998 and carried 1,270,600 passengers in 1999.

Shipping
Regular services connect Macao with Hong Kong, 65 km to the northeast.

In 2002 merchant shipping totalled 4,000 GRT. In 2003 cargo vessel departures by flag totalled 2,451,106 NRT.

Telecommunications
In 2003 there were 538,652 telephone subscribers (1,201 per 1,000 inhabitants), 364,031 mobile phone subscribers and 59,401 Internet subscribers. There were 5,500 fax machines and 92,000 PCs in use (210·2 for every 1,000 persons) in 2002.

Postal Services
21,076,438 letters and parcels were posted in 2003.

SOCIAL INSTITUTIONS

Justice
There is a judicial district court, a criminal court and an administrative court with 24 magistrates in all.

In 2003 there were 9,920 crimes, of which 5,445 were against property. There were 928 persons in prison in 2003.

Education
There are three types of schools: public, church-run and private. In 2002–03 there were 142 schools and colleges with 110,266 students and 5,324 teachers. Numbers of schools and colleges by category (number of students at the end of the 2002–03 academic year): pre-primary, 62 (12,737); primary, 83 (41,535); secondary, 56 (41,551); technical/professional secondary, 4 (2,448); higher, 12 (11,995). In 2002–03 there were 132 adult education institutions with a total of 86,578 students enrolled.

In 2003 total expenditure on education came to 2·9% of GNP and 15·2% of total government spending.

Health
In 2003 there were 986 doctors, 91 dentists and 1,010 nurses. In 2003 there were 444 inhabitants per doctor and 447 per hospital bed.

RELIGION

Non-religious persons account for 62% of the population. About 17% are Buddhists and 7% Roman Catholics.

CULTURE

Broadcasting
One government and one private commercial radio station are in operation on medium-waves broadcasting in Portuguese and Chinese. Number of receivers (2000), 215,300. Macao receives television broadcasts from Hong Kong and in 1984 a public bilingual TV station began operating. There were, in 2001, 126,600 receivers (colour by PAL).

Press
In 2003 there were 11 daily newspapers (three in Portuguese and eight in Chinese) and six weekly newspapers (one in Portuguese and five in Chinese), plus four Chinese periodicals.

Tourism
Tourism is one of the mainstays of the economy. In 2003 there were 11·9m. visitors. 5·7m. were from mainland China, 4·6m. from Hong Kong and 1·0m. from Taiwan. Receipts in 2003 totalled US$4,836m.

FURTHER READING
Direcção de Serviços de Estatística e Censos. *Anuário Estatístico/ Yearbook of Statistics Macau in Figures.* Macao, Annual.
Porter, J., *Macau, the Imaginary City: Culture and Society, 1557 to the Present.* Oxford, 1996
Roberts, E. V., *Historical Dictionary of Hong Kong and Macau.* Metuchen (NJ), 1993

Statistics and Census Service Website: http://www.dsec.gov.mo

TAIWAN[1]

'Republic of China'

Capital: Taipei
Population: 22·1m.
GDP per capita: not available

KEY HISTORICAL EVENTS

Taiwan, christened Ilha Formosa (beautiful island) by the Portuguese, was ceded to Japan by China by the Treaty of Shimonoseki in 1895. After the Second World War the island was surrendered to Gen. Chiang Kai-shek who made it the headquarters for his crumbling Nationalist Government. Until 1970 the USA supported Taiwan's claims to represent all of China. Only in 1971 did the government of the People's Republic of China manage to replace that of Chiang Kai-shek at the UN. In Jan. 1979 the UN established formal diplomatic relations with the People's Republic of China, breaking off all formal ties with Taiwan. Taiwan itself has continued to reject all attempts at reunification, and although there have been frequent threats from mainland China to precipitate direct action (including military manoeuvres off the Taiwanese coast) the prospect of confrontation with the USA supports the status quo.

In July 1999 President Lee Teng-hui repudiated Taiwan's 50-year-old One China policy—the pretence of a common goal of unification—arguing that Taiwan and China should maintain equal 'state to state' relations. This was a rejection of Beijing's view that Taiwan is no more than a renegade Chinese province which must be reunited with the mainland, by force if necessary. In the Presidential election of 18 March 2000 Chen Shui-bian, leader of the Democratic Progressive Party, was elected, together with Annette Lu Hsiu-lien as his Vice President. Both support independence although Chen Shui-bian has made friendly gestures towards China and has distanced himself from colleagues who want an immediate declaration of independence.

TERRITORY AND POPULATION

Taiwan lies between the East and South China Seas about 160 km from the coast of Fujian. The territories currently under the control of the Republic of China include Taiwan, Penghu (the Pescadores), Kinmen (Quemoy), and the Matsu Islands, as well as the archipelagos in the South China Sea. Off the Pacific coast of Taiwan are Green Island and Orchid Island. To the northeast of Taiwan are the Tiaoyutai Islets. The total area of Taiwan Island, the Penghu Archipelago and the Kinmen area (including the fortified offshore islands of Quemoy and Matsu) is 36,188 sq. km (13,973 sq. miles). Population (2001), 22,405,568. The ethnic composition is 84% native Taiwanese (including 15% of Hakka), 14% of Mainland Chinese, and 2% aborigine of Malayo-Polynesian origin. There are also 420,892 aboriginals of Malay origin. Population density: 619 per sq. km.

Taiwan's administrative units comprise (with 2001 populations): two special municipalities: Taipei, the capital (2·69m.) and Kaohsiung (1·48m.); five cities outside the county structure: Chiayi (265,109), Hsinchu (361,958), Keelung (390,966), Taichung (983,694), Tainan (740,846); 16 counties (*hsien*): Changhwa (1,313,994), Chiayi (563,365), Hsinchu (446,300), Hualien (353,139), Ilan (465,799), Kaohsiung (1,236,958), Miaoli (560,640), Nantou (541,818), Penghu (92,268), Pingtung (909,364), Taichung (1,502,274), Tainan (1,109,397), Taipei (3,610,252), Taitung (244,612), Taoyuan (1,792,962), Yunlin (743,562).

SOCIAL STATISTICS

In 2001 the birth rate was 11·65 per 1,000 population; death rate, 5·71 per 1,000; rate of growth, 0·56% per annum. Life expectancy: males, 72·87 years; females, 78·79 years. Infant mortality, 6·62 per 1,000 live births.

CLIMATE

The climate is subtropical in the north and tropical in the south. The typhoon season extends from July to Sept. The average monthly temperatures of Jan. and July in Taipei are 59·5°F (15·3°C) and 83·3°F (28·5°C) respectively, and average annual rainfall is 84·99" (2,158·8 mm). Kaohsiung's average monthly temperatures of Jan. and July are 65·66°F (18·9°C) and 83·3°F (28·5°C) respectively, and average annual rainfall is 69·65" (1,769·2 mm).

CONSTITUTION AND GOVERNMENT

The ROC Constitution is based on the Principles of Nationalism, Democracy and Social Wellbeing formulated by Dr Sun Yat-sen, the founding father of the Republic of China. The ROC government is divided into three main levels: central, provincial/municipal and county/city each of which has well-defined powers.

The central government consists of the Office of the President, the National Assembly, which is specially elected only for constitutional amendment, and five governing branches called '*yuan*', namely the Executive Yuan, the Legislative Yuan, the Judicial Yuan, the Examination Yuan and the Control Yuan. The additional Article 4 of the Constitution stipulates that, beginning with the fourth Legislative Yuan (1999), the Legislative Yuan shall have 225 members.

From 5 May to 23 July 1997 the *Additional Articles of the Constitution of the Republic of China* underwent yet another amendment. As a result a resolution on the impeachment of the President or Vice President is no longer to be instituted by the Control Yuan but rather by the Legislative Yuan. The Legislative Yuan has the power to pass a no-confidence vote against the premier of the Executive Yuan, while the president of the Republic has the power to dissolve the Legislative Yuan. The premier of the Executive Yuan is now directly appointed by the president of the Republic. Hence the consent of the Legislative Yuan is no longer needed.

In Dec. 2003 a law came into effect allowing for referendums to be held.

National Anthem

'San Min Chu I'; words by Dr Sun Yat-sen, tune by Cheng Mao-yun.

RECENT ELECTIONS

Presidential elections took place on 20 March 2004. Incumbent Chen Shui-bian (Democratic Progressive Party) won 50·1% of the vote against 49·9% for Lien Chan (Nationalist Party/Kuomintang). Turnout was 80·3%. Chen Shui-bian was sworn in for a second term on 20 May 2004 but Lien Chan made an appeal to the High Court to overturn the result. The High Court judged against Lien Chan, who in Feb. 2005 declared an intention to challenge the ruling.

Elections to the Legislative Yuan were held on 11 Dec. 2004. The Democratic Progressive Party won 89 seats with 35·7% of votes cast; the Nationalist Party, 79 seats (32·8%); the People First Party, 34 seats (13·9%); the Taiwan Solidarity Union, 12 seats (7·8%); the Non-Partisan Solidarity Union, 6 seats (3·9%); the New Party, 1 seat (0·1%); ind., 4 seats (3·9%).

Elections for an *ad hoc* National Assembly charged with amending the constitution were held on 14 May 2005. The Democratic Progressive Party took 127 of 300 seats (with 42·5% of the vote), the Nationalist Party 117 (38·9%), the Taiwan Solidarity Union 21 (7·1%), the People First Party 18 (6·1%) and the Jhang Ya Jhong Union 5 (1·7%). Turnout was 23·4%.

---

[1]See note on transcription of names in CHINA: Territory and Population.

CURRENT ADMINISTRATION

President: Chen Shui-bian; b. 1951 (Democratic Progressive Party; sworn in 20 May 2000 and re-elected in March 2004).

Vice President: Annette Lu Hsiu-lien.

Prime Minister and *President of the Executive Yuan:* Su Tseng-chang; b. 1947 (Democratic Progressive Party; sworn in 25 Jan. 2006). There are eight ministries under the Executive Yuan: Interior; Foreign Affairs; National Defence; Finance; Education; Justice; Economic Affairs; Transport and Communications.

Vice-President of the Executive Yuan and Minister for the Consumer Protection Commission: Tsai Ing-wen. *President, Control Yuan:* Vacant. *President, Examination Yuan:* Yao Chia-wen. *President, Judicial Yuan:* Yueh-sheng Weng. *President, Legislative Yuan:* Wang Jin-ping. *Secretary General, Executive Yuan:* Liu Yuh-san. *Minister of Foreign Affairs:* James Huang. *Defence:* Lee Jye. *Interior:* Lee Yi-yang. *Finance:* Joseph Lyu. *Education:* Tu Cheng-shen. *Economic Affairs:* Hwang Ing-san. *Justice:* Shih Mao-lin. *Transport and Communications:* Kuo Yao-chi. *Minister, Department of Health:* Hou Sheng-mou. *Ministers without Portfolio:* Hu Sheng-cheng; Lin Si-yao; Ho Mei-yueh; Wu Frank Feng-shan; Lin Ferng-ching; Fu Li-yeh; Wu Tse-Tung (also *Chair of the Public Construction Commission*).

In addition to the Mongolian and Tibetan Affairs Commission and the Overseas Chinese Affairs Commission, a number of commissions and subordinate organizations have been formed with the resolution of the Executive Yuan Council and the Legislature to meet new demands and handle new affairs. Examples include the Environmental Protection Administration, which was set up in 1987 as public awareness of pollution control rose; the Mainland Affairs Council, which was established in 1990 to handle the thawing of relations between Taiwan and the Chinese mainland; and the Fair Trade Commission, which was established in 1992 to promote a fair trade system. Since 1995 even more commissions have been set up to provide a wider scope of services: the Public Construction Commission was set up in July 1995, the Council of Aboriginal Affairs in Dec. 1996, and the National Council on Physical Fitness and Sports in July 1997.

These commissions and councils are headed by:

Agricultural Council: Su Jia-chyuan. *Atomic Energy Council:* Ouyang Min-shen. *Central Election Commission:* Masa Chang. *Coast Guard Administration:* Wang Ginn-wang. *Council for Hakka Affairs:* Lee Yung-te. *Cultural Affairs:* Chiu Kin-liang. *Economic Planning and Development Council:* Hu Sheng-cheng. *Environmental Protection Administration:* Chang Kow-lung. *Fair Trade Commission:* Hwang Tzong-leh. *Indigenous Peoples' Council:* Pelin Walis. *Labour Affairs Council:* Lee Ying-yuan. *Mainland Affairs Council:* Wu Jau-shieh. *Mongolian and Tibetan Affairs Commission:* Hsu Chih-hsiung. *National Council on Physical Fitness and Sports:* Chen Chuan-show. *National Palace Museum:* Lin Mun-lee. *National Science Council:* Chen Chien-jen. *National Youth Commission:* Cheng Li-chiun. *Overseas Chinese Affairs Commission:* Chang Fu-mei. *Research, Development and Evaluation Commission:* Yeh Jiunn-rong. *Veterans Affairs Commission:* Kao Hua-chu.

Government Website: http://www.gio.gov.tw

DEFENCE

Conscription is for two years. Defence expenditure in 2003 totalled US$6,632m. (US$293 per capita), representing 2·4% of GDP.

Army

The Army was estimated to number about 190,000 in 2000, including military police. Army reserves numbered 2·7m. In addition the Ministry of Justice, Ministry of Interior and the Ministry of Defence each command paramilitary forces totalling 25,000 personnel in all. The Army consists of Army Corps, Defence Commands, Airborne Cavalry Brigades, Armoured Brigades, Motorized Rifle Brigades, Infantry Brigades, Special Warfare Brigades and Missile Command.

Navy

Active personnel in the Navy in 2000 totalled 50,000. There are 425,000 naval reservists. The operational and land-based forces consist of four submarines, 16 destroyers and 21 frigates. There is a naval air wing operating 31 combat aircraft and 21 armed helicopters.

Air Force

Units in the operational system are equipped with aircraft that include locally developed IDF, F-16, Mirage 2000-5 and F-5E fighter-interceptors. There were 50,000 Air Force personnel in 2000 and 334,000 reservists.

INTERNATIONAL RELATIONS

By a treaty of 2 Dec. 1954 the USA pledged to defend Taiwan, but this treaty lapsed one year after the USA established diplomatic relations with the People's Republic of China on 1 Jan. 1979. In April 1979 the Taiwan Relations Act was passed by the US Congress to maintain commercial, cultural and other relations between USA and Taiwan through the American Institute in Taiwan and its Taiwan counterpart, the Co-ordination Council for North American Affairs in the USA, which were accorded quasi-diplomatic status in 1980. The People's Republic took over the China seat in the UN from Taiwan on 25 Oct. 1971. In May 1991 Taiwan ended its formal state of war with the People's Republic. Taiwan became a member of the World Trade Organization on 1 Jan. 2002.

In Nov. 2000 Taiwan had formal diplomatic ties with 29 countries and maintained substantive relations with over 100 countries and territories around the globe.

ECONOMY

Overview

Taiwan has made a successful transition from an agricultural economy to one based on sophisticated high-tech electronics. The agricultural, industrial and service sectors account for approximately 2%, 20% and 68% of GDP respectively. Taiwan has experienced average economic growth of 8% during the last three decades; economic growth has been driven primarily by high value added manufacturing and exports, mainly in electronics and computers. Government intervention in investment and foreign trade has decreased since the early 1990s. In 1989 the government began a programme to privatize government-owned enterprises, including banks, telecommunication firms and industrial firms. The Asian financial crisis had a relatively little effect on Taiwan. The economy has, however, suffered recent setbacks, partly owing to policy co-ordination problems and bad debts in the banking system. The economy went into a recession in 2001, when the economy experienced the first year of negative growth ever recorded and unemployment reached record levels. Strong export performance has stimulated a recovery.

Currency

The unit of currency is the *New Taiwan dollar* (TWD) of 100 *cents*. Gold reserves were 13·55m. oz in Oct. 2000. There was deflation in both 1999 and 2000, of 1·4% and 1·6% respectively. Foreign exchange reserves were US$241·7bn. in Dec. 2004.

Budget

As a result of the constitutional amendment to abolish the provincial government from the fiscal year 2000 the central government budget has been enlarged to include the former provincial government. The central government's general budget for the fiscal year 2002 (beginning on 1 Jan.) was NT$1,518,724m. Expenditure planned: 18·1% on education, science and culture; 17·6% on economic development; 17·5% on social security; 15% on defence.

Performance

Taiwan sustained rapid economic growth at an annual rate of 9·2% from 1960 up to 1990. The rate slipped to 6·4% in the 1990s and 5·9% in 2000; Taiwan suffered from the Asian financial crisis, though less than its neighbours. Consumer prices showed increasing stability, rising at an average annual rate of 6·3% from 1960 to 1989, 2·9% in the 1990s and 1·3% in 2000. In 2001 global economic sluggishness and the events of 11 Sept. in the USA severely affected Taiwan's economy, which contracted by 2·2%. Per capita GNP stood at US$12,876, while consumer prices remained almost unchanged. Subsequent economic recovery led to growth of 3·9% in 2002, 3·3% in 2003 and 5·7% in 2004.

Banking and Finance

The Central Bank of China (reactivated in 1961) regulates the money supply, manages foreign exchange and issues currency. The *Governor* is Perng Fai-nan. The Bank of Taiwan is the largest commercial bank and the fiscal agent of the government. There are seven domestic banks, 38 commercial banks and 36 foreign banks. The Bank of Taiwan is scheduled for privatization by 2008 and it is proposed that the government will sell its commercial bank holdings by 2010.

There are two stock exchanges in Taipei.

ENERGY AND NATURAL RESOURCES

Environment

Taiwan's carbon dioxide emissions from the consumption and flaring of fossil fuels in 2002 were the equivalent of 10·2 tonnes per capita. An *Environmental Sustainability Index* compiled for the World Economic Forum meeting in Jan. 2005 ranked Taiwan 145th in the world out of 146 countries analysed, with 32·7%. Only North Korea was ranked lower. The index measured the ability of countries to maintain favourable environmental conditions and examined various factors including pollution levels and the use or abuse of natural resources.

Electricity

Output of electricity in 2001 was 188·5m. MWh; total installed capacity was 35,568 MW, of which 77·1% is held by the Taiwan Power Company. There were six units in three nuclear power stations in 2003. Consumption per capita stood at 4,257 litres of oil equivalent in 2001.

Oil and Gas

Crude oil production in 2001 was 40·6m. litres; natural gas, 849m. cu. metres.

Minerals

Coal production ceased by 2001 because of competitive imports and increasing local production costs.

Agriculture

In 2001 the cultivated area was 848,743 ha., of which 438,974 ha. were paddy fields. Rice production totalled 1,396,274 tonnes. Livestock production was valued at more than NT$101,205m., accounting for 28·67% of Taiwan's total agricultural production value.

Forestry

Forest area, 2001: 2,101,719 ha. Forest reserves: trees, 357,492,423 cu. metres; bamboo, 1,109m. poles. Timber production, 26,401 cu. metres.

Fisheries

In 2001 Taiwan's fishing fleet totalled 27,018 vessels (12,942 were powered craft); the catch was approximately 1·32m. tonnes. NT$89,813m. worth of fish was produced. Of this, 52% came from far-sea fishing, 26% from inland aquaculture, 14% from offshore fishing and 5% from coastal fishing. More than 40% of the catch was exported, with the biggest items being big eye tuna and albacore (long-finned tuna).

INDUSTRY

The largest companies in Taiwan by market capitalization in Nov. 2005 were Taiwan Semicon. Mnfg (US$43·2bn.), Hon Hai Precision Industry (US$19·5bn.) and Cathay Financial Holdings (US$15·1bn.).

Output (in tonnes) in 1999: cement, 18·2m.; steel bars, 1·4m.; pulp, 0·3m.; sugar, 0·3m.; cotton fabrics, 1,061m. sq. metres; portable computers, 9·95m. units; desktop computers, 3·01m. units. Taiwan is the third largest information technology producer after the USA and Japan. The IT sector has replaced traditional industries as the engine for growth.

Labour

In Sept. 2002 the total labour force was 9·97m., of whom 9·44m. were employed. Of the employed population, 55·09% worked in the service sector (including 22·70% in trade and 16·11% in accommodation and eating and drinking establishments); 37·28% in industry (including 27·05% in manufacturing and 7·64% in construction); and 7·63% in agriculture, forestry and fisheries. The unemployment rate was 5·32%.

INTERNATIONAL TRADE

Restrictions on the repatriation of investment earnings by foreign nationals were removed in 1994.

Imports and Exports

Total trade, in US$1m.:

	1996	1997	1998	1999	2000	2001
Imports	102,370	114,425	104,665	110,690	140,011	107,237
Exports	115,942	122,081	110,582	121,591	148,321	122,866

In 2001 the main import suppliers were Japan (24·1%), the USA (17·0%), South Korea (6·3%) and Germany (4·0%). The main export markets were the USA (22·5%), Hong Kong (21·9%), Japan (10·4%) and Germany (3·6%).

Principal imports, in US$1bn.: machinery and electrical equipment, 47·55; minerals, 12·76; chemicals, 10·23; basic metals and articles, 7·78; precision instruments, clocks and watches, and musical instruments, 6·21; vehicles and transport equipment, 4·24; textile products, 2·36.

Principal exports, in US$1bn.: machinery and electrical equipment, 66·85; textiles, 12·63; basic metals and articles, 11·33; plastic and rubber products, 7·99; vehicles and transport equipment, 4·44; toys, games and sports equipment, 1·79; footwear, headwear and umbrellas, 0·79. By 2001 high-tech products were responsible for more than 54% of exports.

COMMUNICATIONS

Roads

In 2002 there were 37,299 km of roads. 17·9m. motor vehicles were registered including 5·0m. passenger cars, 25,000 buses, 700,000 trucks and 12·0m. motorcycles. 1,091m. passengers and 301m. tonnes of freight were transported (including urban buses) in 2001. There were 64,264 road accidents, resulting in 3,344 fatalities.

Rail

In 2001 freight traffic amounted to 16·9m. tonnes and passenger traffic to 165m. Total route length was 2,363 km. A metro system opened in Taipei in 1996.

Civil Aviation

There are currently two international airports: Chiang Kai-shek International at Taoyuan near Taipei, and Kaohsiung International in the south. In addition there are 14 domestic airports: Taipei, Hualien, Taitung, Taichung, Tainan, Chiayi, Pingtung, Makung, Chimei, Orchid Island, Green Island, Wangan, Kinmen and Matsu (Peikan). A second passenger terminal at Chiang Kai-shek International Airport opened in July 2000 as part of a

US$800m. expansion project, which included aircraft bays, airport connection roads, a rapid transit link with Taipei, car parks and the expansion of air freight facilities, begun in 1989. The planned facilities are designed to allow the airport to handle an additional 14m. passengers annually by the year 2010.

In June 2002, 38 airlines including code-share airlines provided flights to destinations in Taiwan, of which 32 foreign and six Taiwanese carriers—China Airlines (CAL), EVA Airways, Far Eastern Air Transport Corp., Mandarin Airlines (MDA; CAL's subsidiary), Trans Asia Airways (TNA) and UNI Airways—operated international services. In 2001, 44·1m. passengers and 1·3m. tonnes of freight were flown.

Taipei–Hong Kong and vice-versa was the most flown airline route in the world in 2001, with 5·43m. passengers flying between the two cities.

Shipping
Maritime transportation is vital to the trade-oriented economy of Taiwan. At the end of 2001 Taiwan's shipping fleet totalled 249 national-flagged ships (over 100 GRT), amounting to 4·7m. GRT and 7·4m. DWT. There are six international ports: Kaohsiung, Keelung, Hualien, Taichung, Anping and Suao. The first two are container centres, Kaohsiung handling 7·54m. 20-ft equivalent units in 2001, making it the world's fourth busiest container port in terms of number of containers handled. Suao port is an auxiliary port to Keelung. In Jan. 2001 the first legal direct shipping links between Taiwanese islands and the Chinese mainland in more than 50 years were inaugurated.

Telecommunications
In 2002 there were 37,004,800 telephone subscribers (1,647·8 per 1,000 inhabitants) and PCs numbered 8·89m. (395·7 per 1,000 inhabitants). Taiwan's biggest telecommunications firm, the state-owned Chunghwa Telecom, lost its fixed-line monopoly in Aug. 2001. In 2002 there were 23,905,400 mobile phone subscribers, equivalent to 1,061·5 per 1,000 persons—the highest rate anywhere in the world. There were approximately 8·59m. Internet users in 2002. In 1997 there were 2,496,090 radio pager subscribers.

SOCIAL INSTITUTIONS

Justice
The Judicial Yuan is the supreme judicial organ of state. Comprising 15 grand justices, since 2003 these have been nominated and, with the consent of the Legislative Yuan, appointed by the President of the Republic. The grand justices hold meetings to interpret the Constitution and unify the interpretation of laws and orders. There are three levels of judiciary: district courts and their branches deal with civil and criminal cases in the first instance; high courts and their branches deal with appeals against judgments of district courts; the Supreme Court reviews judgments by the lower courts. There is also the Supreme Administrative Court, high administrative courts and a Commission on the Disciplinary Sanctions of Public Functionaries. Criminal cases relating to rebellion, treason and offences against friendly relations with foreign states are handled by high courts as the courts of first instance.

The death penalty is still in force. There were three confirmed executions in 2005. The population in penal institutions on 30 Sept. 2002 was approximately 39,000 (135 per 100,000 of national population).

Education
Since 1968 there has been compulsory education for six to 15 year olds with free tuition. The illiteracy rate dropped to 4·21% in 2001 and is still falling. In 2001 there were 2,611 elementary schools with 103,501 teachers and 1,925,491 pupils; 1,181 secondary schools with 98,609 teachers and 1,684,499 students; 154 schools of higher education, including 57 universities, 78 colleges and 19 junior colleges, with 44,769 teachers and 1,189,225 students. Almost one-quarter of the total population attend an educational institution.

Health
In 2001 there was one physician serving every 733 persons, one doctor of Chinese medicine per 5,631 persons and one dentist per 2,505 persons. Some 114,179 beds were provided by the 92 public and 501 private hospitals, averaging nearly 57 beds per 10,000 persons. In addition to the 492 public and 17,136 private clinics, there were 369 health stations and 503 health rooms serving residents in the sparsely populated areas. In 2001 acute infectious diseases were no longer the number one killer. Malignant neoplasms, cerebrovascular diseases, heart diseases and accidents and adverse effects were the first four leading causes of death.

Welfare
A universal health insurance scheme came into force in March 1995 as an extension to 13 social insurance plans which cover only 59% of Taiwan's population. Premium shares among the government, employer and insured are varied according to the insured statuses. By the end of 2001 about 21·65m. people or 96% of the population were covered by the National Health Insurance programme.

RELIGION
According to the registered statistics of Municipality, County and City Government there were 827,135 Taoists in 2001 (and 7,714 temples), 382,437 Protestants (and 2,387 churches), 216,495 Buddhists (and 1,966 temples) and 182,814 Catholics (and 728 churches). In May 2005 there was one cardinal.

CULTURE

Broadcasting
At Oct. 2002 there were 174 radio stations, one public and four commercial TV services and 65 cable systems. June 1997 saw the inauguration of a fourth over-the-air television station—The Kaohsiung-based Formosa Television—which is affiliated with the Democratic Progressive Party and telecasts on VHF low-band. A Public Television Law was promulgated on 18 June 1997. In 2001 there were 9·9m. TV receivers (colour by NTSC).

Press
There were 267 domestic news agencies, 454 newspapers and 7,236 periodicals in 2001.

Tourism
In 2002, 2,617,137 tourists visited Taiwan and 7,189,334 Taiwanese made visits abroad.

FURTHER READING

Statistical Yearbook of the Republic of China. Taipei, annual. *The Republic of China Yearbook.* Taipei, annual. *Taiwan Statistical Data Book.* Taipei, annual. *Annual Review of Government Administration, Republic of China.* Taipei, annual.

Arrigo, L. G., et al., *The Other Taiwan: 1945 to the Present Day.* New York, 1994

Cooper, J. F., *Historical Dictionary of Taiwan.* Metuchen (NJ), 1993

Hughes, C., *Taiwan and Chinese Nationalism: National Identity and Status in International Society.* London, 1997

Lee, W.-C., *Taiwan.* [Bibliography] ABC-Clio, Oxford and Santa Barbara (CA), 1990

Long, S., *Taiwan: China's Last Frontier.* London, 1991

Moody, P. R., *Political Change in Taiwan: a Study of Ruling Party Adaptability.* New York, 1992

Smith, H., *Industry Policy in Taiwan and Korea in the 1980s.* Edward Elgar, Cheltenham, 2000

Tsang, S. (ed.) *In the Shadow of China: Political Developments in Taiwan since 1949.* Farnborough, 1994

National library: National Central Library, Taipei (established 1986).
National Statistics Website: http://www.stat.gov.tw

COLOMBIA

Caribbean Sea
Barranquilla
Cartagena
PANAMA
VENEZUELA
Medellín
PACIFIC OCEAN
BOGOTÁ
Cali
COLOMBIA
Pasto
ECUADOR
BRAZIL
PERU
0   125 mi
0   200 km
© Research Machines plc 2006

República de Colombia

Capital: Bogotá
Population projection, 2010: 48·93m.
GDP per capita, 2003: (PPP$) 6,702
HDI/world rank: 0·785/69

KEY HISTORICAL EVENTS

In 1564 the Spanish Crown appointed a President of New Granada, which included the territories of Colombia, Panama and Venezuela. In 1718 a viceroyalty of New Granada was created. This viceroyalty gained its independence from Spain in 1819, and together with the present territories of Panama, Venezuela and Ecuador was officially constituted as the state of 'Greater Colombia'. This new state lasted only until 1830 when it split up into Venezuela, Ecuador and the republic of New Granada, later renamed *Estados Unidos de Colombia*. The constitution of 5 Aug. 1886, forming the Republic of Colombia, abolished the sovereignty of the states, converting them into departments with governors appointed by the President of the Republic. The department of Panama, however, became an independent country in 1903. Conservatives and Liberals fought a civil war from 1948 to 1957 (*La Violencia*) during which some 300,000 people were killed. Subsequently, powerful drugs lords have made violence endemic. Two Marxist guerrilla forces are active, the Colombian Revolutionary Armed Forces (FARC), and the smaller National Liberation Army (ELN). They are opposed by a well-armed paramilitary organization which emerged after

the setting up of rural self-defence groups. Killings and other abuses by paramilitary squads, guerrillas and the military in 1996 made it the most infamous year in the nation's history for human rights violations. On average, ten Colombians were killed every day for political or ideological reasons, while one person disappeared every two days.

There were hopes of a fresh start in 1998 when Andrés Pastrana was elected president. Offers to talk peace were taken up by the rebels and by their paramilitary enemies. But political differences are wide, with FARC demanding sweeping agrarian reform and a redistribution of wealth. FARC controls around 40% of the country including areas which produce the bulk of illegal drugs. Approximately 80% of the cocaine and 60% of the heroin sold in the USA originates in Colombia. In Feb. 2002, following the kidnapping of a prominent senator, President Pastrana broke off three years of peace talks. In May 2002 Álvaro Uribe Vélez became president, but within days of his inauguration, amidst mounting violence, he called a state of emergency.

TERRITORY AND POPULATION

Colombia is bounded in the north by the Caribbean Sea, northwest by Panama, west by the Pacific Ocean, southwest by Ecuador and Peru, northeast by Venezuela and southeast by Brazil. The estimated area is 1,141,748 sq. km (440,829 sq. miles). Population census (1993), 33,109,840; density, 29·0 per sq. km. Population estimate, 2005: 45·60m.

The UN gives a projected population for 2010 of 48·93m.

In 2003, 76·4% lived in urban areas. Bogotá, the capital (estimate 1999): 6,276,000.

The following table gives population estimates for departments and their capitals for 1999:

Departments	Area (sq. km)	Population	Capital	Population
Amazonas	109,665	69,000	Leticia	30,000[1]
Antioquia	63,612	5,300,000	Medellín	1,958,000
Arauca	23,818	232,000	Arauca	69,000[1]
Atlántico	3,388	2,081,000	Barranquilla	1,226,000
Bogotá[2]	1,587	6,276,000	—	
Bolívar	25,978	1,951,000	Cartagena	877,000
Boyacá	23,189	1,355,000	Tunja	118,000[1]
Caldas	7,888	1,094,000	Manizales	362,000
Caquetá	88,965	410,000	Florencia	115,000[1]
Casanare	44,640	278,000	Yopal	69,000[1]
Cauca	29,308	1,234,000	Popayán	218,000[1]
César	22,905	944,000	Valledupar	297,000[1]
Chocó	46,530	406,000	Quibdó	123,000[1]
Córdoba	25,020	1,308,000	Montería	321,000
Cundinamarca	22,623	2,099,000	Bogotá[1]	—
Guainía	72,238	36,000	Puerto Inírida	20,000[1]
Guaviare	42,327	114,000	San José del Guaviare	54,000[1]
Huila	19,890	911,000	Neiva	322,000
La Guajira	20,848	475,000	Riohacha	115,000[1]
Magdalena	23,188	1,260,000	Santa Marta	343,000[1]
Meta	85,635	686,000	Villavicencio	314,000
Nariño	33,268	1,603,000	Pasto	379,000
Norte de Santander	21,658	1,316,000	Cúcuta	624,000
Putumayo	24,885	324,000	Mocoa	30,000[1]
Quindío	1,845	552,000	Armenia	284,000[1]
Risaralda	4,140	928,000	Pereira	457,000
San Andrés y Providencia	44	71,000	San Andrés	61,000[1]
Santander	30,537	1,939,000	Bucaramanga	521,000
Sucre	10,917	779,000	Sincelejo	214,000[1]
Tolima	23,562	1,293,000	Ibagué	420,000[1]
Valle del Cauca	22,140	4,104,000	Cali	2,111,000

Departments	Area (sq. km)	Population	Capital	Population
Vaupés	65,268	29,000	Mitú	14,000[1]
Vichada	100,242	80,000	Puerto Carreño	12,000[1]

[1]1997. [2]Capital District.

Ethnic divisions (2000): Mestizo 47%, Mulatto 23%, White 20%, Black 6%, Indian 3%, mixed Black-Indian 1%.

The official language is Spanish.

SOCIAL STATISTICS

2000 estimates: births, 734,000; deaths, 184,000. Rates, 2000 estimates (per 1,000 population): births, 17·4; deaths, 4·4. Annual population growth rate, 1992–2002, 1·8%. Life expectancy at birth, 2003, was 69·3 years for men and 75·4 years for women. Infant mortality, 2001, 19 per 1,000 live births; fertility rate, 2001, 2·7 children per woman. Abortion is illegal.

CLIMATE

The climate includes equatorial and tropical conditions, according to situation and altitude. In tropical areas, the wettest months are March to May and Oct. to Nov. Bogotá, Jan. 58°F (14·4°C), July 57°F (13·9°C). Annual rainfall 42" (1,052 mm). Barranquilla, Jan. 80°F (26·7°C), July 82°F (27·8°C). Annual rainfall 32" (799 mm). Cali, Jan. 75°F (23·9°C), July 75°F (23·9°C). Annual rainfall 37" (915 mm). Medellín, Jan. 71°F (21·7°C), July 72°F (22·2°C). Annual rainfall 64" (1,606 mm).

CONSTITUTION AND GOVERNMENT

Simultaneously with the presidential elections of May 1990, a referendum was held in which 7m. votes were cast for the establishment of a special assembly to draft a new constitution. Elections were held on 9 Dec. 1990 for this 74-member 'Constitutional Assembly' which operated from Feb. to July 1991. The electorate was 14·2m.; turnout was 3·7m. The Liberals gained 24 seats, M19 (a former guerrilla organization), 19. The Assembly produced a new constitution which came into force on 5 July 1991. It stresses the state's obligation to protect human rights, and establishes constitutional rights to health care, social security and leisure. Indians are allotted two Senate seats. Congress may dismiss ministers, and representatives may be recalled by their electors.

The *President* is elected by direct vote. In Oct. 2005 the constitution was amended to allow a president to be re-elected for a second term. A vice-presidency was instituted in July 1991.

The legislative power rests with a *Congress* of two houses, the *Senate*, of 102 members (including two elected from a special list set aside for American Indian communities), and the *House of Representatives*, of 166 members, both elected for four years by proportional representation. Congress meets annually at Bogotá on 20 July.

National Anthem

'O! Gloria inmarcesible' ('Oh unfading Glory!'); words by R. Núñez, tune by O. Síndici.

GOVERNMENT CHRONOLOGY

Heads of State since 1945. (PLC = Liberal Party; PSC = Colombian Conservative Party/Colombian Social Conservative Party; n/p = non-partisan)

Presidents

1945–46	PLC	Alberto Lleras Camargo
1946–50	PSC	Luis Mariano Ospina Pérez
1950–51	PSC	Laureano Eleuterio Gómez Castro
1951–53	PSC	Roberto Urdaneta Arbeláez
1953	PSC	Laureano Eleuterio Gómez Castro
1953–57	military	Gustavo Rojas Pinilla

Military Junta

1957–58		Gabriel Paris Gordillo (chair); Rubén Piedrahíta Arango; Deogracias Fonseca Espinosa; Luis Ernesto Ordóñez Castillo; Rafael Navas Pardo

Presidents

1958–62	PLC	Alberto Lleras Camargo
1962–66	PSC	Guillermo León Valencia Muñoz
1966–70	PLC	Carlos Lleras Restrepo
1970–74	PSC	Misael Eduardo Pastrana Borrero
1974–78	PLC	Alfonso López Michelsen
1978–82	PLC	Julio César Turbay Ayala
1982–86	PSC	Belisario Betancur Cuartas
1986–90	PLC	Virgilio Barco Vargas
1990–94	PLC	César Augusto Gaviria Trujillo
1994–98	PLC	Ernesto Samper Pizano
1998–2002	PSC	Andrés Pastrana Arango
2002–	n/p	Álvaro Uribe Vélez

RECENT ELECTIONS

Presidential elections were held on 26 May 2002, in which Álvaro Uribe Vélez (independent) won with 53·1% of votes cast, against 31·8% for his nearest rival, Horacio Serpa (Colombian Liberal Party). Turnout was 46·8%.

Congressional elections were held on 12 March 2006. In elections to the House of Representatives the Colombian Liberal Party won 38 seats, the Social National Unity Party 30, the Colombian Conservative Party 29, the Radical Change Party 20, the Democratic Alternative Pole Party 9, the Citizens' Convergence Party 8 and the Wings Colombia Team 7, with the remaining seats going to smaller parties. In the elections to the Senate the Social National Unity Party won 20 seats, the Colombian Conservative Party 18, the Colombian Liberal Party 17, the Radical Change Party 15 and the Democratic Alternative Pole Party 11, with smaller parties accounting for the remainder.

Presidential elections were scheduled to take place on 28 May 2006.

CURRENT ADMINISTRATION

President: Álvaro Uribe Vélez; b. 1952 (ind.; sworn in 7 Aug. 2002).

Vice President: Francisco Santos Calderón.

In March 2006 the government comprised:

Minister of Interior and Justice: Sabas Pretelt de la Vega. *Finance:* Alberto Carrasquilla Barrera. *Defence:* Camilo Ospina Bernal. *Agriculture and Rural Development:* Andrés Felipe Arias Leyva. *Social Welfare:* Diego Palacio Betancourt. *Mines and Energy:* Luis Ernesto Mejía Castro. *National Education:* Cecilia María Vélez White. *Communications:* Martha Pinto de De Hart. *Trade, Industry and Tourism:* Jorge Humberto Botero. *Foreign Relations:* Carolina Barco Isakson. *Environment, Housing and Territorial Development:* Sandra Suárez Pérez. *Transport:* Andrés Uriel Gallego Henao. *Culture:* Elvira Cuervo de Jaramillo.

Office of the President (Spanish only):
http://www.presidencia.gov.co

CURRENT LEADERS

Álvaro Uribe Vélez

Position
President

Introduction
Álvaro Uribe Vélez was elected president of Colombia in May 2002 in an outright first-round victory. An independent candidate, his hardline mandate of combating left-wing guerrillas and right-wing paramilitaries found popularity with the electorate after

attempts at peace talks by his predecessor Andrés Pastrana had failed.

Early Life

Uribe was born on 4 July 1952 in Medellín. After completing a law degree at the Universidade de Antioquia, he studied management at Harvard University in the USA and worked as an associate professor at Oxford University in England.

At the age of 24 he began working for Medellín's public works, following which he was secretary general of the labour ministry (1977–78), worked for the civil aeronautics department (1980–82) and was then mayor of Medellín. His career in his native region continued between 1995–97 when he served as governor of the Antioquia region. As such he streamlined the local government department and increased spending on education, health and road infrastructure.

Uribe set up the 'Convivirs' security networks which diminished the presence of the left-wing guerrilla Fuerzas Armadas Revolucionarias de Colombia (FARC; Colombian Revolutionary Armed Forces) in Antioquia. But he was criticized for allowing the right-wing paramilitary Autodefensas Unidas de Colombia (AUC; United Self-Defence Forces of Colombia) to take advantage of the reduced FARC profile.

Uribe's hardline view on guerrilla activity in part stems from his father's assassination in 1983 by FARC members during a bungled kidnapping attempt. Combating terrorism was made the central issue of his 2002 presidential campaign. Peace talks between incumbent president Pastrana and FARC leaders had failed to stem violence and kidnappings, and Uribe's pledge to forcefully oppose terrorist activity was well received among voters. Violence increased in the lead up to the polls, including numerous assassination attempts on Uribe and the kidnapping of the independent candidate Ingrid Betancourt. The election itself passed relatively peacefully and, with a turnout of 47%, Uribe beat the Colombian Liberal Party candidate Horacio Serpa by 53% of votes to 32%. Despite a military presence of 20,000, Uribe's inauguration in Aug. 2002 was marred by explosions around Bogotá which killed 20 people and injured 60.

Career in Office

On election Uribe planned to double the size of the army and create a 1m.-strong civil militia. He also sought to amend the constitution to allow for martial law and states of siege. His plans received a positive response from the USA, with the possibility of increased military aid, although FARC promised to resist the government forces. Unlike his predecessor, Uribe demanded a full FARC ceasefire and halt in kidnappings before any peace talks could be brokered. FARC demanded control of two southern provinces, Caquetá and Putumayo, in return. Although Uribe also targeted terrorism by the smaller left-wing Ejército de Liberación Nacional (ELN; National Liberation Army) and the AUC, the latter responded positively to the president's election and formal peace talks began in mid-2003, leading to an AUC commitment to demobilize by the end of 2005 in exchange for amnesty.

In July 2005 the Justice and Peace Law won congressional approval, making generous concessions to illegal fighters in return for laying down their arms. Human rights groups have been critical of the law, however, viewing it as a charter of impunity for war criminals.

Uribe's other aims during his presidency have included eliminating corruption, targeting crime and drug trafficking (both closely linked to guerrilla and paramilitary activities), and, on his Antioquia model, reducing expenditure on public administration.

In Oct. 2005 the Constitutional Court upheld an amendment to the constitution allowing presidential re-election and the following month set out conditions under which an incumbent can stand, so allowing Uribe to campaign for a second term in elections scheduled for May 2006.

DEFENCE

Selective conscription at 18 years is for two years' service. In 2003 defence expenditure totalled US$3,234m. (US$73 per capita), representing 4·2% of GDP. In 1985 expenditure had been US$823m.

Army

Personnel (2002) 136,000 (conscripts, 63,800); reserves number 54,700. The national police numbered (2002) 104,600.

Navy

The Navy has two diesel powered submarines, two midget submarines and four small frigates. Naval personnel in 2002 totalled 15,000. There are also two brigades of marines numbering 10,000. An air arm operates light reconnaissance aircraft.

The Navy's main ocean base is Cartagena with Pacific bases at Buenaventura and Málaga. There are in addition numerous river bases.

Air Force

The Air Force has been independent of the Army and Navy since 1943, when its reorganization began with US assistance. It has 58 combat aircraft and 23 combat helicopters. There are two fighter-bomber squadrons (one with Mirage 5s and one with Kfirs). Total strength (2002), 7,000 personnel (3,900 conscripts).

INTERNATIONAL RELATIONS

Colombia is a member of the UN, WTO, OAS, Inter-American Development Bank, the Andean Group, ALADI/LAIA, ACS, IOM and the Antarctic Treaty.

It was announced in Aug. 2000 that Colombia would receive US$1·3bn. in anti drug-trafficking aid (mostly of a military nature) from the USA as part of 'Plan Colombia', a five-year long series of projects intended to serve as a foundation for stability and peace of which the focal point is the fight against drugs. By Aug. 2003 the USA had given aid amounting to US$2·4bn.

ECONOMY

In 2002 agriculture accounted for 13·9% of GDP, industry 30·2% and services 55·9%.

Overview

Colombia's economic progress has been blighted by guerrilla insurgencies, drug cartels, human rights violations and an unsustainable fiscal deficit. The country produces 80% of the world's cocaine and a third of the world's marijuana. It is estimated that trade in illegal drugs accounts for 3% of GDP.

Colombia has a diversified economic base. The second largest exporter of coffee in the world, it is endowed with substantial oil reserves and is a major producer of gold, silver, emeralds, platinum and coal. Until 1996, Colombia enjoyed relatively high and stable rates of growth but has subsequently suffered its worst economic crisis since the 1930s. The economy was pushed to crisis point in 1998–99 as poverty and unemployment escalated.

Since the 1970s violence and crime have significantly diminished the economy, with the World Bank estimating that ongoing conflict has reduced growth by 2% per year, reducing GDP per capita by two thirds. After 20 years of sustained poverty reduction, the situation reversed in the late 1990s with over 65% of the population below the poverty line by mid-2000. However, there has been strong growth since 2002 with private investment rebounding to pre-crisis levels in 2004–05 and inflation falling to 5·9% in 2004.

Currency

The unit of currency is the *Colombian peso* (COP) of 100 *centavos*. Inflation rates (based on IMF statistics):

1997	1998	1999	2000	2001	2002	2003	2004
18·5%	18·7%	10·9%	9·2%	8·0%	6·3%	7·1%	5·9%

In June 2002 gold reserves were 327,000 troy oz and foreign exchange reserves were US$10,188m. Total money supply was 17,289bn. pesos in June 2002.

Budget
In 2003 budgetary central government revenue was 42,446bn. pesos (34,476bn. pesos in 2002) and expenditure 51,849bn. pesos (43,315bn. pesos in 2002).

Performance
Real GDP growth rates (based on IMF statistics):

1995	1996	1997	1998	1999	2000	2001	2002	2003	2004
5·2%	2·1%	3·4%	0·6%	−4·2%	2·9%	1·5%	1·9%	4·1%	4·1%

When GDP shrank by 4·2% in 1999, Colombia experienced its worst recession since the 1930s. Total GDP in 2004 was US$97·4bn.

Banking and Finance
In 1923 the Bank of the Republic (*Governor*, José Dario Uribe Escobar) was inaugurated as a semi-official central bank, with the exclusive privilege of issuing banknotes. Its note issues must be covered by a reserve in gold of foreign exchange of 25% of their value. Interest rates of 40% plus are imposed.

There are 24 commercial banks, of which 18 are private or mixed, and six official. There is also an Agricultural, Industrial and Mining Credit Institute, a Central Mortgage Bank and a Social Savings Bank. Demand deposits totalled 11,256bn. pesos in Dec. 2002. The Superintendencia Bancaria acts as a supervising body.

There are stock exchanges in Bogotá, Medellín and Cali.

Weights and Measures
The metric system is standard but traditional Spanish weights and measures are still used, *e.g., botella* (750 grammes), *galón* (5 *botellas*), *vara* (70 cm) and *fanegada* (1,000 square varas).

ENERGY AND NATURAL RESOURCES

Environment
In 2002 Colombia's carbon dioxide emissions from the consumption and flaring of fossil fuels were the equivalent of 1·4 tonnes per capita.

Electricity
Installed capacity of electric power (2002) was 13·8m. kW. In 2001 production was 43·68bn. kWh and consumption per capita 1,010 kWh.

Oil and Gas
Crude oil production (2003) 27·9m. tonnes. Natural gas production in 2002 totalled 6·2bn. cu. metres. In 2002 there were proven oil reserves of 1·9bn. bbls. and proven gas reserves of 130bn. cu. metres.

Minerals
Production (2001): gold, 21,813 kg; silver, 7,242 kg; platinum (1998), 14,016 troy oz. Other important minerals include: copper, lead, mercury, manganese, nickel and emeralds (of which Colombia accounts for about half of world production).

Coal production (2000): 38·36m. tonnes; iron ore (2000): 660,000 tonnes; salt production (1998): 159,621 tonnes.

Agriculture
There is a wide range of climate and, consequently, crops. In 2001 there were 2·52m. ha. of arable land and 1·73m. ha. of permanent crops.

Production, 2000 (in 1,000 tonnes): sugarcane, 37,000; potatoes, 2,705; plantains, 2,689; rice, 2,100; cassava, 1,956; bananas, 1,570; maize, 1,010; coffee, 630. Colombia is the third largest coffee producer in the world after Brazil and Vietnam. Coca was cultivated in 2000 on approximately 135,000 ha., up from 40,000 ha. in 1992. Coca leaf production in 2000 totalled 88,000 tonnes, making Colombia the world's largest producer of coca leaves, the raw material for cocaine.

Livestock (2000): 26,000,000 cattle; 2,800,000 pigs; 2,200,000 sheep; 2,450,000 horses; 100m. chickens. Meat production, 2000: beef and veal, 754,000 tonnes; poultry meat, 520,000 tonnes; pork, bacon and ham, 152,000 tonnes.

Forestry
In 2000 the area under forests was 49·6m. ha., or 47·8% of the total land area. Timber production in 2003 was 9·96m. cu. metres.

Fisheries
Total catch (2003) was 157,794 tonnes, of which 62% was from marine waters.

INDUSTRY
Production, 2002 (in tonnes): cement (2001), 6,776,000; petrol, 4,680,000; distillate fuel oil, 3,275,000; residual fuel oil, 3,136,000; sugar, 2,522,637; steel ingots (1998), 264,466; soft drinks (2001), 1,832·5m. litres; beer (2001), 1,421·3m. litres; passenger cars (1998), 49,807 units; industrial vehicles (1998), 14,162 units.

Labour
The economically active workforce in 2001 was 18·65m., of which 16·62m. were employed. The main areas of activity in 2001 were: wholesale and retail trade, restaurants and hotels (employing 4·19m. persons); community, social and personal services (3·74m.); and agriculture, hunting, forestry and fishing (3·49m.). The unemployment rate in 2002 was 15·7%.

INTERNATIONAL TRADE
Foreign companies are liable for basic income tax of 30% and surtax of 7·5%. Since 1993 tax on profit remittance has started at 12%, reducing (except for oil companies) to 7% after three years. Foreign debt was US$33,853m. in 2002.

The Group of Three (G-3) free trade pact with Mexico and Venezuela came into effect on 1 Jan. 1995.

Imports and Exports
In US$1m.:

	1999	2000	2001	2002
Imports f.o.b.	10,262	11,090	12,269	12,077
Exports f.o.b.	12,037	13,620	12,772	12,303

Major import suppliers, 2000: USA (33·7%), Venezuela (8·2%), Japan (4·6%), Brazil (4·4%). Main export markets, 2000: USA (50·0%), Venezuela (9·9%), Ecuador (3·5%), Germany (3·2%). Main exports in 1999 were (in US$1m.): crude oil (3,334·4), chemicals and related products (1,163·7), coal (835·2), bananas (559·5), cut flowers (550·4) and clothing (426·6).

COMMUNICATIONS

Roads
Total length of roads was 114,271 km in 2002 (including 17,819 km of main roads), of which 15·1% were paved. Of the 3,700-km Simón Bolívar highway, which runs from Caracas in Venezuela to Guayaquil in Ecuador, the Colombian portion is complete. Motor vehicles in 1999 numbered 2,122,495, of which 1,803,201 were passenger cars, 184,495 vans and trucks, and 134,799 buses and coaches.

Rail

The National Railways (2,532 km of route, 914 mm gauge) went into liquidation in 1990 prior to takeover of services and obligations by three new public companies in 1992. Freight tonne-km came to 374m. in 2002. Total rail track, 3,304 km. A metro system operates in Medellín.

Civil Aviation

There are international airports at Barranquilla, Bogotá (Eldorado), Cali, Cartagena, Medellín and San Andrés. The main Colombian carrier is Avianca which, in 1998, flew 48·5m. km and carried 3,924,100 passengers. The busiest airport is Bogotá, which in 2000 handled 7,154,312 passengers (5,234,807 on domestic flights) and 372,957 tonnes of freight.

Shipping

Vessels entering Colombian ports in 1995 unloaded 13,806,000 tonnes of imports and loaded 26,284,000 tonnes of exports. In 2000 vessels totalling 52,442,000 NRT entered ports and vessels totalling 50,787,000 NRT cleared. The merchant marine totalled 68,000 GRT in 2002, including oil tankers 6,000 GRT.

The Magdalena River is subject to drought, and navigation is always impeded during the dry season, but it is an important artery of passenger and goods traffic. The river is navigable for 1,400 km; steamers ascend to La Dorada, 953 km from Barranquilla.

Telecommunications

In 2002 there were 12,363,000 telephone subscribers (285·6 for every 1,000 inhabitants) and 2,133,000 PCs in use (49·3 for every 1,000 persons). The number of Internet users was 2·0m. in 2002. Mobile phone subscribers numbered 4,596,000 in 2002 and there were 335,000 fax machines.

Postal Services

In 2003 there were 2,174 post offices.

SOCIAL INSTITUTIONS

Justice

The July 1991 constitution introduced the offices of public prosecutor and public defence. There is no extradition of Colombians for trial in other countries. The Supreme Court, at Bogotá, of 20 members, is divided into three chambers—civil cassation (six), criminal cassation (eight), labour cassation (six). Each of the 61 judicial districts has a superior court with various sub-dependent tribunals of lower juridical grade.

In 2003 there were 23,013 murders (a rate of around 52 per 100,000 persons), down 20% on the 2002 total. Colombia's murder rate is among the highest in the world. In 2003 the reported number of kidnappings numbered 2,200, the highest in the world, albeit down 26% on the 2002 total.

Colombia abolished the death penalty in 1997. The population in penal institutions in May 2001 was 54,034 (126 per 100,000 of national population).

Education

Primary education is free but not compulsory. Schools are both state and privately controlled. In 2000–01 there were 53,357 teachers for 1,070,482 children in pre-primary schools; 197,374 teachers for 5,221,018 pupils in primary schools; and 3,568,889 pupils with 185,588 teachers in secondary schools. In 1995 there were 235 higher education establishments with 562,716 students.

In 1995–96 in the public sector there were 20 universities, one open university, three technological universities, and universities of education, educational technology and industry. There were also two colleges of public administration, one school of police studies, one institute of fine art, one polytechnic and one conservatory. In the private sector there were 25 universities,

four Roman Catholic universities, one college of education and one school of administration. There were eight public, and 44 private, other institutions of higher education. In 1994–95 there were 208,394 university students.

Adult literacy in 2003 was 94·2% (93·7% among males and 94·6% among females).

In 2000–01 total expenditure on education came to 5·2% of GNP and represented 17·4% of total government expenditure.

Health

In 1997 there were 1,165 hospitals with 47,236 beds. Medical personnel (2002) was as follows: doctors, 58,761; dentists, 33,951; nurses and midwives, 103,158.

Welfare

The retirement age is 60 (men), or 55 (women); to be eligible for a state pension 1,000 weeks of contributions are required. The minimum social insurance pension is equal to the minimum wage. If a private pension is less than the minimum pension set by law, the government makes up the difference.

Unemployment benefit is a month's wage for every year of employment.

RELIGION

The religion is Roman Catholic (39·59m. adherents in 2001), with the Cardinal Archbishop of Bogotá as Primate of Colombia and nine other archbishoprics. There are also 44 bishops, 8 apostolic vicars, 5 apostolic prefects and 2 prelates. In 1990 there were 1,546 parishes and 4,020 priests. In May 2005 there were three cardinals. Other forms of religion are permitted so long as their exercise is 'not contrary to Christian morals or the law'. In 2001 there were 3·48m. followers of other religions.

CULTURE

World Heritage Sites

Colombia's heritage sites as classified by UNESCO (with year entered on list) are: the Port, Fortresses and Group of Monuments, Cartagena (1984)—on the Caribbean coast, Cartagena was one of the first cities to be founded in South America; Los Katios National Park (1994); the Historic Centre of Santa Cruz de Mompox (1995), or Mompós, was a focal point for colonization and a vital trade post between the Caribbean coast and the interior; the National Archaeological Park of Tierradentro (1995) contains statues and elaborately decorated underground tombs dating from the 6th–10th centuries; the San Agustín Archaeological Park (1995) protects religious monuments and sculptures from the 1st–8th centuries.

Broadcasting

There are five radio companies overseen by the Dirección General de Radiocomunicaciones. Instituto Nacional de Radio y Televisión transmits on three networks (colour by NTSC) and rents air time to 26 commercial companies. In 2000 there were 21·6m. radio sets and in 2001 there were 12·3m. TV sets. There are 33 television broadcast stations.

Press

There were 23 daily newspapers in 2002, with daily circulation totalling 1·1m.

Tourism

In 2002 there were 541,000 foreign tourists, bringing revenue of US$962m.

DIPLOMATIC REPRESENTATIVES

Of Colombia in the United Kingdom (Flat 3a, 3 Hans Cres., London, SW1X 0LN)
Ambassador: Dr Alfonso Lopez-Cabellero.

Of the United Kingdom in Colombia (Edificio Ing. Barings, Carrera 9 No 76–49, Piso 9, Bogotá)
Ambassador: Haydon Warren-Gash.

Of Colombia in the USA (2118 Leroy Pl., NW, Washington, D.C., 20008)
Ambassador: Andrés Pastrana Arango.

Of the USA in Colombia (Carrera 45 # 22D-45, Bogotá)
Ambassador: William B. Wood.

Of Colombia to the United Nations
Ambassador: María Angela Holguín-Cuellar.

Of Colombia to the European Union
Ambassador: Nicolas Echavarría Mesa.

FURTHER READING

Departamento Administrativo Nacional de Estadística. *Boletín de Estadística.* Monthly.

Davis, Robert H., *Historical Dictionary of Colombia.* 2nd ed. Metuchen (NJ), 1994.—*Colombia.* [Bibliography] ABC-Clio, Oxford and Santa Barbara (CA), 1990

Dudley, Steven, *Walking Ghosts: Murder and Guerrilla Politics in Colombia.* Routledge, London, 2004

Thorp, R., *Economic Management and Economic Development in Peru and Colombia.* London, 1991

National Statistical Office: Departamento Administrativo Nacional de Estadística (DANE), AA 80043, Zona Postal 611, Bogotá.
Website (Spanish only): http://www.dane.gov.co/

COMOROS

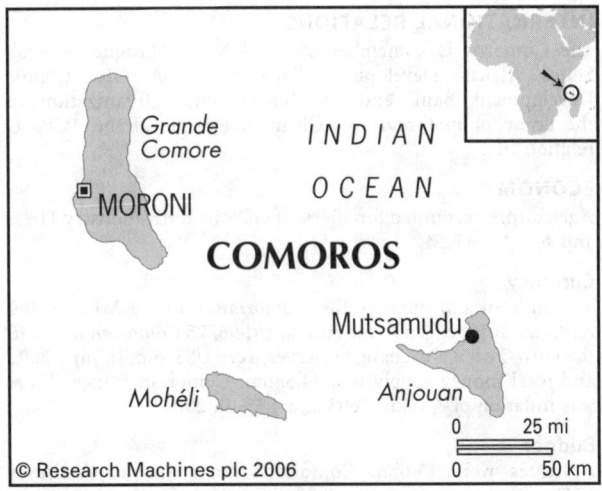

© Research Machines plc 2006

	Area (sq. km)	Population (2003 census, provisional)	Chief town
Njazídja (Grande Comore)	1,148	295,655	Moroni
Nzwani (Anjouan)	424	259,099	Mutsamudu
Mwali (Mohéli)	290	35,378	Fomboni

Estimated population of the chief towns (2002): Moroni, 40,275; Mutsamudu, 21,558; Domoni, 13,254; Fomboni, 13,053.

The indigenous population are a mixture of Malagasy, African, Malay and Arab peoples; the vast majority speak Comorian, an Arabized dialect of Swahili, but a small proportion speak Makua (a Bantu language) or one of the official languages, French and Arabic.

SOCIAL STATISTICS

2000 births (estimates), 26,600; deaths, 6,000. Estimated birth rate in 2000 was 37·7 per 1,000 population; estimated death rate, 8·5. Annual population growth rate, 1992–2002, 3·0%. Infant mortality, 59 per 1,000 live births (2001). Expectation of life in 2003 was 61·1 years among men and 65·4 among females. Fertility rate, 2001, 5·1 children per woman.

CLIMATE

There is a tropical climate, affected by Indian monsoon winds from the north, which gives a wet season from Nov. to April. Moroni, Jan. 81°F (27·2°C), July 75°F (23·9°C). Annual rainfall, 113" (2,825 mm).

CONSTITUTION AND GOVERNMENT

At a referendum on 23 Dec. 2001, 77% of voters approved a new constitution that keeps the three islands as one country while granting each one greater autonomy.

The *President of the Union* is Head of State.

There used to be a *Federal Assembly* comprised of 42 democratically elected officials and a 15-member *Senate* chosen by an electoral college, but these were dissolved after the 1999 coup. A new 33-member *Federal Parliament* was established following the elections of April 2004 (15 deputies selected by the individual islands' parliaments and 18 by universal suffrage).

National Anthem

'Udzima wa ya Masiwa' ('The union of the islands'); words by S. H. Abderamane, tune by K. Abdallah and S. H. Abderamane.

RECENT ELECTIONS

In the first round of presidential elections held on 16 April 2006 on Anjouan, Ahmed Abdallah Mohamed Sambi won 23·7% of the votes, Mohamed Djaanfari 13·1%, Ibrahim Halidi 10·4% and Caabi El-Yachroutu 9·6%. Turnout was 54·9%. The top three candidates qualified for the run-off election on 14 May. Provisional results gave Ahmed Abdallah Mohamed Sambi 58% of votes cast, against 28% for Ibrahim Halidi and 14% for Mohamed Djaanfari.

Parliamentary elections were held on 18 and 25 April 2004. Supporters of the three regional presidents won 12 of the 18 elected seats; supporters of Federal President Azaly Assoumani won six. Holding a majority, the regional presidents each appointed five legislators.

CURRENT ADMINISTRATION

President of the Union: Ahmed Abdallah Mohamed Sambi; b. 1958.

In March 2006 the government comprised:

Vice President of the Union Responsible for Administrative Services in Anjouan and Minister of Solidarity, Health, Population,

Union des Iles Comores
(Union of Comoros Islands)

Capital: Moroni
Population projection, 2010: 907,000
GDP per capita, 2003: (PPP$) 1,714
HDI/world rank: 0·547/132

KEY HISTORICAL EVENTS

The three islands forming the present state became French protectorates at the end of the 19th century and were proclaimed colonies in 1912. With neighbouring Mayotte they were administratively attached to Madagascar from 1914 until 1947 when the four islands became a French Overseas Territory, achieving internal self-government in Dec. 1961. In referendums held on each island on 22 Dec. 1974, the three western islands voted overwhelmingly for independence, while Mayotte voted to remain French. There have been more than 20 coups or attempted takeovers since independence, with recent years being marked by political disruption. In 1997 the islands of Anjouan and Mohéli attempted to secede from the federation.

In April 1999 an agreement was brokered on a federal structure for the three main islands—Grand Comore, Anjouan and Mohéli—to be known as the Union of Comoros Islands. However, the delegates from Anjouan did not sign the agreement. Violence broke out in the capital, Moroni, against Anjouans living there. A military coup followed on 30 April 1999, led by Col. Azaly Assoumani. He subsequently dissolved the government and the constitution, declaring a transitional government.

TERRITORY AND POPULATION

The Comoros consist of three islands in the Indian Ocean between the African mainland and Madagascar with a total area of 1,862 sq. km (719 sq. miles). The population at the 1991 census was 446,817; provisional census population, 2003, 590,151, giving a density of 317 per sq. km. The United Nations population estimate for 2003 was 757,000.

The UN gives a projected population for 2010 of 907,000.

In 2003, 65·0% of the population were rural.

Women's Affairs, Labour and State Reform: Vacant. *Vice President of the Union Responsible for Administrative Services in Mohéli and Minister of Justice, Islamic Affairs and Human Rights:* Ben Massoundi Rachidi.

Minister of State for Foreign Affairs, Co-operation and Francophonie, in Charge of Comorians Abroad: Aboudou Soefo. *Finance and Budget:* Oubeidi Mzé Chei. *Defence, Homeland Security, Communication and Decentralization, in Charge of Relations with Assemblies:* Abdou Madi Mari. *Economy, Foreign Trade, Industrial Development and Employment:* Maoulana Charif. *Rural Development, Fisheries, Handicrafts and Environment:* Mohamed Abdoulhamid. *Planning, Land Management, Energy and Town Planning:* Rehema Boinali. *National and Higher Education and Research:* Laïddine Ahamadi. *Transport, Tourism, Post and Telecommunications:* Badaoui Mohamed Chatur.

CURRENT LEADERS

Ahmed Abdallah Mohamed Sambi

Position
President

Introduction
Known as the 'Ayatollah' after studying in Iran, Ahmed Abdallah Sambi was elected president in May 2006, marking the country's first peaceful handover of power. A moderate Islamist, Sambi defeated two other candidates from the island of Anjouan, in accordance with the federal power-rotation agreement between the three islands.

Early Life
Ahmed Abdallah Mohamed Sambi was born on the 5 June 1958 at Mutsamadu on the Comorian island of Anjouan (Nzwani), where he attended primary and secondary school. He later studied in Saudi Arabia, Sudan and Iran. In 1980 he launched the first Comorian periodical, *Retour à la Source.* His preaching took him to Madagascar in 1982 and Mauritius in 1984 before he returned to the Comoros in 1986. On Anjouan he founded a girls' school and organized evening lectures which were banned by the police and led to his arrest. In 1987 he lectured on Grande Comore (Njazídja) and met Comorian scholars in Cairo.

In 1990 Sambi entered politics, helping to form the Front National pour la Justice, which supported Mohamed Taki Abdoulkarim (who later became president). In 1993 Sambi was active in raising money for Bosnian Muslims and the following year opposed the establishment of diplomatic relations with Israel. He was elected to the federal assembly in Dec. 1996 and was appointed president of the law commission. Sambi opposed the central government's crackdown on Anjouan in Aug. 1997 and was forced to resign his seat in the assembly. Despite urging Anjouan's separatists to negotiate, he fled to Madagascar in Jan. 1999 amid accusations of separatist sympathies. He went into manufacturing in 2000, producing mattresses and perfume. In May 2005 he announced his candidacy for the presidency and came first in the April 2006 primary, held only on Anjouan.

Career in Office
Supervised by South African peacekeepers, Sambi defeated two secular candidates, Deputy Speaker Mohamed Djaanfari and the veteran politician Ibrahim Halidi, in a national vote in May 2006, although his rivals alleged fraud. Sambi has voiced support for the reinstitution of an Islamic state in the Comoros, sparking fears of Islamic radicalization and restrictions on women's freedoms. Doubts have been raised concerning the authority of an Anjouanais over the central government bureaucracy, which is dominated by Grande Comorians.

DEFENCE

Army
The Army was reorganized after a failed coup in Sept. 1995.

Navy
One landing craft with ramps was purchased in 1981. Two small patrol boats were supplied by Japan in 1982. Personnel in 1996 numbered about 200.

INTERNATIONAL RELATIONS
The Comoros is a member of the UN, the League of Arab States, African Development Bank, COMESA, OIC, Islamic Development Bank and the International Organization of the Francophonie, and an ACP member state of the ACP-EU relationship.

ECONOMY
Agriculture accounted for 40·9% of GDP in 2002, industry 11·9% and services 47·2%.

Currency
The unit of currency is the *Comorian franc* (KMF) of 100 *centimes.* It is pegged to the euro at 491·96775 *Comorian francs* to the euro. Foreign exchange reserves were US$76m. in June 2002 and total money supply was 24,586m. Comorian francs. There was inflation of 3·8% in 2003 and 4·5% in 2004.

Budget
Revenues were 15·6bn. Comorian francs and expenditures 17·7bn. Comorian francs in 2000.

Performance
Real GDP growth was 2·1% in 2003 and 1·9% in 2004. In 2004 total GDP was US$0·4bn.

Banking and Finance
The Central Bank is the bank of issue. Chief commercial banks include the Banque Internationale des Comores, the Banque de Développement des Comores and the Banque pour l'Industrie et le Commerce-Comores.

ENERGY AND NATURAL RESOURCES
Environment
Carbon dioxide emissions from the consumption and flaring of fossil fuels were the equivalent of 0·1 tonnes per capita in 2002.

Electricity
In 2000 installed capacity was 6,000 kW. Production was around 19m. kWh in 2000; consumption per capita was an estimated 27 kWh in 2000.

Agriculture
80% of the economically active population depends upon agriculture, which (including fishing, hunting and forestry) contributed 41% to GDP in 2002. There were 80,000 ha. of arable land in 2001 and 52,000 ha. of permanent crops. The chief product was formerly sugarcane, but now vanilla, copra, maize and other food crops, cloves and essential oils (citronella, ylang-ylang, lemon grass) are the most important products. Production (2000 in 1,000 tonnes): coconuts, 75; bananas, 59; cassava, 53; rice, 17; copra, 9; taro, 9; sweet potatoes, 6.

Livestock (2000): goats, 140,000; cattle, 52,000; sheep, 20,000; asses, 5,000.

Forestry
In 2000 the area under forest was 8,000 ha., or 4·3% of the total land area. The forested area has been severely reduced because of the shortage of cultivable land and ylang-ylang production. In 2001, 9,000 cu. metres of timber were cut.

Fisheries
Fishing is on an individual basis, without modern equipment. The catch totalled 12,180 tonnes in 2001.

INDUSTRY
Branches include perfume distillation, textiles, furniture, jewellery, soft drinks and the processing of vanilla and copra.

Labour

The workforce in 1996 was 286,000 (58% males).

INTERNATIONAL TRADE

Total foreign debt was US$270m. in 2002.

Imports and Exports

In 2000 imports amounted to US$43·7m. and exports to US$11·9m.

Main import suppliers, 2000: France, 36·6%; Pakistan, 13·7%; Kenya, 10·8%. Main export markets, 2000: France, 38·6%; USA, 19·9%; Germany, 6·6%. The principal imports are rice (US$14·1m. in 1995), petroleum products (US$7·7m. in 1995), cement, meat, vehicles, and iron and steel. Main exports are vanilla (US$6·2m. in 1995), cloves, ylang-ylang, essences, cocoa, copra and coffee.

COMMUNICATIONS

Roads

In 2002 there were 880 km of roads, of which 76·5% were paved.

Civil Aviation

There is an international airport at Moroni (International Prince Said Ibrahim). In 2001 it handled 108,000 passengers (78,000 on international flights).

Shipping

In 2002 the merchant marine totalled 407,000 GRT.

Telecommunications

There were 10,300 telephone main lines in 2002 (13·5 per 1,000 persons) and 4,000 PCs in use (5·5 per 1,000 persons). In 1995 there were 200 fax machines. Internet users numbered 3,200 in 2002.

Postal Services

In 2001 there were 29 post offices.

SOCIAL INSTITUTIONS

Justice

French and Muslim law is in a new consolidated code. The Supreme Court comprises seven members, two each appointed by the President and the Federal Assembly, and one by each island's Legislative Council. The death penalty is authorized for murder. The last execution was in 1996.

Education

After two pre-primary years at Koran school, which 50% of children attend, there are six years of primary schooling for seven- to 13-year-olds followed by a four-year secondary stage attended by 25% of children. Some 5% of 17- to 20-year-olds conclude schooling at *lycées*. There were 97,706 pupils with 2,723 teachers in primary schools in 2000–01 and 24,324 pupils at secondary schools in 1999–2000. There were 714 students in tertiary education in 1999–2000.

The adult literacy rate in 2002 was 56·2% (63·5% among males and 49·1% among females).

In 1998–99 total expenditure on education came to 3·8% of GNP.

Health

In 1997 there were 64 physicians, 180 nurses and 74 midwives. In 1995 there were 29 hospital beds per 10,000 inhabitants.

RELIGION

Islam is the official religion: 98% of the population are Muslims; there is a small Christian minority. Following the coup of April 1999 the federal government discouraged the practice of religions other than Islam, with Christians especially facing restrictions on worship.

CULTURE

Broadcasting

The state-controlled Radio Comoros broadcasts in French and Comorian. In 1997 there were 90,000 radio and 1,000 television receivers.

Press

There was one weekly newspaper in 2002.

Tourism

In 2000 there were 24,000 foreign tourists (around a third from France), bringing revenue of US$15m.

DIPLOMATIC REPRESENTATIVES

Of the United Kingdom in the Comoros
Ambassador: Anthony Godson (resides in Port Louis, Mauritius).

Of the Comoros in the USA (Temporary: c/o the Permanent Mission of the Union of the Comoran Islands to the United Nations, 420 E 50th St., N.Y. 10022)
Ambassador: Vacant.

Of the USA in the Comoros
Ambassador: Vacant (resides in Port Louis, Mauritius).
Chargé d'Affaires a.i.: Stephen Schwartz.

Of the Comoros to the United Nations
Ambassador: Mahmoud M. Aboud.

Of the Comoros to the European Union
Ambassador (Designate): Sultan Chouzour.

FURTHER READING

Ottenheimer, M. and Ottenheimer, H. J., *Historical Dictionary of the Comoro Islands.* Metuchen (NJ), 1994

CENTRAL AFRICAN REP. SUDAN
UGANDA
RWANDA
CONGO
Kisangani
DEMOCRATIC
REPUBLIC OF
THE CONGO
BURUNDI
KINSHASA
Kananga
Lake
Tanganyika
TANZANIA
ANGOLA
Kolwezi Likasi
0   150 mi
0   250 km
© Research Machines plc 2006
ZAMBIA

République Démocratique du Congo

Capital: Kinshasa
Population projection, 2010: 67·13m.
GDP per capita, 2003: (PPP$) 697
HDI/world rank: 0·385/167

KEY HISTORICAL EVENTS

Bantu tribes migrated to the Congo basin from the northwest in the first millennium AD, forming several kingdoms and many smaller forest communities. Congo emerged as a kingdom on the Atlantic coast in the 14th century. King Nzinga Mbemba entered into diplomatic relations with Portugal after 1492. Christian missionaries, who baptized the king Affonso, caused divisions in Kongo society; the Portuguese were expelled in 1526, only to be welcomed back after attacks by the Jagas in the late 16th century.

The Luba kingdom was centred on the marshy Upemba depression in the southeast. Expansion began in the late 18th century under Ilungu Sungu. A tribute system extended Luba power and established trading relations with East Africa. In central Congo the Kuba kingdom was established in the 17th century as a federation of Bantu groups. Agriculture became the mainstay of the Kuba economy, strengthened by the introduction of American crops by Europeans. Trade made the Kuba elite, especially the Bushoong group, wealthy and encouraged the development of art and decorated cloth. Kuba thrived until the incursions of the Nsapo in the late 19th century.

King Leopold II of the Belgians claimed the Congo Basin as a personal possession in 1885. Exploitation of the native population provoked international condemnation. The Belgian government responded by annexing the Congo in 1908. Political representation was denied the Congolese until 1957, when the colonial administration introduced the *statut des villes* in response to the revolutionary demands of the *Alliance*

des BaKongo (Abako). Political violence increased, instigated by the *Mouvement National Congolais* (MNC), led by Patrice Lumumba. Local elections were held in Dec. 1959 and in Jan. 1960 the Belgian government announced a rapid independence programme. After general elections in May, the Republic of the Congo became independent on 1 June 1960, with Lumumba as prime minister and Joseph Kasavubu, the Abako leader, as president.

Independence and Anarchy

The country descended into anarchy, with the mineral-rich Katanga region declaring independence. Lumumba was ousted and in 1961 was assassinated. Only in 2002 did Belgium admit to participating in his murder. Lieut.-Gen. Joseph-Désiré Mobutu (later Sese Seko) seized power in 1965. At first he was seen as a strongman who could hold together a huge, unstable country comprising hundreds of tribes and language groups. He changed the country's name to Zaïre in 1971. In the 1970s he was feted by the USA, which used Zaïre as a springboard for operations into neighbouring Angola where western-backed Unita rebels were locked in civil war with a Cuban and Soviet backed government. Because Mobutu was useful in the fight against Communism the brutality and repressiveness of his regime was ignored.

After armed insurrection by Tutsi rebels in the province of Kivu, the government alleged pro-Tutsi intervention by the armies of Burundi and Rwanda and on 25 Oct. 1996 declared a state of emergency. By Dec. the secessionist forces of Laurent-Désiré Kabila, the *Alliance des Forces Démocratiques pour la Libération du Congo-Zaïre* (AFDL), had begun to drive the regular Zaïrean army out of Kivu and an attempt was made to establish a rebel administration, called 'Democratic Congo'. In the face of continuing rebel military successes and the disaffection of the army, the Government accepted a UN resolution demanding the immediate cessation of hostilities. The Security Council asked the rebels to make a public declaration of their acceptance. However, they continued in their victorious advance westwards, capturing Kisangani on 15 March 1997, then Kasai and Shaba, giving Kabila control of eastern Zaïre, and crucially the country's mineral wealth. After a futile attempt to deploy Serbian mercenaries, Mobutu succumbed to pressure—particularly from the USA and South Africa—agreeing to meet Kabila, an occasion that had all the trappings of a symbolic surrender. Mobutu fled on the night of 15–16 May 1997. He died of cancer four months later. Described as one of the most destructive tyrants of the African independence era, it is said that his personal fortune, if ever recovered, could wipe out his country's national debt.

On coming to power Kabila changed the name of the country to the Democratic Republic of the Congo. Hopes for democratic and economic renewal were soon disappointed. The Kabila regime relied too closely on its military backup, mainly Rwandans and eastern Congolese from the Tutsi minority. Those supporters seemed more interested in eliminating tribal enemies in eastern border areas than in establishing democracy. As a result, Rwanda and Uganda switched support to rebel forces. When Zimbabwe and Angola sent in troops to help President Kabila, full-scale civil war threatened. A ceasefire was negotiated at a Franco-African summit in Nov. 1998 but the military build-up continued into the new year and violence intensified.

A ceasefire was signed by leaders from more than a dozen African countries in July 1999 to bring the civil war between the government of President Kabila and rebel forces to an end. Rival factions of the *Rassemblement Congolais pour la Démocratie* (RCD), the main rebel group opposed to the president, also signed the accord, but not until Sept. The threat remained of an early return to outright civil war.

Violence and Collapse

'On the third anniversary of Kabila's assumption of power, a dispatch from the Panafrican News Agency reviewed the Democratic Republic of the Congo's condition:– Basic infrastructure is in total decay. Major sections of trunk "A" roads ... are not usable. Proposals for the rehabilitation of other facilities, such as hospitals, industries, manufacturing, and other structures, have also been stalled. On the social front, dirt and environmental decay have spewed all sorts of diseases. Smallpox, diarrhoea, sleeping sickness, among others, have come back in force while AIDS, malaria and poliomyelitis continue to devastate a population already weakened by under-nourishment... More than 60 per cent of the country's working population is not at work...' (The New Yorker, 25 Sept. 2000).

On 16 Jan. 2001 President Kabila was assassinated, allegedly by one of his own bodyguards. Kabila was succeeded by his son Joseph.

Prospects for peace improved dramatically in Feb. 2001 when the UN Security Council approved a plan for the disengagement of the warring factions that would allow the eventual deployment of 3,000 UN-supported peacekeepers. In early 2002 talks between the government and rebels on how to end the conflict ended without a satisfactory agreement embracing all factions. However, talks were resumed and in July 2002 the presidents of the Democratic Republic of the Congo and neighbouring Rwanda signed a peace deal that was expected to be the first stage towards ending the war which has claimed more than 3m. lives. In Oct. 2002 Rwanda completed the withdrawal of its forces. The Democratic Republic of the Congo and Uganda also signed a peace agreement.

Peace Settlement

The conflict, described as Africa's first continental war, had drawn in Zimbabwe, Angola and Namibia (and, for a time, Sudan and Chad) on the side of the government, which controls the west of the country, while Rwanda and Uganda backed other rival factions. The RCD, which controls areas in the east, was backed by Rwanda, while Uganda supported the Mouvement de Libération du Congo (MLC), based in the north and northeast of the country. Burundi also had troops in the country, allied to the Rwandans, although they stayed close to the border with Burundi. In Dec. 2002 the government and leading rebel forces reached an agreement on power-sharing. Its terms allowed for Joseph Kabila to remain as president, with a transitional power-sharing government, until elections which, after several postponements, were scheduled to be held in June 2006. The war is now more or less over, with the government having made peace with most of the principal rebel groups.

TERRITORY AND POPULATION

The Democratic Republic of the Congo is bounded in the north by the Central African Republic, northeast by Sudan, east by Uganda, Rwanda, Burundi and Lake Tanganyika, south by Zambia, southwest by Angola and northwest by the Republic of the Congo. There is a 37-km stretch of coastline which gives access to the Atlantic Ocean, with the Angolan exclave of Cabinda to the immediate north, and Angola itself to the south. Area, 2,344,798 sq. km (905,327 sq. miles). At the last census, in 1988, the population was 34·7m. Estimate (2005) 57,549,000 (68·2% rural in 2003); density, 24 per sq. km.

The UN gives a projected population for 2010 of 67·13m.

More than 200,000 refugees who escaped the fighting between Hutus and Tutsis in Rwanda and Burundi in 1994 are still in the Democratic Republic of the Congo (out of 1m. who came originally), and there are also 100,000 Angolan and 100,000 Sudanese refugees in the country.

Area and populations (1998 estimate) of the provinces (plus Kinshasa City), with their chief towns (1994 population estimates):

Region	Area (sq. km)	Population (in 1,000)	Chief town	Population
Bandundu	295,658	5,201	Bandundu	—
Bas-Congo	53,920	2,835	Matadi	172,730
Equateur	403,292	4,820	Mbandaka	169,841
Kasai Occidental	154,742	3,337	Kananga	393,030
Kasai Oriental	170,302	3,830	Mbuji-Mayi	806,475
Katanga	496,877	4,125	Lubumbashi	851,381
Maniema	132,250	1,247	Kindu	—
Nord-Kivu	59,483	3,564	Goma	109,094
Orientale	503,239	5,566	Kisangani	417,517
Sud-Kivu	65,070	2,838	Bukavu	201,569
Kinshasa City[1]	9,965	4,787	Kinshasa	4,885,000[2]

[1]Neutral city. [2]1999 figure.

Other large cities (with estimated 1994 population): Kolwezi (417,810), Likasi (299,118), Kikwit (182,142), Tshikapa (180,860).

The population is Bantu, with minorities of Sudanese (in the north), Nilotes (northeast), Pygmies and Hamites (in the east). French is the official language, but of more than 200 languages spoken, four are recognized as national languages: Kiswahili, Tshiluba, Kikongo and Lingala. Lingala has become the lingua franca after French.

SOCIAL STATISTICS

2000 estimates: births, 2,293,000; deaths, 661,000. Rates (2000 estimates, per 1,000 population); birth, 47·2; death, 13·6. Annual population growth rate, 1992–2002, 2·4%. Infant mortality in 2001 was 129 per 1,000 live births. Expectation of life in 2003 was 42·1 years for men and 44·1 for females. Fertility rate, 2001, 6·7 children per woman.

CLIMATE

The climate is varied, the central region having an equatorial climate, with year-long high temperatures and rain at all seasons. Elsewhere, depending on position north or south of the Equator, there are well-marked wet and dry seasons. The mountains of the east and south have a temperate mountain climate, with the highest summits having considerable snowfall. Kinshasa, Jan. 79°F (26·1°C), July 73°F (22·8°C). Annual rainfall 45" (1,125 mm). Kananga, Jan. 76°F (24·4°C), July 74°F (23·3°C). Annual rainfall 62" (1,584 mm). Kisangani, Jan. 78°F (25·6°C), July 75°F (23·9°C). Annual rainfall 68" (1,704 mm). Lubumbashi, Jan. 72°F (22·2°C), July 61°F (16·1°C). Annual rainfall 50" (1,237 mm).

CONSTITUTION AND GOVERNMENT

A new constitution was adopted by the transitional parliament on 16 May 2005. It limits the powers of the president, who may now serve a maximum of two five-year terms and lowers the minimum age for presidential candidates from 35 to 30. It allows a greater degree of federalism and recognises as citizens all ethnic groups at the time of independence in 1960. It also called for presidential elections by June 2006. In a referendum held on 18–19 Dec. 2005, 83% of voters approved the constitution in the country's first free vote in 40 years. The constitution was promulgated on 18 Feb. 2006.

Gen. Laurent-Désiré Kabila seized power on 17 May 1997 but the civil war that had started the previous year continued. He assumed the powers of both chief of state and head of government. A new constitution came into force in 1998. A ceasefire, brokered by President Frederick Chiluba of Zambia, was signed by Sept. 1999 by all major groups involved in the civil war. All parties agreed to administer the areas under their control at the time. Kabila was assassinated in Jan. 2001 and was succeeded by his son, Joseph. The ban on political parties was lifted in May 2001. In Dec. 2002 the commitments laid down in the Lusaka peace agreement of 1999 were settled by the main groups. In April 2003 a new constitution was adopted, providing for the installation of a provisional government agreed by rival factions, to rule for two years. A power-sharing transitional government was announced on 30 June 2003.

The 240-member *Constituent and Legislative Assembly* was appointed in Aug. 2000 by former President Laurent Désiré Kabila. In Aug. 2003 a new bicameral parliament of 500 members and 120 senators met in Kinshasa. The representatives were chosen from the groups that comprise the new transitional government.

National Anthem

'Debout Congolais' ('Stand up, Congolese'); words and tune by J. Lutumba and S. Boka di Mpasi Londi.

RECENT ELECTIONS

Presidential and parliamentary elections, the first since the Democratic Republic of the Congo's became independent in 1960, were scheduled to take place on 18 June 2006.

CURRENT ADMINISTRATION

President: Joseph Kabila; b. 1971 (in office since 17 Jan. 2001).

On 30 June 2003 a new transitional government was announced, composed of members of the former government (f.g.), the political opposition (p.o.), the Rassemblement Congolais pour la Démocratie (RCD-Goma), the Rassemblement Congolais pour la Démocratie-Nationale (RCD-N), the Rassemblement Congolais pour la Démocratie-Mouvement de Libération (RCD-ML), the Mouvement de Libération du Congo (MLC) and the Mayi-Mayi. Several members of civil society (c.s.) were also appointed. In March 2006 the government comprised:

Vice-Presidents: Jean-Pierre Bemba (MLC), Abdoulaye Yerodia Ndombasi (f.g.), Arthur Z'ahidi Ngoma (p.o.) and Azarias Ruberwa (RCD-Goma).

Minister for the Interior, Decentralization and Security: Théophile Mbemba Fundu (f.g.). *Foreign Affairs and International Co-operation:* Raymond Ramazani Baya (MLC). *Regional Co-operation:* Mbusa Nyamwisi (RCD-ML). *Defence, Demobilization and War Veterans:* Adolphe Onusumba (RCD-Goma). *Family and Women's Affairs:* Faida Mwangila (RCD-Goma). *Justice:* Honorius Kisimba Ngoy (p.o.). *Human Rights:* Marie-Madeleine Kalala (c.s.). *Press and Information:* Henri Mova Sakanyi (f.g.). *Planning:* Alexis Thambwe Mwamba (MLC). *Budget:* François Mwamba Tshishimbi (RCD-Goma). *Finance:* Marco Banguli (f.g.). *Economy:* Pierre Manoka (RCD-Goma). *Industry and Small and Medium Enterprises:* Mukendi Tshambula (f.g.). *Mines:* Ingele Ifoto (p.o.). *Energy:* Salomon Banamuhere (f.g.). *External Trade:* Chantal Ngalula Mulumba (RCD-N). *State Properties:* Célestin Mvunabandi (RCD-Goma). *Civil Service:* Athenase Matenda Kyelu (c.s.). *Agriculture:* Constant Ndom Nda Ombel (MLC). *Rural Development:* Pardonne Kaliba Munanga (Mayi-Mayi). *Posts and Telecommunications:* Gertrude Kitembo (RCD-Goma). *Scientific Research:* Gérard Kamanda Wa Kamanda (p.o.). *Public Works and Infrastructure:* José Makila (MLC). *Transport and Communications:* Eva Makasa (p.o.). *Environment:* Anselme Enerunga (Mayi-Mayi). *Tourism:* José Engbanda (MLC). *Land Affairs:* Venant Tshipasa (p.o.). *Health:* Emile Bongeli Yekolo (f.g.). *University and Higher Education:* Theo Baruti (RCD-Goma). *Primary, Secondary and Professional Education:* Paul Musafiri (MLC). *Labour and Social Welfare:* Balamage Nkolo (RCD-Goma). *Social Affairs:* Laurent-Charles Otete (p.o.). *Youth and Sports:* Jacques Lunguana (MLC). *Humanitarian Affairs and Solidarity:* Catherine Nzuzi Wa Mbombo (p.o.). *Culture and Arts:* Philémon Mukendi (f.g.). *Urban Affairs:* John Tibasima (RCD-ML).

CURRENT LEADERS

Joseph Kabila

Position
President

Introduction
Joseph Kabila is the son of the former president Laurent Kabila who was assassinated on 16 Jan. 2001. Despite being little known outside his own group, Joseph Kabila was appointed president. He inherited a country divided by civil war which had spanned his father's tenure. Although promising unification in Congo, many need to be persuaded that Kabila has the necessary authority to restore peace to a country split along tribal lines and, despite its rich natural resources, suffering from poverty and economic instability.

Early Life
Joseph Kabila was born on 4 Dec. 1971 at Laurent Kabila's guerrilla movement's headquarters (Hewa Bora) in the Fizi territory of Sud-Kivu, Congo. He was educated at a French-language school in Tanzania and then studied at the Makerere University in Uganda. He also did military training in China. In 1996 his father sent him to join the rebels against the country's dictator, Mobutu Sese Seko. In 1996–97, during the 'liberation war', Kabila was appointed commander of the Northern front (Kisangani).

Career in Office
Following his father's death, Kabila replaced him as president. At first, the identity of his father's assassin was unclear, but in 2002 two military officers, Gen. Yav Nawej and Col. Eddy Kapend, were charged with conspiracy and murder.

In his inaugural speech in 2001, Joseph Kabila promised a ceasefire with the rebels, an end to corruption and an improvement in living standards. He pledged to lead the country into peace and multi-party democracy, and in May 2001 he lifted restrictions on political parties.

Peace negotiations brokered by South Africa in 2002 between the Kabila government and rebel factions led to agreement in July on a withdrawal of foreign forces from the country and in Dec. on a power-sharing accord. Kabila was to remain as president pending future democratic elections, while his supporters, the civilian political opposition and the two main rebel groups would each appoint a vice-president and seven ministers to serve under him on an interim basis. On 30 June 2003 Kabila announced the composition of the new power-sharing government, in line with the Dec. 2002 accord. Although this was a major breakthrough, members of the new transitional government expressed fears for their safety in Kinshasa and stressed the continuing atmosphere of mistrust between the various factions. The new government was inaugurated in Kinshasa in July, and Kabila announced that elections should be held in June 2005. However, political progress has since been very slow and lawlessness and human rights abuses have continued, particularly in the east and northeast of the country. Following a referendum on a new constitution in Dec. 2005, elections were scheduled to be held in June 2006.

DEFENCE

Following the overthrow of the Mobutu regime in May 1997, the former Zaïrean armed forces were in disarray. In June 2003 command of ground forces and naval forces were handed over to the RCD-Goma and MLC factions respectively as part of the power-sharing transitional government. Supreme command of the armed forces will remain in the hands of the former government faction.

A UN mission, MONUC, has been in the Democratic Republic of the Congo since 1999. It currently numbers 16,200 and is the largest peacekeeping force in the world.

Defence expenditure totalled US$946m. in 2002 (US$18 per capita), representing 21·7% of GDP.

Army

The total strength of the Army was estimated at 79,000 (2002). There is an additional paramilitary National Police Force of unknown size. There are thought to be ten infantry brigades, one presidential guard brigade, one mechanized infantry brigade and one commando brigade.

Navy

Naval strength is estimated at 900. The main coastal base is at Matadi.

INTERNATIONAL RELATIONS

The Democratic Republic of the Congo is a member of the UN, WTO, the African Union, African Development Bank, COMESA, IOM, International Organization of the Francophonie and is an ACP member state of the ACP-EU relationship.

ECONOMY

Agriculture accounted for 57·1% of GDP in 2002 (one of the highest percentages of any country), industry 12·1% and services 30·8%. Following the end of the civil war in 2002, several donor countries and institutions agreed to a development aid package worth US$2·5bn.

Overview

The Democratic Republic of the Congo (DRC) has suffered severe economic difficulties since the mid-1980s owing to extreme socio-political unrest. Per capita income has dropped steadily since independence, from US$250 in 1960 to US$100 in 2001. Ceasefire agreements in 1999 and 2001 saw a series of economic and social reforms put into place. The government launched the Interim Post–Conflict Program in 2000, with the aim of rehabilitating the economic sector and rebuilding infrastructure. Stabilization measures launched in May 2001 succeeded in breaking hyperinflation, bringing inflation down from 630% in 2000 to an unstable 26% in 2005. After a decade of contraction, growth has increased since 2002 to nearly 7% in 2005. The economy is dominated by the oil sector, accounting for over 25% of GDP and 75% of export earnings. The DRC is one of the most debt-laden countries in the world, with external debt representing 225% of GDP and 1,280% of exports.

Currency

The unit of currency is the *Congo franc* which replaced the former *zaïre* in July 1998. The value of the new currency fell by two-thirds in the six months following its launch. Foreign exchange reserves were US$83m. in Dec. 1996. Gold reserves were 54,000 troy oz in 1997. Inflation, which reached 23,760% in 1994, had declined to 3·9% by 2004. In May 2001 the franc was floated in an effort to overcome the economic chaos caused by three years of state control and inter-regional war.

Budget

In 2001 total revenue was 66,644m. Congo francs and total expenditure was 139,200m. Congo francs. International economic aid has been made dependent on a coherent plan to revive the economy and progress on democracy and human rights.

Performance

GDP growth was −4·3% in 1999, −6·2% in 2000 and −2·1% in 2001. However, following the end of the five-year long war the economy grew by 3·5% in 2002, 5·7% in 2003 and 6·8% in 2004. Total GDP in 2004 was US$6·6bn.

Banking and Finance

The central bank, the Banque Centrale du Congo (*Governor*, Jean-Claude Masangu), achieved independence in May 2002. There are 14 commercial banks. The largest is the Banque Commerciale Congolaise, in which the Société Générale of Belgium has a 25% stake through its subsidiary, Belgolaise. Other banks include Citibank and Stanbic. A 40% state-owned investment bank, Société Financière de Développement (Sofide), lends mainly to agriculture and manufacturing.

ENERGY AND NATURAL RESOURCES

Electricity

Production (2000), 5·5bn. kWh. A dam at Inga, on the River Congo near Matadi, has a potential capacity in excess of 42,000 MW. Installed capacity was 3·2m. kW in 2000. Consumption per capita was 87 kWh in 2000.

Oil and Gas

Offshore oil production began in Nov. 1975; crude production (1999) was 1·1m. tonnes. Reserves in 2002 were 187m. bbls. There is an oil refinery at Kinlao-Muanda.

Minerals

Production, 2001 (in 1,000 tonnes): coal (2000), 96; copper, 23; cobalt, 5; gold, 50 kg; diamonds (2002), 18·2m. carats. Only Australia, Botswana and Russia produce more diamonds. The country holds an estimated 80% of the world's coltan (columbite-tantalite) reserves. Coal, tin and silver are also found. The most important mining area is in the province of Katanga.

Agriculture

There were, in 2001, 6·70m. ha. of arable land and 1·18m. ha. of permanent crops. 11,000 ha. were irrigated in 2001. There were 2,430 tractors in 2001. The main agricultural crops (2000 production in 1,000 tonnes) are: cassava, 15,959; plantains, 1,800; sugarcane, 1,669; maize, 1,184; rice, 383; groundnuts, 382; sweet potatoes, 370; bananas, 312; yams, 255; papayas, 213; mangoes, 206; pineapples, 196; oranges, 185; palm oil, 157; dry beans, 122; palm kernels, 63; taro, 62.

Livestock (2000): goats, 4,131,000; pigs, 1,049,000; sheep, 925,000; cattle, 882,000; poultry, 22m.

Forestry

Forests covered 135·21m. ha. in 2000, or 59·6% of the land area. Timber production in 2001 was 69·73m. cu. metres.

Fisheries

The catch for 2001 was approximately 208,448 tonnes, almost entirely from inland waters.

INDUSTRY

The main manufactures are foodstuffs, beverages, tobacco, textiles, rubber, leather, wood products, cement and building materials, metallurgy and metal extraction, metal items, transport vehicles, electrical equipment and bicycles. Main products in 1,000 tonnes: cement (1999), 100; steel (2001), 80; sugar (2002), 65; soap (1995), 47; tyres (1995), 50,000 units; printed fabrics (1995), 15·73m. sq. metres; shoes (1995), 1·6m. pairs; beer (2003), 149·6m. litres.

Labour

In 1996 the workforce was 19·62m. (56% males). Agriculture employs around 65% of the total economically active population.

INTERNATIONAL TRADE

With Burundi and Rwanda, the Democratic Republic of the Congo forms part of the Economic Community of the Great Lakes. External debt was US$8,726m. in 2002.

Imports and Exports

Imports in 2001 were US$703·9m. (US$697·1m. in 2000); exports were US$868·2m. (US$823·5m. in 2000). Main commodities for import are consumer goods, foodstuffs, mining and other machinery, transport equipment and fuels; and for export:

diamonds, copper, coffee, cobalt and crude oil. Principal import suppliers in 1999 were South Africa, 22·0%; Belgium, 15·8%; Nigeria, 10·0%; Zambia, 5·3%. Principal export markets were Belgium-Luxembourg, 63·8%; USA, 19·0%; Finland, 4·1%; Italy, 3·0%.

COMMUNICATIONS

Roads
In 2002 there were approximately 33,130 km of motorways and main roads, 40,500 km of secondary roads and 83,400 km of other roads. There were an estimated 26,200 passenger cars in use in 2000 plus 20,400 trucks and vans.

Rail
There was 5,138 km of track on three gauges in 1995, of which 858 km was electrified. However, the length of track in use was severely reduced by the civil strife in late 1996 and the early part of 1997. In 2000, 1·3m. passengers were carried and 1·5m. tonnes of freight.

Civil Aviation
There is an international airport at Kinshasa (Ndjili). Other major airports are at Lubumbashi (Luano), Bukavu, Goma and Kisangani. The national carrier is Congo Airlines. In 2001 Kinshasa handled 278,000 passengers (142,000 on international flights) and 41,500 tonnes of freight.

Shipping
The River Congo and its tributaries are navigable to 300-tonne vessels for about 14,500 km. Regular traffic has been established between Kinshasa and Kisangani as well as Ilebo, on the Lualaba (*i.e.*, the river above Kisangani), on some tributaries and on the lakes. The Democratic Republic of the Congo has only 37 km of sea coast. In 2002 merchant shipping totalled 13,000 GRT. Matadi, Kinshasa and Kalemie are the main seaports.

Telecommunications
There is a ground satellite communications station outside Kinshasa. Telephone subscribers numbered 570,000 in 2002, or 10·8 per 1,000 inhabitants, including 560,000 mobile phone subscribers. With 98·2% of all telephone subscribers being mobile users, no other country has such a high ratio of mobile subscribers to landline subscribers. In 1995 there were 5,000 fax machines. In 2002 there were 50,000 Internet users.

Postal Services
In 2003 there were 280 post offices.

SOCIAL INSTITUTIONS

Justice
There is a Supreme Court at Kinshasa, 11 courts of appeal, 36 courts of first instance and 24 'peace tribunals'. The death penalty is in force.

The population in penal institutions in Jan. 2004 was approximately 30,000 (57 per 100,000 of national population).

Education
In 1994–95 there were 14,885 primary schools with 121,054 teachers for 5·4m. pupils, and 1·5m. pupils in secondary schools. In 1994–95 there were 93,266 students at university level. In higher education there were three universities (Kinshasa, Kisangani and Lubumbashi) in 1994–95, 14 teacher training colleges and 18 technical institutes in the public sector; and 13 university institutes, four teacher training colleges and 49 technical institutes in the private sector. Adult literacy rate was 65·3% in 2003 (male, 79·8%; female, 51·9%).

Health
In 1996 there were 3,224 physicians, 514 dentists and 20,652 nurses.

The Democratic Republic of the Congo has been one of the least successful countries in the battle against undernourishment in the past 15 years. The proportion of the population classified as undernourished increased from 32% in 1990–92 to 71% by 2000–02.

RELIGION
In 2001 there were 21·99m. Roman Catholics, 16·95m. Protestants, 7·17m. Kimbanguistes (African Christians) and 0·75m. Muslims. Animist beliefs persist. In May 2005 there was one cardinal.

CULTURE

World Heritage Sites
Sites under Democratic Republic of the Congo jurisdiction which appear on UNESCO's world heritage list are (with year entered on list): Virunga National Park (1979); Kahuzi-Biega National Park (1980); Garamba National Park (1980); Salonga National Park (1984); and Okapi Wildlife Reserve (1996).

Broadcasting
Broadcasting is provided by government-controlled radio and television stations (colour by SECAM V). There is also an educational radio station. There were 18·7m. radio sets in 2000 and 6·5m. TV receivers in 1997.

Press
In 1998 there were nine daily newspapers with a combined circulation of 129,000.

Tourism
In 2000 there were 103,000 foreign tourists; spending by tourists in 1998 totalled US$2m.

DIPLOMATIC REPRESENTATIVES
Of the Democratic Republic of the Congo in the United Kingdom (281 Gray's Inn Rd, London, WC1X 8QF)
Ambassador: Eugenie Tshiela Compton.

Of the United Kingdom in the Democratic Republic of the Congo (83 Ave. du Roi Baudouin, Kinshasa)
Ambassador: Andrew Sparkes.

Of the Democratic Republic of the Congo in the USA (1800 New Hampshire Ave., NW, Washington, D.C., 20009)
Ambassador: Faida Mitifu.

Of the USA in the Democratic Republic of the Congo (310 Ave. des Aviateurs, Kinshasa)
Ambassador: Roger A. Meece.

Of the Democratic Republic of the Congo to the United Nations
Ambassador: Ileka Atoki.

Of the Democratic Republic of the Congo to the European Union
Ambassador: Jean-Pierre Mavungu-di-Ngoma.

FURTHER READING
Hochschild, Adam, *King Leopold's Ghost: A Study of Greed, Terror and Heroism in Colonial Africa.* Macmillan, London, 1999
Leslie, W. J., *Zaïre: Continuity and Political Change in an Oppressive State.* Boulder (CO), 1993
Williams, D. B., *et al.*, *Zaïre.* [Bibliography] 2nd ed. ABC-Clio, Oxford and Santa Barbara (CA), 1995
Wrong, Michaela, *In the Footsteps of Mr Kurtz: Living on the Brink of Disaster in the Congo.* Fourth Estate, London, 2000

CONGO, REPUBLIC OF THE

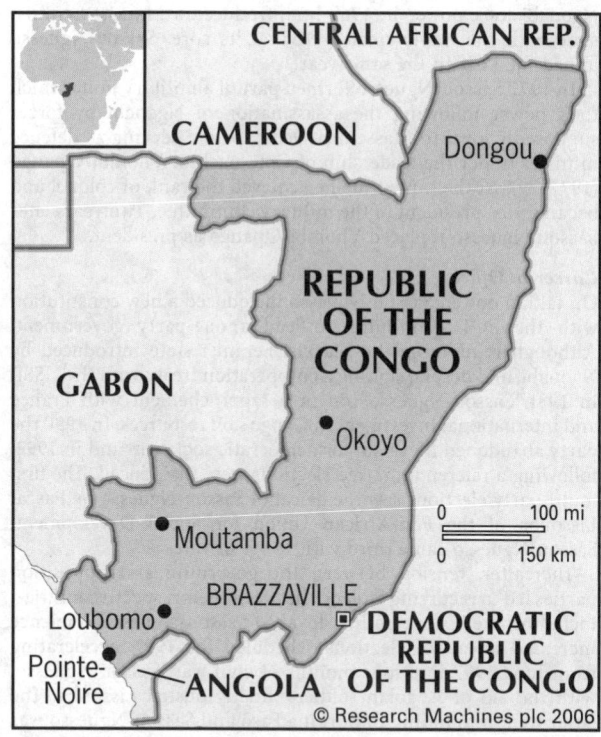

République du Congo

Capital: Brazzaville
Population projection, 2010: 4·63m.
GDP per capita, 2003: (PPP$) 965
HDI/world rank: 0·512/142

KEY HISTORICAL EVENTS

First occupied by France in 1882, the Congo became a territory of French Equatorial Africa from 1910–58, and then a member state of the French Community. Between 1940 and 1944, thanks to Equatorial Africa's allegiance to Gen. de Gaulle, he named Brazzaville the capital of the Empire and Liberated France. Independence was granted in 1960. A Marxist-Leninist state was introduced in 1970. Free elections were restored in 1992 but violence erupted when in June 1997 President Lissouba tried to disarm opposition militia ahead of a fresh election. There followed four months of civil war with fighting concentrated on Brazzaville which became a ghost town. In Oct. Gen. Sassou-Nguesso proclaimed victory, having relied upon military support from Angola. President Lissouba went into hiding in Burkina Faso. A peace agreement signed in Nov. 1999 between President Sassou-Nguesso and the 'Cocoye' and 'Ninja' militias brought a period of relative stability.

TERRITORY AND POPULATION

The Republic of the Congo is bounded by Cameroon and the Central African Republic in the north, the Democratic Republic of the Congo to the east and south, Angola and the Atlantic Ocean to the southwest and Gabon to the west, and covers 341,821 sq. km. At the census of 1996 the population was 2,591,271. Estimated population in 2005, 3,999,000; density, 11·7 per sq. km.

The UN gives a projected population for 2010 of 4·63m.

In 2003, 53·5% of the population were urban. Census population of major cities in 1996: Brazzaville, the capital, 856,410; Pointe-Noire, 455,131; Loubomo (Dolisie), 79,852; N'Kayi, 46,727; Ouesso, 17,784; Mossendjo, 16,458.

Area, census population and county towns of the regions in 1996 were:

Region	Sq. km	Population	County town
Bouenza	12,258	236,566	Madingou
Capital District	100	856,410	Brazzaville
Cuvette	} 74,850	{ 112,946	Owando
Cuvette Ouest		49,422	Ewo
Kouilou	13,650	532,179	Pointe-Noire
Lékoumou	20,950	75,734	Sibiti
Likouala	66,044	66,252	Impfondo
Niari	25,918	199,988	Loubomo (Dolisie)
Plateaux	38,400	139,371	Djambala
Pool	33,955	265,180	Kinkala
Sangha	55,795	57,223	Ouesso

Main ethnic groups are: Kongo (48%), Sangha (20%), Teke (17%) and M'Bochi (12%).

French is the official language. Kongo languages are widely spoken. Monokutuba and Lingala serve as lingua francas.

SOCIAL STATISTICS

2000 estimates: births, 152,000; deaths, 48,000. Rates, 2000 estimates (per 1,000 population): births, 44·2; deaths, 14·0. Infant mortality, 2001 (per 1,000 live births), 81. Expectation of life in 2003 was 50·7 years for males and 53·2 for females. Annual population growth rate, 1992–2002, 3·2%. Fertility rate, 2001, 6·3 children per woman.

CLIMATE

An equatorial climate, with moderate rainfall and a small range of temperature. There is a long dry season from May to Oct. in the southwest plateaux, but the Congo Basin in the northeast is more humid, with rainfall approaching 100" (2,500 mm). Brazzaville, Jan. 78°F (25·6°C), July 73°F (22·8°C). Annual rainfall 59" (1,473 mm).

CONSTITUTION AND GOVERNMENT

A new constitution was approved in a referendum held in Jan. 2002. Under the new constitution the president's term of office is increased from five to seven years. The constitution provides for a new two-chamber assembly consisting of a house of representatives and a senate. The president may also appoint and dismiss ministers. 84·3% of voters were in favour of the draft constitution and 11·3% against. Turnout was 78%, despite calls from opposition parties for a boycott. The new constitution came into force in Aug. 2002.

There is a 137-seat *National Assembly*, with members elected for a five-year term in single-seat constituencies, and a 66-seat *Senate*, with members elected for a six-year term (one third of members every two years).

National Anthem

'La Congolaise'; words by Levent Kimbangui, tune by Français Jacques Tondra.

RECENT ELECTIONS

Presidential elections were held on 10 March 2002. Incumbent Denis Sassou-Nguesso won with 89·4% of votes cast, against 2·7% for Joseph Kignoumbi Kia Mboungou. The turnout was 74·7%. The election represented the first time that Sassou-Nguesso was elected to the presidency, having seized power in 1979 and again in 1997.

Parliamentary elections were held on 26 May and 22 June 2002. President Denis Sassou-Nguesso's Congolese Labour Party won 52 out of 137 seats; his allies, 31; the Union for Democracy and Republic, 6; the Pan-African Union for Social Development, 4. Non-partisans and other political formations won the remaining seats.

CURRENT ADMINISTRATION

President: Denis Sassou-Nguesso; b. 1943 (Congolese Labour Party; sworn in 25 Oct. 1997 for a second time and re-elected in March 2002, having previously held office 1979–92).

In March 2006 the government comprised:

Prime Minister: Isidore Mvouba; b. 1954 (Congolese Labour Party; since 7 Jan. 2005).

State Minister of Planning, Economic Integration and Territorial Development: Pierre Moussa. *Foreign Affairs and Francophonie Affairs:* Rodolphe Adada. *Civil Service and State Reform:* Jean-Martin Mbemba. *Hydrocarbons:* Jean-Baptiste Tati Loutard.

Minister of Agriculture, Livestock and Fisheries: Jeanne Dambedzet. *Commerce, Consumer Affairs and Supplies:* Adélaïde Moundélé-Ngollo. *Communications, in Charge of Relations with Parliament and Government Spokesperson:* Alain Akoualat. *Construction, Urbanism and Housing:* Claude Alphonse Nsilou. *Culture, Arts and Tourism:* Jean Claude Gakosso. *Economy, Finance and Budget:* Pacifique Issoïbéka. *Energy and Water Resources:* Bruno Jean-Richard Itoua. *Equipment and Public Works:* Florent Ntsiba. *Forestry and the Environment:* Henri Djombo. *Health and Population:* Dr Alphonse Gando. *Higher Education:* Henri Ossebi. *Industrial Development and Promotion of the Private Sector:* Emile Mabondzot. *Justice, Guardian of the Seals and Human Rights:* Gabriel Entcha-Ebia. *Labour, Employment and Social Security:* Gilbert Ondongo. *Land Reform:* Lamyr Nguelé. *Maritime Economy and Merchant Marine:* Louis-Marie Nombo Mavoungou. *Mines, Mining Industry and Geology:* Pierre Oba. *Posts and Telecommunications, in Charge of Technological Development:* Philippe Mvouvo. *Primary and Secondary Education and Literacy:* Rosalie Kama. *Promotion of Women and the Involvement of Women in Development:* Jeanne Françoise Lekomba. *Scientific Research and Technical Innovation:* Pierre Ernest Abandzounou. *Security and Public Order:* Paul Mbot. *Small and Medium-Sized Businesses, and Handicrafts:* Martin Parfait Aimé Coussoud-Mavoungou. *Social Affairs, Solidarity, Humanitarian Action, Disabled War Veterans and Family Affairs:* Emilienne Raoul. *Sports and Youth Affairs:* Marcel Mbani. *Technical and Vocational Training:* Pierre Michel Nguimbi. *Territorial Administration and Decentralization:* François Ibovi. *Transport and Civil Aviation:* André Okombi Salissa. *Presidency, in Charge of Co-operation and Development:* Justin Ballay Megot. *Presidency, in Charge of Defence:* Brig.-Gen. Jacques Yvon Ndolou.

CURRENT LEADERS

Denis Sassou-Nguesso

Position
President

Introduction
A military leader from the 1960s, Denis Sassou-Nguesso ruled the Republic of the Congo between 1979–92, regaining power in 1997 in a coup. He maintained Congo's one-party Marxist-Leninist state—through the Congolese Labour Party (PCT; Parti Congolais du Travail)—until 1992, when he introduced free elections in which he was defeated. His latest tenure since 1997 has been marred by civil war and economic crises.

Early Life
Sassou-Nguesso was born in 1943 in Edou. Joining the army in 1960, he trained at the General Leclerc military school in

the Congo and the Saint-Maixent military school in France. In 1963 he was involved in the overthrow of Fulbert Youlou, the first president of independent Congo from 1959, and then of his successor Alphonse Massemba-Débat (1963–68). When Marien Ngouabi took power in 1969 he introduced a Marxist-Leninist state with the newly-created PCT at its core. Sassou-Nguesso joined the PCT in the same year.

In 1977 Sassou-Nguesso formed part of a military junta which took power following the assassination of Ngouabi by forces supposedly loyal to Massemba-Débat, before serving as defence minister under the leadership of Col. Joachim Yhombi-Opango (1977–79). At the same time he achieved the rank of colonel and became vice president of the military committee. Two years later Sassou-Nguesso replaced Yhombi-Opango as president.

Career in Office
On taking power, Sassou-Nguesso introduced a new constitution with the PCT continuing to lead a one-party government. Although reinforcing the Marxist-Leninist state introduced by Ngouabi, and despite signing a co-operation treaty with the USSR in 1981, Sassou-Nguesso sought a rapprochement with France and international investment in Congo's oil resources. In 1990 the party abandoned Marxism for democratic socialism and in 1992, following a referendum, free elections were introduced. The first multi-party elections saw the defeat of Sassou-Nguesso by Pascal Lissouba of the Pan-African Union for Social Development. Sassou-Nguesso came third with 16·9% of votes.

Thereafter, tension between the governing and opposition parties led to recurring violence between their respective militias, including the 'Cobra' militia loyal to Sassou-Nguesso. Violence increased ahead of elections scheduled for 1997, accelerating from June 1997 into four months of civil war. Sassou-Nguesso, with the aid of Angolan soldiers, finally ousted Lissouba. The latter went into hiding in Burkina Faso and Sassou-Nguesso was sworn in as president again in Oct. 1997. Between 10,000–15,000 people were killed in the conflict and the capital's infrastructure was destroyed.

Fighting erupted in Jan. 1999 as 'Cocoye' rebels loyal to Lissouba attacked Brazzaville. In April there was an attack on Pointe-Noire by the 'Ninja' rebels loyal to former prime minister Bernard Kolélas. The conflict caused many to flee to the Democratic Republic of the Congo. In Aug. 1999 peace talks were held by Sassou-Nguesso, Lissouba and Kolélas at which a ceasefire was agreed. Congo's economy, still affected by the civil war of 1997, suffered further.

In Jan. 2001 Sassou-Nguesso passed a new constitution which increased the president's term from five to seven years and strengthened presidential powers. In presidential elections held in March 2002, Sassou-Nguesso won 89·4% of votes. The new constitution deemed Lissouba and Kolélas ineligible to stand, while another opposition candidate, Andre Milongo, refused to stand claiming 'irregularities'. The elections were marred by violence between the 'Ninja' rebels and government forces in the Pool area of the country, which caused the displacement of around 66,000 people. Legislative elections which followed in May and June 2002 resulted in a large parliamentary majority for the PCT and its allies. The results were criticized by international observers and provoked further widespread militia violence. A peace agreement reached in March 2003 remains fragile.

DEFENCE

In 2003 military expenditure totalled US$112m. (US$30 per capita), representing 3·1% of GDP.

Army

Total personnel (2002) 8,000. There is a Gendarmerie of 2,000.

Navy

Personnel in 2002 totalled about 800. The Navy is based at Pointe Noire.

Air Force

The Air Force had (2002) about 1,200 personnel and 12 combat aircraft, most of which are in store.

INTERNATIONAL RELATIONS

The Republic of the Congo is a member of the UN, WTO, the African Union, African Development Bank, IOM, International Organization of the Francophonie and is an ACP member state of the ACP-EU relationship.

ECONOMY

Agriculture produced 6·3% of GDP in 2002, industry 63·3% and services 30·4%.

Currency

The unit of currency is the *franc CFA* (XAF) with a parity of 655·957 francs CFA to one euro. Total money supply in April 2002 was 238,885m. francs CFA and foreign exchange reserves were US$51m. Gold reserves were 11,000 troy oz in June 2002. There was inflation of 1·5% in 2003 and 3·6% in 2004.

Budget

Budgetary central government revenue totalled 642·50bn. francs CFA in 2002 (630·30bn. francs CFA in 2001) and expenditure 564·10bn. francs CFA (440·60bn. francs CFA in 2001).

Performance

Total GDP in 2004 was US$4·4bn. Real GDP growth was 0·3% in 2003 and 3·6% in 2004.

Banking and Finance

The *Banque des Etats de l'Afrique Centrale* (Governor, Jean-Félix Mamalepot) is the bank of issue. There are four commercial banks and a development bank, in all of which the government has majority stakes. There is also a co-operative banking organization (Mutuelle Congolaise de l'Epargne et de Crédit).

ENERGY AND NATURAL RESOURCES

Environment

Carbon dioxide emissions from the consumption and flaring of fossil fuels in 2002 were the equivalent of 0·9 tonnes per capita.

Electricity

Installed capacity was 0·1m. kW in 2000. Total production in 2000 was 300m. kWh and consumption per capita 162 kWh.

Oil and Gas

Oil was discovered in the mid-1960s when Elf Aquitaine was given exclusive rights to production. Elf still has the lion's share but Agip Congo is also involved in oil exploitation. In 2000 production was 13·2m. tonnes. Proven reserves in 2002 were 1·5bn. bbls., including major off-shore deposits. Oil provides about 90% of government revenue and exports. There is a refinery at Pointe-Noire, the second largest city. Gas reserves were estimated at 119bn. cu. metres in 2002.

Minerals

A government mine produces several metals; gold and diamonds are extracted by individuals. There are reserves of potash (4·5m. tonnes), iron ore (1,000m. tonnes), and also clay, bituminous sand, phosphates, zinc and lead.

Agriculture

In 2001 there were 175,000 ha. of arable land and 45,000 ha. of permanent crops. There were some 700 tractors and 85 thresher-harvesters in use in 2001. Production (2000, in thousand tonnes): cassava, 790; sugarcane, 450; plantains, 78; bananas, 52; avocados, 25; groundnuts, 22; sweet potatoes, 22; palm oil, 17; yams, 14.

Livestock (2000): cattle, 77,000; pigs, 46,000; sheep, 116,000; goats, 285,000; poultry, 2m.

Forestry

In 2000 equatorial forests covered 22·06m. ha. (64·6% of the total land area). In 2001, 2·42m. cu. metres of timber were produced, mainly okoumé from the south and sapele from the north. Timber companies are required to replant, and to process at least 60% of their production locally. Before the development of the oil industry, forestry was the mainstay of the economy.

Fisheries

The catch for 2001 was an estimated 42,000, of which approximately half was from inland waters and half from marine waters.

INDUSTRY

There is a growing manufacturing sector, located mainly in the four major towns, producing processed foods, textiles, cement, metal goods and chemicals. Industry produced 65·2% of GDP in 2001, including 4·1% from manufacturing. Production (2000): residual fuel oil, 206,000 tonnes; distillate fuel oil, 62,000 tonnes; petrol, 40,000 tonnes; kerosene, 21,000 tonnes; cigarettes (1994), 655m. cartons; beer (2003), 66·0m. litres; veneer sheets (2001), 12,000 cu. metres; cotton textiles (1993), 1·8m. metres.

Labour

In 1996 the labour force was 1,105,000 (57% males). More than 50% of the economically active population were engaged in agriculture.

Trade Unions

In 1964 the existing unions merged into one national body, the Confédération Syndicale Congolaise. The 40,000-strong *Confédération Syndicale des Travailleurs Congolais* split off from the latter in 1993.

INTERNATIONAL TRADE

Foreign debt was US$5,152m. in 2002.

Imports and Exports

Imports and exports for calendar years in US$1m.:

	1998	1999	2000	2001	2002
Imports f.o.b.	558	523	455	681	691
Exports f.o.b.	1,368	1,560	2,492	2,055	2,289

Principal imported commodities are intermediate manufactures, capital equipment, construction materials, foodstuffs and petroleum products. Apart from crude oil, other significant commodities for export are lumber, plywood, sugar, cocoa, coffee and diamonds. Main import suppliers in 1999 were France, 23·2%; Italy, 7·8%; USA, 7·8%; Hong Kong, 4·9%; Belgium, 3·8%. Main export markets were Taiwan, 31·5%; USA, 22·8%; South Korea, 15·3%; Germany, 6·7%; France, 2·6%.

COMMUNICATIONS

Roads

In 2002 there was an estimated 12,800 km of roads, of which 9·7% were surfaced. Vehicles in use in 1996 numbered 53,000, including approximately 37,240 passenger cars (14 per 1,000 inhabitants). There were 124 deaths in road accidents in 1994.

Rail

A railway (510 km, 1,067 mm gauge) connects Brazzaville with Pointe-Noire via Loubomo and Bilinga, and a branch links Mont-Belo with Mbinda on the Gabon border. Total length is 900 km. In 2000 railways carried 84m. passenger-km and 85m. tonne-km of freight.

Civil Aviation

The principal airports are at Brazzaville (Maya Maya) and Pointe-Noire. In 2003 Trans Air Congo operated services to Abidjan, Cotonou and Lomé, as well as domestic services. Trans

African Airlines flew to Abidjan, Bamako, Cotonou, Dakar and Lomé. In 2001 Brazzaville handled 433,000 passengers (341,000 on domestic flights) and 27,000 tonnes of freight.

Shipping
The only seaport is Pointe-Noire. The merchant marine totalled 3,000 GRT in 2002. There are some 5,000 km of navigable rivers, and river transport is an important service for timber and other freight as well as passengers. There are hydrofoil connections from Brazzaville to Kinshasa.

Telecommunications
There were 243,800 telephone subscribers in 2002 (74·1 per 1,000 persons) and 13,000 PCs were in use (4·0 per 1,000 persons). In 2002 there were 221,800 mobile phone subscribers. There were 5,000 Internet users in 2002. In 1995 there were 100 fax machines.

Postal Services
There were 37 post offices in 2003.

SOCIAL INSTITUTIONS

Justice
The Supreme Court, Court of Appeal and a criminal court are situated in Brazzaville, with a network of *tribunaux de grande instance* and *tribunaux d'instance* in the regions.

Education
In 2000–01 there were 9,880 teachers for 500,921 pupils at primary schools; 7,668 secondary school teachers for 197,184 pupils; and 13,403 students at university level. Adult literacy rate in 2002 was 82·8% (male, 88·9%; female, 77·1%).

In 1999–2000 total expenditure on education came to 5·5% of GNP and 12·6% of total government spending.

Health
In 2001 there were 103 hospitals with 5,195 beds. In 2000 there were 540 physicians, 75 pharmacists, 1,439 nurses and 579 midwives.

RELIGION

In 2001 there were 1·43m. Roman Catholics, 0·49m. Protestants and 0·36m. Kimbanguistes (African Christians). Traditional animist beliefs are still widespread.

CULTURE

Broadcasting
Broadcasting is under the aegis of the government-controlled Radiodiffusion-Télévision Congolaise, which transmits a national and a regional radio programme and a programme in French. There were 424,000 radio and 114,000 TV receivers in 2000.

Press
In 1998 there were six daily newspapers with a combined circulation of 20,600.

Tourism
There were 19,000 foreign tourists in 2000, bringing revenue of US$12m.

DIPLOMATIC REPRESENTATIVES

Of the Republic of the Congo in the United Kingdom
Ambassador: Henri Marie Joseph Lopes (resides in Paris).
Honorary Consul: Louis Muzzu (4 Wendle Court, 131–137 Wandsworth Rd, London, SW8 2LH).

Of the United Kingdom in the Republic of the Congo
Ambassador: Andrew Sparkes (resides in Kinshasa, Democratic Republic of the Congo).

Of the Republic of the Congo in the USA (4891 Colorado Ave., NW, Washington, D.C., 20011)
Ambassador: Serge Mombouli.

Of the USA in the Republic of the Congo (Rue Léon Jacob, Brazzaville)
Ambassador: Vacant.
Chargé d'Affaires a.i.: Mark J. Biedlingmaier.

Of the Republic of the Congo to the United Nations
Ambassador: Basile Ikouebe.

Of the Republic of the Congo to the European Union
Ambassador: Jacques Obia.

FURTHER READING
Fegley, Randall, *Congo*. [Bibliography] ABC-Clio, Oxford and Santa Barbara (CA), 1993
Thompson, V. and Adloff, R., *Historical Dictionary of the People's Republic of the Congo*. 2nd ed. Metuchen (NJ), 1984

National Statistical Office: Centre National de la Statistique et des Etudes Economiques, BP 2031, Brazzaville.
Website (French only): http://www.cnsee.org

COSTA RICA

República de Costa Rica

Capital: San José
Population projection, 2010: 4·66m.
GDP per capita, 2003: (PPP$) 9,606
HDI/world rank: 0·838/47

KEY HISTORICAL EVENTS

Discovered by Columbus in 1502 on his last voyage, Costa Rica (Rich Coast) was part of the Spanish viceroyalty of New Spain from 1540 to 1821, then of the Central American Federation until 1838 when it achieved full independence. Coffee was introduced in 1808 and became a mainstay of the economy, helping to create a peasant land-owning class. In 1948 accusations of election fraud led to a six-week civil war, at the conclusion of which José Figueres Ferrer won power at the head of a revolutionary junta. A new constitution abolished the Army. In 1986 Oscar Arias Sánchez was elected president. He promised to prevent Nicaraguan anti-Sandinista (*contra*) forces using Costa Rica as a base. In 1987 he received the Nobel Peace Prize as recognition of his Central American peace plan, agreed to by the other Central American states. Costa Rica was beset with economic problems in the early 1990s when several politicians, including President Calderón, were accused of profiting from drug trafficking.

TERRITORY AND POPULATION

Costa Rica is bounded in the north by Nicaragua, east by the Caribbean, southeast by Panama, and south and west by the Pacific. The area is estimated at 51,100 sq. km (19,730 sq. miles). The population at the census of July 2000 was 3,810,179; density, 71·4 per sq. km. The estimated population in 2005 was 4·33m. In 2003, 60·6% of the population were urban.

The UN gives a projected population for 2010 of 4·66m.

There are seven provinces (with 2000 population): Alajuela (716,286); Cartago (432,395); Guanacaste (264,238); Heredia (354,732); Limón (339,295); Puntarenas (357,483); San José (1,345,750). The largest cities, with estimated 2000 populations, are San José (346,600); Limón (62,000); and Alajuela (53,900).

Ethnic divisions (2000): White 77%, Mestizo 17%, Mulatto 3%, East Asian (predominantly Chinese) 2%, Amerindian 1%. Spanish is the official language.

SOCIAL STATISTICS

Statistics for calendar years:

	Marriages	Births	Deaths
1998	24,831	76,982	14,708
1999	25,613	78,526	15,052
2000	24,436	78,178	14,944
2001	23,730	76,401	15,609

2001 rates per 1,000 population: births, 19·2; deaths, 3·9. Annual population growth rate, 1992–2002, 2·4%. Life expectancy at birth, 2003, was 75·9 years for men and 80·6 years for women. Infant mortality, 2000, 10·2 per 1,000 live births; fertility rate, 2000, 2·4 children per woman.

CLIMATE

The climate is tropical, with a small range of temperature and abundant rain. The dry season is from Dec. to April. San José, Jan. 66°F (18·9°C), July 69°F (20·6°C). Annual rainfall 72" (1,793 mm).

CONSTITUTION AND GOVERNMENT

The Constitution was promulgated on 7 Nov. 1949. The legislative power is vested in a single-chamber *Legislative Assembly* of 57 deputies elected for four years. The *President* and two *Vice-Presidents* are elected for four years; the candidate receiving the largest vote, provided it is over 40% of the total, is declared elected, but a second ballot is required if no candidate gets 40% of the total. Since 2003 former presidents have been permitted to stand again. Elections are normally held on the first Sunday in Feb.

The President may appoint and remove members of the cabinet.

National Anthem

'Noble patria, tu hermosa bandera' ('Noble fatherland, thy beautiful banner'); words by J. M. Zeledón Brenes, tune by M. M. Gutiérrez.

GOVERNMENT CHRONOLOGY

Presidents since 1944. (PLN = National Liberation Party; PRD = Party of the Democratic Renewal; PRN = National Republican Party; PUN = National Union Party; PUSC = Social Christian Unity Party)

1944–48	PRN	Teodoro Picado Michalski
1948–49	military	José María Figueres Ferrer
1949–53	PUN	Luis Otilio Ulate Blanco
1953–58	PLN	José María Figueres Ferrer
1958–62	PUN	Mario José Echandi Jiménez
1962–66	PLN	Francisco José Orlich Bolmarcich
1966–70	PUN	José Joaquín Trejos Fernández
1970–74	PLN	José María Figueres Ferrer
1974–78	PLN	Daniel Oduber Quirós
1978–82	PRD	Rodrigo José Carazo Odio
1982–86	PLN	Luis Alberto Monge Álvarez
1986–90	PLN	Óscar Rafael Arias Sánchez
1990–94	PUSC	Rafael Ángel Calderón Fournier
1994–98	PLN	José María Figueres Olsen
1998–2002	PUSC	Miguel Ángel Rodríguez Echeverría
2002–06	PUSC	Abel Pacheco de la Espriella
2006–	PLN	Óscar Rafael Arias Sánchez

RECENT ELECTIONS

In presidential elections held on 5 Feb. 2006 former president Óscar Arias Sánchez of the National Liberation Party (PLN) won 40·9% of the vote, Ottón Solís of the Citizens' Action Party (PAC) 39·8%, Otto Guevara of the Libertarian Movement (ML) 8·5% and Ricardo Toledo of the Social Christian Unity Party (PUSC) 3·6%. There were ten other candidates. Turnout was 65·4%. In parliamentary elections held on the same day the PLN won 25 of 57 seats with 36·4% of votes cast, the PAC 17 (25·8%), the ML 6 (9·1%) and the PUSC 5 (7·6%), with four parties each winning one seat.

CURRENT ADMINISTRATION

President: Óscar Arias Sánchez; b. 1940 (PLN; sworn in 8 May 2006).

In May 2006 the government comprised:

First Vice-President and Minister of Justice: Laura Chinchilla. *Second Vice-President and Minister of Planning:* Kevin Casas Zamora. *Culture, Youth and Sports:* María Elena Carballo. *Environment and Energy:* Roberto Dobles. *Finance:* Guillermo Zúñiga. *Foreign Relations and Religion:* Bruno Stagno Ugarte. *Foreign Trade:* Marco Vinicio Ruiz. *Housing and the Fight against Poverty:* Fernando Zumbado. *Labour and Social Security:* Francisco Morales. *Production:* Alfredo Volio. *Public Education:* Leonardo Garnier. *Public Health:* María Luisa Ávila Agüero. *Public Security and the Interior:* Fernando Berrocal. *Public Works and Transportation:* Karla González. *Science and Technology:* Eugenia Flores. *Tourism:* Carlos Ricardo Benavides. *Minister of the Presidency:* Rodrigo Arias Sánchez. *Minister Delegate at the Presidency:* Marco Vargas Díaz.

Government Website (Spanish only): http://www.casapres.go.cr

CURRENT LEADERS

Óscar Arias Sánchez

Position
President

Introduction
Dr Óscar Arias became president of Costa Rica for the second time in May 2006, claiming victory over his rival, Otton Solís, after weeks of recounts. The centrist politician, who previously held the presidency from 1986–90, is best known for his economic reforms and his contribution to peace in Central America.

Early Life
Óscar Rafael Arias Sánchez was born on 13 Sept. 1940 in Heredia, central Costa Rica. He was educated at St Francis College and the University of Costa Rica, where he read law and economics. He received a doctorate from the University of Essex, Britain, before working for José Figueres, a National Liberation Party leader who had served as president from 1970–74. Appointed minister of planning and political economy in 1972, in 1979 Arias was named general secretary of the PLN, helping Luis Alberto Monge to victory in the elections of 1982. Arias himself was elected president on 8 May 1986, easily beating Rafael Calderón of the United Coaltion.

Arias drafted a plan to promote peace and democracy in war-ravaged Central America, which led to the signing of the Esquipulas II Accords on 7 Aug. 1987 and for which he subsequently received the Nobel peace prize. He liberalized the Costa Rican economy, promoting tourism while reducing dependence on exports of bananas and coffee. Steady growth was maintained and unemployment fell to a regional low. After the end of his presidential term in May 1990, he served on the boards of various organizations including the International Crisis Group, Transparency International and the Stockholm International Peace Research Institute. Arias was widely recognized as a champion of democracy and demilitarization and became a prominent spokesman for the developing world.

Arias contested the 5 Feb. 2006 presidential election, promising a 'fresh start' for the country after a series of corruption scandals. However, his early lead in the opinion polls was eroded by a surge in support for Ottón Solís of the left-leaning Citizens' Action Party. The two candidates clashed regularly over the ratification of the controversial Central American Free-Trade Agreement (CAFTA), with Arias favouring approval. The election was followed by a manual recount and weeks of tension. On 7 March 2006 Arias was declared the victor with 40·9% of the vote and was sworn in on 8 May 2006.

Career in Office
Arias has pledged to stamp out corruption and to implement economic reforms but his narrow victory and weak position in Congress suggests a struggle to win support for policies such as confirmation of CAFTA. Costa Rica is to date the only country among the seven signatory countries yet to endorse the agreement.

DEFENCE

In 2003 defence expenditure totalled US$101m. (US$25 per capita), representing 0·6% of GDP.

Army

The Army was abolished in 1948, and replaced by a Civil Guard numbering 4,400 in 2002. In addition there is a Border Security Police of 2,000 and a Rural Guard, also 2,000-strong.

Navy

The paramilitary Maritime Surveillance Unit numbered (2002) 300.

Air Wing

The Civil Guard operates a small air wing equipped with 11 light planes and helicopters.

INTERNATIONAL RELATIONS

Costa Rica is a member of the UN, WTO, OAS, Inter-American Development Bank, CACM, ACS and IOM.

ECONOMY

Agriculture accounted for 8·4% of GDP in 2002, industry 29·1% and services 62·4%.

Currency

The unit of currency is the *Costa Rican colón* (CRC) of 100 *céntimos*. The official rate is used for all imports on an essential list and by the government and autonomous institutions, and a free rate is used for all other transactions. In June 2002 total money supply was 641,189m. colones, foreign exchange reserves were US$1,426m. and gold reserves were 2,000 troy oz. Inflation was 9·4% in 2003 and 12·3% in 2004.

Budget

In 2001 total revenue was 1,202·00bn. colones (1,025·89bn. colones in 2000) and total expenditure was 1,269·56bn. colones (1,095·16bn. colones in 2000).

Performance

Costa Rica, said to be the most stable country in Central America, experienced GDP growth of 8·4% in 1998 and 8·2% in 1999, although then only 1·8% in 2000, 1·1% in 2001 and 2·8% in 2002. GDP growth was 6·5% in 2003 and 4·2% in 2004. Total GDP in 2004 was US$18·4bn.

Banking and Finance

The bank of issue is the Central Bank (founded 1950) which supervises the national monetary system, foreign exchange dealings and banking operations. The bank has a board of seven directors appointed by the government, including *ex officio* the Minister of Finance and the Planning Office Director. The *Governor* is Francisco de Paula Gutiérrez Gutiérrez.

There are three state-owned banks (Banco de Costa Rica, Banco Nacional de Costa Rica and Banco Popular y de Desarrollo Comunal), 17 private banks and one credit co-operative.

There is a stock exchange in San José.

Weights and Measures

The metric system is obligatory but Imperial Spanish measurements are still used.

ENERGY AND NATURAL RESOURCES

Environment

Costa Rica's carbon dioxide emissions from the consumption and flaring of fossil fuels in 2002 were the equivalent of 1·3 tonnes per capita.

Electricity

Installed capacity was 1·7m. kW in 2000. Production was 7·23bn. kWh in 2000; consumption per capita in 2000 was 1,889 kWh.

Minerals

In 2001 gold output was 100 kg and salt production was 37,000 tonnes.

Agriculture

Agriculture is a key sector, with 243,000 people (including hunting, forestry and fisheries) being economically active in 2002. There were 0·23m. ha. of arable land in 2001 and 0·3m. ha. of permanent crops. The principal agricultural products are coffee, bananas and sugar. Cattle are also of great importance. Production figures for 2000 (in 1,000 tonnes): sugarcane, 4,000; bananas, 2,700; rice, 264; melons, 177; coffee, 164; palm oil, 134; oranges, 126; plantains, 90; watermelons, 77; potatoes, 74; pineapples, 43; papayas, 36.

Livestock (2000): cattle, 1·71m.; pigs, 390,000; horses, 115,000; chickens, 17m.

Forestry

In 2000 forests covered 1·97m. ha., or 38·5% of the land area. Timber production in 2001 was 5·16m. cu. metres.

Fisheries

Total catch in 2001 amounted to 34,733 tonnes, mostly from sea fishing.

INDUSTRY

The main manufactured goods are foodstuffs, palm oil, textiles, fertilizers, pharmaceuticals, furniture, cement, tyres, canning, clothing, plastic goods, plywood and electrical equipment.

Labour

In July 2001 there were 1,552,920 people in employment. In July 2001 there were 100,397 unemployed persons, or 6·1% of the workforce. The main area of employment is transport, storage and communications (303,000 people in 2002), followed by agriculture, hunting, forestry and fisheries (243,000 in 2002).

Trade Unions

There are two main trade unions, *Rerum Novarum* (anti-Communist) and *Confederación General de Trabajadores Costarricenses* (Communist).

INTERNATIONAL TRADE

A free trade agreement was signed with Mexico in March 1994. Some 2,300 products were freed from tariffs, with others to follow over ten years. External debt was US$4,834m. in 2002.

Imports and Exports

The value of imports and exports in US$1m. was:

	1999	2000	2001	2002
Imports c.i.f.	5,996	6,025	5,745	6,523
Exports f.o.b.	6,577	5,813	4,923	5,259

Chief exports: manufactured goods and other products, coffee, bananas, sugar, cocoa. Main import suppliers, 2000: USA, 33·5%; Mexico, 8·4%; Venezuela, 7·2%; Japan, 4·5%. Major export markets, 2000: USA, 33·9%; Nicaragua, 6·9%; Guatemala, 6·8%; Germany, 5·3%.

COMMUNICATIONS

Roads

In 2002 there were 35,303 km of roads, including 7,270 km of main roads. On the Costa Rica section of the Inter-American Highway it is possible to motor to Panama during the dry season. The Pan-American Highway into Nicaragua is metalled for most of the way and there is now a good highway open almost to Puntarenas. Motor vehicles, 2002, numbered 651,030 (367,832 passenger cars). There were 336 fatalities as a result of road accidents in 2000.

Rail

The nationalized railway system *(Incofer)* was closed in 1994.

Civil Aviation

There is an international airport at San José (Juan Santamaria). The national carrier is Líneas Aéreas Costarriquenses (LACSA), which in 1999 flew 23·9m. km and carried 922,600 passengers. In 2001 San José handled 2,108,713 passengers (1,972,606 on international flights) and 67,858 tonnes of freight.

Shipping

The chief ports are Limón on the Atlantic and Caldera on the Pacific. The merchant marine totalled 4,000 GRT in 2002. In 2002 vessels totalling 2,101,000 NRT entered ports and vessels totalling 2,101,000 NRT cleared.

Telecommunications

There were 1,497,700 telephone subscribers in 2002 (361·5 per 1,000 inhabitants) and 817,000 PCs in use (197·2 for every 1,000 persons). The government has 202 telegraph offices and 88 official telephone stations. In 2002 mobile phone subscribers numbered 459,800 and there were 12,200 fax machines. Costa Rica had 800,000 Internet users in 2002.

Postal Services

In 2003 there were 121 post offices.

SOCIAL INSTITUTIONS

Justice

Justice is administered by the Supreme Court and five appeal courts divided into five chambers—the Court of Cassation, the Higher and Lower Criminal Courts, and the Higher and Lower Civil Courts. There are also subordinate courts in the separate provinces and local justices throughout the republic. There is no capital punishment.

The population in penal institutions in Nov. 2004 was 7,619 (177 per 100,000 of national population).

Education

The adult literacy rate in 2002 was 95·8% (95·7% among males and 95·9% among females). Primary instruction is compulsory and free from six to 15 years; secondary education (since 1949) is also free. Primary schools are provided and maintained by local school councils, while the national government pays the teachers, besides making subventions in aid of local funds. In 2002 there were 3,904 public and private primary schools with 31,266 teachers and administrative staff and 537,191 enrolled pupils, and 580 public and private secondary schools with 20,549 teachers and 284,841 pupils. In 1999 there was one university and one technological institute in the public sector, and eight universities, one Adventist university and one university of science and technology in the private sector. There were also four other institutions of higher education. In 1999 there were 59,947 university students.

In 2000–01 total expenditure on education came to 4·8% of GNP, representing 20·0% of total government expenditure.

Health
In 2000 there were 3,333 doctors, 346 dentists, 1,214 nurses, 272 pharmacists and (1999) 29 hospitals. In 1997 there were 14 beds per 10,000 inhabitants.

RELIGION
Roman Catholicism is the state religion; it had 3·38m. adherents in 2001. There is entire religious liberty under the constitution. The Archbishop of Costa Rica has six bishops at Alajuela, Ciudad Quesada, Limón, Puntarenas, San Isidro el General and Tilarán. There were 360,000 Protestants in 2001. The remainder of the population are followers of other religions.

CULTURE

World Heritage Sites
Costa Rica's two UNESCO protected sites are: Cocos Island National Park (1997); and the Area de Conservación Guanacaste (1999), an important dry forest habitat. Costa Rica also shares a UNESCO site with Panama: the Talamanca Range-La Amistad Reserves (1983), an important cross-breeding site for North and South American flora and fauna.

Broadcasting
There were 980,000 radio sets in 1997 and 930,000 television receivers in 2000 (colour by NTSC).

Press
There were six daily newspapers in 2002 with a combined circulation of 288,000, at a rate of 72 per 1,000 inhabitants.

Tourism
In 2002 there were 1,113,000 foreign tourists, bringing revenue of US$1,078m.

Theatre and Opera
There are eight national theatres.

Museums and Galleries
Costa Rica has three museums.

DIPLOMATIC REPRESENTATIVES
Of Costa Rica in the United Kingdom (Flat 1, 14 Lancaster Gate, London, W2 3LH)
Ambassador: Vacant.
Chargé d'Affaires a.i.: Sylvia Ugalde.

Of the United Kingdom in Costa Rica (Edificio Centro Colón, 11th Floor, Apartado 815, San José 1007)
Ambassador: Georgina Butler.

Of Costa Rica in the USA (2114 S St., NW, Washington, D.C., 20008)
Ambassador: Tomás Dueñas.

Of the USA in Costa Rica (Pavas, Frente Centro Comercial, San José)
Ambassador: Mark Langdale.

Of Costa Rica to the United Nations
Ambassador: Bruno Stagno.

Of Costa Rica to the European Union
Ambassador: María Salvadora Ortíz Ortíz.

FURTHER READING
Biesanz, R., *et al.*, *The Costa Ricans*. Hemel Hempstead, 1982
Bird, L., *Costa Rica: Unarmed Democracy*. London, 1984
Creedman, T. S., *Historical Dictionary of Costa Rica*. 2nd ed. Metuchen (N.J.), 1991
Stansifer, Charles L., *Costa Rica*. [Bibliography] ABC-Clio, Oxford and Santa Barbara (CA), 1991

National Statistical Office: Instituto Nacional de Estadística y Censos, San José.
Website (Spanish only): http://www.inec.go.cr/

CÔTE D'IVOIRE

MALI

BURKINA FASO

GUINEA

Boundiali

Korhogo

CÔTE D'IVOIRE

GHANA

Man

YAMOUSSOUKRO

Daloa

Adzopé

LIBERIA

Abidjan

Gulf of Guinea

© Research Machines plc 2006

0 100 mi
0 150 km

République de la Côte d'Ivoire
(Republic of the Ivory Coast)

Capital: Yamoussoukro
Seat of government: Abidjan
Population projection, 2010: 19·78m.
GDP per capita, 2003: (PPP$) 1,476
HDI/world rank: 0·420/163

KEY HISTORICAL EVENTS

France obtained rights on the coast in 1842 but did not occupy the territory until 1882. In the early 1870s a French offer to exchange Côte d'Ivoire with the British for the Gambia, which bisected the French colony of Senegal, was refused. Rumours of gold later rekindled French interest and in 1889 Côte d'Ivoire was declared a French protectorate. Governors appointed from France administered the colony using a system of centralized rule that allowed little room for local participation. In 1946 Côte d'Ivoire's first political party, the Democratic Party of Côte d'Ivoire, was created under the leadership of Félix Houphouët-Boigny who eventually adopted a policy of co-operation with the French authorities. By the mid-1950s the country had become the wealthiest in French West Africa and in 1958 Côte d'Ivoire became an autonomous republic within the French Community. Côte d'Ivoire achieved full independence on 7 Aug. 1960, with Félix Houphouët-Boigny as its first president.

On 23 Dec. 1999 President Henri Konan Bédié was ousted in a military coup led by Gen. Robert Guéï, the country's military chief from 1990 to 1995. On 6 Oct. 2000 a state of emergency was declared ahead of a Supreme Court announcement on the candidates allowed to stand for the presidential election on 22 Oct. 2000. After Robert Guéï declared himself the winner in the election, a violent uprising in which over 2,000 people were killed resulted in Gen. Guéï fleeing to Benin. The veteran opposition candidate Laurent Gbagbo was then declared the rightful winner. In Sept. 2002 there was a failed coup by mutinous

soldiers that claimed more than 20 lives, including those of both Gen. Guéï and the interior minister. Since then, Côte d'Ivoire has descended further into civil war, with the country divided between the rebel-held north and the government-held south. In April 2005 government, rebel and opposition leaders signed a deal to end the civil war and pledged to hold elections in Oct., but these were subsequently postponed for a further year owing to the ongoing crisis. In Dec. 2005 the governor of the Central Bank of West African States, Charles Konan Banny, was named as interim prime minister for a transition period that is scheduled to end in Oct. 2006.

TERRITORY AND POPULATION

Côte d'Ivoire is bounded in the west by Liberia and Guinea, north by Mali and Burkina Faso, east by Ghana, and south by the Gulf of Guinea. It has an area (including inland water) of 322,460 sq. km. The population at the 1998 census was 15,366,672; density, 47·7 per sq. km. The population was 55·1% rural in 2003. Population estimate (2005): 18·14m.

The UN gives a projected population for 2010 of 19·78m.

Since 2000 the country has been divided into 19 regions comprising 58 departments.

Areas, populations (1998 census) and capitals of the regions are:

Region	Area (in sq. km)	Population	Capital
Agnéby	9,080	525,211	Agboville
Bafing	8,720	139,251	Touba
Bas-Sassandra	25,800	1,395,251	San-Pédro
Denguélé	20,600	222,446	Odienné
Dix-Huit Montagnes	16,600	936,510	Man
Fromager	6,900	542,992	Gagnoa
Haut-Sassandra	15,200	1,071,977	Daloa
Lacs	8,920	476,235	Yamoussoukro
Lagunes	14,200	3,733,413	Abidjan
Marahoué	8,500	554,807	Bouaflé
Moyen-Cavally	14,150	508,733	Guiglo
Moyen-Comoé	6,900	394,761	Abengourou
N'zi-Comoé	19,560	633,927	Dimbokro
Savanes	40,323	929,673	Korhogo
Sud-Bandama	10,650	682,021	Divo
Sud-Comoé	6,250	459,487	Aboisso
Vallée du Bandama	28,530	1,080,509	Bouaké
Worodougou	21,900	378,463	Séguéla
Zanzan	38,000	701,005	Bondoukou

In 2000 the population of Abidjan stood at 3,790,000. Other major towns (with 1998 census population): Bouaké, 461,618; Yamoussoukro, 299,243; Daloa, 173,107; Korhogo, 142,093.

There are about 60 ethnic groups, the principal ones being the Baoulé (23%), the Bété (18%) and the Sénoufo (15%). A referendum held in July 2000 on the adoption of a new constitution set eligibility conditions for presidential candidates (the candidate and both his parents had to be Ivorian). This excluded a northern Muslim leader and in effect made foreigners out of millions of Ivorians. The north of the country is predominantly Muslim and the south predominantly Christian and animist.

Approximately 30% of the population are immigrants, in particular from Burkina Faso, Mali, Guinea and Senegal.

French is the official language.

SOCIAL STATISTICS

2000 estimates: births, 559,000; deaths, 242,000. Rates (2000 estimates, per 1,000 population): birth, 35·3; death, 15·3. Expectation of life in 2003 was 45·2 years for males and 46·7 for females. Annual population growth rate, 1992–2002, 2·1%. Infant mortality, 2001, 102 per 1,000 live births; fertility rate, 2001, 4·8 births per woman. 29% of the population are migrants.

CLIMATE

A tropical climate, affected by distance from the sea. In coastal areas, there are wet seasons from May to July and in Oct. and Nov., but in central areas the periods are March to May and July to Nov. In the north, there is one wet season from June to Oct. Abidjan, Jan. 81°F (27·2°C), July 75°F (23·9°C). Annual rainfall 84" (2,100 mm). Bouaké, Jan. 81°F (27·2°C), July 77°F (25°C). Annual rainfall 48" (1,200 mm).

CONSTITUTION AND GOVERNMENT

The 1960 Constitution was amended in 1971, 1975, 1980, 1985, 1986, 1990, 1998 and 2000. The sole legal party was the Democratic Party of Côte d'Ivoire, but opposition parties were legalized in 1990. There is a 225-member *National Assembly* elected by universal suffrage for a five-year term. The *President* is also directly elected for a five-year term (renewable). He appoints and leads a Council of Ministers.

In Nov. 1990 the National Assembly voted that its Speaker should become President in the event of the latter's incapacity, and created the post of Prime Minister to be appointed by the President. Following the death of President Houphouët-Boigny on 7 Dec. 1993, the speaker, Henri Konan Bédié, proclaimed himself head of state till the end of the presidential term in Sept. 1995.

Following the coup of Dec. 1999 a referendum was held on 23 July 2000 on the adoption of a new constitution, which set eligibility conditions for presidential candidates (the candidate and both his parents must be Ivorian), reduced the voting age from 21 to 18, and abolished the death penalty. It also offered an amnesty to soldiers who staged the coup and the junta, but committed the junta to hand over power to an elected civilian head of state and parliament within six months of the proclamation of the text. Approximately 87% of votes cast were in favour of the new constitution. This was subsequently adopted on 4 Aug. 2000.

National Anthem

'L'Abidjanaise' ('Song of Abidjan'); words by M. Ekra, J. Bony and P. M. Coty, tune by P. M Pango.

GOVERNMENT CHRONOLOGY

Presidents since 1960. (PDCI-RDA = Democratic Party of Ivory Coast-African Democratic Rally; FPI = Ivorian Popular Front)

1960–93	PDCI-RDA	Félix Houphouët-Boigny
1993–99	PDCI-RDA	Aimé Henri Konan Bédié
1999–2000	military	Robert Guéï
2000–	FPI	Laurent Gbagbo

RECENT ELECTIONS

Presidential elections were held on 22 Oct. 2000, but were boycotted by the former ruling Parti Démocratique de Côte d'Ivoire/Democratic Party of Ivory Coast and the Rassemblement des Républicains/Rally of the Republicans. Laurent Gbagbo (Front Populaire Ivorienne/Ivorian Popular Front) obtained 59·4% of votes cast against 32·7% for Robert Guéï, who had seized power in a coup in Dec. 1999. Initially Robert Guéï claimed victory but following a violent uprising accepted defeat (the first time in Africa that a popular rising had succeeded in toppling a military regime). There were three other candidates.

Presidential and parliamentary elections scheduled for 30 Oct. 2005 were postponed in view of the continuing instability. In order to avert a constitutional crisis, the UN Security Council recommended that the president remain in office for a further year and that an interim prime minister be appointed. On 4 Dec. 2005 international mediators chose Charles Konan Banny, governor of the Central Bank of West African States, as prime

minister for a ten-month period that is scheduled to end in Oct. 2006.

The National Assembly elections were held on 10 Dec. 2000 and 14 Jan. 2001. The Ivorian Popular Front (FPI) won 96 seats; the Democratic Party of Ivory Coast (PDCI) won 94 seats; Rally of the Republicans (RDR), 5. There were also two vacant seats.

CURRENT ADMINISTRATION

President: Laurent Gbagbo; b. 1945 (FPI; assumed office 26 Oct. 2000).

The transitional government appointed in Dec. 2005 was composed mainly of members of the president's party (FPI), the former ruling Parti Démocratique de Côte d'Ivoire (PDCI), the opposition Rassemblement des Républicains (RDR) and the main rebel group, the Forces Nouvelles (FN). Four ministerial positions went to smaller parties and several members of civil society (c.s.) were also appointed. In March 2006 the transitional government comprised:

Interim Prime Minister, Minister for the Economy and Finance, and for Communications: Charles Konan Banny; b. 1942 (ind.; sworn in 7 Dec. 2005).

Minister of State for Planning and Development: Paul Antoine Bohoun Bouabré (FPI). *Minister of State, Responsible for Reconstruction and Reintegration:* Guillaume Soro (FN). *Minister of Agriculture:* Amadou Gon Coulibaly (RDR). *Animal Production and Fishery Resources:* Alphonse Douaty (FPI). *Civil Service, Employment and Administrative Reform:* Hubert Oulaye (FPI). *Commerce:* Moussa Dosso (FN). *Construction, Housing and Town Planning:* Marcel Amon Tanoh (RDR). *Co-operation and African Integration:* Albert Mabri Toikeusse (Union démocratique pour la paix en Côte d'Ivoire). *Culture and Francophonie:* Théodore Mel Eg (Union Démocratique Citoyenne). *Defence:* René Aphing Kouassi (c.s.). *Economic Infrastructure:* Patrick Achi (PDCI). *Environment, Water and Forests:* Jacques Andoh (Parti Ivorien des Travailleurs). *Family and Social Affairs:* Jeanne Peuhmond Adjoua Brou (RDR). *Fight Against AIDS:* Christine Adjobi (FPI). *Foreign Affairs:* Youssouf Bakayoko (PDCI). *Health and Population:* Rémi Allah Kouadio (PDCI). *Higher Education and Scientific Research:* Ibrahim Cissé Bacongo (RDR). *Industry and Promotion of the Private Sector:* Marie Tehoua Amah (PDCI). *Interior:* Joseph Dja Blé (c.s.). *Justice, Human Rights and Keeper of the Seals:* Mamadou Koné (FN). *Mines and Energy:* Léon Monnet (FPI). *National Education:* Michel Amani N'Guessan (FPI). *National Reconciliation and Relations with Institutions:* Sébastien Danon Djédjé (FPI). *New Information Technologies and Telecommunications:* Hamed Bakayoko (RDR). *Solidarity and War Victims:* Louis-André Dakoury Tabley (FN). *Technical Education and Professional Training:* Youssouf Soumahoro (FN). *Tourism and Handicrafts:* Amadou Koné (FN). *Transport:* Innocent Kobena Anaky (Mouvement des Forces de l'Avenir). *Youth, Civic Education and Sports:* Dagobert Banzio (PDCI). *Minister Delegate in the Office of the Prime Minister in Charge of the Economy and Finance:* Charles Diby Koffi (c.s.). *Minister Delegate in the Office of the Prime Minister in Charge of Communications:* Martine Studer Coffi (c.s.).

Government Website (French only): http://www.primature.gov.ci

CURRENT LEADERS

Laurent Gbagbo

Position
President

Introduction
Laurent Gbagbo took over the presidency in Oct. 2000, succeeding Robert Guéï who had been forced into exile after claiming victory in a disputed presidential election. Gbagbo has since overseen a period of political and economic instability and

fighting between the rebel, largely Muslim, north of the country and the government-controlled and mainly Christian south.

Early Life

Gbagbo was born on 31 May 1945 in Gagnoa in the mid-west of the country. He graduated in history and was jailed in the early 1970s for subversive teaching. Increasingly involved in trade union politics, he was a critic of the regime of Félix Houphouët-Boigny who had been in power since 1960.

In the 1980s Gbagbo went into exile in France, from where he established the Ivorian Popular Front (FPI) and developed a nationalist agenda. Gbagbo returned to the country in 1988 and two years later Houphouët-Boigny agreed to multi-party elections. In 1993 Houphouët-Boigny was succeeded by Henri Konan Bédié, who remained in power until 1999, when he was deposed by Gen. Robert Guéï in a military coup.

Guéï announced new presidential elections in which he excluded anyone unable to prove 'pure' Ivorian heritage from running. This removed 15 candidates, including a major opposition leader, Alassane Ouattara of the Rally of the Republicans (RDR), which had widespread support in the Muslim north. Guéï claimed victory although Gbagbo was widely believed to have polled most votes. Popular protests forced Guéï to resign and Gbagbo assumed the presidency on 26 Oct. 2000.

Career in Office

Ouattara immediately urged Gbagbo to call new elections, but Gbagbo refused. Fighting broke out between Ouattara's Muslim supporters in the north and Gbagbo's Christian supporters in the south. In parliamentary elections held at the end of 2000, the FPI emerged as the largest party, although only one third of those eligible voted. In Jan. 2001 Gbagbo survived an attempted coup.

As well as increasing ethnic friction, he was confronted by an economy suffering from a decline in the global cocoa market (Côte d'Ivoire being the world's largest producer of cocoa). Also, his broad nationalist position led him to announce a ban on foreign ownership of property, causing unease among the country's immigrants making up around 30% of the population.

Gbagbo's human rights record has received widespread criticism. Leading opposition politicians have been arrested on disputed charges, and from 2001 the US embassy and Amnesty International voiced concerns over arbitrary detention and mistreatment. Alleged use of child slave labour further tarnished Gbagbo's regime. Côte d'Ivoire consequently suffered cuts in international aid, with the UN refusing to resume assistance until a domestic reconciliation process was in place.

In Sept. 2002 fighting erupted in Abidjan when 700 troops, believed to be loyal to Guéï, mutinied. Guéï was killed by government forces. There was further violence in Bouaké and several other towns which had been seized by rebels. ECOWAS agreed to broker negotiations between the government and the rebel factions and a short-lived ceasefire was signed in Oct. In Jan. 2003 the French authorities brokered another ceasefire and a power-sharing agreement to end the civil war (despite violent anti-French protests in Abidjan by pro-government supporters). Under the agreement Gbagbo would remain president, with a prime minister approved by consensus serving alongside. Seydou Diarra was chosen to serve as prime minister until elections scheduled for 2005. However, little progress was made in disarming militia forces or implementing political reform before a serious resurgence of conflict in Nov. 2004. Following an attack by government forces across the ceasefire line against the rebels and on French peacekeeping troops, the French military retaliated by destroying the Ivorian air force, provoking more rioting by pro-government supporters in Abidjan. Further attempts at reconciliation, brokered by South Africa, resulted in a new agreement in April 2005 to revitalize power sharing, but it remains fragile and elections scheduled for late 2005 were postponed.

DEFENCE

There is selective conscription for six months. Defence expenditure totalled US$172m. in 2003 (US$10 per capita), representing 1·2% of GDP.

Army

Total strength (2002), 6,500. In addition there is a Presidential Guard of 1,350, a Gendarmerie of 7,600 and a Militia of 1,500.

Navy

Personnel in 2002 totalled 900 with the force based at Locodjo (Abidjan).

Air Force

There are five Alpha Jet light strike combat aircraft, although only one or two are operational. Personnel (2002) 700.

INTERNATIONAL RELATIONS

Côte d'Ivoire is a member of the UN, WTO, the African Union, African Development Bank, UEMOA, ECOWAS, IOM, OIC, Islamic Development Bank, International Organization of the Francophonie and is an ACP member state of the ACP-EU relationship.

ECONOMY

Agriculture accounted for 26·2% of GDP in 2002, industry 20·4% and services 53·4%.

Overview

Austerity measures were introduced in May 1990. A privatization programme, concentrating on the agro-industrial sectors, was introduced in 1992. 54 companies from an initial list of 60 had been privatized by mid-1999, when 20 additional companies were listed.

Currency

The unit of currency is the *franc CFA* (XOF) with a parity of 655·957 francs CFA to one euro. Foreign exchange reserves were US$1,273m. in May 2002 and total money supply was 1,338·30bn. francs CFA. In 2000 gold reserves were 45,000 troy oz. Inflation was 3·3% in 2003 and 1·5% in 2004.

Budget

Government revenue and expenditure (in 1bn. francs CFA):

	1998	1999	2000	2001
Revenue	1,392·2	1,283·3	1,238·1	1,335·9
Expenditure	1,557·3	1,521·5	1,351·2	1,297·3

VAT is 18%.

Performance

Real GDP growth was 0·3% in 2001 but there was then a recession with the economy contracting by 1·6% in both 2002 and 2003. However, 2004 saw positive growth of 1·6%. Total GDP in 2004 was US$15·3bn.

Banking and Finance

The regional *Banque Centrale des Etats de l'Afrique de l'Ouest* is the central bank and bank of issue. The *Acting Governor* is Justin Baro Damo. In 2002 there were 13 commercial banks and six credit institutions. The African Development Bank is based in Abidjan.

ENERGY AND NATURAL RESOURCES

Environment

Carbon dioxide emissions from the consumption and flaring of fossil fuels in 2002 were the equivalent of 0·3 tonnes per capita.

Electricity

The electricity industry was privatized in 1990. Installed capacity was 1·2m. kW in 2000. Production in 2000 amounted to 3·62bn. kWh, with consumption per capita 221 kWh.

Oil and Gas

Petroleum has been produced (offshore) since Oct. 1977. Production (1999), 1·5m. tonnes. Oil reserves, 2002, 100m. bbls. Natural gas reserves, 2002, 30bn. cu. metres; production (2000), 1,550m. cu. metres.

Minerals

Côte d'Ivoire has large deposits of iron ores, bauxite, tantalite, diamonds, gold, nickel and manganese, most of which are untapped. Gold production has steadily increased with 3·2 tonnes being produced in 2000. In 2001 diamond production totalled 320,000 carats.

Agriculture

In 2002 the agricultural population was 9·09m., of whom 3·13m. were economically active. In 1998 agriculture accounted for 66% of exports. There were 3·10m. ha. of arable land in 2001 and 4·40m. ha. of permanent crops. 73,000 ha. were irrigated in 2001. There were 3,800 tractors in 2001 and 70 harvester-threshers. Côte d'Ivoire is the world's largest producer and exporter of cocoa beans, with an output of 1·30m. tonnes in 2000 (more than 41% of the world total). It is also a leading coffee producer, with 365,000 tonnes in 2000. The cocoa and coffee industries have for years relied on foreign workers, but tens of thousands have left the country since the 1999 coup resulting in labour shortages. Other main crops, with 2000 production figures in 1,000 tonnes, are: yams (2,923), cassava (1,673), plantains (1,405), rice (1,162), sugarcane (1,155), maize (571), taro (365), seed cotton (270), palm oil (242), bananas (241), pineapples (226), coconuts (193), groundnuts (144), cottonseed (140), cotton lint (130), tomatoes (130) and natural rubber (119). Côte d'Ivoire is the biggest producer of rubber in Africa.

Livestock, 2000: 1·35m. cattle, 1·39m. sheep, 1·09m. goats, 280,000 pigs and 30m. chickens.

Forestry

In 2000 the rainforest covered 7·12m. ha., or 22·4% of the total land area. Products include teak, mahogany and ebony. In 2001, 12·08m. cu. metres of roundwood were produced.

Fisheries

The catch in 2001 amounted to 73,556 tonnes, of which 63,026 tonnes were from marine waters.

INDUSTRY

Industrialization has developed rapidly since independence, particularly food processing, textiles and sawmills. Output in 2000 (in 1,000 tonnes): distillate fuel oil, 1,103; cement (2001), 650; petrol, 554; kerosene, 536; residual fuel oil, 443; sugar, 189; sawnwood (2001), 630,000 cu. metres; veneer sheets (2001), 296,000 cu. metres.

Labour

In 1996 the workforce was 5·7m. (67% males).

Trade Unions

The main trade union is the *Union Générale des Travailleurs de Côte d'Ivoire*, with over 100,000 members.

INTERNATIONAL TRADE

External debt was US$11,816m. in 2002.

Imports and Exports

Imports and exports for calendar years in US$1m.:

	1998	1999	2000	2001	2002
Imports f.o.b.	2,886·5	2,766·0	2,401·8	2,417·7	2,432·0
Exports f.o.b.	4,606·5	4,661·4	3,888·0	3,945·9	5,166·5

Principal imports, 2001: crude and refined petroleum, 28·8%; food products, 22·5%; machinery and transport equipment, 20·4%. Principal exports, 2001: cocoa beans and products, 33·2%; crude petroleum and petroleum products, 13·7%; wood and wood products, 7·1%.

Main import suppliers, 1999: France, 25·9%; Italy, 5·6%; USA, 5·2%; Germany, 4·3%; Japan, 4·3%. Main export markets, 1999: France, 14·4%; Netherlands, 13·4%; USA, 8·5%; Brazil, 7·7%; Mali, 4·7%.

COMMUNICATIONS

Roads

In 1999 roads totalled about 50,400 km, of which 4,900 km were paved. There were about 456,000 motor vehicles in 1996 (293,000 cars, or 18·1 per 1,000 inhabitants, and 163,000 trucks and vans).

Rail

From Abidjan a metre-gauge railway runs to Léraba on the border with Burkina Faso (639 km), and thence through Burkina Faso to Ouagadougou and Kaya. Operation of the railway in both countries is franchised to the mixed public-private company Sitarail.

Civil Aviation

There is an international airport at Abidjan (Félix Houphouët-Boigny Airport), which in 2001 handled 912,000 passengers (all on international flights) and 19,100 tonnes of freight. The national carrier is the state-owned Air Ivoire, which in 1997 flew 1·3m. km and carried 72,100 passengers. It provides domestic services and in 2003 operated international flights to Accra, Bamako, Conakry, Cotonou, Dakar, Douala, Libreville, Lomé, Niamey and Ouagadougou. There were direct flights in 2003 with other airlines to Addis Ababa, Banjul, Beirut, Bobo Dioulasso, Brazzaville, Brussels, Cairo, Casablanca, Freetown, Johannesburg, Lagos, Monrovia, Nairobi, Nouakchott, Paris, Pointe-Noire and Tripoli.

Shipping

The main ports are Abidjan and San-Pédro. Abidjan handled 15m. tonnes of cargo for the first time in 1998 and is the busiest port in West Africa. Some US$200m. have been earmarked for continued expansion of the port. In 2002 the merchant marine totalled 9,000 GRT, including oil tankers 1,000 GRT.

Telecommunications

In 2002 there were 1,363,200 telephone subscribers, or 82·7 per 1,000 inhabitants, and there were 154,000 PCs in use (9·3 per 1,000 persons).

Since liberalization in 1995 the telecommunications sector has quickly progressed to become the West African leader and second only to that in South Africa in the continent as a whole. Mobile phone subscribers numbered 1,027,100 in 2002. In 2002 there were 90,000 Internet users.

Postal Services

In 2003 there were 194 post offices.

SOCIAL INSTITUTIONS

Justice

There are 28 courts of first instance and three assize courts in Abidjan, Bouaké and Daloa, two courts of appeal in Abidjan and Bouaké, and a supreme court in Abidjan. Côte d'Ivoire abolished the death penalty in 2000.

The population in penal institutions in March 2002 was 10,355 (62 per 100,000 of national population).

Education

The adult literacy rate in 2003 was 48·1% (60·1% among males and 38·2% among females). There were, in 2000–01, 2,046,861 pupils with 44,424 teachers in primary schools and 663,636 pupils with 23,184 teachers at secondary schools. In 2000–01 there were 115,413 students at higher education institutions. In 1995–96 there was one university with 21,000 students and 730 academic staff, and three university centres. There were six other institutions of higher education.

In 2000–01 expenditure on education came to 4·9% of GNP and 21·5% of total government spending.

Health

In 1993 there were five hospital beds per 10,000 inhabitants. In 1996 there were 1,318 physicians, 4,568 nurses and 2,196 midwives.

RELIGION

In 2001 there were 6·3m. Muslims (mainly in the north) and 4·3m. Christians (chiefly Roman Catholics in the south). Although Christians are in the majority among Ivorians, when Côte d'Ivoire's large immigrant population is taken into account Muslims are in the majority. Traditional animist beliefs are also practised. In May 2005 the Roman Catholic church had one cardinal.

CULTURE

World Heritage Sites

UNESCO world heritage sites in Côte d'Ivoire are: Taï National Park (inscribed on the list in 1982), an important fragment of the West African primary tropical forest, containing pygmy hippopotami; and the Comoé National Park (1983), containing shrub savannah and rainforest in one of West Africa's largest protected areas.

Broadcasting

The government-controlled Radiodiffusion Télévision Ivoirienne is responsible for broadcasting. There were 1m. television sets (colour by SECAM V) in 2001 and 2·2m. radio receivers in 2000.

Press

In 1998 there were 12 daily newspapers with a combined circulation of 238,000, at a rate of 16 per 1,000 inhabitants.

Tourism

There were 479,000 foreign tourists in 2002; spending by tourists totalled US$74m.

DIPLOMATIC REPRESENTATIVES

Of Côte d'Ivoire in the United Kingdom (2 Upper Belgrave St., London, SW1X 8BJ)
Ambassador: Yousoufou Bamba.

Of the United Kingdom in Côte d'Ivoire
Ambassador: Gordon Wetherell (resides in Accra, Ghana).

Of Côte d'Ivoire in the USA (2424 Massachusetts Ave., NW, Washington, D.C., 20008)
Ambassador: Daouda Diabate.

Of the USA in Côte d'Ivoire (Riviera Golf, 01 B.P. 1712, Abidjan)
Ambassador: Aubrey Hooks.

Of Côte d'Ivoire to the United Nations
Ambassador: Djessan Philippe Djangone-Bi.

Of Côte d'Ivoire to the European Union
Ambassador: Marie Gosset.

FURTHER READING

Direction de la Statistique. *Bulletin Mensuel de Statistique.*
Daniels, Morna, *Côte d'Ivoire.* [Bibliography] ABC-Clio, Oxford and Santa Barbara (CA), 1996

National Statistical Office: Institut National de la Statistique, BP V 55, Abidjan 01.
Website (French only): http://www.ins.ci

CROATIA

Republika Hrvatska

Capital: Zagreb
Population projection, 2010: 4·53m.
GDP per capita, 2003: (PPP$) 11,080
HDI/world rank: 0·841/45

KEY HISTORICAL EVENTS

Croatia was united with Hungary in 1091 and remained under Hungarian administration until the end of the First World War. On 1 Dec. 1918 Croatia became a part of the new Kingdom of Serbs, Croats and Slovenes, which was renamed Yugoslavia in 1929. During the Second World War an independent fascist (Ustaša) state was set up under the aegis of the German occupiers. During the Communist period Croatia became one of the six 'Socialist Republics' constituting the Yugoslav federation led by Marshal Tito. With the collapse of Communism, an independence movement gained momentum.

In a referendum on 19 May 1991, 94·17% of votes cast were in favour of Croatia becoming an independent sovereign state with the option of joining a future Yugoslav confederation as opposed to remaining in the existing Yugoslav federation. The Krajina and other predominantly Serbian areas of Croatia wanted union with Serbia and seized power. Croatian forces and Serb insurgents backed by federal forces became embroiled in a conflict throughout 1991 until the arrival of a UN peacekeeping mission at the beginning of 1992 and the establishment of four UN peacekeeping zones ('pink zones'). In early May 1995 Croatian forces re-took Western Slavonia from the Serbs and opened the Zagreb-Belgrade highway. In a 60-hour operation mounted on 4 Aug. 1995 the former self-declared Serb Republic of Krajina was occupied, provoking an exodus of 180,000 Serb refugees. Croats who had left the area in 1991 began to return. On 12 Nov. 1995 the Croatian government and Bosnian Serbs reached an agreement to place Eastern Slavonia, the last Croatian territory still under Bosnian Serb control, under UN administration.

TERRITORY AND POPULATION

Croatia is bounded in the north by Slovenia and Hungary and in the east by Serbia and Montenegro and Bosnia-Herzegovina. It includes the areas of Dalmatia, Istria and Slavonia which no longer have administrative status. Its area is 56,542 sq. km. Population at the 2001 census was 4,437,460 (4,784,265 in 1991), of whom the predominating ethnic groups were Croats (90%) and Serbs (5%); population density, 78·5 per sq. km. The estimated population in 2005 was 4·55m.

The UN gives a projected population for 2010 of 4·53m.

In 2003, 59·0% of the population lived in urban areas.

The area and population (2001 census) of the 20 counties and one city:

County	Area (in sq. km)	Population	Capital
Bjelovarska-Bilogorska	2,638	133,084	Bjelovar
Brodsko-Posavska	2,027	176,765	Slavonski Brod
Dubrovačko-Neretvanska	1,782	122,870	Dubrovnik
Istarska	2,813	206,344	Pazin
Karlovačka	3,622	141,787	Karlovac
Koprivničko-Križevačka	1,734	124,467	Koprivnica
Krapinsko-Zagorska	1,230	142,432	Krapina
Ličko-Senjska	5,350	53,677	Gospić
Međimurska	730	118,426	Čakovec
Osječko-Baranjska	4,149	330,506	Osijek
Požeško-Slavonska	1,821	85,831	Požega
Primorsko-Goranska	3,590	305,505	Rijeka
Šibensko-Kninska	2,994	112,891	Šibenik
Sisačko-Moslavačka	4,448	185,387	Sisak
Splitsko-Dalmatinska	4,524	463,676	Split
Varaždinska	1,260	184,769	Varaždin
Virovitičko-Podravska	2,021	93,389	Virovitica
Vukovarsko-Srijemska	2,448	204,768	Vukovar
Zadarska	3,643	162,045	Zadar
Zagrebačka	3,078	309,696	Zagreb
Zagreb (city)	640	779,145	Zagreb

Zagreb, the capital, had a 2001 population of 691,724. Other major towns (with 2001 census population): Split (188,694), Rijeka (143,800) and Osijek (90,411).

At the beginning of 1991 there were some 0·6m. resident Serbs. A law of Dec. 1991 guaranteed the autonomy of Serbs in areas where they are in a majority after the establishment of a permanent peace.

The official language is Croatian.

SOCIAL STATISTICS

2004: births, 40,307 (9·1 per 1,000 population); deaths, 49,756 (11·2); marriages, 22,700 (5·1); divorces, 4,985 (1·1); suicides, 871 (19·6 per 100,000). Infant mortality, 2004, 6·1 per 1,000 live births. Annual population growth rate, 1992–2002, –0·6%. In 2004 the most popular age range for marrying was 25–29 for males and 20–24 for females. Life expectancy at birth, 2003, was 71·4 years for males and 78·4 years for females. Fertility rate, 2004, 1·3 children per woman.

CLIMATE

Inland Croatia has a central European type of climate, with cold winters and hot summers, but the Adriatic coastal region experiences a Mediterranean climate with mild, moist winters and hot, brilliantly sunny summers with less than average rainfall. Average annual temperature and rainfall: Dubrovnik, 16·6°C and 1,051 mm. Zadar, 15·6°C and 963 mm. Rijeka, 14·3°C and 1,809 mm. Zagreb, 12·4°C and 1,000 mm. Osijek, 11·3°C and 683 mm.

CONSTITUTION AND GOVERNMENT

A new constitution was adopted on 22 Dec. 1990 and was revised in both 2000 and 2001. The *President* is elected for renewable five-year terms. There is a unicameral Parliament (*Hrvatski Sabor*), consisting of 152 deputies. It has 140 members elected from multi-seat constituencies for a four-year term, five seats are reserved for national minorities and six members representing Croatians abroad are chosen by proportional representation. The upper house, the *Chamber of Counties*, was abolished in 2001.

National Anthem

'Lijepa nasva domovino' ('Beautiful our homeland'); words by A. Mihanović, tune by J. Runjanin.

GOVERNMENT CHRONOLOGY

(HDZ = Croatian Democratic Union; SDP = Social Democratic Party of Croatia; n/p = non-partisan)

Presidents since 1990.

1990–99	HDZ	Franjo Tudjman
2000–	n/p	Stjepan (Stipe) Mesić

Prime Ministers since 1990.

1990	HDZ	Stjepan (Stipe) Mesić
1990–91	HDZ	Josip Manolić
1991–92	HDZ	Franjo Greguric
1992–93	HDZ	Hrvoje Šarinić
1993–95	HDZ	Nikica Valentić
1995–2000	HDZ	Zlatko Mateša
2000–03	SDP	Ivica Račan
2003–	HDZ	Ivo Sanader

RECENT ELECTIONS

Presidential elections were held on 2 Jan. 2005. Incumbent Stipe Mesić (Croatian People's Party) received 48·9% of the vote, Jadranka Kosor (Croatian Democratic Union) 20·3% and Boris Mikšić (ind.) 17·8%. There were ten other candidates. Turnout was 50·6%. As a result a second round was required. In the run-off on 16 Jan. 2005 Stipe Mesić received 65·9% of votes cast, against 34·1% for Jadranka Kosor.

Elections to the Sabor were held on 23 Nov. 2003. The Croatian Democratic Union (HDZ) won 66 of 152 seats (33·9% of the vote); an alliance of the Social Democratic Party of Croatia, the Istrian Democratic Assembly, Libra and the Liberal Party won 43 seats with 22·6% (of which the Social Democratic Party of Croatia 34 seats); an alliance of the Croatian People's Party and the Littoral and Highland Region Alliance won 11 with 8·0%; the Croatian Peasant Party won 10 with 7·2%; the Croatian Party of Rights won 8 seats with 6·4%. Other parties won three seats or fewer; non-partisans took four seats. Turnout was 61·7%.

CURRENT ADMINISTRATION

President: Stipe Mesić; b. 1934 (ind.; sworn in 18 Feb. 2000 and re-elected on 2 Jan. 2005).

Following the election of 23 Nov. 2003 a coalition government was formed between the Croatian Democratic Union and the alliance of the Croatian Social Liberal Party and Democratic Centre.

In March 2006 the government comprised:

Prime Minister: Ivo Sanader; b. 1953 (Croatian Democratic Union; sworn in on 23 Dec. 2003).

Deputy Prime Ministers: Jadranka Kosor (also *Minister of the Family, Veterans' Affairs and Intergenerational Solidarity*); Damir Polančec.

Minister of Foreign Affairs and European Integration: Kolinda Grabar-Kitarović. *Finance:* Ivan Šuker. *Defence:* Berislav Rončević. *Interior:* Ivica Kirin. *Economy, Labour and Entrepreneurship:* Branko Vukelić. *Sea, Tourism, Transport and Development:* Božidar Kalmeta. *Agriculture, Forestry and Water Management:* Petar Čobanković. *Environmental Protection, Physical Planning and Construction:* Marina Matulović Dropulić. *Health and Social Welfare:* Neven Ljubičić. *Culture:* Božo Biškupić. *Justice:* Vesna Škare Ožbolt. *Science, Education and Sports:* Dragan Primorac.

Government Website: http://www.vlada.hr/

CURRENT LEADERS

Stipe Mesić

Position
President

Introduction
Stipe Mesić became Croatian president in Feb. 2000, having previously been prime minister and the Croatian representative for the revolving Yugoslav presidency. Occupying the political centre, he favours rapid integration into NATO and the EU. He has attempted to move away from the autocratic style of his predecessor Franjo Tudjman and has received international support for his co-operation with the Hague War Crimes Tribunal.

Early Life
Mesić was born on 24 Dec. 1934 in Orahovica. He graduated in law from Zagreb University in 1961, where he was active in student politics. He entered the Croatian parliament in the early 1970s but served a year-long prison sentence for his role in the anti-Tito Croatian Spring of 1971.

As a member of the Croatian Democratic Union (HDZ), he served as Croatia's prime minister from 30 May–24 Aug. 1990 and was president of the collective Yugoslav presidency from July–Oct. 1991, resigning a few weeks before Croatia declared independence. From 1992–94 he was speaker of the Croatian parliament, but resigned his office and his membership of the HDZ in 1994. Unhappy with HDZ policy, especially concerning Bosnia-Herzegovina, he founded the Independent Croatian Democrats (HND). Three years later he moved to the Croatian People's Party (HNS), becoming its vice-president.

Following Tudjman's death in Dec. 1999, he stood for the Croatian presidency. Despite being out of frontline politics for six years, his progressive agenda and personal charisma proved popular with voters. In a run-off Mesić defeated Dražen Budiša of the Croatian Social Liberal Party and was sworn into office on 18 Feb. 2000.

Career in Office
Mesić resigned his party membership on assuming office. He promised to prune back presidential powers in a bid to avert the autocratic presidency epitomized by Tudjman. Mesić also vowed to clamp down on corruption within the country. He has pressed the government to institute the necessary reforms to achieve membership of NATO and the EU. Further to this end he has encouraged co-operation with the UN War Crimes Tribunal and in mid-2001 supported the extradition of two Croatians suspected of war crimes. The decision to allow extradition met with considerable hostility, particularly from war veterans, but the government narrowly survived a confidence vote over the issue. In addition, Mesić made known his willingness to testify for the prosecution at the trial of Slobodan Milošević.

Mesić has made headway in improving relations with neighbouring countries. After meetings with his Serbian counterpart, Vojislav Koštunica, the two leaders agreed to improve diplomatic ties between their countries following the downgrading of relations during the 1999 Kosovo conflict. Mesić indicated that 300,000 ethnic Serbs displaced during the 1990s would be accepted back into Croatia. Agreements to improve relations with Bosnia and Slovenia have also been signed.

In Jan. 2005 Mesić was re-elected as president with 66% of the vote in a run-off poll against Jadranka Kosor of the HDZ.

Ivo Sanader

Position
Prime Minister

Introduction
Ivo Sanader was elected prime minister in Dec. 2003. A member of President Tudjman's right-wing administration throughout the 1990s, the former literary agent aims to steer the country to EU membership in 2009.

Early Life
Ivo Sanader was born on 8 June 1953 in Split, Yugoslavia. He studied comparative literature and Romansch languages at Innsbruck University in Austria, graduating with a PhD in 1982. Returning to Split, he began work as a literary agent for the *Logo* publishing house, becoming editor-in-chief in 1988. In 1991, following a three-year spell as a freelance writer and publisher in Innsbruck, Sanader was appointed general manager of the Croatian National Theatre. In Aug. 1992, having been elected to represent the right-wing Croatian Democratic Union (HDZ) in the Republic of Croatia's new parliament, Sanader became minister of science and technology. Appointed deputy foreign minister in early 1993, he participated in the bilateral talks which led to the establishment of the Croat–Muslim Federation of Bosnia and Herzegovina.

Following the signing of the Dayton Peace Accord in Nov. 1995, Sanader was named chief of staff to the president (and then leader of the HDZ), Franjo Tudjman. Sanader was appointed to the defence and national security council, serving as deputy foreign minister from 1996 until the parliamentary elections of Jan. 2000, when the ruling HDZ was defeated by a coalition of the Social Democratic Party and the Croatian Social-Liberal Party. Subsequently elected leader of the HDZ, Sanader brought in sweeping reforms, attempting to root out corruption and draw a line under its authoritarian past. He was re-elected president of the HDZ at the party's congress in April 2002 and led the party to victory in the Nov. 2003 parliamentary elections (winning 66 seats of 152). President Mesić named Sanader prime minister designate on 9 Dec. 2003 and, following parliamentary consent, he was sworn in two weeks later.

Career in Office
Sanader has pledged his commitment to democracy, the rule of law and free market economics. He has promised to cut taxes, fight corruption and prepare Croatia for membership of NATO and the EU. However, burdened with a minority government, economic reforms have been slower than expected. After a series of delays, formal EU accession talks began in Oct. 2005.

DEFENCE

Conscription is for six months. Defence expenditure in 2003 totalled US$596m. (US$134 per capita), representing 2·1% of GDP.

Army
The country is divided into six operations zones. Personnel, 2002, 45,000 (around 20,000 conscripts). Paramilitary forces include an armed police of 10,000. There are 40,000 reserves in 27 Home Defence regiments and 100,000 regular Army reservists.

Navy
In 2002 the fleet included one submarine for special operations and one missile-armed corvette. Total personnel in 2002 numbered about 3,000 including two companies of marines.

Air Force
Personnel, 2002, 3,000 (including Air Defence and 1,320 conscripts). There are 24 combat aircraft including 20 MiG-21s, and 22 armed helicopters.

INTERNATIONAL RELATIONS

Croatia is a member of the UN, WTO, BIS, NATO Partnership for Peace, the Council of Europe, OSCE, the Central European Initiative, the Danube Commission, the Inter-American Development Bank and the IOM. Croatia applied for European Union membership in 2003 and was accepted as an official candidate country in 2004.

ECONOMY

Agriculture contributed 8·9% of GDP in 2002, industry 29·3% and services 61·8%.

Overview
Croatia has experienced average growth rates of 4·5% per annum and consistently low inflation since the mid-1990s. The country witnessed strong industrial production and retail sales in 2003 although private sector activity started to slow down in 2004. Structural reforms including privatization have been successfully undertaken in the last decade. Bankruptcy, company and labour laws have been modernized in a bid to harmonize with EU standards. According to the OECD, deeper reforms are needed in the legal system and in the labour market, and greater privatization is needed outside the telecommunications and banking sectors in order to boost corporate governance and competitiveness. The external position has been gradually worsening despite good performances in other areas. External debt increased to 75% of GDP in 2003; according to the IMF this is more than twice the average of that in emerging markets and higher than that in the other Central and Eastern European countries. Domestic investment has grown faster than savings since the mid-1990s, creating persistent current account deficits, leaving the debt profile increasingly vulnerable to external shocks, particularly in the event of currency depreciation. In 2003 fiscal discipline waned as the fiscal deficit increased to 6·3% of GDP, overshooting its target of 4·5%. In 2004 the newly elected government resumed efforts to maintain fiscal consolidation, to improve transparency in the fiscal accounts, to rein in quasi-fiscal operations and to strengthen public expenditure and debt management.

Currency
On 30 May 1994 the *kuna* (HRK; a name used in 1941–45) of 100 *lipa* replaced the Croatian dinar at one kuna = 1,000 dinars. Foreign exchange reserves were US$5,506m. in June 2002. Gold reserves have been negligible since Sept. 2001. Inflation was 1·7% in 2002, 1·8% in 2003 and 2·1% in 2004. Total money supply was 26,715m. kuna in May 2002.

Budget
Government revenue and expenditure (1m. kuna):

	1996	1997	1998	1999	2000	2001
Revenue	47,696	52,945	63,173	61,358	63,817	65,843
Expenditure	48,407	54,362	63,079	68,889	73,269	73,796

Expenditure by function (2001, in 1m. kuna): social security and welfare, 31,610; health, 11,815; education, 5,896. VAT at 22% was introduced in 1997.

Performance
Real GDP growth was 4·3% in 2003 and 3·8% in 2004. Total GDP was US$34·2bn. in 2004.

Banking and Finance
The National Bank of Croatia (*Governor*, Zeljko Rohatinski) is the bank of issue. In 2001 there were 43 registered banks. The largest banks are Zagrebačka Banka, with assets in 2000 of US$2·8bn., and Privredna Banka Zagreb. There are stock exchanges in Zagreb and Varaždin.

Total foreign direct investments from 1993 to Sept. 2001 amounted to US$5,927·5m., mainly from Austria (US$1,739m.), Germany (US$1,199m.) and the USA (US$1,189m).

ENERGY AND NATURAL RESOURCES

Environment

Croatia's carbon dioxide emissions from the consumption and flaring of fossil fuels in 2002 were the equivalent of 4·4 tonnes per capita.

Electricity

Installed capacity in 2000 was 3·8m. kW. Output was 10·70bn. kWh in 2000, with consumption per capita 3,356 kWh in 2000.

Oil and Gas

In 2000, 1·1m. tonnes of crude oil were produced. Natural gas output in 2000 totalled 1·7bn. cu. metres and reserves were 34bn. cu. metres in 2002.

Minerals

Production (in 1,000 tonnes): salt (2001), 33.

Agriculture

Agriculture and fishing generate approximately 9% of GDP. At the 1993 census 409,647 persons subsisted on agriculture. Agricultural land totals 3·15m. ha. (63·4% is cultivated). There were 1·46m. ha. of arable land in 2001 and 127,000 ha. of permanent crops. Production (in 1,000 tonnes, 2000): wheat, 1,080; maize, 800; sugarbeets, 770; potatoes, 500; grapes, 394; wine, 209; barley, 125.

Livestock, 2000: cattle, 427,000; sheep, 528,000; pigs, 1,233,000; chickens, 11m. Animal products, 2000: milk, 641,000 tonnes; meat, 125,000 tonnes; eggs, 49,000 tonnes; cheese, 19,000 tonnes.

Forestry

Forests covered 1·96m. ha. in 2002, of which 80% are state owned. In 2001, 3·47m. cu. metres of roundwood were produced.

Fisheries

In 2002 there were 15 fish-processing factories. Total catch in 2001 was 18,090 tonnes, almost exclusively from sea fishing.

INDUSTRY

The largest company in Croatia in Jan. 2003 was Pliva (market capitalization of 9,360·3m. kuna), a pharmaceuticals company.

In 2001 industrial production growth totalled 6% in comparison with 2000. Output, 2000: cement, 3·25m. tonnes; cotton fabrics and blankets (1998), 16·75m. sq. metres; wool fabrics and blankets (1998), 6·55m. sq. metres; beer (2001), 379·9m. litres.

Labour

In 2001 the number of employees was 1,469,500 and unemployment was 24·7%. Among 15 to 30-year-olds unemployment is around 40%. The main areas of activity in 2001 were manufacturing (employing 305,600 persons), agriculture, hunting and forestry (224,500), wholesale and retail trade/repair of motor vehicles, motorcycles and personal and household goods (211,300) and public administration and defence/compulsory social security (105,500).

INTERNATIONAL TRADE

Croatia has accepted responsibility for 29·5% of the US$4,400m. commercial bank debt of the former Yugoslavia. Total foreign debt was US$15,347m. in 2002.

Imports and Exports

Imports for 2004 came to US$16,589m. Exports in 2004 were valued at US$8,024m.

Principal imports in 2004 were: machinery and transport equipment, 34·9%; manufactured goods, 19·6%; mineral fuels, 12·0%; miscellaneous manufactured articles, 11·9%; chemicals, 11·2%; food and live animals, 7·2%. Main exports in 2004 were: machinery and transport equipment, 32·3%; miscellaneous

manufactured articles, 17·8%; manufactured goods, 14·8%; mineral fuels, 11·3%; chemicals, 9·4%; food and live animals, 6·3%. In 2004 the main import suppliers were (in US$1m.): Italy (2,819); Germany (2,569); Russia (1,206); Slovenia (1,179); Austria (1,131). Main export markets (in US$1m.): Italy (1,834); Bosnia-Herzegovina (1,154); Germany (895); Austria (757); Slovenia (601).

COMMUNICATIONS

Roads

There were 28,344 km of roads in 2004 (including 742 km of motorways). In 1999, 84·6% of roads were paved. In 2004 there were 1,337,538 passenger cars, 4,869 buses and coaches, and 154,790 vans and trucks. 65m. passengers and 55·3m. tonnes of freight were carried by road transport in 2004. There were 608 deaths in road accidents in 2004.

Rail

There were 2,726 km of 1,435 mm gauge rail in 2004 (984 km electrified). In 2004 railways carried 36·7m. passengers and 12·2m. tonnes of freight.

Civil Aviation

The biggest international airports are Zagreb (Pleso), Split and Dubrovnik. The national carrier is Croatia Airlines. In 2004 scheduled airline traffic of Croatian-based carriers flew 12m. km, carrying 1,336,411 passengers (886,215 on international flights). In 2004 Zagreb handled 1,389,537 passengers (926,011 on international flights) and 7,692 tonnes of freight, Dubrovnik 860,672 passengers (704,331 on international flights) and Split 768,706 passengers (575,019 on international flights).

Shipping

The main port is Rijeka, which handled 2·1m. tonnes of freight in 2004. Figures for 2004 show that 22·6m. passengers and 25·2m. tonnes of cargo were transported. In 2002 merchant shipping totalled 835,000 GRT, including oil tankers 8,000 GRT. In 2004 vessels totalling 212,282,000 GRT entered ports and vessels totalling 214,231,000 GRT cleared.

Telecommunications

The telephone density (the number of lines per 1,000 population) rose from 17·2% in 1990 to 42% in 2004.

In 2004 there were 1,676,482 fixed telephone subscribers and 2,842,377 mobile subscribers (pre-paid included). The number of Internet subscribers in 2004 was 834,468 (excluding 87,152 subscribers using the services of the non-profit Croatian Academic and Research Network).

Postal Services

In 2004 there were 1,158 post offices.

SOCIAL INSTITUTIONS

Justice

The population in penal institutions in Dec. 2001 was 2,584 (59 per 100,000 of national population).

Education

In 2004–05 there were 1,190 pre-school institutions with 104,987 children and 8,476 childcare workers; 2,141 primary schools with 391,744 pupils and 29,485 teachers; 665 secondary schools with 192,076 pupils and 20,701 teachers. In 2004–05 there were 103 institutes of higher education with 134,583 students and 8,764 academic staff. In 2004–05 there were six universities (Zagreb, Osijek, Rijeka, Split, Dubrovnik and Zadar). Adult literacy rate in 2003 was 98·1% (male, 99·3%; female, 97·1%).

In 2002–03 total expenditure on education came to 4·6% of GNP; in 1998–99 expenditure on education accounted for 10·4% of total government expenditure.

Health

In 2003 there were 73 hospitals with 25,000 beds. In 2001 there were 10,552 physicians, 3,021 dentists, 22,185 nurses, 2,235 pharmacists and 1,491 midwives.

Welfare

The official retirement age is 63 years (men) and 58 years (women). However, this is set to rise gradually until 2008 when it will be 65 (men) and 60 (women). The old-age pension is dependent on wages earned in relation to the average wage of all employed persons. The minimum old-age pension is defined for every year of the qualifying period as 0·825% of the average gross salary of all employees in 1998. This amount (39·86 kuna from Jan. 2002) is adjusted for inflation. The minimum unemployment benefit was 725 kuna a month in 2002 and the maximum benefit was 900 kuna a month.

RELIGION

In 2001 there were 3,890,000 Roman Catholics, 250,000 Serbian Orthodox and 100,000 Sunni Muslims. The remainder of the population were followers of other religions. In May 2005 there was one cardinal.

CULTURE

World Heritage Sites

Croatia has six UNESCO protected sites: the Old City of Dubrovnik (entered on the List in 1979), known as the 'Pearl of the Adriatic' and medieval Ragusa, an important maritime republic; the Historic Complex of Split with the Palace of Diocletian (1979), including Roman Emperor Diocletian's mausoleum, now the cathedral; Plitvice Lakes National Park (1979), a series of lakes and waterfalls and a habitat for bears and wolves; the Episcopal Complex of the Euphrasian Basilica in the Historical Centre of Poreč (1997); the Historic City of Trogir (1997), a Venetian city based on a Hellenistic plan; and the Cathedral of St James in Šibenik (2000), built in the Gothic and Renaissance styles between 1431–1535.

Broadcasting

Broadcasting is controlled by the state Croatian Radio-Television (colour by PAL). In 2004 there were 129 radio and 16 television stations. In 2004 there were 1·19m. radio subscribers and 1·11m. television subscribers.

Cinema

In 2004 there were 141 cinemas (of which two were multiplexes, one with 13 screens and one with five screens) with a total attendance of 3·0m. Four feature films were made in 2004.

Press

In 2003 there were 12 daily newspapers; in 2002 the dailies had a circulation of 597,000, at a rate of 135 per 1,000 inhabitants. In 2003 a total of 6,447 book titles and brochures were published.

Tourism

In 2000 there were a total of 6·62m. tourists (5·34m. foreign tourists, including 920,000 Germans and 886,000 Italians) staying 38·41m. tourist nights. In 2002 there were 160,000 hotel beds and 306,000 beds in private accommodation. The tourist industry is now recovering following the 1991–95 war, although the events in neighbouring Yugoslavia in 1999 resulted in the number of tourists for the year declining to 4·75m. In 2000 tourism accounted for more than 15% of GDP. The industry directly employs about 10% of the population.

Festivals

Croatia has a number of cultural and traditional festivals, including the Zagreb Summer Festival (July–Aug.); the International Folk Dance Festival in Zagreb (July); Dubrovnik Summer Festival (July–Aug.); Split Summer (July–Aug.); Alka Festival (traditional medieval tilting), Sinj (Aug.).

Libraries

In 2001 there were 248 public libraries, one National library and 129 Higher Education libraries, two university libraries, five scientific and 195 special libraries. They held a combined 14·8m. volumes for 6·3m. registered users.

DIPLOMATIC REPRESENTATIVES

Of Croatia in the United Kingdom (21 Conway St., London, W1T 6BN)
Ambassador: Josip Paro.

Of the United Kingdom in Croatia (Ivana Lucica 4, 10000 Zagreb)
Ambassador: Sir John Ramsden.

Of Croatia in the USA (2343 Massachusetts Ave., NW, Washington, D.C., 20008)
Ambassador: Neven Jurica.

Of the USA in Croatia (Thomasa Jeffersona 2, 10010 Zagreb)
Ambassador: Ralph Frank.

Of Croatia to the United Nations
Ambassador: Mirjana Mladineo.

Of Croatia to the European Union
Ambassador: Branco Baričević.

FURTHER READING

Central Bureau of Statistics. *Statistical Yearbook, Monthly Statistical Report, Statistical Information, Statistical Reports.*

Carmichael, Cathie, *Croatia.* [Bibliography] ABC-Clio, Oxford and Santa Barbara (CA), 1999

Jovanovic, Nikolina, *Croatia: A History.* Translated from Croatian. C. Hurst, London, 2000

Stallaerts, R. and Laurens, J., *Historical Dictionary of the Republic of Croatia.* Metuchen (NJ), 1995

Tanner, M. C., *A Nation Forged in War.* Yale, 1997

National Statistical Office: Central Bureau of Statistics, 3 Ilica, 10000 Zagreb. *Director (acting):* Darko Jukić.
Website: http://www.dzs.hr/

CUBA

República de Cuba

Capital: Havana
Population projection, 2010: 11·38m.
GDP per capita, 2000: (PPP$) 5,259
HDI/world rank: 0·817/52

KEY HISTORICAL EVENTS

Cuba's first inhabitants were the Taíno, Ciboney and Guanahatabey tribes. Christopher Columbus arrived in Cuba in 1492 and a permanent settlement was established by Diego Velázquez in 1511. Oppression and European diseases virtually exterminated the indigenous population within 50 years and African slaves were imported as replacements. In 1607 Havana was declared the capital.

Resistance to Spanish rule grew after the removal of Cuban delegates from the Spanish Cortes in 1837. Repeated offers by the USA to buy Cuba were rejected. Slavery was suppressed from the 1850s though not abolished until 1886. The first rebellion, the Ten-Year War, broke out in 1868 and was led by Gen. Máximo Gómez. An assembly was granted in 1869. However, José Martí y Pérez created the Cuban Revolutionary Party from New York and launched an invasion of Cuba in 1895 with Gómez and Antonio Maceo. The USA intervened in 1898, winning control of Cuba from Spain at the Treaty of Paris. Municipal elections in 1900 rejected annexationist policies and Cuba achieved independence in 1902. The Platt Amendment allowed for US intervention to preserve independence and stability and awarded the USA control of Guantánamo Bay. At the request of President Estrada Palma, US forces were installed on the island between 1906 and 1909. In 1912 and 1917 there were further instances of American intervention to protect national interests.

Gerardo Machado's dictatorial presidency began in 1925 and was ended by a coup in 1933. The Revolt of the Sergeants brought Fulgencio Batista y Zaldívar to power. The Platt Amendment was revoked and in 1940 a socially progressive constitution was inaugurated. Batista was returned at disputed elections in 1940 but was voted out of office four years later. He ran for re-election in 1952 but, with little chance of victory, led a bloodless coup before elections could be held, suspending the constitution and instigating a repressive and corrupt regime.

Fidel Castro, imprisoned in 1953 after a failed revolt, arrived from Mexico with 80 men in 1956. Castro and Che Guevara led a guerrilla war from the Sierra Maestra mountains and, despite US financial support, Batista fled after revolutionaries seized Havana in Jan. 1959. The USA recognized the new regime but relations soon deteriorated. Castro, as prime minister, launched a nationalization programme, seizing American assets and outlawing foreign land ownership. In Oct. 1960 the USA's trade embargo began and diplomatic relations were broken in Jan.

1961. Close relations between Cuba and the USSR provoked covert US support for the doomed Bay of Pigs invasion in April 1961, in which an offensive by a group of exiled Cubans was defeated by Castro's troops. Castro declared Cuba to be a socialist state. In 1962 the USA and USSR neared nuclear conflict during the Cuban Missile Crisis, with the US Navy imposing a blockade on Cuba from 22 Oct. until 22 Nov. to force the USSR to withdraw Soviet missile bases. In return, the USA guaranteed not to invade Cuba.

Between 1965 and 1973, 250,000 Cubans left for America on Freedom Flights agreed between the two nations. In 1976 a new constitution consolidated Castro's power as head of state, government and the Armed Forces.

Cuba continued to receive financial aid and technical advice from the USSR until the early 1990s when subsidies were suspended. This led to a 40% drop in GDP between 1989 and 1993. The USA has maintained an economic embargo against the island and relations between Cuba and the USA have remained embittered, although contact between the two countries has been growing in recent years. From Jan. 2002 suspected al-Qaeda and Taliban prisoners were brought from Afghanistan to the military prison at the American naval base at Guantánamo Bay.

TERRITORY AND POPULATION

The island of Cuba forms the largest and most westerly of the Greater Antilles group and lies 215 km (135 miles) south of the tip of Florida, USA. The area is 110,861 sq. km, and comprises the island of Cuba (104,748 sq. km); the Isle of Youth (Isla de la Juventud, formerly the Isle of Pines; 2,398 sq. km); and some 1,600 small isles ('cays'; 3,715 sq. km). Population, census (2002), 11,177,743, giving a density of 100·8 per sq. km. In 2003, 75·7% of the population were urban.

The UN gives a projected population for 2010 of 11·38m.

The area, population and density of population of the 14 provinces and the special Municipality of the Isle of Youth (Isla de la Juventud) were as follows (2002):

	Area sq. km	Population
Ciudad de La Habana	727	2,201,610
Santiago de Cuba	6,170	1,036,281
Holguín	9,301	1,021,321
Villa Clara	8,662	817,395
Granma	8,372	822,452
Camagüey	15,990	784,178
Pinar del Río	10,925	726,574
La Habana	5,731	711,066
Matanzas	11,978	670,427
Las Tunas	6,589	525,485
Guantánamo	6,186	507,118
Sancti Spíritus	6,744	460,328
Ciego de Avila	6,910	411,766
Cienfuegos	4,178	395,183
Isla de la Juventud	2,398	86,559

The capital city, Havana, had a population in 2002 of 2,201,610. Other major cities (2002 census populations in 1,000): Santiago de Cuba (423), Camagüey (302), Holguín (270), Santa Clara (210), Guantánamo (208), Bayamo (145), Las Tunas (144), Cienfuegos (141), Pinar del Río (139) and Matanzas (127).

The official language is Spanish.

SOCIAL STATISTICS

2001 births, 138,718; deaths, 79,395; marriages, 54,345; divorces, 37,260; suicides (1996), 2,015. Rates, 2001: birth, 12·4 per 1,000 population; death, 7·1; marriage, 4·8; divorce, 3·3; suicide (1996), 18·3. Infant mortality rate, 2001, 6·2 per 1,000 live births. Annual population growth rate, 1992–2002, 0·4%. Life expectancy in 2003 was 75·5 years for males and 79·2 for females. The fertility rate in 2001 was 1·6 births per woman.

CLIMATE

Situated in the sub-tropical zone, Cuba has a generally rainy climate, affected by the Gulf Stream and the N.E. Trades, although winters are comparatively dry after the heaviest rains in Sept. and Oct. Hurricanes are liable to occur between June and Nov. Havana, Jan. 72°F (22·2°C), July 82°F (27·8°C). Annual rainfall 48" (1,224 mm).

CONSTITUTION AND GOVERNMENT

A Communist Constitution came into force on 24 Feb. 1976. It was amended in July 1992 to permit direct parliamentary elections and in June 2002 to make the country's socialist system 'irrevocable'.

Legislative power is vested in the *National Assembly of People's Power*, which meets twice a year and consists of 609 deputies elected for a five-year term by universal suffrage. Lists of candidates are drawn up by mass organizations (trade unions, etc.). The National Assembly elects a 31-member *Council of State* as its permanent organ. The Council of State's President, who is head of state and of government, nominates and leads a Council of Ministers approved by the National Assembly.

National Anthem

'Al combate corred bayameses' ('Run, Bayamans, to the combat'); words and tune by P. Figueredo.

RECENT ELECTIONS

Elections to the National Assembly were held on 19 Jan. 2003. All 609 candidates were from the National Assembly of People's Power and received the requisite 50% of votes for election. No other parties are allowed.

CURRENT ADMINISTRATION

President: Dr Fidel Castro Ruz (b. 1927) became *President* of the Council of State on 3 Dec. 1976; re-elected for five years on 24 Feb. 1998 and again on 6 March 2003. He is also First Secretary of the Cuban Communist Party, President of the Council of Ministers and C.-in-C. of the National Defence Council.

In March 2006 the government comprised:

First Vice-President of the Council of State and of the Council of Ministers, Minister of the Revolutionary Armed Forces: Gen. Raúl Castro Ruz (Fidel Castro's younger brother and his designated successor).

Vice-Presidents of the Council of Ministers: Osmany Cienfuegos Gorriarán, José Ramón Fernández Alvarez, José Luis Rodríguez García (also *Minister of Economy and Planning*), Pedro Miret Prieto, Otto Rivero Torres. *Secretary of the Council of Ministers:* Carlos Lage Dávila.

Minister of Agriculture: Vacant. *Auditing and Control:* Lina Olinda Pedraza Rodríguez. *Basic Industries:* Yadira García Vera. *Construction:* Fidel Figueroa de la Paz. *Culture:* Abel Prieto Jiménez. *Domestic Trade:* Marino Murillo Jorge. *Education:* Luis Gómez Gutiérrez. *Finance and Prices:* Georgina Barreiro Fajardo. *Fishing Industry:* Alfredo López Valdés. *Food Industry:* Alejandro Roca Iglesias. *Foreign Investment and Economic Co-operation:* Marta Lomas Morales. *Foreign Relations:* Felipe Pérez Roque. *Foreign Trade:* Raúl de la Nuez Ramírez. *Higher Education:* Fernando Vecino Alegret. *Information Science and Communications:* Roberto Ignacio González Planas. *Interior:* Gen. Abelardo Colomé Ibarra. *Iron, Steel and Engineering Industries:* Fernando Acosta Santana. *Justice:* Roberto Díaz Sotolongo. *Labour and Social Security:* Alfredo Morales Cartaya. *Light Industry:* Jesús Pérez Othón. *Public Health:* José Ramón

Balaguer Cabrera. *Science, Technology and Environment:* Vacant. *Sugar Industry:* Div. Gen. Ulises Rosales del Toro. *Tourism:* Manual Marrero Cruz. *Transport:* Carlos Manuel Pazo Torrado. *Minister without Portfolio:* Ricardo Cabrisas Ruiz.

The Congress of the Cuban Communist Party (PCC) elects a Central Committee of 225 members, which in turn appoints a Political Bureau comprising 26 members.

Government Website: http://www.cubagob.cu

CURRENT LEADERS

Fidel Castro

Position
President

Introduction
Lawyer and revolutionary guerrilla, Fidel Alejandro Castro Ruz has led Cuba since he headed the 1959 revolution that overthrew the military dictatorship of Fulgencio Batista. Premier until 1976 when a new constitution created a presidency, Castro set up a socialist state, implemented agrarian reforms, nationalized industries and imposed single party rule. Full employment, free education and universal health care were promised, although all opposition was repressed and freedoms restricted. Strong Soviet links bolstered Cuba in the face of US hostility, but since the collapse of the USSR Castro has become increasingly isolated.

Early Life
Castro was born on 13 Aug. 1926 (his official birthday, although some sources dispute this date) in the Oriente province (now Santiago de Cuba) in eastern Cuba, the illegitimate son of a prosperous Spanish sugarcane farmer and his cook. From the age of six, Castro was educated at Jesuit schools in Santiago de Cuba, and in 1945 went to study law at the capital's Universidad de la Habana, where he became politically active. He was a supporter of Eduardo Chibas who formed the Ortodoxos party (Cuban People's Party) in 1947. After joining the party, Castro was involved with preparations for a coup to depose the Dominican Republic's leader Gen. Rafael Trujillo.

After graduating in 1950, Castro set up a law firm in Havana to help the poor and his political allies. He continued his involvement with Ortodoxos and was their candidate for Havana in the 1952 elections. Before they could take place former premier Batista deposed Prime Minister Carlos Prío Socarrás and set up a military dictatorship. Following unsuccessful legal challenges, Castro began recruiting for a revolutionary movement. After a failed raid on the Moncada army barracks on 26 July 1953, Castro was sentenced to 13 years imprisonment.

He was pardoned in 1955 following an amnesty and went to Mexico where he formed the revolutionary Movimiento 26 de Julio. There he met Ernesto 'Che' Guevara Lynch, who became the Movimiento's doctor. On 2 Dec. 1956 Castro and his followers attacked his native Oriente province. After losing nearly all of their number, the remaining few fighters took refuge in the Sierra Maestra mountains where Castro continued to recruit, gathering together as many as 800 volunteers. Following numerous battles, Batista was forced into exile on 1 Jan. 1959. Castro became commander-in-chief of the army while the premiership was taken by Manuel Urrutia. Forcing the latter out, in July 1959 Castro appointed himself premier, promising to restore civil and political liberties.

Career in Office
Despite promising moderate reforms, Castro's radicalism soon intensified, as did his affiliation to Marxism. Communists were favoured for governmental positions while enforced land distribution ended tenancy and private ownership. Foreign investors left and all industry and commerce was nationalized. By early 1960 Castro had established a favourable trade agreement

with the USSR which provided Cuba with oil, weapons and loans while importing Cuban sugarcane at an advantageous price. In 1961 the Organizaciones Revolucionarias Integradas was created (the Cuban Communist Party—Partido Comunista de Cuba; PCC—from 1965), comprising Castro's Movimiento 26 de Julio, the Popular Socialist Party (Partido Socialista Popular) and the Revolutionary Directorate (Directorio Revolucionario). All opposition was outlawed. The immediate effect of Castro's reforms was the improvement of life for the poorest Cubans. Social services were made available, full employment was promised and illiteracy decreased. However, civil rights abuses led many middle class Cubans to flee the country.

In 1960 US suspicion of Castro and his links to communism led the USA to suspend trade agreements, impose an embargo and sever diplomatic relations. In April 1961 the US government supported and financed an attempted coup by 1,300 Cuban exiles. The unsuccessful invasion at the Bay of Pigs was soon contained by the Cuban army. The USA also mounted several assassination attempts. In 1962 Soviet ballistic missiles were secretly placed in Cuba in range of US cities. In retaliation the US navy surrounded Cuba. The world hovered on the brink of nuclear war until the Soviet leader Nikita Khrushchev agreed to remove the missiles in exchange for a removal of US missiles based in Turkey and a promise of an end to hostilities with Cuba.

In 1976 Castro created a new constitution and national assembly and appointed himself president. His brother Raúl was appointed minister of armed forces becoming *de facto* vice president. In 1980 Castro opened the northern port of Mariel for five months allowing thousands of Cubans to flee, including 125,000 who emigrated to the USA.

On an international level, Castro supported revolutionary activity in Bolivia, Venezuela and the Dominican Republic. Between 1975–89 the Cuban army aided communists in the Angolan civil war and helped Ethiopia combat Somalia's invasion in 1978. But Cuba's military expenditure was detrimental to its economic progress. Castro was unable to stimulate the country's industry or agriculture. In 1991 Cuba suffered heavily from the withdrawal of Soviet trade and rationing had to be imposed, leading to economic and social unrest in 1993. After public demonstrations, Castro agreed to relax restrictions on leaving the country. In 1994 the Cuban economy reached its nadir. Although Castro refused to change his regime after the fall of the USSR (free speech is still effectively banned), he was forced to adopt a pragmatic approach and to open up the economy and encourage a tourist industry. A two-tier financial system has meant plentiful supplies in tourist dollar shops but shortages for most Cubans.

At the end of the 1990s Castro formed an alliance with the Venezuelan premier Hugo Chávez and agreed a preferential trade arrangement exchanging Venezuelan oil for Cuban goods and services. Castro and Chávez also signed a co-operation agreement on agriculture and tourism. In Nov. 1999 relations with the USA were further strained by the Elián González affair, in which the two governments were involved in a custody battle over the fate of a six-year old Cuban refugee.

Castro was re-elected for his sixth presidential term in 2003 with 100% of the 609 available parliamentary votes. In March 2003 relations with the USA deteriorated further when Castro arrested several dozen political dissidents who had met with the US envoy, James Cason. Castro accused Cason of subversion and restricted the movement of diplomats within the country in a tit-for-tat response after the USA imposed similar restrictions in Washington. The EU threatened sanctions in June 2003, but the following month promised to continue aid despite Castro attacking the EU as a 'Trojan horse' of the USA. Diplomatic contacts with the EU were restored in Jan. 2005. In May 2005 Castro unusually allowed a dissident group to hold a public meeting, although foreigners seeking to attend were turned away.

Castro retains a tight grip on the country, but his health has been failing noticeably—with Parkinson's disease according to US officials, although this has been denied in Cuba—and there are concerns that the absence of a recognized successor could lead to civil unrest.

DEFENCE

The National Defence Council is headed by the president of the republic. Conscription is for two years.

In 2003 defence expenditure totalled US$1,200m. (US$106 per capita), representing 4·0% of GDP.

Army

The strength was estimated at 35,000 (including conscripts and Ready Reservists) in 2002. Border Guard and State Security forces total 26,500. The Territorial Militia is estimated at 1m. (reservists), all armed. In addition there is a Youth Labour Army of 70,000 and a Civil Defence Force of 50,000.

Navy

Personnel in 1999 totalled about 5,000 conscripts including about 550 marines. The Navy has five patrol and coastal combatants, six mine warfare vessels and one support vessel. Main bases are at Cabañas and Holguín. The USA still occupies the Guantánamo naval base.

Air Force

In 2002 the Air Force had a strength of some 8,000 and about 130 combat aircraft of which only around 25 are thought to be operational. They include MiG-29, MiG-23 and MiG-21 jet fighters.

INTERNATIONAL RELATIONS

Cuba is a member of the UN, WTO, OAS, LAIA, ACS, Antarctic Treaty and SELA (Latin American Economic System).

ECONOMY

Services account for about 68% of GDP, industry 27% and agriculture 5%.

Overview

Cuba is classified as a middle income country with a GDP per capita of US$2,500. Since the withdrawal of subsidies worth US$4–6bn. from the USSR in 1990, the economy has had to cope with falling tourism, low export prices and hurricane damage. Cuba fell into deep economic recession in the early 1990s, from which it is only now emerging. The government has undertaken limited reforms to alleviate food and goods shortages, with recent growth aided by the legalization of the use of US currency and the promotion of dollar-based tourism with a parallel dollar economy.

Tourism accounts for 12% of GDP and provides 40% of foreign exchange revenue. The US trade embargo on Cuba, imposed in 1963, blocks the island's access to funds from the IMF and the World Bank but the UN is able to continue operating in Cuba. Agriculture accounts for 6% of GDP and employs 24% of the active workforce. The chief export crops are sugar and tobacco, with 10% of the country's population employed in the sugar sector. The industrial sector accounts for 27% of GDP. The black market is bigger than the legal economy and basic economic activities (such as the sale of milk and bread) take place in the informal sector. There are no joint ventures with foreigners or foreign ownership of property. The currency is not convertible. The government employs 75% of the labour force, who receive housing and food subsidies but low wages.

Currency

The unit of currency is the *Cuban peso* (CUP) of 100 *centavos*, which is not convertible, although an official exchange rate is announced daily reflecting any changes in the strength of the US dollar. The US dollar ceased to be legal tender in 2004. 9,710m. pesos were in circulation in 1998. Inflation is low, averaging 1·8% between 1995–2002.

Budget
The 2002 revenue totalled 16,051bn. pesos and expenditure 17,051bn. pesos. Hard-currency earners and the self-employed became liable to a 10–50% income tax in Nov. 1995.

Performance
A combination of poor commodity export prices and a poor sugar harvest slowed down Cuba's economic growth in 1998 to 1·2%, below the government's original target of 2·5–3·5%. In 1999, however, growth was an impressive 6·2% and in 2000 growth remained high at 5·6%. Since 2001, however, growth has slowed with rates of 1·2% in 2002 and 2·6% in 2003.

Banking and Finance
The Central Bank of Cuba (*Governor*, Francisco Soberón Valdés) replaced the National Bank of Cuba as the central bank in June 1997. On 14 Oct. 1960 all banks were nationalized. Changes to the banking structure beginning in 1996 divested the National Bank of its commercial functions, and created new commercial and investment institutions. The Grupa Nueva Banca has majority holdings in each institution of the new structure. There were eight commercial banks in March 2002 and 18 local non-banking financial institutions. In addition, there were 13 representative offices of foreign banks and four representative offices of non-banking financial institutions. All insurance business was nationalized in Jan. 1964. A National Savings Bank was established in 1983.

Weights and Measures
The metric system is legally compulsory, but the American and old Spanish systems are much used. The sugar industry uses the Spanish long ton (1·03 tonnes) and short ton (0·92 tonne). Cuba sugar sack = 329·59 lb or 149·49 kg. Land is measured in *caballerías* (of 13·4 ha. or 33 acres).

ENERGY AND NATURAL RESOURCES

Environment
Cuba's carbon dioxide emissions from the consumption and flaring of fossil fuels were the equivalent of 3·0 tonnes per capita in 2002.

Electricity
Installed capacity was 4·3m. kW in 2000. Production was 15·7bn. kWh in 2002; consumption per capita in 2000 was 1,343 kWh.

Oil and Gas
Crude oil production (2000), 2·7m. tonnes. There were known natural gas reserves of 14bn. cu. metres in 2002. Natural gas production (2000), 589m. cu. metres.

Minerals
Iron ore abounds, with deposits estimated at 3,500m. tonnes. In 2000 output of salt was 177,000 tonnes; refractory chrome, 56,300 tonnes; copper concentrate, 1,346 tonnes. Other minerals are nickel (2001, 72,619 tonnes), cobalt, silica and barytes. Nickel is Cuba's second largest foreign exchange earner, after tourism. Gold and silver are also worked.

Agriculture
In 1959 all land over 30 *caballerías* was nationalized and eventually turned into state farms. In 2001 there were 3·63m. ha. of arable land and 0·84m. ha. of permanent crops. 870,000 ha. were irrigated in 2001. Under legislation of 1993, state farms were re-organized as 'units of basic co-operative production'. Unit workers select their own managers, and are paid an advance on earnings. 294,700 persons were employed in these units in 1995. In 1963 private holdings were reduced to a maximum of five *caballerías*. In 1994 farmers were permitted to trade on free market principles after state delivery quotas had been met.

The most important product is sugar and its by-products, but in 1998 the harvest suffered a series of weather disasters reducing production to 3·2m. tonnes (3·4m. tonnes in 1995–96), the smallest crop for 50 years. By 2000 production had risen again to 3·6m. tonnes. Production of other important crops in 2000 was (in 1,000 tonnes): oranges, 441; rice, 369; potatoes, 344; plantains, 329; grapefruit and pomelos, 233; cassava, 210; sweet potatoes, 195; maize, 185; bananas, 133; tomatoes, 129.

In 2000 livestock included 4·7m. cattle; 2·8m. pigs; 450,000 horses; 310,000 sheep; 140,000 goats; 15m. chickens.

Forestry
Cuba had 2·35m. ha. of forests in 2000, representing 21·4% of the land area. These forests contain valuable cabinet woods, such as mahogany and cedar, besides dye-woods, fibres, gums, resins and oils. Cedar is used locally for cigar boxes, and mahogany is exported. In 2001, 1·70m. cu. metres of roundwood were produced.

Fisheries
Fishing is the third most important export industry, after sugar and nickel. The total catch was approximately 56,000 tonnes in 2001, of which 51,400 tonnes were from marine waters.

INDUSTRY
The gross value of the manufacturing industry in 1998 was 4,290·7m. pesos. All industrial enterprises had been state-controlled, but in 1995 the economy was officially stated to comprise state property, commercial property based on activity by state enterprises, joint co-operative and private property. Production (in 1,000 tonnes): sugar (2002), 3,522; cement (2000), 1,633; residual fuel oil (2000), 780; petrol (2000), 492; distillate fuel oil (2000), 405; sulphuric acid (1989), 381; steel (1998), 278; complete fertilizers (1998), 157; tobacco (1998), 40. Also in 1998: 160m. cigars; textiles, 54m. sq. metres. The sugar industry, the backbone of the country's economy for much of its history, is being restructured. Up to half of Cuba's sugar mills are facing closure.

Labour
In 1998 the labour force was 6,621,522, with 3,753,600 in employment. Self-employment was legalized in 1993. Under legislation of Sept. 1994 employees made redundant must be assigned to other jobs or to strategic social or economic tasks; failing this, they are paid 60% of former salary.

Trade Unions
The Workers' Central Union of Cuba groups 23 unions.

INTERNATIONAL TRADE
Foreign debt to non-communist countries was US$12·3bn. in 2000. Since July 1992 foreign investment has been permitted in selected state enterprises, and Cuban companies have been able to import and export without seeking government permission. Foreign ownership is recognized in joint ventures. A free-trade zone opened at Havana in 1993. In 1994 the productive, real estate and service sectors were opened to foreign investment. Legislation of 1995 opened all sectors of the economy to foreign investment except defence, education and health services. 100% foreign-owned investments and investments in property are now permitted.

The Helms-Burton Law of March 1996 gives US nationals the right to sue foreign companies investing in Cuban estate expropriated by the Cuban government.

Imports and Exports
In 2001 imports totalled US$4,788m. and exports US$1,661m. The principal exports are sugar, minerals, tobacco, fish and

coffee. Sugar accounts for more than half of Cuba's export revenues, but revenues have been gradually declining and are now only a tenth of the 1990 total.

In 1999 the chief import sources (as % of total) were: Spain, 19·5; France, 8·2; Canada, 8·1; China, 7·7; Italy, 7·0. The chief export markets (as % of total) were: Russia, 23·3; Canada, 14·5; Netherlands, 12·9; Spain, 8·0; China, 3·6.

COMMUNICATIONS

Roads

In 2002 there were estimated to be 60,856 km of roads (including 638 km of motorways), of which 29,819 km were paved. Vehicles in use in 1997 included 172,500 passenger cars (15·6 per 1,000 inhabitants) and 156,600 trucks and vans. There were 1,309 fatalities as a result of road accidents in 1997.

Rail

There were (2000) 4,807 km of public railway (1,435 mm gauge), of which 147 km was electrified. Passenger-km travelled in 2000 came to 1,853m. and freight tonne-km to 804m. In addition, the large sugar estates have 7,162 km of lines in total on 1,435 mm, 914 mm and 760 mm gauges.

Civil Aviation

There is an international airport at Havana (Jose Martí). The state airline Cubana operates all services internally, and in 2003 had international flights from Havana to Bogotá, Buenos Aires, Cancún, Caracas, Curaçao, Fort de France, Guatemala City, Guayaquil, Kingston, Las Palmas, London, Madrid, Mexico City, Montego Bay, Montreal, Moscow, Panama City, Paris, Pointe-à-Pitre, Quito, Rome, San José (Costa Rica), Santiago, Santo Domingo, São Paulo and Toronto. Cubana flew 26·2m. km in 1999 and carried 1,259,000 passengers (683,000 on international flights). In 2001 Havana Jose Martí International handled 2,472,300 passengers (2,056,500 on international flights) and 19,302 tonnes of freight.

Shipping

There are 11 ports, the largest being Havana, Cienfuegos and Mariel. The merchant marine in 2002 totalled 103,000 GRT, including oil tankers 5,000 GRT.

Telecommunications

There were 583,000 telephone subscribers in 2001 (51·9 for every 1,000 persons) and 359,000 PCs in use in 2002 (31·8 for every 1,000 persons). Mobile phone subscribers numbered 17,900 in 2002 and there were 400 fax machines in 1995. There were 12,000 Internet users in 2001.

Postal Services

In 2001 there were 1,044 post offices, or one for every 10,800 persons.

SOCIAL INSTITUTIONS

Justice

There is a Supreme Court in Havana and seven regional courts of appeal. The provinces are divided into judicial districts, with courts for civil and criminal actions, and municipal courts for minor offences. The civil code guarantees aliens the same property and personal rights as those enjoyed by nationals.

The 1959 Agrarian Reform Law and the Urban Reform Law passed on 14 Oct. 1960 have placed certain restrictions on both. Revolutionary Summary Tribunals have wide powers.

The death penalty is still in force. In 2003 there were three executions.

The population in penal institutions in 2003 was approximately 55,000 (487 per 100,000 of national population).

Education

Education is compulsory (between the ages of six and 14), free and universal. In 1996–97 there were 154,520 pre-primary pupils with 6,970 teachers; in 2002–03 there were 9,397 elementary schools with 93,000 teachers for 873,700 pupils; and 2,032 secondary schools with 85,600 teachers for 992,000 pupils. There were 192,000 students in higher education in 2002–03.

There are four universities, and ten teacher training, two agricultural, four medical and ten other higher educational institutions.

The adult literacy rate was 96·9% in 2002 (97·0% among males and 96·8% among females).

In 2000–01 total expenditure on education came to 8·7% of GNP and 15·1% of total government spending.

Health

In 2002 there were 67,079 physicians, 9,955 dentists and 83,880 nurses. There were 266 hospitals in 2002 with 63 beds per 10,000 population. Free medical services are provided by the state poly-clinics, though a few doctors still have private practices.

Welfare

The official retirement age is 60 (men) or 55 (women). However, the qualifying age falls to 55 (men) or 50 (women) if the last 12 years of employment or 75% of employment was in dangerous or arduous work. The minimum pension in 2003 was 59 pesos a month, or 79 pesos a month, or 80% of wages, depending on average earnings and the number of years of employment. The maximum pension is 90% of average earnings.

Cuba has a sickness and maternity support programme.

RELIGION

Religious liberty was constitutionally guaranteed in July 1992. 40% of the population were estimated to be Roman Catholics in 2001. In 1994 Cardinal Jaime Ortega (b. 1936) was nominated Primate by Pope John Paul II. In May 2005 there was one cardinal. In 2002 there were 180 Roman Catholic priests, approximately half of them foreign nationals. There is a seminary in Havana which had 61 students in 1996. There is a bishop of the American Episcopal Church in Havana; there are congregations of Methodists in Havana and in the provinces as well as Baptists and other denominations. Cults of African origin (mainly Santería) still persist.

CULTURE

World Heritage Sites

There are eight sites in Cuba that appear on the UNESCO World Heritage List. They are (with the year entered on list): Old Havana and its fortifications (1982), Trinidad and the Valley de los Ingenios (19th century sugar mills; 1988), San Pedro de la Roca Castle in Santiago de Cuba (1997), Desembarco del Granma National Park (marine terraces; 1999), Vinales Valley (1999), the 19th-century coffee plantations at Sierra Maestra (2000), Alejandro de Humboldt National Park (2001) and the urban historic centre of Cienfuegos (2005).

Broadcasting

Broadcasting is the responsibility of the state-controlled Instituto Cubano de Radio y Televisión. There are five national radio networks, provincial and local stations and an external service, Radio Habana (Spanish, Arabic, Creole, English, Esperanto, French, Guaraní, Portuguese and Quechua). There are two TV channels (colour by NTSC). There were 5·32m. radio receivers in 2000 and 2·82m. TV sets in 2001.

Press

There were (2000) two daily newspapers with a combined circulation of 600,000.

Tourism

Tourism is Cuba's largest foreign exchange earner, and for some years was growing by nearly 20% per year. Ironically, with Cuba's sympathy for rebel causes, the country was one of the most seriously affected by the huge drop in visitors following the attacks on New York and Washington of 11 Sept. 2001. There were 1,656,000 foreign tourists in 2002 (1,741,000 in 2000 and 1,735,900 in 2001). Total receipts from tourism in 2002 amounted to US$1,633m.

DIPLOMATIC REPRESENTATIVES

Of Cuba in the United Kingdom (167 High Holborn, London, WC1 6PA)
Ambassador: René Juan Mujica Cantelar.

Of the United Kingdom in Cuba (Calle 34, No. 702/4, entre 7 ma Avenida y 17 Miramar, Havana)
Ambassador: John Dew.

Of Cuba to the United Nations
Ambassador: Rodrigo Malmierca Díaz.

Of Cuba to the European Union
Ambassador: Vacant.

The USA broke off diplomatic relations with Cuba on 3 Jan. 1961 but Cuba has an Interests Section in the Swiss Embassy in Washington, D.C., and the USA has an Interests Section in the Swiss Embassy in Havana.

FURTHER READING

Bethell, L. (ed.) *Cuba: a Short History.* CUP, 1993

Bunck, J. M., *Fidel Castro and the Quest for a Revolutionary Culture in Cuba.* Pennsylvania State Univ. Press, 1994

Cabrera Infantye, G., *Mea Cuba*; translated into English from Spanish. London, 1994

Cardoso, E. and Helwege, A., *Cuba after Communism.* Boston (Mass.), 1992

Eckstein, S. E., *Back from the Future: Cuba under Castro.* Princeton Univ. Press, 1994

Fursenko, A. and Naftali, T., *'One Hell of a Gamble': Khrushchev, Castro and Kennedy, 1958–1964.* New York, 1997

Gott, Richard, *Cuba: A New History.* Yale Univ. Press, 2004

Levine, Robert, *Secret Missions to Cuba: Fidel Castro, Bernardo Benes, and Cuban Miami.* Palgrave Macmillan, Basingstoke, 2002

May, E. R. and Zelikow, P. D., *The Kennedy Tapes: Inside the White House during the Cuban Missile Crisis.* Belknap Press/Harvard Univ. Press, 1997

Mesa-Lago, C. (ed.) *Cuba: After the Cold War.* Pittsburgh Univ. Press, 1993

Stubbs, J., *et al.,* *Cuba.* [Bibliography] ABC-Clio, Oxford and Santa Barbara (CA), 1996

Sweig, Julia, *Inside the Cuban Revolution.* Harvard Univ. Press, 2002

Thomas, Hugh, *Cuba, or the Pursuit of Freedom.* Eyre & Spottiswoode, London, 1971; Picador, London, 2001

CYPRUS

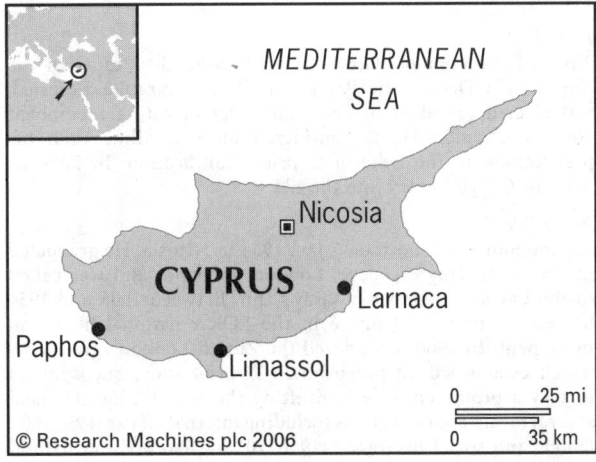

© Research Machines plc 2006

Kypriaki Dimokratia—Kibris Çumhuriyeti
(Republic of Cyprus)

Capital: Nicosia
Population projection, 2010: 881,000
GDP per capita, 2001: (PPP$) 21,190
HDI/world rank: 0·891/29

KEY HISTORICAL EVENTS

About the middle of the second millennium BC, Greek colonies were established in Cyprus and later it formed part of the Persian, Roman and Byzantine empires. In 1193 the island became a Frankish kingdom, in 1489 a Venetian dependency, and in 1751 was conquered by the Turks. In 1914 the island was annexed by Great Britain and on 1 May 1925 it was given the status of a Crown Colony. In the 1930s the Greek Cypriots began to agitate for *enosis* (union with Greece). In 1955 they started a guerrilla movement (EOKA) against the British, with Archbishop Makarios, the head of the Greek Orthodox Church in Cyprus, as leader. In 1959 the Greek and Turkish Cypriots agreed on a constitution for an independent Cyprus and Makarios was elected President.

On 16 June 1960 Cyprus became an independent state. In Dec. 1963 the Turkish Cypriots withdrew from the government. Fighting between Turkish and Greek Cypriots led to a UN peacekeeping force being sent in. Turkey invaded the island on 20 July 1974, eventually occupying the northern part. 0·2m. Greek Cypriots fled to live as refugees in the south.

In 1975 a Turkish Cypriot Federated State was proclaimed. Rauf Denktaş was appointed President. In 1983 the Turkish state unilaterally proclaimed itself the 'Turkish Republic of Northern Cyprus' (TRNC). In 1991 the UN rejected Rauf Denktaş' demands for the recognition of sovereignty for the TRNC, including a right to secession. In 1998 a proposal by Denktaş that the Greek and Turkish communities should join in a federation that recognizes 'the equal and sovereign status of Cyprus' Greek and Turkish parts' was rejected by the Greek and Cypriot governments.

In 2002 Cyprus was nominated as one of ten countries eligible for EU membership in 2004; the TRNC would be included only if UN-brokered talks to reunify the country succeeded. In Nov. 2002 the UN presented a peace plan to the Greek Cypriot and Turkish Cypriot leaders for a 'common' state with two 'component' states, along the lines of Switzerland and its cantons. In March 2003 UN-brokered talks to pave the way for the reunification of Cyprus collapsed. However, as a goodwill measure the 'Turkish Republic of Northern Cyprus' opened the Green Line separating the island's two sections in April 2003. In a referendum held in both the Greek-speaking and the Turkish-speaking areas of Cyprus on 24 April 2004, Greek Cypriots rejected a UN plan to reunite the island while Turkish Cypriots voted in favour. As a result, in the short term, EU benefits and laws will apply only to the Greek Cypriot community. Cyprus became a member of the European Union on 1 May 2004.

TERRITORY AND POPULATION

The island lies in the Mediterranean, about 60 km off the south coast of Turkey and 90 km off the coast of Syria. Area, 9,251 sq. km (3,572 sq. miles). The Turkish-occupied area is 3,335 sq. km. Population by ethnic group:

Ethnic group	1960 census	1973 census	1992	2000
Greek Cypriot	452,291	498,511	599,200	647,100
Turkish Cypriot	104,942	116,000	94,500	87,800
Others	16,333	17,267	20,000	24,200
Total	573,566	631,778	713,700	759,100

The United Nations population estimate for 2005 was 835,000; density, 90 per sq. km.

The UN gives a projected population for 2010 of 881,000.

69·2% of the population lived in urban areas in 2003. Principal towns with populations (2000 estimate): Nicosia (the capital), 199,100; Limassol, 159,800; Larnaca, 70,500; Paphos, 40,900.

As a result of the Turkish occupation of the northern part of Cyprus, 0·2m. Greek Cypriots were displaced and forced to find refuge in the south. The urban centres of Famagusta, Kyrenia and Morphou were completely evacuated. *See below* for details on the 'Turkish Republic of Northern Cyprus'. (The 'TRNC' was unilaterally declared as a 'state' in 1983 in the area of the Republic of Cyprus, which has been under Turkish occupation since 1974, when Turkish forces invaded the island. The establishment of the 'TRNC' was declared illegal by UN Security Resolutions 541/83 and 550/84. The 'TRNC' is not recognized by any country in the world except Turkey). Nicosia is a divided city, with the UN-patrolled Green Line passing through it.

Greek and Turkish are official languages. English is widely spoken.

SOCIAL STATISTICS

2000 births, 9,557; deaths, 6,059; marriages, 9,775; divorces, 1,337. Rates, 2000 (per 1,000 population): birth, 12·6; death, 8·0; marriage, 12·6; divorce, 1·8. Life expectancy at birth, 2003, was 76·1 years for males and 81·1 years for females. Annual population growth rate, 1992–2002, 1·2%; infant mortality, 2000, 5·6 per 1,000 live births; fertility rate, 2000, 1·8 children per woman. In 2000 the average age of first marriage was 28·9 years for men and 26·1 years for women.

CLIMATE

The climate is Mediterranean, with very hot, dry summers and variable winters. Maximum temperatures may reach 112°F (44·5°C) in July and Aug., but minimum figures may fall to 22°F (–5·5°C) in the mountains in winter, when snow is experienced. Rainfall is generally between 10" and 27" (250 and 675 mm) and occurs mainly in the winter months, but it may reach 48" (1,200 mm) in the Troodos mountains. Nicosia, Jan. 50°F (10·0°C), July 83°F (28·3°C). Annual rainfall 19·6" (500 mm).

CONSTITUTION AND GOVERNMENT

Under the 1960 Constitution executive power is vested in a *President* elected for a five-year term by universal suffrage, and exercised through a Council of Ministers appointed by him or her.

The *House of Representatives* exercises legislative power. It is elected by universal suffrage for five-year terms, and consists of 80 members, of whom 56 are elected by the Greek Cypriot and 24 by the Turkish Cypriot community. Voting is compulsory, and is by preferential vote in a proportional representation system with reallocation of votes at national level. As from Dec. 1963 the Turkish Cypriot members have ceased to attend.

National Anthem

'Imnos eis tin Eleftherian' ('Hymn to Freedom'); words by Dionysios Solomos, tune by N. Mantzaros.
(Same as Greece.)

GOVERNMENT CHRONOLOGY

Presidents since 1960. (DIKO = Democratic Party; DISI = Democratic Rally; EOKA = National Organization of Cypriot Fighters; n/p = non-partisan)

1960–74	n/p	Makarios III
1974	EOKA	Nikolaos (Nikos) Sampson
1974–77	n/p	Makarios III
1977–88	DIKO	Spyros Achilleos Kyprianou
1988–93	n/p	Georgios Vasou Vasiliou
1993–2003	DISI	Glafcos Ioannou Clerides
2003–	DIKO	Tassos Nikolaou Papadopoulos

RECENT ELECTIONS

Parliamentary elections were held on 27 May 2001. The Communist Progressive Party of the Working People (AKEL) won 34·7% of the vote and 20 seats, the Democratic Rally (DISI) won 34·0% and 19 seats, the Democratic Party (DIKO) 14·8% and 9 seats and the Social Democrats Movement (KISOS) 6·5% and 4 seats. Four other parties won a single seat each. The electorate was 467,182 and turnout 91·8%. For the first time in a parliamentary election those aged 18 to 21 were able to vote.

Presidential elections held on 16 Feb. 2003 were won by Tassos Papadopoulos (DIKO), with 51·5% of the vote, against 38·8% for incumbent Glafcos Clerides and 6·6% for Alekos Markidis. Turnout was 95·9%.

Parliamentary elections were scheduled to take place on 21 May 2006.

European Parliament

Cyprus has six representatives. At the June 2004 elections turnout was 71·4%. The DISI won 2 seats with 28·2% of votes cast (political affiliation in European Parliament: European People's Party–European Democrats); AKEL, 2 with 27·9% (European Unitary Left/Nordic Green Left); DIKO, 1 with 17·1% (Alliance of Liberals and Democrats for Europe); Gia tin Evropi (For Europe), 1 with 10·8% (European People's Party–European Democrats).

CURRENT ADMINISTRATION

President: Tassos Papadopoulos; b. 1934 (Democratic Party; sworn in on 28 Feb. 2003).

In March 2006 the Council of Ministers consisted of:
Minister of Foreign Affairs: George Iacovou. *Interior:* Andreas Christou. *Defence:* Kyriacos Mavronicolas. *Agriculture, Natural Resources and Environment:* Efthimios Efthimiou. *Commerce, Industry and Tourism:* George Lillikas. *Health:* Andreas Gavrielides. *Communications and Works:* Charis Thrasou. *Finance:* Michalakis Sarris. *Education and Culture:* Pefkios Georgiades. *Labour and Social Insurance:* Christos Taliadoros. *Justice and Public Order:* Doros Thedorou.

Government Website: http://www.cyprus.gov.cy

CURRENT LEADERS

Tassos Papadopoulos

Position
President

Introduction
Tassos Papadopoulos, Greek Cypriot nationalist leader of the centre-right Democratic Party (DIKO; Dimokratiko Komma), was elected president in Feb. 2003 after defeating incumbent Glafcos Clerides. He is considered more hardline than his predecessor on the issue of Cypriot reunification. In 2004 he oversaw Cyprus' entry into the EU.

Early Life
Papadopoulos was born on 7 Jan. 1934 in Nicosia. He graduated in law from King's College, London, England, and was called to the Bar as a member of Gray's Inn. Between 1955 and 1959 he was an important figure in the EOKA national liberation movement. In 1960 he opposed the Zurich-London agreements which established an independent Cypriot state, but went on to play a prominent role in drafting the constitution. He held several ministerial portfolios including internal affairs (1959–60), labour and social insurance (1960–70), agriculture and natural resources (1964–67) and health (1967–70).

In 1970 he entered parliament as the Eniaion (Unified) Party representative for Nicosia. He was re-elected in 1976 as a non-partisan and acted as the intercommunal negotiator on behalf of President Clerides in talks over Cyprus' future following the establishment of the Turkish Republic of Northern Cyprus (TRNC) two years earlier. In 1991 he was elected to parliament for the Democratic Party (DIKO) and was the party spokesman in parliament until 2001. He also represented Cyprus in several international organizations, including the UN general assembly and the ILO, and helped negotiate the country's passage to EU membership.

In 2000 Papadopoulos was elected chairman of DIKO, and in Feb. 2003 defeated Clerides for the state presidency with 51·5% of the vote in the first round in a high turn-out.

Career in Office
Among Papadopoulos' first tasks was to oversee continuing negotiations to reunify the TRNC with the rest of the country, having been critical of the soft negotiating line previously adopted by Clerides. In March 2004 the UN Secretary-General proposed a revised plan for Cypriot reunification based on a federation of two largely autonomous states. A referendum on the plan was held the following month, in which Papadopoulos urged the Greek Cypriot community to vote no, insisting that the provisions for their return to their former homes in the north were not good enough. Although the Turkish Cypriot community endorsed the UN plan, Greek Cypriots rejected it by a large majority. Consequently, Cyprus joined the EU in May 2004 as a partitioned state.

DEFENCE

Conscription is for 25 months. Defence expenditure in 2003 totalled US$294m. (US$382 per capita), representing 2·3% of GDP.

National Guard

Total strength (2002) 10,000 (8,700 conscripts). There is also a paramilitary force of 500 armed police.

There are two British bases (Army and Royal Air Force) and some 3,190 personnel. Greek (1,250) and UN peacekeeping (1,270; UNFICYP) forces are also stationed on the island.

There are approximately 36,000 Turkish troops stationed in the occupied area of Cyprus. The Turkish Cypriot army amounts to 5,000 troops, with 26,000 reservists and a paramilitary armed police of approximately 150.

Navy

The Maritime Wing of the National Guard operates two vessels. In the Turkish-occupied area of Cyprus the Coast Guard operates six patrol craft.

Air Force

The Air Wing of the National Guard operates a handful of aircraft and helicopters.

INTERNATIONAL RELATIONS

Cyprus is a member of the UN, WTO, the Commonwealth, EU, Council of Europe, OSCE, IOM and ILO. It became a member of the EU on 1 May 2004.

On 30 June 2005 Cyprus became the eleventh European Union member to ratify the proposed EU constitution. The parliament approved the treaty by 30 votes to 19 with one abstention.

ECONOMY

Overview

Core exports are agricultural products (vegetables and citrus fruits), transport equipment and textiles. Tourism accounts for 20% of the economy. With one of southern Europe's highest rates of Internet penetration, the country is promoting investment in information technology and financial and medical services. The financial sector accounts for 20% of GDP. There is a wide economic divide between the Turkish-occupied area of Cyprus and the government-controlled area. The government-controlled area, with a per capita income of 83% of the EU average, has potential for strong economic growth. Per capita income in the Turkish-occupied area is 30% of that in the government-controlled area. Using the new Turkish lira as currency, the Turkish-controlled area lacks an independent monetary policy, suffers from high inflation and relies on Turkey for fiscal transfers and trade. The informal economy accounts for 30–40% of GDP.

Since the start of the EU accession negotiations, a tight fiscal policy has reduced the budget deficit by 50%. The government aims to balance the budget by 2009. The Cypriot pound has been pegged to the euro since Jan. 1999, and previously to the ECU since 1992. Following the referendum of April 2004, €259m. were earmarked to Cyprus if there was a solution to the island's problem. The EU is discussing ways of channelling this aid to the Turkish Cypriots in order to raise their economy, mainly by funding infrastructure projects.

Currency

The *Cyprus pound* (CYP) is divided into 100 *cents*. Inflation was 2·8% in 2002, rising to 4·1% in 2003. In June 2004 gold reserves were 465,310 troy oz and foreign exchange reserves were US$3,127m. In Dec. 2003 total money supply was £C1,377m.

Budget

Revenue in 2003 (2002) was £C2·4bn. (£C2·1bn.) and expenditure £C2·8bn. (£C2·4bn.). Main sources of revenue in 2003 (in £C1m.) were: tax revenue, 1,700; non-tax revenue, 377.

Main divisions of expenditure in 2003 (in £C1m.): wages and salaries, 727; social security payments, 387; other goods and services, 242.

Capital expenditure for 2003 totalled £C305m., of which £C219m. was investment expenditure.

The outstanding domestic debt at 31 Dec. 2003 was £C3,681·7m. and the foreign debt was £C1,063·0m.

VAT is 15·0% (reduced rate, 5·0%).

Performance

Real GDP growth was 2·2% in 2003, up from 1·8% in 2002. Total GDP in 2004 was US$15·4bn. GDP per capita in 2000 was 83% of the European Union average, the highest percentage of any of the EU candidate countries.

Banking and Finance

The Central Bank of Cyprus, established in 1963, is the bank of issue. It regulates money supply, credit and foreign exchange and supervises the banking system. The *Governor* is Christodoulos Christodoulou.

In 2004 there were 14 domestic banks, 29 International Banking Units and one representative office of a foreign bank. The leading banks are Bank of Cyprus, Cyprus Popular Bank and Hellenic Bank.

At 30 Sept. 2004 banks' total deposits and lending amounted to £C13,054m. and £C9,003m. respectively. Cyprus has a fast-growing offshore sector—in 2000 there were more than 40,000 offshore companies registered on the island.

There is a stock exchange in Nicosia.

ENERGY AND NATURAL RESOURCES

Environment

Carbon dioxide emissions from the consumption and flaring of fossil fuels in Cyprus were the equivalent of 10·4 tonnes per capita in 2002.

Electricity

Installed capacity was 1·0m. kW in 2003. Production in 2003 was 3·70bn. kWh and consumption 4,044m. kWh.

Water

In 2004, £C16·3m. was spent on water dams, water supplies, hydrological research and geophysical surveys. A further £C16·7m. was spent on the production of desalinated sea water. Existing dams had (2004) a capacity of 327m. cu. metres.

Minerals

The principal minerals extracted in 2004 were (in tonnes): gypsum, 234,000; bentonite, 170,000; umber and other ochres (2000), 12,000; copper (2000), 5,000.

Agriculture

28% of the government-controlled area is cultivated. There were 72,000 ha. of arable land in 2001 and 41,000 ha. of permanent crops. 40,000 ha. were irrigated in 2001. About 6·9% (2002) of the economically active population were engaged in agriculture.

Chief agricultural products in 2002 (1,000 tonnes): milk, 200·6; potatoes, 148·5; cereals (wheat and barley), 141·3; citrus fruit, 137·8; meat, 104·1; grapes, 62·4; fresh fruit, 38·3; olives, 27·5; carobs, 7·2; almonds, 2·0; carrots, 1·9; other vegetables, 141·2; eggs, 12·3.

Livestock in 2002: cattle, 58,300; sheep, 294,000; goats, 459,500; pigs, 491,400; poultry, 3·59m.

Forestry

Total forest area in 2004 was 172,000 ha. (18·6% of the land area). In 2001, 18,000 cu. metres of timber were produced.

Fisheries

Catches in 2004 totalled 1,782 tonnes; aquaculture production in 2004 amounted to 1,820 tonnes.

INDUSTRY

The most important industries in 2003 were: food, beverages and tobacco, metal products, machinery and equipment, other non-metallic mineral products, refined petroleum products, chemicals, chemical products and plastic, wood and wood products, textiles and leather products. The manufacturing industry in 2003 contributed about 9·0% of the GDP.

Labour

Out of 303,206 people in employment in the period March–June 2001, 53,839 were in wholesale and retail trade/repair of motor vehicles, motorcycles and personal and household goods; 37,720 in manufacturing; and 29,439 in construction. The unemployment rate was 3·1% in Sept. 2003.

Trade Unions

About 80% of the workforce is organized and the majority of workers belong either to the Pancyprian Federation of Labour or the Cyprus Workers Confederation.

INTERNATIONAL TRADE

Imports and Exports

Trade figures for calendar years were (in £C1,000):

	2000	2001	2002	2003
Imports	2,401,826	2,528,720	2,486,612	2,314,248
Exports	591,864	628,029	511,277	476,799

Chief imports, 2003 (in £C1,000):

Machinery, electrical equipment, sound and television recorders	384,280
Vehicles, aircraft, vessels and equipment	288,300
Mineral products	233,282
Products of chemical or allied industries	208,729
Prepared foodstuffs, beverages and tobacco	168,799
Textiles and textile articles	163,621
Base metal and articles of base metal	161,095
Plastics and rubber and articles thereof	88,161
Pulp, waste paper and paperboard and articles thereof	82,046
Vegetable products	71,507
Articles of stone, plaster, cement, etc., ceramic and glass products	65,414
Optical, photographic, medical, musical and other instruments, clocks and watches	48,568
Wood and articles, charcoal, cork, etc.	43,077
Footwear, headgear, umbrellas, prepared leathers, etc.	32,640
Live animals and animal products	32,640
Pearls, precious stones and metals, semi-precious stones and articles	22,310

Chief domestic exports, 2003 (in £C1,000):

Medicinal and pharmaceutical products		Cement	9,110
	38,742	Cigarettes	6,839
Citrus fruit	19,018	Wine	6,127
Potatoes	15,051	Fruit, preserved and	
Cheese	11,656	juices	4,869
Clothing	9,810	Footwear	1,374

Main import suppliers, 2003: Greece, 11·9%; Italy, 9·8%; UK, 8·3%; Germany, 7·5%. Main export markets, 2003: UK, 32·0%; Greece, 9·2%; Germany, 3·9%; Lebanon, 3·4%.

COMMUNICATIONS

Roads

In 2003 the total length of roads in the government-controlled area was 11,593 km. The asphalted roads maintained by the Ministry of Communications and Works (Public Works Department) by the end of 2004 totalled 2,353 km. Construction of new asphalted roads in 2000 totalled 240 km. In 2004 there were 321,634 passenger cars, 3,199 buses and coaches, 117,819 trucks and vans and 41,396 motorcycles and mopeds. There were 117 deaths as a result of road accidents in 2004.

The area controlled by the government of the Republic and that controlled by the 'TRNC' are now served by separate transport systems, and there are no services linking the two areas.

Civil Aviation

Nicosia airport has been closed since the Turkish invasion in 1974. It is situated in the UN controlled buffer zone. There are international airports at Larnaca (the main airport) and Paphos. In 2003, 6,483,037 passengers, 58,358 aircraft and 31,725 tonnes of commercial freight went through these airports. Both are set to be expanded with a view to increasing annual capacity by 3m. In 2003 Larnaca handled 4,804,471 passengers (all on international flights) and (2000) 32,077 tonnes of freight. In 2003 Paphos handled 1,679,566 passengers (all on international flights) and (2000) 1,396 tonnes of freight. The national carrier is Cyprus Airways, which is 69·62% state-owned. Cyprus Airways flew 21·1m. km in 2000, carrying 1,452,608 passengers (all on international flights).

Shipping

The two main ports are Limassol and Larnaca. In 2000, 5,289 ships of 20,570,975 net registered tons entered Cyprus ports carrying 6,901,088 tonnes of cargo from, to and via Cyprus. In 2002 the merchant marine totalled 23·0m. GRT, including oil tankers 3·6m. GRT. In 2004 the fleet consisted of 1,400 vessels (150 tankers). In 2004 vessels totalling 18,465,000 NRT entered ports. The port in Famagusta has been closed to international traffic since the Turkish invasion in 1974.

Telecommunications

Telephone subscribers numbered 845,400 in 2002 (1,207·7 for every 1,000 inhabitants) and there were 193,000 PCs in use (275·7 per 1,000 persons). There were 417,900 mobile phone subscribers in 2002. Cyprus had 210,000 Internet users in 2002 and 14,200 fax machines. The Cyprus Telecommunications Authority provides telephone and data transmission services nationally, and to 253 countries automatically. The liberalization of the telecommunications market began in Aug. 2003 when the Electricity Authority of Cyprus was awarded a licence to provide landline telephone services.

Postal Services

In 2003 there were 52 post offices and 912 postal agencies.

SOCIAL INSTITUTIONS

Justice

There is a Supreme Court, Assize Courts and District Courts. The Supreme Court is composed of 13 judges, one of whom is the President of the Court. The Assize Courts have unlimited criminal jurisdiction, and may order the payment of compensation up to £C3,000. The District Courts exercise civil and criminal jurisdiction, the extent of which varies with the composition of the Bench.

A Supreme Council of Judicature, consisting of the President and Judges of the Supreme Court, is entrusted with the appointment, promotion, transfers, termination of appointment and disciplinary control over all judicial officers, other than the Judges of the Supreme Court. The Attorney-General (Petros Clerides) is head of the independent Law Office and legal advisor to the President and his Ministers.

The population in penal institutions in Sept. 2002 was 345 (49 per 100,000 of national population).

The death penalty was abolished for all crimes in 2002.

Education

Greek-Cypriot Education. Elementary education is compulsory and is provided free in six grades to children between 5 years 8 months and 11 years 8 months. There are also schools for the deaf and blind, and nine schools for handicapped children. In 2004 the Ministry of Education and Culture ran 238 kindergartens for children in the age group 3–5 years 8 months; there were also 70 communal and 89 private kindergartens. There were 348 primary schools in 2004 with 58,373 pupils and 4,409 teachers.

Secondary education is also free and attendance for the first cycle is compulsory. The secondary school is six years—three years at the gymnasium followed by three years at the *lykeion* (lyceum) or three years at one of the technical schools which provide technical and vocational education for industry. In 2004 there were 120 secondary schools with 6,200 teachers and 56,634 pupils.

Post-secondary education is provided at seven public institutions: the University of Cyprus, which admitted its first students in Sept. 1992 and had 4,603 students in 2004; the Higher Technical Institute, which provides courses lasting three to four years for technicians in civil, electrical, mechanical and marine engineering; the Cyprus Forestry College (administered by the Ministry of Agriculture, Natural Resources and Environment); the Higher Hotel Institute (Ministry of Labour and Social Insurance); the Mediterranean Institute of Management (Ministry of Labour and Social Insurance); the School of Nursing (Ministry of Health) which runs courses lasting two to three years; the Cyprus Police Academy which provides a three-year training programme.

There are also various public and private institutions which provide courses at various levels. These include the Apprenticeship Training Scheme and Evening Technical Classes, and other vocational and technical courses organized by the Human Resources Development Authority.

In 2003 the adult literacy rate was 96·8% (98·6% among males, 95·1% among females). The percentage of the population aged 20 years and over that has attended school was 88·0% in 2003. In 2002–03 total expenditure on education came to 6·4% of GNP.

Health

In 2004 there were 1,952 doctors, 714 dentists, 3,613 nurses and 800 pharmacists. There were 84 registered private hospitals/clinics, five government hospitals, three rural hospitals, 25 rural health centres and one government psychiatric hospital.

Welfare

Cyprus has a compulsory earnings-related Social Insurance Scheme financed by tripartite contributions, which covers all the gainfully employed population. Employees in the broader public sector are covered by supplementary mandatory pension schemes or provident funds. A large proportion of the private sector's employees have supplementary coverage under non-statutory provident funds established by collective agreements.

RELIGION

The Greek Cypriots are Greek Orthodox Christians, and the Turkish Cypriots are Muslims (mostly Sunnis of the Hanafi sect). There are also small groups of the Armenian Apostolic Church, Roman Catholics (Maronites and Latin Rite) and Protestants (mainly Anglicans). *See also* CYPRUS: Territory and Population.

CULTURE

World Heritage Sites

There are three sites under Cypriot jurisdiction in the World Heritage List: Paphos (entered on the list in 1980); the churches of the Troodos region (1985, 2001); and Choirokoitia (1998). Paphos was a site of worship of the goddess Aphrodite. The Troodos region has one of the largest groups of Byzantine churches and monasteries. The Neolithic settlement of Choirokoitia dates from the 7th to the 4th millennium BC.

Broadcasting

Cyprus Broadcasting Corporation has three radio channels and broadcasts mainly in Greek, but also in Turkish, English and Armenian. The Corporation also broadcasts on two TV channels (colour by SECAM H). A law of June 1990 permits the operation of commercial radio and TV stations. In 2004 there were five independent radio stations broadcasting nationwide and numerous radio stations broadcasting locally. There were also four private TV stations operating and two private Pay-TV. There are also two foreign broadcasting stations. There were 310,000 radio sets in 1997 and 266,000 TV sets in 2001.

Cinema

In the government-controlled area there were 11 cinemas and 33 screens in 2004. In 1999 gross box office receipts came to £C2·6m.

Press

In 2004 there were six daily newspapers with a circulation of 120,000; and 60 other newspapers with a circulation of 250,000.

Tourism

There were 2,418,000 tourist arrivals in 2002, a fall of 0·1% on 2001. Visitors from the UK account for some 50% of all tourist arrivals. Tourist spending in 2002 totalled US$1,863m.

Libraries

In 2004 there were 162 public libraries and one National library, holding a combined 580,000 volumes for 60,000 registered users.

Museums and Galleries

In 2003 there were 27 museums which received 1,227,519 visitors.

DIPLOMATIC REPRESENTATIVES

Of Cyprus in the United Kingdom (93 Park St., London, W1K 7ET)
High Commissioner: Petros Eftychiou.

Of the United Kingdom in Cyprus (Alexander Pallis St., Nicosia)
High Commissioner: Peter Millett.

Of Cyprus in the USA (2211 R St., NW, Washington, D.C., 20008)
Ambassador: Euripides L. Evriviades.

Of the USA in Cyprus (Metochiou and Ploutarchou Streets, Engomi, Nicosia)
Ambassador: Ronald L. Schlicher.

Of Cyprus to the United Nations
Ambassador: Andreas Mavroyiannis.

Of Cyprus to the European Union
Ambassador: Nicos Emiliou.

FURTHER READING

Calotychos, V., *Cyprus and Its People: Nation, Identity and Experience in an Unimaginable Community 1955–1997.* Westview, Oxford, 1999
Christodolou, D., *Inside the Cyprus Miracle: the Labours of an Embattled Mini-Economy.* Univ. of Minnesota Press, 1992
Kitromilides, P. M. and Evriviades, M. L., *Cyprus.* [Bibliography] 2nd ed. ABC-Clio, Oxford and Santa Barbara (CA), 1995
Salem N. (ed.) *Cyprus: a Regional Conflict and its Resolution.* London, 1992

Statistical Information: Statistical Service of the Republic of Cyprus, Michalakis Karaolis Street, 1444 Nicosia.
Website: http://www.mof.gov.cy/mof/cystat/statistics.nsf

'Turkish Republic of Northern Cyprus (TRNC)'

KEY HISTORICAL EVENTS

See CYPRUS: Key Historical Events.

TERRITORY AND POPULATION

The Turkish Republic of Northern Cyprus occupies 3,355 sq. km (about 33% of the island of Cyprus) and its census population in

1996 was 200,587. The population was estimated to be 219,000 in 2004. Distribution of population by districts (1996): Nicosia, 89,818; Famagusta, 72,054; Kyrenia, 38,715.

CONSTITUTION AND GOVERNMENT
The Turkish Republic of Northern Cyprus was proclaimed on 15 Nov. 1983. The 50 members of the Legislative Assembly are elected under a proportional representation system.

RECENT ELECTIONS
Presidential elections were held on 17 April 2005. Prime Minister Mehmet Ali Talat (Republican Turkish Party-United Forces) won 55·6% against Derviş Eroğlu (National Unity Party), who claimed 22·7%. Turnout was 69·6%.

In parliamentary elections on 20 Feb. 2005 the Republican Turkish Party-United Forces (CTP-BG) won 24 seats and 44·5% of the vote, ahead of the National Union Party with 19 and 31·7%, the Democrat Party with 6 and 13·5% and the Peace and Democracy Movement with 1 and 5·8%. Turnout was 80·8%.

CURRENT ADMINISTRATION
President: Mehmet Ali Talat; b. 1952 (sworn in 24 April 2005).

Following the parliamentary election of Feb. 2005 the CTP-BG and the DP renewed their coalition. After the presidential election of April 2005 Mehmet Ali Talat resigned his premiership to take up the presidency and approved a new CTP-BG/DP cabinet consisting in March 2006 of:

Prime Minister: Ferdi Sabit Soyer; b. 1952 (CTP; took office on 26 April 2005).

Deputy Prime Minister and Foreign Minister: Serdar Denktaş (DP).

Minister for Public Works and Transport: Salih Usar (CTP). *Finance:* Ahmet Uzun (CTP). *Youth and Sports:* Özkan Yorgancıoğlu (CTP). *Health and Social Aid:* Eşref Vaiz (CTP). *Interior:* Özkan Murat (CTP). *Agriculture and Forestry:* Hüseyin Öztoprak (DP). *Education and Culture:* Canan Öztoprak (CTP). *Labour and Social Security:* Sonay Adem (CTP). *Economy and Tourism:* Derviş Kemal Deniz (DP).

President of Legislative Assembly: Fatma Ekenoğlu.

Government Website: http://www.trncgov.com

DEFENCE
In 2004, 35,000 members of Turkey's armed forces were stationed in the TRNC with 441 main battle tanks. TRNC forces comprise seven infantry battalions with a total personnel strength of 5,000. Conscription is for two years.

INTERNATIONAL RELATIONS
In April 2004 the European Union pledged to release almost US$310m. as a reward for approval of a UN plan to reunify the island, although it will not be coming into force as it was rejected by the Greek Cypriot south.

ECONOMY
Currency
The Turkish lira is used.

Budget
Revenue in 2003 (in US$1m.) was 696·1 (of which local revenues 404·3 and foreign aid and loans 291·8); expenditure, 691·4.

Banking and Finance
46 banks, including 21 offshore banks, were operating in 2004. Control is exercised by the Central Bank of the TRNC.

ENERGY AND NATURAL RESOURCES
Agriculture
Agriculture accounted for 10·6% of GDP in 2003 (provisional figure).

INTERNATIONAL TRADE
Exports earned US$49·3m. in 2003. Imports cost US$415·2m. Customs tariffs with Turkey were reduced in July 1990. There is a free port at Famagusta.

COMMUNICATIONS
Civil Aviation
There is an international airport at Ercan. In 2004 there were flights to Adana, Ankara, Antalya, Dalaman, İstanbul and İzmir with Turkish Airlines and Cyprus Turkish Airlines.

SOCIAL INSTITUTIONS
Education
In 2003 there were 15,482 pupils and 1,156 teachers in primary schools; 15,910 pupils and 1,504 teachers in secondary and general high schools; 1,985 students and 435 teachers in technical and vocational schools; and 29,054 students in higher education. There are four private colleges and five universities.

Health
In 2002 there were 338 doctors, 115 dentists, 167 pharmacists and 1,121 beds in state hospitals and private clinics.

CULTURE
Broadcasting
There are five local radio stations: Radio Bayrak (BRTK) broadcasts in several languages including Greek, Arabic and English. There are five local television channels. Colour is by PAL. In 1994 there were 108,800 TV and radio sets.

Press
In 2004 there were ten daily and three weekly newspapers.

Tourism
There were 469,867 tourists in 2003, of which 340,083 were from Turkey and 129,784 from other countries. Tourist earnings totalled US$388·3m. in 1995.

FURTHER READING
North Cyprus Almanack, London, 1987
Dodd, C. H. (ed.) *The Political, Social and Economic Development of Northern Cyprus.* Huntingdon, 1993
Hanworth, R., *The Heritage of Northern Cyprus.* Nicosia, 1993
Ioannides, C. P., *In Turkey's Image: the Transformation of Occupied Cyprus into a Turkish Province.* New Rochelle (NY), 1991

CZECH REPUBLIC

Scale: 0 — 50 mi / 0 — 75 km

POLAND · GERMANY · Liberec · PRAGUE · Plzeň · CZECH REPUBLIC · Ostrava · Olomouc · Brno · AUSTRIA · SLOVAKIA

© Research Machines plc 2006

Česká Republika

Capital: Prague
Population projection, 2010: 10·16m.
GDP per capita, 2003: (PPP$) 16,357
HDI/world rank: 0·874/31

KEY HISTORICAL EVENTS

The area that is today the Czech Republic was originally inhabited by Celts around the 4th century BC. The Celtic Boii tribe gave the country its Latin name—Boiohaemum (Bohemia)—but was driven out by Germanic tribes. Slav tribes migrated to central Europe during the period known as the Migration of Peoples and were well established by the 6th century. The first half of the 7th century saw allied Slavonic tribes defending their territory from the Avar Empire in the Hungarian lowlands and from Frank attackers to the West.

Mojmír established The Great Moravian Empire in 830, comprising Bohemia, Moravia and Slovakia. The Empire reached its height under Moravian ruler Svatopluk, but was engulfed and destroyed by the Magyars around 903–07. In 1041, after the defeat of Prince Břetislav the Restorer by the German Emperor Henry III, Bohemia became a fief of the Holy Roman Empire. Dynastic squabbles, exacerbated by German interference, weakened the power of the dukes, but in 1212 Otakar I (1197–1230) was granted a hereditary kingship from the Holy Roman Emperor who also declared the indivisibility of Bohemia which became a key independent state within the realm.

A period of prosperity followed, aided by the immigration of German miners and merchants. Bohemia expanded under the last Přemysl kings: Wenceslas I (1230–53) seized Austria in 1251, though it passed to the Habsburgs when Otakar II was killed at the battle of Marchfeld in 1278. His son Wenceslas II was elected king of Poland in 1300. Wenceslas III was assassinated in 1306, thus ending the Přemysl line. After four years of struggle John of Luxemburg succeeded in 1310.

John's son Charles (1346–78) became Holy Roman Emperor as Charles IV (Charles I of Bohemia) in 1355. He declared Prague the capital of the German Empire and decreed the realm the Crownlands of Bohemia which included parts of modern Germany and Poland. The Golden Bull of Nürnberg in 1356 granted the king of Bohemia first place among the empire's electors.

In what became known as the Golden Age, Charles fostered the commercial and cultural development of Bohemia. In 1348 he founded Prague University, the first university in Central Europe. Work started on the building of St Vitus cathedral, Charles Bridge and the Czech castle of the Grail in Karlstejn during his reign.

Hussite Revolution

Dissatisfaction with the Catholic church in the 14th and 15th centuries climaxed with the Hussite Revolution, the clerical reform movement associated with Jan Hus. The movement had undertones of anti-German Czech nationalism and found support amongst the urban middle classes and lesser rural gentry as well as the urban poor and peasantry. Hus was condemned as a heretic and burnt at the stake in Constance in 1415. Anti-Hussite rulings by Wenceslas IV led to the first 'Defenestration of Prague' in 1419, when Catholic councillors were thrown from the Town Hall windows. In the ensuing Hussite wars Sigismund, the Hungarian Holy Roman Emperor, failed to recover the Bohemian crown. Five crusades were launched against the Hussites in the years 1420–31, all of which were defeated.

The Hussites were eventually weakened by divisions between moderates, the Utraquists, and radicals, the Taborites (originating from the town of Tabor in South Bohemia). The latter's militant leader, Jan Žižka, was defeated in the battle of Lipany in 1434 by the Prague faction supported by Sigismund. This victory allowed for a temporary agreement between Hussite Bohemia and Catholic Europe, known as the Compacts of Basle, which reunited the Utraquist faction with Rome in 1436. A degree of post-war recovery followed under the moderate Hussite king, George of Poděbrady (1457–71), who crushed the radical Taborite dissidents.

In 1471 Vladislav Jagełłon, son of King Cazimir of Poland, was elected King of Bohemia. His son Louis inherited the throne but was killed at Mohás fighting the Turks in 1526. From 1490, Hungary and Bohemia were both ruled by the Jagełłonian Dynasty. Under their rule, the provincial diet of three estates (nobility, gentry and burgesses) acted to enhance the power of the nobility and diminish that of the burgesses. Religious struggles between the Hussite church and the minority Catholic Church continued.

In 1526, after the extinction of the Jagełłonian line, Czech nobles elected Archduke Ferdinand. The advent of the Habsburgs saw Roman Catholicism re-introduced and the Crownlands of Bohemia remained in the Habsburg empire until 1918. When Rudolf II (1576–1611) left Vienna to make Prague the capital of the German Empire and the seat of a papal nuncio, the city became a centre of European culture. However, religious divisions with the beginnings of the Counter-Reformation led to the second Defenestration of Prague. Two Catholic governors and their secretary were thrown from a window of Prague Castle, an action which sparked off the Thirty Years' War (1618–48). This brought political disorder and economic devastation to the country with the Habsburg forces wiping out a third of the Bohemian population. The estates deposed Emperor Ferdinand II in favour of the Calvinist Frederick V but the latter's forces were defeated at the battle of White Mountain in 1620. A period of Habsburg hegemony ensued.

After the suppression of the Taborites, the only remaining Protestant Church in Bohemia was the Unity of Czech Brethren, to which Catholics, Utraquists and Lutherans were opposed. The Czech nobility was replaced by German-speaking adventurers, the burgesses lost their rights, the peasantry suffered severe hardships and citizens were forced to embrace the Catholic faith or emigrate. The throne of Bohemia was made hereditary in the Habsburg Dynasty and the most important offices transferred to Vienna. Risings were savagely repressed. The next two centuries became known as the Dark Ages.

Enlightened Despotism
In the Enlightenment era of the late 18th century, Empress Maria Theresa and her son Joseph II granted freedom of worship and movement to the peasantry in 1781, a precondition for the industrial revolution of the next century which made Bohemia the most developed economy within the Empire. Bohemia and Moravia each became independent parts of the Habsburg Monarchy, although conversely the reforms led to greater Germanization and centralization of power, threatening the Slavic identities of the Empire's subjects.

The revival of the Czech nation, which began as a cultural movement, soon progressed into a struggle for political emancipation. Calls for the promotion of the Czech language encouraged Czech nationalists to campaign for the formation of a new Czechoslovakia. It was a concept fostered by Tomáš Garrigue Masaryk, a philosophy professor at the University of Prague and Professor for Slavonic Studies at King's College London, who was to become the first president of the Czechoslovak Republic.

Male suffrage was granted in 1906 but the chamber of deputies was constantly bypassed by the emperor. The First World War brought estrangement between the Czechs and the Germans, the latter supporting the war effort, the former seeing it as a clash of monarchy versus democracy. Masaryk went into exile in London, where he committed himself to enlisting the support of Britain, France, Russia and the United States in founding a post-war independent Czechoslovak state. He worked with other exiled Czechs and Slovaks, including Dr Edvard Beneš, who later also became president of Czechoslovakia. In 1916 a Czechoslovak National Council was set up in Paris under Masaryk's chairmanship.

In 1918 Masaryk secured the support of US president Woodrow Wilson for Czech and Slovak unity and in May the Pittsburgh agreement was signed in the USA by exiles of both lands. On 18 Oct. 1918 the National Council transformed itself into a provisional government, and was recognized by the Allies.

Creation of the State
Austria accepted President Wilson's terms on 27 Oct. 1918, and the next day a republic was proclaimed with Masaryk, almost 70, as president, and Beneš as foreign minister. In drawing up the frontiers of the new state the principles of Wilsonian self-determination were defeated by the ethnic mix; other criteria employed were the partial restoration of the historic provinces and the need to establish an economically viable and defensible state. Among the minorities were 3·25m. Sudeten Germans. Borders were confirmed in the Treaty of Versailles in June 1919 (although Hungary subsequently called for these to be reformed) along with the official recognition of the state of Czechoslovakia by the international community.

The constitution of 1920 provided for a two-chamber parliament with adult suffrage. The French Constitution and the American Declaration of Rights were both used as models. The electoral system worked so that all governments were coalitions. Slovakia was granted an assembly in 1927, but the state was basically centralist, and the Slovaks maintained their own parties. Between the wars Czechoslovakia became one of the ten most developed and stable countries of the world, although it suffered severe economic depression in the 1930s.

In Nov. 1935 Masaryk was succeeded by Beneš. Meanwhile in Germany, Hitler's designs on expanding the Third Reich stirred up nationalist agitation among the Sudeten Germans. The 1930 census showed 22·3% of the Czechoslovak population were ethnic Germans. In 1933 the German National Socialist Worker's Party in Czechoslovakia, directly affiliated to the Nazi party in Germany, was banned. The Sudeten German Party, led by Konrad Henlein, was formed in its place and won 67% of the German vote in the parliamentary elections of 1935. Czechoslovakia had relied on its 1925 pact with France to defend it against the threat of German aggression, but in the Munich Conference of 29 Sept. 1938 France sided with Britain and Italy in stipulating that all districts with a German population of more than 50% should be ceded to Germany. This legitimized the annexing of the Czech Sudetenland to Germany.

On 5 Oct. 1938 Beneš resigned and went into exile in Britain, and on 15 March 1939 Hitler's troops invaded Prague, contravening the Munich agreement. Slovakia declared itself independent under the fascist leadership of Jozef Tiso, though it was allied to the Germans, and the Czech lands became the German Protectorate of Bohemia-Moravia.

Czechoslovakia suffered further territorial losses to Poland and Hungary under the Vienna Arbitration of 2 Nov. 1938. Altogether it had lost 30% of its territory and almost 34% of its population. Over 1m. Czechs, Slovaks and Ukrainians came under German, Polish and Hungarian rule. Hitler's declared aim was to drive the Czechs out of Central Europe. The Protectorate became a centre for arms production.

Nazi Occupation
Initial attempts at resistance were brutally crushed. On 17 Nov. 1939 German occupiers closed down all Czech universities, executed nine of the leaders of the student movement and transported scores of other students to concentration camps. In 1940 the Gestapo transformed the town of Terezín (Theresienstadt) near Prague into a concentration camp, evacuating the pre-war population to accommodate 140,000 Jews from all parts of the Reich, the majority from the Protectorate of Bohemia-Moravia. 85,000 were then transported to death camps in the East, chiefly to Auschwitz, and over 30,000 prisoners were held in the fortress. Many Communists and Czech resistance fighters also met their deaths there.

Mass expulsions were a regular feature of the Protectorate. In 1942, 30,000 people were forced to leave their homes in order to make way for the military. In another case around 5,000 families were expelled from around 30 villages in Moravia in an attempt to create an ethnic German enclave.

Growing resistance led to the appointment of SS General Reinhard Heydrich, head of the Reich's Security Office, who launched a savage offensive against underground organizations, and executed general Alois Elias, head of the Protectorate's government, for his connections with the Beneš government in Britain. The latter, along with the Allies, were in turn behind the assassination of Heydrich, carried out on 27 May 1942 by two paratroopers. The Nazis responded with a frenzy of terror known as the 'Heydrichiade'. Revenge murders of the entire populations of Lidice (on 10 June 1942) and Lezáky (24 June 1942) were carried out.

The Beneš government in exile in London, with Jan Šrámek as prime minister, was officially recognized by Britain and the USSR on 18 June 1941. A 20-year treaty of alliance with the USSR was signed on 12 Dec. 1943 and, in March 1945, Beneš went to Moscow to prepare for post-war government in the wake of the Soviet Army advance. Liberation by the Soviet Army and US forces was completed in 1945 following an insurrection on 5 May. Territories taken by Germans, Poles and Hungarians were restored to Czechoslovakia. Subcarparthian Ruthenia (now in Ukraine) was transferred to the USSR, creating a common border with the Soviet state.

The Sudeten Germans suffered brutal expulsions, during which up to 250,000 died, 6,000 of whom were murdered. The 'resettlement' of ethnic Germans was officially approved at the Potsdam Conference on 1 Aug. 1945, when the USA and Britain insisted on humane transfer, subsequently supervised by the

Allies and the Red Cross. German or Hungarian Czechs had their citizenship taken away unless they were naturalized Czechs or Slovaks. In order to stay, German or Hungarian Czechs had to prove that they had remained faithful to the Czechoslovak Republic, had fought in the resistance, or had personally suffered at the hands of fascists. Further decrees expropriated property and agricultural land. A total of 2,700,000 Germans were expelled, and in the Czech census of March 1991 only 47,000 claimed German as their nationality. A Czech–German Declaration of 21 Jan. 1997 saw both sides admit to and apologize for their atrocities during the period.

Soviet Domination

Beneš once again became president of Czechoslovakia but, under pressure from the USSR, measures were taken to confiscate and redistribute property and to take key industries into public ownership. Before 1939 the Communist party of Czechoslovakia (CPCz) had never gained more than 13% of the vote, but its patriotic stance in the late 1930s as well as its clear affiliation with the country's main liberators, the USSR, led to a sharp increase in popularity. In the elections of 26 May 1946 the Communists won almost 40% of the vote in Czech areas and 30% in Slovakia. This made the party the largest group in the new Constituent National Assembly, with 114 of the 300 seats and Klement Gottwald as premier. Its leaders pledged commitment to democratic traditions while pursuing a 'specific Czechoslovak road to socialism'.

The party's independence was first put into question when Czechoslovakia was pressurized by Stalin into withdrawing from the American Marshall plan for economic rejuvenation, seen from Moscow as a threat to its own influence. Stalin's encouragement of the CPCz grew in the autumn of 1947 when a people's militia was formed and non-communist parties in the governing coalition found their influence eroded. In protest, 12 non-communist ministers handed in their resignations. The CPCz adroitly handled this situation to its own advantage, forcing President Beneš to appoint a predominantly communist government on 25 Feb. 1948.

A new constitution, declaring Czechoslovakia a 'people's democracy' was approved on 9 May 1948, and elections were held on 30 May with a single list of candidates, resulting in an 89% majority for the government. Beneš resigned on 2 June after refusing to ratify the Communist Constitution. 12 days later Gottwald succeeded him as President. Civil rights were severely restricted; from 1950 monasteries and convents were nationalized, with 219 monasteries being taken over by the People's Militia on the night of 13 April alone; monastic orders were abolished.

The secret service became one of the most systematic and omnipresent in the Soviet bloc. Unsubstantiated charges of treason and resistance to the communist cause led to a series of show trials and executions, with many victims from the CPCz itself. It is estimated that between 200,000 and 280,000 suffered death or persecution during the Stalin era. Stalin died on 5 March 1953, and Gottwald just a week later, but the communists maintained their grip. Workers' demonstrations in Plzeň and other Czech towns against price rises and currency reform, which devalued savings, were brutally suppressed by the military in June that year. Political trials of 'Slovak nationalists' in 1954 had many Slovak Communists imprisoned, including Gustáv Husák, who later went on to become secretary-general of the CPCz and president of Czechoslovakia.

The Soviet five-year economic plans emphasized engineering, arms production and heavy industry. A third of Czechoslovak output came from the arms industry. The service and consumer goods industries were virtually abolished and all farms collectivized. The founding of COMECON on 1 Jan. 1949 and the signing of the Warsaw Pact in 1955 limited Czechoslovakia's trading partners to the Eastern bloc.

A new constitution, introduced in 1960, reinforced the power of the Communist Party and changed the country's name to the Socialist Republic of Czechoslovakia (ČSSR).

Prague Spring

The failure of the third five-year plan to meet its targets gave a push to economic reform. A mixed economy was introduced, which led to a period of cultural liberalization. Support for political reform grew within party ranks. Antonín Novotný was persuaded to resign as CPCz leader on 5 Jan. 1968. He was replaced by Alexander Dubček, leader of the Communist Party of Slovakia. On 22 March, Novotný resigned as president in favour of Gen. Ludvík Svoboda, who was elected by the National Assembly. Precipitating what became known as the Prague Spring, Dubček introduced many reforms in his pursuit of 'socialism with a human face'. New political bodies were formed, breaking up the monopoly of the Communist Party. Press censorship was abolished and restraints on freedom of expression relaxed.

The reforms caused unrest in Moscow. Brezhnev unsuccessfully put pressure on Czechoslovakia between May and August. He then ordered the invasion of Czechoslovakia by troops of the Warsaw Pact countries (with the exception of Romania), whose tanks rolled in on 20–21 Aug. The Soviet intention of replacing Dubček and his government with more hard-line Communists failed when President Svoboda turned down Soviet nominees. Dubček and other party leaders were then abducted to Moscow and forced to sign an agreement to keep Soviet troops stationed in Czechoslovakia. The Prague Spring all but withered. The only surviving measure of reform was the introduction of the federal system on 1 Jan. 1969. Separate Czech and Slovak states came into force within a Czechoslovak federation, a move that satisfied the Slovaks who had been seeking autonomy for some time. Each state was awarded its own administration and a national council, and the National Assembly divided into two chambers. All other reforms of the Dubček administration were stamped out or reversed and the Soviet policy of 'normalization' took hold.

In protest at the Soviet repression, student Jan Palach set fire to himself in Wenceslas Square on 16 Jan. 1969. On 20 March when the Czech National ice hockey team beat the Russians, celebrations turned into anti-Soviet demonstrations which led to many arrests. On 17 April Dubček was forced from office and replaced with the hard-liner, Gustáv Husák. Repression led to mass emigrations. So-called 'enemies of the state' were put under constant surveillance, blacklisted for jobs and their children denied university places. Freedom to travel abroad was no longer granted to ordinary citizens. Protest resurfaced again in 1977, with the signing of Charter 77 and founding of the Committee for the Defence of the Rights of the Unjustly Persecuted (VONS). These two organizations, led by artists and intellectuals, alerted the public to civil rights abuses and campaigned for civil and political rights.

Velvet Revolution

The advent of Mikhail Gorbachev's *glasnost* and *perestroika* in the mid-1980s initially changed little. Husák was replaced as leader of the CPCz by Miloš Jakeš, who had been responsible for Party purges in 1970. But there were renewed demonstrations in Aug. 1988 on the 20th anniversary of the Soviet invasion, in Oct. on the 70th anniversary of the founding of Czechoslovakia and in Jan. 1989 on the 20th anniversary of Jan Palach's suicide when the crowd was brutally dispersed and leading dissidents, including Václav Havel, arrested and imprisoned. Protests, petitions and further demonstrations followed in May, Aug. and Oct. of 1989. The fall of the Berlin Wall on 9 Nov. 1989 galvanized the pro-democracy movement. Another major demonstration by students on 17 Nov. led to further protests until the entire CPCz leadership resigned on 24 Nov. Civic Forum (OF) in the Czech Republic and the Public Against Violence (VPN) in Slovakia were formed to co-ordinate all pro-democratic forces, and an interim broad coalition 'Government of National Understanding' with a minority of Communists took over. These non-violent events became known as the Velvet Revolution. Václav Havel was unanimously elected president of Czechoslovakia by the Federal Assembly on 29 Dec. 1989.

The first free elections since the Second World War were held in June 1990, with a turn-out of 96·4%. The Communists were roundly defeated, and Civic Forum won 52% of the votes. Second parliamentary elections were fixed for mid-1992, by which time neither Civic Forum (OF) nor VPN any longer existed, having been replaced by fully-fledged parties across the political spectrum. In the Czech lands, the right wing emerged as the strongest element, with the Civic Democratic party (ODS) the largest coalition party. Its leader, Václav Klaus, who was also finance minister, became prime minister and stayed in the post until Nov. 1997.

By contrast, in Slovakia, Vladimír Mečiar's Democratic Slovakia party and other post-communists were successful in the elections. A continuing Slovak desire for independence from Prague, along with differences in opinion on economic policy and the role of the state, strained relations between the two federal partners. An agreement to a 'velvet divorce' was reached and from 1 Jan. 1993 the two devolved into separate sovereign states. Economic property was divided in accordance with a federal law of 13 Nov. 1992 and real estate became the property of the republic in which it was located. Other property was divided by specially-constituted commissions in the proportion of 2 (Czech Republic) to 1 (Slovakia) on the basis of population. Military material was also divided on the 2:1 principle, and regular military personnel were invited to choose in which army they would serve.

The Czech Republic showed greater eagerness than its former partner to become westernized. Although many feared a precipitous move towards a market economy, Klaus argued that danger lay in delaying reform, and that the creation of a market economy would lead the 'return to Europe' and the opening up of new markets.

Klaus immediately embarked on a series of radical reforms, impressing Western investors with his Thatcherite rhetoric, policies and publications. A programme of mass privatization was implemented, at first successfully, and the early to mid-nineties were a time of economic boom, with the Czech Republic a leading contender for Western trade and investment. However, many of the tough policies were not fully implemented and an increasing number of financial scandals were associated with the Klaus administration. 1997 also saw a currency crisis, where the crown devalued 12% against the dollar. Klaus was forced to resign as prime minister on 18 Nov. 1997.

Josef Tošovský formed a caretaker government until 1998 when Miloš Zeman formed a minority Social Democratic government, the country's first left-wing government since the fall of socialism. The Czech Republic joined NATO in 1999 and in 2001 Vladimír Špidla succeeded Zeman as party leader and prime minister. The Czech Republic became a member of the EU on 1 May 2004.

TERRITORY AND POPULATION

The Czech Republic is bounded in the west by Germany, north by Poland, east by Slovakia and south by Austria. Minor exchanges of territory to straighten their mutual border were agreed between the Czech Republic and Slovakia on 4 Jan. 1996, but the Czech parliament refused to ratify them on 24 April 1996. Its area is 78,866 sq. km (30,450 sq. miles). At the 2001 census the population was 10,230,060 (51·3% female); density, 129·7 per sq. km. The estimated population in 2005 was 10·22m. In 2003, 74·3% of the population lived in urban areas.

The UN gives a projected population for 2010 of 10·16m.

There are 14 administrative regions *(Kraj)*, one of which is the capital, Prague (Praha).

Region	Chief city	Area in sq. km	Population 2001 census
Jihočeský	České Budějovice	10,056	625,267
Jihomoravský	Brno	7,067	1,127,718
Karlovarský	Karlovy Vary	3,315	304,343
Královéhradecký	Hradec Králové	4,757	550,724
Liberecký	Liberec	3,163	428,184
Moravskoslezský	Ostrava	5,555	1,269,467
Olomoucký	Olomouc	5,139	639,369
Pardubický	Pardubice	4,519	508,281
Plzeňský	Plzeň (Pilsen)	7,560	550,688
Praha (Prague)	—	496	1,169,106
Středočeský	Praha (Prague)	11,014	1,122,473
Ústecký	Ústí nad Labem	5,335	820,219
Vysočina	Jihlava	6,925	519,211
Zlínský	Zlín	3,965	595,010

The estimated population of the principal towns in 2002 (in 1,000):

Prague (Praha)	1,162	Liberec	98	Havířov	85
Brno	371	České Budějovice	96	Zlín	80
Ostrava	314	Hradec Králové	96	Kladno	70
Plzeň	164	Ústí nad Labem	95	Most	68
Olomouc	102	Pardubice	90	Karviná	64

At the 2001 census 90·4% of the population was Czech, 3·7% Moravian and 1·9% Slovak. There were also (in 1,000): Poles, 52; Germans, 39; Roma (Gypsies), 12; Silesians, 11.

The official language is Czech.

SOCIAL STATISTICS

2002 births, 92,786; deaths, 108,243; marriages, 52,732; divorces, 31,758. Rates (per 1,000 population), 1999: birth, 9·1; death, 10·6; marriage, 5·2; divorce, 3·1. Life expectancy at birth, 2003, 72·3 years for males and 78·7 years for females. In 2002 the most popular age for marrying was 26 for males and 25 for females. Annual population growth rate, 1995–2002, –0·2%. Infant mortality, 2002, 4·1 per 1,000 live births; fertility rate, 2002, 1·2 children per woman.

CLIMATE

A humid continental climate, with warm summers and cold winters. Precipitation is generally greater in summer, with thunderstorms. Autumn, with dry clear weather, and spring, which is damp, are each of short duration. Prague, Jan. 29·5°F (–1·5°C), July 67°F (19·4°C). Annual rainfall 19·3" (483 mm). Brno, Jan. 31°F (–0·6°C), July 67°F (19·4°C). Annual rainfall 21" (525 mm).

CONSTITUTION AND GOVERNMENT

The Constitution of 1 Jan. 1993 provides for a parliament comprising a 200-member *Chamber of Deputies*, elected for four-year terms by proportional representation, and an 81-member *Senate* elected for six-year terms in single-member districts, 27 senators being elected every two years. The main function of the Senate is to scrutinize proposed legislation. Senators must be at least 40 years of age, and are elected on a first-past-the-post basis, with a run-off in constituencies where no candidate wins more than half the votes cast. For the House of Representatives there is a 5% threshold; votes for parties failing to surmount this are redistributed on the basis of results in each of the eight electoral districts.

There is a *Constitutional Court* at Brno, whose 15 members are nominated by the President and approved by the Senate for ten-year terms.

The *President* of the Republic is elected for a five-year term by both chambers of parliament. He or she must be at least 40 years of age. The President names the Prime Minister at the suggestion of the Speaker.

National Anthem
'Kde domov můj?' ('Where is my homeland?'); words by J. K. Tyl, tune by F. J. Škroup.

GOVERNMENT CHRONOLOGY

(ČSSD = Czech Social Democratic Party; ODS = Civic Democratic Party; n/p = non-partisan)

Presidents since 1993.

1993–2003	n/p	Václav Havel
2003–	ODS	Václav Klaus

Prime Ministers since 1993.

1993–97	ODS	Václav Klaus
1997–98	n/p	Josef Tošovský
1998–2002	ČSSD	Miloš Zeman
2002–04	ČSSD	Vladimír Špidla
2004–05	ČSSD	Stanislav Gross
2005–	ČSSD	Jiří Paroubek

RECENT ELECTIONS

Former prime minister Václav Klaus (Civic Democratic Party/ODS) was elected president on 28 Feb. 2003 by parliament. He won the lower house 115–81 over Jan Sokol (Czech Social Democratic Party), but Sokol won the Senate 47–32. A second round was also inconclusive. In the third round, in which votes from both chambers were counted together, Klaus won a majority with 142 votes against 124 for Sokol. Previous attempts to elect a president on 15 Jan. and 24 Jan. 2003 had both failed.

Elections to the National Assembly were held on 14 and 15 June 2002; turnout was 58·0%. The Czech Social Democratic Party (ČSSD) gained 70 seats with 30·2% of votes cast; the Civic Democratic Party (ODS) gained 58 with 24·5%; the Communist Party of Bohemia and Moravia (KSČM), 41 with 18·5%; and Koalice, the coalition of the Christian and Democratic Union (KDU), the Czechoslovak People's Party (ČSL), the Freedom Union (US) and the Democratic Union (DU), 31 with 14·3%. Following the elections a coalition government was formed between ČSSD and Koalice.

Elections for a third of the seats in the Senate were held on 5, 6, 12 and 13 Nov. 2004. As a result ODS had 34 seats in the Senate; ind. 19; Koalice (the coalition of four), 15; ČSSD, 6; and a number of parties held either one or two seats.

Parliamentary elections were scheduled to take place on 2 and 3 June 2006.

European Parliament
The Czech Republic has 24 representatives. At the June 2004 elections turnout was 27·9%. The ODS won 9 seats with 30·0% of votes cast (political affiliation in European Parliament: European People's Party–European Democrats); KSČM, 6 with 20·3% (European Unitary Left/Nordic Green Left); SN–ED (Association of Independents–European Democrats Alliance), 3 with 11·0% (European People's Party–European Democrats); KDU–ČSL, 2 with 9·6% (European People's Party–European Democrats); ČSSD, 2 with 8·8% (Party of European Socialists); Klub Nezavisli (Independent), 2 with 8·2% (one non-attached; one Independence and Democracy Group).

CURRENT ADMINISTRATION

President: Václav Klaus; b. 1941 (ODS; sworn in on 7 March 2003).

In March 2006 the ČSSD-Koalice government comprised:

Prime Minister: Jiří Paroubek; b. 1952 (ČSSD; appointed on 25 April 2005).

First Deputy Prime Minister and Minister of Finance: Bohuslav Sobotka. *Deputy Prime Minister and Minister of Labour and Social Affairs:* Zdeněk Škromach. *Deputy Prime Minister and Minister of Justice:* Pavel Němec. *Deputy Prime Minister and Minister of Transport:* Milan Šimonovský. *Deputy Prime Minister:* Jiří Havel.

Minister of Agriculture: Jan Mládek. *Culture:* Vítězslav Jandák. *Defence:* Karel Kühnl. *Education, Youth and Sports:* Petra Buzková. *Environment:* Libor Ambrozek. *Foreign Affairs:* Cyril Svoboda. *Health:* David Rath. *Industry and Trade:* Milan Urban. *Information Technology:* Dana Bérová. *Interior:* František Bublan. *Regional Development:* Radko Martínek. *Minister without Portfolio for Legislation:* Pavel Zářecký.

Government Website: http://www.vlada.cz

CURRENT LEADERS

Václav Klaus

Position
President

Introduction
Dr Václav Klaus, a member of the Civic Forum movement and later the centre-right Civic Democratic Party (ODS; Obcanská Demokratická Strana), was Czechoslovakia's first minister of finance following the Velvet Revolution of 1989. He was elected prime minister in 1992 and oversaw the Czech Republic's transition from a state-planned economy to a free market system. His reforms led initially to economic growth unparalleled among any of the other post-communist nations in the region. However, by the late 1990s the economy was suffering and Klaus resigned in 1997 following a party financing scandal. He succeeded Václav Havel as president in Feb. 2003.

Early Life
Born on 19 April 1941 in Prague, Klaus graduated from the Prague School of Economics in 1963, continuing his education in Naples, Italy and at Cornell University in New York. He was then employed as a researcher at the Institute of Economics of the Czechoslovak Academy of Sciences until 1970, when he was removed as an anti-socialist element. During that time he came into contact with Václav Havel, the dissident writer and future Czech president, when both were on the editorial board of a magazine.

From 1971 until 1987, Klaus held a succession of posts at the Czechoslovak State Bank before joining the Academy of Sciences' Economic Forecasting Institute. On 17 Nov. 1989, while the Velvet Revolution was in its infancy, Klaus returned from lecturing in Vienna to find that his son had only just escaped a serious beating from police in Prague's Wenceslas Square. Two days later he became a founder member of the Civic Forum, the movement that would be instrumental in the overthrow of the Communist regime in the coming days. He was appointed finance minister in the first post-revolution government in Dec. 1989, implementing a range of reformist policies influenced by the free market economists Milton Friedman and F. A. Hayek and also the then British prime minister Margaret Thatcher.

The Civic Forum, which had been a loose alliance of anti-communists, began to splinter and Klaus became a prominent member of the centre-right ODS, which had an ambitious agenda to restructure, deregulate and liberalize the market. In April 1991 he became party chairman, in Oct. 1991 he was appointed deputy premier and following the ODS victory at the general elections of June 1992 he became prime minister.

Career in Office
The newly independent Czech Republic, following the split with Slovakia, underwent a programme of rapid reform and privatization that saw the economy eclipse those of its former communist neighbours. Klaus was acclaimed internationally as the architect of an economic miracle and praised for his

publications (such as *Ten Commandments of Systematic Reform* and *Rebirth of a Nation*).

However, the ODS faired less well than expected at the elections of July 1996 and the governing coalition lost their majority in the House of Representatives. For the first time, Klaus' authority within the ODS had been challenged and was further weakened during that year when his foreign minister, Josef Zieleniec, made public a feud between them. The economy was also beginning to suffer, and there followed a series of crisis budgets, austerity measures and ultimately devaluation in 1997. A number of further problems for Klaus included the resignation of Zieleniec, popular protests against the government and, most damagingly, the re-emergence of corruption allegations concerning ODS party funding. The charges concerned improper donations in return for preferential treatment in relation to privatization, but Klaus vigorously denied all knowledge. Zieleniec publicly declared that Klaus had been aware of a number of certain key donations, and President Havel called for the government to step down. Klaus resigned on 29 Nov. 1997, still denying any wrongdoing.

Although corruption allegations were the catalyst for Klaus' fall from power, his government had been under considerable pressure for some time as the Czech Republic failed to increase its economic lead over its former communist rivals. In July 1998 he was elected speaker of the Chamber of Deputies for a four-year-term and remained one of the country's most significant political figures. In Jan. 2003 he twice stood for election to the presidency in succession to Havel but, despite winning most votes on both occasions, failed to secure the requisite 50%. Havel resigned on 3 Feb. 2003 and Klaus was chosen to succeed him at the third attempt at the end of the month.

In June 2003 membership of the EU, scheduled for 2004, won 77% approval in a national referendum. Klaus, however, had described entry into the EU as a 'marriage of convenience rather than love' and refused to reveal which way he had voted.

Jiří Paroubek

Position
Prime Minister

Introduction
The Czech Republic's third prime minister in nine months, Jiří Paroubek's appointment on 25 April 2005 followed the resignation of his controversial party colleague, Stanislav Gross. Paroubek is an economist who worked for various state-owned industries under communist rule and became a consultant following the sweeping reforms and upheavals of the early 1990s. Although he worked as the deputy mayor of Prague for six years, Paroubek has little ministerial experience. He is faced with the task of holding together the fractious centre-left coalition government.

Early Life
Jiří Paroubek was born in Olomouc, central Czechoslovakia on 21 Aug. 1952. He attended the School of Economics in the capital, Prague, from 1970–76 and in 1970 joined the 'revived National Front', although it had no influence while the country was ruled by the Communist Party of Czechoslovakia (CPCz). Having graduated in 1976, Paroubek worked as an economist at several state-owned organizations including Prefa Malešice, Obuv Praha (a shoe company) and Jídelny a Restaurace (restaurants and food facilities), where he was head of the planning and financial department.

Following the dramatic 'Velvet Revolution' in Nov. 1989 that culminated in the playwright and former dissident Václav Havel being elected president, Paroubek joined the newly reborn Czech Social Democratic Party (ČSSD). In 1990 he was elected as central secretary of the ČSSD and contributed to establishing its organizational structure and financial base. In the same year he was also elected as a member of the municipal assembly of Prague's city hall. In 1991 Paroubek established EPC, an economic consultancy that advised small businesses. At this time, sweeping reforms to the Czechoslovak economy were leading to serious hardship, particularly in the east of the country. A separatist movement in Slovakia led eventually to a formal split into independent states on 1 Jan. 1993.

Paroubek was elected the deputy mayor of Prague in 1998, the year in which Václav Havel was re-elected president. Miloš Zeman led the ČSSD to its first victory in the ensuing legislative elections, promising to prevent a repeat of the 1997 economic downturn and vowing to slow privatization and restore more control to the state. As deputy mayor, responsible for financial policy, Paroubek organized the funding for the renovation of Prague's Congress Centre and secured loans and bonds to improve the city's infrastructure. However, he was criticized for his decision to have bonds worth €170m. issued in euros rather than Czech koruny, which allegedly caused heavy losses for the city in interest-rate speculation. He was also accused of selling off the city's stake in the water utility, Pražské Vodovody a Kanalizace (PVK), to the French company, Vivendi Water, for less than the market rate. Paroubek countered that the funds from the sale were required to repair buildings and roads that were ruined in the floods of Aug. 2002.

In Aug. 2004 he was appointed minister for regional development in Stanislav Gross' new ČSSD-led coalition. Despite his reputation for deal-making and his energetic approach, Gross came under fire just six months into his term of office when it was revealed that in 1999 he had bought a luxury apartment costing far more than his government salary. Gross' attempts to explain the purchase, combined with controversy over his wife's business dealings, led to his resignation. On 25 April 2005 the president, Václav Klaus, named Paroubek prime minister of the Czech Republic. On 13 May 2005 the government (which remained the coalition of the ČSSD and Koalice) passed a motion of confidence in Paroubek.

Career in Office
Paroubek is generally seen as politically to the left of his predecessor, but no major policy changes are expected from his government. He is a strong advocate for the European Constitution, but accepts that it is 'impossible at present' to continue with plans for a referendum to ratify the constitution in the light of its rejection by voters in France and the Netherlands. Paroubek has also pledged to bring in tax cuts for the poor and deregulate state-owned property. Joining the euro is also an objective, although to meet the criteria the country would need to reduce public spending and reform healthcare and education.

DEFENCE

Conscription ended in Dec. 2004 when the armed forces became all-volunteer. Defence expenditure in 2003 totalled US$1,871m. (US$183 per capita), representing 2·2% of GDP.

Army
Strength (2002) 36,370 (15,500 conscripts). There are also paramilitary Border Guards (4,000-strong) and Internal Security Forces (1,600).

Air Force
The Air Force has a strength of some 11,300 and is organized into two main structures—Tactical Air Force and Air Defence. There are 44 combat aircraft (L-159s and MiG-21s) and 34 attack helicopters in all.

INTERNATIONAL RELATIONS

In 1974 the Federal Republic of Germany and Czechoslovakia annulled the Munich agreement of 1938. On 14 Feb. 1997 the

Czech parliament ratified a declaration of German–Czech reconciliation, with particular reference to the Sudeten German problems.

The Czech Republic is a member of the UN, WTO, BIS, NATO, OECD, EU, Council of Europe, OSCE, CEFTA, CERN, CEI, IOM, and the Antarctic Treaty, and is an associate partner of the WEU. The Czech Republic became a member of the EU on 1 May 2004. A referendum held on 13–14 June 2003 approved accession, with 77·3% of votes cast for membership and 22·7% against. In 2000 a visa requirement for Russians entering the country was introduced as one of the conditions for EU membership.

ECONOMY

Agriculture accounted for 3·7% of GDP in 2002, industry 39·6% and services 56·7%. In 2002 an estimated 82·2% of economic output was produced by the private sector.

Overview

Until 1996 the Czech Republic was viewed as the most successful European transition economy. Industrial production and employment declined significantly during the transition from communism but job losses were contained by rising service sector employment and soft loans given to loss-making enterprises by state-banks. After four years of 3% average annual growth, the economy fell into recession in 1997–98. In May 1997 large current account deficits fuelled a speculative attack on the *koruna*, forcing the country to adopt a tight monetary policy and fiscal austerity. With a financial sector no longer able to subsidize loss-making industrial enterprises, industry was forced to make costly financial and enterprise reforms. Foreign direct investment began flowing into the country from the West in 1999 and solid growth resumed in the 2000s without high inflation.

With strength in engineering, low labour costs, good infrastructure and a favourable geographical position, the Czech Republic's diversified industrial export sector has been a key engine of growth. Export markets have been found primarily in Western Europe but also in Central and Eastern Europe and Russia. Despite a strengthening *koruna*, the Czech Republic posted a significant trade surplus in 2005 (US$1·8bn. from Jan.–Sept.) which cut into the persistent current account deficit. The private sector accounted for 80% of GDP in 2001 owing to bank privatization and the sale of the major utilities. Further privatization was planned for 2006. In 2004 fiscal health improved with stricter social benefit eligibility. With an aging population more fiscal adjustments are necessary for the long-term sustainability of public finances.

Currency

The unit of currency is the *koruna* (CEK) or crown of 100 *haler*, introduced on 8 Feb. 1993 at parity with the former Czechoslovakian koruna. Gold reserves were 443,000 troy oz in June 2002; foreign currency reserves were US$21,136m.

Inflation rates (based on OECD statistics):

1995	1996	1997	1998	1999	2000	2001	2002	2003	2004
9·1%	8·8%	8·5%	10·7%	2·1%	3·9%	4·7%	2·0%	−0·1%	2·8%

The koruna became convertible on 1 Oct. 1995. In May 1997 the koruna was devalued 10% and allowed to float. Total money supply was Kč. 692,300m. in Dec. 2002.

Budget

Budgetary central government revenue and expenditure in Kč. 1bn.:

	2001	2002	2003
Revenue	617·55	674·38	702·25
Expenditure	668·30	727·82	783·90

Principal sources of revenue in 2003: social security contributions, Kč. 273·11bn.; taxes on goods and services, Kč. 203·10bn.; taxes on income, profits and capital gains, Kč. 172·91bn. Main items of expenditure by economic type in 2003: social benefits, Kč. 305·03bn.; grants, Kč. 170·74bn.; compensation of employees, Kč. 79·26bn.

VAT, introduced on 1 Jan. 1993, is 19% (reduced rate, 5%).

Performance

Real GDP growth rates (based on OECD statistics):

1995	1996	1997	1998	1999	2000	2001	2002	2003	2004
5·9%	4·2%	−0·7%	−1·1%	1·2%	3·9%	2·6%	1·5%	3·2%	4·4%

Total GDP was US$107·0bn. in 2004.

Banking and Finance

The central bank and bank of issue is the Czech National Bank (*Governor*, Zdeněk Tůma), which also acts as banking supervisor and regulator. Decentralization of the banking system began in 1991, and private banks began to operate. The Czech banking sector accounted for 78·3% of total financial sector assets at the end of 2002, representing Kč. 2,504bn. or 110% of GDP in 2002. The only legal form of domestically operating banks are joint stock companies (27 at 30 June 2003) and branches of foreign banks (nine at 30 June 2003). The Commercial Bank and Investment Bank are privatized nationwide networks with a significant government holding. Specialized banks include the Czech Savings Bank and the Czech Commercial Bank (for foreign trade payments). Private banks tend to be on a regional basis, many of them agricultural banks. In Nov. 1997 the cabinet agreed to sell off large stakes in three of the largest state-held banks to individual foreign investors through tenders, in preparation for European Union entry. In June 2000 the country's fourth largest bank, Československá obchodní banka (CSOB), acquired the operations of the third largest bank, Investiční a Poštovní banka (IPB). The newly-formed institution became the country's largest bank, with assets of US$16·6bn. in Dec. 1999. Other major banks are Komerční banka (assets of US$10·8bn. in Dec. 1999) and Česká Spořitelna (assets of US$9·6bn.). Foreign shareholders controlled 94·5% of the total assets of the banking sector at June 2003, most of them from EU countries. Other capital market participants are subject to the supervision of the Czech Securities Commission. Savings deposits were Kč. 1,467,270m. in 2002.

Foreign direct investment, which was only US$1·29bn. in 1997, rose to US$39·4bn. in 2002.

A stock exchange was founded in Prague in 1992.

ENERGY AND NATURAL RESOURCES

Environment

The Czech Republic's carbon dioxide emissions from the consumption and flaring of fossil fuels in 2002 were the equivalent of 10·1 tonnes per capita.

Electricity

Installed capacity was 16·3m. kW in 2002. Production in 2002 was 76·35bn. kWh. 72% of electricity was produced by thermal power stations (mainly using brown coal), 25% was nuclear and the rest was from hydro-electric generation and autoproduction. In 2003 there were six nuclear reactors in operation. Consumption per capita in 2002 was 4,836 kWh.

Oil and Gas

Natural gas reserves in 2002 totalled 2·1bn. cu. metres. Production in 2000 was 207m. cu. metres. In 2002 crude petroleum reserves were 15m. bbls.; production was 175,000 tonnes in 2000.

Minerals

There are hard coal and lignite reserves (chief fields: Most, Chomutov, Kladno, Ostrava and Sokolov). Lignite production in 2002 was 48·9m. tonnes; coal production in 2002 was 14·5m. tonnes.

Agriculture

In 2002 there were 4,273,000 ha. of agricultural land. In 2002 there were 3·07m. ha. of arable land and 0·97m. ha. of permanent crops. Approximately 24,000 ha. were irrigated in 2001. 31% of agricultural land was state-owned and 61% co-operative. Agriculture employs just 4·9% of the workforce—the smallest proportion of any of the ex-Communist countries in eastern Europe.

A law of May 1991 returned land seized by the Communist regime to its original owners, to a maximum of 150 ha. of arable to a single owner.

Main agricultural production figures, 2002 (1,000 tonnes): wheat, 3,867; sugarbeets, 3,833; barley, 1,793; potatoes, 901; rapeseed, 710; apples, 339; maize, 304; rye, 119.

Livestock, 2003: cattle, 1·47m.; pigs, 3·36m.; sheep, 103,000; poultry, 27m. In 2002 production of meat was 787,000 tonnes; cheese, 146,000 tonnes; milk, 2,728m. litres; 1,829m. eggs.

Forestry

In 2002 forests covered 2,643,000 ha. (34% of the total land area). Timber production in 2002 was 14·54m. cu. metres.

Fisheries

Ponds created for fish-farming number 21,800 and cover about 41,000 ha., the largest of them being two lakes in southern Bohemia. Fish landings in 2002 amounted to 24,193 tonnes, entirely from inland waters.

INDUSTRY

The leading companies by market capitalization in the Czech Republic, excluding banking and finance, in Jan. 2002 were: Český Telecom a.s. (Kč. 111bn.); ČEZ (České Energetické Závody a.s.), Kč. 45bn.; and Philip Morris CR a.s. (Kč. 23bn.), a tobacco company.

In 2002 there were 1,607,151 small private businesses (of which 21,331 were incorporated), 220,461 companies and partnerships (of which 15,260 were joint-stock companies), 12,085 co-operatives and 995 state enterprises. Output, 2002, included: crude steel, 6·5m. tonnes; pig iron, 4·8m. tonnes; cement (2001), 3·6m. tonnes; 1,141,000 TV sets (2000); 428,000 motor cars (2000); beer, 1,798·7m. litres; soft drinks (2001), 1,601·7m. litres.

Labour

In 2002 the economically active population numbered 5,139,000. The major areas of activity were 1·32m. persons employed in mining and manufacturing; 619,800 in trade; 425,200 in construction; 367,600 in transport, storage and communications; and 325,700 in public administration and defence. In Dec. 2005 the unemployment rate was 7·8%. Workers in the Czech Republic put in among the longest hours of any country in the world. In 2002 the average worker put in 1,980 hours. The average monthly wage was Kč. 18,133 in 2002. Pay increases are regulated in firms where wages grow faster than production. Fines are levied if wages rise by more than 15% over four years. In 1996, 11,500 employees were involved in industrial disputes resulting in a loss of 16,400 working days.

INTERNATIONAL TRADE

A memorandum envisaging a customs union and close economic co-operation was signed with Slovakia in Oct. 1992. An agreement of Dec. 1992 with Hungary, Poland and Slovakia abolished tariffs on raw materials and goods, where exports do not compete directly with locally produced items, and envisaged tariff reductions on agricultural and industrial goods in 1995–97.

Foreign debt was US$26,281m. in 2002. There were 10,599 joint ventures in June 1993.

Imports and Exports

Trading with EU and EFTA countries has increased significantly while trading with all post-communist states has decreased.

Trade, 2004, in US$1m. (2003 in brackets): imports f.o.b., 67,750 (51,224); exports f.o.b., 66,874 (48,705). Main import suppliers, 2002: Germany, 32·5%; Italy, 5·4%; Slovakia, 5·2%; France, 4·8%; China, 4·6%; Russia, 4·5%. Main export markets, 2002: Germany, 36·5%; Slovakia, 7·7%; United Kingdom, 5·8%; Austria, 5·5%; France, 4·7%; Poland, 4·7%. In 2002 the EU accounted for 60·1% of Czech imports and 68·3% of exports.

Main imports in 1999 were: machinery and transport equipment, 40·3% (10·1% was electrical machinery and 7·7% was road vehicles); manufactured goods, 21·0%; chemicals, 11·2%; foodstuffs, 4·6%; petroleum products, 4·2%. Main exports in 1999 were: machinery and transport equipment, 43·1% (15·1% was road vehicles and 9·7% was electrical machinery); manufactured goods, 26·5%; chemicals, 6·6%.

COMMUNICATIONS

Roads

In 2002 there were 518 km of motorways, 6,102 km of highways and main roads, 14,668 km of secondary roads and 34,134 km of other roads, forming a total network of 55,422 km. Passenger cars in use in 2002 numbered 3,647,067 (356 per 1,000 inhabitants), and there were also 323,434 commercial vehicles and 21,340 buses and coaches. Motorcycles numbered 760,219. In 2000 passenger transport totalled 73,392m. passenger-km (63,840m. passenger-km private transport) and freight 39,036m. tonne-km. There were 1,431 deaths as a result of road accidents in 2002.

Rail

In 2002 Czech State Railways had a route length of 9,600 km (1,435 mm gauge), of which 2,926 km were electrified. Passenger-km travelled in 2002 came to 6·60bn. and freight tonne-km to 15·81bn. There is a metro (44 km) and tram/light rail system (496 km) in Prague, and tram/light rail networks in Brno, Liberec, Most, Olomouc, Ostrava, Plzeň and Teplice-Trecianské.

Civil Aviation

There are international airports at Prague (Ruzyné), Ostrava (Mosnov) and Brno (Turany). The national carrier is Czech Airlines, 56·43% of which is owned by the Czech National Property Fund. In 2002 it flew 68·0m. km and carried 4,243,000 passengers (all on international flights). In 2001 Prague handled 6,077,658 passengers (6,014,412 on international flights) and 29,571 tonnes of freight, Ostrava handled 116,836 passengers and Brno 110,335 passengers.

Shipping

1·7m. tonnes of freight were carried by inland waterways in 2002. Merchant shipping totalled 16,000 GRT in 1997.

Telecommunications

In 2002 there were 12,285,600 telephone subscribers, or 1,211·1 for every 1,000 inhabitants, and 1·8m. PCs (177·4 per 1,000 persons). Český Telecom and České Radiokomunikace, the two main telecommunications companies, are partly privatized. The government privatized Český Telecom in April 2005 by agreeing to sell a 51·1% stake to the Spanish telecommunications firm Telefónica. Mobile phone subscribers numbered 8·61m. in 2002 (848·8 per 1,000 population) and there were 111,000 fax machines. There were 2·60m. Internet users in 2002.

Postal Services

In 2002 there were 3,407 post offices.

SOCIAL INSTITUTIONS

Justice

The post-Communist judicial system was established in July 1991. This provides for a unified system of civil, criminal, commercial and administrative courts. Commercial courts arbitrate in disputes arising from business activities. Administrative courts examine the legality of the decisions of state institutions when appealed by citizens. In addition, there are military courts which operate under the jurisdiction of the Ministry of Defence. There is a Supreme Court, and a hierarchy of courts under the Ministry of Justice at republic, region and district level. District courts are courts of first instance. Cases are usually decided by senates comprising a judge and two associate judges, though occasionally by a single judge. (Associate judges are citizens in good standing over the age of 25 who are elected for four-year terms). Regional courts are courts of first instance in more serious cases and also courts of appeal for district courts. Cases are usually decided by a senate of two judges and three associate judges, although occasionally by a single judge. There is also a Supreme Administrative Court. The Supreme Court interprets law as a guide to other courts and functions also as a court of appeal. Decisions are made by senates of three judges. Judges are appointed for life by the National Council.

There is no death penalty. In 2002, 372,341 crimes were reported, of which 40·7% were solved. The population in penal institutions in Oct. 2003 was 17,360.

Education
Elementary education up to age 15 is compulsory. 52% of children continue their education in vocational schools and 48% move on to secondary schools.

In 2003–04 there were nine universities, four technical universities, one university for economics, one for agriculture, one for agriculture and forestry, one for veterinary sciences, one for pharmaceutical sciences, one for chemical technology, four academies for performing arts, music and dramatic arts, fine arts and arts, architecture and industrial design, and a higher school of teacher training. Together, these 24 higher education institutions had 219,514 students in 2002–03 and 13,641 teaching staff.

In 2002 total expenditure on education came to Kč. 106,569m., or 4·68% of GNP.

The adult literacy rate is at least 99%.

Health
In 2002 there were 201 hospitals with a provision of 65 beds per 10,000 inhabitants. There were 35,222 physicians, 6,698 dentists, 97,077 nurses, 5,199 pharmacists and 4,895 midwives in 2001. In 2001 the Czech Republic spent 7·3% of its GDP on health.

Welfare
Since 1 Jan. 1996 the retirement age has been gradually increasing by two months per year for men and by four months per year for women. The target retirement age, from 1 Jan. 2007, is 62 years (men) and 57 to 61 (women), according to the number of children raised.

The old-age pension is calculated as a flat-rate basic amount of Kč. 1,310 plus an earnings-related percentage calculated on personal assessment and the number of years of insurance. In 2002 the minimum monthly pension was Kč. 2,080.

To qualify for unemployment benefit the applicant must have been in employment for at least 12 months in the previous three years. The maximum unemployment benefit in 2002 was Kč. 10,250 per month.

RELIGION
In 2003 there were 25 registered churches and religious societies. In 2001 church membership was estimated to be: Roman Catholic, 2,740,800; Evangelical Church of the Czech Brethren, 117,200; Hussites, 99,100; Eastern Orthodox, 23,000; Silesian Evangelicals, 14,000. 6,040,000 persons were classified as atheist or non-religious, and there were 331,000 adherents of other religions.

Miloslav Vlk (b. 1932) was installed as Archbishop of Prague and Primate of Czechoslovakia in 1991. The national Czech church, created in 1918, took the name 'Hussite' in 1972. In 1991

it had a patriarch, five bishops and 300 pastors (40% women). In 1991 there were also around a dozen other Protestant churches, the largest being the Evangelical which unites Calvinists and Lutherans, and numbered about 200,000. In May 2005 the Roman Catholic church had two cardinals.

CULTURE
World Heritage Sites
Sites under Czech jurisdiction which appear on UNESCO's world heritage list are (with year entered on list): Historic Centre of Prague (1992); Historic Centre of Český Krumlov (1992); Historic Centre of Telč (1992); Pilgrimage Church of St John of Nipomuk at Zelena Hora in Zdar nad Sazavou (1994); Kutná Hora—the Historical Town Centre with the Church of Saint Barbara and the Cathedral of our Lady at Sedlec (1995); Lednice-Valtice Cultural Landscape (1996); Holašovice Historical Village Reservation (1998); Gardens and Castle at Kroměříž (1998); Litomyšl Castle (1999); Holy Trinity Column in Olomouc (2000); Tugendhat Villa in Brno (2001); and the Jewish Quarter and St Procopius' Basilica in Třebíč (2003).

Broadcasting
Broadcasting is the responsibility of the independent Board for Radio and Television. Czech Television (CTV, colour by SECAM H) and Czech Radio are public corporations. The former Czechoslovakian broadcasting stations in the Czech Republic have become a second service. There is also a nationwide private TV company and two radio companies as well as local private stations. There were 5·5m. TV receivers in 2001 and 8·23m. radio receivers in 2000.

Cinema
In 2002 there were 665 cinemas; attendance for the year was 10·7m.

Press
There were 93 daily newspapers in 2002 with a total readership of 2,620,000 (256 per 1,000 inhabitants). There were also 3,636 non-dailies with total readership of 4,200,000 (410 per 1,000 inhabitants).

Tourism
There were 16,031,000 foreign tourists in 1999; foreign currency income from tourism in 2002 was US$2,941m.

Libraries
In 2002 there were 6,043 libraries, one National library and 1,096 national libraries. They held a combined 51,178,000 volumes for 1,600,000 registered users.

Museums and Galleries
In 2002 there were 331 museums hosting a combined 8,726,000 visitors.

DIPLOMATIC REPRESENTATIVES
Of the Czech Republic in the United Kingdom (26 Kensington Palace Gdns, London, W8 4QY)
Ambassador: Jan Winkler.

Of the United Kingdom in the Czech Republic (Thunovská 14, 118 00 Prague 1)
Ambassador: Linda Duffield.

Of the Czech Republic in the USA (3900 Spring of Freedom St., NW, Washington, D.C., 20008)
Ambassador: Petr Kolar.

Of the USA in the Czech Republic (Tržiste 15, 118 01 Prague 1)
Ambassador: William J. Cabaniss, Jr.

Of the Czech Republic to the United Nations
Ambassador: Hynek Kmoníček.

Of the Czech Republic to the European Union
Ambassador: Pavel Telička.

FURTHER READING

Czech Statistical Office. *Statistical Yearbook of the Czech Republic*.

Havel, V., *Disturbing the Peace*. London, 1990.—*Living in Truth: Twenty-Two Essays*. London, 1990.—*Summer Meditations*. London, 1992

Krejcí, Jaroslav and Machonin, Pavel, *Czechoslovakia 1918–1992: A Laboratory for Social Change*. Macmillan, London, 1996

Leff, C. S., *National Conflict in Czechoslovakia: The Making and Remaking of a State, 1918–1987*. Princeton, 1988

Lunt, Susie, *Prague*. [Bibliography] ABC-Clio, Oxford and Santa Barbara (CA), 1997

Simmons, M., *The Reluctant President: a Political Life of Vaclav Havel*. London, 1992

Turner, Barry, (ed.) *Central Europe Profiled*. Macmillan, London, 2000

National Statistical Office: Czech Statistical Office, Na Padesátém 81, 100 82 Prague 10.

Website: http://www.czso.cz

DENMARK

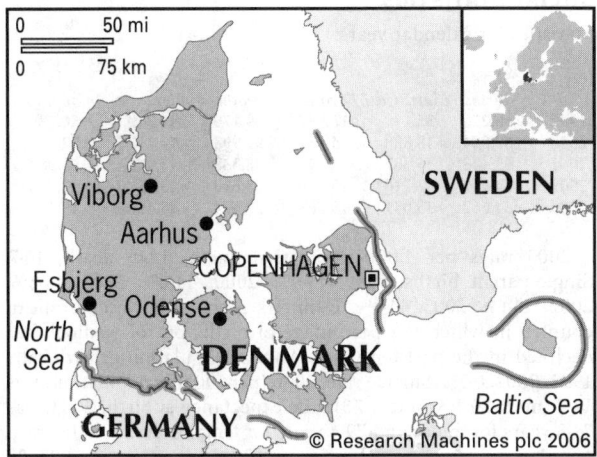

**Kongeriget Danmark
(Kingdom of Denmark)**

Capital: Copenhagen
Population projection, 2010: 5·50m.
GDP per capita, 2003: (PPP$) 31,465
HDI/world rank: 0·941/14

KEY HISTORICAL EVENTS

Evidence of habitation exists from the Bølling period (12500–12000 BC). By 7700 BC reindeer hunters were settled on the Jutland Peninsula and around 3900 BC agriculture developed. Metal tools and weapons were imported in the Dagger Period (*c.* 2000 BC) but trading stations on the coast did not appear until around AD 300. The first towns developed in the Germanic Iron Age (AD 400–750). The first trading market was held in the 8th century in Hedeby. Denmark was converted to Christianity in 860 when Ansgar built churches in Hedeby and Ribe.

Danish Vikings first attacked England's northeast coast in 793. In about 900 Harold Bluetooth became the first king of Denmark and Skåne. His grandson, Canute the Great, fought successfully to incorporate England into his North Sea Empire and from 1018–35, Denmark, England and Norway were one nation. However, civil war broke out and in 1146 the kingdom was divided between Magnus the Strong and Knud Lavard. In 1157 Knud's son Valdemar was recognized as the ruler of Denmark. By 1200 Skåne, Halland and Blekinge in the South of Sweden were part of the Danish kingdom. The southern border of Denmark extended to the Eider in what is today northern Germany. In 1219 Valdemar conquered Estonia. He also established a code of law and a land register (Jordebog). The first written constitution was a coronation charter signed by Erik V in 1282.

In the 13th century, agriculture was supplemented by the expansion of fishing to supply inland Europe. Other industries also benefited and this brought with it a passion for building, particularly cathedrals and churches. Economic growth strengthened German influence. The Hanseatic League of German entrepreneurs was granted trade concessions for herring, salt and grain and also played a leading role in the country's political affairs. Valdemar IV Atterdag was crowned king in 1340. He challenged the privileges of the Hanseatic League, and was brought into conflict with Sweden over the southern provinces

of Skåne, Halland and Blekinge. In 1361 Valdemar Atterdag took Gotland in one of the bloodiest Nordic battles. When the king died in 1375, his daughter Margaret (married to King Håkon of Norway) claimed the throne on behalf of her five-year-old son Olav. After Håkon's death in 1388 she also became regent of Norway. While resisting the Hanseatic League, she succeeded in defeating her opponent Albrecht of Mecklenburg, king of Sweden, thus clearing the way to a Nordic union. In 1397, after Olav's death, Margaret's nephew Erik of Pomerania became king of Denmark, Norway and Sweden. In 1412 Erik was opposed by the Swedish nobles, who resented being taxed to finance Danish wars in northern Germany. When Erik abdicated, Christian I was elected king of Denmark and Norway in 1448.

By the 16th century Scandinavia was divided between Denmark–Norway (including Iceland and Greenland) and Sweden–Finland. In 1520 a power struggle in Sweden made the country vulnerable to a Danish invasion. Christian II was crowned king of Sweden but was soon challenged by Gustav Vasa, who replaced Christian II in 1521 as king of Sweden. In 1523 Christian was succeeded by Frederick I, who ended the union with Sweden. Following the Lutheran Reformation, the monarchy enhanced its power by confiscating the property of the Roman Catholic Church.

Imperial Rise and Fall

Christian IV (1577–1648) is regarded as one of Denmark's greatest rulers. Around this time overseas colonies were established, including Tranquebar (India), Danish Gold Coast (Ghana) and the Danish West Indies (the US Virgin Islands). However, in 1626 Denmark was defeated in the Thirty Years' War. Denmark lost Gotland and the Norwegian territories of Jämtland and Härjedalen to Sweden. In 1660 Sweden gained Skåne, Halland and Blekinge. A new constitution proclaimed the Danish king absolute sovereign. In 1661 the Supreme Court was established and in 1683 the law was codified.

In the Great Northern War, Denmark allied itself with Russia, the Netherlands and France, a policy which lasted for the rest of the 18th century. In the Napoleonic Wars, Denmark, smarting under the British bombardment of Copenhagen, allied itself to Napoleon. The price Denmark had to pay was signing away its rights to Norway, which it did by the treaty of Kiel in 1814. Danish possessions were now reduced to Iceland, Greenland, the Faeroes and Schleswig-Holstein. Holstein was lost to Germany in 1863 and Schleswig a year later. The surrender of so much rich agricultural land, with nearly 1m. inhabitants, brought Denmark to the edge of bankruptcy. But within a few years the country managed to pull itself back from one of the lowest points in its history. The economy benefited from a land-reclamation programme in Jutland. Socially, Bishop Grundtvig (founder of the folk high-schools), who reconciled patriotism with a reduced status for Denmark in European affairs, had a great influence. There were demands for a liberal constitution. In 1846 Anton Frederik Tscherning founded the Society of the Friends of the Peasant (Bondevennernes Selskab), which later became the Liberal Party (Venstre).

Social Reform

In 1901 the Left Reform Party (Venstrereformparti) came to power to introduce free-trade , popular education and changes in the revenue system to make income rather than land the criterion for taxation. The First World War gave neutral Denmark an improved export market but there was a shortage of raw materials. In 1929 a Social Democrat government, with Thorvald Stauning as prime minister, combined rural and urban interests in one of the most ambitious programmes of social reforms ever mounted. The 1930s Great Depression led to unemployment made worse when Britain favoured Commonwealth food imports over those from Denmark. In the late 1930s trade improved and industry expanded.

In 1939 when the Second World War broke out, Denmark again declared neutrality. On 9 April 1940 German troops entered and occupied the country. The Germans permitted Danish self-government until growing resistance led to a state of emergency. After the liberation a Liberal government was elected with Knud Kristensen as prime minister. Kristensen's campaign for the return of southern Schleswig from Germany brought down his government in 1947. Denmark joined NATO in 1949.

With its share of the Marshall Plan, Denmark entered on a new industrial revolution. By the mid-1950s the value of manufacturing equalled that of agriculture. However, there was a high rate of inflation. In 1953 the Social Democrats came back to power where they remained until the mid-1960s. By then the rate of inflation was higher than in any comparable country. In 1968 a centre-right coalition was elected, led by Hilmar Baunsgaard. But the change of government did not signify a change in strategy. Taxes were kept high and the budget expanded to increase social welfare. After the 1971 election, the Social Democrat leader Jens Otto Krag negotiated entry into the European Union, making Copenhagen the bridge between the Nordic capitals and Brussels. In 1982 a Conservative-led minority government was formed, led by Poul Schlüter, the first Conservative prime minister since 1901. He remained in power until 1993 when a Social Democratic coalition led by Poul Nyrup Rasmussen took office. Following the 2001 election, a right-wing government came to power. The new prime minister, Anders Fogh Rasmussen, advocated joining EMU (European Monetary Union) but this was rejected in a referendum in 2000.

TERRITORY AND POPULATION

Denmark is bounded in the west by the North Sea, northwest and north by the Skagerrak and Kattegat straits (separating it from Norway and Sweden), and south by Germany. A 16-km long fixed link with Sweden was opened in July 2000 when the Øresund motorway and railway bridge between Copenhagen and Malmö was completed.

Administrative divisions		Area (sq. km) 2004	Population 1 Jan. 2004	Population per sq. km 2004
København (Copenhagen)	(city)	88	501,664	5,684·6
Frederiksberg	(borough)	9	91,721	10,458·5
Københavns	(county)	528	618,407	1,170·6
Frederiksborg	(county)	1,347	373,688	277·3
Roskilde	(county)	891	237,089	266·0
Vestsjælland	(county)	2,984	302,479	101·4
Storstrøm	(county)	3,398	261,884	77·1
Bornholm	(county)	589	43,774	74·4
Fyn	(county)	3,486	475,082	136·3
Sønderjylland	(county)	3,939	252,936	64·2
Ribe	(county)	3,132	224,595	71·7
Vejle	(county)	2,997	355,691	118·7
Ringkøbing	(county)	4,854	274,830	56·6
Aarhus	(county)	4,561	653,472	143·3
Viborg	(county)	4,123	234,659	56·9
Nordjylland	(county)	6,173	492,669	80·3
Total		43,098	5,397,640	125·2

The UN gives a projected population for 2010 of 5·50m.

In 2004 an estimated 85·4% of the population lived in urban areas. In 2004, 92·8% of the inhabitants were born in Denmark, including the Faroe Islands and Greenland.

On 1 Jan. 2004 the population of the capital, Copenhagen (comprising Copenhagen, Frederiksberg and Gentofte munici-palities), was 662,089; Aarhus, 228,547; Odense, 145,554; Aalborg,

121,549; Esbjerg, 72,550; Randers, 55,739; Kolding, 54,941; Vejle, 49,917; Horsens, 49,652; Roskilde, 44,205.

The official language is Danish.

SOCIAL STATISTICS

Statistics for calendar years:

	Live births	Marriages	Divorces	Deaths	Emigration	Immigration
1999	66,220	35,439	13,537	59,179	41,340	50,236
2000	67,084	38,388	14,381	57,998	43,417	52,915
2001	65,458	36,567	14,597	58,338	43,980	55,984
2002	64,149	37,210	15,304	58,610	43,481	52,778
2003	64,682	35,041	15,763	57,574	43,466	49,754

2003 rates per 1,000 population: birth, 12·0; death, 10·7. Single-parent births: 1999, 44·9%; 2000, 44·6%; 2001, 44·6%; 2002, 44·6%; 2003, 44·9%. Denmark is the only west European country in which the percentage of births out of wedlock has declined in the past ten years. Annual population growth rate, 1992–2002, 0·3%. Suicide rate, 2000 (per 100,000 population) was 13·7 (men, 20·2; women, 7·3). Life expectancy at birth, 2003, was 74·8 years for males and 79·4 years for females. In 2003 the most popular age range for marrying was 30–34 for males and 25–29 for females. Infant mortality, 2003, 4·4 per 1,000 live births. Fertility rate, 2003, 1·8 births per woman. In 2003 Denmark received 4,593 asylum applications, equivalent to 0·9 per 1,000 inhabitants. In July 2002 a controversial new immigration law was introduced in an attempt to deter potential asylum seekers.

A UNICEF report published in 2005 showed that 2·4% of children in Demark live in poverty (in households with income below 50% of the national median), the lowest percentage of any country.

CLIMATE

The climate is much modified by marine influences and the effect of the Gulf Stream, to give winters that may be both cold or mild and often cloudy. Summers may be warm and sunny or chilly and rainy. Generally the east is drier than the west. Long periods of calm weather are exceptional and windy conditions are common. Copenhagen, Jan. 33°F (0·5°C), July 63°F (17°C). Annual rainfall 650 mm. Esbjerg, Jan. 33°F (0·5°C), July 61°F (16°C). Annual rainfall 800 mm. In general 10% of precipitation is snow.

CONSTITUTION AND GOVERNMENT

The present constitution is founded upon the Basic Law of 5 June 1953. The legislative power lies with the Queen and the *Folketing* (parliament) jointly. The executive power is vested in the monarch, who exercises authority through the ministers.

The reigning Queen is **Margrethe II**, b. 16 April 1940; married 10 June 1967 to Prince Henrik, b. Count de Monpezat. She succeeded to the throne on the death of her father, King Frederik IX, on 14 Jan. 1972. *Offspring:* Crown Prince Frederik, b. 26 May 1968, married 14 May 2004 Mary Elizabeth Donaldson, b. 5 Feb. 1972 (*offspring:* Prince Christian Valdemar Henri John, b. 15 Oct 2005); Prince Joachim, b. 7 June 1969; married 18 Nov. 1995 Alexandra Manley, b. 30 June 1964, divorced 8 April 2005 (*offspring:* Prince Nikolai William Alexander Frederik, b. 28 Aug. 1999; Prince Felix Henrik Valdemar Christian, b. 22 July 2002).

Sisters of the Queen. Princess Benedikte, b. 29 April 1944; married 3 Feb. 1968 to Prince Richard of Sayn-Wittgenstein-Berleburg; Princess Anne-Marie, b. 30 Aug. 1946; married 18 Sept. 1964 to King Constantine of Greece.

The crown was elective from the earliest times but became hereditary by right in 1660. The direct male line of the house of Oldenburg became extinct with King Frederik VII on 15 Nov. 1863. In view of the death of the king, without direct heirs, the

Great Powers signed a treaty at London on 8 May 1852, by the terms of which the succession to the crown was made over to Prince Christian of Schleswig-Holstein-Sonderburg-Glücksburg, and to the direct male descendants of his union with the Princess Louise of Hesse-Cassel. This became law on 31 July 1853. Linked to the constitution of 5 June 1953, a new law of succession, dated 27 March 1953, has come into force, which restricts the right of succession to the descendants of King Christian X and Queen Alexandrine, and admits the sovereign's daughters to the line of succession, ranking after the sovereign's sons.

The Queen receives a tax-free annual sum of 59·7m. kroner from the state (2004).

The judicial power is with the courts. The monarch must be a member of the Evangelical-Lutheran Church, the official Church of the State, and may not assume major international obligations without the consent of the Folketing. The Folketing consists of one chamber. All men and women of Danish nationality of more than 18 years of age and permanently resident in Denmark possess the franchise, and are eligible for election to the Folketing, which is at present composed of 179 members; 135 members are elected by the method of proportional representation in 17 constituencies. In order to attain an equal representation of the different parties, 40 additional seats are divided among such parties which have not obtained sufficient returns at the constituency elections. Two members are elected for the Faroe Islands and two for Greenland. The term of the legislature is four years, but a general election may be called at any time. The Folketing convenes every year on the first Tuesday in Oct. Besides its legislative functions, every six years it appoints judges who, together with the ordinary members of the Supreme Court, form the *Rigsret*, a tribunal which can alone try parliamentary impeachments.

National Anthem

'Kong Kristian stod ved højen mast' ('King Christian stood by the lofty mast'); words by J. Ewald, tune by D. L. Rogert.

GOVERNMENT CHRONOLOGY

Prime Ministers since 1945. (KF = Conservative Party; RV = Radical Liberal Party; SD = Social Democratic Party; V = Liberal Party)

1945	SD	Vilhelm Buhl
1945–47	V	Knud Kristensen
1947–50	SD	Hans Hedtoft
1950–53	V	Erik Eriksen
1953–55	SD	Hans Hedtoft
1955–60	SD	Hans Christian Hansen
1960–62	SD	Viggo Kampmann
1962–68	SD	Jens Otto Krag
1968–71	RV	Hilmar Baunsgaard
1971–72	SD	Jens Otto Krag
1972–73	SD	Anker Jørgensen
1973–75	V	Poul Hartling
1975–82	SD	Anker Jørgensen
1982–93	KF	Poul Holmskov Schlüter
1993–2001	SD	Poul Nyrup Rasmussen
2001–	V	Anders Fogh Rasmussen

RECENT ELECTIONS

Parliamentary elections were held on 8 Feb. 2005; turnout was 84·5%. The Liberal Party (V) won 52 seats, with 29·1% of votes cast (56 seats with 31·3% in 2001); the Social Democratic Party (SD) 47 with 25·9% (52 with 29·1%); the Danish People's Party (DF) 24 with 13·2% (22 with 12·0%); the Conservative Party (KF) 18 with 10·3% (16 with 9·1%); the Radical Liberal Party (RV) 17 with 9·2% (9 with 5·2%); the Socialist People's Party (SF) 11 with 6·0% (12 with 6·4%); the Unity List—the Red Greens (E) 6 with 3·4% (4 with 2·4%). Four remaining seats go to representative parties from the Faroe Islands and Greenland.

European Parliament

Denmark has 14 (16 in 1999) representatives. At the June 2004 elections turnout was 47·9% (49·9% in 1999). The SD won 5 seats with 32·7% of votes cast (political affiliation in European Parliament: Party of European Socialists); V, 3 with 19·4% (Alliance of Liberals and Democrats for Europe); KF, 1 with 11·3% (European People's Party–European Democrats); the June Movement, 1 with 9·1% (Independence and Democracy Group); the SF, 1 with 8·0% (Greens/European Free Alliance); DF, 1 with 6·8% (Union for a Europe of Nations); RV, 1 with 6·4% (Alliance of Liberals and Democrats for Europe); the People's Anti-EU Movement, 1 with 5·2% (European Unitary Left/Nordic Green Left).

CURRENT ADMINISTRATION

Following the 2001 election a coalition government of the Liberal Party (V) and Conservatives (KF) was formed. The coalition was re-elected in Feb. 2005. The government relies on the support of the far-right, anti-immigrant Danish People's Party, although it is not represented in the cabinet. In March 2006 the government comprised:

Prime Minister: Anders Fogh Rasmussen; b. 1953 (V; sworn in on 27 Nov. 2001).

Minister of Culture: Brian Mikkelsen (KF). *Defence:* Søren Gade (V). *Development Co-operation:* Ulla Tørnæs (V). *Economic and Business Affairs:* Bendt Bendtsen (KF). *Education and Ecclesiastical Affairs:* Bertel Haarder (V). *Employment:* Claus Hjort Frederiksen (V). *Environment and Nordic Co-operation:* Connie Hedegaard (KF). *Family and Consumer Affairs:* Lars Barfoed (KF). *Finance:* Thor Pedersen (V). *Food, Agriculture and Fisheries:* Hans Christian Schmidt (V). *Foreign Affairs:* Dr Per Stig Møller (KF). *Interior and Health:* Lars Løkke Rasmussen (V). *Justice:* Lene Espersen (KF). *Refugees, Immigration and Integration:* Rikke Hvilshøj (V). *Science, Technology and Innovation:* Helge Sander (V). *Social Affairs and Gender Equality:* Eva Kjer Hansen (V). *Taxation:* Kristian Jensen (V). *Transport and Energy:* Flemming Hansen (KF).

Office of the Prime Minister: http://www.statsministeriet.dk

CURRENT LEADERS

Anders Fogh Rasmussen

Position
Prime Minister

Introduction
Anders Fogh Rasmussen became Denmark's prime minister in Nov. 2001. His Liberal Party (Venstre or V) had the largest representation in parliament, but to form a government he had to form a coalition with the Conservatives. Although espousing a centre-right line, his government is supported by the far-right Danish People's Party. Following the 2005 general election, he was the first Liberal leader to win a second consecutive term of office.

Early Life
Fogh Rasmussen was born on 26 Jan. 1953 in Ginnerup, Jutland. He joined the Young Liberals (Venstres Ungdom) in 1970 and stood unsuccessfully as the Liberal parliamentary candidate for Viborg in Jan. 1973. The following year he was elected chairman of the Young Liberals, a post he held for two years.

In 1978 Fogh Rasmussen graduated with a masters degree in economics from Aarhus University. In the same year he joined the Folketing as a replacement member for Viborg County. He had previously been in parliament for three months as cover for another member on sick leave.

From 1981–86 Fogh Rasmussen was vice chairman of the Folketing's housing committee, and in 1985 was appointed the

Liberal Party's deputy chairman. After re-election at the 1987 general election, he became taxation minister, adding the role of finance minister in 1990. However, he was forced to resign two years later after a government commission concluded he had provided misleading information to parliament, although he denied the allegations.

In April 1998 he was elected Liberal chairman, having been its spokesman since 1992. Following the attacks on the USA in Sept. 2001, the incumbent Social Democrat prime minister, Poul Nyrup Rasmussen, called a snap election when his popularity ratings were high. The election campaign was fought largely on the issue of immigration, with Fogh Rasmussen gaining popular support for his proposed hard line. Having defeated the Social Democrats, he took office on 27 Nov. 2001.

Career in Office
Forming a minority coalition with the Conservatives, Fogh Rasmussen's key pledges for his first term in office were health reforms, better care provisions for the elderly, an increase in maternity leave, stiffer sentences for criminals and a ceiling on taxes. He also promised a tightening up of immigration laws. There were concerns, however, among Denmark's European neighbours about the parliamentary backing for (and potential influence on) his government from the far-right Danish People's Party (which had doubled its parliamentary representation in 2001). In foreign policy, Fogh Rasmussen was supportive of the US-led military campaign in Iraq in 2003. In Feb. 2005 he was re-elected as prime minister, again in coalition with the Conservatives with the parliamentary support of the Danish People's Party.

Fogh Rasmussen is a strong advocate of the European Union. Under Denmark's presidency from July–Dec. 2002 the EU concluded negotiations for the accession to membership of ten new candidate countries. A referendum in Denmark on the proposed new EU constitutional treaty was postponed indefinitely following the European Council meeting in June 2005.

DEFENCE

Pursuant to the new Defence Agreement covering 2005–09 the Danish defence system will be completely restructured. A new security mechanism is being built from scratch to make it relevant in today's security environment. The entire transformation process centres on increasing Denmark's deployable capabilities. The composition of armed forces personnel has changed to 60:40 in favour of operational elements. Change has been accomplished by establishing so-called functional services in a number of areas formerly run by each individual service, and by reducing the staff- and support structure.

Denmark will be able simultaneously to deploy 2,000 soldiers on international missions and offer considerable High Readiness forces to NATO or coalition partners. The Armed Forces as a whole have been professionalized. Formal conscription still exists, but no specific combat training takes place. New conscripts train for four months in basic Homeland Defence, for example fire fighting, relief work during *force majeure* and basic weapons handling. The 20% of conscripts expected to sign up for additional time undergo military training focussing on participation in international operations for eight months and then deploy on an international assignment for six months.

The overall organization of the Danish Armed Forces includes the Ministry of Defence (MoD), the Danish Defence Command, the Army, the Navy, the Air Force and several joint service institutions and authorities; to this should be added the Home Guard, which is an integral part of Danish military defence. The Chief of Defence (CHOD), answering to the Minister of Defence, is in full command of the Army, the Navy and the Air Force.

Denmark has a compulsory military service with mobilization based on The Constitution of 1849. This states that it is the duty of every fit man to contribute to the national defence. In 2004 defence expenditure totalled US$2,750m. (US$519 per capita), representing 1·2% of GDP.

Army
The Danish Army is comprised of field army formations and local defence forces. The peacetime strength of the Danish Army is approximately 13,200. The Army's military wartime establishment would be about 46,000. The Danish Army is organized in two brigades, the first made up of professional soldiers and the second functioning as a training structure for conscripts.

Navy
The peacetime strength of the Royal Danish Navy is approximately 4,100. The naval wartime establishment would be about 7,300. The two main naval bases are located at Frederikshavn and Korsør.

Air Force
The peacetime strength of the Royal Danish Air Force is approximately 4,100. The wartime establishment would be about 11,600. The Royal Danish Air Force consists of Tactical Air Command Denmark and the Danish Air Materiel Command.

Home Guard (Hjemmeværnet)
The overall Home Guard organization comprises the Home Guard Command, the Army Home Guard, the Naval Home Guard, the Air Force Home Guard and supporting institutions. The personnel are recruited on a voluntary basis. The personnel establishment of the Home Guard is approximately 57,000 soldiers.

INTERNATIONAL RELATIONS

In a referendum in June 1992 the electorate voted against ratifying the Maastricht Treaty for closer political union within the EU. Turn-out was 82%. 50·7% of votes were against ratification, 49·3% in favour. However, a second referendum on 18 May 1993 reversed this result, with 56·8% of votes cast in favour of ratification and 43·2% against. Turn-out was 86·2%. In a referendum held on 28 Sept. 2000 Danish voters rejected their country's entry into the common European currency, 53·2% opposing membership of the euro against 46·8% voting in favour. Turn-out was 87·6%.

Denmark gave US$2·0bn. in international aid in 2004, which at 0·85% of GNI made it the second most generous country as a percentage of its gross national income, after Norway.

Denmark is a member of the UN, WTO, BIS, NATO, OECD, the EU, Council of Europe, OSCE, CERN, Nordic Council, Council of the Baltic Sea States, Inter-American Development Bank, Asian Development Bank, IOM and the Antarctic Treaty. On 19 Dec. 1996 Denmark acceded to the Schengen accord of June 1990 which abolishes border controls between Denmark, Austria, Belgium, Finland, France, Germany, Greece, Iceland, Italy, Luxembourg, the Netherlands, Norway, Portugal, Spain and Sweden.

ECONOMY

In 2002 agriculture accounted for 2·6% of GDP, industry 26·5% and services 70·9%.

According to the Berlin-based organization *Transparency International*, in 2005 Denmark ranked fourth in the world in a 2005 survey of countries with the least corruption in business and government. It received 9·5 out of 10 in the corruption perceptions index.

Overview
After weak growth during the Scandinavian banking crisis of 1991–93, the Danish economy grew robustly from 1994–2004. During the period 2001–03 Denmark avoided recession in the face of a global economic slowdown but averaged annual growth

of less than 1%. The growth of both foreign and domestic demand was instrumental in the economic revival from 2004. Income tax cuts passed in 2004 and a hot real estate market boosted consumer demand in 2005. Investment growth and a strong export performance also helped growth. Denmark has enjoyed a comfortable balance of payments surplus in recent years and is a net exporter of both food and energy.

Until the 1960s Denmark's economy was heavily based on its competitive agricultural sector. In 1960 roughly a fifth of the labour force was employed in agriculture while 40% were employed in manufacturing and construction. Since then the percentage of total employment in the manufacturing and agriculture and fishing sectors has shrunk while employment in public and private services has grown. By 2003 agriculture accounted for only 4% of employment and manufacturing and construction 23%. Almost three-quarters of Denmark's current workforce are employed in services. The segment of the economy with the greatest proportional gain in employment in the last half-century is public services, which accounted for only 10% of total employment in 1960 and now accounts for a third.

Denmark's research and development (R&D) expenditure to GDP ratio was below the EU and OECD average in the early 1990s but has since increased substantially. In the period 1993–2003 total R&D expenditure nearly doubled. Expenditure grew particularly in the private sector, which has come to account for over two-thirds of total R&D expenditure. In 2002 R&D expenditure as a share of GDP reached 2·5%, a level below that of Sweden and Finland but well above both the EU and OECD averages. R&D is particularly high in manufacturing and is also high in knowledge services such as information and communications technologies and, increasingly, financial services.

In 2005 *Transparency International* ranked Denmark the fourth least corrupt country in the world. It also has one of the world's lowest Gini coefficients, a measure of income inequality. Income taxes were cut by the centre-right governing coalition in 2004 but Denmark retains a high tax rate and a large public sector, which are generally not thought to be a drag on the economy. In the 2005 *World Economic Forum* Competitiveness Report, Denmark was ranked fourth, close behind third-placed Sweden. Denmark's low corruption environment has ensured that government revenues have helped to build world-class educational establishments and a social safety net that does not create a disincentive to work. In the latter half of the 1990s unemployment fell from double-digits and since 1998 has remained within the range of 4–6%. However, the OECD recommends that measures involving lower taxes and less public spending would increase labour supply.

Currency

The monetary unit is the *Danish krone* (DKK) of 100 øre. Inflation rates (based on OECD statistics):

1995	1996	1997	1998	1999	2000	2001	2002	2003	2004
2·1%	2·1%	2·2%	1·8%	2·5%	2·9%	2·4%	2·4%	2·1%	1·2%

The inflation rate in 2005 according to Statistics Denmark was 1·8%.

Foreign exchange reserves were 236,300m. kroner in 2003 and gold reserves 2·14m. troy oz. In June 2000 the money supply was 387,135m. kroner.

While not participating directly in EMU, the Danish krone is pegged to the new currency in ERM-2, the successor to the exchange rate mechanism.

Budget

The following shows the actual revenue and expenditure in central government accounts for the calendar years 2002 and 2003, the approved budget figures for 2004 and the budget for 2005 (in 1,000 kroner):

	2002	2003	2004	2005
Revenue[1]	438,721,400	436,932,600	454,819,900	476,544,600
Expenditure[1]	409,903,800	420,626,700	440,347,700	451,486,600

[1]Receipts and expenditures of special government funds and expenditures on public works are included.

The 2005 budget envisaged revenue of 142,312·7m. kroner from income and property taxes and 228,720·0m. kroner from consumer taxes. The central government debt on 31 Dec. 2003 amounted to 535,838m. kroner.

VAT is 25%.

Performance

Real GDP growth rates (based on OECD statistics):

1995	1996	1997	1998	1999	2000	2001	2002	2003	2004
3·1%	2·8%	3·2%	2·2%	2·6%	3·5%	0·7%	0·5%	0·6%	2·1%

Total GDP was US$243·0bn. in 2004. Denmark was placed fourth in both the Growth Competitiveness Index and the Business Competitiveness Index in the World Economic Forum's *Global Competitiveness Report 2005–2006*.

The *OECD Economic Survey* of July 2003 reported: 'The Danish economy has continued to perform well despite the weak international economic climate. The macroeconomic policy framework provides a sound underpinning for a policy stance that aims to guide the country safely through short-term developments by steadfastly focusing on medium-term priorities rather than allowing itself to be blown off course. This steady-as-she goes approach enables policymakers to concentrate most of their efforts on addressing the longer-term challenges it faces.'

Banking and Finance

On 31 Dec. 2001 the accounts of the National Bank (*Chairman of the Board of Governors*, Nils Bernstein) balanced at 295,286m. kroner. The assets included official net foreign reserves of 148,427m. kroner. The liabilities included notes and coins totalling 47,299m. kroner. On 31 Dec. 2000 there were 97 commercial banks and savings banks, with deposits of 757,625m. kroner.

The two largest commercial banks are Den Danske Bank and Unibank, which merged with MeritaNordbanken in 2000 and now forms part of the Stockholm-based Nordea group. The supervisory boards of all banks must include public representation.

There is a stock exchange in Copenhagen.

ENERGY AND NATURAL RESOURCES

Environment

Denmark's carbon dioxide emissions from the consumption and flaring of fossil fuels in 2002 were the equivalent of 10·3 tonnes per capita.

Electricity

Installed capacity was 12·9m. kW in 2003. Production (2003), 43,757m. kWh. Consumption per capita in 2003 was 6,378 kWh. In 2003 some 5,560 wind turbines produced 13% of output.

Oil and Gas

Oil production was (2003) 18·3m. tonnes with 1,700m. bbls. of proven reserves. Production of natural gas was (2003) 7·1bn. cu. metres with 136bn. cu. metres of proven reserves.

Wind

Denmark is one of the world's largest wind-power producers, with an installed capacity of 2,886 MW at the end of 2002. Denmark generates 13% of its electricity from wind, the highest proportion of any country.

Agriculture

Agriculture accounted for 11·0% of exports and 2·6% of imports in 2001. Land ownership is widely distributed. In May 2003 there were 48,613 holdings with at least 5 ha. of agricultural area (or at least a production equivalent to that from 5 ha. of barley). There were 9,829 small holdings (with less than 10 ha.), 21,605 medium-sized holdings (10–50 ha.) and 17,181 holdings with more than 50 ha. Approximately 5·0% of all agricultural land is used for organic farming. There were 28,232 agricultural workers in 2003. In 2003 Denmark had 2·29m. ha. of arable land and 8,000 ha. of permanent crops.

In 2003 the cultivated area was (in 1,000 ha.): grain, 1,487; green fodder and grass, 622; set aside, 207; root crops, 94; other crops, 217; pulses, 31; total cultivated area, 2,658.

Chief crops	Area (1,000 ha.)				Production (in 1,000 tonnes)			
	2000	2001	2002	2003[1]	2000	2001	2002	2003[1]
Wheat	628	634	577	664	4,693	4,664	4,059	4,701
Barley	741	744	825	710	3,980	3,966	4,121	3,776
Potatoes	39	38	38	36	1,645	1,543	1,504	1,412
Oats	45	60	55	50	233	292	276	260
Rye	51	65	46	33	263	332	230	169
Other root crops	77	70	68	58	4,498	4,048	4,102	3,404

[1]Provisional figures.

Livestock, 2002 (in 1,000): pigs, 12,732; cattle, 2,000; sheep, 131; horses, 38; poultry, 20,580.

Production (in 1,000 tonnes) in 2002: pork and bacon, 1,892; beef, 169; milk, 4,445; cheese, 318; eggs, 81; butter, 47.

In 2001 tractors numbered 123,000 and harvester-threshers 23,300.

Forestry

The area under forests in 2000 was 486,000 ha., or 11·3% of the total land area. Timber production in 2003 was 1·81m. cu. metres.

Fisheries

The total value of the fish caught was (in 1m. kroner): 1950, 156; 1955, 252; 1960, 376; 1965, 650; 1970, 854; 1975, 1,442; 1980, 2,888; 1985, 3,542; 1990, 3,485; 1995, 3,020; 2000, 3,141; 2003, 2,748.

In 2003 the total catch was 1,035,857 tonnes, almost exclusively from sea fishing. Denmark is the leading fishing nation in the EU.

INDUSTRY

The leading companies by market capitalization in Denmark in Nov. 2005 were: A. P. Møller-Mærsk (US$38·1bn.), a shipping company; Den Danske Bank (US$20·5bn.); and Novo Nordisk A/S (US$15·0bn.), a health care company.

The following table is of gross value added by kind of activity (in 1m. kroner; 1995 constant prices):

	2001	2002[1]	2003[1]
Total	1,017,068	1,026,029	1,031,246
Agriculture, fishing and quarrying	50,709	49,822	51,301
Manufacturing	168,651	168,472	168,614
Electricity, gas and water supply	22,551	21,147	20,330
Construction	51,335	51,666	50,285
Trade, hotels and restaurants	163,810	166,055	167,569
Transport, storage and communications	94,756	97,430	99,960
Financial intermediation, business activities	250,356	253,699	254,808
Public and personal services	256,357	260,939	262,407
Financial intermediation services indirectly measured	−41,457	−43,201	−44,028

[1]Provisional or estimated figures.

In the following table 'number of jobs' refers to 18,530 local activity units including single-proprietor units (Nov. 2002):

Branch of industry	Number of jobs
Food, beverages and tobacco	84,425
Textiles, wearing apparel, leather	12,022
Wood and wood products	14,898
Paper products	55,170
Refined petroleum products	646
Chemicals and man-made fibres	29,806
Rubber and plastic products	22,296
Non-metallic mineral products	17,560
Basic metals	53,669
Machinery and equipment	67,004
Electrical and optical equipment	53,118
Transport equipment	15,158
Furniture, other manufactures	30,379
Total manufacturing	456,511

Labour

In 2003 the labour force was 2,860,636. 35·2% of the working population in 2002 were in public and personal services; 18·0% in wholesale and retail trade, hotels and restaurants; 16·7% in manufacturing; 13·7% in financial intermediation, commerce, etc.; 6·4% in transport, storage and telecommunications; 6·1% in construction; 3·7% in agriculture, fisheries and quarrying; and 0·5% in electricity, gas and water supply. In 2003, 439,120 persons were employed in manufacturing. Retirement age is 67. In Dec. 2005 the unemployment rate was 4·4%. In 2003 Denmark lost 22 working days to strikes per 1,000 employees.

INTERNATIONAL TRADE

Imports and Exports

In 2003 imports totalled 369,700·9m. kroner and exports 429,272·2m. kroner.

Imports and exports (in 1m. kroner) for calendar years:

Leading commodities	2002[1]		2003[1]	
	Imports	Exports	Imports	Exports
Live animals, meat and meat preparations	4,146	29,335	4,575	27,270
Dairy products and eggs	2,927	11,051	2,840	10,797
Fish, crustaceans, etc. and preparations	9,599	16,250	9,197	15,365
Cereals and cereal preparations	3,287	5,185	3,275	5,164
Fodder for animals	5,387	4,435	5,344	4,205
Wood and cork	4,492	980	4,699	771
Textile fibres, yarns, fabrics, etc.	8,523	8,501	8,060	8,210
Mineral fuels, lubricants, etc.	15,127	28,346	16,063	28,857
Chemicals and plastics	18,190	13,944	17,601	14,313
Medicine and pharmaceutical products	10,564	30,374	11,296	32,190
Metals, manufacture of metals	28,298	19,598	28,079	19,614
Machinery, electrical, equipment, etc.	102,951	110,380	94,723	101,124
Transport equipment	41,632	19,320	36,201	17,117
Furniture, etc.	5,653	15,754	6,068	15,773
Clothing and clothing accessories	17,985	14,931	17,780	15,048

[1]Excluding trade not distributed.

Distribution of foreign trade (in 1m. kroner) according to countries of origin and destination for 2003:

Countries	Imports[1]	Exports[1]
Austria	4,643·5	4,440·9
Belgium	12,814·5	7,879·7
Canada	1,220·8	3,612·8
China	13,622·5	5,010·4
Finland	8,568·2	13,713·0
France and Monaco	17,926·7	21,706·6
Germany	85,582·6	79,685·1
Greece	900·8	3,388·5

Countries	Imports[1]	Exports[1]
Greenland	2,117·4	2,405·0
Hong Kong	1,589·3	3,984·5
Ireland	4,466·1	6,485·4
Italy	15,340·5	14,397·1
Japan	3,154·6	13,322·4
Netherlands	25,616·2	19,960·8
Norway	16,688·9	24,538·3
Poland	6,721·2	6,777·0
Russia	3,966·3	5,703·5
Singapore	3,119·9	1,853·4
South Korea	4,228·6	2,389·0
Spain	6,478·5	13,466·4
Sweden	47,708·5	54,381·0
Switzerland	4,184·0	4,882·7
Turkey	3,368·4	2,006·2
United Kingdom	25,947·0	36,454·0
United States of America	11,988·6	26,178·0

[1]Excluding trade not distributed.

In 2003 other European Union member countries accounted for 70·1% of imports and 64·8% of exports.

COMMUNICATIONS

Roads

Denmark proper had (1 Jan. 2004) 1,027 km of motorways, 649 km of other state roads, 9,682 km of other provincial roads and 60,717 km of commercial roads. Motor vehicles registered at 1 Jan. 2004 comprised 1,894,649 passenger cars, 34,896 trucks, 365,112 vans, 17,217 taxi cabs (including 11,296 for private hire), 14,132 buses and 87,779 motorcycles. There were 8,844 road accidents in 2003, resulting in 432 fatalities.

Rail

In 2003 there were 2,273 km of State railways of 1,435 mm gauge (641 km electrified), which carried 154m. passengers and 7·71m. tonnes of freight. There were also 495 km of private railways. A metro system was opened in Copenhagen in 2002.

Civil Aviation

The main international airport is at Copenhagen (Kastrup), and there are also international flights from Aalborg, Aarhus, Billund and Esbjerg. The Scandinavian Airlines System (SAS) resulted from the 1950 merger of the three former Scandinavian airlines. SAS Denmark A/S is the Danish partner (SAS Norge ASA and SAS Sverige AB being the other two). Denmark and Norway each hold two-sevenths of the capital of SAS and Sweden three-sevenths.

On 1 Jan. 2001 Denmark had 1,089 aircraft with a capacity of 23,110 seats. In 2001 there were 305,636 take-offs and landings to and from abroad, and 335,392 to and from Danish airports, including local flights. Copenhagen (Kastrup) handled 9,124,447 departing passengers in 2001, Billund 849,761, Aalborg 348,390 and Aarhus 327,399.

Shipping

On 1 Jan. 2004 the merchant fleet consisted of 660 vessels (above 20 GRT) totalling 7·3m. GRT. In 2003, 45m. tonnes of cargo were unloaded and 35m. tonnes were loaded in Danish ports; traffic by passenger ships and ferries is not included.

Telecommunications

In 2003 there were 8,380,100 telephone subscribers (1,552 per 1,000 persons), including 4,767,300 mobile phone subscribers. In June 2002 there were 3·37m. Internet users (62·73% of the population). There were 3·1m. PCs in use in 2002 (576·8 per 1,000 persons).

Postal Services

In 2003 there were 1,019 post offices.

SOCIAL INSTITUTIONS

Justice

The lowest courts of justice are organized in 82 tribunals (byretter), where minor cases are dealt with by a single judge. The tribunal at Copenhagen has one president and 49 other judges; and Aarhus one president and 15 other judges; the other tribunals have one to 11 judges. Cases of greater consequence are dealt with by the two High Courts (Landsretterne); these courts are also courts of appeal for minor cases. The Eastern High Court in Copenhagen has one president and 65 other judges; and the Western in Viborg one president and 38 other judges. From these an appeal lies to the Supreme Court in Copenhagen, composed of a president and 18 other judges. Judges under 65 years of age can be removed only by judicial sentence.

In 2003 there were 15,735 convictions for males and 1,722 for females for violations of the criminal code, fines not included. In 2003 the daily average population in penal institutions was 3,641 (67·6 per 100,000 of national population).

Education

Education has been compulsory since 1814. The first stage of the Danish education system is the basic school (education at first level). This starts with an optional pre-school year (education preceding the first level) and continues up to and including the optional 10th year in the folkeskole (municipal primary and lower secondary school). In 2003, 704,668 pupils attended education at first level and second level, first stage. Of this group, 69,165 began their education at pre-school, while 156,953 attended grades 8 to 10.

Of all students leaving basic school in 1997–98, 76·1% had commenced further education after a period of three months. Almost half the students had elected to attend general upper-secondary education (general programmes of education at secondary level, second stage), while 27% opted for a vocational education at secondary level, second stage.

Education that qualifies students for tertiary level education is called general upper-secondary education and comprises general upper-secondary education (general programmes of education at second level, second stage), such as gymnasium (upper-secondary school), higher preparatory examination, and adult upper-secondary level courses as well as general/vocational upper secondary education at the vocational education institutions. In 2003, 103,674 students attended general upper-secondary education.

Higher education is divided into three levels: short-cycle higher education involves two years of training, sometimes practical, after completion of upper-secondary education (31,350 students in 2003); medium-cycle higher education involves two–four years of mainly theoretical training (71,580 students in 2003); long-cycle higher education requires more than four years of education, mainly theoretical, divided between a bachelors' degree and a candidate programme (51,196 students in bachelors' programmes in 2003 and 57,030 in the candidate programme). Universities, 1997–98: the University of Copenhagen (founded 1479), 29,389 students; the University of Aarhus (founded in 1928), 17,901 students; the University of Odense (founded in 1964), 9,127 students; the University of Aalborg (founded in 1974), 8,927 students; Roskilde University Centre (founded in 1972), 5,719 students. The Technical University of Denmark had 6,372 students in 1997–98. Eight engineering colleges had 6,126 students.

Other types of post-secondary education (2002): the Royal Veterinary and Agricultural University had 3,240 students; the Danish School of Pharmacy, 1,189 students; 7 colleges of economics, business administration and modern languages, 17,354 students; 2 schools of architecture, 2,326 students; 7 academies of music, 1,399 students; 2 schools of library and information science, 958 students; the Educational University of

Denmark, 2,737 students; 4 schools of social work, 2,213 students; the Danish School of Journalism, 963 students; 9 colleges of physiotherapy, 3,794 students; 2 schools of Midwifery Education, 294 students; 2 colleges of home economics, 873 students; the School of Visual Arts, 186 students; 23 schools of nursing, 9,772 students; 3 military academies, 586 students.

In 2002 total expenditure on education came to 15% of total government spending.

The adult literacy rate in 2003 was at least 99%.

Health

In 2001 there were 15,598 doctors (292 per 100,000 persons), 4,619 dentists, 51,669 nurses, 39,197 auxiliary nurses and 1,308 midwives. There were 68 hospitals in 2002 (provision of 18,683 beds in 2000). In 2003 Denmark spent 9·0% of its GDP on health. In 2004 an estimated 31% of men and 32% of women smoked. The rate among women is one of the highest in the world.

Welfare

The main body of Danish social welfare legislation is consolidated in seven acts concerning: (1) public health security, (2) sick-day benefits, (3) social pensions (for early retirement and old age), (4) employment injuries insurance, (5) employment services, unemployment insurance and activation measures, (6) social assistance including assistance to handicapped, rehabilitation, child and juvenile guidance, daycare institutions, care of the aged and sick, and (7) family allowances.

Public health security, covering the entire population, provides free medical care, substantial subsidies for certain essential medicines together with some dental care, and a funeral allowance. Hospitals are primarily municipal and treatment is normally free. All employed workers are granted daily sickness allowances; others can have limited daily sickness allowances. Daily cash benefits are granted in the case of temporary incapacity because of illness, injury or childbirth to all persons in paid employment. The benefit is paid up to the rate of 100% of the average weekly earnings. There is, however, a maximum rate of 3,016 kroner a week.

Social pensions cover the entire population. Entitlement to the old-age pension at the full rate is subject to the condition that the beneficiary has been ordinarily resident in Denmark for 40 years. For a shorter period of residence, the benefits are reduced proportionally. The basic amount of the old-age pension in Jan. 2004 was 163,968 kroner a year to married couples and 111,924 to single persons. Various supplementary allowances, depending on age and income, may be payable with the basic amount. The retirement age is 65, or 67 for those born before 1 July 1939. Depending on health and income, persons aged 60–64 (60–66 for those born before 1 July 1939) may apply for an early retirement pension. Persons over 65 (or 67) years of age are entitled to the basic amount. The pensions to a married couple are calculated and paid to the husband and the wife separately. Early retirement pension to a disabled person is payable at ages 18–64 (or 66) years, at a rate of 166,740 kroner to a single person. Early retirement pensions may be subject to income regulation. The same applies to the old-age pension.

Employment injuries insurance provides for disability or survivors' pensions and compensations. The scheme covers practically all employees.

Employment services are provided by regional public employment agencies. Insurance against unemployment provides daily allowances and covers about 85% of the unemployed. The unemployment insurance system is based on state subsidized insurance funds linked to the trade unions. The unemployment insurance funds had a membership of 2,147,015 in Nov. 2004.

The *Social Assistance Act* comprises three acts (the act on active social policy, the act on social service and the act on integration of foreigners). From these acts individual benefits are applied, in contrast to the other fields of social legislation which apply to fixed benefits. Total social expenditure, including hospital and health services, statutory pensions, etc. amounted in the financial year 2003 to 420,123·7m. kroner.

RELIGION

There is complete religious liberty. The state church is the Evangelical-Lutheran to which 84·3% of the population belonged in 2002. It is divided into ten dioceses, each with a Bishop. The Bishop together with the Chief Administrative Officer of the county make up the diocesan-governing body, responsible for all matters of ecclesiastical local finance and general administration. Bishops are appointed by the Crown after an election by the clergy and parish council members. Each diocese is divided into a number of deaneries (111 in the whole country), each with its own Dean and Deanery Committee, who have certain financial powers.

CULTURE

World Heritage Sites

Denmark has four sites on the UNESCO World Heritage List: the burial mounds, runic stones and church at Jelling (inscribed on the list in 1994); Roskilde Cathedral (1995); Kronborg Castle (2000); and Ilulissat Icefjord (2004), the sea mouth of Sermeq Kujalleq in Greenland.

Broadcasting

Danmarks Radio is the government broadcasting station and is financed by household licence fees. Television is broadcast by *Danmarks Radio* and *TV2* with colour programmes by PAL system. Number of licences (2003): TV, 2·15m., including 2·14m. colour sets. Denmark had 1·28m. cable TV subscribers in 2003. There were 7·2m. radio receivers in 2000 and 4·6m. television receivers in 2001.

Cinema

In 2003 there were 379 auditoria. Total attendance in 2003 was 12·3m.; in 2003 net box office receipts came to 582m. kroner. 33 full-length films were made in 2003.

Press

In 2003 there were 32 daily newspapers with a combined circulation of 1·38m. The newspaper with the largest average circulation in the period Jan.–June 2003 was *Jyllands-Posten* (172,000 on weekdays and 231,000 on Sundays), followed by *Berlingske Tidende* (142,000 on weekdays and 165,000 on Sundays) and *Politiken* (137,000 on weekdays and 173,000 on Sundays).

Tourism

In 2003, 3,352,000 foreign tourists visited Denmark. In 2001 tourists spent some 39,078m. kroner. Foreigners spent 5,925,000 nights in hotels and 3,557,000 nights at camping sites in 2003.

Libraries

In 2002 there were 764 public libraries, one National library and 43 Higher Education libraries. They held a combined 100,385,000 volumes.

DIPLOMATIC REPRESENTATIVES

Of Denmark in the United Kingdom (55 Sloane St., London, SW1X 9SR)
Ambassador: Tom Risdahl Jensen.

Of the United Kingdom in Denmark (Kastelsvej 36–40, DK-2100, Copenhagen Ø)
Ambassador: Sir Nicholas Browne, KBE, CMG.

Of Denmark in the USA (3200 Whitehaven St., NW, Washington, D.C., 20008)
Ambassador: Friis Arne Petersen.

Of the USA in Denmark (Dag Hammarskjölds Allé 24, DK-2100, Copenhagen Ø)
Ambassador: James Cain.

Of Denmark to the United Nations
Ambassador: Ellen Margrethe Løj.

FURTHER READING

Statistical Information: Danmarks Statistik (Sejrøgade 11, DK-2100 Copenhagen Ø. *Website:* http://www.dst.dk/) was founded in 1849 and reorganized in 1966 as an independent institution; it is administratively placed under the Minister of Economic Affairs. Its main publications are: *Statistisk Årbog* (Statistical Yearbook). From 1896: *Statistiske Efterretninger* (Statistical News). *Konjunkturstatistik* (Main indicators); *Statistisk Tiårsoversigt* (Statistical Ten-Year Review).

Dania polyglotta. Annual Bibliography of Books . . . in Foreign Languages Printed in Denmark. State Library, Copenhagen. Annual
Kongelig Dansk Hof og Statskalender. Copenhagen. Annual
Jespersen, Knud J. V., *History of Denmark.* Palgrave Macmillan, Basingstoke, 2004
Larsen, Henrik, *Analysing Small State Foreign Policy in the EU: The Case of Denmark.* Palgrave Macmillan, Basingstoke, 2005
Petersson, O., *The Government and Politics of the Nordic Countries.* Stockholm, 1994
Turner, Barry, (ed.) *Scandinavia Profiled.* Macmillan, London, 2000

National library: Det kongelige Bibliotek, P.O.B. 2149, DK-1016 Copenhagen K. *Director:* Erland Kolding Nielsen.
National Statistical Office: Statistics Denmark, Copenhagen. *Director General:* Jan Plovsing.
Website: http://www.dst.dk/

The Faroe Islands

Føroyar/Færøerne

KEY HISTORICAL EVENTS

A Norwegian province until the peace treaty of 14 Jan. 1814, the islands have been represented by two members in the Danish parliament since 1851. In 1852 they were granted an elected parliament which in 1948 secured a degree of home-rule. The islands are not part of the EU. Recently, negotiations for independence were given a push by the prospect of exploiting offshore oil and gas.

TERRITORY AND POPULATION

The archipelago is situated due north of Scotland, 300 km from the Shetland Islands, 675 km from Norway and 450 km from Iceland, with a total land area of 1,399 sq. km (540 sq. miles). There are 17 inhabited islands (the main ones being Streymoy, Eysturoy, Vágoy, Suðuroy, Sandoy and Borðoy) and numerous islets, all mountainous and of volcanic origin. Population in Dec. 2004 was 48,400; density, 34·6 per sq. km. In 2003 an estimated 61·4% of the population lived in rural areas. The capital is Tórshavn (12,600 residents in 2004) on Streymoy.
The official languages are Faroese and Danish.

SOCIAL STATISTICS

Birth rate per 1,000 inhabitants (2002), 15·0; death rate, 8·3. Life expectancy at birth for total population (1996 est.), 77·83.

CONSTITUTION AND GOVERNMENT

The parliament comprises 32 members elected by proportional representation by universal suffrage at age 18. Parliament elects a government of at least three members which administers home rule. Denmark is represented in parliament by the chief administrator. A referendum was to be held on 26 May 2001 on the government's plan to move towards full sovereignty, but it was called off after the Danish prime minister at the time Poul Nyrup Rasmussen stated that subsidies would cease after four years if the islanders voted for independence.

RECENT ELECTIONS

Parliamentary elections were held on 20 Jan. 2004: the Party for People's Government (TF) won 8 seats with 21·7% of the vote; the Union Party (SF) won 7 seats (23·7%); the Equality Party/Social Democrats (JF) won 7 seats (21·8%); the People's Party (FF) won 7 seats (20·6%); the Centre Party (MF) won 2 seats (5·2%); and the Self-Government Party (SSF) won 1 seat (4·6%).

CURRENT ADMINISTRATION

High Commissioner: Søren Christiansen (b. 1940; appointed 2005).
  Prime Minister: Jóannes Eidesgaard; b. 1951 (JF; took office on 3 Feb. 2004).

ECONOMY

Currency
Since 1940 the currency has been the Faroese *króna* (kr.) which remains freely interchangeable with the Danish krone.

Budget
In 2002 revenues totalled 3,726m. kr. and expenditures 3,586m. kr.

Banking and Finance
The largest bank is the state-owned Føroya Banki. There are four other banks.

ENERGY AND NATURAL RESOURCES

Environment
Carbon dioxide emissions from the consumption and flaring of fossil fuels in 2002 were the equivalent of 14·7 tonnes per capita.

Electricity
Installed capacity was 93,000 kW in 2000. Total production in 2000 was estimated at 188m. kWh, of which approximately 44% was hydro-electric. There are five hydro-electric stations at Vestmanna on Streymoy and one at Eiði on Eysturoy. Consumption per capita was an estimated 4,087 kWh in 2000.

Agriculture
Only 2% of the surface is cultivated; it is chiefly used for sheep and cattle grazing. Potatoes are grown for home consumption. Livestock (2002): sheep, 68,000; cattle, 2,000.

Fisheries
Deep-sea fishing now forms the most important sector (90%) of the economy, primarily in the 200-mile exclusive zone, but also off Greenland, Iceland, Svalbard and Newfoundland and in the Barents Sea. Total catch (2001) 524,837 tonnes, primarily cod, coalfish, redfish, mackerel, blue whiting, capelin, prawns and herring.

INTERNATIONAL TRADE

Imports and Exports
Trade, 2003, in US$1m. (2002 in brackets): imports f.o.b., 684 (472); exports f.o.b., 594 (537). In 2002 goods for household consumption accounted for 28·3% of imports, machinery and transport equipment 21·3% and industrial goods 19·0%. Chilled and frozen fish excluding salmon constituted 50·4% of exports in 2002, salted fish 16·3% and salmon 14·8%. Denmark supplied 31·4% of imports in 2002, Norway 18·7% and Germany 7·6%; the United Kingdom took 24·4% of exports in 2002, Denmark 20·5% and Spain 11·7%.

COMMUNICATIONS

Roads

In 1995 there were 458 km of highways, 11,528 passenger cars and 2,901 commercial vehicles.

Civil Aviation

The airport is on Vágoy, from which there are regular services to Aberdeen, Billund, Copenhagen and Reykjavík.

Shipping

The chief port is Tórshavn, with smaller ports at Klaksvik, Vestmanna, Skálafjørður, Tvøroyri, Vágur and Fuglafjørður. In 2002 merchant shipping totalled 200,000 GRT, including oil tankers 80,000 GRT.

Telecommunications

In 2002 there were 23,000 telephone main lines in use. There were 30,700 mobile phone subscribers in 2002 and 25,000 Internet users.

SOCIAL INSTITUTIONS

Education

In 2000–01 there were 5,570 primary and 2,507 secondary school pupils (total of 670 teachers).

Health

In 2003 there were 83 physicians, 38 dentists and 360 nurses. In 2003 there were three hospitals with 290 beds.

RELIGION

About 80% are Evangelical Lutherans and 20% are Plymouth Brethren, or belong to small communities of Roman Catholics, Pentecostalists, Adventists, Jehovah's Witnesses and Bahais.

CULTURE

Broadcasting

Radio and TV broadcasting (colour by PAL) are provided by Utvarp Føroya and Sjónvarp Føroya respectively. In 2000 there were 102,000 radio and 46,800 TV receivers.

Press

In 2004 there were 13 newspapers per week, with a combined circulation of 22,100.

FURTHER READING

Árbók fyri Føroyar. Annual.
Rutherford, G. K. (ed.) *The Physical Environment of the Færoe Islands.* The Hague, 1982
Wylie, J., *The Faroe Islands: Interpretations of History.* Lexington, 1987

National Statistical Office: Hagstova Føroya, Statistics Faroe Islands.
Website (Faroese only): http://www.hagstova.fo

Greenland

Grønland/Kalaallit Nunaat

KEY HISTORICAL EVENTS

A Danish possession since 1380, Greenland became an integral part of the Danish kingdom on 5 June 1953. Following a referendum in Jan. 1979, home rule was introduced from 1 May 1979.

TERRITORY AND POPULATION

Area, 2,166,086 sq. km (840,000 sq. miles), made up of 1,755,437 sq. km of ice cap and 410,449 sq. km of ice-free land. The population, 1 Jan. 2005, numbered 56,969; density, 0·03 sq. km. In 2000, 45,714 persons were urban (81%); 49,369 were born in Greenland and 6,755 were born outside Greenland. 2000 population of West Greenland, 51,069; East Greenland, 3,462; North Greenland (Thule/Qaanaaq), 864; and 729 not belonging to any specific municipality. The capital is Nuuk (Godthåb), with a population in 2004 of 14,501.

The predominant language is Greenlandic. Danish is widely used in matters relating to teaching, administration and business.

SOCIAL STATISTICS

Registered live births (2001), 936; deaths (1999), 482. Number of abortions (2001): 809. Birth rate per 1,000 population (1999), 16·9; death rate per 1,000 population (1999), 8·6. In 1999 suicide was the cause of death in 11% of all deaths. Annual growth rate (2000), 0·1%.

CONSTITUTION AND GOVERNMENT

There is a 31-member Home Rule Parliament, which is elected for four-year terms and meets two to three times a year. The seven-member cabinet is elected by parliament. Ministers need not be members of parliament. In accordance with the Home Rule Act, the Greenland Home Rule government is constituted by an elected parliament, *Landstinget* (The Greenland Parliament), and an administration headed by a local government, *Landsstyret* (The Cabinet).

Greenland elects two representatives to the Danish parliament (*Folketing*). Denmark is represented by an appointed High Commissioner.

RECENT ELECTIONS

At parliamentary elections held on 15 Nov. 2005 Siumut (Social Democratic) won 10 of 31 seats and 30·7% of votes cast, the Democrats 7 and 22·8%, Inuit Ataqatigiit (leftist) 7 and 22·6%, Atássut (Liberal) 6 and 19·1%, and independents 1 with 4·1%. Turnout was 74·9%.

CURRENT ADMINISTRATION

A coalition government of Siumut, Inuit Ataqatigiit and Atássut was formed in Nov. 2005.

Prime Minister: Hans Enoksen; b. 1956 (Siumut; in office since 14 Dec. 2002).

High Commissioner: Søren Hald Møller (appointed 2005).

Greenland Homerule Website: http://www.nanoq.gl

ECONOMY

Currency

The Danish krone is the legal currency.

Budget

The budget (*finanslovsforslag*) for the following year must be approved by the Home Rule Parliament (*Landstinget*) no later than 31 Oct.

The following table shows the actual revenue and expenditure as shown in Home Rule government accounts for the calendar years 1997–99 and the approved budget figures for 2000 and 2001. Figures are in 1,000 kroner.

	1997	1998	1999	2000	2001
Revenue	4,178	4,304	4,511	4,646	4,687
Expenditure	4,089	4,366	4,393	4,342	4,652

Performance

Following a period of recession between 1990–93, the economy has been growing since 1994, although at a rate well below the OECD average in recent years. In 2001 GDP at market prices was 9,088m. kroner and gross national disposable income was 12,281m. kroner. In 1998 the real GNP growth rate was 7·8%.

Banking and Finance

There are two private banks, Grønlandsbanken and Sparbank Vest.

ENERGY AND NATURAL RESOURCES

Environment
Greenland's carbon dioxide emissions from the consumption and flaring of fossil fuels in 2002 were the equivalent of 10·2 tonnes per capita.

Electricity
Installed capacity was 0·1m. kW in 2000. Production in 2000 was about 263m. kWh.

Oil and Gas
Imports of fuel and fuel oil (1999), 171,523 tonnes worth 256m. kroner.

Agriculture
Livestock, 1999: sheep, 21,007; reindeer, 2,106. There are about 57 sheep-breeding farms in southwest Greenland.

Fisheries
Fishing and product-processing are the principal industry. The total catch in 2001 was 158,485 tonnes. In 1999 prawns accounted for almost 64% of the country's economic output. Greenland halibut and other fish made up around 26%. In 1999, 190 large whales were caught and 3,981 smaller cetacean mammals, such as porpoise (subject to the International Whaling Commission's regulations); and in 1998, 167,506 seals.

INDUSTRY
Six shipyards repair and maintain ships and produce industrial tanks, containers and steel constructions for building.

Labour
At 1 Jan. 2000 the potential labour force was 36,434.

INTERNATIONAL TRADE

Imports and Exports
In 2001 imports totalled 2,466m. kroner and exports 2,251m. kroner. Principal import commodities were food, beverages and tobacco products (17·3%); mineral fuels (16·6%); goods for construction industry (9·2%). Main export commodities were fish and fish products (87·2%), notably shrimp and crab.

Principal import sources, 2000: Denmark, 72·8%; Norway, 8·9%; Japan, 2·6%; Germany, 2·4%. Main export markets, 2000: Denmark, 86·0%; Japan, 6·6%; USA, 4·7%; Thailand, 1·4%.

COMMUNICATIONS

Roads
There are no roads between towns. Registered vehicles (1999): passenger cars, 2,226; lorries and trucks, 1,332; total (including others), 4,026.

Civil Aviation
Number of passengers to/from Greenland (1999): 100,094. Domestic flights—number of passengers (1999): aeroplanes, 169,732; helicopters, 62,155. Air Greenland operates domestic services and international flights to Denmark. There are international airports at Kangerlussuaq (Søndre Strømfjord), Narsarsuaq and Kulusuk and 18 local airports/heliports with scheduled services.

Shipping
There are no overseas passenger services. In 1998, 100,969 passengers were carried on coastal services. There are cargo services to Denmark, Iceland and St John's (Canada).

Telecommunications
In 2002 there were 45,300 telephone subscribers (798·5 per 1,000 inhabitants). There were 19,900 mobile phone subscribers in 2002. In Dec. 2000 Internet users numbered 17,800.

SOCIAL INSTITUTIONS

Justice
The High Court in Nuuk comprises one professional judge and two lay magistrates, while there are 18 district courts under lay assessors.

The population in penal institutions in 2000 was 74 (131 per 100,000 of national population).

Education
Education is compulsory from six to 15 years. A further three years of schooling are optional. Primary schools (2001–02) had 11,368 pupils and 1,191 teachers; secondary schools, 682 pupils.

Health
The medical service is free to all citizens. There is a central hospital in Nuuk and 15 smaller district hospitals. In 2001 there were 89 doctors.

Non-natural death occurred in approximately one-fifth of all deaths in 1999. Suicide is the most dominant non-natural cause of death. There were 104 reported cases of tuberculosis in 2001, 1,942 cases of chlamydia and 707 cases of gonorrhoea. Reported cases of syphilis had decreased from 37 in 1991 to one in 2001. In 2000, seven new cases of HIV were reported while a total of six new HIV-positive cases were reported in 2001.

Welfare
Pensions are granted to persons who are 63 or above. The right to maternity leave has been extended to two weeks before the expected birth and up to 20 weeks after birth against a total of 21 weeks in earlier regulations. The father's right to one week's paternity leave in connection with the birth has been extended to three weeks as from 1 Jan. 2000. Wage earners who are members of SIK (The National Workers' Union) receive financial assistance (unemployment benefit) according to fixed rates, in case of unemployment or illness.

RELIGION
About 80% of the population are Evangelical Lutherans. In 1998 there were 17 parishes with 81 churches and chapels, and 22 ministers.

CULTURE

Broadcasting
The government Kalaallit Nunaata Radioa provides broadcasting services, and there are also local services. In 1997 there were estimated to be 27,000 radio and 22,000 TV sets (colour by NTSC). Several towns have local television stations.

Press
There are two national newspapers with a combined circulation of 7,500.

Tourism
In 1999 visitors stayed 205,573 nights in hotels (including 105,227 Greenlandic visitors) at 31 hotels.

FURTHER READING
Greenland 19xx and *Greenland 20xx: Statistical Yearbook* has been published annually since 1989 by Statistics Greenland in Greenlandic/Danish. *Greenland 2001–2002* in English

Gad, F., *A History of Greenland*. 2 vols. London, 1970–73

Miller, K. E., *Greenland*. [Bibliography] ABC-Clio, Oxford and Santa Barbara (CA), 1991

Greenland National Library, P.O. Box 1011, DK-3900 Nuuk

National Statistical Office: Statistics Greenland, PO Box 1025, DK-3900 Nuuk.

Website: http://www.statgreen.gl

DJIBOUTI

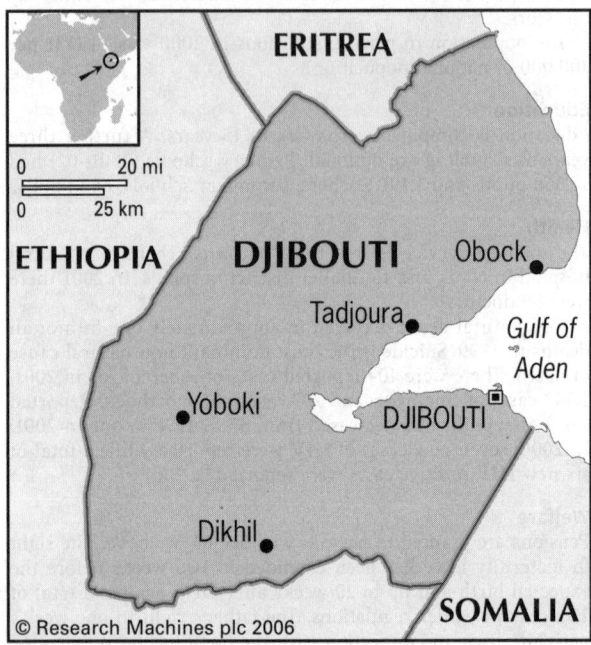

Jumhouriyya Djibouti
(Republic of Djibouti)

Capital: Djibouti
Population projection, 2010: 859,000
GDP per capita, 2003: (PPP$) 2,086
HDI/world rank: 0·495/150

KEY HISTORICAL EVENTS

At a referendum held on 19 March 1967, 60% of the electorate voted for continued association with France rather than independence. France affirmed that the Territory of the Afars and the Issas was destined for independence but no date was fixed. Independence as the Republic of Djibouti was achieved on 27 June 1977. Afar rebels in the north, belonging to the Front for the Restoration of Unity and Democracy (FRUD), signed a 'Peace and National Reconciliation Agreement' with the government on 26 Dec. 1994, envisaging the formation of a national coalition government, the redrafting of the electoral roll and the integration of FRUD militants into the armed forces and civil service.

TERRITORY AND POPULATION

Djibouti is in effect a city-state surrounded by a semi-desert hinterland. It is bounded in the northwest by Eritrea, northeast by the Gulf of Aden, southeast by Somalia and southwest by Ethiopia. The area is 23,200 sq. km (8,958 sq. miles). The population was estimated in 2002 at 688,000 (83·6% urban in 2003), of whom about half were Somali (Issa, Gadaboursi and Issaq), 35% Afar, and some Europeans (mainly French) and Arabs. 2002 density, 30 per sq. km.

The UN gives a projected population for 2010 of 859,000.

There are five administrative districts (areas in sq. km): Ali-Sabieh (2,400); Dikhil (7,200); Djibouti (600); Obock (5,700); Tadjoura (7,300). The capital is Djibouti (1999 population, 523,000).

French and Arabic are official languages; Somali and Afar are also spoken.

SOCIAL STATISTICS

1999 estimates: births, 24,000; deaths, 10,000. Rates (1999 estimates, per 1,000 population); birth, 37; death, 15. Annual population growth rate, 1992–2002, 2·3%. Infant mortality, 2001, 100 per 1,000 live births. Expectation of life, 2003: 51·6 years for men, 54·0 for women. Fertility rate, 2001, 5·9 children per woman.

CLIMATE

Conditions are hot throughout the year, with very little rain. Djibouti, Jan. 78°F (25·6°C), July 96°F (35·6°C). Annual rainfall 5″ (130 mm).

CONSTITUTION AND GOVERNMENT

After a referendum at which turnout was 70%, a new constitution was approved on 4 Sept. 1992 by 96·63% of votes cast, which permits the existence of up to four political parties. Parties are required to maintain an ethnic balance in their membership. The *President* is directly elected for a renewable six-year term. Parliament is a 65-member *Chamber of Deputies* elected for five-year terms.

National Anthem

'Hinjinne u sara kaca' ('Arise with strength'); words by A. Elmi, tune by A. Robleh.

RECENT ELECTIONS

In the presidential election on 8 April 2005 Ismail Omar Guelleh was re-elected with 100% of the votes cast. There were no other candidates. Turnout was 78·9%.

At the parliamentary elections of 10 Jan. 2003—the first free multi-party general elections since independence—the Union for a Presidential Majority, a coalition of RPP (People's Rally for Progress) and FRUD (Front for the Restoration of Unity and Democracy), won all 65 seats with 62·2% of votes cast, against 36·9% for the Union for a Democratic Alternative. Turnout was 48%.

CURRENT ADMINISTRATION

President: Ismail Omar Guelleh; b. 1947 (RPP; sworn in 8 May 1999 and re-elected in April 2005).

In March 2006 the Council of Ministers comprised:

Prime Minister: Dilleita Mohamed Dilleita; b. 1958 (RPP; sworn in 7 March 2001).

Minister of Agriculture, Fisheries and Livestock: Abdoulkader Kamil Mohamed. *Commerce and Industry:* Rifki Abdoulkader Bamakhrama. *Communications, Culture, Post and Telecommunications, Government Spokesperson:* Ali Abdi Farah. *Defence:* Ougoureh Kifleh Ahmed. *Economy, Finance and Privatization:* Ali Farah Assoweh. *Employment and National Solidarity:* Houmed Mohamed Dini. *Energy and Natural Resources:* Mohamed Ali Mohamed. *Equipment and Transport:* Ismael Ibrahim Houmed. *Foreign Affairs and International Co-operation:* Mahamoud Ali Youssouf. *Health:* Abdallah Abdillahi Miguil. *Housing, Town Planning, Environment and Parliamentary Relations:* Elmi Obsieh Waiss. *Interior and Decentralization:* Yacin Elmi Bouh. *Justice, Penal and Muslim Affairs, and Human Rights:* Mohamed Barkat Abdillahi. *National and Higher Education:* Abdi Ibrahim Absieh. *Presidential Affairs and Investment Promotion:* Osman

Ahmed Moussa. *Youth, Sports, Leisure and Tourism:* Hassan Farah Miguil.

Government Website (French only): http://www.presidence.dj

CURRENT LEADERS

Ismail Omar Guelleh

Position
President

Introduction
Ismail Omar Guelleh was elected unopposed for a second six-year term as president in April 2005. He succeeded his uncle in 1999, becoming the country's second president since independence in 1977. He has proved an able diplomat, brokering peace between Djibouti's two main ethnic groups and participating in peace talks in neighbouring Somalia.

Early Life
Ismail Omar Guelleh was born on 27 Nov. 1947 in Dire Dawa, Ethiopia. He is the grandson of Guelleh Batal, one of the chiefs of the Issa clan who signed the 1917 agreement placing the Issa territories under French administration. From 1974 Guelleh became increasingly involved in the fight for independence as a member of the African Popular League for Independence (LPAI). Following Djibouti's declaration of independence on 27 June 1977, Guelleh was appointed principal private secretary to the president, his uncle, Hassan Gouled Aptidon.

Guelleh became head of the security services and joined the People's Rally for Progress (RPP) when it was established in March 1979. He became head of the party's cultural commission in 1981, the year in which Gouled made the Issa-dominated RPP the country's only legal political party, causing resentment among the Afar community. Civil war followed in 1991. When Gouled announced that he would not contest the April 1999 presidential elections, Guelleh stood as the RPP candidate. He was sworn in as president on 8 May 1999.

Career in Office
In Feb. 2000 Guelleh signed a peace agreement with the radical faction of the Afar party, the Front for the Restoration of Unity and Democracy (FRUD), ending nine years of civil war. In Sept. 2002, in support of the US-led 'War on Terror', Guelleh allowed 900 US troops to be based in Djibouti. During the multi-party elections of Jan. 2003 the coalition supporting Guelleh (the Union for a Presidential Majority) won all 65 seats, prompting opposition accusations of vote-rigging. In the run-up to the April 2005 presidential election, Guelleh pledged to reduce poverty and the country's dependence on food imports while boosting women's rights and institutional accountability. The election was boycotted by the opposition and Guelleh was sworn in for a second six-year term with 100% of votes cast.

DEFENCE

France maintains a naval base and forces numbering 2,900 under an agreement renewed in Feb. 1991. Defence expenditure totalled US$24m. in 2003 (US$34 per capita), representing 3·9% of GDP.

Army

There are three Army commands: North, Central and South. The strength of the Army in 2002 was 8,000. There is also a paramilitary Gendarmerie of some 1,400, and an Interior Ministry National Security Force of 2,500.

Navy

A coastal patrol is maintained. Personnel (2002), 200.

Air Force

There is a small Air Force with no combat aircraft. Personnel (2002), 250.

INTERNATIONAL RELATIONS

Djibouti is a member of the UN, WTO, the African Union, African Development Bank, COMESA, OIC, Islamic Development Bank, the League of Arab States, the Intergovernmental Authority on Development, the International Organization of the Francophonie and is an ACP member state of the ACP-EU relationship.

ECONOMY

Agriculture accounted for 3·6% of GDP in 1997, industry 20·5% and services 75·8%.

Currency

The currency is the *Djibouti franc* (DJF), notionally of 100 *centimes*. Foreign exchange reserves were US$72m. in June 2002 and total money supply was 31,286m. Djibouti francs. Inflation was 2·0% in 2003 and 3·1% in 2004.

Budget

Revenues in 2000 were 23·7bn. Djibouti francs and expenditures 38·2bn. Djibouti francs.

Performance

Real GDP growth was 3·2% in 2003 and 3·0% in 2004. Total GDP in 2004 was US$0·7bn.

Banking and Finance

The Banque Nationale de Djibouti is the bank of issue (*Governor*, Djama Mahamoud Haid). There are three commercial banks and a development bank.

ENERGY AND NATURAL RESOURCES

Environment

Djibouti's carbon dioxide emissions from the consumption and flaring of fossil fuels in 2002 were the equivalent of 2·8 tonnes per capita.

Electricity

Installed capacity in 2000 was 88,000 kW. Production in 2000 was around 192m. kWh; consumption per capita was an estimated 304 kWh in 2000.

Agriculture

Approximately 1·3m. ha. were permanent pasture in 1994. There were 1,000 ha. of arable land in 2001. Production is dependent on irrigation which in 2000 covered 1,000 ha. Vegetable production (2000) 24,000 tonnes. The most common crops are tomatoes and dates. Livestock (2000): cattle, 269,000; sheep, 465,000; goats, 513,000; camels, 67,000. Livestock products, 2000: meat, 9,000 tonnes; milk, 8,000 tonnes.

Forestry

In 2000 the area under forests was 6,000 ha., or 0·3% of the total land area.

Fisheries

In 2001 the catch was approximately 350 tonnes, entirely from sea fishing.

INDUSTRY

Labour

In 1991 the estimated labour force totalled 282,000, with 75% employed in agriculture, 14% in services and 11% in industry. A 40-hour working week is standard. Unemployment in 1994 was estimated at 30%.

INTERNATIONAL TRADE

Foreign debt totalled US$335m. in 2002.

Imports and Exports

The main economic activity is the operation of the port; in 1990 only 36% of imports were destined for Djibouti. Exports are largely re-exports. In 1998 imports totalled US$238·8m. and exports US$59·1m. The chief imports are cotton goods, sugar, cement, flour, fuel oil and vehicles; the chief exports are hides, cattle and coffee (transit from Ethiopia).

Main import suppliers, 1998 (% of total trade): France, 12·5%; Ethiopia, 12·0%; Italy, 9·2%. Main export markets, 1998: Somalia, 53·0%; Yemen, 22·5%; Ethiopia, 5·0%.

COMMUNICATIONS

Roads

In 2002 there were estimated to be 2,890 km of roads, of which 12·6% were hard-surfaced. An estimated 15,700 passenger cars were in use in 2002 (23·5 per 1,000 inhabitants), plus 3,200 vans and trucks.

Rail

For the line from Djibouti to Addis Ababa, of which 97 km lie within Djibouti, *see* ETHIOPIA: Communications. Traffic carried is mainly in transit to and from Ethiopia.

Civil Aviation

There is an international airport at Djibouti (Ambouli), 5 km south of Djibouti. Djibouti-based carriers are Daallo Airlines and Djibouti Airlines. They operated flights in 2003 to Addis Ababa, Asmara, Borama, Bossaso, Burao, Dire Dawa, Dubai, Galcaio, Hargeisa, Jeddah, London, Mogadishu, Paris and Ta'iz.

Shipping

Djibouti is a free port and container terminal. 1,138 ships berthed in 1999 (including 117 warships), totalling 5·93m. NRT. 7,238 passengers embarked or disembarked, and 3·88m. tonnes of cargo were handled. In 2002 the merchant marine totalled 3,000 GRT.

Telecommunications

There were 25,100 telephone subscribers in 2002 (38·3 for every 1,000 inhabitants) and 10,000 PCs in use. Mobile phone subscribers numbered 15,000 in 2002. In 2002 there were 100 fax machines and 4,500 Internet users.

Postal Services

There were ten post offices in 2003.

SOCIAL INSTITUTIONS

Justice

There is a Court of First Instance and a Court of Appeal in the capital. The judicial system is based on Islamic law. The death penalty was abolished for all crimes in 1994.

The population in penal institutions in Dec. 1999 was 384 (61 per 100,000 of national population).

Education

Adult literacy in 2001 was 65·5% (76·1% of men; 55·5% of women). In 2000–01 there were 42,692 pupils and 1,199 teachers in primary schools, and 18,808 pupils and 791 teachers in secondary schools. In 2000–01 there were 496 students at tertiary education institutions.

In 1998–99 total expenditure on education came to 3·4% of GNP.

Health

In 1999 there were seven hospitals and medical centres with a total of 1,159 beds. There were 86 physicians, ten dentists, 424 nurses and 12 pharmacists in 1999.

RELIGION

In 2001, 96% of the population were Muslim; there were small Roman Catholic, Protestant and Orthodox minorities.

CULTURE

Broadcasting

The state-run *Radiodiffusion-Télévision de Djibouti* broadcasts in French, Somali, Afar and Arabic. There is a television transmitter in Djibouti, broadcasting for 35 hours a week. Number of receivers: radio (2000), 38,000; TV (2001), 50,000 (colour by SECAM V).

Tourism

There were 17,000 foreign tourists in 2002; tourist spending totalled US$4m. in 1998.

DIPLOMATIC REPRESENTATIVES

Of Djibouti in the United Kingdom
Ambassador: Rachad Farah (resides in Paris).

Of the United Kingdom in Djibouti
Ambassador: Robert Dewar (resides in Addis Ababa, Ethiopia).

Of the USA in Djibouti (Plateau du Serpent Blvd, Djibouti)
Ambassador: Marguerita Ragsdale.

Of Djibouti to the United Nations and in the USA (1156 15th St., NW, Suite 515, Washington, D.C., 20005)
Ambassador: Roble Olhaye.

Of Djibouti to the European Union
Ambassador: Mohamed Moussa Chehem.

FURTHER READING

Direction Nationale de la Statistique. *Annuaire Statistique de Djibouti*
Schraeder, Peter J., *Djibouti*. [Bibliography] ABC-Clio, Oxford and Santa Barbara (CA), 1991

National Statistical Office: Direction Nationale de la Statistique, Ministère du Commerce, des Transports et du Tourisme, BP 1846, Djibouti.

DOMINICA

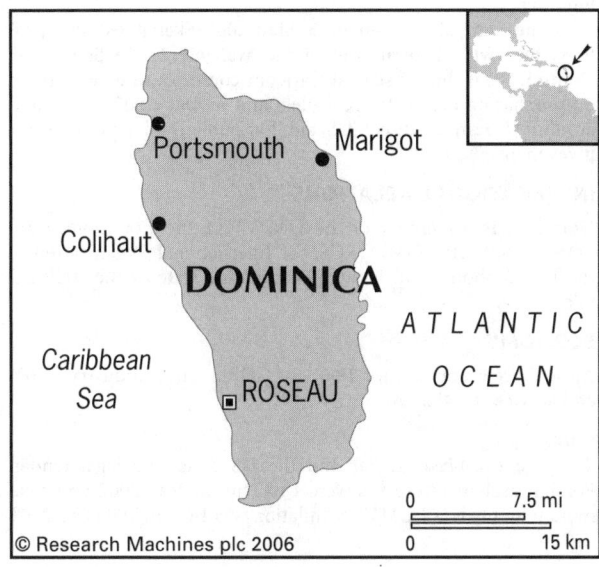

Portsmouth · Marigot · Colihaut · **DOMINICA** · Caribbean Sea · □ROSEAU · ATLANTIC OCEAN

© Research Machines plc 2006

0   7.5 mi
0   15 km

Commonwealth of Dominica

Capital: Roseau
Population, 2001: 72,000
GDP per capita, 2003: (PPP$) 5,448
HDI/world rank: 0·783/70

KEY HISTORICAL EVENTS

When Christopher Columbus sighted Dominica on 3 Nov. 1493 it was occupied by Carib Indians, who are thought to have overrun the previous inhabitants, the Arawak, from around 1300. Dominica remained a 'Carib Isle' until the 1630s, when French farmers and missionaries established sugar plantations. Control was contested between the British and French until it was awarded to the British by the Treaty of Versailles in 1783. In March 1967 Dominica became a self-governing state within the West Indies Associated States, with Britain retaining control of external relations and defence. The island became an independent republic, the Commonwealth of Dominica, on 3 Nov. 1978.

TERRITORY AND POPULATION

Dominica is an island in the Windward group of the West Indies situated between Martinique and Guadeloupe. It has an area of 750 sq. km (290 sq. miles) and a population at the 2001 census of 71,474. The population density in 2001 was 95·0 per sq. km.

In 2003, 72·0% of the population were urban. The chief town, Roseau, had 14,539 inhabitants in 2001.

The population is mainly of African and mixed origins, with small white and Asian minorities. There is a Carib settlement of about 500, almost entirely of mixed blood.

The official language is English, although 90% of the population also speak a French Creole.

SOCIAL STATISTICS

Births, 2000, 1,199 (rate of 16·8 per 1,000 population); deaths, 503 (rate of 7·0); marriages (1999), 339 (rate of 4·7); divorces (1999), 61 (rate of 0·9). Life expectancy, 2003: male, 71·0 years; female, 76·0 years. Annual population growth rate, 1992–2002, 0·0%.

Infant mortality rate, 2001, 14 per 1,000 live births. Fertility rate, 2001, 1·8 births per woman.

CLIMATE

A tropical climate, with pleasant conditions between Dec. and March, but there is a rainy season from June to Oct., when hurricanes may occur. Rainfall is heavy, with coastal areas having 70" (1,750 mm) but the mountains may have up to 225" (6,250 mm). Roseau, Jan. 76°F (24·2°C), July 81°F (27·2°C). Annual rainfall 78" (1,956 mm).

CONSTITUTION AND GOVERNMENT

The head of state is the *President*, nominated by the Prime Minister and the Leader of the Opposition, and elected for a five-year term (renewable once) by the House of Assembly. The *House of Assembly* has 30 members, of whom 21 members are elected and nine nominated by the President.

National Anthem

'Isle of beauty, isle of splendour'; words by W. Pond, tune by L. M. Christian.

RECENT ELECTIONS

Elections were held on 5 May 2005. The Dominica Labour Party (DLP) won 12 of the 21 available seats (10 in 2000), the United Workers Party (UWP) won 8 seats (9 in 2000) and independent candidates won 1 seat (0 in 1995). The Dominica Freedom Party (DFP), previously part of the coalition government, did not win any seats. The DLP formed the government without the need for a coalition partner.

CURRENT ADMINISTRATION

President: Dr Nicholas Liverpool; b. 1934 (took office on 2 Oct. 2003).

Prime Minister, Minister of Finance and Planning, and Overseas Nationals: Roosevelt Skerrit; b. 1972 (DLP; sworn in 8 Jan. 2004). He is currently the youngest head of government in the world.

In March 2006 the cabinet comprised:

Minister of Foreign Affairs, Trade, Labour and Public Services: Charles Savarin. *Housing, Lands, Communications, Energy and Ports:* Reginald Austrie. *Tourism, Industry and Public Sector Affairs:* Yvor Nassief. *Health and Social Security:* John Fabien. *Community Development, Gender Affairs, Culture and Information:* Matthew Walters. *Agriculture, Fisheries and the Environment:* Colin McIntyre. *Education, Human Resource Development, Sports and Youth Affairs:* Vince Henderson. *Public Works and Public Utilities:* Ambrose George. *Immigration, Legal Affairs and Attorney General:* Ian Douglas.

CURRENT LEADERS

Dr Nicholas Liverpool

Position
President

Introduction
Dr Nicholas Liverpool became Dominica's eighth president in Oct. 2003. He has called for national unity and emphasized the importance of focusing on the needs of the nation's youth. In Aug. 2005 he opened a debate on constitutional and political reform.

Early Life
Nicholas Joseph Orville Liverpool was born in the village of Grand Bay, Dominica in 1934. After studying law, he was called to the Bar in London in 1961 and completed a doctorate at Sheffield

University in 1965. Returning to the Caribbean, he spent 18 years as a law lecturer at the University of the West Indies in Barbados and in 1992 became dean of its law school. He served as a regional judge and then an appeal court judge in several countries in the Caribbean including Belize and Grenada. He also served as a high court judge in Antigua and Montserrat and has served on a number of tribunals and commissions for legal reform. In 2002 he was chairman of the constitutional review commission for Grenada.

In 1998 Liverpool became Dominica's ambassador to the USA, serving under the United Workers Party administration and the succeeding Dominica Labour Party–Dominica Freedom Party (DLP–DFP) coalition. In Oct. 2003 all three main political parties backed his appointment as president.

Career in Office
Liverpool took office on 2 Oct. 2003, announcing his intention to explore changes to the constitution. After becoming president he was awarded the Dominican award of honour for his contribution to law and jurisprudence in the Caribbean.

When Prime Minister Pierre Charles died suddenly in Jan. 2004 it fell to Liverpool to appoint his successor. He selected Roosevelt Skerrit on the recommendation of the ruling DLP–DFP coalition.

In Aug. 2005 Liverpool suggested changes to the constitution and the structure and role of parliament. Among his proposals was the merging of the presidential and prime ministerial roles into a single directly elected executive presidency. He also advocated changing the name of 'Leader of the Opposition' to 'Leader(s) of the Minority Party(ies)' to reflect the collaborative nature of parliament.

Roosevelt Skerrit

Position
Prime Minister

Introduction
Roosevelt Skerrit became Dominica's youngest ever prime minister in Jan. 2004 when he took office following the sudden death of his predecessor, Pierre Charles. Appointed by parliamentary recommendation to lead the coalition government, he was returned as prime minister in the May 2005 general election when the Dominica Labour Party (DLP) won an outright majority.

Early Life
Roosevelt Skerrit was born in 1972 and grew up in the village of Vieille Case in northeast Dominica. From 1994–97 he studied psychology and English at the University of Mississippi and New Mexico State University. On his return to Dominica he worked as a teacher, first in a high school then at the Dominica community college. In 1999 he entered politics and in 2000 was elected as a DLP representative to the house of assembly.

In the coalition government of the DLP and the Dominica Freedom Party (DFP), Skerrit served as minister for sports and youth affairs and later also for education. When Pierre Charles died of a heart attack in Jan. 2004, President Nicholas Liverpool appointed Skerrit as his replacement.

Career in Office
Skerrit inherited a small working majority and sought to maintain unity in the coalition government. Against a background of economic troubles, the government introduced unpopular austerity measures, with a combination of spending cuts and higher taxes prompting strikes.

During his first year in office Skerrit pursued a Caricom initiative to raise US$50m. of aid and has subsequently been involved in developing a regional stabilization fund under the auspices of the Caribbean Development Bank.

In March 2004 Skerrit reversed Dominica's traditional policy of pursuing diplomatic ties with Taiwan in preference to relations with China, obtaining a six-year aid package from China worth US$117m. In an attempt to reduce Dominica's dependence on agriculture, the government has invested in tourism (including eco-tourism) and major infrastructure projects, notably road-building.

In the general election of 5 May 2005 Skerrit led the DLP to victory with 12 seats out of the available 21. In Sept. 2005 Dominica was one of several Caricom countries to enter into an oil-purchasing deal with Venezuela and in Oct. 2005 he secured around US$2m of direct US aid for public and private sector investment.

INTERNATIONAL RELATIONS

Dominica is a member of the UN, WTO, the Commonwealth, OAS, ACS, CARICOM, OECS, the International Organization of the Francophonie and is an ACP member state of the ACP-EU relationship.

ECONOMY

Agriculture accounted for 18·6% of GDP in 2002, industry 21·0% and services 60·4%.

Currency
The *East Caribbean dollar* and the US dollar are legal tender. Foreign exchange reserves were US$34m. in May 2002 and total money supply was EC$113m. Inflation was 1·6% in 2003 and 2·4% in 2004.

Budget
Revenues for the fiscal year 2000–01 were EC$194·9m. and expenditures EC$270·8m.

Performance
Real GDP growth was 0·3% in 2000 but Dominica then went into recession, with the economy contracting by 3·9% in 2001 and 3·7% in 2002. GDP growth was 0·9% in 2003 followed by 3·7% in 2004. In 2004 total GDP was US$0·3bn.

Banking and Finance
The East Caribbean Central Bank based in St Kitts and Nevis functions as a central bank. The *Governor* is Sir Dwight Venner. In 2001 there were five commercial banks (four foreign, one domestic), a development bank and a credit union. Dominica is affiliated to the Eastern Caribbean Securities Exchange in Basseterre, St Kitts and Nevis.

ENERGY AND NATURAL RESOURCES

Environment
Carbon dioxide emissions from the consumption and flaring of fossil fuels in 2002 were the equivalent of 1·4 tonnes per capita.

Electricity
Installed capacity was 13,000 kW in 2000. Production in 2000 was 77m. kWh. Consumption per capita in 2000 was 1,069 kWh. There is a hydro-electric power station.

Agriculture
Agriculture employs 26% of the labour force. In 2001 there were 5,000 ha. of arable land and 15,000 ha. of permanent crops. Production (2000, in 1,000 tonnes): bananas, 31; grapefruit and pomelos, 21; coconuts, 12; taro, 11; oranges, 8; plantains, 8; yams, 8. Livestock (2000): cattle, 13,000; goats, 10,000; sheep, 8,000; pigs, 5,000.

Forestry
In 2000 forests covered 46,000 ha., or 61·3% of the total land area.

Fisheries
In 2001 fish landings were estimated at 1,150 tonnes, exclusively from sea fishing.

INDUSTRY

Manufactures include soap (10,500 tonnes in 2001), coconut oil, copra, cement blocks, furniture and footwear.

Labour

Around 25% of the economically active population are engaged in agriculture, fishing and forestry. In 2003 the minimum wage was US$0·75 an hour. The unemployment rate in 2003 was 15·7%.

INTERNATIONAL TRADE

Total foreign debt was US$207m. in 2002.

Imports and Exports

In 2001 imports (c.i.f.) totalled US$115·3m. and exports (f.o.b.) US$44·4m. Main imports in 1999: machine and transport equipment (US$34·4m.), food (US$23·8m.), manufactured goods (US$23·8m.), chemicals (US$16·7m.) and refined petroleum products (US$7·4m.). Main exports (1999): soap (US$17·0m.), bananas (US$16·7m.), fruit, perfumes and sand. Main import suppliers, 2000: USA, 37·5%; Trinidad and Tobago, 16·3%; UK, 7·7%; Japan, 6·3%; Canada, 4·2%. Main export markets, 2000: UK, 24·8%; Jamaica, 23·7%; France, 8·5%; Antigua and Barbuda, 7·4%; USA, 7·4%.

COMMUNICATIONS

Roads

In 2002 there were an estimated 788 km of roads, of which 50·4% were paved. Approximately 10,300 passenger cars and 3,500 commercial vehicles were in use in 2002.

Civil Aviation

There are international airports at Melville Hall and Cane Field. In 2003 there were direct flights to Anguilla, Antigua, Barbados, British Virgin Islands, Grenada, Guadeloupe, Martinique, Puerto Rico, St Kitts, St Lucia, St Maarten, St Vincent, Trinidad and the US Virgin Islands.

Shipping

There are deep-water harbours at Roseau and Woodbridge Bay. Roseau has a cruise ship berth. In 2002 merchant shipping totalled 4,000 GRT. In 1998 vessels totalling 2,218,000 NRT entered ports.

Telecommunications

There were 34,800 telephone subscribers in 2002, equivalent to 445·7 per 1,000 inhabitants, and 7,000 PCs were in use (89·7 for every 1,000 persons). In 2002 there were 9,400 mobile phone subscribers and in 1995 approximately 300 fax machines were in use. Dominica had 12,500 Internet users in 2002.

Postal Services

In 2001 there were 72 post offices, or one for every 1,090 persons.

SOCIAL INSTITUTIONS

Justice

There is a supreme court and 14 magistrates courts. Law is based on UK common law as exercised by the Eastern Caribbean Supreme Court on St Lucia. Final appeal lies to the UK Privy Council. Dominica was one of twelve countries to sign an agreement establishing a Caribbean Court of Justice to replace the British Privy Council as the highest civil and criminal court. The court was inaugurated at Port-of-Spain, Trinidad on 16 April 2005.

The police force has a residual responsibility for defence. The population in penal institutions in Dec. 2003 was 243 (equivalent to 337 per 100,000 of national population).

Education

In 1998 adult literacy was 94%. Education is free and compulsory between the ages of five and 15 years. In 2000–01 there were 552 teachers and 11,430 pupils in primary schools, and 374 teachers and 7,456 pupils in general secondary level education. In 1992–93 there were 484 students and 34 teaching staff at higher education institutions. In 1999–2000 total expenditure on education came to 5·6% of GNP.

Health

In 1994 there were 53 hospitals and health centres with 25 beds per 10,000 inhabitants. There were 38 physicians, ten dentists and 361 nurses in 1998. Large numbers of professional nurses take up employment abroad, especially in the USA, causing a shortage of health care workers in Dominica.

RELIGION

70% of the population was Roman Catholic in 2001.

CULTURE

World Heritage Sites

Dominica has one site on the UNESCO World Heritage List: Morne Trois Pitons National Park (1997), a tropical forest centred on the Morne Trois Pitons volcano.

Broadcasting

Radio and television broadcasting is provided by the part government-controlled, part-commercial Dominica Broadcasting Corporation. There are also two religious radio networks, two commercial TV channels (colour by NTSC) and a commercial cable service. There were 46,000 radios in 1997 and 15,700 TV sets in 2000.

Cinema

There is one cinema with a seating capacity of 1,000.

Press

In 1994 there were three newspapers, including one government and one independent weekly.

Tourism

In 2003 there were 72,948 stop-over and 177,044 cruise ship visitors. Tourism receipts in 2002 totalled US$36m.

DIPLOMATIC REPRESENTATIVES

Of Dominica in the United Kingdom (1 Collingham Gdns, South Kensington, London, SW5 0HW)
Acting High Commissioner: Agnes Adonis.

Of the United Kingdom in Dominica
High Commissioner: Duncan Taylor (resides in Bridgetown, Barbados).

Of Dominica in the USA (3216 New Mexico Ave., NW, Washington, D.C., 20016)
Ambassador: Vacant.

Of the USA in Dominica
Ambassador: Mary E. Kramer (resides in Bridgetown, Barbados).

Of Dominica to the United Nations
Ambassador: Crispin Gregoire.

Of Dominica to the European Union
Ambassador: George Bullen.

FURTHER READING

Baker, P. L., *Centring the Periphery: Chaos, Order and the Ethnohistory of Dominica.* McGill-Queen's Univ. Press, 1994

Honychurch, L., *The Dominica Story: a History of the Island.* 2nd ed. London, 1995

Myers, R. A., *Dominica.* [Bibliography] ABC-Clio, Oxford and Santa Barbara (CA), 1987

National Statistical Office: Central Statistical Office, Kennedy Avenue, Roseau.

DOMINICAN REPUBLIC

República Dominicana

Capital: Santo Domingo
Population projection, 2010: 9·52m.
GDP per capita, 2003: (PPP$) 6,823
HDI/world rank: 0·749/95

KEY HISTORICAL EVENTS

In 1492 Columbus discovered the island of Hispaniola, which he called La Isla Española, and which for a time was also known as Santo Domingo. The city of Santo Domingo, founded by his brother, Bartholomew, in 1496, is the oldest city in the Americas. The western third of the island—now the Republic of Haiti—was later occupied and colonized by the French, to whom the Spanish colony of Santo Domingo was also ceded in 1795. In 1808 the Dominican population routed the French at the battle of Palo Hincado. Eventually, with the aid of a British naval squadron, the French were forced to return the colony to Spanish rule, from which it declared its independence in 1821. It was invaded and held by the Haitians from 1822 to 1844, when the Dominican Republic was founded and a constitution adopted.

Thereafter the rule was dictatorship interspersed with brief democratic interludes. Between 1916 and 1924 the country was under US military occupation. From 1930 until his assassination in 1961, Rafael Trujillo was one of Latin America's legendary dictators. The conservative pro-American Joaquin Balaguer was president from 1966 to 1978. In 1986 Balaguer returned to power at the head of the Socialist Christian Reform Party, leading the way to economic reforms. But there was violent opposition to spending cuts and general austerity. The 1996 elections brought in a reforming government pledged to act against corruption.

TERRITORY AND POPULATION

The Dominican Republic occupies the eastern portion (about two-thirds) of the island of Hispaniola, the western division forming the Republic of Haiti. The area is 48,137 sq. km (18,586 sq. miles). The area and 2002 census populations of the provinces and National District (Santo Domingo area) were:

	Area (in sq. km)	Population
La Altagracia	2,474	182,020
Azua	2,532	208,857
Bahoruco	1,282	91,480

	Area (in sq. km)	Population
Barahona	1,739	179,239
Dajabón	1,021	62,046
Distrito Nacional (Santo Domingo area)	1,401	2,731,294
Duarte	1,605	283,805
Elías Piña	1,426	63,879
Espaillat	839	225,091
Hato Mayor	1,329	87,631
Independencia	2,006	50,833
María Trinidad Sánchez	1,272	135,727
Monseñor Nouel	992	167,618
Monte Cristi	1,924	111,014
Monte Plata	2,632	180,376
Pedernales	2,075	21,207
Peravia	998	232,233
Puerto Plata	1,857	312,706
La Romana	654	219,812
Salcedo	440	96,356
Samaná	854	91,875
Sánchez Ramírez	1,196	151,179
San Cristóbal	1,266	532,880
San José de Ocoa[1]	650	—
San Juan	3,569	241,105
San Pedro de Macorís	1,255	301,744
Santiago	2,839	908,250
Santiago Rodríguez	1,111	59,629
Santo Domingo[2]	1,296	—
El Seíbo	1,787	89,261
Valverde	823	158,293
La Vega	2,287	385,101

[1]Created in 2002; formerly part of Peravia.
[2]Created in 2001; formerly part of Distrito Nacional.

Census population (2002), 8,562,541 (4,297,326 females). In 2003 the population was 59·3% urban.

The UN gives a projected population for 2010 of 9·52m.

Population of the main towns (1993, in 1,000): Santo Domingo, the capital, 3,523 (1999); Santiago de los Caballeros, 1,289 (1995); La Romana, 140; San Pedro de Macorís, 125; San Francisco de Macorís, 108.

The population is mainly composed of a mixed race of European (Spanish) and African blood. The official language is Spanish; about 0·18m. persons speak a Haitian-French Creole.

SOCIAL STATISTICS

2004 estimates: births, 210,000; deaths, 61,000. Rates, 2004 estimates (per 1,000 population): birth, 24; death, 7. Annual population growth rate, 1992–2002, 1·7%. Life expectancy, 2003, 63·9 years for males and 71·0 for females. Infant mortality, 2001, 41 per 1,000 live births. Fertility rate, 2001, 2·8 children per woman.

CLIMATE

A tropical maritime climate with most rain falling in the summer months. The rainy season extends from May to Nov. and amounts are greatest in the north and east. Hurricanes may occur from June to Nov. Santo Domingo, Jan. 75°F (23·9°C), July 81°F (27·2°C). Annual rainfall 56" (1,400 mm).

CONSTITUTION AND GOVERNMENT

The constitution dates from 28 Nov. 1966 and was amended on 25 July 2002. The *President* is elected for four years, by direct vote, and has executive power. A constitutional amendment of Aug. 1994 prohibits the president from serving consecutive terms. In 1994 the constitution was amended to allow for a second round of voting in a presidential election, when no candidate secures an absolute majority in the first ballot. There is a bicameral legislature, the *Congress*, comprising a 32-member Senate (one member for each province and one for the National District of Santo Domingo) and a 150-member *Chamber of Deputies*, both elected for four-year terms. Citizens are entitled to vote at the age of 18, or less when married.

National Anthem

'Quisqueyanos valientes, alcemos' ('Valiant Quisqueyans, Let us raise our voices'); words by E. Prud'homme, tune by J. Reyes.

GOVERNMENT CHRONOLOGY

Heads of State since 1942. (PD = Dominican Party; PLD = Dominican Liberation Party; PR = Reformist Party; PRD = Dominican Revolutionary Party; PRSC = Social Christian Reformist Party; REP = Republican Party; UCN = National Civic Union; n/p = non-partisan)

Presidents

1942–52	PD/military	Rafael Leonidas Trujillo Molina
1952–60	PD	Héctor Bienvenido Trujillo Molina
1960–62	PD	Joaquín Antonio Balaguer Ricardo
1962–63	REP	Rafael Filiberto Bonelly Fondeur
1963	PRD	Juan Emilio Bosch Gaviño

Chairmen of the Triumvirate

1963	n/p	Emilio de los Santos
1963–65	UCN	Donald Joseph Reid Cabral

Chairman of Military Junta of Government

1965	military	Pedro Bartolomé Benoit Vanderhorst

President of the Government of National Reconstruction

1965	military	Antonio Cosme Imbert Barrera

Presidents

1965	military	Francisco Alberto Caamaño Deñó
1965–66	PR	Héctor Federico García-Godoy Cáceres
1966–78	PR	Joaquín Antonio Balaguer Ricardo
1978–82	PRD	Silvestre Antonio Guzmán Fernández
1982	PRD	Jacobo Majluta Azar
1982–86	PRD	Salvador Jorge Blanco
1986–96	PRSC	Joaquín Antonio Balaguer Ricardo
1996–2000	PLD	Leonel Antonio Fernández Reyna
2000–04	PRD	Rafael Hipólito Mejía Domínguez
2004–	PLD	Leonel Antonio Fernández Reyna

RECENT ELECTIONS

Presidential elections were held on 16 May 2004. Leonel Antonio Fernández Reyna of the Dominican Liberation Party/PLD won 57·1% of the votes, incumbent Rafael Hipólito Mejía Domínguez of the Dominican Revolutionary Party/PRD 33·6% and Eduardo Estrella of the Social Christian Reformist Party/PRSC 8·8%. Turnout was 72·8%.

Parliamentary elections were held on 16 May 2002. In the election to the Chamber of the Deputies the PRD won 73 seats, the PLD 41 and the PRSC 36. In the Senate elections on the same day, the PRD won 29 seats, the PLD 2 and the PRSC 1.

CURRENT ADMINISTRATION

President: Leonel Antonio Fernández; b. 1953 (PLD; sworn in 16 Aug. 2004, having previously been president from 1996–2000).

Vice-President: Rafael Alburquerque.

In March 2006 the government comprised:

Secretary of State for Agriculture: Amílcar Romero. *Armed Forces:* Rear Adm. Sigfrido Pared Pérez. *Culture:* José Rafael Lantigua. *Education:* Alejandrina Germán. *Environment and Natural Resources:* Maximiliamo Puig. *Finance:* Vicente Bengoa. *Foreign Relations:* Carlos Morales Troncoso. *Higher Education, Science and Technology:* Ligia Amada de Melo. *Industry and Commerce:* Francisco Javier García. *Interior and Police:* Franklin Almeyda. *Labour:* José Ramón Fadul. *Presidency:* Danilo Medina. *Public Health and Social Welfare:* Bautista Rojas Gómez. *Public Works and Communications:* Manuel de Jesús Pérez. *Sport:* Felipe Jay Payano. *Tourism:* Félix Jiménez. *Women:* Gladis Gutiérrez.

Youth: Manuel Crespo. *Without Portfolio:* Miguel Mejía; Eduardo Selman.

Office of the President (Spanish only):
http://www.presidencia.gov.do

CURRENT LEADERS

Dr Leonel Fernández

Position
President

Introduction
Dr Leonel Fernández first became president in 1996 and won a second four-year term in May 2004. He has won plaudits for easing the country's economic crisis but there is little evidence of reductions in poverty, unemployment and corruption.

Early Life
Leonel Antonio Fernández Reyna was born on 26 Dec. 1953 in Santo Domingo, the capital city. In 1962 his family moved to New York, where he attended school before returning to Santo Domingo in 1971. He enrolled at the Independent University of Santo Domingo (UASD) to study law. In 1973 Fernández joined the leftist Dominican Liberation Party (PLD), the movement founded by his professor and mentor, the former president, Juan Bosch. Following his graduation with a doctorate in 1978, Fernández worked as a political journalist. He subsequently lectured at the UASD and the Latin American Faculty of Social Science in Santo Domingo. Elected to the PLD's central committee in 1985, he rose through the party's administrative ranks and stood as Bosch's running mate at the 1994 presidential election (won by Joaquin Balaguer). Balagauer was barred from running in the May 1996 elections and Fernández defeated José Francisco Peña Gómez in a run-off a month later.

Career in Office
Sworn in as president on 16 Aug. 1996, Fernández brought in sweeping economic and judicial reforms. Despite increased foreign investment, economic growth and infrastructural improvements, Hipólito Mejía of the Dominican Revolutionary Party (PRD) was elected president in Aug. 2000 amid discontent over power cuts in the recently privatized electric industry. Mejía presided over a deepening economic crisis and spiralling crime and unemployment. Fernández was re-elected president on 16 May 2004 and sworn in three months later. He introduced austerity measures and succeeded in stabilizing inflation and the currency. However, attempts to tackle poverty and corruption, and to resolve the energy crisis have been less successful.

DEFENCE

In 2003 defence expenditure totalled US$162m. (US$19 per capita), representing 1·0% of GDP.

Army

There are three defence zones. The Army has a strength (2002) of about 15,000 and includes a special forces unit and a Presidential Guard. There is a paramilitary National Police 15,000-strong.

Navy

The Navy is equipped with former US vessels. Personnel in 2002 totalled 4,000, based at Santo Domingo and Las Calderas.

Air Force

The Air Force, with HQ at San Isidoro, has 16 combat aircraft. Personnel strength (2002), 5,500.

INTERNATIONAL RELATIONS

The Dominican Republic is a member of the UN, WTO, OAS, Inter-American Development Bank, ACS, IOM and is an ACP member state of the ACP-EU relationship.

ECONOMY

In 2002 agriculture accounted for 11·8% of GDP, industry 32·9% and services 55·2%.

Currency

The unit of currency is the *peso* (DOP) of 100 *centavos*. Gold reserves were 18,000 troy oz in June 2002 and foreign exchange reserves US$876m. Total money supply was RD$37,826m. in March 2002. Inflation was 27·4% in 2003 and 51·5% in 2004. Only Zimbabwe had a higher annual inflation rate in 2004.

Budget

Budgetary central government revenue in 2002 totalled RD$66,779m. (RD$60,416m. in 2001) and expenditure RD$53,208m. (RD$46,095m. in 2001). Tax revenues in 2002 were RD$63,101m. (including RD$24,419m. in taxes on goods and services; RD$22,194m. in taxes on international trade and transactions; and RD$14,904m. in taxes on income, profits and capital gains).

Performance

Real GDP growth was –1·6% in 2003, but there followed a recovery, with growth of 2·0% in 2004. Total GDP in 2004 was US$18·7bn.

Banking and Finance

In 1947 the Central Bank was established (*Governor*, Héctor Valdez Albizu). Its total assets were RD$34,958·7m. in 1993. In 2002 there were 12 commercial banks, two foreign banks and nine development banks.

The Santo Domingo Securities Exchange is a member of the Association of Central American Stock Exchanges (Bolcen).

Weights and Measures

The metric system is in force but US units are in common use. Rural land is measured with the *tarea* (624 sq. metres).

ENERGY AND NATURAL RESOURCES

Environment

Carbon dioxide emissions from the consumption and flaring of fossil fuels in 2002 were the equivalent of 2·1 tonnes per capita.

Electricity

Installed capacity was 3·6m. kW in 2000. Production was 9·70bn. kWh in 2000; consumption per capita was 1,139 kWh.

Minerals

Bauxite output in 1988 was 167,800 tonnes, but had declined to nil by 1992. Output: nickel (2002), 38,859 tonnes; gold (1999), 651 kg. Gold production had been declining over the previous few years and has since been suspended.

Agriculture

Agriculture and processing are the chief sources of income, sugar cultivation being the principal industry. In 2001 there were 1·1m. ha. of arable land and 500,000 ha. of permanent cropland. 275,000 ha. were irrigated in 2001.

Production, 2000 (in 1,000 tonnes): sugarcane, 4,785; rice, 527; bananas, 422; plantains, 343; tomatoes, 286; mangoes, 180; coconuts, 173; oranges, 131.

Livestock in 2000: 1·90m. cattle; 539,000 pigs; 330,000 horses; 170,000 goats; 46m. chickens. Livestock products, 2000 (in 1,000 tonnes): poultry meat, 254; beef and veal, 69; pork, bacon and ham, 61; eggs, 61; milk, 398.

Forestry

Forests and woodlands covered 1·38m. ha. in 2000, representing 28·4% of the total land area. In 2001, 562,000 cu. metres of timber were cut.

Fisheries

The total catch in 2001 was 13,217 tonnes, mainly from sea fishing.

INDUSTRY

Production, 2000 (in 1,000 tonnes): cement (2001), 2,758; residual fuel oil, 599; sugar (2002), 516; kerosene, 394; distillate fuel oil, 385; petrol, 345; rum (1995–96), 395·6m. litres; beer (2003), 337·0m. litres; cigarettes (1999), 4·0bn. units.

Labour

In 2001 the labour force was 3,710,000. In 1997 the unemployment rate was 15·9%.

INTERNATIONAL TRADE

Foreign debt was US$6,256m. in 2002.

Imports and Exports

Imports f.o.b. in 2002 totalled US$8,882·5m. (US$8,779·3m. in 2001); exports in 2002 totalled US$5,183·4m. (US$5,276·3m. in 2001). Main imports, 1995: oil and products, 21·7%; agricultural products, 17·2%. Main exports: ferronickel, 31·6%; raw sugar, 13·3%; coffee, 10·6%; cocoa, 7·1%; gold, 5·4%.

Main import suppliers, 1997: USA, 56%; Venezuela, 23%; Mexico, 9%. Main export markets: USA, 54%; Belgium, 12%; Puerto Rico, 7%.

COMMUNICATIONS

Roads

In 2002 the road network covered an estimated 19,705 km, of which 51·2% were paved. In 2002 there were 378,500 passenger cars (43·6 per 1,000 inhabitants), 178,600 trucks and vans, and 14,550 buses and coaches (1996). In 1998 there were 1,494 road accidents resulting in 1,683 deaths.

Rail

In 1995 the total length was 757 km, comprising 375 km of the Central Romana Railroad, 142 km of the Dominican Republic Government Railway between Guayubin and the port of Pepillo, and 240 km operated by the sugar industry.

Civil Aviation

There are international airports at Santo Domingo (Las Americas), Puerto Plata and Punta Cana. Air Santo Domingo operates scheduled domestic services and international services to Puerto Rico. In 2000 Santo Domingo was the busiest airport, handling 4,652,000 passengers, followed by Puerto Plata (estimated at 2,023,000 passengers) and Punta Cana (1,745,000).

Shipping

The main ports are Santo Domingo, Puerto Plata, La Romana and Haina. In 2002 the merchant marine totalled 9,000 GRT. In 2001 vessels totalling 13,892,000 NRT entered and vessels totalling 2,507,000 NRT cleared.

Telecommunications

In 2002 there were 2,609,600 telephone subscribers (299·7 for every 1,000 inhabitants). Mobile phone subscribers numbered 1,700,600 in 2002 and there were 2,500 fax machines in 1995. The number of Internet users in 2002 was 300,000.

Postal Services

In 2003 there were 278 post offices.

SOCIAL INSTITUTIONS

Justice

The judicial power resides in the Supreme Court of Justice, the courts of appeal, the courts of first instance, the communal courts and other tribunals created by special laws, such as the land courts. The Supreme Court, consisting of a president and eight judges chosen by the Senate, and the procurator-general, appointed by the executive, supervises the lower courts. Each province forms a judicial district, as does the National District, and each has its own procurator fiscal and court of first instance;

these districts are subdivided, in all, into 97 municipalities, each with one or more local justices. The death penalty was abolished in 1924.

The population in penal institutions in June 2003 was 16,789 (193 per 100,000 of national population).

Education

Primary instruction is free and compulsory for children between seven and 14 years of age; there are also secondary, normal, vocational and special schools, all of which are either wholly maintained by the State or state-aided. In 2001–02 there were 1,399,844 primary school pupils and 756,240 pupils at secondary level. There are four universities, three Roman Catholic universities, one Adventist university, three technological universities and one Roman Catholic university college, and five other higher education institutions. Adult literacy was 87·7% in 2003 (88·0% among males and 87·3% among females).

In 1999–2000 total expenditure on education came to 2·6% of GNP and 15·7% of total government spending.

Health

In 2000 there were 15,670 physicians, 7,000 dentists, 15,352 nurses and 3,330 pharmacists. There were 723 government hospitals in 1992.

RELIGION

The religion of the state is Roman Catholic; there were 7·11m. adherents in 2001. Protestants numbered 560,000 in 2001. In May 2005 there was one cardinal.

CULTURE

World Heritage Sites

The Dominican Republic has one site on the UNESCO World Heritage List: the Colonial City of Santo Domingo (1990)— founded in 1492, it is the site of the first cathedral and university in the Americas.

Broadcasting

There were (1994) more than 170 broadcasting stations in Santo Domingo and other towns; this includes the two government stations. There were seven television stations (colour by NTSC). In 2000 there were 1·51m. radio and 810,000 television receivers.

Press

In 2000 there were nine dailies with a combined circulation of 230,000.

Tourism

In 2003 there were 3,268,182 non-resident air arrivals and 398,263 cruise ship visitors. Tourism receipts in 2002 totalled US$2,736m. For some 15 years the Dominican Republic has been experiencing annual growth of 10% or more in both tourist arrivals and hotel capacity. In Dec. 1998 there were 41,600 hotel rooms (11,400 in 1987).

DIPLOMATIC REPRESENTATIVES

Of the Dominican Republic in the United Kingdom (139 Inverness Terrace, London, W2 6JF)
Ambassador: Anibal de Castro.

Of the United Kingdom in the Dominican Republic (Edificio Corominas Pepin, Ave. 27 de Febrero 233, Santo Domingo)
Ambassador: Andy Ashcroft.

Of the Dominican Republic in the USA (1715 22nd St., NW, Washington, D.C., 20008)
Ambassador: Flavio Dario Espinal.

Of the USA in the Dominican Republic (Calle Cesar Nicolas Penson, Santo Domingo)
Ambassador: Hans H. Hertell.

Of the Dominican Republic to the United Nations
Ambassador: Erasmo Lara-Peña.

Of the Dominican Republic to the European Union
Ambassador: Clara Quiñones de Longo.

FURTHER READING

Black, J. K., *The Dominican Republic: Politics and Development in an Unsovereign State.* London, 1986
Schoenhals, K., *Dominican Republic.* [Bibliography] ABC-Clio, Oxford and Santa Barbara (CA), 1990

National Statistical Office: Oficina Nacional de Estadística, Av. México esq. Leopoldo Navarro, Edificio Oficinas Gubernamentales 'Juan Pablo Duarte' Pisos 8 y 9 Gazcue, Santo Domingo.
Website (Spanish only): http://www.one.gov.do/

EAST TIMOR

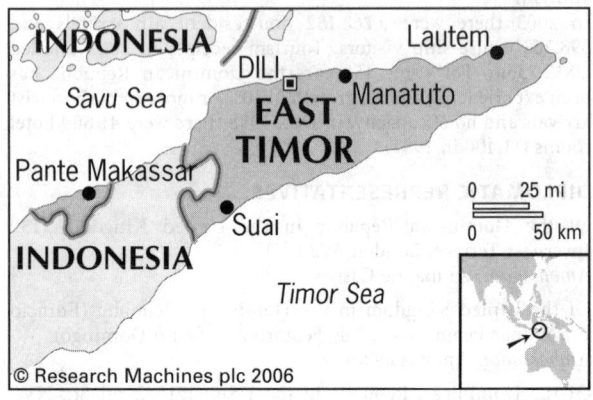

República Democrática de Timor-Leste
(Democratic Republic of East Timor)

Capital: Dili
Population projection, 2010: 1,244,000
GDP per capita: not available
GNI per capita: $430
HDI/world rank: 0·513/140

KEY HISTORICAL EVENTS

Portugal abandoned its former colony, with its largely Roman Catholic population, in 1975, when it was occupied by Indonesia and claimed as the province of Timor Timur. The UN did not recognize Indonesian sovereignty over the territory. An independence movement, the Revolutionary Front for an Independent East Timor (FRETILIN), maintained a guerrilla resistance to the Indonesian government which resulted in large-scale casualties and alleged atrocities. On 24 July 1998 Indonesia announced a withdrawal of troops from East Timor and an amnesty for some political prisoners, although no indication was given of how many of the estimated 12,000 troops and police would pull out. On 5 Aug. 1998 Indonesia and Portugal reached agreement on the outlines of an autonomy plan which would give the Timorese the right to self-government except in foreign affairs and defence.

In a referendum on the future of East Timor held on 30 Aug. 1999 the electorate was some 450,000 and turn-out was nearly 99%. 78·5% of voters opted for independence, but pro-Indonesian militia gangs wreaked havoc both before and after the referendum. The militias accused the UN of rigging the poll. There was widespread violence in and around Dili, the provincial capital, with heavy loss of life, and thousands of people were forced to take to the hills after intimidation. East Timor's first democratic election took place on 30 Aug. 2001 in a ballot run by the UN, with FRETILIN winning 57% of the vote and 55 of the 88 seats in the new constituent assembly. East Timor became an independent country on 20 May 2002 but unrest continues.

TERRITORY AND POPULATION

East Timor has a total land area of 17,222 sq. km (6,649 sq. miles), consisting of the mainland (14,609 sq. km), the enclave of Oscússu-Ambeno in West Timor (2,461 sq. km), and the islands of Ataúro to the north (144 sq. km) and Jaco to the east (8 sq. km). The mainland area incorporates the eastern half of the island of Timor. Oscússu-Ambeno lies westwards, separated from the main portion of East Timor by a distance of some 100 km. The island is bound to the south by the Timor Sea and lies approximately 500 km from the Australian coast.

The UN population estimate for East Timor in 2005 was 947,000; density, 55 per sq. km. The largest city is Dili, East Timor's capital. In 1999 its population was an estimated 180,000. In 2003, 92·3% of the population was rural (the highest percentage of any country).

The UN gives a projected population for 2010 of 1,244,000.

The ethnic East Timorese form the majority of the population. Non-East Timorese, comprising Portuguese and West Timorese as well as persons from Sumatra, Java, Sulawesi and other parts of Indonesia, are estimated to constitute approximately 20% of the total population.

During Indonesian occupation the official language was Bahasa Indonesia. East Timor's new constitution designates Portuguese and Tetum (the region's *lingua franca*) as the official languages, and English and Bahasa Indonesia as working languages.

SOCIAL STATISTICS

2002 estimates: births, 21,000; deaths, 11,000. Rates, 2002 estimates (per 1,000 population): births, 27·7; deaths, 14·0. Based on UN figures for the period 1995–2000: fertility rate, 4·3 births per woman; annual population growth rate, 1·7%. In 2003 life expectancy at birth was 54·5 years for males and 56·6 years for females.

From having the world's highest rate of infant mortality in the early 1980s, East Timor's infant mortality rate has dropped to around 60 per 1,000 live births in 1999, although the figure varies widely between urban and rural areas.

CLIMATE

In the north there is an average annual temperature of over 24°C (75°F), weak precipitation—below 1,500 mm (59") annually—and a dry period lasting five months. The mountainous zone, between the northern and southern parts of the island, has high precipitation—above 1,500 mm (59")—and a dry period of four months. The southern zone has precipitation reaching 2,000 mm (79") and is permanently humid. The monsoon season extends from Nov. to May.

CONSTITUTION AND GOVERNMENT

There is a 88-seat *National Parliament*, with 13 members elected in single-seat constituencies and 75 by proportional representation. After the expiry of the first term the number of seats will be reduced, with a minimum requirement of 52 seats and a maximum of 65.

The *President*, who is elected for a period of five years, is appointed by the *National Parliament*.

National Anthem

'Pátria, Pátria, Timor-Leste, nossa Nação' ('Fatherland, fatherland, East Timor our Nation'); words by F. Borja da Costa, tune by A. Araujo.

RECENT ELECTIONS

Presidential elections were held on 14 April 2002. Former separatist guerrilla leader Xanana Gusmão (FRETILIN) won a landslide victory with 82·6% of votes cast against 17·3% for Xavier do Amaral, his single rival. Turnout was 86%. Amaral, who served as president of East Timor for nine days in 1975, in the short period between Portuguese withdrawal and Indonesian occupation, declared that his intention to run for the presidency was solely to provide the electorate with a choice of candidates.

Elections to the 75-member national assembly took place on 30 Aug. 2001, the anniversary of the referendum for independence two years earlier. The Frente Revolucionária do Timor Leste Independente (FRETILIN; Revolutionary Front for an Independent East Timor) won 57·37% of the vote and took 43 seats with 208,531 votes. The Partido Democrático (PD; Democratic Party) won 8·72% of votes cast and 7 seats; the Partido Social Democrata (PSD; Social Democratic Party) won 8·18% and 6 seats; the Associação Social-Democrata Timorense (ASDT) 7·84% and 6 seats; the União Democrática Timorense (UDT) 2·36% and 2 seats; the Partido do Povo de Timor (PPT) 2·01% and 2 seats. Other parties won less than 2% of the vote. In elections to the district assembly, held on the same day, FRETILIN secured 12 of the 13 seats, giving them a total of 55 seats in the 88-seat constituent assembly. Turnout for the elections was 91·3%. 23 of the seats went to women.

CURRENT ADMINISTRATION

President: Xanana Gusmão; b. 1946 (ind.; sworn in 20 May 2002).

In March 2006 the government was comprised as follows:
Prime Minister and Minister for Development and the Environment: Marí Bim Amude Alkatiri (FRETILIN).

Deputy Prime Minister: Ana Maria Pessoa Pereira da Silva Pinto.

Minister for Foreign Affairs and Co-operation: José Ramos Horta. *Justice:* Domingos Maria Sarmento. *Finance:* Madalena Brites Boavida. *Internal Administration:* Rogerio Tiago Lobato. *Health:* Rui Maria de Araujo. *Education, Culture and Youth:* Armindo Maia. *Agriculture and Fisheries:* Estanislau Aleixo da Silva. *Transportation, Communications and General Employment:* Ovidio Amaral.

Government Website: http://www.gov.east-timor.org

CURRENT LEADERS

Xanana Gusmão

Position
President

Introduction
Independent East Timor's first president, Xanana Gusmão, having led the independence movement for over two decades, came to power in a landslide victory in elections held in April 2002. A poet and painter, Gusmão won the national poetry prize in 1974 and earned the nickname of 'poet-warrior' whilst imprisoned by the Indonesian government.

Early Career
Xanana Gusmão was born José Alexandre Gusmão on 20 June 1946 in the town of Laleia, Manatuto. After studying at a Jesuit seminary in Soibade and then at Dare, he joined the local department of forestry and agriculture as a civil servant.

In 1974 he joined FRETILIN (the Revolutionary Front for an Independent East Timor), replacing Nicolau Lobato as its leader in 1978. In 1981 he was elected commander-in-chief of the organization's military front. Leading the guerrilla movement from the mountains, Gusmão worked to integrate the various groups fighting for independence.

On 20 Nov. 1992 he was captured by the Indonesian army and sentenced to life imprisonment on charges of subversion. Serving only six years, Gusmão remained the figurehead of the independence movement. Following an appeal from UN Secretary-General Kofi Annan, Gusmão was released after the referendum of Sept. 1999 in which an overwhelming majority of East Timorese voted for independence.

East Timor gained independence on 20 May 2002 and Gusmão was inaugurated as president, having won a landslide victory in elections the previous month.

Career in Office
In office Gusmão plays a largely ceremonial role, with decision-making reserved for the FRETILIN-dominated government, but he has appealed for reconciliation and an end of violence against those who opposed independence. He has also stressed that poverty and unemployment are the most serious problems facing the country.

DEFENCE

Training began in 2001 with the aim of deploying 1,500 full-time personnel and 1,500 reservists by 2004. A 650-strong East Timor Defence Force became operational in 2002.

INTERNATIONAL RELATIONS

East Timor is a member of the UN, the IMF and the Asian Development Bank.

ECONOMY

Currency
The official currency is the US dollar. The Australian dollar and the Indonesian rupiah, both previously used, no longer serve as legal tender. Inflation was 7·1% in 2003 and 3·3% in 2004.

Performance
Total GDP in 2004 was US$0·3bn. The economy contracted by 6·2% in 2003 but expanded by 1·8% in 2004.

ENERGY AND NATURAL RESOURCES

Electricity
In 1996 only a quarter of households in East Timor had electricity.

Oil and Gas
Although current production is small, the Timor Gap, an area of offshore territory between East Timor and Australia, is one of the richest oilfields in the world outside the Middle East. Potential revenue from the area is estimated at US$11bn. The area is split into three zones with a central 'zone of occupation' (occupying 61,000 sq. km). Royalties on oil discovered within the central zone were split equally between Indonesia and Australia following the Timor Gap Treaty which came into force on 9 Feb. 1991. Questions over East Timor's rights to oil revenue from the area have arisen following the 1999 independence referendum.

Minerals
Gold, iron sands, copper and chromium are present.

Agriculture
Although the presence of sandalwood was one of the principal reasons behind Portuguese colonization, its production has declined in recent years. In 2001 there were 70,000 ha. of arable land and 10,000 ha. of permanent crops. Coffee is grown extensively.

Fisheries
The total fish catch in 2001 was 356 tonnes.

INDUSTRY

Labour
In 2000 the unemployment rate exceeded 80% of the labour force.

INTERNATIONAL TRADE

Imports and Exports
All basic goods such as rice, sugar and flour are imported. Coffee and cattle are important exports.

COMMUNICATIONS

Civil Aviation

There is an international airport at Dili.

SOCIAL INSTITUTIONS

Health

Plans for a medical system include 64 community health centres, 88 health posts, 117 mobile clinics and 21 doctors.

RELIGION

Over 90% of East Timor's population are Roman Catholic, with Protestants, Muslims, Hindus and Buddhists accounting for the remainder.

CULTURE

Press

In 2004 there were two daily newspapers, the *Timor Post* and *Suara Timor Lorosae*.

DIPLOMATIC REPRESENTATIVES

Of the United Kingdom in East Timor (Pantai Kelapa, PO Box 194, The Post Office, Dili)
Ambassador: Tina Redshaw.

Of East Timor in the USA (4201 Connecticut Ave., NW, Suite 504, Washington, D.C., 20008)
Ambassador: José Luis Guterres.

Of the USA in East Timor (Avenido do Portugal, Farol, Dili)
Ambassador: Grover Joseph Rees, III.

Of East Timor to the United Nations
Ambassador: José Luis Guterres.

Of East Timor to the European Union
Ambassador: José Antonio Amorim Dias.

FURTHER READING

Nevins, Joseph, *A Not-So-Distant Horror: Mass Violence in East Timor.* Cornell Univ. Press, Ithaca (NY), 2005

ECUADOR

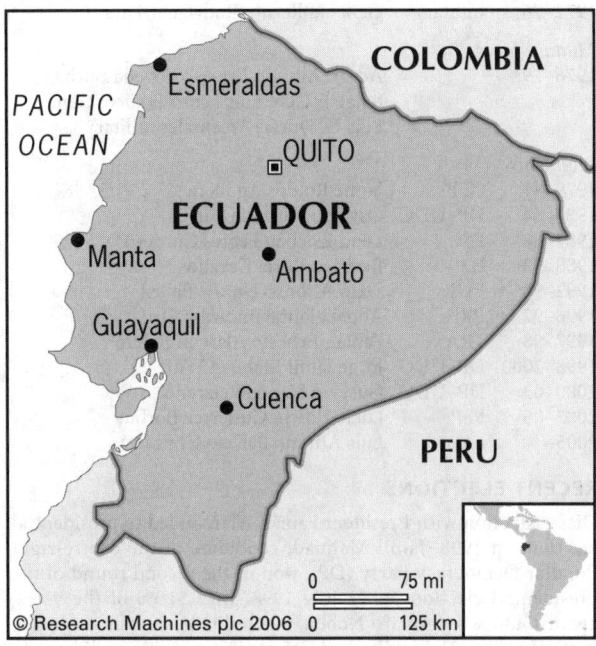

República del Ecuador

Capital: Quito
Population projection, 2010: 14·19m.
GDP per capita, 2003: (PPP$) 3,641
HDI/world rank: 0·759/82

KEY HISTORICAL EVENTS

In 1532 the Spaniards founded a colony in Ecuador, then called Quito. In 1821 a revolt led to the defeat of the Spaniards at Pichincha and thus independence from Spain. On 13 March 1830, Quito became the Republic of Ecuador. Political instability was endemic. From the mid-1930s, President José Maria Velasco Ibarra was deposed by military coups from four of his five presidencies.

From 1963 to 1966 and from 1976 to 1979 military juntas ruled the country. The second of these juntas produced a new constitution which came into force on 10 Aug. 1979. Presidencies were more stable but civil unrest continued in the wake of economic reforms and attempts to combat political corruption.

In Jan. 2000 President Mahaud declared a state of emergency when protesters demanded his resignation over his handling of an economic crisis. There was a coup on 21 Jan. but, after five hours in control, the military junta handed power to the former vice-president, Gustavo Noboa.

In April 2005 President Lucio Gutiérrez was ousted by Ecuador's congress after public protest at his attempts to implement IMF-backed economic policies and his substitution of 27 out of 31 Supreme Court judges with his allies. The replacement judges promptly dropped corruption charges against two former presidents, increasing public outcry. Four days after being dismissed, Gutiérrez fled to Brazil. He was replaced by Alfredo Palacio, who immediately issued a warrant for Gutiérrez's arrest.

TERRITORY AND POPULATION

Ecuador is bounded in the north by Colombia, in the east and south by Peru and in the west by the Pacific ocean. The frontier with Peru has long been a source of dispute. It was delimited in the Treaty of Rio, 29 Jan. 1942, when, after being invaded by Peru, Ecuador lost over half her Amazonian territories. Ecuador unilaterally denounced this treaty in Sept. 1961. Fighting between Peru and Ecuador began again in Jan. 1981 over this border issue but a ceasefire was agreed in early Feb. Following a confrontation of soldiers in Aug. 1991 the foreign ministers of both countries signed a pact creating a security zone, and took their cases to the UN in Oct. 1991. On 26 Jan. 1995 further armed clashes broke out with Peruvian forces in the undemarcated mutual border area ('Cordillera del Cóndor'). On 2 Feb. talks were held under the auspices of the guarantor nations of the 1942 Protocol of Rio de Janeiro (Argentina, Brazil, Chile and the USA), but fighting continued. A ceasefire was agreed on 17 Feb., which was broken, and again on 28 Feb. On 25 July 1995 an agreement between Ecuador and Peru established a demilitarized zone along their joint frontier. The frontier was re-opened on 4 Sept. 1995. Since 23 Feb. 1996 Ecuador and Peru have signed three further agreements to regulate the dispute. The dispute was settled in Oct. 1998. Confirming the Peruvian claim that the border lies along the high peaks of the Cóndor, Ecuador gained navigation rights on the Amazon within Peru.

No definite figure of the area of the country can yet be given. One estimate of the area of Ecuador is 272,045 sq. km, excluding the litigation zone between Peru and Ecuador, which is 190,807 sq. km, but including the **Galápagos** Archipelago (8,010 sq. km), situated in the Pacific ocean about 960 km west of Ecuador, and comprising 13 islands and 19 islets. These were discovered in 1535 by Fray Tomás de Berlanga and had a population of 10,207 in 1996. They constitute a national park, and had about 80,000 visitors in 1995.

The population is an amalgam of European, Amerindian and African origins. Some 41% of the population is Amerindian: Quechua, Swiwiar, Achuar and Zaparo. In May 1992 they were granted title to the 1m. ha. of land they occupy in Pastaza.

The official language is Spanish. Quechua and other languages are also spoken.

Census population in 2001, 12,156,608; density, 45 per sq. km. In 2003, 61·8% lived in urban areas. The estimated population in 2005 was 13·23m.

The UN gives a projected population for 2010 of 14·19m.

The population was distributed by provinces as follows in 2001 (census figures):

Province	Sq. km	Population	Capital	Population
Azuay	8,124·7	599,546	Cuenca	277,374
Bolívar	3,939·9	169,370	Guaranda	20,742
Cañar	3,122·1	194,529	Azogues	27,866
Carchi	3,605·1	206,981	Tulcán	47,359
Chimborazo	6,569·3	403,632	Riobamba	124,807
Cotopaxi	6,071·9	349,540	Latacunga	51,689
El Oro	5,850·1	525,763	Machala	204,578
Esmeraldas	15,239·1	385,223	Esmeraldas	95,124
Guayas	20,502·5	3,309,034	Guayaquil	1,985,379
Imbabura	4,559·3	344,044	Ibarra	108,535
Loja	11,026·5	404,835	Loja	118,532
Los Ríos	7,175·0	650,178	Babahoyo	76,869
Manabí	18,878·8	1,186,025	Portoviejo	171,847
Morona-Santiago	25,690·0	115,412	Macas	13,602
Napo	11,430·9	79,139	Tena	16,669
Orellana	22,500·0	86,493	Francisco de Orellana	18,298
Pastaza	29,773·7	61,779	Puyo	24,432

Province	Sq. km	Population	Capital	Population
Pichincha	12,914·7	2,388,817	Quito	1,399,378
Sucumbíos	18,327·5	128,995	Nueva Loja	34,106
Tungurahua	3,334·8	441,034	Ambato	154,095
Zamora-Chinchipe	23,110·8	76,601	Zamora	10,355
Galápagos	8,010·0	18,640	Puerto Baquerizo Moreno	4,908
Non-delimited zones	2,288·8	72,588		

SOCIAL STATISTICS

2001 estimates: births, 328,000; deaths, 68,000. Rates, 2001 estimates (per 1,000 population): birth, 26·0; death, 5·4. Life expectancy at birth, 2003, was 71·4 years for males and 77·3 years for females. Annual population growth rate, 1992–2002, 1·8%. Infant mortality, 2001, 24 per 1,000 live births; fertility rate, 2001, 2·9 children per woman. In 1998 the most popular age for marrying was 20–24 for both men and women.

CLIMATE

The climate varies from equatorial, through warm temperate to mountain conditions, according to altitude, which affects temperatures and rainfall. In coastal areas, the dry season is from May to Dec., but only from June to Sept. in mountainous parts, where temperatures may be 20°F colder than on the coast. Quito, Jan. 59°F (15°C), July 58°F (14·4°C). Annual rainfall 44" (1,115 mm). Guayaquil, Jan. 79°F (26·1°C), July 75°F (23·9°C). Annual rainfall 39" (986 mm).

CONSTITUTION AND GOVERNMENT

A new constitution came into force on 10 Aug. 1998. It provides for an executive president and a vice-president to be directly elected by universal suffrage. The president appoints and leads a *Council of Ministers*, and determines the number and functions of the ministries that comprise the executive branch. The new constitution strengthened the executive branch by eliminating mid-term congressional elections and by restricting congress' power to challenge and remove cabinet ministers.

Legislative power is vested in a *National Congress* of 100 members, popularly elected by province. Voting is obligatory for all literate citizens of 18–65 years.

National Anthem

'Salve, Oh Patria, mil veces, Oh Patria' ('Hail, Oh Fatherland, a thousand times, Oh Fatherland'); words by J. L. Mera, tune by A. Neumane.

GOVERNMENT CHRONOLOGY

Heads of State since 1944. (AD = Democratic Alliance; CFP = Concentration of Popular Forces; CID = Democratic Institutional Coalition; DP–UDC = People's Democracy–Christian Democratic Union; FNV = National Velasquista Federation; FRA = Alfarista Radical Front; ID = Democratic Left; MCDN = Nacional Democratic Civic Movement; MSC = Social Christian Party (called PSC since 1967); PRE = Ecuadorian Roldosist Party; PSC = Social Christian Party; PSP = January 21 Patriotic Society; PUR = Republican Union Party; n/p = non-party)

Presidents

1944–47	AD	José María Velasco Ibarra
1947–48	n/p	Carlos Julio Arosemena Tola
1948–52	MCDN	Galo Plaza Lasso
1952–56	FNV	José María Velasco Ibarra
1956–60	MSC	Camilo Ponce Enríquez
1960–61	FNV	José María Velasco Ibarra
1961–63	FNV	Carlos Julio Arosemena Monroy

Military Junta

1963–66		Adm. Ramón Castro Jijón (chair); Gen. Luis Cabrera Sevilla; Col. Guillermo Freile Posso; Gen. Mario Gándara Enríquez

Presidents

1966	n/p	Clemente Yerovi Indaburu
1966–68	CID	Otto Arosemena Gómez
1968–72	FNV	José María Velasco Ibarra
1972–76	military	Gen. Guillermo Rodríguez Lara

Military Junta

1976–79		Admr. Alfredo Ernesto Poveda Burbano (chair); Gen. Luis Leoro Franco; Gen. Luis G. Durán Arcentales military

Presidents

1979–81	CFP	Jaime Roldós Aguilera
1981–84	DP–UDC	Osvaldo Hurtado Larrea
1984–88	PSC	León Esteban Febres Cordero
1988–92	ID	Rodrigo Borja Cevallos
1992–96	PUR	Sixto Alfonso Durán-Ballén
1996–97	PRE	Abdalá Jaime Bucaram Ortiz
1997–98	FRA	Fabián Ernesto Alarcón Rivera
1998–2000	DP–UDC	Jorge Jamil Mahuad Witt
2000–03	DP–UDC	Gustavo Noboa Bejarano
2003–05	PSP	Lucio Edwin Gutiérrez Borbúa
2005–	n/p	Luis Alfredo Palacio González

RECENT ELECTIONS

Dissatisfaction with President Fabián Alarcón led to presidential elections in 1998. Jamil Mahuad, candidate of the centre-right Popular Democracy party (DP), won in the second round of the presidential election on 12 July 1998, with 51·3% of the votes, against 48·7% for Alvaro Noboa, a populist businessman. In the first round on 31 May he had defeated five other candidates to win 35·3% of the vote. After a coup in Jan. 2000 Noboa (who was elected vice-president) replaced Jamil Mahuad as president. In the first round of presidential elections held on 20 Oct. 2002 Col. Lucio Gutiérrez (the instigator of the coup) won 20·3% of the vote, against 17·4% for Alvaro Noboa. In the run-off held on 24 Nov. 2002 Gutiérrez won 54·3% against 45·7% for Noboa.

In National Congress elections on 20 Oct. 2002 the Social Christian Party (PSC) won 25 seats, the Democratic Left (ID) 16, the Ecuadorian Roldosist Party (PRE) 15, the National Action Institutional Renewal Party (PRIAN) 10, the 21 January Patriotic Society (PSP) 9, the Pluri–National Pachakutik Movement–New Country (MUPP–NP) 6, the Popular Democratic Movement (MPD) 5, the People's Democracy–Christian Democrat Union (DP–UDC) 4 and the Socialist Party of Ecuador–Wide Front (PS–FA) 3. Independent candidates won the remaining seven seats.

Presidential and parliamentary elections are scheduled to take place on 15 Oct. 2006.

CURRENT ADMINISTRATION

President: Dr Alfredo Palacio; b. 1939 (sworn in 20 April 2005).

Vice-President: Alejandro Serrano.

In March 2006 the cabinet comprised:

Minister of Agriculture and Livestock: Pablo Rizzo. *Defence:* Gen. Oswaldo Jarrín. *Economy and Finance:* Diego Borja Cornejo. *Education and Culture:* Raúl Vallejo. *Energy and Mines:* Iván Rodríguez. *Environment:* Anita Albán. *Foreign Relations:* Francisco Carrión. *Foreign Trade, Industrialization, Fishing and Competitiveness:* Jorge Illingworth. *Government and Police:* Felipe Vega. *Labour and Employment:* Galo Chiriboga. *Public Health:* Iván Zambrano. *Public Works and Communications:* Derliz Palacios. *Social Welfare:* Atahualpa Medina. *Tourism:* María Isabel Salvador. *Urban Development and Housing (acting):* Héctor Vélez.

Office of the President (Spanish only):
  http://www.presidencia.gov.ec

CURRENT LEADERS

Dr Alfredo Palacio

Position
President

Introduction
Dr Alfredo Palacio, a cardiologist with little ministerial experience, was elected by the national congress to be the country's president on 20 April 2005. His appointment came amid a week of mass protests that resulted in the sacking of Lucio Gutiérrez as president. Palacio was faced with the task of introducing economic reforms, fighting poverty and quelling unrest in the oil-producing east of the country.

Early Life
Luis Alfredo Palacio González was born on 22 Jan. 1939 in the port-city of Guayaquil. He attended the Abdón Calderón primary school and the Colegio San José La Salle, before graduating in medicine from the Guayaquil University in 1967. He moved to Cleveland, Ohio in June 1969 to work as an intern specializing in cardiology at the city's Mount Sinai hospital. Two years later he relocated to Missouri, first working at the state's Veteran's Administration hospital and, from July 1972, at Barnes Hospital, Washington University in St Louis. Returning to Ecuador in 1979, Palacio practised at the National Institute of Cardiology. He maintained an academic career, lecturing in cardiology and public health at Guayaquil University's faculty of medicine and publishing numerous papers and books. By 1989 he was the faculty's principal professor in cardiology.

Although not a member of a political party, Palacio became minister for public health in 1994, in the government of the moderate-conservative Sixto Durán-Ballén, who had won the presidential election of July 1992. Durán's government ushered in a new economic programme, which included cutting state subsidies, joining the World Trade Organization and encouraging foreign investment. However, interest rates remained high and a resumption of the border war with Peru in early 1995 left the country with a crippling debt. When Durán was ousted in the presidential election of July 1996, Palacio left the political stage to continue his academic work and cardiology practice. The late 1990s saw an economic downturn and increasing political instability, which culminated in a bloodless military coup in Jan. 2000, led by Lucio Gutiérrez (although Gustavo Noboa became the president). Dollarization of the currency and an IMF structural-adjustment programme followed, as did widespread emigration. Palacio re-entered the political scene in late 2002, as the running mate for Gutiérrez in the Nov. presidential elections. They campaigned on a left-wing, populist platform, promising to tackle poverty, social problems and corruption. When Gutiérrez won the run-off, Palacio took up the post of vice-president.

Gutiérrez attempted to reduce Ecuador's debt by cutting subsidies on food and cooking gas, leading to widespread resentment. The president's popularity plunged and, though he survived an attempt to impeach him in Nov. 2004, he lost further support when he was accused of intervening in the affairs of the Supreme Court. By mid-April 2005 the country was gripped by mass protest. When the presidential palace in the capital, Quito, was engulfed by over 100,000 protestors on 20 April 2005, congress sacked Gutiérrez and named Alfredo Palacio as the new president.

Career in Office
Palacio was critical of Gutiérrez during the final months of his presidency, and Palacio's lack of an affinity with a political party was seen by many in congress as a strength, although analysts observed that many of the ministers he chose hailed from the Izquierda Democratia (Democratic Left). Palacio promised to fight poverty and implement reform programmes, including

amendments to the country's 1998 constitution. Unrest continued, however, particularly in the oil-producing areas in the east of the country. Protesters sabotaged drilling equipment and blocked roads, demanding that foreign oil companies provide money and jobs for local people. In Aug. 2005 Palacio declared a state of emergency in the provinces of Sucumbíos and Orellana and granted some concessions to protesters.

DEFENCE

Military service is selective, with a one-year period of conscription. The country is divided into four military zones, with headquarters at Quito, Guayaquil, Cuenca and Pastaza.

In 2003 defence expenditure totalled US$640m. (US$49 per capita), representing 2·4% of GDP.

Army
Strength (2002) 50,000, with about 100,000 reservists.

Navy
Navy combatant forces include two diesel submarines and two ex-UK frigates. The Maritime Air Force has eight aircraft but no combat aircraft. Naval personnel in 2002 totalled 5,500 including some 1,700 marines.

Air Force
The Air Force had a 2002 strength of about 4,000 personnel and 79 combat aircraft, and includes Jaguars, Mirage F-1s and Kfirs.

INTERNATIONAL RELATIONS

Ecuador is a member of the UN, WTO, OAS, Inter-American Development Bank the Andean Group, LAIA, IOM and the Antarctic Treaty.

ECONOMY

Agriculture accounted for 9·0% of GDP in 2002, industry 28·3% and services 62·6%.

Overview
Up to the 1970s Ecuador's GDP and GDP per capita both grew steadily. In the 1980s and most of the 1990s per capita income stagnated at a level above the Latin American average but below the world average. With its economy heavily dependent on oil exports, the fall in oil prices in the late 1990s combined with natural disasters to trigger a momentary but sharp collapse in GDP and income levels. The economy rebounded in the early 2000s and has since maintained modest growth on the back of strong oil prices. Whilst public debt as a percentage of GDP has fallen, the pace of repayment stalled as government priorities shifted towards social spending, causing friction with the World Bank and foreign investors. Economic reforms and privatization plans have been on the agenda for over a decade, but no significant progress has been made and political instability and corruption remain obstacles. Corruption is endemic and poverty continues to afflict much of the population. Violent protests are a threat to the maintenance of oil output levels and a potential hindrance to further investment in the country's oil industry.

Currency
The monetary unit is the US dollar. Inflation was 2·7% in 2004, down from 7·9% in 2003. In March 2000 the government passed a law to phase out the former national currency, the *sucre*, to be replaced by the US dollar, and in April bank cash machines began dispensing dollars instead of sucres. On 11 Sept. 2000 the dollar became the only legal currency. Foreign exchange reserves were US$880m. in June 2002 and gold reserves 845,000 troy oz.

Budget
Revenues in 2002 were US$4,526m. and expenditures US$4,694m.

In 2000 VAT was increased from 10% to 12% and corporate tax from 15% to 25%.

Performance

Ecuador experienced a recession in 1999, with the economy shrinking by 6·3%, partly owing to years of mismanagement and partly to El Niño (periodic warm current of water that brings about temporary climate change). There was a recovery in 2000, however, with the growth rate reaching 2·8%. In 2001 growth was 5·1%, the highest in Latin America, followed in 2002 by growth of 3·4%. In 2003 GDP growth was 2·7% followed by 6·9% in 2004. Total GDP in 2004 was US$30·3bn.

Banking and Finance

The Central Bank of Ecuador (*President of the Directorate*, Eduardo Cabezas), the bank of issue, with a capital and reserves of US$1,557m. at 31 Dec. 1995, is modelled after the Federal Reserve Banks of the USA; through branches opened in 16 towns, it now deals in mortgage bonds. There are five other state banks, 16 commercial banks, four foreign banks and a *Multibanco*. All commercial banks must be affiliated to the Central Bank. Legislation of May 1994 liberalized the financial sector. The national monetary board is based in Quito.

There are stock exchanges in Quito and Guayaquil.

Weights and Measures

The metric system is standard but some US measures are used.

ENERGY AND NATURAL RESOURCES

Environment

Ecuador's carbon dioxide emissions from the consumption and flaring of fossil fuels were the equivalent of 1·7 tonnes per capita in 2002.

Electricity

Installed capacity was 3·49m. kW in 2000. Production was 10·61bn. kWh in 2000; consumption per capita was 839 kWh.

Oil and Gas

Production of crude oil in 2000 was 20·9m. tonnes. Estimated reserves, 2002, 4,600m. bbls. In 1999 natural gas production was 772m. cu. metres. Estimated reserves (2002), 109bn. cu. metres.

Minerals

Main products are silver, gold, copper and zinc. The country also has some iron, uranium, lead, coal, cobalt, manganese and titanium.

Agriculture

There were 1·62m. ha. of arable land in 2001 and 1·37m. ha. of permanent crops. In 2002, 24·5% of the economically active population worked in agriculture.

50,000 ha. of rich virgin land in the Santo Domingo de los Colorados area has been set aside for settlement by medium and large landowners. A law of 1994 restricts the redistribution of land to small farmers to land which has lain fallow for more than three years.

The staple export products are bananas and coffee. Main crops, in 1,000 tonnes, in 2000: bananas, 6,816; sugarcane, 6,200; rice, 1,520; potatoes, 788; maize, 747; plantains, 476; palm oil, 268; cassava, 184; soybeans, 170; oranges, 157; coffee, 133. Ecuador's annual banana crop is exceeded only by that of India.

Livestock, 2000: cattle, 5·11m.; sheep, 2·13m.; pigs, 2·87m.; horses, 521,000; goats, 284,000; asses, 269,000; chickens, 130m.

Forestry

Excepting the agricultural zones and a few arid spots on the Pacific coast, Ecuador is a vast forest. 10·56m. ha., or 38·1% of the land area, was forested in 2000. In 2001, 10·92m. cu. metres of roundwood were produced.

Fisheries

In 1993 primary sea export products were valued at US$498·9m. Fish landings in 2001 were 586,570 tonnes (almost entirely from sea fishing).

INDUSTRY

Industry produced 29·4% of GDP in 2001, including 11·7% from manufacturing. Manufacturing showed an annual increase of 2·9% in 2001. Main products include (2000, in 1,000 tonnes): residual fuel oil, 3,914; cement (1999), 2,262; distillate fuel oil, 1,751; petrol, 1,302.

Labour

Out of 3,673,200 people in urban employment in 2001, 1,026,700 were in wholesale and retail trade/repair of motor vehicles, motorcycles and personal and household goods; 610,600 in manufacturing; 244,600 in transport, storage and communications; and 239,800 in agriculture, hunting and forestry. In June 2001, 10·4% of the workforce was unemployed.

Trade Unions

The main trade union federation is the United Workers' Front.

INTERNATIONAL TRADE

Most restrictions on foreign investment were removed in 1992 and the repatriation of profits was permitted. Foreign debt was US$16,452m. in 2002.

Imports and Exports

Imports and exports for calendar years, in US$1m.:

	1998	1999	2000	2001	2002
Imports f.o.b.	5,458	3,028	3,743	5,325	6,196
Exports f.o.b.	4,326	4,615	5,137	4,862	5,192

Main imports in 1999 were (in US$1m.): machinery and transport equipment, 869·8; chemicals, 663·8; manufactured goods, 498·4; petroleum and petroleum products, 143·1; cereals, 134·8. Ecuador is the world's leading exporter of bananas (US$954·4m. in 1999), with approximately a third of world banana exports. Other major exports (1999, in US$1m.): crude oil, 1,312·3; shrimps, 608·5; fish, 256·1; cut flowers, 180·4; cocoa, 102·7. Main import suppliers, 1999: USA, 918·5 (30·4%); Colombia, 363·4; Venezuela, 193·2; Japan, 142·0; Germany, 126·0. Main export markets (in US$1m.): USA, 1,708·2 (38·4%); Colombia, 227·2; Panama, 219·5; South Korea, 213·5; Italy, 208·1.

COMMUNICATIONS

Roads

In 2002 there were 43,197 km of roads. In 2001 there were 529,359 passenger cars (43·5 per 1,000 inhabitants) and 54,698 lorries and vans. There were 1,177 fatalities in road accidents in 1999.

In 1998 storms and floods on the coast, caused by El Niño, resulted in 2,000 km of roads being damaged or destroyed.

Rail

The railway network, once 971 km long, now has a total length of just 204 km. In 2002 passenger-km travelled came to 33m.

Civil Aviation

There are international airports at Quito (Mariscal Sucre) and Guayaquil (Simon Bolivar). The main Ecuadorian carriers are Tame Linea Aerea del Ecuador and Icaro. In 2001 Quito handled 2,213,000 passengers (1,140,000 on domestic flights) and 105,400 tonnes of freight, and Guayaquil handled 1,416,000 passengers (749,000 on domestic flights) and 40,500 tonnes of freight.

Shipping

Ecuador has three major seaports, of which Guayaquil is the most important, and six minor ones. In 2002 the merchant navy totalled 313,000 GRT of ocean-going vessels, including oil tankers 219,000 GRT. In 2001 vessels totalling 3,064,000 NRT entered ports and vessels totalling 18,761,000 NRT cleared.

Telecommunications
In 2002 there were 2,987,000 telephone subscribers, equivalent to 230·8 for every 1,000 persons, and 403,000 PCs were in use (31·1 for every 1,000 persons). Mobile phone subscribers numbered 1,560,900 in 2002 and there were 58,000 fax machines. Ecuador had 537,900 Internet users in 2002.

Postal Services
In 2003 there were 254 post offices.

SOCIAL INSTITUTIONS

Justice
The Supreme Court in Quito, consisting of a President and 30 Justices, comprises ten chambers each of three Justices. It is also a Court of Appeal. There is a Superior Court in each province, comprising chambers (as appointed by the Supreme Court) of three magistrates each. The Superior Courts are at the apex of a hierarchy of various tribunals. There is no death penalty.

The population in penal institutions in June 2002 was 7,716 (59 per 100,000 of national population).

Education
In 2000–01 there were 199,588 pre-primary pupils with 13,755 teachers. Primary education is free and compulsory. Private schools, both primary and secondary, are under some state supervision. In 2000–01 there were 1·96m. pupils and 84,758 teachers in primary schools; and 936,406 pupils with 79,231 teachers in secondary schools. In the public sector in 2000–01 there were: 9 universities, 8 technical universities, 2 institutes of technology, 1 polytechnical university, 1 military polytechnic and 1 agricultural university; and in the private sector: 9 universities, 3 Roman Catholic universities, 4 institutes of technology, 2 polytechnic institutes and 1 technical university. Adult literacy was 91·0% in 2003 (male, 92·3%; female, 89·7%).

In 2000–01 total expenditure on education came to 1·7% of GNP and 8·0% of total government spending.

Health
In 2002 there were 3,496 hospitals and clinics with 14 beds per 10,000 inhabitants. There were 18,335 physicians, 2,062 dentists, 19,549 nurses and 1,037 midwives in 2000.

Welfare
Those who qualify for a pension must be aged 55 and have 360 months of contributions if born before 30 Nov. 1946, or be aged 65 with 180 months of contributions. A scheme to change the age of retirement to 60 with 360 months of contributions is being phased in gradually. In 2003 the minimum monthly pension was US$25, and the maximum pension was US$125.

RELIGION
The state recognizes no religion and grants freedom of worship to all. In 2001 there were 11·91m. Roman Catholics. There were also small numbers of Protestants and followers of other faiths. In May 2005 there was one cardinal.

CULTURE

World Heritage Sites
Ecuador has four sites on the UNESCO World Heritage List: the Galápagos Islands (inscribed on the list in 1978 and 2001); the City of Quito (1978); Sangay National Park (1983); and the Historic Centre of Santa Ana de los Ríos de Cuenca (1999).

Broadcasting
There were 5·2m. radio sets in 2000 and 2·9m. TV receivers in 2001 (colour by NTSC).

Press
There were 36 daily newspapers in 2000, with a circulation of 1,220,000.

Tourism
Foreign tourists numbered 654,000 in 2002, with spending of US$447m.

DIPLOMATIC REPRESENTATIVES
Of Ecuador in the United Kingdom (Flat 3b, 3 Hans Cres., London, SW1X 0LS)
Ambassador: Vacant.
Chargé d'Affaires a.i.: Déborah Salgado Campaña.

Of the United Kingdom in Ecuador (Citiplaza Bldg, Naciones Unidas Ave., & Republica de El Salvador, 14th Floor, Quito)
Ambassador: Richard Lewington.

Of Ecuador in the USA (2535 15th St., NW, Washington, D.C., 20009)
Ambassador: Luis Gallegos Chiriboga.

Of the USA in Ecuador (Avenida 12 de Octubre y Avenida Patria, Quito)
Ambassador: Linda J. Jewell.

Of Ecuador to the United Nations
Ambassador: Diego Cordovez.

Of Ecuador to the European Union
Ambassador: Méntor Villagomez Merino.

FURTHER READING
Hidrobo, J. A., *Power and Industrialization in Ecuador.* Boulder (CO), 1993
Martz, J. D., *Politics and Petroleum in Ecuador.* New Brunswick, 1987
Pineo, R. F., *Social and Economic Reform in Ecuador.* Univ. Press of Florida, 1996
Roos, W. and van Renterghem, O., *Ecuador in Focus: A Guide to the People, Politics and Culture.* Interlink Publishing Group, Northampton (MA), 1997
Selverston-Scher, M., *Ethnopolitics in Ecuador: Indigenous Rights and the Strengthening of Democracy.* Lynne Rienner Publishers, 2001

National Statistical Office: Instituto Nacional de Estadistica y Censos (INEC), Juan Larrea 534 y Riofrío, Quito.
Website (Spanish only): http://www.inec.gov.ec/

EGYPT

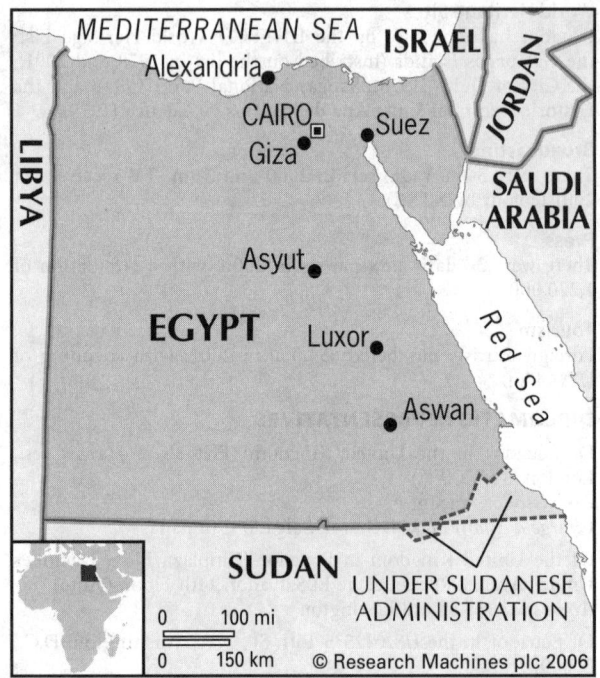

MEDITERRANEAN SEA
ISRAEL
JORDAN
Alexandria
CAIRO
Giza
Suez
LIBYA
SAUDI ARABIA
EGYPT
Asyut
Luxor
Red Sea
Aswan
SUDAN
UNDER SUDANESE ADMINISTRATION
0   100 mi
0   150 km
© Research Machines plc 2006

Jumhuriyat Misr al-Arabiya
(Arab Republic of Egypt)

Capital: Cairo
Population projection, 2010: 81·13m.
GDP per capita, 2003: (PPP$) 3,950
HDI/world rank: 0·659/119

KEY HISTORICAL EVENTS

There is evidence of Neolithic habitation along the Nile and there was agricultural activity by 6000 BC. Around 3100 BC Menes united Upper and Lower Egypt and so began the rule of 31 successive pharaonic dynasties. This period was marked by three phases. The Old Kingdom, which lasted from *c.* 2575–2150 BC, was governed centrally from Memphis and saw the construction of the Giza pyramids. The Middle Kingdom (*c.* 2050–1650 BC) saw Egypt reach its zenith culturally and intellectually. The era finished with the incursions of the Hyksos, a nomadic Asiatic tribe. The New Kingdom came into being with the expulsion of the Hyksos around 1550 BC and lasted until 1050 BC. It saw Egypt achieve its greatest territorial dominance, with Syria, Palestine and northern Iraq all under Egyptian jurisdiction.

The last Pharaoh was ousted by Persian invading forces under Cambyses in 525 BC. The Persians remained in power until overrun by Alexander the Great around 330 BC. He founded the port city of Alexandria, including its great lighthouse, and made it the commercial and cultural centre of the Greek world. On his death in 305 BC, Ptolemy of Macedonia seized power, establishing a dynasty which lasted until 30 BC and the suicide of Cleopatra. Egypt then became a province of the Roman empire until Islamic forces took control in AD 642.

Under the successive rule of Turkish, Arabic and Mameluke leaders, Egypt gained an increasingly Arabic Islamic culture. In 1517 it was absorbed into the Ottoman empire. Napoleonic forces

seized the country between 1798 and 1801, but were forced to flee by a combined Anglo-Ottoman force. Muhammad Ali (1805–40) succeeded in establishing a hereditary dynasty of Khedives but with the opening of the Suez Canal in 1869 and Britain's purchase of the Khedives' shares, Egypt's strategic importance paved the way for foreign intervention and domination. Egypt came under the control of Britain after 1882 until limited independence in 1922.

In the Second World War (1939–45) Egypt supported the Allies. Following a revolution in July 1952 led by Gen. Neguib, King Farouk abdicated in favour of his son but in 1953 the monarchy was abolished. Neguib became president but encountered opposition from the military when he attempted to move towards a parliamentary republic. Col. Gamal Abdel Nasser became head of state on 14 June 1954 (president from 1956), and remained in office until he died on 28 Sept. 1970. In 1956 Egypt nationalized the Suez Canal, a move which led Britain, France and Israel to mount military attacks against Egypt until forced by the UN and the USA to withdraw.

The 1960s and 1970s saw constant conflict with Israel until President Muhammad Anwar Sadat, who succeeded Nasser, made a dramatic peace treaty with Israel in March 1979. Sadat was assassinated on 6 Oct. 1981, and was succeeded by the vice-president, Lieut.-Gen. Muhammad Hosni Mubarak.

TERRITORY AND POPULATION

Egypt is bounded in the east by Israel and Palestine, the Gulf of Aqaba and the Red Sea, south by Sudan, west by Libya and north by the Mediterranean. The total area (including inland waters) is 1,001,450 sq. km, but the cultivated and settled area, that is the Nile Valley, Delta and oases, covers only 35,189 sq. km. A number of new desert cities are being developed to entice people away from the overcrowded Nile valley. Population density in this latter, 1992, 1,557·9 per sq. km. The 1996 census population was 61,492,914; in 2005 the estimated population was 74·03m. In 2003, 57·8% of the population were rural.

The UN gives a projected population for 2010 of 81·13m.

1·9m. Egyptians were living abroad in 2002.

Area, population and capitals of the governorates (1986 and 1996 censuses):

Governorate	Area (in sq. km)	Population (1986 census)	(1996 census)	Capital
Alexandria	2,679	2,917,327	3,339,076	Alexandria
Aswan	679	801,408	974,068	Aswan
Asyut	1,553	2,223,034	2,802,334	Asyut
Behera	10,130	3,257,168	3,994,297	Damanhur
Beni Suef	1,322	1,442,981	1,859,214	Beni Suef
Cairo	214	6,052,836	6,800,992	Cairo
Dakahlia	3,471	3,500,470	4,223,919	Mansura
Damietta	589	741,264	913,555	Damietta
Fayum	1,827	1,544,047	1,989,774	Fayum
Gharbia	1,942	2,870,960	3,406,020	Tanta
Giza	85,153	3,700,054	4,784,099	Giza
Ismailia	1,442	544,427	714,828	Ismailia
Kafr El Shaikh	3,437	1,800,129	2,223,659	Kafr El Shaikh
Kalyubia	1,001	2,514,244	3,301,244	Benha
Luxor	55	—	361,138	Luxor
Matruh	212,112	160,567	212,001	Matruh
Menia	2,262	2,648,043	3,310,129	Menia
Menufia	1,532	2,227,087	2,760,431	Shibin Al Kom
New Valley	376,505	113,838	141,774	Al Kharija
Port Said	72	399,793	472,335	Port Said
Qena	1,796	2,252,315	2,442,016	Qena
Red Sea	203,685	90,491	157,315	El Gurdakah
Sharkia	4,180	3,420,119	4,281,068	Zagazig
North Sinai	27,574	171,505	252,160	Al Arish

Governorate	Area (in sq. km)	Population (1986 census)	(1996 census)	Capital
South Sinai	33,140	28,988	54,826	At Tur
Suez	17,840	326,820	417,527	Suez
Suhag	1,547	2,455,134	3,125,115	Suhag

Principal cities, with estimated 2005 populations (in 1,000): Cairo, 7,765; Alexandria, 3,821; Giza (1998), 2,326; Shubra Al Khayma (1998), 912; Port Said, 538; Suez, 489.

Smaller cities, with 1996 populations (in 1,000): Mahalla Al Kubra, 395; Hulwan, 372; Tanta, 371; Mansura, 369; Luxor (Uqsur), 361; Asyut, 343; Zagazig, 267; Fayum, 261; Ismailia, 254; Kafr Ad Dawwar, 232; Aswan, 219; Damanhur, 212; Menia, 201; Beni Suef, 172; Qena, 171; Suhag, 170; Shibin Al Kom, 160; Benha, 146; Kafr Ash Shaikh, 125.

The official language is Arabic, although French and English are widely spoken.

SOCIAL STATISTICS

Births, 1999, 1,693,025 (27·0 per 1,000 population); deaths, 401,433 (6·4); marriages, 525,000 (rate per 1,000 population, 8·4); divorces, 73,000 (1·2). Annual population growth rate, 1992–2002, 1·9%. In 1991 the average family size was 4·3 and 40% of the population was under 40 years. Life expectancy at birth, 2004, was 68·4 years for males and 72·8 years for females. Fertility rate, 2001, 3·0 births per woman; infant mortality, 2001, 35 per 1,000 live births. Egypt has made some of the best progress in recent years in reducing child mortality. The number of deaths per 1,000 live births among children under five was reduced from more than 100 in 1990 to only just over 50 in 1999.

In the Human Development Index, or HDI (measuring progress in countries in longevity, knowledge and standard of living), Egypt's index achieved the second largest improvement during the last quarter of the 20th century, rising from 0·430 in 1975 to 0·635 in 1999. Only Indonesia recorded a greater increase.

CLIMATE

The climate is mainly dry, but there are winter rains along the Mediterranean coast. Elsewhere, rainfall is very low and erratic in its distribution. Winter temperatures are comfortable everywhere, but summer temperatures are very high, especially in the south. Cairo, Jan. 56°F (13·3°C), July 83°F (28·3°C). Annual rainfall 1·2" (28 mm). Alexandria, Jan. 58°F (14·4°C), July 79°F (26·1°C). Annual rainfall 7" (178 mm). Aswan, Jan. 62°F (16·7°C), July 92°F (33·3°C). Annual rainfall (trace). Giza, Jan. 55°F (12·8°C), July 78°F (25·6°C). Annual rainfall 16" (389 mm). Ismailia, Jan. 56°F (13·3°C), July 84°F (28·9°C). Annual rainfall 1·5" (37 mm). Luxor, Jan. 59°F (15°C), July 86°F (30°C). Annual rainfall (trace). Port Said, Jan. 58°F (14·4°C), July 78°F (27·2°C). Annual rainfall 3" (76 mm).

CONSTITUTION AND GOVERNMENT

The Constitution was approved by referendum on 11 Sept. 1971 and was amended on 22 May 1980. It defines Egypt as 'an Arab Republic with a democratic, socialist system' and the Egyptian people as 'part of the Arab nation'. The *President* was to be nominated by the People's Assembly and confirmed by plebiscite for a six-year term. However, In March 2005 parliament approved a proposal by President Mubarak to amend the constitution to allow for multi-candidate presidential elections. This was approved in a referendum on 25 May 2005. The President may appoint one or more *Vice-Presidents*.

The *People's Assembly* consists of 454 members, 444 directly elected and ten appointed by the president. An upper house, the *Shura Council*, was established in 1980, but it has a consultative role only. It has 264 members, 176 elected by popular vote and 88 appointed by the president. There is a *Constitutional Court*.

The President appoints the Prime Minister and a Council of Ministers. It is traditional for two ministers to be Coptic Christians.

National Anthem

'Biladi' ('My homeland'); words and tune by S. Darwish.

GOVERNMENT CHRONOLOGY

Heads of State since 1953. (ASU = Arab Socialist Union; LR = Liberation Rally; NDP = National Democratic Party; NU = National Union)

President
1953–54	military, LR	Muhammad Neguib

Chairman of the Revolutionary Command Council
1954	military, LR	Gamal Abdel Nasser

President
1954	military, LR	Muhammad Neguib

Chairman of the Revolutionary Command Council
1954–56	military, LR	Gamal Abdel Nasser

Presidents
1956–70	NU, ASU	Gamal Abdel Nasser
1970–81	ASU, NDP	Muhammad Anwar Sadat
1981–	NDP	Muhammad Hosni Mubarak

RECENT ELECTIONS

Elections for the People's Assembly were held in six rounds between 9 Nov. 2005 and 7 Dec. 2005. Turnout was 26·2%. The National Democratic Party (NDP) gained 388 seats; ind., 112 (of which 88 with the Muslim Brotherhood); New Wafd Party, 6; Al-Tagamu, 2; Al-Ghad 1.

On 26 Sept. 1999 a referendum was held to confirm the People's Assembly's nomination of Hosni Mubarak for a fourth term as president. Turnout was 79% with Mubarak gaining 93·97% support. The first multiparty election in Egypt's history took place on 7 Sept. 2005 when Hosni Mubarak was re-elected with 88·6% of the votes against 7·3% for Ayman Nour and 2·8% for Noaman Gomaa. There were some allegations of ballot stuffing, vote buying and voter intimidation. Turnout was 23%.

CURRENT ADMINISTRATION

President: Hosni Mubarak; b. 1928 (NDP; first sworn in on 14 Oct. 1981 and most recently re-elected in Sept. 2005).

In March 2006 the cabinet comprised:

Prime Minister: Ahmad Mahmoud Nazif; b. 1952 (NDP; sworn in on 14 July 2004).

Minister of Agriculture and Land Reclamation: Amin Abaza. *Civil Aviation:* Ahmed Mohammed Shafique. *Transport:* Mohamed Mansour. *Electricity and Energy:* Hassan Ahmed Younis. *Defence and Military Production:* Field Marshal Mohamed Hussein Tantawi. *Information:* Anas el-Fiqqi. *Foreign Affairs:* Ahmed Ali Ahmed Abou Elgheit. *International Co-operation:* Fayza Abu el-Naga. *Justice:* Mahmoud Abo Elleil Rashed. *Culture:* Farouk Abdel Aziz Hosni. *Finance:* Yousef Boutrous Ghali. *Religious Affairs (Awqaf):* Mahmoud Hamdi Zakzouk. *Health:* Hatem el-Gabali. *Trade and Industry:* Rasheed Mohamed Rasheed Hussein. *Education:* Yousri Saber Hussein al-Gamal. *Higher Education and Scientific Research:* Hani Helal. *Petroleum:* Amin Sameh Fahmy. *Interior:* Habib Ibrahim Al-Adly. *Tourism:* Zuheir Garana. *Irrigation and Water Resources:* Mahmoud Abd Al-Halim Abu-Zeid. *Housing:* Ahmed el-Maghrabi. *Communications and Information Technology:* Tarek Mohamed Kamel Mahmoud. *Investment:* Mahmoud Safwat Mohyee El-Din. *Manpower and Immigration:* Aicha Abdel Hadi. *Planning:* Osman Mohammed Osman. *Social Solidarity:* Ali Al-Sayed Al-Moselhi.

Office of the President: http://www.presidency.gov.eg

CURRENT LEADERS

Muhammad Hosni Mubarak

Position
President

Introduction
Following a career in the Air Force, Hosni Mubarak was appointed vice-president of Egypt in April 1975 and then became president in Oct. 1981 shortly after the assassination of Anwar Sadat by militant Islamic fundamentalists. He has since been re-elected as president on four occasions—in 1987, 1993, 1999 and 2005—and remains chairman of the dominant National Democratic Party (NDP). Mubarak kept faith with most of his predecessor's policies, in particular reconciliation with the Western powers (after Gamal Abdel Nasser's pro-Soviet stance) and Egypt's controversial peace accord with Israel. However, he also sought to re-establish links with Arab states. He has taken a hard line with Muslim extremists and has been the target of several assassination plots.

Early Life
Born in Kafr al Musailha on 4 May 1928, Mubarak attended high school and graduated from the military academy in Cairo before joining the Egyptian Air Force in 1950. He was promoted successively to squadron leader, base commander, director of the Air Force Academy (1967–69) and chief of staff (1969–72), before his appointment as commander of the Air Force and deputy minister for military affairs in 1972. In the 1973 war with Israel he was acclaimed for his command of Egyptian air operations. Two years later Sadat made Mubarak his vice-president.

Career in Office
Following Sadat's assassination, Mubarak was inaugurated as president and prime minister on 14 Oct. 1981 (although he relinquished the latter post in Jan. 1982). Under his presidency, Egypt's isolation in the Arab world in the wake of Sadat's peace treaty with Israel came to an end. By the end of the 1980s the country had resumed a leading role in regional politics. Mubarak supported UN sanctions against Iraq after its occupation of Kuwait in 1990, and Egypt participated in the Gulf War of 1991 in support of the Western-led coalition against the Iraqi president Saddam Hussein. Thereafter, Egypt's foreign policy focused on a comprehensive settlement between Israel and other neighbouring Arab states, with particular emphasis on resolving Palestinian grievances. This policy, however, was undermined by the outbreak from Sept. 2000 of the Palestinian intifada in opposition to Israeli occupation.

Since the 11 Sept. 2001 attacks on the USA, Mubarak has been a key supporter of the US campaign against terrorism, and Egypt itself has been the target of several terrorist attacks directed mainly against the tourism industry, a major source of revenue. Mubarak hosted summits on the Middle East peace process in 2000–03, and worked with Israel and the Palestinian Authority during 2004–05 to facilitate stability following Israel's withdrawal from Gaza.

Domestically Mubarak has maintained the political status quo, albeit with a measure of liberalization. However, his economic reforms have struggled to keep pace with inflation and rapid population growth, and he has alienated poorer sections of society. There was a resurgence of violent Islamic fundamentalism in the 1990s, targeted in particular at foreign tourists. Mubarak narrowly survived an assassination attempt by Egyptian militants in Addis Ababa, Ethiopia, in June 1995. His NDP government responded with a security crackdown on activists.

In early 2005 political reformers and opposition activists mounted a series of anti-government demonstrations. In Feb. Mubarak proposed amending the constitution to allow for the country's first multi-candidate presidential elections. That amendment was approved in a referendum in May, albeit with restrictions including a five-year registration for parties wanting to nominate candidates. As expected, Mubarak was re-elected for a fifth consecutive term in Sept. with 88·6% of the vote. However, only 23% of the eligible electorate turned out and there were allegations of vote buying and intimidation. In Dec. 2005 parliamentary elections ended with clashes between police and opposition supporters. Although the NDP retained its parliamentary majority, the Muslim Brotherhood won a record number of seats.

DEFENCE

Conscription is selective, and for one–three years (followed by refresher training over a period of up to nine years). Military expenditure totalled US$2,732m. in 2003 (US$40 per capita), representing 4·0% of GDP. According to *Deadly Arsenals*, published by the Carnegie Endowment for International Peace, Egypt has a chemical and biological weapons programme.

Army

Strength (2002) 320,000 (250,000 conscripts). In addition there were 250,000 reservists, a Central Security Force of 150,000, a National Guard of 60,000 and 20,000 Border Guards.

Navy

Major surface combatants include one destroyer and ten frigates. A small shore-based naval aviation branch operates 24 helicopters. There are naval bases at Al Ghardaqah, Alexandria, Hurghada, Mersa Matruh, Port Said, Port Tewfik, Safaqa and Suez. Naval personnel in 2002 totalled 19,000.

Air Force

Until 1979 the Air Force was equipped largely with aircraft of USSR design, but subsequent re-equipment involves aircraft bought in the West, as well as some supplied by China. Strength (2002) is about 29,000 personnel (10,000 conscripts), 128 attack helicopters and 608 combat aircraft including F-16s, MiG-21s, *Alpha Jets* and *Mirages*.

INTERNATIONAL RELATIONS

Egypt is a member of the UN, WTO, the League of Arab States, OAPEC (Organization of Arab Petroleum Exporting Countries), the African Union, African Development Bank, COMESA, IOM, OIC, Islamic Development Bank and the International Organization of the Francophonie.

ECONOMY

In 2002 agriculture accounted for 16·5% of GDP, industry 34·8% and services 48·7%.

Overview

The 1980s was a decade of macroeconomic disorder in Egypt. In the 1990s the government implemented an IMF-backed reform programme and the economy achieved stability. Reform started with a privatization push in the early 1990s and by the end of 2000 around 50% of state-owned enterprises were fully privatized. However, the late 1990s saw an economic downturn and privatization efforts stalled in the early 2000s. Egypt's economy has a consistent growth record but the pace is moderate for a developing country. Though Egypt's economy is the largest in North Africa, its per capita income is well below the region's average. In 2004 an economically liberal cabinet was appointed and the reform agenda was revived, with President Mubarak investing political capital in structural reforms to generate jobs and promote foreign investment. Cuts have been made in customs duties and income taxes and the government has tackled problems in the banking system, which accumulated large amounts of non-performing loans during the economic slowdown of the late 1990s. Since 2004 the government has sold off shares of state banks in joint ventures with foreign banks and taken steps to consolidate and strengthen them through mergers. The OECD argues that 'unemployment remains a serious problem for Egypt' and financial sector reform is seen as fundamental to achieving the growth rates necessary to generate significant employment. Two natural gas projects are under way that could make Egypt the sixth largest exporter of liquefied gas.

Currency

The monetary unit is the *Egyptian pound* (EGP) of 100 *piastres*. Inflation rates (based on IMF statistics) for fiscal years:

1997	1998	1999	2000	2001	2002	2003	2004
6·2%	4·7%	3·7%	2·8%	2·4%	2·4%	3·2%	8·1%

Faced with slowing economic activity, the country devalued the Egyptian pound four times in 2001. In Jan. 2003 the Egyptian pound was allowed to float against the dollar after years of a government-controlled foreign exchange regime. In May 2002 foreign exchange reserves were US$12,587m. and gold reserves 2·43m. troy oz. Total money supply in May 2002 was £E70,345m.

Budget

The financial year runs from 1 July. Revenues in 2000–01 were £E97,938m. and expenditures £E111,669m. Main sources of revenue were income and profits taxes, 28·4%; sales taxes, 18·4%; customs duties, 13·3%; oil revenue, 4·7%. Current expenditure accounted for 76·7% of total expenditures and capital expenditure 23·3%.

Performance

Real GDP growth rates (based on IMF statistics):

1997	1998	1999	2000	2001	2002	2003	2004
5·9%	7·5%	6·1%	5·4%	3·5%	3·2%	3·1%	4·1%

Total GDP in 2004 was US$75·1bn.

Banking and Finance

The Central Bank of Egypt (founded 1960) is the central bank and bank of issue. The *Governor* is Farouk el-Okdah.

In 2003, four major public-sector commercial banks accounted for some 77% of all banking assets: the National Bank of Egypt (the largest bank, with assets of nearly £E74bn in 1999), the Banque Misr, the Bank of Alexandria and the Banque du Caïre. There were 62 banks in total in 2002. Foreign banks have only been allowed to operate since 1996.

Foreign direct investment inflows, which were US$1,235m. in 2000, fell to just US$237m. in 2003.

There are stock exchanges in Cairo and Alexandria.

Weights and Measures

The metric system is official with the exception of the *feddan* (= 0·42 ha.) to measure land. However, other traditional measures are still in use: *Kadah* = 1·91 litres; *Rob* = 4 kadahs; *Keila* = 8 kadahs; *Ardeb* = 96 kadahs; *Dirhem* = 3·12 grammes; *Rotl* = 144 dirhems (0·449 kg); *Oke* = 400 dirhems; *Qantar* = 100 rotls or 36 okes.

ENERGY AND NATURAL RESOURCES

Environment

Egypt's carbon dioxide emissions from the consumption and flaring of fossil fuels in 2002 were the equivalent of 2·0 tonnes per capita.

Electricity

Installed capacity was 17·0m. kW in 2002. Electricity generated in 2003–04 was 95·18bn. kWh. Consumption per capita was an estimated 1,287 kWh in 2002. Electricity sector investments reached approximately £E2·7bn. in 2002–03. The use of solar energy is expanding.

Oil and Gas

Oil was discovered in 1909. Oil policy is controlled by the state-owned Egyptian General Petroleum Corporation, whole or part-owner of the production and refining companies. Oil reserves in 2002 were 3·7bn. bbls. Production of crude oil has been declining from a record 45·0m. tonnes in 1992 to 29·8m. tonnes in 2003–04.

As a result of a series of new discoveries in 1999 and 2000 gas reserves have been steadily increasing. Annual revenue from future natural gas exports could exceed US$1·5bn. 2002 total production amounted to 22·7bn. cu. metres. There were proven natural gas reserves of 1,533bn. cu. metres in 2002.

Water

The Aswan High Dam, completed in 1970, allows for a perennial irrigation system.

The Mubarak Pumping Station, the world's largest, has been operational since Jan. 2003. Located behind the Aswan High Dam at Lake Nasser, since its inauguration it has been pumping 14·5m. cu. metres of water per day into a 67 km canal to irrigate approximately 540,000 feddans of desert land in Toshka.

Minerals

Production (2003–04, in tonnes): phosphate, 2·08m.; iron ore, 1·98m.; salt, 1·55m.; kaolin, 221,000; aluminium (2002 estimate), 190,000; quartz, 19,000; asbestos (2002 estimate), 2,000.

Agriculture

There were 2·86m. ha. of arable land in 2001 and 0·48m. ha. of permanent crops. In 1996, of the total cultivated area 18·4% was reclaimed desert. Irrigation is vital to agriculture and is being developed by government programmes; it now reaches most cultivated areas and in 2001 covered 3·34m. ha. The Nile provides 85% of the water used in irrigation, some 55,000m. cu. metres annually. There were 89,527 tractors in 2001 and 2,370 harvester-threshers.

In 1994 there were 5,214 agricultural co-operatives. 0·71m. feddan of land had been distributed by 1991 to 0·35m. families under an agrarian reform programme. In 2001, 5·07m. persons were engaged in agriculture. Cotton, sugarcane and rice are subject to government price controls and procurement quotas.

Output (in 1,000 tonnes), 2000: sugarcane, 15,668; wheat, 6,564; maize, 6,395; tomatoes, 6,354; rice, 5,597; sugarbeets, 2,560; melons and watermelons, 2,225; potatoes, 1,784; oranges, 1,550; grapes, 1,008; dry onions, 1,000; sorghum, 950; dates, 890; pumpkins and squash, 650; seed cotton, 644; bananas, 620; aubergines, 562; cabbages, 500; tangerines and mandarins, 450; apples, 410; peaches and nectarines, 400; cottonseed, 389; chillies and green peppers, 369; broad beans, 354; garlic, 301. Egypt is Africa's largest producer of a number of crops, including wheat, rice, tomatoes, potatoes and oranges.

Livestock, 2000: cattle, 3·18m.; sheep, 4·45m.; buffaloes, 3·20m.; goats, 3·30m.; asses, 3·05m.; camels, 120,000; chickens, 88m. Livestock products in 2000 (in 1,000 tonnes): buffalo milk, 2,079; cow milk, 1,645; meat, 1,391; eggs, 170. 464,000 tonnes of cheese were produced in 2000, making Egypt the largest cheese producer in Africa.

Forestry

In 2003, 16·91m. cu. metres of roundwood were produced.

Fisheries

The catch in 2003 was 430,809 tonnes, of which 313,371 tonnes were freshwater fish.

INDUSTRY

According to the Financial Times Survey (FT 500), the largest companies by market capitalization in Egypt on 4 Jan. 2001 were MobiNil (US$1,860·4m.), the Egyptian mobile phone provider; and Orascom Telecom (US$1,375·3m.).

Almost all large-scale enterprises are in the public sector, and these account for about two-thirds of total output. The private sector, dominated by food processing and textiles, consists of about 150,000 small and medium businesses, most employing fewer than 50 workers. Industrial production in 2001 showed a growth rate of 0·7% compared to 2000, although manufacturing grew by 4·5%.

Production, 2002, in 1,000 tonnes: cement (2001), 26,811; residual fuel oil, 10,003; distillate fuel oil, 7,702; petrol, 6,046; fertilizers (1997–98), 4,634; crude steel, 4,300; sugar (2001–02), 1,555; tobacco (1997–98), 595; paper and paperboard (2001), 460; cotton yarn (1997–98), 275. Motor vehicles (2002), 46,479 units; washing machines (1999), 252,000 units; cigarettes (2000), 53·0bn. units.

Labour

In 2002–03 the labour force was 19·9m. In 1999, 27·6% of the economically active workforce were engaged in wholesale and retail trade, restaurants and hotels; 14·9% in transport, storage and communication; 13·2% in mining and quarrying; and 9·9% in agriculture, hunting, forestry and fishing. Unemployment was 9·9% in 2003. The high birth rate of the 1980s has meant that there are now some 800,000 new entrants into the job market annually.

INTERNATIONAL TRADE

Foreign debt totalled US$28,938m. in 2004.

Imports and Exports

In 2002 imports (f.o.b.) were valued at US$12,879m.; exports (f.o.b.) were valued at US$7,118m. Services accounted for 64·1% of exports in 1998—mainly from travel and tourism—the highest percentage of any country.

Imports of principal commodities in 1999: machinery and transport equipment, 26·2%; foodstuffs, 18·3%; manufactured goods, 18·0%; chemical products, 11·5%; mineral fuels, 6·1%. Exports, 1999: petroleum and petroleum products, 36·0%; cotton yarn and fabrics, 10·1%; clothing, 7·9%; foodstuffs, 7·9%; chemicals, 7·5%; cotton, 6·8%; aluminium, 3·3%. Egypt exports less than 20% of its manufactured goods. Much higher exports are deemed necessary to accelerate growth and job creation.

Main import suppliers in 2001: USA, 18·6%; Italy, 6·6%; Germany, 6·5%; France, 4·9%; China, 4·4%. Main export markets, 2001: Italy, 15·0%; USA, 14·4%; UK, 9·3%; France, 4·7%; Germany, 4·1%. Trade between Egypt and the European Union represented 35% of Egypt's foreign trade in 1999.

COMMUNICATIONS

Roads

In 2003–04 there were 24,992 km of highways and main roads, 50,204 km of secondary roads and 17,049 km of other roads. The road link between Sinai and the mainland across the Suez Canal was opened in 1996. Vehicles (in 1,000): passenger cars (2004), 1,960 (27 per 1,000 inhabitants); trucks and vans (2003), 646; motorcycles (2003), 564; buses (2003), 68.

Rail

In 2000 there were 5,062 km of state railways (1,435 mm gauge), of which 62 km were electrified. Passenger-km travelled in 2000 came to 73·6bn. and freight tonne-km to 4·0bn.

There are tramway networks in Cairo, Heliopolis and Alexandria, and a metro (88 km) opened in Cairo in 1987.

Civil Aviation

There are international airports at Cairo, Luxor, Alexandria and Marsa Alam. The national carrier is Egyptair, which flew 67·7m. km in 1999 and carried 4,620,100 passengers (3,064,000 on international flights). In 2000 Cairo handled 8,633,307 passengers (6,384,961 on international flights) and 170,329 tonnes of freight. Luxor was the second busiest in 2000, with 2,313,000 passengers.

Shipping

In 2002 the merchant marine totalled 1,275,000 GRT, including oil tankers 223,000 GRT. In 2000 vessels totalling 69,801,000 NRT entered ports and vessels totalling 54,142,000 NRT cleared. Dockyards for containerized shipping were constructed in Alexandria, Dekheila, Damietta and Port Said in 1995–96, with two more planned for Adabeya and the Suez Canal. Egypt's largest port is Damietta, which handles 14m. tonnes of cargo annually.

Suez Canal

The Suez Canal was opened for navigation on 17 Nov. 1869 and nationalized in June 1956. By the convention of Constantinople of 29 Oct. 1888, the canal is open to vessels of all nations and is free from blockade, except in time of war. It is 190 km long, connecting the Mediterranean with the Red Sea. It has a maximum depth of 22·5 metres and a maximum width of 365 metres. Vessels of up to 210,000 DWT fully laden are able to pass through the canal.

In 2004, 16,850 vessels (net tonnage, 621m.) went through the canal. In 2004, 521m. tonnes of cargo were transported. Toll revenue in 2004 was US$3,085m. Tolls for tankers were increased by 3% from Feb. 2005.

Telecommunications

In 2004 there were 9,461,100 main telephone lines (135·2 per 1,000 persons); 2·30m. PCs were in use in 2004 (32·9 per 1,000 persons). In Dec. 2005 the Egyptian government sold 20% of its holding in Telecom Egypt. In 2005 mobile phone subscribers numbered 7·93m. and there were 3·90m. Internet users. There were 37,300 fax machines in 2002.

Postal Services

There were 5,530 post offices in 2003, or one for every 13,000 persons.

SOCIAL INSTITUTIONS

Justice

The court system comprises: a Court of Cassation with a bench of five judges which constitutes the highest court of appeal in both criminal and civil cases; five Courts of Appeal with three judges; Assize Courts with three judges which deal with all cases of serious crime; Central Tribunals with three judges which deal with ordinary civil and commercial cases; Summary Tribunals presided over by a single judge which hear minor civil disputes and criminal offences. Contempt for religion and what is judged to be a false interpretation of the Koran may result in prison sentences.

The population in penal institutions in 1998 was approximately 80,000 (121 per 100,000 of national population). The death penalty is in force. There were six confirmed executions in 2004.

Education

The adult literacy rate in 2001 was 56·1% (67·2% among males and 44·8% among females). Free compulsory education is provided in primary schools (eight years). Secondary and technical education is also free. In 2002–03, 53·9% of girls and 46·1% of boys were enrolled in the primary school system. In 2001–02 there were 4,312 pre-primary schools with 413,725 pupils. In 2004–05 there were 8,634,115 primary school pupils at 16,369 schools, 8,757 preparatory schools with 2,889,212 pupils and 2,170 general secondary schools with 1,299,233 pupils. In 2004–05 there were 788,017 students in 841 commercial secondary schools, 1,050,970 in 855 industrial secondary schools and 251,021 in 172 agricultural secondary schools.

Al Azhar institutes educate students who intend enrolling at Al Azhar University, one of the world's oldest universities and

Sunni Islam's foremost seat of learning. In 2003–04 in the Al Azhar system there were 6,690 institutes with 1,449,048 pupils.

In 2002–03 there were 12 state universities, the Al Azhar university and five private universities including a French and a German university. There were 2·0m. students enrolled in university and higher education.

Education expenditure in 1998 was between 6% and 7% of GDP.

Health

At 1 Jan. 2002 there were 1,112 hospitals with 80,519 beds. There were 143,555 physicians, 18,438 dentists and 187,017 nurses in 2000. In 2004–05 health expenditure represented 3·4% of GDP.

Welfare

In 2003–04 there were 18·7m. welfare beneficiaries including, in 2002–03, 7·4m. recipients of pensions.

RELIGION

Islam is constitutionally the state religion. In 2001 there were 58·1m. Sunni Muslims (84% of the population); some 9% of the population are Coptic Christians, the remainder being Roman Catholics, Protestants or Greek Orthodox, with a small number of Jews. A Patriarch heads the Coptic Church, and there are 25 metropolitans and bishops in Egypt; four metropolitans for Ethiopia, Jerusalem, Khartoum and Omdurman, and 12 bishops in Ethiopia. The Copts use the Diocletian (or Martyrs') calendar, which begins in AD 284. In May 2005 the Roman Catholic church had one cardinal.

CULTURE

World Heritage Sites

There are seven sites under Egyptian jurisdiction that appear on the UNESCO World Heritage List. The first five were entered on the list in 1979. They are: Memphis and its Necropolis (the Pyramid Fields from Giza to Dahshur); Ancient Thebes with its Necropolis; Nubian Monuments from Abu Simbel to Philae; Islamic Cairo; and Abu Mena. Memphis was considered one of the Seven Wonders of the World. Ancient Thebes was the capital of Egypt during the period of the middle (c. 2000 BC) and new (c. 1600 BC) kingdoms. The Nubian monuments include the temples of Ramses II in Abu Simbel and the Sanctuary of Isis in Philae. Islamic Cairo, founded in the 10th century, became the centre of the Islamic world. Abu Mena was an early Christian holy city.

The Saint Catherine Area was added to the list in 2002. It included Saint Catherine's Monastery, an outstanding example of an Orthodox Christian monastic settlement, dating from the 6th century AD. The area is centred on Mount Sinai (Jebel Musa or Mount Horeb). In 2005 Wadi Al-Hitan (Whale Valley) was inscribed on the list. The site is an area rich in fossil remains in Egypt's western desert.

Broadcasting

The Ministry of Information operates domestic television and radio stations through the Egyptian Radio and Television Union. Two private satellite stations have been broadcasting since 2001, Dream TV and al-Mihwar. The state holds a monopoly on radio broadcasting. Number of radio receivers in 2000, 21·9m.; TV receivers (2001), 14·9m. Colour is by SECAM V.

Cinema

There were 146 cinemas in 2003. Attendances totalled 15,602.

Press

In 2003 there were 16 dailies with a total average circulation of 1·28m. To set up a newspaper requires permission from the prime minister. In 2002 a total of 976 book titles were published.

Tourism

There were 8·10m. foreign tourists in 2004; tourist spending reached a record US$5·3bn in 2003. Tourism is the leading source of foreign revenue and employs nearly 150,000 people.

Libraries

In 2003 there were 357 public libraries and 36 National libraries. They held a combined 2,558,000 volumes.

DIPLOMATIC REPRESENTATIVES

Of Egypt in the United Kingdom (26 South St., London, W1K 1DW)
Ambassador: Gehad Refaat Madi.

Of the United Kingdom in Egypt (Ahmed Ragheb St., Garden City, Cairo)
Ambassador: Sir Derek Plumbly, KCMG.

Of Egypt in the USA (3521 International Court, NW, Washington, D.C., 20008)
Ambassador: Nabil Fahmy.

Of the USA in Egypt (8 Kamal el-Din Salah St., Garden City, Cairo)
Ambassador: Francis J. Ricciardone.

Of Egypt to the United Nations
Ambassador: Maged Abdelfattah Abdelaziz.

Of Egypt to the European Union
Ambassador: Soliman Awaad.

FURTHER READING

CAPMAS, *Statistical Year Book, Arab Republic of Egypt*

Abdel-Khalek, G., *Stabilization and Adjustment in Egypt.* Edward Elgar, Cheltenham, 2001

Daly, M. W. (ed.) *The Cambridge History of Egypt.* 2 vols. CUP, 2000

Hopwood, D., *Egypt: Politics and Society 1945–1990.* 3rd ed. London, 1992

Ibrahim, Fouad N. and Ibrahim, Barbara, *Egypt: An Economic Geography.* I. B. Tauris, London, 2001

King, J. W., *Historical Dictionary of Egypt.* 2nd ed. Revised by A. Goldschmidt. Metuchen (NJ), 1995

Malek, J. (ed.) *Egypt.* Univ. of Oklahoma Press, 1993

Raymond, André, *Cairo.* Harvard Univ. Press, 2001

Rodenbeck, M., *Cairo—the City Victorious.* Picador, London, 1998

Rubin, Barry, *Islamic Fundamentalism in Egyptian Politics.* Palgrave Macmillan, Basingstoke, 2002

Vatikiotis, P. J., *History of Modern Egypt: from Muhammad Ali to Mubarak.* London, 1991

National Statistical Office: Central Agency for Public Mobilization and Statistics (CAPMAS), Nasr City, Cairo.

EL SALVADOR

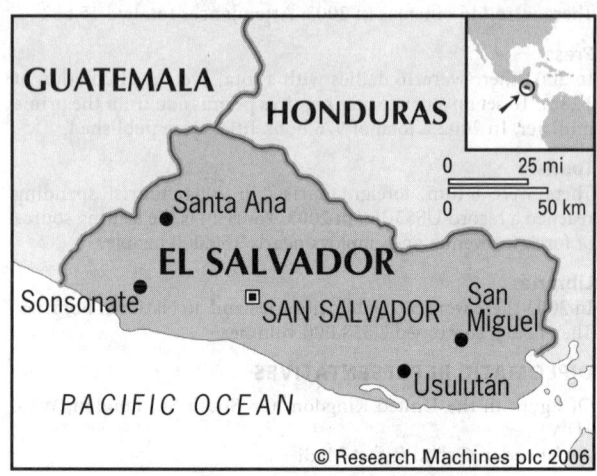

Department	Area	Population	Chief town	Population
Ahuachapán	1,240	354,600	Ahuachapán	38,100
Cabañas	1,104	157,000	Sensuntepeque	16,900
Chalatenango	2,017	203,600	Chalatenango	16,200
Cuscatlán	756	212,500	Cojutepeque	47,500
La Libertad	1,653	784,500	Nueva San Salvador	161,500
La Paz	1,224	318,100	Zacatecoluca	33,800
La Unión	2,074	302,500	La Unión	23,600
Morazán	1,447	178,900	San Francisco	14,200
San Miguel	2,077	533,700	San Miguel	183,200
San Salvador	886	2,198,200	San Salvador	507,700[1]
San Vicente	1,184	170,900	San Vicente	34,600
Santa Ana	2,023	606,800	Santa Ana	178,600
Sonsonate	1,226	506,400	Sonsonate	65,100
Usulatán	2,130	347,900	Usulután	45,300

[1]Greater San Salvador conurbation (2005), 2,232,300.

The official language is Spanish.

República de El Salvador

Capital: San Salvador
Population projection, 2010: 7·46m.
GDP per capita, 2003: (PPP$) 4,781
HDI/world rank: 0·722/104

KEY HISTORICAL EVENTS

Conquered by Spain in 1526, El Salvador remained under Spanish rule until 1821. Thereafter, El Salvador was a member of the Central American Federation comprising the states of El Salvador, Guatemala, Honduras, Nicaragua and Costa Rica until this federation was dissolved in 1839. In 1841 El Salvador declared itself an independent republic.

The country's history has been marked by political violence. The repressive dictatorship of President Maximiliano Hernandez Martínez lasted from 1931 to 1944 when he was deposed as were his successors in 1948 and 1960. The military junta that followed gave way to more secure presidential succession although left-wing guerrilla groups were fighting government troops in the late 1970s. As the guerrillas grew stronger and gained control over a part of the country, the USA sent economic aid and assisted in the training of Salvadorean troops. A new constitution was enacted in Dec. 1983 but the presidential election was boycotted by the main left-wing organization, the Favabundo Marti National Liberation Front (FMLN). Talks between the government and the FMLN in April 1991 led to constitutional reforms in May, envisaging the establishment of civilian control over the armed forces and a reduction in their size. On 16 Jan. 1992 the government and the FMLN signed a peace agreement.

TERRITORY AND POPULATION

El Salvador is bounded in the northwest by Guatemala, northeast and east by Honduras and south by the Pacific Ocean. The area (including 247 sq. km of inland lakes) is 21,041 sq. km. Population (1992 census), 5,118,599 (female 52%); 2005 estimate, 6·88m., giving a population density of 327 per sq. km.

The UN gives a projected population for 2010 of 7·46m.

In 2003, 59·4% of the population were urban. In 2004, 2m. Salvadoreans were living abroad, mainly in the USA.

The republic is divided into 14 departments. Areas (in sq. km) and 2005 estimated populations:

SOCIAL STATISTICS

2001 births, 138,354; deaths, 29,559. Rates (2001, per 1,000 population): births, 21·6; deaths, 4·6. Life expectancy at birth in 2003 was 67·8 years for males and 73·9 years for females. Annual population growth rate, 1992–2002, 1·9%. Infant mortality, 2001, 33 per 1,000 live births; fertility rate, 2001, 3·0 births per woman. Abortion is illegal.

CLIMATE

Despite its proximity to the equator, the climate is warm rather than hot, and nights are cool inland. Light rains occur in the dry season from Nov. to April, while the rest of the year has heavy rains, especially on the coastal plain. San Salvador, Jan. 71°F (21·7°C), July 75°F (23·9°C). Annual rainfall 71" (1,775 mm). San Miguel, Jan. 77°F (25°C), July 83°F (28·3°C). Annual rainfall 68" (1,700 mm).

CONSTITUTION AND GOVERNMENT

A new Constitution was enacted in Dec. 1983. Executive power is vested in a *President* and *Vice-President* elected for a non-renewable term of five years. There is a *Legislative Assembly* of 84 members elected by universal suffrage and proportional representation: 64 locally and 20 nationally, for a term of three years.

National Anthem

'Saludemos la patria orgullosos' ('We proudly salute the Fatherland'); words by J. J. Cañas, tune by J. Aberle.

GOVERNMENT CHRONOLOGY

Heads of State since 1944. (ARENA: Nationalist Republican Alliance; PCN: National Conciliation Party; PDC: Christian Democratic Party; PRUD: Revolutionary Party of Democratic Unification; n/p: non-party)

Presidents
1944–45	military	Osmín Aguirre y Salinas
1945–48	military	Salvador Castaneda Castro

Military Junta
1948–50		Manuel de Jesús Córdova; Óscar Osorio Hernández; Reinaldo Galindo Pohl; Óscar A. Bolaños; Humberto Costa.

Presidents
1950–56	military, PRUD	Óscar Osorio Hernández
1956–60	military, PRUD	José María Lemus López

Junta

1960–61		Miguel Ángel Castillo; César Yanes Urías; Rubén Alonso Rosales; Ricardo Falla Cáceres; Fabio Castillo Figueroa; Rene Fortín Magaña.

Civic-Military Directory

1961–62		José Antonio Rodríguez Porth; José Francisco Valiente; Feliciano Avelar; Aníbal Portillo; Julio Adalberto Rivera Carballo; Mariano Castro Morán.

Presidents

1962	n/p	Eusebio Rodolfo Cordón Cea
1962–67	military, PCN	Julio Adalberto Rivera Carballo
1967–72	military, PCN	Fidel Sánchez Hernández
1972–77	military, PCN	Arturo Armando Molina Barraza
1977–79	military, PCN	Carlos Humberto Romero Mena

Revolutionary Junta of Government (I)

1979–80		Adolfo Arnaldo Majano Ramos; Jaime Abdul Gutiérrez Avendaño; Román Mayorga Quirós; Guillermo Manuel Ungo Revelo; Mario Antonio Andino.

Revolutionary Junta of Government (II)

1980		Adolfo Arnaldo Majano Ramos (military); Jaime Abdul Gutiérrez Avendaño (military); José Antonio Morales Ehrlich (PDC); Héctor Miguel Dada Hirezi (PDC); José Napoleón Duarte Fuentes (PDC); José Ramón Ávalos Navarrete (n/p).

Chairman of the Revolutionary Junta of Government

1980–82	PDC	José Napoleón Duarte Fuentes

Presidents

1982–84	n/p	Álvaro Alfredo Magaña Borja
1984–89	PDC	José Napoleón Duarte Fuentes
1989–94	ARENA	Alfredo Félix Cristiani Burkard
1994–99	ARENA	Armando Calderón Sol
1999–2004	ARENA	Francisco Guillermo Flores Pérez
2004–	ARENA	Elías Antonio Saca González

RECENT ELECTIONS

Presidential elections were held on 21 March 2004. Antonio Saca (Nationalist Republican Alliance; ARENA) received 57·7% of votes cast, ahead of Schafik Hándal (National Liberation Front) with 35·7%, Héctor Silva Argüello (United Democratic Centre–Christian Democratic Party) with 3·9% and José Rafael Machuca Zelaya (National Conciliation Party) with 2·7%.

In parliamentary elections on 12 March 2006 the Nationalist Republican Alliance (ARENA) gained 34 of a possible 84 seats in the Legislative Assembly ahead of the FMLN (Farabundo Martí National Liberation Front) with 32, the National Conciliation Party 10, the Christian Democratic Party 6 and the United Democratic Centre 2. Turnout was 41·4%.

CURRENT ADMINISTRATION

President: Antonio Saca; b. 1965 (ARENA; sworn in 1 June 2004).

In March 2006 the cabinet comprised:

Vice-President: Ana Vilma de Escobar.

Minister of Agriculture and Livestock: Mario Salaverría. *Defence:* Gen. Otto Romero. *Economy:* Yolanda de Gavidia. *Education:* Darlyn Meza. *Environment:* Hugo Barrera. *Finance:* Guillermo López Suárez. *Foreign Affairs:* Francisco Laínez. *Governance:* René Figueroa. *Health:* José Guillermo Maza. *Labour and Social Welfare:* José Espinal. *Public Works:* David Gutiérrez. *Tourism:* Rubén Rochi.

Office of the President (Spanish only):
   http://www.casapres.gob.sv

CURRENT LEADERS

Elías Antonio Saca

Position
President

Introduction
Antonio Saca, a sports broadcaster and media mogul with limited political experience, was elected president in March 2004. His conservative administration has strengthened ties with the USA through a free-trade agreement.

Early Life
Elías Antonio Saca González was born on 9 March 1965 in Usulután, the son of Palestinian immigrants. Educated at the San Agustin school in Usulután and the Cervantes Institute in the capital, San Salvador, Saca began working in the media, initially for Radio Vanguardia. From 1980, against the backdrop of civil war, Saca specialized in sports commentary for radio while studying journalism at the University of El Salvador. In 1983 he became head of sports coverage at El Salvador's Channel 4 television station, a position he held for ten years. By the mid-1990s he was a well-known national figure, as well as the owner of several radio stations. In 1997 he became president of the Salvadorean Association of Radio Broadcasters (ASDER) and was later elected to the presidency of the Association of Private Businessmen.

Saca contested the presidential election of March 2004 as candidate for the conservative Nationalist Republican Alliance (ARENA). Despite his lack of political experience, he easily defeated the National Liberation Front candidate, Schafik Hándal. Opponents were critical of Saca's influence over the media.

Career in Office
Sworn in as president on 1 June 2004, Saca has since built on the conservative, pro-US policies of his predecessor, Francisco Flores. Saca pledged to fight poverty and unemployment and attract inward investment. In Dec. 2004 the government ratified a free-trade agreement with the USA, along with Honduras, Nicaragua and Guatemala.

DEFENCE

There is selective conscription for one year. In 2003 defence expenditure totalled US$106m. (US$16 per capita), representing 0·7% of GDP.

Army

Strength (2002): 15,000 (4,000 conscripts). The National Civilian Police numbers 12,000 and is scheduled to be increased to 16,000.

Navy

A small coastguard force based largely at Acajutla, with 700 (2002) personnel. There was also (2002) one company of Naval Infantry numbering 90.

Air Force

Strength (2002): 1,100 personnel (200 conscripts). There are 23 combat aircraft and 21 armed helicopters.

INTERNATIONAL RELATIONS

El Salvador is a member of the UN, WTO, OAS, Inter-American Development Bank, CACM, ACS and IOM.

ECONOMY

Agriculture accounted for 8·7% of GDP in 2002, industry 30·3% and services 61·0%.

Currency

The *dollar* (USD) replaced the *colón* as the legal currency of El Salvador in 2003. Inflation was 2·5% in 2003 and 5·4% in 2004. Foreign exchange reserves were US$1,669m. and gold reserves 469,000 troy oz in June 2002. Total money supply was ₡9,608m. in Dec. 2000.

Budget

Central government budgetary revenue totalled US$1,922·6m. in 2003; expenditure, US$1,679·1m.

Performance

Real GDP growth was 1·8% in 2003 and 1·5% in 2004. Total GDP in 2004 was US$15·8bn.

Banking and Finance

The bank of issue is the Central Reserve Bank (*President*, Luz María Serpas de Portillo), formed in 1934 and nationalized in 1961. There are 15 commercial banks (two foreign). Individual private holdings may not exceed 5% of the total equity.

There is a stock exchange in San Salvador, founded in 1992.

Weights and Measures

The metric system is standard with US gallons.

ENERGY AND NATURAL RESOURCES

Environment

El Salvador's carbon dioxide emissions from the consumption and flaring of fossil fuels were the equivalent of 0·9 tonnes per capita in 2002.

Electricity

Installed capacity in 2000 was 601,000 kW, of which 395,000 kW hydro-electric. Production in 2000 was 3·55bn. kWh; consumption per capita was 676 kWh in 2000.

Minerals

El Salvador has few mineral resources. In 2002 an estimated 3·2m. tonnes of limestone were produced. Annual marine salt production averages 30,000 tonnes.

Agriculture

27% of the land surface is given over to arable farming. There were 660,000 ha. of arable land in 2001 and 250,000 ha. of permanent crops. In 2002, 27·8% of the working population was engaged in agriculture. Large landholdings have been progressively expropriated and redistributed in accordance with legislation initiated in 1980. By 1994 some 12,000 individuals had received plots of 4–5 ha.

Since the mid-19th century El Salvador's economy has been dominated by coffee. Cotton is the second main commercial crop. Production, in 1,000 tonnes (2000): sugarcane, 5,145; maize, 588; sorghum, 157; coffee, 138; coconuts, 86; dry beans, 71; bananas, 70; rice, 48.

Livestock (2000): 1,212,000 cattle, 300,000 pigs, 96,000 horses, 8m. chickens. Livestock products (2000, in 1,000 tonnes): beef and veal, 34; pork, bacon and ham, 8; poultry, 48; milk, 401; eggs, 53.

Forestry

Forest area was 121,000 ha. (5·8% of the land area) in 2000. In the national forests, dye woods are found, and valuable hardwoods including mahogany, cedar and walnut. Balsam trees abound: El Salvador is the world's principal source of this medicinal gum. In 2001, 5·20m. cu. metres of roundwood were cut.

Fisheries

The catch in 2001 was 17,747 tonnes (90% from marine waters).

INDUSTRY

Production, in 1,000 tonnes: cement (2001), 1,174; residual fuel oil (2000), 537; sugar (2002), 476; distillate fuel oil (2000), 163; petrol (2000), 140; paper and paperboard (2001), 56. Traditional industries include food processing and textiles.

Labour

Out of 2,412,800 people in employment in 2002, 688,500 were in wholesale and retail trade/repair of motor vehicles, motorcycles and personal and household goods/hotels and restaurants; 458,400 in agriculture, forestry and hunting; 434,100 in manufacturing; and 155,400 in health and social work, and other community, social and personal service activities. There were 160,200 unemployed persons, or 6·2% of the workforce, in 2002.

INTERNATIONAL TRADE

In May 1992 El Salvador, Guatemala and Honduras agreed to create a free trade zone for almost all goods and capital. External debt was US$5,828m. in 2002.

Imports and Exports

Imports and exports in calendar years (in US$1m.):

	1998	1999	2000	2001	2002
Imports f.o.b.	3,765·2	3,890·4	4,702·8	4,796·0	4,922·3
Exports f.o.b.	2,459·5	2,534·3	2,963·2	2,890·8	3,016·8

Principal import suppliers, 1999: USA, 37·5%; Guatemala, 11·8%; Mexico, 8·4%; Japan, 4·1%. Principal export markets, 1999: Guatemala, 23·4%; USA, 21·3%; Honduras, 14·7%; Germany, 9·0%. Main import commodities are chemicals and chemical products, transport equipment, and food and beverages; main export commodities are coffee, paper and paper products, and clothing.

COMMUNICATIONS

Roads

In 2002 there were an estimated 10,029 km of roads, including 327 km of motorways. Vehicles in use in 2002: passenger cars, 112,700; trucks and vans, 234,500. There were 656 fatalities in road accidents in 1997.

Rail

The railways are run by the National Railways of El Salvador. Route length (operational) in 2002: 283 km. There is a link to the Guatemalan system. Passenger-km travelled in 1999 came to 8m. and freight tonne-km to 19m.

Civil Aviation

The international airport is El Salvador International in San Salvador. The national carrier is Taca International Airlines, which flew 27·6m. km in 1999, carrying 1,624,100 passengers. It flies to various destinations in the USA, Mexico and all Central American countries. In 2001 El Salvador International handled 1,294,864 passengers on international flights and 26,276 tonnes of international freight.

Shipping

The main ports are Acajutla and Cutuco. Merchant shipping totalled 6,000 GRT in 2002. In 1999 vessels totalling 3,374,000 NRT entered ports and vessels totalling 566,000 NRT cleared.

Telecommunications

The telephone system has been privatized and is owned by two international telephone companies. In 2002 there were 1,556,500 telephone subscribers (241·0 per 1,000 inhabitants) and 163,000 PCs in use (25·2 for every 1,000 persons). There were 888,800 mobile phone subscribers in 2002. Internet users numbered 30,000 in 2002.

Postal Services

In 2003 there were 313 post offices.

SOCIAL INSTITUTIONS

Justice

Justice is administered by the Supreme Court (six members appointed for three-year terms by the Legislative Assembly and six by bar associations), courts of first and second instance, and minor tribunals.

Following the disbanding of security forces in Jan. 1992 a new National Civilian Police Force was created which numbered 12,000 by 2002.

El Salvador has among the highest annual murder rates in the world, at 55 per 100,000 people.

The population in penal institutions in July 2002 was 10,278 (158 per 100,000 of national population).

Education

The adult literacy rate in 2002 was 79·7% (82·4% among males and 77·1% among females). Education, run by the state, is free and compulsory. In 2000–01 there were 203,133 pupils in nursery schools, 940,457 in primary schools and 429,579 in secondary schools. In 1995–96 in the public sector there were three universities; in the private sector there were 21 universities and 14 specialized universities (1 American, 3 Evangelical, 1 Roman Catholic, 1 Open and 1 each for business, integrated education, polytechnic, science and development, teaching, science and technology, technical studies and technology). In 2000–01 there were 118,491 students and 7,285 academic staff in tertiary education.

In 1999–2000 total expenditure on education came to 2·4% of GNP and 13·4% of total government spending.

Health

In 2003 there were 30 hospitals with nine beds per 10,000 inhabitants. There were 8,171 physicians, 3,573 dentists and 11,777 nurses in 2002.

Welfare

The Social Security Institute now administers the sickness, old age and death insurance, covering industrial workers and employees earning up to ₡700 a month. Employees in other private institutions with higher salaries are included but are excluded from the medical and hospital benefits.

RELIGION

In 2001 there were 4,880,000 Roman Catholics. Under the 1962 Constitution, churches are exempted from the property tax; the Catholic Church is recognized as a legal person, and other churches are entitled to secure similar recognition. There is an archbishop in San Salvador and bishops at Santa Ana, San Miguel, San Vicente, Santiago de María, Usulután, Sonsonate and Zacatecoluca. There were about 1,070,000 Protestants in 2001 and 290,000 followers of other religions.

CULTURE

World Heritage Sites

El Salvador has one site on the UNESCO World Heritage List: the Joya de Cerén Archaeological Site (1993), a pre-Hispanic farming community preserved under volcanic ash.

Broadcasting

Broadcasting is under the control of the Administración Nacional de Telecomunicaciones. There are six commercial television channels, a government-owned channel and two educational channels sponsored by the Ministry of Education. There were 2·97m. radio receivers in 2000 and 1·49m. television sets in 2001 (colour by NTSC).

Press

In 1998 there were four daily newspapers with a combined circulation of 171,000, at a rate of 28 per 1,000 inhabitants.

Tourism

There were 951,000 foreign tourists in 2002, spending US$342m.

DIPLOMATIC REPRESENTATIVES

Of El Salvador in the United Kingdom (Mayfair House, 39 Great Portland St., London, W1W 7JZ)
Ambassador: Dr Vladimiro P. Villalta.

Of the United Kingdom in El Salvador (embassy in San Salvador closed in July 2003)
Ambassador: Richard Lavers (resides in Guatemala City).

Of El Salvador in the USA (2308 California St., NW, Washington, D.C., 20008)
Ambassador: Rene A. León Rodríguez.

Of the USA in El Salvador (Urbanización Santa Elena, Antiguo Cuscatlán, San Salvador)
Ambassador: Hugh Douglas Barclay.

Of El Salvador to the United Nations
Ambassador: Carmen María Gallardo Hernández.

Of El Salvador to the European Union
Ambassador: Héctor Gonzalez Urrutia.

FURTHER READING

Kufeld, A., *El Salvador.* NY, 1991
Montgomery, T. S., *Revolution in El Salvador: Origins and Evolution.* Boulder (CO), 1982

National Statistical Office: Dirección General de Estadística y Censos, Calle Arce, San Salvador.

EQUATORIAL GUINEA

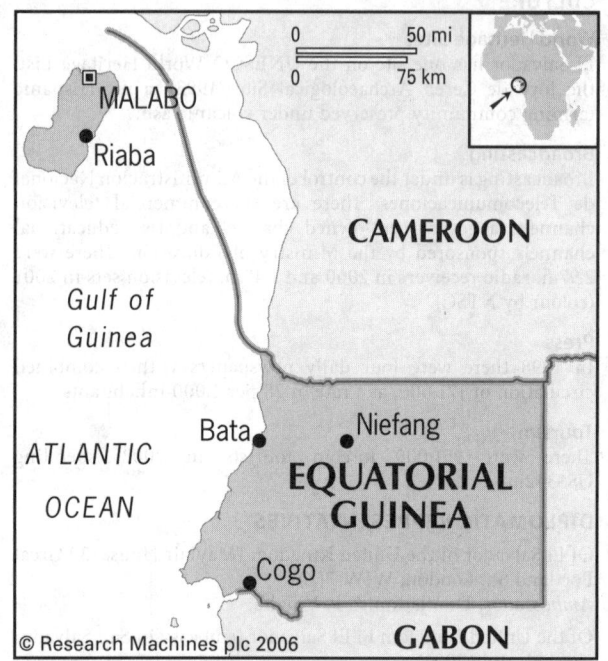

© Research Machines plc 2006

República de Guinea Ecuatorial

Capital: Malabo
Population projection, 2010: 563,000
GDP per capita, 2000: (PPP$) 15,073
HDI/world rank: 0·655/121

KEY HISTORICAL EVENTS

Equatorial Guinea consists of the island of Bioko, for centuries called Fernando Po; other smaller islands and the mainland territory of Rio Muni. Fernando Po was named after the Portuguese navigator Fernão do Po. The island was then ruled for three centuries by Portugal until 1778 when it was ceded to Spain. For some decades after taking possession of Fernando Po, Spain did not effectively occupy it and allowed Britain to establish a naval base at Clarence (later Santa Isabel), which was important for the suppression of slave trading over a wide area. Spain asserted its rule from the 1840s. On Fernando Po the Spanish grew cocoa on European-owned plantations using imported African labour. This traffic led to an international scandal in 1930 when Liberians were found to be held in virtual slavery.

African nationalist movements began in the 1950s. Internal self-government was granted in 1963. In 1969 Spain suspended the constitution but then, under pressure to grant independence, agreed on condition of its approval by a referendum, which was given on 11 Aug. 1969. The two parts of Equatorial Guinea were united under Macías Nguema who established single-party rule. Up to a third of the population was killed or else left the country. Macías was declared President-for-Life in July 1972 but was overthrown by a military coup on 3 Aug. 1979.

A constitution approved by a referendum on 3 Aug. 1982 restored some institutions but a Supreme Military Council remained the sole political body until constitutional rule was resumed on 12 Oct. 1982.

TERRITORY AND POPULATION

The mainland part of Equatorial Guinea is bounded in the north by Cameroon, east and south by Gabon, and west by the Gulf of Guinea, in which lie the islands of Bioko (formerly Macías Nguema, formerly Fernando Póo) and Annobón (called Pagalu from 1973 to 1979). The total area is 28,051 sq. km (10,831 sq. miles) and the population at the 1994 census was 406,151. Estimate (July 2003), 510,500; density, 18 per sq. km. Another 110,000 are estimated to remain in exile abroad.

The UN gives a projected population for 2010 of 563,000.

In 2003, 52·0% of the population were rural.

The seven provinces are grouped into two regions—Continental (C), chief town Bata; and Insular (I), chief town Malabo—with areas and populations as follows:

		Census 1994	
	Sq. km	(estimate)	Chief town
Annobón (I)	17	2,800	San Antonio de Palea
Bioko Norte (I)	776	75,100	Malabo
Bioko Sur (I)	1,241	12,600	Luba
Centro Sur (C)	9,931	60,300	Evinayong
Kié-Ntem (C)	3,943	92,800	Ebebiyin
Litoral (C)	6,665[1]	100,000	Bata
Wele-Nzas (C)	5,478	62,500	Mongomo

[1]Including the adjacent islets of Corisco, Elobey Grande and Elobey Chico (17 sq. km).

In 2003 the capital, Malabo, had an estimated population of 92,900.

The main ethnic group on the mainland is the Fang, which comprises 85% of the total population; there are several minority groups along the coast and adjacent islets. On Bioko the indigenous inhabitants (Bubis) constitute 60% of the population there, the balance being mainly Fang and coast people. On Annobón the indigenous inhabitants are the descendants of Portuguese slaves and still speak a Portuguese patois. The official language is Spanish.

SOCIAL STATISTICS

2000 estimates: births, 19,700; deaths, 6,900. Rates (2000 estimates, per 1,000 population); birth, 43·2; death, 15·1. Life expectancy (2003): male, 42·6 years; female, 43·9. Annual population growth rate, 1992–2002, 2·6%. Infant mortality, 2001, 101 per 1,000 live births; fertility rate, 2001, 5·9 births per woman.

CLIMATE

The climate is equatorial, with alternate wet and dry seasons. In Rio Muni, the wet season lasts from Dec. to Feb.

CONSTITUTION AND GOVERNMENT

A Constitution was approved in a plebiscite in Aug. 1982 by 95% of the votes cast and was amended in Jan. 1995. It provided for an 11-member Council of State, and for a 41-member House of Representatives of the People, the latter being directly elected on 28 Aug. 1983 for a five-year term and re-elected on 10 July 1988. The President appointed and leads a Council of Ministers.

On 12 Oct. 1987 a single new political party was formed as the *Partido Democrático de Guinea Ecuatorial.*

A referendum on 17 Nov. 1991 approved the institution of multi-party democracy, and a law to this effect was passed in Jan. 1992. The electorate is restricted to citizens who have resided in Equatorial Guinea for at least ten years. A parliament created as a result, the *Cámara de Representantes del Pueblo (House of*

People's Representatives), has 100 seats, with members elected for a five-year term by proportional representation in multi-member constituencies.

National Anthem

'Caminemos pisando las sendas' ('Let us journey treading the pathways'); words by A. N. Miyongo, tune anonymous.

RECENT ELECTIONS

At the National Assembly elections on 25 April 2004, boycotted by most opposition parties, the ruling Democratic Party of Equatorial Guinea (PDGE) won 68 of the 100 seats with 47·5% of the vote, its allies (the so-called 'democratic opposition') won 30 with 40·5% and the Convergence for Social Democracy won 2 with 6·0%.

Presidential elections were held on 15 Dec. 2002. President Nguema Mbasogo was re-elected with 97·1% of votes cast, against 2·2% for Celestino Bonifacio Bacalé. Opposition parties withdrew their candidates during polling, citing irregularities.

CURRENT ADMINISTRATION

President of the Supreme Military Council: Brig.-Gen. Teodoro Obiang Nguema Mbasogo; b. 1943 (PDGE; in office since 1979, most recently re-elected in 2002).

In March 2006 the government comprised:

Prime Minister: Miguel Abia Biteo Borico; b. 1961 (PDGE; sworn in 14 June 2004).

First Deputy Prime Minister and Minister of Internal Affairs: Marcelino Oyono Ntutumu. Second Deputy Prime Minister, in Charge of Social Affairs and Human Rights: Ricardo Mangue Obama Nfubea.

Minister of Foreign Affairs and International Co-operation: Micha Ondo Bilé. Justice and Religion: Angel Masié Mibuy. Economy, Commerce and Promotion: Jaime Ela Ndong. Interior and Local Corporations: Clemente Engonga Nguema Onguene. National Defence: Gen. Antonio Mba Nguema. National Security: Col. Manuel Nguema Mba. Planning, Economic Development and Public Investment: Carmelo Modu Acusé Bindang. Mines, Industry and Energy: Atanasio Ela Ntugu Nsa. Finance and Budget: Marcelino Owono Edu. Women's Development: Jesusa Obono Engono. Health and Social Welfare: Justino Obama Nvé. Fisheries and Environment: Fortunato Ofa Mbo. Labour and Social Security: Enrique Mercader Costa. Transport, Technology, Posts and Communications: Demetrio Elo Ndong Nsefumu. Education, Science and Sports: Cristobal Meñana Ela. Agriculture and Forestry: Teodoro Nguema Obiang Mangue. Information, Tourism, Culture and Government Spokesperson: Alfonso Nsue Mokuy. Infrastructure and Urban Planning: Aniceto Ebiaka Muete. Minister of State at the Presidency: Alejandro Evuna Owono Asangono. Secretary General of the Government in Charge of Administrative Co-ordination and Relations with Parliament: Antonio Martin Ndong Ntutumu.

CURRENT LEADERS

Brig.-Gen. Teodoro Obiang Nguema Mbasogo

Position
President

Introduction
Brig.-Gen. Teodoro Obiang Nguema Mbasogo became president of Equatorial Guinea in Aug. 1979, having led a coup d'état against the dictatorial regime of his uncle, Macías Nguema. After introducing some liberalizing reforms, Obiang himself adopted an authoritarian form of government, leading to widespread allegations of civil rights abuses and electoral fraud. The discovery of major fossil fuel reserves in the mid-1990s has created an economic boom, although Obiang has been criticized for the government's lack of transparency in administering this new wealth.

Early Life
Obiang, an ethnic Fang, was born on 5 June 1942 into the Esangui clan of Acoacán. He undertook military training in Spain and, following the election of his uncle as president of the newly-independent country, was made a lieutenant. He had stints as governor of Bioko, presidential aide-de-camp and head of the military, while Macías Nguema's regime became increasingly repressive, with around a third of the population leaving the country during the 1970s.

In Aug. 1979 Obiang ousted his uncle, who was subsequently put on trial and executed.

Career in Office
On assuming the presidency on 3 Aug. 1979 it was hoped that Obiang would implement a more liberal and democratic approach to government. One of his first acts was to call an amnesty on refugees and to free 5,000 political prisoners. However, he retained many of the powers of his uncle and soon came under criticism for his style of government. Local and national political appointments have been blighted by nepotism, which has led to some interfamilial feuding within the political and military establishments.

The discovery of large oil and gas reserves off Bioko in the mid-1990s led to a massive upturn in the economy as Equatorial Guinea became one of sub-Saharan Africa's leading oil exporters. However, it has been widely claimed that the benefits of this oil money have failed to reach the population at large. In 1997 the growth rate was around 151% and Equatorial Guinea had the fastest-growing economy on the continent (although subsequently dropping to 33% by 2004). The IMF and the World Bank demanded increased transparency concerning government oil revenues, which Obiang claimed were a state secret, and warned against an over-reliance on the oil reserves (although they are not expected to start running out until 2012 at the earliest). It was also reported that the US senate was investigating several hundred million dollars worth of deposits in US accounts belonging to members of Obiang's family.

The country's first multi-party elections in 1993 were won by Obiang's Democratic Party of Equatorial Guinea (PDGE), but boycotted by most of the opposition parties. Then, in the presidential election in Feb. 1996, he was returned with a reported 99% of the vote. At the presidential election of Dec. 2002 he again claimed over 97% of the vote and opposition parties accused the government of vote rigging. A government-in-exile formed by Obiang's opponents was established in Spain. Obiang's treatment of opposition politicians has received condemnation from, among others, the EU and Amnesty International and the president has been accused of using torture on political prisoners. There have also been high-profile public trials such as that in 2002 which resulted in the one-year imprisonment of opposition leader Fabian Nseu Guema for insulting Obiang on a website.

In foreign policy, Obiang has been in dispute with Gabon over the latter's long-term occupation of Mbagne, an island in the Bay of Corisco thought to contain further significant oil supplies. In 2000 he called on the people of Equatorial Guinea to be permanently vigilant against unspecified neighbouring countries accused of attempting to destabilize the nation. In 2002 he signed an agreement with Nigeria for the development of the Zafiro-Ekanga oil field along their joint maritime border.

In 2004 a plane flying from Zimbabwe was intercepted after Obiang announced it was carrying mercenaries preparing a coup against him. Those arrested for involvement included Mark Thatcher (in South Africa), son of former British prime minister Margaret Thatcher. Obiang claimed the arrests were evidence of a plot by the secret services of the USA, UK and Spain to overthrow him.

The PDGE retained its dominance in parliamentary elections in April 2004, but most opposition parties boycotted the poll and foreign observers claimed that there were serious irregularities.

DEFENCE

In 2003 defence expenditure totalled US$6m. (US$12 per capita), representing 0·2% of GDP.

Army

The Army consists of three infantry battalions with (2002) 1,100 personnel. There is also a paramilitary Guardia Civil.

Navy

A small force, numbering 120 in 2002 and based at Malabo and Bata, operates four inshore patrol craft.

Air Force

There are no combat aircraft or armed helicopters. Personnel (2002), 100.

INTERNATIONAL RELATIONS

Equatorial Guinea is a member of the UN, the African Union, African Development Bank and the International Organization of the Francophonie, and is an ACP member state of the ACP-EU relationship.

ECONOMY

Agriculture accounted for 8·9% of GDP in 2002, industry 86·0% (the highest percentage of any country) and services 5·0%.

Overview

Overseas investment, especially in the oil industry, has transformed the economy.

Currency

On 2 Jan. 1985 the country joined the Franc Zone and the *ekpwele* was replaced by the *franc CFA* (XAF) which now has a parity value of 655·957 francs CFA to one euro. Foreign exchange reserves were US$77m. in April 2002 and total money supply was 68,514m. francs CFA. Inflation was 7·3% in 2003 and 4·2% in 2004.

Budget

In 2002 revenue was 414,484m. francs CFA and expenditure 227,236m. francs CFA. Oil revenue accounts for more than 80% of revenues.

Performance

Equatorial Guinea is one of the world's fastest-growing economies thanks to the rapid expansion of its oil sector. The economy grew by a record 151·4% in 1997. The growth rate was 48·1% in 2001, 9·7% in 2002, 21·3% in 2003 and 32·8% in 2004. In 1997, 1998, 1999, 2000, 2001, 2003 and 2004 Equatorial Guinea's real GDP growth was the highest in the world. However, the bulk of the population remains in poverty. In 2004 total GDP was US$3·2bn.

Banking and Finance

The *Banque des Etats de l'Afrique Centrale* (*Governor*, Jean-Félix Mamalepot) became the bank of issue in Jan. 1985. There are two commercial banks (Caisse Commune d'Epargne et d'Investissement Guinea Ecuatorial; Société Générale des Banques GE) and two development banks.

ENERGY AND NATURAL RESOURCES

Environment

Carbon dioxide emissions from the consumption and flaring of fossil fuels in 2002 were the equivalent of 8·3 tonnes per capita.

Electricity

There are two hydro-electric plants. Installed capacity was 18,000 kW in 2000. Production was around 23m. kWh in 2000; consumption per capita in 2000 was an estimated 50 kWh.

Oil and Gas

Oil production started in 1992, and in 2003 totalled 12·3m. tonnes, up from 5·6m. tonnes in 2000. In 2002 Equatorial Guinea's oil production increased at a faster rate than that of any other country. Mobil is the biggest operator in the country but other US-based oil companies are investing heavily. Since oil in commercial quantities was discovered in 1995 Equatorial Guinea has attracted more than US$3bn. in foreign direct investment.

Natural gas reserves were 100bn. cu. metres in 2002.

Minerals

There is some small-scale alluvial gold production.

Agriculture

There were 130,000 ha. of arable land in 2001 and 100,000 ha. of permanent crops. Subsistence farming predominates, and in 2002 approximately 69% of the economically active population were engaged in agriculture. Production (in 1,000 tonnes, in 2000): cassava, 45; sweet potatoes, 36; bananas, 20; coconuts, 6; cocoa beans, 4; coffee, 4. Plantations in the hinterland have been abandoned by their Spanish former owners and, except for cocoa and coffee, commercial agriculture is in serious difficulties. Livestock (2000): cattle, 5,000; goats, 8,000; pigs, 5,000; sheep, 36,000.

Forestry

In 2000 forests covered 1·75m. ha., or 62·5% of the total land area. Timber production in 2001 totalled 811,000 cu. metres.

Fisheries

The total catch in 2001 was estimated to be 3,500 tonnes (71% from sea fishing). Tuna and shellfish are caught.

INDUSTRY

The once-flourishing light industry collapsed under the Macías regime. Oil production is now the major activity. Production of veneer sheets, 2001, 15,000 cu. metres. Food processing is also being developed.

Labour

In 1996 the labour force was 171,000 (65% males). The wage-earning non-agricultural workforce is small. The average monthly wage was 14,000 francs CFA in 1992.

INTERNATIONAL TRADE

Foreign debt was US$260m. in 2002.

Imports and Exports

In 2001 imports were 593·4bn. francs CFA and exports 1,346·7bn. francs CFA.

Main import suppliers, 1998: USA, 35·4%; France, 15·0%; Cameroon, 9·9%; Spain, 9·9%; UK, 6·2%. Main export markets, 1998: USA, 62·0%; Spain, 17·3%; China, 8·9%; France, 3·4%; Japan, 3·4%. Principal import commodities are machinery and transport equipment, and petroleum and petroleum products; principal export commodities are petroleum, cocoa and timber.

COMMUNICATIONS

Roads

In 2002 the road network covered 2,880 km. Most roads are in a state of disrepair. There were 4,700 passenger cars (9·6 per 1,000 inhabitants) and 3,600 vans and trucks in 2002.

Civil Aviation

There is an international airport at Malabo. There were international flights in 2003 to Cotonou, Douala, Libreville, Madrid, Yaoundé and Zürich. In 1998 Malabo handled 54,000 passengers.

Shipping

Bata is the main port, handling mainly timber. The other ports are Luba, formerly San Carlos (bananas, cocoa), in Bioko, and Malabo, Evinayong and Mbini on the mainland. Ocean-going shipping totalled 29,000 GRT in 2002.

Telecommunications

Telephone services are rudimentary. In 2002 there were 35,800 telephone subscribers (73·4 for every 1,000 persons) and the number of PCs in use was 4,000 (7·2 per 1,000 persons). There were 32,000 mobile phone subscribers in 2002. In 1995 there were around 100 fax machines. In 2002 Internet users numbered 1,800.

SOCIAL INSTITUTIONS

Justice

The Constitution guarantees an independent judiciary. The Supreme Tribunal, the highest court of appeal, is located at Malabo. There are Courts of First Instance and Courts of Appeal at Malabo and Bata.

Education

In 2000–01 there were 596 teachers for 16,654 children in pre-primary schools; 1,754 teachers for 72,791 pupils in primary schools; and (1999–2000) 20,679 secondary pupils with 836 teachers. In 1993 there were 2 teacher training colleges, 2 post-secondary vocational schools and 1 agricultural institute. Adult literacy was 84·2% in 2003 (male, 92·1%; female, 76·4%). The rate for males is second only to Zimbabwe among African countries. In 2000–01 total expenditure on education came to 1·9% of GNP.

Health

In 1988 there were 29 hospital beds per 10,000 inhabitants. There were 105 physicians, four dentists, 169 nurses and nine midwives in 1996.

RELIGION

Christianity was proscribed under President Macías but reinstated in 1979. In 2001 there were 390,000 Roman Catholics with the remainder of the population followers of other religions.

CULTURE

Broadcasting

Two radio programmes are broadcast by the state-controlled Radio Nacional de Guinea Ecuatorial and Televisión Nacional. There is also a commercial radio network, and a cultural programme produced with Spanish collaboration. In 1997 there were 180,000 radio and 4,000 TV receivers (colour by SECAM).

Press

In 1998 there was one daily newspaper with a circulation of 2,000, at a rate of 4·6 per 1,000 inhabitants.

Tourism

Foreign tourists brought in revenue of US$14m. in 2001.

DIPLOMATIC REPRESENTATIVES

Of Equatorial Guinea in the United Kingdom (13 Park Place, London, SW1A 1LP)
Ambassador: Agustin Nze Nfumu.

Of the United Kingdom in Equatorial Guinea
Ambassador: Richard Wildash, LVO (resides in Yaoundé, Cameroon).

Of Equatorial Guinea in the USA (2020 16th St., NW, Washington, D.C., 20009)
Ambassador: Purificación Angue Ondo.

Of Equatorial Guinea to the United Nations
Ambassador: Lino Sima Ekua Avomo.

Of Equatorial Guinea to the European Union
Ambassador: Victorino Nka Obiang Maye.

The USA does not have an embassy in Equatorial Guinea; US relations with Equatorial Guinea are handled through the US Embassy in Yaoundé, Cameroon.

FURTHER READING

Fegley, Randall, *Equatorial Guinea, an African Tragedy.* New York, 1989
Liniger-Goumaz, M., *Guinea Ecuatorial: Bibliografía General.* Geneva, 1974–91
Molino, A. M. del, *La Ciudad de Clarence.* Madrid, 1994

National Statistical Office: Dirección General de Estadísticas y Cuentas Nacionales.
Website (Spanish only): http://www.dgecnstat-ge.org

ERITREA

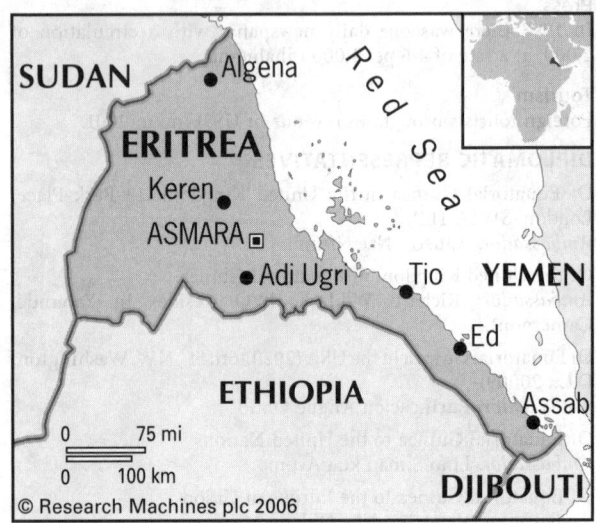

Capital: Asmara
Population projection, 2010: 5·13m.
GDP per capita, 2003: (PPP$) 849
HDI/world rank: 0·444/161

KEY HISTORICAL EVENTS

Italy was the colonial ruler from 1890 until 1941 when Eritrea fell to British forces and a British protectorate was set up. This ended in 1952 when the UN sanctioned federation with Ethiopia. In 1962 Ethiopia became a unitary state and Eritrea was incorporated as a province. Eritreans began an armed struggle for independence under the leadership of the Eritrean People's Liberation Front (EPLF) which culminated successfully in the capture of Asmara on 24 May 1991. Thereafter the EPLF maintained a de facto independent administration recognized by the Ethiopian government. Sovereignty was proclaimed on 24 May 1993. In 1999 fighting broke out along the border with Ethiopia. After the failure of international mediation, the 13-month long-truce between Eritrea and Ethiopia ended in May 2000. Ethiopia launched a major offensive in the ongoing war over territorial disputes and claimed victory. In June both sides agreed to an Organization of African Unity peace deal to end the two-year border war.

TERRITORY AND POPULATION

Eritrea is bounded in the northeast by the Red Sea, southeast by Djibouti, south by Ethiopia and west by Sudan. Some 300 islands form the Dahlak Archipelago, most of them uninhabited. For the dispute with Yemen over the islands of Greater and Lesser Hanish see YEMEN: Territory and Population. Its area is 121,100 sq. km (46,800 sq. miles). Population, 2005 estimate, 4,401,000 (80·0% rural in 2003); density, 36·3 per sq. km.

The UN gives a projected population for 2010 of 5·13m.

There are six regions: Anseba, Debub, Debubawi Keyih Bahri, Gash Barka, Maekel and Semenawi Keyih Bahri. The capital is Asmara (2002 estimated population, 500,600). Other large towns (with 2002 populations) are Keren (74,800) and Adi Ugri (25,700). An agreement of July 1993 gives Ethiopia rights to use the ports of Assab and Massawa.

49% of the population speak Tigrinya and 32% Tigré, and there are seven other indigenous languages. Arabic is spoken on the coast and along the Sudanese border, and English is used in secondary schools. Arabic and Tigrinya are the official languages.

SOCIAL STATISTICS

2000 births (estimates), 143,000; deaths, 49,000. Estimated birth rate in 2000 was 38·5 per 1,000 population; estimated death rate, 13·3. Annual population growth rate, 1992–2002, 2·4%. Life expectancy at birth, 2003, was 51·8 years for males and 55·7 years for females. Infant mortality, 2001, 72 per 1,000 live births; fertility rate, 2001, 5·4 births per woman.

CLIMATE

Massawa, Jan. 78°F (25·6°C), July 94°F (34·4°C). Annual rainfall 8" (193 mm).

CONSTITUTION AND GOVERNMENT

A referendum to approve independence was held on 23–25 April 1993. The electorate was 1,173,506. 99·8% of votes cast were in favour.

The transitional government consists of the President and a 150-member National Assembly. It elects the President, who in turn appoints the State Council made up of 14 ministers and the governors of the ten provinces. The President chairs both the State Council and the National Assembly.

National Anthem

'Ertra, Ertra, Ertra' ('Eritrea, Eritrea, Eritrea'); words by S. Beraki, tune by I. Meharezghi and A. Tesfatsion.

RECENT ELECTIONS

In the presidential and legislative elections in May 1997, President Afewerki was re-elected to office.

National Assembly elections, postponed in 1998, were initially set to take place before the end of 2003 but have been put back indefinitely. In the meantime several dissident politicians have been jailed.

CURRENT ADMINISTRATION

President: Issaias Afewerki; b. 1945 (People's Front for Democracy and Justice, formerly the Eritrean People's Liberation Front; elected 22 May 1993 and re-elected in May 1997).

In March 2006 the ministers in the State Council were:

Minister of Agriculture: Arefaine Berhe. Construction: Abraha Asfaha. Defence: Sebhat Ephrem. Education: Osman Saleh. Energy and Mining: Tesfai Ghebreselassie. Finance: Berhane Abrehe. Fisheries and Maritime Resources: Ahmed Haj Ali. Foreign Affairs (acting): Mohammed Omar. Health: Saleh Meki. Information: Ali Abdu. Justice: Fozia Hashim. Labour and Human Welfare: Askalu Menkerios. Land, Water and Environment: Woldemichael Ghebremariam. Tourism: Amna Nur Husayn. National Development: Wolday Futur. Trade and Industry: Giorgis Teklemikael. Transport and Communications: Woldemikael Abraha.

CURRENT LEADERS

Issaias Afewerki

Position
President

Introduction
Issaias Afewerki has been president of Eritrea since it achieved independence from Ethiopia in 1993, having been a leading

campaigner for secession since the mid-1960s. However, his tenure has been marked by civil rights abuses. In foreign policy he has overseen a bloody war with Ethiopia in 1999–2000, which threatened to reignite in late 2005 over an unresolved border dispute.

Early Life
Issaias Afewerki was born in 1945 in Asmara, Eritrea's capital, which was then under British administration. Eritrea became part of Ethiopia in 1962 and in 1966 Afewerki joined the secessionist Eritrean Liberation Front (ELF). Having received military training in China, he became a deputy divisional commander. In 1970 he helped found the Eritrean People's Liberation Front (EPLF), becoming its general secretary in 1987.

Following the collapse of the Mengistu military regime in Ethiopia in 1991, the new government agreed to a referendum on Eritrean independence. The referendum was held in 1993 and Eritrea declared independence in May of that year. Eritrea's National Assembly selected Afewerki as the country's first president.

Career in Office
The EPLF initially suggested a multi-party political system and in the early stages of his tenure Afewerki advocated close economic relations with Ethiopia. However, in Feb. 2002 the National Assembly, composed of EPLF representatives, refused to ratify a bill on the establishment of new political parties. Multi-party elections, previously scheduled for the end of 2001, were shelved.

In 2001 Afewerki authorized the arrest of critical journalists and political opponents. The move was condemned internationally and the Italian ambassador, who had voiced concerns over human rights violations, was expelled. International aid was consequently cut. In 2002 Afewerki set out his plans for the creation of a 'responsible' press, soon after an opposition party—the Eritrean People's Liberation Front Democratic Party—had emerged to challenge him. The party was believed to have been co-founded by Mesfin Hagos, Afewerki's former defence minister.

In 1999 border disputes escalated into full-scale war between Ethiopian and Eritrean forces which resulted in 70,000 deaths. A ceasefire was agreed in June 2000, with Ethiopia withdrawing its forces under UN supervision. A formal peace treaty was signed in Dec. 2000. Tensions remained, particularly concerning the ownership of the small border settlement of Badame, and in May 2001 the countries agreed to abide by the decision of an international boundary commission. The commission awarded Badame to Eritrea, but Ethiopia refused to accept the decision. Fears of a renewed conflict mounted in late 2005 after Eritrea expelled UN observers policing the militarized border region.

Afewerki has meanwhile overseen the restoration of diplomatic ties with Sudan and Djibouti, although relations with both countries remain unsettled. Eritrea claims that Islamic fundamentalist groups active within the country have received backing from Khartoum, while the Sudanese government resents Eritrean support for the opposition coalition. Eritrea has also accused Djibouti of providing military support to Ethiopia, a claim denied by Djibouti.

DEFENCE

Conscription for 18 months was introduced in 1994 for all Eritreans between the ages of 18 and 40, with some exceptions. It has since been reduced to 16 months. The total strength of all forces was estimated at 172,200 in 2002.

Defence expenditure totalled US$73m. in 2003 (US$17 per capita and 9·2% of GDP).

Army
The Army had a strength of around 170,000 in 2002. There were an additional 120,000 reservists available.

Navy
Most of the former Ethiopian Navy is now in Eritrean hands. The main bases and training establishments are at Massawa, Assab and Dahlak. Personnel numbered 1,400 in 2002.

Air Force
Personnel numbers were estimated at 800 in 2002. There were over 17 combat aircraft including MiG-23s, MiG-21s and MiG-29s.

INTERNATIONAL RELATIONS

A border dispute between Eritrea and Ethiopia broke out in May 1998. Eritrean troops took over the border town of Badame after a skirmish between Ethiopian police units and armed men from Eritrea. Ethiopia maintained that Badame and Sheraro, a nearby town, had always been part of Ethiopia and called Eritrea's action an invasion. An agreement ending hostilities was signed in June 2000, followed by a peace accord in Dec. A buffer zone has been created to separate the armies, but tensions do still arise from time to time, notably in late 2005 following a further dispute between the two countries over Badame.

Eritrea is a member of the UN, the African Union, African Development Bank, COMESA, the Intergovernmental Authority on Development and is an ACP member state of the ACP-EU relationship.

ECONOMY

In 2002 agriculture accounted for 12·9% of GDP, industry 25·0% and services 62·1%.

Eritrea's resources are meagre, the population small and poorly-educated; communications are difficult and there is a shortage of energy.

Currency
A new currency, the *nakfa*, has replaced the Ethiopian currency, the *birr*. However, its introduction led to tensions with Ethiopia, adversely affecting cross-border trade. Inflation was 22·7% in 2003 and 25·1% in 2004.

Budget
Revenues in 2001 were 3,362m. nafka and expenditures 4,545m. nafka.

Performance
Total GDP in 2004 was US$0·9bn. The economy expanded by 9·2% in 2001 following the end of the conflict with neighbouring Ethiopia but then by only 0·7% in 2002. Real GDP growth rate 3·0% in 2003 and 1·8% in 2004.

Banking and Finance
The central bank is the National Bank of Eritrea (*Governor*, Tequie Beyene). All banks and financial institutions are state-run. There is a Commercial Bank of Eritrea with 15 branches, an Eritrean Investment and Development Bank with 13 branches, a Housing and Commercial Bank of Eritrea with seven branches and an Insurance Corporation.

ENERGY AND NATURAL RESOURCES

Environment
Carbon dioxide emissions from the consumption and flaring of fossil fuels were the equivalent of 0·2 tonnes per capita in 2002.

Electricity
Installed capacity was 0·2m. kW in 2000. Electricity is provided to only some 10% of the population. Total production was around 216m. kWh in 2000.

Minerals
There are deposits of gold, silver, copper, zinc, sulphur, nickel, chrome and potash. Basalt, limestone, marble, sand and silicates

are extracted. Oil exploration is taking place in the Red Sea. Salt production totals 200,000 tonnes annually.

Agriculture

Agriculture engaged approximately 77% of the economically active population in 2002. Several systems of land ownership (state, colonial, traditional) co-exist. In 1994 the PFDJ proclaimed the sole right of the state to own land. There were 500,000 ha. of arable land in 2001 and 3,000 ha. of permanent crops. 21,000 ha. were irrigated in 2001. There were 463 tractors in 2001 and 125 harvester-threshers. Main agricultural products, 2000 (in 1,000 tonnes): sorghum, 100; potatoes, 35; barley, 25; millet, 25; maize, 12; wheat, 10. Livestock, 2000: cattle, 1·80m.; sheep, 1·54m.; goats, 1·50m.; camels, 73,000; chickens, 1m.

Forestry

In 2000 forests covered 1·59m. ha., or 13·5% of the total land area. Timber production in 2001 was 2·29m. cu. metres.

Fisheries

The total catch in 2001 was 8,820 tonnes, exclusively from marine waters, but a joint French–Eritrean project to assess fish stocks in the Red Sea suggests a sustainable yield of up to 70,000 tonnes a year.

INDUSTRY

Light industry was well developed in the colonial period but capability has declined. Processed food, textiles, leatherwear, building materials, glassware and oil products are produced. Industrial production accounted for 22·5% of GDP in 2001, with the manufacturing sector providing 10·8%.

Labour

In 1996 the labour force was 1,649,000 (53% males).

INTERNATIONAL TRADE

Eritrea is dependent on foreign aid for most of its capital expenditure. Total external debt in 2002 was US$528m.

Imports and Exports

In 2000 imports were valued at US$471·4m. and exports at US$36·8m. The leading imports are machinery and transport equipment, basic manufactures, and food and live animals. The main exports are drinks, leather and products, textiles and oil products. Principal import suppliers in 1998 were Italy, 17·4%; United Arab Emirates, 16·2%; Germany, 5·7%; UK, 4·5%; USA, 4·2%. Principal export markets, 1998: Sudan, 27·2%; Ethiopia, 26·5%; Japan, 13·2%; United Arab Emirates, 7·3%; Italy, 5·3%.

COMMUNICATIONS

Roads

There were some 4,010 km of roads in 1999, around 875 km of which were paved. A tarmac road links the capital Asmara with one of the main ports, Massawa. In 1996 passenger cars in use numbered 5,940 (1·5 per 1,000 inhabitants). About 500 buses operate regular services.

Rail

In 2000 the reconstruction of the 117 km Massawa–Asmara line reached Embatkala, thus opening up an 80 km stretch from Massawa on the coast. In 2003 the line was re-built right through to Asmara.

Civil Aviation

There is an international airport at Asmara (Yohannes IV Airport). In 2003 there were scheduled flights to Cairo, Djibouti, Dubai, Frankfurt, Jeddah, Milan, Nairobi and Sana'a. In 2001 Asmara handled 140,000 passengers (129,000 on international flights) and 3,200 tonnes of freight.

Shipping

Massawa is the main port; Assab used to be the main port for imports to Ethiopia. Both were free ports for Ethiopia until the onset of hostilities. Merchant shipping totalled 21,000 GRT in 2002.

Telecommunications

International telephone links were restored in 1992. There were 35,900 telephone subscribers in 2002 (9·0 for every 1,000 inhabitants) and 10,000 PCs were in use (2·5 per 1,000 inhabitants). Eritrea had 9,000 Internet users in 2002 and there were 2,200 fax machines.

Postal Services

In 2003 there were 64 post offices, equivalent to one for every 64,700 persons.

SOCIAL INSTITUTIONS

Justice

The legal system derives from a decree of May 1993.

Education

Adult literacy was about 56·7% in 2001 (68·2% among males and 34·6% among females). In 2000–01 there were 298,691 pupils and 6,668 teachers in primary schools, and 142,124 pupils at secondary schools with 2,710 teachers. There is one university, with 3,200 students and 250 academic staff in 1994–95. In 1998–99 total expenditure on education came to 4·1% of GNP.

Health

In 1993 there were 10 small regional hospitals, 32 health centres and 65 medical posts. In 1996 there were 108 physicians, 4 dentists, 574 nurses and 79 midwives.

Eritrea has one of the highest rates of undernourishment of any country. The proportion of the population classified as undernourished was 73% in the period 2000–02, up from 68% in 1995–97.

RELIGION

Half the population are Sunni Muslims (along the coast and in the north), and half Coptic Christians (in the south).

CULTURE

Broadcasting

There is daily radio and TV broadcasting. In 2001 there were 150,000 TV receivers and in 2000 there were 1,650,000 radio receivers.

Press

There is a government daily in Arabic and Tigrinya. In Sept. 2001 the government closed down the country's eight independent newspapers. A number of journalists have been jailed.

Tourism

There were 101,000 foreign tourists in 2002. Receipts totalled US$73m.

DIPLOMATIC REPRESENTATIVES

Of Eritrea in the United Kingdom (96 White Lion St., London, N1 9PF)
Ambassador: Negassi Sengal Ghebrezghi.

Of the United Kingdom in Eritrea (66–68 Mariam Ghimbi St., PO Box 5584, Asmara)
Ambassador: Mike Murray.

Of Eritrea in the USA (1708 New Hampshire Ave., NW, Washington, D.C., 20009)
Ambassador: Girma Asmerom.

Of the USA in Eritrea (Franklin D. Roosevelt St., PO Box 211, Asmara)
Ambassador: Scott H. DeLisi.

Of Eritrea to the United Nations
Ambassador: Araya Desta.

Of Eritrea to the European Union
Ambassador: Aldebrhan Weldegiorgis.

FURTHER READING

Henze, Paul, *Eritrea's War: Confrontation, International Response, Outcome, Prospects.* Shama, Addis Ababa, 2001

Negash, Tekeste and Tronvoll, Kjetil, *Brothers at War: Making Sense of the Eritrean–Ethiopian War.* Ohio Univ. Press and James Currey, Oxford, 2001

Wrong, Michaela, *I Didn't Do It For You: How the World Betrayed a Small African Nation.* Fourth Estate, London, 2005

ESTONIA

Eesti Vabariik
(Republic of Estonia)

Capital: Tallinn
Population projection, 2010: 1·31m.
GDP per capita, 2003: (PPP$) 13,539
HDI/world rank: 0·853/38

KEY HISTORICAL EVENTS

Estonia was part of the Holy Roman Empire until it became a Swedish possession in the 17th century. On Sweden's defeat by Peter the Great, Estonia passed to the Russian Empire in 1721. The workers' and soldiers' Soviets, which came to prominence in 1917, were overthrown with the assistance of British naval forces in May 1919 and a democratic republic proclaimed. In March 1934 this regime was, in turn, overthrown by a fascist coup. The secret protocol of the Soviet-German agreement of 23 Aug. 1939 assigned Estonia to the Soviet sphere of interest. An ultimatum (16 June 1940) led to the formation of the Estonian Soviet Socialist Republic. At a referendum in March 1991, 77·8% of votes cast were in favour of independence. A fully independent status was conceded by the USSR State Council on 6 Sept. 1991. Estonia was admitted to the Council of Europe in 1993, and became a member of NATO in March 2004 and the European Union in May 2004.

TERRITORY AND POPULATION

Estonia is bounded in the west and north by the Baltic Sea, east by Russia and south by Latvia. There are 1,521 offshore islands, of which the largest are Saaremaa and Hiiumaa, but only 12 are permanently inhabited. Area, 45,227 sq. km (17,462 sq. miles); population, 1,370,052 (2000 census), giving a density of 30·3 per sq. km. Estimate, 2005: 1,330,000.

The UN gives a projected population for 2010 of 1·31m.

In 2003, 69·5% of the population lived in urban areas. Of the whole population, Estonians accounted for 67·9%, Russians 25·6%, Ukrainians 2·1%, Belarusians 1·3% and Finns 0·9%. The capital is Tallinn (population, 397,200 or 29·3%). Other large towns are Tartu (101,200), Narva (67,800), Kohtla-Järve (46,800) and Pärnu (44,800). There are 15 counties, 47 towns and 202 rural municipalities.

The official language is Estonian.

SOCIAL STATISTICS

2003 registered births, 13,198; deaths, 18,231. Rates (per 1,000 population): birth, 9·7; death, 13·4. There were 10,834 induced abortions in 2002. Expectation of life in 2003 was 65·6 years for males and 77·0 for females. The annual population growth rate in the period 1992–2002 was –1·4%, giving Estonia one of the fastest declining populations of any country. The suicide rate, at 27·3 per 100,000 population in 2002, is one of the highest in the world. Among males it was 47·7 per 100,000 population in 2002. Infant mortality in 2002 was 5·7 per 1,000 births. In 2002 total fertility rate was 1·37 births per woman.

CLIMATE

Because of its maritime location Estonia has a moderate climate, with cool summers and mild winters. Average daily temperatures in 2000: Jan. –2·5°C; July 16·3°C. Rainfall is heavy, 500–700 mm per year, and evaporation low.

CONSTITUTION AND GOVERNMENT

A draft constitution drawn up by a constitutional assembly was approved by 91·1% of votes cast at a referendum on 28 June 1992. Turnout was 66·6%. The constitution came into effect on 3 July 1992. It defines Estonia as a 'democratic state guided by the rule of law, where universally recognized norms of international law are an inseparable part of the legal system.' It provides for a 101-member national assembly (*Riigikogu*) elected for four-year terms. There are 12 electoral districts with eight to 12 mandates each. Candidates may be elected: a) by gaining more than 'quota', i.e. the number of votes cast in a district divided by the number of its mandates; b) by standing for a party which attracts for all of its candidates more than the quota, in order of listing; c) by being listed nationally for parties which clear a 5% threshold and eligible for the seats remaining according to position on the lists. The head of state is the *President*, elected by the Riigikogu for five-year terms. Presidential candidates must gain the nominations of at least 20% of parliamentary deputies. If no candidate wins a two-thirds majority in any of three rounds, the Speaker convenes an electoral college, composed of parliamentary deputies and local councillors. At this stage any 21 electors may nominate an additional candidate. The electoral college elects the President by a simple majority.

Citizenship requirements are two years residence and competence in Estonian for existing residents. For residents immigrating after 1 April 1995, five years qualifying residence is required.

National Anthem

'Mu isamaa, mu õnn ja rõõm' ('My native land, my pride and joy'); words by J. V. Jannsen, tune by F. Pacius (same as Finland).

GOVERNMENT CHRONOLOGY

Heads of State since independence.

Chairman of the Supreme Council
1991–92   Arnold Rüütel

Presidents
1992–2001   Lennart Georg Meri
2001–   Arnold Rüütel

Prime Ministers since independence. (IERSP (Isamaaliit) = Pro Patria Union; KMÜ-K = Estonian Coalition Party; n/p = non-party; Rahvarinne = Popular Front of Estonia; RE (Reformierakond) = Estonian Reform Party; ResP = Union for the Republic-Res Publica; RK Isamaa = National Coalition Party Pro Patria)

1990–92	Rahvarinne	Edgar Savisaar
1992	n/p	Tiit Vähi
1992–94	RK Isamaa	Mart Laar
1994–95	n/p	Andres Taran
1995–97	KMÜ-K	Tiit Vähi
1997–99	KMÜ-K	Mart Siimann
1999–2002	IERSP	Mart Laar
2002–03	RE	Siim Kallas
2003–05	ResP	Juhan Parts
2005–	RE	Andrus Ansip

RECENT ELECTIONS

Parliamentary elections were held on 2 March 2003; turnout was 58·2%. The Estonian Centre Party (Kesk) won 28 of the 101 seats (with 25·4% of the total votes); Union for the Republic-Res Publica (ResP), 28 seats (24·6%); Estonian Reform Party (Reform), 19 seats (17·7%); Estonian People's Union (Rahvaliit), 13 (13·3%); Pro Patria Union (Isamaa), 7 seats (7·3%); People's Party Moderates (Mõõdukad), 6 seats (7·0%). Two other parties failed to win seats.

A special government assembly elected the president after two rounds of votes on 21 Sept. 2001. There were four candidates. In the run-off for the presidency Arnold Rüütel won with 186 votes against 155 for Toomas Savi.

European Parliament

Estonia has six representatives. At the June 2004 elections turnout was 26·9%. The Social Democratic Party (was Mõõdukad) won 3 seats with 36·8% of votes cast (political affiliation in European Parliament: Party of European Socialists); Kesk, 1 with 17·5% (Alliance of Liberals and Democrats for Europe); Reform, 1 with 12·2% (Alliance of Liberals and Democrats for Europe); Isamaa, 1 with 10·5% (European People's Party–European Democrats).

CURRENT ADMINISTRATION

President: Arnold Rüütel; b. 1928 (sworn in 8 Oct. 2001).

In March 2006 the Reform-Kesk-Rahvaliit coalition government comprised:

Prime Minister: Andrus Ansip; b. 1956 (Reform; in office since 13 April 2005).

Minister of Agriculture: Ester Tuiksoo (Rahvaliit). *Culture:* Raivo Palmaru (Kesk). *Defence:* Jürgen Ligi (Reform). *Economic Affairs and Communications:* Edgar Savisaar (Kesk). *Education and Research:* Mailis Reps (Kesk). *Environment:* Villu Reiljan (Rahvaliit). *Finance:* Aivar Sõerd (Rahvaliit). *Foreign Affairs:* Urmas Paet (Reform). *Internal Affairs:* Kalle Laanet (Kesk). *Justice:* Rein Lang (Reform). *Population Affairs:* Paul-Eerik Rummo (Reform). *Regional Affairs:* Jaan Õunapuu (Rahvaliit). *Social Affairs:* Jaak Aab (Kesk).

Government Website: http://www.riik.ee

CURRENT LEADERS

Arnold Rüütel

Position
President

Introduction
Arnold Rüütel was elected president by an electoral college in Sept. 2001. He is yet to confirm if he will run for a further term at the 2006 presidential elections.

Early Life
Arnold Rüütel was born in Saaremaa, Estonia on 10 May 1928. He graduated from agricultural college in 1949 and from 1949–57 worked in agronomics and as a teacher of agriculture. In 1957 he became director and livestock expert of an experimental farm owned by the Estonian livestock breeding and veterinary institute. In 1963 he was appointed director of the Tartu Model Sovkhoz state farm. He was also studying during this period and

graduated from the Estonian academy of agriculture in 1964. In 1969 he was appointed rector of the academy, a position he held for eight years. He continued his studies into the 1990s, being awarded his doctorate in agriculture in 1991.

Rüütel's political career began in 1977 when he took the first of a series of posts in the communist institutions of the Estonian Soviet Socialist Republic (ESSR). In 1983 he was selected as chairman of the presidium of the supreme council of the ESSR (effectively head of state). He held the position until Oct. 1992 and was key in the preparation of the Estonian declaration of sovereignty adopted on 16 Nov. 1988.

Estonia declared independence on 20 Aug. 1991. Rüütel was a member of the constitutional assembly from 1991–92 and was instrumental in drafting the new Republic's constitution. In 1992 Rüütel stood for the presidency but lost to Lennart Meri. In 1995 he was elected to parliament as vice-speaker. From 1994–2000 he was party chairman of the People's Union of Estonia.

Career in Office
When Rüütel came to power in 2001 Estonia was aiming to join NATO and the EU. To this end and to benefit the third of Estonians who are native Russian speakers Rüütel ratified a law in Dec. 2001 opening public office to permitting non-Estonian speakers. In Nov. 2002 NATO invited Estonia to join the alliance, with the EU issuing a similar invitation a month later. In Sept. 2003 EU membership won overwhelming backing in a referendum and Estonia was one of ten new states to join the EU in May 2004. Full NATO membership was granted in March 2004,

Although the presidency is largely ceremonial, the president has been much involved with a ruling coalition subject to inter-party hostility. In 2002, Prime Minister Mart Laar resigned after parliamentary confusion threatened entry into NATO and the EU. In April 2003 Rüütel invited Juhan Parts, leader of the conservative Res Publica party, to be prime minister in a coalition with the Reform Party and the People's Union. In Feb. 2005 he sacked foreign minister Kristina Ojuland after secret files, mostly concerned with Estonia's position at EU summits, had disappeared from her ministry. Parts submitted the government's resignation after a vote of no confidence in the justice minister over a tough anti-corruption programme. Rüütel invited Reform Party leader Andrus Ansip to take over the premiership.

In March 2005 Rüütel declined an invitation to attend Moscow's celebrations to mark the anniversary of the end of the Second World War as a protest against the suffering and loss experienced by Estonia during the Soviet occupation.

Andrus Ansip

Position
Prime Minister

Introduction
When Andrus Ansip was sworn in as prime minister of Estonia on 13 April 2005, he took charge of the country's 12th government since its independence in 1991. A right-leaning former investment banker who was mayor of the second-largest city, Tartu, for six years, Ansip has pledged to implement policies that will attract investment and strengthen Estonia's position as a dynamic, post-industrial economy.

Early Life
Ansip was born in Tartu in the Soviet Republic of Estonia (ESSR) on 1 Oct. 1956. He attended local schools and graduated from the University of Tartu with a diploma in chemistry in 1979. He remained at the historic university to undertake further academic study, and later joined the municipal Committee of the Estonian Communist Party (ECP), which had been led, since 1978, by Karl Vaino, a Russian-born Estonian. The ESSR experienced increased Russification and 'Sovietization' in the early 1980s, in accordance with the policy of the Soviet leader,

Leonid Brezhnev. By 1988 however, there was growing opposition to the communist leadership and, against a backdrop of gradual economic liberalization, Ansip joined Estkompexim, a 'joint-venture' specializing in the import and export of foodstuffs. He was head of Estkompexim's Tartu office during 1991, when, following the collapse of the USSR, Estonia was internationally recognized as an independent nation. The following year Ansip attended a business management course at the University of York in Toronto, Canada.

On his return to Estonia in 1993, Ansip entered the rapidly evolving banking and investment sector, serving as a member of the board of directors of Rahvapank (the People's Bank) until 1995 and then chairman of the board of Livonia Privatization. In 1997 he was chief executive officer of the investment fund, Fondiinvesteeringu Maakler AS, as well as chairman of the board of Radio Tartu. The following year he was elected Mayor of Tartu as a candidate of the centre-right Estonian Reform Party (Reform), established in 1994 by Siim Kallas, a former governor of Estonia's central bank. A popular mayor, Ansip was credited with attracting investment to the country's second city and overseeing developments such as the Baltic Defence College and a new biomedical research institute which capitalized on Tartu's long-standing reputation as an academic centre.

On 13 Sept. 2004, shortly after Estonia joined the EU and NATO, Ansip was nominated to replace Meelis Atonen as the minister of economic affairs and communications. Two months later, he became chairman of Reform, which had formed part of the Res Publica-led coalition government under Juhan Parts since March 2003. His appointment followed the departure of Reform's leader (and former prime minister), Siim Kallas, to Brussels to become an EU commissioner. When, in March 2005, the *Riigikogu* (parliament) passed a vote of no confidence in the country's justice minister over proposed anti-corruption measures, Parts resigned as prime minister. On 31 March 2005 the president, Arnold Rüütel, asked Ansip to form a new government. He succeeded in forging a coalition with the Estonian Centre Party (Kesk) and the Estonian Peoples' Union (Rahvaliit). Ansip was backed by 53 out of 101 members of the *Riigikogu*, and was inaugurated as prime minister on 13 April 2005.

Career in Office
Ansip has said that he will continue steering Estonia towards membership of the euro in 2007. He acknowledges that it will be tough to fulfil the criterion of holding inflation to no more than 1·5 percentage points above that of the three lowest-inflation EU countries, given that Estonia's economy is growing at around 7% a year and its exports had risen by 20% in its first 12 months in the EU. He pledges to maintain the previous government's tax-cutting agenda, as well as increasing social welfare measures to bridge the gap between the relatively wealthy, young urban population and poorer rural citizens whose skills date from the Soviet period.

DEFENCE
The President is the head of national defence. Conscription is eight to 11 months for men and voluntary for women. Conscientious objectors may opt for 16 months civilian service instead.

Defence expenditure in 2003 totalled US$203m. (US$150 per capita), representing 2·0% of GDP.

The Estonian Defence Forces (EDF) regular component is divided into the Army, the Air Force and the Navy.

Army
The Army consists of nine army-training battalions (six for infantry, one for air defence, one for artillery and one for peace operations). Annually around 3,000 conscripts are trained for reserve. The total number of personnel in the Army in 2000 was 4,535 (1,420 officers and NCOs and contract soldiers; 2,290 conscripts and 825 civilians).

Navy
The Navy consists of the Naval Staff (Naval HQ), the Naval Base, and the Mine Countermeasures (MCM) Squadron. The total number of personnel in the Navy in 2000 was 385 (110 officers and NCOs and contract soldiers, 220 conscripts and 55 civilians). Estonia, Latvia and Lithuania have established a joint naval unit 'BALTRON' (Baltic Naval Squadron), with bases at Tallinn in Estonia, Liepāja, Riga and Ventspils in Latvia, and Klaipėda in Lithuania.

Air Force
The Air Force consists of an Air Force Staff, Air Force Base, and Air Surveillance Battalion. The total number of personnel in the Air Force is 200 (120 officers and NCOs and contract soldiers, 50 conscripts and 30 civilians).

INTERNATIONAL RELATIONS
Estonia is a member of the UN, WTO, BIS, NATO, EU, the Council of Europe, OSCE, Council of the Baltic Sea States, IOM and is an associate partner of the WEU. Estonia became a member of NATO on 29 March 2004 and of the EU on 1 May 2004.

Estonia held a referendum on EU membership on 14 Sept. 2003, in which 66·9% of votes cast were in favour of accession, with 33·1% against.

ECONOMY
Agriculture contributed 4% of GDP in 2003, industry 21% and services 75%.

Overview
According to the IMF 'the Estonian experience has demonstrated clearly that a free and open trade regime is key to strong economic performance'. Since independence, Estonia has been among the fastest growing of the EU accession countries, with per capita GDP almost doubling between 1993–2003 to reach about 45% of the EU average in purchasing power parity terms. Exports include machinery, electrical equipment, wood and textile products. Tourism is important. Finland and Sweden are core business partners in investment and tourism. The transition to a market economy was helped by proximity to Nordic countries. The cornerstone of economic reform was the introduction of the new currency, tight budgetary policies, privatization and trade liberalization. In 1999 many tariff and non-tariff barriers were abolished in line with WTO rules. Privatization of large and medium-sized enterprises has been successful with the private sector contributing 80% of GDP in 2002. Telecommunications and banking industries have been opened up.

Currency
The unit of currency is the *kroon* (EKR) of 100 *sents*. The kroon is pegged to the euro at a rate of 15·6466 *krooni* to one euro. Estonia is set to adopt the euro as its currency on 1 Jan. 2007. Foreign exchange reserves were US$914m. in June 2002 and gold reserves 8,000 troy oz. Inflation was 3·0% in 2004, up from 1·3% in 2003 although down on the rate of 3·6% in 2002. Total money supply in June 2002 was 25,936m. krooni. In June 2004 the kroon was included in the Exchange Rate Mechanism II (ERM II); the fixed exchange rate with the euro remains unchanged. There are no restrictions on the free movement of capital between Estonia and foreign countries.

Budget
Government budgetary revenue and expenditure in 1m. krooni for calendar years:

	2000	2001	2002	2003[1]
Revenue	26,773·0	31,285·6	36,125·2	41,382·1
Expenditure	27,373·3	30,295·7	34,103·6	37,001·9

[1]Provisional.

Tax revenue provided 32,372·9m. krooni in 2002, non-tax revenue totalled 3,215·7m. krooni and grants 536·6m. krooni. The standard rate of income tax is 23%; VAT is 18% (reduced rate, 5%).

Performance
The real GDP growth rate was 7·8% in 2004 and 6·7% in 2003—among the highest rates in the region—following growth of 7·2% in 2002 and 6·5% in 2001. Growth was supported by the increasing import demand of the European Union. Total GDP in 2004 was US$10·8bn.

Banking and Finance
A central bank, the Bank of Estonia, was re-established in 1990 (*Governor*, Andres Lipstok). The Estonian Investment Bank was established in 1992 to provide financing for privatized and private companies. Since 1 Jan. 1996 banks have been required to have an equity of at least 50m. krooni. As of Dec. 2004 there were six Estonian authorized commercial banks, three foreign banks' branches and five foreign banks' representative offices. As a result of a wave of mergers the two largest groups, Hansabank and the Union Bank of Estonia, control 80% of the market. Total assets and liabilities of commercial banks at Nov. 2004 were 128,211m. krooni. The Estonian Banking Association was founded in 1992.

A stock exchange opened in Tallinn in 1996.

ENERGY AND NATURAL RESOURCES
Environment
Estonia's carbon dioxide emissions from the consumption and flaring of fossil fuels in 2002 were the equivalent of 9·1 tonnes per capita.

Electricity
Estonia is a net electricity exporter. In 2001 installed capacity was 3·2m. kW in 2001, with production of 7·9bn. kWh. Consumption per capita was 5,540 kWh in 2000. In 1999, 92% of electricity was produced by burning oil shale. Wind power is being utilized on a small scale on Saaremaa and Hiiumaa.

Oil and Gas
Recoverable oil shale deposits were estimated at 1,500m. tonnes in 2000. A factory for the production of gas from shale and a 208 km-pipeline from Kohtla-Järve supplies shale gas to Tallinn, and exports to St Petersburg. Natural gas is imported from Russia.

Minerals
Oil shale is the most valuable mineral resource. Production volume has decreased (from 21m. tonnes in 1990 to 12m. tonnes in 2001) because of falls in exports and domestic electricity consumption, and an increase in the use of natural gas. Peatlands occupy about 22% of Estonia's territory; there are extensive deposits, of which an estimated 1·5bn. tonnes were classed as recoverable reserves in 2001. Phosphorites and super-phosphates are found and refined, and lignite (11·73m. tonnes in 2000), limestone, dolomite, clay, sand and gravel are mined.

Agriculture
In the course of the 1990s the proportion of agriculture in the gross national product decreased from 15% to 4%. Farming employed 6·1% of the population in 2003. At 1 Jan. 2001 there were 60,895 private farms and 709 state agricultural enterprises and co-operatives. In 2000 there were 1·43m. ha. of agricultural land of which 1·12m. ha. were arable and 0·30m. ha. were natural grassland. There were 19,000 ha. of permanent crops in 2001. Total agricultural output in 2003 was valued at 7,044m. krooni, including: animal production 3,388m. krooni; crop production, 2,616m. krooni; agricultural services and other non-agricultural production, 1,040m. krooni.

Output of main agricultural products (in 1,000 tonnes) in 2003: barley, 254; potatoes, 244; wheat, 145; oats, 63; rye, 23.

In 2003 there were 253,900 cattle, 29,900 sheep, 340,800 pigs and 2,096,000 chickens.

Livestock products (in 1,000 tonnes), 2003: meat, 105; milk, 611; eggs, 15.

Forestry
In 2000, 2·06m. ha. were covered by forests, which provide material for sawmills, furniture, and the match and pulp industries, as well as wood fuel. Private, municipal and state ownership of forests is allowed. In 2001 the annual timber cut was 10·20m. cu. metres, of which approximately 55% was from private forests.

Fisheries
In 2000 the Estonian fishing fleet numbered 170 vessels over 12 metres; 6,690 people were employed in active fishing. The total catch in 2001 was 126,902 tonnes.

INDUSTRY
The leading companies by market capitalization in Estonia, excluding banking and finance, in Jan. 2002 were: Eesti Telekom (12bn. krooni); Norma (830m. krooni), a car seatbelt producer; and Merko Ehitus (719m. krooni), a construction company.

Important industries are engineering, metalworking, food products, wood products, furniture and textiles. In 2001 manufacturing accounted for 16·5% of GDP.

Labour
The workforce in 2003 totalled 660,500, of whom 594,300 were employed. The monthly average gross wage in 2003 was 6,723 krooni. The unemployment rate in 2003 was 10·0%, compared with 13·7% in 2000.

Retirement age was 63 years for both men and women in 2004.

Trade Unions
The main trade union organization in Estonia is the Estonian Association of Trade Unions, which represents the interests of industrial, service, trade, public and agricultural employees.

INTERNATIONAL TRADE
Direct investment position in Estonia by countries as of 31 Dec. 2003: Sweden, 42·8%; Finland, 27·0%; USA, 5·5%; Netherlands, 3·0%; Denmark, 2·6%; Germany, 2·5%; Norway, 2·5%. Estonia's direct investment position abroad by countries as of 31 Dec. 2004: Lithuania, 45·4%; Latvia, 28·4%; Cyprus, 14·0%; Italy, 4·4%; Ukraine, 2·5%. Direct foreign investment in Estonia as at 31 Dec. 2003 totalled 80,792·3m. krooni. Estonia's direct investment abroad as at 31 Dec. 2003 totalled 12,668m. krooni.

External debt was US$3,703m. in 2002.

Imports and Exports
Imports in 2003 (and 2002) were valued at US$7,602·5m. (US$6,734·9m.); exports, US$5,299·3m. (US$4,829·7m.).

Main import suppliers in 2003: Finland, 15·9%; Germany, 11·3%; Sweden, 8·8%; Russia, 8·6%; China, 4·5%. Main export markets, 2003: Finland, 25·9%; Sweden, 15·3%; Germany, 9·9%; Latvia, 7·0%; UK, 4·2%.

Around 80% of Estonian trade is with EU member countries, and 41% with Finland and Sweden alone.

COMMUNICATIONS
Roads
As of 1 Jan. 2004 there were 16,452 km of national roads (29·4% of the total Estonian road and street network of 55,592 km), of which 52·3% were paved. In 2003 there were 433,982 registered passenger cars in use, plus 83,400 trucks and vans, 5,400 buses and coaches, and 8,100 motorcycles and mopeds. There were 1,928 road accidents and 164 fatalities in 2003.

Rail

Length of railways in 2002 was 968 km (1,520 mm gauge), of which 132 km was electrified. In 2003, 5·06m. passengers and 65·6m. tonnes of freight were carried.

Civil Aviation

In 2002 there were 38 airports in Estonia. There is an international airport at Tallinn (Ulemiste), which handled 570,919 passengers (566,551 on international flights) and 2,181 tonnes of freight in 2001. Estonian aviation companies handled 336,200 passengers and 5,500 tonnes of goods in 1999. The national carrier is Estonian Air, 34% state-owned. In 2003 Estonian Air operated services to Copenhagen, Frankfurt, Hamburg, Kyiv, London, Moscow, Paris, Riga, Stockholm and Vilnius. In 1999 it flew 6·0m. km, carrying 291,300 passengers (all on international flights). In Jan. 2000 there were 124 aircraft in Estonia.

Shipping

There are six major shipping companies, all of which are privatized. There are ice-free, deep-water ports at Tallinn and Muuga (state-owned). Tallinn handled 85% of the total turnover of goods in Estonia in 2000. The port of Tallinn makes most of its money by shipping out Russian oil and importing goods destined for Russia. In 2002 the merchant shipping fleet comprised 33 vessels of 1,000 GRT or over.

Telecommunications

Estonia had 1,356,000 telephone subscribers in 2002 (1,000·7 per 1,000 persons) and 285,000 PCs (210·3 per 1,000 persons). There were 881,000 mobile phone subscribers in 2002 and 52,000 fax machines. In Feb. 2000 the Estonian parliament voted to guarantee Internet access to its citizens. The number of Internet users in 2002 was 444,000.

Postal Services

As of 1 Jan. 2004, the state-owned Eesti Post had 12 main post offices, 395 other post offices and 154 postal agencies, employing 4,237.

SOCIAL INSTITUTIONS

Justice

A post-Soviet criminal code was introduced in 1992. There is a three-tier court system with the State Court at its apex, and there are both city and district courts. The latter act as courts of appeal. The State Court is the final court of appeal, and also functions as a constitutional court. There are also administrative courts for petty offences. Judges are appointed for life. City and district judges are appointed by the President; State Court judges are elected by Parliament.

In 2003, 53,595 crimes were recorded; there were 38 murders and attempted murders (down from 200 in 1999). There are nine prisons; in May 2003, 4,874 persons were in custody (361 per 100,000 of national population—one of the highest rates in Europe).

The death penalty was abolished for all crimes in 1998.

Education

Adult literacy rate in 2003 was 99·8% (99·8% for both males and females). There are nine years of comprehensive school starting at age six, followed by three years secondary school. In 2002–03 there were 636 general education schools: 65 nursery/primary, 52 primary, 279 basic and 240 secondary/upper secondary. Of these, 525 were Estonian-language, 89 Russian-language and 22 mixed-language. There were 45 schools for children with special needs. The total number of pupils at basic school level in general education in 2002–03 was 165,486 (115,204 at urban schools and 50,282 at rural schools). At the start of the 2003–04 academic year there were 65,659 higher education students studying at six public universities, six private universities, seven state higher schools and 17 private higher schools; 11 vocational educational institutions also provide higher education.

In 2001 central government expenditure on education came to 2,136·9m. krooni. In 1999–2000 total education expenditure came to 7·6% of GNP.

Health

Estonia had 51 hospitals (14 private) in 2002, down from 78 hospitals (28 private) in 1999. There were 8,248 hospital beds in 2002. In 2003 there were 4,293 doctors (1,245 in private medicine).

Welfare

In 2003 there were 0·37m. pensioners. The average monthly pension was 1,816 krooni in 2003. An official poverty line was introduced in 1993 (then 280 krooni per month). Persons receiving less are entitled to state benefit. Unemployment benefit was 400 krooni a month in 2003.

RELIGION

There is freedom of religion in Estonia and no state church, although most of the population is Lutheran. The Estonian Orthodox Church owed allegiance to Constantinople until it was forcibly brought under Moscow's control in 1940; a synod of the free Estonian Orthodox Church was established in Stockholm. Returning from exile, it registered itself in 1993 as the Estonian Apostolic Orthodox Church. By an agreement in 1996 between the Moscow and Constantinople Orthodox Patriarchates, there are now two Orthodox jurisdictions in Estonia. In 2000 there were 152,000 Lutherans and 144,000 Orthodox. Other Christian denominations, including Methodist, Baptist and Roman Catholic, are also represented.

CULTURE

World Heritage Sites

Estonia has two sites on the UNESCO World Heritage List: the Historic Centre (Old Town) of Tallinn (1997) and the Struve Geodetic Arc (2005). The Arc is a chain of survey triangulations spanning from Norway to the Black Sea that helped establish the exact shape and size of the earth and is shared with nine other countries.

Broadcasting

There were over 30 radio stations in Estonia in 2000. Public service radio, Estonian Radio, operates four channels, three in Estonian and one in languages of national minorities, mainly Russian. In 2000 there were four TV channels with nationwide networks (colour by PAL): Estonian State Television and three commercial channels. The Broadcasting Council is the regulatory body for public service broadcasting and has nine members nominated by Riigikogu (the Estonian Parliament). There were 900,000 TV receivers in 2001 and 1·50m. radio receivers in 2000.

Cinema

In 2003 there were 69 cinemas (81 screens); attendances totalled 1·27m. Three full-length films were released in 2003.

Press

In 2000 there were 109 officially registered newspapers, including 82 in Estonian; and 956 periodicals, including 778 in Estonian. *The Baltic Times* is an English-language weekly.

Tourism

There were 1·4m. foreign visitors in 2002 who spent US$555m.

Festivals

Festivals include: International Folklore Festival, BALTICA, which is staged every three years; Festival of Baroque Music; Jazz festival, JAZZKAAR; Pärnu International Documentary and Anthropology Film Festival and the Viljandi Folk Music Festival. Estonia's Song Festival, which was first held in 1869, is held every five years and is next scheduled to take place in 2009. *Baltoscandal*, an international theatre festival which takes place every two years, was scheduled to celebrate its 9th staging in June–July 2006.

Libraries

The Eesti Rahvusraamatukogu (National Library of Estonia) opened in 1993. Other libraries include the Tallinn Tartu University Library (1802); Technical University Library (1919); and the Estonian Academic Library (1946). In 1997 there were 743 public libraries, two National libraries and 33 Higher Education libraries. They held a combined 18,116,000 volumes for 1,073,000 registered users.

Theatre and Opera

Most performances are in the Estonian language with the exception of the Russian Drama Theatre, and the Estonia Opera and Ballet Theatre which sometimes performs operas in their original language. There were nine state theatres and one municipal in 2000.

DIPLOMATIC REPRESENTATIVES

Of Estonia in the United Kingdom (16 Hyde Park Gate, London, SW7 5DG)
Ambassador: Vacant.
Chargé d'Affaires a.i.: Aivar Tsarski.

Of the United Kingdom in Estonia (Wismari 6, 10136 Tallinn)
Ambassador: Nigel Haywood.

Of Estonia in the USA (2131 Massachusetts Ave., NW, Washington, D.C., 20008)
Ambassador: Juri Luik.

Of the USA in Estonia (Kentmanni 20, 15099 Tallinn)
Ambassador: Aldona Zofia Wos.

Of Estonia to the United Nations
Ambassador: Tiina Intelmann.

Of Estonia to the European Union
Ambassador: Väino Reinart.

FURTHER READING

Statistical Office of Estonia. *Statistical Yearbook.*
Ministry of the Economy. *Estonian Economy.* Annual
Hood, N., *et al.*, (eds.) *Transition in the Baltic States.* London, 1997
Lieven, A., *The Baltic Revolution: Estonia, Latvia, Lithuania and the Path to Independence.* 2nd ed. Yale Univ. Press, 1994
Misiunas, R.-J. and Taagepera, R., *The Baltic States: Years of Dependence 1940–1991.* 2nd ed., Farnborough, 1993
Smith, I. A. and Grunts, M. V., *The Baltic States.* [Bibliography] ABC-Clio, Oxford and Santa Barbara (CA), 1993
Taagepera, R., *Estonia: Return to Independence.* Boulder (CO), 1993

National Statistical Office: Statistical Office of Estonia, Tallinn.
Website: http://www.stat.ee/

ETHIOPIA

Federal Democratic Republic of Ethiopia

Capital: Addis Ababa
Population projection, 2010: 87·00m.
GDP per capita, 2003: (PPP$) 711
HDI/world rank: 0·367/170

KEY HISTORICAL EVENTS

The ancient empire of Ethiopia has its legendary origin in the meeting of King Solomon and the Queen of Sheba. The empire developed at Askum in the north in the centuries before and after the birth of Christ as a result of Semitic immigration from South Arabia. Ethiopia's subsequent history is one of sporadic expansion southwards and eastwards, checked from the 16th to early 19th centuries by devastating wars with Muslims and Gallas. Modern Ethiopia dates from the reign of the Emperor Theodore (1855–68). Menelik II (1889–1913) defeated the Italians in 1896 and thereby safeguarded the empire's independence in the scramble for Africa.

In 1923 the heir to the throne, Ras Tafari (crowned Emperor Haile Selassie five years later), succeeded in getting Ethiopia admitted as an independent country to the League of Nations. However, the League was ineffective in preventing a second Italian invasion in 1936. The emperor fled the country, only returning when the Allied forces defeated the Italians in 1941.

In 1950 the former Italian colony of Eritrea, from 1941 under British military administration, was handed over to Ethiopia. Thereafter, a secessionist movement fought a guerrilla war for independence under the Eritrean Peoples' Liberation Front (EPLF). A military government, known as the Dirgue, assumed power on 12 Sept. 1974 under the leadership of Lieut. Col. Mengistu Haile Miriam. It deposed the emperor, abolished the monarchy and mounted an agricultural collectivization programme. In 1977 Somalia invaded Ethiopia and took control of the Ogaden region. After a counter offensive with Soviet and Cuban support the area was recaptured. Following ever-increasing territorial gains by the insurgent Ethiopian People's Revolutionary Democratic Front (EPRDF) and the EPLF, Mengistu fled the country. In July 1991 a conference of 24 political groups, called to appoint a transitional government, agreed a democratic

charter. Eritrea seceded, and became independent, on 24 May 1993. In 1999 fighting broke out along Ethiopia's border with Eritrea. After the failure of international mediation, the 13-month long-truce between Ethiopia and Eritrea ended in May 2000. Ethiopia launched a major offensive in the ongoing war over territorial disputes and claimed victory. In June both sides agreed to an Organization of African Unity peace deal to end the two-year border war. Economic progress, including market-led reforms, raised hopes of higher living standards until three successive years of drought left food resources seriously depleted. Widespread malnutrition was alleviated by international aid.

TERRITORY AND POPULATION

Ethiopia is bounded in the northeast by Eritrea, east by Djibouti and Somalia, south by Kenya and west by Sudan. It has a total area of 1,127,127 sq. km. The secession of Eritrea in 1993 left Ethiopia without a coastline. An Eritrean–Ethiopian agreement of July 1993 gives Ethiopia rights to use the Eritrean ports of Assab and Massawa.

The first census was carried out in 1984: population, 42,019,418 (without Eritrea, 39,570,266). 1994 census population: 49,218,178. Estimate (2005), 77·43m. (84·3% rural in 2003); density, 69 per sq. km.

The UN gives a projected population for 2010 of 87·00m.

Ethiopia has eleven administrative divisions—eight states (Afar, Amhara, Benshangul/Gumaz, Gambella, Oromia, the Peoples of the South, Somalia and Tigre) and three cities (Addis Ababa, Dire Dawa and Harar).

The population of the capital, Addis Ababa, was 2,534,000 in 1999. Other large towns (1994 populations): Dire Dawa, 164,851; Nazret, 127,842; Harar, 122,932; Mekele, 119,779; Jimma, 119,717.

There are six major ethnic groups (in % of total population in 1996): Oromo, 31%; Amhara, 30%; Tigrinya, 7%; Gurage, 5%; Somali, 4%; Sidamo, 3%. There are also some 60 minor ethnic groups and 286 languages are spoken. The *de facto* official language is Amharic (which uses its own alphabet), though Oromo-speakers form the largest group.

SOCIAL STATISTICS

Births, 1999, 2,186,000; deaths, 1,062,000. Rates per 1,000 population, 1999: births, 34·2; deaths, 16·6. Expectation of life at birth in 2003 was 46·6 years for males and 48·7 years for females. Annual population growth rate, 1992–2002, 2·8%; infant mortality, 2001, 116 per 1,000 live births; fertility rate, 2001, 6·8 births per woman.

CLIMATE

The wide range of latitude produces many climatic variations between the high, temperate plateaus and the hot, humid lowlands. The main rainy season lasts from June to Aug., with light rains from Feb. to April, but the country is very vulnerable to drought. Addis Ababa, Jan. 59°F (15°C), July 59°F (15°C). Annual rainfall 50" (1,237 mm). Harar, Jan. 65°F (18·3°C), July 64°F (17·8°C). Annual rainfall 35" (897 mm). Massawa, Jan. 78°F (25·6°C), July 94°F (34·4°C). Annual rainfall 8" (193 mm).

CONSTITUTION AND GOVERNMENT

A 548-member constituent assembly was elected on 5 June 1994; turnout was 55%. The EPRDF gained 484 seats. On 8 Dec. 1994 it unanimously adopted a new federal Constitution which became effective on 22 Aug. 1995. It provided for the creation of a federation of nine regions based (except the capital and the southern region) on a predominant ethnic group. These regions have the right of secession after a referendum. The *President*, a largely ceremonial post, is elected by parliament, the 548-member *Council of People's Representatives*. There is also an upper house, the 108-member *Federal Council*.

National Anthem

'Yazegennat keber ba-Ityop yachchen santo' ('In our Ethiopia our civic pride is strong'); words by D. M. Mengesha, tune by S. Lulu Mitiku.

RECENT ELECTIONS

Parliamentary elections were held on 15 May 2005 with repeat elections on 21 Aug. where irregularities had been reported or results were challenged. The Ethiopian People's Revolutionary Democratic Front (EPRDF) won 327 seats, followed by the Coalition for Unity and Democracy (CUD) with 109 seats, United Ethiopian Democratic Front (UEDF) with 52, Somali People's Democratic Party (SPDP) 23, Oromo Federalist Democratic Movement (OFDM) 11, Afar National Democratic Party (ANDP) 8, Benishangul Gumuz People's Democratic Unity Front (BGPDUF) 8, Gambella Peoples' Democratic Movement (GPDM) 3, Argoba National Democratic Organization (ANDO) 1, Hareri National League (HNL) 1, Sheko and Mezenger People's Democratic Unity Organization (SMPDUO) 1, ind. 1.

CURRENT ADMINISTRATION

President: Girma Wolde-Giyorgis; b. 1925 (elected 8 Oct. 2001).

In March 2006 the government comprised:

Prime Minister: Meles Zenawi; b. 1955 (EPRDF; appointed 22 Aug. 1995).

Deputy Prime Minister: Adisu Legesse (also *Minister of Agriculture and Rural Development*).

Minister of Capacity Building: Tefera Walwa. *Culture and Tourism:* Mahmud Dirir. *Defence:* Kuma Demeksa. *Education:* Sintayehu Woldemikael. *Federal Affairs:* Siraj Fegeta. *Finance and Economic Development:* Sufyan Ahmad. *Foreign Affairs:* Seyoum Mesfin. *Health:* Dr Tewodros Adhanom. *Information:* Berhan Hailu. *Justice:* Assefa Keseto. *Labour and Social Affairs:* Hassan Abdella. *Mines and Energy:* Alemayehu Tegenu. *Revenue:* Melaku Fenta. *Trade and Industry:* Girma Birru. *Transport and Communications:* Junedi Sado. *Water Resources:* Asefaw Dingam. *Women's Affairs:* Hirut Dilebo. *Works and Urban Development:* Kasu Ilala. *Youth and Sports:* Aster Mamo.

CURRENT LEADERS

Meles Zenawi

Position
Prime Minister

Introduction
Meles Zenawi headed Ethiopia's transitional government from 1991–95. He was then appointed prime minister, the most important executive position in the country. He has had to cope with one of the world's weakest economies threatened by famine. His tenure has witnessed a border war with Eritrea, which officially ended in 2000 but remains a source of contention. Relations with Sudan have improved under Meles' guidance, but he remains troubled by separatist fighters in western Ethiopia.

Early Life
Meles Zenawi Asres was born in Adwa, in Ethiopia's Tigre region in 1955. He attended school in Adwa and Addis Ababa. In 1972 he began studying medicine at Addis Ababa University but left two years later to join the Tigre People's Liberation Front (TPLF) to fight against the Dirgue military government of Lieut. Col. Mengistu Haile Miriam. He served on the organization's central committee between 1979 and 1983 and sat on the executive council from 1983 until 1989. In 1989 he was elected chairman of

the TPLF and of the Ethiopian People's Revolutionary Democratic Front (EPRDF), an alliance formed that year between the TPLF and the Ethiopian People's Democratic Movement.

Career in Office
Alongside his role as EPRDF chair, Meles was president of Ethiopia's transitional government, established after the overthrow of the Mengistu regime, from 1991 until 1995. During this period he oversaw the secession of Eritrea and the drafting of a new constitution which divided Ethiopia into ethnic regions. In 1995 the EPRDF-dominated elections were boycotted by the major opposition groups. In Aug. 1995 Meles was elected prime minister of the newly established Federal Democratic Republic of Ethiopia, while Negasso Gidada took the largely ceremonial role of president. Meles was also voted chairman of the Organization of African Unity (now the African Union) for 1995–96.

In 2000 the EPRDF again dominated parliamentary elections and Meles was confirmed in office as prime minister. Despite the liberalization of the media and a move away from the human rights abuses of the Mengistu years, there remained opposition to Meles' government, and in 2001 there were mass protests in the capital against police brutality and political and academic oppression. In May 2005 Meles won a third term of office in further elections that were bitterly contested. Following allegations of fraud, there were violent protests and elections were re-run in some constituencies in Aug. In Sept. the Election Board confirmed the final results giving the EPRDF and its affiliates a solid parliamentary majority. Meanwhile, however, opposition parties and demonstrators continued to contest the outcome, clashing in June with security forces in Addis Ababa where 36 people were killed. In Nov. at least 46 more protesters died during renewed violence between security forces and opposition supporters.

On the economic front, Meles—formerly an advocate of Marxist-Leninism—has adopted free market reforms that have generated considerable growth, although the country remains among the world's poorest. In 2002 an Economic Commission for Africa report highlighted excessive bureaucracy and the HIV/AIDS pandemic as major obstacles to sustained development.

In 1999 border fighting between Ethiopian and Eritrean forces escalated into a full-scale war, which cost 70,000 lives. A ceasefire was agreed in June 2000, with Ethiopia withdrawing its forces under UN supervision. A formal peace treaty was signed in Dec. 2000. Tensions remained, particularly concerning the control of the small border settlement of Badame. In May 2001 the countries agreed to abide by the decision of an international boundary commission. The commission awarded Badame to Eritrea, but Meles' government refused to accept the decision. Fears of a renewed conflict mounted in late 2005 after Eritrea expelled UN observers policing the militarized border region.

In other disputes, Somalia has accused Ethiopia of backing Somalian rebel factions, while Ethiopia has claimed Somalian backing of Islamic terrorist groups within Ethiopia. However, relations improved when Ethiopia agreed to support reconciliation between Somalia's warring factions in Nov. 2001. Ethiopian–Sudanese relations have also been strained, principally over Sudan's alleged involvement in an assassination attempt on Egyptian President Hosni Mubarak in Addis Ababa in 1995.

DEFENCE

In 2003 defence expenditure totalled US$326m. (US$5 per capita), representing 4·9% of GDP.

Army

Following the overthrow of President Mengistu's government Ethiopian armed forces were constituted from former members of the Tigray People's Liberation Front. The strength of the armed forces is estimated at 252,500 (2002).

Air Force

Owing to its role in the war with Eritrea aircraft operability has improved. There were 55 combat aircraft in 2002, including MiG-21s and MiG-23s, and 30 armed helicopters. Personnel were estimated at 2,500 in 2002.

INTERNATIONAL RELATIONS

A border dispute between Ethiopia and Eritrea broke out in May 1998. Eritrean troops took over the border town of Badame after a skirmish between Ethiopian police units and armed men from Eritrea. Ethiopia maintained that Badame and Sheraro, a nearby town, had always been part of Ethiopia and called Eritrea's action an invasion. An agreement ending hostilities was signed in June 2000, followed by a peace accord in Dec. A buffer zone has been created to separate the armies but tensions do still arise from time to time, notably in late 2005 following a further dispute between the two countries over Badame.

Ethiopia is a member of the UN, the African Union, African Development Bank, COMESA, the Intergovernmental Authority on Development and is an ACP member state of the ACP-EU relationship.

ECONOMY

Agriculture accounted for 42·3% of GDP in 2002, industry 11·1% and services 46·5%.

Overview

An Economic Reform Programme, instituted in 1992, aimed at stabilizing the economy and deregulating economic activities to prepare for a free-market economy. An Economic Rehabilitation and Reconstruction Programme (ERRP), launched in 1991–92, eased foreign exchange regulations and a privatization programme began in 1995. Economic growth has been hampered by drought, leading to widespread food shortages.

Currency

The *birr* (ETB), of 100 *cents*, is the unit of currency. The birr was devalued in Oct. 1992. In May 2002 total money supply was 12,976m. birr, foreign exchange reserves were US$638m. and gold reserves 205,000 troy oz. There was inflation in 2003 of 15·1% and in 2004 of 8·6%.

Budget

The fiscal year ends on 6 July. Revenue, 1999–2000, 11,222m. birrs; expenditure, 17,184m. birrs.

Performance

Real GDP growth was 11·5% in 2004 (–4·2% in 2003). Total GDP was US$8·1bn. in 2004.

Banking and Finance

The central bank and bank of issue is the National Bank of Ethiopia (founded 1964; *Governor*, Teklewold Atnafu). The country's largest bank is the state-owned Commercial Bank of Ethiopia. The complete monopoly held by the bank ended with deregulation in 1994, but it still commands about 90% of the market share. There are eight other banks. On 1 Jan. 1975 the government nationalized all banks, mortgage and insurance companies.

Weights and Measures

The metric system is official. Traditional units include the *feresula* (= approximately 17 kg), and the *gasha* (based on family land-ownership), which is officially 40 ha. but can be up to 120 ha.

ENERGY AND NATURAL RESOURCES

Environment

Carbon dioxide emissions from the consumption and flaring of fossil fuels were the equivalent of 0·1 tonnes per capita in 2002.

Electricity

Installed capacity in 2000 was 0·5m. kW. Production in 2000 was 1·70bn. kWh. Hydro-electricity accounts for 97% of generation. Consumption per capita was 28 kWh in 2000. Supply: 220 volts; 50 Hz.

Oil and Gas

The Calub gas field in the southeast of Ethiopia had reserves estimated at 25bn. cu. metres in 2002.

Minerals

Gold and salt are produced. Lege Dembi, an open-pit gold mine in the south of the country, has proven reserves of over 62 tonnes and produces more than five tonnes a year.

Agriculture

Small-scale farmers make up about 85% of Ethiopia's population. There were 10·7m. ha. of arable land in 2001 and 750,000 ha. of permanent crops. 190,000 ha. were irrigated in 2001. There were 3,000 tractors in 2001 and 100 harvester-threshers. By 1993, 96% of agricultural land was worked by smallholdings averaging 0·5–1·5 ha. Land remains the property of the state, but individuals are granted rights of usage which can be passed to their children, and produce may be sold on the open market instead of compulsorily to the state at low fixed prices.

Coffee is by far the most important source of rural income. Main agricultural products (2000, in 1,000 tonnes): maize, 2,600; sugarcane, 2,300; wheat, 1,220; sorghum, 1,190; barley, 750; potatoes, 340; millet, 320; broad beans, 280; yams, 250; coffee, 230. Teff (*Eragrastis abyssinica*) and durra are also major products.

Livestock, 2000: cattle, 35·0m.; sheep, 21·0m.; goats, 16·8m.; asses, 5·20m.; horses, 2·75m.; camels, 1·06m.; chickens, 56m.

Forestry

In 2000 forests covered 4·59m. ha., representing 4·2% of the land area. Ethiopia is Africa's leading roundwood producer, with removals totalling 91·28m. cu. metres in 2001.

Fisheries

The catch in 2001 was 15,390 tonnes, entirely from inland waters.

INDUSTRY

Most public industrial enterprises are controlled by the state. Industrial activity is centred around Addis Ababa. Processed food, cement, textiles and drinks are the main commodities produced. Industrial production accounted for 11·1% of GDP in 2001, including 7·0% from manufacturing.

Labour

The labour force in 1996 was 25,392,000 (59% males); it was estimated by the UN that 30% were unemployed. Coffee provided a livelihood to a quarter of the population.

INTERNATIONAL TRADE

Foreign debt was US$6,522m. in 2002.

Imports and Exports

Imports and exports for calendar years in US$1m.:

	1998	1999	2000	2001	2002
Imports f.o.b.	1,359·8	1,387·2	1,131·4	1,625·8	1,455·0
Exports f.o.b.	560·3	467·4	486·0	455·6	480·2

Principal imports (2000): machinery and apparatus (19·8%); refined petroleum (19·6%); road vehicles (12·0%); chemicals and chemical products (11·3%). Principal exports: coffee (53·0%); leather (8·5%). Other important exports include sugar, pulses and cattle.

Coffee accounts for about half of the country's export earnings. In 1997, 103,000 tonnes of coffee were exported, earning around US$360m. (£220m.) compared to just US$160m. (£100m.) in 1993.

Major import suppliers, 2000: Yemen, 19·1%; Italy, 8·9%; Japan, 8·2%; China, 7·7%. Main export markets: Germany, 19·6%; Japan, 11·7%; Djibouti, 10·7%; Saudi Arabia, 8·1%.

COMMUNICATIONS

Roads
There were 33,297 km of roads in 2002, only 12% of which were paved. Passenger cars in use in 2002 numbered 67,614 (one per 1,000 inhabitants) and there were also 34,102 trucks and vans, and 18,067 buses and coaches. In 1999 there were 1,274 deaths in road accidents.

In 1998 a US$500m. deal was signed with the World Bank for road and power development projects.

Rail
The Ethiopian-Djibouti Railway has a length of 782 km (metre-gauge), but much of the route is in need of renovation. Passenger-km travelled in 1998–99 came to 151m. and freight tonne-km to 90m.

Civil Aviation
There are international airports at Addis Ababa (Bole) and Dire Dawa. The national carrier is the state-owned Ethiopian Airlines. In 2003 it served 43 international and 25 domestic destinations. In 1999 scheduled airline traffic of Ethiopian-based carriers flew 28·5m. km, carrying 861,000 passengers (617,000 on international flights). In 2001 Addis Ababa (Bole) handled 1,096,500 passengers and 26,490 tonnes of freight.

Shipping
Merchant shipping totalled 82,000 GRT in 2002, including oil tankers 2,000 GRT.

Telecommunications
All the main centres are connected with Addis Ababa by telephone or radio telegraph. In 2002 there were 404,200 telephone subscribers (6·0 per 1,000 persons), including 50,400 mobile phone subscribers. There were 100,000 PCs in use in 2002 (1·5 per 1,000 persons) and 4,900 fax machines. In 2002 Ethiopia had 50,000 Internet users.

Postal Services
In 2003 there were 611 post offices, or one for every 116,000 persons.

SOCIAL INSTITUTIONS

Justice
The legal system is based on the Justinian Code. A new penal code came into force in 1958 and Special Penal Law in 1974. Codes of criminal procedure, civil, commercial and maritime codes have since been promulgated. Provincial and district courts have been established, and High Court judges visit the provincial courts on circuit. The Supreme Court at Addis Ababa is presided over by the Chief Justice.

The population in penal institutions in 2003 was approximately 65,000 (92 per 100,000 of national population).

Education
The adult literacy rate in 2002 was 41·5% (49·2% among males and 33·8% among females). Primary education commences at seven years and continues with optional secondary education at 13 years. Up to the age of 12, education is in the local language of the federal region. In 2000–01 there were 6,650,841 pupils at primary schools with 121,077 teachers, and 1,495,445 pupils with 25,984 (1995–96) teachers at secondary schools. During the period 1990–95 only 19% of females of primary school age were enrolled in school. In 1994–95 there was one university with 19,200 students and 900 academic staff, and one agricultural university with 1,551 students and 324 academic staff. There were two institutes of health sciences and water technology; and two colleges—one of teacher training and one of town planning.

In 2000–01 expenditure on education came to 4·8% of GNP and 13·8% of total government spending.

Health
In 2002 there were 1,971 physicians, 61 dentists, 13,018 nurses, 1,142 midwives and 125 pharmacists. In 2000 only 24% of the population had access to safe drinking water.

RELIGION

About 59% of the population are Christian, mainly belonging to the Ethiopian Orthodox Church, and 32% Sunni Muslims. Amhara, Tigreans and some Oromos are Christian. Somalis, Afars and some Oromos are Muslims. About 5% of the population follow traditional animist beliefs.

CULTURE

World Heritage Sites
There are seven sites in Ethiopia that appear on the UNESCO World Heritage List. They are (with the year entered on list): the Rock-hewn Churches at Laibela (1978), 11 monolithic 13th century churches; Simien National Park (1978); Fasil Ghebbi, Gondar Region (1979), a 16th century fortress city; Aksum (1980), the capital of the ancient Kingdom of Aksum, containing tombs and castles dating from the first millennium AD; the Lower Valley of the Awash (1980), an important palaeontological site; the Lower Valley of the Omo (1980), where *Homo gracilis* was discovered; and Tiya (1980), a group of archeological sites south of Addis Ababa.

Broadcasting
The government-run Voice of Ethiopia broadcasts a national programme and an external service in English. The government-controlled Ethiopian Television (colour by PAL) transmits about 28 hours a week. Private radio stations have been permitted since 2004. In 2000 there were 11·8m. radio receivers and in 2001 there were 370,000 TV receivers.

Press
In 1998 there were two daily newspapers with a combined circulation of 23,000 and 78 non-dailies and periodicals.

Tourism
In 2001 there were 148,000 foreign visitors. Revenue from tourists totalled US$75m.

Calendar
The Julian calendar remains in use; the year has 13 months (12 months with 30 days and one month with five or six, depending on the leap-year). It begins on 11 Sept. (Gregorian) and is seven or eight years behind the Gregorian calendar.

DIPLOMATIC REPRESENTATIVES

Of Ethiopia in the United Kingdom (17 Prince's Gate, London, SW7 1PZ)
Ambassador: Fisseha Adugna.

Of the United Kingdom in Ethiopia (Fikre Mariam Abatechan St., Addis Ababa)
Ambassador: Robert Dewar.

Of Ethiopia in the USA (3506 International Drive, NW, Washington, D.C., 20008)
Ambassador: Ayele Kassahun.

Of the USA in Ethiopia (Entoto St., Addis Ababa)
Ambassador: Vacant.
Chargé d'Affaires a.i.: Vicki J. Huddleston.

Of Ethiopia to the United Nations
Ambassador: Vacant.
Chargé d'Affaires a.i.: Zenna Teruneh.

Of Ethiopia to the European Union
Ambassador: Ato Berhane Gebre-Christos.

FURTHER READING

Araia, G., *Ethiopia: the Political Economy of Transition.* Univ. Press of America, 1995

Crummey, Donald, *Land and Society in the Christian Kingdom of Ethiopia: From the Thirteenth to the Twentieth Century.* Univ. of Illinois Press and James Currey, Oxford, 2000

Henze, Paul B., *Layers of Time: A History of Ethiopia.* C. Hurst, London, 2000

Mekonnen, T. (ed.) *The Ethiopian Economy: Structure, Problems and Policy Issues.* Addis Ababa, 1992

Munro-Hay, Stuart and Pankhurst, Richard, *Ethiopia.* [Bibliography] ABC-Clio, Oxford and Santa Barbara (CA), 1995

Negash, Tekeste and Tronvoll, Kjetil, *Brothers at War: Making Sense of the Eritrean–Ethiopian War.* Ohio Univ. Press and James Currey, Oxford, 2001

Pankhurst, Richard, *The Ethiopians.* Oxford, 1999

Tiruneh, A., *The Ethiopian Revolution: a Transformation from an Aristocratic to a Totalitarian Autocracy.* CUP, 1993

National Statistical Office: Central Statistical Office, Addis Ababa.

FIJI ISLANDS

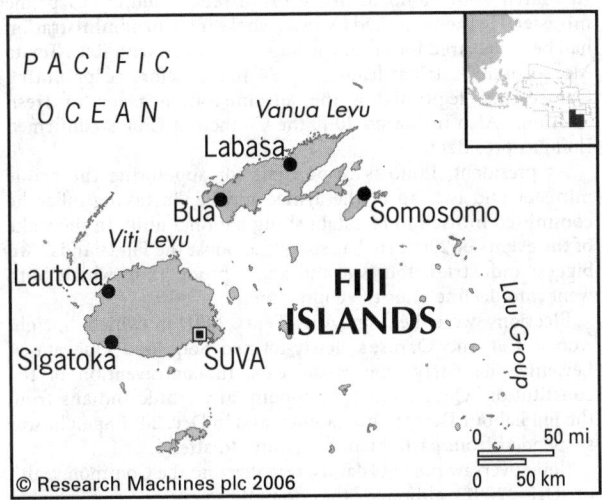

© Research Machines plc 2006

Capital: Suva
Population projection, 2010: 878,000
GDP per capita, 2003: (PPP$) 5,880
HDI/world rank: 0·752/92

KEY HISTORICAL EVENTS

The Fiji Islands were first recorded in detail by Capt. Bligh after the mutiny of the *Bounty* (1789). In the 19th century the demand for sandalwood attracted merchant ships. Deserters and shipwrecked men stayed. Tribal wars were bloody and widespread until Fiji was ceded to Britain on 10 Oct. 1874. Fiji gained independence on 10 Oct. 1970. It remained an independent state within the Commonwealth with a Governor-General appointed by the Queen until 1987. In the general election of 12 April 1987 a left-wing coalition came to power with the support of the Indian population who outnumbered the indigenous Fijians by 50% to 44%. However, it was overthrown in a military coup. A month later, Fiji declared itself a Republic and Fiji's Commonwealth membership lapsed.

In 1990 a new coalition restored civilian rule but made it impossible for Fijian Indians to hold power. A rapprochement with Indian leaders led to an agreement to restore multi-racial government in 1998. Fiji rejoined the Commonwealth in 1997. On 27 July 1998 a new constitution changed the country's name from Fiji to Fiji Islands.

A coup was staged in May 2000 under the leadership of George Speight, a failed businessman. His main aim was to exclude Indians from the government. An interim government, excluding Speight supporters, was appointed on 3 July 2000 to rule for 18 months. On 26 July George Speight and 400 of his supporters were arrested. On 18 Feb. 2002 Speight was sentenced to death although this was subsequently commuted to life imprisonment.

TERRITORY AND POPULATION

The Fiji Islands comprise 332 islands and islets (about one-third are inhabited) lying between 15° and 22° S. lat. and 174° E. and 177° W. long. The largest is Viti Levu, area 10,429 sq. km (4,027 sq. miles); next is Vanua Levu, area 5,556 sq. km (2,145 sq. miles). The island of Rotuma (47 sq. km, 18 sq. miles), about 12° 30′ S. lat., 178° E. long., was added to the colony in 1881. Total area, 18,272 sq. km (7,055 sq. miles). Total population

(1996 census), 775,077 (females, 381,146); ethnic groups: Fijian, 393,575; Indian, 338,818; part-European/European, 14,788; other Pacific islanders, 10,463; Rotuman, 9,727; Chinese, 4,939; other, 2,767. Population density (1996), 42·4 per sq. km. 2005 population estimate: 848,000. In 2003, 51·7% of the population lived in urban areas.

The UN gives a projected population for 2010 of 878,000.

Population estimate of the capital, Suva, in 1999 was 196,000. Other large towns, with 1996 populations, are Lautoka (42,917), Nadi (30,791) and Labasa (24,187).

English is the official language; Fijian and Hindustani are also spoken.

SOCIAL STATISTICS

Births, 1999, 16,916; deaths, 3,603; marriages (1998), 8,058. 1999 birth rate per 1,000 population, 21·0; death rate per 1,000 population, 4·5. Annual population growth rate, 1992–2002, 1·2%. Life expectancy at birth in 2003 was 65·7 years for males and 70·1 years for females. Infant mortality, 2001, 18 per 1,000 live births; fertility rate, 2001, 3·0 births per woman.

CLIMATE

A tropical climate, but oceanic influences prevent undue extremes of heat or humidity. The S. E. Trades blow from May to Nov., during which time nights are cool and rainfall amounts least. Suva, Jan. 80°F (26·7°C), July 73°F (22·8°C). Annual rainfall 117″ (2,974 mm).

CONSTITUTION AND GOVERNMENT

The executive authority of the State is vested in the *President*, who is appointed by the Bose Levu Vakaturaga (Great Council of Chiefs). The *Prime Minister* is appointed by the President. The Prime Minister must establish a multi-party cabinet. The President's term of office is five years.

A new Constitution unanimously passed by Parliament and assented to by H.E. the President came into force on 27 July 1998. The country's name was changed from Fiji to Fiji Islands and the people were to be known as Fiji Islanders instead of Fijians. The new Constitution also does away with an indigenous Prime Minister and has a 71-seat *House of Representatives* (Lower House), with 46 elected on a communal role and 25 from an open electoral roll. Of the 46, 23 will be elected from a roll of voters registered as Fijians, 19 from a roll of voters registered as Indians, one from a roll of voters registered as Rotumans and three from a roll of voters registered who are none of these. The Upper House or *Senate* has 34 members, 24 appointed by the Great Council of Chiefs, nine appointed by the president, and one appointed by the Council of Rotuma.

Parliament was reopened in Oct. 2001, having been suspended following a coup in May 2000. In July 2003 the supreme court declared that, according to the constitution, the government must include members of the opposition. Laisenia Qarase, who replaced Mahendra Chaudhry as prime minister after the 2000 coup, had excluded MPs from the Indian-dominated Labour party following general elections in 2001. In Nov. 2004 the Labour party leadership declined the offered cabinet positions, preferring instead to form an official opposition.

National Anthem

'Meda Dau Doka' ('God Bless Fiji'); words and tune by M. Prescott.

RECENT ELECTIONS

Mahendra Chaudhry, the Fiji Labour Party leader, became the country's first Indian prime minister in 1999, but was ousted in the coup of May 2000 after just over a year in office. In parliamentary elections held between 25 Aug.–2 Sept. 2001 Soqosoqo Duavata ni Lewenivanua (Fiji United Party) won 32 out of 71 seats ahead of the Fiji Labour Party with 27. Other parties won six seats or fewer.

CURRENT ADMINISTRATION

President: Ratu Josefa Iloilo; b. 1920 (appointed as interim president on 18 July 2000; re-appointed as president for a five-year term on 15 March 2001 and again on 8 March 2006).

Vice President: Ratu Joni Madraiwiwi.

In March 2006 the government comprised:

Prime Minister, Minister for National Reconciliation and Unity, Fijian Affairs, Culture and Heritage: Laisenia Qarase (sworn in 10 Sept. 2001, having previously been interim prime minister from 4 July 2000 to 14 March 2001 and from 16 March 2001 until officially taking office). He named a cabinet that did not include any members of the Indian-dominated Fiji Labour party in defiance of the constitution, which states that any party with eight or more seats is entitled to ministerial positions.

Minister of Agriculture, Sugar and Land Resettlement: Ilaitia Tuisese. *Commerce, Business Development and Investment:* Tomasi Vuetilovoni. *Education:* Ro Teimumu Kepa. *Finance and National Planning:* Ratu Jone Kubuabola. *Fisheries and Forests:* Konisi Yabaki. *Foreign Affairs and External Trade:* Kaliopate Tavola. *Health:* Solomone Naivalu. *Home Affairs, Immigration and National Disaster Management:* Josefa Vosanibola. *Information and Media Relations:* Marieta Rigamoto. *Justice and Attorney General:* Qoriniasi Bale. *Labour, Industrial Relations and Productivity:* Kenneth Zinck. *Lands and Mineral Resources:* Samisoni Tikoinasau. *Local Government, Housing, Squatter Settlement and Environment:* Pio Wong. *Multi-Ethnic Affairs:* George Shiu Raj. *Public Enterprises and Public Sector Reform:* Jonetani Galuinadi. *Regional Development:* Ted Young. *Tourism:* Pita Nacuva. *Transport and Civil Aviation:* Ratu Naiqama Lalabalavu. *Women, Social Welfare and Poverty Alleviation:* Asenaca Caucau. *Works and Energy:* Savenaca Draunidalo. *Youth, Employment Opportunities and Sports:* Isireli Leweniqila.

Fiji Islands Government Online: http://www.fiji.gov.fj

CURRENT LEADERS

Ratu Josefa Iloilo

Position
President

Introduction
Ratu Josefa Iloilo became acting president following the nationalist coup of 2000 and was given the job on a permanent basis in March 2001. He has had to contend with a racially-divided, economically and politically unstable environment.

Early Life
Iloilo was born in 1920. He was the Fiji Islands' vice president when in May 2000 indigenous Fijian George Speight and his supporters took hostage the government of ethnic Indian prime minister, Mahendra Chaudhry. Chaudhry's administration was subsequently dismissed by decree of the Great Council of Chiefs. Speight, a bankrupt businessman, pronounced himself prime minister. The affair was the culmination of years of rising tensions between the ethnic Fijian population and the Fiji Islands' financially and politically powerful ethnic Indian minority. The Fiji Islands were suspended from the Commonwealth's councils in June 2000. The following month, with Chaudhry and his supporters having been released, Iloilo, father-in-law of Speight's brother, was chosen by the Council of Chiefs to be interim president. Speight was arrested in July 2000 by the military authorities under Commodore J. V. Bainimarama and

Laisenia Qarase, an ethnic Fijian, was named interim prime minister.

Career in Office
In March 2001 Iloilo formally dismissed Chaudhry as prime minister. He then replaced Qarase, whose interim administration had been declared illegal by the Supreme Court, with Ratu Tevita Momoedonu, a tribal leader, for 24 hours before reappointing Qarase and legitimizing the administration prior to fresh elections. Also in March 2001 the Council of Chiefs confirmed Iloilo as president.

As president, Iloilo is responsible for appointing the prime minister and is head of the armed forces. On taking office he committed himself to re-establishing national unity in the wake of the events of 2000. He has sought to boost the Fiji Islands' two biggest industries, tourism and sugar production, which both went into decline after the coup attempt.

Elections were held in Aug.–Sept. 2001 in which Speight won a seat and Qarase's newly-formed Soqosoqo Duavata ni Lewenivanua party won most seats. In contravention of the constitution, Qarase failed to appoint any ethnic Indians from the Fiji Labour Party to his cabinet, and in Dec. 2001 Speight was suspended from parliament for failure to attend.

Iloilo oversaw the Fiji Islands' re-entry into the Commonwealth in Dec. 2001, although the domestic political environment remained unstable. In Jan. 2002 a constitutional court demanded the inclusion of Labour members in the cabinet and the following month Speight received a death sentence, later commuted by Iloilo to life imprisonment, for treason. In 2004 Iloilo's vice president, Ratu Jope Seniloli, was found guilty of treason for his involvement in the Speight coup. Seniloli had been named president by Speight during the 2000 crisis and was elected vice president by indigenous leaders after Speight's arrest. Iloilo was reappointed president for a further five-year term in March 2006.

Laisenia Qarase

Position
Prime Minister

Introduction
Laisenia Qarase was appointed prime minister of an interim government following the collapse of Mahendra Chaudhry's government in a coup in May 2000. Qarase formed a new party, Soqosoqo Duavata ni Lewenivanua, and won the elections of Aug.–Sept. 2001. An ethnic Fijian, he ruled out a return to the pre-coup situation of government by the Indian minority. His major challenges were to return the Fiji Islands to political stability and revitalize the economy.

Early Life
Qarase was born in 1941 in Mavana on the eastern Lau islands. He was schooled in Suva and graduated in commerce from the University of Auckland in New Zealand. He returned to the Fiji Islands and took a job with the Fijian Affairs Board. He then became deputy secretary of the finance department, permanent secretary for commerce and industry, and secretary of the Public Service Commission. Between 1983 and 1998 he headed the Fiji Development Bank and in 1998 moved into the private sector to take charge of a merchant bank.

In 1999 he was appointed to the Senate, where he gained a reputation for his vociferous criticism of the regime of Mahendra Chaudhry, the Fiji Islands' first ethnic Indian prime minister. In May 2000 George Speight, an indigenous Fijian, stormed parliament with his supporters and took the government hostage. Chaudry's administration was dismissed by decree of the Great Council of Chiefs and Speight, a bankrupt businessman, pronounced himself prime minister. Qarase was named prime minister of an interim government in July 2000 as part of the deal which saw the release of Chaudhry and his colleagues. The affair was the culmination of years of rising tensions between the ethnic Fijian population and the Fiji Islands' financially and politically powerful ethnic Indian minority.

Career in Office

During Qarase's first month in office the hostages were freed and Speight was arrested. The Fiji Islands had been suspended from the Commonwealth's councils the previous month and was subject to sanctions by Australia, New Zealand, France and the USA. Qarase was charged with restoring stability to the political scene. He was to pave the way for new elections, prepare a new constitution and revive the badly-hit economy.

In March 2001 the Supreme Court declared the interim government illegal. President Iloilo, who had come to power after the coup, formally dismissed Chaudhry (who had been effectively excluded from political life since the coup) and replaced Qarase with Ratu Tevita Momoedonu, a tribal leader, for 24 hours. He then reappointed Qarase, thus legitimizing the new administration, despite Chaudhry's protests that his sacking was unconstitutional.

In the build-up to the elections of Aug.–Sept. 2001 Qarase formed a new nationalist party, Soqosoqo Duavata ni Leweniavanua (SDL). He announced that a new constitution would not be of the multi-racial nature of the 1997 document which allowed for the appointment of Chaudhry. Instead Qarase stated that 'there must be better guarantees…for indigenous Fijians to be in control of their political destiny'. The SDL won 32 out of 71 seats, against 27 for Chaudhry's Fiji Labour Party.

Qarase was constitutionally required to invite Chaudhry into the new government but actively encouraged his opponent not to accept any posts, claiming a joint government would be unworkable. Chaudhry announced plans to establish an opposition group within the government. In his first 18-man cabinet Qarase failed to appoint any Labour members but did include two allies of Speight, whose Matanitu Vanua had won six seats. Chaudhry claimed his party was entitled to six cabinet posts, a view upheld by an appeal court in Feb. 2002 and by the Supreme Court in July 2003.

Qarase oversaw the Fiji Islands' re-entry into the Commonwealth in Dec. 2001, although the domestic political environment remained unstable. In Jan. 2002 a gang was arrested for plotting Qarase's kidnapping in order to secure the freedom of Speight who in Feb. 2002 received a death sentence, later commuted to life imprisonment, for treason. In June 2002 Qarase came under investigation for vote-buying at the previous year's elections. The political fall-out from the Speight-led coup was again evident in 2004 when the vice president, Ratu Jope Seniloli, was found guilty of treason for his involvement.

Meanwhile, negotiation had not resolved the problem of the number of cabinet posts to which the Labour Party was entitled. In 2004 Chaudry declined any seats and took the position of leader of the opposition. In 2005 Qarase's government introduced the Promotion of Reconciliation, Tolerance and Unity Bill. This generated considerable opposition from many sections of society towards the proposed amnesty for those who were involved in the 2000 coup, and has led to friction between the government and the military.

In Nov. 2002 Qarase's government announced plans for the comprehensive modernization of the nation's sugar industry, upon which a quarter of the population are economically reliant.

DEFENCE

In 2003 defence expenditure totalled US$33m. (US$40 per capita), representing 1·5% of GDP.

Army

Personnel in 2002 numbered 3,200 including 300 recalled reserves. More than 600 of these are actively involved in UN and peacekeeping operations. There is an additional reserve force of 6,000.

Navy

A small naval division of the armed forces numbered 300 in 2002.

INTERNATIONAL RELATIONS

The Fiji Islands are a member of the UN, WTO, the Commonwealth, the Asian Development Bank, the Colombo Plan, the Pacific Community, the Pacific Islands Forum and is an ACP member state of the ACP-EU relationship.

ECONOMY

Agriculture accounted for 16·2% of GDP in 2002, industry 27·0% and services 56·8%.

Currency

The unit of currency is the *Fiji dollar* (FJD) of 100 *cents*. In June 2002 total money supply was $F661m., foreign exchange reserves were US$332m. and gold reserves 1,000 troy oz. Inflation in 2004 was 2·8%. The Fiji dollar was devalued by 20% in Jan. 1998.

Budget

Revenues in 2003 totalled $F1,079·1m. and expenditures $F1,083·3m.

VAT of 10% was introduced in 1992 (increased to 12·5% in 2003).

Performance

There was a recession in 2000, with the economy shrinking by 3·2%, but 2001 saw a recovery, with growth of 4·3%. In 2004 there was real GDP growth of 4·1% (4·8% in 2003 and 4·4% in 2002). Total GDP in 2004 was US$2·6bn.

Banking and Finance

The central bank and bank of issue is the Reserve Bank of Fiji (*Governor*, Savenaca Narube). Total assets were $F493·07m. in June 1996. The National Bank is a government-owned commercial bank. The Fiji Development Bank has assets totalling $F356·01m. There are six foreign banks in the country, one commercial bank, one development bank and two merchant banks. Total assets of commercial banks were $F1,797·92m. in June 1996.

The South Pacific Stock Exchange is based in Suva.

ENERGY AND NATURAL RESOURCES

Environment

Carbon dioxide emissions from the consumption and flaring of fossil fuels in 2002 were the equivalent of 1·1 tonnes per capita.

Electricity

The Fiji Electricity Authority is responsible for the generation, transmission and distribution of electricity in the country. It operates six separate supply systems. The largest energy project is one of hydro-electricity generating 95% of the main island's electric needs. Two rural hydro schemes have been completed, one generating 100 kW and the other 800 kW. In 1994 there were seven thermal and one hydro-electric power stations.

Installed capacity in 2000 was 0·2m. kW. Production in 2000 was 545m. kWh with consumption per capita an estimated 670 kWh.

Minerals

The main gold-mine accounts for almost one tenth of the country's exports and employs about 1,700 people. Gold is one of the Fiji Islands' main exports. Gold production, 2001, was 3,858 kg.

Agriculture

With a total land area of 1·8m. ha., only 16% is suitable for farming. In 2001 there were 200,000 ha. of arable land and

85,000 ha. of permanent crops. Arable land: 24% sugarcane, 23% coconut and 53% other crops. Production figures for 2000 (in 1,000 tonnes): sugarcane, 2,250; coconut, 215; cassava, 30; taro, 27; rice, 18; copra, 14; sweet potatoes, 8. Ginger is becoming increasingly important.

Livestock (2000): cattle, 350,000; horses, 44,000; goats, 235,000; pigs, 115,000; chickens, 4m. Products, 2000 (in 1,000 tonnes): beef and veal, 10; pork, bacon and ham, 4; poultry meat, 8; eggs, 4. Total production of milk was 58,000 tonnes in 2000.

Forestry

Forests covered 815,000 ha—44·6% of the land area—in 2000. Forestry contributed around 1·2% of GDP in 1998. It is the fifth most important export commodity, valued at $F34m. in 1996. Hardwood plantations covered over 48,000 ha. in 1996. In 2000 Fiji Pine Ltd had nearly 42,000 ha. of softwood plantations. Roundwood production in 2001 was 510,000 cu. metres.

Fisheries

The catch in 2001 was 42,972 tonnes, of which 37,051 tonnes came from sea fishing. In 1997 fisheries accounted for 2% of GDP. Mainstay of export fisheries are the skipjack and albacore tuna for canning. There was an increase in export of fresh and chilled tuna from 53 tonnes in 1989 to over 3,000 tonnes in 1995.

INDUSTRY

The Tax Free Factory scheme was instituted in 1987 as an encouragement to industry. In 1991 it was replaced by the Trade Free Zones (TFZ), of which there were 131 in 2001. However, the scheme is being gradually phased out. The main industries are tourism, garments (a major beneficiary of the TFZ scheme) and sugar, which in 2001 accounted for 19·2%, 12·3% and 8·5% of GDP respectively. In 1987 garments accounted for less than 1% of GDP.

Output (in tonnes): sugar (2002), 334,200; cement (2003), 100,000; flour (2003), 63,559; animal feed (2003), 41,095; coconut oil (2003), 7,523; soap, washing powder and detergents (2003), 3,192; beer (2003), 15·0m. litres; soft drinks (2003), 79·4m. litres; cigarettes (2001), 389m. (units). Garment production was valued at $F129·1m. in 2003.

Labour

Approximately 301,500 persons were in paid employment in 1996. In 2002 there were 23,000 people out of work and seeking employment—the number of unemployed people doubled between 1996 and 2002.

INTERNATIONAL TRADE

The Tax Free Factory/Tax Free Zone Scheme was introduced in 1987 to stimulate investment and encourage export-oriented businesses.

Foreign debt was US$210m. in 2002.

Imports and Exports

Imports totalled $F2·2m. in 2003; exports $F1·3m.

Chief exports are sugar, gold, prepared and preserved fish, timber, ginger and molasses. Principal import suppliers, 2001: Australia, 39·8%; New Zealand, 18·7%; Singapore, 5·5%. Main export markets, 2001: Australia, 25·6%; USA, 22·5%; UK, 15·1%.

COMMUNICATIONS

Roads

Total road length in 2002 was an estimated 3,440 km, of which almost half were surfaced. There were a total of 72,100 passenger cars and 44,500 lorries and vans in 2002. In 1997, 73 fatalities were caused by road accidents.

Rail

Fiji Sugar Cane Corporation runs 600 mm gauge railways at four of its mills on Viti Levu and Vanua Levu, totalling 595 km.

Civil Aviation

There are international airports at Nadi and Suva. The national carrier is Air Pacific (51% government-owned). In 2003 it provided services to Australia, Japan, New Zealand, USA and a number of Pacific island nations. Air Fiji only operates on domestic routes. In 2001 Nadi handled 911,000 passengers (808,000 on international flights).

Shipping

The three ports of entry are Suva, Lautoka and Levuka. Ocean-going shipping totalled 27,000 GRT in 2000, including oil tankers 1,000 GRT. Inter-island shipping fleet is a mix of private and government vessels. A total of 620 foreign vessels called into the Suva port in 1995, 318 and 109 respectively in Lautoka and Levuka. Altogether 7,189 ships including local ships, yachts and foreign vessels called into the three major ports.

Telecommunications

There were 187,400 telephone subscribers in 2002 (224·7 for every 1,000 population). In 2002, 40% of subscribers were business customers and 60% residential. There were over 500 cardphones located around the country in 1998 and approximately 80 in rural areas. In 2002 there were 89,900 mobile phone subscribers, 40,000 PCs in use (48·0 per 1,000 persons) and 50,000 Internet users. There were 2,000 fax machines in 2002.

Postal Services

There were 142 post offices in 2003, or one for every 5,910 persons. A total of 37m. pieces of mail were processed in 2003.

SOCIAL INSTITUTIONS

Justice

An independent Judiciary is guaranteed under the constitution. A High Court has unlimited original jurisdiction to hear and determine any civil or criminal proceedings under any law. The High Court also has jurisdiction to hear and determine constitutional and electoral questions including the membership of the House of Representatives. The Chief Justice of the Fiji Islands is appointed by the President after consultation with the Prime Minister.

The Fiji Islands' Court of Appeal, of which the Chief Justice is *ex officio* President, is formed by three specially appointed Justices of Appeal, appointed by the President after consultation with the Judicial and Legal Services Commission. Generally, any person convicted of an offence has a right of appeal from the High Court of Appeal. The final appellant court is the Supreme Court. Most matters coming before the Superior Courts originate in Magistrates' Courts.

The population in penal institutions in 2002 was 897 (108 per 100,000 of national population).

Police

In 1997 the Royal Fiji Police Force had a total strength of 1,915.

Education

Adult literacy rate was 93·2% in 2001 (95·2% among males and 91·2% among females). Total enrolment in 2003: primary schools, 142,781 (with 5,107 teachers); secondary schools, 68,178 (with 3,935 teachers). Enrolment in 1996: teacher training, 903 (with 92 teachers); vocational/technical education, 1,876. The number of registered schools totalled 1,261. Of these there were 391 pre-schools, 16 special schools, 698 primary schools, 151 secondary schools and 5 post secondary schools.

The University of the South Pacific, which is located in Suva, serves 12 countries in the South Pacific region. The Fiji Islands also has a college of agriculture, school of medicine and nursing, an institute of technology, a primary school teacher training college and an advanced college of education.

In 2000–01 total expenditure on education came to 5·1% of GNP and 17·0% of total government spending.

Health

There were 25 hospitals with 1,805 beds in 1997; and 271 doctors, 32 dentists and 1,576 nurses in 1999.

Through its national health service system, the government continues to provide the bulk of health services both in the curative and public health programmes. In 1998, 41% of adults in the Fiji Islands aged 15 and over smoked—the second highest percentage of any country, after Russia.

RELIGION

In 2001 the population consisted of 53% Christians, 38% Hindus, 8% Muslims and 1% others.

CULTURE

Broadcasting

There are two major radio stations, Island Network Corporation Ltd and Communications Fiji Ltd. Fiji Television Company is a commercial network that has one free to air and two pay channels (colour by NTSC). In 2001 there were 95,100 TV receivers and in 1997 there were 500,000 radio receivers.

Press

There are two daily newspapers, *Fiji Times and Herald* and *The Daily Post*. Vernacular newspapers are also published by these two, including *Nai Lalakai, Nai Volasiga* and *Shanti Dut*. Other locally produced periodicals are the *Review, Island's Business, Fiji First, Pacific Islands Monthly* and *Marama Vou*.

Tourism

Visitor arrivals in 2003 totalled 431,000; earnings from tourism in 2000 amounted to US$171m.

DIPLOMATIC REPRESENTATIVES

Of the Fiji Islands in the United Kingdom (34 Hyde Park Gate, London, SW7 5DN)
High Commissioner: Emitai Lausiki Boladuadua.

Of the United Kingdom in the Fiji Islands (Victoria House, 47 Gladstone Rd, Suva)
High Commissioner: Charles Mochan.

Of the Fiji Islands in the USA (2233 Wisconsin Ave., NW, Washington, D.C., 20007)
Ambassador: Jesoni Vitusagavulu.

Of the USA in the Fiji Islands (31 Loftus St., Suva)
Ambassador: Larry M. Dinger.

Of the Fiji Islands to the United Nations
Ambassador: Isikia Savua.

Of the Fiji Islands to the European Union
Ambassador: Isikeli Uluinairai Mataitoga.

FURTHER READING

Bureau of Statistics. *Annual Report; Current Economic Statistics.* Quarterly
Reserve Bank of Fiji. *Quarterly Review*
Gorman, G. E. and Mills, J. J., *Fiji.* [Bibliography] ABC-Clio, Oxford and Santa Barbara (CA), 1994
Lal, B. J., *Broken Waves: a History of the Fiji Islands in the Twentieth Century.* Univ. of Hawaii Press, 1992
Sutherland, W., *Beyond the Politics of Race: an Alternative History of Fiji to 1992.* Australian National Univ. Press, 1992

National Statistical Office: Bureau of Statistics, POB 2221, Government Buildings, Suva.

FINLAND

© Research Machines plc 2006

Suomen Tasavalta—Republiken Finland

Capital: Helsinki
Population projection, 2010: 5·31m.
GDP per capita, 2003: (PPP$) 27,619
HDI/world rank: 0·941/13

KEY HISTORICAL EVENTS

Finland's first inhabitants moved northwards at the end of the Ice Age. Further waves of settlement came in 4000 BC and 1000 BC and although the population was spread out, distinct social groups began to develop. During the Viking era Finland's location on the trade route between Russia and Sweden brought prosperity and conflict in equal measure, with attacks frequently made on Finnish trading posts by the Swedes and the Danes.

In the 12th century economic and religious rivalry between Sweden and Russia was centred on Finland. Sweden, supported by the Papacy in Rome, began a succession of crusades to draw Finland into its sphere of control. The defeat of Birger Jarl in 1240 marked the end of the Swedish incursions into Finland but efforts at strengthening the Swedish presence in areas it already

held were intensified. By 1323 Russia was forced to recognize a boundary marking off those parts of Finland which were under Swedish control including all of western and southern Finland. Finland remained a duchy of Sweden until 1581 when it was made a grand duchy.

In the 18th century Russian forces conquered the southeast territory. The rest of the country was ceded to Russia by the treaty of Hamina in 1809 when Finland became an autonomous grand duchy, retaining its laws and institutions but owing allegiance to the tsar of Russia.

Throughout the 19th century Finland remained in Russia's shadow. Under Alexander II Finland built on her status as a grand duchy, so that by the 1880s she had control over her own army. This proved too much for the Russian military, who feared that moves towards Finnish separatism would make more difficult their task of defending the long western border. With the appointment of Gen. Bobrikov as governor general in 1898 a start was made on bringing Finland back into the imperial fold. The army was put under Russian command, the Russian language was made compulsory for the civil service and for schools and decision-making reverted to the tsar's appointees.

Resistance first took the form of non-cooperation but as the Russian revolutionary movement gathered pace, their allies in Finland became bolder. In June 1904 Bobrikov was assassinated and in 1916 the Marxists won an absolute majority in parliamentary elections. It was a short-lived victory but the far left held its popular appeal.

Civil War
Following the revolution, on 6 Dec. 1917 Finland declared independence. This was recognized by the Russian Bolsheviks on 31 Dec. By this time, however, a breach between the left and right parties in Finland had become irreconcilable. In Jan. 1918 the Whites (the government forces) took the western, Russian-controlled province of Ostrobothnia while the Reds (the left-wing forces, supported by the Bolsheviks) seized power in the south. At the end of Jan. the Reds staged a coup and the Whites were forced to abandon Helsinki, relocating to Vaasa. Civil war ensued which the government forces won, led by Gen. Gustaf Mannerheim and aided by German troops.

Parliament approved a new constitution in which a German prince, Friedrich Karl, would become regent. However, such plans were halted with the collapse of Germany at the end of the First World War. In the summer of 1919 Finland became a republic with K. J. Ståhlberg elected as its first president.

Throughout the 1920s and early 1930s the class antagonism inherited from the civil war remained the dominant political issue. As a conciliatory measure the Social Democrats were brought into government and the party formed a minority government in 1926–27. In the early 1930s fascism entered domestic politics with the emergence of the Lapua Movement. After an unsuccessful coup attempt in 1932 the movement was banned. In common with its Scandinavian neighbours, Finland was hit by the Great Depression but cushioned by the dominant role of agriculture in the Finnish economy, industrialization and urbanization both continued throughout the inter-war years.

Winter War
As Europe was anticipating German aggression, the Finns were taking up arms to resist Moscow's territorial demands. Outnumbered and outmatched in arms and equipment, their hopes were pinned on foreign involvement. When this failed to materialize, there was no option but to give the Russians all

they wanted, including the Karelian Isthmus. The 1940 treaty, which ended the Winter War, required the resettlement of 12% of the Finnish population. Fearing worse to come from the Soviet Union, Helsinki opened up contacts with the Germans, allowing transit for military traffic in return for food and armaments.

There followed the German invasion of Russia, a campaign which Mannerheim, in justifying the active participation of his army, described as a 'holy war' to restore Finnish borders. Having achieved this objective with remarkable ease, the Finns wanted out, a desire which became all the more determined as the German advance ground to a halt at Stalingrad. But there was no basis for a settlement and the Finns could only wait for the inevitable Russian counter-attack. When it came, retreating Germans took revenge by devastating everything in their path.

Having fought first against Russia then against Germany, the country emerged from the Second World War defeated, demoralized and in political disarray. The peace treaty with the Soviet Union was still to be agreed, but the terms of the 1944 armistice—the surrender of one-twelfth of Finnish territory and reparations to be paid in goods valued at US$300m. at 1938 prices—suggested that Russia had no inhibitions about leaning heavily on her weaker neighbour.

If the public looked anywhere for a lead it was to the presidency, and to Field-Marshal Mannerheim. Revered as a national hero by the right, Mannerheim extended his reputation by bringing his country through the Winter War and by his initial success in the renewed hostilities with Russia in 1941. Though he was not much loved by the Soviets they acknowledged Mannerheim's unique personal authority. Carl Enckell, a close and trusted associate of Mannerheim for many years, took charge of foreign affairs while Juho Paasikivi was appointed premier. The 1945 election confirmed Paasikivi and Enckell in their jobs and a cabinet was formed giving roughly equal representation to the social democrats, communists and the farmers' party. When Mannerheim, who had turned 78 and was ailing fast, was persuaded to stand down in mid-term of his presidency, Paasikivi was the obvious successor.

The peace treaty with Russia was signed in Feb. 1947. Though severe, the terms confirmed what had already been provisionally agreed by the 1944 armistice. Finland lost 12% of her border territory to the Soviet Union, including the country's second largest city, Viipuri, and the port and province of Petsamo on the Arctic coast. With a large part of the province of Karelia taken over by the Russians the frontier was moved back from a distance of only 31 km from Leningrad to a new line 180 km from the former Russian capital. 400,000 people had to be resettled. The Åland Islands were to remain demilitarized and limitations were imposed on the size of the Finnish armed forces and its weaponry.

Pacifying Russia

The Russians then raised the stakes with an 'invitation' to negotiate a mutual assistance agreement. It seemed as if nothing less than an administration directly answerable to Moscow would satisfy the Russians. Paasikivi opened negotiations by arguing that the interests of the Soviet Union on her northwestern border (the only part of Finland that really mattered to the Russian military) could best be served by a sovereign Finland whose sympathetic relations with her eastern neighbour precluded her territory being used as a platform for attack. Skilfully, Paasikivi shifted the emphasis away from Russian ambitions for making Finland an ally towards the far more attractive prospect of the two countries' entering into a joint security arrangement which would allow Finland to stand aside from big power politics. In the end it was a matter of interpretation. Finland promised to defend herself against an attack from Germany or an allied state, to confer with Russia in case of war or threat of war and, if necessary, to accept Russian aid. Great play was made of Finland's ambition 'to remain outside the conflicting interests of the great powers'.

The popular view in Europe was that Finland had tied herself to the Soviet Union and was as much under the control of Moscow as any of the communist satellites. Paasikivi did his best to counteract this impression and reacted decisively if there was any hint of a threat to his own authority. When in the spring of 1948 there were rumours that the communists were planning to seize power, he dismissed the powerful minister of internal affairs, Yrjö Leino. But the president was hyper-sensitive to Moscow's needs for reassurances of Finnish good faith. The press was told to tone down criticism of the Soviet Union. In this uncertain political climate the economy entered its first painful stage of recovery. Fortunately, most of the nation's productive capacity had survived the war intact, and the export demand for wood products was strong. But paying off reparations in goods the Russians wanted meant a big transfer of resources to the engineering industry. All this had to be achieved without a share in Marshall Aid, though US loans totalling $150m. were channelled in other ways. Skilled labour and consumer goods were both in short supply, with the inevitable consequence that wages and prices climbed steeply, each one feeding off the other to send inflation soaring. In 1948 prices were eight times their pre-war level.

The communists were well placed to take advantage of the government's troubles. In the summer of 1949 they disrupted industry with a series of strikes, splitting the trade union movement and raising fears of an imminent coup. Paasikivi promptly replaced the social democrat government with one formed by the agrarians under the leadership of Urho Kekkonen. Like Paasikivi, Kekkonen worked hard to establish good personal relations with the USSR. But he was not content to be merely an echo of his master's voice. In 1952 he put up a plan for 'a neutral alliance between the Scandinavian countries', which 'would remove even the theoretical threat of an attack ... via Finland's territory'. In reality, a Scandinavian alliance, neutral or otherwise, was impracticable since Denmark and Norway had only recently joined NATO. But the gain to Kekkonen was approval from the Soviet Union. Moscow was delighted by an unsolicited rejection of the Atlantic pact by a north European state and congratulated Finland on pursuing the course of 'strict neutrality'. This was one of the strongest indications so far that Russia was prepared to recognize Finland as neutral, and though Soviet commentators generally referred to that country as 'striving for neutrality' rather than having achieved the objective, Kekkonen's initiative put relations between the two nations on an entirely new footing.

Defending Neutrality

In 1955, two years after the death of Stalin had brought the first signs of an easing in the cold war, Finland negotiated the return of the Porkkala base near Helsinki, which had been leased to the Soviet Union for 50 years. This meant the departure of the last Soviet troops on Finnish territory—the most powerful boost to national morale of the early post-war years. That same year Finland joined the United Nations but stayed out of the latest formation of Soviet defence, the Warsaw Pact. In 1956 Kekkonen succeeded Paasikivi as president. A succession of weak governments consolidated presidential power and confirmed Kekkonen as the only leader capable of handling the Russians. Enjoying his enhanced prestige he was soon back on course with his policy of trying to establish Finland as an independent neutral.

His first move was to assert his country's freedom of action, by suggesting that Finland might come to a deal with the European Community. In response, the Soviet Union activated article 2 of the 1948 Treaty by demanding consultation on measures to ensure the defence of their frontiers. It was the most serious challenge yet to Finnish neutrality. It had been said that article

2 could be acted upon only when *both* parties agreed that a threat existed; it came as a shock to realize that a unilateral declaration of interest by the stronger partner was sufficient to start the process of military consultation. If the Soviet claim went uncontested Finnish independence would be seen as a sham.

Western observers expected the worst; nothing less than military bases on Finnish soil would satisfy Moscow. But Kekkonen remained placid. His compromise strategy called for a postponement of military talks in favour of discussions aimed at reassuring the Kremlin that Finland would remain true to her foreign policy. This was accompanied by a warning that if military consultations went ahead there would be a war scare in Scandinavia, possibly leading to counter-measures by the West. When the Soviet Union backed down Kekkonen was feted as the country's saviour. He was elected for a second six-year term by an overwhelming majority on the first round of voting.

In 1981 the ailing Kekkonen was replaced by Mauno Koivisto. At first he adopted the foreign policy of his predecessor but with the collapse of the Soviet Union at the end of the 1980s he was able to move Finland towards closer ties with Western Europe. Koivisto played a major role in dismantling the 1948 Treaty and in the early 1990s fostered close relations with the EU. A referendum held in 1995 paved the way for Finland to join the EU.

TERRITORY AND POPULATION

Finland, a country of lakes and forests, is bounded in the northwest and north by Norway, east by Russia, south by the Baltic Sea and west by the Gulf of Bothnia and Sweden. The most recent ten-yearly census took place on 31 Dec. 2000. The area and the population of Finland on 31 Dec. 2003 (Swedish names in brackets):

Provinces (in italics) and Regions	Area (sq. km)[1]	Population	Population per sq. km
Etelä-Suomi (Södra Finland)	*30,173*	*2,116,914*	*70·2*
Uusimaa (Nyland)	6,366	1,338,180	210·2
Itä-Uusimaa (Östra Nyland)	2,747	91,689	33·4
Kanta-Häme (Egentliga Tavastland)	5,204	166,648	32·0
Päijät-Häme (Päijänne-Tavastland)	5,133	198,434	38·7
Kymenlaakso (Kymmenedalen)	5,106	185,662	36·4
Etelä-Karjala (Södra Karelen)	5,618	133,301	24·3
Itä-Suomi (Östra Finland)	*48,727*	*582,781*	*12·0*
Etelä-Savo (Södra Savolax)	14,137	162,296	11·5
Pohjois-Savo (Norra Savolax)	16,808	251,356	15·0
Pohjois-Karjala (Norra Karelen)	17,782	169,129	9·5
Länsi-Suomi (Västra Finland)	*74,185*	*1,848,269*	*24·9*
Varsinais-Suomi (Egentliga Finland)	10,624	452,444	42·6
Satakunta	8,289	234,777	28·3
Pirkanmaa (Birkaland)	12,272	457,317	37·3
Keski-Suomi (Mellersta Finland)	16,582	266,082	16·0
Etelä-Pohjanmaa (Södra Österbotten)	13,458	193,954	14·4
Pohjanmaa (Österbotten)	7,675	173,111	22·6
Keski-Pohjanmaa (Mellersta Österbotten)	5,286	70,584	13·4
Lappi (Lappland)	*93,004*	*186,917*	*2·0*
Oulu (Uleåborg)	*56,857*	*458,504*	*8·1*
Pohjois-Pohjanmaa (Norra Österbotten)	35,290	371,931	10·5
Kainuu (Kajanaland)	21,567	86,573	4·0
Ahvenanmaa (Åland)	*1,527*	*26,347*	*17·3*
Total	304,473	5,219,732	17·1

[1]Excluding inland water area which totals 33,672 sq. km.

The semi-autonomous province of the **Åland Islands** (Ahvenanmaa) occupies a special position as a demilitarized area and is 93% Swedish-speaking. **Åland** elects a 30-member parliament (*Lagting*), which in turn elects the provincial government (*Landskapsstyrelse*). It has a population of 26,000. The capital is Mariehamn (Maarianhamina).

The growth of Finland's population, which was 421,500 in 1750, has been:

End of year	Urban[1]	Semi-urban[2]	Rural	Total	Percentage urban
1800	46,600	—	786,100	832,700	5·6
1900	333,300	—	2,322,600	2,655,900	12·5
1950	1,302,400	—	2,727,400	4,029,800	32·3
1970	2,340,300	—	2,258,000	4,598,300	50·9
1980	2,865,100	—	1,922,700	4,787,800	59·8
1990	2,846,220	803,224	1,349,034	4,998,500	56·9
2000	3,167,668	898,860	1,114,587	5,181,115	61·1
2001	3,190,897	899,120	1,104,884	5,194,901	61·4
2002	3,225,913	882,617	1,097,765	5,206,295	62·0
2003	3,242,443	884,308	1,092,981	5,219,732	62·1

The classification urban/rural has been revised as follows: [1]Urban—at least 90% of the population lives in urban settlements, or in which the population of the largest settlement is at least 15,000. [2]Semi-urban—at least 60% but less than 90% live in urban settlements, or the population of the largest settlement is more than 4,000 but less than 15,000.

The population on 31 Dec. 2003 by language spoken: Finnish, 4,803,343; Swedish, 289,868; Lappish, 1,704; other languages, 124,817.

The projected population for 2010 is 5·31m.

The principal towns with resident population, 31 Dec. 2003, are (Swedish names in brackets):

Helsinki (Helsingfors)—capital	559,330	Rauma (Raumo)	36,869
Espoo (Esbo)	224,231	Lohja (Lojo)	36,004
Tampere (Tammerfors)	200,966	Kokkola (Karleby)	35,756
Vantaa (Vanda)	184,039	Kajaani	35,713
Turku (Åbo)	175,059	Rovaniemi	35,081
Oulu (Uleåborg)	125,928	Tuusula	33,952
Lahti	98,253	Seinäjoki	31,696
Kuopio	88,250	Kouvola	31,339
Jyväskylä	82,409	Kerava (Kervo)	31,170
Pori (Björneborg)	76,189	Imatra	29,969
Lappeenranta (Villmanstrand)	58,897	Nokia	28,090
Vaasa (Vasa)	56,953	Savonlinna (Nyslott)	27,536
Kotka	54,618	Riihimäki	26,654
Joensuu	52,659	Salo	24,794
Hämeenlinna (Tavastehus)	46,909	Raisio (Reso)	23,430
Mikkeli (St Michel)	46,511	Kemi	23,056
Porvoo (Borgå)	46,217	Varkaus	22,761
Hyvinkää (Hyvinge)	43,169	Iisalmi	22,647
Järvenpää	37,114	Tornio (Torneå)	22,198

In 2003, 61·0% of the population lived in urban areas. Nearly one-fifth of the total population lives in the Helsinki metropolitan region.

Finnish and Swedish are the official languages. Sami is spoken in Lapland.

SOCIAL STATISTICS

Statistics in calendar years:

	Living births	Of which outside marriage	Still-born	Marriages	Deaths (exclusive of still-born)	Emigration
1996	60,723	21,484	231	24,464	49,167	10,587
1997	59,329	21,659	221	23,444	49,108	9,854
1998	57,108	21,244	211	24,023	49,262	10,817
1999	57,574	22,273	177	24,271	49,345	11,966
2000	56,742	22,247	231	26,150	49,339	14,311
2001	56,189	22,222	185	24,830	48,550	13,153
2002	55,555	22,156	176	26,969	49,418	12,891
2003	56,630	22,649	178	25,815	48,996	12,083

In 2003 the rate per 1,000 population was: births, 11; deaths, 9; marriages, 5; infant deaths (per 1,000 live births), 3·1. Annual population growth rate, 1994–2003, 0·3%. In 2003 the suicide rate per 100,000 population was 32·0 among men and 9·8 among women, giving Finland one of the highest suicide rates in Europe. Life expectancy at birth, 2003, 75·1 years for males and 81·7 years for females. In 2003 the most popular age range for marrying was 25–29 for both males and females. Fertility rate, 2003, 1·7 births per woman. In 2003 Finland received 3,221 asylum applications, equivalent to 0·6 per 1,000 inhabitants.

A UNICEF report published in 2005 showed that 2·8% of children in Finland live in poverty (in households with income below 50% of the national median), the second lowest percentage of any country behind Denmark.

CLIMATE

A quarter of Finland lies north of the Arctic Circle. The climate is severe in winter, which lasts about six months, but mean temperatures in the south and southwest are less harsh, 21°F (–6°C). In the north, mean temperatures may fall to 8·5°F (–13°C). Snow covers the ground for three months in the south and for over six months in the far north. Summers are short but quite warm, with occasional very hot days. Precipitation is light throughout the country, with one third falling as snow, the remainder mainly as rain in summer and autumn. Helsinki (Helsingfors), Jan. 30·2°F (–1·0°C), July 68·4°F (20·2°C). Annual rainfall 27·9″ (708·7 mm).

CONSTITUTION AND GOVERNMENT

Finland is a republic governed by the constitution of 1 March 2000 (which replaced the previous constitution dating from 1919). Although the president used to choose who formed the government, under the new constitution it is the responsibility of parliament to select the prime minister. The government is in charge of domestic and EU affairs with the president responsible for foreign policy 'in co-operation with the government'.

Parliament consists of one chamber (*Eduskunta*) of 200 members chosen by direct and proportional election by all citizens of 18 or over. The country is divided into 15 electoral districts, with a representation proportional to their population. Every citizen over the age of 18 is eligible for parliament, which is elected for four years, but can be dissolved sooner by the president.

The *president* is elected for six years by direct popular vote. In the event of no candidate winning an absolute majority, a second round is held between the two most successful candidates.

National Anthem

'Maamme'/'Vårt land' ('Our land'); words by J. L. Runeberg, tune by F. Pacius (same as Estonia).

GOVERNMENT CHRONOLOGY

(KESK = Centre Party; KOK = National Rally Party; ML = Agrarian League; SDP = Social Democratic Party; SFP = Swedish People's Party; SKDL = Finnish People's Democratic League; VL = Liberal League; n/p = non-partisan)

Presidents of the Republic

1944–46	military	Carl Gustaf Emil Mannerheim
1946–56	KOK	Juho Kusti Paasikivi
1956–82	ML/KESK	Urho Kaleva Kekkonen
1982–94	SDP	Mauno Henrik Koivisto
1994–2000	SDP	Martti Oiva Kalevi Ahtisaari
2000–	SDP	Tarja Kaarina Halonen

Prime Ministers

1944–46	KOK	Juho Kusti Paasikivi
1946–48	SKDL	Mauno Pekkala
1948–50	SDP	Karl-August Fagerholm
1950–53	ML	Urho Kaleva Kekkonen
1953–54	VL	Sakari Severi Tuomioja
1954	SFP	Ralf Johan Gustaf Törngren
1954–56	ML	Urho Kaleva Kekkonen
1956–57	SDP	Karl-August Fagerholm
1957	ML	Väinö Johannes Sukselainen
1957–58	n/p	Berndt Rainer von Fieandt
1958	n/p	Reino Iisakki Kuuskoski
1958–59	SDP	Karl-August Fagerholm
1959–61	ML	Väinö Johannes Sukselainen
1961–62	ML	Martti Juhani Miettunen
1962–63	ML	Ahti Kalle Samuli Karjalainen
1963–64	n/p	Reino Ragnar Lehto
1964–66	ML/KESK	Johannes Virolainen
1966–68	SDP	Kustaa Rafael Paasio
1968–1970	SDP	Mauno Henrik Koivisto
1970	n/p	Teuvo Ensio Aura
1970–71	KESK	Ahti Kalle Samuli Karjalainen
1971–72	n/p	Teuvo Ensio Aura
1972	SDP	Kustaa Rafael Paasio
1972–75	SDP	Taisto Kalevi Sorsa
1975	n/p	Keijo Antero Liinamaa
1975–77	KESK	Martti Juhani Miettunen
1977–79	SDP	Taisto Kalevi Sorsa
1979–81	SDP	Mauno Henrik Koivisto
1982–87	SDP	Taisto Kalevi Sorsa
1987–91	KOK	Harri Hermanni Holkeri
1991–95	KESK	Esko Tapani Aho
1995–2003	SDP	Paavo Tapio Lipponen
2003	KESK	Anneli Tuulikki Jäätteenmäki
2003–	KESK	Matti Taneli Vanhanen

RECENT ELECTIONS

Presidential elections were held on 15 Jan. 2006 with a second round on 29 Jan. In the first round incumbent president and Social Democratic Party candidate Tarja Halonen came first with 46·3% of the vote, followed by Sauli Niinistö (National Rally Party) with 24·1%, Prime Minister Matti Vanhanen (Centre Party) 18·6% and Heidi Hautala (Green League) 3·5%. There were five other candidates. In the run-off Halonen won with 51·8% against 48·2% for Niinistö. Turnout was 70·8% in the first round and 74·0% in the run-off.

At the elections for the 200-member parliament on 16 March 2003, turnout was 69·6%. The Centre Party (KESK) won 55 seats with 24·7% of votes cast (48 seats in 1999), the ruling Social Democratic Party (SDP) 53 with 24·5% (51 seats in 1999), the National Rally Party (KOK) 40 with 18·5%, the Left Wing League 19 with 9·9% (19), the Green League 14 with 8·0%, the Christian Democrats 7 with 5·3% and the Swedish People's Party (SFP) 8 with 4·6%. Turnout was 69·6%. Following the March 2003 election 37·5% of the seats in parliament were held by women.

European Parliament
Finland has 14 (16 in 1999) representatives. At the June 2004 elections turnout was 41·1% (30·1% in 1999). The KOK won 4 seats with 23·7% of votes cast (political affiliation in European Parliament: European People's Party–European Democrats); Centre Party, 4 with 23·3% (Alliance of Liberals and Democrats for Europe); the SDP, 3 with 21·1% (Party of European Socialists); Green League, 1 with 10·4% (Greens/European Free Alliance); Left Wing League, 1 with 9·1% (European Unitary Left/Nordic Green Left); the SFP, 1 with 5·7% (Alliance of Liberals and Democrats for Europe).

CURRENT ADMINISTRATION

President: Tarja Halonen; b. 1943 (Social Democrat; sworn in 1 March 2000 and re-elected Jan. 2006).

The Council of State (Cabinet) is composed of a coalition of the Centre Party (KESK), the Social Democratic Party (SDP) and the Swedish People's Party (SFP). Former Prime Minister Anneli Jäätteenmäki, who took office following the March 2003 elections on 17 April 2003, resigned on 18 June and was deputized by Antti Kalliomäki. Defence Minister Matti Vanhanen was elected prime minister by parliament on 24 June. The 18-member cabinet, consisting of ten men and eight women, comprised in March 2006:

Prime Minister: Matti Vanhanen; b. 1955 (KESK; sworn in on 24 June 2003).

Deputy Prime Minister and Minister of Finance: Eero Heinäluoma (SDP). *Foreign Affairs:* Erkki Tuomioja (SDP). *Justice:* Leena Luhtanen (SDP). *Education:* Antti Kalliomäki (SDP). *Culture:* Tanja Karpela (KESK). *Interior:* Kari Rajamäki (SDP). *Trade and Industry:* Mauri Pekkarinen (KESK). *Transport and Communications:* Susanna Huovinen (SDP). *Social Affairs and Health:* Tuula Haatainen (SDP). *Health and Social Services:* Liisa Hyssälä (KESK). *Labour:* Tarja Filatov (SDP). *Defence:* Seppo Kääriäinen (KESK). *Environment:* Jan-Erik Enestam (SFP). *Regional and Municipal Affairs:* Hannes Manninen (KESK). *Foreign Trade and Development:* Paula Lehtomäki (KESK). *Agriculture and Forestry:* Juha Korkeaoja (KESK). *Minister at the Ministry of Finance:* Ulla-Maj Wideroos (SFP).

The *Speaker* is Paavo Lipponen.

Government Website: http://www.valtioneuvosto.fi

CURRENT LEADERS

Tarja Halonen

Position
President

Introduction
The first woman president in Finnish history, Tarja Kaarina Halonen began her term in office on 1 March 2000. She won a second term in Jan. 2006. A member of parliament from 1979 until her election to the presidency, she has also served as a minister in three governments since 1987. From 1995–2000 she was the country's foreign minister.

Early Life
Tarja Halonen was born on 24 Dec. 1943. She was educated at the University of Helsinki where she received a degree in law. She was actively involved in student politics and served as the General Secretary for the National Union of Finnish Students. From 1970–74 she was a lawyer with the central organization of Finnish Trade Unions. In 1974 she changed from a professional to a political career by becoming the parliamentary secretary to prime minister, Kalevi Sorsa. She held this position until the following year when Sorsa's term ended. Halonen was elected to the Helsinki City council in 1977 (she remained a councillor until 1996) and two years later she was elected a member of the Finnish parliament. She was chairman of the parliamentary social affairs committee from 1984–87. Having fulfilled this office, she was appointed minister of social affairs and health. She went on to hold two further ministerial positions, serving as minister for Nordic co-operation (1989–91) and minister of justice (1990–91), before becoming the minister of foreign affairs in April 1995. In this role she oversaw Finland's assimilation into the European Union. In Jan. 2000 Halonen stood for election as the Social Democratic Party candidate for the presidency, campaigning on a liberal and feminist manifesto. She received 51·6% of the total votes cast in the second round of the presidential elections on 6 Feb. 2000, narrowly defeating the Centre Party's Esko Aho.

Career in Office
On the day of her inauguration, a new national constitution came into effect which reduced presidential powers and expanded and emphasized parliament as the most important body in the Finnish political system. The president was still granted a significant role in foreign policy, a fact which suited Halonen's diplomatic and linguistic skills. Halonen has continued her country's pro-European Union policies, although her position on NATO has been less certain, with some commentators suggesting that she is opposed to Finnish membership of the organization.

In Nov. 2005 the SDP nominated Halonen for re-election as its presidential candidate in Jan. 2006. Having failed to secure a majority in the first round of voting, she narrowly defeated the Conservative candidate, Sauli Niinistö, in a run-off.

Matti Vanhanen

Position
Prime Minister

Introduction
Matti Vanhanen took over as Finland's prime minister in June 2003 when the three-month tenure of Anneli Jäätteenmäki ended amid political scandal. A member of the Centre Party like his predecessor, Vanhanen is widely regarded as a cautious and reliable politician.

Early Life
Matti Taneli Vanhanen was born 4 Nov. 1955 in Jyväskylä, Finland. From 1980–83 he was chairman of the Centre Party's youth organization, and in 1989 completed a university degree in political science. His early career as a journalist, working as editor-in-chief of Kehäsanomat from 1988–91, won him a reputation as a European Union expert. In 1991 he was elected to the Finnish parliament, where he became vice-president of the party and, later, defence minister.

On 18 June 2003 Anneli Jäätteenmäki resigned from both her role as prime minister and as leader of the Centre Party, following allegations over her use of information concerning her predecessor, Paavo Lipponen, in the build-up to the elections of March 2003. Jäätteenmäki was in office for just 63 days.

Career in Office
Observers viewed the appointment of Vanhanen as an attempt to restore calm to Finnish national politics and one of his principal tasks was to win back public trust. He heads a coalition comprising the Centre Party, the Social Democrats and the Swedish People's Party.

Vanhanen was expected to pursue a similar programme to that of Jäätteenmäki, aiming to reduce unemployment which topped 10% in 2003. Within the EU he has spoken out against plans for a proposed common defence policy. He is a leading advocate of ecological and environmental issues and has voiced his opposition to plans to build a fifth nuclear reactor in Finland.

During 2005 a seven-week industrial dispute in the paper mill industry over pay and conditions caused nationwide strikes before being settled by mediation. Losses in export earnings were expected to reach €5bn. and Vanhanen's government faced considerable losses in tax revenue.

In Oct. 2005 Vanhanen was nominated as the presidential candidate of the Centre Party for the Jan. 2006 election—he came third in the election with just under 19% of the vote.

DEFENCE

Conscript service is 6–12 months. Total strength of trained and equipped reserves is about 485,000 (to be 350,000).

Defence expenditure totalled about US$2·2bn. in 2004 (1·4% of GDP).

Army

The Army consists of 1 armoured training brigade, 3 readiness brigades, 3 infantry training brigades, 3 jaeger regiments, 1 artillery brigade, 3 brigade artillery regiments, 2 air defence regiments, 1 engineer regiment (including ABC school), 3 brigade engineer battalions, 1 signals regiment, 4 brigade signals battalions and a reserve officer school. Total strength of 27,300 (21,600 conscripts).

Frontier Guard

This comes under the purview of the Ministry of the Interior, but is militarily organized to participate in the defence of the country. It is in charge of border surveillance and border controls. It is also responsible for conducting maritime search and rescue operations. If necessary in the interests of defence capability, the frontier troops or parts thereof may be attached to the Defence Forces. Personnel, 2004, 3,200 (professional) with a potential mobilizational force of 22,000 (to be 8,500).

Navy

The organization of the Navy was changed on 1 July 1998. The Coastal Defence, comprising the coast artillery and naval infantry, was merged into the Navy.

About 50% of the combatant units are kept manned, with the others on short-notice reserve and re-activated on a regular basis. Naval bases exist at Upinniemi (near Helsinki), Turku and Kotka. Naval Infantry mobile troops are trained at Tammisaari. Total personnel strength (2004) was 6,800, of whom 4,500 were conscripts.

Air Force

Personnel (2004), 4,500 (1,500 conscripts). Equipment included 63 F-18 Hornets.

INTERNATIONAL RELATIONS

Finland is a member of the UN, WTO, BIS, NATO Partnership for Peace, OECD, EU, Council of Europe, OSCE, CERN, Nordic Council, Council of the Baltic Sea States, Inter-American Development Bank, Asian Development Bank, IOM and the Antarctic Treaty. Finland has acceded to the Schengen accord, which abolishes border controls between Finland, Austria, Belgium, Denmark, France, Germany, Greece, Iceland, Italy, Luxembourg, the Netherlands, Norway, Portugal, Spain and Sweden.

ECONOMY

Agriculture accounted for 4% of GDP in 2003, industry 31% and services 65%.

According to the Berlin-based organization *Transparency International*, Finland ranked equal second in a 2005 survey of countries with the least corruption in business and government. It received 9·6 out of 10 in the corruption perceptions index.

Overview

Finland's economy, once based on basic metals and forestry, has evolved to become a leading force in knowledge-based, high-tech production. Finland is one of the world's leading information and communications technology (ICT) producers. The emergence of venture capital financing in the 1990s created opportunities for high-risk technology start-ups and the rapid increase in research and development (R&D) also pushed the economic transformation. Expenditure on R&D has risen significantly since the 1980s. Its share of GDP was 3·5% in 2004, one of the highest levels in the world. The economy's structural transition began to produce significant economic results after the Scandinavian banking crisis and four years of negative annual growth in the period 1990–93. Strong global demand in the ICT sector in the late 1990s helped boost the economy. From 1994–2000 real GDP growth averaged a robust 3·9% annually. By 2000 almost one third of Finnish exports were from the ICT sector.

The downturn in the demand for ICT goods beginning in 2001 slowed real GDP growth from 2001–03. In 2004 an investment led recovery once again pushed annual growth above 3%. Key sectors in the 2004 rebound were electronics, paper, forestry and metals. Growth slowed in the first half of 2005 owing to a falling demand for metal and electronics in the first quarter and a strike in the forestry industry in the second quarter. In the second half of the 2005 economic activity accelerated but not enough to bring annual growth up to 2004 levels.

In 2005 Finland was ranked first in the world in the *World Economic Forum*'s Competitiveness Report and rated the second least corrupt country in the world by *Transparency International*. However, Finland's own ministry of finance estimates that in the medium-term the pace of economic growth will be less than 2%. The three factors impeding growth are an ageing population, the relocation of production overseas and the slow rate of production capacity increases. The combination of a decrease in labour supply owing to an increase in the number of pensioners and high structural unemployment will limit economic growth on the demand side. On the supply side there are fears that Finnish companies will increasingly look to outsource production to areas either closer to large markets or with lower labour costs. The key to Finland's growth performance will be the pace of productivity gains. Yet productivity growth is not expected to grow strongly as the economy is increasingly service-based where productivity gains are harder to achieve while the contracting supply of skilled labour threatens to raise labour costs.

Finland has been running fiscal surpluses since 1998, which are necessary to finance the growing number of pensioners. The Vanhanen government has taken measures to boost employment by seeking to reduce non-wage labour costs, raise skills levels and foster co-operation between regional employment agencies. A pension reform package aimed at encouraging older workers to stay employed longer was passed in 2005.

Currency

On 1 Jan. 1999 the euro (EUR) became the legal currency in Finland; irrevocable conversion rate 5·94573 marks to one euro. The euro, which consists of 100 cents, has been in circulation since 1 Jan. 2002. There are seven euro notes in different colours and sizes denominated in 500, 200, 100, 50, 20, 10 and 5 euros, and eight coins denominated in 2 and 1 euros, then 50, 20, 10, 5, 2 and 1 cents. On the introduction of the euro there was a 'dual circulation' period before the mark ceased to be legal tender on 28 Feb. 2002. Euro banknotes in circulation on 1 Jan. 2002 had a total value of €8·0bn.

Inflation rates (based on OECD statistics):

1995	1996	1997	1998	1999	2000	2001	2002	2003	2004
0·4%	1·1%	1·2%	1·4%	1·3%	3·0%	2·7%	2·0%	1·3%	0·1%

Foreign exchange reserves were US$7,904m. in June 2002 and gold reserves 1·58m. troy oz. Total money supply was €5,189m. in June 2002.

Budget

Revenue and expenditure for the calendar years 2000–04 in €1m:

	2000	2001	2002	2003	2004[1]
Revenue	37,756	35,426	36,353	36,413	37,065
Expenditure	38,472	36,072	35,511	36,897	37,065

[1]Proposed figure.

Of the total revenue in 2003, 34% derived from income and property tax, 28% from value added tax, 13% from excise duties, 6% from other taxes and similar revenue and 19% from miscellaneous sources. Of the total expenditure, 2003, 23% went to health and social security, 16% to education and culture, 7% to agriculture and forestry, 5% to defence, 5% to transport and 44% to other expenditure.

VAT is 22% (reduced rates, 17% and 8%).

At the end of Dec. 2003 the central government debt totalled €63,320m. Domestic debt amounted to €62,079m.; foreign debt, €1,241m.

Performance

Real GDP growth rates (based on OECD statistics):

1995	1996	1997	1998	1999	2000	2001	2002	2003	2004
3·5%	3·6%	6·2%	5·0%	3·3%	5·3%	0·9%	2·2%	2·4%	3·5%

The real GDP growth rate in 2005 (provisional) according to Statistics Finland was 2·1%. Total GDP was US$186·6bn. in 2004.

Finland was placed first in the world in the Growth Competitiveness Index and second behind the USA in the Business Competitiveness Index in the World Economic Forum's *Global Competitiveness Report 2005–2006*. In both indexes it had been in the same positions in the 2004–2005 index.

Banking and Finance

The central bank is the Bank of Finland (founded in 1811), operating under the guarantee and supervision of parliament. The Bank is a member of the European System of Central Banks. As a member of the euro area, the Bank issues euro banknotes and coins in Finland by permission of the European Central Bank. The *Governor* is Erkki Liikanen.

At the end of 2003 the deposits in banking institutions totalled €66,424m. and the loans granted by them €81,842m.

The most important groups of banking institutions in 2003 were:

	Number of institutions	Number branches	Deposits (€1m.)	Loans (€1m.)
Commercial banks	11	493	36,747	49,303
Savings banks	40	232	5,737	5,504
Co-operative banks	284	509	21,392	21,570
Foreign banks	8	29	1,975	5,465

The three largest banks are Nordea Bank Finland (formed in 1997 as MeritaNordbanken when Nordbanken of Sweden merged with Merita of Finland), Sampo Bank (formerly Leonia) and OKO Bank. In March 2000 MeritaNordbanken acquired Denmark's Unidanmark, thereby becoming the Nordic region's biggest bank in terms of assets. It has also become Europe's leading Internet bank, by July 2000 having 1·4m. Internet banking clients. By early 2001 approximately 40% of the Finnish population were using e-banking, the highest percentage in any country.

In 2003 Finland received US$2·8bn. worth of foreign direct investment.

There is a stock exchange in Helsinki.

ENERGY AND NATURAL RESOURCES

Environment

Finland's carbon dioxide emissions in 2002 were the equivalent of 12·0 tonnes per capita. An *Environmental Sustainability Index* compiled for the World Economic Forum meeting in Jan. 2005 ranked Finland first in the world, with 75·1%. The index measured the ability of countries to maintain favourable environmental conditions and examined various factors including pollution levels and the use or abuse of natural resources.

Electricity

Installed capacity was 17·7m. kW at the beginning of 2004. Production was 71,617m. kWh. in 2002 (15% hydro-electric) and 71,229m. kWh in 2001 (18% hydro-electric). Consumption per capita in 2002 was an estimated 16,047 kWh. In 2003 there were four nuclear reactors, which contributed 30% of production in 2002. In May 2002 parliament approved the construction of a fifth reactor. Supply: 220 volts; 50 Hz.

Water

Finland has abundant surface water and groundwater resources relative to its population and level of consumption. The total groundwater yield is estimated to be 10–30m. cu. metres a day, of which some 6m. is suitable for water supplies. Approximately 15% of this latter figure is made use of at the present time. A total of 2–4% of Finland's exploitable water resources are utilized each year.

Minerals

Notable of the mines are Pyhäsalmi (zinc–copper), Orivesi (gold ore), Hitura (nickel) and Keminmaa (chromium). In 2002 the metal content (in tonnes) of the output of zinc ore was 34,100; of copper ore, 11,200; of nickel ore, 2,500; of chromium, 248,000.

Agriculture

The cultivated area covers only 7% of the land, and of the economically active population 5% were employed in agriculture and forestry in 2003. In 2003 there were 2·21m. ha. of arable land. The arable area was divided in 2003 into 73,714 farms (including 636 farms with under one hectare of arable land). The distribution of this area by the size of the farms was: less than 5 ha. cultivated, 6,031 farms; 5–20 ha., 27,486 farms; 20–50 ha., 27,904 farms; 50–100 ha., 10,063 farms; over 100 ha., 2,230 farms.

Agriculture accounted for 0·9% of exports and 1·9% of imports in 2001.

The principal crops (area in 1,000 ha., yield in 1,000 tonnes) were in 2003:

Crop	Area	Yield	Crop	Area	Yield
Barley	530·7	1,697·4	Hay	101·2	344·6
Oats	425·5	1,294·5	Wheat	191·6	679·0
Potatoes	28·7	617·4	Rye	30·7	72·8

The total area under cultivation in 2003 was 2,212,100 ha. Approximately 7·2% of all agricultural land is used for organic farming. Production of dairy butter in 2003 was 58,402 tonnes; and of cheese, 97,486 tonnes.

Livestock (2003): horses, 60,200 (including trotting and riding horses, and ponies); cattle, 1,000,200; pigs, 1,374,900; poultry, 3,947,100; reindeer, 197,000.

Forestry

Forests covered 23·1m. ha. in 2002, or 75·8% of the total land area. The productive forest land covers 20·3m. ha. Timber production in 2003 was 55·0m. cu. metres. Finland is one of the largest producers of roundwood in Europe. Finland's per capita consumption of roundwood is the highest in the world, at 12·32m. cu. metres per person in 2001.

Fisheries

The catch in 2002 was 103,640 tonnes, of which 98,423 tonnes came from sea fishing. In 2003 there were 223 food fish production farms in operation, of which 69 were freshwater farms. Their total production amounted to 12,558 tonnes. In addition there were 104 fry-farms and 294 natural food rearers, most of these in freshwater.

INDUSTRY

The leading companies by market capitalization in Finland in Nov. 2005 were: Nokia Oyj (US$76·7bn.), the world's leading mobile phone producer; Fortum (US$15·2bn.), an energy company; and Stora Enso (US$10·6bn.), a forest-products company.

Forests are still Finland's most crucial raw material resource, although the metal and engineering industry has long been Finland's leading branch of manufacturing, both in terms of value added and as an employer. In 2002 there were 29,224 establishments in industry (of which 26,766 were manufacturing concerns) with 439,089 personnel (of whom 418,736 were in manufacturing). Gross value of industrial production in 2002 was €102,207m., of which manufacturing accounted for €96,179m.

Labour

In 2003 the labour force was 2,365,000 (52% males). In 2003, 68·3% of the economically active population worked in services, 19·9% in manufacturing and 15·3% in trade and restaurants. In 2005 unemployment was 8·4%, up from 3·2% in 1990, but down from 16·6% in 1994.

Trade Unions

There are three labour organizations: the Confederation of Unions for Academic Professionals—Akateemisten Toimihenkilöiden Keskusjarjesto (AKAVA); the Finnish Confederation of Salaried Employees—Toimihenkilokeskusjarjesto (STTK); and the Central Organization of Finnish Trade Unions (SAK). According to an incomes policy agreement reached by the central labour market organizations in Nov. 2004, which is in force until Sept. 2007, wages and salaries were to be raised by 1·9% in March 2005 and by 1·4% in June 2006. The government has undertaken to cut taxes on wages and salaries to support moderate pay increases.

INTERNATIONAL TRADE

At the start of the 1990s a collapse in trade with Russia led to the worst recession in the country's recent history. Today, exports to Russia are less than 8% of the total.

Imports and Exports

In 1960 wood and paper industry dominated exports with their 69% contribution, but today the metal and engineering industry is the largest export sector.

Imports and exports for calendar years, in €1m.:

	2000	2001	2002	2003
Imports	36,837	35,891	35,611	36,775
Exports	49,484	47,800	47,245	46,378

Use of Goods	Imports 2003
Raw materials, production necessities	38%
Investment goods	22%
Durable consumer goods	12%
Energy	12%
Other	16%

Industry	Exports 2003
Metal, Engineering, Electronics	55%
Forest Industry	26%
Chemical Industry	6%
Other	13%

Region	Imports 2003	Exports 2003
European Union	55%	53%
Other Europe	23%	20%
Developing Countries	12%	14%
EFTA	4%	4%
Other Countries	6%	9%

Trade with principal partners in 2003 was as follows (in €1m.):

	Imports	Exports		Imports	Exports
Australia	283	333	Italy	1,376	1,845
Austria	398	462	Japan	1,507	985
Belgium	872	1,296	Netherlands	1,466	2,169
Brazil	214	212	Norway	1,012	1,118
Canada	123	510	Poland	353	863
China	1,582	1,283	Portugal	166	272
Czech Republic	251	214	Russia	4,367	3,477
Denmark	1,541	1,030	South Korea	329	316
Estonia	1,032	1,138	Spain	604	1,297
France	1,777	1,732	Sweden	4,064	4,590
Germany	5,513	5,491	Switzerland	430	449
Greece	104	392	Taiwan	264	295
Hong Kong	101	408	Turkey	217	374
Hungary	377	357	UK	1,936	3,740
Ireland	386	234	USA	1,711	3,760

COMMUNICATIONS

Roads

In Jan. 2004 there were 78,197 km of public roads, of which 50,539 km were paved. At the end of 2003 there were 2,274,577 registered cars, 77,015 lorries, 250,107 vans and pick-ups, 10,358 buses and coaches and 14,942 special automobiles. Road accidents caused 379 fatalities in 2003.

Rail

In 2003 the total length of the line operated was 5,851 km (2,400 km electrified), all of it owned by the State. The gauge is 1,524 mm. In 2003, 55·9m. passengers and 43·5m. tonnes of freight were carried. There is a metro (17 km) and tram/light rail network (75 km) in Helsinki.

Civil Aviation

The main international airport is at Helsinki (Vantaa), and there are also international airports at Turku, Tampere, Rovaniemi and Oulu. The national carrier is Finnair. Scheduled traffic of Finnish airlines covered 98m. km in 2003. The number of passengers was 7·6m. and the number of passenger-km 14,008,000; the air transport of freight and mail amounted to 278·8m. tonne-km. Helsinki-Vantaa handled 9,710,920 passengers in 2003 (7,026,302 on international flights) and 88,116 tonnes of freight and mail. Oulu is the second busiest airport, handling 669,882 passengers in 2003, and Rovaniemi the third busiest, with 364,898 in 2003.

Shipping

The total registered mercantile marine in 2003 was 626 vessels of 1,484,711 GRT. In 2003 the total number of vessels arriving in Finland from abroad was 30,037 and the goods discharged amounted to 51·8m. tonnes. The goods loaded for export from Finnish ports amounted to 39·9m. tonnes.

The lakes, rivers and canals are navigable for about 6,300 km. Timber floating has some importance, and there are about 9,149 km of floatable inland waterways. In 2000 bundle floating was about 0·9m. tonnes.

Telecommunications

In 2003 there were 2,568,000 telephone main lines in use and 4,747,000 mobile telephone subscribers. In spring 2004 around 94% of Finnish households owned at least one mobile phone. The rate among 18- and 19-year-olds is almost 100%. In mid-1999 approximately 19% of Finnish households only had a mobile phone and did not have a fixed-line phone at all. The Finnish company Nokia is the world's biggest manufacturer of mobile phones, having a 30% share of the world mobile phone market. It is by far the biggest company in Finland, accounting for 4·5% of the country's GDP in 2000 and more than half the value of its stock exchange. The biggest operator is Sonera (formerly Telecom Finland). Approximately 50% of all voice and data traffic streams through the company's networks, and approximately 60% of all mobile users are Sonera customers. In 2003 Sonera and the Swedish telecommunications operator Telia merged. Finland has the lowest rates in Europe for both fixed and mobile phone calls.

There were 2·3m. PCs in use in 2002 (441·7 per 1,000 persons) and 304,000 fax machines. Finland had 2·73m. Internet users in May 2004.

Postal Services

In 2003 there were 293 primary post offices and 1,053 agents providing postal services in Finland. Finland Post Group is now exposed to competition in its business operations, with the exception of addressed letter mail for which it holds a licence for nationwide delivery.

SOCIAL INSTITUTIONS

Justice

The lowest court of justice is the District Court. In most civil cases a District Court has a quorum of three legally qualified members. In criminal cases as well as in some cases related to family law the District Court has a quorum with a chair and three lay judges. In the preliminary preparation of a civil case and in a criminal case concerning a minor offence, a

District Court is composed of the chair only. From the District Court an appeal lies to the courts of appeal in Turku, Vaasa, Kuopio, Helsinki, Kouvola and Rovaniemi. The Supreme Court sits in Helsinki. Appeals from the decisions of administrative authorities are in the final instance decided by the Supreme Administrative Court, also in Helsinki. Judges can be removed only by judicial sentence. Two functionaries, the Chancellor of Justice and the Ombudsman or Solicitor-General, exercise control over the administration of justice. The former acts also as counsel and public prosecutor for the government; the latter is appointed by Parliament.

At the end of 2003 the daily average number of prisoners was 3,578 of which 205 were women. The number of convictions in 2003 was 283,768, of which 218,883 were for minor offences with a maximum penalty of fines, and 26,678 with penalty of imprisonment. 11,604 of the prison sentences were unconditional.

Education
Number of institutions, teachers and students (2003).

Primary and Secondary Education

	Number of institutions	Teachers[1]	Students
First-level Education (Lower sections of the comprehensive schools, grades I–VI)			400,368[2]
Second-level Education General education (Upper sections of the comprehensive schools, grades VII–IX, and upper secondary general schools)	4,248	51,263	318,862
Vocational and Professional Education	281[3]	13,548[3, 4]	174,659

[1]Data for teachers refers to 2002.
[2]Including pre-primary education (12,434 pupils) in comprehensive schools.
[3]Numbers of institutions for vocational and professional education refer to secondary and tertiary education.
[4]Number of teachers for vocational and professional education refer to secondary and tertiary education.

Tertiary Education
Vocational and professional education at tertiary education level was provided for 154 students in 2003. In 2003 polytechnic education was provided at 31 polytechnics with 129,875 students and 5,844 teachers (2002). In 2003, 24·6% of the population aged 15 years or over had been through tertiary education.

University Education
Universities with the number of teachers and students in 2003:

			Students	
	Founded[1]	Teachers	Total	Women
Universities				
Helsinki	1640	1,648	37,486	23,886
Turku (Swedish)	1918	362	6,725	4,116
Turku (Finnish)	1922	793	15,226	9,715
Tampere	1925	608	14,800	9,761
Jyväskylä	1934	702	13,668	8,728
Oulu	1958	848	15,127	7,333
Vaasa	1968	164	4,850	2,652
Joensuu	1969	403	7,561	4,844
Kuopio	1972	336	5,938	3,917
Lapland	1979	192	4,099	2,835
Universities of Technology				
Helsinki	1849	514	14,599	3,094
Tampere	1965	332	11,889	2,408
Lappeenranta	1969	213	5,549	1,482
Schools of Economics and Business Administration				
Helsinki (Swedish)	1909	100	2,375	1,020
Helsinki (Finnish)	1911	152	4,206	1,836
Turku (Finnish)	1950	100	2,122	1,068

			Students	
Universities of Art				
Academy of Fine Arts	1848	25	220	119
University of Art and Design	1871	147	1,507	925
Sibelius Academy	1882	239	1,481	815
Theatre Academy	1943	55	418	232
Total		7,933	169,846	90,786

[1]Year when the institution was founded regardless of status at the time.

Adult Education
Adult education provided by educational institutions in 2003.

Type of institution	Participants[1]
General education institutions[2]	1,914,000
Vocational and professional education institutions	558,000
Permanent polytechnics	90,500
Universities[3]	141,100
Summer universities	75,400
	2,779,000

[1]Participants are persons who have attended adult education courses run by educational institutions in the course of the calendar year. The same person may have attended a number of different courses and has been recorded as a participant in each one of them.
[2]Including study centres.
[3]Adult education at continuing education centres of universities.

In 2002 total expenditure on education came to 6·4% of GNP and 12·8% of total government spending.

The adult literacy rate in 2003 was almost 100%.

Health
In 2003 there were 16,433 physicians, 4,607 dentists and 37,656 hospital beds. The average Finnish adult smokes 3·5 cigarettes a day and drinks 9·4 litres of alcohol a year.

In 2003 Finland spent 7·4% of its GDP on health.

Welfare
The Social Insurance Institution administers general systems of old-age pensions (to all persons over 65 years of age and disabled younger persons) and of health insurance. An additional system of compulsory old-age pensions paid for by the employers is in force and works through the Central Pension Security Institute. Systems for other public aid are administered by the communes and supervised by the National Social Board and the Ministry of Social Affairs and Health.

The total cost of social security amounted to €36,908m. in 2002. Out of this €16,593m. (45%) was spent on old age and disability, €8,879m. (24%) on health, €5,557m. (15%) on family allowances and child welfare, €3,509m. (10%) on unemployment and €2,372m. (6%) on general welfare purposes and administration. Out of the total expenditure, 39·2% was financed by employers, 23·7% by the State, 19·6% by local authorities, 11·0% by the insured and 6·5% by property income.

RELIGION
Liberty of conscience is guaranteed to members of all religions. National churches are the Lutheran National Church and the Greek Orthodox Church of Finland. The Lutheran Church is divided into eight bishoprics (Turku being the archiepiscopal see), 80 provostships and 567 parishes. The Greek Orthodox Church is divided into three bishoprics (Kuopio being the archiepiscopal see) and 27 parishes, in addition to which there are a monastery and a convent.

Percentage of the total population at the end of 2003: Lutherans, 84·2; Greek Orthodox, 1·1; others, 0·6; not members of any religion, 13·5.

CULTURE
World Heritage Sites
Finland has six sites on the UNESCO world heritage list: Old Rauma harbour (1991); the sea fortress of Suomenlinna (1991); the old church of Petäjävesi (1994); Verla groundwood and board

mill (1996); the Bronze Age burial site of Sammallahdenmäki (1999); and the Struve Geodetic Arc (2005). The Arc is a chain of survey triangulations spanning from Norway to the Black Sea that helped establish the exact shape and size of the earth and is shared with nine other countries.

Broadcasting

There are four national television channels: *TV1*, *TV2*, *MTV3* and *Channel Four*. The Finnish Broadcasting Company, YLE, is the biggest national radio and television service provider. YLE operates two analogue and five digital national television channels. The second biggest television broadcaster, the privately owned Commercial *MTV3*, has one nationwide channel and one cable channel. The private TV channel, *Channel Four Finland*, started in 1997. In addition, the coverage of the Swedish-language channel *SVT Europa* with programmes from the Swedish channels 1 and 2 extends over southern Finland. There are some 38 local TV stations that mainly relay foreign and domestic programmes over cable and radio waves, in addition to locally produced material. On 31 Dec. 2003 the number of television licences was 2,016,753. The government decided upon the digitalization of the distribution of television and radio broadcasting in the mid 1990s. In 2004 the transmission area covered 94% of Finnish households. Examples of the commercial digital channels are the sports channel (*Urheilukanava*), *SubTV* and the shopping channel *TV5*. There were 3·52m. TV receivers in 2001.

The only radio broadcaster with full nationwide coverage is YLE. It transmits three analogue national channels in Finnish and two in Swedish, as well as various regional channels, including one in Sami in Lapland. In addition YLE has three digital radio channels. At the end of 2003 there were 67 local radio stations. Two of them, the news and music stations Nova and Classic, cover almost 60% of the population. There were 8·4m. radio receivers in 2000.

Cinema

In 2003 there were 338 cinema halls. In 2003 total attendance was 7·7m. and gross box office receipts came to €56·4m. 177 films premiered of which fourteen were Finnish.

Press

Finland has 53 newspapers that are published four to seven times a week, nine of which are in Swedish, and 150 with one to three issues per week. The total circulation of all newspapers is 3·2m. There are 5,042 registered periodicals with a total circulation of over 17m. In terms of total circulation of dailies relative to population, Finland ranks second in Europe after Norway. Most newspapers are bought on subscription rather than from newsstands. Only two newspapers depend entirely on newsstand sales. The five bestselling newspapers in 2003 were: *Helsingin Sanomat* (average daily circulation, 439,618 copies), *Ilta-Sanomat* (198,829), *Aamulehti* (136,331), *Iltalehti* (121,267) and *Turun Sanomat* (111,517). The bestselling newspaper in the Swedish language is *Hufvudstadsbladet*, 50,094. In 2003 a total of 12,309 book titles were published.

Tourism

There were 21,047,444 foreign tourists in 2003; the income from tourism was €1,656m. and the expenses were €2,150m.

Spas, leisure centres and amusement parks are popular tourism destinations for the Finns, while international tourists favour churches and other religious attractions as well as spas and leisure centres. Major international tourist attractions include Uspensky Cathedral, Helsinki Cathedral and Suomenlinna (all in Helsinki). Helsinki's churches and Santa Park in Rovaniemi are particularly popular among foreigners, who account for the majority of their visitors.

Festivals

Major festivals are the Helsinki Festival Week, the Maritime Festival in Kotka, the Lakeside Blues Festival in Järvenpää, Pori Jazz Festival, Kaustinen Folk Music Festival, Tampere Theatre Festival and Seinäjoki's Tango Festival.

Libraries

The Helsinki University Library doubles as a National Library. The collections of the university libraries and major research libraries comprise in total 53·9m. volumes (of which the university libraries have 21·8m.). In total, they issued 19·4m. loans (university libraries 14·0m.) in 2003.

The revised Public Library Act, which came into force on 1 Jan. 1999, requires each municipality to provide basic library services free of charge. The public library network is comprehensive with 968 libraries altogether. These are complemented by 191 mobile units with over 15,807 service stops. The Helsinki City Library doubles as a Central Library in this sector. Additionally the country is divided into 19 regions with a Regional Central Library providing supplementary services. In 2003 there were over 2·4m. registered borrowers, who represent 47% of the population. The number of loans issued totalled 108·4m.

Theatre and Opera

A new Opera House and a new 14,000-seat Arena Show Hall opened in 1999 in Helsinki. The city hosts both the National Theatre and the National Opera. All major cities have theatres and showhalls. In 2003 there were 13,239 performances in total with over 2·5m. tickets sold.

Museums and Galleries

The National Museum as well as the National Gallery (the Atheneum) are located in Helsinki. The new Museum of Modern Art (Kiasma) was opened in Helsinki in 1998 and a new Ethnographic Museum and a media centre, also in Helsinki, opened in 1999. Major cities all host their own art galleries and local museums. The Alvar Aalto Museum is located in Jyväskylä in central Finland. In 2003 there were 163 museums with full-time personnel. The number of exhibitions was 1,275 and there were 4·5m. visitors.

DIPLOMATIC REPRESENTATIVES

Of Finland in the United Kingdom (38 Chesham Pl., London, SW1X 8HW)
Ambassador: Jaako Laajava.

Of the United Kingdom in Finland (Itäinen Puistotie 17, 00140 Helsinki)
Ambassador: Matthew Kirk.

Of Finland in the USA (3301 Massachusetts Ave., NW, Washington, D.C., 20008)
Ambassador: Pekka Lintu.

Of the USA in Finland (Itäinen Puistotie 14B, Helsinki 00140)
Ambassador: Marilyn Ware.

Of Finland to the United Nations
Ambassador: Kirsti Lintonen.

FURTHER READING

Statistics Finland. *Statistical Yearbook of Finland* (from 1879).—*Bulletin of Statistics* (quarterly, from 1971).
Constitution Act and Parliament Act of Finland. Helsinki, 1984
Suomen valtiokalenteri—Finlands statskalender (State Calendar of Finland). Helsinki. Annual
Facts About Finland. Helsinki. Annual (Union Bank of Finland)
Finland in Figures. Helsinki, Annual
Kirby, D. G., *Finland in the Twentieth Century.* 2nd ed. London, 1984
Klinge, M., *A Brief History of Finland.* Helsinki, 1987
Petersson, O., *The Government and Politics of the Nordic Countries.* Stockholm, 1994
Singleton, F., *The Economy of Finland in the Twentieth Century.* Univ. of Bradford Press, 1987.—*A Short History of Finland.* 2nd edition. CUP, 1998
Tillotson, H. M., *Finland at Peace and War, 1918–1993.* London, 1993
Turner, Barry, (ed.) *Scandinavia Profiled.* Macmillan, London, 2000

National Statistical Office: Statistics Finland, FIN-00022.
Website: http://www.stat.fi/

FRANCE

République Française

Capital: Paris
Population projection, 2010: 61·54m.
GDP per capita, 2003: (PPP$) 27,677
HDI/world rank: 0·938/16

KEY HISTORICAL EVENTS

The Dordogne has evidence of Mousterian industry from 40,000 BC and of Cro-Magnon man of the Upper Paleolithic period. With the end of the Ice Age, agricultural settlement appeared around 7000 BC. By the beginning of the 8th century BC, Celtic tribes from Central Europe were inhabiting the Rhône valley of Gaul (now France) while the Greeks were building cities such as Massalia (Marseilles) along the southern coast. The Romans crossed the Alps into southern France in 121 BC and Gaul was conquered by Julius Caesar in 52 BC. The country benefited from protected trade routes and from Roman infrastructure, speech and government. Roman rule was consolidated by the reign of Augustus at the end of the 1st century AD. But the Empire was threatened by Germanic ('barbarian') incursions from the north and east. Many of these tribes were assimilated as *foederati* (treaty nations) into the Gallo-Roman Empire but they assumed authority in their domains as Roman government receded in the 4th and 5th centuries. After the repulse of Attila and his Huns in 451, the Salian Franks emerged as the strongest of the Germanic tribes—their leader, Merovius, was the progenitor of the Merovingian dynasty that ruled France until the beginning of the 8th century.

On the death of Merovius' grandson, Clovis, the kingdom was divided between his three sons. The Merovingians remained in power for two centuries but their rule, weakened by internecine warfare, gave way to the Carolingian dynasty in 751. Having extended his empire over Germany and Italy, Charlemagne was crowned emperor of the West by the pope in 800. He moved his seat of government to Aix-la-Chapelle (Aachen) where he presided over a revival of learning and education.

Charlemagne died in 814 and his empire was fought over by his grandsons before the 843 Treaty of Verdun officially split the territories. Charles le Chauve (823–77) inherited the western territories, an area roughly corresponding to modern day France. But by 912 Vikings had settled in Rouen, having laid siege to Paris. Further threats came from Muslim Saracens in the south and Hungarian Magyars in the east. The Carolingians struggled to keep their power for another century but they were weakened by unrest and disunity. In 987 Hugh Capet, the duke of the Franks, ousted the legitimate claimant to the throne, Charles of Lorraine, and appointed himself king. To control a diverse country, power was centralized on Paris.

Between 1150 and 1300 France underwent a period of economic expansion, though the 12th century also saw the Holy Land crusades and the expulsion of the Jews, followed by the bloody Albigensian Crusade against the heretical Cathars of Languedoc in 1209. The last Capetian king, Charles IV, died in 1328 (leaving only daughters) and the Capetian dynasty gave way to the House of Valois. However, King Edward III of England disputed Philippe de Valois' claim to the French throne, prompting the start of the Hundred Years War (1337–1453). With his son the Black Prince, Edward III's successful invasion led to the Treaty of Brétigny in 1360, which ceded Aquitaine to England. Edward renounced all claims to the French throne but the warfare continued until Charles V (ruled 1364–80) won back most of their territories. In 1415 Henry V of England, with the backing of the Burgundians, defeated the French at Agincourt. He married the daughter of Charles IV and obtained the right of succession to the French throne. The war continued between his son Henry VI and the dauphin Charles (VI) who enlisted the help of Joan of Arc (Jeanne d'Arc). After leading a series of successful campaigns against the English, she was captured, tried as a heretic by a court of Burgundian ecclesiastics and burnt at the stake in Rouen in 1431. Nevertheless, French successes continued and eventually the English were driven from all their French possessions except Calais.

Rising Power

The reign of Louis XI (1461–83) saw a change from a medieval social system to a more modern state. Provincial governments were set up in major cities and nobles wielding independent power were crushed. In 1494 Charles VIII, encouraged to pursue his claim to the crown of Naples by Ludovico Sforza, duke of Milan, invaded Italy. The speed of his advance shocked the Italian cities into an alliance to expel his army. The appearance of Spanish power in Naples began the Habsburg-Valois wars that used Italy as a battlefield until the Peace of Cateau-Cambrésis in 1559. François I is considered the first Renaissance French king. He patronized some of Italy's greatest artists, commissioning palaces such as the Château de Chambord and rebuilding the Louvre and Château de Fontainebleau. To finance his cultural interests and his military failures in Italy—he was captured by Spanish forces at the Battle of Pavia in 1525—François imposed huge tax rises, severely straining the French economy.

Between 1562–98 the Wars of Religion raged in France between the Protestant Huguenots and the Spanish-supported Catholic League. The civil war reached its peak with the 1572 St Bartholomew's Day massacre, in which 20,000 Huguenots were killed, before ending with Henry of Navarre's conversion to Catholicism. He did not abandon his Huguenot roots, however, and the 1598 Edict of Nantes guaranteed Protestants political and religious rights.

After Henry's assassination in 1610 the young Louis XIII took the throne with his mother, Marie de Médicis, acting as regent. Between 1624–42 Cardinal Richelieu held the reins of government and set about establishing absolute royal power in France, with the suppression of Protestant influences. This policy was continued for the next twenty years by his successor Cardinal Mazarin. On Mazarin's death Louis XIV (1643–1715) was able to govern alone. Louis, the 'Sun King', attempted to impose a centralized absolutism—symbolized by his Palais de Versailles—gathering the aristocracy around him and thus denying it traditional regional power. The king formally revoked the Edict of Nantes, Protestant churches were destroyed and religious minorities persecuted. His successor, Louis XV, married Maria, the daughter of the deposed king of Poland, who drew France into the War of the Polish Succession. Further costly military disasters followed including the Seven Years' War, in which France lost her colonies in India, North America and the West Indies.

When Louis XVI succeeded to the throne in 1774, financial crises caused by prolonged military failure coupled with a succession of bad harvests led to grain riots in 1787–88 in Paris, Lyons, Nantes and Grenoble. The subsequent reforms were rejected by the aristocracy (*les privilégiés*), the upper ranks of the clergy (the First Estate) and the majority of the nobility (the Second Estate), who feared a reduction in their tax-levying privileges. Meanwhile, Louis XVI supported the American colonies in their struggle for independence from Britain, a policy that was financially disastrous and also did much to disseminate revolutionary and democratic ideals in France.

Revolution

The French Revolution erupted in 1789 when the Third Estate (the non-privilégiés) assumed power in the National Assembly and overthrew the government. Riots broke out across France, culminating in the storming of the Bastille in Paris on 14 July 1789. A new legislative assembly was formed and although the moderate Girondins held power at the start, the more extreme followers of Danton, Robespierre and Marat—the Jacobins—seized power and in 1792 declared a republic.

On 21 Jan. 1793 Louis XVI was guillotined in the Place de la Révolution. After his death a reign of terror led by Maximilien Robespierre followed in which thousands of people were guillotined. Despite the efforts of the royalists to re-establish a monarchy, in 1795 the 'Directory of Five' was appointed to run the country. As one of these five, Paul Barras had been responsible for the promotion of a young Corsican, Napoleon Bonaparte, to the rank of general. Over four years, Napoleon commanded the French troops in a series of successful campaigns against the Austrians and the British. On his return to Paris, he found the Directory in disarray and in 1799 overthrew the government and declared himself first consul. Napoleon immediately faced a hostile coalition of England, Austria and Russia. In 1805 he defeated Austria and Russia at the Battle of Austerlitz but the British naval victory at the Battle of Trafalgar earlier the same year gave Britain maritime supremacy. Napoleon's best troops were bogged down supporting his brother Joseph in the Peninsula War in Spain and his success at Borodino, Russia in 1812 was followed by the army's forced retreat from Moscow during the harsh winter months. The Prussian army retaliated at Leipzig, entered France and forced the surrender of Paris in March 1814. Napoleon abdicated at Fontainebleau on 20 April 1814 and retired to Elba. But when Louis XVIII returned from exile in England later that year, Napoleon left Elba to attempt to recover his empire. He marched north towards Paris, gathering support on the way. But his defeat in 1815 at Waterloo by the Allies led by the duke of Wellington ended his 'Hundred Days' reign. He was exiled to the island of St Helena where he died in 1821.

Second Empire

The monarchy was restored with the Bourbon family. A revolution in 1830 brought Louis Philippe, son of the duke of Orléans, to the throne as a constitutional monarch. This 'July Monarchy' was overthrown in 1848 and superseded by the Second Republic, with Louis Napoleon (nephew of Napoleon I) elected president. In 1852 he took the title of Emperor Napoleon III, and hence began the Second Empire. However, the early military failures of France in the Franco-Prussian War (1870–71) led to Napoleon being deposed and the proclamation of the Third Republic in 1870. But German troops were advancing on Paris and after a four-month siege and much suffering and starvation, Paris capitulated in Jan. 1871. By Sept. 1873 the occupying troops had gone and France was left to pick up the pieces. Alsace and Lorraine had been lost and French politics, embittered by the Dreyfus Affair (1894–1906), in which forged evidence resulted in the Jewish general staff captain being imprisoned for spying, went from crisis to crisis. An entente cordiale was established between France and Britain in 1904, putting an end to colonial rivalry and paving the way for future co-operation. In 1905 the Church was separated from the State, a measure to counteract ecclesiastical influence over education.

European War

Although Paris was saved from occupation during the First World War, ten departments were overrun and four long years of trench warfare followed. The tide began to turn against Germany in 1916 with the Battle of the Somme, the French stand at Verdun and the arrival of the Americans in 1917; the Armistice was finally signed on 11 Nov. 1918. By the end of the war France had lost a total of 1·3m. men. The main thrust of France's efforts to rebuild her defences after the First World War was concentrated on the 'Maginot Line'—a supposedly impregnable barrier running along the German frontier, but which was sidestepped by the advancing German forces in 1939. Demoralized French troops, unable to resist the German advance, were forced to retreat towards Dunkerque (Dunkirk). The French government capitulated and a pro-German government presided over by Marshal Pétain (a hero of the Battle of Verdun) was established at Vichy. A truce was signed with Germany agreeing German occupation in the northern third of the country and collaborationist government control in the south. Gen. Charles de Gaulle established the Forces Françaises Libres (Free French Forces) and declared the Comité National Français to be the true French government-in-exile with its headquarters first in London and then in Algiers. With help from the Resistance in France, in Aug. 1944 de Gaulle returned at the head of the allied armies and liberated Paris. An armistice with Germany was signed in March 1945.

In Oct. 1946 the Fourth Republic, institutionally similar to the Third Republic, was established but during prolonged wrangling over the form of the new constitution Gen. de Gaulle retired. Despite frequent changes of government and defeat in Indo-China, France achieved economic recovery. In 1957 a European common market was established of which France, West Germany, Italy and the Benelux countries were founder members.

Fifth Republic

Between 1954–62 France was embroiled in a war of independence with Algeria that split public and political opinion. In 1958 de Gaulle prepared a new constitution and was persuaded to return first as prime minister and then, by universal suffrage, as the first president of the newly declared Fifth Republic. The new constitution greatly enhanced the power of the president. The politics of the early Fifth Republic was dominated by the centre-right, with a succession of parties (including the Union of Democrats for the Republic, Union of Democrats for the V Republic, Union for the New Republic, Union for the French Republic-Democratic Union of Labour) working to a Gaullist agenda. There was an emphasis on national independence, government involvement in the economy and broadly conservative social policies.

In 1962 Algeria gained independence. De Gaulle continued to preside over a period of relative stability and economic growth but serious student riots in Paris in 1968 precipitated reforms to the authoritarian system of education. The students were joined by workers wanting better pay and conditions. The National Assembly was dissolved and, although the Gaullists were returned to power in the new election, de Gaulle's referendum proposing decentralization was defeated and in 1969 he resigned. Georges Pompidou, who had been de Gaulle's prime minister, succeeded him. Pompidou attempted to consolidate de Gaulle's legacy by concentrating on economic reform. When he died in office in 1974 he was succeeded by Valéry Giscard d'Estaing who continued right-wing policies, eventually precipitating a swing to the left. In 1981 the Socialist leader François Mitterrand was elected president. He immediately implemented widespread social reforms but a deep recession in 1983 forced him to take a series of unpopular deflationary measures.

When the ailing Mitterrand's term of office expired in 1995, Jacques Chirac was elected president with Alain Juppé as prime minister. After the Socialists won an assembly majority in 1997, Juppé resigned making way for the Socialist leader Lionel Jospin to take over as prime minister. The right and leftwing *cohabitation* lasted five years until Jospin retired after a disastrous result in the first round presidential elections. Chirac's second electoral success was consolidated by the moderate right taking an assembly majority in the 2002 legislative elections.

In Oct. 2005 the death of two youths of African origin led to several days of nationwide rioting in immigrant ghettoes, prompting the government to declare a state of emergency, which was lifted in Jan. 2006.

TERRITORY AND POPULATION

France is bounded in the north by the English Channel (*La Manche*), northeast by Belgium and Luxembourg, east by Germany, Switzerland and Italy, south by the Mediterranean (with Monaco as a coastal enclave), southwest by Spain and Andorra, and west by the Atlantic Ocean. The total area is 543,965 sq. km. Paris is the most populous agglomeration in Europe, with a population of over 9·7m. More than 14% of the population of Paris are foreign and 19% are foreign born.

Population (1999 census), 58,518,748; density, 108 persons per sq. km. Population estimate, 2002: 59,492,000.

The UN gives a projected population for 2010 of 61·54m.

In 2003, 76·3% of the population lived in urban areas.

The growth of the population has been as follows:

Census	Population	Census	Population	Census	Population
1801	27,349,003	1946	40,506,639	1975	52,655,802
1861	37,386,313	1954	42,777,174	1982	54,334,871
1901	38,961,945	1962	46,519,997	1990	56,615,155
1921	39,209,518	1968	49,778,540	1999	58,518,748
1931	41,834,923				

According to the 1999 census, there were 3·26m. people of foreign extraction in France (5·6% of the population). The largest groups of foreigners with residence permits in 1999 were: Portuguese (573,000), Algerians (545,000) and Moroccans (445,000). France's Muslim population, at 5m., is the highest in Europe.

Controls on illegal immigration were tightened in July 1991. Automatic right to citizenship for those born on French soil was restored in 1997 by the new left-wing coalition government. New immigration legislation, which came into force in 1998, brought in harsher penalties for organized traffic in illegal immigrants and extended asylum laws to include people whose lives are at risk from non-state as well as state groups. It also extended nationality at the age of 18 to those born in France of non-French

parents, provided they have lived a minimum of five years in France since the age of 11.

The areas, populations and chief towns of the 22 metropolitan regions at the 1999 census were as follows:

Regions	Area (sq. km)	Population	Chief town
Alsace	8,280	1,734,145	Strasbourg
Aquitaine	41,309	2,908,359	Bordeaux
Auvergne	26,013	1,308,878	Clermont-Ferrand
Basse-Normandie	17,589	1,422,193	Caen
Bourgogne (Burgundy)	31,582	1,610,067	Dijon
Bretagne (Brittany)	27,209	2,906,197	Rennes
Centre	39,151	2,440,329	Orléans
Champagne-Ardenne	25,606	1,342,363	Reims
Corse (Corsica)	8,680	260,196	Ajaccio
Franche-Comté	16,202	1,117,059	Besançon
Haute-Normandie	12,318	1,780,192	Rouen
Île-de-France	12,011	10,925,011	Paris
Languedoc-Roussillon	27,376	2,295,648	Montpellier
Limousin	16,942	710,939	Limoges
Lorraine	23,542	2,310,376	Nancy
Midi-Pyrénées	45,348	2,551,687	Toulouse
Nord-Pas-de-Calais	12,414	3,996,588	Lille
Pays de la Loire	32,082	3,222,061	Nantes
Picardie	19,399	1,857,834	Amiens
Poitou-Charentes	25,809	1,640,068	Poitiers
Provence-Alpes-Côte d'Azur	31,400	4,506,151	Marseilles
Rhône-Alpes	43,698	5,645,407	Lyons

The 22 regions are divided into 96 metropolitan *départements*, which, in 2001, consisted of 36,565 communes.

Populations of the principal conurbations (in descending order of size) and towns at the 1999 census:

	Conurbation	Town
Paris	9,644,507[1]	2,147,857
Marseilles–Aix-en-Provence	1,349,772[2]	807,071
Lyons	1,348,832[3]	453,187
Lille	1,000,900[4]	191,164
Nice	888,784	345,892
Toulouse	761,090	398,423
Bordeaux	753,931	218,948
Nantes	544,932	277,728
Toulon	519,640	166,442
Douai–Lens	518,727	...[5]
Strasbourg	427,245	267,051
Grenoble	419,334	156,203
Rouen	389,862	108,758
Valenciennes	357,395	42,343
Nancy	331,363	105,830
Metz	322,526	127,498
Tours	297,631	137,046
Saint-Étienne	291,960	183,522
Montpellier	287,981	229,025
Rennes	272,263	212,494
Orléans	263,292	116,559
Béthune	259,198	28,522
Clermont-Ferrand	258,541	141,004
Avignon	253,580	88,312
Le Havre	248,547	193,259
Dijon	236,953	153,815
Mulhouse	234,445	112,002
Angers	226,843	156,327
Reims	215,581	191,325
Brest	210,055	156,217
Caen	199,490	117,157
Le Mans	194,825	150,605
Dunkerque	191,173	72,333
Pau	181,413	80,610
Bayonne	178,965	41,778
Limoges	173,299	137,502
Perpignan	162,678	107,241
Amiens	160,815	139,210
Nîmes	148,889	137,740
Saint-Nazaire	136,886	68,616
Annecy	136,815	52,100
Besançon	134,376	122,308

	Conurbation	Town
Thionville	130,480	42,205
Troyes	128,945	62,612
Poitiers	119,371	87,012
Valence	117,448	66,568
Lorient	116,174	61,844
La Rochelle	116,157	80,055
Chambéry	113,457	57,592
Montbéliard	113,059	28,766
Genève–Annemasse	106,673	. . .[6]
Calais	104,852	78,170
Angoulême	103,746	46,324

[1]Including Boulogne-Billancourt (107,042), Argenteuil (95,416), Montreuil (91,146), Versailles (88,476), Saint-Denis (86,871), Nanterre (86,219), Créteil (82,630), Aulnay-sous-Bois (80,315), Vitry-sur-Seine (79,322).
[2]Including Aix-en-Provence (137,067).
[3]Including Villeurbanne (127,299), Vénissieux (56,487).
[4]Including Roubaix (98,039), Tourcoing (94,204).
[5]Including Douai (44,742), Lens (36,823).
[6]Including Annemasse (27,659).

France has 6 national parks, 35 regional national parks and 132 nature reserves.

Languages

The official language is French. Breton and Basque are spoken in their regions. The *Toubon* legislation of 1994 seeks to restrict the use of foreign words in official communications, broadcasting and advertisements (a previous such decree dated from 1975). The Constitutional Court has since ruled that imposing such restrictions on private citizens would infringe their freedom of expression.

SOCIAL STATISTICS

Statistics for calendar years:

	Births	Deaths	Marriages	Divorces
1999	744,791	537,661	286,191	116,813
2000	774,782	530,864	297,922	114,005
2001	770,945	531,073	288,255	112,631
2002	761,630	535,144	279,087	115,861
2003	761,464	552,339	275,963	125,175
2004	767,816[1]	510,532[1]	271,598[1]	—

[1]Provisional.

Live birth rate (2003) was 12·7 per 1,000 population; death rate, 9·2; marriage rate, 4·6; divorce rate, 2·1. 44·3% of births in 2002 were outside marriage. In 1999 the most popular age range for marrying was 25–29 for both males and females. Abortions were legalized in 1975; there were an estimated 205,600 in 2002. Life expectancy at birth, 2003, 75·9 years for males and 83·0 years for females. Annual population growth rate, 1992–2002, 0·4%. In 1999 the suicide rate per 100,000 population was 17·5 (males, 26·1; females, 9·4). Infant mortality, 2001, 4 per 1,000 live births; fertility rate, 2001, 1·8 births per woman. In 2003 France received 59,770 asylum applications (58,970 in 2002 and 54,290 in 2001).

CLIMATE

The northwest has a moderate maritime climate, with small temperature range and abundant rainfall; inland, rainfall becomes more seasonal, with a summer maximum, and the annual range of temperature increases. Southern France has a Mediterranean climate, with mild moist winters and hot dry summers. Eastern France has a continental climate and a rainfall maximum in summer, with thunderstorms prevalent. Paris, Jan. 37°F (3°C), July 64°F (18°C). Annual rainfall 22·9" (573 mm). Bordeaux, Jan. 41°F (5°C), July 68°F (20°C). Annual rainfall 31·4" (786 mm). Lyons, Jan. 37°F (3°C), July 68°F (20°C). Annual rainfall 31·8" (794 mm).

CONSTITUTION AND GOVERNMENT

The Constitution of the Fifth Republic, superseding that of 1946, came into force on 4 Oct. 1958. It consists of a preamble, dealing with the Rights of Man, and 89 articles.

France is a decentralized republic, indivisible, secular, democratic and social; all citizens are equal before the law (Art. 1). National sovereignty resides with the people, who exercise it through their representatives and by referendums (Art. 3). Constitutional reforms of July 1995 widened the range of issues on which referendums may be called. Political parties carry out their activities freely, but must respect the principles of national sovereignty and democracy (Art. 4).

A constitutional amendment of 4 Aug. 1995 deleted all references to the 'community' (*communauté*) between France and her overseas possessions, representing an important step towards the constitutional dismantling of the former French colonial empire.

The head of state is the *President*, who sees that the Constitution is respected; ensures the regular functioning of the public authorities, as well as the continuity of the state; is the protector of national independence and territorial integrity (Art. 5). As a result of a referendum held on 24 Sept. 2000 the President is elected for five years by direct universal suffrage (Art. 6). Previously the term of office had been seven years. The President appoints (and dismisses) a Prime Minister and, on the latter's advice, appoints and dismisses the other members of the government (*Council of Ministers*) (Art. 8); presides over the Council of Ministers (Art. 9); may dissolve the National Assembly, after consultation with the Prime Minister and the Presidents of the two Houses (Art. 12); appoints to the civil and military offices of the state (Art. 13). In times of crisis, the President may take such emergency powers as the circumstances demand; the National Assembly cannot be dissolved during such a period (Art. 16).

Parliament consists of the National Assembly and the Senate. The National Assembly is elected by direct suffrage by the second ballot system (by which candidates winning 50% or more of the vote in their constituencies are elected, candidates winning less than 12·5% are eliminated and other candidates go on to a second round of voting); the Senate is elected by indirect suffrage (Art. 24). Since 1996 the National Assembly has convened for an annual nine-month session. It comprises 577 deputies, elected by a two-ballot system for a five-year term from single-member constituencies (555 in Metropolitan France, 22 in the overseas departments and dependencies), and may be dissolved by the President.

The *Senate* comprises 321 senators elected for nine-year terms (one-third every three years) by an electoral college in each Department or overseas dependency, made up of all members of the Departmental Council or its equivalent in overseas dependencies, together with all members of Municipal Councils within that area. The *Speaker* of the Senate deputizes for the President of the Republic in the event of the latter's incapacity. Senate elections were last held on 26 Sept. 2004.

The *Constitutional Council* is composed of nine members whose term of office is nine years (non-renewable), one-third every three years; three are appointed by the President of the Republic, three by the President of the National Assembly, three by the President of the Senate; in addition, former Presidents of the Republic are, by right, life members of the Constitutional Council (Art. 56). It oversees the fairness of the elections of the President (Art. 58) and Parliament (Art. 59), and of referendums (Art. 60), and acts as a guardian of the Constitution (Art. 61). Its *President* is Pierre Mazeaud (appointed 27 Feb. 2004).

The *Economic and Social Council* advises on Government and Private Members' Bills (Art. 69). It comprises representatives of employers', workers' and farmers' organizations in each Department and Overseas Territory.

Constitutional amendments of 25 March 2003 and 1 March 2005 added provisions for European Union arrest warrants and allowed for a referendum on the European Union constitution.

Ameller, M., *L'Assemblée Nationale*. Paris, 1994

Duhamel, O. and Mény, Y., *Dictionnaire Constitutionnel*. Paris, 1992

Elgie, R., (ed.) *Electing the French President: the 1995 Presidential Election*. Macmillan, London, 1996

National Anthem

'La Marseillaise'; words and tune by C. Rouget de Lisle.

GOVERNMENT CHRONOLOGY

(CD = Democratic Centre; CNIP = National Centre of Independents and Peasants; DL = Liberal Democracy; FNRI = National Federation of Independent Republicans; MRP = People's Republican Movement; PR= Republican Party; PS = Socialist Party; Rad. = Radical Party; RPR = Rally for the Republic; SFIO = French Section of the Workers International; UDF = Union for the French Democracy; UDR = Union of Democrats for the Republic; UDSR = Democratic and Social Union of the Resistance; UDT = Democratic Union of Labour; UDVe = Union of Democrats for the V Republic; UMP = Union for a Popular Movement; UNR = Union for the New Republic; UNR-UDT = Union for the French Republic-Democratic Union of Labour; n/p = non-partisan)

Presidents of the French Republic since the Second World War.

1947–54	SFIO	Vincent Auriol
1954–59	CNIP	René Coty

With the advent of the Fifth Republic the power of the president gained at the expense of the prime minister.

1959–69	UNR, UNR-UDT, UDVe, UDR	Charles de Gaulle
1969	CD	Alain Poher
1969–74	UDR	Georges Pompidou
1974	CD	Alain Poher
1974–81	FNRI, PR-UDF	Valéry Giscard d'Estaing
1981–95	PS	François Mitterrand
1995–	RPR, UMP	Jacques Chirac

Heads of Government since 1944.

Chairmen of the Provisional Government of the French Republic

1944–46	n/p	Charles de Gaulle
1946	SFIO	Félix Gouin
1946	MRP	Georges Bidault
1946–47	SFIO	Léon Blum

Chairmen of the Council of Ministers

1947	SFIO	Paul Ramadier
1947–48	MRP	Robert Schuman
1948	Rad.	André Marie
1948	MRP	Robert Schuman
1948–49	Rad.	Antoine Henri Queuille
1949–50	MRP	Georges Bidault
1950	Rad.	Antoine Henri Queuille
1950–51	UDSR	René Pleven
1951	Rad.	Antoine Henri Queuille
1951–52	UDSR	René Pleven
1952	Rad.	Edgar Faure
1952–53	CNIP	Antoine Pinay
1953	Rad.	René Mayer
1953–54	CNIP	Joseph Laniel
1954–55	Rad.	Pierre Mendès France
1955–56	Rad.	Edgar Faure
1956–57	SFIO	Guy Mollet
1957	Rad.	Maurice Bourgès-Maunoury
1957–58	Rad.	Félix Gaillard
1958	MRP	Pierre Pflimlin
1958–59	UNR	Charles de Gaulle

Prime Ministers

1959–62	UNR	Michel Debré
1962–68	UNR, UNR-UDT, UDVe	Georges Pompidou
1968–69	UDVe, UDR	Maurice Couve de Murville
1969–72	UDR	Jacques Chaban-Delmas
1972–74	UDR	Pierre Messmer
1974–76	UDR	Jacques Chirac
1976–81	n/p, UDF	Raymond Barre
1981–84	PS	Pierre Mauroy
1984–86	PS	Laurent Fabius
1986–88	RPR	Jacques Chirac
1988–91	PS	Michel Rocard
1991–92	PS	Edith Cresson
1992–93	PS	Pierre Bérégovoy
1993–95	RPR	Édouard Balladur
1995–97	RPR	Alain Juppé
1997–2002	PS	Lionel Jospin
2002–05	DL, UMP	Jean-Pierre Raffarin
2005–	UMP	Dominique de Villepin

RECENT ELECTIONS

At the first round of presidential elections on 21 April 2002 Jacques Chirac gained the largest number of votes (19·87% of those cast) against 15 opponents. His nearest rivals were the National Front leader Jean-Marie Le Pen, who came second with 16·86% of votes cast, and incumbent prime minister Lionel Jospin, with 16·17%. The result caused a series of anti-Le Pen protest rallies across France. Socialist leaders urged their supporters to vote for Chirac in the second round run-off between Chirac and Le Pen in order that the extreme right-wing leader might be kept from gaining power. In the second round of voting, held on 5 May 2002, Jacques Chirac won a second consecutive presidential term in a landslide victory, with 82·21% of votes cast against 17·79% for Le Pen. Turnout was 79·7% in the second round (71·6% in the first round).

Elections to the National Assembly were held on 9 and 16 June 2002. The Union for the Presidential Majority (UMP)—formed by the Rassemblement pour la République (Rally for the Republic) and the Démocratie Libérale (Liberal Democracy)—the allies of President Jacques Chirac, gained an overwhelming parliamentary majority with 357 seats, winning 33·7% of votes cast; the Socialist Party (PS), 140 seats with 24·1%; the Union for French Democracy (UDF), 29 seats with 4·8%; the Communist Party (PCF), 21 seats with 4·8%; the Left Radical Party (PRG), 7 seats with 1·5%; the Greens, 3 seats with 4·5%; the Rally for France (RPF), 2 seats with 0·4%; the Movement for France (MPF), 1 seat with 0·8%; others, 17 seats with 14·1%. Despite winning 11·3% of votes cast, the National Front (FN) failed to gain a single seat. The result brought to an end five years of 'cohabitation', with a right-wing president and a socialist prime minister. Only 70 of the 577 deputies elected in June 2002 were women.

Following the election held on 26 Sept. 2004, the Senate was composed of (by group, including affiliates): UMP, 155; the Socialist Group, 97; the Centrist Group, 33; Républicain, Communiste et Citoyen (RCC), 23; Democratic and Social European Rally, 15; Unattached, 8. In Oct. 1998 Christian Poncelet (RPR) was elected *Speaker* for a three-year term. He was re-elected for a further term in Oct. 2001 and again in Oct. 2004.

European Parliament

France has 78 (87 in 1999) representatives. At the June 2004 elections turnout was 43·1% (47·0% in 1999). The PS won 31 seats with 28·9% of votes cast (political affiliation in European Parliament: Party of European Socialists); Union pour un Mouvement Populaire, 17 with 16·6% (European People's Party–European Democrats); UDF, 11 with 12·0% (Alliance of Liberals and Democrats for Europe); the FN, 7 with 9·8% (non-attached); the Greens, 6 with 7·4% (Greens/European Free Alliance); Mouvement pour la France, 3 with 6·7% (Independence and Democracy Group); PCF, 2 with 5·3% (European Unitary Left/Nordic Green Left); Union de la Gauche, 1 with 1·4% (European Unitary Left/Nordic Green Left).

CURRENT ADMINISTRATION

President: Jacques Chirac; b. 1932 (RPR; sworn in 17 May 1995 and re-elected 5 May 2002).

In March 2006 the cabinet comprised:

Prime Minister: Dominique de Villepin; b. 1953 (Union for a Popular Movement; sworn in 31 May 2005).

Minister of State, Minister of the Interior and Land Management: Nicolas Sarkozy.

Minister of the Economy, Finance and Industry: Thierry Breton. *National Education, Higher Education and Research:* Gilles de Robien. *Employment, Labour and Social Cohesion:* Jean-Louis Borloo. *Justice and Keeper of the Seals:* Pascal Clément. *Defence:* Michèle Alliot-Marie. *Foreign Affairs:* Philippe Douste-Blazy. *Health and Solidarity:* Xavier Bertrand. *Transportation, Capital Works, Tourism and Marine Affairs:* Dominique Perben. *Civil Service:* Christian Jacob. *Agriculture and Fisheries:* Dominique Bussereau. *Environment and Sustainable Development:* Nelly Olin. *Culture and Communication:* Renaud Donnedieu de Vabres. *Overseas Departments and Territories:* François Baroin. *Youth, Sport and Community:* Jean-François Lamour. *Small and Medium-Sized Enterprises, Trade, Small-Scale Industry and the Professions:* Renaud Dutreil.

President of the National Assembly: Jean-Louis Debré.

Office of the Prime Minister:
   http://www.premier-ministre.gouv.fr/

CURRENT LEADERS

Jacques Chirac

Position
President

Introduction
President Jacques René Chirac was elected president in 1995 on the ticket of the right-wing Gaullist party, Rassemblement pour la République (Rally for the Republic; RPR), of which he was the founder. He was prime minister under the right-wing Républicains Indépendants president Valéry Giscard d'Estaing between 1974–76 before resigning to form the RPR. Between 1986–88 he was again prime minister under Socialist Party (PS) president François Mitterrand. He was mayor of Paris between 1977–95. In the 2002 presidential elections he stood for re-election as the candidate of the UMP (Union pour la Majorité Presidentielle) right-wing coalition. Following the shock success of National Front candidate Jean-Marie Le Pen, popular opinion rallied around Chirac in the second round run-off, which he won with a landslide majority. He subsequently disbanded the RPR and formalized the UMP as the Union pour un Mouvement Populaire (Union for a Popular Movement). His opposition to US pressure for a war on Iraq in 2003 won him domestic popularity but led to a deterioration of relations with the USA and UK.

The French electorate's rejection in a referendum in May 2005 of the proposed EU constitution was a major political setback for Chirac, prompting his appointment of a new government. Later in the year, confronting the social devastation left by rioting during Oct.–Nov., Chirac asked parliament to extend a national state of emergency and pledged to fight unemployment and discrimination among disadvantaged sections of the population.

Early Life
Chirac was born in Paris on 29 Nov. 1932. The son of a banker, he was educated at the Institut d'Études Politiques de Paris before studying business at a Harvard University summer school. He was in Algeria for his national service between 1956–57. From 1957–59 he studied at the École Nationale d'Administration, the elite training institution for civil servants. As a young man Chirac was inclined to left-wing politics but his sympathies shifted right when he embarked on his career in the civil service. Chirac rose swiftly through the ranks of the civil service, becoming head of department and secretary of state. In 1967 he was elected parliamentary representative of his family's native Corrèze in Limousin, a post he held until he became president in 1995. Chirac was a close ally and protégé of former president Georges Pompidou, who supported Chirac's rise through the party and his election to the National Assembly in 1967. During Pompidou's premiership under the presidency of Charles de Gaulle, Chirac aided Pompidou in resolving the May 1968 student-worker revolts.

Chirac's career advanced further after Pompidou became president. He served as minister for parliamentary relations (1971–72), agriculture minister (1972–74) and minister for the interior (1974). In the 1974 presidential elections Chirac refused to support the candidature of the official Gaullist candidate, Jacques Chaban-Delmas, choosing instead to support the successful right-wing Républicains Indépendants candidate, Valéry Giscard d'Estaing. The latter appointed Chirac prime minister in 1974 but he was soon at odds with the president and resigned in 1976. He then founded the RPR, based on de Gaulle's Rassemblement du Peuple Français (Rally of the French People) party. Between 1976–81 the RPR was well represented in the National Assembly.

In 1977 Chirac was elected Mayor of Paris, the first since the post was abolished in 1871. In 1981 Chirac stood in his first presidential election against François Mitterrand and Giscard d'Estaing. The right divided, Mitterrand won and Chirac came third. Between 1981–86 Chirac led the right-wing opposition in the Assembly. In 1986 the PS lost its majority and Chirac was appointed prime minister in the first *cohabitation* (power sharing). Over the next two years Chirac reversed Mitterrand's policy of nationalization, implementing widespread privatization schemes. In 1988 he stood again for the presidency. In a run-off with Mitterrand, Chirac came second with 46% of votes. Over the next seven years he remained mayor of Paris.

Career in Office
In 1995 Chirac stood for his third presidential election against the PS candidate Lionel Jospin and the prime minister and fellow RPR member Édouard Balladur. The latter had proved a popular prime minister and had the support of the right-wing Union pour la Démocratie Française (Union for the French Democracy). Chirac lost some right-wing support by defending the Maastricht Treaty which allowed for a closer European Union. But with strong campaigning, helped by a financial scandal involving Balladur, he came out ahead in the first round. In the second round run-off with Jospin, Chirac gained 52·6% of votes. Alain Juppé replaced Chirac as RPR president.

The first few months of Chirac's presidency were overshadowed by international condemnation of France for controversial nuclear tests in the Pacific Ocean. Reaction was such that Chile and New Zealand recalled their ambassadors and riots broke out in Tahiti. A poll showed 60% of French people against the testing and Chirac's popularity suffered. The timing of the testing was all the more controversial as it threatened the 1996 Comprehensive Nuclear Test-Ban Treaty.

Chirac went on to end conscription and to reform the military and the health service. To qualify for the European Monetary Union, the government needed to reduce budget deficits. He began a series of spending cuts including a reduction in welfare and a freezing of public-sector wages. Public discontent was coupled with rising unemployment which reached 12·6% by 1997. Chirac dissolved the Assembly and called early elections, hoping to gain support for his policies. The result was the loss of the parliamentary majority to a coalition of Socialists, Communists and Greens. Chirac was forced to appoint the Socialist Lionel Jospin prime minister in a second *cohabitation*.

The end of 2000 was difficult for Chirac. Allegations of corruption centred on the claim that when Chirac was mayor of Paris, bribes from building companies had been taken in exchange for construction and maintenance contracts. An estimated €95m. was extorted, 70% of which went to the RPR, the rest being divided between the PS and the Parti Communiste Français (French Communist Party). In Sept. 2000 a posthumous confession from a former property developer and RPR official, Jean-Claude Méry, claimed the RPR had been bolstered by €5·5–6·5m. a year. Although Chirac as the head of state is exempt from prosecution, his former aide, Michel Roussin, was investigated and imprisoned for refusing to answer questions.

Chirac's chairmanship of the 2000 EU summit in Nice was widely criticized. It was claimed that he was too much concerned with national interest, fighting hard to retain France's voting power against demands for votes to be allocated relative to population.

The 18 March 2001 municipal elections led to a shock left-wing victory in Paris, traditionally held by the right. The alleged corruption of the Chirac years was a major factor. In June 2001 an investigation began into how Chirac spent an alleged 2·4m. francs on family air travel tickets while he was mayor in the early 1990s.

Chirac entered the first round presidential elections in April 2002 expecting to fight Jospin in the second round. But in a shock result, the National Front leader Jean-Marie Le Pen came in second with 16·86% of votes to Chirac's 19·87%. Jospin, who came third with 16·17%, promptly resigned as prime minister and leader of the PS. The result caused a series of anti-Le Pen protest rallies across France and jolted voter apathy for the second round, for which the turnout was 79·7%. Socialist leaders urged their supporters to vote for Chirac and moderate voters, frightened by the prospect of a far-right government, rallied to the president. In a landslide victory, Chirac took 82·21% of votes. The success was consolidated in parliamentary elections the following month, giving Chirac control of policy for the first time in five years. He appointed Jean-Pierre Raffarin as his prime minister.

For his second presidential term, Chirac pledged to tackle crime and bolster national security—both issues which Le Pen had highlighted to his advantage—with increased prison capacity and a strengthened police force. He proposed a business-friendly fiscal policy and a more flexible integration of the 35-hour working week, which had troubled many businesses. He also pledged to cut taxes by a third over his term. On the international stage, Chirac won domestic support but courted US anger for his refusal to support the US stance on Iraq. As one of the five countries in the UN with the power of veto, Chirac held the right to block UN-supported military action in Iraq. His position also found support in Algeria, which he visited in March 2003 on the first official visit by a French head of state since the end of the Franco–Algerian War in 1962. In May 2003 there were widespread strikes in protest at plans to increase pension contributions, raise the retirement age and to reduce benefits.

On Bastille Day 2002 Chirac survived an assassination attempt by a far-right extremist. In 2003 he came under the international spotlight again by threatening to veto any US-brokered UN resolution supporting an armed attack on Iraq. US-led troops invaded Iraq in March 2003 without a clear UN mandate and overthrew the Saddam Hussein regime the following month. France, Germany and Russia were among the most vociferous opponents of the war and the breakdown in relations between the USA and what it called 'Old Europe' led to renewed questions over the role of the UN, NATO and the EU in international politics. However, in May 2003 France voted to accept a UN resolution on Iraq's future which had been jointly proposed by the USA, UK and Spain. Chirac justified this acceptance as France's responsibility to the world, although he continued to emphasize the importance of the UN as an organization to prevent countries acting in isolation. In return for the immediate ending of sanctions, the UN was to co-operate with the occupying forces to form a new government. In addition France would be able to complete longstanding contracts with Iraq.

In July 2003 voters in a referendum in Corsica narrowly rejected plans to increase regional autonomy. Under the proposals, Corsica would have established a single regional assembly (streamlining three existing institutions) and would have won limited control over energy, transport and regional aid. Chirac had declared his support for the motion, but campaigning became dominated by the question of eventual full independence. In the same month Chirac caused consternation among several of the EU's smaller nations by calling for a relaxation of the stability and growth pact rules, under which the budget deficit of euro-zone countries is not to exceed 3% of GDP.

Despite the EU's emphasis on France reducing its deficit, the government endorsed €3·3bn. worth of tax cuts in Sept. 2003. In March 2004 the governing party suffered local election defeats, resulting in the UMP holding on to only one of the 21 mainland regions. Despite the losses, Chirac urged ministers to press on with reforms aiming to boost economic growth, create more jobs and improve the healthcare system.

At the June 2004 European summit clashes occurred between France and the UK as Chirac and Prime Minister Tony Blair disagreed on the proposed new EU constitution and on candidates for the European Commission presidency. Also in June, Chirac rejected tentative US calls for NATO to become more involved in Iraq following the handover of power.

In May 2005 the French electorate voted against the new EU constitution in a referendum. Although it was a bitter defeat for Chirac, he resisted calls to stand down and responded by appointing a new government with Dominique de Villepin as the prime minister. Further discontent with his government was apparent during Oct.–Nov. in a 24-hour national strike against the privatization programme and pension reform plans and in rioting across many French towns and cities. The riots started in the poorer suburbs of Paris before spreading more widely, leading to extensive destruction and the introduction of emergency security powers. Having been criticized for his silence during the riots, Chirac made his first formal speech on the subject as the disturbances subsided in mid-Nov. He confirmed that the government would extend the state of emergency by three months, but also pledged to improve life in the deprived suburbs. Acknowledging that the violence had highlighted a 'profound malaise' in France, he spoke of the need to recognise 'the diversity of French society'.

In Sept. 2005 Chirac spent a few days in hospital after what officials called a vascular incident affecting his sight.

Dominique de Villepin

Position
Prime Minister

Introduction
Dominique de Villepin, a flamboyant former diplomat and poet, was appointed prime minister of France by the president, Jacques Chirac, on 31 May 2005 following the electorate's dramatic rejection in a referendum of the European Union constitution that had been championed by the government. Villepin faces an uphill struggle to revive the French economy and reduce the high

level of unemployment. Critics questioned his ability to unite the country, given that he is a member of the political elite who has never stood for election to public office and with little experience of domestic economic or social policy. Nevertheless, faced with the worst civil unrest in France since the troubles of 1968, he took tough emergency measures in Oct.–Nov. 2005 to deal with widespread rioting across the country.

Early Life
Dominique Marie François René Galouzeau de Villepin was born on 14 Nov. 1953 in Rabat, Morocco (then a French protectorate), the son of a senior civil servant and a businessman. The family moved from Morocco to Caracas, Venezuela, where Villepin attended the French lycée, and then New York, USA.

Villepin attended university in France, first studying literature in Toulouse in the early 1970s, followed by a law degree in Paris at the Institute of Political Studies. His military service included a spell as a naval officer on the aircraft carrier *Clemenceau*. In 1977 he joined the Rassemblement pour la République (RPR), which had been launched the year before by the former prime minister, Jacques Chirac. Villepin consolidated his place among France's governing elite by attending the prestigious École Nationale d'Administration (ENA) in Paris—graduating in May 1980 and being swiftly recruited by the ministry for foreign affairs. He spent three years as an adviser at the department for African and Malagasy affairs, before being posted to Washington, D.C. to work as press officer for the French embassy in 1984. He was responsible for dealing with enquiries on French policy in the Middle East at the time of 'Irangate' and the arms-for-hostages scandal. In 1987 Villepin was promoted to head of the press and information unit at the embassy.

Two years later he was transferred to the French embassy in New Delhi, India, serving as second councillor and then first councillor, before returning to Paris in 1992 to resume work at the ministry for foreign affairs. Villepin was assistant director in the department for African and Malagasy affairs in 1993, the year in which France offered support to the government of its former colony, Algeria, in its 'struggle against terrorism and religious fanaticism'. Later that year he became principal private secretary to Alain Juppé, the minister for foreign affairs. Following Jacques Chirac's victory in the presidential elections of May 1995, Villepin was appointed secretary-general of the presidency of the republic, a post he retained until May 2002. He became one of the president's closest confidants, and is thought to have advised Chirac to dissolve parliament in 1997, a year earlier than necessary, in an attempt to give the by then unpopular prime minister, Juppé, a mandate to see through an economic austerity package. However, Villepin and Chirac misjudged the mood of voters, who delivered an outright majority for the left and forced the appointment of Lionel Jospin as prime minister, heralding five years of *cohabitation* with the left.

When the centre-right regained control of the government in the 2002 legislative elections, Villepin was appointed minister for foreign affairs. He is credited with negotiating a peace settlement between the government and rebels in Côte d'Ivoire, which was enforced by 3,000 French troops. In early 2003, in the build-up to the US-led invasion of Iraq, Villepin became known internationally as one of the war's main opponents, particularly after his impassioned address to the United Nations on 14 Feb. 2003. Less well publicized, however, was his backing for French military intervention in the Central African Republic a few weeks later, following a coup in the former colony.

In a reshuffle in March 2004 Villepin succeeded Nicolas Sarkozy as minister for the interior, internal security and local freedoms. He built on Sarkozy's police service reforms and won plaudits for tightening visa regulations and cracking down on Islamic militancy. When, in a referendum on 29 May 2005, the French public voted against the ratification of the new EU constitution, the government, which had campaigned for the 'yes' vote, was forced to make changes. President Chirac accepted the resignation of his unpopular prime minister, Jean-Pierre Raffarin, on 30 May and immediately appointed Villepin as his successor.

Career in Office
Villepin formally took over from Raffarin in a brief handover ceremony at the prime minister's official residence on 31 May 2005. On 2 June the deputy secretary-general of the Elysée Palace unveiled the new cabinet of 31 ministers appointed by Villepin. In a television interview, Villepin gave himself 100 days to 'restore the confidence of the people', and promised to make reducing France's high rate of unemployment his priority. In his general policy declaration to parliament on 8 June, Villepin restated his desire to 'win the battle for jobs'. He added that France, as 'a founding country, will occupy a full place in the European Union. It will respect its commitments. It will continue to pull the European adventure upwards ….. Europe has been built on the economy and pragmatism. People are now demanding more humanity and more protection: greater job security, increased attention to environmental issues, better defence of the values of respect and equal opportunities.' He continued: 'The meaning of Europe can be found in these values. It cannot be constructed through market forces alone'. Villepin's speech was followed by a vote of confidence from the National Assembly which he won by 363 votes to 178 (with 4 abstentions).

In Sept. 2005 Villepin announced his economic recovery plan. This included proposals for tax reform, financial incentives to encourage job seekers and to reduce the numbers of people receiving state benefits, and tighter controls on welfare payments. He also introduced new employment contracts with easier-dismissal rules for companies with fewer than 20 employees. Despite opposition from the trade unions, Villepin accelerated the privatization programme, selling a first government stake in Gaz de France. In Oct. there was a national strike in protest at new labour laws and welfare reforms. Later in the month rioting began in the largely immigrant suburbs of northeastern Paris. As the unrest escalated and the destruction spread across the country, Villepin declared a state of emergency, invoking a 1955 law that allowed local authorities to impose curfews and restrict movements in troubled areas. The government extended the state of emergency for three months as the country gradually calmed down after three weeks of unrest. Villepin acknowledged that the government had made mistakes in its treatment of its immigrants and promised to improve life in the suburbs for poorer communities with high levels of unemployment.

DEFENCE

The President of the Republic is the supreme head of defence policy and exercises command over the Armed Forces. He is the only person empowered to give the order to use nuclear weapons. He is assisted by the Council of Ministers, which studies defence problems, and by the Defence Council and the Restricted Defence Committee, which formulate directives.

Legislation of 1996 inaugurated a wide-ranging reform of the defence system over 1997–2002, with regard to the professionalization of the armed forces (brought about by the ending of military conscription and consequent switch to an all-volunteer defence force), the modification and modernization of equipment and the restructuring of the defence industry. In 2003 defence expenditure totalled US$45,695m. (equivalent to US$765 per capita). Defence spending as a proportion of GDP has fallen from 3·9% in 1985 to 2·6% in 2003.

French forces are not formally under the NATO command structure, although France signed the NATO strategic document on eastern Europe in Nov. 1991. The Minister of Defence attends informal NATO meetings which have an agenda of French interest, but not the formal twice-yearly meetings. Since Dec. 1995 France has taken a seat on the NATO Military Committee.

In early 2004 there were 33,441 French military personnel stationed outside France, in a number of countries including Afghanistan, Bosnia-Herzegovina, Côte d'Ivoire, the Democratic Republic of the Congo and Macedonia.

Conscription was for ten months, but France officially ended its military draft on 27 June 2001 with a reprieve granted to all conscripts (barring those serving in civil positions) on 30 Nov. 2001.

Nuclear Weapons

Having carried out its first test in 1960, there have been 210 tests in all. The last French test was in 1996 (this compares with the last UK test in 1991 and the last US test in 1993). The nuclear arsenal consisted of approximately 348 warheads in Jan. 2005 according to the Stockholm International Peace Research Institute.

Arms Trade

France was the world's fourth largest exporter after the USA, the UK and Russia in 2002, with sales worth US$1,800m., or 7·1% of the world total.

Army

The Army comprises the Logistic Force (CFLT), based in Montlhéry with two logistic brigades, and the Land Force Command (CFAT), based in Lille. Apart from the Franco-German brigade, there are 12 brigades, each made up of between four and seven battalions, including one airmobile brigade.

Personnel numbered (2004) 137,000 including 14,700 marines and a Foreign Legion of 7,700. There were 28,000 army reservists in 2004. The 1997–2002 Programming Act provided for the following force at the end of the transitional period: 16,000 officers, 50,000 NCOs, 66,500 army enlistees, 5,500 volunteers, 34,000 civilians and 30,000 reservists. Equipment levels in 2004 included 614 main battle tanks and 418 helicopters.

Gendarmerie

The paramilitary police force exists to ensure public security and maintain law and order, as well as participate in the operational defence of French territory as part of the armed forces. It consisted in 2004 of 101,399 personnel including 7,250 women and 1,966 civilians. It comprises a territorial force of 64,659 personnel throughout the country, a mobile force of 17,715 personnel and specialized formations including the Republican Guard, the Air Force and Naval Gendarmeries, and an anti-terrorist unit.

Navy

The missions of the Navy are to provide the prime element of the French independent nuclear deterrent through its force of strategic submarines; to assure the security of the French offshore zones; to contribute to NATO's missions; and to provide on-station and deployment forces overseas in support of French territorial interests and UN commitments. French territorial seas and economic zones are organized into two maritime districts (with headquarters in Brest and Toulon).

The strategic deterrent force comprises four nuclear-powered strategic-missile submarines, including three new-generation vessels of a much larger class (*Le Triomphant*, *Le Téméraire* and *Le Vigilant*, which entered service in 1997, 1999 and 2004 respectively).

Until it was withdrawn from service in 2000, the *Foch*, of 33,000 tonnes, was the principal surface ship. The 40,000-tonne nuclear-powered replacement *Charles de Gaulle*, which was launched at Brest in 1994, commissioned in Oct. 2000. There is one cruiser, the *Jeanne d'Arc*, completed in 1964 and used in peacetime as a training vessel. Other surface combatants include 12 destroyers and 20 frigates.

The naval air arm, *Aviation Navale*, numbers some 6,800 personnel. Operational aircraft include Super-Etendard nuclear-capable strike aircraft, Etendard reconnaissance aircraft and maritime Rafale combat aircraft. A small Marine force of 1,700 *Fusiliers Marins* provides assault groups.

Personnel in 2004 numbered 44,250, including 10,296 civilians. There were 97,000 reserves in 2002.

Air Force

Created in 1934, the Air Force was reorganized in June 1994. The Conventional Forces in Europe (CFE) Agreement imposes a ceiling of 800 combat aircraft. In 2002 there were 355 combat aircraft, 100 transport aircraft and 290 aircraft for training purposes.

Personnel (2004) 64,000. Air Force reserves in 2002 numbered 79,500.

INTERNATIONAL RELATIONS

France is a member of the UN, WTO, BIS, the Council of Europe, WEU, EU, OSCE, OECD, CERN, Inter-American Development Bank, Asian Development Bank, the Pacific Community, IOM, Antarctic Treaty and the International Organization of the Francophonie. France is a signatory to the Schengen accord, which abolishes border controls between France, Austria, Belgium, Denmark, Finland, Germany, Greece, Iceland, Italy, Luxembourg, the Netherlands, Norway, Portugal, Spain and Sweden.

At a referendum in Sept. 1992 to approve the ratification of the Maastricht treaty on European union of 7 Feb. 1992, 12,967,498 votes (50·81%) were cast for and 12,550,651 (49·18%) against. On 29 May 2005 France became the first European Union member to reject the proposed EU constitution, with 54·67% of votes cast in a referendum against the constitution and only 45·33% in favour.

France is the focus of the *Communauté Francophone* (French-speaking Community) which formally links France with many of its former colonies in Africa. A wide range of agreements, both with members of the Community and with other French-speaking countries, extend to economic and technical matters, and in particular to the disbursement of overseas aid.

ECONOMY

Agriculture accounted for 2·7% of GDP in 2002, industry 24·9% and services 72·4%.

According to the Berlin-based organization *Transparency International*, France ranked 18th in a 2005 survey of countries with the least corruption in business and government. It received 7·5 out of 10 in the corruption perceptions index.

Overview

France enjoys high per capita income and is one of the world's largest economies. Recent growth performance has compared favourably with European neighbours. Since 1998 annual GDP growth marginally outperformed the European Big Four and euro zone averages. Since 2003, however, growth rates have fallen short of OECD and G7 averages. Business sector productivity is high and in the period 1996–2005 labour productivity (output per hour worked) grew at an average annual rate of 1·23% according to the Economist Intelligence Unit, higher than Germany's average of 1·05%. By 2000 labour productivity surpassed that of the USA. Per capita income in France has remained below that of the USA primarily because the French, like other European countries, work shorter hours. Total factor productivity, however, grew at only 0·47% on average over the decade, lower than Germany's average of 0·64%.

The agricultural sector is larger than that of other developed countries. While agriculture accounts for an average 1·3% of GDP among G7 countries, it accounts for twice as much in France and employs 4% of the total workforce. France demanded the formation of the Common Agricultural Policy (CAP), which subsidizes European agriculture, as a condition for establishing the EU and is the largest beneficiary of CAP subsidies. France receives around 25% of all EU farm subsidies, over €40bn. a year (or roughly 40% of the total EU budget). The share of the EU budget devoted to farm subsidies has declined from 70% in the mid-1980s and in 2003 the CAP was reformed so that most subsidies were converted from price supports to direct income payments which distort trade less. France has received international criticism for its resoluteness on the issue of farm support, a major point of contention in EU budget and WTO trade negotiations.

The tax burden in France is one of the highest in Europe (nearly 50% of GDP in 2005). France also has particularly low labour force participation and high structural unemployment. In the mid-1990s the unemployment rate hovered around 12%. In 2001 unemployment fell to 8·5% before rising to 9·6% in 2004. In 2005 unemployment fell marginally but only a third of new jobs were created by the private sector. A two-year job contract introduced by Prime Minister Villepin in 2005 gave employers of fewer than 20 workers more flexibility, but the number of firms and employees that have benefited from the legislation has been limited. Unemployment remains slightly higher than the euro zone average and over 3% higher than the OECD average.

High unemployment is linked to another key challenge for France, reducing its persistently high budget deficit. Since 2002 France has breached the 3% GDP budget deficit limit set by the euro zone's Growth and Stability Pact, causing public debt to exceed 60% of GDP in 2003. There is a high correlation between the country's unemployment cycles and its public deficit levels. Low employment adversely affects the government's revenue stream, increases its welfare expenditure and generates political pressure to use fiscal stimulus to generate employment. According to the IMF some key elements for a general government budget deficit of less than 3% of GDP have been put in place such as 'the announced freeze in real spending of the central government…, the postponement of promised income tax cuts, and the pursuit of a nominal target for health care spending in line with trend GDP growth.' But unless spending is increased, taxes raised or structural reforms implemented to generate higher economic growth, it is unlikely that the budget deficit will significantly reverse the trend of growing public debt. Although France's demographics compare favourably with other developed countries, its population is ageing and, unless public debt is tackled and structural reforms implemented, this will dampen future growth.

The IMF suggests introducing further product market reforms to boost consumer welfare. In July 2005 the IMF wrote: 'the impending modification of rules governing margins in the distribution sector (loi Galland), the successful public flotation of Gaz de France, and the planned opening of the capital of the electricity utility will be helpful. At the same time, it is important to increase the autonomy of regulatory agencies in setting tariffs and combating abuse of market power. The recent focus of the authorities on increasing the transparency of switching costs in the utilities, financial services and telecommunications sectors will foster competition at the benefit of the consumer. Important strides are being made in reducing the administrative burden on businesses, and similar determined efforts in economic deregulation would be welcome.' Service sector liberalization, exposing services markets to competition, is also mentioned by the IMF as likely to raise economic efficiency though such liberalization in the EU context was a primary reason for the rejection of the EU constitution in a referendum in 2005. In recent years the French government has increasingly taken conservative stances on EU issues. In late 2005 the government announced its intention to protect eleven sectors of the economy from foreign acquisitions.

Currency

On 1 Jan. 1999 the euro (EUR) became the legal currency in France; irrevocable conversion rate 6·55957 francs to one euro. The euro, which consists of 100 cents, has been in circulation since 1 Jan. 2002. There are seven euro notes in different colours and sizes denominated in 500, 200, 100, 50, 20, 10 and 5 euros, and eight coins denominated in 2 and 1 euros, then 50, 20, 10, 5, 2 and 1 cents. On the introduction of the euro there was a 'dual circulation' period before the franc ceased to be legal tender on 17 Feb. 2002. Euro banknotes in circulation on 1 Jan. 2002 had a total value of €84·2bn.

Foreign exchange reserves were US$23,338m. in June 2002 and gold reserves 97·25m. troy oz (81·89m. troy oz in 1997). Total money supply was €62,266m. in June 2002. Inflation rates (based on OECD statistics):

1995	1996	1997	1998	1999	2000	2001	2002	2003	2004
1·8%	2·1%	1·3%	0·7%	0·6%	1·8%	1·8%	1·9%	2·2%	2·3%

Franc Zone

13 former French colonies (Benin, Burkina Faso, Cameroon, Central African Republic, Chad, Comoros, the Republic of the Congo, Côte d'Ivoire, Gabon, Mali, Niger, Senegal and Togo), the former Spanish colony of Equatorial Guinea and the former Portuguese colony of Guinea-Bissau are members of a Franc Zone, the CFA (Communauté Financière Africaine). Comoros uses the Comorian franc. The franc CFA is pegged to the euro at a rate of 655·957 francs CFA to one euro. The franc CFP (Comptoirs Français du Pacifique) is the common currency of French Polynesia, New Caledonia and Wallis and Futuna. It is pegged to the euro at 119·3317422 francs CFP to the euro.

Budget

Receipts and expenditure in €1m.:

	2001	2002	2003
Revenue	662,110	674,870	688,770
Expenditure	683,500	723,130	749,390

Principal sources of revenue in 2003: social security contributions, €258·90bn.; taxes on goods and services, €165·61bn.; taxes on income, profits and capital gains, €159·99bn. Main items of expenditure by economic type in 2003: social benefits, €367·54bn.; compensation of employees, €167·86bn.; grants, €70·26bn.

The standard rate of VAT is 19·6% (reduced rates, 5·5% and 2·1%). In 2004 the top rate of income tax was 48·09% and corporate tax was 33·3%.

Ministère de l'Economie, des Finances et du Plan. Le Budget de l'Etat: de la Préparation à l'Exécution. Paris, 1995

Performance

Real GDP growth rates (based on OECD statistics):

1995	1996	1997	1998	1999	2000	2001	2002	2003	2004
2·0%	1·1%	2·3%	3·4%	3·2%	4·1%	2·1%	1·3%	0·9%	2·1%

The real GDP growth rate in 2005 (provisional) according to BNP Paribas was 1·4%. Total GDP in 2004 was US$2,002·6bn.

The Sept. 2005 OECD Economic Survey reported: 'After a weak performance in 2000–03 output growth recovered in 2004, somewhat more strongly than in most euro zone countries. It reached 2¼ per cent but, as in the rest of the euro zone, weaker growth is likely in 2005–06, while unemployment remains stubbornly high, currently around 10%. The origins of poor labour market performance, a central challenge for French policymakers, lie in a combination of measures themselves designed to protect workers, notably a high minimum cost of labour and strict employment protection legislation, as well as high tax wedges on labour; a lack of competition in a number of service sectors further inhibits employment creation.'

Banking and Finance

The central bank and bank of issue is the Banque de France (Governor, Christian Noyer, appointed 2003), founded in 1800, and nationalized on 2 Dec. 1945. The Governor is appointed for a six-year term (renewable once) and heads the nine-member Council of Monetary Policy.

The National Credit Council, formed in 1945 to regulate banking activity and consulted in all political decisions on monetary policy, comprises 51 members nominated by the government; its president is the Minister for the Economy; its Vice-President is the Governor of the Banque de France.

In 2003 there were 1,518 banks and other credit institutions, including 304 banks and 593 investment firms. Four principal deposit banks were nationalized in 1945, the remainder in 1982; the latter were privatized in 1987. The banking and insurance sectors underwent a flurry of mergers, privatizations, foreign investment, corporate restructuring and consolidation in 1997, in both the national and international fields. The largest banks in 2003 by assets were: Crédit Agricole (US$989,863m.), BNP Paribas (US$986,128m.) and Société Générale (US$679,250m.). In 2004 the largest banks by market value were BNP Paribas (US$53,143m.), Société Générale (US$37,405m.) and Crédit Agricole (US$37,069m.).

The state savings organization *Caisse Nationale d'Epargne* is administered by the post office on a giro system. There are also commercial savings banks (*caisses d'epargne et de prévoyance*). Deposited funds are centralized by a non-banking body, the *Caisse de Dépôts et Consignations*, which finances a large number of local authorities and state-aided housing projects, and carries an important portfolio of transferable securities.

France attracted a record US$50·48bn. worth of foreign direct investment in 2001, although in 2002 and 2003 this fell slightly to US$48·91m. and US$46·98m. respectively.

There is a stock exchange (Bourse) in Paris; it is a component of Euronext, which was created in Sept. 2000 through the merger of the Paris, Brussels and Amsterdam bourses.

ENERGY AND NATURAL RESOURCES

Environment
France's carbon dioxide emissions from the consumption and flaring of fossil fuels in 2002 were the equivalent of 6·8 tonnes per capita. An *Environmental Sustainability Index* compiled for the World Economic Forum meeting in Jan. 2005 ranked France 36th in the world, with 55·2%. The index measured the ability of countries to maintain favourable environmental conditions and examined various factors including pollution levels and the use or abuse of natural resources.

Electricity
Electricité de France is responsible for power generation and supply. It was privatized in Nov. 2005 when the government sold a 15% stake in the company. Installed capacity was 116·3m. kW in 2002. Electricity production in 2002: 560·21bn. kWh, of which 80·0% was nuclear. Hydro-electric power contributes about 11·8% of total electricity output. Consumption per capita in 2002 was 8,123 kWh. In 2002 France was the European Union's biggest exporter of electricity with 93·7bn. kWh. Electricité de France is Europe's leading electricity producer, generating 486bn. kWh in 2002.

France, not rich in natural energy resources, is at the centre of Europe's nuclear energy industry. In 2003 there were 59 nuclear reactors in operation—more than in any other country in the world apart from the USA—with a generating capacity of 63,473 MW. Only Lithuania has a higher percentage of its electricity generated through nuclear power.

Oil and Gas
In 2000, 1·4m. tonnes of crude oil were produced. The greater part came from the Parentis oilfield in the Landes. Reserves in 2002 totalled 148m. bbls. The importation and distribution of natural gas is the responsibility of Gaz de France, in which the government holds a 79·45% stake following the company's part privatization in June 2005. Production of natural gas (2000) was 1·6bn. cu. metres. Gas reserves were 14bn. cu. metres in 2002.

Minerals
France is a significant producer of nickel, uranium, iron ore, bauxite, potash, pig iron, aluminium and coal. Société Le Nickel extracts in New Caledonia and is the world's third largest nickel producer.

Coal production in 2002 was 2·1m. tonnes. Coal reserves in Dec. 2001 were 36m. tonnes, but France's last coal mine closed in April 2004. Production of other principal minerals and metals, in 1,000 tonnes: salt (2002), 7,100; aluminium (2001), 462; potash salts (2001), 257; gold (2000), 2,632 kg.

Agriculture
France has the highest agricultural production in Europe. In 2004 the agricultural sector employed about 929,000 people, down from 1,869,000 in 1980. Agriculture accounts for 14·5% of exports and 11·4% of imports.

In 2003 there were 590,000 holdings (average size 45 ha.), down from over 1m. in 1988. Co-operatives account for between 30–50% of output. There were 1,264,000 tractors and 91,000 harvester-threshers in 2001. Although the total number of tractors has been declining steadily in recent years, increasingly more powerful ones are being used. In 2000, 427,000 tractors in use were of 80 hp or higher, compared to 96,000 in 1979.

Of the total area of France (54·9m. ha.), the utilized agricultural area comprised 29·68m. ha. in 2003. 18·30m. ha. were arable, 10·12m. ha. were under pasture and 1·12m. ha. were under permanent crops including vines (0·88m. ha.).

Area under cultivation and yield for principal crops:

	Area (1,000 ha.)			Production (1,000 tonnes)		
	2001	2002	2003	2001	2002	2003
Wheat	4,767	5,230	4,905	31,540	38,934	30,582
Sugarbeets	429	438	402	26,841	33,450	29,238
Maize	1,916	1,831	1,667	16,408	16,440	11,898
Barley	1,705	1,643	1,750	9,799	10,988	9,818
Potatoes	162	162	156	6,078	6,877	6,235
Rapeseeds	1,083	1,036	1,080	2,878	3,317	3,341
Peas	417	339	367	2,134	2,085	2,013
Sunflower seeds	708	616	689	1,584	1,497	1,494

Production of principal fruit crops (in 1,000 tonnes) as follows:

	2001	2002	2003
Apples	2,397	2,478	2,402
Melons	318	282	297
Plums	272	253	247
Pears	260	268	210
Peaches	263	264	192

Total fruit and vegetable production in 2003 was 18,371,000 tonnes. Other important vegetables include tomatoes (834,000 tonnes in 2003), carrots (682,000 tonnes), onions (393,000 tonnes) and cauliflowers (390,000 tonnes). France is the world's leading producer of sugarbeets. Total area under cultivation and yield of grapes from the vine (2003): 851,000 ha.; 6·31m. tonnes. Wine production (2003): 4,735,000 tonnes. France is the largest wine producer in the world, having overtaken Italy in 1999. Consumption in France has declined dramatically in recent times, from nearly 120 litres per person in 1966 to 57 litres per person in 2001.

Figures compiled by the Soil Association, a British organization, show that in 1999 France set aside 220,000 ha. (1% of its agricultural land) for the growth of organic crops, compared to the EU average of 2·2%.

Livestock (2003, in 1,000): cattle, 19,517; pigs, 15,058; sheep, 9,204; goats, 1,214; horses, 345; chickens, 220,000; turkeys, 42,000; ducks, 25,000. Livestock products (2002, in 1,000 tonnes): pork, bacon and ham, 2,346; beef and veal, 1,640; lamb and mutton, 128; horse, 10; poultry, 2,105; eggs, 989. Milk production, 2002 (in 1,000 tonnes): cow, 25,197; goat, 536; sheep, 257. Cheese production, 1,783,000 tonnes. France is the second largest cheese producer in the world after the USA.

Source: SCEES/Agreste

Forestry

Forestry is France's richest natural resource and employs 550,000 people. In 2000 forest covered 15·05m. ha. (27·4% of the land area). In 1990 the area under forests had been 14·23m. ha., or 25·9% of the land area. 65% of forest is privately owned. 51,000 ha. of land in France is reforested annually. Timber production in 2003 was 36·85m. cu. metres.

Fisheries

In 2002 there were 8,088 fishing vessels totalling 229,762 GRT, and (in 1996) 16,556 fishermen. Catch in 2003 was 632,149 tonnes, of which 630,019 tonnes were from marine waters.

INDUSTRY

The leading companies by market capitalization in France in Nov. 2005 were: Total (US$149·2bn.), an integrated oil company; Sanofi-Aventis (US$107·9bn.), a pharmaceuticals and biotechnology company; and BNP Paribas (US$66·0bn.).

The industrial sector employs about 19% of the workforce. In 2000 capacity utilization in industry was approaching 88%. Chief industries: steel, chemicals, textiles, aircraft, machinery, electronic equipment, tourism, wine and perfume.

Industrial production, 2002 (in 1,000 tonnes): distillate fuel oil, 33,301; cement (2001), 20,652; crude steel, 20,300; petrol, 16,970; pig iron, 13,500; residual fuel oil, 10,626; jet fuel, 5,238; sulphuric acid (2001), 2,051; caustic soda (1999), 777. France is one of the biggest producers of mineral water, with 6,283m. litres in 2001; soft drinks production in 2000, 2,276m. litres; beer production in 2001, 1,572m. litres; cigarette production in 2001, 41·8bn. units.

Engineering production (in 1,000 units): passenger cars (2002), 3,009; car tyres (2001), 63,790; television sets (2002), 5,375; radio sets (2002), 3,357.

Labour

Out of an economically active population of 23,529,000 in March 2000, 44·7% were women. By sector, 71·5% worked in services (58·1% in 1980), 24·4% in industry and construction (33·1% in 1980) and 4·1% in agriculture (8·8% in 1980). Some 5m. people work in the public sector at national and local level. It was estimated in 1997 that 51% of households have no-one working in the private sector.

A new definition of 'unemployed' was adopted in Aug. 1995, omitting persons who had worked at least 78 hours in the previous month. The unemployment rate rose from 8·5% in 2001 to 9·6% in 2004, but has declined slightly since then and was down to 9·2% in Dec. 2005. The rate among the under 25s is more than double the overall national rate.

Conciliation boards (Conseils de Prud'hommes) mediate in labour disputes. They are elected for five-year terms by two colleges of employers and employees. There were 2,131 strikes in 2001. Between 1997 and 2001 strikes cost France an average of 71 days per 1,000 employees a year. In July 2005 the minimum wage (SMIC) was raised to €8·03 an hour (€1,217·88 a month for a 35-hour week); it affected about 2·1m. wage-earners in July 2003. The net average annual wage was 130,790 francs (€19,938) in 1999. Retirement age is 60, although the average actual age for retirement is 57. A five-week annual holiday is statutory.

In March 2005 the National Assembly voted by 350 to 135 to amend the working hours law restricting the legal working week to 35 hours, introduced by the former Socialist government between 1998–2000. Under the new proposals employees can, in

agreement with their employer, work up to 48 hours per week. There is no change in the legal working week: any increased hours are on a voluntary basis. The proposal also allows for the increase of overtime hours from 180 to 220 per year, payable at 125% of the normal hourly rate (110% for businesses employing fewer than 20 people until 2008).

Trade Unions

The main trade union confederations are as follows: the Communist-led CGT (Confédération Générale du Travail), founded 1895; the CGT-FO (Confédération Générale du Travail–Force Ouvrière) which broke away from the CGT in 1948; the CFTC (Confédération Française des Travailleurs Chrétiens), founded in 1919 and divided in 1964, with a breakaway group retaining the old name and the main body continuing under the new name of CFDT (Confédération Française Démocratique du Travail); and the CGC-CFE (Confédération Générale des Cadres-Confédération Française de l'Encadrement) formed in 1946, which represents managerial and supervisory staff. The main haulage confederation is the FNTR; the leading employers' association is the CNPF, often referred to as the Patronat. Unions are not required to publish membership figures, but in 2002 the two largest federations, the CFDT and CGT, had an estimated 0·89m. and 0·65m. members respectively.

Although France has the lowest rate of trade union membership in Europe (9% in 2000, compared to 29% in the UK, 30% in Germany and over 90% in Sweden), its trade unionists have considerable clout: they run France's welfare system; staff the country's dispute-settling industrial tribunals (conseils de prud'hommes); and fix national agreements on wages and working conditions. A union call to strike is invariably answered by more than a union's membership.

INTERNATIONAL TRADE

Imports and Exports

In 2003 imports (c.i.f.) totalled US$363·60bn. (US$309·03bn. in 2002); exports (f.o.b.), US$358·81bn. (US$307·48bn. in 2002). Principal imports include: oil, machinery and equipment, chemicals, iron and steel, and foodstuffs. Major exports: metals, chemicals, industrial equipment, consumer goods and agricultural products.

In 2003 chemicals, manufactured goods classified chiefly by material and miscellaneous manufactured articles accounted for 42·3% of France's imports and 39·4% of exports; machinery and transport equipment 36·9% of imports and 42·9% of exports; food, live animals, beverages and tobacco 8·4% of imports and 13·1% of exports; mineral fuels, lubricants and related materials 9·6% of imports and 2·6% of exports; and crude materials, inedible, animal and vegetable oil and fats 2·8% of imports and 2·0% of exports.

In 2002 the chief import sources (as % of total imports) were as follows: Germany, 17·3%; Italy, 9·1%; USA, 7·9%; UK, 7·4%; Spain, 7·2%. The chief export markets (as % of total) were: Germany, 14·5%; UK, 10·4%; Spain, 9·8%; Italy, 9·1%; USA, 8·0%. Imports from fellow European Union members accounted for 60·0% of all imports, and exports to other European Union members constituted 62·3% of the total.

Trade Fairs

Paris ranks as the most popular convention city in the world according to the Union des Associations Internationales (UAI), hosting 2·5% of all international meetings held in 2002.

COMMUNICATIONS

Roads

In 2002 there were 893,100 km of road, including 12,000 km of motorway. France has the longest road network in the EU. Around 90% of all freight is transported by road. In 2002 there were 29,160,000 passenger cars, 5,903,000 lorries and vans,

81,000 buses, and 2,321,000 motorcycles and scooters (1998). The average distance travelled by a passenger car in 2002 was 14,000 km. Road passenger traffic in 1998 totalled 753·1bn. passenger-km. In 2002 there were 7,655 road deaths (12·9 per 100,000 population), down from 8,160 in 2001.

Rail

In 1938 all the independent railway companies were merged with the existing state railway system in a Société Nationale des Chemins de Fer Français (SNCF), which became a public industrial and commercial establishment in 1983. Legislation came into effect in 1997 which vested ownership of the railway infrastructure (track and signalling) in a newly established public corporation, the French Rail Network (RFF). The RFF is funded by payments for usage from the SNCF, government and local subventions and authority capital made available by the state derived from the proceeds of privatization. The SNCF remains responsible for maintenance and management of the rail network. The legislation also envisages the establishment of regional railway services which receive funds previously given to the SNCF as well as a state subvention. These regional bodies negotiate with SNCF for the provision of suitable services for their area. SNCF is the most heavily indebted and subsidized company in France.

In 2001 the RFF-managed network totalled 31,385 km of track (14,464 km electrified). High-speed TGV lines link Paris to the south and west of France, and Paris and Lille to the Channel Tunnel (Eurostar). The high-speed TGV line appeared in 1983; it had 2,110 km of track in 2001, and another 4,000 km planned by 2015. Services from London through the Channel Tunnel began operating in 1994. Rail passenger traffic in 2001 totalled 71·6bn. passenger km and freight tonne-km came to 50·4bn.

The Paris transport network consisted in 2000 of 211·3 km of metro (297 stations), 115 km of regional express railways and 20 km of tramway. There are metros in Lille (28·3 km), Lyons (27·0 km), Marseilles (19·0 km), Rennes (9·4 km) and Toulouse (9·7 km), and tram/light railway networks in Bordeaux (21·3 km), Grenoble (18·5 km), Lille (19·0 km), Lyons (18·7 km), Marseilles (3·0 km), Montpellier (15·2 km), Nantes (38·5 km), Orléans (17·9 km), Rouen (15·8 km), St Étienne (9·3 km) and Strasbourg (28·0 km).

Civil Aviation

The main international airports are at Paris (Charles de Gaulle), Paris (Orly), Bordeaux (Mérignac), Lyons (Satolas), Marseilles-Provence, Nice-Côte d'Azur, Strasbourg (Entzheim), Toulouse (Blagnac), Clermont-Ferrand (Aulnat) and Nantes (Atlantique). The following had international flights to only a few destinations in 2003: Brest, Caen, Carcassonne, Le Havre, Le Touquet, Lille, Pau, Rennes, Rouen and Saint-Étienne. The national airline, Air France, was 54·4% state-owned but merged in Oct. 2003 with the Dutch carrier KLM to form Air France-KLM. In the process the share owned by the French state fell to 44·2%. In Dec. 2004 the government sold off a further 18·4% to reduce its stake to 25·8%, and in the meantime the government's share has come down still further to 18·6%. In 1999 Air France flew 636·8m. km, carrying 37,027,900 passengers (19,141,000 on international flights). In 2001 Charles de Gaulle airport handled 47,930,187 passengers (42,859,153 on international flights) and 1,069,677 tonnes of freight. Only Heathrow handled more international passengers in 2001. Orly was the second busiest airport, handling 23,010,946 passengers (17,336,729 on domestic flights) and 80,491 tonnes of freight. Nice was the third busiest for passengers, with 8,992,373 (4,607,370 on international flights).

In April 2003 Air France announced that Concorde, the world's first supersonic jet which began commercial service in 1976, would be permanently grounded from Oct. 2003.

Shipping

In 2000 the merchant fleet comprised 808 vessels (of 100 gross tons or more) totalling 4·82m. GRT, including 68 tankers of 2·70m. GRT. In 2001 vessels totalling 2,225m. NRT entered ports. In 1993 from a total of 215 vessels (all sizes; GRT: 3,928,000), 212m. tonnes of cargo were unloaded, including 130m. tonnes of crude and refined petroleum products, 93m. tonnes were loaded; total passenger traffic was 29·2m. Chief ports: Marseilles, Le Havre, Dunkerque, Saint-Nazaire and Calais.

France has extensive inland waterways. Canals are administered by the public authority France Navigable Waterways (VNF). In 1993 there were 8,500 km of navigable rivers, waterways and canals (of which 1,647 km were accessible to vessels over 3,000 tons), with a total traffic of 59·8m. tonnes.

Telecommunications

France Télécom became a limited company on 1 Jan. 1997. In 2002 there were 72,579,700 telephone subscribers, or 1,217·0 for every 1,000 inhabitants, and there were 20·7m. PCs in use (equivalent to 347·1 per 1,000 persons). Mobile phone subscribers numbered 38,585,300 in 2002. The largest operators are Orange France, with a 48% share of the market, and SFR, with a 34% share. In 2002 there were 4·3m. fax machines in use. France had 16·97m. Internet users in May 2002—just over 28% of the population.

Postal Services

There were 16,992 post offices in 2003. A total of 17,201m. pieces of mail were processed in 2003, or 286 items per person. La Poste is a public enterprise under autonomous management responsible for mail delivery and financial services.

SOCIAL INSTITUTIONS

Justice

The system of justice is divided into two jurisdictions: the judicial and the administrative. Within the judicial jurisdiction are common law courts including 473 lower courts (*tribunaux d'instance*, 11 in overseas departments), 181 higher courts (*tribunaux de grande instance*, 5 *tribunaux de première instance* in the overseas territories) and 454 police courts (*tribunaux de police*, 11 in overseas departments).

The *tribunaux d'instance* are presided over by a single judge. The *tribunaux de grande instance* usually have a collegiate composition, but may be presided over by a single judge in some civil cases. The *tribunaux de police*, presided over by a judge on duty in the *tribunal d'instance*, deal with petty offences (*contraventions*); correctional chambers (*chambres correctionelles*, of which there is at least one in each *tribunal de grande instance*) deal with graver offences (*délits*), including cases involving imprisonment up to five years. Correctional chambers normally consist of three judges of a *tribunal de grande instance* (a single judge in some cases). Sometimes in cases of *délit*, and in all cases of more serious *crimes*, a preliminary inquiry is made in secrecy by one of 569 examining magistrates (*juges d'instruction*), who either dismisses the case or sends it for trial before a public prosecutor.

Within the judicial jurisdiction are various specialized courts, including 191 commercial courts (*tribunaux de commerce*), composed of tradesmen and manufacturers elected for two years initially, and then for four years; 271 conciliation boards (*conseils de prud'hommes*), composed of an equal number of employers and employees elected for five years to deal with labour disputes; 437 courts for settling rural landholding disputes (*tribunaux paritaires des baux ruraux*, 11 in overseas departments); and 116 social security courts (*tribunaux des affaires de sécurité sociale*).

When the decisions of any of these courts are susceptible of appeal, the case goes to one of the 35 courts of appeal (*cours d'appel*), composed each of a president and a variable number of members. There are 104 courts of assize (*cours d'assises*), each composed of a president who is a member of the court of appeal, and two other magistrates, and assisted by a lay jury of nine members. These try crimes involving imprisonment of over five years. The decisions of the courts of appeal and the courts of assize are final. However, the Court of Cassation (*cour de cassation*) has discretion to verify if the law has been correctly interpreted and if the rules of procedure have been followed exactly. The Court of Cassation may annul any judgment, following which the cases must be retried by a court of appeal or a court of assizes.

The administrative jurisdiction exists to resolve conflicts arising between citizens and central and local government authorities. It consists of 36 administrative courts (*tribunaux administratifs*, of which eight are in overseas departments and territories) and 15 administrative courts of appeal (*cours administratives d'appel*, of which eight are in overseas departments and territories). The Council of State is the final court of appeal in administrative cases, though it may also act as a court of first instance.

Cases of doubt as to whether the judicial or administrative jurisdiction is competent in any case are resolved by a *Tribunal de conflits* composed in equal measure of members of the Court of Cassation and the Council of State. In 1997 the government restricted its ability to intervene in individual cases of justice.

Penal code
A revised penal code came into force on 1 March 1994, replacing the *Code Napoléon* of 1810. Penal institutions consist of: (1) *maisons d'arrêt*, where persons awaiting trial as well as those condemned to short periods of imprisonment are kept; (2) punishment institutions – (a) central prisons (*maisons centrales*) for those sentenced to long imprisonment, (b) detention centres for offenders showing promise of rehabilitation, and (c) penitentiary centres, establishments combining (a) and (b); (3) hospitals for the sick. Special attention is being paid to classified treatment and the rehabilitation and vocational re-education of prisoners including work in open-air and semi-free establishments. Juvenile delinquents go before special judges in 139 (11 in overseas departments and territories) juvenile courts (*tribunaux pour enfants*); they are sent to public or private institutions of supervision and re-education.

The first Ombudsman (*Médiateur*) was appointed for a six-year period in Jan. 1973. The present incumbent is Jean-Paul Delevoye (appointed April 2004).

Capital punishment was abolished in Aug. 1981. In metropolitan France the detention rate in July 2001 was 84·3 prisoners per 100,000 population, up from 50 per 100,000 in 1975. The average period of detention in 2001 was 10·2 months. The principal offences committed were: theft, 27·2%; rape and other sexual assaults, 21·0%; drug-related offences, 16·8%. The population of the 186 penal establishments (three for women) in July 2001 was 49,718 including 1,746 women.

Weston, M., *English Reader's Guide to the French Legal System.* Oxford, 1991

Education
The primary, secondary and higher state schools constitute the 'Université de France'. Its Supreme Council of 84 members has deliberative, administrative and judiciary functions, and as a consultative committee advises respecting the working of the school system; the inspectors-general are in direct communication with the Minister. For local education administration France is divided into 25 academic areas, each of which has an Academic Council whose members include a certain number elected by the professors or teachers. The Academic Council deals with all grades of education. Each is under a Rector, and each is provided with academy inspectors, one for each department.

Compulsory education is provided for children of 6–16. The educational stages are as follows:

1. Non-compulsory pre-school instruction for children aged 2–5, to be given in infant schools or infant classes attached to primary schools.

2. Compulsory elementary instruction for children aged 6–11, to be given in primary schools and certain classes of the *lycées*. It consists of three courses: preparatory (one year), elementary (two years) and intermediary (two years). Children with special needs are cared for in special institutions or special classes of primary schools.

3. Lower secondary education (*Enseignement du premier cycle du Second Degré*) for pupils aged 11–15, consists of four years of study in the *lycées* (grammar schools), *Collèges d'Enseignement Technique* or *Collèges d'Enseignement Général*.

4. Upper secondary education (*Enseignement du second cycle du Second Degré*) for pupils aged 15–18: (1) *Long, général* or *professionel* provided by the *lycées* and leading to the *baccalauréat* or to the *baccalauréat de technicien* after three years; and (2) *Court*, professional courses of three, two and one year are taught in the *lycées d'enseignement professionel*, or the specialized sections of the *lycées*, CES or CEG.

The following table shows the number of schools in 2002–03 and the numbers of teachers and pupils in 2000–01:

	Number of Schools	Teachers	Pupils
Nursery	18,460	132,447	2,443,116
Primary	39,329	204,727	3,837,902
Secondary	11,389	506,304	5,876,047

Higher education is provided by the state free of charge in universities and in special schools, and by private individuals in the free faculties and schools. Legislation of 1968 redefined the activities and workings of universities. Bringing several disciplines together, 780 units for teaching and research (*UER— Unités d'Enseignement et de Recherche*) were formed which decided their own teaching activities, research programmes and procedures for checking the level of knowledge gained. They and the other parts of each university must respect the rules designed to maintain the national standard of qualifications. The UERs form the basic units of the 69 state universities and three national polytechnic institutes (with university status), which are grouped into 25 *Académies*. There are also five Catholic universities in Paris, Angers, Lille, Lyons and Toulouse; and private universities. There were 2,031,743 students in higher education in 2000–01.

Outside the university system, higher education (academic, professional and technical) is provided by over 400 schools and institutes, including the 177 *Grandes Écoles*, which are highly selective public or private institutions offering mainly technological or commercial curricula. These have an annual output of about 20,000 graduates, and in 2004–05 there were also 73,147 students in preparatory classes leading to the *Grandes Écoles*; 230,275 students were registered in the Sections de Techniciens Supérieurs and 100,899 in the Écoles d'Ingénieurs.

The adult literacy rate is at least 99%.

In 2000–01 total expenditure on education came to 5·7% of GNP and represented 11·4% of total government expenditure.

Health
Ordinances of 1996 created a new regional regime of hospital administration and introduced a system of patients' records to prevent abuses of public health benefits. In 2002 there were 4,671 hospitals with a provision of 115 beds per 10,000 persons. There were 196,000 physicians, 40,426 dentists, 397,506 nurses, 60,366 pharmacists and 14,725 midwives in 2001.

In 2003 France spent 10·1% of its GDP on health; public spending in 2002 amounted to 76·0% of the total. A survey published by the World Health Organization in June 2000 to measure health systems in all of the sovereign countries and find which country has the best overall health care ranked France in first place.

The average French adult smokes 4·0 cigarettes a day and drinks 14·1 litres of alcohol a year.

Welfare

An order of 4 Oct. 1945 laid down the framework of a comprehensive plan of Social Security and created a single organization which superseded the various laws relating to social insurance, workmen's compensation, health insurance, family allowances, etc. All previous matters relating to Social Security are dealt with in the Social Security Code, 1956; this has been revised several times. The Chamber of Deputies and Senate, meeting as Congress on 19 Feb. 1996, adopted an important revision of the Constitution giving parliament powers to review annually the funding of social security (previously managed by the trade unions and employers' associations), and to fix targets for expenditure in the light of anticipated receipts.

In 2002 the welfare system accounted for €381bn., representing 35% of GDP. In 1997, 6m. people were dependent on the welfare system. The Social Security budget had a deficit of some 13bn. francs in 1998.

Contributions. The general social security contribution (CSG) introduced in 1991 was raised by 4% to 7·5% in 1997 by the Jospin administration in an attempt to dramatically reduce the deficit on social security spending, effectively almost doubling the CSG. All wage-earning workers or those of equivalent status are insured regardless of the amount or the nature of the salary or earnings. The funds for the general scheme are raised mainly from professional contributions, these being fixed within the limits of a ceiling and calculated as a percentage of the salaries. The calculation of contributions payable for family allowances, old age and industrial injuries relates only to this amount; on the other hand, the amount payable for sickness, maternity expenses, disability and death is calculated partly within the limit of the 'ceiling' and partly on the whole salary. These contributions are the responsibility of both employer and employee, except in the case of family allowances or industrial injuries, where they are the sole responsibility of the employer.

Self-employed Workers. From 17 Jan. 1948 allowances and old-age pensions were paid to self-employed workers by independent insurance funds set up within their own profession, trade or business. Schemes of compulsory insurance for sickness were instituted in 1961 for farmers, and in 1966, with modifications in 1970, for other non-wage-earning workers.

Social Insurance. The orders laid down in Aug. 1967 ensure that the whole population can benefit from the Social Security Scheme; at present all elderly persons who have been engaged in the professions, as well as the surviving spouse, are entitled to claim an old-age benefit.

Sickness Insurance refunds the costs of treatment required by the insured and the needs of dependants.

Maternity Insurance covers the costs of medical treatment relating to the pregnancy, confinement and lying-in period; the beneficiaries being the insured person or the spouse.

Insurance for Invalids is divided into three categories: (1) those who are capable of working; (2) those who cannot work; (3) those who, in addition, are in need of the help of another person. According to the category, the pension rate varies from 30 to 50% of the average salary for the last ten years, with additional allowance for home help for the third category.

Old-Age Pensions for workers were introduced in 1910 and are now fixed by the Social Security Code of 28 Jan. 1972. Since 1983 people who have paid insurance for at least 37½ years (150 quarters) receive at 60 a pension equal to 60% of basic salary. People who have paid insurance for less than 37½ years but no less than 15 years can expect a pension equal to as many 1/150ths of the full pension as their quarterly payments justify. In the event of death of the insured person, the husband or wife of the deceased person receives half the pension received by the latter. Compulsory supplementary schemes ensure benefits equal to 70% of previous earnings. In 2003 the duration an employee had to work in order to qualify for a pension was raised from 37½ years to 40 years, to take effect by 2008.

Family Allowances. A controversial programme of means-testing for Family Allowance was introduced in 1997 by the new administration. The Family Allowance benefit system comprises: (a) Family allowances proper, equivalent to 25·5% of the basic monthly salary for two dependent children, 46% for the third child, 41% for the fourth child, and 39% for the fifth and each subsequent child; a supplement equivalent to 9% of the basic monthly salary for the second and each subsequent dependent child more than ten years old, and 16% for each dependent child over 15 years. (b) Family supplement for persons with at least three children or one child aged less than three years. (c) Ante-natal grants. (d) Maternity grant is equal to 260% of basic salary. Increase for multiple births or adoptions, 198%; increase for birth or adoption of third or subsequent child, 457%. (e) Allowance for specialized education of handicapped children. (f) Allowance for orphans. (g) Single parent allowance. (h) Allowance for opening of school term. (i) Allowance for accommodation, under certain circumstances. (j) Minimum family income for those with at least three children. Allowances (b), (g), (h) and (j) only apply to those whose annual income falls below a specified level.

Workmen's Compensation. The law passed by the National Assembly on 30 Oct. 1946 forms part of the Social Security Code and is administered by the Social Security Organization. Employers are invited to take preventive measures. The application of these measures is supervised by consulting engineers (assessors) of the local funds dealing with sickness insurance, who may compel employers who do not respect these measures to make additional contributions; they may, in like manner, grant rebates to employers who have in operation suitable preventive measures. The injured person receives free treatment, the insurance fund reimburses the practitioners, hospitals and suppliers chosen freely by the injured. In cases of temporary disablement, the daily payments are equal to half the total daily wage received by the injured. In case of permanent disablement, the injured person receives a pension, the amount of which varies according to the degree of disablement and the salary received during the past 12 months.

Unemployment Benefits vary according to circumstances (full or partial unemployment) which are means-tested.

Ambler, J. S., (ed.) *The French Welfare State: Surviving Social and Ideological Change.* New York Univ. Press, 1992

RELIGION

A law of 1905 separated church and state. In 2005 there were 96 Roman Catholic dioceses in metropolitan France and 106 bishops. In May 2005 there were seven cardinals. In 2001 there were 38·69m. Roman Catholics (over 65% of the population), 4·18m. Muslims, 0·72m. Protestants and 0·59m. Jews. France has both the highest number of Muslims and of Jews of any EU member country. An estimated 9·23m. people were non-religious in 2001 and there were 2·38m. atheists.

CULTURE

World Heritage Sites

There are 28 sites under French jurisdiction that appear of the UNESCO world heritage list. They are (with year entered on list): Mont-Saint-Michel and its Bay, the Versailles Palace and

Park, the church and hill at Vézelay (Burgundy), the Decorated Grottoes of the Vézère Valley (Dordogne) and Chartres Cathedral (all 1979); Fontainebleau Palace and Park, Amiens Cathedral, Orange's Roman theatre and Arch de Triomphe, the Roman and Romanesque monuments of Arles and Fontenay's Cistercian Abbey (all 1981); the Royal Saltworks of Arc-et-Senans, Franche-Comté (1982); Nancy's Place Stanislas, Place de la Carrière and Place d'Alliance, the Church of Saint-Savin, Poitou-Charentes, and Cape Girolata, Cape Porto, Scandola Nature Reserve and the Piana Calanches in Corsica (all 1983); the Pont du Gard Roman aqueduct, Languedoc (1985); Strasbourg-Grande île (1988); the Banks of the Seine and Reims' Notre Dame Cathedral, Abbey of Saint-Remi and Tau Palace (both 1991); Bourges Cathedral (1992); Avignon's historic centre (1995); the Canal du Midi, Languedoc (1996); the Historic Fortified City of Carcassonne (1997); Lyons' historic sites and the route of Santiago de Compostela (both 1998); Saint-Emilion Jurisdiction (1999); the Loire Valley between Sully-sur-Loire and Chalonnes (2000); Provins, the Town of Medieval Fairs (2001); and the city of Le Havre (2005).

France also shares the Pyrénées–Mount Perdu site (1997) with Spain and the Belfries of Belgium and France (1998) with Belgium.

Broadcasting

The broadcasting authority (an independent regulatory commission) is the *Conseil Supérieur de l'Audiovisuel (CSA)*. Public radio is provided by *Radio France*, *Réseau France outre-mer* (*RFO*) and *Radio France Internationale* (*RFI*). *Radio France* broadcasts nationwide on *France Info, France Inter, France Musiques, France Culture, France Bleu*; locally via 40 radio stations plus *FIP* and *Le Mouv'*, both of which serve a number of cities; and Europe-wide on *Hector, France Culture Europe* and *Elisa*. In Oct. 1998 there were 3,229 private local radio stations. *Réseau France outre-mer* has two networks, *RFO 1* and *RFO 2*, which broadcast in the French Overseas Departments and Territories. An external service, *Radio France Internationale*, was founded in 1931 (as 'Poste Coloniale'), and broadcasts in 18 languages.

There are three public national TV channels that together form the *France Télévision* group—*France 2, France 3* and *France 5*. Until the mid-1990s, French state controlled television was protected from competition by legislation but under pressure from the private sector and cable companies, the two public channels were re-named and *France Télévision* was created in 1992 to manage them. The third channel, *La Cinquième*, started up in 1994, mainly as an education service and was renamed *France 5* in 2002. The four main terrestrial private channels broadcasting nationwide are: TF1, a former state channel privatized in 1987; M6, established in 1987; Arte, a joint Franco-German cultural channel; and Canal+, a subscription channel. Colour is by SECAM H. French TV broadcasts (terrestrial and satellite) must contain at least 60% EU-generated programmes and 50% of these must be French.

France has been broadcasting via satellite since 1984 with a combined service relaying programmes from Belgian and Swiss as well as French satellites. More satellites have been added including TDF1 and TDF2 broadcasting for Arte, Canal+ and Radio France. Télécom A and Télécom B transmit for the principal TV stations and from 1995, Astra, Eutelsat and Télécom satellites have been broadcasting to the majority of households able to receive television. Digital Television arrived in 1996 and three new satellites, Canal Satellite, Télévision par Satellite and AB Sat, were launched. There were 853 TV channels altogether in 2002. In 2002 there were 8·8m. satellite and cable TV subscribers.

In addition to specialized French national channels, foreign channels are also transmitted to approximately 1·5m. French households via cable.

There were about 55·9m. radio receivers in use in 2000 and 37·5m. TV sets in 2001.

Cinema

There were 5,280 cinema screens in 2002. Attendances totalled 184·5m. in 2002 (130·2m. in 1995); gross box office receipts came to €1,027·9m. in 2002. A record 183 full-length films of French initiative were produced in 2003. In 2003 French films took 35% of the national market.

Press

There were 74 daily papers (11 nationals, 63 provincials) in 2002. The leading dailies are: *Ouest France* (average circulation, 762,000); *Le Parisien* (average circulation, 458,000); *L'Équipe* (average circulation, 384,000); *Le Monde; Le Figaro; Sud Ouest; Voix du Nord; Le Dauphiné Libéré*. The *Journal de Dimanche* is the only national Sunday paper. In 2002 total daily press circulation was 12·7m. copies. In 1999 a total of 49,808 book titles were published.

Tourism

There were 77,012,000 foreign tourists in 2002; tourism receipts in 2002 were US$32·7bn. France is the most popular tourist destination in the world, and receipts from tourism in 2002 were exceeded only in the USA and Spain. The most visited tourist attractions in 2002 were Disneyland Paris (13·1m.), the Eiffel Tower (6·2m.) and the Louvre (5·8m.). Around 11m. foreigners a year visit Paris. Countries of origin of visitors to France in 2002: UK, 19·4%; Germany, 18·6%; Netherlands, 16·4%; Belgium and Luxembourg, 11·0%; Italy, 10·2%; Switzerland, 4·0%; Spain, 3·9%; USA, 3·9%. There were 583,578 classified hotel rooms in 18,563 hotels in 2000. 39,000 new jobs were created in 2000 through tourism.

Festivals

Religious Festivals
Assumption of the Blessed Virgin Mary (15 Aug.) and All Saints Day (1 Nov.) are both Public Holidays.

Cultural Festivals
The Grande Parade de Montmartre, Paris (1 Jan.); the Carnival of Nice (Feb.–March); the Fête de la Victoire (8 May), celebrates victory in World War Two; the May Feasts take place in Nice regularly throughout May; the prestigious Cannes Film Festival, which has been running since 1946, lasts two weeks in mid-May; the Avignon Festival is a celebration of theatre that attracts average attendances of 140,000 each year and runs for most of July; Bastille Day (14 July) sees celebrations, parties and fireworks across the country. The Festival International d'Art Lyrique, focusing on classical music, opera and ballet, takes place in Aix-en-Provence every July. There are also annual festivals of opera at Orange (July–Aug.) and baroque music at Ambronay (Sept.–Oct.).

Libraries

In 2001 there were 3,884 public libraries, one National library and 396 Higher Education Libraries. Public and Higher Education libraries held 152,185,000 volumes.

Museums and Galleries

In 2001, 12m. people visited France's 33 national museums: the Musée du Louvre received 5·16m. visitors; the Château de Versailles, 2·59m.; the Musée d'Orsay, 1·67m.

DIPLOMATIC REPRESENTATIVES

Of France in the United Kingdom (58 Knightsbridge, London, SW1X 7JT)
Ambassador: Gérard Errera.

Of the United Kingdom in France (35 rue du Faubourg St Honoré, 75383 Paris Cedex 08)
Ambassador: Sir John Eaton Holmes, KBE, CVO, CMG.

Of France in the USA (4101 Reservoir Rd, NW, Washington, D.C., 20007)
Ambassador: Jean-David Levitte.

Of the USA in France (2 Ave. Gabriel, Paris)
Ambassador: Craig R. Stapleton.

Of France to the United Nations
Ambassador: Jean-Marc de la Sablière.

FURTHER READING

Institut National de la Statistique et des Études Économiques: *Annuaire statistique de la France* (from 1878); *Bulletin mensuel de statistique* (monthly); *Documentation économique* (bi-monthly); *Economie et Statistique* (monthly); *Tableaux de l'Économie Française* (biennially, from 1956); *Tendances de la Conjoncture* (monthly).

Agulhon, Maurice, *De Gaulle: Histoire, Symbole, Mythe.* Plon, Paris, 2000

Agulhon, M., and Nevill, A., *The French Republic, 1879–1992.* Blackwell, Oxford, 1993

Ardagh, John, *France in the New Century: Portrait of a Changing Society.* Viking, London, 1999

Ardant, P., *Les Institutions de la Ve République.* Paris, 1992

Balladur, E., *Deux Ans à Matignon.* Paris, 1995

Bell, David, *Presidential Power in Fifth Republic France.* Berg, Oxford, 2000.—*Parties and Democracy in France: Parties under Presidentialism.* Ashgate, Aldershot, 2000

Chafer, Tony and Sackur, Amanda, (eds.) *French Colonial Empire and the Popular Front.* Macmillan, London, 1999

Chazal, C., *Balladur.* [in French] Paris, 1993

Cole, Alistair, Le Galès, Patrick and Levy, Jonah, (eds.) *Developments in French Politics 3.* Palgrave Macmillan, Basingstoke, 2005

Cubertafond, A., *Le Pouvoir, la Politique et l'État en France.* Paris, 1993

L'État de la France. Paris, annual

Friend, Julius W., *The Long Presidency: France in the Mitterrand Years, 1981–95.* Westview, Oxford, 1999

Gildea, R., *France since 1945.* OUP, 1996

Guyard, Marius-François, (ed.) *Charles de Gaulle: Mémoires.* Gallimard, Paris, 2000

Hollifield, J. F. and Ross, G., *Searching for the New France.* Routledge, London, 1991

Hudson, G. L., *Corsica.* [World Bibliographic Series, vol. 202] Oxford, 1997

Jack, A., *The French Exception.* Profile Books, London, 1999

Jones, C., *The Cambridge Illustrated History of France.* CUP, 1994

Knapp, Andrew, *Parties and the Party System in France: A Disconnected Democracy?* Palgrave Macmillan, Basingstoke, 2004

Lacoutre, Jean, *Mitterrand: Une histoire de Français.* 2 vols. Seuil, Paris, 1999

Lewis-Beck, Michael S., *The French Voter: Before and After the 2002 Elections.* Palgrave Macmillan, Basingstoke, 2004

MacLean, Mairi, *The Mitterrand Years: Legacy and Evaluation.* Macmillan, London, 1999

McMillan, J. F., *Twentieth-Century France: Politics and Society in France, 1898–1991.* 2nd ed. [of *Dreyfus to De Gaulle*]. Arnold, London, 1992

Menon, Anand, *France, NATO and the Limits of Independence, 1918–97.* Macmillan, London, 1999

Milner, Susan and Parsons, Nick, (eds.) *Reinventing France: State and Society in the 21st Century.* Palgrave Macmillan, Basingstoke, 2004

Noin, D. and White, P., *Paris.* John Wiley, Chichester, 1998

Peyrefitte, Alain, *C'était de Gaulle.* Fayard, Paris, 2000

Popkin, J. D., *A History of Modern France.* New York, 1994

Price, Roger, *A Concise History of France.* CUP, 1993

Raymond, Gino G. (ed.) *Structures of Power in Modern France.* Macmillan, London, 1999

Stevens, Anne, *Government and Politics of France.* Palgrave Macmillan, Basingstoke, 2003

Tiersky, Ronald, *Mitterrand in Light and Shadow.* Macmillan, London, 1999.—*François Mitterrand: The Last French President.* St Martin's Press, New York, 2000

Tippett-Spiritou, Sandy, *French Catholicism.* Macmillan, London, 1999

Turner, Barry, (ed.) *France Profiled.* Macmillan, London, 1999

Zeldin, T., *The French.* Harvill Press, London, 1997

(Also see specialized titles listed under relevant sections, above.)

National Statistical Office: Institut National de la Statistique et des Études Économiques (INSEE), 75582 Paris Cedex 12.
Website: http://www.insee.fr/

DEPARTMENTS AND TERRITORIES OVERSEAS

Départements (DOM) et Territoires (TOM) d'Outre-Mer

GENERAL DETAILS

These fall into six categories: *Overseas Departments* (French Guiana, Guadeloupe, Martinique, Réunion); *Departmental Collectivities* (Mayotte); *Territorial Collectivities* (New Caledonia, St Pierre and Miquelon); *Overseas Countries* (French Polynesia); *Overseas Territories* (Southern and Antarctic Territories, Wallis and Futuna); and *Dependencies* (Bassas da India, Clipperton Island, Europa Island, Glorieuses Islands, Juan de Nova Island, Tromelin Island).

FURTHER READING

Aldrich, R. and Connell, J., *France's Overseas Frontier: Départements et Territoires d'Outre-Mer.* CUP, 1992

OVERSEAS DEPARTMENTS

Départements d'Outre-Mer

French Guiana
Guyane Française

KEY HISTORICAL EVENTS

A French settlement on the island of Cayenne was established in 1604 and the territory between the Maroni and Oyapock rivers finally became a French possession in 1817. Convict settlements were established from 1852, that on Devil's Island being the most notorious; all were closed by 1945. On 19 March 1946 the status of French Guiana was changed to that of an Overseas Department.

TERRITORY AND POPULATION

French Guiana is situated on the northeast coast of Latin America, and is bounded in the northeast by the Atlantic Ocean, west by Suriname, and south and east by Brazil. It includes the offshore Devil's Island, Royal Island and St Joseph, and has an area of 85,534 sq. km. Population at the 1999 census: 157,213. The estimated population in 2005 was 187,000. The UN gives a projected population for 2010 of 209,000. In 1999, 77·6% lived in urban areas. The chief towns are (with 1999 census populations): the capital, Cayenne (50,594 inhabitants), Saint-Laurent-du-Maroni (19,210) and Kourou (19,107). About 58% of inhabitants are of African descent.

The official language is French.

SOCIAL STATISTICS

2002 births, 5,276; deaths, 665. 49% of the population are migrants. Annual growth rate, 1995–2002, 3·5%.

CLIMATE

Equatorial type climate with most of the country having a main rainy season between April and July and a fairly dry period between Aug. and Dec. Both temperatures and humidity are high the whole year round. Cayenne, Jan. 26°C, July 29°C. Annual rainfall 3,202 mm.

CONSTITUTION AND GOVERNMENT

French Guiana is administered by a General Council of 19 members directly elected for five-year terms, and by a Regional Council of 31 members. It is represented in the National Assembly by two deputies; in the Senate by one senator. The French government is represented by a Prefect. There are two *arrondissements* (Cayenne and Saint Laurent-du-Maroni) sub-divided into 22 communes and 19 cantons.

CURRENT ADMINISTRATION

Prefect: Ange Mancini.
   President of the General Council: Pierre Désert (Entente Démocratique).
   President of the Regional Council: Antoine Karam (Parti Socialiste de Guyanais).

ECONOMY

Currency

Since 1 Jan. 2002 the euro has been the official currency as in metropolitan France.

Performance

In 2000 GDP was €1,729m.; GDP per capita was €10,550. Real GDP growth was –10·5% in 2000.

Banking and Finance

The Caisse Centrale de Coopération Economique is the bank of issue. In 2001 commercial banks included the Banque Nationale de Paris-Guyane, Crédit Populaire Guyanais and Banque Française Commerciale.

ENERGY AND NATURAL RESOURCES

Electricity

Installed capacity was 0·1m. kW in 2000. Production in 2000 was about 455m. kWh.

Minerals

Placer gold mining is the most important industry in French Guiana. In 2001, 3,971 kg of gold were produced.

Agriculture

There were 12,000 ha. of arable land in 2001 and 4,000 ha. of permanent crops. Principal crops (2002 estimates, in 1,000 tonnes): rice, 20; cassava, 10; cabbages, 6; sugarcane, 5.
   Livestock (2002): 9,000 cattle; 10,000 pigs; 3,000 sheep; 220,000 poultry (1993).

Forestry

The country has immense forests which are rich in many kinds of timber. In 2000 forests covered 79,260 sq. km, or 89·9% of the total land area. Roundwood production (2001) 139,000 cu. metres. The trees also yield oils, essences and gum products.

Fisheries

The catch in 2001 was an estimated 5,194 tonnes. Shrimp account for nearly 55% of the total catch.

INDUSTRY

Important products include rum, rosewood essence and beer. The island has sawmills and one sugar factory.

Labour

The economically active population (1993) was 46,300. In July 2005 the minimum wage (SMIC) was raised to €8·03 an hour (€1,217·88 a month for a 35-hour week). 8,324 persons were registered unemployed in 1994.

INTERNATIONAL TRADE

Imports and Exports

Imports (2000), €1,910m.; exports (2000), €1,274m. Main import suppliers are France, the USA and Trinidad and Tobago. Leading export markets are France, Switzerland and the USA.

COMMUNICATIONS

Roads

There were (1996) 356 km of national and 366 km of departmental roads. In 2002 there were 30,000 passenger cars and 11,200 commercial vehicles.

Civil Aviation

In 2001 Rochambeau International Airport (Cayenne) handled 386,687 passengers and 5,104 tonnes of freight. The base of the European Space Agency (ESA) is located near Kourou and has been operational since 1979.

Shipping

359 vessels arrived and departed in 1993; 249,160 tonnes of petroleum products and 230,179 tonnes of other products were discharged, and 69,185 tonnes of freight loaded. Chief ports: Cayenne, St-Laurent-du-Maroni and Kourou. There are also inland waterways navigable by small craft.

Telecommunications

In 2001 there were 51,000 telephone main lines (302·2 per 1,000 population). There were 138,200 mobile phone subscribers in 2002 and 70,000 PCs in use (291·6 for every 1,000 persons). In Dec. 2003 there were 31,000 Internet users.

SOCIAL INSTITUTIONS

Justice

At Cayenne there is a *tribunal d'instance* and a *tribunal de grande instance*, from which appeal is to the regional *cour d'appel* in Martinique.
   The population in penal institutions in April 2003 was 5,900 (324 per 100,000 population).

Education

Primary education is free and compulsory. In 2001–02 there were 33,813 pupils at pre-elementary and primary schools, and 21,439 at secondary level. In 1993, 644 students from French Guiana attended the Henri Visioz Institute, which forms part of the University of Antilles-Guyana (8,290 students in 1993).

Health

In 1996 there were 25 hospitals with a provision of 143 beds per 10,000 inhabitants. There were (2003) 319 doctors, 38 dentists, 70 pharmacists, 47 midwives and 371 nursing personnel.

RELIGION

In 2001 approximately 55% of the population was Roman Catholic.

CULTURE

Broadcasting

Radiodiffusion Française d'Outre-Mer-Guyane broadcasts for 133 hours each week on medium- and short-waves, and FM in French. Television is broadcast for 60 hours each week on two channels. There were 104,000 radio receivers in 1997 and 37,000 TV receivers in 1998; colour is by SECAM.

Press

There was (1996) one daily newspaper with a circulation of 1,000, and a second paper published four times a week has a circulation of 5,500.

Tourism

Total number of tourists (2002), 65,000; receipts totalled US$45m.

FURTHER READING

Crane, Janet, *French Guiana*. [Bibliography] ABC-Clio, Oxford and Santa Barbara (CA), 1998

Guadeloupe

KEY HISTORICAL EVENTS

The islands were discovered by Columbus in 1493. The Carib inhabitants resisted Spanish attempts to colonize. A French colony was established on 28 June 1635, and apart from short periods of occupancy by British forces, Guadeloupe has since remained a French possession. On 19 March 1946 Guadeloupe became an Overseas Department.

TERRITORY AND POPULATION

Guadeloupe consists of a group of islands in the Lesser Antilles with a total area of 1,705 sq. km. The two main islands, Basse-Terre (to the west) and Grande-Terre (to the east), are joined by a bridge over a narrow channel. Adjacent to these are the islands of Marie-Galante (to the southeast), La Désirade (to the east), and the Îles des Saintes (to the south); the islands of St Martin and St Barthélemy lie 250 km to the northwest.

Island	Area (sq. km)	1999 populations	Chief town
St Martin[1]	53[2]	29,078	Marigot
St Barthélemy	21	6,852	Gustavia
Basse-Terre	848	172,693	Basse-Terre
Grande-Terre	590	196,767	Pointe-à-Pitre
Îles des Saintes	13	2,998	Terre-de-Bas
La Désirade	22	1,620	Grande Anse
Marie-Galante	158	12,488	Grand-Bourg

[1]Northern part only; the southern third is Dutch.
[2]Includes uninhabited Tintamarre.

Population at the last census (1999), 422,496. The estimated population in 2005 was 448,000. The UN gives a projected population for 2010 of 462,000. An estimated 99·6% of the population were urban in 1999. Population of principal towns (1999): Les Abymes, 63,054; Saint-Martin, 29,078; Pointe-à-Pitre, 20,948; Basse-Terre, 12,410. Basse-Terre is the seat of government, while larger Pointe-à-Pitre is the department's main economic centre and port; Les Abymes is a 'suburb' of Pointe-à-Pitre.

French is the official language, but Creole is spoken by the vast majority, except on St Martin.

SOCIAL STATISTICS

2000: live births, 7,659; deaths, 2,602; marriages (1998), 3,510. 1998 estimates (per 1,000 population): birth rate, 15·5; death rate, 6·0. Annual growth rate, 1995–99, 1·5%. Life expectancy at birth, 1990–95, 71·1 years for males and 78·0 years for females.

CLIMATE

Warm and humid. Pointe-à-Pitre, Jan. 74°F (23·4°C), July 80°F (26·7°C). Annual rainfall 71" (1,814 mm).

CONSTITUTION AND GOVERNMENT

Guadeloupe is administered by a General Council of 42 members directly elected for six-year terms (assisted by an Economic and Social Committee of 40 members) and by a Regional Council of 41 members. It is represented in the National Assembly by four deputies; in the Senate by two senators; and on the Economic and Social Council by one councillor. There are four *arrondissements*, sub-divided into 42 cantons and 34 communes, each administered by an elected municipal council. The French government is represented by an appointed Prefect.

CURRENT ADMINISTRATION

Prefect: Paul Girot de Langlade.
　　President of the General Council: Jacques Gillot.
　　President of the Regional Council: Victorin Lurel.

ECONOMY

Currency

Since 1 Jan. 2002 the euro has been the official currency as in metropolitan France.

Performance

In 2000 GDP was €5,593m.; GDP per capita was €13,071. Real GDP growth was 4·9% in 2000.

Banking and Finance

The Caisse Française de Développement is the official bank of the department. The main commercial banks in 1995 (with number of branches) were: Banque des Antilles Françaises (six), Banque Régionale d'Escompte et de Depôts (five), Banque Nationale de Paris (eight), Crédit Agricole (18), Banque Française Commerciale (eight), Société Générale de Banque aux Antilles (five), Crédit Lyonnais (six), Crédit Martiniquais (three), Banque Inschauspé et Cie (one).

ENERGY AND NATURAL RESOURCES

Electricity

Total production (2000): 1·22bn. kWh. Installed capacity was 0·4m. kW in 2000.

Agriculture

Chief products (2002 estimates, in 1,000 tonnes): sugarcane, 798; bananas, 115; yams, 10; plantains, 9; pineapples, 7. Other fruits and vegetables are also grown for both export and domestic consumption.

　　Livestock (2002): cattle, 85,000; goats, 28,000; pigs, 19,000.

Forestry

In 2000 forests covered 82,000 ha., or 48·5% of the total land area. Timber production in 2001 was 15,000 cu. metres.

Fisheries

Total catch in 2001 amounted to an estimated 10,100 tonnes, exclusively from sea fishing.

INDUSTRY

The main industries are sugar refining, food processing and rum distilling, carried out by small and medium-sized businesses. Other important industries are cement production and tourism.

Labour

The economically active population in 1997 was approximately 125,900. In July 2005 the minimum wage (SMIC) was raised to €8·03 an hour (€1,217·88 a month for a 35-hour week). 46,360 persons were registered unemployed in 1994.

INTERNATIONAL TRADE

Imports and Exports

Total imports (2000): €2,010m.; total exports (2000): €538m. Main export commodities are bananas, sugar and rum. Main import sources in 1998 were France, 63·4%; Germany, 4·4%; Italy, 3·5%; Martinique, 3·4%. Main export markets were France, 68·5%; Martinique, 9·4%; Italy, 4·8%; Belgium-Luxembourg, 3·3%.

COMMUNICATIONS

Roads

In 1996 there were 3,200 km of roads. In 1993 there were 101,600 passenger cars and 37,500 commercial vehicles. There were 83 road-related fatalities in 1996.

Civil Aviation

Air France and six other airlines call at Guadeloupe airport. In 2001 there were 30,043 arrivals and departures of aircraft, and 1,815,285 passengers, at Le Raizet (Pointe-à-Pitre) airport. There are also airports at Marie-Galante, La Désirade, St Barthélemy and St Martin. Most domestic services are operated by Air Caraibes.

Shipping

In 1996 Port Autonome was visited by 2,014 cargo vessels carrying 2·9m. tonnes of freight and by 1,328 passenger ships.

Telecommunications

Guadeloupe had 204,900 main telephone lines in 2000 and 323,500 mobile phone subscribers in 2002. There were 111,000 PCs in use in 2001 and 3,400 fax machines in 1995. Internet users numbered 63,000 in Dec. 2003.

SOCIAL INSTITUTIONS

Justice

There are four *tribunaux d'instance* and two *tribunaux de grande instance* at Basse-Terre and Pointe-à-Pitre; there is also a court of appeal and a court of assizes.

The population in penal institutions in April 2003 was 695 (159 per 100,000 population).

Education

Education is free and compulsory from six to 16 years. In 2001–02 there were 63,310 pupils at pre-elementary and primary schools, and 52,770 at secondary level. In 1993 there were 4,308 students from Guadeloupe at the University of Antilles-Guyana (out of total number of 8,290).

Health

In 1995 there were 13 public hospitals and 16 private clinics. In 2003 there were 924 physicians, 151 dentists, 1,957 nurses, 265 pharmacists and 148 midwives.

RELIGION

The majority of the population are Roman Catholic.

CULTURE

Broadcasting

Radiodiffusion Française d'Outre-Mer broadcasts for 17 hours a day in French. There is a local region radio station, and several private stations. There are two television channels (one regional; one satellite) broadcasting for six hours a day (colour by SECAM V). There were (1997) 113,000 radio and (1999) 118,000 TV receivers.

Press

There was (1996) one daily newspaper with a circulation of 30,000.

Tourism

Tourism is the chief economic activity. In 2001 there were 521,000 tourists (excluding the north islands of St Martin and St Bartholémy). Tourism receipts in 2000 totalled US$418m.

Martinique

KEY HISTORICAL EVENTS

Discovered by Columbus in 1502, Martinique became a French colony in 1635 and apart from brief periods of British occupation the island has since remained under French control. On 19 March 1946 its status was altered to that of an Overseas Department.

TERRITORY AND POPULATION

The island, situated in the Lesser Antilles between Dominica and St Lucia, occupies an area of 1,128 sq. km. Population at last census (1999), 381,427; density, 338 per sq. km. The estimated population in 2005 was 396,000. The UN gives a projected population for 2010 of 401,000. An estimated 94·6% of the population were urban in 1999. Population of principal towns (1999 census): the capital and main port Fort-de-France, 94,049; Le Lamentin, 35,460; Schoelcher, 20,845; Sainte-Marie, 20,098; Rivière-Pilote, 13,057; La Trinité, 12,890.

French is the official language but the majority of people speak Creole.

SOCIAL STATISTICS

2002: live births, 5,446; deaths, 2,681. 2002 estimates per 1,000 population: birth rate, 14·0; death rate, 6·9. Annual growth rate, 1995–2002, 0·8%. Life expectancy at birth, 2002, 75·4 years for males and 82·2 years for females.

CLIMATE

The dry season is from Dec. to May, and the humid season from June to Nov. Fort-de-France, Jan. 74°F (23·5°C), July 78°F (25·6°C). Annual rainfall 72" (1,840 mm).

CONSTITUTION AND GOVERNMENT

The island is administered by a General Council of 45 members directly elected for six-year terms and by a Regional Council of 42 members. The French government is represented by an appointed Prefect. There are four *arrondissements*, sub-divided into 45 cantons and 34 communes, each administered by an elected municipal council. Martinique is represented in the National Assembly by four deputies, in the Senate by two senators and on the Economic and Social Council by one councillor.

CURRENT ADMINISTRATION

Prefect: Yves Dassonville; b. 1948 (took office on 8 Feb. 2004).
   President of the General Council: Claude Lise.
   President of the Regional Council: Alfred Marie-Jeanne.

ECONOMY

Main sectors of activity: tradeable services, distribution, industry, building and public works, transport and telecommunications, agriculture and tourism.

Currency

Since 1 Jan. 2002 the euro has been the official currency as in metropolitan France.

Performance

In 2000 GDP was €5,496m.; GDP per capita was €14,283. Real GDP growth was 0·7% in 2000.

Banking and Finance

The Agence Française de Développement is the government's vehicle for the promotion of economic development in the region. There were five commercial banks, four co-operative banks, one savings bank, five investment companies and two specialized financial institutions in 1999.

ENERGY AND NATURAL RESOURCES

Electricity

A network of 4,262 km of cables covers 98% of Martinique and supplies more than 142,000 customers. Electricity is produced by two fuel-powered electricity stations. Total production (2000): 1·09bn. kWh. Installed capacity (2000): 0·4m. kW.

Agriculture

In 1997 there were 3,035 ha. under sugarcane, 11,200 ha. under bananas and 600 ha. under pineapples. Production (2002 estimates, in 1,000 tonnes): bananas, 310; sugarcane, 207; plantains, 16; pineapples, 10.

Livestock (2002): 25,000 cattle; 34,000 sheep; 35,000 pigs; 17,000 goats; 295,000 poultry (1997).

Forestry

In 2000 there were 47,000 ha. of forest, or 43·9% of the total land area. Timber production in 2001 was 12,000 cu. metres.

Fisheries

The catch in 2001 was 6,200 tonnes, exclusively from sea fishing.

INDUSTRY

Some food processing and chemical engineering is carried out by small and medium-size businesses. There were 14,839 businesses in 2000. There is an important cement industry; 11 rum distilleries and an oil refinery, with an annual treatment capacity of 0·75m. tonnes. Martinique has five industrial zones.

Labour

In 1998, 6·6% of the working population were in agriculture; 15·1% in industry; 23·8% in retail; 34·1% in services; 16·9% in distribution. In July 2005 the minimum wage (SMIC) was raised to €8·03 an hour (€1,217·88 a month for a 35-hour week). The economically active population in 1999 was 166,800. In 1999, 48,667 persons were unemployed.

INTERNATIONAL TRADE

Imports and Exports

Martinique has a structural trade deficit owing to the nature of goods traded. It imports high-value-added goods (foodstuffs, capital goods, consumer goods and motor vehicles) and exports agricultural produce (bananas) and refined oil.

In 2000 imports were valued at €1,958m.; exports at €585m. Main trading partners: France, EU, French Guiana and Guadeloupe. Trade with France accounted for 63% of imports and 61% of exports in 1995.

COMMUNICATIONS

Roads

Martinique has 2,176 km of roads. In 1993 there were 108,300 passenger cars and 32,200 commercial vehicles.

Civil Aviation

There is an international airport at Fort-de-France (Lamentin). In 2001 it handled 1,408,526 passengers and 14,958 tonnes of freight.

Shipping

The island is visited regularly by French, American and other lines. The main sea links to and from Martinique are ensured by CGM Sud. It links Martinique to Europe and some African and American companies. Since 1995 new scheduled links have been introduced between Martinique, French Guiana, Haiti and Panama. These new links facilitate exchanges between Martinique, Latin America and the Caribbean, especially Cuba. In 1993, 2,856 vessels called at Martinique and discharged 80,605 passengers and 1,612,000 tonnes of freight, and embarked 82,119 passengers and 789,000 tonnes of freight.

Telecommunications

In 2001 there were 458,100 telephone subscribers, or 1,145·3 per 1,000 inhabitants, and 54,000 PCs in use (equivalent to 133·3 for every 1,000 persons). There were 319,900 mobile phone subscribers in 2002 and 20,000 fax machines in 1995. The main operator is France Télécom. In Dec. 2003 there were 80,000 Internet users.

SOCIAL INSTITUTIONS

Justice

Justice is administered by two lower courts (*tribunaux d'instance*), a higher court (*tribunal de grande instance*), a regional court of appeal, a commercial court and an administrative court.

The population in penal institutions in April 2003 was 643 (164 per 100,000 population).

Education

Education is compulsory between the ages of six and 16 years. In 2002–03 there were 51,926 pupils in nursery and primary schools, and 47,770 pupils in secondary schools. There were 29 institutes of higher education in 1994. In 1993, 3,670 students from Martinique were registered at the University of Antilles-French Guyana (out of a total of 8,290).

Health

In 1995 there were eight hospitals, three private clinics and seven nursing homes. Total number of beds, 2,100. There were 909 physicians, 148 dentists, 2,229 nurses, 271 pharmacists and 149 midwives in 2003.

RELIGION

In 2001, 87% of the population was Roman Catholic.

CULTURE

Broadcasting

Radio Diffusion Française d'Outre-Mer broadcasts on FM wave, and operates two channels (one satellite). There are also two commercial TV stations. There were 82,000 radio receivers in 1997 and 66,000 TV receivers in 1999 (colour by SECAM V).

Press

In 1996 there was one daily newspaper with a circulation of 30,000.

Tourism

In 2002 there were 447,891 staying visitors and 200,847 cruise ship arrivals. Tourism receipts totalled US$302m. in 2000. In 1999 there were 122 hotels, with 6,051 rooms.

FURTHER READING

Crane, Janet, *Martinique*. [Bibliography] ABC-Clio, Oxford and Santa Barbara (CA), 1995

Réunion

KEY HISTORICAL EVENTS

Réunion (formerly Île Bourbon) became a French possession in 1638 and remained so until 19 March 1946, when its status was altered to that of an Overseas Department.

TERRITORY AND POPULATION

The island of Réunion lies in the Indian Ocean, about 880 km east of Madagascar and 210 km southwest of Mauritius. It has an area of 2,507 sq. km. Population on 1 Jan. 2001: 728,400, giving a density of 291 per sq. km. The estimated population in 2005 was 785,000. An estimated 82·7% of the population were urban in 1999. The capital is Saint-Denis (population, 1999: 132,338); other large towns are Saint-Pierre (69,358), Saint-Paul (88,254) and le Tampon (60,701).

The UN gives a projected population for 2010 of 838,000.

French is the official language, but Creole is also spoken.

SOCIAL STATISTICS

2001: births, 14,541; deaths, 3,740; marriages, 3,344; divorces, 934. Birth rate per 1,000 population (2001), 19·8; death rate, 5·1. Annual growth rate, 1995–99, 1·3%. Life expectancy at birth, 2000, 70·6 years for males and 78·7 years for females. Infant mortality, 1998, 8·0 per 1,000 live births; fertility rate, 1998, 2·8 births per woman.

CLIMATE

There is a sub-tropical maritime climate, free from extremes of weather, although the island lies in the cyclone belt of the Indian Ocean. Conditions are generally humid and there is no well-defined dry season. Saint-Denis, Jan. 80°F (26·7°C), July 70°F (21·1°C). Annual rainfall 56" (1,400 mm).

CONSTITUTION AND GOVERNMENT

Réunion is administered by a General Council of 47 members directly elected for six-year terms, and by a Regional Council of 45 members. Réunion is represented in the National Assembly in Paris by five deputies; in the Senate by three senators; and in the Economic and Social Council by one councillor. There are four *arrondissements* sub-divided into 47 cantons and 24 communes, each administered by an elected municipal council. The French government is represented by an appointed Commissioner.

CURRENT ADMINISTRATION

Prefect: Laurent Cayrel.
President of the General Council: Nassimah Dindar-Mangrolia.
President of the Regional Council: Paul Vergès.

ECONOMY

Currency

Since 1 Jan. 2002 the euro has been the official currency as in metropolitan France. Owing to its geographical location, Réunion was by two hours the first territory to introduce the euro.

Performance

GDP was €7,615m. in 1998; real GDP growth was 4·1% in 1998. GDP per capita (1998) was €10,907.

Banking and Finance

The Institut d'Émission des Départements d'Outre-mer has the right to issue bank-notes. Banks operating in Réunion are the Banque de la Réunion (Crédit Lyonnais), the Banque Nationale de Paris Intercontinentale, the Crédit Agricole de la Réunion, the Banque Française Commerciale (BFC) CCP, Trésorerie Générale and the Banque de la Réunion pour l'Économie et le Développement (BRED).

ENERGY AND NATURAL RESOURCES

Electricity

Production (2001), 1,871m. kWh. Consumption per capita (2000), 2,208 kWh. Installed capacity (2000): 0·4m. kW.

Agriculture

There were 34,000 ha. of arable land in 2001 and 3,000 ha. of permanent crops. Main agricultural products: sugarcane, 1,835,000 (2001); maize, 17,000 (2001 estimate); pineapples, 10,000 (2001 estimate); cabbages, 8,000 (2001 estimate); cauliflowers, 8,000 (2001 estimate).

Livestock (2002): 78,000 pigs, 30,000 cattle, 37,000 goats, 12,000 poultry (1997). Meat production (1999, in tonnes): pork, 11,810; beef and veal, 1,660; poultry, 13,550. Milk production (1999), 19,726 hectolitres.

Forestry

There were 71,000 ha. of forest in 2000, or 28·4% of the total land area. Timber production in 2001 was 36,000 cu. metres.

Fisheries

In 2001 the catch was 5,406 tonnes, almost entirely from marine waters. Deep-sea fishing (1999) is mainly for blue marlin, sailfish, blue-fin tuna and sea bream.

INDUSTRY

The major industries are electricity and sugar. Food processing, chemical engineering, printing and the production of perfume, textiles, leathers, tobacco, wood and construction materials are carried out by small and medium-sized businesses. At the beginning of 1994 there were 9,465 craft businesses employing about 20,000 persons. Production of sugar was 215,600 tonnes in 1999; rum, 74,154 hectolitres (pure alcohol) in 1999.

Labour

The workforce was 284,300 in 2000. In July 2005 the minimum wage (SMIC) was raised to €8·03 an hour (€1,217·88 a month for a 35-hour week). In 2000, 130,400 persons were registered unemployed, a rate of 42·1%. Among the under 25s the unemployment rate is nearly 60%.

INTERNATIONAL TRADE

Imports and Exports

Trade in 1m. French francs:

	1996	1997	1998	1999	2000	2001
Imports	14,214	14,262	15,310	15,828	17,908	18,728
Exports	1,071	1,250	1,215	1,267	1,489	1,502

The chief export is sugar, accounting for 53·7% of total exports (1999). In 1999, 62·2% of trade was with France.

COMMUNICATIONS

Roads

There were, in 2001, 2,914 km of roads and 258,400 registered vehicles. In 1999 the County Council was operating bus services to all towns.

Civil Aviation

In 2001, 712,941 passengers and 17,933 tonnes of freight arrived at, and 707,807 passengers and 8,858 tonnes of freight departed from, Roland Garros Saint-Denis airport.

Shipping

753 vessels visited the island in 2000, unloading 2,783,700 tonnes of freight and loading 482,300 tonnes at Port-Réunion.

Telecommunications

There were 300,000 telephone main lines in 2001, or 410·4 per 1,000 inhabitants, and 32,000 PCs were in use (46·3 per 1,000 persons) in 1999. There were 489,800 mobile phone subscribers in 2002. In 1995 there were 1,900 fax machines. Internet users numbered 180,000 in Dec. 2003.

Postal Services

In 1996 there were 824 post offices.

SOCIAL INSTITUTIONS

Justice

There are three lower courts (*tribunaux d'instance*), two higher courts (*tribunaux de grande instance*), one appeal, one administrative court and one conciliation board.

The population in penal institutions in April 2003 was 1,071 (143 per 100,000 population).

Education

In 2002–03 there were 121,926 pupils in primary schools and 100,020 in secondary schools. In 1999–2000 secondary education was provided in 27 *lycées*, 73 colleges and 13 technical *lycées*. The *Université Française de l'Océan Indien* (founded 1971) had 13,371 students in 1999–2000.

Health

In 2000 there were 17 hospitals with 2,734 beds, 1,595 doctors, 364 dentists, 342 pharmacists, 221 midwives and 2,906 nursing personnel.

RELIGION

In 2001, 82% of the population was Roman Catholic.

CULTURE

Broadcasting

Radiodiffusion Française d'Outre-Mer broadcasts in French on medium- and short-waves for more than 18 hours a day. There are two national television channels (*RFD1* and *Tempo*) and three independent channels (*Antenne Réunion, Canal Réunion/Canal + and Parabole Réunion*). Colour transmission is by SECAM V. There were 130,000 TV receivers in 1998 and 173,000 radio receivers in 1997.

Press

There were (2000) three daily newspapers (*Quotidien, Journal de l'Île, Témoignages*), two weekly (*Visu, Télé Magazine*), three monthly (*Memento, Via, l'Eco Austral*) and two fortnightly magazines (*Leader* and *Attitude*), with a combined circulation of 57,000.

Tourism

Tourism is a major resource industry. There were 430,000 visitors in 2000 (81·6% French). Receipts (2000) totalled €276m. In Jan. 2001 accommodation included 60 hotels, 126 country lodges (*gîtes ruraux*), 269 bed and breakfast houses, 22 stopover lodges (*gîtes d'étape*) and 22 mountain huts.

FURTHER READING

Institut National de la Statistique et des Etudes Économiques: *Tableau Économique de la Réunion*. Paris (annual)

Bertile, W., *Atlas Thématique et Régional*. Réunion, 1990

DEPARTMENTAL COLLECTIVITIES

Collectivités Départementales

Mayotte

KEY HISTORICAL EVENTS

Mayotte was a French colony from 1843 until 1914 when it was attached, with the other Comoro islands, to the government-general of Madagascar. The Comoro group was granted administrative autonomy within the French Republic and became an Overseas Territory. When the other three islands voted to become independent (as the Comoro state) in 1974, Mayotte voted against and remained a French dependency. In Dec. 1976 it became a Territorial Collectivity. On 11 July 2001 Mayotte became a Departmental Collectivity—a constitutional innovation—as a result of a referendum. This was denounced by the Comorian authorities, who claim Mayotte as part of the Union of the Comoro Islands.

TERRITORY AND POPULATION

Mayotte, east of the Comoro Islands, had a total population at the 2002 census of 160,265 (population density of 426 persons per sq. km). The estimated population for 2003 was 183,400. The whole territory covers 376 sq. km (144 sq. miles). It consists of a main island (362 sq. km) with (2003 estimate) 158,500 inhabitants, containing the chief town, Mamoudzou (45,485 inhabitants in 2002); and the smaller island of Pamanzi (11 sq. km) lying 2 km to the east (24,900 estimated for 2003) containing the old capital of Dzaoudzi (12,066 in 2002).

The spoken language is Shimaoré (akin to Comorian, an Arabized dialect of Swahili), but French remains the official, commercial and administrative language.

CLIMATE

The dry and sunniest season is from May to Oct. The hot but rainy season is from Nov. to April. Average temperatures are 27°C from Dec. to March and 24°C from May to Sept.

CONSTITUTION AND GOVERNMENT

The island is administered by a General Council of 19 members, directly elected for a six-year term. The French government is represented by an appointed Prefect. In accordance with the legislation of 11 July 2001 executive powers were transferred from the prefect to the president of the General Council in March 2004. Mayotte is represented by one deputy in the National Assembly and by one member in the Senate. There are 17 communes, including two on Pamanzi.

RECENT ELECTIONS

At the General Council elections on 21 and 28 March 2004 the Union pour un Mouvement Populaire (UMP) won nine seats (with 22·8% of the vote), the Mouvement Départmentaliste Mahorais (MDM) won six (23·3%) and the Mouvement Républicain et Citoyen (MRC) won two (8·9%). The Mouvement Populaire Mahorais (MPM) and Diverse Gauche (DVG) took one seat each. The Parti Socialiste (PS) took 10·2% of the vote but no seats.

CURRENT ADMINISTRATION

Prefect: Jean-Paul Kihl.
　　President of the General Council: Saïd Omar Oili (ind.).

ECONOMY

Currency

Since 1 Jan. 2002 the euro has been the official currency as in metropolitan France.

Banking and Finance

The Institut d'Emission d'Outre-mer and the Banque Française Commerciale both have branches in Dzaoudzi and Mamoudzou.

ENERGY AND NATURAL RESOURCES

Agriculture

The area under cultivation in 1998 was 14,400 ha. Mayotte is the world's second largest producer of ylang-ylang essence. Important cash crops include cinnamon, ylang-ylang, vanilla and coconut. The main food crops (1997) were bananas (30,200 tonnes) and cassava (10,000 tonnes). Livestock (1997): cattle, 17,000; goats, 25,000; sheep, 2,000.

Forestry

There are some 19,750 ha. of forest, of which 1,150 ha. is primary, 15,000 ha. secondary and 3,600 ha. badlands (uncultivable or eroded).

Fisheries

A lobster and shrimp industry has been created. Fish landings in 2001 totalled 5,500 tonnes.

INDUSTRY

Labour

In 1994, 18·5% of the active population was engaged in public building and works. Unemployment rate, 1997, 41%.

INTERNATIONAL TRADE

Imports and Exports

In 1999 imports totalled US$96·2m. and exports US$1·9m. Main export commodities are ylang-ylang, vanilla, cinnamon and coconut.

Main imports sources in 1997: France, 66%; South Africa, 14%. Main export destinations, 1997: France, 80%; Comoros, 15%.

COMMUNICATIONS

Roads

In 2002 there were 224 km of main roads, all of which are paved, and 1,528 motor vehicles.

Civil Aviation

There is an airport at Pamandzi, with scheduled services in 2002 provided to the Comoros, Kenya, Madagascar, Mozambique, Réunion, Seychelles and South Africa.

Shipping

There are services provided by Tratringa and Ville de Sima to Anjouan (Comoros) and Moroni (Comoros).

Telecommunications

In 2001 there were 10,000 telephone main lines, or 69·8 per 1,000 inhabitants. There were 21,700 mobile phone subscribers in 2002.

SOCIAL INSTITUTIONS

Justice

There is a *tribunal de première instance* and a *tribunal supérieur d'appel.*

Education

In 1994 there were 25,805 pupils in nursery and primary schools, and 6,190 pupils at seven *collèges* and one *lycée* at secondary level. There were also 1,922 pupils enrolled in pre-professional classes and professional *lycées.* There is a teacher training college.

Health

There were two hospitals with 100 beds in 1994. In 1985 (latest data available) there were nine doctors, one dentist, one pharmacist, two midwives and 51 nursing personnel.

RELIGION

The population is 97% Sunni Muslim, with a small Christian (mainly Roman Catholic) minority.

CULTURE

Broadcasting

Broadcasting is conducted by *Radio-Télévision Française d'Outre-Mer* (RFO-Mayotte) with one hour a day in Shimaoré. *Télé Mayotte RFO* on Petite Terre transmits from 6 a.m. to around midnight every day. There are two private radio stations. In 2000 there were an estimated 40,000 radio and 5,000 TV receivers; colour is by SECAM.

Press

There are two newspapers: *Kwezi*, published twice a week, and *Mayotte Hebdo*, published once a week.

Tourism

In 2001 there were 23,000 visitors.

TERRITORIAL COLLECTIVITIES

Collectivités Territoriales

New Caledonia

Nouvelle-Calédonie

KEY HISTORICAL EVENTS

From the 11th century Melanesians settled in the islands that now form New Caledonia and dependencies. Capt. James Cook was the first European to arrive on Grande Terre on 4 Sept. 1774. The first European settlers (English Protestants and French Catholics) came in 1840. In 1853 New Caledonia was annexed by France and was used as a penal colony, taking in 21,000 convicts by 1897. Nickel was discovered in 1863, the mining of which provoked revolt among the Kanak tribes. During the Second World War, New Caledonia was used as a military base by the USA. Having fought for France during the war, the Kanaks were awarded citizenship in 1946. Together with most of its former dependencies, New Caledonia was made an Overseas Territory in 1958. It became a Territorial Collectivity under the Nouméa Accord of May 1998, which agreed on a gradual handover of responsibilities and the creation of New Caledonian citizenship. A referendum on independence will be held between 2013 and 2018.

TERRITORY AND POPULATION

The territory comprises Grande Terre (New Caledonia mainland) and various outlying islands, all situated in the southwest Pacific (Melanesia) with a total land area of 18,575 sq. km (7,172 sq. miles). New Caledonia has the second biggest coral reef in the world. The population (2004 census) was 230,789; density, 12·4 per sq. km. The census population of 196,836 in 1996 included 67,151 Europeans (majority French), 86,788 Melanesians (Kanaks), 7,825 Vietnamese and Indonesians, 5,171 Polynesians, 17,763 Wallisians and Futunians, 1,318 others. In 2000 an estimated 60·7% of the population lived in urban areas. The UN gives a projected population for 2010 of 257,000. The capital, Nouméa, had 91,386 inhabitants in 2004.

There are four main islands (or groups of):

Grande Terre An area of 16,372 sq. km (about 400 km long, 50 km wide) with a population (2004 census) of 205,939. A central mountain range separates a humid east coast and a drier temperate west coast. The east coast is predominantly Melanesian; the Nouméa region predominantly European; and the rest of the west coast is of mixed population.

Loyalty Islands 100 km (60 miles) east of New Caledonia, consisting of four large islands: Maré, Lifou, Uvéa and Tiga. It has a total area of 1,981 sq. km and a population (2004) of 22,080.

Isle of Pines A tourist and fishing centre 50 km (30 miles) to the southeast of Nouméa, with an area of 152 sq. km and a population (2004) of 1,840.

Bélep Archipelago About 50 km northwest of New Caledonia, with an area of 70 sq. km and a population (2004) of 930.

The remaining islands are very small and have no permanent inhabitants.

At the 1996 census there were 341 tribes (which have legal status under a high chief) living in 160 reserves, covering a surface area of 392,550 ha. (21% of total land), and representing about 28·7% of the population. 80,443 Melanesians belong to a tribe.

New Caledonia has a remarkable diversity of Melanesian languages (29 vernacular), divided into four main groups (Northern, Central, Southern and Loyalty Islands). There were 53,556 speakers (1996). In 2000 six Melanesian languages were taught in schools.

SOCIAL STATISTICS

2000: live births, 4,564; deaths, 1,075; marriages, 995; divorces, 159. Annual growth rate, 1·65%. Life expectancy at birth, 2001, 70·5 years for males and 76·1 years for females. Infant mortality, 1990–95, 22 per 1,000 live births; fertility rate, 2·7 births per woman.

CLIMATE

2000: Nouméa, Jan. 25·8°C, July 20·4°C (average temperature, 23·8°C; max. 33·5°C, min. 14·3°C). Annual rainfall 1,294 mm.

CONSTITUTION AND GOVERNMENT

Subsequent to the referendum law of 9 Nov. 1988, the organic and ordinary laws of 19 March 1999 define New Caledonia's new statute. Until then an 'Overseas Territory', New Caledonia became a Territorial Collectivity with specific status endowed with wide autonomy.

New Caledonia's institutions comprise the congress, government, economic and social council (CES), the customary senate and customary councils. The congress is made up of 54 members called 'Councillors of New Caledonia', from the provincial assemblies. The 11-member government is elected by congress on a proportional ballot from party lists. The president is elected by majority vote of all members. Each member is allocated to lead and control a given sector in the administration. The government's mandate ends when the mandate of the Congress that elected it comes to an end.

New Caledonia is represented by two deputies and one senator in the French parliament.

RECENT ELECTIONS

On 8 Nov. 1998 there was a referendum for the agreement of the Nouméa accords. Nearly 72% of those who voted approved. Turnout was 74·2%. Voting was restricted to those people resident in New Caledonia before 1998.

In elections to the Territorial Congress on 9 May 2004, the conservative Rassemblement-UMP and Our Future Together (Avenir Ensemble; AE) won 16 seats each, the National Union for Independence/National Liberation Front of the Socialist Kanaks (UNI/FLNKS) 8, the Caledonian Union 7 and the National Front 4. Turnout was 76%.

CURRENT ADMINISTRATION

High Commissioner: Michel Mathieu; b. 1944 (took office on 9 Sept. 2005).

Congress elected Marie-Noëlle Thémereau as president of the government on 10 June 2004 but the resignation of three ministers brought down the government. The congressional vote on 24 June was split between Thémereau and her predecessor, Pierre Frogier. Thémereau won the vote on 29 June.

President: Marie-Noëlle Thémereau; b. 1949 (AE; took office on 10 June 2004).

Vice-President: Déwé Gorodey (UNI/FLNKS).
President of the Congress: Harold Martin (AE).

ECONOMY

Currency

The unit of currency is the franc CFP (XPF), with a parity of 119·3317422 francs CPF to the euro. 211,396m. francs CFP were in circulation in Dec. 2000.

Budget

The budget for 2000 balanced at 74,904m. francs CFP.

Performance

Total GDP was US$2·7bn in 2001.

Banking and Finance

In 2000 the banks were: Banque Calédonienne d'Investissement (BCI), the Bank of Hawaii-Nouvelle-Calédonie (BoH-NC), the Banque Nationale de Paris/Nouvelle-Calédonie (BNP/NC), the Société Générale Calédonienne de Banque (SGCB) and the Caisse d'Epargne.

ENERGY AND NATURAL RESOURCES

Environment

Carbon dioxide emissions from the consumption and flaring of fossil fuels in 2002 were the equivalent of 8·6 tonnes per capita.

Electricity

Production (2000): 1,645m. kWh. Installed capacity was 0·4m. kW in 2000.

Minerals

A wide range of minerals has been found in New Caledonia including: nickel, copper and lead, gold, chrome, gypsum and platinum metals. The nickel deposits are of special value, being without arsenic, and constitute between 20–40% of the world's known nickel resources located on the mainland.

Production of nickel ore (2000): 128,289 tonnes, of which garnieritic ore (108,302 tonnes) and lateritic ore (19,987).

Agriculture

According to the 1996 census, 4,663 persons worked in the agricultural sector. In 2001 there were an estimated 7,000 ha. of arable land and 6,000 ha. of permanent crops. In 1999 livestock numbered: pigs, 38,000; goats, 16,000; deer, 13,000; horses, 11,000; poultry, 877,000; cattle (2000), 122,000. The chief products are beef, pork, poultry, coffee, copra, maize, fruit and vegetables. Production (2002 estimates, in 1,000 tonnes): coconuts, 16; yams, 11; cassava, 3; sweet potatoes, 3.

Forestry

There were 372,000 ha. of forest in 2000, or 20·4% of the total land area. Timber production (2001), 5,000 cu. metres.

Fisheries

Total catch in 2001 was approximately 3,337 tonnes. In 1998 there were 291 fishing boats (1,950 GRT). Aquaculture (consisting mainly of saltwater prawns) provides New Caledonia's second highest source of export income after nickel.

INDUSTRY

Up until the end of the 1970s the New Caledonia economy was almost totally dependent on the nickel industry. Subsequently transformation or processing industries gained in importance to reach levels similar to those in metallurgic industries.

Labour

The employed population (1996) was 64,377. In July 2001 the guaranteed monthly minimum wage was 100,000 francs CFP. In 2002 the unemployment rate stood at 10·5%.

INTERNATIONAL TRADE

Imports and Exports

Trade, 2004, in US$1m. (2003 in brackets): imports f.o.b., 1,473 (1,408); exports f.o.b., 1,009 (783). In 2003, 50·0% of imports came from France, 10·4% from Singapore and 10·2% from Australia. In 2003, 26·0% of exports went to France, 21·4% to Japan and 16·6% to Taiwan. In 1999 machinery and apparatus accounted for 20·0% of imports, food 16·2% and transportation equipment 15·6%. Ferro-nickel accounted for 54·8% of exports, nickel ore 18·8% and nickel matte 13·9%.

COMMUNICATIONS

Roads

In 2000 there were 5,432 km of roads and 83,554 vehicles. In 1999 road accidents injured 983 and killed 58 persons.

Civil Aviation

New Caledonia is connected by air routes with Australia, Japan, Vanuatu, Wallis and Futuna, Fiji Islands and French Polynesia. Regular domestic air services are provided by Air Calédonie from Magenta aerodrome in Nouméa. In 2000 there were 288,322 passengers recorded at Magenta Aerodrome. Internal services with Air Calédonie link Nouméa to a number of domestic airfields.

In 2001, 346,774 passengers and 5,061 tonnes of freight were carried via La Tontouta International Airport, near Nouméa.

Shipping

In 1999, 510 vessels entered New Caledonia, unloading 1,254,662 tonnes of freight, loading 4,007,049 tonnes (including 3·8m. tonnes of nickel ore).

Telecommunications

In 2002 there were 132,000 telephone subscribers (589·3 per 1,000 inhabitants). There were 80,000 mobile phone subscribers in 2002 and 4,600 fax machines. New Caledonia has had Internet access since 1995. In 2002 there were 30,000 Internet users.

Postal Services

In 2003 there were 54 post offices.

SOCIAL INSTITUTIONS

Justice

There are courts at Nouméa, Koné and Wé (on Lifou Island), a court of appeal, a labour court and a joint commerce tribunal. There were 4,054 cases judged in the magistrates courts in 1999; 280 went before the court of appeal, 26 were sentenced in the court of assizes.

The population in penal institutions in April 2003 was 315 (139 per 100,000 population).

Education

In 1999 there were 36,667 pupils and 1,628 teachers in 284 primary schools; 27,877 pupils and 2,212 teachers in 85 secondary schools; and 1,866 students at university with 89 teaching staff. By decree of 1999 the New Caledonia campus of the French University of the Pacific (UFP), established in 1987, was separated from the campus, to become University of New Caledonia (UNC).

Health

In 1999 there were 418 doctors, 106 dentists, 91 pharmacists and 1,209 paramedical personnel. There were 26 socio-medical districts, with four hospitals, three private clinics for a total of 838 beds.

Welfare

There are two main forms of social security cover: Free Medical Aid provides total sickness cover for non-waged persons and low-income earners; the Family Benefit, Workplace Injury and Contingency Fund for Workers in New Caledonia (CAFAT). There are also numerous mutual benefit societies. In 1999 Free Medical Aid had 56,894 beneficiaries; CAFAT had approximately 150,000 beneficiaries.

RELIGION

There were about 130,000 Roman Catholics in 2001.

CULTURE

Broadcasting

Television broadcasting was, for a long time, limited to one or two state-owned stations (today Télé Nouvelle-Calédonie and Tempo). A private channel (Canal+) began broadcasting in 1994, and in late 1999 a digital selection of 13 pay-channels (Canal'Sat) was launched. By the end of 2001 Canal Calédonie had 17,000 Canal'Sat subscribers and 18,000 Canal+ subscribers.

There were 111,000 TV sets in 2001 and 107,000 radio receivers in 1997.

Press

In 2001 there was one daily newspaper, *Les Nouvelles Calédoniennes*.

Tourism

In 2000 New Caledonia welcomed 109,587 tourists (Japan, 23·8%; Australia, 16·4%; France, 16·4%; New Zealand, 8·7%). Spending by tourists totalled US$110m. in 2000. In 1999 there were 82 hotels providing 2,398 beds.

FURTHER READING

Institut de la Statistique et des Etudes Économiques: *Tableaux de l'Économie Calédonienne/New Caledonia: Facts & Figures (TEC 2003)* (every three years); *Informations Statistiques Rapides de Nouvelle-Calédonie* (monthly).

Imprimerie Administrative, Nouméa: *Journal Officiel de la Nouvelle Calédonie.*

Local Statistical Office: Institut Territorial de la Statistique et des Études Économiques, BP 823, 98845 Nouméa.

St Pierre and Miquelon

Îles Saint-Pierre et Miquelon

KEY HISTORICAL EVENTS

The only remaining fragment of the once-extensive French possessions in North America, the archipelago was settled from France in the 17th century. It was a French colony from 1816 until 1976, an overseas department until 1985, and is now a Territorial Collectivity.

TERRITORY AND POPULATION

The archipelago consists of two islands off the south coast of Newfoundland, with a total area of 242 sq. km, comprising the Saint-Pierre group (26 sq. km) and the Miquelon-Langlade group (216 sq. km). The population (1999 census) was 6,316 of whom 3,169 were female. This total population figure represents a decrease of 76 from the 1990 census. Approximately 88% of the population lives on Saint-Pierre. The chief town is St Pierre.

The official language is French.

SOCIAL STATISTICS

2000: births, 51; deaths, 35; marriages, 24; divorces, 7.

CONSTITUTION AND GOVERNMENT

The Territorial Collectivity is administered by a General Council of 19 members directly elected for a six-year term. It is represented in the National Assembly in Paris by one deputy, in the Senate by one senator and in the Economic and Social Council by one councillor. The French government is represented by a Prefect.

RECENT ELECTIONS

At the General Council elections on 19 and 26 March 2000, 11 seats went to Défense des Intérêts de l'Archipel, 3 to Volonté

Insulaire, 2 to Expérience et Innovation, 2 to Cap sur l'Avenir and 1 to Miquelon 2000.

CURRENT ADMINISTRATION

Prefect: Albert Dupuy.
    President of the General Council: Marc Plantegenest.

ECONOMY

Currency
Since 1 Jan. 2002 the euro has been the official currency as in metropolitan France.

Budget
The budget for 2000 balanced at 270m. French francs.

Banking and Finance
Banks include the Banque des Îles Saint-Pierre et Miquelon, the Crédit Saint-Pierrais and the Caisse d'Épargne.

    A Development Agency was created in 1996 to help with investment projects.

ENERGY AND NATURAL RESOURCES

Environment
Carbon dioxide emissions from the consumption and flaring of fossil fuels in 2002 were the equivalent of 10·9 tonnes per capita.

Electricity
Production (2000): 39m. kWh. Installed capacity (2000): 27,000 kW.

Agriculture
The islands, being mostly barren rock, are unsuited for agriculture, but some vegetables are grown and livestock is kept for local consumption.

Fisheries
In June 1992 an international tribunal awarded France a 24-mile fishery and economic zone around the islands and a 10·5-mile-wide corridor extending for 200 miles to the high seas. The 2000 catch amounted to 1,261 tonnes, chiefly snow crab, cod, lumpfish, shark and scallops. A Franco-Canadian agreement regulating fishing in the area was signed in Dec. 1994. The total annual catch has declined dramatically in the past 15 years.

INDUSTRY

In 1994 there were 351 businesses (including 144 services, 69 public works, 45 food trade, 8 manufacturing and 2 agriculture). The main industry, fish processing, resumed in 1994 after a temporary cessation due to lack of supplies in 1992. Diversification activities are in progress (aquaculture, sea products processing, scallops plant).

Labour
The economically active population in 2000 was 3,261. In July 2005 the minimum wage (SMIC) was raised to €8·03 an hour

(€1,217·88 a month for a 35-hour week). In 1996, 11% of the labour force was registered as unemployed.

INTERNATIONAL TRADE

Imports and Exports
Trade in 1m. French francs (2000): imports, 371 (51% from Canada); exports, 50.

COMMUNICATIONS

Roads
In 2000 there were 117 km of roads, of which 80 km were surfaced. There were 2,508 passenger cars and 1,254 commercial vehicles in use.

Civil Aviation
Air Saint-Pierre connects St Pierre with Halifax, Montreal, Sydney (Nova Scotia) and St John's (Newfoundland). In addition, a new airport capable of receiving medium-haul aeroplanes was opened in 1999.

Shipping
St Pierre has regular services to Fortune and Halifax in Canada. In 1999, 893 vessels called at St Pierre; 17,067 tonnes of freight were unloaded and 3,020 tonnes were loaded.

Telecommunications
There were 4,900 telephones in 2000.

SOCIAL INSTITUTIONS

Justice
There is a court of first instance and a higher court of appeal at St Pierre.

Education
Primary instruction is free. In 2000 there were three nursery and five primary schools with 799 pupils; three secondary schools with 564 pupils; and two technical schools with 199 pupils.

Health
In 2000 there was one hospital with 45 beds, one convalescent home with 20 beds, one retirement home with 40 beds; 15 doctors and one dentist.

RELIGION

The population is chiefly Roman Catholic.

CULTURE

Broadcasting
Radio Télévision Française d'Outre Mer (RFO) broadcasts in French on medium waves and on two television channels (one satellite). In 2000 there were 35 cable television channels from Canada and USA. In 2000 there were also approximately 4,900 radio and 4,500 television sets in use.

Tourism
In 2000 there were 10,090 visitors.

OVERSEAS COUNTRIES

Pays d'Outre-Mer

French Polynesia

Territoire de la Polynésie Française

KEY HISTORICAL EVENTS

French protectorates since 1843, these islands were annexed to France 1880–82 to form 'French Settlements in Oceania', which

opted in Nov. 1958 for the status of an overseas territory within the French Community.

TERRITORY AND POPULATION

The total land area of these five archipelagoes, comprising 130 volcanic islands and coral atolls (76 inhabited) scattered over a wide area in the eastern Pacific, is 4,167 sq. km. The population (2002 census) was 245,516; density, 59 per sq. km. At Dec. 1998 French forces stationed in Polynesia numbered 2,119 (based mostly on Tahiti and the Hao atoll) and employed 1,162 Polynesian citizens. In 2000 an estimated 52·7% of the population lived in urban areas.

The UN gives a projected population for 2010 of 274,000.

The official languages are French and Tahitian.

The islands are administratively divided into five *circon-scriptions* as follows:

Windward Islands (Îles du Vent) (184,224 inhabitants, 2002) comprise Tahiti with an area of 1,042 sq. km and 150,707 inhabitants in 1996; Mooréa with an area of 132 sq. km and 11,682 inhabitants in 1996; Maiao (Tubuai Manu) with an area of 9 sq. km; and the smaller Mehetia and Tetiaroa. The capital is Papeete, Tahiti (79,024 inhabitants in 1996, including suburbs).

Leeward Islands (Îles sous le Vent) comprise the five volcanic islands of Raiatéa, Tahaa, Huahine, Bora-Bora and Maupiti, together with four small atolls (Tupai, Mopelia, Scilly, Bellinghausen), the group having a total land area of 404 sq. km and 30,221 inhabitants in 2002. The chief town is Uturoa on Raiatéa. The Windward and Leeward Islands together are called the Society Archipelago (Archipel de la Société). Tahitian, a Polynesian language, is spoken throughout the archipelago and used as a *lingua franca* in the rest of the territory.

Marquesas Islands 12 islands lying north of the Tuamotu Archipelago, with a total area of 1,049 sq. km and 8,712 inhabitants in 2002. There are six inhabited islands: Nuku Hiva, Ua Pou, Ua Uka, Hiva Oa, Tahuata, Fatu Hiva; and six smaller (uninhabited) ones; the chief centre is Taiohae on Nuku Hiva.

Austral or Tubuai Islands lying south of the Society Archipelago, comprise a 1,300 km chain of volcanic islands and reefs. There are five inhabited islands (Rimatara, Rurutu, Tubuai, Raivavae and, 500 km to the south, Rapa), with a combined area of 148 sq. km (6,386 inhabitants in 2002); the chief centre is Mataura on Tubuai.

Tuamotu Archipelago consists of two parallel ranges of 76 atolls (53 inhabited) lying north and east of the Society Archipelago, and has a total area of 690 sq. km, with 15,973 inhabitants in 2002. The most populous atolls are Rangiroa (1,913 inhabitants in 1996), Hao (1,356 in 1996) and Manihi (769 in 1996).

The Mururoa and Fangataufa atolls in the southeast of the group were ceded to France in 1964 by the Territorial Assembly, and were used by France for nuclear tests from 1966–96. The Pacific Testing Centre (CEP) was dismantled in 1998. A small military presence remains to ensure permanent radiological control.

SOCIAL STATISTICS

2000: births, 4,900; deaths, 1,013 (estimate). Annual population growth rate, 2·2%. Life expectancy at birth, 1990–95, 68·3 years for males and 73·8 years for females. Infant mortality, 1990–95, 11 per 1,000 live births; fertility rate, 3·1 births per woman.

CLIMATE

Papeete, Jan. 81°F (27·1°C), July 75°F (24°C). Annual rainfall 83" (2,106 mm).

CONSTITUTION AND GOVERNMENT

Under the 1984 Constitution, the Territory is administered by a Council of Ministers, whose President is elected by the Territorial Assembly from among its own members; the President appoints a Vice-President and 14 other ministers. French Polynesia is represented in the French Assembly by two deputies and in the Senate by one senator. The French government is represented by a High Commissioner. The Territorial Assembly comprises 41 members elected every five years from five constituencies by universal suffrage, using the same proportional representation system as in metropolitan French regional elections. To be elected a party must gain at least 5% of votes cast.

In Dec. 2003 French Polynesia's status was changed from that of an Overseas Territory to an Overseas Country within the French Republic. The statute gives the government in Papeete more powers and allows it to change some laws.

RECENT ELECTIONS

Elections were held on 23 May 2004. The People's Front-Rally for the Republic (TH-RPR), the party of President Gaston Flosse, won 28 seats and the Union for Democracy (UPD) won 27 seats. New Star (Fetia Api) and the Nicole Bouteau List took one seat each. Following by-elections on 13 Feb. 2005 after elections in one of the districts had been declared invalid the TH-RPR and the UPD each held 27 seats and the Alliance for a New Democracy (alliance of New Star and the Nicole Bouteau List) 3 seats. In the presidential vote held on 3 March 2005 in the Territorial Assembly, Oscar Temaru (UPD) defeated Gaston Tong Sang (TH-RPR) by 29 votes to 26.

CURRENT ADMINISTRATION

High Commissioner: Anne Boquet; b. 1952 (took office on 10 Sept. 2005).

President: Oscar Temaru; b. 1944 (UPD; took office for a second time on 3 March 2005).

ECONOMY

Currency

The unit of currency is the franc CFP (XPF). Up to 31 Dec. 1998, its parity was to the French franc: 1 franc CFP = 0·055 French francs; from 1 Jan. 1999 parity was linked to the euro: 119·3317422 francs CPF = one euro.

Budget

Revenues totalled 108·0bn. francs CPF in 2001 and expenditures 140·7bn. francs CPF.

Performance

Total GDP in 2001 was US$3·4bn.

Banking and Finance

There are four commercial banks: Banque de Tahiti, Banque de Polynésie, Société de Crédit et de Développement de l'Océanie and the Banque Westpac.

ENERGY AND NATURAL RESOURCES

Electricity

Production (2000) was 407m. kWh, of which approximately 29% was hydro-electric. Consumption per capita in 2000 was 1,747 kWh.

Oil and Gas

In 1997 over 236,000 tonnes of combustible products were imported (with a value of 346m. French francs), mainly from Australia and Hawaii; 8,600 tonnes of gas was imported.

Agriculture

Agriculture used to be the primary economic sector but now accounts for only a modest 8% (1997) of GDP. Production in 1,000 tonnes (2002 estimates): coconuts, 88; copra, 10; cassava, 6; sugarcane, 3. Livestock (2002): cattle 11,000; pigs 34,000; goats 16,000; poultry (1995) 297,700.

Forestry

In 1999 there was between 4,000 and 5,000 ha. of forest, around half of it exploitable. The industry remains embryonic.

Fisheries

Polynesia has an exclusive zone of 5·2m. sq. km, one of the largest in the world. Catch (2001): 15,404 tonnes, almost exclusively from sea fishing.

INDUSTRY

Some 2,218 industrial enterprises employ 5,800 people. Principal industries include food and drink products, cosmetics, clothing and jewellery, furniture-making, metalwork and shipbuilding.

INTERNATIONAL TRADE

Imports and Exports

French Polynesia imports a great deal and exports very little. Trade, 2004, in US$1m. (2003 in brackets): imports f.o.b., 1,440 (1,530); exports f.o.b., 179 (149).

The chief exports are coconut oil, fish, nono juice, mother of pearl and cultured pearls. Representing 27% of the world market, Polynesia is the world's second largest producer of pearls after Australia.

The major trading partner overall is France, although Japan (66% of pearl exports) is the leading export market. France accounted for nearly 36% of imports and more than 14% of exports in 2001.

COMMUNICATIONS

Roads

There were estimated to be 2,590 km of roads in 1999, 67% bitumenized.

Civil Aviation

The main airport is at Papeete (Tahiti-Faa'a). Air France and nine other international airlines connect Tahiti International Airport with Paris, Auckland, Honolulu, Los Angeles, Osaka, Santiago, Tokyo and many Pacific islands. In 2000 Papeete handled 1,553,132 passengers (849,540 on domestic flights) and 11,429 tonnes of freight.

Shipping

In 1997, 727,000 tonnes of cargo were unloaded and 28,000 tonnes loaded at Papeete's main port. Around 1·4m. people pass through the port each year.

Telecommunications

Number of telephone subscribers in 2002 was 142,500 (593·7 per 1,000 inhabitants); mobile phone subscribers (2002), 90,000. In 2002 there were 4,400 fax machines and 35,000 Internet users.

Postal Services

In 2002 there were 94 post offices.

SOCIAL INSTITUTIONS

Justice

There is a *tribunal de première instance* and a *cour d'appel* at Papeete. The population in penal institutions in April 2003 was 291 (120 per 100,000 population).

Education

In 1998–99 there were 77,300 pupils and 5,200 teachers in 316 schools (46,800 in 255 primary schools; 30,500 in secondary school). The French University of the Pacific (UFP) has a campus on Tahiti. The South Pacific University Institute for Teacher Training (part of UFP) has three colleges: in French Polynesia, Wallis and Futuna, and in Nouméa (New Caledonia), where it is headquartered. In 1997–98, 2,200 students followed university courses.

Health

In 1999 there were one territorial hospital centre, four general hospitals, one specialist hospital and two private clinics, with a total of 855 beds. Medical personnel numbered 1,590 persons, including 384 doctors (175 per 100,000 inhabitants), 94 dentists and 51 pharmacists. Health spending accounted for 10·2% of GDP in 1997.

Welfare

In 1997, 202,760 people benefited from social welfare.

RELIGION

In 2001 there were approximately 119,000 protestants (about 49% of the population) and 94,000 Roman Catholics (39%).

CULTURE

Broadcasting

There are three TV broadcasters (one public, two independent): *Radio Télévision Française d'Outre-mer* (RFO) which broadcasts on two channels in French, Tahitian and English; *Canal + Polynésie*; and *Telefenua* which broadcasts across 16 channels. There are also 11 private radio stations. Number of receivers: radio (1999), 40,350; TV (2001), 54,400 (colour by SECAM H).

Press

In 1999 there were two daily newspapers.

Tourism

Tourism is the main industry. There were 189,000 tourist arrivals in 2002. Total revenue (1999) US$394m

FURTHER READING

Local Statistical Office: Institut Statistique de Polynésie Française, Papeete.

Website (French only): http://www.ispf.pf

OVERSEAS TERRITORIES

Territoires d'Outre-Mer

Southern and Antarctic Territories

Terres Australes et Antarctiques Françaises (TAAF)

GENERAL DETAILS

The Territory of the TAAF was created on 6 Aug. 1955. It comprises the Kerguelen and Crozet archipelagoes, the islands of Saint-Paul and Amsterdam (formerly Nouvelle Amsterdam), all in the southern Indian Ocean, and Terre Adélie. Since 2 April 1997 the administration has had its seat in Saint-Pierre, Réunion; before that it was in Paris. The Administrator is assisted by a seven-member consultative council which meets twice yearly in Paris; its members are nominated by the government for five years. The 15-member Polar Environment

Committee, which in 1993 replaced the former Consultative Committee on the Environment (est. 1982), meets at least once a year to discuss all problems relating to the preservation of the environment.

The French Institute for Polar Research and Technology was set up to organize scientific research and expeditions in Jan. 1992. The staff of the permanent scientific stations of the TAAF (120 in 1998) is renewed every 6 or 12 months and forms the only population.

Administrateur Supérieur Michel Champon.

Kerguelen Islands Situated 48–50° S. lat., 68–70° E. long.; consists of one large and 85 smaller islands, and over 200 islets and rocks, with a total area of 7,215 sq. km (2,786 sq. miles) of which Grande Terre occupies 6,675 sq. km (2,577 sq. miles). It was discovered in 1772 by Yves de Kerguelen, but was effectively occupied by France only in 1949. Port-aux-Français has several scientific research stations (56 members). Reindeer, trout and sheep have been acclimatized.

Crozet Islands Situated 46° S. lat., 50–52° E. long.; consists of five larger and 15 tiny islands, with a total area of 505 sq. km (195 sq. miles). The western group includes Apostles, Pigs and Penguins islands; the eastern group, Possession and Eastern islands. The archipelago was discovered in 1772 by Marion Dufresne, whose first mate, Crozet, annexed it for Louis XV. A meteorological and scientific station (17 members) at Base Alfred-Faure on Possession Island was built in 1964.

Amsterdam and **Saint-Paul Islands** Situated 38–39° S. lat., 77° E. long. Amsterdam, with an area of 54 sq. km (21 sq. miles) was discovered in 1522 by Magellan's companions; Saint-Paul, lying about 100 km to the south, with an area of 7 sq. km (2·7 sq. miles), was probably discovered in 1559 by Portuguese sailors. Both were first visited in 1633 by the Dutch explorer, Van Diemen, and were annexed by France in 1843. They are both extinct volcanoes. The only inhabitants are at Base Martin de Vivies (est. 1949 on Amsterdam Island), including several scientific research stations, a hospital, communication and other facilities (20 members). Crayfish are caught commercially on Amsterdam.

Terre Adélie Comprises that section of the Antarctic continent between 136° and 142° E. long., south of 60° S. lat. The ice-covered plateau has an area of about 432,000 sq. km (166,800 sq. miles), and was discovered in 1840 by Dumont d'Urville. A research station (27 members) is situated at Base Dumont d'Urville, which is maintained by the French Institute for Polar Research and Technology.

Wallis and Futuna

Wallis et Futuna

KEY HISTORICAL EVENTS

French dependencies since 1842, the inhabitants of these islands voted on 22 Dec. 1959 by 4,307 votes out of 4,576 in favour of exchanging their status to that of an overseas territory, which took effect from 29 July 1961.

TERRITORY AND POPULATION

The territory comprises two groups of islands in the central Pacific (total area 274 sq. km, provisional census population 14,944 in 2003). The Îles de Hoorn lie 255 km northeast of the Fiji Islands and consist of two main islands: Futuna (64 sq. km, 4,873 inhabitants) and uninhabited Alofi (51 sq. km). The Wallis Archipelago lies another 160 km further northeast, and has an area of 159 sq. km (10,071 inhabitants). It comprises the main island of Uvéa (60 sq. km) and neighbouring uninhabited islands, with a surrounding coral reef. The capital is Mata-Utu (2003 provisional census population of 1,191) on Uvéa. Wallisian and Futunian are distinct Polynesian languages.

SOCIAL STATISTICS

Estimates per 1,000 population, 1998: birth rate, 23·0; death rate, 4·8.

CONSTITUTION AND GOVERNMENT

A Prefect represents the French government and carries out the duties of head of the territory, assisted by a 20-member Territorial Assembly directly elected for a five-year term, and a six-member Territorial Council, comprising the three traditional chiefs and three nominees of the Prefect agreed by the Territorial Assembly. The territory is represented by one deputy in the French National Assembly, by one senator in the Senate, and by one member on the Economic and Social Council. There are three districts: Singave and Alo (both on Futuna), and Wallis; in each, tribal kings exercise customary powers assisted by ministers and district and village chiefs.

RECENT ELECTIONS

Territorial Assembly elections were held on 10 March 2002. Rassemblement pour la République–La Voix des Peuples Wallisens et Futuniens won 13 of the 20 seats, with 7 going to Parti Socialiste–Union Populaire pour Wallis et Futuna.

CURRENT ADMINISTRATION

Senior Administrator: Xavier de Furst.
　　President of the Territorial Assembly: Apeleto Likuvalu.

ECONOMY

Currency

The unit of currency is the franc CFP (XPF), with a parity of 119·3317422 francs CPF to the euro.

Budget

The budget for 1997 balanced at 120,100m. French francs.

Banking and Finance

There is a branch of Banque Indosuez at Mata-Utu.

ENERGY AND NATURAL RESOURCES

Electricity

There is a thermal power station at Mata-Utu.

Agriculture

The chief products are bananas, coconuts, copra, cassava, yams and taro.
　　Livestock (2002): 25,000 pigs; 7,000 goats.

Fisheries

The catch in 2001 was estimated at 300 tonnes.

COMMUNICATIONS

Roads

There are about 100 km of roads on Uvéa.

Civil Aviation

There is an airport on Wallis, at Hihifo, and another near Alo on Futuna. Eight flights a week link Wallis and Futuna. Air Calédonie International operates two flights a week to Nouméa (three in the summer) and two flights a week to Nadi.

Shipping

A regular cargo service links Mata-Utu (Wallis) and Singave (Futuna) with Nouméa (New Caledonia). In 2002 merchant shipping totalled 158,000 GRT.

Telecommunications

There were 1,890 main telephone lines in 2001.

Postal Services

There were five post offices in 2000.

SOCIAL INSTITUTIONS

Justice

There is a court of first instance, from which appeals can be made to the court of appeal in New Caledonia.

Education

In 1993 there were 3,624 pupils in primary schools and 1,777 in secondary schools. The South Pacific University Institute for Teacher Training, founded in 1992 (part of the French University of the Pacific, UFP) has three colleges: in Wallis and Futuna,

French Polynesia and Nouméa (New Caledonia), where it is headquartered.

Health

In 1991 there was one hospital with 60 beds, and four dispensaries.

RELIGION

The majority of the population is Roman Catholic.

CULTURE

Broadcasting

Since Aug. 2000 Réseau Français d'Outre-Mer (RFO) Wallis et Futuna radio has broadcast 24 hours a day. Télé Wallis et Futuna is the only television station.

DEPENDENCIES

Dépendances

Bassas da India

Île Bassas da India

KEY HISTORICAL EVENTS

The island was annexed by France in 1897. Its present status, an entity administered by France but not part of any other French territory, was established in 1960. The island is claimed by Madagascar.

TERRITORY AND POPULATION

Bassas da India is an uninhabited Indian Ocean atoll surrounded by reefs. It lies 380 km west of Madagascar and 460 km from the African mainland, and covers an area of 0·2 sq. km. The entire surface of the atoll is made of volcanic rock. Most of the island is submerged under water at high tide.

CONSTITUTION AND GOVERNMENT

The island is administered from St Denis, in Réunion, although it is not legally part of that territory.

Clipperton Island

Île Clipperton

KEY HISTORICAL EVENTS

In the 18th century the island was the hideout of a pirate, John Clipperton, for whom it was named. In 1855 it was claimed by France, and in 1897 by Mexico. It was awarded to France by international arbitration in 1935.

TERRITORY AND POPULATION

Clipperton Island is a Pacific atoll, 3 km long, some 1,120 km southwest of the coast of Mexico. It covers an area of 7 sq. km and is uninhabited.

CONSTITUTION AND GOVERNMENT

The island is administered from Papeete, in French Polynesia, although it is not legally part of that territory.

ECONOMY

The island is occasionally visited by tuna fishermen.

Europa Island

Île Europa

KEY HISTORICAL EVENTS

The island was annexed by France in 1897. Its present status, an entity administered by France but not part of any other French territory, was established in 1960. The island is claimed by Madagascar.

TERRITORY AND POPULATION

The island, which lies 350 km west of Madagascar, is low and flat. It covers an area of 28 sq. km. There is no permanent population, although there is a small French military garrison and a meteorological station.

CONSTITUTION AND GOVERNMENT

The island is administered from St Denis, in Réunion, although it is not legally part of that territory.

Glorieuses Islands

Îles Glorieuses

KEY HISTORICAL EVENTS

The islands were claimed by France in 1892. Their present status, an entity administered by France but not part of any other French territory, was established in 1960. The islands are claimed by Madagascar.

TERRITORY AND POPULATION

The Glorieuses Islands (also known as Glorioso) are two lush tropical islands, Ile du Lys and Grande Glorieuse, plus a number of rocky outcrops, Les Rochers. The group lies between Madagascar and Mayotte and have an area of 5 sq. km. There is no permanent population although there is a French military garrison, a meteorological station and a radio station on Grande Glorieuse.

CONSTITUTION AND GOVERNMENT

The islands are administered from St Denis, in Réunion, although they are not legally part of that territory.

Juan de Nova Island

Île Juan de Nova

KEY HISTORICAL EVENTS

The island was discovered by a 15th century Spanish navigator for whom it was named. In 1897 it was claimed by France. Its present status, an entity administered by France but not part of any other French territory, was established in 1960. The island is claimed by Madagascar.

TERRITORY AND POPULATION

Situated between Madagascar and Mozambique, the island has an area of 4·4 sq. km. There is no permanent population although there is a meteorological station. There is also a small civilian workforce to mine the island's guano.

CONSTITUTION AND GOVERNMENT

The island is administered from St Denis, in Réunion, although it is not legally part of that territory.

Tromelin Island

Île Tromelin

KEY HISTORICAL EVENTS

The island was explored by French navigators in 1776. In 1814 it was claimed by France and annexed to Réunion. Its present status, an entity administered by France but not part of any other French territory, was established in 1960. The island is claimed by Madagascar.

TERRITORY AND POPULATION

Tromelin, which is situated in the Mascarene Basin 535 km northwest of Réunion and 350 km east of Madagascar, covers an area of 1 sq. km. There is no permanent population although there is a meteorological station.

CONSTITUTION AND GOVERNMENT

The island is administered from St Denis, in Réunion, although it is not legally part of that territory.

GABON

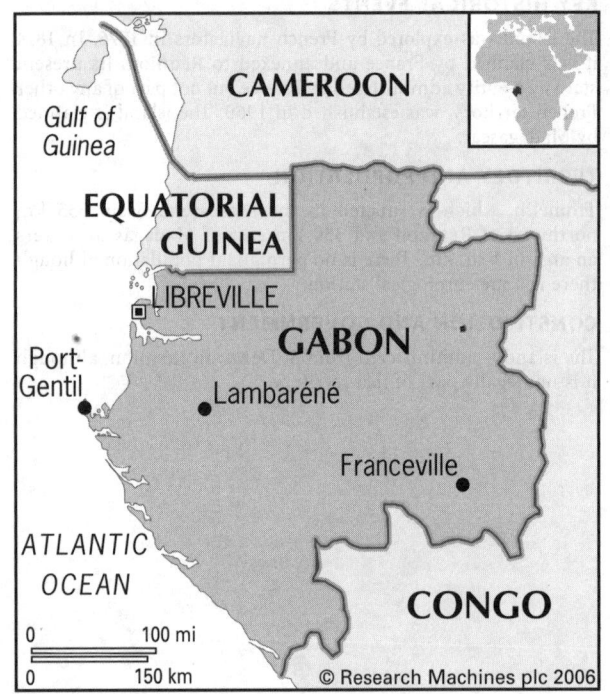

Province	Area in sq. km	Population 1993 census	Capital
Estuaire	20,740	463,187	Libreville
Haut-Ogooué	36,547	104,301	Franceville (Masuku)
Moyen-Ogooué	18,535	42,316	Lambaréné
Ngounié	37,750	77,781	Mouila
Nyanga	21,285	39,430	Tchibanga
Ogooué-Ivindo	46,075	48,862	Makokou
Ogooué-Lolo	25,380	43,915	Koulamoutou
Ogooué-Maritime	22,890	97,913	Port-Gentil
Woleu-Ntem	38,465	97,271	Oyem

The largest ethnic groups are the Fangs (25%) in the north and the Bapounou (24%) in the south. There are some 40 smaller groups. French is the official language.

SOCIAL STATISTICS

2003 estimates: births, 41,000; deaths, 16,000. Estimated rates, 2003 (per 1,000 population): births, 31; deaths, 12. Annual population growth rate, 1992–2002, 2·6%. Expectation of life at birth, 2003, 53·7 years for males and 55·2 years for females. Infant mortality, 2001, 60 per 1,000 live births; fertility rate, 2001, 5·4 births per woman.

CLIMATE

The climate is equatorial, with high temperatures and considerable rainfall. Mid-May to mid-Sept. is the long dry season, followed by a short rainy season, then a dry season again from mid-Dec. to mid-Feb., and finally a long rainy season once more. Libreville, Jan. 80°F (26·7°C), July 75°F (23·9°C). Annual rainfall 99" (2,510 mm).

CONSTITUTION AND GOVERNMENT

On 21 March 1997 the government presented to the Parliament legislation aimed at reforming the constitution in a number of key areas: notably, the bill mandated the creation of a Vice-President of the Republic, the extension of the presidential term of office from five to seven years, and the transformation of the Senate into an Upper Chamber of Parliament. Gabon has a bicameral legislature, consisting of a 120-member *National Assembly* (with members elected by direct, popular vote to serve five-year terms) and a 91-member *Senate* (elected for six-year terms in single-seat constituencies by local and departmental councillors). At a referendum on electoral reform on 23 July 1995, 96·48% of votes cast were in favour; turnout was 63·45%. The 1991 Constitution provides for an Executive *President* directly elected for a five-year term (renewable once only). In July 2003 Gabon's parliament approved an amendment to the constitution that allows the president to seek re-election indefinitely. The head of government is the *Prime Minister*, who appoints a Council of Ministers.

National Anthem

'La concorde' ('The Concord'); words and tune by G. Damas Aleka.

RECENT ELECTIONS

Presidential elections were held on 27 Nov. 2005. President Bongo was re-elected against four opponents with 79·2% of votes cast.

Elections for the National Assembly were held in two rounds on 9 and 23 Dec. 2001. The Gabonese Democratic Party (PDG) won 85 seats, the National Woodcutters' Rally 6, the Gabonese Party of Progress 3, the Social Democratic Party 2 and the People's Unity Party 1. Non-partisans took 11 seats.

République Gabonaise

Capital: Libreville
Population projection, 2010: 1·50m.
GDP per capita, 2003: (PPP$) 6,397
HDI/world rank: 0·635/123

KEY HISTORICAL EVENTS

Between the 16th and 18th centuries, the Fang and other peoples in the region of present-day Gabon were part of a federation of chiefdoms. The country's capital, Libreville, grew from a settlement of slaves who were rescued from captivity by the French in 1849. Colonized by France around this period, the territory was annexed to French Congo in 1888. There was resistance by the indigenous people between 1905 and 1911 to the depredations of colonial rule, but the country became a separate colony in 1910 as one of the four territories of French Equatorial Africa. Gabon became an autonomous republic within the French Community on 28 Nov. 1958 and achieved independence on 17 Aug. 1960.

TERRITORY AND POPULATION

Gabon is bounded in the west by the Atlantic Ocean, north by Equatorial Guinea and Cameroon and east and south by the Republic of the Congo. The area covers 267,667 sq. km. Its population at the 1993 census was 1,014,976; density, 3·8 per sq. km. In 2003, 83·7% of the population were urban. 2005 estimate, 1,384,000; density, 5·2 per sq. km.

The UN gives a projected population for 2010 of 1·50m.

The capital is Libreville (523,000 inhabitants, 1999 estimate), other large towns (1993 census) being Port-Gentil (79,225), Franceville (31,183), Oyem (22,404) and Moanda (21,882).

Provincial areas, populations (in 1,000) and capitals:

CURRENT ADMINISTRATION

President: El Hadj Omar Bongo Ondimba; b. 1935 (PDG; succeeded 2 Dec. 1967, re-elected in 1973, 1979, 1986, 1993, 1998 and 2005).

Vice President: Didjob Divungi Di Ndinge.

In March 2006 the Council of Ministers comprised:

Prime Minister: Jean Eyeghe Ndong; b. 1946 (sworn in 20 Jan. 2006).

Deputy Prime Ministers: Emmanuel Ondo-Metogho (also *Minister Responsible for Relations with Parliament and Co-ordination of Interministerial Commissions*); Georgette Koko (also *Minister of the Environment, Nature Protection, Research and Technology*); Paul Mba Abessole (also *Minister of Transport and Civil Aviation*); Louis Gaston Mayila (also *Minister of National Solidarity, Social Affairs, Well-Being and the Fight Against Poverty*).

Minister of State for Economy, Finance, Budget and Privatization: Paul Toungui. *Foreign Affairs, Co-operation, Francophonie Affairs and Regional Integration:* Jean Ping. *Housing, Town Planning and Land Registry:* Jacques Adiahénot. *Restructuring, Human Rights, Fight Against Corruption and Illicit Enrichment:* Pierre Claver Maganga Moussavou. *Planning and Development Programmes:* Casimir Oyé Mba. *Public Health:* Paulette Missambo. *Culture, Arts and Popular Education:* Pierre Marie Mdong. *Public Works, Equipment and Construction:* Gen. Idriss Ngari. *Defence:* Ali Bongo Ondimba. *Interior, Public Security and Immigration:* André Mba Obame. *Technical Education, Professional Training and Rehabilitation:* Pierre André Kombila.

Minister of Agriculture, Livestock and Rural Development: Faustin Boukoubi. *Civil Service, Administrative Reform and State Modernization:* Jean Boniface Assélé. *Commerce and Industrial Development:* Paul Biyoghé-Mba. *Communications, Posts, Telecommunications, Information Technology and Government Spokesperson:* René Ndemezo Obiang. *Decentralization and Land Management:* Dieudonné Pambo. *Family, Child Welfare and Women's Affairs:* Angélique Ngoma. *Fight Against AIDS, and Responsible for AIDS Orphans:* Alice Lamou. *Forest Economy, Water, Fisheries and National Parks:* Emile Doumba. *Justice and Keeper of the Seals:* Honorine Dossou Naki. *Labour and Employment:* Christiane Bitoughat. *Merchant Marine and Harbour Equipment:* Martin Mabala. *Mines, Energy, Oil and Hydraulic Resources:* Richard Onouviet. *National and Higher Education:* Albert Ondo Ossa. *Prevention and Management of Natural Disasters:* Jean Massima. *Private Sector Promotion, Social Economy and Handicrafts:* Marie Missouloukagne. *Small and Medium-Sized Enterprises and Industries:* Senturel Ngoma Madoungou. *State Control and Inspections:* Francine Meviane. *Towns, Promotion of Associative Life and Protection of Widows and Orphans:* Pierre Amoughe Mba. *Youth, Sports and Leisure:* Egide Boundono Simangoye.

CURRENT LEADERS

Omar Bongo

Position
President

Introduction
El Hadj Omar Bongo Ondimba, Africa's longest serving head of state, has been president of Gabon since 1967. His period in office has been characterized by political stability, with Gabon having the highest per capita wealth in West Africa. Despite introducing multi-party democracy in the early 1990s, he has been widely accused of corruption and a flawed electoral system has given concern to the international community.

Early Life
Bongo, given the name Albert-Bernard, was born in 1935 in what was then French Equatorial Africa. He was educated in Brazzaville, went to Chad for military training and served in the French air force. He joined the civil service in 1958 and developed a close relationship with Leon M'ba, who became president following Gabon's independence in 1960. M'ba appointed Bongo director of the president's office in 1962.

The military attempted a coup in 1964 and held both M'ba and Bongo in custody until M'ba was returned to power with the support of French forces. Bongo was appointed minister of defence in 1965 and minister of information and tourism the following year. Bongo then became vice president and assumed the presidency following the death of M'ba in Nov. 1967.

Career in Office
Bongo declared Gabon a one-party state in 1968 and under this system was re-elected to the presidency in 1973, 1979 and 1986. In 1973 he converted to Islam and took the name Omar. In 1982 an opposition group, the Movement for National Renewal (MORENA), was founded and pushed for the return of a multi-party system. Gabon's economy had benefited greatly from oil revenues but was affected by declining world oil prices in the late 1980s. Popular dissatisfaction spilled over into violent protests in 1990, during which French forces entered the country to protect its nationals. With the democratic movement newly invigorated, Bongo agreed to a national conference which included opposition figures. Multi-party politics were formally reintroduced in 1991.

Bongo was again victorious at the presidential elections of 1993 but his leading rival, Father Paul M'ba Abessole, voiced widely-held suspicions of electoral irregularities. Serious civil unrest was narrowly averted when Bongo agreed a deal, known as the Paris agreement, which allowed for the establishment of an electoral commission and improved electoral processes. In 1997 a constitutional amendment extended the presidential tenure from five to seven years, and Bongo's victory at the 1998 presidential polls was again widely questioned. An offer by Bongo to meet for talks with Pierre Mamboundou of the Gabonese People's Union (UPG) was rejected. The UPG called for a boycott of the 2001 parliamentary elections, which were dominated by Bongo's Gabonese Democratic Party (PDG). In an apparent gesture of reconciliation, the PDG invited opposition figures into the government.

A controversial constitutional amendment was then passed allowing the president to serve two consecutive seven-year terms, potentially granting power to Bongo until 2012. This was followed in June 2003 by further revisions permitting the president to contest the presidency as many times as he wished. In the following elections in Nov. 2005, Bongo was again re-elected with 79·2% of the popular vote.

In foreign policy, he has been involved in attempts to resolve regional conflicts, notably in Burundi, the Central African Republic, and in both the Republic of the Congo and Democratic Republic of the Congo. In March 2003 Cándido Muatetema Rivas, then prime minister of Equatorial Guinea, claimed Gabon's occupation of the oil-rich island of Mbagne, close to the coast of both countries, was illegal. In April 2001 Bongo signed agreements with Russia on military and technical co-operation as well as trade and culture.

Despite Gabon's relatively prosperous economy, boosted by oil sales and high levels of foreign investment, Bongo's lavish expenditure has attracted international criticism.

Jean Eyeghe Ndong

Position
Prime Minister

Introduction
Jean Eyeghe Ndong was appointed prime minister in Jan. 2006. The French-educated civil servant and politician is a member of the ruling Gabonese Democratic Party (PDG) and an ally

of the president, Omar Bongo, who has ruled the country since 1967.

Early Life

Jean Eyeghe Ndong was born on 12 Feb. 1946 in Libreville, Gabon, then part of the federation of French Equatorial Africa. A nephew of Leon M'ba, Gabon's first post-independence president, he was educated at l'Ecole Mont-Fort, Libreville, followed by the Collège Saint-Gabriel de Mouila and the Collège Moderne d'Oyem. He studied for a diploma at the School of Social Sciences in Paris in the early 1960s and subsequently obtained a doctorate in political science from the University of Paris X-Nanterre.

Entering Gabon's public administration in 1980 as a civil servant, Ndong worked as director of administrative services and human resources in Libreville's city hall. Four years later he was promoted to director of pensions at the national office for social security, a post he occupied until he was made director of the national office of social insurance in 1990. That year saw widespread protests against the regime of President Bongo and subsequent constitutional amendments that restored the multi-party political system. Elections for a new national assembly took place in Oct. 1990.

Following his election to the national assembly in 1996 as a PDG representative, Ndong entered the government as secretary of state for finances, responsible for privatization. He was also elected to be a consultant to the municipal council of Libreville. President Bongo, who won a further seven year term in Nov. 2005, appointed Ndong to replace Jean-François Ntoutoume-Emane as prime minister on 20 Jan. 2006.

Career in Office

Ndong has said the government will work to promote economic development, social justice, public security, public health and education. 'It will be an open government, and it will work hard and earnestly to gain the people's trust.'

DEFENCE

In 2003 military expenditure totalled US$15m. (US$12 per capita), representing 0·2% of GDP.

Army

The Army totalled (2002) 3,200. A referendum of 23 July 1995 favoured the transformation of the Presidential Guard into a republican guard. There is also a paramilitary Gendarmerie of 2,000. France maintains a 750-strong marine infantry battalion.

Navy

There is a small naval flotilla, 500 strong in 2002.

Air Force

Personnel (2002) 1,000. There are ten combat aircraft including nine Mirage 5s and five armed helicopters.

INTERNATIONAL RELATIONS

Gabon is a member of the UN, WTO, IMF, World Bank, African Development Bank, the African Union, IOM, Islamic Development Bank, Economic and Monetary Community of Central Africa (CEMAC), Economic Community of the Central African States (CEEAC), Islamic Conference, International Organization of the Francophonie, Movement of Non-Aligned Countries and is an ACP member state of the ACP-EU relationship.

ECONOMY

Agriculture accounted for 7·6% of GDP in 2002, industry 46·4% and services 46·0%.

Overview

Five-year development plans, of which there were five after 1966, have been replaced by three-year rolling investment plans.

Currency

The unit of currency is the *franc CFA* (XAF) with a parity of 655·957 francs CFA to one euro. Foreign exchange reserves were US$38m. in April 2002 and total money supply was 343,048m. francs CFA. Gold reserves were 13,000 troy oz in June 2002. Inflation was 2·1% in 2003 and 0·4% in 2004.

Budget

In 2000 revenue totalled 1,207·6bn. francs CFA and expenditure 786bn. francs CFA. Oil revenues account for nearly two-thirds of all revenues.

Performance

Gabon experienced a recession in 1999 and 2000, with the economy shrinking by 8·9% and 1·9% respectively, but there has been a slight recovery since then. Growth was 2·4% in 2003, followed by 1·4% in 2004.

Total GDP in 2004 was US$7·2bn.

Banking and Finance

The *Banque des États de l'Afrique Centrale* (Governor, Jean-Félix Mamalepot) is the bank of issue. There are five commercial banks. The largest are Banque Internationale pour le Commerce et l'Industrie du Gabon, BGFIBANK and Union Gabonaise de Banque, which between them had 80% of the market share in 2003.

ENERGY AND NATURAL RESOURCES

Environment

Gabon's carbon dioxide emissions from the consumption and flaring of fossil fuels in 2002 were the equivalent of 3·7 tonnes per capita.

An *Environmental Sustainability Index* compiled for the World Economic Forum meeting in Jan. 2005 ranked Gabon 12th in the world, with 61·7%. The index measured the ability of countries to maintain favourable environmental conditions and examined various factors including pollution levels and the use or abuse of natural resources.

Electricity

Installed capacity was 0·4m. kW in 2000. The semi-public *Société d'énergie et d'eau du Gabon* produced 1·35bn. kWh in 2000 (approximately 52% hydro-electric and 48% thermal). Consumption per capita was 1,123 kWh in 2000.

Oil and Gas

Proven oil reserves (2002), 2·5bn. bbls. Production, 2003, 12·0m. tonnes. There were proven natural gas reserves of 99bn. cu. metres in 2002. Natural gas production (2000) was 1·1bn. cu. metres.

Minerals

There are an estimated 200m. tonnes of manganese ore and 850m. tonnes of iron ore deposits. Gold, zinc and phosphates also occur. Output, 2001: manganese ore, 1·57m. tonnes.

Agriculture

There were 325,000 ha. of arable land in 2001 and 170,000 ha. of permanent crops. 15,000 ha. were irrigated in 2001. The major crops (estimated production, 2000, in 1,000 tonnes) are: plantains, 280; cassava, 225; sugarcane, 176; yams, 150; taro, 59; maize, 31; groundnuts, 17; bananas, 12. Other important products include palm oil, sweet potatoes and soybeans.

Livestock (2000): 36,000 cattle, 198,000 sheep, 91,000 goats, 213,000 pigs.

Forestry

Equatorial forests covered 21·83m. ha. in 2000, or 84·7% of the total land area. Timber production in 2001 was 3·10m. cu. metres.

In 2002 President Bongo announced that a tenth of the country would be transformed into 13 national parks covering nearly 30,000 sq. km. Gabon is likely to need US$85m. over a seven-year period to build the national parks.

Fisheries

The catch in 2001 was 40,457 tonnes, of which 30,607 tonnes were from marine waters. Industrial fleets account for about 25% of the catch.

INDUSTRY

Most manufacturing is based on the processing of food (particularly sugar), timber and mineral resources, cement and chemical production and oil refining. Production figures (2000) in 1,000 tonnes: residual fuel oil, 283; cement (2001), 240; distillate fuel oil, 185; kerosene, 23; beer (2001), 86·7m. litres; soft drinks (2001), 57·8m. litres.

Labour

The workforce in 1996 numbered 519,000 (56% males). Around 60% of the economically active population are engaged in agriculture.

In 1993 the legal minimum monthly wage was 1,200 francs CFA. There is a 40-hour working week.

INTERNATIONAL TRADE

Foreign debt was US$3,533m. in 2002. The government retains the right to participate in foreign investment in oil and mineral extraction.

Imports and Exports

In 2003 imports totalled 602bn. francs CFA and exports 1,842bn. francs CFA.

Machinery and mechanical equipment accounted for 26·4% of imports in 1997, food and agricultural products 23·1%, consumer products 15·5% and transport equipment 11·5%. Crude petroleum and petroleum products constituted 77·1% of exports in 1997, and wood 14·5%.

Main import suppliers, 1997: France, 39·1%; Belgium, 9·7%; USA, 8·1%. Main export markets: USA, 68·2%; France, 8·1%; Japan, 3·2%.

COMMUNICATIONS

Roads

In 2000 there were an estimated 8,464 km of roads (9·9% asphalted); and in 2002 some 25,600 passenger cars plus 17,000 trucks and vans. There were 293 deaths in road accidents in 2000.

Rail

The 657-km standard gauge Transgabonais railway runs from the port of Owendo to Franceville. Total length of railways, 2000, 649 km. In 2000, 237,000 passengers and 3·1m. tonnes of freight were transported.

Civil Aviation

There are international airports at Libreville (Léon M'Ba Airport), Port-Gentil and Franceville (Masuku); scheduled internal services link these to a number of domestic airfields. The national carrier is Air Gabon (80% state-owned). Libreville, the main airport, handled 757,000 passengers and 17,700 tonnes of freight in 2001. In 1999 scheduled airline traffic of Gabonese-based carriers flew 8·0m. km, carrying 423,000 passengers (226,000 on international flights).

Shipping

In 2002 the merchant marine totalled 13,000 GRT, including oil tankers 1,000 GRT. Owendo (near Libreville), Mayumba and Port-Gentil are the main ports. In 2000, 18m. tonnes of cargo were handled at the ports. Rivers are an important means of inland transport.

Telecommunications

In 2003 Gabon had 338,400 telephone subscribers (300,000 mobile and 38,400 landline) and 30,000 PCs were in use. There were 28·7 main telephone lines per 1,000 inhabitants and 224·4 mobile phone subscribers per 1,000 inhabitants. There were 600 fax machines in 2002 and 25,000 Internet users.

Postal Services

There were 59 post offices in 2003.

SOCIAL INSTITUTIONS

Justice

There are *tribunaux de grande instance* at Libreville, Port-Gentil, Lambaréné, Mouila, Oyem, Franceville (Masuku) and Koulamoutou, from which cases move progressively to a central Criminal Court, Court of Appeal and Supreme Court, all three located in Libreville. Civil police number about 900.

Education

The adult literacy rate in 2000 was 71·0%. Education is compulsory between 6–16 years. In 2000–01 there were 265,714 pupils and 5,399 teachers in primary schools, and 101,681 pupils with 2,727 (1996–97) teachers at secondary schools; in 1996–97 there were 6,703 students in 11 technical and professional schools and 76 students in two teacher-training establishments.

In 1996–97 there was one university at Libreville (the Omar Bongo University) and one university of science and technology at Franceville (Masuku), with a total of 6,800 students and 506 academic staff. In 2004 a university of health sciences (previously part of the Omar Bongo University) was created in Libreville.

In 2000–01 total expenditure on education came to 4·6% of GNP.

Health

In 1995 there were 292 doctors, eight dentists and 23 pharmacists; and in 1989 (latest data available), 240 midwives and 759 nurses. In 1999 there were 25 hospitals, 63 medical centres and 413 dispensaries.

RELIGION

In 2001 there were 0·69m. Roman Catholics, 0·22m. Protestants and 0·17m. followers of African Christian sects. The majority of the remaining population follow animist beliefs. There are about 12,000 Muslims.

CULTURE

Broadcasting

Broadcasting is the responsibility of the state-controlled Radiodiffusion Télévision Gabonaise (RTG), which transmits two national radio programmes and provincial services. RTG has two TV channels (one national). In 2000 there were eight private radio stations and two private TV channels. There were 630,000 radio sets in 2000 and 400,000 TV sets in 2001 (colour by SECAM).

Press

In 2000 there was one government-controlled daily newspaper (*L'Union*).

Tourism

There were 169,000 foreign tourists in 2001, spending US$7m.

DIPLOMATIC REPRESENTATIVES

Of Gabon in the United Kingdom (27 Elvaston Place, London, SW7 5NL)
Ambassador: Alain Mansah-Zoguelet.

Of the United Kingdom in Gabon
Ambassador: Richard Wildash, LVO (resides in Yaoundé, Cameroon).

Of Gabon in the USA (2034 20th St., NW, Suite 200, Washington, D.C., 20009)
Ambassador: Jules M. Ogouebandja.

Of the USA in Gabon (Blvd de la Mer, Libreville)
Ambassador: Barrie R. Walkley.

Of Gabon to the United Nations
Ambassador: Denis Dangue Réwaka.

Of Gabon to the European Union
Ambassador: René Makongo.

FURTHER READING

Barnes, J. F. G., *Gabon: Beyond the Colonial Legacy.* Boulder (Colo.), 1992

Gardinier, David E. (ed.) *Historical Dictionary of Gabon.* 2nd ed. Metuchen (NJ), 1994.—*Gabon.* [Bibliography] ABC-Clio, Oxford and Santa Barbara (CA), 1992

Saint Paul, M. A., *Gabon: the Development of a Nation.* London, 1989

National Statistical Office: Direction Générale de la Statistique et des Études Économiques, Ministère de la Planification et de la Programmation du Développement, Libreville.

THE GAMBIA

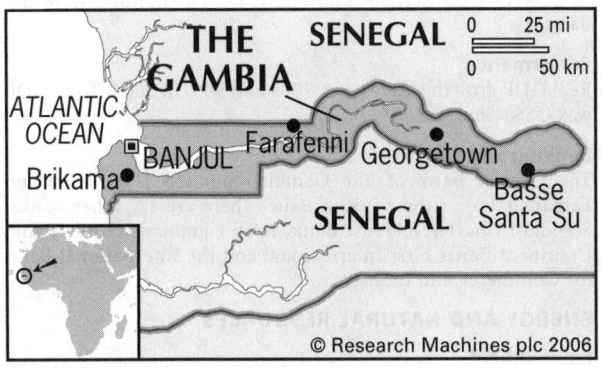

Republic of The Gambia

Capital: Banjul
Population projection, 2010: 1·71m.
GDP per capita, 2003: (PPP$) 1,859
HDI/world rank: 0·470/155

KEY HISTORICAL EVENTS

Stone circles thought to have been constructed by ancestors of the Jola people are estimated to date from 600 AD. Kingdoms of Mandinka-speaking people were established near the Gambia River from around 1100. State-building by the Jolof and Serer groups gathered pace from around 1400. Portuguese mariners entered the Gambia River in 1455 but the first permanent European settlement was founded by traders from the Baltic Duchy of Courland (Latvia) in 1651. English and French merchants subsequently vied for control of the region (Senegambia). The British Captain, Alexander Grant, established Bathurst (Banjul) as a garrison in 1816 and it was controlled from the Freetown Colony (Sierra Leone). The Gambia became an independent member of the British Commonwealth on 18 Feb. 1965 and an independent republic on 24 April 1970.

TERRITORY AND POPULATION

The Gambia takes its name from the River Gambia, and consists of a strip of territory never wider than 10 km on both banks. It is bounded in the west by the Atlantic Ocean and on all other sides by Senegal. The area is 10,689 sq. km, including 2,077 sq. km of inland water. Population (census provisional, 2003), 1,364,507; density, 128 per sq. km. In 2003, 73·8% of the population were rural.

The UN gives a projected population for 2010 of 1·71m.

The largest ethnic group is the Mandingo, followed by the Wolofs, Fulas, Jolas and Sarahuley. The country is administratively divided into the capital, Banjul (2003 census provisional, 357,238) plus five other administrative divisions.

The five rural divisions, with their areas, populations and chief towns are (listed west to east, or upriver):

Division	Area in sq. km	Population 2003 census	Chief town
Western	1,764	392,987	Brikama
North Bank	2,256	172,806	Kerewan/Farafenni
Lower River	1,618	72,546	Mansa Konko
Central River	2,894	185,897	Jangjangbureh
Upper River	2,069	183,033	Basse

The official language is English.

SOCIAL STATISTICS

2000 estimates: births, 49,000; deaths, 22,000. Estimated birth rate in 2000 was 37·2 per 1,000 population; estimated death rate, 17·0. Annual population growth rate, 1992–2002, 3·3%. Expectation of life, 2003, was 54·3 years for males and 57·1 for females. Fertility rate, 2001, 4·9 births per woman; infant mortality, 2001, 91 per 1,000 live births. The Gambia has made some of the best progress in recent years in reducing child mortality. The number of deaths per 1,000 live births among children under five was reduced from around 130 in 1990 to approximately 80 in 1999.

CLIMATE

The climate is characterized by two very different seasons. The dry season lasts from Nov. to May, when precipitation is very light and humidity moderate. Days are warm but nights quite cool. The SW monsoon is likely to set in with spectacular storms and produces considerable rainfall from July to Oct., with increased humidity. Banjul, Jan. 73°F (22·8°C), July 80°F (26·7°C). Annual rainfall 52" (1,295 mm).

CONSTITUTION AND GOVERNMENT

The 1970 constitution provided for an executive *President* elected directly for renewable five-year terms. The President appoints a *Vice-President* who is the government's chief minister. The single-chamber *National Assembly* has 53 members (48 elected by universal adult suffrage for a five-year term and five appointed by the President).

A referendum of 8 Aug. 1996 approved a new constitution by 70·4% of votes cast. It took effect in Jan. 1997 and thereby created the Second Republic. Under this, the ban on political parties imposed in July 1994 was lifted. Members of the ruling Military Council resigned from their military positions before joining the Alliance for Patriotic Reorientation and Construction (APRC).

National Anthem

'For the Gambia, our homeland'; words by V. J. Howe, tune traditional.

RECENT ELECTIONS

Presidential elections were held on 18 Oct. 2001. President Jammeh was re-elected against four opponents with 53·0% of votes cast. Turnout was 89·9%.

Parliamentary elections were held on 17 Jan. 2002. The Alliance for Patriotic Reorientation and Construction (APRC) won 45 seats (33 of which were unopposed because of boycotting by opposition parties), the People's Democratic Organization for Independence and Socialism 2, and the National Reconciliation Party 1.

CURRENT ADMINISTRATION

President, and Acting Minister of Works, Construction and Infrastructure: Col. (retd) Yahya Jammeh; b. 1965 (APRC; seized power 22 July 1994; elected 26 Sept. 1996 and re-elected in 2001).

In March 2006 the government comprised:

Vice-President and Secretary of State for Women's Affairs: Isatou Njie Saidy.

Secretary of State for Agriculture: Yankuba Touray. *Local Government and Lands:* Ismaila Sambou. *Finance and Economic Affairs:* Musa Gibril Balal Gaye. *Foreign Affairs:* Lamin Karba Bajo. *Interior:* Baboucarr Jatta. *Trade, Industry and Employment:* Alieu Ngum. *Communications, Information and Technology:* Neneh Macdoull-Gaye. *Forestry and Environment:* Edward

Singhatey. *Education:* Fatou Faye. *Fisheries and Water Resources:* Bai Mass Taal. *Health and Social Affairs:* Tamsir Mbowe. *Justice and Attorney General:* Sheikh Tijan Hydara. *Tourism and Culture:* Susan Waffa-Ogoo. *Youth and Sports:* Samba Faal.

Office of the President: http://www.statehouse.gm/

CURRENT LEADERS

Retd Col. Yahya Jammeh

Position
President

Introduction
Former army colonel Yahya Jammeh came to power in a military coup in July 1994 and led his party to electoral victories in 1997 and 2001. He intends to run for a third term in elections scheduled for Oct. 2006.

Early Life
Yahya A. J. J. Jammeh was born in the Foni Kansala district of The Gambia on 25 May 1965, the year in which the country gained independence from Great Britain. Jammeh joined the army in 1984, rising to captain by 1992. On 22 July 1994 Jammeh led a successful coup against Sir Dawda Jawara, president since 1970.

While Jammeh was unelected head of state, all political parties were banned and the constitution revoked. In 1996 a new constitution was approved by national referendum and in Jan. 1997 presidential elections completed a return to civilian rule. Jammeh was confirmed as president and his Alliance for Patriotic Reorientation and Construction (APRC) secured a comfortable majority of seats in parliament. Jammeh was re-elected president in Oct. 2001. The 2002 parliamentary elections, in which the APRC won nearly all the seats, were boycotted by the main opposition party.

Career in Office
After Jammeh's electoral victory in 1997, The Gambia emerged from its isolation to accept a two-year seat on the UN Security Council. Economic and political relations damaged by the 1994 coup have gradually improved and trading partners now include India, Thailand and the UK. A blanket ban on political activities was lifted in Aug. 1996 but, with the approach of presidential elections in late 2006, the government announced the arrest of three opposition leaders for alleged involvement in subversive activities. Legislation passed in 2004 set jail terms for journalists guilty of libel while broadcast news is tightly controlled.

DEFENCE

The Gambian National Army, 800 strong, has two infantry battalions and one engineer squadron.

The marine unit of the Army consisted in 2002 of 70 personnel operating three inshore patrol craft, based at Banjul.

Defence expenditure totalled US$2m. in 2003 (US$1 per capita), representing 0·6% of GDP.

INTERNATIONAL RELATIONS

The Gambia is a member of the UN, WTO, the Commonwealth, the African Union, African Development Bank, ECOWAS, IOM, OIC, Islamic Development Bank and is an ACP member state of the ACP-EU relationship.

ECONOMY

Agriculture accounted for 25·8% of GDP in 2002, industry 14·2% and services 60·0%.

Currency

The unit of currency is the *dalasi* (GMD), of 100 *butut*. Inflation was 17·0% in 2003 and 14·2% in 2004. Foreign exchange reserves

were US$94m. in May 2002. Total money supply in May 2002 was 1,343m. dalasis.

Budget

In 1999 revenues were 944·5m. dalasis and expenditures 1,118·2m. dalasis.

Performance

Real GDP growth was 6·9% in 2003 and 5·1% in 2004. Total GDP was US$0·4bn. in 2004.

Banking and Finance

The Central Bank of The Gambia (founded 1971; *Governor,* Famara Jatta) is the bank of issue. There are six other banks: Standard Chartered, Trust Bank, Arab Gambian Islamic Bank, Continent Bank, First International and the International Bank for Commerce and Industry.

ENERGY AND NATURAL RESOURCES

Environment

Carbon dioxide emissions from the consumption and flaring of fossil fuels in 2002 were the equivalent of 0·2 tonnes per capita.

Electricity

Installed capacity was 29,000 kW in 2000. Production was 132m. kWh in 2000; consumption per capita in 2000 was 95 kWh.

Oil and Gas

President Jammeh announced in Feb. 2004 that large quantities of oil had been discovered in waters off The Gambia's coast.

Minerals

Heavy minerals, including ilmenite, zircon and rutile, have been discovered in Sanyang, Batokunku and Kartong areas.

Agriculture

About 68% of the population depend upon agriculture. There were 0·25m. ha. of arable land in 2001 and 5,000 ha. of permanent crops. Almost all commercial activity centres upon the marketing of groundnuts, which is the only export crop of financial significance; in 2000 an estimated 126,000 tonnes were produced. Cotton is also exported on a limited scale. Rice is of increasing importance for local consumption. Major products (2000 estimates, in 1,000 tonnes), are: groundnuts, 126; millet, 76; rice, 29; maize, 21; sorghum, 18; cassava, 6; palm oil, 3; palm kernels, 2.

Livestock (2000): 370,000 cattle, 270,000 goats, 195,000 sheep and 1m. poultry.

Forestry

In 2000 forests covered 481,000 ha., or 48·1% of the land area. Timber production in 2001 was 724,000 cu. metres.

Fisheries

The total catch in 2001 was estimated at 34,527 tonnes, of which 32,027 tonnes were from marine waters.

INDUSTRY

Labour

The labour force in 1996 totalled 579,000 (55% males). Around 78% of the economically active population are engaged in agriculture.

INTERNATIONAL TRADE

Foreign debt was US$573m. in 2002.

Imports and Exports

Imports and exports in US$1m.:

	1995	1996	1997	1998	1999
Imports c.i.f.	214·6	219·2	256·0	257·2	193·7
Exports f.o.b.	18·7	12·8	8·6	25·6	8·2

Chief imports in 1998 were: machinery and transport equipment, US$52·9m.; rice, US$40·7m.; and manufactured goods, US$37·1m. In 1998, US$13·2m. of groundnuts were exported, US$2·5m. of fish and seafood and US$2·5m. of vegetables and fruit. Main import suppliers in 1999 were (in US$1m.): Germany, 26·8; UK, 20·6; France, 13·0; China, 12·4. Leading export destinations in 1999 were (in US$1m.): Belgium, 2·1; UK, 1·4; Germany, 0·9; Spain, 0·7.

COMMUNICATIONS

Roads
There were some 2,700 km of roads in 2002, of which 956 km were paved. Number of vehicles (2002): 7,200 passenger cars; 3,600 trucks and vans.

Civil Aviation
There is an international airport at Banjul (Yundum). The national carrier is Gambia International Airlines. Banjul handled 300,000 passengers in 2001 and 2,700 tonnes of freight.

Shipping
The chief port is Banjul. Ocean-going vessels can travel up the Gambia River as far as Kuntaur. The merchant marine totalled 2,000 GRT in 2002.

Telecommunications
The Gambia had 138,300 telephone subscribers in 2002, or 100·8 per 1,000 population, and there were 19,000 PCs in use (13·8 per 1,000 persons). Mobile phone subscribers numbered 100,000 in 2002 and there were 1,200 fax machines. In 2002 there were 25,000 Internet users.

Postal Services
There were 14 post offices in 2003.

SOCIAL INSTITUTIONS

Justice
Justice is administered by a Supreme Court consisting of a chief justice and puisne judges. The High Court has unlimited original jurisdiction in civil and criminal matters. The Supreme Court is the highest court of appeal and succeeds the judicial committee of the Privy Council in London. There are Magistrates Courts in each of the divisions plus one in Banjul and two in nearby Kombo St Mary's Division—eight in all. There are resident magistrates in provincial areas. There are also Muslim courts, district tribunals dealing with cases concerned with customary law, and two juvenile courts.

The death penalty, last used in 1981, was abolished in 1993 but restored by decree in 1995. The population in penal institutions in Sept. 2002 was 450 (32 per 100,000 of national population).

Education
The adult literacy rate in 2001 was 37·8% (45·0% among males and 30·9% among females). In 2000–01 there were 156,839 pupils with 4,186 teachers at primary schools and 56,179 pupils with 2,207 teachers at secondary schools. In 1993–94 there were 1,591 students at 155 institutions of higher education, which comprise The Gambia College, a technical training institute, a management development institute, a multi-media training institute, a hotel training school, and centres for self-development and skills training, and continuing education.

In 2000–01 total expenditure on education came to 2·7% of GNP and 14·2% of total government spending.

Health
In 1994 there were two hospitals, one clinic, ten health centres and some 60 dispensaries. There were 43 physicians, 155 nurses, six pharmacists and 102 midwives in 1997.

RELIGION
More than 90% of the population is Muslim. Banjul is the seat of an Anglican and a Roman Catholic bishop. There is a Methodist mission. A few sections of the population retain their original animist beliefs.

CULTURE

World Heritage Sites
The Gambia has one site on the UNESCO World Heritage List: James Island and Related Sites (inscribed on the list in 2003), containing important evidence of early Afro-European encounters and the slave trade.

Broadcasting
Gambia Radio and Television Services (GRTS) broadcasts radio and television programmes in English and some other local languages. There are four private commercial radio stations and three community radio stations. TV operations started in 1995 and programmes are transmitted countrywide and beyond (colour by PAL). There were 520,000 radio receivers in 2000 and 20,000 television receivers in 2001.

Press
There is a government-owned daily; an independent newspaper appears five times a week, there are two weeklies, several news-sheets and a monthly.

Tourism
Tourism is The Gambia's biggest foreign exchange earner. In 2002 there were 113,000 foreign tourists; spending by tourists totalled US$43m.

DIPLOMATIC REPRESENTATIVES

Of The Gambia in the United Kingdom (57 Kensington Ct., London, W8 5DG)
High Commissioner: Gibril Seman Joof.

Of the United Kingdom in The Gambia (48 Atlantic Rd, Fajara, Banjul)
High Commissioner: Eric Jenkinson.

Of The Gambia in USA (1156 15th St., Suite 1000, NW, Washington, D.C., 20005)
Ambassador: Dodou Bammy Jagne.

Of the USA in The Gambia (Fajara (East), Kairaba Ave., Banjul)
Ambassador: Joseph D. Stafford, III.

Of The Gambia to the United Nations
Ambassador: Crispin Grey-Johnson.

Of The Gambia to the European Union
Ambassador: Yusupha Alieu Kah.

FURTHER READING

Hughes, A. and Perfect, D., *Political History of The Gambia, 1816–1992.* Farnborough, 1993

GEORGIA

Sakartvelos Respublika
(Republic of Georgia)

Capital: Tbilisi
Population projection, 2010: 4·30m.
GDP per capita, 2003: (PPP$) 2,588
HDI/world rank: 0·732/100

KEY HISTORICAL EVENTS

The independent Georgian Social Democratic Republic was declared on 26 May 1918 and was recognized by the Russian Soviet Federal Socialist Republic on 7 May 1920. In 1936 the Georgian Soviet Socialist Republic became one of the constituent republics of the USSR. Following nationalist successes at elections in Oct. 1990, the Supreme Soviet resolved on a transition to full independence and on 9 April 1991 unanimously declared the republic an independent state. President Zviad Gamsakhurdia was deposed by armed insurrection on 6 Jan. 1992 and a military council took control. After elections in which he gained 95% of votes cast, Eduard Shevardnadze became *de facto* head of state in Oct. 1992. On 22 Oct. 1993 Georgia joined the Commonwealth of Independent States. Supporters of the deposed president Gamsakhurdia were in intermittent conflict with the government, mainly in Mingrelia, but suffered heavy defeats once Russian support became available via the CIS. Ethnic conflict has been rife in the two autonomous republics of South Ossetia and Abhkazia. Civil war broke out with South Ossetia in 1990 and Abhkazia in 1992 and 1998. Georgia has since moved closer to the West but economic reforms have been slow in coming and industry and agriculture are both in need of investment. In Nov. 2003 Eduard Shevardnadze resigned after opposition forces stormed parliament in protest against alleged fixing of elections three weeks earlier.

TERRITORY AND POPULATION

Georgia is bounded in the west by the Black Sea and south by Turkey, Armenia and Azerbaijan. Area, 69,700 sq. km (26,900 sq. miles). Its census population in 2002 was 4,371,535 (excluding Abkhazia and South Ossetia); density (excluding Abkhazia and South Ossetia), 76 per sq. km.

The UN gives a projected population for 2010 of 4·30m.

In 2003, 52·0% of the population lived in urban areas. The capital is Tbilisi (2002 population estimate, 1·08m.). Other important towns are Kutaisi (186,000; 2002), Batumi (122,000; 2002), Sukhumi (121,000; 1991), Rustavi (116,500; 2002), Gori (49,500; 2002) and Poti (47,000; 2002).

Georgians accounted for 83·8% of the 2002 census population; others included 6·5% Azerbaijanis, 5·7% Armenians and 1·5% Russians. Georgia includes the Autonomous Republics of Abkhazia and Adjaria and the former Autonomous Region of South Ossetia.

Georgian is the official language. Armenian, Russian and Azeri are also spoken.

SOCIAL STATISTICS

2001 estimates: births, 40,400; deaths, 39,300. Rates, 2001 estimates: birth, 7·8 per 1,000 population; death, 7·5 per 1,000. Annual population growth rate, 1992–2002, –0·5%. Life expectancy, 2003, 66·6 years for males and 74·3 years for females. Infant mortality, 2001, 24 per 1,000 live births; fertility rate, 2001, 1·4 births per woman.

CLIMATE

The Georgian climate is extremely varied. The relatively small territory covers different climatic zones, ranging from humid sub-tropical zones to permanent snow and glaciers. In Tbilisi summer is hot: 25–35°C. Nov. sees the beginning of the Georgian winter and the temperature in Tbilisi can drop to –8°C; however, average temperature ranges from 2–6°C.

CONSTITUTION AND GOVERNMENT

A new Constitution of 24 Aug. 1995 defines Georgia as a presidential republic with federal elements. The head of state is the *President*, elected by universal suffrage for not more than two five-year terms. The 235-member *Supreme Council* is elected by a system combining 85 single-member districts with proportional representation based on party lists. There is a 5% threshold.

National Anthem

'Tavisupleba' ('Freedom'); words by Dawit Magradse, tune by Zakaria Paliashvili.

RECENT ELECTIONS

At the presidential election held on 4 Jan. 2004 Mikhail Saakashvili of the United National Movement was elected president with 96·3% of the vote. Teimuraz Shashiashvili took 1·9%. Turnout was 88·0%.

The parliamentary elections of 2 Nov. 2003 were declared invalid. At the parliamentary elections of 28 March 2004 the National Movement–Democrats (formed through the merger of the United National Movement and the United Democrats) won 67·0% of the vote (135 of the 235 seats). The Rightist Opposition won 7·6% (15 seats). No other party achieved the 7% necessary to win a seat. 75 seats were taken in single-seat constituencies in Nov. 2003 and ten seats represent Abkhazians.

CURRENT ADMINISTRATION

President: Mikhail Saakashvili; b. 1967 (National Movement–Democrats; sworn in on 25 Jan. 2004).

In March 2006 the government comprised:

Prime Minister: Zurab Noghaideli; b. 1964 (National Movement–Democrats; sworn in on 17 Feb. 2005).

Minister of Agriculture: Mikhail Svimonishvili. *Culture and Sports:* Giorgi Gabashvili. *Defence:* Irakli Okruashvili. *Economic Development:* Irakli Chogovadze. *Education and Science:* Kakha Lomaia. *Energy:* Nika Gilauri. *Environment:* Giorgi Papuashvili. *Finance and Revenue:* Alexi Alexishvili. *Foreign Affairs:* Gela Bezhuashvili. *Interior:* Vano Merabishvili. *Justice:* Gia Kvataradze. *Labour, Health and Social Welfare:*

Vladimir Chipashvili. *Refugees and Resettlement:* Giorgi Kheviashvili.

The *Speaker* is Nino Burjanadze.

Georgian Parliament: http://www.parliament.ge

CURRENT LEADERS

Mikhail Saakashvili

Position
President

Introduction
Mikhail Saakashvili was elected president of Georgia on 4 Jan. 2004. A former protégé of President Eduard Shevardnadze, he led opposition to the rigged parliamentary elections of Nov. 2003 and forced the president to resign. Saakashvili's peaceful management of the 'rose revolution' earned him respect at home and abroad and even the support of the ousted Shevardnadze. Fluent in Georgian, Russian, English, French and Ukrainian, Saakashvili's juridical training is seen as appropriate for the state-building made necessary by Georgia's territorial fragmentation of the 1990s.

Early Life
Mikhail (Mikheil in Georgian) Saakashvili was born on 21 Dec. 1967 in Tbilisi. He received law degrees from Kyiv University, Ukraine in 1992 and Columbia University, New York in 1994 and completed a doctorate in juridical science at George Washington University, Washington, D.C. He pursued further studies in Florence and Strasbourg.

While working for a New York law firm, Saakashvili was approached by Zurab Zhvania, speaker of the Georgian parliament. The Georgian leader, Eduard Shevardnadze, was seeking potential parliamentary candidates, unconnected to the Soviet system. Saakashvili returned home and was elected to parliament in Dec. 1995. As a member of Shevardnadze's Citizens' Union and a trained jurist, Saakashvili's political career developed rapidly. He served as chairman of the parliamentary committee on electoral reform and contributed to the drafting of the 1995 constitution. He led the Citizens' Union in parliament from 1998–99 and was appointed vice-president of the Council of Europe's parliamentary assembly in Jan. 2000.

Appointed justice minister in Oct. 2000, Saakashvili attempted an overhaul of the judicial system, condemned by international observers as highly corrupt. He also tried to reform the prison system and proposed a bill on illegal property confiscation, which was blocked by Shevardnadze. His programme was cut short when he openly accused the ministers for economics and state security and Tbilisi's head of police of corruption and profiteering. Shevardnadze, then president, refused to act on these charges, forcing Saakashvili to resign in Sept. 2001.

Having left the government, he continued his anti-corruption programme by forming a party, the United National Movement, to represent Georgia's reformist elements. Coalition partners included the small ideological Republican Party and the Union of National Forces. Support was widened by alliances with Zurab Zhvania's United Democrats and the Burjanadze-Democrats, led by Nino Burjanadze, Zhvania's replacement as speaker. Saakashvili was elected chairman of the Tbilisi Assembly in June 2002.

Saakashvili campaigned for the Nov. 2003 parliamentary elections on an anti-Shevardnadze platform, drawing large crowds with his energetic rhetoric, especially in Adjaria, in the southwest, and Kvemo Kartli, a province in the southeast with a large Azeri minority. Despite OSCE sponsorship, the elections on 2 Nov. were chaotic and heavily rigged by the ruling Citizens' Union. The delayed announcement of provisional results provoked accusations of electoral fraud. Burjanadze and Zhvania agreed to form a coalition with Saakashvili—the United Opposition Front—and massive demonstrations were

organized night after night in Tbilisi. After the results were announced, putting Saakashvili's National Movement in third place, a boycott of parliament was declared by the coalition. Shevardnadze refused to compromise and opened parliament on 22 Nov. Saakashvili responded by summoning his national supporters to Tbilisi and demanded the president's resignation. During Shevardnadze's opening address Saakashvili burst into the assembly, brandishing a rose, the symbol of the peaceful demonstrations. His supporters occupied the chancellery, causing the president to declare a state of emergency.

Bereft of support from abroad and in his own government, Shevardnadze finally resigned on 23 Nov. His avoidance of a military solution was praised internationally and by the opposition leaders. In the wake of his resignation, Saakashvili, Burjanadze and Zhvania agreed to present a united front in immediate presidential elections, the former gaining the support from the other two in exchange for senior government positions. On 4 Jan. 2004 Saakashvili won the presidential election with just over 96% of the votes. His electoral promises were broad and ambitious: the abolition of taxes on small businesses, doubling of pensions and public sector salaries and swift punishment for the worst abuses of the previous regime. His campaign was strengthened by the co-operation of Shevardnadze, who voted for his successor.

Career in Office
Saakashvili declared his priorities in office as maintaining the territorial integrity of Georgia and his anti-corruption programme. He consolidated his political position in March 2004 when the National Movement–Democrats bloc won the parliamentary elections with a substantial majority of seats. Tension increased with Adjaria's president, Aslan Abashidze, who declared a state of emergency in his jurisdiction and rejected the new central government's authority. Saakashvili reasserted direct control over Adjaria in May 2004 after popular demonstrations in Batumi forced Abashidze to step down. Elsewhere, Saakashvili has proposed giving greater autonomy—but not full independence—to the separatist regions of South Ossetia and Abkhazia, which have continued to provide a serious challenge to his leadership. Although Russia's links with these regions are a cause of friction, as are the issue of the remaining Russian bases in Georgia and the conflict in Chechnya, Saakashvili has sought to improve relations between the two countries.

DEFENCE

The total strength of the Armed Forces consists of 17,500 personnel. In 2002 some 4,000 Russian military personnel and 12,130 peacekeeping forces were stationed in Georgia. The UN has some 107 observers from 23 countries. Russia and Georgia signed an agreement in May 2005 on the withdrawal of all remaining Russian troops from Georgia by 2008.

Defence expenditure in 2003 totalled US$350m. (US$68 per capita), representing 2·7% of GDP.

Army
The Army totals 8,620. In addition there are 250,000 reservists and a paramilitary border guard estimated at 5,400.

Navy
Former Soviet facilities at Poti have been taken over. The headquarters are at Tbilisi. Personnel, 2002, 1,830.

Air Force
Personnel, 2002, 1,250. Equipment includes Su-17 and Su-25 fighter-bombers.

INTERNATIONAL RELATIONS

Georgia is a member of the UN, WTO, CIS, NATO Partnership for Peace, Council of Europe, OSCE, BSEC and IOM.

ECONOMY

Agriculture accounted for 20·6% of GDP in 2002, industry 24·3% and services 55·0%.

Overview

Georgia is a small lower-income transition economy. After independence in 1991, civil war and the loss of markets in the former Soviet Union led to economic collapse. Georgia suffered the worst declines experienced by any of the transition economies, with exports declining by 90% and output falling by 70%. Georgia's economy suffered political tensions, declining standards of living and low tax revenues that undermined the funding of basic state functions. The 1996–99 programme of reforms, supported by the IMF, focused on building national institutions, privatization, energy sector rehabilitation, land reform and fiscal consolidation. Georgia made progress towards macroeconomic stabilization in the late 1990s although this progress was thwarted by internal fragmentation, drought and the 1998 financial crisis in Russia. The second round of IMF supported programmes, from 2001–04, brought the recovery of growth and of price stability. The IMF notes that several areas of weakness still remain, notably a lack of fiscal consolidation, strong interest groups and corruption hampering reforms, the under-development of financial markets and the slow progress of privatization.

Currency

The unit of currency is the *lari* (GEL) of 100 *tetri*, which replaced coupons at 1 lari = 1m. coupons on 25 Sept. 1995. Inflation was 5·7% in 2004, having been 163% in 1995 and 15,606% in 1994. Gold reserves are negligible. Total money supply was 394m. laris in June 2002.

Budget

Revenues in 2002 totalled 928·6m. laris and expenditures 920·5m. laris. Tax revenue accounted for 83·1% of total revenues; current expenditure accounted for 99·7% of total expenditures.

Performance

Real GDP growth was 4·7% in 2001, 5·5% in 2002, 11·1% in 2003 and 6·2% in 2004. In both 1996 and 1997 growth had exceeded 10%, but prior to that the economy had suffered a sharp downturn, contracting by 45% in 1992, 29% in 1993 and 10% in 1994. Of all the former Soviet republics Georgia's economy, along with that of Moldova, has suffered the most since 1989 when political and economic reforms took place across central and eastern Europe. In 2002 the level of GDP was estimated to be only 38% of that in 1989. Total GDP was US$5·1bn. in 2004.

Between 1990 and 1996 the average annual real growth in GNP per capita was −19·3% (the lowest of any country in the world).

Banking and Finance

The *President* of the Central Bank is Roman Gotsiridze. In 1996 there were 65 commercial banks. One foreign bank had a representative office.

ENERGY AND NATURAL RESOURCES

Environment

Carbon dioxide emissions from the consumption and flaring of fossil fuels in Georgia were the equivalent of 1·7 tonnes per capita in 2002.

Electricity

The many fast-flowing rivers provide an important hydro-electric resource. Installed capacity was 4·6m. kW in 2000. Production in 2000 was 7·40bn. kWh; consumption per capita in 2000 was 1,452 kWh.

Oil and Gas

Output (2000) of crude petroleum, 110,000 tonnes. A 920 km long oil pipeline is under construction from an offshore Azerbaijani oilfield in the Caspian Sea across Azerbaijan and Georgia to a new oil terminal at Supsa, near Poti, on the Black Sea Coast. The US$600m. pipeline started pumping oil in early 1999 and allowed Georgia to create 25,000 new jobs. However, Georgia is still heavily dependent on Russia for natural gas. Accords for the construction of a second oil pipeline through Georgia were signed in Nov. 1999, to take oil from Azerbaijan to Turkey via Georgia. Work on the pipeline began in Sept. 2002 and it was officially opened in May 2005. Natural gas production was 61m. cu. metres in 2000.

Minerals

Manganese deposits are calculated at 250m. tonnes. Other important minerals are coal, barytes, clays, gold, diatomite shale, agate, marble, alabaster, iron and other ores, building stone, arsenic, molybdenum, tungsten and mercury. Output of coal in 2000 was estimated to be 7,000 tonnes.

Agriculture

Agriculture plays an important part in Georgia's economy, contributing 20·6% of GDP in 2002. In 2001 there were 795,000 ha. of arable land and 268,000 ha. permanent crops. 469,000 ha. were irrigated in 2001.

Output of main agricultural products (in 1,000 tonnes) in 2000: potatoes, 480; tomatoes, 325; maize, 225; grapes, 200; cabbages, 125; wine, 116; apples, 115; wheat, 84; watermelons (including melons, pumpkins and squash), 70.

Livestock, 2000: cattle, 1,122,000; sheep, 560,000; pigs, 411,000; chickens, 8m. Livestock products, 2000 (in 1,000 tonnes): meat, 105; milk, 721; eggs, 24.

Forestry

There were 2·99m. ha. of forest in 2000, or 43·7% of the total land area.

Fisheries

The catch in 2001 was 1,830 tonnes, down from 147,688 tonnes in 1989.

INDUSTRY

Industry accounted for 24·3% of GDP in 2002. There is a metallurgical plant and a motor works. There are factories for processing tea, creameries and breweries. There are also textile and silk industries.

Production (in 1,000 tonnes): cement (2001), 335; nitrogenous fertilizer (2000), 99; flour (2002), 78; steel (2000), 49; footwear (2001), 45,000 pairs; beer (2002), 27·0m. litres; spirits (2002), 2·1m. litres; cigarettes (2001), 1,615m. units.

Labour

The economically active workforce numbered 1,877,600 in 2001 (966,600 males), including: 989,600 in agriculture, hunting and forestry; 181,500 in wholesale and retail trade/repair of motor vehicles, motorcycles and personal and household goods; 138,700 in education; 105,600 in public administration and defence/ compulsory social security; and 102,400 in manufacturing. The unemployment rate was 11·5% in 2003. Approximately 500,000 Georgians, or a tenth of the population, work in Russia, but in Dec. 2000 Russia began requiring Georgians to have a visa to visit the country.

INTERNATIONAL TRADE

Total foreign debt was US$1,838m. in 2002. The debt was mainly as a result of the importing of natural gas from Turkmenistan.

Imports and Exports

In 2002 Georgian imports (f.o.b.) amounted to US$1,041·6m. and exports (f.o.b.) US$583·4m. Major commodities imported are fuel, grain and other foods, machinery and parts, and transport equipment. Major commodities for export are iron and steel products, food and beverages, machinery, textiles and chemicals. Main import suppliers, 2000: Turkey, 16·0%; Russia, 14·1%; USA, 10·1%; Azerbaijan, 8·5%. Main export markets, 2000: Turkey, 22·7%; Russia, 21·1%; Germany, 10·4%; Azerbaijan, 6·4%.

COMMUNICATIONS

Roads

There were 20,229 km of roads in 2002 (93·5% hard-surfaced). Passenger cars in use in 2002 numbered 251,961 (56·3 per 1,000 inhabitants), and there were also 45,470 trucks and vans and 24,134 buses and coaches. In 2002 there were 515 road deaths.

Rail

Total length is 1,562 km of 1,520 mm gauge (1,544 km electrified). In 2000 railways carried 2·3m. tonnes of freight and 11·5m. passengers. There is a metro system in Tbilisi.

Civil Aviation

The main airport is at Tbilisi (Novo-Alexeyevka). The main Georgian carrier is Airzena Georgian Airlines. In 2003 it had flights to Amsterdam, Frankfurt, Kyiv, Paris, Prague, Tel Aviv and Vienna. In 2001 Tbilisi airport handled 250,000 passengers (all on international flights) and 4,300 tonnes of freight.

Shipping

In 2002 sea-going shipping totalled 569,000 GRT, of which oil tankers accounted for 41,000 GRT.

Telecommunications

There were 1,152,100 telephone subscribers in 2002, or 233·5 per 1,000 persons, and PCs numbered 156,000. Mobile phone subscribers numbered 503,600 in 2002 and there were 500 fax machines in 1995. In 2002 there were 73,500 Internet users.

Postal Services

There were 1,025 post offices in 2003.

SOCIAL INSTITUTIONS

Justice

The population in penal institutions in Sept. 2002 was 7,343 (198 per 100,000 of national population). The death penalty was abolished in 1997.

Education

In 2000–01 there were 1,195 pre-primary schools with 6,958 teachers for 72,790 pupils; and 3,409 primary schools with 17,732 teachers for 276,389 pupils. In 1999–2000 there were 467,249 pupils at secondary level with 62,517 teachers; and 140,627 students at institutions of higher education. There is one university and one technical university, with (1996) a total of 34,590 students and 6,464 academic staff. Adult literacy rate in 2001 was over 99%.

Health

Georgia had 18,200 hospital beds in 2003. In 2002 there were 20,225 physicians, 1,532 dentists, 19,298 nurses, 364 pharmacists and 1,500 midwives.

Welfare

In 1994 there were 804,000 age and 355,000 other pensioners.

RELIGION

The Georgian Orthodox Church has its own organization under Catholicos (patriarch) Ilya II who is resident in Tbilisi. In 2001 there were 1·8m. Georgian Orthodox, 550,000 Sunni Muslims, 280,000 Armenian Apostolic (Orthodox) and 130,000 Russian Orthodox.

CULTURE

World Heritage Sites

Georgia has three sites on the UNESCO World Heritage List: City-Museum Reserve of Mtskheta (inscribed on the list in 1994), churches of the former Georgian capital; Bagrati Cathedral and Gelati Monastery (1994); and Upper Svaneti (1996), a mountainous area of medieval villages.

Broadcasting

The government-controlled Georgian Radio broadcasts two national and three regional programmes, and a foreign service, Radio Georgia (English, Russian). There are local independent TV stations in ten towns. The main independent TV station is *Rustavi-2*. Colour is by SECAM V. There were 2·79m. radio receivers in 2000 and 1·76m. TV receivers in 2001.

Press

In 2000 there were 35 dailies with a combined daily circulation of 25,705.

Tourism

Investment in tourism has increased substantially in recent years, and large numbers of hotels have been built. In 2002 there were 298,000 foreign tourists bringing in receipts of US$472m.

DIPLOMATIC REPRESENTATIVES

Of Georgia in the United Kingdom (4 Russell Gdns, London, W14 8EZ)
Ambassador: Amiran Kavadze.

Of the United Kingdom in Georgia (Sheraton Metechi Palace Hotel, 380003 Tbilisi)
Ambassador: Donald MacLaren of MacLaren.

Of Georgia in the USA (1101 15th St., NW, Suite 602, Washington, D.C., 20005)
Ambassador: Levan Mikeladze.

Of the USA in Georgia (11 George Balanchine St., 0131 Tbilisi)
Ambassador: John Tefft.

Of Georgia to the United Nations
Ambassador: Revaz Adamia.

Of Georgia to the European Union
Ambassador: Konstantin Zaldastanishvili.

FURTHER READING

Brook, S., *Claws of the Crab: Georgia and Armenia in Crisis.* London, 1992
Gachechiladze, R., *The New Georgia: Space, Society, Politics.* London, 1995
Nasmyth, P., *Georgia: a Rebel in the Caucasus.* London, 1992
Suny, R. G., *The Making of the Georgian Nation.* 2nd ed. Indiana Univ. Press, 1994

State Department for Statistics Website: http://www.statistics.ge

---

Abkhazia

All statistics are the latest data available. Area, 8,600 sq. km (3,320 sq. miles); population (Jan. 2004 est.), 178,600. Capital Sukhumi (1990 population, 121,700). This area, the ancient Colchis, saw the establishment of a West Georgian kingdom in the 4th century and a Russian protectorate in 1810. In March 1921 a congress of local Soviets proclaimed it a Soviet Republic, and its status as an Autonomous Republic, within Georgia, was confirmed on 17 April 1930 and again by the Georgian Constitution of 1995.

Ethnic groups at the 1989 census were Georgians, 45·7%; Abkhazians, 17·8%; Armenians, 14·6%; and Russians, 14·3%. Around 300,000 ethnic Georgians were displaced as a result of the 1992–94 war and ethnic Abkhazians are now thought to constitute the majority population.

In July 1992 the Abkhazian parliament declared sovereignty under the presidency of Vladislav Ardzinba and the restoration of its 1925 constitution. Fighting broke out as Georgian forces moved into Abkhazia. On 3 Sept. and on 19 Nov. ceasefires were agreed, but fighting continued into 1993 and by Sept. Georgian forces were driven out. On 15 May 1994 Georgian and Abkhazian delegates under Russian auspices signed an agreement on a ceasefire and deployment of 2,500 Russian troops as a peacekeeping force. On 26 Nov. 1994 parliament adopted a new Constitution proclaiming Abkhazian sovereignty. CIS economic sanctions were imposed in Jan. 1996. Parliamentary elections were held on 23 Nov. 1996. Neither the constitution nor the elections were recognized by the Georgian government or the international community.

Fighting flared up between rival militia forces again in May 1998 after Abkhazian forces ejected thousands of ethnic Mingrelian and Georgian refugees who had returned to the southern Abkhazian region of Gali. After the fighting in 1998, the worst in five years, both sides declared a ceasefire. Up to 20,000 Georgians lost their homes. Abkhazia has expressed a desire to join the Russian Federation, but Russia is wary of the request.

Abkhazia, and notably Sukhumi, the capital, have seen living standards plunge dramatically. There are no Internet links, no mobile phones and no hotels. There is very little work and practically no money.

President: Sergei Bagapsh (elected on 3 Oct. 2004). Georgian officials declared the election illegal. The Supreme Court eventually decided to hold new elections within two months, although parliament voted on 26 Nov. 2004 to recognize Sergei Bagapsh as the winner of the election. In the new elections held on 12 Jan. 2005 Sergei Bagapsh was elected with 90·1% of the votes, against 4·5% for Yakub Lakoba.

Prime Minister: Akeksandr Ankvab (appointed on 14 Feb. 2005).

The republic has coal, electric power, building materials and light industries. Main crops are tobacco, tea, grapes, oranges, tangerines and lemons. Crop area: 43,900 ha.

Livestock, 1 Jan. 1987: 147,300 cattle, 127,900 pigs, 28,800 sheep and goats.

In 1990–91 there were 16,700 children attending pre-school institutions. There is a university at Sukhumi with 3,000 students and 270 academic staff in 1995–96. In 1990 there were 2,100 students at colleges and 7,700 students at other institutions of higher education.

In Jan. 1990 there were 2,500 doctors and 6,600 junior medical personnel.

Adjaria

All statistics are the latest data available. Area, 2,900 sq. km (1,160 sq. miles); provisional census population (2002): 376,016. Capital, Batumi (2002 population, 121,806, mostly Sunni

Muslim). Adjaria fell under Turkish rule in the 17th century, and was annexed to Russia (rejoining Georgia) after the Berlin Treaty of 1878.

On 16 July 1921 the territory was constituted as an Autonomous Republic within the Georgian SSR, a status confirmed by the Georgian Constitution of 1995. In Jan. 2004 Adjarian leader Aslan Abashidze refused to acknowledge the central government of Mikhail Saakashvili and declared a state of emergency. Fearing a Georgian invasion, Abashidze destroyed road and rail links to the rest of Georgia but was forced to step down on 6 May after popular demonstrations in Batumi. Saakashvili imposed direct rule over Adjaria. Elections were held on 20 June 2004. Saakashvili's Victorious Adjaria group took 72·1% of the vote and 28 of the 30 seats in the *Supreme Council*, Adjaria's parliament. Two seats went to the Republican Party (13·5% of the vote).

Russia has agreed to withdraw from its military base in Batumi by 2008.

Ethnic groups at the 1989 census: Georgians, 82·8%; Russians, 7·7%; Armenians, 4%.

Chairman of the Supreme Council: Mikheil Makharadze.

Prime Minister: Levan Varshalomidze.

Elections were held in Sept. 1996. A coalition of the Citizens' Union of Georgia and the All-Georgian Union of Revival gained a majority of seats.

Adjaria specializes in sub-tropical agricultural products. These include tea, citruses, bamboo, eucalyptus, tobacco, etc. Livestock (Dec. 2003): 128,400 cattle, 1,900 pigs, 16,100 sheep and goats.

There is a port and a shipyard at Batumi, oil-refining, food-processing and canning factories, clothing, building materials, pharmaceutical factories, etc.

Approximately 166,300 persons were in paid employment in 2003; the unemployment rate was 12·1%.

In 1990–91, 77,239 pupils were engaged in study at all levels.

In Jan. 1990 there were 1,700 doctors and 4,400 junior medical personnel.

South Ossetia

All statistics are the latest data available. Area, 3,900 sq. km (1,505 sq. miles); population (Jan. 2004 est.), 49,200. At the 1989 census the ethnic groups were Ossetians (66%) and Georgians (29%). The capital, Tskhinvali, had a population of 42,934 in Jan. 1989. It is estimated that around 45,000 Ossetians have fled to North Ossetia (in the Russian Federation) since 1990.

This area was populated by Ossetians from across the Caucasus (North Ossetia), driven out by the Mongols in the 13th century. The region was set up within the Georgian SSR on 20 April 1922. Formerly an Autonomous Region, its administrative autonomy was abolished by the Georgian Supreme Soviet on 11 Dec. 1990, and it has been named the Tskhinvali Region.

Fighting broke out in 1990 between insurgents wishing to unite with North Ossetia and Georgian forces. By a Russo-Georgian agreement of July 1992 Russian peacekeeping forces moved into a seven-km buffer zone between South Ossetia and Georgia pending negotiations. An OSCE peacekeeping force has been deployed since 1992.

At elections not recognized by the Georgian government on 10 Nov. 1996, Lyudvig Chibirov was elected president. Though maintaining a commitment to independence, President Chibirov came to a political agreement with the Georgian government in 1996 that neither force nor sanctions should be applied. In July 2003 his successor, President Eduard Kokoyty, asked Vladmir

Putin to let South Ossetia become a member of the Russian Federation. Georgian President Mikhail Saakashvili, who took office in Jan. 2004, has made clear his wish to revive the authority of the Georgian government in the regions.

President: Eduard Kokoyty (elected on 6 Dec. 2001).

Prime Minister: Yuri Morozov (appointed on 5 July 2005).

Main industries are mining, timber, electrical engineering and building materials.

In 1989–90 there were 21,200 pupils in elementary and secondary schools. There were 6,525 children in pre-school institutions.

In Jan. 1987 there were 511 doctors and 1,400 hospital beds.

© Research Machines plc 2006

Bundesrepublik Deutschland
(Federal Republic of Germany)

Capital: Berlin
Seat of Government: Berlin/Bonn
Population projection, 2010: 82·70m.
GDP per capita, 2003: (PPP$) 27,756
HDI/world rank: 0·930/20

KEY HISTORICAL EVENTS

From the 8th century BC the Celtic peoples inhabited a vast proportion of present-day Germany but by about 500 BC warlike Germanic tribes had pushed their way north and settled in the Celtic lands. The expanding Roman Empire established its boundaries along the Rhine and the Danube rivers but attempts to move further east had to be abandoned after the Roman provincial Governor Varius was defeated in AD 9 by the Germanic forces under Arminius. For the next thousand years the towns of Trier, Regensburg, Augsburg, Mainz and Cologne, founded by the Romans, formed the main centres of urban settlement. Christianity was introduced under Emperor Constantine and the first bishopric north of the Alps was established in Trier in AD 314.

At the start of the 5th century the Huns forced the indigenous Saxons north, towards Britain. However, the Franks, who came from the lowlands and were to become the founders of a civilized German state, gradually asserted themselves over all the other Germanic people. Towards the end of the 5th century a powerful Rhenish state was founded under King Clovis, a descendant of Merovech (Merovius), a Salian Frankish king. The powerful Merovingian dynasty eventually gave way to the Carolingians, whose authority was strengthened by papal support.

Charlemagne succeeded to the throne in 768, founding what was later known as the First Reich (Empire). The Franks continued to thrive until their influence stretched from Rome to the North Sea and from the Pyrenees to the River Elbe. The Pope crowned Charlemagne emperor on Christmas Day 800, creating what was to become known as the Holy Roman Empire. But the empire was too unwieldy to survive Charlemagne. On his death in 814 it began to break up. The Treaty of Verdun in 843 divided the French and German people for the first time, creating a Germanic Central Europe and a Latin Western Europe. The first king of the newly formed eastern kingdom was Ludwig the German and under him a specific German race and culture began to take shape. The last of Charlemagne's descendants died in 911 and with it the Carolingian dynasty. Power shifted, via Conrad I, duke of Franconia, to Henry I, duke of Saxony. Henry's son Otto the Great crushed the increasing power of the hereditary duchies and by making grants of land to the Church he strengthened ties with Rome. His coronation as emperor of the Romans in 962 was the first to associate German kingship with the office of the Holy Roman Emperor.

Over two centuries, powerful dynasties emerged to threaten the position of the emperor. After an intense feud the Hohenstaufens (of Swabia) gained supremacy over the Guelfs (the counts of Bavaria; later denoting anti-imperial loyalties and the papal faction) and managed to keep the upper hand for well over a century. Frederick Barbarossa, descended from both dynasties, led several expeditions to subjugate Italy and died on the Third Crusade. The Knights of the Teutonic Order set about converting Eastern Europe to Christianity and by the 14th century they had conquered much of the Baltic. By controlling the lucrative grain trade Germany grew rich.

Habsburg Rule

The Golden Bull of 1356 established the method for electing an emperor by setting up an Electoral College composed of seven princes or *electors*. Three of these were drawn from the church (the archbishops of Cologne, Mainz and Trier), and four from the nobility (the king of Bohemia, the duke of Saxony, the margrave of Brandenburg and the count palatine of the Rhine), all of whom had the right to build castles, mint their own coinage, impose taxes and act as judges. The title of Holy Roman Emperor nearly always went to an outsider and increasingly to members of the Austrian Habsburg dynasty. In 1273 Count Rudolph IV was the first Habsburg to be crowned king of the Germans. The Great Schism of 1378–1417, which resulted in rival popes holding court in Rome and Avignon, effectively ended the church's residual power over German affairs.

The Hundred Years War between France and England benefited the growing number of Free Imperial Cities along the German trading routes. Merchants and craftsmen organized themselves into guilds, wresting control of civic life away from the nobility and laying the foundations for a capitalist economy. Founded as a defence and trading league at Lübeck, the Hanseatic League combated piracy and established Germanic economic and political domination of the Baltic and North Sea. German communities were founded in Scandinavia and along the opposite coast as far as Estonia.

In the 14th century the bubonic plague wiped out a quarter of the German population. Rather than put the onus on their own tradesmen returning from Asia, it was the Jews, living in tightly-knit segregated communities, who were blamed. Excluded from guilds and trades they took to money lending, an occupation forbidden to Christians, and one which engendered envy and suspicion.

In 1273 Count Rudolph IV was the first Habsburg to be crowned king of the Germans. Over two centuries the Habsburg dynasty became increasingly powerful, retaining the title of Holy Roman Emperor from 1432 until its abolition nearly four centuries later. Succeeding to the title in 1493 Maximilian I gained the Netherlands by his marriage to Mary of Burgundy and control of Hungary and Bohemia by other marital alliances. Spain was added to the Habsburg dominions by the marriage of Maximilian's son, Philip, to Juana the Mad.

Reformation

In the early part of the 15th century the unpopularity of the church was linked to corruption coupled with a growing trade in the sale of indulgences. Huge land taxes were levied to pay for St Peter's Church and other sacred buildings in Rome. In 1517 an Augustinian monk named Martin Luther, professor of theology at the University of Wittenberg, made his famous protest with 95 Theses or arguments against indulgences nailed to the door of the Schlosskirche in Wittenberg. This was seen as an open attack on the Church of Rome and marked the beginning of the Reformation. Luther challenged the power of the pope, the privileged position of the priests and the doctrine of transubstantiation that had always been at the heart of Catholic dogma. But for the death of Maximilian I in 1519 and the subsequent power struggle for the title of Holy Roman Emperor, Luther might well have been executed as a heretic.

Following Maximilian's death, Francis I of France staked a claim to the succession in an attempt to avoid the concentration of power that would result in the election of the Habsburg candidate, Charles I of Spain. To placate the electors of Germany, the pope named Luther's patron, Frederick the Wise of Saxony, as a compromise candidate. This gained Luther only a temporary reprieve as, after much intrigue, the king of Spain was elected. Although Luther was excommunicated in 1520, he had the right to a hearing before an Imperial Diet (court). This was convened at Worms and although he was branded an outlaw and his books were ordered to be burned, he was given safe haven in Wartburg Castle where he translated the Bible into German, with the help of Philipp Melanchthon. Thanks to the revolutionary system of printing invented by Johannes Gutenberg, Luther's ideas spread quickly throughout Germany. His doctrine of 'justification by faith alone', with its apparent invitation to resist the authority of the church, was one of the main causes of the Peasants' War of 1524–25 that led to wholesale destruction of monasteries and castles. To the surprise of the rebels, Luther aligned himself with the authorities and so the uprising was brutally crushed. The Reformation thus gained political authority. By 1555 many of the small independent German states had joined the Protestant (as it was now known) cause that Charles V admitted defeat and abdicated, retiring to a monastery in Spain. His brother Ferdinand succeeded him and signed the Peace of Augsburg. This agreement gave the secular rulers of each state the right to decide on their own religious practices (*cuius regio, eius religio*), so dividing Germany between Catholics and Lutherans.

Thirty Years War

Martin Luther died in 1546. The Catholics then launched a Counter-Reformation following the church reforms agreed at the Council of Trent. Bavaria's annexation of the mostly Protestant free city of Donauwörth in 1608 led to the formation of the Protestant Union, an armed alliance under the leadership of the Palatinate. The Catholic League, set up by the Bavarians the following year, created a sharp division in Germany. Rudolf II, who reigned as emperor for 36 years, chose Prague as his power base, thus weakening his authority over his more distant territories. After he was deposed in 1611 a series of dynastic and religious conflicts set in train what came to be known as the Thirty Years' War. Germany was devastated; the countryside was laid waste, towns were pillaged and mass slaughter reduced the population by as much as a third. Although the Catholics were the early victors, Denmark and Sweden as well as Catholic France (who preferred the Protestants to the Habsburgs) backed the Protestants while Spain supported the Catholics. After repeated attempts to end the war, the Peace of Westphalia (signed in 1648) brought peace but deprived the emperor of much of his authority. Power was divided between 300 principalities, and over 1,000 other territories.

During the 17th and 18th centuries the German princes consolidated their power, building vast palaces to bolster their claim to divine right. The Hanoverian branch of the Welf family inherited the British Crown in 1714; a royal union that was to last until 1837.

Meanwhile, the Habsburgs were struggling to hold on to the title of Holy Roman Emperor. The Turks reached Vienna in 1683 but after they were repulsed, the Austrians pushed eastwards and began to build up an empire in the Balkans. This left their western borders vulnerable where the French, who had long regarded the Rhine as the natural limit of their territory to their east, annexed Alsace and Strasbourg in 1688 and 1697. To the north, the presence of Brandenburg-Prussia under the Hohenzollern family was beginning to be felt. Throughout the 18th century Prussia was built up into a powerful independent state with its capital in Berlin. Strong militarism and a strict class-dominated society helped Prussia to become a major European power. When Frederick the Great came to the throne in 1740, he softened his country's military image by introducing reforms and by creating a cultured life at his court. His main preoccupation, however, continued to be expansion by force. His annexation of Silesia (under an old Brandenburg claim) provoked the Habsburgs to retaliate and, backed by Russia and France, they launched the Seven Years' War. Frederick had only the tacit support of Hanover and Britain to fall back on and, within three years, the Prussian armies were seriously overextended. But Frederick engineered a dramatic change in his fortunes by swelling the ranks of his armies with fresh recruits and in 1772, helped by the collapse of the alliance between Austria and Russia, he annexed most of Poland, achieving his goal of establishing his version of Austria in north Germany.

Unification

Revolutionary France had expanded east and when the left bank of the Rhine fell under French control during the War of the first Coalition of 1792–97 the way was paved for the unification of Germany. After Napoleon Bonaparte defeated Austria in 1802 he redrew the map of Germany. All but a few of the free German cities and all the ecclesiastical territories were stripped of their independence. In their place he created a series of buffer states. Bavaria, Württemberg and Saxony were raised to the status of kingdoms, with Baden and Hesse-Darmstadt as duchies. In 1806 the Holy Roman Empire was officially abolished. The Habsburgs promoted themselves from archdukes to emperors of Austria and set about consolidating their position in the Balkans. After the defeat of Prussia and the occupation of Berlin by Napoleon, the country was forced to sign away half its territory. In the aftermath, Prussia abolished serfdom and allowed the cities to develop their own municipal governments. Prussia played a critical role in the defeat of Napoleon at Waterloo in 1815. The Congress of Vienna, which met to determine the structure of post-Napoleon Europe, established Prussian dominance in German affairs. Westphalia and the Rhineland were added to its territories and although there were still 39 independent states, much of Napoleon's original vision for the reorganization of the Holy Roman Empire was ratified. A German Confederation was established, each state was represented in the Frankfurt-based Diet and Austria held the permanent right to the presidency with Prussia holding the vice-presidency.

The dominant political forces in Germany after the Congress of Vienna were still extremely conservative, but the rapid advance of the industrial revolution brought about the emergence of a new social order, with wage-earning workers and a growing bourgeoisie. The workers were quick to agitate for better working conditions and the middle classes for political representation. Adding to the social unrest was the peasant class, whose poor living standards were made worse by the failed harvests of the late 1840s. By 1848 violence had erupted all over Europe, forcing the Prussian king to allow elections to the National Assembly in Frankfurt. Although this presented an opportunity for the electorate to introduce widespread liberal social reforms, the middle class members of the Assembly blocked all radical measures. When armed rebellions broke out in 1849, the National Assembly was disbanded and the Prussian army, backed by other German kingdoms and principalities, seized power. From the 1850s, Prussia was in an unassailable position. Realizing the importance of industrial might, Prussia became the driving force for creating a single German market.

Bismarck

In 1862 Wilhelm I appointed Otto von Bismarck as chancellor. Although a leading member of the Junker class, he set about introducing widespread reforms. In order to unite the liberal and conservative wings, he backed the demands for universal male suffrage and, in return for the Chancellor's support for a united Germany, the liberals supported his plans for modernizing the army. Bismarck persuaded Austria to back him in a war against Denmark, which resulted in the recapture of Schleswig and Holstein, and in a subsequent row with Austria over the spoils (the Seven Years' War) Austria was crushed by the superior strength of Prussian arms and military organization. Austria was forced out of German affairs and the previously neutral Hanover and Hesse-Kassel joined the other small German states under Prussia to form a North German Confederation. Bismarck still needed to bring the southern German states into the fold and, in 1870, he rallied all the German states to provoke a war with France. The outcome of the Franco-Prussian War of 1870–71 was the defeat of France and the creation of a united Germany (including the long disputed provinces of Alsace and Lorraine). Wilhelm I of Prussia was named kaiser and the empire was dubbed the

Second Reich, commemorating the revival of German imperial tradition after a hiatus of 65 years.

At home, Bismarck continued with his liberal reforms. Uniform systems of law, currency, banking and administration were introduced nationwide, restrictions on trade and labour movements were lifted and the cities were given civic autonomy. These measures were designed to contain the liberals while he set about trying to undermine the influence of the Catholic Church. Although he forced the Catholics to support his agricultural policies designed to protect the interests of the Junker landowners, he had to back down on other issues. Despite the introduction of welfare benefits, opposition to Bismarck grew with the formation of the Social Democratic Party (SPD) in 1870.

Meanwhile, Bismarck was competing with Britain and France in the acquisition of colonies in Africa and the Pacific. In Germany he managed a political balancing act, on one hand creating an alliance of the three great imperial powers of Germany, Russia and Austria and on the other a Mediterranean alliance with Britain to prevent Russia from expanding into the Balkans. When Wilhelm I died in 1888, he was succeeded by his son, Friedrich III, who died after only a few months, and then by his grandson Kaiser Wilhelm II, a firm believer in the divine right of kings. After dismissing Bismarck from office in 1890, he appointed a series of 'yes men' to run his government, thereby seriously undermining the strength and stability that had been built up under Bismarck in the previous decade. Britain had long been an ally of Germany, bound by the ties of dynasty and common distrust of France but after the Kaiser came out in open support of the South African Boers, with whom Britain was in conflict, relations between the two countries plummeted, and the European arms race accelerated. Bismarck's juggling of alliances collapsed and Europe was divided into two hostile camps. On one side, Germany was allied once more with Austria (who needed help in propping up her collapsing Eastern Empire) and with Italy. On the other, France and Russia, united in common mistrust of the German-speaking nations, drew Britain closer to them. The European war that was brewing was set in motion in 1914 when a Bosnian nationalist assassinated the Austrian Archduke Franz Ferdinand at Sarajevo. Austria sent a threatening memo falsely accusing Serbia of causing the assassination. This led Russia to mobilize in defence of her Slavic neighbours. Seeing this as an excuse to strike first, Germany attacked France. Belgium's neutrality (which had been guaranteed by Britain) was violated when the German armies marched through on their way to France and Britain declared war on Germany in 1914.

First World War

The German generals miscalculated the strength of the resistance from France and Russia. They had counted on a capitulation within a short time and when this did not happen, they found they were fighting a war on two fronts. A new form of warfare emerged with the digging of trenches all along Northern France and Belgium. The injury and loss of life suffered by both sides during the next four years was to damage an entire generation of young men all over Europe. In 1917 the United States entered the war and although the Bolshevik revolution in Russia that same year gained Germany a reprieve, allowing the transfer of vast numbers of troops from the eastern to western fronts, the respite was short-lived. Troops returning from Russia agitated against the war. At the same time, the German lines were weakened by over-extension. On 8 Aug. 1918 the German defences were finally broken and the armies routed. In 1916 the Kaiser had handed over military and political power to Generals Paul von Hindenburg and Erich Ludendorff. As the threat of defeat came closer and in an attempt to minimize the potential damage of a harsh peace treaty, Ludendorff decided to leave the peace negotiations to a parliamentary delegation. He felt they would be more likely to gain lenient terms and this might serve to nip a possible Bolshevik-style revolution in the bud. Two months

of frenzied political activity followed which resulted in the abdication of the kaiser and the announcement of a new German republic. The First World War ended on 11 Nov. 1918.

The Elections that followed confirmed the Social Democratic Party as the new political force in Germany. Friedrich Ebert, leader of the SPD, was made president, with Philip Scheidmann as chancellor. In 1919 a new constitution was drawn up at Weimar and a republican government under Chancellor Ebert attempted to restore political and economic stability. But the Treaty of Versailles had exacted painful losses. The rich industrial regions of Saarland and Alsace-Lorraine were ceded to France and Upper Silesia was given to a resurrected Poland. A Polish corridor to the sea effectively cut off East Prussia from the rest of the country and all Germany's overseas colonies were confiscated. The Rhineland was declared a demilitarized zone and the size of the armed forces was severely limited. The German economy was burdened with a heavy reparation bill.

Feeling betrayed by what they saw as a harsh settlement, the German military fostered the 'stab in the back' excuse for failure, which was readily accepted by a disillusioned public. Scheidmann was forced to resign and in the elections of 1920 the SPD withdrew altogether, leaving power in the hands of minorities drawn from the liberal and moderate conservative parties. The reparation payments were having such an effect on the economy that payments were withheld, giving France the excuse to occupy the industrial region of the Ruhr in 1923. Passive resistance by the German workers meant that production ground to a halt and galloping inflation quickly ruined the middle class as the currency became worthless. Although the Weimar Republic seemed bound to fail, a new chancellor, Gustav Stresemann, realised the danger of economic collapse and ended the passive resistance to the allies in the Ruhr. He also negotiated enormous loans from the United States to help rebuild Germany's economy.

Rise of Hitler

By Oct. 1924 the currency was re-established at more or less its former value and (very nearly) full employment and general prosperity followed. Scheidmann went on to serve as foreign secretary when he re-established Germany as a world power. Reparation payments were scaled down and more US aid was negotiated. Even though in 1925 the ailing and aged Hindenburg was elected president, the German Republic seemed secure.

The National Socialist German Workers' Party was founded in 1918. Its first leader, a locksmith named Anton Drexler, was soon ousted by Adolf Hitler, a former soldier from Austria whose fanaticism had been fed by defeat in 1918. The party attracted political extremists and misfits, whose views mixed the extremes of right and left wing opinion. The party's constitution was based on a combination of Communism and Italian fascism.

After forming its own army, the Brown Shirts or Storm Troopers (SA), Hitler led a failed *Putsch* in Bavaria in 1923. He was arrested and convicted of high treason. He served only nine months of his sentence and emerged having used his time in prison to write his political manifesto, *Mein Kampf*. Initially, sales of Mein Kampf were negligible and Hitler's views were treated as something of a joke. Only the power of his personality, and Joseph Goebbels' propaganda skills, sustained the National Socialists on the German political scene.

The recession of the late 1920s proved fertile ground for Hitler's ideas, which began to appeal to wounded national pride and seemed to offer an attractive solution to the growing economic crisis. Elections were held in 1930 and the Nazi party gained an astonishing 6·4m. votes, becoming the country's second largest party.

The young, the unemployed and the impoverished middle classes were Hitler's main supporters but it was the decision of the right wing traditionalists to back Hitler in order to gain control over his supporters that gave him respectability.

Financial support from leading industrialists and giant corporations followed, enabling the Nazi party to fight a strong campaign in the 1932 presidential elections. Hindenburg, backed by the SPD and other democratic parties, scraped a victory. Appointed chancellor, Heinrich Brüning introduced a series of economic reforms, negotiated the end of reparation payments and regained Germany's right to arms equality. But his attempt to introduce land reform lost him the support of the landowners, who undermined his efforts to make the Republic work. Two short-term chancellors followed—Franz von Papen and Gen. Kurt von Schleicher. In 1932 one inconclusive election followed another. Hitler, greatly helped by a campaign of terror by his storm troopers, won increased support. Von Papen, who plotted to persuade Hindenburg to declare Hitler chancellor, mistakenly believed that his party's majority in the Reichstag would enable him to retain control. Hitler was sworn in as chancellor on 30 Jan. 1933.

No sooner had Hitler assumed power than he set about destroying all opposition, stepping up the campaign of terror, which was now backed by the apparatus of the state. He was greatly helped by Hermann Göring who, as Prussian minister of the interior, had control of the police. A month later, the Reichstag was burned down and Hindenburg was obliged to declare a state of emergency, giving Hitler the excuse to silence his opponents legally. Hitler was now the country's dictator, declaring himself president of the Third Reich in 1934.

Race to War

Hitler's policies embraced a theory of Aryan racial supremacy by which, during the following decade, millions of Jews, gypsies, and other non-Aryan 'undesirables' were persecuted, used as slave labour, shipped off to concentration camps, murdered and their assets confiscated. Hitler's expansionism led to his annexation of Austria (the *Anschluss*) and German-speaking Czechoslovakia (the Sudetenland) in 1938. The following year he declared all of Bohemia-Moravia a German protectorate and invaded Poland, attempting to restore the authority exercised there by Prussia before 1918. After the invasion of Czechoslovakia, Britain and France signed an agreement with Germany sacrificing Czech national integrity in return for what they believed would be world peace. Interpreting this as a sign of weakness, Hitler ordered the invasion of Poland, signed a non-aggression pact with Russia and expected a similar collapse of resistance on the part of other western powers. However, by now Britain and France had realized that the Munich agreement was a humiliating sham and that Hitler's invasion of Poland on 1 Sept. 1939 meant that he would pursue his policy of 'Lebensraum'. Two days after German tanks rolled into Poland, Britain and France declared war on Germany and the Second World War began.

Germany was well prepared for conflict and to begin with the war went well for Hitler. The fall of Poland was quickly followed by the defeat of the Low Countries and in 1940 France was forced to sign an armistice with Germany and to set up a puppet government in Vichy. Hitler bombarded Britain from the air but held back from invasion. Instead, he turned to the east, subduing the Balkans and, in 1941, planned an invasion of the Soviet Union. In Dec. 1941, after Hitler's Japanese allies attacked the United States naval base at Pearl Harbor, America declared war on the Axis powers. By this time, Germany was hopelessly overextended. Defeat in North Africa, in May 1943, was followed by the halt of German advance on Russia. The Allies invaded France in June 1944, liberating Paris in Aug. while Russian troops advanced from the east. Hitler was faced with certain defeat but refused to surrender, ordering the German people to defend every square inch of German territory to the death. On 30 April 1945, as Soviet forces marched into Berlin, Hitler committed suicide in his bunker. Germany surrendered unconditionally on 7 May 1945, bringing the Third Reich to an end.

Post War

The Allied forces occupied Germany—the UK, the USA and France holding the west and the USSR the east. By the Berlin Declaration of 5 June 1945 each was allocated a zone of occupation. The zone commanders-in-chief together made up the Allied Control Council in Berlin. The area of Greater Berlin was also divided into four sectors.

At the Potsdam Conference of 1945 northern East Prussia was transferred to the USSR. It was also agreed that, pending a final peace settlement, Poland should administer the areas east of the rivers Oder and Neisse, with the frontier fixed on the Oder and Western Neisse down to the Czechoslovak frontier.

By 1948 it had become clear that there would be no agreement between the occupying powers as to the future of Germany. Accordingly, the western allies united their zones into one unit in March 1948. In protest, the USSR withdrew from the Allied Control Council, blockaded Berlin until May 1949, and consolidated control of eastern Germany, establishing the German Democratic Republic (GDR).

A People's Council appointed in 1948 drew up a constitution for the GDR that came into force in Oct. 1949, providing for a communist state of five Länder with a centrally planned economy. In 1952 the government marked the division between its own territory and that of the Federal Republic (West Germany), with a three-mile cordon fenced along the frontier. Berlin was closed as a migration route by the construction of a concrete boundary wall in 1961. In 1953 there were popular revolts against food shortages and the pressure to collectivize. In 1954 the government eased economic restraints, the USSR ceased to collect reparation payments, and sovereignty was granted. The GDR signed the Warsaw Pact in 1955. Socialist policies were stepped up in 1958, leading to flight to the West of skilled workers.

Meanwhile, a constituent assembly met in Bonn in Sept. 1948 and drafted a Basic Law, which came into force in May 1949. In Sept. 1949 the occupation forces limited their own powers and the Federal Republic of Germany came into existence. The occupation forces retained some powers, however, and the Republic did not become a sovereign state until 1955 when the Occupation Statute was revoked.

The Republic consisted of the states of Schleswig-Holstein, Hamburg, Lower Saxony, Bremen, North Rhine-Westphalia, Hessen, Rhineland-Palatinate, Baden-Württemberg, Bavaria and Saarland, together with West Berlin.

The first chancellor, Konrad Adenauer (1949–63), was committed to the ultimate reunification of Germany and refused to acknowledge the German Democratic Republic. It was not until 1972 that the two German states signed an agreement of mutual recognition and intent to co-operate, forged by West German Chancellor Willy Brandt.

The most marked feature of post-war West Germany was rapid population and economic growth. Immigration from the German Democratic Republic, about 3m. since 1945, stopped when the Berlin Wall was built in 1961; however, there was a strong movement of German-speaking people from German settlements in countries of the Soviet bloc. Industrial growth also attracted labour from Turkey, Yugoslavia, Italy and Spain.

Reunification

The Paris Treaty, which came into force in 1955, ensured the Republic's contribution to NATO and NATO forces were stationed along the Rhine in large numbers, with consequent dispute about the deployment of nuclear missiles on German soil. Even before sovereignty, the Republic had begun negotiations for a measure of European unity, and joined in creating the European Coal and Steel Community in 1951 and the European Economic Community in 1957. In Jan. 1957 the Saarland was returned to full German control. In 1973 the Federal Republic entered the UN.

In the autumn of 1989 movements for political liberalization in the GDR and reunification with Federal Germany gathered strength. Erich Honecker and other long-serving Communist leaders were dismissed in Oct.–Nov. The Berlin Wall was breached on 9 Nov. Following the reforms in the GDR in Nov. 1989 the Federal Chancellor Helmut Kohl issued a plan for German confederation. The ambassadors of the four wartime allies met in Berlin in Dec. After talks with Chancellor Kohl on 11 Feb. 1990, President Gorbachev said the USSR would raise no objection to German reunification. The Allies agreed a formula for reunification talks to begin after the GDR elections on 18 March. On 18 May Federal Germany and the GDR signed a treaty extending Federal Germany's currency, together with its economic, monetary and social legislation, to the GDR as of 1 July. On 23 Aug. the *Volkskammer* (the parliament of the GDR) by 294 votes to 62 'declared its accession to the jurisdiction of the Federal Republic as from 3 Oct. according to article 23 of the Basic Law', which provided for the Länder of pre-war Germany to accede to the Federal Republic. On 12 Sept. the Treaty on the Final Settlement with Respect to Germany was signed by the Federal Republic of Germany, the GDR and the four wartime allies: France, the USSR, the UK and the USA.

The single most important event in German post-war history took place on 3 Oct. 1990 with the reunification of the Federal Republic and the former GDR. That it happened at all was remarkable enough but that it was achieved without major social and political disruption was a huge tribute to the strength of a still young democracy. That is not to say that reunification has been trouble free. Notwithstanding the injection of billions of deutschemarks of public subsidy which has transformed the infrastructure and restored urban areas, the easterners found the transition from communism to capitalism more painful than they had anticipated. Part of the problem was the adoption of the deutschemark which, by virtue of its strength as an international currency, inspired confidence but at the same time made it harder for export markets in central and eastern Europe to afford to buy German. The collapse of much traditional industry in the east has been hastened by wage equalization deals, pushing up labour costs. As a result, unemployment has soared.

But there are signs that an economic revival may not be far off. The automotive and information technology sectors are doing well and the chemicals industry, which contracted sharply after reunification, is beginning once more to expand.

The Federal Assembly (*Bundestag*) moved from Bonn to the renovated *Reichstag* in Berlin in 1999. The government move to Berlin is calculated to do much to bring eastern Germany back into the centre of national life as an equal part of the country.

TERRITORY AND POPULATION

Germany is bounded in the north by Denmark and the North and Baltic Seas, east by Poland, east and southeast by the Czech Republic, southeast and south by Austria, south by Switzerland and west by France, Luxembourg, Belgium and the Netherlands. Area: 357,043 sq. km. Population estimate, 31 Dec. 2004: 82,501,000 (42,147,000 females). Of the total population, 65,680,000 lived in the former Federal Republic of Germany (including West Berlin) and 16,821,000 in the five new states of the former German Democratic Republic (including East Berlin); density, 231 per sq. km. In 2003, 88.1% of the population lived in urban areas. There were 39.12m. households in March 2004 of which 14.56m. were single-person. Germany has an ageing population. The proportion of the population over 60 has been steadily rising, and that of the under 20s steadily declining. By the mid-1990s the number of over 60s had surpassed the number of under 20s and now stands at 25% of the total population.

The UN gives a projected population for 2010 of 82.70m.

On 14 Nov. 1990 Germany and Poland signed a treaty confirming Poland's existing western frontier and renouncing German claims to territory lost as a result of the Second World War.

The capital is Berlin; the Federal German government moved from Bonn to Berlin in 1999.

The Federation comprises 16 *Bundesländer* (states). Area and population:

Bundesländer	Area in sq. km	Population (in 1,000) 1987 census	2004 estimate	Density per sq. km (2004)
Baden-Württemberg (BW)	35,752	9,286	10,718[1]	300[1]
Bavaria (BY)	70,549	10,903	12,444	176
Berlin (BE)[2]	892	—	3,388	3,798
Brandenburg (BB)[3]	29,478	—	2,568	86
Bremen (HB)	404	660	663	1,642
Hamburg (HH)	755	1,593	1,735	2,298
Hessen (HE)	21,115	5,508	6,098	289
Lower Saxony (NI)	47,618	7,162	8,006[4]	168[4]
Mecklenburg-West Pomerania (MV)[3]	23,178	—	1,720	74
North Rhine-Westphalia (NW)	34,082	16,712	18,075	530
Rhineland-Palatinate (RP)	19,853	3,631	4,061	205
Saarland (SL)	2,570	1,056	1,056	411
Saxony (SN)[3]	18,415	—	4,296	233
Saxony-Anhalt (ST)[3]	20,447	—	2,494	122
Schleswig-Holstein (SH)	15,763	2,554	2,829	179
Thuringia (TH)[3]	16,172	—	2,355	146

[1]March 2005. [2]1987 census population of West Berlin: 2,013,000. [3]Reconstituted in 1990 in the Federal Republic. [4]June 2005.

On 31 Dec. 2004 there were 6,717,100 resident foreigners, including 1,764,300 Turks, 548,200 Italians, 316,000 Greeks and 125,800 Serbs and Montenegrins. More than 1·6m. of these were born in Germany. Germany's Muslim population, at 3·2m., is the second highest in Europe after that of France. In 2004 Germany received 35,607 asylum applications, compared to 438,200 in 1992. The main countries of origin in 2004 were Turkey, Serbia and Montenegro, Russia, Vietnam, Iran and Azerbaijan. 127,153 persons were naturalized in 2004, of whom 44,465 were from Turkey. In 2003 there were 626,300 emigrants and 769,000 immigrants. New citizenship laws were introduced on 1 Jan. 2000, whereby a child of non-Germans will have German citizenship automatically if the birth is in Germany, if at the time of the birth one parent has made Germany his or her customary legal place of abode for at least eight years, and if this parent has had an unlimited residence permit for at least three years. Previously at least one parent had to hold German citizenship for the child to become a German national.

Populations of the 82 towns of over 100,000 inhabitants in Dec. 2003 (in 1,000):

Town (and Bundesland)	Population in 1,000	Ranking by Population	Town (and Bundesland)	Population in 1,000	Ranking by Population
Aachen (NW)	256·6	27	Cottbus (BB)	107·5	75
Augsburg (BY)	259·2	26	Darmstadt (HE)	139·7	55
Bergisch Gladbach (NW)	106·1	77	Dortmund (NW)	589·7	6
Berlin (BE)	3,388·5	1	Dresden (SN)	483·6	15
Bielefeld (NW)	328·5	18	Duisburg (NW)	506·5	12
Bochum (NW)	387·3	16	Düsseldorf (NW)	572·5	9
Bonn (NW)	311·1	19	Erfurt (TH)	201·6	37
Bottrop (NW)	120·3	62	Erlangen (BY)	102·4	80
Braunschweig (NI)	245·1	29	Essen (NW)	589·5	7
Bremen (HB)	544·9	10	Frankfurt am Main (HE)	643·4	5
Bremerhaven (HB)	118·3	67	Freiburg im Breisgau (BW)	212·5	36
Chemnitz (SN)	249·9	28	Fürth (BY)	111·9	70
Cologne (NW)	966·0	4			

Town (and Bundesland)	Population in 1,000	Ranking by Population	Town (and Bundesland)	Population in 1,000	Ranking by Population
Gelsenkirchen (NW)	272·4	22	Munich (BY)	1,247·9	3
Gera (TH)	106·4	76	Münster (NW)	269·6	24
Göttingen (NI)	122·9	59	Neuss (NW)	152·1	51
Hagen (NW)	200·0	38	Nuremberg (BY)	493·6	14
Halle (ST)	240·1	30	Oberhausen (NW)	220·0	34
Hamburg (HH)	1,743·1	2	Offenbach am Main (HE)	119·2	65
Hamm (NW)	185·0	42	Oldenburg (NI)	158·3	50
Hanover (NI)	516·2	11	Osnabrück (NI)	165·5	46
Heidelberg (BW)	143·0	53	Paderborn (NW)	141·8	54
Heilbronn (BW)	120·7	61	Pforzheim (BW)	119·0	66
Herne (NW)	172·9	44	Potsdam (BB)	145·0	52
Hildesheim (NI)	103·2	78	Recklinghausen (NW)	123·1	58
Ingolstadt (BY)	119·5	64	Regensburg (BY)	128·6	57
Jena (TH)	102·6	79	Remscheid (NW)	117·7	68
Karlsruhe (BW)	282·6	21	Reutlingen (BW)	112·3	69
Kassel (HE)	194·3	40	Rostock (MV)	198·3	39
Kiel (SH)	233·0	32	Saarbrücken (SL)	181·9	43
Koblenz (RP)	107·6	74	Salzgitter (NI)	109·9	71
Krefeld (NW)	238·6	31	Siegen (NW)	107·8	73
Leipzig (SN)	497·5	13	Solingen (NW)	164·5	47
Leverkusen (NW)	161·5	49	Stuttgart (BW)	589·2	8
Lübeck (SH)	212·8	35	Trier (RP)	100·2	82
Ludwigshafen am Rhein (RP)	162·8	48	Ulm (BW)	119·8	63
Magdeburg (ST)	227·5	33	Wiesbaden (HE)	272·0	23
Mainz (RP)	185·5	41	Witten (NW)	101·8	81
Mannheim (BW)	308·4	20	Wolfsburg (NI)	122·7	60
Moers (NW)	107·9	72	Wuppertal (NW)	362·1	17
Mönchengladbach (NW)	262·4	25	Würzburg (BY)	132·7	56
Mülheim a. d. Ruhr (NW)	170·7	45			

The official language is German. Minor orthographical amendments were agreed in 1995. An agreement between German-speaking countries in Vienna on 1 July 1996 provided for minor orthographical changes and established a Commission for German Orthography in Mannheim. There have been considerable objections within Germany, particularly in the North, and many *Bundesländer* are to decide their own language programmes for schools. Generally, both old and new spellings are acceptable.

SOCIAL STATISTICS

Calendar years:

	Marriages	Live births	Of these to single parents	Deaths	Divorces
1999	430,674	770,744	170,634	846,330	190,590
2000	418,550	766,999	179,574	838,797	194,630
2001	389,591	734,475	183,816	828,541	197,498
2002	391,963	719,250	187,961	841,686	204,214
2003	382,911	706,721	190,641	853,946	214,274

Of the 382,911 marriages in 2003, 35,583 involved a foreign male and 45,751 involved a foreign female. The average age of bridegrooms in 2003 was 35·8 years, and of brides 32·5. The average first-time marrying age for men was 32 and for women 29.

Rates (per 1,000 population), 2003: birth, 8·6; death, 10·3; marriage, 4·6; infant mortality, 4·2 per 1,000 births; stillborn rate, 3·8 per 1,000 births. Life expectancy, 2003: men, 75·7 years; women, 81·5. Suicide rates, 2002, per 100,000 population, 13·5 (men, 20·3; women, 7·0). Annual population growth rate, 1992–2002, 0·2%; fertility rate, 2001, 1·3 births per woman.

Legislation of 1995 categorizes abortions as illegal, but stipulates that prosecutions will not be brought if they are performed in the first three months of pregnancy after consultation with a doctor. The annual abortion rate, at under ten per 1,000 women aged 15–44, is among the lowest in the world.

Since 1 Aug. 2001 same-sex couples have been permitted to exchange vows at registry offices. The law also gives them the same rights as heterosexual couples in inheritance and insurance law.

A UNICEF report published in 2005 showed that 10·2% of children in Germany live in poverty (in households with income below 50% of the national median). A similar report from 2000 had shown that the poverty rate of children in lone-parent families in Germany was 51·2%, compared to 6·2% in two-parent families.

CLIMATE

Oceanic influences are only found in the northwest where winters are quite mild but stormy. Elsewhere a continental climate is general. To the east and south, winter temperatures are lower, with bright frosty weather and considerable snowfall. Summer temperatures are fairly uniform throughout. Berlin, Jan. 31°F (−0·5°C), July 66°F (19°C). Annual rainfall 22·5" (563 mm). Cologne, Jan. 36°F (2·2°C), July 66°F (18·9°C). Annual rainfall 27" (676 mm). Dresden, Jan. 30°F (−0·1°C), July 65°F (18·5°C). Annual rainfall 27·2" (680 mm). Frankfurt, Jan. 33°F (0·6°C), July 66°F (18·9°C). Annual rainfall 24" (601 mm). Hamburg, Jan. 31°F (−0·6°C), July 63°F (17·2°C). Annual rainfall 29" (726 mm). Hanover, Jan. 33°F (0·6°C), July 64°F (17·8°C). Annual rainfall 24" (604 mm). Munich, Jan. 28°F (−2·2°C), July 63°F (17·2°C). Annual rainfall 34" (855 mm). Stuttgart, Jan. 33°F (0·6°C), July 66°F (18·9°C). Annual rainfall 27" (677 mm).

CONSTITUTION AND GOVERNMENT

The Basic Law (*Grundgesetz*) was approved by the parliaments of the participating *Bundesländer* and came into force on 23 May 1949. It is to remain in force until 'a constitution adopted by a free decision of the German people comes into being'. The Federal Republic is a democratic and social constitutional state on a parliamentary basis. The federation is constituted by the 16 *Bundesländer* (states). The Basic Law decrees that the general rules of international law form part of the federal law. The constitutions of the *Bundesländer* must conform to the principles of a republican, democratic and social state based on the rule of law. Executive power is vested in the *Bundesländer*, unless the Basic Law prescribes or permits otherwise. Federal law takes precedence over state law.

Legislative power is vested in the *Bundestag* (Federal Assembly) and the *Bundesrat* (Federal Council). The Bundestag is currently composed of 614 members and is elected in universal, free, equal and secret elections for a term of four years. A party must gain 5% of total votes cast in order to gain representation in the Bundestag, although if a party has three candidates elected directly, they may take their seats even if the party obtains less than 5% of the national vote. The electoral system combines relative-majority and proportional voting; each voter has two votes, the first for the direct constituency representative, the second for the competing party lists in the *Bundesländer*. All directly elected constituency representatives enter parliament, but if a party receives more 'indirect' than 'direct' votes, the first name in order on the party list not to have a seat becomes a member—the number of seats is increased by the difference ('overhang votes'). Thus the number of seats in the Bundestag varies, but is 598 regular members (for the 2005 election, the same as in 2002, but down from 656 for the previous elections since reunification) plus the 'overhang votes' (16 at the 2005 election, giving a total of 614 members). The Bundesrat consists of 69 members appointed by the governments of the *Bundesländer* in proportions determined by the number of inhabitants. Each *Bundesland* has at least three votes.

The Head of State is the Federal *President,* who is elected for a five-year term by a *Federal Convention* specially convened for this purpose. This Convention consists of all the members of the Bundestag and an equal number of members elected by the *Bundesländer* parliaments in accordance with party strengths, but who need not themselves be members of the parliaments. No president may serve more than two terms. Executive power is vested in the Federal government, which consists of the Federal *Chancellor*, elected by the Bundestag on the proposal of the Federal President, and the Federal Ministers, who are appointed and dismissed by the Federal President upon the proposal of the Federal Chancellor.

The Federal Republic has exclusive legislation on: (1) foreign affairs; (2) federal citizenship; (3) freedom of movement, passports, immigration and emigration, and extradition; (4) currency, money and coinage, weights and measures, and regulation of time and calendar; (5) customs, commercial and navigation agreements, traffic in goods and payments with foreign countries, including customs and frontier protection; (6) federal railways and air traffic; (7) post and telecommunications; (8) the legal status of persons in the employment of the Federation and of public law corporations under direct supervision of the Federal government; (9) trade marks, copyright and publishing rights; (10) co-operation of the Federal Republic and the *Bundesländer* in the criminal police and in matters concerning the protection of the constitution, the establishment of a Federal Office of Criminal Police, as well as the combating of international crime; (11) federal statistics.

In the field of finance the Federal Republic has exclusive legislation on customs and financial monopolies and concurrent legislation on: (1) excise taxes and taxes on transactions, in particular, taxes on real-estate acquisition, incremented value and on fire protection; (2) taxes on income, property, inheritance and donations; (3) real estate, industrial and trade taxes, with the exception of the determining of the tax rates.

Federal laws are passed by the Bundestag and after their adoption submitted to the Bundesrat, which has a limited veto. The Basic Law may be amended only upon the approval of two-thirds of the members of the Bundestag and two-thirds of the votes of the Bundesrat.

Die Bundesrepublik Deutschland: Staatshandbuch. Cologne, annual

National Anthem

'Einigkeit und Recht und Freiheit' ('Unity and right and freedom'); words by H. Hoffmann, tune by J. Haydn.

GOVERNMENT CHRONOLOGY

Federal Republic of Germany (prior to re-unification).
Chancellors since 1949 (CDU = Christian Democratic Union; FDP = Free Democratic Party; SPD = Social Democratic Party)

1949–63	CDU	Konrad Adenauer
1963–66	CDU	Ludwig Erhard
1966–69	CDU	Kurt Georg Kiesinger
1969–74	SPD	Willy Brandt
1974	FDP	Walter Scheel
1974–82	SPD	Helmut Schmidt
1982–90	CDU	Helmut Kohl

German Democratic Republic = Presidents of the Republic (1949–60) then Leaders of the Council of State. (LDPD = Liberal Democratic Party of Germany; SED = Socialist Unity Party of Germany)

1949	LDPD	Johannes Dieckmann
1949–60	SED	Willhelm Pieck
1960	LDPD	Johannes Dieckmann
1960–73	SED	Walter Ulbricht
1973	SED	Friedrich Ebert
1973–76	SED	Willi Stoph
1976–89	SED	Erich Honecker
1989	SED	Egon Krenz
1989–90	LDPD	Manfred Gerlach

Federal Republic of Germany.
Chancellors since re-unification.

1990–98	CDU	Helmut Kohl
1998–2005	SPD	Gerhard Schröder
2005–	CDU	Angela Merkel

Presidents since 1949.

1949–59	FDP	Theodor Heuss
1959–69	CDU	Karl Heinrich Lübke
1969–74	SPD	Gustav Heinemann
1974–79	FDP	Walter Scheel
1979–84	CDU	Karl Carstens
1984–94	CDU	Richard von Weizsäcker
1994–99	CDU	Roman Herzog
1999–2004	SPD	Johannes Rau
2004–	CDU	Horst Köhler

RECENT ELECTIONS

On 23 May 2004 Horst Köhler was elected Federal President by the Federal Convention, defeating Gesine Schwan, the government's candidate, in the first round.

Bundestag elections were held on 18 Sept. 2005. The opposition Christian Democratic Union/Christian Social Union (CDU/CSU; the CSU is a Bavarian party where the CDU does not stand) won 226 seats with 35·2% of votes cast (248 with 38·5% in 2002); the Social Democratic Party (SPD) of Chancellor Gerhard Schröder won 222 with 34·2% (251 seats with 38·5%); the Free Democratic Party (FDP), 61 with 9·8% (47 with 7·4%); the Left Party (former Party for Democratic Socialism), 54 with 8·7% (2 with 4·0%); the Greens/Alliance 90, 51 with 8·1% (55 with 8·6%). Turnout was 77·7%. With neither major party winning a clear majority, either alone or with their traditional coalition partners, the CDU and the SPD agreed after lengthy negotiations to form a 'Grand Coalition' for only the second time in German history and the first since 1966–69. CDU leader Angela Merkel became Chancellor, although the SPD was given eight of the 14 ministerial posts.

European Parliament

Germany has 99 representatives. At the June 2004 elections turnout was 43·0% (45·2% in 1999). The CDU won 40 seats with 36·5% of votes cast (political affiliation in European Parliament: European People's Party–European Democrats); the SPD, 23 with 21·5% (Party of European Socialists); the Greens, 13 with 11·9% (Greens/European Free Alliance); the CSU, 9 with 9·0% (European People's Party–European Democrats); the FDP, 7 with 6·1% (Alliance of Liberals and Democrats for Europe); PDS, 7 with 6·1% (European Unitary Left/Nordic Green Left).

CURRENT ADMINISTRATION

Federal President: Horst Köhler; b. 1943 (CDU; sworn in 1 July 2004).

A 'Grand Coalition' between the CDU and the SPD was formed following the election of Sept. 2005. The cabinet was composed as follows in March 2006:

Chancellor: Angela Merkel; b. 1954 (CDU; sworn in on 22 Nov. 2005).

Vice-Chancellor and Minister of Labour and Social Affairs: Franz Müntefering (SPD). *Foreign Minister:* Frank-Walter Steinmeier (SPD). *Interior:* Wolfgang Schäuble (CDU). *Justice:* Brigitte Zypries (SPD). *Finance:* Peer Steinbrück (SPD). *Economy and Technology:* Michael Glos (CSU). *Consumer Protection, Food and Agriculture:* Horst Seehofer (CSU). *Defence:* Franz Josef Jung (CDU). *Family Affairs, Senior Citizens, Women and Youth:* Ursula von der Leyen (CDU). *Health:* Ulla Schmidt (SPD). *Transport, Housing and Construction:* Wolfgang Tiefensee (SPD). *Environment, Nature Conservation and Nuclear Safety:* Sigmar Gabriel (SPD). *Education and Research:* Annette Schavan (CDU). *Economic Co-operation and Development:* Heidemarie Wieczorek-Zeul (SPD). *Head of the Federal Chancellery:* Thomas de Maizière (CDU).

President of the Bundestag: Norbert Lammert (CDU; elected Oct. 2005).

Government Website: http://www.bundesregierung.de

CURRENT LEADERS

Horst Köhler

Position
President

Introduction
Horst Köhler took office as federal president of Germany on 1 July 2004, having previously served as the first German managing director of the International Monetary Fund (IMF) from 2000–04. Prior to the IMF, he was involved in German financial politics, particularly in regard to German reunification and the European Union Maastricht Treaty negotiations in 1991.

Early Life
Köhler was born on 22 Feb. 1943 in Skierbieszów, Poland. Following the Soviet invasion in the Second World War, his family fled to East Germany. In 1953 they moved into West Germany. He earned a doctorate in economics and politics from the University of Tübingen, where he was a scientific research assistant at the Institute for Applied Economic Research during 1969–76. Between 1976–89 he held various posts in Germany's ministries of economics and finance. He played an important role in the economic planning for Germany's reunification and assisted in providing aid to Russia after the collapse of the USSR. In 1991 Köhler was Germany's lead official in the negotiations that led to the Maastricht Treaty. From 1990–93 he served as Germany's deputy finance minister and from 1993–98 he was president of the German Savings Bank Association. In 1998 Köhler was appointed president of the European Bank for Reconstruction and Development (EBRD). He took part in focusing the EBRD's priorities on small businesses rather than large infrastructure projects. During his presidency the EBRD improved its finances, from having lost US$2,528m. in 1998 to making a profit of US$41m. in 1999. In addition he was deputy governor for Germany at the World Bank and was the personal representative of the federal chancellor in the preparation of the Group of Seven (G7) economic summits from 1990–93.

On 23 March 2000 Köhler was elected managing director and chairman of the Executive Board of the IMF, the first German to hold the post. His appointment came after the then chancellor, Gerhard Schröder, had campaigned to persuade European nations to back him. In 2002 his plan to allow indebted countries to file for bankruptcy caused protests from international financial markets.

Career in Office
Relinquishing his position at the IMF, Köhler was elected federal president of Germany on 23 May 2004. In his inaugural speech he encouraged the government to persevere with its economic reform programme, despite the short-term hardships that it would present. Following inconclusive parliamentary elections in Sept. 2005, he formally appointed Angela Merkel of the CDU as the first female federal chancellor at the head of a new coalition government in Nov. 2005.

Angela Merkel

Position
Chancellor

Introduction
Angela Merkel became Germany's first female chancellor in Nov. 2005. Her appointment came after three weeks of negotiations following elections that failed to give a parliamentary majority to either her party, the Christian Democrats (CDU), or the Social Democrats (SPD) of incumbent Gerhard Schröder. Merkel is expected to spearhead fundamental reforms to energize Germany's moribund economy.

Early Life
Angela Dorothea Kasner was born on 17 July 1954 in Hamburg, West Germany, the daughter of a Lutheran pastor and a teacher. Later in 1954 her father received a pastorship in East Germany (GDR) and the family moved to Templin, 50 km north of Berlin. Merkel was educated in Templin before studying physics at the University of Leipzig from 1973–78. Having married Ulrich Merkel in 1977, she continued her studies at the Academy of Sciences in East Berlin, receiving a doctorate in 1986, and subsequently combined research in quantum chemistry with lecturing. While a student, she was secretary for propaganda in the FDJ, an East German youth organization loyal to the ruling Socialist Unity Party of Germany. Following the fall of the Berlin Wall in Nov. 1989 she joined the new Democratic Awakening party.

Following democratic elections in the GDR on 18 March 1990, Merkel became a member of the East German Christian Democratic Union (CDU) and deputy spokesperson of the new government under Lothar de Maizière. She was elected to the *Bundestag* in the first post-unification general elections in Dec. 1990, representing the united CDU in a Baltic coast constituency encompassing Rügen and the city of Stralsund. She was also appointed to Chancellor Helmut Kohl's cabinet as minister for women and youth, a position she held until being promoted to minister for the environment in 1994.

Merkel lost ministerial office in 1998 when the CDU were defeated in federal elections but later that year was appointed secretary-general of the CDU. She oversaw a string of CDU provincial election victories in 1999, although it was a party funding scandal implicating the CDU's chairman, Wolfgang Schäuble, and Kohl himself, which thrust Merkel into the limelight. She criticized Kohl (who was later stripped of his title of the CDU's honorary chairman), called for a fresh start for the party and was duly elected president of the CDU on 10 April 2000.

Unable to garner sufficient support to challenge Chancellor Schröder in the 2002 federal elections, Merkel ceded that role to Edmund Stoiber, leader of the CDU's sister party, the Bavarian Christian Social Union (CSU). Following Stoiber's narrow defeat, Merkel became leader of the conservative opposition in the *Bundestag*. She advocated institutional reform through simplifying the tax code and lowering taxes, simplifying health care and radically overhauling pensions. She also argued for a loosening of German labour law and, in 2003, controversially backed the US-led invasion of Iraq.

On 30 May 2005 Merkel won the CDU/CSU nomination as challenger to Schröder in the 2005 elections. The CDU began with a 21% lead in opinion polls but Merkel trailed Schröder in terms of personal popularity. In the elections on 18 Sept. the CDU/CSU won 35·2% of the vote to the SPD's 34·2%. Both Merkel and Schröder claimed victory and weeks of wrangling ensued. A deal for a grand coalition was eventually reached whereby Merkel would become chancellor and the SPD would hold eight of the fourteen cabinet posts. Merkel was elected chancellor by a majority of delegates in the *Bundestag* on 22 Nov. 2005.

Career in Office
Merkel won plaudits for brokering an EU budget deal between France's Jacques Chirac and Britain's Tony Blair within weeks of becoming chancellor. Early opinion polls in Germany were favourable but persuading the potentially fractious grand coalition to agree on reforms to the labour market, healthcare and pension funding is likely to prove difficult.

DEFENCE

Conscription was reduced from ten months to nine months from Jan. 2002. In July 1994 the Constitutional Court ruled that German armed forces might be sent on peacekeeping missions abroad. Germany has increased the number of professionals available for military missions abroad and sent troops to Afghanistan as part of the international alliance against terrorism in the aftermath of 11 Sept. 2001. The first time that German armed forces were deployed in this way since the Second World War, the move provoked controversy in Germany. Since Jan. 2001 women have been allowed to serve in all branches of the military on the same basis as men.

In 2003 defence expenditure totalled US$35,145m. (US$426 per capita), representing 1·5% of GDP.

Army

The Army is organized in the Army Forces Command. The equipment of the former East German army is in store. Total strength was (2004) 284,500 (conscripts 94,500). There are Army reserves of 297,300.

The Territorial Army is organized into five Military Districts, under three Territorial Commands. Its main task is to defend rear areas and remains under national control even in wartime.

Navy

The Fleet Commander operates from a modern Maritime Headquarters at Glücksburg, close to the Danish border.

The fleet includes 12 diesel coastal submarines, one destroyer and 12 frigates. The main naval bases are at Wilhelmshaven, Olpenitz, Kiel, Eckernförde and Warnemünde.

The Naval Air Arm, 3,700 strong, is organized into two wings and includes 65 combat aircraft (Tornados and Atlantics) and 22 armed helicopters.

Personnel in 2004 numbered 25,650, including 4,950 conscripts.

Air Force

Since 1970 the *Luftwaffe* has comprised the following commands: German Air Force Tactical Command, German Air Force Support Command (including two German Air Force Regional Support Commands—North and South) and General Air Force Office. Personnel in 2004 was 67,500 (16,100 conscripts). There were 384 combat aircraft, including *Tornados*, F-4Fs, T-37Bs and T-38As.

INTERNATIONAL RELATIONS

A treaty of friendship with Poland signed on 17 June 1991 recognized the Oder-Neisse border and guaranteed minorities' rights in both countries.

Germany is a member of the UN, WTO, NATO, BIS, OECD, EU, Council of Europe, WEU, OSCE, CERN, Council of the Baltic Sea States, Danube Commission, Inter-American Development Bank, Asian Development Bank, IOM and the Antarctic Treaty. Germany is a signatory to the Schengen accord which abolishes border controls between Germany, Austria, Belgium, Denmark, Finland, France, Greece, Iceland, Italy, Luxembourg, the Netherlands, Norway, Portugal, Spain and Sweden.

In May 2005 Germany became the ninth country to ratify the proposed EU constitution when the *Bundestag* voted in favour by 569 votes to 23 with two abstentions on 12 May and the *Bundesrat* ratified the constitution by 66 votes to nil with three abstentions on 27 May.

ECONOMY

Services accounted for 69·2% of GDP in 2002, industry (manufacturing and construction) 29·6% and agriculture 1·2%.

According to the anti-corruption organization *Transparency International*, Germany ranked 16th in the world in a 2005 survey of the countries with the least corruption in business and government. It received 8·2 out of 10 in the annual index.

Overview

Measured on an international exchange rate basis, Germany is the third largest economy in the world after the USA and Japan, and is home to several of Europe's most successful companies.

However, its GDP growth in the 2000s ranked with Italy as the worst performing in the euro zone. GDP growth averaged 4·5% per annum in the 1960s but slowed to under 1% in the first half of the 2000s. Germany's principal manufacturing industries are the automotive and chemical industries, with telecommunications an increasingly important sector. Although the share of overall industrial output (excluding construction) in GDP has declined over the years, manufacturing and related services are still of greater importance to the economy than to other advanced economies. The traditionally important steelmaking sector in the Ruhr valley has faced sharp decline, while agriculture's economic importance has diminished significantly.

The country's post-war economic miracle (*Wirtschaftswunder*) was marked by prudent fiscal and monetary policy, the growth of a globally competitive manufacturing sector and good relations between social partners. The German economy is described as a 'social market' in that it embraces industrial relations and enlightened company management, as well as social welfare and other aspects of government policy. An important element is the 'stakeholder' concept, with companies not only responsible to their shareholders but also to employees, customers, suppliers and local communities. However, the system is changing as a result of the internationalization of German companies, corporate mergers, the revitalization of the stock exchange and the ending of large cross-shareholdings by companies and banks. This has meant a weakening of previously interlocking structures in commerce and finance.

Low growth in recent years has been attributed to weaknesses in the labour market and the high cost of restructuring the economy of the former GDR. Labour utilization has diminished owing to high and inflexible labour costs, generous unemployment benefits and early retirement policies. Household income and consumption were stagnant from 2002–05 as a result of structural difficulties, with private consumption growth significantly beneath the euro zone average. Unemployment benefits are generous by international standards and unemployment in Germany has been persistently high, almost twice the OECD average. In June 2003 Chancellor Schröder won support for Agenda 2010, a series of reforms to pensions, the labour market and health care, aimed at reducing key structural weaknesses. Unemployment benefits and social security have been amalgamated for long-term claimants (known as the Hartz IV reforms).

The IMF suggests that further reforms are needed to support higher growth and fiscal consolidation in the long run. In June 2005 the IMF wrote: 'The Hartz IV reforms are boosting labour supply, but by themselves are not sufficient for durable employment growth. The new system has improved incentives to work and the government's perseverance in introducing these difficult reforms is commendable. However, employment growth has so far been limited to temporary work and self-employment, and high labour costs still hold back demand for full-time employment … As more workers are now looking for jobs, greater emphasis needs to be put on reforms that increase labour demand: wage setting needs to respond better to labour market imbalances and more closely reflect productivity differentials. With the majority of unemployed having low productivity, it will be important to reduce wage floors for entry-level and low-skill jobs. Reducing central controls on wage bargaining in favour of more decentralized and firm-level bargaining is a priority. Cutting employment protection legislation would boost participation and employment, in particular for the young, old, and unskilled. A loosening of the existing legislation could improve conditions for hiring those with little work experience or skills.'

Labour market rigidities have contributed to Germany's recent budget deficit problems. As tax and social security revenues rely heavily on wage income, the revenue base of the public sector is eroding while high and long-lasting unemployment benefits and social transfers put pressure on expenditure. From 2002–05 the government's annual budget deficit exceeded the 3% GDP euro zone limit by roughly 0·75%. From 1996–2002 public debt hovered around 60% of GDP but has grown since 2003, nearing 70% in 2005. According to the IMF: 'Germany is at the cusp of a powerful demographic shift and long-run simulations show that public finances and long-standing welfare programs are not sustainable under current policies... In view of the increasing pressure from aging, policies should aim to eliminate the structural deficit by 2010.'

The Merkel government formed in late 2005 made reduction of the budget deficit a key short-term objective. Despite fears of stifling consumer spending, an increase in VAT from 16% to 19% will take effect in 2007. Aside from tax reform the IMF suggests recalibrating social security benefits, given the demographic profile of the country, and implementing durable expenditure cuts.

In 2004–05 the economy experienced modest recovery after two years of stagnation. The manufacturing export sector performed exceptionally well. Business confidence in Jan. 2006 was at its highest level since 1999–2000. In recent years exporters have benefited from a mild EU recovery, strong US growth and increasingly close export relations with developing countries in Eastern Europe and Asia. Yet the industrial sector's revival has not been matched by a similar buoyancy in consumer spending or broad-based economic growth. Dependence on the manufacturing sector could leave the country vulnerable to slowdowns or recessions in its principal export markets. The IMF regards product and services market reforms as essential to improving Germany's economic performance by increasing competition and enhancing productivity. The growth of labour productivity and total factor productivity has decelerated over the last decade, with both growing at less than 1% in the 2000s.

Currency

On 1 Jan. 1999 the euro (EUR) became the legal currency in Germany; irrevocable conversion rate 1·95583 DM (deutschemark) to one euro. The euro, which consists of 100 cents, has been in circulation since 1 Jan. 2002. There are seven euro notes in different colours and sizes denominated in 500, 200, 100, 50, 20, 10 and 5 euros, and eight coins denominated in 2 and 1 euros, then 50, 20, 10, 5, 2 and 1 cents. It was still possible to make cash transactions in German marks until 28 Feb. 2002, although formally the mark had ceased to be legal tender on 31 Dec. 2001. Euro banknotes in circulation on 1 Jan. 2002 had a total value of €254·2bn.

Foreign exchange reserves were US$42,260m. in June 2002 and gold reserves were 110·79m. troy oz (95·18m. troy oz in 1997). Only the USA, with 262·00m. troy oz, had more in June 2002. Total money supply was €93,977m. in June 2002.

Inflation rates (based on OECD statistics):

1995	1996	1997	1998	1999	2000	2001	2002	2003	2004
2·7%	1·2%	1·5%	0·6%	0·6%	1·4%	1·9%	1·3%	1·0%	1·8%

The inflation rate in 2005 according to Destatis, the Federal Statistical Office, was 2·0%.

Budget

In July 2000 Chancellor Schröder pushed through a tax-cutting package which included from 2001 a reduction in corporation tax from 40%/30% to 25%. The top rate of income tax was to be reduced gradually from 51% to 42% by 2005. In March 2003 Schröder announced 'Agenda 2010', to include cuts in unemployment benefits, an easing of job protection rules and trimmed state pensions. The health system, among the world's most expensive, was also a core target. 'Agenda 2010' encountered criticism from trade unionists and left-wingers within the SPD. In July 2003 the German government announced that it would bring forward the tax cuts scheduled for 2005 and combine them

with those planned for 2004, bringing the total tax cut for 2004 to €15·5bn.

Since 1 Jan. 1979 tax revenues have been distributed as follows: *Federal government.* Income tax, 42·5%; capital yield and corporation tax, 50%; turnover tax, 67·5%; trade tax, 15%; capital gains, insurance and accounts taxes, 100%; excise duties (other than on beer), 100%. *Bundesländer.* Income tax, 42·5%; capital yield and corporation tax, 50%; turnover tax, 32·5%; trade tax, 15%; other taxes, 100%. *Local authorities.* Income tax, 15%; trade tax, 70%; local taxes, 100%.

VAT is currently 16% (reduced rate, 7%) but is set to rise to 19% from 1 Jan. 2007.

Budget for 2004 (in €1m.):

	All public authorities	Federal portion
Revenue	*Current*	
Taxes	439,721	197,677
Economic activities	18,111	4,193
Interest	4,059	1,028
Current allocations and subsidies	136,936	4,307
Other receipts	34,796	8,577
minus equalising payments	120,504	—
	513,119	215,782
Revenue	*Capital*	
Sale of assets	15,602	7,783
Allocations for investment	21,933	2
Repayment of loans	9,015	4,163
Public sector borrowing	326	—
minus equalising payments	17,348	—
	29,528	11,948
Excess revenue	702	—
Total revenues	543,349	227,730
Expenditure	*Current*	
Staff	173,208	27,325
Materials	68,630	17,536
Interest	67,284	37,655
Allocations and subsidies	353,556	152,786
minus equalising payments	120,504	—
	542,174	235,302
Expenditure	*Capital*	
Construction	25,728	5,517
Acquisition of property	8,021	1,613
Allocations and subsidies	41,023	13,636
Loans	10,325	3,685
Acquisition of shares	2,354	565
Repayments in the public sector	701	—
minus equalising payments	17,348	—
	70,804	25,016
Excess expenditure	-4,505	-3,019
Total expenditures	608,473	257,299

Performance

Real GDP growth rates (based on OECD statistics):

1995	1996	1997	1998	1999	2000	2001	2002	2003	2004
2·0%	1·0%	1·9%	1·8%	1·9%	3·5%	1·4%	0·1%	−0·2%	1·1%

In 2002 real GDP growth was just 0·1%, the lowest since 1993, and in 2003 the economy contracted by 0·2%, although Germany came out of recession in the second half of the year. The real GDP growth rates in 2004 and 2005 according to Destatis, the Federal Statistical Office, were 1·6% and 0·9% respectively. Total GDP in 2004 was US$2,714·4bn., the third highest behind USA and Japan. Germany was ranked third in the Business Competitiveness Index in the World Economic Forum's *Global Competitiveness Report 2005–2006.* It had also been third in the 2004–2005 index.

According to the Sept. 2004 *OECD Economic* Survey: 'Poor labour market performance continues to weigh on consumer sentiment and business confidence remains volatile. The labour market suffers from weak growth and distorted incentives, with both contributing to problems in taking up work and providing employment....Cyclical weakness and the structural problems of the economy impact strongly on public budgets, while uncertainty about how public finances will be put on a durably sustainable path is a further factor undermining confidence. Re-establishing Germany's traditional economic strength requires a comprehensive policy response within a coherent framework.'

Banking and Finance

The Deutsche Bundesbank (German Federal Bank) is the central bank and bank of issue. Its duty is to protect the stability of the currency. It is independent of the government but obliged to support the government's general policy. Its Governor is appointed by the government for eight years. The *President* is Axel Weber. Its assets were US$874,706m. in June 2001. Ranked by total assets it is the third largest bank in the world. Its market capitalization in June 2001 was US$45·7bn. The largest private banks are the Deutsche Bank, HypoVereinsbank, Dresdner Bank and Commerzbank. The former GDR central bank Staatsbank has become a public commercial bank. In April 2001 Dresdner Bank accepted a takeover offer from Allianz, the country's largest insurance company. In June 2005 Italy's UniCredit finalized an agreement to acquire HypoVereinsbank in Europe's biggest cross-border banking takeover.

In 2004 there were 2,400 credit institutes, including 357 banks, 477 savings banks, 27 mortgage lenders and 1,338 credit societies. They are represented in the wholesale market by the 13 public sector *Bundesländer* banks. Total assets, 2003, €6,470,882m. Savings deposits were €600,378m. in 2004. By Oct. 2000 approximately 6% of the German population were using e-banking.

A single stock exchange, the Deutsche Börse, was created in 1992, based on the former Frankfurt stock exchange in a union with the smaller exchanges in Berlin, Bremen, Düsseldorf, Hamburg, Hanover, Munich and Stuttgart. Frankfurt processes 90% of equities trading in the country.

Germany attracted US$12·87bn. worth of foreign direct investment in 2003, compared to a record US$198·28bn. in 2000.

Gull, L., et al., *The Deutsche Bank, 1870–1995*. London, 1996

ENERGY AND NATURAL RESOURCES

Environment

Germany's carbon dioxide emissions from the consumption and flaring of fossil fuels were the equivalent of 10·2 tonnes per capita in 2002. An *Environmental Sustainability Index* compiled for the World Economic Forum meeting in Jan. 2005 ranked Germany 31st in the world, with 56·9%. The index measured the ability of countries to maintain favourable environmental conditions and examined various factors including pollution levels and the use or abuse of natural resources.

Germany is one of the world leaders in recycling. In 2001, 51% of all household waste was recycled.

Electricity

Installed capacity in 2003 was 112·78m. kW. In 2003 there were 18 nuclear reactors in operation, but in Dec. 2001 the German parliament decided to decommission the country's nuclear reactors over the next two decades. Production of electricity was 581·07bn. kWh in 2003, of which about 19% was nuclear. There is a moratorium on further nuclear plant construction. Consumption per capita was 7,729 kWh in 2001. In April 1998 the electricity market was liberalized, leading to huge cuts in bills for both industrial and residential customers. In June 2000 Veba and Viag merged to form E.ON, which became the world's largest private energy service provider.

By 2010 it is hoped that renewable energy sources, which currently account for 6% of electric power, will constitute 10% of the total.

Oil and Gas

The chief oilfields are in Emsland (Lower Saxony). In 2004, 3·5m. tonnes of crude oil were produced. Natural gas production was 17·4bn. cu. metres in 2002. Natural gas reserves were 320bn. cu. metres and crude petroleum reserves 364m. bbls. in 2002.

Wind

Germany is the world's leading producer of wind-power. By the end of 2003 there were 15,387 wind turbines with a total rated power of 14,609 MW (37% of the world total).

Minerals

The main production areas are: North Rhine-Westphalia (for coal, iron and metal smelting-works), Central Germany (for lignite) and Lower Saxony (Salzgitter for iron ore; the Harz for metal ore).

Production (in 1,000 tonnes), 2004: lignite, 181,903; coal, 28,859; salt (2003), 15,700. In 2000 recoverable coal reserves were estimated at 67bn. tonnes. Germany is the world's largest lignite producer and the third largest salt producer after the USA and China.

Agriculture

In 2004 there were 11·89m. ha. of arable land and 207,000 ha. of permanent crops. Sown areas in 2004 (in 1,000 ha.) included: wheat, 3,111·7; barley, 1,979·4; fodder, 1,659·6; rape, 1,283·4; rye, 624·9; maize, 461·7; sugarbeets, 440·5; potatoes, 295·3; oats, 227·8. Crop production, 2003 (and 1994) (in 1,000 tonnes): fodder, 47,017·5 (52,187·9); sugarbeets (2002), 26,464·8 (24,211·3); wheat, 19,287·9 (16,480·5); barley, 10,636·5 (10,902·5); potatoes, 9,812·8 (9,668·6); rapeseed, 3,637·7 (2,895·5); maize, 3,455·7 (2,446·0); rye, 2,278·7 (3,450·6); oats, 1,196·0 (1,663·0). Germany is the world's largest producer of hops (30,000 tonnes in 2000) and the second largest producer of both barley and rye.

In 2003 Germany set aside 4·1% of its agricultural land for the growth of organic crops. Organic food sales for Germany in 2004 were valued at €3·5bn. (the second highest in the world behind the USA).

In 2003 there were 420,697 farms, of which 70,642 were between two and five ha. and 28,463 over 100 ha. In 2003 there were 388,600 farmers assisted by 434,100 household members and 480,600 hired labourers (289,200 of them seasonal).

In 2004 wine production was 1,000·7m. litres.

Livestock, 2004 (in 1,000): beef cattle, 13,031·3; milch cows, 4,286·6; sheep, 2,713·5; pigs, 26,334·8; horses (2003), 524·8; poultry (2003), 109,793·5. Livestock products, 2004 (in 1,000 tonnes): milk, 28,245; meat, 5,586; cheese (2003), 1,816; eggs (2002), 870.

Forestry

Forest area in 2003 was 9,042,600 ha., of which about half was owned by the State. Timber production was 51·18m. cu metres in 2003. In recent years depredation has occurred through pollution with acid rain.

Fisheries

The total catch in 2003 was 260,867 tonnes (238,256 tonnes from marine waters). In 2000 the fishing fleet consisted of 44 ocean-going vessels and 2,247 coastal cutters.

INDUSTRY

The leading companies by market capitalization in Germany in Nov. 2005 were: Deutsche Telekom (US$69·8bn.); Siemens AG, an electronic and electric equipment producer (US$67·6bn.); and E.ON, an energy service provider (US$62·8bn.).

In 2004 a total of 960,533 firms were registered, 800,587 of which were classified as sole traders.

Output of major industrial products, 2004 (in 1,000 tonnes): distillate fuel oil (2002), 47,455; crude steel (2003), 44,800; cement, 32,082; pig iron (2003), 29,400; unleaded petrol, 24,936; rolled steel (2001), 23,757; household plastics (2003), 13,531; residual fuel oil (2002), 12,183; paper, 10,970; flour, 4,762; jet fuels (2002), 4,157; sulphuric acid, 1,916; nitrogenous fertilizers, 1,245; synthetic fibre, 400; passenger cars, 5,773,000 units; household dishwashing machines, 3,884,000 units; refrigerators, 2,669,000 units; glass bottles, 9,714m. units; radio sets (2001), 4,746,000; TV sets, 2,703,000; beer, 9,775m. litres; soft drinks (excluding milk-based beverages), 26,698m. litres.

Labour

Retirement age is normally 65 years. At March 2004 the workforce was 40·05m. (17·81m. females), of whom 35·66m. (15·98m. females) were working and 4·38m. (1·84m. females) were unemployed. In March 2004 there were 29·16m. employees, 3·85m. self-employed, 2·24m. civil servants and 402,000 helping other family members. 3·60m. foreign workers were employed in 2004, making up 9% of the workforce. Of the 2004 workforce the year average for the number of employees in each industry was as follows: 8,255,000 in the mining, processing and manufacturing industries, 8,159,000 in the public and private service sector, 6,217,000 in the retail, 3,276,000 in real estate and corporate services, hotel and catering industries, 2,922,000 in the civil service, 2,435,000 in the construction industry, 1,971,000 in transport and communications, 1,296,000 in banking and insurance, 835,000 in agriculture, forestry and fisheries and 296,000 in energy and water services. In 2003 there were 354,726 job vacancies. By 2000 there was a shortfall of 75,000 people in the information technology industry. In Aug. 2000 Germany launched a 'Green Card' project, aimed at attracting 20,000 telecommunication and information technology specialists from non-European Union countries in a bid to make up for the shortfall in qualified personnel. The card will authorize the holder to unrestricted employment in Germany for five years. By Aug. 2001 more than 8,000 recruits had found work. The standardized unemployment rate was 9·5% in 2005 (9·5% in 2004 and 9·1% in 2003); the rate in the former GDR is more than double that in the states of the former Federal Republic of Germany. In Jan. 2005 the number of people out of work reached 5m., the highest total since the 1930s.

Trade Unions

Germany's largest trade union is *Vereinigte Dienstleistungsgewerkschaft*, or *ver.di*, created in March 2001 as a result of the merger of five smaller unions. Representing 3m. workers in the service industry, it is the largest trade union outside of China.

The majority of trade unions belong to the *Deutscher Gewerkschaftsbund* (DGB, German Trade Union Federation), which had 7,013,037 (2,237,666 women) members in Dec. 2004. It functions as an umbrella organization for its eight member unions. DGB unions are organized in industrial branches such that only one union operates within each enterprise. The official GDR trade union organization (FDGB) was merged in the Deutscher Gewerkschaftsbund. Trade union membership declined significantly during the 1990s, from 11·8m. in 1991 to 8·3m. in 1999. Strikes are not legal unless called by a union with the backing of 75% of members. Certain public service employees are contractually not permitted to strike. 163,281 days were lost through strikes in 2003, up substantially from 2001 (26,833 days lost). Between 1994 and 2003 strikes cost Germany an average of four days per 1,000 employees a year, one of the lowest rates in the EU.

INTERNATIONAL TRADE

In 2004 Germany had its highest ever annual trade surplus, at €156·1bn. for the year compared to €129·9bn. a year earlier.

Imports and Exports
Trade in €1m.:

	2001	2002	2003	2004
Imports	542,774	518,532	534,534	577,375
Exports	638,268	651,320	664,455	733,456

Most important trading partners in 2004 (trade figures in €1m.). Imports: France, 52,204; Netherlands, 47,865; USA, 40,265; Italy, 34,963; UK, 34,313; Belgium, 28,500; Austria, 24,237; Switzerland, 21,415; Japan, 21,094. Exports: France, 75,301; USA, 64,802; UK, 61,058; Italy, 52,441; Netherlands, 45,491; Belgium, 41,164; Austria, 39,434; Spain, 36,810; Switzerland, 27,952.

Distribution of imports and exports by commodities in 2004 (in €1m.): finished goods, 403,478 and 624,196; semi-finished goods, 37,356 and 29,819; foodstuffs, 42,423 and 31,629; raw materials, 48,088 and 8,727; drinks and tobacco, 5,885 and 4,982; live animals, 543 and 635.

Germany is the second largest trading nation in the world after the USA, but in 2003 took over from the USA as the world's leading exporter.

Trade Fairs

Germany has a number of major annual trade fairs, among the most important of which are Internationale Grüne Woche Berlin (International Green Week Berlin—Exhibition for the Food Industry, Agriculture and Horticulture), held in Berlin in Jan.; Ambiente (for high quality consumer goods and new products), held in Frankfurt in Feb.; ITB Berlin (International Tourism Exchange), held in Berlin in March; CeBit (World Business Fair for Office Automation, Information Technology and Telecommunications), held in Hanover in March; Hannover Messe (the World's Leading Fair for Industry, Automation and Innovation), held in Hanover, in April; Internationale Funkausstellung Berlin (Your World of Consumer Electronics), held in Berlin in late Aug./early Sept.; and Frankfurter Buchmesse (Frankfurt Book Fair) held in Frankfurt in Oct. Hanover's trade fair site is the largest in Europe and Frankfurt's the second largest.

COMMUNICATIONS

Roads

In 2004 the total length of the road network was 231,420 km, including 12,044 km of motorway (*Autobahn*), 41,139 km of federal highways and 86,809 km of secondary roads. The motorway network is the largest in Europe. On 1 Jan. 2005 there were 54,519,700 motor vehicles, including: passenger cars, 45,375,500 (approximately one car for every two persons); trucks, 2,572,100; buses, 85,500; motorcycles, 3,827,900. In 2003, 8,034m. passengers were transported by long-distance road traffic. The average distance travelled by a passenger car in the year 2003 was 12,900 km. In 2004, 339,310 motorists were arrested at the scene of an accident (resulting in injury) for driving offences, of which 21,096 were alcohol related and 72,372 for exceeding speed limits. Road casualties in 2004 (and 2003) totalled 445,968 (468,783), with 440,126 injured (462,170) and 5,842 killed (6,613). In 2002 there were 8·3 fatalities per 100,000 population.

Rail

Legislation of 1993 provides for the eventual privatization of the railways, but in 2004 DB Regio, part of Deutsche Bahn, still had almost 90% of the market. On 1 Jan. 1994 West German Bundesbahn and the former GDR Reichsbahn were amalgamated as the Deutsche Bahn, a joint-stock company in which track, long-distance passenger traffic, regional passenger traffic, goods traffic and railway stations/services are run as five separate administrative entities. These were intended after 3–5 years to become themselves companies, at first under a holding company, and ultimately independent. Initially the government will hold all the shares. Length of railway in 2003 was 43,793 km (1,435 mm gauge) of which 19,882 km were electrified. There were 5,046 stations in 2003. 1,955m. passengers were carried in 2004 and 310·3m. tonnes of freight.

There are metros in Berlin (143 km), Hamburg (100 km), Munich (75 km), Frankfurt am Main (51 km) and Nuremberg (25 km), and tram/light rail networks in 56 cities.

Civil Aviation
Lufthansa, the largest carrier, was set up in 1953 and was originally 75% state-owned. The government sold its final shares in 1997. Other airlines include Condor, Deutsche-British Airways, Hapag Lloyd, Eurowings, LTU International Airways, Air Berlin and Germanwings. Lufthansa flew 629·9m. km in 1999, carrying 41,892,700 passengers (27,276,400 on international flights). The total number of passengers carried in 2005 was 51·3m. In 2004 civil aviation had 652 aircraft over 20 tonnes (619 jets).

In 2004 there were 78·29m. passenger arrivals and 78·36m. departures. Main international airports: Bremen, Cologne-Bonn, Düsseldorf, Frankfurt am Main, Hamburg (Fuhlsbüttel), Hanover, Leipzig, Munich, Nuremberg, Stuttgart and three at Berlin (Tegel, Tempelhof and Schönefeld). Airports at Dortmund, Dresden, Frankfurt (Hahn), Lübeck, Paderborn, Rostock and Saarbrücken are used for only a few scheduled international flights in addition to domestic flights.

In 2004 Frankfurt am Main handled 50,703,000 passengers (37,087,000 on international flights in 1999) and 1,713,000 tonnes of freight. It is the busiest airport in Europe in terms of freight handled. Munich was the second busiest German airport in terms of passenger traffic in 2004 (26·6m.) but third for freight. Cologne-Bonn was the second busiest in 2004 for freight, with 611,000 tonnes, but only seventh for passenger traffic.

Shipping
At 31 Dec. 2004 the mercantile marine comprised 998 ocean-going vessels of 7,894,000 GRT. Sea-going ships in 2004 carried 271·87m. tonnes of cargo. Navigable rivers and canals have a total length of 7,476 km. The inland-waterways fleet on 31 Dec. 2004 included 956 motor freight vessels totalling 1·13m. tonnes and 344 tankers of 536,556 tonnes. 235·86m. tonnes of freight were transported in 2004. In 2002 vessels totalling 958,945,000 NRT entered ports and vessels totalling 958,503,000 NRT cleared. The busiest port, Hamburg, handled 99·5m. tonnes of cargo in 2004, ranking it third in Europe behind Rotterdam and Antwerp. Hamburg is Europe's second busiest container port after Rotterdam.

Telecommunications
Telecommunications were deregulated in 1989. On 1 Jan. 1995, three state-owned joint-stock companies were set up: Deutsche Telekom, Postdienst and Postbank. The partial privatization of Deutsche Telekom began in Nov. 1996.

In 2002 there were 113,763,000 telephone subscribers, equivalent to 1,378·3 per 1,000 population. In 2001, 96·4% of all households had a private telephone. There were 35·6m. PCs in use in 2002 (431·3 per 1,000 persons). In 2002 Germany had 60,043,000 mobile phone subscribers, the highest number in any European country. T-Mobile and D2 Vodafone are the largest networks, each having around 40% of the market share. Germany is the country with the second highest number of Internet users in Europe after the UK, with approximately 32·1m. in Aug. 2002 (nearly 39% of the population). In 2002, 16·4% of households had fax transmitters.

Postal Services
In 2003 there were 13,514 post offices and 5,513 affiliated agents. A total of 18,120m. pieces of mail were processed in 2003.

SOCIAL INSTITUTIONS

Justice
Justice is administered by the federal courts and by the courts of the *Bundesländer*. In criminal procedures, civil cases and procedures of non-contentious jurisdiction the courts on the state level are the local courts (*Amtsgerichte*), the regional courts (*Landgerichte*) and the courts of appeal (*Oberlandesgerichte*). Constitutional federal disputes are dealt with by the Federal Constitutional Court (*Bundesverfassungsgericht*) elected by the Bundestag and Bundesrat. The *Bundesländer* also have constitutional courts. In labour law disputes the courts of the first and second instance are the labour courts and the *Bundesland* labour courts, and in the third instance the Federal Labour Court (*Bundesarbeitsgericht*). Disputes about public law in matters of social security, unemployment insurance, maintenance of war victims and similar cases are dealt with in the first and second instances by the social courts and the *Bundesland* social courts and in the third instance by the Federal Social Court (*Bundessozialgericht*). In most tax matters the finance courts of the *Bundesländer* are competent, and in the second instance the Federal Finance Court (*Bundesfinanzhof*). Other controversies of public law in non-constitutional matters are decided in the first and second instance by the administrative and the higher administrative courts (*Oberverwaltungsgerichte*) of the *Bundesländer*, and in the third instance by the Federal Administrative Court (*Bundesverwaltungsgericht*).

For the inquiry into maritime accidents the admiralty courts (*Seeämter*) are competent on the state level and in the second instance the Federal Admiralty Court (*Bundesoberseeamt*) in Hamburg.

The death sentence was abolished in the Federal Republic of Germany in 1949 and in the German Democratic Republic in 1987.

The population in penal institutions in 2004 was 63,373. 1,794 prisoners were serving life sentences.

Education
Education is compulsory for children aged 6 to 15. After the first four (or six) years at primary school (*Grundschulen*) children attend post-primary (*Hauptschulen*), secondary modern (*Realschulen*), grammar (*Gymnasien*), or comprehensive schools (*Integrierte Gesamtschulen*). Secondary modern school lasts six years and grammar school nine. Entry to higher education is by the final Grammar School Certificate (*Abitur*—Higher School Certificate). There are also schools for physically disabled children and those with other special needs (*Sonderschulen*).

In 2003–04 there were 3,217 kindergartens with 53,970 pupils and 3,909 teachers; 16,992 primary schools with 3,146,879 pupils and 188,789 teachers; 3,479 special schools with 429,325 pupils and 70,937 teachers; 10,050 secondary modern schools with 2,676,295 pupils and 170,708 teachers; 3,139 grammar schools with 2,316,263 pupils and 157,443 teachers; 938 comprehensive schools with 618,782 pupils and 47,542 teachers.

In 2003–04 there were 678,101 working teachers, of whom 455,008 were female.

The adult literacy rate is at least 99%.

In 2002 total expenditure on education came to €88.39bn. In 2000–01 total expenditure on education came to 4·6% of GNP and represented 9·9% of total government expenditure.

Vocational education is provided in part-time, full-time and advanced vocational schools (*Berufs-, Berufsaufbau-, Berufsfach-* and *Fachschulen*, including *Fachschulen für Technik* and *Schulen des Gesundheitswesens*). Occupation-related, part-time vocational training of six to 12 hours per week is compulsory for all (including unemployed) up to the age of 18 years or until the completion of the practical vocational training. Full-time vocational schools comprise courses of at least one year. They prepare for commercial and domestic occupations as well as specialized occupations in the field of handicrafts. Advanced full-time vocational schools are attended by pupils over 18. Courses vary from six months to three or more years.

In 2003–04 there were 8,812 full- and part-time vocational schools with 2,725,523 students and 119,174 teachers.

Higher Education. In the winter term of the 2004–05 academic year there were 370 institutes of higher education (*Hochschulen*) with 1,957,330 students, including 100 universities (1,339,887 students), six teacher training colleges (21,129), 15 theological seminaries (2,397), 52 schools of art (31,204), 168 technical colleges (526,312) and 29 management schools (36,401). Only 300,142 students (15·3%) were in their first year.

Health

In 2003 there were 304,117 doctors (368 doctors for every 100,000 people), 64,609 dentists and 53,804 pharmacists. In 2003 there were 2,197 hospitals with 541,901 beds (66 for every 10,000 people). In 2003 Germany spent 11·1% of its GDP on health; public spending in 2002 amounted to 78·5% of the total. In 2002 total expenditure on health came to €134·96bn.

Welfare

Social Health Insurance (introduced in 1883). Wage-earners and apprentices, salaried employees with an income below a certain limit and social insurance pensioners are compulsorily insured within the state system. Voluntary insurance is also possible.

Benefits: medical treatment, medicines, hospital and nursing care, maternity benefits, death benefits for the insured and their families, sickness payments and out-patients' allowances. Economy measures of Dec. 1992 introduced prescription charges related to recipients' income.

As part of a series of measures to tackle a funding shortfall in the health service, a patient charge of €10 was introduced from Jan. 2004, payable for the first visit only per quarter to a doctor.

50·62m. persons were insured in 2004 (28·75m. compulsorily). Number of cases of incapacity for work (2003) totalled 34·41m., and the number of working days lost were 252·37m. (men) and 213·36m. (women). Total disbursements in 2003 were €136,223m.

Accident Insurance (introduced in 1884). Those insured are all persons in employment or service, apprentices and the majority of the self-employed and the unpaid family workers.

Benefits in the case of industrial injuries and occupational diseases: medical treatment and nursing care, sickness payments, pensions and other payments in cash and in kind, surviving dependants' pensions.

Number of insured in 2003, 57·36m.; number of current pensions, 1,106,517; total disbursements, €10,009m.

Workers' and Employees' Old-Age Insurance Scheme (introduced in 1889). All wage-earners and salaried employees, the members of certain liberal professions and—subject to certain conditions— self-employed craftsmen are compulsorily insured. The insured may voluntarily continue to insure when no longer liable to do so or increase the insurance.

Benefits: measures designed to maintain, improve and restore the earning capacity; pensions paid to persons incapable of work, old age and surviving dependants' pensions.

Number of insured in May 2000, 43·13m. (20·28m. women); number of current pensions (in July 2004), 24·08m.; pensions to widows and widowers, 5·43m. Total disbursements in 2003, €251,644m. There are plans to raise the statutory retirement age gradually from 65 to 67 starting in 2011.

There are also special retirement and unemployment pension schemes for miners and farmers, assistance for war victims and compensation payments to members of German minorities in East European countries expelled after the Second World War and persons who suffered damage because of the war or in connection with the currency reform.

Family Allowances. €29·02bn. were dispensed to 9·19m. recipients (1·06m. foreigners) in 2004 on behalf of 15·26m. children. Paid child care leave is available for three years to mothers or fathers.

Unemployment Allowances. In 2004, 1·84m. persons (0·80m. women) were receiving unemployment benefit and 2·19m. (0·85m. women) earnings-related benefit. Total expenditure on these and similar benefits (e.g. short-working supplement, job creation schemes) was €54·49bn. in 2004. Unemployment assistance was abolished in Jan. 2005 and replaced with a new so-called 'Unemployment benefit II'. The new benefit is no longer tied to the former income of the recipient but is around the same flat-rate level as the social assistance benefit. The time an unemployed person can receive an earnings-related benefit will be reduced to a standard 12 months.

Public Welfare (introduced in 1962). In 2003, €25·59bn. were distributed to 2·82m. recipients (1·56m. women).

Public Youth Welfare. For supervision of foster children, official guardianship, assistance with adoptions and affiliations, social assistance in juvenile courts, educational assistance and correctional education under a court order. A total of €18·40bn. was spent on recipients in 2003.

Pension Reform. A major reform of the German pension system became law on 11 May 2001. The changes entail a cut in the value of the average state pension from 70% to approximately 67% of average final earnings by 2030. There will be incentives in the form of tax concessions and direct payments to encourage individuals to build up supplementary provision by contributing up to 4% of their earnings into private-sector personal pensions. In the long term these could supply up to 40% of overall pension income, with 60% coming from the state as opposed to 85% prior to the changes.

RELIGION

In 2003 there were 25,836,000 Protestants in 16,279 parishes, 26,165,000 Roman Catholics in 12,998 parishes; and in 2004, 105,733 Jews with 32 rabbis and 74 synagogues.

There are seven Roman Catholic archbishoprics (Bamberg, Berlin, Cologne, Freiburg, Hamburg, Munich and Freising, Paderborn) and 27 bishoprics. Chairman of the German Bishops' Conference is Cardinal Karl Lehmann, Bishop of Mainz. A concordat between Germany and the Holy See dates from 10 Sept. 1933. In April 2005 Cardinal Joseph Ratzinger, former archbishop of Munich and Freising, was elected Pope as Benedict XVI. In May 2005 there were seven cardinals.

The Evangelical (Protestant) Church (EKD) consists of 24 member-churches including seven Lutheran Churches, eight United-Lutheran-Reformed, two Reformed Churches and one Confederation of United member Churches: 'Church of the Union'. Its organs are the Synod, the Church Conference and the Council under the chairmanship of Dr Wolfgang Huber. There are also some 12 Evangelical Free Churches.

CULTURE

World Heritage Sites

Germany has 31 sites on the UNESCO World Heritage List (date of inscription on the list in brackets): Aachen Cathedral (1978), begun in the 8th century under Charlemagne; Speyer Cathedral (1981), founded in 1030 and constructed in the Romanesque style; Würzburg Residence, with the Court Gardens and Residence Square (1981), an 18th century Baroque palace; Pilgrimage Church of Wies (1983), an 18th century Baroque-

Rococo church; Castles of Augustusburg and Falkenlust at Brühl (1984), early examples of 18th century Rococo architecture; St Mary's Cathedral and St Michael's Church at Hildesheim (1985), Romanesque constructions from the 11th century; Roman Monuments in Trier (1986), a Roman colony from the 1st century, and the Cathedral of St Peter and Church of Our Lady; Hanseatic City of Lübeck (1987), founded in the 12th century; Palaces and Parks of Potsdam and Berlin (1990), an eclectic mix of 150 buildings covering 500 hectares built between 1730 and 1916; Mines of Rammelsberg and Historic Town of Goslar (1991), with a well-preserved historic centre; Abbey and Altenmünster of Lorsch (1992), an example of Carolignian architecture; Town of Bamberg (1993), the country's biggest intact historical city core; Maulbronn Monastery Complex (1993), a former Cistercian abbey over 850 years old; Collegiate Church, Castle, and Old Town of Quedlinburg (1994), capital of the East Franconian German Empire; Völklingen Ironworks (1994), a preserved 19th/20th centuries ironworks; Messel Pit Fossil site (1995), containing important fossils from 57m.–36m. BC; Cologne Cathedral (1996), a Gothic masterpiece begun in 1248; Bauhaus and its sites in Weimar and Dessau (1996), buildings of the influential early-20th century architectural movement; Luther Memorials in Eisleben and Wittenberg (1996), including his birthplace, baptism church, and religious sites; Classical Weimar (1998), a cultural epicentre during the 18th and early 19th centuries; Museumsinsel (Museum Island), Berlin (1999), including Altes Museum, Bodemuseum, Neues Museum and Pergamonmuseum; Wartburg Castle (1999), dating from the feudal period and rebuilt in the 19th century—Luther translated the New Testament here; Garden Kingdom of Dessau-Wörlitz (2000), an 18th century landscaped garden in the Enlightenment style; Monastic Island of Reichenau (2000), on Lake Constance, incorporating medieval churches and the remains of an 8th century Benedictine monastery; Zollverein Coal Mine Industrial Complex in Essen (2001), a 20th century mining complex with modernist buildings; Upper Middle Rhine Valley (2002), a 65 km-stretch of one of Europe's most important historical transport conduits; Historic Centres of Stralsund and Wismar (2002), Hanseatic towns; Dresden Elbe Valley (2004); Town Hall and Roland on the Marketplace of Bremen (2004).

Germany and Poland are jointly responsible for Muskauer Park/Park Muzakowski (2004), a landscaped park astride the Neisse river. Germany and the United Kingdom share the Frontiers of the Roman Empire sites (1987 and 2005), which contain the border line of the Roman Empire at its greatest extent in the 2nd century AD.

Broadcasting

There are two public service broadcasting companies—ARD (*Arbeitsgemeinschaft der öffentlich-rechtlichen Rundfunkanstalten der Bundesrepublik Deutschland*) and ZDF (*Zweites Deutsches Fernsehen*)—plus many private and regional stations, notably RTL and SAT1. ARD is the co-ordinating body for television and radio. It represents public-right broadcasters and organizes co-operation between them. Deutsche Welle Fernsehen (DW-tv) is the foreign service broadcaster. Most German households now subscribe to cable television. In 2004 there were 36·75m. TV licences. There were 21·8m. cable TV subscribers in 2001.

Public service radio is provided by ARD and ZDF via DeutschlandRadio. Private radio stations also broadcast in the regions. Deutsche Welle (DW-radio) broadcasts overseas. In 2004 there were 42·17m. radio licences.

Cinema

In 2004 there were 4,681 cinemas with a total seating capacity of 878,665. In 2004, 87 feature films were made. A total of 157m. visits to the cinema were made in 2004; gross box office receipts came to €829·9m. in 2004. In 2001 German films took 18% of the national market, up from 10% in 1998.

Press

The daily press is mainly regional. The dailies with the highest circulation are (average figures for Oct.–Dec. 2005): the tabloid *Bild* (3·81m. copies per day); *Die Welt* (0·65m.); *Süddeutsche Zeitung* (Munich, 0·45m.); and *Frankfurter Allgemeine Zeitung* (0·37m.). Other important opinion leaders are the weeklies *Die Zeit, Die Woche* and *Rheinischer Merkur*. *Bild* has the highest circulation of any paper in Europe. In 2002 almost 400 quality daily newspapers, 845 popular newspapers and around 1,000 professional journals were published with respective circulations of 30m., 130m. and 18m. The six main Sunday papers sold 3·7m. copies. The total circulation of daily newspapers in Germany is the highest in Europe. 78% of the population over the age of 14 regularly read a daily newspaper. There are also 410 online newspapers. Among magazines the most widely read are *Der Spiegel* (1·04m. weekly) and *Stern* (1·02m. weekly). In 2004 a total of 74,074 book titles were published.

Tourism

In 2004 there were 52,967 places of accommodation with 2,510,664 beds (including 13,078 hotels with 949,381 beds). 20,136,979 foreign visitors and 96,274,438 tourists resident in Germany spent a total of 338,768,840 nights in holiday accommodation. Berlin is the most visited city with 5,923,793 visitors in 2004, and Bavaria the most visited *Bundesland* with 23,871,216 (3,805,685 visited Munich). More foreign visitors were from the Netherlands (2,883,669) than any other country, with the USA second (1,925,626) followed by 1,787,943 visitors from the UK. In 2004 tourism brought in €22,234m.

Festivals

The Munich Opera Festival takes place annually in June–July, and the Wagner Festspiele (the Wagner Festival) in Bayreuth is held from late July to the end of Aug. The Oberammergau Passion Play, which takes place every ten years, was last held in 2000. Karneval (Fasching in some areas), in Jan./Feb./March, is a major event in the annual calendar in cities such as Cologne, Munich, Düsseldorf and Mainz. The Berlin Love Parade, which takes place in mid-July, is Europe's second largest street party. Oktoberfest, Munich's famous beer festival which first began in 1810, takes place each year in late Sept. and early Oct. and regularly attracts 7m. visitors.

Libraries

In 2003 there were 10,577 public libraries, six national libraries and 256 Higher Education libraries; they and other libraries held a combined 357,354,000 volumes. There were 11,808,000 active users in 2003, with 405,820,000 loans.

Theatre and Opera

In 2002–03 there were 122 theatre companies, performing on 747 stages. Audiences totalled 19·68m.

Museums and Galleries

In 2003 there were 4,929 museums which attracted 98,362,000 visitors.

DIPLOMATIC REPRESENTATIVES

Of Germany in the United Kingdom (23 Belgrave Sq., 1 Chesham Place, London, SW1X 8PZ)
Ambassador: Thomas Matussek.

Of the United Kingdom in Germany (Wilhelmstrasse 70, 10117 Berlin)
Ambassador: Sir Peter J. Torry, KCMG.

Of Germany in the USA (4645 Reservoir Rd, NW, Washington, D.C., 20007)
Ambassador: Wolfgang Ischinger.

Of the USA in Germany (Neustädtische Kirchstr. 4, 10117 Berlin)
Ambassador: William R. Timken, Jr.

Of Germany to the United Nations
Ambassador: Gunter Pleuger.

FURTHER READING

Statistisches Bundesamt. *Statistisches Jahrbuch für die Bundesrepublik Deutschland; Wirtschaft und Statistik* (monthly, from 1949); *Das Arbeitsgebiet der Bundesstatistik* (latest issue 1997; Abridged English version: *Survey of German Federal Statistics*).

Ardagh, J., *Germany and the Germans*. 3rd ed. London, 1996

Balfour, M., *Germany: the Tides of Power*. Routledge, London, 1992

Bark, D. L. and Gress, D. R., *A History of West Germany, 1945–1991*. 2nd ed. 2 vols. Oxford, 1993

Betz, H. G., *Postmodern Politics in Germany*. London, 1991

Blackbourn, D., *Fontana History of Germany, 1780–1918: The Long Nineteenth Century*. Fontana, London, 1997

Blackbourn, D. and Eley, G., *The Peculiarities of German History*. Oxford University Press, 1985

Carr, W., *A History of Germany, 1815–1990*. 4th ed. Edward Arnold, London, 1995

Childs, D., *Germany in the 20th Century*. London, 1991.—*The Stasi: The East German Intelligence and Security Service*. Macmillan, London, 1999

Dennis, M., *The German Democratic Republic: Politics, Economics and Society*. Pinter, London, 1987

Edinger, L. J., *West German Politics*. Columbia Univ. Press, New York, 1986

Eley, G., *From Unification to Nazism: Reinterpreting the German Past*. London, 1986

Fulbrook, Mary, *A Concise History of Germany*. CUP, 1991.—*The Divided Nation: A History of Germany, 1918–1990*. CUP, 1992.—*German National Identity After the Holocaust*. Polity, Oxford, 1999.—*Interpretation of the Two Germanies, 1945–1997*. Macmillan, London, 1999

Glees, A., *Reinventing Germany: German Political Development since 1945*. Berg, Oxford, 1996

Heneghan, Tom, *Unchained Eagle: Germany After the Wall*. Reuters, London, 2000

Huelshoff, M. G., *et al.*, (eds.) *From Bundesrepublik to Deutschland: German Politics after Reunification*. Michigan Univ. Press, 1993

Kielinger, T., *Crossroads and Roundabouts, Junctions in German-British Relations*. Bonn, 1997

Langewiesche, Dieter, *Liberalism in Germany*. Macmillan, London, 1999

Lees, Charles, *Party Politics in Germany*. Palgrave Macmillan, Basingstoke, 2005

Loth, W., *Stalin's Unwanted Child—The Soviet Union, the German Question and the Founding of the GDR*. St Martin's Press, New York, 1998

Maier, C. S., *Dissolution: The Crisis of Communism and the End of East Germany*. Princeton Univ. Press, N.J., 1997

Marsh, D., *The New Germany: At the Crossroads*. London, 1990

Maull, Hanns W., *German Foreign Policy Since Reunification*. Palgrave Macmillan, Basingstoke, 2005

Merkl, Peter H. (ed.) *The Federal Republic of Germany at Fifty: The End of a Century of Turmoil*. Macmillan, London, 1999

Müller, Jan-Werner, *Another Country: German Intellectuals, Unification and National Identity*. Yale, New Haven (CT) and London, 2000

Neville, P., *Appeasing Hitler: The Diplomacy of Sir Neville Henderson*. Macmillan, London, 1999

Nicholls, A. J., *The Bonn Republic: West German Democracy, 1945–1990*. Addison-Wesley, Harlow, 1998

Olsen, Jonathan, *Nature and Nationalism: Right-wing Ecology and the Politics of Identity in Contemporary Germany*. Macmillan, London, 2000

Orlow, D., *A History of Modern Germany, 1871 to the Present*. 4th ed. Prentice Hall, New York, 1994

Padgett, Stephen, Paterson, William E. and Smith, Gordon, (eds.) *Developments in German Politics 3*. Palgrave Macmillan, Basingstoke, 2003

Parkes, K. S., *Understanding Contemporary Germany*. Routledge, London, 1996

Pulzer, P., *German Politics, 1945–1995*. OUP, 1995

Sa'adah, Anne, *Germany's Second Chance: Trust, Justice and Democratization*. Harvard Univ. Press, 1999

Schmidt, H., *Handeln für Deutschland*. Berlin, 1993

Schwartz, H-P., translator, Willmot, L., *Konrad Adenauer Vol 1: From the German Empire to the Federal Republic, 1876–1952*. Berghahn Books, Oxford and New York, 1995

Schwartz, H.-P., translator, Willmot, L., *Konrad Adenauer Vol 2: The Statesman: 1952–1967*. Berghahn Books, Oxford and New York, 1997

Schweitzer, C.-C., Karsten, D., Spencer, R., Cole, R. T., Kommers, D. P. and Nicholls, A. J. (eds.) *Politics and Government in Germany, 1944–1994: Basic Documents*. 2nd ed. Berghahn Books, Oxford, 1995

Sereny, Gitta, *The German Trauma: Experiences and Reflections, 1938–99*. Penguin Press, London, 2000

Sinn, G. and Sinn, H.-W., *Jumpstart: the Economic Reunification of Germany*. MIT Press, Boston (MA), 1993

Smyser, W. R., *The Economy of United Germany: Colossus at the Crossroads*. New York, 1992.—*From Yalta to Berlin: The Cold War Struggle over Germany*. St Martin's, New York and Macmillan, London, 1999

Speirs, Ronald and Breuilly, John, (eds.) *Germany's Two Unifications: Anticipations, Experiences, Responses*. Palgrave Macmillan, Basingstoke, 2005

Stürmer, M., *Die Grenzen der Macht*. Berlin, 1992

Taylor, R., *Berlin and its Culture*. Yale Univ. Press, 1997

Thompson, W. C., *et al.*, *Historical Dictionary of Germany*. Scarecrow Press, Metuchen (NJ), 1995

Turner, Barry, (ed.) *Germany Profiled*. Macmillan, London, 1999

Turner, H. A., *Germany from Partition to Reunification*. 2nd ed. [of *Two Germanies since 1945*]. Yale Univ. Press, 1993

Tusa, A., *The Last Division – A History of Berlin, 1945–1989*. Perseus Books, Reading, Mass., 1997

Wallace, I., *East Germany: the German Democratic Republic*. [Bibliography] ABC-Clio, Oxford and Santa Barbara (CA), 1987

Watson, A., *The Germans: Who Are They Now?* 2nd ed. London, 1994

Wende, Peter, *History of Germany*. Palgrave Macmillan, Basingstoke, 2004

Williams, C., *Adenauer: The Father of the New Germany*. Little, Brown, London, 2000

Other more specialized titles are listed under CONSTITUTION AND GOVERNMENT *and* BANKING AND FINANCE, *above.*

National Statistical Office: Statistisches Bundesamt, 65189 Wiesbaden, Gustav Stresemann Ring 11. *President:* Johann Hahlen. *Website:* http://www.destatis.de

National libraries: Deutsche Bibliothek, Zeppelinallee 4–8; Frankfurt am Main. *Director:* Elisabeth Niggemann; (Berliner) Staatsbibliothek Preussischer Kulturbesitz, Potsdamer Str. 33, Postfach 1407, 10785 Berlin. *Director:* Barbara Schneider-Kempf.

THE BUNDESLÄNDER

Baden-Württemberg

KEY HISTORICAL EVENTS

The *Bundesland* is a combination of former states. Baden (the western part of the present *Bundesland*) became a united margravate in 1771, after being divided as Baden-Baden and Baden-Durlach since 1535; Baden-Baden was predominantly Catholic, and Baden-Durlach predominantly Protestant. The margrave became an ally of Napoleon, ceding land west of the Rhine and receiving northern and southern territory as compensation. In 1805 Baden became a grand duchy and in 1806 a member state of the Confederation of the Rhine, extending from the Main to Lake Constance. In 1815 it was a founder-state of the German Confederation. A constitution was granted by the grand duke in 1818, but later rulers were less liberal and there was revolution in 1848, put down with Prussian help. The grand Duchy was abolished and replaced by a *Bundesland* in 1919.

In 1949 Baden was combined with Württemberg to form three states; the three joined as one in 1952.

Württemberg, having been a duchy since 1495, became a kingdom in 1805 and joined the Confederations as did Baden. A constitution was granted in 1819 and the state remained liberal. In 1866 the king allied himself with Austria against Prussia, but in 1870 joined Prussia in war against France. The liberal monarchy came to an end with the abdication of William II in 1918, and Württemberg became a state of the German Republic. In 1945 the state was divided between Allied occupation authorities but the divisions ended in 1952.

TERRITORY AND POPULATION

Baden-Württemberg comprises 35,752 sq. km, with a population (at 31 March 2005) of 10,718,327 (5,456,361 females, 5,261,966 males).

The *Bundesland* is divided into four administrative regions, nine urban and 35 rural districts, and numbers 1,111 communes. The capital is Stuttgart.

SOCIAL STATISTICS

Statistics for calendar years:

	Live births	Marriages	Divorces	Deaths
2001	101,366	51,382	22,774	94,096
2002	99,604	51,946	23,794	95,110
2003	97,596	50,693	25,091	97,229
2004	96,655	51,382	25,166	91,646

CONSTITUTION AND GOVERNMENT

Baden-Württemberg is a merger of Baden, Württemberg-Baden and Württemberg-Hohenzollern, which were formed after 1945. The merger was approved by a plebiscite held on 9 Dec. 1951, when 70% of the population voted in its favour. It has six votes in the Bundesrat.

RECENT ELECTIONS

At the elections to the 139-member Diet of 26 March 2006, turnout was 53·4%. The Christian Democrats won 69 seats with 44·2% of the vote, the Social Democrats 38 with 25·2%, the Greens 17 with 11·7% and the Free Democrats 15 with 10·7%. The Election Alternative Labour and Social Justice only received 3·1% of the vote, and therefore won no seats.

CURRENT ADMINISTRATION

Günther Oettinger (CDU) is *Prime Minister.*

Government Website: http://www.baden-wuerttemberg.de

ECONOMY

Performance
GDP in 2004 was €292,293m., which amounted to 14·5% of Germany's total GDP. Manufacturing industries (*Verarbeitendes Gewerbe*) provide around 28·8% of GDP (33·1% in 1991). Real GDP growth in 2003 was −0·2%. Services enterprises account for nearly 61·3% of GDP, compared to 51·8% as recently as 1991.

Banking and Finance
There is a stock exchange in Stuttgart. Turnover of shares and bonds in 2004 was €63·2bn.

ENERGY AND NATURAL RESOURCES

Electricity
Hydro-electric power is a significant source of electricity in the *Bundesland.*

Agriculture
Area and yield of the most important crops:

	Area (in 1,000 ha.)			Yield (in 1,000 tonnes)		
	2002	2003	2004	2002	2003	2004
Wheat	222·6	206·4	224·3	1,511·7	1,219·3	1,734·6
Sugarbeet	22·3	20·6	20·9	1,484·4	988·7	1,351·3

	Area (in 1,000 ha.)			Yield (in 1,000 tonnes)		
	2002	2003	2004	2002	2003	2004
Barley	195·1	201·7	192·6	1,058·9	1,021·6	1,174·4
Potatoes	7·9	6·8	6·3	269·4	183·5	226·0
Oats	41·5	44·0	38·2	204·5	216·9	209·6
Rye	8·9	6·7	7·4	48·0	30·2	43·5

Livestock in May 2005 (in thousands): cattle, 1,057·5 (including 379·8 milch cows); pigs, 2,227·3; sheep, 301·2; poultry, 5,061·8 (May 2003).

Forestry
Total area covered by forests is 13,630 sq. km or 38·1% of the total area.

INDUSTRY

Baden-Württemberg is one of Germany's most industrialized states. In 2004, 8,588 establishments (with 20 or more employees) employed 1,211,628 persons; of these, 267,917 were employed in machine construction (excluding office machines, data processing equipment and facilities); 242,673 in car manufacture; 195,997 in electrical engineering; 18,385 in the textile industry.

Labour
Economically active persons totalled 4,944,900 at the 1%-EU-sample survey of May 2004: 4·37m. were employees and 572,600 were self-employed (including family workers); 1,928,900 were engaged in power supply, mining, manufacturing and building; 987,500 in commerce and transport; 95,700 in agriculture and forestry; 1,932,900 in other industries and services. There were 340,284 unemployed in 2004, a rate of 6·2%.

INTERNATIONAL TRADE

Imports and Exports
Total imports (2004): €91,292m. Total exports: €114,323m., of which €66,646m. went to the EU. Machinery exports totalled €27,110m. and automotive exports €26,537m.

COMMUNICATIONS

Roads
On 1 Jan. 2004 there were 27,416 km of 'classified' roads, comprising 1,028 km of Autobahn, 4,408 km of federal roads, 9,908 km of first-class and 12,072 km of second-class highways. Motor vehicles, at 1 Jan. 2005, numbered 7,463,426, including 6,150,096 passenger cars, 9,500 buses, 298,483 lorries, 339,437 tractors and 567,299 motorcycles.

Civil Aviation
The largest airport in Baden-Württemberg is at Stuttgart, which in 2004 handled 8,651,000 passengers and 17,301 tonnes of freight. There are two further airports, Baden-Baden and Friedrichshafen.

Shipping
The harbour in Mannheim is the largest in Baden-Württemberg. In 2004 it handled 7·7m. tonnes of freight, compared to 6·7m. tonnes in Karlsruhe.

SOCIAL INSTITUTIONS

Justice
There are a constitutional court (*Staatsgerichtshof*), two courts of appeal, 17 regional courts, 108 local courts, a *Bundesland* labour court, nine labour courts, a *Bundesland* social court, eight social courts, a finance court, a higher administrative court (*Verwaltungsgerichtshof*) and four administrative courts.

Education
In 2004–05 there were 2,721 primary schools (*Grund- und Hauptschulen*) with 35,869 teachers and 656,393 pupils; 585 special schools with 10,937 teachers and 54,823 pupils; 467

intermediate schools with 12,880 teachers and 247,564 pupils; 452 high schools with 20,085 teachers and 320,846 pupils; 46 *Freie Waldorf* schools with 1,519 teachers and 22,088 pupils. Other general schools had 656 teachers and 10,983 pupils in total; there were also 772 vocational schools with 406,971 pupils. There were 38 *Fachhochschulen* (colleges of engineering and others) with 73,637 students in winter term 2004–05.

In the winter term 2004–05 there were nine universities (Freiburg, 21,026 students; Heidelberg, 24,089; Konstanz, 9,662; Tübingen, 22,139; Karlsruhe, 17,002; Stuttgart, 19,732; Hohenheim, 5,326; Mannheim, 11,711; Ulm, 7,075); six teacher-training colleges with 21,244 students; five colleges of music with 2,772 students; and three colleges of fine arts with 1,380 students.

Health

In 2004 the 316 hospitals in Baden-Württemberg had 62,387 beds and treated 1,913,648 patients. The average occupancy rate was 74·3%.

Welfare

At 31 Dec. 2004 there were 232,669 persons receiving benefits of all kinds. 2003 expenditure on social welfare was €2,323m.

RELIGION

In 2003, 38·3% of the population were Roman Catholics and 34·3% were Protestants.

CULTURE

Tourism

In 2004, 14,336,025 visitors spent a total of 40,023,300 nights in Baden-Württemberg. Only Bavaria of the German *Bundesländer* recorded more overnight stays.

FURTHER READING

Statistical Information: Statistisches Landesamt Baden-Württemberg (P.O.B. 10 60 33, 70049 Stuttgart) (*President:* Dr Gisela Meister-Scheufelen), publishes: *Statistisches Monatsheft* (monthly); *Trends und Fakten* (latest issue 2004); *Statistisches Taschenbuch* (latest issue 2005).

State libraries: Württembergische Landesbibliothek, Konrad-Adenauer-Str. 8, 70173 Stuttgart. Badische Landesbibliothek Karlsruhe, Erbprinzenstr. 15, 76133 Karlsruhe.

Bavaria

Bayern

KEY HISTORICAL EVENTS

Bavaria was ruled by the Wittelsbach family from 1180. The duchy remained Catholic after the Reformation, which made it a natural ally of Austria and the Habsburg Emperors.

The present boundaries were reached during the Napoleonic wars, and Bavaria became a kingdom in 1806. Despite the granting of a constitution and parliament, radical feeling forced the abdication of King Ludwig I in 1848. Maximilian II was followed by Ludwig II who allied himself with Austria against Prussia in 1866, but was reconciled with Prussia and entered the German Empire in 1871. In 1918 the King Ludwig III abdicated. The first years of republican government were filled with unrest, attempts at the overthrow of the state by both communist and right-wing groups culminating in an unsuccessful coup by Adolf Hitler in 1923.

The state of Bavaria included the Palatinate from 1214 until 1945, when it was taken from Bavaria and added to the Rhineland. The present *Bundesland* of Bavaria was formed in 1946. Munich became capital of Bavaria in the reign of Albert IV (1467–1508) and remains capital of the *Bundesland*.

TERRITORY AND POPULATION

Bavaria has an area of 70,549 sq. km. The capital is Munich. There are seven administrative regions, 25 urban districts, 71 rural districts, 216 unincorporated areas and 2,056 communes, 991 of which are members of 314 administrative associations (as of 31 Dec. 2004). The population (31 Dec. 2004) numbered 12,443,893 (6,088,805 males, 6,355,088 females).

SOCIAL STATISTICS

Statistics for calendar years:

	Live births	Marriages	Divorces	Deaths
2001	115,964	60,226	28,347	117,930
2002	113,818	60,686	29,503	119,755
2003	111,536	59,009	29,992	121,778
2004	111,164	60,712	29,748	116,460

CONSTITUTION AND GOVERNMENT

The Constituent Assembly, elected on 30 June 1946, passed a constitution on the lines of the democratic constitution of 1919, but with greater emphasis on state rights; this was agreed upon by the Christian Social Union (CSU) and the Social Democrats (SPD). Bavaria has six seats in the Bundesrat. The CSU replaces the Christian Democratic Party in Bavaria.

RECENT ELECTIONS

At the Diet elections on 21 Sept. 2003 the CSU won 124 seats with 60·7% of votes cast, the SPD 41 with 19·6% and the Greens 15 with 7·7%. The Free Democratic Party took 2·6% but won no seats. Turnout was 57·1%.

CURRENT ADMINISTRATION

The *Prime Minister* is Dr Edmund Stoiber (CSU).

Government Website: http://www.bayern.de

ECONOMY

Performance

Real GDP growth in 2003 was 0·2%, compared to the national growth rate of –0·1%. Real GDP growth in 2004 was 1·9%.

ENERGY AND NATURAL RESOURCES

Agriculture

Area and yield of the most important products:

	Area (in 1,000 ha.)			Yield (in 1,000 tonnes)		
	2002	2003	2004	2002	2003	2004
Sugarbeet	74·1	71·7	73·4	5,272·8	3,979·5	5,112·3
Wheat	468·1	435·9	491·6	3,103·0	2,559·7	4,001·6
Barley	451·2	466·7	457·1	2,382·6	2,174·2	2,827·7
Potatoes	51·6	51·0	51·8	2,094·6	1,576·4	2,037·4
Rye	42·4	31·1	40·4	212·1	120·8	258·5
Oats	51·4	57·4	49·0	217·0	262·6	247·8

Livestock, 2004: 3,632,200 cattle (including 1,291,700 milch cows); 85,000 horses (2003); 470,300 sheep; 3,632,500 pigs; 10,329,300 poultry (2003).

INDUSTRY

In 2004, 7,786 establishments (with 20 or more employees) employed 1,164,433 persons; of these, 192,189 were employed in the manufacture of machinery and equipment, 182,637 in the manufacture of motor vehicles and 32,075 in the manufacture of textiles and textile products.

Labour

The economically active persons totalled 5,827,000 at the 1% sample survey of the microcensus of 2004. Of the total, 5,046,000 were employees, 693,000 were self-employed, 88,000 were unpaid family workers; 1,985,000 worked in power supply, mining, manufacturing and building; 1,273,000 in commerce, hotels and restaurants, and transport; 175,000 in agriculture and forestry; 2,394,000 in other services.

COMMUNICATIONS

Roads
There were, on 1 Jan. 2005, 41,778 km of 'classified' roads, comprising 2,298 km of Autobahn, 6,757 km of federal roads, 13,941 km of first-class and 18,782 km of second-class highways. Number of motor vehicles on 1 Jan. 2005 was 9,183,729, including 7,300,847 passenger cars, 378,935 lorries, 14,627 buses and 757,859 motorcycles.

Civil Aviation
Munich airport handled 26,602,776 passengers (17,940,776 on international flights) and 171,142 tonnes of freight in 2004. Nuremberg handled 3,548,996 (2,300,567 on international flights) and 10,854 tonnes of freight in 2004.

SOCIAL INSTITUTIONS

Justice
There are a constitutional court (Verfassungsgerichtshof), a supreme Bundesland court (Oberstes Landesgericht), three courts of appeal, 22 regional courts, 72 local courts, two Bundesland labour courts, 11 labour courts, a Bundesland social court, seven social courts, two finance courts, a higher administrative court (Verwaltungsgerichtshof) and six administrative courts. The supreme Bundesland court (Oberstes Landesgericht) was scheduled to be abolished in mid-2006. Since 1 Jan. 2005 new cases have been transferred to the courts of appeal.

Education
In 2004–05 there were 2,874 primary schools with 47,616 teachers and 804,898 pupils; 375 special schools with 8,199 teachers and 61,326 pupils; 346 intermediate schools with 12,141 teachers and 220,397 pupils; 405 high schools with 22,831 teachers and 349,203 pupils; 229 part-time vocational schools with 7,991 teachers and 292,571 pupils, including 49 special part-time vocational schools with 1,074 teachers and 15,354 pupils; 811 full-time vocational schools with 5,268 teachers and 75,007 pupils including 357 schools for public health occupations with 1,648 teachers and 21,402 pupils; 343 advanced full-time vocational schools with 1,810 teachers and 24,242 pupils; 132 vocational high schools (Berufsoberschulen, Fachoberschulen) with 2,496 teachers and 42,012 pupils.

In 2004–05 there were 12 universities with 173,513 students (Augsburg, 14,821; Bamberg, 8,364; Bayreuth, 9,138; Eichstätt, 4,706; Erlangen-Nürnberg, 24,137; München, 44,865; Passau, 8,422; Regensburg, 17,022; Würzburg, 18,565; the Technical University of München, 19,627; University of the Federal Armed Forces, München (Universität der Bundeswehr), 2,932; the college of politics, München, 914); plus the college of philosophy, München, 449, and two philosophical-theological colleges with 207 students in total (Benediktbeuern, 96; Neuendettelsau, 111). There were also five colleges of music, two colleges of fine arts and one college of television and film, with 3,485 students in total; 23 vocational colleges (Fachhochschulen) with 71,477 students including one for the civil service (Bayerische Beamtenfachhochschule) with 3,496 students.

Welfare
In Dec. 2004 there were 237,145 persons receiving benefits of all kinds.

RELIGION
In 2003, 58·5% of the population were Roman Catholics and 21·9% were Protestants.

CULTURE

Tourism
In June 2004 there were 13,865 places of accommodation (with nine beds or more) providing beds for 555,198 people. In 2004 they received 22,781,104 guests of whom 4,677,722 were foreigners. They stayed an average of 3·0 nights each, totalling 69,365,163 nights (9,774,592 nights stayed by foreign visitors).

Festivals
Oktoberfest, Munich's famous beer festival, takes place each year from the penultimate Saturday in Sept. through to the first Sunday in Oct. (extended to 3 Oct. if the last Sunday of the festival falls on 1 or 2 Oct.). There were 6·1m. visitors at the 172nd Oktoberfest in 2005.

FURTHER READING
Statistical Information: Bayerisches Landesamt für Statistik und Datenverarbeitung, Neuhauser Str. 8, 80331 Munich. *President:* Dr Peter Bauer. It publishes: *Statistisches Jahrbuch für Bayern.* 1894 ff.—*Bayern in Zahlen.* Monthly (from Jan. 1947).—*Zeitschrift des Bayerischen Statistischen Landesamts.* July 1869–1943; 1948 ff.—*Beiträge zur Statistik Bayerns.* 1850 ff.—*Statistische Berichte.* 1951 ff.—*Kreisdaten.* 1972–2001 (from 2003 incorporated in *Statistisches Jahrbuch für Bayern).—Gemeindedaten.* 1973 ff.

State Library: Bayerische Staatsbibliothek, Munich. *Director General:* Dr Hermann Leskien.

Berlin

KEY HISTORICAL EVENTS
After the end of World War II, Berlin was divided into four occupied sectors, each with a military governor from one of the victorious Allied Powers (the USA, the Soviet Union, Britain and France). In March 1948 the USSR withdrew from the Allied Control Council and in June blockaded West Berlin until May 1949. In response, the allies flew food and other supplies into the city in what became known as the Berlin Airlift. On 30 Nov. 1948 a separate municipal government was set up in the Soviet sector which led to the political division of the city. In contravention of the special Allied status agreed for the city, East Berlin became 'Capital of the GDR' in 1949 and thus increasingly integrated into the GDR as a whole. In West Berlin, the formal authority of the western allies lasted until 1990.

On 17 June 1953 the protest by workers in East Berlin against political oppression and economic hardship was suppressed by Soviet military forces. To stop refugees, the east German government erected the Berlin Wall to seal off West Berlin's borders on 13 Aug. 1961.

The Berlin Wall was breached on 9 Nov. 1989 as the regime in the GDR bowed to the internal pressure which had been building for months. East and West Berlin were amalgamated on the re-unification of Germany in Oct. 1990. In April 1994 the *Bundesland* governments of Berlin and Brandenburg agreed to merge the two *Bundesländer* in 1999 or 2002, subject to the approval of their respective parliaments, and of their electorates in referendums held in May 1996. In Berlin 53·4% of votes were cast in favour, but in Brandenburg 62·8% were against. A further referendum on the proposed merger is likely to take place in the next few years.

With the move of the national government, the parliament (Bundestag), and the federal organ of the *Bundesländer* (Bundesrat) in 1999, Berlin is once again a capital city.

TERRITORY AND POPULATION
The area is 891·82 sq. km. Population, 31 Dec. 2004, 3,387,828 (1,734,771 females), including 454,545 foreign nationals; density, 3,798·8 per sq. km.

SOCIAL STATISTICS

Statistics for calendar years:

	Live births	Marriages	Divorces	Deaths
2000	29,695	14,119	9,631	33,335
2001	28,624	12,903	8,731	32,826
2002	28,801	12,800	9,322	33,492
2003	28,723	12,390	10,102	33,146
2004	29,446	12,569	10,245	31,792

CONSTITUTION AND GOVERNMENT

According to the constitutions of Sept. 1950 and Oct. 1995, Berlin is simultaneously a *Bundesland* of the Federal Republic and a city. It is governed by a House of Representatives (of at least 130 members); executive power is vested in a Senate, consisting of the Governing Mayor, two Mayors and not more than eight senators. Since 1992 adherence to the constitution has been watched over by a Constitutional Court.

After a proposed merger was rejected by Brandenburg in the 1996 referendum, a Joint Berlin-Brandenburg Co-operation Council was set up.

Berlin has four seats in the Bundesrat.

RECENT ELECTIONS

In Dec. 1999 a CDU–SPD coalition government was formed, but the 'grand coalition' that had held power for more than ten years collapsed on 7 June 2001. The Social Democrats announced their withdrawal after the authorities had accumulated huge debts. At the elections of 21 Oct. 2001 turnout was 68·1%. The Social Democratic Party (SPD) won 44 seats with 29·7% of votes cast; the Christian Democratic Union (CDU) 35, with 23·8%; the Party of Democratic Socialism (former Communists) 33, with 22·6%; the Free Democratic Party 15, with 9·9%; and the Greens 14, with 9·1%. Initially the SPD had coalition talks with the Free Democratic Party and the Greens, but these broke down. Thus the SPD formed a coalition with the Party of Democratic Socialism, the successor to the former German Democratic Republic's Communist Party, who thereby had their first share of power in Berlin since the fall of the Wall.

CURRENT ADMINISTRATION

The *Governing Mayor* is Klaus Wowereit (SPD).

Government Website: http://www.berlin.de

ECONOMY

Berlin's real GDP growth was 0·5% in 2004.

INDUSTRY

In 2004 there were 860 industrial concerns employing 102,100 people. The main industries in terms of percentage of the labour force employed were: electronics, 28·1%; paper, printing and publishing, 13·3%; food and tobacco, 12·4%; chemicals, 11·6%; machine-building, 10·7%; vehicle production, 8·8%; metallurgy, 8·3%.

Labour

In 2004 the workforce was 1,533,500. There were 297,947 persons registered unemployed in 2004 and 3,505 on short time. An average of 6,801 jobs were available at any one time in 2004. The unemployment rate in 2004 was 17·6%.

COMMUNICATIONS

Roads

On 1 Jan. 2005 there were 5,341·7 km of roads (251·0 km of 'classified' roads, made up of 68·1 km of Autobahn and 182·9 km of federal roads). In Jan. 2005, 1,419,217 motor vehicles were registered, including 1,218,019 passenger cars, 81,522 lorries, 2,468 buses and 93,144 motorcycles. There were 124,514 road accidents in 2004 of which 14,948 involved badly damaged vehicles or injured persons, of whom there were 16,599.

Civil Aviation

196,303 flights were made from Berlin's three airports—Tegel, Tempelhof and Schönefeld—in 2004, carrying a total of 14,710,551 passengers.

SOCIAL INSTITUTIONS

Justice

There are a court of appeal *(Kammergericht)*, a regional court, nine local courts, a *Bundesland* Labour court, a labour court, a *Bundesland* social court, a social court, a higher administrative court, an administrative court and a finance court.

Education

In the autumn of 2004 there were 340,658 pupils attending schools. There were 447 primary schools with 148,630 pupils, 60 schools for practical education with 14,538 pupils, 95 special schools with 13,558 pupils, 83 secondary modern schools with 27,066 pupils, 122 grammar schools with 85,297 pupils and 63 comprehensive schools with 48,037 pupils. In 2004–05 there were two universities and two technical universities, four arts colleges and 12 technical colleges. There were an estimated 141,010 students in higher education.

Health

In 2004 there were 71 hospitals with 20,531 beds, 6,918 doctors, 3,124 dentists and 869 pharmacies.

RELIGION

In Dec. 2004 membership and number of places of worship for major religions was as follows:

Religion	Members	Places of Worship
Protestant	756,866	461[1]
Roman Catholic	312,398	114
Jewish	12,165	8
Muslim	212,723	123
	[1]2003.	

CULTURE

Tourism

In 2004 Berlin had 558 places of accommodation providing 75,009 beds for 5,923,793 visitors.

FURTHER READING

Statistical Information: The Statistisches Landesamt Berlin was founded in 1862 (Alt-Friedrichsfelde 60, 10315 Berlin (Lichtenberg)). *Director:* Prof. Dr Ulrike Rockmann. It publishes: *Statistisches Jahrbuch* (from 1867): *Berliner Statistik* (monthly, from 1947).—*100 Jahre Berliner Statistik* (1962).
Website (German only): http://www.statistik-berlin.de

Read, A., and Fisher, D., *Berlin, Biography of a City.* London, 1994
Taylor, R., *Berlin and its Culture.* London, 1997
Wallace, Ian, *Berlin.* [Bibliography] ABC-Clio, Oxford and Santa Barbara (CA), 1993

State Library: Zentral- und Landesbibliothek, Blücherplatz 1, 10961 Berlin. *Director:* Dr Claudia Lux.

Brandenburg

KEY HISTORICAL EVENTS

For the proposed merger with Berlin *see* BERLIN: Key Historical Events.

Brandenburg surrounds the capital city of Germany, Berlin, but the people of the state voted against the recommendations of the Berlin House of Representatives and the Brandenburg State Parliament that the two states should merge around the year 2000. The state capital, Potsdam, is the ancient city of the

Emperor Frederic II 'The Great' who transformed the garrison town of his father Frederic I 'The Soldier' into an elegant city.

TERRITORY AND POPULATION

The area is 29,478 sq. km. Population on 31 Dec. 2004 was 2,567,704 (1,297,357 females). There are four urban districts, 14 rural districts and 421 communes (31 Dec. 2004). The capital is Potsdam.

SOCIAL STATISTICS

Statistics for calendar years:

	Live births	Marriages	Divorces	Deaths
2001	17,692	9,774	6,043	25,889
2002	17,704	9,650	5,829	26,494
2003	17,970	9,974	6,107	26,862
2004	18,148	11,285	5,773	25,859

CONSTITUTION AND GOVERNMENT

The *Bundesland* was reconstituted on former GDR territory on 14 Oct. 1990. Brandenburg has four seats in the Bundesrat and 16 in the Bundestag.

After a proposed merger was rejected by Brandenburg in the 1996 referendum, a Joint Berlin-Brandenburg Co-operation Council was set up.

At a referendum on 14 June 1992, 93·5% of votes cast were in favour of a new constitution guaranteeing direct democracy and the right to work and housing.

RECENT ELECTIONS

At the Diet elections on 19 Sept. 2004 the Social Democrats (SPD) won 33 seats with 31·9% of the vote; the Party of Democratic Socialism (PDS, former Communists) 29, with 28·0%; the Christian Democrats (CDU) 20, with 19·4%; the extreme right-wing German People's Union (DVU) 6, with 6·1%. Turnout was 56·6%.

CURRENT ADMINISTRATION

The *Prime Minister* is Matthias Platzeck (SPD).

Government Website: http://www.brandenburg.de

ECONOMY

Performance
GDP in 2004 was €45,018m. (nominal).

ENERGY AND NATURAL RESOURCES

Electricity
Power stations in Brandenburg produced 38,124m. kWh in 2004. A minimal amount was produced from hydro-electric power.

Agriculture
Area and yield of the most important crops:

	Area (in 1,000 ha.)			Yield (in 1,000 tonnes)		
	2002	2003	2004	2002	2003	2004
Wheat	139·2	145·4	153·3	828·8	574·3	1,057·9
Rye	231·0	170·9	197·3	945·6	504·2	1,059·4
Sugarbeet	12·1	11·2	12·1	597·2	465·3	642·1
Potatoes	11·5	11·4	13·1	345·5	303·8	503·5
Barley	78·2	82·9	74·6	375·2	245·4	469·3
Rape	111·3	112·3	110·3	296·0	223·6	451·2
Oats	16·2	20·2	18·3	55·7	42·2	79·2

Livestock on 3 May 2003: cattle, 614,337 (including 181,472 milch cows); pigs, 769,084; sheep, 140,287; horses, 17,633; poultry, 8,273,000.

INDUSTRY

In 2004, 1,114 establishments (20 or more employees) in the mining and manufacturing industries employed 85,257 persons,

the main areas being: vehicle construction (11,900); the food industry (10,450); manufacturing of metal products (8,939); machine construction (6,779); glassworks, ceramics, processing stones and earthenware (5,289); mining and quarrying (4,739); and chemical industries (4,630). There were 679 companies (with 20 or more employees) in the building industry, employing 28,109 persons.

Labour
In March 2004 at the 1%-sample of the microcensus, 1,102,000 persons were economically active, of which 524,800 white-collar and 384,100 manual workers, 115,600 self-employed and family assistants, and 77,400 civil servants. At 31 Dec. 2004 there were 250,032 unemployed persons (20·3%).

INTERNATIONAL TRADE

Imports and Exports
Total imports (2004): €6,643m. Total exports: €5,466m.

COMMUNICATIONS

Roads
On 1 Jan. 2005 there were 1,697,839 registered vehicles including 1,429,114 passenger cars.

SOCIAL INSTITUTIONS

Education
In 2004–05 there were 978 schools providing general education (including special schools) with 260,977 pupils and 67 vocational schools with 76,692 pupils.

In the winter term 2004–05 there were three universities and ten colleges with 41,036 students.

RELIGION

In 2003, 19·6% of the population were Protestants and 3·1% were Roman Catholics.

CULTURE

Tourism
In 2004 there were 1,502 places of accommodation (with nine or more beds), including 482 hotels, providing a total of 78,290 beds (31 July 2004). 3,053,906 visitors spent a total of 8,501,348 nights in Brandenburg in 2004.

FURTHER READING

Statistical office: Landesbetrieb für Datenverarbeitung und Statistik Land Brandenburg, Dortustrasse 46, 14467 Potsdam. It publishes *Statistisches Jahrbuch Land Brandenburg* (since 1991). *Website (German only):* http://www.lds-bb.de/sixcms/list.php/lds

---

Bremen

Freie Hansestadt Bremen

KEY HISTORICAL EVENTS

The state is dominated by the Free City of Bremen and its port, Bremerhaven. In 1815, when it joined the German Confederation, Bremen was an autonomous city and Hanse port with important Baltic trade. In 1827 the expansion of trade inspired the founding of Bremerhaven on land ceded by Hanover at the confluence of the Geest and Weser rivers. Further expansion followed the founding of the Nord-deutscher Lloyd Shipping Company in 1857. Merchant shipping, associated trade and fishing were dominant until 1940 but there was diversification in the post-war years. In 1939 Bremerhaven was absorbed by the Hanoverian town of Wesermünde. The combined port was returned to the jurisdiction of Bremen in 1947.

TERRITORY AND POPULATION

The area of the *Bundesland*, consisting of the two urban districts and ports of Bremen and Bremerhaven, is 404 sq. km. Population, 31 Dec. 2004, 663,213 (321,206 males, 342,007 females).

SOCIAL STATISTICS

Statistics for calendar years:

	Live births	Marriages	Divorces	Deaths
2000	6,070	3,275	1,814	7,638
2001	5,831	3,153	1,805	7,473
2002	5,484	3,130	1,742	7,668
2003	5,577	3,094	1,797	7,658

CONSTITUTION AND GOVERNMENT

Political power is vested in the 100-member House of Burgesses (*Bürgerschaft*) which appoints the executive, called the Senate. Bremen has three seats in the Bundesrat.

RECENT ELECTIONS

At the elections of 25 May 2003 the Social Democratic Party won 40 seats with 42·3% of votes cast; the Christian Democratic Union 29 with 29·9%; the Greens 12 with 12·8%; the Free Democratic Party 1 with 4·2%; and the German People's Union 1 with 2·3%. The *Partei Rechtsstaatlicher Offensive* took 4·3% of the vote but secured no seats. Turnout was 61·4%.

CURRENT ADMINISTRATION

The Burgomaster is Jens Böhrnsen (Social Democrat).

Government Website: http://www.bremen.de

ENERGY AND NATURAL RESOURCES

Agriculture

Agricultural area comprised (2001) 11,741 ha. Livestock (2 May 1999): 12,612 cattle (including 3,502 milch cows); 1,792 pigs; 301 sheep; 1,099 horses; 10,866 poultry.

INDUSTRY

In 2002, 355 establishments (20 or more employees) employed 64,005 persons; of these, 24,891 were employed in the production of cars and car parts and other vehicles; 5,388 were employed in machine construction; 3,524 in electrical engineering; 1,996 in shipbuilding (except naval engineering); 1,278 in coffee and tea processing.

Labour

The economically active persons totalled 276,000 at the microcensus of April 2001. Of the total, 248,000 were employees, 26,000 self-employed; 83,000 in commerce, trade and communications, 68,000 in production industries, 122,000 in other industries and services.

COMMUNICATIONS

Roads

On 1 Jan. 2003 there were 98 km of 'classified' roads, of which 59 km were Autobahn and 39 km federal roads. Registered motor vehicles on 1 Jan. 2003 numbered 339,583, including 292,885 passenger cars, 18,433 lorries, 520 buses, 2,918 tractors and 19,648 motorcycles.

Civil Aviation

Bremen airport handled 1,639,834 passengers (1,004,261 on international flights) in 2003.

Shipping

Vessels entered in 2004, 9,236 of 146,903,356 GRT; cleared, 9,069 of 145,989,781 GRT. Sea traffic, 2004, incoming 27,874,000 tonnes; outgoing, 24,445,000 tonnes.

SOCIAL INSTITUTIONS

Justice

There are a constitutional court (*Staatsgerichtshof*), a court of appeal, a regional court, three local courts, a *Bundesland* labour court, two labour courts, a *Bundesland* social court, a finance court, a higher administrative court and an administrative court.

Education

In 2004 there were 354 new system schools with 4,865 teachers and 72,664 pupils; 22 part-time vocational schools with 17,387 pupils; 24 full-time vocational schools with 2,554 pupils; five advanced vocational schools (including institutions for the training of technicians) with 778 pupils; seven schools for public health occupations with 812 pupils. In 2004 there were 25 special schools with 634 teachers and 2,493 pupils.

In the winter term 2004–05, 22,008 students were enrolled at the University of Bremen and 796 at the International University of Bremen. In addition to the universities there were four other colleges in 2004–05 with 11,784 students.

RELIGION

In 2003, 44·4% of the population were Protestants and 12·1% Roman Catholics.

CULTURE

Tourism

Bremen had 95 places of accommodation providing 9,554 beds for 795,446 visitors in 2004.

FURTHER READING

Statistical Information: Statistisches Landesamt Bremen (An der Weide 14–16, P. B. 101309, D-28195 Bremen), founded in 1850. *Director:* Reg. Dir. Jürgen Dinse. Its current publications include: *Statistisches Jahrbuch Bremen* (from 1992).—*Statistische Mitteilungen* (from 1948).—*Statistische Monatsberichte* (from 1954).—*Statistische Berichte* (from 1956).—*Statistisches Handbuch Bremen* (1950–60, 1961; 1960–64, 1967; 1965–69, 1971; 1970–74, 1975; 1975–80, 1982; 1981–85, 1987).—*Bremen im statistischen Zeitvergleich 1950–1976.* 1977.—*Bremen in Zahlen,* 2005.

State and University Library: Bibliotheksstr., 28359 Bremen. *Director:* Annette Rath-Beckmann.

Hamburg

Freie und Hansestadt Hamburg

KEY HISTORICAL EVENTS

Hamburg was a free Hanse town owing nominal allegiance to the Holy Roman Emperor until 1806. In 1815 it became part of the German Confederation, sharing a seat in the Federal Diet with Lübeck, Bremen and Frankfurt. During the Empire it retained its autonomy. By 1938 it had become the third largest port in the world and its territory was extended by the cession of land (three urban and 27 rural districts) from Prussia. After World War II, Hamburg became a *Bundesland* of the Federal Republic with its 1938 boundaries.

TERRITORY AND POPULATION

Total area, 755·3 sq. km (2004), including the islands Neuwerk and Scharhörn (7·6 sq. km). Population (31 Dec. 2004), 1,734,800 (843,600 males; 891,300 females). The *Bundesland* forms a single urban district (*Stadtstaat*) with seven administrative subdivisions.

SOCIAL STATISTICS

Statistics for calendar years:

	Live births	Marriages	Divorces	Deaths
2001	15,786	7,020	4,328	17,869
2002	15,707	6,999	4,560	18,424
2003	15,916	6,959	4,989	18,072
2004	16,103	6,793	4,892	17,562

CONSTITUTION AND GOVERNMENT

The constitution of 6 June 1952 vests the supreme power in the House of Burgesses *(Bürgerschaft)* of 121 members. The executive is in the hands of the Senate, whose members are elected by the Bürgerschaft. Hamburg has three seats in the Bundesrat.

RECENT ELECTIONS

The elections of 29 Feb. 2004 had the following results: Christian Democrats, 63 seats with 47·2% of votes cast; Social Democrats, 41 with 30·5%; the Greens, 17 with 12·3%; Pro DM/Schill, no seats (3·1%); Free Democrats, no seats (2·8%). 11 other parties stood. Turnout was 68·7%.

CURRENT ADMINISTRATION

The First Burgomaster is Ole von Beust (Christian Democrat).

Government Website: http://www.hamburg.de

ENERGY AND NATURAL RESOURCES

Agriculture

The agricultural area comprised 13,736 ha. in 2003.

Livestock (2003): cattle, 7,129 (including 1,087 milch cows); pigs, 1,441; horses, 3,268; sheep, 2,848; poultry, 7,507.

INDUSTRY

In June 2004, 535 establishments (with 20 or more employees) employed 94,270 persons; of these, 25,407 were employed in manufacturing transport equipment (including motor vehicles, aircraft and ships), 13,329 in manufacturing machinery, 11,964 in manufacturing electrical and optical equipment, 6,934 in manufacturing chemical products and 5,143 in the mineral oil industry.

Labour

Economically active persons totalled 777,000 at the 1%-sample survey of the microcensus of May 2004. Of the total, 668,000 were employees and 109,000 were self-employed or unpaid family workers; 219,000 were engaged in commerce and transport, 148,000 in power supply, mining, manufacturing and building, 5,000 in agriculture and forestry, 405,000 in other industries and services.

COMMUNICATIONS

Roads

In 2004 there were 3,956 km of roads, including 82 km of Autobahn, 123 km of federal roads. Number of motor vehicles (1 Jan. 2005), 961,043, of which 835,828 were passenger cars, 54,296 lorries, 1,579 buses, 48,038 motorcycles and 21,302 other motor vehicles.

Civil Aviation

Hamburg airport handled 9,764,529 passengers (5,426,971 on international flights) and 25,044 tonnes of freight in 2004.

Shipping

Hamburg is the largest sea port in Germany.

Vessels		2002	2003	2004
Entered:	Number	11,606	11,503	11,491
	Tonnage (gross)	120,683,288	129,782,091	137,044,773
Cleared:	Number	11,650	11,514	11,522
	Tonnage (gross)	120,970,345	128,961,988	136,625,739

SOCIAL INSTITUTIONS

Justice

There is a constitutional court *(Verfassungsgericht)*, a court of appeal *(Oberlandesgericht)*, a regional court *(Landgericht)*, eight local courts *(Amtsgerichte)*, a *Bundesland* labour court, a labour court, a *Bundesland* social court, a social court, a finance court, a higher administrative court and an administrative court.

Education

In 2004 there were 415 schools of general education (not including *Internationale Schule*) with 181,600 pupils; 45 special schools with 7,527 pupils; 41 part-time vocational schools with 33,961 pupils; 38 schools with 4,451 pupils in manual instruction classes; 48 full-time vocational schools with 13,138 pupils; nine economic secondary schools with 2,303 pupils; two technical *Gymnasien* with 412 pupils; 19 advanced vocational schools with 3,460 pupils; 25 schools for public health occupations with 2,431 pupils; and 19 technical superior schools with 1,643 pupils.

In the winter term 2004–05 there was one university with 36,574 students; one technical university with 5,689 students; one college of music and one college of fine arts with 1,649 students in total; one university of the *Bundeswehr* (Helmut Schmidt University) with 1,888 students; one university of economics and political sciences with 2,753 students; four professional colleges with a total of 20,092 students.

Health

In 2004 there were 47 hospitals with 11,848 beds, 9,404 doctors and 1,754 dentists.

RELIGION

In 2004, 32·2% of the population went to the Evangelical Church and Free Churches, whilst 10·1% were Roman Catholic.

CULTURE

Broadcasting

In 2003 there was one public broadcasting service as well as seven private broadcasters.

Tourism

At Dec. 2004 there were 279 places of accommodation with 33,439 beds. Of the 3,247,048 visitors in 2004, 19·1% were foreigners.

FURTHER READING

Statistical Information: Statistisches Amt für Hamburg und Schleswig-Holstein (Standort Hamburg, Steckelhörn 12, 20457 Hamburg). *Directors:* Dr Wolfgang Bick, Dr Hans-Peter Kirschner. Publications: *Statistische Berichte, Statistisches Jahrbuch, Hamburger Statistische Porträts, Statistik Magazin.*

Hamburger Sparkasse, *Hamburg: von Altona bis Zollspieker.* Hamburg, 2002

Hamburgische Gesellschaft für Wirtschaftsförderung mbH, *Hamburg.* Oldenburg, 1993

Klessmann, E., *Geschichte der Stadt Hamburg.* 7th ed. Hamburg, 1994

Kopitzsch, F. and Brietzke, D., *Hamburgische Biografie, Personenlexikon.* Vol. 1. Hamburg, 2001

Kopitzsch, F. and Tilgner, D., *Hamburg Lexikon.* Hamburg, 1998

Möller, I., *Hamburg.* 2nd ed. Stuttgart, 1999

Schubert, D. and Harms, H., *Wohnen am Hafen.* Hamburg, 1993

Schütt, E. C., *Die Chronik Hamburgs.* Hamburg, 1991

State Library: Staats- und Universitätsbibliothek, Carl von Ossietzky, Von-Melle-Park 3, 20146 Hamburg. *Director:* Prof. Dr Peter Rau.

Hessen

KEY HISTORICAL EVENTS

The *Bundesland* consists of the former states of Hesse-Darmstadt and Hesse-Kassel, and Nassau. Hesse-Darmstadt was ruled by the

Landgrave Louis X from 1790. He became grand duke in 1806 with absolute power, having dismissed the parliament in 1803. However, he granted a constitution and bicameral parliament in 1820. Hesse-Darmstadt lost land to Prussia in the Seven Weeks' War of 1866, but retained its independence, both then and as a state of the German Empire after 1871. In 1918 the grand duke abdicated and the territory became a state of the German Republic. In 1945 areas west of the Rhine were incorporated into the new *Bundesland* of Rhineland-Palatinate, areas east of the Rhine became part of the *Bundesland* of Greater Hesse.

Hesse-Kassel was ruled by the Landgrave William IX from 1785 until he became Elector in 1805. In 1807 the Electorate was absorbed into the Kingdom of Westphalia (a Napoleonic creation), becoming independent again in 1815 as a state of the German Confederation. In 1831 a constitution and parliament were granted but the Electors remained strongly conservative.

In 1866 the Diet approved alliance with Prussia against Austria; the Elector nevertheless supported Austria. He was defeated by the Prussians and exiled and Hesse-Kassel was annexed to Prussia. In 1867 it was combined with Frankfurt and some areas taken from Nassau and Hesse-Darmstadt to form a Prussian province (Hesse-Nassau). In 1801 Nassau west of the Rhine passed to France; Napoleon also took the northern state in 1806. The remnant of the southern states allied in 1803 and three years later they became a duchy. In 1866 the duke supported Austria against Prussia and the duchy was annexed by Prussia as a result. In 1944 the Prussian province of Hesse-Nassau was split in two: Nassau and Electoral Hesse, also called Kurhessen. The following year these were combined with Hesse-Darmstadt as the *Bundesland* of Greater Hesse which became known as Hessen.

TERRITORY AND POPULATION

Area, 21,115 sq. km. The capital is Wiesbaden. There are three administrative regions with five urban and 21 rural districts and 426 communes. Population, 31 Dec. 2004, was 6,097,765 (2,986,543 males, 3,111,222 females).

SOCIAL STATISTICS

Statistics for calendar years:

	Live births	Marriages	Divorces	Deaths
2001	56,228	29,832	15,078	59,370
2002	55,324	30,472	15,785	60,367
2003	54,400	29,613	16,288	61,508
2004	54,332	29,727	16,573	58,507

CONSTITUTION AND GOVERNMENT

The constitution was put into force by popular referendum on 1 Dec. 1946. Hessen has five seats in the Bundesrat.

RECENT ELECTIONS

At the Diet elections on 2 Feb. 2003 the Christian Democratic Union (CDU) won 56 of 110 seats, with 48·8% of votes cast (up from 43·4% in 1999), the Social Democratic Party (SPD) 33 with 29·1% (down from 39·4% in 1999), the Greens 12 with 10·1% and the Free Democratic Party (FDP) 9 with 7·9%.

CURRENT ADMINISTRATION

The cabinet is headed by *Prime Minister* Roland Koch (Christian Democrats; CDU).

Government Website (German only): http://www.hessen.de

ECONOMY

Performance

In 2004 the gross domestic product at market prices (GDP) was unchanged at 1995 constant prices in comparison with the previous year. The total amount was €183·8bn. in 2004. The GDP per person engaged in labour productivity was €61,411 in 2004 (€60,569 in 2003).

ENERGY AND NATURAL RESOURCES

Electricity

Electricity production in 2004 was 31,015m. kWh (gross) and 27,984m. kWh (net). Total electricity consumption in 2004 was 35,143m. kWh.

Oil and Gas

Gas consumption in 2004 was 70,413m. kWh. All gas was imported from other parts of Germany

Agriculture

Area and yield of the most important crops:

	Area (in 1,000 ha.)			Yield (in 1,000 tonnes)		
	2002	2003	2004	2002	2003	2004
Wheat	148·9	147·5	154·7	1,054·9	1,030·5	1,324·3
Sugarbeet	18·8	18·6	18·8	1,108·9	995·8	1,182·0
Barley	105·0	104·2	100·0	594·9	541·3	657·4
Potatoes	4·7	5·1	5·6	153·0	172·2	225·9
Rape	53·5	56·3	55·8	173·6	161·4	195·4
Rye	17·5	13·8	14·6	103·6	74·3	101·7
Oats	16·9	19·1	16·5	72·7	103·7	86·5

Livestock, May 2005: cattle, 476,182 (including 157,494 milch cows); pigs, 802,257; sheep, 177,204; horses, 32,207; poultry, 1·42m.

INDUSTRY

In Sept. 2005, 3,084 establishments (with 20 or more employees) employed 414,306 persons; of these, 59,923 were employed in the chemical industry; 56,524 in machine construction; 50,955 in car building; 35,655 in production of metal products.

Labour

The economically active persons totalled 2,701,600 at the 1% sample survey of the microcensus of March 2004. Of the total, 2,364,000 were employees, 306,000 self-employed, 32,000 unpaid family workers; 754,000 were engaged in power supply, mining, manufacturing and building, 641,000 in commerce, transport, hotels and restaurants, 38,000 in agriculture and forestry and 1,268,000 in other services.

COMMUNICATIONS

Roads

On 1 Jan. 2005 there were 16,718 km of 'classified' roads, comprising 957 km of Autobahn, 3,479 km of federal highways, 7,251 km of first-class highways and 5,032 km of second-class highways. Motor vehicles licensed on 1 Jan. 2005 totalled 4,245,303, including 3,563,518 passenger cars, 6,278 buses, 183,038 lorries, 137,444 tractors and 303,146 motorcycles.

Civil Aviation

Frankfurt/Main airport is one of the most important freight airports in the world. In 2004, 477,475 aeroplanes took off and landed, carrying 51,106,647 passengers, 1,750,996 tonnes of air freight and 117,825 tonnes of air mail.

Shipping

Frankfurt/Main harbour and Hanau harbour are the two most important harbours. In 2004, 10·2m. tonnes of goods were imported into the *Bundesland* and 2·5m. tonnes were exported.

SOCIAL INSTITUTIONS

Justice

There are a constitutional court (*Staatsgerichtshof*), a court of appeal, nine regional courts, 58 local courts, a *Bundesland* labour court, 12 labour courts, a *Bundesland* social court, seven social courts, a finance court, a higher administrative court (*Verwaltungsgerichtshof*) and five administrative courts.

Education

In 2004 there were 1,258 primary schools with 281,798 pupils (including *Förderstufen*); 166 intermediate schools with 53,089 pupils; 19,344 teachers in primary and intermediate schools; 233 special schools with 4,386 teachers and 26,118 pupils; 167 high schools with 9,213 teachers and 146,932 pupils; 209 *Gesamtschulen* (comprehensive schools) with 11,999 teachers and 189,285 pupils; 119 part-time vocational schools with 129,820 pupils; 264 full-time vocational schools with 52,349 pupils; 108 advanced vocational schools with 11,255 pupils; 8,484 teachers in the vocational schools.

In the winter term 2004–05 there were four universities (Frankfurt/Main, 34,658 students; Giessen, 20,477; Kassel, 15,847; Marburg/Lahn, 17,668); one technical university in Darmstadt (17,626); two private *Wissenschaftliche Hochschulen* (1,871); 16 *Fachhochschulen* (49,208); two Roman Catholic theological colleges and one Protestant theological college with a total of 299; one college of music and two colleges of fine arts with 1,372 students in total.

RELIGION

In 2004 the churches in Hessen reported 2,557,000 (41·9%) Protestants and 1,564,000 (25·6%) Roman Catholics.

CULTURE

Press

In 2004 there were 80 newspapers published in Hessen with a combined circulation of 1·9m.

Tourism

In 2004, 9·8m. visitors stayed 23·9m. nights in Hessen.

FURTHER READING

Statistical Information: The Hessisches Statistisches Landesamt (Rheinstr. 35–37, 65175 Wiesbaden). *President:* Eckart Hohmann. Main publications: *Statistisches Jahrbuch für das Land Hessen* (biannual).—*Staat und Wirtschaft in Hessen* (monthly).—*Statistische Berichte.*—*Hessische Gemeindestatistik* (annual, 1980 ff.). Website (German only): http://www.statistik-hessen.de

State Library: Hessische Landesbibliothek, Rheinstr. 55–57, 65185 Wiesbaden. *Director:* Dr Marianne Dörr.

Lower Saxony

Niedersachsen

KEY HISTORICAL EVENTS

The *Bundesland* consists of the former states of Hanover, Oldenburg, Schaumburg-Lippe and Brunswick. It does not include the cities of Bremen or Bremerhaven. Oldenburg, Danish from 1667, passed to the bishopric of Lübeck in 1773; the Holy Roman Emperor made it a duchy in 1777. As a small state of the Confederation after 1815 it supported Prussia, becoming a member of the Prussian Zollverein (1853) and North German Confederation (1867). The grand duke abdicated in 1918 and was replaced by an elected government.

Schaumburg-Lippe was a small sovereign principality. As such it became a member of the Confederation of the Rhine in 1807 and of the German Confederation in 1815. Surrounded by Prussian territory, it also joined the Prussian-led North German Confederation in 1867. Part of the Empire until 1918, it then became a state of the new republic.

Brunswick, a small duchy, was taken into the Kingdom of Westphalia by Napoleon in 1806 but restored to independence in 1814. In 1830 the duke, Charles II, was forced into exile and replaced in 1831 by his more liberal brother, William. The succession passed to a Hanoverian claimant in 1913 but the duchy ended with the Empire in 1918.

As a state of the republican Germany, Brunswick was greatly reduced under the Third Reich. Its boundaries were restored by the British occupation forces in 1945.

Hanover was an autonomous Electorate of the Holy Roman Empire whose rulers were also kings of Great Britain from 1714 to 1837. From 1762 they ruled almost entirely from England. After Napoleonic invasions Hanover was restored in 1815. A constitution of 1819 made no radical change and had to be followed by more liberal versions in 1833 and 1848. Prussia annexed Hanover in 1866; it remained a Prussian province until 1946. On 1 Nov. 1946 all four states were combined by the British military administration to form the *Bundesland* of Lower Saxony.

TERRITORY AND POPULATION

Lower Saxony has an area of 47,618 sq. km, and is divided into eight urban districts, 38 rural districts and 1,023 communes; capital, Hanover.

Population, on 30 June 2005, was 8,005,927 (3,924,183 males; 4,081,744 females).

SOCIAL STATISTICS

Statistics for calendar years:

	Live births	Marriages	Divorces	Deaths
2001	75,239	41,781	19,485	82,517
2002	73,193	42,391	21,044	83,512
2003	70,563	40,827	21,921	85,336
2004	70,371	41,794	21,872	81,487

CONSTITUTION AND GOVERNMENT

The *Bundesland* Niedersachsen was formed on 1 Nov. 1946 by merging the former Prussian province of Hanover with Brunswick, Oldenburg and Schaumburg-Lippe. Lower Saxony has seven seats in the Bundesrat.

RECENT ELECTIONS

At the Diet elections on 2 Feb. 2003 the Christian Democratic Union won 91 of 183 seats, receiving 48·3% of votes cast (up from 35·9% in 1998), the Social Democratic Party 63 with 33·4% (down from 47·9% in 1998), the Free Democrats 15 with 8·1% and the Greens 14 with 7·6%.

CURRENT ADMINISTRATION

The *Prime Minister* is Christian Wulff (CDU).

Government Website (German only):
http://www.niedersachsen.de

ECONOMY

Banking and Finance

209 credit institutions were operating in 2004. Deposits totalled €50,741m.

ENERGY AND NATURAL RESOURCES

Electricity

Electricity production in 2004 was 52,973m. kWh. Consumption in 2003 was 53,141m. kWh.

Agriculture

Area and yield of the most important crops:

	Area (in 1,000 ha.)			Yield (in 1,000 tonnes)		
	2002	2003	2004	2002	2003	2004
Sugarbeet	117	114	108	6,369	6,627	6,421
Potatoes	123	126	127	4,948	4,588	6,069
Wheat	412	405	423	2,925	2,972	3,577
Barley	295	297	278	1,548	1,631	1,835

	Area (in 1,000 ha.)			Yield (in 1,000 tonnes)		
	2002	2003	2004	2002	2003	2004
Rye	132	104	120	761	582	820
Oats	24	26	24	96	129	117

Livestock, 3 May 2005: cattle, 2,581,500 (including 728,300 milch cows); pigs, 7,835,700; sheep, 234,500; horses, 81,600; poultry, 53,766,200.

INDUSTRY

In Sept. 2004, 3,790 establishments employed 521,481 persons; of these 52,821 were employed in electrical engineering; 50,673 in machine construction.

Labour

The economically active persons totalled 3,325,000 in April 2004. Of the total, 2,917,000 were employees, 356,600 self-employed, 51,700 unpaid family workers; 992,300 were engaged in power supply, mining, manufacturing and building, 785,300 in commerce and transport, 118,100 in agriculture and forestry, and 1,429,600 in other industries and services.

COMMUNICATIONS

Roads

At 1 Jan. 2005 there were 28,217 km of 'classified' roads, comprising 1,392 km of Autobahn, 4,833 km of federal roads, 8,309 km of first-class and 13,683 km of second-class highways. Number of motor vehicles, 1 Jan. 2005, was 5,404,796 including 4,461,355 passenger cars, 241,978 lorries, 8,445 buses, 233,545 tractors and 382,722 motorcycles.

Rail

In 2004, 28·1m. tonnes of freight came into the *Bundesland* by rail and 21·3m. tonnes left by rail.

Civil Aviation

77,514 planes landed at Hanover airport in 2004, which saw 2,562,660 passenger arrivals and 2,560,635 departures. 3,038 tonnes of freight left by air and 2,275 tonnes came in.

SOCIAL INSTITUTIONS

Justice

There are a constitutional court (*Staatsgerichtshof*), three courts of appeal, 11 regional courts, 79 local courts, a *Bundesland* labour court, 15 labour courts, a *Bundesland* social court, eight social courts, a finance court, a higher administrative court and seven administrative courts.

Education

In 2004–05 there were 1,861 primary schools with 346,296 pupils; 502 post-primary schools with 116,965 pupils; 295 special schools with 39,940 pupils; 461 secondary modern schools with 180,497 pupils; 244 grammar schools with 231,207 pupils; 34 co-operative comprehensive schools with 37,449 pupils; and 33 integrated comprehensive schools with 27,964 pupils.

In the winter term 2004–05 there were seven universities (Göttingen, 23,465 students; Hanover, 23,769; Hildesheim, 3,970; Lüneburg, 6,818; Oldenburg, 11,293; Osnabrück, 10,739; Vechta, 2,697); two technical universities (Braunschweig, 13,444; Clausthal, 2,771); the medical college of Hanover (3,248); the veterinary college in Hanover (2,048).

Health

At Dec. 2004 there were 25,863 doctors and 206 hospitals with 5·7 beds per 1,000 population.

RELIGION

In 2003 there were 52·4% Protestants and 17·9% Roman Catholics.

CULTURE

Broadcasting

Norddeutscher Rundfunk is the public broadcasting service for Lower Saxony.

Tourism

In 2004, 9,392,384 guests spent 31,504,197 nights in Lower Saxony.

FURTHER READING

Statistical Information: The Niedersächsisches Landesamt für Statistik, Postfach 910764, 30427 Hanover. *Head of Division:* President Karl-Ludwig Strelen. Main publications are: *Statistische Monatshefte Niedersachsen* (from 1947).—*Statistische Berichte Niedersachsen.*—*Statistisches Taschenbuch Niedersachsen 2004* (biennial).

State Libraries: Niedersächsische Staats- und Universitätsbibliothek, Platz der Göttinger Sieben 1, 37073 Göttingen. *Director:* Prof. Dr Elmar Mittler; Niedersächsische Landesbibliothek, Waterloostr. 8, 30169 Hanover. *Director:* Dr Georg Ruppelt.

Mecklenburg-West Pomerania

Mecklenburg-Vorpommern

KEY HISTORICAL EVENTS

Pomerania was at one time under Swedish control while Mecklenburg was an independent part of the German Empire. The two states were not united until after the Second World War, and after a short period when it was subdivided into three districts under the GDR, it became a state of the Federal Republic of Germany in 1990. The people of the region speak a dialect known as Plattdeutsch (Low German). The four main cities of this state are Hanseatic towns from the period when the area dominated trade with Scandinavia. Rostock on the North Sea coast became the home of the GDR's biggest shipyards.

TERRITORY AND POPULATION

The area is 23,178 sq. km. It is divided into six urban districts, 12 rural districts and 871 communes. Population on 31 Dec. 2004 was 1,719,653 (867,510 females). It is the most sparsely populated of the German *Bundesländer*, with a population density of 74 per sq. km in 2004. The capital is Schwerin.

SOCIAL STATISTICS

Statistics for calendar years:

	Live births	Marriages	Divorces	Deaths
2001	12,968	7,869	4,021	17,179
2002	12,504	7,901	3,505	17,333
2003	12,782	7,872	3,677	17,715
2004	13,045	9,567	3,940	17,134

CONSTITUTION AND GOVERNMENT

The *Bundesland* was reconstituted on former GDR territory in 1990. It has three seats in the Bundesrat.

RECENT ELECTIONS

At the Diet elections of 22 Sept. 2002 the Social Democrats (SPD) won 33 seats with 40·6% of the vote; the Christian Democrats (CDU), 25, with 31·3%; and the Party of Democratic Socialism (PDS, former Communists), 13, with 16·4%.

CURRENT ADMINISTRATION

The *Prime Minister* is Dr Harald Ringstorff (SPD).

Government Website: http://www.mecklenburg-vorpommern.de

ENERGY AND NATURAL RESOURCES

Agriculture

Area and yield of the most important crops:

	Area (in 1,000 ha.)			Yield (in 1,000 tonnes)		
	2002	2003	2004	2002	2003	2004
Wheat	324·2	338·6	339·8	2,309·0	2,153·4	2,671·2
Sugarbeet	27·8	27·0	25·5	1,357·4	1,381·0	1,380·0
Rape	237·1	227·3	234·2	755·9	756·9	1,055·1
Barley	115·9	140·9	137·0	712·8	764·0	971·4
Potatoes	15·4	16·3	17·5	555·1	543·6	770·5
Rye	87·1	54·3	66·9	467·4	263·0	423·1
Oats	12·0	13·2	12·0	50·9	56·5	66·5

Livestock in 2004: cattle, 556,200 (including 181,400 milch cows); pigs, 688,400; sheep, 116,300; horses, 12,480 (2003); poultry, 8,235,352 (2003).

Fisheries

Sea catch, 2004: 44,472 tonnes (26,772 tonnes frozen, 17,700 tonnes fresh). Freshwater catch, 2004: 396 tonnes (mainly carp, pike, perch and eels). Fish farming, 2004: 500 tonnes.

INDUSTRY

In 2004 there were 704 enterprises (with 20 or more employees) employing 49,195 persons.

Labour

700,500 persons (322,000 females) were employed at the 1%-sample survey of the microcensus of March 2004, including 353,200 white-collar workers, 235,000 manual workers and 68,100 self-employed and family assistants. 40,100 persons were employed as officials. Employment by sector (on average for the year 2004): public and private services, 264,500; trade, guest business, transport and communications, 185,400; financing, leasing and services for enterprises, 94,500; manufacturing, 72,700; construction, 55,200; agriculture, forestry and fisheries, 31,200; mining, energy and water resources, 7,000; total, 710,500.

COMMUNICATIONS

Roads

In 2004 there were 9,930 km of 'classified' roads, comprising 477 km of Autobahn, 2,071 km of federal roads, 3,258 km of first-class and 4,124 km of second-class highways. Number of motor vehicles at 1 Jan. 2005 was 1,061,532, including 897,144 passenger cars, 71,996 lorries, 1,893 buses and 51,649 motorcycles.

Shipping

There is a lake district of some 554 lakes greater than 0·1 sq. km. The ports of Rostock, Stralsund and Wismar are important for ship-building and repairs. In 2004 the cargo fleet consisted of 99 vessels (including one tanker) of 1,499,000 GT. Sea traffic, 2004; incoming 12,309,393 tonnes; outgoing 11,064,141 tonnes.

SOCIAL INSTITUTIONS

Justice

There is a court of appeal (*Oberlandesgericht*), four regional courts (*Landgerichte*), 21 local courts (*Amtsgerichte*), four labour courts, four social courts, a finance court and two administrative courts.

Education

In 2003 there were 257 primary schools, 26 comprehensives, 96 secondary schools and 92 special needs schools. There are universities at Rostock and Greifswald with (in 2004–05) 24,678 students and 4,695 academic staff, and five institutions of equivalent status with 10,305 students and 1,077 academic staff.

RELIGION

In 2004 the Evangelical Lutheran Church of Mecklenburg had 214,300 adherents, 233 pastors and 308 parishes. Roman Catholics numbered 58,200, with 51 priests and 58 parishes. The Pomeranian Evangelical Church had 106,000 adherents, 128 pastors and 258 parishes in 2004.

CULTURE

Tourism

In July 2004 there were 2,651 places of accommodation (with nine or more beds) providing a total of 164,970 beds. 4,944,969 guests stayed an average of 4·3 nights each in 2004.

FURTHER READING

Statistical office: Statistisches Landesamt Mecklenburg-Vorpommern, Postfach 120135, 19018 Schwerin.

Main publications are: *Statistische Hefte* (formerly *Statistische Monatshefte*) *Mecklenburg-Vorpommern* (since 1991); *Gemeindedaten Mecklenburg-Vorpommern* (since 1999; electronic); *Statistische Berichte* (since 1991; various); *Statistisches Jahrbuch Mecklenburg-Vorpommern* (since 1991); *Statistische Sonderhefte* (since 1992; various). *Website (German only):* http://www.statistik-mv.de

---

North Rhine-Westphalia

Nordrhein-Westfalen

KEY HISTORICAL EVENTS

Historical Westphalia consisted of many small political units, most of them absorbed by Prussia and Hanover before 1800. In 1807 Napoleon created a Kingdom of Westphalia for his brother Joseph. This included Hesse-Kassel, but was formed mainly from the Prussian and Hanoverian lands between the rivers Elbe and Weser.

In 1815 the kingdom ended with Napoleon's defeat. Most of the area was given to Prussia, with the small principalities of Lippe and Waldeck surviving as independent states. Both joined the North German Confederation in 1867. Lippe remained autonomous after the end of the Empire in 1918; Waldeck was absorbed into Prussia in 1929.

In 1946 the occupying forces combined Lippe with most of the Prussian province of Westphalia to form the *Bundesland* of North Rhine-Westphalia. On 1 March 1947 the allied Control Council formally abolished Prussia.

TERRITORY AND POPULATION

The *Bundesland* comprises 34,082 sq. km. It is divided into five administrative regions, 23 urban districts, 31 rural districts and 396 communes. Capital: Düsseldorf. Population, 31 Dec. 2004, 18,075,352 (9,272,097 females, 8,803,255 males).

SOCIAL STATISTICS

Statistics for calendar years:

	Live births	Marriages	Divorces	Deaths
2000	175,144	97,508	45,201	187,736
2001	167,752	89,529	46,913	184,824
2002	163,434	89,803	47,208	188,333
2003	159,883	87,768	50,962	190,793
2004	158,054	88,105	51,139	184,449

CONSTITUTION AND GOVERNMENT

Since Oct. 1990 North Rhine-Westphalia has had six seats in the Bundesrat.

RECENT ELECTIONS

The Diet elected on 22 May 2005 consisted of 89 Christian Democrats (44·8% of votes cast), 74 Social Democrats (37·1%—their worst showing in North Rhine-Westphalia in 50 years), 12 Free Democrats (6·2%) and 12 Greens (6·2%). Turnout was 63·0%.

CURRENT ADMINISTRATION

North Rhine-Westphalia is governed by the Christan Democrats (CDU) and the Free Democrats (FDP).

Prime Minister: Jürgen Rüttgers (CDU).

Government Website (German only): http://www.nrw.de

ECONOMY

North Rhine-Westphalia has the highest GDP of any German *Bundesland*—€481·4bn. in 2004 out of a total of €2,177·0bn. Foreign direct investment is also higher than in any other *Bundesland.*

Budget

The predicted total revenue for 2005 was €49,264·7m. and the predicted total expenditure was also €49,264·7m.

ENERGY AND NATURAL RESOURCES

Agriculture

Area and yield of the most important crops:

	Area (in 1,000 ha.)			Yield (in 1,000 tonnes)		
	2002	2003	2004	2002	2003	2004
Sugarbeet	71·3	69·9	69·2	4,045·6	4,089·5	4,398·9
Wheat	259·1	260·8	270·4	2,132·6	2,091·0	2,366·3
Potatoes	29·9	30·8	33·7	1,298·4	1,329·2	1,612·9
Barley	189·2	200·3	196·0	1,273·5	1,249·7	1,383·1
Rye	22·9	17·6	18·9	156·6	112·5	125·3
Oats	22·0	26·3	22·5	103·1	146·9	121·3

Livestock, 3 May 2004: cattle, 1,375,121 (including 384,002 milch cows); pigs, 6,064,677; sheep, 231,070; poultry (2003), 11,198,984.

INDUSTRY

In Sept. 2004, 10,566 establishments (with 20 or more employees) employed 1,302,113 persons: 286,115 were employed in metal production and manufacture of metal goods; 209,217 in machine construction; 144,301 in manufacture of office machines, computers, electrical and precision engineering and optics; 113,298 in the chemical industry; 97,882 in motor vehicle manufacture; 94,826 in production of food and tobacco. 68% of the workforce is now employed in the services industry. Of the total population, 7·2% were engaged in industry.

Labour

The economically active persons totalled 7,401,000 at the 1%-sample survey of the microcensus of March 2004. Of the total, 6,579,000 were employees, 742,000 self-employed and 80,000 unpaid family workers; 2,256,000 were engaged in power supply, mining, manufacturing, water supply and building, 1,735,000 in commerce, hotel trade and transport, 113,000 in agriculture, forestry and fishing, and 3,296,000 in other industries and services.

COMMUNICATIONS

Roads

There were (1 Jan. 2005) 29,707 km of 'classified' roads, comprising 2,175 km of Autobahn, 5,053 km of federal roads, 12,672 km of first-class and 9,807 km of second-class highways. Number of motor vehicles (1 Jan. 2005): 11,426,553, including 9,733,822 passenger cars, 497,064 lorries, 18,114 buses and 818,808 motorcycles.

Civil Aviation

In 2004, 94,290 aircraft landed at Düsseldorf, bringing 7,542,666 incoming passengers; and 67,876 aircraft landed at Cologne-Bonn, bringing 4,126,213 incoming passengers.

SOCIAL INSTITUTIONS

Justice

There are a constitutional court *(Verfassungsgerichtshof),* three courts of appeal, 19 regional courts, 130 local courts, three *Bundesland* labour courts, 30 labour courts, one *Bundesland* social court, eight social courts, three finance courts, a higher administrative court and seven administrative courts.

Education

In 2004 there were 4,186 primary schools with 60,888 teachers and 1,051,979 pupils; 708 special schools with 17,499 teachers and 104,400 pupils; 554 intermediate schools with 18,742 teachers and 344,387 pupils; 265 *Gesamtschulen* (comprehensive schools) with 18,281 teachers and 248,147 pupils; 627 high schools with 33,200 teachers and 557,038 pupils; there were 300 part-time vocational schools with 356,884 pupils; 197 vocational preparatory year schools with 22,672 pupils; 306 full-time vocational schools with 132,723 pupils; 192 full-time vocational schools leading up to vocational colleges with 22,501 pupils; 260 advanced full-time vocational schools with 44,911 pupils; 508 schools for public health occupations with 15,464 teachers and 43,329 pupils.

In the winter term 2004–05 there were 14 universities (Bielefeld, 17,707 students; Bochum, 30,220; Bonn, 29,974; Cologne (Köln), 44,240; Dortmund, 21,130; Düsseldorf, 18,021; Duisburg-Essen, 32,849; Münster, 37,916; Paderborn, 13,345; Siegen, 11,797; Witten/Herdecke, 1,058; Wuppertal, 12,163; the Technical University of Aachen, 28,210; Fernuniversität at Hagen, 31,435); the College for physical education in Cologne, 4,465; four Roman Catholic and two Protestant theological colleges with a total of 659 students. There were also four colleges of music, three colleges of fine arts with 4,795 students in total; 24 *Fachhochschulen* (vocational colleges) with 109,419 students.

Health

In 2004 there were 456 hospitals in North Rhine-Westphalia with 130,489 beds, which had an average occupancy rate of 74·6%.

RELIGION

In 2003 there were 43·4% Roman Catholics and 28·7% Protestants.

CULTURE

Tourism

At Dec. 2004 there were 5,247 places of accommodation (nine beds or more) providing 272,468 beds altogether. In 2004, 15,506,126 visitors (2,937,154 foreigners) spent 37,692,445 nights in North Rhine-Westphalia.

FURTHER READING

Statistical Information: The Landesamt für Datenverarbeitung und Statistik Nordrhein-Westfalen (Mauerstr. 51, 40476 Düsseldorf) was founded in 1946, by amalgamating the provincial statistical offices of Rhineland and Westphalia. *President:* Jochen Kehlenbach. The Landesamt publishes (from 1949): *Statistisches Jahrbuch Nordrhein-Westfalen.* More than 550 other publications yearly. *Website (German only):* http://www.lds.nrw.de

Bundesland Library: Universitätsbibliothek, Universitätsstr. 1, 40225 Düsseldorf. *Director:* Dr Irmgard Siebert.

Rhineland-Palatinate

Rheinland-Pfalz

KEY HISTORICAL EVENTS

The *Bundesland* was formed from the Rhenisch Palatinate and the Rhine valley areas of Prussia, Hesse-Darmstadt, Hesse-Kassel and Bavaria.

From 1214 the Palatinate was ruled by the Bavarian house of Wittelsbach, with its capital as Heidelberg. In 1797 the land west of the Rhine was taken into France, and Napoleon divided the eastern land between Baden and Hesse. In 1815 the territory taken by France was restored to Germany and allotted to Bavaria. The area and its neighbours formed the strategically important Bavarian Circle of the Rhine. The rule of the Wittelsbachs ended in 1918 but the Palatinate remained part of Bavaria until the American occupying forces detached it in 1946. The new *Bundesland*, incorporating the Palatinate and other territory, received its constitution in April 1947.

TERRITORY AND POPULATION

Rhineland-Palatinate has an area of 19,853 sq. km. It comprises 12 urban districts, 24 rural districts and 2,306 other communes. The capital is Mainz. Population (at 31 Dec. 2004), 4,061,105 (2,069,130 females).

SOCIAL STATISTICS

Statistics for calendar years:

	Live births	Marriages	Divorces	Deaths
2001	35,781	20,608	10,301	42,222
2002	34,741	20,800	11,187	42,669
2003	34,083	20,123	11,567	43,933
2004	33,421	21,039	11,298	41,563

CONSTITUTION AND GOVERNMENT

The constitution of the *Bundesland* Rheinland-Pfalz was approved by the Consultative Assembly on 25 April 1947 and by referendum on 18 May 1947, when 579,002 voted for and 514,338 against its acceptance. It has four seats in the Bundesrat.

RECENT ELECTIONS

At the elections of 26 March 2006 the Social Democratic Party won 53 seats of the 101 in the state parliament with 45·6% of votes cast; the Christian Democrats 38 with 32·8% (their worst result ever in Rheinland-Pfalz); the Free Democrats 10 with 8·0%. The Greens only received 4·6% of the vote and the Election Alternative Labour and Social Justice 3·1%; therefore neither party won any seats. Turnout was 58·2%.

CURRENT ADMINISTRATION

The coalition cabinet is headed by Kurt Beck (b. 1949; Social Democrat).

Government Website: http://www.rlp.de

ENERGY AND NATURAL RESOURCES

Agriculture

Area and yield of the most important products:

	Area (1,000 ha.)			Yield (1,000 tonnes)		
	2002	2003	2004	2002	2003	2004
Sugarbeet	21·8	21·7	22·1	1,449·5	1,006·4	1,346·7
Wheat	95·0	87·1	96·6	650·5	522·6	725·2
Barley	104·1	112·0	103·5	511·7	538·5	623·0
Potatoes	9·6	8·8	8·9	310·9	252·4	302·6
Rye	12·3	8·5	11·2	73·9	41·3	72·5
Oats	10·4	11·2	10·0	39·7	47·4	48·8
Wine	61·8	61·4	61·3	6,635·4[1]	5,585·0[1]	6,596·1[1]

[1]1,000 hectolitres.

Livestock (2004, in 1,000): cattle, 397·4 (including milch cows, 125·2); sheep, 128·8; pigs, 324·0; horses (2003), 23·4; poultry (2003), 1,676·7.

Forestry

Total area covered by forests in Dec. 2004 was 8,236·0 sq. km or 41·5% of the total area.

INDUSTRY

In 2004, 2,179 establishments (with 20 or more employees) employed 282,410 persons; of these 56,954 were employed in the chemical industry; 34,291 in machine construction; 19,653 in processing stoneware and earthenware; 17,175 in electrical equipment manufacture; 3,594 in leather goods and footwear.

Labour

The economically active persons totalled 1,743,700 in 2004. Of the total, 1,533,000 were employees, 184,300 were self-employed, 26,500 were unpaid family workers; 548,800 were engaged in power supply, mining, manufacturing and building, 398,900 in commerce, transport, hotels and restaurants, 49,300 in agriculture and forestry, 746,700 in other industries and services.

COMMUNICATIONS

Roads

In 2005 there were 18,427 km of 'classified' roads, comprising 869 km of Autobahn, 2,969 km of federal roads, 7,197 km of first-class and 7,392 km of second-class highways. Number of motor vehicles, 1 Jan. 2005, was 2,911,846, including 2,389,094 passenger cars, 123,885 lorries, 5,359 buses, 136,538 tractors and 221,389 motorcycles.

SOCIAL INSTITUTIONS

Justice

There are a constitutional court (*Verfassungsgerichtshof*), two courts of appeal, eight regional courts, 46 local courts, a *Bundesland* labour court, five labour courts, a *Bundesland* social court, four social courts, a finance court, a higher administrative court and four administrative courts.

Education

In 2004 there were 996 primary schools with 8,963 teachers and 171,368 pupils; 584 secondary schools with 17,926 teachers and 301,934 pupils; 141 special schools with 2,538 teachers and 17,513 pupils; 105 vocational and advanced vocational schools with 5,405 teachers and 127,776 pupils.

In higher education, in the winter term 2005–06 (provisional figures) there were the University of Mainz (34,391 students), the University of Kaiserslautern (9,397 students), the University of Trier (13,326 students), the University of Koblenz-Landau (11,018 students), the *Deutsche Hochschule für Verwaltungswissenschaften* in Speyer (435 students), the *Wissenschaftliche Hochschule für Unternehmensführung* (Otto Beisheim Graduate School) in Vallendar (439 students), the Roman Catholic Theological College in Trier (311 students) and the Roman Catholic Theological College in Vallendar (99 students). There were also nine *Fachhochschulen* with 30,290 students and three *Verwaltungsfachhochschulen* with 1,810 students.

RELIGION

In 2003 there were 47·0% Roman Catholics and 32·0% Protestants.

CULTURE

Tourism

In 2004, 3,706 places of accommodation provided 156,652 beds for 6,396,968 visitors.

FURTHER READING

Statistical Information: Statistisches Landesamt Rheinland-Pfalz (Mainzer Str., 14–16, 56130 Bad Ems). *President:* Jörg Berres. Its publications include: *Statistisches Taschenbuch Rheinland-Pfalz* (from 1948); *Statistische Monatshefte Rheinland-Pfalz* (from 1958); *Statistik von Rheinland-Pfalz* (from 1946) 390 vols. to date; *Rheinland-Pfalz im Spiegel der Statistik* (from 1968); *Rheinland-Pfalz—seine kreisfreien Städte und Landkreise* (1992); *Rheinland-Pfalz heute* (from 1973).

Saarland

KEY HISTORICAL EVENTS

Long disputed between Germany and France, the area was occupied by France in 1792. Most of it was allotted to Prussia at the close of the Napoleonic wars in 1815. In 1870 Prussia defeated France and when, in 1871, the German Empire was founded under Prussian leadership, it was able to incorporate Lorraine. This part of France was the Saar territory's western neighbour so the Saar was no longer a vulnerable boundary state. It began to develop industrially, exploiting Lorraine coal and iron.

In 1919 the League of Nations took control of the Saar until a plebiscite of 1935 favoured return to Germany. In 1945 there was a French occupation, and in 1947 the Saar was made an international area, but in economic union with France. In 1954 France and Germany agreed that the Saar should be a separate and autonomous state, under an independent commissioner. This was rejected by referendum and France agreed to return Saarland to Germany; it became a *Bundesland* of the Federal Republic on 1 Jan. 1957.

TERRITORY AND POPULATION

Saarland has an area of 2,570 sq. km. Population, 31 Dec. 2004, 1,056,417 (513,460 males, 542,957 females). It comprises six rural districts and 52 communes. The capital is Saarbrücken.

SOCIAL STATISTICS

Statistics for calendar years:

	Live births	Marriages	Divorces	Deaths
2001	8,196	5,417	3,100	12,316
2002	7,879	5,289	2,981	12,371
2003	7,598	5,141	2,867	12,852
2004	7,660	5,265	2,786	12,015

CONSTITUTION AND GOVERNMENT

Saarland has three seats in the Bundesrat.

RECENT ELECTIONS

At the elections to the Saar Diet of 5 Sept. 2004 the Christian Democrats (CDU) won 27 seats with 47·5% of votes cast and the Social Democrats (SDP) 18 with 30·8%. The Greens and the Free Democrats each won 3 seats. Turnout was 55·5%.

CURRENT ADMINISTRATION

Saarland is governed by Christian Democrats in Parliament. The *Prime Minister* is Peter Müller (Christian Democrat).

Government Website: http://www.saarland.de

ENERGY AND NATURAL RESOURCES

Electricity

In 2004 electricity production was 10,699m. kWh. End-user consumption totalled 7,699m. kWh in 2004.

Oil and Gas

7,916m. kWh of gas was used in 2004.

Agriculture

The cultivated area (2005) occupied 113,501 ha. or 44·2% of the total area.

Area and yield of the most important crops:

	Area (in 1,000 ha.)			Yield (in 1,000 tonnes)		
	2003	2004	2005	2003	2004	2005
Wheat	8·2	8·7	8·3	44·1	61·1	56·6
Barley	7·0	7·2	6·0	31·7	36·3	35·4
Rye	3·3	3·9	3·7	14·5	25·4	20·6
Oats	3·5	3·3	2·7	13·9	15·4	11·5
Potatoes	0·2	0·2	0·2	4·4	5·8	5·8

Livestock, May 2003: cattle, 58,460 (including 14,801 milch cows); pigs, 20,700; sheep, 14,872; horses, 5,594; poultry, 194,357.

Forestry

The forest area comprises nearly 33·4% of the total (256,974 ha.).

INDUSTRY

In June 2005, 496 establishments (with 20 or more employees) employed 97,882 persons; of these 25,046 were engaged in manufacturing of motor vehicles, parts and accessories, 11,868 in machine construction, 11,192 in iron and steel production, 6,986 in coalmining, 2,521 in steel construction and 2,427 in electrical engineering. In 2004 the coalmines produced 6·0m. tonnes of coal. Two blast furnaces and seven steel furnaces produced 4·4m. tonnes of pig iron and 5·6m. tonnes of crude steel.

Labour

The economically active persons totalled 425,800 at the 1%-sample survey of the microcensus of May 2004. Of the total, 382,200 were employees and 43,600 self-employed; 137,200 were engaged in power supply, mining, manufacturing and building, 101,000 in commerce and transport, 5,300 in agriculture and forestry, and 182,200 in other industries and services.

COMMUNICATIONS

Roads

At 1 Jan. 2004 there were 2,037 km of classified roads, comprising 240 km of Autobahn, 329 km of federal roads, 848 km of first-class and 620 km of second-class highways. Number of motor vehicles, 31 Dec. 2003, 749,303, including 634,792 passenger cars, 33,304 lorries, 1,341 buses, 15,158 tractors and 56,788 motorcycles.

Shipping

During 2004, 1,665 ships docked in Saarland ports, bringing 2·2m. tonnes of freight. In the same period 1,662 ships left the ports, carrying 905,000 tonnes of freight.

SOCIAL INSTITUTIONS

Justice

There are a constitutional court (*Verfassungsgerichtshof*), a regional court of appeal, a regional court, ten local courts, a *Bundesland* labour court, three labour courts, a *Bundesland* social court, a social court, a finance court, a higher administrative court and an administrative court.

Education

In 2004–05 there were 268 primary schools with 39,414 pupils; 41 special schools with 4,094 pupils; 55 *Realschulen, Erweiterte Realschulen* and *Sekundarschulen* with 29,136 pupils; 35 high schools with 30,435 pupils; 15 comprehensive high schools with 10,993 pupils; four *Freie Waldorfschulen* with 1,314 pupils; four business and technical grammar schools with 645 pupils; two evening intermediate schools with 349 pupils; one evening high school and one Saarland College with 287 pupils; 44 part-time vocational schools with 20,827 pupils; year of commercial basic training: 52 institutions with 2,974 pupils; 16 advanced full-time vocational schools and schools for technicians with 2,236 pupils; 42 full-time vocational schools with 3,647 pupils; 33 *Fachoberschulen* (full-time vocational schools leading up to vocational colleges) with 6,945 pupils; 39 schools for public health occupations with 2,556 pupils. The number of pupils attending the vocational schools amounts to 40,042.

In the winter term 2004–05 there was the University of the Saarland with 14,718 students; one academy of fine art with 285 students; one academy of music and theatre with 329 students; one vocational college (economics and technics) with 3,326 students; one vocational college for social affairs with 286 students; and one vocational college for public administration with 391 students.

Health

In 2003 the 26 hospitals in the Saarland contained 7,395 beds and treated 266,731 patients. The average occupancy rate was 81·3%. There were also 21 out-patient and rehabilitation centres which treated 35,433 patients in 2003. On average they were using 77·4% of their capacity.

RELIGION

In 2003, 65·7% of the population were Roman Catholics and 19·7% were Protestants.

CULTURE

Tourism

In 2004, 14,742 beds were available in 268 places of accommodation (of nine or more beds). 698,469 guests spent 2,079,922 nights in the Saarland, staying an average of 3·0 days each.

FURTHER READING

Statistical Information: Statistisches Landesamt Saarland (Virchowstrasse 7, 66119 Saarbrücken). *Director*: Michael Sossong. The most important publications are: *Statistisches Jahrbuch Saarland* (annual).—*Saarland in Zahlen* (special issues).—*Einzelschriften zur Statistik des Saarlandes* (special issues).—*Statistik-Journal* (quarterly magazine). *Website (German only)*: http://www.statistik.saarland.de

Born, M., *Geographische Inselkunde des Saarlandes.* Saarbrücken, 1980
Herrmann, H.-W., *et al.*, *Das Saarland: Politische, wirtschaftliche und kulturelle Entwicklung.* Saarbrücken, 1989
Matthias, K., *Wirtschaftsgeographie des Saarlandes.* Saarbrücken, 1980.—*Wirtschaftsraum Saarland* (published in collaboration with the Industrie- und Handelskammer des Saarlandes). Oldenburg, 1990
Staerk, D., *Das Saarlandbuch.* Saarbrücken, 1981

Saxony

Freistaat Sachsen

KEY HISTORICAL EVENTS

The former kingdom of Saxony was a member state of the German Empire from 1871 until 1918, when it became the state of Saxony and joined the Weimar Republic. After the Second World War it was one of the five states in the German Democratic Republic until German reunification in 1990. It has been home to much of Germany's cultural history. In the 18th century, the capital of Saxony, Dresden, became the cultural capital of northern Europe earning the title 'Florence of the North', and the other great eastern German city, Leipzig, was a lively commercial city with strong artistic trends. The three cities of Dresden, Chemnitz and Leipzig formed the industrial heartland of Germany which, after World War II, was the manufacturing centre of the GDR.

TERRITORY AND POPULATION

The area is 18,415 sq. km. It is divided into three administrative regions, seven urban districts, 22 rural districts and 515 communes. Population on 31 Dec. 2004 was 4,296,284 (2,204,463 females, 2,091,821 males); density, 233 per sq. km. The capital is Dresden.

SOCIAL STATISTICS

Statistics for calendar years:

	Live births	Marriages	Divorces	Deaths
2001	31,943	15,421	8,430	49,244
2002	31,518	15,188	8,515	50,096
2003	32,079	14,778	8,946	50,669
2004	33,044	16,851	8,842	48,254

CONSTITUTION AND GOVERNMENT

The *Bundesland* was reconstituted as the Free State of Saxony on former GDR territory in 1990. It has four seats in the Bundesrat.

RECENT ELECTIONS

At the Diet elections of 19 Sept. 2004 the Christian Democratic Union won 55 seats, with 41·1% of the vote; the Party of Democratic Socialism (former Communists), 31, with 23·6%; the Social Democratic Party, 13, with 9·8%; the extreme right-wing National Democratic Party, 12, with 9·2%; the Free Democrats, 7, with 5·9%; and the Greens, 6, with 5·1%. Turnout was 59·6%.

CURRENT ADMINISTRATION

The *Prime Minister* is Georg Milbradt (b. 1945; Christian Democrat).

Government Website (German only): http://www.sachsen.de

ENERGY AND NATURAL RESOURCES

Agriculture

Area and yield of the most important crops:

	Area (in 1,000 ha.)			Yield (in 1,000 tonnes)		
	2003	2004	2005	2003	2004	2005
Maize	77·7	79·3	75·4	2,106·6	2,605·3	2,742·7
Fodder	180·9	185·2	197·4	987·3	1,545·7	1,619·1
Wheat	167·4	174·7	177·5	823·4	1,414·1	1,315·8
Barley	141·1	134·9	142·2	602·3	911·9	836·7
Potatoes	8·0	8·1	7·4	221·0	322·4	312·7
Rye	31·9	39·6	30·9	119·3	266·1	168·5

Livestock in May 2005 (in 1,000): cattle, 501 (including milch cows, 203); pigs, 630; sheep, 128.

INDUSTRY

In Sept. 2005, 2,927 establishments (with 20 or more employees) employed 232,030 persons.

Labour

The unemployment rate was 19·5% in Aug. 2005.

COMMUNICATIONS

Roads

On 1 Jan. 2005 there were 468·5 km of autobahn and 2,481·0 km of main roads. On 1 Jan. 2005 there were 2,675,304 registered motor vehicles, including 2,293,752 motor cars, 227,273 lorries and tractors, 4,288 buses and 126,980 motorcycles.

Civil Aviation

Leipzig airport handled 2,026,550 passengers in 2004.

SOCIAL INSTITUTIONS

Education

In 2005–06 there were 854 primary schools (*Grundschulen*) with 110,220 pupils and 9,489 teachers; 424 secondary schools (*Mittelschulen*) with 112,823 pupils and 11,222 teachers; 146 grammar schools (*Gymnasien*) with 95,622 pupils and 8,189 teachers; and 166 high schools (*Förderschulen*) with 20,848 pupils and 3,454 teachers. There were three *Freie Waldorfschulen* (private) with 1,202 pupils and 105 teachers and, in 2004–05, 834 professional training schools with 169,366 students and 7,184 teachers. In 2004–05 there were seven universities with 76,727 students, 12 polytechnics with 26,018 students, seven art schools with 2,700 students and two management colleges with 1,107 students.

Health

In 2004 there were 86 hospitals with 28,507 beds. There were 14,220 doctors and 3,806 dentists.

RELIGION

In 2004, 21·5% of the population belonged to the Evangelical Church and 3·6% were Roman Catholic.

CULTURE

Tourism

In 2004 there were 111,543 beds in places of accommodation (totalling 2,170 in 2004). There were 5,436,572 visitors during the year.

FURTHER READING

Statistical office: Statistisches Landesamt des Freistaates Sachsen, Postfach 1105, 01911 Kamenz. It publishes *Statistisches Jahrbuch des Freistaates Sachsen* (since 1990).

Saxony-Anhalt

Sachsen-Anhalt

KEY HISTORICAL EVENTS

Saxony-Anhalt has a short history as a state in its own right. Made up of a patchwork of older regions ruled by other states, Saxony-Anhalt existed between 1947 and 1952 and then, after reunification in 1990, it was re-established. Geographically, it lies at the very heart of Germany and despite the brevity of its federal status, the region has some of the oldest heartlands of German culture.

TERRITORY AND POPULATION

The area is 20,447 sq. km. It is divided into three administrative regions, three urban districts, 21 rural districts and 1,197 communes. Population in 2004 was 2,494,437. The capital is Magdeburg.

SOCIAL STATISTICS

Statistics for calendar years:

	Live births	Marriages	Divorces	Deaths
2001	18,073	9,359	5,829	29,621
2002	17,617	9,274	5,838	30,159
2003	16,889	9,314	5,863	29,632
2004	17,337	10,748	5,866	29,008

CONSTITUTION AND GOVERNMENT

The *Bundesland* was reconstituted on former GDR territory in 1990. It has four seats in the Bundesrat.

RECENT ELECTIONS

At the Diet election on 26 March 2006 the CDU received 36·2% of votes cast giving them 40 of 97 seats, the Left Party (former Party for Democratic Socialism) 24·1% (26 seats), the SPD 21·4% (24 seats) and the Free Democratic Party 6·7% (7). The Green Party only received 3·6% of the vote, and therefore won no seats. Turnout was 44·4%.

CURRENT ADMINISTRATION

The *Prime Minister* is Wolfgang Böhmer (CDU).

Government Website: http://www.sachsen-anhalt.de

ENERGY AND NATURAL RESOURCES

Agriculture

Area and yield of the most important crops:

	Area (in 1,000 ha.)			Yield (in 1,000 tonnes)		
	2002	2003	2004	2002	2003	2004
Cereals	587·2	559·5	574·8	3,577·2	3,312·3	4,499·5
Sugarbeet	51·8	50·3	50·7	2,618·8	2,246·4	2,716·9
Potatoes	13·8	14·1	13·8	556·1	465·1	600·5
Maize	13·6	23·7	20·9	120·1	122·8	172·1

Livestock in 2003 (in 1,000): cattle, 352·1 (including milch cows, 140·9); pigs, 849·2; sheep, 122·7.

INDUSTRY

In 2003, 1,360 establishments (with 20 or more employees) employed 110,871 persons; of these, 50,032 were employed in basic industry, 31,776 in the capital goods industry and 20,668 in the food industry. Major sectors are extraction of metal, metal working, metal articles, the nutrition industry, mechanical engineering and the chemical industry.

Labour

The economically active persons totalled 1,018,300 in March 2004. Of the total, 927,100 were employees, 85,800 self-employed, 5,400 unpaid family workers; 295,100 were engaged in power supply, mining, manufacturing and building, 237,500 in commerce and transport, 32,500 in agriculture and forestry, 453,200 in other industries and services.

COMMUNICATIONS

Roads

In 2004 there were 374 km of motorways, 2,376 km of main and 3,819 km of local roads. At 1 Jan. 2005 there were 1,540,769 registered motor vehicles, including 1,318,773 passenger cars, 97,305 lorries, 2,562 buses and 73,641 motorcycles.

SOCIAL INSTITUTIONS

Education

In 2004–05 there were 1,098 schools with 230,484 pupils. There were ten universities and institutes of equivalent status with 52,439 students.

RELIGION

In 2003, 15·9% of the population were Protestants and 4·3% were Roman Catholics.

CULTURE

Tourism

1,071 places of accommodation provided 54,624 beds in Dec. 2004. There were 2,348,778 visitors during the year.

FURTHER READING

Statistical office: Statistisches Landesamt Sachsen-Anhalt, Postfach 20 11 56, 06012 Halle (Saale). It publishes *Statistisches Jahrbuch des Landes Sachsen-Anhalt* (since 1991).

Schleswig-Holstein

KEY HISTORICAL EVENTS

The *Bundesland* is formed from two states formerly contested between Germany and Denmark. Schleswig was a Danish dependency ruled since 1474 by the King of Denmark as Duke of Schleswig. He also ruled Holstein, its southern neighbour, as Duke of Holstein, but he did so recognizing that it was a fief of the Holy Roman Empire. As such, Holstein joined the German Confederation which replaced the Empire in 1815.

Disputes between Denmark and the powerful German states were accompanied by rising national feeling in the duchies, where the population was part-Danish and part-German. There was war in 1848–50 and in 1864, when Denmark surrendered its claims to Prussia and Austria. Following her defeat of Austria in 1866 Prussia annexed both duchies.

North Schleswig (predominantly Danish) was awarded to Denmark in 1920. Prussian Holstein and south Schleswig became the present *Bundesland* in 1946.

TERRITORY AND POPULATION

The area of Schleswig-Holstein is 15,763 sq. km. It is divided into four urban and 11 rural districts and 1,127 communes. The capital is Kiel. The population (estimate, 31 Dec. 2004) numbered 2,828,760 (1,382,531 males, 1,446,229 females).

SOCIAL STATISTICS

Statistics for calendar years:

	Live births	Marriages	Divorces	Deaths
2001	25,681	16,773	7,604	29,667
2002	24,914	17,037	8,194	29,902
2003	24,216	16,985	8,293	30,543
2004	24,093	17,514	8,180	29,828

CONSTITUTION AND GOVERNMENT

The *Bundesland* has four seats in the Bundesrat.

RECENT ELECTIONS

At the elections of 20 Feb. 2005 the Christian Democrats won 30 of the 69 available seats with 40·2% of votes cast, the Social Democrats 29 with 38·7%, the Free Democrats 4 with 6·6%, the Greens 4 with 6·2% and the (Danish) South Schleswig Voters Association 2 with 6·6%. Turnout was 66·6%.

CURRENT ADMINISTRATION

The *Prime Minister* is Peter Harry Carstensen (b. 1947; CDU).

Government Website (German only):
  http://www.schleswig-holstein.de

ENERGY AND NATURAL RESOURCES

Agriculture

Area and yield of the most important crops:

	Area (in 1,000 ha.)			Yield (in 1,000 tonnes)		
	2002	2003	2004	2002	2003	2004
Wheat	219	217	208	1,776	1,866	1,879
Sugarbeet	14	13	12	744	686	710
Barley	50	69	69	323	514	534
Potatoes	6	6	6	187	200	252
Rye	24	16	17	154	108	119
Oats	10	9	9	52	54	59

Livestock, Nov. 2003: 1,228,174 cattle (including 375,129 milch cows); 1,397,664 pigs. May 2003: 363,075 sheep; 53,050 horses; 2,515,593 poultry.

Fisheries

In 2003 the yield of small-scale deep-sea and inshore fisheries was 62,844 tonnes valued at €63·4m.

INDUSTRY

In 2004 (average), 1,376 mining, quarrying and manufacturing establishments (with 20 or more employees) employed 128,877 persons; of these, 21,377 were employed in machine construction; 20,212 in food and related industries; 9,133 in electrical engineering; 5,472 in shipbuilding (except naval engineering).

Labour

The economically active persons totalled 1,216,000 in 2004. Of the total, 1,060,000 were employees, 143,000 were self-employed, 12,000 unpaid family workers; 320,000 were engaged in commerce and transport, 283,000 in power supply, mining, manufacturing and building, 41,000 in agriculture and forestry, and 572,000 in other industries and services.

COMMUNICATIONS

Roads

There were (1 Jan. 2002) 9,888 km of 'classified' roads, comprising 485 km of Autobahn, 1,673 km of federal roads, 3,631 km of first-class and 4,098 km of second-class highways. In 2004 the number of motor vehicles was 1,886,816, including 1,552,152 passenger cars, 94,580 lorries, 2,979 buses, 71,460 tractors and 132,183 motorcycles.

Shipping

The Kiel Canal (*Nord-Ostsee-Kanal*) is 98·7 km long; in 2002, 38,562 vessels of 49m. NRT passed through it.

SOCIAL INSTITUTIONS

Justice

There are a court of appeal, four regional courts, 27 local courts, a *Bundesland* labour court, five labour courts, a *Bundesland* social court, four social courts, a finance court, an upper administrative court and an administrative court.

Education

In 2004–05 there were 657 primary schools with 7,440 teachers and 120,417 pupils; 286 elementary schools with 3,168 teachers and 45,725 pupils; 171 intermediate schools with 4,239 teachers and 65,246 pupils; 105 grammar schools (*Gymnasien*) with 5,611 teachers and 75,828 pupils; 27 comprehensive schools with 1,469 teachers and 17,970 pupils; 168 other schools (including special schools) with 1,933 teachers and 11,907 pupils; 298 vocational schools with 4,377 teachers and 91,015 pupils.

In the winter term of the academic year 2004–05 there were 27,426 students at the three universities (Kiel, Flensburg and Lübeck) and 19,139 students at 11 further education colleges.

RELIGION

In 2003, 56·9% of the population were Protestants and 6·1% Roman Catholics.

CULTURE

Tourism

4,610 places of accommodation provided 174,112 beds in 2004 for 4,445,537 visitors.

FURTHER READING

Statistical Information: Statistisches Amt für Hamburg und Schleswig-Holstein (Fröbel Str. 15–17, 24113 Kiel). *Directors:* Dr Hans-Peter Kirschner, Wolfgang Bick. Publications: *Statistisches Taschenbuch Schleswig-Holstein,* since 1954.—*Statistisches Jahrbuch Schleswig-Holstein,* since 1951.—*Statistische Monatshefte Schleswig-Holstein,* since 1949.—*Statistische Berichte,* since 1947.—*Beitrage zur historischen Statistik Schleswig-Holstein,* from 1967.—*Lange Reihen,* from 1977. *Website (German only):* http://www.statistik-nord.de

Baxter, R. R., *The Law of International Waterways*. Harvard Univ. Press, 1964

Brandt, O., *Grundriss der Geschichte Schleswig-Holsteins*. 5th ed. Kiel, 1957

Handbuch für Schleswig-Holstein. 28th ed. Kiel, 1996

State Library: Schleswig-Holsteinische Landesbibliothek, Kiel, Schloss. *Director:* Prof. Dr Dieter Lohmeier.

Thuringia

Thüringen

KEY HISTORICAL EVENTS

Thuringia with its capital Erfurt is criss-crossed by the rivers Saale, Werra and Weisse Elster and dominated in the south by the mountains of the Thuringian Forest. Martin Luther spent his exile in Eisenach where he translated the New Testament into German while he lived in protective custody in the castle. Weimar became the centre of German intellectual life in the 18th century. In 1919 Weimar was the seat of a briefly liberal Republic. Only ten miles from Weimar lies Buchenwald, the site of a war-time Nazi concentration camp, which is now a national monument to the victims of fascism.

TERRITORY AND POPULATION

The area is 16,172 sq. km. Population on 31 Dec. 2004 was 2,355,280 (1,196,824 females); density, 146 per sq. km. It is divided into six urban districts, 17 rural districts and 998 communes. The capital is Erfurt.

SOCIAL STATISTICS

Statistics for calendar years:

	Live births	Marriages	Divorces	Deaths
2001	17,351	8,575	4,748	25,499
2002	17,007	8,597	5,301	26,000
2003	16,911	8,372	5,558	26,220
2004	17,310	9,691	5,454	25,325

CONSTITUTION AND GOVERNMENT

The *Bundesland* was reconstituted on former GDR territory in 1990. It has four seats in the Bundesrat.

RECENT ELECTIONS

At the Diet elections of 13 June 2004 the Christian Democrats (CDU) won 45 seats, with 43·0% of the vote; the Party of Democratic Socialism (PDS) 28, with 26·1%; and the Social Democrats (SPD) 15, with 14·5%. Turnout was 53·8%.

CURRENT ADMINISTRATION

The *Prime Minister* is Dieter Althaus (CDU).

Government Website: http://www.thueringen.de

ENERGY AND NATURAL RESOURCES

Agriculture

Area and yield of the most important crops:

	Area (in 1,000 ha.)			Yield (in 1,000 tonnes)		
	2002	2003	2004	2002	2003	2004
Wheat	217·2	208·0	221·9	1,335·6	1,277·7	1,749·5
Barley	118·9	124·4	114·6	644·6	637·7	745·0
Sugarbeet	11·2	10·8	10·9	609·7	537·0	593·6
Potatoes	2·7	2·6	2·9	105·1	75·3	114·0
Rye	13·7	9·1	12·1	88·3	51·9	91·6
Oats	6·9	8·6	6·8	33·3	40·6	39·7

Livestock, 3 May 2004: 354,510 cattle (including 124,028 milch cows); 742,942 pigs; 228,205 sheep; 8,645 horses (2003); 4,679,089 poultry (2003).

INDUSTRY

In 2004, 1,950 establishments (with 20 or more employees) employed 146,211 persons; of these, 68,277 were employed by producers of materials and supplies, 40,613 by producers of investment goods, 8,883 by producers of durables and 28,439 by producers of non-durables.

Labour

The economically active persons totalled 1,027,500 in March 2004, including 483,800 professional workers, 394,200 manual workers and 95,300 self-employed. 350,200 were engaged in production industries, 226,300 in commerce, transport and communications, 27,900 persons in agriculture and forestry, and 423,000 in other sectors. There were 210,243 persons registered unemployed in Dec. 2004 (103,315 females) and 6,509 on short time; the unemployment rate was 18·5%.

COMMUNICATIONS

Roads

At 1 Jan. 2005 there were 383 km of motorways, 1,870 km of federal roads, 5,307 km of first- and second-class highways and 2,602 km of district highways. Number of motor vehicles, Jan. 2005, 1,518,916, including 1,282,001 private cars, 99,165 lorries, 2,726 buses, 41,037 tractors and 79,963 motorcycles.

SOCIAL INSTITUTIONS

Education

In 2004–05 there were 476 primary schools with 58,104 pupils, 272 core curriculum schools with 68,328 pupils, 108 grammar schools with 62,549 pupils and 99 special schools with 14,874 pupils; there were 86,191 pupils in technical and professional education, and 5,175 in professional training for the disabled.

In 2004–05 there were 11 universities and colleges with 48,683 students enrolled.

Health

In 2004 there were 50 hospitals with 16,759 beds. There were 7,795 doctors (one doctor per 302 population).

Welfare

2004 expenditure on social welfare was €506m.

RELIGION

In 2003, 632,102 persons were Protestant and 191,173 persons were Roman Catholic. In 2004, 590 were Jewish.

CULTURE

Tourism

In July 2004 there were 1,376 places of accommodation (with nine or more beds). There were 2,864,300 visitors who stayed 8,143,400 nights in 2004.

FURTHER READING

Statistical information: Thüringer Landesamt für Statistik (Postfach 900163, 99104 Erfurt; Europaplatz 3, 99091 Erfurt). *President:* Günter Krombholz. Publications: *Statistisches Jahrbuch Thüringen*, since 1993. *Kreiszahlen für Thüringen*, since 1995. *Gemeindezahlen für Thüringen*, since 1998. *Thüringen-Atlas*, since 1999. *Statistische Monatshefte Thüringen*, since 1994. *Statistische Berichte*, since 1991. *Faltblätter*, since 1991. *Website (German only):* http://www.tls.thueringen.de

State library: Thüringer Universitäts- und Landesbibliothek, Jena.

GHANA

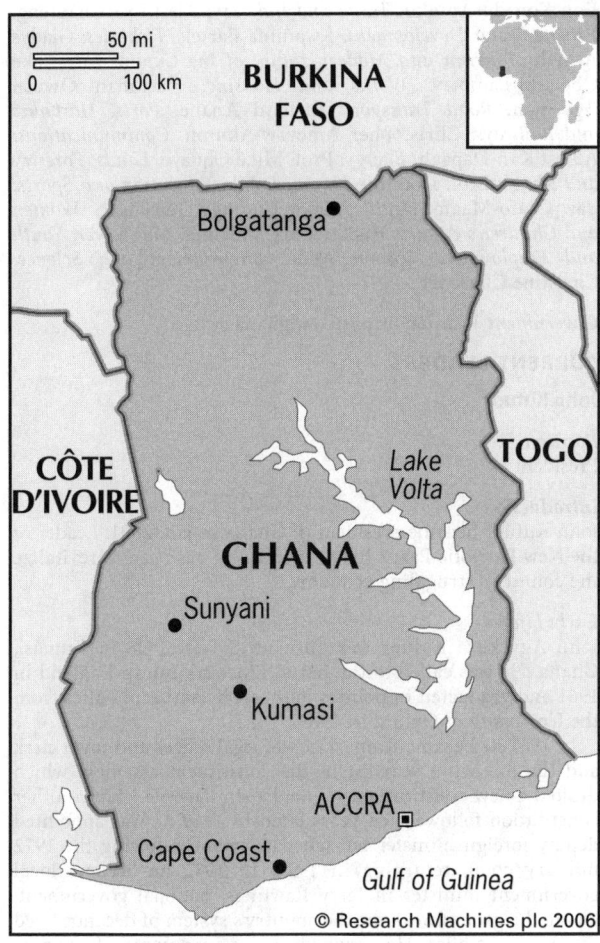

© Research Machines plc 2006

Republic of Ghana

Capital: Accra
Population projection, 2010: 24·31m.
GDP per capita, 2003: (PPP$) 2,238
HDI/world rank: 0·520/138

KEY HISTORICAL EVENTS

By the 17th century, strong chiefdoms and warrior states, notably the Ashanti, dominated the territory. The Ashanti state was strengthened by its collaboration with the slave trade but by 1874 it had been conquered by Britain and made a colony. The hinterland became a protectorate in 1901. British rule was challenged after the Second World War by Kwame Nkrumah and the Convention People's Party (CPP), formed in 1949. The state of Ghana came into existence on 6 March 1957 when the former Colony of the Gold Coast with the Trusteeship Territory of Togoland attained Dominion status. The country was declared a Republic within the Commonwealth on 1 July 1960 with Dr Kwame Nkrumah as the first President.

In 1966 the Nkrumah regime was overthrown by the military who ruled until 1969 when they handed over to a civilian regime under a new constitution. On 13 Jan. 1972 the armed forces regained power. In 1979 the Supreme Military Council

(SMC) was toppled in a coup led by Flight-Lieut. J. J. Rawlings. The new government permitted elections already scheduled and these resulted in a victory for Dr Hilla Limann and his People's National Party. However, on 31 Dec. 1981 another coup led by Rawlings dismissed the government and Parliament, suspended the constitution and established a Provisional National Defence Council to exercise all government powers. A new pluralist democratic constitution was approved by referendum in April 1992. The Fourth Republic was proclaimed on 7 Jan. 1993.

TERRITORY AND POPULATION

Ghana is bounded west by Côte d'Ivoire, north by Burkina Faso, east by Togo and south by the Gulf of Guinea. The area is 238,533 sq. km; the 2000 census population was 18,845,265, giving a density of 79·0 persons per sq. km. The United Nations population estimate for 2005 was 22,113,000.

The UN gives a projected population for 2010 of 24·31m.

In 2003, 54·6% of the population was rural. 1m. Ghanaians lived abroad in 1995.

Ghana is divided into ten regions:

Regions	Area (sq. km)	Population, census 2000	Capital
Ashanti	24,389	3,600,358	Kumasi
Brong-Ahafo	39,557	1,798,058	Sunyani
Central	9,826	1,593,888	Cape Coast
Eastern	19,323	2,101,650	Koforidua
Greater Accra	3,245	2,903,753	Accra
Northern	70,384	1,805,428	Tamale
Upper East	8,842	919,549	Bolgatanga
Upper West	18,476	575,579	Wa
Volta	20,570	1,630,254	Ho
Western	23,921	1,916,748	Sekondi-Takoradi

In 1999 the capital, Accra, had a population of 1,904,000. Other major cities are Kumasi, Tamale, Tema and Sekondi-Takoradi.

About 42% of the population are Akan. Other tribal groups include Moshi (23%), Ewe (10%) and Ga-Adangme (7%). About 75 languages are spoken; the official language is English.

SOCIAL STATISTICS

2000 estimates: births, 639,000; deaths, 204,000. Rates, 2000 estimates (per 1,000 population): births, 32·6; deaths, 10·4. 2003 life expectancy, 56·3 years for men and 57·3 for women. Infant mortality, 57 per 1,000 live births (2001). Annual population growth rate, 1992–2002, 2·4%; fertility rate, 2001, 4·3 births per woman.

CLIMATE

The climate ranges from the equatorial type on the coast to savannah in the north and is typified by the existence of well-marked dry and wet seasons. Temperatures are relatively high throughout the year. The amount, duration and seasonal distribution of rain is very marked, from the south, with over 80" (2,000 mm), to the north, with under 50" (1,250 mm). In the extreme north, the wet season is from March to Aug., but further south it lasts until Oct. Near Kumasi, two wet seasons occur, in May and June and again in Oct., and this is repeated, with greater amounts, along the coast of Ghana. Accra, Jan. 80°F (26·7°C), July 77°F (25°C). Annual rainfall 29" (724 mm). Kumasi, Jan. 77°F (25°C), July 76°F (24·4°C). Annual rainfall 58" (1,402 mm). Sekondi-Takoradi, Jan. 77°F (25°C), July 76°F (24·4°C). Annual rainfall 47" (1,181 mm). Tamale, Jan. 82°F (27·8°C), July 78°F (25·6°C). Annual rainfall 41" (1,026 mm).

CONSTITUTION AND GOVERNMENT

After the coup of 31 Dec. 1981, supreme power was vested in the Provisional National Defence Council (PNDC), chaired by Flight-Lieut. Jerry John Rawlings.

A new constitution was approved by 92·6% of votes cast at a referendum on 28 April 1992. The electorate was 8,255,690; turnout was 43·8%. The constitution sets up a presidential system on the US model, with a multi-party parliament and an independent judiciary. The *President* is elected by universal suffrage for a four-year term renewable once.

The unicameral *Parliament* has 230 members, elected for a four-year term in single-seat constituencies.

National Anthem

'God bless our Homeland, Ghana'; words by the government, tune by P. Gbeho.

GOVERNMENT CHRONOLOGY

Heads of State since 1960. (CPP = Convention People's Party; PNP = People's National Party; NDC = National Democratic Congress; NPP = New Patriotic Party; n/p = non-partisan)

President of the Republic
1960–66   CPP   Kofi Kwame Nkrumah

Chairmen of the National Liberation Council
1966–69   military   Joseph Arthur Ankrah
1969   military   Akwasi Amankwaa Afrifa

Presidential Commission
1969–1970   Akwasi Amankwaa Afrifa (chairman),
          John Willie Kofi Harlley, Albert Kwesi Ocran

Presidents of the Republic
1970–72   n/p   Edward Akufo-Addo

Chairman of the National Redemption Council
1972–75   military   Ignatius Kutu Acheampong

Chairmen of the Supreme Military Council
1975–78   military   Ignatius Kutu Acheampong
1978–79   military   Frederick Kwasi Akuffo

Chairman of the Armed Forces Revolutionary Council
1979   military   Jerry John Rawlings

President of the Republic
1979–81   PNP   Hilla Limann

Chairman of the Provisional National Defence Council
1981–93   military   Jerry John Rawlings

Presidents of the Republic
1993–2001   NDC   Jerry John Rawlings
2001–   NPP   John Agyekum Kufuor

RECENT ELECTIONS

Presidential elections were held on 7 Dec. 2004. Incumbent John Agyekum Kufuor of the New Patriotic Party (NPP) won 52·5% of the vote and John Atta Mills of the National Democratic Congress (NDC) 44·6%. There were two other candidates. In parliamentary elections, the NPP won 128 of 230 seats, the NDC 94, the People's National Convention 4, the Convention People's Party 3 and ind. 1.

CURRENT ADMINISTRATION

President: John Agyekum Kufuor; b. 1938 (NPP; sworn in 7 Jan. 2001 and re-elected in Dec. 2004).

Vice-President: Aliu Mahama.

In March 2006 the government comprised the following:

Senior Minister and Leader of Government Economic Team: Joseph Henry Mensah. *Minister of Defence:* Dr Kwame Addo-Kufuor. *Local Government and Rural Development:* Charles Bintim. *Foreign Affairs:* Nana Akufo Addo. *Interior:* Papa Owusu

Ankomah. *Information:* Dan Botwe. *Justice and Attorney General:* Ayikoi Otoo. *Parliamentary Affairs:* Felix Owusu-Adjapong. *Food and Agriculture:* Ernest Debrah. *Finance and Economic Planning:* Kwadwo Baah Wiredu. *Regional Co-operation and NEPAD:* Kofi Konadu Apraku. *Trade and Industry:* Alan Kyeremanteng. *Private Sector Development:* Kwamina Bartels. *Fisheries:* Gladys Asmah. *Tourism and Modernization of the Capital City:* Jake Obetsebi-Lamptey. *Works and Housing:* Hackman Owusu Agyeman. *Road Transport:* Richard Anane. *Ports, Harbours and Railways:* Christopher Ameyaw-Akumfi. *Communications:* Albert Kan-Dapaah. *Energy:* Prof. Mike Oquaye. *Lands, Forestry and Mines:* Prof. Dominic Kwaku Fobih. *Education and Sports:* Yaw Osafo-Maafo. *Health:* Major Courage Quashigah. *Women and Children's Affairs:* Hajia Alima Mahama. *Manpower, Youth and Employment:* Joseph Adda. *Environment and Science:* Christine Churcher.

Government Website: http://www.ghana.gov.gh

CURRENT LEADERS

John Kufuor

Position
President

Introduction
John Kufuor became president of Ghana in Jan. 2001. Leader of the New Patriotic Party, his principal aim has been to revitalize the country's struggling economy.

Early Life
John Agyekum Kufuor was born on 8 Dec. 1938 in Kumasi, Ghana. He was called to the Bar at Lincoln's Inn in England in 1961 and graduated in politics, philosophy and economics from the University of Oxford in 1964.

In 1967 he became Kumasi's chief legal officer and town clerk and the following year sat in the constituent assembly which drafted a new constitution. He held a similar role when another constitution followed ten years later. In 1969 he was appointed deputy foreign minister but left parliament following the 1972 military coup, returning in 1979. In 1982 he became local government minister in Jerry Rawlings' national government, laying the groundwork for the country's system of decentralized district assemblies. He resigned after seven months to pursue business interests.

In 1996 Kufuor unsuccessfully challenged Rawlings for the presidency, standing as the NPP candidate. In Oct. 1998 he was selected as leader of the NPP and again stood for the presidency in Dec. 2000. When no candidate achieved the 50% threshold for victory after the first round, Kufuor went into a run-off against the National Democratic Congress' John Atta Mills. Kufuor won the support of the five candidates who dropped out after the first round and won the election with 57%.

Career in Office
Taking office in Jan. 2001, Kufuor aimed to lead Ghana into an economic 'golden age.' He faced inflation at over 40%, interest rates at over 50% and the collapse of the cedi, the national currency. By May 2002 inflation was down to 14%, interest rates down to 26% and the cedi had stabilized. However, the government's withdrawal of fuel subsidies saw petrol prices increase by 60% and the price of utilities also rocketed. In April 2001 Ghana received major debt relief under a World Bank/IMF scheme and in May 2002 the African Development Bank wrote off 80% of the country's debts. The relief was seen as a reward for Kufuor's handling of the economy.

His tenure has been marked by continued tribal conflict, particularly in the north of the country, where a state of emergency was declared in April 2002. In May 2001 Kufuor declared a national day of mourning after 126 people died during a stampede at a soccer match, for which the police were heavily criticized.

Kufuor has done much to distance himself from the Jerry Rawlings era. In 2001 the government abandoned public holidays celebrating Rawlings' 1979 coup. In May 2002 he instituted a reconciliation committee to investigate allegations of human rights abuses during Rawlings' rule. He has also attempted to improve relations with Ghana's West African neighbours.

In Dec. 2004 Kufuor was re-elected as president with 52·5% of the vote in the second round. The NPP meanwhile secured a majority of seats in parliamentary elections.

DEFENCE

Defence expenditure totalled US$23m. in 2003 (US$1 per capita), representing 0·3% of GDP.

Army

Total strength (2002), 5,000.

Navy

The Navy, based at Sekondi and Tema, numbered 1,000 in 2002 including support personnel.

Air Force

There are air bases at Takoradi and Tamale. Personnel strength (2002), 1,000. There were 19 combat aircraft.

INTERNATIONAL RELATIONS

Ghana is a member of the UN, WTO, the Commonwealth, the African Union, African Development Bank, ECOWAS and is an ACP member state of the ACP-EU relationship.

ECONOMY

Agriculture accounted for 36·0% of GDP in 2002, industry 24·3% and services 39·7%.

Overview

Ghana is committed to the reform programmes of the IMF and World Bank and is one of Africa's biggest borrowers. In 1996 aid amounted to 11% of GDP, or four times the value of Ghana's exports. A privatization programme was inaugurated in 1988. By April 2000, 132 state-owned enterprises had been sold off to become 232 privately-owned companies. A further 168 were set to be privatized. Privatization deals raised US$804m. between 1990 and 1996, including the Ashanti Goldfields sell-off worth more than US$400m. On 27 April 2004 Ashanti Goldfields completed its merger with South Africa's AngloGold to form the world's largest gold mining company in terms of reserves, under the new name of AngloGold Ashanti. Only South Africa among sub-Saharan African nations has raised more from privatization. Building, tourism, technology and financial services account for more than 46% of national income.

Currency

The monetary unit is the *cedi* (GHC) of 100 *pesewas* (P). Inflation was 26·7% in 2003 and 12·6% in 2004. Foreign exchange reserves were US$238m. in April 2002 and gold reserves 281,000 troy oz in May 2002. Total money supply in Sept. 2001 was ₵3,867·83bn.

Budget

In 2000 revenues totalled ₵5,385bn. and expenditures ₵7,525bn.

Performance

Real GDP growth was 5·2% in 2003 and 5·8% in 2004. Total GDP was US$8·6bn. in 2004.

Banking and Finance

The Bank of Ghana (*Governor,* Dr Paul Acquah) was established in 1957 as the central bank and bank of issue. At Dec. 1995 its total assets were ₵3,272,946·6m. There were in 1998 nine commercial banks, four merchant banks and 130 rural banks.

There are two discount houses. Banks are required to have a capital base of at least 6% of net assets. At Dec. 1995 assets of commercial banks totalled ₵1,900,327·1m.

Foreign investment is actively encouraged with the Ghana Free Zone Scheme offering particular incentives such as full exemption of duties and levies on all imports for production and exports from the zones, full exemption on tax on profits for ten years, and no more than 8% after ten years. It is a condition of the scheme that at least 70% of goods made within the zones must be exported. Within 18 months of the scheme being set up in 1995, 50 projects had been registered.

There is a stock exchange in Accra.

ENERGY AND NATURAL RESOURCES

Ghana is facing an energy crisis, with power cuts of up to 12 hours a day because drought has caused the level of Lake Volta to drop to below the danger level.

Environment

Ghana's carbon dioxide emissions from the consumption and flaring of fossil fuels in 2002 were the equivalent of 0·3 tonnes per capita.

Electricity

Installed capacity was 1·2m. kW in 2000. Production (2000) 7·55bn. kWh, mainly from two hydro-electric stations operated by the Volta River Authority, Akosombo (six units) and Kpong (four units). Consumption per capita was 417 kWh in 2000. A drought in 1998 caused power cuts, with over 99% of electricity being hydro-electric. It is planned that electricity production will become less dependent on hydro-electric stations and more so on gas, with the construction of a 600 km pipeline forming part of the proposed West African Gas Pipeline Project.

Oil and Gas

Ghana is pursuing the development of its own gas fields and plans to harness gas at the North and South Tano fields located off the western coast. Natural gas reserves, 2002, totalled 23bn. cu. metres. Oil reserves in 2002 were 17m. bbls.

Minerals

Gold is one of the mainstays of the economy; Ghana ranks second only to South Africa among African gold producers. Production in 2001 was 68,700 kg. In 2002 diamond production was 963,000 carats; manganese, 1·14m. tonnes; bauxite, 684,000 tonnes; aluminium, 117,000 tonnes.

Agriculture

The rural poor earn little and many small farmers have reverted to subsistence farming. The agricultural population in 2002 was 12·97m., of whom 5·74m. were economically active. There were 3·70m. ha. of arable land in 2001 and 2·20m. ha. of permanent crops. 11,000 ha. were irrigated in 2001. There were 3,600 tractors in 2001. In southern and central Ghana main food crops are maize, rice, cassava, plantains, groundnuts, yam and taro, and in northern Ghana groundnuts, rice, maize, sorghum, millet and yams. Agriculture presently operates at only 20% of its potential and is an area that is to be a major focus of investment.

Production of main food crops, 2000 (in 1,000 tonnes): cassava, 7,845; yams, 3,249; plantains, 2,046; taro, 1,707; maize, 1,014; cocoa beans, 398; coconuts, 305; sorghum, 302; chillies and green peppers, 270; oranges, 270. Cocoa is the main cash crop. The government estimates that more than 40% of the population relies either directly or indirectly on cocoa as a source of income. It contributes approximately 13% of GDP. Ghana is the second largest cocoa bean producer in the world after Côte d'Ivoire, and the second largest producer of both yams and taro, after Nigeria.

Livestock, 2000: cattle, 1·28m.; sheep, 2·56m.; pigs, 350,000; goats, 2·80m.; chickens, 18m.

Forestry

There were 6·34m. ha. of forest in 2000, or 27·8% of the total land area. Reserves account for some 30% of the total forest lands. Timber production in 2001 was 21·98m. cu. metres.

Fisheries

In 2001 total catch was 445,287 tonnes, of which 370,787 tonnes came from sea fishing.

INDUSTRY

Ghana's industries include mining, lumbering, light manufacturing and food processing.

Labour

In 1996 the labour force was 8,393,000. Females constituted 51% of the workforce in 1999. Only Cambodia had a higher percentage of females in its workforce.

In 1994 there were 37,000 persons registered as unemployed.

INTERNATIONAL TRADE

Foreign debt was US$7,338m. in 2002.

Imports and Exports

In 2002 imports (f.o.b.) were valued at US$2,705·1m.; exports (f.o.b.) totalled US$2,015·2m. Principal imported commodities, 1999: machinery and transport equipment, 38%; petroleum, 16%; manufactured goods, 13%; foodstuffs, 11%. Principal exports: cocoa, 35%; manufactured goods (including wood products, aluminium, iron and steel), 18%; timber, 8%; and gold, 8%. Main import suppliers, 1999: UK, 10%; USA, 9%; Nigeria, 8%; Belgium, 7%; Germany, 7%; Netherlands, 7%. Main export markets: UK, 23%; Netherlands, 14%; Italy, 6%; Burkina Faso, 5%; USA, 5%.

COMMUNICATIONS

Roads

In 2001 there were 46,179 km of roads, including 21 km of motorways. About 18·4% of all roads are hard-surfaced. A Road Sector Strategy and Programme to develop the road network ran from 1995 to 2000. There were 93,700 passenger cars in use in 2002, equivalent to 4·3 per 1,000 inhabitants.

Rail

Total length of railways in 2000 was 953 km of 1,067 mm gauge. In 2000 railways carried 1·0m. tonnes of freight and 2·2m. passengers.

Civil Aviation

There is an international airport at Accra (Kotoka). In 1999 scheduled airline traffic of Ghana-based carriers flew 9·1m. km, carrying 304,000 passengers (all on international flights). Accra handled 623,000 passengers (all on international flights) in 2001.

Shipping

The chief ports are Tema and Takoradi. In 2002, 6·8m. tonnes of cargo were handled at Tema and 3·4m. tonnes at Takoradi. There is inland water transport on Lake Volta. In 2002 the merchant marine totalled 126,000 GRT, including oil tankers 8,000 GRT. The Volta, Ankobra and Tano rivers provide 168 km of navigable waterways for launches and lighters.

Telecommunications

Ghana Telecom was privatized in 1996. In 2002 Ghana had 723,800 telephone subscribers, or 33·4 for every 1,000 inhabitants, and there were 82,000 PCs in use (3·8 per 1,000 persons). Mobile phone subscribers numbered 449,400 in 2002. There were 170,000 Internet users in 2002 and 6,700 fax machines.

Postal Services

In 2003 there were 730 post offices.

SOCIAL INSTITUTIONS

Justice

The Courts are constituted as follows:

Supreme Court. The Supreme Court consists of the Chief Justice who is also the President, and not less than four other Justices of the Supreme Court. The Supreme Court is the final court of appeal in Ghana. The final interpretation of the constitution is entrusted to the Supreme Court.

Court of Appeal. The Court of Appeal consists of the Chief Justice with not less than five other Justices of the Appeal court and such other Justices of Superior Courts as the Chief Justice may nominate. The Court of Appeal is duly constituted by three Justices. The Court of Appeal is bound by its own previous decisions and all courts inferior to the Court of Appeal are bound to follow the decisions of the Court of Appeal on questions of law. Divisions of the Appeal Court may be created, subject to the discretion of the Chief Justice.

High Court of Justice. The Court has jurisdiction in civil and criminal matters as well as those relating to industrial and labour disputes including administrative complaints. The High Court of Justice has supervisory jurisdiction over all inferior Courts and any adjudicating authority and in exercise of its supervisory jurisdiction has power to issue such directions, orders or writs including writs or orders in the nature of habeas corpus, certiorari, mandamus, prohibition and quo warranto. The High Court of Justice has no jurisdiction in cases of treason. The High Court consists of the Chief Justice and not less than 12 other judges and such other Justices of the Superior Court as the Chief Justice may appoint.

Under the Provisional National Defence Council which ruled from 1981 to 2001 public tribunals were established in addition to the traditional courts of justice.

The population in penal institutions in 2002 was 11,624 (58 per 100,000 of national population).

Education

Schooling is free and compulsory, and consists of six years of primary, three years of junior secondary and three years of senior secondary education. In 1990, 75% of eligible children attended primary, and 39% secondary, school. In 2000–01 there were 2·48m. pupils in primary schools with 75,087 teachers; and 1·03m. pupils with 55,549 teachers in secondary schools. University education is free. There are two universities, one university each for development studies, and science and technology. In 1994–95 there were 11,225 university students and 779 academic staff. There were also six polytechnics, seven colleges and 38 teacher training colleges. Adult literacy in 2003 was 54·1% (62·9% among men and 45·7% among women). In 1970 adult literacy was just 31%.

In 1999–2000 total expenditure on education came to 4·2% of GNP.

Health

In 2002 there were 1,842 physicians, 13,102 nurses, 4,094 midwives and 1,433 pharmacists. In 2003 there were an estimated 350,000 people living with HIV, mainly women.

Ghana has been one of the most successful countries in reducing undernourishment in the past 15 years. Between 1990–92 and 2000–02 the proportion of undernourished people declined from 37% of the population to just 13%.

RELIGION

An estimated 30% of the population are Muslim and 24% Christian, with 38% adherents to indigenous beliefs and 8% other religions. In May 2005 the Roman Catholic church had one cardinal.

CULTURE

World Heritage Sites

Ghana has two sites on the UNESCO World Heritage List: Forts and Castles, Volta, Greater Accra, Central and Western Regions (inscribed on the list in 1979), Portuguese trading posts built between 1482 and 1786 along the coast; Asante Traditional Buildings (1980), the remains of the Asante civilization that peaked in the 18th century.

Broadcasting

The Ghana Broadcasting Corporation is an autonomous statutory body. In April 2000 there were three free television stations, three satellite/cable services and 49 commercial radio stations. There were 1·1m. TV receivers (colour by PAL) in 2001 and 13·9m. radio receivers in 2000.

Press

There were (1998) four daily newspapers with a combined circulation of 260,000.

Tourism

There were 483,000 foreign tourists in 2002, spending US$358m

DIPLOMATIC REPRESENTATIVES

Of Ghana in the United Kingdom (13 Belgrave Sq., London, SW1X 8PN)
High Commissioner: Isaac Osei.

Of the United Kingdom in Ghana (Osu Link, off Gamel Abdul Nasser Ave., Accra)
High Commissioner: Gordon Wetherell.

Of Ghana in the USA (3512 International Dr., NW, Washington, D.C., 20008)
Ambassador: Fritz Kwabena Poku.

Of the USA in Ghana (Ring Rd. East, Accra)
Ambassador: Pamela E. Bridgewater.

Of Ghana to the United Nations
Ambassador: Nana Effah-Apentang.

Of Ghana to the European Union
Ambassador: Kobina Wudu.

FURTHER READING

Carmichael, J., *Profile of Ghana.* London, 1992.—*African Eldorado: Ghana from Gold Coast to Independence.* London, 1993

Herbst, J., *The Politics of Reform in Ghana, 1982–1991.* California Univ. Press, 1993

Petchenkine, Y., *Ghana in Search of Stability, 1957–1992.* New York, 1992

Rathbone, R., *Nkrumah and the Chiefs: The Politics of Chieftaincy in Ghana.* Currey, Oxford, 2000

Ray, D. I., *Ghana: Politics, Economics and Society.* London, 1986

Rimmer, D., *Staying Poor: Ghana's Political Economy, 1950–1990.* Oxford, 1993

National Statistical Office: Statistical Service, Accra.

GREECE

© Research Machines plc 2006

Elliniki Dimokratia
(Hellenic Republic)

Capital: Athens
Population projection, 2010: 11·20m.
GDP per capita, 2003: (PPP$) 19,954
HDI/world rank: 0·912/24

KEY HISTORICAL EVENTS

The land which is now Greece was first inhabited between 2000–1700 BC by tribes from the North. This period was followed by the Mycenaean Civilization which was overthrown by the Dorians at the end of the 12th century BC. Its dominant citadels were at Tiryns and Mycenae. What little is known about this period is from stories such as those by Homer written in the 9th or 8th century BC.

The following period, known as the Greek Dark Ages, ended by the 6th century BC when the *polis*, or city state, was formed. Built mainly on coastal plains, the two principal cities were Sparta and Athens. With government based on consensus of a ruling class, and rich in theatre, art and philosophy, the *polis* was the pinnacle of the Greek Classical Age. It was the era of Euripides, Theusidades and Socrates. With strong trade links, Greece also had territories in Southern Italy, Sicily, Southern France and Asia Minor.

Two Persian invasions in the 5th century were checked at Marathon (490 BC) and Thermopylae (480 BC) where Spartans held off a great force of Persian soldiers. In 431 BC rivalry between the dominant city states erupted into the Peloponnesian War. In 404 BC Sparta defeated Athens, but in the next century Sparta itself fell to Thebes (371 BC).

Led by Philip II of Macedon, the Macedonians defeated the city states in 338 BC. The *poleis* were forced to unify under his rule. With Plato and Aristotle active at this time, the latter serving as a tutor to Philip's son Alexander, this was a period of cultural enrichment. When Philip was assassinated in 336 BC, Alexander, then aged of 20, succeeded him. He spent the next thirteen years on a relentless campaign to expand the Macedonian territories. The Greek Empire stretched to the edge of India and encompassed most of the known civilized world.

Following Alexander's death in 323 BC, the empire gradually disintegrated. By the end of the 2nd century AD, the Romans had defeated the Macedonians and Greece was incorporated into the Roman Empire. It remained in Roman hands until it became part of the Byzantine Empire in the 4th century AD. A population of Greek-speaking Christians had its power base in Constantinople.

Over the next six centuries Greece was invaded by Franks, Normans and Arabs but remained part of the Byzantine Empire. Following the Empire's decline in the 11th century, Greece was incorporated into the Ottoman Empire in 1460. Apart from a period under Venetian control between 1686–1715, Greece was part of Turkey until the Greek War of Independence.

Greece broke away from the Ottoman Empire in the 1820s and was declared a kingdom under the protection of Great Britain, France and Russia. Many Greeks were left outside the new state but Greece's area increased by 70%, the population growing from 2·8m. to 4·8m., after the Treaty of Bucharest (1913) recognized Greek sovereignty over Crete.

King Constantine opted for neutrality in the First World War, while Prime Minister Venezelos favoured the Entente powers. This National Schism led to British and French intervention which deposed Constantine on 11 June 1917. When his son Alexander died on 25 Oct. 1920, he returned and reigned until 1922. He was forced to abdicate by a coup after defeat by Turkey and the loss of Smyrna. The Treaty of Lausanne (1923) recognized Smyrna as Turkish with Eastern Thrace and the islands of Imvros and Tenedos, all of which had been ceded to Greece by the 1920 Treaty of Sevres. An exchange of Christian and Muslim populations followed. Resistance to Italian demands brought Greece into the Second World War when Germany had to come to the aid of the hard-pressed Italians. Athens was occupied on 27 April 1941. The occupation lasted until 15 Oct. 1944.

A communist led insurrection in 1946–47 was put down with the help of British and, later, US troops. Peace came after 1949.

The late 1950s saw the emergence of the Left, capitalizing on the movement for union with Cyprus and unease over NATO membership (1952). A military coup in 1967 led to the authoritarian rule of the 'Colonels' headed by George Papadopoulos. A republic was declared on 29 July 1973. The dictatorship collapsed in 1974 giving way to a civilian government of national unity. The monarchy was abolished by a referendum on 8 Dec. 1974. The 1981 election brought Andreas Papandreou to power at the head of a socialist government. Earlier that year Greece had become the tenth member of the EU. Re-elected in 1985, Papandreou imposed economic austerity to combat inflation and soaring budgets but industrial unrest and evidence of widespread corruption led to his fall and a succession of weak governments. Papandreou returned to power in Oct. 1993 but ill-health forced his resignation two years later. His successor Constantinos Simitis took a more pro-European stance, instituting economic reforms to prepare the way for entry into European Monetary Union (EMU).

TERRITORY AND POPULATION

Greece is bounded in the north by Albania, the Former Yugoslav Republic of Macedonia (FYROM) and Bulgaria, east by Turkey and the Aegean Sea, south by the Mediterranean and west by the Ionian Sea. The total area is 131,957 sq. km (50,949 sq. miles), of which the islands account for 25,026 sq. km (9,663 sq. miles).

The population was 10,964,020 (5,536,338 females) according to the census of March 2001; density, 83·1 per sq. km. The estimated population in 2005 was 11·12m.

The UN gives a projected population for 2010 of 11·20m.

In 2003, 60·9% of the population lived in urban areas. There were 166,031 resident foreign nationals in 1991. A further 5m. Greeks are estimated to live abroad.

In 1987 the territory of Greece was administratively reorganized into 13 *regions* comprising in all 51 *departments*. Areas and populations according to the 2001 census:

Geographic Region/ Department	Area in sq. km	Population[1]	Chief town
Aegean Islands	*9,122*	*508,807*	
Chios	904	53,408	Chios
Cyclades	2,572	112,615	Hermoupolis
Dodecanese	2,714	190,071	Rhodes
Lesbos	2,154	109,118	Mytilene
Samos	778	43,595	Samos
Attica[2]	*3,808*	*3,761,810*	*Athens*
Central Greece and Euboea	*21,010*	*829,758*	
Aetolia and Acarnania	5,461	224,429	Messolonghi
Boeotia	2,952	131,085	Levadeia
Euboea	4,167	215,136	Chalcis
Evrytania	1,869	32,053	Karpenissi
Phocis	2,121	48,284	Amphissa
Phthiotis	4,440	178,771	Lamia
Crete	*8,336*	*601,131*	
Canea	2,376	150,387	Canea
Heraklion	2,641	292,489	Heraklion
Lassithi	1,823	76,319	Aghios Nikolaos
Rethymnon	1,496	81,936	Rethymnon
Epirus	*9,203*	*353,820*	
Arta	1,662	78,134	Arta
Ioannina	4,990	170,239	Ioannina
Preveza	1,036	59,356	Preveza
Thesprotia	1,515	46,091	Hegoumenitsa
Ionian Islands	*2,307*	*212,984*	
Cephalonia	904	39,488	Argostoli
Corfu	641	111,975	Corfu
Leucas	356	22,506	Leucas
Zante	406	39,015	Zante
Macedonia	*34,178*	*2,424,765*	
Cavalla	2,112	145,054	Cavalla
Chalcidice	2,918	104,894	Polygyros
Drama	3,468	103,975	Drama
Florina	1,925	54,768	Florina
Grevena	2,291	37,947	Grevena
Imathia	1,701	143,618	Veroia
Kastoria	1,728	53,483	Kastoria
Kilkis	2,519	89,056	Kilkis
Kozani	3,516	155,324	Kozani
Mount Athos[3]	336	2,262	Karyai
Pella	2,506	145,797	Edessa
Pieria	1,517	129,846	Katerini
Serres	3,958	200,916	Serres
Thessaloniki (Salonika)	3,683	1,057,825	Thessaloniki
Peloponnese	*21,379*	*1,155,019*	
Achaia	3,272	322,789	Patras
Arcadia	4,419	102,035	Tripolis
Argolis	2,154	105,770	Nauplion
Corinth	2,290	154,624	Corinthos
Elia	2,618	193,288	Pyrgos
Laconia	3,636	99,637	Sparti
Messenia	2,991	176,876	Calamata
Thessaly	*14,036*	*753,888*	
Karditsa	2,636	129,541	Karditsa
Larissa	5,381	279,305	Larissa
Magnesia	2,636	206,995	Volos
Trikala	3,383	138,047	Trikala
Thrace	*8,578*	*362,038*	
Evros	4,242	149,354	Alexandroupolis
Rhodope	2,543	110,828	Comotini
Xanthi	1,793	101,856	Xanthi

[1]*De facto* population. [2]Attica is both region and department.
[3]Autonomous region.

The largest cities (2001 census populations) are Athens (the capital), 745,514; Thessaloniki, 363,987; Piraeus, 175,697; Patras, 160,400; Peristerion, 137,918; Heraklion, 130,914; Larissa, 124,394; Kallithea, 109,609; Volos, 82,439. The department of Attica, composed of Athens, the port of Piraeus and a number of suburbs, contains about one third of the Greek population. It also contains about 50% of the country's industry and is the principal commercial, financial and diplomatic centre. Efforts have, however, been made to decentralize the economy. The second city, Thessaloniki, with its major port, has grown rapidly in population and industrial development.

The Monastic Republic of **Mount Athos** (or Agion Oros, i.e. 'Holy Mountain'), the easternmost of the three prongs of the peninsula of Chalcidice, is a self-governing community composed of 20 monasteries. The peninsula is administered by a Council of four members and an Assembly of 20 members, one deputy from each monastery. The Constitution of 1927 gives legal sanction to the Charter of Mount Athos, drawn up by representatives of the 20 monasteries on 20 May 1924, and its status is confirmed by the 1952 and 1975 Constitutions. Women are not permitted to enter. Population, 2001, 2,262.

The modern Greek language had two contesting literary standard forms, the archaizing *Katharevousa* ('purist'), and a version based on the spoken vernacular, 'Demotic'. In 1976 Standard Modern Greek was adopted as the official language, with Demotic as its core.

SOCIAL STATISTICS

2002: 103,569 live births; 103,915 deaths; 57,872 marriages; 11,080 divorces; 510 still births; 4,600 births to unmarried mothers. 2002 rates: birth (per 1,000 population), 9·4; death, 9·5; marriage, 5·3; divorce, 1·0. Annual population growth rate, 1992–2002, 0·7%. In 1999 the suicide rate per 100,000 population was 3·6 (men, 5·7; women, 1·6). Expectation of life at birth, 2003, 75·6 years for males and 80·9 years for females. In 1998 the most popular age range for marrying was 25–29 for both males and females. Infant mortality, 2002, five per 1,000 live births; fertility rate, 2002, 1·3 births per woman. In 2002 Greece received 5,664 asylum applications, equivalent to 0·5 per 1,000 inhabitants.

CLIMATE

Coastal regions and the islands have typical Mediterranean conditions, with mild, rainy winters and hot, dry, sunny summers. Rainfall comes almost entirely in the winter months, though amounts vary widely according to position and relief. Continental conditions affect the northern mountainous areas, with severe winters, deep snow cover and heavy precipitation, but summers are hot. Athens, Jan. 48°F (8·6°C), July 82·5°F (28·2°C). Annual rainfall 16·6" (414·3 mm).

CONSTITUTION AND GOVERNMENT

Greece is a presidential parliamentary democracy. A new Constitution was introduced in June 1975 and was amended in March 1986 and April 2001. The 300-member *Chamber of Deputies* is elected for four-year terms by proportional representation. There is a 3% threshold. Extra seats are awarded to the party which leads in an election. The Chamber of Deputies elects the head of state, the *President*, for a five-year term.

National Anthem

'Imnos eis tin Eleftherian' ('Hymn to Freedom'); words by Dionysios Solomos, tune by N. Mantzaros.
 (Same as Cyprus.)

GOVERNMENT CHRONOLOGY

(EEK = National Unionist Party; EK, Center Union; EPEK = National Progressive Center Union; ERE = National Radical Union;

ES = Hellenic Union; FDK = Liberal Democratic Center; KF = Liberal Party; LK = People's Party; ND = New Democracy; Pasok = Panhellenic Socialist Movement; n/p = non-partisan)

Presidents since 1973.

1973	n/p	Georgios C. (George) Papadopoulos
1973–74	military	Phaidon D. Gizikis
1974–75	n/p	Michail D. Stasinopoulos
1975–80	ND	Konstantinos D. Tsatsos
1980–85	ND	Konstantinos G. Karamanlis
1985–90	n/p	Christos A. Sartzetakis
1990–95	ND	Konstantinos G. Karamanlis
1995–2005	n/p	Konstantinos (Kostis) Stephanopoulos
2005–	Pasok	Karolos G. Papoulias

Prime Ministers since 1945.

1945	military	Nikolaos Plastiras
1945	military	Petros Voulgaris
1945	EEK	Panagiotis Kanellopoulos
1945–46	KF	Themistoklis P. Sophoulis
1946	n/p	Panagiotis Poulitsas
1946–47	LK	Konstantinos S. Tsaldaris
1947	n/p	Dimitrios E. Maximos
1947	LK	Konstantinos S. Tsaldaris
1947–49	KF	Themistoklis P. Sophoulis
1949–50	n/p	Alexandros N. Diomidis
1950	LK	Ioannis G. Theotokis
1950	KF	Sophoklis E. Venizelos
1950	EPEK	Nikolaos Plastiras
1950–51	KF	Sophoklis E. Venizelos
1951–52	EPEK	Nikolaos Plastiras
1952	n/p	Dimitrios Kiousopoulos
1952–55	ES	Alexandros L. Papagos
1955–58	ES, ERE	Konstantinos G. Karamanlis
1958–61	ERE	Konstantinos G. Karamanlis
1961–63	ERE	Konstantinos G. Karamanlis
1963	ERE	Panagiotis Pipinelis
1963	n/p	Stilianos Mavromichalis
1963	EK	Georgios A. Papandreou (sr.)
1963–64	n/p	Ioannis Paraskevopoulos
1964–65	EK	Georgios A. Papandreou (sr.)
1965	EK	Georgios T. Athanasiadis-Novas
1965	n/p	Elias I. Tsirimokos
1965–66	FDK	Stephanos C. Stephanopoulos
1966–67	n/p	Ioannis Paraskevopoulos
1967	ERE	Panagiotis Kanellopoulos
1967	n/p	Konstantinos V. Kollias
1967–73	military	Georgios C. (George) Papadopoulos
1973	n/p	Spiros V. Markezinis
1973–74	n/p	Adamantios Androutsopoulos
1974–80	ND	Konstantinos G. Karamanlis
1980–81	ND	Georgios I. Rallis
1981–89	Pasok	Andreas G. Papandreou
1989	ND	Tzannis P. Tzannetakis
1989–90	n/p	Xenophon E. Zolotas
1990–93	ND	Konstantinos K. Mitsotakis
1993–96	Pasok	Andreas G. Papandreou
1996–2004	Pasok	Costantinos G. (Kostas) Simitis
2004–	ND	Konstantinos A. (Kostas) Karamanlis

RECENT ELECTIONS

Karolos Papoulias was elected president by the 300-member parliament on 8 Feb. 2005, receiving 279 votes. No other candidates stood.

Parliamentary elections were held on 7 March 2004. Turnout was 76.5%. Seats gained (and % of vote): New Democracy (ND), 165 (45.4%); Pasok (Panhellenic Socialist Movement), 117 (40.6%); Communist Party, 12 (5.9%); Coalition of the Left and Progress (SIN), 6 (3.3%).

European Parliament

Greece has 24 (25 in 1999) representatives. At the June 2004 elections turnout was 62.8% (70.1% in 1999). ND won 11 seats with 43.1% of votes cast (political affiliation in European Parliament: European People's Party–European Democrats); Pasok, 8 with 34.0% (Party of European Socialists); Communist Party, 3 with 9.5% (European Unitary Left/Nordic Green Left); the SIN, 1 with 4.2% (European Unitary Left/Nordic Green Left); the Populist Orthodox Rally (LAOS), 1 with 4.1% (Independence and Democracy Group).

CURRENT ADMINISTRATION

President: Karolos Papoulias; b. 1929 (Pasok; sworn in 12 March 2005).

In March 2006 the government comprised:

Prime Minister: Dr Konstantinos 'Kostas' Karamanlis; b. 1956 (New Democracy; sworn in 10 March 2004).

Minister of Economy and Finance: Georgios Alogoskoufis. *Foreign Affairs:* Dora Bakoyannis. *National Defence:* Evangelos Meimarakis. *Interior, Public Administration and Decentralization:* Prokopis Pavlopoulos. *Development:* Dimitris Sioufas. *Environment, Land Planning and Public Works:* Giorgos Souflias. *Education and Religion:* Marietta Giannakou. *Employment:* Savvas Tsitouridis. *Health and Social Solidarity:* Dimitri Avramopoulos. *Rural Development and Food:* Evangelos Basiakos. *Justice:* Anastasios Papaligouras. *Transport and Communications:* Michalis Liapis. *Public Order:* Vyron Polydoras. *Culture:* Georgios Voulgarakis. *Mercantile Marine:* Manolis Kefalogiannis. *Macedonia and Thrace:* Georgios Kalatzis. *Tourism:* Fanny Palli-Petralia. *Aegean and Island Policy:* Aristotelis Pavlidis. *Minister of State and Government Spokesman:* Thodoris Rousopoulos.

Office of the Prime Minister: http://www.primeminister.gr

CURRENT LEADERS

Karolos Papoulias

Position
President

Introduction
Karolos Papoulias was sworn in as president of Greece on 12 March 2005, having been elected by an unprecedented parliamentary majority of 279 out of the 300 available votes. A founding member of the Panhellenic Socialist Movement (Pasok) and foreign minister throughout the 1980s and 1990s, Papoulias succeeded Kostis Stephanopoulos in this largely ceremonial role.

Early Life
Papoulias was born on 4 June 1929 in the northwestern city of Ioannina and went on to study law at the University of Athens and at the University of Milan in Italy, followed by a doctorate in private international law at the University of Cologne in Germany.

In 1967, following a coup that saw the right-wing Greek government replaced by a military dictatorship under Georgios Papadopoulos, Papoulias left Greece for Cologne. There he founded the resistance organization, the Overseas Socialist Democratic Union, which mobilized exiled Greeks against the military regime. From 1967–74 Papoulias broadcast regularly on Deutsche Welle Radio's Greek programme, denouncing the military government. With the fall of the Papadopoulos dictatorship and the establishment of the democratic Third Hellenic Republic in 1974, Papoulias returned to Greece, where, with fellow returned exile Andreas Papandreou, he helped to found Pasok. With its principles of 'National Independence, Popular Sovereignty, Social Emancipation and Democratic Process', Pasok was to dominate Greek political life throughout the 1980s and 1990s.

At the Nov. 1974 elections Pasok won 13·5% of the vote, coming third in the electoral battle behind the Liberal Party and the conservative New Democracy Party. By Nov. 1977, however, Pasok had doubled its percentage of the votes and become the official opposition. In the elections of Oct. 1981 Pasok won a resounding 48% of the vote and, with Papoulias' long-time associate Andreas Papandreou as prime minister, formed the first socialist government in the history of Greece. Papoulias served as secretary of Pasok's International Relations Committee from 1975–85, and from 1976–80 he was also a member of the party's Co-ordinating Council. In 1977 Papoulias entered parliament for the first time, representing Ioannina as a Pasok member. He was to be re-elected eight times, serving a total of 27 years continuously until 2004. In Oct. 1981 Papoulias gave up his law practice to take up a full-time post as deputy foreign minister in the Pasok government. He held his post until 1984, becoming foreign minister from 1985–90, and again from 1993–96. Arguably his most significant legacy was the signing of the Single European Act in 1985, by which Papoulias committed Greece to full membership of the EU, a move with huge consequences for the country's foreign policy and economic development.

Under the leadership of Papoulias, Pasok foreign policy in the Balkan states contributed significantly to the stability of at least some parts of this historically volatile area. In 1976 the Greek government initiated an inter-Balkan conference on economic and technical co-operation, attended by representatives of Yugoslavia, Romania, Bulgaria and Turkey. Similar conferences followed in 1979 and 1982, leading in 1984 to talks on the denuclearization of the Balkan region. Despite the two counties having been officially at war since 1940, Greco-Albanian relations improved dramatically during the mid-1980s and, in 1985, the Greco-Albanian border was reopened for the first time in 45 years, with full normalization of relations in 1987.

Following the death of Andreas Papandreou in June 1996, and the general election of Sept. of that year, Papoulias left the cabinet to become the Greek representative at the Organization for Security and Co-operation in Europe (OSCE).

On 12 Dec. 2004 Prime Minister Karamanlis (New Democracy) and leader of the opposition George Papandreou (Pasok) named Papoulias as the only presidential candidate in the Feb. 2005 election. Gaining 279 out of 300 votes Papoulias was elected by a huge majority of MPs representing all the parliamentary parties. He is expected to serve a full five-year term.

Career in Office

The appointment of Papoulias to the role of president of the Third Hellenic Republic ended months of speculation that Pasok MPs might withhold the votes required for the endorsement of a new president, forcing early elections just one year after the centre-right New Democracy Party came to power. In Oct. 2005 Papoulias, who enjoys popularity across the political spectrum, spoke of his desire to see a united Cyprus and expressed hope that Turkey's EU membership talks would be a trigger for progress on the issue.

Kostas Karamanlis

Position
Prime Minister

Introduction
Dr Konstantinos 'Kostas' Karamanlis became prime minister after leading the New Democracy (ND) to victory at the general election of March 2004, ending over ten years rule by Pasok (the Panhellenic Socialist Movement). Karamanlis has promised to streamline Greece's bureaucracy, fight corruption in government and reduce taxation while increasing social welfare spending. Among his first tasks on assuming office was to ensure that preparations for the 2004 Athens Olympics were completed on time.

Early Life
Karamanlis was born on 14 Sept. 1956 in Athens. His uncle was Konstantinos Karamanlis, the founder of ND and three times prime minister of Greece. Karamanlis graduated from Athens University Law School, then undertook further study at the private Deree College before taking a doctorate in international relations and political science from the Fletcher School of Law and Diplomacy in the USA.

From 1974–79 Karamanlis served in ONNED, the youth arm of ND. Following his period of study in America, he practised as a lawyer from 1984–89. At the same time he was active within the infrastructures of ND and ONNED and was teaching politics at Deree College. In 1989 he entered parliament as the ND member for Thessaloniki, which he represented until 2004 when he became member for Larissa. Following electoral defeat in 1996, Karamanlis was chosen as party leader the following year. At the general election of 2000 Pasok defeated ND by less that one percentage point.

By early 2004 opinion polls were showing ND with an eight-point advantage over Pasok. The gap narrowed after Pasok's appointment of George Papandreou in Jan. 2004 and observers predicted a close-run election. At the polls on 7 March 2004, however, the ND won a sweeping victory and secured a large majority in parliament.

Career in Office
Although lacking ministerial experience, Karamanlis had been in frontline politics as leader of ND for eight years when he took office. With preparations for the Athens Olympics in Aug. 2004 behind schedule and international concern over security arrangements, Karamanlis assumed control of the culture ministry, and thus responsibility for Olympics affairs. He announced his intention to reduce taxes, lower unemployment and increase spending on reforming the agricultural and education sectors. He also declared plans to privatize many of the larger state-owned industries and promised to encourage foreign investment. Despite pre-election pledges to reduce the size of government, his first cabinet comprised 47 members.

In foreign affairs he was expected to continue to pursue a negotiated agreement with Turkey over the future of Cyprus, despite the rejection in April 2004 by the Greek Cypriot population of the UN-backed plan for the island's future.

DEFENCE

Prior to 2001 conscription was generally: (Army) 18 months, (Navy) 21 months, (Air Force) 20 months. However, following a gradual shortening of military service, by 2003 conscription was 12 months in the Army, 14 in the Air Force and 15 in the Navy.

In 2003 defence expenditure totalled US$7,169m. (US$671 per capita), representing 4·1% of GDP (the highest percentage in the EU). In the period 1999–2003 Greece's spending on major conventional weapons, at US$4·4bn., was the third highest behind China and India.

Army
The Field Army is organized in three military regions, with one Army, two command, five corps and five divisional headquarters. Total Army strength (2002) 114,000 (81,000 conscripts, 2,700 women). There is also a Territorial Defence Force/National Guard of 35,000 whose role is internal security.

Navy
The current strength of the Hellenic Navy includes eight diesel submarines, two destroyers and 12 frigates. Main bases are at Salamis, Patras and Soudha Bay (Crete). Personnel in 2002 totalled 19,000 (9,800 conscripts, 1,300 women).

Air Force

The Hellenic Air Force (HAF) had a strength (2002) of 33,000 (7,521 conscripts, 1,520 women). There were 418 combat aircraft including A-7s, F-4s, F-5s, F-16s, Mirage F-1s and Mirage 2000s. The HAF is organized into Tactical and Air Training Commands.

INTERNATIONAL RELATIONS

Greece is a member of the UN, WTO, BIS, NATO, OECD, EU, WEU, Council of Europe, OSCE, CERN, BSEC, IOM, the Antarctic Treaty and the International Organization of the Francophonie. Greece is a signatory to the Schengen accord which abolishes border controls between Greece, Austria, Belgium, Denmark, Finland, France, Germany, Iceland, Italy, Luxembourg, the Netherlands, Norway, Portugal, Spain and Sweden. On 19 April 2005 Greece became the fifth European Union member to ratify the proposed EU constitution. The parliament approved the treaty by 268 votes to 17, with 15 abstentions.

ECONOMY

Agriculture accounted for 7·3% of GDP in 2002 (the highest percentage in the EU), industry 22·4% and services 70·3%.

Overview

Greece's economy is the smallest of the old EU-15 and its income per capita is the lowest among the group. As a reflection of its relative backwardness, agriculture's share of GDP is roughly twice the OECD average. Greece's industrial base is also small compared to other developed countries. Until the early 1990s the state was responsible for up to 70% of all industrial assets, but in 1998 the government began a programme of privatization to meet EU membership criteria. The mining and extractive metallurgy sectors have traditionally been important to the economy. Most industries are located around Athens and Thessaloniki and the government's attempt to decentralize industry has not reached Greece's northern regions or its islands owing to poor infrastructure. However, financial aid from the EU's Community Support Framework programmes has brought improvements in road, rail, harbour and airport links. Tourism is also an important sector, as is property management. Greece ranks among the top 15 tourism destinations in the world according to the UNWTO and in 2004 attracted over 16m. foreign tourists, the vast majority from Western Europe. In 2004 the tourism industry accounted for roughly one-seventh of total GDP and provided nearly one-sixth of the country's total employment.

The economy has grown strongly in recent years, outstripping both EU and OECD average growth rates. It has benefited substantially from EU aid over the years and growth was boosted by spending on the 2004 Olympic Games. Private consumption has grown with the rapid development in private sector credit. The combination of low interest rates inherited when joining the euro and financial market reform has also helped boost investment spending. In 2004 it was revealed that since 1997 the deficit-to-GDP ratio had been understated by close to two percentage points, in breach of the euro zone's Growth and Stability Pact. For 2004 the deficit was revised to 6% of GDP.

On the supply side the economy has benefited from strong capital formation, immigration and productivity gains. GDP growth slowed in 2005 as a result of high oil prices and the end of expenditure on the Olympics. The IMF warns that the Greek economy will slow in the future as a result of the erosion of international competitiveness and the diminishing benefits of joining the euro. A positive prospect for Greece could be the opportunities arising from the development of neighbouring southeast European countries.

OECD reports have long argued that the Greek tax system is one of the most complex and inequitable among developed countries. In 2005 the ministry of economy and finance began simplifying tax regulations, speeding up bureaucratic procedures and reducing the corporate tax rate from 35% to 25% by 2007. The OECD has also warned that rigidities in the labour market must be tackled if unemployment is to fall significantly below 10%.

Currency

In June 2000 EU leaders approved a recommendation for Greece to join the European single currency, the euro, and on 1 Jan. 2001 the euro (EUR) became the legal currency; irrevocable conversion rate 340·750 drachmas to 1 euro. The euro, which consists of 100 cents, has been in circulation since 1 Jan. 2002. There are seven euro notes in different colours and sizes denominated in 500, 200, 100, 50, 20, 10 and 5 euros, and eight coins denominated in 2 and 1 euros, then 50, 20, 10, 5, 2 and 1 cents. On the introduction of the euro there was a 'dual circulation' period before the drachma ceased to be legal tender on 28 Feb. 2002. Euro banknotes in circulation on 1 Jan. 2002 had a total value of €13·4bn.

Inflation rates (based on OECD statistics):

1995	1996	1997	1998	1999	2000	2001	2002	2003	2004
8·9%	7·9%	5·4%	4·5%	2·1%	2·9%	3·7%	3·9%	3·4%	3·0%

Foreign exchange reserves were US$6,509m. and gold reserves 3·86m. troy oz in June 2002. Total money supply in June 2002 was €7,683m.

Budget

Ordinary budget revenue in 2002 (in €1m.): 38,920 (tax revenue, 35,284); expenditure: 36,637.

VAT is 18% (reduced rates, 8% and 4%).

Performance

Real GDP growth rates (based on OECD statistics):

1995	1996	1997	1998	1999	2000	2001	2002	2003	2004
2·1%	2·4%	3·6%	3·4%	3·4%	4·5%	4·6%	3·8%	4·6%	4·7%

Greece has had economic growth above the EU average every year since 1996. Total GDP in 2004 was US$203·4bn.

Banking and Finance

The central bank and bank of issue is the Bank of Greece. Its *Governor* is Nicholas Garganas. There were 39 commercial banks in 2002 (17 Greek and 22 foreign). Total assets of all banks were 41,819bn. drachmas in 1999. The six leading banks in 2000 accounted for nearly 80% of assets of all Greek banks. Ranked by size of assets the largest banks were National Bank of Greece, Alpha Bank, Agricultural Bank, Commercial Bank of Greece, EFG Eurobank and Piraeus Bank. Foreign direct investment is extremely low, at just US$47m. in 2003.

There is a stock exchange in Athens.

ENERGY AND NATURAL RESOURCES

Environment

Carbon dioxide emissions from the consumption and flaring of fossil fuels in Greece were the equivalent of 9·5 tonnes per capita in 2002.

Electricity

Installed capacity in 2002 was 11·3m. kW. A national grid supplies the mainland, and islands near its coast. Power is produced in remoter islands by local generators. Total production in 2002 was 54·76bn. kWh; consumption per capita in 2002 was 5,247 kWh. 91% of electricity was produced in 2002 by thermal power stations (mainly using lignite) and the rest was from hydro-electric generation. Electricity supply is: domestic, 220v, 50 cycles AC; industrial, 280v, AC 3 phase.

Oil and Gas

Output of crude petroleum, 2000, 256,000 tonnes; proven reserves, 2002, 9m. bbls. The oil sector plays a critical role in the Greek economy, accounting for more than 70% of total energy demand. Supply is mostly imported but oil prospecting is intensifying. Natural gas was introduced in Greece in 1997 through a pipeline from Russia, and an additional source of supply is liquefied natural gas from Algeria. Demand for natural gas is in its infancy; however, in 2000 production ran to 51m. cu. metres. The public monopoly in natural gas, DEPA, has developed only a few sales contracts to some large industrial groups, outside a large contract with DEH.

Minerals

Greece produces a variety of ores and minerals, including (with production, in tonnes): asbestos ore (4·0m. in 1998), bauxite (1,931,497 in 2001), magnesite (483,296 in 2001), aluminium (168,000 in 2000), caustic magnesia (115,000 in 2002), nickel ore (22,670 in 2002), iron-pyrites (18,737 in 1995), zinc (16,900 in 2000), chromite (2,273 in 1999), silver (62 in 2001), marble (white and coloured) and various other earths. There is little coal, and the lignite is of indifferent quality (70·47m. tonnes, 2002). Salt production (2000) 244,709 tonnes.

Agriculture

In 2001 there were 2·72m. ha. of arable land and 1·13m. ha. of permanent crops.

The Greek economy was traditionally based on agriculture, with small-scale farming predominating, except in a few areas in the north. There were 817,100 farms in 2000. However, there has been a steady shift towards industry and although agriculture still employs nearly 17% of the population, it accounted for only 7% of GDP in 2002. Nevertheless, prior to the accession of the ten new member countries in May 2004 Greece had a higher percentage of its population working in agriculture than any other European Union member country. Agriculture accounts for 33·1% of exports and 17·9% of imports.

Production (2000, in 1,000 tonnes):

Sugarbeets	2,906	Oranges	950
Olives	2,000	Peaches and nectarines	900
Tomatoes	1,960	Potatoes	890
Maize	1,850	Cottonseed	650
Wheat	1,770	Watermelons	650
Seed cotton	1,250	Olive oil	443
Grapes	1,200	Wine	430

Livestock (2000, in 1,000): 590 cattle, 9,041 sheep, 5,293 goats, 906 pigs, 78 asses, 37 mules, 33 horses, 28,000 poultry. Livestock products, 2000 (in 1,000 tonnes): milk, 1,990; meat, 499; cheese, 240.

Forestry

Area covered by forests in 2000 was 3·60m. ha., or 27·9% of the total land area. Timber production in 2003 was 1·67m. cu. metres.

Fisheries

Total catch in 2003 was 93,383 tonnes, mainly from sea fishing. In 1998, 17,093 fishermen were active. 10,000 kg of sponges were produced in 1998.

INDUSTRY

The leading companies by market capitalization in Greece in Nov. 2005 were the National Bank of Greece (NBG), US$13·0bn.; and Hellenic Telecommunications Organization SA (OTE), US$10·5bn.

The main products are canned vegetables and fruit, fruit juice, beer, wine, alcoholic beverages, cigarettes, textiles, yarn, leather, shoes, synthetic timber, paper, plastics, rubber products, chemical acids, pigments, pharmaceutical products, cosmetics, soap, disinfectants, fertilizers, glassware, porcelain sanitary items, wire and power coils and household instruments.

Production in 1,000 tonnes (2002): cement, 14,981; residual fuel oil, 6,560; distillate fuel oil, 5,666; petrol, 4,001; crude steel, 1,840; jet fuels, 1,766; iron (concrete-reinforcing bars), 1,454; fertilizers, 1,374; alumina, 750; sulphuric acid, 468; packing materials, 318; soap, washing powder and detergents, 239; textile yarns, 130; soft drinks, 573·6m. litres; beer, 465·1m. litres; wine, 167·2m. litres; cigarettes, 30·5bn. units; glass (2001), 382,343 sq. metres.

Although manufacturing accounts for more than 21% of GDP, Greece's performance is hampered by the proliferation of small, traditional, low-tech firms, often run as family businesses. Food, drink and tobacco processing are the most important sectors, but there are also some steel mills and several shipyards. Shipping is of prime importance to the economy. In addition, there are major programmes under way in the fields of power, irrigation and land reclamation.

Labour

Of the total workforce of 4,822,800 in the period April–June 2004, 4,329,700 persons were employed. 748,200 were engaged in wholesale and retail trade; 569,700 in manufacturing; 533,100 in agriculture, animal breeding, hunting and forestry; and 350,000 in construction. Automatic index-linking of wages was abolished at the end of 1990. Since 1989 a statutory minimum of wage-bills must be spent on training (0·45%). Retirement age is 65 years for men and 60 for women, although most men retire before the age of 60. Unemployment was 10·1% in Sept. 2005; youth unemployment in the period April–June 2004 was 26·5%.

Trade Unions

The status of trade unions is regulated by the Associations Act 1914. Trade union liberties are guaranteed under the Constitution, and a law of June 1982 altered the unions' right to strike.

The national body of trade unions is the Greek General Confederation of Labour.

INTERNATIONAL TRADE

Following the normalization of their relations, Greece lifted its trade embargo (imposed in Feb. 1994) on Macedonia on 13 Oct. 1995. There are quarrels with Turkey over Cyprus, oil rights under the Aegean and ownership of uninhabited islands close to the Turkish coast.

Imports and Exports

In 2002 imports (f.o.b.) were valued at US$31,320m. and exports (f.o.b.) at US$9,868m. In 2000 principal imports were: machinery and apparatus, 18·6%; chemicals and chemical products, 11·5%; crude petroleum, 10·1%; road vehicles, 9·5%; food products, 9·1%. Principal exports in 2000 were: food, 14·6% (notably fruit and nuts); clothing and apparel, 12·8%; refined petroleum, 12·5%; machinery and apparatus, 9·8%; aluminium, 4·2%.

In 2001 Italy was the principal supplier of imports (13·5% of the total), ahead of Germany (13·4%), France (7·1%) and the Netherlands (5·7%). Germany was the leading export market (12·3% of the total), followed by Italy (9·2%), UK (6·4%) and USA (5·3%). Fellow EU member countries accounted for 54·8% of imports in 2001 and 46·7% of all exports.

COMMUNICATIONS

Roads

There were, in 1999, an estimated 117,000 km of roads, including 470 km of motorways, 9,100 km of national roads and 31,300 km of secondary roads. Number of motor vehicles in 2000: 3,195,065 passenger cars, 1,057,422 trucks and vans, 781,361 motorcycles and 27,037 buses. There are approximately 312 passenger cars per 1,000 population. There were 1,654 road deaths in 2002. With 15·7 deaths per 100,000 population in 2002, Greece has among the highest death rates in road accidents of any industrialized country. Road projects include improved links to Turkey and Bulgaria.

Rail

In 1997 the state network, Hellenic Railways (OSE), totalled 2,503 km including 1,565 km of 1,435 mm gauge, 887 km of 1,000 mm gauge, and 51 km of 750 mm gauge. Railways carried 3·2m. tonnes of freight and 14·9m. passengers in 2000. The Greek Railways Organization is investing US$23bn. in the link from Athens to the northern Bulgarian border. A 52-km long metro opened in Athens in Jan. 2000.

Civil Aviation

There are international airports at Athens (Spata 'Eleftherios Venizelos') and Thessaloniki-Makedonia. The airport at Spata opened in March 2001. The old airport at Hellenikon has now closed down. The national carrier is Olympic Airlines, serving some 30 towns and islands. Several failed attempts to privatize its predecessor, Olympic Airways, by selling a 51% stake led to the establishment of Olympic Airlines in Dec. 2003. Apart from the international airports there are a further 25 provincial airports. 6·27m. passengers were carried in 1999, of whom 3·64m. were on domestic and 2·63m. on international flights. Olympic Airlines operates routes from Athens to all important cities of the country, Europe, the Middle East and USA. In 1999 Athens airport (Hellenikon) handled 10,335,000 passengers (6,164,000 on international flights).

Shipping

In 2002 the merchant navy totalled 30,821,000 GRT, of which oil tankers 16,113,000 GRT. Greek-owned ships under foreign flags numbered 127 of 2,785,865 GRT in 1997. In 2001 vessels totalling 45,973,000 NRT entered ports and vessels totalling 23,970,000 NRT cleared.

There is a canal (opened 9 Nov. 1893) across the Isthmus of Corinth (about 7 km). The principal seaports are Piraeus, Thessaloniki, Patras, Volos, Igoumenitsa and Heraklion. Greece has 123 seaports with cargo and passenger handling facilities. Container terminals at the port of Piraeus are to be expanded to 1m. TEUs (twenty-foot equivalent units).

Telecommunications

In 2001 Greece had 13,569,700 telephone subscribers (equivalent to 1,280·6 per 1,000 inhabitants) and 900,000 PCs were in use (or 81·7 per 1,000 persons). Mobile phone subscribers numbered 9,314,300 in 2002 and there were 1,704,900 Internet users. In 1999 there were 40,000 fax machines.

Postal Services

In 2003 there were 2,218 post offices, or one for every 4,950 persons. A total of 622m. pieces of mail were processed, or 57 items per person.

SOCIAL INSTITUTIONS

Justice

Judges are appointed for life by the President after consultation with the judicial council. Judges enjoy personal and functional independence. There are three divisions of the courts—administrative, civil and criminal—and they must not give decisions which are contrary to the Constitution. Final jurisdiction lies with a Special Supreme Tribunal.

The Ombudsman (*Synigoros*), Giorgos Kaminis, was appointed for a five-year term in April 2003. In the period 1998–2002 a total of 41,865 complaints were submitted, relating to: State–Citizen Relations (36·10%), Social Welfare (28·97%), Quality of Life (22·00%) and Human Rights (12·93%).

The population in penal institutions in Dec. 2002 was 8,500 (80 per 100,000 of national population). The death penalty was abolished for ordinary crimes in 1993.

Education

Public education is provided in nursery, primary and secondary schools, starting at 5½–6½ years of age and free at all levels. Adult literacy rate, 2003, 91·0% (male 94·0%; female 88·3%).

In 2003–04 there were 5,722 nursery schools with 10,992 teachers and 140,535 pupils; 5,955 primary schools with 54,131 teachers and 655,369 pupils; 3,214 high schools (lycea) with 57,806 teachers and 563,337 pupils; 663 secondary technical, vocational and ecclesiastic schools with 16,128 teachers and 144,234 students. In 2002–03 there were 68 technical, vocational and ecclesiastic schools in third level education with 11,357 teachers and 146,270 students; and 19 universities with 11,079 academic staff and 175,597 students. In 1998–99 there was also one teacher training school with 159 teachers and 895 students.

In 2000–01 total expenditure on education came to 3·7% of GNP and in 1999–2000 represented 7·0% of total government expenditure.

Health

Doctor and hospital treatment within the Greek national health system is free, but patients have to pay 25% of prescription charges. Those living in remote areas can reclaim a proportion of private medical expenses. In 2000 there were 337 hospitals and sanatoria with a total of 51,500 beds; there were 180 health centres. In 2001 there were 47,944 doctors and 12,394 dentists. In 2003 Greece spent 9·9% of its GDP on health. Greeks smoke on average 3,020 cigarettes a year.

Welfare

The majority of employees are covered by the Social Insurance Institute, financed by employer and employee contributions. Benefits include pensions, medical expenses and long-term disability payments. Social insurance expenditure in 2000 totalled 8,215bn. drachmas.

RELIGION

The Christian Eastern (Greek) Orthodox Church is the established religion to which 91% of the population belong. It is under an archbishop and 67 metropolitans, one archbishop and seven metropolitans in Crete, and four metropolitans in the Dodecanese. The head of the Greek Orthodox Church is Archbishop Christodoulos Paraskevaides of Athens and All Greece (b. 1939). Roman Catholics have three archbishops (in Naxos and Corfu and, not recognized by the State, in Athens) and one bishop (for Syra and Santorin). The Exarchs of the Greek Catholics and the Armenians are not recognized by the State. There are 360,000 Muslims.

Complete religious freedom is recognized by the Constitution of 1974, but proselytizing from, and interference with, the Greek Orthodox Church is forbidden.

CULTURE

Patras is the European Capital of Culture for 2006. The title attracts large European Union grants.

World Heritage sites

Greece has 16 sites on the UNESCO World Heritage List, they are: the Temple of Apollo Epicurius at Bassae (1986); the archaeological site of Delphi (1987); The Acropolis, Athens (1987); Mount Athos (1988); Meteora (1988); the Paleochristian and Byzantine monuments of Thessaloniki (1988); the Archaeological Site of Epidaurus (1988); the Medieval City of Rhodes (1988); the archaeological site of Olympia (1989); Mystras (1989); Delos (1990); the monasteries of Daphni, Hossios Luckas and Nea Moni of Chios (1990); the Pythagoreion and Heraion of Samos (1992); the archaeological site of Vergina (1996); the archaeological sites of Mycenae and Tiryns (1999); and the historical sites on the Island of Patmos (1999).

Broadcasting
Elliniki Radiophonia Tileorasis (ERT), the Hellenic National Radio and Television Institute, is the government broadcasting station. There are four national and regional programmes, and an external service, Voice of Greece (16 languages). ERT broadcasts two TV programmes (colour by SECAM H). Number of receivers: radio (2000), 5·2m.; television (2001), 5·5m.

Press
There were 32 daily newspapers published in 2002 with a combined daily circulation of 628,000. A total of 6,826 book titles were published.

Tourism
Tourism is Greece's biggest industry with an estimated revenue for 2002 of US$10·20bn.; in 2004 tourism contributed approximately 14% of GDP. Tourists in 2002 numbered 12·0m. There were 606,330 hotel beds in 2002 (285,956 in 1981). A total of 52,249,768 nights were spent in hotels in 2002, 39,118,775 by foreigners and 13,130,993 by nationals.

Festivals
There are many festivals throughout the year, notably: The feast of St. Basil (1 Jan.); Gynaecocracy (8 Jan., female dominion); Carnival Season (mid-Feb. to mid-March); Independence Day (25 March); Feast of St George (23 April); Anastenaria (21–23 May, firewalking); Navy Week (end of June/beginning of July); Athens Lycabettus Theatre artistic performances (June–Aug.); Athens Festival (June–Sept.); Epidaurus Festival (July–Sept.); Philipi and Thasos Festival (July–Sept.); Dodoni Festival (July–Sept.); Athens Wine Festival and Ithaca Music Festival (end of July); Olympus Festival (Aug.); Epirotika Festival (Aug.); Kos Hippokrateia Festival (Aug.); Thessaloniki Film Festival and Festival of Popular Song (Sept.–Oct.); National Anniversary Procession (28 Oct.).

Libraries
In 1997 there were 829 public libraries, two National libraries and 64 Higher Education libraries; they held a combined 18,159,000 volumes. There were 7,521,000 visits to the libraries in 1997.

Theatre and Opera
There are two National Theatres and one Opera House.

Museums and Galleries
Amongst Greece's most important museums are the Acropolis Museum, the Museum of the City of Athens, the National Archaeological Museum and the National Historical Museum. In 1999 there were 89 museums and 182 galleries visited by 1,814,823 guests.

DIPLOMATIC REPRESENTATIVES
Of Greece in the United Kingdom (1A Holland Park, London, W11 3TP)
Ambassador: Anastase Scopelitis.

Of the United Kingdom in Greece (1 Ploutarchou St., 106 75 Athens)
Ambassador: Simon Gass.

Of Greece in the USA (2221 Massachusetts Ave., NW, Washington, D.C., 20008)
Ambassador: Alexandros Mallias.

Of the USA in Greece (91 Vasilissis Sophias Blvd, 101 60 Athens)
Ambassador: Charles P. Ries.

Of Greece to the United Nations
Ambassador: Adamantios Th. Vassilakis.

FURTHER READING
Clogg, Richard, *A Concise History of Greece.* 2nd ed. CUP, 2002
Jougnatos, G. A., *Development of the Greek Economy, 1950–91: an Historical, Empirical and Econometric Analysis.* London, 1992
Legg, K. R. and Roberts, J. M., *Modern Greece: A Civilization on the Periphery.* Oxford, 1997
Pettifer, J., *The Greeks: the Land and the People since the War.* London, 1994
Sarafis, M. and Eve, M. (eds.) *Background to Contemporary Greece.* London, 1990
Tsakalotos, E., *Alternative Economic Strategies: the Case of Greece.* Aldershot, 1991
Veremis, T., *The Military in Greek Politics: From Independence to Democracy.* C. Hurst, London, 1997
Woodhouse, C. M., *Modern Greece: a Short History.* rev. ed. London, 1991

National Statistical Office: National Statistical Service; 14–16 Lycourgou St., Athens.
Website: http://www.statistics.gr/

GRENADA

Capital: St George's
Population, 2001: 101,000
GDP per capita, 2003: (PPP$) 7,959
HDI/world rank: 0·787/66

KEY HISTORICAL EVENTS

Carib Indians inhabited Grenada when it was sighted by Christopher Columbus in 1498. The Caribs prevented European settlement until French forces landed in 1654. The British took control of Grenada in 1783 and established sugar plantations using African slave labour. Eric Gairy led a violent uprising of impoverished plantation workers in 1951 and became the island's dominant political figure in the lead-up to independence on 7 Feb. 1974. He was ousted by a leftist coup on 13 March 1979. The army took control on 19 Oct. 1983 after a power struggle led to the killing of the prime minister, Maurice Bishop. At the request of a group of Caribbean countries, Grenada was invaded by US-led forces on 25–28 Oct. On 1 Nov. a state of emergency was imposed which ended later in the year with the restoration of the 1973 constitution.

TERRITORY AND POPULATION

Grenada is the most southerly island of the Windward Islands with an area of 344 sq. km (133 sq. miles); the state also includes the Southern Grenadine Islands to the north, chiefly Carriacou (58·3 sq. km) and Petit Martinique. The total population at the 2001 census was 102,632; density, 298 per sq. km.

In 2003, 59·3% of the population were rural. The Borough of St George's, the capital, had 35,559 inhabitants in 2001. 52% of the population is Black, 40% of mixed origins, 4% Indian and 1% White.

The official language is English. A French-African patois is also spoken.

SOCIAL STATISTICS

Births, 2001, 1,899; deaths, 727. Rates per 1,000 population, 2001: birth, 18·8; death, 7·2. Life expectancy, 2000: 68 years for males, 73 years for females. Infant mortality, 2001, 20 per 1,000 live births. Annual population growth rate, 1995–2001, 0·4%; fertility rate, 2001, 3·5 births per woman.

CLIMATE

The tropical climate is very agreeable in the dry season, from Jan. to May, when days are warm and nights quite cool, but in the wet season there is very little difference between day and night temperatures. On the coast, annual rainfall is about 60" (1,500 mm) but it is as high as 150–200" (3,750–5,000 mm) in the mountains. Average temperature, 27°C.

CONSTITUTION AND GOVERNMENT

The head of state is the British sovereign, represented by an appointed Governor-General. There is a bicameral legislature, consisting of a 13-member *Senate*, appointed by the Governor-General, and a 15-member *House of Representatives*, elected by universal suffrage.

National Anthem

'Hail Grenada, land of ours'; words by I. M. Baptiste, tune by L. A. Masanto.

RECENT ELECTIONS

At the elections of 27 Nov. 2003 for the House of Representatives the New National Party (NNP) won 8 seats, with 49·9% of the votes cast, against 7 and 45·1% for the National Democratic Congress.

CURRENT ADMINISTRATION

Governor-General: Sir Daniel Williams.

In March 2006 the government comprised:

Prime Minister, Minister of Information, National Security, Business and Private Sector Development, Youth Development and Information Communication Technology: Dr Keith Mitchell; b. 1946 (NNP; in office since 22 June 1995).

Minister of Health, Social Security and the Environment: Ann David Antoine. *Foreign Affairs and International Trade, Carriacou and Petit Martinique Affairs, Legal Affairs and Attorney General:* Elvin Nimrod. *Finance and Planning:* Anthony Boatswain. *Agriculture, Lands, Forestry, Fisheries, Public Utilities, Energy and the Marketing and National Importing Board:* Gregory Bowen. *Education and Labour:* Claris Charles. *Tourism, Civil Aviation, Culture and the Performing Arts:* Brenda Hood. *Social Development:* Yolande Bain Joseph. *Sports, Community Development and Co-operatives:* Roland Bhola. *Communications, Works and Transport:* Clarice Modeste-Curwen. *Youth Development:* Emmalin Pierre.

CURRENT LEADERS

Dr Keith Mitchell

Position
Prime Minister

Introduction
Dr Keith Mitchell is prime minister of Grenada and leader of the New National Party (NNP). Elected prime minister in 1995, he was re-elected in a landslide victory in 1999 when his party took all 15 seats in parliament. He retained power with a reduced majority in Nov. 2003.

Early Life

Keith Mitchell was born on 12 Nov. 1946 in St George's, Grenada. He graduated in mathematics and chemistry from the University of the West Indies in Barbados in 1971. After briefly teaching at a boys' college he continued his studies, first in Barbados then in the USA where he gained a PhD in mathematics from the American University. From 1977–83 he was professor of mathematics at Howard University in Washington, D.C. He also acted as a statistical consultant to government agencies and private corporations in the USA.

In 1984 Mitchell returned to Grenada and became a member of parliament, representing the ruling NNP. He served as minister of works, communications and public utilities from 1984 until the NNP lost power in 1989. He became prime minister when the NNP returned to power in 1995.

Career in Office

In his first term Mitchell successfully diversified Grenada's agriculture-reliant economy by expanding the offshore banking sector. In 1999 he became the first Grenadian prime minister to win two consecutive terms, claiming all 15 parliamentary seats. Despite generally strong economic growth, the agricultural sector (especially the banana industry) suffered a crisis and in 2000 Mitchell was confronted by tense industrial relations. The situation was exacerbated by longstanding political and social tensions arising from Grenada's 'Revolutionary Years' of 1976–83 and in 2000 Mitchell established a Truth and Reconciliation Commission with the help of South Africa.

The late 1990s saw growing international concern over the lack of regulation in offshore banking. In 2001 Grenada was placed on a blacklist of international money-laundering and tax havens compiled by the Financial Action Task Force (set up by the G7 group of major industrialized nations). Mitchell's government revoked the licences of more than 20 offshore banks and strengthened regulations on financial services. After the 11 Sept. attacks on New York and Washington, further international pressure led Mitchell to suspend the sale of passports to non-citizens. Grenada was removed from the blacklist in 2003.

Mitchell has been a vigorous lobbyist for the Caribbean region. He chaired CARICOM in 1998 and has been responsible for its science, technology and human resource development since 1995. In 2001, with aid declining from the USA and the UK, he campaigned with the OECS for a sustained programme of economic help. In Sept. 2004 Hurricane Ivan killed 39 in Grenada and damaged 90% of its housing and infrastructure. Mitchell called on the UN to set up a special fund for small countries in crisis.

Mitchell was re-elected for a third term in Nov. 2003 though with a slimmer majority.

DEFENCE

Royal Grenada Police Force

Modelled on the British system, the 730-strong police force includes an 80-member paramilitary unit and a 30-member coastguard.

INTERNATIONAL RELATIONS

Grenada is a member of the UN, WTO, OAS, ACS, CARICOM, OECS, IOM, the Commonwealth and is an ACP member state of the ACP-EU relationship.

ECONOMY

Agriculture accounted for 7·5% of GDP in 2002, industry 22·6% and services 69·8%.

Currency

The unit of currency is the *Eastern Caribbean dollar* (EC$). Foreign exchange reserves were US$69m. in May 2002. Total money supply in May 2002 was EC$228m. Inflation was 2·2% in 2003 and 2·3% in 2004.

Budget

In 2001 current revenue was EC$326·4m. and current expenditure EC$257·0m. Capital expenditure was EC$125·0m. Income tax has been abolished. VAT is 25% (reduced rate, 5%).

Performance

Real GDP growth was 5·8% in 2003 but there then followed a recession, with the economy shrinking by 3·0% in 2004. Total GDP in 2004 was US$0·4bn.

Banking and Finance

Grenada is a member of the Eastern Caribbean Central Bank. The *Governor* is Sir Dwight Venner. In 2002 there were three commercial banks and four foreign banks. The Grenada Agricultural Bank was established in 1965 to encourage agricultural development; in 1975 it became the Grenada Agricultural and Industrial Development Corporation. In 1995 bank deposits were EC$666·8m. (US$249·7m.). Total foreign currency deposits in 1995 amounted to US$11·8m.

Grenada is affiliated to the Eastern Caribbean Securities Exchange in Basseterre, St Kitts and Nevis.

ENERGY AND NATURAL RESOURCES

Environment

Grenada's carbon dioxide emissions from the consumption and flaring of fossil fuels in 2002 were the equivalent of 2·3 tonnes per capita.

Electricity

Installed capacity in 2000 was 27,000 kW. Production in 2000 was 118m. kWh, with consumption per capita 1,168 kWh.

Agriculture

There were 2,000 ha. of arable land in 2001 and 10,000 ha. of permanent crops. Principal crop production (2000, in 1,000 tonnes): coconuts, 7; sugarcane, 7; bananas, 5; avocados, 2; grapefruit and pomelos, 2; mangoes, 2. Nutmeg, corn, pigeon peas, citrus, root-crops and vegetables are also grown, in addition to small scattered cultivations of cotton, cloves, cinnamon, pimento, coffee and fruit trees. Grenada is the second largest producer of nutmeg in the world, after Indonesia.

Livestock (2000): cattle, 4,000; sheep, 13,000; goats, 7,000; pigs, 5,000.

Forestry

In 2000 the area under forests was 5,000 ha., or 14·7% of the total land area.

Fisheries

The catch in 2001 was 2,247 tonnes, entirely from marine waters.

INDUSTRY

Main products are wheat flour, soft drinks, beer, animal feed, rum and cigarettes.

Labour

In 1993 the labour force was estimated at 27,820. Unemployment was 11% in Dec. 2000.

INTERNATIONAL TRADE

Total external debt amounted to US$339m. in 2002.

Imports and Exports

In 2002 imports totalled US$233·2m. and exports US$59·7m. Major import commodities were: machinery and transport equipment, 27·4%; food, 16·6%; chemicals and chemical products, 11·1%. The principal exports were: electronic components, 36·1%; nutmeg, 19·7%; fish, 6·8%.

In 1999 the main import suppliers were the USA (41·8%), Trinidad and Tobago (21·4%), the UK (8·0%), Japan (5·4%), Canada (3·5%) and Barbados (2·8%). Main export destinations were the Netherlands (19·8%), the USA (18·7%), Germany (11·0%), St Lucia (6·9%), France (5·5%) and Barbados (5·2%).

COMMUNICATIONS

Roads
In 1999 there were about 1,040 km of roads, of which 638 km were hard-surfaced.

Civil Aviation
The main airport is Point Salines International. Union Island and Carriacou have smaller airports. There were direct flights from Point Salines in 2003 to Anguilla, Antigua, Barbados, the British Virgin Islands, Dominica, Frankfurt, London, Montego Bay, New York, Philadelphia, Puerto Rico, St Kitts, St Lucia, St Maarten, St Vincent, Tobago and Trinidad. In 2001 Point Salines handled 344,064 passengers (342,124 on international flights) and 2,747 tonnes of freight.

Shipping
The main port is at St George's; there are eight minor ports. Total number of containers handled in 1991 was 5,161; cargo landed, 187,039 tonnes; cargo loaded, 24,786 tonnes. Sea-going shipping totalled 1,000 GRT in 2002.

Telecommunications
Telephone subscribers numbered 41,100 in 2002 (387·7 per 1,000 persons) and there were 14,000 PCs in use (132·1 for every 1,000 persons). There were 7,600 mobile phone subscribers in 2002 and 300 fax machines in 1999. In 2002 Grenada had 15,000 Internet users.

Postal Services
In 2003 there were 52 post offices.

SOCIAL INSTITUTIONS

Justice
The Grenada Supreme Court, situated in St George's, comprises a High Court of Justice, a Court of Magisterial Appeal (which hears appeals from the lower Magistrates' Courts exercising summary jurisdiction) and an Itinerant Court of Appeal (to hear appeals from the High Court). Grenada was one of ten countries to sign an agreement in Feb. 2001 establishing a Caribbean Court of Justice to replace the British Privy Council as the highest civil and criminal court. In the meantime the number of signatories has risen to twelve. The court was inaugurated at Port-of-Spain, Trinidad on 16 April 2005. For police see DEFENCE, *above*.

The population in penal institutions in June 2002 was 297 (equivalent to 333 per 100,000 of national population).

Education
Adult literacy was 96% in 1998. In 2000–01 there were 15,974 pupils in primary schools (765 teachers) and 8,312 pupils (439 teachers) in secondary schools. In 2000–01 the teacher-pupil ratio was 1:21 in primary schools and 1:19 in secondary schools.

The Grenada National College was established in 1988. There is also a branch of the University of the West Indies. 12·3% of the 2001 budget was allocated to education.

Health
In 1996 there were three general hospitals with a provision of 35 beds per 10,000 inhabitants. There were 96 physicians, 14 dentists, 232 nurses and 47 pharmacists in 1996. 16·2% of the 2001 budget was allocated to health.

RELIGION
At the 2001 census 53% of the population were Roman Catholic, 14% Anglican and the remainder other religions.

CULTURE

Broadcasting
The government-owned Grenada Broadcasting Corporation operates Radio Grenada and Grenada Television. There are also four independent radio stations. Grenada Television transmits on three channels (colour by NTSC). A private cable TV company provides services on 25 channels, and there is a religious TV service. In 1997 there were 57,000 radio and (1999) 33,000 TV sets.

Press
In 1993 there were five weekly, one monthly and two bi-monthly newspapers.

Tourism
In 2001 there were 123,351 overnight visitors and 147,300 cruise ship arrivals. Tourism receipts totalled US$84m. in 2002.

DIPLOMATIC REPRESENTATIVES
Of Grenada in the United Kingdom (5 Chandos St., London, W1G 9DG)
High Commissioner: Joslyn R. Whiteman.

Of the United Kingdom in Grenada
High Commissioner: Duncan Taylor (resides in Bridgetown, Barbados).

Of Grenada in the USA (1701 New Hampshire Ave., NW, Washington, D.C., 20009)
Ambassador: Denis Antoine.

Of the USA in Grenada
Ambassador: Mary E. Kramer (resides in Bridgetown, Barbados).

Of Grenada to the United Nations
Ambassador: Ruth Elizabeth Rouse.

Of Grenada to the European Union
Ambassador: Joan Marie Coutain.

FURTHER READING
Ferguson, J., *Grenada: Revolution in Reverse.* London, 1991
Heine, J. (ed.) *A Revolution Aborted: the Lessons of Grenada.* Pittsburgh Univ. Press, 1990

GUATEMALA

República de Guatemala

Capital: Guatemala City
Population projection, 2010: 14·21m.
GDP per capita, 2003: (PPP$) 4,148
HDI/world rank: 0·663/117

KEY HISTORICAL EVENTS

From 1524 Guatemala was part of a Spanish captaincy-general, comprising the whole of Central America. It became independent in 1821 and formed part of the Confederation of Central America from 1823 to 1839. The overthrow of the right-wing dictator Jorge Ubico in 1944 opened a decade of left-wing activity. In 1954 the leftist regime of Jacobo Arbenz Guzmán was overthrown by a CIA-supported coup. A series of right-wing governments failed to produce stability while the toll on human life and the violation of human rights was such as to cause thousands of refugees to flee to Mexico. Elections to a National Constituent Assembly were held on 1 July 1984, and a new constitution was promulgated in May 1985. Amidst violence and assassinations, the presidential election was won by Marco Vinicio Cerezo Arévalo. On 14 Jan. 1986 Cerezo's civilian government was installed—the first for 16 years and only the second since 1954. Violence continued, however, and there were frequent reports of torture and killings by right-wing 'death squads'. The elections of Nov. 1995 saw the return of open politics for the first time in over 40 years. Meanwhile the Guatemalan Revolutionary Unit declared a ceasefire. On 6 May and 19 Sept. 1996 the government agreed reforms to military, internal security, judicial and agrarian institutions. A ceasefire was concluded in Oslo on 4 Dec. 1996 and a final peace treaty was signed on 29 Dec. 1996. In Nov. 1999 the country's first presidential elections took place since the end of the 36-year-long civil war, which had claimed over 200,000 lives.

TERRITORY AND POPULATION

Guatemala is bounded on the north and west by Mexico, south by the Pacific ocean and east by El Salvador, Honduras and Belize, and the area is 108,889 sq. km (42,042 sq. miles). In March 1936 Guatemala, El Salvador and Honduras agreed to accept the peak of Mount Montecristo as the common boundary point.

The population was 11,237,196 at the census of Nov. 2002; density, 103 per sq. km.

The UN gives a projected population for 2010 of 14·21m.

In 2003, 53·7% of the population were rural. In 2000, 33% were Amerindian, of 21 different groups descended from the Maya; 64% Mestizo (mixed Amerindian and Spanish). 51% speak Spanish, with the remainder speaking one or a combination of the 23 Indian dialects.

Guatemala is administratively divided into 22 departments, each with a governor appointed by the president. Population, 2002:

Departments	Area (sq. km)	Population	Departments	Area (sq. km)	Population
Alta Verapaz	8,686	776,246	Petén	35,854	366,735
Baja Verapaz	3,124	215,915	Quezaltenango	1,951	624,716
Chimaltenango	1,979	446,133	Quiché	8,378	655,510
Chiquimula	2,376	302,485	Retalhuleu	1,858	241,411
El Progreso	1,922	139,490	Sacatepéquez	465	248,019
Escuintla	4,384	538,746	San Marcos	3,791	794,951
Guatemala City	2,126	2,541,581	Santa Rosa	2,955	301,370
Huehuetenango	7,403	846,544	Sololá	1,061	307,661
Izabal	9,038	314,306	Suchitepéquez	2,510	403,945
Jalapa	2,063	242,926	Totonicapán	1,061	339,254
Jutiapa	3,219	389,085	Zacapa	2,690	200,167

In 1999 Guatemala City, the capital, had a population of 3,119,000. Populations of other major towns, 1995 estimates (in 1,000): Quezaltenango, 104; Escuintla, 70; Mazatenango, 43; Retalhuleu, 40; Puerto Barrios, 39.

SOCIAL STATISTICS

Births, 2002, 297,885; deaths, 46,224. 2002 rates per 1,000 population: birth, 26·5; death, 4·1. Life expectancy, 2003: male 63·6 years, female 71·0. Annual population growth rate, 1992–2002, 2·7%. Infant mortality, 2001, 43 per 1,000 live births; fertility rate, 2001, 4·6 births per woman.

CLIMATE

A tropical climate, with little variation in temperature and a well marked wet season from May to Oct. Guatemala City, Jan. 63°F (17·2°C), July 69°F (20·6°C). Annual rainfall 53" (1,316 mm).

CONSTITUTION AND GOVERNMENT

A new Constitution, drawn up by the Constituent Assembly elected on 1 July 1984, was promulgated in June 1985 and came into force on 14 Jan. 1986. In 1993, 43 amendments were adopted, reducing *inter alia* the President's term of office from five to four years. The President and Vice-President are elected by direct election (with a second round of voting if no candidate secures 50% of the first-round votes) for a non-renewable four-year term. The unicameral *Congreso de la República* comprises 158 members, elected partly from constituencies and partly by proportional representation to serve four-year terms.

National Anthem

'¡Guatemala! Feliz' ('Happy Guatemala'); words by J. J. Palma, tune by R. Alvárez.

GOVERNMENT CHRONOLOGY

Heads of State since 1944. (DCG = Guatemalan Christian Democracy; FRG = Guatemalan Republican Front; GANA = Grand National Alliance; MAS = Solidarity Action Movement; MLN = National Liberation Movement; PAN = National Advancement Party; PAR = Revolutionary Action Party; PID =

Democratic Institutional Party; PR = Revolutionary Party; PRDN = National Democratic Reconciliation/Redemption Party; n/p = non-partisan)

Military Junta

1944–45		Maj. Francisco Javier Arana; Capt. Jacobo Arbenz Guzmán; Jorge Toriello Garrido.

Presidents

1945–51	PAR	Juan José Arévalo Bermejo
1951–54	PAR	Jacobo Arbenz Guzmán
1954	military	Carlos Enrique Díaz de León

Military Juntas

1954		Col. Elfego Hernán Monzón Aguirre; Col. José Ángel Sánchez; Col. José Luis Cruz Salazar; Col. Carlos Enrique Díaz de León; Col Mauricio Dubois.
1954		Col. Carlos Castillo Armas; Col. Mauricio Dubois; Maj. Enrique Trinidad Oliva; Col. Elfego Hernán Monzón Aguirre; Col. José Luis Cruz Salazar.

Presidents

1954–57	military	Carlos Castillo Armas
1957–58	military	Guillermo Flores Avendaño
1958–63	PRDN	José Ramón Ydígoras Fuentes
1963–66	military	Alfredo Enrique Peralta Azurdia
1966–70	PR	Julio César Méndez Montenegro
1970–74	military, MLN	Carlos Manuel Arana Osorio
1974–78	military, MLN/PID	Kjell Eugenio Laugerud García
1978–82	military, PID/PR	Fernando Romeo Lucas García
1982–83	military	José Efraín Ríos Montt
1983–86	military	Óscar Humberto Mejía Víctores
1986–91	DCG	Marco Vinicio Cerezo Arévalo
1991–93	MAS	Jorge Antonio Serrano Elías
1993–96	n/p	Ramiro de León Carpio
1996–2000	PAN	Álvaro Enrique Arzú Yrigoyen
2000–04	FRG	Alfonso Antonio Portillo Cabrera
2004–	GANA	Óscar Rafael Berger Perdomo

RECENT ELECTIONS

In a run-off for the presidency on 28 Dec. 2003 Óscar Berger Perdomo of the Gran Alianza Nacional (GANA, Grand National Alliance) won with 54·1% of the vote against Álvaro Colom Caballeros of the Unidad Nacional de la Esperanza (UNE, National Union of Hope). A further seven candidates had participated in the first round of voting on 9 Nov. 2003. Combined turnout was 45·8%.

Congressional elections were held on 9 Nov. 2003: the Gran Alianza Nacional (composed of the Patriotic Party, the Reformist Movement and the National Solidarity Party) won 47 seats with 24·3% of the vote; the Frente Republicano Guatemalteco (FRG, Guatemalan Republican Front) won 43 seats (19·7%); the UNE won 32 seats (17·9%); the Partido de Avanzade Nacional (PAN, National Advancement Party) won 17 seats (10·9%); the Partido Unionista (PU; Unionist Party) won 7 seats (6·2%); the Alianza Nueva Nación (ANN; New National Alliance won 6 seats (4·9%). Four other parties won six seats between them. Turnout was 57·9%.

CURRENT ADMINISTRATION

President: Óscar Berger Perdomo; b. 1946 (GANA; sworn in 14 Jan. 2004).

Vice-President: Dr Eduardo Stein Barillas; b. 1945 (took office on 14 Jan. 2004).

In March 2006 the government comprised:

Minister of Agriculture, Livestock and Food: Alvaro Aguilar. *Communications, Transportation and Public Works:* Eduardo Castillo. *Culture:* Manuel Salazar. *Defence:* Brig.-Gen. Francisco Bermúdez Amado. *Economy:* Marcio Cuevas. *Environment and Natural Resources:* Mario Dary. *Education:* María del Carmen Aceña. *Energy and Mining:* Luis Romero Ortíz Peláez. *External Relations:* Jorge Briz Abularach. *Government:* Carlos Vielman. *Labour:* Jorge Gallardo. *Public Finance:* María Antonieta de Bonilla. *Public Health and Social Assistance:* Marco Tulio Sosa.

Government Website (Spanish only):
   http://www.guatemala.gob.gt

CURRENT LEADERS

Óscar Berger Perdomo

Position
President

Introduction
President of Guatemala since Jan. 2004, Óscar Berger Perdomo of the Grand National Alliance (GANA) was previously twice mayor of the capital, Guatemala City.

Early Life
Born into a wealthy family on 11 Aug. 1946 in Guatemala City, Berger received a private education culminating in his graduation from the Jesuit Rafael Landívar University as a lawyer and notary. Having supported Álvaro Arzú, a classmate from university and later president of Guatemala, in his successful campaign in the mid-1980s to become mayor of Guatemala City, Berger then held this position himself from 1991–99. At the end of the 1980s, Berger and Arzú formed the National Advancement Party (PAN) to take advantage of what they saw as a gap in the political spectrum, hitherto dominated by conservative and far-right parties. Standing for the PAN in the Nov.–Dec. 1999 presidential elections, Berger lost to the FRG candidate, Alfonso Cabrera, in the second round of voting.

Career in Office
In late 2003 Berger stood again as a presidential election candidate, this time for the GANA, and won the second round run-off with 54·1% of the vote. He was sworn in on 14 Jan. 2004. Despite his personal victory, his GANA coalition failed to secure a congressional majority and he has faced political opposition to his government's programme. He has introduced improvements in education and health programmes and also initiated reductions in the armed forces. However, his greatest challenge is the high level of violent crime in the country. In Oct. 2005 a state of emergency was declared following a hurricane.

DEFENCE

There is selective conscription for 30 months. In 2003 defence expenditure totalled US$102m. (US$8 per capita), representing 0·4% of GDP.

Army

The Army numbered (2002) 29,200 (23,000 conscripts) and is organized in 15 military zones. It includes a special forces unit. There is a paramilitary national police of 7,000, treasury police of 2,500 and a trained reserve of 35,000.

Navy

A naval element of the combined armed forces was (2002) 1,500 strong of whom 650 are marines for maintenance of riverine security. Main bases are Santo Tomás de Castilla (on the Atlantic Coast) and Puerto Quetzal (Pacific).

Air Force

There is a small Air Force with 10 combat aircraft and 12 armed helicopters (although fewer than half are operational). Strength was (2002) 700.

INTERNATIONAL RELATIONS

Guatemala is a member of the UN, WTO, OAS, Inter-American Development Bank, CACM, ACS and IOM.

ECONOMY

In 2002 agriculture accounted for 22·5% of GDP, industry 19·3% and services 58·2%.

Overview

Guatemala has the third highest per capita income in Central America. However, owing to a highly unequal income distribution with approximately 50% of the overall population living in poverty, Guatemala's social indicators rank among the lowest in the region. The signing of the UN-sponsored peace accords in 1996, which ended 36 years of civil war, was followed by an ambitious programme aimed at addressing social problems, improving social capital, raising productivity and mobilizing domestic resources. The progress of the programme was, however, slower than forecast. The Guatemalan authorities have presented revised programmes incorporating the agenda of the 1996 peace accords. In early 2002 a medium-term poverty reduction strategy (PRS) was introduced to enhance economic growth and improve social conditions. The strategy set specific goals to be reached by 2005 such as reducing extreme poverty by 3%, raising economic growth to more than 4% per year and improving the quality of education, health and rural development. Despite significant accomplishments since 1996, overall compliance with the peace commitments has been uneven. According to the World Bank, to achieve growth targets Guatemala needs to strengthen its institutions by improving property rights, dismantling excessive regulation and reducing crime rates.

Currency

The unit of currency is the *quetzal* (CTQ) of 100 *centavos*, established on 7 May 1925. In June 2002 foreign exchange reserves were US$2,222m., total money supply was Q.20,561m. and gold reserves were 222,000 troy oz. Inflation was 5·6% in 2003 and 7·6% in 2004.

Budget

Budgetary central government revenue and expenditure (in Q.1m.):

	2001	2002	2003
Revenue	18,191·3	20,715·6	21,694·4
Expenditure	19,380·4	20,758·7	24,968·6

VAT is 12%.

Performance

Real GDP growth was 2·1% in 2003 and 2·7% in 2004. Total GDP in 2004 was US$27·5bn.

Banking and Finance

The Banco de Guatemala is the central bank and bank of issue (*President*, Lizardo Sosa López). Constitutional amendments of 1993 placed limits on its financing of government spending. In 2002 there were 27 national banks (four state-owned and 23 private). The international banks and the foreign banks are authorized to operate as commercial banks.

There are two stock exchanges.

Weights and Measures

The metric system is official but the imperial is still used locally.

ENERGY AND NATURAL RESOURCES

Environment

Carbon dioxide emissions from the consumption and flaring of fossil fuels in 2002 were the equivalent of 0·8 tonnes per capita.

Electricity

Installed capacity in 2000 was 1·3m. kW. Production, 2000, 6·05bn. kWh. Consumption per capita in 2000 was 469 kWh.

Oil and Gas

There were proven natural gas reserves in 2002 of 2·8bn. cu. metres. Production (1998), 11m. cu. metres. In 2002 crude petroleum reserves were 526m. bbls.; in 2000 output was 1·0m. tonnes.

Minerals

There are deposits of gold, silver and nickel.

Agriculture

There were 1·36m. ha. of arable land in 2001 and 0·55m. ha. of permanent crops. 130,000 ha. were irrigated in 2001. Production, 2000 (in 1,000 tonnes): sugarcane, 17,150; maize, 1,109; bananas, 733; coffee, 295; tomatoes, 150; lemons and limes, 117; melons, 115. Rubber development schemes are under way, assisted by US funds. Guatemala is one of the largest sources of essential oils (citronella and lemongrass). Arable land: 12%; permanent crops: 4%; meadows and pastures: 12%; forest and woodland: 40%; other: 32%.

Livestock (2000): cattle, 2·30m.; pigs, 825,000; sheep, 551,000; horses, 120,000; goats, 110,000; chickens, 24m.

Forestry

In 2000 the area under forests was 2·85m ha., or 26·3% of the total land area. Mahogany and cedar are grown, and chick, a chewing gum base, is produced. Timber production in 2001 was 15·34m. cu. metres.

Fisheries

In 2001 the total catch was approximately 10,100 tonnes (7,300 tonnes from inland waters).

INDUSTRY

Manufacturing contributed 12·9% of GDP in 2001. The principal industries are food and beverages, tobacco, chemicals, hides and skins, textiles, garments and non-metallic minerals. Cement production in 2000 was 2,039,000 tonnes; raw sugar production was 1,661,000 tonnes in 2001. New industries include electrical goods, plastic sheet and metal furniture.

Labour

In 1995 the workforce totalled 3,316,723 including: agriculture, 1,513,600; commerce, 572,011; services, 439,719; manufacturing, 439,121; building, 214,102; transport and communications, 77,476; finance, 40,474.

There is a working week of a maximum of 44 hours.

Trade Unions

There are three federations for private sector workers.

INTERNATIONAL TRADE

In May 1992 Guatemala, El Salvador and Honduras agreed to create a free trade zone and standardize import duties. External debt was US$4,676m. in 2002.

Imports and Exports

Values in US$1m. were:

	1998	1999	2000	2001	2002
Imports f.o.b.	4,255·7	4,225·7	4,742·0	5,142·0	5,578·4
Exports f.o.b.	2,846·9	2,780·6	3,085·1	2,859·8	2,628·4

In 1999 the main imports were: machinery and transport equipment, 35·4%; manufactured goods, 16·6%; chemicals, 16·3%; foodstuffs, 10·2%; petroleum and related products, 8·9%. Principal exports were: coffee, 22·9%; chemicals, 13·1%; manufactured goods, 11·3%; sugar, 7·9%; bananas, 5·9%.

Main import suppliers, 1999: USA, 41·6%; Mexico, 11·0%; El Salvador, 5·6%; Venezuela, 4·5%; Japan, 4·0%. Main export markets: USA, 34·3%; El Salvador, 14·5%; Honduras, 8·5%; Costa Rica, 4·9%; Nicaragua, 4·2%.

COMMUNICATIONS

Roads
In 2002 there were 14,891 km of roads, of which 74 km were motorways. 37·6% of all roads were paved in 2002. There is a highway from coast to coast via Guatemala City. There are two highways from the Mexican to the Salvadorean frontier: the Pacific Highway serving the fertile coastal plain and the Pan-American Highway running through the highlands and Guatemala City. Passenger cars numbered 578,733 in 2000, and there were 42,219 trucks and vans and 11,017 buses and coaches.

Rail
The state-owned Ferrocarriles de Guatemala operated 903 km of railway in 2000, linking east and west coast seaports to Guatemala City, with branch lines to the north and south borders. Passenger-km travelled in 1994 came to 991m. and freight tonne-km in 2000 to 2·2bn.

Civil Aviation
There are international airports at Guatemala City (La Aurora) and Flores. In 2000 La Aurora handled 1,258,919 passengers and 58,118 tonnes of freight. In 1999 scheduled airline traffic of Guatemalan-based carriers flew 5·3m. km, carrying 506,000 passengers (472,000 on international flights).

Shipping
The chief ports on the Atlantic coast are Puerto Barrios and Santo Tomás de Castilla: on the Pacific coast, Puerto Quetzal and Champerico. Merchant shipping totalled 9,000 GRT in 2002. In 1997 vessels totalling 4,505,000 NRT entered ports and vessels totalling 3,815,000 NRT cleared.

Telecommunications
The government own and operate the telecommunications services. In 2002 there were 2,423,100 telephone subscribers, or 202·0 for every 1,000 persons, and 173,000 PCs were in use (14·4 for every 1,000 persons). There were 1,577,100 mobile phone subscribers in 2002 and 10,000 fax machines in use in 1999. Guatemala had 400,000 Internet users in 2002.

Postal Services
There were 434 post offices in 2003.

SOCIAL INSTITUTIONS

Justice
Justice is administered in a Constitution Court, a Supreme Court, six appeal courts and 28 courts of first instance. Supreme Court and appeal court judges are elected by Congress. Judges of first instance are appointed by the Supreme Court.

The death penalty is authorized for murder and kidnapping. Two executions were carried out in 2000.

A new National Civil Police force under the authority of the Minister of the Interior was created in 1996. It was 19,000-strong in 2002.

The population in penal institutions in Feb. 2003 was 8,307 (68 per 100,000 of national population).

Education
In 2000–01 there were 1,909,389 pupils at primary schools and 503,884 pupils at secondary level. The adult literacy rate in 2003 was 69·1% (male, 75·4%; female, 63·3%). In 1994–95 there were five universities with 70,233 students and 4,450 academic staff.

In 2000–01 total public expenditure on education came to 1·7% of GNP and 11·4% of total government spending.

Health
Guatemala had 9,965 physicians and 2,046 dentists in 1999. There were 49 hospitals, 257 country health centres and 1,288 community health clinics in 2000.

Welfare
A comprehensive system of social security was outlined in a law of 30 Oct. 1946.

RELIGION

Roman Catholicism is the prevailing faith (8·9m. adherents in 2001) and there is a Roman Catholic archbishopric. In May 2005 there was one cardinal. The remainder of the population are followers of other religions (mainly Evangelical Protestantism).

CULTURE

World Heritage Sites
Guatemala has three sites on the UNESCO World Heritage List: Tikal National Park (inscribed on the list in 1979); Antigua Guatemala (1979); and the Archaeological Park and Ruins of Quiriguá (1981).

Broadcasting
There are five government, six educational and 84 commercial radio broadcasting services. There are four commercial TV stations and one government station. There is also reception by US television satellite.

There were 1·7m. TV receivers (colour by NTSC) in 2001 and 902,000 radio sets in 2000.

Press
In 2002 there were 11 daily newspapers.

Tourism
Tourism is an important source of foreign exchange (US$612m. in 2002). There were 884,000 foreign tourists in 2002.

DIPLOMATIC REPRESENTATIVES

Of Guatemala in the United Kingdom (13 Fawcett St., London, SW10 9HN)
Ambassador: Vacant.
Chargé d'Affaires a.i.: Rodrigo Vielmann.

Of the United Kingdom in Guatemala (Avenida La Reforma 16-00, Zona 10, Edificio Torre Internacional, Nivel 11, Guatemala City)
Ambassador: Richard Lavers.

Of Guatemala in the USA (2220 R. St., NW, Washington, D.C., 20008)
Ambassador: Guillermo Castillo.

Of the USA in Guatemala (7-01 Avenida de la Reforma, Zone 10, Guatemala City)
Ambassador: James M. Derham.

Of Guatemala to the United Nations
Ambassador: Jorge Skinner-Klée Arenales.

Of Guatemala to the European Union
Ambassador: Edmond Mulet-Lesieur.

FURTHER READING

Jonas, Susanne, *Of Centaurs and Doves: Guatemala's Peace Process.* Westview Press, Boulder (CO), 2001
Woodward, R. L., *Guatemala.* [Bibliography] 2nd ed. ABC-Clio, Oxford and Santa Barbara (CA), 1992

National library: Biblioteca Nacional, 5a Avenida y 8a Calle, Zona 1, Guatemala City.
National Institute of Statistics Website (Spanish only): http://www.segeplan.gob.gt/ine

GUINEA

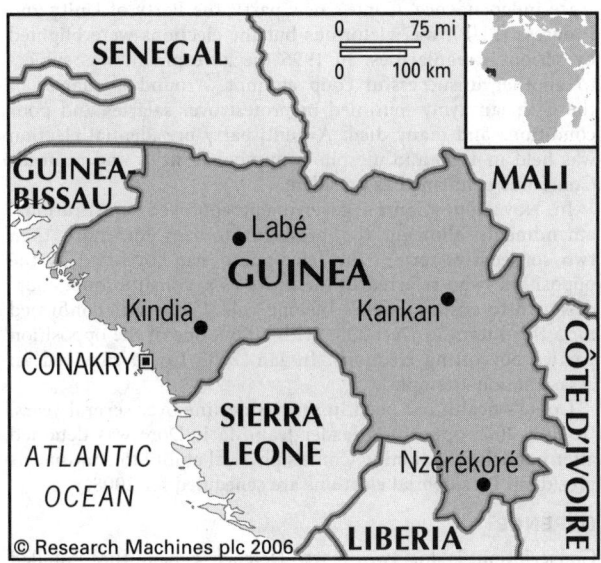

República de Guinée

Capital: Conakry
Population projection, 2010: 10·48m.
GDP per capita, 2003: (PPP$) 2,097
HDI/world rank: 0·466/156

KEY HISTORICAL EVENTS

In 1888 Guinea became a French protectorate, in 1893 a colony, and in 1904 a constituent territory of French West Africa. Forced labour and other colonial depredations ensued, although a form of representation was introduced in 1946. The independent Republic of Guinea was proclaimed on 2 Oct. 1958, after the territory of French Guinea had decided to leave the French community. Guinea became a single-party state. In 1980 the armed forces staged a coup and dissolved the National Assembly. Following popular disturbances a multi-party system was introduced in April 1992.

In 2000 fierce fighting broke out between Guinean government troops and rebels, believed to be a mix of Guinean dissidents and mercenaries from Liberia and Sierra Leone. More than 250,000 refugees were caught up in what the United Nations High Commissioner for Refugees described as the world's worst refugee crisis.

TERRITORY AND POPULATION

Guinea is bounded in the northwest by Guinea-Bissau and Senegal, northeast by Mali, southeast by Côte d'Ivoire, south by Liberia and Sierra Leone, and west by the Atlantic Ocean.

The area is 245,857 sq. km (94,926 sq. miles). In 1996 the census population was 7,164,823 (density 29·1 per sq. km). 2005 estimate: 9,402,000.

The UN gives a projected population for 2010 of 10·48m.

The capital is Conakry. In 2003, 65·1% of the population were rural.

Guinea is divided into seven provinces and a special zone (national capital). These are in turn divided into 33 administrative regions. The major divisions (with their areas in sq. km) are: Boké, 34,231; Conakry (special zone—national capital), 308;

Faranah, 38,272; Kankan, 71,085; Kindia, 26,749; Labé, 21,150; Mamou, 13,560; Nzérékoré, 40,502.

The main towns are Conakry (population estimate, 1999, 1,764,000), Kindia, Nzérékoré, Kankan and Labé.

The ethnic composition is Fulani (38·6%, predominant in Moyenne-Guinée), Malinké (or Mandingo, 23·2%, prominent in Haute-Guinée), Susu (11·0%, prominent in Guinée-Maritime), Kissi (6·0%) and Kpelle (4·6%) in Guinée-Forestière, and Dialonka, Loma and others (16·6%).

The official language is French.

SOCIAL STATISTICS

2000 estimates: births, 352,000; deaths, 136,000. Rates, 2000 estimates (per 1,000 population): births, 43·4; deaths, 16·8. infant mortality, 2001, 109 per 1,000 live births. Life expectancy, 2003, 53·4 years for males and 54·1 for females. Annual population growth rate, 1992–2002, 2·4%; fertility rate, 2001, 6·0 births per woman.

CLIMATE

A tropical climate, with high rainfall near the coast and constant heat, but conditions are a little cooler on the plateau. The wet season on the coast lasts from May to Nov., but only to Oct. inland. Conakry, Jan. 80°F (26·7°C), July 77°F (25°C). Annual rainfall 172" (4,293 mm).

CONSTITUTION AND GOVERNMENT

There is a 114-member *National Assembly*, 38 of whose members are elected on a first-past-the-post system, and the remainder from national lists by proportional representation.

On 11 Nov. 2001 a referendum was held in which 98·4% of votes cast were in favour of President Conté remaining in office for a third term, requiring an amendment to the constitution (previously allowing a maximum two presidential terms). The referendum, which also increased the presidential mandate from five to seven years, was boycotted by opposition parties.

National Anthem

'Peuple d'Afrique, le passé historique' ('People of Africa, the historic past'); words anonymous, tune by Fodeba Keita.

RECENT ELECTIONS

Presidential elections were held on 21 Dec. 2003. President Lansana Conté of the Party of Unity and Progress (PUP) was re-elected with 95·6% of the vote against 4·4% won by Mamadou Bhoye Barry of the Union for National Progress (UPR). Opposition parties boycotted the elections. Turnout was reported to be 82·8%.

Parliamentary elections took place on 30 June 2002. The PUP gained 85 out of 114 seats with 61·6% of votes cast and the Union for Progress and Revival gained 20 seats with 26·6%. The turnout was 72·5%.

CURRENT ADMINISTRATION

President: Gen. Lansana Conté; b. 1934 (PUP; seized power 3 April 1984, most recently re-elected 21 Dec. 2003).

In April 2006 the cabinet comprised:

Minister of Agriculture and Animal Husbandry: Jean Paul Sarr. *Commerce, Industry and Small- and Medium-Scale Enterprise:* Dr Djéné Saran Camara. *Co-operation:* Elhadj Thierno Habib Diallo. *Economy and Finance:* Mady Kaba Camara. *Employment and Public Administration:* Alpha Ibrahima Kéira. *Environment:* Abdel Kader Sangaré. *Fishing and Aquaculture:* Ibrahima Sory Touré. *Foreign Affairs:* Fatoumata

Kaba. *Higher Education and Scientific Research:* Sékou Décasy Camara. *Information:* Hadja Aïssatou Bella Diallo. *Justice and Keeper of the Seals:* Sylla Mamadou Syma. *Mining and Geology:* Ahmed Tidiane Souaré. *Planning:* Eugène Camara. *Posts and Telecommunications:* Jean-Claude Sultan. *Public Works:* Bana Sidibé. *Pre-University and Civic Education:* Galéma Guilavogui. *Public Health:* Dr Amara Cissé. *Security:* Ousmane Camara. *Social Affairs and Promotion of Women and Children:* Mariama Aribot. *Technical Teaching and Professional Training:* Ibrahima Soumah. *Territorial Administration and Decentralization:* Kiridi Bangoura. *Tourism, Hotels and Handicrafts:* Hadja Koumba Diakité. *Transport:* Aliou Condé. *Urban Planning and Housing:* Ouo-Ouo Blaise Foromou. *Water Power and Energy:* Dioubaté Hadj Fatoumata Binta. *Youth, Sports and Culture:* Fodé Soumah. *Secretary General of the Government:* Elhadj Oury Baïlo Diallo.

Government Website (French only): http://www.guinee.gov.gn

CURRENT LEADERS

Gen. Lansana Conté

Position
President

Introduction
Gen. Lansana Conté won a third term as president on 21 Dec. 2003. Many opposition parties boycotted the election claiming fraud and irregularities. With his health in serious decline, it is unsure whether Conté will survive a full term of office.

Early Life
Lansana Conté was born in 1934 in Dubréka, Guinea. He was educated in Dubréka before completing his military training at preparatory schools in France and West Africa.

In 1955 he enlisted in the French Army and was posted to Algeria during the war of independence. Guinea gained independence from France on 2 Oct. 1958 and when Conté returned home from military service he joined the new national army as a sergeant. In 1962 he attended the Camp Alpha Officer's School in Conakry, Guinea and became a second lieutenant the following year before a promotion to lieutenant in 1965. In Nov. 1970 Guinean exiles invaded the country in an attempt to overthrow President Ahmed Sékou Touré. Conté was part of the military team that repelled the invasion and, in recognition of his contribution, was promoted to captain in 1971. Four years later he became assistant chief of staff of the army.

In 1977 Conté began his political career when he headed Guinea's delegation during negotiations to resolve a border dispute with Guinea-Bissau. In 1980 he was elected to the National Assembly.

On 3 April 1984, following the death of President Touré, Conté led a bloodless coup to overthrow the interim government of Prime Minister Louis Lansana Beaogui. Conté created the Military Committee for National Recovery (CMRN), suspended the constitution and the national assembly and banned all political activity. He denounced the Touré regime, released over 200 political prisoners and encouraged those Guineans exiled during Touré's rule to return to the country. He was proclaimed president two days later.

Career in Office
Conté's presidency has been plagued by controversy. In July 1985 Prime Minister Diarra Traoré tried to seize power while Conté was attending an ECOWAS summit in Togo. Conté's troops prevented the coup and on his return 100 military personnel, including Traoré, were executed.

Conté became army general in 1990 and shortly afterwards the government introduced a new constitution which included provision for the establishment of civilian government. In June 1991 the CMRN was replaced by the Transitional Committee for National Recovery (CTRN).

In 1992 Conté legalized political parties in the build-up to presidential elections in Dec. 1993, the first multi-party election since independence. Conté's new party, the Party of Unity and Progress (PUP), was victorious but the elections were blighted by serious irregularities. In 1996 the government was subject to another unsuccessful coup attempt. Around a quarter of the Guinean army mutinied in protest over salaries and poor conditions and many died. A multi-party presidential election was held in 1998 and, despite a number of flaws and protests, Conté was confirmed as president.

In Nov. 2001 Conté's government approved constitutional amendments allowing the president to run for more than two consecutive terms. The referendum was boycotted by the opposition, who referred to the move as a 'constitutional coup' designed to ensure Conté's lifelong rule. Conté was confirmed for a third term in Dec. 2003 with all but one of the opposition parties boycotting elections. In Jan. 2005 Conté survived an assassination attempt.

Conté's health has been in serious decline over several years. In Nov. 2003 opposition leader Jean-Marie Dore was detained after publicly questioning Conté's physical ability to continue as president. Presidential elections are scheduled for 2008.

DEFENCE

Conscription is for two years. Defence expenditure totalled US$71m. in 2003 (US$9 per capita), representing 1·9% of GDP.

Army
The Army of 8,500 (2002) includes 7,500 conscripts. There are also three paramilitary forces: People's Militia (7,000), Gendarmerie (1,000) and Republican Guard (1,600).

Navy
A small force of 400 (2002) operates from bases at Conakry and Kakanda.

Air Force
Personnel (2002) 800. There were eight combat aircraft including MiG-17s and MiG-21s.

INTERNATIONAL RELATIONS

Guinea is a member of the UN, WTO, the African Union, African Development Bank, ECOWAS, IOM, OIC, Islamic Development Bank, International Organization of the Francophonie and is an ACP member state of the ACP-EU relationship.

ECONOMY

Agriculture produced 24·2% of GDP in 2002, industry 36·6% and services 39·1%.

Currency
The monetary unit is the *Guinean franc* (GNF). Inflation was 12·9% in 2003 and 17·5% in 2004. In June 2002 foreign exchange reserves were US$192m. and total money supply was 600,100m. Guinean francs.

Budget
Revenue for 2002 was 909,700m. Guinean francs and expenditure 1,281,800m. Guinean francs.

Of total government revenue in 2002, tax revenue accounted for 76·2%, grants 16·0% and non-tax revenue 7·8%. Current expenditure accounted for 61·5% of total expenditure and capital expenditure 38·5%. VAT was applied to non-essential goods in July 1996.

Performance
Real GDP growth in 2004 was 2·7% (1·2% in 2003). Total GDP in 2004 was US$3·5bn.

Banking and Finance

In 1986 the Central Bank (*Governor*, Mohamed Alkhaly Daffé) and commercial banking were restructured, and commercial banks returned to the private sector. There were seven commercial banks in 2002. There is an Islamic bank.

ENERGY AND NATURAL RESOURCES

Environment

Guinea's carbon dioxide emissions from the consumption and flaring of fossil fuels in 2002 were the equivalent of 0·2 tonnes per capita.

Electricity

In 2000 installed capacity was 0·2m. kW. Production was approximately 569m. kWh in 2000; consumption per capita was an estimated 70 kWh.

Minerals

Mining produced 16% of GDP in 1999. Guinea possesses over 25% of the world's bauxite reserves and is the second largest producer after Australia. Output: bauxite (2001), 15,700,000 tonnes; alumina (2002), 701,936 tonnes; diamonds (2001), 370,000 carats; gold (2000), 13,104 kg. There are also deposits of granite, iron ore, chrome, copper, lead, manganese, molybdenum, nickel, platinum, uranium and zinc.

Agriculture

Subsistence agriculture supports about 70% of the population. There were 890,000 ha. of arable land in 2001 and 635,000 ha. of permanent crops. 95,000 ha. were irrigated in 2001. The chief crops (production, 2000, in 1,000 tonnes) are: cassava, 870; rice, 750; plantains, 429; sugarcane, 220; groundnuts, 182; bananas, 150; sweet potatoes, 135; maize, 90; yams, 88; mangoes, 83; pineapples, 72; palm kernels, 52; palm oil, 50; seed cotton, 50; taro, 29; coffee, 21; cotton lint, 21.

Livestock (2000): cattle, 2·37m.; goats, 864,000; sheep, 687,000; pigs, 54,000; chickens, 9m.

Forestry

The area under forests in 2000 was 6·93m. ha., or 28·2% of the total land area. In 2001, 12·14m. cu. metres of roundwood were cut.

Fisheries

In 2001 the total catch was approximately 90,000 tonnes, almost entirely from sea fishing.

INDUSTRY

Manufacturing accounted for 4·4% of GDP in 2001. Cement, corrugated and sheet iron, beer, soft drinks and cigarettes are produced.

Labour

In 1996 the labour force was 3,565,000 (53% males). The agricultural sector employs 80% of the workforce.

INTERNATIONAL TRADE

Foreign debt was US$3,401m. in 2002. Imports require authorization and there are restrictions on the export of capital.

Imports and Exports

Imports and exports for calendar years in US$1m.:

	1998	1999	2000	2001	2002
Imports f.o.b.	572·0	581·7	587·1	561·9	668·4
Exports f.o.b.	693·0	635·7	666·3	731·0	886·0

Main imports by value, 2000: refined petroleum, 25%; food, 18%; machinery and apparatus, 10%; road vehicles, 9%. Principal import suppliers, 2000: Côte d'Ivoire, 21%; France, 20%; Belgium,

8%; USA, 8%; Japan, 6%. Main exports by value, 1998: bauxite, 46%; gold, 18%; alumina, 14%; diamonds, 7%. Principal export markets, 2000: France, 33%; USA, 13%; Spain, 10%; Ireland, 9%; Germany, 6%.

COMMUNICATIONS

Roads

In 2002 there were about 4,368 km of main and national roads, 7,979 km of secondary roads and 18,153 km of other roads; 16·5% of all roads were paved. In 2002 there were 26,800 passenger cars, or 3·5 per 1,000 inhabitants, and 13,300 trucks and vans.

Rail

A railway connects Conakry with Kankan (662 km). A line 134 km long linking bauxite deposits at Sangaredi with Port Kamsar was opened in 1973 (carried 12·5m. tonnes in 1993), a third line links Conakry and Fria (144 km; carried 1m. tonnes in 1993) and a fourth, the Kindia Bauxite Railway (102 km) linking Débéle with Conakry, carried 3m. tonnes in 1994.

Civil Aviation

There is an international airport at Conakry (Gbessia). In 2003 there were scheduled flights to Abidjan, Accra, Bamako, Banjul, Bissau, Brussels, Casablanca, Dakar, Freetown, Lagos and Paris. In 2001 Conakry handled 240,000 passengers (219,000 on international flights) and 3,700 tonnes of freight. In 1999 scheduled airline traffic of Guinean-based carriers flew 800,000 km, carrying 59,000 passengers (all on international flights).

Shipping

There are ports at Conakry and for bauxite exports at Kamsar (opened 1973). Merchant shipping totalled 12,000 GRT in 2002.

Telecommunications

The Société des Télécommunications de Guinée is 40% state-owned. In 2002 there were 116,800 telephone subscribers, equivalent to 15·2 per 1,000 population, and 42,000 PCs in use (5·5 per 1,000 persons). There were 90,800 mobile phone subscribers in 2002 and 4,600 fax machines. In 2002 Guinea had 35,000 Internet users.

Postal Services

In 2003 there were 61 post offices, or one for every 139,000 persons.

SOCIAL INSTITUTIONS

Justice

There are *tribunaux du premier degré* at Conakry and Kankan, and a *juge de paix* at Nzérékoré. The High Court, Court of Appeal and Superior Tribunal of Cassation are at Conakry. The death penalty is in force, and was used in 2001 for the first time in 17 years.

The population in penal institutions in 2002 was 3,070 (37 per 100,000 of national population).

Education

In 1998 adult literacy was 36·0%. In 2000–01 there were 853,623 pupils with 19,244 teachers in primary schools; and 232,567 pupils with 5,099 teachers (1997–98) in general education in secondary schools. In 1995 there were 28,311 pupils (6,143 girls) and 1,407 teachers in 61 *lycées* and 8,569 pupils (3,013) and 1,268 teachers in 55 institutions of professional education. In 1996 there were two universities with 5,735 students and 525 academic staff.

Besides French, there are eight official languages taught in schools: Fulani, Malinké, Susu, Kissi, Kpelle, Loma, Basari and Koniagi.

In 2000–01 total expenditure on education came to 2·0% of GNP and 25·6% of total government spending.

Health
In 2003 there were 48 hospitals. There were (2000) 764 doctors, 38 dentists, 199 pharmacists, 299 midwives and 3,506 trained nursing personnel.

RELIGION
79% of the population are Muslim, 9% Christian. Traditional animist beliefs are still found.

CULTURE

World Heritage Sites
Guinea shares one site with Côte d'Ivoire on the UNESCO World Heritage List: Mount Nimba Strict Nature Reserve (inscribed on the list in 1981). The dense forested slopes are home to viviparous toads and chimpanzees among other fauna.

Broadcasting
Broadcasting is the responsibility of the state-controlled Radiodiffusion Télévision Guinéenne. There were 357,000 TV receivers (colour by SECAM H) in 2001 and 422,000 radio receivers in 2000.

Press
There is one daily newspaper (circulation 20,000).

Tourism
There were 43,000 foreign tourists in 2002 bringing in revenue of US$31m.

DIPLOMATIC REPRESENTATIVES
Of Guinea in the United Kingdom (83 Victoria St., London, SW1H 0HW)
Ambassador: Lansana Keïta.

Of the United Kingdom in Guinea (4th Floor, ETI-Bull Building, Boulevard du Commerce, Commune de Kaloum, Conakry)
Ambassador: John McManus.

Of Guinea in the USA (2112 Leroy Pl., NW, Washington, D.C., 20008)
Ambassador: Alpha Oumar Rafiou Barry.

Of the USA in Guinea (Rue KA 038, Conakry)
Ambassador: Jackson McDonald.

Of Guinea to the United Nations
Ambassador: Alpha Ibrahima Sow.

Of Guinea to the European Union
Ambassador: Kazaliou Balde.

FURTHER READING

Bulletin Statistique et Economique de la Guinée. Monthly. Conakry

Binns, Margaret, *Guinea.* [Bibliography] ABC-Clio, Oxford and Santa Barbara (CA), 1996

National Statistical Office: Direction Nationale de la Statistique, BP 221, Conakry.
Website (French only): http://www.stat-guinee.org

GUINEA-BISSAU

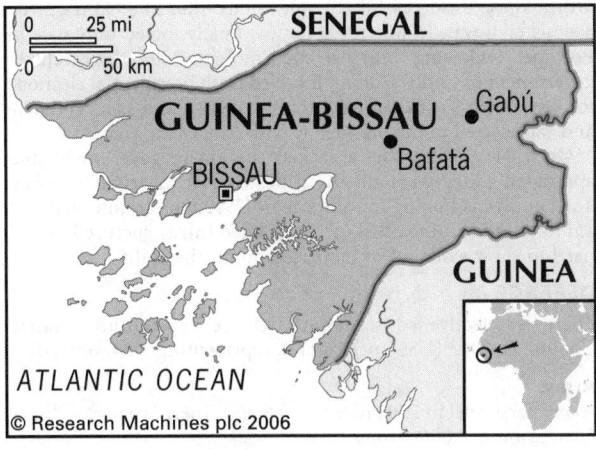

Republica da Guiné-Bissau

Capital: Bissau
Population projection, 2010: 1·83m.
GDP per capita, 2003: (PPP$) 711
HDI/world rank: 0·348/172

KEY HISTORICAL EVENTS

Portugal was the major power in the area throughout the colonial period. In 1974, after the Portuguese revolution, Portugal abandoned the struggle to keep Guinea-Bissau and independence was formally recognized on 10 Sept. 1974. In 1975 Cape Verde also became independent but the two countries remained separate sovereign states. On 14 Nov. 1980 a coup d'état was in part inspired by resentment in Guinea-Bissau over the privileges enjoyed by Cape Verdians. Guineans obtained a more prominent role under the new government. On 16 May 1984 a new constitution was approved based on Marxist principles but after 1986 there was a return to private enterprise in an attempt to solve critical economic problems and to lift the country out of poverty. A year-long civil war broke out in 1998 between army rebels and the country's long-time ruler. Neighbouring Senegal and Guinea sent troops in to aid the government. On 7 May 1999 President João Bernardo Vieira was ousted in a military coup led by former chief of staff Gen. Ansumane Mané, whom the president had dismissed in 1998. Following the coup Mané briefly headed a military junta before National Assembly speaker Malam Bacai Sanhá took power as acting president. After presidential elections in Nov. 1999 and Jan. 2000 Kumba Ialá gained the presidency in a landslide victory. Marking a change towards a democratic future in Guinea-Bissau's politics, Ialá rejected a demand made by the outgoing junta for special consultative status following the elections. Kumba Ialá was overthrown in a coup in Sept. 2003 led by army chief of staff Gen. Veríssimo Correia Seabra.

TERRITORY AND POPULATION

Guinea-Bissau is bounded by Senegal in the north, the Atlantic Ocean in the west and by Guinea in the east and south. It includes the adjacent archipelago of Bijagós. Area, 36,125 sq. km (13,948 sq. miles). Population (1991 census), 983,367. Population estimate, 2005: 1,586,000 (803,000 females); density, 43·9 per sq. km. The capital, Bissau, had an estimated 274,000 inhabitants in 1999. In 2003, 66·0% of the population were rural.

The UN gives a projected population for 2010 of 1·83m.

The area, population, and chief town of the capital and the eight regions:

Region	Area in sq. km	Population (1991 census)	Chief town
Bissau City	78	197,610	—
Bafatá	5,981	143,377	Bafatá
Biombo	838	60,420	Quinhámel
Bolama	2,624	26,691	Bolama
Cacheu	5,175	146,980	Cacheu
Gabú	9,150	134,971	Gabú
Oio	5,403	156,084	Farim
Quinara	3,138	44,793	Fulacunda
Tombali	3,736	72,441	Catió

The main ethnic groups were (1998) the Balante (30%), Fulani (20%), Manjaco (14%), Mandingo (13%) and Papeis (7%). Portuguese remains the official language, but Crioulo is spoken throughout the country.

SOCIAL STATISTICS

2000 births (estimates), 61,000; deaths, 26,000. Estimated birth rate in 2000 was 44·6 per 1,000 population; estimated death rate, 19·3. Annual population growth rate, 1992–2002, 3·0%. Life expectancy in 2003 was 46·2 years for women and 43·2 for men. Infant mortality, 2001, 130 per 1,000 live births; fertility rate, 2001, 6·0 births per woman.

CLIMATE

The tropical climate has a wet season from June to Nov., when rains are abundant, but the hot, dry Harmattan wind blows from Dec. to May. Bissau, Jan. 76°F (24·4°C), July 80°F (26·7°C). Annual rainfall 78" (1,950 mm).

CONSTITUTION AND GOVERNMENT

A new Constitution was promulgated on 16 May 1984 and has been amended five times since, most recently in 1996. The Revolutionary Council, established following the 1980 coup, was replaced by a 15-member Council of State, while in April 1984 a new National People's Assembly was elected comprising 150 representatives elected by and from the directly-elected regional councils for five-year terms. The sole political movement was the *Partido Africano da Independência da Guiné e Cabo Verde* (PAIGC), but in Dec. 1990 a policy of 'integral multi-partyism' was announced, and in May 1991 the National Assembly voted unanimously to abolish the law making the PAIGC the sole party. The *President* is Head of State and Government and is elected for a five-year term. The *National Assembly* has 100 members.

After the coup of Sept. 2003 a transitional government was appointed by the National Transition Council (CNT) which governed until elections in March 2004. The CNT, which was to function as the parliament until the elections, comprised 25 military officers and 31 representatives of 23 political parties and eight groups from civil society.

National Anthem

'Sol, suor, o verde e mar' ('Sun, sweat, the green and the sea'); words and tune by A. Lopes Cabral.

RECENT ELECTIONS

Presidential elections were held in two rounds on 19 June and 24 July 2005. In the first round former acting president Malam Bacai Sanhá (African Party for the Independence of Guinea and Cape Verde) took 35·5% of votes cast, ahead of former military ruler and president João Bernardo Vieira with 28·9%, a further former president Kumba Ialá (Party for Social Renewal) with 25·0% and former prime minister Francisco Fadul (United Social Democratic Party) with 2·9%. Turnout was 87·3%. In the second round turnout was 78·6%. João Bernardo Vieira won with 52·4% of the vote, against 47·6% for Malam Bacai Sanhá.

At the parliamentary elections on 28 March 2004 turnout was 76·3%. The African Party for the Independence of Guinea and Cape Verde (PAIGC) won 33·9% of the vote (45 of 100 seats), the Party for Social Renewal (PRS) 26·5% (35 seats) and the United Social Democratic Party (PUSD) 17·6% (17 seats). The Electoral Union (UE) took two seats and the United Popular Alliance (APU) one seat.

CURRENT ADMINISTRATION

President: João Bernardo Vieira; b. 1939 (took office on 1 Oct. 2005; he had previously ruled from 1980 to 1999 after initially assuming power through a bloodless military coup).

In March 2006 the government comprised:

Prime Minister: Aristides Gomes (ind.); b. 1954 (since 2 Nov. 2005).

Minister for the Presidency of the Council of Ministers, for Social Communication and Relations with Parliament: Rui Diã de Sousa. *Foreign Affairs, International Co-operation and Communities:* António Isaac Monteiro. *Defence:* Hélder Proença. *Interior:* Ernesto Carvalho. *Territorial Administration:* Braima Embaló. *Civil Service and Labour:* Carlos Costa. *Economy:* Issuf Sanhá. *Finance:* Vítor Mandinga. *Social Solidarity, Family and the Fight against Poverty:* Adelina Na Tamba. *National and Higher Education:* Tcherno Djaló. *Agriculture and Rural Development:* Sola Nkilin Na Bitchita. *Public Works, Construction and Urbanization:* Carlitos Barai. *Transport and Communications:* Admiro Nelson Belo. *Fisheries and Maritime Economy:* Abdú Mané. *Natural Resources:* Aristides Ocante da Silva. *Commerce, Industry and Handicrafts:* Pascoal Domingos Baticã. *Justice:* Namuano Dias Gomes. *Tourism:* Francisco Conduto de Pina. *Public Health:* Antónia Mendes Teixeira.

President of the Assembly: Francisco Benante (PAIGC).

CURRENT LEADERS

João Bernardo Vieira

Position
President

Introduction
After leading a military coup in 1980 João Vieira held the presidency until 1999, when he was ousted by the army. After six years in exile he returned to Guinea-Bissau to contest the 2005 presidential elections, modelling himself as a 'soldier of peace'. He narrowly won with 52% of the vote and took office in Oct. 2005.

Early Life
João Bernardo (Nino) Vieira was born on 27 April 1939 in Bissau, then part of Portuguese Guinea. He trained as an electrician and in 1960 joined the African Party for the Independence of Guinea and Cape Verde (PAIGC). From 1961 Vieira was the party's political commissioner in the Catio region and from 1964 he was military head of the Southern Front in the war of independence. In 1970 he was promoted to head of military operations in the War Council. Following independence in Sept. 1974, Vieira became commander in chief of the armed forces under President Luis Cabral. On 14 Nov. 1980 Vieira overthrew Cabral in a coup and appointed himself president, chair of the revolutionary council and, the following year, secretary general of the PAIGC.

Career in Office
For the next 18 years Vieira led the country towards a market economy and a multi-party system. Having retired from the army

in May 1994, he stood as the PAIGC candidate in the country's first free presidential elections, narrowly defeating Kumba Ialá of the Party for Social Renewal. Criticized for his increasingly autocratic style of leadership, Vieira came under fire from sections of the army, whose unsuccessful attempt to oust him in 1998 triggered a short civil war. In May 1999 he was finally forced into exile in Portugal. Following a further coup in Sept. 2003, the caretaker government of Carlos Gomes, Jr tabled fresh presidential elections for Oct. 2005. Vieira returned from exile to stand as a candidate and was elected to the presidency with 52% of the vote.

On 1 Nov. 2005 Vieira sacked the entire government and appointed a long-term ally, Aristides Gomes, as prime minister. The country is hoping for more than US$200m. in international aid to rebuild Guinea-Bissau's devastated infrastructure but will need to show evidence of increased political stability.

DEFENCE

There is selective conscription. Defence expenditure totalled US$9m. in 2003 (US$6 per capita), representing 4·0% of GDP.

Army

Army personnel in 2002 numbered 6,800. There is a paramilitary Gendarmerie 2,000 strong.

Navy

The naval flotilla, based at Bissau, numbered 350 in 2002.

Air Force

Formation of a small Air Force began in 1978. Personnel (2002) 100 with three combat aircraft (MiG-17s).

INTERNATIONAL RELATIONS

Guinea-Bissau is a member of the UN, WTO, the African Union, African Development Bank, ECOWAS, IOM, OIC, Islamic Development Bank, International Organization of the Francophonie and is an ACP member state of the ACP-EU relationship.

ECONOMY

In 2002 agriculture accounted for 62·4% of GDP (one of the highest percentages of any country), industry 13·1% and services 24·5%.

Currency

On 2 May 1997 Guinea-Bissau joined the French Franc Zone, and the *peso* was replaced by the franc CFA at 65 pesos = one franc CFA. The *franc CFA* (XOF) has a parity rate of 655·957 francs CFA to one euro. Foreign exchange reserves were US$84m. in May 2002. Inflation was 3·0% in both 2003 and 2004. Total money supply in May 2002 was 77,011m. francs CFA.

Budget

Revenue in 2001 was 47,530m. francs CFA; expenditure totalled 63,162m. francs CFA.

Performance

Real GDP growth in 2004 was 4·3% (0·6% in 2003). Total GDP in 2004 was US$0·3bn.

Banking and Finance

The bank of issue and the central bank is the regional Central Bank of West African States (BCEAO). The *Acting Governor* is Justin Baro Damo. There are four other banks (Banco da Africa Occidental; Banco Internacional de Guiné-Bissau; Caixa de Crédito de Guiné; Caixa Económica Postal).

The stock exchange of the Economic and Monetary Union of West Africa is in Abidjan.

ENERGY AND NATURAL RESOURCES

Environment

Carbon dioxide emissions from the consumption and flaring of fossil fuels in 2002 were the equivalent of 0·3 tonnes per capita.

Electricity

Installed capacity in 2000 was 21,000 kW. Production was about 58m. kWh in 2000; consumption per capita was an estimated 48 kWh.

Minerals

Mineral resources are not exploited. There are estimated to be 200m. tonnes of bauxite and 112m. tonnes of phosphate.

Agriculture

Agriculture employs 80% of the labour force. There were 300,000 ha. of arable land in 2001 and 248,000 ha. of permanent crops. Chief crops (production, 2000, in 1,000 tonnes) are: rice, 138; coconuts, 46; cashew nuts, 42; plantains, 38; millet, 35; sorghum, 26; groundnuts, 19; cassava, 17; maize, 10; copra, 9; palm kernels, 9; sugarcane, 6.

Livestock (2000): cattle, 530,000; pigs, 345,000; goats, 325,000; sheep, 285,000; chickens, 1m.

Forestry

The area covered by forests in 2000 was 2·19m. ha., or 60·5% of the total land area. In 2001, 592,000 cu. metres of roundwood were cut.

Fisheries

Total catch in 2001 came to approximately 5,000 tonnes, of which 96% was from sea fishing. Revenue from fishing licences may be worth as much as 45% of government revenue.

INDUSTRY

Manufacturing accounted for 10·1% of GDP in 2001. Output of main products: vegetable oils (3·4m. litres in 2000), sawnwood (16,000 tonnes in 2001), soap (2,500 tonnes in 2000) and animal hides and skins (1,400 tonnes in 2001).

Labour

The labour force in 1996 was 514,000 (60% males).

INTERNATIONAL TRADE

Foreign debt totalled US$699m. in 2002.

Imports and Exports

Trade, 2003, in US$1m. (2002 in brackets): imports f.o.b., 65·3 (58·5); exports f.o.b., 65·0 (54·4). Main imports in 2001 were: foodstuffs, 18·7%; transport equipment, 13·2%; equipment and machinery, 7·7%. Exports: cashew nuts, 95·6%; cotton, 2·3%; logs, 1·5%. Guinea-Bissau supplies more than 10% of the world market of cashew nuts.

Main import suppliers, 2001: Portugal, 30·9%; Senegal, 28·3%; China, 11·3%; Netherlands, 6·8%. Main export markets, 2001: India, 85·6%; Portugal, 3·8%; Senegal, 2·5%; France, 1·7%.

COMMUNICATIONS

Roads

In 2002 there were about 4,400 km of roads, of which 2,400 km were national roads. There were 3,400 passenger cars (2·6 per 1,000 inhabitants) and 2,500 trucks in 2002.

Civil Aviation

The national carrier is Transportes Aéreos de Guiné-Bissau. There is an international airport serving Bissau (Osvaldo Vieira). In 2003 there were scheduled flights to Banjul, Conakry, Dakar, Lisbon, Nouakchott, Praia and Sal.

Shipping

The main port is Bissau; minor ports are Bolama, Cacheu and Catió. In 2002 the merchant marine totalled 6,000 GRT.

Telecommunications

Telephone subscribers numbered 11,200 in 2002 (8·9 per 1,000 persons) and there were 600 fax machines. In 2002 there were 5,000 Internet users.

Postal Services

In 2003 there were 20 post offices.

SOCIAL INSTITUTIONS

Justice

The death penalty was abolished for all crimes in 1993.

Education

Adult literacy was 39·6% in 2001 (male, 55·2%; female, 24·7%). Some 60% of children of primary school age attend school. In 1999–2000 there were 150,041 pupils at primary schools (3,405 teachers), 25,736 at secondary schools (1,226 teachers) and 463 students in tertiary education. In 1999–2000 total expenditure on education came to 2·3% of GNP and 4·8% of total government spending.

Health

In 1999 there were two national, seven regional hospitals and 26 prefectorial hospitals. In 2003 there were 893 physicians and dentists, 1,092 nurses and 193 pharmacists.

RELIGION

In 2001 about 38% of the population were Muslim and about 12% Christian (mainly Roman Catholic). The remainder held traditional animist beliefs.

CULTURE

Broadcasting

In 2000 there were 56,000 radio receivers. A television service started in 1989 (colour by SECAM V). In 2001 there were 44,000 TV receivers.

Press

In 1996 there were three newspapers, including one privately owned.

Tourism

There were 8,000 foreign visitors in 2001.

DIPLOMATIC REPRESENTATIVES

Of Guinea-Bissau in the United Kingdom
Chargé d'Affaires a.i.: Fali Embalo (resides in Paris).
Honorary Consul: Mabel Figueirdo da Fonseca Smith (PO Box 393, Tunbridge Wells, Kent, TN4 9YZ).

Of the United Kingdom in Guinea-Bissau
Ambassador: Peter Newall (resides in Dakar, Senegal).

Of Guinea-Bissau in the USA (PO Box 33813, Washington, D.C., 20033)
Ambassador: Vacant.
Chargé d'Affaires a.i.: Henrique Adriano Da Silva.

Of the USA in Guinea-Bissau
Ambassador: Richard Jackson (resides in Dakar, Senegal).

Of Guinea-Bissau to the United Nations
Ambassador: Alfredo Lopes Cabral.

Of Guinea-Bissau to the European Union
Ambassador: Vacant.
Chargé d'Affaires a.i.: Serafim Ianga.

FURTHER READING

Forrest, J. A., *Guinea-Bissau: Power, Conflict and Renewal in a West African Nation.* Boulder (CO), 1992
Galli, Rosemary, *Guinea-Bissau.* [Bibliography] ABC-Clio, Oxford and Santa Barbara (CA), 1990

National Statistical Office: Instituto Nacional de Estadística e Censos (INEC), CP 06 Bissau.
Website (Portuguese only): http://www.stat-guinebissau.com

GUYANA

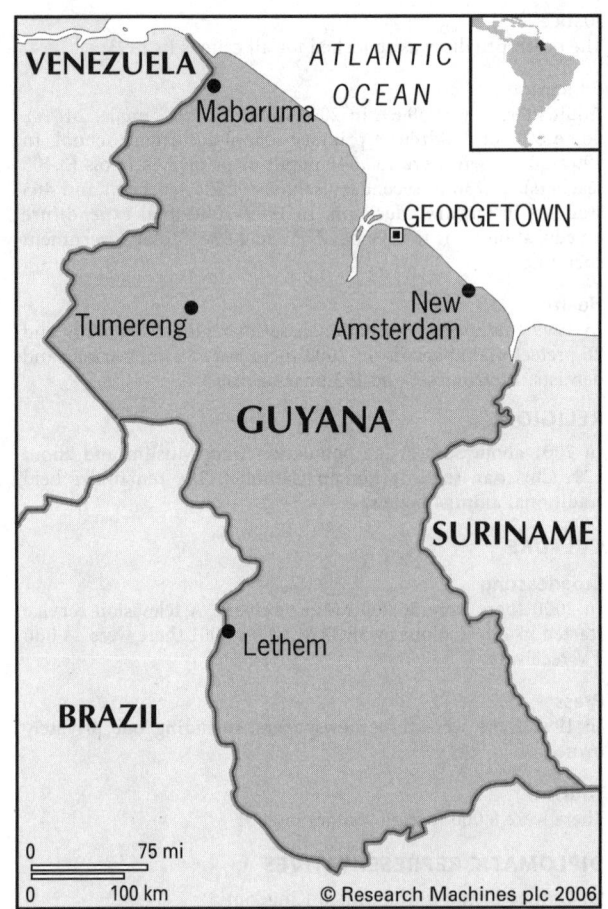

Co-operative Republic of Guyana

Capital: Georgetown
Population projection, 2010: 751,000
GDP per capita, 2003: (PPP$) 4,230
HDI/world rank: 0·720/107

KEY HISTORICAL EVENTS

First settled by the Dutch West Indian Company about 1620, the territory was captured by Britain to whom it was ceded in 1814 and named British Guiana. African slaves were transported to Guyana in the 18th century to work the sugar plantations, with East Indian and Chinese indentured labourers following in the 19th century. From 1950 the anti-colonial struggle was spearheaded by the People's Progressive Party (PPP) led by Cheddi Jagan and Forbes Burnham. By the time internal autonomy was granted in 1961 Burnham had split with Jagan to form the more moderate People's National Congress (PNC). Guyana became an independent member of the Commonwealth in 1966 with Burnham as the first prime minister, later president. By the 1980s, desperate economic straits had forced Guyana to seek outside help which came on condition of restoring free elections. Dr Jagan returned to power in 1992. Following his death in March 1997 his wife, Janet Jagan, was sworn in as President.

TERRITORY AND POPULATION

Guyana is situated on the northeast coast of Latin America on the Atlantic Ocean, with Suriname on the east, Venezuela on the west and Brazil on the south and west. Area, 214,999 sq. km (83,013 sq. miles). In 2002 the census population was 751,223; density 3·5 per sq. km. Estimated population (2005), 751,000.

The UN gives a projected population for 2010 of 751,000.

Guyana has the highest proportion of rural population in South America, with only 37·6% living in urban areas in 2003. Ethnic groups by origin: 49% Indian, 36% African, 7% mixed race, 7% Amerindian and 1% others. The capital is Georgetown (2002 provisional census population, 34,179; urban agglomeration, 137,330); other towns are Linden, New Amsterdam, Anna Regina and Corriverton.

Venezuela demanded the return of the Essequibo region in 1963. It was finally agreed in March 1983 that the UN Secretary-General should mediate. There was also an unresolved claim (1984) by Suriname for the return of an area between the New River and the Corentyne River.

The official language is English.

SOCIAL STATISTICS

2004 estimates: births, 16,000; deaths, 7,000. Rates, 2004 estimates (per 1,000 population): birth, 21; death, 9. Life expectancy at birth in 2003; male 60·0 years and female 66·1 years. Annual population growth rate, 1992–2002, 0·4%. Infant mortality, 2001, 54 per 1,000 live births; fertility rate, 2001, 2·4 births per woman.

CLIMATE

A tropical climate, with rainy seasons from April to July and Nov. to Jan. Humidity is high all the year but temperatures are moderated by sea-breezes. Rainfall increases from 90" (2,280 mm) on the coast to 140" (3,560 mm) in the forest zone. Georgetown, Jan. 79°F (26·1°C), July 81°F (27·2°C). Annual rainfall 87" (2,175 mm).

CONSTITUTION AND GOVERNMENT

A new Constitution was promulgated in Oct. 1980. There is an *Executive Presidency*, and a 68-member *National Assembly*, with 65 members elected by popular vote, one elected Speaker of the National Assembly and two non-voting members appointed by the president. Elections for five-year terms are held under the single-list system of proportional representation, with the whole of the country forming one electoral area and each voter casting a vote for a party list of candidates.

National Anthem

'Dear land of Guyana'; words by A. L. Luker, tune by R. Potter.

RECENT ELECTIONS

Bharrat Jagdeo and the People's Progressive Party (PPP) won the presidential and parliamentary elections of 19 March 2001. In the presidential election incumbent Bharrat Jagdeo received 209,031 votes (53·1% of the vote), with former president Desmond Hoyte of the People's National Congress (PNC) receiving 164,074 (41·7%). The PPP won 35 seats with 52·6% of votes in the parliamentary election, compared to 27 and 41·5% for the PNC.

CURRENT ADMINISTRATION

President: Bharrat Jagdeo; b. 1964 (PPP; sworn in 11 Aug. 1999 and re-elected in March 2001).

In March 2006 the government comprised:

Prime Minister and Minister of Public Works: Samuel Hinds; b. 1943 (PPP; first sworn in 9 Oct. 1992 and now in office for the third time).

Minister in the Office of the President with Responsibility for Parliamentary Affairs: Reepu Daman Persaud. *Attorney General and Minister of Legal Affairs:* Doodnauth Singh. *Cabinet Secretary:* Roger Luncheon. *Minister of Finance:* Sasenarine Kowlessar. *Foreign Affairs:* Samuel Rudolph Insanally. *Foreign Trade:* Clement Rohee. *Health:* Leslie Ramsammy. *Education:* Henry Jeffrey. *Home Affairs:* Gail Teixeira. *Culture, Youth and Sports:* Carl Anthony Xavier. *Trade, Industry and Tourism:* Manzoor Nadir. *Amerindian Affairs:* Carolyn Rodrigues. *Housing and Water:* Shaik Baksh. *Information:* Vacant. *Local Government:* Harripersaud Nokta. *Human Services, Social Security and Labour:* Dale Bisnauth. *Public Service:* Jennifer Westford. *Agriculture:* Satyadeow Sawh. *Fisheries, Crops and Livestock:* Satyadeow Sawah. *Transport and Hydraulics:* Harry Narine Nawbatt.

Government Information Agency Website:
  http://www.gina.gov.gy

CURRENT LEADERS

Bharrat Jagdeo

Position
President

Introduction
Bharrat Jagdeo, representing the People's Progressive Party (PPP), took over from President Janet Jagan in 1999, when the latter retired on health grounds, and was re-elected in 2001. Jagdeo's main challenges have been placating civil unrest caused by rivalry between supporters of the PPP and the opposition People's National Congress (PNC) and negotiating settlements of border disputes with Suriname and Venezuela.

Early Life
Jagdeo was born on 23 Jan. 1964. He studied economics before taking a masters degree at the Friendship University in Moscow, Russia. In 1977 he joined the PPP's youth group, the Progress Youth Organization, becoming a full PPP member three years later. In 1990 he worked as an economist in the state planning secretariat. When the PPP came to power in 1992 he was appointed special advisor to the finance ministry from which he progressed to the post of junior finance minister the following year. He also served on various PPP committees. In 1995 he became finance minister (occasionally acting as prime minister), a position he kept when Janet Jagan came to power in 1997. In April 1999 Jagdeo negotiated with workers from the Guyana Public Service Union who went on strike for a 40% wage increase. The strike eventually ended after eight weeks of suspended public services.

Career in Office
Favoured by Jagan as her successor, Jagdeo took over the presidency following her resignation in 1999. However, he inherited ongoing political and civil disputes between politicians and followers of the PPP and those of the PNC, despite both being socialist parties. The PNC claimed that the 1997 elections had been fixed and had never accepted Jagan, subsequently refusing to recognize the Jagdeo presidency. During negotiations in 1998 directed by CARICOM, the PPP agreed to shorten the presidential term by two years.

In 2001 the two parties and their followers were caught up in more widespread racial tensions that traditionally erupted around elections (the PPP representing the Indo-Guyanese population and the PNC the Afro-Guyanese community). For this reason the elections that year were closely monitored by international observers and a special commission. They passed off without too much trouble, and Jagdeo was elected with 53·1% of the vote against 41·7% for Desmond Hoyte of the PNC. Hoyte accused the PPP of fraud, claiming many voters had disappeared from the electoral role. Jagdeo admitted this, but said that both parties had been affected by the discrepancies.

On the international level, there remain continuing border disputes with Venezuela and Suriname. In June 2000 a Surinamese naval ship expelled a Canadian-owned oil rig which had been granted a licence for oil exploration by Guyana but was said to be in waters claimed by Suriname. Talks between Jagdeo and the then Surinamese president under the mediation of then Jamaican prime minister P. J. Patterson failed. At the same time, Jagdeo agreed the construction of a rocket launch site by a US company 40 km from the Venezuelan border. Claiming a large portion of Guyanese land up to the Essequibo River, Venezuela argued that the project could be used for military purposes. The PNC also voiced its opposition to the proposed site.

DEFENCE

In 2003 defence expenditure totalled US$5m. (US$7 per capita), representing 0·7% of GDP. The army, navy and air force are combined in a 1,600-strong Guyana Defence Force.

Army
The Guyana Army had (2002) a strength of 1,400 including 500 reserves. There is a paramilitary Guyana People's Militia 1,500 strong.

Navy
The Maritime Corps is an integral part of the Guyana Defence Force. In 2002 it had 100 personnel and one patrol and coastal combatant plus two boats. It is based at Georgetown and New Amsterdam.

Air Force
The Air Command has no combat aircraft. It is equipped with light aircraft and helicopters. Personnel (2002) 100.

INTERNATIONAL RELATIONS

In June 2000 a maritime dispute arose between Guyana and Suriname over offshore oil exploration.

Guyana is a member of the UN, WTO, the Commonwealth, OAS, Inter-American Development Bank, ACS, CARICOM, OIC and is an ACP member state of the ACP-EU relationship.

ECONOMY

Agriculture accounted for 30·8% of GDP in 2002, industry 28·6% and services 40·6%.

Overview
State control was reduced during the 1990s, with some privatization.

Currency
The unit of currency is the *Guyana dollar* (GYD) of 100 *cents*. Inflation was 6·0% in 2003 and 4·7% in 2004. Foreign exchange reserves were US$280m. in June 2002 and total money supply was G$26·31bn.

Budget
Revenues in 1999 totalled G$36,544m. (tax revenue, 91·6%) and expenditures G$41,983m. (current expenditure, 71·2%).

Performance
GDP growth in 2003 was negative, at −0·7%, but was followed by a recovery, with growth in 2004 of 1·6%. Total GDP was US$0·8bn. in 2004.

Banking and Finance
The bank of issue is the Bank of Guyana (*Governor*, Lawrence Williams), established 1965. There are five commercial banks

and three foreign-owned. At March 1996 the total assets of commercial banks were G$62,587·9m. Savings deposits were G$26,564·2m.

ENERGY AND NATURAL RESOURCES

Environment
Guyana's carbon dioxide emissions from the consumption and flaring of fossil fuels were the equivalent of 2·2 tonnes per capita in 2002. An *Environmental Sustainability Index* compiled for the World Economic Forum meeting in Jan. 2005 ranked Guyana eighth in the world, with 62·9%. The index measured the ability of countries to maintain favourable environmental conditions and examined various factors including pollution levels and the use or abuse of natural resources.

Electricity
Capacity in 2000 was 0·3m. kW. In 2000 production was 894m. kWh and consumption per capita 1,158 kWh.

Minerals
Placer gold mining commenced in 1884, and was followed by diamond mining in 1887. In 2001 output of bauxite was 1,985,000 tonnes, and of gold 14,183 kg. Other minerals include copper, tungsten, iron, nickel, quartz and molybdenum.

Agriculture
In 2001 Guyana had 480,000 ha. of arable land and 30,000 ha. of permanent crops. 150,000 ha. were irrigated in 2001. Agricultural production, 2000 (in 1,000 tonnes): sugarcane, 3,000; rice, 600; coconuts, 56; cassava, 26; plantains, 14; bananas, 12; pineapples, 7.

Livestock (2000): cattle, 220,000; sheep, 130,000; goats, 79,000; pigs, 20,000; chickens, 13m. Livestock products, 2000 (in 1,000 tonnes): meat, 17; milk, 13; eggs, 7.

Forestry
In 2000 the area under forests totalled 16·88m. ha. (78·5% of the land area). 25% of the country's energy needs are met by wood fuel. Timber production in 2001 was 1·19m. cu. metres.

Fisheries
Fish landings in 2001 came to 53,405 tonnes, of which 99% was from sea fishing.

INDUSTRY

The main industries are agro-processing (sugar, rice, timber and coconut) and mining (gold and diamonds). There is a light manufacturing sector, and textiles and pharmaceuticals are produced by state and private companies. Production: sugar (2002), 331,068 tonnes; rum (2002), 14·6m. litres; beer (2001), 8·1m. litres; soft drinks (2002), 4,251,000 cases; textiles (1995), 322m. metres; footwear (1995), 54,132 pairs; margarine (1995), 1,262,420 kg; edible oil (1995), 2,388,120 litres; refrigerators (1995), 2,763 units; paint (1995), 923,847 litres.

Labour
In 1996 the labour force was 353,000 (67% males).

INTERNATIONAL TRADE

Guyana's external debt in 2002 was US$1,459m.

Imports and Exports
In 2002 imports were valued at US$563·1m. and exports at US$494·9m. Main commodities imported, 2002: consumer goods, 28·0%; fuels and lubricants, 22·3%; capital goods, 20·1%. Principal commodities exported, 2002: gold, 27·5%; sugar, 24·1%; shrimps, 10·6%. Rice, timber and bauxite are also exported. Major import suppliers, 1999: USA, 29%; Trinidad and Tobago, 18%; Netherlands Antilles, 16%; UK, 7%. Main export markets in 1999: Canada, 22%; USA, 22%; UK, 18%; Netherlands Antilles, 11%.

COMMUNICATIONS

Roads
In 2002 there were an estimated 7,970 km of roads, of which 590 km were paved. Passenger cars numbered 25,300 in 2002 and commercial vehicles 10,600.

Rail
There is a government-owned railway in the North West District, while the Guyana Mining Enterprise operates a standard gauge railway of 133 km from Linden on the Demerara River to Ituni and Coomacka.

Civil Aviation
There is an international airport at Georgetown (Timehri). In 2003 there were direct flights to Anguilla, Antigua, Barbados, Dominica, Miami, New York, Paramaribo, Port of Spain, St Kitts and the British Virgin Islands. In 1999 scheduled airline traffic of Guyana-based carriers flew 1·7m. km, carrying 70,000 passengers.

Shipping
The major port is Georgetown; there are two other ports. In 2002 merchant shipping totalled 15,000 GRT. There are 217 nautical miles of river navigation. There are ferry services across the mouths of the Demerara, Berbice and Essequibo rivers.

Telecommunications
The inland public telegraph and radio communication services are operated by the Guyana Telephone and Telegraph Company Ltd. In 2002 there were 167,700 telephone subscribers, equivalent to 190·8 per 1,000 population, and 24,000 PCs in 2000 (or 27·3 for every 1,000 persons). Mobile phone subscribers numbered 87,300 in 2002. There were 125,000 Internet users in 2002.

Postal Services
In 2003 there were 89 post offices.

SOCIAL INSTITUTIONS

Justice
The law, both civil and criminal, is based on the common and statute law of England, save that the principles of the Roman–Dutch law have been retained for the registration, conveyance and mortgaging of land.

The Supreme Court of Judicature consists of a Court of Appeal, a High Court and a number of courts of summary jurisdiction. Guyana was one of ten countries to sign an agreement in Feb. 2001 establishing a Caribbean Court of Justice to replace the British Privy Council as the highest civil and criminal court. In the meantime the number of signatories has risen to twelve. The court was inaugurated at Port-of-Spain, Trinidad on 16 April 2005.

In 1996 there were 4,563 reported serious crimes, including 88 homicides. The population in penal institutions in July 2001 was 1,507 (175 per 100,000 of national population).

Education
In 1999–2000 there were 407 pre-primary schools with 2,218 teachers for 36,955 pupils; 428 primary schools with 3,951 teachers for 105,800 pupils; and 408 secondary schools with 3,371 teachers for 62,495 pupils. In 1999–2000 there were 7,496 students at university level.

Adult literacy in 2001 was 98·6% (male, 99·0%; female, 98·2%). The literacy rates are the highest in South America. An OECD report published in 2005 showed that Guyana loses a greater proportion of its graduates (83%) to OECD member countries than any other non-OECD member.

In 1999–2000 total expenditure on education came to 4·5% of GNP and 8·6% of total government spending.

Health

In 1994 there were 30 hospitals (five private), 162 health centres and 14 health posts. In 1997 there were 38·8 hospital beds per 10,000 population. There were 366 physicians, 30 dentists and 1,738 nurses and midwives in 2000.

RELIGION

In 2001, 40% of the population were Protestant and Roman Catholic, 35% Hindu and 9% Muslim.

CULTURE

Broadcasting

The Guyana Broadcasting Corporation has two radio programmes. There were 85,000 TV receivers (colour by PAL) in 2001 and 420,000 radio receivers in 1997. The Guyana Television Broadcasting Company (GTV) is state-owned and there are 12 private stations relaying US satellite services.

Press

In 2000 there were two daily newspapers with a combined circulation of 56,750.

Tourism

There were 104,000 foreign visitors in 2002; receipts totalled US$49m.

Festivals

There are a number of Christian, Hindu and Muslim festivals throughout the year.

Libraries

There is a National Library in Georgetown.

Museums and Galleries

The Guyana National Museum contains a broad selection of animal life and Guyanese heritage. Castellani House, the National Gallery, is home to the finest art collection in Guyana.

DIPLOMATIC REPRESENTATIVES

Of Guyana in the United Kingdom (3 Palace Ct., London, W2 4LP)
High Commissioner: Laleshwar K. N. Singh.

Of the United Kingdom in Guyana (44 Main St., Georgetown)
High Commissioner: Stephen Hiscock.

Of Guyana in the USA (2490 Tracy Pl., NW, Washington, D.C., 20008)
Ambassador: Bayney R. Karran.

Of the USA in Guyana (99–100 Young and Duke Streets, Kingston, Georgetown)
Ambassador: Roland W. Bullen.

Of Guyana to the United Nations
Ambassador: Samuel Rudolph Insanally.

Of Guyana to the European Union
Ambassador: Kenneth F. S. King.

FURTHER READING

Braveboy-Wagner, J. A., *The Venezuela-Guyana Border Dispute: Britain's Colonial Legacy in Latin America.* London, 1984
Daly, V. T., *A Short History of the Guyanese People.* 3rd. ed. London, 1992
Williams, B. F., *Stains on My Name, War in My Veins: Guyana and the Politics of Cultural Struggle.* Duke Univ. Press, 1992

National Statistical Office: Bureau of Statistics, Avenue of the Republic and Brickdam, Georgetown.

HAITI

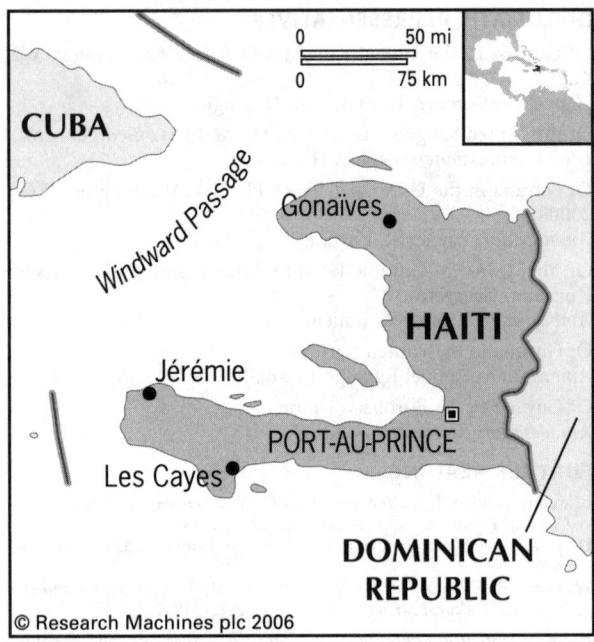

© Research Machines plc 2006

République d'Haïti

Capital: Port-au-Prince
Population projection, 2010: 9·14m.
GDP per capita, 2003: (PPP$) 1,742
HDI/world rank: 0·475/153

KEY HISTORICAL EVENTS

In the 16th century, Spain imported large numbers of African slaves whose descendants now populate the country. The colony subsequently fell under French rule. In 1791 a slave uprising led to the 13-year-long Haitian Revolution. In 1801 Toussaint Louverture, one of the leaders of the revolution, succeeded in eradicating slavery. He proclaimed himself governor-general for life over the whole island. He was captured and sent to France, but Jean-Jacques Dessalines, one of his generals, led the final battle that defeated Napoleon's forces. The newly-named Haiti declared its independence on 1 Jan. 1804, becoming the first independent black republic in the world. Ruled by a succession of self-appointed monarchs, Haiti became a republic in the mid-19th century. From 1915 to 1934 Haiti was under United States occupation.

A corrupt regime was dominated by François Duvalier from 1957 to 1964 when he was succeeded by his son, Jean-Claude Duvalier. He fled the country on 7 Feb. 1986. After a period of military rule, Father Jean-Bertrand Aristide was elected president in Dec. 1990.

On 30 Sept. 1991 President Aristide was deposed by a military junta and went into exile. Under international pressure, parliament again recognized Aristide as president in June 1993. However, despite a UN led naval blockade, the junta showed no sign of stepping down. 20,000 US troops moved into Haiti on 19 Sept. in an uncontested occupation. President Aristide returned to office on 15 Oct. 1994 and on 1 April 1995 a UN peacekeeping force (MANUH) took over from the US military mission. Aristide was succeeded by René Préval who was generally assumed to be a stand-in for his predecessor. Jean-Bertrand Aristide subsequently won the presidential elections held in Nov. 2000. In Dec. 2001 there was an unsuccessful coup led by former police and army officers. After armed rebels took control of the north of the country President Aristide stood down in Feb. 2004 and fled into exile.

TERRITORY AND POPULATION

Haiti is bounded in the east by the Dominican Republic, to the north by the Atlantic and elsewhere by the Caribbean Sea. The area is 27,700 sq. km (10,695 sq. miles). The Île de la Gonave, some 40 miles long, lies in the gulf of the same name. Among other islands is La Tortue, off the north peninsula. Provisional census population (2003), 7,929,048. Population density, 286 per sq. km. In 2003, 62·5% of the population were rural.

The UN gives a projected population for 2010 of 9·14m.

Areas, provisional census populations (2003) and chief towns of the nine departments:

Department	Area (in sq. km)	Population	Chief town
Artibonite	4,984	1,070,397	Gonaïves
Centre	3,675	566,043	Hinche
Grande Anse	3,310	603,894	Jérémie
Nord	2,106	773,546	Cap Haïtien
Nord-Est	1,805	300,493	Fort-Liberté
Nord-Ouest	2,176	445,080	Port-de-Paix
Ouest	4,827	3,093,699	Port-au-Prince
Sud	2,794	627,311	Les Cayes
Sud-Est	2,023	449,585	Jacmel

The capital is Port-au-Prince (2003 provisional census population, 703,023; urban agglomeration, 1,977,036); other towns are Cap Haïtien (111,094 in 2003), Gonaïves (104,825 in 2003), Saint-Marc (49,128 in 1997) and Les Cayes (48,095 in 2003). Most of the population is of African or mixed origin.

The official languages are French and Créole. Créole is spoken by all Haitians; French by only a small minority.

SOCIAL STATISTICS

2004 estimates: births, 247,000; deaths, 107,000. Rates, 2004 estimates (per 1,000 population): birth, 30; death, 13. Annual population growth rate, 1992–2002, 1·4%. Expectation of life at birth, 2003, 50·8 years for males and 52·4 years for females. Infant mortality, 2001, 79 per 1,000 live births; fertility rate, 2001, 4·1 births per woman.

In the Human Development Index, or HDI (measuring progress in countries in longevity, knowledge and standard of living), Haiti is the lowest-ranked country outside of Africa.

CLIMATE

A tropical climate, but the central mountains can cause semi-arid conditions in their lee. There are rainy seasons from April to June and Aug. to Nov. Hurricanes and severe thunderstorms can occur. The annual temperature range is small. Port-au-Prince, Jan. 77°F (25°C), July 84°F (28·9°C). Annual rainfall 53" (1,321 mm).

CONSTITUTION AND GOVERNMENT

The 1987 constitution, ratified by a referendum, provides for a bicameral legislature (an 99-member *Chamber of Deputies* and a 30-member *Senate*), and an executive *President*, directly elected for a five-year term. The President can stand for a second term but only after a five-year interval. The constitution was suspended in 1988 but the country returned to constitutional rule in Oct. 1994.

National Anthem

'La Dessalinienne' ('The Dessalines Song'); words by J. Lhérisson, tune by N. Geffrard.

RECENT ELECTIONS

After several postponements presidential elections were held on 7 Feb. 2006. Former president René Préval won 51·2% of the vote, former president Leslie Manigat 12·4% and Charles Henry Baker 8·2%. There were 32 other candidates. Initial results gave Préval less than the 50% needed to avoid a second round run-off, but following several days of protests amid claims of irregularities the provisional results were amended and Préval was declared the winner.

Delayed parliamentary elections were held on 7 Feb. and 21 April 2006. In the vote for the Chamber of Deputies, Lespwa won 20 seats, Fusion Social and Democratic party 19, Democratic Alliance party 14, the Lavalas Family party 5 with the remaining seats going to a number of smaller parties. 15 seats were still to be decided in areas where the run-off vote was cancelled because of violence or other problems. In elections for the Senate also held on 7 Feb. and 21 April 2006, Lespwa took 12 of the 27 available seats, Struggling People's Organization 4 and Fusion Social and Democratic party 3, with the remaining seats going to smaller parties. Three Senate seats were still to be decided.

CURRENT ADMINISTRATION

President: René Préval; b. 1943 (Front for Hope; sworn in 14 May 2006 having previously been president from Feb. 1996 to Feb. 2001).

In March 2006 the interim government comprised:

Prime Minister: Gérard Latortue; b. 1934 (sworn in 12 March 2004).

Minister of Foreign Affairs: Hérard Abraham. *Justice and Public Security:* Henri Dorleans. *Education, Youth, Sport and Culture:* Pierre Buteau. *Economy and Finance:* Henry Bazin. *Planning and International Co-operation:* Roland Pierre. *Commerce, Industry and Tourism:* Jacques Fritz Kénol. *Environment:* Yves André Wainwright. *Agriculture, Natural Resources and Rural Development:* Philippe Mathieu. *Public Health and Population:* Dr Josette Bijoux. *Public Works, Transport and Communications:* Fritz Adrien. *Social Affairs:* Franck Charles. *Interior and National Security:* Paul Gustave Magloire. *Haitians Living Abroad:* Alix Baptiste. *Women's Affairs and Rights:* Adeline Magloire Chancy. *Minister without Portfolio, Responsible for Liaison with the Presidency:* Robert Ulysse.

CURRENT LEADERS

René Préval

Position
President

Introduction
René Préval won a controversial election in Feb. 2006 to become president of Haiti for the second time. A former ally of ousted president, Jean-Bertrand Aristide, and with a strong following among the poor, Préval is charged with restoring stability and hope to the nation.

Early Life
René Garcia Préval was born on 17 Jan. 1943 in the Haitian capital, Port-au-Prince. The son of a politician, Préval's family were forced into exile in 1963 by the dictator, François 'Papa Doc' Duvalier. Préval studied agronomy at the College of Gembloux, Belgium, before moving to New York, USA in 1970, where he lived for five years. Returning to Haiti, Préval worked at the national institute for mineral resources. He became active in politics and charity work following the fall of Jean-Claude 'Baby Doc' Duvalier in Feb. 1986. During this period he grew close to the radical slum preacher, Jean-Bertrand Aristide, who in Dec. 1990 was elected president. Préval was appointed prime minister on 13 Feb. 1991 but was forced to flee the country shortly after a military coup led by Gen. Raoul Cedras on 29 Sept. 1991.

Joining the exiled constitutional government in Washington, D.C., USA in 1992, Préval held the prime minister's portfolio, as well as those of the interior and defence. Aristide was reinstated as president in Oct. 1994 but was constitutionally barred from running in the Dec. 1995 presidential election. Préval emerged victorious with 88% of the vote and took office on 7 Feb. 1996, inheriting a country with a devastated economy and crippling poverty. In Jan 1999, following a series of disagreements with legislators, Préval declared that their terms had expired and began a rule by decree. Following Aristide's return to power after a controversial presidential election in Nov. 2000, Préval, whose relationship with Aristide deteriorated from the mid-1990s, retreated to a farm in the north of the country.

Poverty and massive unemployment, together with Aristide's increasingly authoritarian rule, led to violent protests which forced the president into exile in Feb. 2004. His successor, the former chief justice, Boniface Alexandre, worked with a US-led international force to stabilize the country and prepare for fresh presidential and legislative elections. Préval unexpectedly returned to the fray, running as the candidate for the Front for Hope and distancing himself from his time as an ally of Aristide and his Lavalas movement. Following repeated delays, the presidential election was held on 7 Feb. 2006. Initially it appeared that Préval would contest a run-off, but on 16 Feb. 2006 he was declared the outright winner, with 51·2% of the vote. He was sworn in as president 14 May 2006.

Career in Office
Préval pledged to create 'cohesion' in Haiti's fractured society and restore peace in an effort to revive the ailing economy and provide employment. He stressed the importance of the Haitian diaspora in providing 'investment, talent and knowledge'.

DEFENCE

After the restoration of civilian rule in 1994 the armed forces and police were disbanded and an Interim Public Security Force formed, although this was later also dissolved. In 1995 a new police force—Police Nationale d'Haiti (PNH)—was recruited from former military personnel and others not implicated in human rights violations. The PNH currently has about 5,300 members.

A UN peacekeeping force, MINUSTAH, consisting of over 8,000 military personnel and civilian police, has been in Haiti since 2004.

In 2003 defence expenditure totalled US$22m. (US$3 per capita), representing 0·8% of GDP.

Army

The Army was disbanded in 1995.

Navy

A small Coast Guard, based at Port-au-Prince, is being developed. It had 30 personnel in 2002.

Air Force

The Air Force was disbanded in 1995.

INTERNATIONAL RELATIONS

In July 2004 international donors pledged more than US$1bn. in aid to help rebuild Haiti in addition to more than US$400m. previously committed. More than US$2bn. in aid had been given to Haiti over the previous ten years.

Haiti is a member of the UN, WTO, OAS, Inter-American Development Bank, ACS, CARICOM, IOM, International

Organization of the Francophonie and is an ACP member state of the ACP-EU relationship.

ECONOMY

Agriculture accounted for 27·1% of GDP in 2002, industry 16·3% and services 56·5%.

Currency

The unit of currency is the *gourde* (HTG) of 100 *centimes*. Total money supply in June 2002 was 10,763m. gourdes. Inflation was 32·5% in 2003 and 27·1% in 2004. In April 2002 foreign exchange reserves were US$185m.

Budget

In 2001 revenues were 6,509m. gourdes (of which general sales tax 31·3% and customs duties 27·2%) and expenditures 8,728m. gourdes (current expenditure 81·9%).

Performance

There was a recession in both 2001 and 2002, with the economy contracting by 1·0% and 0·5% respectively. There was positive growth in 2003 with the economy expanding by 0·5%, but then a further recession in 2004 with the economy shrinking by 3·8%. Total GDP in 2004 was US$3·5bn.

Banking and Finance

The Banque Nationale de la République d'Haïti is the central bank and bank of issue (*Governor*, Raymond Magloire). In 1999 there were 12 commercial banks (three foreign-owned) and a development bank.

Weights and Measures

The metric system and British imperial and US measures are in use.

ENERGY AND NATURAL RESOURCES

Environment

Carbon dioxide emissions from the consumption and flaring of fossil fuels in 2002 were the equivalent of 0·2 tonnes per capita. An *Environmental Sustainability Index* compiled for the World Economic Forum meeting in Jan. 2005 ranked Haiti 141st in the world out of the 146 countries analysed, with 34·8%. The index measured the ability of countries to maintain favourable environmental conditions and examined various factors including pollution levels and the use or abuse of natural resources.

Electricity

Most of the country is only provided with around four hours of electricity a day, supplied by the state-owned Electricité d'Haiti. Installed capacity was 0·3m. kW in 2000. Production in 2000 was 635m. kWh, with consumption per capita 80 kWh.

Minerals

Until the supply was exhausted in the 1970s, a small quantity of bauxite was mined.

Agriculture

There were 780,000 ha. of arable land in 2001 and 320,000 ha. of permanent crops. 65% of the workforce, mainly smallholders, make a living by agriculture carried on in seven large plains, from 0·2m. to 25,000 acres, and in 15 smaller plains down to 2,000 acres. Irrigation is used in some areas and in 2001 covered 75,000 ha. The main crops are (2000 production, in 1,000 tonnes): sugarcane, 800; cassava, 338; bananas, 323; plantains, 290; mangoes, 250; maize, 203; yams, 200; sweet potatoes, 180; rice, 130; sorghum, 98. Livestock (2000): cattle, 1·43m.; goats, 1·94m.; pigs, 1·0m.; horses, 500,000; chickens, 6m.

Forestry

The area under forests in 2000 was 88,000 ha., or 3·2% of the total land area. In 2001, 2·21m. cu. metres of roundwood were cut.

Fisheries

The total catch in 2001 was estimated to be 5,000 tonnes, of which 90% was from marine waters.

INDUSTRY

Manufacturing is largely based on the assembly of imported components: toys, sports equipment, clothing, electronic and electrical equipment. Textiles, steel, soap, chemicals, paint and shoes are also produced. Many jobs were lost to other Central American and Caribbean countries during the 1991–94 trade embargo, after President Aristide was deposed.

Labour

In 1996 the labour force was 3,209,000 (57% males). The unemployment rate in July 1998 was around 60%.

Trade Unions

Whilst at least six unions exist, their influence is very limited.

INTERNATIONAL TRADE

Foreign debt was US$1,248m. in 2002.

Imports and Exports

In 2003 imports totalled US$1,115·8m. and exports US$333·2m. The leading imports are petroleum products, foodstuffs, textiles, machinery, animal and vegetable oils, chemicals, pharmaceuticals, raw materials for transformation industries and vehicles. The USA is by far the leading trading partner. Main import suppliers in 1999 were USA, 60%; Dominican Republic, 4%; France, 3%; Japan, 3%. The USA accounted for 90% of exports in 1999.

COMMUNICATIONS

Roads

Total length of roads was estimated at 4,160 km in 2002, of which 1,010 km were surfaced. There were 58,100 passenger cars in 2002 (7·1 per 1,000 inhabitants), plus 39,100 trucks and vans.

Civil Aviation

There is an international airport at Port-au-Prince. Cap Haïtien also has scheduled flights to the Turks and Caicos Islands. In 2003 there were international flights to Aruba, Boston, Cayenne, Curaçao, Fort de France, Kingston, Miami, Montego Bay, Montreal, New York, Panama City, Paramaribo, Pointe-à-Pitre, Raleigh/Durham, Sint Maarten, Santiago (Cuba), Santiago (Dominican Republic), Santo Domingo and Washington, D.C. In 2001 Port-au-Prince handled 913,022 passengers (771,656 on international flights) and 13,455 tonnes of freight.

Shipping

Port-au-Prince and Cap Haïtien are the principal ports, and there are 12 minor ports. In 2002 the merchant marine totalled 1,000 GRT. In 1997 vessels totalling 1,304,000 NRT entered ports.

Telecommunications

The state telecommunications agency is Teleco. Telephone subscribers in 2002 numbered 270,000 (32·5 for every 1,000 inhabitants), including 140,000 mobile phone subscribers. In 2002 there were approximately 80,000 Internet users.

Postal Services

There were 24 post offices in 2003, equivalent to one for every 347,000 persons (the lowest ratio of any country). The postal service is fairly reliable in the capital and major towns. Many businesses, however, prefer to use express courier services (DHL and Federal Express).

SOCIAL INSTITUTIONS

Justice

The Court of Cassation is the highest court in the judicial system. There are four Courts of Appeal and four Civil Courts. Judges are appointed by the President. The legal system is basically French.

The population in penal institutions in 2003 was 3,519 (42 per 100,000 of national population).

Education

The adult literacy rate in 2002 was 51·9% (53·8% among males and 50·0% among females). Education is divided into nine years 'education fondamentale', followed by four years to 'Baccalaureate' and university/higher education. The school system is based on the French system and instruction is in French and Créole. About 20% of education is provided by state schools; the remaining 80% by private schools, including Church and Mission schools.

In 1994–95 there were 360 primary schools (221 state, 139 religious), 21 public *lycées*, 123 private secondary schools, 18 vocational training centres and 42 domestic science centres.

There is a state university, several private universities and an Institute of Administration and Management.

In 2000–01 total expenditure on education came to 1·1% of GNP and 10·9% of total government spending.

Health

In 1996 there were 773 physicians and 2,630 nurses. There were 49 hospitals with a provision of ten beds per 10,000 population in 1994.

RELIGION

Since the Concordat of 1860 Roman Catholicism has been given special recognition, under an archbishop with nine bishops. The Episcopal Church has one bishop. 60% of the population are nominally Roman Catholic, while other Christian churches number perhaps 20%. Probably two-thirds of the population to some extent adhere to Voodoo, recognized as an official religion in 2003.

CULTURE

World Heritage Sites

Haiti has one site on the UNESCO World Heritage List: National History Park—Citadel, Sans-Souci, Ramiers (inscribed on the list in 1982), 19th century monuments to independence.

Broadcasting

Under the aegis of the Conseil National des Télécommunications, radio and TV programmes (colour by SECAM V) are broadcast by Radio Nationale and Télévision Nationale. There is a privately-owned cable TV company, and several privately-owned radio stations. There were 395,000 radio and 36,000 TV sets in 2000.

Cinema

There are ten cinemas in Port-au-Prince.

Press

There were two daily newspapers in 1998. In 1995 the press had a combined circulation of 45,000, at a rate of six per 1,000 inhabitants.

Tourism

In 2001 there were 142,000 foreign tourists, spending US$54m. Cruise ship arrivals in 1998 numbered 246,000. There are only about 1,000 hotel rooms in the whole country.

Libraries

There is a public library, Bibliothèque Nationale, in Port-au-Prince. A private library open to scholars, Bibliothèque des Frères de l'Instruction Chrétienne, is nearby.

Theatre and Opera

The Théâtre National is in Port-au-Prince.

Museums and Galleries

The main museums are MUPANAH and the Musée de l'Art Haïtien, both in Port-au-Prince. There are at least 20 private art shops in Port-au-Prince and major towns.

DIPLOMATIC REPRESENTATIVES

Of Haiti in the United Kingdom. The Embassy closed on 30 March 1987.

Of the United Kingdom in Haiti
Ambassador: Andy Ashcroft (resides in Santo Domingo, Dominican Republic).

Of Haiti in the USA (2311 Massachusetts Ave., NW, Washington, D.C., 20008)
Ambassador: Raymond Alcide Joseph.

Of the USA in Haiti (Harry Truman Blvd, Port-au-Prince)
Ambassador: Timothy M. Carney.

Of Haiti to the United Nations
Ambassador: Leo Merores.

Of Haiti to the European Union
Ambassador: Yolette Azor-Charles.

FURTHER READING

Chambers, F., *Haiti.* [Bibliography] 2nd ed. ABC-Clio, Oxford and Santa Barbara (CA), 1994

Heinl, Robert & Nancy, revised by Michael Heinl, *Written in Blood.* Univ. Press of America, 1996

Nicholls, D., *From Dessalines to Duvalier: Race, Colour and National Independence in Haiti.* 2nd ed. CUP, 1992.

Thomson, I., *Bonjour Blanc: a Journey through Haiti.* London, 1992

Weinstein, B. and Segal, A., *Haiti: the Failure of Politics.* New York, 1992

National library: Bibliothèque Nationale, Rue du Centre, Port-au-Prince.

HONDURAS

República de Honduras

Capital: Tegucigalpa
Population projection, 2010: 8·00m.
GDP per capita, 2003: (PPP$) 2,665
HDI/world rank: 0·667/116

KEY HISTORICAL EVENTS

Discovered by Columbus in 1502, Honduras was ruled by Spain until independence in 1821. Political instability was endemic throughout the 19th and most of the 20th century. The end of military rule seemed to come in 1981 when a general election gave victory to the more liberal and non-military party, PLH (Partido Liberal de Honduras). However, power remained with the armed forces. Internal unrest continued into the 1990s with politicians and military leaders at loggerheads, particularly over attempts to investigate violations of human rights. In Oct. 1998 Honduras was devastated by Hurricane Mitch, the worst natural disaster to hit the area in modern times.

TERRITORY AND POPULATION

Honduras is bounded in the north by the Caribbean, east and southeast by Nicaragua, west by Guatemala, southwest by El Salvador and south by the Pacific Ocean. The area is 112,492 sq. km (43,433 sq. miles). In 2001 the census population was 6,535,344 (3,304,386 females), giving a density of 58 per sq. km. The estimated population in 2005 was 7·20m. In 2003, 54·4% of the population were urban.

The UN gives a projected population for 2010 of 8·00m.

The chief cities and towns are (2001 census populations): Tegucigalpa, the capital (819,867), San Pedro Sula (483,384), La Ceiba (126,721), Choloma (126,042), El Progreso (94,797), Choluteca (76,135), Comayagua (60,078), Danlí (47,310), Catacamas (35,995), Juticalpa (33,698).

Areas and 2001 populations of the 18 departments:

Department	Area (in sq. km)	Population
Atlántida	4,372	344,099
Choluteca	3,923	390,085
Colón	4,360	246,708
Comayagua	8,249	352,881
Copán	5,124	288,766
Cortés	3,242	1,202,510

Department	Area (in sq. km)	Population
El Paraíso	7,489	350,054
Francisco Morazán	8,619	1,180,676
Gracias a Dios	16,997	67,384
Intibucá	3,123	179,862
Islas de la Bahía	236	38,073
La Paz	2,525	156,560
Lempira	4,228	250,067
Ocotepeque	1,630	108,029
Olancho	23,905	419,561
Santa Bárbara	5,024	342,054
Valle	1,665	151,841
Yoro	7,781	465,414

The official language is Spanish. The Spanish-speaking population is of mixed Spanish and Amerindian descent (87%), with 6% Amerindians.

SOCIAL STATISTICS

2004 estimates: births, 204,000; deaths, 42,000. Rates, 2004 estimates (per 1,000 population): birth, 29; death, 6. 2003 life expectancy, 65·8 years for men and 69·9 for women. Annual population growth rate, 1992–2002, 2·8%. Infant mortality, 2001, 31 per 1,000 live births; fertility rate, 2001, 3·9 births per woman. Abortion is illegal.

CLIMATE

The climate is tropical, with a small annual range of temperature but with high rainfall. Upland areas have two wet seasons, from May to July and in Sept. and Oct. The Caribbean Coast has most rain in Dec. and Jan. and temperatures are generally higher than inland. Tegucigalpa, Jan. 66°F (19°C), July 74°F (23·3°C). Annual rainfall 64" (1,621 mm).

CONSTITUTION AND GOVERNMENT

The present Constitution came into force in 1982 and was amended in 1995. The *President* is elected for a single four-year term. Members of the *National Congress* (total 128 seats) and municipal mayors are elected simultaneously on a proportional basis, according to combined votes cast for the Presidential candidate of their party.

National Anthem

'Tu bandera' ('Thy Banner'); words by A. C. Coello, tune by C. Hartling.

RECENT ELECTIONS

Presidential and parliamentary elections took place on 27 Nov. 2005. In the presidential elections Manuel Zelaya (Liberal Party/Partido Liberal; PL) won with 49·9% of votes cast, against 46·2% for his chief rival, Porfirio Lobo Salsa. There were three other candidates. In the elections to the National Congress, the Liberal Party won 62 of 128 seats, the National Party 55, the Democratic Unification Party 5, the Christian Democratic Party 4 and the Innovation and Unity Party–Social Democracy 2.

CURRENT ADMINISTRATION

President: Manuel Zelaya; b. 1952 (PL; sworn in 27 Jan. 2006).
Vice-President: Elvin Santos.

In March 2006 the government consisted of:

Minister of Agriculture and Livestock: Héctor Hernández. *Culture, Arts and Sports:* Rodolfo Pastor. *Defence:* Arístides Mejía. *Education:* Rafael Pineda Ponce. *Finance:* Hugo Noé Pino. *Foreign Relations:* Milton Jiménez Puerto. *Industry and Commerce:* Lizzy Azcona. *Interior and Justice:* Jorge Arturo Reina. *Labour and Social Security:* Riccy Moncada. *Natural Resources and Environment:* Mayra Mejía del Cid. *Presidency:* Yani Rosenthal. *Public Health:* Orison Velásquez. *Public Works, Transportation and Housing:* Saro Bonano. *Science and Technology:* Miriam Mejía. *Security:* Gen. (retd) Alvaro Romero. *Social Investment Fund:* Marlon Lara. *Tourism:* Ricardo Martínez.

Honduran Parliament (Spanish only):
http://www.congreso.gob.hn

CURRENT LEADERS

Manuel Zelaya

Position
President

Introduction
Manuel Zelaya was sworn in as president in Jan. 2006 after a bitterly contested election. A wealthy landowner and member of the Liberal Party (PL), Zelaya confronts high levels of unemployment, widespread poverty and a serious crime wave.

Early Life
José Manuel Zelaya Rosales was born on 20 Sept. 1952 in Catacamas in the Olancho department of Honduras and studied civil engineering at the National University of Honduras in the capital, Tegucigalpa. He inherited land in Olancho and worked there as a rancher during the 1970s, when Honduras was under military rule. In 1980 he began working as a co-ordinator for the PL, which won the 1981 presidential election with its candidate, Roberto Suazo Cordova. Zelaya was elected a deputy in the national congress at the elections of Nov. 1985, a position he held until 1998. From 1987–94 he was on the board of the national council for private enterprise and was president of the industrial association of Medera.

Following the victory of Carlos Roberto Reina (PL) in the presidential election of Nov. 1993, Zelaya was appointed minister for investment in charge of the social investment fund. From late 1997, under the PL-led government of Carlos Roberto Flores, Zelaya introduced a programme to return power to local communities. Selected as the PL candidate to contest the presidential election of 27 Nov. 2005, Zelaya campaigned on a platform of tackling crime by doubling police numbers and introducing re-education programmes for criminals. This contrasted with the approach of his National Party rival, Porfirio Lobo Sosa, who promised the death penalty for convicted gang members. Results were delayed for a week but Zelaya emerged victorious with 49·9% of the vote to Lobo Sosa's 46·2%. He was sworn in as president in Tegucigalpa on 27 Jan. 2006.

Career in Office
In addition to his vow to fight gang violence and drug trafficking, Zelaya has pledged more job training, reforms to the education system and cuts in red tape. He has also laid out plans for 'civil assemblies' to monitor government and has guaranteed food for the poor and the creation of 400,000 new jobs. He is banking on expanded trade under the US-Central America free trade agreement and on debt relief under the World Bank's heavily indebted poor countries initiative.

DEFENCE

Conscription was abolished in 1995. In 2003 defence expenditure totalled US$53m. (US$8 per capita), representing 0·8% of GDP.

Army
The Army numbered (2002) 5,500. There is also a paramilitary Public Security Force of 6,000.

Navy
Personnel (2002), 1,000 including 400 marines. Bases are at Puerto Cortés, Puerto Castilla and Amapala.

Air Force
There were 49 combat aircraft in 2002 including F-5E/F Tiger II fighters. Total strength was (2002) about 1,800 personnel.

INTERNATIONAL RELATIONS

Honduras is a member of the UN, WTO, OAS, Inter-American Development Bank, CACM, ACS and IOM.

ECONOMY

Agriculture accounted for 13·4% of GDP in 2002, industry 30·6% and services 56·0%.

Currency
The unit of currency is the *lempira* (HNL) of 100 *centavos*. Foreign exchange reserves were US$1,526m. and gold reserves 21,000 troy oz in June 2002. Inflation was 7·7% in 2003 and 8·1% in 2004. Total money supply in May 2002 was 11,610m. lempiras.

Budget
In 1999 revenues were 14,621m. lempiras and expenditures 18,198m. lempiras.

Performance
Real GDP growth was 3·5% in 2003 and 4·6% in 2004. Total GDP in 2004 was US$7·4bn.

Banking and Finance
The central bank of issue is the Banco Central de Honduras (*President,* Gabriela Núñez). It had total reserves at Dec. 2002 of US$1,531m. There is an agricultural development bank, Banadesa, for small grain producers, a state land bank and a network of rural credit agencies managed by peasant organizations. The Central American Bank for Economic Integration (CABEI) has its head office in Tegucigalpa. In 1999 there were 40 private banks, including four foreign.

There are stock exchanges in Tegucigalpa and San Pedro Sula.

Weights and Measures
The metric system is official but some local measures are used, such as the *manzana* (= 0·7 ha.) and the *vara* (= 88 mm).

ENERGY AND NATURAL RESOURCES

Environment
Carbon dioxide emissions from the consumption and flaring of fossil fuels in 2002 were the equivalent of 0·8 tonnes per capita.

Electricity
Installed capacity was 0·9m. kW in 2000 (0·4m. kW hydro-electric). Production in 2000 was 3·68bn. kWh (77% hydro-electric); consumption per capita (2000) was 617 kWh.

Minerals
Output in 2002: zinc, 46,339 tonnes; lead (1998), 10,400 tonnes; silver, 52,877 kg. Small quantities of gold are mined, and there are also deposits of tin, iron, copper, coal, antimony and pitchblende.

Agriculture
There were 1·07m. ha. of arable land in 2001 and 0·36m. ha. of permanent crops. Legislation of 1975 provided for the compulsory redistribution of land, but in 1992 the grounds for this were much reduced, and a 5-ha. minimum area for land titles was abolished. Members of the 2,800 co-operatives set up in 1975 received individual shareholdings which can be broken up into personal units. Since 1992 women may have tenure in their own right. The state monopoly of the foreign grain trade was abolished in 1992. In 1996 the Agricultural Incentive Program was created (Ley de Incentivo Agrícola, LIA) which involves the redistribution of land for agricultural development.

Crop production in 2000 (in 1,000 tonnes): sugarcane, 3,896; maize, 534; bananas, 453; plantains, 250; coffee, 196; palm oil, 150; melons, 102; dry beans, 85; oranges, 80; pineapples, 71; sorghum, 65.

Livestock (2000): cattle, 1·95m.; pigs, 800,000; horses, 179,000; mules, 70,000; chickens, 18m.

Forestry
In 2000 forests covered 5·38m. ha., or 48·1% of the total land area. In 2001, 9·55m. cu. metres of roundwood were cut.

Fisheries
Shrimp and lobster are important catches. The total catch in 2001 was 7,451 tonnes, almost entirely from sea fishing.

INDUSTRY
Industry is small-scale and local. 2001 output (in 1,000 tonnes): cement, 1,100; raw sugar, 316; wheat flour (1996), 100; fabrics (1995), 11,641 metres; beer (2003), 96·1m. litres; rum (1995), 2·37m. litres.

Labour
The workforce was 2,438,000 in Sept. 2001. Of 2,334,600 persons in employment in Sept. 2001, 766,800 were in agriculture, hunting, forestry and fishing, 559,200 in wholesale and retail trade and restaurants and hotels, 380,300 in community, social and personal services and 356,000 in manufacturing. Unemployment rate, Sept. 2001: 4·2%.

Trade Unions
About 346,000 workers were unionized in 1994.

INTERNATIONAL TRADE
In May 1992 Honduras, El Salvador and Guatemala agreed to create a free trade zone and standardize import duties. Foreign debt was US$5,395m. in 2002.

Imports and Exports
Imports (f.o.b.) in 2002 were valued at US$2,804·4m. and exports (f.o.b.) at US$1,930·4m.

Main imports are machinery and electrical equipment, industrial chemicals, and mineral products and lubricants. Main exports are bananas, coffee, shrimps and lobsters, fruit, lead and zinc, timber, and refrigerated meats. Principal import suppliers, 1999: USA, 48·8%; Guatemala, 7·7%; El Salvador, 6·1%; Mexico, 5·2%; Panama, 4·3%; Japan, 4·0%. Principal export markets, 1999: USA, 57·3%; El Salvador, 10·1%; Guatemala, 7·7%; Germany, 4·6%; Japan, 3·5%; Spain, 1·8%.

COMMUNICATIONS

Roads
Honduras is connected with Guatemala, El Salvador and Nicaragua by the Pan-American Highway. Out of a total of 13,603 km of roads in 2002, 20·4% were paved. In 1999 there were 326,541 passenger cars, 18,419 buses and coaches, 40,903 trucks and vans, and 90,890 motorcycles and mopeds.

Rail
The small government-run railway was built to serve the banana industry and is confined to the northern coastal region and does not reach Tegucigalpa. In 1995 there were 595 km of track in three gauges, which in 1994 carried 1m. passengers and 1·2m. tonnes of freight.

Civil Aviation
There are four international airports: San Pedro Sula (Ramon Villeda) and Tegucigalpa (Toncontín) are the main ones, plus Roatún and La Ceiba, with over 80 smaller airstrips in various parts of the country. In addition to domestic flights and services to other parts of central America and the Caribbean, there were flights in 2003 to Barcelona, Dallas/Fort Worth, Houston, Las Vegas, Los Angeles, Madrid, Miami, New Orleans, New York, Oklahoma City, Orange County, Phoenix and San Jose. In 2001 San Pedro Sula handled 496,000 passengers (386,000 on international flights) and 7,500 tonnes of freight, and Tegucigalpa handled 451,000 passengers (327,000 on international flights) and 3,800 tonnes of freight.

Shipping
The largest port is Puerto Cortés on the Atlantic coast. There are also ports at Henecán (on the Pacific) and Puerto Castilla and Tela (northern coast). In 2002 the merchant marine totalled 933,000 GRT, including oil tankers 214,000 GRT. Honduras is a flag of convenience registry.

Telecommunications
In 2002 there were 649,000 telephone subscribers, or 96·7 for every 1,000 persons, and 91,000 PCs were in use (13·6 for every 1,000 persons). There were 326,500 mobile phone subscribers in 2002. Honduras had 168,600 Internet users in 2002.

Postal Services
There were 290 post offices in 2003.

SOCIAL INSTITUTIONS

Justice
Judicial power is vested in the Supreme Court, with nine judges elected by the National Congress for four years; it appoints the judges of the courts of appeal, and justices of the peace.

There were 2,155 homicides in 2000. Honduras has among the highest murder rates in the world.

The population in penal institutions in June 2002 was 11,502 (172 per 100,000 of national population).

Education
Adult literacy in 2003 was 80·0% (male, 79·8%; female, 80·2%). Education is free, compulsory (from 7 to 12 years) and secular. There is a high drop-out rate after the first years in primary education. In 2000–01 there were 120,141 children in pre-primary schools (6,167 teachers); 1,094,792 children in primary schools (32,144 teachers); 310,053 pupils in general education in secondary schools (12,480 teachers in 1995); and 90,620 students in tertiary education (5,549 academic staff). In 1995 there were eight universities or specialized colleges.

In 1998–99 expenditure on education came to 4·2% of GNP.

Health
In 1997 there were 4,896 physicians, 989 dentists and 6,152 nurses. In 1994 there were 29 public hospitals and 32 private, with 4,737 beds, and 849 health centres.

RELIGION
Roman Catholicism is the prevailing religion (5,740,000 followers in 2001), but the constitution guarantees freedom to all creeds, and the State does not contribute to the support of any. In 2001 there were 690,000 Evangelical Protestants with the remainder of the population followers of other faiths. In May 2005 there was one cardinal.

CULTURE

World Heritage Sites
Honduras has two sites on the UNESCO World Heritage List: Maya Site of Copán (inscribed on the list in 1980), a centre of the Mayan civilization abandoned in the early 10th century; and Río Plátano Biosphere Reserve (1982), one of the few remains of the Central American rain forest.

Broadcasting
There were six commercial TV channels in 1993 (colour by NTSC) and various radio stations (mostly local). There were 640,000 TV sets in 2001 and 2·62m. radio receivers in 2000.

Press

Honduras had eight national daily papers in 1998, with a combined circulation of 240,000.

Tourism

In 2002 there were 550,000 foreign tourists, spending US$342m.

Festivals

Honduras has a number of annual festivals and religious celebrations. The Fiesta de San Isidro is a week-long carnival held every May in La Ceiba to honour the city's patron saint.

DIPLOMATIC REPRESENTATIVES

Of Honduras in the United Kingdom (115 Gloucester Pl., London, W1U 6JT)
Ambassador: Vacant.
Chargé d'Affaires a.i.: Iván Romero-Nasser.

Of the United Kingdom in Honduras. The embassy closed on 28 Nov. 2003.
Ambassador: Richard Lavers (resides in Guatemala City).

Of Honduras in the USA (3007 Tilden St., NW, Washington, D.C., 20008)
Ambassador: Norman García.

Of the USA in Honduras (Av. La Paz, Tegucigalpa)
Ambassador: Charles A. Ford.

Of Honduras to the United Nations
Ambassador: Manuel Acosta Bonilla.

Of Honduras to the European Union
Ambassador: Teodolinda Banegas de Makris.

FURTHER READING

Banco Central de Honduras. *Honduras en Cifras 1990–92.* Tegucigalpa, 1993

Howard-Reguindin, Pamela F., *Honduras.* [Bibliography] ABC-Clio, Oxford and Santa Barbara (CA), 1992

Meyer, H. K. and Meyer, J. H., *Historical Dictionary of Honduras.* 2nd ed. Metuchen (NJ), 1994

National Statistical Office: Instituto Nacional de Estadísticas, Tegucigalpa.
Website (Spanish only): http://www.ine-hn.org

HUNGARY

Magyar Köztársaság
(Hungarian Republic)

Capital: Budapest
Population projection, 2010: 9·96m.
GDP per capita, 2003: (PPP$) 14,584
HDI/world rank: 0·862/35

KEY HISTORICAL EVENTS

Records date back to 9 BC, when the Romans subdued the Celts to establish Pannonia. From the 5th century both Romans and Celts retreated before attacks from the Huns who were followed by the Avars in the 7th century and the Magyars in the 9th. It was then that the name *On ogur* ('ten arrows') was adopted for the country that was to become Hungary. The founding date of Hungary is put at 896 after which Árpád, leader of one of the Magyar tribes, forged a dynasty which ruled Hungary until 1301. Forays into Italy, Germany, the Balkans and Spain ended after the Magyars were defeated by Holy Roman Emperor Otto I at the battle of Lechfeld in 955, and the Ostmark (Austria) was returned to Germanic control.

In seeking a truce with Otto I, the Árpád leader Géza invited him to send Catholic missionaries into Hungary. He had his son István (Stephen) crowned as King of Hungary and replaced the tribal structure with a system of counties (*megye*), administered by royal officials. A disputed succession led to intervention by the Holy Roman Emperor who established temporary suzerainty over Hungary. By the end of the 11th century, Slovakia, Carpathian Ruthenia and Transylvania were all under the crown of St Stephen. In a struggle for control of the ports on the Adriatic, Venice and Hungary went to war on 21 occasions between 1115–1420.

Andrew III, the last Árpád monarch, could do little to hold the country together against the opposition of feuding nobles. His death in 1301 led to a seven-year interregnum, after which, with two exceptions, Hungary was ruled by foreign kings. Linked to the Árpáds through marriage, Charles Robert of Anjou was elected to the throne. His primary task was to restore royal authority over the nobles. An economic boom coincided with

Hungary becoming the leading gold producer in Europe and trade links with European neighbours were fostered.

Ottoman Threat

His successors had to contend with the growing power of the Ottoman Empire. Assaults on Hungary increased after the fall of Constantinople in 1453, but in 1456 János Hunyadi, acting as military regent, broke the siege of Belgrade to keep the Turks at bay for another 70 years.

Rival magnates reacted to Hunyadi's death from the plague in 1456 by trying to wipe out the omnipotent Hunyadi clan, but in 1457 the Diet appointed his 15-year-old son Matthias Corvinus as king. Matthias was an enlightened despot. He built up one of Europe's finest libraries—destroyed a century later by the Ottomans—and encouraged writers and artists, many of whom were Italian, to come and work in Hungary. The heirless Matthias was succeeded in 1490 by Bohemia's ruler Vladislav, or King Ulászló II (1490–1516), known as 'Rex Bene', as 'dobre', or 'good' was his reply to almost everything. He managed to repel a Habsburg invasion of Hungary but indulged the nobles with disproportionate powers and relied heavily on foreign financing. Vladislav II was succeeded in 1516 by his son Louis II, who held both the Hungarian and Bohemian thrones. A ten-year-old, he could do little to discourage the onslaught of the Turks, to whom Belgrade was lost in 1521. The Hungarians were defeated ignominiously by the Turks under Suleiman II at the battle of Mohács on 29 Aug. 1526. Louis was killed in battle and Hungary lost its independence, not to be regained until 1918.

Hungary was partitioned, the largest section going to the Turks, royal Hungary to the Habsburgs and Transylvania, though theoretically autonomous, becoming a vassal state of the Ottomans. The Transylvanians were at constant war with the Habsburgs, who in turn fought the Ottomans. The economy along with the Magyar language declined and much agricultural land, mainly the Hungarian Plain, went to waste.

The Treaty of Vienna of 1606 was meant to set peaceful boundaries, but was soon violated. A series of costly territorial struggles culminated in the Ottoman siege of Vienna in 1683. Repelled by the Habsburgs, it marked a turning point for the Turks who, by 1699, had ceded most of their Hungarian territory. The Habsburgs became hereditary rulers pursuing a policy of divide and rule which led to anti-Habsburg risings. The second, under Ferenc Rákóczi, the last independent prince of Transylvania, united both nobles and peasants, and lasted from 1703–11. It was concluded by the signing of the Peace of Szatmár, in which the Habsburgs guaranteed political freedom for the three 'nations'—the ethnic Magyar, Saxon and Székelys groups. State education, introduced by Maria Theresa and Joseph II, led to greater Germanization.

Challenge to Habsburg Rule

Power was concentrated on the Magyar nobility, descendents of the Árpád royal line, who owned vast estates and were exempt from land tax. In March 1848 the Hungarian Diet renounced Viennese rule and legislated for a sovereign Magyar state, which was approved by Emperor Ferdinand. However, what began peacefully soon deteriorated as national minorities such as the Croats, the Romanians, Serbs and Slovaks demanded the same rights. In the War of Independence, heavy fighting broke out between the Hungarians and the Austrians, the Hungarians being led by Lajos Kossuth (1802–94).

When Emperor Franz Joseph I took the throne in 1848, the Hungarians refused to recognize him. This provoked an

Austrian invasion, which was repelled, and in Feb. 1849 the diet in Debrecen declared Hungary an independent republic under Kossuth's leadership. Franz Joseph reacted by accepting the assistance of Tsar Nicholas I of Russia in suppressing the revolution. The Magyars chose to surrender to the Russians rather than the Austrians but the aftermath of the war witnessed mass executions and imprisonment of rebel factions. Kossuth escaped into exile. Direct rule was imposed from Vienna.

Dual Monarchy

Having lost territory to Sardinia in 1859 and to Prussia in 1866, Austria recognized the need for a compromise with Hungary. What became known as the 'Ausgleich' created a dual monarchy to preside over the Austro-Hungarian Empire. Hungary gained internal autonomy but while the Ausgleich profited Magyars and Austro-Germans it did little to benefit national minorities.

Bosnia-Herzegovina was annexed in 1908, which outraged Serbia, but Austria tried a number of tricks to prevent retaliation including the Zagreb Treason Trial of 1909, when evidence was produced of a Serb-Croat conspiracy to bring down the Habsburgs. It was the Czech professor and future president Tomáš Masaryk who proved the evidence to be fake.

On 28 June 1914 the heir to the Habsburg throne, Archduke Franz Ferdinand, and his wife were shot in Sarajevo by a Bosnian Serb. Austria-Hungary declared war on Serbia a month later, precipitating the First World War. The Entente of France, Britain and Russia united against the Central Powers of Germany and Austria-Hungary, with other nations soon joining in one or other alliance. By the Treaty of Versailles, the territories of Hungary and Austria were reduced drastically. Hungary became a republic in Nov. 1918, with Mihály Károlyi as president. Transylvania was handed over to Romania. New countries including Czechoslovakia and Yugoslavia were created, all of which gained former Hungarian territory.

On 21 March 1919, Károlyi was replaced by the Bolshevik leader, Béla Kun, who was in power for 133 days. His downfall was brought about by a non-communist revolutionary movement fighting to regain Slovakia and Romania. The Allies persuaded Romania to retreat, and Hungary's borders were finalized by the Treaty of Trianon on 4 June 1920. Two-thirds of Hungary's territory and over half of the population were assigned to neighbouring countries.

In 1919 the Hungarian Kingdom was restored under Count Miklós Horthy, who ruled as regent and appointed a chiefly aristocratic government. Despite Horthy's efforts to amend the Trianon treaty, Hungary's boundaries remained unchanged until the Second World War. Germany and Italy backed the 'Vienna awards' of Nov. 1938 which restored to Hungary southern Slovakia and southern Subcarparthian Ruth, and in Aug. 1940, Transylvanian and Romanian territory. Hitler's support, including favourable trading terms, drew Hungary into fighting with Germany against the Soviet army in 1941, a tactical error which led to enormous losses.

In March 1944 the Germans occupied Hungary. Horthy was forced to abdicate and Hitler appointed a government of Ferenc Szálasi and his fascist Arrow Cross movement. Large-scale deportation of Jews and political dissidents began. Around 400,000 Jews are estimated to have been murdered. With civilian and military losses, almost a million Hungarians died in the war.

Soviet Rule

With the Soviets as the occupying power, post-war Communist rule was established in 1948–49 after a three-year multi-party democracy which the Communists conspired to undermine. Mátyás Rákosi and his Hungarian Workers' Party headed a dictatorship which went unchallenged until 1953, the year of Stalin's death. Rákosi was ousted by reformers led by Imre Nagy. Appointed prime minister, Nagy began what he called

'the new stage in building socialism', which entailed industrial and economic reforms and the restoration of human rights. But disagreements within the Soviet leadership gave an advantage to Rákosi who was still general secretary of the Workers' Party. Nagy was forced out of office in April 1955.

On 23 Oct. 1956 a student-led demonstration demanded democratic reforms and Nagy's reinstatement as prime minister. Soviet troops fired into crowds trying to occupy the radio station. The next day Imre Nagy was reappointed prime minister but was unable to quell the riots. Revolutionary committees were set up and there was a general strike to promote the three aims of the revolution: national independence, a democratic political structure and the protection of social benefits. All of this, along with armed rebels in the capital, put pressure on the hardliners in the party to accept reform.

A ceasefire, called by Nagy on 28 Oct., was honoured and Soviet troops retreated from Budapest. A multi-party democracy was announced, and the State Security Authority abolished. Even so, there were continuing demands for a clean sweep of all Stalinist-Rákosist ministers and total Soviet withdrawal. Nagy believed that such a transition should occur gradually and peacefully, but when he voiced the nation's support for neutrality and a withdrawal from the Warsaw pact, it was a step too far for Moscow. János Kádár was encouraged to form a counter-government with Soviet military backing. The Soviet Army marched into Budapest on 4 Nov., crushing all resistance.

Soviet hopes that Nagy would resign after this resounding defeat and support Kádár were disappointed. Kádár returned from Moscow on 7 Nov. after the heaviest fighting was over, to be confronted by a less than compromising nation. The re-named Hungarian Socialist Workers' Party declared all Oct. events as a counter-revolution, and began a series of revenge attacks. Nagy was hanged on 16 June 1958 along with several of his reformist associates. Many opponents of the regime were deported to labour camps in the Soviet Union and over 200,000 people fled the country.

Gradual Reform

János Kádár was party leader from 1956–89, and prime minister in the years 1956–58 and 1961–65. In the early '60s Kádár made a gradual shift towards liberalization. After the wave of executions, a distinction was made between political crime and mere error, and people were no longer required to be active in the party in order to succeed professionally. Trade unions were allowed to play a more active role, as was the press, so long as the government was not openly criticized.

The now-recognized need to loosen state control of the economy gave rise to the New Economic Mechanism (NEM) in 1968, which relaxed price controls, acknowledged the profit motive, improved manufacturing quality and shifted the emphasis from heavy to light industry. Subsidies were reduced and enterprise encouraged. Growing demands for a more open market economy coincided with the first signs of a weakening of the Soviet system. A group of Hungarian dissidents were sufficiently encouraged by the liberal trend in Moscow to form the Hungarian Democratic Forum. Led by their secretary general, Imre Pozsgay, they produced a manifesto 'Turn and Reform' which argued for a total overhaul of the economy.

The subsequent debate re-opened divisions between hardliners and reformists, and throughout the country there were demonstrations and strikes. The conservative old school of the Hungarian Socialist Workers' Party was gradually phased out by the reformists. A committee was set up to investigate the events of 1956, which concluded that it had been a popular uprising and not a counter-revolution. This called for the ceremonial reburial of Imre Nagy's remains on 16 June 1989, an event attended by a quarter of a million people who gathered in Heroes' Square, Budapest.

Post Communism

When prime minister Miklós Németh opened the borders with Austria, the flood of refugees from East Germany precipitated the fall of the Berlin wall. Multi-party democracy was enshrined in law in Sept. 1989 and Hungary ceased to be a People's Republic on 23 Oct. A unicameral National Assembly was formed and the first free elections took place on 25 March 1990. Of the 386 members elected to the National Assembly, only 21 had ever served in parliament before, and of the six successful parties, three were entirely new. The Hungarian Democratic Forum (MDF) and Alliance of Free Democrats advocated democracy, political pluralism, a market economy and a 'return' to Europe. The MDF came out ahead but having failed to secure a majority, formed a coalition with the Independent Smallholders' Party and the Christian Democratic People's Party.

A largely inexperienced government set about economic reform while trying to contain trade and budget deficits and high inflation. Social unrest prompted the government to slow down its privatization programme which proved popular with the electorate until they realized that the economy was stalling. In 1993 Iván Szabó became finance minister and adopted much stricter policies, cutting social budgets and devaluing the forint. This again led to domestic hardship. Unemployment, a hitherto unknown phenomenon, grew to over 12%. A nostalgia for a Communist past where jobs, housing and benefits were secure was perceptible in voting patterns at the 1994 elections.

Although the MDF's 'shock tactic' policies were praised by the West, and attracted foreign investment, the electorate opted for an updated version of the Hungarian Socialist Party (MSzP). Former Communist and leader Gyula Horn touted the party as one free of ideological limitations, playing down the traditional left and promising a higher standard of living along with continued economic reform under the guidance of László Bekesy, finance minister of the former Communist government. Horn became prime minister of a coalition led by the Alliance of Free Democrats (SzDSz) and the MSzP. Economic reforms were put back on the agenda but the government moved cautiously in an effort to carry public opinion.

The 1998 elections produced another coalition led by Viktor Orbán of the Federation of Young Democrats (later called Fidesz). He was succeeded in May 2002 by Péter Medgyessy, the Socialists' candidate, who formed a coalition with the SzDSz. In June 2002 revelations that Medgyessy had worked as a counter-intelligence agent for the communist regime highlighted the transitional problems for former Eastern Bloc nations. Hungary became a member of NATO in 1999 and of the EU on 1 May 2004.

TERRITORY AND POPULATION

Hungary is bounded in the north by Slovakia, northeast by Ukraine, east by Romania, south by Croatia and Serbia and Montenegro, southwest by Slovenia and west by Austria. The peace treaty of 10 Feb. 1947 restored the frontiers as of 1 Jan. 1938. The area of Hungary is 93,030 sq. km (35,919 sq. miles).

At the census of 1 Feb. 2001 the population was 10,198,315 (5,347,665 females); 2005 estimate, 10,098,000.

The UN gives a projected population for 2010 of 9.96m.

Hungary's population has been falling at such a steady rate since 1980 that its 2005 population was the same as that in the early 1960s.

65.2% of the population was urban in 2003; population density, 2001, 109.6 per sq. km. Ethnic minorities, 2000: Roma (Gypsies), 5.3%; Ruthenians, 2.9%; Germans, 2.4%; Romanians, 1.0%; Slovaks, 0.9%. A law of 1993 permits ethnic minorities to set up self-governing councils. There is a worldwide Hungarian diaspora of nearly 2.5m. (1.5m. in the USA; 200,000 in Israel; 140,000 in Canada; 140,000 in Germany), and Hungarian minorities (totalling 3.2m. in 1992) in Romania (1.7m.), Slovakia

(0.6m.), Serbia and Montenegro (0.35m., mainly in Vojvodina) and Ukraine (0.16m.).

Hungary is divided into 19 counties (*megyék*) and the capital, Budapest, which has county status.

Area (in sq. km) and population (in 1,000) of counties and county towns:

Counties	Area	2003 population	Chief town	2003 population
Bács-Kiskun	8,445	544	Kecskemét	108
Baranya	4,430	405	Pécs	159
Békés	5,631	396	Békéscsaba	66
Borsod-Abaúj-Zemplén	7,247	744	Miskolc	180
Csongrád	4,263	427	Szeged	163
Fejér	4,359	428	Székesfehérvár	103
Győr-Moson-Sopron	4,089	439	Győr	129
Hajdú-Bihar	6,211	552	Debrecen	206
Heves	3,637	325	Eger	57
Jász-Nagykún-Szolnok	5,582	416	Szolnok	77
Komárom-Esztergom	2,265	316	Tatabánya	71
Nógrád	2,544	219	Salgótarján	44
Pest	6,393[1]	1,105[2]	Budapest	1,719
Somogy	6,036	336	Kaposvár	68
Szabolcs-Szatmár-Bereg	5,936	586	Nyíregyháza	117
Tolna	3,703	249	Szekszárd	35
Vas	3,336	267	Szombathely	81
Veszprém	4,613	370	Veszprém	62
Zala	3,784	298	Zalaegerszeg	62
Budapest	525	1,719	(has county status)	

[1]Excluding area of Budapest. [2]Excluding population of Budapest.

The official language is Hungarian. 98.5% of the population have Hungarian as their mother tongue. Ethnic minorities have the right to education in their own language.

SOCIAL STATISTICS

2001: births, 97,047; deaths, 132,183; marriages, 43,583; divorces, 24,379. In 2000 the number of births rose for the first time in a decade. There were 2,979 suicides in 2001. Rates (per 1,000 population), 2001: birth, 9.5; death, 13.0; marriage, 4.3; divorce, 2.4. Annual population growth rate, 1992–2002, –0.4%. In 2002 the suicide rate per 100,000 population was 28.0, with the rate among men nearly four times as high as that among women. In 2001 the most popular age range for marrying was 25–29 for males and 20–24 for females. Expectation of life at birth, 2003, 68.6 years for males and 76.8 years for females (the lowest of any OECD member country). Infant mortality, 2001, 8 per 1,000 live births. Fertility rate, 2001, 1.3 births per woman.

CLIMATE

A humid continental climate, with warm summers and cold winters. Precipitation is generally greater in summer, with thunderstorms. Dry, clear weather is likely in autumn, but spring is damp and both seasons are of short duration. Budapest, Jan. 32°F (0°C), July 71°F (21.5°C). Annual rainfall 25" (625 mm). Pécs, Jan. 30°F (–0.7°C), July 71°F (21.5°C). Annual rainfall 26.4" (661 mm).

CONSTITUTION AND GOVERNMENT

On 18 Oct. 1989 the National Assembly approved by an 88% majority a constitution which abolished the People's Republic, and established Hungary as an independent, democratic, law-based state. The constitution was amended in 1997.

The head of state is the *President*, who is elected for five-year terms by the National Assembly.

The single-chamber *National Assembly* has 386 members, made up of 176 individual constituency winners, 152 allotted by proportional representation from county party lists and 58 from a national list. It is elected for four-year terms. A

Constitutional Court was established in Jan. 1990 to review laws under consideration.

National Anthem

'Isten áldd meg a magyart' ('God bless the Hungarians'); words by Ferenc Kölcsey, tune by Ferenc Erkel.

GOVERNMENT CHRONOLOGY

(Fidesz-MPP = Fidesz-Hungarian Civic Party; FKgP = Independent Party of Smallholders, Agrarian Workers and Citizens; MDF = Hungarian Democratic Forum; MDP = Hungarian Workers' Party; MKP = Hungarian Communist Party; MSzMP = Hungarian Socialist Workers' Party; MSzP = Hungarian Socialist Party; SzDSz = Alliance of Free Democrats; n/p = non-partisan)

Presidents since 1946.

1946–48	FKgP	Zoltán Tildy
1948–50	MDP	Árpád Szakasits
1950–52	MDP	Sándor Rónai
1952–67	MSzMP	István Dobi
1967–87	MSzMP	Pál Losonczi
1987–88	MSzMP	Károly Németh
1988–89	MSzMP	Bruno Ferenc Straub
1989–90	MSzP	Mátyás Szürös
1990–2000	SzDSz	Árpád Göncz
2000–05	n/p	Ferenc Mádl
2005–	n/p	László Sólyom

Prime Ministers since 1946.

1946–47	FKgP	Ferenc Nagy
1947–48	FKgP	Lajos Dinnyés
1948–52	MDP	István Dobi
1952–53	MDP	Mátyás Rákosi
1953–55	MDP	Imre Nagy
1955–56	MDP	András Hegedüs
1956	MDP	Imre Nagy
1956–58	MSzMP	János Kádár
1958–61	MSzMP	Ferenc Münnich
1961–65	MSzMP	János Kádár
1965–67	MSzMP	Gyula Kállai
1967–75	MSzMP	Jenö Fock
1975–87	MSzMP	György Lázár
1987–88	MSzMP	Károly Grósz
1988–90	MSzP	Miklós Németh
1990–93	MDF	József Antall
1993–94	MDF	Péter Boross
1994–98	MSzP	Gyula Horn
1998–2002	Fidesz-MPP	Viktor Orbán
2002–04	n/p (MSzP)	Péter Medgyessy
2004–	MSzP	Ferenc Gyurcsány

Leaders of the Communist Party, 1945–89.

General Secretary of MKP/MDP

1945–	Mátyás Rákosi

First Secretaries of MDP/MSzMP

1953–56	Mátyás Rákosi
1956	Ernö Gerö
1956–88	János Kádár
1988–89	Károly Grósz

Collective Chairmanship of MSzMP

1989	Rezsö Nyers, Miklós Németh, Károly Grósz, Imre Pozsgay

RECENT ELECTIONS

László Sólyom was elected president by the National Assembly on 7 June 2005 by 185 votes to 182. In two previous rounds he had failed to achieve the required two-thirds majority.

In the Hungarian parliamentary elections on 9 and 23 April 2006 the Socialist Party won 186 seats in the 386-seat National Assembly with 48·2% of the vote, followed by the Fidesz-Hungarian Civic Union (Fidesz-MPP) with 164 seats and 42·5% of the vote, the Alliance of Free Democrats with 18 seats and 4·7%, the Hungarian Democratic Forum (MDF) with 11 seats and 2·8%, the Hungarian Socialist Party-Alliance of Free Democrats with 6 seats and 1·5%, and Somogyért with 1 seat and 0·3%. Turnout in the first round was 67·8% and in the second round 64·4%.

European Parliament

Hungary has 24 representatives. At the June 2004 elections turnout was 38·5%. Fidesz-MPP won 12 seats with 47·4% of votes cast (political affiliation in European Parliament: European People's Party–European Democrats); the MSzP, 9 with 34·3% (Party of European Socialists); the SzDSz, 2 with 7·7% (Alliance of Liberals and Democrats for Europe); the MDF, 1 with 5·3% (European People's Party–European Democrats).

CURRENT ADMINISTRATION

President: László Sólyom; b. 1942 (in office since 5 Aug. 2005).

In March 2006 the MSzP-SzDSz coalition government consisted of:

Prime Minister: Ferenc Gyurcsány; b. 1961 (MSzP; acting from 27 Aug. to 28 Sept. 2004 and sworn in on 29 Sept. 2004).

Head of Prime Minister's Office: Péter Kiss. *Minister of Agriculture and Regional Development:* József Gráf. *Cultural Heritage:* András Bozóki. *Defence:* Ferenc Juhász. *Economic Affairs and Transport:* János Kóka. *Education:* Bálint Magyar. *Employment and Labour:* Gábor Csizmár. *Environment and Water Management:* Miklós Persányi. *Finance:* János Veres. *Foreign Affairs:* Ferenc Somogyi. *Health, Social and Family Affairs:* Jenő Rácz. *Information Technology and Telecommunications:* Kálmán Kovács. *Interior:* Mónika Lamperth. *Justice:* József Petrétei. *Youth, Family Affairs and Equal Opportunities:* Kinga Göncz. *Minister without Portfolio in Charge of EU Affairs:* Etele Baráth. *Minister without Portfolio in Charge of Regional Development and Housing:* István Kolber.

Office of the Prime Minister: http://www.meh.hu

CURRENT LEADERS

László Sólyom

Position
President

Introduction
As a professor of law and an environmental activist, László Sólyom was closely involved in the negotiations between opposition civic groups and the Communist regime that led to the fall of the Iron Curtain. For most of the 1990s Sólyom was chief justice in Hungary's newly-established constitutional court, overseeing sweeping reforms to the country's legal system. He became president on 5 Aug. 2005.

Early Life
László Sólyom was born in the southern Hungarian city of Pécs on 3 Jan. 1942. In 1965 he graduated in law from the University of Pécs. Later that year he qualified as a librarian at the National Széchenyi Library in Budapest. Between 1966 and 1969 he studied for a doctorate and worked as assistant lecturer at the institute of civil law at the Friedrich Schiller University in Jena in East Germany, an institution known as a dissident stronghold. Returning to Budapest in 1969, Sólyom became a fellow of the institute of political and legal sciences at the Hungarian Academy of Sciences (MTA). He also worked as a librarian at the library of parliament. In 1978 Sólyom joined the Eötvös Loránd University in Budapest as an assistant professor in the department of civil law. Five years later he became a professor at the university. He specialized in the field of the right to privacy, and was largely responsible for the introduction of

data protection legislation in Hungary. Sólyom also worked as a legal adviser to some of the country's new and radical civil and environmental organizations during the 1980s.

Sólyom was one of a group of dissident intellectuals that met at the town of Lakitelek in Sept. 1987 and formed the Hungarian Democratic Forum (MDF), which became a fully-fledged political party six months later. As a member of the MDF's executive committee, Sólyom participated in roundtable negotiations that precipitated the end of Hungary's Communist regime and the dismantling of the Iron Curtain between Hungary and Austria in May 1989. Sólyom was elected onto the newly-established constitutional court of Hungary on 24 Nov. 1989, and was made the court's chief justice shortly afterwards. He remained in this post for nine years, playing a key role in strengthening democracy in Hungary. Highly activist, with the power to review and invalidate parliamentary acts, the court did much to promote freedom of opinion and the removal of capital punishment.

When his mandate expired in 1998 Sólyom continued his academic career, lecturing at universities throughout Hungary and internationally, including the University of Cologne (Köln), Germany, where he was visiting professor in 1999 and 2000. He joined numerous boards and committees, including the Council of Europe's Commission for Democracy through Law, the Hungarian Accreditation Commission and the Geneva-based International Commission of Jurists. He became a member of the Védegylet (an environmental and civil-society organization) when it was founded in early 2000 and it was this group which nominated him to replace Ferenc Mádl as the country's president in 2005. Backed by the right-leaning opposition MDF and Fidesz, Sólyom went head-to-head with Katalin Szili, the parliamentary speaker and candidate of the Socialist-led coalition government. In a third-round run-off on 7 June 2005, Sólyom emerged victorious with 185 votes to Szili's 182.

Career in Office

Sólyom was inaugurated as president on 5 Aug. 2005. He has been critical of some politicians, accusing them of spending their time attacking each other instead of dealing with the key issues at hand. Although the position of president is largely a ceremonial role in Hungary, Sólyom is expected to exercise his right to forward legislation to the constitutional court for review.

Ferenc Gyurcsány

Position

Prime Minister

Introduction

Multi-millionaire businessman Ferenc Gyurcsány became Hungary's prime minister on 29 Sept. 2004 after just two years in mainstream politics. His promotion came when his mentor and fellow Socialist Péter Medgyessy unexpectedly resigned.

Early Life

Gyurcsány was born in the town of Pápa in western Hungary on 4 June 1961. He entered the Janus Pannonius University in Pécs in 1980 and graduated with a teaching qualification in 1984. He remained at the university and studied economics for the next six years. During this time he was an active member of the Association of Young Communists (KISZ), becoming the president of its university wing in 1988. The forced resignation of Hungary's long-serving communist leader, János Kádár, in March 1988 led to the formation of a raft of opposition groups and political parties including the Hungarian Democratic Youth Association (DEMISZ), which Gyurcsány joined. He became its vice-president in 1989. Prime Minister Miklós Németh's decision to open Hungary's western border with Austria in Sept. 1989 precipitated the fall of the Iron Curtain and ushered in a new era. Gyurcsány graduated in economics in 1990 and worked

as a financial consultant, establishing various companies and becoming Chief Executive Officer of ALTUS Investment and Assets Management Inc. in 1992, a post he held for the next ten years.

Rumoured to be one of the wealthiest men in Hungary, Gyurcsány entered politics in 2002 as strategic adviser to the prime minister, Péter Medgyessy. Gyurcsány was promoted the following year to be the minister for sport and youth development. He was nominated as president of the Hungarian Socialist Party (MSzP) for the northwestern county of Győr-Moson-Sopron in Jan. 2004. Opinion polls suggested that public support for the MSzP was dwindling and, in Aug. 2004, tensions flared between the Socialists and their coalition partners, the Free Democrats, over a cabinet reshuffle. Medgyessy resigned and, a week later, Gyurcsány was nominated to succeed his mentor by members of the MSzP. He was formally approved as Hungary's prime minister on 29 Sept. 2004.

Career in Office

Gyurcsány has pledged to boost Hungary's economic growth, cut the spiralling budget deficit and steer the country on a course for euro zone membership in 2010. Although he hails from the social democratic wing of the MSzP and advocates pro-market policies, Gyurcsány says that his party should be responsive to the poor in society. He gained a further term in office when the Socialists won the elections of April 2006, thereby becoming the first Hungarian party to retain power at an election since the fall of socialism in 1989.

DEFENCE

The President of the Republic is C.-in-C. of the armed forces.

Men between the ages of 18 and 23 are liable for six months' conscription, or two years of civilian service.

Defence expenditure in 2003 totalled US$1,589m. Per capita spending in 2003 was US$157. The 2003 expenditure represented 1·9% of GDP, compared to 6·8% in 1985.

Army

The strength of the Army was (2002) 23,600 (including 16,500 conscripts). There is an additional force of 12,000 border guards. Army reserves number 74,950.

Navy

The Danube Flotilla, the maritime wing of the Army, consisted of some 290 personnel in 1999. It is based at Budapest.

Air Force

The Air Force had a strength (2002) of 7,700 (including conscripts). There were 37 combat aircraft in 2002, including MiG-21s, MiG-23s, MiG-29s and Su-22s, plus 55 in store, and 49 attack helicopters.

INTERNATIONAL RELATIONS

Hungary is a member of the UN, WTO, BIS, NATO, OECD, EU, Council of Europe, OSCE, CEFTA, CERN, CEI, Danube Commission, IOM, Antarctic Treaty, and is an Associate Partner of the WEU. Hungary held a referendum on EU membership on 12 April 2003, in which 83·8% of votes cast were in favour of accession, with 16·2% against, although turn-out was only 45·6%. It became a member of the EU on 1 May 2004. On 20 Dec. 2004 Hungary became the second European Union member to ratify the proposed EU constitution. The parliament approved the treaty by 304 votes to nine. In 2000 Hungary introduced a visa requirement for Russians entering the country as one of the conditions for EU membership.

Hungary has had a long-standing dispute with Slovakia over the Gabčíkovo-Nagymaros Project, involving the building of dam structures in both countries for the production of electric power, flood control and improvement of navigation on the Danube as agreed in a treaty signed in 1977 between Hungary and Czechoslovakia. In late 1998 Slovakia and Hungary signed a protocol easing tensions between the two nations and settling differences over the dam.

ECONOMY

Agriculture accounted for 4·3% of GDP in 2002, industry 31·2% and services 64·5%. In 2003 the private sector was responsible for an estimated 80% of economic output.

Overview

Hungary's transition from communism has been among the smoothest of the former Eastern Bloc nations, aided by market-oriented policy changes during the last two decades of communist rule and structural and stabilization measures implemented in the 1990s. Since the collapse of communism services have accounted for an increasing share of GDP while the contribution of industry has fallen. However, manufacturing, concentrated in low-cost industrial assembly and processing, has been the main engine of growth and the largest part of both import and export bills.

Hungary has attracted the most foreign direct investment in the region after the Czech Republic, helping to modernize production and redirect trade from east to west. Since the mid-1990s the majority of state assets have been privatized and the private sector now accounts for over 80% of GDP. Exports of goods and services accounted for 65% of GDP in 2004 and inflation has been brought under control. Unemployment levels are low, averaging 6% in the first half of the 2000s, but the labour force participation rate is among the lowest in the OECD. Structural and fiscal reforms of the late 1990s have lost momentum and fiscal and current account deficits are persistent. Adoption of the euro is likely to be postponed as a result of the failure to reign in spending combined with popular opposition.

Currency

A decree of 26 July 1946 instituted a new monetary unit, the *forint* (HUF) of 100 *fillér*. The forint was made fully convertible in Jan. 1991 and moves in a 15% band against the euro either side of a central rate of €1=276·1 forints. Inflation rates (based on OECD statistics):

1995	1996	1997	1998	1999	2000	2001	2002	2003	2004
28·3%	23·5%	18·3%	14·2%	10·0%	9·8%	9·1%	5·2%	4·7%	6·7%

The inflation rate of 4·7% in 2003 was the lowest rate in more than 20 years. Foreign exchange reserves were US$9,695m. in June 2002 and gold reserves 101,000 troy oz. Total money supply in April 2002 was 2,662·29bn. forints.

Budget

Central government revenues totalled 6,338·1bn. forints in 2002 (5,707·5bn. forints in 2001); expenditures totalled 7,161·8bn. forints in 2002 (5,968·6bn. forints in 2001). Principal sources of revenue in 2002: social security contributions, 2,159·1bn. forints; taxes on goods and services, 2,032·0bn. forints; taxes on income, profits and capital gains, 1,355·4bn. forints. Main items of expenditure by economic type in 2002: social benefits, 2,598·5bn. forints; grants, 1,028·2bn. forints; compensation of employees, 996·8bn. forints.

VAT is 20·0% (reduced rate, 15·0% and 5%).

Performance

Real GDP growth rates (based on OECD statistics):

1995	1996	1997	1998	1999	2000	2001	2002	2003	2004
1·5%	1·3%	4·6%	4·9%	4·2%	5·2%	3·8%	5·1%	3·4%	4·6%

Total GDP was US$99·7bn. in 2004.

Banking and Finance

In 1987 a two-tier system was established. The National Bank (*Director*, Zsigmond Járai) remained the central state financial institution. It is responsible for the operation of monetary policy and the foreign exchange system. In Sept. 2004 the Hungarian financial system comprised 32 banks, 5 specialized credit institutions, 178 co-operatives, 199 financial enterprises, 18 investment enterprises, 24 investment funds, 65 insurance companies and 168 pension/health related funds. They are all supervised by the Hungarian Financial Supervisory Authority (HFSA).

The largest bank is OTP Bank Rt. (the National Savings and Commercial Bank of Hungary), with assets in 2002 of 2,393bn. forints. Other leading banks are K+H (Hungarian Commercial and Credit Bank) and MKB (Hungarian Foreign Trade Bank). A law of June 1991 sets capital and reserve requirements, and provides for foreign investment in Hungarian banks. Permission is needed for investments of more than 10%. Privatization of the banking system is well under way.

At the end of 2002 foreign direct investments totalled US$35·9bn.

The Hungarian International Trade Bank opened in London in 1973. In 1980 the Central European International Bank was set up in Budapest with seven western banks holding 66% of the shares.

A stock exchange was opened in Budapest in Jan. 1989.

ENERGY AND NATURAL RESOURCES

Environment

Hungary's carbon dioxide emissions from the consumption and flaring of fossil fuels in 2002 were the equivalent of 5·7 tonnes per capita.

Electricity

Installed capacity in 2002 was 8·5m. kW, about a fifth of which is nuclear. There is an 880 MW nuclear power station at Paks with four reactors. It produced an estimated 36% of total output in 2002.

In 2003 Hungary produced 34·1bn. kWh of electricity and 8·9bn. kWh were imported. Total consumption in 2003 (including domestic consumption, power station consumption, network losses and exports) was 43bn. kWh. Consumption per capita in 2002 was 3,972 kWh.

Oil and Gas

Oil and natural gas are found in the Szeged basin and Zala county. Oil production in 2000 was 1·1m. tonnes. Gas production in 2000 was 3·0bn. cu. metres, with proven reserves of 65bn. cu. metres in 2002.

Minerals

Production in 1,000 tonnes: lignite (2002), 13,027; bauxite (2001), 1,000; hard coal (2002), 660.

Agriculture

Agricultural land was collectivized in 1950. It was announced in 1990 that land would be restored to its pre-collectivization owners if they wished to cultivate it. A law of April 1994 restricts the area of land that may be bought by individuals to 300 ha., and prohibits the sale of arable land and land in conservation zones to companies and foreign nationals. Today, although 90% of all cultivated land is in private hands, most farms are little more than smallholdings. In 2003 the agricultural area was 5·87m. ha. (equivalent to 63% of the total land area); arable land constituted 4·52m. ha.

Agricultural production has dropped drastically since 1989. Production figures (2003, in 1,000 tonnes): maize, 4,532 (6,747 in 1989); wheat, 2,941 (6,509 in 1989); sugarbeets, 1,812 (5,277 in 1989); sunflower seeds, 992; barley, 810; potatoes, 582; grapes, 581; apples, 508.

Livestock has also drastically decreased since 1989 from 7·7m. pigs to 5·1m. by 2003, from 1·6m. cattle to 770,000, and from

2·1m. sheep to 1·1m. Thus the pig stock, cattle stock and sheep stock have all declined to levels not seen in fifty years.

The north shore of Lake Balaton and the Tokaj area are important wine-producing districts. Wine production in 2002 was 380,000 tonnes.

Forestry

The forest area in 2003 was 1·77m. ha., or 19·1% of the land area. Timber production in 2003 was 5·79m. cu. metres.

Fisheries

There are fisheries in the rivers Danube and Tisza and Lake Balaton. In 2003 there were 33,100 ha. of commercial fishponds. In 2003 total catch was 6,536 tonnes, exclusively from inland fishing.

INDUSTRY

The leading companies by market capitalization in Hungary, excluding banking and finance, in Jan. 2002 were: Magyar Távközlési Rt. (MATÁV), the telecommunications company (1trn. forints); MOL Magyar Olaj-és Gázipari Rt (Hungarian Oil and Gas Plc), 489bn. forints; and Richter Gedeon Rt. (335bn. forints), a pharmaceuticals company.

Manufacturing output grew by an average of 8·5% annually between 1992 and 2002.

Important items include food and beverages, chemicals and chemical products, motor vehicles, refined petroleum products, base metals and computers. Production (in 1,000 tonnes): cement (2001), 3,500; distillate fuel oil (2002), 3,096; crude steel (2000), 1,969; rolled steel (2001), 1,900; petrol (2002), 1,573; plastics (2002), 1,136; fertilizers (2000), 781; residual fuel oil (2002), 358; alumina (2001), 300; sulphuric acid (2001), 80; radio sets (2001), 3,459,000 units; refrigerators (2001), 1,058,000 units; beer (2003), 750·0m. litres.

Labour

In 2001 out of an economically active population of 4,093,000 there were 3,860,000 employed persons, of which 3,296,000 were employees. Among the employed persons, 59·6% worked in services, 34·2% in industry and construction, and 6·2% in agriculture. Average gross monthly wages in 2001: 103,558 forints. Minimum monthly wage, 2004, 53,000 forints. In Dec. 2005 Hungary had an unemployment rate of 7·3%. Retirement age: men, 60; women, 55.

Trade Unions

The former official Communist organization (National Council of Trade Unions), renamed the National Confederation of Hungarian Trade Unions (MSZOSZ), groups 70 organizations and claimed 240,000 members in 2003. Other major workers' organizations are (with 2003 membership): the Association of Autonomous Trade Unions (ASZSZ, 150,000); Co-operation Forum of Trade Unions (SZEF, 270,000); Confederation of Unions of Professionals (ESZT, 85,000); Democratic League of Independent Trade Unions (Liga, 100,000); National Federation of Workers' Councils (MOSZ, 56,000).

INTERNATIONAL TRADE

Hungary is a member of CEFTA, along with the Czech Republic, Poland, Slovakia and Slovenia. Foreign debt was US$34,958m. in 2002. An import surcharge imposed in March 1995 was abolished in July 1997.

Imports and Exports

In 2004 the value of imports was US$58,290m. and that of exports US$55,368m. (up from US$46,753m. and US$43,475m. respectively in 2003). Hungary's foreign trade has been expanding at a very fast rate, with the value of both its imports and its exports trebling between 1996 and 2004. Machinery and transport equipment accounted for 51·5% of imports and 57·5%

of exports in 2001, and manufactured goods 35·3% of imports and 31·0% of exports. 75% of exports go to European Union member countries, the highest share of any of the central and eastern European countries that joined the EU in May 2004. The share of CIS countries is only around 2%. In 2001, 26·4% of imports came from Germany and 34·9% of exports went to Germany. Italy was the second biggest supplier of imports in 2001 (8·3% of the total) and Austria the second biggest market for exports (8·7%). In 2001, 1·5% of exports went to Russia, down from 13·1% in 1992.

COMMUNICATIONS

Roads

In 2002 there were 159,568 km of roads, including 533 km of motorways and 30,460 km of main roads. Passenger cars numbered (2002) 2,629,500; trucks, vans and special-purpose vehicles, 369,300; buses, 17,900; and motorcycles, 10,200. In 2003 there were 19,976 road accidents with 1,135 fatalities.

Rail

In 2003 the rail network was 7,685 km in length; 49·9m. tonnes of freight and 159·8m. passengers were carried. There is a metro in Budapest (30·1 km), and tram/light rail networks in Budapest (332·0 km), Debrecen, Miskolc and Szeged.

Civil Aviation

Budapest airport (Ferihegy) handled 4,482,000 passengers in 2002 (all on international flights) and 42,380 tonnes of freight. The national carrier is Malév, which is 99·95% owned by the state. It carried 2,354,080 passengers in 2003.

Shipping

There are 1,622 km of navigable waterways. In 2002, along the Hungarian section of the Danube River, 4,801 vessels entered the country on their way to a Hungarian destination, 4,916 vessels left Hungary for other countries and 3,331 vessels were in transit. In 2003, 2·06m. tonnes of cargo and 1·42m. passengers were carried. Merchant shipping totalled 4,000 GRT in 2002. The Hungarian Shipping Company (MAHART) has agencies at Amsterdam, Alexandria, Algiers, Beirut, Rijeka and Trieste. It has 23 ships and runs scheduled services between Budapest and Esztergom.

Telecommunications

There were 10,288,400 main telephone subscribers in 2002, equivalent to 1,007·5 per 1,000 population, and 1,100,000 PCs in use (108·4 per 1,000 persons). Matav, the privatized former national telephone company, still has more than 80% of the fixed line market. Hungary had 6,862,800 mobile phone subscribers in 2002 (68% of the population). Internet users numbered 1·6m. in 2002 and there were 425,000 fax machines in use.

Postal Services

In 2001 there were 2,581 post offices.

SOCIAL INSTITUTIONS

Justice

The administration of justice is the responsibility of the Procurator-General, elected by Parliament for six years. There are 111 local courts, 20 labour law courts, 20 county courts, six district courts and a Supreme Court. Criminal proceedings are dealt with by the regional courts through three-member councils and by the county courts and the Supreme Court in five-member councils. A new Civil Code was adopted in 1978 and a new Criminal Code in 1979.

Regional courts act as courts of first instance; county courts as either courts of first instance or of appeal. The Supreme Court acts normally as an appeal court, but may act as a court of first instance in cases submitted to it by the Public Prosecutor. All courts, when acting as courts of first instance, consist of one professional judge and two lay assessors, and, as courts of appeal, of three professional judges. Local government Executive Committees may try petty offences.

Regional and county judges and assessors are elected by the appropriate local councils; members of the Supreme Court by Parliament.

The Office of Ombudsman was instituted in 1993. He or she is elected by parliament for a six-year term, renewable once.

There are also military courts of the first instance. Military cases of the second instance go before the Supreme Court.

The death penalty was abolished in Oct. 1990.

The population in penal institutions in Nov. 2003 was 16,700 (165 per 100,000 of national population). There were 87,476 convictions of adults and 6,726 of juvenile offenders in 2003; 34% of convictions resulted in custodial sentences (most of them suspended). 18,000 crimes against the person were detected in 2003, including 227 homicides.

Education

Adult literacy rate in 2003 was 99·3% (male, 99·4%; female, 99·3%). Education is free and compulsory from six to 14. Primary schooling ends at 14; thereafter education may be continued at secondary, secondary technical or secondary vocational schools, which offer diplomas entitling students to apply for higher education, or at vocational training schools which offer tradesmen's diplomas. Students at the latter may also take the secondary school diploma examinations after two years of evening or correspondence study. Optional religious education was introduced in schools in 1990.

In 2003–04 there were: 4,610 kindergartens with 31,383 teachers and 327,500 pupils; 3,748 primary schools with 89,784 teachers and 913,600 pupils; and 1,622 secondary schools (including vocational schools) with 38,479 teachers and 531,400 pupils (of which 438,100 were full-time). 409,075 students were enrolled in tertiary education at 68 institutions in 2003–04: of these, 366,947 were at university and college level (204,910 full-time and 162,037 part-time). In 1990 only 11% of 18- to 23-year-olds were enrolled in higher education. By 2000 the proportion had risen to 35% and the target for 2010 is 50%.

There were, in 1999–2000, 201 schools for special needs with 45,245 pupils and 7,244 teachers. Schools for ethnic minorities, 1997–98: kindergartens, 386, with 20,440 pupils and 993 teachers; primary schools, 390, with 53,021 pupils and 1,357 teachers; secondary schools, 27, with 2,310 pupils and 179 teachers.

In 2000–01 total expenditure on education came to 5·2% of GNP and 14·1% of total government spending.

Health

In 2003 there were 32,877 doctors, 5,347 dentists, 5,125 pharmacists, 4,949 midwives and 87,381 nurses. While there is an excess supply of doctors, there are too few nurses and wages for both groups are exceptionally low. In 2003 there were 178 hospitals with 79,368 beds. Spending on health accounted for 6·8% of GDP in 2001.

Welfare

In 1998 the Hungarian parliament decided to place the financial funds of health and pension insurance under government supervision. The self-governing bodies which had previously been responsible for this were dissolved. Medical treatment is free. Patients bear 15% of the cost of medicines. Sickness benefit is 75% of wages, old age pensions (at 60 for men, 55 for women) 60–70%. In 2003, 1·9trn. forints was spent on pensions and pension-like benefits for 3·05m. recipients (old age 53%, disability or reduced working ability 34%, and widows and other pensions 13%); the average monthly amount of benefit per capita was 50,428 forints. Family and child benefits totalled about 2·5% of GDP in 2001. On a monthly basis as of Jan. 2004, 1·3m. families were receiving family allowance on behalf of

2·1m. children, child care allowance was being paid for 164,000 children and 82,000 were receiving child care fee.

RELIGION

Church-state affairs are regulated by a law of Feb. 1990 which guarantees freedom of conscience and religion and separates church and state by prohibiting state interference in church affairs. Religious matters are the concern of the Department for Church Relations, under the auspices of the Prime Minister's Office.

According to the 2001 census, 51·9% of the population was Roman Catholic (5·3m. people), 15·9% Calvinist (1·6m.), 3·0% Lutheran (0·3m.) and 2·6% Greek Catholic (0·27m.). Adherents to smaller Christian faiths, including Baptists, other Protestant groups, Adventists and a range of Orthodox denominations, numbered around 98,000. About 0·1% of the population was Jewish in 2001.

The Primate of Hungary is Péter Erdő, Archbishop of Esztergom-Budapest, installed in Jan. 2003. There are 11 dioceses, all with bishops or archbishops. There is one Uniate bishopric. In May 2005 the Roman Catholic church had two cardinals.

CULTURE

World Heritage Sites

Sites under Hungarian jurisdiction which appear on UNESCO's world heritage list are (with year entered on list): the Cultural Landscape of Fertö/Neusiedlersee (2001), an area on the border with Austria that has acted as a meeting place for different cultures for 8,000 years; Budapest, and specifically the Banks of the Danube and the Buda Castle Quarter (1987); Hollókő (1987), a preserved settlement developed during the 17th and 18th centuries; Millenary Benedictine Monastery of Pannonhalma and its Natural Environment (1996), first settled by Benedictine monks in 996; Hortobágy National Park (1999), a large area of plains and wetlands in eastern Hungary; Pécs (Sopianae) Early Christian Cemetery (2000), a series of decorated tombs dating from the 4th century; Tokaj Wine Region Historic Cultural Landscape (2002).

Hungary also shares a UNESCO site with Slovakia: the Caves of Aggtelek and Slovak Karst (1995 and 2000), a complex of 712 temperate-zone karstic caves.

Broadcasting

The government network *Magyar Rádió* broadcasts four programmes on medium wave and FM and also regional programmes, including transmissions in German, Romanian and Serbo-Croat. There are four other networks, three of them commercial. There are five national television channels, three of which are state-owned. *Magyar Televízió* operates two TV channels (colour by PAL). *Duna Televízió* broadcasts to Hungarians abroad. The two national private TV channels are *tv2* and *RTL-KLUB*. There are approximately 220 other commercial television stations and 30 private radio stations. There were 7·05m. radios in use and 4·45m. TV sets in 2000.

Cinema

There were 326 cinema screens in 2002; attendances in 2001 totalled 14·1m. In 2002, 24 full-length feature films were made.

Press

In 2002 there were 38 daily newspapers with a combined circulation of 1,595,000, at a rate of 158 per 1,000 inhabitants. The most widely read newspaper is the free tabloid *Metro*. In 2000 there were 167 non-dailies. A total of 8,837 book titles were published in 2001 in 32·62m. copies.

Tourism

In 2000 there were 15·57m. foreign tourists. 11·1m. Hungarians travelled abroad in 2001. Revenue from foreign tourists in 2002 was US$3·27bn. 5% of GDP is produced by tourism.

Festivals

The Budapest Spring Festival, comprising music, theatre, dance etc., takes place in March. The Balaton Festival is in May and the Szeged Open-Air Theatre Festival is in July–Aug.

Libraries

In 2001 there were 3,429 public libraries and three National libraries. They held a combined 45,630,000 volumes for 1,416,000 registered users.

Theatre and Opera

Hungary had 54 theatres in 2003.

Museums and Galleries

There were 776 museums and galleries in 1997. 466,000 people visited museums in 2003.

DIPLOMATIC REPRESENTATIVES

Of Hungary in the United Kingdom (35 Eaton Pl., London, SW1X 8BY)
Ambassador: Béla Szombati.

Of the United Kingdom in Hungary (Harmincad Utca 6, Budapest 1051)
Ambassador: John Nichols.

Of Hungary in the USA (3910 Shoemaker St., NW, Washington, D.C., 20008)
Ambassador: András Simonyi.

Of the USA in Hungary (Szabadság Tér 12, Budapest V)
Ambassador: George Herbert Walker.

Of Hungary to the United Nations
Ambassador: Gábor Bródi.

Of Hungary to the European Union
Ambassador: Péter Balázs.

FURTHER READING

Central Statistical Office. *Statisztikai ,Évkönyv.* Annual since 1871.—*Magyar Statisztikai Zsebkönyv.* Annual.—*Statistical Yearbook.*—*Statistical Handbook of Hungary.*—*Monthly Bulletin of Statistics.*

Bozóki, A., *et al.*, (eds.) *Post-Communist Transition: Emerging Pluralism in Hungary.* London, 1992

Burawoy, M. and Lukács, J., *The Radiant Past: Ideology and Reality in Hungary's Road to Capitalism.* Chicago Univ. Press, 1992

Cox, T. and Furlong, A. (eds.) *Hungary: the Politics of Transition.* London, 1995

Geró, A., *Modern Hungarian Society in the Making: the Unfinished Experience;* translated from Hungarian. Budapest, 1995

Kontler, László, *A History of Hungary.* Palgrave Macmillan, Basingstoke, 2002

Mitchell, K. D. (ed.) *Political Pluralism in Hungary and Poland: Perspectives on the Reforms.* New York, 1992

Molnár, Miklós, *A Concise History of Hungary.* CUP, 2001

Sárközi, Mátyás, *Budapest.* [Bibliography] ABC-Clio, Oxford and Santa Barbara (CA), 1997

Szekely, I. P., *Hungary: an Economy in Transition.* CUP, 1993

Turner, Barry, (ed.) *Central Europe Profiled.* Macmillan, London, 2000

National library: Széchenyi Library, Budapest.

National Statistical Office: Központi Statisztikai Hivatal/Central Statistical Office, Keleti Károly u. 5/7, H-1024 Budapest. *Director:* Dr Péter Pukli.

Website: http://www.ksh.hu/

ICELAND

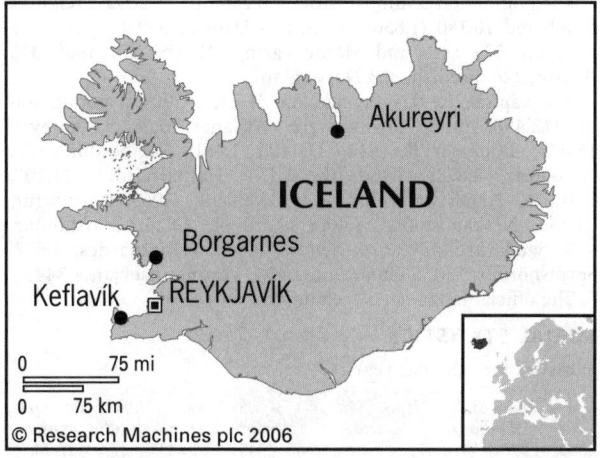

© Research Machines plc 2006

Lyðveldið Ísland
(Republic of Iceland)

Capital: Reykjavík
Population projection, 2010: 307,000
GDP per capita, 2003: (PPP$) 31,243
HDI/world rank: 0·956/2

KEY HISTORICAL EVENTS

Scandinavia's North Atlantic outpost was first settled in 874. According to the *Landnámabók* or 'book of settlements', the first to land was Ingólfr Arnarson, who came from Norway to live on the site of present-day Reykjavík. He was followed by some 400 migrants, mainly from Norway but also from other Nordic countries and from Norse settlements in the British Isles.

A ruling class was soon formed by chieftains, known as the *godar*. In 930 they established the first ever democratic national assembly, the *Alþingi* (Althing). Primarily an adjudicating body, it also served as a legislature and as a fair, a marriage mart and as a national celebration in which a large proportion of the Icelandic population participated for two weeks each June. The first notable event in its history occurred in 1000 when, by majority decision, Christianity was adopted as Iceland's official religion. Despite the change, the *godar* remained politically important and some of them were ordained. Bishoprics were established at Skálholt in 1056 and at Hólar in 1106. It was not until the 1800s, after the bishoprics were united, that Reykjavík became the new episcopal see, making it the leading community.

Trade flourished with homespun woollen cloth as the chief export, although certain materials such as grain and timber had to be imported. Iceland's only indigenous wood, birchwood, which grew in abundance yet proved unsuitable for building, later became valuable in making charcoal.

In the mid-13th century there were power struggles between the *godar*. With the 'Old Treaty' of 1262, the *godar* were persuaded to swear allegiance to the king of Norway, bringing Iceland under Norwegian rule but leaving it with internal autonomy. When Norway was joined with Denmark in 1380, Iceland still retained the Althing as well as its own code of law.

In the 14th century, the expansion of fishing to satisfy European demand stimulated agriculture and other basic industries. Iceland's newfound prosperity encouraged trade between the Icelandic fisherman and traders in Bergen, Norway. English

traders in Bergen were keen to bypass Norwegian importers and instead began trading directly with Iceland. The Danish were largely unsuccessful in preventing this and it was not until the 16th century, when the English turned to the North American fishing grounds, that hostilities ceased.

Iceland's economic progress was checked when birchwood became depleted. Coupled with over-grazing, this led to soil erosion and put an end to crop growth. Further troubles came in the 15th century when Iceland fell victim to the Black Death, on two occasions losing around half of the population.

With the advent of Lutheranism in the first half of the 16th century, Iceland resisted Denmark's efforts to impose the Reformation on their North Atlantic possession. The bishoprics of Skálholt and Hólar were eventually overcome in 1550, marking the consolidation of Danish power over Iceland. In 1602 a royal decree gave all foreign trading rights in Iceland exclusively to Danish merchants. This restriction, which lasted until 1787, virtually ended Iceland's contacts with England and Germany, their one-time trading partners. Absolutism in Denmark and Norway under King Frederick III was recognized by Iceland in 1662, further strengthening external rule, and after economic hardship in the 18th century (in the 1780s famine killed one-fifth of the population) Iceland's receding status was confirmed. When Norway split from Denmark in 1814 there were no similar calls for secession from Iceland.

Home Rule

In the 1830s a Danish consultative assembly was formed in which Iceland was given two seats. Denmark's transition to a system of representative democratic government after Frederick VII relinquished absolute power in 1848 did not extend to Iceland. After failures to reach agreement over the country's status, the Althing decided that 1874, the year that marked a thousand years of settlement, should be chosen as the year when it gained a new constitution. This was to provide the Althing with legislative if not executive control. During this period Iceland's economy continued to fare badly. With soil erosion still a problem, the strains of population growth forced mass emigration to North America. Around 15,000 emigrants left Iceland between 1870 and 1914. In 1904, after several decades of pressure for autonomy and, from 1901 onwards, support from the governing Danish Liberal party, Iceland finally achieved home rule.

Economic progress was led by the motorization of the fishing industry and an expanded labour force. In 1916 a national trade unions organization was established and a process of urbanization began as the population moved towards the coastal fishing villages. Educational reform brought the introduction of compulsory education and in 1911, the establishment of the University of Iceland at Reykjavík.

In 1918 Iceland became a separate state under the Danish crown, with only foreign affairs remaining under Danish jurisdiction. The following decades were overshadowed by the influence of the 1930s' depression and the Spanish Civil War in 1936, the latter bringing an end to the lucrative fish trade with Spain.

In 1944 Iceland declared independence since Denmark was then occupied by Nazi Germany. The termination of the union was little more than a formality, the German invasion of Denmark in 1940 having effectively ended that country's responsibility for Iceland's foreign relations.

Iceland was occupied peacefully by Britain in 1940 but US troops took over a year later. They improved roads and docks, built an airport and paid high wages. An American request for a long-term lease on three military bases was reviewed sympathetically. But the continuing presence of American forces somehow gave the lie to the independence so recently celebrated. The answer was for Iceland to join NATO. Objections to the American-run Keflavík airbase were gradually withdrawn and in 1951 a defence agreement with the United States allowed for an increase in the number of troops brought in 'to defend Iceland and ... to ensure the security of the seas around the country'. Greater integration with Europe came with joining the European Free Trade Association in 1970.

Fish remained central to the economy, accounting for 90% of the export trade. But there were worries about over-dependence on a single product and concern that other nations were taking too large a share of the Icelandic catch. In 1948 the demarcation of new fishing zones was made subject to Icelandic jurisdiction. Two years later one mile was added to the three-mile offshore zone which Iceland had administered since 1901. This was just acceptable to other fishing nations but when, in 1958, the limit was extended to 12 miles, Britain sent naval vessels to protect trawlers from harassment and arrest. This was the first Cod War, a cat-and-mouse game between the British navy and coastguard patrols which continued to 1961. At that point Britain and West Germany, the other fishing nation involved in the dispute, accepted the 12-mile zone on condition that if Iceland intended to widen her jurisdiction still further she had to give six months' notice of her intention and, if challenged, refer her claims to the International Court of Justice at The Hague.

In 1971, however, the government fulfilled its promise to do something about over-fishing by unilaterally extending the offshore zone to 50 miles. Despite a clear contravention of treaty commitment, Iceland gained sympathy as the tiny nation fighting the giants. Also in Iceland's favour was the move by Britain and members of the European Community to extend their jurisdiction over the continental shelf. A law officially expanding the Icelandic fishery limits to 50 miles came into force on 1 Sept. 1972. However, a second Cod War began shortly after as British and German trawlers continued to fish within the new zone. Hostility quickly intensified, with the Icelandic Coast Guard deploying net cutters to prevent the ships securing their catch. An agreement was signed on 8 Nov. 1973 confining British trawlers to specific areas within the 50 mile catch zone, and limiting their annual catch to 130,000 tonnes.

This agreement expired in Nov. 1975, after which Iceland declared the ocean up to 200 miles from its coast to be under Icelandic authority, and a third Cod War began. Britain protested at the 200-mile limit but when the talks reached stalemate in Dec. 1976, British vessels were nevertheless banned from Icelandic waters.

TERRITORY AND POPULATION

Iceland is an island in the North Atlantic, close to the Arctic Circle. Area, 102,819 sq. km (39,698 sq. miles).

There are eight regions:

Region	Inhabited land (sq. km)	Mountain pasture (sq. km)	Waste-land (sq. km)	Total area (sq. km)	Popula-tion (31 Dec. 2003)
Capital area					181,917
Southwest	1,266	716	—	1,982	
Peninsula					16,953
West	5,011	3,415	275	8,701	14,438
Western Peninsula	4,130	3,698	1,652	9,470	7,837
Northland West	4,867	5,278	2,948	13,093	9,145
Northland East	9,890	6,727	5,751	22,368	26,835
East	16,921	17,929	12,555	21,991	11,887
South				25,214	21,558
Iceland	42,085	37,553	23,181	102,819	290,570

Of the population of 290,570 in 2003, 21,109 were domiciled in rural districts and 269,461 (92·7%) in towns and villages (of over 200 inhabitants). Population density (2003), 2·8 per sq. km.

The UN gives a projected population for 2010 of 307,000.

The population is almost entirely Icelandic. In 2003 foreigners numbered 10,180 (1,856 Polish, 870 Danish, 609 Filipino, 551 German, 529 Serb and Montenegrin, 521 US, 474 Thai, 370 British, 326 Swedish, 323 Norwegian).

The capital, Reykjavík, had on 31 Dec. 2003 a population of 112,490; other towns were: Akranes, 5,588; Akureyri, 16,086; Bolungarvík, 944; Dalvík, 1,461; Eskifjörður, 972; Garðabær, 8,878; Grindavík, 2,434; Hafnarfjörður, 21,207; Húsavík, 2,368; Ísafjörður, 2,596; Keflavík, 7,963; Kópavogur, 25,352; Neskaupstaður, 1,400; Njarðvík, 2,825; Ólafsfjörður, 994; Sauðárkrókur, 2,620; Selfoss, 5,068; Seltjarnarnes, 4,577; Seyðisfjörður, 730; Siglufjörður, 1,434; Vestmannaeyjar, 4,344.

The official language is Icelandic.

SOCIAL STATISTICS

Statistics for calendar years:

	Live births	Still-born	Marriages	Divorces	Deaths	Infant deaths	Net immi-gration
2000	4,329	14	1,777 (12 same sex)	545	1,823	13	1,714
2001	4,091	11	1,484 (13 same sex)	551	1,725	11	968
2002	4,090	7	1,652 (9 same sex)	529	1,821	9	−275
2003	4,143	4	1,473 (12 same sex)	531	1,827	10	−133

2003 rates per 1,000 population: births, 14·3; deaths, 6·3. 64% of births are to unmarried mothers, the highest percentage in Europe. Population growth rate, 2003, 0·7%. In 2003 the most popular age range for marrying was 30–34 for both males and females. Life expectancy, 2003: males, 78·7 years; females, 82·6. Infant mortality, 2003, 2·4 per 1,000 live births (one of the lowest rates in the world); fertility rate, 2003, 1·99 births per woman.

CLIMATE

The climate is cool temperate oceanic and rather changeable, but mild for its latitude because of the Gulf Stream and prevailing S.W. winds. Precipitation is high in upland areas, mainly in the form of snow. Reykjavík, Jan. 33·8°F (1·0°C), July 51·6°F (10·9°C). Annual rainfall 31·4" (792 mm).

CONSTITUTION AND GOVERNMENT

The present constitution came into force on 17 June 1944 and has been amended four times since, most recently on 24 June 1999. The President is elected by direct, popular vote for a period of four years.

The *Alþingi* (parliament) is elected in accordance with the electoral law of 1999, which provides for an *Alþingi* of 63 members. The country is divided into a minimum of six and a maximum of seven constituencies. There are currently six constituencies: Northwest (10 seats); Northeast (10 seats); South (10); Southwest (11); Reykjavík north (11); and Reykjavík south (11).

National Anthem

'Ó Guð vors lands' ('Oh God of Our Country'); words by M. Jochumsson, tune by S. Sveinbjörnsson.

GOVERNMENT CHRONOLOGY

Presidents since 1944.

1944–52	Sveinn Björnsson
1952–68	Ásgeir Ásgeirsson
1968–80	Kristján Thórarinsson Eldjárn
1980–96	Vigdís Finnbogadóttir
1996–	Ólafur Ragnar Grímsson

Prime Ministers since 1944. (AF = People's Party; FSF= Progressive Party; SSF = IndependenceParty)

1944–47	SSF	Ólafur Thors
1947–49	AF	Stefán Jóhann Stefánsson

1949–50	SSF	Ólafur Thors
1950–53	FSF	Steingrímur Steinthórsson
1953–56	SSF	Ólafur Thors
1956–58	FSF	Hermann Jónasson
1958–59	AF	Emil Jónsson
1959–63	SSF	Ólafur Thors
1963–70	SSF	Bjarni Benediktsson
1970–71	SSF	Jóhann Hafstein
1971–74	FSF	Ólafur Jóhannesson
1974–78	SSF	Geir Hallgrímsson
1978–79	FSF	Ólafur Jóhannesson
1979–80	AF	Benedikt Gröndal
1980–83	SSF	Gunnar Thoroddsen
1983–87	FSF	Steingrímur Hermannsson
1987–88	SSF	Thorsteinn Pálsson
1988–91	FSF	Steingrímur Hermannsson
1991–2004	SSF	Davíð Oddsson
2004–	FSF	Halldór Ásgrímsson

RECENT ELECTIONS

President Ólafur Ragnar Grímsson was reappointed for a second term on 1 Aug. 2000, no opposing candidates having come forward. On 26 June 2004 he stood for popular election and gained 85·6% of the vote. Baldur Ágústsson won 12·5% and Ástþór Magnússon won 1·9%. Turnout was 63·0%.

In the parliamentary election held on 10 May 2003, the conservative Independence Party (SSF) won 22 of the 63 seats with 33·7% of the votes cast, the Alliance (SF)—consisting of the People's Alliance, the People's Party and the Alliance of the Women's List—20 with 31·0%, the Progressive Party (FSF) 12 with 17·7%, the Left-Green Alliance (VG) 5 with 8·8% and the Liberal Party (FF) 4 with 7·4%. Turnout was 87·5%.

CURRENT ADMINISTRATION

President: Ólafur Ragnar Grímsson; b. 1943 (People's Alliance; sworn in 1 Aug. 1996, reappointed 1 Aug. 2000 and re-elected on 26 June 2004).

In March 2006 the government, formed by the Independence Party (SSF/IP) and the Progressive Party (FSF/PP), comprised:

Prime Minister: Halldór Ásgrímsson; b. 1947 (PP; sworn in 15 Sept. 2004).

Minister of Foreign Affairs: Geir H. Haarde (IP). *Finance:* Árni Mathiesen (IP). *Social Affairs:* Jón Kristjánsson (PP). *Fisheries:* Einar Kristinn Guðfinnsson (IP). *Justice and Ecclesiastical Affairs:* Björn Bjarnason (IP). *Agriculture:* Guðni Ágústsson (PP). *Environment:* Sigríður Anna Þórðardóttir (IP). *Health and Social Security:* Siv Friðleifsdóttir (PP). *Education, Science and Culture:* Þorgerður Katrín Gunnarsdóttir (IP). *Industry, Commerce and Nordic Co-operation:* Valgerður Sverrisdóttir (PP). *Communications:* Sturla Böðvarsson (IP).

Government Offices of Iceland Website: http://www.stjr.is

CURRENT LEADERS

Ólafur Ragnar Grímsson

Position
President

Introduction
Ólafur Ragnar Grímsson was leader of the People's Alliance until becoming president in 1996. Observers feared his background would politicize the presidency, which is traditionally a non-partisan, ceremonial post. His relationship with Davíð Oddsson, the prime minister until Aug. 2004, was strained following several years as high-profile party political opponents.

Early Life
Grímsson was born on 14 May 1943 in Ísafjörður. He studied economics and political science at Manchester University in the UK, graduating with a doctorate in 1970. He took up a lecturing post at the University of Iceland and was appointed professor in 1973. From 1966 until 1973 he was on the board of the youth wing of the Progressive Party and between 1971 and 1973 he sat on the party's executive board.

He moved to the People's Alliance and was elected to the *Alþingi* (Parliament) in 1978 as a member for Reykjavík. From 1980 until 1983, when he failed to win re-election to parliament, Grímsson led the People's Alliance in the *Alþingi*. During 1987–96 he was party chairman and between 1988–91 served as the minister of finance. Between 1984–90 he held senior posts with Parliamentarians for Global Action, an international organization with a membership of 1,800 throughout the world. Grímsson also held positions in the Council of Europe during the 1980s and 1990s.

In 1995 he led the People's Alliance to a poor showing at the polls, in which they secured less than 15% of the vote. Shortly afterwards Grímsson announced his candidacy for the presidency at the following year's elections. In June 1996 he was elected with 41% of the vote, defeating three other candidates.

Career in Office
The presidency is a largely ceremonial office and Grímsson's election prompted some observers to fear he would politicize the position. His relationship with the then prime minister, Davíð Oddsson, had been poor ever since the two had clashed as leaders of rival parties. Nevertheless, Grímsson was reappointed as president for a second term (without an election as there were no opposing candidates) and then re-elected by popular vote on 26 June 2004 with nearly 86% of the poll. During his presidency Grímsson has used his international profile to vigorously promote Iceland and its industrial potential, particularly in emerging sectors such as information technology.

Halldór Ásgrímsson

Position
Prime Minister

Introduction
When Iceland's prime minister of 13 years, Davíð Oddsson, became ill in Aug. 2004, Halldór Ásgrímsson was chosen to replace him. The accountant-turned-politician, who had been minister for foreign affairs since 1995, took office on 15 Sept. 2004.

Early Life
Halldór Ásgrímsson was born in Vopnafjörður in eastern Iceland on 8 Sept. 1947. He attended the Co-operative College of Iceland in Reykjavík and graduated in 1965. He then specialized in finance and commerce and received a licence as a certified public accountant in 1970. The following year he undertook further studies abroad at the universities of Bergen and Copenhagen. Returning to Reykjavík in 1973, Ásgrímsson began working at the University of Iceland, lecturing at the faculty of economics and business administration. A year later, in the general election that was brought about by a split in the ruling coalition over economic policies, Ásgrímsson was elected as a member of the *Alþingi* (Parliament) for the moderate Progressive Party (PP). In 1976 Ásgrímsson became a member of the board of the Central Bank of Iceland. He served as a member of the Icelandic delegation to the Copenhagen-based Nordic Council in 1977–78.

In 1980 he became vice-chairman of the PP, which had joined the People's Alliance (PA) in a coalition led by the former Independence Party (IP) leader Gunnar Thoroddsen. The presidential election of 1980 was won by Vigdís Finnbogadóttir, who became the world's first popularly elected female head of state. Ásgrímsson became the minister for fisheries in May 1983 following the general election which resulted in the PP leader Steingrímur Hermannsson becoming prime minister. Ásgrímsson later served as minister for Nordic co-operation (1985–87) and minister for justice and ecclesiastical affairs (1988–89). He took over as leader of the PP when Hermannsson stepped down in 1994. From 1995–2004 Ásgrímsson was minister for foreign affairs and external trade in a coalition government of the PP and the IP led by prime minister Davíð Oddsson. The period was broadly characterized by strong economic growth underpinned by fisheries and the production of aluminium. Oddsson emerged victorious in the May 2004 general election, but decided to make way for Ásgrímsson following a period of ill-health in Aug. Oddsson took the job of minister of foreign affairs until Sept. 2005.

Career in Office

According to an agreement between the two coalition parties (IP and PP), Ásgrímsson became prime minister of Iceland on 15 Sept. 2004. In his opening policy address he outlined his commitment to diversifying the Icelandic economy away from its dependence on fisheries by expanding the country's power-intensive industries and taking full advantage of abundant supplies of free geothermal energy. He also pledged to cut income tax over three years, raise child allowance and promised a review of the constitution. His government also aims to promote more active international co-operation following the announcement of Iceland's candidacy for a seat on the UN Security Council for the period 2009–10 with elections taking place in 2008. Iceland is not a member of the European Union, although Ásgrímsson has indicated that the country should not preclude EU membership.

DEFENCE

Iceland possesses no armed forces. Under the North Atlantic Treaty, US forces are stationed in Iceland as the Iceland Defence Force.

Navy

There is a paramilitary coastguard of 120.

INTERNATIONAL RELATIONS

Iceland is a member of the UN, WTO, BIS, NATO, OECD, EFTA, OSCE, the Council of Europe, the Nordic Council and Council of the Baltic Sea States, and is an Associate Member of the WEU. Iceland has acceded to the Schengen accord, which abolishes border controls between Iceland, Austria, Belgium, Denmark, Finland, France, Germany, Greece, Italy, Luxembourg, the Netherlands, Norway, Portugal, Spain and Sweden.

ECONOMY

Agriculture and fishing contributed 11·1% of GDP in 2003, industry 21·4%, and services 67·5%.

According to the anti-corruption organization *Transparency International*, Iceland has the least corruption in business and government of any country in the world. It received 9·7 out of 10 in the annual index in 2005.

Overview

The economy experienced strong growth since the mid-1990s as a result of privatization and deregulation. Per capita income has approximately doubled over the last two decades. In 2004 the government opened the mortgage market to the country's three commercial banks, causing a sharp appreciation in real estate prices. The strong housing market, in combination with a tight job market, subsequently fuelled domestic demand. Inflation more than doubled in three years to 4·5% in March 2006, well above the central bank's 2·5% target. Until Feb. 2006 Iceland experienced strong capital inflows as a result of international investors borrowing money at low interest rates in the USA, the eurozone and Japan and investing them in Iceland's currency

and high yielding bonds. Capital inflows generated a substantial current account deficit and in Feb. 2006 Iceland's debt was downgraded by Fitch Ratings, sparking a fall in the Icelandic króna. The króna lost 9·3% against the US dollar in less than two days. Government finances are healthy, however, and the central bank has proved ready to raise interest rates aggressively.

Currency

The unit of currency is the *króna* (ISK) of 100 *aurar* (singular: *eyrir*). Foreign exchange markets were deregulated on 1 Jan. 1992. The krona was devalued 7·5% in June 1993. Inflation rates (based on OECD statistics):

1995	1996	1997	1998	1999	2000	2001	2002	2003	2004
1·7%	2·3%	1·8%	1·7%	3·2%	5·1%	6·4%	5·2%	2·1%	3·2%

Foreign exchange reserves were US$366m. and gold reserves 62,000 troy oz in June 2002. Note and coin circulation at 31 Dec. 2003 was 8,391m. kr.

Budget

Total central government revenue and expenditure for calendar years (in 1m. kr.):

	1998	1999	2000	2001	2002	2003
Revenue	170,500	198,900	212,600	227,100	237,000	251,500
Expenditure	164,300	183,300	195,600	222,600	241,700	266,100

Central government debt was 277,000m. kr. on 31 Dec. 2003, of which the foreign debt amounted to 112,005m. kr. VAT is 24·5% (reduced rate, 14%).

Performance

Real GDP growth rates (based on OECD statistics):

1995	1996	1997	1998	1999	2000	2001	2002	2003	2004
0·1%	5·2%	4·7%	5·7%	4·2%	5·0%	3·3%	−1·3%	3·6%	6·2%

GDP in 2004 totalled US$12·4bn.

Banking and Finance

The Central Bank of Iceland (founded 1961; *Chairman of the Board of Governors*, Davíð Oddsson) is responsible for note issue and carries out the central banking functions. There were 27 savings banks in 2002. The government had by 2003 sold to the public its shares in two banks. On 31 Dec. 2003 the accounts of the Central Bank balanced at 87,307m. kr. Commercial bank deposits were 369,605m. kr., and deposits in the 29 savings banks 87,307m. kr.

There is a stock exchange in Reykjavík.

ENERGY AND NATURAL RESOURCES

Iceland is aiming to become the world's first 'hydrogen economy'; its buses started to convert to fuel cell-powered vehicles in late 2003. Ultimately it aims to run all its transport and even its fishing fleet on hydrogen produced in Iceland.

Environment

Iceland's carbon dioxide emissions from the consumption and flaring of fossil fuels in 2002 were the equivalent of 10·8 tonnes per capita. An *Environmental Sustainability Index* compiled for the World Economic Forum meeting in Jan. 2005 ranked Iceland fifth in the world, with 70·8%. The index measured the ability of countries to maintain favourable environmental conditions and examined various factors including pollution levels and the use or abuse of natural resources.

Electricity

The installed capacity of public electrical power plants at the end of 2003 totalled 1·5m. kW; installed capacity of hydro-electric plants was 1,150,700 kW. Total electricity production in public-owned plants in 2003 amounted to 8,495m. kWh;

in privately owned plants, 5m. kWh. Virtually all of Iceland's electricity is produced from hydro power and geothermal energy. Consumption per capita was estimated in 2003 to be 29,367 kWh (one of the highest in the world).

Agriculture

Of the total area, about six-sevenths is unproductive, but only about 1·3% is under cultivation, which is largely confined to hay and potatoes. Arable land totalled 15,500 ha. in 2003. In 2003 the total hay crop was 2,287,936 cu. metres; the crop of potatoes, 7,090 tonnes; of tomatoes, 1,074 tonnes; and of cucumbers, 896 tonnes. Livestock (end of 2003): sheep, 463,006; horses, 71,412; cattle, 66,035 (milch cows, 24,904); pigs, 3,852; poultry, 48,953. Livestock products (2003, in tonnes): lamb, 8,792; milk, 108,384; cheese, 4,190; butter and dairy margarines, 1,447.

Forestry

In 2000 forests covered 31,000 ha., or approximately 0·3% of the total land area.

Fisheries

Fishing is of vital importance to the economy. Fishing vessels at the end of 2003 numbered 1,872, with a gross tonnage of 183,725. Total catch in 2000: 1,980,163; 2001: 1,986,584; 2002: 2,133,327; 2003: 1,979,545. Virtually all the fish caught is from marine waters. Iceland has received international praise for its management system which aims to avoid the over-fishing that has decimated stocks in other parts of the world. In 2003 fisheries accounted for 9·7% of GDP, down from 16·8% in 1996. The per capita consumption of fish and fishery products is the second highest in the world, after that of the Maldives.

Fishery limits were extended from 12 to 50 nautical miles in 1972 and to 200 nautical miles in 1975.

INDUSTRY

Production, 2002, in 1,000 tonnes: aluminium, 285·3; ferro-silicon, 120·6; diatomite, 26·4; and 82·6 of cement was sold.

Labour

In 2003 the economically active population was 162,400, of which 3·4% were unemployed. In the period 1993–2002 Iceland averaged 554 working days lost to strikes per 1,000 employees—the highest number in any western European country. In 2003 agriculture and fishing employed 6·9% of the economically active population, industry 21·7% (including manufacturing except fish processing 10·4%) and services 71·4% (including health services and social work 15·8% and wholesale, retail trade and repairs 13·1%).

Trade Unions

In 2002 trade union membership was 85·4% of the workforce.

INTERNATIONAL TRADE

The economy is heavily trade-dependent.

Imports and Exports

Total value of imports (c.i.f.) and exports (f.o.b.) in 1m. kr.:

	1999	2000	2001	2002	2003
Imports	182,322	203,222	220,874	207,608	216,525
Exports	144,928	149,273	196,582	204,303	182,580

Main imports, 2003 (in 1m. kr.): road vehicles, 20,959; petroleum and products, 15,605; electrical machinery and appliances, 14,197. Main exports, 2003 (in 1m. kr.): fish, crustaceans, molluscs and preparations thereof, 97,950; non-ferrous metals, 34,280; fodder for animals (excluding unmilled cereals), 11,938; iron and steel, 6,071.

Value of trade with principal countries for three years (in 1,000 kr.):

	2001 Imports (c.i.f.)	2001 Exports (f.o.b.)	2002 Imports (c.i.f.)	2002 Exports (f.o.b.)	2003 Imports (c.i.f.)	2003 Exports (f.o.b.)
Belgium	4,120,900	2,798,900	3,683,600	3,209,700	4,828,200	3,215,800
China	6,352,400	905,200	6,112,300	1,310,100	7,719,200	1,327,300
Denmark	19,077,600	8,282,100	17,654,200	9,417,400	17,389,000	9,315,300
Finland	3,724,200	1,326,500	3,478,300	1,867,100	3,188,900	1,336,000
France	6,982,600	7,687,900	6,436,300	7,500,700	6,919,100	7,381,500
Germany	26,908,800	29,292,200	22,165,400	37,747,900	25,578,800	31,829,300
Italy	6,802,900	2,517,100	6,206,700	2,762,900	10,100,700	2,464,700
Japan	7,297,600	6,838,600	6,514,200	6,766,400	8,266,600	5,914,800
Netherlands	14,554,400	21,442,100	12,504,900	22,059,400	13,355,200	20,459,900
Norway	17,234,600	10,384,300	16,600,600	9,332,600	15,009,000	8,157,400
Portugal	1,223,400	10,816,300	1,011,500	8,865,000	1,022,500	6,916,400
Russia	3,551,200	715,700	7,898,200	1,704,600	6,054,000	1,034,000
Spain	4,341,800	10,538,600	3,852,800	10,693,900	3,936,300	11,546,500
Sweden	12,757,400	2,084,700	12,294,300	2,174,300	13,995,000	2,348,900
Switzerland	3,039,300	6,400,000	2,225,500	3,056,400	2,610,300	3,555,900
UK	16,609,600	35,839,100	15,459,600	35,739,000	16,096,600	31,990,100
USA	24,505,600	20,329,900	23,024,800	21,988,800	16,122,900	16,927,300

COMMUNICATIONS

Roads

On 31 Dec. 2003 the length of the public roads (including roads in towns) was 13,004 km. Of these 8,208 km were main and secondary roads and 4,796 km were provincial roads. Total length of surfaced roads was 4,331 km. A ring road of 1,400 km runs just inland from much of the coast; about 80% of it is smooth-surfaced. Motor vehicles registered at the end of 2003 numbered 183,813, of which 168,578 were passenger cars and 21,235 lorries; there were also 2,747 motorcycles. There were 20 fatal road accidents in 2003 with 23 persons killed.

Civil Aviation

Icelandair is the national carrier. In 2003 it served 13 destinations in western Europe and six in north America as well as operating domestic services. In 1999 it carried 1·3m. passengers. The main international airport is at Keflavík (Leifsstöd), with Reykjavík for flights to the Faroe Islands, Greenland and domestic services. Keflavík handled 1,368,496 passengers in 2003 (of which 211,904 transit passengers) and 40,554 tonnes of freight.

Shipping

Total registered vessels, 1,129 (228,231 gross tonnage) in 2003; of these, 943 were sea-going fishing vessels.

Telecommunications

In 2003 the number of telephone main lines was 192,552; mobile phone subscribers, 279,670 (more than 95% of the population—among the highest penetration rates in the world). In 2002 there were 130,000 PCs (451·4 per 1,000 persons) and 6,300 fax machines. There were 195,000 Internet users in 2003, 67·5% of the total population (the highest percentage in the world).

Postal Services
At the end of 2003 the number of post offices was 100.

SOCIAL INSTITUTIONS

Justice
In 1992 jurisdiction in civil and criminal cases was transferred from the provincial magistrates to eight new district courts, separating the judiciary from the prosecution. From the district courts there is an appeal to the Supreme Court in Reykjavík, which has eight judges. The population in penal institutions in Sept. 2002 was 107 (37 per 100,000 of national population).

Education
Primary education is compulsory and free from 6–15 years of age. Optional secondary education from 16 to 19 is also free. In 2003 there were 44,809 pupils in primary schools, 21,901 in secondary schools (18,885 on day courses) and 15,466 tertiary-level students (12,800 on day courses). Some 14% of tertiary-level students study abroad.

There are eight universities and specialized colleges at the tertiary level in Iceland. The largest is the University of Iceland in Reykjavík (founded 1911). There is also a university in Akureyri (founded 1987). Total enrolment of these two institutions was 6,100 students in 1997–98. In Reykjavík there are a teachers' university, a technical college, business colleges and an agricultural university.

In 2003 public sector spending on education was 6·5% of GNP.

The adult literacy rate is at least 99%.

Health
In 2002 there were 23 hospitals with 2,228 beds, equivalent to 78 per 10,000 population. There were 1,047 doctors in 2003, 2,342 nurses and 273 pharmacists in 2002 and 283 dentists in 2000. In 2003 there were 3·6 doctors per 1,000 inhabitants. Iceland has one of the lowest alcohol consumption rates in Europe, at 6·52 litres of alcohol per adult per year (2003). In 2003 Iceland spent 10·5% of its GDP on health.

Welfare
The main body of social welfare legislation is consolidated in six acts:

(i) The social security legislation (a) health insurance, including sickness benefits; *(b)* social security pensions, mainly consisting of old age pension, disablement pension and widows' pension, and also children's pension; *(c)* employment injuries insurance.

(ii) The unemployment insurance legislation, where daily allowances are paid to those who have met certain conditions.

(iii) The subsistence legislation. This is controlled by municipal government.

(iv) The tax legislation/ Prior to 1988 children's support was included in the tax legislation. Since 1988 family allowances are paid directly to all children age 0–15 years. The amount is increased with the second child in the family, and children under the age of seven get additional benefits. Single parents receive additional allowances.

(v) The rehabilitation legislation.

(vi) Child and juvenile guidance.

Health insurance covers the entire population. Citizenship is not demanded and there is a six-month waiting period. Most hospitals are both municipally and state run, a few solely state run and all offer free medical help. Medical treatment out of hospitals is partly paid by the patient; the same applies to medicines, except medicines of lifelong necessary use, which are paid in full by the health insurance. Dental care is partly paid by the state for children under 17 years old and also for old age and disabled pensioners. Sickness benefits are paid to those who lose income because of periodical illness.

The pension system is composed of the public social security system and some 90 private pension funds. The social security system pays basic old age and disablement pensions of a fixed amount regardless of past or present income, as well as supplementary pensions to individuals with low present income. The pensions are index-linked, i.e. are changed in line with changes in wage and salary rates in the labour market. In the public social security system, entitlement to old age and disablement pensions at the full rates is subject to the condition that the beneficiary has been resident in Iceland for 40 years at the age period of 16–67. For shorter periods of residence, the benefits are reduced proportionally. Entitled to old age pension are all those who are 67 years old, and have been residents in Iceland for three years of the age period of 16–67. Old age and disablement pension are of equally high amount; in the year 2004 the total sum was 254,988 kr. for an individual. Married pensioners receive double the basic pension. Pensioners with little or no other income are entitled to an income supplement; in 2004 the maximum annual income supplement was 520,688 kr.

The employment injuries insurance covers medical care, daily allowances, disablement pension and survivors' pension and is applicable to practically all employees.

RELIGION
The national church, the Evangelical Lutheran, is endowed by the state. There is complete religious liberty. The affairs of the national church are under the superintendence of a bishop. In 2004, 250,661 (86·3%) of the population were members of it (93·2% in 1980). 13,155 persons (4·5%) belonged to Lutheran free churches. 22,331 persons (7·7%) belonged to other religious organizations and 7,144 persons (2·5%) did not belong to any religious community.

CULTURE

World Heritage Sites
There is one UNESCO site in Iceland: Þingvellir National Park (2004), located on an active volcanic site.

Broadcasting
The state-owned public service, The Icelandic State Broadcasting Service, broadcasts two national and three regional radio programmes and one national TV channel. In addition, 27 privately owned radio stations and ten private TV stations were in operation in 2003. At 31 Dec. 2003, 93,501 colour TV sets were licensed (497 black and white).

Cinema
There were 23 cinemas with 46 screens in 2003 of which the capital had seven cinemas and 27 screens. Total admissions numbered 1,445,783 in 2003, with the Reykjavík area accounting for 1,277,546. In 2002 gross box office receipts came to 1,149·9m. kr. Four full-length Icelandic films were released in 2002; the most successful was Baltasar Kormákur's *The Sea*.

Press
In 2002 there were three daily newspapers and 22 non-daily newspapers (13 paid-for and nine free).

Iceland publishes more books per person than any other country in the world. In 2002, 1,192 volumes of books and 775 volumes of booklets were published.

Tourism
There were 308,768 visitors in 2003; revenue totalled 37,285m. kr. Overnight stays in hotels and guest houses in 2003 numbered

1,260,501 (of which foreign travellers, 970,256; and Icelanders, 290,245). Tourism accounts for more than 13% of foreign currency earnings.

Festivals
The Reykjavík Arts Festival, an annual programme of international artists and performers, is held every May–June.

Libraries
The National and University Library of Iceland is in Reykjavík and contains 901,000 volumes. The seven University libraries contain 205,074 volumes, the 43 special libraries 360,854 volumes. There are 57 public libraries with 2,235,658 volumes.

Theatre and Opera
In 2003 there were six professional theatres operated on a yearly basis (of which five were in the capital region) and 18 professional theatre groups (all in the capital region). In 2003 there were 188,869 admissions to performances of the professional theatres, 67,044 admissions to the National Theatre and 78,106 admissions to the City Theatre and Idno Theatre. Total audience of the Icelandic Opera was 11,907.

Museums and Galleries
In 2002 there were 107 museums, botanical gardens, aquariums and zoos in operation, with a total of 1,108,259 visitors. The National Museum re-opened in Sept. 2004 after extensive renovation, so received no visitors in 2002. The National Gallery received 28,459 visitors and 97,878 attended the Reykjavík Municipal Art Museum.

DIPLOMATIC REPRESENTATIVES

Of Iceland in the United Kingdom (2A Hans St., London, SW1X 0JE)
Ambassador: Sverrir Hakur Gunnlaugsson.

Of the United Kingdom in Iceland (Laufásvegur 31, 101 Reykjavík)
Ambassador: Alp Mehmet, MVO.

Of Iceland in the USA (1156 15th St. NW, Suite 1200, Washington, D.C., 20005)
Ambassador: Helgi Ágústsson.

Of the USA in Iceland (Laufásvegur 21, 101 Reykjavík)
Ambassador: Carol van Voorst.

Of Iceland to the United Nations
Ambassador: Hjálmar W. Hannesson.

Of Iceland to the European Union
Ambassador: Kjartan Jóhansson.

FURTHER READING

Statistics Iceland, *Landshagir* (Statistical Yearbook of Iceland).—*Hagtíðindi* (Statistical Series)
Central Bank of Iceland. *Monetary Bulletin.—The Economy of Iceland.* (Latest issue 2005)
Byock, Jesse, *Viking Age Iceland.* Penguin, London, 2001
Hastrup, K., *A Place Apart: An Anthropological Study of the Icelandic World.* Clarendon Press, Oxford, 1998
Karlsson, G., *The History of Iceland.* Univ. of Minnesota Press, 2000
Lacy, T., *Ring of Seasons: Iceland—Its culture and history.* University of Michigan Press, 1998
McBride F. R., *Iceland.* [Bibliography] 2nd ed. ABC-Clio, Oxford and Santa Barbara (CA), 1996
Smiley, Jane, (ed.) *The Sagas of Icelanders: A Selection.* Penguin, London, 2002
Turner, Barry, (ed.) *Scandinavia Profiled.* Macmillan, London, 2000

National Statistical Office: Statistics Iceland, Bogartúni 21a, IS-150 Reykjavík.
Website: http://www.hagstofa.is
National library: Landsbókasafn Islands.—Háskólabókasafn, Reykjavík, *Librarian:* Sigrún Klara Hannesdóttir.

INDIA

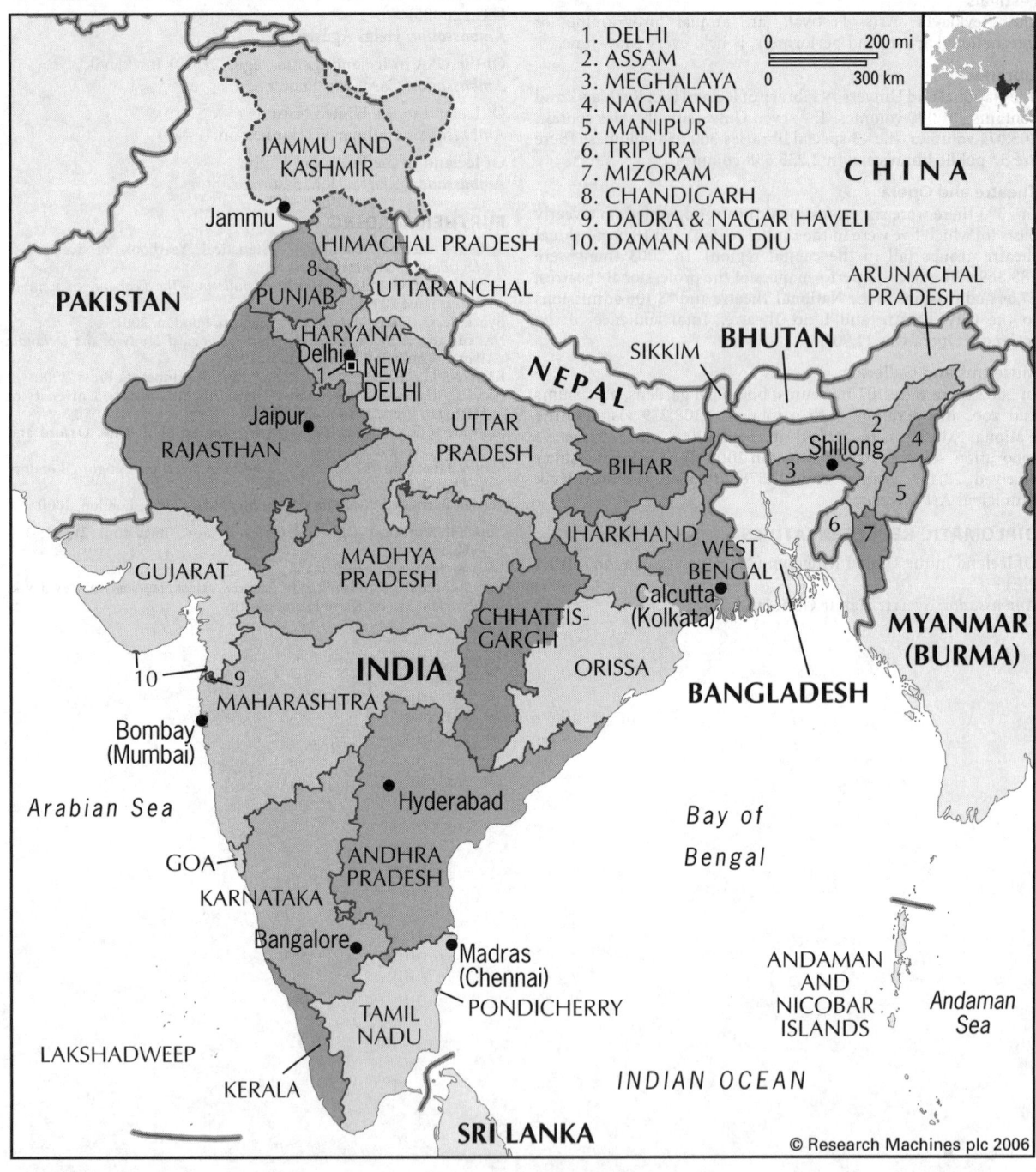

1. DELHI
2. ASSAM
3. MEGHALAYA
4. NAGALAND
5. MANIPUR
6. TRIPURA
7. MIZORAM
8. CHANDIGARH
9. DADRA & NAGAR HAVELI
10. DAMAN AND DIU

0   200 mi
0   300 km

CHINA

PAKISTAN

JAMMU AND KASHMIR

Jammu

HIMACHAL PRADESH

8

PUNJAB

UTTARANCHAL

HARYANA

Delhi
1 NEW DELHI

Jaipur

RAJASTHAN

UTTAR PRADESH

NEPAL

SIKKIM

BHUTAN

ARUNACHAL PRADESH

2

Shillong

4

3

BIHAR

5

JHARKHAND

GUJARAT

MADHYA PRADESH

WEST BENGAL

6   7

Calcutta (Kolkata)

CHHATTIS-GARGH

INDIA

ORISSA

BANGLADESH

MYANMAR (BURMA)

10

9

MAHARASHTRA

Bombay (Mumbai)

Arabian Sea

Hyderabad

GOA

ANDHRA PRADESH

KARNATAKA

Bangalore

Madras (Chennai)

PONDICHERRY

TAMIL NADU

LAKSHADWEEP

KERALA

SRI LANKA

Bay of Bengal

ANDAMAN AND NICOBAR ISLANDS

Andaman Sea

INDIAN OCEAN

© Research Machines plc 2006

Map. Based upon Survey of India Map with the permission of the Surveyor General of India. The responsibility for the correctness of internal details rests with the publisher. The territorial waters of India extend into the sea to a distance of 12 nautical miles measured from the appropriate base line. The external boundaries and coatlines of India agree with the Record/Master Copy certified by the Survey of India.

Bharat
(Republic of India)

Capital: New Delhi
Population projection, 2010: 1,183·29m.
GDP per capita, 2003: 2,892 (PPP$)
HDI/world rank 0·602/127

KEY HISTORICAL EVENTS

The valley of the Indus and its tributaries is divided today between India and Pakistan. Some 7,000 years ago the valley was one of the cradles of civilization. From the Indus Valley, Dravidian peoples spread agriculture and fixed settlements gradually across India, arriving in the far south by about 4,000 years ago. The Indus Valley Harappan civilization, a Bronze Age culture, flourished from around 2300 to 1500 BC and had links with western Asian civilizations in Iran. The two great cities of the Harappan civilization—Mohenjo-Daro and Harappa—were in what is now Pakistan, but Harappan culture also thrived in modern-day northwestern India. Writing, fine jewellery and textile production, town planning, metalworking and pottery were the hallmarks of an advanced urban society, which collapsed for reasons that are still not fully understood.

At the same time, another Bronze Age civilization existed in the Ganges Valley. This civilization, whose links were with southeastern Asia, was based on a rice-growing rural economy, which supported a number of city-states. Around 1500 BC a pastoral people, the Aryans, invaded the Indus Valley from Iran and Central Asia. Their arrival completed the destruction of the Harappan civilization and shifted the balance of power in the subcontinent to the Ganges Valley.

The Aryans took over northern and central India, merging their culture with that of the Dravidians. The caste system, still a feature of Indian society, dates back to the Dravidians, but the languages of northern and central India, and the polytheistic religion that is now followed by the majority of the inhabitants of the subcontinent, are both Aryan in origin. From these two cultures, a Hindu civilization emerged.

By 800 BC a series of Hindu kingdoms had developed in the Ganges Valley. This region gave birth to one of the world's great religions: Buddhism. Prince Gautama, the Buddha (c. 563–483 BC), renounced a life of wealth to seek enlightenment. His creed of non-violence was spread throughout India and, later, southeastern Asia. However, Buddhism was partly instrumental in destroying the most powerful of ancient states of the Ganges Valley: Magdalha.

Magdalha was ruled by the Nanda dynasty in the 4th century BC. In 321 BC the Nandas were replaced by the Mauryans under Chandragupta Maurya (reigned 321–297 BC). Chandragupta conquered most of northern India before his ascetic death from self-imposed starvation. His grandson, Ashoka, ruled an empire that stretched from the Deccan to Afghanistan from c. 272–c. 231, but he is mainly remembered for his enthusiasm for Buddhist pacifism. Attacked by enemies who did not share this creed, the Mauryan empire collapsed soon after Ashoka's death.

To the west, the Indus Valley had passed to the Persian Empire by the 5th century BC and then fell to Alexander the Great. After Alexander's death in 323 BC, Greek influences continued to be felt in the northwest of the subcontinent where an Indo-Greek civilization flourished for at least 200 years. This was brought to an end by nomadic invasions from Central Asia between the 1st and 5th centuries AD. By then, India had been divided into many small warring states, most of which were short-lived.

Empire Building

However, two strong states emerged briefly to reunite much of India: the Gupta empire and the Harsa empire. The Gupta empire was founded in the Ganges Valley by Chandragupta I (reigned c. 320–30). His warrior son, Samudragupta (reigned c. 330–80), won most of north India, but the empire was destroyed by succession disputes and a Hun invasion in the middle of the 5th century. The Harsa empire was the personal creation of a Buddhist convert, Harsa (reigned 606–47), who briefly ruled most of the north of the subcontinent. With his death, his empire fell apart and India was once more divided into many rival kingdoms.

Although no Hindu state managed to unite India, the Hindu religion and culture proved powerful influences throughout the region. The agents of Hinduism were not kings or soldiers but merchants. By about 500 BC Sri Lanka was within the Hindu sphere of influence. Over the next 800 years Hindu kingdoms were established in Burma, Cambodia, Sumatra, Thailand and Java. From the 4th century BC, Indian merchants also spread Buddhism through southeastern Asia. The great Hindu kingdoms flourished far beyond the subcontinent. The most splendid were the Khmer kingdom based on Angkor Wat in Cambodia and the maritime kingdom of Sriwijaya, based in Sumatra.

While Indian religion and culture spread south and east, an invasion from the west threatened to change the subcontinent. In 713 a Muslim army conquered Sind. For the next 300 years, Islamic rulers were largely confined to what is now Pakistan, but in 1000 a raid by the ruler of Ghazni (now in Afghanistan) overran the Punjab. During the 11th and 12th centuries the Hindu states of the Ganges Valley were toppled by Muslim invaders.

The principal Islamic state of India, following the Muslim conquest of northern India, was the sultanate of Delhi. This powerful state was founded by Qutb-ud-Din Aybak (reigned c. 1208–10), a former slave, who united the Indus and Ganges valleys and founded the Mu'izzi dynasty. Under the short-lived Khaljis dynasty, the sultanate became the leading power in India, largely owing to the military prowess of Sultan 'Ala-ud-Din Khalji (reigned 1296–1316). But by 1388, following the inept rule of the three sultans of the Tughluq dynasty, the sultanate had ceased to be important.

The Delhi sultanate was eventually replaced in the north by the Mughal Empire, which was founded by Babur (reigned 1526–30), a descendant of Timur and Genghis Khan. Akbar the Great (reigned 1556–1605) extended the Mughal Empire, conquering Baluchistan, Gujarat, Bengal, Orissa, Rajasthan, Afghanistan and Bihar. In his campaign against Gujarat, Akbar marched his army 800 km (500 miles) in only 11 days. His grandson, Shah Jahan (reigned 1628–58), was a pleasure-seeking ruler, who is remembered for constructing the Taj Mahal as a memorial to his favourite wife.

The decline of the Mughal Empire began under Shah Jahan's son, Aurangzeb I (reigned 1658–1707). Aurangzeb persecuted Hindus with a vengeance. Inter-community violence and wars against Hindu states weakened the empire. Throughout the 18th century, disputed successions and fears of assassination diverted the Mughal emperors. By the close of the 18th century the last emperor was nominal ruler of the environs of Delhi.

The main Hindu state of the subcontinent from the 14th century to the 17th century was the kingdom of Vijayanagar, which occupied most of southern India. Harihara I (reigned 1336–54), who had been governor of part of central India for the Mughal emperor, rebelled and established his own kingdom. Under Devaraya II (reigned 1425–47), Vijayanagar included virtually all of southern India and much of Sri Lanka. This kingdom reached its zenith under Krsnadevaraya (reigned 1509–29), who encouraged good relations with the Portuguese who had founded trading posts on his shores. Vijayanagar collapsed in civil wars (1614–46).

The Bahmani sultanate of the Deccan was an Islamic state, which dominated central India from the mid-14th century until the 16th century. This state was founded by 'Ala-ud-Din Hasan Bahmani Shah (reigned 1347–58), the local governor for the sultan of Delhi who rebelled against Delhi and established his own dynasty. For a time the Bahmani sultanate was the most powerful state in central India, but defeats at the hands of the kingdom of Vijayanagar in the 15th century weakened the Bahmani sultans. Upon the death of the last Bahmani sultan in 1518 this extensive kingdom was divided by the provincial governors into small states.

European Influence

By the 16th century European traders had established centres along India's coasts. The first to arrive were the Portuguese in 1498. In 1510 the Portuguese took Goa, which was to remain the centre of the fragmented possessions of Portuguese India until 1962. The creation of the (English) East India Company in 1600 heralded the beginning of what was to become the British Indian Empire. Forts were established on the coast in 1619 and in 1661 England took possession of Bombay.

Initially the Europeans were only interested in trade, but they soon became involved in local politics, in particular the disputed successions that bedevilled Indian states. Portugal and England were not alone in attempting to establish themselves in India. The Dutch were active in the 17th century but were effectively eliminated from the competition long before 1759, when Britain took Chinsura, the headquarters of Dutch administration in India. Two small Danish colonies lasted from 1618 until 1858. However, the main threat to British rule in India was France. Although the East India Company controlled parts of Bengal and the Ganges Valley, France was supreme in the Deccan where French forces, and Indian rulers allied to France, held sway over an area twice the size of France itself.

In the 1750s Britain and France fought out their European wars overseas. The defeat of French forces, and France's Indian allies, at the battle of Plassey (1757), by British forces led by Robert Clive (1725–74), confirmed British rule in Bengal and Bihar and ejected France from the Deccan. Henceforth, France was restricted to five small coastal possessions.

The Maratha state was the major power in central and southern India in the 17th and 18th centuries. This empire was founded by Sivaji (1627–80), who built the state between 1653 and 1660. The Hindu Sivaji came into conflict with the fanatical Muslim Mughal emperor Aurangzeb, who imprisoned Sivaji. After his famous escape from captivity, concealed in a fruit basket, Sivaji made himself emperor of his Maratha state in 1674. This pious monarch ruled competently, establishing an efficient administration, but by the time of his grandson, Shahu (reigned 1707–27), the power of the Maratha emperors had been eclipsed by that of their hereditary chief minister, the Peshwa. In 1727 the Peshwa Baji Rao I (reigned 1720–40) effectively replaced the emperor and established his own dynasty. Baji Rao made the Maratha state the strongest in India. His descendant, Baji Rao II (reigned 1795–1817), raised a weakened state against the British and was crushed. He was the last important Indian monarch outside British influence.

East India Company

In the first half of the 19th century, wars against Sind (1843) and the Sikhs in Punjab (1849) extended the borders of British India. By the middle of the 19th century about 60% of the subcontinent was controlled by the East India Company. The remaining 40% was divided between about 620 Indian states, which were, in theory, still sovereign and ruled by their own maharajas, sultans, nawabs and other monarchs, each advised by a British resident. The Indian states ranged from large entities the size of European countries (such as Hyderabad, Baroda, Mysore and Indore) to tiny states no bigger than an English parish.

British rule brought land reform in the areas controlled by the East India Company. The traditional patterns of land holdings was broken up and private land ownership was introduced. This had the unintended result of concentrating ownership in the hands of a small number of powerful landlords. As a result, landless peasants and dispossessed princes united in their opposition to British rule. In 1857 a mutiny by soldiers of the East India Company quickly spread into full-scale rebellion. Throughout India those who resented the speed and nature of the changes brought about by British rule made one final attempt to eject the occupiers. The Indian Mutiny took 14 months to put down.

After the Mutiny the British government replaced the East India Company as the ruler of an Indian colonial empire (1858), and the modernization of India began apace. Emphasis was placed on building up an Indian infrastructure, particularly roads and railways. The participation of Indians within the civil administration, the construction of a vast national railway system and the imposition of the English language, through the many new schools, colleges and universities, did much to forge a national identity overriding the divisions of local state and caste. But industry in India was not modernized, in part through fear of competition. In 1877 the Indian Empire was proclaimed and Queen Victoria became Empress of India (Kaiser-i-Hind).

Growing Nationalism

The (Hindu-dominated) Indian National Congress, the forerunner of the Congress Party, first met in 1885, and in 1906 the rival Muslim League was founded. Demands for Home Rule grew in the early years of the 20th century, and nationalist feeling was fuelled when British troops fired without warning on a peaceful nationalist protest meeting—the Amritsar Massacre (1919).

Realizing that change was inevitable, the British government reformed the administration through two Acts of Parliament in 1919 and 1935. These created an Indian federation, effectively removing many of the differences between the Crown territories and the Indian states. These acts granted a new Indian government limited autonomy. The pace of reform was, however, too slow for Indian popular opinion.

In 1920 the Congress party began a campaign of non-violence and non-cooperation with the British colonial authorities. Congress was led in its struggle by the charismatic figure of Mahatma Gandhi (1869–1948). The British authorities were forced to concede Gandhi's moral influence and invited him to a conference to discuss India's future. However, Gandhi found himself opposed by the traditional rulers of the Indian states, whose own positions were at risk.

By the start of the Second World War (1939–45), relations between the Hindu and Muslim communities in India had broken down, and the Muslims were demanding a separate independent Islamic state, later, Pakistan. During the war, Assam and other northeastern areas were faced with the threat of a Japanese invasion. Although many Indians served in the Allied forces during the war, a minority supported Japan as a possible liberator of India from colonial rule.

In 1945 Britain had neither the will nor the resources to maintain the Indian Empire. But although Britain had accepted independence as unavoidable, religious tension had made partition inevitable. In 1947 the sub-continent was divided between India, a predominantly Hindu state led by Jawaharlal (Pandit) Nehru (1889–1964) of the Congress Party, and Pakistan, a Muslim state led by Mohammad Ali Jinnah (1876–1948) of the Muslim League. The rulers of the Indian states were entitled to choose their allegiance while British Crown territories were assigned to either India or Pakistan.

Partitions

Partition brought enormous upheaval. More than 70m. Hindus and Muslims became refugees as they trekked across the new boundaries. Many thousands were killed in intercommunal violence. The Muslim ruler of the large, mainly Hindu, southern Indian state of Hyderabad declared independence, and the adherence of his state to India was only achieved through Indian military intervention. The Hindu ruler of mainly Muslim Kashmir opted to join India, against the wishes of his people. Elsewhere the border remained disputed in many places. Tension increased when Gandhi was assassinated by a Hindu fundamentalist (1948). In 1950 India became a republic.

Tension between India and Pakistan erupted into war in 1947–49 when the two countries fought over Kashmir. The region was divided along a ceasefire line, although neither side recognized this as an international border. India and Pakistan went to war again over Kashmir in 1965, and again in 1971 when Bangladesh (formerly East Pakistan) gained its independence as a result of Indian military intervention. Indian forces saw action in 1961 when Indian troops invaded and annexed Portuguese India and in 1962 in a border war with China. France had already ceded its small enclaves to India in 1950 and 1955. In 1975 India annexed the small Himalayan kingdom of Sikkim.

Despite its involvement in several wars, India assumed joint leadership of the non-aligned world. Pandit Nehru, who was premier from 1947 to 1964, was briefly succeeded by Lal Bahadur Shastri. In 1966 Nehru's daughter Indira Gandhi (1917–84) became premier. Under Mrs Gandhi, India continued to assert itself as a regional power and the rival of Pakistan. Although non-aligned, India developed close relations with the Soviet Union.

In 1971 Mrs Gandhi's government abolished the titles, pensions and privileges guaranteed to the Indian princes at independence as compensation for merging their states into India. India was wracked by local separatism and communal unrest, which brought instability. From 1975 to 1977 Mrs Gandhi imposed a much-criticized state of emergency. Her actions split the Congress Party, allowing Morarji Desai (1896–1995) of the Janata Party to form India's first non-Congress administration. However, his coalition soon shattered and a wing of Congress, led by Mrs Gandhi, was returned to power in 1980.

Violence in Sikh areas, fanned by demands by militant Sikhs for an independent homeland (called Khalistan) increased tensions. In 1984 Mrs Gandhi ordered that the Golden Temple in Amritsar be stormed after it had been turned into a storehouse for weapons by Sikh extremists. Soon afterwards, Mrs Gandhi was assassinated by her Sikh bodyguards.

Mrs Gandhi was succeeded as premier by her son, Rajiv (1944–91), during whose period of office India became involved in Sri Lanka, supporting the central government against the separatist Tamil Tigers movement. Rajiv Gandhi was assassinated by a Tamil Tiger suicide bomber during the 1991 election campaign.

Recent Politics

By 1989 personality clashes and separatists tendencies had shattered the unity of the once all-powerful Congress Party. Regional parties and Hindu nationalist parties came to the fore and, since 1989, when Rajiv Gandhi left office, multi-party coalitions have held office. Seven prime ministers have led India since 1989: the longest periods in office were enjoyed by P. V. Narasimha Rao (born 1921), who led a coalition from 1991 to 1996, and Atal Bihari Vajpayee (born 1924), who was premier in 1996 and held office again from 1998–2004. The right-wing Hindu nationalist Bharatiya Janata Party (BJP) has been part of most of these coalitions. Support for the BJP increased following violence between Hindus and Muslims over a campaign, which began in 1990, to build a Hindu temple on the site of a mosque in the holy city of Ayodhya.

Since the fall of the Soviet Union (1991), India has gradually abandoned state ownership and protectionism. Privatization has been accompanied by an economic revolution that has seen the development of high tech industries. At the same time, India has become a nuclear power. Although India exploded its first nuclear device in 1974, tests in 1998 confirmed the nation's capability to deliver these weapons.

There have been 35,000 deaths since the outbreak of the Kashmir insurgency in 1988. Negotiations with Pakistan over the future of the disputed territory began in July 1999. Hopes of avoiding further violence were set back in Dec. 2001, in an attack on the Indian parliament by suicide bombers. 13 people died. Although no group claimed responsibility, Kashmiri separatists were blamed. However, Pakistani President Pervez Musharraf's subsequent crackdown on militants helped to bring the two countries back from the brink of war. Tension between India and Pakistan increased following an attack on an Indian army base in Indian-occupied Kashmir on 14 May 2002. The attack, which killed 31 people, was linked to Islamic terrorists infiltrating the Kashmir valley from Pakistan. It drew widespread criticism of President Musharraf for failing to combat terrorism in the disputed region. In Feb. 2002, 58 Hindu pilgrims returning from Ayodhya were killed when their train was set on fire following a confrontation with a Muslim crowd at Godhra in Gujarat. The incident led to three months of intermittent communal rioting, during which at least 800 Muslims died in attacks by Hindus. Relations between India and Pakistan cooled following terrorist bombings in Bombay (Mumbai). Since then, however, the situation has improved, with the two countries embarking on the most promising, if uncertain, path to peace for years. In May 2004 India elected Manmohan Singh as its first Sikh prime minister.

TERRITORY AND POPULATION

India is bounded in the northwest by Pakistan, north by China (Tibet), Nepal and Bhutan, east by Myanmar, and southeast, south and southwest by the Indian Ocean. The far eastern states and territories are almost separated from the rest by Bangladesh. The area (excluding the Pakistan and China-occupied parts of Jammu and Kashmir) is 3,166,414 sq. km. A Sino-Indian agreement of 7 Sept. 1993 settled frontier disputes dating from the war of 1962. Population (excluding occupied Jammu and Kashmir), 2001 census population: 1,027,015,247 (495,738,169 females), giving a density of 324 persons per sq. km. There are also 20m. Indians and ethnic Indians living abroad, notably in Malaysia, the USA, Saudi Arabia, the UK and South Africa. 71·7% of the population was rural in 2003. Goa is the most urban state, at 49·8% in 2001; and Himachal Pradesh the most rural, at 90·2% in 2001. More than 45% of Indians are under 20. The estimated population in 2005 was 1,103·37m.

The UN gives a projected population for 2010 of 1,183·29m.

By 2050 India is expected to have a population of 1·59bn. It is projected to overtake China as the world's most populous country around 2030.

Area and population of states and union territories:

States	Area in sq. km	Population 2001 census	Density per sq. km (2001)
Andhra Pradesh (And P)	275,069	75,727,541	275
Arunachal Pradesh (Arun P)	83,743	1,091,117	13
Assam (Ass)	78,438	26,638,407	340
Bihar (Bih)	94,163	82,878,796	880
Chhattisgarh (Chh)	135,191	20,795,956	154
Goa	3,702	1,343,998	363
Gujarat (Guj)	196,022	50,596,992	258
Haryana (Har)	44,212	21,082,989	477
Himachal Pradesh (Him P)	55,673	6,077,248	109
Jammu and Kashmir (J and K)[1]	101,387	10,069,917	99
Jharkhand (Jha)	79,714	26,909,428	338
Karnataka (Kar)	191,791	52,733,958	275
Kerala (Ker)	38,863	31,838,619	819
Madhya Pradesh (MP)	308,245	60,385,118	196
Maharashtra (Mah)	307,713	96,752,247	314
Manipur (Man)	22,327	2,388,634	107
Meghalaya (Meg)	22,429	2,306,069	103
Mizoram (Miz)	21,081	891,058	42
Nagaland (Nag)	16,579	1,988,636	120
Orissa (Or)	155,707	36,706,920	236
Punjab (Pun)	50,362	24,289,296	482
Rajasthan (Raj)	342,239	56,473,122	165
Sikkim (Sik)	7,096	540,493	76
Tamil Nadu (TN)	130,058	62,110,839	478
Tripura (Tri)	10,486	3,191,168	304
Uttar Pradesh (UP)	240,928	166,052,859	689
Uttaranchal (Uan)	53,483	8,479,562	159
West Bengal (WB)	88,752	80,221,171	904

Union Territories	Area in sq. km	Population 2001 census	Density per sq. km (2001)
Andaman and Nicobar Islands (ANI)	8,249	356,265	43
Chandigarh (Chan)	114	900,914	7,903
Dadra and Nagar Haveli (DNH)	491	220,451	449
Daman and Diu (D and D)	112	158,059	1,411
Delhi (Del)	1,483	13,782,976	9,294
Lakshadweep (Lak)	32	60,595	1,894
Pondicherry (Pon)	480	973,829	2,029

¹Excludes the area occupied by Pakistan and China.

Urban agglomerations with populations over 2m., together with their core cities at the 2001 census:

	State/ Union Territory	Urban agglomeration	Core city
Bombay (Mumbai)	Maharashtra	16,368,084	11,914,348
Calcutta (Kolkata)	West Bengal	13,216,546	4,580,544
Delhi	Delhi	12,791,458	9,817,439
Madras (Chennai)	Tamil Nadu	6,424,624	4,216,268
Bangalore	Karnataka	5,686,844	4,292,223
Hyderabad	Andhra Pradesh	5,533,640	3,449,878
Ahmedabad	Gujarat	4,519,278	3,515,361
Pune (Poona)	Maharashtra	3,755,525	2,540,069
Surat	Gujarat	2,811,466	2,433,787
Kanpur	Uttar Pradesh	2,690,486	2,532,138
Jaipur	Rajasthan	2,324,319	2,324,319
Lucknow	Uttar Pradesh	2,266,933	2,207,340
Nagpur	Maharashtra	2,122,965	2,051,320

Smaller urban agglomerations and cities with populations over 250,000 (with 2001 census populations, in 1,000):

Agra (UP)	1,321		Gaya (Bih)	394	
Ahmadnagar (Mah)	347		Ghaziabad (UP)	969	
Ajmer (Raj)	490		Gorakhpur (UP)	625	
Akola (Mah)	400		Gulbarga (Kar)	436	
Alappuzha (Ker)	283		Guntur (And P)	515	
Aligarh (UP)	668		Guwahati (Ass)	815	
Allahabad (UP)	1,050		Gwalior (MP)	866	
Alwar (Raj)	266		Hisar (Har)	263	
Amravati (Mah)	549		Hubli-Dharwad (Kar)	786	
Amritsar (Pun)	1,011		Ichalkaranji (Mah)	286	
Asansol (WB)	1,090		Indore (MP)	1,639	
Aurangabad (Mah)	892		Jabalpur (MP)	1,117	
Barddhaman (WB)	286		Jalandhar (Pun)	709	
Bareilly (UP)	730		Jalgaon (Mah)	369	
Belgaum (Mah)	506		Jammu (J and K)	608	
Bellary (Kar)	317		Jamnagar (Guj)	558	
Bhagalpur (Bih)	350		Jamshedpur (Jha)	1,102	
Bhavnagar (Guj)	518		Jhansi (UP)	463	
Bhilai (Chh)	924		Jodhpur (Raj)	856	
Bhilwara (Raj)	280		Junagadh (Guj)	252	
Bhiwandi (Mah)	621		Kakinada (And P)	369	
Bhopal (MP)	1,455		Kharagpur (WB)	296	
Bhubaneswar (Or)	657		Kochi (Ker)	1,355	
Bijapur (Kar)	253		Kolhapur (Mah)	498	
Bikaner (Raj)	529		Kollam (Ker)	380	
Bilaspur (Chh)	330		Korba (Chh)	316	
Bokaro Steel City (Jha)	498		Kota (Raj)	705	
Brahmapur (OR)	290		Kozhikode (Ker)	880	
Chandigarh (Chan)	809		Kurnool (And P)	321	
Chandrapur (Mah)	298		Latur (Mah)	300	
Coimbatore (TN)	1,446		Ludhiana (Pun)	1,395	
Cuddapah (And P)	261		Madurai (TN)	1,195	
Cuttack (Or)	588		Malegaon (Mah)	409	
Darbhanga (Bih)	267		Mangalore (Kar)	539	
Davangere (Kar)	364		Mathura (UP)	319	
Dehra Dun (Uan)	528		Meerut (UP)	1,074	
Dhanbad (Jha)	1,064		Moradabad (UP)	641	
Dhule (Mah)	341		Muzaffarnagar (UP)	331	
Durgapur (WB)	493		Muzaffarpur (Bih)	305	
Erode (TN)	391		Mysore (Kar)	786	
Faridabad Complex (Har)	1,055		Nanded (Mah)	431	
Firozabad (UP)	432		Nashik (Mah)	1,152	

Nellore (And P)	405	Shillong (Meg)	268
Nizamabad (And P)	287	Shimoga (Kar)	274
Panipat (Har)	354	Sholapur (Mah)	873
Parbhani (Mah)	259	Srinagar (J and K)	971
Patiala (Pun)	323	Thalassery (Ker)	498
Patna (Bih)	1,707	Thiruvananthapuram (Ker)	889
Pondicherry (Pon)	506	Thrissur (Ker)	330
Raipur (Chh)	699	Tiruchirapalli (TN)	847
Rajahmundry (And P)	408	Tirunelveli (TN)	432
Rajkot (Guj)	1,002	Tirupati (And P)	302
Rampur (UP)	282	Tiruppur (TN)	543
Ranchi (Jha)	863	Udaipur (Raj)	389
Rohtak (Har)	295	Ujjain (MP)	431
Rourkela (OR)	484	Vadodara (Guj)	1,492
Sagar (MP)	309	Varanasi (UP)	1,212
Saharanpur (UP)	453	Vellore (TN)	388
Salem (TN)	749	Vijayawada (And P)	1,011
Sangli-Miraj (Mah)	448	Visakhapatnam (And P)	1,329
Shahjahanpur (UP)	323	Warangal (And P)	577
Shiliguri (WB)	470	Yamunanagar (Har)	307

SOCIAL STATISTICS

Many births and deaths go unregistered. The Registrar General's data suggests a birth rate for 2003 of 23·3 per 1,000 population and a death rate of 8·5, which would indicate in a year approximately 24,860,000 births and 9,070,000 deaths. The growth rate is, however, slowing, and by 2003 had dropped below 1·5%, having been over 2% in 1991. Expectation of life at birth, 2003, 61·8 years for males and 65·0 years for females.

Marriages and divorces are not registered. The minimum age for a civil marriage is 18 for women and 21 for men; for a sacramental marriage, 14 for females and 18 for males. Population growth rate, 1991–2001, 21·35% (the lowest since 1961–71). Infant mortality, 2002, 60 per 1,000 live births; fertility rate, 2002, 2·9 births per woman. Child deaths (under the age of five) were more than halved between 1980 and 2001, from 172 per 1,000 in 1980 to only 72 per 1,000 in 2001.

CLIMATE

India has a variety of climatic sub-divisions. In general, there are four seasons. The cool one lasts from Dec. to March, the hot season is in April and May, the rainy season is June to Sept., followed by a further dry season until Nov. Rainfall, however, varies considerably, from 4" (100 mm) in the N.W. desert to over 400" (10,000 mm) in parts of Assam.

Range of temperature and rainfall: New Delhi, Jan. 57°F (13·9°C), July 88°F (31·1°C). Annual rainfall 26" (640 mm). Bombay, Jan. 75°F (23·9°C), July 81°F (27·2°C). Annual rainfall 72" (1,809 mm). Calcutta, Jan. 67°F (19·4°C), July 84°F (28·9°C). Annual rainfall 64" (1,600 mm). Cherrapunji, Jan. 53°F (11·7°C), July 68°F (20°C). Annual rainfall 432" (10,798 mm). Darjeeling, Jan. 41°F (5°C), July 62°F (16·7°C). Annual rainfall 121" (3,035 mm). Hyderabad, Jan. 72°F (22·2°C), July 80°F (26·7°C). Annual rainfall 30" (752 mm). Kochi, Jan. 80°F (26·7°C), July 79°F (26·1°C). Annual rainfall 117" (2,929 mm). Madras, Jan. 76°F (24·4°C), July 87°F (30·6°C). Annual rainfall 51" (1,270 mm). Patna, Jan. 63°F (17·2°C), July 90°F (32·2°C). Annual rainfall 46" (1,150 mm).

On 26 Dec. 2004 an undersea earthquake centred off the Indonesian island of Sumatra caused a huge tsunami that flooded coastal areas in southern India resulting in 16,000 deaths. In total there were 290,000 deaths in twelve countries.

CONSTITUTION AND GOVERNMENT

The Constitution was passed by the Constituent Assembly on 26 Nov. 1949 and came into force on 26 Jan. 1950. It has since been amended 93 times.

India is a republic and comprises a Union of 28 States and seven Union Territories. Each State is administered by a

Governor appointed by the President for a term of five years while each Union Territory is administered by the President through a Lieut.-Governor or an administrator appointed by him. The head of the Union (head of state) is the *President* in whom all executive power is vested, to be exercised on the advice of ministers responsible to Parliament. The President, who must be an Indian citizen at least 35 years old and eligible for election to the House of the People, is elected by an electoral college of all the elected members of Parliament and of the state legislative assemblies, holds office for five years and is eligible for re-election. There is also a *Vice-President* who is *ex officio* chairman of the Council of States.

There is a *Council of Ministers* to aid and advise the President; this comprises Ministers who are members of the Cabinet and Ministers of State and deputy ministers who are not. A Minister who for any period of six consecutive months is not a member of either House of Parliament ceases to be a Minister at the expiration of that period. The *Prime Minister* is appointed by the President; other Ministers are appointed by the President on the Prime Minister's advice. The salary of each Minister is Rs 12,000 per month.

Parliament consists of the President, the *Council of States* (*Rajya Sabha*) and the *House of the People* (*Lok Sabha*). The Council of States, or the Upper House, consists of not more than 250 members; in July 2005 there were 233 elected members and 11 members nominated by the President. The election to this house is indirect; the representatives of each State are elected by the elected members of the Legislative Assembly of that State. The Council of States is a permanent body not liable to dissolution, but one-third of the members retire every second year. The House of the People, or the Lower House, normally consists of 545 members, 543 directly elected on the basis of adult suffrage from territorial constituencies in the States, and the Union territories; in July 2005 there were 540 elected members, two nominated members and three vacancies. The House of the People unless sooner dissolved continues for a period of five years from the date appointed for its first meeting; in emergency, Parliament can extend the term by one year.

State Legislatures

For every State there is a legislature which consists of the Governor, and (a) two Houses, a Legislative Assembly and a Legislative Council, in the States of Bihar, Jammu and Kashmir, Karnataka, Madhya Pradesh (where it is provided for but not in operation), Maharashtra and Uttar Pradesh, and (b) one House, a Legislative Assembly, in the other States. Every Legislative Assembly, unless sooner dissolved, continues for five years from the date appointed for its first meeting. In emergency the term can be extended by one year. Every State Legislative Council is a permanent body and is not subject to dissolution, but one-third of the members retire every second year. Parliament can, however, abolish an existing Legislative Council or create a new one, if the proposal is supported by a resolution of the Legislative Assembly concerned.

Legislation

The various subjects of legislation are enumerated in three lists in the seventh schedule to the constitution. List I, the Union List, consists of 97 subjects (including defence, foreign affairs, communications, currency and coinage, banking and customs) with respect to which the Union Parliament has exclusive power to make laws. The State legislature has exclusive power to make laws with respect to the 66 subjects in list II, the State List; these include police and public order, agriculture and irrigation, education, public health and local government. The powers to make laws with respect to the 47 subjects (including economic and social planning, legal questions and labour and price control) in list III, the Concurrent List, are held by both Union and State governments, though the former prevails. But Parliament may legislate with respect to any subject in the State List in circumstances when the subject assumes national importance or during emergencies.

Fundamental Rights

Two chapters of the constitution deal with fundamental rights and 'Directive Principles of State Policy'. 'Untouchability' is abolished, and its practice in any form is punishable. The fundamental rights can be enforced through the ordinary courts of law and through the Supreme Court of the Union. The directive principles cannot be enforced through the courts of law; they are nevertheless fundamental in the governance of the country.

Citizenship

Under the Constitution, every person who was on the 26 Jan. 1950 domiciled in India and (a) was born in India or (b) either of whose parents was born in India or (c) who has been ordinarily resident in the territory of India for not less than five years immediately preceding that date became a citizen of India. Special provision is made for migrants from Pakistan and for Indians resident abroad. The right to vote is granted to every person who is a citizen of India and who is not less than 18 years of age on a fixed date and is not otherwise disqualified.

Parliament

Parliament and the state legislatures are organized according to the following schedule (figures show distribution of seats in July 2005 for the Lok Sabha, the Rajya Sabha and the State Legislatures):

| | Parliament | | State Legislatures | |
	House of the People (Lok Sabha)	Council of States (Rajya Sabha)	Legislative Assemblies (Vidhan Sabhas)	Legislative Councils (Vidhan Parishads)
States:				
Andhra Pradesh	42	18	295	—
Arunachal Pradesh	2	1	60	—
Assam	14	7	126	—
Bihar	40	16	243	96
Chhattisgarh	11	5	90	—
Goa	2	1	40	—
Gujarat	26	11	182	—
Haryana	9	5	90	—
Himachal Pradesh	4	3	68	—
Jammu and Kashmir	6	4	89[1,2]	36[3]
Jharkhand	14	6	81	—
Karnataka	28	12	225[4]	75
Kerala	19	9	141[4]	—
Madhya Pradesh	29	11	231[4]	—
Maharashtra	47	19	289[4]	78
Manipur	2	1	60	—
Meghalaya	2	1	60	—
Mizoram	1	1	40	—
Nagaland	1	1	60	—
Orissa	21	10	147	—
Punjab	13	7	117	—
Rajasthan	25	10	200	—
Sikkim	1	1	32	—
Tamil Nadu	39	18	235[4]	—
Tripura	2	1	60	—
Uttar Pradesh	80	31	404[4]	100
Uttaranchal	5	3	70	—
West Bengal	42	16	295[4]	—
Union Territories:				
Andaman and Nicobar Islands	1	—	—	—
Chandigarh	1	—	—	—
Dadra and Nagar Haveli	1	—	—	—
Daman and Diu	1	—	—	—
Delhi	7	3	70	—
Lakshadweep	1	—	—	—
Pondicherry	1	1	30	—

	Parliament		State Legislatures	
	House of the People (Lok Sabha)	Council of States (Rajya Sabha)	Legislative Assemblies (Vidhan Sabhas)	Legislative Councils (Vidhan Parishads)
Union Territories: Nominated by the President under Article 80 (1) (a) of the Constitution	—	11	—	—
Total	542[5]	244	4,130	393

[1]Includes two nominated members.
[2]Excludes 24 seats for Pakistan-occupied areas of the State which are in abeyance.
[3]Excludes seats for the Pakistan-occupied areas.
[4]Includes one nominated member.
[5]Includes two nominated members to represent Anglo-Indians.

Language

The Constitution provides that the official language of the Union shall be Hindi in the Devanagari script. Hindi is spoken by over 30% of the population. It was originally provided that English should continue to be used for all official purposes until 1965. But the Official Languages Act 1963 provides that, after the expiry of this period of 15 years from the coming into force of the Constitution, English might continue to be used, in addition to Hindi, for all official purposes of the Union for which it was being used immediately before that day, and for the transaction of business in Parliament. According to the Official Languages (Use for official purposes of the Union) Rules 1976, an employee may record in Hindi or in English without being required to furnish a translation thereof in the other language and no employee possessing a working knowledge of Hindi may ask for an English translation of any document in Hindi except in the case of legal or technical documents.

The 58th amendment to the Constitution (26 Nov. 1987) authorized the preparation of a Constitution text in Hindi.

The following 18 languages are included in the Eighth Schedule to the Constitution (with 2003 estimate of speakers): Assamese (16·6m.), Bengali (88·6m.), Gujarati (51·7m.), Hindi (429·1m.), Kannada (41·7m.), Kashmiri (1·1m.), Konkani (2·2m.), Malayalam (38·6m.), Manipuri (1·6m.), Marathi (79·5m.), Nepali (2·7m.), Oriya (35·7m.), Punjabi (29·8m.), Sanskrit (fewer than 1m.), Sindhi (2·7m.), Tamil (67·4m.), Telugu (84·0m.), Urdu (55·3m.).

Thakur, R., *The Government and Politics of India*. London, 1995

National Anthem

'Jana-gana-mana' ('Thou art the ruler of the minds of all people'); words and tune by Rabindranath Tagore.

GOVERNMENT CHRONOLOGY

Prime Ministers since 1947. (BJP = Bharatiya Janata Party; BLD = Indian People's Party/Bharatiya Lok Dal; INC = Indian National Congress (a.k.a. Indian Congress Party); INC(i) = Indian National Congress-Indira Gandhi faction; JD = People's Party/Janata Dal; JD(s) = Janata Dal-Chandra Shekhar faction; JP = People's Party/Janata Dal)

1947–64	INC	Jawaharlal Nehru
1964	INC	Gulzarilal Nanda
1964–66	INC	Lal Bahadur Shastri
1966	INC	Gulzarilal Nanda
1966–77	INC	Indira Gandhi
1977–79	JP	Morarji Desai
1979–80	JP/BLD	Charan Singh
1980–84	INC(i)	Indira Gandhi
1984–89	INC(i)	Rajiv Gandhi
1989–90	JD	Vishwanath Pratap Singh
1990–91	JD(s)	Chandra Shekhar
1991–96	INC(i)	Pamulaparti Venkata Narasimha Rao
1996	BJP	Atal Bihari Vajpayee
1996–97	JD	Haradanahalli Dodde Deve Gowda
1997–98	JD	Inder Kumar Gujral
1998–04	BJP	Atal Bihari Vajpayee
2004–	INC	Manmohan Singh

Presidents of the Union since 1950.

1950–62	Rajendra Prasad
1962–67	Sarvepalli Radhakrishnan
1967–69	Zakir Husain
1969–74	Varahgiri Venkata Giri
1974–77	Fakhruddin Ali Ahmed
1977–82	Neelam Sanjiva Reddy
1982–87	Zail Singh
1987–92	Ramaswamy Iyer Venkataraman
1992–97	Shankar Dayal Sharma
1997–2002	Kocheril Raman Narayanan
2002–	Avul Pakir Jainulabdeen Abdul Kalam

RECENT ELECTIONS

Presidential elections were held on 18 July 2002. A. P. J. Abdul Kalam was elected against one opponent with 89·6% of votes cast.

Parliamentary elections were held in four phases between 20 April and 10 May 2004. Turnout was 57·9%. The Indian National Congress and its allies gained 217 seats and received 34·6% of votes cast (112 seats in 1999), with the Indian National Congress (INC) winning 145 seats; the National Democratic Alliance gained 185 seats and received 35·3% of the vote (182 seats in 1999), with the Bharatiya Janata Party (BJP) winning 138 seats; the Left Front (LF) won 59 seats; Samajwadi Party (SP) 36; Bahujan Samaj Party (BSP) 19; Janata Dal (Secular) (JD(S)) 4; ind. 4; Rashtriya Lok Dal (RLD) 3. A total of ten other parties won either one or two seats and two members were nominated by the president.

Singh, V. B., *Elections in India: Data Handbook on Lok Sabha Elections, 1986–91*. Delhi, 1994

CURRENT ADMINISTRATION

President: A. P. J. Abdul Kalam; b. 1931 (sworn in 25 July 2002).

Vice-President: Bhairon Singh Shekhawat.

After the 2004 elections, despite emotional appeals from her supporters, Congress President Sonia Gandhi declined the premiership on 18 May. Manmohan Singh became India's first Sikh prime minister on 22 May.

In March 2006 the INC-led 12-party coalition government was composed as follows:

Prime Minister and Minister of Personnel, Public Grievances and Pensions, Planning, Atomic Energy, Space, and Foreign Affairs: Manmohan Singh; b. 1932 (INC; sworn in 22 May 2004).

Minister of Defence: Pranab Mukherjee (INC). *Human Resource Development:* Arjun Singh (INC). *Agriculture, Food and Civil Supplies, Consumer Affairs and Public Distribution:* Sharad Pawar (Nationalist Congress Party). *Railways:* Lalu Prasad Yadav (Rashtriya Janata Dal; RJD). *Home Affairs:* Shivraj Patil (INC). *Chemicals and Fertilizers, and Steel:* Ram Vilas Paswan (Lok Jan Shakti Party). *Urban Development:* S. Jaipal Reddy (INC). *Labour and Employment:* Chandra Shekhar Rao (Telangana Rashtra Samithi). *Finance:* P. Chidambaram (INC). *Mines:* Sish Ram Ola (INC). *Small-Scale, Agro and Rural Industries:* Mahavir Prasad (INC). *Tribal Affairs and Development of the North East:* P. R. Kyndiah (INC). *Shipping, Road Transport and Highways:* T. R. Baalu (Dravida Progressive Federation; DMK). *Textiles:* Shankersinh Vaghela (INC). *Commerce and Industry:* Kamal Nath (INC). *Law and Justice:* H. R. Bhardwaj (INC). *Power:* Sushil Kumar Shinde (INC). *Rural Development:* Raghubansh Prasad Singh (Rashtriya Janata Dal; RJD). *Information and Broadcasting, and Parliamentary Affairs:*

Priya Ranjan Dasmunsi (INC). *Petroleum and Natural Gas:* Murli Deora (INC). *Social Justice and Empowerment:* Meira Kumar (INC). *Environment and Forests:* A. Raja (Dravida Progressive Federation; DMK). *Communication and Information Technology:* Dayanidhi Maran (Dravida Progressive Federation; DMK). *Health and Family Welfare:* Anbumani Ramadoss (Pattali Makkal Katchi). *Youth, Sports and Panchayati Raj:* Mani Shankar Aiyar (INC). *Minority Affairs:* Abdul Rehman Antulay (INC). *Indians Abroad:* Vayalar Ravi (INC). *Tourism and Culture:* Ambika Soni (INC). *Water Resources:* Saif-uddin Soz (INC). *Coal:* Shibu Soren (Jharkhand Mukti Morcha; JMM). *Heavy Industries and Public Enterprises:* Santosh Mohan Dev (INC). *Company Affairs:* Prem Chand Gupta (Rashtriya Janata Dal; RJD). *Science, Technology and Ocean Development:* Kapil Sibal (INC).

Office of the Prime Minister: http://www.pmindia.nic.in

CURRENT LEADERS

Abdul Kalam

Position
President

Introduction
On 25 July 2002 Abdul Kalam succeeded K. R. Narayanan to become India's president. Credited with founding and developing the country's nuclear missile programme, Kalam has promoted a plan for India's economic development by 2020. A Muslim brought up in impoverished circumstances, his desire for social unity has drawn criticism from Muslim leaders. His non-political background and concern for the people's social and economic welfare on the other hand have made him a popular and respected public figure.

Early Life
Avul Pakir Jainulabdeen Abdul Kalam was born on 15 Oct. 1931 in the Rameswaram district of Tamil Nadu. He was educated at a missionary institute in Ramanathapuram and at St Joseph College in Tiruchirrapalli before going on to study aeronautical engineering at the Madras Institute of Technology.

Kalam joined the Defence Research and Development Organisation (DRDO) in 1958 and the Indian Space Research Organization (ISRO) in 1963, when he was also invited to spend four months in the USA working for the National Aeronautics and Space Administration (NASA). Ten years after rejoining DRDO in 1982 Kalam became scientific adviser to the defence minister and secretary until 1999. From 1999 to 2001 he acted as principal scientific adviser to the government with the rank of cabinet minister.

In 1998, under Kalam's scientific direction, India detonated its first nuclear bomb. While this increased tension with neighbouring Pakistan and earned international condemnation and sanctions, many Indians have felt that this marked out India as an emerging world power.

Nominated by both Prime Minister Vajpayee's National Democratic Alliance and its primary opposition party, the Indian National Congress, Kalam was elected president on 18 July 2002. He defeated his chief rival, Lakshmi Sahgal, by a margin of over 800,000 votes.

Career in Office
While his powers of office are largely nominal and ceremonial, India's 'Missile Man' has taken advantage of his high profile to advocate the development and the promotion of science and technology. He upholds his pre-presidential vision of India as an economically developed country by 2020, largely through the exploitation of natural resources and education.

A practising Muslim, Kalam is said to be equally familiar with the Koran and the Bhagvad Gita. However, his endorsement of tolerance and pluralism has met with disapproval by Muslim leaders, which has led to accusations of affiliation with the Hindu militant group, Sangh Parivar. Although at first seen as an extension of India's military, Kalam's secular and humanitarian approach has attracted wider support.

Manmohan Singh

Position
Prime Minister

Introduction
After three decades as a civil servant, the quietly-spoken former academic and economist was sworn in as India's first Sikh prime minister on 22 May 2004. His appointment followed the general election victory of the Indian National Congress over the Bharatiya Janata Party (BJP; Indian People's Party) and Sonia Ghandhi's unexpected rejection of the top job. A low-profile technocrat and adviser throughout the 1970s and 1980s, Singh came to the fore in 1991 when he was appointed finance minister in the cabinet of P. V. Narasimha Rao. India was in severe financial crisis and Manmohan Singh is credited with bringing about a fundamental change of direction, becoming known as the 'architect of India's economic reform'.

Early life
Manmohan Singh was born in Gah, West Punjab (now in Pakistan), on 26 Sept. 1932, the son of a shopkeeper. He was educated at Punjab University in the newly-established city of Chandigarh (built to replace Lahore as the capital of the Indian state of Punjab following the formation of Pakistan in 1947). He also attended the universities of Cambridge and Oxford in England on scholarships and won Cambridge's prestigious Adam Smith Prize in 1956. Returning to India as an economics lecturer, he remained at Punjab University before being made professor in 1963. Three years later he joined UNCTAD (the UN Conference on Trade and Development) at the United Nations Secretariat in New York, as economic affairs officer. In 1969 Singh returned to India and joined the School of Economics at the University of Delhi as professor of international trade.

Cutting short his academic career in 1971, Singh joined Indira Gandhi's New Congress Party-led government to serve as an economic adviser to the ministry of foreign trade and, from 1972–76, as chief economic adviser in the finance ministry. Stronger ties with the USSR, which influenced Indian economic policy and brought in new aid agreements, marked this period. In 1976 Singh became director of the Reserve Bank of India, a post he held for four years. From 1982–85 he was governor of the Reserve Bank of India and then deputy chairman of the Planning Commission from 1985–87, undertaking various assignments at the International Monetary Fund and the Asian Development Bank. He was first selected for the Rajya Sabha (the upper house of parliament) in 1991, representing the Congress.

In 1991, with India in financial crisis, Singh was appointed finance minister in P. V. Narasimha Rao's cabinet. Foreign exchange reserves were nearly exhausted and the country was close to defaulting on its international debt. In his maiden speech as finance minister, Singh quoted Victor Hugo—'No power on earth can stop an idea whose time has come'—and brought in an ambitious and unprecedented economic reform programme. He slashed red tape, simplified the tax system and ended the 'license Raj' regulations that forced businesses to get government approval for most decisions. He also devalued the rupee, cut subsidies for domestically produced goods, and privatized some state-run companies. Singh spoke of wanting to 'release the innovative, entrepreneurial spirit which was always there in India in such a manner that our economy would grow at a much faster pace, sooner than most people believed.' The recipe worked; industry picked up, inflation was checked, and growth rates remained consistently high through the 1990s (his policies were broadly continued by the BJP-led coalition after they were elected in 1996).

Career in Office

When Singh was sworn in as prime minister on 22 May 2004, he took on a healthy economy: GDP growth was at 7%, foreign exchange reserves were comfortable at US$118bn. and inflation stood at just 4%. However, hundreds of millions of Indians still live in poverty and Singh has a tough task in bringing about improvements in living standards, while balancing the demands of leftist and communist parties in the coalition. His first address as prime minister called for 'economic reforms with a human face' stressing the need to achieve friendly relations with neighbouring countries, especially Pakistan. Singh has a reputation for honesty and even-handedness, but there are some questions about his lack of election-winning political experience—he failed to win a seat in the Lok Sabha (Lower House) elections for South Delhi in 1999.

DEFENCE

The Supreme Command of the Armed Forces is vested in the President. As well as armed forces of 1,325,000 personnel in 2004, there are nearly 1,090,000 active paramilitary forces including 174,000 members of the Border Security Force based mainly in the troubled Jammu and Kashmir region. Military service is voluntary but, under the amended constitution, it is regarded as a fundamental duty of every citizen to perform National Service when called upon. Defence expenditure in 2003 was US$15,508m. (US$15 per capita and 2·6% of GDP). In the period 1999–2003 India's spending on major conventional weapons was second only to that of China, at US$7·8bn.—in 2000, 2001 and 2002 China's expenditure was higher, although in 2003 that of India (at US$3·6bn.) was the highest in the world. In Sept. 2003 India announced that it would be buying 66 Hawk trainer fighter jets, with delivery expected by 2009. In Oct. 2003 agreement was reached for India to purchase Israel's sophisticated US$1bn. Phalcon early-warning radar system.

Nuclear Weapons

India's first nuclear test was in 1974. Its most recent tests were a series of five carried out in May 1998. According to the Stockholm International Peace Research Institute, India's nuclear arsenal was estimated to consist of between 30 and 40 nuclear warheads in Jan. 2005. India, known to have a nuclear weapons programme, has not signed the Comprehensive Nuclear-Test-Ban-Treaty, which is intended to bring about a ban on any nuclear explosions. According to *Deadly Arsenals*, published by the Carnegie Endowment for International Peace, India has chemical weapons and has a biological weapons research programme.

Army

The Army is organized into five commands each divided into areas, which in turn are subdivided into sub-areas.

The strength of the Army in 2004 was 1·1m. There are 4 'RAPID' divisions, 18 infantry divisions, three armoured divisions and two artillery divisions: in all there are 355 infantry battalions, 300 artillery regiments, 62 tank battalions and 22 helicopter squadrons. Officers are trained at the Indian Military Academy, Dehra Dun (Uttaranchal). An Aviation Corps of 14 squadrons operates helicopters locally-built under licence. Army reserves number 300,000 with a further 500,000 personnel available as a second-line reserve force. There is a volunteer Territorial Army of 40,000. There are numerous paramilitary groups including the Ministry of Defence *Rashtriya Rifles* (numbering 40,000), the Indo-Tibetan Border Police (32,400), the State Armed Police

(400,000), the Civil Defence (453,000), the Central Industrial Security Force (95,000) and the Ministry of Home Affairs Assam Rifles (52,500).

Navy

The Navy has three commands; Eastern (at Visakhapatnam), Western (at Bombay) and Southern (at Kochi), the latter a training and support command. The fleet is divided into two elements, Eastern and Western; and well-trained, all-volunteer personnel operate a mix of Soviet and western vessels. In May 2003 India held joint naval exercises with Russia in the Arabian Sea for the first time since the collapse of the Soviet Union.

The principal ship is the light aircraft carrier, *Viraat*, formerly HMS *Hermes*, of 29,000 tonnes, completed in 1959 and transferred to the Indian Navy in 1987 after seeing service in the Falklands War. In 2003 India began construction of another aircraft carrier and began negotiations to purchase a third from the Russian navy. The fleet includes 12 Soviet-built diesel submarines and four new German-designed boats. There are also 24 destroyers and frigates. The Naval Air force, 5,000 strong, operates 35 combat aircraft (including 20 Sea Harriers) and 32 armed helicopters. Main bases are at Bombay (main dockyard), Goa, Visakhapatnam and Calcutta on the sub-continent and Port Blair in the Andaman Islands.

Naval personnel in 2004 numbered 55,000 including 5,000 Naval Air Arm and 1,200 marines.

Air Force

Units of the IAF are organized into five operational commands—Central at Allahabad, Eastern at Shillong, Southern at Thiruvananthapuram, South-Western at Gandhinagar and Western at Delhi. The air force has 170,000 personnel.

Equipment includes nearly 680 combat aircraft, in 46 squadrons of aircraft, and about 40 armed helicopters. Major combat types include Su-30s, MiG-21s, MiG-23s, MiG-27s, MiG-29s, *Jaguars* and Mirage 2000s. Air Force reserves numbered 140,000 in 2004.

INTERNATIONAL RELATIONS

India is a member of the UN, WTO, BIS, the Commonwealth, Asian Development Bank, Colombo Plan, SAARC and the Antarctic Treaty.

ECONOMY

Agriculture accounted for 22·7% of GDP in 2002, industry 26·6% and services 50·7%.

In the late 1990s there were ever-increasing signs of a divide between the south and west, where a modern economy is booming in cities such as Bangalore, Hyderabad and Madras, and the poorer and politically volatile areas in the north and east.

Overview

After gaining independence in 1947 India adopted a policy of import substituting industrialization (ISI). Protected by tariffs from international competition, a broad industrial base was built that initially generated strong growth. However, the Indian economy was plagued by inefficient bureaucracy and insufficient competition, hindering sustained productivity growth. In 1991 a balance of payments and foreign currency reserve crisis pushed India to initiate a reform process that has helped it become one of the world's fastest-growing economies. Industrial licensing (determining how much entrepreneurs could manufacture) has been abolished and trade barriers lowered. Foreign direct investment rose from almost nothing to over US$5bn. in 2004. The liberalization reform programme has contributed to increased foreign participation and growth in durable consumer goods production, including cars, scooters, consumer electronics, computer systems and white goods. The service sector experienced the most significant liberalization and has become the economy's most dynamic sector, particularly the telecommunications and information technology (IT) segments. India's well educated and English-speaking skilled labour force seized the opportunities that came with the global boom in IT service demand over the last decade and has helped the country become a leader in IT services. India serves as a vast services outsourcing centre for developed countries, particularly the USA. Yet the economy as a whole remains fairly closed and is rated amongst the most restrictive by the IMF. A large proportion of heavy industry remains publicly-owned and inefficient state-owned enterprises, chiefly in the banking sector, hinder greater growth.

Two-thirds of the workforce is employed in agriculture, which accounts for roughly one-quarter of the country's total output. Yields per hectare in India are low by international standards, with many workers at subsistence level. The majority of the total workforce employed in unproductive agriculture significantly limits the potential for non-agricultural demand and the development of other sectors. Poverty declined from 36% of the population in 1993–94 to 26% in the early 2000s and social indicators have improved but there are still over 250m. poor in the country according to the World Bank. Human development indicators remain among the lowest in the world, especially in rural areas. Sustained poverty reduction will be difficult until agricultural productivity is raised and the rural infrastructure developed. Many economists argue that stronger growth in the manufacturing sector, which remains protected in many segments and hindered by poor infrastructure, is essential to generate sufficient productive employment for the rapidly growing population.

Yet with an already worrisome level of fiscal deficits, India cannot afford a large increase in social and infrastructure expenditure. A positive step was taken in Nov. 2005 when the government approved the establishment of the India Infrastructure Finance Company to raise funds in financial markets for long-term mega infrastructure projects. Economic data released by the Central Statistical Organisation in New Delhi in 2005 also showed an encouraging surge in manufacturing production. The Economist Intelligence Unit argues, however, that unless the large fiscal deficits, rigid labour laws and weak regulatory system are tackled, the economy will continue to grow below potential.

Currency

A decimal system of coinage was introduced in 1957. The Indian *rupee* (INR) is divided into 100 *paise*. The paper currency consists of Reserve Bank notes and Government of India currency notes.

Foreign exchange reserves were US$54,703m. in June 2002 and gold reserves 11·50m. troy oz. Inflation rates (based on IMF statistics):

1995	1996	1997	1998	1999	2000	2001	2002	2003	2004
10·2%	9·0%	7·2%	13·2%	4·7%	4·0%	3·8%	4·3%	3·8%	3·8%

The official exchange rate was abolished on 1 March 1993; the rupee now has a single market exchange rate and is convertible. The pound sterling is the currency of intervention. Total money supply in May 2002 was Rs 4,191·12bn.

Budget

Revenue and expenditure of the central government for years ending 31 March, in Rs 1m.:

	2001–02	2002–03	2003–04
Revenue	2,573,600	2,958,000	3,222,300
Expenditure	3,559,200	4,041,100	4,446,100

Breakdown of revenue and expenditure of the central government for 1999–2000, in Rs 1m.:

Revenue		Expenditure	
Current Revenue	2,326,900	Economic Affairs and	
Tax	*1,717,500*	Services	492,600
including:		Defence	467,900
Domestic taxes on		General Public Services	
goods and services	653,500	including Public Order	195,900
Tax on incomes,		Housing and Community	
profits and capital		Amenities	156,200
gains	575,600	Other	1,700,500
Non-tax	*609,400*	including Interest	
Capital Revenue	22,800	Payments	868,800

VAT was introduced on 1 April 2005, at 12·5% (reduced rate, 4%).

Performance

India has one of the fastest-growing economies in Asia. Real GDP growth rates (based on IMF statistics):

1995	1996	1997	1998	1999	2000	2001	2002	2003	2004
7·6%	7·5%	5·0%	5·8%	6·7%	5·4%	3·9%	4·7%	7·4%	7·3%

The 5·8% growth rate in 1998 demonstrates that India managed to avoid the worst of the Asian crisis. In spite of impressive growth in recent years critics claim that growth needs to be at least 8% in order to tackle the country's poverty. Recent years have seen a growing disparity between the performance of India's richest states, mainly in the south and the west, and the poorest states, generally in the east and the north.

Total GDP in 2004 was US$691·9bn.

Banking and Finance

The Reserve Bank, the central bank for India, was established in 1934 and started functioning on 1 April 1935 as a shareholder's bank; it became a nationalized institution on 1 Jan. 1949. It has the sole right of issuing currency notes. The *Governor* is Yaga Venugopal Reddy. The Bank acts as adviser to the government on financial problems and is the banker for central and state governments, commercial banks and some other financial institutions. It manages the rupee public debt of central and state governments and is the custodian of the country's exchange reserve.

The commercial banking system consisted of 298 scheduled banks (*i.e.*, banks which are included in the 2nd schedule to the Reserve Bank Act) in Dec. 1999. 223 of these were in the public sector, of which 196 were Regional Rural Banks. The other 27 (which comprise the State Bank of India and its seven associate banks and 19 nationalized banks) were regular commercial banks and account for more than 75% of deposits and about 75% of bank credit of all scheduled commercial banks. Total deposits in commercial banks, March 2002, stood at Rs 11,234,160m. The business of non-scheduled banks forms less than 0·1% of commercial bank business. The State Bank of India acts as the agent of the Reserve Bank for transacting government business as well as undertaking commercial functions. In 2002 India received US$3·4bn. worth of foreign direct investment.

There are stock exchanges in Ahmedabad, Bombay, Calcutta, Delhi, Madras and 18 other centres.

Weights and Measures

The metric system is official but Imperial measurements are still used in commerce. Frequent use is made in figures of the terms *lakh* (=100,000) and *crore* (= 10m.).

ENERGY AND NATURAL RESOURCES

Environment

India's carbon dioxide emissions from the consumption and flaring of fossil fuels were equivalent to 0·98 tonnes per capita in 2002, well below the global average and the lowest figure for any major industrial country. A 2003 report issued by the US Department of Energy stated that India was the world's fifth largest emitter of carbon dioxide but that in 2000 emissions decreased by 0·6% to 292m. tonnes of carbon. An *Environmental Sustainability Index* compiled for the World Economic Forum meeting in Jan. 2005 ranked India 101st in the world out of 146 countries analysed, with 45·2%. The index measured the ability of countries to maintain favourable environmental conditions and examined various factors including pollution levels and the use or abuse of natural resources.

Electricity

Installed capacity in 2004 was 114m. kW. In 2002 nearly 520,000 villages out of 600,000 had electricity. Production of electricity in 2001 was 533·3bn. kWh, of which approximately 81·7% came from thermal stations, 3·4% from nuclear stations and 14·5% from hydro-electric stations. In 2003 there were 14 nuclear reactors in use. An additional eight reactors were either under construction or approved to start construction. Electricity consumption per capita in 2001 was 473 kWh. Electricity demand exceeds supply, making power surges and cuts frequent. India aims to have electricity in every household by 2012.

Oil and Gas

The Oil and Natural Gas Corporation Ltd and Oil India Ltd are the only producers of crude oil. Production 2001–02, 32·0m. tonnes. The main fields are in Assam and Gujarat and offshore in the Gulf of Cambay (the Bombay High field). India imports 70% of its annual oil requirement. There were proven reserves of 5·4bn. bbls. in 2002. Oil refinery capacity, 2002, was 2·3m. bbls. daily. Natural gas production, 2002, 28·4bn. cu. metres with 760bn. cu. metres of proven reserves in 2002.

Water

By 2000, 76·34m. ha. of irrigation potential had been created of which 57·24m. ha. was utilized. Irrigation projects have formed an important part of all the Five-Year Plans. The possibilities of diverting rivers into canals being nearly exhausted, the emphasis is now on damming the monsoon surplus flow and diverting that. Ultimate potential of irrigation is assessed at 110m. ha. by 2025, total cultivated land being 185m. ha.

A Ganges water-sharing accord was signed with Bangladesh in 1997, ending a 25-year dispute which had hindered and dominated relations between the two countries.

Minerals

The coal industry was nationalized in 1973. Production, 2000, 316m. tonnes; recoverable reserves were estimated at 102bn. tonnes (2002). Production of other minerals (in 1,000 tonnes): iron ore (2001), 79,200; lignite (2002), 25,038; salt (2002), 14,800; bauxite (2001), 8,585; chromite (2002), 1,900; manganese ore (2002–03), 1,662; aluminium (2001), 624; silver (2001), 49,500 kg; gold (2001), 3,700 kg. Other important minerals are lead, zinc, limestone, apatite and phosphorite, dolomite, magnesite and uranium. Value of mineral production, 2002–03, Rs 635,403·5m.; mineral fuels produced Rs 513,172·4m., metallic minerals Rs 45,405·8m. and non-metallic Rs 22,081·0m.

Agriculture

About 70% of the people are dependent on the land for their living. The farming year runs from July to June through three crop seasons: kharif (monsoon); rabi (winter) and summer. In 2001 there were 161,750,000 ha. of arable land and 8,150,000 ha. of permanent cropland. 54,800,000 ha. were irrigated in 2001. There were 1,525,000 tractors and 4,200 harvester-threshers in 2001. The average size of holdings for the whole of India in 1996 was 1·41 ha.

Agricultural production, 2000 (in 1,000 tonnes): sugarcane, 315,000; rice, 134,150; wheat, 74,251; potatoes, 23,500; mangoes, 15,642; bananas, 13,900; maize, 11,500; coconuts, 11,100; sorghum, 9,500; millet, 9,000; seed cotton, 6,172; rapeseed, 6,120; aubergines, 6,100; groundnuts, 6,100; cassava, 5,800;

tomatoes, 5,500; onions, 5,467; soybeans, 5,400; chick-peas, 5,350; cauliflowers, 5,250; dry beans, 4,340; cabbages, 4,250; cottonseed, 4,115; pumpkins and squash, 3,400. Jute is grown in West Bengal (70% of total yield), Bihar and Assam: total yield, 1,740,000 tonnes. The coffee industry is growing: the main cash varieties are Arabica and Robusta (main growing areas Karnataka, Kerala and Tamil Nadu). India is the world's leading producer of a number of agricultural crops, including mangoes, millet, bananas and chick-peas.

The tea industry is important, with production concentrated in Assam, West Bengal, Tamil Nadu and Kerala. India is the world's largest tea producer. The 2000 crop was 749,000 tonnes; exports in 2001–02, 180,100 tonnes, valued at US$360m.

Livestock (2000): cattle, 218·8m.; goats, 123·0m.; buffaloes, 93·8m.; sheep, 57·9m.; pigs, 16·5m.; asses, 1·0m.; camels, 1·0m.; horses, 990,000; chickens, 402m. There are more cattle and buffaloes in India than in any other country.

Fertilizer use in 2001 was 17·36m. tonnes.

Opium

By international agreement the poppy is cultivated under licence, and all raw opium is sold to the central government. Opium, other than for wholly medical use, is available only to registered addicts.

Forestry

The lands under the control of the state forest departments are classified as 'reserved forests' (forests intended to be permanently maintained for the supply of timber, etc., or for the protection of water supply, etc.), 'protected forests' and 'unclassed' forest land. In 2000 the total forest area was 64·11m. ha. (21·6% of the land area). Main types are teak and sal. About 16% of the area is inaccessible, of which about 45% is potentially productive. In 2003, 321·03m. cu. metres of roundwood were produced, making India the second largest producer after the USA (9·6% of the world total in 2003). Most states have encouraged planting small areas around villages.

Fisheries

Total catch (2003) was 3,688,994 tonnes, of which Kerala, Tamil Nadu and Maharashtra produced about half. Of the total catch, 2,911,721 tonnes were marine fish. There were 46,918 mechanized boats in 1994–95. There were also 31,726 motorized traditional crafts and 159,481 traditional crafts in 1994–95. There were 11,440 fishermen's co-operatives with 1,250,379 members in 1995–96; total sales, Rs 1,495m. (1994–95).

INDUSTRY

The leading companies by market capitalization in India, excluding banking and finance, in May 2004 were: the Oil & Natural Gas Corporation Ltd (ONGC), US$19·7bn.; Reliance Industries, a chemical production company (US$13·2bn.); and Indian Oil (US$8·6bn.).

The information technology industry has become increasingly important, leading Prime Minister Atal Vajpayee to state in 1999 that 'I believe that IT is India's tomorrow'. In 1994–95 the software industry had been valued at just Rs 63,450m., but by 1998–99 it was worth Rs 247,815m., with a forecast for 1999–2000 of a further rapid expansion, making it worth Rs 361,000m. (US$8,390m.).

There is expansion in petrochemicals, based on the oil and associated gas of the Bombay High field, and gas from Krishna-Godavari Basin, Rajasthan, Tripura, Assam and Bassein field. Small industries numbering 2·72m. (initial outlay on capital equipment of less than Rs 30m.) are important; they employ about 15·26m. and produced (1995–96) goods worth Rs 3,164,210m.

Industrial production, 2002 unless otherwise indicated (in 1,000 tonnes): cement (2000), 99,227; distillate fuel oil, 39,373; crude steel, 28,800; pig iron, 24,300; sugar, 19,525; residual fuel oil, 12,246; nitrogenous fertilizers (2000), 11,025; petrol, 10,133; kerosene, 10,062; sulphuric acid (2000), 5,540; paper and paperboard (2001), 3,973; phosphate fertilizer (2000), 3,745; jute goods (1995–96), 1,114; man-made fibre and yarn (1995–96), 468; 3,756,000 motorcycles, mopeds and scooters (2000); 2,854,719 diesel engines (2001); 1,648,000 electric motors (2001); 859,927 cars and lorries; 60·58bn. cigarettes (2001).

Labour
At the 2001 census there were 402·5m. workers, of whom 127·6m. were cultivators; 107·4m. agricultural labourers; and 16·4m. worked in household industry, manufacturing, processing, servicing and repairs. Workdays lost by industrial disputes, 2000, 28·76m., through strikes and lockouts.

The unemployment rate was 4·3% of the workforce in Jan. 2000.

Companies
The total number of companies limited by shares at work as on 31 March 2002 was 589,246; estimated paid-up capital was Rs 3,870,239m. Of these, 76,279 were public limited companies with an estimated paid-up capital of Rs 2,587,149m., and 512,967 private limited companies (Rs 1,283,090m.).

During 2001–02 there were 21,059 new limited companies registered in the Indian Union under the Companies Act 1956 with a total authorized capital of Rs 53,156m.; 14 were government companies (Rs 5,781m.). There were 479 companies with unlimited liability and 3,007 companies with liability limited by guarantee and association not for profit also registered in 2001–02. During 2001–02, 760 non-government companies with an aggregate paid-up capital of Rs 144·7m. went into liquidation or were struck off the register.

On 31 March 2002 there were 1,261 government companies at work with a total paid-up capital of Rs 1,099,155m.; 658 were public limited companies and 603 were private limited companies. There were 587,985 non-government companies at work on 31 March 2002. Of these 75,621 were public limited companies and 512,364 were private limited companies.

On 31 March 2002, 1,285 companies incorporated elsewhere were reported to have a place of business in India; 241 were of UK and 286 of US origin.

Co-operative Movement
In 1995–96 there were 411,000 co-operative societies with a total membership of 197·8m. These included Primary Co-operative Marketing Societies, State Co-operative Marketing Federations and the National Agricultural Co-operative Marketing Federation of India. There were also State Co-operative Commodity Marketing Federations, and 29 general purpose and 16 Special Commodities Marketing Federations.

There were, in 1995–96, 28 State Co-operative Banks, 362 District Central Co-operative Banks, 90,783 Primary Agricultural Credit Societies, 20 State Land Development Banks, and 2,970 Primary Land Development Banks which provide long-term credits.

Trade Unions
The Indian National Trade Union Congress (INTUC) had 3,987 affiliated unions with a total membership of 6,726,569 in March 2000.

INTERNATIONAL TRADE
Foreign investment is encouraged by a tax holiday on income up to 6% of capital employed for five years. There are special depreciation allowances, and customs and excise concessions, for export industries. Proposals for investment ventures involving up to 51% foreign equity require only the Reserve Bank's approval under new liberalized policy. In Feb. 1991 India resumed transfrontier trade with China, which had ceased in 1962.

Foreign debt was US$104,429m. in 2002.

Imports and Exports
The external trade of India (excluding land-borne trade with Tibet and Bhutan) was as follows (in Rs 100,000):

	Imports	Exports and Re-exports
1999–2000	21,552,844	15,956,139
2000–01	23,087,276	20,357,101
2001–02	24,519,972	20,901,797

The distribution of commerce by countries was as follows in the year ended 31 March 2002 (in Rs 100,000):

Countries	Imports from	Exports to
Afghanistan	8,357	11,623
Argentina	207,937	30,818
Australia	622,903	199,363
Austria	37,113	36,405
Bahrain	63,912	36,052
Bangladesh	28,194	477,958
Belgium	1,317,727	663,213
Brazil	146,974	104,450
Canada	252,497	278,910
China	971,192	454,004
Czech Republic	18,423	19,594
Denmark	57,523	72,424
Egypt	47,664	220,686
France	402,640	450,689
Germany	967,238	852,901
Hong Kong	347,609	1,128,560
Hungary	11,406	22,270
Indonesia	494,476	254,535
Iran	135,360	120,676
Israel	204,001	204,131
Italy	336,125	575,415
Japan	1,023,680	720,355
Jordan	100,038	38,582
North Korea	1,523	76,339
South Korea	544,341	224,807
Kuwait	35,143	98,364
Malaysia	540,605	368,989
Mexico	29,681	113,243
Morocco	127,045	26,494
Myanmar	178,572	29,041
Nepal	169,756	102,280
Netherlands	222,467	412,001
New Zealand	39,189	29,669
Nigeria	41,548	268,574
Norway	22,881	25,895
Pakistan	30,883	68,679
Philippines	45,233	118,175
Poland	14,972	51,653
Qatar	43,730	23,371
Romania	23,094	5,429
Russia	255,393	380,669
Saudi Arabia	221,284	394,142
Senegal	63,715	10,985
Singapore	621,945	463,713
South Africa	687,191	168,326
Spain	80,494	322,972
Sri Lanka	32,134	300,885
Sweden	191,821	73,575
Switzerland	1,369,115	195,109
Taiwan	266,729	171,742
Tanzania	36,290	43,295
Thailand	201,779	301,954
Tunisia	49,675	22,115
Turkey	33,078	104,471
UAE	436,423	1,188,381
UK	1,222,440	1,030,561
Ukraine	79,588	38,353
USA	1,502,112	4,060,175
Vietnam	9,019	104,051
Yemen	22,802	70,460

The value (in Rs 100,000) of the leading articles of merchandise was as follows in the year ended 31 March 2002:

Imports	Value
Artificial resins, plastic materials etc.	321,480
Chemical materials and products	211,964
Coal, coke and briquettes, etc.	545,274
Computer software in physical form	103,272
Electronic goods	1,803,719
Fertilizers, manufactured	216,879
Gold	1,988,920
Inorganic chemicals	568,157
Iron and steel	375,877
Machinery other than electric and electronic	1,416,846
Manufactures of metals	194,124
Medicinal and pharmaceutical products	202,658
Metalliferous ores and metal scrap	545,462
Newsprint	117,055
Non-ferrous metal	308,686
Organic chemicals	767,028
Pearls, precious and semi-precious stones	2,204,599
Petroleum, crude oil and related products	6,676,986
Professional instruments other than electronic	496,507
Project goods	271,355
Pulp and waste paper	140,525
Pulses	316,016
Silver	196,460
Textile yarn, fabrics and made-up articles	140,745
Transport equipment	548,187
Vegetable oils (edible)	646,497
Wood and wood products	258,387

Exports	Value
Carpet products (excluding silk)	178,759
Cashew nuts	164,713
Coffee	109,492
Cotton yarn, fabrics and made-up articles	1,465,492
Drugs, pharmaceuticals and fine chemicals	983,292
Dyes, intermediates and coal tar chemicals	262,199
Electronic goods	558,599
Engineering goods	2,740,621
Gems and jewellery	3,484,506
Handicrafts (excluding handmade carpets)	261,806
Inorganic and organic agro-chemicals	392,827
Iron ore	203,355
Leather garments	180,635
Leather goods	194,182
Man-made yarn, fabrics and made-up articles	507,892
Marine products	589,686
Meat preparations	119,304
Oil meals	226,293
Petroleum, crude oil and related products	994,815
Plastics and linoleum	470,889
Processed minerals	167,550
Ready-made garments, including clothing accessories of all textile materials	2,387,762
Residual chemicals and allied products	182,562
Rice	317,414
Rubber manufactured products (except footwear)	178,074
Spices	149,697
Tea	171,922

Technology industries have become increasingly important in recent years, with software exports having grown more than 50% annually each year during the 1990s. In 1998–99 software exports were worth Rs 109,400m. (US$2,650m.), with 61% going to the USA and Canada, and 23% to Europe. Exports grew by 67·5% in 1998–99 compared to 1997–98.

In 2001–02 the main import suppliers (percentage of total trade) were: USA, 6·1%; Switzerland, 5·6%; Belgium, 5·4%; UK, 5·0%; Japan, 4·2%. Main export markets in 2001–02 were: USA, 19·4%; United Arab Emirates, 5·7%; Hong Kong, 5·4%; UK, 4·9%; Japan, 3·4%.

COMMUNICATIONS

Roads

In 2002 there were 3·91m. km of roads, of which 1·57m. km were surfaced. Roads are divided into six main administrative classes, namely: national highways, state highways, other public works department (PWD) roads, *Panchayati Raj* roads, urban roads and project roads. The national highways (54,289 km in 2002) connect capitals of states, major ports and foreign highways. The national highway system is linked with the UN Economic and Social Commission for Asia and the Pacific international highway system. The state highways are the main trunk roads of the states, while the other PWD roads and *Panchayati Raj* roads connect subsidiary areas of production and markets with distribution centres, and form the main link between headquarters and neighbouring districts. A US$12bn. ten-year highway plan is currently under way that aims to have India's main cities, ports and regions linked by more than 13,000 km of highways by 2009.

There were (2000) 6,042,000 passenger cars, 35,490,000 motorcycles and scooters, 559,000 buses and coaches, and 2,681,000 trucks and vans. In 1998 there were 298,052 road accidents resulting in 62,721 deaths.

Rail

The Indian railway system is government-owned (under the control of the Railway Board). Following reconstruction there are 16 zones, seven of which were created in 2002:

Zone	Headquarters	Year of Creation
Central	Bombay	1951
Southern	Madras	1951
Western	Bombay	1951
Eastern	Calcutta	1952
Northern	Delhi	1952
North Eastern	Gorakhpur	1952
South Eastern	Calcutta	1955
North East Frontier	Guwahati	1958
South Central	Secunderabad	1966
East Central	Hajipur	2002
East Coast	Bhubaneswar	2002
North Central	Allahabad	2002
North Western	Jaipur	2002
South East Central	Bilaspur	2002
South Western	Hubli	2002
West Central	Jabalpur	2002

The total length of the Indian railway network is 63,000 km (14,600 electrified), with the Northern zone having the longest network, at 11,040 km.

The Konkan Railway (760 km of 1,676 mm gauge) linking Roha and Mangalore opened in 1996. It is operated as a separate entity.

Principal gauges are 1,676 mm (40,620 km) and 1 metre (18,501 km), with networks also of 762 mm and 610 mm gauge (3,794 km).

Passenger-km travelled in 2002–03 came to 515·0bn. and freight tonne-km to 353·2bn. Revenue (2002–03) from passengers, Rs 125,754m. (including the Calcutta Metro, which is part of Indian Railways); from goods, Rs 262,315m.

There are metros in Calcutta (16·5 km), Delhi (23·0 km) and Madras (15·5 km).

Civil Aviation

The main international airports are at Bombay, Calcutta, Delhi (Indira Gandhi), Madras and Thiruvananthapuram, with some international flights from Ahmedabad, Amritsar, Bangalore, Calicut, Goa and Hyderabad. Air transport was nationalized in 1953 with the formation of two Air Corporations: Air India for long-distance international air services, and Indian Airlines for air services within India and to adjacent countries. Domestic air transport has been opened to private companies, the largest of which is Jet Airways. In 1999 Indian Airlines carried 5,912,100 passengers, Jet Airways 4,647,400 and Air India 3,132,600 passengers.

In 2003 Air India operated routes to Africa (Dar es Salaam and Nairobi); to Mauritius; to Europe (Frankfurt, London, Moscow,

Paris, Vienna and Zürich); to western Asia (Abu Dhabi, Al Ain, Bahrain, Damman, Doha, Dubai, Jeddah, Kuwait, Muscat and Riyadh); to east Asia (Bangkok, Hong Kong, Jakarta, Kuala Lumpur, Osaka, Seoul, Singapore and Tokyo); and to North America (Chicago and New York). Indian Airlines operated international flights in 2003 to Almaty, Bahrain, Bangkok, Bishkek, Colombo, Dhaka, Doha, Dubai, Fujairah, Kathmandu, Kuala Lumpur, Kuwait, Malé, Muscat, Rangoon (Yangon), Ras-al-Khaimah, Sharjah and Singapore. Flights from Delhi to Lahore were restored in Jan. 2004. India's first budget airline, Air Deccan, began operations in 2003.

In 2001 Bombay was the busiest airport, handling 11,113,639 passengers (6,634,620 on domestic flights) and 278,185 tonnes of freight, followed by Delhi, with 8,453,398 passengers (4,884,012 on domestic flights) and 227,703 tonnes of freight. Plans have been announced for the privatization of both Bombay and Delhi airports.

Shipping
In 2000 the merchant fleet comprised 987 vessels (of 100 gross tons or more) totalling 6·66m. GRT, including 122 oil tankers of 3·00m. GRT. Cargo traffic of major ports, 2001–02, was as follows:

Port	Total (1m. tonnes)	Unloaded (1m. tonnes)	Loaded (1m. tonnes)	Transshipment (1m. tonnes)
Bombay	26·71	16·14	9·21	1·38
Cochin	12·21	10·15	2·07	0·00
Haldia	25·12	18·50	6·62	0·01
Jawaharlal Nehru	24·09	12·18	11·01	0·91
Kandla	37·85	28·52	7·77	1·57
Madras	36·46	23·22	13·14	0·10
Mormugao	22·93	4·60	18·31	0·02
New Mangalore	17·51	8·77	8·75	0·00
Paradip	21·13	6·66	14·48	0·00
Tuticorin	13·23	9·91	3·32	0·00
Visakhapatnam	44·37	17·87	16·91	9·57

There are about 3,700 km of major rivers navigable by motorized craft, of which 2,000 km are used. Canals, 4,300 km, of which 900 km are navigable by motorized craft.

Telecommunications
The telephone system is in the hands of the Telecommunications Department, except in Delhi and Bombay, which are served by a public corporation. Telephone subscribers numbered 53,903,000 in 2002, equivalent to 51·7 for every 1,000 persons; 1·65m. people were still on the waiting list for a line in 2001. There were 12·69m. mobile phone subscribers and 7·50m. PCs in use in 2002. There were 230,000 fax machines in 2002 and 16,580,000 Internet users.

Postal Services
In 2003 there were 155,618 post offices. India has more post offices than any other country. In 2003 a total of 9,126m. pieces of mail were processed, or nine items per person.

SOCIAL INSTITUTIONS

Justice
All courts form a single hierarchy, with the Supreme Court at the head, which constitutes the highest court of appeal. Immediately below it are the High Courts and subordinate courts in each state. Every court in this chain administers the whole law of the country, whether made by Parliament or by the state legislatures.

The states of Andhra Pradesh, Assam (in common with Nagaland, Meghalaya, Manipur, Mizoram, Tripura and Arunachal Pradesh), Bihar, Gujarat, Himachal Pradesh, Jammu and Kashmir, Karnataka, Kerala, Madhya Pradesh, Maharashtra (in common with Goa and the Union Territories of Daman and Diu, and Dadra and Nagar Haveli), Orissa, Punjab (in

common with the state of Haryana and the Union Territory of Chandigarh), Rajasthan, Tamil Nadu (in common with the Union Territory of Pondicherry), Uttar Pradesh, West Bengal and Sikkim each have a High Court. There is a separate High Court for Delhi. For the Andaman and Nicobar Islands the Calcutta High Court, for Pondicherry the High Court of Madras and for Lakshadweep the High Court of Kerala are the highest judicial authorities. The Allahabad High Court has a Bench at Lucknow, the Bombay High Court has Benches at Nagpur, Aurangabad and Panaji, the Gauhati High Court has Benches at Kohima, Aizwal, Imphal and Agartala, the Madhya Pradesh High Court has Benches at Gwalior and Indore, the Patna High Court has a Bench at Ranchi and the Rajasthan High Court has a Bench at Jaipur. Judges and Division Courts of the Guwahati High Court also sit in Meghalaya. Similarly, judges and Division Courts of the Calcutta High Court also sit in the Andaman and Nicobar Islands. High Courts have also been established in the new states of Chhattisgarh, Jharkhand and Uttaranchal. Below the High Court each state is divided into a number of districts under the jurisdiction of district judges who preside over civil courts and courts of sessions. There are a number of judicial authorities subordinate to the district civil courts. On the criminal side magistrates of various classes act under the overall supervision of the High Court.

In Oct. 1991 the Supreme Court upheld capital punishment by hanging. In 2004 there were two executions, the first ones since 1995.

The population in penal institutions in June 2002 was 304,893 (29 per 100,000 of national population).

Police
The states control their own police forces. The Home Affairs Minister of the central government co-ordinates the work of the states. The Indian Police Service provides senior officers for the state police forces. The Central Bureau of Investigation functions under the control of the Cabinet Secretariat.

The cities of Pune, Ahmedabad, Nagpur, Bangalore, Calcutta, Madras, Bombay, Delhi and Hyderabad have separate police commissionerates.

Education
Adult literacy was 58·0% in 2001 (69·0% among males and 46·4% among females). Of the states and territories, Kerala and Mizoram have the highest rates.

Educational Organization. Education is the concurrent responsibility of state and Union governments. In the Union Territories it is the responsibility of the central government. The Union government is also directly responsible for the central universities and all institutions declared by parliament to be of national importance; the promotion of Hindi as the federal language and co-ordinating and maintaining standards in higher education, research, science and technology. Professional education rests with the Ministry or Department concerned. There is a Central Advisory Board of Education to advise the Union and the State governments on any educational question which may be referred to it.

School Education. The school system has four stages: primary, middle, secondary and senior secondary.

Primary education is imparted either at independent primary (or junior basic) schools or primary classes attached to middle or secondary schools. The period of instruction varies from four to five years and the medium of instruction is in most cases the mother tongue of the child or the regional language. Free primary education is available for all children. Legislation for compulsory education has been passed by some state governments and Union Territories but it is not practicable to enforce compulsion when the reasons for non-attendance are socio-economic. There are residential schools for country children. The period for the middle stage varies from two to three years.

Higher Education. Higher education is given in arts, science or professional colleges, universities and all-India educational or research institutions. In 1995–96 there were 166 universities, four institutes established under state legislature act, 11 institutions of national importance and 37 institutions deemed as universities. Of the universities, 13 are central: Aligarh Muslim University; Banaras Hindu University; Delhi University; Hyderabad University; Jamia Millia Islamia, New Delhi; Jawaharlal Nehru University; North Eastern Hill University; Visva Bharati; Pondicherry University; Baba Sahib B. R. Ambedkar University; Assam University; Tezpur University; and Nagaland University. The rest are state universities. Total enrolment at universities, 1995–96, 6,425,624, of which 5,667,400 were undergraduates. Women students numbered 2,191,138.

Technical Education. The number of institutions awarding degrees in engineering and technology in 1996–97 was 418, and those awarding diplomas, 1,029; the former admitted 328,399 students, the latter 357,891 including 58,454 female students.

Adult Education. The Directorate of Adult Education, established in 1971, is the national resource centre.

There is also a National Literacy Mission.

Educational statistics for 2001–02:

Type of recognized institution	No. of institutions	No. of students on rolls	No. of teachers
Primary/junior basic schools	664,041	113,900,000	1,928,000
Middle/senior basic schools	219,626	44,800,000	1,468,000
High/higher secondary schools[1]	133,492	30,500,000	1,777,000
Colleges for professional education	2,409	237,509[2]	—
Colleges for general education	8,737	6,425,624[2]	239,488[2]

[1]Including Junior Colleges. [2]1996–97.

Expenditure. Total budgeted central expenditure on revenue account of education and other departments 1997–98 was estimated at Rs 46,383m. Total public expenditure on education, sport, arts and youth welfare during the Eighth (1992–97) Plan, Rs 212,170·2m.; Seventh Plan spending on adult education, Rs 3,007m. in the central and Rs 6,098m. in the state sectors. In 1999–2000 total expenditure on education came to 4·1% of GNP and 12·7% of total government spending.

Health

Medical services are primarily the responsibility of the states. The Union government has sponsored major schemes for disease prevention and control which are implemented nationally.

Total central expenditure on health and family welfare in 1997–98 was Rs 14,166·2m. on revenue account. In 2002 there were 15,741 hospitals and 607,100 doctors. In 2002 there were 15 beds per 10,000 inhabitants.

In 2001 approximately 221m. people, representing 21% of the population, were undernourished. In 1979, 38% of the population had been undernourished.

Approximately 3·7m. Indians are HIV-infected, a number only exceeded in South Africa (and equivalent to nearly 9% of all the people believed to be infected worldwide). Some suggestions indicate that there may be as many as 15m. HIV-positive people by 2010.

RELIGION

India is a secular state; any worship is permitted, but the state itself has no religion. The principal religions in 2001 were: Hindus, 759m.; Sunni Muslims, 92m.; Shia Muslims, 31m.; Sikhs, 22m.; Protestants, 15m.; Roman Catholics, 14m.; Buddhists, 7m.; Jains, 4m. In addition to having the largest Hindu population of any country, India has the third highest number of Muslims, after Indonesia and Pakistan. In May 2005 the Roman Catholic church had five cardinals.

CULTURE

World Heritage Sites

There are 26 sites under Indian jurisdiction that appear on the UNESCO World Heritage List. They are (with year entered on list): Ajanta Caves (1983), Ellora Caves (1983), Agra Fort (1983), Taj Mahal (1983), Sun Temple, Konarak (1984), Monuments at Mahabalipuram (1985), Kaziranga National Park (1985), Manas Wildlife Sanctuary (1985), Keoladeo National Park (1985), Churches and Convents of Goa (1986), Monuments at Khajuraho (1986), Monuments at Hampi (1986), Fatehpur Sikri (1986), Monuments at Pattadakal (1987), Elephanta Caves (1987), Brihadisvara Temple, Thanjavur (1987), Sundarbans National Park (1987), Nanda Devi National Park (1988 and 2005), Buddhist Monuments at Sanchi (1989), Humayan's Tomb, Delhi (1993), Qutb Minar and its Monuments, Delhi (1993), Darjeeling Himalayan Railway (1999), Mahabodhi Temple Complex at Bodh Gaya (2002), the Rock Shelters of Bhimbetka (2003), Champaner-Pavagadh Archaeological Park (2004) and the Chhatrapati Shivaji Terminus—formerly Victoria Terminus (2004) in Bombay.

Broadcasting

The national television (Doordarshan) and radio (All India Radio, or Akashwani) networks are state-owned. Satellite broadcasting is dominated by AajTak, Star and Zee TV. In March 1997 there were 187 radio stations and 297 transmitters, 19 channels and 41 programme production centres. Television reached 85·8% of the population, through a network of 834 transmitters (colour by PAL). There were estimated to be 123m. radio sets and 79m. TV sets in 2000. There were 18m. cable TV subscribers in 1997—approximately 29% of households that had TV licences. By 2001 the number of TV sets had increased to 85m. and cable subscribers to 40m.

Cinema

In 2001 there were 11,962 cinema screens with a total attendance of 2·8bn. In 2002, 1,233 feature films were certified (943 Indian, 290 foreign).

Press

There were 58,469 registered newspapers in March 2004, with a total circulation of 133·1m. In 2002 there were 402 dailies with a total circulation of 31·1m. Hindi papers have the highest number and circulation, followed by English, then Urdu, Bengali and Marathi. The newspaper with the highest circulation is the *Times of India* (daily average of 2·1m. copies in 2002). In 2002 a total of 17,038 book titles were published.

It was estimated in 1999 that 29% of the electorate of 620m. for the general election had no access to any sort of news media.

Tourism

In 2002 there were 2,384,000 foreign tourists, spending US$2·92bn. Of these, over 387,000 were from the UK, 348,000 from the USA and 108,000 from Sri Lanka.

Calendar

The Indian National Calendar, adopted in 1957, is dated from the Saka era (Indian dynasty beginning AD 78). It uses the same year-length as the Gregorian calendar (also used for administrative and informal purposes) but begins on 22 March. Local and religious variations are also used.

DIPLOMATIC REPRESENTATIVES

Of India in the United Kingdom (India House, Aldwych, London, WC2B 4NA)
High Commissioner: Kamalesh Sharma.

Of the United Kingdom in India (Chanakyapuri, New Delhi 110021)
High Commissioner: Sir Michael Arthur, KCMG.

Of India in the USA (2107 Massachusetts Ave., NW, Washington, D.C., 20008)
Ambassador: Ronen Sen.

Of the USA in India (Shanti Path, Chanakyapuri, New Delhi 110021)
Ambassador: David C. Mulford.

Of India to the United Nations
Ambassador: Nirupam Sen.

Of India to the European Union
Ambassador: Pradeep Kumar Singh.

FURTHER READING

Bhambhri, C. P., *The Political Process in India, 1947–91.* Delhi, 1991
Bose, S. and Jalal, A. (eds.) *Nationalism, Democracy and Development: State and Politics in India.* OUP, 1997
Brown, J., *Modern India: The Origins of an Asian Democracy.* 2nd ed. OUP, 1994
Derbyshire, I., *India.* [Bibliography] 2nd ed. ABC-Clio, Oxford and Santa Barbara (CA), 1995
Gupta, D. C., *Indian Government and Politics.* 3rd ed. London, 1992

Jaffrelot, C. (ed.) *L'Inde Contemporain de 1950 à nos Jours.* Paris, 1996
James, L., *Raj: The Making and Unmaking of British India.* Little, Brown, London, 1997
Joshi, V. and Little, I. M. D., *India's Economic Reforms, 1991–2000.* Oxford, 1996
Keay, John, *India: A History.* HarperCollins, London, 2000
Khilnani, S., *The Idea of India.* London, 1997
King, R., *Nehru and the Language Politics of India.* OUP, 1997
Metcalf, Barbara D. and Metcalf, Thomas R., *A Concise History of India.* CUP, 2001
Mohan, C. Raja, *Crossing the Rubicon: The Shaping of India's New Foreign Policy.* Penguin India, New Delhi, 2003
New Cambridge History of India. 2nd ed. 5 vols. CUP, 1994–96
Robb, Peter, *A History of India.* Palgrave Macmillan, Basingstoke, 2002
Vohra, R., *The Making of India: A Historical Survey.* Armonk (NY), 1997

National Statistical Office: Ministry of Statistics and Programme Implementation.
Website: http://mospi.nic.in
Census India Website: http://www.censusindia.net
Other more specialized titles are listed under CONSTITUTION AND GOVERNMENT *and* RECENT ELECTIONS, *above.*

STATES AND TERRITORIES

GENERAL DETAILS

The Republic of India is composed of the following 28 States and seven centrally administered Union Territories:

States	Capital	States	Capital
Andhra Pradesh	Hyderabad	Maharashtra	Bombay
Arunachal Pradesh	Itanagar	Manipur	Imphal
Assam	Dispur	Meghalaya	Shillong
Bihar	Patna	Mizoram	Aizawl
Chhattisgarh	Raipur	Nagaland	Kohima
Goa	Panaji	Orissa	Bhubaneswar
Gujarat	Gandhinagar	Punjab	Chandigarh
Haryana	Chandigarh	Rajasthan	Jaipur
Himachal Pradesh	Shimla	Sikkim	Gangtok
Jammu and Kashmir	Srinagar	Tamil Nadu	Madras
Jharkhand	Ranchi	Tripura	Agartala
Karnataka	Bangalore	Uttar Pradesh	Lucknow
Kerala	Thiruvananthapuram	Uttaranchal	Dehra Dun
Madhya Pradesh	Bhopal	West Bengal	Calcutta

Union Territories. Andaman and Nicobar Islands; Chandigarh; Dadra and Nagar Haveli; Daman and Diu; Delhi; Lakshadweep; Pondicherry.

Andhra Pradesh

KEY HISTORICAL EVENTS

Constituted a separate state on 1 Oct. 1953, Andhra Pradesh was the undisputed Telugu-speaking area of Madras. To this region was added, on 1 Nov. 1956, the Telangana area of the former Hyderabad State, comprising the districts of Hyderabad, Medak, Nizamabad, Karimnagar, Warangal, Khammam, Nalgonda and Mahbubnagar, parts of the Adilabad district, some taluks of the Raichur, Gulbarga and Bidar districts and some revenue circles of the Nanded district. On 1 April 1960, 221·4 sq. miles in the Chingleput and Salem districts of Madras were transferred to Andhra Pradesh in exchange for 410 sq. miles from Chittoor district. The district of Prakasam was formed on 2 Feb. 1970. Hyderabad was split into two districts on 15 Aug. 1978 (Ranga Reddy and Hyderabad). A new district, Vizianagaram, was formed in 1979.

TERRITORY AND POPULATION

Andhra Pradesh is in south India and is bounded in the south by Tamil Nadu, west by Karnataka, north and northwest by Maharashtra, northeast by Chhattisgarh and Orissa and east by the Bay of Bengal. The state has an area of 275,069 sq. km and a population (2001 census) of 75,727,541; density, 275 per sq. km. The principal language is Telugu. Cities with over 250,000 population (2001 census), *see* INDIA: Territory and Population. Other large cities (2001): Anantapur, 243,359; Ramagundam, 236,623; Karimnagar, 215,782; Eluru, 215,343; Khamman, 196,763; Vizianagaram, 195,462; Machilipatnam, 183,370; Chirala, 166,877; Proddutur, 164,932; Adoni, 161,125; Nandyal, 156,216; Chittoor, 152,966; Ongole, 152,945; Tenali, 149,839; Bheemavaram, 141,975; Mahbubnagar, 139,483; Adilabad, 128,196; Hindupur, 125,056; Mancherial, 118,047; Guntakal, 117,403; Srikakulam, 117,066; Gudivada, 112,245; Nalgonda, 111,745; Madanapalle, 107,262; Kottagudem, 105,265; Dharmavaram, 103,400; Tadepalligudem, 102,303.

SOCIAL STATISTICS

Growth rate 1991–2001, 13·86%.

CONSTITUTION AND GOVERNMENT

Andhra Pradesh has a unicameral legislature; the Legislative Council was abolished in June 1985. There are 295 seats in the Legislative Assembly. For administrative purposes there are 23 districts in the state. The capital is Hyderabad.

RECENT ELECTIONS

At the State Assembly elections held on 20 and 26 April 2004 the Congress Alliance won 226 seats—of which 185 (38·2% of the vote) for the INC, 26 (6·6%) for Telangana Rashtra Samithi, 9 (2·0%) for the CPI-M and 6 (1·5%) for the CPI. The Telugu Desam Party won 47 seats (37·1%) and the BJP 2 (2·6%). Four other parties received a total of 8 seats and 11 independents were elected.

CURRENT ADMINISTRATION

Governor: Rameshwar Thakur; b. 1927 (took office on 29 Jan. 2006).
 Chief Minister: Y. S. Rajasekhara Reddy; b. 1949 (took office on 14 May 2004).

ECONOMY

Budget
Budget estimate, 2002–03: receipts on revenue account, Rs 256,747·9m.; expenditure, Rs 281,205·0m. Annual plan, 2002–03: Rs 112,995·0m.

ENERGY AND NATURAL RESOURCES

Electricity
There are 13 hydro-electric plants, 11 thermal stations and two gas-based units. Installed capacity, 2000, 7,341 MW; power generated (1999) 6,480m. kWh. By Nov. 1996 all 27,358 villages had electricity and 1·74m. electric pump sets were energized.

Oil and Gas
Crude oil is refined at Visakhapatnam in Andhra Pradesh. Oil/gas structures are found in Krishna-Godavari basin which encompasses an area of 20,000 sq. km on land and 21,000 sq. km up to 200 metres isobath off-shore. In 2001, 1,604m. cu. metres of natural gas were produced. Reserves of the land basin are estimated at 760 metric tonnes of oil and oil equivalent of gas.

Water
In 2000 more than 120 irrigation projects had created irrigation potential of 6m. ha. The Telugu Ganga joint project with Tamil Nadu, begun in the early 1980s, will eventually irrigate about 233,000 ha., besides supplying drinking water to Madras city (Tamil Nadu).

Minerals
The state is an important producer of asbestos and barytes. The Cuppadah basin is a major source of uranium and other minerals. Other important minerals are copper ore, coal, iron and limestone, steatite, mica and manganese.

Agriculture
There were (1999) about 10·7m. ha. of cropped land, of which 6·8m. ha. were under foodgrains. Irrigated area, 2000, 6m. ha. Production in 1999 (in tonnes): bananas, 13·73m.; pulses, 10·94m.; foodgrains, 10·37m. (rice, 8·51m.); oil seeds, 1·3m.; sugarcane, 0·2m.

Livestock (1993): cattle, 10·95m.; buffaloes, 9·13m.; sheep, 7·77m.; goats, 4·32m. There are also an estimated 100m. chickens.

Forestry
In 1999 it was estimated that forests occupy 15·7% of the total area of the state, or 43,290 sq. km; main forest products are teak, eucalyptus, cashew, casuarina, softwoods and bamboo.

Fisheries
Production 2001–02, 578,000 tonnes of marine and freshwater fish and crustaceans. This represents 10% of India's catch. The state has a coastline of 974 km.

INDUSTRY

The main industries are textile manufacture, sugar-milling, machine tools, pharmaceuticals (Andhra Pradesh commands 40% of India's pharmaceuticals industry), electronic equipment, heavy electrical machinery, aircraft parts and paper-making. There is an oil refinery at Visakhapatnam, where India's major shipbuilding yards are situated. A major steel plant at Visakhapatnam and a railway repair shop at Tirupati are functioning. At 31 March 1997 there were 1,536 large and medium industries employing 644,480 persons, and 124,209 small-scale industries employing 1m. There are cottage industries and sericulture. District Industries Centres have been set up to promote small-scale industry. Tourism is growing; the main centres are Hyderabad, Nagarjunasagar, Warangal, Arakuvalley, Horsley Hills and Tirupati.

COMMUNICATIONS

Roads
In 2002 there were 198,000 km of roads in the state including national roads. Number of vehicles as of 31 March 1997 was 2,783,220, including 2,287,029 motorcycles and scooters, 187,863 goods vehicles and 177,516 cars and jeeps.

Rail
There are 5,073 route-km of railway.

Civil Aviation
There are airports at Hyderabad, Tirupati, Vijayawada and Visakhapatnam, with regular scheduled services to Bombay, Delhi, Calcutta, Bangalore, Madras and Bhubaneswar. International flights are operated from Hyderabad to Bangkok, Dubai, Jeddah, Kuala Lumpur, Kuwait, Muscat, Sharjah and Singapore.

Shipping
The chief port is Visakhapatnam, which handles 44·6m. tonnes of cargo annually. There are minor ports at Kakinada, Machilipatnam, Bheemunipatnam, Narsapur, Krishnapatnam, Nizampatnam, Vadarevu and Kalingapatnam.

SOCIAL INSTITUTIONS

Justice
The high court of Judicature at Hyderabad has a Chief Justice and a sanctioned strength of 39 judges.

Education
In 2001, 61·11% of the population were literate (70·85% of men and 51·17% of women). There were, in 1999, 51,836 primary schools (6,237,700 students); 8,713 upper primary (2,440,000); 8,819 high schools (3,732,000). Education is free for children up to 14.

In 1995–96 there were 1,818 junior colleges (676,455 students). In 1996–97 there were 805 degree colleges (427,652 students); 46 oriented colleges and 18 universities: Osmania University, Hyderabad; Andhra University, Waltair; Sri Venkateswara University, Tirupati; Kakatiya University, Warangal; Nagarjuna University, Guntur; Sri Jawaharlal Nehru Technological University, Hyderabad; Hyderabad University, Hyderabad; N. G. Ranga Agricultural University, Hyderabad; Sri Krishnadevaraya University, Anantapur; Smt. Padmavathi Mahila Vishwavidyalayam (University for Women), Tirupati; Dr B. R. Ambedkar Open University, Hyderabad; Patti Sriramulu Telugu University, Hyderabad; N. T. R. University of Health Science, Vijayawada; Moulana Azad National Urdu University, Hyderabad; Dravidian University, Chittoor; Rashtriya Sanskrit Vidyapeeth, Tirupati; Sri Satya Sai Institute of Higher Learning, Prashanti Nilayam; National Academy of Legal Studies and Research University, Hyderabad.

Health
There were (1996) 1,947 allopathic hospitals and dispensaries, 550 Ayurvedic hospitals and dispensaries, 193 Unani and 283 homoeopathy hospitals and dispensaries. There were also 181 nature cure hospitals and (in 1999) 1,360 primary health centres. Number of beds in hospitals was 32,116.

RELIGION

At the 2001 census Hindus accounted for 89·14% of the population, Muslims 8·91%, Christians 1·83%, Jains 0·04%, Buddhists 0·03% and Sikhs 0·03%.

Arunachal Pradesh

KEY HISTORICAL EVENTS

Before independence the North East Frontier Agency of Assam was administered for the viceroy by a political agent working through tribal groups. After independence it became the North East Frontier Tract, administered for the central government by the Governor of Assam. In 1972 the area became the Union Territory of Arunachal Pradesh; statehood was achieved in Dec. 1986.

TERRITORY AND POPULATION

The state is in the extreme northeast of India and is bounded in the north by China, east by Myanmar, west by Bhutan and south by Assam and Nagaland. It has 13 districts and comprises the former frontier divisions of Kameng, Tirap, Subansiri, Siang and Lohit; it has an area of 83,743 sq. km and a population (2001 census) of 1,091,117; density, 13 per sq. km.

The state is mainly tribal; there are 106 tribes using about 50 tribal dialects.

SOCIAL STATISTICS

Growth rate 1991–2001, 26·21%.

CONSTITUTION AND GOVERNMENT

There is a Legislative Assembly of 60 members. The capital is Itanagar (population, 2001, 34,970).

RECENT ELECTIONS

At the State Assembly elections held on 7 Oct. 2004 the India National Congress Party won 34 seats; the Bharatiya Janata Party, 9; the Nationalist Congress Party, 2; the Arunachal Congress, 2; ind., 13.

CURRENT ADMINISTRATION

Governor: Shailendra Kumar Singh; b. 1932 (since 16 Dec. 2004).

Chief Minister: Gegong Apang (since 3 Aug. 2003; previously in office from 1980–99).

ECONOMY

Budget

Total estimated receipts, 2000–01, Rs 11,843m.; total estimated expenditure, Rs 11,451m. Plan outlay, 2000–01, Rs 6,400m.

ENERGY AND NATURAL RESOURCES

Electricity

Total installed capacity (1999), 45·43 MW. Power generated (1999): 66·28m. units. 2,188 out of 3,257 villages have electricity.

Oil and Gas

Production, 2001, 31,000 tonnes of crude oil and 23m. cu. metres of gas. Crude oil reserves are estimated at nearly 30m. tonnes.

Minerals

Coal reserves are estimated at 90·23m. tonnes; dolomite, 154·13m. tonnes; limestone, 409·35m. tonnes.

Agriculture

Production of foodgrains, 1999, 204,000 tonnes.

Forestry

Area under forest, 51,540 sq. km; revenue from forestry (1995–96) Rs 402m.

INDUSTRY

In 1996 there were 18 medium and 3,306 small industries, 80 craft or weaving centres and 225 sericulture centres. Most of the medium industries are forest-based. Industries include coal, textiles, jute, iron and steel, chemicals, tea and leather.

COMMUNICATIONS

Roads

Total length of roads in the state, 12,280 km of which 9,855 km are surfaced. There were 14,821 vehicles in 1995–96. The state had 393 km of national highway in 2000. Four towns are linked by air services.

SOCIAL INSTITUTIONS

Education

In 2001, 54·74% of the population were literate (64·07% of men and 44·24% of women). There were (1996–97) 1,256 primary schools with 147,676 students, 301 middle schools with 42,197 students, 157 high and higher secondary schools with 24,951 students, six colleges and two technical schools. Arunachal University, established in 1985, had four colleges and 3,240 students in 1994–95.

Health

There were (2004) 14 hospitals, 19 community health centres, 58 primary health centres and 273 sub-centres. In 1996 there were two TB hospitals and 11 leprosy and other hospitals. Total number of beds (2002), 2,641.

RELIGION

At the 2001 census Hindus accounted for 37·04% of the population, Buddhists 12·88%, Christians 10·29%, Muslims 1·38%, Sikhs 0·14%, Jains 0·01%, others 36·22%.

FURTHER READING

Bose, M. L., *History of Arunachal Pradesh.* Concept Publications, New Delhi, 1997

Assam

KEY HISTORICAL EVENTS

Assam first became a British Protectorate at the close of the first Burmese War in 1826. In 1832 Cachar was annexed; in 1835 the Jaintia Hills were included in the East India Company's dominions, and in 1839 Assam was annexed to Bengal. In 1874 Assam was detached from Bengal and made a separate chief commissionership. On the partition of Bengal in 1905, it was united to the Eastern Districts of Bengal under a Lieut.-Governor. From 1912 the chief commissionership of Assam was revived, and in 1921 a governorship was created. On the partition of India almost the whole of the predominantly Muslim district of Sylhet was merged with East Bengal (Pakistan). Dewangiri in North Kamrup was ceded to Bhutan in 1951. The Naga Hill district, administered by the Union government since 1957, became part of Nagaland in 1962. The autonomous state of Meghalaya within Assam, comprising the districts of Garo Hills and Khasi and Jaintia Hills, came into existence on 2 April 1970, and achieved full independent statehood in Jan. 1972, when it was also decided to form a Union Territory, Mizoram (now a state), from the Mizo Hills district.

TERRITORY AND POPULATION

Assam is in northeast India, almost separated from central India by Bangladesh. It is bounded in the west by West Bengal, north by Bhutan and Arunachal Pradesh, east by Nagaland, Manipur and Myanmar, south by Meghalaya, Bangladesh, Mizoram and Tripura. The area of the state is now 78,438 sq. km. Population (2001 census) 26,638,407; density, 340 per sq. km. Principal towns with population (2001 census): Guwahati, 814,575; Silchar, 184,285; Dibrugarh, 137,879; Jorhat, 135,091; Nagaon, 123,054; Tinsukia, 108,102; Tezpur, 83,028; Bongaigaon, 76,397; Dhubri, 63,965. The principal language is Assamese.

The central government is surveying the line of a proposed boundary fence to prevent illegal entry from Bangladesh.

SOCIAL STATISTICS

Growth rate 1991–2001, 18·85%.

CONSTITUTION AND GOVERNMENT

Assam has a unicameral legislature of 126 members. The capital is Dispur. The state has 23 districts.

RECENT ELECTIONS

In the elections of 10 May 2001 the Indian National Congress (INC) took 70 seats, Asom Gana Parishad 20 and Bharatiya Janata Party (BJP) 8.

CURRENT ADMINISTRATION

Governor: Lieut.-Gen. (retd) Ajai Singh (took office on 5 June 2003).

Chief Minister: Tarun Gogoi; b. 1936 (took office on 18 May 2001).

ECONOMY

Budget

The budget estimates for 2001 showed receipts of Rs 91,576m. and expenditure of Rs 100,124m.

ENERGY AND NATURAL RESOURCES

Electricity

In 2000 there was an installed capacity of 574 MW. In 1998, 77% of villages had electricity. New power stations are under construction at Lakwa, and Karbi-Langpi hydro-electricity project.

Oil and Gas

Assam contains important oilfields and produces about 16% of India's crude oil. Production (1999): crude oil, 5·00m. tonnes; gas (1999), 1,333m. cu. metres.

Minerals

Coal production (2002–03), 633,000 tonnes. The state also has limestone, refractory clay, dolomite and corundum.

Agriculture

Assam produces 50% of India's tea—in 2003 there were 1,196 registered tea estates in the state. Production in 1998 was 425·4m. kg. 82% of the cultivable area is used. Over 72% of the cultivated area is under food crops, of which the most important is rice. Total foodgrains, 1997, 3·53m. tonnes. Main cash crops: tea, jute, cotton, oilseeds, sugarcane, fruit and potatoes. Wheat production, 100,000 tonnes in 2000; rice, 3·9m. tonnes; pulses, 64,688 tonnes. Cattle are important.

Forestry

In 2000 there were 17,420 sq. km of reserved forests under the administration of the Forest Department and 6,000 sq. km of unclassed forests, altogether about 39% of the total area of the state. Revenue from forests, in 1999, Rs 9,590m.

INDUSTRY

Sericulture and hand-loom weaving, both silk and cotton, are important home industries together with the manufacture of brass, cane and bamboo articles. The main heavy industry is petro-chemicals; there are four oil refineries in the region. Other industries include manufacturing paper, nylon, electronic goods, cement, fertilizers, sugar, jute and plywood products, rice and oil milling.

There were 23,218 small-scale industries in 2000. In 1999, 1·1m. persons were employed in state-run enterprises.

COMMUNICATIONS

Roads

In 1998 there were 33,064 km of road maintained by the Public Works Department. There were 2,034 km of national highway in 1999. There were 373,962 motor vehicles in the state in 1998–99.

Rail

The route-km of railways in 1999 was 3,722 km, of which 2,392 km was broad gauge.

Civil Aviation

Daily scheduled flights connect the principal towns with the rest of India. There are airports at Guwahati, Tezpur, Jorhat, North Lakhimpur, Silchar and Dibrugarh.

Shipping

Water transport is important in Lower Assam; the main waterway is the Brahmaputra River. Cargo carried in 1998 was 50,334 tonnes.

SOCIAL INSTITUTIONS

Justice

The seat of the High Court is Guwahati. It has a Chief Justice and Justice and a sanctioned strength of 19 judges.

Education

In 2001, 64·28% of the population were literate (71·93% of men and 56·03% of women). In 1999–2000 there were 31,888 primary/junior basic schools with 3,293,835 students; 8,019 middle/senior basic schools with 1,406,818 students; 4,514 high/higher secondary schools with 1,465,518 students. There were 247 colleges for general education, six medical colleges, three engineering and one agricultural, 24 teacher-training colleges, and a fisheries college at Raha. There were five universities: Assam Agricultural University, Jorhat; Dibrugarh University, Dibrugarh with 86 colleges and 55,982 students (1992–93); Gauhati University, Guwahati with 128 colleges and 80,363 students (1992–93); and two central universities, at Silchar and Tezpur.

Health

In 2000 there were 164 hospitals (12,900 beds), 618 primary health centres and 323 dispensaries.

RELIGION

At the 1991 census Hindus numbered 15,047,293; Muslims, 6,373,204; Christians, 744,367; Buddhists, 64,008; Sikhs, 21,910; Jains, 20,645.

Bihar

KEY HISTORICAL EVENTS

Bihar was part of Bengal under British rule until 1912 when it was separated together with Orissa. The two were joined until 1936 when Bihar became a separate province. As a state of the Indian Union it was enlarged in 1956 by the addition of land from West Bengal.

The state contains the ethnic areas of North Bihar, Santhal Pargana and Chota Nagpur. In 1956 some areas of Purnea and Manbhum districts were transferred to West Bengal. In 2000 the state of Jharkhand was carved from the mineral-rich southern region of Bihar, substantially reducing the state's revenue-earning power.

TERRITORY AND POPULATION

Bihar is in north India and is bounded north by Nepal, east by West Bengal, south by the new state of Jharkhand, southwest and west by Uttar Pradesh. After the formation of Jharkhand the area of Bihar is 94,163 sq. km (previously 173,877 sq. km). Population (2001 census), 82,878,796, with a density of 880 per sq. km. Population of principal towns, *see* INDIA: Territory and Population. Other large towns (2001): Biharsharif, 231,972; Arrah, 203,395; Munger, 187,311; Chapra, 178,835; Katihar, 175,169; Purnea, 171,235; Sasaram, 131,042; Dinapur Nizamat, 130,339; Saharsa, 124,015; Hajipur, 119,276; Dehri, 119,007; Bettiah, 116,692; Siwan, 108,172; Motihari, 101,506.

The state is divided into 37 districts. The capital is Patna.

The official language is Hindi (spoken by 80·9% at the 2001 census), the second, Urdu (9·9%), and the third, Bengali (2·9%).

SOCIAL STATISTICS

Growth rate 1991–2001, 28·43%.

CONSTITUTION AND GOVERNMENT

Bihar has a bicameral legislature. The Legislative Assembly consists of 243 elected members, and the Council 96. In March 2005 the state was put under president's rule after the elections had resulted in a hung assembly.

RECENT ELECTIONS

In elections held on 18 and 26 Oct., and 13 and 19 Nov. 2005 the Janata Dal (United) won 88 of 243 seats; Bharatiya Janata Party, 55; the ruling Rashtriya Janata Dal, 54; Lok Janshakti Party, 10; Indian National Congress, 9; Communist Party of India (Marxist-Leninist) (Liberation), 5; Bahujan Samaj Party, 4; Communist Party of India, 3; Samajwadi Party, 2; Akhil Jan Vikas Dal, 1; Communist Party of India (Marxist), 1; Nationalist Congress Party, 1; ind., 10.

CURRENT ADMINISTRATION

Governor: Gopalkrishna Gandhi; b. 1945 (took office on 31 Jan. 2006).

Chief Minister: Nirtish Kumar; b. 1951 (took office for a second time on 25 Nov. 2005).

ECONOMY

Budget

The budget estimates for 2001–02 showed total receipts of Rs 68,020m. and expenditure of Rs 66,806m. The creation of Jharkhand in 2000 removed two-thirds of Bihar's revenue.

ENERGY AND NATURAL RESOURCES

Electricity

Installed capacity (2000–01) 3,170 MW. Power generated in Bihar and Jharkhand (1994–95), 2,700m. kWh. There were (2001) 26,115 villages with electricity. Bihar has a higher percentage of villages without electricity than most Indian states. Hydro-electric projects in hand will add about 149·2 MW capacity.

Minerals

Before the creation of the new state of Jharkhand, Bihar was very rich in minerals. The truncated state has only deposits of bauxite, mica, glass sand and salt.

Agriculture

(Including Jharkhand). The irrigated area was 4·13m. ha. in 1993–94. Cultivable land, 11·6m. ha., of a total area of 17·4m. ha. Total cropped area, 1991–92, 9·79m. ha. Production (1995–96): rice, 6·91m. tonnes; wheat, 4·18m.; total foodgrains, 13·07m. Other food crops are maize, rabi and pulses. Main cash crops are jute, sugarcane, oilseeds, tobacco and potatoes.

Forests in 1995 covered 26,561 sq. km. There are 12 protected forests.

INDUSTRY

(Including Jharkhand). Iron, steel and aluminium are produced and there is an oil refinery. Other important industries are heavy engineering, machine tools, fertilizers, electrical engineering, manufacturing drugs and fruit processing. There were 500 large and medium industries and 163,000 small and handicraft units in 1996–97.

COMMUNICATIONS

Roads

(Including Jharkhand). In March 1997 the state had 87,836 km of roads, including 2,118 km of national highway, 4,192 km of state highway and 15,526 km of district roads. Passenger transport has been nationalized. There were 1,329,709 motor vehicles registered in March 1996.

Rail

(Including Jharkhand). The North Eastern, South Eastern and Eastern railways traverse the state; route-km, 1995–96, 5,283 km.

Civil Aviation

There are airports at Patna and Gaya with regular scheduled services to Calcutta and Delhi.

Shipping

(Including Jharkhand). The length of waterways open for navigation is 1,300 km.

SOCIAL INSTITUTIONS

Justice

There is a High Court (constituted in 1916) at Patna with a Chief Justice, 31 puisne judges and four additional judges.

Police

The police force is under a Director General of Police; in 1990 there were 1,097 police stations.

Education

At the census of 2001, 47·53% of the population were literate (60·32% of males and 33·57% of females). There were, 1996–97, 4,149 high and higher secondary schools with 1,080,321 pupils, 13,834 middle schools with 2·42m. pupils and 53,652 primary schools with 9,626,855 pupils. Education is free for children aged 6–11.

There are 12 universities: Patna University (founded 1917) with 14,699 students (1994–95); Babasaheb Bhimrao Ambedkar Bihar University, Muzaffarpur (1952) with 95 colleges, and 84,873 students (1989–90); Tilka Manjhi Bhagalpur University (1960) with 140,718 students (1990–91); Kameshwara Singh Darbhanga Sanskrit University (1961); Magadh University, Gaya (1962) with 186 colleges and 122,019 students (1994–95); Lalit Narayan Mithila University (1972), Darbhanga; Rajendra Agricultural University, Samastipur (1970); Nalanda Open University, Nalanda; BN Mandal University, Madhepura; Indira Gandhi University of Medical Sciences, Sheikhpura; Jai Prakash University, Chapra; and Veer Kunwar Singh University, Arrah. Including Jharkhand, there were 742 degree colleges, 11 engineering colleges, 31 medical colleges and 15 teacher training colleges in 1996–97. Ranchi University, Bisra Agricultural College and Sidhu Kanhu University, all formerly in Bihar, are now part of Jharkhand.

Health

(Including Jharkhand). In 2000 there were 1,636 hospitals and dispensaries with 12,123 beds.

RELIGION

At the 2001 census Hindus numbered 82·4% of the population.

CULTURE

Tourism

The main tourist centres are Bodh Gaya, Patna, Nalanda, Sasaram, Rajgir and Vaishali.

Chhattisgarh

KEY HISTORICAL EVENTS

The state was carved from sixteen mainly tribal districts of Madhya Pradesh and became the twenty-sixth state of India on 1 Nov. 2000. Chhattisgarh has been under the administrative control of many different rulers during its history, which can be traced back to the 4th century. Originally known as South Kosala, archaeological excavations made in recent times indicate that the region was a hive of artistic and cultural experimentation in ancient times. During the Sarabhapuriyas, Nalas, Pandavamsis and Kalchuris dynasties between the 6th and 8th centuries vast numbers of brick temples were built in the area. The British took control of the area from the Mahrattas in the early 19th century. Despite possessing its own cultural identity Chhattisgarh was constantly swallowed up by other regions and in 1956, as a direct result of the Indian Union of 1949, it was made part of the new region of Madhya Pradesh. For several years locals in Chhattisgarh voiced the grievance that their region was effectively a 'colony' of Madhya Pradesh, maintaining that the revenue generated by their region, which was termed the 'rice bowl of Madhya Pradesh' and was also rich in minerals, was insufficiently re-invested in the area itself. In 2000 the National Democratic Alliance successfully negotiated the passage of a bill through both houses of the Indian parliament which carved out three new Indian states, Chhattisgarh among them.

TERRITORY AND POPULATION

Chhattisgarh is in central eastern India and is bounded by the new state of Jharkhand to the east, Orissa to the southeast, Andhra Pradesh to the south and Maharashtra and Madhya Pradesh to the west. Chhattisgarh has an area of 135,191 sq. km. Population (2001 census) 20,795,956; density, 154 per sq. km. The principal languages are Hindi and Chhattisgarhi.

Cities with over 250,000 population, *see* INDIA: Territory and Population. Other large cities (2001): Rajnandgaon, 143,727; Raigarh, 115,740; Jagdalpur, 103,216.

SOCIAL STATISTICS

Growth rate 1991–2001, 18·06%.

CONSTITUTION AND GOVERNMENT

Chhattisgarh is the twenty-sixth state of India. In creating Chhattisgarh it was decided that the 90 members of the Madhya Pradesh Legislative Assembly from Chhattisgarhi districts would become the members of the new state's legislative assembly. For administrative purposes the region is divided into 16 districts. The council of ministers consists of 15 cabinet ministers and eight ministers of state.

The capital and seat of government is at Raipur.

RECENT ELECTIONS

At elections in Dec. 2003 the Bharatiya Janata Party won 50 seats and the Congress (I) Party took 36. Other parties won three seats.

CURRENT ADMINISTRATION

Governor: Lieut.-Gen. (retd) Krishna Mohan Seth; b. 1939 (since 2 June 2003).

Chief Minister: Dr Raman Singh; b. 1952 (took office 8 Dec. 2003).

ENERGY AND NATURAL RESOURCES

Electricity

Of the 19,720 villages in Chhattisgarh, 18,070 have electricity.

Water

1·21m. ha. of land is under irrigation. 44,750 residential areas have sufficient drinking water supplies while 7,315 residential areas only have partial supplies and 2,751 areas have insufficient supplies. In total there were 102,063 hand pumps in the state and 701 water fulfilment plans in place in 1999.

Minerals

The state has extensive mineral resources including (1999 estimates): over 27,000m. tonnes of tin ore, 2,000m. tonnes of iron ore, 525m. tonnes of dolomite (accounting for 24% of India's entire share) and 73m. tonnes of bauxite. There are also significant deposits of limestone, copper ore, rock phosphate, corundum, tin, coal and manganese ore. Deobogh in the Raipur district contains deposits of diamonds.

Agriculture

Agriculture is the occupation for 1·7m. of the population (around 80%). 5·8m. ha. of land is agricultural and the area provides food grain for over 600 rice mills. The great plains of Chhattisgarh produce 10,000 varieties of rice. Other crops include maize, millet, groundnuts, soybeans and sunflower. More than 25% of the land in Chhattisgarh is double cropped.

COMMUNICATIONS

Roads

Total length of roads (1999) was 33,182 km. State highways connect Raipur to neighbouring states and to Jagdalpur and Kondagaon in the south of Chhattisgarh and Durg and Rajnandgaon in the west.

Rail

Raipur is at the centre of the state's railway network, linking Chhattisgarh to the states of Orissa and Madhya Pradesh.

SOCIAL INSTITUTIONS

Education

In 2001, 65·18% of the population were literate (77·86% of men and 52·40% of women). There are three universities in Chhattisgarh. Ravishankar University (founded 1964), at Raipur, had 89 affiliated colleges (1992–93); Indira Gandhi Krishi Vishwavidyalaya, Raipur, a music and fine arts institution (founded in 1956); and Guru Ghasidas University, Bilaspur which had 58 colleges and 34,717 students (1992–93).

Health

In 2004 there were 138 hospitals with 5,565 beds and 285 doctors.

Goa

KEY HISTORICAL EVENTS

The coastal area was captured by the Portuguese in 1510 and the inland area was added in the 18th century. In Dec. 1961 Portuguese rule was ended and Goa incorporated into the Indian Union as a Territory together with Daman and Diu. Goa was granted statehood as a separate unit on 30 May 1987. Daman and Diu remained Union Territories.

TERRITORY AND POPULATION

Goa, bounded on the north by Maharashtra and on the east and south by Karnataka, has a coastline of 105 km. The area is 3,702 sq. km. Population (2001 census) 1,343,998; density, 363 per sq. km. Marmagao is the largest town; population (urban agglomeration, 2001) 104,689. The capital is Panaji; population (urban agglomeration, 2001) 98,915. The state has two districts. There are 183 village Panchayats. The languages spoken are Konkani (official language; 51·5%), Marathi 33·4%, Kannada 4·6%, Hindi and English.

SOCIAL STATISTICS

Growth rate 1991–2001, 14·89%.

CONSTITUTION AND GOVERNMENT

The Indian Parliament passed legislation in March 1962 by which Goa became a Union Territory with retrospective effect from 20 Dec. 1961. On 30 May 1987 Goa attained statehood. There is a Legislative Assembly of 40 members. In March 2005 the state was put under president's rule following a controversy over a vote of confidence in the Legislative Assembly. It was lifted in June 2005 after Pratapsingh Rane was sworn in as the new chief minister.

RECENT ELECTIONS

Of the 40 seats available at the elections for the State Assembly on 30 May 2002, the Bharatiya Janata Party won 17; Indian National Congress, 16; United Goans Democratic Party, 3; Maharashtrawadi Gomantak Party, 2; Nationalist Congress Party, 1; ind., 1.

CURRENT ADMINISTRATION

Governor: S. C. Jamir; b. 1931 (took office on 17 July 2004).

Chief Minister: Pratapsingh Rane; b. 1939 (took office for a fourth time on 7 June 2005).

ECONOMY

Budget

The total budget for 2001–02 was Rs 21,377m.; receipts, Rs 22,125m.

ENERGY AND NATURAL RESOURCES

Electricity

In 1996 installed capacity was 0·16m. MW, but Goa receives most of its power supply from the states of Maharashtra and Karnataka. In 2001, 360 villages and 44 towns had electricity.

Minerals

Resources include bauxite, ferro-manganese ore and iron ore, all of which are exported. Iron ore production (2002–03) 17,502,000 tonnes. There are also reserves of limestone and clay.

Agriculture

Agriculture is the main occupation, important crops being rice, pulses, ragi, mango, cashew and coconuts. Area under rice (2001) 57,207 ha.; production, 128,100 tonnes. Area under pulses 13,250 ha., sugarcane 1,250 ha., cashew nuts 53,767 ha. Total production of foodgrains, 2001, 138,000 tonnes.

Government poultry and dairy farming schemes produced 94m. eggs and 29,000m. litres of milk in 1992–93. Poultry (2001), 780,000; cattle (2001), 88,000.

Forestry

Forests covered 1,250 sq. km in 1995.

Fisheries

Fish is the state's staple food. In 1995–96 the catch of seafish was 84,210 tonnes. There is a coastline of about 104 km and about 2,850 (1994–95) active fishing vessels.

INDUSTRY

In 2001 there were 891 factories registered with a workforce of 39,938. There were 6,127 small-scale industries registered employing 43,312 persons. Production included: automotive components, electronic goods, fertilizers, footwear, nylon fishing nets, pesticides, pharmaceuticals, ready made clothing, ship-building and tyres.

COMMUNICATIONS

Roads

There were 7,419 km of roads in 1993–94 (National Highway, 224 km). Motor vehicles numbered 211,756 in March 1996.

Rail

In 1995–96 there were 79 km of route. In 2003 plans were announced for a monorail system.

Civil Aviation

An airport at Dabolim is connected with Agatti, Bangalore, Bombay, Delhi, Kochi, Kozhikode, Pune and Madras. It also receives international charter flights and scheduled flights from Kuwait and Sharjah.

Shipping

There are seaports at Panaji, Marmagao and Margao.

SOCIAL INSTITUTIONS

Justice

There is a bench of the Bombay High Court at Panaji.

Education

In 2001, 82·32% of the population were literate (88·88% of men and 75·51% of women). In 2001 there were 1,268 primary schools (97,457 students), 440 middle schools (72,726 students) and 445 high and higher secondary schools (85,217 students). In 1996–97 there were also two engineering colleges, four medical colleges, two teacher-training colleges, 21 other colleges and six polytechnic institutes. Goa University, Taleigao (1985) had 33 colleges and 16,977 students in 1994–95.

Health

In 2001 there were 120 hospitals (4,865 beds), 201 rural medical dispensaries, health and sub-health centres and 268 family planning units.

RELIGION

At the 2001 census 65% of the population were Hindus, 30% Christians and 5% Muslims.

FURTHER READING

Hutt, A., *Goa: A Traveller's Historical and Architectural Guide.* Buckhurst Hill, 1988

Gujarat

KEY HISTORICAL EVENTS

The Gujarati-speaking areas of India were part of the Moghul empire, coming under Mahratta domination in the late 18th century. In 1818 areas of present Gujarat around the Gulf of Cambay were annexed by the British East India Company. The remainder consisted of a group of small principalities, notably Baroda, Rajkot, Bhavnagar and Nawanagar. British areas became part of the Bombay Presidency.

At independence all the area now forming Gujarat became part of Bombay State except for Rajkot and Bhavnagar which formed the state of Saurashtra until incorporated in Bombay in 1956. In 1960 Bombay State was divided and the Gujarati-speaking areas became Gujarat.

In early 2002 at least 800 people, mostly Muslims, were killed in Gujarat in ethnic violence involving Hindus and the Muslim minority.

TERRITORY AND POPULATION

Gujarat is in western India and is bounded in the north by Pakistan and Rajasthan, east by Madhya Pradesh, southeast by Maharashtra, south and west by the Indian ocean and Arabian sea. The area of the state is 196,022 sq. km and the population (2001 census) 50,596,992; density, 258 per sq. km. The chief cities, see INDIA: Territory and Population. Other important towns (2001 census) are: Navsari (232,420), Surendranagar (219,828), Anand (218,064), Porbandar (197,414), Nadiad (196,679), Gandhinagar (195,891), Morbi (178,148), Bharuch (176,531), Veraval (157,869), Gandhidham (151,475), Valsad (145,650), Mehesana (141,367), Bhuj (136,327), Godhra (131,144), Palanpur (122,279), Patan (113,568), Anklesvar (112,648), Dahod (112,087), Kalol (112,025), Jetpur (104,301), Botad (100,059). Gujarati and Hindi in the Devanagari script are the official languages.

SOCIAL STATISTICS

Growth rate 1991–2001, 22·48%.

CLIMATE

Summers are intensely hot: 33–45°C. Winters: 7–13°C. Monsoon season: 22–36°C. Annual rainfall varies from 35 cm to 189 cm.

CONSTITUTION AND GOVERNMENT

Gujarat has a unicameral legislature, the *Legislative Assembly*, which has 182 elected members.

The capital is Gandhinagar. There are 25 districts.

RECENT ELECTIONS

In elections held in Dec. 2002 the Bharatiya Janata Party retained power with an increased majority, winning 126 seats against 51 for Congress, with ind. and others winning four seats.

CURRENT ADMINISTRATION

Governor: Nawal Kishore Sharma; b. 1925 (took office on 24 July 2004).

Chief Minister: Shri Narendrabhai Modi; b. 1950 (took office on 7 Oct. 2001).

ECONOMY

Budget

The budget estimates for 2004–05 showed revenue receipts of Rs 208,136·7m. and revenue expenditure of Rs 237,863·3m.

Banking and Finance

At March 2004 there were 3,668 branches of commercial banks in the State with combined deposits of Rs 846,810m. Total credit advanced was Rs 366,820m.

ENERGY AND NATURAL RESOURCES

Electricity

In March 2004 total installed capacity was 8,713 MW and 17,940 villages had electricity.

Oil and Gas

There are large crude oil and gas reserves. Production, 2002–03: crude oil, 6·0m. tonnes; gas, 3,324m. cu. metres.

Water

Water resources are limited. In 2003 irrigation potential was 6·49m. ha.

Minerals

Chief minerals produced in 2002–03 (in tonnes) included limestone (18m.), lignite (5·7m.), bauxite (1·7m.), quartz and silica (865,305), crude china clay (129,084), dolomite (128,519), calcareous and sea sand (4,000 in 1999–2000) and agate stone (68). Value of production (2002–03) Rs 51,221m. Reserves of coal lie under the Kalol and Mehsana oil and gas fields. The deposit, mixed with crude petroleum, is estimated at 100,000m. tonnes.

Agriculture

3·5m. ha. of the cropped area was irrigated in June 2003.

Production of principal crops, 2002–03: foodgrains, 3·6m. tonnes (wheat, 0·86m. tonnes); rice, 0·6m. tonnes from 481,000 ha.; pulses, 327,000 tonnes; cotton, 1·69m. bales of 170 kg. Tobacco and groundnuts are important cash crops.

Livestock (1997): buffaloes, 6·29m.; other cattle, 6·75m.; sheep and goats, 6·54m.; horses and ponies, 14,381.

Forestry

Forests covered 18,940 sq. km in March 2003 (9·66% of total area). The State has four National Parks and 21 sanctuaries.

Fisheries

There were (1997) 158,000 people engaged in fisheries. In 2002–03 there were 30,098 fishing vessels and the catch was 777,905 tonnes.

INDUSTRY

Gujarat ranks among India's most industrialized states. In 2003 there were 286,185 small-scale units and (2001) 18,880 factories including 3,293 chemical and chemical products factories, 2,275 textile factories, 1,736 non-metallic mineral products factories, 1,700 machinery and equipment factories and 876 rubber and plastic products factories. There were 251 industrial estates in 2002–03. Principal industries are textiles, general and electrical engineering, oil-refining, fertilizers, petrochemicals, machine tools, automobiles, heavy chemicals, pharmaceuticals, dyes, sugar, soda ash, cement, man-made fibres, salt, sulphuric acid, paper and paperboard.

In 2002 state production of soda-ash was 1·88m. tonnes, salt production was 13·08m. tonnes and cement production 10·78m. tonnes.

COMMUNICATIONS

Roads

At March 2002 there were 74,018 km of roads. Gujarat State Road Transport Corporation operated 18,507 routes. Number of vehicles at the end of March 2004, 7,087,490.

Rail

In 2002–03 the state had 5,186 route-km of railway line.

Civil Aviation

Sardar Vallabhbhai Patel International Airport at Ahmedabad is the main airport. There are some international flights and regular internal services between Ahmedabad and Bombay, Delhi and Jaipur, and within Gujarat between Ahmedabad and Bhavnagar, Bhuj, Rajkot and Vadodara (Baroda). There are five other airports: Jamnagar (which also has some international flights), Kandla, Keshod, Porbandar and Surat.

Shipping

The largest port is Kandla. There are 40 other ports. Cargo handled at the ports in 2003–04 totalled 130·9m. tonnes (41·5m. tonnes at Kandla).

Telecommunications

There were 2,775,500 telephone connections and 2,073,035 mobile phone connections in the state at the end of March 2004.

Postal Services

There were 9,023 post offices and 1,258 telegraph offices at the end of March 2004.

SOCIAL INSTITUTIONS

Justice

The High Court of Judicature at Ahmedabad has a Chief Justice and 30 puisne judges.

Education

In 2001, 69·97% of the population were literate (80·50% of males and 58·60% of females). Primary and secondary education up to Standard XII are free. Education above Standard XII is free for girls. In 2002–03 there were 41,339 primary schools with 8·47m. students and 7,308 secondary schools with 2·48m. students.

There are 11 universities in the state. Gujarat University, Ahmedabad, founded in 1950, is teaching and affiliating; it has 154 affiliated colleges and 143,692 students (all student figures for 1998–99). The Maharaja Sayajirao University of Vadodara (1949) is residential and teaching; it has 12 colleges and 26,511 students. The Sardar Patel University, Vallabh-Vidyanagar (1955), has 20 constituent and affiliated colleges and 17,913 students. Saurashtra University at Rajkot (1968) has 113 affiliated colleges and 72,234 students. South Gujarat University at Surat (1967) has 58 colleges and 59,600 students. Bhavnagar University (1978) is residential and teaching with 15 affiliated colleges and 11,195 students. North Gujarat University was established at Patan in 1986 and has 73 colleges and 54,720 students. Gujarat Vidyapith at Ahmedabad is deemed a university under the University Grants Commission Act. There are also Gujarat Agricultural University, Banaskantha, Gujarat Ayurved University, Jamnagar and Dr Babasaheb Ambedkar Open University, Ahmedabad.

There are 31 engineering and technical colleges, 36 polytechnics, 50 medical colleges and nine agricultural colleges. There are also 339 arts, science and commerce colleges, 42 teacher-training colleges and 31 law colleges. There were 0·4m. students enrolled in 1998–99 in all colleges.

Health

At March 2004 there were 271 community health centres, 1,067 primary health centres and 7,274 sub-centres. There were 25 general hospitals, 23 cottage hospitals (2000) and 22 Taluka-level hospitals. In 2003–04, 41·3m. patients were treated.

RELIGION

At the 2001 census Hindus numbered 89% of the population; Muslims, 9%; Jains, 1%; Christians, 0·6%.

CULTURE

Press

At June 2004 there were 2,445 newspapers and periodicals of which 2,255 were published in Gujarati, 85 in English and 75 in Hindi.

Tourism

There are many sights of religious pilgrimage as well as archaeological sights, attractive beaches, the Lion Sanctuary of Gir Forest and the Wild Ass Sanctuary in Kachchh. Mahatma Gandhi's birthplace at Porbandar is also a popular tourist attraction.

FURTHER READING

Desai, I. F., *Untouchability in Rural Gujarat.* Bombay, 1977
Sharma, R. N., *Gujrat Holocaust (Communalism in the Land of Gandhi).* Delhi, 2002

Haryana

KEY HISTORICAL EVENTS

The state of Haryana, created on 1 Nov. 1966 under the Punjab Reorganization Act, 1966, was formed from the Hindi-speaking parts of the state of Punjab (India). It comprises the districts of Ambala, Bhiwani, Faridabad, Fatehabad, Gurgaon, Hisar, Jhajjar, Jind, Kaithal, Karnal, Kurukshetra, Mahendragarh, Panchkula, Panipat, Rewari, Rohtak, Sirsa, Sonipat and Yamunanagar.

TERRITORY AND POPULATION

Haryana is in north India and is bounded north by Himachal Pradesh, east by Uttar Pradesh, south and west by Rajasthan and northwest by Punjab. Delhi forms an enclave on its eastern boundary. The state has an area of 44,212 sq. km and a population (2001 census) of 21,082,989; density, 477 per sq. km. Principal cities, *see* INDIA: Territory and Population. Other large towns (2001) are: Gurgaon (229,243), Sonipat (225,151), Karnal (222,017), Bhiwani (169,424), Ambala (168,003), Sirsa (160,129), Panchkula Urban Estate (140,992), Jind (136,089), Bahadurgarh (131,924), Thanesar (122,704), Kaithal (117,226). The principal language is Hindi.

SOCIAL STATISTICS

Growth rate 1991–2001, 28·06%.

CONSTITUTION AND GOVERNMENT

The state has a unicameral legislature with 90 members. The capital (shared with Punjab) is Chandigarh. Its transfer to Punjab, intended for 1986, has been postponed. There are 19 districts.

RECENT ELECTIONS

In the elections of 3 Feb. 2005 the Indian National Congress won 67 seats, the Indian National Lok Dal 9, the Bharatiya Janata Party 2, the Bahujan Samaj Party 1, the Nationalist Congress Party 1 and ind. 10.

CURRENT ADMINISTRATION

Governor: A. R. Kidwai; b. 1920 (took office on 7 July 2004).
Chief Minister: Bhupinder Singh Hooda; b. 1947 (took office on 5 March 2005).

ECONOMY

Budget

Budget estimates for 2002–03 show revenue income of Rs 104,091·4m. and revenue expenditure of Rs 114,057·9m.

ENERGY AND NATURAL RESOURCES

Electricity

Approximately 1,000 MW are supplied to Haryana, mainly from the Bhakra Nangal system. In 1999 installed capacity was 8,301 MW and all the villages had electric power.

Minerals

Minerals include placer gold, barytes, tin and rare earths. Value of production, 2002–03, Rs 1,487m.

Agriculture

Haryana has sandy soil and erratic rainfall, but the state shares the benefit of the Sutlej-Beas scheme. Agriculture employs over 82% of the working population; in 1995–96 there were about 1·7m. holdings (average 2·1 ha.), and the gross irrigated area was 2·05m. ha. in 1993–94. Area under foodgrains, 1995–96, 4·02m. ha. Foodgrain production, 1999–2000, 10·36m. tonnes (rice 2·59m. tonnes in 2000, wheat 7·35m. tonnes in 1995–96); pulses, 416,400 tonnes in 1995–96; cotton, 1·5m. bales of 170 kg in 1995–96; sugar (gur) and oilseeds are important. Haryana produces a surplus of wheat and rice.

Forestry

Forests covered 603 sq. km in 1995.

INDUSTRY

Haryana has a large market for consumer goods in neighbouring Delhi. In 1996–97 there were 916 large and medium scale industries and 138,759 small units providing employment to about 1m. persons, and 56,012 rural industrial units. The main industries are cotton textiles, agricultural machinery and tractors, woollen textiles, scientific instruments, glass, cement, paper and sugar milling, cars, tyres and tubes, motorcycles, bicycles, steel tubes, engineering goods, electrical and electronic goods. An oil refinery at Panipat was commissioned in 1999 and includes a diesel hydro desulphurization plant.

COMMUNICATIONS

Roads
There were (2002) 29,524 km of metalled roads—including 656 km of national highways, 3,135 km of state highways and 1,587 km of district highways—linking all villages. Road transport is nationalized. There were 954,563 motor vehicles in 1995–96. Haryana roadways carried 1·75m. passengers daily in 2002 with a fleet of 3,411 buses.

Rail
The state is crossed by lines from Delhi to Agra, Ajmer, Ferozepur and Chandigarh. Route km, 1995–96, 1,452 km. The main stations are at Ambala and Kurukshetra.

Civil Aviation
There is no airport within the state but Delhi is on its eastern boundary.

SOCIAL INSTITUTIONS

Justice
Haryana shares the High Court of Punjab and Haryana at Chandigarh.

Education
In 2001, 68·59% of the population were literate (79·25% of men and 56·31% of women). In 1996–97 there were 5,651 primary schools with 1,981,993 students, 3,233 high and higher secondary schools with 511,377 students, 1,631 middle schools with 832,886 students and 129 colleges of arts, science and commerce, nine engineering and technical colleges and ten medical colleges. There are four universities: Haryana Agricultural University, Hisar; Kurukshetra University, Kurukshetra with 70 colleges and 80,000 students (1999); Maharshi Dayanand University, Rohtak; and Guru Jambeshwar University, Hisar.

Health
In 2003 there were 49 hospitals, 64 community health centres, 402 primary health centres and 2,299 health sub-centres. A further 12 primary health centres were under construction.

RELIGION
At the 2001 census Hindus numbered 89% of the population; Sikhs, 5·8%; Muslims, 4·6%.

Himachal Pradesh

KEY HISTORICAL EVENTS
Thirty small hill states were merged to form the Territory of Himachal Pradesh in 1948; the state of Bilaspur was added in 1954 and parts of the Punjab in 1966. The whole territory became a state in Jan. 1971. The state is a Himalayan area of hill-tribes, rivers and forests. Its main component areas are Chamba, a former princely state, dominated in turn by Moghuls and Sikhs before coming under British influence in 1848; Bilaspur, an independent Punjab state until it was invaded by Gurkhas in 1814 (the British East India Company forces drove out the Gurkhas in 1815); Simla district around the town built by the

Company near Bilaspur on land reclaimed from Gurkha troops (the summer capital of India from 1865 until 1948); Mandi, a princely state until 1948; Kangra and Kullu districts, originally Rajput areas which had become part of the British-ruled Punjab. They were incorporated into Himachal Pradesh in 1966 when the Punjab was reorganized.

TERRITORY AND POPULATION
Himachal Pradesh is in north India and is bounded north by Kashmir, east by Tibet, southeast by Uttaranchal, south by Haryana, southwest and west by Punjab. The area of the state is 55,673 sq. km and the population (2001 census) 6,077,248; density, 109 per sq. km. Principal languages are Hindi and Pahari. The capital is Shimla, population (2001 census) of the urban agglomeration, 144,578.

SOCIAL STATISTICS
Growth rate 1991–2001, 17·53%.

CONSTITUTION AND GOVERNMENT
Full statehood was attained, as the 18th State of the Union, on 25 Jan. 1971. On 1 Sept. 1972 districts were reorganized and three new districts created, Solan, Hamirpur and Una, making a total of 12.

There is a unicameral *Legislative Assembly*.

RECENT ELECTIONS
Elections were held in Feb. 2003 in 65 of the 68 constituencies. Congress won 40 seats; Bharatiya Janata Party (BJP), 16; ind., 6; other parties, 3.

CURRENT ADMINISTRATION
Governor: Vishnu Sadashiv Kokje; b. 1939 (took office on 8 May 2003).

Chief Minister: Virbhadra Singh; b. 1934 (since 6 March 2003, for a third time).

ECONOMY

Budget
Budget estimates for 2000–01 showed receipts of Rs 39,854m. and expenditure of Rs 48,860m.

ENERGY AND NATURAL RESOURCES

Electricity
All 16,881 villages have electricity. Installed capacity (1995–96), 288·7 MW. The state has huge hydropower potential—there is an estimated potential of 20,376 MW (14·5% of India's potential). In 2003 there was an installed capacity of 3,942 MW, expected to rise to 11,000 MW. There were 13,436 substations and 70,323 km of power lines in 2003. The Nathpa Jhakri project is India's largest hydroelectric power plant. The plant, which incorporates a 28 km power tunnel, came online in Oct. 2003. Electricity generated (1999), 1,485m. kWh.

Water
An artificial confluence of the Sutlej and Beas rivers has been made, directing their united flow into Govind Sagar Lake.

Minerals
The state has rock salt, slate, gypsum, limestone, barytes, dolomite, pyrites, copper, gold and sulphur. However, Himachal Pradesh supplies only 0·2% of the national mineral output.

Agriculture
Farming employs 71% of the people. Irrigated area is 17% of the area sown. There are about 2,000 tea planters cultivating 2,063 ha. Main crops are seed potatoes, off season vegetables, wheat, maize, rice and fruits such as apples, peaches, apricots, hops, kiwi fruit, strawberries and flowers; 436,000 tonnes of fruits were produced in 1999.

Production (2001): foodgrains 1,599,000 tonnes (of which maize 768,000 tonnes, wheat 637,000 tonnes and rice 137,000 tonnes), plus vegetables 627,000 tonnes and ginger 2,900 tonnes.

Livestock (1992 census): buffaloes, 701,000; other cattle, 2,152,000; goats and sheep, 2·19m.

Forestry

Himachal Pradesh forests cover 66·2% of the state and supply the largest quantities of coniferous timber in northern India. The forests also ensure the safety of the catchment areas of the Yamuna, Sutlej, Beas, Ravi and Chenab rivers. Commercial felling of green trees has been totally halted and forest working nationalized. Area under forests, 37,033 sq. km.

INDUSTRY

The main sources of employment are the forests and their related industries; there are factories making turpentine and rosin. The state also makes fertilizers, cement, electronic items, TV sets, watches, computer parts, electronic toys and video cassettes. Sericulture is a major industry. There is a foundry and a brewery. Other industries include salt production and handicrafts, including weaving. The state has 173 large and medium units, 27,000 small scale units (providing employment for 140,000 people), seven industrial estates and 21 industrial areas. 300 mineral based industries have also been established.

COMMUNICATIONS

Roads

The national highway from Chandigarh runs through Shimla; other main highways from Shimla serve Kullu, Manali, Kangra, Chamba and Pathankot. The rest are minor roads. Pathankot is also on national highways from Punjab to Kashmir. Length of roads (1999), 25,773 km; number of vehicles (1995–96), 119,037; number of transport buses (1995–96), 1,692.

Rail

There is a line from Chandigarh to Shimla, and the Jammu-Delhi line runs through Pathankot. A Nangal-Talwara rail link has been approved by the central government. There are two narrow gauge lines, from Shimla to Kalka (96 km) and Jogindernagar to Pathankot (103 km), and a broad gauge line from Una to Nangal (16 km). Route-km in 2003, 256 km.

Civil Aviation

The state has airports at Bhuntar near Kullu, at Jubbarhatti near Shimla and at Gaggal in Kangra district. There are also 12 state-run helipads across the state.

SOCIAL INSTITUTIONS

Justice

The state has its own High Court at Shimla with eight judges.

Education

In 2001, 77·13% of the population were literate (86·02% of men and 68·08% of women). There were (1996–97) 7,732 primary schools with 728,870 students, 1,037 middle schools with 371,622 students, 1,228 high and higher secondary schools with 271,596 students, 62 (including 18 private) arts, science and commerce colleges, one engineering college, two medical colleges, one teacher training college and three universities. The universities are Himachal Pradesh University, Shimla (1970) with 48 affiliated colleges and 32,773 students (1992–93), Himachal Pradesh Agricultural University, Palampur (1978) and Dr Y. S. Parmar University of Horticulture and Forestry, Solan (1985).

Health

There were (2005) 50 hospitals (8,832 beds), 505 primary and community health centres and 2,068 sub-health centres.

RELIGION

At the 2001 census Hindus accounted for 96% of the population; Muslims, 1·7%; Buddhists, 1·2%.

FURTHER READING

Verma, Vishwashwar, *The Emergence of Himachal Pradesh: A Survey of Constitutional Development.* Indus Publishing Company, New Delhi, 1995

Jammu and Kashmir

KEY HISTORICAL EVENTS

The state of Jammu and Kashmir was brought into being in 1846 at the close of the First Sikh War. By the Treaty of Amritsar, Gulab Singh, *de facto* ruler of Jammu and Ladakh, added Kashmir to his existing territories, in consideration of his agreeing to pay the indemnity imposed by the British on the defeated Sikh empire. Of the state's three component parts, Ladakh and Kashmir were ancient polities, Ladakh having been an independent kingdom since the tenth century AD until its conquest by Gulab Singh's armies in 1834–42. Kashmir lost its independence to the Mughal empire in 1586, and was conquered in turn by the Afghans (1756) and the Sikhs (1819). Jammu was a collection of small principalities, until these were consolidated by Gulab Singh and his brothers in the early nineteenth century.

British supremacy was recognized until the Indian Independence Act, 1947, when all states decided on accession to India or Pakistan. Kashmir asked for standstill agreements with both. Pakistan agreed, but India wanted further discussion with the government of Jammu and Kashmir State. Meantime the state was subject to armed attack from Pakistan and the Maharajah acceded to India on 26 Oct. 1947 by signing the Instrument of Accession. India approached the UN in Jan. 1948, and the conflict ended by ceasefire in Jan. 1949, the major part of the state remaining with India, but a significant amount of territory in the north and west going to Pakistan. Hostilities between the two countries broke out in 1965 and again in 1971, but notwithstanding bilateral agreements—the Tashkent Declaration (Jan. 1966) and the Simla Agreement (July 1972)—the issue remains unresolved. With Muslims a majority of its population, both India and Pakistan regard the state as a touchstone of their divergent political raisons d'être—Pakistan as a Muslim nation, and India a secular one—and hence their position as non-negotiable. Intermittent violence between nationalistic factions has led to further negotiations between India and Pakistan with both sides pledging a peaceful solution. In Dec. 2002 the new provincial government promised to open talks with separatist groups.

TERRITORY AND POPULATION

The state is in the extreme north and is bounded north by China, east by Tibet, south by Himachal Pradesh and Punjab and west by Pakistan. The area is 222,236 sq. km, of which about 84,100 sq. km is occupied by Pakistan and 36,749 sq. km by China; the population of the territory on the Indian side of the line in the 2001 census, was 10,069,917. Srinagar (population, 2001, 971,357) is the summer and Jammu (607,642) the winter capital. The official language is Urdu; other commonly spoken languages are Kashmiri, Hindi, Dogri, Gujri, Pahari, Ladakhi and Punjabi.

SOCIAL STATISTICS

Growth rate 1991–2001, 29·04%.

CONSTITUTION AND GOVERNMENT

The Maharajah's son, Yuvraj Karan Singh, took over as Regent in 1950 and, on the ending of hereditary rule (17 Oct. 1952), was sworn in as Sadar-i-Riyasat. On his father's death (26 April 1961) Yuvraj Karan Singh was recognized as Maharajah by the Indian government. The permanent Constitution of the state came into force in part on 17 Nov. 1956 and fully on 26 Jan. 1957. There is a bicameral legislature; the Legislative Council has 36 members and the Legislative Assembly has 89 (two of which are nominated). Since the 1967 elections the six representatives of Jammu and Kashmir in the central House of the People are directly elected; there are four representatives in the Council of States. After a period of President's rule, a National Conference–Indira Congress coalition government was formed in March 1987. The government was dismissed and the state was brought under President's rule on 18 July 1990.

The state has 14 districts.

RECENT ELECTIONS

Elections to the State Assembly were held in four rounds between 16 Sept. and 8 Oct. 2002. The ruling pro-India National Conference won 28 of the 87 seats (57 in 1996); the Indian Congress Party won 20 (7 in 1996); the People's Democratic Party, 16; and the Bharatiya Janata Party, 1 (8 in 1996). Despite ongoing violence and voter intimidation throughout the elections, turnout was estimated at 46%. Following the elections, a coalition government was formed by the Indian Congress Party, the People's Democratic Party and other smaller parties.

CURRENT ADMINISTRATION

Governor: Lieut.-Gen. (retd) Sriniwas Kumar Sinha; b. 1926 (since 4 June 2003).

Chief Minister: Ghulam Nabi Azad; b. 1949 (took office on 2 Nov. 2005).

ECONOMY

Budget
Budget estimates for 2000–01 show total receipts of Rs 57,158m. and total expenditure of Rs 77,483m.

ENERGY AND NATURAL RESOURCES

Electricity
The state has exploitable hydropower potential of about 15,000 MW. The gas turbine station at Srinagar is an important contributor. Installed capacity (2002) 1,781 MW; 95% of the villages had electricity in 2000.

Minerals
Minerals include coal, bauxite and gypsum.

Agriculture
About 80% of the population are supported by agriculture. Rice, wheat and maize are the major cereals. The total area under foodgrains (1998–99) was estimated at 908,000 ha. Total foodgrains produced, 1998–99, 1·45m. tonnes (rice, 0·55m. tonnes; wheat, 0·43m. tonnes); pulses, 17,000 tonnes. Fruit is important: production, 1994–95, 0·9m. tonnes; exports, 0·76m. tonnes.

Irrigated area, 1993–94, 442,000 ha.

Livestock (1982; latest data available): cattle, 2,325,200; buffaloes, 5,631,000; goats, 1,003,900; sheep, 1,908,700; horses, 973,000; and poultry, 2,406,760.

Forestry
Forests cover about 20,443 sq. km (1995), forming an important source of revenue, besides providing employment to a large section of the population.

INDUSTRY

There are two central public sector industries and 30 medium-scale. There are 35,576 small units (1994–95) employing over 125,000. There are industries based on horticulture; traditional handicrafts are silk spinning, wood-carving, papier mâché and carpet-weaving. 750 tonnes of silk cocoons were produced in 1994–95.

The handicraft sector employed 0·26m. persons and had a production turnover of Rs 2,500m. in 1995–96.

COMMUNICATIONS

Roads
Kashmir is linked with the rest of India by the motorable Jammu–Pathankot road. The Jawahar Tunnel, through the Banihal mountain, connects Srinagar and Jammu, and maintains road communication with the Kashmir Valley during the winter months. In 2000 there were 13,093 km of roads.

There were 195,125 motor vehicles in 1995–96.

Rail
Kashmir is linked with the Indian railway system by the line between Jammu and Pathankot; route-km of railways in the state, 2002, 77 km.

Civil Aviation
Major airports are at Srinagar and Jammu. There is a third airport at Leh. There are services connecting Jammu with Amritsar, Chandigarh, Delhi and Srinagar; and services connecting Srinagar with Ahmedabad, Amritsar, Bombay, Chandigarh, Delhi, Jammu and Leh.

Telecommunications
There were 328,700 telephones in 2004 of which 40,100 were mobile phones.

Postal Services
There were 1,665 post offices at 31 March 2001.

SOCIAL INSTITUTIONS

Justice
The High Court, at Srinagar and Jammu, has a Chief Justice and four puisne judges.

Education
The proportion of literate people was 54·46% in 2001 (65·75% of men and 41·82% of women). Education is free. There were (1996–97) 1,351 high and higher secondary schools with 227,699 students, 3,104 middle schools with 405,598 students and 10,483 primary schools with 893,005 students. Jammu University (1969) has five constituent and 13 affiliated colleges, with 15,278 students (1992–93); Kashmir University (1948) has 18 colleges (17,000 students, 1992–93); there are two other universities: Sher-E-Kashmir University of Agricultural Sciences and Technology and Hemwati Nandan Bahuguna Garhwal University at Srinagar. There are four medical colleges, two engineering and technology colleges, four polytechnics, eight oriental colleges and an Ayurvedic college, 34 arts, science and commerce colleges and four teacher training colleges.

Health
In 2001 there were 43 hospitals with (2000) 2,076 beds, 337 primary health centres and 1,700 sub-centres, and 53 community health centres. There is a National Institute of Medical Sciences.

RELIGION

The majority of the population, except in Jammu, are Muslims (making it the only Indian state to have a Muslim majority). In 2003, 65% of the population of the state was estimated to be Muslim and 30% Hindu.

FURTHER READING

Lamb, A., *Kashmir: a Disputed Legacy, 1846–1990.* Hertingfordbury, 1991.
Wirsing, R. G., *India, Pakistan and the Kashmir Dispute: on Regional Conflict and its Resolution.* London, 1995

Jharkhand

KEY HISTORICAL EVENTS

The state was carved from Bihar and became the twenty-eighth state of India on 15 Nov. 2000. Located in the plateau regions of eastern India, Jharkhand (literally meaning land of forests) is mentioned in ancient Indian texts as an area inaccessible to the rest of India owing to its unforgiving terrain and the warring nature of the tribes living in its forests. The Mughals attacked the region in 1385 and again in 1616, arresting the King of Jharkhand and imprisoning him while they collected money from local chieftains. During the 17th century Jharkhand was a part of the Mughal empire and spread over areas of present-day Madhya Pradesh and Bihar. The East India Company was granted revenue-collecting power of the area in 1765 and the permanent settlement of 1796 increased the company's grip on the area. In 1858 sovereignty was transferred to the English crown. From 1793 until 1915 there were periodic tribal rebellions throughout Jharkhand against the British. In 1912 Jharkhand was constituted as part of the province of Bihar and Orissa after the former was separated from West Bengal. The Jharkhand Party submitted a request for Jharkhand to become a separate state to the State Reorganisation Committee in 1955. In 2000 a separate Jharkhand state was formed after legislation initiated by the National Democratic Alliance. The new state comprised a large area of southern Bihar but not any parts of West Bengal or Orissa as had been originally proposed.

TERRITORY AND POPULATION

Jharkhand is in central eastern India and is bounded by Bihar to the north, West Bengal to the east, Orissa to the south and the new state of Chhattisgarh to the west. Jharkhand has an area of 79,714 sq. km. Population (2001 census) 26,909,428; density: 338 per sq. km. Cities with over 250,000 population, *see* INDIA: Territory and Population. Other large cities (2001): Phusro (174,367), Hazaribag (135,446), Adityapur (119,221), Deogar (112,501), Ramgarh (110,497), Chirkunda (106,200), Giridih (105,212).

SOCIAL STATISTICS

Growth rate 1991–2001, 23·19%.

CONSTITUTION AND GOVERNMENT

Jharkhand is the twenty-eighth state of India. After the region was carved from Bihar it was decided that the 81 Members of the Legislative Assembly (MLAs) from Jharkhandi districts would become the members of the new state's legislative assembly. For administrative purposes the region is divided into 18 districts.

The capital and seat of government is at Ranchi.

RECENT ELECTIONS

In elections held on 3, 15 and 23 Feb. 2005 the Bharatiya Janata Party won 30 of 81 seats; Jharkhand Mukti Morcha, 17; Indian National Congress, 9; Rashtriya Janata Dal, 7; Janata Dal (United), 6; ind. and other parties, 12.

CURRENT ADMINISTRATION

Governor: Syed Sibtey Razi; b. 1939 (took office on 10 Dec. 2004).

Chief Minister: Arjun Munda; b. 1968 (took office on 12 March 2005).

ECONOMY

Budget

Budget estimates for Jharkhand in 2002 showed it had receipts of Rs 37,070m. and expenditure of Rs 36,560m. The formation of Jharkhand in 2000 substantially weakened the economy of Bihar, which lost 55% of its revenue but only 45% of its population. Jharkhand's annual plan of outlay for 2001–02 was Rs 19,000m.

ENERGY AND NATURAL RESOURCES

Minerals

Jharkhand is very rich in minerals, with about 40% of national production, including 90% of the country's cooking coal deposits, 40% of its copper, 37% of known coal reserves and 2% of iron ore. Other important minerals: bauxite, quartz, building stones and ceramics, graphite, limestone, kyanite, manganese, lead and silver. The state has 176 coal mines with an annual production of 78·7m. tonnes. Annually the state mines 8·6m. tonnes of iron ore, 1·2m. tonnes of copper ores, 1·0m. tonnes of bauxite, 50,000 tonnes of fire clays and 18,700 tonnes of manganese.

INDUSTRY

There is a major engineering corporation in Jharkhand as well as India's largest steel plant at Bokaro. Other important industries are aluminium and copper plants, forging, explosives, refractories and glass production. Jharkhand contains large thermal plants at Patratu, Tenughat, Chandrapura and Bokaro.

COMMUNICATIONS

Roads

National highways connect Ranchi to the neighbouring states of Bihar in the north, West Bengal to the east and Orissa to the south. State highways connect to the new state of Chhattisgarh in the west. Jharkhand has a total length of about 6,450 km of state highways, 1,660 km of national highways and 400 km of district highways.

Rail

Ranchi and the steel city of Bokaro are at the hub of the state's railway network linking Jharkhand to its neighbouring states as well as to Calcutta.

SOCIAL INSTITUTIONS

Education

In 2001, 54·13% of the population were literate (87·94% of men and 39·38% of women). There are five universities: Ranchi University (founded 1960), with 106 colleges and 55,731 students (1994–95); Bisra Agricultural University at Ranchi (1980); Sidhu Kanhu University at Dumka; Binova Bhave University at Hazaribag; B. I. T. Mesra University at Ranchi (formerly Birla Institute of Technology). There are two law colleges, two agricultural colleges, five engineering colleges and ten medical colleges.

Health

There were 83 hospitals in 2003.

CULTURE

Tourism

The main tourist centre is Ranchi.

Karnataka

KEY HISTORICAL EVENTS

The state of Karnataka, constituted as Mysore under the States Reorganization Act, 1956, brought together the Kannada-speaking people distributed in five states, and consisted of the territories of the old states of Mysore and Coorg, the Bijapur, Kanara and Dharwar districts and the Belgaum district (except one taluk) in former Bombay, the major portions of the Gulbarga, Raichur and Bidar districts in former Hyderabad, the South Kanara district (apart from the Kasaragod taluk) and the Kollegal taluk of the Coimbatore district in Madras. The state was renamed Karnataka in 1973.

TERRITORY AND POPULATION

The state is in south India and is bounded north by Maharashtra, east by Andhra Pradesh, south by Tamil Nadu and Kerala, west by the Indian ocean and northeast by Goa. The area of the state is 191,791 sq. km, and its population (2001 census), 52,733,958; density, 275 per sq. km. Principal cities, see INDIA: Territory and Population. The capital is Bangalore. Other large towns (2001) are: Tumkur (248,592), Raichur (205,634), Bidar (172,298), Hospet (163,284), Bhadravati (160,392), Robertson Pet (156,961), Hassan (133,317), Mandya (131,211), Udupi (127,060), Chitradurga (125,060), Kolar (113,299), Gangawati (101,397), Chikmagalur (101,022).

Kannada is the language of administration and is spoken by about 66% of the people. Other languages include Urdu (9%), Telugu (8·2%), Marathi (4·5%), Tamil (3·6%), Tulu and Konkani.

SOCIAL STATISTICS

Growth rate 1991–2001, 17·25%.

CONSTITUTION AND GOVERNMENT

Karnataka has a bicameral legislature. The Legislative Council has 75 members. The Legislative Assembly consists of 225 members (one of which is nominated).

The state has 27 districts grouped in four divisions: Bangalore, Belgaum, Gulbarga and Mysore.

RECENT ELECTIONS

At the state elections on 20 and 26 April 2004 the BJP won 79 seats (with 28·3% of the vote); the INC, 65 (35·3%); the Janata Dal (Secular), 58 (20·8%); Janata Dal (United), 5 (2·1%). 13 independents were elected. Turnout was 64·8%.

CURRENT ADMINISTRATION

Governor: Triloki Nath Chaturvedi; b. 1928 (took office on 21 Aug. 2002).

Chief Minister: H. D. Kumaraswamy; b. 1959 (since 3 Feb. 2006).

ECONOMY

Budget

Budget estimates, 2000–01: revenue receipts, Rs 200,252m.; revenue expenditure, Rs 200,615m.

ENERGY AND NATURAL RESOURCES

Electricity

In 1999 the state's installed capacity was 6,652·1 MW. Electricity generated, 1994–95, 16,830m. kWh. 26,483 villages had electricity in March 1996.

Minerals

Karnataka is an important source of gold and silver. The state produces 84% of India's gold. The estimated reserves of high grade iron ore are 8,798m. tonnes. These reserves are found mainly in the Chitradurga belt. The National Mineral Development Corporation of India has indicated total reserves of nearly 332m. tonnes of magnesite and iron ore (with an iron content ranging from 25 to 40) which have been found in Kudremukh Ganga-Mula region in Chikmagalur District. Value of production (2002–03) Rs 10,580m. The estimated reserves of manganese are over 320m. tonnes.

Limestone is found in many regions; production (2002–03) was about 12·2m. tonnes.

Karnataka is the largest producer of chromite. It is one of only two states in India producing magnesite. The other minerals of industrial importance are corundum and garnet. Karnataka produces 63% of India's moulding sand annually and 57% of the country's quartzite, and is the only producer of felsite.

Agriculture

Agriculture forms the main occupation of more than three-quarters of the population. Physically, Karnataka divides into four regions—the coastal region, the southern and northern plains, comprising roughly the districts of Bangalore, Tumkur, Chitradurga, Kolar, Bellary, Mandya and Mysore, and the hill country, comprising the districts of Chikmagalur, Hassan and Shimoga. Rainfall is heavy in the hill country, and there is dense forest. The greater part of the plains are cultivated. Coorg district is essentially agricultural.

The main food crops are rice paddy and jowar, and ragi which is also about 30% of the national crop. Total foodgrains production (1998–99), 8·80m. tonnes (including rice 3·33m. tonnes); pulses 0·48m. tonnes. Sugar, groundnut, castor-seed, safflower, mulberry silk and cotton are important cash crops. The state grows about 70% of the national coffee crop.

Production, 1998–99: sugarcane, 28·33m. tonnes; cotton, 985,000 tonnes.

Livestock (1992–93): buffaloes, 4·07m.; other cattle, 10·18m.; sheep, 4·73m.; goats, 3·89m.

Forestry

Total forest in the state (2000) is 38,284 sq. km, producing sandalwood, bamboo and other timbers.

Fisheries

The catch in 1998 totalled 140,000 tonnes. Catches are declining rapidly owing to overfishing and pollution.

INDUSTRY

There were 7,765 factories, 125 industrial estates and 5,176 industrial sheds employing 818,000 in March 1994. In 1994–95, 163,524 small industries employed 1,076,312 persons. The Vishveshwaraiah Iron and Steel Works is situated at Bhadravati, while at Bangalore are national undertakings for the manufacture of aircraft, machine tools, telephones, light engineering and electronics goods. The Kudremukh iron ore project is of national importance. An oil refinery is in operation at Mangalore. Other industries include textiles, vehicle manufacture, cement, chemicals, sugar, paper, porcelain and soap. In addition, much of the world's sandalwood is processed, the oil being one of the most valuable products of the state. Sericulture is a more important cottage industry giving employment, directly or indirectly, to about 2·7m. persons; production of raw silk, 2000, 9,000 tonnes, over two-thirds of national production.

COMMUNICATIONS

Roads

In 1999 the state had 137,520 km of roads, including 2,000 km of national highway and 73,000 km of state highway. There were (31 March 1996) 2,249,890 motor vehicles.

Rail

In 1999 there were 3,192 km of railway (including 149 km of narrow gauge) in the state.

Civil Aviation

There are airports at Bangalore, Hubli, Mysore, Mangalore, Bellary and Belgaum, with regular scheduled services to Bombay, Calcutta, Delhi and Madras. Bangalore is being upgraded to an international airport—the present airport already receives international flights from a number of destinations. A new Bangalore international airport is under construction at Devanahalli, 34 km from the city.

Shipping

Mangalore is a deep-water port for the export of mineral ores. Karwar is being developed as an intermediate port.

SOCIAL INSTITUTIONS

Justice
The seat of the High Court is at Bangalore. It has a Chief Justice and 42 puisne judges.

Education
In 2001, 67·04% of the population were literate (76·29% of men and 57·50% of women). In 1996–97 the state had 22,870 primary schools with 6,507,805 students, 18,485 middle schools with 2,158,487 students, 7,644 high and higher secondary schools with 1,270,794 students, 172 polytechnic and 125 medical colleges, 49 engineering and technology colleges, 761 arts, science and commerce colleges, 12 universities and the National Law School of India. Education is free up to pre-university level.

Universities: Mysore (1916); Karnataka (1949) at Dharwar; University of Agricultural Sciences (1964) at Hebbal, Bangalore; Bangalore; Gulbarga; Kannada; Mangalore; University of Agricultural Sciences, Dharwad; Kuvempu University, Shimoga; Karnataka State Open University, Mysore; Rajiv Gandhi University of Health Sciences, Bangalore; and Visveswaraiah Technological University, Nehrunagar.

Mysore has six university and 125 affiliated colleges; Karnataka, five and 240; Bangalore, 204 affiliated; Hebbal, eight constituent colleges.

The Indian Institute of Science, Bangalore and the Manipal Academy of Higher Education have the status of a university.

Health
There were in 2003, 293 hospitals, 622 primary health units and dispensaries, 1,297 primary health centres and 7,793 health subcentres. Total number of beds in 2003, about 50,000.

RELIGION
At the 2001 census Hindus were 85·6% of the population; Muslims, 11·6%; Christians, 1·5%.

Kerala

KEY HISTORICAL EVENTS
The state of Kerala was created in 1956, bringing together the Malayalam-speaking areas. It includes most of the former state of Travancore-Cochin and small areas from the state of Madras. Cochin, a safe harbour, was an early site of European trading in India. In 1795 the British took it from the Dutch and British influence remained dominant. Travancore was a Hindu state which became a British protectorate in 1795, having been an ally of the British East India Company for some years. Cochin and Travancore were combined as one state in 1947, reorganized and renamed Kerala in 1956.

TERRITORY AND POPULATION
Kerala is in south India and is bounded north by Karnataka, east and southeast by Tamil Nadu, southwest and west by the Indian ocean. The state has an area of 38,863 sq. km. The 2001 census showed a population of 31,838,619; density, 819 per sq. km. Chief cities, see INDIA: Territory and Population. Other principal towns (2001): Palakkad (197,281), Kottayam (172,867), Malappuram (170,364), Cherthala (141,512), Guruvayur (138,676), Kanhangad (129,364), Vadakara (123,965).

Languages spoken in the state are Malayalam, Tamil and Kannada.

SOCIAL STATISTICS
The growth rate during the period 1991–2001, at 9·42%, was the lowest of any Indian state.

CONSTITUTION AND GOVERNMENT
The state has a unicameral legislature of 141 members (one of which is nominated) including the Speaker.

The state has 14 districts. The capital is Thiruvananthapuram.

RECENT ELECTIONS
At the elections of 10 May 2001 the Indian National Congress party won 62 seats, the Communist Party of India (Marxist) (CPM) 23 and the Muslim League Kerala State Committee 16.

CURRENT ADMINISTRATION
Governor: Raghunandan Lal Bhatia; b. 1921 (took office on 23 June 2004).

Chief Minister: Oommen Chandy; b. 1943 (took office on 31 Aug. 2004).

ECONOMY

Budget
Budget estimates for 2000–01 showed revenue receipts of Rs 135,665m.; expenditure Rs 135,761m.

ENERGY AND NATURAL RESOURCES

Electricity
Installed capacity (1999–2000), 1,775·5 MW. The Idukki hydro-electric plant produced 3,064m. kWh and the Sabarigiri scheme 1,674m. kWh. All villages have electricity. The state had a power deficit until the inauguration of the Kayamkulam thermal power plant in 1999.

Minerals
The beach sands of Kerala contain monazite, ilmenite, rutile, zircon, sillimanite, etc. There are extensive white clay deposits; other minerals of commercial importance include titanium, copper, magnesite, china clay, limestone, quartz sand and lignite. Iron ore has been found at Kozhikode (Calicut).

Agriculture
Area under irrigation in 1995–96 was 644,000 ha.; six irrigation projects were under execution in 1996–97. The chief agricultural products are rice, tapioca, coconut, arecanut, cashew nut, oilseeds, pepper, sugarcane, rubber, tea, coffee and cardamom. About 98% of Indian black pepper and about 95% of Indian rubber is produced in Kerala. Production of principal crops, 2000: total rice, 770,686 tonnes (from 349,774 ha.); tapioca, 2,563,512 tonnes; coconuts, 5,167m. nuts; rubber, 572,820 tonnes; pepper, 56,431 tonnes; coffee, 60,470 tonnes; tea, 71,295 tonnes; cashew nuts, 46,366 tonnes; ginger, 38,607 tonnes; sugarcane, 47,767 tonnes.

Livestock (1987): buffaloes, 329,000; other cattle, 3·4m.; goats, 1·6m. In 1995–96 milk production was 2·24m. tonnes; egg production, 1,991m.

Forestry
Forest occupied 10,815 sq. km in 2000, including teak, sandalwood, ebony and blackwood and varieties of softwood. Net forest revenue, 1995–96, Rs 1,607·7m.

Fisheries
Fishing is a flourishing industry; the total catch in 1995–96 was 582,000 tonnes (of which marine, 532,000 tonnes). Fish exports, 78,896 tonnes in 1995–96.

INDUSTRY
There are numerous cashew and coir factories. Important industries are rubber, tea, coffee, tiles, automotive tyres, watches, electronics, oil, textiles, ceramics, fertilizers and chemicals, pharmaceuticals, zinc-smelting, sugar, cement, rayon, glass, matches, pencils, monazite, ilmenite, titanium oxide, rare earths, aluminium, electrical goods, paper, shark-liver oil, etc.

The state has a refinery and a shipyard at Kochi (Cochin).

The number of factories registered under the Factories Act 1948 in 2000 was 18,340, with daily average employment of 0·41m. There were 20,006 small-scale units in 2000; 0·78m. persons were employed in small-scale units on 31 March 1996.

COMMUNICATIONS

Roads
In 2000 there were 21,730 km of roads in the state (national and state highways, 4,113 km; district roads, 4,992 km). There were 1·91m. motor vehicles in 2000.

Rail
There is a coastal line from Mangalore in Karnataka which connects with Tamil Nadu. In 1995–96 there were 1,053 route-km of track.

Civil Aviation
There are airports at Kozhikode, Kochi and Thiruvananthapuram with regular scheduled internal services to Delhi, Bombay and Madras. In addition Kochi has international flights to a number of destinations in the Gulf states plus Colombo and Singapore, and Kozhikode and Thiruvananthapuram also have flights to the Gulf.

Shipping
Port Kochi, administered by the central government, is one of India's major ports; in 1983 it became the out-port for the Inland Container Depot at Coimbatore in Tamil Nadu. There are 12 other ports and harbours.

SOCIAL INSTITUTIONS

Justice
The High Court at Ernakulam has a Chief Justice and 29 puisne judges.

Education
Kerala is the most literate Indian state, with 25·63m. literate people at the 2001 census (90·92%; 94·20% of men and 87·86% of women). Education is free up to the age of 14.

In 2000 there were 6,726 primary schools with 2·79m. students, 2,968 upper primary schools with 1·84m. students and 3,511 high and higher secondary schools with 1·07m. students. There were 169 junior colleges in 1996–97 with 210,074 pupils.

Kerala University (established 1937) at Thiruvananthapuram is affiliating and teaching; in 1995–96 it had 52 affiliated colleges with 113,569 students. The University of Kochi is federal, and for post-graduate studies only. The University of Calicut (established 1968) is teaching and affiliating and has 95 affiliated colleges with 122,343 students (1995–96). Kerala Agricultural University (established 1971) has seven constituent colleges. Mahatma Gandhi University at Kottayam was established in 1983 and has 64 affiliated colleges with 112,992 students (1995–96). There are two other universities, Sree Sankaracharya University at Ernakulam and Kannur (formerly Malabar) University. There were also (2000) seven medical colleges, 20 pharmacy colleges, three dental colleges, four homeopathy colleges, 32 engineering colleges, 59 technology colleges, three nursing colleges, 19 teacher training colleges and 191 arts and science colleges.

Health
In 2000 there were 1,425 hospitals and health centres, including 113 Ayurvedic hospitals and 30 homeopathic hospitals. There were 41,462 hospital beds plus 2,604 beds in Ayurvedic hospitals and 970 beds in homeopathic clinics and hospitals.

RELIGION
At the 2001 census Hindus accounted for 57·5% of the population, Muslims 23·5% and Christians 18·5%.

FURTHER READING
Jeffrey, R., *Politics, Women and Well-Being: How Kerala Became a Model.* London, 1992

Madhya Pradesh

KEY HISTORICAL EVENTS
The state was formed in 1956 to bring together the Hindi-speaking districts of the area including the 17 Hindi districts of the old Madhya Pradesh, most of the former state of Madhya Bharat, the former states of Bhopal and Vindhya Pradesh and a former Rajput enclave, Sironj. This was an area which the Mahrattas took from the Moghuls between 1712 and 1760. The British overcame Mahratta power in 1818 and established their own Central Provinces. Nagpur became the Province's capital and was also the capital of Madhya Pradesh until in 1956 boundary changes transferred it to Maharashtra. The present capital, Bhopal, was the centre of a Muslim princely state from 1723. An ally of the British against the Mahrattas, Bhopal (with neighbouring small states) became a British-protected agency in 1818. After independence Bhopal acceded to the Indian Union in 1949. The states of Madhya Bharat and Vindhya Pradesh were then formed as neighbours, and in 1956 were combined with Bhopal and Sironj and renamed Madhya Pradesh. In 2000 sixteen mainly tribal districts were carved from Madhya Pradesh to form the new state of Chhattisgarh.

TERRITORY AND POPULATION
The state is in central India and is bounded north by Uttar Pradesh, east by the new state of Chhattisgarh, south by Maharashtra, and west by Gujarat and Rajasthan. Owing to the creation of Chhattisgarh, Madhya Pradesh is no longer the largest Indian state in size. Its revised area is 308,245 sq. km (previously 443,446 sq. km), making it the second largest state in the country (after Rajasthan). Population (2001 census), 60,385,118 (31,456,873 males); density, 196 per sq. km.

Cities with over 250,000 population, *see* INDIA: Territory and Population. Other large cities (2001): Ratlam, 233,480; Dewas, 230,658; Satna, 229,323; Burhanpur, 194,360; Murwara, 186,738; Singrauli, 185,580; Rewa, 183,232; Khandwa, 171,976; Bhind, 153,768; Chhindwara, 153,635; Morena, 150,890; Shivpuri, 146,859; Guna, 137,132; Damoh, 127,939; Vidisha, 125,457; Mandsaur, 117,532; Nimach, 112,691; Itarsi, 109,288; Chhatarpur, 109,021; Khargone, 103,980.

Hindi, Marathi, Urdu and Gujarati are spoken. In April 1990 Hindi, which predominates in the state, became the sole official language.

SOCIAL STATISTICS
Growth rate 1991–2001, 24·34%.

CONSTITUTION AND GOVERNMENT
Madhya Pradesh is one of the nine states for which the Constitution provides a bicameral legislature, but the Vidhan Parishad or Upper House (to consist of 90 members) has yet to be formed. The Vidhan Sabha or Lower House has 231 members (one of which is nominated).

For administrative purposes the state has been split into nine revenue divisions with a Commissioner at the head of each; the headquarters of these are located at Bhopal, Gwalior, Hoshangabad, Indore, Jabalpur, Morena, Rewa, Sagar and Ujjain. There are 22,029 *gram* (village) panchayats, 313 *janpad* (intermediate) panchayats and 45 *zila* (district) panchayats, following the creation of 16 new districts in administrative reforms of 1999 and the creation of Chhattisgarh in 2000.

The seat of government is at Bhopal.

RECENT ELECTIONS

Following the election in Dec. 2003, the Bharatiya Janata Party (BJP) won power with 173 seats (117 in 1998). The Congress (I) Party declined from 170 seats in 1998 to 38. Other parties won 19 seats.

CURRENT ADMINISTRATION

Governor: Balram Jakhar; b. 1923 (took office on 30 June 2004).

Chief Minister: Shivraj Singh Chauhan; b. 1959 (took office on 29 Nov. 2005).

ECONOMY

Budget

Budget estimates for 2001–02 showed revenue receipts of Rs 125,184m. and expenditure of Rs 162,770m. Annual plan, 2002–03, Rs 48,209m.

ENERGY AND NATURAL RESOURCES

Electricity

Madhya Pradesh is rich in low-grade coal suitable for power generation, and also has immense potential for hydro-electric energy. Total installed capacity, 2000–01, 2,941 MW. Power generated, 14,009m. kWh in 2000–01. There are eight hydro-electric power stations of 747·5 MW installed capacity. 50,306 out of 51,806 villages had electricity by 2000–01.

Water

Major irrigation projects include the Chambal Valley scheme (started in 1952 with Rajasthan), the Tawa project in Hoshangabad district, the Barna and Hasdeo schemes, the Mahanadi canal system and schemes in the Narmada valley at Bargi and Narmadasagar. Area under irrigation, 1999–2000, 4·28m. ha.

Minerals

Much of the state's extensive mineral deposits were in the area that has now become the new state of Chhattisgarh. In 2000–01 (1996 figures in brackets) there were 25·04m. tonnes (8,001m.) of limestone, 0·25m. tonnes (126·8m.) of bauxite, 4·04m. tonnes (26,853m.) of coal, and 0·92m. tonnes (2,186·2m.) of iron ore. In 2001–02 the output of diamonds was 73,981 carats and manganese ore 0·43m. tonnes. In 2001–02 revenue from minerals was Rs 5·39m. (Rs 8,500m. in 1997–98) and coal output was 4·4m. tonnes (43·0m. in 1999–2000).

Agriculture

The creation of the new state of Chhattisgarh, previously known as the 'rice bowl' of Madhya Pradesh, in 2000 had serious implications for the state. Agriculture is the mainstay of the state's economy and 76·8% of the people are rural. 43·7% of the land area is cultivable, of which 16·6% is irrigated. Production of principal crops, 2001–02 (in tonnes): foodgrains, 8·93m.; pulses, 3·96m.; cotton, 0·23m. bales of 170 kg.

Livestock (1997; Madhya Pradesh and Chhattisgarh combined): buffaloes, 6·64m.; other cattle, 34·88m.; sheep, 6·56m.; goats, 6·47m.

Forestry

The forested area totals 95,200 sq. km, or about 30·9% of the state. The forests are chiefly of sal, saja and teak species. They are the chief source in India of best-quality teak; they also provide firewood for about 60% of domestic fuel needs, and form valuable watershed protection. Forest revenue, 2001–02, Rs 32·5m.

INDUSTRY

The major industries are steel, aluminium, paper, cement, motor vehicles, ordnance, textiles and heavy electrical equipment. Other industries include electronics, telecommunications, sugar, fertilizers, straw board, vegetable oil, refractories, potteries, textile machinery, steel casting and re-rolling, industrial gases, synthetic fibres, drugs, biscuit manufacturing, engineering, optical fibres, plastics, tools, rayon and art silk. The number of heavy and medium industries in the state is 805; the number of small-scale establishments in production is 497,000.

There are 23 'growth centres' in operation, and five under development. The Government of India has proposed setting up a Special Economic Zone at Indore.

COMMUNICATIONS

Roads

Total length of roads is 68,100 km. The length of national highways is 4,720 km and state highway 6,500 km. In March 2002 there were 3,173,000 motor vehicles.

Rail

The main rail route linking northern and southern India passes through Madhya Pradesh. Bhopal, Bina, Gwalior, Indore, Itarsi, Jabalpur, Katni, Khandwa, Ratlam and Ujjain are important junctions for the central, south, eastern and western networks. Route length (1998–99), 5,764·8 km.

Civil Aviation

There are domestic airports at Bhopal, Gwalior, Indore and Khajuraho with regular scheduled services to Bombay, Delhi, Agra, Varanasi and Raipur.

SOCIAL INSTITUTIONS

Justice

The High Court of Judicature at Jabalpur has a Chief Justice and 29 puisne judges. Its benches are located at Gwalior and Indore. A National Institute of Law and a National Judicial Academy have been set up at Bhopal.

Education

In 2001, 64·11% of the population were literate (76·80% of men and 50·28% of women). Education is free for children aged up to 14.

In 1998 there were 81,000 primary schools (63,712 in 2001) with 10·33m. students, 20,000 middle schools with 3·46m. students and 7,000 high and higher secondary schools (8,471 in 2001) with 2·03m. students.

Universities: Dr Harisingh Gour University (established 1946), at Sagar, had 97 affiliated colleges and 74,386 students in 1992–93; Rani Durgavati University at Jabalpur (1957) had 46 affiliated colleges and 45,315 students; Vikram University (1957), at Ujjain, had 83 affiliated colleges and 39,723 students; Devi Ahilya University at Indore (1964) had 32 affiliated colleges and 28,196 students; Jiwaji University (1963), at Gwalior, had 60 affiliated colleges and (1991–92) 58,825 students; Awadhesh Pratap Singh University, Rewa had 81 colleges and 24,960 students; Barkatullah Vishwavidyalaya, Bhopal had 44 colleges and 18,817 students; Makhanlal Chaturvedi Rashtriya Patrakarita Vishwavidhyalaya Bhopal; Mahatma Gandhi Chitrakoot Gramodoya Vishwavidhayalaya, Chitrakoot; Rajiv Gandhi Technology University, Bhopal; Indira Kala Sangeet Vishwavidyalaya, Khairagarh; Jawaharlal Nehru Krishi University, Jabalpur; Bhoj Open University, Bhopal; the Maharshi Mahesh Yogi Vedic Vishwavidyalaya, Jabalpur. In 1999 there were 413 government colleges (15 of which were lost to Chhattisgarh in 2000), 252 private colleges (14 of which were lost to Chhattisgarh in 2000), 30 engineering colleges (all to be affiliated to the Rajiv Ghandi Technology University), seven medical colleges, 44 polytechnics, five institutions of architecture and 30 management institutes.

Health

In 2001–02 there were 45 district hospitals, 57 urban civil hospitals, 1,194 primary health centres, 8,835 sub-health centres, 229 community health centres, seven TB hospitals and two TB sanatoriums.

RELIGION

At the 2001 census Hindus numbered 92%; Muslims, 5%.

Maharashtra

KEY HISTORICAL EVENTS

The Bombay Presidency of the British East India Company began with a trading factory, made over to the Company in 1668. The Presidency expanded, overcoming the surrounding Mahratta chiefs until Mahratta power was finally conquered in 1818. After independence Bombay State succeeded the Presidency; its area was altered in 1956 by adding Kutch and Saurashtra and the Marathi-speaking areas of Hyderabad and Madhya Pradesh, and taking away Kannada-speaking areas (which were added to Mysore). In 1960 the Bombay Reorganization Act divided Bombay State between Gujarati and Marathi areas, the latter becoming Maharashtra. The state of Maharashtra consists of the following districts of the former Bombay State: Ahmadnagar, Akola, Amravati, Aurangabad, Bhandara, Bhir, Buldana, Chanda, Dhulia (West Khandesh), Greater Bombay, Jalgaon (East Khandesh), Kolaba, Kolhapur, Nagpur, Nanded, Nashik, Osmanabad, Parbhani, Pune, Ratnagiri, Sangli, Satara, Sholapur, Thane, Wardha, Yeotmal; certain portions of Thane and Dhulia districts have become part of Gujarat.

TERRITORY AND POPULATION

Maharashtra is in central India and is bounded north by Madhya Pradesh, east by Chhattisgarh, south by Andhra Pradesh, Karnataka and Goa, west by the Indian ocean and northwest by Daman and Gujarat. The state has an area of 307,713 sq. km. The population in 2001 (census) was 96,752,247; density, 314 per sq. km. In 2001 the area of Greater Bombay was 603 sq. km and its population 16·4m. For other principal cities, *see* INDIA: Territory and Population. Other large towns (2001): Jalna (235,529), Bhusawal (187,524), Vasai (174,382), Yavatmal (141,970), Bid (138,091), Kamthi (137,056), Gondia (120,878), Virar (118,945), Wardha (110,070), Satara (108,043), Achalpur (107,304), Barsi (104,786), Panvel (104,031).

The official language is Marathi.

SOCIAL STATISTICS

Growth rate 1991–2001, 22·57%.

CONSTITUTION AND GOVERNMENT

Maharashtra has a bicameral legislature. The Legislative Council has 78 members. The Legislative Assembly has 288 elected members and one member nominated by the Governor to represent the Anglo-Indian community.

The Council of Ministers consists of the Chief Minister, 16 other Ministers and 19 Ministers of State.

The capital is Bombay (Mumbai). The state has 35 districts.

RECENT ELECTIONS

At the elections held on 13 Oct. 2004 the Nationalist Congress Party won 71 of the 288 seats, the Indian National Congress 69, Shiv Sena 62, the Bharatiya Janata Party 54, the Communist Party of India (Marxist) 3, other parties 10 and ind. 19. Turnout was 63·4%.

CURRENT ADMINISTRATION

Governor: S. M. Krishna; b. 1932 (took office on 6 Dec. 2004).

Chief Minister: Vilasrao Deshmukh; b. 1945 (since 1 Nov. 2004; first in office 1999–2003).

ECONOMY

Budget

Budget estimates, 2000–01: revenue receipts, Rs 374,303m.; revenue expenditure, Rs 366,869m.

ENERGY AND NATURAL RESOURCES

Electricity

Installed capacity, 1998, 8,231 MW. All villages have electricity. Output, 2001, 53,013m. kWh.

Oil and Gas

Bombay High (offshore) produced 14·25m. tonnes of crude oil and 17,200,000 cu. metres of natural gas in 2001. Oil production has declined by one-third since the early 1990s. A recovery plan for the ageing field began in 2001. This involves drilling 145 new wells and laying about 245 km of sub-sea pipeline. The plan is scheduled to be completed in the course of 2006.

Minerals

The state has coal, silica sand, dolomite, kyanite, chromite, limestone, iron ore, manganese and bauxite. Value of mineral production, 2001, Rs 21,340m. of which 94% is contributed by coal. Coal production in 2000–01 was 28·8m. tonnes. Manganese is the second most valuable mineral.

Agriculture

3·3m. ha. of the cropped area of 21·4m. ha. are irrigated. In normal seasons the main food crops are rice, wheat, jowar, bajra and pulses. Main cash crops: cotton, sugarcane, groundnuts. Production, 2000–01 (in tonnes): sugarcane, 36·5m.; foodgrains, 11·9m. (rice, 2·4m., wheat, 1·11m.); pulses, 1·7m.; groundnuts, 0·6m.; cotton, 476,000.

Livestock (1992 census, in 1,000): buffaloes, 5,447; other cattle, 17,441; sheep and goats, 13,015; poultry, 32,189.

Forestry

Forests occupied 64,300 sq. km in 1995–96. Value of forest products in 1996–97, Rs 2,820m.

Fisheries

In 2000–01 the marine fish catch was estimated at 403,000 tonnes and the inland fish catch at 123,000 tonnes; in 1995–96, 18,038 boats, including 8,552 mechanized, were used for marine fishing.

INDUSTRY

Industry is concentrated mainly in Bombay, Nashik, Pune and Thane. The main groups are chemicals and products, textiles, electrical and non-electrical machinery, petroleum and products, aircraft, rubber and plastic products, transport equipment, automobiles, paper, electronic items, engineering goods, pharmaceuticals and food products. The state industrial development corporation invested Rs 77,020m. in 21,452 industrial units in 1994–95. In June 1995 there were 26,642 working factories employing 1·2m. people. In Dec. 1996 there were 203,882 small scale industries employing 1·63m. people.

COMMUNICATIONS

Roads

In 2001 there were 260,000 km of roads, of which nearly 200,000 km were surfaced. There were 7,194,000 motor vehicles on 1 Jan. 2001, of which about 25% were in Greater Bombay. Passenger and freight transport has been nationalized.

Rail

The total length of railway in 2001 was 5,459 km; 66% was broad gauge, 14% metre gauge and 20% narrow gauge. The main junctions and termini are Bombay, Dadar, Manmad, Akola, Nagpur, Pune and Sholapur.

Civil Aviation

The main airport is Bombay, which has national and international flights. Nagpur airport is on the route from Bombay to Calcutta and there are also airports at Pune and Aurangabad.

Shipping

Maharashtra has a coastline of 720 km. Bombay is the major port, and there are 48 minor ports.

SOCIAL INSTITUTIONS

Justice

The High Court has a Chief Justice and 60 judges. The seat of the High Court is Bombay, but it has benches at Nagpur, Aurangabad and Panaji (Goa).

Education

The number of literate people, according to the 2001 census, was 64·57m. (77·27%; 86·27% of men and 67·51% of women). In 2001 there were 10,225 high and 3,981 higher secondary schools with (1995) 2,795,567 pupils; 15,070 middle schools with (1995) 4,753,257 pupils; and 66,369 primary schools with (1995) 11,685,598 pupils. There are 111 engineering and technology colleges, 156 medical colleges (including dental and Ayurvedic colleges), 244 teacher training colleges, 152 polytechnics and 820 arts, science and commerce colleges.

Bombay University, founded in 1857, is mainly an affiliating university. It has 276 colleges with a total (1993–94) of 234,469 students. Nagpur University (1923) is both teaching and affiliating. It has 258 colleges with 95,664 students. Pune University, founded in 1948, is teaching and affiliating; it has 167 colleges and 151,990 students. The SNDT Women's University had 33 colleges with a total of 33,343 students. Dr B. R. Ambedkar Marathwada University, Aurangabad was founded in 1958 as a teaching and affiliating body to control colleges in the Marathwada or Marathi-speaking area, previously under Osmania University; it has 190 colleges and 195,806 students. Shivaji University, Kolhapur, was established in 1963 to control affiliated colleges previously under Pune University. It has 205 colleges and 115,553 students. Amravati University has 130 colleges and 74,484 students. Other universities are: Marathwada Krishi Vidyapeeth, Parbhani; Y. Chavan Maharashtra Open University, Nashik; North Maharashtra University, Jalgaon, with 101 colleges and 66,092 students; Mahatma Phule Krishi University, Rahuri; Dr Punjabrao Deshmukh Krishi University, Akola; Konkan Krishi University, Dapoli; Dr Babasaheb Ambedkar Technological University, Lonere; Swami Ramanand Teerth Marathwad University, Nanded; Tilak Maharashtra Vidyapeeth, Pune; Bharati Vidyapeeth, Pune; Gokhale Institute of Politics and Economics, Pune; Deccan College, Pune; Indian Institute of Technology, Bombay; Indira Gandhi Institute of Developmental Research, Bombay; International Institute for Population Sciences, Bombay; Tata Institute of Social Sciences, Bombay. The Central Institute of Fisheries Education in Bombay also has university-equivalent status.

Health

There were 3,446 hospitals with 99,062 beds in 2000; there were also 1,768 primary health centres, 9,725 sub-health centres and 351 community health centres in 2001.

RELIGION

At the 2001 census 81% of the population were Hindus, 9·7% Muslims and 6·3% Buddhists.

Manipur

KEY HISTORICAL EVENTS

Formerly a state under the political control of the government of India, Manipur entered into interim arrangements with the Indian Union on 15 Aug. 1947 and the political agency was abolished. The administration was taken over by the government of India on 15 Oct. 1949 under a merger agreement, and it was centrally administered by the government of India through a Chief Commissioner. In 1950–51 an Advisory form of government was introduced. In 1957 this was replaced by a Territorial Council of 30 elected and two nominated members. Later, in 1963, a Legislative Assembly of 30 elected and three nominated members was established under the government of Union Territories Act 1963. Because of the unstable party position in the Assembly, it had to be dissolved on 16 Oct. 1969 and president's rule introduced. The status of the administrator was raised from Chief Commissioner to Lieut.-Governor with effect from 19 Dec. 1969. On 21 Jan. 1972 Manipur became a state and the status of the administrator was changed from Lieut.-Governor to Governor. In June 2001 Manipur was placed under central rule, but ceased to be so after the 2002 elections.

TERRITORY AND POPULATION

The state is in northeast India and is bounded north by Nagaland, east by Myanmar, south by Myanmar and Mizoram, and west by Assam. Manipur has an area of 22,327 sq. km and a population (2001 census) of 2,388,634; density, 107 per sq. km. The valley, which is about 1,813 sq. km, is 800 metres above sea-level. The largest city is Imphal with a population of 245,967 (2001 census). The hills rise in places to 3,000 metres, but are mostly about 1,500–1,800 metres. The average annual rainfall is 165 cm. The hill areas are inhabited by various hill tribes who constitute about one-third of the total population of the state. There are about 30 tribes and sub-tribes falling into two main groups of Nagas and Kukis. Manipuri and English are the official languages. A large number of dialects are spoken.

SOCIAL STATISTICS

Growth rate 1991–2001, 30·02%.

CONSTITUTION AND GOVERNMENT

Manipur has a Legislative Assembly of 60 members, of which 19 are from reserved tribal constituencies. There are nine districts. The capital is Imphal.

RECENT ELECTIONS

Elections were held in Feb. 2002. The Indian National Congress party (INC) won 19 seats; the Federal Party of Manipur (FPM), 13; the Manipur State Congress Party (MSCP), 6; the Bharatiya Janata Party (BJP), 4; Samata Party, 3; others, 15. Following the elections a Secular Progressive Front (SPF) was installed in government, comprising the INC, the MSCP, the Nationalist Congress Party and the Communist Party of India.

CURRENT ADMINISTRATION

Governor: Shivinder Singh Sidhu; b. 1929 (took office on 6 Aug. 2004).

Chief Minister: Okram Ibobi Singh; b. 1948 (took office on 7 March 2002).

ECONOMY

Budget

Budget estimates for 2000–01 show revenue of Rs 12,220·2m. and expenditure of Rs 12,453·3m.

ENERGY AND NATURAL RESOURCES

Electricity
Installed capacity (2002) is 45 MW from diesel and hydro-electric generators. This has been augmented since 1981 by the North Eastern Regional Grid and by the Lotak and Irang Hep schemes. In March 1996 there were 2,015 villages with electricity.

Water
The main power, irrigation and flood-control schemes are the Loktak Lift Irrigation scheme (irrigation potential, 40,000 ha.); the Singda scheme (potential 4,000 ha., and improved water supply for Imphal); the Thoubal scheme (potential 34,000 ha.); and four other large projects. By 1994–95, 59,100 ha. had been irrigated.

Minerals
Chromite is the only significant mineral resource—it is extracted from a single mine.

Agriculture
Rice is the principal crop; with wheat, maize and pulses. Total foodgrains, 1998, 365,000 tonnes (rice, 352,000 tonnes).

Agricultural workforce, 453,040. Only 0·21m. ha. are cultivable, of which 158,000 ha. are under paddy. Fruit and vegetables are important in the valley, including pineapples, oranges, bananas, mangoes, pears, peaches and plums. Soil erosion, produced by shifting cultivation, is being halted by terracing. Fruit production in 1993–94, 0·11m. tonnes.

Forestry
Forests occupied about 17,418 sq. km in 1998. The main products are teak, jurjan and pine; there are also large areas of bamboo and cane, especially in the Jiri and Barak river drainage areas, yielding about 0·3m. tonnes annually. Total revenue from forests, 1990–91, Rs 9·95m.

Fisheries
Landings in 1995–96, 12,500 tonnes.

INDUSTRY
Handloom weaving is a cottage industry. Manipur is one of the least industrialized states of India. Location, limited infrastructure and insufficient power hold back industrial development. Larger-scale industries include the manufacture of bicycles and TV sets, sugar, cement, starch, vegetable oil and glucose. Sericulture produces about 45 tonnes of raw silk annually. Estimated non-agricultural workforce, 229,000.

COMMUNICATIONS

Roads
Length of road (1995), 7,003 km; number of vehicles (1996–97) 65,223. A national highway from Kaziranga (Assam) runs through Imphal to the border with Myanmar. The total length of national highway in 2000 was 954 km.

Rail
A railway link was opened in 1990, linking Karong with the Assamese railway system.

Civil Aviation
There is an airport at Imphal with regular scheduled services to Delhi and Calcutta.

SOCIAL INSTITUTIONS

Education
In 2001, 68·87% of the population were literate (77·87% of men and 59·70% of women). In 1996–97 there were 2,548 primary schools with 230,230 students, 555 middle schools with 106,200 students, 553 high and higher secondary schools with 66,160 students, 50 colleges, one medical college, two teacher training colleges, three polytechnics, Manipur University with 62 colleges and 52,352 students (1997–98) and an agricultural university (Central Agricultural University, Imphal).

Health
In 2001 there were 85 hospitals and public health centres, 28 dispensaries, 16 community health centres, 420 sub-centres and 26 other facilities.

RELIGION
At the 2001 census Hindus numbered nearly 58% of the population; Christians, 34%; Muslims, 7%.

Meghalaya

KEY HISTORICAL EVENTS
The state was created under the Assam Reorganization (Meghalaya) Act 1969 and inaugurated on 2 April 1970. Its status was that of a state within the State of Assam until 21 Jan. 1972 when it became a fully-fledged state of the Union. It consists of the former Garo Hills district and United Khasi and Jaintia Hills district of Assam.

TERRITORY AND POPULATION
Meghalaya is bounded in the north and east by Assam, south and west by Bangladesh. The area is 22,429 sq. km and the population (2001 census) 2,306,069; density, 103 per sq. km. The people are mainly of the Khasi, Jaintia and Garo tribes. The main languages of the state are Khasi, Jaintia, Garo and English.

SOCIAL STATISTICS
Growth rate 1991–2001, 29·94%.

CONSTITUTION AND GOVERNMENT
Meghalaya has a unicameral legislature. The Legislative Assembly has 60 seats.

There are seven districts. The capital is Shillong (population, 2001 census, 267,881 in the urban agglomeration).

RECENT ELECTIONS
In elections held in Feb. 2003 the Indian National Congress won 22 seats; Nationalist Congress Party, 14; United Democratic Party, 9; ind., 5; other parties, 10.

CURRENT ADMINISTRATION
Governor: Mundakkal Matthew Jacob; b. 1928 (took office on 19 June 1995).

Chief Minister: D. D. Lapang; b. 1934 (since 4 March 2003; also 1992–93).

ECONOMY

Budget
Budget estimates for 2001–02 showed revenue receipts of Rs 13,211·3m. and expenditure of Rs 13,548·3m.

ENERGY AND NATURAL RESOURCES

Electricity
Total installed capacity (2000–01) was 185·2 MW. 2,580 villages out of 4,902 had electricity in March 2001.

Minerals
The Khasi Hills, Jaintia Hills and Garo Hills districts produce coal, sillimanite (95% of India's total output), limestone, fire clay, dolomite, feldspar, quartz and glass sand. The state also has deposits of coal (estimated reserves 600m. tonnes), limestone

(3,000m.), fire clay (6m.) and sandstone which are so far virtually untapped. Coal production in 2000–01 was 5,149,000 tonnes; limestone production in 2000–01 was 585,000 tonnes.

Agriculture

About 71% of the people depend on agriculture. Principal crops are rice, maize, potatoes, cotton, oranges, ginger, tezpata, areca nuts, jute, mesta, bananas and pineapples. Production 2000–01 (in tonnes) of principal crops: rice, 179,000; potatoes, 144,000; ginger, 45,000; jute, 36,000; citrus fruits, 32,000; maize, 24,000; cotton, 8,000; rape and mustard, 5,000. Poultry and pigs are the principal livestock.

Forestry

Forests covered 9,496 sq. km in 2002. Forest products are one of the state's chief resources.

INDUSTRY

Apart from agriculture the main source of employment is the extraction and processing of minerals; there are also important timber processing mills and cement factories. Other industries include electronics, tantalum capacitors, beverages and watches. The state has five industrial estates, two industrial areas and one growth centre. In 1995–96 there were 58 registered factories and 2,533 small-scale industries. In 2000, 17,800 workers were involved in manufacturing and processing. There were also, in 2001–02, 1,812 sericultural villages, six sericultural farms, eight silk units and nine weaving centres. In 2000 there were more than 5,400 *khadi* and village industrial units.

COMMUNICATIONS

Roads

Three national highways run through the state for a distance of 520 km. In 2000–01 there were 7,598 km of surfaced and unsurfaced roads, of which 3,523 km were surfaced. Total number of motor vehicles in 2000–01 was 67,076, including 13,464 trucks, 12,853 private cars and 2,463 buses.

Rail

The state has only 1 km of railways, but this does not connect the state with the national network. The nearest station is 103 km outside the state. There is a plan to extend the national network to Byrnihat, 20 km inside Meghalaya.

Civil Aviation

Umroi airport (35 km from Shillong) connects the state with main air services. There are regular flights to Calcutta. Umroi is to be upgraded to receive larger aircraft. However, the main airport serving the state is Borjhar, at Guwahati, 21 km across the state border but only 124 km from Shillong. Guwahati has air links with several major north Indian cities.

SOCIAL INSTITUTIONS

Justice

The Guwahati High Court is common to Assam, Meghalaya, Nagaland, Manipur, Mizoram, Tripura and Arunachal Pradesh—there are 19 judges. There is a bench of the Guwahati High Court at Shillong.

Education

In 2001, 63·31% of the population were literate (66·14% of men and 60·41% of women). In 2000–01 the state had 4,685 primary and middle schools with 445,443 students, and 1,613 senior middle, secondary and higher secondary schools with 181,068 students. There were 35 colleges and other institutions of higher education including ten teacher training schools, one college and one polytechnic, with a total enrolment of 31,975 students. The North Eastern Hill University started functioning at Shillong in 1973; in 1993–94 it had 41 colleges and 54,803 students.

Health

In 2000–01 there were ten government hospitals, 88 primary health centres and 12 additional health centres, 38 government dispensaries and 413 sub-centres. Total beds (hospitals and health centres), 2,377. There were 389 doctors, 384 staff nurses and 915 paramedics.

RELIGION

At the 2001 census Christians numbered 64·8% of the population; Hindus, over 14·5%; Khasi, 6·2%.

Mizoram

KEY HISTORICAL EVENTS

On 21 Jan. 1972 the former Mizo Hills District of Assam was created a Union Territory. A long dispute between the Mizo National Front (originally Separatist) and the central government was resolved in 1986. Mizoram became a state by the Constitution (53rd Amendment) and the State of Mizoram Acts, July 1986.

TERRITORY AND POPULATION

Mizoram is one of the easternmost Indian states, lying between Bangladesh and Myanmar, and having on its northern boundaries Tripura, Assam and Manipur. There are eight districts. The area is 21,081 sq. km and the population (2001 census) 891,058; density, 42 per sq. km. The main languages spoken are Mizo and English.

SOCIAL STATISTICS

Growth rate 1991–2001, 29·18%.

CONSTITUTION AND GOVERNMENT

Mizoram has a unicameral Legislative Assembly with 40 seats. The capital is Aizawl (population, 2001, 229,714 in the urban agglomeration).

RECENT ELECTIONS

In the elections of Nov. 2003 distribution of seats was: Mizo National Front, 20; Indian National Congress, 11; Mizoram People's Conference, 5; others and ind., 4.

CURRENT ADMINISTRATION

Governor: Amolak Rattan Kohli; b. 1942 (took office on 18 May 2001).

Chief Minister: Pu Zoramthanga; b. 1944 (took office on 3 Dec. 1998).

ECONOMY

Budget

Budget estimates for 2000–01 show revenue receipts of Rs 9,227m. and expenditure of Rs 9,848m.

ENERGY AND NATURAL RESOURCES

Electricity

There are 19 power stations and an installed capacity (2002) of 87·75 MW. 631 out of 764 villages had electricity in 2002.

Agriculture

About 60% of the people are engaged in agriculture, either on terraced holdings or in shifting cultivation. Total production of foodgrains, 1998–99, 127,000 tonnes (rice, 111,000 tonnes; oilseeds, 12,000).

Forestry

Total forest area, 2000, 18,576 sq. km.

INDUSTRY

Handloom weaving and other cottage industries are important. The state had (1992) 2,300 small scale industrial units, including furniture industries, steel fabrication, TV manufacturing, truck and bus body building.

COMMUNICATIONS

Roads

Aizawl is connected by road with Silchar in Assam. Total length of roads in 2000, about 6,840 km of which 885 km are national highways, 225 km are state highways, 3,471 km are classed as major highways and 935 km as village roads. 341 of Mizoram's 764 villages are served by all-weather roads, although 85 villages do not have any roads. There were 29,353 motor vehicles in 2000 of which 767 were buses, 12,847 private cars, and 357 tractors and trailers.

Rail

There is a metre-gauge rail link at Bairabi, 130 km from Aizawl.

Civil Aviation

Lengpui Airport, Aizawl is connected by air with Silchar in Assam and with Calcutta three days a week.

SOCIAL INSTITUTIONS

Education

In 2001, 88·49% of the population were literate (90·69% of men and 86·13% of women). In 1998–99 there were 1,318 primary schools with over 130,000 students, 733 middle schools with 45,000 students, and 345 high and higher secondary schools with 23,000 students; there were 29 colleges, one teacher training college, three teacher training schools, one polytechnic and 29 junior colleges. Mizoram does not have any universities.

Health

In 2000–01 there were ten hospitals, 60 health centres and over 300 health sub-centres. Total beds, over 1,450. The state pays particular attention to immunization programmes.

RELIGION

At the 2001 census Christians numbered over 85·5% of the population; Buddhists, 8%; Hindus, 5%.

Nagaland

KEY HISTORICAL EVENTS

The state was created in 1961, effective 1963. It consisted of the Naga Hills district of Assam and the Tuensang Frontier Agency. The agency was a British-supervised tribal area on the borders of Myanmar. Its supervision passed to the government of India at independence, and in 1957 Tuensang and the Naga Hills became a Centrally Administered Area, governed by the central government through the Governor of Assam.

A number of Naga leaders fought for independence until a settlement was reached with the Indian government at the Shillong Peace Agreement of 1975. However, calls for a greater Naga state, potentially incorporating parts of neighbouring Manipur, Arunachal Pradesh and Assam, continued to be voiced, notably through the National Socialist Council of Nagaland (NSCN), which had been active since 1954. The national government and NSCN met in Delhi in early Jan. 2003 to hold their first joint talks in 37 years, after which the NSCN declared 'the war is over'.

TERRITORY AND POPULATION

The state is in the northeast of India and is bounded in the north by Arunachal Pradesh, west by Assam, east by Myanmar and south by Manipur. Nagaland has an area of 16,579 sq. km and a population (2001 census) of 1,988,636; density, 120 per sq. km. The major towns are the capital, Kohima (2001 population, 78,584) and Dimapur (107,382). Other towns include Wokha, Mon, Zunheboto, Mokokchung and Tuensang. The chief tribes in numerical order are: Angami, Ao, Sumi, Konyak, Chakhesang, Lotha, Phom, Khiamngan, Chang, Yimchunger, Zeliang-Kuki, Rengma, Sangtam and Pochury. The main languages of the state are English, Hindi and Nagamese.

SOCIAL STATISTICS

Growth rate 1991–2001, 64·41% (the highest rate of any Indian state).

CONSTITUTION AND GOVERNMENT

An Interim Body (Legislative Assembly) of 42 members elected by the Naga people and an Executive Council (Council of Ministers) of five members were formed in 1961, and continued until the State Assembly was elected in Jan. 1964. The Assembly has 60 members. The Governor has extraordinary powers, which include special responsibility for law and order.

The state has eight districts (Dimapur, Kohima, Mon, Zunheboto, Wokha, Phek, Mokokchung and Tuensang). The capital is Kohima.

RECENT ELECTIONS

At the elections to the State Assembly in Feb. 2003 the Indian National Congress party won 20 seats (53 in 1998); Nagaland People's Front, 19; BJP, 6; Nagaland Democratic Movement, 5; ind., 4; other parties, 4. Results for two seats were not available.

CURRENT ADMINISTRATION

Governor: Shyamal Datta; b. 1941 (took office on 28 Jan. 2002).

Chief Minister: Neiphi-u Rio; b. 1950 (took office on 6 March 2003).

ECONOMY

Budget

Budget estimates for 2000–01 showed total receipts of Rs 15,283m. and expenditure of Rs 14,998m.

ENERGY AND NATURAL RESOURCES

Electricity

Installed capacity in 1997 was 4·26 MW—five projects under construction or nearing completion will add 27 MW of installed capacity; all towns and villages have electricity.

Oil and Gas

Oil has been located in three districts. Reserves are estimated at 600m. tonnes.

Minerals

In addition to oil, other minerals include: coal, limestone, marble, chromite, magnesite, nickel, cobalt, chromium, iron ore, copper ore, clay, glass sand and slate.

Agriculture

90% of the people derive their livelihood from agriculture. The Angamis, in Kohima district, practise a fixed agriculture in the shape of terraced slopes, and wet paddy cultivation in the lowlands. In the other two districts a traditional form of shifting cultivation (*jhumming*) still predominates, but some farmers have begun tea and coffee plantations and horticulture. About 61,000 ha. were under terrace cultivation and 74,040 ha. under *jhumming* in 1994–95. Production of rice (1999) was 187,000 tonnes, total foodgrains 227,300 tonnes and pulses 13,000 tonnes.

Forestry

Forests, including open forests, covered 14,221 sq. km in 1999, of which forest area excluding open forest was 8,630 sq. km.

INDUSTRY

There is a forest products factory at Tijit; a paper-mill (100 tonnes daily capacity) at Tuli, a distillery unit and a sugar-mill (1,000 tonnes daily capacity) at Dimapur, and a cement factory (50 tonnes daily capacity) at Wazeho. Bricks and TV sets are also made, and there are 1,850 small units. There is a ceramics plant and sericulture is also important.

COMMUNICATIONS

Roads

There is a national highway from Kaziranga (Assam) to Kohima and on to Manipur. There are state highways connecting Kohima with the district headquarters. Total length of roads in 1999, over 15,500 km, of which 365 km are national highway and 1,094 km state highway. There were 95,020 motor vehicles registered in 1994–95.

Rail

Dimapur has a rail-head. Railway route-km in 2000, 60 km.

Civil Aviation

Dimapur has a daily air service to Calcutta. The state government plans to upgrade the airport to receive international flights.

SOCIAL INSTITUTIONS

Justice

A permanent bench of the Guwahati High Court has been established in Kohima. There are 19 judges.

Education

In 2001, 67·11% of the population were literate (71·77% of men and 61·92% of women). In 1996–97 there were 1,414 primary schools with 271,932 students, 416 middle schools with 63,437 students, 244 high and higher secondary schools with 24,547 students, 36 colleges, two teacher training colleges and two polytechnics. The North Eastern Hill University opened at Kohima in 1978. Nagaland University was established in 1994.

Health

In 2005 there were eight hospitals (1,300 beds), 93 primary and 21 community health centres, 16 dispensaries, 412 sub-centres, ten TB centres and 36 leprosy centres.

RELIGION

At the 2001 census Christians formed 87% of the population; Hindus 10% and Muslims under 2%.

FURTHER READING

Aram, M., *Peace in Nagaland*. New Delhi, 1974

Orissa

KEY HISTORICAL EVENTS

Orissa was divided between Mahratta and Bengal rulers when conquered by the British East India Company, the Bengal area in 1757 and the Mahratta in 1803. The area which now forms the state then consisted of directly controlled British districts and a large number of small princely states with tributary rulers. The British districts were administered as part of Bengal until 1912 when, together with Bihar, they were separated from Bengal to form a single province. Bihar and Orissa were separated from each other in 1936. In 1948 a new state government took control of the whole state, including the former princely states (except Saraikella and Kharswan which were transferred to Bihar, and Mayurbhanj which was not incorporated until 1949).

In Oct. 1999 Orissa was hit by a devastating cyclone which resulted in more than 10,000 deaths.

TERRITORY AND POPULATION

Orissa is in eastern India and is bounded north by Jharkhand, northeast by West Bengal, east by the Bay of Bengal, south by Andhra Pradesh and west by Chhattisgarh. The area of the state is 155,707 sq. km, and its population (2001 census), 36,706,920; density 236 per sq. km. Cities with over 250,000 population at 2001 census, *see* INDIA: Territory and Population. Other large cities (2001): Sambalpur, 226,966; Puri, 157,610; Baleshwar, 156,274; Baripada, 100,593. The principal and official language is Oriya.

SOCIAL STATISTICS

Growth rate 1991–2001, 15·94%.

CONSTITUTION AND GOVERNMENT

The Legislative Assembly has 147 members.
The state consists of 30 districts.
The capital is Bhubaneswar (18 miles south of Cuttack).

RECENT ELECTIONS

At the state elections of 20 and 26 April 2004 the Biju Janata Dal won 61 seats (with 27·4% of the vote); the INC, 28 (34·8%); the BJP, 32 (17·1%); the Jharkhand Mukti Morcha, 4 (1·8%); and the Orissa Gana Parishad, 2 (1·3%). Eight independents were elected and two other parties received one seat each.

CURRENT ADMINISTRATION

Governor: Rameshwar Thakur; b. 1927 (took office on 17 Nov. 2004).
Chief Minister: Naveen Patnaik; b. 1946 (took office on 5 March 2000).

ECONOMY

Budget

Budget estimates, 2000–01, showed total receipts of Rs 124,216m. and total expenditure of Rs 121,046m.

ENERGY AND NATURAL RESOURCES

Electricity

The Hirakud Dam Project on the river Mahanadi irrigates 628,000 acres and has an installed capacity of 307·5 MW. There are other projects under construction; hydro-electric power is now serving a large part of the state. Other hydro-power projects are Balimela (360 MW), Upper Kolab (320 MW) and Rengali (250 MW). Total installed capacity (2002) 1,693 MW. In March 1996, 32,068 villages had electricity.

Minerals

Orissa is India's leading producer of chromite (97% of national output), bauxite (71%), iron ore (33% of national reserves), dolomite (50%), manganese ore (32%), graphite (80%), iron ore (16%), fire-clay (34%), limestone (20%) and quartz-quartzite (18%). Kaliapani is the centre of chromite mining and processing. Daitari is the major centre for iron production.

Production in 2002–03 (1,000 tonnes): coal, 52,229; iron ore, 21,518; bauxite, 4,904; chromite, 3,047; limestone, 2,362; dolomite, 959; manganese ore, 616. Value of production in 2002–03 was Rs 33,560m.

Agriculture

The cultivation of rice is the principal occupation of about 80% of the workforce, and only a very small amount of other cereals is grown. Production of foodgrains (1998–99) totalled 6·35m.

tonnes from 4·7m. ha. (rice 6·2m. tonnes, wheat 60,000 tonnes); pulses, 0·28m. tonnes; oilseeds, 0·21m. tonnes; sugarcane, 1·14m. tonnes. Turmeric is cultivated in the uplands of the districts of Ganjam, Phulbani and Koraput, and is exported.

Livestock (1993): buffaloes, 1·04m.; other cattle, 9·2m.; sheep, 1·87m.; goats, 5·4m.; 15·91m. poultry including ducks (1995).

Forestry

Forests occupied 58,135 sq. km in 1999 (37·3% of the state). The most important species are sal, teak, kendu, sandal, sisu, bija, kusum, kongada and bamboo.

Fisheries

There were, in 1999, over 600 fishery co-operative societies. Fish production in 2002 was 1·3m. tonnes of marine fish (including crustaceans) and 140,000 tonnes of freshwater fish. About 170,000 people depend upon sea fishing for a living. Hundreds of fishing boats are engaged in illegal shrimp fishing. The state has four fishing harbours.

INDUSTRY

289 large and medium industries are in operation (1995–96), mostly based on minerals: steel, pig iron, ferrochrome, ferro-manganese, ferrosilicon, aluminium, cement, automotive tyres and synthetic fibres.

Other industries of importance are sugar, glass, paper, fertilizers, caustic soda, salt, industrial explosives, heavy machine tools, a coach-repair factory, a re-rolling mill, textile mills and electronics. There is an oil refinery. In the past decade there has been much investment and expansion in biotechnology, electronics, leather and marine-based industries. Also, there were 49,611 small-scale industries in 1995–96 employing 349,800 persons, and 1,342,561 artisan units providing employment to 2·33m. persons. Handloom weaving and the manufacture of baskets, wooden articles, hats and nets, silver filigree work and hand-woven fabrics are specially well known.

COMMUNICATIONS

Roads

On 31 March 1996 length of roads was: state highway, 4,360 km; national highway, 1,625 km; other roads, 212,490 km. There were 658,401 motor vehicles in 1995–96. A 144-km expressway, part national highway, connects the Daitari mining area with Paradip Port.

Rail

The route-km of railway in 2001 was 2,261 km, of which 143 km was narrow gauge.

Civil Aviation

There is an airport at Bhubaneswar with regular scheduled services to New Delhi, Calcutta, Visakhapatnam and Hyderabad.

Shipping

Paradip was declared a 'major' port in 1966; it handled 23·9m. tonnes of traffic in 2002–03. There are minor ports at Bahabalpur and Gopalpur.

SOCIAL INSTITUTIONS

Justice

The High Court of Judicature at Cuttack has a Chief Justice and 16 puisne judges.

Education

The percentage of literate people in the population in 2001 was 63·61% (males, 75·95%; females, 50·97%).

In 1996–97 there were 42,104 primary schools with 3·95m. students, 12,096 middle schools with 1·3m. students and 6,198 high and higher secondary schools with 945,000 students. There are ten engineering and technology colleges, 20 medical

colleges, 13 teacher training colleges, 15 engineering schools/polytechnics, 497 arts, science and commerce colleges and 440 junior colleges.

Utkal University was established in 1943 at Cuttack and moved to Bhubaneswar in 1962; it is both teaching and affiliating. It has 368 affiliated colleges and 14,000 students (1993–94). Berhampur University has 33 affiliated colleges with 33,755 students, and Orissa University of Agriculture and Technology has eight constituent colleges with 641 students. Sambalpur University has 97 affiliated colleges and 43,982 students. Sri Jagannath Sanskrit Viswavidyalaya at Puri was established in 1981 for oriental studies.

Health

There were (1999–2000) 180 hospitals, 150 dispensaries, 1,351 primary health centres and units, and 5,929 health subcentres, with a total of 13,786 beds. There were also 462 homeopathic and 519 Ayurvedic dispensaries.

RELIGION

At the 2001 census Hindus numbered 94·7% of the population, Christians 2·1% and Muslims 1·8%.

CULTURE

Tourism

Tourist traffic is concentrated mainly on the 'Golden Triangle' of Konark, Puri, and Bhubaneswar and its temples. Tourists also visit Gopalpur, the Similipal National Park, Nandankanan and Chilka Lake, Bhiar-Kanika and Ushakothi Wildlife Sanctuary.

Punjab (India)

KEY HISTORICAL EVENTS

The Punjab was constituted an autonomous province of India in 1937. In 1947 the province was partitioned between India and Pakistan into East and West Punjab respectively. The name of East Punjab was changed to Punjab (India) under the Constitution of India. On 1 Nov. 1956 the erstwhile states of Punjab and Patiala and East Punjab States Union (PEPSU) were integrated to form the state of Punjab. On 1 Nov. 1966, under the Punjab Reorganization Act, 1966, the state was reconstituted as a Punjabi-speaking state comprising the districts of Gurdaspur (excluding Dalhousie), Amritsar, Kapurthala, Jullundur, Ferozepur, Bhatinda, Patiala and Ludhiana; parts of Sangrur, Hoshiarpur and Ambala districts; and part of Kharar tehsil. The remaining area comprising 47,000 sq. km and an estimated (1967) population of 8·5m. was shared between the new state of Haryana and the Union Territory of Himachal Pradesh. The existing capital of Chandigarh was made joint capital of Punjab and Haryana; its transfer to Punjab alone (scheduled for 1986) has been delayed while the two states seek agreement as to which Hindi-speaking districts shall be transferred to Haryana in exchange.

TERRITORY AND POPULATION

The Punjab is in north India and is bounded at its northernmost point by Kashmir, northeast by Himachal Pradesh, southeast by Haryana, south by Rajasthan, west and northwest by Pakistan. The area of the state is 50,362 sq. km, with a population (2001 census) of 24,289,296; density, 482 per sq. km. Cities with over 250,000 population at 2001 census, see INDIA: Territory and Population. Other principal towns (2001): Bathinda (217,389); Pathankot (168,275); Hoshiarpur (148,243); Batala (147,753); Moga (124,624); Abohar (124,303); S.A.S. Nagar (123,284); Maler Kotla (106,802); Khanna (103,059); Phagwara (102,111). The official language is Punjabi.

SOCIAL STATISTICS

Growth rate 1991–2001, 19·76%.

CONSTITUTION AND GOVERNMENT

Punjab (India) has a unicameral legislature, the Legislative Assembly, of 117 members. Presidential rule was imposed in May 1987 after outbreaks of communal violence. In March 1988 the Assembly was officially dissolved. Presidential rule was lifted in Feb. 1992.

There are 17 districts. The capital is Chandigarh.

RECENT ELECTIONS

Legislative Assembly elections were held on 13 Feb. 2002. The Congress Party (INC) won 62 seats, the Shiromani Akali Dal (SAD) 41, the Bharatiya Janata Party (BJP) 3, ind. 9 and the Communist Party of India (CPI) 2.

CURRENT ADMINISTRATION

Governor: Gen. S. F. Rodrigues; b. 1933 (took office on 16 Nov. 2004).

Chief Minister: Capt. Amarinder Singh; b. 1942 (took office on 27 Feb. 2002).

ECONOMY

Budget

Budget estimates, 2000–01, showed revenue receipts of Rs 159,597m. and revenue expenditure of Rs 159,725m.

ENERGY AND NATURAL RESOURCES

Electricity

Installed capacity, 2001–02, was 4,743 MW; all villages had electricity. There are nine major hydro electric plants—Shanan, UBDC, Anandpur Sahib, RSDHEP, Mukerian, Nadampur, Daudhar, Rohti and Thuhi. The per capita consumption of electricity in Punjab is higher than in any other Indian state, at 821 units (kWh) per annum in 2000–01.

Agriculture

About 75% of the population depends on agriculture, which is technically advanced. The irrigated area rose from 2·2m. ha. in 1950–51 to 4·2m. ha. in 1996–97. 95·1% of cropland in Punjab is irrigated. In 2001 wheat production was 15·5m. tonnes; potatoes, 10·0m.; rice, 9·1m.; kinnow, 0·2m.; plus large amounts of chillies, mangoes, grapes, pears, peaches and lemons. Total foodgrains, 24·90m. tonnes; sugarcane, 1·3m. tonnes; oilseeds, 61,000 tonnes. Cotton, 1·91m. bales of 170 kg, representing 12·4% of India's cotton. Punjab contributes 22·6% of India's wheat.

Agriculture in Punjab is more advanced and mechanized than in most other parts of India. Emphasis has recently been on diversification with new crops including hyola seeds, soybeans, sunflower, spring maize and floriculture, and the use of bio-fertilizers.

Livestock (2003 census): buffaloes, 5,995,000; other cattle, 2·04m.; sheep and goats, 498,300; horses and ponies, 29,300; poultry, 10·5m.

Forestry

In 1999 there were 1,387 sq. km of forest land.

INDUSTRY

In March 2001 the number of registered industrial units was 202,356, employing about 1,184,550 people. In 2001 there were 620 large and medium industries and 201,736 small industrial units, investment Rs 43,310m. The chief manufactures are metals, textiles (especially hosiery and fabrics), yarn, sports goods, hand tools, sugar, bicycles, electronic goods, machine tools, hand tools, automobiles and vehicle parts, surgical goods, vegetable oils, tractors, chemicals and pharmaceuticals, fertilizers, food processing, electronics, railway coaches, paper and newsprint, cement, engineering goods and telecommunications items. There is an oil refinery.

COMMUNICATIONS

Roads

The total length of roads in 2001 was 50,389 km, including 1,729 km national highways—seven national highways pass through the state. All villages in the state are connected to metalled roads. State transport services cover 1·9m. effective km daily with a fleet of 3,426 buses carrying a daily average of over 1·2m. passengers. Coverage by private operators is estimated at 40%. There were 1,915,059 vehicles in 1995–96.

Rail

The Punjab possesses an extensive system of railway communications, served by the Northern Railway. Route-km (1995–96), 2,121 km.

Civil Aviation

There is an airport at Amritsar, and Chandigarh airport is on the northeastern boundary; both have regular scheduled services to Delhi, Jammu, Srinagar and Leh. There are also Vayudoot services to Ludhiana. Amritsar is now an international airport with charter flights from Europe and from several Middle East destinations.

SOCIAL INSTITUTIONS

Justice

The Punjab and Haryana High Court exercises jurisdiction over the states of Punjab and Haryana and the territory of Chandigarh. It is located in Chandigarh. In 2003 it consisted of a Chief Justice and 40 puisne judges.

Education

Compulsory education was introduced in April 1961; at the same time free education was introduced up to 8th class for boys and 9th class for girls as well as fee concessions. The aim is education for all children of 6–11. In 2001, 69·95% of the population were literate (75·63% of men and 63·55% of women).

In 1996–97 there were 12,590 primary schools with 2,081,965 students, 2,545 middle schools with 968,762 students, 2,159 high schools with 490,888 students and 1,134 higher secondary schools with 259,718 students.

Punjab University was established in 1882 at Lahore as an examining, teaching and affiliating body. It divided in 1947 with the Indian part moving to Shimla, and in 1956 moved again to Chandigarh (in 1993–94 it had 94 colleges and 77,868 students). In 1962 Punjabi University was established at Patiala (it had 66 colleges with 40,712 students) and Punjab Agricultural University at Ludhiana. Guru Nanak Dev University was established at Amritsar in 1969 to mark the 500th anniversary celebrations for Guru Nanak Dev, first Guru of the Sikhs (it had 85 colleges and 80,330 students, 1992–93). The Thapar Institute of Engineering and Technology, at Patiala, has university status and there is also the Baba Farid University of Health Science, at Faridkot. Altogether there are 293 affiliated colleges.

Health

There were (2000) 207 hospitals, 12 hospitals/health centres, 55 community health centres, 38 community primary health centres, 446 primary health centres, and 1,470 dispensaries and clinics. There were six Ayurvedic hospitals and 507 Ayurvedic dispensaries, plus one homeopathic hospital and 105 homeopathic dispensaries. There were over 25,000 hospital beds in 2000.

RELIGION

At the 2001 census Sikhs numbered 63% of the population; Hindus, 34·5%; Muslims, over 1·5%.

FURTHER READING

Singh, Khushwant, *A History of the Sikhs*. 2 vols. OUP, 1999
Singh Tatla, Darshan and Talbot, Ian, *Punjab*. [Bibliography] ABC-Clio, Oxford and Santa Barbara (CA), 1995

Rajasthan

KEY HISTORICAL EVENTS

The state is in the largely desert area formerly known as Rajputana. The Rajput princes were tributary to the Moghul emperors when they were conquered by the Mahrattas' leader, Mahadaji Sindhia, in the 1780s. In 1818 Rajputana became a British protectorate and was recognized during British rule as a group of princely states including Jaipur, Jodhpur and Udaipur. After independence the Rajput princes surrendered their powers and in 1950 were replaced by a single state government. In 1956 the state boundaries were altered; small areas of the former Bombay and Madhya Bharat states were added, together with the neighbouring state of Ajmer. Ajmer had been a Moghul power base; it was taken by the Mahrattas in 1770 and annexed by the British in 1818. In 1878 it became Ajmer-Merwara, a British province, and survived as a separate state until 1956.

TERRITORY AND POPULATION

Rajasthan is in northwest India and is bounded north by Punjab, northeast by Haryana and Uttar Pradesh, east by Madhya Pradesh, south by Gujarat and west by Pakistan. Since the area of Madhya Pradesh was reduced by the creation of Chhattisgarh in 2000, Rajasthan has become the largest Indian state in size, with an area of 342,239 sq. km. Population (2001 census), 56,473,122; density 165 per sq. km. For chief cities, *see* INDIA: Territory and Population. Other major towns (2001): Ganganagar (222,833), Bharatpur (205,104), Pali (187,571), Sikar (185,506), Tonk (135,663), Hunumangarh (129,654), Beawar (125,923), Kishangarh (116,156), Gangapur (105,336), Churu (101,853), Jhunjhunun (100,476). The main languages spoken are Rajasthani and Hindi.

SOCIAL STATISTICS

Growth rate 1991–2001, 28·33%.

CONSTITUTION AND GOVERNMENT

There is a unicameral legislature, the Legislative Assembly, having 200 members. The capital is Jaipur. There are 32 districts.

RECENT ELECTIONS

After the election in Dec. 2003 the Bharatiya Janata Party came to power. BJP, 120 seats; Congress (I), 56; others, 24.

CURRENT ADMINISTRATION

Governor: Pratibha Patil; b. 1934 (took office on 8 Nov. 2004).
   Chief Minister: Vasundhara Raje; b. 1953 (took office on 8 Dec. 2003).

ECONOMY

Budget
The budget estimates for 2000–01 showed total revenue receipts of Rs 172,340m., and expenditure of Rs 172,403m.

ENERGY AND NATURAL RESOURCES

Electricity
Installed capacity in March 2001, 4,000 MW; 30,620 villages (March 1996) and 514,758 wells had electric power.

Minerals
There are 64 different minerals mined in the state. It is the sole producer of garnet and jasper in India, and by far the leading producer of zinc, calcite, gypsum and asbestos. Others include silver, tungsten, granite, marble, kaolin (44% of India's production), dolomite, lignite, lead (80% of India's production), fluorite (59% of India's production), emeralds, soapstone, feldspar (70% of India's production), copper, barytes (53% of India's production), limestone and salt. Total revenue from minerals in 2002, Rs 3,000m. Four blocs are being explored for mineral oils and gas.

Agriculture
The state has suffered drought and encroaching desert for several years. The cultivable area is (1999) about 25·6m. ha., of which 4·65m. ha. is irrigated. Production of principal crops (in tonnes), 1999: pulses, 2·64m.; total foodgrains, 11·40m. (wheat, 6·7m.; rice, 190,000); cotton, 868,000 tonnes.
   The total irrigable area of the state is 13·6m. ha., which is 53% of the cultivable area. The Indira Gandhi Nahar Canal—India's largest irrigation project—is the main canal system, of which 189 km of main canal, 204 km of feeder and more than 3,400 km of distributors have been built. There were 37,560 villages with full or partial drinking water facilities in Jan. 2004, out of 37,889 villages.
   Livestock (1992): buffaloes, 7·75m.; other cattle, 11·6m.; sheep, 12·17m.; goats, 15·06m.; horses and ponies, 28,000; camels, 731,000.

Forestry
Forests covered 13,353 sq. km in 1999, of which 9,632 sq. km was protected.

INDUSTRY

In 2001 there were 221,369 small industrial units with an investment of Rs 31,160·6m. and employment of 857,000. Of these units 45,705 were agro-based, 26,842 forest-based, 27,397 metal-working and 24,861 textiles. There were 212 industrial estates in 2001. 10,244 medium-size and large factories were recorded in 2001. Total capital investment (1993–94) Rs 13,160m. Chief manufactures are textiles, dyeing, printing cloth, cement, glass, sugar, sodium, oxygen and acetylene units, pesticides, insecticides, dyes, caustic soda, calcium, carbide, synthetic fibres, fertilizers, shaving equipment, automobiles and automobile components, tyres, watches, nylon tyre cords and refined copper. The state is a major textile centre and is the leading producer of polyester and viscose yarns in India and the second largest producer of suiting material; out of 862 spinning mills in India, 69 are in Rajasthan.

COMMUNICATIONS

Roads
In 2001 there were 150,870 km of roads in Rajasthan including 61,520 km of good and surfaced roads. The state government gives a road length of 85,008 km in 1999 for surfaced roads—there were 4,453 km of national highways and 8,898 km of state highways. A total of 12 national highways crossed the state. Motor vehicles numbered 3·6m. in 2003.

Rail
Jodhpur, Marwar, Udaipur, Ajmer, Jaipur, Kota, Bikaner and Sawai Madhopur are important junctions of the northwestern network. Route km (2003) 5,924. The major cities of the state are integrated with the national broad-gauge network.

Civil Aviation
There are airports at Jaipur (Sanganer Airport), Jodhpur, Kota and Udaipur with regular scheduled services by Indian Airlines to Delhi, Bombay and Ahmedabad. Sanganer has been upgraded

and now receives charter international flights as well as scheduled flights from Dubai and other gulf destinations.

SOCIAL INSTITUTIONS

Justice
The seat of the High Court is at Jodhpur. There is a Chief Justice and 32 puisne judges. There is also a bench of High Court judges at Jaipur.

Education
The proportion of literate people to the total population was 61·03% at the 2001 census; 76·46% of men and 44·34% of women.

In 2001 there were 35,015 primary schools with 7,540,000 students, 16,336 middle schools with 2,327,000 students, 4,124 high schools and 1,923 higher secondary schools with 1,560,000 students between them. Elementary education is free but not compulsory.

In 2001 there were 280 colleges. Rajasthan University, established at Jaipur in 1947, is teaching and affiliating; in 1993–94 it had 135 colleges and 160,000 students. There are 11 other universities: Rajasthan Agricultural University, Bikaner; Mohanlal Sukhadia University, Udaipur; Maharishi Dayanand Saraswati University, Ajmer; Jai Narayan Vyas University, Jodhpur; Kota Open University, Kota; National Law University, Jodhpur; Rajasthan Sanskrit University, Jaipur; Birla Institute of Science and Technology, Pilani; Jain Vishwa Bharti, Ladnu; Rajasthan Vidyapeeth, Udaipur; Vanasthali Vidyapeeth, Vanasthali. There are also 280 colleges: 111 government colleges (including teacher-training colleges and 27 polytechnics), 75 government colleges and research institutes, 92 non-aided colleges and two other institutes.

Health
In 2001 there were 113 hospitals with 17,459 beds, 263 community health centres, 1,674 primary health centres and 9,926 sub-centres.

RELIGION
At the 2001 census Hindus numbered 89% of the population; Muslims, 8%; Sikhs, nearly 1·5%.

FURTHER READING
Sharma, S. K. and Sharma, Usha (eds.) *History and Geography of Rajasthan*. New Delhi, 2000

Sikkim

KEY HISTORICAL EVENTS
A small Himalayan kingdom between Nepal and Bhutan, Sikkim was independent in the 1830s although in continual conflict with larger neighbours. In 1839 the British took the Darjeeling district. British political influence increased during the 19th century, as Sikkim was the smallest buffer between India and Tibet. However, Sikkim remained an independent kingdom ruled by the 14th-century Namgyal dynasty. In 1950 a treaty was signed with the government of India, declaring Sikkim an Indian Protectorate. Indian influence increased from then on. Internal political unrest came to a head in 1973, and led to the granting of constitutional reforms in 1974. Agitation continued until Sikkim became a 'state associated with the Indian Union' later that year. In 1975 the king was deposed and Sikkim became an Indian state, a change approved by referendum.

TERRITORY AND POPULATION
Sikkim is in the Eastern Himalayas and is bounded north by Tibet, east by Tibet and Bhutan, south by West Bengal and west Nepal. Area, 7,096 sq. km. It is inhabited chiefly by the Lepchas, a tribe indigenous to Sikkim, the Bhutias, who originally came from Tibet, and the Nepalis, who entered from Nepal in large numbers in the late 19th and early 20th century. Population (2001 census), 540,493; density, 76 per sq km. The capital is Gangtok (population of 29,162 at the 2001 census).

English is the principal language. Lepcha, Bhutia, Nepali and Limboo also have official status.

SOCIAL STATISTICS
Growth rate 1991–2001, 32·98%.

CONSTITUTION AND GOVERNMENT
The Assembly has 32 members.

The official language of the government is English. Lepcha, Bhutia, Nepali and Limboo have also been declared official languages.

Sikkim is divided into four districts for administration purposes, Gangtok, Mangan, Namchi and Gyalshing being the headquarters for the Eastern, Northern, Southern and Western districts respectively.

RECENT ELECTIONS
At the State Assembly election of 10 May 2004 the Sikkim Democratic Front won 31 seats (71·1% of the vote) and the INC took one seat (26·1%).

CURRENT ADMINISTRATION
Governor: V. Rama Rao; b. 1926 (took office on 25 Oct. 2002).

Chief Minister: Pawan Kumar Chamling; b. 1950 (took office on 12 Dec. 1994).

ECONOMY

Budget
Budget estimates for 2000–01 showed receipts of Rs 114,360m. and expenditure of Rs 116,300m.

ENERGY AND NATURAL RESOURCES

Electricity
Installed capacity (1999) 35·9 MW. There are four hydro-electric power stations. All villages had electricity in 1991.

Minerals
Copper, zinc and lead are mined.

Agriculture
There are 70,000 ha. of cultivable land. The economy is mainly agricultural; main food crops are cardamom, ginger, rice, maize, millet, wheat and barley; cash crops are mandarin oranges, apples, potatoes and buckwheat. Foodgrain production, 1999, 98,000 tonnes (maize, 56,000; rice, 21,000 tonnes; wheat, 14,000 tonnes); potatoes, 28,000 tonnes; pulses, 6,000 tonnes. Tea is grown. Medicinal herbs are exported. Sericulture produces 179 kg of silk per annum.

Forestry
Forests occupied about 3,127 sq. km in 1995 and the potential for a timber and wood-pulp industry is being explored.

INDUSTRY
Small-scale industries include cigarettes, distilling, tanning, fruit preservation, carpets and watchmaking. Local crafts include carpet weaving, making handmade paper, wood carving and silverwork. The State Trading Corporation of Sikkim stimulates trade in indigenous products.

COMMUNICATIONS

Roads
There are 2,376 km of roads, all on mountainous terrain. Of these 40 km are national highways and 678 km state highways. 1,445 km are surfaced and 931 km unsurfaced. There are 18 major bridges. Public transport and road haulage is nationalized. There were 8,997 motor vehicles in 1995–96.

Rail
The nearest railhead is at Shiliguri (115 km from Gangtok).

Civil Aviation
The nearest airport is at Bagdogra (128 km from Gangtok), linked to Gangtok by helicopter service.

Telecommunications
At 31 Dec. 2002 there were 33,884 telephone subscribers.

SOCIAL INSTITUTIONS

Education
In 2001, 69·68% of the population were literate (76·73% of men and 61·46% of women). Sikkim had (1999) 739 pre-primary schools with 23,538 students, 335 primary schools with 84,986 students, 122 junior high schools with 23,949 students, 72 high schools with 3,331 students and 27 higher secondary schools with 1,484 students. Education is free up to class XII; text books are free up to class V. There are 500 adult education centres. There is also a training institute for primary teachers, two degree colleges and a teacher training college.

Health
In 2002 there was one state hospital, four community health centres, 24 primary health centres and 147 sub-primary health centres, with a total of 920 beds. Some 28,244 patients were treated in 2000–01.

RELIGION
At the 2001 census Hindus accounted for 68% of the population, Buddhists 27% and Christians just over 3%.

CULTURE

Broadcasting
A radio broadcasting station, Akashvani Gangtok, was built in 1982, and a permanent station in 1983. Gangtok also has a low-power TV transmitter.

Tamil Nadu

KEY HISTORICAL EVENTS
The first trading establishment made by the British in the Madras State was at Peddapali (now Nizampatnam) in 1611 and then at Masulipatnam. In 1639 the English were permitted to make a settlement at the place which is now Madras, and Fort St George was founded. By 1801 the whole of the country from the Northern Circars to Cape Comorin (with the exception of certain French and Danish settlements) had been brought under British rule.

Under the provisions of the States Reorganization Act, 1956, the Malabar district (excluding the islands of Laccadive and Minicoy) and the Kasaragod district taluk of South Kanara were transferred to the new state of Kerala; the South Kanara district (excluding Kasaragod taluk and the Amindivi Islands) and the Kollegal taluk of the Coimbatore district were transferred to new state of Mysore; and the Laccadive, Amindivi and Minicoy Islands were constituted a separate Territory. Four taluks of the

Trivandrum district and the Shencottah taluk of Quilon district were transferred from Travancore-Cochin to the new Madras State. On 1 April 1960, 1,049 sq. km from the Chittoor district of Andhra Pradesh were transferred to Madras in exchange for 844 sq. km from the Chingleput and Salem districts. In Aug. 1968 the state was renamed Tamil Nadu.

TERRITORY AND POPULATION
Tamil Nadu is in south India and is bounded north by Karnataka and Andhra Pradesh, east and south by the Indian Ocean and west by Kerala. Area, 130,058 sq. km. Population (2001 census), 62,110,839; density 478 per sq. km. Tamil is the principal language and has been adopted as the state language with effect from 14 Jan. 1958. For the principal towns, see INDIA: Territory and Population. Other large towns (2001 census): Tuticorin (242,860), Thanjavur (215,725), Nagercoil (208,149), Dindigul (196,619), Kanchipuram (188,349), Kumbakonam (160,827), Cuddalore (158,569), Karur (153,123), Neyveli (138,387), Tiruvannamalai (130,301), Pollachi (127,993), Arcot (126,975), Karaikkudi (125,185), Rajapalaiyam (121,982), Sivakasi (121,312), Pudukkottai (108,947), Bhavani (104,285), Vaniyambadi (103,841), Coonoor (101,234), Gudiyatham (100,021). The capital is Madras (Chennai).

SOCIAL STATISTICS
Growth rate 1991–2001, 15·39%.

CONSTITUTION AND GOVERNMENT
There is a unicameral legislature; the Legislative Assembly has 235 members (one of which is nominated). There are 30 districts.

RECENT ELECTIONS
In elections held on 10 May 2001 the All India Anna Dravida Munnetra Kazagam gained 132 seats, Dravida Munnetra Kazagam 31, the Tamil Maanila Congress (Moopanar) 23 and the Pattali Makkal Katchi 20.

CURRENT ADMINISTRATION
Governor: Surjit Singh Barnala; b. 1925 (since 3 Nov. 2004; in office for the second time).

Chief Minister: Jayaram Jayalalitha; b. 1948 (since 2 March 2002; in office for the third time).

ECONOMY

Budget
2003–04 revenue receipts, Rs 228,505·3m.; expenditure, Rs 265,500·4m. Annual plan outlay, 2003–04, Rs 70,000m. Budget estimates for 2004–05: revenue receipts, Rs 247,923m.; revenue expenditure, Rs 281,287m.

ENERGY AND NATURAL RESOURCES

Electricity
Installed capacity in Jan. 2005 was 10,139 MW, of which 1,995 MW was hydro-electric, 6,424 MW thermal, 1,362 MW wind powered and 358 MW nuclear (the Kalpakkam nuclear power plant became operational in 1983). All villages are supplied with electricity.

Minerals
The state has magnesite, lignite, bauxite, limestone, manganese, fireclay and feldspar.

Agriculture
The land is a fertile plain watered by rivers flowing east from the Western Ghats, particularly the Cauvery and the Tambaraparani. Temperature ranges between 6°C and 40°C, rainfall between 442 mm and 934 mm. Of the total land area (13m. ha.), 6,519,000 ha. were cropped and 349,000 ha. of wasteland were cultivable

in 1999–2000. Total area under irrigation in 2000–01, 3·49m. ha. The staple food crops grown are paddy, maize, jowar, bajra, pulses and millets. Important commercial crops are sugarcane, oilseeds, cotton, tobacco, coffee, rubber and pepper. In 2003–04, 3·2m. tonnes of paddy, 1·76m. tonnes of sugarcane, 918,000 tonnes of groundnuts, 888,000 tonnes of millets and other cereals, and 201,000 tonnes of pulses were produced.

Livestock (1997): buffaloes, 2,741,263; other cattle, 9,046,542; sheep, 5,258,884; goats, 6,416,204; poultry, 26,511,075.

Forestry
Forest area, 2000, 22,871 sq. km. Products include timber, teak, wattle, sandalwood, pulp wood and sapwood.

Fisheries
In 2003–04 marine production totalled 381,148 tonnes and inland production 77,304 tonnes; there were 591 marine fishing villages.

INDUSTRY

In 2002–03 there were 448,905 registered small-scale industrial units, employing 3,142,335 workers; the number of working factories totalled 25,000, with 1,238,000 workers. The biggest central sector project is Salem steel plant. Textiles constitute one of the major industries; in 2003 Tamil Nadu produced nearly 40% of India's cotton textiles and accounted for 42% of Indian leather exports. Other important industries are automobile ancillaries (constituting 27·5% of exports from India as at mid-2003), chemicals and petrochemicals, agricultural and food processing, biotechnology and computer software (accounting for about 17% of India's software exports).

Trade Unions
In 2004 there were 9,685 registered trade unions.

COMMUNICATIONS

Roads
In March 2003 the state had 178,545 km of national and state highways, major and other district roads; there were 6,752,473 registered motor vehicles.

Rail
In March 2003 there were 4,016 route-km. Madras and Madurai are the main centres.

Civil Aviation
There are airports at Madras, Coimbatore, Tiruchirapalli and Madurai, with regular scheduled services to Bombay, Calcutta and Delhi. Madras is an international airport and the main centre of airline routes in south India. In 2003–04 Madras handled 2,054,043 international passengers, 2,501,778 domestic passengers and 154,123 tonnes of freight.

Shipping
Madras, Tuticorin and Ennore are the chief ports. Important minor ports are Cuddalore and Nagapattinam.

Telecommunications
In 2003–04 there were 3,871,900 telephones in use, with 123,706 public call facilities; there were 521,690 cellular phones.

Postal Services
Post offices numbered 8,692 in 2003–04.

SOCIAL INSTITUTIONS

Justice
There is a High Court at Madras with a Chief Justice and 26 judges.

Police
In 2003–04 the strength of the police force was 95,412, with 1,217 police stations.

Education
At the 2001 census 73·47% of the population were literate (82·33% of men and 64·55% of women).

Education is free up to pre-university level. In 2003–04 there were 32,242 primary schools with 4·3m. students, 6,825 middle schools with 2·2m. students, 4,859 high schools with 1·9m. students and 4,136 higher secondary schools with 4·5m. students. There were 18 universities in 2003–04: Madras University (founded in 1857); Annamalai University, Annamalainagar (1929); Gandhigram Rural Institute, Gandhigram (1956); Madurai Kamaraj University, Palkalainagar (1966); Tamil Nadu Agricultural University, Coimbatore (1971); Anna University, Madras (1978); Tamil University, Thanjavur (1981); Bharathidasan University, Tiruchirapalli (1982); Bharathiyar University, Coimbatore (1982); Mother Teresa Women's University, Kodaikanal (1984); Alagappa University, Karaikkudi (1985); Sri Ramachandra Medical College and Research Institute, Madras (1985); Tamil Nadu Dr M. G. R. Medical University, Madras (1987); Avinashilingam Institute for Home Science and Higher Education for Women, Coimbatore (1988); Tamil Nadu Veterinary and Animal Sciences University, Madras (1989); Manonmaniam Sundaranar University, Tirunelveli (1990); Sri Chandrasekarendra Saraswathi Viswa Mahavidyalaya University, Enathur (1993); Thanthai Periyar University, Salem (1997).

Health
In 2002 there were 408 hospitals and 512 dispensaries, with about 61,000 beds.

RELIGION

At the 2001 census Hindus numbered 54,985,079 (88·0%); Christians, 3,786,060 (6·0%); Muslims, 3,470,647 (5·6%).

CULTURE

Press
In 2002–03 there were 3,093 newspapers and periodicals.

Tourism
In 2004, 1,058,012 foreign tourists visited the state.

FURTHER READING

Statistical Information: The Department of Statistics (Fort St George, Madras) was established in 1948 and reorganized in 1953. Main publications: *Annual Statistical Abstract; Decennial Statistical Atlas; Season and Crop Report; Quinquennial Wages Census; Quarterly Abstract of Statistics.*

Tripura

KEY HISTORICAL EVENTS

Tripura is a Hindu state of great antiquity having been ruled by the Maharajahs for 1,300 years before its accession to the Indian Union on 15 Oct. 1949. With the reorganization of states on 1 Sept. 1956 Tripura became a Union Territory, and was so declared on 1 Nov. 1957. The Territory was made a State on 21 Jan. 1972.

TERRITORY AND POPULATION

Tripura is bounded by Bangladesh, except in the northeast where it joins Assam and Mizoram. The major portion of the state is hilly and mainly jungle. It has an area of 10,486 sq. km. Population, 3,191,168 (2001 census); density, 304 per sq. km.

The official languages are Bengali and Kokbarak. Manipuri is also spoken.

SOCIAL STATISTICS

Growth rate 1991–2001, 15·74%.

CONSTITUTION AND GOVERNMENT

The territory has four districts, namely Dhalai, North Tripura, South Tripura and West Tripura. The capital is Agartala (population, 2001, 189,327).

The Legislative Assembly has 60 members.

RECENT ELECTIONS

The Communist Party of India (Marxist) won the Legislative Assembly elections in Feb. 2003 with 38 seats; Congress won 13; Indigenous National Party of Tripura (INPT), 6; others, 3.

CURRENT ADMINISTRATION

Governor: Dinesh Nandan Sahaya; b. 1936 (took office on 2 June 2003).

Chief Minister: Manik Sarkar; b. 1949 (took office on 11 March 1998).

ECONOMY

Budget

Budget estimates, 2004–05, showed expenditure of Rs 31,829m. and receipts of Rs 30,972m.

ENERGY AND NATURAL RESOURCES

Electricity

Installed capacity in 2005 was 220·46 MW, of which 76·11 MW were hydro-electric and 144·35 MW were thermal. There were (March 2003) 817 villages with electricity out of a total of 855.

Oil and Gas

The state has significant natural gas resources in non-associate form, with established reserves of 31bn. cu. metres.

Agriculture

About 24% of the land area is cultivable. The tribes practise shifting cultivation, but this is being replaced by modern methods. The main crops are rice, wheat, jute, mesta, potatoes, oilseeds and sugarcane. In 2002–03 there were 246,000 ha. under cereal cultivation. In 2001 tea gardens covered 6,700 ha.

Forestry

Forests covered 6,293 sq. km in 2000, 3,588 sq. km of which were reserved and 509 sq. km protected. Commercial rubber plantation is being encouraged and in 2001–02 the state produced 12,000 tonnes of natural rubber.

INDUSTRY

Main small industries: aluminium utensils, rubber, saw-milling, soap, piping, fruit canning, handloom weaving and sericulture. In 1999–2000 there were 1,363 registered factories which employed 31,250 persons and 500 notified factories with 2,000 workers. 384,000 persons were employed in handloom and handicrafts industries in 2003–04.

COMMUNICATIONS

Roads

Total length of roads (2003–04), 10,242 km. In March 2002 vehicles registered totalled 57,428, of which 1,985 were buses and 5,775 were goods vehicles.

Rail

There is a railway between Kumarghat and Kalkalighat (Assam). Route-km in 2003–04, 66 km.

Civil Aviation

There is one airport and three airstrips. The airport (Agartala) has regular scheduled services to Calcutta.

SOCIAL INSTITUTIONS

Education

In 2001, 73·66% of the population were literate (81·47% of men and 65·41% of women). In Sept. 2003 there were 1,776 primary schools (451,731 pupils), 1,001 middle schools (186,651), and 652 high and higher secondary schools (118,006). There were 14 colleges of general education, two engineering and technical institutes, and five professional and other colleges. Tripura University, established in 1987, has 20 affiliated colleges.

Health

There were (2002) 27 hospitals, with 2,000 beds. There were 58 primary health centres, 539 sub-centres and 11 community health centres in 2001.

RELIGION

At the 2001 census Hindus numbered 2,739,310; Muslims, 254,422; Christians, 102,489; Buddhists, 98,922; Sikhs, 1,182; Jains, 477.

Uttar Pradesh

KEY HISTORICAL EVENTS

In 1833 the then Bengal Presidency was divided into two parts, one of which became the Presidency of Agra. In 1836 the Agra area was styled the North-West Province and placed under a Lieut.-Governor. In 1877 the two provinces of Agra and Oudh were placed under one administrator, styled Lieut.-Governor of the North-West Province and Chief Commissioner of Oudh. In 1902 the name was changed to 'United Provinces of Agra and Oudh', under a Lieut.-Governor, and the Lieut.-Governorship was altered to a Governorship in 1921. In 1935 the name was shortened to 'United Provinces'. On independence, the states of Rampur, Banaras and Tehri-Garwhal were merged with United Provinces. In 1950 the name of the United Provinces was changed to Uttar Pradesh. In 2000 the new state of Uttaranchal was carved from the northern, mainly mountainous, region of Uttar Pradesh.

TERRITORY AND POPULATION

Uttar Pradesh is in north India and is bounded north by the new state of Uttaranchal and Nepal, east by Bihar and Jharkhand, south by Madhya Pradesh and Chhattisgarh and west by Rajasthan, Haryana and Delhi. After the formation of Uttaranchal the area of Uttar Pradesh is 240,928 sq. km (previously 294,411 sq. km). Population (2001 census), 166,052,859; density, 689 per sq. km. Despite the decline in the population caused by the creation of Uttaranchal, Uttar Pradesh still has the highest population of any of the Indian states. If Uttar Pradesh were a separate country it would have the sixth highest population (after China, India, USA, Indonesia and Brazil). Cities with more than 250,000 population, *see* INDIA: Territory and Population. Other important towns (2001 census): Farrukhabad (242,558), Hapur (211,987), Etawah (211,460), Maunath Bhanjan (210,071), Faizabad (208,164), Mirzapur (205,264), Sambhal (182,930), Bulandshahr (176,256), Rae Bareli (169,285), Bahraich (168,376), Amroha (164,890), Jaunpur (159,996), Sitapur (151,827), Fatehpur (151,757), Budaun (148,138), Unnao (144,917), Modinagar (139,642), Orai (139,444), Banda (139,387), Hathras (126,352), Pilibhit (124,082), Gonda (122,164), Lakhimpur (120,566), Mughal Sarai (116,246), Hardoi (112,474), Lalitpur (111,810), Etah (107,098), Basti (106,985), Azamgarh (104,943), Deoria (104,222), Chandausi (103,757), Ghazipur (103,283), Ballia (102,226), Mainpuri (102,007), Sultanpur (100,085). The sole official language has been Hindi since April 1990.

SOCIAL STATISTICS

Growth rate 1991–2001, 25·85%.

CONSTITUTION AND GOVERNMENT

Uttar Pradesh has had an autonomous system of government since 1937. There is a bicameral legislature. The Legislative Council has 108 members; the Legislative Assembly has 404.

There are 17 administrative divisions, each under a Commissioner, and 70 districts.

The capital is Lucknow.

RECENT ELECTIONS

Elections were held in Feb. 2002. The Samajwadi Party (SP) won 145 seats; the Bharatiya Janata Party (BJP), 107; the Bahujan Samaj Party (BSP), 98; the Indian National Congress (INC), 25; ind. and others, 26.

CURRENT ADMINISTRATION

Governor: Tanjavelu Rajeshwar; b. 1926 (took office on 8 July 2004).

Chief Minister: Mulayam Singh Yadav; b. 1939 (took office on 29 Aug. 2003).

ECONOMY

Budget

Budget estimates for 2004–05 showed revenue receipts of Rs 372,590m.; expenditure, Rs 427,860m.

ENERGY AND NATURAL RESOURCES

Electricity

Installed capacity in Jan. 2005 was 8,102·6 MW, of which 829·6 MW were hydro-electric, 7,135·0 MW thermal and 138·0 MW nuclear. In March 2004 there were 57,115 villages with electricity out of a total of 97,942.

Minerals

The state's minerals include magnesite, granite, dolomite, coal, marble, limestone, bauxite, uranium and silica sand. In 2003–04, 15·8m. tonnes of coal were produced.

Agriculture

In 2003–04 Uttar Pradesh had almost 19·2m. ha. of land under foodgrain cultivation. It is India's largest producer of foodgrains: production (2002–03), 38·3m. tonnes (wheat, 23·7m. tonnes; rice, 9·6m. tonnes). The state is also one of India's main producers of sugar and potatoes: 2002–03 production of sugarcane, 120·9m. tonnes; and potatoes, 10·2m. tonnes.

Forestry

Forests covered 16,887 sq. km in 2002, 11,078 sq. km of which were reserved and 2,425 sq. km protected. In 1995 forests had accounted for 51,663 sq. km, but much of this area is now in the new state of Uttaranchal.

INDUSTRY

Sugar production is important; other industries include cement, vegetable oils, textiles, cotton yarn, jute and glassware. In 2000–01 there were 9,635 factories employing 401,676 workers.

COMMUNICATIONS

Roads

Total length of roads in 1999, 284,765 km, of which 163,908 km were surfaced. In March 2003 vehicles registered totalled 5,928,395, of which 4,488,426 were two-wheelers.

Rail

Lucknow is the main junction of the northern network; other important junctions are Agra, Kanpur, Allahabad, Mughal Sarai and Varanasi. Route-km in 1995–96, 8,934 km.

Civil Aviation

The main airports are at Lucknow, Kanpur, Varanasi, Allahabad, Agra and Gorakhpur.

SOCIAL INSTITUTIONS

Justice

The High Court of Judicature at Allahabad (with a bench at Lucknow) has a Chief Justice and 63 puisne judges including additional judges. The state is divided into 46 judicial districts.

Education

At the 2001 census 75·77m. people were literate (56·3%; 68·8% of men and 42·2% of women). In 2002–03 there were 98,220 primary schools with 15·60m. students, 23,696 middle schools with 5·54m. students and 11,524 higher secondary schools with 3·87m. students.

Universities: Allahabad University (founded 1887); the Banaras Hindu University, Varanasi (1916); Aligarh Muslim University (1920); Lucknow University (1921); Agra University (1927); Roorkee University (1949), formerly Thomason College of Civil Engineering (established in 1847); Gorakhpur University (1957); Sampurnanand Sanskrit Vishwavidyalaya, Varanasi (1958); Ch. Charan Singh University (1966); Kanpur University (1966); H. N. Bahuguna Garhwal University, Srinagar (1973); Bundelkhand University, Jhansi (1975); C. S. Azad University of Agriculture and Technology, Kanpur (1975); Dr Ram Manohar Lohia Awadh, Faizabad (1975); Narendra Deva University of Agriculture and Technology, Faizabad (1975); Rohilkhand University, Bareilly (1975); Purvanchal University, Jaunpur (1987).

In 2005 there were also four institutions with university status: Indian Veterinary Research Institute; Central Institute of Higher Tibetan Studies; Sanjai Gandhi Post Graduate Institute of Medical Sciences; and Dayal Bagh Educational Institute. There were 42 medical colleges, 42 veterinary colleges, 24 engineering colleges, eight agricultural colleges, two law colleges, five teacher training colleges, 635 arts, science and commerce colleges, and 491 oriental learning colleges in 2000–01.

Health

In 2003 there were 4,236 allopathic, 2,210 Ayurvedic and Unani and 1,342 homoeopathic hospitals and dispensaries. There were 3,808 primary health centres, 20,153 sub-centres and 310 community health centres in 2001. In Dec. 2003 there were 44,927 doctors registered with the state medical council.

RELIGION

At the 2001 census Hindus numbered 133,979,263; Muslims, 30,740,158; Sikhs, 678,059; Buddhists, 302,031; Christians, 212,478; Jains, 207,111.

FURTHER READING

Hasan, Z., *Quest for Power: Oppositional Movements and Post-Congress Politics in Uttar Pradesh*. OUP, 1998

Lieten, G. K. and Srivastava, R., *Unequal Partners: Power Relations, Devolution and Development in Uttar Pradesh*. Sage Publications, New Delhi, 1999

Misra, S., *A Narrative of Communal Politics, Uttar Pradesh, 1937–39*. Sage Publications, New Delhi, 2001

Uttaranchal

KEY HISTORICAL EVENTS

The state was carved from Uttar Pradesh and became the twenty-seventh state of India on 9 Nov. 2000. It is located in the hilly and mountainous region of the northern border of the Indian subcontinent. The regions of Kumaon and Garhwal contained in the new state were referred to as Uttarakhand in ancient Hindu scriptures. The Chinese suppression of revolt in Tibet in 1959 saw a rapid influx of Tibetan exiles to the region and the Indo-Chinese conflict of 1962 persuaded the Indian government to initiate a modernization programme throughout the Indian Himalayas that resulted in the development of roads and communication networks in the previously backward region. From the 1970s the hill people began to agitate for their districts to be separated from Uttar Pradesh, which had been established in 1950. On 1 Aug. 2000 the Uttar Pradesh Reorganisation bill was passed, allowing for a separate state, called Uttaranchal, to incorporate 12 hill districts and, controversially, the lowland area of Udham Singh Nagar.

TERRITORY AND POPULATION

Uttaranchal is located in northern India and is bounded in the northeast by China and in the east by Nepal. The state of Uttar Pradesh is to the southwest, Haryana to the west and Himachal Pradesh to the northwest. Uttaranchal has an area of 53,483 sq. km. Population (2001 census), 8,479,562; density, 159 per sq. km. The principal languages are the Hindi dialects of Garhwali and Kumaoni. Cities with over 250,000 population, *see* INDIA: Territory and Population. Other large cities (2001 census): Hardwar (220,433), Haldwani (159,020), Roorkee (114,811).

SOCIAL STATISTICS

Growth rate 1991–2001, 19·20%.

CONSTITUTION AND GOVERNMENT

Uttaranchal is the twenty-seventh state of India. After the region was carved from Uttar Pradesh it was decided that the 22 members of the Legislative Assembly from Uttaranchali districts would become the members of the new state's Legislative Assembly. Subsequently this was increased to 30 when the provisional assembly was established, and to 70 as a result of the elections to the Legislative Assembly of Feb. 2002. For administrative purposes the region is divided into 13 districts.

The interim capital and seat of government is at Dehra Dun.

RECENT ELECTIONS

On the formation of the new state the Bharatiya Janata Party (BJP) was the single largest party with 17 seats, enabling them to form a majority administration in the 23-seat assembly with Nityanand Swamy becoming the state's first chief minister.

State assembly elections were held in Feb. 2002. The Indian National Congress party (INC) won 36 seats; the Bharatiya Janata Party (BJP), 19; the Bahujan Samaj Party (BSP), 7; the Uttarakhand Kranti Dal (UKKD), 4; the Nationalist Congress Party (NCP), 1; ind. and others, 3.

CURRENT ADMINISTRATION

Governor: Sudarshan Agarwal; b. 1931 (took office on 8 Jan. 2003).

Chief Minister: Narain Dutt Tiwari; b. 1925 (took office on 2 March 2002).

ENERGY AND NATURAL RESOURCES

Electricity
The state has a potential hydro-electric capacity of 40,000 MW. Government figures claim that more than 75% of the state's 17,000 villages have electricity.

Water
Uttaranchal suffers from an acute shortage of water for drinking and irrigation. Only 10% of the water potential is currently utilized.

Minerals
There are deposits of limestone, gypsum, iron ore, graphite and copper.

Agriculture
Agriculture is the occupation for approximately 50% of the population. Subsistence farming is the norm, as only 9% of the land in the state is cultivable.

Forestry
Approximately 65%–70% of the state's area is covered in forest.

INDUSTRY

Tourism is by far the most important industry. The state can offer ski resorts, adventure tourism, mountaineering, hiking and several areas of religious interest. Other industries include: horticulture, floriculture, fruit-processing and medicine production. In the Terai region there are around 350 industrial units and 130 in the Doon Valley.

COMMUNICATIONS

Roads
There are 23 km of roads for every 100 sq. km of land in the state. State highways link Uttaranchal to the neighbouring states of Himachal Pradesh, Haryana and Uttar Pradesh. The state remains very inaccessible in parts.

Rail
Four main railway lines in the south of the state link several districts to Uttar Pradesh and Himachal Pradesh. Railways along the foothills connect Dehra Dun, Hardwar, Rishikesh, Roorkee, Kotdwaar, Ram Nagar, Kathgodam and Tanakpur. The rest of the state is not connected to the rail network.

Civil Aviation
There are airports at Dehra Dun and Udham Singh Nagar.

SOCIAL INSTITUTIONS

Education
In 2001, 77·28% of the population were literate (84·01% of men and 60·26% of women).

West Bengal

KEY HISTORICAL EVENTS

Bengal was under the overlordship of the Moghul emperor and ruled by a Moghul governor (*nawab*) who declared himself independent in 1740. The British East India Company based at Calcutta was in conflict with the *nawab* from 1756 until 1757 when British forces defeated him at Plassey and installed their own *nawab* in 1760. The French were also in Bengal; the British captured their trading settlement at Chandernagore in 1757 and in 1794, restoring it to France in 1815.

The area of British Bengal included modern Orissa and Bihar, Bangladesh and (until 1833) Uttar Pradesh. Calcutta was the capital of British India from 1772 until 1912.

The first division into East and West took place in 1905–11 and was not popular. However, at Partition in 1947 the East (Muslim) chose to join what was then East Pakistan (now Bangladesh), leaving West Bengal as an Indian frontier state and promoting a steady flow of non-Muslim Bengali immigrants from the East. In 1950 West Bengal received the former princely state of Cooch Behar and, in 1954, Chandernagore. Small areas were transferred from Bihar in 1956.

TERRITORY AND POPULATION

West Bengal is in northeast India and is bounded north by Sikkim and Bhutan, east by Assam and Bangladesh, south by the Bay of Bengal, southwest by Orissa, west by Jharkhand and Bihar and northwest by Nepal. The total area of West Bengal is 88,752 sq. km. Population (2001 census), 80,221,171; density, 904 per sq. km. The capital is Calcutta (Kolkata). Population of chief cities, *see* INDIA: Territory and Population. Other major towns (2001): Habra, 239,170; Ingraj Bazar (English Bazar), 224,392; Raiganj, 175,064; Haldia, 170,695; Baharampur, 170,343; Medinipur, 153,349; Krishnanagar, 148,645; Ranaghat, 145,172; Balurghat, 143,095; Santipur, 138,195; Bankura, 128,811; Navadvip, 125,346; Khardaha, 116,252; Birnagar, 115,104; Alipur Duar, 114,069; Puruliya, 113,766; Basirhat, 113,120; Darjiling (Darjeeling), 109,163; Cooch Behar, 102,922; Bangaon, 102,115; Chakdaha, 101,278; Jalpaiguri, 100,212.

The principal language is Bengali.

SOCIAL STATISTICS

Growth rate 1991–2001, 17·84%.

CONSTITUTION AND GOVERNMENT

The state of West Bengal came into existence as a result of the Indian Independence Act, 1947. The territory of Cooch Behar State was merged with West Bengal on 1 Jan. 1950, and the former French possession of Chandernagore became part of the state on 2 Oct. 1954. Under the States Reorganization Act, 1956, certain portions of Bihar State (an area of 3,157 sq. miles with a population of 1,446,385) were transferred to West Bengal.

The Legislative Assembly has 295 seats (294 elected and one nominated).

For administrative purposes there are three divisions (Jalpaiguri, Burdwan and Presidency), under which there are 18 districts, including Calcutta. The Calcutta Metropolitan Development Authority has been set up to co-ordinate development in the metropolitan area (1,350 sq. km). For the purposes of local self-government there are 16 *zilla parishads* (district boards) excluding Darjeeling, 328 *panchayat samities* (regional boards), one *siliguri mahakuma parishad* and 3,247 *gram* (village) *panchayats*. There are 113 municipalities, six Corporations and 11 Notified Areas. The Calcutta Municipal Corporation is headed by a mayor in council.

RECENT ELECTIONS

In elections held on 10 May 2001, 143 seats went to the Communist Party of India (Marxist), 60 went to the All India Trinamool Congress, 26 to the Indian National Congress, 25 to the All India Forward Bloc and 17 to the Revolutionary Socialist Party. In winning the election the Communists retained power for a sixth consecutive term.

CURRENT ADMINISTRATION

Governor: Gopalkrishna Gandhi; b. 1945 (took office on 14 Dec. 2004).

Chief Minister: Buddhadeb Bhattacharjee; b. 1944 (since 6 Nov. 2000).

ECONOMY

Budget

2003–04 revenue receipts, Rs 174,045m.; expenditure, Rs 267,800·7m. Budget estimates for 2004–05: revenue receipts, Rs 204,981·3m.; expenditure, Rs 277,984·4m.

ENERGY AND NATURAL RESOURCES

Electricity

Installed capacity as at Jan. 2005 was 6,761·8 MW, of which 261 MW were hydro-electric, 6,499 MW thermal and 2·2 MW wind powered. In March 2003, 31,367 (82·7%) villages were supplied with electricity.

Water

The largest irrigation and power scheme under construction is the Teesta Barrage (irrigation potential, 533,520 ha.). Other major irrigation schemes are the Mayurakshi Reservoir, Kangsabati Reservoir, Mahananda Barrage and Aqueduct and Damodar Valley.

In 2000–01, 1·4m. ha. of land were under irrigation from tubewells and other wells, 434,000 ha. from canals and 523,000 ha. from other sources.

Minerals

Value of production, 2002–03, Rs 23,933m.

The state has coal (the Raniganj field is one of the three biggest in India) including coking coal. Coal production (2002–03), 20·48m. tonnes.

Agriculture

About 5·84m. ha. were under rice-paddy in 2002–03. Total foodgrain production, 2002–03, 15·52m. tonnes (rice 14·39m. tonnes, wheat 887,000 tonnes, pulses 167,000 tonnes). Other principal crops (2002–03): potatoes, 6·9m. tonnes; sugarcane, 1·28m. tonnes; oilseeds, 476,000 tonnes; jute, 8·5m. bales of 180 kg (76·3% of the national output). The state produces around 200,000 tonnes of tea each year.

Livestock (2000–01): 18,274,000 cattle; 1,008,000 buffaloes; 1,451,000 sheep; 17,225,000 goats; and 50,470,000 poultry.

Forestry

Forests covered 11,879 sq. km in 2000, 7,054 sq. km of which were reserved and 3,772 sq. km protected.

Fisheries

Landings, 1997–98, 950,000 tonnes, of which inland 786,000 tonnes.

During 1997–98 a total of Rs 318·6m. was invested in fishery schemes. West Bengal is the largest inland fish producer in the country.

INDUSTRY

There were 6,195 factories in 2001–02 employing 432,930 workers. There were 99 coal-mines in 2002–03.

There is a large automobile factory at Uttarpara, and an aluminium rolling-mill at Belur. There is a steel plant at Burnpur (Asansol) and a spun pipe factory at Kulti. Durgapur has a large steel plant and other industries under the state sector—a thermal power plant, coke oven plant, fertilizer factory, alloy steel plant and ophthalmic glass plant. There is a locomotive factory at Chittaranjan and a cable factory at Rupnarayanpur. A refinery and fertilizer factory are operating at Haldia. Other industries include chemicals, engineering goods, electronics, textiles, automobile tyres, paper, cigarettes, distillery, aluminium foil, tea, pharmaceuticals, carbon black, graphite, iron foundry, silk and explosives.

Small industries are important; 490,158 units were registered at 31 March 1998, employing 3m. persons.

The silk industry is also important; 667,000 persons were employed in the handloom industry in the organized sector in 1997–98.

COMMUNICATIONS

Roads

Total length of roads in 1999: 79,255 km, of which 44,970 km were surfaced.

As at end-March 2002 there were 1,689,805 registered vehicles, including 366,043 cars, 41,298 taxis, 22,336 buses, 189,568 goods vehicles and 1,036,009 two-wheelers.

Rail

The route-km of railways within the state was 3,784·96 km in 1997–98. The main centres are Asansol, New Jalpaiguri and Kharagpur. There is a metro in Calcutta (16·4 km).

Civil Aviation

The main airport is Calcutta, which has national and international flights. In 2001 it handled 2,549,965 passengers (1,990,746 on domestic flights) and 55,089 tonnes of freight. The second airport is at Bagdogra in the extreme north, which has regular scheduled services to Calcutta and Delhi.

Shipping

Calcutta is the chief port: a barrage has been built at Farakka to control the flow of the Ganges and to provide a rail and road link between North and South Bengal. A second port has been developed at Haldia, between the present port and the sea, which is intended mainly for bulk cargoes. West Bengal has about 800 km of navigable canals.

SOCIAL INSTITUTIONS

Justice

The High Court of Judicature at Calcutta has a Chief Justice and 45 puisne judges. The Andaman and Nicobar Islands come under its jurisdiction.

Police

In 2001 the police force numbered 83,466, under a director-general and an inspector-general. Calcutta has a separate force under a commissioner directly responsible to the government; its strength was about 26,000 in 2002.

Education

In 2001, 69·22% of the total population were literate (men, 77·58%; women, 60·22%). There were 52,426 primary schools, 2,883 junior high schools and 9,620 high and higher secondary schools in 2001 with (1998–99) 1,881,226 students. Education is free up to higher secondary stage.

In 2001 there were nine universities: the University of Calcutta (founded 1857); University of Jadavpur, Calcutta (1955); Burdwan University (1960); Kalyani University (1960); University of North Bengal (1962); Rabindra Bharati University (1962); Vidyasagar University, Medinipur (1981); Bengal Engineering College (deemed to have university status from 1992); Netaji Subhas Open University. The enrolment of students in universities for 2001 totalled 37,461. There were 36 government degree colleges and institutes in 2001 and 370 non-government colleges and institutes; enrolment of students, 550,989.

Health

As at 1 Jan. 2002 there were 411 hospitals with 55,279 beds. There were 1,262 primary health centres, 8,126 sub-centres and 99 community health centres in 2001.

RELIGION

At the 2001 census Hindus numbered 58,104,835; Muslims, 20,240,543; Christians, 515,160; Buddhists, 243,364; Sikhs, 66,391; Jains, 55,223.

FURTHER READING

Chatterjee, P., *The Present History of West Bengal: Essays in Political Criticism*. OUP, 1997

UNION TERRITORIES

Andaman and Nicobar Islands

The Andaman and Nicobar Islands are administered by the President of the Republic of India acting through a Lieut.-Governor. There is a 30-member Pradesh Council, five members of which are selected by the Administrator as advisory counsellors.

The seat of administration is at Port Blair, which is connected with Calcutta (1,255 km away) and Madras (1,190 km) by steamer service which calls about every ten days; there are air services from Calcutta and Madras. Roads in the islands, 733 km black-topped and 48 km others. There are two districts.

The population (2001 census) was 356,265. The area is 8,249 sq. km and the density 43 per sq. km. There are 457 villages and one town. Growth rate 1991–2001, 26·94%. Port Blair (2001), 100,186.

The climate is tropical, with little variation in temperature. Heavy rain (125″ annually) is mainly brought by the southwest monsoon. Humidity is high. The islands were severely affected by the tsunami of 26 Dec. 2004.

Budget figures for 2002–03 show total revenue receipts of Rs 885m., and total expenditure on revenue account of Rs 3,850m.

There is installed capacity of 38,805 KW. 479 villages have electricity.

In 2001, 26,524 ha. were under cultivation, of which 10,885 ha. were under rice. 48,167 tonnes of rice were grown. There were 70,923 goats, 60,180 cattle and 42,836 pigs in 2001.

In 2002, 25,561 tonnes of fish were landed. There were 1,966 registered fishing boats in 2002 and 2,721 fishermen.

There are 7,171 sq. km of forests, of which 4,242 sq. km are protected. In 2002, 4,712 cu. metres of sawn timber were extracted.

There are 1,502 km of paved roads and 45 km of other roads.

In 2003 there were 48 factories and 1,479 small-scale industrial units, employing 5,032 people.

In 2001 there were 207 primary schools with 43,000 students, 56 middle schools with 23,000 students, 45 high schools with 11,000 students and 48 higher secondary schools with 4,000 students. There is a teachers' training college, two polytechnics and two colleges. Literacy (2001 census), 81·18% (86·07% of men and 75·29% of women).

In 2003 there were three hospitals, 28 health centres and 107 primary health sub-centres.

Lieut.-Governor: Ram Kapse; b. 1933 (sworn in 5 Jan. 2004).

The **Andaman Islands** lie in the Bay of Bengal, 193 km from Cape Negrais in Myanmar, 1,255 from Calcutta and 1,190 from Madras. Five large islands grouped together are called the Great Andamans, and to the south is the island of Little Andaman. There are some 239 islets and a total of 572 islands, islets and rocks, the two principal groups being the Ritchie Archipelago and the Labyrinth Islands. The Great Andaman group is about 467 km long and, at the widest, 51 km broad.

The original inhabitants live in the forests by hunting and fishing. The total population of the Andaman Islands (including about 430 aboriginals) was 240,089 in 1991. Main aboriginal tribes: Andamanese, Onges, Jarawas and Sentinelese.

The Great Andaman group, densely wooded (forests covered 7,615 sq. km in 1995), contains hardwood and softwood and supplies the match and plywood industries. Annually the

Forest Department export about 25,000 tonnes of timber to the mainland. Coconut, coffee and rubber are cultivated. The islands are slowly being made self-sufficient in paddy and rice, and now grow approximately half their annual requirements. Livestock (1982): 27,400 cattle, 9,720 buffaloes, 17,600 goats and 21,220 pigs. Fishing is important. There is a sawmill at Port Blair and a coconut-oil mill. Little Andaman has a palm-oil mill.

The islands possess a number of harbours and safe anchorages, notably Port Blair in the south, Port Cornwallis in the north and Elphinstone and Mayabandar in the middle.

The **Nicobar Islands** are situated to the south of the Andamans, 121 km from Little Andaman. The Danes were in possession 1756–1869, and then the British until 1947. There are 19 islands, seven uninhabited; total area, 1,841 sq. km. The islands are usually divided into three sub-groups (southern, central and northern), the chief islands in each being respectively Great Nicobar, Camotra with Nancowrie and Car Nicobar. There is a harbour between the islands of Camotra and Nancowrie, Nancowrie Harbour.

The population numbered, in 1991, 39,208, including about 22,200 of Nicobarese and Shompen tribes. The coconut and areca nut are the main items of trade, and coconuts are a major item in the people's diet.

Chandigarh

On 1 Nov. 1966 the city of Chandigarh and the area surrounding it was constituted a Union Territory. Population (2001), 900,914; density, 7,903 per sq. km; growth rate 1991–2001, 40·33%. Area, 114 sq. km. It serves as the joint capital of both Punjab (India) and the state of Haryana, and is the seat of a High Court. The city, which had a population of 808,796 inhabitants at the 2001 census, will ultimately be the capital of just the Punjab; joint status is to last while a new capital is built for Haryana.

Budget for 2000–01 showed revenue of Rs 4,730m. and expenditure of Rs 6,327m.

There is some cultivated land and some forest (27·5% of the territory).

In 2001 there were 280 factories, of which 15 were large and medium scale factories and about 2,100 small scale industries, employing 24,000 people.

In 1996–97 there were 44 primary schools (60,012 students), 33 middle schools (34,095 students), 50 high schools (18,510 students) and 47 higher secondary schools (16,710 students). There were also two engineering and technology colleges, 12 arts, science and commerce colleges, two polytechnic institutes and a university (Panjab University). Other institutes have university status: Chandigarh College of Architecture; the Chandigarh Government College of Art; Chandigarh Institute of Postgraduate Medicinal Education and Research; Punjab Engineering College.

In 2001, 81·76% of the population were literate (85·65% of men and 78·65% of women).

In 2000 there were 43 dispensaries, 16 general hospitals and 72 private hospitals with a total of 2,530 beds.

Administrator: Gen. S. F. Rodrigues; b. 1933 (took office as Governor of Punjab on 16 Nov. 2004).

Dadra and Nagar Haveli

GENERAL DETAILS

Formerly Portuguese, the territories of Dadra and Nagar Haveli were occupied in July 1954 by nationalists, and a pro-India administration was formed; this body made a request for incorporation into the Union on 1 June 1961. By the 10th amendment to the constitution the territories became a centrally administered Union Territory with effect from 11 Aug. 1961, forming an enclave at the southernmost point of the border between Gujarat and Maharashtra, approximately 30 km from the west coast. Area 491 sq. km; population (census 2001), 220,451; density 449 per sq. km; growth rate 1991–2001, 59·20%. There is an Administrator appointed by the government of India. The day-to-day business is done by various departments, co-ordinated by the Secretaries, Assistant Secretary, Collector and Resident Deputy Collector. The capital is Silvassa, which had a population of 21,890 at the 2001 census.

78·82% of the population is tribal and organized in 140 villages.

Languages used are dialects classified under Bhilodi (91·1%), Bhilli, Gujarati, Marathi and Hindi.

CURRENT ADMINISTRATION

Administrator: O. P. Kelkar (since 19 July 1999).

ECONOMY

Budget

The budget for 2001–02 shows revenue receipts of Rs 1,178·3m. and revenue expenditure of Rs 507 was Rs 1,212·2m.; budget estimate was Rs 552·8m. under Plan Sector and Rs 3,688·4m. under Non-Plan Sector.

ENERGY AND NATURAL RESOURCES

Electricity

Electricity is supplied from Central Grid, and all villages have been electrified. A major sub-station at Kharadpada village has been completed.

Water

As a result of a joint project with the governments of Gujarat, Goa and Daman and Diu there is a reservoir at Damanganga with irrigation potential of 5,900 ha. Drinking water is made available through wells and piped water supply schemes.

Minerals

There are few natural mineral resources although there is some ordinary sand and quarry stone.

Agriculture

Farming is the chief occupation, and 22,352 ha. were under net crop in 2001–02. Much of the land is terraced and there is a 100% subsidy for soil conservation. The major food crops are rice and ragi; wheat, small millets and pulses are also grown. There is a coverage of lift irrigation over 6,736 ha. There are nine veterinary aid centres, a veterinary hospital, an agricultural research centre and breeding centres to improve strains of cattle and poultry. During 2001–02 the administration distributed 152 tonnes of high-yielding paddy and wheat seed and 1,574 tonnes of manures and fertilizers.

Forestry

20,359 ha. or 40·8% of the total area is forest, mainly of teak, sadad and khair. In 1985 a moratorium was imposed on commercial felling to preserve the environmental function of the forests and ensure local supplies of firewood, timber and fodder. The tribals have been given exclusive right to collect minor forest produce from the reserved forest area for domestic use. 92 sq. km of reserved forest was declared a wildlife sanctuary in 2000.

Fisheries

There is some inland fishing in water reservoir project areas and individual ponds. During 2001–02 the total catch was 55 tonnes.

INDUSTRY

There is no heavy industry, and the Territory is a 'No Polluting Industry District'. Industrial estates for small and medium scales have been set up at Pipariya, Masat and Khadoli. In March 2002 there were 1,317 small scale and 383 medium scale units employing 37,297 people.

Labour

The Labour Enforcement Office ensures the application of the Monitoring of Minimum Wages Act (1948), the Industrial Disputes Act (1947), the Contract Labour (Regulation and Abolition) Act (1970) and the Workmen's Compensation Act (1923). During 2001–02, 81 cases under the Industrial Disputes Act were settled. Under the Contract Labour (Regulation and Abolition) Act (1970), 53 certificates of registration and 56 licences were issued to the industrial establishment. 19 cases under the Workman's Compensation Act (1923) were settled.

Trade Unions

There is one trade union registered under the Trade Union Act.

COMMUNICATIONS

Roads

In 2002 there were 580 km of road of which 545·45 km were surfaced. Out of 72 villages, 68 are connected by all-weather road. There were 27,300 motor vehicles in 2001–02. The National Highway no. 8 passes through Vapi, 18 km from Silvassa.

Rail

Although there are no railways in the territory the line from Bombay to Ahmedabad runs through Vapi, 18 km from Silvassa.

Civil Aviation

The nearest airport is at Bombay, 180 km from Silvassa.

Telecommunications

There are six telephone exchanges, one telex exchange and one wireless station. The Telephone Department has provided over 6,000 telephone connections.

Postal Services

There is currently one post and telegraph office with three sub-post offices and 41 branch post offices covering 66 villages.

SOCIAL INSTITUTIONS

Justice

The territory is under the jurisdiction of the Bombay (Maharashtra) High Court. There is a District and Sessions Court and one Junior Division Civil Court at Silvassa.

Education

Literacy was 60·03% of the population at the 2001 census (73·32% of men and 42·99% of women). In 2001–02 there were 195 primary and middle schools (35,637 students) and 17 high and higher secondary schools (8,887 students).

Health

The territory had (2001–02) a civil hospital, 6 primary health centres, 36 sub-centres, three dispensaries and a mobile dispensary. A Community Health Centre has been established at Khanvel, 20 km from Silvassa. The Pulse Polio Immunisation programme was organized in 1999 and 54,128 polio doses were provided to children below five years of age. There has been a sharp fall in the incidence of malaria, especially cerebral malaria, owing to the sustained efforts of the administration. Hepatitis B vaccination of all inmates in the social welfare hostels was completed with the co-operation of voluntary organizations. A blood testing centre has been established for HIV testing.

Welfare

The Social Welfare Department implements the welfare schemes for poor Scheduled castes, Scheduled tribes, women and physically disabled persons, etc.

RELIGION

Numbers of religious followers (2001 census): Hindu, 95% of the population; Muslims, 2·5%; Christians, 1·5%.

CULTURE

Broadcasting

There is a low power Government of India TV transmission centre.

Press

One weekly newspaper and two fortnightly news magazines are published.

Tourism

The territory is a rural area between the industrial centres of Bombay and Surat-Vapi. The Tourism Department is developing areas of natural beauty to promote eco-friendly tourism. Several gardens and the Madhuban Dam are among the tourist sites. A lion safari park has been set up at Vasona over 20 ha. About 380,000 visitors came to Dadra and Nagar Haveli during 2000. The government completed a tourist accommodation complex at Silvassa in 1999.

Daman and Diu

GENERAL DETAILS

Daman (Damão) on the Gujarat coast, 100 miles (160 km) north of Bombay, was seized by the Portuguese in 1531 and ceded to them (1539) by the Shar of Gujarat. The island of Diu, captured in 1534, lies off the southeast coast of Kathiawar (Gujarat); there is a small coastal area. Former Portuguese forts on either side of the entrance to the Gulf of Cambay, in Dec. 1961 the territories were occupied by India and incorporated into the Indian Union; they were administered as one unit together with Goa, to which they were attached until 30 May 1987, when Goa was separated from them and became a state.

TERRITORY AND POPULATION

The territory has an area of 112 sq. km and a population of 158,059 at the 2001 census. Density, 1,411 sq. km. Daman has an area of 72 sq. km, population (2001) 113,949; Diu, 40 sq. km, population 44,110. Daman is the capital of the territory. The main language spoken is Gujarati.

The chief towns are (with 2001 populations) Daman (35,743) and Diu (21,576).

Daman and Diu have been governed as parts of a Union Territory since Dec. 1961, becoming the whole of that Territory on 30 May 1987. There are two districts.

The main activities are tourism, fishing and tapping the toddy palm (preparing palm tree sap for consumption). In Daman there is rice-growing, some wheat and dairying. Diu has fine tourist beaches, grows coconuts and pearl millet, and processes salt.

SOCIAL STATISTICS

Growth rate 1991–2001, 55·59%.

CURRENT ADMINISTRATION

Administrator: O. P. Kelkar (since 19 July 1999).

ECONOMY

Fishing is the main economic activity. Tourism is developing.

Budget

The budget for 2000–01 shows revenue receipts of Rs 713·0m. and revenue expenditure of Rs 553·5m.

SOCIAL INSTITUTIONS

Education

In 2001, 81·09% of the population were literate (88·40% of men and 70·37% of women). In 1996–97 there were 53 primary schools with 14,531 students, 20 middle schools with 6,834 students, 20 high schools with 3,220 students and 3 higher secondary schools with 1,202 students. There is a degree college and a polytechnic.

Delhi

GENERAL DETAILS

Delhi became a Union Territory on 1 Nov. 1956 and was designated the National Capital Territory in 1995.

TERRITORY AND POPULATION

The territory forms an enclave near the eastern frontier of Haryana and the western frontier of Uttar Pradesh in north India. Delhi has an area of 1,483 sq. km. Its population (2001 census) is 13,782,976 (density per sq. km, 9,294). Growth rate 1991–2001, 46·31%. In the rural area of Delhi there are 231 villages and 27 census towns. They are distributed in five community development blocks.

CONSTITUTION AND GOVERNMENT

The Lieut.-Governor is the Administrator. Under the New Delhi Municipal Act 1994 New Delhi Municipal Council is nominated by central government and replaces the former New Delhi Municipal Committee.

RECENT ELECTIONS

Elections for the 70-member Legislative Assembly were held in Dec. 2003; the Congress Party formed the government. The Indian National Congress won 47 seats (52 in 1998); Bharatiya Janata Party, 15 (20 in 1998); others, 3.

CURRENT ADMINISTRATION

Lieut.-Governor: B. L. Joshi (took office 9 June 2004).
   Chief Minister: Sheila Dikshit (took office on 3 Dec. 1998).

ECONOMY

Budget

Estimates for 2003–04 show revenue receipts of Rs 98,000m. and expenditure of Rs 98,000m.

ENERGY AND NATURAL RESOURCES

Minerals

The Union Territory has deposits of kaolin (chine clay), quartzite and fire clay.

Agriculture

The contribution to the economy is not significant. In 2003–04 about 41,500 ha. were cropped (of which 22,700 ha. were irrigated). Animal husbandry is increasing and mixed farms are common. Chief crops are wheat, bajra, paddy, sugarcane, gram, jowar and vegetables. Buffaloes are kept as a source of milk; pigs and goats are kept for meat.

INDUSTRY

The modern city is the largest commercial centre in northern India and an important industrial centre. Since 1947 a large number of industrial units have been established; these include factories for the manufacture of razor blades, sports goods, electronic goods, bicycles and parts, plastic and PVC goods including footwear, textiles, chemicals, fertilizers, medicines, hosiery, leather goods, soft drinks and hand tools. The largest single industry is the manufacture of garments. There are also metal forging, casting, galvanizing, electro-plating and printing enterprises. The number of industrial units functioning was about 126,000 in 1996–97; average number of workers employed was 1·14m. Production was worth Rs 63,100m. and investment was about Rs 25,240m. in 1996–97.

Some traditional handicrafts, for which Delhi was formerly famous, still flourish; among them are ivory carving, miniature painting, gold and silver jewellery and papier mâché work. The handwoven textiles of Delhi are particularly fine; this craft is being successfully revived.

Delhi is a major market for manufactures, imports and agricultural goods; there are specialist fruit and vegetable, food grain, fodder, cloth, bicycle, hosiery, dry fruit and general markets.

COMMUNICATIONS

Roads

Five national highways pass through the city. There were (2000–01) 3,456,579 registered motor vehicles. There were 41,483 buses in 2000–01.

Rail

Delhi is an important rail junction with three main stations: New Delhi, Delhi Junction and Hazrat Nizamuddin. There is an electric ring railway for commuters (route-km in 1995–96, 214). The first of three lines of the Delhi metro system opened in 2002: when complete it will consist of 34·5 km subway, 35·5 km elevated and 111 km surface running.

Civil Aviation

Indira Gandhi International Airport operates international flights; Palam airport operates internal flights.

SOCIAL INSTITUTIONS

Education

The proportion of literate people to the total population was 81·82% at the 2001 census (87·37% of males and 75·00% of females). In 2003–04 there were 2,126 primary schools with 924,493 students and 22,930 teachers, 681 middle schools with 230,362 students and 9,192 teachers, 1,678 high schools and higher secondary schools with 1,747,884 students and 59,064 teachers. In 1996–97 there were nine engineering and technology colleges, nine medical colleges and 25 polytechnics.

The University of Delhi was founded in 1922; it had 78 affiliated colleges in 2002–03 and 189,332 students in 1994–95. There are also Jawaharlal Nehru University, Indira Gandhi National Open University, the Jamia Millia Islamia University, the Guru Gobind Singh Indraprastha University, Jamia Hamdard University and Shri Lal Bahadur Shastri Rashtriya Sanskrit Vidyapeeth University; the Indian Institute of Technology at Hauz Khas; the Indian Agricultural Research Institute at Pusa; the All India Institute of Medical Science at Ansari Nagar and the Indian Institute of Public Administration are the other important institutions.

Health

In 2001 there were 11 government hospitals plus 71 private hospitals, 167 government dispensaries plus 489 other dispensaries, 73 mobile health clinics and 64 school health clinics.

RELIGION

At the 2001 census Hindus accounted for 82·0% of the population; Muslims, 11·7%; Sikhs, 4·0%; Jains, 1·1%; Christians, 0·9%; Buddhists, 0·2%.

CULTURE

Press

Delhi publishes major daily newspapers, including the *Times of India*, *Hindustan Times*, *The Hindu*, *Indian Express*, *National Herald*, *Patriot*, *Economic Times*, *The Pioneer*, *The Observer of Business and Politics*, *Financial Express*, *Statesman*, *Asian Age* and *Business Standard* (all in English); *Nav Bharat Times*, *Rashtriya Sahara*, *Jansatta* and *Hindustan* (all in Hindi); and three Urdu dailies.

Lakshadweep

The territory consists of an archipelago of 36 islands (ten inhabited), about 300 km off the west coast of Kerala. It was constituted a Union Territory in 1956 as the Laccadive, Minicoy and Amindivi Islands, and renamed in Nov. 1973. The total area of the islands is 32 sq. km. The northern portion is called the Amindivis. The remaining islands are called the Laccadives (except Minicoy Island). The inhabited islands are: Androth (the largest), Amini, Agatti, Bitra, Chetlat, Kadmat, Kalpeni, Kavaratti, Kiltan and Minicoy. Androth is 4·8 sq. km, and is nearest to Kerala. An Advisory Committee associated with the Union Home Minister and an Advisory Council to the Administrator assist in the administration of the islands; these are constituted annually.

Population (2001 census), 60,595, nearly all Muslims. Density, 1,894 per sq. km; growth rate 1991–2001, 17·19%. The language is Malayalam, but the language in Minicoy is Mahl. Budget for 2000–01 showed revenue of Rs 90·3m. and expenditure of Rs 1,370m. Installed electric capacity (1998) 8,120 kW. A solar power plant is under construction at Kadmat and wind generated plants at Kavaratti and Agatti. Guaranteeing supplies of potable water is problematic in most islands. Rain water harvesting schemes have been introduced as well as desalination plants. There are several small factories processing fibre from coconut husks: in 2002 these employed 316 workers. There are two handicraft training centres. The islands have great tourist potential. The major industry is fishing—in 1999 there were 375 registered fishing boats. The principal catches are tuna and shark. Tuna is canned at a factory at Minicoy. There is an experimental pearl culture scheme at the uninhabited island of Bangarem.

In 2001, 87·52% of the population were literate (93·15% of men and 81·56% of women). There were, in 1996–97, nine high schools (2,043 students) and nine nursery schools (1,197 students), 19 junior basic schools (9,015 students), four senior basic schools (4,797 students) and two junior colleges. There are two hospitals and four primary health centres plus 14 health sub-centres. The staple products are copra and fish; coconut is the only major crop. Headquarters of administration, Kavaratti, population 10,113 (2001 census), on Kavaratti Island. An airport, with Vayudoot services, opened on Agatti Island in April 1988. The islands are also served by ship from the mainland and have helicopter inter-island services. There are two catamaran-type high-speed inter-island ferries and four barges. The islands have 253 km of roads, of which 124 km have paved surfaces.

Administrator: K. S. Mehra (took office on 19 June 2001).

Pondicherry

GENERAL DETAILS

Formerly the chief French settlement in India, Pondicherry was founded by the French in 1673, taken by the Dutch in 1693 and restored to the French in 1699. The English took it in 1761, restored it in 1765, re-took it in 1778, restored it a second time in 1785, re-took it a third time in 1793 and finally restored it to the French in 1816. Administration was transferred to India on 1 Nov. 1954. A Treaty of Cession (together with Karaikal, Mahé and Yanam) was signed on 28 May 1956; instruments of ratification were signed on 16 Aug. 1962 from which date (by the 14th amendment to the Indian Constitution) Pondicherry, comprising the four territories, became a Union Territory.

TERRITORY AND POPULATION

The territory is composed of enclaves on the Coromandel Coast of Tamil Nadu and Andhra Pradesh, with Mahé forming two enclaves on the coast of Kerala. The total area of Pondicherry is 480 sq. km, divided into 11 enclaves that are grouped into four Districts. On Tamil Nadu coast: Pondicherry (290 sq. km; population, 2001 census, 735,004), Karaikal (161; 170,640). On Kerala coast: Mahé (9; 36,823). On Andhra Pradesh coast (although the enclave lies back from the shore but at no point does its territory touch the coast): Yanam (20; 31,362). Total population (2001 census), 973,829; density, 2,029 per sq. km. Pondicherry Municipality had (2001) 220,748 inhabitants and the urban agglomeration had 505,715 inhabitants. The principal languages spoken are Tamil, Telugu, Malayalam, French and English.

SOCIAL STATISTICS

Growth rate 1991–2001, 20·56%. In 2001 the birth rate was 17·9 per 1,000 and the infant mortality rate was 23 per 1,000 live births.

CONSTITUTION AND GOVERNMENT

By the government of Union Territories Act 1963 Pondicherry is governed by a Lieut.-Governor, appointed by the President, and a Council of Ministers responsible to a Legislative Assembly.

RECENT ELECTIONS

In the elections of 10 May 2001 the Indian National Congress–Tamil Maanila Congress (Moopanar) gained 13 seats, Dravida Munnetra Kazhagam plus allies 12, All India Anna Dravida Munnetra Kazhagam plus allies 3, and others 2.

CURRENT ADMINISTRATION

Lieut.-Governor: M. M. Lakhera; b. 1937 (sworn in 7 July 2004).

Chief Minister: N. Rangaswamy; b. 1950 (took office on 27 Oct. 2001).

ECONOMY

Budget

Budget estimates for 2000–01 showed expenditure of Rs 8,534·7m. Total expenditure Rs 8,304·2m.

ENERGY AND NATURAL RESOURCES

Electricity

Power is bought from neighbouring states. All 11 towns and 263 villages have electricity. Consumption, 2002–03, 1,629 units per head. Total consumption, 1999–2000, 1,239·7m. units.

Agriculture

Nearly 45% of the population is engaged in agriculture and allied pursuits; 90% of the cultivated area is irrigated. The main food crop is rice. Foodgrain production, 58,785 tonnes in 2003. Rice production, 2003, 57,514 tonnes from 24,142 ha. Principal cash crops are sugarcane (209,496 tonnes in 2003) and groundnuts; minor food crops include cotton, ragi, bajra and pulses.

Fisheries

In 2003 the marine catch was 40,105 tonnes. There was also a prawn catch of 4,310 tonnes.

INDUSTRY

In March 2003 there were 55 large and 139 medium-scale enterprises manufacturing items such as textiles, sugar, cotton yarn, spirits and beer, potassium chlorate, rice bran oil, vehicle parts, soap, amino acids, paper, plastics, steel ingots, washing machines, glass and tin containers and bio polymers. These factories employed 25,095 people. There were also 6,876 small industrial units (2003) engaged in varied manufacturing.

COMMUNICATIONS

Roads

There were (2002–03) 2,498 km of roads of which 2,114 km were surfaced. Motor vehicles (March 2003) 293,248.

Rail

Pondicherry is connected to Villupuram Junction. Route-km in 2001, 38 km.

Civil Aviation

The nearest main airport is Madras.

SOCIAL INSTITUTIONS

Education

In 2001, 81·24% of the population were literate (88·62% of men and 73·90% of women). There were, in 2000–01, 223 pre-primary schools (22,462 pupils), 337 primary schools (38,405), 110 middle schools (34,034), 128 high schools (65,451) and 65 higher secondary schools (76,726). There were (2000–01) eight general education colleges, three medical colleges, a law college, five engineering colleges, an agricultural college and a dental college, and five polytechnics. Pondicherry University had around 1,600 students in 2005.

Health

There were 14 hospitals in 2004 (with 3,064 beds); and 39 primary health centres, 75 sub-centres and four community health centres in 2001.

INDONESIA

Republik Indonesia

Capital: Jakarta
Population projection, 2010: 235·75m.
GDP per capita, 2003: (PPP$) 3,361
HDI/world rank: 0·697/110

KEY HISTORICAL EVENTS

In the 16th century Portuguese traders settled in some of the islands which now comprise Indonesia but were ejected by the British who in turn were ousted by the Dutch in 1595. From 1602 the Netherlands East India Company controlled the area until the dissolution of the Company in 1798. The Netherlands government then ruled the colony from 1816 until 1941 when it was occupied by the Japanese until 1945. On 17 Aug. 1945 nationalist leaders proclaimed an independent republic. On 27 Dec. 1949 the Netherlands conceded unconditional sovereignty.

In 1960 President Sukarno assumed power and dissolved political parties. In their place he set up the National Front and a supreme state body called the Provisional People's Consultative Assembly. On 11–12 March 1966 the military commanders under the leadership of Lieut.-Gen. Suharto took over executive power while leaving President Sukarno as the head of state. The Communist party, which had twice attempted to overthrow the government, was outlawed. On 22 Feb. 1967 Sukarno handed over all his powers to Gen. Suharto.

Re-elected president at five-year intervals, on the final occasion on 10 March 1998, Suharto presided over a booming economy but one which was characterized by corruption and croneyism. The weaknesses became apparent when, in 1997, a failure of economic confidence spread from Japan across Asia. By May 1998 Indonesia had regressed to the verge of civil war. As food prices doubled, then trebled, riots broke out in Jakarta destroying homes and shops. The risk of society fragmenting along ethnic and religious lines was emphasized by the particular sufferings of the Chinese community. President Suharto was forced to stand down on 21 May 1998 and was succeeded by his Vice-President, Bacharuddin Jusuf Habibie, who promised political and economic reforms. Continuing protest centred on the Suharto family which until recently exercised control over large parts of the Indonesian economy. Several of the country's discontented regions are wanting to break free.

In Aug. 1999 East Timor, the former Portuguese colony which Indonesia invaded in 1975, voted for independence, a move that was eventually approved by the Indonesian parliament after violent clashes between independence supporters and pro-Indonesian militia groups. It gained independence from Indonesia on 20 May 2002.

In Nov. 1999 up to 1m. people took to the streets in the province of Aceh, in the far west of the country, seeking a referendum on independence. One of the founder provinces of the Republic of Indonesia, there were fears that Aceh's possible secession would threaten the break-up of the country. More than 5,000 people were killed there during the 1990s, and rebellions in a number of other Indonesian provinces were suppressed with heavy loss of life. In Dec. 2002 the government and the separatist Free Aceh Movement signed a peace deal to end the violence. In exchange for disarmament, Aceh was granted autonomy and self-government from 2004. All non-local Indonesian army troops left the province in Dec. 2005 as part of the peace agreement.

In Oct. 2002 around 200 people, mainly foreign nationals, died in a car bomb explosion outside a nightclub in Bali. A second bomb exploded near a US consulate. The Indonesian and Australian governments blamed al-Qaeda.

On 26 Dec. 2004 Indonesia, along with a number of other south Asian countries, was hit by a devastating tsunami following an undersea earthquake. The death toll in Indonesia alone was put at 237,000, almost exclusively in the province of Aceh.

TERRITORY AND POPULATION

Indonesia, with a land area of 1,890,754 sq. km (730,020 sq. miles), consists of 17,507 islands (6,000 of which are inhabited) extending about 3,200 miles east to west through three time-zones (East, Central and West Indonesian Standard time) and 1,250 miles north to south.

The largest islands are Sumatra, Java, Kalimantan (Indonesian Borneo), Sulawesi (Celebes) and Papua, formerly West Papua (the western part of New Guinea). Most of the smaller islands except Madura and Bali are grouped together. The two largest groups of islands are Maluku (the Moluccas) and Nusa Tenggara (the

Lesser Sundas). On the island of Timor, Indonesia is bounded in the east by East Timor.

Population at the 2000 census was 206,264,595 (54·5% rural in 2003); density, 102 per sq. km. Indonesia has the fourth largest population in the world, after China, India and the USA. The estimated population in 2005 was 222·78m.

The UN gives a projected population for 2010 of 235·75m.

Area, population and chief towns of the provinces, autonomous districts and major islands:

The capital, Jakarta, had a population of 8·35m. in 2000. Other major cities (2000 estimates in 1m.): Surabaya, 2·60; Bandung, 2·14; Medan, 1·90; Bekasi, 1·66; Palembang, 1·45; Semarang, 1·35.

The principal ethnic groups are the Acehnese, Bataks and Minangkabaus in Sumatra, the Javanese and Sundanese in Java, the Madurese in Madura, the Balinese in Bali, the Sasaks in Lombok, the Menadonese, Minahasans, Torajas and Buginese in Sulawesi, the Dayaks in Kalimantan, the Irianese in Papua and

	Area (in sq. km)	Population (2000 census)	Chief town	Population (1990 census)
Bali	5,633	3,151,162	Denpasar	261,263[1]
Nusa Tenggara Barat	20,153	4,009,261	Mataram	141,387[1]
Nusa Tenggara Timur	47,351	3,952,279	Kupang	403,110[1]
Bali and Nusa Tenggara	73,137	11,112,702		
Banten	8,651	8,098,780	Serang	—[2]
DKI Jakarta[3]	664	8,389,443	Jakarta	8,259,266
Jawa Barat	34,597	35,729,537	Bandung	2,026,893
Jawa Tengah	32,549	31,228,940	Semarang	1,005,316
Jawa Timur	47,922	34,783,640	Surabaya	2,421,016
Yogyakarta[3]	3,186	3,122,268	Yogyakarta	412,392
Java	127,569	121,352,608		
Kalimantan Barat	146,807	4,034,198	Pontianak	387,112
Kalimantan Selatan	43,546	2,985,240	Banjarmasin	443,738
Kalimantan Tengah	153,564	1,857,000	Palangkaraya	60,447[1]
Kalimantan Timur	230,277	2,455,120	Samarinda	335,016
Kalimantan	574,194	11,331,558		
Irian Jaya Barat[4]	—	—	Manokwari	—[2]
Maluku	46,975	1,205,539	Amboina	206,260
Maluku Utara	30,895	785,059	Ternate	—[2]
Papua[4]	365,466	2,220,934	Jayapura	149,618[1]
Maluku and Papua	443,336	4,211,532		
Gorontalo	12,215	835,044	Gorontalo	—[2]
Sulawesi Barat[5]	—	—	—	—[2]
Sulawesi Selatan[5]	62,365	8,059,627	Makassar	913,196
Sulawesi Tengah	63,678	2,218,435	Palu	298,584[1]
Sulawesi Tenggara	38,140	1,821,284	Kendari	41,021[1]
Sulawesi Utara	15,273	2,012,098	Menado	275,374
Sulawesi	191,671	14,946,488		
Aceh[3,6]	51,937	3,930,905	Banda Aceh	143,409
Bangka-Belitung	16,171	900,197	Pangkalpinang	—[2]
Bengkulu	19,789	1,567,432	Bengkulu	146,439
Jambi	53,437	2,413,846	Jambi[7]	301,359
Kepulauan Riau[8]	—	—	Tanjung Pinang	—[2]
Lampung	35,384	6,741,439	Bandar Lampung	457,900[9]
Riau[8]	94,560	4,957,627	Pakanbaru	341,328
Sumatera Barat	42,899	4,248,931	Padang	477,344
Sumatera Selatan	93,083	6,899,675	Palembang	1,084,483
Sumatera Utara	73,587	11,649,655	Medan	1,685,972
Sumatra	480,847	43,309,707		

[1]1980 census. [2]Province created since 1990. [3]Autonomous District. [4]Irian Jaya Barat, formerly part of Papua, was created in 2003. [5]Sulawesi Barat, formerly part of Sulawesi Selatan, was created in 2004. [6]The population of Aceh was reduced by about 237,000 as a result of the tsunami that struck Indonesia on 26 Dec. 2004. [7]Formerly Telanaipura. [8]Kepulauan Riau, formerly part of Riau, was created in 2002. [9]Estimate.

the Ambonese in the Moluccas. There were some 6m. Chinese resident in 1991.

Bahasa Indonesia is the official language; Dutch is spoken as a colonial inheritance.

SOCIAL STATISTICS

Estimated births, 2001, 4,620,000; deaths, 1,533,000. 2001 birth rate, 22·0 per 1,000 population; death rate, 7·3. Life expectancy in 2003 was 64·9 years for men and 68·8 for women. Annual population growth rate, 1992–2002, 1·4%. Infant mortality, 2001, 33 per 1,000 live births; fertility rate, 2001, 2·4 births per woman.

In the Human Development Index, or HDI (measuring progress in countries in longevity, knowledge and standard of living), Indonesia's index improved the most of any country during the last quarter of the 20th century, rising from 0·456 in 1975 to 0·677 in 1999.

CLIMATE

Conditions vary greatly over this spread of islands, but generally the climate is tropical monsoon, with a dry season from June to Sept. and a wet one from Oct. to April. Temperatures are high all the year and rainfall varies according to situation on lee or windward shores. Jakarta, Jan. 78°F (25·6°C), July 78°F (25·6°C). Annual rainfall 71" (1,775 mm). Padang, Jan. 79°F (26·1°C), July 79°F (26·1°C). Annual rainfall 177" (4,427 mm). Surabaya, Jan. 79°F (26·1°C), July 78°F (25·6°C). Annual rainfall 51" (1,285 mm).

On 26 Dec. 2004 an undersea earthquake centred off Sumatra caused a huge tsunami that flooded large areas along the coast of northwestern Indonesia resulting in 237,000 deaths. In total there were 290,000 deaths in twelve countries.

CONSTITUTION AND GOVERNMENT

The constitution originally dates from Aug. 1945 and was in force until 1949; it was restored on 5 July 1959.

The political system is based on *pancasila*, in which deliberations lead to a consensus. There is a 550-member *Dewan Perwakilan Rakyat* (House of People's Representatives), with members elected for a five-year term by proportional representation in multi-member constituencies. The constitution was changed on 10 Aug. 2002 to allow for direct elections for the president and the vice-president.

There is no limit to the number of presidential terms. Although predominantly a Muslim country, the constitution protects the religious beliefs of non-Muslims.

National Anthem

'Indonesia, tanah airku' ('Indonesia, our native land'); words and tune by W. R. Supratman.

GOVERNMENT CHRONOLOGY

Presidents since 1949. (Golkar = Party of the Functional Groups; PD = Democrat Party; PDIP = Indonesian Democratic Party of Struggle; PKB = National Awakening Party; PNI = Indonesian National Party)

1949–67	PNI	(Ahmed) Sukarno
1967–98	Golkar	(Mohamed) Suharto
1998–99	Golkar	Bacharuddin Jusuf Habibie
1999–2001	PKB	Abdurrahman Wahid
2001–04	PDIP	Megawati Sukarnoputri
2004–	PD	Susilo Bambang Yudhoyono

RECENT ELECTIONS

Elections to the House of People's Representatives were held on 5 April 2004. The Party of the Functional Groups (Golkar) won 128 seats with 21·6% of the vote; the Indonesian Democratic Party of Struggle (PDIP) won 109 seats with 18·5%; United Development Party (PPP) 58 with 8·2%; Democrat Party (PD) 57 with 7·5%; National Awakening Party (PKB) 52 with 10·6%; National Mandate Party (PAN) 52 with 6·4%; Prosperous Justice Party (PKS) 45 with 7·3%; Reform Star Party (PBR) 13 with 2·4%; Crescent Star Party (PBB) 11 with 2·6%; National Democracy Unity Party (PDK) 5 with 1·2%. The Concern for the Nation Functional Party (PKPB) and the Pioneers' Party (PP) won two seats each. The Indonesian National Party-Marhaenisme, Freedom Bull National Party (PNBK), Justice and Unity Party of Indonesia (PKPI) and the Indonesian Democratic Vanguard Party (PPDI) won one seat each. Turnout was 84·5%.

Indonesia's first direct presidential election took place in 2004. In the first round held on 5 July 2004 Susilo Bambang Yudhoyono (PD) won 33·6% of the vote, incumbent Megawati Sukarnoputri (PDIP) 26·2%, Wiranto (Golkar) 22·2%, Amien Rais (PAN) 14·9% and Hamzah Haz (PPP) 3·1%. The run-off held on 20 Sept. 2004 was won by Susilo Bambang Yudhoyono, with 60·9% of votes cast, against 39·1% for Megawati Sukarnoputri.

CURRENT ADMINISTRATION

President: Susilo Bambang Yudhoyono; b. 1949 (PD; sworn in 20 Oct. 2004).

Vice-President: Jusuf Kalla.

In March 2006 the cabinet was composed as follows:

Co-ordinating Ministers: (Political, Legal and Security Affairs) Widodo Adi Sucipto; *(Economic Affairs)* Boediono; *(People's Welfare)* Aburizal Bakrie.

Minister of Foreign Affairs: Hassan Wirajuda. *Justice and Human Rights:* Hamid Awaluddin. *Defence:* Juwono Sudarsono. *Religious Affairs:* Muhammad Maftuh Basyuni. *Education:* Bambang Soedibyo. *Health:* Fadilah Supari. *Finance:* Sri Mulyani Indrawati. *Trade:* Mari E. Pangestu. *Manpower and Transmigration:* Fahmi Idris. *Agriculture:* Anton Apriyantono. *Forestry:* M. S. Kaban. *Industry:* Adung Nitimiharja. *Transportation:* Hatta Radjasa. *Maritime Affairs and Fisheries:* Freddy Numberi. *Social Services:* Bachtiar Chamsyah. *Energy and Mineral Resources:* Purnomo Yusgiantoro. *Home Affairs:* Mohamed Maaruf. *Public Works:* Joko Kirmanto. *Culture and Tourism:* Jero Wacik.

Government Website (Indonesian only):
  http://www.indonesia.go.id

CURRENT LEADERS

Susilo Bambang Yudhoyono

Position
President

Introduction
Retired general Susilo Bambang Yudhoyono, known widely by his acronym SBY, succeeded Megawati Sukarnoputri as president of Indonesia on 20 Oct. 2004. In the country's first direct presidential election he polled 61% of an estimated 125m. votes.

Early Life
Susilo Bambang Yudhoyono was born on 9 Sept. 1949 in the small town of Pacitan, in the east of the Indonesian island of Java. His family were observant Muslims and he attended a traditional *pesantren* (Muslim boarding school). He graduated from Indonesia's military academy in 1973 and joined the army, which was then, with Gen. Suharto as president, the country's dominant authority. He served as a senior officer in Indonesia's 1975 invasion of East Timor, then a Portuguese colony. Gen. Suharto's 'New Order' political system was characterized by a strongly anti-communist foreign policy and relatively good relations with the USA. Yudhoyono travelled to the USA in 1976 and 1982, attending military training programmes at Fort Benning, Georgia. He later took a masters degree in business management from Webster University in Missouri and has since described the USA as his 'second home'. Between 1984–87 Yudhoyono returned to East Timor and commanded Battalion 744 in the city of Dili.

By the mid-1990s he had risen through the ranks to become chief-of-staff in the Jakarta command. Questions have been asked about his knowledge of a raid by security forces on the Jakarta offices of the Indonesian Democratic Party (PDI) on 27 July 1996 (then chaired by Megawati Sukarnoputri), which left five dead and 23 missing.

In 1996 Yudhoyono served as chief military observer with the United Nations force in Bosnia. Two years later, with Indonesia in turmoil following the ousting of President Suharto in March 1998, he left the army and was appointed the minister for mining and energy in the administration of Abdurrahman Wahid. When the Muslim cleric was succeeded as president in 2001 by Mrs Megawati, daughter of former president Sukarno, Yudhoyono joined her cabinet as chief security minister.

He was praised for the way he handled the aftermath of the Oct. 2002 Bali bombing that killed 202 people. He subsequently helped draft Indonesia's first counter-terrorist law and attempted to broker a peace agreement with separatist rebels in the historically troubled province of Aceh in Sumatra in 2003, which collapsed in May of that year. In March 2004 Yudhoyono resigned from Megawati's increasingly unpopular cabinet to establish the Democrat Party (PD). In the first round of elections in early April (for choosing the members of parliament and three tiers of local officials) the PD had a strong showing. On 5 July, when Yudhoyono, along with his running mate Jusuf Kalla—a business tycoon with ties to many of the country's Islamic clerics—fought in the country's first direct presidential elections, no candidate won more than 50% of the vote. This forced a run-off election between Yudhoyono and Megawati on 20 Sept. which Yudhoyono won with 60·9% of the vote. He was officially sworn in as president on 20 Oct. 2004.

Career in Office
In interviews with the international media Yudhoyono vowed to fight terrorism and eradicate corruption in his five-year term. He also promised to restore Indonesian institutions and the rule of law and to rebuild the economy. The president has set himself the goal of creating jobs for 50m. unemployed Indonesians. He also pledged to repair the often fractious relationship with Australia. In the aftermath of the Indian Ocean tsunami of 26 Dec. 2004, which is estimated to have killed over 237,000 people on the Indonesian island of Sumatra, Yudhoyono was quick to accept aid and expertise from the international community. Handling relief and reconstruction was an opportunity for him to be a more decisive and approachable leader than his predecessor. It was also an opportunity for him to improve relations between Jakarta and Aceh—the region worst-affected by the tsunami—and in Aug. 2005 his government signed a peace agreement with separatist leaders granting greater political autonomy to the province.

DEFENCE
There is selective conscription for two years. Defence expenditure in 2003 totalled US$6,443m. (US$30 per capita), representing 3·0% of GDP.

Army
Army strength in 2002 was estimated at 230,000 with a strategic reserve (KOSTRAD) of 30,000 and further potential mobilizable reserves of 400,000.

There is a paramilitary police some 194,000 strong; and a part-time local auxiliary forces, KAMRA (People's Security), which numbers around 40,000.

Navy
The Navy in 2002 numbered about 40,000, including 12,000 in the Commando Corps and 1,000 in the Naval Air Arm. Combatant strength includes two diesel submarines and 17 frigates. The Naval Air Arm operates 17 armed helicopters.

The Navy's principal command is split between the Western Fleet, at Teluk Ratai (Jakarta), and the Eastern Fleet, at Surabaya.

Air Force
Personnel (2002) approximately 27,000. There were 90 combat aircraft, including A-4s, F-16s, F-5s and British Aerospace *Hawks*.

INTERNATIONAL RELATIONS
Indonesia is in dispute with Malaysia over sovereignty of two islands in the Celebes Sea. Both countries have agreed to accept the Judgment of the International Court of Justice.

Indonesia is a member of the UN, WTO, OPEC, Asian Development Bank, Colombo Plan, APEC, ASEAN, Mekong Group, OIC and Islamic Development Bank.

ECONOMY
Agriculture accounted for 17·1% of GDP in 2002, industry 44·2% and services 38·7%.

Overview
In the 1970s the country's economy was largely based on agriculture, fishing and forestry. Its main exports consisted of a few primary products such as crude oil, natural rubber, coconut oil, copra and tin. The fall of oil prices after 1983 encouraged industrialization. From the mid-1980s the strongest growth was in manufacturing, which averaged 13% real annual growth in the half decade from 1984–88 according to the Economist Intelligence Unit (EIU). In 1991 the manufacturing share of GDP moved ahead of agriculture for the first time. The country's mining sector also grew strongly during this period, exploiting the country's vast mineral resources. Services grew in importance too, led by a push to develop the tourism sector. By the first half of the 2000s the growth rates of the various sectors converged, with the EIU estimating that mining and manufacturing output grew between 6–7% and services and agriculture near 4% in 2004.

Indonesia was the country worst hit by the Asian financial crisis that began in 1997. The dual banking and foreign exchange crisis caused real GDP to contract by over 13% in 1998. With high levels of non-performing loans in a structurally weak banking sector and an over-reliance on short-term dollar-denominated loans by Indonesian enterprise, the sharp devaluation of the *rupiah* caused severe banking and economic distress. Inflation surged by close to 60% during 1998 and the country's debt-to-GDP ratio jumped. In 1998 the Indonesian Bank Restructuring Agency (IBRA) was established to recapitalize state banks. Interest rates were increased radically to reduce inflation. Regulatory, institutional and other reforms were initiated in order to help regain investor confidence. In 1999 the economy stabilized and in 2000 it managed to resume growth at a solid pace. Despite a strong recovery, Indonesia's recent growth performance does not match the 7·6% annual growth averaged in the half-decade from 1992–96 or the 8·9% averaged in the half decade from 1987–91. From 2000–04 the economy averaged 4·6% annual growth.

Macroeconomic performance in 2004 and 2005 was encouraging. Growth was solid, the country's debt-to-GDP ratio lower and inflation under control. However the IMF warns that the macroeconomic health of the country remains delicate and that stronger growth is necessary for high unemployment and poverty to be overcome. In 2005 there was a recovery in investment but investment levels are significantly lower than in other developing countries in the region. The IMF urges Indonesia to accelerate privatization and financial sector reform in order to boost investment. It also encourages an increase in pace of tax and labour market reform, as well as the upgrading of infrastructure and the strengthening of the legal framework. Corruption remains rife.

Currency
The monetary unit is the *rupiah* (IDR) notionally of 100 *sen*. Inflation rates (based on IMF statistics):

1995	1996	1997	1998	1999	2000	2001	2002	2003	2004
9·4%	7·9%	6·2%	58·0%	20·7%	3·8%	11·5%	11·8%	6·8%	6·1%

Foreign exchange reserves were US$28,127m. and gold reserves 3·10m. troy oz in June 2002. Total money supply in Dec. 2001 was 170,509·0bn. rupiahs.

Budget
The fiscal year used to start 1 April but since 2001 has been the calendar year. Revenue in 2001 was 307,927bn. rupiahs and expenditure was 359,038bn. rupiahs. Tax accounted for 63·9% of revenue. Main items of expenditure: social security and welfare,

8·6%; general public services, 4·6%; education, 3·7%; and defence, 3·0%.

Performance

Real GDP growth rates (based on IMF statistics):

1995	1996	1997	1998	1999	2000	2001	2002	2003	2004
8·2%	8·0%	4·5%	−13·1%	0·8%	4·9%	3·8%	4·4%	4·9%	5·1%

The Asian economic crisis of 1997 affected Indonesia more than any other country. In 2004 total GDP was US$257·6bn.

Banking and Finance

The Bank Indonesia, successor to De Javasche Bank established by the Dutch in 1828, was made the central bank of Indonesia on 1 July 1953. Its *Governor* is Burhanuddin Abdullah. It had an original capital of 25m. rupiahs, a reserve fund of 18m. rupiahs and a special reserve of 84m. rupiahs. In Jan. 2000 independent auditors declared that the bank was technically bankrupt. In response the IMF stated that future loans would probably depend on recapitalization and an internal reorganization.

In 2003 there were 138 commercial banks, 26 regional government banks, 76 private national banks and 31 foreign banks and joint banks. The leading banks are Bank Madiri (with assets of US$27·9bn. in Dec. 2002), Bank Central Asia and Bank BNI. All state banks are authorized to deal in foreign exchange.

The government owns one Savings Bank, Bank Tabungan Negara and 1,000 Post Office Savings Banks. There are also over 3,500 rural and village savings banks and credit co-operatives. At least 16 banks closed in the wake of the 1997 financial crisis.

There is a stock exchange in Jakarta.

ENERGY AND NATURAL RESOURCES

Environment

Indonesia's carbon dioxide emissions from the consumption and flaring of fossil fuels in 2002 were the equivalent of 1·4 tonnes per capita.

Electricity

Installed capacity in 2002 was 25·3m. kW and production 97·77bn. kWh (13·83bn. kWh hydro-electric). Consumption per capita was 463 kWh in 2002. 68,045 villages were supplied with electricity in 1999.

Oil and Gas

The importance of oil in the economy is declining. The 2003 output of crude oil was 57·5m. tonnes. Proven reserves in 2002 totalled 5·0bn. bbls. Natural gas production, 2002, was 70·6bn. cu. metres with 2,620bn. cu. metres of proven reserves. In Jan. 2001 a 640-km gas pipeline linking Indonesia's West Natuna field with Singapore came on stream. It is expected to provide Singapore with US$8bn. worth of natural gas over a 20-year period.

Minerals

The high cost of extraction means that little of the large mineral resources outside Java is exploited; however, there is copper mining in Papua, nickel mining and processing on Sulawesi, and aluminium smelting in northern Sumatra. Open-cast coal mining has been conducted since the 1890s, but since the 1970s coal production has been developed as an alternative to oil. Reserves are estimated at 28,000m. tonnes. Coal production (2000), 76·8m. tonnes. Other minerals: copper concentrate (1998), 2·9m. tonnes; bauxite (2001), 1,237,000 tonnes; salt (1998 estimate), 650,000 tonnes; iron ore (2000), 489,000 tonnes; nickel (2002), 122,000 tonnes (content of nickel ores and concentrates); tin (1998), 50,833 tonnes; silver (2001), 348 tonnes; gold (2001), 166 tonnes.

Agriculture

There were 20·50m. ha. of arable land in 2001 and 13·1m. ha. of permanent crops. 4·82m. ha. were irrigated in 2001. Production

(2000, in 1,000 tonnes): rice, 51,000; sugarcane, 21,400; cassava, 16,347; coconuts, 16,235; maize, 9,169; bananas, 3,377; cabbages, 1,750; sweet potatoes, 1,627; palm kernels, 1,600; natural rubber, 1,488; copra, 1,380; soybeans, 1,198; groundnuts, 1,000; potatoes, 924; dry beans, 900; mangoes, 827; onions, 805; oranges, 645; cucumbers and gherkins, 580. Annual nutmeg production is 6,000 tonnes, more than two-thirds of the world total. Indonesia is the world's largest producer of coconuts.

Livestock (2000): goats, 14·12m.; cattle, 12·10m.; pigs, 9·35m.; sheep, 7·50m.; buffaloes, 2·86m.; horses, 579,000; chickens, 800m.; ducks, 26m.

Forestry

In 2000 the area under forests was 104·99m. ha., or 58·0% of the total land area. The annual loss of 1,312,000 ha. between 1990 and 2000 was exceeded during the same period only in Brazil. In 2003, 112·00m. cu. metres of roundwood were cut, most of it fuelwood and charcoal.

Fisheries

In 2003 total catch was 4,675,100 tonnes, of which 4,349,860 tonnes were sea fish. In 1997 there were 191,270 motorized and 371,007 other fishing vessels.

INDUSTRY

The largest company in Indonesia by market capitalization in May 2004 was Telekomunikasi Indonesia (US$8·0bn.).

There are shipyards at Jakarta Raya, Surabaya, Semarang and Amboina. There are textile factories, large paper factories, match factories, automobile and bicycle assembly works, large construction works, tyre factories, glass factories, a caustic soda and other chemical factories. Production (2002, in 1,000 tonnes): cement (2000), 22,789; distillate fuel oil, 13,724; residual fuel oil, 11,951; petrol, 8,344; kerosene, 7,263; fertilizers, 7,038; paper and paperboard (2001), 6,995; palm oil (2000), 6,900; sugar (1998), 1,493; plywood (2001), 7·3m. cu. metres; 4,937,000 radio sets (1999); 804,000 TV sets (1998); 342,500 cars and lorries; 254·3bn. cigarettes (1999). Indonesia is the third largest producer of plywood after the USA and China.

Labour

In 2001 the labour force was 98,812,000. 43·8% of employed persons worked in agriculture, forestry, hunting and fisheries, 19·2% in trade, restaurants and hotels, 13·3% in manufacturing and 12·1% in community, social and personal services. National daily average wage, 1996, 4,073 rupiahs. Unemployment in 2001 was 8·1%.

Trade Unions

Workers have a constitutional right to organize and under a law passed in Feb. 2003 have a right to be paid during lawful strikes. Until the fall of Suharto in 1998 unions were expected to affiliate to the All Indonesia Trade Union (SPSI), which enjoyed government approval and was affiliated to the ruling party. Between 1994 and 1996 there were more than 2,000 strikes involving 1m. workers. In Feb. 2003 the Indonesian Trade Union Congress (KSPI), supported by the International Confederation of Free Trade Unions, was inaugurated. It represents 3·1m. members and encompasses 12 industrial federations.

INTERNATIONAL TRADE

Since 1992 foreigners have been permitted to hold 100% of the equity of new companies in Indonesia with more than US$50m. part capital, or situated in remote provinces. Foreign debt was US$132,208m. in 2002.

Pressure on Indonesia's currency and stock market led to an appeal to the IMF and World Bank for long-term support funds in Oct. 1997. A bail-out package worth US$38,000m. was eventually agreed on condition that Indonesia tightened financial controls and instituted reforms, including the establishment of an independent privatization board, liberalizing foreign investment, cutting import tariffs and phasing out export levies.

Imports and Exports

Imports and exports in US$1m.:

	1998	1999	2000	2001	2002
Imports f.o.b.	31,942	30,598	40,366	34,669	35,652
Exports f.o.b.	50,371	51,242	65,406	57,364	58,773

Principal import items: machinery and transport equipment, basic manufactures and chemicals. Principal export items: gas and oil, forestry products, manufactured goods, rubber, coffee, fishery products, coal, copper, tin, pepper, palm products and tea. Main import suppliers, 2001: Japan, 18·8%; Singapore, 10·2%; South Korea, 9·8%. Main export markets, 2001: Japan, 20·0%; USA, 15·0%; Singapore, 10·8%.

COMMUNICATIONS

Roads

In 1999 there were about 342,700 km of roads (27,357 km of highways or main roads in 1997), of which 158,700 km were surfaced. Motor vehicles, 1998: passenger cars, 2,772,500; buses and coaches, 628,000; trucks and vans, 1,592,600; motorcycles, 12,651,800. There were 272 fatalities in road accidents in 1996.

Rail

In 1997 the national railways totalled 6,458 km of 1,067 mm gauge, comprising 4,967 km on Java (of which 125 km electrified) and 1,491 km on Sumatra. Passenger-km travelled in 2002 came to 21·3bn. and freight tonne-km to 5·0bn.

Civil Aviation

Garuda Indonesia is the state-owned national flag carrier. Merpati Nusantara Airlines is their domestic subsidiary. Domestic services are also provided by Bouraq Indonesia. There are international airports at Jakarta (Sukarno-Hatta), Denpasar (on Bali), Medan (Sumatra), Pekanbaru (Sumatra), Ujung Pandang (Sulawesi), Manado (Sulawesi), Solo (Java) and Surabaya Juanda (Java). Jakarta is the busiest airport, in 2001 handling 11,192,000 passengers (6,685,000 on domestic flights) and 280,900 tonnes of freight. Denpasar handled 4,431,000 passengers in 2001 and Surabaya Juanda 2,380,000. In 1999 scheduled airline traffic of Indonesia-based carriers flew 121·8m. km, carrying 8,047,000 passengers (1,927,000 on international flights).

Shipping

There are 16 ports for ocean-going ships, the largest of which is Tanjung Priok, which serves the Jakarta area and has a container terminal. In 2002 cargo traffic at Tanjung Priok totalled 39·3m. tonnes. The national shipping company Pelajaran Nasional Indonesia (PELNI) maintains inter-island communications. Jakarta Lloyd maintains regular services between Jakarta, Amsterdam, Hamburg and London. In 1995 the merchant marine comprised 535 ocean-going ships totalling 4·13m. DWT. 95 vessels (36·22% of total tonnage) were registered under foreign flags. In 2002 total tonnage registered came to 3·72m. GRT, including oil tankers 827,000 GRT. In 2002 vessels totalling 361,246,000 net registered tons entered ports and vessels totalling 86,554,000 NRT cleared.

Telecommunications

In 2002 there were 19,450,000 telephone subscribers (91·7 per 1,000 population) and 2,519,000 PCs in use (11·9 for every 1,000 persons). There were 11,700,000 mobile phone subscribers in 2002 and 314,000 fax machines. Indonesia had 8·0m. Internet users in 2002, up from 400,000 in 2000.

Postal Services

In 2003 there were 20,073 post offices.

SOCIAL INSTITUTIONS

Justice

There are courts of first instance, high courts of appeal in every provincial capital and a Supreme Court of Justice for the whole of Indonesia in Jakarta.

In civil law the population is divided into three main groups: Indonesians, Europeans and foreign Orientals, to whom different law systems are applicable. When, however, people from different groups are involved, a system of so-called 'inter-gentile' law is applied.

The present criminal law, which has been in force since 1918, is codified and is based on European penal law. This law is equally applicable to all groups of the population. The death penalty is still in use; in 2005 there were two executions.

The population in penal institutions in 2001 was 62,886 (29 per 100,000 of national population).

Education

Adult literacy in 2002 was 87·9% (92·5% among males and 83·4% among females). In 2000–01 there were 28,690,131 pupils and 1,289,720 teachers at primary schools, and 14,828,085 pupils and 1,040,081 teachers at secondary schools. Number of students in higher education (2000–01), 3,017,887. In 1994–95 in the state sector there were 31 universities and one open university, and 13 institutes of higher education, including ten teacher training colleges. In the private sector there were 66 universities and the following specialized universities: Adventist, one; Christian, seven; Islamic, ten; Methodist, one; Roman Catholic, five; Veterans', one. There were 19 institutes of higher education in the private sector, including 12 teacher training colleges.

In 2000–01 total expenditure on education came to 1·6% of GNP and 9·6% of total government spending.

Health

In 2000 there were 34,347 doctors, 92,371 nurses, 11,547 midwives and 2,406 dentists. There were 1,162 hospitals in 2002, with a provision of six beds per 10,000 population.

Welfare

The official retirement age is 55. There are currently no unemployment benefits or family allowance programmes.

RELIGION

Religious liberty is granted to all denominations. In 2001 there were 185·1m. Muslims (making Indonesia the world's biggest Muslim country), 12·8m. Protestants and 7·6m. Roman Catholics. There were also significant numbers of Hindus and Buddhists. In May 2005 there was one cardinal.

CULTURE

World Heritage Sites

There are seven UNESCO sites in Indonesia (the first four inscribed in 1991): Borobudur Temple Compounds, Ujung Kulon National Park, Komodo National Park, Prambanan Temple Compounds, Sangiran Early Man Site (1996), Lorentz National Park (1999) and the Tropical Rainforest Heritage of Sumatra (2004).

Broadcasting

Radio Republik Indonesia, under the Department of Information, operates 49 stations. There were 32m. television receivers (colour by PAL) in 2001 and 33m. radio sets in 2000.

Cinema

There were 850 cinema screens in 2002.

Press

In 2002 there were 176 daily newspapers (total average circulation of 4,665,000 at a rate of 22 per 1,000 inhabitants). In 2002 a total of 3,823 book titles were published.

Tourism

In 2002 there were 5,033,000 foreign tourists, spending US$4·31bn.

Festivals

Independence from the Dutch is celebrated on 17 Aug. with musical and theatrical performances, carnivals and sporting events. The military parades on Armed Forces Day (5 Oct.) and women are celebrated on Kartini Day (21 April) in memory of Raden Ajeng Kartini, a symbol of female emancipation. In Bali the Hindu new year is marked by a day of silence, *Nyepi*, followed by a day of feasting. Muslim, Hindu, Buddhist and Christian festivals are marked throughout the country.

DIPLOMATIC REPRESENTATIVES

Of Indonesia in the United Kingdom (38 Grosvenor Sq., London, W1X 9AD)
Ambassador: Dr Raden Mohammad Marty Muliana Natalegawa.

Of the United Kingdom in Indonesia (Jalan M.H. Thamrin 75, Jakarta 10310)
Ambassador: Charles Humfrey, CMG.

Of Indonesia in the USA (2020 Massachusetts Ave., NW, Washington, D.C., 20036)
Ambassador: Sudjadnan Parnohadiningrat.

Of the USA in Indonesia (Medan Merdeka Selatan 5, Jakarta)
Ambassador: B. Lynn Pascoe.

Of Indonesia to the United Nations
Ambassador: Rezlan Ishar Jenie.

Of Indonesia to the European Union
Ambassador: Abdurachman Mattalitti.

FURTHER READING

Central Bureau of Statistics. *Statistical Yearbook of Indonesia.—Monthly Statistical Bulletin: Economic Indicator.*
Cribb, R., *Historical Dictionary of Indonesia*. Metuchen (NJ), 1993.—and Brown, C., *Modern Indonesia: a History since 1945*. Harlow, 1995
Elson, R. E., *Suharto; a Political Biography*. CUP, 2001
Forrester, Geoff, (ed.) *Post-Soeharto Indonesia: Renewal or Chaos?* St Martin's Press, New York, 1999
Forrester, Geoff and May, R. J. (eds.) *The Fall of Soeharto*. C. Hurst, London, 1999
Friend, Theodore, *Indonesian Destinies*. Belknap Press, Harvard Univ. Press, 2003
Kingsbury, Damien, *The Politics of Indonesia*. 2nd ed. OUP, 2002
Krausse, G. H. and Krausse, S. C. E., *Indonesia*. [Bibliography] ABC-Clio, Oxford and Santa Barbara (CA), 1994
Ricklefs, M. C., *A History of Modern Indonesia since c. 1200*. 3rd ed. Palgrave, Basingstoke, 2001
Schwarz, Adam, *A Nation in Waiting: Indonesia's Search for Stability*. Revised ed. Westview Press, Boulder (CO), 1999
Schwarz, Adam and Paris, Jonathan, (eds.) *The Politics of Post-Suharto Indonesia*. New York, 1999
Vatikiotis, M. R. J., *Indonesian Politics under Suharto: Order, Development and Pressure for Change*. 2nd ed. London, 1994

National Statistical Office: Central Bureau of Statistics, POB 1003, Jakarta, 10010.
Website: http://www.bps.go.id

IRAN

Jomhuri-e-Eslami-e-Iran
(Islamic Republic of Iran)

Capital: Tehran
Population projection, 2010: 74·28m.
GDP per capita, 2003: (PPP$) 6,995
HDI/world rank: 0·736/99

KEY HISTORICAL EVENTS

Persia was ruled by the Shahs as an absolute monarchy from the 16th century until 1906, when the first constitution was granted and a national assembly established. After a coup in 1921, Reza Khan began his rise to power. He was declared Shah on 12 Dec. 1925 and as closer relations with Europe were developed in the mid-1930s so the name Iran began to be used in the west instead of Persia. When in the Second World War Iran supported Germany, the Allies occupied the country and forced Reza Shah to abdicate in favour of his son. The British controlled oil industry was nationalized in March 1951 in line with the policy of the National Front Party, whose leader, Dr Muhammad Mussadeq, became prime minister in April 1951. He was opposed by the Shah who fled the country until Aug. 1953 when the monarchists staged a coup which led to Mussadeq being deposed. The Shah's policy, which included the redistribution of land to small farmers and the enfranchisement of women, was opposed by the Shia religious scholars who considered it to be contrary to Islamic teaching. Despite economic growth, unrest was caused by the Shah's repressive measures and his extensive use of the Savak, the secret police. The opposition led by Ayatollah Ruhollah Khomeini, the Shia Muslim spiritual leader who had been exiled in 1965, was particularly successful. Following intense civil unrest in Tehran, the Shah left Iran with his family on 17 Jan. 1979 (and died in Egypt on 27 July 1980). The Ayatollah Khomeini returned from exile on 1 Feb. 1979, the

Shah's government resigned and parliament dissolved itself on 11 Feb. Following a referendum in March, an Islamic Republic was proclaimed. The constitution gave supreme authority to a religious leader (*wali faqih*), a position held by Ayatollah Khomeini for the rest of his life. In Sept. 1980 border fighting with Iraq escalated into full-scale war. A UN-arranged ceasefire took place on 20 Aug. 1988, and in Aug. 1990, following Iraq's invasion of Kuwait, Iraq offered peace terms and began the withdrawal of troops from Iranian soil. Approximately 30,000 political opponents of the regime are believed to have been executed shortly after the end of the war.

In 1997 the election of Mohammad Khatami as president signalled a shift away from Islamic extremism. A clampdown on Islamic vigilantes who wage a violent campaign against western 'decadence' is the latest sign of a cautiously liberal integration of the constitution. But the conservative faction led by the spiritual leader Ayatollah Ali Khamenei retains huge power including the final say on defence and foreign policy.

In July 1999 riot police fought pitched battles with pro-democracy students in Tehran in the worst unrest since the revolution in 1979. Islamic leaders remain divided on the degree of overlap between politics and religion.

Following the election of President Mahmoud Ahmadinejad in June 2005, Iran recommenced uranium conversion research. Despite Tehran's insistence that the research programme was for peaceful purposes only, increasing international disquiet saw the International Atomic Energy Agency report Iran to the UN Security Council in Feb. 2006. Iran has since resumed uranium enrichment.

TERRITORY AND POPULATION

Iran is bounded in the north by Armenia, Azerbaijan, the Caspian Sea and Turkmenistan, east by Afghanistan and Pakistan, south by the Gulf of Oman and the Persian Gulf, and west by Iraq and Turkey. It has an area (including inland water) of 1,648,195 sq. km (636,368 sq. miles), but a vast portion is desert. Population (1996 census): 60,055,488 (2003, 66·6% urban). Population density: 36 per sq. km. The United Nations population estimate for 2005 was 69,515,000.

The UN gives a projected population for 2010 of 74·28m.

In 2003 Iran had 985,000 refugees, mostly from Afghanistan (although the number of Afghan refugees in Iran was at its lowest at the end of 2003 for a decade). Only Pakistan has more refugees.

The areas, populations and capitals of the 28 provinces (*ostan*) were:

Province	Area (sq. km)	Census 1996	Estimate 2002	Capital
Ardabil	17,881	1,168,011	1,204,410	Ardabil
Azarbayejan, East	47,830	3,325,540	3,378,242	Tabriz
Azarbayejan, West	39,487	2,496,320	2,774,804	Orumiyeh
Bushehr	23,191	743,675	796,639	Bushehr
Chahar Mahal and Bakhtyari	16,201	761,168	794,077	Shahr-e-Kord
Esfahan	107,027	3,923,255	4,316,767	Esfahan
Fars	122,416	3,817,036	4,135,251	Shiraz
Gilan	14,106	2,241,896	2,310,033	Rasht
Golestan	20,891	1,426,288	1,555,058	Gorgan
Hamadan	19,547	1,677,957	1,718,627	Hamadan
Hormozgan	71,193	1,062,155	1,235,816	Bandar-e-Abbas
Ilam	20,151	487,886	550,971	Ilam
Kerman	181,814	2,004,328	2,215,376	Kerman
Kermanshah	24,641	1,778,596	1,962,176	Kermanshah
Khorasan	302,766	6,047,661	6,094,888	Mashhad
Khuzestan	63,238	3,746,772	4,506,816	Ahvaz

Province	Area (sq. km)	Census 1996	Estimate 2002	Capital
Kohgiluyeh and Boyer Ahmad	15,563	544,356	627,517	Yasuj
Kordestan	29,151	1,346,383	1,492,007	Sanandaj
Lorestan	28,392	1,584,434	1,671,706	Khorramabad
Markazi	29,406	1,228,812	1,300,778	Arak
Mazandaran	23,064	2,602,008	2,742,885	Sari
Qazvin	15,502	968,257	1,066,317	Qazvin
Qom	11,237	853,044	971,280	Qom
Semnan	96,816	501,447	563,959	Semnan
Sistan and Baluchestan	178,431	1,722,579	2,086,170	Zahedan
Tehran	18,637	10,343,965	11,689,301	Tehran
Yazd	73,467	750,769	841,370	Yazd
Zanjan	21,841	900,890	936,985	Zanjan

At the 1996 census the populations of the principal cities were:

	Population		Population
Tehran	6,758,845[1]	Arak	380,755
Mashhad	1,887,405	Ardabil	340,386
Esfahan	1,266,072	Yazd	326,776
Tabriz	1,191,043	Qazvin	291,117
Shiraz	1,053,025	Zanjan	286,295
Karaj	940,968	Sanandaj	277,808
Ahvaz	804,980	Bandar-e-Abbas	273,578
Qom	777,677	Khorramabad	272,815
Kermanshah	692,986	Eslamshahr	265,450
Orumiyeh	435,200	Borujerd	217,804
Zahedan	419,518	Abadan	206,073
Rasht	417,748	Dezful	202,639
Hamadan	401,281	Khorramshahr	105,636
Kerman	384,991		

[1]1999 population, 6,934,750.

The national language is Farsi or Persian, spoken by 45·6% of the population in 2003. 28·5% spoke related languages, including Kurdish (9·1%) and Luri in the west, Gilaki and Mazandarami in the north, and Baluchi in the southeast; 22·3% speak Turkic languages, primarily in the northwest. Iranians, who are Persians, not Arabs, are less emotionally connected to the plight of the Arab Palestinians than people in other parts of the Middle East.

SOCIAL STATISTICS

1999 births, 1,177,557; deaths, 374,838. Rates (1999, per 1,000 population): birth, 18·8; death, 6·0. Abortion is illegal, but a family planning scheme was inaugurated in 1988. Expectation of life at birth, 2003, 71·9 years for females and 69·0 years for males. Infant mortality, 2001, 35 per 1,000 live births. Annual population growth rate, 1992–2002, 1·4%; fertility rate, 2001, 2·9 births per woman. Iran has had one of the largest reductions in its fertility rate of any country in the world over the past 30 years, having had a rate of 6·4 births per woman in 1975. The suicide rate is 25 for every 100,000 people—more than twice the world average.

CLIMATE

Mainly a desert climate, but with more temperate conditions on the shores of the Caspian Sea. Seasonal range of temperature is considerable, as is rain (ranging from 2" in the southeast to 78" in the Caspian region). Winter is normally the rainy season for the whole country. Abadan, Jan. 54°F (12·2°C), July 97°F (36·1°C). Annual rainfall 8" (204 mm). Tehran, Jan. 36°F (2·2°C), July 85°F (29·4°C). Annual rainfall 10" (246 mm).

CONSTITUTION AND GOVERNMENT

The Constitution of the Islamic Republic was approved by a national referendum in Dec. 1979. It was revised in 1989 to expand the powers of the presidency and eliminate the position of prime minister. It gives supreme authority to the Spiritual Leader (wali faqih), a position which was held by Ayatollah Khomeini until his death on 3 June 1989. Ayatollah Seyed Ali Khamenei was elected to succeed him on 4 June 1989. Following the death of the previous incumbent, Ayatollah Ali Khamenei was proclaimed the Source of Knowledge (Marja e Taghlid) at the head of all Shia Muslims in Dec. 1994.

The 86-member Assembly of Experts was established in 1982. It is popularly elected every eight years. Its mandate is to interpret the constitution and select the Spiritual Leader. Candidates for election are examined by the Council of Guardians.

The Islamic Consultative Assembly has 290 members, elected for a four-year term in single-seat constituencies. All candidates have to be approved by the 12-member Council of Guardians.

The President of the Republic is popularly elected for not more than two four-year terms and is head of the executive; he appoints Ministers subject to approval by the Islamic Consultative Assembly (Majlis).

Legislative power is held by the Islamic Consultative Assembly, directly elected on a non-party basis for a four-year term by all citizens aged 17 or over. A new law passed in Oct. 1999 raised the voting age from 16 to 17, thus depriving an estimated 1·5m. young people from voting. Two-thirds of the electorate is under 30. Voting is secret but ballot papers are not printed; electors must write the name of their preferred candidate themselves. Five seats are reserved for religious minorities. All legislation is subject to approval by the Council of Guardians who ensure it is in accordance with the Islamic code and with the Constitution. The Spiritual Leader appoints six members, as does the judiciary.

National Anthem

'Sar zad az ofogh mehr-e khavaran' ('Rose from the horizon the affectionate sun of the East'); words by a group of poets, tune by Dr Riahi.

GOVERNMENT CHRONOLOGY

Spiritual Leaders of the Islamic Republic since 1980.
1980–89	Ayatollah Seyed Ruhollah Mousavi Khomeini
1989–	Ayatollah Seyed Mohammad Ali Hoseyn Khamenei

Heads of State since 1941.
Emperor (Shah)
1941–79	Mohammad Reza Pahlavi

Leader of the Revolution (Rahbar-e Enqelab)
1979–80	Ayatollah Seyed Ruhollah Mousavi Khomeini

President of the Republic
1980–81	Abolhasan Bani-Sadr

Interim Presidential Commission
1981

President of the Republic
1981	Mohammad Ali Rajai

Interim Presidential Commission
1981

Presidents of the Republic
1981–89	Ayatollah Seyed Mohammad Ali Hoseyn Khamenei Hodjatoleslam
1989–97	Ali Akbar Hashemi Rafsanjani Hodjatoleslam Seyed
1997–2005	Mohammad Khatami
2005–	Mahmoud Ahmadinejad

RECENT ELECTIONS

In presidential elections held on 17 June 2005 former president Ali Akbar Hashemi Rafsanjani took 21·0% of the vote, ahead of Mahmoud Ahmadinejad with 19·5%, Mehdi Karroubi 17·3%, Mohammad Baqer Qalibaf 13·9%, Mostafa Moin 13·8%, Ali Larijani 5·9% and Mohsen Mehralizadeh 4·4%. Turnout was 62·7%. As a result a second round run-off was required, in which

Mahmoud Ahmadinejad was elected with 61·7% of the vote on 24 June 2005 against 35·9% for Ali Akbar Hashemi Rafsanjani. Turnout was 59·6%.

Elections to the Islamic Consultative Assembly were held on 20 Feb. 2004. Conservatives won 156 seats, allies of President Mohammad Khatami 40 and ind. 30. In the second round of elections held on 7 May 2004 conservatives won 40 of 57 seats, reformists 8 and ind. 9.

Elections to the Assembly of Experts were held on 23 Oct. 1998; turnout was 46%. Conservative candidates won 54 seats, 13 went to moderates and the remaining 21 went to conservative-allied independents.

CURRENT ADMINISTRATION

In March 2006 the cabinet was composed as follows:

President: Mahmoud Ahmadinejad; b. 1956 (sworn in 6 Aug. 2005).

First Vice-President: Parviz Dawoodi.

Vice-President and Head of National Atomic Energy Organization: Gholamreza Aghazedeh-Khoi. *Vice-President and Head of Cultural Heritage and Tourism Organization:* Esfandiar Rahim Mashaei. *Vice-President and Head of Environmental Protection Organization:* Fatemeh Javadi. *Vice-President and Head of Foundation for Martyrs and Veterans Affairs:* Hossein Dehghan. *Vice-President and Head of Physical Education Organization:* Mohammad Aliabadi. *Vice-President and Head of Management and Planning Organization:* Farhad Rahbar. *Vice-President and Head of National Youth Organization:* Hojatoleslam Ali Akbari. *Vice-President for Legal and Parliamentary Affairs:* Ahmad Mousavi. *Vice-President for Executive Affairs:* Ali Saeedlou. *Secretary of the Cabinet:* Massoud Zaribafan.

Minister of Foreign Affairs: Manouchehr Mottaki. *Oil:* Kazem Vaziri-Hamaneh. *Interior:* Hojjatol-Islam Mostafa Pour-Mohammadi. *Economy:* Davoud Danesh-Jaafari. *Agriculture Jihad:* Mohammad-Reza Eskandari. *Commerce:* Masoud Mir-Kazemi. *Energy:* Parviz Fattah. *Transport:* Mohammad Rahmati. *Industry and Mines:* Ali-Reza Tahmasbi. *Housing and Urban Development:* Mohammad Saeedi-Kia. *Labour and Social Affairs:* Mohammad Jahromi. *Health:* Kamran Lankarani. *Education:* Mahmud Farshidi. *Science, Research and Technology:* Mohammad-Mehdi Zahedi. *Justice:* Jamal Karimi-Rad. *Defence:* Mostafa Mohammad-Najjar. *Culture and Islamic Guidance:* Mohammad-Hossein Saffar-Harandi. *Co-operatives:* Mohammad Nazemi Ardakani. *Intelligence and Security:* Hojjatol-Islam Gholam-Hossein Mohseni Ezhei. *Communications and Information Technology:* Mohammad Soleymani. *Welfare and Social Security:* Parviz Kazemi.

Speaker of the Islamic Consultative Assembly (*Majlis*): Gholam Ali Hadad-Adel.

Presidency Website: http://www.president.ir

CURRENT LEADERS

Ayatollah Seyed Ali Khamenei

Position
Spiritual Leader (wali faqih)

Introduction
Seyed Ali Khamenei succeeded Ayatollah Khomeini as Iran's supreme spiritual leader on the latter's death in June 1989, having previously served from 1981 as the third president of the Islamic Republic.

Early Life
Khamanei was born in Mashhad on 15 July 1939. He attended theological colleges in Qom, where he was a pupil of Ayatollah Khomeini, and Mashhad. From 1963 he was involved with the Islamic opposition to the regime of the Shah, for which he spent three years in prison and a year in exile. Active in the Islamic

revolution of 1979, Khamenei was appointed to the Revolutionary Council and became deputy minister of defence. He was also leader of the Friday congregational prayers in Tehran from mid-1980 and, from Aug. 1981, was appointed secretary-general of the Islamic Republican Party (IRP), dissolved in 1987. He was injured in a bomb blast in June 1986.

Career in Office
On 2 Oct 1981, as the IRP candidate, Khamenei was the first cleric to be elected as president, with 95% of the popular vote. Ayatollah Khomeini had previously barred the clergy from the office. He succeeded Mohammad Ali Radjai who had been assassinated in Aug. In Aug. 1985 he was re-elected, again overwhelmingly, for a second four-year term. On the death of Khomeini, Khamenei was elected to succeed him on 4 June 1989 by an Assembly of Experts. Previously a middle-ranking cleric (Hojatolislam), he assumed the title of Ayatollah, a constitutional precondition of appointment to the Islamic republic's spiritual leadership. In Dec. 1994 he was proclaimed the Marja e Taghlid (Source of Knowledge) at the head of all Shia Muslims.

Khamenei became directly involved in negotiations with the International Atomic Energy Agency (IAEA) in 2003, denying that the government sought nuclear weapons. However, the acceptance of IAEA inspections in Oct. was attributed to the leader's inclination to avoid further confrontation with the international community, specifically the USA.

The standoff between President Khatami's reformist government and the hard-line conservative Council of Guardians reached a critical point in the run-up to the Feb. 2004 parliamentary elections. The Council's disqualification of over 2,000 reformist candidates provoked threats of resignations in government and boycott in the electorate. Khamenei intervened in Jan. 2004 on state television, calling for review of the Council's decisions and backing the 83 Majlis deputies whose candidacies had been rejected. However, over a third of the Majlis' deputies resigned in protest on 1 Feb. 2004 and in the subsequent election religious conservatives regained parliamentary control.

Khamenei has since presided over a deterioration in relations with the Western powers over Iran's uranium enrichment activities and its alleged ambitions to acquire nuclear weapons. Western concerns were further heightened by the election in June 2005 of the hard-line Islamic conservative Mahmoud Ahmadinejad as state president and his formal endorsement in Aug. by Khamenei.

Mahmoud Ahmadinejad

Position
President

Introduction
Mahmoud Ahmadinejad won the run-off in Iran's presidential election on 24 June 2005. The ultra-conservative former Revolutionary Guard and mayor of Tehran promised to tackle poverty and corruption. Analysts expect an end to the fragile social reforms made under his predecessor, President Mohammad Khatami, and a hardening of Iran's foreign policy towards the West, particularly over its nuclear programme.

Early Life
The son of a blacksmith, Mahmoud Ahmadinejad was born in 1956 in the village of Aradan, near Qa-emshahr in northern Iran. The family moved to Tehran a year later, where he attended school. In 1976 he took up a place to study civil engineering at the Iran University of Science and Technology (IUST). A conservative, he was supportive of Ayatollah Khomeini's Islamic revolution in 1979 and was a student representative of the Office for the Strengthening of Unity between Universities and Theological Seminaries (OSU). Some of the 52 Americans who were held hostage in the US embassy after the revolution allege

that Ahmadinejad was among those who captured them, though he strongly denies the claim. He remained at the IUST until the late 1980s, taking a masters degree in civil engineering, followed by a PhD in traffic and transportation engineering and planning, and then winning a professorship.

Ahmadinejad was drawn into the long-running Iran–Iraq war in 1986, when he joined the Islamic Revolutionary Guards and fought on the Iraqi border near Kirkuk. He later served as chief engineer in the sixth division. When the war ended in 1988, Ahmadinejad worked as an engineer in the local government offices of Maku and Khvoy in the province of West Azarbayejan, near the Turkish border. In 1993 he became governor of the northwestern province of Ardabil until he was ousted following the election of the reform-minded President Mohammad Khatami in 1997. Returning to Tehran, Ahmadinejad rejoined the IUST's civil engineering faculty, where he remained until May 2003. There has been speculation that he assisted at this time with the organization of the conservative Islamist group, Ansar-e Hizbollah.

Ahmadinejad was elected mayor of Tehran on 3 May 2003, and pursued conservative policies, strengthening the role of religious activities in many of the city's cultural centres. He closed down some fast-food restaurants and banned an advertising campaign that featured a Western celebrity. His conservative views were at odds with President Khatami, who barred him from attending cabinet meetings, a privilege normally accorded to mayors of the capital. With the backing of conservative groups including the Alliance of Developers of an Islamic Iran, Ahmadinejad contested the June 2005 presidential elections. His campaign was aimed at the poor and disadvantaged, as well as religious conservatives. He emphasized his working-class upbringing and promised to redistribute the country's income from oil. In a run-off against the former president, Ali Akbar Hashemi Rafsanjani, on 24 June 2005, Ahmadinejad emerged victorious, with 61·7% of the vote, although there were complaints of voting irregularities.

Career in Office

On 3 Aug. Ahmadinejad received the formal approval of the Supreme Leader, Ayatollah Khamenei, and, having taken the vow before the Majlis to protect Shia Islam and the constitution, he became the president on 6 Aug. 2005. In his inaugural address, Ahmadinejad called for unity and said he was going to build a model state based on principles of 'modern, advanced, and strong Islamic government'. However, he quickly caused consternation both at home and abroad. Within Iran, he seemingly instituted a purge of various branches of government, state economic agencies and the diplomatic service, drawing accusations that he was exceeding his constitutional powers. On the international stage, Iran's resumption of uranium enrichment at its Esfahan plant in Aug. intensified Western concerns over nuclear weapon proliferation, and a vehemently anti-Israeli speech by Ahmadinejad in Oct. provoked worldwide condemnation.

DEFENCE

Two years' military service is compulsory. Military expenditure totalled US$3,051m. in 2003 (equivalent to US$46 per capita), representing 2·4% of GDP, compared to 7·7% in 1985.

Nuclear Weapons

Although Iran is a member of the Non-Proliferation Treaty (NPT), United Nations inspectors have found enriched uranium in environmental samples, increasing US suspicion that Iran is developing nuclear weapons. In Aug. 2005 Iran rejected proposals from France, Germany and the UK for economic incentives in return for an indefinite suspension of uranium enrichment and resumed nuclear conversion activities at its plant in Esfahan.

Iran has successfully tested Shahab-3 medium-range ballistic missiles with a known range of 1,300 km, and in Aug. 2004 tested a new version that analysts believe may have a range of 2,000 km. According to *Deadly Arsenals*, published by the Carnegie Endowment for International Peace, Iran has a chemical and biological weapons programme.

Army

Strength (2002), 325,000 (about 220,000 conscripts). Reserves are estimated to be around 350,000, made up of ex-service volunteers.

Revolutionary Guard (*Pasdaran Inqilab*)

Numbering some 125,000, the Guard is divided between ground forces (100,000), naval forces (some 20,000) and marines (5,000). It controls the Basij, a volunteer 'popular mobilization army' of about 300,000, which can number 1m. strong in wartime.

Navy

The fleet includes six submarines (including three ex-Soviet *Kilo* class) and three ex-UK frigates. Personnel numbered 18,000 in 2002 including 2,000 in Naval Aviation and 2,600 marines.

The Naval Aviation wing operated five combat aircraft and 19 armed helicopters.

The main naval bases are at Bandar-e-Abbas, Bushehr and Chah Bahar.

Air Force

In 2002 there were 306 combat aircraft including US F-14 Tomcat, F-5E Tiger II and F-4D/E Phantom II fighter-bombers, and a number of MiG-29 interceptors and Su-24 strike aircraft. The serviceability of the aircraft varies with only 60–80% operational.

Strength (2002) estimated at 52,000 personnel (about 15,000 air defence).

INTERNATIONAL RELATIONS

In April 2001 Iran and Saudi Arabia signed a security pact to fight drug trafficking and terrorism, 13 years after the two countries had broken off relations. Currently there is a standoff between Iran and the international community on the question of nuclear development.

Iran is a member of the UN, OPEC, ECO, Colombo Plan, IOM, OIC and Islamic Development Bank.

ECONOMY

Agriculture accounted for 11·7% of GDP in 2002, industry 40·6% and services 47·7%.

Overview

Iran's macroeconomic performance has been strong in recent years. In the first half of the 2000s GDP grew by an average annual rate of 5·1%. This growth is largely owing to rising oil prices but the private sector has also seen strong growth. Manufacturing and construction have been key growth sectors, along with the wholesale, retail trade, restaurants and hotels sectors. According to the World Bank, strong private sector performance was a result of high oil prices, expansionary macroeconomic policy and a positive private sector reaction to structural reforms implemented by the government of Mohammad Khatami. However, the economy remains reliant on oil and the Ahmadinejad government's commitment to pushing through further structural reform is uncertain. Inconsistent implementation of privatization and liberalization reforms has hindered the growth of private sector activity. Price subsidies and controls continue to distort the economy. Inflation averaged 14·2% in the first half of the 2000s and has not been brought under control. Unemployment has fallen but job creation remains a major challenge. With strong labour force growth resulting from the post-revolution baby boom of the 1980s, unemployment is likely to rise in future years.

Currency

The unit of currency is the *rial* (IRR) of which 10 = 1 *toman*. In March 2005 the Iranian rial was fixed at a rate of IRR 9,090 to the US dollar. Gold reserves were 5·42m. troy oz in March 1996. Total money supply in Feb. 2002 was 130,015bn. rials. Inflation rates (based on IMF statistics) for fiscal years:

1995	1996	1997	1998	1999	2000	2001	2002	2003	2004
49·4%	23·2%	17·3%	18·1%	20·1%	12·6%	11·4%	15·8%	15·6%	15·6%

Budget

The financial year runs from 21 March. Revenues in 2001–02 totalled 180,975bn. rials and expenditures 168,992bn. rials. Petroleum and natural gas revenues accounted for 57·0% of all revenues and taxes 23·0%. Current expenditure accounted for 66·6% of all expenditures.

Performance

Real GDP growth rates (based on IMF statistics):

1997	1998	1999	2000	2001	2002	2003	2004
3·4%	2·7%	1·9%	5·1%	3·7%	7·5%	6·7%	5·6%

Total GDP in 2004 was US$162·7bn.

Banking and Finance

The Central Bank is the note issuing authority and government bank. Its *Governor* is Ebrahim Sheibani. All other banks and insurance companies were nationalized in 1979, and re-organized into new state banking corporations. In April 2000 the government announced that it would permit the establishment of private banks for the first time since the revolution in 1979, ending the state monopoly on banking. The first private bank since the revolution came into existence in Aug. 2001 with the creation of Bank-e-Eqtesadi Novin (Modern Economic Bank). A further three private banks have opened in the meantime. In 2002 there were 11 commercial banks, two development banks, one housing bank and around 30 foreign banks.

A stock exchange re-opened in Tehran in 1992.

ENERGY AND NATURAL RESOURCES

Environment

Iran's carbon dioxide emissions from the consumption and flaring of fossil fuels were the equivalent of 5·3 tonnes per capita in 2002.

Electricity

Total installed capacity in 2002 was 35·4m. kW; production (2002), 136·00bn. kWh (130·92bn. kWh thermal and 5·08bn. kWh hydro-electric). Consumption per capita in 2002 was about 2,075 kWh. Iran's first nuclear reactor is being built by Russia at Bushehr and is scheduled to be commissioned before the end of 2006.

Oil and Gas

Iran has 11·4% of proven global oil reserves. Oil is its chief source of revenue. The main oilfields are in the Zagros Mountains where oil was first discovered in 1908. Oil companies were nationalized in 1979 and operations of crude oil and natural gas exploitation are now run by the National Iranian Oil Company. Refining operations of crude oil are run by the National Company for Refining and Distribution of Oil Products. Iran produced 166·9m. tonnes of oil in 2002 (4·7% of the world total oil output); in 2003 it had reserves amounting to 130·7bn. bbls. (only Saudi Arabia had more). In 1999 the most important discovery in more than 30 years was made, with the Azadegan oilfield in the southwest of the country being found to have reserves of approximately 26bn. bbls. In 2001 revenue from oil exports amounted to US$14bn. (US$19bn. in 2000). Iran depends on oil for some 86% of its exports, but domestic consumption has been increasing to such an extent that it is now as high as exports.

Iran has nearly 15% of proven global gas reserves. A deal reached in Nov. 1997 between Gazprom, the Russian gas company, and Total, the French energy group, involved the investment of US$2,000m. into the development of a gas field.

In Dec. 1997 the first natural gas pipeline linking Iran with the Caspian Sea via Turkmenistan was opened. The 200-km line links gas fields in western Turkmenistan to industrial markets in northern Iran. Natural gas production (2002): 64·5bn. cu. metres. Natural gas reserves in 2002 were 23,000bn. cu. metres, the second largest behind Russia.

Minerals

Production (in 1,000 tonnes): gypsum (1999–2000), 10,834; iron ore (1999–2000), 10,776; decorative stone (1999), 7,700; crude steel (2002), 7,300; salt (1999), 1,600; coal (2000), 1,394; chromite (1999), 255; zinc and lead (1999), 182; bauxite (2000), 140; copper (2001), 140; aluminium (1999), 137; manganese (1999), 104. It was announced in Feb. 2003 that uranium deposits had been discovered in central Iran. In Nov. 2003 the International Atomic Energy Agency announced that Iran had admitted to enriching uranium at an electric plant outside Tehran.

Agriculture

Agriculture accounted for approximately 12·7% of GDP in 2000. There were 14·27m. ha. of arable land in 2001 and 2·28m. ha. of permanent crops. 7·5m. ha. were irrigated in 2001.

Crop production (2000, in 1,000 tonnes): wheat, 8,088; sugarbeets, 4,332; potatoes, 3,658; tomatoes, 3,191; grapes, 2,505; sugarcane, 2,367; rice (paddy), 1,971; barley, 1,686; watermelons, 1,650; onions, 1,344; cucumbers and gherkins, 1,343; maize, 1,036; dates, 870; pistachios, 304. Iran's annual production of dates and pistachios is the highest in the world.

Livestock (2000): 55·0m. sheep; 26·0m. goats; 8·1m. cattle; 500,000 buffaloes; 1·6m. asses; 386m. chickens.

Forestry

Approximately 4·5% of Iran is forested (7·30m. ha.), much of it in the Caspian region. Timber production in 2003 was 693,000 cu. metres.

Fisheries

In 2003 the total catch was 349,121 tonnes (299,128 tonnes from sea fishing).

INDUSTRY

Major industries: petrochemical, automotive, food, beverages and tobacco, textiles, clothing and leather, wood and fibre, paper and cardboard, chemical products, non-metal mining products, basic materials, machinery and equipment, copper, steel and aluminium. The textile industry uses local cotton and silk; carpet manufacture is an important industry. The country's steel industry is the largest in the Middle East; crude steel production in 2002 totalled 7·3m. tonnes.

Production includes: cement (2000), 23·3m. tonnes; cottonseed oil (1998), 994,000 tonnes; sugar (1998), 863,200 tonnes; stockings (2000), 18·5m. pairs; building bricks (2000), 10,077m. units.

Labour

The economically active population numbered 20m. in 2002, of which 17·6m. were employed. Approximately 12·2% of the workforce are unemployed and 800,000 Iranians enter the workforce every year.

INTERNATIONAL TRADE

There had been a limit on foreign investment, but legislation of 1995 permits foreign nationals to hold more than 50% of the equity of joint ventures with the consent of the Foreign Investment Board. Foreign debt was US$9,154m. in 2002.

Imports and Exports

Imports and exports for calendar years in US$1m.:

	1996	1997	1998	1999	2000
Imports f.o.b.	14,989	14,123	14,286	13,433	15,207
Exports f.o.b.	22,391	18,381	13,118	21,030	28,345

Main imports: machinery and motor vehicles, iron and steel, chemicals, pharmaceuticals, food. Main exports: oil, carpets, pistachios, leather and caviar. Petroleum and crude oil exports (1996): 2,620,000 bbls. a day. Crude oil exports account for 85% of hard currency earnings. Carpet exports are the second largest hard currency earner. Main import suppliers, 1998–99: Germany, 11·6%; Italy, 8·3%; Japan, 7·0%; Belgium, 6·3%; United Arab Emirates, 5·3%; Argentina, 4·4%. Main export markets in 1998–99: UK, 16·8%; Japan, 15·7%; Italy, 8·6%; United Arab Emirates, 6·7%; Greece, 5·0%; South Korea, 5·0%.

COMMUNICATIONS

Roads

In 2002 the total length of roads was 167,394 km, of which 811 km were motorways, 24,875 km main roads, 68,062 km secondary regional roads and 73,646 km other local roads. In 2002 there were 1,513,000 passenger cars; 590,000 vans and lorries; 2,565,000 motorcycles and mopeds (1996). In 1999 there were 16,858 road accidents resulting in 2,313 deaths.

Rail

The State Railways totalled 6,688 km in 2000, of which 148 km were electrified. In 2000 the railways carried 11·7m. passengers and 25·2m. tonnes of freight. An isolated 1,676 mm gauge line (94 km) in the southeast provides a link with Pakistan Railways. A rail link to Turkmenistan was opened in May 1996. A metro system was opened in Tehran in 1999.

Civil Aviation

There are international airports at Tehran (Mehrabad), Shiraz and Bandar-e-Abbas. Tehran is the busiest airport, in 2000 handling 8,474,000 passengers (6,473,000 on domestic flights). The Imam Khomeini International Airport, construction of which began in 1977 before being halted in 1979, was inaugurated in Feb. 2004. The first flight arrived at the airport in May 2004 but it was then shut down by Iran's Revolutionary Guard, citing breaches of security by the foreign operators. The state-owned Iran Air carried 5·8m. passengers and 38,343 tonnes of freight in 1998–99.

Shipping

In 2002 the merchant fleet totalled 4·13m. GRT, including oil tankers totalling 2·14m. GRT. In 1998–99, 4,447 ships loaded and unloaded 31·0m. and 41·1m. tonnes of goods respectively (including oil products). In 2001 vessels totalling 67,267,000 NRT entered ports.

Telecommunications

In 2002 there were 14,387,100 telephone main lines, equivalent to 220·1 per 1,000 population, and 4·9m. PCs in use (75·0 for every 1,000 persons). In 2002 mobile phone subscribers numbered 2,187,000 and there were 48,000 fax machines in use. Iran had 3,168,000 Internet users in 2002.

Postal Services

In 2003 there were 5,843 post offices. 521m. pieces of mail were processed during the year, or seven items per person.

SOCIAL INSTITUTIONS

Justice

A legal system based on Islamic law (Sharia) was introduced by the 1979 constitution. A new criminal code on similar principles was introduced in Nov. 1995. The President of the Supreme Court and the public Prosecutor-General are appointed by the Spiritual Leader. The Supreme Court has 16 branches and 109 offences carry the death penalty. To these were added economic crimes in 1990.

The population in penal institutions in April 2002 was 163,526 (226 per 100,000 of national population). There were 94 confirmed executions in 2005. Executions are frequently held in public.

Police

Women rejoined the police force in 2003 for the first time since the 1979 revolution.

Education

Adult literacy in 2003 was 77·0% (83·5% among males and 70·4% among females). Most primary and secondary schools are state schools. Elementary education in state schools and university education is free; small fees are charged for state-run secondary schools. In 2001–02 there were 7,513,015 pupils and 309,260 teachers at 68,836 primary schools, 9,416,272 pupils and 344,042 teachers at secondary schools, and 1,566,509 pupils and 79,235 academic staff at institutions of higher education. Female students now outnumber male students at the state universities.

In 1994–95 there were 30 universities, 30 medical universities, 12 specialized universities (one agriculture, one art, one oil engineering, four teacher training, five technology) and two open (distance-learning) universities. There were 733,527 students and 46,747 academic staff in tertiary education in 2000–01.

In 2000–01 total expenditure on education came to 4·4% of GNP and represented 20·4% of total government expenditure.

Health

There were 717 hospitals in 2001, with 109,152 beds. In 2001 medical personnel totalled 295,325 of which 152,396 were paramedics. There were 25,988 nurses and 8,105 midwives.

Welfare

The official retirement ages are 60 years (men) or 55 (women). However, these ages drop to 50 years (men) or 45 (women) if the individual has spent between 20 and 25 years of work in an unhealthy or physically demanding environment. The minimum old-age pension is 50% of earnings but not less than 696,460 rials a month (the minimum wage of an unskilled labourer), plus food coupons. The maximum pension is 100% of earnings up to 1,970,000 rials a month.

The minimum unemployment benefit is 55% of average earnings. The maximum cannot exceed 80% of average earnings.

RELIGION

The official religion is the Shia branch of Islam. Adherents numbered approximately 85% of the population in 2001; 5% were Sunni Muslims. However, less than 2% of the population now attend Friday prayers.

CULTURE

World Heritage Sites

There are seven sites in Iran (all inscribed in 1979 except for Takht-e Soleyman, in 2003, Bam and Pasargadae in 2004 and Soltaniyeh in 2005): Tchogha Zanbil, the ruins of the holy city of the kingdom of Elam founded around 1250 BC; Persepolis, the palace complex founded by Darius I in 518 BC and capital of the Achaemenid empire (the first Persian empire); Meidan Imam, the square built in Esfahan by Abbas I in the early 17th century, which is bordered on all sides by monumental buildings linked by a series of arcades; Takht-e Soleyman, a Sasanian royal residence with important Zoroastrian religious architecture and decoration; Bam and its Cultural Landscape, a fortified medieval town where 26,000 people lost their lives in the earthquake of Dec. 2003; Pasargadae, the first dynastic capital of the great multicultural Achaemenid Empire in Western Asia; and Soltaniyeh, the capital of the Ilkhamid dynasty that stands as a monument to Persian and Islamic architecture.

Broadcasting

Broadcasting is controlled by the government agency, Islamic Republic of Iran Broadcasting (IRIB). Both television and radio operate under a single organization, the National Iranian Radio and Television Organization (NIRT), established by an Act of Parliament in 1967, which in 1990 employed some 11,620 people. There are two national radio stations (Radio One and Radio Two) and 27 regional radio stations, including a Koran service and an external service (Voice of the Islamic Republic of Iran, which broadcasts in 20 languages). There are no commercial radio stations; radio broadcasting is a state monopoly. There were (1997) 138 radio transmitters in operation. There are four television networks (colour by SECAM H). There were 17·9m. radio receivers in 2000 and 11·1m. television receivers in 2001.

Cinema

There were 312 cinemas with an attendance in 2001 of 33m.

Press

In 2000 there were 117 daily and 259 weekly newspapers. Approximately 80% of the Iranian press is printed in Farsi; much of the remaining 20% is in English or Arabic. As the power struggle continues between the conservative religious establishment and the Khatami government more than 70 reform-minded newspapers have been closed down since 1999.

In 1999 a total of 14,783 book titles were published.

Tourism

There were 1,402,160 foreign tourists in 2001, spending US$1,122m.

Calendar

The Iranian year is a solar year starting on varying dates between 19 and 22 March. The current solar year is 1385 (21 March 2006 to 20 March 2007). The Islamic *hegira* (622 AD, when Mohammed left Makkah for Madinah) year 1427 corresponds to 31 Jan. 2006–19 Jan. 2007, and is the current lunar year.

Libraries

In 2001 there were 1,502 libraries affiliated to the Ministry of Culture and Islamic Guidance.

DIPLOMATIC REPRESENTATIVES

Of Iran in the United Kingdom (16 Prince's Gate, London, SW7 1PT)
Ambassador: Vacant.
Chargé d'Affaires a.i.: Hamid Reza Nafez Arefi.

Of the United Kingdom in Iran (143 Ferdowsi Ave., Tehran 11344)
Ambassador: Richard Dalton, CMG.

The USA does not have diplomatic relations with Iran, but Iran has an Interests Section in the Pakistani Embassy in Washington, D.C., and the USA has an Interests Section in the Swiss Embassy in Tehran.

Of Iran to the United Nations
Ambassador: M. Javad Zarif.

Of Iran to the European Union
Ambassador: Abolghasem Delfi.

FURTHER READING

Abdelkhah, Fariba, *Being Modern in Iran.* Columbia Univ. Press, 1999
Abrahamian, E., *Khomeinism: Essays on the Islamic Republic.* Univ. of California Press, 1993
Amuzegar, J., *Iran's Economy Under the Islamic Republic.* London, 1992
Ansari, Ali M., *Modern Iran Since 1921: The Pahlavis and After.* Pearson Longman, Harlow, 2003
Daneshvar, P., *Revolution in Iran.* London, 1996
Ehtesami, A., *After Khomeini: the Iranian Second Republic.* London, 1994
Foran, J., *Fragile Resistance: Social Transformation in Iran from 1500 to the Revolution.* Boulder (Colo.), 1993
Kamrava, M., *Political History of Modern Iran: from Tribalism to Theocracy.* London, 1993
Kinzer, Stephen, *All the Shah's Men: an American Coup and the Roots of Middle East Terror.* John Wiley, Indianapolis, 2003
Martin, Vanessa, *Creating an Islamic State: Khomeini and the Making of a New Iran.* I. B. Tauris, London and New York, 2000
Mir-Hosseini, Ziba, *Islam and Gender: The Religious Debate in Contemporary Iran.* Princeton Univ. Press, 1999
Moin, Baqer, *Khomeini: Life of the Ayatollah.* I. B. Tauris, London, 1999
Omid, H., *Islam and the Post-Revolutionary State in Iran.* London, 1994
Rahnema, A. and Behdad, S. (eds.) *Iran After the Revolution: the Crisis of an Islamic State.* London, 1995

National Statistical Office: Statistical Centre of Iran, Dr Fatemi Avenue, Tehran 1414663111, Iran.
Website: http://www.sci.org.ir/

IRAQ

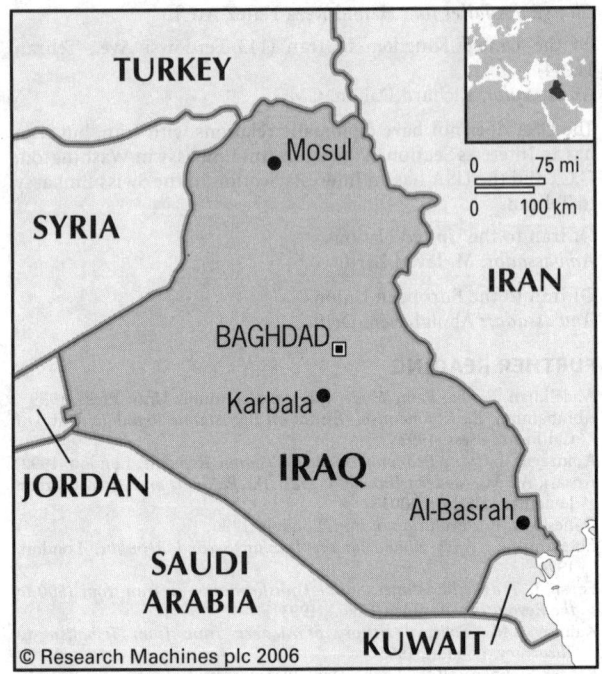

TURKEY

Mosul

SYRIA

IRAN

BAGHDAD

Karbala

JORDAN

IRAQ

Al-Basrah

SAUDI
ARABIA

KUWAIT

0   75 mi
0   100 km

© Research Machines plc 2006

Jumhouriya al 'Iraqia
(Republic of Iraq)

Capital: Baghdad
Population projection, 2010: 32·53m.
GDP per capita, 1998: (PPP$) 3,197

KEY HISTORICAL EVENTS

Around 3000 BC the Sumerian culture flourished in Mesopotamia—the part of the Fertile Crescent between and around the Tigris and Euphrates rivers. Incursions from Semitic peoples of the Arabian Peninsula led to Akkadian supremacy after the victory of Sargon the Great (*c.* 2340 BC). The Sumerian cities, such as Ur, reasserted their independence until 1700 BC, when King Hammurabi established the first dynasty of Babylon. Hammurabi and his son, Samsu-iluna, presided over the political and cultural apogee of Babylon; it was a time of great prosperity and relative peace. Babylonia was challenged by the Anatolian Hittites, who sacked Babylon in 1595 BC. A weakened Babylonia fell to the Kassites from the Zagros mountains, who held sway for over 400 years. The power-vacuum in northern Babylonia was filled by the Hurrian kingdom of Mitanni until Assyria's dominance in the 13th century BC. The Semitic Assyrians built an empire that stretched from Tarsus on the Mediterranean to Babylon, which they sacked in 1240 BC.

Elamite invasions in the 12th century BC allowed the establishment of a second Babylonian dynasty—Isin, or Pashe—but the assertiveness of its king, Nebuchadnezzar I, provoked Assyrian retaliation. Assyrian control of Babylonia was regained but tempered by massive immigration of Aramaeans from Upper Mesopotamia and Syria. Nevertheless, the Assyrians achieved considerable imperial expansion under Ashurnasirpal II in the early ninth century BC. Assyrian decline and revival was repeated in the eighth century. Babylon was recaptured in 729

BC and most of the Fertile Crescent, from the Nile Delta to the Persian Gulf, was subjugated. However, the empire soon crumbled after the death of the great King Ashurbanipal in 627 BC. Revolts in Babylonia were led by the Chaldeans, who had settled in the south from the ninth century. An alliance of old enemies—the Medes and the Scythians—ravaged the Assyrian Empire and in 612 BC, the capital, Nineveh, fell to the Medes.

Babylonia, known at this time as Chaldea, assumed control of much of the Fertile Crescent. In 586 BC, Nebuchadnezzar II conquered Phoenicia and Judah, destroying Jerusalem and deporting 15,000 Judaeans as labourers for Babylon. This Babylonian revival withered under his successors, who were defeated by Achaemenid Persia. Cyrus the Great captured Babylon in 539 BC. His rule was strengthened by his self-association with the Babylonian throne and by his religious tolerance; the Babylonian deity Bel-Marduk was restored and the Temple of Jerusalem rebuilt. Xerxes I (485–465 BC) styled himself the Persian Emperor and seized the Bel-Marduk statue, provoking several Babylonian rebellions.

Alexander

The last of the Achaemenids, Darius III, was defeated at the Battle of Gaugamela (near Mosul) in 331 BC by Alexander the Great of Macedon, who established the Hellenistic Age of the Near East. Having assumed the Persian throne, he died at Babylon in 323 BC. His empire was split in four; Seleucus took control of Mesopotamia and Persia and declared himself king in 305 BC. Babylon was soon eclipsed by a new capital at Seleucia on the Tigris and was abandoned during the third century. Parthia, Bactria and Anatolia were lost by Seleucus' successors until Antiochus III (223–187 BC) reasserted his lordship over the lost provinces. However, his foray into Greece was repulsed by Rome, which forced a heavy indemnity on the Seleucid Empire. Rapid territorial losses to Rome, Ptolemaic Egypt and local rebellions led to a Parthian invasion of Babylonia in 129 BC.

The Parthian Empire, with its winter capital at Ctesiphon on the Tigris, reached its territorial zenith under Mithridates II (123–88 BC), who defeated Armenia and repelled the Scythians. Though a looser political unit than the Seleucid state, Mithridates' empire was a conscious inheritor of the great traditions—Persian, Babylonian and Hellenistic—in culture, language and symbolism. Intrigue over its nominal vassal, Armenia, brought Parthia into conflict with Rome. At Carrhae the Parthians inflicted a crushing defeat on a Roman army under Crassus in 53 BC. Several wars followed until Vologases I achieved a settlement with Emperor Nero over the Armenian buffer-state in 63 AD. Dynastic disputes bedevilled Parthia and its vassal kingdoms. The invasion of Armenia by Osroes I (109–129 AD) sparked a Roman invasion in 113 AD under Trajan, who annexed Armenia and occupied most of Mesopotamia. Roman control ended after Trajan's death but Vologases IV was forced to cede western Mesopotamia to Rome. However, Mesopotamia remained a battleground, such as the 195 AD invasion by the Emperor Severus, who looted Ctesiphon, further weakening the Parthian state. In 224 AD Artabanus IV, the last of the Parthian kings, was defeated by Ardashir (Artaxerxes), ruler of Persia and founder of the Sassanid Dynasty.

The Sassanian Persians emulated the Achaemenids and attempted to regain their empire, leading to inevitable conflict with Rome. Ardashir's son, Shapur I, continued his father's expansion in the east and attacked Rome's Levantine provinces. Syria and Armenia were overrun and the Roman Emperor Valerian captured at Edessa in 259. Shapur II (309–379) consolidated Sassanid power, defeating threats from Arabia and

Central Asia and wresting control of the Tigris and Armenia from the Romans. The religious policies of the Zoroastrian Sassanids fluctuated from tolerance to persecution. Khosrau I (531–579) revived imperial expansion; his grandson, Khosrau II, was restored to the throne by the Byzantine Emperor Maurice, who was rewarded with Armenia and northeastern Mesopotamia. However, Khosrau retook Mesopotamia after Maurice's murder, beginning a Persian rampage through the Byzantine East. The sack and pillage of Jerusalem provoked Emperor Heraclius, who struck the Persian heartland. In 627 Heraclius entered Ctesiphon and destroyed the palace of Khosrau, who was murdered. Sassanid Persia, exhausted by conflict with Rome, quickly fell to the Arab invasion.

Led by Sa'd ibn Abi Waqqas, the Arab forces of Islam defeated the Sassanians at the Battle of Al-Qadisiyyah (c. 636) on the Euphrates and at Nahavand, western Iran, in 642. By 639 most of Iraq (Erak, 'lower Iran'), comprising the centre and south of modern republic, had been conquered; as had Al-Jazirah ('The Island'), the area north of Tikrit. Mass Arab immigration saw the establishment of garrison towns at Kufa (near Babylon) and Al-Basrah and later at Mosul. After the first four caliphs, the Caliphate effectively became hereditary under the Ummayads, based at Damascus. However, their rule was disputed, especially in Iraq. The death of Ali's second son, Husayn, at Karbala in 680 left a body of opposition, the Shias, or 'partisans' of Ali. Iraq was controlled by a governor and, from the 690s, Arabic became the language of administration.

Rise of Baghdad

In 743 civil war came to the Caliphate. Having failed to resolve the tensions between rival Arab military groups, the Umayyads succumbed to the rebellion of the Abbasids, who called for a return to strong Islamic leadership. In 750 the last Ummayad caliph, Marwan II, was deposed by Abu al-'Abbas (As-Saffah), supported by Iranian and Iraqi Shias. However, As-Saffah installed himself as caliph, rejecting a Shia imam. In 754 he was succeeded by his brother Al-Mansur, who moved the capital to Baghdad on the Tigris. This move symbolized the end of the hegemony of Syrian and Yemeni Arabs over the Caliphate. Nevertheless, an overburdened Iraq provided numerous threats to Abbasid authority; Al-Mansur had to quell Shia revolts in Iraq in 763. Caliph Al-Mu'tasim moved his capital to Samarra in 836 to remove his Turkic Mamluk soldiers from Baghdad. The suppression of the Zanj Revolt (869–879) of African slaves around Al-Basrah prompted the return to Baghdad.

Political fragmentation came quickly in the 930s and broke the Caliphate. The Shia Buyids took Iraq in 946, depriving the Abbasid caliphs of temporal power. From the 970s, Egypt was ruled by a rival caliphate, the Ismaili Fatimids. Baghdad was taken by the Seljuk Turks under Toghrül, the Sultan of Iran, in 1055. Although the Seljuk territories fragmented after the death of Malik Shah I in 1092, Iraq remained under Seljuk authority until the Mongol invasion. In 1258 Baghdad was sacked by the Mongol Hulagu Khan; the city was ravaged, its people slaughtered and its Grand Library destroyed. The sack ended the Abbasid Caliphate and Baghdad's role as a major cultural centre. Hulagu established the Il-Khanid Dynasty of Iran. Buddhism and Nestorian Christianity flourished under the patronage of Hulagu's successors until the conversion of Khan Ghazan to Sunni Islam in 1292. The Il-Khanate fragmented in the 1330s and Iraq was ruled by the Mongol Jalayirids.

Ottoman Rule

Baghdad was once again viciously sacked in 1401 by Timur. His death in 1405 allowed the Black Sheep Turkmen (Kara Koyunlu) to overthrow their Jalayirid masters. However, their rapid expansion ended in defeat in 1466 at the hands of the White Sheep Turkmen (Ak Koyunlu). Rivalry with the Ottoman

Turks in Anatolia weakened the White Sheep Turkmen, who were forced to withdraw from Iraq by the Turkic Safavid rulers of Iran. Shah Ismail I took Baghdad in 1509 and made Shi'ism the state religion; all other creeds were banned. However, Iraq soon fell to the Sunni Ottomans, with Sultan Suleyman the Magnificent taking Baghdad in 1534. Shah Abbas reclaimed Iraq for Iran in 1603, brutally suppressing a major Kurdish rebellion in 1610. Ottoman authority was re-imposed by Sultan Murad IV, who led his army into Baghdad in 1638.

Centuries of neglect and war had devastated the irrigation systems and agricultural wealth of Iraq. The Ottomans treated Iraq as a buffer state against Iran and allowed Kurdish and Bedouin tribes to dominate. Mamluks asserted their power in Iraq until 1831, when Baghdad was devastated by flooding. Serious administrative reform (tanzimat) came in 1869 with the appointment of Midhat Pasha as governor of Baghdad, with great improvements in the army, the law and education. The Young Turks revolution of 1908 gave Iraq limited political representation.

British Mandate

Anglo-German rivalry led to a British invasion of southern Iraq in Nov. 1914. Although Al-Basrah fell in 1915, the British suffered a major defeat at Al-Kut in 1916. Nevertheless, Baghdad was taken in March 1917. After the First World War the Allies entrusted Iraq to Britain under the Sykes-Picot Agreement, which protected British oil interests in the region. The State of Iraq became a League of Nations mandate under British Control in Nov. 1920. Rebellions in Kurdish and southern areas were suppressed with bombing campaigns. A Hashemite monarchy was installed, under Amir Faysal ibn Husayn from Mecca, a wartime ally, and an indigenous army created. The monarchy was supported by a plebiscite in 1921. Kurdish-dominated Mosul province—vital for its massive oil reserves—was granted to Iraq by the League of Nations in 1925. Britain's mandate ended in 1932. Rebellions followed in Kurdish areas, led by Mustafa Barzani until he fled to the USSR in 1945. Rejecting the partition of Palestine, Iraq went to war with Israel in 1948, leading to the emigration of 120,000 Iraqi Jews.

The monarchy was overthrown in a military coup on 14 July 1958. King Faisal II and Nuri al Said, the prime minister, were killed. A republic was established, controlled by a military-led Council of Sovereignty under Gen. Abdul Karim Qassim. In 1963 Qassim was overthrown and Gen. Abdul Salam Aref became president, with a partial return to a civilian government, but on 17 July 1968 a successful coup was mounted by the Pan-Arabist Ba'ath Party. Gen. Ahmed Al Bakr became president, prime minister, and chairman of a newly established nine-member Revolutionary Command Council. In July 1979 Saddam Hussein, the vice-president and a Sunni Muslim, became president in a peaceful transfer of power.

The 1979 Iranian Revolution was perceived as a threat to the delicate Sunni-Shia balance in Iraq. In Sept. 1980 Iraq invaded Iran, ostensibly over territorial rights in the Shatt-al-Arab waterway. The war claimed over a million lives and saw the use of chemical weapons by the Iraqi army. The al-Anfal campaign (1986–89) countered Kurdish rebellions, killing 182,000 Kurds. Chemical weapons were prominent, most notably at Halabja, where 5,000 died in one day. A UN-arranged ceasefire took place on 20 Aug. 1988 and UN-sponsored peace talks continued in 1989. On 15 Aug. 1990 Iraq accepted the pre-war border and withdrew troops from Iranian soil.

1991 War

On 2 Aug. 1990 Iraqi forces invaded and rapidly overran Kuwait, on the pretext of alleged Kuwaiti 'slant-drilling' across the Iraqi border. The UN Security Council voted to impose economic sanctions on Iraq until it withdrew from Kuwait and the USA sent a large military force to Saudi Arabia. Further Security

Council resolutions included authorization for the use of military force if Iraq did not withdraw by 15 Jan. 1991.

On the night of 16–17 Jan. coalition forces (US and over 30 allies) began an air attack on strategic targets in Iraq. A land offensive followed on 24 Feb. The Iraqi army was routed and Kuwait City was liberated on 28 Feb. Iraq agreed to the conditions of a provisional ceasefire, including withdrawal from Kuwait. Subsequent Kurdish and Shia rebellions were brutally suppressed.

In June 1991 UNSCOM, the United Nations Special Commission, conducted its first chemical weapons inspection in Iraq in accordance with UN Resolution 687. In Sept. a UN Security Council resolution permitted Iraq to sell oil worth US$1,600m. to pay for food and medical supplies. In Oct. the Security Council voted unanimously to prohibit Iraq from all nuclear activities. Imports of materials used in the manufacture of nuclear, biological or chemical weapons were banned, and UN weapons inspectors received wide powers to examine and retain data throughout Iraq.

In Aug. 1992 the USA, UK and France began to enforce air exclusion zones over southern and northern Iraq in response to the government's persecution of Shias and Kurds. Following Iraqi violations of this zone and incursions over the Kuwaiti border, US, British and French forces made air and missile attacks on Iraqi military targets in Jan. 1993. On 10 Nov. 1994 Iraq recognized the independence and boundaries of Kuwait. In the first half of 1995 UN weapons inspectors secured information on an extensive biological weapons programme. At the beginning of Sept. 1996 Iraqi troops occupied the town of Arbol in a Kurdish safe haven in support of the Kurdish Democratic Party faction which was at odds with another Kurdish faction, the Patriotic Union of Kurdistan. On 3 Sept. 1996 US forces fired missiles at targets in southern Iraq and extended the no-fly area northwards to the southern suburbs of Baghdad.

Weapons Inspection

Relations with the USA deteriorated still further in 1997 when Iraq refused co-operation with UN weapons inspectors. The USA and the UK threatened retaliatory action and a renewal of hostilities looked probable until late Feb. 1998 when Kofi Annan, the UN Secretary General, forged an agreement in Baghdad allowing for 'immediate, unconditional and unrestricted access' to all suspected weapons sites. In Aug. 1998 Saddam Hussein engineered another stand-off with the UN arms inspectors, demanding a declaration that Iraq had rid itself of all weapons of mass destruction. This was refused by the UN chief inspector. In Nov. all UN personnel left Iraq as the USA threatened air strikes unless Iraq complied with UN resolutions. Russia and France urged further diplomatic efforts, but on 16 Dec. the USA and Britain launched air and missile attacks aimed at destroying Saddam Hussein's suspected arsenal of nuclear, chemical and biological weapons.

In Feb. 2000 the UN Security Council nominated Sweden's Hans Blix to head the new arms inspectorate to Iraq but he was refused entry into the country. In Feb. 2001 the USA and Britain launched a further series of air attacks on military targets in and around Baghdad. A new UN Security Council resolution was passed in May 2002. Constituting the biggest change since the introduction in 1966 of a UN-administered Oil-for-Food scheme to alleviate the suffering among the civilian population, the new resolution limited import restrictions to a number of specific sensitive goods. In Nov. 2002 the UN Security Council adopted Resolution 1441, holding Iraq in 'material breach' of disarmament obligations. Weapons inspectors, under the leadership of Hans Blix, returned to Iraq four years after their last inspections, but US and British suspicion that the Iraq regime was failing to comply led to increasing tension, resulting in the USA, the UK and Spain reserving the right to disarm Iraq without the need for a further Security Council resolution. Other Security Council members, notably China, France, Germany and Russia, opposed the proposed action.

Fall of Saddam

On 20 March 2003 US forces, supported by the UK, began a war aimed at 'liberating Iraq'. UK troops entered Iraq's second city, Al-Basrah, on 6 April. On 9 April 2003 American forces took control of central Baghdad, effectively bringing an end to Saddam Hussein's rule. Widespread looting and disorder followed the fall of the capital. The bloodless capture of Tikrit, Saddam Hussein's hometown, on 14 April marked the end of formal Iraqi resistance. An interim government was planned until democratic elections could be held. On 22 May the UN Security Council voted to lift economic sanctions against Iraq and to support the US and UK occupation 'until an internationally recognized, representative government is established by the people of Iraq'. Only Syria opposed the resolution by boycotting the session. A 25-man Iraqi-led governing council (IGC) met in Baghdad for the first time in July 2003.

Resistance to the occupying forces increased from late summer. Bomb attacks in Aug. targeted the UN's Baghdad office, killing the UN special representative. Ayatollah Mohammed Baqr al-Hakim, the most senior Shia cleric in Iraq, was assassinated with 100 others in Najaf. Saddam Hussein was captured by American forces at Al-Dawr, near Tikrit, on 13 Dec. 2003. His trial for crimes against humanity, war crimes and genocide began in July 2004. In Feb. 2004 over 100 Kurds were killed in attacks in Irbil and the Shia community suffered 270 deaths in Baghdad and Karbala. In May 2004 accusations surfaced of abuse of Iraqi prisoners by American and British soldiers.

On 30 Jan. 2005 the first democratic elections to a Transitional National Assembly were won by the Shia-dominated United Iraqi Alliance. Jalal Talabani became the country's new president on 6 April 2005, and on 3 May 2005 Iraq's first democratically elected government under Prime Minister Ibrahim al-Jaafari was sworn in. In Oct. 2005 a new federal constitution was approved in a nationwide referendum (although without the support of the Sunni community) and the trial of former dictator Saddam Hussein for mass murder opened in Baghdad. Despite the political advances, insurgent violence has continued against foreign troops, domestic security forces and civilians. In Dec. 2005 a general election for a new parliament was won by the United Iraqi Alliance. In April 2006 after months of deadlock Nouri al-Maliki was appointed the new prime minister. Insurgent violence continues against foreign troops, domestic security forces and civilians. At least 25,000 civilians have been killed since the start of the US-led invasion in March 2003.

TERRITORY AND POPULATION

Iraq is bounded in the north by Turkey, east by Iran, southeast by the Persian Gulf, south by Kuwait and Saudi Arabia, and west by Jordan and Syria. In April 1992 the UN Boundary Commission redefined Iraq's border with Kuwait, moving it slightly northwards in line with an agreement of 1932. Area, 434,128 sq. km. Population, 1997 census, 22,046,244; density, 50·8 per sq. km. 2005 population estimate: 28,807,000. In 2000, 67·9% of the population lived in urban areas.

The UN gives a projected population for 2010 of 32·53m.

The areas, populations and capitals of the governorates:

Governorate	Area in sq. km	Population 1997 census	Capital
Al-Anbar	138,501	1,023,776	Ar-Ramadi
Babil (Babylon)	6,468	1,181,751	Al-Hillah
Baghdad	734	5,423,964	Baghdad
Al-Basrah	19,070	1,556,445	Al-Basrah
Dahuk	6,553	402,970	Dahuk
Dhi Qar	12,900	1,184,796	An-Nasiriyah
Diyala	19,076	1,135,223	Ba'qubah
Irbil	14,471	1,095,992	Irbil

Governorate	Area in sq. km	Population 1997 census	Capital
Karbala	5,034	594,235	Karbala
Maysan	16,072	637,126	Al-Amarah
Al-Muthanna	51,740	436,825	As-Samawah
An-Najaf	28,824	775,042	An-Najaf
Ninawa (Nineveh)	37,323	2,042,852	Mosul
Al-Qadisiyah	8,153	751,331	Ad-Diwaniyah
Salah ad-Din	24,751	904,432	Samarra
As-Sulaymaniyah	17,023	1,362,739	As-Sulaymaniyah
Ta'mim	10,282	753,171	Kirkuk
Wasit	17,153	783,614	Al-Kut

The most populous cities are Baghdad (the capital), population of 4,689,000 in 1999, Irbil and Mosul. Other large cities included Kirkuk, Al-Basrah, As-Sulaymaniyah and An-Najaf.

The population is approximately 80% Arab, 17% Kurdish (mainly in the north of the country) and 3% Turkmen, Assyrian, Chaldean or other. Shia Arabs (predominantly in the south of the country) constitute approximately 60% of the total population and Sunni Arabs (principally in the centre) 20%.

The national language is Arabic. Other languages spoken are Kurdish (official in Kurdish regions), Assyrian and Armenian.

SOCIAL STATISTICS

2000 estimates: births, 792,000; deaths, 177,000; marriages, 171,000. Birth and death rates, 2000 (per 1,000 population): births, 34·1; deaths, 7·6. Life expectancy in 2000: 61·7 years for males and 64·7 for females. Annual population growth rate, 1992–2002, 2·9%. Infant mortality, 2003: 107 per 1,000 live births. Fertility rate, 2002: 4·9 births per woman. Maternal mortality rate per 10,000 live births, 2003: 29·4.

CLIMATE

The climate is mainly arid, with limited and unreliable rainfall and a large annual range of temperature. Summers are very hot and winters are cold. Al-Basrah, Jan. 55°F (12·8°C), July 92°F (33·3°C). Annual rainfall 7" (175 mm). Baghdad, Jan. 50°F (10°C), July 95°F (35°C). Annual rainfall 6" (140 mm). Mosul, Jan. 44°F (6·7°C), July 90°F (32·2°C). Annual rainfall 15" (384 mm).

CONSTITUTION AND GOVERNMENT

Until the fall of Saddam Hussein, the highest state authority was the Revolutionary Command Council (RCC) but some legislative power was given to the 220-member *National Assembly*. The only legal political grouping was the National Progressive Front (founded 1973) comprising the Arab Socialist Renaissance (Ba'ath) Party and various Kurdish groups, but a law of Aug. 1991 legalized political parties provided they were not based on religion, racism or ethnicity.

In July 2003 a 25-man Iraqi-led governing council met in Baghdad for the first time since the US-led war in an important staging post towards full self-government. The temporary Coalition Provisional Authority was dissolved on 28 June 2004. Power was handed over to the interim Iraqi government which assumed full sovereign powers for governing Iraq. It became a transitional government after elections in Jan. 2005. The 275-member Transitional National Assembly approved a draft new constitution on 29 Aug. 2005, 14 days after the original deadline. It was approved in a nationwide referendum held on 15 Oct., with 78·6% of votes cast in favour. Shias and Kurds generally supported the constitution. Most Sunnis opposed it because of its reference to federalism and the risk that Iraq could ultimately break up, as Iraq's oil resources are in the Shia and Kurdish areas. The constitution states that Iraq is a democratic, federal, representative republic and a multi-ethnic, multi-religious and multi-sect country. Islam is the official religion of the state and a basic source of legislation. Elections were held in Dec. 2005 for the new 275-member *Council of Representatives*. The newly-elected Council of Representatives is expected to determine the composition of a proposed upper chamber.

National Anthem

'Mawtini' ('My Homeland'); words by I. Touqan, tune by W. G. Gholmieh.

RECENT ELECTIONS

In parliamentary elections to the permanent Iraqi National Assembly held on 15 Dec. 2005 the United Iraqi Alliance won 41·2% of the votes, taking 128 of 275 seats, ahead of the Kurdistan Alliance with 21·7% and 53 seats, the Iraqi Accord Front (15·1% and 44), the Iraqi National List (8·0% and 25), the Iraqi Front for National Dialogue (4·1% and 11) and the Kurdistan Islamic Union (1·3% and 5). A further six parties won three seats or fewer.

CURRENT ADMINISTRATION

President: Jalal Talabani; b. 1933 (sworn in 7 April 2005).

Vice Presidents: Tariq al-Hashemi; Adil Abdel-Mahdi.

Prime Minister: Nouri al-Maliki (nominated 22 April 2006).

On 6 April 2005 Iraq's parliament chose Jalal Talabani, a Kurd, as the country's new interim president, with Sheikh Ghazi al-Yawer, a Sunni Arab, and Adil Abdel-Mahdi, a Shia, as the vice presidents. On 3 May, Ibrahim al-Jaafari from the Shia-dominated United Iraqi Alliance was sworn in as Prime Minister of Iraq's first democratically elected government. Following the narrow approval of a new federal constitution in Oct., fresh parliamentary elections were held in Dec. 2005, which again returned the United Iraqi Alliance as the leading political force. Subsequent negotiations on forming a broad-based national unity government then went on inconclusively for the next four months against a background of sectarian violence. However, the United Iraqi Alliance's continuing nomination of al-Jaafari as Prime Minister remained the principal stumbling block until he agreed on 22 April 2006 to step aside in favour of Nouri al-Maliki, also from the Alliance but a less contentious choice for the Sunni and Kurdish communities. Despite the renewed political optimism, violence continued into May, and at the time of going to press al-Maliki had yet to forge a new government.

CURRENT LEADERS

Jalal Talabani

Position
President

Introduction
Jalal Talabani, an experienced Iraqi Kurdish politician, was named state president of Iraq on 6 April 2005 by the Iraqi National Assembly. He was elected to a second term on 22 April 2006. He was previously the founder and secretary general of one of the main Iraqi Kurdish political parties, the Patriotic Union of Kurdistan (PUK), and later a prominent member of the Iraqi Governing Council which was established following the US-led invasion of Iraq in 2003.

Early Life
Jalal Talabani was born in the village of Kelkan, Irbil province in Iraqi Kurdistan in 1933, the year after Britain surrendered its mandate over Iraq. Talabani joined the Kurdistan Democratic Party (KDP) at the age of 14 and was elected to its central committee six years later. He attended secondary schools in Irbil and Kirkuk and the Law College in Baghdad from 1952 to 1955, when he was forced to leave the college because of his political activities. Following the Iraqi revolution in 1958, when the monarchy was overthrown by a military coup led by Abdul Karim Qassim, Talabani rejoined the college, and graduated in 1959. He subsequently served in the Iraqi army as

the commander of a tank unit, before working as a journalist for various Kurdish publications.

When the Kurdish north launched an armed uprising against the Iraqi government in Sept. 1961, Talabani joined the forces led by Mulla Mustafa al-Barzani (the *peshmerga*) and fought in the Kirkuk and As-Sulaymaniyah areas. He also led Kurdish diplomatic delegations to Europe and the Middle East and negotiated with the leftist, secular Ba'ath party, whose members dominated Iraq's governing council following a coup led by Abdul Salam Aref in Feb. 1963.

By 1964, when profound disagreements were emerging within the KDP, Talabani established a more secular, urban and left-leaning faction, criticizing al-Barzani for 'conservative and tribal' politics. Arguments between the two factions rumbled throughout the late 1960s and early 1970s, occasionally erupting into armed confrontations. Although deals that secured some autonomy for the Kurds were struck between the KDP and the ruling Ba'ath party (the so-called March Manifesto of 1970), arguments broke out over access to the region's oil supplies and whether Kurds could maintain an army. When the Kurdish revolt collapsed in 1975 (partly as a result of Iran withdrawing its support), Talabani formed a new party, the Patriotic Union of Kurdistan (PUK), based in As-Sulaymaniyah.

The PUK bitterly opposed the Ba'ath party's enforced resettlement of Kurds to Arab areas of Iraq in the late 1970s. At this time there were also numerous armed confrontations between the PUK and the KDP. In 1983, while the KDP was fighting Saddam Hussein's Ba'ath party, Talabani was prepared to negotiate. However, hostilities were resumed by the PUK in 1985, after Saddam failed to implement an agreement. In the aftermath of Saddam's chemical weapons attack that killed around 5,000 Kurds at Halabja in 1988 and the subsequent military action that led to more than 100,000 Kurds fleeing to Turkey, Talabani made efforts to bring unity to Kurdish politics. He improved relations between the PUK and the KDP (then led by Mas'ud al-Barzani) and later formed the Iraqi Kurdistan Front, travelling widely to gain international support for Kurdish autonomy. He became an increasingly powerful and vocal critic of Saddam Hussein's regime.

When a haven was created for Kurds by the Western alliance after the first Gulf War, elections were held there, and a PUK-KDP joint administration was formed in 1992. However, tensions resurfaced and led to serious confrontations between the two groups in 1994. Both parties signed a peace deal in Washington, D.C. in 1998 and the accord was cemented in Oct. 2002 when the regional parliament reconvened in a session attended by both parties' MPs.

Following the US-led invasion of Iraq and the fall of Saddam in April 2003, Talabani joined the US-appointed Iraqi Governing Council (IGC), holding the organization's rotating presidency for the month of Nov. 2003. He distanced himself from the movement for Kurdish independence, pledging to support Iraqi federalism.

In the Iraqi elections on 30 Jan. 2005, a Shia alliance won a slim majority in parliament and the Kurdish coalition came second in the polls. For over two months, with the country under sustained attacks from insurgents, both groups argued about the formation of the new government before electing Talabani as the president (a largely ceremonial role) on 6 April 2005. Adil Abdel-Mahdi, a Shia, and interim president Ghazi al-Yawer, a Sunni Arab, were elected as vice-presidents.

Career in Office

A presidential council of Talabani and his two deputies appointed Ibrahim al-Jaafari, a conservative Islamist from the majority Shia community, as prime minister on 7 April 2005. Speaking as Iraq's new president, Talabani promised to represent all Iraqis and to reach out to the country's ethnic and religious groups as well as to Iraq's Arab and Islamic neighbours. In a letter to the British prime minister, Tony Blair, Talabani wrote: 'We honour those who sacrificed their lives for our liberation. We are determined out of respect to create a tolerant and democratic Iraq, an Iraq for all the Iraqi people. It will take time and much patience, but I can assure you it will be worthwhile, not only for Iraq, but for the whole of the Middle East.' He went on to describe his election to president as 'a symbol of the promise, integration and unity of the new Iraq.'

Against a backdrop of continuing violence in Iraq, many analysts questioned the strength of the Shia-Kurdish alliance, pointing out that the two groups have little common ground other than a shared past of resistance against Saddam Hussein. In Oct. 2005 a new Iraqi constitution was approved narrowly in a national referendum, heralding fresh parliamentary elections on 15 Dec. 2005.

After months of political deadlock, Iraq's parliament convened on 22 April 2006 to fill the top leadership posts and Talabani was elected to a second presidential term. Talabani named the Shia politician Nouri al-Maliki as prime minister designate after the latter was nominated by his Shia coalition, the United Iraqi Alliance (UIA). Talabani asked the new prime minister to form a government within 30 days, as stipulated by the new Iraqi constitution.

Nouri al-Maliki

Position
Prime Minister

Introduction
Nouri al-Maliki was appointed Iraq's prime minister designate by the president, Jalal Talabani, on 22 April 2006. He succeeded his close ally and fellow member of the conservative Shia Muslim al-Dawa group, Ibrahim al-Jaafari, who had been unable to curb the violent insurgency or create alliances with Sunni and Kurdish factions since elections in Dec. 2005. Al-Maliki, who once commanded Shia forces against Saddam Hussein's regime from exile in Syria, promised an inclusive government comprising 'all components of Iraqi society.'

Early Life
Nouri Kamel al-Maliki was born in Hindiyah, near Hillah, southern Iraq in 1950. While studying Arabic at Baghdad University in the early 1970s he joined al-Dawa, a conservative Shia Muslim group that was deeply opposed to the secular politics of the ruling Ba'ath party. In 1980, following a crackdown on al-Dawa by Saddam Hussein's administration, al-Maliki was forced into exile, initially in Iran and from 1990 in Damascus, Syria. He organized resistance against Saddam as a political officer for al-Dawa, at a time when the party was developing close ties with the militant Hizbollah group in Lebanon and with the Iranian authorities, who were then waging war with Saddam's Iraq.

Following the US-led invasion of Iraq in March 2003 and the fall of Saddam, al-Maliki returned to his homeland. In July 2003 he was selected as a member of the US-backed Iraqi Interim Governing Council, serving as deputy chairman of a committee formed to purge Saddam's Ba'athist allies from political life. The de-Ba'athification committee was criticized for being heavy-handed and many Sunni Muslims resented what they saw as a Shia plot to deny them a role in post-Saddam Iraq. In April 2004 the then top US official in Iraq, Paul Bremer, conceded the de-Ba'athification committee had overstepped its boundaries and returned some teachers and army officers to their old jobs. As a senior member of al-Dawa, al-Maliki worked closely with his party's leader, Ibrahim al-Jaafari, to forge a coalition of Shia parties, known as the United Iraqi Alliance (UIA). The coalition was endorsed by Iranian-born Grand Ayatollah Ali al-Sistani, Iraq's most influential Shia cleric, and it won a parliamentary majority (140 of the available 275 seats) in the Iraqi elections of 30 Jan. 2005.

Having been elected to the transitional National Assembly, al-Maliki became the senior Shia member of the committee charged with drafting the new constitution. He took a tough line in the protracted negotiations and resisted efforts by Sunnis to reduce the autonomy given to Kurds in the north and Shias in the south of the country. Attempts by the prime minister, Ibrahim al-Jaafari, to form a broad-based coalition government to reflect the results of the elections on 15 Dec. 2005 became deadlocked, against a backdrop of increasing sectarian violence. Faced by strong opposition from Sunni and Kurdish factions, al-Jaafari stepped down on 21 April 2006 and al-Maliki emerged as the UIA's candidate for the premiership. He was named prime minister designate by President Jalal Talabani on 22 April 2006.

Career in Office

Al-Maliki called for an end to sectarian divisions and a commitment to unity and began the task of appointing 32 cabinet members, a process with a 30-day deadline. A key challenge was assigning control of the defence and interior ministries, responsible for the army and the police, said to have been infiltrated by militias. Al-Maliki signalled that he would work to curb the Sunni insurgency by requiring militias to be integrated into the nation's security services.

Al-Maliki is seen by some Sunni leaders as more independent of Iran than his predecessor, a situation which some observers see as a cause for optimism. However, it remains uncertain whether Iraqi leaders representing religiously- and ethnically-based parties can set aside their individual interests and rise to the challenge of managing a nation that remains on the brink of civil war.

DEFENCE

Following the downfall of Saddam Hussein, recruitment began in July 2003 for a new professional army run by the US military. Saddam Hussein's forces numbered 400,000 at their peak. Foreign troops in Iraq in Aug. 2005 numbered 162,000 (139,000 American).

Army

A New Iraqi Army is being created to replace Saddam's army with a professional force. In Jan. 2006 army personnel numbered 105,600.

In July 2004 the Civil Defense Corps (23,100 personnel in April 2004) was disbanded and converted into a National Guard. It has an end-strength objective of 61,900.

Navy

An 800-strong Coastal Defense Force has been established. It began operations in Oct. 2004.

Air Force

An Army Air Corps has been established and, at Feb. 2005, had a total of 14 fully trained Iraqi pilots. There were a total of 500 personnel in Jan. 2006.

INTERNATIONAL RELATIONS

Iraq is a member of the UN, the League of Arab States, OPEC, OIC and Islamic Development Bank.

ECONOMY

The oil sector accounted for 76·1% of GDP in 2001; agriculture accounted for 7·8%, manufacturing 1·6% and services 13·8%.

Overview

The military victory of the US-led coalition in 2003 led to the shutdown of much of Iraq's administrative structure. Looting, insurgent attacks and sabotage, targeted especially at oil pipelines and facilities, have since undermined efforts to rebuild the economy. World Bank estimates indicate that Iraq's GDP declined by 30% in 2003. In Nov. 2004 the Paris Club of official creditors agreed to write off 80% of Iraq's external debt, subject to Iraq concluding an economic stabilization programme with the IMF.

Currency

From 15 Oct. 2003 a new national currency, the new *Iraqi dinar* (NID), was introduced to replace the existing currencies in circulation in the south and north of the country.

Budget

In Oct. 2003 the Iraqi minister of finance announced the post-Saddam Iraqi national budget for 2004, projecting total revenues of about 19·26trn. new Iraqi dinars (US$13bn.) and total expenditures of 20·15trn. new Iraqi dinars (US$13·5bn.). The deficit was to be funded through refunds from cancelled Oil-for-Food contracts. The UN terminated the Oil-for-Food programme in Nov. 2003, with surplus funds being transferred to the Development Fund for Iraq (administered by the Coalition Provisional Authority). An international conference was held in Madrid, Spain in Oct. 2003 to help raise additional funds for reconstruction and development. A follow-up conference was held in Brussels in June 2005, at which the Iraqi government outlined its priorities for reconstruction and the international community reinforced pledges made at Madrid.

Banking and Finance

All banks were nationalized in 1964. Following the Gulf War in 1991 the formation of private banks was approved, although they were prohibited from conducting international transactions. A new post-Saddam banking law in Oct. 2003 authorized private banks to process international payments, remittances and foreign currency letters of credit. The Trade Bank of Iraq has been established as an export credit agency to facilitate trade financing. The independent Central Bank of Iraq is the sole bank of issue; its *Governor* is Dr Sinan Mohammed Rida Al-Shabibi. All domestic interest rates were liberalized on 1 March 2004.

ENERGY AND NATURAL RESOURCES

Environment

Iraq's carbon dioxide emissions from the consumption and flaring of fossil fuels were the equivalent of 3·2 tonnes per capita in 2002. An *Environmental Sustainability Index* compiled for the World Economic Forum meeting in Jan. 2005 ranked Iraq 143rd in the world out of 146 countries analysed, with 33·6%. The index measured the ability of countries to maintain favourable environmental conditions and examined various factors including pollution levels and the use or abuse of natural resources.

Electricity

Before the war in March–April 2003 installed capacity was 4,400 MW. Despite post-war looting and sabotage, production had recovered and by Oct. 2003 the generating capacity was back to pre-war levels. The estimated available power generating capacity in 2005 was about 6,000 MW.

Oil and Gas

Proven oil reserves at the end of 2004 totalled 115·0bn. bbls. Only Saudi Arabia and Iran have more reserves. Crude oil production in 2002 totalled 99·7m. tonnes. The restoration of significant oil production and the resumption of exports have been priorities since the war in March–April 2003. Production in March 2005 was 2·1m. bbls. a day and exports 1·4m. bbls. a day.

At the end of 2004 Iraq had natural gas reserves of 3,170bn. cu. metres.

Minerals

The principal minerals extracted are phosphate rock (100,000 tonnes in 2002) and sulphur (98,000 tonnes in 2002).

Agriculture

There were 5·75m. ha. of arable land in 2001 and 0·34m. ha. of permanent crops. 3·53m. ha. were irrigated in 2001. Production (2003 estimates, in 1,000 tonnes): wheat, 2,553; barley, 1,316; tomatoes, 1,000; dates, 910; potatoes, 625; melons and watermelons, 575; cucumbers and gherkins, 350; oranges, 310.

Livestock (2000): cattle, 1·35m.; sheep, 6·78m.; goats, 1·60m.; asses, 380,000; chickens, 23m.

Forestry

In 2000 forests covered 799,000 ha., representing 1·8% of the land area. Timber production in 2001 was 111,000 cu. metres.

Fisheries

Catches in 2001 totalled approximately 20,800 tonnes, of which about 60% from marine waters.

INDUSTRY

Iraq remains under-developed industrially. Production figures (2000, in 1,000 tonnes): residual fuel oil, 7,710; distillate fuel oil, 6,800; petrol, 3,011; cement (2001), 2,000; kerosene, 1,005; jet fuel, 557.

Labour

In 1996 the labour force was 5,573,000 (75% males). Unemployment was 33% in Aug. 2005, down from 55% in Aug. 2003. In Sept. 2003 the US civil administrator signed an order implementing a new 11-tier salary scale for all public employees, replacing a temporary scale in effect since the collapse of the Saddam regime.

INTERNATIONAL TRADE

Imports and Exports

Imports and exports (in US$1m.):

	2000	2001	2002
Imports (c.i.f.)	3,330	5,190	9,817
Exports (f.o.b.)	14,289	11,041	9,990

Manufactures and food are the main import commodities. Crude oil is the main export commodity. Post-war crude oil exports are estimated to have risen from 0·2m. bbls. a day in June 2003 to 1·5m. bbls. a day by Dec. 2003. Imports and exports have both increased significantly since the Saddam era.

COMMUNICATIONS

Roads

In 2002 there were an estimated 44,900 km of roads, of which 84·3% were paved. Vehicles in use in 2002 included 637,500 passenger cars and 375,000 lorries and vans. In 1996 there were 1,338 road accidents resulting in 1,573 deaths. Considerable post-war road reconstruction since 2003 reflects heavy military use and lack of maintenance.

Rail

In 2000 railways comprised 2,603 km of 1,435 mm gauge route. Passenger-km travelled in 2000 came to 0·38bn. and freight tonne-km to 0·87bn. In 2003, five main lines were in operation, serving 107 stations.

Civil Aviation

In 2000 there were international flights for the first time since the 1991 Gulf War, with air links being established between Iraq and Egypt, Jordan and Syria. Since 2003 the two international airports at Baghdad and Al-Basrah have undergone post-war reconstruction. Major domestic airports are at Mosul, Kirkuk and Irbil.

Shipping

The merchant fleet in 2002 had a total tonnage of 188,000 GRT, including oil tankers 59,000 GRT. A 565-km canal was opened in 1992 between Baghdad and the Persian Gulf for shipping, irrigation, the drainage of saline water and the reclamation of marsh land.

Iraq has three oil tanker terminals at Al-Basrah, Khor Al-Amaya and Khor Al-Zubair. Its single deep-water port is at Umm Qasr.

Telecommunications

In 2002 there were 675,000 main telephone lines (28 per 1,000 population). Since the end of the Saddam regime the number of telephone subscribers has increased fivefold. There were 20,000 mobile phone subscribers in 2002. Internet users in 2002 numbered 25,000. Satellite connections are the primary international telecommunications link. The Coalition Provisional Authority awarded three regional mobile telecommunications licences in Oct. 2003.

Postal Services

In 2003 there were 331 post offices.

SOCIAL INSTITUTIONS

Justice

Up until the war in March–April 2003, for civil matters: the court of cassation in Baghdad; six courts of appeal at Al-Basrah, Baghdad (2), Babil (Babylon), Mosul and Kirkuk; 18 courts of first instance with unlimited powers and 150 courts of first instance with limited powers, all being courts of single judges. In addition, six peace courts had peace court jurisdiction only. 'Revolutionary courts' dealt with cases affecting state security.

For religious matters: the Sharia courts at all places where there were civil courts, constituted in some places of specially appointed Qadhis (religious judges) and in other places of the judges of the civil courts. For criminal matters: the court of cassation; six sessions courts (two being presided over by the judge of the local court of first instance and four being identical with the courts of appeal). Magistrates' courts at all places where there were civil courts, constituted of civil judges exercising magisterial powers of the first and second class. There were also a number of third-class magistrates' courts, powers for this purpose being granted to municipal councils and a number of administrative officials.

The death penalty was introduced for serious theft in 1992; amputation of a hand for theft in 1994. It is believed that during the Saddam era there were hundreds of executions annually. The death penalty was suspended in April 2003 after the fall of Saddam, but reinstated in Aug. 2004. There were three executions in 2005.

In the immediate aftermath of the war, the justice system was idle but by July 2003 an estimated 100 courts were functioning. All Baghdad criminal court functions were consolidated into two operational courthouses. In Dec. 2003 the Governing Council established the Iraqi Special Tribunal to try senior members of the Saddam regime for war crimes, crimes against humanity and genocide.

The population in penal institutions in April 2004 was approximately 15,000 (60 per 100,000 of national population).

Police

A new post-war national police force has been established and numbered 82,400 in Jan. 2006. The personnel includes both former officers who are being retrained and new recruits.

Education

Primary education became compulsory in 1976. Primary school age is 6–12. Secondary education is for six years, of which the first three are termed intermediate. The medium of instruction is Arabic; Kurdish is used in primary schools in northern districts.

According to UNESCO, in 2000–01 there were: 68,400 kindergarten pupils; 4·03m. primary school children with 190,650 teachers; and 1·36m. secondary school pupils with 81,500 teachers. Adult literacy rate was 56% in 2000 (male, 68%; female, 43%). Most schools were closed in March–April 2003 when UNICEF estimates that 200 were destroyed and a further 2,750 looted. By Oct. 2003 all 22 universities and 43 technical institutes and colleges were open, as were nearly all primary and secondary schools. School enrolment has increased by 20% since 2000. Expenditure on education in 2003 was an estimated US$384·5m.

Health

According to the World Health Organization, in 2003 there were (per 10,000 population): 6·3 physicians, 1·2 dentists, 1·0 pharmacists, 13·1 hospital beds, and 12·1 nurses and midwifery personnel. There are approximately 240 hospitals and 1,200 primary health care clinics operating in post-war Iraq.

RELIGION

The constitution proclaims Islam the state religion, but also stipulates freedom of religious belief and expression. In 2001 the population was 97% Muslim; there were also 750,000 Christians. *See also* TERRITORY AND POPULATION.

CULTURE

World Heritage Sites

Iraq has two UNESCO World Heritage Sites: Hatra (inscribed on the list in 1985), a large fortified city of the Parthian (Persian) Empire; and Ashur (Qal'at Sherqat) (2003), the first capital and the religious centre of the Assyrians from the 14th to the 9th centuries BC.

Broadcasting

In 2000 there were 5·03m. radio and 1·88m. TV receivers (colour by SECAM H). The ban on satellite dishes, enforced while Saddam Hussein was in power, has since been lifted. By Aug. 2005 there were 29 independent TV stations.

Press

In 1996 there were four main daily newspapers (one of which is in English) with a combined circulation of 407,000.

Tourism

In 2001 there were 127,000 foreign tourists.

DIPLOMATIC REPRESENTATIVES

Of Iraq in the United Kingdom (9 Holland Villas Rd, London, W14 8BP)
Ambassador: Salah Al-Shaikhly.

Of the United Kingdom in Iraq (International Zone, Baghdad)
Ambassador: William Patey, CMG.

Of Iraq in the USA (1801 P St., NW, Washington., D.C., 20036)
Ambassador: Vacant.
Chargé d'Affaires a.i.: Said Shihab Ahmad.

Of the USA in Iraq (APO AE 09316, Baghdad)
Ambassador: Zalmay Khalilzad.

Of Iraq to the United Nations
Ambassador: Samir Shakir Mahmood Sumaidaie.

Of Iraq to the European Union
Ambassador: Vacant.

FURTHER READING

Aburish, S. K., *Saddam Hussein: The Politics of Revenge*. Bloomsbury, London, 2000
Anderson, Liam and Stansfield, Gareth, *The Future of Iraq: Dictatorship, Democracy or Division?* Palgrave Macmillan, Basingstoke, 2004
Blix, Hans, *Disarming Iraq: The Search for Weapons of Mass Destruction*. Bloomsbury, London, 2004
Butler, R., *Saddam Defiant: The Threat of Weapons of Mass Destruction and the Crisis of Global Security*. Weidenfeld & Nicolson, London, 2000
Mackey, Sandra, *The Reckoning: Iraq and the Legacy of Saddam Hussein*. W. W. Norton, New York, 2002
Shahid, Anthony, *Night Draws Near: Iraq's People in the Shadow of America's War*. Henry Holt, New York, 2005
Sluglett, Marion Farouk and Sluglett, Peter, *Iraq Since 1958: From Revolution to Dictatorship*. 3rd ed. I. B. Tauris, London, 2001
Tripp, Charles, *A History of Iraq*. 2nd ed. CUP, 2002

IRELAND

Letterkenny

NORTHERN IRELAND

Sligo

Dundalk

IRELAND

Galway

DUBLIN

Irish Sea

ATLANTIC OCEAN

Limerick

Killarney

Cork

0   25 mi

0   50 km

© Research Machines plc 2006

Éire

Capital: Dublin
Population projection, 2010: 4·42m.
GDP per capita, 2003: (PPP$) 37,738
HDI/world rank: 0·946/8

KEY HISTORICAL EVENTS

Ireland was first inhabited around 7500 BC by Mesolithic hunter-gatherers who travelled across the land bridge that connected southwest Scotland with the northern part of Ireland (it was submerged around 6700 BC). The earliest settlement, at Mount Sandel near Coleraine, has been dated to 5935 BC. Farmers from the Middle-East arrived in Ireland around 3500 BC. Their elaborate graves are also a feature of Neolithic communities in Brittany and the Iberian peninsula. From the sixth century BC, the island was invaded by waves of Celtic tribes from central Europe, including the Gaels, who established pastoral communities within massive stone forts. By AD 200 the Gaels dominated the island, though there was no central control: society was based on a complex structure of hundreds of small kingdoms. The Romans, who dominated much of northern Europe, never reached Ireland. The Gaels traded with other Celtic peoples and sent raiding parties to form settlements in Scotland (Dál Riata) and west Wales.

Christian missionaries reached Ireland during the third century AD. St Patrick, born on the west coast of Britain, was consecrated as a bishop in Gaul and lived and preached in Ireland from *c.* 432 until his death *c.* 465. Monasteries were founded and, in an overwhelmingly agrarian society, they became important centres of learning and the dissemination of the written word. In contrast to much of northern Europe, ravaged by fragmentary forces following the collapse of the Roman Empire, Christianity found a haven in Ireland. Later, Irish missionaries took Celtic Christianity to Britain and continental Europe. By the fifth

century AD there were five leading Gaelic kingdoms, which roughly correspond to the latter-day provinces of Ulster, Leinster, Munster and Connacht (the fifth kingdom occupied land in the modern counties of Meath and Westmeath). Each kingdom was dominated by one or two families—the Uí Néill clan was especially powerful in the north and east. The south (Munster) was dominated by the Eóganachta family.

Nordic Invasion

Viking longboats first appeared off the Irish coast in the late seventh century. 795 saw a full-scale Viking invasion, which heralded more than two hundred years of Scandinavian influence. The Vikings were great traders and established the first towns along the east and south coasts—the towns of Wexford, Waterford, Cork and Limerick became prosperous centres of manufacturing and commerce. Dublin, said to be founded in 841 by the Norse king Thurgesius, became a key outpost in a Viking diaspora stretching as far as Sicily and Russia. Gaelic kings made military alliances with the Viking settlers to support their struggles with neighbouring dynasties. In 976 the warrior Brian Boru (Bóruma) became king of Munster following a series of victories against the powerful Eóganachta. Following Boru's defeat of the Leinster groups and their Norse allies at Clontarf in 1014 he seemed destined to be the first high king of all Ireland, but was murdered shortly after his famous victory.

In the mid-12th century the Pope gave his blessing to an expedition of Anglo-Normans to Ireland. They were sent by the English King Henry II, who had been approached for military support by the deposed king of Leinster, Dermot MacMurrough (Díarmait Mac Murchada). Returning to Ireland in 1169 with Norman barons and Welsh mercenaries, MacMurrough recovered part of his former territories and captured Dublin. Richard de Clare (Strongbow), a powerful Norman invader, became MacMurrough's heir after marrying his daughter. During the 13th century various Anglo-Norman adventurers began to establish themselves in Ireland. Dublin Castle was built in 1204 on the site of a Norse fort and the first parliament sat there in 1264. After his decisive defeat of English forces at the Battle of Bannockburn in 1314, Edward Bruce, the brother of Robert Bruce, king of Scotland, dreamed of establishing a Celtic kingdom. In 1315 he landed in Ulster and attempted to overthrow the English. Within a year he controlled most of Ireland north of Dublin, but his troops left a trail of destruction and soon lost support. Bruce was defeated and killed at Dundalk in 1317 by a Norman-Irish army reinforced from England under orders from King Edward II.

The descendants of the Anglo-Norman settlers gradually became identified with the native Irish, whose language, habits, and laws they adopted. To counteract this, the Anglo-Irish Parliament passed the Statute of Kilkenny in 1366, decreeing heavy penalties against all who allied themselves with the Irish. This statute, however, remained inoperative; although Richard II went to Ireland in 1394 and 1399 to reassert royal authority, he failed to achieve any practical result. During the subsequent Wars of the Roses in England the authority of the English crown became limited to the Pale, a coastal district around Dublin.

King Edward IV, of the House of York, came to the English throne in 1461 and appointed Gerald (Gearóid Mór) FitzGerald, 8th earl of Kildare as viceroy of Ireland. The FitzGeralds were wealthy Yorkists, well-connected to a network of Anglo-Norman and Gaelic families. Gearóid Mór wielded considerable power, and managed to hold onto it even after the return of the Lancastrians in 1485. He was eventually replaced in 1494 by Sir Edward Poynings, who, representing English interests, brought in legislation providing for the reduction of the power of the Anglo-Irish lords. The Poynings Laws removed the legal rights of the Irish parliament to legislate independently.

Henry VII re-appointed Gearóid Mór as viceroy in 1496. For the next 38 years the FitzGeralds (Geraldines) ruled Ireland from Maynooth Castle, paying deference to the English crown. Henry VIII was determined to centralize power and reduce the influence of provincial magnates. He introduced the Reformation to Ireland in 1537 and began to dissolve the monasteries with little resistance.

Ulster Rebellion

Elizabeth I, through her deputy in Ireland, Sir Henry Sidley, removed the Irish chiefdoms from their positions of power. An uprising in Munster in the early 1570s was quickly suppressed and only Ulster now provided a stumbling block to Tudor domination. It was from Ulster that Hugh O'Neill and Red Hugh O'Donnell launched an open rebellion. In 1598 O'Neill ambushed and defeated a government force of over 4,000 at the Battle of Yellow Ford near Armagh. Spoken of as 'Prince of Ireland', his ambitions were thwarted by the arrival of 20,000 troops under Lord Mountjoy in 1600. Reinforcements of Spanish soldiers in 1601 were insufficient and O'Neill left for the Continent with his followers in the 1607 'Flight of the Earls'.

The Earls' lands were seized by the English crown and in 1609 Ulster-Scottish and English settlers were invited to colonize. Swathes of land were cleared of farms and woodland, and 23 walled new towns were created, including Belfast. By the early 1620s the Anglo-Scottish population of Ulster was more than 20,000. English politics in the 1630s was dominated by struggles between the crown and parliament (the Puritans) and the Irish in Ulster took advantage, rebelling against the planters in late 1641 in a series of vicious attacks in which thousands of Protestants were killed. The following year Owen Roe O'Neill, who had fled to Spain with his uncle Hugh in 1607, returned to Ireland and led the Confederate forces. A provisional government was established at Kilkenny and by the end of 1642 O'Neill controlled the whole island apart from Dublin and parts of Ulster.

Victory for the English parliamentarians under Oliver Cromwell and the execution of Charles I in 1649 had a profound impact on Ireland. Cromwell was determined to avenge the 1641 massacre of the Ulster planters. With his New Model Army, Cromwell stormed Drogheda and murdered its garrison of 2,000 men. Wexford then fell, and by 1652 all of Ireland was in Cromwellian hands. Hundreds of thousands of acres of land were confiscated and given to a new wave of Protestant settlers.

Following the restoration of the English monarchy in 1660, Catholics in Ireland hoped to be rewarded for their former loyalty, but Charles II restored only a small number of Catholic estates. King James II, however, was a declared Catholic and under his viceroy in Ireland, Richard Talbot, earl of Tyrconnel, Catholics were advanced to positions of state and placed in control of the military. Protestant power was on the wane in England and the Protestant aristocracy invited William of Orange (the Dutch husband of James II's daughter Mary) to claim the English crown. James II fled to France, then travelled to Ireland with French soldiers. They moved north, aiming to subjugate Protestant Ulster. In the spring of 1689 only the walled towns of Derry/Londonderry and Enniskillen remained in Protestant hands. Derry/Londonderry was besieged, but it held out for 15 weeks until the arrival of William's forces, which defeated James at the Battle of the Boyne. The Jacobites retreated to Limerick, where they negotiated the Treaty of Limerick of 1691. Catholics were permitted some religious freedom, and the restoration of their lands. However, the treaty was not honoured by the English parliament and 11,000 Irish Jacobites set sail to join the French army.

Religious Divide

The defeat of the Catholic cause was followed by more confiscation of land and the introduction of the Penal Laws, which prevented Catholics from buying freehold land, holding public office or bearing arms. During the American revolution, fear of a French invasion led Irish Protestants to form the Protestant Volunteer army. Led by Henry Grattan, they used their military strength to extract concessions from Britain. Trade concessions were granted in 1779 and the Poynings Laws repealed three years later. However, Catholics continued to be denied the right to hold political office.

The principles of the French Revolution found their most powerful expression in Ireland in the Society of United Irishmen, which, led by the protestant lawyer Theobald Wolfe Tone, mounted a rebellion in 1798. Without the expected French assistance, the rebellion was crushed by crown troops led by Gen. Lake. The British prime minister, William Pitt, was convinced that the 'Irish problem' could be solved by the abolition of the Irish parliament, legislative union with Britain and Catholic emancipation. The first two goals were achieved in 1801, but the opposition of George III and British Protestants prevented the enactment of the Catholic Emancipation act until 1829, when it was accomplished largely through the efforts of Daniel O'Connell.

After 1829 the Irish representatives in the British Parliament, led by O'Connell, sought a repeal of the Act of Union. Calls for land reforms were drowned out by a disastrous potato famine. Between 1845–49 a blight wiped out the potato crop, the staple food of the Irish population and resulted in mass starvation. Of a population of 8·5m. almost 1m. died and well over 1m. emigrated, mostly to the United States. Irish Catholics in the United States formed the secret Fenian movement, dedicated to achieving full Irish independence.

Home Rule Campaign

Charles Parnell, a Home Rule League MP, came to the fore of the nationalist movement in 1877 as president of the Home Rule Confederation of Great Britain. Parnell led parliamentary obstruction in response to the House of Lords' rejection of limited land reform in Ireland. Parnell's Irish Land League saw limited gains in Gladstone's 1881 Land Act but Parnell, voicing continuing discontent, was imprisoned in Dublin. His release in 1882 and the subsequent Kilmainham Treaty, granting more concessions to tenants, was seen by London as the quickest solution to an increasingly anarchic Ireland.

The Home Rule Party, led by Parnell, brought down the Conservative government at Westminster by voting with the Liberals, allowing William Gladstone to form a government in 1886. Gladstone attempted to resolve the 'Irish problem' by introducing a Home Rule Bill—seen as Parnell's greatest achievement—which would give the Irish Parliament the right to appoint the executive of Ireland. However, Home Rule was greatly opposed in Ulster and England and failed at Westminster in 1886 and 1893. Parnell's domination of Irish politics came to end with the disclosure of his affair with Kitty O'Shea in 1890. After Gladstone rejected him, he lost control of the Irish parliamentarians and was condemned by the Catholic clergy.

During the 1880s a new pride in traditional Irish culture took root, symbolized by the establishment of the Gaelic Athletic Association in 1884 and the Gaelic League in 1893, which successfully campaigned for the return of the Irish language to the school curriculum. Though not political organizations, they provided a link between the conservative Catholic church and the Fenians (nationalists). In 1905 the Irish political leader and journalist Arthur Griffith founded Sinn Féin to promote Irish economic welfare and achieve complete political independence. However, at the time the dominant nationalist group remained the Home Rule party of John Redmond.

A Home Rule Bill was finally passed in 1914 but the act was suspended for the duration of the First World War. Redmond pledged the support of Ireland to the British war effort, which angered some nationalists. The Irish Republican Brotherhood (IRB) plotted a rebellion while Britain was at war, soliciting German support. On Easter Monday 1916 the IRB seized the General Post Office in Dublin and Patrick Pearse read out the proclamation of the Republic of Ireland. Though the Easter Rising was over in under a week, the emotional impact was heightened when the British executed 16 of the rebel leaders. Sinn Féin, linked in the Irish public's mind with the rising, scored a dramatic victory in the parliamentary elections of 1918. Its members refused to take their seats in Westminster, declared the *Dáil Éireann* ('Diet of Ireland') and proclaimed the Irish republic. The British outlawed Sinn Féin and the Dáil, which went underground and associated military groups including the Irish Republican Army (IRA) engaged in guerrilla warfare against the local authorities representing the Union. The British sent troops (the Black and Tans) who further inflamed the situation.

Civil War

A new Home Rule Bill was passed in 1920, establishing two parliaments, one in Belfast and the other in Dublin. The Unionists of the six counties accepted this scheme, and a Northern Parliament was duly elected in May 1921. Sinn Féin rejected the plan, but in autumn 1921 British Prime Minister Lloyd George negotiated with Griffith and Michael Collins of the Dáil a treaty granting Catholic Ireland dominion status within the British Empire. Collins managed to gain approval in the Dáil by a slim majority. The Republicans in the Dáil, led by Eamonn de Valera, rejected the treaty, which had divided Ireland and fell short of full independence. A brutal civil war ensued; Collins, who had assumed command of the army, was assassinated in Aug. 1922 by anti-treaty rebels. The treaty supporters emerged as victors and the Irish Free State was established in Jan. 1922. William Cosgrave became the first prime minister and his Fine Gael party led for ten years. In 1932 de Valera, leader of the Fianna Fáil party, became prime minister (*taoiseach*). Five years later he brought in a new constitution establishing the sovereign nation of Ireland and abolishing the oath of allegiance sworn by Irish parliamentarians to the British crown.

Independence

Ireland remained neutral in the Second World War, though in the harsh economic conditions of the time tens of thousands of people emigrated to Britain for work and many thousands joined the war effort. In 1948 Prime Minister John Costello demanded total independence from Britain and reunification with the six counties of Northern Ireland. Independence came the following year and in 1955 the Republic of Ireland was admitted to the United Nations, but nothing came of the claim to the six Ulster counties under British rule. Economic relations between the Republic and Northern Ireland improved in the 1950s and '60s, though both decades were marked by large-scale emigration from the Republic, chiefly to the United States. Trouble in the North flared up in the late '60s over Catholic demands for civil rights and equality in the allocation of housing. Confrontation between the two religious communities intensified and in 1969 British troops were deployed to keep the peace. The British military soon lost the confidence of the Catholic community, the IRA increased its activity and more violence ensued. In 1972 the Unionist government in Belfast resigned and direct rule from London was imposed.

On 1 Jan. 1973 The Republic of Ireland became a member state of the European Economic Community. Jack Lynch led Fianna Fáil into power in 1977, though over the next decade there were party splits while general elections were held against a backdrop of soaring unemployment. Emigration increased, especially among young people, reaching a peak of 44,000 in 1989 under Charles

Haughey's premiership. The 1990s were marked by an economic upturn, buoyed by EU subsidies and foreign investment. The legalization of divorce in 1995 symbolized the Irish Republic's embrace of modern European values. In the north, a ceasefire between the IRA and Protestant militias in 1994 formed the basis for the signing of the Good Friday Agreement in April 1998. On 2 Dec. 1999 the Irish constitution was amended to remove the articles laying claim to Northern Ireland. Prime minister Bertie Ahern, who came to power in the 1997 general election, took Ireland into the single European currency in Jan. 2002. In Oct. 2002 the Northern Irish Assembly was suspended for the fourth time in its history over allegations of IRA spying at the Northern Ireland Office. Direct rule from London was subsequently re-imposed.

TERRITORY AND POPULATION

The Republic of Ireland lies in the Atlantic Ocean, separated from Great Britain by the Irish Sea to the east, and bounded in the northeast by Northern Ireland (UK). In 2003, 59·9% of the population lived in urban areas. The population at the 2002 census was 3,917,203 (1,971,039 females), giving a density of 55·7 persons per sq. km. The total population in April 2003 was estimated at 3·98m., the highest figure since 1871 when the census recorded a population of 4·05m.

The UN gives a projected population for 2010 of 4·42m.

The capital is Dublin (Baile Átha Cliath). Town populations, 2002: Greater Dublin, 1,004,614; Cork, 186,239; Limerick, 83,147; Galway, 66,163; Waterford, 46,736.

Counties and Cities[1]	Area in ha[2]	Population, 2002		
		Males	Females	Totals
Province of Leinster				
Carlow	89,655	23,403	22,611	46,014
Dublin City	11,758	237,813	257,968	495,781
Dun Laoghaire-Rathdown	12,638	91,337	100,455	191,792
Fingal	45,467	97,409	99,004	196,413
Kildare	169,540	82,735	81,209	163,944
Kilkenny	207,289	40,540	39,799	80,339
Laoighis	171,990	30,131	28,643	58,744
Longford	109,116	15,794	15,274	31,068
Louth	82,613	50,489	51,332	101,821
Meath	234,207	67,733	66,272	134,005
Offaly	200,117	32,185	31,478	63,663
South Dublin	22,364	117,516	121,319	238,835
Westmeath	183,965	35,960	35,898	71,858
Wexford	236,685	58,170	58,426	116,596
Wicklow	202,662	56,800	57,876	114,676
Total of Leinster	1,980,066	1,038,015	1,067,564	2,105,579
Province of Munster				
Clare	345,004	52,063	51,214	103,277
Cork City	3,953	59,263	63,799	123,062
Cork	746,042	163,054	161,713	324,767
Kerry	480,689	66,572	65,955	132,527
Limerick City	2,087	26,128	27,895	54,023
Limerick	273,504	61,503	59,778	121,281
Tipperary, N. R.	204,627	30,864	30,146	61,010
Tipperary, S. R.	225,845	39,999	39,122	79,121
Waterford City	4,103	21,782	22,812	44,594
Waterford	181,556	28,890	28,062	56,952
Total of Munster	2,467,410	550,118	550,496	1,100,614
Province of Connacht				
Galway City	5,057	31,015	34,817	65,832
Galway	609,820	73,352	69,893	143,245
Leitrim	159,003	13,324	12,475	25,799
Mayo	558,605	59,149	58,297	117,446
Roscommon	254,819	27,583	26,1918	53,774
Sligo	183,752	28,771	29,429	58,200
Total of Connacht	1,771,056	233,194	231,102	464,296

Counties and Cities[1] Province of Ulster (part of)	Area in ha[2]	Population, 2002 Males	Females	Totals
Cavan	193,177	29,015	27,531	56,546
Donegal	486,091	69,016	68,559	137,575
Monaghan	129,508	26,806	25,787	52,593
Total of Ulster (part of)	808,776	124,837	121,877	246,714
Total	7,027,308	1,946,164	1,971,039	3,917,203

[1]Cities were previously known as County Boroughs.
[2]Area details provided by Ordnance Survey.

The official languages are Irish (the national language) and English; according to the National Survey of Languages of 1994, Irish is spoken as a mother tongue only by 2% of the population, in certain western areas (Gaeltacht), and is no longer a compulsory subject at school.

SOCIAL STATISTICS

Statistics for six calendar years:

	Births	Marriages	Deaths		Births	Marriages	Deaths
1998	53,551	16,783	31,352	2001	57,882	19,246	29,812
1999	53,354	18,526	31,683	2002	60,521	20,556	29,348
2000	54,239	19,168	31,115	2003	61,517	20,302	28,823

2003 rates: birth, 15·5; death, 7·2; marriage, 5·1. Annual population growth rate, 1993–2003, 1·1%. Expectation of life at birth, 2003, 75·1 years for males and 80·3 years for females.

In 2002 the suicide rate per 100,000 population (provisional) was 11·5 (men, 19·1; women, 4·1). Infant mortality in 2002, 5·1 per 1,000 live births; fertility rate (2002), 2·0 births per woman.

At a referendum on 24 Nov. 1995 on the legalization of civil divorce the electorate was 1,628,580; 818,852 votes were in favour, 809,728 against. In 2002 Ireland received 11,634 asylum applications, equivalent to 3·1 per 1,000 inhabitants.

The estimated number of immigrants in the year to April 2003 was 50,500 while emigrants numbered 20,700 in the same period. Immigration is estimated to have peaked at 66,900 in the twelve months to April 2002. 40% of emigrants went to countries other than the EU and the USA, while 45% of all immigrants originated from outside the EU and USA.

A UNICEF report published in 2005 showed that 15·7% of children in Ireland live in poverty (in households with income below 50% of the national median), compared to 2·4% in Denmark. A similar report from 2000 had shown that the poverty rate of children in lone-parent families was 46·4%, compared to 14·2% in two-parent families.

CLIMATE

Influenced by the Gulf Stream, there is an equable climate with mild southwest winds, making temperatures almost uniform over the whole country. The coldest months are Jan. and Feb. (39–45°F, 4–7°C) and the warmest July and Aug. (57–61°F, 14–16°C). May and June are the sunniest months, averaging 5·5 to 6·5 hours each day, but over 7 hours in the extreme southeast. Rainfall is lowest along the eastern coastal strip. The central parts vary between 30–44" (750–1,125 mm), and up to 60" (1,500 mm) may be experienced in low-lying areas in the west. Dublin, Jan. 40°F (4°C), July 59°F (15°C). Annual rainfall 30" (750 mm). Cork, Jan. 42°F (5°C), July 61°F (16°C). Annual rainfall 41" (1,025 mm).

CONSTITUTION AND GOVERNMENT

Ireland is a sovereign independent, democratic republic. Its parliament exercises jurisdiction in 26 of the 32 counties of the island of Ireland. The first Constitution of the Irish Free State came into operation on 6 Dec. 1922. Certain provisions which were regarded as contrary to the national sentiments were gradually removed by successive amendments, with the result that at the end of 1936 the text differed considerably from the original document. On 14 June 1937 a new Constitution was approved by Parliament and enacted by a plebiscite on 1 July 1937. This Constitution came into operation on 29 Dec. 1937. Under it the name Ireland (Éire) was restored. In its original form the Irish Constitution provided that the territory of Ireland comprised the whole island, and thus included that of Northern Ireland. This position was modified by referendum in 1998 following the Good Friday Agreement of that year. The former territorial claim has now been replaced with a statement that, while it is the aspiration of the Irish nation to unite the peoples of the island and the current territory of Ireland is not final, unification shall not take place without the consent of majorities in both jurisdictions.

The head of state is the *President*, whose role is largely ceremonial, but who has the power to refer proposed legislation which might infringe the Constitution to the Supreme Court.

The *Oireachtas* or National Parliament consists of the President, a House of Representatives (*Dáil Éireann*) and a Senate (*Seanad Éireann*). The *Dáil*, consisting of 166 members, is elected by adult suffrage on the Single Transferable Vote system in constituencies of three, four or five members. Of the 60 members of the Senate, 11 are nominated by the *Taoiseach* (Prime Minister), six are elected by the universities and the remaining 43 are elected from five panels of candidates established on a vocational basis, representing the following public services and interests: (1) national language and culture, literature, art, education and such professional interests as may be defined by law for the purpose of this panel; (2) agricultural and allied interests, and fisheries; (3) labour, whether organized or unorganized; (4) industry and commerce, including banking, finance, accountancy, engineering and architecture; (5) public administration and social services, including voluntary social activities. The electing body comprises members of the *Dáil*, Senate, county boroughs and county councils.

A maximum period of 90 days is afforded to the Senate for the consideration or amendment of Bills sent to that House by the *Dáil*, but the Senate has no power to veto legislative proposals.

No amendment of the Constitution can be effected except with the approval of the people given at a referendum.

National Anthem

'Amhrán na bhFiann' ('The Soldier's Song'); words by P. Kearney, tune by P. Heeney and P. Kearney.

GOVERNMENT CHRONOLOGY

(FF = Fianna Fáil; FG = Fine Gael; n/p = non-partisan)

Presidents since 1938.

1938–45	FF	Douglas Hyde
1945–59	FF	Séan Thomas O'Kelly
1959–73	FF	Eamon de Valera
1973–74	FF	Erskine Hamilton Childers
1974–76	FF	Cearbhall O'Dalaigh
1976–90	FF	Patrick John Hillery
1990–97	n/p	Mary Terese Robinson
1997–	FF	Mary Patricia McAleese

Prime Ministers

1932–48	FF	Eamon de Valera
1948–51	FG	John Aloysius Costello
1951–54	FF	Eamon de Valera
1954–57	FG	John Aloysius Costello
1957–59	FF	Eamon de Valera
1959–66	FF	Séan Francis Lemass
1966–73	FF	John (Jack) Mary Lynch
1973–77	FG	Liam Thomas Cosgrave
1977–79	FF	John (Jack) Mary Lynch
1979–81	FF	Charles James Haughey

1981–82	FG	Garret Michael FitzGerald
1982	FF	Charles James Haughey
1982–87	FG	Garret Michael FitzGerald
1987–92	FF	Charles James Haughey
1992–94	FF	Albert Reynolds
1994–97	FG	John Gerard Bruton
1997–	FF	Bartholomew (Bertie) P. Ahern

RECENT ELECTIONS

A general election was held on 17 May 2002: Fianna Fáil (FF) gained 81 seats with 41·5% of votes cast (in 1997, 77 seats); Fine Gael (FG), 31 with 22·5% (54); Labour Party (L), 21 with 10·8% (17); Progressive Democrats (PD), 8; Green Party (G), 6; Sinn Féin, 5; Socialist Party, 1; ind., 13.

Following elections to the Senate on 16 and 17 July 2002, FF held 30 of the 60 seats, FG had 15, L had 5, PD had 4 and non-partisans and others held 6 seats.

Presidential elections would have taken place on 22 Oct. 2004, but incumbent Mary McAleese (FF) was reappointed unopposed as no other candidates secured the necessary backing for an election to take place.

European Parliament
Ireland has 13 (15 in 1999) representatives. At the June 2004 elections turnout was 59·7%. Fine Gael won 5 seats with 27·8% of votes cast (political affiliation in European Parliament: European People's Party–European Democrats); Fianna Fáil, 4 with 29·5% (Union for a Europe of Nations); Sinn Féin, 1 with 11·1% (European Unitary Left/Nordic Green Left); Labour Party, 1 with 10·6% (Party of European Socialists). Two independents were elected (one Alliance of Liberals and Democrats for Europe; one Independence and Democracy Group).

CURRENT ADMINISTRATION

President: Mary McAleese (b. 1951; FF), elected out of five candidates on 30 Oct. 1997 and inaugurated 11 Nov. 1997, and appointed for a second term on 1 Oct. 2004.

Following the 2002 election the coalition government that had held office since 1997 between Fianna Fáil (FF) and the Progressive Democrats (PD) was renewed. In March 2006 it was composed as follows:

Taoiseach (Prime Minister): Bertie Ahern; b. 1951 (FF; sworn in 26 June 1997 and re-elected in 2002).

Tánaiste (Deputy Prime Minister), Minister for Health and Children: Mary Harney (b. 1953; PD). *Defence:* Willie O'Dea (b. 1952; FF). *Agriculture and Food:* Mary Coughlan (b. 1965; FF). *Finance:* Brian Cowen (b. 1960; FF). *Foreign Affairs:* Dermot Ahern (b. 1955; FF). *Education and Science:* Mary Hanafin (b. 1959; FF). *Communications, Marine and Natural Resources:* Noel Dempsey (b. 1953; FF). *Community, Rural and Gaeltacht Affairs:* Eamon Ó Cuív (b. 1952; FF). *Enterprise, Trade and Employment:* Micheál Martin (b. 1960; FF). *Transport:* Martin Cullen (b. 1954; FF). *Justice, Equality and Law Reform:* Michael McDowell (b. 1949; PD). *Environment and Local Government:* Dick Roche (b. 1947; FF). *Arts, Sport and Tourism:* John O'Donoghue (b. 1956; FF). *Social and Family Affairs:* Séamus Brennan (b. 1948; FF).

There are 17 Ministers of State.

Attorney General: Rory Brady.

Speaker of Dail Éireann: Rory O'Hanlon.

Government Website: http://www.irlgov.ie

CURRENT LEADERS
Mary McAleese

Position
President

Introduction
Mary McAleese became Ireland's president in 1997, the first person from Northern Ireland to fill the post. A lawyer by profession, she is a devout Catholic with a conservative stance on social issues. Her campaign for the presidency was dogged by claims that she was a supporter of the nationalist Sinn Féin movement, allegations she strongly refuted.

Early Life
Mary McAleese (*née* Leneghan) was born in Belfast on 27 June 1951. Her father was a pub landlord in Catholic West Belfast. The outbreak of sectarian violence in the late 1960s resulted in the family moving to County Down.

In 1973 she graduated in law from Queen's University, Belfast, and was called to the Bar the following year. In 1975 she took up a law professorship at Trinity College Dublin. She stayed in this position until 1987, although between 1979–81 she worked as a television broadcaster and journalist.

In 1987 she unsuccessfully stood as a Fianna Fáil candidate for a Dublin seat at the general election. In 1994 she was appointed pro-vice chancellor of Queen's University, the first female to hold the post. Three years later she was selected by Fianna Fáil to stand in the presidential elections, defeating former prime minister Albert Reynolds for the candidacy. Unpopular with many unionists, she was accused of having links to Sinn Féin, the political arm of the paramilitary Irish Republican Army (IRA). Having denied the accusations, she presented herself as a 'builder of bridges' and won an overwhelming majority at the polls.

Career in Office
McAleese was inaugurated as president on 11 Nov. 1997. Her role is largely ceremonial and non-partisan. A practising Catholic, she is opposed to abortion and aligns herself with the Vatican on such issues as divorce and contraception. She has voiced support for the ongoing peace initiatives in Northern Ireland and for continued cross-border co-operation. In Oct. 2004 she was appointed unopposed for a second presidential term.

Bertie Ahern

Position
Prime Minister

Introduction
Bertie Ahern became the Irish *taoiseach* (prime minister) in 1997, heading a coalition comprising his party, Fianna Fáil, and the Progressive Democrats. He was instrumental in brokering the Good Friday Agreement, the framework accord for peace in Northern Ireland. Staunchly pro-European, he has encouraged the expansion and closer unity of the EU.

Early Life
Bartholemew Ahern was born on 12 Sept. 1951 in Dublin. After school he studied economics and computer science at University College Dublin and the London School of Economics. In 1977 he entered the Irish parliament (the *Dáil*) as the republican Fianna Fáil member for a Dublin seat. Two years later he joined the Dublin City Council, serving as lord mayor for a year in the late 1980s.

He first obtained government office in 1980 as a chief whip under prime minister Charles Haughey. Junior ministerial posts followed until 1987 when he was appointed minister for labour. In this post until 1991 he gained a reputation as a skilled and pragmatic negotiator. In 1991 he took over the finance portfolio. In Nov. 1994, after 11 years as Fianna Fáil's deputy leader, Ahern was voted Albert Reynolds' successor. He led Fianna Fáil in opposition until 1997.

As Ireland's biggest party following the June 1997 elections, Ahern was prepared to form a coalition government with the Labour Party, but following last minute realignments he went into government with the Progressive Democrats.

Career in Office

Within a month of Ahern taking office the Irish Republican Army (IRA) renewed its ceasefire, and all-party peace talks resumed in Sept. These culminated in the Good Friday Agreement of April 1998. Amongst the agreement's key provisions were the creation of the Northern Irish assembly, a North–South ministerial council and a Council of the Isles (also known as the British-Irish Council). It also laid out guidelines for weapons decommissioning by paramilitary groups, which became a major stumbling block to progress. Although the IRA promised to put weapons 'beyond use', peace negotiations were stalled on several occasions over the issue of disarmament. Ahern meanwhile acknowledged that getting paramilitary violence out of the way was only a first step, the chief problem in his view being deep-rooted 'tribalism'.

Ahern's handling of the peace talks and Ireland's healthy economy maintained his popularity, although support fell in the Catholic community after his separation from his wife. Also, within a year of Ahern taking office, two of his long-term allies—former *taosieach* Charles Haughey and former minister Ray Burke—were involved in embarrassing funding scandals.

Ahern has been a leading advocate for the EU. He oversaw the transition from the Irish pound to the euro in 2002 and expressed a wish that the UK would also adopt the new currency, thus facilitating commerce between the Republic of Ireland and the North. In Oct. 2002 he oversaw the endorsement via referendum of the Nice Treaty, allowing ten new countries to join the EU in 2004 (the treaty having been rejected in an earlier Irish referendum in 2001). Elsewhere on the international stage, in 1998 Ahern became the first Irish prime minister to visit China.

Ahern won another term of office when Fianna Fáil won the elections of May 2002. In Oct. 2002 the Northern Irish Assembly executive was suspended over allegations of IRA spying at the Northern Ireland Office. Direct rule from London was reimposed and shortly afterwards the IRA cut off its links with the international weapons decommissioning body. In May 2003 UK Prime Minister Blair postponed elections to the Northern Irish Assembly, defending the move on the grounds that Sinn Féin leader Gerry Adams' assurance that the IRA would not do anything to undermine the peace process did not provide a specific guarantee. Ahern refused to endorse Blair's position but restated his commitment to working with the UK government towards a lasting peace. Subsequently, in July 2005, the IRA declared formally that it was ending its armed campaign to pursue peaceful political dialogue—a move confirmed by the international decommissioning body in Sept. despite Unionist scepticism.

DEFENCE

Supreme command of the Defence Forces is vested in the President. Exercise of the supreme command is regulated by law (Defence Act 1954). Military Command is exercised by the government through the Minister for Defence, who is the overall commander of the Defence Forces.

The Defence Forces comprise the Permanent Defence Force (the regular Army, the Air Corps and the Naval Service) and the Defence Reserve (comprising a First Line Reserve of members who have served in the Permanent Defence Force, a second-line Territorial Army Reserve and a second-line Naval Reserve).

The total strength of the Permanent Defence Force in Oct. 2005 was 10,541 (including 524 women). The total strength of the Reserve in Aug. 2005 was 11,218. In Dec. 2005, 768 Defence Forces personnel were involved in 19 peace-support missions throughout the world.

Defence expenditure in 2005 totalled €760m. (US$913m.), equivalent to €190 (US$228) per capita, representing 0·6% of GDP.

Army

The Army strength in Oct. 2005 was 8,623 personnel with 10,810 reservists. There is a Training Centre at the Curragh, Co. Kildare and a Logistics Base, with elements located at the Curragh and Dublin for force level logistical support.

Navy

The Naval Service is based at Haulbowline in Co. Cork. The strength in Oct. 2005 was 1,061 with 408 reservists. It operates eight patrol vessels.

Air Corps

The Air Corps has its headquarters at Casement Aerodrome, Baldonnel, Co. Dublin. The Air Corps is a stand-alone Corps which does not form an intrinsic part of the new Army Brigade structure. The Air Corps strength in Oct. 2005 was 857 personnel. The Corps operates 18 fixed-wing aircraft and 12 helicopters.

INTERNATIONAL RELATIONS

Ireland is a member of the UN, WTO, BIS, OECD, EU, the Council of Europe, the OSCE and IOM.

ECONOMY

Agriculture accounted for 3·3% of GDP in 2002, industry 41·2% and services 55·5%.

According to the anti-corruption organization *Transparency International*, Ireland ranked equal 19th in the world in a 2005 survey of the countries with the least corruption in business and government. It received 7·4 out of 10 in the annual index.

Overview

Previously one of Western Europe's least developed economies, Ireland is now the region's second richest economy per capita after Luxembourg. The engine of Irish growth in the last decade has been its high-tech export sector (chiefly chemicals and computer hardware and software). A magnet for US investment in Europe, investors have been attracted by Ireland's favourable corporate tax environment for manufacturers and its skilled, English-speaking labour force. Net inflows of foreign direct investment accelerated significantly in 1998, peaking in 2000 at roughly 26% of GDP. In 2001 the slowdown in the US brought foreign direct investment down from its record high but inflows remained strong and picked up in 2002–03. Foreign investment was up again in 2005 at around 8% of GDP, after hitting its lowest level since 1997 in 2004. Real GDP growth averaged 9·8% between 1997 and 2000. Though growth has since slowed, it remains above the OECD average.

Ireland's dependence on the USA for investment and as an export market makes the economy potentially vulnerable to a collapse in the US dollar. Exports remain Ireland's primary growth engine but healthy income growth and consumer spending have also boosted construction and business investment. Rapid growth has led to infrastructure bottlenecks and inflationary pressures. Strong domestic demand has kept inflation above the euro zone average, but steps have been taken to combat price pressures, such as the deregulation of the retail market in 2005.

Currency

On 1 Jan. 1999 the euro (EUR) became the legal currency in Ireland; irrevocable conversion rate 0·787564 Irish pounds to 1 euro. The euro, which consists of 100 cents, has been in circulation since 1 Jan. 2002. There are seven euro notes in different colours and sizes denominated in 500, 200, 100, 50, 20, 10 and 5 euros, and eight coins denominated in 2 and 1 euros, then 50, 20, 10, 5, 2 and 1 cents. On the introduction of the euro there was a 'dual circulation' period before the Irish pound ceased to be legal tender on 9 Feb. 2002. Euro banknotes in circulation on 1 Jan. 2002 had a total value of €6·8bn.

Inflation rates (based on OECD statistics):

1995	1996	1997	1998	1999	2000	2001	2002	2003	2004
2·5%	2·2%	1·2%	2·1%	2·5%	5·3%	4·0%	4·7%	4·0%	2·3%

The Central Bank has the sole right of issuing legal tender notes; token coinage is issued by the Minister for Finance through the Bank. Gold reserves were 176,000 troy oz in June 2002 and foreign exchange reserves US$4,648m. Total money supply was €3,616m. in June 2002.

Budget
Current revenue and expenditure (in €1m.):

Current Revenue	2002	2003
Customs duties	134	137
Excise duties	4,441	4,572
Capital taxes	778	1,657
Stamp duties	1,167	1,688
Income tax	9,063	9,162
Corporation tax	4,803	5,161
Value-added tax	8,885	9,721
Levies	23	5
Non-tax revenue	2,231	1,054
Total	31,525	33,157
Current expenditure		
Debt service	1,669	2,027
Industry and labour	1,228	1,212
Agriculture	1,317	1,227
Fisheries, Forestry, Tourism	253	283
Health	7,788	8,729
Education	4,808	5,449
Social Welfare	9,529	10,515
Other (voted)	5,302	5,611
Other (non-voted)	1,143	1,276
Gross current	33,037	36,330
Less: Receipts, e.g. social security	6,880	7,539
Net total (including non-voted central fund)	26,157	28,791

VAT is 21·0% (reduced rate 13·5%).

Total public capital programme expenditure amounted to €5,290m. (net voted capital expenditure) in 2003, with provision for €5,481m. in 2004. The general government debt at the end of 2003 is estimated at €36·3bn., 33·1% of GDP, and is forecast to remain around 33% of GDP in the medium term.

Performance
Real GDP growth rates (based on OECD statistics):

1995	1996	1997	1998	1999	2000	2001	2002	2003	2004
9·6%	8·3%	10·8%	8·6%	10·7%	9·2%	6·2%	6·1%	4·4%	4·5%

During the late 1990s Ireland had the fastest-growing economy in the European Union, with real GDP growth in 2000 of 9·2% following growth averaging 9·6% over the previous five years. Real GDP growth has slowed since then, but at 4·5% in 2004 is still one of the best performing economies in the EU. From a GDP per head of only 69% of the EU average in 1987, it was estimated to have risen to 136% of the EU average by 2003. GNP in Ireland is much lower than GDP owing to profit repatriations by multi-nationals and foreign debt servicing. Ireland's GNP per head is about 99% of the EU average. Total GDP in 2004 was US$183·6bn.

Banking and Finance
The Central Bank (founded in 1943) replaced the Currency Commission as the note-issuing authority. In 2003 the Central Bank was renamed the Central Bank and Financial Services Authority of Ireland (CBFSAI). The CBFSAI has two component entities: the Central Bank and the Irish Financial Services Regulatory Authority. It has the power of receiving deposits from banks and public authorities, of rediscounting Exchequer bills and bills of exchange, of making advances to banks against such bills or against government securities, of fixing and publishing rates of interest for rediscounting bills, or buying and selling certain government securities and securities of any international bank or financial institution formed wholly or mainly by governments. The CBFSAI also collects and publishes information relating to monetary and credit matters. The Central Bank Acts, 1971, 1989 and 1997, together with the Building Societies Act, 1989, the Investment Intermediaries Act, 1995 and the Stock Exchange Act, 1995, gave further powers to the CBFSAI in the regulation and supervision of financial institutions and payment systems.

The Board of Directors of the Central Bank consists of a Governor, appointed for a seven-year term by the President on the advice of the government, and twelve directors, all appointed by the Minister for Finance. The Governor is John Hurley. In 2003 the Bank's net profit was €60·04m.; €321·73m. was paid to the Exchequer.

In 2004 the Irish Financial Services Regulatory Authority was responsible for the regulation of 80 credit institutions (including branches). There are three State banks—ICC Bank, ACC Bank and the Trustee Savings Bank.

At 30 April 2004 total assets of within-the-State offices of all credit institutions amounted to €629·5bn.

The Dublin stock exchange has been affiliated to the London exchange since 1973.

ENERGY AND NATURAL RESOURCES

Environment
Ireland's carbon dioxide emissions from the consumption and flaring of fossil fuels in 2002 were the equivalent of 11·5 tonnes per capita.

Electricity
The total generating capacity in 2004 was 5,592 MW, as averaged on a daily basis. This included wind generation, small renewable and small Combined Heat and Power (CHP). In 2003 there were approximately 1,804,680 customers connected to the network consuming 22,286 GWh.

Oil and Gas
Over 0·6m. sq. km of the Irish continental shelf has been designated an exploration area for oil and gas; at the furthest point the limit of jurisdiction is 520 nautical miles from the coast. It has been established that there is potential for discoveries both offshore and onshore. In the offshore there is a vast Continental Shelf in which a number of major basins and troughs have been identified. Much of the shelf remains unexplored but since 1971 a total of 166 wells have been drilled (121 offshore exploration wells and 45 appraisal/development wells), and since 1965 a total of 381 offshore surveys have been carried out.

Natural gas reserves in 2002 totalled 20bn. cu. metres. Production in 2000 was 1·2bn. cu. metres and consumption 4·2bn. cu. metres. 80% of natural gas supplies for the Irish Market are imported through the two sub-sea interconnectors connecting Ireland with Scotland and the remaining 20% is supplied from the Kinsale Head gas field, 50 km off the south coast of Ireland.

Natural gas transmission and distribution is currently carried out by Bord Gáis Éireann (Irish Gas Board). The liberalization of the Irish gas market is underway; in July 2004 all non-domestic natural gas customers became eligible to choose their own natural gas supplier. Full market opening is anticipated to take place during 2006, when all remaining end users will be eligible to choose any licensed natural gas supplier.

Peat

The country has very little indigenous coal, but possesses large reserves of peat, the development of which is handled largely by Bord na Móna (Peat Board). To date, the Board has acquired and developed 85,000 ha. of bog and has 27 locations around the country. In the year ending 31 March 2001 the Board sold 2·8m. tonnes of milled peat for use in five milled peat electricity generating stations. 301,000 tonnes of briquettes were produced for sale to the domestic heating market. Bord na Móna also sold 136m. cu. metres of horticultural peat, mainly for export. It is estimated that some 1m. tonnes of privately-produced peat was consumed in the same period.

Minerals

Ireland has three zinc-lead mines, which in 2004 produced a combined total of 438,000 tonnes of zinc in concentrate and 64,000 tonnes of lead in concentrate, together with some silver (in lead). Ireland is Europe's leading zinc mine producer (44% of European output in 2004) and ranks seventh in the world for total zinc production. The total value of production in 2003 was €260m. Production of gypsum is significant and the aggregates sector has expanded dramatically in recent years. Aggregate production in 2004 was an estimated 120m. tonnes. About 30 companies hold 285 prospecting licences; a total of €8m. was spent on exploration in 2003. The main target is base metals but there is also interest in gold.

Agriculture

The CSO's Quarterly National Household Survey showed in the quarter of March–May 2003 that there were 113,200 people whose primary source of income was from agriculture. A total of 240,100 people worked on farms on a regular basis, working the equivalent of 158,100 full-time jobs. There were 136,500 farm holdings in Ireland, almost all of which were family farms. Average farm size was 32·0 ha. 43% of farms were under 20 ha. 13% of farmers were under 35 and 41% were over 55. In 2001 there were 1·05m. ha. of arable land in Ireland and 2,000 ha. of permanent crops.

Agriculture, fisheries and forestry represented 3·5% of GDP in 2002 (provisional). 90% of the agricultural area was devoted to grass in 2002. In 2003 beef and milk production accounted for 57% of goods output at producer prices.

Figures at June 2002: barley accounted (in ha.) for 176,000; wheat, 102,700; oats, 18,800; other cereals, 1,800; potatoes, 15,400. Production figures (in 1,000 tonnes): sugarbeets, 1,313; barley, 963; wheat, 867; potatoes, 519; oats, 134.

Goods output at producer prices including changes in stock for 2003 was estimated at €4·7bn.; operating surplus (aggregate income) was €2·5bn. Direct income payments, financed or co-financed by the EU, amounted to €1·6bn. It is estimated that net subsidies (subsidies on products plus subsidies on production less taxes on products and taxes on production) represented 63% of aggregate income.

Livestock: (June 2003 provisional) 6,924,100 cattle, 6,964,400 sheep; (June 2002) 1,769,500 pigs, 12,708,600 poultry.

Forestry

Total forest area by the end of 2000 was 699,166 ha. (10·1% of total land area). Timber production in 2004 was 2·82m. cu. metres.

Fisheries

In 1999 approximately 17,600 people were engaged full- or part-time in the sea fishing industry; in 2004 the fishing fleet consisted of 1,425 vessels. The quantities and values of fish landed during 2004 were: wetfish, 256,170 tonnes, value €106·2m.; shellfish, 62,331 tonnes, value €80·1m. Total quantity (2004): 318,501 tonnes; total value, €186·4m. The main types of fish caught in 2004 were mackerel (63,000 tonnes), blue whiting (49,000 tonnes), horse mackerel (37,000 tonnes) and herring (29,000 tonnes). More than 98% of fish caught is from sea fishing.

INDUSTRY

The leading companies by market capitalization in Ireland in Nov. 2005 were: Allied Irish Banks (€15·9bn.); Bank of Ireland (€12·7bn.); and CRH plc (US$12·0bn.), a building materials company.

Enterprise Ireland. Enterprise Ireland was established in 1998 to provide an integrated development package specifically for indigenous firms. Its mission is 'to accelerate the development of world-class Irish companies to achieve strong positions in global markets resulting in increased national and regional prosperity'. Enterprise Ireland brings together the key marketing, technology, enterprise development, business training and science and innovation initiatives through which the government supports the growth of Irish manufacturing and internationally traded sectors.

County Enterprise Boards. The 35 City and County Enterprise Boards (CEB's), which were established in Oct. 1993, are locally controlled enterprise development companies established in each county and local authority area in Ireland. The function of the Boards is to develop indigenous enterprise potential and to stimulate economic activity at a local level. This is primarily achieved through the provision of financial support for the development of micro enterprise (ten employees or fewer).

IDA Ireland. IDA Ireland, founded in 1949 as the Industrial Development Authority, is an autonomous Irish government agency with responsibility for the attraction of foreign direct investment into Ireland and the develop-ment of the existing base of more than 1,000 IDA-supported overseas companies.

IDA Ireland's success in attracting leading global companies from all business sectors has led to Ireland being acknowledged as one of the world's leading locations for higher-value, knowledge-intensive and skills-driven activities in biopharmaceutical, pharmaceutical, ICT, international services and financial services, in all areas of business including innovative R&D, high-value manufacturing, leading-edge international services and financial services.

Shannon Development. Shannon Development, which was established in 1959, is the regional economic development company responsible for industrial, tourism and rural development in the Shannon region. Its regional mandate covers Counties Clare, Limerick, North Tipperary, South Offaly and North Kerry.

Forfás. Forfás is the policy advisory and co-ordination board for industrial development and science and technology. It is the statutory agency through which powers are delegated to Enterprise Ireland for the promotion of indigenous enterprise and to IDA Ireland for the promotion of inward investment.

The main functions of Forfás are to advise the Minister on matters relating to industrial policy, to advise on the development and co-ordination of policy for Enterprise Ireland and IDA Ireland, and encourage the development of industry, technology, marketing and human resources.

The Chairman of Forfás is Eoin O'Driscoll and its Chief Executive is Martin Cronin.

The census of industrial production for 2002 gives the following details of the values (in €1m.) of gross and net output for the principal manufacturing industries.

	Gross output	Net output
Mining and quarrying	1,070·2	546·0
Manufacture of food products, beverages and tobacco	16,689·4	8,366·7
Manufacture of textiles and textile products	672·0	325·1

	Gross output	Net output
Manufacture of leather and leather products	53·1	14·3
Manufacture of wood and wood products	881·6	367·8
Manufacture of pulp, paper and paper products; publishing and printing	10,577·8	8,180·5
Manufacture of chemicals, chemical products and man-made fibres	30,206·1	25,556·9
Manufacture of rubber and plastic products	1,092·8	532·4
Manufacture of other non-metallic mineral products	1,471·9	757·2
Manufacture of basic metals and fabricated metal products	1,746·4	773·4
Manufacture of machinery and equipment n.e.c.	1,650·9	769·2
Manufacture of electrical and optical equipment	27,591·0	11,112·6
Manufacture of transport equipment	1,058·7	467·2
Manufacturing n.e.c.	1,905·9	661·3
Electricity, gas and water supply	3,298·8	1,942·1
Total (all industries)	99,966·5	60,372·7

In 2001 gross output was €98,373m. and net output €56,139m.

Labour

The total labour force for 2003 was estimated to be 1,859,700, of which 81,400 were out of work. With the birth rate having peaked around 1980 there is currently a marked increase in the numbers entering the workforce. The unemployment rate in 2005 was 4·3% (among the lowest in the EU), down from nearly 16% in 1993. Of those at work in 2003, 1,172,600 were employed in the services sector, 492,600 in the industrial sector and 113,200 in the agricultural sector. Employment rose by approximately 51% between 1991 and 2001—more than twice as much as in any other industrialized country. The retirement age is 65 years.

Trade Unions

The number of trade unions affiliated to the Irish Congress of Trade Unions and based exclusively in Ireland was 31 in 2005; total membership, 557,000. There were also approximately 40,000 union members unaffiliated to the Congress. The six largest unions accounted for 68% of total membership in 2002. A series of three-year social pacts, which, in addition to covering a range of economic and social policy measures, include provision for pay increases, have been negotiated between the government, trade unions and employees' organizations since 1987. The fifth such agreement concluded in Feb. 2000, the Programme for Prosperity and Fairness (PPF), provided pay increases of 15% of basic pay in the public and private sectors of the economy over the period of the agreement, 2000–02. Owing to escalating inflation a further compensatory 1% lump sum payment was negotiated, for payment in March 2001. The third phase increase (4%) in the public service was not to be paid earlier than Oct. 2002 and was dependent on the establishment of performance indicators by April 2001 and the achievement of sectoral targets by April 2002.

The PPF agreement expired for some workers in the private sector in Dec. 2002; depending on start dates, for others the agreement continued into 2003. The PPF pay element expired in Oct. 2003 for the public service. The successor agreement, Sustaining Progress, was in operation between 1 Jan. 2003 and 31 Dec. 2005. The programme allowed for a cumulative increase in actual pay of 13·6%, in six separate increases, over that period.

INTERNATIONAL TRADE

Imports and Exports

In 2002 exports accounted for 94% of GDP (both merchandise and service). This showed a slight decrease on the 2001 level which was just over 96% of GDP. Value of imports and exports of merchandise for calendar years (in €1m.):

	1999	2000	2001	2002
Imports	44,327	55,909	57,384	53,303
Exports	66,956	83,889	92,690	93,724

The values of the chief imports and total exports are shown in the following table (in €1m.):

	Imports		Exports	
	2001	2002	2001	2002
Animal and vegetable oils and waxes	123	115	24	28
Beverages and tobacco	679	757	985	1,001
Chemicals	6,341	6,998	32,281	39,313
Live animals and food	3,116	3,135	5,801	5,679
Machinery and transport equipment	30,224	27,892	37,607	32,759
Manufactured articles	6,300	6,068	8,969	8,068
Manufactured goods	4,391	4,290	1,955	1,839
Mineral fuels and lubricants	2,219	1,740	297	361
Raw materials	799	788	953	855

Ireland is one of the most trade-dependent countries in the world. Exports constitute an increasing share of the economy's output of goods and services. In 2002 the total value of merchandise exports amounted to just over €93·7bn. (the highest ever level), which generated a trade surplus of €38·4bn. In 2002 merchandise imports from other European Union countries accounted for 59·4% of total imports while merchandise exports to other EU countries accounted for 63·7% of total exports. Information technology has become increasingly important, and by 1999 Ireland had become the largest exporter of software products in the world.

Import and export totals for Ireland's top ten export markets in 2002 (€1m.):

	Imports		Exports	
	2001	2002	2001	2002
Belgium	864	791	4,431	3,519
France	2,752	2,252	5,532	4,668
Germany	3,521	3,533	11,671	6,744
Italy	1,185	1,092	3,309	3,593
Japan	1,991	2,012	3,261	2,642
Netherlands	1,860	1,822	4,237	3,410
Spain	646	676	2,283	2,231
Switzerland	530	557	2,706	3,121
United Kingdom	20,481	19,860	22,630	22,431
United States of America	8,700	8,504	15,694	16,385

COMMUNICATIONS

Roads

At 31 Dec. 2003 there were 95,811 km of public roads, consisting of 2,746 km of National Primary Roads (including 176 km of motorway), 2,685 km of National Secondary Roads, 11,607 km of Regional Roads and 78,773 km of Local Roads.

Number of licensed motor vehicles at 31 Dec. 2002: private cars, 1,447,908; public-service vehicles, 25,342; goods vehicles, 233,069; agricultural vehicles, 66,665; motorcycles, 33,147; other vehicles, 43,915. In 2002 a total of 376 people were killed in 346 fatal accidents.

Rail

The total length of railway open for traffic at 31 Dec. 1993 was 1,919 km (478 km electrified), all 1,600 mm gauge. A massive investment in public transport infrastructure is taking place in Ireland. The National Development plan that runs from Jan. 2000 to Dec. 2006 allows for €235m. to be invested in Dublin suburban rail alone.

Railway statistics for years ending 31 Dec.	2001	2002
Passengers (journeys)	34,206,000	35,370,000
Km run by passenger train	12,356,000	12,602,000
Freight (tonne-km)	515,754,000	426,307,000
Km run by freight trains	4,133,000	2,895,000

Railway statistics for years ending 31 Dec.	2001	2002
Receipts (IR£)	197,088,000	198,780,000
Expenditure (IR£)	378,843,000	396,127,000

A light railway system was launched in Dublin in 2004.

Civil Aviation

Aer Lingus and Ryanair are the two major airlines operating in Ireland.

Aer Lingus was founded in 1936 as a State-owned enterprise. Its principal business is the provision of passenger and cargo services to the UK, Europe and the USA. Ryanair began operations in 1985 and now operates to a range of destinations in the UK and Europe.

In addition to Aer Lingus and Ryanair, there are 16 other independent air transport operators. The main operators in this group are Aer Arann Express and Cityjet.

The principal airports (Dublin, Shannon and Cork) are operated by the Dublin Airport Authority plc. In 2002 Dublin handled 15·08m. passengers and 116,700 tonnes of freight. Shannon handled 2·35m. passengers and 48,100 tonnes of freight. Cork was the third busiest, with 1·87m. passengers and 12,900 tonnes of freight. In 2003 Ireland's three state airports catered for almost 16m. passengers in Dublin, 2·4m. in Shannon and 2·2m. in Cork to give over 20m. passengers, up almost 6% on 2002.

There are six privately owned regional airports. The government part funds the scheduled services from Dublin to five of these airports and to the City of Derry airport in Northern Ireland to ensure efficient and speedy access to the more isolated regions of the state for both business and tourist travellers. The principal focus of growth during 2003 was the European market with the Dublin–London air route amongst the busiest in Europe.

Shipping

The merchant fleet totalled 269,693 GRT in 2002. Total cargo traffic passing through the country's ports amounted to 44,919,000 tonnes in 2002. Dublin handled 22·2m. tonnes of cargo in 2002 and Cork 9·4m. tonnes.

Inland Waterways

The principal inland waterways open to navigation are the Shannon Navigation (270 km), which includes the Shannon-Erne Waterway (Ballinamore/Ballyconnell Canal), and the Grand Canal and Barrow Navigation (249 km). The Waterways Service of the Department of Arts, Culture and the Gaeltacht is responsible for the waterways system as a public amenity. Merchandise traffic has now ceased and navigation is confined to pleasure craft operated either privately or commercially. The Royal Canal (146 km) from Dublin to Mullingar (53 km) was reopened for navigation in 1995.

Telecommunications

The Minister for Public Enterprise, a member of the government, has overall policy responsibility for the development of the sector. Among the key elements of the government's policy is the objective of creating a fully open and competitive telecommunications market that will stimulate investment in advanced information infrastructure and services in Ireland and develop Ireland as a global leader in the growth of Internet-based industries and electronic commerce.

The Director of Telecommunications Regulation, established by legislation as an independent officer with a separate office and staff in June 1997, is responsible for licensing of operators, allocation of numbers and radio frequency spectrum, supervision of network interconnection arrangements and other regulatory functions.

Ireland's telecommunications sector has been fully liberalized with effect from 1 Dec. 1998 when the last remaining elements of Telecom Éireann's (now called Eircom) exclusive privilege were removed. All elements of the market are now open to competition from other licensed operators. The three licensed mobile telephone operators are Vodafone, O2 and Meteor.

The Government has also sold the state's entire remaining stake of 50·1% in Eircom by way of an initial public offering of shares in the company. The sale took place in July 1999.

eircom plc—Operational Information

The dominant operator in the telecommunications sector is eircom plc (previously Telecom Éireann). Telecom Éireann was a statutory body set up under the Postal and Telecommunications Services Act, 1983. In 1996, 20% of the State's holding was sold to KPN/Telia, a Dutch–Swedish consortium, who had an option of a further 15%, which was taken up in July 1999. In 1998 the government concluded an Employee Share Ownership Scheme under which 14·9% of the company was to be made available to employees and also held an Initial Public Offer (IPO) of shares in the company in July 1999. In Oct. 1999 the newly-privatized Telecom Éireann became eircom plc.

The level of network digitalization is 100%. In 2002 there were 4,944,000 telephone subscribers, equivalent to 1,257·7 per 1,000 inhabitants. Mobile phone customers numbered 3·0m. in 2002 and there were 1,654,000 PCs in use (420·8 per 1,000 persons). In 2004 Irish mobile phone subscribers sent 3·74bn. text messages in total (89 messages per subscriber per month). There were 1·31m. Internet users in Sept. 2002 and 132,500 were connected to broadband in Dec. 2004.

Postal Services

Postal services are provided by An Post, a statutory body established under the Postal and Telecommunications Services Act, 1983. In 2003 there were 1,658 post offices. A total of 830m. pieces of mail were handled during 2003, equivalent to 183 per person. An Post also offers a range of services to the business community through a dedicated unit, Special Delivery Services, and subsidiaries PostGEM, PrintPost and Precision Marketing Information. A range of services are provided through the Post Office network including Savings and Investments, passport applications, bill payments, National Lottery products and the payment of Social Welfare benefits on an agency basis for the State.

SOCIAL INSTITUTIONS

Justice

The Constitution provides that justice shall be administered in public in Courts established by law by Judges appointed by the President on the advice of the government. The jurisdiction and organization of the Courts are dealt with in the Courts (Establishment and Constitution) Act, 1961, the Courts (Supplemental Provisions) Acts, 1961–91, and the Courts and Court Officers Acts, 1995–2002. These Courts consist of Courts of First Instance and a Court of Final Appeal, called the Supreme Court. The Courts of First Instance are the High Court with full original jurisdiction and the Circuit and the District Courts with local and limited jurisdictions. A judge may not be removed from office except for stated misbehaviour or incapacity and then only on resolutions passed by both Houses of the Oireachtas. Judges are appointed by the President on the advice of Government. Judges of the Supreme Court and High Court are appointed from among practising Barristers or Solicitors of not less than 12 years standing or by the elevation of an existing member of the judiciary. Judges of the Circuit Court are appointed from among practising Barristers or Solicitors of not less than ten years standing or a County Registrar who has practised as a Barrister or Solicitor for not less than ten years before being appointed to that post or by the elevation of a District Court Judge. Judges of the District Court are appointed from among practising Barristers or Solicitors of not less than ten years standing.

The Supreme Court, which consists of the Chief Justice (who is *ex officio* an additional judge of the High Court) and seven ordinary judges, may sit in two Divisions and has appellate jurisdiction from all decisions of the High Court. The President may, after consultation with the Council of State, refer a Bill, which has been passed by both Houses of the Oireachtas (other than a money bill and certain other bills), to the Supreme Court for a decision on the question as to whether such Bill or any provision thereof is repugnant to the Constitution.

The High Court, which consists of a President (who is *ex officio* an additional Judge of the Supreme Court) and 31 ordinary judges (or 32 when a High Court Judge is appointed as a Commissioner of the Law Reform Commission, as is currently the case), has full original jurisdiction in and power to determine all matters and questions, whether of law or fact, civil or criminal. In all cases in which questions arise concerning the validity of any law having regard to the provisions of the Constitution, the High Court alone exercises original jurisdiction. The High Court on Circuit acts as an appeal court from the Circuit Court.

The Court of Criminal Appeal consists of the Chief Justice or an ordinary Judge of the Supreme Court, together with either two ordinary judges of the High Court or the President and one ordinary judge of the High Court. It deals with appeals by persons convicted on indictment where the appellant obtains a certificate from the trial judge that the case is a fit one for appeal, or, in case such certificate is refused, where the court itself, on appeal from such refusal, grants leave to appeal. The decision of the Court of Criminal Appeal is final, unless that court, the Attorney-General or the Director of Public Prosecutions certifies that the decision involves a point of law of exceptional public importance, in which case an appeal is taken to the Supreme Court.

The Offences against the State Act, 1939 provides in Part V for the establishment of Special Criminal Courts. A Special Criminal Court sits without a jury. The rules of evidence that apply in proceedings before a Special Criminal Court are the same as those applicable in trials in the Central Criminal Court. A Special Criminal Court is authorized by the 1939 Act to make rules governing its own practice and procedure. An appeal against conviction or sentence by a Special Criminal Court may be taken to the Court of Criminal Appeal. On 30 May 1972 Orders were made establishing a Special Criminal Court and declaring that offences of a particular class or kind (as set out) were to be scheduled offences for the purposes of Part V of the Act, the effect of which was to give the Special Criminal Court jurisdiction to try persons charged with those offences.

The High Court exercising criminal jurisdiction is known as the Central Criminal Court. It consists of a judge or judges of the High Court, nominated by the President of the High Court. The Court tries criminal cases which are outside the jurisdiction of the Circuit Court.

The Circuit Court consists of a President (who is *ex officio* an additional judge of the High Court) and 33 ordinary judges. The country is divided into eight circuits. The jurisdiction of the court in civil proceedings is subject to a financial ceiling, save by consent of the parties, in which event the jurisdiction is unlimited. In criminal matters it has jurisdiction in all cases except murder, treason, piracy, rape, serious and aggravated sexual assault and allied offences. The Circuit Court acts as an appeal court from the District Court. The Circuit Court also has jurisdiction in the Family Law area such as divorce.

The District Court, which consists of a President and 54 ordinary judges, has summary jurisdiction in a large number of criminal cases where the offence is not of a serious nature. In civil matters the Court has jurisdiction in contract and tort (except slander, libel, seduction, slander of title and false imprisonment) where the claim does not exceed €6,348·69; in proceedings founded on hire-purchase and credit-sale agreements, the jurisdiction is also

€6,348·69. The District Court also has jurisdiction in Family Law matters such as maintenance, custody, access and the issuing of barring orders. The District Court also has jurisdiction in a large number of licensing (intoxicating liquor) matters.

All criminal cases, except those of a minor nature, and those tried in the Special Criminal Court, are tried by a judge and a jury of 12. Generally, a verdict need not be unanimous in a case where there are not fewer than 11 jurors if ten of them agree on the verdict.

The Courts Service Act, 1998, provided for the transfer of responsibility for the day to day management of the Courts from the Minister for Justice, Equality and Law Reform to a new body known as the Courts Service. The Board of the Courts Service consists of 17 members including members of the judiciary, the legal profession, staff and trade union representatives, a representative of court users, a person with commercial/financial experience and a Chief Executive Officer. The Courts Service was formally established on 9 Nov. 1999. While the Minister retains political responsibility to the Oireachtas, the courts are now administered independently by the Board and CEO.

At 31 Dec. 2003 the police force, the Garda Síochána, had a total staff of 12,210. There were 103,360 headline offences recorded in 2003, of which 37,184 were detected, and non-headline offences resulted in proceedings against 292,279 persons; there were 45 murders in 2003 (1·24 per 100,000 population). The National Juvenile Office received 19,915 referrals relating to 17,043 individual children during 2003. The population in penal institutions in Sept. 2003 was 3,366 (85 per 100,000 of national population).

Education

In 2001 total expenditure on education came to 5·1% of GNP and 13·0% of total government spending. The adult literacy rate is at least 99%.

Elementary. Elementary education is free and was given in about 3,283 national schools (including 128 special schools) in 2002–03. The total number of pupils on rolls in 2002–03 was 443,720, including pupils in special schools and classes; the number of teachers of all classes was about 24,700 in 2002–03, including remedial teachers and teachers of special classes. The total expenditure for first level education during the financial year ended 31 Dec. 2003 was €2,119·7m. The total salaries for teachers for 2003, including superannuation etc., was €1,509·0m.

Special. Special provision is made for children with disabilities in special schools which are recognized on the same basis as primary schools, in special classes attached to ordinary schools and in certain voluntary centres where educational services appropriate to the needs of the children are provided. Integration of children with disabilities in ordinary schools and classes is encouraged wherever possible, if necessary with special additional support. There are also part-time teaching facilities in hospitals, child guidance clinics, rehabilitation workshops, special 'Saturday-morning' centres and home teaching schemes. Special schools (2002–03) numbered 128 with approximately 6,807 pupils. There were also some 9,384 pupils enrolled in about 1,001 special classes within ordinary schools. There is a National Education Officer for travelling children.

Secondary. Voluntary secondary schools are under private ownership and are conducted in most cases by religious orders. These schools receive grants from the State and are open to inspection by the Department of Education. The number of recognized secondary schools during the school year 2002–03 was 410, and the number of pupils in attendance was 189,093. There were 12,447 teachers in 2002–03.

Vocational Education Committee schools provide courses of general and technical education. Pupils are prepared for State examinations and for entrance to universities and institutes of further education. The number of vocational schools during the school year 2002–03 was 247, the number of full-time students in attendance was 98,233 and the number of teachers 5,933. These schools are controlled by the local Vocational Education Committees; they are financed mainly by State grants and also by contributions from local rating authorities and Vocational Education Committee receipts. These schools also provide adult education facilities for their own areas.

Comprehensive and Community Schools. Comprehensive schools which are financed by the State combine academic and technical subjects in one broad curriculum so that pupils may be offered educational options suited to their needs, abilities and interests. Pupils are prepared for State examinations and for entrance to universities and institutes of further education. The number of comprehensive and community schools during the school year 2002–03 was 89 and the number of students in attendance was 51,905. These schools also provide adult education facilities for their own areas and make facilities available to voluntary organizations and to the adult community generally.

The total current expenditure from public funds for second level and further education for 2003 was €2,304·8m.

Education Third-Level. Traditionally, the third-level education system in Ireland has comprised the university sector, the technical and technological colleges and the colleges of education, all of which are substantially funded by the State and are autonomous. In the mid- and late 1990s a number of independent private colleges came into existence, offering a range of mainly business-related courses conferring professional qualifications and, in some instances, recognized diplomas and certificates. Numbers in third-level education have expanded dramatically since the mid-1960s, from 21,000 full-time students in 1965 to over 129,000 in 2002–03.

University education is provided by the National University of Ireland, founded in Dublin in 1908, by the University of Dublin (Trinity College), founded in 1592, and by the Dublin City University and the University of Limerick established in 1989. The National University comprises four constituent universities—NUI Dublin, NUI Cork, NUI Galway and NUI Maynooth.

St Patrick's College, Maynooth, Co. Kildare is a national seminary for Catholic priests and a pontifical university with the power to confer degrees up to doctoral level in philosophy, theology and canon law.

Besides the University medical schools, the Royal College of Surgeons in Ireland (a long-established independent medical school) provides medical qualifications which are internationally recognized. Courses to degree level are available at the National College of Art and Design, Dublin.

There are five Colleges of Education for training primary school teachers. For degree awarding purposes, three of these colleges are associated with Trinity College, one with Dublin City University and one with the University of Limerick. There are also two Home Economics Colleges for teacher training, one associated with Trinity College and the other with the National University of Ireland, Galway.

Institutes of Technology in 14 centres (Athlone, Blanchardstown, Carlow, Cork, Dundalk, Dun Laoghaire, Galway, Letterkenny, Limerick, Sligo, Tallaght, Tipperary, Tralee and Waterford) provide vocational and technical education and training for trade and industry from craft to professional level through certificate, diploma and some degree courses. These colleges (with the exception of Blandchardstown, Dun Laoghaire and Tipperary) were established on a statutory basis on 1 Jan. 1993. Prior to this they operated under the aegis of the Vocational Education Committees (VECs) for their areas. Dun Laoghaire College of Art and Design was designated under the RTC Act

1992, from 1 April 1997. The Dublin Institute of Technology (DIT) was also established on a statutory basis on 1 Jan. 1993. Prior to this it operated under the aegis of City of Dublin VEC. The DIT provides certificate, degree and diploma level courses in engineering, architecture, business studies, catering, music, etc. The Hotel and Catering College in Killybegs continues to operate under the aegis of Co. Donegal VEC.

Total full-time enrolments in the Institutes of Technology/Other Technological Colleges in the 2002–03 academic year were approximately 51,507. The Higher Education and Training Awards Council (HETAC) was established by the Government on 11 June 2001, under the Qualifications (Education and Training) Act 1999. HETAC is the qualifications awarding body for third-level educational and training institutes outside the university sector.

The total full-time enrolment at third-level in institutions aided by the Department of Education and Science in 2002–03 was 129,283. Whereas in the late 1970s only one in five school leavers went on to university, now at least six out of ten are doing so.

The total current expenditure from public funds on third-level education during the financial year ended 31 Dec. 2003 was approximately €1,388·3m.

Agricultural. Teagasc, the Agriculture and Food Development Authority, is the State agency responsible for providing advisory, training, research and development services for the agriculture and food industries. Full-time instruction in agriculture is provided for all sections of the farming community. Training for young entrants, adult farmers, rural dwellers and the food industry is provided from eight colleges, local training centres and research centres.

Health

Health boards are responsible for administering health services in Ireland. There are currently ten health boards established: three area health boards located in the eastern region under the guidance of the Eastern Regional Health Authority (ERHA) and seven regional health boards covering the rest of the country. Each health board is responsible for the provision of health and social services in its area. The boards provide many of the services directly and they arrange for the provision of other services by health professionals, private health service providers, voluntary hospitals and voluntary/community organizations.

A health service reform programme is currently being implemented which will result in the most significant structural changes in the Irish health services in recent decades. The existing health boards will be replaced by a single Health Service Executive (HSE) with four regional administrative areas. A Health Information and Quality Authority (HIQA) will also be established.

Everybody ordinarily resident in Ireland has either full or limited eligibility for the public health services.

A person who satisfies the criteria of a means test receives a medical card, which confers Category 1 or full eligibility on them and their dependants. This entitles the holder to the full range of public health and hospital services, free of charge, i.e. family doctor, drugs and medicines, hospital and specialist services as well as dental, aural and optical services. Maternity care and infant welfare services are also provided.

The remainder of the population has Category 2 or limited eligibility. Category 2 patients receive public consultant and public hospital services subject to certain charges. Persons in Category 2 are liable for a hospital in-patient charge of €55 per night up to a maximum of €550 in any 12 consecutive months (with effect from 1 Jan. 2005). There is no charge for out-patient services. However, persons in Category 2 are liable for a charge of €55 if they attend the Accident and Emergency Department of a hospital without a letter from a General Practitioner.

The *Long Term Illness Scheme* entitles persons to free drugs and medicines, which are prescribed in respect of 15 specific illnesses. The needs of individuals with significant or ongoing medical expenses are met by a range of other schemes, which provide assistance towards the cost of prescribed drugs and medicines. The *Drug Payment Scheme* was introduced on 1 July 1999 and replaced the Drug Cost Subsidisation Scheme (DCSS) and the Drug Refund Scheme (DRS). Under this scheme no individual or family will have to pay more than €78 in any calendar month for approved prescribed drugs, medicines and appliances for use by the person or his/her family in that month.

Services for People with Disabilities: The Department of Health and Children provides, through the health boards and the Eastern Regional Health Authority, a wide range of services for people with disabilities. These include day care, home support (including personal assistance services), therapy services, training, employment, sheltered work and residential respite care. The following allowances and grants for eligible people with disabilities come under the aegis of the Department of Health and Children and are administered by the health boards and the Eastern Regional Health Authority:

Blind Welfare Allowance—provides supplementary financial support to unemployed blind persons who are not maintained in an institution and who are in receipt of a Department of Social, Community and Family Affairs payment, such as Disability Allowance, Blind Pension or Old Age Pension.

Rehabilitative Training Bonus—payable to persons who are attending approved rehabilitative training programmes. The payment of €31·80 replaced the Disabled Persons Rehabilitation Allowance (DPRA) from 1 Aug. 2001.

Domiciliary Care Allowance (DCA)—provides home care for severely disabled or mentally handicapped children up to the age of 16. The maximum rate of DCA in Jan. 2005 was €225·20 per month.

Infectious Diseases Maintenance Allowance (IDMA)—payable to a person who is unable to make reasonable and proper provision for their own maintenance or the maintenance of their dependants because they are undergoing treatment for one of the infectious diseases specified in the IDMA regulations. The personal adult rate in Jan. 2005 was €134·80 per week.

Mobility Allowance—provides assistance to severely disabled persons who are unable to walk or use public transport in order to finance the occasional taxi journey. At Jan. 2005 the monthly higher rate, payable only to those who do not benefit from the 'Disabled Drivers and Disabled Passengers Scheme', was €156. The lower rate was €78.

Motorized Transport Grant—provides financial assistance to disabled persons who require a car to obtain or retain employment or who have transport needs because they live in very isolated areas. The maximum grant in Jan. 2005 was €4,690.

Respite Care Grant (RCG)—an annual payment of €835 to help carers obtain respite care (at June 2004).

Spending Allowance for Persons in Long-Stay Institutions— provides basic spending money for people with disabilities and other eligible people in long stay institutions (e.g. residential accommodation) who have no other source of income to help them meet the cost of basic necessities. The maximum rate in Jan. 2005 was €24·40 per week.

Health Contributions—A health contribution of 2% of income is payable by those with Category 2 eligibility. Employers meet the levy in respect of those employees who have a medical card.

In 2003 there were 59 publicly funded acute hospitals in operation with an 85% occupancy rate. The average number of in-patient beds available for use over the year was 12,300. There were 96,499 wholetime equivalent numbers employed in health board/regional authority and voluntary/joint board hospitals and homes for the mentally handicapped at 31 Dec. 2003. Of these 6,792 were medical/dental staff, 12,690 were health and social care professionals and 33,766 were nursing staff. In 2002 Ireland spent 7·3% of its GDP on health.

Welfare
The Department of Social and Family Affairs is responsible for the day-to-day administration and delivery of social welfare schemes and services through a network of local, regional and decentralized offices. The Department's local delivery of services is structured on a regional basis. There are a total of ten regions, with offices in Waterford, Cork, Limerick, Galway, Longford, Sligo, Dundalk and three in the Dublin area.

Social Welfare Schemes. The social welfare supports can be divided into three categories:
—*Social Insurance (Contributory)* payments made on the basis of a Pay Related Social Insurance (PRSI) record. Such payments are funded by employers, employees and the self-employed. Any deficit in the fund is met by Exchequer subvention.
—*Social Assistance (Non Contributory)* payments made on the basis of satisfying a means test. These payments are financed entirely by the Exchequer.
—*Universal payments* such as Child Benefit or Free Travel which do not depend on PRSI or a means test.

The Social Welfare Appeals Office (SWAO) is an independent office responsible for determining appeals against decisions on social welfare entitlements.

There are, in addition, five statutory agencies under the aegis of the Department:
—*the Combat Poverty Agency* which has responsibilities in the areas of advice to the Minister, research, action programmes and public information in relation to poverty.
—*the Pensions Board* which has the function of promoting the security of occupational pensions, their development and the general issue of pensions coverage.
—*Comhairle* which has the function of ensuring that all citizens have easy access to the highest quality of information, advice and advocacy on social services.
—*Family Support Agency* which aims to support families, promote the continuity of stability in family life, prevent marital breakdown and foster a supportive community environment for families at a local level.
—*Office of the Pensions Ombudsman* which investigates and decides complaints and disputes involving occupational pension schemes and Personal Retirement Savings Accounts (PRSAs). The Ombudsman is independent of the Minister and the Department in the performance of his functions.

In 2003 social welfare expenditure accounted for 9·6% of GNP.

RELIGION
According to the census of population taken in 2002 the principal religious professions were as follows:

	Leinster	Munster	Connacht	Ulster (part of)	Total
Roman Catholics	1,828,097	995,728	424,019	214,762	3,462,606
Church of Ireland (including Protestants)	67,877	26,183	9,773	11,778	115,611
Other Christian religion n.e.c.	13,892	5,036	1,672	803	21,403
Presbyterians	8,447	2,056	1,086	8,984	20,582

	Leinster	Munster	Connacht	Ulster (part of)	Total
Muslims (Islamic)	13,233	3,683	1,731	500	19,147
Methodists	5,778	2,574	812	869	10,033
Orthodox	7,570	1,884	657	326	10,437
Other stated religions	24,803	10,003	3,599	1,621	40,026
Not stated or no religion	135,882	53,458	20,947	7,071	217,358

Seán Brady (b. 1939) is the Roman Catholic Cardinal of Armagh and Primate of All Ireland. In May 2005 there were two cardinals.

In May 1990 the General Synod of the Church of Ireland voted to ordain women.

CULTURE

World Heritage Sites

There are two sites under Irish jurisdiction which appear on the UNESCO world heritage list. They are (with year put on list): Archaeological Ensemble of the Bend of the Boyne (1993), the three principal sites of the Brúna Bóinne Complex, a major centre of prehistoric megalithic art; Skellig Michael (1996), a monastic complex on a craggy island from the 7th century.

Broadcasting

Public service broadcasting is provided by Radio Telefís Éireann (RTÉ), a statutory body established under the Broadcasting Authority Acts 1960–2001. RTÉ is financed principally by TV licence and advertising. Its TV channels, RTÉ One and RTÉ Two, both provide 24-hour-a-day broadcasts seven days a week. In 2004 a total of 1,241,381 TV licences were issued. Legislation enacted in 1988 provided for the establishment of the Independent Radio and Television Commission to arrange provision of independent commercial radio stations and an independent TV service. There were (2005) one national independent TV station (TV3), one national independent radio station, one regional station, 26 local commercial radio stations, 19 community radio stations, one special interest radio station and six hospital/institutional radio stations.

There were 2·66m. radio receivers in 2000 and 1·52m. TV receivers (colour by PAL) in 2001. An Irish-language TV channel, TG4, was launched in 1996. At the end of Sept. 2004, 857,000 persons subscribed to pay TV via cable/MMDS and satellite, 55% of which subscribed to digital TV.

Cinema

As at April 2004 there were 321 cinema screens. 66 new films were made in 2001.

Press

In 2004 there were six weekday newspapers and six Sunday newspapers (all in English) with a combined circulation of 1,492,099 for Jan. to June 2004.

Tourism

Total number of overseas tourists in 2002 was 6,065,000 compared to 5,990,000 in 2001 (a 1·3% increase). In 2002 earnings from all visits to Ireland, including cross-border visits, amounted to €3,985m. In 2002, 59% of visits were from Great Britain. In 2002 Irish residents made 4,634,000 visits abroad (a 9·9% increase on 2001).

Festivals

Ireland's national holiday, St Patrick's Day (17 March), is celebrated annually.

Libraries

In 2003 there were 32 public library authorities with 365 service points open to the public (including 29 mobile libraries). They held 13·2m. items of stock. Total registered membership stood at 843,000. 12·3m. visits were made to public libraries in 2003 and 14·3m. items were borrowed. There were 52 academic libraries in 2003 including seven university libraries. There is one national library—the National Library of Ireland.

DIPLOMATIC REPRESENTATIVES

Of Ireland in the United Kingdom (17 Grosvenor Pl., London, SW1X 7HR)
Ambassador: Dáithí O'Ceallaigh.

Of the United Kingdom in Ireland (29 Merrion Rd, Ballsbridge, Dublin, 4)
Ambassador: Stewart Eldon CMG, OBE.

Of Ireland in the USA (2234 Massachusetts Ave., NW, Washington, D.C., 20008)
Ambassador: Noel Fahey.

Of the USA in Ireland (42 Elgin Rd, Ballsbridge, Dublin)
Ambassador: James C. Kenny.

Of Ireland to the United Nations
Ambassador: David Cooney.

FURTHER READING

Central Statistics Office. *National Income and Expenditure* (annual), *Statistical Abstract* (annual), *Census of Population Reports* (quinquennial), *Census of Industrial Production Reports* (annual), *Trade and Shipping Statistics* (annual and monthly), *Trend of Employment and Unemployment, Reports on Vital Statistics* (annual and quarterly), *Statistical Bulletin* (quarterly), *Labour Force Surveys* (annual), *Trade Statistics* (monthly), *Economic Series* (monthly).

Ardagh, J., *Ireland and the Irish: a Portrait of a Changing Society.* London, 1994

Chubb, B., *Government and Politics in Ireland.* 3rd ed. London, 1992

Collins, N. (ed.) *Political Issues in Ireland Today.* Manchester Univ. Press, 1994

Cronin, Mike, *A History of Ireland.* Palgrave, Basingstoke, 2001

Delanty, G. and O'Mahony, P., *Rethinking Irish History: Nationalism, Identity and Ideology.* London, 1997

Foster, R. F., *The Oxford Illustrated History of Ireland.* OUP, 1991

Garvin, T., *1922 The Birth of Irish Democracy.* Dublin, 1997

Harkness, D., *Ireland in the Twentieth Century: a Divided Island.* London, 1995

Hussey, G., *Ireland Today: Anatomy of a Changing State.* Dublin, 1993

Institute of Public Administration, *Ireland: a Directory.* Dublin, annual

Kostick, C., *Revolution in Ireland – Popular Militancy 1917–1923.* London, 1997

Munck, R., *The Irish Economy: Results and Prospects.* London, 1993

O'Beirne Ranelagh, J., *A Short History of Ireland.* 2nd ed. CUP, 1999

O'Hagan, J. W. (ed.) *The Economy of Ireland: Policy and Performance of a Small European Country.* London, 1995

Vaughan, W. E. (ed.) *A New History of Ireland,* 6 vols. Oxford, 1996

Wiles, J. L. and Finnegan, R. B., *Aspirations and Realities: a Documentary History of Economic Development Policy in Ireland since 1922.* London, 1992.

National Statistical Office: Central Statistics Office, Skehard Road, Cork.
Director-General: Donal Garvey, M.Sc., M.Sc. (Mgt).
Website: http://www.cso.ie/

ISREAL

© Research Machines plc 2006

Medinat Israel
(State of Israel)

Capital: Jerusalem
Population projection, 2010: 7·31m.
GDP per capita, 2003: (PPP$) 20,033
HDI/world rank: 0·915/23

KEY HISTORICAL EVENTS

A settled agricultural community by 6000 BC, the oasis of Jericho is possibly the world's oldest continuously inhabited settlement. Canaan—probably derived from 'Land of Purple', from the purple sea snail dye—described the Eastern Mediterranean coast and hinterland from the 3rd millennium BC. As part of the Fertile Crescent, it became an important caravan route between Egypt and Mesopotamia. 'Canaanite' has come to be associated with the Semitic group of languages and peoples of the pre-Classical Levant.

In the reign of Pharaoh Pepi I (*c.* 2313–2279 BC), Canaan was invaded five times by Egyptian forces. Egyptian authority collapsed in the 17th century, marking the end of the Middle

Kingdom. Egyptian control was re-established with the reunification of Egypt in the 16th century. Thutmose III (1479–1425 BC), campaigning against the Mitanni Kingdom in Syria, defeated a Canaanite coalition at the Battle of Megiddo, subjugating Canaan and deporting thousands to Egypt. Egyptian power was challenged by the Hittites of Anatolia until Ramesses II concluded a peace treaty (the first recorded in the world) with the Hittite King Hattusilis III in 1258 BC, setting the border in northern Canaan.

The Israelite (or Hebrew) group occupied the hills of southern Canaan by the late 13th century. Around 1200 BC the Eastern Mediterranean littoral was attacked by the 'Sea Peoples' (probably including the Philistines), who destroyed coastal cities and settled on the coastal plain. The Israelite kingdom was formed from tribes supposedly returned from captivity in Egypt. In the late 11th century, Saul became king but it was his successor, David, who greatly expanded the Israelite state over most of southern Canaan. With Hittite and Egyptian power at low ebb, David conquered the trans-Jordanian states of Ammon, Edom and Moab, subjected Aram (lower Syria) to vassalage and made Jerusalem his capital. After the reign of Solomon (mid-10th century), who built the Temple of Jerusalem, the kingdom split into two: Judah in the south and the more populous Israel, centred on Samaria, in the north.

Having refused to pay tribute, Israel was conquered by Assyria's Sargon II in 722 BC and many of its people were deported; subsequent inhabitants of the Assyrian province of 'Samerina' became known as Samaritans, a mixed race of Israelites and immigrants from Mesopotamia and Persia. Sargon also besieged Jerusalem but was distracted by a Babylonian uprising. The resurgent Babylonians conquered Judah in 586 BC, having utterly destroyed Philistia in 605 to clear access to Egypt. Nebuchadnezzar II had taken Jerusalem the previous year, deporting much of the Judaean (Jewish) nobility to Babylon. Having conquered Babylon in 539 BC, Cyrus II of Persia allowed the return of the Jews to Jerusalem, as Persian vassals, and the rebuilding of the Temple. Persia's defeat by Alexander the Great of Macedon brought the region, by then known as Palestine (derived from Philistia), under Hellenistic control. The Hellenistic period saw an influx of Arab groups, including the Nabataeans, who replaced the Edomites south of the Dead Sea.

Roman Rule

A revolt against the religious intolerance of the Seleucid King Antiochus IV began in 167 BC, led by Judas Maccabaeus, who established the Hasmonean Dynasty in Judaea. Relations with the Samaritans, who also followed the Torah (the first five books of the Hebrew bible), deteriorated when the Hasmonean King John Hyrcanus destroyed the Samaritan Temple at Mount Gerizim in 128 BC. The entire region was conquered for Rome by Pompey in 67 BC; Judaea, including Samaria, was administered as a client kingdom. After the Parthian invasion of Judaea in 40 BC, an Idumaean, Herod, was installed by Rome as king of Judaea. On Herod's death in 4 BC, the kingdom was split amongst three of his sons, who ruled as tetrarchs. Herod's grandson, Herod Agrippa, was granted a reunited Judaea by Emperor Claudius in 41 AD, as a reward for supporting Claudius' claim to the imperial throne. However, Herod Agrippa was assassinated in 44 AD and Judaea placed under a Roman procurator. Jewish resentment against loss of autonomy grew until the Great Jewish Revolt (66–73 AD), which was brutally suppressed. Jerusalem was destroyed and hundreds of thousands were massacred or sold into slavery. Jewish rebellions across the

East in 115 (the Kitos War) were quickly suppressed. Emperor Hadrian's attempts to enforce cultural uniformity across the Empire included rebuilding Jerusalem as Aelia Capitolina and forbidding Jewish custom. Simon Bar Kokhba, supported by the Sanhedrin (Jewish sages), led a major revolt in 132 AD and established a Jewish government in Jerusalem. However, Roman armies prevailed in 135, with the death of around half a million Jews. Hadrian reacted to the rebellion by suppressing Judaism, banning Jews from Aelia Capitolina, deporting large numbers as slaves and renaming the province (*Syria*) *Palaestina*; the province was split in three around 390.

Christianity

Under the Christian Byzantine Empire, Palestine became a centre of Christianity (Jerusalem was recognized as a patriarchate in 451), bringing pilgrims and prosperity. It also received lavish imperial patronage, such as Constantine's Church of the Holy Sepulchre (*c.* 326). The Samaritans made a bid for independence in 529 but were crushed by Justinian I and the Ghassanid Arabs. Persecuted by Christians, Jews and later by Muslims, Samaritan numbers dwindled over the following centuries. Byzantine administration of Palestine ended temporarily during the Persian occupation of 614–28; Jerusalem was sacked, its churches burned and the city turned over to the Jews. A spectacular campaign in 628, led by Emperor Heraclius, forced the Persians to cede Palestine and Syria. However, Byzantine rule ended permanently after the Arabs conquered the region; Jerusalem was taken in 638.

The Arabs retained the existing system of administration in the provinces of Jund Filastine (the south) and Jund Urdunn (the north). Taxes and restrictions on religious practice and office-holding imposed on non-Muslims caused large-scale conversions. The Ummayad caliphs moved the capital to Damascus and built the Dome of the Rock on the site of the Jewish Temple in Jerusalem in the 690s. The Christian and Jewish communities of Palestine were partly administered by their own religious leaders. Under the Ummayads' successors, the Abbasids, the capital moved to Baghdad in 762, drawing Asian trade away from Palestine. Fragmentation of the Caliphate in the 9th century saw Egyptian independence under the Tulunids, who seized Palestine and Syria in 878. Although Palestine was retaken in 906 for the Caliphate, in 935 it again fell to Egypt, this time under the Ikhshid Dynasty and, in 970, to its successors, the Fatimids.

Crusades

1070 saw the arrival of the Seljuk Turks, who rapidly overran the Byzantine East. Seljuk restrictions on Christian pilgrimage led to the European Crusader invasions of Palestine and Syria in the 12th century. Having been wrested from the Seljuks by the Fatimids in 1098, Jerusalem was taken the following year by a Crusader army, which massacred the population. Baldwin, count of Edessa, became king of Jerusalem in 1100. Responding to Crusader threats to Mecca (Makkah), Saladin (Salah ad-Din), the Kurdish sultan of Egypt, recaptured Jerusalem in 1187, bringing Palestine under the Ayyubid Dynasty. A treaty in 1192 with Richard I of England allowed Christian pilgrimage to Jerusalem and secured the rump Crusader states along the coast. A treaty of 1229 gave much of Palestine (the Kingdom of Jerusalem) to the Holy Roman Emperor, Frederick II, though Jerusalem was destroyed by Central Asian Khwarezmians in 1244, on behalf of the Ayyubids. The fall of Acre (Akko) to the Mamluks, rulers of Egypt, in 1291 ended Crusader rule in the Holy Land.

Under Mamluk suzerainty, Palestine was administered by Muslim emirates. Economic decline was exacerbated by the arrival of the Black Death in 1351. Although the Mamluk sultanate successfully held off Mongol invasions, Palestine fell to the Ottomans in 1516, bringing it (as part of the Damascus-Syria province) and most of the Islamic world under the rule of Turkish İstanbul. Suleyman the Magnificent rebuilt Jerusalem's walls in 1537.

Zionism

Palestine was briefly invaded in 1799 by Napoleon Bonaparte of France, who had occupied Egypt. Muhammad Ali, the renegade Ottoman viceroy of Egypt, invaded Palestine and Syria in 1831, defeating the Ottoman army. However, British intervention at Beirut, on behalf of the sultan, forced the viceroy's withdrawal to Egypt. Jews from central and eastern Europe arrived in Palestine from the 1880s as part of a nascent Zionist movement. In 1897 the first Zionist Congress met in Basle, Switzerland. Attempts were made in vain to gain the approval of Sultan Abdul Hamid II for Jewish settlement. However, by 1914, about 85,000 Jews were living in Palestine, many on agricultural collectives (*kibbutz*), in part funded by Western Europe's Jewry. Tel Aviv (originally called Ahuzat Bayit) was founded by Jews in 1909 as a dormitory settlement for workers in Jaffa.

Britain, France and Russia declared war on the Ottoman Empire in Nov. 1914, in retaliation for its co-operation with Germany. Having repelled Ottoman attacks on the Suez Canal, British forces invaded Ottoman Palestine, seizing Rafah in Jan. 1917. Two abortive attacks on Gaza were followed by British-led success at Beersheba in Oct. 1917, leading to the fall of Gaza in Nov. and Jerusalem in Dec. The British won a major victory at Megiddo in Sept. 1918, effectively ending Ottoman rule in Palestine. The British were granted Palestine and Transjordan as mandates under the League of Nations, established in 1919 at the Versailles Peace Conference.

Britain supported a 'national home' for the Jews in Palestine, as laid out in the Balfour Declaration of 1917. Jewish immigration, though limited by the British authorities, increased in the 1920s. Land ownership disputes aggravated Jewish-Arab relations, leading to paramilitary communal attacks. While Transjordan was granted independence in 1928, proposals for an Arab-Jewish partition in Palestine were rejected. In 1936 an Arab strike degenerated into insurrection—the 'Great Uprising' or 'Great Revolt'—under the leadership of Amin al-Husayni, the Grand Mufti of Jerusalem. The revolt was suppressed by the British by 1939, aided informally by the Jewish paramilitary *Haganah*. Al-Husayni fled to Germany, where he declared *jihad* on the Allies during the Second World War. The Italian air force bombed Haifa and Tel Aviv in 1940. Some Jewish groups, such as the Lehi, fought the British during the war on account of the British ban on Jewish immigration to Palestine.

Arab Israeli Wars

In 1947 the United Nations intervened, recommending partition of Palestine and an international administration for Jerusalem. The plan was accepted by the Jewish Agency (not representative of all Jewish groups) but rejected by the Palestinian Arab leadership; inter-communal war followed. On 14 May 1948 the British Government terminated its mandate and the Jewish leaders proclaimed the State of Israel. No independent Arab state was established in Palestine. Instead the neighbouring Arab states invaded Israel on 15 May 1948. The Jewish state defended itself successfully, and the ceasefire in Jan. 1949 left Israel with one-third more land than had been originally assigned by the UN.

In 1967, following some years of uneasy peace, local clashes on the Israeli–Syrian border were followed by Egyptian mass concentration of forces on the borders of Israel. Israel struck out at Egypt on land and in the air on 5–9 June 1967. Jordan joined in the conflict which spread to the Syrian borders. By 11 June the Israelis had occupied the Gaza Strip and the Sinai peninsula as far as the Suez Canal in Egypt, West Jordan as far as the Jordan valley and the heights east of the Sea of Galilee, including the Syrian city of Quneitra, which was destroyed during the conflict.

A further war broke out on 6 Oct. 1973 when Egyptian and Syrian offensives were launched. Following UN Security Council resolutions a ceasefire came into force on 24 Oct. In Sept. 1978 Egypt and Israel agreed on frameworks for peace in the Middle East. A treaty was signed in Washington on 26 March 1979 whereby Israel withdrew from the Sinai Desert in two phases; part was achieved on 26 Jan. 1980 and the final withdrawal by 26 April 1982.

In June 1982 Israeli forces invaded the Lebanon. On 16 Feb. 1985 the Israeli forces started a withdrawal, leaving behind an Israeli trained and equipped Christian Lebanese force to act as a buffer against Muslim Shia or Palestinian guerrilla attacks.

Peace Process

In 1993, following declarations by Prime Minister Yitzhak Rabin recognizing the Palestine Liberation Organization (PLO) as representative of the Palestinian people, and by Yasser Arafat, leader of the PLO, renouncing terrorism and recognizing the State of Israel, an agreement was signed in Washington providing for limited Palestinian self-rule in the Gaza Strip and Jericho. Negotiations on the permanent status of the West Bank and Gaza began in 1996. On 4 Nov. 1995 Yitzhak Rabin was assassinated by a Jewish religious extremist. In the subsequent election, a right-wing coalition led by Binyamin Netanyahu took office. Peace talks with the Palestinians then stalled. In Oct. 1998 Israel accepted partial withdrawal from the West Bank on condition that the Palestinians cracked down on terrorism. The following month, 2% of the West Bank was handed over to Palestinian control. Further moves were put on hold after the collapse of the Netanyahu coalition and the announcement of early elections.

In Sept. 1999 Ehud Barak provided the first evidence that the Middle East peace process was back on track by releasing nearly 200 Palestinian prisoners and by handing over 430 sq. km of land on the West Bank. In May 2000 Israel completed its withdrawal from south Lebanon, 22 years after the first invasion. By Oct. 2000 violence had broken out again between Israelis and Palestinians, fuelled by the conflict over control of Jerusalem, with terrorist acts a daily occurrence, leading to heavy casualties on both sides. With peace talks stalled once again, Barak called for a nationwide vote of confidence by putting himself up for re-election as prime minister. Defeated by the right-wing Ariel Sharon in Feb. 2001, he retired from politics. As violence escalated, in Dec. 2001 Israel ended all contact with Yasser Arafat, besieging his compound at Ramallah and putting him under virtual house arrest. Israeli incursions into Palestinian-controlled areas of the West Bank and the Gaza Strip, and suicide attacks by Palestinians, continued unabated in early 2002 with heavy loss of life. In June 2002 Israel began constructing a barrier to cut off the West Bank, with the aim of shielding the country from suicide bombers. Arafat died on 11 Nov. 2004 and was succeeded by Mahmoud Abbas in Jan. 2005. In Feb. 2005 Israeli prime minister Ariel Sharon and Mahmoud Abbas agreed to a 'cessation of hostilities' between the two peoples, a move which encouraged hopes of a resumption of the peace process. In Aug. 2005 Israeli troops and police evicted the 8,500 Jewish settlers from the Gaza Strip in accordance with an agreement between Israel and the Palestinians. This was the first time Israel had withdrawn from Palestinian land captured in the 1967 war.

TERRITORY AND POPULATION

The area of Israel, including the Golan Heights (1,154 sq. km) and East Jerusalem, is 22,072 sq. km (8,522 sq. miles), of which 21,643 sq. km (8,357 sq. miles) are land. The population in 2002 was estimated to be 6·6m., including East Jerusalem, the Golan Heights and Israeli settlers in the occupied territories. Population density, 299 per sq. km.

The UN gives a projected population for 2010 of 7·31m.

In 2003, 91·6% of the population lived in urban areas.

Population by place of origin as of 1995: Europe and America, 1·8m.; former USSR, 0·66m.; Morocco, 0·5m.; Iraq, 0·25m.; Poland, 0·25m.; Romania, 0·25m.; Yemen, 0·15m.; Iran, 0·13m.; Algeria and Tunisia, 0·12m.

The Jewish Agency, which, in accordance with Article IV of the Palestine Mandate, played a leading role in establishing the State of Israel, continues to organize immigration.

Israel is administratively divided into six districts:

District	Area (sq. km)	Population[1]	Chief town
Northern	4,473	1,127,200	Nazareth
Haifa	866	838,900	Haifa
Central	1,294	1,541,100	Ramla
Tel Aviv	172	1,161,100	Tel Aviv
Jerusalem[2]	653	794,100	Jerusalem
Southern	14,185	948,500	Beersheba

[1]2002. [2]Includes East Jerusalem.

On 23 Jan. 1950 the Knesset proclaimed Jerusalem the capital of the State and on 14 Dec. 1981 extended Israeli law into the Golan Heights. Population of the main towns (2002): Jerusalem, 680,400; Tel Aviv/Jaffa, 360,400; Haifa, 270,800; Rishon le-Ziyyon, 211,600; Ashdod, 187,500; Beersheba, 181,500; Petach Tikva, 172,600; Holon, 165,800; Netanya, 164,800; Bene Berak, 138,900; Bat Yam, 133,900; Ramat Gan, 126,600.

The official languages are Hebrew and Arabic.

SOCIAL STATISTICS

2001 births, 136,638; deaths, 37,173; marriages, 38,924; divorces, 11,164. 2001 crude birth rate per 1,000 population of Jewish population, 18·3; Non-Jewish: Muslims, 36·8; Christians, 20·0; Druzes, 26·2. Crude death rate per 1,000 (2001), Jewish, 6·6; Muslims, 2·8; Christians, 4·7; Druzes, 3·0. Infant mortality rate per 1,000 live births (2001), Jewish, 4·1; Muslims, 8·2; Christians, 4·9 (1996–99); Druzes, 8·7 (1996–99). Life expectancy, 2003, 77·6 years for males and 81·7 for females. Average annual population growth rate, 1992–2002, 2·7%. Fertility rate, 2001, 2·8 births per woman.

Immigration. The following table shows the numbers of immigrants entering Palestine/Israel.

1997	66,221	1999	76,766	2001	43,580
1998	56,730	2000	60,192	2002	33,567

There were 199,516 immigrants in 1990 and 176,100 in 1991 following the fall of communism in eastern Europe and the break-up of the former Soviet Union.

CLIMATE

From April to Oct., the summers are long and hot, and almost rainless. From Nov. to March, the weather is generally mild, though colder in hilly areas, and this is the wet season. Jerusalem, Jan. 12·8°C, July 28·9°C. Annual rainfall, 657 mm. Tel Aviv, Jan. 17·2°C, July 30·2°C. Annual rainfall, 803 mm.

CONSTITUTION AND GOVERNMENT

Israel is an independent sovereign republic, established by proclamation on 14 May 1948.

In 1950 the Knesset (*Parliament*), which in 1949 had passed the Transition Law dealing in general terms with the powers of the Knesset, President and Cabinet, resolved to enact from time to time fundamental laws, which eventually, taken together, would form the Constitution. The eleven fundamental laws that have been passed are: the Knesset (1958), Israel Lands (1960), the President (1964), the State Economy (1975), the Army (1976), Jerusalem, capital of Israel (1980), the Judicature (1984), the State Comptroller (1988), Human Dignity and Liberty (1992), Freedom of Occupation (1994) and the Government (2001).

The *President* (head of state) is elected by the Knesset by secret ballot by a simple majority; his term of office is five years. He may be re-elected once.

The Knesset, a one-chamber Parliament, consists of 120 members. It is elected for a four-year term by secret ballot and universal direct suffrage. Under the system of election introduced in 1996, electors vote once for a party and once for a candidate for Prime Minister. To be elected Prime Minister, a candidate must gain more than half the votes cast, and be elected to the Knesset. If there are more than two candidates and none gain half the vote, a second round is held 15 days later. The Prime Minister forms a cabinet (no fewer than eight members and no more than 18) with the approval of the Knesset.

National Anthem

'Hatikvah' ('The Hope'); words by N. H. Imber; folk-tune.

GOVERNMENT CHRONOLOGY

Prime Ministers since 1948. (Avoda = Labour Party; Herut = Freedom Movement; Kadima = 'Forward'; Likud = 'Consolidation'; Mapai = Israeli Workers' Party)

1948–53	Mapai	David Ben-Gurion
1953–55	Mapai	Moshe Sharett
1955–63	Mapai	David Ben-Gurion
1963–69	Mapai	Levi Eshkol
1969–74	Avoda	Golda Meir
1974–77	Avoda	Yitzhak Rabin
1977–83	Herut/Likud	Menahem Begin
1983–84	Herut/Likud	Yitzhak Shamir
1984–86	Avoda	Shimon Peres
1986–92	Likud	Yitzhak Shamir
1992–95	Avoda	Yitzhak Rabin
1995–96	Avoda	Shimon Peres
1996–99	Likud	Binyamin Netanyahu
1999–2001	Avoda	Ehud Barak
2001–06	Likud, Kadima	Ariel Sharon
2006–	Kadima	Ehud Olmert

RECENT ELECTIONS

Ariel Sharon of Likud won the election for *Prime Minister* on 6 Feb. 2001 with 62·4% of the vote, against 37·6% for the incumbent Prime Minister Ehud Barak of Avoda (Labor). Sharon quit Likud in Nov. 2005 to found the Kadima ('Forward') party. In the parliamentary (Knesset) elections on 28 March 2006, Kadima won 29 of 120 seats with 21·8% of votes cast, Labour 19 (15·1%), Shas 12 (9·6%), Likud 12 (8·9%), Yisrael Beytenu 11 (9·0%), the National Union/National Religious Party 9 (6·9%), Gil 7 (5·9%), United Torah Judaism 6 (4·8%), Meretz-Yachad 5 (3·6%), the United Arab List 4 (3·1%), Hadash 3 (2·8%) and Balad 3 (2·4%). Turnout was 63·2%.

In a parliamentary vote for the presidency on 31 July 2000, Moshe Katzav defeated Shimon Peres in the second round. He claimed 63 votes against 57 for Peres.

CURRENT ADMINISTRATION

President: Moshe Katzav; b. 1945 (Likud; sworn in 1 Aug. 2000).

Following the election of 6 Feb. 2001 Ariel Sharon formed an eight-party coalition. In Oct. 2002 Labour Party ministers resigned from the cabinet following a dispute over the funding of Jewish settlements in the West Bank. Unable to maintain the coalition without Labour support, Ariel Sharon was forced to call early elections which were held on 28 Jan. 2003. A national unity government was formed after two parties left the previous coalition in late 2004. In Nov. 2005 the Labour ministers again resigned. Sharon also quit Likud to found the Kadima ('Forward') party. Owing to Sharon's ill health Ehud Olmert became acting prime minister in March 2006. He was

confirmed as prime minister in April 2006, following which the cabinet was composed as follows:

Prime Minister and Minister of Welfare: Ehud Olmert; b. 1945 (Kadima; since 4 Jan. 2006).

Vice-Prime Minister and Minister for the Development of the Negev and the Galilee: Shimon Peres.

Acting Prime Minister and Minister of Foreign Affairs: Tzipi Livni. *Deputy Prime Minister and Minister of Defence:* Amir Peretz. *Deputy Prime Minister and Minister of Industry, Trade and Labour:* Eli Yishai. *Deputy Prime Minister and Minister of Transportation and Road Safety:* Shaul Mofaz.

Minister of Communications: Ariel Atias. *Immigrant Absorption:* Zeev Boim. *National Infrastructures:* Binyamin Ben-Eliezer. *Health:* Yaakov Ben-Yizri. *Interior:* Roni Bar-On. *Internal Security:* Avi Dichter. *Finance:* Avraham Hirschson. *Tourism:* Yitzhak Herzog. *Environment:* Gideon Ezra. *Science and Technology:* Ofir Pines-Paz. *Justice:* Haim Ramon. *Construction and Housing:* Meir Sheerit. *Agriculture and Rural Development:* Shalom Simhon. *Education, Culture and Sport:* Yuli Tamir. *Minister in the Prime Minister's Office, Responsible for Pensioners' Affairs:* Rafi Eitan. *Ministers without Portfolio:* Yaakov Edri; Eitan Cabel; Yitzhak Cohen; Meshulam Nahari.

Office of the Prime Minister: http://www.pmo.gov.il

CURRENT LEADERS

Ehud Olmert

Position
Prime Minister

Introduction
Ehud Olmert was thrust into the political limelight in Jan. 2006 when the prime minister, Ariel Sharon, suffered a severe stroke. Olmert, a lawyer and close aide to Sharon, was appointed acting prime minister and led the newly established Kadima party to a narrow victory in the Knesset elections of March 2006. He officially replaced Sharon as prime minister in mid-April 2006.

Early Life
Ehud Olmert was born on 30 Sept. 1945 near Binyamina in the British Mandate of Palestine. His parents were Zionists who joined the right-wing Herut Party after Israel's independence in 1948. A member of the Betar Youth Organisation, Ehud Olmert studied philosophy, psychology and law at the Hebrew University of Jerusalem and later served in the Israeli Defense Forces (IDF) as a combat infantry unit officer and a military correspondent.

In 1973 Olmert was elected to the Knesset as a member of Gahal, the parliamentary bloc of Herut and the Liberals led by Menachem Begin, which later became the Likud bloc in opposition to the governing Labour Alignment. Olmert served on the law and justice committee, campaigning against corruption in public life. From 1974 he built a successful legal practice, despite facing allegations of corruption himself in the 1980s.

Begin led Likud to victory in the 1977 elections but Olmert opposed his stance on withdrawal from land captured from Egypt in the Six Day War and voted against the 1978 Camp David Peace Accords. However, he was to become a staunch supporter of the pullout of Israeli settlers from Gaza in 2005. From 1981–88 Olmert was a member of the foreign affairs and security committee. Under Prime Minister Yitzhak Shamir, he served as minister without portfolio (responsible for minority affairs) from 1988–90 and then as minister of health until 1992.

In Nov. 1993 Olmert became mayor of Jerusalem, on a platform of unifying the city. He initiated projects to improve the road and rail infrastructure as well as reforming the education system. However, on resigning in Jan. 2003 to run for the Knesset his critics pointed to the gulf between the level of services in Palestinian East Jerusalem and those in wealthier Jewish areas.

In Jan. 2003 Ariel Sharon, the Likud leader, won a landslide re-election to the premiership, doubling his party's parliamentary representation. Olmert became minister of trade and industry and deputy prime minister. By Dec. 2003 Olmert had abandoned the dream of a Greater Israel including Gaza and the West Bank. Working with Sharon, he formulated plans for Israeli settlers to leave Gaza. After Binyamin Netanyahu resigned in Aug. 2005 in protest at 'disengagement', Olmert became finance minister. In Nov. 2005 Olmert followed Sharon from Likud to form the Kadima Party ahead of elections in March 2006. On 4 Jan. 2006 Sharon suffered a severe hemorrhagic stroke and Olmert assumed the powers of acting prime minister, holding a cabinet meeting on 5 Jan. to signal the transfer of power.

Career in Office

Olmert was elected acting chairman of Kadima on 16 Jan. 2006. In a speech on 24 Jan. 2006 he backed the creation of a Palestinian State, arguing that Israel would have to relinquish control of parts of the West Bank to maintain its Jewish majority. In elections on 28 March Kadima won most votes, taking 29 of 120 seats, but lacked an outright majority with turnout at a record low. With Sharon declared 'permanently incapacitated', Olmert took over as prime minister outright on 14 April 2006 and formed a four-party coalition cabinet which took office on 4 May 2006.

Olmert has declared that he will attempt to settle the final borders of Israel in an agreement with the Palestinians. However, analysts see little hope of progress towards a negotiated two-state solution, given that the Palestinians' Hamas government refuses to recognize Israel's right to exist. Selling Kadima's plans to potential coalition partners, none of whom stood for unilateral withdrawals before the election, also poses a serious challenge to Olmert's tenure.

DEFENCE

Conscription (for Jews and Druze only) is three years (usually four years for officers; two years for women). The Israel Defense Forces is a unified force, in which army, navy and air force are subordinate to a single chief-of-staff. The Minister of Defence is *de facto* C.-in-C.

Defence expenditure in 2003 totalled US$10,325m., representing 9·5% of GDP. Expenditure per capita in 2003 was US$1,544, a figure exceeded only by Qatar and Kuwait.

Nuclear Weapons

Israel has an undeclared nuclear weapons capability. Although known to have a nuclear bomb, it pledges not to introduce nuclear testing to the Middle East. According to the Stockholm International Peace Research Institute, the nuclear arsenal was estimated to have approximately 200 warheads in Jan. 2005. Israel has never admitted possessing biological or chemical weapons, but according to *Deadly Arsenals*, published by the Carnegie Endowment for International Peace, it does have a chemical and biological weapons programme.

Army

Strength (2004) 125,000 (conscripts 85,000). There are also 380,000 reservists available on mobilization. In addition there is a paramilitary border police of about 8,000.

Navy

The Navy, tasked primarily for coastal protection and based at Haifa, Ashdod and Eilat, includes three small diesel submarines and three corvettes.

Naval personnel in 2004 totalled about 8,000 (including a Naval Commando of 300) of whom 2,500 are conscripts. There are also 11,500 naval reservists available on mobilization.

Air Force

The Air Force (including air defence) has a personnel strength (2004) of 35,000, with 399 combat aircraft, all jets, of Israeli and US manufacture including F-4E *Phantoms*, F-15s and F-16s, and 95 armed helicopters. There are 24,500 Air Force reservists.

INTERNATIONAL RELATIONS

Israel is a member of the UN, WTO, Inter-American Development Bank and IOM. It is the largest recipient of foreign aid in absolute terms, in 2002 receiving US$2·8bn., representing around US$435 per person.

ECONOMY

Services account for about 82% of GDP, industry 16% and agriculture 2%.

Overview

Israel has a diversified economy relative to its neighbours. Over the past two decades electronics manufacturing has replaced traditional industries such as footwear and clothing. In the 1990s traditional industries benefited from protectionist policies but have since undergone structural changes, including labour outsourcing to neighbouring countries with lower wages. As a result, Israeli manufacturers have focused on product design and on trade agreements with the USA and the EU.

In 2000 the government opened the telecommunications sector to foreign competition. Israel's high standard of education and investment in military research and development have boosted high-tech industries over the years. The 1990s saw strong growth and in 2000 the economy grew by 7·7%. However, in 2001 and 2002 Israel experienced its worst recession in 50 years, a result of high security costs arising from the second *intifada*, a sharp decline in tourism and difficulties in the high-tech sector. The collapse of the US financial markets, especially the NASDAQ, hurt Israel's technology sectors, which were reliant on US market financing. The economy subsequently emerged from recession, expanding at a rate of 1·7% in 2003 and 4·4% in 2004. Aided by competitive labour costs and a significant depreciation of the *shekel*, many areas of the high-tech sector, notably electronic component production and exports, have rebounded strongly.

Currency

The unit of currency is the *shekel* (ILS) of 100 *agorot*. Foreign exchange reserves were US$24,782m. in June 2002. Gold reserves have been negligible since 1998. There was inflation in 2003 of 0·7%, but deflation in 2004 of 0·4%. Total money supply in May 2002 was 37,702m. shekels.

Budget

Budget revenue and expenditure (in 1m. shekels), year ending 31 Dec.:

	1996	1997	1998	1999	2000	2001
Revenue	123,796	145,110	159,911	173,187	194,736	195,376
Expenditure	149,571	165,250	183,046	197,954	208,603	224,287

Performance

Real GDP growth rates (based on IMF statistics):

1997	1998	1999	2000	2001	2002	2003	2004
3·6%	3·7%	2·3%	7·7%	−0·3%	−1·2%	1·7%	4·4%

Total GDP was US$117·5bn. in 2004.

Banking and Finance

The Bank of Israel was established by law in 1954 as Israel's central bank. Its Governor is appointed by the President on the recommendation of the Cabinet for a five-year term. He acts as economic adviser to the government and has ministerial status. The *Governor* is Prof. Stanley Fischer. Central bank reserves in Dec. 2002 were US$24·1bn. The government raised some US$4bn. from bank privatizations during the 1990s.

In 2001 there were 23 commercial banks headed by Bank Leumi Le Israel, Bank Hapoalim and Israel Discount Bank, two merchant banks, three foreign banks, eight mortgage banks and nine lending institutions specifically set up to aid industry and agriculture.

There is a stock exchange in Tel Aviv.

Weights and Measures

The metric system is in general use. The (metrical) *dunam* = 1,000 sq. metres.

ENERGY AND NATURAL RESOURCES

Environment

Carbon dioxide emissions from the consumption and flaring of fossil fuels in 2002 were the equivalent of 9·5 tonnes per capita.

Electricity

Installed capacity in 2002 was 10·0m. kW. Electric power production amounted to 45·39bn. kWh in 2002; consumption per capita was 6,698 kWh in 2002.

Oil and Gas

The only significant hydrocarbon is oil shale. Crude petroleum reserves in 2002 were 4m. bbls.

Water

In the northern Negev farming has been aided by the Yarkon–Negev water pipeline. This has become part of the overall project of the 'National Water Carrier', which is to take water from the Sea of Galilee (Lake Kinnereth) to the south. The plan includes a number of regional projects such as the Lake Kinnereth–Negev pipeline which came into operation in 1964; it has an annual capacity of 320m. cu. metres. Total water production in 2001 amounted to 1,885m. cu. metres, of which 1,800m. cu. metres was consumed.

Minerals

The most valuable natural resources are the potash, bromine and other salt deposits of the Dead Sea. Production figures (2000) in 1,000 tonnes: phosphate rock, 4,110; potash, 1,748; salt, 526; lignite (2002), 458.

Agriculture

In the coastal plain mixed farming, poultry raising, citriculture and vineyards are the main agricultural activities. The Emek (the Valley of Jezreel) is the main agricultural centre of Israel. Mixed farming is to be found throughout the valleys; the sub-tropical Beisan and Jordan plainlands are also centres of banana plantations and fish breeding. In Galilee mixed farming, olive and tobacco plantations prevail. The Hills of Ephraim are a vineyard centre; many parts of the hill country are under afforestation.

There were 338,000 ha. of arable land in 2001 and 86,000 ha. of permanent crops.

Production, 2000 (in 1,000 tonnes): tomatoes, 550; melons and watermelons, 447; grapefruit and pomelos, 370; potatoes, 349; oranges, 300; tangerines and mandarins, 140; bananas, 130; cucumbers and gherkins, 108; chillies and green peppers, 97; onions, 90.

Livestock (2000): 388,000 cattle; 350,000 sheep; 163,000 pigs; 70,000 goats; 28m. poultry.

Types of rural settlement: (1) The *Kibbutz* and *Kvutza* (communal collective settlement), where all property and earnings are collectively owned and work is collectively organized. (115,700 people lived in 268 *Kibbutzim* in 1999.) (2) The *Moshav* (workers' co-operative smallholders' settlement) which is founded on the principles of mutual aid and equality of opportunity between the members, all farms being equal in size (184,500 in 411). (3) The *Moshav Shitufi* (co-operative settlement), which is based on collective ownership and economy as in the *Kibbutz*, but with each family having its own house and being responsible for its own domestic services (18,200 in 43). (4) Other rural settlements in which land and property are privately owned and

every resident is responsible for his own well-being. In 1999 there were a total of 259 non-cooperative villages with a population of 314,900.

Forestry

In 2000 forests covered 132,000 ha. or 6·4% of the total land area. Timber production was 27,000 cu. metres in 2003.

Fisheries

Catches in 2003 totalled 4,055 tonnes, of which 2,991 tonnes were from marine waters.

INDUSTRY

The leading companies by market capitalization in Israel, excluding banking and finance, in Jan. 2002 were: Teva Pharmaceutical Industries Ltd (40bn. shekels); Check Point Software Technologies Ltd (20bn. shekels); and BEZEQ—The Israel Telecommunications Corporation Ltd (12bn. shekels).

Products include chemicals, metal products, textiles, tyres, diamonds, paper, plastics, leather goods, glass and ceramics, building materials, precision instruments, tobacco, foodstuffs, electrical and electronic equipment.

Labour

The economically active workforce was 2,270,500 in 2001 (1,236,200 males). The principal areas of activity were: manufacturing, mining and quarrying, 394,200; wholesale and retail trade/repair of motor vehicles, motorcycles and personal and household goods, 299,800; education, 283,700; real estate, renting and business activities, 277,200; and health and social work, 225,100. Unemployment was 10·5% in 2002, up from 6·4% in 1996.

Trade Unions

New Histadrut (The New General Federation of Workers), founded in 1920 as Histadrut, had 700,000 members in 2000. Several trades unions also exist representing other political and religious groups.

INTERNATIONAL TRADE

Imports and Exports

External trade, in US$1m., for calendar years:

	2000	2001	2002	2003	2004
Imports f.o.b.	34,059	31,014	31,229	32,338	38,473
Exports f.o.b.	31,188	27,967	27,535	30,098	36,585

Main imports in 1999 were: machinery and transport equipment, 35·2%; manufactured goods, 30·7% (of which 60% was diamonds); chemicals and related products, 8·9%; mineral fuels, 6·9%; foodstuffs, 4·9%. Main import suppliers in 2002: USA, 18·5%; Belgium, 9·1%; Germany, 7·1%; UK, 6·7%.

The main exportable commodities are citrus fruit and by-products, fruit juices, flowers, wines and liquor, sweets, polished diamonds, chemicals, tyres, textiles, metal products, machinery, electronic and transportation equipment. The main exports in 1999 were: machinery and equipment, 32·6% (of which a third was telecommunication equipment); worked diamonds, 24·7%; chemicals and chemical products, 12·8%. In 2002 the main export markets were: USA, 40·2%; Belgium, 6·3%; Hong Kong, 4·7%; UK, 3·9%.

COMMUNICATIONS

Roads

There were 16,903 km of paved roads in 2002, including 74 km of motorway. Registered motor vehicles in 2002 totalled 1,522,112 passenger cars, 19,140 buses and coaches and 335,724 lorries and vans. There were 525 fatalities as a result of road accidents in 2002.

Rail

There were 676 km of standard gauge line in 2002. 17·5m. passengers were carried in 2002 and 10·3m. tonnes of freight in 2000. One of the smallest metro systems in the world (1,800 metres) was opened in Haifa in 1959.

Civil Aviation

There are international airports at Tel Aviv (Ben Gurion), Eilat (J. Hozman), Haifa and Ovda. Tel Aviv is the busiest airport, in 2001 handling 8,305,950 passengers (7,864,200 on international flights) and 296,054 tonnes of freight. El Al is the state-owned airline. In 1999 it flew 79·5m. km and carried 2,972,400 passengers (all on international flights). In 2003 services (mainly domestic) were also provided by another Israeli airline, Arkia, and by over 40 international carriers.

Shipping

Israel has three commercial ports—Haifa, Ashdod and Eilat. In 2002, 5,984 ships departed from Israeli ports; 45,810,000 tonnes of freight and 137,000 passengers were handled. The merchant fleet totalled 765,000 GRT in 2002.

Telecommunications

A public company responsible to the Ministry of Communications administers the telecommunications service. In 2002 there were 9,434,000 telephone subscribers (equivalent to 1,421·7 per 1,000 population) and 1·61m. PCs were in use (242·6 for every 1,000 persons). Israel had 6,334,000 mobile phone subscribers in 2002 (954·5 per 1,000 inhabitants—among the highest penetration rates in the world) and 388,000 fax machines were in use. There were 2·0m. Internet users in 2002.

Postal Services

The Ministry of Communications supervises the postal service. In 2003 there were 668 post offices, or one for every 9,630 persons.

SOCIAL INSTITUTIONS

Justice

Law. Under the Law and Administration Ordinance, 5708/1948, the first law passed by the Provisional Council of State, the law of Israel is the law which was obtaining in Palestine on 14 May 1948 in so far as it is not in conflict with that Ordinance or any other law passed by the Israel legislature and with such modifications as result from the establishment of the State and its authorities.

Capital punishment was abolished in 1954, except for support given to the Nazis and for high treason.

The law of Palestine was derived from Ottoman law, English law (Common Law and Equity) and the law enacted by the Palestine legislature, which to a great extent was modelled on English law.

Civil Courts. Municipal courts, established in certain municipal areas, have criminal jurisdiction over offences against municipal regulations and bylaws and certain specified offences committed within a municipal area. Magistrates courts, established in each district and sub-district, have limited jurisdiction in both civil and criminal matters. District courts, sitting at Jerusalem, Tel Aviv and Haifa, have jurisdiction, as courts of first instance, in all civil matters not within the jurisdiction of magistrates courts, and in all criminal matters, and as appellate courts from magistrates courts and municipal courts. The 14-member Supreme Court has jurisdiction as a court of first instance (sitting as a High Court of Justice dealing mainly with administrative matters) and as an appellate court from the district courts (sitting as a Court of Civil or of Criminal Appeal).

In addition, there are various tribunals for special classes of cases. Settlement Officers deal with disputes with regard to the ownership or possession of land in settlement areas constituted under the Land (Settlement of Title) Ordinance.

Religious Courts. The rabbinical courts of the Jewish community have exclusive jurisdiction in matters of marriage and divorce, alimony and confirmation of wills of members of their community and concurrent jurisdiction with the civil courts in all other matters of personal status of all members of their community with the consent of all parties to the action.

The courts of the several recognized Christian communities have a similar jurisdiction over members of their respective communities.

The Muslim religious courts have exclusive jurisdiction in all matters of personal status over Muslims who are not foreigners, and over Muslims who are foreigners, if under the law of their nationality they are subject in such matters to the jurisdiction of Muslim religious courts.

Where any action of personal status involves persons of different religious communities, the President of the Supreme Court will decide which court shall have jurisdiction, and whenever a question arises as to whether or not a case is one of personal status within the exclusive jurisdiction of a religious court, the matter must be referred to a special tribunal composed of two judges of the Supreme Court and the president of the highest court of the religious community concerned in Israel.

In 2001 government expenditure on public security and justice totalled 7,238m. shekels. The population in penal institutions in Jan. 2002 was 10,164 (163 per 100,000 of national population).

Education

The adult literacy rate in 2003 was 96·9% (male, 98·3%; female, 95·6%). There is free and compulsory education from five to 16 years and optional free education until 18. There is a unified state-controlled elementary school system with a provision for special religious schools. The standard curriculum for all elementary schools is issued by the Ministry with a possibility of adding supplementary subjects comprising not more than 25% of the total syllabus. Most schools in towns are maintained by municipalities, a number are private and some are administered by teachers' co-operatives or trustees.

In 2000–01 there were 1,485,000 Hebrew pupils and 353,000 Arab pupils in the education system. In primary schools and kindergartens in 2000–01 there were 800,000 Hebrew children and 247,000 Arab children. There were 45,000 Hebrew teachers and 11,000 Arab teachers in 1999–2000. In secondary education there were 454,000 Hebrew pupils and 106,000 Arab pupils in 2000–01, with 47,000 Hebrew teachers and 7,000 Arab teachers in 1999–2000. In special education there were 31,060 pupils in 1998–99. In post-secondary education, such as colleges, universities and vocational institutions, there were 235,000 pupils, of which 231,000 were Hebrew.

The Hebrew University of Jerusalem, founded in 1925, comprises faculties of the humanities, social sciences, law, science, medicine and agriculture. In 2002–03 it had 22,600 students. The Technion in Haifa had 13,118 students. The Weizmann Institute of Science in Rehovoth, founded in 1949, had 760 students in 1995–96.

Tel Aviv University had 26,100 students in 1995–96. In 2002–03 the religious Bar-Ilan University at Ramat Gan, opened in 1965, had 31,200 students, the Haifa University had about 13,000 students and the Ben Gurion University had more than 15,000 students.

In 2001 government expenditure on education totalled 28,279m. shekels. In 2000–01 total expenditure on education came to 7·6% of GNP.

Health

In 2002 there were 367 hospitals with 61 beds per 10,000 inhabitants. There were 24,140 physicians, 7,387 dentists, 38,029 nurses, 4,176 pharmacists and 1,108 midwives in 2001. In 2001 government expenditure on health totalled 12,960m. shekels.

Welfare

The National Insurance Law of 1954 provides for old-age pensions, survivors' insurance, work-injury insurance, maternity insurance, family allowances and unemployment benefits. In 2001 recipients of allocations from the National Insurance Institute included (monthly averages): child allowances, 2,154,735; old age pensions, 571,200; general disability allowances, 142,440; income support benefits, 142,011; maternity grants, 129,089; survivors' pensions, 105,818; unemployment benefits, 104,707.

RELIGION

Religious affairs are under the supervision of a special Ministry, with departments for the Christian and Muslim communities. The religious affairs of each community remain under the full control of the ecclesiastical authorities concerned: in the case of the Jews, the Ashkenazi and Sephardi Chief Rabbis, in the case of the Christians, the heads of the various communities, and in the case of the Muslims, the Qadis. The Druze were officially recognized in 1957 as an autonomous religious community.

In 2001 there were: Jews, 4,960,000; Muslims, 930,000; others (mainly Christians and Druze), 360,000.

The Chief Rabbis are Yona Metzger (Ashkenazi) and Shlomo Amar (Sephardi).

CULTURE

World Heritage Sites

There are five sites under Israeli jurisdiction in the World Heritage List: Masada and the old city of Acre were both inscribed in 2001. Masada was built as a palace complex and fortress by Herod the Great. It was the site of the mass suicide of about 1,000 Jewish patriots in the face of a Roman army in the 1st century AD and is a symbol of the ancient kingdom of Israel. The port city of Acre preserves remains of its medieval Crusader buildings beneath the existing Muslim fortified town dating from the 18th and 19th centuries. The White City of Tel Aviv—the Modern Movement (2003) is an example of early 20th century town planning, based on the plan of Sir Patrick Geddes. The Biblical Tels, a series of prehistoric settlement mounds with biblical connections, and the Incense Route, four Nabatean towns along the spice and incense trail, were added to the list in 2005.

Broadcasting

Television and the state radio station, Kol Israel (Voice of Israel), are controlled by the Israel Broadcasting Authority. There is a national programme, two commercial programmes, a music programme and a service in Arabic. There were 2·15m. TV sets (colour by PAL) in 2001 and 3·21m. radio receivers in 2000.

Press

In 1996 there were 34 daily newspapers. Combined circulation was 1,650,000, at a rate of 291 per 1,000 inhabitants.

Tourism

In 2002 there were 862,000 foreign tourists, bringing revenue of US$1·20bn.

Calendar

The Jewish year 5766 corresponds to 4 Oct. 2005–22 Sept. 2006; 5767 corresponds to 23 Sept. 2006–12 Sept. 2007.

Libraries

In 1995 there was one National Library with 3m. volumes and 2,176 registered users. In 1993 there were 1,180 public libraries with 11,242,000 volumes and 737,565 registered users.

DIPLOMATIC REPRESENTATIVES

Of Israel in the United Kingdom (2 Palace Green, Kensington, London, W8 4QB)
Ambassador: Zvi Heifetz.

Of the United Kingdom in Israel (192 Hayarkon St., Tel Aviv 63405)
Ambassador: Simon McDonald.

Of Israel in the USA (3514 International Dr., NW, Washington, D.C., 20008)
Ambassador: Daniel Ayalon.

Of the USA in Israel (71 Hayarkon St., Tel Aviv)
Ambassador: Richard H. Jones.

Of Israel to the United Nations
Ambassador: Dan Gillerman.

Of Israel to the European Union
Ambassador: Oded Eran.

FURTHER READING

Central Bureau of Statistics. *Statistical Abstract of Israel.* (Annual)— *Statistical Bulletin of Israel.* (Monthly)
Beitlin, Y., *Israel: a Concise History.* London, 1992
Bleaney, C. H., *Israel.* [Bibliography] 2nd ed. ABC-Clio, Oxford and Santa Barbara (CA), 1994
Bregman, Ahron, *History of Israel.* Palgrave Macmillan, Basingstoke, 2002
Freedman, R. (ed.) *Israel Under Rabin.* Boulder (CO), 1995
Garfinkle, A., *Politics and Society in Modern Israel: Myths and Realities.* Armonk (NY), 1997
Gilbert, Martin, *Israel: A History.* New York, 1998
Sachar, H. M., *A History of Israel.* 2 vols. OUP, 1976–87
Schlör, Joachim, *Tel Aviv: From Dream to City.* Reaktion, London, 1999
Segev, T., *1949: The First Israelis.* New York, 1986
Tessler, M., *A History of the Israeli-Palestinian Conflict.* Indiana Univ. Press, 1994
Thomas, Baylis, *How Israel Was Won: A Concise History of the Arab–Israeli Conflict (1900–1999).* Lexington Books, Pennsylvania, 2000
Wasserstein, Bernard, *Israel and Palestine: Why They Fight and Can They Stop?* Profile Books, London, 2003

Other more specialized titles are entered under PALESTINIAN-ADMINISTERED TERRITORIES.

National Statistical Office: Central Bureau of Statistics, Prime Minister's Office, POB 13015, Jerusalem 91130.
Website: http://www.cbs.gov.il/
National library: The Jewish National and University Library, Jerusalem

---

Palestinian-Administered Territories

KEY HISTORICAL EVENTS

Under the Israeli-Palestinian agreement of 28 Sept. 1995 the Israeli army redeployed from six of the seven largest Palestinian towns in the West Bank and from 460 smaller towns and villages. Following this in April 1996 an 82-member *Palestinian Council* was elected and also a head (*Rais*) of the executive authority of the Council. The rest of the West Bank stayed under Israeli army control with some progressive redeployments at six-month intervals, although Palestinian civil affairs here too were administered by the Palestinian Council. Negotiations on the permanent status of the West Bank and Gaza began in May 1996. Issues to be resolved include the position of 0·17m. Israelis in the West Bank and 0·18m. in East Jerusalem, the status of Jerusalem, military locations and water supplies.

Following the opening of an archaeological tunnel in Jerusalem, armed clashes broke out at the end of Sept. 1996 between demonstrators and Palestinian police on the one hand and Israeli troops. On 18 Nov. 1996 the Israeli Minister of Defence approved plans for an expansion of Jewish settlement in the West Bank. Under an agreement brokered by King Hussein of Jordan and signed by the Prime Minister of Israel and the President of the Palestinian Authority on 15 Jan. 1997, Israeli troop withdrawals from 80% of Hebron and all rural areas of the

West Bank were scheduled to take place in three phases between 28 Feb. 1996 and 31 Aug. 1998.

The Israeli decision in Feb. 1997 to continue to promote Jewish settlement in the Jerusalem suburb of Har Homa was seen by the Palestinian authorities as a hostile move and caused a setback to peace negotiations. In 1998 an American proposal that Israel should withdraw from 13·1% of the West Bank was not agreed on, but at a meeting in the USA in Oct. Israel accepted partial withdrawal on condition that the Palestinians cracked down on terrorism.

President Netanyahu's defeat by Ehud Barak in Israel's 1999 elections led to improved relations with the Palestine Liberation Organization. Israel and the PLO signed the Sharm el-Sheikh Memorandum in Sept. 1999 which established a time-frame for the implementation of outstanding commitments from earlier Palestinian-Israeli agreements. Israel conducted two more phases of redeployment from the West Bank in Sept. 1999 and Jan. 2000. The permanent status negotiations, having commenced in May 1996, began in earnest in Nov. 1999. In March 2000 Yasser Arafat accepted Israel's plan for a further expansion of self-rule in the West Bank, involving the transfer of another 6·1% of the West Bank to the control of the Palestinian Authority. As a result, 39·8% of the West Bank is under full or partial Palestinian control. But violence escalated, and in Dec. 2001 Israel ended all direct contact with Yasser Arafat, besieging his compound and putting him under virtual house arrest. In March 2002 the UN Security Council endorsed a Palestinian state for the first time. Israeli incursions into Palestinian-controlled areas of the West Bank and the Gaza Strip, and suicide attacks by Palestinians, continued unabated in early 2002 with heavy loss of life.

In March 2003 the Palestinian parliament approved the creation of the post of prime minister. Mahmoud Abbas was nominated the Palestinian Authority's first premier, resulting in Yasser Arafat losing many of his powers. Yasser Arafat died on 11 Nov. 2004. Mahmoud Abbas was elected president in Jan. 2005. In Feb. 2005 he and Israeli prime minister Ariel Sharon agreed to a 'cessation of hostilities' between the two peoples, a move which encouraged hopes of a resumption of the peace process. In Aug. 2005 Israeli troops and police evicted the 8,500 Jewish settlers from the Gaza Strip in accordance with an agreement between Israel and the Palestinians. This was the first time Israel had withdrawn from Palestinian land captured in the 1967 war. Although representing less than 0·5% of the population of the Gaza Strip the Jewish settlers had occupied around a fifth of the total area.

In Jan. 2006 the legislative elections were won by the militant party Change and Reform (Hamas), which does not recognize Israel and has called for its destruction.

TERRITORY AND POPULATION

The 1997 census population of the Palestinian territory was 2,895,683; 2005 estimate 3,702,000. In 2003, 71·1% of the population was urban. Life expectancy at birth, 2003, was 74·0 years for females and 70·9 years for males. The UN gives a projected population for 2010 of 4·33m.

The West Bank (preferred Palestinian term, Northern District) has an area of 5,651 sq. km; 1997 census population was 1,873,476. The estimated population in 2004 was 2,311,000, in addition to 365,000 Jewish settlers and 10,000 troops deployed there. 99·8% of the population in 1997 were Palestinians. In 2001 there were 1,860,000 Muslims, 230,000 Jews and 200,000 Christians and others. In 2004 there was a Palestinian diaspora of 4·8m. The birth rate in 2004 was estimated at 39·6 per 1,000 population and the death rate 4·8 per 1,000. In 1995–99 the infant mortality rate was 24·4 per 1,000 live births. The fertility rate in 1999 was 5·5 births per woman. In 2003 there were 31,646 private cars and 14,521 commercial vehicles and trucks registered. There were (2003–04) 542,520 pupils in basic stage

education and 59,909 in secondary stage. In 1998–99 there were 36,224 students in institutions of higher education. In 2003 there were 54 hospitals.

The Gaza Strip (preferred Palestinian term, Gaza District) has an area of 365 sq. km; 1997 census population was 1,022,207. The population doubled between 1975 and 1995. Estimate, 2004, 1,325,000. Crude birth rate in 2004 was 43·7 per 1,000 population. The death rate was estimated at 3·9 per 1,000 population. The fertility rate in 1999 was 6·8 births per woman. Infant mortality, 1995–99, 27·3 per 1,000 live births. Agricultural production, 2002 estimates, in 1,000 tonnes: oranges, 105; tomatoes, 48; potatoes, 35; cucumbers and gherkins, 18; grapefruit and pomelos, 10. Total fish catch in 2001 was 2,144 tonnes. In 2003–04 there were 374,713 students in basic stage education, 41,185 in secondary stage and 30,058 students in higher education (1998–99). In 2003 there were 17 hospitals.

The chief town is Gaza itself. Over 98% of the population are Arabic-speaking Muslims. In 1995 an estimated 94·2% of the population lived in urban areas. In 2003 there were 38,677 private cars and 9,392 commercial vehicles and trucks registered. Gaza International Airport, at the southern edge of the Gaza Strip, opened in Nov. 1998. Telecommunications development has been rapid, the number of fixed line telephone subscribers more than trebling between 1997 and 2000. In 2003 there were 243,494 subscribers. In 2003 life expectancy at birth was 71·7 years.

CONSTITUTION AND GOVERNMENT

In April 1996 the Palestinian Council removed from its Charter all clauses contrary to its recognition by Israel, including references to armed struggle as the only means of liberating Palestine, and the elimination of Zionism from Palestine. The *President* is directly elected and heads the executive organ, the Palestinian National Authority, one fifth of whose members he appoints, while four fifths are elected by the *Legislative Council*. The latter comprises 132 members (88 until 2005), of which 66 members are chosen by district voting and the other 66 by proportional representation. The Palestinian Authority was created by agreement of the PLO and Israel as an interim instrument of self-rule for Palestinians living on the West Bank and Gaza Strip. The failure of the PLO and Israel to strike a permanent status agreement has resulted in the Authority retaining its powers. It is entitled to establish ministries and subordinate bodies, as required to fulfil its obligations and responsibilities. It possesses legislative and executive powers within the functional areas transferred to it in the 1995 Interim Agreement. Its territorial jurisdiction is restricted to Areas A and B in the West Bank and approximately two-thirds of the Gaza Strip.

Following an Israeli-Palestinian agreement on customs duties and VAT in Aug. 1994 the Palestinians set up their own customs and immigration points into Gaza and Jericho. Israel collects customs dues on Palestinian imports through Israeli entry points and transfers these to the Palestinian treasury.

A special committee is working on drafting a new Palestinian constitution. In March 2003 parliament approved the creation of the position of prime minister. Yasser Arafat nominated Mahmoud Abbas, the PLO Secretary General, to be the first premier.

There is a Palestinian *Council for Reconstruction and Development*.

RECENT ELECTIONS

Legislative Council elections were held on 25 Jan. 2006. Change and Reform (Hamas) won 74 seats; Fatah Movement, 45; Popular Front for the Liberation of Palestine, 3; the Alternative, 2; Independent Palestine, 2; Third Way, 2; ind. and others, 4. Turnout was 74·6%.

Presidential elections were held on 9 Jan. 2005. Mahmoud Abbas was elected president by 67·4% of votes cast, ahead of Mustafa Barghouti with 21·0%. There were five other candidates.

CURRENT ADMINISTRATION

President of the Palestinian Authority: Mahmoud Abbas; b. 1935.

Prime Minister: Ismail Haniya; b. 1962.

Palestinian Authority Website: http://www.pna.gov.ps

ECONOMY

Currency
Israeli currency is in use.

Banking and Finance
Banking is regulated by the Palestinian Monetary Authority. Palestine's leading bank is Arab Bank. A securities exchange, the Palestine Securities Exchange, opened in Nablus in Feb. 1997.

COMMUNICATIONS

Telecommunications
In 2003 there were 243,494 telephone subscribers, or 71·0 per 1,000 inhabitants. In March 2001 there were 60,000 Internet users.

SOCIAL INSTITUTIONS

Justice
The Palestinian police consists of some 15,000; they are not empowered to arrest Israelis, but may detain them and hand them over to the Israeli authorities. There were five executions in 2005.

Education
Adult literacy was 91·9% in 2003 (96·3% among males and 87·4% among females).

CULTURE

Tourism
In 2001 there were 7,000 foreign visitors; receipts from tourism totalled US$9m.

FURTHER READING

Kimmerling, B. and Migdal J. S., *Palestinians: the Making of a People.* Harvard Univ. Press, 1994.—*The Palestinian People: A History.* Harvard Univ. Press, 2003
Stendel, O., *The Arabs in Israel.* Brighton, 1996
Wasserstein, Bernard, *Israel and Palestine: Why They Fight and Can They Stop?* Profile Books, London, 2003

Statistical office: Palestinian Central Bureau of Statistics.
Website: http://www.pcbs.gov.ps

Repubblica Italiana

Capital: Rome
Population projection, 2010: 58·18m.
GDP per capita, 2003: (PPP$) 27,119
HDI/world rank: 0·934/18

KEY HISTORICAL EVENTS

Excavations at Isernia have uncovered remains of Palaeolithic Neanderthal man that date back 70,000 years. New Stone Age settlements have been found across the Italian peninsula and at the beginning of the Bronze Age there were several Italic tribes, including the Ligurians, Veneti, Apulians, Siculi and the Sardi. The Etruscans were established in Italy by around 1200 BC. Their highly civilized society flourished between the Arno and Tiber valleys, with other important settlements in Campania, Lazio and the Po valley. The Etruscans were primarily navigators and travellers competing for the valuable trading routes and markets with the Phoenicians and Greeks. During the 8th century BC the Greeks had begun to settle in southern Italy and presented a challenge to Etruscan domination of sea trade routes. Greek settlements were established along the southern coast, on the island of Ischia in the Bay of Naples and in Sicily where the Corinthians founded the city of Syracuse. These colonies were known as *Magna Graecia* and flourished for about six centuries. Magna Graecia eventually succumbed to the growing power of Rome where the impact of the Hellenic culture had already been felt.

According to legend, Rome was founded on 21 April 753 BC by Romulus (a descendant of Aeneas, a Trojan) who, after killing his twin brother, Remus, declared himself the first king of Rome. The Etruscan dynasty of Tarquins gained control in 616 BC and

expanded Roman agriculture and trade to rival the Greeks. The Romans overthrew the Tarquins in 510 BC and the first Roman Republic was born.

With the Republic came the establishment of the 'Roman Code', a collection of principles of political philosophy that enshrined the sovereign rights of Roman citizens. The early Roman Senate was dominated by a few patrician families, who held a monopoly on public office with the *equites* (the highest class of non-noble rich).

With the exception of the Greek city-states, Italy was unified by the Romans, who then set their sights on the Mediterranean, controlled by Carthage. Between 264–146 BC Carthage and Rome fought three wars (the Punic Wars) for supremacy of the Mediterranean trade routes. At the start Carthage was the more powerful, with a colonial empire that stretched as far as Morocco and included Sicily, Corsica, Sardinia and parts of Spain. Rome was also inexperienced in maritime war. In 218 BC the second Punic War started when Hannibal crossed the Alps and marched south, defeating the Romans in a series of battles in Italy. Without taking Rome itself, he crossed over to Zama in North Africa where he was finally defeated by Scipio in 202 BC. But by the end of the third Punic War in 146 BC the destruction of Carthage was total and Macedonian Greece was added to Rome's provinces. Rome incorporated Spain into her colonies and became the dominant power in the Mediterranean.

This dominance of trade routes led to great riches for Rome and the ensuing corruption among the upper ruling classes gave rise to social unrest. Sulla, a patrician general, marched on Rome in 82 BC, took the city in a bloody coup and instituted a new constitution. Nine years later Spartacus, an escaped slave, led 70,000 of his fellow slaves in a rampage throughout the peninsula. Out of the ensuing chaos, Julius Caesar emerged as leader. He had already conquered Gaul and declared southern Britain a part of Rome in 54 BC. His disregard for the Senate led to his legions being disbanded but he remained popular and returned to Rome a hero. His great strength and charisma led to his assassination by jealous members of the Senate on the Ides of March 44 BC. After his death, various rival successors fought to gain control, including Mark Anthony (Marcus Antonius), Marcus Junius Brutus and Gaius Cassius. But it was Caesar's nephew Octavian, having defeated Mark Anthony in 31 BC, who was crowned the first emperor of Rome in 27 BC, assuming the title Augustus.

Roman Domination

Augustus reigned for 45 years. With the aid of a professional army and an imperial bureaucracy he established the *Pax Romana* while extending the empire and disseminating its laws and civic culture. The arts thrived with writers, dramatists and philosophers such as Cicero, Plautus, Terence, Virgil, Horace and Ovid developing Latin into an expressive and poetic language. In 100 BC Rome itself had more than 1·5m. inhabitants and the Roman Empire was a unified diversity of many races and creeds. It had more than 100,000 km of paved roads, a complex of sophisticated aqueducts, and an efficient army and administrative system.

In AD 14 Augustus was succeeded by his stepson, Tiberius, who ruled in an era that saw the rise of Christianity. Successive emperors tried to suppress the new religion, which spread quickly throughout the empire. The deranged and corrupt Emperor Nero, who came to power in AD 54, initiated violent persecution of the Christians and was accused of setting Rome on fire. His death in AD 68 brought the Julio-Claudian dynasty to a close and, after a period of instability, Vespasian, the son of a provincial civil servant, took the throne and began some of the most ambitious building projects the Empire had seen. He started the Colosseum (completed by his son Titus) and the Arco di Tito (where the Via Sacra joins the Forum).

In AD 98 the Senate elected Trajan as emperor. Beginning a century of successful rule by the Antonine dynasty, he expanded the empire with the conquests of Dacia (Romania), Mesopotamia, Persia, Syria and Armenia. By the end of his reign the Roman Empire stretched from the Persian Gulf to Britain, from the Caspian Sea to Morocco and from the Sahara to the Danube. Trajan was responsible for several great architectural projects. A huge column depicting his Dacian campaigns served as his tomb in Rome. Trajan's successor, Hadrian, continued this programme of huge constructions, including Hadrian's Wall in Britain. After his death in 138, his tomb was converted into the fortress of Castel Sant'Angelo on the banks of the Tiber.

Under pressure from Teutonic tribes along the Danube and as a result of the increasingly strong influence of the Eastern religions, Rome began to lose control of its empire at the start of the 3rd century. In 306 Constantine became emperor. After he converted to Christianity in 313 his Edict of Milan established Rome as the headquarters of the Christian religion. A new building programme of Christian cathedrals and churches began throughout Italy. At the same time, Constantine cultivated the wealthy eastern regions of the Empire and, in 324, he moved his capital to Constantinople (now Istanbul). The decline of the Roman Empire continued when, after the death of Constantine, two brothers, Valens and Valentian, divided the Empire. The west and east gradually became alienated, separated by invaders, language and religious interpretation. 'Rome' endured in the east as the Byzantine Empire, the most powerful medieval state in the Mediterranean.

Fall of Rome

The western half of the Roman Empire, having embraced Christianity as the state religion, came under repeated attacks from Central European ('Barbarian') tribes. The Germanic Vandals had cut off Rome's corn supplies from North Africa, and the Visigoths, a Teutonic tribe, controlled the northern Mediterranean coast and northern Italy. In 452 Attila the Hun, from the steppes of Central Asia, invaded and forced the people of northeastern Italy onto a lagoon haven that became Venice. Rome was captured and sacked in 455 by the Vandals and in 476 a Germanic mercenary captain, Odovacar, deposed Romulus Augustus, the last of the Western Roman Emperors. This date is generally accepted as the end of the Roman Empire in the West.

In 493 Odovacar was succeeded by Theodoric, an Ostrogoth who had spent time as a hostage in Constantinople and who had acquired a taste for Roman culture. Theodoric ruled from Ravenna and by the time he died in 527 he had managed to restore peace to Italy. On his death, Italy was re-conquered by an emperor of the Eastern Roman Empire, Justinian, who together with his wife Theodora laid the foundations of the Byzantine period. Although the Lombards drove back the Justinian conquest, Byzantine emperors managed to retain control of parts of southern Italy until the 11th century.

In the mid-5th century Attila the Hun had been persuaded not to attack Rome by Pope Leo I ('The Great'). This and a document known as the 'Donation of Constantine' secured the Western Roman Empire for the Catholic Church. In 590 Gregory I became pope and set about an extensive programme of reforms, including improved conditions for slaves and the distribution of free bread in Rome. He oversaw the Christianization of Britain, repaired Italy's network of aqueducts and created the foundations for Catholic services and rituals and church administration.

The invasion of Italy by the Lombards began before Gregory became pope and, although they eventually penetrated as far south as Spoleto and Benevento, they were unable to take Rome.

They settled around Milan, Pavia and Brescia and abandoned their own language and customs in favour of the local culture. However, they were sufficiently threatening to cause the pope to invite the Franks under King Pepin to invade. In 756 the Franks overthrew the Lombards and established the Papal States (which survived until 1870). Pepin issued his 'Donation of Pepin', which gave the land still controlled by the Byzantine Empire to Pope Stephen II, proclaiming him and future popes the heirs of the Roman emperors. Pepin's son, Charlemagne, succeeded him and was crowned emperor on Christmas Day 800 by Pope Leo III in St Peter's Basilica in Rome. The installation of a 'Roman' emperor in the West—what was to become the Holy Roman Empire—endorsed the separation between Rome and Byzantium and moved the seat of European political power north of the Alps.

After Charlemagne's death it proved impossible to keep the enormous Carolingian Empire intact. In the period of anarchy that followed, many small independent rival states were established while in Rome the aristocratic families fought over the Papacy. Meanwhile, southern Italy was prospering under Muslim rule. By 831 Muslim Arabs had invaded Sicily and made Palermo their capital. Syracuse fell to them in 878. They created a Greek style civilization with Muslim philosophers, physicians, astronomers, mathematicians and geographers. Cotton, sugarcane and citrus fruits appeared for the first time in Italy and taxes were lowered. Hundreds of mosques were built and all over the region centres of academic and medical learning sprang up. Southern Italy lived harmoniously under Arab influence for more than 200 years while the north remained unsettled. After the collapse of the Carolingian Empire, warfare broke out between local rulers, forcing many people to take refuge in fortified hill towns. In 962 Otto I, a Saxon, was crowned Holy Roman Emperor, the first of a succession of Germanic emperors that was to continue until 1806.

At the beginning of the 11th century the Normans began to enter southern Italy in great numbers, where they had originally been recruited to fight the Arabs. Establishing themselves in Apulia and Calabria, they assimilated much of the eastern culture, coexisting peacefully with the Arabs. The architecture of churches and cathedrals built during this period shows the merging of the two cultural and religious influences. Roger II of Sicily (reigned 1112–54), nephew of the adventurer Robert Guiscard, extended Norman Hauteville power over southern Italy and his navy was dominant in the Mediterranean. He presided over a famous court of scholars and artists, many from the Muslim world, making Palermo a model of tolerance and learning.

North South Divide

Meanwhile, the delicate relationship between the Holy Roman Empire based in the north of Europe and the Papacy in the south was maintained by a common desire to recapture the Holy Land from the Muslims. Crusades were launched, mostly from the northern states, but achieved little. Germanic claims to the southern territories grew and after Frederick I (known as Barbarossa) was crowned Holy Roman Emperor in 1155, he married off his son Henry to the heir to the Norman throne in Sicily. Frederick II, Frederick Barbarossa's grandson, came to the throne of Sicily as a child in 1197 and was crowned Holy Roman Emperor in 1220. An enlightened and tolerant ruler, he was known as 'Stupor Mundi' ('Wonder of the World'). An accomplished warrior, he valued scholarship and the Arab culture and allowed Muslims and Jews freedom to follow their own religions. He founded the University of Naples in 1224 with the intention of producing a generation of administrators for his kingdom and moved the court of the Holy Roman Empire to the newly built octagonal masterpiece, Castel del Monte, in Apulia.

During this period a new middle class emerged; with the seat of government so far south, some of the northern cities began to free themselves from feudal control and set themselves up as autonomous states under the protection of either the pope or the emperor. Milan, Cremona, Bologna, Florence, Pavia, Modena, Parma and Lodi were the most important of these new states, each dominated by a powerful family, exercising governmental power in the form of *signorie*. These states functioned autonomously within larger regional areas: Veneto, Lombardy, Tuscany, the Papal States and the Southern Kingdom. In 1265 Charles of Anjou (a Frenchman who had beheaded Frederick II's grandson) was crowned king of Sicily. Greatly increased taxes, especially on rich landowners, made him unpopular despite his programme of road building, reform of the monetary system, improvement of the ports and the opening of silver mines. In 1282 an uprising known as the Sicilian Vespers was sparked off by a French soldier assaulting a Sicilian woman. As a consequence of the opposition to the French in southern Italy, Palermo declared itself an independent republic while supporting the Spaniard Peter of Aragon as king. By 1302 the Anjou dynasty had established itself in Naples.

Plague

The Black Death (La Peste), the deadly plague that swept throughout Europe towards the end of the 13th century, ravaged the populations of the major cities, which were already struggling with famine after years of war. Despite this, the strength of the northern and central Italian city-states was increasing. The rival maritime republics of Venice and Genoa had their own fleets. Venice had added the ports of Dalmatia, the Peloponnese and Cyprus to its possessions and Genoa's influence stretched as far as the Black Sea. Meanwhile, the pope and the Church turned their crusading zeal from the East towards European heretics. Pope Boniface, elected in 1294, came from Italian nobility and was determined to safeguard the interests of his own family. He claimed papal supremacy in worldly and spiritual affairs with his Papal Bull (*Unam Sanctam*) in 1302.

Meanwhile, a rival Papacy had appeared in Avignon, where John XXII was based. Rome had lost most of her former glory and had become little more than a battleground for the power struggles between the Orsini and Colonna families. The Papal claim to be temporal rulers of Rome was under threat and the Papal States began to fall apart. The period 1305–77, when seven successive popes ruled in Avignon, became known as the 'Babylonian Captivity'. In 1377 Pope Gregory XI returned to Rome after Cardinal Egidio d'Albornoz managed to restore the Papal States with his Egidian Constitutions. Rome was in such a ruined state that Gregory was obliged to set up his court in the Vatican, which was fortified and protected by the proximity of the Castel Sant'Angelo. Gregory died a year later and the Roman cardinals elected one of their own, Urban VI, as his successor. Urban's unpopularity was such that the French cardinals rebelled, electing their own pope, Clement VII, who set up his rival claim in Avignon. Yet another rival pope set himself in Pisa and thus began the Great Schism that would separate the papacy from Rome for nearly half a century.

Renaissance

In 1418 the Great Schism was brought to an end by the Council of Constance and Rome began to recapture her previous glory. Italy was at the forefront of the Renaissance, a flowering of artistic and intellectual humanist expression in the city-states. After the Peace of Lodi in 1454, the powerful ruling families—among others the Medici in Florence, the Gonzaga in Mantua and the d'Este in Ferrara—were at leisure to sponsor the Renaissance and Rome became again the centre of Italian political, cultural and intellectual life. In Florence the Signoria was taken over by a wealthy merchant, Cosimo de Medici. His nephew, Lorenzo II Magnifico, became one of the great patrons of the arts. Feudal lords like Lorenzo de Medici frequently switched allegiance between the popes and the emperors, becoming wealthy bankers and captains of adventure in the process. Having defeated its arch-rival, Genoa, in 1381, Venice grew enormously, transforming its commercial maritime empire into a territorial empire that stretched almost to Milan.

The peace was shattered in 1494 by the invasion of Charles VIII, king of France. Encouraged to pursue his claim to the crown of Naples by Ludovico Sforza, duke of Milan, Charles shocked the Italian cities into an alliance to expel his army. As cities competed to become the richest and most cultured, a Dominican monk, Girolamo Savonarola, preached against humanism in Florence. He persuaded Charles VIII to overthrow the Medici family and declare a Florentine republic. Although he was eventually excommunicated, hanged and burned at the stake, Savonarola exerted a lasting influence on Florentine politics. The Venetian expansion, through diplomatic and military guile, had alienated Venice's neighbours, who formed in 1508 the League of Cambrai, which came close to eradicating the Venetian Republic.

The appearance of Spanish power in Naples began the Habsburg-Valois wars that used Italy as a battlefield until the Peace of Cateau-Cambrésis in 1559. These Italian Wars radically altered the political landscape of the peninsula, leaving Spain dominant in Italy. Florence's time as a republic was brief. The Emperor Charles V, who had sacked Rome in 1527, reinstated the Medici, who went on to rule Florence for the next 210 years.

By the second half of the 16th century, the Church of Rome was obliged to respond to the rise of the Protestant movement (the Reformation), inspired in Germany by Martin Luther. During the Counter-Reformation, the Inquisition, backed by Catholic Spain, was used to suppress heresy. Spain succeeded in dominating Italy during the second half of the 16th century but when Charles II (the last of the Spanish Habsburgs) died in 1700, the War of the Spanish Succession saw Italy become a prize for the dominant European powers. Italy was divided amongst the Austrian Habsburgs, the Spanish Bourbons, Savoy and the independent states. The papacy became less influential, the Jesuits were expelled from Portugal, France and Spain and, thanks to intermarriage between many of the ruling houses of Europe and new trading laws, many national barriers were broken down. The 18th century Age of Enlightenment gave Italy some of its greatest thinkers and writers as well as liberal legal reforms.

Unification

In 1796 Napoleon Bonaparte invaded Italy and declared an Italian Republic under his personal rule. In creating a single political entity, he laid the basis for modern Italy. The Congress of Vienna, which met after the defeat of Napoleon in 1815, reinstated Italy's former rulers. Secret societies, made up of disillusioned middle class intellectuals, fought for a new constitution to reunify the country. One such was founded in 1830 by a Genoan, Giuseppe Mazzini. His 'Young Italy' was committed to liberating the country from foreign dominance and to establishing a unified state under a republican government, a campaign that came to be known as *Il Risorgimento*. During the 1830s and 1840s Mazzini instigated a series of unsuccessful uprisings until he was exiled. By 1848 revolutionary uprisings were taking place all over Europe and the Italian Nationalist movement was gaining ground. Two supporters of the Nationalist cause, Cesare Balbo and Count Camillo Benso di Cavour, published a document—*Statuto*—that proposed a bicameral legislature and would become the basis of a new Italian constitution.

As nationalist feeling increased, Giuseppe Garibaldi, whose terrorist activities for Young Italy had obliged him to flee to South America, returned to Italy and allied himself with the Italian National Society. Cavour, the prime minister of Sardinia-Piedmont, attempted to remove Austria from Italy with French help but it was not until Garibaldi and 1,000 volunteers (the Red Shirts) took Sicily and Naples from the Bourbons in 1860 that unification became a real possibility. Garibaldi handed over these kingdoms to Victor Emmanuel II, king of Sardinia-

Piedmont. This was to the relief of Cavour, who had feared that Garibaldi might institute a rival republican government in the south. Although Italy was declared a kingdom in 1861 under Victor Emmanuel II, the country was still not unified. Venice was in the hands of the Austrians while France held Rome. In 1866 the Italians took the Veneto from the Prussians and in 1870 Rome was recaptured from the French. Only the Papal troops resisted the advance of the Italian army in 1870 and Pope Pius IX refused to recognize the Kingdom of Italy. In retaliation, the government stripped the pope of his temporal powers. Thus Italy was fully unified.

Twentieth Century

The turn of the 20th century saw popular support fluctuate between left-wing socialist and right-wing imperialist political parties. When the First World War broke out in 1914, Italy remained neutral although the State was associated with the British, French and Russian allies while the Papacy declared for Catholic Austria. In 1919 Benito Mussolini founded the Italian Fascist Party, whose black shirts and Roman salutes were to become the symbols of aggressive nationalism in Italy for the next two decades. In the elections of 1921 the Fascist Party won 35 of the 135 seats in the Italian parliament. A year later, Mussolini raised a militia of 40,000 'Black Shirts' and marched on Rome to 'liberate' it from the socialists. In 1922 the king asked Mussolini to form a government. His Fascist party won the elections of 1924 and Mussolini assumed the title *Il Duce*. By the end of 1925 Mussolini had expelled all opposition parties from parliament and gained control of the trade unions. Four years later, he signed a pact with Pope Pius XI declaring Catholicism the sole religion of Italy and recognizing the Vatican as an independent state. In return, the pope finally recognized the United Kingdom of Italy.

Mussolini's aggressive foreign policy resulted in disputes with Greece over Corfu and military campaigns in the Italian colony of Libya. In 1935 Italy invaded Abyssinia (now Ethiopia) and captured Addis Ababa. The newly formed League of Nations condemned this action and imposed sanctions. In the face of international isolation, Mussolini formed an alliance with the German dictator, Adolf Hitler, and in 1936 the Rome-Berlin Axis was formed. Having annexed Albania in April 1939, Italy entered the Second World War in June 1940. Mussolini's armies invaded Greece from Albania in Oct. 1940 but were repelled, forcing Hitler to invade Yugoslavia and Greece in April 1941. This diversion of German troops has been seen as a critical factor in the ultimate failure of the invasion of the USSR, delayed from May to June 1941. The Italian colonies of East Africa were lost in 1941 and Italian forces in North Africa surrendered in May 1943. The Allied armies landed in Sicily in July 1943 and, in the face of diminishing popular support for fascism and Hitler's refusal to assign more troops to the defence of Italy, the king led a coup against Mussolini and had him arrested. In the 45 days that followed, Italy exploded in a series of uprisings against the war. The king signed an armistice with the Allies and declared war on Germany but Nazi troops had already overrun northern Italy. The Germans rescued Mussolini from prison and installed him as a puppet ruler. In 1945 after trying to flee the country, Mussolini was recaptured by Italian partisans and shot. After the Italian Resistance suffered huge losses against the Germans, the allies liberated northern Italy in May 1945.

Post War

In the years following the end of the Second World War, Italy's political forces attempted to regroup. The Marshall Plan, America's post-war aid programme, exerted considerable political and economic influence. The constitutional monarchy was abolished in 1946 by referendum and a republic was formed with a president (elected for a seven-year term by an electoral college), a two-chamber parliament and a separate judiciary.

Initially the newly formed Christian Democrats under Alcide De Gasperi were in power with both the Communist Party and the Socialist Party, participating in a series of coalition governments until they were both excluded by De Gasperi in 1947. More than 300 separate political factions have struggled for power throughout the post-war era and no government has lasted longer than four years. Despite this instability, the war-damaged Italian economy began to pick up in the early 1950s. The industrialized northern regions thrived while the less industrialized south remained underdeveloped. The Cassa per il Mezzogiorno (a state fund for the South) was founded to try to redress the balance but with limited success.

In 1957 Italy became a founder member of the European Economic Community (EEC). The rapid growth of the motor industry, most notably Fiat in Turin, saw huge migrations of peasants from the south to work in the factories. By the mid-1960s the Communist Party, which had been gradually increasing its share of the poll at each election, had more card carrying members than the Christian Democrats and was exerting considerable influence over Italian politics without actually managing to participate in government. Social unrest was commonplace and in 1969 a series of strikes, demonstrations and riots followed on the heels of unrest elsewhere in Europe. Various terrorist groups were active including the extreme left-wing socialist group, the Red Brigade, founded in 1970. Extreme right-wing neo-fascist terrorists were also in action, and in the less developed south, the Mafia, a loose coalition of crime 'families', flourished. Most of Italy's social, economic and political structures were manipulated by these unofficial organizations. In 1963 Aldo Moro, a Christian Democrat, was appointed prime minister (a post he held until 1968) and invited the Socialists into his government. Later on, in the 1970s, he was working towards a compromise to allow the Communists to enter government when he was captured, held hostage and finally murdered by the Red Brigade. This national outrage prompted the government to appoint Carabinieri Gen. Carlo Alberto dalla Chiesa to wipe out the terrorist groups. He instituted a system of *pentiti* (informants) who, in return for collaboration, would receive greatly reduced prison sentences. In 1980 he was asked to expand his area of operations to include the Mafia but was assassinated in Palermo a few months later. Throughout the 1970s Italy experienced radical social and political change. The country was divided into regional administrative areas with their own elected governments. Divorce became legal, women's rights were expanded (Italian women only achieved full suffrage after the Second World War) and abortion was legalized. In 1983 the minority Christian Democratic government handed the premiership to the Socialists under Bettino Craxi.

Italy was well on its way to becoming one of the world's leading economic powers but the 1990s brought fresh crises in the economic and political arenas. Unemployment and inflation rose sharply which, combined with a huge national debt and unstable lira, led to instability. On the political front, the Communist Party split with the hard-liners forming the Rifondazione Communista, led by Fausto Bernotti, while the more moderate members set up the Democratic Party of the Left. In early 1992 the arrest of a Socialist Party worker on charges of accepting bribes in exchange for public works contracts sparked off Italy's largest ever political corruption scandal. Investigations into *'Tangentopoli'* ('kick-back city') implicated thousands of politicians, public officials and businessmen. Former Prime Minister Bettino Craxi was forced to resign as party secretary after he came under investigation for bribery. Allied to Italy's humiliating exit from Europe's Exchange Rate Mechanism (ERM), the old political establishment was driven out of office. In the April 1992 elections, the Christian Democrat share of the vote dropped by 5% while the Lega Nord (the Northern League), under Umberto Bossi, took 9% of the vote on an anti-corruption, federalist platform. Oscar Luigi Scalfaro was elected president on a promise to set about reforming electoral laws and clearing up the Tangentopoli scandal. Investigations into corruption continued, despite reprisals from the Mafia. Craxi was convicted *in absentia* while Giulio Andreotti, who was prime minister three times between 1972 and 1992, was brought to trial in 1995 on charges of dealing with the Sicilian Mafia.

In the 1994 elections a right-wing coalition was elected. The Freedom Alliance, including the neo-fascist National Alliance and the federalist Northern League, was led by Silvio Berlusconi, a multi-millionaire media tycoon. Berlusconi lost his majority when the Northern League withdrew after nine months. Under mounting criticism for his failure to disassociate himself from his business interests and after receiving a vote of no confidence, Berlusconi resigned. After leaving the Freedom Alliance, the Northern League became more fanatical, advocating a 'Northern Republic of Padania', a separation of the rich northern regions from the poorer southern ones. The 1996 elections brought to power the centre-left 'Olive Tree' alliance with Romano Prodi as prime minister. Prodi aimed to balance the budget and create a stable political environment. He gained his first objective with a succession of economic measures that prepared the way for Italy's entry into EMU.

Prodi was succeeded by Massimo D'Alema in 1998 who, in turn, was replaced by Giuliano Amato in 2000. By the time of the 2001 elections Berlusconi's popularity had revived and he formed a new centre-right coalition. He introduced the first major constitutional reforms in 55 years, allowing the nation's 20 regions increased responsibility for their own tax, education and environmental programmes.

TERRITORY AND POPULATION

Italy is bounded in the north by Switzerland and Austria, east by Slovenia and the Adriatic Sea, southeast by the Ionian Sea, south by the Mediterranean Sea, southwest by the Tyrrhenian Sea and Ligurian Sea and west by France.

The area is 301,277 sq. km. Populations at successive censuses were as follows:

10 Feb. 1901	33,778	15 Oct. 1961	50,624
10 June 1911	36,921	24 Oct. 1971	54,137
1 Dec. 1921	37,856	25 Oct. 1981	56,557
21 April 1931	41,043	20 Oct. 1991	56,778
21 April 1936	42,399	21 Oct. 2001	56,996
4 Nov. 1951	47,516		

Population estimate, 1 Jan. 2005, 58,462,375 (30,085,571 females). Density: 194 per sq. km.

The UN gives a projected population for 2010 of 58·18m.

In 2003, 67·4% of the population lived in urban areas.

The following table gives area and population of the Autonomous Regions (censuses 1991 and 2001):

Regions	Area in sq. km	Resident pop. census, 1991	Resident pop. census, 2001	Density per sq. km, 2001
Piemonte (Piedmont)	25,399	4,302,565	4,214,677	166
Valle d'Aosta[1]	3,262	115,938	119,548	37
Lombardia (Lombardy)	23,857	8,856,074	9,032,554	379
Trentino-Alto Adige[1]	13,618	890,360	940,016	69
Bolzano-Bozen	7,400	440,508	462,999	63
Trento	6,218	449,852	477,017	77
Veneto	18,364	4,380,797	4,527,694	247
Friuli-Venezia Giulia[1]	7,845	1,197,666	1,183,764	151
Liguria	5,418	1,676,282	1,571,783	290
Emilia Romagna	22,123	3,909,512	3,983,346	180
Toscana (Tuscany)	22,992	3,529,946	3,497,806	152
Umbria	8,456	811,831	825,826	98
Marche	9,693	1,429,205	1,470,581	152
Lazio	17,203	5,140,371	5,112,413	297
Abruzzi	10,794	1,249,054	1,262,392	117
Molise	4,438	330,900	320,601	72

Regions	Area in sq. km	Resident pop. census, 1991	Resident pop. census, 2001	Density per sq. km, 2001
Campania	13,595	5,630,280	5,701,931	419
Puglia	19,348	4,031,885	4,020,707	208
Basilicata	9,992	610,528	597,768	60
Calabria	15,080	2,070,203	2,011,466	133
Sicilica (Sicily)[1]	25,709	4,966,386	4,968,991	193
Sardegna (Sardinia)[1]	24,090	1,648,248	1,631,880	68

[1]With special statute.

Communes of more than 100,000 inhabitants, with population resident at the censuses of 20 Oct. 1991 and 21 Oct. 2001:

	1991	2001
Roma (Rome)	2,775,250	2,733,416
Milano (Milan)	1,369,231	1,256,211
Napoli (Naples)	1,067,365	1,004,500
Torino (Turin)	962,507	865,263
Palermo	698,556	686,722
Genova (Genoa)	678,771	610,307
Bologna	404,376	371,217
Firenze (Florence)	403,294	356,118
Bari	342,309	316,532
Catania	333,075	313,110
Venezia (Venice)	309,422	271,073
Verona	255,824	253,208
Taranto	232,334	202,033
Messina	231,693	252,026
Trieste	213,100	211,184
Padova (Padua)	215,137	204,870
Cagliari	204,237	164,249
Brescia	194,502	187,567
Reggio di Calabria	177,580	180,353
Modena	176,990	175,502
Parma	170,520	163,457
Livorno	167,512	156,274
Prato	165,707	172,499
Foggia	156,268	155,203
Salerno	148,932	138,188
Perugia	144,732	149,125
Ferrara	138,015	130,992
Ravenna	135,844	134,631
Reggio nell'Emilia	132,030	141,877
Rimini	127,960	128,656
Siracusa (Syracuse)	125,941	123,657
Sassari	122,339	120,729
Pescara	122,236	116,286
Monza	120,651	120,204
Bergamo	114,936	113,143
Forlì	109,541	108,335
Terni	108,248	105,018
Vicenza	107,454	107,223
Latina	106,203	107,898
Piacenza	102,268	95,594
Trento	101,545	104,946
La Spezia	101,442	91,391
Torre del Greco	101,361	90,607
Ancona	101,285	100,507
Novara	101,112	100,910
Lecce	100,884	83,303

The official language is Italian, spoken by 92·8% of the population in 2003. There are 0·3m. German-speakers in Bolzano and 30,000 French-speakers in Valle d'Aosta.

In addition to Sicily and Sardinia, there are a number of other Italian islands, the largest being Elba (363 sq. km), and the most distant Lampedusa, which is 205 km from Sicily but only 113 km from Tunisia.

SOCIAL STATISTICS

Vital statistics (and rates per 1,000 population), 2002: births, 535,538 (9·4); deaths, 558,270 (9·8); marriages, 265,635 (4·7). 2000: divorces, 37,573 (0·7). Infant deaths, 2002 (up to one year of age): 2,400 (4·5 per 1,000 live births). Expectation of life, 2003: females, 83·1 years; males, 76·9. At the 2001 population census 18·68% of the population was over 65, the highest percentage of any country in the world.

Annual population growth rate, 1992–2002, 0·1%; fertility rate, 2001, 1·2 births per woman. With only 10·2% of births being to unmarried mothers, Italy has one of the lowest rates of births out of wedlock in Europe.

In 2002 there were 2,947 suicides; 76·6% were men.

In Jan. 2002 there were 1,448,392 legal immigrants living in Italy, up from 1,379,749 a year earlier. In 2000, 56,601 people emigrated from Italy and there were 226,968 immigrants into the country. Italy received 7,281 asylum applications in 2002, equivalent to 0·1 per 1,000 inhabitants. New legislation was introduced in 2002 to tighten up immigration rules.

CLIMATE

The climate varies considerably with latitude. In the south, it is warm temperate, with little rain in the summer months, but the north is cool temperate with rainfall more evenly distributed over the year. Florence, Jan. 47·7°F (8·7°C), July 79·5°F (26·4°C). Annual rainfall 33" (842 mm). Milan, Jan. 38·7°F (3·7°C), July 73·4°F (23·0°C). Annual rainfall 38" (984 mm). Naples, Jan. 50·2°F (10·1°C), July 77·4°F (25·2°C). Annual rainfall 36" (935 mm). Palermo, Jan. 52·5°F (11·4°C), July 78·4°F (25·8°C). Annual rainfall 35" (897 mm). Rome, Jan. 53·4°F (11·9°C), July 76·3°F (24·6°C). Annual rainfall 31" (793 mm). Venice, Jan. 43·3°F (6·3°C), July 70·9°F (21·6°C). Annual rainfall 32" (830 mm).

CONSTITUTION AND GOVERNMENT

The Constitution dates from 1948. Italy is 'a democratic republic founded on work'. Parliament consists of the *Chamber of Deputies* and the *Senate*. The Chamber is elected for five years by universal and direct suffrage and consists of 630 deputies. The Senate is elected for five years on a regional basis by electors over the age of 25, each Region having at least seven senators. The total number of senators is 315. The Valle d'Aosta is represented by one senator only, the Molise by two. The President of the Republic can nominate 11 senators for life from eminent persons in the social, scientific, artistic and literary spheres. The President may become a senator for life. The *President* is elected in a joint session of Chamber and Senate, to which are added three delegates from each Regional Council (one from the Valle d'Aosta). A two-thirds majority is required for the election, but after a third indecisive scrutiny the absolute majority of votes is sufficient. The President must be 50 years or over; term of office, seven years. The Speaker of the Senate acts as the deputy President. The President can dissolve the chambers of parliament, except during the last six months of the presidential term. An attempt to create a new constitution, which had been under consideration for 18 months, collapsed in June 1998.

A *Constitutional Court*, consisting of 15 judges who are appointed, five each by the President, Parliament (in joint session) and the highest law and administrative courts, can decide on the constitutionality of laws and decrees, define the powers of the State and Regions, judge conflicts between the State and Regions and between the Regions, and try the President and Ministers.

The revival of the Fascist Party is forbidden. Direct male descendants of King Victor Emmanuel are excluded from all public offices and have no right to vote or to be elected; their estates are forfeit to the State. For 56 years they were also banned from Italian territory until the constitution was changed in 2002 to allow them to return from exile. Titles of nobility are no longer recognized, but those existing before 28 Oct. 1922 are retained as part of the name.

A referendum was held in June 1991 to decide whether the system of preferential voting by indicating four candidates by their listed number should be changed to a simpler system, less open to abuse, of indicating a single candidate by name. The electorate was 46m. Turnout was 62·5% (there was a 50% quorum). 95·6% of votes cast were in favour of the change. As a result, an electoral reform of 1993 provides for the replacement of proportional representation by a system in which 475 seats in the Chamber of Deputies are elected by a first-past-the-post single-round vote and 155 seats by proportional representation in a separate single-round vote on the same day. There are 27 electoral regions. There is a 4% threshold for entry to the Chamber of Deputies.

At a further referendum in April 1993, turnout was 77%. Voters favoured the eight reforms proposed, including a new system of election to the Senate and the abolition of some ministries. 75% of the Senate is now elected by a first-past-the-post system, the remainder by proportional representation; no party may present more than one candidate in each constituency. In July 1997 an all-party parliamentary commission on constitutional reform proposed a directly elected president with responsibility for defence and foreign policy, the devolving of powers to the regions, a reduction in the number of seats in the Senate and in the lower house and the creation of a third chamber to speak on behalf of the regions.

National Anthem

'Fratelli d'Italia' ('Brothers of Italy'); words by G. Mameli, tune by M. Novaro, 1847.

GOVERNMENT CHRONOLOGY

Presidents of the Council of Ministers (Prime Ministers) since 1944. (DC = Christian Democrats; DS = Democrats of the Left-Party of the European Socialism; FI = Forza Italia; PA = Action Party; PRI = Italian Republican Party; PSI = Italian Socialist Party; Ulivo = Olive Tree; n/p = non-partisan)

1944–45	n/p	Ivanoe Bonomi
1945	PA	Ferruccio Parri
1945–53	DC	Alcide De Gasperi
1953–54	DC	Giuseppe Pella
1954	DC	Amintore Fanfani
1954–55	DC	Mario Scelba
1955–57	DC	Antonio Segni
1957–58	DC	Adone Zoli
1958–59	DC	Amintore Fanfani
1959–60	DC	Antonio Segni
1960	DC	Fernando Tambroni
1960–63	DC	Amintore Fanfani
1963	DC	Giovanni Leone
1963–68	DC	Aldo Moro
1968	DC	Giovanni Leone
1968–70	DC	Mariano Rumor
1970–72	DC	Emilio Colombo
1972–73	DC	Giulio Andreotti
1973–74	DC	Mariano Rumor
1974–76	DC	Aldo Moro
1976–79	DC	Giulio Andreotti
1979–80	DC	Francesco Cossiga
1980–81	DC	Arnaldo Forlani
1981–82	PRI	Giovanni Spadolini
1982–83	DC	Amintore Fanfani
1983–87	PSI	Benedettino Craxi
1987	DC	Amintore Fanfani
1987–88	DC	Giovanni Giuseppe Goria
1988–89	DC	Ciriaco De Mita
1989–92	DC	Giulio Andreotti
1992–93	PSI	Giuliano Amato
1993–94	n/p	Carlo Azeglio Ciampi
1994–95	FI	Silvio Berlusconi
1995–96	n/p	Lamberto Dini
1996–98	n/p	Romano Prodi
1998–2000	DS	Massimo D'Alema
2000–01	n/p	Giuliano Amato
2001–06	FI	Silvio Berlusconi
2006–	Ulivo	Romano Prodi

RECENT ELECTIONS

Parliamentary elections were held on 9–10 April 2006. The turnout was 83·6%. The centre-left Union coalition (comprised of Ulivo, the Communist Refoundation Party, Rose in the Fist and 12 smaller parties) won 348 seats in the Chamber of Deputies and 158 in the Senate, against Prime Minister Silvio Berlusconi's centre-right House of Freedoms Alliance (comprised of Forza Italia, the National Alliance, the Union of Christian and Centre Democrats, and ten other parties) with 281 and 156 seats respectively.

European Parliament

Italy has 78 (87 in 1999) representatives. At the June 2004 elections turnout was 73·1% (70·6% in 1999). Ulivo won 25 seats—the DS, 12 (political affiliation in European Parliament: Party of European Socialists), La Margherita, 7 (Alliance of Liberals and Democrats for Europe), Social Democrats, 2 (Party of European Socialists), the European Republican Movement, 1 (Alliance of Liberals and Democrats for Europe), South Tyrolean People's Party, 1 (European People's Party–European Democrats), ind. 2 (Party of European Socialists)—with 31·1% of votes cast; Forza Italia gained 16 seats with 21·0% of votes cast (European People's Party–European Democrats); the National Alliance, 9 with 11·5% (Union for a Europe of Nations); the RC, 5 with 6·1% (European Unitary Left/Nordic Green Left); the Union of Christian and Centre Democrats, 5 with 5·9% (European People's Party–European Democrats); the Northern League, 4 with 5·0% (Independence and Democracy Group); Federation of Greens, 2 with 2·5% (Greens/European Free Alliance); Italian Communist Party, 2 with 2·4% (European Unitary Left/Nordic Green Left); Lista Bonino (Radicals), 2 with 2·3% (Alliance of Liberals and Democrats for Europe); Società Civile di Pietro, 2 with 2·1% (Alliance of Liberals and Democrats for Europe); United Socialists for Europe, 2 with 2·0% (non-attached); Alleanza Populare Udeur, 1 with 1·3% (European People's Party–European Democrats); Alternativa Sociale-Alessandra Mussolini, 1 with 1·2% (non-attached); the Pensioners Party, 1 with 1·1% (European People's Party–European Democrats); Social Movement Fiamma Tricolore, 1 with 0·7% (non-attached).

CURRENT ADMINISTRATION

President: Giorgio Napolitano; b. 1925 (sworn in 15 May 2006).

Following the April 2006 elections, Silvio Berlusconi refused to accept the results, claiming there were irregularities particularly in the votes of Italians abroad. Romano Prodi meanwhile rejected Berlusconi's suggestion of forming a grand coalition and continued with plans to establish a new centre-left government. On 2 May Berlusconi finally agreed to resign as Prime Minister, after the centre-left secured the election of its nominees to the powerful parliamentary speakerships of both the Chamber of Deputies and the Senate. However, Prodi's mandate to form an administration then hinged on the election of a new President (the largely ceremonial head of state formally appoints the Prime Minister), to succeed the retiring incumbent, Carlo Azeglio Ciampi, who had been in office since 1999. At the end of four rounds of voting by the Senate, Chamber of Deputies and regional council representatives, a veteran politician and former Communist, Giorgio Napolitano, was elected President on 10 May and sworn in on 15 May (three days before the end of Ciampi's term). At the time of going to press, President Napolitano has asked Prodi to form a government.

Government Website (Italian only): http://www.governo.it

CURRENT LEADERS

Romano Prodi

Position
Prime Minister

Introduction
In April 2006 Romano Prodi was elected prime minister for the second time, defeating his arch-rival Silvio Berlusconi by a slim majority. Leading a diverse leftist coalition, Prodi faces a struggle to build a government strong enough to maintain power for a full term of office. He was previously prime minister from 1996–98 and was credited with steering the Italian economy towards European Monetary Union (EMU). As president of the European Commission between 1999–2004 he was instrumental in working towards the expansion of the European Union and closer unity between the member states.

Early Life
Romano Prodi was born on 9 Aug. 1939 in Scandiano, Reggio Emilia. On completion of his schooling in Reggio Emilia, he studied law at the Catholic University of Milan before undertaking postgraduate studies at the London School of Economics in the UK. He went on to hold the post of professor of industrial organization and policy at the University of Bologna for over 25 years. He was also a visiting professor at Harvard University and had a long association with the Stanford Research Institute, both in the USA. In 1978 he commenced his political career, holding an array of posts including minister for industry (in the government of Giulio Andreotti) and chairman of the institute for industrial reconstruction (a government holding company). While in the latter position, he was subject to allegations of conflict of interest in relation to his private business concerns, but was acquitted of any wrongdoing.

In 1995 Prodi became chairman of the *Ulivo* (Olive Tree) centre-left coalition and stood in the 1996 elections against the then prime minister, media millionaire and owner of AC Milan football club, Silvio Berlusconi. *Ulivo* won the election with a narrow majority and in May 1996 Prodi was appointed prime minister. During his 28-month premiership he introduced a swathe of financial reforms and reduced the public sector deficit. He also introduced changes in the areas of public administration, fiscal planning and corporate governance law. On 9 Oct. 1998 Prodi lost a vote of no confidence, initiated by the leader of the Communist Refoundation party, Fausto Bertinotti.

Prodi was elected president of the European Commission in May 1999. In this role he promoted increased powers for the European Union (EU) and common foreign and immigration policies. He also oversaw increased EU involvement in national economic policies. When his tenure expired in Nov. 2004, he was replaced as president of the European Commission by José Manuel Durão Barroso.

Following the end of his European Commission presidency Prodi returned to the national political arena, leading the opposition against Silvio Berlusconi's ruling right-wing coalition, *Forza Italia*. In Oct. 2004 the centre-left opposition coalition, formerly known as *Ulivo*, was refounded and renamed the Great Democratic Alliance (GAD). Key to this restructuring was the inclusion of the far-left Communist Refoundation party led by Fausto Bertinotti. On 6 Oct. 2005, 4m. people voted in primary elections to choose the opposition candidate to stand against Berlusconi in general elections planned for April 2006. Prodi claimed a landslide victory, winning 73·5% of the vote, while Bertinotti polled 15·4%.

A general election took place on 10 April 2006. Following a record-breaking electoral turnout of 83%, the result was a knife-edge victory for Prodi and his Union coalition. Recent changes to the electoral system provided the winner of the lower house with a working majority, 348 seats against 281 for *Forza Italia*. Less comfortably, the Union coalition won only 158 seats in the upper house against 156 for *Forza Italia*. With both houses holding equal power, the government is vulnerable.

Career in Office
Berlusconi contested the results of the election, demanding a recount in several areas. However, Prodi's victory was confirmed by the judiciary on 22 April 2006. There were further delays before Prodi was able to take office. The new government had

to wait until Giorgio Napolitano, the newly-elected president, had formally replaced outgoing president Carlo Azeglio Ciampi on 15 May. Chosen after four rounds of voting, 80-year-old Napolitano was Prodi's favoured candidate. The speakers of both houses of parliament were also elected following several rounds of close voting, with the position in the lower house going to Fausto Bertinotti and in the upper house to moderate trade union leader Franco Marini. In both cases the speakers were Prodi's chosen candidates.

With a public debt that has ballooned to 106·5% of gross domestic product, and a budget deficit that has exceeded European Union limits for the past two years, Italians have chosen a prime minister who promises to improve tax collection, slim down the country's overweight bureaucracy, increase competition and gradually reduce the budget deficit.

However, the far-left factions of the GAD look set to complicate any plans to privatize state industries and drive consolidation in areas such as the banking sector. Additionally, Prodi has long been an outspoken opponent to the war in Iraq and there are fears that a review on refinancing for troops in Iraq, scheduled for June 2006, could lead to splits within the already fragile coalition.

As leader of a rainbow coalition of parties ranging from communists to Catholic centrists, and with a majority in the upper house so small that the absence of a single senator could change the outcome of a vote, there is a consensus among opinion-formers that Prodi's government may be unable or unwilling to implement the reforms necessary for the long-term revitalization of the Italian economy.

DEFENCE

Head of the armed forces is the Defence Chief of Staff. Conscription was abolished at the end of 2004 with the military becoming all-professional from 2005. In Aug. 1998 the government voted to allow women into the armed forces.

In 2003 defence expenditure totalled US$27,751m. (US$481 per capita), representing 1·9% of GDP.

Army

Strength (2004) 116,000 (6,000 conscripts). Equipment includes 715 *Leopard,* 378 *Centauro* and 200 *Ariete* tanks. First line Army reserves number 11,900 with a further 500,000 personnel available for mobilization.

The paramilitary Carabinieri number 111,800. In addition there were 79,000 public security guards run by the Ministry of the Interior and 63,500 Finance Guards run by the Treasury.

Navy

The principal ships of the Navy are the light aircraft carrier *Giuseppe Garibaldi* and the helicopter-carrying cruiser *Vittorio Veneto.* The combatant forces also include six diesel submarines, four destroyers and 12 frigates. The Naval Air Arm, 2,000 strong, operates 17 combat aircraft and 63 armed helicopters.

Main naval bases are at La Spezia, Brindisi, Taranto and Augusta. The personnel of the Navy in 2004 numbered 34,000 (1,500 conscripts), including the naval air arm and the marine battalion. There were 21,000 naval reservists.

Air Force

Control is exercised through two regional headquarters near Taranto and Milan.

Air Force strength in 2004 was about 48,000 (3,200 conscripts). There were 220 combat aircraft in operation in 2004 including Typhoons and Tornados. There were 30,300 Air Force reservists in 2004.

INTERNATIONAL RELATIONS

Italy is a member of the UN, WTO, NATO, BIS, OECD, EU, Council of Europe, WEU, OSCE, CERN, CEI, Inter-American Development Bank, Asian Development Bank, IOM and the Antarctic Treaty. Italy is a signatory to the Schengen accord of June 1990 which abolishes border controls between Italy, Austria, Belgium, Denmark, Finland, France, Germany, Greece, Iceland, Luxembourg, the Netherlands, Norway, Portugal, Spain and Sweden. On 6 April 2005 Italy ratified the proposed EU constitution. The Senate approved the treaty by 217 votes to 16; it had already been approved by the Chamber of Deputies in Jan. 2005.

In 2004 Italy gave US$2·5bn. in international aid. In terms of a percentage of GNI, however, Italy was the least generous major industrialized country, giving just 0·15%.

ECONOMY

Agriculture accounted for 2·6% of GDP, industry 27·3% and services 70·1% in 2002.

Overview

Italy has a diversified industrial base and is one of the world's largest economies. Italians enjoy average income levels roughly equal to those of other leading economies. However, since 1988 Italy's economic performance has trailed that of other developed countries. In the last few years in particular, Italy has been at the bottom of the OECD country group in terms of economic growth. The economic structure is similar to that of most advanced OECD economies, with a diminishing and small primary sector and a large gross value added contribution by the service sector. However, with the exceptions of design and tourism, Italy is not internationally competitive in most service sectors.

Manufacturing has been a key sector for the economy, encompassing mainly small- and medium-sized companies specializing in products requiring skilled engineering and design. Manufacturing accounts for roughly 90% of total merchandise exports and 25% of GDP. Small and medium-sized family-owned companies are the strongest component of the economy, producing mainly high-quality consumer goods such as clothing, furniture and white goods. These companies have resisted becoming publicly funded companies but face pressure from global economic integration and competition and are vulnerable to acquisition by foreign firms looking for brand power and high-quality production capabilities. A few large companies play an important role in the economy, including Fiat (still controlled by the Agnelli family), Pirelli, Telecom Italia (controlled by Marco Tronchetti Provera, heir to the Pirelli family) and Mediaset (controlled by the family of ex-Prime Minister Silvio Berlusconi). These families have cross-shareholding pacts with industrial and financial allies that allowed them to maintain control of companies even with small direct shareholdings. Recent legislation requiring more open dealing by listed companies and better minority shareholder rights has so far had little impact.

The northeast is Italy's most dynamic region and where most value added production is concentrated. Despite progress in the *Mezzogiorno* (the south and Sicily and Sardinia) the economic gap between north and south remains. Unemployment rates in the north are low while the south faces some of the highest rates in the EU. In addition to regional imbalance, Italy's economy suffers from other structural weaknesses. The country's public debt has been reduced from over 120% in the mid-1990s to under 110% but it is still among the highest in the world. Fiscal deficits were found to have significantly exceeded the 3% euro zone limit in recent years and fiscal reform remains a policy challenge. According to the Economist Intelligence Unit productivity growth has been negative since 2001. Since joining the euro Italy has enjoyed low borrowing costs and enhanced macroeconomic security but has no longer been able to rely on competitive devaluations of its currency. Labour market reforms in the 1990s have helped reduce unemployment significantly but the labour market remains one of the most rigid in western

Europe and the corporate tax system discourages firms from employing workers in the formal labour market.

Public pensions account for roughly 15% of GDP (nearly twice as high as the EU average) and 40% of public sector spending. The country faces one of the most unfavourable demographic situations in the world. Birth rates are low and the percentage of people over 65 years old is high and rising rapidly. The IMF believes that population ageing will increase annual pension spending by approximately 2% of GDP over coming years and annual health spending by 3% per year. Pension reforms in 2004, which increase the effective retirement age from 2008, are considered by the IMF and OECD to be significant but insufficient in addressing the fiscal liability problem presented by rising pension and healthcare costs. Since 1993 privatization initiatives have reduced the state's direct involvement in the economy and enhanced competition but the OECD notes that further regulatory reform and liberalization efforts are needed in the electricity, transportation, road freight, professional services and retail trade sectors.

Currency
On 1 Jan. 1999 the euro (EUR) became the legal currency in Italy; irrevocable conversion rate 1,936·27 lire to 1 euro. The euro, which consists of 100 cents, has been in circulation since 1 Jan. 2002. There are seven euro notes in different colours and sizes denominated in 500, 200, 100, 50, 20, 10 and 5 euros, and eight coins denominated in 2 and 1 euros, then 50, 20, 10, 5, 2 and 1 cents. On the introduction of the euro there was a 'dual circulation' period before the lira ceased to be legal tender on 28 Feb. 2002. Euro banknotes in circulation on 1 Jan. 2002 had a total value of €97·4bn.

Inflation rates (based on OECD statistics):

1995	1996	1997	1998	1999	2000	2001	2002	2003	2004
5·4%	4·0%	1·9%	2·0%	1·7%	2·6%	2·3%	2·6%	2·8%	2·3%

The inflation rate in 2005 according to BNP Paribas was 2·0%. In June 2002 gold reserves were 78·83m. troy oz (66·67m. troy oz in 1997) and foreign exchange reserves US$20,533m. (US$45,307m. in Dec. 1999). Total money supply in June 2002 was €54,958m.

Budget
In 2000 revenues totalled €444·50bn. (€441·16bn. in 1999) and expenditures €462·35bn. (€454·00bn. in 1999). Principal sources of revenue in 2000: taxes on income, profits and capital gains, €153·60bn.; social security contributions, €144·47bn.; taxes on goods and services, €103·64bn. Main items of expenditure by economic type in 2000: social benefits, €193·61bn.; interest, €73·77bn.; compensation of employees, €72·29bn.

VAT is 20% (reduced rates, 10% and 4%).

The public debt at 31 Dec. 2002 totalled €1,220,956m. Between 1992 and 2002 the public deficit came down from more than 10% to 2·4%, or possibly less, of gross domestic product. Interest rates have also declined significantly.

Performance
Real GDP growth rates (based on OECD statistics):

1995	1996	1997	1998	1999	2000	2001	2002	2003	2004
3·0%	1·0%	2·0%	1·7%	1·7%	3·2%	1·7%	0·4%	0·4%	1·0%

Total GDP was US$1,672·3bn. in 2004. Italy's average economic growth since 1990 has been the slowest in the EU.

In May 2005 the OECD reported: 'In recent years, Italy's GDP growth has been below the euro-area average, and…potential growth rate of GDP…has fallen below 1½ per cent. Consumer price inflation has been faster than in the euro-area and relative unit labour costs…have been rising steeply.…The challenges are

thus to…raise real per capita income growth rates and improve the public finances.'

Banking and Finance
The bank of issue is the Bank of Italy (founded 1893). It is owned by public-sector banks. Its *Governor* (Mario Draghi) is selected without fixed term by the 13 directors of the Bank's non-executive board. In 1991 it received increased responsibility for the supervision of banking and stock exchange affairs, and in 1993 greater independence from the government.

The number of banks has gradually been declining in recent years, from 1,176 in 1990 to 778 in 2004. Of these, 439 were mutual banks and 37 were co-operative banks. Italy's largest bank in terms of assets is Banca Intesa, following its merger with Banca Commerciale Italiana in 1999. In June 2000 it had assets of 643,000bn. lire. Other major banks are Sanpaolo IMI and UniCredito Italiano. In June 2005 UniCredito Italiano finalized an agreement to acquire Germany's HypoVereinsbank in Europe's biggest cross-border banking takeover.

The 'Amato' law of July 1990 gave public sector banks the right to become joint stock companies and permitted the placing of up to 49% of their equity with private shareholders. In 1999 the last state-controlled bank was sold off.

On 31 Dec. 2000 the post office savings banks had deposits of 270,011bn. lire. In the same year credit institutions had deposits of 1,005,484bn. lire.

Legislation reforming stock markets came into effect in Dec. 1990. In 1996 local stock exchanges, relics of pre-unification Italy, were closed, and stock exchange activities concentrated in Milan.

ENERGY AND NATURAL RESOURCES
Environment
Italy's carbon dioxide emissions from the consumption and flaring of fossil fuels in 2002 were the equivalent of 7·8 tonnes per capita.

Electricity
In 2001 installed capacity was 78,787 MW and the total power generated was 279·0bn. kWh (19·3% hydro-electric). Consumption in 2001 was 285·5bn. kWh, of which: industry, 151·0bn. kWh; services, 67·8bn. kWh; domestic use, 61·5bn. kWh; agriculture, 5·2bn. kWh. Consumption per capita was 5,768 kWh in 2001. Italy has four nuclear reactors in permanent shutdown, the last having closed in 1990.

Oil and Gas
Oil production, 2002, 5,394,197 tonnes. Proven oil reserves in 2002 were 0·6bn. bbls. In 2002 natural gas production was 15·1bn. cu. metres with proven reserves of 230bn. cu. metres.

Minerals
Fuel and mineral resources fail to meet needs. Only sulphur and mercury yield a substantial surplus for exports.

Production of metals and minerals (in tonnes) was as follows:

	1998	1999	2000	2001	2002
Sulphur	3,413,522	3,338,162	3,339,761	—	—
Feldspar	2,503,541	2,493,846	2,851,289	3,240,457	3,159,569
Bentonite	580,209	562,674	636,589	579,029	463,231
Lead	10,102	9,734	5,961	4,016	4,709
Zinc	5,242	—	—	—	—

Agriculture
In 2000, 1,120,000 persons were employed in agriculture, of whom 451,000 were dependent (148,000 female); independently employed were 669,000 (203,000 female). At the fifth agricultural census, held on 22 Oct. 2000, there were 13,212,652 sq. km of agricultural and forest lands, distributed as follows (in 1,000 ha.): woods, 4,711; cereals, 4,052; forage and pasture, 3,414; olive

trees, 1,081; vines, 676; leguminous plants, 66. In 2001 there were 8·17m. ha. of arable land and 2·80m. ha. of permanent crops. In 2003 organic crops were grown in an area covering 1·17m. ha. (the third largest area after Australia and Argentina), representing 8·0% of all farmland.

At the 2000 census agricultural holdings numbered 2,593,090 and covered 19,607,094 ha. 2,457,960 owners (95·7%) farmed directly 13,868,478 ha. (70·3%); 132,935 owners (3·9%) worked with hired labour on 5,706,993 ha. (29·1%); the remaining 2,195 holdings (0·4%) of 31,623 ha. (0·6%) were operated in other ways. 97,307 share-croppers tilled 1,445,826 ha. Only 13,212,652 sq. km was in active agricultural use.

Agriculture and fishing accounted for 1·5% of exports and 3·4% of imports in 2001.

Figures compiled by the Soil Association, a British organization, show that in 1999 Italy set aside 900,000 ha. (5·3% of its agricultural land) for the growth of organic crops.

In 2001, 1,650,000 tractors were in use and 51,000 harvester-threshers.

Output of principal crops (in 1,000 tonnes) in 2002: sugarbeets, 12,726; maize, 10,824; wheat, 7,444; grapes, 7,394; tomatoes, 5,748; olives, 3,079; apples, 2,203; potatoes, 1,961; oranges, 1,687; peaches and nectarines, 1,587; rice, 1,371; barley, 1,177; pears, 924; soybeans, 566; lemons, 501.

Wine production in 2002 totalled 44,604,000 hectolitres (17% of the world total). Italy is the second-largest wine producer in the world after France. In 2002 Italy was the leading producer of grapes, but France produced more wine. Wine consumption in Italy has declined dramatically in recent times, from more than 110 litres per person in 1966 to 52·9 litres per person in 2001.

Livestock, 2001: cattle, 6,232,000; sheep and goats, 12,279,000; pigs, 8,766,000; horses, 280,000; buffaloes, 173,000; chickens, 100m.; turkeys, 23m. Livestock products, 2000 (in 1,000 tonnes): cow milk, 11,741; sheep milk, 850; buffalo milk, 158; goat milk, 140; pork, bacon and ham, 1,475; beef and veal, 1,160; poultry meat, 1,140; cheese, 1,011; butter, 101; eggs, 768. Italy is the second largest producer of sheep milk, after China.

Forestry

In 2001 forests covered 6·85m. ha. or 22·7% of the total land area. Timber production was 8·22m. cu. metres in 2003.

Fisheries

The fishing fleet comprised, in 2002, 16,045 motor boats of 215,247 gross tonnes. The catch in 2003 was 295,694 tonnes, of which more than 98% were from marine waters.

INDUSTRY

The leading companies by market capitalization in Italy in Nov. 2005 were: Ente Nazionale Idrocarburi (ENI), an integrated oil company (US$108·6bn.); UniCredito Italiano (US$64·4bn.); and Telecom Italia (US$51·9bn.).

The value added at factor cost in 2001 was €1,098,992m. The percentage of industrial value at factor cost by activity sector was: agriculture, forestry and fishing: 2·93%; construction: 4·92%; financial activity, currency and real activities: 26·13%; strictly industry: 22·74%; trade, transport, hotels and restaurants: 24·21%; other services: 19·07%. Main strictly industry items (% of overall total) in 2001 were: metal production and metallic products: 2·69%; machines and mechanical apparatus: 2·50%; textiles and clothing: 2·40%; electric energy—production and distribution: 2·20%; food, beverages and tobacco: 2·10%; electric machines, electric apparatus and optical instruments: 1·74%; chemicals and synthetic fibres: 1·70%.

Production, 2001: cement, 38,965,000 tonnes; crude steel (2002), 26,100,000 tonnes; polyethylene resins, 1,100,114 tonnes; artificial and synthetic fibres (including staple fibre and waste), 627,482 tonnes; motor vehicles, 1,272,000 units; TV sets, 1,208,000 units.

Labour

In 2003 the workforce was 24,150,000 (69·3% males and 42·7% females) of whom 21,829,000 were employed. 2,096,000 were unemployed and looking for work. The unemployment rate over the past four years has been regularly declining; in 2003 it was 8·6%, down from 10·8% in 2000. By Sept. 2005 it had declined further, to 7·5%. In 2002, 63·2% of the workforce were in services, 31·8% in industry and 5·0% in agriculture. There are strong indications of labour markets having become less rigid, especially in the north. In the northeast unemployment was 3·3% in 2003, in the northwest 4·4% and in the centre 6·6%; in the south it was 18·3%. In 1996 the difference in the unemployment rates in the north and in the south was 12%, compared to a difference of just 2% in the 1960s. Nearly 60% of Italy's jobless have been out of work for more than a year, the highest rate in any industrialized country. Pensionable retirement age was 60 for men and 55 for women in 1991, but this is being progressively raised to 65 for both sexes. In 2002 the rate of employment among people aged 55–64 was just 4·1%.

In 1997 parliament approved the so-called 'Treu Package', which involves a large number of institutional changes regarding working hours and apprenticeships, mainly for young people from the south, and the introduction of employment agencies. As a consequence, the share of temporary workers over total employees had grown from 6·2% in 1993 to 9·9% in 2002.

Trade Unions

There are three main groups: the Confederazione Generale Italiana del Lavoro (CGIL; formerly Communist-dominated), the Confederazione Italiana Sindacati Lavoratori (CISL; Catholic) and the Unione Italiana del Lavoro (UIL). Membership (2002): CGIL, 5·5m.; CISL, 4·2m.; UIL, 1·6m. In referendums held in June 1995 the electorate voted to remove some restrictions on trade union representation, end government involvement in public sector trade unions and end the automatic deduction of trade union dues from wage packets.

INTERNATIONAL TRADE

Imports and Exports

The following table shows the value of Italy's foreign trade (in US$1bn.):

	2000	2001	2002	2003	2004
Imports	230·9	229·4	239·2	286·6	341·3
Exports	240·5	244·9	252·6	298·1	352·2

Percentage of trade with EU countries in 2002: imports, 72·5%; exports, 69·2%. Principal import suppliers, 2002 (% of total trade): Germany, 17·76%; France, 11·28%; UK, 4·94%; USA, 4·87%. Principal export markets: Germany, 13·68%; France, 12·16%; USA, 9·74%; UK, 6·90%.

Imports/exports by category, 2001 (% volume):

	Imports	Exports
Chemicals and artificial fibres	12·9	9·5
Electric and precision instruments	14·1	10·1
Food, beverages and tobacco	6·9	5·1
Leather and leather products	2·5	5·4
Machinery and mechanical equipment	7·9	19·8
Metals and metal products	9·8	8·0
Minerals	10·2	0·0
Textiles and clothing	5·3	10·6
Transport equipment	14·3	10·9
Other products	16·1	19·8

COMMUNICATIONS

Roads

Roads totalled 479,688 km in 1999, of which 6,621 km were motorways, 46,009 km were highways and main roads, 114,909 km were secondary roads and 312,149 km other roads. In 2001 there were 40,743,777 motor vehicles, including: passenger cars, 33,239,029 (563 per 1,000 inhabitants); buses and coaches, 89,858; vans and trucks, 3,541,545. There were 6,682 fatalities in road accidents in 2001.

Rail
The length of state-run railway (*Ferrovie dello Stato*) in 2002 was 15,985 km (10,891 km electrified). In 2001 the state railways carried 491·8m. passengers and 83·2m. tonnes of freight. There are metros in Naples (79·0 km), Milan (68·7 km), Rome (33·5 km), Genoa (5·0 km) and Catania (3·8 km), and tram/light rail networks in Genoa, Messina, Milan (206 km), Naples, Trieste and Turin (123 km).

Civil Aviation
There are major international airports at Bologna (G. Marconi), Genoa (Cristoforo Colombo), Milan (Linate and Malpensa), Naples (Capodichino), Pisa (Galileo Galilei), Rome (Leonardo da Vinci/Fiumicino), Turin (Caselle) and Venice (Marco Polo). A number of other airports have a small selection of international flights. The national carrier, Alitalia, is 49·9% owned by the state. As a response to severe economic struggles, the company announced plans in 2004 to split into two and reduce the workforce by 2,700. As part of this restructuring, Alitalia received €400m. from the government. In Jan. 2005 the EU Commission launched an investigation into complaints that the finance constituted illegal state aid. In 1997 it flew 297·2m. km and carried 24,551,600 passengers. There are a number of other Italian airlines, most notably Meridiana, which flew 24·4m. km and carried 2,935,400 passengers in 1998. The busiest airport for passenger traffic is Rome (Fiumicino), which in 2001 handled 24,331,558 passengers (12,244,136 on international flights), plus 381,956 passengers in transit and 169,648 tonnes of freight. Milan Malpensa was the second busiest for passengers, handling 18,457,037 (14,169,573 on international flights), plus 109,652 passengers in transit, but the busiest for freight, with 289,382 tonnes. Linate, which handled 7,131,604 passengers in 2001 (4,995,000 on domestic flights), plus 738 passengers in transit, had been the principal Milan airport and for many years Italy's second busiest for passenger traffic, but in 1998 a new terminal was opened at Malpensa with many foreign operators subsequently using it instead of Linate.

Shipping
The mercantile marine in 2000 totalled 9·60m. GRT, including oil tankers 1·10m. GRT. In 2000 vessels totalling 211,242,000 NRT entered ports and vessels totalling 137,864,000 NRT cleared. 2,039,697 passengers embarked and 2,185,645 departed in 1995. The chief ports are Genoa (51,748,000 tonnes of cargo handled in 2002), Trieste, Venice, Livorno, Gioia Tauro and Ravenna.

Telecommunications
There were 79,767,900 telephone subscribers in 2002, or 1,412·7 per 1,000 persons. In May 1999 Olivetti bought a controlling stake in the telephone operator Telecom Italia, and in July 2001 Pirelli, backed by the Benetton clothing empire, in turn paid €7bn. (US$6·1bn.) to take over control of Telecom Italia. In 2002 mobile phone subscribers numbered 53,003,000, equivalent to 938·7 per 1,000 population (among the highest penetration rates in the world). TIM (Telecom Italia Mobile) is the largest operator, with a 45% share of the market. There were 13·0m. PCs in use (230·7 per 1,000 persons) in 2002 and 2·5m. fax machines. There were 19·9m. Internet users in 2002.

Postal Services
In 2003 there were 13,728 post offices, or one for every 4,180 persons.

SOCIAL INSTITUTIONS

Justice
Italy has one court of cassation, in Rome, and is divided for the administration of justice into 29 appeal court districts,

subdivided into 164 tribunal *circondari* (districts). There are also 93 first degree assize courts and 29 assize courts of appeal. For civil business, besides the magistracy above mentioned, *Giudici di pace* have jurisdiction in petty plaints.

2,231,550 crimes were reported in 2002; 768,771 persons were indicted in 2002. On 31 Dec. 2002 there were 55,670 persons in prison (2,469 females). There were 16,788 foreigners in prison (1,008 females). In 1947 the re-established democracy rewrote the Legislative Order; the constitution of the Italian Republic abolished the death penalty sanctioned in 1930 by Codice Penale, commonly known as Codice Rocco. Although the death penalty was abolished for ordinary crimes in 1947, it was not until 1994 that it was abolished for all crimes.

Education
Five years of primary and three years of secondary education are compulsory from the age of six. In 2000–01 there were 25,044 pre-school institutions with 1,576,562 pupils and 128,972 teachers (state and non-state schools); 18,854 primary schools with 2,810,337 pupils and 287,344 teachers (state and non-state schools); 7,908 compulsory secondary schools (*scuole medie*) with 1,776,889 pupils and 209,971 teachers (state and non-state schools); and 6,624 higher secondary schools with 2,570,509 pupils and 307,279 teachers (state and non-state schools).

Higher secondary education is subdivided into classical (*ginnasio* and classical *liceo*), scientific (scientific *liceo*), language lyceum, professional institutes and technical education: agricultural, industrial, commercial, technical, nautical institutes, institutes for surveyors, institutes for girls (five-year course) and teacher-training institutes (four-year course).

In 2001–02 there were 59 universities, of which two are universities of Italian studies for foreigners, three specialized universities (commerce; education; Roman Catholic), three polytechnical university institutes and six Free Universities; seven specialized university institutes (architecture; bio-medicine; modern languages; naval studies; oriental studies; social studies; teacher training). In 2001–02 there were 1,702,575 university students and 56,060 academic staff.

Adult literacy rate, 2001, 98·5% (male 98·9%; female 98·1%).

In 2000–01 total expenditure on education came to 4·7% of GNP and in 1999–2000 accounted for 9·5% of total government spending.

Health
The provision of health services is a regional responsibility, but they are funded by central government. Medical consultations are free, but a portion of prescription costs are payable. In 2000 the National Health Service included 1,425 hospitals of which 785 were public with 212,165 beds and 640 private hospitals with 56,359 beds. In 2000 there were 112,332 doctors and 273,520 auxiliary medical personnel.

A survey published by the World Health Organization in June 2000 to measure health systems in all of the sovereign countries and find which country has the best overall health care ranked Italy in second place, behind France. In 2003 Italy spent 8·4% of its GDP on health.

Welfare
Social expenditure is made up of transfers which the central public departments, local departments and social security departments make to families. Payment is principally for pensions, family allowances and health services. Expenditure on subsidies, public assistance to various classes of people and people injured by political events or national disasters are also included.

Italians currently receive a state pension at 57 or after 35 years of work, whichever comes first. From 2008 workers will only be able to draw a state pension from the age of 60 (for women—65 for men), providing they have made 35 years of pension contributions. The age restriction will not apply in the case of workers who have made 40 years of pension contributions.

Public pensions are indexed to prices; 22,210,241 pensions were paid in 2001, with payments totalling €170,779·0m. (including 16,910,061 private sector, with payments totalling €130,169·7m.). Current social security expenditure in 2001 was €381m. Social contributions totalled €154,731m.

RELIGION

The treaty between the Holy See and Italy of 11 Feb. 1929, confirmed by article 7 of the Constitution of the republic, lays down that the Catholic Apostolic Roman Religion is the only religion of the State. Other creeds are permitted, provided they do not profess principles, or follow rites, contrary to public order or moral behaviour.

The appointment of archbishops and of bishops is made by the Holy See; but the Holy See submits to the Italian government the name of the person to be appointed in order to obtain an assurance that the latter will not raise objections of a political nature. In May 2005 there were 38 cardinals.

Catholic religious teaching is given in elementary and intermediate schools. Marriages celebrated before a Catholic priest are automatically transferred to the civil register. Marriages celebrated by clergy of other denominations must be made valid before a registrar.

There were 46,260,000 Roman Catholics in 2001, 680,000 Muslims, 1,350,000 adherents of other religions and 9,600,000 non-religious and atheists.

CULTURE

World Heritage Sites

Italy has 40 sites that have been included on UNESCO's World Heritage List. They are listed here in the order in which they were designated world heritage sites: the Rock Drawings in Valcamonica near Brescia (1979); Santa Maria delle Grazie with 'The Last Supper' by Leonardo da Vinci (1980); the Historic Centre of Rome, the properties of the Holy See in that city enjoying extraterritorial rights (1980); San Paolo Fuori le Mura Historic Centre of Florence (1982); Venice and its Lagoon (1987); Piazza del Duomo, Pisa (1987); Historic Centre of San Gimignano (1990); I Sassi di Matera (1993); Vicenza, the City of Palladio and the Villas of the Veneto (1994); Historic Center of Siena (1995); Historic Center of Naples (1995); Ferrara (1995); Crespi d'Adda (1995); Castel del Monte (1996); Trulli of Alberobello (1996); Early Christian Monuments and Mosaics of Ravenna (1996); Historic Centre of the City of Pienza (1996); The 18th-Century Royal Palace at Caserta with the Park, the Aqueduct of Vanvitelli and the San Leucio Complex (1997); Residences of the Royal House of Savoy (1997); Botanical Garden (Orto Botanico), Padua (1997); Cathedral, Torre Civica and Piazza Grande, Modena (1997); Archaeological Areas of Pompeii, Ercolano and Torre Annunziata (1997); Villa Romana del Casale (1997); Su Nuraxi di Barumini (1997); Portovenere, Cinque Terre and the Islands (Palmaria, Tino and Tinetto) (1997); The Costiera Amalfitana (1997); Archaeological Area of Agrigento (1997); Cilento and Vallo di Diano National Park (1998); Historic Centre of Urbino (1998); Archaeological Area and the Patriarchal Basilica of Aquileia (1998); Villa Adriana (1999); Aeolian Islands (2000); Assisi (2000); the City of Verona (2000); Villa d'Este, Tivoli (2001); the Late Baroque Towns of the Val di Noto (2002); and Sacri Monti of Piedmont and Lombardy (2003); Val d'Orcia (2004), part of the agricultural hinterland of Siena; the Etruscan Necropolises of Cerveteri and Tarquinia (2004); and Syracuse and the Rocky Necropolis of Pantalica (2005).

Broadcasting

Broadcasting is regulated by the Public Radio-Television Administration Council.

Questions have been raised over the impartiality of state-owned *Radiotelevisione Italiana* (RAI) but all attempts at privatization have been rejected. RAI, the public television company, broadcasts three public channels, RAI 1, RAI 2 and RAI 3. Mediaset, a private company controlled by Fininvest, produces three commercial channels: Canale 5, Italia 1 and Rete 4. RAI 1 has the highest viewing figures, followed by Canale 5, RAI 2 and Italia 1. There are 15 national and about 820 local private TV networks. There were 50·0m. radio receivers and 28·3m. TV sets (colour by PAL) in 2000. In 2002, 16,216,006 television licences were bought.

Cinema

In 2001 there were 2,243 cinemas and 3,198 screens, and 110m. admissions. In 2001 gross box office receipts came to €589m. and 103 full-length films were made.

Press

There were (2002) 91 dailies with a combined circulation of 5·9m. copies. Several of the papers are owned or supported by political parties. The church and various economic groups exert strong right of centre influence on editorial opinion. Most newspapers are regional but *Corriere della Sera* (which has the highest circulation of any Italian newspaper), *La Repubblica*, *Il Sole 24 Ore* and *La Stampa* are the most important of those papers that are nationally circulated. In 2001 a total of 53,131 book titles were published in 275m. copies.

Tourism

In 2002, 39,799,000 foreigners visited Italy; receipts from tourism in 2002 were US$26·92bn.

Festivals

One of the most traditional festivals in Italy is the Carnival di Ivrea which lasts for a week in late Feb. or early March. Among the famous arts festivals is the Venice Film Festival in Sept. Venice also plays host, in the ten days before Ash Wednesday, to a large carnival. Major music festivals are the Maggio Musicale Fiorentino in Florence (May–June), the Ravenna Festival (June–July), the Spoleto Festival (June–July), the Rossini Opera Festival at Pesaro (Aug.) and the Verona Summer Opera Festival (July–Sept.).

Libraries

In 2002 there were 12,614 public libraries, four National libraries and 1,924 Higher Education libraries; they held a combined 93,629,000 volumes. There were 274,425,000 visits to the public libraries in 1997.

Museums and Galleries

In 2002 there were 192 museums and galleries and 198 archeological sites. There were 31,041,436 visitors, up from 29,543,020 in 2001.

DIPLOMATIC REPRESENTATIVES

Of Italy in the United Kingdom (14 Three Kings Yard, Davies St., London, W1K 4EH)
Ambassador: Giancarlo Aragona.

Of the United Kingdom in Italy (Via XX Settembre 80A, 00187, Rome)
Ambassador: Sir Ivor Roberts, KCMG.

Of Italy in the USA (3000 Whitehaven St., NW, Washington, D.C., 20008)
Ambassador: Giovanni Castellaneta.

Of the USA in Italy (Via Veneto 119/A, Rome)
Ambassador: Ronald P. Spogli.

Of Italy to the United Nations
Ambassador: Marcello Spatafora.

FURTHER READING

Istituto Nazionale di Statistica. *Annuario Statistico Italiano.—Compendio Statistico Italiano* (Annual).—*Italian Statistical Abstract* (Annual).—*Bollettino Mensile di Statistica* (Monthly).

Absalom, R., *Italy since 1880: a Nation in the Balance?* Harlow, 1995

Bufacchi, Vittorio and Burgess, Simon, *Italy since 1989*. Macmillan, London, 1999

Burnett, Stanton H. and Mantovani, Luca, *The Italian Guillotine: Operation 'Clean Hands' and the Overthrow of Italy's First Republic.* Rowman and Littlefield, Oxford, 1999

Di Scala, S. M., *Italy from Revolution to Republic: 1700 to the Present.* Boulder (CO), 1995

Duggan, Christopher, *A Concise History of Italy.* CUP, 1994

Frei, M., *Italy: the Unfinished Revolution.* London, 1996

Furlong, P., *Modern Italy: Representation and Reform.* London, 1994

Gilbert, M., *Italian Revolution: the Ignominious End of Politics, Italian Style.* Boulder (CO), 1995

Ginsborg, Paul, *Italy and its Discontents, 1980–2001.* Penguin, London, 2002

Gundie, S. and Parker, S. (eds.) *The New Italian Republic: from the Fall of the Berlin Wall to Berlusconi.* London, 1995

McCarthy, P., *The Crisis of the Italian State: from the Origins of the Cold War to the Fall of Berlusconi.* London, 1996

OECD, *OECD Economic Surveys 1998–99: Italy.* Paris, 1998

Plant, Margaret, *Venice: Fragile City 1797–1997.* Yale Univ. Press, 2002

Putnam, R., *et al.*, *Making Democracy Work: Civic Traditions in Modern Italy.* Princeton Univ. Press, 1993

Richards, C., *The New Italians.* London, 1994

Smith, D. M., *Modern Italy: A Political History.* Yale Univ. Press, 1997

Sponza, L. and Zancani, D., *Italy.* [Bibliography] ABC-Clio, Oxford and Santa Barbara (CA), 1995

Turner, Barry, (ed.) *Italy Profiled.* Macmillan, London, 1999

Volcanasek, Mary L., *Constitutional Politics in Italy.* Macmillan, London, 1999

National Statistical Office: Istituto Nazionale di Statistica (ISTAT), 16 Via Cesare Balbo, 00184 Rome.

Website: http://www.istat.it

National library: Biblioteca Nazionale Centrale, Vittorio Emanuele II, Viale Castro Pretorio, Rome.

JAMAICA

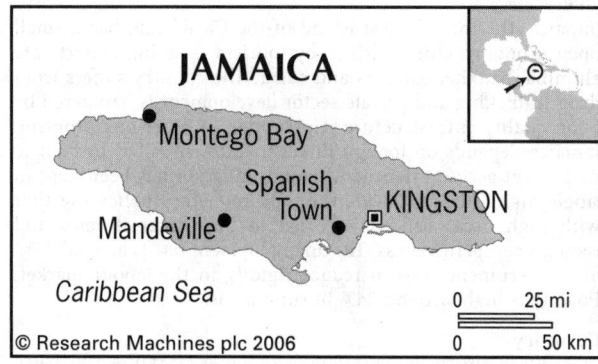

Capital: Kingston
Population projection, 2010: 2·70m.
GDP per capita, 2003: (PPP$) 4,104
HDI/world rank: 0·738/98

KEY HISTORICAL EVENTS

Jamaica was discovered by Columbus in 1494 and was occupied by the Spaniards from 1509 until 1655 when the island was captured by the English. In 1661 a representative constitution was established consisting of a governor, privy council, legislative council and legislative assembly. The slavery introduced by the Spanish was augmented as sugar production increased in value and extent in the 18th century. The plantation economy collapsed with the abolition of the slave trade in the late 1830s. The 1866 Crown Colony government was introduced with a legislative council. In 1884 a partially elective legislative council was instituted. Women were enfranchised in 1919. By the late 1930s, demands for self-government increased and the constitution of Nov. 1944 stated that the governor was to be assisted by a freely-elected house of representatives of 32 members, a legislative council (the upper house) of 15 members, and an executive council. In 1958 Jamaica joined with Trinidad, Barbados, the Leeward Islands and the Windward Islands to create the West Indies Federation. In 1959 internal self-government was achieved. Jamaica withdrew from the West Indies Federation in 1961 and became an independent state within the British Commonwealth in 1962.

TERRITORY AND POPULATION

Jamaica is an island which lies in the Caribbean Sea about 150 km south of Cuba. The area is 10,991 sq. km (4,244 sq. miles). The population at the census of Sept. 2001 was 2,607,632, distributed on the basis of the 13 parishes of the island as follows: Kingston and St Andrew, 651,880; St Thomas, 91,604; Portland, 80,205; St Mary, 111,466; St Ann, 166,762; Trelawny, 73,066; St James, 175,127; Hanover, 67,037; Westmoreland, 138,947; St Elizabeth, 146,404; Manchester, 185,801; St Catherine, 482,308; Clarendon, 237,024. 2001 density: 237 per sq. km. There is a worldwide Jamaican diaspora of more than 2m. The estimated population in 2005 was 2·65m.

The UN gives a projected population for 2010 of 2·70m.

Chief towns: Kingston, 579,137 (in 2001), metropolitan area; (2001 figures) Spanish Town, 131,515; Montego Bay, 96,488; Portmore (1995), 93,800; May Pen, 57,334; Mandeville (1995), 39,900.

In 2003, 52·2% of the population were urban. The population is about 92% of African ethnic origin.

SOCIAL STATISTICS

Vital statistics (2002): births, 52,300 (20·0 per 1,000 population); deaths, 16,900 (6·5); marriages (1999), 26,871 (10·4); divorces (1999), 1,131 (0·4). There were 17,669 emigrants in 1995, mainly to the USA. Expectation of life at birth, 2003, 69·0 years for males and 72·5 years for females. Annual population growth rate, 1991–2002, 0·8%; infant mortality, 2001, 17 per 1,000 live births; fertility rate, 2001, 2·4 births per woman.

CLIMATE

A tropical climate but with considerable variation. High temperatures on the coast are usually mitigated by sea breezes, while upland areas enjoy cooler and less humid conditions. Rainfall is plentiful over most of Jamaica, being heaviest in May and from Aug. to Nov. The island lies in the hurricane zone. Kingston, Jan. 76°F (24·4°C), July 81°F (27·2°C). Annual rainfall 32" (800 mm).

CONSTITUTION AND GOVERNMENT

Under the Constitution of Aug. 1962 the Crown is represented by a Governor-General appointed by the Crown on the advice of the Prime Minister. The Governor-General is assisted by a Privy Council of six appointed members. The Legislature comprises the *House of Representatives* and the *Senate.* The Senate consists of 21 senators appointed by the Governor-General, 13 on the advice of the Prime Minister, eight on the advice of the Leader of the Opposition. The House of Representatives (60 members) is elected by universal adult suffrage for a period not exceeding five years. Electors and elected must be Jamaican or Commonwealth citizens resident in Jamaica for at least 12 months before registration. It is likely that Jamaica will become a republic in the early part of the 21st century, with Queen Elizabeth II being replaced as head of state by a ceremonial president.

National Anthem

'Eternal Father, bless our land'; words by H. Sherlock, tune by R. Lightbourne.

RECENT ELECTIONS

In parliamentary elections held on 16 Oct. 2002 the People's National Party (PNP) won a fourth consecutive term (the third under Prime Minister Percival J. Patterson) with 34 seats (down from 50 in 1997) and 52·2% of votes cast, while the Jamaica Labour Party (JLP) took 26 (up from 10 in 1997), with 47·2% of the vote. Turnout was 56·3%.

CURRENT ADMINISTRATION

Governor-General: Kenneth Hall.

In March 2006 the cabinet comprised:

Prime Minister and Minister of Defence, Sports and Women's Affairs: Portia Simpson-Miller; b. 1945 (PNP; sworn in on 30 March 2006).

Minister of Agriculture and Land: Roger Clarke. *Education and Youth:* Maxine Henry-Wilson. *Finance and Planning:* Omar Davies. *Foreign Affairs and Foreign Trade:* Anthony Hylton. *Health:* Horace Dalley. *Housing, Transportation and Works:* Robert Pickersgill. *Industry, Commerce, Science and Technology:* Phillip Paulwell. *Information and Development:* Colin Campbell. *Justice and Attorney General:* Arnold Nicholson. *Labour and Social Security:* Derrick Kellier. *Local Government and Environment:* Dean Peart. *National Security:* Peter Phillips. *Tourism, Entertainment and Culture:* Aloun N'dombet Assamba.

Cabinet Website: http://www.cabinet.gov.jm

CURRENT LEADERS

Portia Simpson-Miller

Position
Prime Minister

Introduction
In Feb. 2005 Portia Simpson-Miller won an internal party election to succeed P. J. Patterson as leader of the ruling People's National Party (PNP), and so became Jamaica's first female prime minister.

Early Life
Portia Simpson-Miller was born on 12 Dec. 1945 in Wood Hall, St Catherine's Parish, Jamaica. She was educated at St Martin's High School and the Union Institute, Miami, USA, from where she graduated with a degree in public administration. She became a councillor for the left-leaning PNP in 1974, winning the inner-city seat of Trench Town West in the Kingston & St Andrew Corporation. In 1977, in the administration of Michael Manley, she was appointed parliamentary secretary in the ministry of local government. Simpson-Miller was elected vice-president of the PNP in 1978, a post she held for the next 27 years. Despite the PNP's crushing defeat in the 1980 general election, she retained her councillor's seat and from 1983–89 served as the party spokesperson on women's affairs and pensions, social security and consumer affairs.

In the 1989 general election, when Manley returned the PNP to power, Simpson-Miller was elected MP for South West St Andrew and appointed minister of labour, social security and sport. Following Manley's resignation in 1992 she unsuccessfully challenged Patterson for the premiership. Promoted to minister for tourism and sport in 2000, Simpson-Miller won plaudits for her work to rebuild the tourism sector in the wake of the 11 Sept. 2001 attacks on the USA. Following the general election of Oct. 2002 she regained the local government portfolio in an expanded ministry of local government, community development and sport.

On 25 Feb. 2006 Simpson-Miller narrowly defeated Peter Phillips to become Patterson's successor as head of the PNP and prime minister-elect. She was sworn in to office on 30 March 2006.

Career in Office
Simpson-Miller has prioritized tackling poverty and Jamaica's high crime rate. She has called for 'a more united, engaged, and spiritually strong nation' to play a dynamic role within the Caribbean Community.

DEFENCE

In 2003 defence expenditure totalled US$52m. (US$20 per capita), representing 0·7% of GDP.

Army
The Jamaica Defence Force consists of a Regular and a Reserve Force. Total strength (Army, 2002), 2,500. Reserves, 950.

Navy
The Coast Guard, numbering 190 in 2002, operates seven inshore patrol craft based at Port Royal.

Air Force
The Air Wing of the Jamaica Defence Force was formed in July 1963 and has since been expanded and trained successively by the British Army Air Corps and Canadian Air Force personnel. There are no combat aircraft. Personnel (2002), 140.

INTERNATIONAL RELATIONS

Jamaica is a member of the UN, WTO, the Commonwealth, IOM, OAS, Inter-American Development Bank, ACS, CARICOM and is an ACP member state of the ACP-EU relationship.

ECONOMY

Agriculture accounted for 5·5% of GDP in 2002, industry 29·1% and services 65·3%.

Overview
Jamaica, the third largest island of the Caribbean, has a small open economy, chiefly driven by tourism. Leading exports are alumina, bauxite, bananas and sugar. The country suffers from drug trafficking and private sector development is hampered by poor quality infrastructure. Corruption is a serious problem. Jamaica depends on foreign direct investment (FDI) to finance its current account deficit. Although inflation has been kept in single digits since 1997–98, the tight monetary policy together with high fiscal deficits have led to high interest rates and reduced competitiveness. The unemployment rate is around 15%. The government aims to reduce rigidity in the labour market. Poverty is high, around 24% in rural areas.

Currency
The unit of currency is the *Jamaican dollar* (JMD) of 100 *cents*. The Jamaican dollar was floated in Sept. 1990. Inflation was 12·9% in 2003 and 12·8% in 2004. Foreign exchange reserves were US$1,839m. in June 2002 and total money supply was J$52,360m.

Budget
Budgetary central government revenue and expenditure for fiscal years ending 31 March (in J$1m.):

	2001	2002	2003
Revenue	108,719	118,266	131,088
Expenditure	121,983	145,944	182,831

The chief items of current revenue are income taxes, consumption taxes and customs duties. The chief items of current expenditure are public debt, education and health.

Performance
Jamaica has been experiencing major economic difficulties in the past decade, with negative growth in 1996, 1997 and 1998. The economy has recovered slightly in the meantime, with growth of 2·0% in 2003 and 2·5% in 2004. Total GDP in 2004 was US$8·0bn.

Banking and Finance
The central bank and bank of issue is the Bank of Jamaica. The *Governor* is Derick Milton Latibeaudiere, OJ.

In 2002 there were five commercial banks, three development banks and two other banks (National Export-Import Bank of Jamaica and the National Investment Bank of Jamaica). Total assets of commercial banks in 1995 were J$121,324·9m.; deposits were J$89,135·4m.

There is a stock exchange in Kingston, which participates in the regional Caribbean exchange.

ENERGY AND NATURAL RESOURCES

Environment
In 2002 carbon dioxide emissions from the consumption and flaring of fossil fuels were the equivalent of 4·2 tonnes per capita.

Electricity
The Jamaica Public Service Co. is the public supplier. Total installed capacity, 2000, 1·4m. kW. Production in 2000 was 6·63bn. kWh; consumption per capita in 2000 was 2,518 kWh.

Oil and Gas
There is an oil refinery in Kingston.

Minerals
Jamaica is the third largest producer of bauxite, behind Australia and Guinea. Ceramic clays, marble, silica sand and gypsum are

also commercially viable. Production in 2001 (in tonnes): bauxite ore, 12·4m.; limestone, 3·5m.; sand and gravel, 2·2m.; gypsum, 320,323.

Agriculture

In 2001 there were 174,000 ha. of arable land and 110,000 ha. of permanent crops.

2000 production (in 1,000 tonnes): sugarcane, 2,600; yams, 196; bananas, 130; coconuts, 115; oranges, 72; grapefruit and pomelos, 42; pumpkins and squash, 42; plantains, 34.

Livestock (2000): cattle, 400,000; goats, 440,000; pigs, 180,000; poultry, 11m. Livestock products, 2000 (in 1,000 tonnes): beef and veal, 15; pork, bacon and ham, 7; poultry meat, 73.

Forestry

Forests covered 325,000 ha. in 2000, or 30·0% of the total land area. Timber production was 874,000 cu. metres in 2001.

Fisheries

Catches in 2001 totalled approximately 5,700 tonnes, of which 92% were sea fish.

INDUSTRY

Alumina production, 2002, 3·6m. tonnes. Output of other products (in tonnes): cement (2002), 621,831; residual fuel oil (2000), 533,000; distillate fuel oil (2000), 193,000; sugar (2002), 174,949; petrol (2000), 135,000; wheat flour (2000), 130,000; molasses (2003), 72,631; fertilizer (1995), 57,500; cigarettes (2000), 991m. units; rum (2003), 25·5m. litres. In 2001 industry accounted for 30·8% of GDP, with manufacturing contributing 13·0%.

Labour

Total labour force (2000), 1·11m., of whom 933,500 were employed. In 1998, 258,600 were employed in community, social and personal services; 204,400 in wholesale and retail trade, restaurants and hotels; 200,100 in agriculture, hunting, forestry and fishing; and 78,400 in construction. In 2000 the unemployment rate was 15·5% (22·3% for females and 10·2% for males).

INTERNATIONAL TRADE

Foreign debt was US$5,477m. in 2002.

Imports and Exports

Value of imports and domestic exports for calendar years (in US$1m.):

	1998	1999	2000	2001	2002
Imports f.o.b.	2,743·9	2,685·6	3,004·3	3,072·6	3,179·6
Exports f.o.b.	1,613·4	1,499·1	1,562·8	1,454·4	1,309·1

Principal imports in 2000 (% of total): machinery and transport equipment 22·6%, mineral fuels, lubricants and related minerals 19·6%, miscellaneous manufactured articles 13·6% and food 13·5%.

Principal domestic exports in 2000 (% of total): crude materials (excluding fuels) 56·9%, food 17·3%, miscellaneous manufactured articles 12·0% and chemicals 5·2%.

Main import suppliers, 2000: USA, 44·8%; Trinidad and Tobago, 10·0%; Japan, 6·0%; France, 5·0%; Venezuela, 3·9%. Main export markets, 2000: USA, 39·1%; UK, 11·5%; Canada, 10·2%; Norway, 9·1%; Japan, 2·3%.

COMMUNICATIONS

Roads

In 2002 the island had about 18,746 km of roads (70·1% surfaced). In 2002 there were 197,500 passenger cars and 56,900 lorries and vans. There were 292 fatalities in traffic accidents in 2002.

Civil Aviation

International airlines operate through the Norman Manley and Sangster airports at Palisadoes and Montego Bay. In 2000 Sangster International was the busiest for passenger traffic, handling 2,739,000 passengers and 6,400 tonnes of freight. Norman Manley airport is busier for freight, handling 20,680 tonnes of freight but only 1,415,862 passengers. Air Jamaica, originally set up in conjunction with BOAC and BWIA in 1966, became a new company, Air Jamaica (1968) Ltd. In 1969 it began operations as Jamaica's national airline. In 1999 scheduled airline traffic of Jamaica-based carriers flew 35·1m. km and carried 1,670,000 passengers.

Shipping

In 2002 the merchant marine totalled 75,000 GRT, including oil tankers 2,000 GRT. In 2001 there were 3,574 visits to all ports; 15·6m. tonnes of cargo were handled. In 2002 Kingston had 2,520 visits and handled 11·1m. tonnes. In 1997 vessels totalling 12,815,000 NRT entered ports and vessels totalling 6,457,000 NRT cleared.

Telecommunications

In 2002 there were 1,850,000 telephone subscribers (706·6 per 1,000 population) and there were 141,000 PCs in use (53·9 for every 1,000 persons). Mobile phone subscribers numbered 1,400,000 in 2002. In 1995 there were 600 fax machines and in 2002 there were 600,000 Internet users.

Postal Services

In 2003 there were 624 post offices, or one for every 4,250 persons.

SOCIAL INSTITUTIONS

Justice

The Judicature comprises a Supreme Court, a court of appeal, resident magistrates' courts, petty sessional courts, coroners' courts, a traffic court and a family court which was instituted in 1975. The Chief Justice is head of the judiciary. Jamaica was one of ten countries to sign an agreement in Feb. 2001 establishing a Caribbean Court of Justice to replace the British Privy Council as the highest civil and criminal court. In the meantime the number of signatories has risen to twelve. The court was inaugurated at Port-of-Spain, Trinidad on 16 April 2005.

In 1995, 54,595 crimes were reported, of which 33,889 were cleared up. The daily average prison population, 1995, was 3,289. In 2004 there were 1,445 murders. The rate of 53·9 per 100,000 persons is more than nine times that of the USA.

The population in penal institutions in Nov. 2003 was 4,744 (176 per 100,000 of national population).

Police

The Constabulary Force in 1995 stood at approximately 5,861 officers, sub-officers and constables (men and women).

Education

Adult literacy was 87·6% in 2003 (91·4% among females but only 83·8% among males).

Education is free in government-operated schools. Schools and colleges in 1994–95 (government-operated and grant-aided): basic, 1,694; infant, 29; primary, 792; primary with infant department, 83; all-age, 430; primary and junior high, 20; new secondary, 47; secondary high, 56; comprehensive high, 23; technical high, 12; agricultural/vocational, 6; special, 11; (independent): kindergarten/preparatory, 126; secondary high with preparatory department, 28; high/vocational, 5; business education, 29; (tertiary): teacher-training, 13.

Enrolment in 2002–03 in primary institutions was 332,900, in secondary institutions 226,500, in tertiary institutions 12,500 and in universities 20,700. Numbers of teachers, 1994–95: infant schools, 299; primary, 5,399; all-age and primary and junior high (grades 1 to 9), 6,424; new secondary, 1,852; secondary high, 4,132; technical high, 831; comprehensive high, 2,393; agricultural/vocational, 119.

The University of the West Indies is at Kingston. In 1994–95 it had 12,630 students, 800 external students and about 900 academic staff. The University of Technology in Kingston had 6,374 students, and the College of Agriculture, Science and Education in Portland, 533 students. Large numbers of educated Jamaicans have left the island over the past 30 years, but in the early part of the 21st century there are signs that young professionals are increasingly returning to Jamaica.

In 2000–01 total expenditure on education came to 6·6% of GNP and 11·1% of total government spending.

Health

In 2001 there were 27 hospitals with 4,606 beds. There were 2,253 physicians, 4,374 nurses and midwives, and 212 dentists in 2003.

Welfare

The official retirement age is 65 years (men) or 60 years (women). The old-age pension is made up of a basic benefit of J$900 a week (reduced to J$675 a week with annual average contributions of between 26 and 38 weeks; J$450 with 13 weeks to 25 weeks), plus an earnings-related benefit of J$0·06 a week for every J$13 of employer-employee contributions paid during the working lifetime.

Jamaica's social welfare projects also cover disability and survivor benefits, sickness and maternity, and work injury. Jamaica has no unemployment programmes.

RELIGION

Freedom of worship is guaranteed under the Constitution. The main Christian denominations are Anglican, Baptist, Roman Catholic, Methodist, Church of God, United Church of Jamaica and Grand Cayman (Presbyterian-Congregational-Disciples of Christ), Moravian, Seventh-Day Adventist, Pentecostal, Salvation Army and Quaker. Pocomania is a mixture of Christianity and African survivals. Non-Christians include Hindus, Jews, Muslims, Bahai followers and Rastafarians.

CULTURE

Broadcasting

There were (1995) seven commercial and one publicly owned broadcasting stations; the latter also operates a television service (colour by NTSC), and there was one commercial television station. There were 2·03m. radio receivers in 2000 and 510,000 TV sets in 2001.

Press

In 1996 there were three daily newspapers with a combined circulation of 158,000, at a rate of 63 per 1,000 inhabitants.

Tourism

In 2003 there were 1,350,284 staying visitors and 1,132,596 cruise ship arrivals. Tourism receipts in 2002 totalled US$1,209m.

DIPLOMATIC REPRESENTATIVES

Of Jamaica in the United Kingdom (1–2 Prince Consort Rd, London, SW7 2BZ)
High Commissioner: Gail Mathurin.

Of the United Kingdom in Jamaica (Trafalgar Rd, Kingston 10)
High Commissioner: Jeremy Cresswell.

Of Jamaica in the USA (1520 New Hampshire Ave., NW, Washington, D.C., 20036)
Ambassador: Gordon Shirley.

Of the USA in Jamaica (2 Oxford Rd, Kingston 5)
Ambassador: Brenda La Grange Johnson.

Of Jamaica to the United Nations
Ambassador: Stafford O. Neil.

Of Jamaica to the European Union
Ambassador: Evadne Coye.

FURTHER READING

Planning Institute of Jamaica. *Economic and Social Survey, Jamaica.* Annual.—*Survey of Living Conditions.* Annual
Statistical Institute of Jamaica. *Statistical Abstract.* Annual.—*Demographic Statistics.* Annual.—*Production Statistics.* Annual

Boyd, D., *Economic Management, Income Distribution, and Poverty in Jamaica.* Praeger Publishers, Westport (CT), 1988
Hart, R., *Towards Decolonisation: Political, Labour and Economic Developments in Jamaica 1938–1945.* Univ. of the West Indies Press, Kingston, 1999
Henke, H. W. and Mills, D., *Between Self-Determination and Dependency: Jamaica's Foreign Relations 1972–1989.* Univ. of the West Indies Press, Kingston, 2000
Ingram, K. E., *Jamaica.* [Bibliography] 2nd ed. ABC-Clio, Oxford and Santa Barbara (CA), 1997

National library: National Library of Jamaica, Kingston.
National Statistical Office: Statistical Institute of Jamaica (STATIN), POB 643, Kingston 5. *Director General:* Sonia Jackson.
Website: http://www.statinja.com

JAPAN

© Research Machines plc 2006

Nihon (or Nippon[1]) Koku
(Land of the Rising Sun)

Capital: Tokyo
Population projection, 2010: 128·46m.
GDP per capita, 2003: (PPP$) 27,967
HDI/world rank: 0·943/11

KEY HISTORICAL EVENTS

When the last ice sheets covered much of Asia, the sea level fell low enough for a land bridge to appear between Japan and the Asian mainland. This route was taken by hunter-gatherers from Asia who crossed into previously uninhabited Japan. By 10,000 BC the first pottery was produced in Japan and there was some cultivation. Rice was introduced, probably from Korea, by about 400 BC, and the use of metals around a century later, but agriculture and fixed settlements were confined to the south for a long period. During this time waves of migrants came from mainland Asia, bringing with them skills and technologies, including the Chinese characters for writing.

Religion, too, came from China: both Buddhism and Confucianism entered Japan, the former gaining a large following. In time traditional beliefs consolidated into Shintoism, which became the national religion. But, until the first millennium AD, there was no Japanese nation, although the legends of Japan tell us otherwise. According to myth, the first Japanese emperor was Jimmu around 600 BC, said to be a descendant of the sun goddess, Amaterasu.

In the first century BC, another wave of migrants entered Japan from Korea. The first Japanese state appeared in the central region of Honshu in the 7th century. This state soon controlled most of the west and centre of the island. In 710 the first permanent Japanese capital was established in Nara by Empress Genmei. In 794 the seat of power moved to Heian-kyo (present-day Kyoto).

Following the court and government tradition of China, Japan cut itself off from the outside world. As the imperial office became increasingly religious the day-to-day power passed into the hands of powerful nobles, such as the Fujiwara clan. Fujiwara Yoshifusa (804–872) was a powerful regent of Japan from 857 until his death, and by the 11th century the Fujiwaras were unchallenged rulers of the country. In the 12th century, however, Japan entered into a period of anarchy. The country passed under the control of barons, the *daimyo*, who exercised power through the warrior class known as the *samurai*.

Shogun

The anarchy ended when Taira Kiyamori seized power and made himself dictator. A civil war, the Gempei War, followed (1180–85). When Taira was defeated, power passed to Minamoto Yoritomo (1147–92), a distant descendant of the imperial family. Yoritomo established a new office, the *shogun*. For the next 700 years Japan was ruled by a military dictator, the shogun, while the emperor lived reclusively as a religious and national symbol.

At first the shogunate was seated in Kamakura, near modern Tokyo. Nine shoguns ruled during the Kamakura epoch (1185–1333) although latterly the Kamakura shogun was a puppet of the Hojo clan. In 1274 and 1281 Mongol attempts to invade Japan were unsuccessful: in 1281 the invasion was thwarted by a sudden typhoon that became known as the 'divine wind' (kami-kaze).

In 1334 a brief restoration of power to the emperor was ended by Ashikaga Takauji (1305–58), who established a strong military government. Subsequent members of the Ashikaga family ruled as shoguns based in Kyoto. Eventually this system, too, collapsed into anarchy, the victim of the ambitions of rival warlords. From 1467 to 1603 Japan suffered the Fighting Principalities (*Sengokujidai*). It was when the country was at its weakest that another powerful outside influence began to exert itself.

From 1543 Portuguese traders and missionaries arrived on the southern and western coasts. At first, trade was welcomed. Christianity, too, made converts after the Spanish Jesuit missionary St Francis Xavier landed in Japan in 1549. Along with western ideas and religion, the Portuguese, and later the Dutch, brought firearms. Three warlords in turn used western weapons to seize power and reunite the country. The last of this trio was Tokugawa Ieyasu (1542–1616), who held power from 1600. Ieyasu ordered the nobles to destroy their fortifications, except their principal residences, and encouraged the arts and learning as a preferred alternative to warfare.

Isolation

As the true rulers of Japan until 1869, the Tokugawa shogunate established itself at Edo (present-day Tokyo). They ruled harshly, subduing the warring lords by holding members of their families hostages. The Tokugawa perceived foreign influences as unsettling and a danger to their supremacy. For this reason, they decreed that Japan should become a closed society. In 1636 Japanese were forbidden to emigrate. Europeans were expelled, except for a single Dutch trading post in Nagasaki, which—after 1639—became Japan's only contact with the outside world. Christianity was suppressed and the ownership of firearms,

[1]Both forms are valid, and derive from different pronunciations of a Chinese character.

except by the central authorities, was made illegal. Japan entered 220 years of self-imposed isolation.

Cut off from outside influences, Japan gained stability and a strong sense of national identity. Yet this isolation came at a price. In 1853 a US fleet led by Commodore Matthew C. Perry appeared off the Japanese coast. Japan was forced to open up to international trade through the threat of invasion. Other western nations followed the American example. Japan was thrust into a modern world for which it was ill suited. The voices for reform grew and the Tokugawa shogunate, humiliated by Perry's mission, collapsed. Reformers seized Kyoto and parts of the west, but they needed a national symbol to legitimize their rule. In 1869 the shadowy figure of the emperor was called out of his cloistered life. His city, Edo, had by then been renamed Tokyo, meaning 'eastern capital'. The emperor surprised the country by his zeal for modernization which led to a period of rapid reform and transformed Japan into a modern nation.

But while a constitution was introduced, the resemblance to a western democracy was skin deep. Though the peasants were freed from serfdom, power remained in the hands of the nobility. Priority was given to developing industry and modern technology. Japan's rise as an industrial state began.

Rise of the Military

Much emphasis was given to modernizing the armed forces. A revitalized Japan defeated China in war in 1894–95 and gained Taiwan. In 1900 Japan intervened alongside the western powers against the Boxer Rebellion in China. An even greater shock was Japan's victory against Russia in 1903–04 in a war over Korea and Manchuria. Having contained Russian land forces in Manchuria, Japan astonished the west when the Japanese fleet appeared in the North Sea on its way to the Baltic. Russia's influence in the region faded and Japan received half of Sakhalin and the Kurile Islands. Later, with Russia removed from the scene, Japan annexed Korea (1910) and took control of parts of Manchuria.

In 1902 Japan made an alliance with Britain. To emphasize Japan's western credentials, Tokyo entered the First World War against Germany in 1914. Japanese forces took the German island colonies in the north and central Pacific and received these archipelagoes as a League of Nations Trust Territory in 1919. But greater rewards for their efforts in the war had been expected and Tokyo's disillusion with the west began. The collapse of world trade at the end of the 1920s brought hardship and helped the rise of political extremism and nationalism.

Japan began a phase of aggressive expansionism. In 1931 Japan invaded Manchuria and, two years later, installed the deposed last emperor of China as puppet emperor of Manchukuo. From 1932 Japanese forces entered various coastal and border areas of China, and in 1937 there was a full-scale war with China. Japanese forces took Shanghai in 1937, Guangzhou in 1938 and Nanjing in 1940. By the end of 1940 Japan had occupied French Indochina and formed a triple alliance (or Axis) with Nazi Germany and Fascist Italy.

Pearl Harbor

Under premier Gen. Tojo Hideki (1884–1948), Japan attacked the US fleet in Pearl Harbor, Hawaii in Dec. 1941. This action brought the United States into the Second World War (1939–45) and ranged Japan against forces that were superior in size and technology. Nevertheless, the war was initially in Japan's favour. Japanese forces swept through the Pacific and into Malaya and the Dutch East Indies (now Indonesia). The speed of Japan's ruthless advance overwhelmed the Allied powers as British and American positions were surrendered. The tide turned with the American victory at Midway in late 1942, but by the time Germany surrendered in May 1945 Japanese forces were still in control of large areas of the Pacific and Southeast Asia. In Aug. 1945 US planes dropped atomic bombs on the Japanese cities of Hiroshima and Nagasaki, devastating the two cities and causing more than 200,000 deaths. The emperor Hirohito (1926–89) surrendered.

The war had cost Japan dearly. Not only had two cities suffered the horror of atomic warfare, but many more Japanese had died in combat. Nearly 2m. Japanese were abandoned in China, most of whom were shipped to Siberia as prisoners. Japan was to be reformed by the occupying US forces under Gen. MacArthur. In 1945 Shintoism, which had become associated with aggressive nationalism, ceased to be the state religion. In the following year, the emperor renounced his divinity.

A new liberal constitution was introduced in 1946. Japan signed a peace treaty in 1951 at San Francisco and the American occupation of Japan ended in April 1952 when the country regained its independence. A separate peace treaty was concluded later between Japan and China. There was, however, no agreement with the Soviet Union, which, at American behest, had declared war against Japan in the closing days of the Second World War. Soviet forces occupied Sakhalin and the Kurile islands to which Japan still lays claim.

The new Japan remained a monarchy, albeit one in which the emperor was a figurehead. Japan renounced war and the threat or use of force, but retained 'Self Defence Forces'. Japanese cities and industry were rebuilt. An astonishing economic recovery was led by an aggressive export policy. Huge investment in new technology gave the country a dominant position in many industries including motor vehicles, shipbuilding, electrical goods, electronics and computers. Japan grew to be the world's second biggest economy. This success is owed, in part, to the protection of domestic markets.

The power of Japanese industry was reflected in the political power of a small number of major corporations. From 1955 until 1993 the political scene was dominated by the centre-right pro-business Liberal Democrats (LDP). However, a series of major financial scandals broke the party's monopoly and coalition governments followed. By 2000 the LDP had resumed its dominant role.

In recent years, Japan has shown more confidence in international relations. The country is a major donor of aid to developing countries. In 1992 the Diet (parliament) approved the contribution of Japanese military personnel and equipment to UN peacekeeping missions and in 2002 Japan contributed naval support vessels to the US-led intervention in Afghanistan. However, the country faces severe economic problems. A heavy international debt and domestic deflation left the Japanese economy in the doldrums at the turn of the century.

TERRITORY AND POPULATION

Japan consists of four major islands, Honshu, Hokkaido, Kyushu and Shikoku, and many small islands, with an area of 377,829 sq. km. Census population (1 Oct. 2000) 126,925,843 (males 62,110,764, females 64,815,079). Oct. 2005 population: 127,757,000; density, 338 per sq. km.

The UN gives a projected population for 2010 of 128·46m.

In 2003, 65·5% of the population lived in urban areas. Foreigners registered on 31 Dec. 2003 were 1,915,030: including 613,791 Koreans, 462,396 Chinese, 274,700 Brazilians, 185,237 Filipinos, 53,649 Peruvians, 47,836 Americans, 34,825 Thais, 23,853 Vietnamese, 22,862 Indonesians, 18,230 British, 14,234 Indians, 11,984 Canadians, 11,582 Australians, 9,707 Bangladeshis, 9,008 Malaysians and 1,846 stateless persons. In 2002 Japan accepted 14 asylum seekers.

Japanese overseas, Oct. 2002, 873,641; of these 315,976 lived in the USA, 72,343 in Brazil, 64,090 in China (26,267 in Hong Kong), 50,864 in the UK, 46,893 in Australia, 36,375 in Canada, 30,384 in France, 27,810 in Germany, 25,329 in Thailand and 20,697 in Singapore.

The official language is Japanese.

A law of May 1997 'on the promotion of Ainu culture' marked the first official recognition of the existence of an ethnic minority in Japan.

The areas, populations and chief cities of the principal islands (and regions) are:

Island/Region	Sq. km	Pop. estimate 2002	Chief cities
Hokkaido	83,454	5,670,000	Sapporo
Honshu/Tohoku	66,889	9,778,000	Sendai
Honshu/Kanto	32,423	40,871,000	Tokyo
Honshu/Chubu	66,790	21,718,000	Nagoya
Honshu/Kinki	33,110	22,754,000	Osaka
Honshu/Chugoku	31,915	7,718,000	Hiroshima
Shikoku	18,803	4,137,000	Matsuyama
Kyushu	42,170	13,447,000	Fukuoka
Okinawa	2,272	1,339,000	Naha

The leading cities, with population in 2003 (in 1,000), are:

Akashi	291	Machida	392
Akita	313	Maebashi	283
Amagasaki	462	Matsudo	466
Aomori	297	Matsuyama	475
Asahikawa	361	Miyazaki	306
Chiba	889	Morioka	281
Fujisawa	386	Nagano	359
Fukui	250	Nagasaki	419
Fukuoka	1,315	Nagoya	2,117
Fukushima	289	Naha	306
Fukuyama	407	Nara	364
Funabashi	557	Niigata	515
Gifu	402	Nishinomiya	442
Hachioji	524	Oita	439
Hakodate	283	Okayama	625
Hamamatsu	576	Okazaki	339
Higashiosaka	496	Osaka	2,490
Himeji	477	Otsu	294
Hirakata	403	Sagamihara	605
Hiratsuka	253	Saitama	1,038
Hiroshima	1,119	Sakai	787
Ibaraki	259	Sapporo	1,838
Ichihara	281	Sendai	991
Ichikawa	450	Shizuoka	469
Ichinomiya	278	Suita	344
Iwaki	363	Takamatsu	334
Kagoshima	546	Takatsuki	352
Kakogawa	266	Tokorozawa	332
Kanazawa	441	Tokushima	262
Kashiwa	328	Tokyo	8,083
Kasugai	291	Toyama	321
Kawagoe	326	Toyohashi	358
Kawaguchi	468	Toyonaka	388
Kawasaki	1,259	Toyota	345
Kitakyushu	997	Utsunomiya	446
Kobe	1,484	Wakayama	390
Kochi	327	Yamagata	251
Koriyama	332	Yao	267
Koshigaya	311	Yokkaichi	289
Kumamoto	656	Yokohama	3,467
Kurashiki	434	Yokosuka	435
Kyoto	1,386		

The Tokyo conurbation, with a population in 2000 of 26·44m., is the largest in the world, having overtaken New York around 1970.

SOCIAL STATISTICS

Statistics (in 1,000) for calendar years:

	1996	1997	1998	1999	2000	2001	2002
Births	1,207	1,192	1,203	1,178	1,191	1,171	1,154
Deaths	896	913	936	982	962	970	982

Crude birth rate of Japanese nationals in present area, 2002, was 9·2 per 1,000 population (1947: 34·3); crude death rate, 7·8; marriage rate per 1,000 persons, 6·0; divorce rate per 1,000

persons, 2·3. In 2002 the most popular age for marrying was 30·8 for males and 28·6 for females. The infant mortality rate per 1,000 live births, 3·0 (2002), is one of the lowest in the world. Expectation of life was 78·4 years for men and 85·4 years for women—the highest rate in the world overall and the highest rate among women—in 2003. The World Health Organization's 2004 World Health Report put the Japanese in first place in a 'healthy life expectancy' list, with an expected 75·0 years of healthy life for babies born in 2002. Japan had 25,606 centenarians in 2005. Japan has a very fast ageing population, stemming from a sharply declined fertility rate and one of the highest life expectancies in the world. The number of centenarians is increasing by more than 2,000 every year. Annual population growth rate, 1992–2002, 0·2%.

In 2003 the average number of children a Japanese woman bears in her life reached a record low of 1·29.

There were a record 34,427 suicides in 2003 (72·5% males).

CLIMATE

The islands of Japan lie in the temperate zone, northeast of the main monsoon region of southeast Asia. The climate is temperate with warm, humid summers and relatively mild winters except in the island of Hokkaido and northern parts of Honshu facing the Sea of Japan. There is a month's rainy season in June–July, but the best seasons are spring and autumn, although Sept. may bring typhoons. Tokyo, Jan. 5·8°C, July 25·4°C. Annual rainfall 1,467 mm. Hiroshima, Jan. 5·3°C, July 26·9°C. Annual rainfall 1,541 mm. Nagasaki, Jan. 6·8°C, July 26·6°C. Annual rainfall 1,960 mm. Osaka, Jan. 5·8°C, July 27·2°C. Annual rainfall 1,306 mm. Sapporo, Jan. −4·1°C, July 20·5°C. Annual rainfall 1,128 mm.

CONSTITUTION AND GOVERNMENT

The Emperor is Akihito (b. 23 Dec. 1933), who succeeded his father, Hirohito on 7 Jan. 1989 (enthroned, 12 Nov. 1990); married 10 April 1959, to Michiko Shoda (b. 20 Oct. 1934). *Offspring:* Crown Prince Naruhito (Hironomiya; b. 23 Feb. 1960); Prince Fumihito (Akishinomiya; b. 30 Nov. 1965); Princess Sayako (Norinomiya; b. 18 April 1969). Prince Naruhito married Masako Owada (b. 9 Dec. 1963) 9 June 1993. *Offspring:* Princess Aiko (b. 1 Dec. 2001). Princess Sayako married Yoshiki Kuroda (b. 17 April 1965) 15 Nov. 2005. The succession to the throne is fixed upon the male descendants. The 1947 constitution supersedes the Meiji constitution of 1889. In it the Japanese people pledge themselves to uphold the ideas of democracy and peace. The Emperor is the symbol of the unity of the people. Sovereign power rests with the people. The Emperor has no powers related to government. Fundamental human rights are guaranteed.

Legislative power rests with the *Diet*, which consists of the *House of Deputies* (Shugi-in), elected by men and women over 20 years of age for a four-year term, and an upper house, the *House of Councillors* (Sangi-in) of 242 members (96 elected by party list system with proportional representation according to the d'Hondt method and 146 from prefectural districts), one-half of its members being elected every three years. The number of members has been reduced in recent years. There had been 252 members until 2001 and 247 members from 2001 until elections of July 2004.

The number of members in the House of Deputies was reduced from 500 to 480 for the election of June 2000, of whom 300 were to be elected from single-seat constituencies, and 180 by proportional representation on a base of 11 regions. There is a 2% threshold to gain one of the latter seats. Donations to individual politicians are to be supplanted over five years by state subsidies to parties.

A new electoral law passed in Oct. 2000 gives voters a choice between individual candidates and parties when casting ballots for the proportional representation seats in the *House of Councillors.*

On becoming prime minister in April 2001 Junichiro Koizumi established a panel to consider introducing the direct election of prime ministers by popular vote.

National Anthem

'Kimigayo' ('The Reign of Our Emperor'); words 9th century, tune by Hayashi Hiromori. On 9 Aug. 1999 a law on the national flag and the national anthem was enacted. The law designates the Hinomaru and 'Kimigayo' as the national flag and national anthem of Japan. The 'Kimi' in 'Kimigayo' indicates the Emperor who is the symbol of the State and of the unity of the people, deriving his position from the will of the people with whom resides sovereign power; 'Kimigayo' depicts the state of being of the country as a whole.

GOVERNMENT CHRONOLOGY

Prime ministers since 1945. (Jt = Liberal Party; Mt = Democratic Party; NSt = Socialist Party of Japan; LDP = Liberal Democratic Party; NSt = New Japan Party; SSt = Renewal Party; SDP = Social Democratic Party; n/p = non party)

1945	military	Kantaro Suzuki
1945	military	Naruhito Kigashi-Kuni
1945–46	n/p	Kijuro Shidehara
1946–47	Jt	Shigeru Yoshida
1947–48	NSt	Tetsu Katayama
1948	Mt	Hitoshi Ashida
1948–54	Jt	Shigeru Yoshida
1954–56	LDP	Ichiro Hatoyama
1956–57	LDP	Tanzan Ishibashi
1957–60	LDP	Nobusuke Kishi
1960–64	LDP	Hayato Ikeda
1964–72	LDP	Eisaku Sato
1972–74	LDP	Kakuei Tanaka
1974–76	LDP	Takeo Miki
1976–78	LDP	Takeo Fukuda
1978–80	LDP	Masayoshi Ohira
1980	LDP	Masayoshi Ito
1980–82	LDP	Zenko Suzuki
1982–87	LDP	Yasuhiro Nakasone
1987–89	LDP	Noboru Takeshita
1989	LDP	Sosuke Uno
1989–91	LDP	Toshiki Kaifu
1991–93	LDP	Kiichi Miyazawa
1993–94	NSt	Morihiro Hosokawa
1994	SSt	Tsutomu Hata
1994–96	SDP	Tomiichi Murayama
1996–98	LDP	Ryutaro Hashimoto
1998–2000	LDP	Keizo Obuchi
2000	LDP	Michio Aoki
2000–01	LDP	Yoshiro Mori
2001–	LDP	Junichiro Koizumi

RECENT ELECTIONS

Elections to the House of Deputies were held on 11 Sept. 2005. Turnout was 67·5%. The Liberal Democratic Party (LDP; Jiyu Minshuto) gained 296 seats (with 38·2% of the vote); Democratic Party (Minshuto), 113 (31·0%); New Clean Government Party (New Komeito), 31 (13·3%); Communist Party of Japan (Nihon Kyosanto), 9 (7·3%); Social Democratic Party (SDP; Shakai Minshuto), 7 (5·5%); People's New Party (Kokumin Shinto), 4; New Party Nippon (Shinto Nippon), 1; New Party Daichi (Shinto Daichi), 1. Non-partisans took 18 seats. The ruling LDP relies on its support primarily from rural areas, with only a tenth of urban voters actively supporting it. Only 43 of the 480 elected MPs were women.

Elections to 121 seats of the House of Councillors were held on 11 July 2004. The Democratic Party gained 50 seats, LDP 49, New Komeito 11, SDP 2, Communist Party of Japan 4, and ind. 5. As a result the LDP held 115 seats, Democratic Party 82, New Komeito 24, Communist Party of Japan 9, Social Democratic Party 5 and ind. 7.

CURRENT ADMINISTRATION

Prime Minister: Junichiro Koizumi; b. 1942 (LDP; appointed 26 April 2001).

In March 2006 the LDP–New Clean Government Party coalition government comprised:

Minister of Justice: Seiken Sugiura. *Foreign Affairs:* Taro Aso. *Finance:* Sadakazu Tanigaki. *Education, Culture, Sports, Science and Technology:* Kenji Kosaka. *Health, Labour and Welfare:* Jiro Kawasaki. *Agriculture, Forestry and Fisheries:* Shoichi Nakagawa. *Economy, Trade and Industry:* Toshihiro Nikai. *Land, Infrastructure and Transport:* Kazuo Kitagawa. *Internal Affairs and Communications, Minister of State for Privatization of the Postal Services:* Heizo Takenaka. *Environment, Minister of State for Okinawa and Northern Territories Affairs, Minister in Charge of Global Environmental Problems:* Yuriko Koike.

Chief Cabinet Secretary: Shinzo Abe. *Minister of State for Defence:* Fukushiro Nukaga. *Chairman of the National Public Safety Commission, Minister of State for Disaster Management and for National Emergency Legislation:* Tetsuo Kutsukake. *Minister of State for Science and Technology Policy, Food Safety and Information Technology:* Iwao Matsuda. *Minister of State for Economic and Fiscal Policy, and Financial Services:* Kaoru Yosano. *Minister of State for Administrative and Regulatory Reform, Special Zones for Structural Reform, and Regional Revitalization:* Kouki Chuma. *Minister of State for Youth Affairs and Measures for Declining Birth Rate, and Gender Equality:* Kuniko Inoguchi.

Office of the Prime Minister: http://www.kantei.go.jp

CURRENT LEADERS

Junichiro Koizumi

Position
Prime Minister

Introduction
Representing the Liberal Democratic Party (LDP), Koizumi became prime minister in 2001 following the resignation of Yoshiro Mori. Faced with a legacy of economic stagnation and a troubled banking system, he has sought, with popular backing, a more radical approach to domestic reform. Internationally, he has tried to effect a thawing of relations with North Korea, but courted wider regional hostility by his visits to Tokyo's Yasukuni shrine honouring Japan's war dead.

Early Life
Born on 8 Jan. 1942 in Yokosuka City in the Kanagawa Prefecture, Koizumi studied economics at Keio University. After graduating in 1967, he became involved in politics, working in 1970 as a secretary for the future prime minister Takeo Fukuda (1976–78). In 1972 he was elected to the Diet, where he served continuously until his premiership. He was appointed to his first cabinet post in Dec. 1988, with responsibility for health and welfare. He served in that capacity for several terms in subsequent governments through the 1990s, and also for a time as minister of posts and telecommunications. Within the LDP, he held senior posts from the early 1980s before being elected party president at his third attempt in 2001.

Following the resignation of Yoshiro Mori in April 2001, Koizumi stood against three other candidates to succeed him as LDP party leader and prime minister. Relatively unknown, and espousing radical proposals to counter Japan's economic problems, he defeated former prime minister Ryutaro Hashimoto (1996–98), whose own term had seen a period of economic decline.

Career in Office

On election, Koizumi attempted to reignite Japan's economy, signalling his intention to privatize the massive postal and savings system (the world's biggest financial institution). Nonetheless, recession continued. His perceived inaction on reform and an inability to stem deflation or the departure of businesses from Japan led the opposition to mount a confidence vote in July 2002. However, Koizumi survived with 280 votes to 185. In Sept. 2002 he reshuffled his cabinet, dismissing his financial services minister to force through a controversial reform to help the banking sector. For the first time, the Bank of Japan allowed the government to use a 15trn. yen emergency fund to invest in commercial banks.

Improvements in the Japanese economy during 2003 eased pressure on Koizumi's leadership, and in the Nov. 2003 parliamentary elections the LDP won 237 seats in the 480-member Diet. Pursuing his policy of privatizing the postal and savings system in the face of broad parliamentary opposition, including from within his own party, Koizumi called a snap election in Aug. 2005. The LDP was returned with an increased mandate in Sept., vindicating his privatization plan and confirming his popular standing in the country.

At the international level, Koizumi has sought to improve relations with North Korea, making two controversial visits to Pyongyang during his premiership. However, the issue of the disappearance of several Japanese citizens in the 1970s and 1980s, attributable to North Korea's intelligence services, remains unresolved to Japan's satisfaction. Koizumi has also visited Seoul and offered an apology for the suffering that South Korea endured under Japanese colonial rule. Relations with China meanwhile deteriorated from April 2005 over Japan's textbook portrayal of its military history. On the wider stage, Koizumi's government launched Japan's application in Sept. 2004 for a permanent Japanese seat on the UN Security Council. In April 2006 Koizumi became Japan's longest-serving prime minister since the early 1970s.

DEFENCE

Japan has renounced war as a sovereign right and the threat or the use of force as a means of settling disputes with other nations. Its troops had not previously been able to serve abroad, but in 1992 the House of Representatives voted to allow up to 2,000 troops to take part in UN peacekeeping missions. A law of Nov. 1994 authorizes the Self-Defence Force to send aircraft abroad in rescue operations where Japanese citizens are involved. Following the attacks on New York and Washington of 11 Sept. 2001, legislation was passed allowing Japan's armed forces to take part in operations in the form of logistical support assisting the US-led war on terror. The legislation permits troops to take part in limited overseas operations but not to engage in combat. In May 2003 parliament passed a series of measures in response to North Korea's nuclear programme. Central government won increased control over the military which now has greater freedom to requisition civilian property in the event of attack.

In Jan. 1991 Japan and the USA signed a renewal agreement under which Japan pays 40% of the costs of stationing US forces and 100% of the associated labour costs. US forces in Japan totalled 43,550 in 2004, nearly half of them on Okinawa. A US-Japanese agreement of Dec. 1996 stipulates that one fifth of the territory on Okinawa occupied by the US military is to be returned to local landowners by 2008.

Total armed forces in 2004 numbered 239,900.

Defence expenditure in 2003 totalled US$42,835m. (US$337 per capita), representing 1·0% of GDP.

Army

The 'Ground Self-Defence Force' is organized in five regional commands and in 2004 had a strength of 148,200 and a reserve of 37,300. The USA maintains an army force of 1,750.

Navy

The 'Maritime Self-Defence Force' is tasked with coastal protection and defence of the sea lanes to 1,000 nautical miles range from Japan. The main elements of the fleet are organized into four escort flotillas based at Yokosuka, Kure, Sasebo, Maizuru and Ominato. The submarines are based at Yokosuka and Kure.

Personnel in 2004 numbered 44,400 including the Naval Air Arm. The combatant fleet, all home-built, includes 16 diesel submarines, 45 destroyers and nine frigates. The Air Arm operated 80 combat aircraft and 102 armed helicopters in 2004. Air Arm personnel was estimated at 9,800 in 2004.

Air Force

An 'Air Self-Defence Force' was inaugurated on 1 July 1954. Its equipment includes (2004) F-15 *Eagles*, F-4E *Phantoms* and Mitsubishi F-1 fighters.

Strength (2004) 45,600 operating 280 combat aircraft.

INTERNATIONAL RELATIONS

In terms of total aid given, Japan was the second most generous country in the world in 2004 after the USA, donating US$8·9bn. in international aid in the course of the year. This represented 0·19% of its GNI.

Japan is a member of the UN, BIS, OECD, WTO, Inter-American Development Bank, Asian Development Bank, Colombo Plan, APEC, IOM and the Antarctic Treaty.

ECONOMY

In 2001 services accounted for 71·0% of GDP, industry 27·6% and agriculture, forestry and fisheries 1·4%.

Overview

The world's second largest economy after the USA, Japan recorded growth of 2·7% in 2004 but has suffered a series of recessions in the past decade. Output per capita, measured on purchasing power parity terms, has fallen from 83% of the US level in the early 1990s to less than 75% in 2004. Weak performance during the late 1990s and early 2000s is attributed to the collapse of the asset price bubble, problems in the banking sector, weak competition and outdated regulations. Growth since 2002 has been robust, with exports initially driving growth before momentum shifted to strong domestic demand and private investment. According to the IMF, longstanding problems of sluggish economic activity, deflation and financial and corporate sector weaknesses are easing. Recent strong investment has allowed for the upgrading of ageing capital stock and strong consumption growth has improved labour market conditions and business confidence. Unemployment has fallen to below 4·5% from record highs of 5·5% in 2002 and 2003.

According to the IMF, the strengthening of the economy is attributable to steady reforms in labour and product markets, success in bank balance sheet restructuring and corporate efforts to eliminate excess capacity and debt. The traditional system of lifetime employment, limiting labour market flexibility, is slowly being replaced by more flexible labour contracts. The system of Keiretsu (closely knit production chains linking manufacturers, suppliers and distributors) is being eroded. Foreign direct investment tripled between 1998–2003, although its level as a percentage of GDP remains the lowest in the OECD.

Labour productivity in Japan is more than 30% below that of the USA, despite Japan having several features characteristic of growth. Japan has the highest proportion of the working age population with at least a secondary school education in the OECD area, research and development (R&D) expenditure is 3% of GDP (third highest in the OECD), and growth in capital investment is 4·5% (second highest in the OECD). Gross fixed investment was 25% of GDP in 2005, considerably above that of other G7 countries.

The Long-Term Trade Agreement (LTTA) led to Japan being China's most important trading partner in the late 1970s, with Japan particularly interested in building closer ties with a regional oil supplier. Since the adoption of market policies in China, domestic demand for energy has increased rapidly, constraining the export market and causing friction between the two countries. Building further international ties has been a priority of the Chinese government, leading to Japan's relative decline as China's major trading partner. Political crises over past Japanese aggressions have mounted since 2004, although the economic impact is yet to be seen.

Monetary easing, with short term interest rates of around 0%, succeeded in boosting the monetary base by 60% between 2002 and 2005, although it failed to end the deflationary period which began in 1999. The savings rate plummeted from 18% in 1981 to 6% in 2002, though a tradition of asceticism allied to land price increases has helped Japanese households retain a high level of net wealth relative to other OECD countries. 85% of the population have savings with Japan Post which, with assets of over US$3trn., is one of the largest financial institutions in the world and the largest life insurer in Japan. Privatization of the postal service, approved in 2005, will split it into four separate units for savings, insurance, postal services and personnel and property management.

A fall in bank lending since 1998 has reduced total bank credit by 30% of GDP. Lending continued to drop in 2005 despite increased mortgage loans from banks that have taken the place of government housing loans. The banking system has been strengthened by tighter regulation introduced in the Program for Financial Revival (PFR). The combination of the PFR and corporate sector improvements have succeeded in halving non-performing loans to below 3% of total loans in major banks in 2005, although the progress of regional banks has been less strong. Despite sectoral improvements, bank profitability remains low by OECD standards, with small profit margins and greater vulnerability to shocks and losses. Poor profitability has been attributed by the IMF to excessive reliance on real-estate collateral, weaknesses in credit allocation and limitations in the nature of client–bank relations.

In 2004 public debt stood at 166% GDP, the highest level in the OECD, following a decade of high deficits. Since long-term interest rates are greater than nominal GDP growth, the size of public debt relative to GDP has continued to rise. High levels of public debt reflect institutional features that promote fiscal recklessness, including lenient budget rules and implicit guarantees by central government to support local jurisdictions. Government revenue stands at 30% of GDP and is among the lowest in the OECD. The budget deficit peaked at 8% in 2002 and 2003, attributable to a 5% rise in spending and a decline in revenues of 3% owing to weak growth. Further use of fiscal instruments is thus constrained. With tax cuts and persistently slow economic growth in the recent past, the share of tax revenue in GDP is the second lowest in the OECD. The authorities aim to constrain fiscal deficit growth and to achieve a budget surplus by the early 2010s. Financial institutions have made progress in strengthening their positions.

The ratio of elderly to young people is increasing more rapidly than in the other OECD countries. Japan is one of the few OECD countries where the working-age population started declining in the early 2000s. The government projects a 0·7% per annum decline in the working-age population between 2004–10, increasing the elderly dependency ratio by 3%. Pension expenditure has doubled from 6% to 12% of national income, putting pressure on public finances. Despite 2004 reforms designed to cut pension benefits, social security outlays will rise by 1·5% of GDP by 2010.

Currency

The unit of currency is the *yen* (JPY). Inflation rates (based on OECD statistics):

1995	1996	1997	1998	1999	2000	2001	2002	2003	2004
−0·1%	0·0%	1·7%	0·7%	−0·3%	−0·8%	−0·8%	−0·9%	−0·3%	0·0%

Japan's foreign exchange reserves totalled US$844·5bn. in Dec. 2004 (US$172·4bn. in 1995)—the highest in the world. Gold reserves in June 2002 were 24·60m. troy oz. In Dec. 2003 the currency in circulation consisted of 76,910,000m. yen Bank of Japan notes and 4,423,000m. yen subsidiary coins.

Budget

Ordinary revenue and expenditure for fiscal year ending 31 March 2004 balanced at 81,789,100m. yen.

Of the proposed revenue (in yen) in 2003, 41,786,000m. was to come from taxes and stamps, 36,445,000m. from public bonds. Main items of expenditure: social security, 18,990,700m.; local government, 16,392,600m.; public works, 8,097,100m.; education, 6,471,200m.; defence, 4,953,000m.

The outstanding national debt incurred by public bonds was estimated in March 2002 to be 448,162,000m. yen.

The estimated 2003 budgets of the prefectures and other local authorities forecast a total revenue of 86,211,000m. yen, to be made up partly by local taxes and partly by government grants and local loans.

Performance

Real GDP growth rates (based on OECD statistics):

1995	1996	1997	1998	1999	2000	2001	2002	2003	2004
2·0%	3·4%	1·8%	−1·0%	−0·1%	2·4%	0·2%	−0·3%	1·4%	2·7%

The real GDP growth rate for 2004 was 2·7% despite negative growth in both the second and third quarters. In 2004 Japan's total GDP was US$4,623·4bn., the second highest in the world after the USA.

The March 2005 OECD Economic Survey noted: 'The Japanese economy is in its best shape in a decade thanks to buoyant external demand, the progress in restructuring the corporate sector and economic reforms. Output has increased at an annual rate of more than 2 per cent since 2002…The pace of growth has been sufficient to boost employment during the past year and reduce the unemployment rate from its record high. Profit margins, as well as confidence in the business and household sectors, are at their highest levels since the early 1990s.'

Banking and Finance

The Nippon Ginko (Bank of Japan), founded 1882, finances the government and the banks, its function being similar to that of a central bank in other countries. The Bank undertakes the management of Treasury funds and foreign exchange control. Its *Governor* is Toshihiko Fukui (appointed March 2003 for a five-year term). Its gold bullion and cash holdings at 31 Dec. 2002 stood at 638,000m. yen.

There were in Feb. 2004, six city banks, 64 regional banks, 27 trust banks, two long-term credit banks, 50 member banks of the second association of regional banks, 309 Shinkin banks (credit associations), 185 credit co-operatives, 72 foreign banks and six others. There is also a public corporation Japan Post handling postal savings which amounted to 229,938,100m. yen in Sept. 2003. Total savings by individuals, including insurance and securities, stood at 1,209,453,100m. yen on 30 Sept. 2003, and about 61% of these savings were deposited in banks and the post office. In 1999 a number of important mergers were announced in the banking sector, most notably the proposed merger of the Industrial Bank of Japan, Dai-Ichi Kangyo and Fuji Bank, which in Sept. 2000 created Mizuho Financial Group, at the time the world's biggest bank in terms of assets, at over 135,000bn. yen (US$1·3trn.). The second and fourth biggest banks, the Mitsubishi Tokyo Financial Group and UFJ Holdings, announced in Aug. 2004 that they had reached a basic agreement to merge to create the world's largest bank. The new bank, named

Bank of Tokyo–Mitsubishi UFJ, came into existence in Jan. 2006 with assets of 190,000bn. yen (US$1·6trn.).

Japan's banks are in a situation where many of them would be insolvent if they admitted the market value of the loans, shares and property they hold. At 31 March 2003 it was estimated that the banking system's bad loans amounted to 21,441bn. yen.

There are five stock exchanges, the largest being in Tokyo.

ENERGY AND NATURAL RESOURCES

Environment
Japan's carbon dioxide emissions from the consumption and flaring of fossil fuels in 2002 accounted for 4·8% of the world total and were equivalent to 9·3 tonnes per capita. An *Environmental Sustainability Index* compiled for the World Economic Forum meeting in Jan. 2005 ranked Japan 30th in the world out of 146 countries analysed, with 57·3%. The index measured the ability of countries to maintain favourable environmental conditions and examined various factors including pollution levels and the use or abuse of natural resources.

Electricity
Japan is poor in energy resources, and nuclear power generation is important in reducing dependence on foreign supplies. In 2003 Japan had a nuclear generating capacity of 44,153 MW. Total installed generating capacity was 260·9m. kW in 2002. Electricity produced in 2002 was 1,097,167m. kWh. In 2003 there were 53 nuclear reactors; in 2002 nuclear reactors produced approximately 39% of electricity. In 2001, ten regional publicly-held supply companies produced 72·3% of output. There are four plants under construction and plans to construct a further eight nuclear power plants. Consumption per capita in 2001 was an estimated 7,567 kWh.

Oil and Gas
Output of crude petroleum, 2002, was 723,000 kilolitres, almost entirely from oilfields on the island of Honshu, but 241·9m. kilolitres of crude oil had to be imported. Output of natural gas, 2002, 2,571m. cu. metres; with reserves of 40bn. cu. metres.

Minerals
Ore production in tonnes, 2002, of coal (2001), 3,208,000; zinc, 42,851; lead, 5,723; copper (2001), 744; iron (2001), 258; silver, 81,416 kg; gold, 8,615 kg. Gypsum production, 2000, 5,917,000 tonnes; salt production, 2001, 1,358,000 tonnes.

Agriculture
Agricultural workers in 2002 on farms with 0·3 ha. or more of cultivated land or 0·5m. yen annual sales were 3·8m. (including 0·22m. subsidiary and seasonal workers), representing 4·5% (2000) of the labour force as opposed to 24·7% in 1962. Land under cultivation in 2002 was 4·8m. ha., down from 6·1m. ha. in 1961. In 2001 Japan had 0·35m. ha. of permanent crops. Average farm size was 1·6 ha. in 2002. In 2001 there were 2,028,000 tractors and 1,042,000 harvester-threshers.

Rice is the staple food, but its consumption is declining. Rice cultivation accounted for 1,689,000 ha. in 2002. Output of rice (in 1,000 tonnes) was 10,748 in 1995, 9,490 in 2000 and 8,889 in 2002.

Production in 2002 (in 1,000 tonnes) of sugarbeets was 4,098; potatoes (2001), 2,959; cabbages (2001), 1,435; sugarcane, 1,328; onions (2001), 1,259; wheat, 829; tomatoes (2001), 798; cucumbers (2001), 736; carrots (2001), 691; aubergines (2001), 448; soybeans, 270; pumpkins and squash (2001), 228; taro (2001), 218; yams (2001), 182. Sweet potatoes, which in the past mitigated the effects of rice famines, have, in view of rice over-production, decreased from 4,955,000 tonnes in 1965 to 1,030,000 tonnes in 2002. Domestic sugar production accounted for only 32% of requirement in 2001. In 2002, 1·48m. tonnes were imported, 52·4% of this being imported from Australia, 27·3% from Thailand, 12·6% from South Africa.

Fruit production, 2002 (in 1,000 tonnes): oranges, 1,229; apples, 926; watermelons (2001), 573; pears, 407; persimmons, 269; grapes, 232.

Livestock (2003): 4·52m. cattle (including about 1·72m. milch cows), 9·72m. pigs, 29,000 goats (2000), 27,000 horses (2000), 16,000 sheep (2000), 284m. chickens. Livestock products (in 1,000 tonnes): milk (2003), 8,400; meat (2000), 3,015; eggs (2000), 2,508.

Forestry
Forests covered 25·11m. ha. in 2000, or 66·4% of the land area. There was an estimated timber stand of 3,758m. cu. metres in 2001. Timber production was 15·29m. cu. metres in 2003.

Fisheries
The catch in 2003 was 4,596,000 tonnes, excluding whaling. More than 98% of fish caught are from marine waters. Japan is the leading importer of fishery commodities, with imports in 2003 totalling US$12·40bn.

INDUSTRY

The leading companies by market capitalization in Japan in Nov. 2005 were: the Toyota Motor Corporation (US$158·2bn.); Mitsubishi UFJ Financial Group (US$126·4bn.); and Mizuho Financial Group (US$76·6bn.).

The industrial structure is dominated by corporate groups (*keiretsu*) either linking companies in different branches or linking individual companies with their suppliers and distributors.

Japan's industrial equipment, 2000, numbered 589,713 plants of all sizes, employing 9·70m. production workers.

Output in 2001 included: watches, 515·3m.; computers, 11·6m.; cameras, 7·91m.; refrigerators, 3·87m.; television sets, 2·86m.; radio sets, 1·9m. The chemical industry ranks fourth in shipment value after machinery, metals and food products. Production, 2001, included (in tonnes): sulphuric acid, 6·7m.; caustic soda, 4·22m.; ammonium sulphate, 1·59m.; calcium superphosphate, 0·25m. A total of 10,257,000 motor vehicles were manufactured in Japan in 2002, making it the second largest producer after the USA. It is the largest producer of passenger cars (8,618,000 in 2002).

Output, in 1,000 tonnes, of crude steel (2002) was 107,745; ordinary rolled steel (2001), 78,927; pig iron (2001), 78,836; cement (2002), 71,828.

2002 production (in 1,000 tonnes): distillate fuel oil, 57,948; petrol, 42,702; residual fuel oil, 33,119; kerosene, 22,866.

In 2001 paper production was 18·39m. tonnes; paperboard, 12·33m. tonnes.

Output of cotton yarn, 2001, 139,000 tonnes, and of cotton cloth, 603m. sq. metres. Output, 2001, 30,000 tonnes of woollen yarns and 95m. sq. metres of woollen fabrics. Output, 2001, of synthetic woven fabrics, 1,484m. sq. metres; rayon woven fabrics, 213m. sq. metres; silk fabrics, 31m. sq. metres.

4,813m. litres of beer were produced in 2001–02; 3,670m. litres of soft drinks and mineral water in 2001.

Shipbuilding orders in 2002 totalled 12,944,000 GRT. In 2001, 11,729,000 GRT were launched, of which 3,092,000 GRT were tankers.

Labour
Total labour force, 2004, was 66·42m., of which 11·50m. were in manufacturing, 11·23m. in wholesale and retail trade, 8·81m. in services, 5·84m. in construction, 5·31m. in health and welfare, 3·47m. in hotels and restaurants, 3·23m. in transport, 2·84m. in education and 2·64m. in agriculture and forestry. Retirement age is being raised progressively from 60 years to reach 65 by 2013. However, in 1995 the average actual retirement age among males was 66.

In Jan. 2003 unemployment stood at 5·5%, the highest rate on record. It had also been 5·5% in Aug. and Oct. 2002. It has fallen since then, and was 4·4% in Dec. 2005. In 2001, 29,000 working days were lost in industrial stoppages. In 2003 the average working week was 38·45 hours.

Trade Unions

In 2002 there were 10,801,000 workers organized in 65,642 unions. In Nov. 1989 the 'Japanese Private Sector Trade Union Confederation' (Rengo), which was organized in 1987, was reorganized into the 'Japan Trade Union Confederation' (Rengo) with the former 'General Council of Japanese Trade Unions' (Sohyo) and other unions, and was the largest federation with 6,829,000 members in 2002. The 'National Confederation of Trade Unions' (Zenroren) had 787,000 members and the 'National Trade Union Council' (Zenrokyo) 169,000 members.

INTERNATIONAL TRADE

Imports and Exports

Trade (in US$1m.):

	1997	1998	1999	2000	2001	2002
Imports	338,705	280,505	311,246	379,718	349,190	337,833
Exports	420,896	387,958	419,358	479,284	403,227	417,015

In 2001 Japanese imports accounted for 5·8% of the world total imports, and exports 6·9% of the world total exports.

Distribution of trade by countries (customs clearance basis) (US$1m.):

	Imports		Exports	
	2001	2002	2001	2002
Africa	4,543	5,698	4,432	4,918
Australia	14,451	14,023	7,683	8,323
Canada	7,751	7,163	6,563	7,331
China	57,786	61,863	30,941	39,985
Germany	12,395	12,435	15,639	14,135
Hong Kong	1,457	1,420	23,248	25,448
Latin America	9,700	9,568	17,855	16,234
ASEAN	54,382	51,708	54,270	55,796
Korea, Republic of	17,210	15,502	25,285	28,629
Taiwan	14,195	13,572	24,214	26,282
UK	6,003	5,419	12,145	11,969
USA	63,171	61,863	121,146	118,875

Principal items in 2002, with value in 1m. yen were:

	Imports, c.i.f.
Machinery and transport equipment	13,434,000
Mineral fuels	8,174,000
Foodstuffs	5,282,000
Metal ores and scrap	950,000

	Exports, f.o.b.
Machinery and transport equipment	37,542,000
Chemicals	4,174,000
Metals and metal products	3,227,000
Textile products	918,000

The importation of rice was prohibited until the emergency importation of 1m. tonnes from Australia, China, Thailand and the USA in 1993–94 to offset a poor domestic harvest. The prohibition was lifted in line with WTO agreements. Until 2000 rice imports had limited access; the market is now fully open.

COMMUNICATIONS

Roads

The total length of roads (including urban and other local roads) was 1,171,647 km at 1 April 2001. There were 53,866 km of national roads of which 53,303 km were paved. In 2001, 77·1% of all roads were paved. Motor vehicles, at 31 Dec. 2002, numbered 72,254,000, including 54,540,000 passenger cars and 17,480,000 commercial vehicles. In 2001 there were 4,289,700 new car registrations. In 2003 there were 7,702 road deaths (10,679 in 1995).

The world's longest undersea road tunnel, spanning Tokyo Bay, was opened in Dec. 1997. The Tokyo Bay Aqualine, built at a cost of 1·44trn. yen (US$11·3bn.), consists of a 4·4 km (2·7 mile) bridge and a 9·4 km tunnel that allows commuters to cross the bay in about 15 minutes.

Rail

The first railway was completed in 1872, between Tokyo and Yokohama (29 km). Most railways are of 1,067 mm gauge, but the high-speed 'Shinkansen' lines are standard 1,435 mm gauge. In April 1987 the Japanese National Railways was reorganized into seven private companies, the Japanese Railways (JR) Group—six passenger companies and one freight company. Total length of railways in March 2001 was 27,501 km, of which the JR had 20,057 km and other private railways 7,444 km. In 2002 the JR carried 8,585m. passengers (other private, 12,976m.) and 38m. tonnes of freight (other private, 18m.). An undersea tunnel linking Honshu with Hokkaido was opened to rail services in 1988.

There are metros in Tokyo (two systems, total 286 km in 2001), Fukuoka (17·8 km), Kobe (41·5 km), Kyoto (26·0 km), Nagoya (76·5 km), Osaka (105·8 km), Sapporo (45·2 km), Sendai (14·8 km) and Yokohama (32·9 km). There are also tram/light rail networks in 19 cities.

Civil Aviation

The main international airports are at Fukuoka, Hiroshima, Kagoshima, Nagoya, Naha, Niigata, Osaka (Kansai International), Sapporo, Sendai and two serving Tokyo—at Narita (New Tokyo International) and Haneda (Tokyo International). The principal airlines are Japan Airlines (JAL), Japan Air System and All Nippon Airways. In the financial year 2002 Japanese companies carried 96·66m. passengers on domestic services and 17·89m. passengers on international services. JAL flew 361·8m. km in 2002 and carried 33,525,752 passengers, All Nippon Airways flew 259·1m. km and carried 43,680,438 passengers, and Japan Air System flew 106·9m. km and carried 21,426,817 passengers.

In 2001 Narita handled 22,933,000 passengers (22,241,000 on international flights) and 1,630,900 tonnes of freight. Osaka (Kansai International) handled 18,500,392 passengers (10,704,867 on international flights) and 837,918 tonnes of freight in 2001. Built on a reclaimed offshore island, it was only opened in Sept. 1994 but in 2001 was the 18th busiest airport in the world for freight, with Narita ranked 4th. Tokyo Haneda is mainly used for domestic flights, but handled 58,657,000 passengers in 2001 (57,736,000 on domestic flights), making it the 5th busiest airport in the world for overall traffic volume.

Shipping

On 1 July 2001 the merchant fleet consisted of 5,733 vessels of 100 GRT and over; total tonnage 14m. GRT; there were 161 ships for passenger transport (203,000 GRT), 1,602 cargo ships (954,000 GRT) and 727 oil tankers (3,331,000 GRT). In 2000 vessels totalling 461,903,000 net registered tons entered ports. The busiest ports are Chiba (158,929,000 freight tonnes handled in 2002), Nagoya, Yokohama, Osaka and Kitakyushu.

Coastguard

The 'Japan Coast Guard' consists of one headquarters, 11 regional headquarters, 66 offices, one maritime guard and rescue office, 53 stations, six info-communication management centres, seven traffic advisory service centres, 14 air stations, one transnational organized crime strike force station, one special security station, one special rescue station, one national strike team station, five district communications centres, four hydrographic observatories, one Loran navigation system centre and 39 aids-to-navigation offices (with 5,604 aids-to-navigation facilities); and controlled 52 large patrol vessels, 44 medium patrol vessels, 23 small patrol vessels, 233 patrol craft, 13 hydrographic service vessels, five large firefighting boats, four medium firefighting boats, 87 special guard and rescue boats, one aids-to-navigation evaluation vessel, four buoy tenders and 50 aids-to-navigation tenders in the financial year 2003. Personnel numbered 12,258. The 'Japan Coast Guard' aviation service includes 29 fixed-wing aircraft and 46 helicopters.

Telecommunications

Telephone services have been operated by private companies (NTT and others) since 1985. There were 152,267,000 telephone subscribers (equivalent to 1,194·9 per 1,000 population) in 2002. In 2002 Japan had 81,118,400 mobile phone subscribers. There were 48·7m. PCs in use in 2002 (382·2 per 1,000 persons) and 21·9m. fax machines. There were 57·2m. Internet users in 2002. Approximately 70% of Internet users are men. Internet commerce, or e-commerce, amounted to US$285bn. in 2001—second only to the USA.

Postal Services

There were 24,752 post offices in 2002, handling a total of 25,647m. items of domestic mail, and foreign items of mail numbering 80m. out of and 262m. into Japan. Privatization of the post office is set to start in 2007 and be completed in 2017.

SOCIAL INSTITUTIONS

Justice

The Supreme Court is composed of the Chief Justice and 14 other judges. The Chief Justice is appointed by the Emperor, the other judges by the Cabinet. Every ten years a justice must submit himself to the electorate. All justices and judges of the lower courts serve until they are 70 years of age.

Below the Supreme Court are eight regional higher courts, district courts in each prefecture (four in Hokkaido) and the local courts.

The Supreme Court is authorized to declare unconstitutional any act of the Legislature or the Executive which violates the Constitution.

In 2002, 3,693,928 penal code offences were reported, including 1,396 homicides. The death penalty is authorized; there was one execution in 2005. The average daily population in penal institutions in 2001 was 63,415 (49·81 per 100,000 population).

Education

Education is compulsory and free between the ages of six and 15. Almost all national and municipal institutions are co-educational. In May 2003 there were 14,174 kindergartens with 108,822 teachers and 1,760,000 pupils; 23,169 elementary schools with 413,890 teachers and 7,227,000 pupils; 11,060 lower secondary schools with 252,050 teachers and 3,748,000 pupils; 5,331 upper secondary schools with 258,537 teachers and 3,810,000 pupils; 525 junior colleges with 13,534 teachers and 250,000 pupils; and 63 technical colleges with 7,000 teachers and 57,875 pupils. There were also 918 special schools for children with physical disabilities (63,228 teachers, 96,473 pupils).

Japan has seven main state universities: Tokyo University (1877); Kyoto University (1897); Tohoku University, Sendai (1907); Kyushu University, Fukuoka (1910); Hokkaido University, Sapporo (1918); Osaka University (1931); and Nagoya University (1939). In addition, there are various other state and municipal as well as private universities. There are 702 colleges and universities altogether with (May 2003) 2,804,000 students and 310,825 teachers (156,155 full-time).

In 2000–01 total expenditure on education came to 3·5% of GNP and 10·5% of total government spending.

The adult literacy rate is at least 99%.

Health

Hospitals on 1 Oct. 2002 numbered 9,187 with 1,642,593 beds. The hospital bed provision of 129 per 10,000 population (2001) was one of the highest in the world. Physicians in 2002 numbered 249,574 (provision of one for every 511 persons); dentists, 90,499. In 2002 Japan spent 7·9% of its GDP on health.

Welfare

There are in force various types of social security schemes, such as health insurance, unemployment insurance and age pensions. The old age pension system in Japan is made up of a two-tiered public benefit. The first tier of the public pension is the basic pension which is payable from age 65 with 25 years' contributions. To receive the full benefit amount, 40 years' contributions to the system are necessary. There is an earnings floor for contributions at approximately 28% of average earnings. The monthly premium of the National Pension is uniformly fixed (13,300 yen in fiscal year 2004). The full basic pension was a flat amount of 804,200 yen in fiscal year 2002. There were a total of 41m. pensioners in 2000.

14 weeks maternity leave is statutory.

In 2000, 12,866,887 persons and 9,015,632 households received some form of regular public assistance, the total of which came to 1,973,420m. yen. A proposed reform of the pension system involves the public making higher payments for lower benefits.

RELIGION

State subsidies have ceased for all religions, and all religious teachings are forbidden in public schools. In Dec. 2002 Shintoism claimed 107·78m. adherents, Buddhism 95·56m.; these figures overlap. Christians numbered 1·92m. In May 2005 the Roman Catholic church had two cardinals.

CULTURE

World Heritage Sites

Japan has 13 sites on the UNESCO World Heritage List (date of inscription on the list in brackets): the Buddhist Monuments in the Horyu-ji Area (1993); Himeji-jo (1993); Yakushima (1993); Shirakami-Sanchi (1993); the Historic Monuments of Ancient Kyoto (Kyoto, Uji and Otsu Cities) (1994), including 13 of Kyoto's Buddhist temples, three Shinto shrines and one castle—temples include Byōdo-in, Daigo-ji, Enryaku-ji, Ginkaku-ji, Kinkaku-ji, Kiyomizu-dera, Kōzan-ji, Ninna-ji, Nishi Hongan-ji, Ryōan-ji, Saihō-ji, Tenryū-ji and Tō-ji; the Historic Villages of Shirakawa-go and Gokayama (1995); Hiroshima Peace Memorial (Genbaku Dome) (1996); Itsukushima Shinto Shrine (1996); the Historic Monuments of Ancient Nara (1998), including five Buddhist temples—Tōdai-ji, Kōfuku-ji, Gango-ji, Yakushi-ji and Tōshōdai-ji—and three listed shrines—Kasuga Taisha, Kasuga Yama Primeval Forest and the remains of Heijō-kyō Palace; Shrines and Temples of Nikko (1999); Gusuku Sites and Related Properties of the Kingdom of Ryukyu (2000); Sacred sites and pilgrimage routes in the Kii mountain range (2004); marine and land ecosystems at Shiretoko (2005).

Broadcasting

Broadcasting is under the aegis of the public Japan Broadcasting Corporation (Nippon Hoso Kyokai) and the National Association of Commercial Broadcasters (Minporen). The former transmits two national networks and an external service, Radio Japan (22 languages). In 2002 there were 127 commercial television companies operating on terrestrial broadcasting waves. There were 93m. TV sets (colour by NTSC) in 2001 and 121m. radio receivers in 2000. In 2002 there were 23·33m. cable TV subscribers, and in 1998 more than 68,000 cable TV stations. The average Japanese watches 300 minutes of television daily—the most of any country.

Cinema

In 2003 cinemas numbered 2,681 with an annual attendance of 162m. (1960: 1,014m.). Of 622 new films shown in 2003, 287 were Japanese.

Press

In 2002 daily newspapers numbered 106 with aggregate circulation of 70·82m. (the highest circulation of daily newspapers in the world) including four major English-language newspapers. The newspapers with the highest circulation are *Yomiuri Shimbun* (daily average of 10·2m. copies in 2002) and *Asahi Shimbun* (daily average of 8·3m. copies in 2002). They are also the two most widely read newspapers in the world.

In 2002, 74,259 book titles were published.

Tourism

In 2002, 5,771,975 foreigners visited Japan, 755,196 of whom came from the USA and 379,832 from the UK. Japanese travelling abroad totalled 16,522,804. Tourism receipts in 2002 totalled US$3·50bn.

Festivals

Japan has a huge number of annual festivals, among the largest of which are the Sapporo Snow Festival (Feb.); Hakata Dontaku, Fukuoka City (May); the Sanja Festival of Asakusa Shrine, Tokyo (May); the Tanabata Festival in Hiratsuka City (July) and Sendai City (Aug.); the Nebuta Festival in Aomori City (Aug.); and Jidai Matsuri, Kyoto (Oct.).

Libraries

In 2002 public libraries numbered 2,742 (including one National Diet Library), holding 308m. books. In addition the 699 university libraries held 179m. Japanese and 92m. foreign books.

Theatre and Opera

In 2003 there were five National Theatres: National Theatre (traditional Japanese performances); Nogakudo (Noh Theatre); Bunraku Theatre (Japanese puppet show); the New National Theatre (Opera House); and National Theatre Okinawa.

Museums and Galleries

In 2002 there were 1,120 museums. These included 383 historical, 383 fine arts and 141 general museums. There were 113,977,000 visitors in 2001.

DIPLOMATIC REPRESENTATIVES

Of Japan in the United Kingdom (101–104 Piccadilly, London, W1J 7JT)
Ambassador: Yoshiji Nogami.

Of the United Kingdom in Japan (1 Ichiban-cho, Chiyoda-ku, Tokyo 102-8381)
Ambassador: Graham Fry.

Of Japan in the USA (2520 Massachusetts Ave., NW, Washington, D.C., 20008)
Ambassador: Ryozo Kato.

Of the USA in Japan (10–5, Akasaka 1-chome, Minato-ku, Tokyo)
Ambassador: John Thomas Schieffer.

Of Japan to the United Nations
Ambassador: Kenzo Oshima.

Of Japan to the European Union
Ambassador: Kazuo Asakai.

FURTHER READING

Statistics Bureau of the Prime Minister's Office (up to 2000) and Statistics Bureau of the Ministry of Public Management, Home Affairs, Posts and Telecommunications (from 2001): *Statistical Year-Book* (from 1949).— *Statistical Abstract* (from 1950).—*Monthly Bulletin* (from April 1950)

Economic Planning Agency (up to 2000) and Economic and Social Research Institute (from 2001) of the Cabinet Office: *Economic Survey* (annual), *Economic Statistics* (monthly), *Economic Indicators* (monthly)

Ministry of International Trade and Industry (up to 2000) and the Ministry of Economy, Trade and Industry (from 2001): *Foreign Trade of Japan* (annual)

Allinson, G. D., *Japan's Postwar History.* London, 1997

Argy, V. and Stein, L., *The Japanese Economy.* London, 1996

Bailey, P. J., *Post-war Japan: 1945 to the Present.* Oxford, 1996

Beasley, W. G., *The Rise of Modern Japan: Political, Economic and Social Change Since 1850.* 2nd ed. London, 1995

Buruma, Ian, *Inventing Japan: 1853–1964.* Weidenfeld & Nicolson, London, 2003

The Cambridge Encyclopedia of Japan. CUP, 1993

Cambridge History of Japan. vols. 1–5. CUP, 1990–93

Campbell, A. (ed.) *Japan: an Illustrated Encyclopedia.* Tokyo, 1994

Clesse, A., *et al.* (eds.) *The Vitality of Japan: Sources of National Strength and Weakness.* London, 1997

Henshall, K. G., *A History of Japan, From Stone Age to Superpower.* Palgrave, Basingstoke, 2001

Japan: an Illustrated Encyclopedia. London, 1993

Johnson, C., *Japan: Who Governs? The Rise of the Developmental State.* New York, 1995

McCargo, Duncan, *Contemporary Japan.* 2nd ed. Palgrave Macmillan, Basingstoke, 2004

McClain, James, *Japan: A Modern History.* W. W. Norton, New York, 2001

Nakano, M., *The Policy-making Process in Contemporary Japan.* London, 1996

Okabe, M. (ed.) *The Structure of the Japanese Economy: Changes on the Domestic and International Fronts.* London, 1994

Perren, R., *Japanese Studies From Pre-History to 1990.* Manchester Univ. Press, 1992

Schirokauer, C., *Brief History of Japanese Civilization.* New York, 1993

Woronoff, J., *The Japanese Economic Crisis.* 2nd ed. London, 1996

National Statistical Office: Statistics Bureau, Prime Minister's Office, Tokyo.
Website: http://www.stat.go.jp/

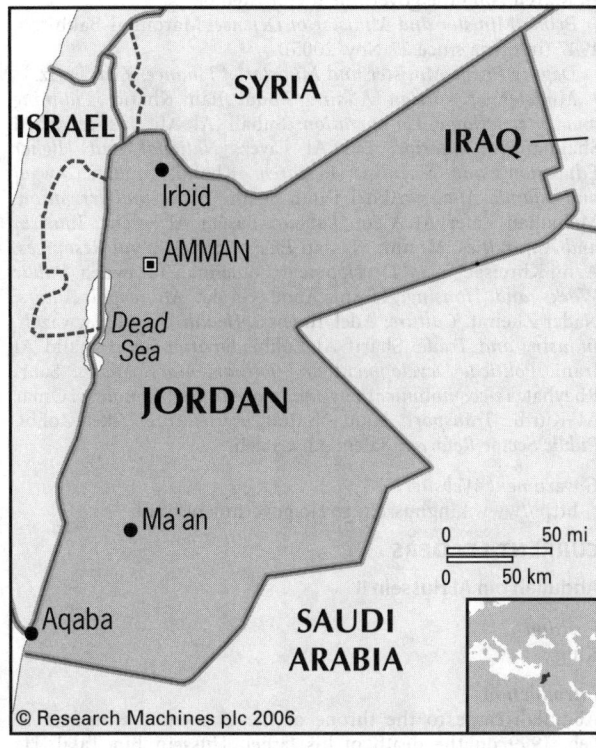

Al-Mamlaka Al-Urduniya Al-Hashemiyah
(Hashemite[1] Kingdom of Jordan)

Capital: Amman
Population projection, 2010: 6·34m.
GDP per capita, 2003: (PPP$) 4,320
HDI/world rank: 0·753/90

KEY HISTORICAL EVENTS

Egyptian control was established over Semitic Amorite tribes in the Jordan valley in the 16th century BC. However, Egypt's conflict with the Hittite Empire allowed the development of autonomous kingdoms such as Edom, Moab, Gilead and Ammon (centred on modern Amman). The Israelites settled on the east bank of the Jordan in the 13th century and crossed into Canaan. David subjugated Moab, Edom and Ammon in the 10th century but the Assyrians wrested control in the 9th century, remaining until 612 BC. Nabataea expanded in the south during the Babylonian and Persian periods until conquered for Rome by Pompey in the 1st century BC. After Trajan's campaign of 106 AD, the Jordan area was absorbed as Arabia Petraea.

Rome (later Byzantium) and Sassanid Persia clashed over the area but a Muslim army under Khalid ibn al-Walid defeated Byzantium in 636 at the Yarmuk River. After the fall of the Umayyad Caliphate in 750, the centre of power moved from Damascus to Baghdad and Jordan was neglected. The principality of Oultre Jourdain, established by the Christian crusader kingdom of Jerusalem in the early 12th century, was destroyed by Saladin in 1187. The Mamluk Empire held power

until the advent of the Turkish Ottoman Empire in the 16th century.

The Arabs of the Ottoman Damascus province rebelled with British support in 1916. The Hashemite Prince Faisal ibn Husayn took Aqaba in 1917 and the British took Amman and Damascus in 1918. The First World War victors decreed two mandates—British Palestine and French Syria. Britain created the Transjordan Emirate in 1922, ruled semi-autonomously by Faisal's brother, Abdullah. Full independence was achieved on 25 May 1946 as the Hashemite Kingdom of Transjordan (Jordan from 1949).

Transjordan declared war on the Israeli state in May 1948, taking the West Bank and East Jerusalem, an occupation supported only by Britain. Palestinian resistance to the annexation culminated in King Abdullah's assassination in 1951. Talal, his son and successor, was deemed mentally unfit in 1952 and Hussein Bin Talal was installed in 1953. After an attempted coup in 1957, instigated by West Bank Palestinians, King Hussein banned political parties and ended Palestinian representation. A brief union with Iraq, ruled by his cousin, ended after an Iraqi republican coup in 1958. Hussein turned to Britain and the USA for military and financial support.

Fatah and the Palestine Liberation Organization (PLO) maintained terrorist attacks on Israel from Jordan, provoking Israeli retaliation in the West Bank. Despite secret co-operation with Israel over containing the Palestinians, Hussein allied with Syria and Egypt in the war of June 1967. Israel repelled Jordanian forces from the West Bank, moving the *de facto* border to the River Jordan. This devastated the Jordanian economy but removed Palestinian opposition to the Hashemite regime. However, Jordan's relations with the Palestinians deteriorated; in Sept. 1970 four airliners were destroyed by Palestinian extremists in the Jordanian desert. Jordan, with US and British assistance, repelled a Syrian invasion and evicted the PLO. Relations with Israel also worsened from 1977 with the Jewish settlement programme in the West Bank.

On 31 July 1988 Hussein dissolved Jordan's legal and administrative ties with the West Bank in reaction to the *intifada*, which he saw as a threat to his regime. Elections in 1989 led the way to the suspension of martial law—in place from 1967–91. Hussein, constrained by Jordan's economic and political ties with Iraq, refused to abandon Saddam Hussein in the 1991 Gulf War, creating a rift with Jordan's Western partners. Multiparty elections were held in 1993, giving Hussein parliamentary support. He signed a peace treaty with Israel in 1994. In Jan. 1999 Hussein replaced as crown prince his brother, Hassan, with his son, Abdullah, who succeeded on his father's death a month later.

TERRITORY AND POPULATION

Jordan is bounded in the north by Syria, east by Iraq, southeast and south by Saudi Arabia and west by Israel. It has an outlet to an arm of the Red Sea at Aqaba. Its area is 89,342 sq. km. The provisional 2004 census population was 5,100,981; density 57·1 per sq. km. The United Nations population estimate for 2004 was 5,561,000.

The UN gives a projected population for 2010 of 6·34m. (including immigrant workers).

In 2003, 79·1% of the population lived in urban areas. Populations of the 12 governorates:

---

[1]'Hashemite' denotes a descendant of the prophet Mohammed.

Governorate	2004 (provisional)	Governorate	2004 (provisional)
Ajloun	118,496	Karak	204,135
Amman	1,939,405	Ma'an	92,672
Aqaba	101,736	Madaba	129,792
Balqa	344,985	Mafraq	240,515
Irbid	925,736	Tafilah	75,290
Jerash	153,650	Zarqa	774,569

The largest towns, with estimated population, 2000: Amman, the capital, 1,147,000; Zarqa, 429,000; Irbid, 247,000.

The official language is Arabic.

SOCIAL STATISTICS

Births, 2003, 148,294; deaths, 16,937. Rates, 2003 per 1,000 population: birth, 27·1; death, 3·1. Annual population growth rate, 1992–2002, 3·9%. Life expectancy at birth in 2003; 69·9 years for men, 72·9 for women. Infant mortality, 2002, 22 per 1,000 live births; fertility rate, 2002, 3·7 births per woman.

CLIMATE

Predominantly a Mediterranean climate, with hot dry summers and cool wet winters, but in hilly parts summers are cooler and winters colder. Those areas below sea-level are very hot in summer and warm in winter. Eastern parts have a desert climate. Amman, Jan. 46°F (7·5°C), July 77°F (24·9°C). Annual rainfall 13·4" (340·6 mm). Aqaba, Jan. 61°F (16°C), July 89°F (31·5°C). Annual rainfall 1·4" (36·7 mm).

CONSTITUTION AND GOVERNMENT

The Kingdom is a constitutional monarchy headed by H. M. King **Abdullah Bin Al Hussein** II, born 30 Jan. 1962, married H. M. Queen Rania (Rania Al-Yassin, b. 31 Aug. 1970) on 10 June 1993. He succeeded on the death of his father, H. M. King Hussein, on 7 Feb. 1999. *Sons:* Hussein, b. 28 June 1994; Hashem, b. 30 Jan. 2005; *daughters:* Iman, b. 27 Sept. 1996; Salma, b. 26 Sept. 2000.

The Constitution ratified on 8 Dec. 1952 provides that the Cabinet is responsible to Parliament. It was amended in 1974, 1976 and 1984. The legislature consists of a *Senate* of 55 members appointed by the King and a *Chamber of Deputies* of 110 members (six are reserved for women elected by an electoral college) elected by universal suffrage. Nine seats are reserved for Christians, six for Bedouin and three for Circassians. A law of 1993 restricts each elector to a single vote.

The lower house was dissolved in 1976 and elections postponed because no elections could be held in the West Bank under Israeli occupation. Parliament was reconvened on 9 Jan. 1984. By-elections were held in March 1984 and six members were nominated for the West Bank, bringing Parliament to 60 members. Women voted for the first time in 1984. On 9 June 1991 the King and the main political movements endorsed a national charter which legalized political parties in return for the acceptance of the constitution and monarchy. Movements linked to, or financed by, non-Jordanian bodies are not allowed.

National Anthem

'Asha al Malik' ('Long Live the King'); words by A. Al Rifai, tune by A. Al Tanir.

GOVERNMENT CHRONOLOGY

Kings since 1946.

1946–51	Abdullah Bin Al Hussein Al Hashimi I
1951–52	Talal Bin Abdullah Al Hashimi
1953–99	Hussein Bin Talal Al Hashimi
1999–	Abdullah Bin Al Hussein Al Hashimi II

RECENT ELECTIONS

Elections to the Chamber of Deputies were held on 17 June 2003, having been postponed three times since 2001. 62 of the 110 seats were won by independents loyal to the king. The Islamic Action Front won 18 seats. Turnout was 59%.

CURRENT ADMINISTRATION

In March 2006 the government consisted of:

Prime Minister and Minister of Defence: Marouf al-Bakhit; b. 1947 (in office since 27 Nov. 2005).

Deputy Prime Minister and Minister of Finance: Ziad Fariz.

Minister of Foreign Affairs: Abdul Ilah Khatib. *Planning and International Co-operation:* Suhair Al Ali. *Justice:* Abed Shakhanbeh. *Interior:* Eid Al Fayez. *National and Higher Education, and Scientific Research:* Khalid Touqan. *Awqaf and Islamic Affairs:* Abdel Fatah Salah. *Water and Irrigation:* Mohamad Zafer Al Alem. *Labour:* Basem Al Salem. *Tourism and Antiquities:* Mounir Nassar. *Energy and Mineral Resources:* Azmi Khreisât. *Social Development:* Souleiman Tarawneh. *Public Works and Housing:* Hosni Abou Ghida. *Municipal Affairs:* Nader Zheirat. *Culture:* Adel Toueissi. *Health:* Saeed Darwazeh. *Industry and Trade:* Sharif Al Zohbi. *Environment:* Khalid Al Irani. *Political Development and Parliamentary Affairs:* Sabri Rbeyhat. *Telecommunications and Information Technology:* Omar Al Kurdi. *Transport:* Soud Nsairat. *Agriculture:* Akef Zohbi. *Public Sector Reforms:* Salem Khazaaleh.

Government Website:
http://www.kinghussein.gov.jo/government.html

CURRENT LEADERS

Abdullah bin Al Hussein II

Position
King

Introduction
Abdullah came to the throne of the Hashemite Kingdom in Feb. 1999 on the death of his father, Hussein Bin Talal. He had been declared Crown Prince and heir by his father the previous month, replacing his uncle, Prince Hassan, who had served in that capacity since 1965. Abdullah has maintained the moderate policies of his late father. He has aimed to reconcile the domestically unpopular 1994 peace agreement with Israel and friendly relations with the USA with the need to appease Jordan's more militant Arab neighbours and its own large Palestinian population.

Early Life
Born in Amman on 30 Jan. 1962, Abdullah was educated at St Edmund's School in Surrey, England, then Eaglebrook School in Massachusetts and Deerfield Academy in the USA. With his uncle holding office as Crown Prince, Abdullah focused on the military, enrolling in the Royal Military Academy Sandhurst, England in 1980. Having then attended Oxford University and Georgetown University in Washington, D.C., for studies in international relations, he moved up through the ranks of Jordan's armed forces to become Major-Gen. in May 1998.

Career in Office
Abdullah became Crown Prince on 25 Jan. 1999 after King Hussein had rescinded the 1965 constitutional amendment in favour of his younger brother Hassan. Two weeks later, on 7 Feb. 1999, Hussein died and Abdullah assumed the throne. Consistent with the policy of his father, Abdullah has deterred Islamic militancy (particularly the activities of the radical Palestinian Hamas group), while extending economic liberalization. He revived the privatization programme, oversaw Jordan's admission to the World Trade Organization and concluded a free trade accord with the USA.

Abdullah has supported the wider Arab-Israeli peace process and maintains a close affinity with the USA. He also backs Palestinian statehood in the West Bank, a policy that takes account of Jordan's large Palestinian population. He made early overtures towards Jordan's moderate Arab neighbours, visiting Egypt, Saudi Arabia, Oman and the United Arab Emirates in the first few months of his reign, and also tried to forge closer relations with Syria, a traditional antagonist. Relations with Iran have wavered since Abdullah's accession. In 2003 Abdullah backed the US intervention in Iraq, a decision not wholly popular with Jordanian citizens. The subsequent insurgency in Iraq spilled over into Jordan in Nov. 2005 when nearly 70 people were killed in the capital, Amman, in co-ordinated suicide bomb attacks apparently perpetrated by an Iraqi wing of the al-Qaeda terrorist network.

Although Abdullah retains the power to rule by decree, there is an elected Chamber of Deputies to which a majority of non-partisan candidates loyal to the King were returned in polling in June 2003 (the previous assembly having been dissolved in 2001). No women were directly elected, but six seats in the chamber were reserved for those women with the most votes. In the wake of the Nov. 2005 terrorist attack on Amman, Abdullah appointed Jordan's national security chief, Marouf al-Bakhit, as the new prime minister, replacing Adnan Badran who had been in office for only seven months.

DEFENCE

Defence expenditure in 2003 totalled US$889m. (US$162 per capita), representing 12·5% of GDP.

Army
Total strength (2002) 84,700. In addition there were 30,000 army reservists, a paramilitary Public Security Directorate of approximately 10,000 and a civil militia 'People's Army' of approximately 35,000.

Navy
The Royal Jordanian Naval Force numbered 540 in 2002 and operates a handful of patrol boats, all based at Aqaba.

Air Force
Strength (2002) 15,000 personnel (including 3,400 Air defence), 101 combat aircraft (including F-5Es, F-16As and Mirage F1s) and 22 armed helicopters.

INTERNATIONAL RELATIONS

A 46-year-old formal state of hostilities with Israel was brought to an end by a peace agreement on 26 Oct. 1994.

Jordan is a member of the UN, WTO, IOM, OIC, Islamic Development Bank and the League of Arab States.

ECONOMY

Services accounted for 71·9% of GDP in 2002, industry 25·9% and agriculture 2·2%.

Overview
Jordan is classified by the World Bank as a small, lower middle-income country. It has no significant natural resources but relies primarily on its human capital for development and growth. Jordan has suffered external shocks related to the situation in Iraq and in the West Bank and Gaza. These have had an impact on exports, tourism and foreign and domestic investment. Despite these difficulties recent growth has been robust with growth of 3·3% in 2003. Reforms have continued and have been accelerated in some areas, including macroeconomic stabilization, private investment and privatization. Despite the strength of recent economic growth, external debt remains high, at 85% of GDP in 2001, with unemployment of around 15% in 2004. The World Bank estimates that the number of Jordanians living in poverty declined by one third between 1997 and 2002, but remains high at 14·2% in 2004. According to the IMF Jordan's main challenges in the medium term concern oil price vulnerability, dependence on foreign loans and the reformation of an incomplete direct tax system.

Currency
The unit of currency is the *Jordan dinar* (JD.) of 1,000 *fils*, pegged to the US dollar since 1995 at a rate of one dinar = US$1·41. Inflation was 1·6% in 2003 and 3·4% in 2004. Foreign exchange controls were abolished in July 1997. Foreign exchange reserves were US$3,650m. and gold reserves 408,000 troy oz in June 2002. Total money supply in March 2002 was JD.2,095m.

Budget
Revenue and expenditure over a six-year period (in JD.1m.):

	1998	1999	2000	2001	2002	2003
Revenue	1,574·9	1,732·1	1,815·9	1,968·0	2,020·8	2,381·2
Expenditure	2,087·7	2,039·5	2,054·1	2,192·3	2,296·7	2,542·6

Performance
Total GDP was US$11·2bn. in 2004. Real GDP growth in 2004 was 7·7% (4·1% in 2003).

Banking and Finance
The Central Bank of Jordan was established in 1964 (*Governor*, Dr Umayya Toukan). In 2002 there were nine national banks, seven foreign banks and 11 specialized credit institutions. Assets and liabilities of the banking system (including the Central Bank, commercial banks, the Housing Bank and investment banks) totalled JD.8,430·4m. in 1995.

There is a stock exchange in Amman (Amman Financial Market).

Weights and Measures
The metric system is in force. Land area is measured in *dunums* (1 dunum = 0·1 ha.).

ENERGY AND NATURAL RESOURCES

Environment
Carbon dioxide emissions in 2003 were the equivalent of 3·39 tonnes per capita.

Electricity
Installed capacity was 1·7m. kW in 2000. Production (2003) 7·99bn. kWh; consumption per capita was 1,509 kWh.

Oil and Gas
Natural gas reserves in 2003 totalled 5·83bn. cu. metres, with production (2000) 237m. cu. metres.

Water
99% of the total population and 100% of the urban population has access to safe drinking water.

Minerals
Phosphate ore production in 2003 was 6·47m. tonnes; potash, 1·96m. tonnes.

Agriculture
The country east of the Hejaz Railway line is largely desert; northwestern Jordan is potentially of agricultural value and an integrated Jordan Valley project began in 1973. In 1993 about 15% of land was given over to agricultural use (including 9% permanent pasture and 4% arable crops). In 2001 there were 73,500 ha. of irrigated land. The agricultural cropping pattern for irrigated vegetable cultivation was introduced in 1984 to regulate production and diversify the crops being cultivated. In 1986 the government began to lease state-owned land in the semi-arid southern regions for agricultural development by private investors, mostly for wheat and barley. In 2001 there were 256,400 ha. of arable land and 87,800 ha. of permanent crops. There were 5,770 tractors in 2001 and 168 harvester-threshers.

Production in 2000 (in 1,000 tonnes): tomatoes, 354; olives, 134; cucumbers and gherkins, 133; potatoes, 97; pumpkins and squash, 49; apples, 37; watermelons, 35; lemons and limes, 29; cauliflowers, 26; bananas, 21; cabbages, 12.

Livestock (2003): 1·5m. sheep; 547,000 goats; 66,000 cattle; 18,000 asses (2000); 18,000 camels (2000); 25m. chickens (2000). Total meat production was 130,810 tonnes in 2000; milk, 214,340 tonnes.

Forestry

Forests covered 86,000 ha. in 2000, or 1·0% of the land area. In 2001, 234,000 cu. metres of roundwood were cut.

Fisheries

Fish landings in 2001 totalled 520 tonnes, mainly from inland waters.

INDUSTRY

According to the Financial Times Survey (FT 500), the largest company by market capitalization in Jordan on 4 Jan. 2001 was Arab Bank (US$1,970·7m.).

The number of industrial units in 2002 was 17,834, employing 124,421 persons in mining, quarrying, manufacturing and the production and distribution of electricity. The principal industrial concerns are the production or processing of phosphates, potash, fertilizers, cement and oil.

Production in 1,000 tonnes: cement (2001), 3,149; residual fuel oil (2000), 1,496; distillate fuel oil (2000), 895; fertilizers (2000), 619; phosphoric acid (2002), 594.

Labour

The workforce in 1996 was 935,000. In 2002, 692,070 persons worked in social and public administration, 150,922 in commerce, 122,741 in mining and manufacturing, and 31,095 in transport and communications. In 1993, 54,995 persons worked in agriculture. Unemployment was officially 12% in Oct. 2000 but was estimated by economists to be more than 20%. In 2000 Jordan had more than 600,000 foreign workers, many of them Iraqis.

INTERNATIONAL TRADE

Foreign debt was US$8,094m. in 2002. Legislation of 1995 eases restrictions on foreign investment and makes some reductions in taxes and customs duties.

Imports and Exports

Imports (f.o.b.) in 2002 totalled US$5,069·2m. and exports (f.o.b.) US$2,766·1m. Major exports are phosphate, potash, fertilizers, foodstuffs, pharmaceuticals, fruit and vegetables, textiles, cement, plastics, detergent and soap.

Principal import sources in 1999 were from: Germany, 9·9%; USA, 8·6%; and Italy, 6·1%. Main exports in 1999 were to: Saudi Arabia, 15·9%; India, 12·6%; and Japan, 5·2%. In 2000 Jordan became the first Arab country to sign a free trade agreement with the USA.

COMMUNICATIONS

Roads

Total length of roads, 2003, 7,364 km, of which 2,972 km were main roads. In 2003 there were 422,904 passenger cars (77·1 per 1,000 inhabitants), 686 motorcycles and mopeds, 8,910 coaches and buses, and 113,223 trucks and vans. There were 832 deaths in road accidents in 2003 (388 in 1992).

Rail

The 1,050 mm gauge Hejaz Jordan and Aqaba Railway runs from the Syrian border at Nassib to Ma'an and Naqb Ishtar and Aqaba Port (total, 618 km). The state railway is only minimally operational. Passenger-km travelled in 2000 came to 2m. and freight tonne-km to 671m.

Civil Aviation

The Queen Alia International airport is at Zizya, 30 km south of Amman. There are also international flights from Amman's second airport. Queen Alia International handled 2,231,806 passengers in 2001 (2,209,168 on international flights) and 87,679 tonnes of freight. The national carrier is Royal Jordanian, which flew 36·2m. km and carried 1,252,200 passengers (all on international flights) in 1999. Royal Jordanian is currently state-owned, but in Oct. 1999 the government announced its intention to sell a 49% stake in the airline.

Shipping

In 2002 sea-going shipping totalled 69,000 GRT. Vessels totalling 2,789,000 NRT entered ports in 2002. The main port is Aqaba.

Telecommunications

There were 1,949,300 telephone subscribers in 2003, or 355·7 per 1,000 persons. In Jan. 2000 the government sold a 40% stake in Jordan Telecommunications Company (Jordan Telecom) to France Telecom for US$508m. Jordan Telecom's monopoly on fixed-line services ended on 1 Jan. 2005. There were 200,000 PCs (37·5 for every 1,000 persons) in 2002 and 83,000 fax machines. Jordan had 1,325,000 mobile phone subscribers in 2003. The number of Internet users in 2002 was 307,500.

Postal Services

In 2003 there were 393 post offices.

SOCIAL INSTITUTIONS

Justice

The legal system is based on Islamic law (Shari'a) and civil law, and administers justice in cases of civil, criminal or administrative disputes. The constitution guarantees the independence of the judiciary. Courts are divided into three tiers: regular courts (courts of first instance, magistrate courts, courts of appeal, Court of Cassation/High Court of Justice); religious courts (Shari'a courts and Council of Religious Communities); special courts (e.g. police court, military councils, customs court, state security court).

The death penalty is authorized; there were ten executions in 2005. The murder rate in 2000 stood at two per 100,000 population. The population in penal institutions in Jan. 2002 was 5,448 (106 per 100,000 of national population).

Education

Adult literacy in 2003 was 89·9% (male, 95·1%; female, 84·7%). Basic primary and secondary education is free and compulsory. In 2002–03 there were 1,366 kindergartens (1,362 private) with 4,871 teachers and 92,244 pupils; 2,789 basic schools (662 private) with 55,911 teachers and 1,222,360 pupils; 1,205 secondary schools (154 private) with 15,213 teachers and 179,842 pupils; and 55 vocational schools with 3,557 teachers and 43,424 pupils. In 1996–97 there were six state and 11 private universities. 19,221 Jordanians were studying abroad in 2003.

In 1999–2000 total expenditure on education came to 5·0% of GNP and 20·6% of total government spending.

Health

There were 10,623 physicians, 14,251 nurses and midwives, 2,850 dentists and 4,975 pharmacists in 2001. In 2003 there were a total of 9,743 hospital beds in 97 hospitals.

Welfare

There are numerous government organizations involved in social welfare projects. The General Union of Voluntary Societies finances and supports the Governorate Unions, voluntary societies, and needy individuals through financial and in-kind aid. There are also 240 day care centres run by non-governmental organizations.

RELIGION

About 94% of the population are Sunni Muslims.

CULTURE

World Heritage Sites

There are three sites on the World Heritage List: the rose-red rock-carved city of Petra and Quseir Amra (both entered on the list in 1985) and Um er-Rasas (2004). Petra is over 2,000 years old and contains more than 800 monuments, some built but most carved out of the natural rock. Quseir Amra is the best preserved of Jordan's 'desert castles' and is noted for its frescoes. Um er-Rasas (Kastron Mefa'a) is an archaeological site largely unexcavated, containing remains from the Roman, Byzantine and Early Muslim periods.

Broadcasting

The Jordan Radio and Television Corporation transmits two national radio services (one in English), a Koran service and an external service, Radio Jordan.

There are two television services (colour by PAL). There were 1·85m. radio receivers in use in 2000 and 852,000 TV sets in 2001.

Press

In 2000 there were five daily newspapers with a combined circulation (1998) of 352,000. Newspapers were denationalized in 1990, although government institutions still hold majority ownership.

In 2002 a total of 791 book titles were published.

Tourism

Tourism accounts for 8·5% of GDP. In 2002 there were 1,622,000 foreign tourists; spending by tourists totalled US$786m.

DIPLOMATIC REPRESENTATIVES

Of Jordan in the United Kingdom (6 Upper Phillimore Gdns, Kensington, London, W8 7HA)
Ambassador: Vacant.
Chargé d'Affaires a.i.: Mohammed N. Zenati.

Of the United Kingdom in Jordan (PO Box 87, Abdoun, Amman)
Ambassador: Christopher Prentice.

Of Jordan in the USA (3504 International Dr., NW, Washington, D.C., 20008)
Ambassador: Karim Tawfiq Kawar.

Of the USA in Jordan (Abdoun, Amman)
Ambassador: David Hale.

Of Jordan to the United Nations
Ambassador: Prince Zeid Raad Al Hussein.

Of Jordan to the European Union
Ambassador: Vacant.
Chargé d'Affaires a.i.: Malek Twal.

FURTHER READING

Department of Statistics. *Statistical Yearbook*
Central Bank of Jordan. *Monthly Statistical Bulletin*

Dallas, R., *King Hussein, The Great Survivor.* Profile Books, London, 1998
Rogan, E. and Tell, T. (eds.) *Village, Steppe and State: the Social Origins of Modern Jordan.* London, 1994
Salibi, Kamal, *The Modern History of Jordan.* I. B. Tauris, London, 1998
Satloff, R. B., *From Abdullah to Hussein: Jordan in Transition.* OUP, 1994

National Statistical Office: National Information Technology Centre, P. O. Box 259 Jubeiha, 11941 Amman.
Website: http://www.nic.gov.jo

KAZAKHSTAN

Qazaqstan Respūblīkasy

Capital: Astana
Population projection, 2010: 14·80m.
GDP per capita, 2003: (PPP$) 6,671
HDI/world rank: 0·761/80

KEY HISTORICAL EVENTS

Turkestan (part of the territory now known as Kazakhstan) was conquered by the Russians in the 1860s. In 1866 Tashkent was occupied, followed in 1868 by Samarkand. Subsequently further territory was conquered and united with Russian Turkestan. In the 1870s Bokhara was subjugated, with the amir, by an agreement of 1873, recognizing Russian suzerainty. In the same year Khiva became a vassal state to Russia. Until 1917 Russian Central Asia was divided politically into the Khanate of Khiva, the Emirate of Bokhara and the Governor-Generalship of Turkestan. In the summer of 1919 the authority of the Soviet Government extended to these regions. The Khan of Khiva was deposed in Feb. 1920, and a People's Soviet Republic was set up, the medieval name of Khorezm being revived. In Aug. 1920 the Amir of Bokhara suffered the same fate and a similar regime was set up in Bokhara. The former Governor-Generalship of Turkestan was constituted an Autonomous Soviet Socialist Republic within the RSFSR on 11 April 1921.

In the autumn of 1924 the Soviets of the Turkestan, Bokhara and Khiva Republics decided to redistribute their territories on a nationality basis; at the same time Bokhara and Khiva became Socialist Republics. The redistribution was completed in May 1925, when the new states of Uzbekistan, Turkmenistan and Tajikistan were accepted into the USSR as Union Republics. The remaining districts of Turkestan populated by Kazakhs were united with Kazakhstan which was established as an Autonomous Soviet Republic in 1925 and became a constituent republic in 1936. Independence was declared on 16 Dec. 1991 when Kazakhstan joined the CIS. Nursultan Nazarbaev became president, and legislation has been introduced to award him privileges for life. Over a million of the country's ethnic Russians and Germans have returned to their homelands in the last ten years. Kazakhstan has been focusing on border disputes with China and Uzbekistan and fighting fundamentalism along with other Central Asian governments.

TERRITORY AND POPULATION

Kazakhstan is bounded in the west by the Caspian Sea and Russia, in the north by Russia, in the east by China and in the south by Uzbekistan, Kyrgyzstan and Turkmenistan. The area is 2,724,900 sq. km (1,052,090 sq. miles). The 1999 census population was 14,952,420 (density of 5·5 per sq. km), of whom Kazakhs accounted for 53·4% and Russians 30·0%. There are also Ukrainians, Uzbeks, Germans, Tatars, Uigurs and smaller minorities. 2005 estimate: 14,825,000. In 1999 the population was 51·8% female; it was 55·9% urban in 2003. During the 1990s some 1·5m. people left Kazakhstan—mostly Russians and Germans returning to their homelands. Approximately 10·8m. Kazakhs live abroad.

The UN gives a projected population for 2010 of 14·80m.

Kazakhstan's administrative divisions consist of 14 provinces and two cities as follows, with area and population:

	Area (sq. km)	Population (1999)
Almaty[1]	223,900	1,558,500
Almaty City	300	1,129,400
Aqmola[2]	121,400	836,300
Aqtöbe	300,600	682,600
Astana City	300	319,300
Atyraū[3]	118,600	440,300
Batys Qazaqstan	151,300	616,800
Mangghystaū	165,600	314,700
Ongtüstik Qazaqstan	117,300	1,978,300
Pavlodar	124,800	807,000
Qaraghandy	428,000	1,410,200
Qostanay	196,000	1,017,700
Qyzylorda	226,000	596,200
Shyghys Qazaqstan	283,300	1,531,000
Soltüstik Qazaqstan	123,200	726,000
Zhambyl[4]	144,300	988,800

[1]Formerly Alma-Ata. [2]Formerly Tselinograd and then Akmola.
[3]Formerly Gurev. [4]Formerly Dzhambul.

In Dec. 1997 the capital was moved from Almaty to Aqmola, which was renamed Astana in May 1998 (the name of the province remained as Aqmola). Astana has a population of 313,000 (2000). Other major cities, with 2000 populations: Almaty (1,129,000); Qaraghandy (437,000); Shymkent (360,000).

The official language is Kazakh.

SOCIAL STATISTICS

2003: births, 247,946; deaths, 155,277; marriages, 110,414. Rates, 2003 (per 1,000 population): births, 16·6; deaths, 10·4. Suicides in 2002 numbered 4,271 (rate of 28·8 per 100,000 population). Expectation of life at birth, 2003, 57·8 years for males and 69·0 years for females. Infant mortality, 2001, 61 per 1,000 live births; fertility rate, 2001, 2·0 births per woman.

CLIMATE

The climate is generally fairly dry. Winters are cold but spring comes earlier in the south than in the far north. Almaty, Jan. −4°C, July 24°C. Annual rainfall 598 mm.

CONSTITUTION AND GOVERNMENT

Relying on a judgement of the Constitutional Court that the 1994 parliamentary elections were invalid, President Nazarbaev dissolved parliament on 11 March 1995 and began to rule by decree. A referendum on the adoption of a new constitution was held on 30 Aug. 1995. The electorate was 8·8m.; turnout was 80%. 89% of votes cast were in favour. The Constitution thus adopted allows the President to rule by decree and to dissolve parliament if it holds a no-confidence vote or twice rejects his nominee for

Prime Minister. It establishes a parliament consisting of a 39-member Senate (two selected by each of the elected assemblies of Kazakhstan's 16 principal administrative divisions plus seven appointed by the president); and a lower house of 77 (67 popularly elected by single mandate districts, with ten members elected by party-list vote). The constitution was amended in Oct. 1998 to provide for a seven-year presidential term.

A Constitutional Court was set up in Dec. 1991 and a new Constitution adopted on 28 Jan. 1993, but President Nazarbaev abolished the Constitutional Court in 1995. In June 2000 a bill to provide President Nazarbaev with life-long powers and privileges was passed into law.

National Anthem

'Mening Qazaqstan' ('My Kazakhstan'); words by Z. Nazhimedenov and N. Nazarbaev, tune by S. Kaldayakov.

GOVERNMENT CHRONOLOGY

Presidents since 1991.
1991–   Nursultan Abishuly Nazarbaev

RECENT ELECTIONS

At the presidential elections of 4 Dec. 2005 Nursultan Nazarbaev was re-elected with 91·2% of votes cast against four other candidates. Turnout was 76·8%.

National Assembly elections were held on 19 Sept. and 3 Oct. 2004. President Nursultan Nazarbaev's Otan (Fatherland) Party won 42 seats. Aist (Agrarian and Industrial Union of Workers Block) won 11 seats, the Asar (All Together) Party 4, the Ak Zhol (Bright Path) Party 1, the Democratic Party 1 and ind. 18. There were widespread allegations that the elections were fraudulent.

CURRENT ADMINISTRATION

President: Nursultan Nazarbaev; b. 1940 (elected in 1991 and re-elected in 1999 and 2005).

In March 2006 the government comprised:

Prime Minister: Daniyal Akhmetov; b. 1954 (sworn in 13 June 2003).

Deputy Prime Minister: Karim Massimov.

Minister of Agriculture: Akhmetzhan Yessimov. *Culture, Information and Sports:* Yermukhamet Yertysbayev. *Defence:* Col. Gen. Mukhtar Altynbayev. *Economy and Budget Planning:* Kairat Kelimbetov. *Education and Science:* Byrganym Aytimova. *Emergency Situations:* Shalbai Kulmakhanov. *Energy and Mineral Resources:* Baktykozha Izmoukhambetov. *Environmental Protection:* Kamaltin Mukhamedzhanov. *Finance:* Natalya Korzhova. *Foreign Affairs:* Kasymzhomart Tokayev. *Health:* Erbolat Dossayev. *Industry and Trade:* Vladimir Shkolnik. *Internal Affairs:* Baurzhan Mukhamedzhanov. *Justice:* Zagipa Baliyeva. *Labour and Social Security:* Gulzhana Karagusova. *Transport and Communications:* Askar Mamin.

Chairman, Senate (*Upper House*): Nurtay Abikaev.

Chairman, Majlis (*Lower House*): Ural Mukhamedzhanov.

CURRENT LEADERS

Nursultan Abishuly Nazarbaev

Position
President

Introduction
Nursultan Nazarbaev, leader of the Otan (Fatherland) Party, was elected president of Kazakhstan in 1991, leading the country to independence after the collapse of the USSR. He has sought to exploit the nation's rich mineral resources although much of the population remains poor. He has sought close ties with regional neighbours as well as Russia, China and the West. His regime, however, has been widely accused of corruption and human rights abuses.

Early Life
Nursultan Nazarbaev was born on 6 July 1940 in Chemolgan in the Almaty region. He was employed by the Karagandy metallurgical works in 1960 and graduated in engineering from a higher technical college in 1967. Having joined the Soviet Communist Party in 1962, he became secretary of the party's regional committee in 1977 and rose through the ranks to the central committee. In 1984 he was appointed chairman of the Republic's council of ministers and became a full member of the Politburo five years later. In the same year Nazarbaev was named first secretary of the Kazakh Communist party. In April 1990 he was chosen by the Supreme Soviet as president of the Republic of Kazakhstan.

Career in Office
Nazarbaev spoke out in support of Soviet leader Mikhail Gorbachev during a coup attempt in Moscow in Aug. 1991. Nevertheless, Kazakhstan seceded from the USSR in Dec. 1991 to join the Commonwealth of Independent States (CIS). In the same month Nazarbaev's position as head of state was consolidated in presidential elections. Earlier in the year he had closed the country's most important nuclear test ground at Semipalatinsk.

In 1992 Nazarbaev secured Kazakhstan's membership of the UN and of the Conference on Security and Co-operation in Europe (the precursor of the OSCE). Despite parliamentary opposition, he implemented a series of economic reforms, including a programme of privatization. He sought close co-operation with his CIS partners and signed up Kazakhstan to the strategic arms reduction treaty and the treaty on the non-proliferation of nuclear weapons. Two years later he signed an agreement on economic and military co-operation with Russia. In the same year his term of office was extended by referendum to 2000 amid accusations that he was becoming increasingly autocratic.

In 1997 Nazarbaev announced the transfer of the national capital from Almata to Aqmola (renamed Astana in 1998) to take advantage of Aqmola's central location and its seismatically less sensitive position. He won presidential elections brought forward to Jan. 1999 with 79·8% of the vote, but earned international criticism for the disqualification of the leading opposition figure, Akezhan Kazhegeldin, from the polls. Kazhegeldin was accused of corruption, went into exile and was sentenced *in absentia* to ten years imprisonment. Parliamentary elections held later in the year were criticized by the OSCE.

In 2000 Nazarbaev's government instituted a ten-year economic programme, winning praise from the World Bank for its reforms. Exploitation of the nation's vast oil reserves offers the best opportunity of economic success, and Kazakhstan aims to become the world's sixth largest oil producer by 2010.

Nazarbaev implemented heightened security measures against Islamist militants following increased activity in the region in 2000. In June 2001 Kazakhstan joined the Shanghai Co-operation Organization (along with China, Russia, Kyrgyzstan, Uzbekistan and Tajikistan) to bolster regional co-operation in economics and against ethnic and religious activism. In the aftermath of the 11 Sept. attacks on Washington and New York in 2001, Nazarbaev met US President George W. Bush to consolidate relations between the two countries.

Nazarbaev's autocratic style of governance has regularly been the focus of international attention. In 2000 the government passed constitutional amendments granting him wide-ranging influence once he has retired from office. In Nov. 2001 he purged his government of founding members of Democratic Choice, a group seeking to reduce presidential powers. Leading Democratic Choice figures were subsequently imprisoned on a variety of disputed charges, as were journalists critical of his regime. In 2002 Nazarbaev was accused of siphoning state monies into a personal bank account, but he denied any wrongdoing.

In Feb. 2003 the government announced plans to work with Russia to develop a national nuclear energy programme. In June 2003 prime minister Imangali Tasmagambetov resigned in protest at land reforms allowing private ownership for the first time in the nation's history. Nazarbaev's Otan Party won a majority of National Assembly seats in parliamentary elections in 2004, and on 4 Dec. 2005 he was re-elected overwhelmingly as president with 91% of the votes cast.

DEFENCE

Defence expenditure in 2003 totalled US$1,500m. (US$101 per capita), representing 1·5% of GDP.

Army

Personnel, 2002, 41,000. Paramilitary units: Presidential Guard (2,000), Government Guard (500), Ministry of the Interior Security Troops (20,000), Frontier Guards (12,000).

Navy

A 3,000-strong Maritime Border Guard operates on the Caspian Sea. Kazakhstan hopes to have a fully-fledged navy by 2013.

Air Force

In 2002 there was an Air Force division with about 19,000 personnel with some 164 combat aircraft, including MiG-29 and Su-27 interceptors and MiG-27, Su-24 and Su-25 strike aircraft.

INTERNATIONAL RELATIONS

In Jan. 1995 agreements were reached for closer integration with Russia, including the combining of military forces, currency convertibility and a customs union.

Kazakhstan is a member of the UN, CIS, OSCE, Asian Development Bank, ECO, IOM, OIC, Islamic Development Bank and the NATO Partnership for Peace. Sandwiched between Russia and China, in 1998 President Nazarbaev signed major treaties with both countries in the hope of improving relations with both.

ECONOMY

Agriculture accounted for 8·6% of GDP in 2002, industry 38·6% and services 52·8%.

Overview

Kazakhstan's economy shrunk drastically after the break-up of the Soviet Union. From 1991 to 1995 both GDP and GDP per capita fell considerably before stabilizing and remaining static over the latter half of the 1990s. In the 2000s a strong recovery was made on the back of economic reform and privatization schemes implemented in the latter half of the 1990s. Economic growth has been strong in recent years and per capita income levels have surpassed the average for ex-Soviet republics and have converged on the world average. The country is a net energy exporter and its industry is heavily geared towards the exploitation of its vast natural resources. Exports of Kazakhstan's resources are strong but so is dependence on imports. Government policy has aimed to increase output in other industrial areas in response but a significant reduction in import dependence has yet to materialize. Despite the recovery and continued growth, economic management remains far from optimal and corruption is endemic. Western-oriented opposition groups with reform agendas have grown over the years and the potential exists for political instability.

Currency

The unit of currency is the *tenge* of 100 *tiyn*, which was introduced on 15 Nov. 1993 at 1 tenge = 500 roubles. It became the sole legal tender on 25 Nov. 1993. Inflation was running at nearly 1,880% in 1994, but dropped dramatically and was only 6·9% in 2004. In June 2002 foreign exchange reserves were US$2,280m. and gold reserves amounted to 1·74m. troy oz. Total money supply in May 2002 was 258,470m. tenge.

Budget

Government revenue and expenditure (in 1m. tenge), year ending 31 Dec.:

	1998	1999	2000	2001
Revenue	262,916	207,765	317,747	393,584
Expenditure	318,253	304,150	372,612	475,710

Performance

The break-up of the Soviet Union triggered an economic collapse as orders from Russian factories for Kazakhstan's metals and phosphates, two mainstays of the economy, dried up. Real GDP growth was –1·9% in 1998 but there was a slight recovery in 1999, with growth of 2·7%. Growth was an impressive 9·8% in 2000, an even more spectacular 13·5% in 2001 and 9·8% in 2002. The economy has continued to expand in 2003 and 2004 with growth of 9·3% and 9·4% respectively. Total GDP in 2004 was US$40·7bn. The size of the economy is expected to double between 2004 and 2008, and triple between 2004 and 2015, as a result of increasing oil production.

Banking and Finance

The central bank and bank of issue is the National Bank (*Governor,* Anvar Saydenov). In 2001 there were 44 domestic banks, with assets totalling US$5·3bn. The largest bank is Kazkommertsbank (KKB), with assets of US$1·8bn. in Dec. 2002. There were also 12 branches or representative offices of foreign banks. Foreign direct investment amounted to US$2·8bn. in 2001, more than double the 2000 total.

ENERGY AND NATURAL RESOURCES

Environment

Carbon dioxide emissions from the consumption and flaring of fossil fuels in 2002 were the equivalent of 9·9 tonnes per capita.

Electricity

Installed capacity was 19·0m. kW in 2000. Output in 2003 was 63·9bn. kWh. There is one nuclear power station. Consumption per capita was an estimated 3,666 kWh in 2000.

Oil and Gas

Proven oil reserves in 2002 were 9·0bn. bbls. The onshore Tengiz field has estimated oil reserves between 6bn. and 9bn. bbls.; the onshore Karachaganak field has oil reserves of 2bn. bbls., and gas reserves of 600,000m. cu. metres. Output of crude oil, 2003, 52·2m. tonnes; natural gas, 2002, 12·3bn. cu. metres with proven reserves (2002) of 1,840bn. cu. metres. The first major pipeline for the export of oil from the Tengiz field was opened in March 2001, linking the Caspian port of Atyraü with the Russian Black Sea port of Novorossiisk. In Sept. 1997 Kazakhstan signed oil agreements with China worth US$9·5bn.; these include a 3,000 km pipeline to Xinjiang province in western China. Oil and gas investment by foreign companies is now driving the economy. In 1997 oil production sharing deals were concluded with two international consortia to explore the North Caspian basin and to develop the Karachaganak gas field. A huge new offshore oilfield in the far north of the Caspian Sea, known as East Kashagan, was discovered in early 2000. The field could prove to be the largest find in the last 30 years, and estimates suggest that it may contain 50bn. bbls. of oil. The various recent discoveries have meant that by 2010 Kazakhstan aims to have become the world's sixth largest oil producer. Oil production is expected to triple in the next ten years.

It is believed that there may be as much as 14bn. tonnes of oil and gas reserves under Kazakhstan's portion of the Caspian Sea.

A state-owned national company, Kazmunaigaz, was created in 2002 to manage the oil and natural gas industries.

Minerals

Kazakhstan is extremely rich in mineral resources, including coal, bauxite, cobalt, vanadium, iron ores, chromium, phosphates, borates and other salts, copper, lead, manganese, molybdenum, nickel, tin, gold, silver, tungsten and zinc. Production figures (2003), in tonnes: coal, 80·60m.; iron ore, 19·28m.; bauxite, 4·74m.; lignite, 4·31m.; copper, 485,000; zinc, 394,000; uranium (2002), 2,800; silver, 827·4; gold, 19·3.

Agriculture

Kazakh agriculture has changed from primarily nomad cattle breeding to production of grain, cotton and other industrial crops. In 2002 agriculture accounted for 9% of GDP. There were 21·54m. ha. of arable land and 0·14m. ha. of permanent crops in 2001. 2·35m. ha. were irrigated in 2001. In 1993, 181·3m. ha. were under cultivation, of which private subsidiary agriculture accounted for 0·3m. ha. and commercial farming 6·3m. ha. in 16,300 farms. Around 60,000 private farms have emerged since independence.

Tobacco, rubber plants and mustard are also cultivated. Kazakhstan has rich orchards and vineyards. Kazakhstan is noted for its livestock, particularly its sheep, from which excellent quality wool is obtained. Livestock (2003): 4·56m. cattle (down from 9·57m. in 1993), 9·79m. sheep (down from 33·63m. in 1993), 1·49m. goats, 1·23m. pigs, 1·02m. horses and 23·79m. chickens.

Output of main agricultural products (in 1,000 tonnes) in 2003: wheat, 11,537; potatoes, 2,308; barley, 2,154; watermelons, 604; tomatoes, 448; maize, 438; sugarbeets, 424; cabbages, 328; onions, 320; sunflower seeds, 293; rice, 273. Livestock products, 2002 (in 1,000 tonnes): cow's milk, 4,110; meat, 676; eggs, 117. Kazakhstan is a major exporter of grain to Russia, but in recent years there has been a significant reduction in the quantity exported as a result of low crop yields coupled with the need to meet domestic demand.

Forestry

Forests covered 12·15m. ha. in 2000, or 4·5% of the land area. In 1999, 315,000 cu. metres of timber were cut.

Fisheries

Catches in 2001 totalled 30,654 tonnes, exclusively freshwater fish.

INDUSTRY

Kazakhstan was heavily industrialized in the Soviet period, with non-ferrous metallurgy, heavy engineering and the chemical industries prominent. Output was valued at 2,000bn. tenge in current prices in 2001, up from 1,798bn. tenge in 2000. Production, 2003 (in 1,000 tonnes) includes: crude steel, 5,069; pig iron, 4,138; residual fuel oil, 3,069; distillate fuel oil, 2,754; cement, 2,581; wheat flour, 2,123; petrol, 1,841; ferroalloys (2002), 1,241; fabrics (1997), 24·6m. sq. metres; leather footwear (2002), 250,000 pairs; TV sets (2001), 347,000 units.

Labour

In 2002 the economically active labour force numbered 6,708,900, with the main areas of activity as follows: agriculture, hunting and forestry, 2,366,700; trade, restaurants and hotels, 1,007,200; industry, 824,000; education, 589,000; transport, storage and communications, 503,700. In 2003 the unemployment rate was 8·8% (down from 13·5% in 1999).

INTERNATIONAL TRADE

In Jan. 1994 an agreement to create a single economic zone was signed with Kyrgyzstan and Uzbekistan. Since Jan. 1992 individuals and enterprises have been able to engage in foreign trade without needing government permission, except for goods 'of national interest' (fuel, minerals, mineral fertilizers, grain, cotton, wool, caviar and pharmaceutical products) which may be exported only by state organizations. Foreign debt was US$17,538m. in 2002.

Imports and Exports

In 2003 imports (c.i.f.) were valued at US$8,408·7m. and exports (f.o.b.) at US$12,926·7m. In 2003, 39·0% of imports came from Russia, 8·7% from Germany, 6·2% from China and 5·6% from the USA. Main export markets in 2003 were Bermuda, 17·0%; Russia, 15·2%; Switzerland, 13·0%; China, 12·8%. Main imports: machinery, mechanical appliances and electrical equipment, transportation equipment, and mineral products. Main exports: mineral products, ferrous and non-ferrous metals, and vegetable products.

COMMUNICATIONS

Roads

In 2002 there were 82,980 km of roads, of which 22,781 were national roads. In 1997 an estimated 1bn. passengers used public transport and 1bn. tonnes of freight were carried. Passenger cars in use in 2003 numbered 1,148,754, and there were also 261,327 trucks and vans and 61,391 buses and coaches. There were 2,147 fatalities as a result of road accidents in 1999.

Rail

In 2000 there were 13,545 km of 1,520 mm gauge railways. Passenger-km travelled in 2003 came to 10·7bn. and freight tonne-km to 147·7bn.

Civil Aviation

The national carrier is Air Kazakhstan. There is an international airport at Almaty. In 1999 scheduled airline traffic of Kazakhstan-based carriers flew 33·2m. km, carrying 667,000 passengers (318,000 on international flights).

Shipping

There is one large port, Aktau. In 1993, 1·2m. passengers and 4m. tonnes of freight were carried on inland waterways. Merchant shipping totalled 11,845 GRT and 20 vessels in 2002.

Telecommunications

Telephone subscribers numbered 2,910,100 in 2002, or 182·2 per 1,000 persons. There were 1,027,000 mobile phone subscribers in 2002 and 3,000 fax machines. Kazakhstan had 250,000 Internet users in 2002.

Postal Services

In 2003 there were 3,791 post offices.

SOCIAL INSTITUTIONS

Justice

In 1994, 201,796 crimes were reported; in 1996 there were 2,986 murders. The population in penal institutions in April 2001 was 84,000 (522 per 100,000 of national population—one of the highest rates in the world). A moratorium on the death penalty was decreed in Dec. 2003 with a view to eventual abolition.

Education

In 2002–03, 147,500 children were attending pre-school institutions, there were 1,120,000 pupils at primary schools, 2,187,700 pupils at secondary schools and 597,500 students at higher education institutions. Adult literacy rate is more than 99%.

Health

In 2002 there were 894 hospitals with a provision of 65 beds per 10,000 inhabitants. There were 51,289 physicians, 4,337 dentists, 88,140 nurses, 2,672 pharmacists and 8,094 midwives in 2001.

Welfare

In Jan. 1994 there were 2·1m. age and 0·9m. other pensioners. Pension contributions are 20% of salary and are payable to the State Pension Fund.

RELIGION

There were some 4,000 mosques in 1996 (63 in 1990). A Roman Catholic diocese was established in 1991. In 2001 there were 6,988,000 Muslims, 1,216,000 Russian Orthodox and 318,000 Protestants. The remainder of the population followed other religions or were non-religious.

CULTURE

World Heritage Sites

Kazakhstan has two sites on the UNESCO World Heritage List: the Mausoleum of Khoja Ahmed Yasawi (inscribed on the list in 2003), an excellent and well preserved example of late 14th century Timurid architecture; and Petroglyphs within the Archaeological Landscape of Tamgaly (2004), a concentration of some 5,000 rock carvings.

Broadcasting

Broadcasting is the responsibility of the Kazakh State Radio and Television Co. There are three national and 13 regional radio programmes, a Radio Moscow relay and a foreign service, Radio Alma-Ata (Kazakh, English). There is one TV channel (colour by SECAM). There were 6·27m. radio receivers in 2000 and 5·44m. television receivers in 2001.

Press

In 1995 there were 472 periodicals in Kazakh, 511 in Russian and 60 in both languages. In 2002 a total of 1,005 book titles were published.

Tourism

In 2002 there were 2,832,000 foreign tourists; spending by tourists totalled US$621m.

DIPLOMATIC REPRESENTATIVES

Of Kazakhstan in the United Kingdom (33 Thurloe Sq., London, SW7 2SD)
Ambassador: Erlan Idrissov.

Of the United Kingdom in Kazakhstan (Ul. Furmanova 173, Almaty 480091)
Ambassador: James Lyall Sharp.

Of Kazakhstan in the USA (1401 16th St., NW, Washington, D.C., 20036)
Ambassador: Kanat B. Saudabayev.

Of the USA in Kazakhstan (Ul. Furmanova 99/97a, Almaty 480091)
Ambassador: John M. Ordway.

Of Kazakhstan to the United Nations
Ambassador: Yerzhan Kazykhanov.

Of Kazakhstan to the European Union
Ambassador: Konstantin Zhigalov.

FURTHER READING

Alexandrov, M., *Uneasy Alliance: Relations Between Russia and Kazakhstan in the Post-Soviet Era, 1992–1997.* Greenwood Publishing Group, Westport (CT), 1999
Nazpary, J., *Post-Soviet Chaos: Violence and Dispossession in Kazakhstan.* Pluto Press, London, 2001
Olcott, Marta Brill, *The Kazakhs.* Stanford, 1987.—*Kazakhstan: Unfilled Promise.* Carnegie Endowment for International Peace, Washington, D.C., 2001

National Statistical Office: Agency of Kazakhstan on Statistics, 125 Abay Ave., 480008 Almaty, Kazakhstan.
Website: http://www.stat.kz

KENYA

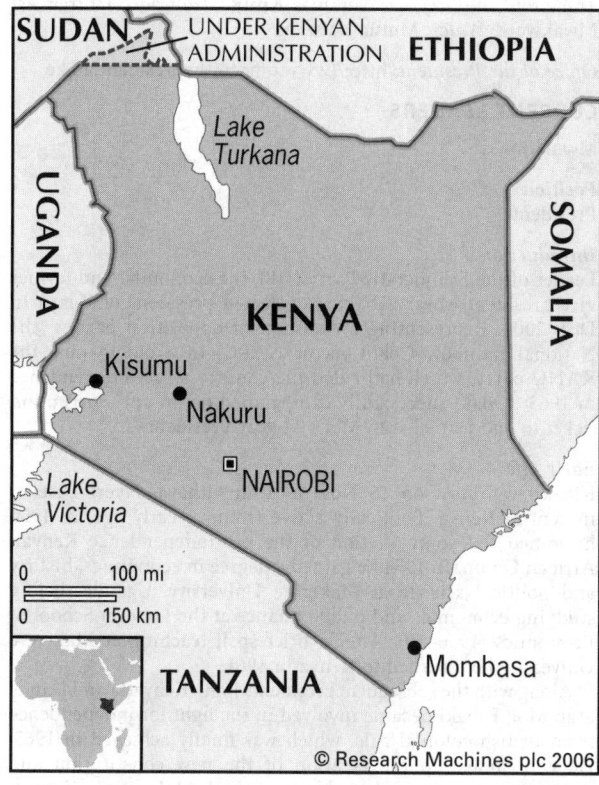

SUDAN · UNDER KENYAN ADMINISTRATION · ETHIOPIA

Lake Turkana

UGANDA

KENYA

SOMALIA

Kisumu

Nakuru

NAIROBI

Lake Victoria

0   100 mi
0   150 km

TANZANIA

Mombasa

© Research Machines plc 2006

Jamhuri ya Kenya
(Republic of Kenya)

Capital: Nairobi
Population projection, 2010: 38·96m.
GDP per capita, 2003: (PPP$) 1,037
HDI/world rank: 0·474/154

KEY HISTORICAL EVENTS

Prior to colonialism, the area comprised African farming communities, notably the Kikuyu and the Masai. From the 16th century through to the 19th, they were loosely controlled by the Arabic rulers of Oman. In 1895 the British declared part of the region the East Africa Protectorate, which from 1920 was known as the Colony of Kenya. The influx of European settlers was resented by Africans not only for the whites' land holdings but also for their exclusive political representation in the colonial Legislative Council. A state of emergency existed between Oct. 1952 and Jan. 1960 during the period of the Mau Mau uprising. Over 13,000 Africans and 100 Europeans were killed. The Kenya African Union was banned and its president, Jomo Kenyatta, imprisoned. The state of emergency ended in 1960. Full internal self-government was achieved in 1962 and in Dec. 1963 Kenya became an independent member of the Commonwealth. In 1982 Kenya became a one-party state and in 1986 party preliminary elections were instituted to reduce the number of parliamentary candidates at general elections. Only those candidates obtaining over 30% of the preliminary vote were eligible to stand. On the death of Kenyatta in Aug. 1978 Daniel T. arap Moi, the vice-president, became acting president and was elected in 1979, and then re-elected in 1983, 1988, 1992 and 1997. An attempted coup in 1982 was unsuccessful. A multi-party election was permitted in 1992 and again in 1997, the first genuinely competitive elections since 1963. In the 2002 elections the opposition united behind Mwai Kibaki, who won a landslide victory against Moi's successor Uhuru Kenyatta. Kibaki became the first non-Kenya African National Union president of independent Kenya.

TERRITORY AND POPULATION

Kenya is bounded by Sudan and Ethiopia in the north, Uganda in the west, Tanzania in the south and Somalia and the Indian Ocean in the east. The total area is 582,646 sq. km, of which 581,677 sq. km is land area. In the 1989 census the population was 21,443,636 (19% urban; up to 39·3% by 2003). The 1999 census gave a population of 28,686,607 (14,481,018 females). 2005 estimate: 34,256,000.

The UN gives a projected population for 2010 of 38·96m.

The land areas, populations and capitals of the provinces are:

Province	Sq. km	Census 1999	Capital	Census 1999
Rift Valley	173,868	6,987,036	Nakuru	219,366
Eastern	159,891	4,631,779	Embu	31,500
Nyanza	16,162	4,392,196	Kisumu	322,734
Central	13,176	3,724,159	Nyeri	98,908
Western	8,360	3,358,776	Kakamega	73,607
Coast	83,603	2,487,264	Mombasa	655,018
Nairobi	684	2,143,254		
North-Eastern	126,902	962,143	Garissa	50,955

Other large towns (1999): Eldoret (167,016), Thika (82,665), Ruiru (79,741).

Most of Kenya's 26·44m. people belong to 13 tribes, the main ones including Kikuyu (about 22% of the population), Luhya (14%), Luo (13%), Kalenjin (12%), Kamba (11%), Gusii (6%), Meru (5%) and Mijikenda (5%).

Swahili is the official language, but people belonging to the different tribes have their own language as their mother tongue. English is spoken in commercial centres.

SOCIAL STATISTICS

2000 births (estimates), 1,042,000; deaths, 419,000. Estimated birth rate in 2000 was 34·1 per 1,000 population; estimated death rate, 13·7. Annual population growth rate, 1992–2002, 2·3%. Expectation of life at birth in 2003 was 48·1 years for males and 46·3 years for females. Infant mortality, 2001, 78 per 1,000 live births. Fertility rate, 2001, 4·3 births per woman, down from 5·8 in 1991. In 2000 more than half of Kenyans lived below the poverty line, up by over 10% in the space of ten years.

CLIMATE

The climate is tropical, with wet and dry seasons, but considerable differences in altitude make for varied conditions between the hot, coastal lowlands and the plateau, where temperatures are very much cooler. Heaviest rains occur in April and May, but in some parts there is a second wet season in Nov. and Dec. Nairobi, Jan. 65°F (18·3°C), July 60°F (15·6°C). Annual rainfall 39" (958 mm). Mombasa, Jan. 81°F (27·2°C), July 76°F (24·4°C). Annual rainfall 47" (1,201 mm).

CONSTITUTION AND GOVERNMENT

There is a unicameral *National Assembly*, which until the Dec. 1997 elections had 200 members, comprising 188 elected by universal suffrage for a five-year term, ten members appointed by the President, and the Speaker and Attorney-General *ex officio*. Following a review of constituency boundaries, the

National Assembly now has 210 elected members, 12 members appointed and the two *ex officio* members, making 224 in total. The President is also directly elected for five years; he appoints a Vice-President and other Ministers to a Cabinet over which he presides. A constitutional amendment of Aug. 1992 stipulates that the winning presidential candidate must receive a nationwide majority and also the vote of 25% of electors in at least five of the eight provinces. The sole legal political party had been the Kenya African National Union (KANU), but after demonstrations by the pro-reform lobby which led to extreme violence, KANU agreed to legalize opposition parties. A Constitutional Review Commission was established in 1997 to amend the Constitution before elections that were scheduled for 2002. In Sept. 2002 the Commission recommended changes to Kenya's system of government, including the curbing of presidential powers and the introduction of an executive prime ministerial position. However, in Oct. 2002 President Daniel arap Moi announced the dissolution of parliament before the Commission had completed its task, preventing a new constitution from being in place in time for the elections. A proposed new constitution was rejected at a referendum held in Nov. 2005, with 57% of votes cast against and only 43% in favour. The new constitution would have introduced the post of prime minister, dealt with land reform and provided greater rights for women.

National Anthem

'Ee Mungu nguvu yetu' ('Oh God of all creation'); words by a collective, tune traditional.

GOVERNMENT CHRONOLOGY

President since 1964. (DP = Democratic Party; KANU = Kenya African National Union; NARC = National Rainbow Coalition)

1964–78	KANU	Jomo Kenyatta
1978–2002	KANU	Daniel arap Moi
2002–	NARC/DP	Mwai Kibaki

RECENT ELECTIONS

Presidential elections held on 27 Dec. 2002 were won by Mwai Kibaki of the opposition National Rainbow Coalition (NARC) with 62·2% of the vote, against 31·3% for Uhuru Kenyatta, candidate of the ruling Kenya African National Union (KANU), and 5·9% for Simeon Nyachae of the Forum for the Restoration of Democracy-People (FORD-People). Turnout was 57·2%. Mwai Kibaki's victory ended nearly 40 years of KANU rule since Kenya became independent in 1963.

In parliamentary elections also held on 27 Dec. 2002 NARC won 125 of 210 seats, KANU 64, FORD-People 14, Sisi Kwa Sisi 2, Safina 2, Forum for the Restoration of Democracy-Asili 2 and Shirikisho Party of Kenya 1.

CURRENT ADMINISTRATION

President: Mwai Kibaki; b. 1931 (NARC; sworn in 30 Dec. 2002).

Following the elections of 27 Dec. 2002 a new cabinet was formed, composed in March 2006 as follows:

Vice President and Minister for Home Affairs: Moodi Awori; b. 1927 (appointed 25 Sept. 2003).

Minister of Agriculture: Kipruto arap Kirwa. *Co-operative Development and Marketing:* Peter Njeru Ndwiga. *Defence:* Njenga Karume. *East African and Regional Co-operation:* John Koech. *Education, Science and Technology (acting):* Noah Wekesa. *Environment and Natural Resources, and Lands (acting):* Kivutha Kibwana. *Finance:* Amos Kimunya. *Foreign Affairs:* Raphael Tuju. *Gender, Sports, Culture and Social Services:* Maina Kamanda. *Health:* Charity Ngilu Kaluki. *Housing:* Soita Shitanda. *Information and Communication:* Mutahi Kagwe. *Justice and Constitutional Affairs:* Martha Karua. *Labour and Human Resource Development:* Dr Newton Kulundu. *Livestock and Fisheries Development:* Joseph Konzolo Munyao.

Local Government: Musikari Kombo. *Planning and National Development, and Energy (acting):* Henry Obwocha. *Regional Development Authorities:* Abdi Mohamed. *Roads and Public Works:* Simeon Nyachae. *Tourism and Wildlife:* Morris Dzoro. *Trade and Industry:* Dr Mukhisa Kituyi. *Transport:* Chirau Ali Mwakwere. *Water:* Mutua Katuku.

Office of the President: http://www.officeofthepresident.go.ke

CURRENT LEADERS

Mwai Kibaki

Position
President

Introduction
Leader of the Democratic Party (DP), the economist and former vice president Mwai Kibaki was elected president of Kenya in Dec. 2002. Representing a coalition of opposition parties (the National Rainbow Coalition, or NARC) in a bid to oust the KANU party, which had ruled the country since independence in 1963, Kibaki successfully campaigned on an anti-corruption ticket to end Daniel arap Moi's 24 year-presidency.

Early Life
Kibaki was born on 15 Nov. 1931 in Othaya, Nyeri District in central Kenya. Politically active from an early age, in 1950 he joined the youth section of the pro-independence Kenyan African Union. In 1954 he gained a degree in economics, history and political science at Makerere University, Uganda, before studying economics and public finance at the London School of Economics (1956–59). After a brief spell teaching at Makerere University he returned to Kenya in 1961.

Along with the subsequent presidents Jomo Kenyatta and Daniel arap Moi, Kibaki became involved in the fight for independence from British colonial rule, which was finally achieved in 1963. He contributed to the creation of the new constitution and was among the original members of the KANU party (Kenyan African National Union). He served as the party's chief executive officer from 1961–63 before being elected representative of Bahati, Nairobi in 1963. From 1963–66 he worked for the finance ministry heading an economic planning commission, after which he was appointed commerce and industry minister. From 1970–81 he served as finance minister. Vice president under Kenyatta and then his successor Moi, he also served as home affairs minister (1982–88) and health minister (1988–91).

A one-party state from 1964, the ban on opposition parties was finally lifted in 1991. Kibaki resigned from his ministerial post in Dec. 1991, and at the beginning of 1992 he and other party members left KANU to form the Democratic Party, of which Kibaki remains leader. Criticizing endemic government corruption, the DP promised a democratic and open leadership. In the 1992 elections, the country's first multi-party elections, Kibaki took third place with around 20% of votes. Moi retained the presidency although the opposition alleged irregularities. In 1997 he again stood against Moi, coming second with 30·9% of votes.

In 2002 he was chosen to head the National Rainbow Coalition (NARC), a coalition of opposition parties. The ruling party was split when Moi announced his chosen successor to be Uhuru Kenyatta, son of the country's first independent president Jomo Kenyatta. Several KANU members joined NARC. Kibaki's campaign focused on corruption within the ruling party and growing discontent with Moi's presidency. In the Dec. 2002 elections Kibaki won a landslide victory with 62·2% to Kenyatta's 31·3%, ending nearly forty years of KANU rule.

Career in Office
On election, Kibaki prioritized the fight against corruption, which had deterred international aid donors and investors since

1997. In a move towards transparent politics, all public figures, including civil servants, were obliged to declare their wealth confidentially to the anti-corruption police. Kibaki also outlined plans to pass a new constitution, previously blocked by Moi, and vowed to provide free universal primary school education and improve healthcare. In July 2003 the World Bank announced a resumption of loans to the Kenyan government in response to successful anti-corruption reforms.

In Oct. 2003 Kibaki suspended six Appeal Court judges, 17 High Court judges and 82 magistrates and appointed two tribunals to investigate them over allegations of corruption and unethical conduct. The suspension of half of Kenya's judges and a third of magistrates was welcomed by opposition leader, Uhuru Kenyatta. Kibaki extended his anti-corruption drive later that month to forestry officers. The environment minister, Dr Newton Kulundu, ordered compulsory leave for the chief conservator of forests and over 800 forestry officials accused of complicity in illegal logging.

On 22 Nov. 2005 a revised constitution proposing a new post of prime minister but allowing Kibaki to retain extensive presidential powers was rejected in a national referendum by a 57% to 43% margin largely reflecting tribal and regional divisions in the country and the government. Kibaki accepted the result but sacked his entire cabinet the following day. On 7 Dec. he named a new cabinet.

DEFENCE

In 2003 defence expenditure totalled US$237m. (US$7 per capita), representing 1·8% of GDP.

Army

Total strength (2002) 20,000. In addition there is a paramilitary Police General Service Unit of 5,000.

Navy

The Navy, based in Mombasa, consisted in 2002 of 1,400 personnel.

Air Force

An air force, formed on 1 June 1964, was built up with RAF assistance. Equipment includes F-5E/F-5F attack jets. Personnel (2002) 3,000, with 29 combat aircraft and 34 armed helicopters.

INTERNATIONAL RELATIONS

Kenya is a member of the UN, WTO, the Commonwealth, the African Union, African Development Bank, COMESA, EAC, the Intergovernmental Authority on Development, IOM and is an ACP member state of the ACP-EU relationship.

In Nov. 1999 a treaty was signed between Kenya, Tanzania and Uganda to create a new East African Community as a means of developing East African trade, tourism and industry and laying the foundations for a future common market and political federation.

ECONOMY

Agriculture contributed 16·9% of GDP in 2002, industry 19·0% and services 64·1%.

Kenya used to have one of the strongest economies in Africa but years of mismanagement and corruption have had a detrimental effect, made worse in 2000 by one of the longest droughts in living memory. Up to US$1bn. in international aid was frozen during the Moi era because Kenya failed to pass anti-corruption legislation.

Overview

Since a privatization programme was launched in 1992, the government has completed the sale of the majority of the 207 enterprises originally targeted. The government's fiscal programme lost track in 2000–01 owing to failure to privatize Kenya Telkom and loss of foreign aid. In July 2003 the World Bank announced a resumption of loans to the Kenyan government in response to successful anti-corruption reforms.

Currency

The monetary unit is the *Kenya shilling* (KES) of 100 *cents*. The currency became convertible in May 1994. The shilling was devalued by 23% in April 1993. The annual rate of inflation was 9·8% in 2003 and 11·6% in 2004. Foreign exchange reserves were US$1,120m. in June 2002. Gold reserves have been negligible since 1998. In May 2002 total money supply was K Sh 133,063m.

Budget

In 2002–03 revenues totalled K Sh 210,798m. and expenditures K Sh 304,063m. Tax revenue accounted for 85·0% of revenues; recurrent expenditure accounted for 89·5% of expenditures. The fiscal year ends on 30 June.

Performance

Real GDP growth was 4·3% in 2004 (2·8% in 2003). Total GDP in 2004 was US$15·6bn.

Banking and Finance

The central bank and bank of issue is the Central Bank of Kenya (*Governor*, Dr Andrew Mullei, appointed March 2003). There are 43 banks, two non-banking financial institutions and a couple of building societies. In Dec. 2003 their combined assets totalled K Sh 567,600m. In 1998 the government offloaded 25% of its stake in the Kenya Commercial Bank, which lowered its shareholding to 35%. In 2004 it further lowered its shareholding, to 25%.

There is a stock exchange in Nairobi.

ENERGY AND NATURAL RESOURCES

Environment

Kenya's carbon dioxide emissions from the consumption and flaring of fossil fuels in 2002 were the equivalent of 0·3 tonnes per capita.

Electricity

Installed generating capacity was 1·14m. kW in 2003; mostly provided by hydropower from power stations on the Tana river, with some from oil-fired power stations and by geothermal power. Production in 2003 was 4·66bn. kWh, with consumption per capita 142 kWh. In 1999 it was decided to encourage the private sector to take part in electricity generation alongside the state-owned Kenya Electricity Generating Company as a means of bringing to an end the shortage of power and the frequent blackouts. In June 2000 a rationing scheme was introduced in much of the country restricting the power supply to 12 hours a day, and sometimes less.

Oil and Gas

Kenya signed an oil and gas exploration deal in 1997 with Canada's Tornado Resources Ltd, who pledged to commit a minimum of US$7m. over a three-year period.

Minerals

Production, 2001 (in 1,000 tonnes): lime and limestone, 31,631; soda ash (2002), 304; fluorite, 119. Other minerals include gold (1,545 kg in 2001), raw soda, diatomite, garnets, salt and vermiculite.

Agriculture

As agriculture is possible from sea-level to altitudes of over 2,500 metres, tropical, sub-tropical and temperate crops can be grown and mixed farming is pursued. In 2001 there were 4·6m. ha. of arable land and 560,000 ha. of permanent crop land. 87,000 ha. were irrigated in 2001. There were 12,568 tractors in 2001 and 800 harvester-threshers. Four-fifths of the country is range-land which produces mainly livestock products and the wild game which is a major tourist attraction.

Tea, coffee and horticultural products, particularly flowers, are all major foreign exchange earners.

Kenya has about 131,450 ha. under tea production, and is the world's fourth largest producer and largest exporter of tea. The production is high quality tea, raised in near-perfect agronomic conditions. It is plucked the whole year round, and almost exclusively by hand. In 2003 production was 294,000 tonnes; exports were worth US$434m.

Coffee output in 2003 was 55,000 tonnes; 170,000 ha. is under coffee production. Some 75% of the total hectarage under coffee is cultivated by smallholders, although their production has been in decline in recent years.

Other major agricultural products (2000, in 1,000 tonnes): sugarcane (2003), 4,200; maize (2003), 2,520; potatoes (2003), 1,000; cassava, 950; sweet potatoes, 535; plantains, 370; pineapples, 280; bananas, 210; sorghum, 133; wheat, 105.

Maize is Kenya's most important food crop with about 1·3m. ha. under cultivation and annual production of over 2·5m. tonnes. Sisal, pyrethrum, maize and wheat are crops of major importance in the Highlands, while coconuts, cashew nuts, cotton, sugar, sisal and maize are the principal crops grown at the lower altitudes.

Livestock (2003): cattle, 12·8m.; goats, 11·5m.; sheep, 9·5m.; camels, 863,000; pigs, 337,000; chickens, 28·6m.

More than half the agricultural labour force is employed in the livestock sector, accounting for 10% of GDP.

Forestry
Forests covered 17·1m. ha. in 2000 (30·0% of the land area), mainly between 1,800 and 3,300 metres above sea-level. There are coniferous, broad-leaved, hardwood and bamboo forests. Timber production was 21·8m. cu. metres in 2001.

Fisheries
Catches in 2003 totalled 147,665 tonnes, of which 139,811 tonnes were freshwater fish (of which 94% from Lake Victoria). Marine fishing has not reached its full potential, despite a coastline of 680 km. Fish landed from the sea totals less than 8,000 tonnes annually, but there is an estimated potential of 200,000 tonnes in tuna and similar species.

INDUSTRY
In 2001 industry accounted for 18·2% of GDP, with manufacturing contributing 12·5%. In 2003 there were 579 manufacturing firms employing more than 50 persons. The main products are textiles, chemicals, vehicle assembly and transport equipment, leather and footwear, printing and publishing, food and tobacco processing and oil refining. Production (2003) included (in tonnes): cement, 1,658,073; distillate fuel oil, 578,344; sugar, 448,489; residual fuel oil, 338,313; kerosene, 278,968; petrol, 254,702; wheat flour, 179,866; maize meal, 120,942; cattle feed, 99,616.

Labour
The labour force in 1998–99 was 12,326,000. In 1998–99 the unemployment level was estimated to be 1·8m. The average Kenyan earns US$350 a year.

INTERNATIONAL TRADE
Foreign debt was US$6,031m. in 2002. Foreign investment on the stock exchange has been permitted since 1 Jan. 1995. Export Processing Zones were introduced in 1990, offering foreign companies exemption from taxes and duties for ten years.

Imports and Exports
Imports and exports for calendar years in US$1m.:

	1999	2000	2001	2002	2003
Imports f.o.b.	2,731·8	3,044·0	3,176·1	3,277·9	3,708·3
Exports f.o.b.	1,756·7	1,782·2	1,894·0	1,671·2	1,798·7

Principal imports in 2003: machinery and transport equipment, 26·1%; petroleum, 23·3%; chemicals, 15·9%; manufactured goods, 13·4%. Exports: horticultural produce, 26·7%; tea, 24·1%; chemicals, 5·2%; coffee, 4·6%.

Main import suppliers, 2003: United Arab Emirates, 11·3%; Saudi Arabia, 8·6%; South Africa, 8·3%; UK, 7·0%; Japan, 6·6%; India, 5·3%; USA, 5·1%; Indonesia, 4·4%; Germany, 3·9%. Main export markets, 2003: Uganda, 16·7%; UK, 11·6%; Tanzania, 8·0%; Netherlands, 7·7%; Pakistan, 5·0%; Rwanda, 3·3%; Egypt, 3·0%.

The UK is the largest foreign investor in Kenya with over US$1,500m. in more than 60 enterprises.

COMMUNICATIONS

Roads
Of some 63,942 km of roads in 2000, only about 12·1% are paved. The network has seriously deteriorated since the mid 1980s through poor maintenance. Urban roads comprise around 7,000 km, or about 5% of the total road network, but less than half of them are classified as 'good' or in 'fair' condition. Yet more than 70% of all vehicles in the country use urban roads because of the heavy concentration of economic activities in urban areas. Overall, more than 80% of passengers and freight are carried on the roads. There were, in 2003, 270,000 passenger cars, 47,000 motorcycles, 227,000 vans and trucks and 47,000 buses and coaches. There were 13,400 road accidents in 2003, resulting in 2,800 fatalities.

Rail
In 2002 route length was 2,597 km of metre-gauge. Passenger-km travelled in 2002 came to 288m. and freight tonne-km to 1,538m. A South African-led consortium signed agreements with the Kenyan and Ugandan governments in Nov. 2005 to take over the management of the Kenya-Uganda railway linking Mombasa to the Ugandan capital, Kampala.

Civil Aviation
There are international airports at Nairobi (Jomo Kenyatta International) and Mombasa (Moi International). The national carrier is the now privatized Kenya Airways. KLM has a 26% share of Kenya Airways. In 1999 Kenya Airways flew 22·5m. km and carried 1,246,000 passengers (807,600 on international flights). In 2000 Jomo Kenyatta International handled 2,734,108 passengers and 135,619 tonnes of freight, and Moi International 853,944 passengers and 2,716 tonnes of freight.

Shipping
The main port is Mombasa, which handled 12·8m. tonnes of cargo in 2002. Container traffic has doubled since 1990 to 246,731 TEUs (twenty-foot equivalent units) in 2001. The merchant marine totalled 19,000 GRT in 2002, including oil tankers 5,000 GRT. In 2001 vessels totalling 10,600,000 NRT entered ports.

Telecommunications
Kenya had 1,653,300 telephone subscribers in 2002, or 51·8 per 1,000 persons. The government aims to improve telephone availability in rural areas from 0·16 lines per 100 persons in 1997 to one line per 100 by 2015, and in urban areas from four lines to 20 lines per 100 persons. In 2002 mobile phone subscribers numbered 1,325,200. There were 204,000 PCs in 2002 (6·4 per 1,000 persons) and 5,200 fax machines. In 2002 there were 400,000 Internet users.

Postal Services
In 2003 there were 877 post offices, or one for every 36,500 persons.

SOCIAL INSTITUTIONS

Justice
The courts of Justice comprises the court of Appeal, the High Court and a large number of subsidiary courts. The court of Appeal is the final Apellant court in the country and is based in

Nairobi. It comprises seven Judges of Appeal. In the course of its Appellate duties the court of Appeal visits Mombasa, Kisumu, Nakuru and Nyeri. The High court with full jurisdiction in both civil and criminal matters comprises a total of 28 puisne Judges. Puisne Judges sit in Nairobi (16), Mombasa (two), Nakuru, Kisumu, Nyeri, Eldoret, Meru and Kisii (one each).

The Magistracy consists of approximately 300 magistrates of various cadres based in all provincial, district and some divisional centres. In addition to the above there are the Kadhi courts established in areas of concentrated Muslim populations: Mombasa, Nairobi, Malindi, Lamu, Garissa, Kisumu and Marsabit. They exercise limited jurisdiction in matters governed by Islamic Law.

There were 17,589 criminal convictions in 1993; the prison population was 35,278 in 2002 (111 per 100,000 of national population).

Education

The adult literacy rate in 2003 was 73·6% (77·7% among males and 70·2% among females). Free primary education was introduced in 2003. In 2002–03 there were 29,465 pre-primary schools with 49,914 teachers and 1,619,401 pupils. 7,185,106 pupils were in primary schools in 2003 with 178,622 teachers. In 2003 there were also 884,950 pupils and 46,445 teachers in secondary schools; 32 teacher training schools with 21,136 students; 24 technical training institutes with 18,611 students. There were three polytechnics with 14,106 students, and six universities (Nairobi, Moi, Kenyatta, Maseno, Egerton and Jomo Kenyatta University College of Agriculture and Technology) with 58,016 students.

In 2003–04 total expenditure on education came to 7·7% of GNP and 20·6% of total government spending.

Health

In 2003 there were 4,813 physicians, 772 dentists, 40,081 nurses and 1,881 pharmacists. There were 526 hospitals (with 63,407 beds), 649 health centres and 3,382 sub-centres and dispensaries in 2003. Free medical service for all children and adult out-patients was launched in 1965.

RELIGION

In 2001 there were 6·78m. Roman Catholics, 6·40m. African Christians, 6·17m. Protestants, 2·90m. Anglicans and 2·24m. Muslims. Traditional beliefs persist.

CULTURE

World Heritage Sites

Kenya has three sites on the UNESCO World Heritage List: Mount Kenya National Park/Natural Forest (1997), including the second highest peak in Africa; Lake Turkana National Parks (1997 and 2001); and Lamu Old Town (2001), the oldest and best-preserved Swahili settlement in East Africa.

Broadcasting

Broadcasting is the responsibility of KBC, which transmits the following services: National (in Swahili), General (English), Central (four languages), Western (six languages), North-Eastern and Coastal (four languages). KBC also provides television programmes, mainly in English and Swahili (colour by PAL).

There are several private broadcasting stations, including Kenya Television Network (which broadcasts CNN), Stellavision (which broadcasts Sky News), Capital Radio and Metro FM. The BBC has been awarded a licence to broadcast on the FM frequency. Number of sets: TV (2001), 813,000; radio (2000), 6·76m.

Press

In 1999 there were four daily papers with a total circulation of 250,000. In May 2002 the Kenyan parliament passed a law making it illegal to sell books, newspapers or magazines that had not been submitted to the government for review.

Tourism

In 2003 there were 1,146,100 foreign visitors. Once Kenya's fastest growing source of foreign exchange, receipts from tourism had dropped from US$500m. a year to US$257m. a year by 2000. A European Union grant is helping to revive the industry; in 2003 receipts from tourism amounted to US$338·6m. In 2000 tourism employed approximately 155,500 people. The industry contributed 9·5% of GDP in 1999.

DIPLOMATIC REPRESENTATIVES

Of Kenya in the United Kingdom (45 Portland Pl., London, W1B 1AS)
High Commissioner: Joseph Kirugumi Muchemi.

Of the United Kingdom in Kenya (Upper Hill Rd, Nairobi)
High Commissioner: Edward Clay, CMG.

Of Kenya in the USA (2249 R. St., NW, Washington, D.C., 20008)
Ambassador: Leonard Ngaithe.

Of the USA in Kenya (United Nations Ave., Gigiri, Nairobi)
Ambassador: William M. Bellamy.

Of Kenya to the United Nations
Ambassador: Judith Mbula Bahemuka.

Of Kenya to the European Union
Ambassador: Peter Nkuraiya.

FURTHER READING

Anderson, David, *Histories of the Hanged: The Dirty War in Kenya and the End of Empire.* W. W. Norton, New York and Weidenfeld & Nicolson, London, 2005

Coger, D., *Kenya.* [Bibliography] 2nd ed. ABC-Clio, Oxford and Santa Barbara (CA), 1996

Elkins, Caroline, *Britain's Gulag.* Jonathan Cape, London, 2005; US title: *Imperial Reckoning: The Untold Story of the End of Empire in Kenya.* Henry Holt, New York, 2005

Haugerud, A., *The Culture of Politics in Modern Kenya.* CUP, 1995

Kyle, Keith, *The Politics of the Independence of Kenya.* Macmillan, London, 1999

Miller, N. N., *Kenya: the Quest for Prosperity.* 2nd ed. Boulder (CO), 1994

Ogot, B. A. and Ochieng, W. R. (eds.) *Decolonization and Independence in Kenya, 1940–93.* London, 1995

Throup, David and Hornsby, Charles, *Multiparty Politics in Kenya.* James Currey, Oxford, 1999

Widner, J. A., *The Rise of a Party State in Kenya: from 'Harambee' to 'Nayayo'.* Univ. of California Press, 1993

National Statistical Office: Central Bureau of Statistics, Ministry of Planning and National Development, POB 30266, Nairobi.

KIRIBATI

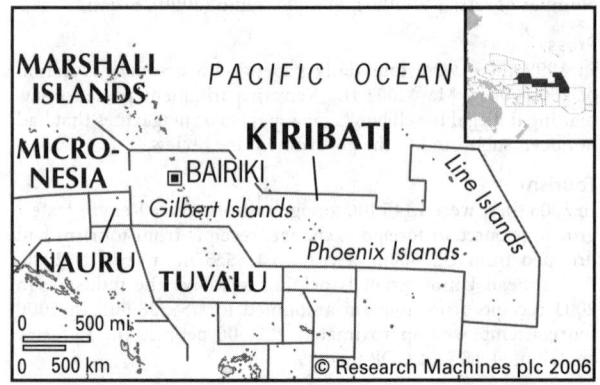

Ribaberikin Kiribati
(Republic of Kiribati)

Capital: Bairiki (Tarawa)
Population, 2000: 84,000
GDP per capita: not available
GNI per capita: $880

KEY HISTORICAL EVENTS

The islands that now constitute Kiribati were first settled by early Austronesian-speaking peoples long before the 1st century AD. Fijians and Tongans arrived about the 14th century and subsequently merged with the older groups to form the traditional I-Kiribati Micronesian society and culture. The Gilbert and Ellice Islands were proclaimed a British protectorate in 1892 and annexed at the request of the native governments as the Gilbert and Ellice Islands Colony on 10 Nov. 1915. On 1 Oct. 1975 the Ellice Islands severed constitutional links with the Gilbert Islands and took on a new name, Tuvalu. The Gilberts achieved full independence as Kiribati in 1979. Internal self-government was obtained on 1 Nov. 1976 and independence on 12 July 1979 as the Republic of Kiribati.

TERRITORY AND POPULATION

Kiribati (pronounced Kiribahss) consists of three groups of coral atolls and one isolated volcanic island, spread over a large expanse of the Central Pacific with a total land area of 811 sq. km (313 sq. miles). It comprises **Banaba** or Ocean Island (6 sq. km), the 16 **Gilbert Islands** (280 sq. km), the eight **Phoenix Islands** (29 sq. km), and eight of the 11 **Line Islands** (496 sq. km), the other three Line Islands (Jarvis, Palmyra Atoll and Kingman Reef) being uninhabited dependencies of the USA. The capital is the island of Bairiki in Tarawa. The gradual rise in sea levels in recent years is slowly reducing the area of the islands.

Population, 2000 census, 84,494 (42,848 females); density, 104 per sq. km.

In 2000 an estimated 57·0% of the population lived in rural areas. Between 1995 and 2000 the number of people living in urban areas increased by 6·4%. Between 1988 and 1993, 4,700 people were resettled on Teraina and Tabuaeran atolls because the main island group was overcrowded. Since then the government's programme has been suspended owing to the need to improve the physical infrastructure and housing.

The population distribution at the 2000 census was 49·4% in the Outer Islands, 42·9% in South Tarawa (urban area) and 7·7% in the Line and Phoenix Islands. Banaba, all 16 Gilbert Islands,

Kanton (or Abariringa) in the Phoenix Islands and three atolls in the Line Islands (Teraina, Tabuaeran and Kiritimati—formerly Washington, Fanning and Christmas Islands respectively) are inhabited; their populations in 2000 (census) were as follows:

Banaba (Ocean Is.)	276	Tabiteuea	4,582
Makin	1,691	North Tabiteuea	3,365
Butaritari	3,464	South Tabiteuea	1,217
Marakei	2,544	Beru	2,732
Abaiang	5,794	Nikunau	1,733
Tarawa	41,194	Onotoa	1,668
North Tarawa	4,477	Tamana	962
South Tarawa	36,717	Arorae	1,225
Maiana	2,048	Kanton	61
Abemama	3,142	Teraina	1,087
Kuria	961	Tabuaeran	1,757
Aranuka	966	Kiritimati	3,431
Nonouti	3,176		

The remaining 12 atolls have no permanent population; the seven Phoenix Islands comprise Birnie, Rawaki (formerly Phoenix), Enderbury, Manra (formerly Sydney), Orona (formerly Hull), McKean and Nikumaroro (formerly Gardner), while the others are Malden and Starbuck in the Central Line Islands, and Millennium Island (formerly Caroline), Flint and Vostok in the Southern Line Islands. The population is almost entirely Micronesian.

English is the official language; I-Kiribati (Gilbertese) is also spoken.

SOCIAL STATISTICS

2000 estimates: births, 2,200; deaths, 800. Rates, 2000 estimates (per 1,000 population): births, 26·4; deaths, 9·0. Infant mortality rate (1997), 51·5 per 1,000 live births; life expectancy (2003), 65·0 years. Annual population growth rate, 1992–2002, 1·5%; fertility rate, 2001, 4·6 births per woman.

CLIMATE

The Line Islands, Phoenix Islands and Banaba have a maritime equatorial climate, but the islands further north and south are tropical. Annual and daily ranges of temperature are small; mean annual rainfall ranges from 50" (1,250 mm) near the equator to 120" (3,000 mm) in the north. Typhoons are prevalent (Nov.–March) and there are occasional tornadoes. Tarawa, Jan. 83°F (28·3°C), July 82°F (27·8°C). Annual rainfall 79" (1,977 mm).

CONSTITUTION AND GOVERNMENT

Under the constitution founded on 12 July 1979 the republic has a unicameral legislature, the *House of Assembly* (Maneaba ni Maungatabu), comprising 42 members, 40 of whom are elected by popular vote, and two (the Attorney-General *ex officio* and a representative from the Banaban community) appointed for a four-year term. The *President* is directly elected and is both Head of State and government.

National Anthem

'Teirake kain Kiribati' ('Stand up, Kiribatians'); words and tune by U. Ioteba.

RECENT ELECTIONS

The last House of Assembly elections were held on 9 and 16 May 2003. Maneaban te Mauri (MTM; 'Protect the Maneaba') won 24 seats and Boutokanto Koaava (BK; 'Pillars of Truth') won 16 seats.

On 28 March 2003 President Teburoro Tito (MTM) was defeated in a no-confidence motion. On 4 July 2003 Anote Tong (BK) won the presidential elections with 47·4% of the vote, defeating his brother, Dr Harry Tong (MTM) who took 43·5%. Banuera Berina of the Maurin Kiribati Pati came third with 9·1%.

CURRENT ADMINISTRATION

President and Minister of Foreign Affairs and Immigration: Anote Tong (elected 4 July 2003).

In March 2006 the government comprised:

Vice President and Minister of Education, Youth and Sport Development: Teima Onorio.

Minister of Commerce, Industry and Co-operatives: Ioteba Redfern. *Communications, Transport and Tourism Development:* Naatan Teewe. *Environment, Land and Agricultural Development:* Martin Tofinga. *Finance and Economic Development:* Nabuti Mwemwenikarawa. *Fisheries and Marine Resources Development:* Tetabo Nakara. *Health and Medical Services:* Natanera Kirata. *Internal Affairs and Social Development:* Amberoti Nikora. *Labour and Human Resources Development:* Bauro Tongaai. *Line and Phoenix Islands:* Tawita Temoku. *Public Works and Utilities:* James Tom.

CURRENT LEADERS

Anote Tong

Position
President

Introduction
Anote Tong became president of the Pacific Ocean republic in July 2003. The president is chief of state and head of government.

Early Life
Anote Tong was born in the British Gilbert and Ellice Islands colony in 1952, the son of a Chinese father and a Gilbertian mother. He was an undergraduate at the University of Canterbury, Christchurch, New Zealand and graduated in 1988 with an MSc from the London School of Economics.

He entered politics in 1976 as an assistant secretary in the ministry of education, then served in the ministry of communications and works during the 1980s. Between 1994–96 he was minister of environment and natural resources in the government of President Teburoro Tito, after which he represented Maiana Island in parliament. When Tito lost a parliamentary confidence motion shortly after being elected to serve for a third term, the speaker, Taomati Iuta, led an interim government until presidential elections in July 2003. Anote Tong stood for the opposition Boutokanto Koaava party (Pillars of Truth) against his older brother, the government candidate Dr Harry Tong. Anote won by 13, 500 to 12,500 votes.

Career in Office
Following Tong's election his brother mounted a court challenge alleging electoral fraud but in Oct. 2003 an Australian judge ruled in President Tong's favour. During his campaign the president had promised to review the lease on a satellite-tracking base used by China. Within six months of taking office the president established relations with Taiwan, which had paid a large sum for fishing rights in Kiribati's territorial waters. China severed relations with Kiribati and abandoned the satellite-tracking base.

During 2004 the political scene was dominated by a dispute between the president and his brother over the extent of Taiwanese influence in Kiribati affairs. The government was also faced by high unemployment and rising sea levels caused by climate change, a pressing threat to the 33-island archipelago, whose land rises only a few metres above sea level.

INTERNATIONAL RELATIONS

Kiribati is a member of the UN, Commonwealth, Asian Development Bank, the Pacific Islands Forum and the Pacific Community (formerly the South Pacific Commission) and is an ACP member state of the ACP-EU relationship.

ECONOMY

Agriculture accounted for 14·2% of GDP in 2002, industry 10·9% and services 74·9%.

Currency

The currency in use is the Australian *dollar*. In 2004 the inflation rate was −0·6%, down from 1·6% in 2003.

Budget

Foreign financial aid, mainly from the UK and Japan, has amounted to 25–50% of GDP in recent years. Revenues in 2000 totalled $A107·8m. and expenditures $A90·0m.

Performance

Real GDP growth was 2·2% in 2003, followed by a recession in 2004 when the economy shrank by 1·4%. Total GDP in 2004 was US$62m.

Banking and Finance

The Bank of Kiribati is 25% government-owned and 75% owned by ANZ Bank. In 1999 it had total assets of $A46·3m. There is also a Development Bank of Kiribati and a network of village lending banks and credit institutions.

ENERGY AND NATURAL RESOURCES

Environment

Carbon dioxide emissions from the consumption and flaring of fossil fuels were the equivalent of 0·3 tonnes per capita in 2002.

Electricity

Installed capacity (2000), 2,000 kW; production (2000), 7m. kWh.

Agriculture

In 2001 there were 2,000 ha. of arable land and 37,000 ha. of permanent crops. Copra and fish represent the bulk of production and exports. The principal tree is the coconut; other food-bearing trees are the pandanus palm and the breadfruit. The only vegetable which grows in any quantity is a coarse calladium (alocasia) with the local name 'bwabwai', which is cultivated in pits; taro and sweet potatoes are also grown. Coconut production (2000), 77,000 tonnes; copra, 12,000 tonnes; bananas, 5,000 tonnes; taro, 2,000 tonnes. Principal livestock: pigs (12,000 in 2000).

Forestry

Forests covered 28,000 ha. in 2000, or 38·4% of the land area.

Fisheries

Tuna fishing is an important industry; licenses are held by the USA, Japan and the Republic of Korea. Catches in 2001 totalled 32,375 tonnes, exclusively from sea fishing.

INDUSTRY

Industry is concentrated on fishing and handicrafts.

Labour

The economically active population in paid employment (not including subsistence farmers) totalled 11,167 in 1990. In 1994, 11% were employed in agriculture, 4% in industry and 85% in services. Some 70% of the labour force are underemployed; 2% unemployed.

INTERNATIONAL TRADE

Imports and Exports

Total imports (1999), $A63·7m.; exports, $A14·0m. Main import sources in 1996: Australia, 46·1%; Fiji Islands, 18·7%; Japan, 8·6%; New Zealand, 8·4%; China, 5·9%. Main export markets in 1994: Japan, 32·9%; USA, 17·1%; Hong Kong, 12·9%; Bangladesh, 8·6%; Germany, 8·6%. Principal exports: copra, seaweed, fish; imports: foodstuffs, machinery and equipment, manufactured goods and fuel.

COMMUNICATIONS

Roads

In 2002 there were 670 km of roads.

Civil Aviation

There were 20 airports in 2002. In 2003 there were scheduled services from Tarawa (Bonriki) to the Marshall Islands, Nauru and the Fiji Islands.

Shipping

The main port is at Betio (Tarawa). Other ports of entry are Banaba, English Harbor and Kanton. There is also a small network of canals in the Line Islands. The merchant marine fleet totalled 4,000 GRT in 2002.

Telecommunications

Main telephone lines numbered 4,500 in 2002, or 51 per 1,000 population. There were 200 fax machines in 1999 and 2,000 PCs in use in 2000 (18·0 per 1,000 persons). Kiribati had 2,000 Internet users in 2002.

Postal Services

In 2003 there were 25 post offices.

SOCIAL INSTITUTIONS

Justice

Kiribati's police force is under the command of a Commissioner of Police who is also responsible for prisons, immigration, fire service (both domestic and airport) and firearms licensing. There is a Court of Appeal and High Court, with judges at all levels appointed by the President.

The population in penal institutions in 2002 was 64 (equivalent to 67 per 100,000 of national population).

Education

In 2002 there were 14,823 pupils and 660 teachers at primary schools and 10,334 pupils in general secondary education with 561 teachers. There is also a teachers' training college with 110 students (1995) and a marine training centre offering training for about 100 merchant seamen a year. The Tarawa Technical

Institute at Betio offers part-time technical and commercial courses.

Health

The government maintains free medical and other services. In 1998 there were 26 physicians, four dentists and 208 nurses. There was one hospital on Tarawa in 1990 with 283 beds, and dispensaries on other islands.

RELIGION

In 2001, 53% of the population were Roman Catholic and 38% Protestant (Congregational); there are also small numbers of Seventh-Day Adventists, Latter-day Saints (Mormons), Bahais and Church of God.

CULTURE

Broadcasting

Radio Kiribati, a division of the Broadcasting and Publications Authority, transmits daily in English and I-Kiribati from Tarawa. A satellite link to Australia was established in 1985. There were 32,600 radio receivers and 3,030 TV receivers in 2000.

Cinema

There are no cinemas. There is a private-owned projector with film shows once a week in every village on South Tarawa.

Press

In 2003 there were two newspapers: the government-owned *Te Uekera* and the independent weekly *Kiribati Newstar*.

Tourism

Tourism is in the early stages of development. In 2001 there were 5,000 foreign tourists, bringing in revenue of US$3m.

DIPLOMATIC REPRESENTATIVES

Of Kiribati in the United Kingdom

Acting High Commissioner: Makurita Baaro (resides in Kiribati).

Honorary Consul: Michael Walsh (The Great House, Llanddewi Rydderch, Monmouthshire, NP7 9UY).

Of the United Kingdom in Kiribati

High Commissioner: Charles Mochan (resides in Suva, Fiji Islands).

Of the USA in Kiribati

Ambassador: Larry M. Dinger (resides in Suva, Fiji Islands).

FURTHER READING

Tearo, T., *Coming of Age.* Tarawa, 1989

National Statistical Office: Kiribati Statistics Office, PO Box 67, Bairiki.

KOREA

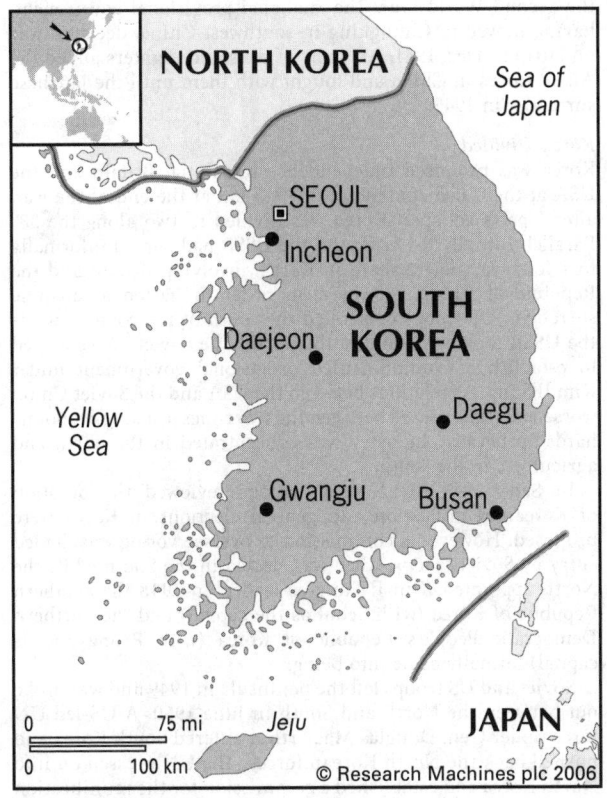

NORTH KOREA

Sea of Japan

□ SEOUL

● Incheon

SOUTH KOREA

● Daejeon

● Daegu

Yellow Sea

● Gwangju

● Busan

Jeju

JAPAN

0 ___ 75 mi

0 ___ 100 km

© Research Machines plc 2006

Daehan Minguk
(Republic of Korea)

Capital: Seoul
Population projection, 2010: 48·57m.
GDP per capita, 2003: (PPP$) 17,971
HDI/world rank: 0·901/28

KEY HISTORICAL EVENTS

The Korean peninsula was first settled by tribal peoples from Manchuria and Siberia who provided the basis for the modern Korean language. By 3000 BC agriculture-based communities had emerged.

The earliest known colony in the region was established at Pyongyang in the 12th century BC. Among the most prominent agricultural communities was Old Choson, which by 194 BC had evolved into a league of tribes ruled by Wiman or 'Wei Man', a leader widely held to have defected from China, although he may have been a native of the Choson region. His realm was taken over by the Han empire of China in 108 BC and replaced by four Chinese colonies.

The rest of the peninsula developed into tribal states; Puyo in the north and Chin south of the Han River. Chin was itself split into three tribal states (Mahan, Chinhan and Pyonhan); these states then evolved into three rival kingdoms, Koguryo, Paekche, and Silla. Three powerful figures, King T'aejo (AD 53–146) of Koguryo, King Koi (AD 234–86) of Paekche and King Naemul (AD 356–402) of Silla, established hereditary monarchies while powerful aristocracies developed from tribal chiefdoms.

With China's support Silla conquered the other two kingdoms; Paekche in 660 and Koguryo in 668. In 676 Silla drove out the Chinese and gained complete control of the peninsula. Survivors from Koguryo established Parhae in the northern region. After a period of conflict with Silla, Parhae grew into a prosperous state in its own right before being taken over by northern nomadic peoples. In Silla an absolute monarchy replaced the council of nobles with a central administrative body called the chancellery (*Chipsabu*), thus undermining aristocratic power. Meanwhile, the capital Kumsong (now Kyongju in South Korea) was developed. The state was divided into administrative units by province (*chu*), prefecture (*kun*), and county (*hyon*), and five provincial capitals prospered as cultural centres. Avatamsaka Buddhism was the dominant religion.

Divisions within the aristocracy in the 8th century led to the restoration of the Council of Nobles and the overthrow of the monarchy. Forced to pay taxes to powerful provincial families and central government, the peasants rebelled. Two provincial leaders, Kyonhwon and Kungye, established the Later Paekche (892) and Later Koguryo (901) as rivals to Silla.

National Unity

The powerful leader Wang Kon founded Koryo (now Kaesong, North Korea) in 918, and established a unified kingdom in the Korean peninsula in 936. Three chancelleries and the royal secretariat formed the supreme council of state and governed the kingdom. Koryo's leaders were then largely aristocratic, and the political system greatly favoured those in the top five tiers of the nine hierarchical levels. That the military was not eligible for any hierarchical position above the second level and received little land, led to a military coup in 1170. Gen. Ch'oe Ch'ung-hon established a military regime which held power for the next sixty years. Zen Buddhism and the allied ideology of Confucianism had grown popular but were suppressed under the Ch'oe regime. Many monks fled to the mountains, where they formed what became Korean Buddhism, the *Chogye*.

In 1231 the Mongols invaded Koryo but were resisted by the Ch'oe leaders for nearly three decades, until a peasant uprising saw the Ch'oe overthrown. A power-sharing agreement between the rebels and the Mongols came into force in 1258. Despite some interference from the Mongols, Koryo retained its identity as a unified state. The aristocracy established seats of power throughout the country, encouraging peasants to seek protection as serfs. This, however, led to reduced tax revenues and when the government did not have sufficient resources to reward its bureaucratic class, a rebellion ensued. Led by General Yi Song-gye, and with the help of the Ming dynasty in China, government officials seized power in 1392 and established a new system of land distribution, thus ending the Koryo dynasty.

Gen. Yi named the state Choson, designating Hanyang (now Seoul, South Korea) as the capital. Buddhism was dropped in favour of a new Chinese-influenced Confucian ethical system and the state was governed by a hereditary aristocracy (the *yangban*), who controlled all aspects of Korean society. In 1420 the Hall of Worthies (*Chiphyonjon*) was established for scholars, and after 1443 the Korean phonetic alphabet (*hangul*) developed. Later in the period, a centralized yangban government was formed and the country divided into eight administrative regions, with standardized laws and a central decision-making and judicial body.

In 1592 Japan, newly unified under the command of Toyotomi Hideyoshi, sent an army to Korea supposedly as part of an invasion of China. Korea's naval forces, under Admiral Yi Sun-shin, were able to repel the invaders. Swelling anti-Japanese sentiment prompted Koreans from all hierarchical divisions to fight in the war alongside troops dispatched from Ming China. However, Japanese forces did not withdraw completely until Toyotomi's death in 1598, leaving Korea in ruins.

Despite joint efforts by China and Korea to stem the advances of the nomadic Manchu in the early 17th century, Seoul was captured in 1636. The Manchu established the Ch'ing dynasty several years later and demanded tribute from Korea.

During the 17th and 18th centuries, Korea's agriculture developed as irrigation improved and rice, tobacco and ginseng became increasingly important crops. By the late 18th century many Korean scholars had turned to Roman Catholicism, leading to government suppression of Christianity in a bid to preserve the dominance of Confucianism. However, European priests maintained strong links in the country.

Japanese Influence

In the 19th century, a succession of monarchs yet to attain the age of majority undermined national stability. In 1864 Taewon'gun, the father of the child-king Kojong, took power and pursued a programme of controversial political reform that increasingly isolated Korea from the outside world. When Taewon'gun was eventually forced to step down, Korea came under pressure from Japan to open up its ports. Nervous of growing Japanese influence, China placed troops in Korea following a failed coup attempt by pro-Taewon'gun forces. There followed a trade agreement which greatly benefited Chinese commercial interests. Further treaties with France, Germany, Russia, the UK and the USA followed in the 1880s. As foreign influence increased, Korea's ruling elite divided between moderates and radicals. The radicals carried out a coup in 1884 but were quickly defeated by Chinese troops. An agreement to maintain a balance of power in the region was signed by Japan and China the following year.

As modernization gathered pace, government spending increased, adding to the burden of reparations payments to Japan. The peasants turned to *Tonghak* ('Eastern Learning'), a new religion established by an old yangban scholar and based on traditional beliefs. A Tonghak rebellion in 1894 caused China to send in troops. Japan responded by sending its own forces and war broke out. By the following year Japan had secured control of the peninsula.

Korea declared neutrality at the outbreak of war between Japan and Russia in 1904 but was pressured by Japan into allowing use of Korean territory. Japan achieved victory in 1905 and made Korea a protectorate. An unsuccessful appeal to the international peace conference at The Hague further undermined relations between Japan and Korea. Anti-Japanese guerrilla fighters in the southern provinces were active during 1908–09 but were crushed the following year when Korea was annexed by Japan.

Japan established a government in Korea and implemented a programme designed to supplant the Korean identity. There were restrictions on freedom of speech, press and assembly and the language and history of Japan was taught in schools at the expense of those of Korea. Many Koreans were dispossessed of their land as Japan built new transport and communications infrastructures. When the Japanese brutally suppressed a 2m.-strong demonstration in 1919, independence leaders established a provisional government in Shanghai and named Syngman Rhee as president. Hoping to calm dissent, Japan lifted certain press restrictions and replaced the gendarmerie with an ordinary police force, but uncompromising colonial rule remained in place.

Korea became a market for Japanese goods and attracted much capital investment but at the expense of agriculture, leading to a long-term shortage of rice. Tokyo reimposed military rule in 1931 when war broke out between Japan and China and attempted to quash all manifestations of a separate Korean identity over the following decade. Magazines, newspapers and academic organisations operating in the Korean language were banned. Hundreds of thousands of Koreans were made to fight in the Japanese army, or work in Japanese mines and factories in order to support Japan's military efforts during the Second World War. The Shanghai provisional government, having moved to Chungking in southwest China, declared war on Japan in Dec. 1941. An army of resistance fighters joined the Allied forces in China and fought with them until the Japanese surrender in 1945.

Korea Divided

Korea was promised independence by China, Britain and the USA at the Cairo conference of 1943 but at the end of the war, after Japan's collapse, Korea was divided in two along the 38° Parallel. Initially the USA and the USSR had agreed informally to a four-way power share in Korea, involving Britain and the Republic of China. However, in order to hasten a Japanese surrender, US troops controlled the south of the country while the USSR took command of the north. The Soviet forces helped to establish a Communist-led provisional government under Kim Il Sung. As relations between the USA and the Soviet Union worsened, trade ceased between the two zones, causing economic hardship because industry was concentrated in the north and agriculture in the south.

In Sept. 1947 the United Nations reviewed the question of Korean reunification and general elections in Korea were proposed. However, a commission to oversee voting was denied entry by Soviet troops. Rhee was elected in the South while the North appointed Kim Il Sung as leader. In 1948 the southern Republic of Korea (with Seoul as the capital) and the northern Democratic People's Republic of Korea (with Pyongyang as capital) formally came into being.

Soviet and US troops left the peninsula in 1949 and war broke out between the North and South in June 1950. A US-led UN force under Gen. Douglas MacArthur entered South Korea and pushed back the North Korean forces. The UN pressed on into North Korea and established a commission for the reunification and rehabilitation of Korea. China, which at that point had no representation in the United Nations, entered the war and contributed 1·2m. troops to the North Korean side. Negotiations to end the war began in 1951 and a new international boundary and demilitarized zone were declared in 1953. The USA offered South Korea financial support and signed a mutual security pact with Rhee, who had been reluctant to accept the division of the country. The issue of prisoner returns, particularly of North Koreans unwilling to return to the communist state, remained a point of contention. The war left 4m. people dead or injured.

Traditionally an agricultural region, South Korea faced severe economic problems after partition. Limited resources, war damage and a flood of refugees from North Korea all pointed towards economic disaster, and the country became dependent on foreign aid, particularly from the USA. The country faced large-scale unemployment, inflation and foreign debt.

The authoritarian rule of President Rhee, marred by corruption and injustice, received widespread condemnation. The elections of 1960 were blighted by violence and fraud and when the police shot 125 students during a demonstration, the government was forced to step down and Rhee was exiled. Subsequent leaders failed to solve the country's problems and in May 1961 Gen. Park Chung-hee led a military coup. As leader of the Democratic Republican Party, he was elected president in 1963, 1967 and, following a constitutional amendment to allow a third term in office, 1971.

Park's government was powerful and efficient, reviving the economy through the development of manufacturing for export and increased foreign investment, especially from America. In 1972 Park proclaimed martial law and abolished the national assembly. In 1979 he was assassinated and the country collapsed into chaos. Chun Doo-hwan became leader in 1980 in another military coup and, as leader of the Democratic Justice Party (DJP), revived the national assembly as the economy continued to grow. Dissatisfaction with the government also grew, however, and a new constitution in 1987 demanded the president be elected by popular vote and his term of office be reduced to five years.

Roh Tae-woo was elected president in 1988 as leader of the DJP and later of the Democratic Liberal Party. Fighting rising inflation, he attempted to establish diplomatic relations with China and the Soviet Union and developed a better relationship with opposition parties in his own country. North and South Korea met several times during the 1980s in a bid to improve relations. In 1991 the two countries signed a treaty of non-aggression, with each country promising not to interfere in the internal affairs of the other.

In 1992 Kim Young-sam, the former opposition leader who had merged his party with Roh's, became the first civilian to be elected president since the Korean War. He launched an anti-corruption campaign and continued to pursue closer relations with North Korea. During the financial crisis that affected East Asia in 1997 South Korea was forced to ask the International Monetary Fund for help, though it largely avoided long-term economic damage and remains one of Asia's most affluent countries.

In Dec. 1997 Kim Dae-jung, a pro-democracy dissident during the years of military dictatorship, was elected president. Kim forged a 'sunshine policy' aimed at closer ties with the North and received the Nobel peace prize for his efforts. The two Koreas have subsequently undertaken a series of joint commercial and infrastructural projects. Constitutionally disqualified from standing for the presidency again in 2002, Kim was replaced by Roh Moo-hyun who continued the 'sunshine policy', despite North Korea's declining relationship with the USA.

TERRITORY AND POPULATION

South Korea is bounded in the north by the demilitarized zone (separating it from North Korea), east by the East Sea, south by the Korea Strait (separating it from Japan) and west by the Yellow Sea. The area is 99,585 sq. km. The population (census, 1 Nov. 2000) was 46,136,101 (22,977,519 females); density, 463·35 per sq. km (one of the highest in the world). In 2003 the urban population was 80·3%. The population estimate for 2005 was 47·82m.

The UN gives a projected population for 2010 of 48·57m.

The official language is Korean. In July 2000 the Korean government introduced a new Romanization System for the Korean Language to romanize Korean words into English.

There are nine provinces (do) and seven metropolitan cities with provincial status. Area and population in 2000:

Province	Area (in sq. km)	Population (in 1,000)
Gyeonggi	10,135	8,984
Gyeongsangnam	10,516	2,909
Gyeongsangbuk	19,024	2,725
Jeollanam	11,987	1,996
Jeollabuk	8,050	1,891
Chungcheongnam	8,586	1,845
Gangwon	16,502	1,487
Chungcheongbuk	7,432	1,467
Jeju	1,846	513
Seoul (city)	606	9,895
Busan (city)	760	3,663
Daegu (city)	886	2,481
Incheon (city)	965	2,475
Daejeon (city)	540	1,368
Gwangju (city)	501	1,353
Ulsan (city)	1,056	1,014

Cities with over 500,000 inhabitants (census 2000):

Seoul	9,895,217	Ulsan	1,014,428	Cheongju	586,700
Busan	3,662,884	Suwon	946,704	Anyang	580,544
Daegu	2,480,578	Seongnam	914,590	Ansan	562,920
Incheon	2,475,139	Goyang	763,971	Changwon	517,410
Daejeon	1,368,207	Bucheon	761,389	Pohang	515,714
Gwangju	1,352,797	Jeonju	616,468		

SOCIAL STATISTICS

2001: births, 557,228; deaths, 242,730; marriages, 320,063; divorces, 135,014. Rates per 1,000 population in 2001: birth, 11·6; death, 5·1; marriage, 6·9; divorce, 2·8. Suicides numbered 12,277 in 2001. Expectation of life at birth, 2003, 80·6 years for females and 73·3 for males. Life expectancy had been 47 in 1955 and 62 in 1971. Infant mortality, 2001, 5·1 per 1,000 live births; fertility rate, 1·3 births per woman. Annual population growth rate in 2002 was 0·6%. In 2001 the average age of first marriage was 29·6 for men and 26·8 for women, with 28·0 years being the average age that women had their first child. South Korea has one of the most rapidly ageing populations in the world, partly owing to an ever-decreasing birth rate. In 2002, 7·9% of the population were over 65, up from 2·9% in 1960. There were 14·31m. households in 2000, with on average 3·1 members per household. 11,584 South Koreans emigrated in 2001, down from 15,307 in 2000. Between 1962 and 1998 a total of 847,714 Koreans emigrated, 77·8% of them to the USA. 5·65m. Koreans lived abroad in 2001, including 2·1m. in the USA, 1·9m. in China and 640,000 in Japan.

CLIMATE

The country experiences continental temperate conditions. Rainfall is concentrated in the period April to Sept. and ranges from 40" (1,020 mm) to 60" (1,520 mm). Busan, Jan. 36°F (2·2°C), July 76°F (24·4°C). Annual rainfall 56" (1,407 mm). Seoul, Jan. 23°F (−5°C), July 77°F (25°C). Annual rainfall 50" (1,250 mm).

CONSTITUTION AND GOVERNMENT

The 1988 constitution provides for a *President*, directly elected for a single five-year term, who appoints the members of the *State Council* and heads it, and for a *National Assembly* (*Gukhoe*), currently of 299 members, directly elected for four years (243 from constituencies and 56 from party lists in proportion to the overall vote). The current constitution created the Sixth Republic. The minimum voting age is 20.

National Anthem

'Aegukga' ('A Song of Love for the Country'); words anonymous, tune by Ahn Eaktay.

GOVERNMENT CHRONOLOGY

Heads of State of South Korea since 1948. (DJP = Democratic Justice Party; DLP = Democratic Liberal Party; DP = Democratic Party; DRP = Democratic Republican Party; LP = Liberal Party; MDP = Millennium Democratic Party; NCNP = National Congress for New Politics; NDP = New Democratic Party; NKP = New Korea Party; UD = Uri Party)

Presidents

1948–60	LP	Syngman Rhee
1960–62	DP, NDP	Yun Po-sun

Chairman of the Supreme Council for National Reconstruction

1962–63	military	Park Chung-hee

Presidents

1963–79	DRP	Park Chung-hee
1979–80	DRP	Choi Kyu-hah
1980–88	military, DJP	Chun Doo-hwan
1988–93	DJP, DLP	Roh Tae-woo
1993–98	DLP, NKP	Kim Young-sam
1998–2003	NCNP, MDP	Kim Dae-jung
2003–	MDP, UD	Roh Moo-hyun

RECENT ELECTIONS

Presidential elections were held on 19 Dec. 2002. Roh Moo-hyun of the ruling Millennium Democratic Party won with 48·9% of votes cast, against 46·6% for Lee Hoi-chang of the Grand National Party. Turnout was 70·2%.

Elections to the National Assembly were held on 15 April 2004. Turnout was 59·9%. Uri Party (UD) won 152 out of 299 seats with 38·3% of votes cast; the Grand National Party (HD) won 121 with 35·8%; the Democratic Labour Party (MDD) 10 with 13·0%; the Millennium Democratic Party (MDP) 9 with 7·1%; the United Liberal Democrats (JMY) 4 with 2·8%. National Alliance 21 won one seat and two seats went to non-partisans.

CURRENT ADMINISTRATION

President: Roh Moo-hyun; b. 1946 (Uri Party, formerly of the Millennium Democratic Party; sworn in on 25 Feb. 2003, suspended on 12 March 2004, following a vote in the National Assembly to impeach him, but reinstated on 14 May 2004).

In April 2006 the cabinet comprised:

Prime Minister: Han Myeong-sook; b. 1944 (Uri Party; since 19 April 2006).

Deputy Prime Minister and Minister of Finance and Economy: Han Duck-soo. *Deputy Prime Minister and Minister of Education and Human Resources Development:* Kim Jin-pyo. *Deputy Prime Minister and Minister of Science and Technology:* Kim Woo-shik.

Minister of Agriculture and Forestry: Park Hong-soo. *Commerce, Industry and Energy:* Chung Sye-kyun. *Construction and Transportation:* Choo Byung-jik. *Culture and Tourism:* Kim Myong-gon. *Environment:* Lee Chi-beom. *Foreign Affairs and Trade:* Ban Ki-moon. *Gender Equality:* Jang Ha-jin. *Government Administration and Home Affairs:* Lee Yong-sup. *Health and Welfare:* Rhyu Si-min. *Information and Communication:* Rho Jun-hyong. *Justice:* Chun Jung-bae. *Labour:* Lee Sang-soo. *Maritime Affairs and Fisheries:* Kim Sung-jin. *National Defence:* Yoon Kwang-ung. *Planning and Budget:* Byeon Yang-kyoon. *Unification:* Lee Jong-seok.

National Assembly Speaker: Park Kwan-yong.

Office of the Prime Minister: http://www.opm.go.kr

CURRENT LEADERS

Roh Moo-hyun

Position
President

Introduction
Roh Moo-hyun won the presidential elections of Dec. 2002 and succeeded incumbent Kim Dae-jung in Feb. 2003. A member of Kim's Millennium Democratic Party (MDP) until Sept. 2003, Roh has continued Kim's policy of closer ties with North Korea. He commands greatest support among young voters who favour a close relationship with the North, although his stance has strained relations with the US leadership, which takes a hardline against Pyongyang until it ends all nuclear activities.

Early Life
Roh was born on 6 Aug. 1946 in Gimhae in the Gyeongsangbuk region, into a peasant farming family. In 1966 he graduated from Busan Commercial High School and undertook various low-paid jobs while teaching himself law. He passed his state bar exams in 1975. In 1977 he was appointed a district court judge in the city of Daejeon, and the following year he opened his own law office. In 1981, after representing a student prosecuted for owning outlawed literature, he committed himself to human rights cases and became a prominent pro-democracy campaigner. In 1987 Roh was imprisoned for three weeks for assisting striking workers.

The following year he entered parliament as part of a grouping led by future president, Kim Young-sam. In the same year he won recognition as a member of a parliamentary committee which investigated the 1980 massacres of protesters during the rule of Chun Doo-hwan. Having lost his parliamentary seat in 1992, Roh re-entered parliament in 1998 after winning a seat in Seoul.

In 2000 he joined the supreme council of the MDP. Between Aug. 2000–March 2001 he was minister for fisheries and maritime affairs. With President Kim Dae-jung constitutionally barred from standing for re-election in 2002, Roh was selected as the MDP's candidate. The election campaign was fought in the shadow of rising tensions between the USA and North Korea over the North's nuclear programmes. Roh and the MDP continued to espouse Kim's 'sunshine policy' of engagement with Pyongyang. Lee Hoi-chang of the Grand National Party (GNP), Roh's chief opponent, favoured the freezing of talks until the North ended all nuclear activities and was thus regarded as Washington's favoured candidate.

Roh's close ties with the MDP and Kim Dae-jung cost him support as several corruption scandals came to light. Roh's campaign was further weakened shortly before polls opened when his running-mate, Chung Moon-jung, pulled out. Chung had a popular following based on the successful staging of the 2002 football World Cup finals but he withdrew from the elections following Roh's perceived anti-US comment that 'if the US and North Korea start a fight, we should dissuade them.' Nonetheless, Roh won large-scale support from young voters and claimed victory at the elections of Dec. 2002 with 49% of the vote against Lee's 46·6%.

Career in Office
Roh was sworn into office in Feb. 2003. He appointed former mayor of Seoul, Goh Kun, as prime minister. Goh Kun had previously held the office in 1997–98. Roh's first major challenge was to establish a policy on North Korea acceptable both domestically and to the USA. Although a vocal supporter of Kim's 'sunshine policy', Roh had to demonstrate a more conciliatory approach towards Washington. In May 2002 he sought to heal rifts with the USA by supporting the continued presence of US forces in the region, having previously called for the removal of 30,000 troops stationed in South Korea. The more aggressive policy of US President George W. Bush towards North Korea—threatening the North by placing it in the 'Axis of Evil' declaration—made the continuation of peaceful engagement with Pyongyang more difficult.

In the domestic sphere, Roh sought on his election to repair the cultural and commercial split between South Korea's south-eastern and south-western regions. Large-scale business and the media were both expected to be subject to major reforms and the president promised to prevent the further rise in property prices, which grew 16% in 2002 despite economic stagnation. Decentralization and autonomy were central to Roh's domestic agenda. To relieve population pressure in the Seoul area, Roh outlined a national development programme, including the construction of a new administrative capital in the central region of Chungcheong. The new capital will have a population of 500,000, many of whom will work in support of the new presidential complex and national assembly. Believing that the concentration of power and money in Seoul has hampered the country's economic recovery, Roh promised to start construction in 2007.

Negotiations for free trade areas with Singapore and Japan made a promising start. Economic relations with North Korea, although strained by tensions with the USA, continued to expand. Inter-Korean ministerial talks in Oct. 2003 focused on the construction of the Kaesong Industrial Complex in North Korea, one of three large-scale economic projects agreed by the Kim Dae-jung government.

Roh's determination to distance himself from the corruption scandals of the previous presidency led him to leave the MDP in Sept. 2003. His decision was anticipated after the departure of parliamentary allies who formed a new party—the Uri Party—with a reformist agenda. In March 2004 Roh was suspended from office following a vote in the National Assembly to impeach him for allegedly trying to influence unfairly the outcome of parliamentary elections due in April 2004. Prime Minister Goh Kun took over as acting president. The pro-Roh Uri Party gained a slim overall majority in the April elections, winning 152 seats in the 299-member Assembly, and the following month Roh was reinstated after the Constitutional Court overturned his impeachment. Goh Kun meanwhile resigned as prime minister and was replaced in June 2004 by Lee Hai-chan. In his new year message at the start of 2005 Roh promised to make revitalizing the flagging South Korean economy his policy priority.

DEFENCE

Peacetime operational control, which had been transferred to the United Nations Command (UNC) under a US general in July 1950 after the outbreak of the Korean War, was restored to South Korea on 1 Dec. 1994. In the event of a new crisis, operational control over the Korean armed forces will revert to the Combined Forces Command (CFC). Conscription is 26 months in the Army, 28 months in the Navy and 30 months in the Air Force. Conscripts may choose or be required to exchange military service for civilian work. There were 37,140 US personnel based in South Korea in 2002. By 2008 the American combat strength is set to decline by a third. Defence expenditure in 2003 totalled US$14,632m. (US$305 per capita), representing 2.8% of GDP.

Army

Strength (2002) 560,000 (140,000 conscripts). Paramilitary Civilian Defence Corps, 6.28m. The armed forces reserves numbered 3.04m.

Navy

In 2002 the Navy had a substantial force of 63,000 (19,000 conscripts), including 28,000 marine corps troops; it continued its steady modernization programme. Current strength includes 160 surface vessels, 20 support vessels, ten submarines/submersibles and 70 aircraft. The main bases are at Jinhae, Incheon and Busan.

Air Force

In 2002 the Air Force had a strength of 63,000 men and 538 combat aircraft including 560 fighters, 40 special aircraft and 210 support aircraft.

INTERNATIONAL RELATIONS

Defections to South Korea from North Korea totalled 1,890 in 2004 (1,281 in 2003, 1,139 in 2002, 583 in 2001, 312 in 2000, 41 in 1995 and 8 in 1993).

South Korea is a member of the UN, WTO, BIS, OECD, Inter-American Development Bank, Asian Development Bank, Colombo Plan, APEC, IOM and the Antarctic Treaty.

The aim of Korea's foreign policy is to secure international support for peace and stability in Northeast Asia, including a means to reunify the Korean Peninsula without confrontation.

ECONOMY

Agriculture, forestry and fishing accounted for 3.6% of GDP in 2002, industry (including mining, construction and power and water supply) 33.8% and services 62.6%.

Overview

South Korea is a recent development success story. Economic development began in the 1960s but it was not until the late 1980s that Korea's convergence with the rest of the developed world began. Characteristic policies were the favouring of raw materials and technology imports at the expense of consumer goods, and the encouragement of domestic savings and investment over consumption (resulting in Korea having an extremely high fixed-investment expenditure share of GDP).

Korea's development model was based on export-oriented industrialization rather than import substituting industrialization (ISI). Export production has long been dominated by *chaebol* (conglomerates), controlled by their founding families with close government ties. However, continued subsidization of businesses and the careers of bureaucrats directing the subsidies were made contingent on export success. Korea's first internationally competitive sector was textile manufacturing but the country is now highly competitive in electronics, automobiles, shipbuilding, chemicals and steel. Korea's success is also closely linked to its role as a key long-term destination for Japanese foreign direct investment (FDI), which provided Korean manufacturing with the transfer of technological know-how as well as capital equipment. Despite currently spending a relatively large share of GDP (nearly 3%) on research and development (R&D) and being home to some of the world's leading business innovators, the OECD notes that research is highly concentrated in only a few companies and market segments. The OECD recommends strengthening links between business, government, universities and researchers and increasing competition, particularly in services, so as to promote the diffusion of new technologies.

The economy was hit hard by the 1997 Asian financial crisis, exposing weaknesses in the country's development model. High debt-to-equity ratios, heavy foreign borrowing and an undisciplined financial sector with a significant amount of non-performing loans weighed heavily on the country. Reforms were implemented, such as strengthening competition and restructuring the financial sector, and growth rebounded strongly in 1999. Strong domestic demand then helped the economy weather the global slowdown in 2001–02. In 2003 the economy was hit by the effects of a credit card crisis. Between 2000 and 2002 Korea experienced a credit card boom which ended with 3.7m. people defaulting by the end of 2003 (10% of the adult population). Household consumption accelerated positively in 2005 but households remain heavily indebted. Rising oil prices are a significant potential threat to Korea's highly oil-intensive economy. China, which has become Korea's chief export and FDI destination, also poses an increasingly competitive threat to many of Korea's leading industries.

Although average incomes and productivity levels have converged on the OECD average over the last two decades, catch-up growth has faded and levels remain well below those of leading economies. Much of Korea's convergence is thought to have resulted from an increase in labour supply. The OECD has highlighted service sector reform as essential for further growth, especially since the country will soon face a reversal of its previously favourable demographics. There is evidence, however, that the political momentum behind reform has weakened.

Currency

The unit of currency is the *won* (KRW). Inflation rates (based on OECD statistics):

1995	1996	1997	1998	1999	2000	2001	2002	2003	2004
4.5%	4.9%	4.4%	7.5%	0.8%	2.3%	4.1%	2.8%	3.5%	3.6%

Foreign exchange reserves were US$111,934m. in June 2002 (US$31,928m. in 1995) and gold reserves 442,000 troy oz. Total money supply in May 2002 was 53,335bn. won.

Budget

Revenue and expenditure (in 1,000,000m. won), including bond issuances, at the 2002 budget: 105.8 and 105.8. Sources of revenue: national tax, 93.8; non-tax, 12.0. Expenditure includes: economic development, 27·4; education, 18·5; defence, 17·1; infrastructure, 13·9; general administration, 10·0; contingency, 2·5.

External liabilities in Dec. 2002 were 154,114m. won.

Performance
Real GDP growth rates (based on OECD statistics):

1995	1996	1997	1998	1999	2000	2001	2002	2003	2004
9·2%	7·0%	4·7%	−6·9%	9·5%	8·5%	3·8%	7·0%	3·1%	4·6%

Real GDP growth was forecast to fall to 3·9% in 2005. Total GDP in 2004 was US$679·7bn.

According to the *OECD Economic Survey* of March 2003 'Korea's economic recovery in 2002…was based on…a broad restructuring programme, accompanied by appropriate macroeconomic policies. However, this should not lead to complacency about resolving remaining structural weaknesses and addressing emerging balances.…The acceleration in wages and the sharp increase in real estate prices risk boosting inflationary pressure.'

Banking and Finance
The central bank and bank of issue is the Bank of Korea (*Governor*, Park Seung). In Oct. 2002 bank deposits totalled 498,886bn. won, of which 447,329bn. won were savings and time deposits.

In Dec. 2001 there were 20 national and provincial commercial banks. The largest bank is Kookmin Bank, with assets in Sept. 2002 of 204,337bn. won (US$171·47bn.). Other major banks are the National Agricultural Cooperative Federation (NACF) and Woori (formerly Hanvit) Bank. There were 40 foreign banks in Dec. 2002. In Dec. 2001 non-bank financial institutions included 44 insurance companies, 45 securities companies and three merchant banks. The use of real names in financial dealings has been required since 1994.

South Korea has started to open up once protected industries to foreign ownership, and in 2002 attracted US$9·1bn. in foreign direct investment.

There is a stock exchange in Seoul.

Weights and Measures
The metric system is in use alongside traditional measures. 1 *gwan* = 3·75 kg. 1 *pyeong* = 3·3 sq. metres.

ENERGY AND NATURAL RESOURCES

Environment
South Korea's carbon dioxide emissions from the consumption and flaring of fossil fuels in 2002 were the equivalent of 9·5 tonnes per capita.

Electricity
Installed capacity in 2001 was 51m. kW. Electricity generated (2001) was 285,224m. kWh. Power sources in 2001: nuclear, 39·3%; coal, 38·7%; liquefied natural gas, 10·7%; oil, 9·8%; hydroelectric, 1·5%. There were 18 nuclear reactors in use in 2003. Consumption per capita in 2001 was estimated at 5,444 kWh.

Oil and Gas
In 2001 the imports of petroleum products amounted to 1,099m. bbls., of which crude oil was 859·4m. bbls. The output of petroleum products was 892·8m. bbls., consumption 743·6m. bbls. and the volume of exports 295·0m. bbls. In 2001, 873·4m. bbls. of crude oil were imported. In Sept. 1999 a massive crude oil terminal was opened at Yeosu, Jeollanam-do. It has a capacity to store more than 30m. bbls.

In 2001 imports of natural gas totalled 16·1m. tonnes, consumption 16·0m. tonnes. The total output of city gas in 2001 was 12,657m. cu. metres as was consumption, of which 8,964m. cu. metres was used for household purposes, 3,376m. cu. metres for industrial use and 1,761m. cu. metres for commercial use. In April 1999 a large underwater gas deposit was discovered off the southeastern coast of the country, which was estimated to contain up to 60bn. cu. metres of natural gas.

Water
Water consumption in 2000 was 33,100m. cu. metres, of which 15,800m. cu. metres was for agricultural purposes, 7,300m. cu. metres was supplied to households and 2,900m. cu. metres was for industrial use. Of the total population, 87·8% had tap water in 2001 and per capita supply was 374 litres per day. As of 2001 there were 1,206 dams with walls higher than 15 metres and containing a total of 17·96bn. cu. metres of water.

Minerals
In 2001, 599 mining companies employed 12,103 people. Output, 2001, included (in tonnes): limestone, 82m.; anthracite coal, 3·82m.; iron ore, 0·2m.; zinc ore, 10,259; lead ore, 1,975; gold, 28,595 kg; silver, 664,533 kg. The largest gold deposits in South Korea were discovered in Suryun Mine near Daegu in June 1999. The mine contained an estimated 9·9 tonnes of gold, worth approximately US$81m. Salt production averages 500,000 tonnes a year.

Agriculture
Cultivated land was 1·88m. ha. in 2001, of which 1·15m. ha. were rice paddies. In 2001 there were 1·70m. ha. of arable land and 193,000 ha. of permanent crops. In 2001 the farming population was 3·93m. and there were 1·35m. farms. The agricultural workforce was 2·1m. in 2001. There were 201,089 tractors in 2001.

In 2001, 1·08m. ha. were sown to rice. Production (2001, in 1,000 tonnes): rice, 5,515; cabbages, 3,450; onions, 1,078; melons and watermelons, 972; tangerines and mandarins, 645; potatoes, 604; barley, 593; grapes, 454; cucumbers and gherkins, 451; pears, 419; chillies and green peppers, 411; garlic, 406; sweet potatoes, 273. Livestock in 2001 (in 1,000): cows, 1,954; pigs, 8,720; sheep, 441; chickens, 102,393.

Forestry
Forest area was 6·42m. ha. in 2001 (64% of the land area). Total stock was 428·3m. cu. metres. In 1997, 70% of the total forest area was privately owned. Timber production was 1·5m. cu. metres in 2001.

Fisheries
In 2001 there were a total of 94,835 boats (864,853 gross tonnes). 482 deep-sea fishing vessels were operating overseas as of Dec. 2002. The fish catch was 1,907,925 tonnes in 2001, mainly from marine waters.

INDUSTRY
The leading companies by market capitalization in South Korea in Nov. 2005 were: Samsung Electronics Company Ltd (US$100·4bn.); Kookmin Bank (US$22·1bn.); and Hyundai Motor (US$21·8bn.).

Manufacturing industry is concentrated primarily on oil, petrochemicals, chemical fibres, construction, iron and steel, mobile phones, cement, machinery, chips, shipbuilding, automobiles and electronics. Tobacco manufacture is a semi-government monopoly. Industry is dominated by giant conglomerates (*chaebol*). There were 3·01m. businesses in 2000, of which 261,119 were incorporated. 916,688 businesses were in wholesale and retail trades, 607,718 in dining and accommodation, 329,488 in services, 313,246 in manufacturing and 265,598 in transport and communications. The leading *chaebol* are Samsung, with assets in April 2002 of 72·4trn. won; LG, with assets of 54·5trn. won; and SK, with assets of 46·8trn. won.

Production in 2001: petroleum products, 857·5m. bbls.; cars (2002), 3·15m.; mobile phones, 90m.; TV sets, 9·32m.; refrigerators, 5·13m. Production in 1,000 tonnes: cement, 52,046; crude steel (2002), 45,400; distillate fuel oil (2002), 28,732; residual fuel oil

(2002), 28,569; pig iron (2002), 26,600; artificial fertilizers, 3,500; soft drinks (1997), 2,514m. litres; beer, 1,776m. litres; cigarettes, 94·1bn. units.

Shipbuilding orders totalled 6·41m. GT in 2001.

Labour

At Dec. 2001 the population of working age (15 to 59 years) was 36·48m. The economically-active population was 22·18m.; 0·82m. (2001) were registered unemployed. At Nov. 2002, 13·9m. persons were employed in services, 4·2m. in manufacturing, 2·2m. in agriculture, fisheries and forestry, 1·8m. in construction and 19,000 in mining. 6·34m. persons were self-employed in Nov. 2002. Unemployment was 3·4% in Sept. 2005. An annual legal minimum wage is set by the *Minimum Wage Act* (enforced from 1988), which applies to all industries. From Sept. 2004 to Aug. 2005 it was 20,080 won per day and 567,260 won per month. In Dec. 2001 the average monthly wage was 1·75m. won. In 2001 the working week averaged 47 hours (including a half day on Saturdays). In July 2004 the working week in the civil service, for financial and insurance firms, and for employers with 1,000 or more staff was reduced from 44 to 40 hours. A five-day working week for smaller companies is being gradually phased in; employers with fewer than 20 workers do not have to introduce the shorter working week until 2011. Workers in South Korea put in the longest hours of any OECD country. In 2003 full- and part-time workers put in an average of 2,390 hours—nearly 46 hours a week.

Trade Unions

At Dec. 2001 there were 6,150 unions with a total membership of 1,568,723. 877,827 workers belong to the government-recognized Federation of Korean Trade Unions. Since 1997 unions have been permitted to engage in political activities. The Korean Confederation of Trade Unions (*President*, Jo Jun-ho), had 644,000 members in 2002.

INTERNATIONAL TRADE

Total external foreign debt was US$110,109m. in 2001. In May 1998 the government removed restrictions on foreign investment in the Korean stock market. It also began to allow foreign businesses to engage in mergers and acquisitions. From July 1998 foreigners were allowed to buy plots of land for both business and non-business purposes. Since Aug. 1990 South Korean businesses and individuals have been permitted to make investments and set up branch offices in North Korea, on an approval basis. According to the Unification Ministry, the overall volume of inter-Korean trade was US$641m. in 2002 (US$342m. in business transactions and US$298m. in non-profit transactions), a 59·3% increase on 2001.

Imports and Exports

In 2004 imports (c.i.f.) totalled US$224,463m. (US$178,827m. in 2003); exports (f.o.b.), US$253,845m. (US$193,817m. in 2003). Leading import sources in 2004 were: Japan, 20·6%; China, 13·2%; USA, 12·9%; Kuwait, 7·0%. The prinicpal export markets in 2004 were: China, 19·6%; USA, 16·9%; Japan, 8·5%; Hong Kong, 7·1%. In 2004 machinery and transport equipment accounted for 33·6% of imports and 63·0% of exports; chemicals, manufactured goods classified chiefly by material and miscellaneous manufactured articles 33·4% of imports and 30·7% of exports; mineral fuels, lubricants and related materials 22·4% of imports and 4·1% of exports; crude materials, inedible, animal and vegetable oil and fats 6·3% of imports and 1·0% of exports; and food, live animals, beverages and tobacco 4·4% of imports and 1·2% of exports.

Rice imports were prohibited until 1994, but following the GATT Uruguay Round the rice market opened to foreign imports in 1995.

Trade Fairs

In 2001 there were about 100 trade fairs hosted by COEX and 30 hosted by BEXCO (Busan). 3,187 Korean companies participated in 145 trade fairs held in other countries supported by KOTRA, the Korea Trade-Investment Agency.

COMMUNICATIONS

Roads

In 2001 there were 91,396 km of roads, of which 77% (70,146 km) were paved. 10·7m. passengers (2000) and 535·76m. tonnes of freight were carried in 2001. In Dec. 2001 motor vehicles registered totalled 12,914,115, including 8,889,327 passenger cars. There were 991,590 new car registrations in 2002 (by Nov.). In 2001 there were 8,097 fatalities as a result of road accidents (9,353 in 2000). At 16·9 deaths per 100,000 people, South Korea has among the highest death rates in road accidents of any industrialized country. The first of two planned cross-border roads between the two Koreas opened in Feb. 2003.

Rail

In 2001 the National Railroad totalled 3,127 km of 1,435 mm gauge (667·5 km electrified) and 20 km of 762 mm gauge. In 2001 railways carried 912m. passengers and 45m. tonnes of freight. In June 2000 it was agreed to start consultations to restore the railway from Seoul to Sinuiju, on the North Korean/Chinese border, by rebuilding a 12 km long stretch from Munsan, in South Korea, to Jangdan, on the South Korean/North Korean border, and an 8 km long stretch in North Korea. Work on the restoration began in Sept. 2000 but has been delayed in part because of the diplomatic crisis between North Korea and the USA, which escalated in Oct. 2002.

There are metros in Seoul (287 km), and smaller ones in Busan (72·5 km), Daegu (25·7 km) and Incheon (24·6 km).

Civil Aviation

There are six international airports in South Korea: at Seoul (Incheon), Busan (Gimhae), Daegu, Jeju, Yangyang and Cheongju. The new Incheon airport, 50 km to the west of Seoul, built on reclaimed land made up of four small islands, opened in March 2001 and is the largest airport in Asia. It has replaced Gimpo Airport as Seoul's International Airport. The national carrier is Korean Air. Another Korean carrier, Asiana Airlines, also provides services, as did in 2002 around 57 foreign airlines. In 2001, 28·5m. passengers and 423,692 tonnes of cargo were carried on domestic routes and 19·7m. passengers and 1·8m. tonnes of cargo on international routes.

In 2001 Seoul's Gimpo airport handled 22,041,099 passengers (17,743,235 on domestic flights) and 588,938 tonnes of freight. Busan handled 9,168,089 passengers (7,662,429 on domestic flights) and 167,024 tonnes of freight. Jeju handled 9,320,337 passengers (8,968,107 on domestic flights) and 285,648 tonnes of freight.

Shipping

In 2002 there were 51 ports (28 for international trade), including Busan, Incheon, Gunsan, Mokpo, Yeosu, Pohang, Donghae, Jeju, Masan, Ulsan, Daesan and Kwangyang. In 1997 the merchant marine comprised 562 vessels totalling 25·15m. DWT, representing 3·4% of the world's tonnage. 298 vessels (66·87% of gross tonnage) were registered under foreign flags. Total GRT in 2002, 7·05m., including oil tankers 841,000 GRT. In 2001 vessels totalling 770,284,000 NRT entered ports and vessels totalling 776,250,000 NRT cleared. The busiest port is Busan, which in 1999 was visited by 69,429 vessels of 450,033,000 GRT. It is the world's third busiest container port, after Hong Kong and Singapore.

In 2001, 9,340,000 domestic passengers and 1,075,000 international passengers took ferries and other ocean-going vessels. There were a total of 6,586 registered vessels in 2001.

Telecommunications

There were 22,725,000 main telephone lines in 2001 (480 per 1,000 persons). In 2001 public telephones totalled 516,000. In

2002 the number of mobile phone subscribers was 32,342,000 (68·0% of the population). The largest operator, SK Telecom, has 39·5% of the market share, ahead of KTF, with 33·7%. 60·1% of households had PCs in 2002. There were approximately 25·6m. Internet users in July 2002.

Postal Services

In 2003 there were 3,702 post offices operating, with each *myon* (administrative unit comprising several villages) having one or more post offices. In 2002 the mail volume totalled 4,498m. items.

SOCIAL INSTITUTIONS

Justice

Judicial power is vested in the Supreme Court, High Courts, District Courts and Family Court, as well as the Administrative Court and Patent Court. The single six-year term Chief Justice is appointed by the President with the consent of the National Assembly. The other 13 Justices of the Supreme Court are appointed by the President with the consent of the National Assembly, upon the recommendation of the Chief Justice, for renewable six-year terms; the Chief Justice appoints other judges. The death penalty is authorized. In Jan. 2002 there were 1,508 judges, 1,134 prosecutors and about 3,800 private practising lawyers.

The population in penal institutions in Oct. 2002 was 60,721 (128 per 100,000 of national population).

Education

The Korean education system consists of a six-year elementary school, a three-year middle school, a three-year high school and college and university (two to four years). Elementary education for 6–11 year olds is compulsory. Mandatory middle school education began in 2002.

The total number of schools has increased sixfold from 3,000 in 1945 to 19,124 in 2002, with 11,957,388 enrolled students. In 2002 there were 8,343 kindergartens with 550,256 pupils and 29,673 teachers; 5,384 elementary schools with 4,138,366 pupils and 147,497 teachers; 1,841,030 pupils and 95,283 teachers at 2,809 middle schools; and 1,995 high schools with 1,795,509 pupils and 44,177 teachers. In 2002 there were 163 colleges and universities with 1,771,738 students and 44,177 teachers; 11 teacher training colleges with 23,259 students and 721 teachers; 945 graduate schools with 262,867 students; and 19 industrial universities with 187,040 students and 2,543 teachers. In 1996, 5·6% of the population was enrolled in tertiary education, up from just 0·6% in 1970. Around 150,000 South Koreans were studying abroad in 2001.

In 2000–01 total expenditure on education came to 3·8% of GNP and 17·4% of total government spending. The adult literacy was 97·9% in 2001 (99·2% of males and 96·6% of females).

Health

In 2000 there were 285 general hospitals (with 113,518 beds), 20,053 other hospitals and clinics (130,162 beds), 7,412 oriental medical hospitals and clinics (8,436 beds) and 10,527 dental hospitals and clinics. In 2000 there were 72,503 physicians (648 people per doctor), 10,108 oriental medical doctors, 18,039 dentists, 8,728 midwives, 160,295 nurses and 50,623 pharmacists. In 2001 South Korea spent 5·9% of its GDP on health. In 1998, 67·6% of all adult men smoked (the highest proportion in any country in the world), but only 6·7% of women were smokers.

Welfare

In Dec. 2001, 16·3m. persons were covered by the National Pension System introduced in 1988. Employers and employees make equal contributions; persons joining by choice or in rural areas pay their own contributions. The System covers age pensions, disability pensions and survivors' pensions.

Under a system of unemployment insurance introduced in July 1995, workers laid off after working at least six months for a member employer are entitled to benefits averaging 50% of their previous wage for a period of 90 up to 240 days.

RELIGION

Traditionally, Koreans have lived under the influence of shamanism, Buddhism (introduced AD 372) and Confucianism, which was the official faith from 1392 to 1910. Catholic converts from China introduced Christianity in the 18th century, but a ban on Roman Catholicism was not lifted until 1882. The Anglican Church was introduced in 1890 and became an independent jurisdiction in 1993 under the Archbishop of Korea. In 1998 it had 110 churches, 175 priests and some 65,000 faithful. Religious affiliations of the population in 2001: Buddhism, 23·3%; Protestantism, 19·8%; Roman Catholicism, 6·7%; Confucianism, 0·5%; others, 0·8%; no religion, 49·6%. In May 2005 there was one Roman Catholic cardinal.

CULTURE

World Heritage Sites

There are seven sites in South Korea that appear on the UNESCO World Heritage List. They are (with year entered on list): the Sokkuram Grotto and Pulguksa Temple (1995), the Temple of Haeinsa (1995), Chongmyo Shrine (1995), Changdeokgung Palace, Seoul (1997), Hwasong fort, Suwon (1997), the dolmens of Kanghwa (2000), Gyeongju historic area (2000).

Broadcasting

The Korean Broadcasting System (KBS) is a public corporation which broadcasts seven radio channels, two terrestrial TV channels and two satellite TV channels. KBS maintains a nationwide network that connects the key station in Seoul with 25 local stations. It also maintains ten bureaux overseas. In addition to KBS, there is a semi-public TV broadcaster, Munhwa Broadcasting Corporation (MBC), and one commercial TV network, Education Broadcasting System (EBS). Cable TV was inaugurated in March 1995. It had 3·5m. paying subscribers in 2000 and provided 44 channels. There were 17·0m. TV sets (colour by NTSC) in 2001 and 48·6m. radio receivers in 2000.

Cinema

In 2000 there were 376 cinemas with a seating capacity of 193,775. 48 full-length films were produced in 1999.

Press

There were 123 dailies in 2001 and 6,913 periodicals. The main dailies are *Chosun Ilbo* (average circulation of 2·4m. per issue), *JoongAng Ilbo* (average circulation of 2·1m. per issue) and *Dong-A Ilbo* (average circulation of 2·0m. per issue).

A total of 36,185 book titles and 118m. books were published in 2002.

Tourism

In 2001, 6,084,476 Koreans travelled abroad. 5,347,000 foreign nationals visited South Korea in 2002 (4,542,000 in 1997). In 2002 tourist revenues from foreign visitors totalled US$5·3bn.; overseas travel expenditure by Koreans going abroad totalled US$7·6bn. On 18 Nov. 1998 the first South Korean tourists to visit North Korea went on a cruise and tour organized by the South Korean firm Hyundai.

Libraries

There were 9,337 libraries in 2001, including one national library, one congressional, 420 public, 420 university and 7,918 libraries at primary, middle and high schools. There were also 578 specialized and professional libraries.

Theatre and Opera

There are 316 theatres nationwide. 47 have 1,200 seats that can accommodate large-scale dramas, operas, dances and musicals. The Seoul Arts Centre has an opera house.

Museums and Galleries

In 2001 there were 249 museums, including 25 national museums, 36 public museums, 107 private museums and 81 university museums. There were an estimated 500 art galleries in 2001.

DIPLOMATIC REPRESENTATIVES

Of the Republic of Korea in the United Kingdom (60 Buckingham Gate, London, SW1E 6AJ)
Ambassador: Dr Yoon-Je Cho.

Of the United Kingdom in the Republic of Korea (4 Jeong-dong, Jung-gu, Seoul 100–120)
Ambassador: Warwick Morris.

Of the Republic of Korea in the USA (2450 Massachusetts Ave., NW, Washington, D.C., 20008)
Ambassador: Lee Tae-Sik.

Of the USA in the Republic of Korea (82 Sejongno, Jongno-gu, Seoul)
Ambassador: Alexander Vershbow.

Of the Republic of Korea to the United Nations
Ambassador: Choi Young-jin.

Of the Republic of Korea to the European Union
Ambassador: Oh Haeng-kyeom.

FURTHER READING

National Bureau of Statistics. *Korea Statistical Yearbook*
Bank of Korea. *Economic Statistics Yearbook*
Castley, R., *Korea's Economic Miracle*. London, 1997
Cumings, B., *Korea's Place in the Sun: A Modern History*. New York, 1997
Hoare, James E., *Korea.* [Bibliography] ABC-Clio, Oxford and Santa Barbara (CA), 1997
Kang, M.-H., *The Korean Business Conglomerate: Chaebol Then and Now.* Univ. of California Press, 1996
Kim, D.-H. and Tat, Y.-K. (eds.) *The Korean Peninsula in Transition.* London, 1997
Simons, G., *Korea: the Search for Sovereignty*. London, 1995
Smith, H., *Industry Policy in Taiwan and Korea in the 1980s*. Edward Elgar, 2000
Song, P.-N., *The Rise of the Korean Economy*. 2nd ed. OUP, 1994
Tennant, R., *A History of Korea*. London, 1996

National Statistical Office: National Bureau of Statistics, Ministry of Finance and Economy, Seoul.
Website: http://www.nso.go.kr/

NORTH KOREA

Chosun Minchu-chui Inmin Konghwa-guk
(Democratic People's Republic of Korea)

Capital: Pyongyang
Population projection, 2010: 22·91m.
GDP per capita: not available

KEY HISTORICAL EVENTS

The Korean peninsula was first settled by tribal peoples from Manchuria and Siberia who provided the basis for the modern Korean language. By 3000 BC agriculture-based communities had emerged. The earliest known colony in the region was established at Pyongyang in the 12th century BC. Among the most prominent agricultural communities was Old Choson, which by 194 BC had evolved into a league of tribes ruled by Wiman or 'Wei Man', a leader widely held to have defected from China, although he may have been a native of the Choson region. His realm was taken over by the Han empire of China in 108 BC and replaced by four Chinese colonies.

The rest of the peninsula developed into tribal states; Puyo in the north and Chin south of the Han River. Chin was itself split into three tribal states (Mahan, Chinhan and Pyonhan); these states then evolved into three rival kingdoms (Koguryo, Paekche and Silla). Three powerful figures, King T'aejo (AD 53–146) of Koguryo, King Koi (AD 234–86) of Paekche and King Naemul (AD 356–402) of Silla, established hereditary monarchies while powerful aristocracies developed from tribal chiefdoms.

With China's support Silla conquered the other two kingdoms; Paekche in 660 and Koguryo in 668. In 676 Silla drove out the Chinese and gained complete control of the peninsula. Survivors from Koguryo established Parhae, under the leadership of Tae Cho-yong, in the northern region. After a period of conflict with Silla, Parhae grew into a prosperous state in its own right before being taken over by northern nomadic peoples. In Silla an absolute monarchy replaced the council of nobles (its former

decision making body) with a central administrative body called the chancellery (*Chipsabu*), thus undermining aristocratic power. Meanwhile, the capital Kumsong (now Kyongju in South Korea) was developed. The state was divided into administrative units by province (*chu*), prefecture (*kun*), and county (*hyon*), and five provincial capitals prospered as cultural centres. Avatamsaka Buddhism was the dominant religion.

Divisions within the aristocracy in the 8th century led to the restoration of the Council of Nobles and the overthrow of the monarchy. Forced to pay taxes to powerful provincial families and central government, the peasants rebelled. Two provincial leaders, Kyonhwon and Kungye, established the Later Paekche (892) and Later Koguryo (901) as rivals to Silla.

National Unity

The powerful leader Wang Kon founded Koryo (now Kaesong, North Korea) in 918, and established a unified kingdom in the Korean peninsula in 936. Three chancelleries and the royal secretariat formed the supreme council of state and governed the kingdom. Koryo's leaders were then largely aristocratic, and the political system greatly favoured those in the top five tiers of the nine hierarchical levels. That the military was not eligible for any hierarchical position above the second level and received little land, led to a military coup in 1170. Gen. Ch'oe Ch'ung-hon established a military regime which held power for the next sixty years. Zen Buddhism and the allied ideology of Confucianism had grown popular but were suppressed under the Ch'oe regime. Many monks fled to the mountains, where they formed what became Korean Buddhism, the *Chogye*.

In 1231 the Mongols invaded Koryo but were resisted by the Ch'oe leaders for nearly three decades, until a peasant uprising saw the Ch'oe overthrown. A power-sharing agreement between the rebels and the Mongols came into force in 1258. Despite some interference from the Mongols, Koryo retained its identity as a unified state. The aristocracy established seats of power throughout the country, encouraging peasants to seek protection as serfs. This, however, led to reduced tax revenues and when the government did not have sufficient resources to reward its bureaucratic class, a rebellion ensued. Led by General Yi Song-gye, and with the help of the Ming dynasty in China, government officials seized power in 1392 and established a new system of land distribution, thus ending the Koryo dynasty.

Gen. Yi named the state Choson, designating Hanyang (now Seoul, South Korea) as the capital. Buddhism was dropped in favour of a new Chinese-influenced Confucian ethical system and the state was governed by a hereditary aristocracy (the *yangban*), who controlled all aspects of Korean society. In 1420 the Hall of Worthies (*Chiphyonjon*) was established for scholars, and after 1443 the Korean phonetic alphabet (*hangul*) developed. Later in the period, a centralized yangban government was formed and the country divided into eight administrative regions, with standardized laws and a central decision-making and judicial body.

In 1592 Japan, newly unified under the command of Toyotomi Hideyoshi, sent an army to Korea supposedly as part of an invasion of China. Korea's naval forces, under Admiral Yi Sun-shin, were able to repel the invaders. Swelling anti-Japanese sentiment prompted Koreans from all hierarchical divisions to fight in the war alongside troops dispatched from Ming China. However, Japanese forces did not withdraw completely until Toyotomi's death in 1598, leaving Korea in ruins.

Despite joint efforts by China and Korea to stem the advances of the nomadic Manchu in the early 17th century, Seoul was captured in 1636. The Manchu established the Ch'ing dynasty several years later and demanded tribute from Korea.

During the 17th and 18th centuries, Korea's agriculture developed as irrigation improved and rice, tobacco and ginseng became increasingly important crops. By the late 18th century many Korean scholars had turned to Roman Catholicism, leading to government suppression of Christianity in a bid to preserve the dominance of Confucianism. However, European priests maintained strong links in the country.

Japanese Influence

In the 19th century, a succession of monarchs yet to attain the age of majority undermined national stability. In 1864 Taewon'gun, the father of the child-king Kojong, took power and pursued a programme of controversial political reform that increasingly isolated Korea from the outside world. When Taewon'gun was eventually forced to step down, Korea came under pressure from Japan to open up its ports. Nervous of growing Japanese influence, China placed troops in Korea following a failed coup attempt by pro-Taewon'gun forces. There followed a trade agreement which greatly benefited Chinese commercial interests. Further treaties with France, Germany, Russia, the UK and the USA followed in the 1880s. As foreign influence increased, Korea's ruling elite divided between moderates and radicals. The radicals carried out a coup in 1884 but were quickly defeated by Chinese troops. An agreement to maintain a balance of power in the region was signed by Japan and China the following year.

As modernization gathered pace, government spending increased, adding to the burden of reparations payments to Japan. The peasants turned to *Tonghak* ('Eastern Learning'), a new religion established by an old yangban scholar and based on traditional beliefs. A Tonghak rebellion in 1894 caused China to send in troops. Japan responded by sending its own forces and war broke out. By the following year Japan had secured control of the peninsula.

Korea declared neutrality at the outbreak of war between Japan and Russia in 1904 but was pressured by Japan into allowing use of Korean territory. Japan achieved victory in 1905 and made Korea a protectorate. An unsuccessful appeal to the international peace conference at The Hague further undermined relations between Japan and Korea. Anti-Japanese guerrilla fighters in the southern provinces were active during 1908–09 but were crushed the following year when Korea was annexed by Japan.

Japan established a government in Korea and implemented a programme designed to supplant the Korean identity. There were restrictions on freedom of speech, press and assembly and the language and history of Japan was taught in schools at the expense of those of Korea. Many Koreans were dispossessed of their land as Japan built new transport and communications infrastructures. When the Japanese brutally suppressed a 2m.-strong demonstration in 1919, independence leaders established a provisional government in Shanghai and named Syngman Rhee as president. Hoping to calm dissent, Japan lifted certain press restrictions and replaced the gendarmerie with an ordinary police force, but uncompromising colonial rule remained in place.

Korea became a market for Japanese goods and attracted much capital investment but at the expense of agriculture, leading to a long-term shortage of rice. Tokyo reimposed military rule in 1931 when war broke out between Japan and China and attempted to quash all manifestations of a separate Korean identity over the following decade. Magazines, newspapers and academic organisations operating in the Korean language were banned and hundred of thousands of Koreans were made to fight in the Japanese army or work in Japanese mines and factories in order to support Japan's military efforts during the Second World War. The Shanghai provisional government, having moved to Chungking in southwest China, declared war on Japan in Dec. 1941. An army of resistance fighters joined the Allied forces in China and fought with them until the Japanese surrender in 1945.

Korea Divided

Korea was promised independence by China, Britain and the USA at the Cairo conference of 1943 but at the end of the war, after Japan's collapse, Korea was divided in two along the 38° Parallel. Initially the USA and the USSR had agreed informally to a four-way power share in Korea, involving Britain and the Republic of China. However, in order to hasten a Japanese surrender, US troops controlled the south of the country while the USSR took command of the north. The Soviet forces helped to establish a Communist-led provisional government under Kim Il Sung. As relations between the USA and the Soviet Union worsened, trade ceased between the two zones, causing economic hardship because industry was concentrated in the north and agriculture in the south.

In Sept. 1947 the United Nations reviewed the question of Korean reunification and general elections in Korea were proposed. However, a commission to oversee voting was denied entry by Soviet troops. Rhee was elected in the South while the North appointed Kim Il Sung as leader. In 1948 the southern Republic of Korea (with Seoul as the capital) and the northern Democratic People's Republic of Korea (with Pyongyang as capital) formally came into being.

Soviet and US troops left the peninsula in 1949 and war broke out between the North and South in June 1950. A US-led UN force under Gen. Douglas MacArthur entered South Korea and pushed back the North Korean forces. The UN pressed on into North Korea and established a commission for the reunification and rehabilitation of Korea. China, which at that point had no representation in the United Nations, entered the war and contributed 1·2m. troops to the North Korean side. Negotiations to end the war began in 1951 and a new international boundary and demilitarized zone were declared in 1953. The USA offered South Korea financial support and signed a mutual security pact with Rhee, who had been reluctant to accept the division of the country. The issue of prisoner returns, particularly of North Koreans unwilling to return to the communist state, remained a point of contention. The war left 4m. people dead or injured.

In the aftermath, Kim set about tightening his grip on his country by purging potential rivals. He established a dictatorship based on a personality cult and introduced his philosophy of *Juche*, by which the country was to develop without any help from outside. Industrialization and military spending gathered pace in the later 1950s and the 1960s despite North Korea's international isolation. However, by the late 1970s North Korea had fallen far behind its southern neighbour and a period of stagnation began.

Kim maintained close relations with China and the Soviet Union, although his allegiance wavered between the two as Sino-Soviet relations deteriorated from the 1960s onwards. When the Soviet Union collapsed in 1990–91, North Korea went into an economic crisis that included widespread famine. Attempts to improve relations with South Korea in the early 1990s faltered over the North's alleged nuclear capacity although in 1994 North Korea agreed to shut down controversial reactors in return for aid and oil. Kim died in 1994 and power passed to his son, Kim Jong Il, who, like his father, has received international condemnation for civil rights abuses.

Under the younger Kim the economy has collapsed to subsistence level although spending on the military remains high. In 1997 the UN World Food Programme estimated that 2m. North Koreans faced starvation. More than 5% of the population starved to death during the 1990s. In 2000 Kim received South Korean President Kim Dae-jung as relations between the North and South appeared to be thawing. The two leaders agreed that reunification was the eventual aim of both Koreas but relations had again deteriorated by 2002 after a naval battle in the Yellow Sea between North and South forces killed four South Korean and around 30 North Korean sailors. Kim Jong Il blamed the USA and South Korea for the attack. South Korean president Kim Dae-jung suspended rice shipments to the north and demanded an apology.

Relations with the USA worsened during 2002 and 2003 after the USA claimed that North Korea had a secret nuclear programme. US president George Bush accused North Korea of forming part of what he called the 'Axis of Evil' along with Iraq and Iran. North Korea subsequently re-activated a nuclear plant and demanded the withdrawal of inspectors from the UN International Atomic Energy Agency. Pyongyang claimed it had been forced to re-open the reactor in response to US plans for a pre-emptive nuclear strike. North Korea then announced its withdrawal from the nuclear non-proliferation treaty, although it denied any intention to produce nuclear weapons. Many observers suggested Kim carried out these manoeuvres to pressurize the USA into direct talks with a view to signing a mutual non-aggression pact. North Korea's nuclear programme has in turn unsettled relations with regional neighbours including South Korea and Japan. In Feb. 2005 North Korea publicly admitted for the first time that it possessed nuclear weapons.

TERRITORY AND POPULATION

North Korea is bounded in the north by China, east by the sea of Japan, west by the Yellow Sea and south by South Korea, from which it is separated by a demilitarized zone of 1,262 sq. km. Its area is 122,762 sq. km.

The census population in 1993 was 20,522,351; density 167·2 per sq. km. In the elections to the Supreme People's Assembly held on 26 July 1998, 687 deputies were elected, as was the case in 1990. The South Korean weekly NEWSREVIEW stated that North Korea has made it a rule that there should be one deputy per 30,000 people, suggesting that the population has remained stable since 1990. 30,000 multiplied by 687 would give a population of 20·61m., more than 1·5m. less than official estimates. 2005 population estimate: 22,488,000.

The UN gives a projected population for 2010 of 22·91m.

The area, 1993 census population (in 1,000) and chief towns of the provinces, special cities and special districts:

	Area in sq. km	Population	Chief Town
Chagang	16,968	1,153	Kanggye
North Hamgyong[1]	17,570	2,061	Chongjin
South Hamgyong	18,970	2,732	Hamhung
North Hwanghae	8,007	1,512	Sariwon
South Hwanghae	8,002	2,011	Haeju
Hyangsan (special district)[2]	—	33	
Kaesong (special city)	1,255	334	
Kangwon	11,152	1,304	Wonsan
Najin Sonbong (special city)[3]	—	—	
Nampo (special city)	753	731	
North Pyongan[4]	12,191	2,404	Sinuiju
South Pyongan	11,577	2,866	Pyongsan
Pyongyang (special city)	2,000	2,741	
Yanggang	14,317	638	Hyesan

[1]Area and population include Najin Sonbong special city.
[2]Area included in North Pyongan. [3]Created in 2001.
[4]Area includes Hyangsan special district.

Pyongyang, the capital, had a 1999 population of 3,136,000. Other large towns (census, 1993): Nampo (731,448); Hamhung (709,730); Chongjin (582,480).

The official language is Korean.

SOCIAL STATISTICS

1995 births, 477,000; deaths, 122,000. 1995 birth rate, 21·6 per 1,000 population; death rate, 5·5. Annual population growth rate, 1990–99, 1·6%. Marriage is discouraged before the age of 32 for men and 29 for women. Life expectancy at birth, 1997, was 59·8 years for males and 64·5 years for females. Infant mortality, 1990–95, 24 per 1,000 live births; fertility rate, 2001, 2·1 births per woman. It was estimated in 1999 that up to 300,000 North Korean food-seeking refugees had gone to China to escape the famine.

27% of the population is classified as 'hostile' by the regime and 45% as 'unstable'.

CLIMATE

There is a warm temperate climate, though winters can be very cold in the north. Rainfall is concentrated in the summer months. Pyongyang, Jan. 18°F (–7·8°C), July 75°F (23·9°C). Annual rainfall 37" (916 mm).

CONSTITUTION AND GOVERNMENT

The political structure is based upon the Constitution of 27 Dec. 1972. Constitutional amendments of April 1992 delete references to Marxism-Leninism but retain the Communist Party's monopoly of rule. The Constitution provides for a 687-seat *Supreme People's Assembly* elected every five years by universal suffrage. Citizens of 17 years and over can vote and be elected. The government consists of the *Administration Council* directed by the Central People's Committee.

The head of state is the *President*, elected for four-year terms. On the death of Kim Il Sung on 8 July 1994 his son and designated successor, Kim Jong Il (b. 1942), assumed all his father's posts. On 5 Sept. 1998 he took over as President and 'Supreme Leader'.

Party membership was 2m. in 1995. There are also the puppet religious Chongu and Korean Social Democratic Parties and various organizations combined in a Fatherland Front.

National Anthem

'A chi mun bin na ra i gang san' ('Shine bright, o dawn, on this land so fair'); words by Pak Se Yong, tune by Kim Won Gyun.

RECENT ELECTIONS

Elections to the Supreme People's Assembly were held on 3 Aug. 2003. Only the list of the Democratic Front for the Reunification of the Fatherland (led by the Korean Workers' Party) was allowed to participate. 687 deputies were elected unopposed.

CURRENT ADMINISTRATION

President: Kim Jong Il. He also holds the posts of *Supreme Commander of the Korean People's Army* and *Chairman of the National Defence Commission.*

In March 2006 the government included:

Prime Minister: Pak Pong-chu (appointed 3 Sept. 2003).

Vice Prime Ministers: Kwak Pom-ki, Chon Sung-hun, No Tu-ch'ol.

Minister of Agriculture: Yi Kyong-sik. *Chemical Industry:* Yi Mu-yong. *City Management:* Ch'oe Chong-kon. *Commerce:* Yi Yong-son. *Construction and Building Materials Industry:* Tong Chong-ho. *Crude Oil Industry:* Ko Chong-sik. *Culture:* Kim Jin-song. *Education:* Kim Yong-chin. *Electronic Industry:* O Su-yong. *Extractive Industries:* Kang Min-chol. *Finance:* Mun Il-pong. *Fisheries:* Yi Song-ung. *Foreign Affairs:* Paek Nam-sun. *Foreign Trade:* Rim Kyong-man. *Forestry:* Sok Kun-su. *Labour:* Jong Yong-su. *Land and Environment Protection:* Chang Il-son. *Land and Marine Transport:* Kim Yong-il. *Light Industry:* Yi Chu-o. *Machine-Building Industry:* Jo Pyong-ju. *Metal Industry:* Kim Sung-hyon. *People's Security:* Ju Sang-song. *Post and Telecommunications:* Ryu Yong-sop. *Power and Coal Industries:* Chu Tong-il. *Procurement and Food Administration:* Choe Nam-kyun. *Public Health:* Kim Su-hak. *Railways:* Kim Yong-sam. *State Construction Control:* Pae Tal-chun. *State Inspection:* Kim Ui-sun.

President, Supreme People's Assembly Praesidium: Kim Yong-nam. *Vice Presidents:* Yang Hyong-sop, Kim Yong-t'ae.

In practice the country is ruled by the Korean Workers' (*i.e.*, Communist) Party which elects a Central Committee which in turn appoints a Politburo.

Office of the President: http://www.korea-dpr.com/

CURRENT LEADERS

Kim Jong Il

Position
President

Introduction
Kim Jong Il is the second ruler of the world's only Communist dynasty. Groomed to succeed his father, Kim Il Sung, the founder of the Democratic People's Republic of Korea (North Korea), Kim junior is commonly known to his countrymen as the 'Dear Leader'. Despite some progress in foreign relations, notably with South Korea, North Korea's nuclear weapons programme continues to cause international unease.

Early Life
According to some accounts, Kim Jong Il was born on 16 Feb. 1941 on Paekdusan, the highest mountain in Korea, although it is probable he was born in the Siberian city of Khabarovsk, where his father was based at the time and where he spent his first four years.

Kim Jong Il returned with his family to Korea after World War II, only to be sent to China for safety at the outbreak of the Korean War (1950–53). Thereafter, he grew up in North Korea, where he has since lived apart from a brief period in East Germany training to be a pilot. On his return he studied at the Kim Il Sung University in Pyongyang.

From the early 1960s Kim Jong Il was groomed to succeed his father. In the mid-1960s he helped his father purge the (Communist) Korean Workers' Party (KWP) and held a variety of posts within the party. In 1973, Kim Jong Il was placed in charge of party propaganda and organization. In 1980 he was named as his father's heir. During the 1970s and 1980s he was appointed to various high offices, beginning with election to the KWP Politburo in 1974. In Dec. 1991 he took over the country's armed forces and three years later, on his father's death, he became president.

Career in Office
Kim Jong Il did not immediately assume any of his father's offices of state. He became general secretary of the KWP in 1997 and chairman of the National Defence Commission, a role that is now effectively head of state.

Kim has ruled in tandem with a group of relatives and some of his father's colleagues. He has presided over the collapse of his country's economy to subsistence level. Kim visited Moscow and Beijing in an attempt to recement old alliances but economic assistance was not forthcoming. He maintained spending on the military, considered the base of his support, and encouraged the development of a missile programme. His regime is widely perceived to have nuclear ambitions and in Jan. 2002 US President George Bush labelled North Korea part of an 'Axis of Evil' with Iraq and Iran.

In 2000 he received South Korean President Kim Dae-jung on an unprecedented visit. Although the two leaders agreed that reunification was the eventual aim of both Koreas, relations deteriorated in late June 2002 after a naval battle in the Yellow Sea between North and South forces killed four South Korean and around 30 North Korean sailors. Kim Jong Il blamed the USA and South Korea for the attack. South Korean president Kim Dae-jung suspended rice shipments to the North and demanded an apology.

In Sept. 2002 some progress was made in ending North Korea's isolation when the Japanese prime minister Junichiro Koizumi

visited the president in a move to re-establish diplomatic relations, although Kim was forced to admit to, and apologize for, the kidnapping of 11 Japanese citizens in 1970s and 1980s. In Oct. 2002 North Korea admitted to developing nuclear technology in contravention of an agreement signed with the USA in 1994. While President Bush advocated a diplomatic solution, the ongoing talks with Japan faltered when Japan accused North Korea of reneging on promises to halt its nuclear development. In late Nov. 2002 the EU, Japan and South Korea suspended fuel oil shipments to North Korea.

The crisis between Kim's regime and the USA intensified in Dec. 2002 and Jan. 2003 when North Korea reactivated a nuclear plant and demanded the withdrawal of inspectors from the UN International Atomic Energy Agency. Pyongyang claimed it had been forced to reopen the reactor in response to US plans for a pre-emptive nuclear strike. North Korea then announced its withdrawal from the Nuclear Non-Proliferation Treaty, although it denied any intention to produce nuclear weapons. Many observers suggested Kim carried out these manoeuvres to pressurize the USA into direct talks with a view to signing a mutual non-aggression pact. President Bush responded with proposals for a 'tailored containment' strategy, potentially involving economic sanctions. South Korea opposed attempts to isolate the North Korean economy and sent diplomats to China and Russia, two of North Korea's traditional allies, in a bid to exert pressure on Pyongyang to reconsider its nuclear policy.

Relations with the international community deteriorated throughout Feb. 2003. The IAEA formally reported North Korea to the UN Security Council for failing to comply with nuclear non-proliferation accords. Pyongyang responded by asserting its capability to attack US interests throughout the world if provoked. It also declared that it would consider UN-imposed sanctions as a declaration of war. Japan in turn said it would use military force to repel any threat from North Korea while China urged the UN to support ongoing negotiations with Pyongyang. The following month Pyongyang launched two short-range anti-ship missiles in the direction of the Sea of Japan. Kim then withdrew from border liaison negotiations with US officials and the North Korean parliament increased its defence budget. Pyongyang had earlier claimed that joint military exercises between the USA and South Korea, which coincided with the invasion of Iraq, were a sign that the USA intended to launch strikes on the North's nuclear establishments. Pyongyang also accused Japan of a 'hostile act' after it launched two spy satellites. In April 2003 Chinese-brokered talks with the USA ended acrimoniously and the following month Pyongyang announced its withdrawal from a 1992 accord with South Korea guaranteeing the Korean peninsula as a nuclear weapon-free zone.

In July 2003 Pyongyang claimed to have produced enough plutonium to start making nuclear bombs. Over the next two years there followed several rounds of inconclusive negotiations between North Korea and the USA, together with South Korea, Japan, China and Russia. During this period Kim's regime admitted publicly in Feb 2005 that it had built nuclear weapons for self-defence before agreeing in principle in Sept. 2005 to give up its development programme in return for aid and security guarantees. However, that accord was almost immediately undermined when North Korea then demanded the delivery of civil nuclear equipment.

DEFENCE

The Supreme Commander of the Armed Forces is Kim Jong Il. Military service is compulsory at the age of 16 for periods of 5–8 years in the Army, 5–10 years in the Navy and 3–4 years in the Air Force, followed by obligatory part-time service in the Pacification Corps to age 40. Total armed forces troops were estimated to number 1,082,000 in 2002, up from 840,000 in

1986 although down from 1,160,000 in 1997. Around 70% of the troops are located along or near the Demilitarized Zone between North and South Korea.

Defence expenditure in 2003 totalled US$5,500m. (US$243 per capita), and represented 25·0% of GDP—the highest percentage of any country in the world.

In 1998 North Korea tested a medium-range nuclear-capable Taepo Dong-1 missile. It has also developed a shorter-range No-Dong ballistic missile in addition to Scud B and Scud C missiles, and is known to be developing a longer-range inter-continental ballistic missile, the two-stage Taepo Dong-2, which experts believe could reach Alaska and the westernmost Hawaiian islands.

Nuclear Weapons

North Korea was for many years suspected of having a secret nuclear-weapons programme, and perhaps enough material to build two warheads. In Oct. 2002 it revealed that it had developed a nuclear bomb in violation of an arms control pact agreed with the USA in 1994. North Korea has not signed the Comprehensive Nuclear-Test-Ban-Treaty, which is intended to bring about a ban on any nuclear explosions. In Feb. 2005 it declared that it had manufactured nuclear weapons—a claim that cannot be verified—and stated that it would not re-enter multilateral negotiations on its disarmament. North Korea is widely suspected of having both biological and chemical weapons.

Army

One of the world's biggest, the Army was estimated at 950,000 personnel in 2002 with around 600,000 reserves. There is also a paramilitary worker-peasant Red Guard of some 3·5m. and a Ministry of Public Security force of 189,000 including border guards. Equipment includes some 3,500 T-34, T-54/55, T-62 and Type-59 main battle tanks.

Navy

The Navy, principally tasked to coastal patrol and defence, comprises 26 diesel submarines, three small frigates and six corvettes. Personnel in 2002 totalled about 46,000 with 65,000 reserves.

Air Force

The Air Force had a total of 621 combat aircraft and 86,000 personnel in 2002. Combat aircraft include J-5/6/7s (Chinese built versions of MiG-17/19/23s), MiG-29s, Su-7s and Su-25s.

INTERNATIONAL RELATIONS

In Sept. 1999 following negotiations between Pyongyang and Washington in Berlin, Pyongyang agreed to put off its plan to test-fire an advanced long-range missile whilst the USA agreed gradually to lift economic sanctions imposed in 1950. The gesture on the part of the USA was the most significant since the end of the Korean War.

In 2000 North Korea received US$220m. in foreign aid, of which US$114m. came from South Korea.

North Korea is a member of the UN and the Antarctic Treaty.

ECONOMY

Agriculture is estimated to account for approximately 25% of GDP, industry 60% and services 15%.

Overview

In Dec. 1993 it was officially admitted that the third seven-year plan had failed to achieve its industrial targets owing to the disappearance of Communist markets and aid. Policy now concentrates on the development of agriculture, light industry and foreign trade but progress is impeded by an all-powerful bureaucracy and a reluctance to depart from the Marxist-Stalinist line. Changes in the economy in July 2002—the revocation of the rationing system for rice and large increases in prices for food, electricity and housing—prompted hopes of an upturn but food shortages became critical in 2003 after the deterioration of relations with international donors.

Currency

The monetary unit is the *won* (KPW) of 100 *chon*. Banknotes were replaced by a new issue in July 1992. Exchanges of new for old notes were limited to 500 won. In July 2002 the government readjusted the value of the won from an artificially set rate of 2·15 won per dollar to 150 won per dollar, although the black market rate is nearer 800 won to the dollar. Inflation was an estimated 5% in 1998.

Budget

Estimated revenue, 1999, 19,801m. won; expenditure, 20,018m. won.

Performance

The real GDP growth rate was 6·2% in 1999 following a decade of negative growth. This was followed in 2000 by growth of 1·3%, rising in 2001 to 3·7%. GDP per head was put at US$741 in 1997, or about a thirteenth of that of South Korea.

Banking and Finance

The bank of issue is the Central Bank of Korea (*Governor*, Kim Wan-su). In 2002 there were seven state banks, seven joint venture banks and two foreign investment banks.

Weights and Measures

While the metric system is in force traditional measures are in frequent use. The *jungbo* = one ha; the *ri* = 3,927 metres.

ENERGY AND NATURAL RESOURCES

Environment

Carbon dioxide emissions from the consumption and flaring of fossil fuels in 2002 were the equivalent of 3·5 tonnes per capita. An *Environmental Sustainability Index* compiled for the World Economic Forum meeting in Jan. 2005 ranked North Korea 146th in the world out of 146 countries analysed, with 29·2%. The index measured the ability of countries to maintain favourable environmental conditions and examined various factors including pollution levels and the use or abuse of natural resources.

Electricity

There are three thermal power stations and four hydro-electric plants. Installed capacity was 9·5m. kW in 2000. Production in 2000 was 19·4bn. kWh. Consumption per capita was 1,474 kWh in 2000. Hydro-electric potential exceeds 8m. kW. A hydro-electric plant and dam under construction on the Pukhan River near Mount Kumgang has been denounced as a flood threat by the South Koreans, who constructed a defensive 'Peace Dam' in retaliation. American aid to increase energy supply slowed after evidence that North Korea had broken its promise to freeze its nuclear weapons programme. But in Oct. 1998 Japan agreed to contribute US$1bn. towards building two nuclear power stations and the US Congress agreed to funds to supply fuel oil on condition that North Korea abandons its nuclear ambitions. In Aug. 2002 work began on the construction of the two western-designed light-water nuclear reactors. In Feb. 2003 North Korea reactivated its nuclear reactor at Yongbyon that had been dormant since 1994.

Oil and Gas

Oil wells went into production in 1957. An oil pipeline from China came on stream in 1976. China's supplies account for 70% of North Korea's oil consumption. Refinery distillation output amounted to 2·5m. tonnes in 1998.

Minerals

North Korea is rich in minerals. Estimated reserves in tonnes: coal, 11,990m.; manganese, 6,500m.; iron ore, 3,300m.; uranium, 26m.; zinc, 12m.; lead, 6m.; copper, 2·15m. 54m. tonnes of coal were mined in 2000, 11m. tonnes of iron ore in 1996, 11m. tonnes of lignite in 2002 and 13,000 tonnes of copper ore in 2002. 2001 production of gold was 2,000 kg; silver (2001 estimate), 40 tonnes; salt (1997 estimate), 590,000 tonnes.

Agriculture

In 2001 there were 2·5m. ha. of arable land and 300,000 ha. of permanent crop land. In 1995 there were 0·65m. ha. of paddy fields. In 2002, 3·32m. persons were economically active in agriculture.

Collectivization took place between 1954 and 1958. 90% of the cultivated land is farmed by co-operatives. Land belongs either to the State or to co-operatives, and it is intended gradually to transform the latter into the former, but small individually-tended plots producing for 'farmers' markets' are tolerated as a 'transition measure'.

There is a large-scale tideland reclamation project. In 2001, 1·46m. ha. were under irrigation, making possible two rice harvests a year. There were 70,000 tractors in 2001. The technical revolution in agriculture (nearly 95% of ploughing, etc., is mechanized) has considerably increased the yield of wheat (sown on 103,000 ha.). Production (2000, in 1,000 tonnes): rice, 1,690; potatoes, 1,402; maize, 1,041; apples, 650; cabbages, 630; sweet potatoes, 468; soybeans, 350; dry beans, 280; melons and watermelons, 214.

Livestock, 2000: pigs, 2·97m.; goats, 2·10m.; cattle, 600,000; sheep, 190,000; 10m. chickens.

A chronic food shortage has led to repeated efforts by UN agencies to stave off famine. In Jan. 1998 the UN launched an appeal for US$378m. for food for North Korea, the largest ever relief effort mounted by its World Fund Programme.

Forestry

Forest area in 2000 was 8·21m. ha. (68·2% of the land area). Timber production was 7·06m. cu. metres in 2001.

Fisheries

In 2001 total catch was approximately 200,000 tonnes, of which 90% were sea fish.

INDUSTRY

Industries were intensively developed by the Japanese occupiers, notably cotton spinning, hydro-electric power, cotton, silk and rayon weaving, and chemical fertilizers. Production: pig iron (2002), 800,000 tonnes; cement (2002), 5·3m. tonnes; crude steel (2000), 1·11m. tonnes; textile fabrics (1994), 350m. metres; TV sets (1995), 240,000 units; motor cars (2000), 6,600 units; ships (1995), 50,000 GRT. Industrial production is estimated to have halved between 1990 and 2000.

Labour

The labour force totalled 11,881,000 (55% males) in 1996. Nearly 29% of the economically active population in 2002 were engaged in agriculture.

INTERNATIONAL TRADE

Joint ventures with foreign firms have been permitted since 1984. A law of Oct. 1992 revised the 1984 rules: foreign investors may now set up wholly-owned facilities in special economic zones, repatriate part of profits and enjoy tax concessions. In 1996 foreign debt was estimated at US$11,830m. The USA imposed sanctions in Jan. 1988 for alleged terrorist activities. Since June 1995 South Korean businesses and individuals have been permitted to make investments and set up branch offices in North Korea.

Imports and Exports

Imports in 2001 were US$1,847m.; exports, US$826m. In 2001 China was the biggest import supplier (31%), followed by Japan (13%) and South Korea (12%); Japan was the main export destination (27%), ahead of South Korea (21%) and China (20%). The chief imports are machinery and petroleum products, the chief exports metal ores and products.

COMMUNICATIONS

Roads

There were around 31,200 km of road in 2002, of which 2,000 km were paved. There were 262,000 passenger cars in 2000. The first of two planned cross-border roads between the two Koreas opened in Feb. 2003.

Rail

The railway network totalled 8,533 km in 1990, of which 3,250 km were electrified. In 1990, 38·5m. tonnes of freight and 35m. passengers were carried. In June 2000 it was agreed to start consultations to restore the railway from Sinuiju, on the North Korean/Chinese border, to Seoul by rebuilding an 8 km long stretch from Pongdong-ni to Changdan, on the North Korean/South Korean border, and a 12 km long stretch in South Korea. The first two rail links between the two Koreas are currently under construction.

There is a metro and two tramways in Pyongyang.

Civil Aviation

There is an international airport at Pyongyang (Sunan). There were flights in 2003 to Bangkok, Beijing, Khabarovsk, Macao, Shenyang and Vladivostok. The national carrier is Air Koryo.

Shipping

The leading ports are Chongjin, Wonsan and Hungnam. Pyongyang is connected to the port of Nampo by railway and river. In 2002 the ocean-going merchant fleet totalled 870,000 GRT, including oil tankers 16,000 GRT.

The biggest navigable river is the Yalu, 698 km up to the Hyesan district.

Telecommunications

An agreement to share in Japan's telecommunications satellites was reached in Sept. 1990. There were 1,100,000 main telephone lines in 2000, or 45·8 per 1,000 population. In 1995 there were 3,000 fax machines. North Korea's first Internet cafe opened in May 2002.

SOCIAL INSTITUTIONS

Justice

The judiciary consists of the Supreme Court, whose judges are elected by the Assembly for three years; provincial courts; and city or county people's courts. The procurator-general, appointed by the Assembly, has supervisory powers over the judiciary and the administration; the Supreme Court controls the judicial administration.

In Jan. 1999 approximately 200,000 political prisoners were being held at ten detention camps in the country. There were five confirmed executions in 2005.

Education

Free compulsory universal technical education lasts 11 years: one pre-school year, four years primary education starting at the age of six, followed by six years secondary. In 1994–95 there were 37 universities, 31 specialized universities and 108 specialized colleges.

The adult literacy rate is 95%.

Health

Medical treatment is free. In 1995 there were 64,006 physicians, 38,792 nurses and 12,931 midwives. The hospital bed provision in 1995 of 136·1 per 10,000 population was one of the highest in the world.

North Korea has been one of the least successful countries in the battle against undernourishment in the past 25 years. Between 1980 and 1996 the proportion of undernourished people rose from 16% of the population to 48%. Many people have had to resort to eating twigs, bark and leaves.

RELIGION

The Constitution provides for 'freedom of religion as well as the freedom of anti-religious propaganda'. In 2001 there were 3·0m. Chondoists. Another 3·4m. followed traditional beliefs. There were also significant numbers of Christians and Buddhists.

CULTURE

World Heritage Sites
There is one UNESCO site in North Korea: the Complex of Koguryo Tombs (2004).

Broadcasting
The government-controlled Korean Central Broadcasting Station and Korean Central Television Station are responsible for radio and TV broadcasting. In 1991 there were 34 radio and 11 TV stations (colour by PAL). There were 3·33m. radio and 1·17m. TV sets in 2000. All radio and television stations being government-run, North Koreans know very little of the outside world. They have been told that the food shortages of recent years were a global catastrophe and that they are comparatively well-off. However, North Korean refugees sheltering with ethnic Koreans in China are learning more about the outside world and word of the South Korean prosperity is filtering back into North Korea.

Press
There were three daily newspapers in 1996. The party newspaper is *Nodong* (or *Rodong*) *Sinmun* (Workers' Daily News). Circulation is about 600,000.

Tourism
A 40-year ban on non-Communist tourists was lifted in 1986. In 1998 there were 130,000 foreign tourists. On 19 Nov. 1998 North Korea received its first tourists from South Korea, on a cruise and tour organized by the South Korean firm Hyundai.

Calendar
A new yearly calendar was announced on 9 July 1997 based on Kim Il Sung's birthday on 15 April 1912. Thus 1912 became *Juche* year 1; 2006 is *Juche* year 96.

DIPLOMATIC REPRESENTATIVES

Of North Korea in the United Kingdom (73 Gunnersbury Ave., London, W5 4LP)
Ambassador: Ri Yong Ho.

Of the United Kingdom in North Korea (Munsu Dong Diplomatic Compound, Pyongyang)
Ambassador: David Slinn, OBE.

Of North Korea to the United Nations
Ambassador: Pak Kil-yon.

Of North Korea to the European Union
Ambassador: Vacant.

FURTHER READING

Becker, Jasper, *Rogue Regime: Kim Jong Il and the Looming Threat of North Korea.* OUP, 2005

Cha, Victor D. and Kang, David C., *Nuclear North Korea: A Debate on Engagement Strategies.* Columbia Univ. Press, 2003

Cumings, Bruce, *North Korea: Another Country.* New Press, New York, 2004

Harrison, S., *Korean Endgame: A Strategy for Reunification and US Disengagement.* Princeton Univ. Press, 2002

Hunter, H., *Kim Il-Song's North Korea.* Praeger Publishers, Westport (CT), 1999

Kleiner, J., *Korea: a Century of Change.* World Scientific Publishing Co., Singapore, 2001

Oh, K. and Hassig, R. C., *North Korea Through the Looking Glass.* Brookings Institution Press, Washington (D. C.), 2000

O'Hanlon, Michael E. and Mochizuki, Mike, *Crisis on the Korean Peninsula: How to Deal with a Nuclear North Korea.* McGraw-Hill, New York, 2003

Sigal, L. V., *Disarming Strangers: Nuclear Diplomacy with North Korea.* Princeton Univ. Press, 1999

National Statistical Office: Central Statistics Bureau, Pyongyang.

KUWAIT

0 25 mi
0 50 km

IRAN

IRAQ

KUWAIT

Jahra

KUWAIT

Ahmadi

Persian Gulf

SAUDI ARABIA

© Research Machines plc 2006

Dowlat al Kuwait
(State of Kuwait)

Capital: Kuwait
Population projection, 2010: 3·05m.
GDP per capita, 2003: (PPP$) 18,047
HDI/world rank: 0·844/44

KEY HISTORICAL EVENTS

The ruling dynasty was founded by Sheikh Sabah al-Awwal, who ruled from 1756 to 1772. In 1899 Sheikh Mubarak concluded a treaty with Great Britain wherein, in return for the assurance of British protection, he undertook to support British interests. In 1914 the British Government recognized Kuwait as an independent government under British protection. On 19 June 1961 an agreement reaffirmed the independence and sovereignty of Kuwait and recognized the Government of Kuwait's responsibility for the conduct of internal and external affairs. On 2 Aug. 1990 Iraqi forces invaded the country. Following the expiry of the date set by the UN for the withdrawal of Iraqi forces, an air offensive was launched by coalition forces, followed by a land attack on 24 Feb. 1991. Iraqi forces were routed and Kuwait City was liberated on 26 Feb. On 10 Nov. 1994 Iraq recognized the independence and boundaries of Kuwait. In 2006 Sheikh Jaber, who had been Amir since 1977, died and was replaced by Sheikh Sabah.

TERRITORY AND POPULATION

Kuwait is bounded in the east by the Persian Gulf, north and west by Iraq and south and southwest by Saudi Arabia, with an area of 17,818 sq. km. In 1992–93 the UN Boundary Commission redefined Kuwait's border with Iraq, moving it slightly northwards in conformity with an agreement of 1932. The population at the census of 1995 was 1,575,570, of whom about 58·5% were non-Kuwaitis. Official population estimate,

2004: 2,638,579; density, 148 per sq. km. In 2003, 96·2% of the population were urban.

The UN gives a projected population for 2010 of 3·05m.

The country is divided into six governorates: the capital (comprising Kuwait City, Kuwait's nine islands and territorial and shared territorial waters) (2004 population, 439,030); Farwaniya (686,116); Hawalli (565,767); Ahmadi (449,716); Jahra (322,783); Mubarak Al-Kabir (175,167). The capital city is Kuwait, with a population in 1995 of 28,747. Other major cities are (1995 populations): as-Salimiya (129,775), Qalib ash-Shuyukh (102,169), Hawalli (82,154), Hitan-al-Janubiyah (62,241).

The Neutral Zone (Kuwait's share, 2,590 sq. km), jointly owned and administered by Kuwait and Saudi Arabia from 1922 to 1966, was partitioned between the two countries in May 1966, but the exploitation of the oil and other natural resources continues to be shared.

Over 78% speak Arabic, the official language. English is also used as a second language.

SOCIAL STATISTICS

Births, 2003, 43,982; deaths, 4,424. The birth rate was 17·6 per 1,000 population. Kuwait's 2003 death rate, at 1·8 per 1,000 population, was the lowest in the world. Expectation of life at birth, 2003, was 75·2 years for males and 79·5 years for females. Infant mortality, 2003, 8·2 per 1,000 live births. Annual population growth rate, 1992–2002, 2·1%.

Total fertility rate for Kuwaiti females was 4·1 births per woman in 2003. Kuwait has had one of the largest reductions in its fertility rate of any country in the world over the past 25 years, having had a rate of 7·2 births per woman in 1975. Kuwait has a young population, with 40·7% of the population being under 15 in June 2004.

CLIMATE

Kuwait has a dry, desert climate which is cool in winter but very hot and humid in summer. Rainfall is extremely light. Kuwait, Jan. 56°F (13·5°C), July 99°F (36·6°C). Annual rainfall 5" (125 mm).

CONSTITUTION AND GOVERNMENT

The ruler is HH Sheikh Sabah Al-Ahmed Al-Jaber Al-Sabah, the 15th Amir of Kuwait, who succeeded on 29 Jan. 2006. *Crown Prince:* Sheikh Nawwaf Al-Ahmed Al-Sabah (b. 1937). The present constitution was approved and promulgated on 11 Nov. 1962.

In 1990 the *National Council* was established, consisting of 50 elected members and 25 appointed by the Amir. It was replaced by a *National Assembly* or *Majlis al-Umma* in 1992, consisting of 50 elected members. The franchise is limited to men over 21 whose families have been of Kuwaiti nationality since before 1920 and the sons of persons naturalized since 1992. In May 1999 the cabinet approved a draft law giving women the right to vote and run for parliament. However, in Dec. 1999 parliament rejected the bill allowing women to vote by a margin of 32 to 20. Women were granted the right to vote and run for office in May 2005 when parliament voted in favour of amending the election law by a margin of 35 votes to 23. Women will be able to vote for the first time in the parliamentary election scheduled for 2007.

Executive authority is vested in the *Council of Ministers*.

National Anthem

'Watanil Kuwait salemta lilmajdi, wa ala jabeenoka tali ossaadi,' ('Kuwait, my fatherland! May you be safe and glorious! May you always enjoy good fortune!'); words by Moshari al-Adwani, tune by Ibrahim Nassar al-Soula.

GOVERNMENT CHRONOLOGY

Amirs since 1950.

1950–65	Sheikh Abdullah al-Salem al-Sabah
1965–77	Sheikh Sabah al-Salem al-Sabah
1977–2006	Sheikh Jaber al-Ahmed al-Jaber al-Sabah
2006–	Sheikh Sabah al-Ahmed al-Jaber al-Sabah

RECENT ELECTIONS

At the all-male National Assembly elections on 5 July 2003 Islamist candidates won 21 seats, supporters of the government 14, liberals 3 (down from 14 at the previous election) and independents 12. Turnout was 80·0%. An alternative election was staged by women, denied the vote. The Amir's decree offering female suffrage in 1999 was opposed by traditionalists, but on 16 May 2005 the National Assembly passed legislation granting women the right to vote and to run for office beginning in 2007, provided they observe Islamic laws.

CURRENT ADMINISTRATION

In March 2006 the government comprised:

Prime Minister: Sheikh Nasser Muhammad Al Ahmad Al-Sabah; b. 1941 (appointed 7 Feb. 2006).

First Deputy Prime Minister, Defence and Interior Minister: Sheikh Jabir Mubarak Al-Hamad Al-Sabah. *Deputy Prime Minister and Minister of Foreign Affairs:* Sheikh Muhammad Sabah Al-Salem Al-Sabah. *Deputy Prime Minister and State Minister for Cabinet Affairs and National Assembly Affairs:* Mohammad Sharar.

Minister of Communications: Ismail al-Shatti. *Social Affairs and Labour:* Sheikh Ali al-Jarrah al-Sabah. *Information:* Anas Al Rashed. *Health:* Sheikh Ahmad Abdallah Al-Ahmad Al-Sabah. *Energy:* Sheikh Ahmad Fahd Al-Ahmad Al-Sabah. *Finance:* Bader Mishari Al-Humaidhi. *Housing and Public Works:* Bader Nasser Al-Humaidhi. *Planning:* Massouma al-Mubarak. *Commerce and Industry:* Youssef al-Zalzalah. *Religious Endowments (Awqaf) and Islamic Affairs, and Justice:* Abdallah Al-Matuq. *Education and Higher Education:* Adel Al Tabtabai.

Speaker: Jasim Al-Khurafi.

Council of Ministers (Arabic only): http://www.fatwa.gov.kw

CURRENT LEADERS

Sheikh Sabah al-Ahmed al-Sabah

Position
Amir

Introduction
Sheikh Sabah became Amir of Kuwait in Jan. 2006, ending a brief constitutional crisis in the wake of the death of Sheikh Jaber. As foreign minister for over 40 years, Sheikh Sabah oversaw the positioning of Kuwait as a key Western ally in the Gulf, allowing the USA to use the country as a launchpad for its invasion of Iraq in 2003.

Early Life
Sabah IV al-Ahmed al-Jaber al-Sabah was born in 1929 in Kuwait, then a British protectorate. He is the fourth son of Sheikh Ahmed Al-Jaber Al-Sabah, the founder of modern Kuwait and the country's leader from 1921–50. Educated at al Mubarakya School and by tutors, Sheikh Sabah entered the emirate's administration in 1954 as a member of the central committee municipality council. He also served as a member of the building and construction council at a time when the Amir, Sheikh Abdullah al-Salem al-Sabah, was pumping much of the state's new oil wealth into an ambitious public works programme.

From 1956–62 Sheikh Sabah chaired the printing and publishing authority and was then appointed minister of information in the first post-independence cabinet. He was promoted to foreign minister in 1963 and headed Kuwait's inaugural delegation to the UN later that year. He presided over a generally low-profile, neutralist foreign policy. Palestinian rights received strong support; Fatah was founded in Kuwait.

On 16 Feb. 1978 Sheikh Sabah was appointed deputy prime minister while keeping the foreign affairs portfolio. A broadly pro-Iraqi orientation was adopted during the early stages of the Iran–Iraq War and Kuwait became a member of the Gulf Co-operation Council. After Iraq's invasion of Kuwait on 2 Aug. 1990, Sheikh Sabah joined other government members in exile in Saudi Arabia, where he lobbied for an international response. The al-Sabahs' flight to Saudi Arabia caused resentment among those left behind in Kuwait but post-liberation elections and the creation of a national assembly in 1992 were well received. In 1996 Sheikh Sabah joined the supreme council of planning. Still foreign minister, he strengthened links with the West and cooled relations with several Arab states, particularly those that had shown indifference to Kuwait's plight at the hands of Saddam Hussein.

The increasingly frail Sheikh Jaber issued a decree separating the posts of crown prince and prime minister on 13 July 2003 and appointed Sheikh Sabah as premier. Endowed with considerable executive powers, he continued the reforms begun by the Amir, appointing the first woman minister and promoting religious tolerance in schools. After the death of Sheikh Jaber in Jan. 2006, the 76-year old crown prince, Sheikh Saad al-Abdullah al Salim al-Sabah, was deemed too ill to take the Amir's oath of office. He was voted out of office by parliament on 24 Jan. 2006 and the cabinet nominated Sheikh Sabah to take over. He was sworn in on 29 Jan. 2006.

Career in Office
Sheikh Sabah has promised to speed up economic and political reforms, including greater economic transparency. He has pledged to grant full political rights to women and vowed to change the electoral map to promote more democratic elections, next scheduled for 2007. He is also expected to push for a law enabling a proposed US$7bn. foreign investment in the northern oilfields.

DEFENCE

In Sept. 1991 the USA signed a ten-year agreement with Kuwait to store equipment, use ports and carry out joint training exercises. Conscription is for two years. There were over 8,000 US and UN personnel based in Kuwait in 2002.

Defence expenditure in 2003 totalled US$3,794m. (US$1,593 per capita), representing 9·4% of GDP. The expenditure per capita in 2003 was the second highest in the world after that of Qatar.

Army

Strength (2002) about 11,000 including 1,600 foreign personnel. In addition there is a National Guard of 6,600.

Navy

Personnel in 2002 numbered 2,000, including 500 Coast Guard personnel.

Air Force

From a small initial combat force the Air Force has grown rapidly, although it suffered heavy losses after the Iraqi invasion of 1990–91. Equipment includes F/A-18 *Hornet* strike aircraft and Mirage F-1s. Personnel strength was estimated (2002) at 2,500, with 81 combat aircraft and 20 armed helicopters.

INTERNATIONAL RELATIONS

Kuwait is a member of the UN, WTO, the League of Arab States, Gulf Co-operation Council, OPEC, OIC and Islamic Development Bank.

ECONOMY

Industry accounted for 59·7% of GDP in 2003 and services 40·3%.

Overview

After the liberation that followed invasion by Iraq in 1991, the economy achieved relative stability. The economy remains dominated by oil production, accounting for 80% of government revenue. High oil prices since 2003 have produced large trade surpluses and growth has been strong as revenues from state oil production have fed into the economy via government spending, primarily on infrastructure. Significant foreign currency reserves, high oil prices and confidence in future economic prospects have led the government to adopt a strong pro-cyclical fiscal policy. With high earnings from oil and with a small population, the government has found it possible to maintain a generous welfare system while resisting pressure to implement structural reforms and to privatize parts of the state-dominated economy. However, the economy has opened up over the years and private business activity has grown. As part of its WTO membership commitments Kuwait has also begun to liberalize its banking sector. Kuwait's economic performance is tied to that of Iraq, where many opportunities exist for Kuwaiti enterprise.

Currency

The unit of currency is the *Kuwaiti dinar* (KD) of 1,000 *fils*. Inflation in 2004 was 1·8%. Foreign exchange reserves were US$10,260m. in June 2002, monetary gold reserves were 2·54m. troy oz and total money supply (M3) was KD 2,156m.

In 2001 the six Gulf Arab states—Kuwait, along with Bahrain, Oman, Qatar, Saudi Arabia and the United Arab Emirates—signed an agreement to establish a single currency by 2010.

Budget

The fiscal year begins on 1 April. Revenues in 2002–03 totalled KD 6,219m. and expenditures KD 4,927m. Oil accounts for 80% of government revenues. Expenditure by function in 2002–03 (in KD 1m.): defence, 1,180; education, 701; public order and safety, 531; social security and welfare, 452; health, 300.

Performance

Real GDP growth was 9·7% in 2003 and 7·2% in 2004. Total GDP in 2003 was US$32·1bn. In 2003 there was a current account surplus of US$7,566m.

Banking and Finance

The *Governor* of the Central Bank is Sheikh Salem Abdulaziz Al-Sabah. There is also the Kuwait Finance House. In 2002 there were eleven national banks and one Islamic banking firm. The combined assets of banks operating in Kuwait totalled KD 18,818m. in Dec. 2003. Foreign banks are banned.

There is a stock exchange, linked with those of Bahrain and Oman.

ENERGY AND NATURAL RESOURCES

Environment

Kuwait's carbon dioxide emissions from the consumption and flaring of fossil fuels were the equivalent of 25·5 tonnes per capita in 2002. An *Environmental Sustainability Index* compiled for the World Economic Forum meeting in Jan. 2005 ranked Kuwait 138th in the world out of the 146 countries analysed, with 36·6%. The index measured the ability of countries to maintain favourable environmental conditions and examined various factors including pollution levels and the use or abuse of natural resources.

Electricity

There are six power stations with a total installed capacity of 9·2m. kW in 2002. Production in 2003 was 38·6bn. kWh; consumption per capita was 15,434 kWh.

Oil and Gas

Crude oil production in 2003, 769·3m. bbls. Kuwait produced 2·6% of the world total oil output in 2002 and had reserves amounting to 96·5bn. bbls. Only Saudi Arabia, Iran, Iraq and the United Arab Emirates have greater reserves. Most of the oil is in the Great Burgan area (reserves of approximately 70bn. bbls.), comprising the Burgan, Maqwa and Ahmadi fields located south of Kuwait City. Natural gas production was 11·0bn. cu. metres in 2002 with 1,490bn. cu metres of proven reserves (2002).

Water

The country depends upon desalination plants. In 1993 there were four plants with a daily total capacity of 216m. gallons. Fresh mineral water is pumped and bottled at Rawdhatain. Underground brackish water is used for irrigation, street cleaning and livestock. Production, 2003, 127,185m. gallons (95,174m. gallons fresh, 32,011m. gallons brackish). Consumption, 2003, 119,521m. gallons (94,987m. gallons fresh, 24,534m. gallons brackish).

Agriculture

There were 10,400 ha. of arable land in 2003 and 2,100 ha. of permanent crops. Production of main crops, 2003 (in 1,000 tonnes): tomatoes, 64; cucumbers and gherkins, 35; potatoes, 21; dates, 16; aubergines, 15; chillies and green peppers, 8; pumpkins and squash, 8; cauliflowers, 7.

Livestock (2003): sheep, 481,000; goats, 194,000; cattle, 27,000; camels, 6,000; poultry, 30m. Milk production (2003), 43,000 tonnes.

Forestry

Forests covered 5,000 ha. in 2000, or 0·3% of the land area.

Fisheries

The total catch in 2001 was 5,846 tonnes, exclusively from sea fishing. In the space of a month in 2001 more than 2,000 tonnes of dead fish were washed ashore. Some experts claimed the cause was the alleged pumping of raw sewage into the Gulf while others attributed it to waste from the oil industry. Shrimp fishing was important, but has declined since the 1990–91 war through oil pollution of coastal waters. Before the discovery of oil, pearls were at the centre of Kuwait's economy, but today pearl fishing is only on a small scale.

INDUSTRY

According to the Financial Times Survey (FT 500), the largest companies by market capitalization in Kuwait on 4 Jan. 2001 were: The National Bank of Kuwait (US$3,579·8m.); Mobile Telephone (US$2,466·7m.); and Kuwait Finance House (US$1,489·6m.).

Industries, apart from oil, include boat building, fishing, food production, petrochemicals, gases and construction. Production figures in 2000 (in 1,000 tonnes): distillate fuel oil, 11,626; residual fuel oil, 8,642; kerosene, 5,789; liquefied petroleum gas, 3,003; jet fuel, 1,745; petrol, 1,377; cement, 1,187.

Labour

In June 2004 the labour force totalled 1,551,342 (81·3% non-Kuwaitis). Of the total labour force, 52·1% worked in social, community and personal services, 15·2% in trade, hotels and restaurants, 7·2% in construction and 5·8% in manufacturing. Registered unemployment in June 2004 was 1·7%. Approximately 95% of nationals work for the government, with around 95% of private jobs being filled by expatriates.

Trade Unions

There is a Kuwaiti Trade Union Federation, but in 2002 only 5·6% of the workforce belonged to a union or labour group.

INTERNATIONAL TRADE

Kuwait, along with Bahrain, Oman, Qatar, Saudi Arabia and the United Arab Emirates began the implementation of a customs union in Jan. 2003.

Imports and Exports

Imports (f.o.b.) were valued at US$16,252m. in 2003 (US$8,117m. in 2002) and exports (f.o.b.) at US$22,427m. (US$15,366m. in 2002). Oil accounts for 91% of revenue from exports, and oil exports account for approximately 46% of GDP. The main non-oil export is chemical fertilizer.

Main import suppliers, 2003: Germany, 10·3%; Japan, 9·9%; USA, 1·6%. Main export markets, 2003: Saudi Arabia, 13·7%; Iraq, 10·8%; UAE, 10·0%.

COMMUNICATIONS

Roads

There were about 5,507 km of roads in 2003, 80·6% of which were paved. Number of vehicles in 2003 was 955,000 (777,000 passenger cars, or 334 per 1,000 inhabitants, and 104,000 trucks and vans). There were 45,376 road accidents in 2003 involving injury with 1,704 fatalities.

Civil Aviation

There is an international airport (Kuwait International). The national carrier is the state-owned Kuwait Airways. In 1999 it flew 36·5m. km and carried 2,130,000 passengers (all on international flights). Kuwait's first low-cost airline, Jazeera Airways, began operations in Oct. 2005. Kuwait International airport handled 4,260,136 passengers in 2003 and 144,727 tonnes of freight.

Shipping

The port of Kuwait formerly served mainly as an entrepôt, but this function is declining in importance with the development of the oil industry. The largest oil terminal is at Mina Ahmadi. Three small oil ports lie to the south of Mina Ahmadi: Mina Shuaiba, Mina Abdullah and Mina Al-Zor. The merchant fleet totalled 2,256,000 GRT in 2002, of which 1,628,000 GRT were oil tankers. In 2002 vessels totalling 2,052,000 NRT entered ports and vessels totalling 1,178,000 NRT cleared.

Telecommunications

Kuwait had 1,708,900 telephone subscribers in 2002, or 722·9 per 1,000 population, and there were 285,000 PCs (120·6 for every 1,000 persons). In 2002 mobile phone subscribers numbered 1,227,000 and there were 86,000 fax machines. The number of Internet users in 2002 was 250,000.

Postal Services

In 2003 there were 113,000 post office boxes, 96,301 rented. There were 31,943 outgoing telegrams and 26,482 incoming.

SOCIAL INSTITUTIONS

Justice

In 1960 Kuwait adopted a unified judicial system covering all levels of courts. These are: Courts of Summary Justice, Courts of the First Instance, Supreme Court of Appeal, Court of Cassation and a Constitutional Court. Islamic Sharia is a major source of legislation. The death penalty is still in use. There were 11 confirmed executions in 2005.

The population in penal institutions in 2003 was approximately 3,700 (148 per 100,000 of national population).

Education

Education is free and compulsory from six to 14 years. In 2002–03 there were 245 pre-primary schools with 4,675 teachers for 62,724 pupils, 314 primary schools with 11,594 teachers for 153,956 pupils, 281 intermediate schools with 11,826 teachers for 134,742 pupils and 12,279 teachers in 215 secondary schools for 110,041 pupils. There were 17,828 students at Kuwait University in 2002–03. A pan-Arab Open University based in Kuwait and with branches in several other Middle Eastern countries was opened in Nov. 2002 with an initial enrolment of 3,000 students.

Adult literacy rate in 2003 was 93·4% (97·7% among men and 89·3% among women). Total expenditure on education in 1995: KD 490,000,000 or 5·7% of GDP.

Health

Medical services are free to all residents. In 2003 there were 15 hospitals and sanatoria, with a provision of 4,712 beds (19 per 10,000 population). There were 3,643 doctors (15 per 10,000 population), 613 dentists, 8,997 nurses and 532 pharmacists in 2003. There were 74 clinics and other health centres and 1,569,549 people were admitted to public hospitals in 2003.

RELIGION

In 2001, 1,020,000 people were Sunni Muslims, 680,000 Shia Muslims, 230,000 other Muslims and 340,000 other (mostly Christian and Hindu).

CULTURE

Broadcasting

The government-controlled Radio Kuwait and Kuwait Television broadcast a main and a second radio programme, a Koran programme and a service in English and four TV programmes (colour by PAL). In 2001 there were 950,000 TV receivers and in 2000 there were 1,400,000 radios.

Press

In 1999 there were eight daily newspapers, with a combined circulation of about 535,000. Formal press censorship was lifted in Jan. 1992.

Tourism

There were 94,000 foreign tourists in 2003, bringing revenue of US$98m. There were 38 hotels providing 5,063 beds in 2003.

Libraries

In 2003 there were 11 non-specialized and 27 public libraries, stocking 461,000 books for 12,500 registered users. The number of school libraries was 585 in 2002–03.

Museums and Galleries

There were three museums attracting 38,000 visitors in 2003.

DIPLOMATIC REPRESENTATIVES

Of Kuwait in the United Kingdom (2 Albert Gate, London, SW1X 7JU)
Ambassador: Khaled Al-Duwaisan, GCVO.

Of the United Kingdom in Kuwait (Arabian Gulf St., Kuwait)
Ambassador: Christopher Wilton, CMG.

Of Kuwait in the USA (2940 Tilden St., NW, Washington, D.C., 20008)
Ambassador: Salem Abdulla Al-Jaber Al-Sabah.

Of the USA in Kuwait (Al-Masjed Al-Aqsa St., Bayan, Kuwait)
Ambassador: Richard LeBaron.

Of Kuwait to the United Nations
Ambassador: Nabeela Abdulla Al-Mulla.

Of Kuwait to the European Union
Ambassador: Abdulazeez A. Al-Sharikh.

FURTHER READING

Al-Yahya, M.A., *Kuwait: Fall and Rebirth.* London, 1993
Clements, F. A., *Kuwait.* [Bibliography] ABC-Clio, 2nd ed. Oxford and Santa Barbara (CA), 1996
Crystal, J., *Kuwait: the Transformation of an Oil State.* Boulder (Colo.), 1992
Finnie, D. H., *Shifting Lines in the Sand: Kuwait's Elusive Frontier with Iraq.* London, 1992

National Statistical Office: Statistics and Census Sector, Ministry of Planning
Website: http://www.mop.gov.kw

KYRGYZSTAN

Kyrgyz Respublikasy

Capital: Bishkek
Population projection, 2010: 5·57m.
GDP per capita, 2003: (PPP$) 1,751
HDI/world rank: 0·702/109

KEY HISTORICAL EVENTS

Kyrgyzstan became part of Soviet Turkestan, which itself became a Soviet Socialist Republic within the Russian Soviet Federal Socialist Republic (RSFSR) in April 1921. In 1924, when Central Asia was reorganized territorially on a national basis, Kyrgyzstan was separated from Turkestan. In Dec. 1936 Kyrgyzstan was proclaimed one of the constituent Soviet Socialist Republics of the USSR. With the collapse of the Soviet Empire, the republic asserted its claim to sovereignty in 1990 and declared independence in Sept. 1991. Askar Akayev became president in 1990 and subsequently expanded presidential powers. Kyrgyzstan became a member of the CIS in Dec. 1991.

Incursions into Kyrgyz territory by Islamic rebels and border skirmishes in the Fergana Valley are a cause for concern for all Central Asian governments. Kyrgyzstan tripled its defence budget for 2001 to combat terrorism. Allegations of widespread government corruption and disputed parliamentary elections in Feb. 2005 led to widespread popular protests. The Supreme Court declared the elections void and Kurmanbek Bakiyev was appointed prime minister and acting president. Akayev, in exile in Russia, resigned as president in April 2005. Bakiyev was confirmed as president by winning the elections held in July 2005.

TERRITORY AND POPULATION

Kyrgyzstan is situated on the Tien-Shan mountains and bordered in the east by China, west by Kazakhstan and Uzbekistan, north by Kazakhstan and south by Tajikistan. Area, 199,900 sq. km (77,180 sq. miles). Population (census 1999), 4,822,938 (2,442,473 females); density, 24 per sq. km. 2005 estimate: 5,264,000. In 2003, 66·0% of the population lived in rural areas.

The UN gives a projected population for 2010 of 5·57m.

The republic comprises seven provinces (Batken, Djalal-Abad, Issyk-Kul, Naryn, Osh, Talas and Chu) plus the city of Bishkek, the capital (formerly Frunze; 1999 census population, 750,327). Other large towns are Osh (208,520), Djalal-Abad (70,401), Przhevalsk (64,322), Tokmak (59,409), Karabalta (47,159), Balykchy (41,342) and Naryn (40,050).

The Kyrgyz are of Turkic origin and formed 64·9% of the population in 1999; the rest included Uzbeks (13·8%), Russians (12·5%), Dungans (1·1%) and Ukrainians (1·0%).

The official languages are Kyrgyz and Russian. After the break-up of the Soviet Union, Russian was only the official language in provinces where Russians are in a majority. However, in May 2000 parliament voted to make it an official language nationwide, mainly in an attempt to stem the ever-increasing exodus of skilled ethnic Russians. The Roman alphabet (in use 1928–40) was re-introduced in 1992.

SOCIAL STATISTICS

2003 births, 105,490; deaths, 35,941; marriages, 34,266. Rates, 2003 (per 1,000 population): birth, 20·9; death, 7·1; infant mortality (per 1,000 live births), 59. Life expectancy, 2003, 62·7 years for males and 71·1 for females. In 2000 the most popular age for marrying was 20–24 for both males and females. Annual population growth rate, 2000–03, 0·9%; fertility rate, 2003, 2·5 births per woman.

CLIMATE

The climate varies from dry continental to polar in the high Tien-Shan, to sub-tropical in the southwest (Fergana Valley) and temperate in the northern foothills. Bishkek, Jan. 9°F (–13°C), July 70°F (21°C). Annual rainfall 14·8" (375 mm).

CONSTITUTION AND GOVERNMENT

A new Constitution was adopted on 5 May 1993. The Presidency is executive, and directly elected for renewable five-year terms. At a referendum on 30 Jan. 1994, 96% of votes cast favoured President Akayev's serving out the rest of his term of office; turnout was 95%. At a referendum on 22–23 Oct. 1994 turnout was 87%. 75% of votes cast were in favour of instituting referendums as a constitutional mechanism, and 73% were in favour of establishing a new bicameral parliament (*Jogorku Kenesh*), with a 35-member directly-elected legislature (Legislative Assembly), and a 70-member upper house (Assembly of People's Representatives) elected on a regional basis and meeting twice a year. At a referendum in Feb. 2003 it was decided to revert to a unicameral parliament of 75 members. 94·5% of votes cast at a referendum on 10 Feb. 1996 were in favour of giving the President the right to appoint all ministers except the Prime Minister without reference to parliament.

National Anthem

'Ak möngülüü aska yoolor, talaalar' ('High mountains, valleys and fields'); words by D. Sadykov and E. Kuluev, tune by N. Davlyesov and K. Moldovasanov.

RECENT ELECTIONS

Parliamentary elections were held on 27 Feb. and 13 March 2005 in which 74 of 75 seats were allocated. However, following protests the Supreme Court annulled the results of the elections and the Upper House of parliament named Kurmanbek Bakiyev acting prime minister and acting president. The new parliament later confirmed Bakiyev as prime minister and the Upper House was dissolved.

Presidential elections were held on 10 July 2005. Acting President Kurmanbek Bakiyev won with 88·9% of the vote, ahead of Bakir Tursunbai with 3·8% and Akbarali Aitikeev with 3·6%. There were four other candidates.

CURRENT ADMINISTRATION

President: Kurmanbek Bakiyev; b. 1949 (ind.; sworn in 14 Aug. 2005, having been acting president since 25 March 2005).

In March 2006 the government comprised:

Prime Minister: Feliks Kulov; b. 1948 (ind.; in office since 15 Aug. 2005—acting until 1 Sept. 2005).

First Deputy Prime Minister: Medetbek Kerimkulov. *Deputy Prime Minister:* Adakhan Madumarov.

Minister of Agriculture and Water Resources: Abdimalik Anarbayev. *Culture:* Sultan Rayev. *Defence:* Ismael Isakov. *Ecology and Emergency Situations:* Janysh Rustenbekov. *Economics and Finance:* Akylbek Japarov. *Education, Science and Youth Policy:* Dosbol Nur Uulu. *Foreign Affairs:* Alikbek Jekshenkulov. *Industry, Trade and Tourism:* Almazbek Atambayev. *Internal Affairs:* Murat Sutalinov. *Justice:* Marat Kayipov. *Labour and Social Welfare:* Yevgeniy Semenenko. *Public Health:* Shailoobek Niyazov. *Transport and Communications:* Nurlan Sulaimanov.

Government Website: http://www.gov.kg/

CURRENT LEADERS

Kurmanbek Bakiyev

Position
President

Introduction
Kurmanbek Bakiyev swept into power with a landslide majority in the presidential election that followed Kyrgyzstan's 'Tulip Revolution' in early 2005.

Early life
Kurmanbek Saliyevich Bakiyev was born on 1 Aug. 1949 in Masadan, Osh province in the Kirghiz Soviet Socialist Republic (Kirghiz SSR). In 1972, having graduated in engineering from the Kuybyshev Polytechnic Institute in Russia, Bakiyev worked at the city's electronics plant. Returning to the Kirghiz SSR in 1979, Bakiyev worked as an engineer in Jalal-Abad and, from 1985, in Kok Jangak. Five years later he entered local politics, serving on Kok Jangak's town council. In 1991, as the Soviet Union collapsed and the Kyrgyz Republic declared independence, Bakiyev was a senior administrator in the Jalal-Abad provincial authority.

In 1994 Bakiyev became deputy chairman of the State Property Fund in the capital, Bishkek. Having become leader of the administration of Chui province in April 1997, Bakiyev was nominated by the president, Askar Akayev, as a prime ministerial candidate. On 21 Dec. 2000 he was elected by parliament but was forced to resign in May 2002 after riot police shot six anti-Akayev protesters in Aksy.

Bakiyev joined the opposition, becoming head of the People's Movement of Kyrgyzstan and an architect of the 'Tulip Revolution' of March 2005. Angered by allegations of vote-rigging by Akayev and continuing poverty and unemployment, demonstrators stormed the presidential palace and forced Akayev into exile. Bakiyev formed a co-ordinating council and set fresh presidential elections for 10 July 2005. He won almost 89% of the vote and appointed a number of opposition leaders to key positions. He was sworn in as the president on 14 Aug. 2005.

Career in Office
Bakiyev has promised social and economic policies to increase prosperity, modernize institutions and 'return respect for authorities and law'.

DEFENCE

Conscription is for 18 months. Defence expenditure in 2003 totalled US$220m. (US$44 per capita), representing 2·6% of GDP. The USA opened a military base in Kyrgyzstan in 2001 to aid the war in Afghanistan against the Taliban. In Sept. 2003 Kyrgyzstan also agreed to allow Russia to open an air force base in the country.

Army

Personnel, 2002, 8,500. In addition there is a combined forces reserve of 57,000 and 5,000 border guards.

Air Force

There is an aviation element with MiG-21 fighters and a variety of other ex-Soviet equipment. Personnel, 2002, 2,400.

INTERNATIONAL RELATIONS

Kyrgyzstan is a member of the UN, WTO, CIS, OSCE, Asian Development Bank, ECO, IOM, OIC, Islamic Development Bank and the NATO Partnership for Peace.

ECONOMY

Agriculture accounted for 37·7% of GDP in 2002, industry 23·3% and services 39·0%.

Currency

On 10 May 1993 Kyrgyzstan introduced its own currency unit, the *som* (KGS), of 100 *tyiyn*, at a rate of 1 som = 200 roubles. Inflation was 5·6% in 2003, falling to 2·8% in 2004. Gold reserves totalled 83,000 troy oz in June 2002 and foreign exchange reserves US$237m. Total money supply in June 2002 was 6,247m. soms.

Budget

Government revenue and expenditure (in 1m. soms), year ending 31 Dec.:

	1998	1999	2000	2001	2002	2003
Revenue[1]	6,090·7	7,873·7	9,280·1	11,917·7	13,588·1	15,747·9
Expenditure[2]	7,298·3	9,312·0	11,308·2	12,255·7	15,188·6	16,890·6

[1]Without official transfers. [2]Without state investment programmes.

Performance

Real GDP growth was 7·0% in 2003 and 7·1% in 2004. Total GDP in 2004 was US$2·2bn.

Banking and Finance

The central bank and bank of issue is the National Bank (*Chairman,* Ulan Sarbanov). There were 22 commercial banks, including three foreign banks, in 2002. There is a stock exchange in Bishkek.

ENERGY AND NATURAL RESOURCES

Environment

Kyrgyzstan's carbon dioxide emissions from the consumption and flaring of fossil fuels were the equivalent of 1·5 tonnes per capita in 2002.

Electricity

Installed capacity was 4·0m. kW in 2004. Production in 2003 was 14·02bn. kWh, around 92·7% hydro-electric; consumption per capita was 2,804 kWh.

Oil and Gas

Output of oil, 2003, 69,500 tonnes; natural gas, 2003, 27·1m. cu. metres.

Minerals

In 2003 lignite production totalled 351,700 tonnes and coal production 63,600 tonnes. Some gold is mined.

Agriculture

Kyrgyzstan is famed for its livestock breeding, in particular the small Kyrgyz horse. In 2004 there were 2,882,000 sheep, 1,003,000 cattle, 795,000 goats, 340,000 horses and 2m. chickens. Yaks are bred as meat and dairy cattle, and graze on high altitudes unsuitable for other cattle. Crossed with domestic cattle, hybrids give twice the yield of milk.

There were 1·34m. ha. of arable land in 2003 and 67,000 ha. of permanent crops. Number of peasant farms (2003), 255,822.

Principal crops include wheat, barley, corn and vegetables. Fodder crops for livestock are grown, particularly lucerne; also sugarbeets, cotton, tobacco and medicinal herbs. Sericulture, fruit, grapes and vegetables are major branches.

Output of main agricultural products (in 1,000 tonnes) in 2003: potatoes, 1,308; wheat, 1,014; sugarbeets, 812; corn for grain, 399; barley, 198; tomatoes, 144; carrots, 126; raw cotton, 106; cabbages, 104; onions, 104; cucumbers, 50. Livestock products, 2003, in 1,000 tonnes: beef and veal, 94; mutton and goat meat, 44; milk, 1,192; eggs, 268m. units.

Forestry
In 2003 forests covered 1,057,000 ha., or 5·3% of the land area. Timber production in 2001 was 26,000 cu. metres.

Fisheries
The catch in 2003 was 93 tonnes, entirely from freshwater fishing.

INDUSTRY
Industrial enterprises include food, timber, textile, engineering, metallurgical, oil and mining. There are also sugar refineries, tanneries, cotton and wool-cleansing works, flour-mills and a tobacco factory. In 2001 industry accounted for 28·3% of GDP, with manufacturing contributing 10·8%. In 2003 output was valued at 48,940·1m. soms at current prices.

Production, 2003: cement, 757,300 tonnes; carpets, 13·4m. sq. metres; woven cotton (2000), 6m. sq. metres; footwear, 238,000 pairs.

Labour
Out of 1,837,000 people in employment in 2003, 951,200 were engaged in agriculture, hunting and forestry; 205,800 in wholesale and retail trade/repair of motor vehicles, motorcycles and personal and household goods; 151,900 in education; and 113,700 in manufacturing. In 2004 the unemployment rate was 2·9%.

INTERNATIONAL TRADE
In Jan. 1994 an agreement to create a single economic zone was signed with Kazakhstan and Uzbekistan. In March 1996 Kyrgyzstan joined a customs union with Russia, Kazakhstan and Belarus. Total external debt was US$1,797m. in 2002.

Imports and Exports
Imports (c.i.f.) were valued at US$717·0m. in 2003 and exports (f.o.b.) at US$581·7m. Principal imports in 2001: petroleum and natural gas, 22·6%; machinery and apparatus, 21·0%; food products, 11·7%; chemicals and chemical products, 9·5%. Principal exports in 2001: nonferrous metals (notably gold), 51·7%; machinery and apparatus, 12·0%; electricity, 9·8%; agricultural products (notably tobacco), 9·5%.

Main import suppliers in 2003: Russia, 24·6%; Kazakhstan, 23·8%; China, 10·8%; USA, 6·7%; Uzbekistan, 5·5%; Germany, 5·3%. Main export markets, 2003: United Arab Emirates, 24·8%; Switzerland, 20·3%; Russia, 16·7%; Kazakhstan, 9·8%; Canada, 5·3%; China, 4·0%.

COMMUNICATIONS

Roads
There were 18,800 km of roads in 2003, including 140 km of motorways. 91·4% of all roads in 2003 were paved. Passenger cars in use in 2003 numbered 188,900 (38 per 1,000 inhabitants). There were 897 road accident fatalities in 2003.

Rail
In the north a railway runs from Lugovaya through Bishkek to Rybachi on Lake Issyk-Kul. Towns in the southern valleys are linked by short lines with the Ursatyevskaya–Andizhan railway in Uzbekistan. Total length of railway, 2000, 417 km. Passenger-km travelled in 2003 came to 49·8m. and freight tonne-km to 562m.

Civil Aviation
There is an international airport at Bishkek (Manas). The national carrier is Kyrgyzstan Airlines. In 2003 Bishkek handled 217,576 passengers (112,487 on international flights) and 1,978 tonnes of freight. In 1999 scheduled airline traffic of Kyrgyzstan-based carriers flew 8·6m. km, carrying 312,000 passengers (136,000 on international flights).

Shipping
The total length of inland waterways was 460 km in 2003. In 2003, 38,700 tonnes of freight were carried.

Telecommunications
There were 539,900 telephone subscribers in 2003, equivalent to 107 for every 1,000 persons, and 65,000 PCs in use in 2002. There were 138,600 mobile phone subscribers in 2003. Internet users numbered 642,300 in 2003.

Postal Services
In 2003 there were 920 post offices.

SOCIAL INSTITUTIONS

Justice
In 2004, 32,616 crimes were reported, including 419 murders and attempted murders. The population in penal institutions in March 2002 was 19,500 (390 per 100,000 of national population). A moratorium on the death penalty, first imposed in 1998, was extended in Jan. 2006 for another year.

Education
In 2003 there were 417 pre-primary schools for 47,464 pupils; in 2004 there were 143 primary schools with 11,769 pupils, 160 basic schools with 32,192 pupils, 1,778 secondary schools with 1,084,922 pupils and 13,337 university level lecturers for 218,273 students. There were 49 higher educational institutions and 75 secondary professional education establishments in 2004–05. Kyrgyz University had 20,855 students in 2004–05. Adult literacy was 98·7% in 1999.

In 1998–99 total expenditure on education came to 5·7% of GNP.

Health
In 2003 there were 13,608 physicians, 1,076 dentists, 21,120 nurses and 2,663 midwives; in 2003 there were 151 hospitals.

Welfare
In Jan. 1994 there were 443,000 age and 196,000 other pensioners.

RELIGION
In 2001, 75% of the population was Sunni Muslim. There were some 1,000 mosques, 30 Russian Orthodox, 17 Evangelical, 9 Seventh Day Adventist and 8 Lutheran churches in 1996.

CULTURE

Broadcasting
Kyrgyz Radio and Kyrgyz Television are state-controlled. There are two national radio programmes, with some broadcasting in English and German. There is one commercial radio station. In 1993 there were three hours of TV broadcasting a day (colour by SECAM). There were 542,000 radio receivers in 2000 and 242,000 television receivers in 2001.

Cinema
In 1999 there were 293 cinemas with an annual attendance of 0·3m.

Press
There were three daily newspapers in 2000, with a combined circulation (1996) of 67,000.

Tourism

In 2002 there were 81,000 foreign tourists; spending by tourists totalled US$5m.

DIPLOMATIC REPRESENTATIVES

Of Kyrgyzstan in the United Kingdom (Ascot House, 119 Crawford St., London, W1H 1AF)
Ambassador: Dilde Sarbagysheva.

Of the United Kingdom in Kyrgyzstan
Ambassador: James Lyall Sharp (resides in Almaty, Kazakhstan).

Of Kyrgyzstan in the USA (1732 Wisconsin Ave., NW, Washington, D.C., 20007)
Ambassador: Zamira Sydykova.

Of the USA in Kyrgyzstan (171 Prospekt Mira, Bishkek 720016)
Ambassador: Marie L. Yovanovitch.

Of Kyrgyzstan to the United Nations
Ambassador: Nurbek Jeenbaev.

Of Kyrgyzstan to the European Union
Ambassador: Tchinguiz Aitmatov.

FURTHER READING

Abazov, Rafis, *Historical Dictionary of Kyrgyzstan.* Scarecrow Press, Lanham, Maryland, 2004
Anderson, J., *Kyrgyzstan: Central Asia's Island of Democracy?* Routledge, London, 1999

National Statistical Office: National Statistical Committee of the Kyrgyz Republic, 374 Frunze Street, Bishkek City 720033.

LAOS

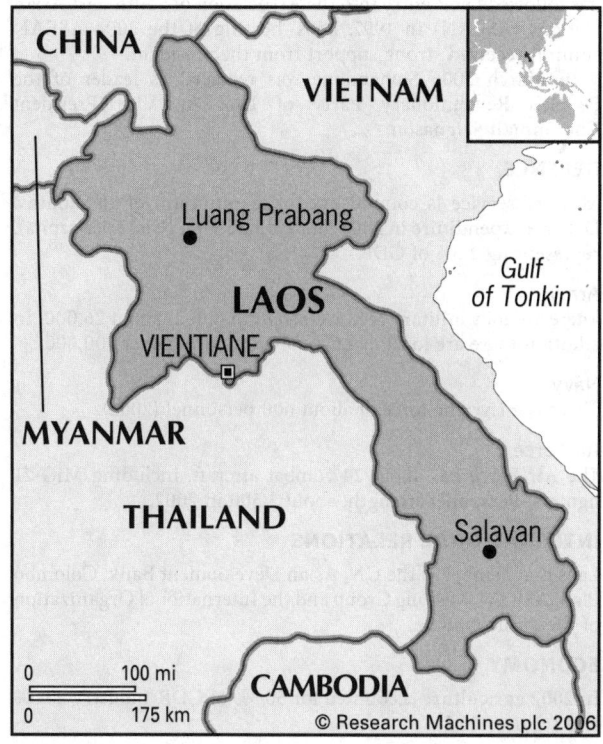

Sathalanalath Pasathipatai Pasasonlao
(Lao People's Democratic Republic)

Capital: Vientiane
Population projection, 2010: 6·60m.
GDP per capita, 2003: (PPP$) 1,759
HDI/world rank: 0·545/133

KEY HISTORICAL EVENTS

The Kingdom of Laos, once called Lanxang (the Land of a Million Elephants), was founded in the 14th century. In 1893 Laos became a French protectorate and in 1907 acquired its present frontiers. In 1945, after French authority had been suppressed by the Japanese, an independence movement known as Lao Issara (Free Laos) set up a government which collapsed with the return of the French in 1946. Under a new constitution of 1947 Laos became a constitutional monarchy under the Luang Prabang dynasty and in 1949 became an independent sovereign state within the French Union. An almost continuous state of war began in 1953 between the Royal Lao Government, supported by American bombing and Thai mercenaries, and the Patriotic Front Pathet Lao, supported by North Vietnamese troops. Peace talks resulted in an agreement on 21 Feb. 1973 providing for the formation of a provisional government of national union and the withdrawal of foreign troops. A provisional coalition government was duly formed in 1974. However, after the Communist victories in neighbouring Vietnam and Cambodia in April 1975, the Pathet Lao took over the running of the whole country, maintaining only a façade of a coalition. On 29 Nov. 1975 HM King Savang Vatthana abdicated and the People's Congress proclaimed a People's Democratic Republic of Laos on 2 Dec. 1975. Since then the country has been run by a regime with zero tolerance for dissent and a fierce distrust of foreigners.

TERRITORY AND POPULATION

Laos is a landlocked country of 236,800 sq. km (91,428 sq. miles) bordered on the north by China, the east by Vietnam, the south by Cambodia and the west by Thailand and Myanmar. Apart from the Mekong River plains along the border of Thailand, the country is mountainous, particularly in the north, and in places densely forested.

The population (1995 census) was 4,581,258 (2,315,931 females); density, 19 per sq. km. Population, 2005 estimate; 5,924,000. In 2003, 79·3% of the population lived in rural areas.

The UN gives a projected population for 2010 of 6·60m.

There are 16 provinces and one prefecture divided into 133 districts and one special region (*khetphiset*). Area, population and administrative centres in 1996:

Province	Sq. km	Population (in 1,000)	Administrative centre
Attopeu	10,320	87·7	Samakhi Xai
Bokeo	6,196	114·9	Ban Houei Xai
Bolikhamxai	14,863	164·9	Paksan
Champassak	15,415	503·3	Pakse
Houa Phan	16,500	247·3	Xam Neua
Khammouane	16,315	275·4	Thakhek
Luang Namtha	9,325	115·2	Luang Namtha
Luang Prabang	16,875	367·2	Luang Prabang
Oudomxai	15,370	211·3	Muang Xai
Phongsali	16,270	153·4	Phongsali
Salavan	10,691	258·3	Salavan
Savannakhet	21,774	674·9	Shanthabouli
Sayabouri	16,389	293·3	Sayabouri
Sekong	7,665	64·2	Sekong
Vientiane	15,927	286·8	Phonghong
Vientiane[1]	3,920	531·8	Vientiane
Xaisomboun[2]	7,105	54·2	Ban Muang Cha
Xieng Khouang	15,880	201·2	Phonsavanh

[1]Prefecture. [2]Special Region (1995 population).

The capital and largest town is Vientiane, with a population of (1999 estimate) 640,000. Other important towns are Savannakhet, Pakse, Xam Neua and Luang Prabang.

The population is divided into three groups: about 67% Lao-Lum (Valley-Lao); 17% Lao-Theung (Lao of the mountain sides); and 7·4% Lao-Sung (Lao of the mountain tops), who comprise the Hmong and Yao (or Mien). Lao is the official language. French and English are spoken.

SOCIAL STATISTICS

2004 estimates: births, 203,000; deaths, 70,000. Rates, 2004 estimates (per 1,000 population): birth, 35; death, 12; infant mortality, 87 per 1,000 live births (2001). Life expectancy, 2003: 53·4 years for men and 55·9 for women. Annual population growth rate, 1992–2002, 2·4%. Fertility rate, 2001, 5·0 births per woman.

CLIMATE

A tropical monsoon climate, with high temperatures throughout the year and very heavy rains from May to Oct. Vientiane, Jan. 70°F (21·1°C), July 81°F (27·2°C). Annual rainfall 69" (1,715 mm).

CONSTITUTION AND GOVERNMENT

In Aug. 1991 the National Assembly adopted a new constitution. The head of state is the President, elected by the National

Assembly, which consists of 109 members (99 prior to the elections of Feb. 2002).

Under the constitution the People's Revolutionary Party of Laos (PPPL) remains the 'central nucleus' of the 'people's democracy'; other parties are not permitted. The PPPL's Politburo comprises 11 members, including Khamtay Siphandone (PPPL, *President*).

National Anthem

'Xatlao tangtae dayma lao thookthuana xeutxoo sootchay' ('For the whole of time the Lao people have glorified their Fatherland'); words by Sisana Sisane, tune by Thongdy Sounthonevichit.

RECENT ELECTIONS

The National Assembly (Fourth Legislature) elected Khamtay Siphandone as president at the first session of the Fourth National Assembly held on 23–26 Feb. 1998. He was re-elected on 24 Feb. 2002.

There were parliamentary elections on 24 Feb. 2002 in which the People's Revolutionary Party of Laos (PPPL) won 108 seats. Only one (approved) non-partisan candidate won a seat.

CURRENT ADMINISTRATION

President: Gen. Khamtay Siphandone; b. 1924 (PPPL; elected 24 Feb. 1998 and re-elected March 2001).

Vice President: Lieut.-Gen. Choummali Saignason.

In March 2006 the government consisted of:

Prime Minister: Boungnang Vorachith (PPPL; in office since 27 March 2001).

First Deputy Prime Minister: Bouasone Bouphavanh. *Deputy Prime Ministers:* Maj. Gen. Asang Laoli; Thongloun Sisoolit (also *Chairman of State Planning Committee*); Somsavat Lengsavad (also *Minister for Foreign Affairs*).

Minister of Agriculture and Forestry: Sian Saphangthong. *Commerce and Tourism:* Soulivong Daravong. *Communications, Transport, Posts and Construction:* Bouathong Vonglokham. *Defence:* Douangchai Phichit. *Education (acting):* Bosengkham Vongdara. *Finance:* Chansy Phosikham. *Industry and Handicrafts:* Onneua Phommachanh. *Information and Culture:* Mounkeo Ouraboun. *Interior and Security:* Thongban Sengaphon. *Justice:* Kham Ouane Boupha. *Labour and Social Welfare:* Le Kakanya. *Public Health:* Ponemek Daraloy.

CURRENT LEADERS

Gen. Khamtay Siphandone

Position
President

Introduction
Re-elected in March 2001, army general Khamtay Siphandone is serving his second term as president.

Early Life
Born on 8 Feb. 1924 in Champassak province, Siphandone joined the Lao revolutionary movement in 1947. In 1952 he became a member of the central committee of the Lao Issara (Free Laos) movement, and between 1952–54 was chairman of the committee of the Central Region. His membership of the People's Revolutionary Party of Laos began in 1956, whilst serving as chief of staff of the Pathet Lao forces. He was soon a member of the central party committee and rapidly became head of its office. In 1960 he took charge of military affairs of the central party committee and became commander-in-chief of the Pathet Lao forces. When the Pathet Lao took over the government in 1975 he was appointed deputy prime minister, minister of national defence and commander-in-chief of the Lao People's Army. He served in all three positions concurrently until the early 1990s. On 15 Aug. 1991 he was elected prime minister. Seven years later he was voted president by the National Assembly.

Career in Office
Since becoming president, Siphandone has done little to further democracy in the country. Tight restrictions on the media are still in force, although some opening of the economy and society has followed Laos' entry into the Association of South East Asian Nations (ASEAN) in 1997. Laos' hosting of the 2004 ASEAN summit received strong support from the president.

In March 2006 Siphandone was replaced as leader of the People's Revolutionary Party of Laos by Vice President Choummali Saignason.

DEFENCE

Military service is compulsory for a minimum of 18 months. Defence expenditure in 2003 totalled US$38m. (US$7 per capita), representing 2·0% of GDP.

Army

There are four military regions. Strength (2002) about 26,000. In addition there are local defence forces totalling over 100,000.

Navy

There is a riverine force of about 600 personnel (2002).

Air Force

The Air Force has about 24 combat aircraft, including MiG-21 fighters. Personnel strength, about 3,500 in 2002.

INTERNATIONAL RELATIONS

Laos is a member of the UN, Asian Development Bank, Colombo Plan, ASEAN, Mekong Group and the International Organization of the Francophonie.

ECONOMY

In 2002 agriculture accounted for 50·3% of GDP, industry 23·5% and services 26·2%.

Overview

The sixth five-year plan (2006–10) aims to reduce poverty by 2010 in a bid to remove Laos from the UN list of least developed countries by 2020.

Currency

The unit of currency is the *kip* (LAK). Inflation was 15·5% in 2003 and 10·5% in 2004. Foreign exchange reserves were US$135m. in May 2002 and total money supply 539,490m. kip. Gold reserves were 66,000 troy oz in June 2002.

Budget

Revenues in 2001–02 met 90% of the targeted 2,335·5bn. kip and expenditure was 3,769bn. kip (93·4% of target).

Performance

Real GDP growth was 5·8% in 2003 and 6·4% in 2004. Total GDP in 2004 was US$2·4bn.

Banking and Finance

The central bank and bank of issue is the State Bank (*Acting Governor*, Phouphet Khamphounvong). There were 17 commercial banks in 2002 (seven foreign; branches only permitted).

ENERGY AND NATURAL RESOURCES

Environment

In 2002 carbon dioxide emissions from the consumption and flaring of fossil fuels were the equivalent of 0·1 tonnes per capita.

Electricity

Total installed capacity in 2001–02 was 644 MW, of which 627 MW was hydro-electric. In 2001 production was 3,590 GWh, almost exclusively hydro-electric. Consumption was 710 GWh; 2,823 GWh were exported and 182 GWh were repurchased.

Minerals

2002 output (in tonnes): gypsum, 160,000; salt, 22,100; tin, 510; coal, 355.

Agriculture

There were 747,000 ha. of arable land in 2001 and 81,000 ha. of permanent crop land. The chief products (2001 output in tonnes) are: rice, 2,334,500; sugarcane, 320,000; maize, 111,869; cassava (2000), 71,000; sweet potatoes (2000), 52,000; tobacco, 36,000; potatoes (2000), 35,000; pineapples (2000), 34,000; soybeans, 33,200; melons (2000), 33,000; coffee, 25,200; cotton, 12,000. Opium is produced, although in ever declining quantities, but its manufacture is controlled by the state.

Livestock (2001): cattle, 1·21m.; pigs, 1·36m.; buffaloes, 1·05m.; goats, 123,800; poultry, 13·87m.

Forestry

Forests covered 12·44m. ha. in 2002, or 47% of the land area, down from 13·18m. ha. in 1990. They produce valuable woods such as teak. Timber production, 2001, 6·46m. cu. metres.

Fisheries

The catch in 2001 was approximately 30,000 tonnes, entirely from inland waters.

INDUSTRY

Production in 2002: cement, 201,000 tonnes; iron bars, 13,000 tonnes; detergent, 650 tonnes; nails, 650 tonnes; corrugated iron, 2·8m. sheets; plywood, 2·1m. sheets; mineral water, 235m. litres; beer, 60·49m. litres; soft drinks, 13·15m. litres; oxygen, 21,500 cylinders; cigarettes, 38·3m. packets; lumber, 155,000 cu. metres.

Labour

The working age is 16–55 for females and 16–60 for males. At the 1995 census there were 1,086,172 females and 1,051,112 males within those age groups. Over 75% of the economically active population in 1995 were engaged in agriculture, fishing and forestry.

INTERNATIONAL TRADE

Since 1988 foreign companies have been permitted to participate in Lao enterprises. Total foreign debt was US$2,665m. in 2002.

Imports and Exports

Imports were estimated at US$534·60m. in 2002 (US$528·27m. in 2001) and exports at US$319·60m. (US$324·89m. in 2001).

The main imports in 2000 were: consumption goods, 50·6%; mineral fuels, 13·9%; materials for garment assembly, 10·6%. Main exports: electricity, 32·0%; garments, 26·1%; wood products, 24·8%. Main import suppliers, 2001: Thailand, 52·0%; Vietnam, 26·5%; China, 5·7%; Singapore, 3·3%. Main export markets, 2001: Vietnam, 41·5%; Thailand, 14·8%; France, 6·1%; Germany, 4·6%.

COMMUNICATIONS

Roads

In 1999 there were 21,716 km of roads, of which 44·5% were paved. In 2002 there were 8,500 passenger cars (1·5 per 1,000 inhabitants), 9,000 trucks and vans and 231,000 motorcycles (1996). There were 1,820 traffic accidents with 600 fatalities in 1992. A bridge over the River Mekong, providing an important north-south link, was opened in 1994.

Rail

The Thai railway system extends to Nongkhai, on the Thai bank of the Mekong River.

Civil Aviation

There are three international airports at Vientiane (Wattay), Pakse and Luang Prabang.

The national carrier is Lao Airlines, which in 2005 operated domestic services and international flights to Bangkok, Chiangmai, Hanoi, Ho Chi Minh City, Kunming, Phnom Penh and Siem Reap (Cambodia). In 1999 scheduled airline traffic of Laos-based carriers flew 2·0m. km, carrying 197,000 passengers (54,000 on international flights).

Shipping

The River Mekong and its tributaries are an important means of transport. 898,000 tonnes of freight were carried on inland waterways in 1995. Merchant shipping totalled 2,000 GRT in 2002.

Telecommunications

In 2002 there were 117,100 telephone subscribers (21·2 per 1,000 persons) and 18,000 PCs in use (3·3 for every 1,000 persons). Laos had 15,000 Internet users in 2002. There were 55,200 mobile phone subscribers in 2002 and 2,700 fax machines.

Postal Services

There were 342 post offices in 2003.

SOCIAL INSTITUTIONS

Justice

Criminal legislation of 1990 established a system of courts and a prosecutor's office. Polygamy became an offence.

Education

In 2000 there were 723 kindergartens with 38,000 pupils and 2,000 teachers, 9,737 primary schools with 891,000 pupils and 27,000 teachers, and 248,000 pupils and 11,400 teachers at general secondary level.

There are eight teacher training institutes (four teacher training colleges and four teacher training schools) and one college of Pali. In June 1995 the National University of Laos (NUOL) was established by merging nine existing higher education institutes and a centre of agriculture. NUOL comprises faculties in agriculture, pedagogy, political science, economics and management, forestry, engineering and architecture, medical science, humanities and social science, science, and literature.

Adult literacy in 2003 was 68·7% (male, 77·0%; female, 60·9%). Laos has only a small educated elite.

In 2000–01 total expenditure on education came to 2·4% of GNP and 8·8% of total government spending.

Health

In 2003 there were 24 hospitals (with 2,711 beds), 125 district-level hospitals and 662 primary health care centres. In 2003 there were 1,283 physicians, 83 dentists and 5,291 nurses.

Only 37% of the population had access to safe drinking water in 2000.

RELIGION

In 2001 some 2·75m. were Buddhists (Hinayana), but about 40% of the population follow tribal religions.

CULTURE

World Heritage Sites

Laos has two sites on the UNESCO World Heritage List: the Town of Luang Prabang (inscribed on the list in 1995), a unique blend of Lao and European colonial architecture; and Vat Phou and Associated Ancient Settlements within the Champasak Cultural Landscape (2001), including a Khmer era Hindu temple complex.

Broadcasting

The government-controlled National Radio of Laos broadcasts a national and six regional programmes and an external service (six languages). Lao National TV transmits for three hours daily. There were 781,000 radio sets in 2000 and 280,000 television receivers in 2001 (colour by PAL).

Press

In 1996 there were three dailies (one in English).

Tourism

There were 673,823 foreign visitors in 2001 (270,000 in 1999); revenue from tourism amounted to US$103·8m.

DIPLOMATIC REPRESENTATIVES

Of Laos in the United Kingdom
Ambassador: Soutsakhone Pathammavong (resides in Paris).

Of the United Kingdom in Laos
Ambassador: David Fall (resides in Bangkok).

Of Laos in the USA (2222 S. St., NW, Washington, D.C., 20008)
Ambassador: Phanethong Phommahaxay.

Of the USA in Laos (Rue Bartholonie, Vientiane)
Ambassador: Patricia M. Haslach.

Of Laos to the United Nations
Ambassador: Alounkèo Kittikhoun.

Of Laos to the European Union
Ambassador: Thongphachanh Sonnasinh.

FURTHER READING

National Statistical Centre. *Basic Statistics about the Socio-Economic Development in the Lao P.D.R.* Annual.
Stuart-Fox, M., *Laos: Politics, Economics and Society.* London, 1986—*History of Laos.* Cambridge Univ. Press, 1997

National Statistical Office: National Statistical Centre, Vientiane.

LATVIA

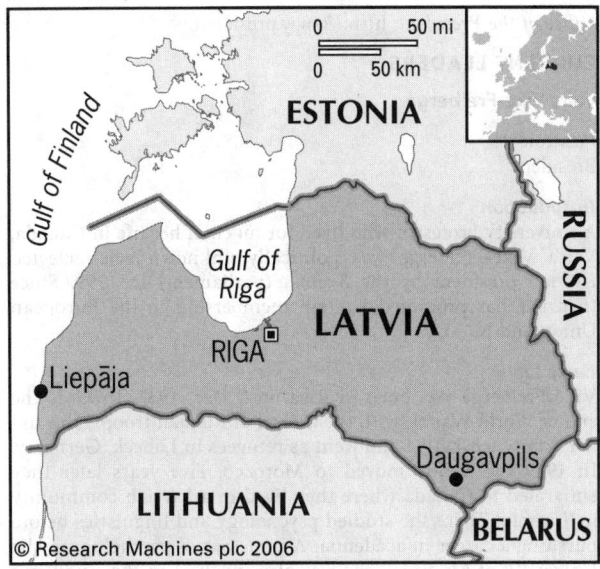

© Research Machines plc 2006

Latvijas Republika

Capital: Riga
Population projection, 2010: 2·25m.
GDP per capita, 2003: (PPP$) 10,270
HDI/world rank: 0·836/48

KEY HISTORICAL EVENTS

The territory that is now Latvia was controlled by crusaders, primarily the German Order of Livonian Knights, until 1561 when Latvia fell into Polish and Swedish hands. Between 1721 and 1795 Latvia was absorbed into the Russian empire. Soviet rule was proclaimed in Dec. 1917, but was overthrown when the Germans occupied all of Latvia (Feb. 1918). Restored when the Germans withdrew (Dec. 1918), the Soviets were again overthrown, this time by combined British naval and German military forces (May–Dec. 1919), and a democratic government was set up. This regime was in turn replaced by a coup which took place in May 1934. The secret protocol of the Soviet–German agreement of 23 Aug. 1939 assigned Latvia to the Soviet sphere of interest. On 4 May 1990 the Latvian Supreme Soviet declared, by 138 votes to nil with 58 abstentions, that the Soviet occupation of Latvia on 17 June 1940 was illegal, and resolved to re-establish the 1922 Constitution. In a referendum in March 1991 the principle of independence was supported by 73·6%. A fully independent status was conceded by the USSR State Council in Sept. 1991. The large Russian minority was initially disadvantaged by the introduction of citizenship and language laws which have since been repealed. President Vīķe-Freiberga was elected as the former Communist bloc's first female president in June 1999. Latvia became a member of NATO in March 2004 and the European Union in May 2004.

TERRITORY AND POPULATION

Latvia is situated in northeastern Europe. It is bordered by Estonia on the north and by Lithuania on the southwest, while on the east there is a frontier with the Russian Federation and to the southeast there is with Belarus. Territory, 64,589 sq. km (larger than Denmark, the Netherlands, Belgium and Switzerland).

Population (2000 census), 2,377,383; density, 37 per sq. km. The estimated population in 2005 was 2,307,000.

The UN gives a projected population for 2010 of 2·25m.

In 2003, 66·3% of the population were urban. Nationalities in 1997: Latvians 55·3%, Russians 32·5%, Belarusians 4·0%, Ukrainians 2·9%, Poles 2·2%, Lithuanians 1·3%, Jews 0·4%, Roma 0·3%, Estonians 0·1%, Germans 0·1%.

There are 26 counties (*rajons*) and seven municipalities with separate status. The capital is Riga (764,329, or nearly a third of the country's total population, at 2000 census); other principal towns, with 2000 populations, are Daugavpils (115,265), Liepāja (89,448), Jelgava (63,652), Jurmala (55,718) and Ventspils (43,928).

The official language is Latvian.

SOCIAL STATISTICS

2001: births, 19,664 (rate of 8·3 per 1,000 population); deaths, 32,991 (14·0 per 1,000 population); marriages, 9,258 (3·9 per 1,000 population); divorces, 5,740 (2·4 per 1,000 population); infant mortality, 17 per 1,000 live births (2001). In 2003 life expectancy was 65·8 years for males but 77·0 years for females. In 2001 the most popular age range for marrying was 25–29 for males and 20–24 for females. The annual population growth rate in the period 1992–2002 was –1·3%, giving Latvia one of the fastest declining populations of any country. Fertility rate, 2001, 1·1 births per woman (one of the lowest rates in the world). The suicide rate, at 28·6 per 100,000 population in 2002, is one of the highest in the world. Among males it was 48·4 per 100,000 population in 2002. In 2001 there were 1,443 immigrants and 6,602 emigrants.

CLIMATE

Owing to the influence of maritime factors, the climate is relatively temperate but changeable. Average temperatures in Jan. range from –2·8°C in the western coastal town of Liepāja to –6·6°C in the inland town of Daugavpils. The average summer temperature is 20°C.

CONSTITUTION AND GOVERNMENT

The Declaration of the Renewal of the Independence of the Republic of Latvia dated 4 May 1990, and the 21 Aug. 1991 declaration re-establishing *de facto* independence, proclaimed the authority of the Constitution (*Satversme*). The Constitution was fully re-instituted as of 6 July 1993, when the fifth Parliament (*Saeima*) was elected.

The head of state in Latvia is the *President*, elected by parliament for a period of four years.

The highest legislative body is the one-chamber parliament comprised of 100 deputies and elected in direct, proportional elections by citizens 18 years of age and over. Deputies serve for four years and parties must receive at least 5% of the national vote to gain seats in parliament.

In a referendum on 3 Oct. 1998, 53% of votes cast were in favour of liberalizing laws on citizenship, which would simplify the naturalization of the Russian-speakers who make up nearly a third of the total population and who were not granted automatic citizenship when Latvia regained its independence from the former Soviet Union in 1991. Around half of the 650,000 ethnic Russians in Latvia have not taken out Latvian citizenship. Ethnic Russians who are not Latvian citizens do not have the right to vote. A seven-member *Constitutional Court* was established in 1996 with powers to invalidate legislation not in conformity with the constitution. Its members are appointed by parliament for ten-year terms.

Executive power is held by the *Cabinet of Ministers*.

National Anthem

'Dievs, svēti Latviju' ('God bless Latvia'); words and tune by Kārlis Baumanis.

GOVERNMENT CHRONOLOGY

(JL = New Era; LC = Latvian Way; LTF = Latvian Popular Front; LZP = Latvian Green Party; LZS = Latvian Farmers' Alliance; TB/LNNK = Fatherland and Freedom Union; TP = People's Party; ZZS = Green and Farmers' Union; n/p = non-partisan)

Heads of State since 1990.
Chairman of the Supreme Council/Head of State

1990–93	n/p, LC	Anatolijs Gorbunovs

Presidents

1993–99	LZS	Guntis Ulmanis
1999–	n/p	Vaira Vīķe-Freiberga

Prime Ministers since 1990.

1990–93	LTF	Ivars Godmanis
1993–94	LC	Valdis Birkavs
1994–95	LC	Māris Gailis
1995–97	n/p	Andris Šķēle
1997–98	TB/LNNK	Guntars Krasts
1998–99	LC	Vilis Krištopāns
1999–2000	TP	Andris Šķēle
2000–02	LC	Andris Bērziņš
2002–04	JL	Einars Repše
2004	ZZS (LZP)	Indulis Emsis
2004–	TP	Aigars Kalvītis

RECENT ELECTIONS

Vaira Vīķe-Freiberga, a Canadian professor who had fled Latvia as a seven-year-old, was elected President of the Republic of Latvia on 17 June 1999. She was re-elected on 20 June 2003.

Parliamentary elections were held on 5 Oct. 2002. Former central bank governor Einars Repše's newly-formed liberal 'New Era' (Jaunais laiks; JL) party won 26 seats with 23·9% of votes cast; For Human Rights in a United Latvia (Par cilvēka tiesībām vienotā Latvijā; PCTVL) won 24 with 18·9%; the People's Party (Tautas partija; TP), 21 with 16·7%; Latvia's First Party (Latvijas Pirmā Partija; LPP), 10 with 9·6%; the Green and Farmers' Union (Zaļo un Zemnieku savienība; ZZS), 12 with 9·5%; and Fatherland and Freedom Alliance/LNNK (Apvienība 'Tēvzemei un Brīvībai'; TB/LNNK), 7 with 5·4%. Prime Minister Andris Bērziņš' Latvian Way party (Savienība 'Latvijas ceļš'; LC) failed to secure a single seat. Turnout was 71·5%.

European Parliament

Latvia has nine representatives. At the June 2004 elections turnout was 41·2%. The TB/LNNK won 4 seats with 29·8% of votes cast (political affiliation in European Parliament: Union for a Europe of Nations); JL, 2 with 19·7% (European People's Party–European Democrats); PCTVL, 1 with 10·7% (Greens/European Free Alliance); TP, 1 with 6·6% (European People's Party–European Democrats); LC, 1 with 6·5% (Alliance of Liberals and Democrats for Europe).

CURRENT ADMINISTRATION

President: Vaira Vīķe-Freiberga; b. 1937 (sworn in 8 July 1999 and re-elected in June 2003).

Prime Minister: Aigars Kalvītis; b. 1966 (TP; took office on 2 Dec. 2004). In April 2006 the coalition government comprised:

Minister for Defence: Atis Slakteris (TP). *Foreign Affairs:* Artis Pabriks (TP). *Economics:* Aigars Štokenbergs (TP). *Finance:* Oskars Spurdziņš (TP). *Interior:* Dzintars Jaundžeikars (LPP). *Education and Science:* Baiba Rivža (ZZS). *Culture:* Helēna Demakova (TP). *Justice:* Guntars Grīnvalds (LPP). *Environment:* Raimonds Vējonis (ZZS). *Agriculture:* Mārtiņš Roze (ZZS). *Transport:* Krišjānis Peters (LPP). *Welfare:* Dagnija Staķe (ZZS). *Health:* Gundars Bērziņš (TP). *Regional Development and Local*

Government: Māris Kučinskis (TP). *Children and Family Affairs:* Ainars Baštiks (LPP). *Special Assignments for Society Integration Affairs:* Karina Pētersone (LC). *Special Assignments for Electronic Government Affairs:* Ina Gudele (ind.).

Office of the President: http://www.president.lv

CURRENT LEADERS

Vaira Vīķe-Freiberga

Position
President

Introduction
A university professor who lived for much of her life in Canada, Vaira Vīķe-Freiberga was politically unknown when elected Latvian president by the *Saeima* (parliament) in 1999. Since then she has promoted Latvian membership to the European Union and NATO.

Early Life
Vīķe-Freiberga was born in Riga on 1 Dec. 1937. Towards the end of World War II, with the arrival of Russian troops, she and her family left Latvia and went as refugees to Lübeck, Germany. In 1949 the family moved to Morocco. Five years later they emigrated to Canada where they lived in a Latvian community in Toronto. There she studied psychology and linguistics before pursuing a career in academia. A professor of psychology at the University of Montreal, she was also involved in the study and promotion of the Latvian language and culture. After Latvia's independence, Vīķe-Freiberga returned to Latvia and between 1998–99 headed the Latvian Institute in Riga.

Career in Office
In 1999, although recently returned to Latvia, Vīķe-Freiberga stood as an independent candidate in the presidential elections. In the seventh round of voting, she took 53 votes to beat the foreign minister Valdis Birkavs and the finance minister Ingrīda Ūdre. She replaced Guntis Ulmanis.

Since her election, Vīķe-Freiberga has worked to promote Latvia to the West and encourage the country's entry into the EU and NATO. After criticism from the EU, the OSCE and Russia, in Dec. 1999 she amended a proposed language law which would have made the Latvian language mandatory in public life and the workplace. The proposals were seen as discriminating against the Russian-speaking population, which constitutes about a third of Latvian inhabitants. In June 2003 she was re-elected president by parliament, receiving 88 votes out of 96. In 2004 Latvia joined both the EU and NATO. Despite protests from Latvian war veterans, Vīķe-Freiberga attended Russia's war anniversary celebrations in Moscow in 2005 (the only Baltic state president to do so).

Aigars Kalvītis

Position
Prime Minister

Introduction
Aigars Kalvītis has been prime minister since 2 Dec. 2004. Prior to this, his ministerial responsibilities included two years as minister of economics and one as minister of agriculture.

Early Life
Born in Riga in 1966, Kalvītis is a former milkman and tractor driver. He first graduated in 1992 from the Latvian University of Agriculture with a degree in agricultural economics. This was supplemented by a masters degree in the same subject gained in 1995. In addition he was awarded a masters degree in food industry business administration from University College Cork in Ireland in 1993 and completed in-service training with

the Holstein Association at the University of Wisconsin, USA. From 1992–98 he was the manager of a variety of agricultural businesses, and began his career in politics in 1997 as one of the founders of the People's Party. He was first elected to parliament in 1998. He served as the minister of agriculture from 1999–2000 and as minister of economics from 2000–02. Kalvītis was re-elected to parliament and became the leader of the parliamentary faction of the People's Party in 2002.

Career in Office

Kalvītis became prime minister on 2 Dec. 2004. He leads a coalition government consisting of his own People's Party, the New Era party, the Green and Farmers' Union, and Latvia's First Party. As prime minister, Kalvītis has identified health issues and inflation as government priorities. In 2005 parliament ratified the proposed new EU constitution.

DEFENCE

Since Latvia gained its independence in Aug. 1991, a renewal process for Latvia's armed forces, including the National Armed forces, the Home Guard and Border Guard, has been under way. Military service is compulsory for male citizens from the age of 19 (women and men 18 years and older can join the national defence forces voluntarily) and the duration of military service is 12 months. Conscientious objectors have the option of serving in non-military service. Latvia has signed a defence co-operation treaty with Lithuania and Estonia to co-ordinate Baltic States' defence and security activities.

In 2003 military expenditure totalled US$194m. (US$84 per capita), representing 1·9% of GDP.

Army

The Army was 4,300 strong in 2002. There is a National Guard reserve of five brigades, and a paramilitary Frontier Guard of 3,200.

Navy

A small coastal protection force, based at Riga and Liepāja, numbered 930 in 2002. Latvia, Estonia and Lithuania have established a joint naval unit 'BALTRON' (Baltic Naval Squadron), with bases at Liepāja, Riga and Ventspils in Latvia, Tallinn in Estonia and Klaipėda in Lithuania.

Air Force

Personnel numbered 270 in 2002. There are no combat aircraft.

INTERNATIONAL RELATIONS

Latvia is a member of the UN, WTO, BIS, NATO, EU, Council of Europe, OSCE, Council of the Baltic Sea States, IOM and an Associate Partner in WEU. Latvia held a referendum on EU membership on 20 Sept. 2003, in which 67·4% of votes cast were in favour of accession, with 32·6% against. It became a member of NATO on 29 March 2004 and the EU on 1 May 2004.

On 2 June 2005 Latvia became the tenth European Union member to ratify the proposed EU constitution. The parliament approved the treaty by 71 votes to five, with six abstentions.

ECONOMY

Agriculture accounted for 4·7% of GDP in 2002, industry 24·7% and services 70·6%.

The Latvian Privatization Agency, established in 1994 to oversee the privatization process, has adopted a case-by-case approach. 97% of all state enterprises have been assigned for privatization. In 2003 the private sector constituted 70% of GDP and 76% of employment.

Overview

Core exports include wood and related products. There is strong export growth in live animals, animal and vegetable products, and metals. Small- and medium-sized enterprises account for over 50% of GDP and employ 70% of the workforce. The private sector accounts for around 67% of GDP. Corruption is still a problem. According to the IMF, the Bank of Latvia has kept monetary developments on track. The currency is pegged to the SDR (Special Drawing Right) and monetary policy has achieved price stability. Inflation has fallen from above 17% in 1996 to under 4%. Unemployment is around 13%. Average incomes are low by EU standards but the gap is closing. Riga has the lowest unemployment rate, while the eastern parts of the country have the highest unemployment.

Currency

The unit of currency is the *lats* (LVL) of 100 *santims*. The lats has been pegged to the SDR basket. In 2004 inflation was 6·3%, down from 109·1% in 1993. Gold reserves were 249,000 troy oz in June 2002 and foreign exchange reserves US$1,145m. Total money supply in June 2002 was 924m. lats.

Budget

The financial year is the calendar year. The fiscal deficit, which had reached 4·0% of GDP (mostly as a consequence of the Russian financial crisis) declined to 2·0% in 2000 and 1·7% of GDP in 2001, but increased to 2·7% in 2002 and 3·2% in 2003.

Government revenue and expenditure (in 1m. lats), year ending 31 Dec.:

	2000	2001	2002	2003
Revenue	1,264·5	1,340·5	1,529·2	1,715·5
Expenditure	1,335·8	1,373·2	1,597·1	1,735·7

The standard rate of VAT is 18·0% (reduced rate, 5·0%).

Performance

GDP growth of 6·9% was recorded in 2000, rising to 8·0% in 2001—the highest rate in Europe. Despite further impressive growth rates in 2002 (6·4%), 2003 (7·5%) and 2004 (8·5%), Latvia has the lowest GDP per capita of any of the ten countries that joined the EU in May 2004. Total GDP was US$13·6bn. in 2004.

Banking and Finance

The Bank of Latvia both legally and practically is a completely independent institution. Governor of the Bank and Council members are appointed by Parliament for office for six years (present *Governor*, Ilmars Rimševičs). In 2002 there were 22 banks in Latvia, including the Riga branches of Société Générale and Vereinsbank. In 1999 the transitional period which had been given for banks to ensure they had capital of €5m. ended with 14 banks fulfilling the requirement. Latvia's largest bank is Parex Bank, with deposits in 2001 of 592·5m. lats. Foreign direct investment inflows in 2003 totalled US$360m. The accumulated FDI at the end of 2002 reached US$2·75bn.

There is a stock exchange in Riga.

ENERGY AND NATURAL RESOURCES

Environment

Latvia's carbon dioxide emissions from the consumption and flaring of fossil fuels in 2002 were the equivalent of 4·2 tonnes per capita.

An *Environmental Sustainability Index* compiled for the World Economic Forum meeting in Jan. 2005 ranked Latvia 15th in the world, with 60·4%. The index measured the ability of countries to maintain favourable environmental conditions and examined various factors including pollution levels and the use or abuse of natural resources.

Electricity

Electricity production in 2001 totalled 4·16bn. kWh. Consumption per capita in 2000 was 2,434 kWh. 68% of electrical power produced in Latvia is generated in hydro-electric power stations.

The largest consumers are industry (34%) and private users (23%). Installed capacity was 2·1m. kW in 2001.

Oil and Gas
Latvia produces virtually no oil and is dependent on imports, although the Latvian Development Agency estimates that there are 733m. bbls. of offshore reserves in the Latvian areas of the Baltic Sea. Oil consumption was 43,000 bbls. per day in 2001. All Latvia's natural gas supplies are imported from Russia. Consumption in 2001 totalled 1·7bn. cu. metres.

Minerals
Peat deposits extend over 645,000 ha. or about 10% of the total area, and it is estimated that total deposits are 3bn.–4bn. tonnes. Peat output in 2001 totalled 555,003 tonnes.

Production of other minerals (in 1,000 tonnes): sand and gravel (2002), 700; limestone (1999), 437; gypsum (2001), 125. Clays and dolomite are also produced.

Agriculture
In 2001 there were 1·84m. ha. of arable land and 29,000 ha. of permanent crops. Cattle and dairy farming are the chief agricultural occupations. Oats, barley, rye, potatoes and flax are the main crops.

In 2001 there were 174,459 farms. 43% of farms have fewer than 5 ha. There were 56,300 tractors and 6,200 harvester-threshers in 2001. Large state and collective farms have been converted into shareholding enterprises; the remainder have been divided into small private holdings for collective farm workers or former owners.

In 2001, 14·7% of the economically active population were employed in agriculture.

Output of crops (in 1,000 tonnes), 2000: grain, 927 (made up of: wheat, 385; barley, 322; oats, 115; rye, 105); potatoes, 747; sugarbeets, 408; cabbages, 66; apples, 24; carrots, 21.

Livestock, 2000: cattle, 378,000; pigs, 405,000; sheep, 27,000; poultry, 3m. Livestock products (2000, in 1,000 tonnes): meat, 61; milk, 825; eggs, 26.

Forestry
In 2000 Latvia's total forest area was 2·9m. ha., or 47·1% of the land area. The overall resources of wood amount to 502m. cu. metres (an increase of 118m. cu. metres since 1984), including 304m. cu. metres of softwood. Private forests account for 44·2% or 1·3m. ha. and comprise about 153,000 holdings. Timber production in 2001 was 12·84m. cu. metres.

The share of the forest sector in gross industrial output is between 13 and 15%. Timber and timber products exports account for 37–38% of Latvia's total exports.

To provide the protection of forests there are three forest categories: commercial forests, 70·4%; restricted management forests, 18·6%; protected forests, 11·0%.

Fisheries
In 2001 the total catch was 125,433 tonnes, of which marine fish 124,852 tonnes. The main types of fish caught are sprat, Baltic herring, cod and salmon. The Latvian fishing fleet consists of almost 400 vessels.

INDUSTRY
Industry accounted for 26·1% of GDP in 2001, with manufacturing contributing 14·8%.

Industrial output in 1,000 tonnes: steel products (1999), 520; cement (2001), 500; crude steel (2000), 500; sugar (2002), 77; sawnwood (2002), 3·95m. cu. metres; wood-based panels (2002), 318,000 cu. metres; beer (2003), 246·6m. litres.

Labour
The total labour force in Nov. 2001 numbered 1,105,500. In Nov. 2000 there were 966,800 persons in employment in Latvia (excluding those in compulsory military service). The leading areas of activity were: manufacturing, 171,300; wholesale and retail trade/repair of motor vehicles, motorcycles and personal and household goods, 154,500; agriculture, hunting, forestry and fishing, 128,400. In 1999 women constituted 50% of the workforce, a higher percentage than in any other European country. In 2004 there was a monthly minimum wage of 80 lats. Average monthly salary was 192 lats in 2003. The official unemployment rate in June 2002 was 12·7%. The average monthly salary in the public sector in early 2000 was 168·39 lats.

Trade Unions
The Free Trade Union Federation of Latvia, LBAS (President: Pēteris Krīgers) was established in 1990. In 2003 there were 28 branch trade unions and professional employee unions representing more than 250,000 members.

INTERNATIONAL TRADE
State debt, as a proportion of GDP, has increased from 14·7% in 2000 to 15·4% in 2001, 16·6% in 2002 and 19·5% in 2003. Total external debt was US$6,690m. in 2002.

Imports and Exports
Imports (f.o.b.) were valued at US$4,020m. in 2002 (US$3,566m. in 2001) and exports (f.o.b.) at US$2,576m. (US$2,216m. in 2001). The leading imports are machinery and mechanical appliances (20·6%), mineral products (12·4%), products of chemical and allied industries (11·1%), metals and products thereof (8·3%). The main exports are wood and wood products (38·8%), textiles and textile articles (13·8%), base metals and articles of base metals (13·3%). Main import suppliers (2002): Germany, 17·2%; Lithuania, 9·8%; Russia, 8·8%; Finland, 8·0%; Sweden, 6·4%. Main export markets (2002): Germany, 15·5%; UK, 14·6%; Sweden, 10·5%, Lithuania, 8·4%; Estonia, 6·0%. In 1997, 53·2% of imports were from the EU and 48·9% of exports went to the EU. Since 1997 trade with the EU has continued to grow and trade with Russia and other former Soviet republics has declined, with trade between Latvia and Russia halving between 1997 and 2001.

COMMUNICATIONS
Roads
In 2001 there were 60,472 km of roads, including 20,279 km of national roads. In 2002 public road transport totalled 2,361m. passenger-km and freight 6,160m. tonne-km. In 2002 there were 518 fatalities in traffic accidents. With 22·1 deaths per 100,000 population in 2002 Latvia has one of the highest death rates in road accidents of any industrialized country. In 1996, 213·5 km of road was repaired and 13·1 km of new road built. Passenger cars in 2002 numbered 619,081 (266 per 1,000 inhabitants), in addition to which there were 102,734 trucks and vans, 22,157 motorcycles and mopeds and 11,164 buses and coaches.

Rail
In 2000 there were 2,331 km of 1,520 mm gauge route (258 km electrified). In 2003, 48·4m. tonnes of cargo and 23·0m. passengers were carried by rail. The main groups of freight transported are oil and oil products, mineral fertilizers, ferrous metals and ferrous alloys.

Civil Aviation
There is an international airport at Riga. A new national carrier, Air Baltic, assumed control of Latavio and Baltic International Airlines in 1995 and began flying in Oct. 1995. It went on to become eastern Europe's first low-cost airline. In 1998 it flew 4·7m. km, carrying 175,000 passengers. In 2003 it operated scheduled services to Berlin, Copenhagen, Hamburg, Helsinki, Kyiv, Moscow, Prague, Stockholm, Tallinn, Vilnius and Warsaw. It is 52·6% state-owned, with SAS owning the remainder. In 2001 Riga handled 622,647 passengers and 4,073 tonnes of freight.

Shipping

There are three large ports (with 51·1m. tonnes of cargo handled, 2002): Ventspils (29m.), Riga (18m.) and Liepāja (4m.). 7,100 ships in all docked at the three ports in 2002. A total of 47·7m. tonnes were loaded at the three ports in 2002 and 3·4m. tonnes unloaded. In 2002 the merchant marine totalled 89,000 GRT, including oil tankers 4,000 GRT (oil tankers 279,000 GRT in 1996 out of a total of 723,000 GRT).

Ventspils can handle up to 100,000 containers a year and it is estimated that it will be able to handle 250,000 a year when the second stage of a US$70m. development project is completed. This project will change Ventspils from a port principally designed for the export of oil and other products from Russia to one which is also a major import centre.

Telecommunications

Telecommunications are conducted by companies in which the government has a 51% stake, under the aegis of the state-controlled Lattelekom. In 2002 telephone subscribers numbered 1,618,400 (694·9 per 1,000 inhabitants) and 400,000 PCs were in use (171·7 per 1,000 persons). There were 917,200 mobile phone subscribers in 2002 and 1,400 fax machines. The number of Internet users in 2002 was 310,000.

Postal Services

In 2003 there were 964 post offices.

SOCIAL INSTITUTIONS

Justice

A new criminal code came into force in 1998. Judges are appointed for life. There are a Supreme Court, regional and district courts and administrative courts. The death penalty is retained but has been subject to a moratorium since Oct. 1996; it was abolished for peacetime offences in 1999. In 2003, 51,773 crimes were reported, 48·8% of which were solved; 13,586 people were convicted for offences. There were 220 murders in 2003 (a 6·3% increase on 2002). In June 2003 there were 8,156 people in penal institutions, giving a prison population rate of 352 per 100,000 population.

Education

Adult literacy rate in 2003 was 99·7% (99·8% among males and 99·7% among females). The Soviet education system has been restructured on the UNESCO model. Education may begin in kindergarten. From the age of six or seven education is compulsory for nine years in comprehensive schools. This may be followed by three years in special secondary school or one to six years in art, technical or vocational schools. In 2003–04 there were 1,044 schools with 327,358 pupils.

State-financed education is available in Latvian and eight national minority languages (Russian, Polish, Hebrew, Ukrainian, Estonian, Lithuanian, Roma and Belarusian), although the use of Latvian in the classroom is being increased. A bilingual curriculum had to be implemented by all minority primary schools from the start of the 2002–03 school year. Secondary schools started to implement minority education curricula with an increased Latvian-language component (60% of all teaching) from Sept. 2004. In 2003–04, 230,212 pupils were taught solely in Latvian, 95,841 received instruction in Russian and 1,305 in other minority languages.

In 2002 there were 37 higher education institutions, with 118,944 students. Courses at state-financed universities are conducted in Latvian. A number of private educational institutions have languages of instruction other than Latvian.

Total expenditure on education in 2000–01 came to 5·9% of GNP.

Health

In 2003 there were 7,900 physicians and dentists. In 2001 there were 11,954 nurses and 501 midwives. There were 131 hospitals in 2003 with a provision of 78 beds per 10,000 persons.

Welfare

The official retirement age is age 62 years (men) or age 59 years 6 months (women). However, the retirement age for women is increasing, by six months each year, so that in 2009 it will also be 62 years. In 2002 the minimum pension was equal to the state social security allowance of 30 lats a month. The minimum pension is increased by 1·1% for an insurance period of at least 20 years, by 1·3% for an insurance period of 20 to 30 years and by 1·5% and for an insurance period of more than 30 years. In 2003 there were 607,000 pension recipients.

The government runs an unemployment benefit scheme in which the amount awarded is determined by the number of insurance contributions and the length of previous employment.

RELIGION

In order to practise in public, religious organizations must be licensed by the Department of Religious Affairs attached to the Ministry of Justice. New sects are required to demonstrate loyalty to the state and its traditional religions over a three-year period. Traditionally Catholics and Lutherans constitute the largest churches, with about 500,000 and 400,000 members respectively in 2002. Congregations in Feb. 2003: Lutherans, 307; Roman Catholics, 252; Russian Orthodox, 117; Baptists, 90; Old Believers, 67; Adventists, 47; Jews, 13; others, 47. In May 2005 the Roman Catholic church had one cardinal.

CULTURE

World Heritage Sites

Latvia has two sites on the UNESCO World Heritage List: the Historic Centre of Riga (inscribed on the list in 1997), a late-medieval Hanseatic centre; and the Struve Geodetic Arc (2005). The Arc is a chain of survey triangulations spanning from Norway to the Black Sea that helped establish the exact shape and size of the earth and is shared with nine other countries.

Broadcasting

Broadcasting is overseen by the nine-member National Radio and Television Council appointed by parliament for four-year terms. There are 26 TV broadcasting companies and 23 radio broadcasting companies. Latvijas Radio broadcasts three programmes and an external service (English, German, Swedish). Latvijas Televizija transmits on two networks (colour by PAL). There were 1·65m. radio receivers in 2000 and 1·97m. television receivers in 2001.

Cinema

In 1999 there were 115 cinemas; attendances totalled 1·4m.

Press

Latvia had 24 daily newspapers in 2002 with a combined circulation of 387,000 (166 per 1,000 inhabitants). 2,178 book titles were published in 1999.

Tourism

In 2002 there were 848,000 foreign tourists; revenue totalled US$161m. In 2003 there were 326 hotels and other accommodation facilities.

Festivals

There is an annual Riga Opera Festival in June. The National Song Festival (held every five years) will next be held in 2008.

Libraries

In 2002 there were 902 public libraries with 613,000 members. There is a National Library of Latvia.

Theatre and Opera

There are a National Opera and Ballet and nine professional theatres.

Museums and Galleries

There are 96 museums.

DIPLOMATIC REPRESENTATIVES

Of Latvia in the United Kingdom (45 Nottingham Place, London, W1U 5LY)
Ambassador: Indulis Bērziņš.

Of the United Kingdom in Latvia (5 Alunana ielā, Riga, LV 1010)
Ambassador: Ian Bond.

Of Latvia in the USA (4325 17th St., NW, Washington, D.C., 20011)
Ambassador: Māris Riekstiņš.

Of the USA in Latvia (7 Raina Blvd, Riga, LV 1510)
Ambassador: Catherine Todd Bailey.

Of Latvia to the United Nations
Ambassador: Solveiga Silkalna.

Of Latvia to the European Union
Ambassador: Andris Kesteris.

FURTHER READING

Central Statistical Bureau. *Statistical Yearbook of Latvia.—Latvia in Figures.* Annual.

Dreifeld, J., *Latvia in Transition.* Riga, 1997

Lieven, A., *The Baltic Revolution: Estonia, Latvia, Lithuania and the Path to Independence.* 2nd ed. Yale Univ. Press, 1994

Misiunas, R. J. and Taagepera, R., *The Baltic States: the Years of Dependence, 1940–91.* 2nd ed. Farnborough, 1993

Smith, I. A. and Grunts, M. V., *The Baltic States.* [Bibliography] ABC-Clio, Oxford and Santa Barbara (CA), 1993

Who is Who in Latvia. Riga, 1996

National Statistical Office: Central Statistical Bureau, Lācplēša ielā 1, 1301 Riga.

Website: http://www.csb.lv/

LEBANON

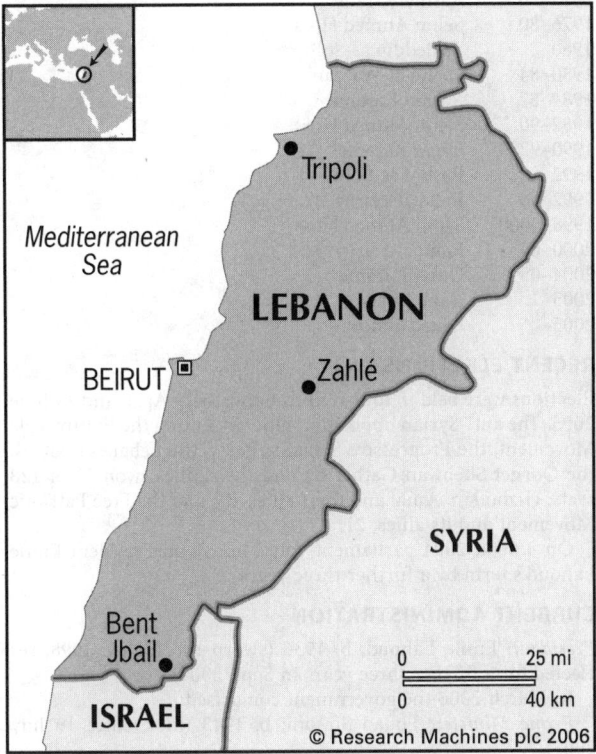

Jumhouriya al-Lubnaniya
(Republic of Lebanon)

Capital: Beirut
Population projection, 2010: 3·77m.
GDP per capita, 2003: (PPP$) 5,074
HDI/world rank: 0·759/81

KEY HISTORICAL EVENTS

The Ottomans invaded Lebanon, then part of Syria, in 1516–17 and held nominal control until 1918. After 20 years' French mandatory regime, Lebanon was proclaimed independent on 26 Nov. 1941. In early May 1958 the Muslim opposition to President Chamoun rose in insurrection and for five months the Muslim quarters of Beirut, Tripoli, Sidon and the northern Bekaa were in insurgent hands. On 15 July the US Government landed army and marines who re-established Government authority. Internal problems were exacerbated by the Palestinian problem. An attempt to regulate the activities of Palestinian fighters through the secret Cairo agreement of 1969 was frustrated both by the inability of the Government to enforce its provisions and by an influx of battle-hardened fighters expelled from Jordan in Sept. 1970. From March 1975 Lebanon was beset by civil disorder by which the economy was brought to a virtual standstill.

By Nov. 1976 large-scale fighting had been brought to an end by the intervention of the Syrian-dominated Arab Deterrent Force. Large areas of the country, however, remained outside governmental control, including West Beirut, which was the scene of frequent conflict between opposing militia groups. In March 1978 there was an Israeli invasion following a Palestinian attack inside Israel. Israeli troops eventually withdrew in June, but

instead of handing over all their positions to UN Peacekeeping Forces, they installed Israeli-controlled Christian Lebanese militia forces in border areas. In June 1982 Israeli forces once again invaded, this time in massive strength, and swept through the country, eventually laying siege to and bombing Beirut. In Sept. Palestinian forces, together with the PLO leadership, evacuated Beirut. Israeli forces started a withdrawal on 16 Feb. 1985 but it was not until the end of 1990 that the various militias which had held sway in Beirut withdrew. A new Government of National Reconciliation was announced on 24 Dec. 1990. The dissolution of all militias was decreed by the National Assembly in April 1991, but the Shia Muslim militia Hizbollah was allowed to remain active. Following a 17-day Israeli bombardment of Hizbollah positions in April 1996, a US-brokered unsigned 'understanding' of 26 April 1996 guaranteed that Hizbollah guerrillas and Palestinian radical groups would cease attacks on civilians in northern Israel and granted Israel the right to self-defence. Hizbollah maintained the right to resist Israel's occupation of Lebanese soil. In May 2000 Israel completed its withdrawal from south Lebanon, 22 years after the first invasion. On 14 Feb. 2005 former Prime Minister Rafiq al-Hariri was assassinated in a bomb attack on his car, sparking international condemnation of the murder and massive public protests at the continued presence of Syrian soldiers in the country. Soon afterwards Syria began withdrawing and redeploying its 14,000 troops and intelligence agents from Beirut. By the end of April 2005 all Syrian troops had been withdrawn from Lebanon.

TERRITORY AND POPULATION

Lebanon is mountainous, bounded on the north and east by Syria, on the west by the Mediterranean and on the south by Israel. The area is 10,452 sq. km (4,036 sq. miles). Population (2005 estimate), 3·58m.; density, 342 per sq. km. In 2003, 87·5% of the population were urban.

The UN gives a projected population for 2010 of 3·77m.

The principal towns, with estimated population (1998), are: Beirut (the capital), 1·5m.; Tripoli, 160,000; Zahlé, 45,000; Saida (Sidon), 38,000.

The official language is Arabic. French and, increasingly, English are widely spoken in official and commercial circles. Armenian is spoken by a minority group.

SOCIAL STATISTICS

2001 estimates: births, 86,000; deaths, 19,000. Estimated rates, 2001 (per 1,000 population): births, 24·3; deaths, 5·4. Infant mortality was 28 per 1,000 live births in 2001; expectation of life (2003), 69·8 years for males and 74·2 for females. Annual population growth rate, 1992–2002, 2·3%; fertility rate, 2001, 2·2 births per woman.

CLIMATE

A Mediterranean climate with short, warm winters and long, hot and rainless summers, with high humidity in coastal areas. Rainfall is largely confined to the winter months and can be torrential, with snow on high ground. Beirut, Jan. 55°F (13°C), July 81°F (27°C). Annual rainfall 35·7" (893 mm).

CONSTITUTION AND GOVERNMENT

The first Constitution was established under the French Mandate on 23 May 1926. It has since been amended in 1927, 1929, 1943 (twice), 1947 and 1990. It is based on a separation of powers, with a President, a single-chamber *National Assembly* elected by universal suffrage at age 21 in 12 electoral constituencies, and an independent judiciary. In Oct. 1995 the National Assembly extended the President's term of office from six to nine years. The executive consists of the President and a Prime Minister and Cabinet appointed after consultation between the President and the National Assembly. The system is adapted to the communal balance on which Lebanese political life depends by an electoral law which allocates deputies according to the religious distribution of the population, and by a series of constitutional conventions whereby, *e.g.,* the President is always a Maronite Christian, the Prime Minister a Sunni Muslim and the Speaker of the Assembly a Shia Muslim. There is no party system. In Aug. 1990, and again in July 1992, the National Assembly voted to increase its membership, and now has 128 deputies with equal numbers of Christians and Muslims.

On 21 Sept. 1990 President Hrawi established the Second Republic by signing constitutional amendments which had been negotiated at Taif (Saudi Arabia) in Oct. 1989. These institute an executive collegium between the President, Prime Minister and Speaker, and remove from the President the right to recall the Prime Minister, dissolve the Assembly and vote in the Council of Ministers.

National Anthem

'Kulluna lil watan lil 'ula lil 'alam' ('All of us for our country, flag and glory'); words by Rashid Nakhlé, tune by W. Sabra.

GOVERNMENT CHRONOLOGY

Presidents since 1943.

1943–52	Béchara Khalil El-Khoury
1952–58	Camille Nemr Chamoun
1958–64	Fouad Abdallah Chehab
1964–70	Charles Alexandre Hélou
1970–76	Soleiman Kabalan Franjieh
1976–82	Elias Sarkis
1982–88	Amine Pierre Gemayel
1989	René Anis Moawad
1989–98	Elias Khalil Haraoui
1998–	Emile Geamil Lahoud

Prime Ministers since 1943.

1943–45	Riyad as-Solh
1945	Abdulhamid Karame
1945–46	Abd' Rashin Sami as-Solh
1946	Saadi al-Munla
1946–51	Riyad as-Solh
1951	Hussein al-Oweini
1951–52	Abdullah Aref al-Yafi
1952	Abd Rashin Sami as-Solh
1952	Nazim al-Akkari
1952	Saeb Sallam
1952	Abdullah Aref al-Yafi
1952–53	Amir Khalid Chehab
1953	Saeb Sallam
1953–54	Abdullah Aref al-Yafi
1954–55	Abd Rashin Sami as-Solh
1955–56	Rashid Karame
1956	Abdullah Aref al-Yafi
1956–58	Abd Rashin Sami as-Solh
1958	Khalil al-Hibri
1958–60	Rashid Karame
1960	Ahmed Daouk
1960–61	Saeb Sallam
1961–64	Rashid Karame
1964–65	Hussein al-Oweini
1965–66	Rashid Karame
1966	Abdullah Aref al-Yafi
1966–68	Rashid Karame
1968–69	Abdullah Aref al-Yafi
1969–70	Rashid Karame
1970–73	Saeb Sallam
1973	Amin al-Hafez
1973–74	Takieddin as-Solh
1974–75	Rashid as-Solh
1975	Nureddin Rifai
1975–76	Rashid Karame
1976–80	Sélim Ahmed Hoss
1980	Takieddin as-Solh
1980–84	Shafiq al-Wazzan
1984–87	Rashid Karame
1987–90	Sélim Ahmed Hoss
1990–92	Omar Karame
1992	Rashid as-Solh
1992–98	Rafiq al-Hariri
1998–2000	Sélim Ahmed Hoss
2000–04	Rafiq al-Hariri
2004–05	Omar Karame
2005	Najib Mikati
2005–	Fouad Siniora

RECENT ELECTIONS

Elections were held in four rounds between 29 April and 19 June 2005. The anti-Syrian opposition bloc (including the Future Tide Movement, the Progressive Socialist Party, the Lebanese Forces, the Qornet Shehwan Gathering and their allies) won 72 of 128 seats; Hizbollah, Amal and their allies, 35; and the Free Patriotic Movement and its allies, 21.

On 3 Sept. 2004 parliament voted to extend President Emile Lahoud's term by a further three years.

CURRENT ADMINISTRATION

President: Emile Lahoud; b. 1936 (sworn in 24 Nov. 1998; re-elected for a further three years in Sept. 2004).

In March 2006 the government comprised:

Prime Minister: Fouad Siniora; b. 1943 (took office 19 July 2005).

Deputy Prime Minister and Minister of Defence: Elias Murr.

Minister of Foreign Affairs and Emigrants: Fawzi Salloukh. *National and Higher Education:* Khaled Kabbani. *Culture:* Tarek Mitri. *Information:* Ghazi Aridi. *Tourism:* Joseph Sarkis. *Justice:* Charles Rizk. *Health:* Mohammed Jawad Khalifé. *Social Affairs:* Nayla Moawad. *Public Works and Transport:* Mohammed Safadi. *Displaced Persons:* Nehmé Tohmé. *Environment:* Yaacoub Sarraf. *Energy and Water:* Mohammed Fneich. *Industry:* Pierre Gemayel. *Finance:* Jihad Azour. *Economy and Commerce:* Sami Haddad. *Telecommunications:* Marwan Hamadé. *Youth and Sport, and Interior and Municipalities (acting):* Ahmed Fatfat. *Labour:* Trad Hamadé. *Agriculture:* Talal Sahili. *Minister of State for Administrative Development:* Jean Oghassapian. *Minister of State for Parliamentary Affairs:* Michel Pharaon.

President's Website: http://www.presidency.gov.lb

CURRENT LEADERS

Emile Lahoud

Position
President

Introduction
Emile Lahoud was sworn in as president on 24 Nov. 1998. As commander of the armed forces, his election on 15 Oct. required a constitutional amendment as serving state officials were formerly prohibited from standing for the presidency. His mandate was extended for a further three years from Sept. 2004 under a constitutional amendment approved by parliament.

Early Life
Born in 1936 in Baabdat, Emile Lahoud was educated at Brumana High School before joining the Military Academy as a cadet

officer in 1956. Between 1958–80 he attended courses at naval academies in the UK and USA as he progressed through the ranks to captain. By 1985 he was a rear-admiral and on 28 Nov. 1989 was promoted to general and commander of the armed forces at the start of Elias Haraoui's presidency.

Career in Office

Credited with rebuilding the Lebanese armed forces and restraining the warring militias that held sway in 1975–90, Lahoud was a respected public figure by the time of his election as president in Nov. 1998. He secured the votes of 118 deputies of the 128-member National Assembly, reflecting his wide acceptance across sectarian lines. The early part of his presidency saw the completion of Israel's military withdrawal from south Lebanon in May 2000. His term of office was originally set to end in late 2004, but was extended for a further three years when the parliament approved a controversial constitutional amendment (believed to have been influenced by Syria) in Sept. 2004. In Feb. 2005 the former prime minister Rafiq al-Hariri was killed by a massive car bomb in Beirut. The assassination caused a series of anti-Syrian rallies, which led to calls for Syria to withdraw its troops, and Lahoud came under pressure to resign. In April Syria claimed to have withdrawn all its military forces, as demanded by the United Nations.

Fouad Siniora

Position
Prime Minister

Introduction
Fouad Siniora became prime minister in July 2005, shortly after the assassination of former prime minister, Rafiq al-Hariri, and the withdrawal of Syrian forces from Lebanese territory. His priorities, to strengthen ties with Syria and to reduce Lebanon's massive foreign debt, are made more challenging by an uncertain political landscape. He is expected to come under pressure to carry out the UN's demands to disarm the militant Hizbollah group.

Early Life
Siniora was born into a Sunni Muslim family in Sidon on Lebanon's southern coast in 1943. He graduated in business studies from the American University in Beirut and began a career in international finance, working for, among others, Citibank. He also taught at the American University during the 1970s.

Between 1977–82 he held a senior position at the country's central bank. Siniora was a close friend of Rafiq al-Hariri, the future prime minister and successful businessman, and in 1982 went to work for his private business empire, holding a number of positions. Al-Hariri became prime minister in 1992 and Siniora served as finance minister in each of his five cabinets in the periods 1992–98 and 2000–04.

In the mid-1990s Siniora unsuccessfully sought to kick-start an economic revival but this increased the national debt. After al-Hariri left office in 1998 Siniora faced charges of corruption and mismanagement, including allegations of the misuse of state funds. His supporters claimed these accusations were an offshoot of the long-running dispute between al-Hariri and President Emile Lahoud. Siniora was cleared of all charges in 2003.

In Feb. 2005 al-Hariri was assassinated by a car bomb. Many Lebanese assumed Syrian involvement in the killing and Beirut witnessed two weeks of large anti-Syrian, and then counter pro-Syrian, demonstrations. In late Feb. 2005 the government of Prime Minister Omar Karame resigned and at the end of April, responding to international pressure, Syria withdrew its troops from Lebanese soil after 29 years of occupancy.

General elections held in April and June 2005 were dominated by the anti-Syrian opposition bloc led by Saad al-Hariri, son

of Rafiq and also a friend of Siniora. Having been asked by President Lahoud to form a government, Siniora resigned from the Group Méditérannée bank. After lengthy negotiations he formed a government that included all the major groupings with the exception of the Christian-based Free Patriotic Movement, led by Gen. Michel Aoun. For the first time the government included a representative of Hizbollah, the subject of a UN resolution ordering it to disarm. Siniora described Hizbollah as 'a natural and honest expression of the Lebanese people's national rights to liberate their land …against Israeli aggression and threats', suggesting that enforcing disarmament was low on his agenda. Siniora was sworn in to office on 19 July 2005, succeeding Najib Mikati.

Career in Office
On taking office Siniora promised to continue the reforms of al-Hariri. Among his primary concerns is the improvement of relations with Syria. Syria closed the border to commercial traffic from Lebanon in early July 2005, costing Lebanon an estimated US$300,000 a day, although Syria claimed the action was to prevent the infiltration of militants across the border. A thaw began when Siniora visited Syria in late July. Other challenges for Siniora include restoring domestic security and electoral and economic reforms. The economy is burdened by public debt of around US$38bn., but by Aug. 2005 there was evidence of an upturn following the relatively smooth transition of power and promises of reform. Bombings aimed at both political and civilian targets, however, continued throughout 2005.

DEFENCE

There were 14,000 Syrian troops in the country in early 2005, but in March 2005 Lebanon and Syria agreed that the troops would be redeployed to the Bekaa Valley in the east of the country. They were subsequently all withdrawn from Lebanon. The United Nations Interim Force in Lebanon (UNIFIL), created in 1978, had a strength of 3,638 in 2002.

Conscription is for 12 months.

Defence expenditure in 2003 totalled US$512m. (US$114 per capita), representing 2·8% of GDP.

Army
The strength of the Army was 70,000 in 2002 and includes a Presidential Guard and five special forces regiments. There is an internal security force, run by the Ministry of the Interior, some 13,000 strong.

Navy
A force of 830 personnel (2002) operate a handful of small craft.

Air Force
The Air Force had (2002) about 1,000 personnel. No combat aircraft were operated.

INTERNATIONAL RELATIONS

A Treaty of Brotherhood, Co-operation and Co-ordination with Syria of May 1991 provides for close relations in the fields of foreign policy, the economy, military affairs and security. The treaty stipulates that Lebanese government decisions are subject to review by six joint Syrian-Lebanese bodies.

Lebanon is a member of the UN, the League of Arab States, OIC, Islamic Development Bank and the International Organization of the Francophonie.

ECONOMY

Agriculture accounted for 11·7% of GDP in 2002, industry 21·0% and services 67·3%.

Overview
The semi-autonomous Council of Development and Reconstruction, originally set up in 1977, was revived in 1991

to oversee a post-civil war rehabilitation programme 'Horizon 2000'. In 1995 this programme was revised and extended up to 2007.

Currency

The unit of currency is the *Lebanese pound* (LBP) of 100 *piastres*. There was inflation of 1·8% in 2002, 1·3% in 2003 and 3·0% in 2004. In June 2002 foreign exchange reserves totalled US$4,604m.; gold reserves were 9·22m. troy oz and total money supply was £Leb.2,231·10bn. There is a fluctuating official rate of exchange, fixed monthly; in practice it is used only for the calculation of *ad-valorem* customs duties on Lebanese imports and for import statistics. For other purposes the free market is used.

Budget

The fiscal year is the calendar year.

In 2002 budgetary central government revenue totalled £Leb.5,385bn. (£Leb.4,260bn. in 2001) and expenditure came to £Leb.8,186bn. (£Leb.7,719bn. in 2001). Principal sources of revenue in 2002: taxes on goods and services, £Leb.2,356bn.; taxes on international trade and transactions, £Leb.596bn.; taxes on income, profits and capital gains, £Leb.590bn. Main items of expenditure by economic type in 2002: interest, £Leb.4,366bn.; compensation of employees, £Leb.2,666bn.; social benefits, £Leb.702bn.

Performance

Total GDP was US$21·8bn. in 2004. Real GDP growth was 5·0% in 2003 and 6·0% in 2004.

Banking and Finance

The Bank of Lebanon (*Governor*, Riad Salameh) is the bank of issue. In 1994 there were 52 domestic banks, 14 subsidiaries and 12 foreign banks, with 590 branches in all. Commercial bank deposits in June 1998 totalled £Leb.41,836,800m. There is a stock exchange in Beirut (closed 1983–95).

ENERGY AND NATURAL RESOURCES

Environment

Lebanon's carbon dioxide emissions from the consumption and flaring of fossil fuels in 2002 were the equivalent of 4·5 tonnes per capita.

Electricity

Installed capacity in 2000 was 2·3m. kW. Production in 2000 was 9·24bn. kWh and consumption per capita 3,041 kWh.

Minerals

There are no commercially viable deposits.

Agriculture

In 2001 there were 170,000 ha. of arable land and 143,000 ha. of permanent crop land. Crop production (in 1,000 tonnes), 2000: tomatoes, 335; sugarbeets, 330; potatoes, 270; grapes, 245; cucumbers and gherkins, 190; oranges, 165; watermelons, 135; apples, 120; lemons and limes, 111; bananas, 110; olives, 105; onions, 85; cabbages, 83.

Livestock (2000): goats, 485,000; sheep, 380,000; cattle, 77,000; pigs, 64,000; chickens, 32m.

Forestry

The forests of the past have been denuded by exploitation and in 2000 covered 36,000 ha., or 3·5% of the total land area. Timber production was 89,000 cu. metres in 2001.

Fisheries

The catch in 2001 was 3,670 tonnes, of which 3,650 tonnes were sea fish.

INDUSTRY

According to the Financial Times Survey (FT 500), the largest company by market capitalization in Lebanon on 4 Jan. 2001 was Solidere (US$1,051·9m.), a Beirut development and reconstruction company.

In 2001 industry accounted for 21·9% of GDP, with manufacturing contributing 10·3%. Industrial production, 2001 (in 1,000 tonnes): cement, 2,890; flour, 420; sulphuric acid, 357; mineral water, 276·8m. litres.

Labour

The workforce was some 650,000 in 1995, of whom 72,000 worked in agriculture. Following considerable labour unrest, an agreement on wage increases and social benefits was concluded between the government and the General Confederation of Lebanese Workers (GCLW) in Dec. 1993.

Trade Unions

The main unions are the General Confederation of Lebanese Workers and the General Confederation of Sectoral Unions.

INTERNATIONAL TRADE

Foreign and domestic trade is the principal source of income. Foreign debt was US$17,077m. in 2002.

Imports and Exports

Imports, 2002: US$6,445m.; exports, US$1,046m. Major imports in 1999 were (in US$1m.): machinery and transport equipment, 1,522·1; manufactured goods, 981·8; foodstuffs, 940·1; chemicals, 666·9; petroleum, 505·6. Major exports were (in US$1m.): foodstuffs, 92·0 (59·1 were vegetables and fruit); chemicals (including phosphoric acids), 91·8; machinery and transport equipment, 80·6; precious metal jewellery, 52·0; gold, 40·3.

In 1999 the main export markets were (in US$1m.): Saudi Arabia, 70·6; UAE, 53·7; France, 52·1; Switzerland, 44·4; USA, 41·9; Syria, 32·1. Main import suppliers (in US$1m.): Italy, 676·0; France, 592·8; Germany, 550·1; USA, 499·1; Switzerland, 440·9; UK, 270·5.

COMMUNICATIONS

Roads

There were 8,530 km of roads in 2002, of which 84·9% were paved. Passenger cars in 2002 numbered 1,253,700, and there were also 97,200 trucks and vans; in 1997 there were 61,470 motorcycles and mopeds and 6,830 buses and coaches. In 1997 there were 3,315 road accidents resulting in 357 deaths.

Rail

Railways are state-owned. There is 222 km of standard gauge track.

Civil Aviation

Beirut International Airport was served in 2003 by nearly 30 airlines. It handled 2,373,056 passengers (all on international flights) in 2001 and 62,789 tonnes of freight. The national airline is the state-owned Middle East Airlines, which in 1999 flew 17·7m. km, carrying 719,400 passengers (all on international flights).

Shipping

Beirut is the largest port, followed by Tripoli, Jounieh and Saida (Sidon). Total GRT in 2002 was 229,000, including oil tankers 1,000 GRT.

Telecommunications

Lebanon had 1,453,900 telephone subscribers in 2002, or 425·8 per 1,000 persons. Mobile phone subscribers numbered 775,100 in 2002 and there were 275,000 PCs in use (80·5 for every 1,000 persons). There were 3,000 fax machines in 1995. The number of Internet users in 2002 was 400,000.

Postal Services

In 2003 there were 349 post offices.

SOCIAL INSTITUTIONS

Justice
The population in penal institutions in March 2003 was 6,382 (172 per 100,000 of national population). The death penalty is still in force. There were three confirmed executions in 2004, the first ones since 1998.

Education
There are state and private primary and secondary schools. In 1999–2000 there were 384,539 pupils with 20,571 teachers at primary schools; and (2000–01) 322,136 pupils with 43,959 teachers in general secondary education. There are 13 universities, including two American and one French, and ten other institutions of higher education. In 2000–01 there were 134,018 students in tertiary education and 9,459 academic staff. Adult literacy was 86·5% in 2001 (92·4% among males and 81·0% among females). In 2000–01 total expenditure on education came to 2·9% of GNP and 11·1% of total government spending.

There is an Academy of Fine Arts.

Health
There were 153 hospitals in 1995 (provision of 22 beds per 10,000 population), and in 2001 there were 11,505 physicians, 4,283 dentists, 4,157 nurses and 3,359 pharmacists.

RELIGION

In 2001 it was estimated that the population was 56·6% Muslim (34·8% Shia and 21·8% Sunni), 36·0% Christian (mainly Maronite) and 7·4% Druze. In 1996 there were 119 Roman Catholic bishops. In May 2005 there was one cardinal.

CULTURE

World Heritage Sites
There are five sites under Lebanese jurisdiction in the World Heritage List. Four were entered on the list in 1984: the ruins of Anjar, a city founded by the Muslim Arab caliph Walid I at the beginning of the 8th century; Baalbek, the most impressive ancient site in Lebanon and one of the most important Roman ruins in the Middle East; Byblos, the site of multi-layered ruins of one of the most ancient cities of Lebanon, dating back to Neolithic times; and Tyre, which has important archaeological remains, principally from Roman times. The Qadisha Valley and Bcharre district, inscribed in 1998, has been the site of monastic communities since the earliest years of Christianity. Its cedar trees, among the most highly prized building materials of the ancient world, are survivors of a sacred forest.

Broadcasting
The government-controlled Radio Lebanon transmits in Arabic, French, English and Armenian. Télé-Liban, which is government-owned, transmits programmes from 13 stations. Colour is by SECAM H. There were 1·20m. TV sets in 2001 and 2·46m. radio receivers in 2000.

Press
In 2002 there were 13 daily newspapers with a combined circulation of 215,000, at a rate of 60 per 1,000 inhabitants.

Tourism
In 2002 there were 956,000 foreign tourists, spending an estimated US$956m. Lebanon has experienced a tourism boom since the attacks on the USA of 11 Sept. 2001, boosted by large numbers of visitors from Arab Gulf countries wary of travelling to Europe and North America.

Festivals
Major annual cultural events are the Al Bustan Festival of music, dance and theatre in Feb.–March; Baalbek International Festival, which reopened in 1997 after an absence of 23 years; Hamra Festival in June; Beiteddine Festival in July–Aug.; Tyre Festival; Byblos Festival; and the Beirut Film Festival.

DIPLOMATIC REPRESENTATIVES

Of Lebanon in the United Kingdom (15–21 Kensington Palace Gdns, London, W8 4QN)
Ambassador: Jihad Mortada.

Of the United Kingdom in Lebanon (Embassies Complex, Army St., Zkak Al-Blat, Serail Hill, PO Box 11–471, Beirut)
Ambassador: James Watt, CVO.

Of Lebanon in the USA (2560 28th St., NW, Washington, D.C., 20008)
Ambassador: Dr Farid Abboud.

Of the USA in Lebanon (P. O. Box 70–840, Antelias, Beirut)
Ambassador: Jeffrey D. Feltman.

Of Lebanon to the United Nations
Ambassador: Sami Kronfol.

Of Lebanon to the European Union
Ambassador: Fawzi Fawaz.

FURTHER READING

Choueiri, Y. M., *State and Society in Syria and Lebanon.* Exeter Univ. Press, 1994
Fisk, R., *Pity the Nation: Lebanon at War.* 2nd ed. OUP, 1992
Gemayel, A., *Rebuilding Lebanon.* New York, 1992
Hiro, D., *Lebanon Fire and Embers: a History of the Lebanese Civil War.* New York, 1993

National library: Dar el Kutub, Parliament Sq., Beirut.
National Statistical Office: Service de Statistique Générale, Beirut.
Website: http://www.cas.gov.lb

LESOTHO

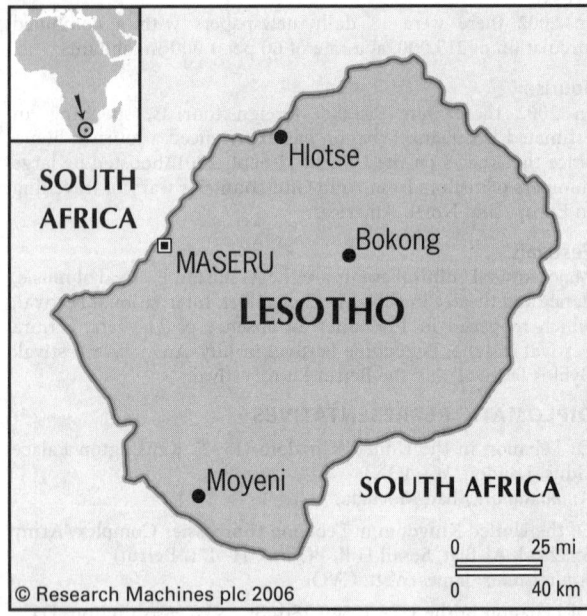

© Research Machines plc 2006

Kingdom of Lesotho

Capital: Maseru
Population projection, 2010: 1·77m.
GDP per capita, 2003: (PPP$) 2,561
HDI/world rank: 0·497/149

KEY HISTORICAL EVENTS

The Basotho nation was constituted in the 19th century under the leadership of Moshoeshoe I, bringing together refugees from disparate tribes scattered by Zulu expansionism in southern Africa. After war with land-hungry Boer settlers in 1856 (and again in 1886), Moshoeshoe appealed for British protection. This was granted in 1868, and in 1871 the territory was annexed to the Cape Colony (now Republic of South Africa), but in 1883 it was restored to the direct control of the British government through the High Commissioner for South Africa. In 1965 full internal self-government was achieved under King Moshoeshoe II. On 4 Oct. 1966 Basutoland became an independent and sovereign member of the British Commonwealth as the Kingdom of Lesotho. Chief Leabua Jonathan, leader of the Basotho National Party and prime minister from 1965, suspended the constitution when the elections of 1970 were declared invalid. On 20 Jan. 1986, after a border blockade by the Republic of South Africa, Chief Jonathan was deposed in a bloodless military coup led by Maj.-Gen. Justin Lekhanya who granted significant powers to the king. King Moeshoeshoe II was deposed in Nov. 1990 and replaced by King Letsie III. Lekhanya was deposed in May 1991. A democratic constitution was promulgated in April 1993. The elections in May 1998 were won by the ruling Lesotho Congress for Democracy. In Sept. 1998 an army mutiny prompted intervention from South Africa to support the government.

TERRITORY AND POPULATION

Lesotho is an enclave within South Africa. The area is 30,355 sq. km (11,720 sq. miles).

The census in 2001 showed a total population of 2,157,580 persons; density, 71·1 per sq. km. In 2003 the population was 82·0% rural. The United Nations population estimate for 2001 was 1,796,000.

The UN gives a projected population for 2010 of 1·77m.

There are ten districts, all named after their chief towns, except Berea (chief town, Teyateyaneng). Area and population:

Region	Area (in sq. km.)	Population (1996 census, in 1,000)	Population (2001 census, in 1,000)
Berea	2,222	240·8	300·6
Butha-Buthe	1,767	109·2	126·9
Leribe	2,828	300·2	362·3
Mafeteng	2,119	212·0	238·9
Maseru	4,279	385·9	477·6
Mohale's Hoek	3,530	184·0	206·8
Mokhotlong	4,075	85·6	89·7
Qacha's Nek	2,349	71·7	80·3
Quthing	2,916	126·3	140·6
Thaba-Tseka	4,270	126·4	133·7

In 1999 the capital, Maseru, had an estimated population of 373,000. Other major towns (with 1996 census population) are: Teyateyaneng, 48,869; Maputsoe, 27,951; Hlotse, 23,122; Mafeteng, 20,804.

The official languages are Sesotho and English.

The population is more than 98% Basotho. The rest is made up of Xhosas, approximately 3,000 expatriate Europeans and several hundred Asians.

SOCIAL STATISTICS

1995 births, 76,000; deaths, 21,000. Rates, 1995: birth (per 1,000 population), 37; death, 10. Annual population growth rate, 1992–2002, 1·1%. Life expectancy at birth in 2003 was 34·6 years for males and 37·7 years for females, largely as a consequence of approximately 31% of all adults being infected with HIV. Only Swaziland has a lower overall life expectancy at birth. Infant mortality, 2001, 91 per 1,000 live births; fertility rate, 2001, 4·5 births per woman.

CLIMATE

A healthy and pleasant climate, with variable rainfall, but averaging 29" (725 mm) a year over most of the country. The rain falls mainly in the summer months of Oct. to April, while the winters are dry and may produce heavy frosts in lowland areas and frequent snow in the highlands. Temperatures in the lowlands range from a maximum of 90°F (32·2°C) in summer to a minimum of 20°F (–6·7°C) in winter.

CONSTITUTION AND GOVERNMENT

Lesotho is a constitutional monarchy with the King as Head of State. Following the death of his father, Moshoeshoe II, **Letsie III** succeeded to the throne in Jan. 1996.

The 1993 constitution provided for a *National Assembly* comprising an elected 80-member lower house and a *Senate* of 22 principal chiefs and 11 members nominated by the King. For the elections of May 2002 a new voting system was introduced, increasing the number of seats in the National Assembly to 120, elected for a five-year term as before, but with 80 members in single-seat constituencies and 40 elected by proportional representation.

National Anthem

'Lesotho fatsela bontat'a rona' ('Lesotho, land of our fathers'); words by F. Coillard, tune by L. Laur.

RECENT ELECTIONS

Following the elections of May 1998 the King swore allegiance to a new constitution and the Military Council was dissolved.

Parliamentary elections were held on 25 May 2002. The ruling Lesotho Congress for Democracy (LCD) won 77 seats with 54·9% of votes cast, the Basotho National Party (BNP) 21 with 22·4%, the Lesotho People's Congress (LPC) 5 with 5·8% and the National Independent Party (NIP) 5 with 5·5%. The remaining seats went to smaller parties with less than 5% of votes cast. Turnout was 68·1%.

CURRENT ADMINISTRATION

In March 2006 the Council of Ministers comprised:

Prime Minister, Minister of Defence and Public Service: Pakalitha Bethuel Mosisili; b. 1945 (LCD; sworn in 29 May 1998).

Deputy Prime Minister and Minister for Home Affairs and Public Safety: Archibald Lesao Lehola. *Minister for Justice, Human Rights and Rehabilitation, and for Law and Constitutional Affairs:* Refiloe Masemene. *Education and Training:* Mohlabi Tsekoa. *Foreign Affairs:* Monyane Moleleki. *Finance and Development Planning:* Timothy Thahane. *Employment and Labour:* Mpeo Mahase-Moiloa. *Local Government:* Dr Ponts'o Suzan 'Matumelo Sekatle. *Gender, Youth and Sports:* Mathabiso Lepono. *Industry, Trade and Marketing:* Mpho Meli Malie. *Health and Social Welfare:* Dr Motloheloa Phooko. *Tourism and Culture:* Lebohang Ntsinyi. *Communications, Science and Technology:* Motsoahae Thomas Thabane. *Natural Resources:* Manphono Khaketla. *Public Works and Transport:* Popane Lebesa. *Agriculture and Food Safety:* Rakoro Phororo. *Forestry and Land Reclamation:* Ralechate Mokose. *Minister in the Prime Minister's Office:* Rammotsi Lehata.

The *College of Chiefs* settles the recognition and succession of Chiefs and adjudicates cases of inefficiency, criminality and absenteeism among them.

Government Website: http://www.lesotho.gov.ls

CURRENT LEADERS

Pakalitha Bethuel Mosisili

Position
Prime Minister

Introduction
Pakalitha Bethuel Mosisili became prime minister in May 1998 after leading Lesotho Congress for Democracy (LCD) to electoral victory. The win was contested by the opposition, resulting in widespread protests and rioting. At the elections of May 2002 Mosisili was confirmed as prime minister despite a parliamentary split led by former deputy Kelebone Maope.

Early Life
Pakalitha Bethuel Mosisili was born on 14 March 1945 in the Qacha's Nek District in Lesotho. He attended the University of Botswana, Lesotho and Swaziland (UBLS) from 1966–70, gaining a BA and a teaching qualification. He studied for an MA at the University of Wisconsin from 1975–76, before claiming a further BA from the University of South Africa (1977–78). In 1982 he gained a masters in education from the Simon Fraser University in Canada.

In 1967, whilst at UBLS, Mosisili joined the Basutoland Congress Party (BCP) and was an active member of its youth league. In 1970 he was detained under emergency regulations and sent to a maximum-security prison for 16 months.

Mosisili's political career began in 1993 when he was elected to parliament representing Qacha's Nek. He was appointed minister of education and training, sports, culture and youth affairs. In Feb. 1995 he became deputy prime minister following the death

of Selometsi Baholo the previous year. He took responsibility for the home affairs and local government portfolios, a role he retained until the 1998 elections. In Feb. 1998 he succeeded Prime Minister Dr Ntsu Mokhele as leader of the LCD.

Career in Office
The victory of the LCD at the elections of May 1998 led to opposition accusations of vote rigging. Mass rioting culminated in protesters seizing the palace grounds. Mosisili called on the Southern African Development Community (SADC) for military assistance to prevent a coup and troops remained in Lesotho until May 1999. In 2001 the government charged 33 protest leaders with treason. The SADC has continued to provide military support and was again called in when, following the LCD's re-election in 2002, the Basotho National Party (BNP) contested the government's legitimacy and stability. In April 2004 the first local elections since independence were held but were boycotted by the opposition in protest at Mosisili's rule.

Mosisili has pledged to tackle Lesotho's severe food shortages, high unemployment rates and rapidly escalating HIV/AIDS problem. Poverty is far reaching, with the UN describing 41% of the population as 'ultra poor', and food output has been affected by deaths of farmers from AIDS and by long periods of severe weather. In Oct. 1998 primary schools received emergency food aid from the UN world food programme. In Feb. 2004 Mosisili declared a state of emergency and requested international food aid, announcing that hundreds of thousands faced shortages following three-years of drought. In March 2004 the first phase of the Lesotho Highlands Water Project was opened, with the long-term aim of supplying water to large areas of southern Africa. During its building, Mosisili called for charges of corruption to be brought against several Western construction companies accused of bribery.

Mosisili aims to tackle unemployment by encouraging foreign investment, emphasising Lesotho's low corporate tax rates and eager work force. Thousands were left unemployed when the textile industry collapsed after the WTO scrapped the global textile quota system in Jan. 2005. Mosisili wants to diversify the economy, focusing on mining and electronics and industrial equipment manufactures.

In 2003, Lesotho hosted an SADC conference on the problem of AIDS in southern Africa. In Lesotho around one in four adults has the virus and Mosisili has campaigned for nationwide testing (himself taking a public test in 2004), the establishment of regional anti-retroviral clinics and a national AIDS commission. In Sept. 2005 he called on the UN to give the same attention to southern Africa's HIV/AIDS plight as to global security.

In April 2005 the government, unable to finance home connections to the national electricity network, decided to privatize the electricity system. The decision followed the government's privatization of its telecoms system in 2000.

DEFENCE

South African and Batswanan troops intervened after a mutiny by Lesotho's armed forces in Sept. 1998. The foreign forces were withdrawn in May 1999.

The Royal Lesotho Defence Force has 2,000 personnel. Defence expenditure totalled US$26m. in 2003 (US$15 per capita), representing 2·3% of GDP.

INTERNATIONAL RELATIONS

Lesotho is a member of the UN, WTO, the Commonwealth, the African Union, African Development Bank, SADC and is an ACP member state of the ACP-EU relationship.

ECONOMY

In 2002 agriculture accounted for 16·3% of GDP, industry 43·1% and services 40·6%.

Overview
The Lesotho National Development Corporation promotes industrial and tourist trade development.

Currency
The unit of currency is the *loti* (plural *maloti*) (LSL) of 100 *lisente*, at par with the South African rand, which is legal tender. Total money supply in June 2002 was 1,471m. maloti. Inflation was 7·6% in 2003 and 5·0% in 2004. Foreign exchange reserves were US$388m. in June 2002.

Budget
Revenues in 2000–01 were 2,752m. maloti and expenditures 2,898m. maloti.

Performance
Real GDP growth was 3·2% in 2003 and 3·0% in 2004. Total GDP in 2004 was US$1·4bn.

Banking and Finance
The Central Bank of Lesotho (*Governor,* Motlatsi Matekane) is the bank of issue, founded in 1982 to succeed the Lesotho Monetary Authority. There are three commercial banks (Lesotho Bank, Nedbank Lesotho, Standard Bank Lesotho) and one development bank (Lesotho Building Finance Corp.). Savings deposits totalled 342·8m. maloti in 1993.

ENERGY AND NATURAL RESOURCES

Environment
Lesotho's carbon dioxide emissions from the consumption and flaring of fossil fuels in 2002 were the equivalent of 0·1 tonnes per capita.

Electricity
Capacity (1993) 13,400 kW (98% supplied by South Africa). Consumption in 1996 was 335m. kWh.

Minerals
Diamonds are the main product; 2000–01 output was 1,140 carats. Sandstone production, 16,000 sq. metres (1996).

Agriculture
Agriculture employs two-thirds of the workforce. The chief crops were (2000 production in 1,000 tonnes): maize, 102; sorghum, 25; wheat, 21; dry beans, 9. Peas and other vegetables are also grown. Soil conservation and the improvement of crops and pasture are matters of vital importance. In 2001 there were 330,000 ha. of arable land and 4,000 ha. of permanent crop land. There were 2,000 tractors in 2001.

Livestock (2000): cattle, 520,000; sheep, 750,000; goats, 580,000; asses, 154,000; horses, 100,000; chickens, 2m.

Forestry
Timber production was 2·03m. cu. metres in 2001.

Fisheries
The catch in 2001 was approximately 24 tonnes, exclusively from inland waters.

INDUSTRY
Important industries are food products, beverages, textiles and chemical products.

Labour
The labour force in 1996 was 847,000 (63% males). In 1998, 76,100 were working in mines in South Africa.

INTERNATIONAL TRADE
Lesotho is a member of the Southern African Customs Union (SACU) with Botswana, Namibia, South Africa and Swaziland. Foreign debt was US$637m. in 2002.

Imports and Exports
In 2002 imports (f.o.b.) were valued at US$736·0m. (US$678·6m. in 2001) and exports (f.o.b.) at US$354·8m. (US$278·6m. in 2001).

Principal exports in 1993 (in 1,000 maloti): machinery and transport equipment, 25,540; wool, 16,853; manufactures, 13,426; cattle, 8,409; mohair, 5,131; canned vegetables, 2,275; wheat flour, 1,717.

The bulk of international trade is with South Africa. In 1998 SACU member countries accounted for 88·7% of imports and 65·5% of exports.

COMMUNICATIONS

Roads
The road network in 2002 totalled 7,091 km, of which 19·8% were paved. In 2002 there were 4,800 passenger cars (2·1 per 1,000 inhabitants) plus 13,000 trucks and vans. In 1999 there were 3,817 traffic accidents with 290 fatalities.

Rail
A branch line built by the South African Railways, one mile long, connects Maseru with the Bloemfontein–Natal line at Marseilles for transport of cargo.

Civil Aviation
There are direct flights from Maseru to Johannesburg. In 2000 Maseru handled 28,613 passengers (28,503 on international flights).

Telecommunications
Lesotho had 126,000 telephone subscribers in 2002, or 58·2 for every 1,000 persons. There were 21,000 Internet users in 2002 and 900 fax machines. Mobile phones have been available since 1996 and in 2002 there were 92,000 subscribers.

Postal Services
In 2003 there were 153 post offices.

SOCIAL INSTITUTIONS

Justice
The legal system is based on Roman-Dutch law. The Lesotho High Court and the Court of Appeal are situated in Maseru, and there are Magistrates' Courts in the districts. 5,888 criminal offences were reported in 1993.

The population in penal institutions in 2002 was 3,000 (143 per 100,000 of national population).

Education
Education levels: pre-school, 3 to 5 years; first level (elementary), 6 to 12; second level (secondary or teacher training or technical training), 7 to 13; third level (university or teacher training college). Lesotho has the highest proportion of female pupils at primary schools in Africa, with 51% in 2000–01. It also has the highest proportion of female pupils in Africa at secondary level education, with 54% in 2000–01, and at tertiary level education, with 63% in 2000–01. In 2002 there were 418,668 pupils in 1,333 primary schools with 8,908 teachers and 81,130 pupils in 224 secondary schools with 3,384 teachers; in 2002 there were 1,739 students in the National Teacher-Training College with 108 teachers and 1,859 students in 8 technical schools with 172 teachers. The National University of Lesotho was established in 1975 at Roma; enrolment in 2001–02, 3,266 students. The adult literacy rate in 2003 was 81·4% (73·7% among males but 90·3% among females). Lesotho has the biggest difference in literacy rates between the sexes in favour of females of any country in the world, and the highest female literacy rate in Africa.

In 1999–2000 total expenditure on education came to 7·9% of GNP and 18·5% of total government spending.

Health

In 1995 there were 105 physicians, 10 dentists, 1,169 nurses and 914 midwives. There were 2,400 hospital beds, equivalent to one bed per 765 persons, in 1992.

RELIGION

In 2001 there were 0·82m. Roman Catholics, 0·28m. Protestants, 0·26m. African Christians and the remainder followed other religions.

CULTURE

Broadcasting

Radio Lesotho transmits daily in English and Sesotho. The broadcasting authority is the Lesotho National Broadcasting Service. In 2000 there were 94,600 radio sets and in 2001 there were 70,000 TV sets (colour by PAL).

Press

There were seven non-daily newspapers and periodicals in 1996. Combined circulation of the two daily papers was 15,000, at a rate of 7·6 per 1,000 inhabitants.

Tourism

In 2002 there were 400,000 foreign tourists; spending by tourists totalled US$29m.

Festivals

The Morija Arts & Cultural Festival is held annually at Morija, where missionaries first arrived in Lesotho in 1833.

DIPLOMATIC REPRESENTATIVES

Of Lesotho in the United Kingdom (7 Chesham Pl., Belgravia, London, SW1 8HN)
High Commissioner: Prince Seeiso Bereng Seeiso.

Of the United Kingdom in Lesotho (PO Box Ms 521, Maseru 100)
High Commissioner: Frank Martin.

Of Lesotho in the USA (2511 Massachusetts Ave., NW, Washington, D.C., 20008)
Ambassador: Molelekeng Ernestina Rapolaki.

Of the USA in Lesotho (254 Kingsway Ave., Maseru 100)
Ambassador: June Carter Perry.

Of Lesotho to the United Nations
Ambassador: Lebohang Fine Maema.

Of Lesotho to the European Union
Ambassador: Moliehi Mathato Adel Matlanyane.

FURTHER READING

Bureau of Statistics. *Statistical Reports.* [Various years]

Haliburton, G. M., *A Historical Dictionary of Lesotho.* Scarecrow Press, Metuchen (NJ), 1977

Johnston, D., *Lesotho.* [Bibliography] 2nd ed. ABC-Clio, Oxford and Santa Barbara (CA), 1996

Machobane, L. B. B. J., *Government and Change in Lesotho, 1880–1966: A Study of Political Institutions.* Macmillan, Basingstoke, 1990

National Statistical Office: Bureau of Statistics, PO Box 455, Maseru.
Website: http://www.bos.gov.ls/

LIBERIA

Republic of Liberia

Capital: Monrovia
Population projection, 2010: 3·80m.
GDP per capita: not available

KEY HISTORICAL EVENTS

The Republic of Liberia was created on the Grain Coast for freed American slaves. In 1822 a settlement was formed near the spot where Monrovia now stands. On 26 July 1847 the State was constituted as the Free and Independent Republic of Liberia.

On 12 April 1980 President Tolbert was assassinated and his government overthrown in a coup led by Master-Sergeant Samuel Doe. At the beginning of 1990 rebel forces entered Liberia from the north and fought their way successfully southwards to confront President Doe's forces in Monrovia. The rebels comprised the National Patriotic Front of Liberia (NPFL) led by Charles Taylor, and the hostile breakaway Independent National Patriotic Front led by Prince Johnson. A peacekeeping force dispatched by the Economic Community of West African States (ECOWAS) disembarked at Monrovia on 25 Aug. 1990. On 9 Sept. President Doe was assassinated by Johnson's rebels. ECOWAS installed a provisional government led by Amos Sawyer. Charles Taylor also declared himself president, as did the former vice-president, Harry Moniba. A succession of ceasefires was negotiated and broken. An ECOWAS-sponsored peace agreement was signed on 17 Aug. 1996 in Abuja, providing for the disarmament of all factions by the end of Jan. 1997 and the election of a president on 31 May 1997. By the end of Jan. 1997 some 20,000 out of approximately 60,000 insurgents had surrendered their arms. It is estimated that up to 200,000 people died in the civil war and up to 1m. were made homeless. Charles Taylor was elected president in July 1997. In Feb. 2002 Taylor declared a state of emergency after an attack by a group of rebels on the town of Kley, where thousands of refugees from Sierra Leone were encamped.

In Aug. 2003 the UN called for the immediate deployment of an ECOWAS peacekeeping force, to be replaced by a full UN force on 1 Oct. Nigerian peacekeepers arrived on 4 Aug. 2003. Taylor relinquished power to his vice-president, Moses Blah, and to a transitional government on 11 Aug. In Nov. 2005 Ellen Johnson-Sirleaf won presidential elections to become Africa's first elected female head of state.

TERRITORY AND POPULATION

Liberia is bounded in the northwest by Sierra Leone, north by Guinea, east by Côte d'Ivoire and southwest by the Atlantic ocean. The total area is 99,065 sq. km. At the last census, in 1984, the population was 2,101,628. Estimate (2005) 3,283,000; density, 33 per sq. km.

The UN gives a projected population for 2010 of 3·80m.

In 2001 an estimated 55% of the population were rural. English is the official language spoken by 20% of the population. The rest belong in the main to three linguistic groups: Mande, West Atlantic and the Kwa. These are in turn subdivided into 16 ethnic groups: Bassa, Bella, Gbandi, Mende, Gio, Dey, Mano, Gola, Kpelle, Kissi, Krahn, Kru, Lorma, Mandingo, Vai and Grebo.

Monrovia, the capital, had (1999) a population of 479,000.

There are 15 counties, whose areas, populations (1999 estimate) and capitals were as follows:

County	Sq. km	1999 population	Chief town
Bomi	1,955	114,316	Tubmanburg
Bong	8,099	299,825	Gbarnga
Gbarpolu[1]	—	—	Bepolu
Grand Bassa	8,759	215,338	Buchanan
Grand Cape Mount	5,827	120,141	Robertsport
Grand Gedeh	17,029	94,497	Zwedru
Grand Kru[2]	—	39,062	Barclayville
Lofa	19,360	351,492	Voinjama
Margibi	3,263	219,417	Kakata
Maryland	5,351	71,977	Harper
Montserrado	2,740	843,783	Bensonville
Nimba	12,043	338,887	Saniquillie
River Gee[1]	—	—	Fish Town
Rivercess	4,385	38,167	Rivercess
Sinoe	10,254	79,241	Greenville

[1]Created since 1999.
[2]Area included in Maryland, of which Grand Kru was formerly a part.

SOCIAL STATISTICS

1997 births, estimate, 110,000; deaths, 30,000. 1997 rates (per 1,000 population), estimate: birth, 42·3; death, 11·5. Annual population growth rate, 1992–2002, 4·3% (the highest of any sovereign country). Life expectancy at birth (2003 estimate): male, 40·0 years; female, 43·0 years. Infant mortality in the period 1990–95 was the highest in the world, at 200 per 1,000 live births, up from 153 per 1,000 live births over the period 1980–85. Fertility rate, 2001, 6·8 births per woman.

CLIMATE

An equatorial climate, with constant high temperatures and plentiful rainfall, although Jan. to May is drier than the rest of the year. Monrovia, Jan. 79°F (26·1°C), July 76°F (24·4°C). Annual rainfall 206" (5,138 mm).

CONSTITUTION AND GOVERNMENT

A Constitution was approved by referendum in July 1984 and came into force on 6 Jan. 1986. Under it the National Assembly consisted of a 26-member Senate and a 64-member House of Representatives. For the elections of Oct. 2005 the number of seats in the Senate was increased to 30.

National Anthem

'All hail, Liberia, hail!'; words by President Daniel Warner, tune by O. Luca.

RECENT ELECTIONS

Presidential and parliamentary elections were held on 11 Oct. 2005. In the presidential elections George Weah of the Congress for Democratic Change (CDC) received 28·3% of the votes cast, ahead of Ellen Johnson-Sirleaf of the Unity Party (UP) with 19·8%, Charles Brumskine of the Liberal Party (LP) with 13·9%, Winston Tubman of the National Democratic Party of Liberia with 9·2% and Varney Sherman of the Coalition for the Transformation of Liberia (COTOL) with 7·8%. There were 17 other candidates. Turnout was 74·9%. As a result a second round run-off was needed, in which Ellen Johnson-Sirleaf received 59·6% of the vote on 8 Nov. 2005 against 40·4% for George Weah. Turnout was 61·0%.

In the elections to the House of Representatives on 11 Oct. 2005 the CDC won 15 of 64 seats, and 3 of 30 Senate seats. The LP won 9 seats (and 3 in the Senate); the UP 8 (3 in the Senate), COTOL 8 (7 in the Senate), the Alliance for Peace and Democracy (APD) 5 (3 in the Senate), and the National Patriotic Party (NPP) 4 (4 in the Senate). Other parties won three seats or fewer in the House of Representatives and two seats or fewer in the Senate.

CURRENT ADMINISTRATION

President: Ellen Johnson-Sirleaf; b. 1938 (Unity Party; sworn in 16 Jan. 2006).

In March 2006 the government comprised:

Vice President: Joseph Boakai.

Minister of Agriculture: Dr Christopher Toe. *Commerce:* Bankie King Akerele. *Defence:* Brownie Samukai. *Education:* Dr Joseph Korto. *Finance:* Dr Antoinette Sayeh. *Foreign Affairs:* George Wallace. *Gender Development:* Varbah Gayflor. *Health and Social Welfare:* Dr Walter Gwenigale. *Information, Culture and Tourism:* Johnny McClain. *Internal Affairs:* Ambullai Johnson. *Justice:* Frances Johnson-Morris. *Labour:* Samuel Kofi Woods. *Land, Mines and Energy:* Dr Eugene Shannon. *National Security:* Fomba Sirleaf. *Planning and Economic Affairs:* Toga McIntosh. *Posts and Telecommunications:* Jackson E. Doe. *Public Works:* Willis Knuckles. *Rural Development:* E. C. B. Jones. *Transport:* Jeremiah Sulunteh. *Youth and Sports:* Jamesetta Howard Wolokollie.

CURRENT LEADERS

Ellen Johnson-Sirleaf

Position
President

Introduction
Ellen Johnson-Sirleaf became Africa's first elected female president in Jan. 2006, having defeated the former footballer, George Weah, in a run-off. A US-educated economist, she returned from exile to attempt to resurrect Liberia's shattered economy after 14 years of civil war.

Early Life
Ellen Johnson-Sirleaf was born in Monrovia, Liberia on 29 Oct. 1938. She was educated at the College of West Africa in Monrovia from 1948–55, before graduating in accountancy in 1964 from the University of Wisconsin in the USA. From 1967 she served as special assistant to the secretary of the treasury before undertaking an MA in public administration at America's Harvard University from 1969–71. Returning to Liberia, Johnson-Sirleaf became assistant minister of finance in the administration of William R. Tolbert, Jr. Following public criticisms of Tolbert's presidency she resigned and left the country, taking up a post as

a loan officer for several Latin American countries at the World Bank. In 1977 she was invited to return home to become deputy minister of finance for fiscal and banking affairs. In Aug. 1979 she replaced James T. Philips as minister of finance.

Shortly after a coup d'etat and Tolbert's assassination on 12 April 1980, the new military leader, Sgt Samuel Doe, appointed Johnson-Sirleaf president of the Liberia Bank for Development and Investment. However, she resigned in Dec. 1980 and returned to the World Bank, before becoming vice president of Citibank in Nairobi, Kenya in mid-1981. She stood in Liberia's general elections in Oct. 1985, at which Doe was controversially elected president. Johnson-Sirleaf was elected senator but was sentenced to ten years in jail as part of Doe's crackdown on 'opponents' following a failed coup in Nov. 1985. Pardoned and released in June 1986, Johnson-Sirleaf again left Liberia for the USA, where she worked for the Equator Bank in Washington, D.C., followed by the UN development programme in New York.

While in the USA Johnson-Sirleaf joined other Liberian exiles in criticizing Doe and helped raise funds for a fellow exile, Charles Taylor, to lead the National Patriotic Front of Liberia (NPFL) into Liberia from the Côte d'Ivoire in late 1989. It triggered a devastating civil war that led to the deaths of over 200,000 people by the time a ceasefire was declared in Aug. 1996. Disillusioned with Taylor, Johnson-Sirleaf resigned as director of the UNDP's Bureau for Africa (a post she held from July 1992) and stood against him on behalf of the Unity Party in presidential elections in 1997. She received only 10% of the vote (against 75% for Taylor) and was later charged with treason by him. Forced into exile again, she became active in various humanitarian projects, including investigations into the 1994 Rwandan genocide for the Organization for African Unity and serving on the board of the International Crisis Group and the Nelson Mandela Foundation. Liberia again descended into civil war but Johnson-Sirleaf returned after Taylor was forced into exile in Aug. 2003. She headed the governance reform commission until resigning in March 2005 to enter the presidential race.

During her campaign, Johnson-Sirleaf criticized the transitional government's inability to fight corruption. She went through to a run-off against George Weah, a former World Footballer of the Year who was representing the Congress for Democratic Change, and on 11 Nov. the national elections commission declared Johnson-Sirleaf the winner. Although Weah accused her of fraud, her victory was confirmed on 23 Nov. Independent observers declared the vote to be free, fair and transparent and her inauguration took place on 16 Jan. 2006.

Career in Office
In her inaugural speech, Johnson-Sirleaf vowed to wage a war on corruption, promising that leading civil servants and ministers would have to declare their assets. She also pledged to work towards reconciliation by bringing former opponents into a government of national unity, and spoke of establishing peaceful relations with neighbouring West African states. She appointed a number of women to ministerial positions and controversially nominated a Nigerian soldier to head Liberia's army. Rebuilding the country's economy—the road network is in ruins, there is no national telephone network, no national electricity grid and no piped water—represents a major challenge but already a US$900m. deal appears to have been reached with Mittal Steel International to mine Liberia's substantial iron ore reserves.

DEFENCE

In June 2003 UN Secretary-General Kofi Annan called for an international peacekeeping force to restore peace after fighting broke out between government forces and Liberians United for Reconciliation and Democracy (LURD). An ECOWAS peacekeeping force of over 3,000 troops was deployed initially, but this has been replaced by the UN Peacekeeping Mission in

Liberia (UNIMIL), which with 15,000 troops in early 2005 is one of the world's largest UN peacekeeping forces.

Defence expenditure totalled US$45m. in 2003 (US$13 per capita), representing 11·4% of GDP.

INTERNATIONAL RELATIONS

Liberia is a member of the UN, the African Union, African Development Bank, ECOWAS, IOM and is an ACP member state of the ACP-EU relationship.

ECONOMY

Agriculture accounts for approximately 77% of GDP (the highest proportion of any country), industry 5% and services 18%.

Currency

US currency is legal tender. There is a *Liberian dollar* (LRD), in theory at parity with the US dollar. Between 1993 and March 2000 different notes were in use in government-held Monrovia and the rebel-held country areas, but on 27 March 2000 a set of new notes went into circulation to end the years of trading in dual banknotes. Inflation was an estimated 11% in 1998. Total money supply was L$1,859m. in May 2002.

Budget

Revenue in 2002 was US$72·7m.; expenditure was US$80·1m.

Performance

The economy is estimated to have contracted by 4% in 1998, but there followed a recovery, with growth in 1999 estimated at 15%. In 2004 total GDP was US$0·4bn.

Banking and Finance

The National Bank of Liberia opened on 22 July 1974 to act as a central bank. The *Governor* of the bank is Elias Saleeby. There were only three banks in operation in Jan. 2004. The banking sector has been badly affected by long-running civil strife.

ENERGY AND NATURAL RESOURCES

Environment

Liberia's carbon dioxide emissions from the consumption and flaring of fossil fuels were the equivalent of 0·1 tonnes per capita in 2002.

Electricity

Installed capacity in 2000 was 0·3m. kW. Production in 2000 was about 524m. kWh. Consumption per capita in 2000 was an estimated 180 kWh.

Minerals

2001 estimates: gold production 1,000 kg and diamond production 170,000 carats.

Agriculture

In 2002, 67% of the economically active population were engaged in agriculture. There were 380,000 ha. of arable land in 2001 and 220,000 ha. of permanent crops. Principal crops (2000) in 1,000 tonnes: cassava, 380; sugarcane, 250; rice, 200; bananas, 95; palm oil, 42. Livestock (2000): cattle, 36,000; pigs, 120,000; sheep, 210,000; goats, 220,000; chickens, 4m.

Forestry

Forest area was 3·48m. ha. (31·3% of the land area) in 2000. In 2001, 5·26m. cu. metres of roundwood were cut. There are rubber plantations.

Fisheries

Fish landings in 2001 were 11,286 tonnes, of which approximately 65% from sea fishing.

INDUSTRY

There are a number of small factories. Production of cement, cigarettes, soft drinks, palm oil and beer are the main industries.

Labour

In 1996 the labour force was 977,000 (61% males).

INTERNATIONAL TRADE

Foreign debt was US$2,324m. in 2002.

Imports and Exports

Imports in 2001 were US$180·9m. and exports US$127·4m. Main import sources in 1999 were South Korea, 27·4%; Japan, 24·8%; Germany, 14·1%; Singapore, 7·1%. Major export destinations in 2001 were Norway, 23·8%; Germany, 10·5%; France, 7·5%; Singapore, 6·5%.

Main imports are food and live animals, petroleum and petroleum products, and machinery and transport equipment. Main exports are rubber, and logs and timber.

COMMUNICATIONS

Roads

There were about 10,600 km of roads in 2002 (only 6·2% of which were paved). In 2002 there were 19,100 passenger cars and 12,500 goods vehicles.

Rail

There is a total of 490 km single track. A 148-km freight line connects iron mines to Monrovia. There is a line from Bong to Monrovia (78 km). All railways have been out of use since 1997 because of the civil war. Large sections have been dismantled.

Civil Aviation

There are two international airports (Roberts International and Sprigg Payne), both near Monrovia. In 2003 there were services to Abidjan, Accra, Brussels, Freetown and Lagos.

Shipping

There are ports at Buchanan, Greenville, Harper and Monrovia. Over 2,000 vessels enter Monrovia each year. The Liberian government requires only a modest registration fee and an almost nominal annual charge and maintains no control over the operation of ships flying the Liberian flag. In 2002 shipping registered totalled 50·40m. GRT (second only to Panama), including oil tankers 18·64m. GRT. In 2000 the fleet consisted of 1,557 vessels of 100 GRT or over, including 585 tankers.

Telecommunications

Telephone main lines numbered 6,700 in 2000, or 2·1 per 1,000 persons. In July 2000 there were 300 Internet users.

Postal Services

In 2000 there were 13 post offices.

SOCIAL INSTITUTIONS

Education

Schools are classified as: (1) Public schools, maintained and run by the government; (2) Mission schools, supported by foreign Missions and subsidized by the government, and operated by qualified Missionaries and Liberian teachers; (3) Private schools, maintained by endowments and sometimes subsidized by the government. Adult literacy in 1995 was 38·3%; 53·9% among males, 22·4% among females.

Health

In 1997 there were 53 physicians (one for every 43,434 inhabitants), two dentists, 136 nurses and 99 midwives. There were 92 hospitals in 1988 (latest data available).

RELIGION

There were (2001) about 1·27m. Christians and 520,000 Sunni Muslims, plus 1·39m. followers of traditional beliefs.

CULTURE

Broadcasting
In 2000 there were 863,000 radio and 78,700 television receivers (colour by PAL).

Press
There were six daily newspapers in 1998 with a combined circulation of 36,600.

DIPLOMATIC REPRESENTATIVES

Of Liberia in the United Kingdom (23 Fitzroy Sq., London, W1 6EW)
Ambassador: Vacant.
Chargé d'Affaires a.i.: Genevieve A. Kennedy.

Of the United Kingdom in Liberia
Ambassador: Dr John Mitchiner (resides in Freetown, Sierra Leone).

Of Liberia in the USA (5201 16th St., NW, Washington, D.C., 20011)
Ambassador: Charles A. Minor.

Of the USA in Liberia (111 United Nations Drive, Mamba Point, Monrovia)
Ambassador: Donald E. Booth.

Of Liberia to the United Nations
Ambassador: Lami Kawah.

Of Liberia to the European Union
Ambassador: Vacant.
Chargé d'Affaires a.i.: Youngor Telewoda.

FURTHER READING

Daniels, A., *Monrovia Mon Amour: a Visit to Liberia.* London, 1992
Elwood Dunn, D., *Liberia.* [Bibliography] ABC-Clio, Oxford and Santa Barbara (CA), 1995
Sawyer, A., *The Emergence of Autocracy in Liberia: Tragedy and Challenge.* San Francisco, 1992

LIBYA

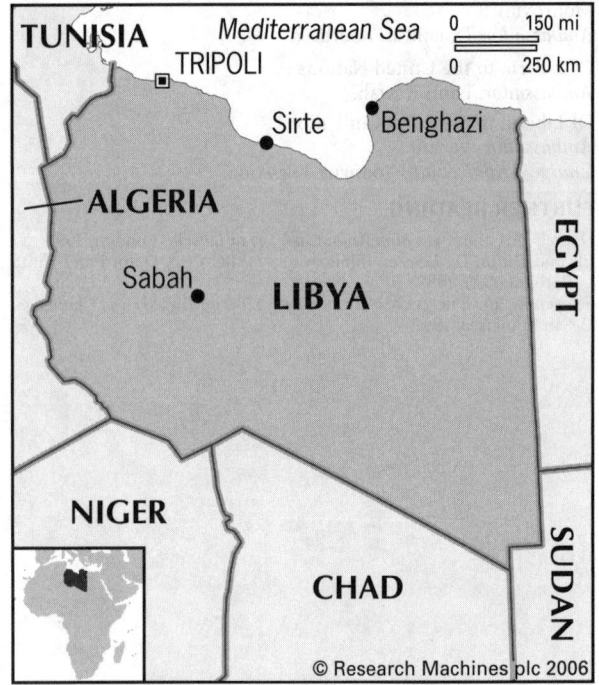

Jamahiriya Al-Arabiya Al-Libiya Al-Shabiya
Al-Ishtirakiya Al-Uzma
(Great Socialist People's Libyan Arab Republic)

Capital: Tripoli
Population projection, 2010: 6·44m.
GDP per capita: not available
GNI per capita: $4,450
HDI/world rank: 0·799/58

KEY HISTORICAL EVENTS

Tripoli fell under Ottoman domination in the 16th century and although in 1711 the Arab population secured some measure of independence, the country came under the direct rule of Turkey in 1835. In 1911 Italy occupied Tripoli and in 1912, by the Treaty of Ouchy, Turkey recognized the sovereignty of Italy in Tripoli. During the Second World War, the British army expelled the Italians and their German allies, and Tripolitania and Cyrenaica were placed under British, and Fezzan under French, military administration. This continued until 1950 under a UN directive. Libya became an independent, sovereign kingdom with the former Amir of Cyrenaica, Muhammad Idris al Senussi, as king on 24 Dec. 1951. King Idris was deposed in Sept. 1969 by a group of army officers, 12 of whom formed the Revolutionary Command Council which, chaired by Col. Muammar Qadhafi, proclaimed the Libyan Arab Republic. In 1977 the Revolutionary Command Council was superseded by a more democratic People's Congress. Qadhafi remained head of state. Throughout the 1980s Libya had constant disagreements with its neighbours and its relations with the USA and other Western countries deteriorated, culminating in the US bombing of the capital in April 1986 to punish Qadhafi for his alleged support of international terrorism. A US trade embargo was enforced in 1986. In 1992 the UN imposed sanctions after

Libya refused to surrender suspects in the 1988 bombing of a Pan Am flight over Lockerbie in Scotland. In April 1999 Libya handed over the two suspects to be tried in the Netherlands but under Scottish law. In Jan. 2001 Abdelbaset Ali Mohmed al Megrahi was sentenced to life imprisonment after being found guilty of murder. The UN had suspended sanctions in 1999, but only formally lifted them in Sept. 2003. In April 2004 the USA eased economic sanctions after Col. Qadhafi pledged to end his weapons of mass destruction programme. Sanctions were formally lifted in Sept. 2004.

TERRITORY AND POPULATION

Libya is bounded in the north by the Mediterranean Sea, east by Egypt and Sudan, south by Chad and Niger and west by Algeria and Tunisia. The area is 1,759,540 sq. km. The estimated population at the 2003 census was 5,678,500; density, 3·2 per sq. km. In 2003, 86·2% of the population lived in urban areas. Ethnic composition, 2000: Libyan Arab and Berber, 64%; other (mainly Egyptians, Sudanese and Chadians), 36%.

The UN gives a projected population for 2010 of 6·44m.

The country was formerly divided into 13 administrative regions, but following reforms in 1998 there are now 26 administrative regions (*Shabiyat*). They are Shabiya Al-Batan, Shabiya Jabal Al-Akhdar, Shabiya Al-Wahad, Shabiya Al-Jofra, Shabiya Wadi Al-Hait, Shabiya Al-Morqib, Shabiya Tripoli, Shabiya Sabrata/Sorman, Shabiya Yefrin, Shabiya Derna, Shabiya Al-Marj, Shabiya Al-Kofra, Shabiya Murzaq, Shabiya Wadi Al-Shaati, Shabiya Ben Walid, Shabiya Al-Jafarah, Shabiya Nikat Al-Khams, Shabiya Nalout, Shabiya Al-Qoba, Shabiya Benghazi, Shabiya Sirte, Shabiya Sabah, Shabiya Musrata, Shabiya Tarhouna/Msallata, Shabiya Zawiyah and Shabiya Gharyan.

The two largest cities are Tripoli, the capital (population of 1,773,000 in 1999), and Benghazi (804,000 in 1995).

The official language is Arabic.

SOCIAL STATISTICS

Estimates, 2001: births, 99,000; deaths, 18,000. Estimated rates, 2001 (per 1,000 population): births, 18·6; deaths, 3·4. Life expectancy (2003), 71·6 years for men and 76·2 for women. Annual population growth rate, 1992–2002, 2·0%; infant mortality, 2001, 16 per 1,000 live births; fertility rate, 2001, 3·5 births per woman.

CLIMATE

The coastal region has a warm temperate climate, with mild wet winters and hot dry summers, although most of the country suffers from aridity. Tripoli, Jan. 52°F (11·1°C), July 81°F (27·2°C). Annual rainfall 16" (400 mm). Benghazi, Jan. 56°F (13·3°C), July 77°F (25°C). Annual rainfall 11" (267 mm).

CONSTITUTION AND GOVERNMENT

The present constitution came into force on 11 Dec. 1969. In 1977 a new form of direct democracy, the state of the masses, was promulgated and the name of the country was changed to Great Socialist People's Libyan Arab Jamahiriya. Under this system, every adult is supposed to be able to share in policy making through the Basic People's Congresses of which there are some 2,000. These Congresses appoint People's Committees to execute policy. Provincial and urban affairs are handled by People's Committees responsible to Municipality People's Congresses, of which there are 26, now called *Shabiyat*. Officials of these Congresses and Committees form at national level the 3,000-member General People's Congress which normally meets for about a week early each year (usually in March). This is the highest policy-making body in the country. The General People's Congress appoints its own General Secretariat and the General People's Committee, whose members (the equivalents of ministers elsewhere) head the government departments which execute policy at national level.

Until 1977 Libya was ruled by a Revolutionary Command Council (RCC) headed by Col. Muammar Qadhafi. Upon its abolition in that year the five surviving members of the RCC became the General Secretariat of the General People's Congress, still under Qadhafi's direction. In 1979 they stood down to be replaced by officials elected by the Congress. Since then, Col. Qadhafi has retained his position as Leader of the Revolution. Neither he nor his former RCC colleagues have any formal posts in the present administration, although they continue to wield considerable authority.

National Anthem

'Allah Akbar' ('God is Great'); words by Abdullah Al-Din, tune by Mahmoud Al-Sharif.

GOVERNMENT CHRONOLOGY

Leaders since 1951.

1951–69	(King) Muhammad Idris I al Senussi
1969–	Col. Muammar Abu Minyar al-Qadhafi (Chairman of the Revolutionary Command Council until 1977; General Secretary of the General People's Congress until 1979; *de facto* leader since 1979)

CURRENT ADMINISTRATION

Leader: Col. Muammar Abu Minyar al-Qadhafi; b. 1942 (came to power 1 Sept. 1969).

In March 2006 the Secretariat for the General People's Congress was headed by:

Secretary: Al-Zanati Muhammad Al-Zanati. *Assistant Secretary:* Ahmed Mohammed Ibrahim.

In March 2006 the General People's Committee comprised:

Secretary: Al-Baghdadi Al-Mahmoudi. *Deputy Secretary:* Mohammad Houij. *Foreign Liaison and International Co-operation:* Abdul Rahman Mohammed Shalgam. *Industry and Electricity:* Fethi Omar bin Chetwane. *Employment:* Ma'tuq Mohammed Ma'tuq. *Planning:* Dr Taher Al-Hadi Al-Jehaimi. *Tourism:* Umar Al-Mabruk Al-Tayyif. *Higher Education:* Abdussalam Abdallah. *Justice:* Ali Al-Hasnaoui. *National Security:* Rajab Al-Mismari. *Finance:* Ahmad Mounsi. *Economy and Trade:* Tayyib Al-Safi. *Youth:* Moustafa Al-Darsi. *Culture:* Nouri Al-Hamid. *Social Affairs:* Bakhita Al-Chalaoui. *Health:* Mohammed Rachid. *Higher Education:* Ibrahim Cherif. *Agriculture:* Abou Bakr Mansouri. *Transport:* Ali Zakri. *Education:* Abdelkader Baghdadi. *Housing:* Abou Zaid Dourda.

CURRENT LEADERS

Col. Muammar Abu Minyar al-Qadhafi

Position

Leader of the Revolution

Introduction

Muammar Qadhafi took power in a military coup against the monarchy in 1969, espousing radical Arab nationalism and Islamic socialist policies. His revolutionary fervour has frequently brought him into conflict with the Western powers, which have held him responsible for acts of international terrorism. There have been improvements in diplomatic and business relations since 2003 as Qadhafi settled the Lockerbie bombing claims and agreed to stop developing weapons of mass destruction.

Early Life

Born into a Bedouin family near Sirte in June 1942, Qadhafi's education was strongly religious and he remains a devout and austere Muslim. He was also influenced in his early life by the Arab nationalist ideology of President Nasser and the Egyptian revolution. In 1965 Qadhafi graduated from the Royal Libyan Military Academy in Benghazi. As he and other officers of like mind rose through the ranks, their radicalism was fuelled by the humiliating defeat of Arab forces by Israel in the Six Day War of 1967. Qadhafi and others in a Revolutionary Command Council (RCC) deposed King Idris on 1 Sept. 1969 in a bloodless coup.

Career in Office

The RCC, with Qadhafi as chairman, instigated a programme of revolutionary reform. British and US military bases in Libya were closed in 1970, foreign-owned oil companies were nationalized and extended welfare provision was funded from oil export revenues. Assuming increasingly dictatorial powers, Qadhafi pursued wider Arab unity, initiating a series of unsuccessful schemes for merging Libya with other Arab countries (including Egypt, Syria, Tunisia, Chad, Morocco and Algeria), while maintaining implacable opposition to Israel. His Islamic socialist ideology was published in *The Green Book*, and in 1977 he promulgated a new constitution. This established the Great Socialist People's Libyan Arab Jamahiriya, which vested power in the masses through the General People's Congress (GPC). In 1979 Qadhafi relinquished his formal posts in the administration but remained Libya's undisputed leader.

With a reputation in international circles for erratic and unpredictable moves, Qadhafi mobilized Libya's oil wealth in support of revolutionary and terrorist groups around the world, and intervening militarily in neighbouring states, particularly Chad. Accusing Qadhafi of sponsoring terrorism, the USA and UK bombed Tripoli and Benghazi in April 1986 in a reprisal air operation. In 1992 United Nations sanctions were imposed on Libya to force the extradition of two Libyan nationals implicated in an aircraft bombing atrocity over Lockerbie in Scotland in Dec. 1988. Qadhafi eventually relented and in 1999 surrendered the two principal suspects for trial in the Netherlands. One of the accused was convicted in 2001 and his subsequent appeal rejected in early 2002.

In Jan. 2003 there was international concern when Libya was nominated to host the annual meeting of the UN Commission on Human Rights. The USA demanded a vote, making Libya the first host country to be approved by vote since the commission was founded in 1947. The ballot by commission members resulted in 33 favourable votes to three, with 17 abstentions.

Also in 2003 Libya signed an agreement to compensate families of the Lockerbie bombing victims. Once the Libyan leader formally took responsibility for the atrocity, the UN Security Council voted to lift sanctions. In March 2004 the UK prime minister Tony Blair met with Qadhafi following the latter's promise to abandon programmes to develop weapons of mass destruction and to allow weapons inspectors into Libya. Diplomatic relations were formally resumed with the USA in June 2004.

Despite an assassination attempt in 1993, Qadhafi remains leader of Libya with no obvious rivals.

DEFENCE

There is selective conscription for one–two years. Defence expenditure in 2003 totalled US$742m. (US$133 per capita), representing 4·2% of GDP.

Nuclear Weapons

In Dec. 2003 Col. Muammar Qadhafi agreed to dismantle his weapons of mass destruction programmes. He also agreed unconditionally to allow inspectors from international organizations to enter Libya.

Army
Strength (2002) 45,000 (25,000 conscripts). In addition there is a People's Militia of 40,000 which acts as a reserve force.

Navy
The fleet, a mixture of Soviet and West European-built ships, includes one diesel submarine, one frigate and one corvette. There is a small Naval Aviation wing operating seven armed helicopters.

Personnel in 2002 totalled 8,000, including coastguard. The main naval bases are at Tripoli, Benghazi, Derna, Tobruk and Al Khums.

Air Force
The Air Force has over 400 combat aircraft, including MiG-21s, MiG-23s, MiG-25s and Mirage 5Ds, but many are in storage. Personnel total (2002) about 23,000.

INTERNATIONAL RELATIONS
Libya is a member of the UN, the African Union, OPEC, Arab Maghreb Union, African Development Bank, OIC, IOM, Islamic Development Bank and COMESA (the Common Market for Eastern and Southern Africa). Libya has declared its desire to join the WTO.

ECONOMY
Agriculture accounted for an estimated 5·3% of GDP in 2002, industry 64·0% and services 30·6%.

Overview
Libya's economy has struggled to achieve solid growth. The economy is based on the production of hydrocarbons, which account for the majority of the government's revenues and the country's export earnings. Oil accounts for roughly a quarter of the country's GDP though the benefits have not been evenly distributed. During the first half of the 2000s the economy posted its most solid growth performance in recent history. In 2003 UN sanctions were lifted after Libya admitted to complicity in the 1988 Lockerbie aircraft bombing and in 2004 the USA lifted almost all its unilateral sanctions after Libya agreed to give up its nuclear weapons programmes. Libya's improved international standing has allowed investment to flow back into the oil sector.

In Nov. 2003 the government announced a liberalization programme incorporating a three-part privatization scheme (including the mineral and chemical industries), scheduled for completion in 2008. Some subsidies have been reduced and the economy's non-oil sectors have expanded but progress is expected to be hampered by excessive bureaucracy and vested interests, except in the oil sector where foreign investment is a high priority. Libya had proven oil reserves of roughly 40bn. bbls. in 2005 but oil companies are convinced that there is more to discover.

Currency
The unit of currency is the *Libyan dinar* (LYD) of 1,000 *millemes*. The dinar was devalued 15% in Nov. 1994, and alongside the official exchange rate a new rate was applied to private sector imports. Foreign exchange reserves were US$13,146m. in June 2002 and total money supply was 7,249m. dinars. Inflation was negative in 2001 (at −8·8%), in 2002 (−9·9%), in 2003 (−2·1%) and again in 2004 (−1·0%).

Budget
In 2001 revenues totalled 5,999m. dinars and expenditures 5,626m. dinars. Oil accounts for 60% of government revenues.

Performance
GDP growth was 9·1% in 2003 and 4·4% in 2004. Total GDP in 2004 was US$29·1bn.

Banking and Finance
A National Bank of Libya was established in 1955; it was renamed the Central Bank of Libya in 1972. The *Governor* is Dr Ahmed M. Menesi. All foreign banks were nationalized by Dec. 1970. In 1972 the government set up the Libyan Arab Foreign Bank whose function is overseas investment and to participate in multinational banking corporations. The National Agricultural Bank has been set up to give loans and subsidies to farmers to develop their land and to assist them in marketing their crops. There are six other banks.

Weights and Measures
Although the metric system has been officially adopted and is obligatory for all contracts, the following weights and measures are still used: *oke* = 1·282 kg; *kantar* = 51·28 kg; *draa* = 46 cm; *handaza* = 68 cm.

ENERGY AND NATURAL RESOURCES
Environment
Libya's carbon dioxide emissions from the consumption and flaring of fossil fuels in 2002 were the equivalent of 8·7 tonnes per capita.

Electricity
Installed capacity in 2000 was 4·6m. kW. Production was about 20·04bn. kWh in 2000 and consumption per capita an estimated 3,789 kWh.

Oil and Gas
Oil accounts for 30% of Libya's GDP. Crude oil production in 2003 totalled 70·0m. tonnes. Reserves (2003) 236·0bn. bbls. Some analysts believe reserves may be as high as 100bn. bbls. The National Oil Corporation (NOC) is the state's organization for the exploitation of oil resources. Libya's first oilfields were discovered in 1959, but the offshore sector remains relatively unexplored although the decision to abandon programmes for developing weapons of mass destruction in 2003 led to greatly increased interest among foreign oil companies. Oil export revenues more than doubled between 1998 and 2003. Production is expected to increase by nearly a third by 2009.

Proven natural gas reserves totalled 1,310bn. cu. metres in 2002. Agip, the Italian oil company, is investing US$3bn. in a project to export natural gas to Europe. Production (2002) 5·7bn. cu. metres.

Water
Since 1984 a US$20bn. project has been under way to bring water from aquifers underlying the Sahara to the inhabited coastal areas of Libya. This scheme, called the 'Great Man-Made River', is intended, on completion, to bring 6,000 cu. metres of water a day along some 4,000 km of pipes. Phase I was completed in Aug. 1991; Phase II of the project (covering the west of Libya) was announced in Sept. 1989. The river is providing Libya's main centres of population with clean water as well as making possible the improvement and expansion of agriculture. The whole project is more than three-quarters complete.

Minerals
Iron ore deposits have been found in the south.

Agriculture
Only the coastal zone, which covers an area of about 17,000 sq. miles, is really suitable for agriculture. Of some 25m. acres of productive land, nearly 20m. are used for grazing and about 1m. for static farming. Agriculture employs around 17% of the workforce. The sub-desert zone produces the alfalfa plant. The desert zone and the Fezzan contain some fertile oases. In 2001 there were 1·82m. ha. of arable land and 0·34m. ha. of permanent crops. 470,000 ha. were irrigated in 2001. There were 34,000 tractors in 2001 and 3,410 harvester-threshers.

Cyrenaica has about 10m. acres of potentially productive land and is suitable for grazing. Certain areas are suitable for dry farming; in addition, grapes, olives and dates are grown. About 143,000 acres are used for settled farming; about 272,000 acres are covered by natural forests. The Agricultural Development Authority plans to reclaim 6,000 ha. each year for agriculture. In the Fezzan there are about 6,700 acres of irrigated gardens and about 297,000 acres are planted with date palms.

Production (2000, in 1,000 tonnes): tomatoes, 250; watermelons, 215; potatoes, 210; olives, 190; onions, 180; wheat, 160; dates, 133; barley, 70; oranges, 43.

Livestock (2000): 5·1m. sheep, 1·9m. goats, 143,000 cattle, 71,000 camels, 25m. chickens.

Forestry

Forest area in 2000 was 358,000 ha. (0·2% of the land area). In 2001, 652,000 cu. metres of roundwood were cut.

Fisheries

The catch in 2001 was approximately 33,239 tonnes, entirely from marine waters.

INDUSTRY

Industry employs nearly 30% of the workforce. Small scale private sector industrialization in the form of partnerships is permitted. Output (2000, in 1,000 tonnes): distillate fuel oil, 4,662; residual fuel oil, 4,330; cement (1997), 2,524; petrol, 2,030.

Labour

The labour force in 1996 was 1,601,000 (79% males).

INTERNATIONAL TRADE

In 1986 the USA applied a trade embargo on the grounds of Libya's alleged complicity in terrorism. Many of the economic sanctions were lifted in April 2004, although Libya remains on Washington's list of state sponsors of terror, as a result of which arms exports are still banned. In 1992 UN sanctions were imposed for Libya's refusal to deliver suspected terrorists for trial in the UK or USA, but these were formally lifted in 2003. In Feb. 1989 Libya signed a treaty of economic co-operation with the four other Maghreb countries: Algeria, Mauritania, Morocco and Tunisia.

Imports and Exports

In 2000 imports were valued at US$7·6bn. and exports at US$13·9bn. Some 80% of GDP derives from trade. Oil accounts for over 95% of exports, worth US$13·4bn. in 2003. Main import suppliers in 2000 were Italy (24%), Germany (12%), Tunisia (9%) and UK (7%); main export markets were Italy (33%), Germany (24%), Spain (10%) and France (5%).

COMMUNICATIONS

Roads

There were 100,024 km of roads in 2002 (57·2% paved). Passenger cars numbered 375,600 in 2002 (64·0 per 1,000 inhabitants), in addition to which there were 350,000 trucks and vans. There were 1,080 deaths as a result of road accidents in 1996.

Civil Aviation

The UN ban on air traffic to and from Libya enforced since April 1992 was lifted in April 1999 following the handing over for trial of two suspected Lockerbie bombers. Libyan Arab Airlines provides both international and domestic services. In 1999 scheduled airline traffic of Libya-based carriers flew 3·8m. km, carrying 571,000 passengers.

Shipping

Sea-going vessels totalled 165,000 GRT in 2002, including oil tankers 7,000 GRT.

Telecommunications

In 2001 telephone subscribers numbered 710,000 (127·2 per 1,000 population). The national operator is the state-run General Posts and Telecommunications Company (GPTC). In 2002 there were 70,000 mobile phone subscribers and 130,000 PCs in use. There are two mobile phone companies, Al-Madar and Libyana, both of which are state-owned. Internet users numbered 125,000 in 2002.

Postal Services

In 2003 there were 351 post offices, or one for every 15,800 persons.

SOCIAL INSTITUTIONS

Justice

The Civil, Commercial and Criminal codes are based mainly on the Egyptian model. Matters of personal status of family or succession matters affecting Muslims are dealt with in special courts according to the Muslim law. All other matters, civil, commercial and criminal, are tried in the ordinary courts, which have jurisdiction over everyone.

There are civil and penal courts in Tripoli and Benghazi, with subsidiary courts at Misurata and Derna; courts of assize in Tripoli and Benghazi, and courts of appeal also in Tripoli and Benghazi.

The population in penal institutions in July 2004 was 11,790 (207 per 100,000 of national population). There were 15 confirmed executions in 2005.

Education

In 2001–02 there were 750,204 primary school pupils and 824,538 secondary level pupils. In 1994–95 there were three universities, one medical and one technological university. There were three other institutes of higher education. In 2001–02 there were 359,146 tertiary level students. Adult literacy in 2002 was 81·7% (male, 91·8%; female, 70·7%).

Health

There were 6,092 physicians in 1997 and 619 dentists, 17,136 nurses and 1,095 pharmacists in 1996. Provision of hospital beds in 1991 was 41 per 10,000 population.

RELIGION

Islam is declared the State religion, but the right of others to practise their religion is provided for. In 2001, 92% were Sunni Muslims.

CULTURE

World Heritage Sites

Libya has five sites on the UNESCO World Heritage List: the Archaeological Site of Leptis Magna (inscribed on the list in 1982); the Archaeological Site of Sabrata (1982); the Archaeological Site of Cyrene (1982); the Rock-art Sites of Tadrart Acacus (1985); and the Old Town of Ghadames (1988).

Broadcasting

Broadcasting is controlled by the government Libyan Jamihiriya Broadcasting and People's Revolution Broadcasting-Television. Radio has a home service, external services in English, French and Arabic and a Holy Koran programme. In 2000 there were 1·43m. radio and 717,000 TV receivers (colour by SECAM H).

Press

In 1998 there were four daily newspapers with a combined circulation of 71,100.

Tourism

In 2000 there were 174,000 foreign tourists; spending by tourists totalled US$35m.

DIPLOMATIC REPRESENTATIVES

Of Libya in the United Kingdom (61–62 Ennismore Gdns, London, SW7 1NH)
Ambassador: Mohammed Abdul Qasim Al-Zwai.

Of the United Kingdom in Libya (PO Box 4206, Tripoli)
Ambassador: Anthony Layden.

The USA has established a Liaison Office in Libya (Corinthia Bab Africa Hotel, Souk al-Thulatha, Al-Gadim, Tripoli)
Principal Officer: Gregory Berry.

Libya has established a Liaison Office in the USA (2600 Virginia Ave., NW, Suite 705, Washington, D.C., 20037)
Chief of Mission: Ali Aujali.

Of Libya to the United Nations
Ambassador: Ali Abd al-Salam al-Turayki.

Of Libya to the European Union
Ambassador: Hamed Ahmed Elhouderi.

FURTHER READING

Blundy, D. and Lycett, A., *Qadhafi and the Libyan Revolution*. London, 1987
Davis, J., *Libyan Politics: Tribe and Revolution*. London, 1988
Harris, L. C., *Libya: Qadhafi's Revolution and the Modern State*. Boulder (CO) and London, 1986
Pazzanita, A. G., *The Maghreb*. [Bibliography] ABC-Clio, Oxford and Santa Barbara (CA), 1998
Simons, G., *Libya: the Struggle for Survival*. London, 1993
Vandewalle, D. (ed.) *Qadhafi's Libya, 1969–1994*. London, 1995

LIECHTENSTEIN

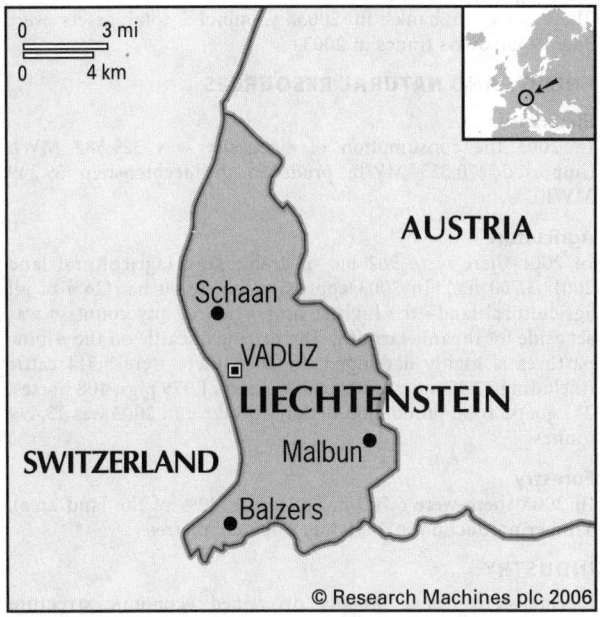

**Fürstentum Liechtenstein
(Principality of Liechtenstein)**

Capital: Vaduz
Population, 2003: 34,300
GDP per capita: not available

KEY HISTORICAL EVENTS

Liechtenstein is a sovereign state with a history dating back to 1342 when Count Hartmann III became ruler of the county of Vaduz. Additions were later made to the count's domains and by 1434 the territory reached its present boundaries. On 23 Jan. 1719 the Emperor Charles VI constituted the two counties as the Principality of Liechtenstein. In 1862 the constitution established an elected diet. After the First World War, Liechtenstein was represented abroad by Switzerland. Swiss currency was adopted in 1921. On 5 Oct. 1921 a new constitution based on that of Switzerland extended democratic rights, but in March 2003 the people of Liechtenstein voted in a referendum to give their prince the power to govern without reference to elected representatives.

TERRITORY AND POPULATION

Liechtenstein is bounded on the east by Austria and the west by Switzerland. Total area 160 sq. km (61·8 sq. miles). The population (Dec. 2003) was 34,294 (17,413 females), including 11,786 resident foreigners, giving a density of 214 per sq. km.

The population of Liechtenstein is predominantly rural. Population of Vaduz (2003) 5,005. The language is German.

SOCIAL STATISTICS

In 2003 there were 347 births and 217 deaths (rates of 10·2 per 1,000 population and 6·4 respectively). The annual population growth rate was 1·4% over the period 1999–2003.

CLIMATE

There is a distinct difference in climate between the higher mountains and the valleys. In summer the peaks can often be foggy while the valleys remain sunny and warm, while in winter the valleys can often be foggy and cold whilst the peaks remain sunny and comparatively warm. Vaduz, Jan. 0°C, July 20°C. Annual rainfall 1,090 mm.

CONSTITUTION AND GOVERNMENT

Liechtenstein is a constitutional monarchy ruled by the princes of the House of Liechtenstein.

The reigning Prince is **Hans-Adam II**, b. 14 Feb. 1945; he succeeded his father Prince Francis Joseph, 13 Nov. 1989 (he exercised the prerogatives to which the Sovereign is entitled from 26 Aug. 1984); married on 30 July 1967 to Countess Marie Kinsky von Wchinitz und Tettau. *Offspring:* Hereditary Prince Alois (b. 11 June 1968), married Duchess Sophie of Bavaria on 3 July 1993 (*offspring:* Prince Joseph Wenzel, b. 24 May 1995; Marie Caroline, b. 17 Oct. 1996; Georg Antonius, b. 20 April 1999; Nikolaus Sebastian, b. 6 Dec. 2000); Prince Maximilian (b. 16 May 1969), married Angela Brown on 29 Jan. 2000 (*offspring:* Alfons, b. 18 May 2001); Prince Constantin (b. 15 March 1972), married Countess Marie Kálnoky de Köröspatak on 17 July 1999 (*offspring:* Moritz, b. 27 May 2003; Georgina, b. 23 July 2005); Princess Tatjana (b. 10 April 1973), married Philipp von Lattorff on 5 June 1999 (*offspring:* Lukas, b. 13 May 2000; Elisabeth, b. 25 Jan. 2002; Marie Teresa, b. 18 Jan. 2004; Camilla Maria, b. 4 Nov. 2005). The monarchy is hereditary in the male line.

The present constitution of 5 Oct. 1921 provided for a unicameral parliament (*Landtag*) of 15 members elected for four years, but this was amended to 25 members in 1988. Election is on the basis of proportional representation. The prince can call and dismiss the parliament, and following a referendum held on 16 March 2003, dismiss the government and veto bills. On parliamentary recommendation, he appoints the ministers. According to the constitution, the Government is a collegial body consisting of five ministers including the prime minister. Each minister has an Alternate who takes part in the meetings of the collegial Government if the minister is unavailable. Any group of 1,000 persons or any three communes may propose legislation (initiative). Bills passed by the parliament may be submitted to popular referendum. A law is valid when it receives a majority approval by the parliament and the prince's signed concurrence. The capital is Vaduz.

National Anthem

'Oben am jungen Rhein' ('Up above the young Rhine'); words by H. H. Jauch; tune, 'God save the Queen'.

RECENT ELECTIONS

At the elections on 13 March 2005 the Progressive Citizens' Party (FBP) gained 12 seats (48·7% of votes cast); the Patriotic Union (VU), 10 (38·2% of votes); Free List (FL), 3 (13·0% of votes). Turnout was 86·5%.

CURRENT ADMINISTRATION

Head of Government, and Minister for Finance, Construction, Public Works and General Government Affairs: Otmar Hasler; b. 1953 (FBP; sworn in 5 April 2001).

In March 2006 the cabinet comprised:

Deputy Head of Government, and Minister for Economic Affairs, Justice and Sport: Klaus Tschütscher. *Education, Environmental Affairs, Land-Use Planning, Agriculture, Forestry and Social Affairs:* Hugo Quaderer. *Foreign Affairs, Family Affairs and Gender Equality, and Culture:* Rita Kieber-Beck. *Health, Interior, Transportation and Telecommunications:* Martin Meyer.

Princely House Website: http://www.fuerstenhaus.li

CURRENT LEADERS

Hans-Adam II

Position
Prince

Introduction
Hans-Adam II succeeded his father, Francis Joseph II, as Prince of Liechtenstein in 1989. A successful banker with a large personal fortune, in March 2003 he was granted extensive legal rights which effectively made him Europe's only absolute monarch. He handed day-to-day responsibility for running the country to his son, Crown Prince Alois, in 2004.

Early Life
Hans-Adam, whose full name is Johannes Adam Pius Ferdinand Alois Josef Maria Marko d'Aviano von und zu Liechtenstein, was born on 14 Feb. 1945. The eldest son of the ruling Prince Francis Joseph II, he was brought up with his three brothers and one sister in Vaduz castle. He was schooled in Austria and Vienna, worked for a short while at a London bank and studied at the St Gallen School of Economics and Social Sciences, graduating with a masters degree in 1969.

In 1970 he was named head of the Prince of Liechtenstein Foundation, a position he retained until 1984. In 1972 his father put him in charge of running the royal estate, during which time he won a reputation for sound management and an interest in the wider economic sphere. In Aug. 1984 Franz Joseph transferred much of his executive power to Hans-Adam, who formally acceded to the throne on his father's death in Nov. 1989.

Career in Office
Hans-Adam has striven to maintain Liechtenstein's strong economy, consolidating its position as a major tax haven. In 1990 he successfully concluded membership talks with the United Nations. A year later, despite having previously declared his support for European unity, he ruled out a bid for membership of the European Union.

In March 2003 Hans-Adam called a national referendum on constitutional amendments which would award him the right to dissolve the government, appoint judges and unilaterally veto legislation. In return he proposed that his right to rule by emergency decree would be reduced to six months, his entitlement to nominate government officials be terminated and that the future of the monarchy be subject to referendum. He threatened to leave for Vienna if the proposals were rejected, a move many Liechtensteiners feared would severely diminish the country's economic standing. Despite the presence of a strong pro-democracy group within Liechtenstein and the threat that the nation might lose its membership of the Council of Europe if the motion was passed, the reforms won 64·3% backing.

In Aug. 2004 Hans-Adam formally transferred responsibility for day to day affairs to his son, Alois. However, he reiterated he had no intention of abdicating the throne.

INTERNATIONAL RELATIONS

Liechtenstein is a member of the UN, WTO, OSCE, EFTA, EEA and the Council of Europe.

ECONOMY

Liechtenstein is one of the world's richest countries with a well diversified economy. Low taxes and bank secrecy laws have made Liechtenstein a successful financial centre.

Currency

Swiss currency has been in use since 1921.

Budget

Budget (in Swiss francs), 2003: revenue, 739,949,279; expenditure, 745,201,777. There is no public debt.

Performance

Real GDP growth was 6·1% in 2002. Total GDP was US$2,345m. in 2001.

Banking and Finance

There were 16 banks in 2003. Combined total assets were 34,908·3m. Swiss francs in 2003.

ENERGY AND NATURAL RESOURCES

Electricity

In 2003 the consumption of electricity was 329,582 MWh (imported 270,333 MWh; produced in Liechtenstein 59,249 MWh).

Agriculture

In 2001 there were 962 ha. of arable land (agricultural land 2001: 3,750 ha.). In 2003 approximately 1,000 ha. (26% of all agricultural land—the highest proportion of any country) was set aside for organic farming. The rearing of cattle on the Alpine pastures is highly developed. In 2003 there were 5,314 cattle (including 2,737 milch cows), 3,070 sheep, 1,979 pigs, 408 horses, 241 goats. Total production of dairy produce in 2003 was 13,499 tonnes.

Forestry

In 2003 there were 6,700 ha. of forest (42% of the land area). Timber production in 2001 was 8,000 cu. metres.

INDUSTRY

Liechtenstein has a broadly diversified economic structure with a significant emphasis on industrial production. The most important branches of the heavily export-oriented industry are mechanical engineering, plant construction, manufacturing of precision instruments, dental technology and the food-processing industry.

Labour

The farming population went down from 70% in 1930 to 1·3% in 2003. The rapid change-over has led to the immigration of foreign workers (Austrians, Germans, Italians, Swiss). The workforce was 29,055 in 2003, including employees commuting from abroad (13,413 in 2003).

INTERNATIONAL TRADE

Liechtenstein has been in a customs union with Switzerland since 1923.

Imports and Exports

Imports in 2000 amounted to 1,456m. Swiss francs. Exports of home produce in 2003 (in Swiss francs), for member companies affiliated to the Chamber of Industry and Commerce, amounted to 4,646m. Swiss francs: 595m. (12·8%) went to Switzerland, 2,000m. (43·1%) went to EEA countries and 2,051m. (44·1%) went to other countries.

COMMUNICATIONS

Roads

There are 400 km of roads. Postal buses are the chief means of public transportation within the country and to Austria and Switzerland. There were 23,524 cars in 2003. There were 582 road accidents in 2002 (none fatal).

Rail

The 10 km of main railway passing through the country is operated by Austrian Federal Railways.

Telecommunications

In 2003 there were 19,945 main telephone lines. In 2002 there were 11,400 mobile phone subscribers and Internet users numbered 20,000.

Postal Services

Post and telegraphs are administered by Switzerland. There were 12 post offices in 2004.

SOCIAL INSTITUTIONS

Justice

The principality has its own civil and penal codes. The lowest court is the county court, *Landgericht*, presided over by one judge, which decides minor civil cases and summary criminal offences. The criminal court, *Kriminalgericht*, with a bench of five judges is for major crimes. Another court of mixed jurisdiction is the court of assizes (with three judges) for misdemeanours. Juvenile cases are treated in the Juvenile Court (with a bench of three judges).

The superior court, *Obergericht*, and Supreme Court, *Oberster Gerichtshof*, are courts of appeal for civil and criminal cases (both with benches of five judges). An administrative court of appeal from government actions and the State Court determines the constitutionality of laws.

The death penalty was abolished in 1989.

Some persons convicted by Liechtenstein are held in Austrian prisons.

Police

The principality has no army. 2003: police force 103, auxiliary police 35.

Education

In 2004 there were 16 primary, three upper, seven secondary and two grammar schools, with approximately 4,300 pupils and 550 teachers. Other schools include an evening technical school and a music school.

Health

There is an obligatory sickness insurance scheme. In 2003 there was one hospital, but Liechtenstein has an agreement with the Swiss cantons of St Gallen and Graubünden and the Austrian Federal State of Vorarlberg that her citizens may use certain hospitals.

In 2003 there were 64 physicians, 26 dentists and two pharmacists.

RELIGION

In 2003, 80·4% of the population was Roman Catholic and 7·1% Protestant; 12·5% belonged to other religions.

CULTURE

Broadcasting

In 1997 there were 21,000 radios and 12,000 TV sets.

Cinema

There were three cinemas in 2003.

Press

In 2003 there were two daily newspapers with a total circulation of 17,652, and one weekly with a circulation of 32,658.

Tourism

In 2003, 50,207 tourists visited Liechtenstein.

DIPLOMATIC REPRESENTATIVES

In 1919 Switzerland agreed to represent the interests of Liechtenstein in countries where it has diplomatic missions and where Liechtenstein is not represented in its own right. In so doing Switzerland always acts only on the basis of mandates of a general or specific nature, which it may either accept or refuse, while Liechtenstein is free to enter into direct relations with foreign states or to set up its own additional diplomatic missions.

Of the United Kingdom in Liechtenstein
Ambassador: Simon Featherstone (resides in Berne).

Of Liechtenstein to the USA (888 17th St., NW, Suite 1250, Washington, D.C., 20006)
Ambassador: Claudia Fritsche.

Of Liechtenstein to the United Nations
Ambassador: Christian Wenaweser.

Of Liechtenstein to the European Union
Ambassador: Prince Nikolaus of Liechtenstein.

FURTHER READING

Amt für Volkswirtschaft. *Statistisches Jahrbuch*. Vaduz

Rechenschaftsbericht der Fürstlichen Regierung. Vaduz. Annual, from 1922

Jahrbuch des Historischen Vereins. Vaduz. Annual since 1901

National library: Landesbibliothek, Vaduz

Beattie, David, *Liechtenstein: A Modern History*. I. B. Tauris, London, 2004

Meier, Regula A., *Liechtenstein*. [Bibliography] ABC-Clio, Oxford and Santa Barbara (CA), 1993

National Statistical Office: Amt für Volkswirtschaft, Vaduz.
Website (German only):
http://www.llv.li/amtsstellen/llv-avw-statistik.htm

LITHUANIA

Lietuvos Respublika

Capital: Vilnius
Population projection, 2010: 3·36m.
GDP per capita, 2003: (PPP$) 11,702
HDI/world rank: 0·852/39

KEY HISTORICAL EVENTS

At the time of Tatar-Mongol domination of Russia, Lithuania annexed Russian lands until by the middle of the 15th century Belorussia, along with those parts of Russia and Ukraine as far as the Black Sea, were under its rule. Lithuania united with Poland dynastically in 1385 and politically in 1569. During the partitions of the Polish-Lithuanian Commonwealth by Russia, Prussia and Austria in the 18th century, Lithuania yielded its Russian territories and was absorbed into the Russian empire in 1795. Following the German occupation during the First World War and the Russian revolution on 16 Feb. 1918, heavy fighting occurred between the Soviet, German, Polish and Lithuanian forces. In April 1919 the Soviets withdrew and the re-formed Lithuanian government established a democratic republic. Lithuanian independence was recognized by the Treaty of Versailles. In Dec. 1926 the democratic regime was overthrown by a coup. The secret protocol of the Soviet-German frontier treaty of 23 Sept. 1939 assigned the greater part of Lithuania to the Soviet sphere of influence. Lithuania became a Soviet Socialist Republic of the USSR on 3 Aug. 1940.

On 11 March 1990 the newly-elected Lithuanian Supreme Soviet proclaimed independence, a decision unacceptable to the USSR government. Initially dispatched to Vilnius to enforce conscription, Soviet army units occupied key buildings in the face of mounting popular unrest. On 13 Jan. 1991 the army fired on demonstrators resulting in a number of casualties. A referendum on independence was held in Feb. 1991 at which 90·5% voted in favour. A fully independent status was conceded by the USSR on 6 Sept. 1991. The first presidential elections were held in 1993 and won by Algirdas Brazauskas, who was subsequently elected to be the current prime minister. Lithuania became a member of NATO in March 2004 and the European Union in May 2004.

TERRITORY AND POPULATION

Lithuania is bounded in the north by Latvia, east and south by Belarus, and west by Poland, the Russian enclave of Kaliningrad and the Baltic Sea. The total area is 65,200 sq. km (25,212 sq. miles) and the population (2001 census) 3,483,972 (1,854,824 females); density, 53·4 per sq. km. The estimated population in 2005 was 3,431,000. In 2003, 66·8% of the population lived in urban areas. Of the 2001 census population, Lithuanians accounted for 83·5%, Poles 6·7%, Russians 6·3% (9·4% in 1989), Belarusians 1·2%, Ukrainians 0·7% and Jews 0·1%.

The UN gives a projected population for 2010 of 3·36m.

There are ten counties (with capitals of the same name): Alytus; Kaunas; Klaipėda; Marijampolė; Panevėžys; Šiauliai; Tauragė; Telšiai; Utena; Vilnius.

The capital is Vilnius (Jan. 2002 population, 553,373). Other large towns are Kaunas (376,575), Klaipėda (192,498), Šiauliai (133,528) and Panevėžys (119,417).

The official language is Lithuanian, but ethnic minorities have the right to official use of their language where they form a substantial part of the population. All residents who applied by 3 Nov. 1991 received Lithuanian citizenship, requirements for which are ten years' residence and competence in Lithuanian.

SOCIAL STATISTICS

2002: births, 30,014; deaths, 41,072; marriages, 16,151; divorces, 10,579; infant deaths, 238. Rates (per 1,000 population): birth, 8·6; death, 11·8; marriage, 4·7; divorce, 3·1. The population started to decline in 1993, a trend which is set to continue. Annual population growth rate, 1990–2003, –0·6%. In 2002, 8,386 births were registered to unmarried mothers and there were 18,907 legally induced abortions. Life expectancy at birth in 2003 was 66·6 years for males and 77·8 years for females. In 2002 the most popular age range for marrying was 20–24 for both males and females. Infant mortality, 2002, 7·9 per 1,000 live births; fertility rate, 1·24 births per woman. In 2002 there were 7,086 emigrants and 5,110 immigrants.

Lithuania has the world's highest suicide rate, at 42·1 per 100,000 inhabitants in 2003 (a rate of 74·3 among males but only 13·9 among women).

CLIMATE

Vilnius, Jan. –2·8°C, July 20·5°C. Annual rainfall 520 mm. Klaipėda, Jan. –0·6°C, July 19·4°C. Annual rainfall 770 mm.

CONSTITUTION AND GOVERNMENT

A referendum to approve a new constitution was held on 25 Oct. 1992. Parliament is the 141-member *Seimas*. Under a new electoral law passed in July 2000, 71 of the parliament's 141 members will defeat rivals for their seats if they receive the most votes in a single round of balloting. Previously they had to win 50% of the votes or face a run-off against the nearest competitor. The parliament's 70 other seats are distributed according to the proportional popularity of the political parties at the ballot box.

The *Constitutional Court* is empowered to rule on whether proposed laws conflict with the constitution or existing legislation. It comprises nine judges who serve nine-year terms, one third rotating every three years.

National Anthem

'Lietuva, tėvyne mūsų' ('Lithuania, our fatherland'); words and tune by V. Kurdirka.

GOVERNMENT CHRONOLOGY

(LDDP = Democratic Labour Party of Lithuania; LDP = Liberal Democratic Party; LKP = Communist Party of Lithuania; LLS = Lithuanian Liberal Union; LSDP = Lithuanian Social Democratic Party; Sajudis = 'Unity'; TS(LK) = Homeland Union (Conservatives of Lithuania); n/p = non-partisan)

Heads of State since 1990.

Chairman of the Supreme Council

1990–92	Sajudis	Vytautas Landsbergis

Chairman of the Seimas (Parliament)

1992–93	LDDP	Algirdas Brazauskas

Presidents of the Republic

1993–98	LDDP	Algirdas Brazauskas
1998–2003	n/p	Valdas Adamkus
2003–04	LDP	Rolandas Paksas
2004–	n/p	Valdas Adamkus

Prime Ministers since 1990.

1990–91	LKP/LDDP	Kazimiera Prunskienė
1991	Sajudis	Albertas Simenas
1991–92	Sajudis	Gediminas Vagnorious
1992	n/p	Aleksandras Abišala
1992–93	LDDP	Bronislovas Lubys
1993–96	LDDP	Adolfas Šleževičius
1996	LDDP	Mindaugas Stankevičius
1996–99	TS(LK)	Gediminas Vagnorius
1999	TS(LK)	Rolandas Paksas
1999–2000	TS(LK)	Andrius Kubilius
2000–01	LLS	Rolandas Paksas
2001–	LSDP	Algirdas Brazauskas

RECENT ELECTIONS

Presidential elections were held in two rounds on 13 and 27 June 2004. In the first round former president Valdas Adamkus won 30·7% of the vote, ahead of former prime minister Kazimiera Prunskienė with 21·4%, Petras Auštrevičius 19·3%, Vilija Blinkevičiūtė 16·6% and Česlovas Juršėnas 11·9%. Turnout was 39·4%. In the second round run-off Adamkus won 52·6% against 47·4% for Prunskienė. Turnout was 52·4%.

Parliamentary elections were held in two rounds on 10 and 24 Oct. 2004. The Labour Party won 38 of the 141 seats (28·4% of the votes cast), Prime Minister Algirdas Brazauskas' coalition 'For a Working Lithuania' (comprising the Lithuanian Social Democratic Party and the New Union) 32 (20·6%), the Homeland Union 25 (14·7%), the Liberal and Centre Union 18 (9·2%), former president Rolandas Paksas' coalition 'For the Order and Justice' 11 (11·4%), the Peasants' and New Democratic Party Union 10 (6·6%), Election Action of Lithuania's Poles 2 (3·8%) and ind. 5 (5·2%). Turnout for the first round was 46·1% and for the second round 40·2%.

European Parliament

Lithuania has 13 representatives. At the June 2004 elections turnout was 48·2%. The Labour Party won 5 seats with 30·2% of votes cast (political affiliation in European Parliament: Alliance of Liberals and Democrats for Europe); Lithuanian Social Democratic Party, 2 with 14·4% (Party of European Socialists); the Homeland Union, 2 with 12·6% (European People's Party–European Democrats); the Liberal and Centre Union, 2 with 11·2% (Alliance of Liberals and Democrats for Europe); the Peasants' and New Democratic Party Union, 1 with 7·4% (Union for a Europe of Nations); the LDP, 1 with 6·8% (Union for a Europe of Nations).

CURRENT ADMINISTRATION

President: Valdas Adamkus; b. 1926 (took office on 12 July 2004; previously held office from Feb. 1998–Feb. 2003).

Prime Minister: Algirdas Mykolas Brazauskas; b. 1932 (LSDP; in office since 3 July 2001).

In March 2006 the cabinet comprised:

Minister of Foreign Affairs: Antanas Valionis. *Defence:* Gediminas Kirkilas. *Finance:* Zigmantas Balčytis. *Economy:* Kęstutis Daukšys. *Social Security and Labour:* Vilija Blinkevičiūtė. *Interior:* Gintaras Jonas Furmanavičius. *Health:* Žilvinas Padaiga. *Justice:* Gintautas Bužinskas. *Agriculture:* Kazimiera Prunskienė. *Environment:* Arūnas Kundrotas. *Transport:* Petras Čėsna. *Culture:* Vladimiras Prudnikovas. *Education and Science:* Remigijus Motuzas.

Seimas Speaker: Artūras Paulauskas.

Government of the Republic of Lithuania: http://www.lrvk.lt

CURRENT LEADERS

Valdas Adamkus

Position

President

Introduction

At the age of 77 Valdas Adamkus was elected president of Lithuania for a second term in 2004, following the impeachment of Rolandas Paksas just 16 months after he took office. Once a blue-collar worker in a Chicago car plant, Adamkus returned to his native Lithuania in 1997 after 48 years in the USA and entered formal politics for the first time. Within a year he had become president.

Early Life

Valdas Adamkus was born in Kaunas on 3 Nov. 1926. His father, Ignas Adamkavicius, was a civil servant and served as a volunteer in battles for Lithuanian independence from Germany (achieved in Nov. 1918, although the capital, Vilnius, came under Polish control in 1920). Kaunas became the country's *de facto* capital in 1922. In the years of the Second World War, when Lithuania was annexed by the USSR (July 1940), and then occupied by Nazi forces (July 1941), Adamkus joined a resistance movement and published an underground newspaper. When Lithuania was again invaded by the Red Army in 1944 he signed up to the National Defence Force and fought against Soviet rule at the battle of Seda in the west of the country. Subsequently Adamkus and his family were among around 60,000 Lithuanians who managed to flee to Germany, where they were liberated by the Western Allies. After graduation from a Lithuanian school in Germany, Adamkus entered the Faculty of Natural Science of the University of Munich. He also worked at the World YMCA organization where he focused on helping displaced Lithuanians. A keen sportsman, Adamkus competed at the Olympic Games of the Enslaved Nations in 1948 and won two gold medals.

Adamkus, along with his parents, brother and sister emigrated to the USA in 1949. He began work in a car factory and later took employment as a draughtsman for an engineering firm. In 1960 he graduated as a construction engineer from the Illinois Institute of Technology in Chicago. Throughout the 1950s and 1960s Adamkus organized demonstrations against the Soviet occupation of Lithuania and initiated numerous petitions. Between 1961–65 he was a member of the board of the Lithuanian Community in the USA. In the late 1960s Adamkus turned his attention to monitoring and protecting the environment, first heading a scientific research centre and later working as deputy administrator of the Environmental Protection Agency's mid-West office. His department's work on improving water quality and the environment in the Great Lakes was widely praised. From 1972 Adamkus became a regular visitor to Lithuania—he established relations with Vilnius University and helped various Soviet institutions to build water purification facilities and set up environmental monitoring projects. When Adamkus resigned as administrator of the Environmental Protection Agency in June 1997 he received the agency's highest award for achievements in service and a letter of thanks from the US president, Bill Clinton.

Following the USSR's recognition of Lithuania's independence on 6 Sept. 1991, Adamkus became increasingly involved in Lithuanian politics. He spearheaded the electoral campaign of Stasys Lozoraitis (the ambassador to the USA) in the 1993 presidential elections, although Lozoraitis lost to the former communist Algirdas Brazauskas who had strong support in the poor, rural areas. Adamkus actively participated in the campaign leading up to the 1996 general election, helping to unite the centre-right Christian Democrats and the Homeland Union. They were guided to victory under Gediminas Vagnorius, who became prime minister. The following year Adamkus returned to Lithuania and was nominated by the Lithuanian Centre Union to represent the council of the northern city of Šiauliai. He stood in the presidential election as an independent candidate on 21 Dec. 1997, winning sufficient votes to contest a run-off with Artûras Paulauskas on 4 Jan. 1998.

Career in Office

Adamkus beat the former prosecutor general by a margin of less than 1% (14,256 votes), with his support coming mostly from the cities of Kaunas and Klaipėda and the west of the country. As president from 1998–2003 he laid the groundwork for Lithuania's membership of NATO and the European Union. Although popular with Lithuania's new middle class, he lost his 2003 bid for re-election to Rolandas Paksas by a narrow margin. However, the Paksas presidency was dogged by financial scandals and allegations of links with the Russian Mafia, and he was impeached in April 2004 for divulging state secrets. In the presidential election in June 2004 Adamkus won a second term after narrowly defeating former prime minister Kazimiera Prunskienė in a run-off.

Adamkus was elected for a five-year term and was expected to make attempts to consolidate rural and urban society. Most analysts predicted that Adamkus would continue to pursue a strongly pro-Western foreign policy with an emphasis on links with neighbouring Nordic states within the EU. In 2005 he declined the invitation to attend the Russian war anniversary celebrations in Moscow.

Algirdas Brazauskas

Position

Prime Minister

Introduction

A former Communist Party first secretary and Lithuanian president (1992–98), Algirdas Mykolas Brazauskas is prime minister of Lithuania, representing the A. Brazauskas Social Democratic Coalition.

Early Life

Brazauskas was born on 22 Sept. 1932 in Rokiškis, northeast Lithuania. He studied engineering and economics at Kaunas Polytechnic, graduating in 1956. Over the next ten years he worked in industry while becoming active in the Lithuanian Communist Party. In 1965 he joined the government of the Lithuanian Soviet Socialist Republic, serving first as construction materials minister and then as deputy chairman of the state planning committee two years later. By 1988 he was the first secretary of the Communist Party's central committee. As Communism weakened throughout the Eastern Bloc, Brazauskas was part of a group of pro-independence Communists who formed the Democratic Labour Party of Lithuania (LDDP), modelling the movement on social democratic lines. As deputy prime minister between 1990–91 he was involved in Lithuania's transition to independence. The Communist Party became illegal in 1991.

A year later the LDDP successfully contested parliamentary elections.

Career in Office

In 1993 Brazauskas stood in Lithuania's first post-independence presidential elections against the independent candidate Stasys Lozoraitis. Winning the presidency with 60·1% of votes, Brazauskas stood down as leader of the LDDP in keeping with the impartiality of the largely ceremonial position. Over the next five years, despite slow progress, Lithuania moved towards a free market economy and forged links with Western governments, including an EU membership application in 1995 and involvement in NATO's Partnership for Peace programme from 1997. In 1994 a national currency, the litas, was introduced. Regionally, Lithuania strengthened its ties with Estonia and Latvia and signed a treaty to cement good relations first with Poland in 1994 and then Belarus the following year. In 1998 Brazauskas was succeeded as president by Valdas Adamkus.

Brazauskas returned to party politics heading the LDDP in opposition. The party joined forces with several other parties (including the Lithuanian Social Democratic Party—LSDP) as the A. Brazauskas Social Democratic Coalition, successfully contesting the 2000 parliamentary elections. The Lithuanian Liberal Union party's Rolandas Paksas became prime minister. The LDDP and the LSDP merged in 2001, and Brazauskas retained the party leadership.

When in June 2001 Paksas' coalition government collapsed over privatization disputes, President Adamkus nominated Brazauskas as Paksas' successor. The following month he was appointed with 84 votes to 45. As prime minister he continued his predecessor's reforms needed for EU membership, which was achieved in May 2004. Two months earlier Lithuania also joined NATO.

The Oct. 2004 elections left no party with a majority of seats in parliament, but Brazauskas agreed to form a broader power-sharing coalition (including the Labour Party which had won the most seats). He was nominated by the president to continue as prime minister and his appointment was approved by parliament in Dec. 2004.

DEFENCE

Conscription is for 12 months. In 2003 military expenditure totalled US$359m., representing 2% of GDP. US$287·7m. went to the ministry of defence with US$71·3m. going to the security agencies, border guard service and anti-terrorism units. In 2002 logistic forces numbered 1,044 and Training and Doctrine Command (TRADOC) numbered 3,353.

Army

The Army numbered 7,332 in 2003 and included one motorized infantry brigade ('Iron Wolf'). First line reserves numbered 25,000 in 2002, including 11,700 in the Volunteer National Defence Service.

There is a 784-strong joint Polish/Lithuanian battalion (LITPOLBAT) which is a component of the EU's rapid reaction forces.

Navy

In 2003 Naval Forces numbered 693 personnel and operated several vessels including two corvettes.

Lithuania, Estonia and Latvia have established a joint naval unit 'BALTRON' (Baltic Naval Squadron), with bases at Klaipėda in Lithuania, Tallinn in Estonia, and Liepāja, Riga and Ventspils in Latvia.

Air Force

The Air Force consisted of 1,172 personnel in 2003. There are no combat aircraft.

The joint Baltic Regional Air Surveillance Network (BALTNET), established in co-operation between the air forces of Estonia, Latvia and Lithuania, has its co-ordination centre in Karmėlava in Lithuania.

INTERNATIONAL RELATIONS

Lithuania is a member of the UN, WTO, BIS, NATO, EBRD, IMF, UNESCO, FAO, IMO, EU, Council of Europe, OSCE, IAEA, Council of the Baltic Sea States, IOM and EAPC and is an Associate Partner of the WEU. Lithuania held a referendum on EU membership on 10–11 May 2003, in which 91·0% of votes cast were in favour of accession, with 9·0% against. It became a member of NATO on 29 March 2004 and the EU on 1 May 2004. On 11 Nov. 2004 Lithuania became the first European Union member to ratify the proposed EU constitution. The parliament approved the treaty by 84 votes to four, with three abstentions.

ECONOMY

Agriculture accounted for 7·1% of GDP in 2002, industry 31·2% and services 61·7%.

Overview

Privatization, co-ordinated by the State Property Fund, is close to completion. The third stage of privatization began in Nov. 1997. In 2002, 963 entities were privatized, the biggest of which was the Lithuanian Agricultural Bank.

Currency

The unit of currency is the *litas* (plural: *litai*) of 100 *cents*, which was introduced on 25 June 1993 and became the sole legal tender on 1 Aug. The litas was pegged to the US dollar on 1 April 1994 at US$1 = four litai, but since 2 Feb. 2002 it has been pegged to the euro at 3·4528 litai = one euro. Lithuania is aiming to adopt the euro as its currency on 1 Jan. 2007. Inflation, which reached a high of 1,161% in the early 1990s, was –1·2% in 2003 and 1·2% in 2004. Total money supply was 6,678m. litai in May 2002. Gold reserves were 186,000 troy oz in June 2002 and foreign exchange reserves US$2,230m.

Budget

Total revenue in 2002 amounted to 10,330m. litai and expenditure to 11,466m. litai. Revenue in 2002 included: VAT, 37%; personal income tax, 24%. Expenditure in 2002 included (in 1m. litai): education, 3,073; social welfare, 1,149; public order, 1,009; general public services, 903; defence, 857; transport and communications, 844; health, 613.

VAT is 18% (reduced rates, 9% and 5%).

Performance

Among the wealthiest provinces of the former Soviet Union, Lithuania has weathered the economic crisis overspilling from Russia. 47·8% of exports in 2001 went to the EU compared to just 11% to Russia. In 1999 Lithuania experienced a recession, with the economy shrinking by 1·7%. There was then a recovery in 2000, with growth of 3·9%, rising to 6·4% in 2001, 6·8% in 2002 and further to 9·7% in 2003. The GDP growth rate in 2004 was 6·7%. Total GDP in 2004 was US$22·3bn. At Nov. 2003 total public debt stood at €3·8bn., of which €2·6bn. was foreign debt.

Banking and Finance

The central bank and bank of issue is the Bank of Lithuania (*Governor*, Reinoldijas Šarkinas). A programme to restructure and privatize the state banks was started in 1996. In 2003 there were ten commercial banks, three foreign bank branches, three foreign bank representative offices, the central credit union of Lithuania and 57 credit unions in operation. The largest private bank in Lithuania is JSC Vilniaus Bankas, which controls approximately 37% of the total banking assets in the country. At Dec. 2003 it was estimated that total assets of domestic commercial banks amounted to 22bn. litai.

A stock exchange opened in Vilnius in 1993. In Oct. 1999 its capitalization was US$3·5bn. The trading volume in 1999 was US$575m.

ENERGY AND NATURAL RESOURCES

Environment

According to Lithuania's Ministry of Environment, carbon dioxide emissions were the equivalent of 4·4 tonnes per capita in 2002.

Electricity

Installed capacity was 6·57m. kW in 2002; production was 17·7bn. kWh. A nuclear power station (with two reactors) in Ignalina was responsible for 79·8% of total output in 2002, and there are also two large hydro-electric, five public and five autoproducer thermal plants. No other country has such a high percentage of its electricity generated through nuclear power. However, at the EU's insistence the government is committed to closing down Ignalina. The process to close the first reactor began on 31 Dec. 2004. The whole facility is scheduled to close by the end of 2009. Electricity consumption per capita in 2002 was 2,827 kWh.

Oil and Gas

Oil production started from a small field at Kretinga in 1990. In Jan. 2003 remaining recoverable reserves were estimated at 3·25m. tonnes; potential recoverable resources, 60–80m. tonnes. Production in 2002 from ten oilfields was 432,000 tonnes.

Minerals

Production in 2002 (in 1,000 tonnes): limestone, 984; peat, 491. Quarrying of stone, clay and sand totalled 1·47m. cu. metres in 1998.

Agriculture

In 2002 agriculture employed about 17·2% of the workforce. As of 1 Jan. 2003 the average farm size was 15·2 ha., one of the lowest in eastern Europe; the agricultural land area was 3,956,200 ha. In 2002 there were 2·93m. ha. of arable land and 59,000 ha. of permanent crops. In 2002, 242,000 persons were employed in agriculture and forestry.

Output of main agricultural products (in 1,000 tonnes) in 2002: potatoes, 1,531; wheat, 1,218; sugarbeets, 1,052; barley, 871; rye, 170; rapeseed, 105; cabbages, 98; oats, 97. Value of agricultural production, 2002 (in 1m. litai), was 4,303·3, of which from individual farm holdings, 3,396·2; and from agricultural partnerships and enterprises, 907·1.

Livestock, Jan. 2003 (in 1,000): cattle, 779·1 (of which milch cows, 443·3); pigs, 1,061·0; sheep and goats, 35·6; horses, 60·7; poultry, 6,848·1. There were 103,000 tractors in use in 2002. Animal products, 2002 (in 1,000 tonnes): meat, 173·6; milk, 770·9; eggs, 779m. units.

Forestry

In 2002 forests covered 2·0m. ha., or 30·6% of Lithuania's territory, and consist of conifers, mostly pine. Timber production in 2002, 5·9m. cu. metres.

Fisheries

In Jan. 2004 the fishing fleet comprised 90 vessels averaging 872 GRT. Total catch in 2002 amounted to 151,530 tonnes (mainly from sea fishing), compared to 57,477 tonnes in 1995.

INDUSTRY

Industrial output included (in 1,000 tonnes): petrol (2000), 1,559; distillate fuel oil (2000), 1,450; residual fuel oil (2000), 798; mineral and chemical fertilizers (2001), 786; cement (2001), 529; sulphuric acid (2001), 465; sugar (2002), 150; cotton fabrics (1998), 63·8m. cu. metres; linen (1998), 15·9m. sq. metres; woollen fabrics (1998), 14·3m. sq. metres; silk (1998), 7·8m. sq. metres; television picture tubes (1998), 1,794,000 units; bicycles (2001),

323,000 units; refrigerators (2001), 260,000 units; TV sets (2001), 143,000 units.

Labour

In 2002 the workforce was 1·6m. (69·9% in private enterprises and 30·1% in the public sector). Employed population by activity (as a percentage): manufacturing, 18·6; wholesale and retail trade, 15·0; education, 9·9; health and social work, 6·7; construction, 6·6; transport and communications, 6·2; real estate, 3·9. Employment skills, 33·2% with tertiary education, 52·5% with upper secondary education, 11·8% with lower secondary. In 2002 the average monthly wage was 1,013·9 litai; legal minimum wage was 450 litai in 2003.

In 2002 old age pension for men started at 62 years and for women at 58. Average number of persons entitled to pensions in 2001 was 636,900. The unemployment rate in Sept. 2003 was 9·3%.

Trade Unions

On 1 Jan. 2001 there were 655 registered unions (339 in operation) affiliated with four federations: the Lithuanian Trade Union Centre (LPSC); the Lithuanian Trade Union Unification (LPSS); the Lithuanian Workers Union (LDS); the Lithuanian Labour Federation (LDF). The LPSC and the LPSS merged on 1 May 2002 to form the Lithuanian Trade Union Confederation (LPSK), now Lithuania's largest trade union organization with 120,000 members.

INTERNATIONAL TRADE

In order to foster export growth, Lithuania maintains a fairly liberal foreign trade regime. There is no quantitative import restriction and the import duties are one of the lowest in central Europe. By the end of 1998 free trade agreements with the European Union, EFTA, neighbouring Latvia and Estonia, as well as with Central European Free Trade Agreement countries (CEFTA) and Ukraine were signed. Meanwhile, most favoured-nation status is applied to trade with Russia.

Foreign investors may purchase up to 100% of the equity companies in Lithuania. By mid-2003, €4·06bn. of foreign capital had been invested. Leading source nations of foreign investment were Denmark, Sweden, Estonia, Germany and the USA.

Total foreign debt was €2·66bn. in 2003.

Individual laws on three free economic zones (namely the laws on Šiauliai, Klaipėda and Kaunas) have been cleared by Lithuania's Parliament, the Seimas.

Imports and Exports

In 2002 imports were valued at 28,220m. litai and exports at 20,280m. litai. Main import suppliers, 2001: Russia, 25·3%; Germany, 17·2%; Poland, 4·9%; Italy, 4·2%. Main export markets, 2001: UK, 13·8%; Germany, 12·6%; Latvia, 12·6%; Russia, 11·0%. Main exports are mineral products, textiles and textile articles, electrical equipment, TV sets, chemical products and prepared foodstuffs.

COMMUNICATIONS

Roads

In 2002 there were 77,148 km of roads, of which 89·7% were paved. The Via Baltica, a US$180m. project, will upgrade a 1,000 km (620 mile) international highway linking Finland, Estonia, Latvia, Lithuania and Poland, and there are plans to continue the link to western and southern Europe.

In 2002 there were 1,180,745 passenger cars, 15,376 buses, 466 trolleybuses, 105,545 goods vehicles and 21,017 motorcycles. In 2002 public transport carried 347·8m. passengers. There were 6,091 traffic accidents in 2002, with 697 fatalities.

Rail

There are 1,775 km of railway track in operation in Lithuania. The majority of rail traffic is diesel propelled, although 122 km of track is electrified. In 2003, 6·7m. passengers and 43·5m. tonnes of freight were carried.

Civil Aviation

The main international airport is based in the capital, Vilnius. Other international airports are at Kaunas, Palanga and Šiauliai. The largest airline is Lithuanian Airlines (a state-owned joint stock company, but scheduled for privatization), which has regular scheduled flights to most of Europe's main transit hubs. In 2003 a number of other international airlines ran regular scheduled flights. In 2003 Lithuanian Airlines flew 8·8m. km, carrying 312,000 passengers (311,500 on international flights). In 2003 Vilnius was the busiest airport for passenger traffic, handling 719,850 passengers, but Kaunas (which handles approximately 6,700 tonnes per annum) was the busiest for freight.

Shipping

The ice-free port of Klaipėda plays a dominant role in the national economy and Baltic maritime traffic. It has the second largest tonnage in the Baltic region and a cargo capacity of 30m. tonnes per annum. A 205 ha. site at the port is dedicated a *Free Economic Zone*, which offers attractive conditions to foreign investors.

In 2003 the merchant fleet numbered 67 ships totalling 362,103 GRT, including eight bulkers, 35 general cargo ships, three tankers and 17 reefers. The turnover of the port in 2003 was 21m. tonnes (up from 12·7m. in 1995).

In 2003 there were 902·3 km of inland waterways, of which 467·7 km were used for carrying freight and passengers. The inland fleet comprised 142 working vessels.

Telecommunications

A majority stake in Lithuanian Telecom (the only fixed telephone service provider) was sold to the Finnish and Swedish consortium SONERA in 1998 and by Jan. 2003 the telecommunications market was fully liberalized. Lithuanian Telecom had 994,000 subscribers in Jan. 2003. In June 2003 there were 1,935,800 mobile phone subscribers (56% penetration). In 2002, 380,000 PCs were in use (109·8 per 1,000 persons). In 2002 there were 10,600 fax machines. The number of Internet users in 2002 was 500,000.

Postal Services

In 2003 there were 945 post offices.

SOCIAL INSTITUTIONS

Justice

The general jurisdiction court system consists of the Supreme Court, the Court of Appeal, five county courts and 54 district courts. Specialized administrative courts were established in 1999. In Jan. 2003 there were 669 judges: 421 in district courts; 139 in county courts; 22 in the Court of Appeal; 33 in the Supreme Court; 41 in the administrative county courts; and 13 in the High Administrative Court.

77,108 crimes were reported in 1999, of which 41·0% were solved. In 2001 there were 378 murders. 2,240 persons were convicted of offences in 1999. Lithuania's murder rate, at 10·8 per 100,000 population in 2001, ranks among the highest in Europe. In Jan. 2003 there were 11,070 prisoners, 8,520 of whom had been convicted. The death penalty was abolished for all crimes in 1998.

Education

Education is compulsory from seven to 16. In 2002–03 there were 686 pre-school establishments with 90,860 pupils and 2,172 general schools with 49,286 teachers and 594,313 pupils, in the following categories:

Type of School	No. of Schools	No. of Pupils
Nursery	148	12,219
Primary	683	35,819
Junior	25	2,326
Basic	645	118,415
Special	67	7,212
Secondary	574	400,566
Adult	27	17,318

119,548 students (70,777 females) attended 19 institutions of higher education and 22,367 (13,735 females) attended vocational colleges in 2002–03. The adult literacy rate in 2003 was 99·6% (99·6% for both males and females).

In 2002 total expenditure on education represented 27·1% of total government expenditure.

Health

In 2002 there were 13,856 physicians, 2,309 dentists and 26,918 nurses. There were 196 hospitals with 31,031 beds in 2002, and 2,238 pharmacists.

Welfare

The social security system is financed by the State Social Insurance Fund. In 2002, 625,000 persons were eligible for retirement pensions, 188,000 for disability provisions and 219,000 for widow's/widower's pensions. In 2002 the average state social insurance old age pension was 323 litai (monthly).

RELIGION

Under the Constitution, the state supports religious groups which have been active in Lithuania for 400 years, i.e., the Roman Catholic, Evangelical Lutheran, Evangelical Reformats and Orthodox Churches. In 2001, 76% of the population were Roman Catholic. As of 1 Jan. 2000 there were 693 Roman Catholic churches with 732 priests, and 43 Orthodox churches with 41 priests. There is an archbishopric of Vilnius and 13 bishops. In 1999 the Lutheran Church had 41 churches, 54 parishes and 23 pastors headed by a bishop. In May 2005 there was one cardinal.

CULTURE

World Heritage Sites

Lithuania has four sites (two shared) on the UNESCO World Heritage List: Vilnius Historic Centre (inscribed on the list in 1994) and Kernave Archaeological Site (2004).

Lithuania shares the Curonian Spit (2000) with the Russian Federation as a UNESCO site. A sand-dune spit between Zelenogradsk, Kaliningrad Region, and Klaipėda, Lithuania, the Spit was subject to massive protective engineering in the 19th century. Lithuania also shares the Struve Geodetic Arc (2005). The Arc is a chain of survey triangulations spanning from Norway to the Black Sea that helped establish the exact shape and size of the earth and is shared with nine other countries.

Broadcasting

In 2002 there were two national and eight commercial radio networks and 57 local commercial radio stations; two national and three commercial TV networks and 28 local TV stations (colour by PAL).

There were 2·1m. radio receivers and 1·41m. television receivers in 2003.

Press

In 2003 there were 337 newspapers (306 in Lithuanian, 19 in Russian, four in Polish, three in English, three in German, one in Yiddish and one in Belarusian) and 391 magazines. 4,859 book titles were published in 2002.

Tourism

There were 4,195,200 foreign tourists in 2001; tourism receipts amounted to US$383m.

DIPLOMATIC REPRESENTATIVES

Of Lithuania in the United Kingdom (84 Gloucester Place, London, W1U 6AU)
Ambassador: Aurimas Taurantas.

Of the United Kingdom in Lithuania (Antakalnio g. 2, 2055 Vilnius)
Ambassador: Colin Roberts.

Of Lithuania in the USA (2622 16th St., NW, Washington, D.C., 20009)
Ambassador: Vygaudas Ušackas.

Of the USA in Lithuania (Akmenu g. 6, 2600 Vilnius)
Ambassador: Stephen D. Mull.

Of Lithuania to the United Nations
Ambassador: Dalius Čekuolis.

Of Lithuania to the European Union
Ambassador: Oskaras Jusys.

FURTHER READING

Department of Statistics to the Government. *Statistical Yearbook of Lithuania – Economic and Social Development in Lithuania.* Monthly.

Hood, N., *et al.* (eds.) *Transition in the Baltic States.* 1997
Lieven, A., *The Baltic Revolution: Estonia, Latvia, Lithuania and the Path to Independence.* 2nd ed. Yale Univ. Press, 1994
Misiunas, R. J. and Taagepera, R., *The Baltic States: the Years of Dependence, 1940–91.* 2nd ed. Farnborough, 1993
Smith, I. A. and Grunts, M. V., *The Baltic States.* [Bibliography] ABC-Clio, Oxford and Santa Barbara (CA), 1993
Vardys, V. S. and Sedaitis, J. B., *Lithuania: the Rebel Nation.* Boulder (CO), 1997

National Statistical Office: Department of Statistics to the Government, Gedimino Pr. 29, LT 01 500 Vilnius. *Director General:* Algirdas Gediminas Semeta.
Website: http://www.std.lt/lt/

LUXEMBOURG

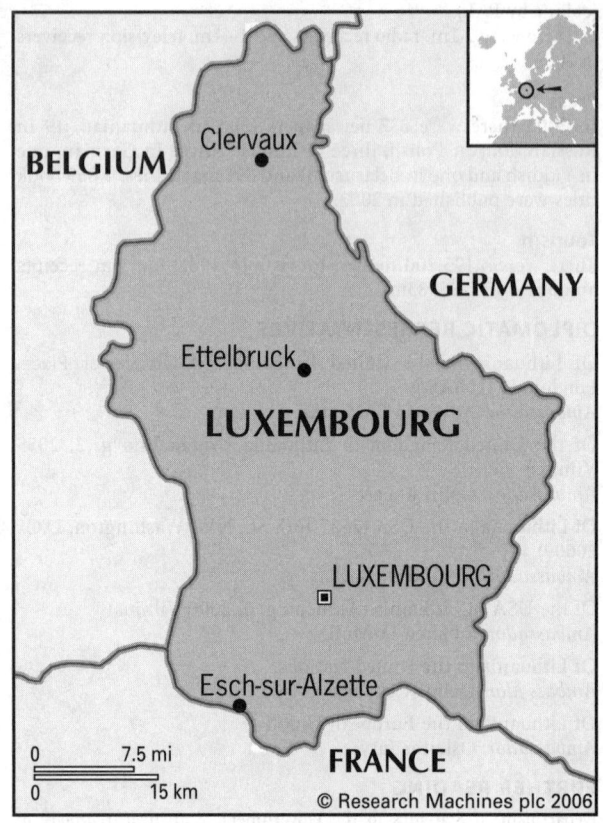

BELGIUM

Clervaux

GERMANY

Ettelbruck

LUXEMBOURG

LUXEMBOURG

Esch-sur-Alzette

FRANCE

| 0 | 7.5 mi |
| 0 | 15 km |

© Research Machines plc 2006

Grand-Duché de Luxembourg

Capital: Luxembourg
Population projection, 2010: 494,000
GDP per capita, 2003: (PPP$) 62,298
HDI/world rank: 0·949/4

KEY HISTORICAL EVENTS

Lying at the heart of Western Europe between Belgium, France and Germany, the Grand-Duchy of Luxembourg has been an independent state ever since the Treaty of London of 19 April 1839. The origins of Luxembourg stretch back to AD 963 when Count Sigfried founded the castle of Lutzilinburhurch. The House of Luxembourg was most prominent on the European scene during the 14th and 15th centuries, when four Counts of the House of Luxembourg became Emperors of the Holy Roman Empire and Kings of Bohemia. The House of Luxembourg subsequently went into decline and was successively occupied by Burgundy, Spain, Austria and finally by revolutionary France. In 1815 the Vienna Treaty decided that the Grand Duchy of Luxembourg would come under the Netherlands ruling house of Orange-Nassau. In 1839 the Walloon-speaking area was joined to Belgium. The union with the Netherlands ended in 1890. In both world wars (1914–18 and 1939–45) Luxembourg, a neutral country, was invaded and occupied by German forces. In June 1942 Luxembourg became the only Nazi-occupied country to stage a general strike against the occupation. In 1948 a Benelux customs union formed by Belgium, the Netherlands and Luxembourg allowed for standardization of prices, taxes

and wages and the free movement of labour among the three countries. Luxembourg was a founder member of the European Union.

TERRITORY AND POPULATION

Luxembourg has an area of 2,586 sq. km (999 sq. miles) and is bounded on the west by Belgium, south by France, east by Germany. A census took place on 15 Feb. 2001; the population was 439,539 (including 162,285 foreigners). In 2005 the population was 455,000 (including 177,400 foreigners); density, 175 per sq. km. The percentage of foreigners living in Luxembourg has increased dramatically in recent years, from 26% in 1986 to 39% in 2005. The main countries of origin of foreigners living in Luxembourg are Portugal (65,700 in 2005), France (22,400) and Italy (18,800).

In 2003, 91·8% of the population were urban. The capital, Luxembourg, has (2005) 76,400 inhabitants; Esch-sur-Alzette, the centre of the mining district, 28,000; Differdange, 20,200; Dudelange, 18,141; Diekirch, 6,460; and Echternach, 4,645.

The UN gives a projected population for 2010 of 494,000. Lëtzebuergesch is spoken by most of the population, and since 1984 has been an official language with French and German.

SOCIAL STATISTICS

Statistics (figures in parentheses indicate births and deaths of resident foreigners):

	Births	Deaths	Marriages	Divorces
2001	5,459 (2,736)	3,719 (531)	1,983	1,029
2002	5,345 (2,653)	3,744 (628)	2,022	1,092
2003	5,303 (2,782)	4,053 (632)	2,001	1,026
2004	5,452 (2,919)	3,578 (571)	1,999	1,055

2004 rates per 1,000 population; birth, 12·0; death, 8·9; marriage, 4·3; divorce, 2·3. Nearly half of annual births are to foreigners. In 2003 the most popular age range for marrying was 25–29 for both males and females. Life expectancy at birth in 2004 was 74·9 years for males and 81·0 years for females. Annual population growth rate, 1992–2003, 1·4%. Infant mortality, 2003, 4·9 per 1,000 live births; fertility rate, 1·6 births per woman. In 2004 Luxembourg received 1,578 asylum applications.

CLIMATE

In general the country resembles Belgium in its climate, with rain evenly distributed throughout the year. Average temperatures are Jan. 0·8°C, July 17·5°C. Annual rainfall 30·8" (782·2 mm).

CONSTITUTION AND GOVERNMENT

The Grand Duchy of Luxembourg is a constitutional monarchy.

The reigning Grand Duke is **Henri**, b. 16 April 1955, son of the former Grand Duke Jean and Princess Joséphine-Charlotte of Belgium; succeeded 7 Oct. 2000 on the abdication of his father; married Maria Teresa Mestre 14 Feb. 1981. (*Offspring:* Prince Guillaume, b. 11 Nov. 1981; Prince Felix, b. 3 June 1984; Prince Louis, b. 3 Aug. 1986; Princess Alexandra, b. 16 Feb. 1991; Prince Sebastian, b. 16 April 1992).

The constitution of 17 Oct. 1868 was revised in 1919, 1948, 1956, 1972, 1983, 1988, 1989, 1994, 1996 and 1998.

The separation of powers between the legislature and the executive is not very strong, resulting in much interaction between the two bodies. Only the judiciary is completely independent.

The 12 cantons are divided into four electoral districts: the South, the East, the Centre and the North. Voters choose between party lists of candidates in multi-member constituencies.

The parliament is the *Chamber of Deputies*, which consists of a maximum of 60 members elected for five years. Voting is compulsory and there is universal suffrage. Seats are allocated according to the rules of proportional representation and the principle of the smallest electoral quote. There is a *Council of State* of 21 members appointed by the Sovereign. Membership is for a maximum period of 15 years, with retirement compulsory at the age of 72. It advises on proposed laws and any other question referred to it.

The head of state takes part in the legislative power, exercises executive power and has a part in the judicial power. The constitution leaves to the sovereign the right to organize the government, which consists of a Minister of State, who is Prime Minister, and of at least three Ministers. Direct consultation by referendum is provided for in the Constitution.

National Anthem
'Ons Hemecht' ('Our Homeland'); words by M. Lentz, tune by J. A. Zinnen.

GOVERNMENT CHRONOLOGY

Prime Ministers since 1937. (CSV = Christian Social Party; DP = Democratic Party)

1937–53	CSV	Pierre Dupong
1953–58	CSV	Joseph Bech
1958–59	CSV	Pierre Frieden
1959–74	CSV	Pierre Werner
1974–79	DP	Gaston Thorn
1979–84	CSV	Pierre Werner
1984–95	CSV	Jacques Santer
1995–	CSV	Jean-Claude Juncker

RECENT ELECTIONS

Elections took place on 13 June 2004. The Christian Social Party (CSV) won 24 seats (with 36·1% of the vote), the Socialist Workers' Party (LSAP) 14 (23·4%), the Democratic Party (DP) 10 (16·1%), the Greens (Déi Gréng) 7 (11·6%) and the Action Committee for Democracy and Pensions Justice (ADR) 7 (9·9%). Turnout was 91·7%. Following the election a coalition government was formed between the Christian Social Party and the Socialist Workers' Party.

European Parliament
Luxembourg has six representatives. At the June 2004 elections turnout was 90·0%. CSV won 3 seats with 37·1% of votes cast (political affiliation in European Parliament: European People's Party–European Democrats); LSAP, 1 with 22·1% (Party of European Socialists); the Greens, 1 with 15·0% (Greens/European Free Alliance); the Democratic Party, 1 with 14·9% (Alliance of Liberals and Democrats for Europe).

CURRENT ADMINISTRATION

In March 2006 the Christian Social Party–Socialist Workers' Party coalition comprised:

Prime Minister, Minister of State, Finance and the Exchequer: Jean-Claude Juncker; b. 1954 (CSV; sworn in 20 Jan. 1995). He is currently Europe's longest-serving prime minister.

Deputy Prime Minister, Minister of Foreign Affairs and Immigration: Jean Asselborn (LSAP). *Agriculture, Viticulture, Rural Development, Middle Classes, Housing and Tourism:* Fernand Boden (CSV). *Treasury and Budget, and Justice:* Luc Frieden (CSV). *The Family, Integration and Equal Opportunities:* Marie-Josée Jacobs (CSV). *Health and Social Security:* Mars Di Bartolomeo (LSAP). *Environment and Transport:* Lucien Lux (LSAP). *Interior and Land Management:* Jean-Marie Halsdorf (CSV). *Economy, External Commerce and Sport:* Jeannot Krecké (LSAP). *Civil Service and Administrative Reform, and Public Works:* Claude Wiseler (CSV). *Co-operation and Humanitarian Action, Communications and Defence:* Jean-Louis Schiltz (CSV).

Labour and Employment, and Religious Affairs: François Biltgen (CSV). *National Education and Professional Training:* Mady Delvaux-Stehres (LSAP).

The *Speaker* is Lucien Weiler.

Government Website (French only): http://www.gouvernement.lu

CURRENT LEADERS

Jean-Claude Juncker

Position
Prime Minister

Introduction
Jean-Claude Juncker was appointed prime minister in Jan. 1995, replacing Jacques Santer who became president of the European Commission. He is the leader of the Christian Social Party (CSV). Having been re-elected as prime minister in 1999 and again in 2004, he is now Europe's longest-serving head of government. He is committed to European integration, and played an important role in the decisions leading up to the creation of the EU's single currency (euro).

Early Life
Juncker was born in Redange-sur-Attert on 9 Dec. 1954. He obtained his primary and secondary education in Luxembourg and Belgium. Having studied law at the University of Strasbourg, he was admitted to the Bar of Luxembourg in Feb. 1980. He was an active member of the CSV and chaired its youth organization from 1979–84. Juncker was appointed state secretary for employment and social affairs in 1982. In 1984 he was elected to Parliament for the first time as minister of labour, minister of social security and minister in charge of the budget. When Luxembourg held the presidency of the European Community in 1985, Juncker chaired the Council of Ministers for social affairs and the budget. In 1990 he was elected party leader of the CSV. As president of the EC Economic and Finance Council in 1991, Juncker was among the core co-authors of the Treaty of Maastricht. He was a governor of the World Bank from 1989–95, and since 1995 has been the country's governor of the European Investment Bank, the European Bank for Reconstruction and Development and the International Monetary Fund.

Career in Office
Juncker concurrently holds the position of prime minister and minister of state, finance and the exchequer. In Oct. 2000 his government oversaw the abdication of the King, Grand Duke Jean, in favour of his son Prince Henri. In Feb. 2002 Juncker was awarded the Légion d'Honneur by French President Jacques Chirac. Following his re-election in mid-2004, he formed a new CSV coalition government with the Socialist Workers' Party. From Jan.–June 2005 he led Luxembourg's six-month presidency of the European Union, and his government secured approval for the proposed new EU constitution in a national referendum in July 2005.

DEFENCE

There is a volunteer light infantry battalion of (2004) 1,000, of which only the career officers are professionals. In recent years Luxembourg soldiers and officers have been actively participating in peacekeeping missions, mainly in the former Yugoslavia. There is also a Gendarmerie of 612. In 2000 the Gendarmerie and the police force merged to form the Police grand-ducale. NATO maintains a squadron of E-3A *Sentries*.

In 2004 military expenditure totalled US$252m. (US$554 per capita), representing 0·9% of GDP.

INTERNATIONAL RELATIONS

Luxembourg is a member of the UN, WTO, NATO, Benelux, the EU, OECD, the Council of Europe, WEU, OSCE, Asian

Development Bank, IOM and the International Organization of the Francophonie. The Schengen accord of June 1990 abolished border controls between Luxembourg, Austria, Belgium, Denmark, Finland, France, Germany, Greece, Iceland, Italy, the Netherlands, Norway, Portugal, Spain and Sweden.

On 10 July 2005 Luxembourg became the thirteenth European Union member to ratify the proposed EU constitution. Voters approved the constitution with 56·5% of votes cast in favour and 43·5% against.

Luxembourg gave US$0·2bn. in international aid in 2004, which at 0·83% of GNI made it the world's third most generous country as a percentage of its gross national income.

ECONOMY

Services accounted for 78·9% of GDP in 2003, industry 20·5% and agriculture 0·6%.

According to the anti-corruption organization *Transparency International*, Luxembourg ranked 13th in the world in a 2005 survey of the countries with the least corruption in business and government. It received 8·5 out of 10 in the annual index.

Overview

A founding member of the European Coal and Steel Community, Luxembourg's post-war economic growth was based primarily upon its highly productive steel industry. The small industrial sector has since become more diversified to include chemical, rubber and other manufactured products. The main engine of recent growth has been the financial services sector, particularly investment fund management. The government is looking to diversify into other financial services. Financial and business services accounted for 43·8% of total gross added value in 2000, well above the developed country norm, while its agricultural and manufacturing sectors accounted for 0·7% and 12·1% respectively, well below the OECD norm.

Other dynamic sectors of the economy include telecommunications, audio-visual and multimedia, industrial plastics and air transport. The strength of the economy has allowed Luxembourg to absorb a significant amount of foreign labour while maintaining low unemployment, although the inflow of people has put a strain on infrastructure. In the half-decade before the global slowdown of 2001, Luxembourg's economy grew faster than its neighbours at an annual average of over 7%. The economy was hit by the slowdown but proved comparatively resilient. Luxembourg is the richest country in the world when measured by per capita GDP and recent growth in the average income level has been very strong for a developed country. Inflation, normally under control, has recently crept above the euro zone average.

Currency

On 1 Jan. 1999 the euro (EUR) became the legal currency in Luxembourg; irrevocable conversion rate 40·3399 Luxembourg francs to 1 euro. The euro, which consists of 100 cents, has been in circulation since 1 Jan. 2002. There are seven euro notes in different colours and sizes denominated in 500, 200, 100, 50, 20, 10 and 5 euros, and eight coins denominated in 2 and 1 euros, then 50, 20, 10, 5, 2 and 1 cents. On the introduction of the euro there was a 'dual circulation' period before the Luxembourg franc ceased to be legal tender on 28 Feb. 2002. Euro banknotes in circulation on 1 Jan. 2002 had a total value of €5·6bn.

Inflation rates (based on OECD statistics):

1995	1996	1997	1998	1999	2000	2001	2002	2003	2004
1·9%	1·2%	1·4%	1·0%	1·0%	3·8%	2·4%	2·1%	2·5%	3·2%

Foreign exchange reserves were US$260m. in Sept. 2005. Gold reserves were 74,000 troy oz in Sept. 2005 and total money supply €505m. in June 2002.

Budget

Revenue and expenditure for calendar years in €1m.:

	2001	2002	2003	2004
Revenue	5,709	5,977	7,211	7,766
Expenditure	5,148	5,999	7,537	8,389

Public debt in 2004 was €614·6m.

VAT is 15%, with reduced rates of 12%, 6% and 3%. According to government projections, the general government surplus was expected to be €14,930,500 in 2001. Income taxes and business taxes have been reduced to preserve competitiveness in the international environment. The normal tax rate for companies at 1 Jan. 2004 was 30·38%, compared with 40·3% in 1996.

Performance

In terms of GDP per head, Luxembourg is the richest country in the world, with a per capita PPP (purchasing power parity) GDP of €49,700 in 2004.

Real GDP growth rates (based on OECD statistics):

1995	1996	1997	1998	1999	2000	2001	2002	2003	2004
1·4%	3·3%	8·3%	6·9%	7·8%	9·0%	1·6%	2·5%	2·9%	4·5%

Total GDP in 2004 was US$31·1bn.

Banking and Finance

Luxembourg's Central Bank (formerly the Monetary Institute) was established in July 1998 (*Director-General*, Yves Mersch). In Dec. 2004 there were 162 banks. German banks make up nearly a third of all the banks. Total deposits in 2004 were €560·7bn.; net assets in unit trusts, €504·0bn.; net assets in investment companies, €600·3bn. There is a stock exchange.

In 2004 the financial sector accounted for 18·1% of gross added value at basic prices and the banks showed a net profit of €2·9bn. The total number of approved insurance companies in 2004 was 95, with reinsurance companies numbering 271; the amount of premiums due was €8,737·5m.

In 2003 Luxembourg received US$91·1bn. worth of foreign direct investment, the highest total of any country.

ENERGY AND NATURAL RESOURCES

Environment

Carbon dioxide emissions from the consumption and flaring of fossil fuels in 2003 were the equivalent of 25·0 tonnes per capita.

Electricity

Apart from hydro-electricity and electricity generated from fossil fuels, Luxembourg has no national energy resources. Installed capacity in 2001 was 1·6m. kW. Net electricity production was 1,592m. kWh in 2001 and consumption per capita 15,654 kWh in 2000.

Agriculture

The contribution of agriculture, viticulture and forestry to the economy has been gradually declining over the years, accounting for only 0·5% of gross added value at basic prices in 2004. However, the actual output of this sector has nearly tripled during the past 30 years, a trend common to many EU countries. There were 4,975 workers engaged in agricultural work (including wine-growing and forestry) in 2004 (726 wage-earners in 2001). In 2001 there were 638 farms with an average area of 55·2 ha.; 128,073 ha. were under cultivation in 2004.

Production, 2004 (in tonnes) of main crops: grassland and pasturage, 707,936; forage crops, 243,782; maize, 184,364; bread crops, 87,899; potatoes, 22,244; colza (rape), 16,526. Production, 2004 (in 1,000 tonnes) of meat, 29·0; milk, 268·5. In 2004–05, 155,800 hectolitres of wine were produced. In 2001 there were 7,534 tractors, 706 harvester-threshers, 1,553 manure spreaders and 1,721 gatherer-presses. Total tractors and other agriculture vehicles, 2005: 14,656.

Livestock (15 May 2004): 3,686 horses, 186,725 cattle, 84,611 pigs, 9,743 sheep.

Forestry
In 2002 there were 89,741 ha. of forests, which in 2003 produced 130,602 cu. metres of broadleaved and 123,483 cu. metres of coniferous wood.

INDUSTRY
According to the Financial Times Survey (FT 500), the largest company by market capitalization in Luxembourg on 4 Jan. 2001 was SES (US$4,557·7m.), a global satellite communications company.

In 2004 there were 3,038 industrial enterprises, of which 1,972 were in the building industry. Production, 2001 (in tonnes): rolled steel products, 4,518,537; steel, 2,724,679. One of the world's largest steel producers, Arcelor, has its headquarters in Luxembourg. Created in Feb. 2002 through the merger of Arbed of Luxembourg, Aceralia of Spain and Usinor of France, it produces in the region of 47m. tonnes of steel annually and accounts for approximately 4·5% of world steel output. The steel industry mainly relies on imported ore.

Labour
In 2004 the estimated total workforce was 301,000. The government fixes a legal minimum wage. Retirement is at 65. Employment creation was 3·2% in 2004–05. In 2005 the standardized unemployment rate was 4·2%. Luxembourg has one of the lowest rates of unemployment of any EU member country. The minimum wage in Jan. 2005 was €8·48 an hour.

Between 1994 and 2003 strikes cost Luxembourg an average of just six days per 1,000 employees a year (the second lowest in the European Union, with Germany having four per 1,000).

There was a 2·6% increase in employment in 2004. Of the new jobs created, around two-thirds went to so-called *frontaliers*, workers living in surrounding countries who commute into Luxembourg to work. More than 100,000 people cross into Luxembourg every day from neighbouring France, Germany and Belgium to work, principally in the financial services industry.

Trade Unions
The main trade unions are the OGB-L (Socialist) and the LCGB (Christian-Social). Other sectorial unions include ALEBA (the banking sector), FNCTTFEL (railworkers) and FEP (private employers). In 2003 employees chose representatives to the 38-member Chamber of Private Sector Staff and the 32-member Chamber of Labour from trade union candidate lists. The next elections are scheduled for 2008.

INTERNATIONAL TRADE
Luxembourg is in the process of turning itself into a centre for electronic commerce, the world's fastest-growing industry.

Imports and Exports
Imports in 2004 (provisional figures) totalled €13,460·8m. and exports €9,783·6m. In 2000 exports reached 156% of GDP. In 2004, 90·6% of imports were from other EU member countries and 87·2% of imports went to other EU member countries.

Principal imports and exports by standard international trade classification (provisional figures) in €1m.:

	Imports 2004	Exports 2004
Food and live animals	963·9	452·7
Beverages and tobacco	460·6	180·3
Crude materials, oils, fats and waxes	987·9	191·3
Mineral fuels and lubricants	1,302·1	56·4
Chemicals and related products	1,289·5	673·3
Manufactured goods in metals	1,641·8	3,038·2

	Imports 2004	Exports 2004
Other manufactured goods classified chiefly by material	1,115·9	1,590·4
Machinery	2,267·9	1,778·5
Transport equipment	1,874·2	594·0
Other manufactured goods	1,557·0	1,228·5
Total	13,460·8	9,783·6

Trade with selected countries (provisional figures) in €1m.:

	Imports 2004	Exports 2004
Austria	111·0	234·5
Belgium	4,811·4	1,170·6
France	1,866·6	1,940·7
Germany	3,641·7	2,564·2
Italy	359·0	658·8
Netherlands	677·8	447·3
Spain	122·4	360·0
UK	220·0	488·3
Total EU	12,203·1	8,535·2
Non-EU Europe	229·1	372·6
Japan	224·8	192·9
NIEA[1]	23·3	90·1
USA	481·2	251·7
Total	13,460·8	9,783·6

[1]New industrialized economies of Asia (Singapore, South Korea, Taiwan, Indonesia, Malaysia and China)

Trade Fairs
The *Foires Internationales de Luxembourg* occurs twice a year, and there are a growing number of specialized fairs.

COMMUNICATIONS

Roads
On 1 Jan. 2005 there were 2,894 km of roads of which 147 km were motorways. Motor vehicles registered at 1 Jan. 2005 numbered 366,480 including 299,759 passenger cars, 23,976 trucks, 1,270 coaches and 13,901 motorcycles. In 2001 there were 774 road accidents with 70 fatalities.

Rail
In 2004 there were 275 km of railway (standard gauge) of which 261 km were electrified; 13·6m. passengers were carried in 2001.

Civil Aviation
Findel is the airport for Luxembourg. 1,517,000 passengers and 730,362 tonnes of freight were handled in 2004. The national carrier is Luxair, 23·1% state-owned. Cargolux has developed into one of the major international freight carriers. In 1999 scheduled airline traffic of Luxembourg-based carriers flew 57·1m. km, carrying 843,000 passengers (all on international flights).

Shipping
A shipping register was set up in 1990. In 2001 merchant shipping totalled 1,591,281 tonnes. 159 vessels were registered at 25 June 2002.

Telecommunications
Luxembourg had 363,267 main telephone lines in 2004, or 798 for every 1,000 population. There were 336,700 PCs in use in 2004 (740 per 1,000 persons) and 546,000 mobile phone subscribers (1,200 per 1,000 persons—the highest rate in any sovereign country). There were 25,000 fax machines in use in 2001. In 2002 Luxembourg had 168,350 Internet users.

Postal Services
In 2003 there were 108 post offices. In 2003 a total of 177·8m. items of mail were processed.

SOCIAL INSTITUTIONS

Justice

The Constitution makes the Courts of Law independent in performing their functions, restricting their sphere of activity, defining their limit of jurisdiction and providing a number of procedural guarantees. The Constitution has additionally laid down a number of provisions designed to ensure judges remain independent of persons under their jurisdiction, and to ensure no interference from the executive and legislative organs. All judges are appointed by Grand-Ducal order and are irremovable.

The judicial organization comprises three Justices of the Peace (conciliation and police courts). The country is, in addition, divided into two judicial districts—Luxembourg and Diekirch. District courts deal with matters such as civic and commercial cases. Offences which are punishable under the Penal Code or by specific laws with imprisonment or hard labour fall within the jurisdiction of the criminal chambers of District Courts, as the Assize Court was repealed by law in 1987. The High Court of Justice consists of a Supreme Court of Appeal and a Court of Appeal.

The judicial organization of the Grand-Duchy does not include the jury system. A division of votes between the judges on the issue of guilt/innocence may lead to acquittal. Society before the Courts of Law is represented by the Public Prosecutor Department, composed of members of the judiciary directly answerable to the government.

In 1999 a new Administrative Tribunal, Administrative Court and Constitutional Court were established.

The population in penal institutions in Dec. 2004 was 455.

Education

The adult literacy rate in 2004 was 100%. Education is compulsory for all children between the ages of six and 15. In 2003–04 there were 13,947 children in pre-primary school (pre-nursery education, 3,535; nursery education, 10,412) with 1,089 teachers; 32,456 pupils in primary schools; 32,520 pupils in secondary schools. In higher education (2002–03) the Higher Institute of Technology (IST) had 358 students and there were 401 students in teacher training. In 2003–04 the University Centre of Luxembourg had 2,849 students. Many students go abroad, predominantly to France, Germany and Belgium. In 2003–04, 6,723 students pursued university studies abroad.

In 1999–2000 total expenditure on education came to 4·0% of GNP and 8·5% of total government spending.

Health

In 2004 there were 1,591 doctors (411 GPs and 840 specialists) and 340 dentists. There were 17 hospitals and 3,045 hospital beds in 2004. In 2003 Luxembourg spent 6·1% of its GDP on health.

Welfare

The official retirement age is 65 years for both men and women. To be eligible, a pensioner must have paid 120 months contributions. The maximum old-age pension is €5,130·08 per month. The minimum pension is €1,108·10 per month if insured for 40 years, reduced by 1/40 for each year less than 40. A minimum pension is not payable if the person has been insured for less than 20 years.

Unemployment benefit is 80% (85% if the insured has a dependant child) of the basis salary during the previous three months, up to 2·5 times the social minimum wage. Recent graduates receive 70% of the social minimum wage whereas self-employed persons receive 80% of the social minimum wage.

RELIGION

The population was 91% Roman Catholic in 2001. There are small Protestant, Jewish, Greek Orthodox, Russian Orthodox and Muslim communities as well.

CULTURE

Luxembourg City will be one of two European Capitals of Culture for 2007. The title attracts large European Union grants.

World Heritage Sites

Luxembourg has one site on the UNESCO World Heritage List: the City of Luxembourg—its Old Quarters and Fortifications (inscribed on the list in 1994).

Broadcasting

The major broadcaster of TV and radio programmes is RTL Group, formerly CLT (*Compagnie Luxembourgeoise de Télédiffusion*), along with local and regional radio stations that have emerged since the 1991 Law on Electronic Media. CLT was set up in 1929 and started broadcasting in 1932. In the same year Radio Luxembourg started broadcasting its multilingual programmes. In 1954 CLT received an exclusive licence for broadcasting radio and TV in the Grand-Duchy, which was extended until the end of 2010 in 1995.

With 31 television and 33 radio stations in ten countries, RTL Group is Europe's largest TV, radio and production company. Listed on the London Stock Exchange, the Luxembourg-based media group operates TV channels and radio stations in Germany, France, Belgium, the Netherlands, UK, Luxembourg, Spain, Hungary, Denmark, Portugal, Croatia, Italy, North America and Australia. CLT-UFA S.A. also broadcast four TV channels and three radio stations via the ASTRA satellite system. The 1991 Law on Electronic Media allowed the creation of four new radio networks and 15 local radio stations, and thus ended the CLT monopoly.

Cinema

In 2000 there were 25 cinema screens throughout the country. Cinema attendances in 2004 totalled 1,357,000.

Press

There were nine daily newspapers in 2005; in 2002 daily newspapers had a circulation of 118,000, equivalent to 265 per 1,000 inhabitants. There are a number of weekly titles with a circulation of 124,166 in 2001.

Tourism

In 2004 there were 933,000 tourists, and 7,424 hotel rooms and 1,279,000 overnight stays. Tourists spent US$2,186m. in 2002. Camping is widespread, and weekend and short-stay tourism accounts for many tourists. There were 1,141,000 overnight stays at campsites in 2004.

Festivals

The Festival International Echternach (May–June) and the Festival of Wiltz (June–July) are annual events. Both feature a variety of classical music, jazz, theatre and recitals.

Libraries

In Dec. 2005 there were 21 public libraries, one national library and six university libraries (which are also open to non-students). In 2004 these libraries held around 2·5m. volumes in total; there were 2,587,201 library loans.

Theatre and Opera

There are several theatres in Luxembourg City, including the *Grand Théâtre de la Ville*, *Théâtre des Capucins*, *Théâtre du Centaure* and *Philharmonie du Luxembourg—Salle de Concerts Grande-Duchesse Joséphine Charlotte*. There are also a number of smaller theatres elsewhere, notably in Esch/Alzette and Echternach.

Museums and Galleries

The main museums in Luxembourg City are the *Musée d'Histoire de la Ville*, the *Villa Vauban*, the *Musée National d'Histoire Naturelle*, the *Musée National d'Histoire et d'Art*, the *Musée d'Art Moderne Grand-Duc Jean*, the *Musée de la Forteresse* and the *Casino Luxembourg—Forum d'Art Contemporain*. There are smaller museums in the rest of the country. In 2000 there were two national museums, 11 public museums and three private museums, which had 189,403 visitors.

DIPLOMATIC REPRESENTATIVES

Of Luxembourg in the United Kingdom (27 Wilton Crescent, London, SWIX 8SD)
Ambassador: Jean-Louis Wolzfeld.

Of the United Kingdom in Luxembourg (14 Blvd Roosevelt, L-2450 Luxembourg)
Ambassador: James Clark.

Of Luxembourg in the USA (2200 Massachusetts Ave., NW, Washington, D.C., 20008)
Ambassador: Joseph Weyland.

Of the USA in Luxembourg (22 Blvd. Emmanuel Servais, L-2535 Luxembourg)
Ambassador: Ann L. Wagner.

Of Luxembourg to the United Nations
Ambassador: Jean-Marc Hoscheit.

FURTHER READING

STATEC. *Annuaire Statistique 2004.*

Christophory, J. and Thoma, E., *Luxembourg.* [Bibliography] 2nd ed. ABC-Clio, Oxford and Santa Barbara (CA), 1997
Newcomer, J., *The Grand Duchy of Luxembourg: The Evolution of Nationhood, 963 AD to 1983.* 2nd ed. Editions Emile Borschette, Luxembourg, 1995

National Library: 37 Boulevard Roosevelt, Luxembourg City.
National Statistical Office: Service Central de la Statistique et des Etudes Economiques (STATEC), CP 304, Luxembourg City, L-2013 Luxembourg. *Director:* Serge Allegrezza.
Website: http://www.statec.public.lu/

MACEDONIA

Republika Makedonija
The Republic of Macedonia
(Former Yugoslav Republic of Macedonia)

Capital: Skopje
Population projection, 2010: 2·05m.
GDP per capita, 2003: (PPP$) 6,794
HDI/world rank: 0·797/59

KEY HISTORICAL EVENTS

The history of Macedonia can be traced to the reign of King Karan (808–778 BC), but the country was at its most powerful at the time of Philip II (359–336 BC) and Alexander the Great (336–323 BC). At the end of the 6th century AD Slavs began to settle in Macedonia. There followed a long period of internal fighting but the spread of Christianity led to consolidation and the creation of the first Macedonian Slav state, the Kingdom of Samuel, 976–1018. In the 14th century it fell to Serbia, and in 1355 to the Turks. After the Balkan wars of 1912–13 Turkey was ousted and Serbia received part of the territory, the rest going to Bulgaria and Greece. In 1918 Yugoslav Macedonia was incorporated into Serbia as South Serbia, becoming a republic in the Socialist Federal Republic of Yugoslavia. Claims to the historical Macedonian territory have long been a source of contention with Bulgaria and Greece. Macedonia declared its independence on 18 Sept. 1991. In April 1999 the Kosovo crisis which led to NATO air attacks on Yugoslavian military targets set off a flood of refugees into Macedonia, although most returned home after the end of the crisis.

In March 2001 there were a series of clashes between government forces and ethnic Albanian separatists near the border between Macedonia and Kosovo. As violence escalated Macedonia found itself on the brink of civil war. In May 2001 the new national unity government gave ethnic Albanian rebels a 'final warning' to end their uprising. As the crisis worsened, a stand-off within the government between the Macedonian and the ethnic Albanian parties was only resolved after the intervention of Javier Solana, the EU's foreign and security policy chief. A number of Macedonian soldiers were killed in clashes with the rebels, and following reverses in the military campaign the commander of the Macedonian army, Jovan Andrevski, resigned in June 2001. In Aug. 2001 a peace accord was negotiated.

TERRITORY AND POPULATION

Macedonia is bounded in the north by Serbia and Montenegro, in the east by Bulgaria, in the south by Greece and in the west by Albania. Its area is 25,713 sq. km. According to the 2002 census final results, the population on 1 Nov. 2002 was 2,022,547. The main ethnic groups in 2002 were Macedonians (1,297,981), Albanians (509,083), Turks (77,959), Romas (53,879), Serbs (35,939) and Vlachs (9,695). Ethnic Albanians predominate on the western side of Macedonia. Minorities are represented in the Council for Inter-Ethnic Relations. In Dec. 2004 density was 79 per sq. km. In 2003, 59·6% of the population lived in urban areas.

The UN gives a projected population for 2010 of 2·05m.

Macedonia is divided into 84 municipalities. The major cities (with 2002 census population) are: Skopje, the capital, 506,926; Kumanovo, 76,275; Bitola, 74,550; Prilep, 69,704; Tetovo, 52,915.

The official language is Macedonian, which uses the Cyrillic alphabet.

SOCIAL STATISTICS

In 2004: births, 23,361; deaths, 17,944; marriages, 14,073; divorces, 1,645; infant deaths, 308. Rates (per 1,000 population): birth, 11·5; death, 8·8; marriage, 6·9; divorce, 0·8. Infant mortality, 2004 (per 1,000 live births), 13·2. Expectation of life at birth in 2003 was 71·3 years for males and 76·3 years for females. Annual population growth rate, 1994–2004, 0·4%. In 2004 the most popular age range for marrying was 25–29 for males and 20–24 for females. Fertility rate, 2004, 1·5 births per woman.

Migration within the Republic of Macedonia, 2004: 9,326. International (external) migration: emigrated persons, 669; immigrated persons 1,381. Net migration in 2004 was 712.

CLIMATE

Macedonia has a mixed Mediterranean-continental type climate, with cold moist winters and hot dry summers. Skopje, Jan. –0·4°C, July 23·1°C.

CONSTITUTION AND GOVERNMENT

At a referendum held on 8 Sept. 1991 turnout was 74%; 99% of votes cast were in favour of a sovereign Macedonia. On 17 Nov. 1991 parliament promulgated a new constitution which officially proclaimed Macedonia's independence. This was replaced by a constitution adopted on 16 Nov. 2001 which for the first time included the recognition of Albanian as an official language. It also increased access for ethnic Albanians to public-sector jobs.

The *President* is directly elected for five-year terms. Candidates must be citizens aged at least 40 years. The parliament is a 120-member single-chamber *Assembly* (*Sobranie*), elected by universal suffrage for four-year terms. There is a *Constitutional Court* whose members are elected by the assembly for non-renewable eight-year terms, and a *National Security Council* chaired by the President. Laws passed by the Assembly must be countersigned by the President, who may return them for reconsideration, but cannot veto them if they gain a two-thirds majority.

Political Parties

The Law on Political Parties makes a distinction between a political party and an association of citizens. The signatures of 500 citizens with the right to vote must be produced for a party to be legally registered. Presently the country has 34 legally registered parties.

National Anthem

'Denes nad Makedonija se radja novo sonce na slobodata' ('Today a new sun of liberty appears over Macedonia'); words by V. Maleski, tune by T. Skalovski.

RECENT ELECTIONS

Following the death of Boris Trajkovski in a plane crash on 26 Feb. 2004, presidential elections were held on 14 April 2004. Branko Crvenkovski (Social Democratic League of Macedonia), the incumbent prime minister, took 42·5% of the vote, Saško Kedev (Internal Macedonian Revolutionary Organization-Democratic Party for Macedonian National Unity) 34·1%, Gzim Ostreni (Democratic Union for Integration) 14·8% and Zidi Xhelili (Democratic Party of Albanians) 8·6%. In the run-off on 28 April Crvenkovski won with 60·6% against Kedev with 39·4%. Turnout was 53·4%.

Parliamentary elections were held on 5 Sept. 2002. The Together for Macedonia coalition, comprising the Social Democratic League of Macedonia (SDSM) and the Liberal-Democratic Party (LDP), won 59 seats with 40·5% of votes cast, defeating Prime Minister Ljubčo Georgievski's Internal Macedonian Revolutionary Organization-Democratic Party for Macedonian National Unity (VMRO-DMPNE-LPM) with 34 seats and 24·4%. The Democratic Union for Integration (DUI) won 16 seats with 11·9%; the Democratic Party of Albanians (PDS), 7 with 5·2%; the Democratic Prosperity Party (PDP), 2 with 2·3%; the National-Democratic Party (NDP), 1 with 2·1%; and the Socialist Party of Macedonia (SPM), 1 with 2·1%. Turnout was 73·5%.

CURRENT ADMINISTRATION

President: Branko Crvenkovski; b. 1962 (SDSM; sworn in 12 May 2004). He was previously prime minister from Aug. 1992–Nov. 1998 and Nov. 2002–May 2004.

Prime Minister: Vlado Buckovski; b. 1962 (SDSM; sworn in 17 Dec. 2004).

Following elections in Sept. 2002, a SDSM-LDP-DUI coalition government was formed, which in March 2006 was composed as follows:

Deputy Prime Minister and Minister of Defence: Jovan Manasievski (LDP). *Deputy Prime Minister for European Integration:* Radmila Shekerinska (SDSM). *Deputy Prime Minister for Political Systems:* Musa Xhaferi (DUI). *Deputy Prime Minister for Economic Systems:* Minco Jordanov (SDSM).

Minister of Agriculture, Forestry and Water Supply: Sadulla Duraku (LDP). *Culture:* Blagoja Stefanovski (SDSM). *Economy:* Fatmir Besimi (DUI). *Education and Science:* Azis Polozani (DUI). *Environment:* Zoran Sapuric (LDP). *Finance:* Nikola Popovski (SDSM). *Foreign Affairs:* Ilinka Mitreva (SDSM). *Health:* Vladimir Dimov (SDSM). *Interior:* Ljubomir Mihajlovski (SDSM). *Justice:* Meri Mladenovska-Gjorgjievska (SDSM). *Labour and Social Policy:* Stevco Jakimovski (LDP). *Local Self-Government:* Rizvan Sulejmani (DUI). *Transport and Communications:* Xhemali Mehazi (DUI). *Minister without Portfolio:* Vlado Popovski (LDP).

Government Website: http://www.vlada.mk

CURRENT LEADERS

Branko Crvenkovski

Position
President

Introduction
Branko Crvenkovski, a former prime minister of Macedonia, became president of the republic in 2004. He was the first to promote Albanian participation in Macedonian politics.

Early Life
Crvenkovski was born 12 Oct. 1962 in Sarajevo. In 1986 he graduated with a degree in computer science and automation from the school of electrical engineering at the St Cyril and Methodius University in Skopje. His political career began when he was elected member of the assembly of the Republic of Macedonia at the first multi-party elections in the former Yugoslavia in 1990, having spent several years as head of department at the Semos company in Skopje. In April 1991, Crvenkovski became the head of the Social Democratic League of Macedonia (SDSM) despite having been a communist.

Career in Office
In Aug. 1992 he became Macedonia's first prime minister after its secession from Yugoslavia. He was then only 29 years old and the youngest government leader in Europe. Re-elected in the Dec. 1994 elections, he retained the premiership until Nov. 1998. At the head of the SDSM, Crvenkovski successfully implemented wide-ranging economic and social reforms, and guided the country out of the immediate post-Yugoslav era. He became prime minister again in 2002 after his SDSM party won parliamentary elections. In April 2004 he won the presidential elections, defeating the centre-right candidate Saško Kedev, and took office on 12 May 2004, resigning as prime minister shortly thereafter.

DEFENCE

The President is the C.-in-C. of the armed forces. There is conscription for nine months.

Defence expenditure in 2003 totalled US$137m. (US$67 per capita), representing 3·1% of GDP.

The European Union's first ever peacekeeping force (EUFOR) officially started work in Macedonia on 1 April 2003, replacing the NATO-led force that had been in the country since 2001.

Army

Army strength was estimated at 11,300 (8,000 conscripts) in 2002 with potential reserves of 60,000. There is a paramilitary police force of 7,600.

Navy

In 2002 the Marine Wing numbered 400, with five river patrol craft.

Air Force

The Army Air Force numbered 800 in 2002, and had four combat aircraft and 12 armed helicopters.

INTERNATIONAL RELATIONS

On 13 Sept. 1995 under the auspices of the UN, Macedonia and Greece agreed to normalize their relations.

Macedonia is a member of the UN, WTO, BIS, the Council of Europe, OSCE, the Central European Initiative, the NATO Partnership for Peace and the International Organization of the Francophonie.

ECONOMY

Agriculture accounted for 12·3% of GDP in 2002, industry 30·2% and services 57·5%.

Currency

The national currency of Macedonia is the *denar* (MKD), of 100 *deni*.

Gold reserves were 196,000 troy oz in May 2002 and foreign exchange reserves US$825m. Inflation was –0·3% in 2004 (1·2% in 2003). Total money supply was 25,725m. denars in June 2002.

Budget

In 2002 revenues totalled 53,089m. denars and expenditures 59,979m. denars.

Performance

In 2000 real GDP growth was 4·5%, but in 2001 the political turmoil in the country resulted in the economy contracting by 4·5%. There was then a slight recovery in 2002, with a growth rate of 0·9%. The economy continued to recover in 2003 and 2004 with growth of 3·5% and 2·4% respectively. Total GDP in 2004 was US$5·2bn.

Banking and Finance

The central bank and bank of issue is the National Bank of Macedonia. Its *Governor* is Petar Goshev (since May 2004). Privatization of the banking sector was completed in 2000. In 2001 there were 20 commercial banks, six of which were majority foreign-owned. As of 31 Dec. 1998 commercial banks' total non-government deposits were 23,136m. denars, and non-government savings deposits were 15,095m. denars. The largest banks are Stopanska Banka, followed by Komercijalna Banka; between them they control more than half the total assets of all banks in Macedonia.

A stock exchange opened in Skopje in 1996.

ENERGY AND NATURAL RESOURCES

Environment

Macedonia's carbon dioxide emissions from the consumption and flaring of fossil fuels were the equivalent of 4·0 tonnes per capita in 2002.

Electricity

Installed capacity in 2000 was 1·5m. kW. Output in 2000: 6·81bn. kWh, of which 1·17bn. kWh were from hydro-electric plants. Consumption per capita was 3,404 kWh in 2000.

Oil and Gas

A 230-km long pipeline bringing crude oil to Macedonia from Thessaloniki in Greece opened in July 2002. Built at a cost of over US$130m., it has the capacity to provide Macedonia with 2·5m. tonnes of crude oil annually.

Minerals

Macedonia is relatively rich in minerals, including lead, zinc, copper, iron, chromium, nickel, antimony, manganese, silver and gold. Output in 2003 (in tonnes): lignite, 8,360,000; copper ore, 1,200,000; lead-zinc ore, 40,000; copper concentrate, 15,000; lead concentrates, 5,000; silver, 10.

Agriculture

In 2002 the agricultural population numbered 833,000 persons, of whom 109,000 were economically active. In 2004 there were 560,264 ha. of arable land, 703,830 ha. of pasture and 44,000 ha. of permanent crops. In 2004, 101,004 ha. of arable land were owned by agricultural organizations and 459,260 ha. by individual farmers.

Crop production, 2004 (in 1,000 tonnes): wheat, 356; grapes, 194; potatoes (2003), 175; barley, 149; wine, 142; maize (2003), 141; watermelons, 115; chillies and green peppers (2003), 111; tomatoes (2002), 109; lucerne, 98; apples, 82; cabbages (2002), 71; sugarbeets, 47; onions (2003), 31; cucumbers and gherkins, 27; plums, 26; tobacco, 22. In 2004, 119,000 tonnes of wine were produced.

Livestock, 2004 (in 1,000): cattle, 255; sheep, 1,432; pigs, 158; horses, 40; chickens, 2,725. Livestock products, 2004 (in 1,000 tonnes): beef, 9; pork, bacon and ham, 9; mutton, 7; poultry, 3; cow's milk, 213m. litres; sheep's milk, 49m. litres; eggs (total), 340m.

There were 65,338 tractors in use in 2004.

Forestry

Forests covered 947,653 ha. in 2004, chiefly oak and beech. 781,000 cu. metres of timber were cut in 2004.

Fisheries

Total catch in 2004 was 1,271 tonnes, entirely from inland waters.

INDUSTRY

In 1999 there were 94,404 enterprises (90,426 private, 1,112 public, 1,257 co-operative, 1,577 mixed and 32 state-owned). Production (in tonnes): cement (2004), 585,000; residual fuel oil (2000), 377,000; distillate fuel oil (2000), 259,000; petrol (2004), 146,377; sulphuric acid (2001), 101,058; ferro-alloys (2004), 72,082; detergents (2004), 14,507.

Labour

In April 2004 there were 522,995 employed persons, including: 116,300 in manufacturing; 87,608 in agriculture, hunting and forestry; 74,218 in wholesale and retail trade/repair of motor vehicles, motorcycles and personal and household goods; and 33,635 in education. The number of unemployed persons in 2004 was 309,286, giving an unemployment rate of 37·2%.

INTERNATIONAL TRADE

The foreign debt of Macedonia, including debt taken over from the former Yugoslavia, was US$1,619m. in 2002.

Imports and Exports

In 2004 imports (f.o.b.) were valued at US$2,903·4m. (US$2,306·4m. in 2003) and exports (f.o.b.) at US$1,673·5m. (US$1,367·0m. in 2003).

Main import suppliers, 2003: Germany (12·6%), Greece (9·7%), Russia (8·7%), Serbia and Montenegro (8·4%) and Bulgaria (7·2%). Main export markets, 2003: Serbia and Montenegro (20·8%), Germany (18·9%), Greece (13·7%), Italy (8·0%) and USA (4·3%).

COMMUNICATIONS

Roads

In 2004 there were 906 km of main roads, 3,801 km of regional roads and 8,417 km of local roads: 1,224 km of roads were paved and 6,939 km asphalted. 9·3m. passengers and 10·5m. tonnes of freight were transported. There were 299,809 cars, 2,478 buses and 19,042 lorries in 2003. In 2004 there were 1,988 road accidents with 155 fatalities.

Rail

In 2004 there were 696 km of railways (233 km electrified). 0·9m. passengers and 2·6m. tonnes of freight were transported.

Civil Aviation

There are international airports at Skopje and Ohrid. The main Macedonia-based carrier is MAT Macedonian Airlines, which flew 4·5m. km and carried 226,000 passengers in 2004. In 2004 Skopje handled 489,942 passengers (all on international flights) and 1,749 tonnes of freight. Ohrid handled 32,497 passengers (all on international flights) and 21 tonnes of freight.

Telecommunications

In 2004 there were 732,468 main telephone lines (360·3 per 1,000 inhabitants) and 997,756 mobile phone subscribers. There were 357,300 Internet users in 2004 and 4,200 fax machines in 2002. In 2002 the Hungarian firm Matav acquired a 51% stake in MakTel, the state monopoly telecommunications provider, in the most significant economic development in the country's history. The deal, worth €618·2m. (US$568·4m.) over two years, is the biggest foreign investment to date.

Postal Services

In 2003 there were 317 post offices.

SOCIAL INSTITUTIONS

Justice

Courts are autonomous and independent. Judges are tenured and elected for life on the proposal of the *Judicial Council*, whose members are themselves elected for renewable six-year terms. The highest court is the Supreme Court. There are 27 courts of first instance and three higher courts.

The population in penal institutions in Sept. 2002 was 1,248 (61 per 100,000 of national population).

Education

The literacy rate was 96·1% in 2003 (98·2% among males and 94·1% among females). Education is free and compulsory for eight years. In 2004, 36,392 children attended 51 pre-school institutions and 486 infant schools of elementary education. In 2004–05 there were 227,254 pupils enrolled in 1,012 primary, 95,268 in 96 secondary schools and (2001–02) 343,587 students in higher education. There are universities at Skopje (Cyril and Methodius, founded in 1949; 36,509 students and 1,314 academic staff in 2004–05) and Bitola (founded 1979; 10,043 students and 233 academic staff in 2004–05). There are two private universities at Skopje (1,075 students and 41 academic staff in 2004–05) and Tetovo (1,737 students and 86 academic staff in 2004–05).

In 1999–2000 total expenditure on education came to 4·2% of GNP.

Health

In 2004 there were 4,490 doctors, 1,134 dentists, 322 pharmacologists and 63 hospitals with 9,699 beds.

Welfare

In 2004 social assistance was paid to 67,260 households. Child care and special supplements went to 46,203 children, and 16,970 underage and 95,053 adults received social benefits. There were 260,075 pensioners in 2004.

RELIGION

Macedonia is traditionally Orthodox but the church is not established and there is freedom of religion. In 2001 there were 1·21m. Serbian (Macedonian) Orthodox and 580,000 Sunni Muslims. In 1967 an autocephalous Orthodox church split off from the Serbian. Its head is the Archbishop of Ohrid and Macedonia whose seat is at Skopje. It has five bishoprics in Macedonia and representatives in USA, Canada and Australia. It has some 300 priests.

The Muslim Religious Union has a superiorate at Skopje. The Roman Catholic Church has a seat at Skopje.

CULTURE

World Heritage Sites

The Former Yugoslav Republic of Macedonia has one site on the UNESCO World Heritage List: Ohrid Region with its Cultural and Historic Aspect and its Natural Environment (inscribed on the list in 1979), a rich repository of Byzantine art and architecture.

Broadcasting

The national Macedonian Radio and Television (colour by PAL) is government-funded. It broadcasts on three TV and seven radio channels. In 2004 there were also 29 local public broadcasting enterprises (state-owned), 18 of which transmitted only radio programmes while the other 11 transmitted radio and TV programmes. In 2004 there were 69 private radio and 54 private TV stations. In 2000 there were 570,000 TV subscribers and 415,000 radio receivers.

Cinema

There were 19 cinemas and 302,653 admissions in 2004; gross box office receipts came to 27m. denars. Five documentary films were made in 2002 and one full-length film in 2004.

Press

There were ten daily newspapers and 11 weeklies in 2004, and 207 other newspapers and periodicals published in Macedonian, Albanian, Turkish, English and other languages.

There are two news agencies in Macedonia, the Macedonian Information Agency (national) and Makfax (privately owned).

Tourism

In 2004 tourists numbered 465,015 spending 1·86m. nights in Macedonia. Total tourist revenue was US$39m. in 2002.

DIPLOMATIC REPRESENTATIVES

Of Macedonia in the United Kingdom (5th floor, 25 James St., London, W1U 1DU)
Ambassador: Gjorgji Spasov.

Of the United Kingdom in Macedonia (Dimitrija Chupovski 26, 1000 Skopje)
Ambassador: Robert Chatterton Dickson.

Of Macedonia in the USA (1101 30th St., NW, Suite 302, Washington, D.C., 20007)
Ambassador: Nikola Dimitrov.

Of the USA in Macedonia (Blvd Ilinden, 1000 Skopje)
Ambassador: Gillian A. Milovanovic.

Of Macedonia to the United Nations
Ambassador: Igor Dzundev.

Of Macedonia to the European Union
Ambassador: Sasko Stefkov.

FURTHER READING

Danforth, L. M., *The Macedonian Conflict: Ethnic Nationalism in a Transnational World.* Princeton Univ. Press, 1996
Poulton, H., *Who Are the Macedonians?* Farnborough, 1996

National Statistical Office: State Statistical Office, Dame Gruev 4, Skopje.
Director: Katerina Kostadinova-Daskalovska.
Website: http://www.stat.gov.mk

MADAGASCAR

Feb. 2002 Ravalomanana declared himself president and imposed a state of emergency. However, incumbent Didier Ratsiraka and his government set up a rival capital in Toamasina. In April 2002 both men agreed to a recount of votes to solve the dispute. Ravalomanana was declared president following the recount.

TERRITORY AND POPULATION

Madagascar is situated 400 km (250 miles) off the southeast coast of Africa, from which it is separated by the Mozambique channel. Its area is 587,041 sq. km (226,658 sq. miles). At the 1993 census the population was 12,092,157 (50·45% female); density, 20·6 per sq. km. Estimate (2005), 18,606,000 (73·4% rural, 2003). Population density, 32 per sq. km.

The UN gives a projected population for 2010 of 21·15m.

Province	Area in sq. km	Population (1993 census)	Chief town	Population (1993 census)
Antananarivo	58,283	3,483,236	Antananarivo	1,432,000[1]
Antsiranana	43,046	942,410	Antsiranana	54,418[2]
Fianarantsoa	102,373	2,671,150	Fianarantsoa	99,005
Mahajanga	150,023	1,330,612	Mahajanga	100,807
Toamasina	71,911	1,935,330	Toamasina	127,441
Toliary	161,405	1,729,419	Toliary	61,460[2]

[1]1999 figure. [2]1990 estimate.

The indigenous population is of Malayo-Polynesian stock, divided into 18 ethnic groups of which the principal are Merina (24%) of the central plateau, the Betsimisaraka (13%) of the east coast and the Betsileo (11%) of the southern plateau. Foreign communities include Europeans (mainly French), Indians, Chinese, Comorians and Arabs.

The official language is Malagasy. French is the language of international communication.

SOCIAL STATISTICS

2000 estimates: births, 663,000; deaths, 211,000. Rates, 2000 estimates (per 1,000 population): births, 41·5; deaths, 13·2. Infant mortality, 2001 (per 1,000 live births), 84. Expectation of life in 2003 was 54·1 years for males and 56·8 for females. Annual population growth rate, 1992–2002, 2·9%. Fertility rate, 2001, 5·8 births per woman.

CLIMATE

A tropical climate, but the mountains cause big variations in rainfall, which is very heavy in the east and very light in the west. Antananarivo, Jan. 70°F (21·1°C), July 59°F (15°C). Annual rainfall 54" (1,350 mm). Toamasina, Jan. 80°F (26·7°C), July 70°F (21·1°C). Annual rainfall 128" (3,256 mm).

CONSTITUTION AND GOVERNMENT

Following a referendum, a Constitution came into force on 30 Dec. 1975 establishing a Democratic Republic. It provided for a National People's Assembly elected by universal suffrage from the single list of the *Front National pour la Défense de la Révolution Socialiste Malgache.* Executive power was vested in the President with the guidance of a Supreme Revolutionary Council.

Under a convention of 31 Oct. 1991 the powers of the National People's Assembly and the Supreme Revolutionary Council were delegated to a High State Authority for a Provisional government. Following a referendum on 19 Aug. 1992 at which turnout was 77·68% and 75·44% of votes cast were in favour, a new Constitution was adopted on 21 Sept. 1992 establishing the Third Republic. Under this the *National Assembly* has 160 seats (increased from 150 for the 2002 election). There is also a *Senate* of 90 members.

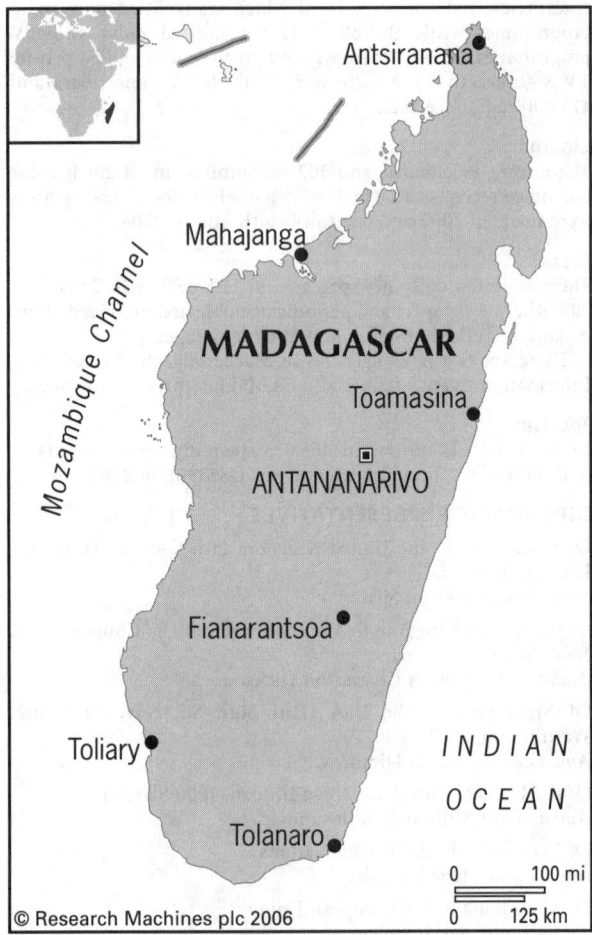

© Research Machines plc 2006

Repoblikan'i Madagasikara

Capital: Antananarivo
Population projection, 2010: 21·15m.
GDP per capita, 2003: (PPP$) 809
HDI/world rank: 0·499/146

KEY HISTORICAL EVENTS

The island was settled by people of African and Indonesian origin when it was visited by the Portuguese explorer, Diego Diaz, in 1500. The island was unified under the Imérina monarchy between 1797 and 1861, but a French protectorate was established in 1895.

Madagascar became a French colony on 6 Aug. 1896 and achieved independence on 26 June 1960.

In Feb. 1975 Col. Richard Ratsimandrava, Head of State, was assassinated. The 1975 Constitution instituted a 'Democratic Republic' in which only a single political party was permitted.

After six months of anti-government unrest an 18-month transitional administration was agreed. A new Constitution instituted the Third Republic in Sept. 1992.

Following the presidential election of Dec. 2001 the opposition candidate Marc Ravalomanana claimed victory, although the High Constitutional Court ruled that a run-off was needed. On 22

A referendum on 17 Sept. 1995 was in favour of the President appointing and dismissing the Prime Minister, hitherto elected by parliament. The electorate was 6m.; turnout was 50%.

National Anthem
'Ry tanindrazanay malala ô!' ('O our beloved Fatherland'); words by Pastor Rahajason, tune by N. Raharisoa.

RECENT ELECTIONS
At the first round of presidential elections on 16 Dec. 2001 there were six candidates. Turnout was 66·7%. Official results gave Marc Ravalomanana 46·2% of votes cast against 40·9% for Didier Ratsiraka, forcing the two men into a run-off, but Marc Ravalomanana himself claimed to have won the election outright. Ravalomanana declared himself president on 22 Feb. 2002 but with Ratsiraka refusing to accept defeat there were effectively two presidents. On 18 April 2002 the two men signed a deal designed to end the bitter power struggle. Following the announcement by the Supreme Court of a recount of the votes cast in the presidential election, the two candidates agreed that in the event of neither obtaining a majority, a referendum would be held to settle the issue. In the recount the High Constitutional Court declared Marc Ravalomanana the winner with 51·5% of votes against 35·9% for Didier Ratsiraka, with others obtaining 12·6% between them, although the result was not recognized by Ratsiraka. On 6 May 2002 Marc Ravalomanana was sworn in as president. In protest, four of Madagascar's six provinces declared independence. In June 2002 US President George W. Bush gave formal recognition of Ravalomanana's claim to the presidency. On 5 July 2002 Ratsiraka left Madagascar for the Seychelles.

In parliamentary elections held on 15 Dec. 2002 President Marc Ravalomanana's I Love Madagascar party won 103 of the 160 seats, his allies within the National Unity coalition 22, independents also 22 and minor parties 13. Turnout was 67·6%.

CURRENT ADMINISTRATION
President: Marc Ravalomanana; b. 1949 (ind., sworn in 6 May 2002).

In March 2006 the cabinet was composed as follows:
Prime Minister: Jacques Sylla; b. 1946 (ind.).

Minister of Foreign Affairs: Gen. Marcel Ranjeva. *Interior:* Charles Rabemananjara. *Defence:* Petera Behajaina. *Agriculture, Livestock and Fisheries:* Harrison Andriarimanana. *Civil Service, Labour and Social Laws:* Théodore Ranjivason. *Tourism and Culture:* Jean Jacques Rabenirina. *Finance and Budget:* Andriamparany Radavidson. *Energy and Mines:* Olivier Donat Andriamahefaparany. *Environment:* Gen. Charles Sylvain Rabotoarison. *Health:* Jean-Louis Robinson. *Industrialization, Commerce and Development of the Private Sector:* Roger Marie Rafanomezantsoa. *Justice:* Henriette Ratsiharivala. *Land Management:* Jean Angelin Randrianarison. *Posts and Telecommunications:* Bruno Ramaroson Andriantavison. *Population, Social Protection and Leisure:* Zafilaza. *Transportation and Public Works:* Roland Randriamampionona. *Basic and Higher Education and Scientific Research:* Hajanirina Razafinjatovo. *Youth and Sports:* Tombo Ramandimbisoa.

Government Website (French only):
http://www.madagascar.gov.mg

CURRENT LEADERS

Marc Ravalomanana

Position
President

Introduction
Marc Ravalomanana became president in May 2002 following disputed presidential elections held in Dec. 2001. Having accused incumbent Didier Ratsiraka of rigging the vote that saw neither man achieve the necessary majority to take office, there followed several months of political and social unrest before Ratsiraka went into exile. Having secured international recognition, Ravalomanana's principal task was to lead an economic recovery.

Early Life
Ravalomanana was born on 12 Dec. 1949 as a member of the Merina ethnic group in Imerikasina, a village outside the capital city, Antananarivo. He was educated at a protestant school in Sweden but finished his academic pursuits in his early twenties to set up a yoghurt manufacturing operation in Antananarivo. Having secured World Bank funding for expansion, his company grew to claim a monopoly of Madagascar's dairy and oil products and to become the biggest locally-owned company in the country.

In 1999 Ravalomanana was elected mayor of Antananarivo and set about a programme of urban redevelopment. Recognized for his dynamism, several of his schemes were also controversial, such as when he ordered the destruction of a hundred habitations on aesthetic grounds. When the first round of presidential elections were held in Dec. 2001, neither Ravalomanana or incumbent President Didier Ratsiraka gained the required 50% plus one vote needed to take office.

Career in Office
A run-off was set to take place in late Feb. 2002 but Ravalomanana accused his opponent of electoral corruption and claimed that he had won 52% of the vote outright. Ravalomanana's supporters took part in mass protests and declared a general strike. In response, Ratsiraka's supporters blockaded the capital. It was estimated that the strike was costing the already-impoverished nation US$14m. per day. An international mediation team, including the secretary of the Organization of African Unity (as was), brokered a deal that saw the run-off postponed. However, on 22 Feb. Ravalomanana declared himself president. Ratsiraka set up a rival government in Tamatave, a port city on the east coast. There followed a suspension from the Organization of African Unity, which claimed the transfer of power from Ratsiraka to Ravalomanana was unconstitutional.

On 29 April the High Constitutional Court ruled that Ravalomanana had indeed won the election and he formally took office on 6 May 2002. Fighting continued between the two camps throughout the country, resulting in extensive casualties. Ravalomanana gradually gained the upper hand and secured international recognition, first from the USA and later from France, the former colonial power and chief trading partner. Having lost control of what had been his provincial heartlands, Ratsiraka went into exile in July 2002. In Feb. 2003 a former head of the armed services was charged with an attempted coup. Six months later Ratsiraka was sentenced *in absentia* to ten years hard labour for embezzlement. In Dec. 2003 former prime minister Tantely Adrianarivo was given 12 years for corruption.

The months of instability following the election had severely weakened what was already a failing economy. Parliamentary elections were held in Dec. 2002 and the strong showing of Ravalomanana's I Love Madagascar party was seen as a reassertion of popular support for the president, who continued to implement free market reforms, provide free primary education for all and oversee improvements in the medical and transport infrastructures. The economy was further hit when two cyclones wreaked havoc and left many thousands homeless in Feb. and March 2004, but received a boost in Oct. 2004 when the World Bank and IMF announced that US$2bn. of Madagascar's debt was to be written off. In March 2005 Madagascar became one of the first beneficiaries of a new development aid scheme designed to reward nations promoting democratic and free market principles.

DEFENCE

There is conscription (including civilian labour service) for 18 months. Defence expenditure totalled US$81m. in 2003 (US$5 per capita), representing 1·5% of GDP.

Army

Strength (2002) 12,500 and gendarmerie 8,100.

Navy

In 2002 the maritime force had a strength of 500 (including 100 marines).

Air Force

Personnel (2002) 500. There are 12 combat aircraft.

INTERNATIONAL RELATIONS

Madagascar is a member of the UN, WTO, the African Union, African Development Bank, COMESA, SADC, IOM, the International Organization of the Francophonie and is an ACP member state of the ACP-EU relationship.

ECONOMY

In 2002 agriculture contributed 31·7% of GDP, industry 14·4% and services 53·8%.

Currency

In July 2003 President Marc Ravalomanana announced that the *Ariary* (MGA) would become the official currency, replacing the *Malagasy franc* (MGFr). The Ariary became legal tender on 1 Aug. 2003 and although the Malagasy franc is no longer legal tender it will remain exchangeable until 2009. The Ariary is subdivided into five *Iraimbilanja*.

In June 2002 foreign exchange reserves were US$393m. Inflation was –1·1% in 2003, but 14·0% in 2004. Total money supply in May 2002 was MGFr5,265·55bn.

Budget

Budget revenue and expenditure (in MGFr1bn.), year ending 31 Dec.:

	1997	1998	1999	2000
Revenue	1,746·8	2,077·0	2,666·8	3,067·8
Expenditure	2,879·4	3,477·5	4,068·8	4,477·7

Performance

Total GDP in 2004 was US$4·4bn. There was a recession in 2002 with the economy contracting by 12·7% as a result of the six-month long political crisis, but a recovery followed in 2003 and 2004 with real GDP growth of 9·8% and 5·3% respectively.

Banking and Finance

A Central Bank, the Banque Centrale de Madagascar, was formed in 1973, replacing the former Institut d'Emission Malgache as the central bank of issue. The *Governor* is Gaston Ravelojaona. All commercial banking and insurance was nationalized in 1975 and privatized in 1988. Of the six other banks, the largest are the Bankin'ny Tantsaha Mpamokatra and the BNI—Crédit Lyonnais de Madagascar.

ENERGY AND NATURAL RESOURCES

Environment

Madagascar's carbon dioxide emissions from the consumption and flaring of fossil fuels in 2002 were the equivalent of 0·1 tonnes per capita.

Electricity

Installed capacity was 0·2m. kW in 2000. Production in 2000 was 807m. kWh, with consumption per capita being 51 kWh.

Oil and Gas

Natural gas reserves (2002), 2·8bn. cu. metres.

Minerals

Mining production in 2000 included: chromite, 118,750 tonnes; graphite, 40,328 tonnes; salt, 25,530 tonnes. There have also been discoveries of precious and semi-precious stones in various parts of the country, in particular sapphires, topaz and garnets.

Agriculture

75–80% of the workforce is employed in agriculture. There were 3·0m. ha. of arable land in 2001 and 0·6m. ha. of permanent crops. 1·09m. ha. were irrigated in 2001. The principal agricultural products in 2000 were (in 1,000 tonnes): rice, 2,300; cassava, 2,228; sugarcane, 2,200; sweet potatoes, 476; potatoes, 293; bananas, 260; mangoes, 204; taro, 155; maize, 150; coconuts, 84; dry beans, 84; oranges, 83. Rice is produced on some 40% of cultivated land.

Cattle breeding and agriculture are the chief occupations. There were, in 2000, 10·36m. cattle, 1·37m. goats, 900,000 pigs, 800,000 sheep and 20m. chickens.

Forestry

In 2000 the area under forests was 11·73m. ha., or 20·2% of the total land area. The forests contain many valuable woods, while gum, resins and plants for tanning, dyeing and medicinal purposes abound. Timber production was 10·01m. cu. metres in 2001.

Fisheries

The catch of fish in 2001 was 135,583 tonnes (78% from marine waters).

INDUSTRY

Industry, hitherto confined mainly to the processing of agricultural products, is now extending to cover other fields.

Labour

In 1996 the workforce was 7,199,000 (55% males). In 1995 approximately 75% of the economically active population were engaged in agriculture, fisheries and forestry.

INTERNATIONAL TRADE

Foreign debt was US$4,518m. in 2002.

Imports and Exports

In 2002 imports (f.o.b.) were valued at US$603m. (US$955m. in 2001) and exports (f.o.b.) at US$486m. (US$928m. in 2001). The principal imports in 1999 were machinery and transport equipment (27%), petroleum products (24%), manufactured goods (15%) and foodstuffs (11%). Principal exports in 1999 were cotton fabrics (13%), cloves (8%), coffee (7%), precious and semi-precious stones (7%) and vanilla (5%). Main import suppliers, 1999: France, 20·7%; Iran, 12·4%; Bahrain, 8·7%; China, 6·7%. Main export markets, 1999: France, 37·8%; Singapore, 7·5%; Germany, 6·4%; USA, 5·4%.

COMMUNICATIONS

Roads

In 2002 there were about 65,663 km of roads, 11·6% of which were paved. There were 52,200 passenger cars in 2002, 39,400 trucks and vans and (1996) 4,850 buses and coaches. 25 people died in road accidents in 1995.

Rail

In 2000 there were 883 km of railways, all metre gauge. In 2000, 0·2m. passengers and 0·1m. tonnes of freight were transported.

Civil Aviation

There are international airports at Antananarivo (Ivato) and Mahajanga (Amborovy). The national carrier is Air Madagascar, which is 89·6% state-owned. In 1999 it flew 8·7m. km, carrying 317,600 passengers (144,800 on international flights). In 2001 Antananarivo handled 699,074 passengers (348,238 on domestic flights) and 15,499 tonnes of freight.

Shipping

The main ports are Toamasina, Mahajanga, Antsiranana and Toliara. In 2002 the merchant marine totalled 35,000 GRT, including oil tankers 5,000 GRT. In 2000 vessels totalling 4,842,000 NRT entered ports.

Telecommunications

Madagascar had 222,500 telephone subscribers in 2002, equivalent to 14·0 per 1,000 persons, and 46,000 PCs were in use (2·9 per 1,000 persons). In 2002 there were 163,000 mobile phone subscribers. In 2002 there were 55,000 Internet users.

Postal Services

There were 957 post offices in 2003, or one for every 18,200 persons.

SOCIAL INSTITUTIONS

Justice

The Supreme Court and the Court of Appeal are in Antananarivo. In most towns there are Courts of First Instance for civil and commercial cases. For criminal cases there are ordinary criminal courts in most towns. In 1996 government expenditure on public order and safety totalled MGFr59,200m.

The population in penal institutions in 2003 was approximately 19,000 (109 per 100,000 of national population).

Education

Education is compulsory from six to 14 years of age. In 2000–01 there were 46,482 teachers for 2·3m. pupils in primary schools, 382,474 pupils in general programmes at secondary level with 16,795 (1995–96) teachers and 31,386 students at university level. In 1994–95 there were six universities. Adult literacy rate in 2003 was 70·6% (male, 76·4%; female, 65·2%). In 2000–01 total expenditure on education came to 3·2% of GNP.

Health

There were nine hospital beds per 10,000 population in 1990. In 2001 there were 1,428 physicians, 76 dentists, 3,088 nurses, 1,472 midwives and eight pharmacists. In 1996 government expenditure on health totalled MGFr191,300m.

Welfare

In 1996 government expenditure on social security and welfare totalled MGFr26,000m.

RELIGION

About 48% of the population practise the traditional religion, 43% are Christians (of whom approximately half are Roman Catholic and half are Protestant, mainly belonging to the Fiangonan'i Jesosy Kristy eto Madagasikara) and 9% are followers of other religions (predominantly Islam). In May 2005 the Roman Catholic church had one cardinal.

CULTURE

World Heritage Sites

Tsingy de Bemaraha Strict Nature Reserve joined the UNESCO World Heritage List in 1990. The undisturbed forests, lakes and mangrove swamps are the habitat for rare and endangered lemurs and birds. The Royal Hill of Ambohimanga was added in 2001, a royal city and burial site and a symbol of Malagasy identity.

Broadcasting

The government-controlled Radio-Télévision Malagasy is responsible for broadcasting. There are radio programmes in Malagasy and French, and 12 hours TV transmission a day (colour by PAL). In 2000 there were 3·35m. radio sets and in 2001 there were 390,000 TV sets.

Press

In 1998 there were five daily newspapers with a total circulation of 68,000.

Tourism

There were 170,000 tourists in 2001. Receipts totalled US$115m.

DIPLOMATIC REPRESENTATIVES

Of Madagascar in the United Kingdom
Ambassador: Vacant.
Chargé d'Affaires a.i.: Guy Rakotomena (resides in Paris).
Honorary Consul: Stephen Hobbs (16 Lanark Mansions, Pennard Rd, London, W12 8DT).

Of the United Kingdom in Madagascar (Lot II 164 Ter, Alarobia-Amboniloha BP 167, Antananarivo)
Ambassador: Anthony Godson (resides in Port Louis, Mauritius).

Of Madagascar in the USA (2374 Massachusetts Ave., NW, Washington, D.C., 20008)
Ambassador: Narisoa Rajaonarivony.

Of the USA in Madagascar (14–16 rue Rainitovo, Antsahavola, Antananarivo)
Ambassador: James D. McGee.

Of Madagascar to the United Nations
Ambassador: Zina Andrianarivelo.

Of Madagascar to the European Union
Ambassador: Jean Beriziky.

FURTHER READING

Banque des Données de l'Etat. *Bulletin Mensuel de Statistique*

Allen, P. M., *Madagascar*. Boulder (CO), 1995

Brandt, H. and Brown, M., *Madagascar*. [Bibliography] ABC-Clio, Oxford and Santa Barbara (CA), 1993

National Statistical Office: Institut National de la Statistique (INSTAT), BP 485 Anosy, Antananarivo 101.

Website (French only): http://www.cite.mg/instat/index.htm

MALAŴI

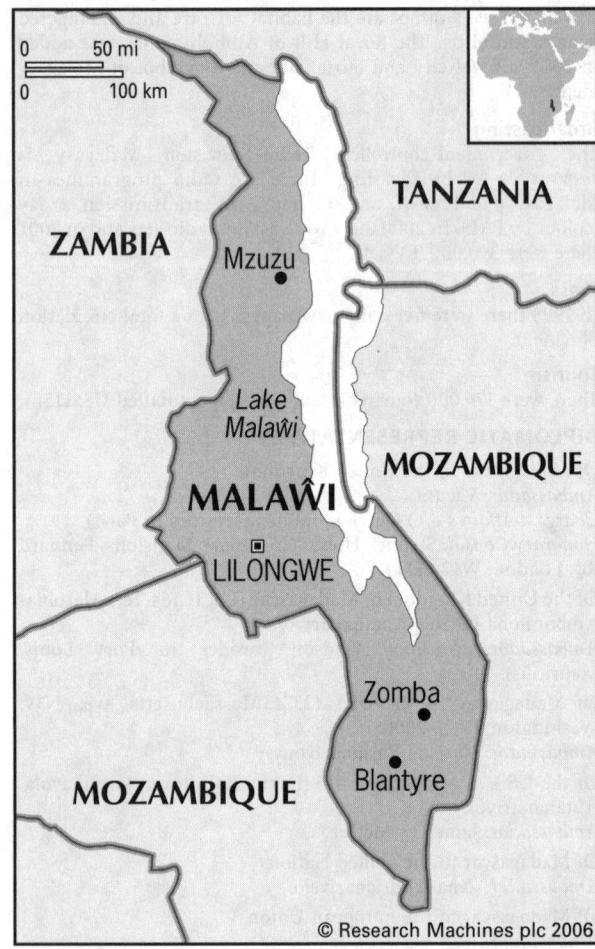

© Research Machines plc 2006

Dziko la Malaŵi
(Republic of Malaŵi)

Capital: Lilongwe
Population projection, 2010: 14·35m.
GDP per capita, 2003: (PPP$) 605
HDI/world rank: 0·404/165

KEY HISTORICAL EVENTS

The explorer David Livingstone reached Lake Nyasa, now Lake Malaŵi, in 1859 and it was the land along the lake's western shore that became, in 1891, the British Protectorate of Nyasaland. In 1884 the British South Africa Company applied for a charter to trade. Pressure on land, the colour bar and other grievances generated Malaŵian resistance. In 1953 Nyasaland was joined with Southern Rhodesia (Zimbabwe) and Northern Rhodesia (Zambia) to form the Federation of Rhodesia and Nyasaland, under British control. This union was dissolved in 1963 when Nyasaland was for a year self-governing, until on 6 July 1964 it became independent, adopting the name of Malaŵi. In 1966 Malaŵi was declared a republic and Dr Hastings Banda became the first president, establishing a one party dictatorship which lasted for 30 years. In 1994 Malaŵi returned to multi-party democracy.

TERRITORY AND POPULATION

Malaŵi lies along the southern and western shores of Lake Malaŵi (the third largest lake in Africa), and is otherwise bounded in the north by Tanzania, south by Mozambique and west by Zambia. Area (including the inland water areas of Lake Malombe, Chilwa, Chiuta and the Malaŵi portion of Lake Malaŵi, which total 24,208 sq. km), 118,484 sq. km (45,747 sq. miles).

Population at census 1998, 9,933,868; density, 83·8 per sq. km. 2005 population estimate: 12,884,000. In 2003, 83·7% of the population was rural.

The UN gives a projected population for 2010 of 14·35m.

Population of main towns (estimated 1998): Blantyre, 2m.; Lilongwe, 1m.; Mzuzu, 100,000; Zomba, 70,000. Population of the regions (1998 census): Northern, 1,233,560; Central, 4,066,340; Southern, 4,633,968.

The official languages are Chichewa, spoken by over 58% of the population, and English.

SOCIAL STATISTICS

2001 estimates: births, 556,000; deaths, 222,000. Estimated rates, 2001 (per 1,000 population): births, 47·8; deaths, 19·1. Annual population growth rate, 1992–2002, 1·9%. Expectation of life at birth in 2003 was 39·8 years for males and 39·6 for females. Infant mortality, 2001, 114 per 1,000 live births; fertility rate, 2001, 6·5 births per woman.

CLIMATE

The tropical climate is marked by a dry season from May to Oct. and a wet season for the remaining months. Rainfall amounts are variable, within the range of 29–100" (725–2,500 mm), and maximum temperatures average 75–89°F (24–32°C), and minimum temperatures 58–67°F (14·4–19·4°C). Lilongwe, Jan. 73°F (22·8°C), July 60°F (15·6°C). Annual rainfall 36" (900 mm). Blantyre, Jan. 75°F (23·9°C), July 63°F (17·2°C). Annual rainfall 45" (1,125 mm). Zomba, Jan. 73°F (22·8°C), July 63°F (17·2°C). Annual rainfall 54" (1,344 mm).

CONSTITUTION AND GOVERNMENT

The *President* is also head of government. Malaŵi was a one-party state, but following a referendum on 14 June 1993, in which 63% of votes cast were in favour of reform, a new Constitution was adopted on 17 May 1994 which ended Hastings Banda's life presidency and provided for the holding of multi-party elections. At these Bakili Muluzi was elected president by 47·16% of votes cast against President Banda and two other opponents. There is a *National Assembly* of 193 members, elected for five-year terms in single-seat constituencies.

National Anthem

'O God Bless our Land of Malaŵi'; words and tune by M.-F. Sauka.

RECENT ELECTIONS

At parliamentary elections of 18 May 2004 the Malaŵi Congress Party (MCP—formerly the only legal party) won 59 seats; the United Democratic Front (UDF), 49; and the Mgwirizano coalition, 27. Independents took 38 seats and others 14, with six districts requiring subsequent by-elections. Turnout was 52%.

At the concurrent presidential elections Bingu wa Mutharika (UDF) won with 35·9% of the vote, ahead of John Tembo (MCP) with 27·1% and Gwanda Chakuamba (Mgwirizano) with 25·7%. Both losing candidates challenged the results and the fairness of the elections.

CURRENT ADMINISTRATION

President and Minister Responsible for Defence, the Civil Service, Statutory Corporations and Privatization: Dr Bingu wa Mutharika; b. 1934 (Democratic Progressive Party; sworn in on 24 May 2004).

President Mutharika was sworn into office despite protests from his two opponents in the May elections. In Feb. 2005 he left the UDF after a power struggle with its chairman, former president Bakili Muluzi, and launched a new party, the Democratic Progressive Party. The 'National Unity' government consisted of the following in March 2006:

Vice President: Dr Cassim Chilumpha.

Minister of Agriculture and Food Security: Uladi Mussa. *Economic Planning and Development:* David Faiti. *Education and Human Resources:* Kate Kainja-Kaluluma. *Finance:* Goodall Gondwe. *Foreign Affairs:* Davis Katsonga. *Health:* Dr Hetherwick Ntaba. *Home Affairs and Internal Security:* Anna Kachikho. *Industry, Science and Technology:* Khumbo Chirwa. *Information, Communications and Tourism:* Patricia Kaliyati. *Irrigation and Water Development:* Sidik Mia. *Justice and Constitutional Affairs:* Henry Phoya. *Labour and Vocational Training:* Ken Lipenga. *Lands, Housing and Surveys:* Bazuka Mhango. *Local Government and Rural Development:* Dr George Chaponda. *Mines, Natural Resources and Environment:* Henry Chimunthu Banda. *Social Development and Persons with Disabilities:* Clement Chiwaya. *Trade and Private Sector Development:* Dr Martin Kansichi. *Transport and Public Works:* Henry Mussa. *Women, Child Welfare and Community Services:* Joyce Banda. *Youth, Sports and Culture:* Jaffali Mussa.

Government Website: http://www.malawi.gov.mw

CURRENT LEADERS

Dr Bingu wa Mutharika

Position
President

Introduction
Dr Bingu wa Mutharika became president of Malaŵi following elections in May 2004, having been nominated by former president (and his former political foe), Bakili Muluzi, who retired after two consecutive terms in office.

Early Life
Bingu wa Mutharika was born in Thyolo, Malaŵi on 24 Feb. 1934. The son of a Catholic primary school teacher, he gained a masters degree in economics from the University of Delhi, India, before studying for a PhD in development economics at Pacific Western University in Los Angeles, USA. He then went to work for the Malaŵian civil service and later for the Zambian government.

In 1978 Mutharika joined the UN, motivated by his opposition to the regime of Hastings Banda, Malaŵi's self-declared 'President for Life'. He was given the post of director for trade and development finance for Africa. In 1991 he became secretary-general of the Common Market for Eastern and Southern Africa (COMESA).

Mutharika was a founding member of the United Democratic Front (UDF), the party led by Muluzi that went on to win Malaŵi's first multi-party elections in 1994. The two became adversaries when Mutharika opposed Muluzi's economic policies. Mutharika left the UDF to form the United Party (UP) in 1997. However, after unsuccessfully contesting the presidency in 1999, he disbanded the UP and returned to the UDF, where he was made minister of economic planning and development in 2002.

Career in Office
In Feb. 2005, following a series of clashes with Muluzi and an alleged assassination attempt in Jan. by UDF members,

Mutharika again resigned from the party, subsequently forming the Democratic Progressive Party (DPP).

His principal challenges are to reduce poverty and to revitalize the economy by encouraging foreign investment. He aims to turn Malaŵi from an import culture to an export one, and so provide trade opportunities for the rural poor. Mutharika has also vowed to continue with his high-profile anti-corruption campaign.

DEFENCE

All services form part of the Army. Defence expenditure totalled US$11m. in 2003 (US$1 per capita), representing 0·7% of GDP.

Army

Personnel (2002) 5,300. In addition there is a paramilitary mobile police force totalling 1,500.

Navy

The Navy, based at Monkey Bay on Lake Nyasa, numbered 220 personnel in 2002.

Air Wing

The Air Wing acts as infantry support and numbered 80 in 1999 with no combat aircraft.

INTERNATIONAL RELATIONS

Malaŵi is a member of the UN, WTO, the Commonwealth, African Development Bank, COMESA (the Common Market for Eastern and Southern Africa), the African Union and SADC and is an ACP member state of the ACP-EU relationship.

ECONOMY

Agriculture accounted for 36·7% of GDP in 2002, industry 14·9% and services 48·4%.

Overview

A privatization programme began in 1996. Of 100 state-owned enterprises, 43 had been privatized by 2005.

Currency

The unit of currency is the *kwacha* (MWK) of 100 *tambala*. Foreign exchange reserves were US$178m. and gold reserves 10,000 troy oz in May 2002. Foreign exchange controls were abolished in Feb. 1994. Inflation fell from 83·1% in 1995 to 9·6% in 2003, but rose to 11·6% in 2004. Total money supply in Dec. 2001 was K.9,829m.

Budget

Budget (in K.1bn.):

	1998	1999	2000	2001
Revenue	10·84	14·63	20·44	22·60
Expenditure	16·41	23·19	35·82	16·05

Performance

Real GDP growth was negative in 2001, at −4·2%, but there was then a slight recovery, with growth of 2·1% in 2002, 3·9% in 2003 and 4·6% in 2004. Total GDP was US$1·8bn. in 2004.

Banking and Finance

The central bank and bank of issue is the Reserve Bank of Malaŵi (founded 1964). The *Governor* is Victor Mbewe. In 2002 there were four commercial banks, one development bank, three merchant banks and a savings bank.

There is a stock exchange in Blantyre.

ENERGY AND NATURAL RESOURCES

Environment

Carbon dioxide emissions from the consumption and flaring of fossil fuels in 2002 were the equivalent of 0·1 tonnes per capita.

Electricity

The Electricity Supply Commission of Malaŵi is the sole supplier. Installed capacity was 0·2m. kW in 2000. Production was approximately 886m. kWh in 2000; consumption per capita was an estimated 78 kWh. Only 4% of the population has access to electricity.

Oil and Gas

In 1997 Malaŵi and Mozambique came to an agreement on the construction of an oil pipeline between the two countries.

Minerals

Mining operations have been limited to small-scale production of coal, limestone, rubies and sapphires, but companies are now moving in to start exploration programmes. Bauxite reserves are estimated at 29m. tonnes and there are proven reserves of clays, diamonds, glass and silica sands, graphite, limestone, mercurate, phosphates, tanzanite, titanium and uranium. Output: limestone (1999), 171,900 tonnes; gemstones (2000), 16,390 kg.

Agriculture

Malaŵi is predominantly an agricultural country. Agricultural produce contributes 90% of export earnings. There were 2·2m. ha. of arable land in 2001 and 140,000 ha. of permanent crops. Maize is the main subsistence crop and is grown by over 95% of all smallholders. Tobacco is the chief cash crop, employing 80% of the workforce, generating 35% of GDP and providing 70% of export earnings. Also important are groundnuts, cassava, millet and rice. There are large plantations which produce sugar, tea and coffee. Production (2000, in 1,000 tonnes): maize, 2,300; sugarcane, 2,000; potatoes, 1,700; cassava, 900; plantains, 200; tobacco, 120; groundnuts, 110; bananas, 93; rice, 87; dry beans, 84; sorghum, 55; tea, 50.

Livestock in 2000: cattle, 760,000; goats, 1,270,000; pigs, 240,000; sheep, 115,000; chickens, 15m.

Forestry

In 2000 the area under forests was 2·56m. ha., or 27·2% of the total land area. Timber production in 2001 was 5·52m. cu. metres.

Fisheries

Landings in 2001 were 40,619 tonnes, entirely from inland waters.

INDUSTRY

Index of industrial production in 2001 (1984 = 100): total general industrial production, 101·9; of this goods for the domestic market were at 73·2 and export goods were at 101·5. Electricity and water were at 231·7.

Labour

The labour force in 1996 was 4,807,000 (51% males). Approximately 85% of the economically active population in 1995 were engaged in agriculture, fisheries and forestry.

INTERNATIONAL TRADE

External debt was US$2·91bn. in 2002.

Imports and Exports

In 2001 imports amounted to K.39·48bn. (K.32·25bn. in 2000) and exports K.36·22bn. (K.23·63bn. in 2000). Major imports, 2001 (in K.1bn.): fuel oils, 5·32. Major exports, 2001 (in K.1bn.): tobacco, 18·36 (more than 50% of the total); sugar, 7·85.

Main sources of imports in 2001 were South Africa (39·7%), Zimbabwe (16·0%), Zambia (10·9%), USA (2·6%). Principal destinations for exports were South Africa (19·1%), USA (15·4%), Germany (11·2%), Japan (7·6%).

Trade Fairs

The annual Malaŵi International Trade Fair takes place in Blantyre, the commercial capital.

COMMUNICATIONS

Roads

The road network consisted of an estimated 40,200 km in 2002, of which 18·5% were paved. There were 16,300 passenger cars (1·4 per 1,000 inhabitants) and 19,100 commercial vehicles in use in 2002.

Rail

Malaŵi Railways operate 797 km on 1,067 mm gauge, providing links to the Mozambican ports of Beira and Nacala. In 1999–2000 passenger-km travelled came to 19m. and freight tonne-km to 62m.

Civil Aviation

The national carrier is Air Malaŵi. It flies to a number of regional centres in Ethiopia, Kenya, South Africa, Zambia and Zimbabwe. In 1999 scheduled airline traffic of Malaŵi-based carriers flew 2·4m. km, carrying 112,000 passengers (63,000 on international flights). There are international airports at Lilongwe (Lilongwe International Airport) and Blantyre (Chileka). In 2000 Lilongwe handled 175,915 passengers (120,575 on international flights) and 4,182 tonnes of freight, and Blantyre had 101,809 passengers (53,426 on international flights) and 680 tonnes of freight.

Shipping

In 1995 lake ships carried 169,000 passengers and 6,000 tonnes of freight.

Telecommunications

Malaŵi had 159,100 telephone subscribers in 2002, or 15·2 for every 1,000 population, and 14,000 PCs were in use (1·3 per 1,000 persons). Mobile phone subscribers numbered 86,000 in 2002 and there were 1,400 fax machines. There were 27,000 Internet users in 2002.

Postal Services

In 2003 there were 324 post offices.

SOCIAL INSTITUTIONS

Justice

Justice is administered in the High Court and in the magistrates' courts. Traditional courts were abolished in 1994. Appeals from magistrates' courts lie to the High Court, and appeals from the High Court to Malaŵi's Supreme Court of Appeal.

The population in penal institutions in Nov. 2003 was 8,566 (70 per 100,000 of national population).

Education

The adult literacy rate in 2001 was 61·0% (75·0% among males and 47·6% among females). Fees for primary education were abolished in 1994. In 2001 the number of pupils in primary schools was 3·19m. (53,444 teachers). The primary school course is of eight years' duration, followed by a four-year secondary course. In 2001 there were 294,638 pupils in secondary schools (7,593 teachers). English is taught from the 1st year and becomes the general medium of instruction from the 4th year.

The University of Malaŵi (consisting of four colleges and one polytechnic) had 4,127 students and 535 academic staff in 2002. A new university at Mzuzu opened in 1998 and provides courses for secondary school teachers.

In 1999–2000 total expenditure on education came to 4·2% of GNP.

Health

In 2003 there were 153 doctors, giving a provision of one doctor for every 68,481 persons—the lowest ratio in the world. In 2003 there were 3,094 nurses, four dentists and 39 pharmacists. In 1998 there were 82 hospitals with 10,251 beds.

RELIGION

2001 estimates: 2,600,000 Roman Catholic; 2,070,000 Protestant (mostly Presbyterian); 1,770,000 African Christian; 1,560,000 Muslim; 820,000 traditional beliefs. The remainder follow other religions.

CULTURE

The dances of the Malaŵi are a strong part of their culture. The National Dance Troupe (formerly the Kwacha Cultural Troupe) formed in Nov. 1987 as a part of the Department of Arts and Crafts of the Ministry of Education.

World Heritage Sites

Malaŵi has one site on the UNESCO World Heritage List: Lake Malaŵi National Park (inscribed on the list in 1984).

Broadcasting

The Malaŵi Broadcasting Corporation, a statutory body, broadcasts in English, Chichewa, Yao, Tumbuka, Lomwe Sena and Tonga. There were 5·4m. radio sets in 2000, up from 260,000 in 1980. No other country had such a large percentage increase in the number of radio receivers in use over the same period. There is a national radio station in Blantyre providing two channels and five private radio stations have been operating since 1997.

A national television station opened in 1999. There were 40,000 sets in use in 2001.

Press

There are more than 16 newspapers in circulation, the main ones being: *The Daily Times* (English, Monday to Friday), 17,000 copies daily; *The Nation* (English, Monday to Friday), 16,000 copies daily; *Malaŵi News* (English and Chichewa, Saturdays), 23,000 copies weekly; and *Weekend Nation* (English and Chichewa, Saturdays), 16,000 copies weekly. In addition there is *Odini* (English and Chichewa), 8,500 copies fortnightly; *Boma Lathu* (Chichewa), 150,000 copies monthly; *Za Alimi* (English and Chichewa), 10,000 copies monthly.

Tourism

There were 285,000 tourists in 2002 bringing in revenue of US$125m.

Museums and Galleries

The main attraction is the Museum of Malaŵi.

DIPLOMATIC REPRESENTATIVES

Of Malaŵi in the United Kingdom (33 Grosvenor St., London, W1K 4QT)
High Commissioner: Dr Francis Moto.

Of the United Kingdom in Malaŵi (PO Box 30042, Lilongwe 3)
High Commissioner: Norman Ling.

Of Malaŵi in the USA (1156 15th St., NW, Suite 320, Washington, D.C., 20005)
Ambassador: Bernardo Sande.

Of the USA in Malaŵi (Area 40, Plot 24, Kenyatta Road, Lilongwe 3)
Ambassador: Alan W. Eastham.

Of Malaŵi to the United Nations
Ambassador: Brown Chimphamba.

Of Malaŵi to the European Union
Ambassador: Dr Jerry Aleksander Alikopaga Jana.

FURTHER READING

National Statistical Office. *Monthly Statistical Bulletin*
Ministry of Economic Planning and Development. *Economic Report.* Annual

Decalo, S., *Malawi.* [Bibliography] 2nd ed. ABC-Clio, Oxford and Santa Barbara (CA), 1995
Kalinga, O. J. M. and Crosby, C. A., *Historical Dictionary of Malawi.* Scarecrow Press, Lanham, Maryland, 1993

National Statistical Office: National Statistical Office, POB 333, Zomba.
Website: http://www.nso.malawi.net/

MALAYSIA

Persekutuan Tanah Malaysia
(Federation of Malaysia)

Capital: Putrajaya (Administrative),
Kuala Lumpur (Financial)
Population projection, 2010: 27·53m.
GDP per capita, 2003: (PPP$) 9,512
HDI/world rank: 0·796/61

KEY HISTORICAL EVENTS

Excavations at Niah in Sarawak, East Malaysia have uncovered evidence of human settlement from 38,000 BC (the oldest relic of *homo sapiens* in southeast Asia). There are numerous sites in the north of Peninsular Malaysia where evidence of hunter-gatherers has been dated to around 10,000 BC. These Hoabinhians were spread across the region from present-day Myanmar to southern China between 12,000 and 3,000 BC. After 3,000 BC Mon-Khmer speaking immigrants moved south into Peninsular Malaysia and introduced a more advanced Neolithic culture, engaging in rudimentary farming. The indigenous people known as Orang Asli, who still live in the remoter, mountainous areas of the northern Malay Peninsula, are considered to be descendents of the Neolithic farmers. Indian traders first visited the Malay Peninsula in the 1st century BC and introduced political ideas, art forms and the Sanskrit language. Hinduism and Buddhism gained a foothold and were practised alongside traditional animist beliefs.

Various Hinduized city-states were established, one of which was located in Kedah. In the 7th century AD Kedah came under the control of the Hinduized Srivijaya empire, centred on Palembang in Sumatra. Srivijaya rule ended in the late 13th century when Sumatra fell to a Javan invasion, after which the king of Sukothai sent forces south into the Malay Peninsula. The Sumatran kingdom of Melayu next ruled over the southern part of the Peninsula, followed by the Madjapahit, the last Hindu empire of Java. In the mid-15th century Melaka emerged as the key trading port in the region—it was host to indigenous Malays, Sumatrans, Javans, Gujaratis, Arabs, Persians, Filipinos and Chinese—and grew rapidly in prosperity. A pattern of government was established in Melaka that became the basis of Malay identity and it was emulated by subsequent Malay kingdoms. Gujarati sailors introduced Islam to the region through Melaka in the 15th century. In 1511 the port was captured by the Portuguese navigator Alfonso de Albuquerque (who had seized Goa in western India the previous year), and who sought to dominate the route by which precious spices were shipped to Europe.

The sultan of Melaka fled to Johor and some of the Muslim mercantile elite relocated to Brunei in northwest Borneo. Sultanates also emerged in Pahang and Perak, which subsequently received large numbers of immigrants from Indonesian islands, notably Acehnese, Bugis and Minangkabau settlers, who displaced the Orang Asli from their coastal communities and drove them to the Malay Peninsula's interior. Conflict arose between the sultanates of Johor and Aceh and the Portuguese as they vied for control over the Straits of Melaka. In the late 16th century the northern Peninsular states of Kedah, Kelantan and Terengganu came under the control of the Thai state of Phetburi. The early 17th century saw the arrival of Dutch traders in the strait of Melaka. As part of the United Netherlands East India Company (Vereenigde Oostindische Compagnie, VOC) they made an alliance with Johor to besiege Melaka, capturing it in 1641. The Dutch brokered a peace deal between Aceh and Johor in the same year, ushering in an era of relative peace and prosperity for Johor under Laksamana Tun Abdul Jamil.

In the late 17th century the Malay Peninsula came under the influence of Bugis merchants from the Indonesian island of Sulawesi, who began settling in Selangor to trade in tin. The Bugis were formidable warriors, renowned for their navigational and commercial skills. By the 1740s they controlled many of the key shipping routes across the Indonesian archipelago and influenced all areas of government in Johor and the Riau archipelago, although Sultan Suliaman was permitted to remain as a figurehead.

British Influence

In the mid-18th century Johor and Melaka became entrepôts for the trade in tea between China and Europe. Ships owned by the British East India Company (EIC) began plying the Melaka straits in greater numbers. The British foothold in India allowed them to expand eastwards, and their control of India's poppy fields enabled them to dominate the lucrative opium trade. In 1786 Francis Light of the EIC leased the island of Penang from the Sultan Abdullah of Kedah, who hoped the British would provide protection against attacks from Siam or Burma. Penang grew swiftly, luring trade away from Melaka (which remained in Dutch control) and Johor-Riau. The British sought to increase their control over the maritime route to China and Sir Thomas Stamford Raffles was ordered to establish an entrepôt in the southern reaches of the Melaka Straits. In 1819 he signed a treaty with Sultan Husein Syah of Johor and founded Singapore. Five years later the British formally acquired Melaka from the Dutch. From 1826 Penang, Singapore and Melaka were ruled by the British authorities in India under a joint administration known as the Straits Settlements. By 1831 the population of Singapore had reached 18,000 (a large proportion of which were Chinese immigrants) and the following year the port replaced Penang as the capital of the Straits Settlements. Meanwhile, the northern provinces of Kedah and Perak came under the influence of the Siamese Chakri dynasty.

The discovery of tin deposits at Larut (western Malay Peninsula) in the 1850s led to large-scale immigration by Chinese miners and labourers. They organized themselves into *hui* (brotherhoods), which eventually became powerful political and economic organizations. Vast profits could be made from tin and clashes broke out between rival developers. At the same time, piracy was on the increase in the Melaka straits, and merchants asked the British to intervene and restore order. A series of agreements in 1874 introduced the British Residential system to Perak, Selangor and Sungei Ujung. In each region, a British Resident functioned as an advisor to the Malay Sultan on all aspects of administration apart from matters relating to the Islamic faith and Malay tradition.

Colonial Rule

In 1896 the three states and Pahang were grouped together as the Federated Malay States, presided over by a British resident general at Kuala Lumpur in the heart of the tin-mining district. By the end of the century, a British colonial infrastructure was taking shape, in the form of public buildings, municipal services, rubber plantations and road and rail construction, which required a stream of low-cost workers. Tamils from south India and Sri Lanka arrived as indentured (and later as licensed) labourers. Negotiations between the British and Siamese in the early years of the 20th century led to British control over the northern states of Kedah, Perlis, Kelantan and Terengganu. Between 1905–08 Malaysia experienced a rubber boom, in line with the expansion of the motor car industry in Europe and North America. Rubber plants, originally from the forests of Brazil and introduced to Malaysia in the 1880s, were planted in every state in Malaysia by 1908 and by 1913 rubber had eclipsed tin as the country's chief export.

Sabah, Sarawak and Brunei, which had come under the control of the North Borneo Chartered Company and was granted protectorate status in 1888, experienced slower economic development than British Malaya but gold, antimony and coal were mined and oil was discovered at Miri in 1910. The colony was hit hard by the global depression of 1929–31 and widespread unemployment in the mines and plantations caused the repatriation of Chinese and Indian workers.

Rubber, tin and oil made Malaya a focus for Imperial Japan from early in the Second World War. When Pearl Harbor and Hong Kong came under attack from Japanese forces in Dec. 1941, other Japanese divisions came ashore at Kota Bharu and Miri. British forces retreated south to Singapore, but the 'impregnable' island capitulated within a few weeks, on 15 Feb. 1942. Japanese troops quickly took over from British colonial officers and controlled Malaya from Singapore (Shonan), meting out harsh treatment to the Chinese population. Thailand allied itself with Japan and was granted control of the northern Malay states in 1943.

Post War

When the British returned in 1946 they reorganized the colony into the Malayan Union. The Malay elite, fearing an end to their privileges by virtue of equal rights for Chinese and Indian subjects, campaigned via the United Malays National Organisation (UMNO, led by Datuk Onn) to demand the continuation of individual sultanates. The British were forced to compromise and established the Federation of Malaya in Feb. 1948, consisting of the nine Malay states, Melaka and Penang and administered by a High Commissioner in Kuala Lumpur. Within months the Federation was under attack, in the form of an armed struggle organized by the Malayan Communist Party (MCP). The Chinese-dominated MCP had grown in strength during the Japanese occupation, when it controlled various anti-Japanese National Salvation Organizations. The High Commissioner Sir Henry Gurney responded to guerrilla attacks by the MCP by putting Malaya on a war-footing in 1950: tightening security, recruiting soldiers from other colonies and dispersing the Chinese squatter settlements that harboured much of the MCP's support. More than 500,000 Chinese were resettled by the mid-1950s. The Communist insurrection, known by the British as 'the Emergency', hastened the transition to Malayan independence and local elections were held in Penang in late 1951. Four years later the first federal-level election was held

and won convincingly by the Alliance Party, a loose coalition of Malay, Chinese and Indian parties, led by Tuanku (Prince) Abdul Rahman. On 31 Aug. 1957 the Federation of Malaya became an independent state and Tuanku Abdul Rahman became the first prime minister.

The concept of Malaysia, as a broader federation including Sabah, Sarawak, Singapore and the British protectorate of Brunei, was first suggested by Abdul Rahman in 1961. It was opposed by neighbouring Indonesia and the Philippines, but public support in Sabah and Sarawak led to Malaysia's formation in Sept. 1963, although Brunei declined to join. The new nation faced continuing hostility from Indonesia, led by Ahmed Sukarno, over the sovereignty of Borneo. There were also disagreements with Singapore's Prime Minister Lee Kuan Yew, leading to Singapore declaring independence in 1965. Tension arose between the Chinese and Malay communities over the use of the Malay language and Malay fears about Chinese economic dominance. The 1969 elections were fought on the highly emotional issues of education and language and the Alliance party failed to obtain a majority. Rioting and serious inter-ethnic violence followed and an emergency government was brought in, led by Deputy Prime Minister Abdul Razak. Parliamentary rule was restored in 1971 and Razak launched the New Economic Policy—a series of five-year plans to eradicate poverty and restructure society to improve ethnic relations, specifically by encouraging ethnic Malays, the *bumiputera*, to shift from subsistence agriculture into the mainstream economy.

Mahathir Mohamad was the first non-royal or non-aristocrat to become prime minister of Malaysia, winning the 1981 elections for the UMNO and leading the National Front coalition to further victories in 1986, 1990, 1995 and 1999. Mahathir shifted the economy away from dependence on commodities and towards manufacturing, services and tourism, aided by substantial Japanese and east Asian investment in manufacturing. The prolonged spell of economic growth and stability was broken by the 1997–98 recession but Mahathir refused to accept financial aid from the International Monetary Fund. In Sept. 1998 Mahathir dismissed Anwar Ibrahim, his finance minister, deputy prime minister and heir apparent. Anwar was found guilty of corruption charges in 1999 and sentenced to prison for six years. In 2002 Mahathir announced that he would resign from the presidency of UMNO and he stepped down as prime minister on 31 Oct. 2003, to be succeeded by Abdullah Ahmad Badawi. Badawi won a landslide victory in the March 2004 general elections for the National Front. In Sept. 2004 he unexpectedly released Anwar from his prison term.

TERRITORY AND POPULATION

The federal state of Malaysia comprises the 13 states and three federal territories of Peninsular Malaysia, bounded in the north by Thailand, and with the island of Singapore as an enclave on its southern tip; and, on the island of Borneo to the east, the state of Sabah (which includes the federal territory of the island of Labuan), and the state of Sarawak, with Brunei as an enclave, both bounded in the south by Indonesia and in the northwest and northeast by the South China and Sulu Seas.

The area of Malaysia is 329,847 sq. km (127,354 sq. miles) and the population (2000 census) 23,274,690; density, 70·6 per sq. km. The estimated population in 2005 was 25,347,000. Malaysia's national waters cover 515,256 sq. km. In 2003, 63·8% of the population lived in urban areas.

The UN gives a projected population for 2010 of 27·53m.

The growth of the population has been:

Year	Peninsular Malaysia	Labuan Sarawak	Sabah/ Labuan	Total Malaysia
1980	11,426,613	1,307,582	1,011,046	13,745,241
1991	14,797,616	1,718,380	1,863,659	18,379,655
2000	18,523,632	2,071,506	2,679,552	23,274,690

The areas, populations and chief towns of the states and federal territories are:

Peninsular States	Area (in sq. km)	Population (2000 census)	Chief Town	Population (1991 census)
Johor	18,987	2,740,625	Johor Bharu	328,436
Kedah	9,425	1,649,756	Alor Setar	124,412
Kelantan	15,024	1,313,014	Kota Bharu	219,582
Kuala Lumpur[1]	243	1,379,310	Kuala Lumpur	1,145,342[1]
Melaka	1,652	635,791	Melaka	75,909
Negeri Sembilan	6,644	859,924	Seremban	182,869
Pahang	35,965	1,288,376	Kuantan	199,484
Perak	21,005	2,051,236	Ipoh	382,853
Perlis	795	204,450	Kangar	14,247
Pulau Pinang	1,031	1,313,449	Penang (Georgetown)	219,603
Putrajaya[1]	50	—[2]	Putrajaya	—
Selangor	7,910	4,188,876[2]	Shah Alam	102,019
Terengganu	12,955	898,825	Kuala Terengganu	228,119
Other states				
Labuan[1]	92	76,067	Victoria	
Sabah	73,619	2,603,485	Kota Kinabalu	76,120
Sarawak	124,450	2,071,506	Kuching	148,059

[1]Federal territory. [2]Putrajaya figure included in population of Selangor.

Other large cities (1997 estimate): Petaling Jaya (254,350), Kelang (243,355), Taiping (183,261), Sibu (126,381), Sandakan (125,841) and Miri (87,167).

Putrajaya, a planned new city described as an 'intelligent garden city', became the administrative capital of Malaysia in 1999 and was created a federal territory on 1 Feb. 2001.

Malay is the national language of the country—53% of the population are Malays. The government promotes the use of the national language to foster national unity. However, the people are free to use their mother tongue and other languages. English as the second language is widely used in business. In Peninsular Malaysia Chinese dialects and Tamil are also spoken. In Sabah there are numerous tribal dialects and Chinese (Mandarin and Hakka dialects predominate). In Sarawak Mandarin and numerous tribal languages are spoken. In addition to Malays, 26% of the population are Chinese, 12% other indigenous ethnic groups, 8% Indians and 1% others.

SOCIAL STATISTICS

2001 births, 535,500; deaths, 105,700. 2001 rates (per 1,000 population): birth, 22·3; death, 4·4. Life expectancy, 2003: males, 70·9 years; females, 75·6 years. Annual population growth rate, 1992–2002, 2·4%. Infant mortality, 2001, seven per 1,000 live births; fertility rate, 2001, 3·0 births per woman. Today only 8% of Malaysians live below the poverty line, compared to 50% in the early 1970s.

CLIMATE

Malaysia lies near the equator between latitudes 1° and 7° North and longitudes 100° and 119° East. Malaysia is subject to maritime influence and the interplay of wind systems which originate in the Indian Ocean and the South China Sea. The year is generally divided into the South-East and the North-East Monsoon seasons. The average daily temperature throughout Malaysia varies from 21°C to 32°C. Humidity is high.

CONSTITUTION AND GOVERNMENT

The Constitution of Malaysia is based on the Constitution of the former Federation of Malaya, but includes safeguards for the special interests of Sabah and Sarawak. It was amended in 1983. The Constitution provides for one of the Rulers of the Malay States to be elected from among themselves to be the *Yang di-Pertuan Agong* (Supreme Head of the Federation). He holds office for a period of five years. The Rulers also elect from among themselves a Deputy Supreme Head of State, also for a period

of five years. In Feb. 1993 the Rulers accepted constitutional amendments abolishing their legal immunity.

Supreme Head of State (Yang di-Pertuan Agong). HRH Syed Sirajuddin ibni al-Marhum Syed Putra Jamalullail, b. 1943, acceded 13 Dec. 2001.

Raja of Perlis. HRH Syed Sirajuddin ibni al-Marhum Syed Putra Jamalullail, b. 1943, acceded 17 April 2000.

Sultan of Kedah. HRH Tuanku Haji Abdul Halim Mu'adzam Shah ibni Al-Marhum Sultan Badlishah, b. 1927, acceded 14 July 1958.

Sultan of Johor. HRH Sultan Mahmood Iskandar ibni Al-Marhum Sultan Ismail, b. 1932, acceded 11 May 1981 (Supreme Head of State from 26 April 1984 to 25 April 1989), returned as Sultan of Johor 26 April 1989.

Sultan of Perak. HRH Sultan Azlan Shah Muhibbuddin Shah ibni Al-Marhum Sultan Yussuf Izzuddin Ghafarullahu-luhu Shah, b. 1928, acceded 3 Feb. 1984.

Yang Di-Pertuan Besar Negeri Sembilan. HRH Tuanku Jaafar ibni Al-Marhum Tuanku Abdul Rahman, b. 1922, acceded 18 April 1967.

Sultan of Kelantan. HRH Sultan Ismail Petra ibni Al-Marhum Sultan Yahya Petra, b. 1949, appointed 29 March 1979.

Sultan of Terengganu. HRH Sultan Mizan Zainal Abidin ibni al-Mahrum Sultan Mahmud Al-Muktafi Billah Shah, b. 1962, acceded 15 May 1998.

Sultan of Pahang. Sultan Haji Ahmad Shah Al-Musta'in Billah ibni Al-Marhum Sultan Abu Bakar Ri'Ayatuddin Al-Mu'Adzam Shah, b. 1930, acceded 8 May 1975.

Sultan of Selangor. HRH Sharafuddin Idris Shah ibni al-Marhum Sultan Salehuddin Abdul Aziz Shah, b. 1945, appointed 22 Nov. 2001.

Yang di-Pertua Negeri Pulau Pinang. HE Datuk Abdul Rahman Haji Abbas, b. 1938, appointed 1 May 2001.

Yang di Pertua Negeri Melaka. HE Tan Sri Khalil Yaakob, b. 1937, appointed 4 June 2004.

Yang di-Pertua Negeri Sarawak. HE Tun Datuk Patinggi Abang Mohamad Salaheddin, b. 1921, acceded 4 Dec. 2000.

Yang di-Pertua Negeri Sabah. HE Datuk Ahmad Shah Abdullah, b. 1946, acceded 1 Jan. 2003.

The federal parliament consists of the *Yang di-Pertuan Agong* and two *Majlis* (Houses of Parliament) known as the *Dewan Negara* (Senate) of 69 members (26 elected, two by each state legislature; and 43 appointed by the *Yang di-Pertuan Agong*) and *Dewan Rakyat* (House of Representatives) of 219 members. Appointment to the Senate is for three years. The maximum life of the House of Representatives is five years, subject to its dissolution at any time by the *Yang di-Pertuan Agong* on the advice of his Ministers.

National Anthem

'Negaraku' ('My Country'); words collective, tune by Pierre de Béranger.

GOVERNMENT CHRONOLOGY

Supreme Heads of State since 1957.

1957–60	Tuanku Abdul Rahman ibni al-Marhum
1960	Tuanku Hisamuddin Alam Shah ibni al-Marhum
1960–65	Syed Harun Petra ibni al-Marhum
1965–70	Tuanku Ismail Nasiruddin Shah ibni al-Marhum
1970–75	Tuanku Abdul Halim Muadzam Shah ibni al-Marhum
1975–79	Tuanku Yahaya Petra ibni al-Marhum
1979–84	Tuanku Ahmad Shah al-Mustain Billah ibni al-Marhum
1984–89	Tuanku Mahmud Iskandar ibni al-Marhum
1989–94	Tuanku Azlan Muhibuddin Shah ibni al-Marhum
1994–99	Tuanku Jaafar ibni al-Marhum
1999–2001	Tuanku Salehuddin Abdul Aziz Shah ibni al-Marhum
2001–	Syed Sirajuddin ibni al-Marhum

Prime Ministers since 1957. (UMNO = United Malays National Organization)

1957–59	UMNO	Tunku Abdul Rahman Putra
1959	UMNO	Tun Abdul Razak bin Hussein
1959–70	UMNO	Tunku Abdul Rahman Putra
1970–76	UMNO	Tun Abdul Razak bin Hussein
1976–81	UMNO	Hussein bin Onn
1981–2003	UMNO	Mahathir bin Mohamad
2003–	UMNO	Abdullah bin Haji Ahmad Badawi

RECENT ELECTIONS

Elections to the *Dewan Rakyat* and 11 state assemblies were held on 21 March 2004. The 14-party National Front Coalition (BN; Barisan Nasional) gained 198 seats, obtaining 64·4% of the votes cast (the predominant partner, the United Malays National Organization (UMNO), won 109 seats). The Democratic Action Party (Parti Tindakan Deomkratik) won 12 seats (9·5%), the Islamic Party of Malaysia (PAS) won seven seats (15·8%) and the People's Justice Party (Parti Keadilan Rakyat) won one seat. One non-partisan was elected. The National Front Coalition also gained a majority in every state assembly except Kelantan, held by PAS, which lost Terengganu. Turnout was 63·6%.

CURRENT ADMINISTRATION

In March 2006 the government comprised:

Prime Minister, Minister of Finance and Internal Security: Dato' Seri Abdullah bin Haji Ahmad Badawi; b. 1939 (UMNO; took office on 31 Oct. 2003).

Deputy Prime Minister and Minister of Defence: Dato' Sri Haji Mohd Najib bin Tun Haji Abdul Razak. *Minister of Transport:* Datuk Seri Chan Kong Choy. *Energy, Water and Communications:* Datuk Seri Dr Lim Keng Yaik. *Entrepreneurial and Co-operative Development:* Datuk Mohamed Khaled Nordin. *Works:* Dato' Seri S. Samy Vellu. *International Trade and Industry:* Dato' Seri Rafidah binti Aziz. *Education:* Datuk Hishammuddin Tun Hussein. *Rural and Regional Development:* Datuk Abdul Aziz Shamsuddin. *Agriculture and Agro-Based Industry:* Tan Sri Muhyiddin Yassin. *Domestic Trade and Consumer Affairs:* Datuk Shafie Apdal. *Health:* Datuk Dr Chua Soi Lek. *Foreign Affairs:* Datuk Seri Syed Hamid bin Syed Jaafar Albar. *Information:* Datuk Zainuddin Maidin. *Arts, Culture and Heritage:* Datuk Seri Dr Rais Yatim. *Human Resources:* Datuk Dr Fong Chan Onn. *Natural Resources and Environment:* Datuk Seri Azmi Khalid. *Housing and Local Government:* Dato' Ong Ka Ting. *Women, Family and Community Development:* Datuk Seri Shahrizat binte Abdul Jalil. *Youth and Sports:* Datuk Azalina Othman Said. *Home Affairs:* Datuk Seri Radzi Sheikh Ahmad. *Higher Education:* Datuk Mustapha Mohamed. *Science, Technology and Innovations:* Datuk Dr Jamaluddin Jarjis. *Tourism:* Datuk Tengku Adnan Tengku Mansor. *Plantation Industries and Commodities:* Datuk Peter Chin Fah Kui. *Federal Territories:* Datuk Zulhasnan Rafique. *Second Minister of Finance:* Tan Sri Nor Mohamed Yakcop. *Ministers in Prime Minister's Department:* Tan Sri Datuk Seri Paglima Bernard Giluk Dompok, Dato' Seri Mohamad Nazri bin Abdul Aziz, Prof. Datuk Dr Abdullah bin Md. Zin, Datuk Dr Maximus Johnity Ongkili; Datuk Seri Dr Mohamed Effendi Norwawi.

Office of the Prime Minister: http://www.pmo.gov.my

CURRENT LEADERS

Tuanku Syed Sirajuddin

Position
King (Yang di-Pertuan Agong)

Introduction
The Yang di-Pertuan Agong (supreme head of state, popularly referred to as the king) serves for a five-year term, having been chosen from the hereditary sultans and rajas who reign in nine of the 13 states. The current head of state is the raja of Perlis, the ruler of the smallest state in Malaysia.

Early Life
Tuanku (Prince) Syed Sirajuddin was born on 16 May 1943 into the royal family of Perlis, in the northeast of what is now Malaysia, during the Japanese occupation of the Malay peninsula. As heir to the raja of Perlis, he went to Wellingborough school in England before entering Sandhurst Military Academy in 1964. Returning to Malaya, then still under British rule, he joined the Malay armed forces and in 1970 the Armed Reserve Force, in which he now holds the rank of colonel.

He succeeded as raja of Perlis on the death of his father on 16 April 2000. As ruler of Perlis, he has made an impression as an unassuming and approachable ruler. When the sultan of Selangor, Tuanku Syed Salahuddin Abdul Aziz Shah, died in office as Yang di-Pertuan Agong on 21 Nov. 2001, the nine royal heads of state met in secret session to elect a new 'king' of Malaysia.

Career in Office
The raja of Perlis was elected and sworn in on 13 Dec. 2001. As head of state of Malaysia, Tuanku Syed Sirajuddin is nominal head of the military, appoints ambassadors and judges, and has discretionary powers to appoint the prime minister. However, the Malaysian monarch is largely a figurehead.

Abdullah Badawi

Position
Prime Minister

Introduction
Dato' Seri Abdullah bin Haji Ahmad Badawi succeeded Mahathir Mohamad as prime minister in Oct. 2003. A less abrasive figure than Mahathir, he espouses moderate Islamic policies and social inclusion. He has continued Mahathir's economic policies, which have made Malaysia's economy one of the most stable in the region, and sought to improve relations with Singapore after decades of fractiousness between the two countries.

Early Life
Badawi was born on 26 Nov. 1939 on the island of Penang. In 1964 he graduated in Islamic studies from the University of Malaya. Badawi then entered the civil service, working in the department for public services until 1969 when he moved to the National Operation Council, which held executive powers after race riots that year. From 1971–73 he served as director general of the Ministry of Culture, Youth and Sports and in 1974 was made deputy secretary general of the department.

Badawi left the civil service in 1978 to pursue his political ambitions, having joined the United Malays National Organization (UMNO) in 1965. His father had been a co-founder of the party. He entered parliament as the member for Kepala Batas and was named parliamentary secretary to the Federal Territory ministry in the government of Mahathir Mohamad. In 1980 he was promoted to deputy minister for the department. From 1981–84 he was minister in the prime minister's department, then minister of education until 1986, minister of defence from 1986–87 and minister of foreign affairs from 1991–99. In 1999 he was made deputy prime minister with responsibility for home affairs, following the sacking and subsequent imprisonment of Mahathir's previous deputy, Anwar Ibrahim. Within UMNO, Badawi had become a member of the party's supreme council in 1981, and was then appointed party vice president three years later and party deputy president in 1999.

When Mahathir resigned after 22 years in power, at the end of Oct. 2003, Badawi assumed the premiership.

Career in Office

On taking office, Badawi was regarded as a less controversial figure than his predecessor. With a buoyant Malaysian economy, he announced few major policy changes. In addition to the premiership and home affairs portfolio (part of which he gave up in March 2004), Badawi also took control of the finance ministry.

Having no electoral mandate, Badawi called elections for March 2004. Though expected to win, many observers believed that the nation's growing Islamic fundamentalist parties (the Islamic Party of Malaysia, or PAS, being the largest) would gain support. The ruling National Front Coalition, of which UMNO is the main element, went on to win by a landslide, with the PAS losing power in one of two states it had previously controlled and only narrowly retaining power in the other. Opposition parties claimed electoral irregularities but failed to provide evidence. Armed with electoral success and a large parliamentary majority, Badawi has continued to espouse moderate Islamic politics.

Badawi has promised to crack down on the official corruption that blighted much of Mahathir's tenure. However, opponents were disappointed when many of Mahathir's key officials were retained in Badawi's first cabinet. In the international arena, he has pursued closer ties with neighbouring Singapore, while at home he has striven to build bridges with non-Malay minorities.

DEFENCE

The Constitution provides for the Head of State to be the Supreme Commander of the Armed Forces who exercises his powers in accordance with the advice of the Cabinet. Under their authority, the Armed Forces Council is responsible for all matters relating to the Armed Forces other than those relating to their operational use. The Ministry of Defence has established bilateral defence relations with countries within as well as outside the region. Malaysia is a member of the Five Powers Defence Arrangement with Australia, New Zealand, Singapore and the UK.

The Malaysian Armed Forces has participated in 16 UN peacekeeping missions in Africa, the Middle East, Indo-China and Europe. Five of the operations are military contingents, the remainder are Observer Groups.

In 2003 defence expenditure totalled US$2,412m. (US$97 per capita), representing 2·3% of GDP.

Army

Strength (2002) about 80,000. There is a paramilitary Police General Operations Force of 18,000 and a People's Volunteer Corps of 240,000 of which 17,500 are armed.

Navy

The Royal Malaysian Navy is commanded by the Chief of the Navy from the integrated Ministry of Defence in Kuala Lumpur. There are four operational areas: No. 1, Kuantan Naval Base, covering the eastern peninsular coast; No. 2, Labuan naval Base, covering the East Malaysia coast; No. 3, Lumut Naval Base, covering the western peninsular coast; and No. 4, Kuching Naval Base, covering Sarawak's coast. The peacetime tasks include fishery protection and anti-piracy patrols. The fleet includes four frigates. A Naval aviation squadron operates six armed helicopters.

Navy personnel in 2002 totalled 12,000 including 160 Naval Air personnel. There were 1,000 naval reserves.

Air Force

Formed on 1 June 1958, the Royal Malaysian Air Force is equipped primarily to provide air defence and air support for the Army, Navy and Police. Its secondary role is to render assistance to government departments and civilian organizations.

Personnel (2002) totalled about 8,000, with 95 combat aircraft including F-5Es, MiG-29s and Bae *Hawks*. There were 600 Air Force reserves.

INTERNATIONAL RELATIONS

Malaysia was in dispute with Indonesia over sovereignty of two islands in the Celebes Sea. Both countries agreed to accept the Judgment of the International Court of Justice which decided in favour of Malaysia in Dec. 2002.

Malaysia is a member of the UN, WTO, BIS, the Commonwealth, Asian Development Bank, Colombo Plan, APEC, ASEAN, Mekong Group, Organization of Islamic Conference and Islamic Development Bank.

ECONOMY

In 2002 agriculture accounted for 9·2% of GDP, industry 47·3% and services 43·5%.

Overview

Malaysia has transformed itself from an economy dependent on mineral production and agriculture into an industrialized, manufacturing-based economy. In the decade prior to the 1997 Asian financial crisis, the economy grew consistently at an annual rate of 7–10%. In 1998, the economy was hit hard by twin currency and banking crises, shrinking by 7·4%. In response, the government sought to boost growth via spending on large infrastructure projects. The Badawi government has since brought spending levels down and has pledged to reduce fiscal deficits in the future.

Manufacturing exports have been the main engine of economic growth, with the Economist Intelligence Unit (EIU) estimating that in 2004 electronic manufacturing made up 37·9% of the country's total exports, making Malaysia vulnerable to fluctuations in global electronics demand. When global recession cut demand in 2001, the country only managed to avoid recession by introducing a US$1·9bn. fiscal stimulus package. Despite continued weak global demand and the outbreak of SARS, the economy rebounded in 2002 and 2003, with growth of 4·4% and 5·4% respectively. According to the EIU, in 2004 Malaysia's total factor productivity grew at 4·8%, its highest rate since 1988. A rebound in the global economy and electronics demand buoyed the economy in 2004–05. Until the depegging of the *ringgit* from the dollar in July 2005 the Malaysian currency followed the decline of the US dollar in 2002–03, giving the export sector a competitive advantage. In Nov. 2005, for the first time since 1998, Malaysia's central bank raised interest rates, to 3%, to combat inflation.

Currency

The unit of currency is the Malaysian *ringgit* (RM) of 100 *sen*. For seven years it was pegged to the US dollar at 3·8 ringgit = 1 US$, but since the revaluation of the Chinese yuan on 21 July 2005 it has been allowed to operate in a managed float. Foreign exchange reserves were US$32,287m. and gold reserves 1·17m. troy oz in June 2002. Inflation rates (based on IMF statistics):

1997	1998	1999	2000	2001	2002	2003	2004
2·7%	5·3%	2·7%	1·5%	1·4%	1·8%	1·1%	1·4%

Total money supply in June 2002 was RM85,913m.

Budget

Revenue and expenditure for calendar years, in RM1bn.:

	1999	2000	2001[1]	2002[1]
Revenue	58·7	61·9	79·6	83·6
Operating expenditure	46·7	56·5	63·8	66·7

[1]Estimate.

Sources of revenue in 2000: direct taxes, 47·2% (55·2%—2002 est.); indirect taxes, 29·1% (25·5%—2002 est.); non-tax revenue, 23·7% (19·3%—2002 est.).

Federal government net development (in addition to operating) expenditure in 2000: RM25,032m. Social services accounted for

33·2% of operating expenditure in 2000, general administration 14·9%, security 12·3% and economic services 11·7%.

Performance
Malaysia was badly affected by the Asian financial crisis, with the economy contracting by 7·4% in 1998. There was also a recession in the second half of 2001 although the economy still expanded by 0·3% in the year as a whole. Real GDP growth rates (based on IMF statistics):

1995	1996	1997	1998	1999	2000	2001	2002	2003	2004
9·8%	10·0%	7·3%	−7·4%	6·1%	8·9%	0·3%	4·4%	5·4%	7·1%

Total GDP in 2004 was US$117·8bn.

Banking and Finance
The central bank and bank of issue is the Bank Negara Malaysia (*Governor*, Dr Zeti Akhtar Aziz). In 2002 there were 47 domestic commercial banks, merchant banks and finance companies. Total deposits of commercial banks, finance companies and merchant banks at 31 Dec. 2005 were RM140·6bn. The largest commercial bank is Malayan Banking Berhad (Maybank), with assets in June 2003 of RM127·6bn. The Islamic Bank of Malaysia began operations in July 1983. In Jan. 2006 there were 54 banks licensed by the Labuan Offshore Financial Services Authority (LOFSA).

There is a stock exchange at Kuala Lumpur, known as BSKL.

ENERGY AND NATURAL RESOURCES

Environment
Malaysia's carbon dioxide emissions from the consumption and flaring of fossil fuels in 2002 were the equivalent of 5·9 tonnes per capita.

Electricity
Installed capacity in 2002, 15·7m. kW. In 2002 an estimated 77,501m. kWh were generated. Consumption per capita in 2002 was 3,234 kWh.

Oil and Gas
Crude petroleum reserves, 2002, 3·0bn. bbls. Oil production, 2003, was 38·8m. tonnes. Natural gas reserves, 2002, 2,120bn. cu. metres. Production of natural gas in 2002 was 50·3bn. cu. metres. In April 1998 Malaysia and Thailand agreed to share equally the natural gas jointly produced in an offshore area which both countries claim as their own territory. It was expected that from 2001 around 18m. cu. metres of natural gas would be produced in the area every day.

Minerals
In 1998 mining contributed 6·9% of GDP. Bauxite production in 2001 was 64,000 tonnes; gold, 3,965 kg. 2000: coal, 382,942 tonnes; iron ore, 259,000 tonnes; tin, 6,307 tonnes.

Agriculture
In 2002 agriculture contributed 9·2% of GDP. There were 1·80m. ha. of arable land in 2001 and 5·79m. ha. of permanent crops. In 2001 approximately 365,000 ha. were irrigated. Production in 2000 (in 1,000 tonnes): palm kernels, 3,163; sugarcane, 1,600; rice, 1,382; rubber, 917; coconuts, 683; bananas, 545; cassava, 380. Livestock (2000): pigs, 1·83m.; cattle, 734,000; goats 238,000; sheep, 145,000; buffaloes, 142,000; chickens, 120m. Malaysia's output of palm kernels is the highest of any country. Only Thailand and Indonesia produce more rubber.

Forestry
In 2000 there were 19·29m. ha. of forests, or 58·7% of the total land area. Timber production in 2003 was 21·34m. cu. metres.

Fisheries
Total catch in 2002 amounted to 1,275,555 tonnes, almost entirely from sea fishing.

INDUSTRY
The leading companies by market capitalization in Malaysia, excluding banking and finance, in May 2004 were: Telekom Malaysia (US$8·5bn.); Tenaga Nasional, an electricity company (US$7·9bn.); and Malaysia International Shipping (US$5·8bn.).

In 2001 industry accounted for 48·3% of GDP, with manufacturing contributing 30·5%. Production figures for 2001 (in 1,000 tonnes): cement, 13,820; palm oil, 11,660; distillate fuel oil (2002), 8,271; petrol (2002), 4,245; residual fuel oil (2002), 2,351; refined sugar, 1,210; wheat flour, 664; plywood (2002), 4,341,000 cu. metres; cigarettes, 25·6bn. units; radio sets, 28·8m. units; pneumatic tyres, 13·1m. units; TV sets, 9·5m. units.

Labour
In 2001 the workforce was 9,892,000 (46·7% female in 2000), of whom 9,535,000 were employed (22·6% in manufacturing, 14·2% in agriculture, forestry and fishing, 10·5% in government services and 8·9% in construction). Unemployment was 3·8% in 2002. It is estimated that Malaysia has some 500,000 illegal workers.

Trade Unions
Membership was 784,881 in 2001, of which the Malaysian Trades Union Congress, an umbrella organization of 235 unions, accounted for 0·5m. Number of unions was 578.

INTERNATIONAL TRADE
Privatization policy permits foreign investment of 25–30% generally; total foreign ownership is permitted of export-oriented projects. External debt was US$48,557m. in 2002.

Imports and Exports
In 2002 imports totalled RM303·5bn. and exports RM354·5bn. The trade surplus in 2002 was RM51·0bn., down from RM73·1bn. in 1999.

Main imports, 2002: microcircuits, transistors and valves, 29·2%; computers, office machines and parts, 6·9%; telecommunications equipment, 4·3%. Chief exports, 2002: microcircuits, transistors and valves, 20·5%; computers, office machines and parts, 18·4%; telecommunications equipment, 5·4%.

The principal import sources in 2002 were: Japan (17·8%), USA (16·4%), Singapore (12·0%). The leading export markets were: USA (20·2%), Singapore (17·1%), Japan (11·2%).

COMMUNICATIONS

Roads
Total road length in 2002 was 70,834 km, of which 54,401 km were paved and 16,433 km were unpaved. In 2002 there were 5,069,412 passenger cars in use, 51,158 buses and coaches, 713,148 trucks and vans and 5,842,617 motorcycles and mopeds. There were 6,035 deaths as a result of road accidents in 2000, which at 29 per 100,000 people ranks among the highest rates in the world.

Rail
In 1999 there were 1,949 km of railway tracks. Passenger-km travelled in 2000 came to 4,800m. and freight tonne-km to 1,230m. There are two metro systems in Kuala Lumpur with a combined length of 56 km.

Civil Aviation
There are a total of 19 airports of which five are international airports and 14 are domestic airports at which regular public air transport is operated. *International airports;* Kuala Lumpur, Penang, Kota Kinabalu, Kuching and Langkawi. *Domestic airports;* Johor Bharu, Alor Setar, Ipoh, Kota Bharu, Kuala Terengganu, Kuantan, Melaka, Sandakan, Lahad Datu, Tawau, Labuan, Bintulu, Sibu and Miri. There are 39 Malaysian airstrips of which ten are in Sabah, 15 in Sarawak and 14 in peninsular Malaysia.

In 2003, 40 international airlines operated through Kuala Lumpur (KLIA-Sepang). Malaysia Airlines, the national airline, is 69% state-owned, and operates domestic flights within Malaysia and international flights to nearly 40 different countries. In 1999 it flew 206·9m. km, carrying 14,984,600 passengers (6,770,550 on international flights). In 2001 Kuala Lumpur handled 14,208,055 passengers (10,044,013 on international flights) and 423,712 tonnes of freight. Kota Kinabalu handled 2,912,802 passengers in 2001 and Kuching 2,544,502.

Shipping
The major ports are Port Kelang, Pulau Pinang, Johor Pasir Gudang, Tanjung Beruas, Miri, Rajang, Pelabuhan Sabah, Port Dickson, Kemaman, Teluk Ewa, Kuantan, Kuching and Bintulu. Port Kelang, the busiest port, handled 82,271,000 freight tonnes of cargo in 2002. In 1996 there were 2,429 marine vessels including 118 oil tankers (0·73m. GRT), 198 passenger carriers (0·03m. GRT) and 426 general cargo ships (0·76m. GRT), with a total GRT of 4·27m. In 1996, 167·9m. tonnes of cargo were loaded and unloaded. Total container throughput in 2002 was 8,716,463 TEUs (twenty-foot equivalent units). In 2002 merchant shipping totalled 5,394,000 GRT, including oil tankers 767,000 GRT.

Telecommunications
In 2002 there were 13,911,300 telephone subscribers, or 567·2 per 1,000 inhabitants, and 3·6m. PCs were in use (146·8 for every 1,000 persons). There were 3,092 telex subscribers in 1999 and 275,000 fax machines in 2002. Malaysia had 7,841,000 Internet users in 2002 and 9,241,400 mobile phone subscribers.

Postal Services
Postal services are the responsibility of the Ministry of Energy, Water and Communications. In 2003 there were 1,211 post offices.

SOCIAL INSTITUTIONS

Justice
The judicial power is vested in the Federal Court, the High Court of Malaya, the High Court of Borneo and subordinate courts: Sessions Courts, Magistrates' Courts and *Mukim* chiefs' Courts.

The Federal Court comprises the Lord President—who is also the head of the Judiciary—the Chief Justice of the High Courts and the Judge of the Federal Court. It has jurisdiction to determine the validity of any law made by Parliament or by a State legislature and disputes between States or between the Federation and any State. It also has jurisdiction to hear and determine appeals from the High Courts.

The death penalty is authorized and was used in 2002. The population in penal institutions in 2002 was 28,804 (125 per 100,000 of national population).

Education
School education is free; tertiary education is provided at a nominal fee. There are six years of primary schooling starting at age seven, three years of universal lower secondary, two years of selective upper secondary and two years of pre-university education. During the Seventh Plan period (1996–2000), a number of major changes were introduced to the education and training system with a view to strengthening and improving the system. These efforts are expected to improve the quality of output to meet the manpower needs of the nation, particularly in the fields of science and technology. In addition, continued emphasis will be given to expand educational opportunities for those in the rural and remote areas. Under the Seventh Plan, the Education Ministry allocated RM8,437,200 on this education programme and RM1,661,600 for training purposes.

In 2000–01 there were 3,017,902 pupils at primary schools with 159,375 teachers, 2,205,426 pupils with 120,002 teachers at secondary schools and 549,205 students and 20,473 academic staff at higher education institutions.

Adult literacy was 88·7% in 2003 (92·0% among males and 85·4% among females).

In 2000 total expenditure on education was RM12,923m. (22·9% from the total budget). In 2000–01 total expenditure on education came to 6·8% of GNP and 26·7% of total government spending.

Health
In 2001 there were 15,619 doctors, 2,144 dentists, 31,129 nurses and 2,333 pharmacists. In 2001 the Ministry of Health ran a total of 855 health clinics and 1,744 dental clinics. In 2002 there were 323 hospitals (provision of 16 beds per 10,000 inhabitants).

Welfare
The Employment Injury Insurance Scheme (SOCSO) provides medical and cash benefits and the Invalidity Pension Scheme provides protection to employees against invalidity as a result of disease or injury from any cause. Other supplementary measures are the Employees' Provident Fund, the pension scheme for all government employees, free medical benefits for all who are unable to pay and the provision of medical benefits particularly for workers under the Labour Code. In 1998 there were 49 welfare service institutions with capacity for 7,170.

RELIGION
Malaysia has a multi-racial population divided between Islam, Buddhism, Taoism, Hinduism and Christianity. Under the Federal constitution, Islam is the official religion of Malaysia but there is freedom of worship. In 2000 there were an estimated 12·30m. Muslims, 4·02m. Buddhists, 2·70m. adherents of Chinese traditional religions, 1·63m. Hindus and 1·49m. Christians.

CULTURE

World Heritage Sites
There are two sites in Malaysia that appear on the UNESCO World Heritage List, both entered in 2000. Both are in Eastern Malaysia. They are the Gunung Mulu National Park with its limestone caves; and Kinabalu Park/Mount Kinabalu.

Broadcasting
There are five TV Stations (colour by PAL). The government-controlled Radio Television Malaysia broadcasts radio and TV programmes nationally. The Voice of Malaysia (broadcasting in eight languages) is beamed internationally. System TV Malaysia Berhad transmits from Kuala Lumpur and is also beamed throughout the country. There were 9·76m. radio receivers in 2000 and 4·77m. television receivers in 2001.

Cinema
In 2002 there were 295 cinema screens with an annual attendance of 10·2m. English, Malay, Chinese, Hindi and Indonesian films are shown.

Press
The Malaysian Media Agencies are comprised of the press, magazine and press agencies/local media, which are further divided into home and foreign news. In 2002 there were 32 daily newspapers with a combined circulation of 2,334,000. A total of 5,123 book titles were published.

Tourism
In 2002 there were 13,292,000 foreign tourists, spending US$6,785m.

Festivals
National Day (31 Aug.) is celebrated in Kuala Lumpur at the Dataran Merdeka and marks Malaysia's independence.

Libraries

The National Library of Malaysia is strong on information technology. The 14 state public libraries and 31 ministry and government department libraries are linked in a Common User Scheme called *Jaringan Ilmu* (Knowledge Network).

Theatre and Opera

Performances by the National Budaya Group include premiere theatre staging, dance drama, national choir concerts, national symphony orchestra, chamber music, and traditional and folk music. Local theatre groups regularly stage contemporary Asian and western dramas, dance dramas and the *bangsawan* (traditional Malay opera).

Museums and Galleries

There is a National Museum for preserving, restoring and imparting knowledge on the historical and cultural heritage of Malaysia. The National Art Gallery promotes Malaysian visual arts through exhibitions, competitions and support programmes which are held locally and abroad.

DIPLOMATIC REPRESENTATIVES

Of Malaysia in the United Kingdom (45 Belgrave Sq., London, SW1X 8QT)
High Commissioner: Dato'Abd Aziz bin Mohammed.

Of the United Kingdom in Malaysia (185 Jalan Ampang, 50450 Kuala Lumpur)
High Commissioner: Bruce Cleghorn, CMG.

Of Malaysia in the USA (3516 International Court, NW, Washington, D.C., 20008)
Ambassador: Dato' Sheikh Abdul Khalid Ghazzali.

Of the USA in Malaysia (376 Jalan Tun Razak, Kuala Lumpur)
Ambassador: Christopher J. LaFleur.

Of Malaysia to the United Nations
Ambassador: Datuk Hamidon Ali.

Of Malaysia to the European Union
Ambassador: Dato' Mohamed Ridzam Deva bin Abdullah.

FURTHER READING

Department of Statistics: Kuala Lumpur. *Yearbook of Statistics, Malaysia* (2005); *Yearbook of Statistics, Sabah* (2004); *Yearbook of Statistics, Sarawak* (2005); *Vital Statistics, Malaysia* (2003).

Prime Minister's Department: Economic Planning Unit. *Malaysian Economy in Figures.* Annual, 2005.

Andaya, B. W. and Andaya, L. Y., *A History of Malaysia.* 2nd ed. Palgrave, Basingstoke, 2001

Drabble, J., *An Economic History of Malaysia, c. 1800–1990.* Palgrave, Basingstoke, 2001

Kahn, J. S. and Wah, F. L. K., *Fragmented Vision: Culture and Politics in Contemporary Malaysia.* Sydney, 1992

BNM: Kuala Lumpur. *Bank Negara Malaysia, Annual Report.* 2005

National Statistical Office: Department of Statistics, Block C6, Parcel C, Federal Government Administrative Centre, 62514 Putrajaya.
Website: http://www.statistics.gov.my/

MALDIVES

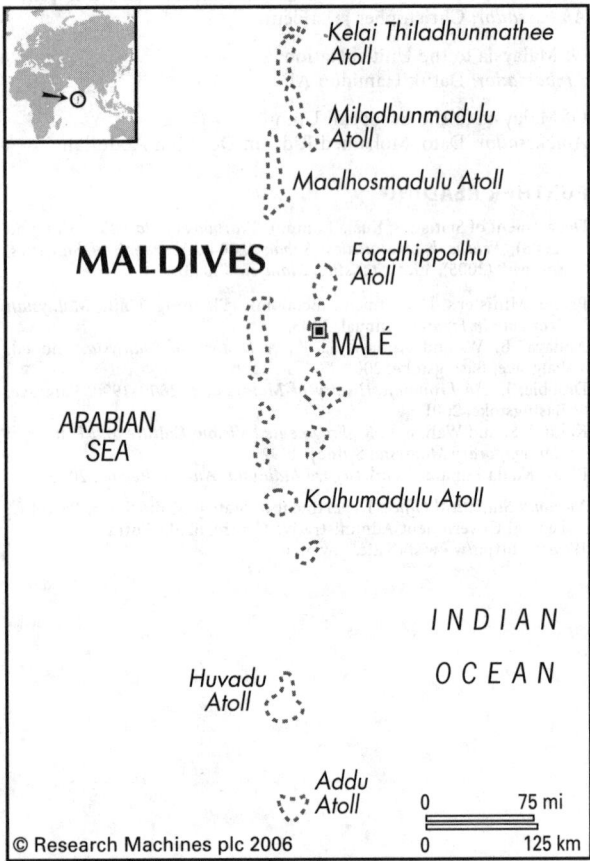

Kelai Thiladhunmathee Atoll

Miladhunmadulu Atoll

Maalhosmadulu Atoll

MALDIVES

Faadhippolhu Atoll

■ MALÉ

ARABIAN SEA

Kolhumadulu Atoll

INDIAN OCEAN

Huvadu Atoll

Addu Atoll

0   75 mi
0   125 km

© Research Machines plc 2006

Divehi Raajjeyge Jumhooriyyaa
(Republic of the Maldives)

Capital: Malé
Population projection, 2010: 371,000
GDP per capita, 2001: (PPP$) 4,798
HDI/world rank: 0·745/96

KEY HISTORICAL EVENTS

Divehi-speaking people (a language related to Sinhalese) have lived on the Maldives since at least 400 AD. Visited by Middle Eastern merchants from around 1000 AD, the archipelago became an Islamic sultanate in 1153. Portuguese explorers occupied the island of Malé (the modern capital) from 1558 until they were expelled by Muhammad Thakurufaanu Al-Azam in 1573. The Dutch, who replaced the Portuguese as the dominant power in Ceylon in the mid-1600s, controlled Maldivian affairs until 1796, although the sultanate held sway over local administration. Thereafter the Maldives came under British protection (formalized in an agreement in 1887) until complete independence was achieved on 26 July 1965. A republic was declared on 11 Nov 1968.

TERRITORY AND POPULATION

The republic, some 650 km to the southwest of Sri Lanka, consists of 1,192 low-lying (the highest point is 2·4 metres above sea-level) coral islands, grouped into 26 atolls. 199 are inhabited. Area 298 sq. km (115 sq. miles). At the 2000 census the population was 270,101 (137,200 males); density, 906·4 per sq. km. The estimated population in 2005 was 329,000.

The UN gives a projected population for 2010 of 371,000.

In 2003, 71·2% of the population lived in rural areas. Capital, Malé (2000 population, 74,000).

The official and spoken language is Divehi.

SOCIAL STATISTICS

2001 births, 4,882; deaths, 1,081. Birth rate, 2001, per 1,000 population, 17·7; death rate, 3·9. Annual population growth rate, 1992–2002, 3·0%. Life expectancy at birth in 2003 was 67·1 years for males and 66·1 years for females. Infant mortality, 2002, 58 per 1,000 live births; fertility rate, 2001, 5·5 births per woman.

CLIMATE

The islands are hot and humid, and affected by monsoons. Malé: average temperature 81°F (27°C), annual rainfall 59" (1,500 mm).

CONSTITUTION AND GOVERNMENT

The present constitution came into effect on 1 Jan. 1998. There is a Citizens' *Majlis* (Parliament) which consists of 50 members, eight of whom are nominated by the President and 42 directly elected (two each from Malé and the 20 administrative districts) for a term of five years. There are no political parties. The President of the Republic is elected by the Citizens' Majlis.

National Anthem

'Gavmii mi ekuverikan matii tibegen kuriime salaam' ('In national unity we salute our nation'); words by M. J. Didi, tune by W. Amaradeva.

RECENT ELECTIONS

President Maumoon Abdul Gayoom was re-elected in a referendum held on 17 Oct. 2003. As sole candidate, he won 90·3% of the votes cast. Turnout was 77%. At the last elections to the *Majlis* on 22 Jan. 2005 only non-partisans were elected, but both the government and the opposition Maldives Democratic Party—which operates in self-imposed exile out of Sri Lanka—claimed victory.

CURRENT ADMINISTRATION

In March 2006 the government consisted of:

President: Maumoon Abdul Gayoom; b. 1937 (in office since 1978; re-elected unopposed for a sixth 5-year term in Oct. 2003).

Minister of Atolls Administration: Mohamed Waheed Deen. *Construction and Public Infrastructure:* Mohamed Mauroof Jameel. *Defence and National Security:* Ismail Shafeeu. *Economic Development and Trade:* Mohammed Jaleel. *Education:* Zaahiya Zareer. *Environment, Energy and Water:* Ahmed Abdullah. *Finance and Treasury:* Gasim Ibrahim. *Fisheries, Agriculture and Marine Resources:* Abdulla Kamaaludeen. *Foreign Affairs:* Ahmed Shaheed. *Gender and Family:* Aishath Mohamed Didi. *Health:* Ilyas Ibrahim. *Higher Education, Employment and Social Security:* Abdulla Yameen. *Home Affairs:* Ahmed Thasmeen Ali. *Housing and Urban Development:* Ibrahim Rafeeq. *Information and Arts:* Mohammed Nasheed. *Justice:* Mahmood Jameel Ahmed. *Planning and National Development:* Hamdoon Hameed. *Presidential Affairs:* Mohamed Hussain. *Tourism and Civil Aviation:* Mahmood Shaugee. *Transportation and Communications:* Mohamed Saeed. *Youth and Sports:*

Hussain Hilmy. *Attorney General:* Hassan Saeed. *Minister to the President's Office:* Aneesa Ahmed.

Speaker of Citizens' Majlis: Ahmed Zahir.

Office of the President: http://www.presidencymaldives.gov.mv

CURRENT LEADERS

Maumoon Abdul Gayoom

Position
President

Introduction
In power as president of the Maldives since 1978, Maumoon Abdul Gayoom was re-elected in a referendum for a sixth consecutive five-year term in office in Oct. 2003. He had succeeded Ibrahim Nasir who served from 1954 and was the premier when the Maldives became independent in 1965. During his tenure he has developed industry, especially the main sectors of fishing and tourism, attracted investment and improved healthcare. But strict censorship and the suppression of opposition has led to international concern.

Early Life
Gayoom was born on 29 Dec. 1937 in Malé where he received his early schooling. After studying in Sri Lanka and Cairo, Egypt, he completed a degree in Islamic studies at the Al-Azhar University, Cairo. He subsequently taught in Nigeria and Malé. He began working for the government in 1972 when he was employed in the shipping department. Two years later he was appointed under-secretary in the prime minister's office before serving a year in Colombo as deputy ambassador to Sri Lanka. After representing the Maldives in the UN from 1976–77, he was made transport minister under Nasir's presidency. When Nasir resigned in 1978, Gayoom was chosen as president, a parliamentary decision ratified by a referendum in which 92·9% supported the appointment.

Career in Office
Gayoom has invested in the nascent tourist industry which has overtaken fishing as the country's chief revenue earner. However, tourism is strictly controlled in an attempt to protect the Maldives' environment and to preserve its culture. As an archipelago of low-lying islands, the Maldives is threatened by the rising sea level caused by global warming. In 1989 Gayoom hosted an international environment conference. The country's relative stability during Gayoom's rule has been one factor in the attraction of foreign investment. He has also invested in the country's health care and aims to reduce the economic disparity between people living on the capital and those on the outer islands. However, Gayoom has led an oligarchic government which has maintained strict control, most notably through media censorship and intolerance of any criticism of the government. Gayoom survived attempted coups in 1980, 1983 and most notably in 1988 when help from Indian troops was needed to suppress a rising supported by Sri Lankan mercenaries.

On the international front, Gayoom has tried to improve relations with India. He was a founder member of the South Asian Association for Regional Co-operation (SAARC) in 1985. In 1996 a Supreme Council for Islamic Affairs, under presidential control, was established to provide advice on matters related to Islam.

In 1980 Gayoom established a Citizens' *Majlis* (Parliament) and, after 17 years of deliberation, it produced guidelines for a new constitution which became operational in Jan. 1998. It extended ministers' executive powers and increased the size of the *Majlis*. It also allowed self-nomination for presidency while stipulating that the candidate be a male Sunni Muslim over 35.

In Oct. 2003 Gayoom was re-elected for a sixth term with 90% of the vote in a referendum.

DEFENCE

In 2003 military expenditure totalled US$40m. (US$138 per capita), representing 6·4% of GDP.

INTERNATIONAL RELATIONS

The Maldives is a member of the UN, WTO, the Commonwealth, Asian Development Bank, Colombo Plan, SAARC, OIC and Islamic Development Bank.

ECONOMY

Fisheries accounts for approximately 7% of GDP, industry 15% and services 78%.

Currency

The unit of currency is the *rufiyaa* (MVR) of 100 *laari*. There was inflation in 2004 of 6·4%. Gold reserves were 1,900 troy oz in Oct. 2004. Foreign exchange reserves were US$192·4m in Oct. 2004. Total money supply was 5,581m. rufiyaa in Oct. 2004.

Budget

In 2002 (year ending 31 Dec.) government total revenue was 2,582·4m. rufiyaa; expenditure 3,135·5m. rufiyaa.

Performance

Real GDP growth was 8·4% in 2003, rising to 8·8% in 2004. Total GDP in 2004 was US$0·8bn.

Banking and Finance

The Maldives Monetary Authority (*Governor*, Gasim Ibrahim), established in 1981, is endowed with the regular powers of a central bank and bank of issue. There is one domestic commercial bank (Bank of Maldives) and branches of four foreign banks.

ENERGY AND NATURAL RESOURCES

Environment

Carbon dioxide emissions from the consumption and flaring of fossil fuels were the equivalent of 1·7 tonnes per capita in 2002.

Electricity

Installed capacity was 36,000 kW in 2000. Production in 2003 was 157m. kWh; consumption per capita in 2000 was 384 kWh. Utilization in Malé was 97m. kWh in 2003.

Minerals

Inshore coral mining has been banned as a measure against the encroachment of the sea.

Agriculture

There were 4,000 ha. of arable land in 2001 and 5,000 ha. of permanent crops. Principal crops in 2000 (in 1,000 tonnes): coconuts, 16; copra, 3; tree nuts, 2; bananas, 1.

Fisheries

The total catch in 2003 was 155,415 tonnes. The Maldives has the highest per capita consumption of fish and fishery products of any country in the world. In the period 1999–2001 the average person consumed 187 kg (412 lb) a year, or more than 11 times the average for the world as a whole.

INDUSTRY

The main industries are fishing, tourism, shipping, lacquerwork and garment manufacturing.

Labour

In 2000 the economically active workforce totalled 87,987 (59,279 males) of whom 86,245 were employed.

INTERNATIONAL TRADE

Total foreign debt amounted to US$270m. in 2002.

Imports and Exports

In 2003 imports (f.o.b.) were valued at US$414·3m. (US$344·7m. in 2002) and exports (f.o.b.) at US$152·0m. (US$132·5m. in 2002). Tuna is the main export commodity. It is exported principally to Thailand, Sri Lanka, Japan and some European markets. Main import suppliers in 2003 were Singapore (24·9%), Sri Lanka (13·7%), India (10·1%), Malaysia (7·7%), UAE (7·6%). Leading export destinations were USA (23·3%), Thailand (16·4%), Sri Lanka (13·6%), Japan (10·3%), UK (9·7%).

COMMUNICATIONS

Roads

In 2003 there were 1,751 cars, 14,370 motorbikes/autocycles, 431 lorries, 127 trucks, 92 tractors, 431 vans, 36 buses, 248 jeeps, 704 pickups and 403 other vehicles.

Civil Aviation

The former national carrier Air Maldives collapsed in April 2000 with final losses in excess of US$50m. In 2003 there were 1,833,620 passenger arrivals, 21m. pieces of cargo and 100,352 pieces of mail handled at Malé's international airport. There are four domestic airports. In 1999 scheduled airline traffic of Maldives-based carriers flew 5·1m. km, carrying 344,000 passengers (273,000 on international flights).

Shipping

The Maldives Shipping Line operated (1992) ten vessels. In 2000 merchant shipping totalled 58,000 GRT.

Telecommunications

In Oct. 2004 telephone subscribers numbered 31,300 (108 fixed lines per 1,000 inhabitants) and mobile phone users 98,300. Landline and mobile usage combined gives an overall density of 447 telephones per 1,000 inhabitants. At the end of 2003 the number of PCs in use was estimated at 25,000. There were approximately 15,000 Internet users in 2003.

Postal Services

At the end of Nov. 2004 there were 197 agency post offices and nine sub-post offices. There are a total of 300 employees.

SOCIAL INSTITUTIONS

Justice

Justice is based on the Islamic Shari'a.

Education

Adult literacy in 2003 was 97·2% (male, 97·3%; female, 97·2%). Education is not compulsory. In 2004 there were 81 government schools (57,139 pupils), 176 community schools (38,043 pupils) and 337 private schools (104,214 pupils) with a total of 5,239 teachers. In 1998–99 total expenditure on education came to 6·5% of GNP and 11·2% of total government spending.

Health

In 2003 there were 236 beds at the Indira Gandhi Memorial Hospital in Malé, six regional hospitals (226 beds) and 27 health centres. In 2003 there were 315 doctors and 785 nurses, 251 pharmacists and 409 midwives.

RELIGION

The State religion is Islam.

CULTURE

Broadcasting

Voice of Maldives and Television Maldives are government-controlled. In 2004 there were an estimated 200,000 radio receivers and 10,800 television sets (colour by PAL).

Press

In 2005 there were 18 newspapers and 77 magazines.

Tourism

Tourism is the major foreign currency earner. There were 563,600 visitors in 2003, spending US$401·6m.

Festivals

The Maldives' National Day in May commemorates the victory of Muhammad Thakurufaanu Al-Azam over the Portuguese in 1573. Victory Day celebrates the defeat of Sri Lankan mercenaries who tried to overthrow the Maldivian government on 3 Nov. 1988. Republic Day is on 11 Nov.

DIPLOMATIC REPRESENTATIVES

Of the Maldives in the United Kingdom (22 Nottingham Pl., London, W1U 5NJ)
High Commissioner: Hassan Sobir.

Of the United Kingdom in the Maldives
High Commissioner: Stephen Evans, CMG, OBE (resides in Colombo, Sri Lanka).

Of the Maldives in the USA (800 2nd Ave., Suite 400E, New York, NY 10017)
Ambassador: Dr Mohamed Latheef.

Of the USA in the Maldives
Ambassador: Jeffrey J. Lunstead (resides in Colombo, Sri Lanka).

Permanent Representative of the Maldives to the United Nations
Ambassador: Dr Mohamed Latheef.

Of the Maldives to the European Union
Ambassador: Vacant.

FURTHER READING

Gayoom, M. A., *The Maldives: A Nation in Peril*. Ministry of Planning, Human Resources and Environment, Republic of Maldives, 1998
Reynolds, Christopher H. B., *Maldives*. [Bibliography] ABC-Clio, Oxford and Santa Barbara (CA), 1993

National Statistical Office: Statistics Section, Ministry of Planning and National Development.
Website: http://www.planning.gov.mv

MALI

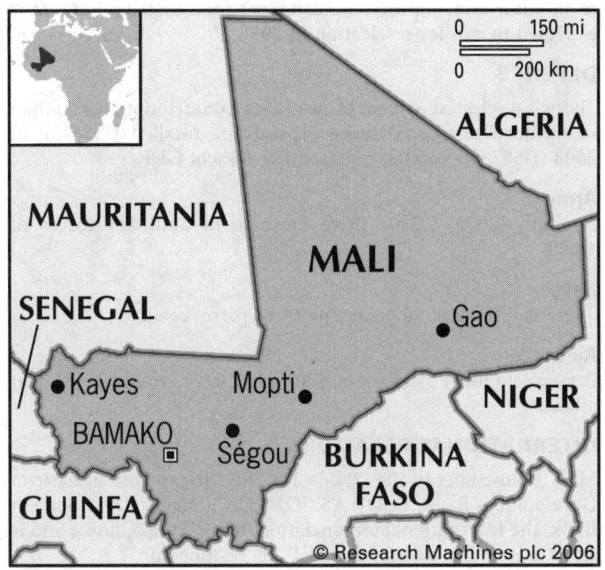

République du Mali

Capital: Bamako
Population projection, 2010: 15·62m.
GDP per capita, 2003: (PPP$) 994
HDI/world rank: 0·333/174

KEY HISTORICAL EVENTS

Mali's power reached its peak between the 11th and 13th centuries when its gold-based empire controlled much of the surrounding area. The country was annexed by France in 1904. As French Sudan it was part of French West Africa. The country became an autonomous state within the French Community on 24 Nov. 1958, and on 4 April 1959 joined with Senegal to form the Federation of Mali. The Federation achieved independence on 20 June 1960, but Senegal seceded on 22 Aug. and Mali proclaimed itself an independent republic on 22 Sept. There was an army coup on 19 Nov. 1968, which brought Moussa Traoré to power. Ruling the country for over 22 years, he wrecked the economy. A further coup followed in March 1991.

In Jan. 1991 a ceasefire was signed with Tuareg insurgents in the north and in April 1992 a national pact was concluded providing for a special administration for the Tuareg north.

Under President Alpha Oumar Konaré, two elections for the National Assembly were held. The first (April 1997) was cancelled by the Constitutional Court and the second, in July 1997, was boycotted by opposition parties. Amadou Toumani Touré, a former military ruler, won presidential elections held in April and May 2002. In July 2005 severe food shortages led to more than 1m. people facing starvation.

TERRITORY AND POPULATION

Mali is bounded in the west by Senegal, northwest by Mauritania, northeast by Algeria, east by Niger and south by Burkina Faso, Côte d'Ivoire and Guinea. Its area is 1,248,574 sq. km (482,077 sq. miles) and it had a population of 10,179,170 at the 1998 census (67·7% rural in 2003). Density, 8·2 per sq. km. 2005 population estimate: 13,518,000.

The UN gives a projected population for 2010 of 15·62m.

The areas, populations and chief towns of the regions are:

Region	Sq. km	1998 population	Chief town
Gao	170,572	495,178	Gao
Kayes	119,743	1,424,657	Kayes
Kidal	151,430	65,524	Kidal
Koulikoro	95,848	1,620,811	Koulikoro
Mopti	79,017	1,405,370	Mopti
Ségou	64,821	1,652,594	Ségou
Sikasso	70,280	1,839,747	Sikasso
Tombouctou	496,611	496,312	Tombouctou
Capital District	252	1,178,977	Bamako

In 1999 the capital, Bamako, had an estimated population of 1,083,000.

In 2000 the principal ethnic groups were: Bambara, 30·6%; Senufo, 10·5%; Fulani, 9·6%; Soninke, 7·4%; Tuareg, 7·0%; Maninka, 6·6%; Songhai, 6·3%; Dogon, 4·3%. The official language is French; Bambara is spoken by about 68% of the population.

SOCIAL STATISTICS

2000 estimates: births, 590,000; deaths, 206,000. Rates, 2000 estimates (per 1,000 population): births, 49·6; deaths, 17·3. Infant mortality, 2001 (per 1,000 live births), 141. Expectation of life in 2003 was 47·2 years for males and 48·5 for females. Annual population growth rate, 1992–2002, 2·8%; fertility rate, 2001, 7·0 children per woman.

CLIMATE

A tropical climate, with adequate rain in the south and west, but conditions become increasingly arid towards the north and east. Bamako, Jan. 76°F (24·4°C), July 80°F (26·7°C). Annual rainfall 45" (1,120 mm). Kayes, Jan. 76°F (24·4°C), July 93°F (33·9°C). Annual rainfall 29" (725 mm). Tombouctou, Jan. 71°F (21·7°C), July 90°F (32·2°C). Annual rainfall 9" (231 mm).

CONSTITUTION AND GOVERNMENT

A constitution was approved by a national referendum in 1974; it was amended by the National Assembly on 2 Sept. 1981. The sole legal party was the *Union démocratique du peuple malien* (UDPM).

A national conference of 1,800 delegates agreed a draft constitution enshrining multi-party democracy in Aug. 1991, and this was approved by 99·76% of votes cast at a referendum in Jan. 1992. Turnout was 43%.

The *President* is elected for not more than two terms of five years.

There is a *National Assembly*, consisting of 147 deputies (formerly 116) plus 13 Malinese living abroad.

A *Constitutional Court* was established in 1994.

National Anthem

'A ton appel, Mali' ('At your call, Mali'); words by S. Kouyate, tune by B. Sissoko.

RECENT ELECTIONS

Presidential elections were held in two rounds on 28 April and 12 May 2002. In the first round Amadou Toumani Touré won 28·0% of votes cast, against 22·7% for Soumaïla Cissé and 20·7% for Ibrahim Boubacar Keita. Turnout was 38·6%. In the run-off between Touré and Cissé on 12 May, Touré won with 64·4% of the vote against 35·7% for Cissé.

Parliamentary elections were held in two rounds on 14 and 28 July 2002. Initial results indicated victory for the Alliance for Democracy in Mali (ADEMA) with 67 seats (down from 128 in

1997) and 47 seats for the Hope 2002 coalition. On 10 Aug. 2002 the Constitutional Court ruled these results invalid and released new results giving 66 seats to the Hope Coalition 2002 against 51 for the Alliance for Democracy in Mali. Turnout was 25·7%.

CURRENT ADMINISTRATION

President: Amadou Toumani Touré; b. 1948 (sworn in 8 June 2002, having previously been president from March 1991–June 1992 following a coup).

In March 2006 the government comprised:

Prime Minister: Ousmane Issoufi Maïga; b. 1945 (sworn in 30 April 2004).

Minister for Environment and Decontamination: Nancouma Kéita. *Planning and National Development:* Marimatia Diarra. *Livestock and Fishing:* Oumar Ibrahima Touré. *Handicrafts and Tourism:* Bah N'Diaye. *Education:* Mohamed Lamine Traoré. *Industry and Commerce:* Choguel Kokala Maïga. *Territorial Administration and Local Collectivities:* Gen. Kafougouna Koné. *Foreign Affairs and International Co-operation:* Moctar Ouane. *Malians Abroad and African Integration:* Oumar Hamadoun Diko. *Agriculture:* Seydou Traoré. *Communications and Information Technology:* Gaoussou Drabo. *Mines, Energy and Water Resources:* Hamed Diane Sémega. *Culture:* Cheick Oumar Sissoko. *Social Development, Solidarity and the Aged:* Djibril Tangara. *Economy and Finance:* Abou-Bacar Traoré. *Civil Service, State Reform and Relations with the Institutions:* Badi Ould Ganfoud. *Employment and Professional Training:* Ba Hawa Keita. *Promotion of Investment and of Small- and Medium-Sized Enterprises:* Ousmane Thiam. *Promotion of Women, Children and the Family:* Diallo M'Bodji Sène. *Defence and Veterans:* Mamadou Clazié Cissouma. *Justice and Keeper of the Seals:* Fanta Sylla. *State Territories and Land Affairs:* Soumaré Aminata Sidibé. *Health:* Maïga Zeinab Mint Youba. *Equipment and Transport:* Abdoulaye Koïta. *Internal Security and Civil Protection:* Col. Sadio Gassama. *Youth and Sports:* Natie Pleah. *Housing and Urbanization:* Modibo Sylla.

CURRENT LEADERS

Amadou Toumani Touré

Position
President

Introduction
In 2002 Amadou Toumani Touré won Mali's election to become the country's second democratically-elected president. He had previously acted as head of state in 1991 when, as an army general, he overthrew military leader Moussa Traoré.

Early Life
Amadou Toumani Touré was born on 4 Nov. 1948 in Mopti. From 1966–69 he studied at Badalabougou Standard Secondary School in Bamako with the intention of becoming a teacher. However, he abandoned teaching in favour of military training and joined the army, enrolling at the Kita-Inter Military College. He then trained in the former USSR and France before joining the parachute corps as a commander in 1984.

Touré led a coup in 1991 against Moussa Traoré after the latter's security forces killed more than a hundred pro-democracy demonstrators. In 1992 Touré handed power back to the newly-elected president Alpha Oumar Konaré, ending 23 years of military dictatorship and earning himself the nickname 'Soldier of Democracy'.

Having retired from the army in Sept. 2001, he decided to return to politics as an independent presidential candidate in 2002, beating Soumaïla Cissé in the second round of elections.

Career in Office
Touré took office with the support of 22 minor parties and a number of other groups. He pledged to promote education and

youth employment and has created a children's foundation. He also pledged to ease poverty and improve the health system. In Aug. 2005 he launched the food security website, developed in conjunction with the Malian food security commission, designed to monitor and improve the country's food distribution. He is expected to run for re-election in 2007.

DEFENCE

There is a selective system of two years' conscription, for civilian or military service. Defence expenditure totalled US$81m. in 2003 (US$7 per capita), representing 1·8% of GDP.

Army

Strength (2002) 7,350. There are also paramilitary forces of 4,800.

Navy

There is a Navy of 50 operating three patrol craft.

Air Force

Personnel (2002) total about 400. There were around 16 combat aircraft.

INTERNATIONAL RELATIONS

Mali is a member of the UN, WTO, the African Union, African Development Bank, ECOWAS, IOM, OIC, Islamic Development Bank, the International Organization of the Francophonie and is an ACP member state of the ACP-EU relationship.

ECONOMY

Agriculture accounted for 34·2% of GDP in 2002, industry 29·7% and services 36·1%.

Currency

The unit of currency is the *franc CFA* (XOF), which replaced the Mali franc in 1984. It has a parity rate of 655·957 francs CFA to one euro. Total money supply in May 2002 was 460,722m. francs CFA and foreign exchange reserves were US$508m. Gold reserves were 19,000 troy oz in June 2000. There was negative inflation in both 2003 and 2004, of –1·3% and –3·1% respectively.

Budget

Revenues for 2002 were 379·4bn. francs CFA and expenditures 601·5bn. francs CFA.

Performance

Real GDP growth was 7·2% in 2003, falling to 2·2% in 2004. In 2004 total GDP was US$4·9bn.

Banking and Finance

The bank of issue and the central bank is the regional Central Bank of West African States (BCEAO). The *Acting Governor* is Justin Baro Damo. In 2002 there were eight commercial and two development banks.

There is a stock exchange in Bamako.

ENERGY AND NATURAL RESOURCES

Environment

Carbon dioxide emissions from the consumption and flaring of fossil fuels were the equivalent of 0·1 tonnes per capita in 2002.

Electricity

Installed capacity in 2000 was 0·1m. kW. Production in 2000 totalled about 412m. kWh, approximately 57% of it hydro-electric. Consumption per capita was an estimated 36 kWh in 2000.

Minerals

Gold (56,026 kg in 2002) is the principal mineral produced. There are also deposits of iron ore, uranium, diamonds, bauxite, manganese, copper, salt, limestone, phosphate, gypsum and lithium.

Agriculture

About 80% of the population depends on agriculture, mainly carried on by small peasant holdings. Mali is second only to Egypt among African cotton producers. In 2001 there were 4·66m. ha. of arable land and 40,000 ha. of permanent cropland. There were 2,600 tractors in 2001 and 650 harvester-threshers.

Production in 2000 included (estimates, in 1,000 tonnes): millet, 953; rice, 810; sorghum, 714; seed cotton, 480; maize, 438; sugarcane, 300; cottonseed, 220; cotton lint, 200; ground-nuts, 140.

Livestock, 2000: cattle, 6·20m.; sheep, 6·00m.; goats, 8·55m.; asses, 652,000; camels, 292,000; chickens, 25m.

138,000 ha. were irrigated in 2001.

Forestry

In 2000 forests covered 13·19m. ha., or 10·8% of the total land area. Timber production in 2001 was 5·20m. cu. metres.

Fisheries

In 2001 approximately 100,000 tonnes of fish were caught, exclusively from inland waters.

INDUSTRY

The main industries are food processing, followed by cotton processing, textiles and clothes. Cement and pharmaceuticals are also produced.

Labour

In 1996 the workforce was estimated to be 5,472,000 (54% males). In 1995 over 80% of the economically active population were engaged in agriculture, fisheries and forestry. Large numbers of Malians emigrate temporarily to work abroad, principally in Côte d'Ivoire.

INTERNATIONAL TRADE

Foreign debt was US$2,803m. in 2002.

Imports and Exports

In 2003 imports (f.o.b.) were valued at US$988·3m. (US$712·5m. in 2002) and exports (f.o.b.) at US$927·8m. (US$875·1m. in 2002).

Principal import commodities are machinery and equipment, foodstuffs, construction materials, petroleum and textiles. Principal export commodities are cotton and livestock (between them accounting for three-quarters of Mali's annual exports) and gold.

The main import suppliers are France and its former colonies (in particular Côte d'Ivoire), western Europe and China. Main export markets are also France and its former colonies, western Europe and China.

COMMUNICATIONS

Roads

There were (2002 estimate) 15,100 km of classified roads, of which 1,830 km were paved. In 2002 there were 19,800 passenger cars (1·6 per 1,000 inhabitants) and 8,600 commercial vehicles. There were 72 road accident deaths in 1994.

Rail

Mali has a railway from Kayes to Koulikoro by way of Bamako, a continuation of the Dakar–Kayes line in Senegal; total length 734 km (metre-gauge). Passenger-km travelled in 2000 came to 204m. and freight tonne-km to 193m.

Civil Aviation

There is an international airport at Bamako (Senou), which handled 312,000 passengers (305,000 on international flights) and 4,400 tonnes of freight in 2001. In 2003 Trans African Airlines operated services to Abidjan, Brazzaville, Cotonou, Dakar, Lomé and Pointe-Noire. There were also international flights to Accra, Addis Ababa, Banjul, Bobo-Dioulasso, Casablanca, Conakry, Douala, Kano, Lagos, Libreville, N'Djaména, Niamey, Nouakchott, Ouagadougou, Paris and Tripoli. In 1999 scheduled airline traffic of Mali-based carriers flew 3·0m. km, carrying 84,000 passengers (all on international flights).

Shipping

For about seven months in the year small steamboats operate a service from Koulikoro to Tombouctou and Gao, and from Bamako to Kouroussa.

Telecommunications

Mali had 102,400 telephone subscribers in 2002, or 9·6 per 1,000 population, and there were 15,000 PCs in use (1·4 per 1,000 persons). In 2002 there were 52,600 mobile phone subscribers. In 2002 Internet users numbered 25,000.

Postal Services

In 2002 there were 117 post offices.

SOCIAL INSTITUTIONS

Justice

The Supreme Court was established at Bamako in 1969 with both judicial and administrative powers. The Court of Appeal is also at Bamako, at the apex of a system of regional tribunals and local *juges de paix*.

The population in penal institutions in Feb. 2002 was 4,040 (34 per 100,000 of national population).

Education

The adult literacy rate in 2001 was 26·4% (36·7% among males and 16·6% among females).

In 2000–01 there were 600 teachers for 15,106 children in pre-primary schools, and 17,788 teachers for 1,127,360 pupils in primary schools; in 1998–99 there were 217,700 secondary school pupils and 18,662 students in tertiary education. During the period 1990–95 only 19% of females of primary school age were enrolled in school.

In 1999–2000 total expenditure on education came to 3·0% of GNP.

Health

In 2001 there were 17 hospitals. In 2000 there were 529 physicians, 1,501 nurses and 284 midwives.

RELIGION

The state is secular, but predominantly Sunni Muslim. About 15% of the population follow traditional animist beliefs and there is a small Christian minority.

CULTURE

World Heritage Sites

Mali has four sites on the UNESCO World Heritage List: Old Towns of Djenné (inscribed on the list in 1988), a market centre established in 250 BC and an important Islamic centre in the 16th century—its buildings are all mudbrick, plastered annually with adobe; Tomboctou (1988) an important Islamic centre, containing the Koranic Sankore University and the famous Djingareyber Mosque; the Cliff of Bandiagara (Land of the Dogons) (1989), for its natural and architectural wonders; and the Tomb of Askia (2004).

Broadcasting

Broadcasting is the responsibility of the autonomous Radiodiffusion Télévision du Mali.

Number of sets: radio (2000), 597,000; TV (2001), 200,000 (colour by SECAM).

Press

In 1998 there were three daily newspapers with a combined circulation of 12,600.

Tourism

There were 86,000 foreign tourists in 2000, bringing in revenue of US$71m.

DIPLOMATIC REPRESENTATIVES

Of Mali in the United Kingdom (resides in Brussels)
Ambassador: Ibrahim Bocar Ba.

Of the United Kingdom in Mali
Ambassador: Peter Newall (resides in Dakar, Senegal).

Of Mali in the USA (2130 R. St., NW, Washington, D.C., 20008)
Ambassador: Abdoulaye Diop.

Of the USA in Mali (Rue Rochester NY and Rue Mohamed V, Bamako)
Ambassador: Terence P. McCulley.

Of Mali to the United Nations
Ambassador: Cheick Sidi Diarra.

Of Mali to the European Union
Ambassador: Ibrahim Bocar Ba.

FURTHER READING

National Statistical Office: Direction National de la Statistique et de l'Informatique, BP 12 rue Adunard, Port 233.
Website (French only): http://www.dnsi.gov.ml

MALTA

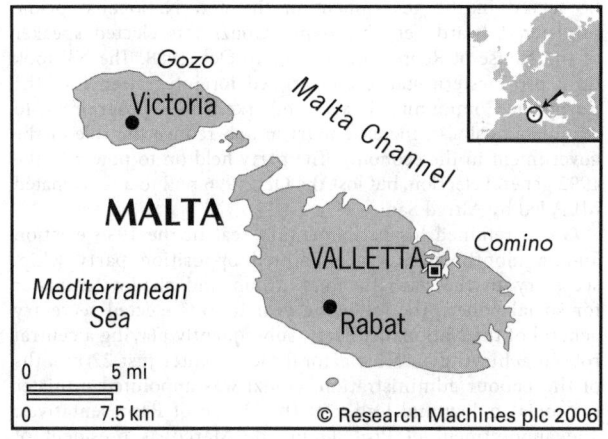

Repubblika ta' Malta

Capital: Valletta
Population projection, 2010: 411,000
GDP per capita, 2003: (PPP$) 17,633
HDI/world rank: 0·867/32

KEY HISTORICAL EVENTS

Malta was held in turn by Phoenicians, Carthaginians and Romans, and was conquered by Arabs in 870. From 1090 it was subject to the same rulers as Sicily until 1530, when it was handed over to the Knights of St John, who ruled until dispersed by Napoleon in 1798. The Maltese rose in rebellion against the French and the island was blockaded by the British, aided by the Maltese from 1798 to 1800. The Maltese people freely requested the protection of the British Crown in 1802 on condition that their rights and privileges be preserved. The island was finally annexed to the British Crown by the Treaty of Paris in 1814. Malta became independent on 21 Sept. 1964 and a republic within the Commonwealth on 13 Dec. 1974. On 1 May 2004 Malta became a member of the European Union.

TERRITORY AND POPULATION

The three Maltese islands and minor islets lie in the Mediterranean 93 km (at the nearest point) south of Sicily and 288 km east of Tunisia. The area of Malta is 246 sq. km (94·9 sq. miles); Gozo, 67 sq. km (25·9 sq. miles) and the virtually uninhabited Comino, 3 sq. km (1·1 sq. miles); total area, 316 sq. km (121·9 sq. miles). The census population in 1995 was 376,335. Population, 31 Dec. 2002, 397,296; Malta island, 366,028; Gozo and Comino, 31,268. Density, 1,257 per sq. km.

The UN gives a projected population for 2010 of 411,000.

In 2003, 91·6% of the population were urban. Chief town and port, Valletta, population 7,173 (2002) but the southern harbour district, 85,562. Other towns: Birkirkara, 22,334; Qormi, 18,553; Mosta, 17,936; Zabbar, 15,057; Sliema, 12,575.

The constitution provides that the national language and language of the courts is Maltese, but both Maltese and English are official languages.

SOCIAL STATISTICS

2002: births, 3,805; deaths, 3,031; marriages, 2,240; emigrants, 96; returned emigrants, 382. 2002 rates per 1,000 population: birth, 9·9; death, 7·8; marriage, 5·8. Divorce and abortion are illegal. In 2002 the most popular age range for marrying was 25–29 for males and 20–24 for females. Life expectancy at birth in 2003: 75·9 years for males and 80·8 years for females. Annual population growth rate, 1992–2002, 0·7%. Infant mortality in 2002: 6·0 per 1,000 live births; fertility rate, 2002, 1·5 births per woman.

CLIMATE

The climate is Mediterranean, with hot, dry and sunny conditions in summer and very little rain from May to Aug. Rainfall is not excessive and falls mainly between Oct. and March. Average daily sunshine in winter is six hours and in summer over ten hours. Valletta, Jan. 12·8°C (55°F), July 25·6°C (78°F). Annual rainfall 578 mm (23").

CONSTITUTION AND GOVERNMENT

Malta is a parliamentary democracy. The Constitution of 1964 provides for a *President*, a *House of Representatives* of members elected by universal suffrage and a Cabinet consisting of the Prime Minister and such number of Ministers as may be appointed. The Constitution makes provision for the protection of fundamental rights and freedom of the individual, and for freedom of conscience and religious worship, and guarantees the separation of executive, judicial and legislative powers. The House of Representatives currently has 65 members directly elected on a plurality basis.

National Anthem

'Lil din l'art helwa, l'omm li tatna isimha' ('Guard her, O Lord, as ever Thou hast guarded'); words by Dun Karm Psaila, tune by Dr Robert Samut.

RECENT ELECTIONS

At the elections of 12 April 2003 the electorate was 294,106; turnout was 96·2%. The Nationalist Party (NP) gained 35 seats with 51·8% of votes cast; the Labour Party (MLP), 30 with 47·5%.

European Parliament
Malta has five representatives. At the June 2004 elections turnout was 82·4%. The MLP won 3 seats with 49·0% of votes cast (political affiliation in European Parliament: Party of European Socialists); and the NP 2 with 40·0% (European People's Party–European Democrats).

CURRENT ADMINISTRATION

President: Dr Edward Fenech Adami; b. 1934 (NP; sworn in 4 April 2004).

In March 2006 the government comprised:

Prime Minister and Minister of Finance: Dr Lawrence Gonzi; b. 1953 (NP; sworn in 23 March 2004).

Deputy Prime Minister, Minister for Justice and Home Affairs and Leader of the House of Representatives: Dr Tonio Borg. *Education, Youth and Employment:* Dr Louis Galea. *Foreign Affairs and Investment Promotion:* Dr Michael Frendo. *Tourism and Culture:* Dr Francis Zammit Dimech. *Competitiveness and Communications:* Censu Galea. *Resources and Infrastructure:* Ninu Zammit. *Gozo:* Giovanna Debono. *Health, the Elderly and Community Care:* Dr Louis Deguara. *Information Technology and Investment:* Dr Austin Gatt. *Rural Affairs and the Environment:* George Pullicino. *Urban Development and Roads:* Jesmond Mugliett. *Family and Social Solidarity:* Dolores Cristina.

Speaker: Anton Tabone.

Government Website: http://www.gov.mt

CURRENT LEADERS

Eddie Fenech Adami

Position
President

Introduction
Dr Edward Fenech Adami, Malta's president since April 2004, was previously twice Malta's prime minister, from May 1987 to Oct. 1996 and Sept. 1998 to March 2004. As head of the Nationalist Party, he instigated programmes of economic liberalization, and he campaigned for entry into the European Union, which Malta joined on 1 May 2004.

Early Life
Edward (Eddie) Fenech Adami was born on 7 Feb. 1934 in Birkirkara. He attended the University of Malta where he studied economics, classics and law. He joined the bar in 1959 and was a newspaper editor between 1962–69, during which time he twice ran unsuccessfully for parliament. In 1969 he won a seat on a Nationalist Party ticket and went on to hold several high profile positions as well as establishing himself in Europe's Christian Democrat community. In 1977 he was elected party leader to succeed Dr Giorgio Borg Olivier. In 1987 Fenech Adami led the Nationalists to victory in the general elections and was sworn in as prime minister.

Career in Office
Fenech Adami's tenure was marked by administrative and economic reform as he tried to steer Malta towards the EU. The banking, telecommunications and trade sectors were deregulated, funding was directed towards improving the national infrastructure and government was decentralized. Within three years of taking office Fenech Adami had overseen the drafting of Malta's application for EU membership.

In 1992 he led the Nationalists to another election victory but lost out to the Labour Party at the 1996 polls. Labour halted the EU application but were only able to maintain power until 1998, when Fenech Adami and the Nationalists returned. The application was immediately revived and in Oct. 2002 Malta was one of ten countries given an entry date of 2004. At a referendum in March 2003, EU entry won 53·6% support. Fenech Adami won a further term of office at the general elections of April 2003; a victory seen as confirmation of the referendum result. He stepped down as prime minister on 23 March 2004 and was elected president on 29 March. He took office as president on 4 April.

Dr Lawrence Gonzi

Position
Prime Minister

Introduction
Appointed Malta's prime minister on 23 March 2004, Lawrence Gonzi oversaw the nation's accession to the EU six weeks later. Leading the right-of-centre Nationalist Party (NP), he advocates seizing the opportunities for trade and investment afforded by Malta's EU membership.

Early Life
Lawrence Gonzi was born on 1 July 1953 in Valletta, Malta. He attended the Circolo Gioventù Cattolica and went on to study law at the University of Malta, graduating in 1975, the year after Malta became a fully independent republic (having achieved independence from Great Britain in 1964). Gonzi took up employment as a junior solicitor in a private firm and subsequently worked as a company lawyer with the Mizzi Organisation. From 1976 he was engaged in the voluntary sector, working with people with disabilities and mental health problems. He was the general president of the Malta Catholic Action Movement between 1976–86.

Gonzi entered politics in 1986, contesting the 1987 general election as a candidate for the Nationalist Party. Duly elected, he served in the government of the new Nationalist prime minister, Edward Fenech Adami. Gonzi was elected speaker of the House of Representatives on 10 Oct. 1988. The NP took up a pro-Western stance and argued for integration into the European Community. It also embarked on a programme to stimulate business, increase tourism and reduce the role of the government in the economy. The party held on to power in the 1992 general election, but lost the Oct. 1996 poll to a rejuvenated MLP, led by Alfred Sant.

Gonzi retained his parliamentary seat in the 1996 election and, a month later, was appointed opposition party whip, secretary to the parliamentary group and shadow minister for social policy. The following year he was elected secretary general of the Nationalist Party, subsequently playing a central role in achieving an NP electoral victory after just 22 months of the Labour administration. Gonzi was appointed minister for social policy and leader of the House of Representatives. The appointment of Prof. Guido de Marco as president of the republic on 2 May 1999 prompted Gonzi to contest the election for the deputy leadership of the NP. He was successful, and shortly afterwards was made deputy to Prime Minister Adami.

During his years at the social policy ministry, Gonzi is remembered for reforms to the industrial relations legislation, his zero-tolerance policy towards benefit fraud and for overseeing the restructuring of Malta's shipyards. In March 2003 Malta's population voted in favour of EU membership in a referendum, and the following month the NP was returned to power in a general election. Adami stepped down as NP leader in March 2004, and in the subsequent leadership contest, Gonzi emerged victorious. On 23 March 2004 he took office as prime minister of Malta.

Career in Office
In his first media briefing in April 2004, Prime Minister Gonzi announced his government's intention to adopt the euro 'when it is advantageous to Malta'. He also promised to boost tourism, the nation's most important source of income, and to create favourable conditions for investment. In June 2004 he ruled out the possibility of a referendum to ratify the proposed new EU constitution, arguing that holding another referendum would cause economic disruption.

DEFENCE

The Armed Forces of Malta (AFM) are made up of a Headquarters and three Regiments. On 1 Jan. 2004 they had a strength of 1,838 uniformed and civilian personnel. An Emergency Volunteer Reserve Force was introduced in 1998 on a small scale. In addition to infantry and light air defence artillery weapons, the AFM are equipped with helicopters, light fixed wing and trainer aircraft. There is no conscription.

Apart from normal military duties, AFM are also responsible for Search and Rescue, airport security, surveillance of Malta's territorial and fishing zones, harbour traffic control and anti-pollution duties.

In 2003 military expenditure totalled US$95m. (US$237 per capita), representing 2·1% of GDP.

Navy

There is a maritime squadron numbering 227 personnel.

Air Force

The Air Squadron operates light aircraft and has a strength of 83 personnel.

INTERNATIONAL RELATIONS

Malta is a member of the UN, WTO, the Commonwealth, EU, the Council of Europe, OSCE, IAEA, the Organization for the Prohibition of Chemical Weapons, the Comprehensive Test-Ban Treaty Organization, IOM and the Inter-Parliamentary Union. Malta held a referendum on EU membership on 9 March 2003, in which 53·6% of votes cast were in favour of accession, with 46·4% against. It became a member of the EU on 1 May 2004.

On 6 July 2005 Malta became the twelfth European Union member to ratify the proposed EU constitution. The parliament approved the treaty with all 65 votes cast in favour of the constitution.

ECONOMY

Services accounted for 71·0% of GDP in 2002, industry 26·2% and agriculture 2·8%.

Overview

The prime objectives of economic strategy are the achievement of a sustainable rate of economic growth, high employment and low stable inflation. To compete internationally, the private sector must be the prime mover of the economy. In the 1999 budget, the government committed itself to reducing the budget deficit to 4% of GDP by 2004. To maximize the benefits from privatization, the government aims at strategic partnerships with international enterprises.

An Institute for the Promotion of Small Enterprises (IPSE) has been established and a number of supporting incentive schemes are being implemented. A Business Promotion Act (BPA) has been enacted to update the Industrial Development Act (IDA) of 1988. The aim is to promote industries that demonstrate growth and employment potential. To maintain Malta's competitive position as a tourist attraction, the Malta Tourism Authority launched its first Strategic Plan for the period 2000–02. The Malta Financial Services Centre regulates and supervises credit and financial institutions with effect from 1 Jan. 2002.

Currency

The unit of currency is the *Maltese lira* (formerly *pound*) (MTL) of 100 *cents*. Total money supply was Lm644m. in March 2002. Inflation was 1·9% in 2003 and 2·7% in 2004. Gold reserves were 4,000 troy oz in June 2002 and foreign exchange reserves US$1,769m.

Budget

Revenue and expenditure (in Lm1m.):

	1998	1999	2000	2001	2002
Revenue	659·1	721·9	642·3	797·4	771·0
Expenditure	666·0	691·0	716·2	766·7	819·3

The most important sources of revenue are Customs and Excise tax, customs and excise duties, income tax, VAT, social security and receipts from the Central Bank of Malta. Also significant in certain years are proceeds from the sale of Government shares, foreign grants and foreign and local loans.

The standard rate of VAT is 18·0%.

Performance

GDP growth in 2003 was negative, at –1·9%, but was followed by a small recovery, with growth in 2004 of 1·0%. Total GDP in 2004 was US$5·4bn.

Banking and Finance

The Central Bank of Malta (*Governor*, Michael C. Bonello) was founded in 1968. In Jan. 2004 there were 16 licensed credit institutions carrying out domestic and international banking activities. In addition 13 local financial institutions licensed in terms of the Financial Institutions Act 1994 also provide services that range from exchange bureau related business to merchant banking.

There is a stock exchange in Valletta.

ENERGY AND NATURAL RESOURCES

Environment

Malta's carbon dioxide emissions from the consumption and flaring of fossil fuels in 2002 were the equivalent of 7·1 tonnes per capita.

Electricity

Electricity is generated at two interconnected thermal power stations located at Marsa (272 MW) and Delimara (305 MW). The primary transmission voltages are 132,000, 33,000 and 11,000 volts while the low-voltage system is 400/230V, 50Hz with neutral point earthed. Installed capacity was 577,000 kW in 2000. Production in 2003 was 2·23bn. kWh; consumption per capita was 5,220 kWh.

Oil and Gas

Malta enjoys a large offshore area, represent geological extensions of southeast Sicily, east Tunisia and northwest Libya where significant hydrocarbon reserves and production exists. Active exploration is at present being carried out by TGS-Nopec, Pancontinental Oil & Gas and TM Services Ltd in offshore areas. Discussions are also underway with oil companies with a view to awarding new licences. The policy of Malta in the oil and gas sector is to intensify exploration by offering oil companies competitive terms and returns that are commensurate with the risk undertaken.

Water

The demand for water during 2003 was 34m. cu. metres. Seawater desalination (Reverse Osmosis Plants) provides 54% of the total potable water requirements.

Agriculture

Malta is self-sufficient in fresh vegetables, pig meat, poultry, eggs and fresh milk. The main crops are potatoes (the spring crop being the country's primary agricultural export), vegetables and fruits, with some items such as tomatoes serving as the main input in the local canning industry. In 2001 there were about 1,524 full-time farmers and 12,589 part-time. There were around 11,959 agricultural holdings and 943 intensive livestock farm units. In 2001 there were 9,000 ha. of arable land and 1,000 ha. of permanent crops.

Agriculture contributes around Lm35·8m. annually towards GDP, or 2·6%. 2001 production figures (in 1,000 tonnes): potatoes, 25; tomatoes, 18; melons, 12; wheat, 10; onions, 7; cauliflowers, 6.

Livestock in 2001: cattle, 18,417; pigs, 80,481; sheep, 10,376; chickens, 1·9m. Livestock produce accounted for 60·7% of the total value of agricultural production during 2001.

Fisheries

In 2001 the fishing industry employed 1,747 power-propelled fishing boats, engaging around 365 full time and 1,598 part-time fishermen. The catch for 2001 was 841 tonnes, valued at Lm1,587,044. It is estimated that during 2001 the local aquaculture industry produced a total of about 1,235 tonnes of sea bass and bream. 95% of the local production was exported to EU countries in 2001, especially to Italy.

INDUSTRY

Besides manufacturing (food, clothing, chemicals, electrical machinery parts and electronic components and products), the mainstays of the economy are ship repair and shipbuilding, agriculture, small crafts units, tourism and the provision of other services such as the freeport facilities. The majority of state-aided manufacturing enterprises operating in Malta are foreign-owned or with foreign interests. The Malta Development Corporation is the government agency responsible for promoting investment, while the Malta Export Trade Corporation serves as a catalyst to the export of local products.

Labour

The labour supply in Dec. 2002 was 144,016 (females, 40,185), including 35,571 in private direct production (agriculture and fisheries, 2,203; manufacturing, 28,970; oil drilling, construction and quarrying, 6,398), 50,059 in private market services, 47,992 in the public sector (including government departments, armed forces, revenue security corps, independent statutory bodies and companies with government majority shareholding) and 1,206 in temporary employment. There were 7,188 registered unemployed (5·0% of labour supply).

Trade Unions

In 2003 there were 33 Trade Unions with a total membership of 86,061 and 23 employers' associations with a total membership of 8,960. In 2003 the largest union was the General Workers' Union with a total membership of 47,254.

INTERNATIONAL TRADE

Imports are being liberalized. Marsaxlokk is an all-weather freeport zone for transhipment activities. The Malta Export Trade Corporation promotes local exports. External debt was US$1,531m. in 2001.

Imports and Exports

In 2002 imports (f.o.b.) were valued at Lm1,222·3m. (Lm1,225·1m. in 2001) and exports (f.o.b.) at Lm905·4m. (Lm880·6m. in 2001). In 2002 the principal items of imports were: machinery and transport equipment, Lm596·3m.; semi-manufactures, Lm151·0m.; manufactures, Lm116·8m.; foodstuffs, Lm109·8m.; fuels, Lm103·0m.; chemicals, Lm96·4m. Of domestic exports: machinery and transport equipment, Lm517·7m.; manufactures, Lm166·8m.; semi-manufactures, Lm50·9m.; foodstuffs, Lm21·4m.; chemicals, Lm13·4m.

In 2000 imports valued at Lm281·9m. came from France; Lm249·7m. from Italy; Lm158·5m. from USA; Lm122·1m. from Germany; Lm119·7m. from UK. Main export markets: USA, Lm286·5m.; Singapore, Lm164·7m.; Germany, Lm96·7m.; France, Lm84·1m.; UK, Lm70·0m.; Italy, Lm33·1m.

Trade Fairs

The Malta Trade Fairs Corporation organizes the International Fair of Malta (early July).

COMMUNICATIONS

Roads

In 2002 there were 2,254 km of roads, including 185 km of motorways. About 94% of roads are paved. Motor vehicles licensed up to 31 Dec. 2002 totalled 261,329 including: private cars, 195,055; commercial vehicles, 43,852; motorcycles, 13,097; self drive cars, 5,454. There were 15 deaths as a result of road accidents in 2000.

Civil Aviation

The national carrier is Air Malta, which is 96·4% state-owned. There were scheduled services in 2003 to around 30 different countries. In 2001 there were 32,652 commercial aircraft movements at Malta International Airport. 2,806,013 passengers and 12,925 tonnes of freight/mail were handled. In 1999 Air Malta flew 24·0m. km and carried 1,421,300 passengers.

Shipping

There is a car ferry between Malta and Gozo. The number of vessels registered on 30 Sept. 2003 was 3,365 totalling 26,702,959

GT, a total only exceeded by Panama, Liberia, the Bahamas and Greece. Ships entering harbour in the period Oct. 2002–Sept. 2003 totalled 9,043. 410 cruise vessels put in during the same period.

The Malta Freeport plays an important role in the economy as it is effectively positioned to act as a distribution centre in the Mediterranean. Apart from providing efficient transhipment operations to the major shipping lines, the Freeport offers warehouse facilities and the storage and blending of oil products.

Telecommunications

The Maltacom plc group is Malta's leading telecommunications and ancillary services provider. Malta's national network consist of 12 AXE10 Ericsson Digital Exchanges and one Siemens EWSD Exchange. Maltacom provides various data services including packet switching, frame relay and high-speed leased lines. The company has an optical fibre-based SDH backbone and large companies are connected to the Network. Maltacom's International Network includes two fully digital gateways, two satellite Standard B Earth Stations (one transmitting to the Atlantic Ocean Region and the other to the Indian Ocean Region) and an optic fibre submarine cable linking Malta to Sicily (Italy) and terrestrially extending to Palermo which is the hub of international submarine cables passing through the Mediterranean.

In 2002 telephone subscribers numbered 484,100 (1,222·5 per 1,000 inhabitants) and there were 101,000 PCs (255·1 per 1,000 persons). Mobile phone subscribers numbered 276,900 in 2002 and there were 12,100 fax machines. In 2002 there were 82,900 Internet users.

Postal Services

In 2003 there were 50 post offices operated by Maltapost plc. Airmail dispatches are forwarded twice daily to the UK, Canada, Australia, USA and Italy. Airmails from most countries are received daily or every other day. There are branch post offices and sub post offices in most towns and villages in Malta and Gozo.

SOCIAL INSTITUTIONS

Justice

The number of persons arrested between 1 Jan. 2001 and 31 Oct. 2001 was 5,451; those found guilty numbered 2,180. 184 persons were committed to prison.

In Jan. 2003 total police strength was 1,841 including 107 officers (92 males and 15 females) and 1,734 other ranks (250 females).

Malta abolished the death penalty for all crimes in 2000.

Education

Adult literacy rate, 2001, 92·3% (male, 91·5%; female, 93·0%).

Education is compulsory between the ages of 5 and 16 and free in government schools from kindergarten to university. Kindergarten education is provided for three- and four-year old children. The primary school course lasts six years. In 2003 there were 19,300 children enrolled in 77 state primary schools. There are education centres for children with special needs, but they are taught in ordinary schools if possible.

Secondary schools, trade schools and junior lyceums provide secondary education in the state sector. At the end of their primary education, pupils sit the 11+ examination to start a secondary education course. Pupils who qualify are admitted in the junior lyceum, while the others attend secondary schools. In 2003–04, 11 junior lyceums had a total of 9,700 students (5,600 girls and 4,100 boys). About 8,200 pupils attend secondary schools. Five centres providing secondary education for under-performing students have a registered student population of about 900, of which 500 are boys. Secondary schools and junior lyceums offer a five-year course leading to the Secondary Education Certificate and the General Certificate of Education, Ordinary Level.

At the end of the five-year secondary course, students may opt to follow a higher academic or technical or vocational course of from one to four years. The academic courses generally lead to Intermediate and Advanced Level examinations set by the British universities. The Matriculation Certificate, which qualifies students for admission to university, is a broad-based holistic qualification covering—among others—the humanities and the sciences, together with systems of knowledge.

About 35% of the student population attend non-state schools, from kindergarten to higher secondary level. In Oct. 2003 there were about 25,700 pupils attending non-state schools, 800 of whom were at post-compulsory secondary level, 17,100 were in schools run by the Roman Catholic Church, while 8,500 students were attending private schools. Under an agreement between the government and the Church, the government subsidizes Church schools and students attending these schools do not pay any fees. During 2001 the government introduced tax rebates for parents whose children attended independent schools.

More than 9,800 students (including 750 from overseas) were following courses at the University in 2003. University students receive a stipend.

A post-compulsory vocational college, the Malta College of Arts, Science and Technology, provides vocational and technical courses up to degree level. In Oct. 2003 about 9,000 students (47% of which were females) were following post-compulsory education in state colleges and institutes.

In 1999–2000 total expenditure on education came to 4·9% of GNP.

Health

In 2003 there were 1,254 doctors, 169 dentists, 799 pharmacists, 1,060 paramedics, 365 midwives and 5,220 nursing personnel. There were eight hospitals (three private) with 2,122 beds. There are also nine health centres.

Welfare

Legislation provides a national contributory insurance scheme and also for the payment of non-contributory allowances, assistances and pensions. It covers the payment of marriage grants, maternity benefits, child allowances, parental allowances, handicapped child allowance, family bonus, sickness benefit, injury benefits, disablement benefits, unemployment benefit, contributory pensions in respect of retirement, invalidity and widowhood, and non-contributory medical assistance, free medical aids, social assistance, a carers' pension and pensions for the handicapped, the blind and the aged.

Malta's average actual retirement age is just 53 years, compared to the EU average of 57.

RELIGION

98% of the population belong to the Roman Catholic Church, which is established by law as the religion of the country, although full liberty of conscience and freedom of worship are guaranteed.

CULTURE

World Heritage Sites

Malta has three sites on the UNESCO World Heritage List (all inscribed on the list in 1980): Hal Saflieni Hypogeum, a prehistoric underground necropolis; the City of Valletta, a highly concentrated centre marked by the influences of Romans, Byzantines and Arabs and the Knights of St John; and the Megalithic Temples of Malta, seven temples on Malta and Gozo.

Broadcasting

Radio and TV services are under the control of the Broadcasting Authority, an independent statutory body. The government-owned Public Broadcasting Services Ltd was set up in 1991 and operates three radio stations and a TV station (colour by PAL). Legislation of 1991 introduced private commercial broadcasting. In 2003 there were 11 radio and four TV services and a cable TV network. In 2001 there were 222,000 television sets and in 1997 there were 255,000 radio receivers.

Cinema

In 2004 there were eight cinemas.

Press

In 2004 there were two English and two Maltese dailies, five Maltese and three English weeklies and two financial weeklies in English.

Tourism

Tourism is the major foreign currency earner, and accounts for more than 25% of Malta's GDP.

In 2002, 1·13m. tourists visited Malta, generating earnings of Lm246·3m. Cruise passenger visits totalled 341,632. Over 40% of tourists are from the UK.

Festivals

Major festivals include the Malta Song Festival; Carnival Festivals at Valletta (Feb.); History and Elegance Festival at Valletta (April); National Folk Singing; Malta International Arts Festival; Malta Jazz Festival; International Food and Beer Festival (June/July); Festa Season (June–Sept.); Malta International Choir Festival (Nov.).

Libraries

The National Library, housed in one of Valletta's 18th-century buildings, is Malta's foremost research Library, founded in 1763. There is a Central Public Library in Floriana, Branch Libraries in government schools in most towns and villages, and the University of Malta Library.

Theatre and Opera

The Manoel Theatre (built 1731) is Malta's National Theatre. There is also the Mediterranean Conference Centre in Valletta, and the Astra Theatre in Victoria, Gozo.

Museums and Galleries

In Valletta: National Museum of Archaeology, National Museum of Fine Arts, Palace Armoury, War Museum (Fort St. Elmo). Mdina and Rabat: National Museum of Natural History, Museum of Roman Antiquities, St Paul's Catacombs, the Cathedral Museum. Paula: Hal Saflieni Hypoguem. Qrendi: Hagar Qim and Mnajra Megalithic Temples. Birzebbuga: Ghar Dalam Cave and Museum. Vittoriosa: Maritime Museum. Gozo (Victoria): Museum of Archaeology, Natural Science Museum, Folklore Museum. Xaghra: Ggantija Megalithic Temples.

DIPLOMATIC REPRESENTATIVES

Of Malta in the United Kingdom (36–38 Piccadilly, London, W1J 0LE)
Acting High Commissioner: Dr Michael Refalo.

Of the United Kingdom in Malta (Whitehall Mansions, Ta'Xbiex Seafront, Msida MSD 11)
High Commissioner: Vincent Fean.

Of Malta in the USA (2017 Connecticut Ave., NW, Washington, D.C., 20008)
Ambassador: John Lowell.

Of the USA in Malta (Development House, St Anne St., Floriana)
Ambassador: Molly Bordonaro.

Of Malta to the United Nations
Ambassador: Victor Camilleri.

Of Malta to the European Union
Ambassador: Vacant.
Chargé d'Affaires a.i.: Tarcisio Zammit.

FURTHER READING

Central Office of Statistics (Lascaris, Valletta). *Statistical Abstracts of the Maltese Islands,* a quarterly digest of statistics, quarterly and annual trade returns, annual vital statistics and annual publications on shipping and aviation, education, agriculture, industry, National Accounts and Balance of Payments.

Department of Information (3 Castille Place, Valletta). *The Malta Government Gazette, Malta Information, Economic Survey [year],*

Reports on the Working of Government Departments, *The Maltese Economy in Figures, 1986–1995, Business Opportunities on Malta, Acts of Parliament and Subsidiary Legislation, Laws of Malta, Constitution of Malta 1992.*

Central Bank of Malta. *Annual Reports.*

Chamber of Commerce (annual). *Trade Directory.*

Berg, W. G., *Historical Dictionary of Malta.* Metuchen (NJ), 1995

Blouet, B., *The Story of Malta.* London, Rev. ed. 1981

Boswell, D. and Beeley, B., *Malta.* [Bibliography] 2nd ed. ABC-Clio, Oxford and Santa Barbara (CA), 1998.

The Malta Yearbook. Valletta

National Statistical Office: Central Office of Statistics, Auberge d'Italie, Valletta.

Website: http://www.nso.gov.mt

MARSHALL ISLANDS

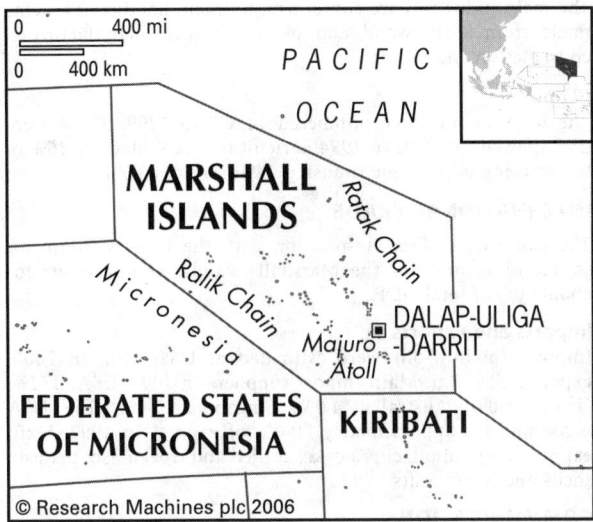

Republic of the Marshall Islands

Capital: Majuro Atoll
Population, 1999: 51,000
GDP per capita: not available
GNI per capita: $2,710

KEY HISTORICAL EVENTS

The Pacific archipelago was populated by emigrants from southeast Asia from around 2000 BC and first documented by Portuguese mariners in 1528. The islands owe their name to the English seafarer, John Marshall, who visited in 1788. They became part of the protectorate of German New Guinea in 1886 and administrative affairs were managed by private German and Australian interests. Japan seized control in 1914 and received a League of Nations mandate over the islands in 1919. The Marshall Islands were occupied by Allied forces in 1944 and became part of the UN Trust Territory of the Pacific Islands on 18 July 1947 (administered by the USA). On 21 Oct. 1986 the islands gained independence. A Compact of Free Association with the USA that came into force at the time was extended by 20 years in May 2004.

TERRITORY AND POPULATION

The Marshall Islands lie in the North Pacific Ocean north of Kiribati and east of Micronesia, and consist of an archipelago of 31 coral atolls, five single islands and 1,152 islets strung out in two chains, eastern and western. Of these, 25 atolls and islands are inhabited. The land area is 181 sq. km (70 sq. miles). The capital is Majuro in the eastern chain (population, 1999 census, 23,682). The principal atoll in the western chain is Kwajalein, containing the only other town, Ebeye (population, 1999 census, 10,903). The two archipelagic island chains of Bikini and Enewetak are former US nuclear test sites; Kwajalein is now used as a US missile test range. The islands lay claim to the US territory of Wake Island. At the census of 1999 the population was 50,840 (26,026 males); density, 281 per sq. km. 2003 estimate: 56,000.

In 1999 some 71% of the population lived in urban areas. About 88% of the population are Marshallese, a Micronesian people.

English is universally spoken and is the official language. Two major Marshallese dialects from the Malayo-Polynesian family, and Japanese, are also spoken.

SOCIAL STATISTICS

2001 births, estimate, 1,511; deaths, 271. 2001 rates per 1,000 population, estimates: birth, 28·0; death, 5·0. Infant mortality rate, 2000, 35 per 1,000 live births; life expectancy, 2000, 68·4 years. Annual population growth rate, 1999–2003, 2·5%; fertility rate, 2001, 5·7 births per woman.

CLIMATE

Hot and humid, with wet season from May to Nov. The islands border the typhoon belt. Jaluit, Jan. 81°F (27·2°C), July 82°F (27·8°C). Annual rainfall 161" (4,034 mm).

CONSTITUTION AND GOVERNMENT

Under the constitution which came into force on 1 May 1979, the Marshall Islands form a republic with a *President* as head of state and government, who is elected for four-year terms by the parliament. The parliament consists of a 33-member *House of Assembly* (Nitijela), directly elected by popular vote for four-year terms. There is also a 12-member appointed *Council of Chiefs* (Iroij) which has a consultative and advisory capacity on matters affecting customary law and practice.

National Anthem

'Forever Marshall Islands'; words and tune by Amata Kabua.

RECENT ELECTIONS

President Kessai Note was re-elected by parliament on 5 Jan. 2004, defeating Justin de Brum. At the House of Assembly elections on 17 Nov. 2003 President Note's United Democratic Party won 20 of the 33 seats.

CURRENT ADMINISTRATION

President: Kessai Note (UDP; elected on 3 Jan. 2000; re-elected 5 Jan. 2004).

In March 2006 the government comprised:

Minister of Assistance to the President: Witten Philippo. *Education:* Wilfred Kendall. *Finance:* Brenson Wase. *Foreign Affairs and Trade:* Gerald Zackios. *Health and Environment:* Alvin Jacklick. *Internal Affairs and Social Welfare:* Rien Morris. *Justice:* Donald Capelle. *Public Works:* Mattlan Zackhras. *Resources, Development and Works:* John Silk. *Transportation and Communications:* Michael Konelios.

CURRENT LEADERS

Kessai Note

Position
President

Introduction
Kessai Note was elected president on 3 Jan. 2000 and was unanimously elected to a second four-year term in Jan. 2004. As president he is both head of state and head of government.

Early Life
Kessai Hesa Note was born on Ailinglaplap Atoll in 1950, then part of the US Trust Territory of the Pacific Islands (TTPI). In 1970 he took up a US government scholarship to study in Papua New Guinea, returning to the Marshall Islands capital, Majuro, in 1974. In 1977 Note was elected to the Constitutional Convention, formed to draft the nation's first constitution.

Following its implementation on 1 May 1979 he was elected to parliament in the country's first constitutional election.

President Amata Kabua appointed Note minister for internal affairs and transportation and communications, portfolios he held for eight years. On 21 Oct. 1986 the US and the Marshall Islands signed a Compact of Free Association, under which the islands became a fully independent republic but received military and economic aid. A year later Note became parliamentary speaker, a post he held until his election as president in Jan. 2000.

Career in Office
He was re-elected in Jan. 2004 and, with the combined support of his United Democratic Party and two opposition members, he holds a virtual two-thirds majority in parliament. He negotiated an amended Compact of Free Trade in May 2004, guaranteeing funding from the USA of around US$800m. over the next 20 years to be used principally on the development of health and education. In return the USA confirmed the long-term use of Kwajalein airbase. Note has pledged to implement wide-ranging economic and administrative reforms and to provide transparent and accountable government.

DEFENCE

The Compact of Free Association gives the USA responsibility for defence in return for US assistance. In 2003 the US lease of Kwajalein Atoll, a missile testing site, was extended by 50 years.

INTERNATIONAL RELATIONS

The Marshall Islands are a member of the UN, Asian Development Bank, Pacific Community (formerly the South Pacific Commission) and the Pacific Islands Forum.

ECONOMY

Agriculture accounts for approximately 15% of GDP, industry 13% and services 72%.

Currency
US currency is used. The average annual inflation rate during the period 1990–96 was 6·4%.

Budget
Revenue in 2002 was US$83·6m.; expenditure was US$74·0m. Under the terms of the Compact of Free Association, the USA provides approximately US$65m. a year in aid.

Performance
Real GDP growth was 0·6% in 2001 (0·7% in 2000). Total GDP in 2004 was US$0·1bn.

Banking and Finance
There are three Banks: the Bank of Marshall Islands, the Marshall Islands Development Bank and the Bank of Guam.

ENERGY AND NATURAL RESOURCES

Electricity
Total installed capacity (1997), 20,200 kW. Production (1999), 63m. kWh.

Minerals
High-grade phosphate deposits are mined on Ailinglaplap Atoll. Deep-seabed minerals are an important natural resource.

Agriculture
A small amount of agricultural produce is exported: coconuts, tomatoes, melons and breadfruit. Other important crops include copra, taro, cassava and sweet potatoes. Pigs and chickens constitute the main livestock. In 2001 there were 3,000 ha. of arable land and 7,000 ha. of permanent crop land.

Fisheries
Total catch in 2001 amounted to 37,098 tonnes. There is a commercial tuna-fishing industry with a canning factory on Majuro. Seaweed is cultivated. Fisheries offers one of the best opportunities for economic growth.

INDUSTRY

The main industries are copra, fish, tourism, handicrafts (items made from shell, wood and pearl), mining, manufacturing, construction and power.

Labour
The total labour force numbered 14,677 in 1999. 30·9% were unemployed in 1999. In 1994 agriculture accounted for 16% of the working population; industry, 14%; services, 70%.

INTERNATIONAL TRADE

The Compact of Free Association with the USA is the major source of income for the Marshall Islands, and accounts for about 70% of total GDP.

Imports and Exports
Imports (mainly oil) were estimated at US$68·2m. in 2000; exports, US$7·3m. Main import suppliers in 1997: USA, 47·2%; Guam, 4·8%; Australia, 4·0%; Singapore, 3·4%. The USA accounted for approximately 80·0% of exports in 1997. Main exports: coconut oil, copra cake, chilled and frozen fish, pet fish, shells and handicrafts.

COMMUNICATIONS

Roads
There are paved roads on major islands (Majuro, Kwajalein); roads are otherwise stone-, coral- or laterite-surfaced. In 1994 there were 1,418 passenger cars and 193 trucks and buses.

Civil Aviation
There were nine paved and seven unpaved airports in 1996. The main airport is Majuro International. In 2003 there were flights to Guam, Honolulu, Johnston Island, Kiribati and Micronesia as well as domestic services. The national carrier is Air Marshall Islands.

Shipping
Majuro is the main port. In 2000 merchant shipping consisted of 302 vessels totalling 9,745,000 GRT, including oil tankers 5,462,000 GRT. The ship's register of the Marshall Islands is a flag of convenience register.

Telecommunications
In 2002 there were 4,900 telephone subscribers (87·2 per 1,000 persons). There is a US satellite communications system on Kwajalein and two Intelsat satellite earth stations (Pacific Ocean). The National Telecommunications Authority provides domestic and international services. Mobile phone subscribers numbered 600 in 2002 and there were 3,000 PCs in use (53·0 per 1,000 persons). There were 1,300 Internet users in 2002.

Postal Services
Postal services are available on the main island of Majuro and also in Ebeye.

SOCIAL INSTITUTIONS

Justice
The Supreme Court is situated on Majuro. There is also a High Court, a District Court and 23 Community Courts. A Traditional Court deals with disputes involving land properties and customs.

Education
In 1998–99 there were 12,421 pupils with 548 teachers in 103 primary schools, and 2,667 pupils with 162 teachers in 16 secondary schools. There is a College of the Marshall Islands, and a subsidiary of the University of the South Pacific, on Majuro. In 1999–2000 total expenditure on education came to 13·8% of GNP.

Health

There were two hospitals in 2003, with a total of 140 beds. There were 31 doctors, 189 nurses and four dentists in 2003; and two pharmacists in 2000.

RELIGION

The population is mainly Protestant, with Roman Catholics next. Other Churches and denominations include Latter-day Saints (Mormons), Jehovah's Witnesses, Baptists, Bahais, Seventh Day Adventists and Assembly of God.

CULTURE

Broadcasting

There are one TV and three radio stations.

Press

There is a publication called Micronitor (The Marshall Islands Journal).

Tourism

In 2002 there were 6,000 foreign tourists; spending by tourists totalled US$4m. Tourism offers one of the best opportunities for economic growth.

Festivals

Custom Day and the Annual Canoe Race are the main festivals.

Libraries

There is one public library.

DIPLOMATIC REPRESENTATIVES

Of the United Kingdom in the Marshall Islands
Ambassador: Peter Beckingham (resides in Manila, Philippines).

Of the Marshall Islands in the USA (2433 Massachusetts Ave., NW, Washington, D.C., 20008)
Ambassador: Banny de Brum.

Of the USA in the Marshall Islands (Oceanside Mejen Weto, Long Island, Majuro)
Ambassador: Greta N. Morris.

Of the Marshall Islands to the United Nations
Ambassador: Alfred Capelle.

Of the Marshall Islands to the European Union
Ambassador: Vacant.

MAURITANIA

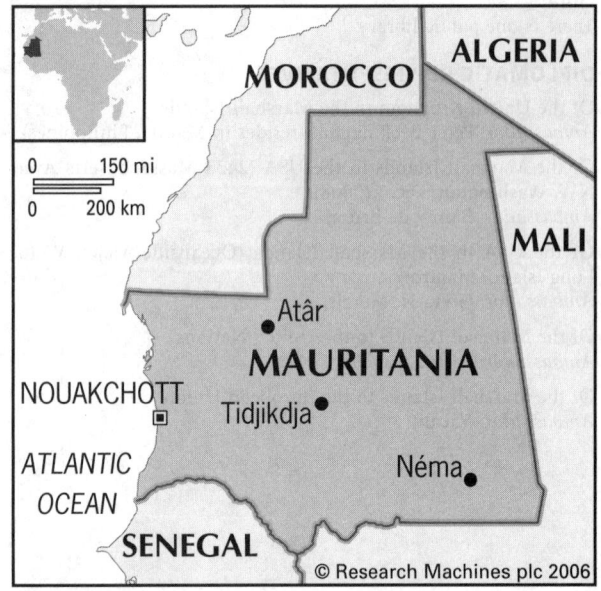

© Research Machines plc 2006

République Islamique Arabe et Africaine de Mauritanie

Capital: Nouakchott
Population projection, 2010: 3·52m.
GDP per capita, 2003: (PPP$) 1,766
HDI/world rank: 0·477/152

KEY HISTORICAL EVENTS

Mauritania became a French protectorate in 1903 and a colony in 1920. It achieved full independence on 28 Nov. 1960. Mauritania became a one-party state in 1964.

The 1980s were characterized by territorial disputes with Morocco and Senegal. Seizing power in 1984, Lieut.-Col. Maaouya Ould Sid'Ahmed Taya prepared the way for a new constitution allowing for a multi-party political system, which also gave extensive powers to the president. A coup attempt against Ould Taya failed in June 2003. But in Aug. 2005 while out of the country he was overthrown in a bloodless coup by a group of army officers who set up a Military Council for Justice and Democracy.

TERRITORY AND POPULATION

Mauritania is bounded west by the Atlantic Ocean, north by Western Sahara, northeast by Algeria, east and southeast by Mali, and south by Senegal. The total area is 1,030,700 sq. km (398,000 sq. miles) of which 47% is desert, and the population at the census of 2000 was 2,548,157; density, 2·47 per sq. km. The estimated population in 2005 was 3,069,000. In 2003, 61·7% of the population was urban.

The UN gives a projected population for 2010 of 3·52m.

Area (in sq. km), population (at the 2000 census) and chief towns of the Nouakchott Capital District and 12 regions:

Region	Area	Population	Chief town
Açâba	36,600	249,596	Kiffa
Adrar	215,300	60,847	Atâr
Brakna	33,800	240,167	Aleg
Dakhlet Nouâdhibou	22,300	75,976	Nouâdhibou

Region	Area	Population	Chief town
Gorgol	13,600	248,980	Kaédi
Guidimaka	10,300	186,697	Sélibaby
Hodh ech-Chargui	182,700	275,288	Néma
Hodh el-Gharbi	53,400	219,167	Aïoun el Atrouss
Inchiri	46,800	11,322	Akjoujt
Nouakchott District	1,000	611,883	Nouakchott
Tagant	95,200	61,984	Tidjikdja
Tiris Zemmour	252,900	53,586	Zouérate
Trarza	67,800	252,664	Rosso

Principal towns (1999 population): Nouakchott, 881,000 including the suburbs of Nouâdhibou and Kaédi.

In 2000 there were also 0·23m. nomads.

The major ethnic groups are (with numbers in 1993): Moors (of mixed Arab, Berber and African origin), 1,513,400; Wolof, 147,000; Tukulor, 114,600; Soninke, 60,000.

Arabic is the official language. French no longer has official status. Pulaar, Soninke and Wolof are national languages.

SOCIAL STATISTICS

2000 estimates: births, 109,000; deaths, 34,000. 2000 rates, estimate (per 1,000 population): births, 42·9; deaths, 13·4. Expectation of life at birth in 2003 was 54·3 years for males and 51·1 for females. Annual population growth rate, 1992–2002, 2·8%. Infant mortality, 2001, 120 per 1,000 live births; fertility rate, 2001, 6·0 births per woman.

CLIMATE

A tropical climate, but conditions are generally arid, even near the coast, where the only appreciable rains come in July to Sept. Nouakchott, Jan. 71°F (21·7°C), July 82°F (27·8°C). Annual rainfall 6" (158 mm).

CONSTITUTION AND GOVERNMENT

A referendum was held in July 1991 to approve a new constitution instituting multi-party politics. Turnout was 85·34%; 97·94% of votes cast were in favour.

The constitution envisages that the President is elected by universal suffrage for renewable six-year terms. There is a 56-member *Senate* and an 81-member *National Assembly*. Parties specifically Islamic are not permitted.

National Anthem

'Kun lil-ilahi nasiran' ('Be a helper for God'); words by Baba Ould Cheikh, tune by Tolia Nikiprowetzky.

RECENT ELECTIONS

Presidential elections were held on 7 Nov. 2003. Col. Maaouya Ould Sid'Ahmed Taya was re-elected with 67·0% of votes cast. Mohamed Khouna Ould Haidalla took 18·7% of the vote, Ahmed Ould Daddah 6·9% and Messaoud Ould Boulkheir 5·0%. Turnout was 60·8%.

Elections for the National Assembly were held on 19 and 26 Oct. 2001. The Democratic and Socialist Republican Party (PRDS) gained 64 seats with 51·0% of votes cast. Turnout was 54·5%. In the Senate elections of 7 and 14 April 2000 the PRDS obtained 52 of the 56 seats.

Parliamentary elections are scheduled to take place on 19 Nov. 2006.

CURRENT ADMINISTRATION

Chairman, Military Council for Justice and Democracy: Col. Ely Ould Mohamed Vall; b. 1952 (assumed office 3 Aug. 2005).

Prime Minister: Sidi Mohamed Ould Boubacar; b. 1957 (PRDS; appointed on 7 Aug. 2005, having previously been prime minister from April 1992–Jan. 1996).

In March 2006 the cabinet comprised:

Minister of Interior: Mohamed Ahmed Ould Mohamed Lemine. *Foreign Affairs and Co-operation:* Ahmed Ould Sid Hamed. *Justice:* Mahfoudh Ould Bettah. *Finance:* Abdallahi Ould Souleymane Ould Cheikh Sidiya. *Economic Affairs and Development:* Mohamed Ould Abed. *Fisheries and Maritime Economy:* Sidi Mohamed Ould Sidina. *Trade, Handicrafts and Tourism:* Ba Abederrahmane. *Mines and Industry:* Mohamed Ould Ismail Ould Abeidna. *Oil and Energy:* Mohamed Ali Ould Sidi Mohamed. *Health and Social Affairs:* Sadna Ould Bouhaida. *Culture, Youth and Sports:* Mehla Mint Ahmed. *Labour and Civil Service:* Mohamed Ould Ahmed Ould Jik. *Equipment and Transportation:* Ba Ibrahima Demba. *Primary and Secondary Education:* Cheikh Ahmed Ould Sid Ahmed. *Higher Education and Scientific Research:* Nagi Ould Mohamed Mahmoud. *Hydraulics:* Ely Ould Ahmedou. *Rural Development and Environment:* Gandega Silly. *Communications:* Cheikh Ould Ebbe. *Literacy and Islamic Orientation:* Yahya Ould Sid El Moustaph.

Government Website (French and Arabic only):
http://www.mauritania.mr

CURRENT LEADERS

Col. Ely Ould Mohamed Vall

Position
Chairman of the Military Council for Justice and Democracy

Introduction
Col. Ely Ould Mohamed Vall deposed Mauritania's President Taya in a bloodless coup in Aug. 2005 and promised to pave the way for genuine multi-party elections within two years.

Early Life
Ely Ould Mohamed Vall was born in 1952 in Nouakchott, Mauritania, then part of the Federation of French West Africa. He was educated in Nouakchott and in the French cities of Aix-en-Provence and Le Mans and in 1973 he joined the Meknès military academy in Morocco. While developing his military career, he also studied law. On his return to Mauritania, Vall served in the war against Western Sahara's pro-independence Polisario Front, commanding military posts at Bir-Mogreïn, Ouadane and Aïn-Benteli. From 1979–81 he commanded the Compagnie du Quartier Général before becoming head of the military district of Rosso.

In 1984, while commander of the military district of Nouakchott, Vall played a key role in the coup led by his ally and fellow military commander, Col. Maaouya Ould Sid'Ahmed Taya. In Nov. 1985 Vall was appointed director of national security. President Taya legalized opposition parties in 1991 but subsequent multi-party presidential elections were nonetheless criticized for irregularities. Taya's regime became increasingly unpopular and reportedly survived three attempted coups during 2003–04.

With the president attending King Fahd's funeral in Saudi Arabia, Vall led a coup against Taya on 3 Aug. 2005 and appeared to have broad domestic backing. However, Vall came under fire from the exiled opposition amid allegations that he had sanctioned torture in jails under his command.

Career in Office
Vall declared that his governing military council would remain in power for up to two years while it created conditions for genuine democratic institutions. The African Union, EU, UN, South Africa and the USA initially denounced Vall's administration as illegitimate. However, in the meantime the international community has engaged with the regime in expectation of democratic elections in Nov. 2006. There remains some scepticism as to whether power will be ceded to civilian rulers, not least because Mauritania is expected to benefit from substantial wealth from its oil and gas reserves in the near future.

DEFENCE

Conscription is authorized for two years. Defence expenditure in 2003 totalled US$19m. (US$7 per capita), representing 1·7% of GDP.

Army

There are six military regions. Army strength was approximately 15,000 in 2002. In addition there was a Gendarmerie of 3,000 and a National Guard of 2,000.

Navy

The Navy, some 500 strong in 2002, is based at Nouâdhibou.

Air Force

Personnel (2002), 250 with eight combat aircraft.

INTERNATIONAL RELATIONS

Mauritania is a member of the UN, WTO, the African Union, the League of Arab States, Arab Maghreb Union, African Development Bank, IOM, OIC, Islamic Development Bank, International Organization of the Francophonie and is an ACP member state of the ACP-EU relationship.

ECONOMY

In 2002 agriculture accounted for 20·8% of GDP, industry 29·4% and services 49·8%.

Currency

The monetary unit is the *ouguiya* (MRO) which is divided into five *khoums*. In Oct. 1992 the ouguiya was devalued 28%. Foreign exchange reserves were US$284m. in Sept. 2000. Gold reserves were 12,000 troy oz in Jan. 2001. Inflation was 5·5% in 2003 and 10·4% in 2004. Total money supply in May 2002 was 29,078m. ouguiya.

Budget

Revenues were 51·8bn. ouguiya in 2001 and expenditures 54·4bn. ouguiya.

Performance

Real GDP growth was 6·4% in 2003 and 6·9% in 2004. Mauritania's total GDP in 2004 was US$1·4bn.

Banking and Finance

The Central Bank (created 1973) is the bank of issue (*Governor,* Zeine Ould Zeidane). In 2002 there were seven commercial banks and two Islamic banks. Bank deposits totalled 12,304m. ouguiya in 1992.

ENERGY AND NATURAL RESOURCES

Environment

In 2002 carbon dioxide emissions from the consumption and flaring of fossil fuels were the equivalent of 1·1 tonnes per capita.

Electricity

Installed capacity was 0·1m. kW in 2000. Production in 2000 was around 163m. kWh; consumption per capita was an estimated 61 kWh.

Oil and Gas

Oil was discovered off the coast of Mauritania in 2001. Production began in Feb. 2006, initially with 75,000 bbls. a day.

Minerals

There are reserves of copper, gold, phosphate, gypsum, platinum and diamonds. Iron ore, 10·3m. tonnes of which were mined in 2001, accounts for about 11% of GNP and 40% of exports. Gold, 1995, 57,900 troy oz. Prospecting licences have also been issued for diamonds.

Agriculture

Only 1% of the country receives enough rain to grow crops, so agriculture is mainly confined to the south, in the Senegal river valley. There were 488,000 ha. of arable land in 2001 and 12,000 ha. of permanent crops. Production (2000, in 1,000 tonnes): sorghum, 134; rice, 103; dates, 22; millet, 13; maize, 11; watermelons, 8; yams, 3.

Herding is the main occupation of the rural population and accounted for 16% of GDP in 1992. In 2000 there were 6·20m. sheep; 4·14m. goats; 1·43m. cattle; 1·21m. camels (1999); 4m. chickens.

Forestry

There were 317,000 ha. of forests in 2000 covering 0·3% of the land area, chiefly in the southern regions, where wild acacias yield the main product, gum arabic. In 2001, 1·47m. cu. metres of roundwood were cut.

Fisheries

Total catch in 2001 was approximately 83,596 tonnes, of which 94% came from marine waters. Mauritania's coastal waters are among the world's most abundant fishing areas, earning it significant amounts of hard currency through licensing agreements. Fishing-related fees account for an estimated 15% of Mauritania's national budget.

INDUSTRY

Output, 2000 (in tonnes): residual fuel oil, 364,000; petrol, 235,000; distillate fuel oil, 153,000; frozen and chilled fish (2001), 27,000; hides and skins (2001), 5,400.

Labour

In 1996 the workforce was 1,072,000 (56% males). In 1994, 430,000 people worked in agriculture, forestry and fishing, 177,000 in services and 80,000 in industry.

INTERNATIONAL TRADE

Total foreign debt was US$2,309m. in 2002. In Feb. 1989 Mauritania signed a treaty of economic co-operation with the four other Maghreb countries—Algeria, Libya, Morocco and Tunisia.

Imports and Exports

In 1998 imports (f.o.b.) were valued at US$318·7m. (US$316·5m. in 1997) and exports (f.o.b.) at US$358·6m. (US$423·6m. in 1997). Main imports are foodstuffs, consumer goods, petroleum products and capital goods. Main exports are fish and fish products (57% of total exports) and iron ore (40%). Main import suppliers in 1997 were France (25·5%), followed by Spain and Germany. Principal export markets were Japan (23·3%), followed by Italy and France.

COMMUNICATIONS

Roads

There were about 7,660 km of roads in 2002, of which 870 km were asphalted. In 2002 there were 7,100 passenger cars and 5,700 commercial vehicles.

Rail

A 704-km railway links Zouérate with the port of Point-Central, 10 km south of Nouâdhibou, and is used primarily for iron ore exports. In 1995 it carried 11·3m. tonnes of freight.

Civil Aviation

There are international airports at Nouakchott, Nouâdhibou and Néma. Air Mauritanie provides domestic services, and in 2003 operated international services to Abidjan, Bamako, Bissau, Casablanca, Cotonou, Dakar, Las Palmas and Paris. In 1997 scheduled airline traffic of Mauritania-based carriers flew 4·3m. km, carrying 245,000 passengers (110,000 on international flights).

Shipping

In 2002 the merchant fleet totalled 48,000 GRT. The major ports are at Point-Central (for mineral exports), Nouakchott and Nouâdhibou.

Telecommunications

In 2002 Mauritania had 278,800 telephone subscribers (103·9 per 1,000 persons) and there were 29,000 PCs in use (10·8 per 1,000 persons). Mobile phone subscribers numbered 247,200 in 2002. There were 10,000 Internet users in 2002 and 5,200 fax machines.

Postal Services

In 1999 there were 61 post offices.

SOCIAL INSTITUTIONS

Justice

There are courts of first instance at Nouakchott, Atâr, Kaédi, Aïoun el Atrouss and Kiffa. The Appeal Court and Supreme Court are situated in Nouakchott. Islamic jurisprudence was adopted in 1980.

The population in penal institutions in 2002 was 1,354 (48 per 100,000 of national population).

Education

Basic education is compulsory for all children between the ages of six and 14. In 2000–01 there were 360,677 pupils and 8,636 teachers in primary schools, 76,658 secondary level pupils with 2,749 teachers and 9,033 tertiary level students with 301 academic staff. The University of Nouakchott had 2,850 students and 70 academic staff in 1994–95. Adult literacy rate in 2003 was 51·2% (male, 59·5%; female, 43·4%).

Total expenditure on education came to 3·6% of GNP in 1999–2000 and 16·6% of total government spending in 1998–99.

Health

In 1990 there were 16 hospitals with a provision of seven beds per 10,000 persons. There were 323 physicians, 47 dentists, 1,461 nurses and 267 midwives in 1995.

In 2000 only 37% of the population had access to safe drinking water.

RELIGION

Over 99% of Mauritanians are Sunni Muslim, mainly of the Qadiriyah sect.

CULTURE

World Heritage Sites

Mauritania has two sites on the UNESCO World Heritage List: Banc d'Arguin National Park (inscribed on the list in 1989), a coastal park of dunes and swamps; and the Ancient *Ksour* of Ouadane, Chinguetti, Tichitt and Oualata (1996), Islamic trading and religious centres in the Sahara.

Broadcasting

The government-controlled Office de Radiodiffusion-Télévision de Mauritanie is responsible for broadcasting. There are two radio and one TV networks. There were 260,000 TV sets (colour by SECAM) in 2001 and 371,000 radio sets in 2000.

Press

In 1996 there were two daily newspapers with a circulation of 1,000.

Tourism

There were 30,000 foreign tourists in 2000; spending by tourists totalled US$25m.

DIPLOMATIC REPRESENTATIVES

Of Mauritania in the United Kingdom (8 Carlos Place, London, W1K 3AS)
Ambassador: Ould Moctar Neche Mélaïnine.

Of the United Kingdom in Mauritania
Ambassador: Charles Gray (resides in Rabat, Morocco).

Of Mauritania in the USA (2129 Leroy Pl., NW, Washington, D.C., 20008)
Ambassador: Tijani Ould Kerim.

Of the USA in Mauritania (Rue Abdallaye, Nouakchott)
Ambassador: Joseph LeBaron.

Of Mauritania to the United Nations
Ambassador: Mohamed Ould Tolba.

Of Mauritania to the European Union
Ambassador: Aliou Ibra Ba.

FURTHER READING

Belvaud, C., *La Mauritanie*. Paris, 1992
Calderini, S., *et al.*, *Mauritania*. [Bibliography] ABC-Clio, Oxford and Santa Barbara (CA), 1992
Pazzanita, A. G., *The Maghreb*. [Bibliography] ABC-Clio, Oxford and Santa Barbara (CA), 1998

National Statistical Office: Office National de la Statistique, BP240, Nouakchott.
Website (French only): http://www.ons.mr

MAURITIUS

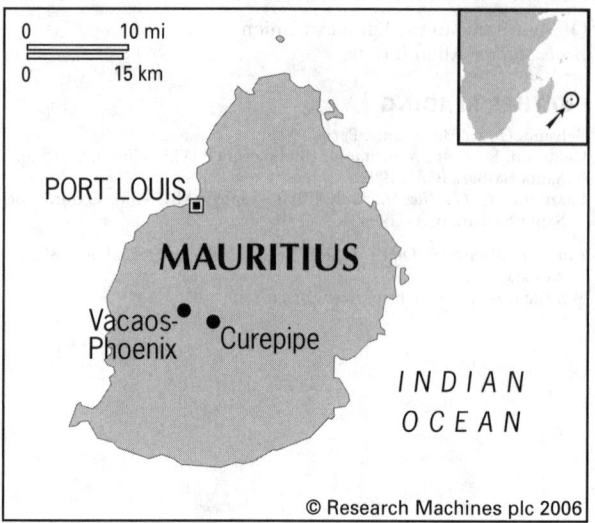

© Research Machines plc 2006

Republic of Mauritius

Capital: Port Louis
Population projection, 2010: 1·30m.
GDP per capita, 2003: (PPP$) 11,287
HDI/world rank: 0·791/65

KEY HISTORICAL EVENTS

Mauritius was visited by Middle Eastern and Malay merchants from around 1000 AD and documented by Portuguese seafarers between 1507 and 1512. In 1598 the Dutch admiral, Van Warwyck, established a settlement and named the island after Prince Maurice of Nassau, the stadtholder of Holland and Zeeland. French forces settled the island in 1722, renamed it Isle de France and brought African slaves to cultivate sugarcane. The British occupied the island in 1810 and it was formally ceded to Great Britain by the Treaty of Paris in 1814. Following the abolition of slavery in 1835, indentured labourers were transported from India. Independence was attained within the Commonwealth on 12 March 1968. Mauritius became a republic on 12 March 1992.

TERRITORY AND POPULATION

Mauritius, the main island, lies 800 km (500 miles) east of Madagascar. Rodrigues is 560 km (350 miles) east. The outer islands are Agalega and the St Brandon Group. Area and population:

Island	Area in sq. km	2003 mid-year population
Mauritius	1,865	1,186,363
Rodrigues	104	36,448
Outer Islands	71	289
Total	2,040	1,223,100

Port Louis is the capital (147,688 inhabitants in 2003). Other towns: Beau Bassin-Rose Hill, 106,978; Vacaos-Phoenix, 103,564; Curepipe, 81,600; and Quatre Bornes, 78,538. In 2003, 56·7% of the population were rural.

The UN gives a projected population for 2010 of 1·30m.

Ethnic composition, 2000: Indo-Pakistani, 67·0%; Creole, 27·4%; Chinese, 3·0%.

The official language is English, although French is widely used. Creole and Bhojpuri are vernacular languages.

SOCIAL STATISTICS

2003: births, 19,343 (rate of 15·8 per 1,000 population); deaths, 8,520 (7·0 per 1,000); marriages, 10,812 (8·8 per 1,000); divorces, 1,190 (1·0 per 1,000). In 2000 the suicide rate was 18·8 per 100,000 population among men and 5·2 per 100,000 among women. Annual population growth rate, 2000–03, 1·0%. In 2003 the most popular age range for marrying was 25–29 for males and 20–24 for females. Life expectancy at birth in 2003 was 68·8 years for males and 75·7 for females. Infant mortality, 2003, 13 per 1,000 live births; fertility rate, 2003, 1·9 births per woman.

CLIMATE

The sub-tropical climate is humid. Most rain falls in the summer. Rainfall varies between 40" (1,000 mm) on the coast to 200" (5,000 mm) on the central plateau, though the west coast only has 35" (875 mm). Mauritius lies in the cyclone belt, whose season runs from Nov. to April, but is seldom affected by intense storms. Port Louis, Jan. 73°F (22·8°C), July 81°F (27·2°C). Annual rainfall 40" (1,000 mm).

CONSTITUTION AND GOVERNMENT

The present constitution came into effect on 12 March 1968 and was amended on 12 March 1992. The head of state is the *President*, elected by a simple majority of members of the National Assembly. The role of *President* is largely a ceremonial one.

The 70-seat *National Assembly* consists of 62 elected members (three each for the 20 constituencies of Mauritius and two for Rodrigues) and eight additional seats in order to ensure a fair and adequate representation of each community within the Assembly. The government is headed by the *Prime Minister* and a Council of Ministers. Elections are held every five years on the basis of universal adult suffrage.

National Anthem

'Glory to thee, Motherland'; words by J. G. Prosper, tune by P. Gentille.

RECENT ELECTIONS

Parliamentary elections were held on 3 July 2005. The Social Alliance won 42 seats with 48·8% of votes cast, followed by the coalition of the Militant Socialist Movement (MSM) and the Mauritian Militant Movement (MMM) with 24 seats (42·6% of votes cast). The Organization of the People of Rodrigues and the Rodrigues Movement won two seats each. Turnout was 81·5%.

CURRENT ADMINISTRATION

President: Sir Aneerood Jugnauth (MSM); b. 1930 (sworn in 7 Oct. 2003; prime minister from June 1982 to Dec. 1995 and Sept. 2000 to Sept. 2003).

In March 2006 the cabinet was composed as follows:

Prime Minister, Minister of Defence, Interior, Civil Service, Administrative Reforms, Rodrigues and Outer Islands: Navin Ramgoolam (Social Alliance); b. 1947 (took office 5 July 2005, having previously been prime minister from Dec. 1995 to Sept. 2000).

Deputy Prime Minister and Minister of Public Infrastructure, Land Transport and Shipping: Ahmed Rashid Beebeejaun. *Deputy Prime Minister and Minister of Tourism, Leisure and External*

Communications: Xavier-Luc Duval. *Deputy Prime Minister and Minister of Finance and Economic Development:* Rama Krishna Sithanen.

Minister of Agro-Industry and Fisheries: Arvin Boolell. *Arts and Culture:* Mahendra Gowressoo. *Education and Human Resources:* Dharambeer Gokhool. *Environment and National Development Unit:* Anil Kumar Bachoo. *Foreign Affairs, International Trade and Co-operation:* Madan Murlidhar Dulloo. *Health and Quality of Life:* Satya Veyash Faugoo. *Housing and Lands:* Mohammed Asraf Ally Dulull. *Industry, Small- and Medium Enterprises, Commerce and Co-operatives:* Rajeshwar Jeetah. *Information Technology and Telecommunications:* Noel-Etienne Ghislain Sinatambou. *Justice and Human Rights:* Jayarama Valayden. *Labour, Industrial Relations and Employment:* Vasant Kumar Bunwaree. *Public Utilities:* Abu Twalib Kasenally. *Regional Administration:* James Burty David. *Security, National Solidarity, Senior Citizen Welfare and Institutional Reform:* Sheilabai Bappoo. *Women's Rights, Child Development, Family Welfare and Consumer Protection:* Indranee Seebun. *Youth and Sports:* Sylvio Hock Tang Wah Hing.

Government Website: http://www.gov.mu

CURRENT LEADERS

Navin Ramgoolam

Position
Prime Minister

Introduction
Navin Ramgoolam was returned as prime minister at the elections of July 2005, defeating Paul Bérenger, leader of the Mauritian Militant Movement. Ramgoolam had previously held the post from Dec. 1995 to Sept. 2000, when he lost to former Mauritian president Sir Aneerood Jugnauth.

Early Life
Navin Ramgoolam was born in Mauritius on 14 July 1947, the son of Seewoosagur Ramgoolam, the country's first president following independence in 1968. The younger Ramgoolam studied sciences at the Royal College at Curepipe in Mauritius before moving to Dublin, Ireland to train as a doctor at the Royal College of Surgeons in 1968. He gained full registration with the UK General Medical Council in 1977. Over the next ten years he worked as a senior medical officer and as a general practitioner in Mauritius, also holding the post of resident medical officer at the Yorkshire Clinic in the UK.

In 1987 Ramgoolam abandoned medicine to study for a masters degree in law at the London School of Economics. However, he subsequently abandoned a legal career in favour of politics, becoming leader of the Mauritius Labour Party in 1991. He went on to succeed Sir Aneerood Jugnauth as prime minister in 1995.

Career in Office
In 2000, towards the end of his first period in office, Mauritius secured a temporary seat on the United Nations Security Council. Rangoolam lost the premiership to his predecessor, Jugnauth, at elections later that year. He then formed the Social Alliance, a coalition led by the Mauritian Labour Party and including the Mauritian Party of Xavier-Luc Duval, the Mauritian Social Democrat Party, the Greens, the Republican Movement and the Mauritian Militant Socialist Movement (MMSM).

At the election of July 2005 the Social Alliance won 42 of a possible 70 seats, giving Ramgoolam a further term as prime minister. On coming to power he announced plans to tackle rising inflation and high levels of unemployment, and sought trade agreements to protect Mauritian exports, particularly sugar and textiles.

In Aug. 2005, Ramgoolam joined forces with the ecological organization Nature Watch to prevent a new highway being built through the endangered Fernley forest. A few weeks later, he implemented a programme of unrestricted free bus travel for the elderly and the handicapped and free bus travel to students during the week.

DEFENCE
The Police Department is responsible for defence. Its strength was (2004) 10,500. In addition there is a special mobile paramilitary force of approximately 1,900, a Coast Guard of about 800 and a helicopter unit of about 100.

Defence expenditure totalled US$13m. in 2003 (US$10 per capita), representing 0·2% of GDP.

INTERNATIONAL RELATIONS
Mauritius is a member of the UN, WTO, the Commonwealth, the African Union, African Development Bank, COMESA, International Organization of the Francophonie, SADC and is an ACP member state of the ACP-EU relationship. Mauritius is also a founder member of the Indian Ocean Rim Association for Regional Co-operation.

ECONOMY
Agriculture accounted for 6·2% of GDP in 2003, industry 30·2% and services 63·6%.

Currency
The unit of currency is the *Mauritius rupee* (MUR) of 100 *cents*. There are Bank of Mauritius notes, cupro-nickel coins, nickel-plated steel coins and copper-plated steel coins. Inflation was 5·1% in 2003 and 4·3% in 2004. In June 2002 foreign exchange reserves were US$964m., gold reserves totalled 62,000 troy oz and total money supply was Rs 15,131m.

Budget
For years ending 30 June: government recurrent revenue in 2004 (revised estimates) was Rs 32,155m. (Rs 29,488m. in 2003). Capital revenue in 2004 (revised estimates) was Rs 7,193m. (Rs 3,153m. in 2003). Recurrent and capital expenditure in 2004 were Rs 36,700m. and Rs 8,500m. respectively (Rs 33,529m. and Rs 8,407m. in 2003). Principal sources of recurrent revenue, 2003–04 (revised estimates): direct taxes, Rs 6,310m.; indirect taxes, Rs 22,505m.; receipts from public utilities, Rs 190m.; receipts from public services, Rs 946m.; rental of government property, Rs 130m.; interest and royalties, Rs 1,826m.; reimbursement, Rs 238m.; miscellaneous income, Rs 10m.

Performance
Real GDP growth was 3·2% in 2003 and 4·3% in 2004. Total GDP in 2004 was US$6·1bn.

Banking and Finance
The Bank of Mauritius (founded 1967) is the central bank. The *Governor* is Rameswurlall Basant Roi. In 2002 there were eight commercial banks, two offshore banks and one development bank. Non-bank financial intermediaries are the Post Office Savings Bank, the State Investment Corporation Ltd, the Mauritius Leasing Company, the National Mutual Fund, the National Investment Trust and the National Pension Fund. Other financial institutions are the Mauritius Housing Company and the Development Bank of Mauritius. There is also a stock exchange in Port Louis.

ENERGY AND NATURAL RESOURCES

Environment
Carbon dioxide emissions were the equivalent of 2·3 tonnes per capita in 2003.

Electricity
Installed capacity was 0·65m. kW in 2003. Production (2003) was 1·86bn. kWh. Consumption per capita in 2003 was 1,330 kWh.

Agriculture

74,117 ha. were planted with sugarcane in 2003; production in 2003 was 5,199,384 tonnes. Main secondary crops (2003, in 1,000 tonnes): tomatoes, 13; bananas, 12; potatoes, 12; pumpkins and squash, 8; cucumbers, 7; cabbages, 6; onions, 4. In 2001 there were 100,000 ha. of arable land and 6,000 ha. of permanent cropland. 21,619 ha. were irrigated in 2003.

Livestock, 2002: cattle, 28,000; goats, 93,000; pigs, 14,000.

Livestock products (2003) in tonnes: beef and veal, 2,580; pork, bacon and ham, 1,040; milk, 4,000; eggs, 12,500.

Forestry

The total forest area was 16,000 ha. in 2000 (7·9% of the land area). In 2003 timber production totalled 14,007 cu. metres.

Fisheries

The catch in 2003 totalled 9,449 tonnes, exclusively sea fish.

INDUSTRY

Manufacturing includes: sugar, textile products, footwear and other leather products, diamond cutting, jewellery, furniture, watches and watchstraps, sunglasses, plastic ware, chemical products, electronic products, pharmaceutical products, electrical appliances, ship models and canned food. There were 11 sugar mills in 2003; sugar production in 2003 was 537,155 tonnes. Production figures for other leading commodities: beer (2003), 38·8m. litres; rum (2003), 7·0m. litres; molasses (2003), 160,041 tonnes; animal feeds (2002), 138,657 tonnes.

Labour

In 2003 the labour force was estimated at 549,500. Manufacturing employed the largest proportion, with 27·1% of total employment; wholesale and retail trade, 14·3%; agriculture, forestry and fishing, 9·4%; construction, 9·3%. In 2003 the unemployment rate was estimated at 10·2%.

Trade Unions

In 1996 there were 330 registered trade unions with a total membership of about 110,000.

INTERNATIONAL TRADE

External debt was US$1,013m. at June 2003.

Imports and Exports

In 2003 imports (c.i.f.) were valued at US$2,301·2m. (US$2,156·5m. in 2002) and exports (f.o.b.) at US$1,850·4m. (US$1,798·8m. in 2002). In 2003 Rs 8,068m. of the imports came from South Africa, Rs 7,841m. from France, Rs 5,539m. from China and Rs 5,438m. from India. In 2003 Rs 15,915m. of the exports went to the UK, Rs 9,403m. to France, Rs 8,772m. to the USA and Rs 3,184m. to Madagascar.

Major imports in 2003 included manufactured goods (paper, textiles, iron and steel), Rs 18,863m.; machinery and transport equipment, Rs 14,241m.; food and live animals, Rs 10,308m. Major exports (2003) included articles of apparel and clothing, Rs 26,759m.; sugar, Rs 8,775m.; fish and fish preparations, Rs 3,167m.; textile yarns, fabrics and make-up articles, Rs 2,055m.

COMMUNICATIONS

Roads

In 2003 there were 75 km of motorway, 950 km of main roads, 990 km of secondary and other roads. In 2003 there were 107,907 cars, 3,418 buses and coaches, 125,602 motorcycles and 33,997 trucks and vans. In 2003 there were 131 deaths as a result of road accidents.

Civil Aviation

In 2000, 1,783,848 passengers and 41,269 tonnes of freight were handled at Sir Seewoosagur Ramgoolam International Airport. The national carrier is Air Mauritius, which is partly state-owned. In 1999 it flew 23·4m. km, carrying 801,700 passengers (743,100 on international flights).

Shipping

A free port was established at Port Louis in Sept. 1991. In 2002 merchant shipping totalled 58,000 GRT. In 2003 vessels totalling 8,309,000 NRT entered ports and vessels totalling 8,843,000 NRT cleared.

Telecommunications

In 2002 there were 677,200 telephone subscribers, equivalent to 559·5 per 1,000 population. Mauritius Telecom, formed in 1992, provided telephone services to 183,902 subscribers in 1996 through 58 exchanges. There were 466,000 mobile phone subscribers in 2003 and 38,000 fax machines in use in 2002. Communication with other parts of the world is by satellite and microwave links. In 2002 there were 141,000 PCs in use (116·5 per 1,000 persons). Mauritius had 120,000 Internet users in 2002.

Postal Services

In 2003 there were 103 post offices.

SOCIAL INSTITUTIONS

Justice

There is an Ombudsman. The death penalty was abolished for all crimes in 1995.

The population in penal institutions in April 2003 was 2,565 (210 per 100,000 of national population).

Education

The adult literacy rate in 2003 was 84·3% (88·2% among males and 80·5% among females). Primary and secondary education is free, primary education being compulsory. Almost all children aged 5–11 years attend schools. In 2003 there were 124,933 pupils in 278 primary schools and 100,447 pupils in 169 secondary schools in the island of Mauritius, and 4,683 pupils in 13 primary schools and 3,400 in six secondary schools in Rodrigues. In 2003, 4,922 teachers were enrolled for training at the Mauritius Institute of Education.

In 2003–04 there were 5,745 students and 383 academic staff at the University of Mauritius.

In 2000–01 total expenditure on education came to 3·7% of GNP and 13·3% of total government spending.

Health

In 2003 there were 1,172 physicians, 154 dentists, 2,795 nurses and midwives, and 279 pharmacists. There were 12 hospitals in 2002 with a provision of 29 beds per 10,000 inhabitants.

RELIGION

In 2001 there were 610,000 Hindus, 330,000 Roman Catholics and 190,000 Muslims. In May 2005 there was one cardinal.

CULTURE

Broadcasting

Broadcasting is run by the commercial Mauritius Broadcasting Corporation. There were 359,000 television sets (colour by SECAM V) in 2001 and 450,000 radio sets in 2000.

Cinema

In 2004 there were 28 cinemas.

Press

There were seven daily papers in French in 2003 (with occasional articles in English), with a combined circulation (2000) of about 138,000.

Tourism

In 2003 there were 702,000 visitors, bringing in US$683m. in tourist revenue.

Festivals

Independence Day is marked by an official celebration at the Champ de Mars racecourse on 12 March. The Hindu festival of Cavadee is celebrated by the Tamil community at the beginning of the year; the major three-day Hindu festival of Maha Shivarati takes place around Feb./March. Other Hindu festivals include Divali and Ganesh Chaturhi, which is celebrated around Aug./Sept. The Spring Festival is celebrated on the eve of the Chinese New Year; Ougadi, the Telegu new year, is celebrated in March; the Tamil new year, Varusha Pirappu, takes place in April. Muslim festivals include Eid El Fitr and Eid El Adha. On 9 Sept. pilgrims visit the grave of the 19th century missionary Père Laval who is regarded as a national saint.

DIPLOMATIC REPRESENTATIVES

Of Mauritius in the United Kingdom (32–33 Elvaston Pl., London, SW7 5NW)
High Commissioner: Abhimanu Mahendra Kundasamy.

Of the United Kingdom in Mauritius (Les Cascades Bldg, Edith Cavell St., Port Louis)
High Commissioner: Anthony Godson.

Of Mauritius in the USA (4301 Connecticut Ave., NW, Washington, D.C., 20008)
Ambassador: Vacant.
Chargé d'Affaires a.i.: Shiu Ching Young Kim Fat.

Of the USA in Mauritius (Rogers House, John Kennedy St., Port Louis)
Ambassador: Vacant.
Chargé d'Affaires a.i.: Stephen Schwartz.

Of Mauritius to the United Nations
Ambassador: Jagdish Dharamchang Koonjul.

Of Mauritius to the European Union
Ambassador: Sutiawan Gunessee.

FURTHER READING

Central Statistical Information Office. *Bi-annual Digest of Statistics.*

Bennett, Pamela R., *Mauritius.* [Bibliography] ABC-Clio, Oxford and Santa Barbara (CA), 1992

Bowman, L. W., *Mauritius: Democracy and Development in the Indian Ocean.* Aldershot, 1991

National Statistical Office: Central Statistics Office, LIC Building, President John Kennedy Street, Port Louis.
Website: http://statsmauritius.gov.mu

MEXICO

Estados Unidos Mexicanos
(United States of Mexico)

Capital: Mexico City
Population projection, 2010: 113·27m.
GDP per capita, 2003: (PPP$) 9,168
HDI/world rank: 0·814/53

KEY HISTORICAL EVENTS

The first settlers of the New World arrived in Alaska from Asia about 15,000 years ago. From about 2000 BC the people of Ancient Mexico began to settle in villages and to cultivate maize and other crops. From about 1000 BC the chief tribes were the Olmec on the Gulf Coast, the Maya in the Yucatán peninsula and modern day Chiapas, the Zapotecs and Mixtecs in Oaxaca, the Tarascans in Michoacán and the Toltecs in central Mexico. One of the largest and most powerful cities in ancient Mexico was Teotihuacán, which in the 6th century AD was one of the six largest cities in the world. By the time the Spanish *conquistadores* arrived in 1519, the dominant people were the Mexica, more commonly known as the Aztecs, whose capital Tenochtitlán became Mexico City after the conquest.

Hernán Cortés landed on the Gulf Coast in 1519 and by 1521 his small band of Spaniards, assisted by an army of indigenous peoples, had destroyed the Aztec state. The land conquered by Cortés was named New Spain, and was ruled by the Spanish Crown for three centuries. The new colony was the personal property of the King, whose representative, the Viceroy, was charged with extracting the maximum income for the Crown. The mainstays of the colonial economy were silver and land. Rich silver mines were discovered and large estates (*haciendas*) were formed. Spain controlled trade with the colonies and discouraged manufacturing to maximize profits for the King. Acapulco became Spain's sole port for trade with Asia.

One early result of the Conquest was a collapse of the indigenous population caused by social dislocation and European diseases. In 1520 the native population was probably 20m. By 1540 it had fallen to 6·5m. and by 1650 the figure was just over 1m.

The beginning of the end of Spanish rule came on 16 Sept. 1810 when the parish priest of Dolores, Miguel Hidalgo y Costilla, called for independence (the 'grito de Dolores') and led a popular army against the Spaniards. Hidalgo's revolution failed as did that of the insurrectionary José María Morelos y Pavón. Independence from Spain was declared in the Plan of Iguala

on 24 Feb. 1821 when Agustín de Iturbide proclaimed himself Emperor of Mexico. He ruled for two years.

There followed half a century of coups and counter coups. Spain invaded Tampico in 1829. Texas declared secession in 1836. The Mexican dictator Antonio de Santa Anna marched north but was defeated by the Texans. France invaded Veracruz in 1838 (the 'Pastry War'). In 1846 the USA declared war on Mexico. The war was ended by the Treaty of Guadalupe in 1848 which forced Mexico to cede a huge swathe of its territory to the USA. Liberals and conservatives fought the War of the Reform from 1858–61. The liberal government of Benito Juárez abolished the *fueros* (clerical and military privileges) and hereditary titles, confiscated the church's lands and attempted far-reaching land reform. This was followed by the French Intervention (1862–67), which installed the Habsburg Archduke Maximilian of Austria as Emperor of Mexico. The French were resisted stubbornly by President Juárez but the republicans were pushed out of productive areas. Napoleon III withdrew his troops from Mexico in 1867 despite a pledge to support Maximilian, allowing the republicans to take back the country virtually unopposed. Asserting Mexico's independence, Juárez ordered the execution of Maximilian.

From 1876–1910, a period known as the *porfiriato*, Mexico was ruled (with one interlude from 1880–84) by General Porfirio Díaz. Díaz imposed a degree of stability and order. He encouraged foreign investment, which funded a rapid expansion of the railways and an export-led economic boom. The economy faltered in the first decade of the 20th century. Díaz was deposed in 1911 by Francisco Madero, whose Plan of San Luís Potosí launched the Mexican Revolution.

Madero was deposed and assassinated in 1913. There followed a civil war fought by the armies of Venustiano Carranza, Pancho Villa and Emiliano Zapata. A new Constitution was written in 1917. Zapata was ambushed and killed in 1919 and Carranza was assassinated in 1920. Villa retired the same year but was assassinated in 1923.

In the 1920s Mexico was ruled by Alvaro Obregón and Plutarco Elías Calles. Obregón's assassination in 1928 led to the formation of the Natural Revolutionary Party (PRN), later the Institutional Revolutionary Party (PRI), which ruled Mexico for the rest of the century. Lázaro Cárdenas was president from 1934–40. He nationalized the oil industry and accelerated the distribution of land to the peasantry. The election of Miguel Alemán in 1946 was opposed unsuccessfully by the last military rebellion in Mexico's history. Alemán's pro-business administration began a long period of relative economic prosperity, the 'Mexican Miracle'.

However, by the late 1960s the Mexican economic and political system was under increasing strain. An uprising led by students ended in a bloody massacre in the Tlatelolco district of Mexico City in 1968. Successive PRI presidents made gestures towards democratization and effective opposition gradually developed. Financial and economic problems in the 1980s increased the strain on the political system. The crisis came in 1988 when the PRI candidate, Carlos Salinas de Gortari, defeated Cuauhtémoc Cárdenas, son of the former president and candidate of the Democratic Revolutionary Party (PRD), in a rigged election. Salinas took Mexico into the North American Free Trade Agreement (NAFTA) with the USA and Canada in 1992. Salinas' choice as the PRI's presidential candidate, Luís Donaldo Colosio, was assassinated in Tijuana on 23 March 1994. He was replaced by Ernesto Zedillo. In the same year the Zapatista National Liberation Army (EZLN) led an uprising in Chiapas, which is ongoing.

Finally, in 2000 Vicente Fox Quesada of the National Action Party (PAN) was elected to the presidency. Fox has attempted to address two key issues: Mexico's economic and financial weakness and illegal migration to the USA. However, the PRI majority in Congress has blocked Fox's fiscal reforms and the Bush administration has been unwilling to support Fox's proposal to liberalize immigration.

TERRITORY AND POPULATION

Mexico is bounded in the north by the USA, west and south by the Pacific Ocean, southeast by Guatemala, Belize and the Caribbean Sea, and northeast by the Gulf of Mexico. It comprises 1,964,375 sq. km (758,464 sq. miles), including uninhabited islands (5,127 sq. km) offshore.

Population at recent censuses: 1970, 48,225,238; 1980, 66,846,833; 1990, 81,249,645; 2000, 97,361,711 (50,007,325 females). Population density, 49·6 per sq. km (2000). The estimated population in 2005 was 107,029,000. 75·5% of the population were urban in 2003.

The UN gives a projected population for 2010 of 113·27m.

Area, population and capitals of the Federal District and 31 states:

	Area (Sq. km)	Population (1995 counting)	Population (2000 census)	Capital
Federal District	1,499	8,489,007	8,591,309	Mexico City
Aguascalientes	5,589	862,720	943,506	Aguascalientes
Baja California Norte	70,113	2,112,140	2,487,700	Mexicali
Baja California Sur	73,677	375,494	423,516	La Paz
Campeche	51,833	642,516	689,656	Campeche
Chiapas	73,887	3,584,786	3,920,515	Tuxtla Gutiérrez
Chihuahua	247,087	2,793,537	3,047,867	Chihuahua
Coahuila de Zaragoza	151,571	2,173,775	2,295,808	Saltillo
Colima	5,455	488,028	540,679	Colima
Durango	119,648	1,431,748	1,445,922	Victoria de Durango
Guanajuato	30,589	4,406,568	4,656,761	Guanajuato
Guerrero	63,794	2,916,567	3,075,083	Chilpancingo de los Bravo
Hidalgo	20,987	2,112,473	2,231,392	Pachuca de Soto
Jalisco	80,137	5,991,176	6,321,278	Guadalajara
México	21,461	11,707,964	13,083,359	Toluca de Lerdo
Michoacán de Ocampo	59,864	3,870,604	3,979,177	Morelia
Morelos	4,941	1,442,662	1,552,878	Cuernavaca
Nayarit	27,621	896,702	919,739	Tepic
Nuevo Léon	64,555	3,550,114	3,826,240	Monterrey
Oaxaca	95,364	3,228,895	3,432,180	Oaxaca de Juárez
Puebla	33,919	4,624,365	5,070,346	Heroica Puebla de Zaragoza
Querétaro de Arteaga	11,769	1,250,476	1,402,010	Santiago de Querétaro
Quintana Roo	50,350	703,536	873,804	Chetumal
San Luis Potosí	62,848	2,200,763	2,296,363	San Luis Potosí
Sinaloa	58,092	2,425,675	2,534,835	Culiacán Rosales
Sonora	184,934	2,085,536	2,213,370	Hermosillo
Tabasco	24,661	1,748,769	1,889,367	Villahermosa
Tamaulipas	79,829	2,527,328	2,747,114	Ciudad Victoria
Tlaxcala	3,914	883,924	961,912	Tlaxcala de Xicohténcatl
Veracruz-Llave	72,815	6,737,324	6,901,111	Xalapa-Enríquez
Yucatán	39,340	1,556,622	1,655,707	Mérida
Zacatecas	75,040	1,336,496	1,351,207	Zacatecas
Total	1,967,183	91,158,290	97,361,711	

The official language is Spanish, the mother tongue of over 93% of the population (2000), but there are some indigenous language groups (of which Náhuatl, Maya, Zapotec, Otomi and Mixtec are the most important) spoken by 6,044,547 persons over five years of age (census 2000).

The populations (2000 census) of the largest cities (250,000 and more) were:

Mexico City	8,591,309	San Nicolás de los Garza	496,878
Guadalajara	1,646,183	Chimalhuacan	482,530
Ecatepcec de Morelos	1,621,827	Ciudad López Mateos	467,544
Heroica Puebla de Zaragoza	1,271,673	Tlaquepaque	458,674
		Toluca de Lerdo	435,125
Ciudad Nezahualcoyotl	1,225,083	Cuautitlan Izcalli	433,830
		Victoria de Durango	427,135
Juárez	1,187,275	Tuxtla Gutiérrez	424,579
Tijuana	1,148,681	Veracruz	411,582
Monterrey	1,110,909	Reynosa	403,718
León de los Aldama	1,020,818	Cancún	397,191
Zapopan	910,690	Heroica Matamoros	376,279
Naucalpan de Juárez	835,053	Xalapa-Enríquez	373,076
Tlalnepantla	714,735	Villahermosa	330,846
Guadalupe	669,842	Mazatlán	327,989
Mérida	662,530	Cuernavaca	327,162
Chihuahua	657,876	Xico	322,784
San Luis Potosí	629,208	Irapuato	319,148
Acapulco de Juárez	620,656	Tonalá	315,278
Aguascalientes	594,092	Nuevo Laredo	308,828
Saltillo	562,587	Tampico	295,442
Morelia	549,996	Celaya	277,750
Mexicali	549,873	Apodaca	270,369
Hermosillo	545,928	Tepic	265,817
Culiacán Rosales	540,823	San Francisco Coalco	252,291
Santiago de Querétaro	536,463	Oaxaca de Juárez	251,846
Torreón	502,964	Ciudad Obregón	250,790

SOCIAL STATISTICS

Statistics for calendar years:

	Births	Deaths	Marriages	Divorces
1999	2,769,089	443,950	743,856	49,721
2000	2,798,339	437,667	707,422	52,358
2001	2,767,610	443,127	665,434	57,370
2002	2,699,084	459,687	616,654	60,641
2003	2,655,894	472,140	584,142	64,248

Rates per 1,000 population, 2003: births, 25·6; deaths, 4·6. In 2000 the most popular age range for marrying was 20–24 for both males and females. Infant mortality was 24 per 1,000 live births in 2001. Life expectancy at birth in 2003 was 72·6 years for males and 77·5 years for females. Annual population growth rate, 1992–2002, 1·7%. Fertility rate, 2001, 2·6 births per woman. Much of the population still lives in poverty, with the gap between the modern north and the backward south constantly growing.

CLIMATE

Latitude and relief produce a variety of climates. Arid and semi-arid conditions are found in the north, with extreme temperatures, whereas in the south there is a humid tropical climate, with temperatures varying with altitude. Conditions on the shores of the Gulf of Mexico are very warm and humid. In general, the rainy season lasts from May to Nov. Mexico City, Jan. 55°F (12·9°C), July 61°F (16·2°C). Annual rainfall 31" (787·6 mm). Guadalajara, Jan. 63°F (17·0°C), July 72°F (22·1°C). Annual rainfall 39" (987·6 mm). La Paz, Jan. 62°F (16·8°C), July 86°F (29·9°C). Annual rainfall 7" (178·3 mm). Mazatlán, Jan. 68°F (20·0°C), July 84°F (29·0°C). Annual rainfall 32" (822·1 mm). Mérida, Jan. 73°F (23·0°C), July 81°F (27·4°C). Annual rainfall 39" (990·0 mm). Monterrey, Jan. 58°F (14·3°C), July 83°F (28·1°C). Annual rainfall 23" (585·4 mm). Puebla de Zaragoza, Jan. 52°F (11·4°C), July 62°F (16·9°C). Annual rainfall 36" (900·8 mm).

CONSTITUTION AND GOVERNMENT

A new Constitution was promulgated on 5 Feb. 1917 and has been amended from time to time. Mexico is a representative, democratic and federal republic, comprising 31 states and a federal district, each state being free and sovereign in all internal affairs, but united in a federation established according to the principles of the Fundamental Law. The head of state and supreme executive authority is the *President*, directly elected for a non-renewable six-year term. The constitution was amended in April 2001, granting autonomy to 10m. indigenous peoples. The amendment was opposed both by the National Congress of Indigenous Peoples and Zapatista rebels who claimed it would leave many indigenous people worse off.

There is complete separation of legislative, executive and judicial powers (Art. 49). Legislative power is vested in a General Congress of two chambers, a *Chamber of Deputies* and a *Senate*. The Chamber of Deputies consists of 500 members directly elected for three years, 300 of them from single-member constituencies and 200 chosen under a system of proportional representation. In 1990 Congress voted a new Electoral Code. This establishes a body to organize elections (IFE), an electoral court (TFE) to resolve disputes, new electoral rolls and introduce a voter's registration card. Priests were enfranchised in 1991.

The Senate comprises 128 members, four from each state and four from the federal district, directly elected for six years. Members of both chambers are not immediately re-eligible for election. Congress sits from 1 Sept. to 31 Dec. each year; during the recess there is a permanent committee of 15 deputies and 14 senators appointed by the respective chambers.

National Anthem

'Mexicanos, al grito de guerra' ('Mexicans, at the war-cry'); words by F. González Bocanegra, tune by Jaime Nunó.

GOVERNMENT CHRONOLOGY

Presidents since 1940. (PRI = Institutional Revolutionary Party; PAN = National Action Party)

1940–46	PRI	Manuel Ávila Camacho
1946–52	PRI	Miguel Alemán Valdés
1952–58	PRI	Adolfo Ruiz Cortines
1958–64	PRI	Adolfo López Mateos
1964–70	PRI	Gustavo Díaz Ordaz Bolaños
1970–76	PRI	Luis Echeverría Álvarez
1976–82	PRI	José López Portillo y Pacheco
1982–88	PRI	Miguel de la Madrid Hurtado
1988–94	PRI	Carlos Salinas de Gortari
1994–2000	PRI	Ernesto Zedillo Ponce de León
2000–	PAN	Vicente Fox Quesada

RECENT ELECTIONS

At the presidential elections of 2 July 2000—the first in Mexico that were deemed free and fair—Vicente Fox of the Partido Acción Nacional (National Action Party/Alliance for Change) won 42·5% of the vote, defeating Francisco Labastida of the Partido Revolucionario Institucional (Institutional Revolutionary Party/PRI) who gained 36·1%. There were four other candidates. It was the first time in 71 years that the PRI had lost power.

Elections were held on 2 July 2000 for the Chamber of Senators (and the Chamber of Deputies). Following the election the composition of the Senate was: PRI, 58 of the 128 seats (45·3%); Alliance for Change (consisting of the National Action Party and the Ecologist Green Party of Mexico), 53 (41·4%); Alianza por México (Alliance for Mexico/AM), 17 (13·3%).

In the elections of 6 July 2003 to the Chamber of Deputies, President Vicente Fox's National Action Party (PAN) won 153 seats (23·1% of the vote), losing a quarter of its seats. The main opposition party, the PRI, won 224 seats (30·6%) and its ally, the Ecologist Green Party (PVEM), won 17 seats (4·0%). The PRI-PVEM joint list took 13·4% of the vote. The Party of the Democratic Revolution (PRD) won 95 seats (17·6%), the Labour Party (PT) won 6 seats (2·4%) and the Convergence for Democracy won 5 seats (2·3%). The Partido de la Sociedad Nacionalista, the Partido Alianza Social, the Partido México

Posible, the Partido Liberal Mexicano and Fuerza Ciudadana failed to win seats. Turnout was 41·8%.

Presidential and parliamentary elections were scheduled to take place on 2 July 2006.

CURRENT ADMINISTRATION

President: Vicente Fox Quesada; b. 1942 (Alliance for Change; sworn in 1 Dec. 2000).

In March 2006 the government comprised:

Minister of Interior: Carlos María Abascal Carranza. *Foreign Affairs:* Luis Ernesto Derbéz Bautista. *Defence:* Gen. Gerardo Clemente Ricardo Vega García. *Naval Affairs:* Adm. Marco Antonio Peyrot González. *Finance and Public Credit:* Francisco Gil Díaz. *Social Development:* Ana Teresa Aranda. *Energy:* Fernando Canales Clariond. *Economy:* Sergio Alejandro García de Alba Zepeda. *Agriculture, Livestock, Rural Development, Fisheries and Food:* Francisco Javier Mayorga Castañeda. *Communication and Transport:* Pedro Cerisola y Weber. *Education:* Reyes Támez Guerra. *Health:* Julio Frenk Mora. *Public Security and Justice Services:* Eduardo Medina-Mora Icaza. *Labour and Social Welfare:* Francisco Javier Salazar Sáenz. *Agrarian Reform:* Florencio Salazar Adame. *Tourism:* Rodolfo Elizondo Torres. *Environment and Natural Resources:* José Luis Luege Tamargo. *Public Service:* Eduardo Romero Ramos. *Attorney General:* Daniel Francisco Cabeza de Vaca Hernández.

Presidency Website: http://www.presidencia.gob.mx

CURRENT LEADERS

Vicente Fox

Position
President

Introduction
Representing the Partido Acción Nacional (PAN; National Action Party), Vicente Fox Quesada was elected president in July 2000 ending 71 years of hegemonic rule by the Partido Revolucionario Institucional (PRI; Institutional Revolutionary Party).

Early Life
Fox was born on 2 July 1942 in Mexico City to an Irish father and a Spanish mother, but grew up in the state of Guanajuato. From a wealthy agricultural family, he studied business at the Universidad Iberoamericana in Mexico City and then at Harvard University in the USA. In 1964 he was employed by Coca-Cola, climbing the ranks to become the company's youngest president for Mexico and Central America.

His political career began in 1987 when he was introduced to the PAN by presidential candidate Manuel J. Clouthier. The following year Fox was elected to congress where he concentrated on agricultural policy. Three years later, hoping to represent his home province of Guanajuato, he stood unsuccessfully in the regional elections, losing out to the PRI candidate, Ramón Aguirre, who claimed 51% of votes against Fox's 39%. Fox accused the government of fraud and protested until the government accepted the PAN victory. Ramón Aguirre was forced to stand down and a PAN representative took his place. Fox was elected at his second attempt in 1995.

Although short on political experience, Fox quickly climbed the ranks of the PAN, establishing a support network called 'Amigos de Fox' (Friends of Fox). In preparation for the 2000 presidential elections the Alianza por el Cambio (Alliance for Change) was formed, comprising the PAN and the small Partido Verde Ecologista de México (PVEM; Ecologist Green Party of Mexico). Fox was nominated the coalition's presidential candidate for the 2000 election. His rival was the PRI candidate Francisco Labastida. Fox's manifesto was based on security, justice, ending corruption and promoting economic growth.

Career in Office

Fox won the 2000 presidential elections with 42·5% of votes against Labastida's 36·1%. His victory ended 71 years of continuous rule by the PRI, often maintained by questionable means, although it was the reforms of outgoing PRI president Ernesto Zedillo that created the environment for democratic elections. On election Fox outlined plans to promote a market-led economy, although he stopped short of privatizing the state oil company Pemex (Petróleos Mexicanos) claiming he was simply looking to attract foreign investment. He also pledged to solve the conflict with the rebel Ejército Zapatista de Liberación Nacional (EZLN; Zapatista Army of Liberation), formed to promote the rights of the indigenous population, especially in the southern Chiapas region. Peace talks under former president Ernesto Zedillo had stalled in 1996. Fox outlined a peace accord that would give the indigenous population more autonomy, and allow recognition of their culture, traditions and language. There were also moves to withdraw the army from the region and release imprisoned Zapatistas. In April 2001 Congress approved legislation granting indigenous communities the right to self-determination. However, despite these measures, the conflict is not yet fully resolved.

Other promised reforms in the policy agenda during Fox's tenure—such as fiscal and energy reform, tackling crime and corruption, and raising educational standards—have failed to materialize. This has reflected the president's lack of a congressional majority, the PAN having lost a quarter of its parliamentary seats in the July 2003 legislative elections. Economically, the slowdown in the early period of Fox's term—largely a consequence of economic difficulties suffered by the USA which takes about 90% of Mexican exports—has more recently improved. This has been mainly as a result of Mexico's standing as a major oil producer and high oil prices on the world market.

On an international level, Fox has sought to promote relations with the USA. In Jan. 2001 he outlined plans to create a 'NAFTA Plus', extending the current trade pact with North America to include more Latin American countries. He has also tried to stimulate trade with Europe.

He was not eligible to stand for re-election in the presidential elections scheduled for July 2006.

DEFENCE

In 2003 defence expenditure totalled US$2,938m. (US$29 per capita), representing 0·5% of GDP.

Army

Enlistment into the regular army is voluntary, but there is also one year of conscription (four hours per week) by lottery. Strength of the regular army (2002) 144,000 (60,000 conscripts). There are combined reserve forces of 300,000. In addition there is a rural defence militia of 14,000.

Navy

The Navy is primarily equipped and organized for offshore and coastal patrol duties. It includes three destroyers and eight frigates. The naval air force, 1,100 strong, operates eight combat aircraft.

Naval personnel in 2002 totalled 37,000, including the naval air force and 8,700 marines.

Air Force

The Air Force had (2002) a strength of about 11,770 with 107 combat aircraft, including PC-7s, AT-33s and F-5Es, and 71 armed helicopters.

INTERNATIONAL RELATIONS

Mexico is a member of the UN (and most UN System organizations), WTO, BIS, OECD, OAS, Inter-American Development Bank (IADB), LAIA, ACS, APEC, NAFTA and IOM.

A free trade agreement was signed with the European Union in 1999.

ECONOMY

Agriculture accounted for 4·0% of GDP in 2002, industry 26·5% and services 69·5%.

Overview

Mexico ranks among the dozen largest economies of the world. Average income levels are the highest in Latin America but remain well below the OECD average. There is a high degree of income inequality, with the World Bank estimating that the richest 10% of the population earns over 40% of total income while the poorest 10% accounts for only 1·1%. Mexico suffered from poor macroeconomic management and economic crises in the 1980s. In 1994–95 it experienced a currency crisis that threw millions of Mexicans into poverty. Yet economic performance over the 1990s compared favourably with that of the previous decade; inflation was significantly reduced and public debt was brought down from 115% in 1986 to 22% in 1999. Since 1995 macroeconomic management has been on a sound footing and further economic crises like those of the past are not expected. The labour market and banking system have been reformed and privatization has reduced the state's direct involvement in the economy. Nonetheless, recent growth is considered to be well below the country's potential growth rate and insufficient to significantly reduce poverty.

Mexico was the world's fifth largest oil producer in 2004 and until 1985 oil was the principal export. Since then manufactured goods exports have come to represent over 80% of total exports while oil now represents roughly 15%. In the domestic economy services account for over two-thirds of GDP, industry for roughly one-quarter and agriculture around 4%. The mining sector was estimated to account for only 1·4% of GDP in 2003 but this understates the importance of oil production to the economy. The transformation of the economy towards manufactured goods export production was initiated by economic liberalization begun in the 1980s and cemented by joining the North American Free-Trade Agreement (a free-trade bloc with the USA and Canada). Nearly half of the country's total exports are produced in *maquiladoras* (in-bond assembly plants for re-export).

From 1993–2000 Mexico's combined exports and imports surged from US$117bn. to US$341bn. but the US economic slowdown of 2001–02 reversed the trend. An export recovery began in July 2002 but its strength was limited by weak productivity growth and stiff competition in the US market. Countries such as China are an increasingly competitive threat to Mexico. The OECD recommends that Mexico's structural reform and economic liberalization programmes be deepened simultaneously in order to benefit from synergies. Educational reform is also highlighted as a policy priority as Mexico's human capital is the lowest in the OECD. Further public finance reform is another priority. The OECD recommends that more oil revenue be saved or spent effectively on development priorities (education, infrastructure, health and poverty alleviation) and that tax reform be implemented to tap alternative revenue sources.

Currency

The unit of currency is the *Mexican peso* (MXP) of 100 *centavos*. A new peso was introduced on 1 Jan. 1993: 1 new peso = 1,000 old pesos. The peso was devalued by 13·94% in Dec. 1994. Foreign exchange reserves were US$45,147m. and gold reserves 191,000 troy oz in June 2002. Inflation rates (based on OECD statistics):

1995	1996	1997	1998	1999	2000	2001	2002	2003	2004
35·0%	34·4%	20·6%	15·9%	16·6%	9·5%	6·4%	5·0%	4·5%	4·7%

Total money supply in June 2002 was 507,075m. new pesos.

Budget

Government revenue and expenditure (in 1m. new pesos), year ending 31 Dec.:

	1995	1996	1997	1998	1999	2000
Revenue	281,138	384,466	468,187	501,231	634,449	811,431
Expenditure	292,479	387,810	516,230	563,990	712,137	875,775

Performance

Real GDP growth rates (based on OECD statistics):

1995	1996	1997	1998	1999	2000	2001	2002	2003	2004
−6·2%	5·1%	6·8%	4·9%	3·9%	6·6%	−0·2%	0·8%	1·4%	4·4%

In 2004 total GDP was US$676·5bn.

The OECD reported in Jan. 2004: 'Fiscal rectitude, progress towards macroeconomic stabilisation, and structural reforms… have not yet been sufficient to raise potential growth to rates that would allow closing the gap in living standards with other OECD countries. Prolonged cyclical weakness, with now unambiguous signs yet of a vigorous upturn, has depressed private investment…Mexico's catching-up is further hindered by low human capital accumulation.'

Banking and Finance

The Bank of Mexico, established 1 Sept. 1925, is the central bank of issue (*Governor*, Guillermo Ortíz Martínez). It gained autonomy over monetary policy in 1993. Exchange rate policy is determined jointly by the bank and the Finance Ministry. Banks were nationalized in 1982, but in May 1990 the government approved their reprivatization. The state continues to have a majority holding in foreign trade and rural development banks. In 1999 Congress approved the removal of regulations limiting foreign holdings to 49%.

In 2000 there were 34 commercial banks, seven major development banks and one foreign bank. Mexico's largest bank is Banamex. In 2001 the American financial services company Citigroup bought Mexico's largest financial group, Banacci, and its second largest bank, Banamex, for US$12·5bn., but retained the name Banamex. Most of Mexico's leading banks are now foreign-owned.

There is a stock exchange in Mexico City.

ENERGY AND NATURAL RESOURCES

Environment

Mexico's carbon dioxide emissions from the consumption and flaring of fossil fuels in 2002 were the equivalent of 3·6 tonnes per capita.

Electricity

Installed capacity, 2002, 47·3m. kW. Output in 2002 was 235·16bn. kWh and consumption per capita 2,280 kWh. In 2003 there were two nuclear reactors in operation.

Oil and Gas

Crude petroleum production was 178·4m. tonnes in 2002. Mexico produced 5·0% of the world total oil output in 2002, and had reserves amounting to 12·6bn. bbls. Revenues from oil exports provide about a third of all government revenues. Natural gas production was 34·8bn. cu. metres in 2002 with 250bn. cu. metres in proven reserves (2002).

Minerals

Output (in 1,000 tonnes): iron ore (2001), 11,500; lignite (2002), 9,238; salt (2002), 8,700; gypsum (2002), 6,500; coal (2000), 2,214; silica (1998), 1,732; sulphur (1998), 913; fluorite (1998), 620; zinc (2001), 429; aluminium (1999), 426; copper (2001), 367; manganese (1998), 203; feldspar (1998), 198; lead (1998), 176; barite (1998), 161; silver (2001), 2·8; gold (2000), 26,375 kg. Mexico is the biggest producer of silver in the world.

Agriculture

In 2001 Mexico had 24·8m. ha. of arable land and 2·5m. ha. of permanent cropland. There were 6·32m. ha. of irrigated land. There were 324,890 tractors and 22,500 harvester-threshers in 2001. In 2002 agriculture contributed 4·0% of GDP (6·0% in 1997). Some 60% of agricultural land belongs to about 30,000 *ejidos* (with 15m. members), communal lands with each member farming his plot independently. *Ejidos* can now be inherited, sold or rented. A land-titling programme (PROCEDE) is establishing the boundaries of 4·6m. plots of land totalling 102m. ha. Other private farmers may not own more than 100 ha. of irrigated land or an equivalent in unirrigated land. There is a theoretical legal minimum of 10 ha. for holdings, but some 60% of private farms were less than 5 ha. in 1990. Laws abolishing the *ejido* system were passed in 1992.

Sown areas, 2000 (in 1,000 ha.) included: maize, 8,661; beans, 2,252; sorghum, 2,170; coffee beans, 757; wheat, 749; sugarcane, 659; barley, 312; chick-peas, 210; chillies and green peppers, 142; safflower seeds, 103; rice, 98.

Production in 2000 (in 1,000 tonnes): sugarcane, 49,275; maize, 18,761; sorghum, 6,400; oranges, 3,390; wheat, 3,300; tomatoes, 2,401; chillies and green peppers, 1,813; bananas, 1,802; potatoes, 1,593; mangoes, 1,529; coconuts, 1,313; lemons and limes, 1,297; beans, 1,219; watermelons, 993; avocados, 939; papayas, 636; barley, 532; melons (excluding watermelons), 500.

Livestock (2000): cattle, 30·29m.; sheep, 5·90m.; pigs, 13·69m.; goats, 9·60m.; horses, 6·25m.; mules, 3·27m.; asses, 3·25m.; chickens, 476m. Meat production, 2000 (in 1,000 tonnes): beef and veal, 1,415; pork, bacon and ham, 1,035; horse, 79; goat, 39; lamb and mutton, 32; poultry meat, 1,896. Dairy production, 2000 (in 1,000 tonnes): cow milk, 9,474; goat milk, 134; eggs, 1,666; cheese, 148; honey, 57.

Forestry

Forests extended over 55·21m. ha. in 2000, representing 28·9% of the land area, containing pine, spruce, cedar, mahogany, logwood and rosewood. There are 14 forest reserves (nearly 0·8m. ha.) and 47 national park forests of 0·75m. ha. Timber production was 45·51m. cu. metres in 2003.

Fisheries

The total catch in 2002 was 1,450,654 tonnes, of which 1,368,006 tonnes came from sea fishing.

INDUSTRY

The leading companies by market capitalization in Mexico in Nov. 2005 were: América Móvil SA de CV (a mobile phone company), US$36·9bn.; Wal-Mart de México SA de CV (general retailers, formerly Cifra), US$23·6bn.; and CEMEX (a cement producing company), US$20·9bn.

In 2001 the manufacturing industry provided 19·6% of GDP. Output in 2001 (in 1,000 tonnes): cement, 32,239; residual fuel oil (2002), 25,599; petrol (2002), 16,654; crude steel (2002), 14,100; distillate fuel oil (2002), 13,165; sugar (2002), 5,073; pig iron, 4,363; wheat flour, 2,611; cigarettes, 56·1bn. units; soft drinks, 13,005·0m. litres; beer, 6,163·2m. litres. Car production has increased from 857,000 in 1994 to 960,000 in 2002.

Labour

In the period March–June 2001 the employed population totalled 39,004,300. The principal areas of activity were (in 1,000): wholesale and retail trade/repair of motor vehicles, motorcycles and personal and household goods, 8,839·2; manufacturing, 7,373·0; agriculture, hunting and forestry, 6,920·7; construction, 2,396·9; hotels and restaurants, 1,982·2; education, 1,971·6. Unemployment rate, March–June 2002, 1·9%. The daily minimum wage at Jan. 2006 ranged from 45·81 new pesos to 48·67 new pesos.

Trade Unions

The Mexican Labour Congress (CTM) is incorporated into the Institutional Revolutionary Party, and is an umbrella organization numbering some 5m. A breakaway from CTM took place in 1997 when rebel labour leaders set up the National Union of Workers (UNT) to combat what they saw as a sharp drop in real wages.

INTERNATIONAL TRADE

In Sept. 1991 Mexico signed the free trade Treaty of Santiago with Chile, envisaging an annual 10% tariffs reduction from Jan. 1992. The North American Free Trade Agreement (NAFTA), between Canada, Mexico and the USA, was signed on 7 Oct. 1992 and came into effect on 1 Jan. 1994. A free trade agreement was signed with Costa Rica in March 1994. Some 8,300 products were free from tariffs, with others to follow over ten years. The Group of Three (G3) free trade pact with Colombia and Venezuela came into effect on 1 Jan. 1995. Total foreign debt was US$141,264m. in 2002, a figure exceeded only by Brazil, China and Russia.

Imports and Exports

Trade for calendar years in US$1m.:

	1998	1999	2000	2001	2002
Imports f.o.b.	125,374	141,975	174,458	168,397	168,679
Exports f.o.b.	117,459	136,391	166,455	158,443	160,763

Of total imports in 1999, 74·3% came from USA, 3·5% from Germany, 3·3% from Japan, 1·9% from Canada and 1·9% from South Korea. Of total exports in 1999, 88·4% went to USA, 1·7% to Canada, 1·5% to Germany, 0·7% to Spain and 0·6% to Japan. In 1998 exports to the USA accounted for 21% of GDP.

The in-bond (*maquiladora*) assembly plants generate the largest flow of foreign exchange. Although originally located along the US border when the programme was introduced in the 1960s, they are now to be found in almost every state. In 2000 there were over 3,000 'foreign to Mexico' manufacturing companies, employing more than 1m. people. Manufactured goods account for 90% of trade revenues.

COMMUNICATIONS

Roads

The total road length in 2002 was 347,667 km, of which 6,796 km were motorways, 44,587 km other main roads, 66,116 km secondary roads and 230,178 km other roads. In 2000 there were 10,443,489 passenger cars, 7,931,590 trucks and vans and 111,756 buses and coaches.

Rail

The National Railway, *Ferrocarriles Nacionales de Mexico*, was split into five companies in 1996 as a preliminary to privatization. It comprises 26,623 km of 1,435 mm gauge (246 km electrified). In 2000 passenger-km travelled came to 91m. and freight tonne-km to 48·9bn. Passenger traffic has declined dramatically over the past ten years and has virtually ceased. There is a 202 km metro in Mexico City with 11 lines. There are light rail lines in Guadalajara (24 km) and Monterrey (23 km).

Civil Aviation

There is an international airport at Mexico City (Benito Juárez) and 55 other international and 29 national airports. Each of the larger states has a local airline which links it with main airports. The national carriers are Aeromexico, Mexicana, Aerocalifornia, Aerolíneas Internacionales and Aviacsa; Aeromexico and Mexicana, both privatized in the late 1980s, are the main ones. In 1999 Aeromexico carried 8,672,000 passengers (1,959,300 on international flights) and Mexicana 7,359,700 passengers (2,901,500 international). In 2001 Mexico City handled 20,599,064 passengers (13,711,141 on domestic flights). Cancún was the second busiest airport for passengers in 2001,

with 7,640,007 (5,905,813 on international flights). Guadalajara handled 5,020,631 passengers (3,337,339 on domestic flights).

Shipping

Mexico had 90 ocean ports in 1998, of which, on the Gulf coast, the most important include Tampico, Coatzacoalcos, Altamira, Progreso, Tuxpan, Morelos and Cozumel. Those on the Pacific Coast include Lázaro Cárdenas, Manzanillo, Guaymas, La Paz-Pichilingue, Ensenada, Topolobampo, Mazatlán and Salina Cruz. Mexico's busiest port is Manzanillo, which handled 13,304,000 tonnes of cargo in 2002. The privatization of port operations has been taking place since the early 1990s.

Merchant shipping loaded 139·5m. tonnes and unloaded 62m. tonnes of cargo in 1996. In 2002 the merchant marine had a total tonnage of 937,000 GRT, including oil tankers 455,000 GRT. In 2002 vessels totalling 51,718,000 NRT entered ports and vessels totalling 130,536,000 NRT cleared.

Telecommunications

Telmex, previously a state-controlled company, was privatized in 1991. It controls about 98% of all the telephone service. There were 40,869,900 telephone subscribers in 2002, or 401·2 for every 1,000 persons, and there were 8,353,000 PCs in use (82·0 per 1,000 population). Mexico had 25,928,300 mobile phone subscribers in 2002 and 10,033,000 Internet users. There were 300,000 fax machines in 2002.

Postal Services

There were 8,681 post offices in 2003 (local administration, offices, agencies), equivalent to one for every 11,900 persons.

SOCIAL INSTITUTIONS

Justice

Magistrates of the Supreme Court are appointed for six years by the President and confirmed by the Senate; they can be removed only on impeachment. The courts include the Supreme Court with 21 magistrates, 12 collegiate circuit courts with three judges each and nine unitary circuit courts with one judge each, and 68 district courts with one judge each.

The penal code of 1 Jan. 1930 abolished the death penalty, except for the armed forces. Mexico abolished the death penalty for all crimes in Dec. 2005—the last execution had been in 1961.

There were 15,596 murders in 1995 (a rate of 17·2 per 100,000 population). The population in penal institutions in June 2000 was 154,765 (156 per 100,000 of national population).

Education

Adult literacy was 90·3% in 2003 (male, 92·0%; female, 88·7%). Primary and secondary education is free and compulsory, and secular, although religious instruction is permitted in private schools. By 2000 Mexicans were attending school for an average of 7·6 years, almost a year more than in 1994.

In 2002–03 there were:

	Establishments	Teachers	Students (in 1,000)
Pre-school	74,758	163,282	3,636
Primary	99,463	557,278	14,857
Secondary	29,749	325,233	5,660
Baccalaureate	9,668	202,161	2,936
Vocational training	1,659	31,683	359
Medium/Professional	664	17,280	167
Higher education	2,539	192,593	1,932
Postgraduate education	1,283	21,685	138

In 2000 total expenditure on education came to 6·1% of GDP, including 1,374m. new pesos on the *Programa de Apoyo Federal a Entidades Federativas* (Federal Support Program to the States).

Health

In 2003 there were 3,039 hospitals, with a total provision of 73,446 beds. In 2001 there were 172,266 physicians, 9,669 dentists and 222,389 nurses. In 2001 Mexico spent 6·6% of its GDP on health.

Welfare

As of 1 July 1997 all workers had to join the private insurance system, while the social insurance system was being phased out. At retirement, employees covered by the social insurance system before 1997 can choose to receive benefits from either the social insurance system or the private insurance system. The official retirement age is 65 years but to be eligible, a pensioner must have paid 1,250 weeks of contributions. The guaranteed minimum pension is equal to the minimum salary in July 1997 indexed to prices. On social insurance, the minimum monthly pension is 100% of the minimum monthly salary in Mexico City (1,357·20 new pesos in 2004).

Unemployment benefit exists under a labour law which requires employers to pay a dismissed employee a lump sum equal to three months' pay plus 20 days' pay for each year of service. Social security pays an unemployment benefit of between 75% and 95% of the old-age pension for unemployed persons aged 60 to 64.

RELIGION

In 2001 an estimated 91% of the population was Roman Catholic, down from 98% in 1950. In May 2005 there were five cardinals. The Church is separated from the State, and the constitution of 1917 provided strict regulation of this and all other religions. In Nov. 1991 Congress approved an amendment to the 1917 constitution permitting the recognition of churches by the state, the possession of property by churches and the enfranchisement of priests. Church buildings remain state property. In 2001 there were estimated to be 3·82m. Protestants, plus followers of various other religions. There were 811,000 Latter-day Saints (Mormons) in 1998.

CULTURE

World Heritage Sites

Mexico has 25 UNESCO world heritage sites. They are (with year entered on list): the Sian Ka'an nature reserve; the historic centre of Mexico City and the canal and island network of Xochimilco; Puebla's historic centre; the pre-Hispanic city of Teotihuacán, now a major archaeological site; the Historic Centre of Oaxaca and archaeological site of Monte Alban; and Palenque—lying in the foothills of the Altos de Chiapas, the Maya ruins of Palenque are surrounded by waterfalls, rainforest and fauna (all 1987); the historic town of Guanajuato and adjacent disused silver mines; and the pre-Hispanic city of Chichen-Itza, Yucatan (both 1988); the historic centre of Morelia, on the southern Pacific coast (1991); the pre-Hispanic city of El Tajin, Veracruz (1992); the El Vizcaino whale sanctuary; the historic centre of Zacatecas, once a major silver mining centre; and the Sierra de San Francisco rock paintings (all 1993); the 14 early 16th-century monasteries on Popocatepetl, to the southeast of Mexico City (1994); the Maya town of Uxmal, Yucatán, with its preserved pyramids and sculptures; and the historic monuments zone of Querétaro (both 1996); the Hospicio (Hospice) Cabañas, Guadalajara (1997); the historic monuments zone of Tlacotalpan; the archeological zone of Paquimé, Casas Grandes in Chihuahua (both 1998); the historic fortified town of Campeche; and Xochicalco's archaeological monuments zone, Morelos state (both 1999); the Ancient Maya City of Calakmul, Campeche (2002); the Franciscan Missions in the Sierra Gorda of Querétaro (2003); Luis Barragán House and Studio in Mexico City (2004); and the islands and protected areas of the Gulf of California (2005).

Broadcasting

In 1997 there were 1,342 radio stations and 580 television stations licensed by the *Dirección General de Concesiones y Permisos de Telecomunicaciones*. Most radio stations carry the 'National Hour' programme. Television services are provided by the Televisa, Televisión Azteca and Multivision. There were 32·3m. radio receivers in 2000 and 28·3m. TV sets (colour by NTSC) in 2001.

Cinema

In 1999 there were 2,320 cinemas and 120m. admissions.

Press

In 2002 there were 299 daily newspapers with a circulation of 8,734,000, equivalent to 88 per 1,000 inhabitants. In 2002 a total of 7,306 book titles were published.

Tourism

There were 19·67m. tourists in 2002, putting Mexico eighth in the world list; gross revenue, including border visitors, amounted to US$8,858m. in 2002.

DIPLOMATIC REPRESENTATIVES

Of Mexico in the United Kingdom (16 St George St., Hanover Sq., London, W1S 1LX)
Ambassador: Juan Bremer de Martino.

Of the United Kingdom in Mexico (Rio Lerma 71, Col. Cuauhtémoc, 06500 México, D.F.)
Ambassador: Giles Paxman.

Of Mexico in the USA (1911 Pennsylvania Ave., NW, Washington, D.C., 20006)
Ambassador: Carlos Alberto de Icaza.

Of the USA in Mexico (Paseo de la Reforma 305, 06500 México, D.F.)
Ambassador: Antonio O. Garza, Jr.

Of Mexico to the United Nations
Ambassador: Enrique Berruga Filloy.

Of Mexico to the European Union
Ambassador: Sergio Ramírez Robles.

FURTHER READING

Instituto Nacional de Estadística, Geografía e Informática. *Anuario Estadístico de los Estados Unidos Mexicanos. Mexican Bulletin of Statistical Information*. Quarterly.

Aspe, P., *Economic Transformation: the Mexican Way*. Cambridge (MA), 1993

Bartra, R., *Agrarian Structure and Political Power in Mexico*. Johns Hopkins Univ. Press, 1993

Bethell, L. (ed.) *Mexico since Independence*. CUP, 1992

Camp, R. A., *Politics in Mexico*. 2nd ed. OUP, 1996

Hamnett, Brian R., *A Concise History of Mexico*. CUP, 1999

Krauze, E., *Mexico, Biography of Power: A History of Modern Mexico, 1810–1996*. London, 1997

Philip, G. (ed.) *The Presidency in Mexican Politics*. London, 1991.— *Mexico*. [Bibliography] 2nd ed. ABC-Clio, Oxford and Santa Barbara (CA), 1993

Rodríguez, J. E., *The Evolution of the Mexican Political System*. New York, 1993

Ruíz, R. E., *Triumphs and Tragedy: a History of the Mexican People*. New York, 1992

Turner, Barry (ed.) *Latin America Profiled*. Macmillan, London, 2000

Whiting, V. R., *The Political Economy of Foreign Investment in Mexico: Nationalism, Liberalism, Constraints on Choice*. Johns Hopkins Univ. Press, 1992

National Statistical Office: Instituto Nacional de Estadística, Geografía e Informática (INEGI), Aguascalientes.
Website (Spanish only): http://www.inegi.gob.mx

MICRONESIA

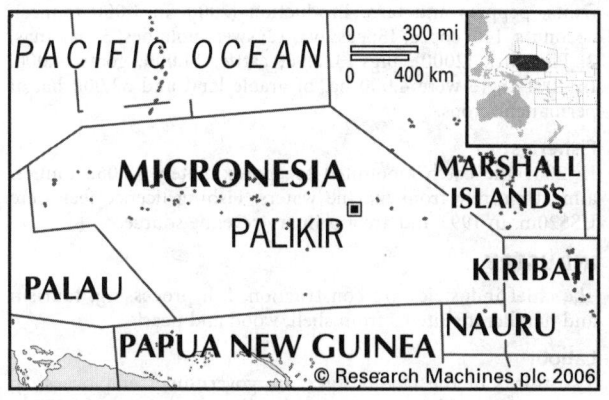

© Research Machines plc 2006

Federated States of Micronesia

Capital: Palikir
Population projection, 2010: 114,000
GDP per capita: not available
GNI per capita: $2,090

KEY HISTORICAL EVENTS

Spain acquired sovereignty over the Caroline Islands in 1886 but sold the archipelago to Germany in 1899. Japan occupied the Islands at the beginning of the First World War and in 1921 they were mandated to Japan by the League of Nations. Captured by Allied Forces in the Second World War, the Islands became part of the UN Trust Territory of the Pacific Islands created on 18 July 1947 and administered by the USA. The Federated States of Micronesia came into being on 10 May 1979. American trusteeship was terminated on 3 Nov. 1986 by the UN Security Council and on the same day Micronesia entered into a 15-year Free Association with the USA. An amended 20-year Compact of Free Association was signed into law on 17 Dec. 2003, guaranteeing US$1·8bn. to Micronesia in grants for a government trust fund.

TERRITORY AND POPULATION

The Federated States lie in the North Pacific Ocean between 137° and 163° E, comprising 607 islands with a total land area of 701 sq. km (271 sq. miles). The population (2000 census) was 107,008; density, 153 per sq. km. The estimated population in 2005 was 110,000.

The UN gives a projected population for 2010 of 114,000.

In 2000 an estimated 71·5% of the population lived in rural areas.

The areas and populations of the four major groups of island states (east to west) are as follows:

State	Area (sq. km)	Population (2000 census)	Headquarters
Kosrae	110	7,686	Tofol
Pohnpei	345	34,486	Kolonia
Chuuk	127	53,595	Weno
Yap	119	11,241	Colonia

Kosrae consists of a single island. Its main town is Lelu (2,591 inhabitants in 2000). Pohnpei comprises a single island (covering 334 sq. km) and eight scattered coral atolls. Kolonia (5,681 inhabitants in 2000) was the national capital until 1989. The new capital, Palikir (6,227 inhabitants in 2000), lies approximately 10 km southwest in the Palikir valley. Chuuk consists of a group of 14 islands within a large reef-fringed lagoon (44,000 inhabitants in 1994); the state also includes 12 coral atolls (8,000 inhabitants), the most important being the Mortlock Islands. The chief town is Weno (16,121 inhabitants in 1994). Yap comprises a main group of four islands (covering 100 sq. km with 7,000 inhabitants in 1994) and 13 coral atolls (4,000 inhabitants in 1994), the main ones being Ulithi and Woleai. Colonia is its chief town (3,161 inhabitants in 1994).

English is used in schools and is the official language. Trukese, Pohnpeian, Yapese and Kosrean are also spoken.

SOCIAL STATISTICS

2004 estimates: births, 3,400; deaths, 700. Rates, 2004 estimates (per 1,000 population): birth, 31; death, 6. Infant mortality rate (2004), 19 per 1,000 live births. 2004 life expectancy, 68 years. Annual population growth rate, 1992–2002, 0·7%; fertility rate, 2001, 5·1 births per woman.

CLIMATE

Tropical, with heavy year-round rainfall, especially in the eastern islands, and occasional typhoons (June–Dec.). Kolonia, Jan. 80°F (26·7°C), July 79°F (26·1°C). Annual rainfall 194" (4,859 mm).

CONSTITUTION AND GOVERNMENT

Under the Constitution founded on 10 May 1979, there is an executive presidency and a 14-member National Congress, comprising ten members elected for two-year terms from single-member constituencies of similar electorates, and four members elected one from each State for a four-year term by proportional representation. The Federal President and Vice-President first run for the Congress before they are elected by members of Congress for a four-year term.

National Anthem

'Patriots of Micronesia'; words anonymous, tune adapted from J. Brahms' 'Academic Festival Overture'.

RECENT ELECTIONS

The last election for Congress was held on 8 March 2005. Only non-partisans were elected. Joseph Urusemal was elected President and Redley Killion was confirmed as Vice-President (elected on 11 May 1999) by Congress on 11 May 2003.

CURRENT ADMINISTRATION

President: Joseph J. Urusemal; b. 1952 (took office 11 May 2003).

Vice-President: Redley Killion.

In March 2006 the government comprised:

Minister of Foreign Affairs: Sebastian Anefal. *Finance and Administration:* Nick Andon. *Health, Education and Social Affairs:* Nena Nena. *Economic Affairs:* Akallino Susaia. *Justice:* Marstella Jack. *Transportation, Communications and Infrastructure:* Andrew Yatilman. *Public Defender:* Beauleen Carl-Worswick.

Speaker of the Congress: Peter Christian.

Government Website: http://www.fsmgov.org

CURRENT LEADERS

Joseph Urusemal

Position
President

Introduction
Elected the sixth president of the Federated States of Micronesia on 11 May 2003, Joseph Urusemal has pledged to tackle poverty

and unemployment and reduce the nation's dependence on foreign aid. He has endeavoured to raise international awareness of the threat posed to Micronesia by global climate change, exemplified by the increasing frequency and intensity of storms in the Pacific.

Early Life

Joseph J. Urusemal was born on 19 March 1952, on Woleai, one of the Yap islands in the US-administered Trust Territory of the Pacific Islands (TPPI). He attended Xavier High School in the Truk islands and graduated from Rockhurst College, Kansas City, Missouri, USA with a BA in administration of justice in 1973. Urusemal then worked for the government of Jackson County for six years. In 1982 he returned to Yap, which in 1979 had become part of the Federated States of Micronesia (FSM), and worked as a teacher at the Outer Islands High School. He also served on the education steering committee.

In 1987 Urusemal was elected Yap States' representative to the FSM Congress. In 1991 he was promoted to floor leader in the congress and held membership of the standing committees for health, education and social affairs, resources and development, transportation and communication and judiciary and government operations. He was elected president by congress on 11 May 2003, succeeding Leo Falcam, who had held office since 1999.

Career in Office

Seven months after Urusemal took office a renewed Compact of Free Association with the USA was signed into law. Its terms ensured the survival of US military bases in the FSM in return for financial assistance worth around US$3·5bn. to the FSM and the Marshall Islands. Urusemal, who has highlighted the need to lessen the FSM's dependency on foreign aid, has focused on developing tourism and improving commercial links with Japan and Australia. He has pledged to oversee the reform and increased accountability of the Chuuk State (formerly Truk) administration, noted for financial and administrative crises for several years.

INTERNATIONAL RELATIONS

Micronesia is a member of the UN, Asian Development Bank, Pacific Community (formerly the South Pacific Commission) and the Pacific Islands Forum.

ECONOMY

Currency

US currency is used. Foreign exchange reserves were US$83m. and total money supply was US$19m. in May 2002.

Budget

US compact funds are an annual US$100m. Revenue (2001–02), US$160m.; expenditure, US$155m.

Performance

Real GDP growth was 2·5% in 2000 and 0·9% in 2001. In 2004 total GDP was US$0·2bn.

Banking and Finance

There are three commercial banks: Bank of Guam, Bank of Hawaii and Bank of the Federated States of Micronesia. There is also a Federated States of Micronesia Development Bank and a regulatory Banking Board.

ENERGY AND NATURAL RESOURCES

Electricity

Capacity (1995), 38,500 kW.

Minerals

The islands have few mineral deposits except for high-grade phosphates.

Agriculture

Agriculture consists mainly of subsistence farming: coconuts, breadfruit, bananas, sweet potatoes and cassava. A small amount of crops are produced for export, including copra, tropical fruits, peppers and taro. Production (2000, in 1,000 tonnes): coconuts, 140; copra, 18; cassava, 12; sweet potatoes, 3; bananas, 2. Livestock (2000): pigs, 32,000; cattle, 14,000; goats, 4,000. In 2001 there were 4,000 ha. of arable land and 32,000 ha. of permanent crops.

Fisheries

In 2001 the catch amounted to approximately 18,062 tonnes, almost entirely from marine waters. Fishing licence fees were US$20m. in 1993 and are a primary revenue source.

INDUSTRY

The chief industries are construction, fish processing, tourism and handicrafts (items from shell, wood and pearl).

Labour

Two-thirds of the labour force are government employees. In 1994, 8,092 people worked in public administration and 7,375 in agriculture, fisheries and farming out of a total labour force of 27,573. The unemployment rate was 15·2%.

INTERNATIONAL TRADE

Imports and Exports

Total imports (2002), US$104·3m.; exports, US$14·4m. Main import suppliers, 2002: USA (excluding Guam), 42·2%; Guam, 20·2%; Japan, 10·6%. Main export markets, 2002: USA (excluding Guam), 29·0%; Japan, 18·7%; Guam, 7·9%. The main imports are foodstuffs and beverages, manufactured goods, machinery and equipment. Main exports: copra, bananas, black pepper, fish and garments.

COMMUNICATIONS

Roads

In 1999 there were 240 km of roads (42 km paved).

Civil Aviation

There are international airports on Pohnpei, Chuuk, Yap and Kosrae. Services are provided by Continental Airlines. In 2003 there were international flights to Guam, Honolulu, Manila, the Marshall Islands and Palau in addition to domestic services. There were five airports in 1996 (four paved).

Shipping

The main ports are Kolonia (Pohnpei), Colonia (Yap), Lepukos (Chuuk), Okat and Lelu (Kosrae). In 2002 merchant shipping totalled 13,000 GRT.

Telecommunications

Micronesia had 10,100 telephone subscribers in 2001, or 86·7 per 1,000 population. Mobile phone subscribers numbered 1,800 in 2002. There were 500 fax machines in 1998. The islands are interconnected by shortwave radiotelephone. There are four earth stations linked to the Intelsat satellite system. There were 6,000 Internet users in 2002.

Postal Services

All four states have postal services.

SOCIAL INSTITUTIONS

Justice

There is a Supreme Court headed by the Chief Justice with two other judges, and a State Court in each of the four states with 13 judges in total.

Education

In 2001–02 there were 26,440 pupils in primary schools; 7,446 pupils in high schools; and 799 students (1999) at the College of

Micronesia in Pohnpei. The Micronesia Maritime and Fisheries Academy in Yap (established in 1990) provides education and training in fisheries technology at secondary and tertiary levels.

In 2001–02 total expenditure on education came to 6·7% of GNP.

Health

In 1994 there were four hospitals with 325 beds. There were 76 physicians, 16 dentists and 368 nurses in 1999.

RELIGION

The population is predominantly Christian. Yap is mainly Roman Catholic; Protestantism is prevalent elsewhere.

CULTURE

Broadcasting

There were five radio and six TV stations in 1996. There were 22,000 radio sets in 1996 and 2,450 TV receivers (colour by NTSC) in 2001.

Tourism

In 2001 there were 15,000 visitors, bringing in US$13m. in tourist revenue.

DIPLOMATIC REPRESENTATIVES

Of the United Kingdom in Micronesia
Ambassador: Peter Beckingham (resides in Manila, Philippines).

Of Micronesia in the USA (1725 N St., NW, Washington, D.C., 20036)
Ambassador: Jesse B. Marehalau.

Of the USA in Micronesia (POB 1286, Kolonia, Pohnpei)
Ambassador: Suzanne K. Hale.

Of Micronesia to the United Nations
Ambassador: Masao Nakayama.

FURTHER READING

Wuerch, W. L. and Ballendorf, D. A., *Historical Dictionary of Guam and Micronesia.* Metuchen (NJ), 1995

MOLDOVA

Republica Moldova

Capital: Chișinău
Population projection, 2010: 4·16m.
GDP per capita, 2003: (PPP$) 1,510
HDI/world rank: 0·671/115

KEY HISTORICAL EVENTS

In Dec. 1991 Moldova became a member of the CIS, a decision ratified by parliament in April 1994. Fighting took place in 1992 between government forces and separatists in the (largely Russian and Ukrainian) area east of the River Nistru (Transnistria). An agreement signed by the presidents of Moldova and Russia on 21 July 1992 brought to an end the armed conflict and established a 'security zone' controlled by peacekeeping forces from Russia, Moldova and Transnistria. On 21 Oct. 1994 a Moldo-Russian agreement obliged Russian troops to withdraw from the territory of Moldova over three years but the agreement was not ratified by the Russian Duma. On 8 May 1997 an agreement between Transnistria and the Moldovan government to end the separatist conflict stipulated that Transnistria would remain part of Moldova as it was territorially constituted in Jan. 1990. In 1997 some 7,000 Russian troops were stationed in Transnistria. In the autumn of 1999 Ion Sturza's centre-right coalition collapsed, along with privatization plans for the wine and tobacco industries. Communist President Vladimir Voronin, who was elected in 2001, has proposed giving the Russian language official status and joining the Russia–Belarus union.

TERRITORY AND POPULATION

Moldova is bounded in the east and south by Ukraine and on the west by Romania. The area is 33,848 sq. km (13,067 sq.

miles). In 2005 the estimated population was 4,206,000 (52·2% female).

The UN gives a projected population for 2010 of 4·16m.

In 2003, 53·9% of the population lived in rural areas. At the last census, in 1989, the population was 4,335,360. Ethnicity (2000): Moldovans accounted for 48·2%, Ukrainians 13·8%, Russians 12·9%, Bulgarians 8·2%, Roma (Gypsy) 6·2%, Gagauz 4·2% and others 6·5%.

Apart from Chișinău, the capital (population of 661,000 in 2003), major towns are Tiraspol (185,000 in 1993), Bălți (146,000 in 2003) and Tighina (133,000 in 1992). The official Moldovan language (i.e. Romanian) was written in Cyrillic prior to the restoration of the Roman alphabet in 1989. It is spoken by 62% of the population; the use of other languages (Russian, Gagauz) is safeguarded by the Constitution.

SOCIAL STATISTICS

2001: births, 36,448; deaths, 40,075. Rates, 2001 (per 1,000 population): births, 10·0; deaths, 11·0. In 2001 the most popular age range for marrying was 20–24 for both males and females. Life expectancy at birth in 2003 was 63·9 years for males and 71·3 years for females. Annual population growth rate, 1992–2002, –0·2%. Infant mortality, 2001, 27 per 1,000 live births; fertility rate, 2001, 1·5 births per woman. By the end of 1998 more than 46% of the population were classified as living in absolute poverty.

CLIMATE

The climate is temperate, with warm summers, crisp, sunny autumns and cold winters with snow. Chișinău, Jan. –7°C, Jul. 20°C. Annual rainfall 677 mm.

CONSTITUTION AND GOVERNMENT

A declaration of republican sovereignty was adopted in June 1990 and in Aug. 1991 the republic declared itself independent. A new Constitution came into effect on 27 Aug. 1994, which defines Moldova as an 'independent, democratic and unitary state'. At a referendum on 6 March 1994 turnout was 75·1%; 95·4% of votes cast favoured 'an independent Moldova within its 1990 borders'. The referendum (and the Feb. parliamentary elections) were not held by the authorities in Transnistria. In a further referendum on 4 June 1999, on whether to switch from a parliamentary system to a presidential one, turnout was 58% with the majority of the votes cast being in favour of the change.

Parliament (*Parlamentul*) has 101 seats and is elected for four-year terms. There is a 4% threshold for election; votes falling below this are re-distributed to successful parties. The *President* is now elected for four-year terms by parliament, after the constitution had been amended to abolish direct presidential elections.

The 1994 Constitution makes provision for the autonomy of Transnistria and the Gagauz (Gagauzi Yeri) region. Work began in July 2003 on the drafting of a new constitution to resolve the conflict between Moldova and Transnistria.

Transnistria. In the predominantly Russian-speaking areas of Transnistria a self-styled 'Dniester Republic' was established in Sept. 1991, and approved by a local referendum in Dec. 1991. A Russo-Moldovan agreement of 21 July 1992 provided for a special statute for Transnistria and a guarantee of self-determination should Moldova unite with Romania. The population in 2001 was 634,000. Romanian here is still written in the Cyrillic alphabet. At a referendum on 24 Dec. 1995, 81% of votes cast were in favour of adopting a new constitution proclaiming independence.

On 17 June 1996 the Moldovan government granted Transnistria a special status as 'a state-territorial formation in the form of a republic within Moldova's internationally recognized border'.

Elections for chief regional executive were held on 9 Dec. 2001. Turnout was 64%. Igor Smirnov (b. 1941) was re-elected for a third five-year term against two opponents winning nearly 82% of votes cast.

At elections to the Supreme Council held on 11 Dec. 2005, which were not internationally recognized as legitimate, the Renovation Party and its allies won 29 of 43 seats and the Republic Party 13.

Gagauz Yeri. This was created an autonomous territorial unit by Moldovan legislation of 13 Jan. 1995. In 2000 the population was 172,000. There is a 35-member *Popular Assembly* directly elected for four-year terms and headed by a *Governor*, who is a member of the Moldovan cabinet. At the elections of 28 May and 11 June 1995 turnout was 68%.

Governor. Gheorghe Tabunscic; b. 1939.

National Anthem

The Romanian anthem was replaced in 1994 by a traditional tune, 'Lîmbă noastră' ('Our Tongue'); words by Alexei Mateevici, tune by Alexandru Cristi.

RECENT ELECTIONS

At the parliamentary elections held on 6 March 2005 the Party of Communists of the Republic of Moldova (PCRM) won 56 seats with 46·0% of the votes, the Democratic Moldova bloc 34 with 28·5% and the Christian Democratic People's Party 11 with 9·1%. Turnout was 63.7%.

Following the parliamentary elections of March 2005 parliament re-elected Vladimir Voronin as president on 4 April 2005. Voronin received 75 votes against one for another communist candidate, Gheorghe Duca.

CURRENT ADMINISTRATION

President: Vladimir Voronin; b. 1941 (PCRM; sworn in 7 April 2001 and re-elected 4 April 2005).

In March 2006 the government comprised:

Prime Minister: Vasile Tarlev; b. 1963 (PCRM; sworn in 19 April 2001 and reappointed 8 April 2005).

First Deputy Prime Minister: Zinaida Greceanîi.

Deputy Prime Ministers: Valerian Cristea; Andrei Stratan (also *Minister of Foreign Affairs*).

Minister of Agriculture and Food Industries: Anatolie Gorodenco. *Culture and Tourism:* Artur Cozma. *Defence:* Valeriu Plesca. *Economy and Commerce:* Valeriu Lazar. *Education, Youth and Sport:* Victor Tvircun. *Environment and Natural Resources:* Constantin Mihailescu. *Finance:* Mihail Pop. *Health and Social Protection:* Ion Ababii. *Industry and Infrastructure:* Vladimir Antosii. *Information Development:* Vladimir Molojen. *Internal Affairs:* Gheorghe Papuc. *Justice:* Victoria Iftodi. *Reintegration:* Vasile Sova. *Transport and Roads Management:* Miron Gagauz.

CURRENT LEADERS

Vladimir Voronin

Position
President

Introduction
Vladimir Voronin was chosen by parliament as Moldova's president following the victory of the Party of Communists of the Republic of Moldova (PCRM) in the Feb. 2001 parliamentary elections. The former Soviet Communist Party bureaucrat is committed to 'modern socialism' by forging closer ties with Russia and increasing the role of the state in improving the economy, which has shrunk by two-thirds since 1991.

Early life
Vladimir Nicolae Voronin was born on 25 May 1941 in the village of Corjova, Chişinău county. He attended the technical co-operatist secondary school in Chişinău and graduated from the USSR's extramural institute of food industry in 1971, having worked as the director of the bread factory in Dubosari from 1966–71. For the next decade, he worked in the regional committee of the PCRM, heading the town councils of Dubosari and Ungheni. Promotion to the central committee of the party came in 1983. In 1985, the year in which Mikhail Gorbachev became leader of the USSR, Voronin was elected as a member of the supreme council of the Moldovan Soviet Socialist Republic (MSSR). Gorbachev's reform programme reversed the suppression of national characteristics within the USSR and by the late 1980s the Romanian language was in common and official use in Moldova. In 1990, when Voronin served as the minister of internal affairs of the MSSR, Moldova achieved *de facto* independence. Full independence followed the dramatic collapse of the USSR in Aug. 1991.

In late 1991 an ex-communist reformer, Mircea Snegur, won an election for the presidency. Four months later Moldova achieved formal recognition as an independent state at the United Nations. But independence brought a guerrilla war to the Transnistria region in the north and east of the country, populated by many ethnic Russians and Ukrainians who feared a Moldovan merger with Romania. A ceasefire in 1992 brought limited autonomy to the region, and Russian 'peacekeeping' troops were stationed there.

Voronin rose through the ranks of the PCRM, becoming first secretary to the central committee in 1994, the year of Moldova's first parliamentary election. Snegur's Agrarian Democratic Party (ADP) won a majority but was subsequently wracked by infighting. In Dec. 1995 residents of Transnistria overwhelmingly voted for independence from Moldova, although the referendum was considered illegal by the central government. Voronin contested a presidential run-off election against Snegur in Dec. 1996 but the eventual victor was Petru Lucinschi, a former communist running as an independent.

In May 1997 Moldova and Transnistria signed an agreement to keep Moldova a single state. During the March 1998 legislative elections the PCRM received the biggest share of the vote but was unable to form a government, leading to a series of short-lived, non-affiliated governments. In 2000 parliament failed to elect a successor to President Lucinschi, leading to early general elections in Feb. 2001. The PCRM won over 50% of the vote and parliament elected Voronin as president on 4 April.

Career in Office
Voronin used his inaugural address to criticize his predecessors, saying they had reduced Moldova to humanitarian catastrophe and dire poverty. He promised major reform in three areas: modernization of the country's ancient administrative structures, liberalization of the economy and the creation of a 'civil society' by strengthening institutions and organizations operating outside state control. Voronin was initially broadly pro-Russian (Russian language lessons having being reintroduced as compulsory in Moldovan schools), but his government has more recently made a fundamental policy change and adopted a pro-European Union position. At the March 2005 parliamentary elections the PCRM was returned to power but with a reduced majority.

The latest attempt to resolve the thorny Transnistria issue was a proposed (June 2002) federal system under which Transnistria and the Turkic enclave of Gagauz Yeri would enjoy constitutional autonomy. However, in the face of violent popular protest, the Moldovan government backed down in Nov. 2003. Despite repeated calls for their departure, Russian military forces remain in Transnistria. Moldova continues to face severe economic problems, especially after the failure of the 2003 harvest (with agriculture, including wine, fruit and tobacco, accounting for nearly a third of GDP). Relations with the IMF and the World Bank have been difficult and the country seems likely to remain the poorest in Europe.

DEFENCE

Conscription is up to 18 months. In 2003 military expenditure totalled US$150m. (US$35 per capita), representing 2·4% of GDP.

Russian troops remained in Transnistria after Moldova gained independence, but in Nov. 1999 the Organization for Security and Co-operation in Europe (OSCE) passed a resolution at its summit requiring Russia to withdraw its troops to Russia by Dec. 2002, unconditionally and under international observation. This deadline was extended to Dec. 2003 but around 1,500 troops remained in the region in 2006.

Army

Personnel, 2002, 5,560 (5,200 conscripts). There is also a paramilitary Interior Ministry force of 2,500, riot police numbering 900 and combined forces reserves of some 66,000.

Air Force

Personnel (including air defence), 2002, 1,400.

INTERNATIONAL RELATIONS

Moldova is a member of the UN, WTO, OSCE, CIS, the Council of Europe, CEI, Danube Commission, BSEC, IOM, International Organization of the Francophonie and the NATO Partnership for Peace.

ECONOMY

Agriculture accounted for 24·1% of GDP in 2002, industry 23·2% and services 52·7%.

Overview

A privatization programme started in 1993. By the end of 2000, 92% of housing had been privatized. The sale of Moldtelecom and its stake in the energy sector are priorities.

Currency

A new unit of currency, the *leu* (MDL), replaced the rouble in Nov. 1993. Inflation was 12·5% in 2004, down from a peak of 2,198% in the early 1990s. Foreign exchange reserves were US$219m. in June 2002 and total money supply 2,607m. lei.

Budget

Total revenue and total expenditure (in 1m. lei), years ending 31 Dec.:

	1998	1999	2000	2001	2002
Revenue	2,808·8	3,064·0	4,033·5	4,078·5	4,977·6
Expenditure	3,271·6	3,660·2	4,738·6	4,335·9	5,756·5

Performance

Moldova's economy has been in dire straits although it is now making a strong recovery. Economic growth was negative in 1998 at −6·5% and again in 1999, at −3·4%. However, more recently there has been growth of 6·6% in 2003 and 7·3% in 2004.

Between 1990 and 1996 the average annual real growth in GNP per capita was −16·8%. Of all the former Soviet republics Moldova's economy, along with that of Georgia, has suffered the most since 1989 when political and economic reforms took place across central and eastern Europe. In 2002 the level of GDP was estimated to be only 38% of that in 1989. Total GDP was US$2·6bn. in 2004 (excluding Transnistria). The private sector accounts for over 50% of official GDP.

Banking and Finance

The central bank and bank of issue is the National Bank (*Governor*, Leonid Talmaci). At June 2002 there were 21 commercial banks and one savings bank. There is a stock exchange in Chişinău.

ENERGY AND NATURAL RESOURCES

Environment

Moldova's carbon dioxide emissions from the consumption and flaring of fossil fuels in 2002 were the equivalent of 2·3 tonnes per capita.

Electricity

Installed capacity in 2000 was 1·0m. kW. Production was about 3·31bn. kWh in 2000; consumption per capita in 2000 was an estimated 1,400 kWh.

Minerals

There are deposits of lignite, phosphorites, gypsum and building materials.

Agriculture

Agriculture employs about 700,000 people. Land under cultivation in 1997 was 2·5m. ha., of which 0·3m. ha. was accounted for by private subsidiary agriculture and 6,700 ha. (in 1993) by commercial agriculture in 3,100 farms. In 2001 there were 1·82m. ha. of arable land and 355,000 ha. of permanent crops. Agriculture is Moldova's biggest exporter, accounting for 75% of total exports.

Output of main agricultural products (in 1,000 tonnes) in 2000: sugarbeets, 1,800; maize, 1,091; wheat, 770; grapes, 450; potatoes, 342; sunflower seeds, 280; wine, 240; tomatoes, 189; barley, 152. Livestock (2000): 416,000 cattle, 974,000 sheep, 705,000 pigs, 14m. chickens. Livestock products, 2000 (in 1,000 tonnes): milk, 571; meat, 88; eggs, 32.

Forestry

In 2000 forests covered 325,000 ha., or 9·9% of the total land area. Timber production in 2001 was 57,000 cu. metres.

Fisheries

The catch in 2001 (exclusively freshwater fish) was estimated at 387 tonnes.

INDUSTRY

There are canning plants, wine-making plants, woodworking and metallurgical factories, a factory of ferro-concrete building materials, footwear, dairy products and textile plants. Manufacturing accounted for 18·2% of GDP in 2001. Production (in tonnes): crude steel (2000), 909,000; cement (2001), 158,000; raw sugar (2002), 125,000; wheat flour (2001), 122,000; canned fruit and vegetables (2001), 86,300; footwear (2001), 1·1m. pairs; 9·4bn. cigarettes (2001); 25,000 washing machines (2001); wine (2001), 155·0m. litres.

Labour

In 2001 the labour force totalled 1,616,700 (810,100 males). A total of 1,499,000 persons were in employment in 2001, including 763,400 engaged in agriculture, hunting, forestry and fisheries, 144,500 in wholesale and retail trade/repair of motor vehicles, motorcycles and personal and household goods, 136,800 in manufacturing and 100,900 in education. In 2002 the unemployment rate was 6·8%.

INTERNATIONAL TRADE

Foreign debt was US$1,349m. in 2002.

Imports and Exports

In 2002 imports (f.o.b.) were valued at US$1,038·1m. (US$878·6m. in 2001) and exports (f.o.b.) at US$659·8m. (US$567·3m. in 2001). Chief import sources in 2002 were: Ukraine, 20·4%; Russia, 15·3%; Romania, 11·4%; Germany, 9·2%. Main export markets in 2002 were: Russia, 35·4%; Italy, 9·1%; Ukraine, 9·1%; Romania, 8·4%. Moldova's leading imports are mineral products and fuel, machinery and equipment, chemicals and textiles. The main export commodity is wine, ahead of tobacco. Fruit and vegetables, textiles and footwear, and machinery are also significant exports.

COMMUNICATIONS

Roads
There were 12,719 km of roads in 2002 (86·3% paved). Passenger cars in use in 2002 numbered 268,822 (74·3 per 1,000 inhabitants), there were 46,277 trucks and vans, 15,777 buses and coaches, and 78,814 motorcycles and mopeds. In 1999 there were 2,669 road accidents resulting in 395 deaths.

Rail
Total length in 2000 was 1,139 km of 1,520 mm gauge. Passenger-km travelled in 2000 came to 315m. and freight tonne-km to 1,538m.

Civil Aviation
The main Moldovan-based airline is Air Moldova, which had flights in 2003 to Amman, Amsterdam, Athens, Bucharest, İstanbul, Larnaca, Moscow, Paris, Prague, Rome and Vienna. In 2000 the airport at Chişinău handled 254,234 passengers (all on international flights) and 2,159 tonnes of freight. In 1999 scheduled airline traffic of Moldovan-based carriers flew 2·3m. km, carrying 43,000 passengers (all on international flights).

Shipping
In 1993, 0·3m. passengers and 0·3m. tonnes of freight were carried on inland waterways.

Telecommunications
There were 864,200 telephone subscribers in 2001 (196·8 per 1,000 persons) and 77,000 PCs in use in 2002 (17·5 per 1,000 persons). There were 338,200 mobile phone subscribers in 2002—up from just 2,200 in 1997—and 900 fax machines in use. In 2002 there were 150,000 Internet users. Privatization of the state-owned telecommunications company, Moldtelecom, is a priority for the government. A majority stake offer from MGTS, Moscow's main telephone company, failed in Nov. 2002.

Postal Services
In 2003 there were 1,270 post offices.

SOCIAL INSTITUTIONS

Justice
47,515 crimes were reported in 1994. The population in penal institutions in Jan. 2003 was 10,903 (301 per 100,000 of national population). The death penalty was abolished for all crimes in 1995.

Education
In 2000–01 there were 77,539 children and 8,508 teachers in pre-schools; 236,763 pupils and 11,648 teachers in primary schools; and 413,029 pupils and 30,518 teachers in secondary schools. There were 102,825 students (7,268 academic staff) in tertiary education in 2000–01. In 1996–97 there were 97 vocational secondary schools, 54 technical colleges and nine higher educational institutions including the state university. Adult literacy rate in 2003 was 96·2% (male, 97·5%; female, 95·0%).

In 2000–01 total expenditure on education came to 3·8% of GNP and represented 15·0% of total government expenditure.

Health
In Jan. 1996 there were 312 hospitals with 54,300 beds, a provision of 125 per 10,000 inhabitants. In 1998 there were 14,959 physicians, 1,761 dentists, 37,355 nurses, 2,885 pharmacists and 3,723 midwives.

Welfare
There were 649,000 age pensioners and 267,000 other pensioners in Jan. 1994.

RELIGION
Religious affiliation in 2001: Romanian Orthodox, 1·26m.; Russian (Moldovan) Orthodox, 342,000.

CULTURE

World Heritage Sites
Moldova has one site on the UNESCO World Heritage List: the Struve Geodetic Arc (inscribed in 2005). The Arc is a chain of survey triangulations spanning from Norway to the Black Sea that helped establish the exact shape and size of the earth and is shared as a UNESCO site with nine other countries.

Broadcasting
The government authority Radioteleviziunea Nationala is responsible for broadcasting. There are two national radio programmes, a Radio Moscow relay, and a foreign service, Radio Moldova International. There is a national state TV service and a private TV network. Romanian and Russian channels are also broadcast. There were 1·3m. television receivers in 2001 and 3·3m. radio receivers in 2000.

Cinema
There were 49 cinemas in 1999, with a total attendance for the year of 100,000.

Press
Moldova has 567 newspapers and magazines. Of these 323 are published in Moldovan, four in English and the rest in Russian.

Tourism
In 2002 there were 18,000 foreign tourists, spending US$47m.

Libraries
There is a National Library and around 1,775 public libraries.

Museums and Galleries
There are 83 museums in Moldova.

DIPLOMATIC REPRESENTATIVES
Of Moldova in the United Kingdom (resides in Brussels)
Ambassador: Mariana Durleşteanu.

Of the United Kingdom in Moldova (ASITO Building, Office 320, 57/1 Banulescu-Bodoni Str, Chişinau 2005)
Ambassador: Bernard Whiteside, MBE.

Of Moldova in the USA (2101 S St., NW, Washington, D.C., 20008)
Ambassador: Mihail Manoli.

Of the USA in Moldova (103 Strada Alexei Matveevici, Chişinau)
Ambassador: Heather M. Hodges.

Of Moldova to the United Nations
Ambassador: Vsevolod Grigore.

Of Moldova to the European Union
Ambassador: Mihai Popov.

FURTHER READING
Gribincea, M., *Agricultural Collectivization in Moldavia.* East European Monographs, Columbia Univ. Press, 1996
King, C., *Post-Soviet Moldova: A Borderland in Transition.* International Specialized Book Service, Portland, Oregon, 1997.—*The Moldovans: Romania, Russia, and the Politics of Culture.* Hoover Institution Press, Stanford, 2000
Mitrasca, M., *Moldova: A Romanian Province Under Russian Rule: Diplomatic History from the Archives of the Great Powers.* Algora Publishing, New York, 2002

National Statistical Office: Department for Statistics and Sociology, MD-2028, Hîncesti 53, Chişinău.
Website: http://www.statistica.md

MONACO

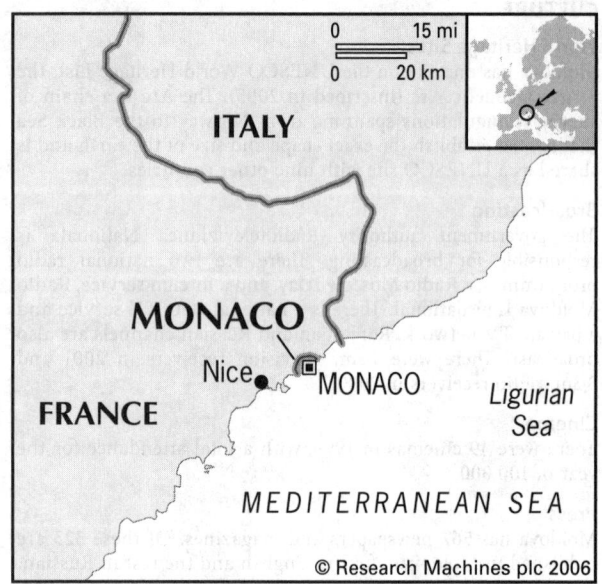

Principauté de Monaco

Capital: Monaco
Population, 2000: 32,000
GDP per capita: not available

KEY HISTORICAL EVENTS

Monaco's natural harbour was settled by Phoenicians, Greeks and Ligurians and later by Saracens. A fortress, built where the palace now stands, was captured by the Grimaldi family of Genoa in 1297. It was passed on through the male line until 1731, when control of Monaco passed to Louise Hippolyte, daughter of Antoine I and wife of Jacques de Goyon Matignon, who took the name of Grimaldi. The Principality was placed under the protection of the Kingdom of Sardinia by the Treaty of Vienna in 1815, and under that of France in 1861. A constitution, signed in 1911, was the first move away from an absolute monarchy. Prince Rainier III succeeded his grandfather, Louis II, in 1949 and ruled the Principality until his death on 6 April 2005.

TERRITORY AND POPULATION

Monaco is bounded in the south by the Mediterranean and elsewhere by France (Department of Alpes Maritimes). The area is 197 ha. (1·97 sq. km). The Principality is divided into four districts: Monaco-Ville, la Condamine, Monte-Carlo and Fontvieille. Population (2000 census), 32,020; there were 6,089 Monegasques (19%), 10,229 French (32%) and 6,410 Italian (20%).

The official language is French.

SOCIAL STATISTICS

2004: births, 825; deaths, 525; marriages, 171; divorces, 82. Rates per 1,000 population, 2000: birth, 23·7; death, 17·1; marriage, 5·0; divorce, 2·6. Annual population growth rate, 2000–04, 0·9%; fertility rate, 2004, 1·9 births per woman.

CLIMATE

A Mediterranean climate, with mild moist winters and hot dry summers. Monaco, Jan. 50°F (10°C), July 74°F (23·3°C). Annual rainfall 30" (758 mm).

CONSTITUTION AND GOVERNMENT

On 17 Dec. 1962 a new constitution was promulgated which maintains the hereditary monarchy.

The reigning Prince is **Albert II**, b. 14 March 1958, son of Prince Rainier III, 1923–2005, and Grace Kelly, 1929–1982. Prince Albert succeeded his father Rainier III, who died on 6 April 2005.

Sisters of the Prince. Princess Caroline Louise Marguerite, b. 23 Jan. 1957; married Philippe Junot on 28 June 1978, divorced 9 Oct. 1980; married Stefano Casiraghi on 29 Dec. 1983 (died 3 Oct. 1990); married Prince Ernst of Hanover on 23 Jan 1999. *Offspring:* Andrea, b. 8 June 1984; Charlotte, b. 3 Aug. 1986; Pierre, b. 7 Sept. 1987; Alexandra, b. 20 July 1999. Princess Stéphanie Marie Elisabeth, b. 1 Feb. 1965, married Daniel Ducruet on 1 July 1995, divorced 4 Oct. 1996; married Adans López Peres on 12 Sept. 2003; separated 2004. *Offspring:* Louis, b. 27 Nov. 1992; Pauline, b. 4 May 1994; Camille, b. 15 July 1998.

Prince Rainier III renounced the principle of divine right. Executive power is exercised jointly by the Prince and a five-member *Council of government*, headed by a Minister of State (a French citizen). A 24-member *National Council* is elected for five-year terms.

The constitution can be modified only with the approval of the National Council. Laws of 1992, 2003 and 2005 permit Monegasque women to give their nationality to their children.

National Anthem

'Principauté Monaco ma patrie' ('Principality of Monaco my fatherland'); words by T. Bellando de Castro, tune by C. Albrecht.

RECENT ELECTIONS

In parliamentary elections held on 9 Feb. 2003 the opposition Union for Monaco won 21 of 24 seats against 3 for the ruling National Democratic Union. Turnout was about 80%.

CURRENT ADMINISTRATION

Chief of State: Prince Albert II.

In March 2006 the cabinet comprised:

Minister of State: Jean-Paul Proust; b. 1940 (sworn in 1 June 2005).

Minister of Finance and Economics: Franck Biancheri. *Environmental Affairs and Town Planning:* Gilles Tonelli. *Social Affairs and Health:* Denis Ravera. *Interior:* Philippe Deslandes. *President of the National Council:* Stéphane Valeri.

Government Website: http://www.monaco.gouv.mc

CURRENT LEADERS

Albert II

Position
Prince

Introduction
Albert II became ruler of Monaco on 6 April 2005 following the death of his father, Prince Rainier III, who had ruled the principality for 56 years. Albert II is expected to maintain the status quo, upholding the low-tax regime that has made Monaco a haven for the super-rich.

Early Life
Albert Alexandre Louis Pierre Grimaldi was born in Monaco on 14 March 1958, the second child and only son of Prince Rainier

III and Grace Kelly, a US cinema actress. He attended the Lycée Albert Ier, the principality's sole secondary school, where he developed a passion for sport. Having received his baccalaureate diploma in 1976, Albert enrolled the following year at Amherst College in Massachusetts, USA, and graduated with a degree in political science in 1981. From Sept. 1981–April 1982 he served in the French Navy as a sub-lieutenant on the aircraft carrier *Jeanne d'Arc*. On 14 Sept. 1982 his mother was killed in a car crash in the mountains near Monaco. Subsequently, he became vice-president of the Princess Grace-USA Foundation, which grants scholarships to talented young musicians, actors and dancers. In the same year he also became president of the Monaco Red Cross

During the mid-1980s Albert undertook work experience at an investment bank and an international law firm in New York, as well as the French luxury goods group, Moet-Hennessy, in Paris. Back in Monaco he chaired the principality's prestigious Yacht Club, the International Television Festival and Monaco's Athletic Federation. Albert also became increasingly involved in the Olympic movement, both as an administrator (as a member of the International Olympic Committee in 1985 and president of Monaco's Olympic Committee in 1993) and competitor (in the principality's bobsleigh team at four Winter Olympics between 1988 and 2002).

During the 1990s he began to increase his involvement in the day-to-day administration of Monaco and in 1997 organized the 700th anniversary celebrations of the Grimaldi family's control over the principality. He also assisted his father and the government in preparing reports that strongly denied allegations by French parliamentarians in 2000 that Monaco's lax policies had facilitated money laundering.

Long described in the press as the world's 'most eligible bachelor', Albert's unmarried status became a matter of political concern, casting doubt on the succession of the Grimaldi family and the independence of the principality. A change to the constitution was formulated in April 2002, however, allowing the throne to continue through the female line. On 31 March 2005 the Palace of Monaco announced that Albert would take over the duties of his father as Regent, after Prince Rainier III, who had been admitted to hospital, was no longer able to rule. Following the death of his father on 6 April 2005, he became Sovereign Prince of Monaco, and was enthroned on 12 July.

Career in Office
In his first public statement as Prince Albert II, he said that the death of his father, who had governed for 56 years, had left the people of the principality feeling orphaned and united in a profound sense of loss. He did not make reference to the future direction of policy, but analysts expect him to retain the famously low-tax regime and continue to develop tourism, as well as nurturing Monaco's precision engineering, fish canning, banking and pharmaceutical industries. He is also expected to rule in a more consensual style than his father.

INTERNATIONAL RELATIONS

Monegasque relations with France are based on conventions of 1963. French citizens are treated as if in France. Monaco is a member of the UN, Council of Europe, OSCE and the International Organization of the Francophonie.

ECONOMY

Currency
On 1 Jan. 1999 the euro (EUR) replaced the French franc as the legal currency in Monaco; irrevocable conversion rate 6·55957 French francs to one euro. The euro, which consists of 100 cents, has been in circulation since 1 Jan. 2002. There are seven euro notes in different colours and sizes denominated in 500, 200, 100, 50, 20, 10 and 5 euros, and eight coins denominated in 2 and

1 euros, then 50, 20, 10, 5, 2 and 1 cents. On the introduction of the euro there was a 'dual circulation' period before the franc ceased to be legal tender on 17 Feb. 2002.

Budget
Revenues in 2004 totalled €636·18m. and expenditures €694·84m.

Performance
Monaco does not publish annual income information. However, the principality's turnover increased from €9,194·42m. in 2003 to €9,815·20m. in 2004, a growth rate of 6·75%.

Banking and Finance
There were 43 banks in 2004 of which 19 were Monegasque banks.

ENERGY AND NATURAL RESOURCES

Electricity
Electricity is imported from France. 503 GWh were supplied to 24,178 customers in 2004. In 2001 output capacity was 83 MW.

Oil and Gas
In 2004, 61 GWh of gas were supplied to 3,935 customers; output capacity was 21 MW.

Water
Total consumption (2004), 5·38m. cu. metres.

INDUSTRY

The main industry is tourism. There is some production of cosmetics, pharmaceuticals, glassware, electrical goods and precision instruments.

Labour
There were 42,637 persons employed in Jan. 2004. 38,773 worked in the private sector; 3,864 in the public sector. 26,017 French citizens worked in Monaco in 2004.

INTERNATIONAL TRADE

Imports and Exports
There is a customs union with France. Imports for 2004 totalled €512m.; exports, €528m. Main imports: pharmaceuticals, perfumes, clothing, paper, synthetic and non-metallic products, and building materials.

COMMUNICATIONS

Roads
There were estimated to be 50 km of roads in 2001. In 2004 there were 33,275 vehicles. Monaco has the densest network of roads of any country in the world. In 2004, 5,141,964 people travelled by bus.

Rail
The 1·7 km of main line passing through the country are operated by the French National Railways (SNCF). In 2004, 3,953,859 people arrived at or departed from Monaco railway station.

Civil Aviation
There are helicopter flights to Nice with Heli Air Monaco and Heli Inter. Helicopter movements (2004) at the Heliport of Monaco (Fontvieille), 37,521; the number of passengers carried was 112,379. The nearest airport is at Nice in France.

Shipping
In 2004 there were 3,829 vessels registered, of which 12 were over 100 tonnes. 2,636 yachts put in to the port of Monaco and 1,193 at Fontvieille in 2004. 178 liners put in to port in Monaco; 10,581 people embarked, 10,195 disembarked and 104,202 were in transit.

Telecommunications

In 2004 there were 33,400 land-based telephone lines and 16,261 mobile phone subscribers. Internet users numbered 16,000 in 2002.

Postal Services

24·19m. items were posted and 27·59m. items were delivered by the Post Office in 2004.

SOCIAL INSTITUTIONS

Justice

There are the following courts: *Tribunal Suprême, Cour de Révision, Cour d'Appel*, a Correctional Tribunal, a Work Tribunal, a Tribunal of the First Instance, two Arbitration Commissions for Rents (one commercial, one domestic), courts for Work-related Accidents and Supervision, a *Juge de Paix*, and a Police Tribunal. There is no death penalty.

Police

In 2004 the police force (Sûreté Publique) comprised 516 personnel. Monaco has one of the highest number of police per head of population of any country in the world.

Education

In 2004, in the public sector, there were six pre-school institutions (*écoles maternelles*) with 750 pupils; four elementary schools with 1,367 pupils; two secondary schools with 2,359 pupils. There were 277 primary teachers and 150 secondary school teachers in total in 2004. In the private sector there were two pre-schools and three primary schools with 179 and 481 pupils respectively; and one secondary school with 700 pupils. In 2005 the government allocated 5·2% of its total budget to education.

The University of Southern Europe in Monaco had 250 students in 2004.

Health

In 2005 the government allocated 6·4% of its total budget to public health. There were 191 doctors and 19 dentists in 2004 and 19 childcare nurses in 2002. There were 503 hospital beds in 2002. Monaco has the highest provision of hospital beds of any country: in 2002 there were 162 per 10,000 population.

RELIGION

90% of the resident population are Roman Catholic. There is a Roman Catholic archbishop.

CULTURE

Broadcasting

Radio Monte Carlo broadcasts FM commercial programmes in French (long- and medium-waves). Radio Monte Carlo owns 55% of *Radio Monte Carlo* Relay Station on Cyprus. The foreign service is dedicated exclusively to religious broadcasts and is maintained by voluntary contributions. It operates in 36 languages under the name 'Trans World Radio' and has relay facilities on Bonaire, West Indies; it is planning to build relay facilities in the southern parts of Africa. *Télé Monte-Carlo* broadcasts TV programmes in French, Italian and English (colour by SECAM H). There is a 30-channel cable service. There were 22,000 radio receivers in 2000 and 25,000 television receivers in 1997.

Press

Monaco had one newspaper in 2004 with a circulation of 8,000, equivalent to 247 per 1,000 inhabitants. There was one weekly magazine in 2004, one monthly newspaper, two monthly magazines, one bimonthly magazine and two quarterly magazines.

Tourism

In 2004, 250,159 foreign visitors spent a total of 695,265 nights in Monaco. The main visitors are Italians, followed by French and Americans. 58,521 people attended 389 congresses in 2004. There are three casinos run by the state, including the one at Monte Carlo attracting 0·4m. visitors a year.

DIPLOMATIC REPRESENTATIVES

British Consul-General (resident in France): Vacant.
British Honorary Consul: Eric G. F. Blair.

Consul-General for Monaco in London: Ivan Bozidar Ivanovic.

Of Monaco to the United Nations
Ambassador: Gilles Noghès.

Of Monaco to the European Union
Ambassador: Jean Pastorelli.

FURTHER READING

Journal de Monaco. Bulletin Officiel. 1858 ff.

Hudson, Grace L., *Monaco.* [Bibliography] ABC-Clio, Oxford and Santa Barbara (CA), 1991

MONGOLIA

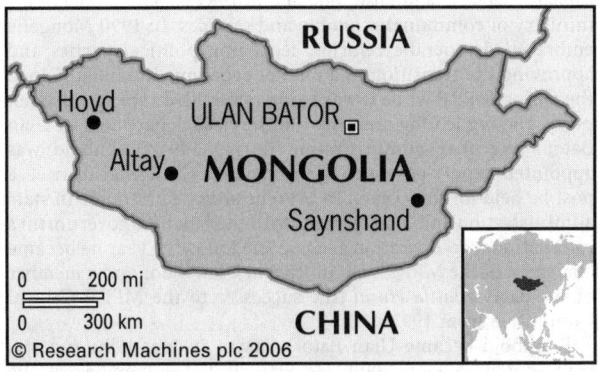

Mongol Uls

Capital: Ulan Bator
Population projection, 2010: 2·81m.
GDP per capita, 2003: (PPP$) 1,850
HDI/world rank: 0·679/114

KEY HISTORICAL EVENTS

Temujin became khan of Hamag Mongolia in 1190. Having united by conquest various Tatar and Mongolian tribes he was confirmed as 'Universal' ('Genghis', 'Chingiz') khan in 1206. The expansionist impulse of his nomadic empire (Beijing captured in 1215; Samarkand in 1220) continued after his death in 1227. Tamurlaine (died 1405) was the last of the conquering khans. In 1368 the Chinese drove the Mongols from Beijing, and for the next two centuries Sino-Mongolian relations alternated between war and trade. In 1691 Outer Mongolia accepted Manchu rule. The head of the Lamaist faith became the symbol of national identity, and his seat ('Urga', now Ulan Bator) was made the Mongolian capital. When the Manchu dynasty was overthrown in 1911 Outer Mongolia declared its independence under its spiritual ruler and turned to Russia for support against China. Soviet and Mongolian revolutionary forces set up a provisional government in March 1921. On the death of the spiritual ruler a people's republic and new constitution were proclaimed in May 1924. With Soviet help Japanese invaders were fended off during the Second World War. The Mongols then took part in the successful Soviet campaign against Inner Mongolia and Manchuria. On 5 Jan. 1946 China recognized the independence of Outer Mongolia. Until 1990 sole power was in the hands of the (Communist) Mongolian People's Revolutionary Party (MPRP), but an opposition Mongolian Democratic Party, founded in Dec. 1989, achieved tacit recognition and held its first congress in Feb. 1990. Following demonstrations and hunger-strikes, on 12 March the entire MPRP Politburo resigned and political opposition was legalized.

TERRITORY AND POPULATION

Mongolia is bounded in the north by the Russian Federation, and in the east and south and west by China. Area, 1,565,008 sq. km (604,250 sq. miles). Population (2000 census), 2,373,493 (1,195,512 females). Density, 2000, 1·5 per sq. km. The estimated population in 2005 was 2,646,000. In 2003, 56·8% of the population were urban.

The UN gives a projected population for 2010 of 2·81m.

The population is predominantly made up of Mongolian peoples (81·5% Khalkh). There is a Turkic Kazakh minority (4·3% of the population) and 20 Mongol minorities. The official language is Khalkh Mongol.

The republic is administratively divided into four municipalities—Ulan Bator, the capital (2000 population, 760,077), Darhan-Uul (83,271 in 2000), Orhon (71,525 in 2000) and Govisumber (12,230 in 2000)—and 18 provinces (*aimag*). The provinces are sub-divided into 334 districts or counties (*suums*).

SOCIAL STATISTICS

Births, 2001, 49,685; deaths, 15,999. 2001 rates: birth, 20·5 per 1,000 population; death, 6·6 per 1,000; marriage, 5·1 per 1,000; divorce, 0·3 per 1,000. Annual population growth rate, 1992–2002, 1·1%. Infant mortality rate, 2001, 61 per 1,000 live births. Expectation of life in 2003 was 62·1 years for males and 66·1 for females. Fertility rate, 2001, 2·4 births per woman.

CLIMATE

A very extreme climate, with six months of mean temperatures below freezing, but much higher temperatures occur for a month or two in summer. Rainfall is very low and limited to the months from mid-May to mid-Sept. Ulan Bator, Jan. –14°F (–25·6°C), July 61°F (16·1°C). Annual rainfall 8" (208 mm).

CONSTITUTION AND GOVERNMENT

The Constitution of 12 Feb. 1992 abolished the 'People's Democracy', introduced democratic institutions and a market economy and guarantees freedom of speech.

The *President* is directly elected for renewable four-year terms.

Since June 1992 the legislature has consisted of a single-chamber 76-seat parliament, the *Great Hural (Ulsyn Ich-Chural)*, which elects the Prime Minister.

National Anthem

'Darkhan manai khuvsgalt uls' ('Our sacred revolutionary country'); words by Tsendiyn Damdinsüren, tune by Bilegin Damdinsüren and Luvsanjamts Murjorj.

RECENT ELECTIONS

At the parliamentary elections of 27 June 2004 turnout was 76·4%. Preliminary results declared that the Mongolian People's Revolutionary Party (MPRP) gained 36 seats (72 in 2000), the Motherland Democracy (EOA, comprising the Democratic Party, the Civic Will Republican Party and the Mongol Democratic New Socialist Party) 34 seats and the Republican Party one seat. Three seats went to non-partisans. Two seats, initially declared for the EOA, were deemed undecided by the electoral commission and required another ballot. One of these went to the MPRP, giving the party 37 seats, and the other to a fourth independent.

In presidential elections on 22 May 2005, Nambaryn Enkhbayar (Mongolian People's Revolutionary Party) won with 53·4% of the vote against Mendsaikhany Enkhsaikhan (Democratic Party) with 19·7%. Turnout was 74·9%.

CURRENT ADMINISTRATION

President: Nambaryn Enkhbayar; b. 1958 (Mongolian People's Revolutionary Party; sworn in 24 June 2005).

The coalition government collapsed in Jan. 2006 following the resignation of the members of the Mongolian People's Revolutionary Party. In March 2006 the coalition government comprised:

Prime Minister: Miyegombo Enkhbold; b. 1964 (Mongolian People's Revolutionary Party; since 25 Jan. 2006).

Deputy Prime Minister: Mendsaikhanii Enkhsaikhan.

Minister of Defence: Mishigiin Sonompil. *Finance:* Nadmidiin Bayartsaikhan. *Foreign Affairs:* Nyamaa Enkhbold. *Health:* Lamjaviin Gundalai. *Industry and Commerce:* Bazarsadiin Jargalsaikhan. *Education, Culture and Science:* Ulziisaikhanii Enkhtuvshin. *Environment:* Ichinkhorloogiin Erdenebaatar. *Fuel and Energy:* Badarchiin Erdenebat. *Food and Agriculture:* Dendeviin Terbishdagva. *Construction and Urban Development:* Janlaviin Naratsatsralt. *Justice and Internal Affairs:* Dorjiin Odbayar. *Professional Control:* Ukhnaagiin Hurelsukh. *Social Welfare and Labour:* Luvsangiin Odoncchimed. *Roads, Transport and Tourism:* Tsegmidiin Tsengel. *Chief of the Cabinet Secretariat:* Sunduin Batbold.

CURRENT LEADERS

Nambaryn Enkhbayar

Position
President

Introduction
Nambaryn Enkhbayar, the candidate of the ruling Mongolian People's Revolutionary Party (MPRP), won presidential elections in May 2005. Enkhbayar, who had been prime minister from 2000 to 2004, has promised to modernize the country and tackle poverty and unemployment.

Early Life
Nambaryn Enkhbayar was born on 1 June 1958 in Ulan Bator. Having graduated from the Gorky Higher Institute of Literature in Moscow in 1980, he returned to Mongolia, working as a literary translator at the Mongolian Writer's Union and then as head of the organization's foreign relations department. He studied European literature at Leeds University in the UK in 1986. Enkhbayar's career in government began with the development committee for culture and art in Nov. 1990, the year in which Mongolia embraced democratic reforms, legalized political parties and approved the transition to a market economy. Elected as the MPRP representative for Ulan Bator's constituency #23 in June 1992, he served as minister of culture until 1996.

When the MPRP was ousted by the National and Social Democrats in the parliamentary elections of June 1996, Enkhbayar was elected to replace Budragchaagiyn Dash-Yondon as leader of the MPRP. He brought in sweeping party reforms, citing Tony Blair's modernization of the UK Labour Party as his inspiration. The MPRP stormed back to power on 2 July 2000, winning 72 out of 76 parliamentary seats, and Enkhbayar was appointed prime minister.

Career in Office
Enkhbayar launched initiatives such as the Millennium Road, a trans-Mongolian highway linking Russia and China, but progress on economic reforms was slow. When the MPRP's majority was slashed in the June 2004 elections, Enkhbayar ceded the premiership to Tsakhiagiin Elbegdorj. Enkhbayar became parliamentary speaker and stood as the MPRP candidate in the 2005 presidential election. On 23 May 2005 he was proclaimed the victor and sworn in on 24 June. He vowed to unite the country after a year of instability and public protests and pledged to reduce unemployment and inflation and tackle corruption.

Miyegombo Enkhbold

Position
Prime Minister

Introduction
Miyegombo Enkhbold succeeded Tsakhia Elbegdorj as prime minister of Mongolia in Jan. 2006, ending two weeks of political crisis. A former mayor of the capital, Ulan Bator, he is also chairman of the ruling Mongolian People's Revolutionary Party (MPRP).

Early Life
Miyegombo Enkhbold was born on 19 July 1964 in Ulan Bator. Graduating from the Mongolia State University with a degree in economics in 1987, he was employed as an economist in the capital's executive administration and in 1989 joined the staff of the ministry of communal economy and services. In 1990 Mongolia embraced democratic reforms, legalizing political parties and approving the transition to a market economy. Enkhbold joined the ruling MPRP while it was being remoulded into a centre-left party. Having led the premises and services department of Ulan Bator's executive administration during 1991, Enkhbold was appointed deputy governor of the capital's Chingeltei district, a post he held for four years. In 1996 he attended a course in state administration and management with the Japanese government's international co-operation agency. The following year he became chairman of the MPRP's committee in Ulan Bator and a member of the party's *Little Hural* (the successor to the MPRP Central Committee from 1992).

Enkhbold became Ulan Bator's mayor in Jan. 1999 and was reappointed in Oct. 2000. He was elected a member of the MPRP's leadership council in March 2001. As mayor, Enkhbold oversaw the introduction of controversial land privatization laws in the capital, which came into force in 2003. In Aug. 2005, Enkhbold was elected to represent Ulan Bator's constituency #65 in the *Great Hural* (parliament) and became chairman of the MPRP.

Mongolia was gripped by crisis in Jan. 2006 when the MPRP withdrew from the governing coalition with the Democratic Party. Enkhbold blamed the Democratic Party prime minister, Tsakhia Elbegdorj, who had overseen rising inflation and a slowdown in economic growth, although members of the Democratic Party claimed the walk-out was because alleged corruption by the MPRP was about to be discussed by parliament. The crisis triggered mass anti-corruption demonstrations, with protesters attempting to storm the MPRP's headquarters in Ulan Bator. Enkhbold's nomination to succeed Elbegdorj was approved by the president, Nambaryn Enkhbayar, and on 25 Jan. 2006 he won 85% support from parliament and duly became prime minister.

Career in Office
Enkhbold formed a 'government of national unity', including several minor parties, which was approved by parliament on 27 Jan. 2006. The MPRP retain ten out of 17 cabinet seats and Enkhbold has promised to focus on speeding up economic development and tackling poverty.

DEFENCE

Conscription is for one year for males aged 18–28 years. Defence expenditure in 2003 totalled US$15m. (US$6 per capita), representing 1·4% of GDP.

Army

Strength (2002) 7,500 (4,000 conscripts). There is a border guard of 6,000, 1,200 internal security troops and 500 Civil Defence Troops.

Air Force

The Air Force had a strength of 800 in 2002 with 11 armed helicopters and nine aircraft in store.

INTERNATIONAL RELATIONS

Mongolia is a member of the UN, WTO, the Asian Development Bank and the Colombo Plan.

ECONOMY

In 2002 agriculture accounted for 29·7% of GDP, industry 15·9% and services 54·4%.

Overview

Mongolia has for centuries had a traditional nomadic pastoral economy which the government aims to transform into a market economy. An Agency for National Development, headed by a minister of cabinet rank, co-ordinates economic policy. A law of May 1991 introduced privatization by the distribution of vouchers worth 10,000 tugriks to 2m. citizens to acquire holdings or to buy small businesses or livestock. About 45% of state-owned assets had been privatized by 2001.

Currency

The unit of currency is the *tugrik* (MNT) of 100 *möngö*. The tugrik was made convertible in 1993. In June 2002 foreign exchange reserves were US$210m., gold reserves totalled 41,000 troy oz and total money supply was 187,680m. tugriks. Inflation, which stood at 268% in 1993, had been brought down to below 10% by 1998 and in 2004 was 7·9%.

Budget

Total revenue and expenditure (in 1m. tugriks):

	1998	1999	2000	2001
Revenue	183,552	196,561	303,215	358,244
Expenditure	201,279	232,795	306,037	353,580

Main sources of revenue, 2001 (in 1m. tugriks): taxes, 265,384 (including: domestic taxes on goods and services, 145,335; social security contributions, 61,306; income, profits and capital gains tax, 27,875; taxes on foreign trade, 27,018); non-tax revenue, 88,457. Major items of expenditure, 2001 (in 1m. tugriks): social security and welfare, 84,093; economic affairs and services, 49,504; health, 30,192; general public services, 29,317.

Performance

Real GDP growth was 5·6% in 2003 and 10·6% in 2004. Total GDP in 2004 was US$1·5bn.

Banking and Finance

The Mongolian Bank (established 1924) is the bank of issue, being also a commercial, savings and development bank: the *Governor* is Ochirbat Chuluunbat. It has 21 main branches. There were 25 other banks in 2002. The largest bank is the state-owned Trade and Development Bank.

A stock exchange opened in Ulan Bator in 1992.

ENERGY AND NATURAL RESOURCES

Environment

In 2002 carbon dioxide emissions from the consumption and flaring of fossil fuels in Mongolia were the equivalent of 2·9 tonnes per capita.

Electricity

Installed capacity was 0·9m. kW in 2000. There are six thermal electric power stations. Production, 2000, 2·93bn. kWh; consumption per capita in 2000 was 1,302 kWh.

Minerals

There are large deposits of copper, nickel, zinc, molybdenum, phosphorites, tin, wolfram and fluorspar; production of the latter in 1996, 565,100 tonnes. There are major coalmines near Ulan Bator and Darhan. In 2000 lignite production was 4·18m. tonnes and coal production was 833,000 tonnes. Copper production, 2001, 133,503 tonnes; gold production, 2001, 13,675 kg.

Agriculture

The prevailing Mongolian style of life is pastoral nomadism. 73% of agricultural production derives from cattle-raising. In 2000 there were 14·0m. sheep, 3·50m. cattle, 3·08m. horses and 360,000 camels. The number of goats rose from 5·5m. to 10m. between 1992 and 2000 as production of cashmere has increased along with the market economy. In late 1999 and early 2000 approximately 3m. animals died as a result of extreme weather and overgrazing, and in late 2000 and early 2001 more than 1·3m. animals died.

The total agricultural area in 1995 was 118·5m. ha. 96% was sown to cereals, 1·6% to fodder and 0·9% to vegetables. In 2001 there were 1·20m. ha. of arable land and 1,000 ha. of permanent crop land. In 2000 output of major crops was 186,000 tonnes of wheat (down from 607,000 in the period 1989–91); 70,000 tonnes of potatoes (down from 128,000 in 1989–91); 4,000 tonnes of barley (down from 83,000 in 1989–91). Livestock products, 2000 (in 1,000 tonnes): meat, 230; cow's milk, 285; goat's milk, 34; sheep's milk, 22. In 2001 there were 5,000 tractors and 1,150 harvester-threshers.

Collectivized farms, set up in the 1950s under Stalin, have been broken up and the land redistributed.

Forestry

Forests, chiefly larch, cedar, fir and birch, occupied 10·65m. ha. in 2000 (6·8% of the land area). Timber production was 631,000 cu. metres in 2001.

Fisheries

The catch in 2001 was 117 tonnes, entirely from inland waters.

INDUSTRY

Industry is still small in scale and local in character. The food industry accounts for 25% of industrial production. The main industrial centre is Ulan Bator; others are at Erdenet and Baga-Nur, and a northern territorial industrial complex is being developed based on Darhan and Erdenet to produce copper and molybdenum concentrates, lime, cement, machinery and wood- and metal-worked products. Production figures: cement (2002), 148,000 tonnes; lime (2002), 41,000 tonnes; bread (2000), 20,000 tonnes; carpets (2000), 705,000 sq. metres; sawnwood (1998), 300,000 cu. metres.

Labour

Out of 870,800 people in employment in Dec. 2002, 381,400 were engaged in agriculture, hunting, fishing and forestry; 104,500 in wholesale and retail trade/repair of motor vehicles, motorcycles and personal and household goods; 59,300 in education; and 55,600 in manufacturing. In July 2003 there were 37,300 registered unemployed persons.

Trade Unions

The Confederation of Mongolian Trade Unions had 450,000 members in 1994.

INTERNATIONAL TRADE

Mongolia is dependent on foreign aid. The largest donor in 1992 was Japan. Foreign debt was US$1,037m. in 2002.

Joint ventures with foreign firms are permitted. Foreign investors may acquire up to 49% of the equity in Mongolian companies. Foreign companies (except in precious metal mining) have a five-year tax holiday and a further five years at 50% of the tax rate.

Imports and Exports

In 2002 imports (f.o.b.) were valued at US$680·2m. (US$623·8m. in 2001) and exports (f.o.b.) at US$524·0m. (US$523·2m. in 2001). Main exports, 2001: copper concentrate, 28·1%; gold, 14·3%; cashmere, 13·4%.

Principal import suppliers in 2002: Russia, 34·1%; China, 24·4%; South Korea, 12·2%; Japan, 6·2%. Main export markets, 2002: China, 42·4%; USA, 31·6%; Russia, 8·6%; South Korea, 4·4%.

COMMUNICATIONS

Roads

The total road network covered 49,250 km in 2002, including 11,121 km of highway. There are 1,185 km of surfaced roads running around Ulan Bator, from Ulan Bator to Darhan, at points on the frontier with the Russian Federation and towards the south. Truck services run where there are no surfaced roads. Vehicles in use in 2002 included 63,224 passenger cars and 26,319 trucks and vans. In 2000 passenger transport totalled 388m. passenger-km and freight 126m. tonne-km. In 2000 there were 5,991 road accidents resulting in 338 fatalities.

Rail
The Trans-Mongolian Railway (1,928 km of 1,524 mm gauge in 1992) connects Ulan Bator with the Russian Federation and China. There are spur lines to Erdenet and to the coalmines at Nalayh and Sharyn Gol. A separate line connects Choybalsan in the east with Borzaya on the Trans-Siberian Railway. Passenger-km travelled in 2000 came to 1,070m. and freight tonne-km to 4,293m.

Civil Aviation
MIAT-Mongolian Airlines operates internal services, and in 2003 flew from Ulan Bator to Beijing, Berlin, Frankfurt, Hohhot, Irkutsk, Moscow, Seoul and Tokyo. In 1999 it flew 6·3m. km, carrying 224,700 passengers (98,300 on international flights). In 2001 Ulan Bator handled 285,399 passengers and 2,660 tonnes of freight.

Shipping
There is a steamer service on the Selenge River and a tug and barge service on Hövsgöl Lake. 70,000 tonnes of freight were carried in 1990.

Telecommunications
Mongolia had 344,000 telephone subscribers in 2002, or 141·6 for every 1,000 persons. There were 216,000 mobile phone subscribers in 2002, up from 2,000 in 1998. There were 69,000 PCs in use (28·4 for every 1,000 persons) in 2002 and 12,500 fax machines. There were 50,000 Internet users in 2002.

Postal Services
There were 385 post offices in 2003.

SOCIAL INSTITUTIONS

Justice
The Procurator-General is appointed, and the Supreme Court elected, by parliament for five years. There are also courts at province, town and district level. Lay assessors sit with professional judges. The death penalty is in force.

The population in penal institutions in 2002 was 7,256 (279 per 100,000 of national population).

Education
Adult literacy was 97·8% in 2003 (male, 98·0%; female, 97·5%). Schooling begins at the age of seven. In 2000–01 there were 79,294 children in pre-primary education; 250,437 pupils and 7,755 teachers in primary education; and 259,888 students and 12,333 teachers in secondary schools. There were 84,970 students in tertiary education in 2000–01. In 1994–95 there were one university and four specialized universities (agricultural; medical; pedagogical; technical). There were also colleges of commerce and business, economics, and railway engineering, and an institute of culture and art.

In 2000–01 total expenditure on education came to 6·6% of GNP.

Health
In 1997 there were 407 hospitals with the equivalent of 78 beds per 10,000 inhabitants. There were 6,823 physicians, 469 dentists, 612 midwives and 7,802 nurses in 2002.

Welfare
In 1995, 102·8m. tugriks were spent on maternity benefits.

RELIGION
Tibetan Buddhist Lamaism is the prevalent religion; the Dalai Lama is its spiritual head. In 1995 there were about 100 monasteries and 2,500 monks.

CULTURE

World Heritage Sites
Mongolia has one site on the UNESCO World Heritage List: the Orkhon Valley Cultural Landscape (inscribed on the list in 2004), an extensive area on both banks of the Orkhon River including the archaeological remains of Kharkhorum, the 13th and 14th century capital of Genghis Khan's vast Empire. A second site falls under joint Mongolian and Russian jurisdiction: Uvs Nuur Basin (2003), an important saline lake system supporting a rich wildlife, especially the snow leopard and Asiatic ibex.

Broadcasting
In 2003 there were four television stations: the government-financed Ulan Bator Broadcasting System (UBS) and Mongol TV and the private Channel 25 and Eagle TV. Ulan Bator Radio (UBS) broadcasts two national programmes and an external service (English, Chinese, Japanese, Russian). Number of sets: TV (2001), 173,000; radio (2000), 368,000.

Press
In 2003 there were five daily newspapers, including *Onoodor* (10,000 regular subscribers) and *Udriin Sonin* (Daily News), and two English-language weeklies, the *UB Post* and the government's *Mongol Messenger*.

Tourism
In 2002 there were 198,000 foreign tourists; spending by tourists totalled US$130m.

DIPLOMATIC REPRESENTATIVES
Of Mongolia in the United Kingdom (7 Kensington Ct, London, W8 5DL)
Ambassador: Davaasambuu Dalrain.

Of the United Kingdom in Mongolia (30 Enkh Taivny Gudamzh, Ulan Bator 13)
Ambassador: Richard Austen, MBE.

Of Mongolia in the USA (2833 M St., NW, Washington, D.C., 20007)
Ambassador: Ravdan Bold.

Of the USA in Mongolia (Micro Region 11, Big Ring Rd, Ulan Bator)
Ambassador: Pamela J. Slutz.

Of Mongolia to the United Nations
Ambassador: Baatar Choisuren.

Of Mongolia to the European Union
Ambassador: Sodoviin Onon.

FURTHER READING
State Statistical Office: *Mongolian Economy and Society in [year]: Statistical Yearbook.— National Economy of the MPR, 1924–1984: Anniversary Statistical Collection.* Ulan Bator, 1984

Akiner, S. (ed.) *Mongolia Today.* London, 1992
Becker, J., *The Lost Country.* London, 1992
Bruun, O. and Odgaard, O. (eds.) *Mongolia in Transition.* Richmond, 1996
Griffin, K. (ed.) *Poverty and the Transition to a Market Economy in Mongolia.* London, 1995
Nordby, Judith, *Mongolia in the Twentieth Century.* Farnborough, 1993.—*Mongolia.* [Bibliography] ABC-Clio, Oxford and Santa Barbara (CA), 1993

National Statistical Office: Government Building 3, Ulan Bator-20A.

MOROCCO

© Research Machines plc 2006

Mamlaka al-Maghrebia
(Kingdom of Morocco)

Capital: Rabat
Population projection, 2010: 33·83m.
GDP per capita, 2003: (PPP$) 4,004
HDI/world rank: 0·631/124

KEY HISTORICAL EVENTS

The native people of Morocco are the Berbers, an ancient race who have suffered the attention of a succession of invaders. When the city of Carthage fell to Rome in the second century BC, the African Mediterranean coast was under Roman dominance for almost six hundred years. When the Roman Empire in turn fell into decline, the area was invaded first by the Vandals in AD 429 and later by Byzantium in AD 533. An Arab invasion of Morocco in AD 682 marked the end of Byzantium dominance and the first Arab rulers, the Idrisid dynasty, ruled for 150 years. Arab and Berber dynasties succeeded the Idrisids until the 13th century when the country was plunged into bitter civil war between Arab and Berber factions. The reign of Ahmed I al-Man-sur in the first Sharifian dynasty stabilized and unified the country between 1579 and 1603. Moors and Jews expelled from Spain settled in Morocco during this time and the country flourished. In 1415 the Moroccan port of Ceuta was captured by Portugal. Moroccan forces defeated the Portuguese in 1578 and by 1700 had regained control of many coastal towns which had previously been in Portuguese hands. During the 18th and early 19th centuries the Barbary Coast became the scene of widespread piracy.

As part of the Entente Cordiale, Britain recognized Morocco as a French sphere of influence and in 1904 Morocco was divided between France and Spain, with the former receiving the larger area. From 1912 to 1956 Morocco was divided into a French protectorate, a Spanish protectorate, and the international zone of Tangier which was established by France, Great Britain and Spain in 1923. On 29 Oct. 1956 the international status of the

Tangier Zone was abolished and Morocco became a kingdom on 18 Aug. 1957, with the Sultan taking the title Mohammed V. Succeeding his father on 3 March 1961, King Hassan tried to combine the various parties in government and established an elected House of Representatives but political unrest led him to discard any attempt at a parliamentary government and to rule autocratically from 1965 to 1977. In 1977 a new Chamber of Representatives was elected and under the constitution Morocco became a constitutional monarchy with a single elected chamber.

TERRITORY AND POPULATION

Morocco is bounded by Algeria to the east and southeast, Mauritania to the south, the Atlantic Ocean to the northwest and the Mediterranean to the north. Excluding the Western Saharan territory claimed and retrieved since 1976 by Morocco, the area is 458,730 sq. km. The population at the 2004 census (including Western Sahara) was 29,891,708; density (including Western Sahara), 42·1 per sq. km. At the 2004 census Western Sahara had an area of 252,120 sq. km and a population of about 356,000. The Moroccan superficie is 710,850 sq. km. The population was 57·4% urban in 2003.

The UN gives a projected population for 2010 of 33·83m.

Morocco has 16 states (*wilaya'at*) divided further into 71 prefectures and provincial units. Areas of the states and census populations in 2004:

State	Area in sq. km	Population
Chaouia-Ouardigha	16,760	1,655,660
Doukkala-Abda	13,285	1,984,039
Fès-Boulemane	19,795	1,573,055
Gharb-Chrarda-Béni Hssen	8,805	1,859,540
Grand Casablanca	1,615	3,631,061
Guelmin-Es Semara	71,970	462,410
Laâyoune-Boujdour-Sakia El Hamra[1]	—	256,152
Marrakesh-Tensift-Al Haouz	31,160	3,102,652
Meknès-Tafilalet	79,210	2,141,527
Oriental	82,820	1,918,094
Oued Eddahab-Lagouira[1]	—	99,367
Rabat-Salé-Zemmour-Zaer	9,580	2,366,494
Souss Massa-Draâ	70,880	3,113,653
Tadla-Azilal	17,125	1,450,519
Tangier-Tétouan	11,570	2,470,372
Taza-Al Hoceima-Taounate	24,155	1,807,113

[1]Laâyoune-Boujdour-Sakia El Hamra and Oued Eddahab-Lagouira correspond roughly to Western Sahara.

The chief cities (with populations in 1,000, 2004) are as follows:

Casablanca	2,934	Tangiers	670	Safi	285
Rabat	1,623	Meknès	536	Mohammedia	189
Fès (Fez)	947	Oujda	401	Khouribga	166
Marrakesh	823	Kénitra	359	Béni Mellal	163
Agadir	679	Tétouan	321		

The official language is Arabic, spoken by 65% of the population. Berber languages, including Tachelhit (or Soussi), Tamazight and Tarafit (or Rifia), are spoken by about half the population. French (widely used for business), Spanish (in the north) and English are also spoken.

SOCIAL STATISTICS

2002 estimates: births, 632,000; deaths, 169,000. Estimated rates, 2002 (per 1,000 population): birth, 21·0; death, 5·6. Annual population growth rate, 1992–2002, 1·7%. Life expectancy at birth in 2003 was 67·5 years for males and 71·9 years for females. Infant mortality, 2001, 39 per 1,000 live births; fertility rate, 2001, 3·1 births per woman.

CLIMATE

Morocco is dominated by the Mediterranean climate which is made temperate by the influence of the Atlantic Ocean in the northern and southern parts of the country. Central Morocco is continental while the south is desert. Rabat, Jan. 55°F (12·9°C), July 72°F (22·2°C). Annual rainfall 23" (564 mm). Agadir, Jan. 57°F (13·9°C), July 72°F (22·2°C). Annual rainfall 9" (224 mm). Casablanca, Jan. 54°F (12·2°C), July 72°F (22·2°C). Annual rainfall 16" (404 mm). Marrakesh, Jan. 52°F (11·1°C), July 84°F (28·9°C). Annual rainfall 10" (239 mm). Tangiers, Jan. 53°F (11·7°C), July 72°F (22·2°C). Annual rainfall 36" (897 mm).

CONSTITUTION AND GOVERNMENT

The ruling King is **Mohammed VI**, born on 21 Aug. 1963, married to Salma Bennani on 21 March 2002; succeeded on 23 July 1999, on the death of his father Hassan II, who reigned 1961–99. *Son:* Hassan, b. 8 May 2003. The King holds supreme civil and religious authority, the latter in his capacity of Emir-el-Muminin or Commander of the Faithful. He resides usually at Rabat, but occasionally in one of the other traditional capitals, Fès (founded in 808), Marrakesh (founded in 1062), or at Skhirat.

A new Constitution was approved by referendum in March 1972 and amendments were approved by referendum in May 1980 and Sept. 1992. The Kingdom of Morocco is a constitutional monarchy. Parliament consists of a *Chamber of Representatives* composed of 325 deputies directly elected for five-year terms. For the Sept. 2002 elections a series of measures were introduced, including a new proportional representation voting system and a national list reserved for women candidates to ensure that at least 10% of new MPs are females.

A referendum on 13 Sept. 1996 established a second *Chamber of Counsellors*, composed of 270 members serving nine-year terms, of whom 162 are elected by local councils, 81 by chambers of commerce and 27 by trade unions. The Chamber of Counsellors has power to initiate legislation, issue warnings of censure to the government and ultimately to force the government's resignation by a two-thirds majority vote. The electorate was 12·3m. and turnout was 82·95%. The King, as sovereign head of State, appoints the Prime Minister and other Ministers, has the right to dissolve Parliament and approves legislation.

A new electoral code of March 1997 fixed voting at 20 and made enrolment on the electoral roll compulsory. In Dec. 2002 King Mohammed VI announced that the voting age was to be lowered from 20 to 18.

National Anthem

'Manbit al Ahrah, mashriq al anwar' ('Fountain of freedom, source of light'); words by Ali Squalli Houssaini, tune by Leo Morgan.

GOVERNMENT CHRONOLOGY

Kings since 1955.
1955–61	Mohammed V ibn Yusuf (sultan from 1955–57)
1961–99	Hassan II ibn Mohammed
1999–	Mohammed VI ibn al-Hasan

RECENT ELECTIONS

Elections to the Chamber of Representatives took place on 27 Sept. 2002. The USFP (Union Socialiste des Forces Populaires) won 50 seats, down from 57 seats in 1997; the PI (Istiqlal/Parti d'Indépendence) gained 48 seats, up from 32 in 1997; and the PJD (Parti de la Justice et du Développement), the only Islamic party taking part in the elections, trebled its representation from 14 to 42 seats. The Rassemblement National des Indépendants won 41 seats, the Mouvement Populaire 27, the Mouvement

Nationale Populaire 18, the Union Constitutionnelle 16, the Parti National-Démocrate 12, the Front des Forces Démocratiques also 12, the Parti du Progrès et du Socialisme 11 and the Union Democratique 10. A further 11 parties obtained fewer than ten seats each. Turnout was 51·6%.

In elections to the Chamber of Counsellors on 5 Dec. 1997 the centre Rassemblement National des Indépendents gained 42 seats, ahead of a second centre party, the Mouvement Démocratique et Social, with 33 seats.

CURRENT ADMINISTRATION

In March 2006 the six-party coalition government comprised:
    Prime Minister: Driss Jettou; b. 1945 (USFP; in office since 9 Oct. 2002).
    Minister for Foreign Affairs and Co-operation: Mohamed Benaissa. *Interior:* Chakib Benmoussa. *Justice:* Mohamed Bouzoubaa. *Finance and Privatization:* Fathallah Oualalou. *'Habous' and Islamic Affairs:* Ahmed Toufiq. *Territorial Development, Water Resources and the Environment:* Mohamed El Yazghi. *Agriculture, Rural Development and Sea Fisheries:* Mohand Laenser. *Employment and Professional Training:* Mustapha Mansouri. *Social Development, Family and Solidarity:* Abderrahim Harouchi. *National Education and Youth Affairs:* Habib El Malki. *Modernization and the Public Sector:* Mohammed Boussaid. *Culture:* Mohammed Achaari. *Equipment and Transport:* Karim Ghellab. *Industry, Commerce and Economic Upgrading:* Salaheddine Mezouar. *Tourism, Handicrafts and Economy:* Adil Douiri. *Health:* Mohammed Cheikh Biadillah. *Relations with Parliament:* Mohammed Saad El Alami. *Energy and Mines:* Mohammed Boutaleb. *Communications and Government Spokesperson:* Nabil Benabdallah. *Foreign Trade:* Mustapha Mechahouri. *Minister of State:* Abbas El Fassi.

Office of the Prime Minister (French only):
    http://www.pm.gov.ma

CURRENT LEADERS

Mohammed VI ibn al-Hasan

Position
King

Introduction
Mohammed Ben VI ibn al-Hasan was crowned King in July 1999 after the death of his father, King Hassan II. Less austere than his father, he has pledged to improve Morocco's democratic institutions and encourage private investment in key economic sectors.

Early Life
King Mohammed VI was born on 21 Aug. 1963 in Rabat, Morocco. In 1985 he graduated from the College of Law in the Rabat Mohammed V University. In 1987 he took a degree in political science and in 1993 was awarded a law doctorate from the French University of Nice-Sophia Antipolis.

Mohammed undertook his first official royal duty, standing in for his father at a commemorative ceremony for French President Georges Pompidou, when he was 11. He was made honorary president of the Socio-Cultural Association of the Mediterranean Basin in 1979 and by the time he was 20 he had led a Moroccan delegation to the Franco-African conference and negotiated with the Organization of African Unity (now the African Union) over the Western Sahara conflict.

Appointed head of the general staff of the Royal Armed Forces in 1985, he succeeded to the throne in 1999.

Career in Office
Mohammed has voiced support for developing a market economy. He has urged increased private sector investment in tourism, sea fishing, agro-industries and handicrafts. In foreign policy, he has

co-operated with the USA in its anti-terror initiatives since the Sept. 2001 attacks. However, Morocco has itself been targeted by terrorist violence, with around 30 people killed in co-ordinated suicide bomb incidents in Casablanca in May 2003. Elsewhere, Mohammed has expressed support for Palestinian claims to their own independent state and spoken out against the use of heavy-handed military force by Israel.

In 2002 the King came into conflict with the Spanish government when Moroccan forces landed on the small, uninhabited island of Perejil (a Spanish possession since 1668), 200 metres off the Moroccan coast. Spain quickly retook the island in a bloodless counter-assault, before withdrawing its troops on the understanding that neither country would occupy the island.

DEFENCE

Conscription is authorized for 18 months. Defence expenditure in 2003 totalled US$1,826m. (US$61 per capita), representing 4·2% of GDP.

Army
The Army is deployed in two commands: Northern Zone and Southern Zone. There is also a Royal Guard of 1,500. Strength (2002), 175,000 (100,000 conscripts). There is also a Royal Gendarmerie of 20,000, an Auxiliary Force of 30,000 and reserves of 150,000.

Navy
The Navy includes two frigates, 27 patrol and coastal combatants and four amphibious craft.

Personnel in 2002 numbered 7,800, including a 1,500 strong brigade of Naval Infantry. Bases are located at Casablanca, Agadir, Al Hoceima, Dakhla and Tangiers.

Air Force
Personnel strength (2002) about 13,500, with 95 combat aircraft, including F-5s and Mirage F-1s, and 24 armed helicopters.

INTERNATIONAL RELATIONS

Morocco is a member of the UN, WTO, the League of Arab States, Arab Maghreb Union, African Development Bank, IOM, OIC, Islamic Development Bank and the International Organization of the Francophonie.

ECONOMY

Agriculture accounted for 16·1% of GDP in 2002, industry 30·3% and services 53·6%.

Overview
Morocco has achieved macroeconomic stability in the last decade, with real growth of 3·0% a year between 1995–2005. However, growth has been insufficient to impact on unemployment and poverty. Poverty levels had risen to 15% of the population in 2005 and reached rates of 40% in particularly vulnerable areas. The government has undertaken structural reforms to deregulate the economy, consolidate macroeconomic and financial stability, increase access to basic social services and fight poverty. The reform process has intensified since 2002 and Morocco's legal and fiscal framework is now close to fulfilling the requirements stipulated by international conventions.

Trade is focused on the EU, which in 2005 accounted for 75% of exports and 56% of imports. The government is abolishing tariffs in preparation for the 2012 implementation of its three-stage free-trade association agreement with the EU, which will liberalize the market for industrialized goods. In 2004 Morocco signed free trade agreements with the United States, Turkey, Egypt, Jordan and Tunisia in a bid to diversify its trade portfolio.

Currency
The unit of currency is the *dirham* (MAD) of 100 *centimes*, introduced in 1959. Foreign exchange reserves were US$9,006m. and gold reserves 708,000 troy oz in June 2002. Since 1993 the dirham has been convertible for current account operations. Inflation was 1·2% in 2003 and 1·5% in 2004. Total money supply in May 2002 was DH248,359m.

Budget
Revenues in 2002 totalled DH98,261m. and expenditures DH118,999m. The main revenue items were VAT (24·4%), taxes on income and profits (16·6%) and excise taxes (16·4%). Current expenditure accounted for 76·2% of total expenditures and capital expenditure 17·8%.

VAT is 20%.

Performance
Real GDP growth was 5·5% in 2003 and 4·2% in 2004. Total GDP in 2004 was US$50·1bn.

Banking and Finance
The central bank is the Bank Al Maghrib (*Governor*, Abdellatif Jouahri) which had assets of DH17,063m. on 31 Dec. 1999. There were 12 other banks in 2002 and three development banks, specializing respectively in industry, housing and agriculture.

There is a stock exchange in Casablanca.

ENERGY AND NATURAL RESOURCES

Environment
Carbon dioxide emissions from the consumption and flaring of fossil fuels in 2002 were the equivalent of 1·0 tonnes per capita.

Electricity
Installed capacity was 4·0m. kW in 2000. Production was 13·27bn. kWh (approximately 95% thermal) in 2000 and consumption per capita 544 kWh.

Oil and Gas
Natural gas reserves in 2002 were 1·3bn. cu. metres; output (2000), 51m. cu. metres.

Minerals
The principal mineral exploited is phosphate (Morocco has the largest reserves in the world), the output of which was 21·98m. tonnes in 2001. Other minerals (in tonnes, 2001) are: barytine, 471,102; salt (2000), 188,000; lead, 110,906; zinc, 89,339; coal (2000), 29,000; manganese, 13,757; copper (2000), 7,125; iron ore (2000), 6,000; silver, 281.

Agriculture
Agricultural production is subject to drought; about 1·35m. ha. were irrigated in 2001. 85% of farmland is individually owned. Only 1% of farms are over 50 ha.; most are under 3 ha. There were 8·75m. ha. of arable land in 2001 and 0·97m. ha. of permanent crops. Main land usage, 2000 (in 1,000 ha.): wheat, 2,902; barley, 2,251; maize, 238. There were 43,226 tractors in 2001 and 3,763 harvester-threshers.

Production in 2000 (in 1,000 tonnes): sugarbeets, 2,883; wheat, 1,381; sugarcane, 1,326; potatoes, 1,090; melons and watermelons, 874; oranges, 870; tomatoes, 764; tangerines and mandarins, 514; barley, 467; olives, 400.

Livestock, 2000: cattle, 2·67m.; sheep, 17·30m.; goats, 5·12m.; asses, 980,000; chickens, 100m. Livestock products in 2000 included (in 1,000 tonnes): milk, 1,212; meat, 540.

Forestry
Forests covered 3·03m. ha. in 2000, or 6·8% of the total land area. Produce includes firewood, building and industrial timber and some cork and charcoal. Timber production was 971,000 cu. metres in 2001.

Fisheries

Total catch in 2001 was 1,083,276 tonnes (sea fish, 1,082,293 tonnes). Morocco's annual catch is the highest of any African country. Total catch value in 1994 was DH3,195m.

INDUSTRY

According to the Financial Times Survey (FT 500), the largest companies in Morocco by market capitalization on 4 Jan. 2001 were: ONA (Omnium Nord Africain), a food and beverages conglomerate, at US$1,805·4m.; and BCM (Banque Commerciale du Maroc), at US$1,100·4m.

In 2001 industry contributed 31·4% of GDP, with manufacturing accounting for 17·3%. Production (in 1,000 tonnes): cement (2001), 8,058; residual fuel oil (2000), 2,365; distillate fuel oil (2000), 2,322; sugar (2000), 556; petrol (2000), 383; paper and paperboard (2002), 129; olive oil (2001), 41.

Labour

Of 9,487,600 persons in employment in 2002, 4,209,300 were engaged in agriculture, hunting, fishing and forestry; 1,371,300 in wholesale and retail trade/repair of motor vehicles, motorcycles and personal and household goods; 1,171,300 in manufacturing; and 871,100 in education, health and social work, and other community, social and personal service activities. The unemployment rate in 2002 was 11·6%. In July 2004 the minimum hourly wage was DH9·66.

Trade Unions

In 1996 there were six trade unions: UMT (Union Marocaine de Travail), CDT (Confédération Démocratique du Travail), UGTM (Union Générale des Travailleurs Marocaine), UNTM (National Union of Moroccan Workers), USP (Union of Popular Workers) and the SNP (National Popular Union).

INTERNATIONAL TRADE

In 1989 Morocco signed a treaty of economic co-operation with the four other Maghreb countries: Algeria, Libya, Mauritania and Tunisia. In 1995 Morocco signed an association agreement with the EU to create a free trade zone in 12 years. Foreign debt was US$18,601m. in 2002.

Imports and Exports

Imports and exports for calendar years in US$1m.:

	1998	1999	2000	2001	2002
Imports f.o.b.	9,463	9,957	10,654	10,164	10,900
Exports f.o.b.	7,144	7,509	7,419	7,142	7,839

Imports in 2002 included: machinery and apparatus, 19·3%; mineral fuels, 15·6%; food, beverages and tobacco, 11·8%; cotton fabric and fibres, 6·4%. Exports included: garments, 21·4%; food, beverages and tobacco, 20·5%; knitwear, 10·4%; phosphoric acid, 6·8%.

Main import suppliers in 2001: France, 24·1%; Spain, 10·3%; UK, 6·2%; Italy, 5·0%. Leading export markets in 2001: France, 32·8%; Spain, 15·3%; UK, 8·6%; Italy, 5·7%.

COMMUNICATIONS

Roads

In 2002 there were 57,694 km of classified roads, including 467 km of motorways and 11,288 km of main roads. A motorway links Rabat to Casablanca. In 2000 freight transport totalled 2,952m. tonne-km. In 2000 there were 1,230,068 passenger cars, 315,550 trucks and vans, 15,019 buses and coaches and 20,397 motorcycles and mopeds. There were 48,371 road accidents in 2000 (3,627 fatalities).

Rail

In 2000 there were 1,907 km of railways, of which 1,003 km were electrified. Passenger-km travelled in 2000 came to 1·96bn. and freight tonne-km to 4·58bn. In 2003 the construction of two 40 km-long rail tunnels under the Straits of Gibraltar was agreed with Spain with an estimated cost of US$30m.

Civil Aviation

The national carrier is Royal Air Maroc. The major international airport is Mohammed V at Casablanca; there are eight other airports. Casablanca handled 3,457,209 passengers in 2001 (2,612,998 on international flights) and 41,140 tonnes of freight; Marrakesh (Menara) handled 1,371,851 passengers and 2,471 tonnes of freight and Agadir (Al Massira) 1,052,181 passengers and 2,351 tonnes of freight. In July 1997 Morocco launched its first private air company, Regional Air Lines, to serve the major regions of the kingdom, in addition to southern Spain and the Canary Islands. In 1999 scheduled airline traffic of Moroccan-based carriers flew 63·1m. km, carrying 3,392,000 passengers (2,587,000 on international flights).

Shipping

There are 12 ports, the largest being Casablanca, Tangiers and Jorf Lasfar. 1·56m. passengers and 40·6m. tonnes of freight were handled in 1994. In 2002 sea-going shipping totalled 502,000 GRT, including oil tankers 4,000 GRT.

Telecommunications

In 2002 there were 7,326,100 telephone subscribers (equivalent to 247·1 per 1,000 population) and 457,000 PCs were in use (15·4 per 1,000 persons). In 2002 there were 29,000 fax machines. French media group Vivendi Universal bought a 35% stake in the state-run operator Maroc Telecom in 2000, and in Jan. 2005 increased its holding to 51%. In 2002 there were 6,198,700 mobile phone subscribers, up from just 74,500 in 1997. Morocco had 700,000 Internet users in 2002.

Postal Services

In 2003 there were 1,623 main post offices.

SOCIAL INSTITUTIONS

Justice

The legal system is based on French and Islamic law codes. There are a Supreme Court, 21 courts of appeal, 65 courts of first instance, 196 centres with resident judges and 706 communal jurisdictions for petty offences.

The population in penal institutions in Dec. 2002 was 54,207 (176 per 100,000 of national population). On ascending to the throne in July 1999, King Mohammed VI pardoned and ordered the release of 7,988 prisoners and reduced the terms of 38,224 others.

Education

The adult literacy rate in 2002 was 50·7% (63·3% among males and 38·3% among females). Education in Berber languages has been permitted since 1994; Berber languages were officially added to the syllabus in 2003. Education is compulsory from the age of seven to 13. In 1993–94 there were 28,335 Koranic schools (33,721 in 1990) with 30,367 teachers and 611,729 pupils. In 2000–01 pre-primary schools had 41,513 teachers for 742,287 pupils and there were 136,558 teachers at primary schools for 3,842,000 pupils. In 1999–2000 there were 90,799 teachers in secondary schools for 1,541,000 pupils. In 1996–97 there were 13 universities with 7,566 teachers and 218,516 students (89,223 women), 8,390 students (1,761 women) in teacher training and (1992–93) 8,967 students and 1,145 teachers in other higher education institutions. An English-language university was opened at Ifrane in Jan. 1995, initially with a staff of 35 and 300 students (scheduled to rise to 3,500).

In 2000–01 total expenditure on education came to 5·6% of GNP.

Health

In 2001 there were 14,293 physicians, 2,304 dentists, 29,462 nurses and 4,901 pharmacists. In 2002 there were 152 hospitals with 28,000 beds, a provision of ten beds per 10,000 inhabitants.

RELIGION

Islam is the established state religion. 98% of the population are Sunni Muslims of the Malekite school and 0·2% are Christians, mainly Roman Catholic, and there is a small Jewish community.

CULTURE

World Heritage Sites

Morocco has eight sites on the UNESCO World Heritage List: the Medina of Fès (inscribed on the list in 1981); the Medina of Marrakesh (1985); the Ksar of Ait-Ben-Haddou (1987); the Historic City of Meknès (1996); the Archaeological Site of Volubilis (1997); the Medina of Tétouan (1997); the Medina of Essaouira/Magador (2001); and the Portuguese City of Mazagan, now part of the city of El Jadida (2004).

Broadcasting

The government-controlled *Radiodiffusion Télévision Marocaine* broadcasts three national (one in French, English and Spanish) and eight regional radio programmes and one TV channel (colour by SECAM V). Broadcasting in Berber languages commenced in 1994. There is also a government commercial radio service and an independent TV channel. There were 4·86m. TV sets in 2001 and 6·92m. radio sets in 2000.

Cinema

There were approximately 160 cinema screens in 2002 and a total attendance of 10·7m. Six full-length films were made in 2000.

Press

In 2000 there were 23 daily newspapers, with a combined circulation of 846,000 (equivalent to 28 per 1,000 inhabitants). In 2000 a number of foreign and local newspapers were banned. Some had been accused of trying to destabilize the country's institutions, including the military.

Tourism

There were 4,193,000 foreign tourists in 2002, spending US$2·15bn. The tourism sector employs some 600,000 people, equivalent to 5·8% of the workforce.

DIPLOMATIC REPRESENTATIVES

Of Morocco in the United Kingdom (49 Queen's Gate Gdns, London, SW7 5NE)
Ambassador: Mohammed Belmahi.

Of the United Kingdom in Morocco (17 Blvd de la Tour Hassan, Rabat)
Ambassador: Charles Gray.

Of Morocco in the USA (1601 21st St., NW, Washington, D.C., 20009)
Ambassador: Aziz Mekouar.

Of the USA in Morocco (2 Ave. de Mohamed el Fassi, Rabat)
Ambassador: Thomas T. Riley.

Of Morocco to the United Nations
Ambassador: Al Mustapha Sahel.

Of Morocco to the European Union
Ambassador: Fath'allah Sijilmassi.

FURTHER READING

Direction de la Statistique. *Annuaire Statistique du Maroc.—Conjoncture Économique.* Quarterly *Bulletin Official.* Rabat.

Bourqia, Rahma and Gilson Miller, Susan (eds.) *In the Shadow of the Sultan: Culture, Power and Politics in Morocco.* Harvard Univ. Press, 2000
Findlay, Anne M. and Allan M., *Morocco.* [Bibliography] 2nd ed. ABC-Clio, Oxford and Santa Barbara (CA), 1995
Pazzanita, A. G., *The Maghreb.* [Bibliography] ABC-Clio, Oxford and Santa Barbara (CA), 1998
Pennell, C. R., *Morocco: From Empire to Independence.* Oneworld Publications, Oxford, 2003

National library: Bibliothèque Générale et Archives, Rabat.

National Statistical Office: Direction de la Statistique, Haute Commissariat au Plan, BP 178, Rabat.

Website (French only): http://www.statistic-hcp.ma

Western Sahara

The Western Sahara was designated by the United Nations in 1975, its borders having been marked as a result of agreements made between France, Spain and Morocco in 1900, 1904 and 1912. Sovereignty of the territory is in dispute between Morocco and the Polisario Front (Popular Front for the Liberation of the Saguia el Hamra and Rio de Oro), which formally proclaimed a government-in-exile of the Sahrawi Arab Democratic Republic (SADR) in Feb. 1976. According to a new UN Security Council resolution adopted in July 2003, Western Sahara should be a semi-autonomous region of Morocco for five years. There would then be a referendum to decide whether it should remain part of Morocco or becomes a separate state. However, the Moroccan government rejected the plan.

Area 252,120 sq. km (97,346 sq. miles). Around 356,000 inhabitants (2004 estimate) are within Moroccan jurisdiction. Another estimated 196,000 Saharawis live in refugee camps around Tindouf in southwest Algeria. The main towns are El-Aaiún (Laâyoune), the capital (184,000 inhabitants in 2004), Dakhla and Es-Semara.

Life expectancy at birth (1997 est.) male, 46·7 years; female, 50·0 years. Birth rate (1997 est.) per 1,000 population: 46·1; death rate: 17·5. The UN gives a projected population for 2010 of 429,000.

The population is Arabic-speaking, and almost entirely Sunni Muslim.

President: Mohammed Abdelaziz.
Prime Minister: Abdelkader Taleb Oumar.

Rich phosphate deposits were discovered in 1963 at Bu Craa. Morocco holds 65% of the shares of the former Spanish state-controlled company. Production reached 5·6m. tonnes in 1975, but exploitation has been severely reduced by guerrilla activity. After a nearly complete collapse, production and transportation of phosphate resumed in 1978, ceased again, and then resumed in 1982. Installed electrical capacity was 58,000 kW in 2000, with production in 2000 of approximately 88m. kWh. There are about 6,100 km of motorable tracks, but only about 500 km of paved roads. There are airports at El-Aaiún and Dakhla. As most of the land is desert, less than 19% is in agricultural use, with about 2,000 tonnes of grain produced annually. There were 56,000 radio receivers and 6,000 television sets in 1997. In 1989 (latest data available) there were 27 primary schools with 14,794 pupils and 18 secondary schools with 9,218 pupils. In 1994 there were 100 physicians, equivalent to one per 2,504 inhabitants.

FURTHER READING

Sheley, Toby, *Endgame in the Western Sahara: What Future for Africa's Last Colony?* Zed Books, London, 2004
Zoubir, Y. H. and Volman, D. (eds.) *The International Dimensions of the Western Sahara Conflict.* New York, 1993

MOZAMBIQUE

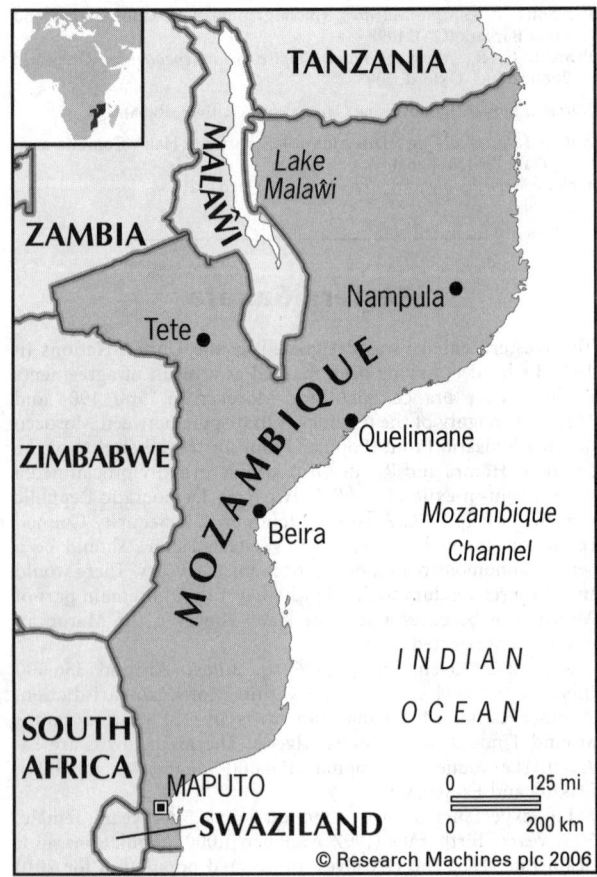

giving a density of 20 per sq. km. Up to 1·5m. refugees abroad and 5m. internally displaced persons during the Civil War have begun to return home. Population estimate, 2005: 19,792,000.

The UN gives a projected population for 2010 of 21·62m.

In 2003, 64·4% of the population were rural. The areas, populations and capitals of the provinces are:

Province	Sq. km	Estimate 2002	Capital
Cabo Delgado	82,625	1,525,634	Pemba
Gaza	75,709	1,266,431	Xai-Xai
Inhambane	68,615	1,326,848	Inhambane
Manica	61,661	1,207,332	Chimoio
City of Maputo	602	1,044,618	
Province of Maputo	25,756	1,003,992	Maputo
Nampula	81,606	3,410,141	Nampula
Niassa	129,056	916,672	Lichinga
Sofala	68,018	1,516,166	Beira
Tete	100,724	1,388,205	Tete
Zambézia	105,008	3,476,484	Quelimane

The capital is Maputo (1997 population, 989,386). Other large cities (with 1997 populations) are Matola (440,927), Beira (412,588) and Nampula (314,965).

The main ethnolinguistic groups are the Makua/Lomwe (52% of the population), the Tsonga/Ronga (24%), the Nyanja/Sena (12%) and Shona (6%).

Portuguese remains the official language, but vernaculars are widely spoken throughout the country. English is also widely spoken.

SOCIAL STATISTICS

2001 estimates: births, 753,000; deaths, 331,000. Estimated rates per 1,000 population, 2001: births, 41·7; deaths, 18·3. Infant mortality per 1,000 live births, 2001, 125. Life expectancy at birth, 2003, was 41·1 years for males and 42·7 years for females. Annual population growth rate, 1992–2002, 2·6%; fertility rate, 2001, 6·0 births per woman.

CLIMATE

A humid tropical climate, with a dry season from June to Sept. In general, temperatures and rainfall decrease from north to south. Maputo, Jan. 78°F (25·6°C), July 65°F (18·3°C). Annual rainfall 30" (760 mm). Beira, Jan. 82°F (27·8°C), July 69°F (20·6°C). Annual rainfall 60" (1,522 mm).

CONSTITUTION AND GOVERNMENT

On 2 Nov. 1990 the People's Assembly unanimously voted a new Constitution, which came into force on 30 Nov. This changed the name of the state to 'Republic of Mozambique', legalized opposition parties, provided for universal secret elections and introduced a bill of rights including the right to strike, press freedoms and *habeas corpus*. The head of state is the *President*, directly elected for a five-year term. Parliament is a 250-member *Assembly of the Republic*, elected for a five-year term by proportional representation.

National Anthem

'Patria Amada' ('Beloved Motherland'); words and tune by J. Sigaulane Chemane.

RECENT ELECTIONS

In the parliamentary elections of 1–2 Dec. 2004 the Liberation Front of Mozambique (FRELIMO) won 160 of the 250 available seats with 62·0% of the vote. The Mozambican National Resistance (RENAMO) won the remaining 90 seats with 29·7%. Turnout was 36·4%.

República de Moçambique

Capital: Maputo
Population projection, 2010: 21·62m.
GDP per capita, 2003: (PPP$) 1,117
HDI/world rank: 0·379/168

KEY HISTORICAL EVENTS

Mozambique was at first ruled as part of Portuguese India but a separate administration was created in 1752. Following a decade of guerrilla activity, independence was achieved on 25 June 1975. A one-party state dominated by the Liberation Front of Mozambique (FRELIMO) was set up but armed insurgency led by the Mozambique National Resistance (RENAMO) continued until 4 Oct. 1992. The peace treaty provided for all weapons to be handed over to the UN and all armed groups to be disbanded within six months. In 1994 the country held its first multi-party elections. In early 2000 some 700 people died in the floods which made thousands homeless.

TERRITORY AND POPULATION

Mozambique is bounded east by the Indian ocean, south by South Africa, southwest by Swaziland, west by South Africa and Zimbabwe and north by Zambia, Malawi and Tanzania. It has an area of 799,380 sq. km (308,642 sq. miles) and a population, according to the 1997 census, of 16,099,246 (7,714,306 males),

In the presidential election, also held on 1–2 Dec. 2004, FRELIMO's Armando Guebuza took 63·7% of the vote against RENAMO's Afonso Marceta Macacho Dhlakama.

CURRENT ADMINISTRATION

President: Armando Guebuza; b. 1943 (FRELIMO; sworn in 2 Feb. 2005).

In March 2006 the government comprised:

Prime Minister: Luísa Dias Diogo; b. 1958 (took office on 17 Feb. 2004).

Minister of Agriculture: Tomás Mandlate. *Defence:* Tobias Dai. *Development and Planning:* Aiuba Cuereneia. *Education:* Aires Bonifácio Ali. *Energy:* Salvador Namburete. *Environmental Action Co-ordinator:* Luciano de Castro. *Finance:* Manuel Chang. *Fisheries:* Cadmiel Muthemba. *Foreign Affairs and Co-operation:* Alcinda Abreu. *Health:* Paulo Ivo Garrido. *Industry and Commerce:* António Fernando. *Interior:* José Pacheco. *Justice:* Esperança Alfredo Machavela. *Labour:* Helena Taipo. *Mineral Resources and Energy:* Esperança Bias. *Public Works and Housing:* Felício Zacarias. *Science and Technology:* Venâncio Massingue. *State Administration:* Lucas Chomera. *Tourism:* Fernando Sumbana. *Transport and Communications:* António Munguambe. *Veterans Affairs:* Feliciano Salomão Gundana. *Women's and Social Affairs:* Virgília Matabele. *Youth and Sport:* David Simango. *Minister of Diplomatic Affairs (President's Office):* Francisco Madeira. *Minister of Parliamentary Affairs (President's Office):* Isabel Manuel Nkavadeka.

Government Website (Portuguese only):
http://www.mozambique.mz

CURRENT LEADERS

Armando Guebuza

Position
President

Introduction
Armando Guebuza, a veteran of Mozambique's fight for independence and one of the nation's wealthiest businessmen, was chosen as the ruling party's candidate for the 2004 presidential elections. He won with a large majority and took office in Feb. 2005.

Early Life
Armando Emílio Guebuza was born on 20 Jan. 1943 in Murrupula, in the northern province of Nampula, Mozambique. He was politically active from an early age and was elected in 1963 as president of the Mozambican Centre of African Students (NESAM), a group created by Eduardo Mondlane, then the leader of Mozambique's fight for independence from Portugal. Later that year Guebuza joined the Liberation Front of Mozambique (FRELIMO) and in 1965 was elected to the organization's central and executive committees. Having undergone military training in Tanzania, Guebuza was involved in guerrilla fighting against the Portuguese administration in northern Mozambique. Following Mondlane's assassination in 1969, FRELIMO was led by Uria Simango and then Samora Moises Machel. Under Machel the organization grew to include over 7,000 guerrillas and by the early 1970s had control over much of northern and central Mozambique. Guebuza became a general and was also an inspector of the schools that were run by FRELIMO.

When Marcello Caetano was overthrown as the Portuguese premier in a military coup on 25 April 1974, independence was assured for Mozambique. Following the signing of the Lusaka Agreements later in 1974, Guebuza was appointed minister of internal administration in the transitional government that led the country to full independence in June 1975. He served as minister of the interior in the single-party Marxist government led by President Machel. Guebuza was responsible for implementing the notorious '20–24' decree, which gave Portuguese settlers 24 hours to leave the country, carrying a maximum of 20 kg of luggage. He went on to serve as vice minister of defence in 1980, against a backdrop of economic decline, drought and warfare with the Mozambique National Resistance (RENAMO), which was backed by the apartheid government in South Africa. While Guebuza was again minister of the interior (1983–85) he was heavily identified with Operation Production, under which thousands of unemployed residents of the cities of Maputo and Beira were forcibly sent to work-camps in the isolated northern province of Niassa.

Joaquim Chissano became president in 1986, following Machel's death in an aircraft crash, and Guebuza was appointed minister of transport. In 1990 he headed the FRELIMO government's delegation to negotiate a peace settlement with RENAMO, leading to the signing of the Rome Peace Agreement in Oct. 1992. By then, however, Mozambique was one of the poorest countries in the world. Having formally renounced Marxism in 1989, the government set about developing a market-oriented economy. Guebuza spearheaded many of these reforms, advocating the need to foster entrepreneurship and a new middle class. He developed business interests in many sectors, including brewing, investment banking and shipping. In the country's first multi-party elections in 1994, won by FRELIMO, Guebuza was elected head of the FRELIMO parliamentary group. He retained that position in the elections of 1999, when Joaquim Chissano again led FRELIMO to victory.

Chissano announced that he would stand down at the 2004 elections. During FRELIMO's national congress in June 2002, Guebuza was elected the party's secretary-general and presidential candidate. His uncompromising nationalist stance and promise to continue the economic reforms of his predecessor won him a large majority in the presidential polling in Dec. 2004 (with 63·7% of the vote), although RENAMO alleged the election had been rigged. In parliamentary elections staged at the same time FRELIMO retained its majority in the National Assembly.

Career in Office
Guebuza was sworn in as president on 2 Feb. 2005 and Lúisa Diogo, the prime minister since Feb. 2004, was reappointed to head the government. Guebuza pledged an 'unrelenting fight against poverty' and promised to tackle corruption, as well as work to attract further foreign investment to build infrastructure. In mid-2005 a trade and investment agreement was signed with the USA, whose officials cited Mozambique as 'a positive model because of its impressive track record on democracy, political stability, economic growth, openness to foreign direct investment and expanding exports'.

DEFENCE

The President of the Republic is C.-in-C. of the armed forces. Defence expenditure totalled US$93m. in 2003 (US$5 per capita), representing 2·2% of GDP.

Army

Personnel numbered 9–10,000 in 2002.

Navy

Naval personnel in 2002 were believed to total 150.

Air Force

Personnel (2002) 1,000 (including air defence units). There were four armed helicopters but no combat aircraft.

INTERNATIONAL RELATIONS

Mozambique is a member of the UN, WTO, the Commonwealth, the African Union, African Development Bank, SADC, Non-Aligned Movement, Organization of the Islamic Conference, Islamic Development Bank, Indian Ocean Rim, Organization of the Portuguese Language Countries and is an ACP member state of the ACP–EU relationship.

IMF projections to 2005 indicated the halving of aid inflows from US$1bn. a year in the 1990s to US$500m. Mozambique is very heavily dependent on foreign aid. In 1996 official aid made up 72% of GDP.

ECONOMY

Agriculture accounted for 26·6% of GDP in 2002, industry 28·9% and services 44·5%.

Overview

A privatization programme launched in 1989 resulted in the partial or total privatization of over 1,200 enterprises by 2002. Heavy flooding in 2000 devastated the economy and infrastructure.

Currency

The unit of currency is the *metical* (MZM) of 100 *centavos*. Inflation was 13·4% in 2003 and 12·6% in 2004. Foreign exchange reserves were US$706m. in June 2002. Total money supply in May 2002 was 10,364·30bn. meticais.

Budget

In 2001 revenues were 19,253m. meticais and expenditures 23,221m. meticais.

Performance

GDP growth has averaged 8·7% since 1997, making Mozambique one of Africa's fastest expanding economies. Mozambique was forecast to be among the fastest growing economies in the world in 2000 but the disastrous floods of early 2000 caused a major setback, resulting in growth for the year of only 1·9%. However, the economy then grew by 13·1% in 2001, one of the highest rates in the world, 8·2% in 2002, 7·8% in 2003 and 7·2% in 2004. Total GDP in 2004 was US$5·5bn.

Banking and Finance

Most banks had been nationalized by 1979. The central bank and bank of issue is the Bank of Mozambique (*Governor*, Adriano Afonso Maleiane) which hived off its commercial functions in 1992 to the newly-founded Commercial Bank of Mozambique. In 1998 the Commercial Bank of Mozambique had 35% of deposits. In 2002 there were ten commercial banks, three foreign banks and a credit fund for agricultural and rural development. The new Mozambique Stock Exchange opened in Maputo in Oct. 1999. By the late 1990s financial services had become one of the fastest-growing areas of the economy.

ENERGY AND NATURAL RESOURCES

Environment

Carbon dioxide emissions from the consumption and flaring of fossil fuels in 2002 were the equivalent of 0·1 tonnes per capita.

Electricity

Installed capacity was 2·1m. kW in 2000. Production in 2000 was 6·97m. kWh; consumption per capita was 88 kWh.

Oil and Gas

Natural gas finds are being explored for potential exploitation, and both onshore and offshore foreign companies are prospecting for oil. In 2002 natural gas reserves were 57bn. cu. metres. Some river basins, especially the Rovuma, Zambezi and Limpopo, are of interest to oil prospectors.

Water

Although the country is rich in water resources, the provision of drinking water to rural areas remains a major concern.

Minerals

There are deposits of pegamite, tantalite, graphite, apatite, tin, iron ore and bauxite. Other known reserves are: nepheline, syenite, magnetite, copper, garnet, kaolin, asbestos, bentonite, limestone, gold, titanium and tin.

Output (in 1,000 tonnes): aluminium (2001), 266; salt (1997 estimate), 60; coal (2000), 19; bauxite (2001), 7.

Agriculture

All land is owned by the state but concessions are given. There were 4·0m. ha. of arable land in 2001 and 0·24m. ha. of permanent crops. 107,000 ha. were irrigated in 2001. There were 5,750 tractors in 2001. Production in 1,000 tonnes (2000): cassava, 4,643; maize, 1,019; sugarcane, 440; coconuts, 300; sorghum, 252; rice, 158; groundnuts, 100; seed cotton, 80; copra, 73; bananas, 59; cottonseed, 51; potatoes, 50.

Livestock, 2000: 1·32m. cattle, 392,000 goats, 125,000 sheep, 180,000 pigs, 28m. chickens.

A quarter of all crops and a third of cattle were lost during the flooding which devastated the country in the early part of 2000.

Forestry

In 2000 there were 30·60m. ha. of forests, or 39·0% of the land area, including eucalyptus, pine and rare hardwoods. In 2001 timber production was 18·04m. cu. metres.

Fisheries

The catch in 2001 was 32,512 tonnes, of which 24,436 tonnes were from sea fishing. Prawn and shrimp are the major exports at 10,000 tonnes per year. The potential sustainable annual catch is estimated at 500,000 tonnes of fish (anchovies 300,000 tonnes, the rest mainly mackerel).

INDUSTRY

Although the country is overwhelmingly rural, there is some substantial industry in and around Maputo (steel, engineering, textiles, processing, docks and railways). A huge aluminium smelter, completed in 2000, is scheduled to produce 250,000 tonnes annually and is a focal point in the country's strategy of attracting foreign investment.

Labour

The labour force in 1996 totalled 9,221,000 (52% males). In 1998, 83% of the economically active population were engaged in agriculture, 8% in industry and 9% in services. Women represent 48% of the total labour force.

Trade Unions

The main trade union confederation is the Organização dos Trabalhadores de Moçambique, but several unions have broken away.

INTERNATIONAL TRADE

Foreign debt was US$4,609m. in 2002.

Imports and Exports

Imports (c.i.f.) totalled US$1,849·7m. in 2004 (US$1,648·1m. in 2003). Exports (f.o.b.) totalled US$1,503·9m. in 2004 (US$1,043·9m. in 2003). Principal imports in 1999 (in US$1m.): machinery and transport equipment, 287·6; foodstuffs, 113·5 (including 76·1 of cereals); manufactured goods, 79·4; chemicals, 73·9; mineral fuels, 73·9. Principal exports in 1999: prawns, 74·8; mineral fuels, 67·8; cashew nuts, 40·2; cotton, 20·0.

Main import suppliers in 1998: Southern African Customs Union, 42·2%; Portugal, 7·9%; USA, 5·3%. Main export markets in 1999: Southern African Customs Union, 28·1%; Zimbabwe, 14·8%; Spain, 12·7%; India, 11·8%; Portugal, 9·0%.

COMMUNICATIONS

Roads

In 2002 there were estimated to be 30,400 km of roads, of which 18·7% were paved. Passenger cars numbered 86,500 in 2002. There were 4,748 road accidents in 1997, with 805 fatalities. The flooding of early 2000 washed away at least one fifth of the country's main road linking the north and the south.

Rail

The state railway consists of five separate networks, with principal routes on 1,067 mm gauge radiating from the ports of Maputo (950 km), Beira (994 km) and Nacala (914 km). Total length in 1995 was 2,983 km of 1,067 mm gauge and 140 km of 762 mm gauge. In 2000, 1·8m. passengers and 2·2m. tonnes of freight were carried. In early 2000 long sections of the railway line linking Mozambique with Zimbabwe were washed away in the floods.

Civil Aviation

There are international airports at Maputo and Beira. The national carrier is the state-owned Linhas Aéreas de Moçambique (LAM). It provides domestic services and in 2003 operated international routes to Comoros, Dar es Salaam, Durban, Harare, Johannesburg and Lisbon. In 2001 Maputo handled 394,671 passengers (213,612 on international flights) and Beira 106,586 (98,590 on domestic flights). In 1999 scheduled airline traffic of Mozambique-based carriers flew 5·3m. km, carrying 235,000 passengers (87,000 on international flights).

Shipping

The principal ports are Maputo, Beira, Nacala and Quelimane. In 2002 the merchant fleet had a total displacement of 37,000 GRT.

Telecommunications

Telephone subscribers numbered 338,500 in 2002 (18·6 per 1,000 persons) and there were 82,000 PCs in use (4·5 per 1,000 persons). There were 254,800 mobile phone subscribers in 2002 and 11,700 fax machines. In 2001 there were 30,000 Internet users.

Postal Services

In 2003 there were 272 post offices. Postal services in Mozambique are provided by a public company, Correios de Moçambique, E.P.

SOCIAL INSTITUTIONS

Justice

The 1990 Constitution provides for an independent judiciary, *habeas corpus*, and an entitlement to legal advice on arrest. The death penalty was abolished in Nov. 1990. The judiciary is riddled with bribery and extortion.

The population in penal institutions in Dec. 1999 was 8,812 (50 per 100,000 of national population).

Education

The adult literacy rate in 2002 was 46·5% (62·3% among males but only 31·4% among females).

In 2003 there were 3,177,586 pupils with 51,912 teachers in 9,027 primary schools; and 160,093 pupils with 4,112 teachers at 154 secondary schools. Private schools and universities were permitted to function in 1990. Eduardo Mondlane University had 3,470 students and 390 academic staff in 1995–96. In the late 1990s a further four institutions of higher education opened: the Higher Institute of International Relations (ISRI), the Pedagogical University (UP), the University and Polytechnic Higher Institute (ISPU) and the Catholic University (UC).

In 1999–2000 total expenditure on education came to 2·5% of GNP and 12·3% of total government spending.

Health

There were (2004) 46 hospitals, 722 health centres and 479 medical posts. There were two psychiatric hospitals. In 2000 there were 435 doctors, 1,414 midwives, 3,664 nursing personnel, 136 dentists and 419 pharmacists. Private health care was introduced alongside the national health service in 1992.

RELIGION

About 55% of the population follow traditional animist religions. In 2001 there were 6·18m. Christians (mainly Roman Catholic) and 2·04m. Muslims. In May 2005 there was one cardinal.

CULTURE

World Heritage Sites

Mozambique has one site on the UNESCO World Heritage List: the Island of Mozambique (inscribed on the list in 1991), a Portuguese trading post with a style of architecture unchanged since the 16th century.

Broadcasting

Radio Moçambique is part state-owned and part commercial. There are three national programmes in Tsonga and Portuguese and an external service in English. Television is at a trial stage (colour by PAL). There were 230,000 TV receivers in 2001 and 778,000 radio sets in 2000.

TVM is the national television station; RTK (Klint Radio and Television) is privately owned.

Cinema

There is a National Institute of Cinema (INC) that was set up in 1975 just after independence. There are at least three cinemas in Maputo.

Press

There are two well-established daily newspapers (*Noticias* and *Diário* in Maputo and Beira respectively). Five additional newspapers were registered in 1998: *Savana, Mediacoop, Demos, Metical* and *Domingo*.

Tourism

Tourism is a potential growth area for the country. Total tourist revenue was US$144m. in 2002. There are 2,500 km of Indian Ocean beaches, coral reefs, diving, deep-sea fishing, wildlife, game parks, highlands and plains.

Festivals

There are annual culture festivals throughout the country.

Libraries

As well as libraries at the higher education institutes, there is an independent public library in Maputo.

Theatre and Opera

In addition to state-owned theatres and opera houses, Avenida and Matchedge are privately owned.

DIPLOMATIC REPRESENTATIVES

Of Mozambique in the United Kingdom (21 Fitzroy Sq., London, W1T 6EL)
High Commissioner: Antonio Gumende.

Of the United Kingdom in Mozambique (Ave. Vladimir I. Lenine 310, Maputo)
High Commissioner: Howard Parkinson, CVO.

Of Mozambique in the USA (1990 M. St., NW, Washington, D.C., 20036)
Ambassador: Armando Alexandre Panguene.

Of the USA in Mozambique (Ave. Kenneth Kaunda 193, Maputo)
Ambassador: Helen R. Meagher La Lime.

Of Mozambique to the United Nations
Ambassador: Filipe Chidumo.

Of Mozambique to the European Union
Ambassador: Maria Manuela dos Santos Lucas.

FURTHER READING

Andersson, H., *Mozambique: a War against the People.* London, 1993
Finnegan, W., *A Complicated War: the Harrowing of Mozambique.* California Univ. Press, 1992
Newitt, M., *A History of Mozambique.* Farnborough, 1996

National Statistical Office: Instituto Nacional de Estatística, Av. Ahmed Sekou Touré, No. 21.
Website: http://www.ine.gov.mz/

MYANMAR

INDIA

CHINA

Mandalay●

MYANMAR

Sittwe●

LAOS

YANGON
(RANGOON)

Bassein●

THAILAND

INDIAN
OCEAN

*Andaman
Sea*

*Gulf of
Thailand*

0   100 mi

0   100 km

© Research Machines plc 2006

Myanmar Naingngandaw
(Union of Myanmar)

Capital: Yangon (Rangoon)

Population projection, 2010: 52·80m.

GDP per capita: not available

GNI per capita: $220

HDI/world rank: 0·578/129

KEY HISTORICAL EVENTS

After Burma's invasion of the kingdom of Assam, the British East India Company retaliated in defence of its Indian interests and in 1826 drove the Burmese out of India. Territory was annexed in south Burma but the kingdom of Upper Burma, ruled from Mandalay, remained independent. A second war with Britain in 1852 ended with the British annexation of the Irrawaddy Delta. In 1885 the British invaded and occupied Upper Burma. In 1886 all Burma became a province of the Indian empire. There were violent uprisings in the 1930s and in 1937 Burma was separated from India and permitted some degree of self-government. Independence was achieved in 1948.

In 1958 there was an army coup, and another in 1962 led by Gen. Ne Win, who installed a Revolutionary Council and dissolved parliament.

The Council lasted until March 1974 when the country became a one-party socialist republic. On 18 Sept. 1988 the Armed Forces seized power and set up the State Law and Order Restoration Council (SLORC). Since then civil unrest has cost more than 10,000 lives. On 19 June 1989 the government changed the name of the country in English to the Union of Myanmar. Aung San Suu Kyi, leader of the National League for Democracy, was put under house arrest in July 1989. In spite of her continuing detention, her party won the 1990 election by a landslide, but the military junta refused to accept the results. She was eventually freed in July 1995, only to be placed under house arrest for a second time in Sept. 2000; she was again released in May 2002, and then again detained in May 2003.

TERRITORY AND POPULATION

Myanmar is bounded in the east by China, Laos and Thailand, and west by the Indian Ocean, Bangladesh and India. Three parallel mountain ranges run from north to south; the Western Yama or Rakhine Yama, the Bagu Yama and the Shaun Plateau. The total area of the Union is 676,577 sq. km (261,228 sq. miles). At the last census, in 1983, the population was 35,307,913. Estimate (2005) 50·52m. (25·44m. female); density, 75 per sq. km. In 2003, 70·5% of the population lived in rural areas.

The UN gives a projected population for 2010 of 52·80m.

The capital is Yangon (Rangoon); its population was 4,101,000 in 1999. Other leading towns are Mandalay, Moulmein, Pegu, Bassein, Sittwe (Akyab), Taunggye and Monywa. In Nov. 2005 the government began moving to a new administrative capital, Pyinmana.

The population of the seven states and seven administrative divisions (2000 estimates): Irrawaddy Division, 6,779,000; Magwe Division, 4,548,000; Mandalay Division, 6,574,000; Pegu Division, 5,099,000; Sagaing Division, 5,488,000; Tenasserim Division, 1,356,000; Yangon Division, 5,560,000; Chin State, 480,000; Kachin State, 1,272,000; Kayah State, 266,000; Karen State, 1,489,000; Mon State, 2,502,000; Rakhine State, 2,744,000; Shan State, 4,851,000. Myanmar is inhabited by many ethnic nationalities. There are as many as 135 national groups with the Bamars, comprising about 68·96% of the population, forming the largest group.

The official language is Burmese; English is also in use.

SOCIAL STATISTICS

2000 estimates: births, 1,165,000; deaths, 550,000. Estimated birth rate in 2002 was 23·7 per 1,000 population; estimated death rate, 11·2. Annual population growth rate, 1992–2002, 1·5%. Life expectancy at birth, 2003, was 57·5 years for males and 63·1 years for females. Infant mortality, 2001, 77 per 1,000 live births; fertility rate, 2001, 3·0 births per woman.

CLIMATE

The climate is equatorial in coastal areas, changing to tropical monsoon over most of the interior, but humid temperate in the extreme north, where there is a more significant range of temperature and a dry season lasting from Nov. to April. In coastal parts, the dry season is shorter. Very heavy rains occur in the monsoon months May to Sept. Rangoon, Jan. 77°F (25°C), July 80°F (26·7°C). Annual rainfall 104" (2,616 mm). Akyab, Jan. 70°F (21·1°C), July 81°F (27·2°C). Annual rainfall 206" (5,154 mm). Mandalay, Jan. 68°F (20°C), July 85°F (29·4°C). Annual rainfall 33" (828 mm).

CONSTITUTION AND GOVERNMENT

The constitution of 3 Jan. 1974 has been suspended since 1988. Following elections in May 1990, the ruling State Law and Order Restoration Council (SLORC) said it would hand over power after the 485-member People's Assembly had agreed on a new constitution, but in July 1990 it stipulated that any such constitution must conform to guidelines which it would itself prescribe.

In May 1991, 48 members of the National League for Democracy (NLD) were given prison sentences on charges of treason. In July 1991 opposition members of the People's Assembly were unseated for alleged offences ranging from treason to illicit foreign exchange dealing. Such members, and unsuccessful candidates in the May 1990 elections, are forbidden to stand in future elections.

On 28 Nov. 1995 the government re-opened a 706-member Constitutional Convention in which the NLD was given 107 places. The NLD withdrew on 29 Nov.

In Nov. 1997 the country's ruling generals changed the name of the government to the State Peace and Development Council (SPDC) and reshuffled the cabinet. In Dec. 1997, following a period when the national currency fell to a record low, there were further changes to the cabinet, while corruption investigations were begun against some former ministers.

National Anthem

'Gba majay Bma' ('We shall love Burma for ever'); words and tune by Saya Tin.

RECENT ELECTIONS

In elections in May 1990 the opposition National League for Democracy (NLD), led by Aung San Suu Kyi (b. 1945), won 392 of the 485 People's Assembly seats contested with some 60% of the valid vote. Turnout was 72%, but 12·4% of ballots cast were declared invalid. The military ignored the result and refused to hand over power.

CURRENT ADMINISTRATION

In March 2006 the government comprised:

Chairman of the State Peace and Development Council (SPCD) and Minister of Defence: Senior Gen. Than Shwe; b. 1933 (in office since 23 April 1992).

Prime Minister: Lieut.-Gen. Soe Win; b. 1948 (appointed 19 Oct. 2004).

Secretary-1 of the SPDC: Lieut.-Gen. Thein Sein. *Secretary-2 of the SPDC:* Vacant.

Minister of Agriculture and Irrigation: Maj.-Gen. Htay Oo. *Industry (No. 1):* Aung Thaung. *Industry (No. 2):* Maj.-Gen. Saw Lwin. *Foreign Affairs:* Maj. Gen. Nyan Win. *National Planning and Economic Development:* Soe Tha. *Transport:* Maj.-Gen. Thein Swe. *Culture:* Maj.-Gen. Kyi Aung. *Co-operatives:* Col. Zaw Min. *Rail Transportation:* Maj.-Gen. Aung Min. *Energy:* Brig.-Gen. Lun Thi. *Education:* Chan Nyein. *Health:* Dr Khaw Myint. *Commerce:* Brig.-Gen. Tin Naing Thein. *Hotels and Tourism, and Communications, Posts and Telegraphs:* Brig.-Gen. Thein Zaw. *Finance and Revenue:* Maj. Gen. Hla Tun. *Religious Affairs:* Brig.-Gen. Thura Myint Maung. *Construction:* Maj.-Gen. Saw Tun. *Immigration and Population, and Social Welfare, Relief and Resettlement:* Maj.-Gen. Sein Htwa. *Labour, and Science and Technology:* U Thaung. *Information:* Brig.-Gen. Kyaw Hsan. *Progress of Border Areas, National Races and Development Affairs:* Col. Thein Nyunt. *Electric Power:* Maj.-Gen. Tin Htut. *Sports:* Brig.-Gen. Thura Aye Myint. *Forestry:* Brig.-Gen. Thein Aung. *Home Affairs:* Maj.-Gen. Maung Oo. *Mines:* Brig.-Gen. Ohn Myint. *Livestock and Fisheries:* Brig.-Gen. Maung Maung Thein.

CURRENT LEADERS

Senior Gen. Than Shwe

Position
Chairman of the State Peace and Development Council

Introduction
Than Shwe became Myanmar's head of state and government in 1992, succeeding Saw Maung as leader of the military junta. Political oppression and widespread civil rights abuses have led to the nation's international isolation. The economy is blighted by corruption and bad management and a reliance on the black market.

Early Life
Than Shwe was born on 2 Feb. 1933 in Kyaukse, Myanmar. He joined the army when he was 20 and had a decorated career, holding several high-profile positions including chief of staff at the ministry of defence and vice chief of staff of the army. In 1990 he was appointed deputy commander-in-chief of the defence services and deputy chairman of the State Law and Order Restoration Council (SLORC). In April 1992 Than Shwe succeeded Saw Maung as chairman of the SLORC, prime minister and minister of defence.

Career in Office
Than Shwe's legitimacy as head of state and government has been challenged by the presence of Aung San Suu Kyi, who led the National League for Democracy (NLD) to a handsome victory in the free elections of 1990 (Myanmar's first since the 1960s). Saw Maung and the army refused to recognize the result, but international dissatisfaction was reflected in 1991 when Aung San Suu Kyi received the Nobel Peace Prize. Put under house arrest after the elections, she was released in 1995 but the Than Shwe regime continued its oppression of the NLD. In Nov. 1997 the SLORC reconstituted itself as the State Peace and Development Council (SPDC).

In 2000 Aung San Suu Kyi began secret negotiations with the SPDC. However, despite Than Shwe authorizing the release of several hundred political prisoners, Myanmar's reputation for human rights abuses has worsened. Amnesty International reported the increased use of torture, and critics suggested that prisoner releases were motivated by the hope of foreign aid rather than the desire to create a more transparent political infrastructure. Myanmar attracted further international condemnation when the International Labour Organization highlighted the used of forced adult and child labour. In June 2001 several opposition parties were allowed to resume operations and in May 2002 Aung San Suu Kyi was released from the house arrest which had been reimposed in 2000. However, she was again put under 'protective custody' in May 2003 after clashes between NLD supporters and government forces.

Than Shwe has overseen the continued decline of the economy, with inflation spiralling and export revenues shrinking. Much of Myanmar's commerce relies on the black market, with heroin among the country's leading revenue earners. Military control of many key industrial sectors has resulted in corruption and bad management.

In foreign policy, the oppressive nature of Than Shwe's regime has seen Myanmar increasingly isolated. However, there have been some successes, notably acceptance into ASEAN in 1997 and the visit of China's President Jiang Zemin in 2001. Relations with neighbouring Thailand have been changeable. Tensions rose in 2001 when conflict between Myanmese troops and Shan separatist rebels spilled onto Thai territory, but subsequent meetings between the two countries helped restrengthen ties. Relations with Bangladesh have been strained since the early 1990s when up to 250,000 Muslim Rohingya refugees entered Bangladesh from Myanmar. However, there was some improvement when, in 2001, Than Shwe abandoned a proposed dam on the Naf River, shared by the two countries, which Bangladesh had claimed would cause widespread damage. In Dec. 2002 talks between Than Shwe and Bangladeshi Prime Minister Khaleda Zia resulted in accords on closer economic co-operation and improved road and shipping links. The first authorized sea route between the two countries was opened in Feb. 2003 and the following month Khaleda Zia made the first official visit to Myanmar by a Bangladeshi prime minister.

In 2002 the international community expressed concern at Than Shwe's deal with Russia to develop nuclear facilities. The USA, EU, China and IAEA all raised doubts about Myanmar's ability to ensure the safety of such enterprises while the NLD suggested that it could lead to the development of nuclear arms.

The renewed detention of Aung San Suu Kyi in May 2003 provoked further hostility from the international community and unprecedented public criticism from ASEAN. Malaysia's then prime minister, Mahathir Mohamad, suggested that Myanmar could be expelled from ASEAN as a last resort, although the then Thai prime minister, Thaksin Shinawatra, emphasized the importance of Myanmar's continued membership for the promotion of democracy in the country. Fresh sanctions were imposed by the USA and the EU, but neither banned all investment in Myanmar and large oil companies have continued to operate there.

In Aug. 2003 the head of intelligence, Gen. Khin Nyunt, was appointed prime minister and unveiled a seven-point road map to democracy. At that time, his appointment suggested a step closer to negotiations with the NLD, and from May–July 2004 a national convention was reconvened for the first time since 1996 to draw up a new constitution for Myanmar. However, in Oct. 2004 Khin Nyunt was removed from office and arrested on charges of corruption. The national convention met again in Feb.–March 2005, but then went into extended recess.

DEFENCE

Military expenditure in 2003 totalled US$6,260m. (US$127 per capita), representing 9·6% of GDP.

Army

The strength of the Army was reported to be about 325,000 in 2002. The Army is organized into 12 regional commands. There are two paramilitary units: People's Police Force (65,000) and People's Militia (35,000).

Navy

Personnel in 2002 totalled about 10,000 including 800 naval infantry.

Air Force

The Air Force is intended primarily for internal security duties. Personnel (2002) 9,000 operating 113 combat aircraft, including F-7s, and 29 armed helicopters.

INTERNATIONAL RELATIONS

Myanmar is a member of the UN, WTO, Asian Development Bank, Colombo Plan, ASEAN and the Mekong Group.

In 2001 tension between Myanmar and neighbouring Thailand escalated amid a series of border skirmishes, in part over the cross-border trade in drugs. In May 2002 the border between the two countries was closed following a diplomatic row. It was re-opened in Oct. 2002.

ECONOMY

Agriculture accounted for 53·2% of GDP in 1998, industry 9·0% and services 37·8%.

Currency

The unit of currency is the *kyat* (MMK) of 100 *pyas*. Total money supply was K.779,984m. in Feb. 2002. Foreign exchange reserves

were US$454m. in March 2002 and gold reserves 231,000 troy oz in June 2002. Inflation was 24·9% in 2003, falling to 10·0% in 2004. Since 1 June 1996 import duties have been calculated at a rate US$1 = K.100.

Budget

Budget revenue and expenditure (in K.1m.), year beginning 1 April:

	1996	1997	1998	1999	2000
Revenue	54,726	86,690	116,066	122,895	134,308
Expenditure	80,120	98,426	124,064	153,497	221,255

State budget estimates are classified into three parts, *viz.* State Administrative Organizations, State Economic Enterprises and Town and City Development Committees.

Performance

Real GDP growth was 13·8% in 2003 and 5·0% in 2004.

Banking and Finance

The Central Bank of Myanmar was established in 1990. Its *Governor* is Kyaw Kyaw Maung. In 2002 there were two state banks (Myanma Economic Bank and Myanma Foreign Trade Bank), two development banks (Myanma Agricultural and Rural Development Bank and Myanma Investment and Commercial Bank) and 17 private banks. Since 1996 foreign banks with representative offices (there were 31 in 1996) have been permitted to set up joint ventures with Myanmese banks. The foreign partner must provide at least 35% of the capital. The state insurance company is the Myanmar Insurance Corporation. Deposits in savings banks were K.30,963m. in 1994.

Myanmar was one of three countries named in a report in June 2005 as failing to co-operate in the fight against international money laundering. The Financial Action Task Force on Money Laundering was set up by the G7 group of major industrialized nations.

A stock exchange opened in Rangoon in 1996.

Weights and Measures

The British Imperial and metric systems are used but in the markets traditional measurements are common: one *tical* (*kyat-tha*) = 16·33 grams; one *viss* (*peit-tha*) = 100 ticals.

ENERGY AND NATURAL RESOURCES

Environment

Myanmar's carbon dioxide emissions from the consumption and flaring of fossil fuels in 2002 were the equivalent of 0·2 tonnes per capita.

Electricity

Total electricity generated, 2000, 5·08bn. kWh; consumption per capita in 2000 was 106 kWh. Installed capacity was 1·5m. kW in 2000.

Oil and Gas

Production (2000) of crude oil was 411,000 tonnes; natural gas (1999), 4·8bn. cu. metres. There were proven natural gas reserves of 346bn. cu. metres in 2002.

Minerals

Production in 2000 (in tonnes): lignite, 524,000; hard coal, 51,000; copper, 26,711. 1995–96: zinc concentrates, 6,070; refined lead, 4,250; tin, tungsten and scheelite mixed, 1,400; tin concentrates, 492; refined tin metal, 310; antimonial lead, 210; tungsten concentrates, 95; nickel speiss, 60; refined silver, 260,000 fine oz; gold (1999), 267 kg.

Agriculture

In 1995–96, 4·5m. peasant families cultivated 10·1m. ha. In 2001 there were 10·0m. ha. of arable land and 635,000 ha. of permanent crops.

Liberalization measures of 1990 permit farmers to grow crops of their choice. 1·99m. ha. were irrigated in 2001. Production (2000, in 1,000 tonnes): rice, 20,000; sugarcane, 5,147; dry beans, 1,229; groundnuts, 640; onions, 507; plantains, 354; maize, 349; sesame seeds, 302; sunflower seeds, 270; coconuts, 263; potatoes, 245. Opium output was 1,097 tonnes in 2001, falling to 828 tonnes in 2002, 810 tonnes in 2003 and 370 tonnes in 2004. Myanmar overtook Afghanistan as the world's largest producer of opium in 2001, but following the fall of the Taliban, opium production in Afghanistan increased to such an extent that output since then has been higher in Afghanistan than in Myanmar.

Livestock (2000): cattle, 10·96m.; buffaloes, 2·44m.; pigs, 3·91m.; goats, 1·39m.; sheep, 390,000; chickens, 44m. There were 6·8m. draught cattle in 1997. In 2001 there were 10,304 tractors and 21,562 harvester-threshers.

Forestry
Forest area in 2000 was 34·42m. ha., covering 52·3% of the total land area. Teak resources cover about 6m. ha. (15m. acres). In 2001, 39·37m. cu. metres of roundwood were cut.

Fisheries
In 2001 the total catch was 1,166,868 tonnes (931,492 tonnes from sea fishing). Aquacultural fish production was 79,851 tonnes in 1995–96. Cultured pearls and oyster shells are produced.

INDUSTRY
Production in 1,000 tonnes: cement (2001), 384; sawnwood (2002), 381; sugar (2000), 75; fertilizers (2001), 60; paper and paperboard (2002), 42; cigarettes (2001), 2,650m. units; clay bricks (2001), 77m. units; bicycles (1995–96), 35,042 units.

Labour
In 1998 the civilian workforce in employment numbered 18,359,000. The leading areas of activity (in 1,000) were: agriculture, hunting, forestry and fishing, 11,507; wholesale and retail trade/repair of motor vehicles, motorcycles and personal and household goods, 1,781; manufacturing, 1,666. In 2001 there were 398,300 persons aged 18 years and over registered as unemployed.

INTERNATIONAL TRADE
In Aug. 1991 the USA imposed trade sanctions in response to alleged civil rights violations. Foreign debt was US$6,556m. in 2002. A law of 1989 permitted joint ventures, with foreign companies or individuals able to hold 100% of the shares.

Imports and Exports
Since 1990, in line with market-oriented measures, firms have been able to participate directly in trade.

Imports (f.o.b.) in 2004 totalled US$1,998·7m. and exports (f.o.b.) US$2,926·6m. Main imports, 1997–98: machinery and transport equipment, 28·6%; intermediate raw materials, 19·9%; basic manufactures, 15·8%; capital construction material, 12·3%; consumer durable goods, 4·3%. Leading import suppliers in 2001 were China, 21·8%; Singapore, 16·6%; Thailand, 13·9%; South Korea, 9·1%. Main exports in 1997–98: pulses and beans, 22·3%; teak, 11·1%; fish and fish products, 4·6%; hardwood, 2·5%; rubber, 2·1%. Main export markets, 2001: Thailand, 20·6%; USA, 16·2%; India, 10·2%; China, 5·0%.

COMMUNICATIONS

Roads
There were 35,892 km of roads in 2002, of which 12·9% were surfaced. An estimated 27,000 passenger cars were in use in 1996 (less than one per 1,000 inhabitants). In 1995–96 the state service ran 951 buses, 197 taxis and 1,969 lorries. There were also 155,107 buses and 29,694 lorries in private co-operative ownership. In 1995–96, 121·28m. passengers and 1·19m. tonnes of freight were carried by road.

Rail
In 1995 there were 3,955 km of route on metre gauge. Passenger-km travelled in 2000 came to 4,451m. and freight tonne-km to 1,122m.

Civil Aviation
Myanma Airways International operates domestic services and in 2003 had international flights to Bangkok, Kuala Lumpur and Singapore. In 1999 it flew 4·0m. km, carrying 392,200 passengers.

Shipping
There are nearly 100 km of navigable canals. The Irrawaddy is navigable up to Myitkyina, 1,450 km from the sea, and its tributary, the Chindwin, is navigable for 630 km. The Irrawaddy delta has approximately 3,000 km of navigable water. The Salween, the Attaran and the G'yne provide about 400 km of navigable waters around Moulmein. In 2002 merchant shipping totalled 402,000 GRT.

In 1995–96, 24·5m. passengers and 1·03m. tonnes of freight were carried on inland waterways. The ocean-going fleet of the state-owned Myanma Five Star Line in 1995 comprised 11 liners, four short-haul vessels and three coastal passenger/cargo vessels. In 1995–96, 60,000 passengers and 1,030,000 tonnes of freight were transported coastally and overseas. In 2000 vessels totalling 4,545,000 NRT entered ports and vessels totalling 2,252,000 NRT cleared. The port is Rangoon.

Telecommunications
Myanmar had 309,000 telephone subscribers in 2001 (6·4 per 1,000 persons) and there were 58,000 PCs in use in 2002 (1·2 for every 1,000 persons). In 2002 mobile phone subscribers numbered 48,000 and there were 4,000 fax machines in use. There were 25,000 Internet users in 2002.

Postal Services
In 2003 there were 1,314 post offices.

SOCIAL INSTITUTIONS

Justice
The highest judicial authority is the Chief Judge, appointed by the government. In 2004 there were approximately 60,000 people (120 per 100,000 of national population) held in prisons. Amnesty International reported in 2000 that there were more than 2,000 political prisoners in the country's jails.

Education
Education is free in primary, middle and vocational schools; fees are charged in senior secondary schools and universities. In 2000–01 there were 4,781,543 pupils at primary schools with 148,231 teachers; and 2,317,834 pupils at secondary schools with 75,272 teachers. In 1995–96 there were 1,578 monastic primary schools (permitted since 1992) with 80,863 pupils.

In higher education in 1995–96 there were 12 teacher training schools with 315 teachers and 2,067 students, five teacher training institutes with 304 teachers and 2,170 students, 17 technical high schools with 498 teachers and 7,145 students, 11 technical institutes with 668 teachers and 12,080 students, ten agricultural high schools with 100 teachers and 1,053 students, seven agricultural institutes with 162 teachers and 1,844 students, 41 vocational schools with 369 teachers and 6,532 students, six universities with 3,050 teachers and 154,680 students, six degree colleges with 705 teachers and 53,362 students, and ten colleges with 629 teachers and 40,327 students.

There was also a University for the Development of the National Races of the Union and institutes of medicine (3), dentistry, paramedical science, pharmacy, nursing, veterinary science, economics, technology (2), agriculture, education (2), foreign languages, computer science and forestry. An institute of remote education maintains a correspondence course at university level.

The adult literacy rate was 89·7% in 2003 (93·7% among males and 86·2% among females).

In 1999–2000 total expenditure on education came to 0·6% of GNP and 8·7% of total government spending.

Health
In 1996 there were 737 hospitals with a provision of seven beds per 10,000 inhabitants. In 2000 there were 14,356 physicians, 12,642 nurses, 10,307 midwives and 871 dentists (1999). Public spending on health is less than 0·2% of GDP.

Welfare
In 1995–96 contributions to social security totalled (K.1m.) 117·5 (from employers, 73·2; from employees, 43·9). Benefits paid totalled 82·6, and included: sickness, 12·9; maternity, 3·9; disability, 3·7; survivors' pensions, 1·3.

RELIGION
About 89·3% of the population—mainly Bamars, Shans, Mons, Rakhines and some Kayins—are Buddhists, while the rest are Christians, Muslims, Hindus and Animists. The Christian population is composed mainly of Kayins, Kachins and Chins. Islam and Hinduism are practised mainly by people of Indian origin.

CULTURE
Broadcasting
The government runs a TV and a radio station. There were 365,000 television receivers (colour by NTSC) in 2001 and 2·8m. radio sets in 2000.

Press
There were four daily newspapers in 1998, with a combined circulation of 400,000, at a rate of nine per 1,000 inhabitants.

Tourism
In 2001 there were 205,000 foreign tourists; spending by tourists totalled US$45m.

DIPLOMATIC REPRESENTATIVES
Of Myanmar in the United Kingdom (19A Charles St., London, W1J 5DX)
Ambassador: U Nay Win.

Of the United Kingdom in Myanmar (80 Strand Rd, Rangoon)
Ambassador: Victoria Bowman.

Of Myanmar in the USA (2300 S. St., NW, Washington, D.C., 20008)
Ambassador: Vacant.
Chargé d'Affaires a.i: Daw Yin Yin Myint.

Of the USA in Myanmar (581 Merchant St., Rangoon)
Ambassador: Shari Villarosa.

Of Myanmar to the United Nations
Ambassador: Kyaw Tint Swe.

Of Myanmar to the European Union
Ambassador: Wunna Maung Lwin.

FURTHER READING
Aung San Suu Kyi, *Freedom from Fear and Other Writings.* London, 1991
Carey, P. (ed.) *Burma: The Challenge of Change in a Divided Society.* London, 1997
Thant Myint-U, *The Making of Modern Burma.* CUP, 2001

National Statistical Office: Ministry of National Planning and Economic Development, Rangoon.

NAMIBIA

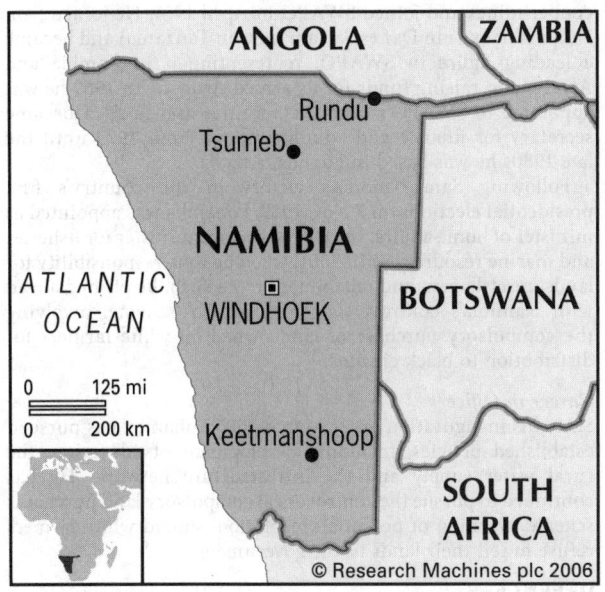

© Research Machines plc 2006

Republic of Namibia

Capital: Windhoek
Population projection, 2010: 2·13m.
GDP per capita, 2003: (PPP$) 6,180
HDI/world rank: 0·627/125

KEY HISTORICAL EVENTS

In 1884 South West Africa was declared a German protectorate. Germany then introduced racial segregation and the exploitation of the diamond mines began. In 1915 the Union of South Africa occupied German South West Africa and on 17 Dec. 1920 the League of Nations entrusted the territory as a Mandate to the Union of South Africa. After World War II South Africa applied for its annexation to the Union and continued to administer the territory in defiance of various UN resolutions. In June 1968 the UN changed the name of the territory to Namibia.

After negotiations between South Africa and the UN, a multi-racial Advisory Council was appointed in 1973 in preparation for independence, but despite several attempts at organizing free elections South Africa remained dominant in the area until the UN Transition Assistance Group supervised elections for the constituent assembly in Nov. 1989. Independence was achieved on 21 March 1990.

TERRITORY AND POPULATION

Namibia is bounded in the north by Angola and Zambia, west by the Atlantic Ocean, south and southeast by South Africa and east by Botswana. The Caprivi Strip (Caprivi Region), about 300 km long, extends eastwards up to the Zambezi river, projecting into Zambia and Botswana and touching Zimbabwe. The area, including the Caprivi Strip and Walvis Bay, is 825,112 sq. km. South Africa transferred Walvis Bay to Namibian jurisdiction on 1 March 1994. Census population, 1991, 1,409,920 (723,593 females; urban, 32·76%). 2001 census population, 1,830,330 (density 2·2 per sq. km). The estimated population in 2005 was 2,031,000. In 2003, 67·6% of the population were rural.

The UN gives a projected population for 2010 of 2·13m.

Population by ethnic group at the censuses of 1970 and 1981 and estimates for 1991:

	1970	1981	1991
Ovambos	342,455	506,114	665,000
Kavangos	49,577	95,055	124,000
Damaras	64,973	76,179	100,000
Hereros	55,670	76,296	100,000
Whites	90,658	76,430	85,000
Namas	32,853	48,541	64,000
Caprivians	25,009	38,594	50,000
Coloureds	28,275	42,254	—
Bushmen	21,909	29,443	—
Basters	16,474	25,181	—
Tswanas	4,407	6,706	—
Other	—	12,403	—
	732,260	1,033,196	1,401,711

Namibia is administratively divided into 13 regions. Area, population and chief towns in 2001:

Region	Area (in sq. km)	Population	Chief town
Caprivi (Liambezi)	19,532	79,826	Katima Mulilo
Erongo	63,719	107,663	Swakopmund
Hardap	109,888	68,249	Mariental
Karas	161,324	69,329	Keetmanshoop
Khomas	36,804	250,262	Windhoek
Kunene	144,254	68,735	Opuwo
Ohangwena	10,582	228,348	Oshikango
Okavango	43,417	202,694	Rundu
Omaheke	84,731	68,039	Gobabis
Omusati	13,637	228,842	Outapi
Oshana	5,290	161,916	Oshakati
Oshikoto	26,607	161,007	Tsumeb
Otjozondjupa	105,327	135,384	Grootfontein

Towns with populations over 5,000 (2001): Windhoek, 233,529; Rundu, 44,413; Walvis Bay, 42,015; Ondangwa, 29,783 (estimate); Oshakati, 28,255; Swakopmund, 25,442 (estimate); Grootfontein, 21,595 (estimate); Rehoboth, 21,300; Otjiwarongo, 19,614; Okahandja, 18,155 (estimate); Keetmanshoop, 15,543; Gobabis, 13,856; Lüderitz, 13,276 (estimate); Tsumeb, 13,108; Mariental, 11,977 (estimate); Khorixas, 10,906 (estimate).

English is the official language. Afrikaans and German are also spoken.

SOCIAL STATISTICS

Estimates, 2000: births, 68,000; deaths, 35,000. Estimated birth rate in 2000 was 34·5 per 1,000 population; estimated death rate, 17·8. Expectation of life, 2003: males, 47·6 years; females, 49·0. Annual population growth rate, 1992–2002, 2·7%; infant mortality, 2001, 55 per 1,000 live births; fertility rate, 2001, 5·0 births per woman.

CLIMATE

The rainfall increases steadily from less than 50 mm in the west and southwest up to 600 mm in the Caprivi Strip. The main rainy season is from Jan. to March, with lesser showers from Sept. to Dec. Namibia is the driest African country south of the Sahara.

CONSTITUTION AND GOVERNMENT

On 9 Feb. 1990 with a unanimous vote the Constituent Assembly approved the Constitution which stipulated a multi-party republic, an independent judiciary and an executive *President* who may serve a maximum of two five-year terms.

The constitution became effective on 12 March 1990 and was amended in 1999 to allow President Sam Nujoma to stand for a third term in office. The bicameral legislature consists of a 78-seat *National Assembly*, 72 members of which are elected for five-year terms by proportional representation and up to six appointed by the president by virtue of position or special expertise, and a 26-seat *National Council* consisting of two members from each Regional Council elected for six-year terms.

National Anthem
'Namibia, land of the brave'; words and tune by Axali Doeseb.

RECENT ELECTIONS

Presidential and parliamentary elections were held on 15–16 Nov. 2004. Hifikepunye Pohamba (South West Africa People's Organization/SWAPO) was elected president with 76·4% of votes cast followed by Ben Ulenga (Congress of Democrats/CoD) with 7·3%, Katuutire Kaura (Democratic Turnhalle Alliance/DTA) with 5·2%, Kuaima Riruako (National Unity Democratic Organization/NUDO) with 4·2% and Chief Justus Garoëb (United Democratic Front/UDF) with 3·7%. Turnout was 85·0%. In the parliamentary elections SWAPO won 55 of the available 72 seats with 75·1% of the vote; the CoD, 5 with 7·2%; DTA, 4 with 5·0%; NUDO, 3 with 4·1%; UDF, 3 with 3·5%; Republican Party, 1 with 1·9%; Monitor Action Group, 1 with 0·8%. Turnout was 84·4%.

CURRENT ADMINISTRATION

President: Hifikepunye Pohamba; b. 1935 (SWAPO; sworn in 21 March 2005).

In March 2006 the government comprised:
Prime Minister: Nahas Angula; b. 1943 (SWAPO; sworn in 21 March 2005).

Deputy Prime Minister: Libertina Amathila.

Minister of Home Affairs and Immigration: Rosalia Ngidinwa. *Presidential Affairs:* Albert Kawana. *Foreign Affairs:* Marco Hausiku. *Defence:* Maj.-Gen. Charles Namoloh. *Finance:* Saara Kuugongelwa-Amadhila. *Education:* Nangolo Mbumba. *Health and Social Services:* Richard Kamwi. *Mines and Energy:* Erkki Nghimtina. *Justice and Attorney General:* Pendukeni Iivula-Iithana. *Regional and Local Government, Housing and Rural Development:* John Pandeni. *Agriculture, Water and Forests:* Nickey Iyambo. *Trade and Industry:* Immanuel Ngatjizeko. *Environment and Tourism:* Willem Konjore. *Works, Transport and Communications:* Joel Kaapanda. *Lands and Rehabilitation:* Jerry Ekandjo. *Fisheries and Marine Resources:* Dr Abraham Iyambo. *Safety and Security:* Peter Tsheehama. *Youth, National Service, Culture and Sport:* John Mutorwa. *Women's Affairs and Child Welfare:* Marlène Mungunda. *Labour and Social Protection:* Alpheus Naruseb. *Information and Broadcasting:* Netumbo Nandi-Ndaitwah. *Minister without Portfolio:* Ngarikutuke Tjiriange.

Office of the Prime Minister: http://www.opm.gov.na

CURRENT LEADERS

Hifikepunye Pohamba

Position
President

Introduction
Lucas Hifikepunye Pohamba, representing the ruling South West Africa People's Organization (SWAPO), won a landslide victory at presidential elections in Nov. 2004 and took office in March 2005. He succeeded Namibia's 'founding father' and former president, Sam Nujoma, and was expected to continue with the same broad political programme.

Early Life
Pohamba was born on 18 Aug. 1935 at Okanghudi in South West Africa (modern Namibia) and educated at the Holy Cross Mission School at Onamunama. He worked in the Tsumeb copper mines and joined SWAPO in April 1959. He joined Sam Nujoma in exile in Dar es Salaam (now in Tanzania) and became a leading figure in SWAPO, representing it in Zambia and Algeria and raising funds for its armed struggle. In 1969 he was appointed to SWAPO's central committee and in 1975 became secretary for finance and administration. From 1979 until the late 1980s he was based in Luanda, Angola.

Following Sam Nujoma's victory in the country's first presidential elections on 7 Nov. 1989, Pohamba was appointed as minister of home affairs. In 1995 he became minister for fisheries and marine resources until 2001, when he took responsibility for lands, resettlement and rehabilitation. As such, he pushed ahead with Namibia's controversial 'land reform' scheme, involving the compulsory purchase of land owned by white farmers for distribution to black citizens.

Career in Office
Since his inauguration on 21 March 2005 Pohamba has pursued established policies, including development of education, the rural water supply and the infrastructure network. He has continued to pursue the controversial compulsory land purchases scheme, warning of potential 'revolution' should white farmers refuse to sell their lands to the government.

DEFENCE

In 2003 defence expenditure totalled US$105m. (US$52 per capita), representing 2·3% of GDP.

Army
Personnel (2002), 9,000.

Coastguard
A force of 200 (2002) is based at Walvis Bay.

Air Force
The Army has a small air wing.

INTERNATIONAL RELATIONS

Namibia is a member of the UN, WTO, the Commonwealth, the African Union, African Development Bank, SADC and is an ACP member state of the ACP-EU relationship.

ECONOMY

Agriculture accounted for 10·6% of GDP in 2002, industry 31·1% and services 58·3%.

The Namibian economy is heavily dependent on mining and fisheries.

Overview
Although the country is dependent on uranium, diamonds, silver, tin and zinc, the majority of the population is employed in agriculture and few benefit from the mineral wealth. The mining sector accounts for 50% of exports. 80% of the manufacturing industry is in food-related industries. There is strong potential for tourism. Since 1990 the government's role in the economy has expanded. It controls the electricity and water utilities, the national airline and a telecommunications company. Namibia is a member of the Southern African Customs Union, which has a 12% common external tariff. The country promotes foreign investment but favours domestic and foreign partnerships. Trade is closely linked to South Africa, although the EU is the country's core export market. Unemployment (including underemployment) is near 60%. The country's history of apartheid policies has led to unequal income distribution, one of the highest in the world, and a shortage of skilled labour. Agriculture employs nearly half of

the workforce. Namibia has one of the highest rates of HIV/ AIDS infection in the world.

Currency

The unit of currency is the *Namibia dollar* (NAD) of 100 *cents*, introduced on 14 Sept. 1993 and pegged to the South African rand. The rand is also legal tender at parity. Inflation was 7·2% in 2003 and 4·1% in 2004. In June 2002 foreign exchange reserves were US$230m. Gold reserves are negligible. Total money supply in June 2002 was N$7,063m.

Budget

The financial year runs from 1 April. Budgetary central government revenue and expenditure (in N$1m.):

	2001	2002	2003
Revenue	7,894	8,953	10,349
Expenditure	7,476	8,724	9,474

Performance

Real GDP growth was 3·7% in 2003 and 4·2% in 2004; total GDP in 2004 was US$5·5bn.

Banking and Finance

The Bank of Namibia is the central bank. Its *Governor* is Tom Alweendo. Commercial banks in 2002 included First National Bank of Namibia, Namibia Banking Corporation, Standard Bank Namibia, Commercial Bank of Namibia, Bank Windhoek (the only locally-owned bank) and City Savings and Investment Bank. There is a state-owned Agricultural Bank and a merchant bank, UAL-Namibia. Total assets of commercial banks were R2,383·2m. at 31 Dec. 1991.

There are two building societies with total assets (31 March 1990) R424·9m. A Post Office Savings Bank was established in 1916. In March 1991 its total assets were R21·8m. A stock exchange (NSE) is in operation in Windhoek.

ENERGY AND NATURAL RESOURCES

Environment

Carbon dioxide emissions from the consumption and flaring of fossil fuels were the equivalent of 1·2 tonnes per capita in 2002.

Electricity

In 2002 electricity production was 1·4bn. kWh. Namibia also imports electricity from South Africa (1·0bn. kWh in 2002). Consumption per capita in 1995 was 584 kWh.

Oil and Gas

Natural gas reserves in 2002 totalled 85bn. cu. metres.

Water

The 12 most important dams have a total capacity of 589·2m. cu. metres. The Kunene, the Okavango, the Zambezi, the Kwando or Mashi and the Orange River are the only permanently running rivers but water can generally be obtained by sinking shallow wells. Except for a few springs, mostly hot, there is no surface water.

Minerals

There are diamond deposits both inshore and off the coast, with production equally divided between the two. Some 3bn. carats of diamonds are believed to be lying in waters off Namibia's Atlantic coast. Namibia produced 1,611,000 carats in 1999, with 98% of the diamonds being of gem quality. Output (in tonnes): salt (1997), 493,000; lead (1996), 67,760; zinc (2001), 31,803; copper (2001), 12,392; silver (2001), 32; gold (2001), 2,851 kg; diamonds (2000), 1,606,000 carats. Uranium production, 2002, 2,333 tonnes.

Agriculture

Namibia is essentially a stock-raising country, the scarcity of water and poor rainfall rendering crop-farming, except in the northern and northeastern parts, almost impossible. There were 816,000 ha. of arable land in 2001 and 4,000 ha. of permanent crops. There were 3,150 tractors in 2001. Generally speaking, the southern half is suited for the raising of small stock, while the central and northern parts are more suited for cattle. Guano is harvested from the coast, converted into fertilizer in South Africa and most of it exported to Europe. In 2002, 40% of the active labour force worked in the agricultural sector and 68% of the population was dependent on agriculture.

Livestock (2000): 2·06m. cattle, 2·10m. sheep, 1·65m. goats, 2m. chickens.

In 2000, 75,000 tonnes of milk and 60,000 tonnes of meat were produced. Principal crops (2000, in tonnes): millet, 79,000; maize, 49,000; sorghum, 7,000; seed cotton, 5,000; wheat, 4,000.

Forestry

Forests covered 8·04m. ha. in 2000, or 9·8% of the land area.

Fisheries

Pilchards, mackerel and hake are the principal fish caught. The catch in 2001 was 547,492 tonnes, of which more than 99% came from marine waters. Conservation policies are in place. The policy aims at ensuring that the country's fisheries resources are utilized on a sustainable basis and also aims to ensure their lasting contribution to the country's economy.

INDUSTRY

Of the estimated total of 400 undertakings, the most important branches are food production (accounting for 29·3% of total output), metals (12·7%) and wooden products (7%). The supply of specialized equipment to the mining industry, the assembly of goods from predominantly imported materials and the manufacture of metal products and construction material play an important part. Small industries (including home industries, textile mills, leather and steel goods) have expanded. Products manufactured locally include chocolates, beer, cement, leather shoes, delicatessen meats and game meat products.

Labour

Of 431,800 people in employment in 2000, 126,500 were engaged in agriculture, hunting and forestry; 46,300 in community, social and personal service activities; 39,300 in real estate, renting and business activities; and 38,900 in wholesale and retail trade/ repair of motor vehicles, motorcycles and personal and household goods. In 2000 the unemployment rate was 33·8%.

INTERNATIONAL TRADE

Total foreign debt was US$140m. in 1996. Export Processing Zones were established in 1995 to grant companies with EPZ status some tax exemptions and other incentives. The Offshore Development Company (ODC) is the flagship of the Export Processing Zone regime. The EPZ regime does not restrict; any investor (local or foreign) enjoys the same or equal advantages in engaging themselves in any choice of business (allowed by law).

Imports and Exports

In 2002 imports (f.o.b.) were valued at US$1,250·5m. (US$1,325·5m. in 2001) and exports (f.o.b.) at US$1,071·6m. (US$1,147·0m. in 2001). Exports in 1996 (in US$1m.) included diamonds (542), fish (289), uranium and other minerals (237), meat products (82), cattle (58), small stock (42). The largest import supplier in 1996 was South Africa with 87%; largest export markets: UK, 34%; South Africa, 27%.

COMMUNICATIONS

Roads

In 2002 the total road network covered 42,237 km, including 4,550 km of national roads. In 2002 there were 160,274 registered motor vehicles, including 82,580 passenger cars and 76,080 trucks and vans. There were 340 deaths as a result of road accidents in 2002.

Rail

The Namibia system connects with the main system of the South African railways at Ariamsvlei. The total length of the line inside Namibia was 2,382 km of 1,065 mm gauge in 1996. In 1995–96 railways carried 124,000 passengers and 1·7m. tonnes of freight.

Civil Aviation

The national carrier is the state-owned Air Namibia. In 2001 the major airport, Windhoek's Hosea Kutako International, handled 379,000 passengers (363,000 on international flights). Eros is used mainly for domestic flights. In 1999 scheduled airline traffic of Namibian-based carriers flew 7·1m. km, carrying 201,000 passengers (165,000 on international flights).

Shipping

The main port is Walvis Bay. During 1997–98, 808 ships called and 1,156,143 tonnes of cargo were landed. There is a harbour at Lüderitz which handles mainly fishing vessels. In 2002 merchant shipping totalled 69,000 GRT.

Telecommunications

Telecom Namibia is the responsible corporation. In 2002 telephone subscribers numbered 271,400 (144·8 per 1,000 inhabitants) and there were 133,000 PCs in use (70·9 per 1,000 persons). Mobile phone subscribers numbered 150,000 in 2002. In 2002 there were 50,000 Internet users.

Postal Services

The national postal service is run by Namibia Post. In 2003 there were 118 post offices, or one for every 16,800 persons.

SOCIAL INSTITUTIONS

Justice

There is a Supreme Court, a High Court and a number of magistrates' and lower courts. An Ombudsman is appointed. Judges are appointed by the president on the recommendation of the Judicial Service Commission.

The population in penal institutions in Dec. 2001 was 4,814 (267 per 100,000 of national population).

Education

Literacy was 85·0% in 2003 (male, 86·8%; female, 83·5%). Primary education is free and compulsory. In 2001–02 there were 398,381 pupils at primary schools, 130,577 at secondary schools and 13,339 students at institutions of higher education (55% female in 1999–2000). The University of Namibia had 3,941 students and 198 academic staff in 2000.

In 1999–2000 total expenditure on education came to 7·7% of GNP.

Health

In 1992 there were 47 hospitals (four private) and 238 clinics and health centres. There were 495 physicians, 67 dentists, 2,817 nurses and 1,954 midwives in 1997.

RELIGION

About 75% of the population is Christian (mainly Protestants).

CULTURE

Broadcasting

The Namibian Broadcasting Corporation operates a national radio service from three stations and vernacular services. It also operates ten TV stations (colour by PAL). In 2001 there were 141,000 TV sets and in 2000 there were 258,000 radios in use. One privately-owned television channel and two privately-owned radio stations operate from Windhoek.

Press

There were four daily and three weekly newspapers in 1997.

Tourism

In 2001 there were 670,000 visitors who spent US$404m. The tourism industry was devastated in 2000 by the Angolan civil war spilling over into the north of Namibia.

DIPLOMATIC REPRESENTATIVES

Of Namibia in the United Kingdom (6 Chandos St., London, W1G 9LU)
High Commissioner: Ringo F. Abed.

Of the United Kingdom in Namibia (116 Robert Mugabe Ave., 9000 Windhoek)
High Commissioner: Alastair MacDermott.

Of Namibia in the USA (1605 New Hampshire Ave., NW, Washington, D.C., 20009)
Ambassador: Hopelong Uushona Ipinge.

Of the USA in Namibia (14 Lossen St., Private Bag 12029, Windhoek)
Ambassador: Joyce A. Barr.

Of Namibia to the United Nations
Ambassador: Martin Andjaba.

Of Namibia to the European Union
Ambassador: Peter Hitjitevi Katjavivi.

FURTHER READING

Herbstein, D. and Evenston, J., *The Devils are Among Us: the War for Namibia.* London, 1989

Kaela, L. C. W., *The Question of Namibia.* London, 1996

Schoeman, Elna and Stanley, *Namibia.* [Bibliography] 2nd ed. ABC-Clio, Oxford and Santa Barbara (CA), 1997

Sparks, D. L. and Green, D., *Namibia: the Nation after Independence.* Boulder, (CO), 1992

National Statistical Office: National Planning Commission.
Website: http://www.npc.gov.na/cbs/index.htm

NAURU

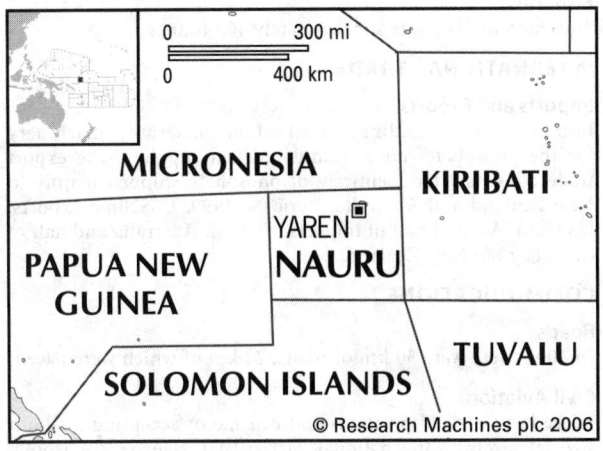

Republic of Nauru

Population, 2003: 13,000
GDP per capita: not available

KEY HISTORICAL EVENTS

Nauru was first settled by Melanesians and Polynesians. The island was discovered by Capt. John Fearn in 1798 and was annexed by Germany in Oct. 1888. Phosphates were discovered in 1900 and exploited by the British Pacific Phosphate Company. Nauru was surrendered to Australian forces in 1914. It was administered by the UK under a League of Nations mandate from 1920 and occupied by Japanese forces from 1942–45. In 1947 the UN approved a trusteeship agreement with Australia, New Zealand and the UK and Nauru was granted independence on 31 Jan. 1968. Phosphate mining provided one of the world's highest GDP per capita rates. In 1993 Australia and the UK agreed to out-of-court settlements for environmental damage during mining. Nauru agreed to hold asylum seekers for Australia in 2001. The depletion of phosphates and mismanagement of revenues caused a financial crisis in the early 21st century. Nauru is almost totally reliant on aid from Australia. In 2003 President Bernard Dowiyogo closed Nauru's offshore banks after US allegations of money-laundering. During 2003 there were six changes of president. In Sept. 2004 a state of emergency was declared after the health minister was suspended and parliament was dismissed for failing to pass the national budget.

TERRITORY AND POPULATION

Nauru is a coral island surrounded by a reef situated 0° 32' S. lat. and 166° 56' E. long. Area, 21·3 sq. km. At the 1992 census the population totalled 9,919, of whom 6,832 were Nauruans. Estimated population in July 2003: 12,570; density, 590 per sq. km.

Nauruan is the official language, although English is widely used for government purposes.

SOCIAL STATISTICS

2000 births (estimates), 270; deaths, 60. Estimated birth rate in 2000 was 22·9 per 1,000 population; estimated death rate, 5·1. Infant mortality (2001), 25 (per 1,000 live births). Annual population growth rate, 1992–2002, 2·5%; fertility rate, 2001, 4·5 births per woman.

CLIMATE

A tropical climate, tempered by sea breezes, but with a high and irregular rainfall, averaging 82" (2,060 mm). Average temperature, Jan. 81°F (27·2°C), July 82°F (27·8°C). Annual rainfall 75" (1,862 mm).

CONSTITUTION AND GOVERNMENT

A Legislative Council was inaugurated on 31 Jan. 1966. The constitution was promulgated on 29 Jan. 1968 and was amended on 17 May 1968. An 18-member Parliament is elected on a three-yearly basis.

National Anthem

'Nauru bwiema, ngabena ma auwe' ('Nauru our homeland, the country we love'); words by M. Hendrie, tune by L. H. Hicks.

RECENT ELECTIONS

At the last elections on 23 Oct. 2004, followers of President Ludwig Scotty won a majority. On 26 Oct. 2004 Scotty was elected president unopposed.

CURRENT ADMINISTRATION

In Aug. 2003 President Ludwig Scotty lost a vote of confidence and left office. His successor, René Harris, was also ousted by a confidence vote on 22 June 2004 and Scotty took office for a second time.

In March 2006 the government comprised:

President and Minister of Public Service and Civil Aviation: Ludwig Scotty (since 22 June 2004, having previously served as president from May–Aug. 2003).

Minister assisting the President and Minister for Foreign Affairs, Internal Affairs, Finance and Customs: David Adeang. *Minister of Education and Vocational Training, Telecommunications, Youth Affairs and Public Works:* Baron Waqa. *Health, Women's Affairs and Shipping:* Dr Kieren Keke. *Island Development, Culture and Tourism, and Nauru Phosphate Royalties Trust:* Frederick Pitcher. *Justice, Nauru Fisheries and Marine Resources, Immigration and Sports:* Godfrey Thoma.

Speaker: Valdon Dowiyogo.

CURRENT LEADERS

Ludwig Scotty

Position
President

Introduction
Scotty has been president of Nauru, the world's smallest republic, since 22 June 2004, having previously held the post for part of 2003. He has attempted to push through financial and legislative reforms necessary to stave off bankruptcy and build the foundations of a sustainable economy.

Early Life
Ludwig Derangadage Scotty was born on 20 June 1948 in Anabar, in the north of Nauru, then a UN Trust Territory under Australian administration. He completed his secondary education in 1964 and studied law at the University of the South Pacific, Suva, Fiji Islands. Returning to Nauru, which gained independence on 31 Jan. 1968, he held several prominent positions including chairman of the Bank of Nauru and member of the executive committee of Air Nauru. The 1970s saw political stability under president Hammer DeRoburt and unprecedented prosperity from the export of the island's valuable phosphorous deposits.

Scotty was elected as one of 18 members of parliament on 15 March 1983, representing the Anabar constituency. He served as parliamentary speaker from the late 1990s and briefly held the ministerial portfolio for health in 2003. During the caretaker administration of Derog Gioura, Scotty was elected president by ten parliamentary votes to seven, defeating the former president, Kinza Clodamur. He was sworn in on 28 May 2003.

Career in Office

With the national phosphate reserves exhausted, Scotty introduced sweeping reforms and unpopular austerity measures to stave off bankruptcy. Following a vote of no confidence on 8 Aug. 2003, he was ousted and replaced by René Harris. Harris himself then lost a vote of confidence and Scotty regained the presidency in June 2004. When the government failed to pass a reform budget by a designated deadline, Scotty dissolved parliament and called a general election for 23 Oct. 2004 and was re-elected unopposed. The reform-minded parliament has subsequently cut government spending and tightened regulations in Nauru's offshore banking industry. Longer-term goals include rehabilitating the devastated environment and developing alternative sources of revenue.

INTERNATIONAL RELATIONS

Nauru is a member of the UN, Asian Development Bank, the Commonwealth, the Pacific Community and the Pacific Islands Forum.

ECONOMY

Currency

The Australian dollar is in use.

Budget

Revenues in 1999 were $A38·7m. and expenditures US$37·2m.

Performance

Real GDP growth was 7·0% in 1995 (4·5% in 1994).

Banking and Finance

The Bank of Nauru is a state bank and there is a commercial bank, Hampshire Bank and Trust Inc.

Nauru was one of three countries named in a report in June 2005 as failing to co-operate in the fight against international money laundering. The Financial Action Task Force on Money Laundering was set up by the G7 group of major industrialized nations.

ENERGY AND NATURAL RESOURCES

Environment

Carbon dioxide emissions from the consumption and flaring of fossil fuels were the equivalent of 13·6 tonnes per capita in 2002.

Electricity

Installed capacity in 2000 was 10,000 kW; production was estimated at 33m. kWh in 2000.

Minerals

A central plateau contained high-grade phosphate deposits. The interests in the phosphate deposits were purchased in 1919 from the Pacific Phosphate Company by the UK, Australia and New Zealand. In 1967 the British Phosphate Corporation agreed to hand over the phosphate industry to Nauru for approximately $A20m. over three years. Nauru took over the industry in July 1969; production in 2001 totalled 266,000 tonnes, compared to 747,000 tonnes in 1992. It is estimated that the deposits will be exhausted by 2008. In May 1989 Nauru filed a claim against Australia for environmental damage caused by the mining. In Aug. 1993 Australia agreed to pay compensation of $A73m. In March 1994 New Zealand and the UK each agreed to pay compensation of $A12m.

Agriculture

Livestock (2000): pigs, 3,000. In 2000 the crop of coconuts was an estimated 2,000 tonnes.

Fisheries

The catch in 2001 was approximately 400 tonnes.

INTERNATIONAL TRADE

Imports and Exports

Imports: food, building construction materials, machinery for the phosphate industry and medical supplies. The export trade consists almost entirely of phosphate shipped mainly to New Zealand and Australia. Imports, 1999, US$20m.; exports, US$40m. Around half of imports are from Australia and half of exports go to New Zealand.

COMMUNICATIONS

Roads

In 2002 there were 30 km of roads, 24 km of which were paved.

Civil Aviation

There is an airfield on the island capable of accepting medium size jet aircraft. The national carrier, Air Nauru, is a wholly owned government subsidiary. It has one aircraft. In 2003 it flew to Brisbane, Melbourne, Nadi and Tarawa. In 1999 scheduled airline traffic of Nauru-based carriers flew 2·5m. km, carrying 143,000 passengers (all on international flights).

Shipping

Deep offshore moorings can accommodate medium-size vessels. Shipping coming to the island consists of vessels under charter to the phosphate industry or general purpose vessels bringing cargo by way of imports.

Telecommunications

There were 1,900 main telephone lines in operation in 2002. International telephone, telex and fax communications are maintained by satellite. A satellite earth station was commissioned in 1990. There were 1,500 mobile phone subscribers in 2001 and 300 Internet users.

SOCIAL INSTITUTIONS

Justice

The highest Court is the Supreme Court of Nauru. It is the Superior Court of record and has the jurisdiction to deal with constitutional matters in addition to its other jurisdiction. There is also a District Court which is presided over by the Resident Magistrate who is also the Chairman of the Family Court and the Registrar of Supreme Court. The laws applicable in Nauru are its own Acts of Parliament. A large number of British statutes and much common law has been adopted insofar as is compatible with Nauruan custom.

Education

Attendance at school is compulsory between the ages of six and 17. In 2003 there were 588 children in pre-primary schools with 44 teachers, 1,375 pupils in primary schools with 63 teachers and 645 pupils in secondary schools with 34 teachers. There is also a trade school with four instructors and an enrolment of 88 trainees. Scholarships are available for Nauruan children to receive secondary and higher education and vocational training in Australia and New Zealand.

In 2000–01 total expenditure on education came to 7·0% of total government spending.

Health

In 1995 there were 17 physicians and 62 nurses.

RELIGION

The population is mainly Roman Catholic or Protestant.

CULTURE

Broadcasting

The government-controlled Nauru Broadcasting Service broadcasts a home service in Nauruan and English for three hours daily. There were 7,000 radio sets in use and 500 television sets in 1997. New Zealand television programmes are received.

DIPLOMATIC REPRESENTATIVES

Of Nauru in the United Kingdom
Honorary Consul: Martin Weston (Romshed Courtyard, Underriver, Nr Sevenoaks, Kent, TN15 0SD).

Of the United Kingdom in Nauru
High Commissioner: Charles Mochan (resides in Suva, Fiji Islands).

Of the USA in Nauru
Ambassador: Larry M. Dinger (resides in Suva, Fiji Islands).

Of Nauru to the United Nations
Ambassador: Marlene Inemwin Moses.

FURTHER READING

Weeremantry, C., *Nauru: Environmental Damage under International Trusteeship.* OUP, 1992

NEPAL

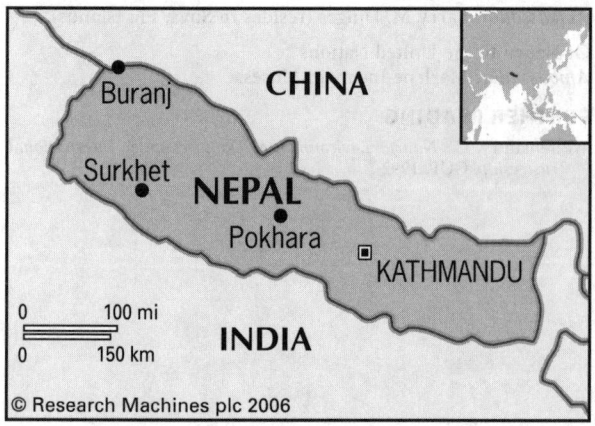

Nepal Adhirajya
(Kingdom of Nepal)

Capital: Kathmandu
Population projection, 2010: 29·89m.
GDP per capita, 2003: (PPP$) 1,420
HDI/world rank: 0·526/136

KEY HISTORICAL EVENTS

Nepal is an independent Himalayan Kingdom located between India and the Tibetan region of China. From the 8th to the 11th centuries many Buddhists fled to Nepal from India, which had been invaded by Muslims. In the 18th century Nepal was a collection of small principalities (many of Rajput origin) and the three kingdoms of the Malla dynasty: Kathmandu, Patan and Bhadgaon. In central Nepal lay the principality of Gurkha (or Gorkha); its ruler after 1742 was Prithvi Narayan Shah, who conquered the small neighbouring states. Fearing his ambitions, in 1767 the Mallas brought in forces lent by the British East India Company. In 1769 these forces were withdrawn and Gurkha was then able to conquer the Malla kingdoms and unite Nepal as one state with its capital at Kathmandu. In 1846 the Rana family became the effective rulers of Nepal, establishing the office of prime minister as hereditary. In 1860 Nepal reached agreement with the British in India whereby Nepali independence was preserved and the recruitment of Gurkhas to the British army was sanctioned.

In 1950 the Shah royal family allied itself with Nepalis abroad to end the power of the Ranas. The last Rana prime minister resigned in Nov. 1951, the king having proclaimed a constitutional monarchy in Feb. 1951. A new constitution, approved in 1959, led to confrontation between the king and his ministers; it was replaced by one less liberal in 1962. In Nov. 1990 the king relinquished his absolute power. The Maoists abandoned parliament in 1996 and launched a 'people's war' in the aim of turning the kingdom into a republic. This has resulted in more than 3,500 deaths.

In June 2001 the king and queen, along with six other members of the royal family, were shot dead by their son and heir to the throne, Crown Prince Dipendra, allegedly following a dispute over his choice of bride. Prince Dipendra then shot himself. The former monarch's younger brother, Gyanendra, was crowned king. In Nov. 2001 King Gyanendra declared a state of emergency and ordered troops to contain a fresh outbreak of Maoist violence. The government lifted the state of emergency in Aug. 2002. In Jan. 2003 the government and Maoist rebels reached a ceasefire agreement, seen as a first step towards bringing to an end the rebels' seven-year insurgency. In Feb. 2005 King Gyanendra dismissed his government and once more declared a state of emergency, taking control of the country and suspending democracy for three years. He lifted the state of emergency on 29 April 2005. In April 2006 he agreed to a return to parliamentary democracy after more than two weeks of unrest.

TERRITORY AND POPULATION

Nepal is bounded in the north by China (Tibet) and the east, south and west by India. Area 147,181 sq. km; population census 2001, 23,151,423 of which 11,587,502 were female; density 157·3 per sq. km. The estimated population in 2005 was 27,133,000. In 2003, 85·0% of the population were rural.

The UN gives a projected population for 2010 of 29·89m.

The country is divided into five regions and subdivided into 14 zones. Area, population and administrative centres:

Zone/Region	Sq. km	Population (2001 census)	Administrative centre
Koshi	9,669	2,110,664	Biratnagar
Mechi	8,196	1,307,669	Ilam
Sagarmatha	10,591	1,926,143	Rajbiraj
East Region	28,456	5,344,476	Dhankuta
Bagmati	9,428	3,008,487	Kathmandu
Janakpur	9,669	2,557,004	Jaleswar
Narayani	8,313	2,466,138	Birganj
Central Region	27,410	8,031,629	Kathmandu
Dhanlagiri	8,148	556,191	Baglung
Gandaki	12,275	1,487,954	Pokhara
Lumbini	8,975	2,526,868	Butwal
West Region	29,398	4,571,013	Pokhara
Bheri	10,545	1,417,085	Nepalganj
Karuali	21,351	309,084	Jumla
Rapti	10,482	1,286,806	Tulsipur
Mid-West Region	42,378	3,012,975	Surkhet
Mahakali	6,989	860,475	Mahendra Nagar
Seti	12,550	1,330,855	Dhangarhi
Far West Region	19,539	2,191,330	Dipayal

Capital, Kathmandu; population (2001) 671,846. Other towns include (2001 census population): Biratnagar, 166,674; Lalitpur, 162,991; Pokhara, 156,312.

The indigenous people are of Tibetan origin with a considerable Hindu admixture. The Gurkha clan became predominant in 1559 and has given its name to men from all parts of Nepal. There are 18 ethnic groups, the largest being: Newars, Indians, Tibetans, Gurungs, Mogars, Tamangs, Bhotias, Rais, Limbus and Sherpas. The official language is Nepalese but there are 20 new languages divided into numerous dialects.

SOCIAL STATISTICS

2002 estimates: births, 790,000; deaths, 247,000. Estimated rates per 1,000 population, 2002: births, 32·0; deaths, 10·0. Annual population growth rate, 1992–2002, 2·3%. Expectation of life was 61·2 years for males and 62·0 years for females in 2003. Infant mortality, 2001, 66 per 1,000 live births; fertility rate, 2001, 4·6 births per woman.

CLIMATE

Varies from cool summers and severe winters in the north to sub-tropical summers and mild winters in the south. The rainfall is high, with maximum amounts from June to Sept., but conditions are very dry from Nov. to Jan. Kathmandu, Jan. 10°C, July, 25°C. Average annual rainfall, 1,424 mm.

CONSTITUTION AND GOVERNMENT

The sovereign is HM Maharajadhiraja **Gyanendra Bir Bikram Shah Dev** (b. 1947), who succeeded Crown Prince Dipendra on 4 June 2001 on the latter's death two days after he had shot and killed his father, the former king Birendra.

Under the constitution of 9 Nov. 1990 Nepal became a constitutional monarchy based on multi-party democracy. *Parliament* has two chambers: a 205-member House of Representatives (*Pratinidhi Sabha*) elected for five-year terms, and a 60-member National Council (*Rastriya Sabha*), of which ten members are nominated by the king.

In Feb. 2005 for the second time since ascending to the throne King Gyanendra dismissed the prime minister and his cabinet and assumed full executive powers. In April 2006, after more than two weeks of protests, he agreed to reinstate the dissolved parliament.

National Anthem

'Sri man gumbhira nepali prachanda pratapi bhupati' ('May glory crown our illustrious sovereign, the gallant Nepalese'); words by C. Chalise, tune by B. Budhapirthi.

RECENT ELECTIONS

In parliamentary elections held on 3 and 17 May 1999 the Nepali Congress Party (NCP) won an absolute majority, winning 110 of the 205 seats and bringing an end to a succession of weak coalition governments. The Communist Party/Unified Marxist-Leninists (NKP-EML) won 68 seats, the National Democratic Party (RPP) 11, Nepalese Goodwill Party (NSP) 5, National People's Front (RJM) 5, United People's Front (SJN) 1, Nepalese Workers' and Farmers' Party (NMKP) 1. Four results were unavailable.

CURRENT ADMINISTRATION

On 4 Oct. 2002 King Gyanendra dismissed Prime Minister Sher Bahadur Deuba's government, following the latter's failure to arrange parliamentary elections for Nov. 2002. On 11 Oct. 2002 King Gyanendra appointed a new cabinet with Lokendra Bahadur Chand of the conservative, royalist RPP as prime minister. However, he resigned on 30 May 2003. His replacement, Surya Bahadur Thapa, resigned on 7 May 2004. Sher Bahadu Deuba was reappointed on 2 June 2004. On 1 Feb. 2005 King Gyanendra again dismissed Prime Minister Sher Bahadur Deuba's government, and assumed power himself. He restored parliament in April 2006.

In May 2006 the cabinet comprised:

Prime Minister and Minister of Defence: Girija Prasad Koirala; b. 1921 (Nepali Congress Party; sworn in 24 April 2006).

Deputy Prime Minister and Minister of Foreign Affairs: Khadka Prasad Sharma Oli (Communist Party of Nepal-Unified Marxist Leninist).

Minister for Home Affairs: Krishna Sitaula (Nepali Congress Party). *Finance:* Dr Ram Sharan Mahat (Nepali Congress Party). *Agriculture and Co-operatives:* Mahant Thakur (Nepali Congress Party). *Physical Planning and Works:* Gopal Man Shrestha (Nepali Congress Party (Democratic)). *Land Reform and Soil Management:* Prabhu Narayan Chaudhary (United Left Front).

Office of the Council of Ministers: http://www.pmo.gov.np

CURRENT LEADERS

King Gyanendra Bir Bikram Shah Dev

Position
King

Introduction
The younger brother of King Birendra, Gyanendra came to the throne in June 2001 when Birendra was murdered by his son, the Crown Prince Dipendra, who then committed suicide.

Gyanendra has advocated the continuation of the constitutional monarchy established in 1990 but in Feb. 2005, faced with the continuing Maoist insurgency, he dismissed Prime Minister Sher Bahadur Deuba's government (for a second time) and assumed direct control.

Early Life
Gyanendra was born on 7 July 1947 in Kathmandu to King Mahendra Bir Bikram Shah and Crown Princess Indra Rajya Laxmi Devi Shah. He studied in Darjeeling in India, graduating in 1966, and three years later completed his studies at Kathmandu's Tribhuvan University. In addition to his business interests, he was involved in high-profile conservation work with the King Mahendra Trust for Nature Conservation and the World Wildlife Fund (now the World Wide Fund for Nature).

On 1 June 2001 Crown Prince Dipendra shot dead King Birendra, Queen Aishwarya and several other family members before turning the gun on himself. Dipendra was declared king, but died from his wounds three days later and Gyanendra succeeded him.

Career in Office
In the early stages of Gyanendra's reign there was public unrest when an official report blamed Dipendra for the royal massacre, claiming that he was under the influence of alcohol and narcotics. However, Dipendra's sister, Ketaki, who was present at the massacre, confirmed the reports findings.

Birendra had ruled as absolute monarch until 1990, when he granted a multi-party democratic constitution. The ensuing years saw frequent changes of government and political instability. A month after Gyanendra came to the throne, Sher Bahadur Deuba became prime minister, amid growing violence by anti-monarchist Maoist rebels. Parliament was suspended in May 2002 in preparation for elections scheduled for Nov. 2002. However, in early Oct. 2002 Deuba, backed by all the leading parliamentary parties, asked for the elections to be suspended so that the political climate could stabilize. For the interim, Deuba proposed an all-party government. On 4 Oct. 2002 Gyanendra responded by dismissing Deuba and his cabinet. He appointed Lokendra Bahadur Chand of the monarchist RPP as prime minister, although opposition figures declared the move illegal. The King assumed the executive powers surrendered by the monarchy in 1990, postponed elections and announced that he would form a non-elected interim government. In a public broadcast he reaffirmed his commitment to the constitutional monarchy, but his actions were widely condemned. In Jan. 2003 government forces and Maoist rebels agreed a ceasefire but this was short-lived. In May 2003 Chand resigned following pressure from opposition parties, which continued to refuse to recognize the legitimacy of his appointment. When his replacement, Surya Bahadur Thapa, also resigned in May 2004, Sher Bahadu Deuba was reappointed the following month as prime minister. Meanwhile, the Maoist insurgency continued, with the rebels gaining control over much of the countryside.

In Feb. 2005 Gyanendra again dismissed Deuba and his government, taking power directly himself and imposing a state of emergency. Although he promised to restore mutli-party democracy within three years, and the emergency was subsequently lifted in April 2005, his actions were criticized abroad, particularly by neighbouring India. In Sept.2005 the Maoist rebels announced a unilateral ceasefire, but this was called off in early Jan. 2006 as explosions rocked the towns of Butwal, Pokhara and Bhairahawa. In April 2006 he agreed to reinstate parliament following more than two weeks of protests.

DEFENCE

The King is commander-in-chief of the armed forces, but shares supreme military authority with the National Defence Council.

Defence expenditure in 2003 totalled US$110m. (US$4 per capita), representing 1·9% of GDP.

Army
Strength (2002) 51,000, and there is also a 40,000-strong paramilitary police force.

Air Force
The Army's air wing has no combat aircraft. Personnel, 2002, 320.

INTERNATIONAL RELATIONS
Nepal is a member of the UN, WTO, the Asian Development Bank, the Colombo Plan, the SAARC and is a founding member of the Non-aligned Movement (NAM).

ECONOMY
Agriculture accounted for 40·7% of GDP in 2002, industry 21·7% and services 37·5%.

Overview
In the past 15 years the government has embarked on economic reform—eliminating business licenses and registration requirements—to encourage trade and foreign investment. The production of textiles and carpets accounts for over two-thirds of foreign exchange earnings. Apart from agricultural land and forests, exploitable natural resources are mica, hydropower and tourism.

Currency
The unit of currency is the *Nepalese rupee* (NPR) of 100 *paisas*. 50 *paisas* = 1 *mohur*. Inflation was 4·7% in 2003 and 4·0% in 2004. Foreign exchange reserves were US$1,034m. in June 2002 and gold reserves totalled 15,000 troy oz (153,000 troy oz in April 2002). Total money supply in Dec. 2001 was NRs 72,161m.

Budget
Revenues and expenditures in NRs 1m. for fiscal years ending 14/15 July:

	1997–98	1998–99	1999–2000	2000–01	2001–02[1]
Revenue	31,492	34,809	40,484	46,607	48,384
Expenditure	51,964	54,720	60,794	73,905	75,705

[1]Provisional.

Performance
Real GDP growth was 3·4% in both 2003 and 2004. Nepal's total GDP in 2004 was US$6·7bn.

Banking and Finance
The Central Bank is the bank of issue (*Governor*, Bijaya Nath Bhattarai). In 2002 there were four domestic commercial banks (Kumari Bank; Nepal Bank; Nepal Industrial and Commercial Bank; Rastriya Banijya Bank), ten joint-venture banks and four development finance organizations (Agricultural Development Bank; Nepal Development Bank; Nepal Housing Development Finance Corporation; Nepal Industrial Development Corporation).

There is a stock exchange in Kathmandu.

ENERGY AND NATURAL RESOURCES

Environment
Nepal's carbon dioxide emissions from the consumption and flaring of fossil fuels in 2002 were the equivalent of 0·1 tonnes per capita.

Electricity
Installed capacity was 0·5m. kW in 2000. Production in 2000 was an estimated 1·43bn. kWh (88% hydro-electric), with consumption per capita about 67 kWh.

Minerals
Production (in tonnes), 2002: limestone, 356,218; coal (2000), 18,000; agricultural lime (2001), 15,587; salt, 5,000; talcum, 2,621; magnesite (2000), 1,640.

Agriculture
Agriculture is the mainstay of the economy, providing a livelihood for over 90% of the population and accounting for 39% of GDP. In 2001 there were 3·1m. ha. of arable land and 92,000 ha. of permanent crops. Cultivated land accounts for 26·5% of land use; forest and woodland 42·4%. Crop production (2000, in 1,000 tonnes): rice, 4,030; sugarcane, 2,103; maize, 1,445; wheat, 1,184; potatoes, 1,183; millet, 295.

Livestock (2000); cattle, 7·03m.; buffaloes, 3·50m.; sheep, 870,000; goats, 6·50m.; pigs, 900,000; chickens, 18m.

Forestry
In 2000 the area under forests was 3·9m. ha., or 27·3% of the total land area. There are eight national parks, covering 1m. ha., five wildlife reserves (170,490 ha.) and two conservation areas (349,000 ha.). Timber production was 14·0m. cu. metres in 2001, mainly for use as fuelwood and charcoal. Expansion of agricultural land has led to widespread deforestation.

Fisheries
The catch in 2001 was 16,700 tonnes, entirely from inland waters.

INDUSTRY
In 2002 industry accounted for 20·9% of GDP, with manufacturing contributing 8·1%. Production (2001–02 unless otherwise stated): cement, 215,000 tonnes; sugar, 65,000 tonnes; soap, washing powder and detergents, 55,100 tonnes; animal feed, 22,000 tonnes; paper and paperboard, 13,000 tonnes; tea (1994), 2,351 tonnes; synthetic textiles (1994), 14·7m. metres; electrical cable (1994), 9·3m. metres; cotton woven fabrics, 2·5m. metres; leather (1994), 1,369,750 sq. metres; shoes, 0·71m. pairs; beer (2003), 23·1m. litres; cigarettes, 6,979m. units. Brewing is one of the successes of Nepal's economy, accounting for some 3% of GDP.

Labour
The labour force in 1996 totalled 10,179,000 (60% males). In 1992, 84% of the economically active population were engaged in agriculture, forestry or fisheries.

INTERNATIONAL TRADE
External debt was an estimated US$2,953m. in 2002.

Imports and Exports
In 2004 imports (f.o.b.) amounted to US$1,812·5m. (US$1,665·9m. in 2003); exports (f.o.b.) US$763·6m. (US$703·2m. in 2003). Principal import commodities are petroleum products, transport equipment and parts, chemical fertilizer and raw wool. Main partners are India, Singapore, Japan, Germany. Principal export commodities are carpets, clothing, leather goods, pulses, raw jute and jute goods, and handicrafts. Hand-knotted woollen carpets are the largest overseas export item constituting almost 32% of foreign exchange earnings. Main partners are India, USA, Germany, UK.

COMMUNICATIONS

Roads
In 1999 there were 13,223 km of roads, of which 30·8% were paved.

Rail
101 km (762 mm gauge) connect Jayanagar on the North Eastern Indian Railway with Janakpur and thence with Bizalpura (54 km). 653,000 passengers and 9,151 tonnes of freight were carried in 1994.

Civil Aviation

There is an international airport (Tribhuvan) at Kathmandu. The national carrier is the state-owned Royal Nepal Airlines. It operates domestic services and in 2003 flew to Bangalore, Bangkok, Bombay, Delhi, Dubai, Hong Kong, Kuala Lumpur, Osaka, Shanghai and Singapore. In 1995 Kathmandu handled 1,357,000 passengers (868,000 on international flights) and 13·9m. tonnes of freight. In 1999 scheduled airline traffic of Nepali-based carriers flew 8·7m. km, carrying 583,000 passengers (452,000 on international flights).

Telecommunications

In 2002 Nepal had 349,600 telephone subscribers (15·1 per 1,000 persons) and there were 85,000 PCs in use (3·7 for every 1,000 persons). There were 80,000 Internet users in 2002 and 11,500 fax machines. Mobile phone subscribers numbered 21,900 in 2002. The mobile phone network was switched off following King Gyanendra's declaration of a state of emergency in Feb. 2005. The network was then restored in May 2005 but was switched off again in Jan. 2006.

Postal Services

In 2000 there were 4,012 post offices.

SOCIAL INSTITUTIONS

Justice

The Supreme Court Act established a uniform judicial system, culminating in a supreme court of a Chief Justice and no more than six judges. Special courts to deal with minor offences may be established at the discretion of the government. The Chief Justice is appointed by the king on recommendation of the Constitutional Council. Other judges are appointed by the king on the recommendation of the Judicial Council.

The death penalty was abolished in 1997. The population in penal institutions in 2002 was 7,132 (29 per 100,000 of national population).

Education

The adult literacy rate in 2003 was 48·6% (62·7% among males but only 34·9% among females). Only Yemen has a bigger difference in literacy rates between the sexes. In 1998 there were 22,994 primary schools; 6,023 lower secondary schools; 3,178 secondary schools; and 310 higher secondary schools. In 2000–01 there were 257,968 children (11,785 teachers) in pre-primary schools, 3,623,150 pupils (97,879 teachers) in primary schools and 1,349,909 pupils (45,655 teachers) in secondary schools. There are five universities; the Tribhuvan University had 93,800 students and 4,300 academic staff in 1995–96.

In 2000–01 total expenditure on education came to 3·6% of GNP and 14·1% of total government spending.

Health

There were 1,259 physicians and 6,216 nurses in 2001. In 2000 there were 133 hospitals, 180 primary health care centres and 711 health posts.

RELIGION

Nepal is a Hindu state. Hinduism was the religion of 82·8% of the people in 2001. Buddhists comprise 8·9% and Muslims 4·2%. Christian missions are permitted, but conversion is forbidden.

CULTURE

World Heritage Sites

Nepal has four sites on the UNESCO World Heritage List: Sagarmatha National Park (inscribed on the list in 1979); Kathmandu Valley (1979); Royal Chitwan National Park (1984); and Lumbini, the Birthplace of the Lord Buddha (1997).

Broadcasting

Radio Nepal is part government-owned and part commercial. It broadcasts in Nepali and English from three stations. The government-owned Nepal Television transmits from one station (colour by PAL). In 2000 there were 883,000 radio sets and in 2001 there were 193,000 TV sets.

Press

In 1998 there were 166 daily newspapers, including the official English-language *Rising Nepal*, three bi-weeklies and 814 weeklies. Press censorship was relaxed in June 1991, but following the imposition of a state of emergency in Feb. 2005 the press was subjected to total censorship.

Tourism

Foreign tourists visiting Nepal numbered 298,100 in 2001, down from 376,500 in 2000, largely as a consequence of the massacre of the royal family and an upsurge in Maoist rebel violence. Revenue from tourism totalled US$107m. in 2002. In 2002, 39,100 hotel beds were available. Tourism accounts for approximately 4% of GDP.

Festivals

Hindu, Buddhist and traditional festivals crowd the Nepali lunar calendar. Dasain (Sept./Oct.) is the longest and most widely observed festival in Nepal. The 15 days of celebration include Dashami, when family elders are honoured. Tihar (Oct./Nov.) celebrates the Hindu goddess Laxmi. During the first three days crows, dogs and cows are worshipped, followed by the spirit, or self. It concludes with Bhai Tika ('Brother's Day'). Buddha Jayanti (May/June) remembers the birth, enlightenment and death of the Buddha. Sherpas gather at Tengboche Monastery near Mount Everest in May to observe Mani Rimdu with meditation, mask dances and Buddhist ceremonies.

DIPLOMATIC REPRESENTATIVES

Of Nepal in the United Kingdom (12A Kensington Palace Gdns, London, W8 4QU)
Ambassador: Prabal S. J. B. Rana, CVO.

Of the United Kingdom in Nepal (Lainchaur, Kathmandu, POB 106)
Ambassador: Keith Bloomfield.

Of Nepal in the USA (2131 Leroy Pl., NW, Washington, D.C., 20008)
Ambassador: Kedar Bhakta Shrestha.

Of the USA in Nepal (Pani Pokhari, Kathmandu)
Ambassador: James Moriarty.

Of Nepal to the United Nations
Ambassador: Madhu Raman Acharya.

Of Nepal to the European Union
Ambassador: Narayan Shumshere Thapa.

FURTHER READING

Central Bureau of Statistics. *Statistical Pocket Book.* [Various years]

Borre, O., *et al., Nepalese Political Behaviour.* Aarhus Univ. Press, 1994
Ghimire, K., *Forest or Farm? The Politics of Poverty and Land Hunger in Nepal.* OUP, 1993
Hutt, Michael, (ed.) *Himalayan 'People's War' Nepal's Maoist Rebellion.* C. Hurst, London, 2004
Sanwal, D. B., *Social and Political History of Nepal.* London, 1993
Whelpton, John, *A History of Nepal.* CUP, 2005

National Statistical Office: Central Bureau of Statistics, National Planning Commission Secretariat, Kathmandu.
Website: http://www.cbs.gov.np

Koninkrijk der Nederlanden
(Kingdom of the Netherlands)

Capital: Amsterdam

Seat of government: The Hague

Population projection, 2010: 16·59m.

GDP per capita, 2003: (PPP$) 29,371

HDI/world rank: 0·943/12

KEY HISTORICAL EVENTS

Flint tools found in the Maastricht area have been estimated to be 250,000 years old. The first definable culture (*c.* 3000 BC) was the Late Stone Age 'Funnel-neck Beaker' culture, named after the objects made by a people known for their monolithic burial monuments. The environment of the 'Low Countries' affected the behaviour of its earliest inhabitants, as demonstrated by the *terpen*—islands of earth and clay—built by the autochthonous Frisians *c.* 500 BC as protection from the sea.

The Romans encountered Celtic tribes to the west and south of the Rhine and Germanic tribes, such as the Frisii, to the north and east. In the 1st century BC Julius Caesar attested to the resistance of the Celtic Eburones and Aduatuci. Roman power beyond the Rhine was limited to isolated forts and client kingdoms.

In the 3rd century AD the stagnant Roman borders began to crumble as military posts were abandoned. Among the most prominent of the encroaching Germanic tribes were the Franks, who settled at first in Toxandria (modern Brabant). Like many 'barbarian' tribes, the Franks entered into agreements with Rome, settling and guarding the border region and assimilating Roman culture. The Frisians (Frisii) became important traders, holding strategic territory between the German (North) Sea and the Meuse and Rhine rivers. With the collapse of Roman government in Gaul and the Rhine in the 5th century, the

Franks extended their power, centred on Austrasia (the central Rhine region). The spread of Christianity in the 7th century, first from the bishoprics of Arras, Tournai and Cambrai, assisted Frankish expansion into the northern Low Countries, where the missionary bishopric of Utrecht was established.

The advent of Viking raids on the North Sea coast devastated the flourishing Frisian economy. The Frisian trading centre of Dorestad was destroyed four times between 834–37 by raiders seeking Carolingian silver. Frisia came under Frankish domination during the reign of Pippin the Short, the founder of the Carolingian Empire.

The High Middle Ages saw the development of independent and semi-autonomous principalities, both secular and ecclesiastical, in the Low Countries. Great landlords established the large counties (Flanders, Hainault, Namur and Holland and Zeeland) and duchies (Brabant, Limburg and Guelders), increasing their authority and size through dynastic alliances and inheritance. The majority fell broadly under the authority of the German king, heirs to the Eastern Frankish realm, though the feudal relationship allowed the growth of a tradition of independence that became a defining characteristic of Dutch politics. The growth of population and its pressure on the land increased the need for land reclamation. Dykes were built from Friesland to Flanders to drain the bogs and marshes for pasturage and, later, agrarian use. The development of urban centres outside the feudal structure was encouraged by the strength of trade and the merchant classes.

The Burgundian era in the Low Countries was born of a series of dynastic matches, most importantly that of Duke Philip II (the Bold) of Burgundy and Margaret, Countess of Flanders and Artois in 1369. Their son, Philip III (the Good), brought most of the northern Low Countries under one lord by inheriting Brabant and Hainault-Holland in the 1430s as well as Luxembourg in 1443. Although the dukes attempted to rule through new centralized bodies, the Burgundian Low Countries were held in a personal union and did not constitute a state. The duke appointed *stadhouders* (stadtholders) and governors to represent him in each of his territories. The summoning of the Estates in 1464 in Brugge (Bruges) represented the first parliamentary assembly in the Low Countries and the importance of the *Nederlands* in the Burgundian realm.

Burgundian Rule

The reign of Charles the Bold, or Rash (1467–77), saw the brief land connection of the realm (by the acquisition of Lorraine) and the first explicit attempt to create a unitary kingdom—an echo of the Middle Frankish Kingdom, Lotharingia. Charles failed in his bid to make himself regent of this kingdom in 1473 and his death at the Battle of Nancy left his domains to his daughter, Mary. The duchess was soon stripped of the Duchy of Burgundy by the French king and was forced to concede privileges to the provinces. Her marriage to Maximilian of Habsburg, the future Holy Roman Emperor, brought the Low Countries into personal union with Austria and, later, Spain. Mary's son, Philip the Handsome, inherited the Spanish throne through his wife, Juana the Mad, forging a massive and disparate empire of kingdoms, principalities and lordships. Philip's son, Charles V, though born in Ghent, spent little time in the Low Countries after succeeding to the Spanish throne. They were administered by governors-general, normally taken from the ruler's family. Centralization, though consistently opposed, continued to be pressed on the inhabitants of the Low Countries. The 17 provinces were brought together formally in 1548 as the 'Burgundian *Kreis*' and the sovereign succession regulated by Pragmatic Sanction the following year. Brussels became the centre of government, being the location of the court and most organs of government.

Philip (II of Spain) imposed a new ecclesiastical hierarchy, sanctioned by papal bull in 1559, in an attempt to use the church as a centralizing force. The traditional resistance of the towns and provinces was given added fervour by the religious controversies attributable to the Reformation. Erasmus, a leading Dutch humanist, openly attacked the abuses and corruptions of the Church but rejected the theology of the reformers such as Martin Luther. However, the works of the radical Jean Calvin arrived in Antwerp in 1545, spreading throughout the region rapidly after their translation in 1560. Calvinism appealed to the intellectual middle classes, as well as the artisans, whose work ethic it extolled.

The government focused its repressive efforts on the Anabaptists, whose refusal to swear allegiance to the prince was an affront to temporal and spiritual authority. The iconoclastic purges of 1566 provoked Philip to send the duke of Alba to restore his authority, thereby sparking full-scale revolt and the Eighty Years War (1568–1648).

Revolt Against Spanish

The causes of the Dutch Revolt were numerous; religious tensions, resentment towards 'Spanish' authority, the heavy burden of taxes and absolutist government and the perceived desecration of traditional privileges were combined with years of hardship caused by climatic conditions and wars with France. However, in the earlier years of the revolt, the 'legitimate' *casus belli* claimed by the Dutch was the influence of 'evil advisors' around the prince—few openly rejected Philip's sovereignty. The *Geuzen*, an army of beggars, pillaging and pirating in the name of William of Orange, took the port of Brielle in 1572. This began the expulsion of Spanish authority from the northern provinces, a process completed by 1574.

The conversion of William (the Silent) to Calvinism in 1572, in response to his selection as stadtholder of Holland and Zeeland, was a political move to gain support for a united Netherlands of Catholics and Protestants. The 1576 Pacification of Ghent brought together predominantly Catholic and Protestant provinces in the face of bloody repression meted out by Alba's Council of Troubles (Council of Blood) and the notorious 'Spanish Fury' massacre in Antwerp. The mainly Catholic southern provinces were largely regained for Philip by the brilliant Alessandro Farnese, duke of Parma in 1578, forcing a 'closer union'—the Union of Utrecht—in the north in 1579, committed to resisting the Spanish. This marked the birth of the United Provinces of the Netherlands, or the 'Dutch Republic', with power concentrated in the hands of the stadtholders, nominally representing the hereditary prince. Philip's refusal to compromise led to his 'forfeiture of sovereignty' in the States-General Act of Abjuration in 1581, on the grounds of persistent tyranny.

The constitutional position of the Republic was unclear. The House of Orange was recognized as the traditional stadtholders of each province, though the lordship of the territories was tendered to both France and England in the 1580s. Maurice of Nassau, the son of William of Orange, was named stadtholder of Holland and Zeeland in 1587. Maurice's victories over Farnese came to be called the 'closing of the garden', giving the United Provinces the approximate borders it has maintained to the modern day. With recognition from England and France, the government negotiated the Twelve Year Truce in 1609 with Spain, which recognized the independence of the United Provinces.

The Calvinist church divided between the followers of two prominent clerics, Jacobus Arminius (the Remonstrants) and Franciscus Gomarus (the Contra-Remonstrants). The Arminians, championed by the elite of Holland and the towns, objected to the repressive orthodoxy of the Gomarists and demanded an inclusive reformed church to protect trade and foreign relations. The execution of the Remonstrant Johan van Oldenbarnvelt, the Advocate of Holland, signified the triumph of Maurice's Contra-Remonstrants and made permanent peace with Spain impossible. After initial Spanish success at Breda in 1621, Maurice's successor, Frederick Henry, turned the tide, taking Maastricht in the far south. Ending the persecution of the Remonstrants, Frederick Henry augmented the authority of his princely house, even earning an honorific royal title from the French King. Lasting peace with Spain was finally won at the 1648 Treaty of Münster, which formally recognized the Dutch Republic.

The 17th century has traditionally been called the Golden Age of the Dutch. From the Twelve Year Truce, the Dutch economy expanded massively, principally through trade in the Baltic and with France, Iberia and the colonies of the West and East Indies. The United East Indies Company, chartered in 1602, held quasi-sovereign authority over its colonies in Sri Lanka, India and Indonesia. Dutch banking financed the northern European markets, chiefly through foreign government bonds. The increase of wealth stimulated a flourishing of the arts. Prosperous life in Dutch towns was painted by Jan Vermeer and Amsterdam's burghers by Rembrandt. Although Calvinism had been officially adopted, Catholics were left unmolested but public worship was prohibited.

After the death of Frederick Henry's bellicose son, William II, in 1650, the republic experienced its first 'stadtholderless' period when the prosperous province of Holland dominated the Netherlands. Relations with Republican England deteriorated because of the execution of Charles I, who was closely related to the House of Orange. More importantly, competition for trade and shipping between the two great maritime powers caused skirmishes in America and Europe and a series of Anglo-Dutch Wars, conducted at sea. The destruction of the English fleet at Chatham in 1667 destroyed relations with Charles II, who had supported Orangist interests in the Netherlands.

The House of Orange reassumed the leadership of the Netherlands when William III took the stadtholdership of Holland in 1672 and defeated the French and the English in naval encounters. The Dutch supported William in his invasion of England—the Glorious Revolution—in 1688, claiming the throne with his wife, Mary Stuart. His death without issue in 1702 heralded the second stadtholderless period, when the councillor pensionaries of Holland asserted the province's leadership. However, the oligarchic nature of government developed little support, especially during Dutch humiliations at the hands of the French in the War of the Austrian Succession (1740–48). William IV of Orange was elected to all provinces in 1747, the House of Orange being seen as the natural leaders of the Dutch people.

Both William IV and William V resisted calls for a more relaxed rule. The Patriot Movement took advantage of the Dutch defeat in the Fourth Anglo-Dutch War of the 1780s to depose William V. However, Prussia's intervention restored the stadtholder and many Patriots fled to France, then on the brink of revolution.

Revolutionary France's invasion of Belgium (the Spanish Netherlands) in 1794 was soon extended to the United Provinces. William V fled to England and the Patriots, supported by the French, assumed control of government. The new 'Batavian Republic', styled after the supposedly original inhabitants, was in reality a protectorate of France.

This truly republican period enabled political modernization, much of which has lasted to the modern day. An elected national assembly was instituted (though the franchise was retained by property owners only), with new electoral constituencies to replace the old provinces. Religious toleration came into force, with all denominations awarded equal treatment. However, the economy declined, partly because of the seizure of the Dutch colonies in the name of William V by Great Britain, which had declared war on France.

Napoleon

The republic was ended in 1806 when Napoleon incorporated the Netherlands into his empire. He installed his brother, Louis, as king of Holland. Louis adopted the cause of his new subjects, frequently defying his brother's orders in favour of Dutch interests. Napoleon ended his brother's reign in 1810 and brought his kingdom under French rule. Gijsbert Karel van Hogendorp, who drew up the new constitution after the French withdrawal in 1813, led the opposition to France. The new constitution provided for a constitutional monarchy, with William V's son proclaimed king (William I), as demanded by the Congress of Vienna. The northern provinces were united with Belgium and Luxembourg under the Kingdom of the Netherlands.

William I saw the revival of the economy as the first priority. Using his personal resources as well as the treasury, he invested heavily in the re-establishment of Dutch shipping, especially to the restored colonies. Domestically, William was not so successful. In 1830 Belgium proclaimed its independence, rejecting a common identity with the predominantly Protestant north—the declaration of Dutch as the sole official language had alienated the French-speaking Walloons in Brussels. Though defeated by the Dutch army, the Belgians gained their independence in 1839 thanks to French and British intervention in 1832.

In response to the European revolutions of 1848, the king granted a liberal constitution. Support for the king was bolstered by the patriotic reaction in the northern provinces to the Belgian secession. The reintroduction of the Catholic hierarchy in 1853 won over a community which made up over a third of the population.

Dutch imperialism was consolidated in the second half of the 19th century. Having lost numerous colonies in the Americas, southern Africa and India, attention focused on the Indonesian archipelago. War with Aceh in northern Sumatra, famous for its piracy, was long and bloody but secured the archipelago for the Netherlands. The division of New Guinea was settled with Germany and Great Britain in 1875. Personal union with Luxembourg came to an end on the accession of Wilhelmina in 1890, barred by Salic Law from inheriting the Grand Duchy.

European War

In 1917 universal male suffrage was granted in return for the secular parties' acceptance of funding for religious schools, thus concluding the thirty-year School Conflict. Female suffrage followed in 1922. Wilhelmina, though less active in government than her father, William III, strongly advocated neutrality in the conflicts of the early 20th century, keeping the Netherlands out of the First World War. The German Kaiser, Wilhelm II, was granted asylum in the Netherlands.

The inter-war years were a period of social and political continuity. The zuilen system expanded, cementing what has been described as a bourgeois consensus, though worldwide depression hit the Netherlands hard in the 1930s. In 1932 the IJsselmeer dam was completed, transforming the Zuider Zee, an inlet of the North Sea, into a freshwater lake, the IJsselmeer.

The neutrality of the Netherlands was not respected by Germany in the Second World War, despite assurances from Hitler after the invasion of Poland. Control of the Netherlands and Belgium was seen as essential to protect the industrial centres of the Ruhr and to gain broader access to the North Sea. The Dutch armed forces were overwhelmed within a week in May 1940. The queen and government went into exile in London. Persecution of the Jews began in Oct. 1941. The first transports left in July 1942, mostly to Auschwitz. 107,000 Dutch Jews died. Dutch resistance took the form of civilian sabotage and the hiding of Jews and onkerduikers ('underdivers')—underground military operatives.

The Netherlands saw some of the bitterest fighting near the close of the war when Allied troops made airborne incursions—Arnhem Bridge in Sept. 1944—to speed victory over Germany. By the end of the war the Dutch were on the brink of famine. The destruction of the economy and much of the infrastructure caused large-scale emigration. In 1947 the Netherlands accepted US$1bn. for reconstruction from the Marshall Plan and entered the Benelux Economic Union with Belgium and Luxembourg (fully established in 1958). The Netherlands abandoned its neutrality when it joined NATO in 1949, the year it granted Indonesia independence. Further changes to Dutch overseas possessions took place in 1954 under the Statute for the Kingdom, which gave the territories in the West Indies equal status. Dutch New Guinea (Irian Jaya) was ceded to Indonesia in 1963 and Suriname was given its independence in 1974.

Dutch politics saw several important changes in the post-war years, such as the introduction of proportional representation in elections. From the end of the war until 1958, a coalition of Catholic and labour parties held power, taking the Netherlands into the Korean War in 1950. The Netherlands was a founder member of the European Coal and Steel Community (ECSC) in 1951, which later merged with the European Economic Community (EEC).

The economy grew rapidly in the late 1950s when the welfare state was greatly expanded. Social unrest in the 1960s was led by youth and labour groups. Social changes in the '70s included the demise of the traditional zuilen and the creation of new political parties across religious divides; most notable of these was the Christian Democratic Appeal (CDA). Newspapers, the voice of the zuilen, disassociated themselves from religious denominations, becoming independent commercial enterprises. The decriminalization of personal cannabis use in the 1970s indicated a policy towards drug use and abuse that focused on rehabilitation (for hard drug users) as opposed to punishment. Vocal youth action was seen most clearly in the confrontations between the police and the krakers—squatters demanding affordable housing.

Opposition to nuclear weapons grew in the 1980s, sparked by the support given by Prime Minister Andreas van Agt to placing US cruise missiles on Dutch soil. In 1986 the pressures of the Netherlands' population density led to creation of the 12th province, Flevoland, from four polders reclaimed from the IJsselmeer.

The Netherlands joined the coalition forces in the 1991 Gulf War, providing two naval frigates. Serious flooding in Gelderland and the threat of worse to come led to the evacuation of 240,000 people from the province in 1995. In 2000 the Netherlands became the first country to legalize euthanasia.

Social liberalization has continued in the Netherlands in recent years. In addition to euthanasia, homosexual marriage and adoption were legalized in 2000. In April 2002, Prime Minister Wim Kok's government resigned in the wake of a report that criticized Dutch inaction in preventing the massacre at Srebrenica in 1995. During the subsequent election campaigning, the right-wing politician Pim Fortuyn was assassinated by an animal-rights activist who opposed Fortuyn's anti-immigration policies. The coalition government led by Jan Peter Balkenende, formed in July, collapsed in Oct., necessitating fresh elections. Balkenende formed a new government in May 2003.

TERRITORY AND POPULATION

The Netherlands is bounded in the north and west by the North Sea, south by Belgium and east by Germany. The area is 41,528 sq. km, of which 33,873 sq. km is land. Projects of sea-flood control and land reclamation (polders) by the construction of dams and drainage schemes have continued since 1920. More than a quarter of the country is below sea level.

The population was 13,060,115 at the census of 1971 and 16,258,000 on 1 Jan. 2004 (8,212,000 females). Population growth in 2003, 0·4%. The population reached 16m. on 8 March 2001.

The UN gives a projected population for 2010 of 16·59m.

On-going 'rolling' censuses have replaced the former decennial counts.

Area, estimated population and density, and chief towns of the 12 provinces on 1 Jan. 2002:

	Area 1995 (in sq. km)	Population 2002	Density 2002 per sq. km land area	Provincial capital
Groningen	2,967·10	570,000	244	Groningen
Friesland	5,740·75	636,000	189	Leeuwarden
Drenthe	2,680·49	479,000	181	Assen
Overijssel	3,420·06	1,094,000	328	Zwolle
Flevoland	2,412·29	342,000	240	Lelystad
Gelderland	5,143·36	1,949,000	391	Arnhem
Utrecht	1,434·24	1,140,000	821	Utrecht
Noord-Holland	4,059·09	2,559,000	958	Haarlem
Zuid-Holland[1]	3,445·75	3,424,000	1,211	The Hague
Zeeland	2,931·91	377,000	209	Middelburg
Noord-Brabant	5,081·83	2,391,000	485	's-Hertogenbosch
Limburg	2,209·29	1,143,000	528	Maastricht
Total	41,526·16	16,105,000	475	

[1]Since 29 Sept. 1994 includes inhabitants of the municipality of The Hague formerly registered in the abolished Central Population Register.

In 2003, 65·8% of the population lived in urban areas.

Population of municipalities with over 50,000 inhabitants on 1 Jan. 2002:

Alkmaar	92,992	Hilversum	83,096
Almelo	71,026	Hoogeveen	53,186
Almere	158,902	Hoorn	66,458
Alphen a/d Rijn	70,649	Kerkrade	50,680
Amersfoort	129,720	Leeuwarden	90,516
Amstelveen	77,256	Leiden	117,170
Amsterdam	735,526	Leidschendam-	
Apeldoorn	154,859	Voorburg	74,085
Arnhem	140,736	Lelystad	66,460
Assen	60,230	Maastricht	122,005
Bergen op Zoom	65,793	Nieuwegein	62,140
Breda	163,427	Nijmegen	154,616
Capelle a/d Ijssel	65,226	Oosterhout	52,968
Delft	96,936	Oss	67,383
Deventer	86,072	Purmerend	73,476
Dordrecht	120,222	Roosendaal	77,640
Ede	103,708	Rotterdam	598,660
Eindhoven	204,776	Schiedam	76,576
Emmen	108,367	Sittard-Geleen	97,953
Enschede	151,346	Smallingerland	53,493
Gouda	71,688	Spijkenisse	75,147
Groningen	175,569	Tilburg	197,358
Haarlem	147,831	Utrecht	260,625
Haarlemmermeer	118,553	Veenendaal	60,669
The Hague	457,726	Velsen	67,407
Hardenberg	57,483	Venlo	91,400
Heerlen	95,004	Vlaardingen	73,935
Den Helder	60,083	Zaanstad	137,669
Helmond	82,853	Zeist	59,682
Hengelo	80,910	Zoetermeer	110,500
's-Hertogenbosch	131,697	Zwolle	109,000

Urban agglomerations as at 1 Jan. 2000: Amsterdam, 1,002,868; Rotterdam, 989,956; The Hague, 610,245; Utrecht, 366,186; Eindhoven, 302,274; Leiden, 250,302; Dordrecht, 241,218; Heerlen, 218,078; Tilburg, 215,419; Groningen, 191,722; Haarlem, 191,079; Breda, 160,615; Amersfoort, 154,890; 's-Hertogenbosch, 154,368; Apeldoorn, 153,261; Nijmegen, 152,200; Enschede, 149,505; Arnhem, 139,576; Sittard-Geleen, 127,322; Maastricht, 122,070; Zwolle, 105,801.

The first national language is Dutch and the second is Friesian.

SOCIAL STATISTICS

Vital statistics for calendar years:

	Live births		Marriages	Divorces	Deaths
	Total	Outside marriage			
1998	199,408	41,439	86,956	32,459	137,482
1999	200,445	45,592	89,428	33,571	140,487
2000	206,619	51,539	88,074	34,650	140,527
2001	202,603	55,108	82,091	37,104	140,377
2002	202,083	58,857	85,808	33,179	142,355

2002 rates per 1,000 population: birth, 12·5; death, 8·8. Annual population growth rate, 1992–2002, 0·6%. In 2000 the suicide rate per 100,000 population was 11·6 (men, 15·8; women, 7·6). In 2001 the average age of marrying was 34·6 years for males and 31·5 for females. Expectation of life, 2003, was 75·7 years for males and 81·1 for females. Infant mortality, 2001, 5·4 per 1,000 live births; fertility rate, 2001, 1·7 births per woman. The annual abortion rate, at under 8 per 1,000 women aged 15–44, is among the lowest in the world. Percentage of population by age in 2001: 0–19 years, 24·5%; 20–64, 61·9%; 65 and over, 13·7%. In 2002 the Netherlands received 18,667 asylum applications, equivalent to 1·2 per 1,000 inhabitants.

CLIMATE

A cool temperate maritime climate, marked by mild winters and cool summers, but with occasional continental influences. Coastal temperatures vary from 37°F (3°C) in winter to 61°F (16°C) in summer, but inland the winters are slightly colder and the summers slightly warmer. Rainfall is least in the months Feb. to May, but inland there is a well-defined summer maximum in July and Aug.

The Hague, Jan. 37°F (2·7°C), July 61°F (16·3°C). Annual rainfall 32·8" (820 mm). Amsterdam, Jan. 36°F (2·3°C), July 62°F (16·5°C). Annual rainfall 34" (850 mm). Rotterdam, Jan. 36·5°F (2·6°C), July 62°F (16·6°C). Annual rainfall 32" (800 mm).

CONSTITUTION AND GOVERNMENT

According to the Constitution (promulgated 1815; last revision, 2002), the Kingdom consists of the Netherlands, Aruba and the Netherlands Antilles. Their relations are regulated by the 'Statute' for the Kingdom, which came into force on 29 Dec. 1954. Each part enjoys full autonomy; they are united, on a footing of equality, for mutual assistance and the protection of their common interests.

The Netherlands is a constitutional and hereditary monarchy. The royal succession is in the direct female or male line in order of birth. The reigning Queen is **Beatrix Wilhelmina Armgard**, born 31 Jan. 1938, daughter of Queen Juliana and Prince Bernhard; married to Claus von Amsberg on 10 March 1966 (born 6 Sept. 1926, died 6 Oct. 2002); succeeded to the crown on 30 April 1980, on the abdication of her mother. *Offspring:* Prince Willem-Alexander, born 27 April 1967, married to Máxima Zorreguieta on 2 Feb. 2002 (*offspring:* Catharina-Amalia, born 7 Dec. 2003; Alexia, born 26 June 2005); Prince Johan Friso, born 25 Sept. 1968, married to Mabel Wisse Smit on 24 April 2004 (*offspring:* Luana, born 26 March 2005); Prince Constantijn, born 11 Oct. 1969, married to Laurentien Brinkhorst on 19 May 2001 (*offspring:* Eloise, born 8 June 2002; Claus-Casimir, born 21 March 2004).

The Queen receives an allowance from the civil list. This was €3,896,000 in 2006; and that of Crown Prince Willem-Alexander, €933,000. Princess Máxima also receives allowances from the civil list.

Sisters of the Queen. Princess Irene Emma Elisabeth, born 5 Aug. 1939, married to Prince Charles Hugues de Bourbon-Parma on 29 April 1964, divorced 1981 (*sons:* Prince Carlos Javier Bernardo, born 27 Jan. 1970; Prince Jaime Bernardo, born 13 Oct. 1972; *daughters:* Princess Margarita Maria Beatriz, born 13 Oct. 1972; Princess Maria Carolina Christina, born 23 June 1974); Princess Margriet Francisca, born in Ottawa, 19 Jan. 1943, married to Pieter van Vollenhoven on 10 Jan. 1967 (*sons:* Prince Maurits, born 17 April 1968; Prince Bernhard, born 25 Dec. 1969; Prince Pieter-Christiaan, born 22 March 1972; Prince Floris, born 10 April 1975); Princess Maria Christina, born 18 Feb. 1947, married to Jorge Guillermo on 28 June 1975 (*sons:* Bernardo, born 17 June 1977; Nicolas, born 6 July 1979; *daughter:* Juliana, born 8 Oct. 1981).

The central executive power of the State rests with the Crown, while the central legislative power is vested in the Crown and Parliament (the *States-General*), consisting of two Chambers. The upper *First Chamber* is composed of 75 members, elected by the members of the Provincial States. The 150-member *Second Chamber* is directly elected by proportional representation for four-year terms. Members of the States-General must be Netherlands subjects of 18 years of age or over. The Hague is the seat of the Court, government and Parliament; Amsterdam is the capital.

The *Council of State*, appointed by the Crown, is composed of a vice-president and not more than 28 members. The monarch is president, but the day-to-day running of the Council is in the hands of the vice-president. The Council has to be consulted on all legislative matters. The Sovereign has the power to dissolve either Chambers, subject to the condition that new elections take place within 40 days, and the new Chamber be convoked within three months. Both the government and the Second Chamber may propose Bills; the First Chamber can only approve or reject them without inserting amendments. The meetings of both Chambers are public, although each of them may by a majority vote decide on a secret session. A Minister or Secretary of State cannot be a member of Parliament at the same time.

The Constitution can be revised only by a Bill declaring that there is reason for introducing such revision and containing the proposed alterations. The passing of this Bill is followed by a dissolution of both Chambers and a second confirmation by the new States-General by two-thirds of the votes. Unless it is expressly stated, all laws concern only the realm in Europe, and not the overseas part of the kingdom, Aruba and the Netherlands Antilles.

National Anthem

'Wilhelmus van Nassaue' ('William of Nassau'); words by Philip Marnix van St Aldegonde, tune anonymous.

GOVERNMENT CHRONOLOGY

Prime Ministers since 1940. (ARP = Anti-Revolutionary Party; CDA = Christian Democratic Appeal; KVP = Catholic People's Party; PvdA = Labour Party; VDB = Liberal Democratic League)

1940–45	ARP	Pieter Sjoerds Gerbrandy
1945–46	VDB/PvdA	Willem Schermerhorn
1946–48	KVP	Louis Jozef Maria Beel
1948–58	PvdA	Willem Drees
1958–59	KVP	Louis Jozef Maria Beel
1959–63	KVP	Jan Eduard de Quay
1963–65	KVP	Victor Gérard Marie Marijnen
1965–66	KVP	Joseph Maria Laurens Theo (Jo) Cals
1966–67	ARP	Jelle Zijlstra
1967–71	KVP	Petrus Josephus Sietse (Piet) de Jong
1971–73	ARP	Barend Willem Biesheuvel
1973–77	PvdA	Johannes Marten (Joop) den Uyl
1977–82	CDA	Andreas Maria (Andries) van Agt
1982–94	CDA	Rudolphus Frans Marie (Ruud) Lubber
1994–2002	PvdA	Willem (Wim) Kok
2002–	CDA	Jan Peter Balkenende

RECENT ELECTIONS

Party affiliation in the First Chamber as elected on 25 May 2003: Christian Democratic Appeal (CDA), 23 seats; Labour Party (PvdA), 19; People's Party for Freedom and Democracy (VVD), 15; Green Left, 5; Socialist Party (SP), 4; Democrats '66 (D66), 3; Christian Union (CU), 2; Political Reformed Party (SGP), 2; List Pim Fortuyn party (LPF), 1; Independent Group in the Senate—Frisian National Party, 1.

Elections to the Second Chamber were held on 22 Jan. 2003. The CDA won 44 seats with 28·6% of votes cast (43 seats at the 2002 election); the PvdA, 42 seats and 27·3% (23 in 2002); the VVD, 28 seats and 17·9% (24); SP, 9 seats and 6·3% (9); the List Pim Fortuyn party (LPF), 8 seats and 5·7% (26); the Green Left, 8 seats and 5·1% (10); D66, 6 seats and 4·1% (7); the Christian Union (CU), 3 seats and 2·1% (4); SGP, 2 seats and 1·6% (2). Turnout was 79·9%.

European Parliament

The Netherlands has 27 (31 in 1999) representatives. At the June 2004 elections turnout was 39·1% (29·9% in 1999). The CDA won 7 seats with 24·4% of votes cast (political affiliation in European Parliament: European People's Party–European Democrats); the PvdA, 7 with 23·6% (Party of European Socialists); the VVD, 4 with 13·2% (Alliance of Liberals and Democrats for Europe); Green Left, 2 with 7·4% (Greens/European Free Alliance); Europa Transparant, 2 with 7·3% (Greens/European Free Alliance); the SP, 2 with 7·0% (European Unitary Left/Nordic Green Left); CU-SGP, 2 with 5·9% (Independence and Democracy Group); D66, 1 with 4·2% (Alliance of Liberals and Democrats for Europe).

CURRENT ADMINISTRATION

A coalition government of CDA, VVD and D66 was sworn in on 27 May 2003. In March 2006 it comprised:

Prime Minister: Jan Peter Balkenende; b. 1956 (CDA).

Deputy Prime Minister and Minister of Finance: Gerrit Zalm (VVD). *Deputy Prime Minister and Minister of Economic Affairs:* Laurens Jan Brinkhorst (D66).

Minister of Foreign Affairs: Bernard Bot (CDA). *Justice:* Piet Hein Donner (CDA). *Interior and Kingdom Relations:* Johan Remkes (VVD). *Government Reform and Kingdom Relations:* Alexander Pechtold (D66). *Education, Culture and Science:* Maria van der Hoeven (CDA). *Defence:* Henk Kamp (VVD). *Housing, Spatial Planning and the Environment:* Sybilla Dekker (VVD). *Transport, Public Works and Water Management:* Karla Peijs (CDA). *Agriculture, Nature Management and Fisheries:* Cees Veerman (CDA). *Health, Welfare and Sport:* Hans Hoogervorst (VVD). *Development Co-operation:* Agnes van Ardenne (CDA). *Immigration and Integration:* Rita Verdonk (VVD). *Social Affairs and Employment:* Aart Jan de Geus (CDA).

Office of the Prime Minister: http://www.minaz.nl

CURRENT LEADERS

Jan Peter Balkenende

Position
Prime Minister

Introduction
Jan Peter Balkenende, head of the Christian Democratic Appeal (CDA), succeeded Wim Kok as Dutch prime minister following the elections of May 2002. He briefly led a right-of-centre coalition which included the People's Party for Freedom and Democracy (VVD) and List Pim Fortuyn (LPF) until Oct. 2002, when LPF in-fighting forced the collapse of the government. Balkenende then led the CDA to victory at the elections of Jan. 2003 and formed a new coalition with the VVD and Democrats '66 (D66).

Early Life
Balkenende was born on 7 May 1956 in Kapelle. He graduated in history and law from the Amsterdam Free University. Between 1982 and 1984 he was a legal affairs policy officer for the Netherlands Universities Council before joining the policy

institute of the CDA, where he stayed until 1998. Between 1993 and 2002 he held a professorship of Christian social thought on society and economics at the Amsterdam Free University. An alderman for Amstelveen, he won a parliamentary seat at the elections of 1998.

When Jaap de Hoop Scheffer resigned the party leadership in late 2001 there was a divisive contest to replace him. Balkenende came under fire for his lack of experience and perceived weak leadership skills, but eventually emerged victorious. In the build-up to the 2002 elections he refused to rule out a coalition with any party, including List Pim Fortuyn, although he distanced himself from some of its extremist policies.

Career in Office

Following the May 2002 elections Balkenende headed a coalition of the CDA, LPF and VVD. His cabinet was sworn nine weeks later. He pledged to tighten up immigration policy, reduce taxes and reduce the number of people receiving disability benefits. In addition, he was expected to instigate a review of the Netherlands' liberal drugs and euthanasia legislation. However, his government was plagued by the instability of the LPF, whose leader, Mat Herben, resigned in Aug. 2002. LPF in-fighting was caused by a personality clash between two of its ministers, Eduard Bomhoff and Herman Heinsbroek, both of whom resigned in Oct. 2002. The CDA and VVD were unable to continue alone and the government resigned on 21 Oct. 2002. Balkenende agreed to remain in place in a caretaker capacity until new elections.

At elections to the Second Chamber in Jan. 2003, the CDA took 44 seats, two ahead of the Labour Party (PvdA). In May 2003, after months of negotiations, Balkenende was sworn in as head of a coalition government comprising the CDA, VVD and D66. His government's policies have since proved unpopular. In Oct. 2004 more than 200,000 people turned out in Amsterdam to protest against public spending cuts and welfare reform, and in June 2005 the electorate voted decisively against the proposed new European Union constitution in a national referendum.

DEFENCE

Conscription ended on 30 Aug. 1996.

The total strength of the armed forces in 2002 was 49,580, including 4,155 women. In 2003 defence expenditure totalled US$8,256m. (US$509 per capita), representing 1·6% of GDP.

Army

The 1st Netherlands Army Corps is assigned to NATO. It consists of ten brigades and Corps troops.

Personnel in 2002 numbered 23,150, including 1,630 women. The National Territorial Command forces consist of territorial brigades, security forces, some logistical units and staffs. Some units in the Netherlands may be assigned to the UN as peacekeeping forces.

There is a paramilitary Royal Military Constabulary, 3,300 strong. In addition there are 22,200 army reservists.

Navy

The principal headquarters and main base of the Royal Netherlands Navy is at Den Helder, with minor bases at Vlissingen (Flushing), Curaçao (Netherlands Antilles) and Oranjestad (Aruba). Command and control in home waters is exercised jointly with the Belgian Navy (submarines excepted).

The combatant fleet includes four diesel submarines, two destroyers and nine frigates. In 2002 personnel totalled 12,130 (1,150 women), including 950 in the Naval Air Service and 3,100 in the Royal Netherlands Marine Corps.

Air Force

The Royal Netherlands Air Force (RNLAF) had 8,850 personnel in 2002 (975 women). It has a first-line combat force of 143 combat aircraft and 30 attack helicopters. Equipment includes F-16A/Bs. All squadrons are operated by Tactical Air Command.

INTERNATIONAL RELATIONS

The Netherlands is a member of the UN, WTO, NATO, BIS, OECD, EU, Council of Europe, WEU, OSCE, CERN, Inter-American Development Bank, Asian Development Bank, IOM and the Antarctic Treaty. The Netherlands is a signatory of the Schengen accord which abolishes border controls between the Netherlands and Austria, Belgium, Denmark, Finland, France, Germany, Greece, Iceland, Italy, Luxembourg, Norway, Portugal, Spain and Sweden.

On 1 June 2005 the Netherlands became the second European Union member after France to reject the proposed EU constitution, with 61·54% of votes cast in a referendum against the constitution and only 38·46% in favour.

The Hague is the seat of several international organizations, including the International Court of Justice.

The Netherlands gave US$4·2bn. in international aid in 2004, which at 0·73% of GNI made it the world's fifth most generous country as a percentage of its gross national income.

ECONOMY

Services accounted for 71·4% of GDP in 2002, industry 25·9% and agriculture 2·7%.

According to the anti-corruption organization *Transparency International*, the Netherlands ranked equal 11th in the world in a 2005 survey of the countries with the least corruption in business and government. It received 8·6 out of 10 in the annual index.

Overview

The Dutch economy is characterized by one of the highest levels of average income in the world and relatively low income inequality. Given the country's small domestic market, its location at the heart of northwest Europe's economic activity and its geography favourable to harbour facilities, the Dutch economy is among the most open and outward-looking economies in the world. Economic vitality depends on foreign trade. Both exports and imports of goods and services account for well over 60% of nominal GDP. Rotterdam is Europe's largest port, handling over twice as much cargo as Antwerp, Europe's second largest port, and generating annual added value equal to nearly one-tenth of total GDP. The scarcity of industrial raw materials also makes the country trade-dependent and has oriented industry towards processing.

The country is one of the most competitive destinations for global foreign direct investment (FDI). A favourable tax environment for multinationals has attracted many foreign companies and significant FDI inflows over the years. FDI was strongest in the period 1998–2002, when inflows totalled €225·5bn. (over €45bn. per year). During this period direct investment inflows were greater than those to countries as large as France and China. Since 2002 FDI has slowed, with the average annual inflow from 2003–05 amounting to less than one-quarter of previous levels but the country remains an important investment destination.

Relative to the European Big Four average the Dutch manufacturing sector share of GDP is small and its agricultural and services sectors are comparatively large. The Netherlands is a leader in horticulture production and a competitive meat and dairy product exporter. The services sector is dominated by the commercial sector, which accounts for nearly half of total GDP. Dutch industrial relations are notably stable with emphasis placed on consensus and pragmatism. The Social Economic Council, a broad-based association representing employers, trade unions and appointees of the central government, is central to Dutch policy-making and has been the main force behind wage moderation over the last two decades. The Dutch welfare system and labour market institutions have similarities with the German model but unemployment is comparatively low.

The financial system is based on shareholding, rather than the German investment banking model. The pension system is mainly financed by pension funds owning shares and other assets but the state's unfunded pension liabilities are nonetheless substantial and dealing with an ageing population is a significant future challenge for the Netherlands. The looming growth of pension payments is a leading reason for the Netherlands' aggressive strengthening of public finances in recent years. The Economist Intelligence Unit estimates that annual budget deficits over the half decade 2000–04 have averaged roughly 1% compared to 3·7% over the previous half decade, despite weaker growth. Public debt has been reduced from over 70% of GDP in the mid-1990s to roughly 55·1% in 2004 and the country consistently runs current account surpluses.

Currency

On 1 Jan. 1999 the euro (EUR) became the legal currency in the Netherlands; irrevocable conversion rate 2·20371 guilders to 1 euro. The euro, which consists of 100 cents, has been in circulation since 1 Jan. 2002. There are seven euro notes in different colours and sizes denominated in 500, 200, 100, 50, 20, 10 and 5 euros, and eight coins denominated in 2 and 1 euros, then 50, 20, 10, 5, 2 and 1 cents. On the introduction of the euro there was a 'dual circulation' period before the guilder ceased to be legal tender on 28 Jan. 2002. Euro banknotes in circulation on 1 Jan. 2002 had a total value of €29·7bn.

Gold reserves were 28·15m. troy oz in June 2002 and foreign exchange reserves US$5,290m. (US$31,060m. in 1995). Total money supply was €16,206m. in June 2002. Inflation rates (based on OECD statistics):

1995	1996	1997	1998	1999	2000	2001	2002	2003	2004
1·4%	1·4%	1·9%	1·8%	2·0%	2·3%	5·1%	3·9%	2·2%	1·4%

The inflation rate in 2005 according to Statistics Netherlands was 1·7%.

Budget

Central government revenues and expenditures in €1m.:

	2001	2002	2003
Revenue	177,914	181,622	184,341
Expenditure	176,548	185,842	195,666

Principal sources of revenue in 2003: social security contributions, €65·71bn.; taxes on goods and services, €52·04bn.; taxes on income, profits and capital gains, €44·61bn. Main items of expenditure by economic type in 2003: social benefits, €86·14bn.; grants, €58·52bn.; compensation of employees, €16·43bn.

As from Jan. 2001 VAT is 19·0% (reduced rate, 6·0%).

Performance

Real GDP growth rates (based on OECD statistics):

1995	1996	1997	1998	1999	2000	2001	2002	2003	2004
3·0%	3·0%	3·8%	4·3%	4·0%	3·5%	1·4%	0·1%	−0·1%	1·7%

Real GDP growth (provisional) in 2005 was 0·9% according to Statistics Netherlands. In 2004 total GDP was US$577·3bn.

The July 2004 *OECD Economic Survey* suggests that: 'The upswing in the world economy will help exports to grow for the first time after two years of stagnation. ... All in all, the recovery is likely to be less strong than after previous recessions as a result of both the domestic factors hampering consumption and the loss of competitiveness.'

Banking and Finance

The central bank and bank of issue is the Netherlands Bank (*President*, Arnout Wellink), founded in 1814 and nationalized in 1948. Its Governor is appointed by the government for seven-year terms. The capital amounted to €500m. in 2002. In 2002 there were 18 leading commercial banks. The largest banks are ABN Amro Holding NV (assets in 2003 of US$707·8bn.) and ING Bank NV (assets in 2003 of US$684·0bn.). There is a stock exchange in Amsterdam; it is a component of Euronext, which was created in Sept. 2000 through the merger of the Amsterdam, Brussels and Paris bourses.

ENERGY AND NATURAL RESOURCES

Environment

Carbon dioxide emissions from the consumption and flaring of fossil fuels in 2002 were the equivalent of 15·9 tonnes per capita.

The Netherlands is one of the world leaders in recycling. In 1998, 46% of all household waste was recycled, including 84% of glass.

Electricity

Installed capacity was 21·0m. kW in 2002. Production of electrical energy in 2002 was 95·98bn. kWh (approximately 4% nuclear); consumption per capita was 6,958 kWh. There was one nuclear reactor in operation in 2003.

Oil and Gas

Production of natural gas in 2002, 59·9bn. cu. metres. Reserves in 2002 were 1,760bn. cu. metres. The Groningen gas field in the north of the country is the largest in continental Europe. In 2001 crude oil production was 1·37m. tonnes; reserves were 107m. bbls. in 2002.

Wind

There were 1,472 wind turbines and an installed capacity of 685 MW at the end of 2002.

Minerals

In 2001, 5·0m. tonnes of salt were produced. Aluminium production in 2001 totalled 294,000 tonnes.

Agriculture

The Netherlands is one of the world's largest exporters of agricultural produce. There were 101,500 farms in 2000. Agriculture accounted for 22·8% of exports and 15·1% of imports in 1998. The agricultural sector employs 2·7% of the workforce. In 2001 there were 905,000 ha. of arable land and 33,000 ha. of permanent crops. The total area of cultivated land in 2001 was 1,931,000 ha.: grassland, 993,000 ha.; arable crops, 798,000 ha.; horticultural crops, 110,000 ha., of which 100,000 ha. was in the open and 11,000 ha. was under glass; fallow land, 30,000 ha. In 2002, 258,000 people were employed in agriculture (89,700 women).

The yield of the more important arable crops, in 1,000 tonnes, was as follows:

Crop	2000	2001	2002
Potatoes	8,127	7,016	—
Sugarbeets	6,728	5,947	—
Wheat	1,143	991	1,111
Sown onions	821	765	883
Barley	288	387	352

Other major fruit and vegetable production in 2000 included (in 1,000 tonnes): tomatoes, 600; apples, 575; cucumbers and gherkins, 465; cabbages, 284; carrots, 274; mushrooms, 263; chillies and green peppers, 250; pears, 125.

Cultivated areas of main flowers (2002) in 1,000 ha.: tulips, 10·6; lilies, 5·1; daffodils, 2·0; gladioli, 1·5; hyacinths, 1·2.

Livestock, 2001 (in 1,000) included: 11,648 pigs; 3,858 cattle; 1,186 sheep; 121 horses and ponies; 102,503 turkeys and chickens.

Animal products in 2000 (in 1,000 tonnes) included: pork, bacon and ham, 1,643; beef and veal, 485; poultry, 713; milk, 10,800; cheese, 690; butter, 126; hens' eggs, 660.

Forestry
Forests covered 375,000 ha. in 2000, or 11·1% of the land area. In 2003, 1·04m. cu. metres of roundwood were cut.

Fisheries
Total catch in 2003 was 526,280 tonnes (chiefly scad, herring, mackerel and plaice), of which 524,130 tonnes were from marine waters. There were 932 fishing vessels in 2002.

INDUSTRY
The leading companies by market capitalization in the Netherlands, excluding banking and finance, in May 2004 were: Royal Dutch Petroleum Company (US$104·9bn.); Unilever NV (US$37·6bn.), a consumer goods firm; and Koninklijke Philips Electronics NV (US$36·0bn.). At 31 Dec. 1999 there were 6,572 enterprises in the manufacturing industry, of which 3,689 had 20–49 employees and 182 had 500 employees or more; total annual sales for 1997 were 151,229m. euros.

The three largest industrial sectors are chemicals, food processing and metal, mechanical and electrical engineering. The food products and beverages industry employed 168,000 people at 30 Sept. 2000 (annual sales for 2000 in €1m., 45,217); machinery and equipment, 101,000 (15,630); electrical machinery and apparatus, 96,000 (17,805); other fabricated metal products, 111,000 (13,831); publishing, printing and reproduction of recorded media, 93,000 (13,412); chemicals and chemical products, 75,000 (35,779); transport equipment, 59,000 (12,461); rubber and plastic products, 39,000 (5,869).

Labour
The total labour force in 2001 was 7,311,000 persons (2,990,000 women) of whom 248,000 (142,000) were unemployed, with 146,000 (69,000) registered unemployed. By education level, the 2001 labour force included (in 1,000): primary education, 633; junior general secondary, 496; pre-vocational secondary, 1,017; senior general secondary, 429; senior vocational secondary, 2,738; vocational colleges, 1,329; university, 664.

The unemployment rate was 4·7% in Dec. 2005, among the lowest rates in the EU. Although the Netherlands has a very low unemployment rate, for every 100 people below the age of 65 who are active in the labour market, 35 are not. In 1995 the average age for retirement among males was 58.

In 2000 the weekly working hours (excluding overtime) of employees were 35·6 for men and 25·5 for women. In 2000 full-time employees' working hours (excluding overtime) totalled 1,710; part-time 945; and flexible 849. Workers in the Netherlands put in among the shortest hours of any industrialized country. In 1996 only 11% of male workers and 4% of female workers worked more than 40 hours a week. In 2004 part-time work accounted for approximately 35% of all employment in the Netherlands— the highest percentage in any major industrialized country. 76·0% of part-time workers in 2004 were women. Average annual gross earnings of employees in 2000 were €26,500 for men and €14,900 for women. In 2001 gross hourly wage earnings by type of employment ranged from €26·42 in mining and quarrying, €22·01 in public utilities and €21·34 in public administration and social security to €10·64 in hotels and restaurants.

Trade Unions
Trade unions are grouped in three central federations: Christian National Trade Union Confederation (CNV), Trade Union Confederation for Middle and Higher Management (MHP) and General Netherlands Trade Union Confederation (FNV). Total membership was 1·92m. in 2001, approximately 25% of waged employees. In Nov. 1993 an agreement on wage restraint was concluded between the trade unions and the employers' federations, in return for an enhancement of the roles of works committees and professional training for employees.

INTERNATIONAL TRADE
On 5 Sept. 1944 and 14 March 1947 the Netherlands signed agreements with Belgium and Luxembourg for the establishment of a customs union. On 1 Jan. 1948 this union came into force and the existing customs tariffs of the Belgium–Luxembourg Economic Union and of the Netherlands were superseded by the joint Benelux Customs Union Tariff. It applied to imports into the three countries from outside sources, and exempted from customs duties all imports into each of the three countries from the other two.

Imports and Exports
In 2004 imports totalled €228,010m. (€206,867m. in 2003); exports, €257,742m. (€234,166m. in 2003).

Value of trade with major partners (in €1m.):

Country	Imports 2001	Exports 2001	Imports (% change on 2000)	Exports (% change on 2000)
Belgium	20,117	28,502	+1	+4
France	12,617	24,944	+3	+2
Germany	40,253	61,697	+5	+3
Ireland	3,809	2,320	–3	+26
Italy	6,173	15,076	+1	+10
Japan	8,696	2,522	–6	+9
Norway	4,504	1,878	–7	+13
Spain	4,742	8,474	+1	+12
Sweden	4,379	4,953	–11	–7
Switzerland	2,379	3,911	–3	–2
UK	19,458	26,884	–6	+7
USA	21,525	10,559	–2	–3

The main imports in 2001 (in €1m.) included machines (including electrical machines), 68,415; chemical products, 24,785; food and live animals, 18,249; road vehicles, 15,046; crude petroleum, 12,245; clothing, 6,348; oil products, 5,367; iron and steel, 4,317; non-ferrous metals, 3,453; paper and paperboard, 3,096. Main exports included machines (including electrical machines), 70,316; chemical products, 36,915; food and live animals, 29,280; oil products, 14,381; raw materials (inedible) except fuels, 11,614; road vehicles, 11,002; fruit and vegetables, 7,633; natural and manufactured gas, 6,864; beverages and tobacco, 5,476; meat, 4,136; iron and steel, 3,879; clothing, 3,608.

COMMUNICATIONS

Roads
In 1999 the length of the Netherlands road network was 116,500 km, including 2,235 km of motorways. 90% of roads are paved. Number of private cars (2002), 6·71m.; trucks and vans, 0·88m.; motorcycles, 461,000. There were 987 fatalities as a result of road accidents in 2002, equivalent to 6·1 fatalities per 100,000 population. Only the UK had a lower death rate from road accidents in 2002.

Rail
All railways are run by the mixed company 'N.V. Nederlandse Spoorwegen'. Route length in 2001 was 2,809 km. Passengers carried (2001), 319m.; goods transported, 26·1m. tonnes. There is a metro (44 km) and tram/light rail network (154 km) in Amsterdam and in Rotterdam (76 km and 67 km). Tram/light rail networks operate in The Hague (128 km) and Utrecht (22 km).

Civil Aviation
There are international airports at Amsterdam (Schiphol), Rotterdam, Maastricht and Eindhoven. The Royal Dutch Airlines (KLM) was founded on 7 Oct. 1919. In Oct. 2003 it merged with Air France to form Air France-KLM, in which the French state

owns a 25·8% stake. In 1999 KLM flew 357·9m. km, carrying 15,568,200 passengers (15,437,400 on international flights). Services were provided in 2003 by around 80 foreign airlines. In 2001 Amsterdam handled 39,309,000 passengers (39,167,000 on international flights) and 1,183,000 tonnes of freight. Rotterdam is the second busiest airport, handling 748,000 passengers in 2001, followed by Maastricht, with 360,000 in 2001.

Sea-going Shipping

Survey of the Netherlands mercantile marine as at 1 Jan. (capacity in 1,000 GRT):

Ships under Netherlands flag	2001 Number	2001 Capacity	2002 Number	2002 Capacity
Passenger ships	17	644	19	734
Freighters (100 GRT and over)	514	3,225	511	3,444
Tankers	61	517	57	477
	592	4,386	587	4,655

In 2001, 42,372 sea-going ships (including 7,418 Dutch-registered ships) of 605·24m. gross tons entered Netherlands ports.

Total goods traffic by sea-going ships in 2001 (with 2000 figures in brackets), in 1m. tonnes, amounted to 326 (325) unloaded and 98 (99) loaded; total seaborne goods traffic in 2001 (and 2000) at Rotterdam was 313·4 (319·6) and at Amsterdam 48·1 (42·1).

The number of containers (including flats) at Dutch ports in 2001 (and 2000) was: unloaded from ships, 1,982,000 (2,001,000), and 1,893,000 (2,005,000) loaded into ships.

Inland Shipping

The total length of navigable rivers and canals is 5,046 km, of which 2,398 km is for ships with a capacity of 1,000 and more tonnes. On 1 Jan. 2002 the inland fleet used for transport (with carrying capacity in 1,000 tonnes) was composed as follows:

	Number	Capacity
Self-propelled barges	3,636	3,879
Dumb barges	549	275
Pushed barges	666	1,347
	4,851	5,501

In 2001, 241·3m. tonnes of goods were transported on rivers and canals, of which 137·7m. tonnes was by international shipping. Goods transport on the Rhine across the Dutch–German frontier near Lobith amounted to 163·3m. tonnes.

Telecommunications

The Netherlands had 22,100,000 telephone subscribers in 2002 (equivalent to 1,364·6 per 1,000 population), and there were 7,557,000 PCs (466·6 per 1,000 persons). Mobile phone subscribers numbered 12,060,000 in 2002 and there were 855,000 fax machines in use. There were 9·73m. Internet users in Sept. 2002.

Postal Services

In 2003 there were 2,577 post offices, equivalent to one for every 6,270 persons.

SOCIAL INSTITUTIONS

Justice

Justice is administered by the High Court (Court of Cassation), by five courts of justice (Courts of Appeal), by 19 district courts and by 61 cantonal courts. The Cantonal Court, which deals with minor offences, comprises a single judge; more serious cases are tried by the district courts, comprising as a rule three judges (in some cases one judge is sufficient); the courts of appeal are constituted of three and the High Court of five judges. All judges are appointed for life by the Sovereign (the judges of the

High Court from a list prepared by the Second Chamber of the States-General). They can be removed only by a decision of the High Court.

At the district court the juvenile judge is specially appointed to try children's civil cases and at the same time charged with administration of justice for criminal actions committed by young persons between 12 and 18 years old, unless imprisonment of more than six months ought to be inflicted; such cases are tried by three judges.

The population in penal institutions at 30 Sept. 2000 was 11,759, of which 5,223 were convicted. The total number of inmates during the year was 43,210 (40,228 men). 1,357,600 crimes were reported in 2001.

Police

The police force is divided into 25 regions. There is also a National Police Service which includes the Central Criminal Investigation Office, which deals with serious crimes throughout the country, and the International Criminal Investigation Office, which informs foreign countries of international crimes.

Education

Statistics for the scholastic year 2001–02:

	Schools	Full-time pupils/students (in 1,000) Total
Primary education	7,036	1,552
Special primary education	361	52
Expertise centres	331	48
Secondary education	795	904
Senior vocational secondary education	70	271
Apprenticeship training	67	162
Vocational colleges	64	258
University education	13	159

Academic Year 2001–02:

	Full-time students Total	% female
University education:		
Agriculture	3,793	49
Behaviour and Social Sciences	34,191	69
Economics	28,414	29
Education	632	54
Engineering	24,888	18
Health	20,807	62
Language and Culture	23,434	64
Law	25,125	55
Science	12,455	32
Other	564	76
Total	174,303	49

In 2001 there were 123,000 participants in adult basic education; and, in 2002, 19,400 Open University students.

In 1999–2000 total expenditure on education came to 4·8% of GNP and 10·4% of total government spending. The adult literacy rate is at least 99%.

Health

On 1 Jan. 2001 there were 7,763 general practitioners, 12,594 physiotherapists, 7,513 dentists, 3,069 pharmacists and 1,627 midwives; on 1 Jan. 2000, a total of 14,712 specialists. There were 131 hospitals and 55,438 licensed hospital beds (excluding mental hospitals) at 1 Jan. 2000.

The 1919 Opium Act (amended in 1928 and 1976) regulates the production and consumption of 'psychoactive' drugs. Personal use of cannabis is effectively decriminalized and the sale of soft drugs through 'coffee shops' is not prosecuted provided certain conditions are met.

Euthanasia became legal when the First Chamber (the Senate) gave its formal approval on 10 April 2001 by 46 votes to 28. The Second Chamber had voted to make it legal by 104 votes to 40 in Nov. 2000. The law came into effect on 1 April 2002. During 2000 euthanasia organizations recorded 2,123 instances of doctors helping patients to die. The Netherlands was the first country to legalize euthanasia.

In 2003 the Netherlands spent 9·8% of its GDP on health.

Welfare

The General Old Age Pension Act (AOW) entitles everyone to draw an old age pension from the age of 65. At 31 Dec. 2001 there were 2,365,600 persons entitled to receive an old age pension, and 163,100 a pension under the Surviving Relatives Insurance; 1,864,300 parents were receiving benefits under the General Family Allowances Act. In 2001 there were 981,300 persons claiming labour disablement benefits and 166,000 persons claiming benefits under the Unemployment Act.

RELIGION

Entire liberty of conscience is granted to the members of all denominations. The royal family belong to the Dutch Reformed Church.

According to estimates of 2001, the population aged 18 years and over was: Roman Catholics, 31%; Dutch Reformed Church, 14%; Calvinist, 7%; other creeds, 9%; no religion, 40%. The government of the Reformed Church is Presbyterian. On 1 July 1992 the Dutch Reformed Church had one synod, nine provincial districts, 75 classes, about 160 districts and about 2,000 parishes. Their clergy numbered 1,735. The Roman Catholic Church had, Jan. 1992, one archbishop (of Utrecht), six bishops, four assistant bishops and about 1,750 parishes and rectorships. In May 2005 there were two Roman Catholic cardinals. The Old Catholics had (1 July 1992) one archbishop (Utrecht), one bishop and 28 parishes. The Jews had, in 1992, 40 communities. At 1 Jan. 2000 there were an estimated 735,600 Muslims (4·6% of the population) and 86,100 Hindus (0·5%).

CULTURE

World Heritage Sites

The Kingdom of the Netherlands has seven sites on the UNESCO World Heritage list: Schokland and its surroundings (inscribed on the list in 1995); the defence line at Amsterdam (1996); the mill network at Kinderdijk-Elshout (1997); the historic area of Willemstad, the inner city and harbour in Curaçao (Netherlands Antilles) (1997); the D. F. Wouda steam pumping station (1998); Droogmakerij de Beemster (Beemster Polder) (1999); and the Rietveld Schröder house (2000).

Broadcasting

Public broadcasting programmes are provided by broadcasting associations representing clearly identifiable social or religious ideals or groupings. The six associations work together in the Netherlands Broadcasting Corporation, *Nederlandse Omroepprogramma Stichting* (NOS). There are three national television channels (colour by PAL) and five radio stations. In addition, there are regional radio stations in every province, a limited number of regional television stations and 400 local radio stations. Commercial broadcasting was introduced in 1992. Dutch-language commercial companies include RTL 4 and 5 which broadcast in Dutch from Luxembourg, Veronica, SBS6, TV10 and the Music Factory. Public broadcasting revenue is obtained from radio and television licences and from advertising.

There were 8·9m. TV receivers in 2001 and 15·6m. radio receivers in 2000. There were 6·32m. cable TV subscribers in 2001.

Cinema

In 2001 there were 558 cinemas and film houses with a seating capacity of 279,000. Total attendance was 23·72m.

Press

In 2002 there were 35 daily newspapers with a combined circulation of 4·3m., equivalent to 267 per 1,000 inhabitants. The most widely read daily is *De Telegraaf,* with average daily sales of 808,000 copies (2003).

Tourism

Tourism is a major sector of the economy, earning US$7,706m. in revenue in 2002. There were 9,595,000 foreign visitors in that year.

Festivals

Floriade, a world-famous horticultural show, takes place every ten years and is the largest Dutch attraction, being attended by 2·3m. people in 2002. The Maastricht Carnival in April attracts many visitors. The Flower Parade from Noordwijk to Haarlem occurs in late April. Koninginnedag on 30 April is a nationwide celebration of Queen Beatrix's birthday. The Oosterparkfestival, a cultural celebration of that district of Amsterdam, runs for three days in the first week of May. Liberation Day is celebrated every five years on 5 May, with the next occurrence being in 2010. An international music festival, the Holland Festival, is held in Amsterdam throughout June each year and the Early Music Festival is held in Utrecht. The North Sea Jazz Festival, the largest in Europe, takes place in The Hague. Each year the most important Dutch and Flemish theatre productions of the previous season are performed at the Theatre Festival in Amsterdam and Antwerp (Belgium). The Holland Dance Festival is held every other year in The Hague and the Springdance Festival in Utrecht annually. Film festivals include the Rotterdam Film Festival in Feb., the World Wide Video Festival in April, the Dutch Film Festival in Sept. and the International Documentary Film Festival of Amsterdam in Dec.

Libraries

In 1997 there were 1,130 public libraries, four National libraries and 856 Higher Education libraries. There were 69,797,000 visits to libraries in 1997.

Theatre and Opera

In 1997–98 there were 56,670 music and theatre performances (including rock and pop concerts) of which 14,530 were plays, 8,240 concerts, 2,900 ballet and dance and 2,390 opera and operetta, with a total attendance of 15,607,000 (excluding rock and pop concerts).

Museums and Galleries

In 1999 there were 902 museums open to the public, to which visits totalled 20,679,000. The Rijksmuseum and Vincent Van Gogh Museums in Amsterdam and the Kröller-Müller Museum in Otterlo attract the most visitors.

DIPLOMATIC REPRESENTATIVES

Of the Netherlands in the United Kingdom (38 Hyde Park Gate, London, SW7 5DP)
Ambassador: Count Jan de Marchant et d'Ansembourg.

Of the United Kingdom in the Netherlands (Lange Voorhout 10, 2514 ED The Hague)
Ambassador: Lyn Parker.

Of the Netherlands in the USA (4200 Linnean Ave., NW, Washington, D.C., 20008)
Ambassador: Boudewijn van Eenennaam.

Of the USA in the Netherlands (Lange Voorhout 102, The Hague)
Ambassador: Vacant.
Chargé d'Affaires a.i.: Chat Blakeman.

Of the Netherlands to the United Nations
Ambassador: Franciscus Antonius Maria Majoor.

FURTHER READING

Centraal Bureau voor de Statistiek. *Statistical Yearbook of the Netherlands.* From 1923/24.— *Statistisch Jaarboek.* From 1899/1924.—*CBS Select (Statistical Essays).* From 1980.— *Statistisch Bulletin.* From 1945; weekly.—*Maandschrift.* From 1944; monthly bulletin.—*90 Jaren Statistiek in Tijdreeksen* (historical series of the Netherlands 1899–1989)

Nationale Rekeningen (National Accounts). From 1948–50.—*Statistische onderzoekingen.* From 1977.—*Regionaal Statistisch Zakboek* (Regional Pocket Yearbook). From 1972

Staatsalmanak voor het Koninkrijk der Nederlanden. Annual. The Hague, from 1814

Staatsblad van het Koninkrijk der Nederlanden. The Hague, from 1814

Staatscourant (State Gazette). The Hague, from 1813

Andeweg, Rudy B. and Irwin, Galen A., *Governance and Politics of the Netherlands.* Palgrave Macmillan, Basingstoke, 2005

Cox, R. H., *The Development of the Dutch Welfare State: from Workers' Insurance to Universal Entitlement.* Pittsburgh Univ. Press, 1994

Gladdish, K., *Governing from the Centre: Politics and Policy-Making in the Netherlands.* London, 1991

King, P. K. and Wintle, M., *The Netherlands.* [Bibliography] ABC-Clio, Oxford and Santa Barbara (CA), 1988

van Os, Andre, *Amsterdam.* [Bibliography] ABC-Clio, Oxford and Santa Barbara (CA), 1997

National library: De Koninklijke Bibliotheek, Prinz Willem Alexanderhof 5, The Hague.

National Statistical Office: Centraal Bureau voor de Statistiek, Netherlands Central Bureau of Statistics, POB 4000, 2270 JM Voorburg.

Statistics Netherlands Website: http://www.cbs.nl

Aruba

KEY HISTORICAL EVENTS

Discovered by Alonzo de Ojeda in 1499, the island of Aruba was claimed for Spain but not settled. It was acquired by the Dutch in 1634, but apart from garrisons, was left to the indigenous Caiquetious (Arawak) Indians until the 19th century. From 1828 it formed part of the Dutch West Indies and, from 1845, part of the Netherlands Antilles with which, on 29 Dec. 1954, it achieved internal self government. Following a referendum in March 1977 the Dutch government announced on 28 Oct. 1981 that Aruba would proceed to independence separately from the other islands. Aruba was constitutionally separated from the Netherlands Antilles from 1 Jan. 1986, and full independence promised by the Netherlands after a ten-year period. However, an agreement with the Netherlands government in June 1990 deletes references to eventual independence at Aruba's request.

TERRITORY AND POPULATION

The island, which lies in the southern Caribbean 32 km north of the Venezuelan coast and 68 km west of Curaçao, has an area of 180 sq. km (75 sq. miles) and a population in Dec. 2000 of 91,065; density 506 inhabitants per sq. km. The chief towns are Oranjestad, the capital (1998 population, 29,000) and San Nicolas. Dutch is the official language, but the language usually spoken is Papiamento, a creole language. Over half the population is of Indian stock, with the balance of Dutch, Spanish and mestizo origin.

SOCIAL STATISTICS

Annual growth rate, 1999, 1·1%. Life expectancy in 2000 was 70 years for males and 76 years for females. Birth rate per 1,000 population (1999), 13·9; death rate, 6·3; infant mortality, 7·2.

CLIMATE

Aruba has a tropical marine climate, with a brief rainy season from Oct. to Dec. Oranjestad (1998), Jan. 28°C (82°F), July 29·4°C (85°F). The annual rainfall in 2000 was 551 mm.

CONSTITUTION AND GOVERNMENT

Under the separate constitution inaugurated on 1 Jan. 1986, Aruba is an autonomous part of the Kingdom of the Netherlands with its own legislature, government, judiciary, civil service and police force. The Netherlands is represented by a Governor appointed by the monarch. The unicameral legislature *(Staten)* consists of 21 members elected for a four-year term of office.

RECENT ELECTIONS

Elections were held on 23 Sept. 2005. The People's Electoral Movement (MEP) won with 11 out of 21 seats (43% of the vote), against 8 seats (32%) for the Aruban People's Party, 1 seat (7%) for the Aruban Patriotic Movement and 1 seat (7%) for Network. Turnout was 85%.

CURRENT ADMINISTRATION

Governor: Fredis Refunjol; b. 1950 (took office on 11 May 2004).
  Prime Minister: Nelson O. Oduber; b. 1947 (sworn in for second term in office on 30 Oct. 2001).

Government Website: http://www.aruba.com

ECONOMY

Currency

Since 1 Jan. 1986 the currency has been the *Aruban florin*, at par with the Netherlands Antilles guilder. Total money supply in 2001 was 1,841m. Aflorins. There were 126m. Aflorins in circulation in 2001. Inflation was 4·2% in 2002. Foreign exchange reserves in June 2002 were US$311m.; gold reserves were 100,000 troy oz. Net foreign assets (including gold and revaluation of gold) in 2000 were 556·3m. Aflorins.

Budget

The 2001 budget totalled 731·8m. Aflorins revenue and grants. Tax revenue was 606·3m. Aflorins in 2001.

Performance

There was a recession in 2002, with negative growth of 3·8%. GDP per capita was 35,966 Aflorins in 2002.

Banking and Finance

There were six domestic and Dutch banks, and one foreign bank, in 2000. There is a special tax regime for offshore banks. The *President* of the Central Bank of Aruba is Robert Henriquez.

ENERGY AND NATURAL RESOURCES

Electricity

In 2001 consumption of electricity was 673,611 MWh.

Fisheries

In 2001 the catch totalled 163 tonnes.

INDUSTRY

The government has established six industrial sites at Oranjestad harbour. The quantity of oil refined in 2001 was 64m. bbls.

Labour

The working age population (15–64 yrs) grew between 1991–2000 from 45,563 to 62,637 persons. The economically active population in 2000 numbered 44,384 persons of which 41,286 were employed and 3,098 unemployed. The employment rate for women grew from 52·8% to 59·2% during the 1990s.

Trade Unions

There are four trade unions: COC, Chambers of Commerce; ATIA, Aruba Trade and Industrial Association; ORMA, Oranjestad Retail and Merchants Association; SNBA, San Nicolas Business Association.

EXTERNAL ECONOMIC RELATIONS

There are two Free Zones at Oranjestad.

Imports and Exports

2002: imports, US$2,050m.; exports, US$1,516m. Leading import suppliers are USA, Netherlands, Venezuela and the Netherlands Antilles. Leading export destinations are USA, Colombia, the Netherlands and the Netherlands Antilles.

COMMUNICATIONS

Roads

In 1984 (latest data available) there were 380 km of surfaced highways. In 2000 there were 39,995 passenger cars and 5,443 commercial vehicles. There were 439 passenger cars per 1,000 inhabitants.

Civil Aviation

There is an international airport (Aeropuerto Internacional Reina Beatrix). There were flights in 2003 to Amsterdam, Atlanta, Barranquilla, Bogotá, Bonaire, Boston, Caracas, Charlotte, Chicago, Curaçao, Harrisburg, Hartford, Las Piedras, Manchester, Maracaibo, Miami, Minneapolis, New York, Paramaribo, Philadelphia, Pittsburgh, Raleigh/Durham, San Juan, Santo Domingo and Washington, D.C. In Dec. 2003 a new airline, Royal Aruban Airlines was launched, with flights to Curaçao and Fort Lauderdale. In 2002 Aruba handled 13,761 commercial landings and 3,113 non-commercial landings. In total 759,285 passengers arrived by air, 751,106 departed and 153,663 were in transit.

Shipping

Oranjestad has a container terminal and cruise ship port. The port at Barcadera services the offshore and energy sector and a deep-water port at San Nicolas services the oil refinery.

Telecommunications

Aruba had 90,100 telephone subscribers in 2001, or 850·3 per 1,000 inhabitants. There were 53,000 mobile phone subscribers in 2001 and 24,000 Internet subscribers.

Postal Services

In 2003 there were five post offices.

SOCIAL INSTITUTIONS

Justice

There is a Common Court of Justice with the Netherlands Antilles. Final Appeal is to the Supreme Court in the Netherlands. The population in penal institutions in Jan. 2005 was 231 (equivalent to 324 per 100,000 population).

Education

In 2000 there were 28 pre-primary, 40 primary, 15 secondary and four middle-level schools, also a teacher training college and law school. Literacy rate (2000 census), 97·3%. The share of education in the 2000–01 budget was 16·0%.

Health

In 2000 there were 123 doctors, 29 dentists, 18 pharmacists and one hospital with 305 beds.

Welfare

All citizens are entitled to an old age pension at the age of 60.

RELIGION

In 2000, 86·2% of the population were Roman Catholic.

CULTURE

Broadcasting

In 2000 there were 18 radio stations and three commercial television stations (colour by NTSC). In 2000 there were 51,000 radio and 20,000 TV sets.

Press

In 1997 there were eight daily newspapers with a combined circulation of 52,000. At more than 700 newspapers per 1,000 inhabitants, Aruba has one of the highest rates of circulation in the world.

Tourism

In 2000 there were 721,224 tourists and 490,148 cruise ship visitors. In 2000 tourist receipts were 1,498·7m. Aflorins. The majority of tourists are from the USA (63·5%), Venezuela (15·5%), Colombia (4·4%) and the Netherlands (4·2%).

FURTHER READING

Schoenhals, K., *Netherlands Antilles and Aruba.* [Bibliography] ABC-Clio, Oxford and Santa Barbara (CA), 1993
Central Bureau of Statistics Website:
   http://www.aruba.com/extlinks/govs/cbstats.html

The Netherlands Antilles

De Nederlandse Antillen

KEY HISTORICAL EVENTS

With Aruba, the islands formed part of the Dutch West Indies from 1828, and the Netherlands Antilles from 1845, with internal self-government being granted on 29 Dec. 1954.

TERRITORY AND POPULATION

The Netherlands Antilles comprise two groups of islands, the Leeward group (Curaçao and Bonaire) being situated 100 km north of the Venezuelan coast and the Windward group (Saba, Sint Eustatius and the southern portion of Sint Maarten) situated 800 km away to the northeast, at the northern end of the Lesser Antilles. The total area is 800 sq. km (308 sq. miles) and the population at the 2001 census was 175,653. The estimated population in 2005 was 183,000. The UN gives a projected population for 2010 of 188,000. An estimated 69·6% of the population were urban in 2001. Willemstad is the capital and had a 1999 population of 123,000.

The areas, populations and chief towns of the islands are:

Island	Sq. km	2001 population	Chief town
Bonaire	288	10,791	Kralendijk
Curaçao	444	130,627	Willemstad
Saba	13	1,349	The Bottom
Sint Eustatius	21	2,292	Oranjestad
Sint Maarten[1]	43	30,594	Philipsburg
[1]The northern portion (St Martin) belongs to France.			

Dutch is the official language, but the languages usually spoken are Papiamento (derived from Dutch, Spanish and Portuguese) on Curaçao and Bonaire, and English in the Windward Islands.

SOCIAL STATISTICS

1999, live births, 2,803; deaths, 1,321; marriages, 956; divorces, 532. Annual growth rate, 1995–99, 1·3%. Expectation of life at birth, 1990–95, was 72·4 years for males and 78·5 for females. Infant mortality, 1990–95, 13 per 1,000 live births; fertility rate, 2·2 births per woman.

CLIMATE

All the islands have a tropical marine climate, with very little difference in temperatures over the year. There is a short rainy season from Oct. to Jan. Willemstad, Feb. 27·7°C, Aug. 29·0°C. Annual rainfall 499 mm.

CONSTITUTION AND GOVERNMENT

On 29 Dec. 1954 the Netherlands Antilles became an integral part of the Kingdom of the Netherlands but are fully autonomous in internal affairs, and constitutionally equal with the Netherlands and Aruba. The Sovereign of the Kingdom of the Netherlands is Head of State and Government, and is represented by a Governor.

The executive power in internal affairs rests with the Governor and the Council of Ministers. The Ministers are responsible to a unicameral legislature *(States)* consisting of 22 members, elected for a four-year term in three multi-seat constituencies and two single-seat constituencies. The executive power in external affairs is vested in the Council of Ministers of the Kingdom, in which the Antilles is represented by a Minister Plenipotentiary with full voting powers.

At a non-binding referendum in Curaçao on 8 April 2005, 68% of votes cast favoured Curaçao seceding from the Netherlands Antilles and becoming a territory of the Netherlands in its own right. At a contemporaneous referendum in Sint Eustatius, 76% voted to remain within the Netherlands Antilles but subject to a federal restructure. In Sept. 2004, 56% of voters in Bonaire voted for direct administration by the Dutch government, as did 86% in Saba in Nov. 2004. Sint Maarten voted for outright autonomy in 2000.

RECENT ELECTIONS

In elections held on 27 Jan. 2006 the Party for the Restructured Antilles (PAR) won 5 seats, the New Antilles Movement 3, the National Alliance 2, the Bonaire Patriotic Union 2, the Party Workers' Liberation Front 30th May 2, National People's Party 2, Forsa Kòrsou 2, with 1 seat each going to four other parties.

CURRENT ADMINISTRATION

Governor: Frits Goedgedrag; b. 1951 (took office on 1 July 2002).

Prime Minister: Emily de Jongh-Elhage; b. 1946 (took office on 26 March 2006).

ECONOMY

Currency

The unit of currency is the *Netherlands Antilles guilder, gulden* (ANG) or *florin* (NAfl.) divided into 100 *cents*. The NA guilder is pegged to the US dollar at US$1 = 1·79 NA guilder. Gold reserves were 548,000 troy oz in June 2000 and foreign exchange reserves US$373m. in May 2002. In 2004 inflation was 1·5%. Total money supply in April 2002 was 1,233m. NA guilders.

Budget

Central government revenues for 2002 were 616·5m. NA guilders and expenditures 768·9m. NA guilders.

Performance

Real GDP growth was 1·7% in 2003 but there then followed a recession, with the economy shrinking by 0·1% in 2004.

Banking and Finance

At 31 Dec. 1994 the Bank of Netherlands Antilles (*President,* Emsley Tromp) had total assets and liabilities of 514·4m. NA guilders; commercial banks, 3,913m. NA guilders.

ENERGY AND NATURAL RESOURCES

Environment

Carbon dioxide emissions from the consumption and flaring of fossil fuels were the equivalent of 52·9 tonnes per capita in 2002.

Electricity

Installed capacity in 2000 was 0·2m. kW. Production in 2000 totalled 1·12bn. kWh and consumption per capita was 5,209 kWh.

Oil and Gas

The economy was formerly based largely on oil refining at the Shell refinery on Curaçao, but following an announcement by Shell that closure was imminent, this was sold to the Netherlands Antilles government in Sept. 1985, and leased to Petróleos de Venezuela to operate on a reduced scale. The refinery has a capacity of 470,000 bbls. a day, but output has not reached this for several years.

Minerals

Calcium carbonate (limestone) has been mined since 1980; production (1991), 0·32m. tonnes. Production of limestone, 1990 (estimate), 0·36m. tonnes; salt, 1996, 0·36m. tonnes.

Agriculture

Livestock (2002): cattle, 1,000; goats, 13,000; pigs, 2,000; sheep, 8,000; asses, 3,000.

Fisheries

Total catch estimate (2001), approximately 950 tonnes.

INDUSTRY

Curaçao has an oil refinery and a large ship-repair dry docks. Bonaire has a textile factory and a modern equipped salt plant. Sint Maarten's industrial activities are primarily based on a rum factory and a fishing factory.

Labour

In 1997 the economically active population numbered 56,200; of which 18,400 were employed in community and social services, 14,600 in trade, 7,300 in financial services and 5,700 in manufacturing. In 1992 the unemployment rate was 15·3% (Curaçao, 1995: 62,236; unemployment rate 13·1%).

EXTERNAL ECONOMIC RELATIONS

Imports and Exports

In 2002 imports totalled US$1,602·7m. and exports US$589·3m. In 1998 crude petroleum made up 54% of imports, aluminium 6% and refined petroleum products 5%. 86% of exports in 1998 was refined petroleum products. Principal import suppliers in 2000: USA, 25·8%; Mexico, 20·7%; Gabon, 6·6%; Italy, 5·8%. Main export markets, 2000: USA, 35·9%; Guatemala, 9·4%; Venezuela, 8·7%; France, 5·4%. There is a Free Zone on Curaçao.

COMMUNICATIONS

Roads

In 1989 (latest data available) the Netherlands Antilles had 845 km of surfaced highway distributed as follows: Curaçao, 590; Bonaire, 226; Sint Maarten, 19. Number of motor vehicles registered in 1994, 166,392.

Civil Aviation

There are international airports on Curaçao (Curaçao-Hato Airport), Bonaire (Flamingo Airport) and Sint Maarten (Princess Juliana Airport). Dutch Caribbean Airways operates on domestic routes, and in 2003 also served Amsterdam, Caracas, Coro, Las Piedras, Maracaibo, Miami, Paramaribo, Port-au-Prince, Port-of-Spain, Santo Domingo and Valencia (Venezuela). In 2001 Sint Maarten handled 1,265,000 passengers and Curaçao 866,000; in 1995 Bonaire handled 286,117, Sint Eustatius 49,369 and Saba (1994) 45,457.

Shipping

5,152 ships (totalling 31,785,000 GRT) entered the port of Curaçao in 1995; 1,011 ships (15,911,000 GRT) entered the port of Bonaire; 1,400 ships entered the port of Sint Maarten. In 1995 Curaçao handled 171,854 passengers; in 1994 Bonaire handled 12,736 and Sint Maarten 718,550. Merchant shipping in 2002 totalled 1,391,000 GRT.

Telecommunications

Number of telephone main lines in 2000 was 80,000 (371·6 per 1,000 population). The number of Internet users in Dec. 1999 was 2,000. There were 20,000 mobile phone subscribers in 2003.

SOCIAL INSTITUTIONS

Justice
There is a Court of First Instance, which sits in each island, and a Court of Appeal in Willemstad. The population in penal institutions in Nov. 1998 was 780 (364 per 100,000 population).

Education
In 2000–01 there were 22,140 pupils in primary schools, 2,337 pupils in special schools, 12,174 pupils in general secondary schools, 3,710 pupils in junior and senior secondary vocational schools, and 928 students in vocational colleges and universities.

In 2000–01 total expenditure on education came to 13·6% of total government spending.

Health
In 2001 there were 12 hospitals with 1,343 beds. There were 333 physicians, 60 dentists, 1,198 nurses, 47 pharmacists (2004) and nine midwives in 2001.

RELIGION
In 2001 about 70% of the population were Roman Catholics and 10% were Protestants (Sint Maarten and Sint Eustatius being primarily Protestant).

CULTURE

World Heritage Sites
The Netherlands Antilles has one site on the UNESCO World Heritage List: the Historic Area of Willemstad, Inner City and Harbour (inscribed on the list in 1997), established on the island of Curaçao in 1634 by Dutch traders.

Broadcasting
In 1995 there were 32 radio transmitters (eight on Bonaire, 17 on Curaçao, two on Saba, one on Sint Eustatius and four on Sint Maarten) and each island had one cable television station, broadcasting in Papiamento, Dutch, English and Spanish. Broadcasting is administered by Landsradio, Telecommunication Administration and Tele Curaçao. In 1997 there were 217,000 radio and 69,000 TV sets (colour by NTSC) in use. In addition, Radio Nederland and Trans World Radio have powerful relay stations operating on medium- and short-waves from Bonaire.

Press
In 1996 there were six daily newspapers (combined circulation of 70,000).

Tourism
In 2001 there were 677,000 foreign visitors. Spending by tourists totalled US$821m. in 2001 (excluding Saba and Sint Eustatius).

DIPLOMATIC REPRESENTATIVES
US Consul-General: Robert E. Sorenson (J. B. Gorsiraweg 1, Curaçao).

FURTHER READING
Central Bureau of Statistics. *Statistical Yearbook of the Netherlands Antilles*

Bank of the Netherlands Antilles. *Annual Report.*

Schoenhals, K., *Netherlands Antilles and Aruba.* [Bibliography] ABC-Clio, Oxford and Santa Barbara (CA), 1993

Statistical office: Central Bureau of Statistics, Fort Amsterdam Z/N, Curaçao.

Website: http://www.central-bureau-of-statistics.an

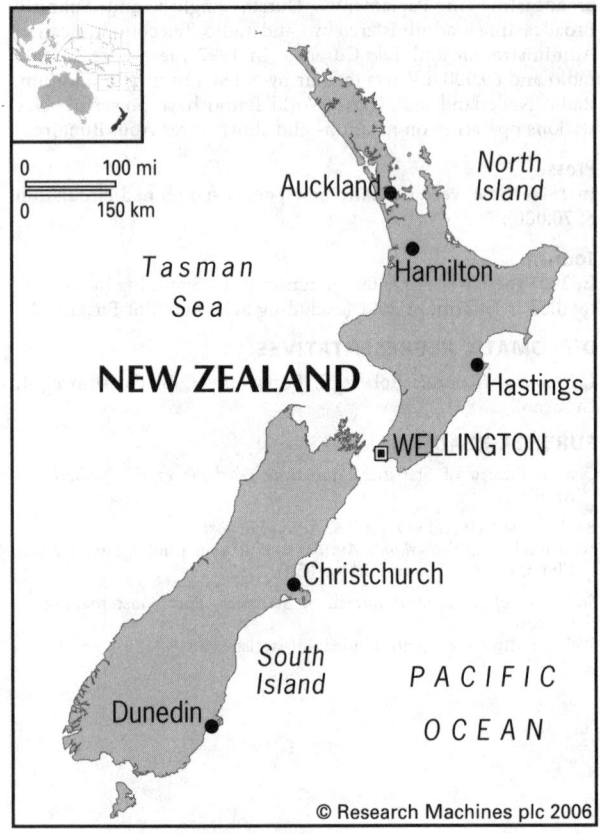

Capital: Wellington
Population projection, 2010: 4·17m.
GDP per capita, 2003: (PPP$) 22,582
HDI/world rank: 0·933/19

KEY HISTORICAL EVENTS

The earliest settlers of New Zealand are thought to have originated from eastern Polynesia, around the turn of the first millennium though some estimates suggest as early as 650 AD or as late as 1400. Maori oral traditions point to discovery of the country by Kupe, who gave New Zealand its first name, Aotearoa, or 'Land of the Long White Cloud'. Oral tradition also refers to seven waka leaving a homeland known as Hawaiiki in a Great Fleet. The waka are still remembered in the names of significant tribal groupings and descent lines: *Aotea, Kurahaupo, Mataatua, Tainui, Takitimu, Te Arawa,* and *Tokomaru*.

By Capt. James Cook's arrival in 1769, substantial settlements existed throughout the North Island, with smaller settlements in the South Island. Despite kinship links, sporadic warfare was common as tribes, or 'iwi', fought for resources and status, or 'mana'.

The first recorded European contact was Dutch explorer Abel Tasman's arrival in 1642. Believing the South Island to be the beginning of a mythical continent connected to Southern Africa, he bequeathed the name 'Staten Land'. A Dutch cartographer corrected Tasman's reasoning, giving the name New Zealand to compliment the larger New Holland, as Australia was known at the time. Tasman had one lasting impact, naming Murderer's Bay

after several crew were cannibalized by local Maori. Earlier on the same voyage Tasman had landed on an island off Australia which he named Van Diemen's Land but which was later called Tasmania in his honour.

Intensive contact between Maori and Europeans, or 'Pakeha', followed Cook's journeys to New Zealand and mapping of the coastline, opening the way for sealing and whaling stations. Coastal trade grew throughout the first decades of the 19th century and trade routes were established between Maori and the new colony of New South Wales as early as the 1820s. The Maori adapted quickly to both a market economy—selling provisions, timber and flax—and to new technologies (notably the musket). Pakeha settlement in the decades following Cook's arrival was often on Maori terms and was used by Maori in the traditional pursuit of mana in the eyes of rivals and neighbours. Mission stations soon appeared: the Church Missionary Society established three stations in the Bay of Islands between 1814 and 1823, and were joined by a Wesleyan Missionary Society station in the Hokianga in the 1820s.

British Ascendency

With greater contact both Maori and Pakeha saw the need to regulate Pakeha settlement. The Colonial Office in London appointed a Resident, James Busby, in 1833; in 1835, prompted by Busby, thirty-five chiefs signed a Declaration of Independence and announced themselves the heads of state of a 'United Tribes of New Zealand'. Colonial Office acknowledgement of the declaration signalled an official but non-interventionist policy. Relations between Maori and Pakeha were formalized by the signing of the Treaty of Waitangi in 1840. In principle—or at least in the Maori text—this treaty guaranteed Maori chieftainship, or 'rangatiratanga', while granting governorship, or 'kawanatanga', to Queen Victoria. Until 1860 Maori outnumbered Pakeha but in practice—and in the English text—sovereignty was transferred, allowing greater British settlement and control.

Established in 1840, Auckland was chosen as the colony's capital by its first governor, Capt. William Hobson. Planned migration occurred through the New Zealand Company with settlements at Wellington and Wanganui (1840), New Plymouth (1841), and Nelson (1842). Scottish immigrants founded Dunedin (1848); and Edward Gibbon Wakefield made plans for a model English settlement—unrealized, he felt, by the New Zealand Company—at Christchurch (1851). In 1852 representative government was established with a constitution providing for a House of Representatives and Legislative Council, as well as six provincial councils. The governor at the time, Sir George Grey, retained the right of veto and was responsible for 'Native' policy. At first the provincial councils exercised extensive powers over what were effectively separate settlements; their abolition in 1876 marked the beginnings of central government. The Legislative Council was disbanded in 1950 leaving New Zealand with a single-tier parliament.

Initially, voting was based on individual land ownership and excluded Maori who traditionally owned land collectively. Participation was extended to Maori in 1867 through four Maori seats. Maori representation in parliament came later: James Carroll, Apirana Ngata, Maui Pomare, and Peter Buck (Te Rangi Hiroa) were all prominent: Carroll was the first Maori to hold the posts of minister of native affairs and later acting prime minister; all made important contributions to Maori policy on issues such as health, education and land development.

Settlement was not always peaceful: war broke out in the 1840s and 1860s in the central and western North Island between settlers, represented by the British army, and Maori opposed to further settlement. British troops fought alongside local militia and friendly Maori, facing some of the earliest forms of trench and guerrilla warfare. Land and the willingness of tribes to provide larger and more productive hinterlands for the growing townships was one issue. Attempts at pan-Maori unity were another: the King movement in the Waikato gained prominence, and the Kotahitanga met as a Maori parliament during the second half of the 19th century.

Confiscating land belonging to tribes who fought against the government was one way in which the Pakeha gained wider possession. They were also helped by the Native Land Court, formed in 1865, to determine the ownership of Maori land according to Pakeha law. Where Maori land and user rights existed communally among a tribe, the Court sought to define parcels of land owned individually, thereby facilitating land sales.

Economic Boom

Earlier land speculation had fuelled an agricultural boom in the 1840s and 1850s providing the colony's first sustainable export commodity. New Zealand provided 8·6% of Britain's wool imports in 1861 and had 8·5m. sheep by 1867. The development of refrigerated shipping in the 1880s bolstered the pastoral economy through meat exports. Gold rushes in the 1860s and 1870s in Otago, the west coast of the South Island, and in Coromandel also contributed to the economy. Gold exports totalled £46m. by 1890. Wealth brought progress; the 1870s administrations of Julius Vogel and Harry Atkinson borrowed heavily to fund work schemes to encourage immigration and settlement. 1,100 miles of rail track were laid by 1879, and telegraphs linked all the main towns. The population had doubled to 500,000 by 1881.

The 1880s saw the beginnings of party politics. Grey's 1879 attempt to form a Liberal party, with policies of 'one man, one vote' and the compulsory purchase of large estates, was popular and succeeded in extending suffrage to all men. Robert Stout and John Ballance's leasehold land policies in the mid-1880s were similarly popular. A Liberal Party was eventually formed in 1889 and, backed by unions and the landless, won the 1890 election with Ballance as its leader. The Conservatives formed the first genuine opposition. Richard John Seddon took over the Liberal leadership in 1892 and remained Premier until his death in 1906. Among the Liberal's achievements were the Land and Income Tax Act 1891 and the Advance to Settlers Act 1894, which assisted 17,000 people on to the land by 1912. Suffrage was extended to women in 1893, New Zealand being the first country to do so. Other reforms included William Pember Reeves' Industrial Conciliation and Arbitration Act of 1894, one of the most radical and extensive labour systems of its time; and one of the world's first pension schemes.

In 1901 New Zealand declined the offer to join the Commonwealth of Australia and remained a British colony until 1907 when it gained Dominion status. Parliament remained subordinate to the British parliament until the adoption in 1947 of the Statute of Westminster under which New Zealand became fully sovereign with the British monarch as head of state. New Zealand exercised its own colonial interests, annexing the Cook Islands in 1901, and being granted administration of Western Samoa at the Treaty of Versailles after capturing it from Germany in the First World War. It administered Samoa until the 1960s. Two world wars tested the spirit of the Australian and New Zealand Army Corps. Both countries saw a duty to fight for the homeland of Britain. New Zealand contributed around 100,000 soldiers in the First World War from a population of little more than a million; nearly 17,000 did not return. Nearly 9,000 New Zealanders died in the influenza epidemic spread by returning soldiers, with a Maori mortality rate six times that of Pakeha. New Zealand's Second World War contribution was even greater; around 200,000 joined Allied forces from a population of 1·6m.

Twentieth Century

Class-based political divisions intensified in the early twentieth century. Worker's unions, early supporters of the Liberal Party, rallied around an embryonic Labour movement while farmers and employers favoured William 'Farmer Bill' Massey's Reform Party. Amid industrial unrest in 1912, the Liberal government fell to a vote of no confidence. Reform took power, introducing anti-union legislation. Strikes in Waihi, Wellington and Huntly were quelled by Massey's 'Cossacks', police forces specially enlisted for the task. Reform governed until 1928, assisted at first by a wartime coalition with the Liberals, and then by tacit Liberal support. Their policies broadly followed the dictates of farmers, creating a national Meat Board (1922) and Dairy Board (1923).

A United–Reform coalition government (1931–35) fought the effect of world recession. Employment reached 12%; the national income fell from an estimated £150m. to £90m., and the value of exports fell by 40%. To balance the budget, cuts were made to pensions, education, health and public works. In the absence of an unemployment benefit, men were sent to rural relief camps to work on low-capital, high-labour tasks. Measures such as creating a Reserve Bank and currency devaluation in 1933 helped farmers but did not address the broader social distress.

Welfare State

Michael Joseph (Micky) Savage's first Labour government (1935–49) reclaimed for New Zealand its title of social laboratory of the world, first bestowed during the Liberal era of the 1890s. Its legacy would be a welfare state which survived until the 1980s. It introduced one of the world's most comprehensive social welfare systems—incorporating pensions, health, education and family benefits—and increased state housing; introduced state guaranteed prices for farm produce to protect farmers from international price fluctuations; and nationalized the Reserve Bank, making it an instrument of state economic policy. By the late 1940s, state finances were healthy enough to allow a £10m. gift to postwar Britain.

Labour lost rural support which rallied around a National Party formed in 1936 from remnants of the United–Reform coalition. Labour retained power in part owing to the support of the four Maori seats, all held by the Ratana Party. The National Party won in 1949, promising to increase spending power and curb creeping socialism in the form of union power and economic controls. 1951 saw militant unions again taking on a conservative government, and losing. National retained power for most of the postwar boom years; brief Labour administrations under Walter Nash (1957–60) and Norman Kirk (1972–75) coincided with unfavourable economic conditions. Keith Holyoake's National government (1960–72) was dominated by international affairs, joining the IMF in 1961 and manoeuvring around Britain's anticipated entry to the EEC. Notable domestic policy included the Equal Pay Act (1972) to address gender-based pay discrimination and the creation of state-funded workplace injury compensation.

Maori demands for recognition of the Treaty of Waitangi grew in the 1970s. The 1975 Land March saw tens of thousands march on parliament and the occupation of Bastion Point in 1977–78 centred on land compulsorily acquired by the government in 1951. Both raised public awareness of disaffection with the way the Treaty had been interpreted. Labour established the Waitangi Tribunal in 1975 to hear Maori claims of Treaty breaches. It lacked authority until 1985 when the next Labour government made its powers retrospective to 1840. Tribunal recommendations have formed the basis for settling several large claims through negotiations between the Crown and tribal authorities.

Britain's entry into the EEC in 1973 was a set-back for an economy dependent on exports to Britain. Robert Muldoon's National government (1975–84) tried to ameliorate the effects through tariff protection, wage and price freezes, and increased borrowing for 'Think Big' public works. Muldoon won a narrow victory in the 1981 election following civil unrest during the 'Springbok' rugby tour. Riot police faced massive demonstrations as many New Zealanders opposed sporting links with the South African apartheid regime. The country found a new direction in the free market policies of David Lange's Labour government, which came to power in 1984. The economic direction of Roger Douglas, 'Rogernomics', radically altered the socio-economic landscape, reducing trade barriers and selling state assets to fund debt recovery.

In international affairs the Labour government was truer to its left-wing support, passing the New Zealand Nuclear Free Zone, Disarmament, and Arms Control Act 1987, which declared the country nuclear free. The legislation—supported by all political parties—led to the end of New Zealand's involvement in the ANZUS military agreement with Australia and the USA. Nuclear issues were high in popular consciousness. In 1973 Australia and New Zealand had tried to halt French nuclear testing in the Pacific through the International Court of Justice, and New Zealand sent two frigates to Mururoa Atoll in protest. The 1985 bombing of the *Rainbow Warrior* in Auckland harbour by French secret service agents reopened the issue.

Internal wrangling over economic direction caused the collapse of the Labour leadership in the late 1980s. Lange resigned and was replaced by Geoffrey Palmer in 1989, who in turn resigned shortly before the 1990 election. He was succeeded by Mike Moore. Labour lost the 1990 election to a National Party led by Jim Bolger who was determined to carry on free market reforms. Social welfare reform, cuts in tertiary education funding and reform of accident compensation legislation cut back state intervention. The Employment Contracts Act (1991) outlawed compulsory union membership and introduced individual contracts, weakening union power. Jenny Shipley led a leadership coup in 1997 and became the country's first female prime minister, though not the first elected female prime minister; that landmark was reserved for Helen Clark who led the Labour Party to victory in the 1999 election.

Electoral reform in the 1990s saw New Zealand move from a first-past-the-post system to proportional representation under the mixed-member-proportional system (MMP). Despite the debacle of the first MMP election in 1996 where a minor party (New Zealand First, formed by disgruntled National supporters) played National off against Labour for two months before forming a coalition with National, the system has provided greater representation for minority interests.

TERRITORY AND POPULATION

New Zealand lies southeast of Australia in the south Pacific, Wellington being 1,983 km from Sydney. There are two principal islands, the North and South Islands, besides Stewart Island, Chatham Islands and small outlying islands, as well as the territories overseas.

New Zealand (*i.e.*, North, South and Stewart Islands) extends over 1,750 km from north to south. Area, excluding territories overseas, 270,534 sq. km: comprising North Island, 115,777 sq. km; South Island, 151,215 sq. km; Stewart Island, 1,746 sq. km; Chatham Islands, 963 sq. km. The minor islands (total area, 829 sq. km or 320 sq. miles) included within the geographical boundaries of New Zealand (but not within any local government area) are the following: Kermadec Islands (34 sq. km), Three Kings Islands (8 sq. km), Auckland Islands (606 sq. km), Campbell Island (114 sq. km), Antipodes Islands (62 sq. km), Bounty Islands (1 sq. km), Snares Islands (3 sq. km), Solander Island (1 sq. km). With the exception of meteorological station staff on Raoul Island in the Kermadec Group and Campbell Island there are no inhabitants.

The Kermadec Islands were annexed to New Zealand in 1887, have no separate administration and all New Zealand laws apply to them. Situation, 29° 10' to 31° 30' S. lat., 177° 45' to 179° W.

long., 1,600 km NNE of New Zealand. The largest of the group is Raoul or Sunday Island, 29 sq. km, smaller islands being Macaulay and Curtis, while Macaulay Island is 5 km in circuit.

Growth in census population, exclusive of territories overseas:

	Total population	Average annual increase (%)		Total population	Average annual increase (%)
1858	115,461	—	1936[2]	1,573,812	1·13
1874	344,985	—	1945[1,2]	1,702,329	0·83
1878	458,007	7·33	1951[1]	1,939,473	2·37
1881	534,030	5·10	1956[1]	2,174,061	2·31
1886	620,451	3·06	1961[1]	2,414,985	2·12
1891	668,652	1·50	1966[1]	2,676,918	2·11
1896	743,214	2·13	1971[1]	2,862,630	1·35
1901[1]	815,862	1·90	1976[1]	3,129,384	1·80
1906	936,309	2·75	1981[1]	3,175,737	0·29
1911	1,058,313	2·52	1986[1]	3,307,083	0·82
1916[1]	1,149,225	1·50	1991[1]	3,434,949	0·76
1921	1,271,667	2·27	1996[1]	3,681,546	1·40
1926	1,408,140	2·06	2001[1]	3,820,749	0·74

[1]Excluding members of the Armed Forces overseas.
[2]The census of New Zealand is quinquennial, but the census falling in 1931 was abandoned as an act of national economy, and owing to war conditions the census due in 1941 was not taken until 25 Sept. 1945.

The latest census took place on 6 March 2001. Of the 3,820,749 people counted, 3,737,277 were usually resident in the country and 83,472 were overseas visitors. Estimated population as at 30 June 2005, 4,098,200.

In 2003, 85·9% of the population lived in urban areas. Density, 14·5 per sq. km (2001).

The usually-resident populations of regional councils (all data conforms with boundaries redrawn after the 1989 re-organization of local government) in 1996 and 2001:

Local Government Region	Total Population 1996 census	Total Population 2001 census	Percentage change 1996–2001 (%)
Northland	137,052	140,133	2·2
Auckland	1,068,657	1,158,891	8·4
Waikato	350,112	357,726	2·2
Bay of Plenty	224,364	239,412	6·7
Gisborne	45,786	43,974	−4·0
Hawke's Bay	142,788	142,947	0·1
Taranaki	106,590	102,858	−3·5
Manawatu-Wanganui	228,771	220,089	−3·8
Wellington	414,048	423,765	2·3
Total North Island	2,718,171	2,829,798	4·1
Tasman	37,971	41,352	8·9
Nelson	40,278	41,568	3·2
Marlborough	38,397	39,558	3·0
West Coast	32,514	30,303	−6·8
Canterbury	468,039	481,431	2·9
Otago	185,082	181,542	−1·9
Southland	97,098	91,005	−6·3
Total South Island	899,385	906,753	0·8
Area outside region	747	726	−2·8
Total New Zealand	*3,618,303*	*3,737,277*	*3·3*

The UN gives a projected population for 2010 of 4·17m.

Between 1991 and 2001 the number of people who identified themselves as being of European ethnicity dropped from 83·2% to 80·0%. Pacific Island people made up 6·5% of the population in 2001 (5·0% in 1991); Asian ethnic groups went from 3·0% in 1996 to 6·6% in 2001. Permanent and long-term arrivals in 2001 totalled 81,094, including 16,844 from the UK, 12,186 from Australia, 11,107 from the People's Republic of China, 4,249 from India and 3,920 from Japan. Permanent and long-term departures in 2001 totalled 71,368, including 36,033 to Australia, 14,852 to the UK, 3,151 to the USA and 1,874 to Japan.

Maori population: 1896, 42,113; 1936, 82,326; 1945, 98,744; 1951, 115,676; 1961, 171,553; 1971, 227,414; 1981, 279,255; 1986, 294,201; 1991, 324,000; 1996, 523,374; 2001, 526,281 (13·8% of the total population, up from 9·4% in 1991). In addition, 604,110 people in 2001 said they have Maori ancestry, compared with 434,847 in 1991. In the 2001 census, 160,527 New Zealanders said they could hold a conversation about everyday matters in Maori. In 2001, one in four people of Maori ethnicity claimed to speak the language.

From the 1970s organizations were formed to pursue Maori grievances over loss of land and resources. The Waitangi Tribunal was set up in 1975 as a forum for complaints about breaches of the Treaty of Waitangi, and in 1984 empowered to hear claims against Crown actions since 1840. Direct negotiations with the Crown have been offered to claimants and a range of proposals to resolve historical grievances launched for public discussion in Dec. 1994. These proposals specify that all claims are to be met over ten years with treaty rights being converted to economic assets. There have been four recent major treaty settlements: NZ$170m. each for Tainui and Ngai Tahu, the NZ$150m. Sealord fishing agreement and NZ$40m. for Whakatohea in the Bay of Plenty. The Maori Land Court has jurisdiction over Maori freehold land and some general land owned by Maoris under the Te Ture Whenue Maori Act 1993.

Resident populations of main urban areas at the 2001 census were as follows:

North Island		Wanganui	39,423
Auckland	1,074,510	Wellington	339,747
Gisborne	31,719	Whangarei	46,050
Hamilton	166,128		
Hastings and Napier	113,673	South Island	
New Plymouth	47,763	Christchurch	334,107
Palmerston North	72,681	Dunedin	107,088
Rotorua	52,608	Invercargill	46,305
Tauranga	95,697	Nelson	53,688

English and Maori are the official languages.

SOCIAL STATISTICS

Statistics for calendar years:

	Total live births	Deaths	Marriages	Divorces (decrees absolute)
1998	57,818	26,206	20,135	10,037
1999	57,053	28,122	21,085	9,931
2000	56,605	26,660	20,655	9,936
2001	55,799	27,825	19,972	9,700
2002	54,021	28,065	20,690	10,300
2003	56,134	28,010	—	—

Birth rate, 2003, 14·14 per 1,000 population; death rate, 7·54 per 1,000 population; infant mortality, 2003, 6·07 per 1,000 live births. Annual population growth rate, 1992–2002, 1·1%. In 2000 there were 458 suicides (516 in 1999). Expectation of life, 2003: males, 76·8 years; females, 81·3. Fertility rate, 2003, 1·79 births per woman.

In the year ending March 2003 there were 97,250 permanent and long-term immigrants (69,490 in 2001) and 54,730 permanent and long-term emigrants (78,760 in 2001).

CLIMATE

Lying in the cool temperate zone, New Zealand enjoys very mild winters for its latitude owing to its oceanic situation, and only the extreme south has cold winters. The situation of the mountain chain produces much sharper climatic contrasts between east and west than in a north-south direction. Mean daily maximum temperatures and rainfall figures:

	Jan (°C)	July (°C)	Annual rainfall (mm) in 2004
Auckland	23·3	14·5	1,331
Christchurch	22·5	11·3	643
Dunedin	18·9	9·8	765
Wellington	20·3	11·4	1,447

The highest extreme temperature recorded in 2004 was 38·4°C, recorded at Darfield on 1 Jan., and the lowest –12·0°C, at Fairlie on 16 Aug.

CONSTITUTION AND GOVERNMENT

Definition was given to the status of New Zealand by the (Imperial) Statute of Westminster of Dec. 1931, which had received the antecedent approval of the New Zealand Parliament in July 1931. The Governor-General's assent was given to the Statute of Westminster Adoption Bill on 25 Nov. 1947.

The powers, duties and responsibilities of the Governor-General and the Executive Council are set out in Royal Letters Patent and Instructions thereunder of 11 May 1917. In the execution of the powers vested in him the Governor-General must be guided by the advice of the Executive Council.

At a referendum on 6 Nov. 1993 a change from a first-past-the-post to a proportional representation electoral system was favoured by 53·9% of votes cast.

Parliament is the *House of Representatives*, consisting of 121 members (for the 2005 election 62 were general seats, 52 party list seats and seven Maori seats), elected by universal adult suffrage on the mixed-member-proportional system (MMP) for three-year terms. The five Maori electoral districts cover the whole country. Maori and people of Maori descent are entitled to register either for a general or a Maori electoral district. As at Oct. 2005 there were 208,003 persons on the Maori electoral roll. There are now seven Maori seats at general elections.

Joseph, P. A., *Constitutional Law in New Zealand*. Sydney, 1993.—(ed.) *Essays on the Constitution*. Sydney, 1995

McGee, D. G., *Parliamentary Practice in New Zealand*. 2nd ed. Wellington, 1994

Ringer, J. B., *An Introduction to New Zealand Government*. Christchurch, 1992

Vowles, J. and Aimer, P. (eds.) *Double Decision: the 1993 Election and Referendum in New Zealand*. Victoria (Wellington) Univ. Press, 1994

National Anthem

'God Defend New Zealand'; words by T. Bracken, tune by J. J. Woods. There is a Maori version, 'Aotearoa', words by T. H. Smith. The UK national anthem has equal status.

GOVERNMENT CHRONOLOGY

Prime Ministers since 1940. (Lab = Labour; Nat = National)

1940–49	Lab	Peter Fraser
1949–57	Nat	Sidney Holland
1957	Nat	Keith Jacka Holyoake
1957–60	Lab	Walter Nash
1960–72	Nat	Keith Jacka Holyoake
1972	Nat	John Ross Marshall
1972–74	Lab	Norman Eric Kirk
1974	Lab	Hugh Watt (acting)
1974–75	Lab	Wallace Edward Rowling
1975–84	Nat	Robert David Muldoon
1984–89	Lab	David Lange
1989–90	Lab	Geoffrey Palmer
1990	Lab	Mike Moore
1990–97	Nat	Jim Bolger
1997–99	Nat	Jenny Shipley
1999–	Lab	Helen Clark

RECENT ELECTIONS

At parliamentary elections on 17 Sept. 2005 turnout was 80·9%. The Labour Party won 50 seats with 41·1%; the National Party

48 with 39·1%; the right-wing New Zealand First Party 7 with 5·7%; the Green Party 6 with 5·3%; the Maori Party 4 with 2·1%; United Future New Zealand 3 with 2·7%; ACT New Zealand 2 with 1·5%; and the Progressive Party 1 with 1·2%.

CURRENT ADMINISTRATION

Governor-General: Dame Silvia Cartwright, DBE (b. 1943; sworn in 4 April 2001).

The government is formed by a centre-left coalition of the Labour Party and the Progressive Party. In March 2006 the cabinet consisted of:

Prime Minister, Minister of Arts, Culture and Heritage: Helen Clark; b. 1950 (Labour; in office since 10 Dec. 1999).

Deputy Prime Minister, Minister of Finance, Tertiary Education, and Attorney General: Michael Cullen (Labour).

Minister of Agriculture, Biosecurity, Fisheries, and Forestry: James (Jim) Anderton (Progressive Party). *State Services, Police, and Food Safety:* Annette King (Labour). *Defence, Trade, Pacific Island Affairs, Disarmament and Arms Control, and Trade Negotiations:* Phil Goff (Labour). *Economic Development, Industry and Regional Development, State Owned Enterprises, and Sport and Recreation:* Trevor Mallard (Labour). *Conservation, Housing, and Ethnic Affairs:* Chris Carter (Labour). *Health, and Land Information:* Peter Hodgson (Labour). *Justice, Local Government, and the Treaty of Waitangi Negotiations:* Mark Burton (Labour). *Internal Affairs, Civil Defence, Courts, and Veterans' Affairs:* Rick Barker (Labour). *Maori Affairs:* Parekura Horomia (Labour). *Education, Broadcasting, Research, Science and Technology, and Crown Research Institutes:* Steven Maharey (Labour). *Labour, Accident Compensation Corporation, Senior Citizens, and Disability Issues:* Ruth Dyson (Labour). *Social Development and Employment, and Environment:* David Benson-Pope (Labour). *Commerce, Women's Affairs, and Small Business:* Lianne Dalziel (Labour). *Corrections, Tourism, and Rural Affairs:* Damien O'Connor (Labour). *Immigration, Communications, and Information Technology:* David Cunliffe (Labour). *Energy, and Transport:* David Parker (Labour). *Customs, and Youth Affairs:* Nanaia Mahuta (Labour). *Building Issues, and Statistics:* Clayton Cosgrove (Labour). *Minister of State:* James Sutton (Labour).

In addition, two ministers were appointed who are not in the cabinet. *Minister of Foreign Affairs, and Racing:* Winston Peters (New Zealand First). *Revenue:* Peter Dunne (United Future New Zealand).

Office of the Prime Minister: http://www.govt.nz

CURRENT LEADERS

Helen Clark

Position
Prime Minister

Introduction
Formerly a university lecturer and the country's second successive female premier, Clark was elected leader of the centre-left Labour Party in Dec. 1993 and came to power as prime minister following the Nov. 1999 election. She is also minister for arts, culture and heritage. Clark joined Labour in 1971, and as the longest serving woman MP is known as 'mother of the house'.

Early Life
Born into a farming family in Hamilton on 26 Feb. 1950, Clark was educated at secondary level in Auckland before reading politics at the University of Auckland. Between 1973–75, while a junior lecturer at the university, she was also president of the Labour Party's Youth Council, and served on the Auckland Labour Regional Council. In 1975 she unsuccessfully contested the safe National Party seat of Piako, and in 1976 represented Labour at an international socialist congress. Clark returned to the University of Auckland to lecture in political studies from

1977–81, during which time she was secretary of the Labour Women's Council (1977). She joined the party's Executive in 1978 and became an MP at Labour's 1981 election victory. In 1985 Clark represented New Zealand at the United Nations conference in Nairobi marking the close of the Decade for Women. As chair of the foreign affairs and defence select committee between 1984–87, and of 1984's *ad hoc* disarmament and arms control select committee, her promotion of international nuclear disarmament earned her the Danish Peace Foundation's 1986 peace prize. During this parliamentary term, Labour introduced 'nuclear free' legislation. Following the party's re-election in 1987, Clark was appointed to the cabinet, initially as conservation minister (Aug. 1987–Jan. 1989) and housing minister (Aug. 1987–Aug. 1989), and then as health minister (Jan. 1989–Oct. 1990) and labour minister (Aug. 1989–Oct. 1990). Her responsibilities during this period included chairing the cabinet's social equity committee, and membership of its economic development and employment committee. As health minister, Clark promoted tobacco control legislation. Aug. 1989 marked her appointment as deputy prime minister, and the following year she joined the Privy Council; she was the first New Zealand woman to hold these positions. Labour's defeat in the 1990 election placed Clark as deputy leader of the opposition. Until replacing Mike Moore as opposition leader on 1 Dec. 1993 she was additionally Labour's spokesperson for health and labour, and sat on the social services and labour select committees.

Career in Office
Clark was elected prime minister on 27 Nov. 1999, when Labour, in partnership with the Alliance Party and supported by the Green Party, won 39% of the vote. She also became minister for arts, culture and heritage, and assumed the ministerial services and security intelligence service portfolios. Advocating a democratic socialist 'third way', her key policies included the allocation of NZ$142m. to the arts over a four-year period; the Employment Relations Act 2000 (intended to foster 'good faith' employment); a five-year NZ$187m. biodiversity conservation strategy; the establishment of an industrial apprenticeship scheme; financial support for Maori land claims; and the implementation in 2001 of a Disability Strategy and Positive Aging Strategy. In 2002 Clark won a second term in office and formed a centre-left government with the Progressive Party. Then, at the following parliamentary elections in Sept. 2005, Labour was again returned to power, but by a narrow margin against a resurgent National Party under Don Brash's leadership. Clark formed a new minority coalition with the Progressive Party, with conditional support from the centrist United Future New Zealand, the populist New Zealand First Party and the Green Party.

DEFENCE

The control and co-ordination of defence activities is obtained through the Ministry of Defence. New Zealand forces serve abroad in Australia, Iraq and Singapore, and with UN peacekeeping missions.

Defence expenditure in 2003 totalled US$1,171m. (US$292 per capita), representing 1·5% of GDP.

Army

Personnel total in 2003: 4,388, plus reserves numbering 2,718 (2,031 territorial, 687 civilians).

Navy

The Navy includes three frigates. The main base and Fleet headquarters is at Auckland.

The Royal New Zealand Navy personnel totalled 1,978 uniformed plus 354 reserve personnel in 2003.

Air Force

Squadrons are based at RNZAF Base Auckland and RNZAF Base Ohakea. Flying training is conducted at Ohakea and

Auckland. Ground training is carried out at RNZAF Base Woodbourne.

The uniform strength in 2003 was 2,200, with six combat aircraft.

INTERNATIONAL RELATIONS

New Zealand is a member of the UN, WTO, the Commonwealth, OECD, Asian Development Bank, the Pacific Community, the Pacific Islands Forum, Colombo Plan, APEC, IOM and the Antarctic Treaty.

ECONOMY

Agriculture accounted for 8% of GDP in 2001, industry 23% and services 69%.

According to the anti-corruption organization *Transparency International*, New Zealand ranked equal second in the world in a 2005 survey of the countries with the least corruption in business and government. It received 9·6 out of 10 in the annual index.

Overview

The New Zealand economy is heavily reliant on agriculture, fishing and forestry. Prior to the 1980s New Zealand had one of the most regulated and protected economies in the developed world. With economic liberalization, the economy has grown every year since 1991 despite the 1997 Asian crisis, periods of drought and the global slowdown which followed the 11 Sept. attacks on the USA. Over the last five years real GDP and per capita income growth rates have been greater than the OECD average, though per capita income remains below the developed world average. According to the IMF, New Zealand's strong economic performance is attributable to the extensive reforms of the 1980s. Inflation has remained within the 1–3% target range set by the Bank of New Zealand. Public sector debt has been reduced by sizeable budget surpluses and unemployment has fallen to exceptionally low levels.

With the economy at full capacity the country has experienced skilled and unskilled labour shortages and infrastructure bottlenecks. New Zealand remains regulated in several areas and voter indecision in the 2005 election may hamper decisive government action. Further growth, says the OECD, needs to come from the increased utilization of under-represented labour groups, intelligent public spending and the removal of barriers to productivity growth.

The country has experienced strong capital inflows in the recent past as international investors have borrowed in low interest-rate areas to invest in high interest-rate economies like New Zealand. The New Zealand dollar suffered a fall following the Feb. 2006 króna collapse in Iceland, a country which has also attracted significant capital inflows in the recent past.

Currency

The monetary unit is the *New Zealand dollar* (NZD), of 100 *cents*. The total value of notes and coins on issue from the Reserve Bank in Dec. 2000 was NZ$2,069m. Inflation rates (based on OECD statistics):

1995	1996	1997	1998	1999	2000	2001	2002	2003	2004
3·8%	2·3%	1·2%	1·3%	–0·1%	2·6%	2·6%	2·7%	1·8%	2·3%

In June 2002 foreign exchange reserves were US$1,843m. Gold reserves are negligible. Total money supply in June 2002 was NZ$18,235m.

Budget

Total central government revenue for 2003 was NZ$57,027m. (NZ$49,979m. in 2002). Central government expenditure in 2003 was NZ$55,224m. (NZ$47,653m. in 2002).

2003 tax revenue was NZ$39,785m. and NZ$2,763m. was earned through levies, fees, fines and penalties. In 2000 income tax on individuals amounted to NZ$15,776m.; company tax, NZ$4,158m.; withholding taxes, NZ$1,563m.

The gross public debt at June 2003 was NZ$38,285m., of which NZ$24,380m. was held in New Zealand currency, NZ$6,697m. in foreign currency and NZ$7,208m. in non-sovereign-guaranteed debt.

Performance

Real GDP growth rates (based on OECD statistics):

1995	1996	1997	1998	1999	2000	2001	2002	2003	2004
3·9%	3·5%	2·9%	0·2%	4·9%	3·7%	2·5%	4·4%	3·7%	4·4%

Total GDP was US$99·7bn. in 2004.

Banking and Finance

The central bank and bank of issue is the Reserve Bank (*Governor*, Dr Alan Bollard).

The financial system comprises a central bank (the Reserve Bank of New Zealand), registered banks and other financial institutions. Registered banks include banks from abroad, which have to satisfy capital adequacy and managerial quality requirements. Other financial institutions include the regional trustee banks, now grouped under Trust Bank, building societies, finance companies, merchant banks and stock and station agents. The number of registered banks was 18 in 2003 of which only four were operating in New Zealand before 1986. Around 99% of the assets of the New Zealand banking system were under the ownership of a foreign bank parent.

The primary functions of the Reserve Bank are the formulation and implementation of monetary policy to achieve the economic objectives set by the government, and the promotion of the efficiency and soundness of the financial system, through the registration of banks, and supervision of financial institutions. Since 1996 supervision has been conducted on a basis of public disclosure by banks of their activities every quarter.

On 30 June 2003 the assets of the Reserve Bank were NZ$11,543m. (including government securities totalling NZ$3,300m. and marketable securities totalling NZ$3,137m.).

The stock exchange in Wellington conducts on-screen trading, unifying the three former trading floors in Auckland, Christchurch and Wellington. There is also a stock exchange in Dunedin.

ENERGY AND NATURAL RESOURCES

Environment

New Zealand's carbon dioxide emissions from the consumption and flaring of fossil fuels were the equivalent of 9·7 tonnes per capita in 2002. An *Environmental Sustainability Index* compiled for the World Economic Forum meeting in Jan. 2005 ranked New Zealand 14th in the world, with 60·9%. The index measured the ability of countries to maintain favourable environmental conditions and examined various factors including pollution levels and the use or abuse of natural resources.

Electricity

On 1 April 1987 the former Electricity Division of the Ministry of Energy became a state-owned enterprise, the Electricity Corporation of N.Z. Ltd, which has since been split into two state-owned enterprises causing a competitive wholesale electricity market to be established. Around 68% of the country's electricity is generated by renewable sources. Hydro-electric plants, mainly based in the South Island, account for some 61% with geothermal power, generated in the North Island, accounting for around 7%. The rest comes from natural gas (25%), coal, wind and landfill gas. Electricity generating capacity, 2002, 8·4m. kW. Consumption per capita was 10,301 kWh in 2002.

Electricity consumption statistics (in GWh) for years ended 31 March are:

	Residential	Commercial	Industrial	Total consumption
1999	11,290	7,334	14,010	32,635
2000	11,057	6,919	14,759	32,735
2001	11,306	6,819	15,142	33,267
2002	11,660	6,965	14,525	33,150

New Zealand also has two wind farms.

Oil and Gas

Crude oil production was estimated at 42,160 bbls. per day in 2001, all from the Taranaki region. Around 75% of production is exported. 119,700 bbls. per day were imported in 2001. Proven reserves were estimated at 90m. bbls. in 2002.

In 2002 gasfields produced 6·1bn. cu. metres. Gas reserves are estimated to last until about 2014, with the Maui field possibly running out in 2007. In 2003 proven natural gas reserves were estimated at 41·77bn. cu. metres.

Minerals

Coal production in 2002 was 4·46m. tonnes. Of the 45 mines operating in 2002, 29 were opencast and 16 underground, responsible for 79·6% and 20·3% of total coal production respectively. Only twelve mines produced over 200,000 tonnes of coal and 14 operations had an output of less than 10,000 tonnes. Around 60% of New Zealand's exported coal goes to India and Japan.

While New Zealand's best known non-fuel mineral is gold (producing about 9·77 tonnes in 2002 worth NZ$212m.) there is also production of silver, ironsand, aggregate, limestone, clay, aluminium, dolomite, pumice, salt, serpentinite, zeolite and bentonite. In addition, there are resources or potential for deposits of titanium (ilmenite beach sands), platinum, sulphur, phosphate, silica and mercury.

Agriculture

Two-thirds of the land area is suitable for agriculture and grazing. The total area of farmland in use in 2002 was 15,640,000 ha. There were 11,967,000 ha. of grazing, arable, fodder and fallow land, 110,000 ha. of land for horticulture and 1,879,000 ha. of plantations of exotic timber. In 2001 there were 1·5m. ha. of arable land and 1·87m. ha. of permanent crops.

The largest freehold estates are held in the South Island. The number of occupied holdings as at 30 June 2002 were as follows:

Regional Council	No. of farms	Total area of farms (1,000 ha.)
Auckland	5,500	302
Bay of Plenty	5,700	600
Gisborne	1,300	653
Hawke's Bay	3,900	962
Manawatu-Wanganui	6,500	1,545
Northland	5,800	836
Taranaki	3,900	496
Waikato	12,000	1,730
Wellington	2,500	504
Total North Island	47,000	7,627
Canterbury	10,000	3,151
Marlborough	1,700	723
Nelson	190	21
Otago	4,100	2,368
Southland	4,300	1,198
Tasman	1,900	277
West Coast	830	225
Total South Island	23,000	8,013
Total New Zealand	70,000	15,640

Production of main crops (2000, in 1,000 tonnes): potatoes, 500; apples, 482; wheat, 360; barley, 281; maize, 174; pumpkins and squash, 155; tomatoes, 85; carrots, 80; grapes, 80; cauliflower, 63.

Livestock, 2002: sheep, 39·54m.; cattle, 9·65m.; pigs, 344,000; goats, 153,000; deer, 1·64m.; chickens, 13m. (2000). Total meat produced in 2002 was 1·40m. tonnes (including 576,000 tonnes of beef and veal, and 521,000 tonnes of lamb and mutton). Meat industry products are New Zealand's second largest export income earner, accounting for about 14% of merchandise exports. New Zealand's main meat exports are lamb, mutton and beef. About 65% of lamb, 61% of beef and 51% of mutton produced in New Zealand in 2001–02 was exported overseas. The domestic market absorbs over 99% of the pigmeat and poultry produced in New Zealand. 54% of the world's exported sheepmeat comes from New Zealand.

Production of wool for the year 2002–03 was 173,000 tonnes. Milk production for 2000–01 totalled a record 12,322m. litres. In 1999–2000 butter production totalled 254,639 tonnes and cheese production 296,745 tonnes.

Forestry

Forests covered 8·0m. ha. in 2002 (30% of New Zealand's land area), up from 7·67m. ha. in 1990. Of this, about 6·2m. ha. are indigenous forest and 1·8m. ha. planted productive forest. New planting and restocking was 65,900 ha. in 2002. Introduced pines form the bulk of the large exotic forest estate and among these radiata pine is the best multi-purpose tree, reaching log size in 25–30 years. Other species planted are Douglas fir and Eucalyptus species. Total roundwood production in 2002–03 was 23·10m. cu. metres. The table below shows production of rough sawn timber in 1,000 cu. metres for years ending 31 March:

	Indigenous			Exotic			All Species
	Rimu and Miro	Beech	Total	Radiata Pine	Douglas Fir	Total	Total
1998	28	5	38	2,995	105	3,157	3,195
1999	30	4	38	2,996	143	3,188	3,226
2000	22	6	30	3,583	134	3,776	3,806
2001	17	8	28	3,625	136	3,820	3,848
2002	13	13	28	3,678	124	3,836	3,864

In 2002–03 forest industries consisted of approximately 360 sawmills, seven plywood and 11 veneer plants, four particle board mills, eight wood pulp mills (four of which also produced paper and paperboard) and six fibreboard mills.

The basic products of the pulp and paper mills are mechanical and chemical pulp which are converted into newsprint, kraft and other papers, paperboard and fibreboard. Production of woodpulp in the year ending 31 March 2002 amounted to 1,523,730 tonnes and of paper (including newsprint paper and paperboard) to 846,727 tonnes.

Fisheries

In 2003 the total catch was 549,146 tonnes, almost entirely from sea fishing. The total value of New Zealand fisheries exports during the year ended Dec. 2002 was NZ$1,530m., of which hoki exports constituted NZ$314·7m.

INDUSTRY

The leading companies by market capitalization in New Zealand, excluding banking and finance, in Jan. 2002 were: Telecom Corporation of New Zealand Ltd (TCNZ), NZ$9bn.; Carter Holt Harvey Ltd (NZ$3bn.), a forest products company; and Lion Nathan Ltd (NZ$3bn.), a brewing company.

Statistics of manufacturing industries (in NZ$1m.):

Production year	Salaries and wages paid	Closing stocks of raw materials	Closing stocks of finished goods	Operating income	Purchases and other operating expenses
2001–02	8,961	2,618	4,945	63,396	47,163
2002–03	9,523	2,595	6,954	65,146	47,770

The following is a statement of the value of the products (including repairs) of the principal industries for the year 2002–03 (in NZ$1m.):

Industry group	Salaries and wages paid	Closing stocks of raw materials	Closing stocks of finished goods	Operating income	Purchases and other operating expenses
Dairy and meat products	1,481	261	3,015	16,057	13,777
Other food	869	213	651	6,939	5,063
Beverage, malt and tobacco	292	154	423	2,926	2,060
Textile and apparel	579	205	296	3,069	2,092
Wood products	674	107	381	4,245	3,227
Paper and paper products	407	110	206	2,870	2,002
Printing, publishing and recorded media	796	84	84	3,392	2,001
Petroleum and industrial chemical	267	195	192	3,202	2,154
Rubber, plastic and other chemical products	728	218	513	4,144	2,840
Non-metallic mineral products	295	52	137	2,041	1,364
Basic metal	314	108	161	2,041	1,524
Structural, sheet and fabricated metal products	780	195	214	4,112	2,849
Transport equipment manufacturing	499	212	145	2,244	1,488
Machinery and equipment	1,138	357	429	5,876	4,010
Furniture and other manufacturing	405	124	106	1,984	1,317

Labour

There were an estimated 1,928,300 persons employed in the quarter ending Sept. 2003. The largest number of employed people worked in the community, social and personal services area (27·4%); followed by wholesale and retail trade, restaurants and hotels (22·9%); and manufacturing (14·7%). Unemployment total for the quarter ending Sept. 2003 was estimated to be 86,300. The unemployment rate for the quarter ending Sept. 2005 was 3·4% of the workforce—the lowest in the developed world.

The weekly average wage in the quarter ended June 2003 was NZ$857 for men, NZ$685 for women. A minimum wage is set by the government annually. As of 1 April 2004 it was NZ$9·00 an hour; a youth rate of NZ$7·20 per hour applies for 16–17 year-olds. In 2002 there were 46 work stoppages (42 in 2001) with 34,398 person-days of work lost (54,440 in 2001).

According to the World Bank's *Doing Business in 2006: Creating Jobs* New Zealand is the easiest country in the world in which to do business.

Trade Unions

In 2000, 19 industrial unions of workers (representing 80% of all union members) were affiliated to the Council of Trade Unions, NZCTU (*President*, Ross Wilson). Compulsory trade union membership was made illegal in 1991, and the national wage award system was replaced by local wage agreements under the Employment Contracts Act 1991. In Dec. 2002 there were 174 unions in total with a combined membership of 334,783.

INTERNATIONAL TRADE

Total overseas debt was NZ$130,615m. in June 2003. In 1990 New Zealand and Australia completed the Closer Economic Relations Agreement (initiated in 1983), which provides for mutual free trade in goods.

Imports and Exports

Trade in NZ$1m. for recent years ending 30 June:

	Imports (c.i.f.)	Exports, including re-exports (f.o.b.)	Balance of Merchandise Trade
1999	24,248	22,582	–1,666
2000	29,193	26,111	–3,082
2001	31,927	32,000	73
2002	31,811	32,332	521
2003	32,161	29,291	–2,870

The principal imports for the 12 months ended 30 June 2003 were:

Commodity	Value (NZ$1m. v.f.d.)
Vehicles, parts and accessories	4,985
Mechanical machinery and equipment	4,333
Mineral fuels	3,152
Electrical machinery and equipment	2,699
Plastics and plastic articles	1,279
Optical, medical and measuring equipment	967
Paper, paperboard and paper articles	924
Aircraft and parts	804
Pharmaceutical products	747
Iron or steel articles	491
Iron and steel	481
Apparel (not knitted or crocheted)	446

The principal exports for the 12 months ended 30 June 2003 were:

Commodity	Value (NZ$1m. f.o.b.)
Dairy produce, eggs and honey	4,714
Meat and edible offal	4,111
Wood and articles of wood	2,386
Machinery and mechanical appliances	1,356
Fish, crustaceans and molluscs	1,215
Albuminoidal substances; modified starches; glues; enzymes	1,148
Fruits and nuts (edible)	1,032
Aluminium and aluminium articles	980
Wool, fine or coarse animal hair	943
Electrical machinery, equipment and parts	938

The principal import suppliers in 2002–03 (imports v.f.d., in NZ$1m.) were: Australia, 7,278; USA, 4,067; Japan, 3,876; China, 2,687; Germany, 1,713; UK, 1,120; Malaysia, 864. The leading export destinations in 2002–03 (exports and re-exports f.o.b., in NZ$1m.) were: Australia, 6,050; USA, 4,366; Japan, 3,354; China, 1,457; UK, 1,361; Republic of Korea, 1,178; Germany, 855.

COMMUNICATIONS

Roads

Total length of roads in 2002 was 92,200 km (62·8% paved), including 190 km of motorways. There were 74 national and provincial state highways comprising 10,570 km of roadway, including the principal arterial traffic routes.

In Feb. 2003 there were 9,830 full-time equivalent persons employed in the provision of road passenger transport and 23,890 persons providing road freight transport.

Total expenditure on roads (including state highways), streets and bridges—by the central government and local authorities combined—amounted to NZ$959m. in 2002.

At 31 March 2003 motor vehicles licensed numbered 2,916,734, of which 2,010,024 were cars. In 2003 there were 7,780 omnibuses/ public taxis and 38,447 motorcycles. In 2002 there were 366,918 trucks and 373,940 trailers.

In 2002 there were 404 deaths in road accidents.

Rail

New Zealand Rail was privatized in 1994 but renationalized in 2004. In 1994 a 24-hour freight link was introduced between Auckland and Christchurch. There were, in 2002, 3,898 km of 1,067 mm gauge railway open for traffic (506 km electrified). New Zealand Rail Limited was renamed Tranz Rail Limited in 1995. In 2003 Tranz Rail carried 14·8m. tonnes of freight and 12·3m. passengers. Total revenue in the financial year 1999–2000 was NZ$594·5m.

At 30 June 2003 Tranz Rail track and rolling stock included 322 diesel, electric and shunting locomotives, 4,048 freight wagons, 177 passenger carriages and commuter units, three rail/road ferries (linking the North and South Islands) and plant and support equipment. After renationalization Tranz Rail was renamed Toll NZ.

Civil Aviation

There are international airports at Wellington, Auckland and Christchurch, with Auckland International being the main airport. The national carrier is Air New Zealand, which was privatized in 1989 but then renationalized in 2001. Trans-Tasman air travel is subject to agreement between Air New Zealand and Qantas.

New Zealand has one of the highest ratios of aircraft to population in the world with 3,530 aircraft in the year to March 2003. Since 1992 air transport flights have increased by about 9% per year. In 1999 scheduled airline traffic of New Zealand-based carriers flew 172·2m. km, carrying 8,892,000 passengers (2,829,000 on international flights). In 2002 there were 113 airports, of which 46 had paved runways.

Shipping

In 2002 merchant shipping totalled 180,000 GRT, including oil tankers 50,000 GRT. In 2003 there were 1,069 km of waterway.

Telecommunications

The provision of telecommunication services is the responsibility of the Telecom Corporation of New Zealand, formed in 1987 and privatized in 1990; and CLEAR Communications, which began operations in Dec. 1990. In 2002 there were 4,201,000 telephone subscribers, or 1,066·5 for every 1,000 persons, and 1,630,000 PCs in use (621·7 per 1,000 persons). There were 141,000 fax machines in 2002. New Zealand had 2·06m. Internet users in Aug. 2002.

Postal Services

On 1 April 1998 the Postal Services Act removed New Zealand Post's former statutory monopoly on the carriage of letters and opened the postal market to full competition. To carry out a business involving the carriage of letters, a person or company must be registered as a postal operator with the Ministry of Commerce.

In 2003 there were 315 post shops, 697 post centre franchises and 2,735 stamp resellers.

SOCIAL INSTITUTIONS

Justice

The judiciary consists of the Court of Appeal, the High Court and District Courts. All exercise both civil and criminal jurisdiction. Final appeal lies to the Privy Council in London. Special courts include the Maori Land Court, the Maori Appellate Court, Family Courts, the Youth Court, Environment Court and the Employment Court. In 2003 there were 5,826 sentenced inmates of whom 274 were women. Of male inmates in 2001, 53% (some 2,499) identified themselves as Maori only compared to 29% who identified themselves as European only. There were 170,999 convictions, including 14,537 for violent offences, in 2002. The

death penalty for murder was replaced by life imprisonment in 1961.

The Criminal Injuries Compensation Act, 1963, which came into force on 1 Jan. 1964, provided for compensation of persons injured by certain criminal acts and the dependants of persons killed by such acts. However, this has now been phased out in favour of the Accident Compensation Act, 1982, except in the residual area of property damage caused by escapees. The Offenders Legal Aid Act 1954 provides that any person charged or convicted of any offence may apply for legal aid which may be granted depending on the person's means and the gravity of the offence etc. Since 1970 legal aid in civil proceedings (except divorce) has been available for persons of small or moderate means. The Legal Services Act 1991 now brings together in one statute the civil and criminal legal aid schemes.

Police

The police are a national body maintained by the central government. In June 2003 there were 7,257 full-time equivalent sworn officers (16% female).

Ombudsmen

The office of Ombudsman was created in 1962. From 1975 additional Ombudsmen have been authorized. There are currently two. Ombudsmen's functions are to investigate complaints under the Ombudsman Act, the Official Information Act and the Local Government Official Information and Meetings Act from members of the public relating to administrative decisions of central, regional and local government. During the year ended 30 June 2003 a total of 4,418 complaints were received. A total of 27 complaints were sustained during the year and 729 were still under investigation

Education

Education is compulsory between the ages of 6 and 15. Children aged three and four years may enrol at the 606 free kindergartens maintained by Free Kindergarten Associations, which receive government assistance. There are also 492 play centres which also receive government subsidy. In 2002 there were 45,169 and 14,879 children on the rolls respectively. There were also 1,612 care centres in 2002 with 76,246 children, 545 *te kohanga reo* (providing early childhood education in the Maori language) with 10,389 children, and a number of other smaller providers of early childhood care and education.

In 2002 there were 2,132 state primary schools (including intermediate and state contributing schools), with 411,850 pupils; the number of teachers was 19,329. A correspondence school for children in remote areas and those otherwise unable to attend school had 7,872 primary and secondary pupils and 242 teachers. In 2003 there were 45 registered private primary and intermediate schools with 6,106 pupils. In 2002 there were 534 teachers at private primary and intermediate schools.

In 2002 there were 320 state secondary schools with 14,577 full-time teachers and 212,426 pupils. There were also 58 state composite area schools with 4,831 scholars in the secondary division. In 2003 there were 2,280 full-time secondary pupils taught by 282 secondary teachers at the Correspondence School. There were 17 registered private secondary schools with 615 teachers and 8,498 pupils in 2002.

New Zealand has eight universities—the University of Auckland, Auckland University of Technology, University of Waikato (at Hamilton), Victoria University of Wellington, Massey University (at Palmerston North), the University of Canterbury (at Christchurch), the University of Otago (at Dunedin) and Lincoln University (near Christchurch). The number of equivalent full-time students attending universities in 2002 was 100,772. There were four teachers' training colleges with 6,338 equivalent full-time students in 2002, and 63,741 equivalent full-time students were enrolled in polytechnic courses in 2002.

Total budgeted expenditure estimated in 2003 on education was NZ$8·2bn. (16·8% of government expenses). The universities are autonomous bodies. All state-funded primary and secondary schools are controlled by boards of trustees. Education in state schools is free for children under 19 years of age. All educational institutions are reviewed every three years by teams of educational reviewers.

A series of reforms is being implemented by the government following reports of 18 working groups on tertiary education. These include a new funding system, begun in 1991 and based solely on student numbers.

The adult literacy rate is at least 99%.

Health

In 2003 there were 10,355 practising doctors. In 2002 there were 85 public hospitals with 12,484 beds and 360 private hospitals with 11,341 beds. In 2003 New Zealand spent 8·1% of its GDP on health. Total budgeted expenditure on health in 2003–04 was NZ$9·6bn.

Welfare

Non-contributory old-age pensions were introduced in 1898. Large reductions in welfare expenditure were introduced by the government in Dec. 1990.

From 1 Oct. 1998 anyone receiving unemployment benefit, sickness benefit, a training benefit, a 55 plus benefit, or a young job seekers allowance has received a benefit called the Community Wage. In return for receiving the Community Wage, recipients are expected to search for work, meet with Work and Income New Zealand when asked, take a suitable work offer and take part in activities that would improve their chances of finding a job.

In the budget of July 1991 it was announced that current rates of Guaranteed Retirement Income Scheme (GRI) payment would be frozen until 1 April 1993, thereafter to be on the previous year's consumer price index. On 1 April 1992 GRI was replaced by the national superannuation scheme which is income-tested. Eligibility has been gradually increased to 65 years. Universal eligibility is available at 70 years. At 1 April 2003 a married couple received NZ$377·38 per week, a single person living alone NZ$245·30 per week.

Social Welfare Benefits.

Benefits	Number in force at 30 June 2003	Total expenditure 2003 (NZ$1,000)
Community Wage—Job Seeker	111,906	1,287,730
Community Wage—Training	4,291	37,942
Community Wage—Sickness	39,902	460,209
Invalids' Benefit	68,507	926,515
Domestic Purposes' Benefit	109,295	1,634,477
Orphans' Benefit/Unsupported Child's Benefit	6,789	47,081
Widows' Benefit	8,659	90,265
Transitional Retirement Benefit	2,110	42,013
New Zealand Superannuation	457,278	5,798,873
Veterans' Pension	7,872	87,625
War Pension	22,271	108,862
Total Income Support	838,880	10,521,592

Reciprocity with Other Countries. New Zealand has overseas social security agreements with the United Kingdom, the Netherlands, Greece, Ireland, Australia, Jersey and Guernsey, Denmark and Canada. The main purpose of these agreements is to encourage free movement of labour and to ensure that when a person has lived or worked in more than one country, each of those countries takes a fair share of the responsibility for meeting the costs of that person's social security coverage. New Zealand also pays people eligible for New Zealand Superannuation or veterans' pensions who live in the Cook Islands, Niue or Tokelau.

RELIGION

No direct state aid is given to any form of religion. For the Church of England the country is divided into seven dioceses, with a separate bishopric (Aotearoa) for the Maori. The Presbyterian Church is divided into 23 presbyteries and the Maori Synod. The Moderator is elected annually. The Methodist Church is divided into ten districts; the President is elected annually. The Roman Catholic Church is divided into four dioceses, with the Archbishop of Wellington as Metropolitan Archbishop. In May 2005 there was one cardinal.

Adherents of leading religions at the 2001 census were as follows:

Religious denomination	Adherents
Anglican	584,793
Catholic	486,012
Presbyterian	417,453
Methodist	120,708
Baptist	51,426
Ratana	48,975
Buddhist	41,664
Latter-day Saints (Mormons)	39,915
Hindu	39,876
Pentecostal	30,222
Islam/Muslim	23,637
Brethren	20,406
Jehovah's Witnesses	17,826
Assemblies of God	16,023
Salvation Army	12,618
Seventh-day Adventist	12,600
All other religious affiliations	398,847
No religion	1,028,052
Object to state	239,241
Not specified	211,638
Total	3,841,932[1]

[1]Where a person reported more than one religious affiliation, they have been counted in each applicable group.

CULTURE

World Heritage Sites

There are three UNESCO World Heritage sites under New Zealand jurisdiction. Te Wahipounamu, on South Island, and the New Zealand Sub-Antarctic Islands were listed in 1990 and 1998 respectively. The Sub-Antarctic Islands consist of the Auckland Islands, Antipodes Islands, Bounty Islands, Campbell Island and the Snares. Tongariro National Park, on North Island, was listed in 1988.

Broadcasting

Legislation of 1995 split the state-owned Radio New Zealand into a government-owned public radio broadcasting company and some 40 commercial stations.

Television New Zealand operates two channels. Two other channels, TV3 and TV4, are commercial. There are also regional TV networks. Pay television was introduced in May 1990—Sky Entertainment operates on more than 70 channels. Maori Television was launched in March 2004. Colour is by PAL. The New Zealand Public Radio Service also includes the Radio New Zealand International, a short-wave which broadcasts to the South Pole. There are 21 regional Maori stations for the promotion of Maori culture. In 2000 there were 3·85m. radio and in 2001 there were 2·13m. television receivers.

Cinema

Cinema admissions totalled 18·3m. in 2003, up from 6·1m. in 1991. Gross box office receipts came to NZ$156·1m. in 2003. In 1999 there were 315 cinema screens.

Press

In 2003 there were 24 daily newspapers with a combined daily average circulation of 740,763, giving a rate of 185 per 1,000 inhabitants. The *New Zealand Herald,* published in Auckland, had the largest daily circulation in 2003, with an average of 210,910 copies. Other major dailies are *The Dominion Post* and *The Press,* with circulations of over 90,000 copies.

There are two Sunday newspapers, *Sunday Star-Times* and *Sunday News,* both published by Fairfax New Zealand Limited and distributed nationwide. The *Sunday Star-Times* is a broadsheet and circulates about 204,000 copies while the *Sunday News* is a tabloid and circulates 115,000 (2000) copies every Sunday.

Tourism

There were 2,062,423 tourists in the year to March 2003 (in 2000, 1,652,000) of whom 638,354 were from Australia, 240,029 were from the UK, 205,796 were from the USA and 172,716 were from Japan. International tourism generated US$3·02bn. in 2002. Domestic travel expenditure for the year ending March 2005 totalled NZ$7·01bn., a fall of 9·5% from the previous year. The leading destination for domestic overnight trips was Auckland (16%), followed by Canterbury (9%) and Wellington (8%).

Festivals

The biennial New Zealand Festival takes place in Wellington in Feb./March in even-numbered years. The biennial Christchurch Arts Festival takes place in July/Aug. in odd-numbered years.

Museums and Galleries

The Museum of New Zealand Te Papa Tongarewa, in Wellington, is the national museum and receives over 1m. visitors per year.

DIPLOMATIC REPRESENTATIVES

Of New Zealand in the United Kingdom (New Zealand House, Haymarket, London, SW1Y 4TQ)
High Commissioner: Jonathan Hunt.

Of the United Kingdom in New Zealand (44 Hill St., Wellington, 1)
High Commissioner: Richard Fell, CVO.

Of New Zealand in the USA (37 Observatory Cir., NW, Washington, D.C., 20008)
Ambassador: Roy Ferguson.

Of the USA in New Zealand (29 Fitzherbert Terr., Wellington)
Ambassador: William P. McCormick.

Of New Zealand to the United Nations
Ambassador: Rosemary Banks.

Of New Zealand to the European Union
Ambassador: Wade Armstrong.

FURTHER READING

Statistics New Zealand. *New Zealand Official Yearbook.—Key Statistics: a Monthly Abstract of Statistics.—Profile of New Zealand.*

Belich, James, *Making Peoples: a History of the New Zealanders from Polynesian Settlement to the End of the Nineteenth century.* London, 1997.—*Paradise Reforged: A History of New Zealanders from the 1880s to the Year 2000.* London, 2002

Harland, B., *On Our Own: New Zealand in a Tripolar World.* Victoria Univ. Press, 1992

Harris, P. and Levine, S. (eds.) *The New Zealand Politics Source Book.* 2nd ed. Palmerston North, 1994

Massey, P., *New Zealand: Market Liberalization in a Developed Economy.* London, 1995

Patterson, B. and K., *New Zealand.* [Bibliography] 2nd ed. ABC-Clio, Oxford and Santa Barbara (CA), 1998

Sinclair, K. (ed.) *The Oxford Illustrated History of New Zealand.* 2nd ed. OUP, 1994

For other more specialized titles see under CONSTITUTION AND GOVERNMENT above.

National Statistical Office: Statistics New Zealand, POB 2922, Wellington, 1.
Website: http://www.stats.govt.nz/

TERRITORIES OVERSEAS

Territories Overseas coming within the jurisdiction of New Zealand consist of Tokelau and the Ross Dependency.

Tokelau

Tokelau is situated some 500 km to the north of Samoa and comprises three dispersed atolls—Atafu, Fakaofo and Nukunonu. The land area is 12 sq. km and the population at the 2001 census was 1,537, giving a density of 128 per sq. km.

The British government transferred administrative control of Tokelau to New Zealand in 1925. Formal sovereignty was transferred to New Zealand in 1948 by act of the New Zealand Parliament. New Zealand statute law, however, does not apply to Tokelau unless it is expressly extended to Tokelau. In practice New Zealand legislation is extended to Tokelau only with its consent.

Under a programme agreed in 1992, the role of Tokelau's political institutions is being better defined and expanded. The process under way enables the base of Tokelau government to be located within Tokelau's national level institutions rather than as before, within a public service located largely in Samoa. In 1994 the Administrator's powers were delegated to the *General Fono* (the national representative body), and when the *General Fono* is not in session, to the *Council of Faipule.* The Tokelau Amendment Act 1996 conferred on the *General Fono* a power to make rules for Tokelau, including the power to impose taxes.

Coconuts (the source of copra) are the only cash crop. Pulaka, breadfruit, papayas, the screw-pine and bananas are cultivated as food crops. Livestock comprises pigs, poultry and goats.

Tokelau affirmed to the United Nations in 1994 that it had under active consideration both the Constitution of a self-governing Tokelau and an act of self-determination. It also expressed a strong preference for a future status of free association with New Zealand. A referendum on self-determination took place in Feb. 2006 with 60% voting in favour of the proposal. As a two-thirds majority was needed for the referendum to succeed, Tokelau remained a New Zealand territory.

Ross Dependency

By Imperial Order in Council, dated 30 July 1923, the territories between 160° E. long. and 150° W. long. and south of 60° S. lat. were brought within the jurisdiction of the New Zealand government. The region was named the Ross Dependency. From time to time laws for the Dependency have been made by regulations promulgated by the Governor-General of New Zealand.

The mainland area is estimated at 400,000–450,000 sq. km and is mostly ice-covered. In Jan. 1957 a New Zealand expedition under Sir Edmund Hillary established a base in the Dependency. In Jan. 1958 Sir Edmund Hillary and four other New Zealanders reached the South Pole.

The main base—Scott Base, at Pram Point, Ross Island—is manned throughout the year, about 12 people being present during winter. The annual activities of 200–300 scientists and support staff are managed by a crown agency, Antarctica New Zealand, based in Christchurch.

SELF-GOVERNING TERRITORIES OVERSEAS

The Cook Islands

KEY HISTORICAL EVENTS

The Cook Islands, which lie between 8° and 23° S. lat., and 156° and 167° W. long., were made a British protectorate in 1888, and on 11 June 1901 were annexed as part of New Zealand. In 1965 the Cook Islands became a self-governing territory in 'free association' with New Zealand.

TERRITORY AND POPULATION

The islands fall roughly into two groups—the scattered islands towards the north (Northern group) and the islands towards the south (Southern group). The islands with their populations at the census of 1996:

Southern Group—	Area sq. km	Population
Aitutaki	18·3	2,389
Atiu	26·9	956
Mangaia	51·8	1,108
Manuae and Te au-o-tu	6·2	—
Mauke (Parry Is.)	18·4	652
Mitiaro	22·3	319
Rarotonga	67·1	11,225
Northern Group—	Area sq. km	Population
Manihiki (Humphrey)	5·4	668
Nassau	1·3	99
Palmerston (Avarua)	2·1	49
Penrhyn (Tongareva)	9·8	606
Pukapuka (Danger)	1·3	779
Rakahanga (Reirson)	4·1	249
Suwarrow (Anchorage)	0·4	4
Total	235·4	19,103

Population density in 1996 was 76 per sq. km. In 1996 an estimated 58·8% of the population lived in urban areas. The 2001 total population (17,700) and the estimated resident population (13,400) have fallen since 1996, the latter by approximately 26%.

SOCIAL STATISTICS

1999: births, 346; deaths, 96. Birth rate (1999, per 1,000 population), 21·1; death rate, 5·9. Life expectancy was estimated in 2003 at: males, 68·0 years; females 74·0. Fertility rate, 2003, 3·2 births per woman.

CLIMATE

Oceanic climate where rainfall is moderate to heavy throughout the year, with Nov. to March being particularly wet. Weather can be changeable from day to day and can end in rainfall after an otherwise sunny day. Rarotonga, Jan. 26°C, July 20°C. Annual rainfall 2,060 mm.

CONSTITUTION AND GOVERNMENT

The Cook Islands Constitution of 1965 provides for internal self-government but linked to New Zealand by a common Head of State and a common citizenship, that of New Zealand. It provides for a ministerial system of government with a Cabinet consisting of a Prime Minister and not more than eight nor fewer than six other Ministers. There is also an advisory council composed of hereditary chiefs, the 15-member House of Ariki, without legislative powers. The New Zealand government is represented by a New Zealand Representative and the Queen, as head of state, by the Queen's Representative. The capital is Avarua on Rarotonga.

The unicameral *Parliament* comprises 25 members elected for a term of five years.

RECENT ELECTIONS

At the elections of 7 Sept. 2004 the centrist Democratic Party won 14 of the 24 seats, the Cook Islands Party won 9 seats and ind. 1 seat.

CURRENT ADMINISTRATION

High Commissioner: John Bryan.
  Prime Minister: Jim Marurai.

ECONOMY

Overview

A package of economic reforms including privatization and deregulation was initiated in July 1996 to deal with a national debt of US$141m., 120% of GDP.

Currency

The Cook Island *dollar* was at par with the New Zealand *dollar*, but was replaced in 1995 by New Zealand currency.

Budget

Revenue, 1996–97, NZ$45·8m.; expenditure, NZ$44·8m. Grants from New Zealand, mainly for medical, educational and general administrative purposes, totalled NZ$11·3m. in 1996–97.

Performance

Real GDP growth was 1·3% in 1995 (1·5% in 1994).

Banking and Finance

There are four banks in the Cook Islands. The Cook Islands Savings Bank is state-owned and has deposit services throughout the islands. The Cook Islands Development Bank is a state-owned corporation funded in part by loans from the Asian Development Bank. The two remaining banks are subsidiaries of the Australia and New Zealand Banking Group Limited and the Westpac Bank, which are both Australian-owned and major banks in Australasia.

ENERGY AND NATURAL RESOURCES

Electricity

Production in 2000 was 25m. kWh. Installed capacity was 8,000 kW in 2000.

Minerals

The islands of the Cook group have no significant mineral resources. However, the seabed, which forms part of the exclusive economic zone, has some of the highest concentrations of manganese nodules in the world. Manganese nodules are rich in cobalt and nickel.

Agriculture

In 2001 there were approximately 4,000 ha. of arable land and 3,000 ha. of permanent crops. Production estimates (2002, in 1,000 tonnes): coconuts, 5; cassava, 3; mangoes, 3. Livestock (2002): 40,000 pigs, 2,000 goats.

Forestry

Timber production was 5,000 cu. metres in 2001.

Fisheries

In 2001 the total catch was estimated at 700 tonnes, entirely from sea fishing.

INDUSTRY

Labour
In 1996 there were 5,230 persons actively employed in the Cook Islands and 764 unemployed. Of those employed, 3,072 were men and 2,158 were women.

INTERNATIONAL TRADE

Imports and Exports
Exports, mainly to New Zealand, were valued at NZ$6·0m. in 1998. Main items exported were fresh fruit and vegetables and black pearls. Imports totalled NZ$70·7m.

COMMUNICATIONS

Roads
In 1992 there were 320 km of roads and, in 1991, 5,015 vehicles.

Civil Aviation
New Zealand has financed the construction of an international airport at Rarotonga which became operational for jet services in 1973. There are nine useable airports. Domestic services are provided by Air Rarotonga, and in 2003 there were also services to Auckland, Honolulu, Los Angeles, the Fiji Islands, French Polynesia and Vancouver.

Shipping
A fortnightly cargo shipping service is provided between New Zealand, Niue and Rarotonga. In 2002 merchant shipping totalled 8,000 GRT.

Telecommunications
In 2002 there were 6,200 telephone lines in service. There were 1,500 mobile phone subscribers in 2002 and 3,600 Internet users.

Postal Services
A full range of postal services are offered and there are post agents in all inhabited islands.

SOCIAL INSTITUTIONS

Justice
There is a High Court and a Court of Appeal, from which further appeal is to the Privy Council in the UK.

The population in penal institutions in 2002 was 24 (equivalent to 120 per 100,000 population).

Education
In March 1998 there were 28 primary schools with 140 teachers and 2,711 pupils, 23 secondary schools with 129 teachers and 1,779 pupils, and 26 pre-schools with 30 teachers and 460 pupils.

In 1998–99 total expenditure on education came to 13·1% of total government spending.

Health
A user pay scheme was introduced in July 1996 where all Cook Islanders pay a fee of NZ$5·00 for any medical or surgical treatment including consultation. Those under the age of 16 years or over the age of 60 years are exempted from payment of this charge. The dental department is privatized except for the school dental health provision. This service continues to be free to all schools.

The Rarotonga Hospital, which is the referral hospital for the outer islands, consists of 80 beds. The hospital has eight doctors, 33 registered nurses and 11 hospital aides.

RELIGION
From the census of 1996, 58% of the population belong to the Cook Islands Christian Church; about 17% are Roman Catholics, and the rest are Latter-day Saints and Seventh-Day Adventists and other religions.

CULTURE

Broadcasting
There are two radio stations (AM and FM) operating in the Cook Islands. In 1997 there were approximately 4,000 TV receivers and 14,000 radio receivers.

Press
The *Cook Islands News* (circulation 1,800 in 1996) is the sole daily newspaper. The *Cook Islands Star*, which is published fortnightly, is sold in the Cook Islands and in New Zealand.

Tourism
In 2002 there were 81,473 tourist arrivals; revenue in 2002 totalled US$36m.

FURTHER READING
Local statistical office: Ministry of Finance and Economic Management, P.O. Box 41, Rarotonga, Cook Islands.

Statistical office: Cook Islands Statistics Office.
Website: http://www.stats.gov.ck

Niue

KEY HISTORICAL EVENTS
Capt. James Cook sighted Niue in 1774 and called it 'Savage Island'. Christian missionaries arrived in 1846. Niue became a British Protectorate in 1900 and was annexed to New Zealand in 1901. Internal self-government was achieved in free association with New Zealand on 19 Oct. 1974, with New Zealand taking responsibility for external affairs and defence. Niue is a member of the South Pacific Forum. In Jan. 2004 Cyclone Heta destroyed the capital, Alofi, and a state of emergency was declared, although it was lifted a month later.

TERRITORY AND POPULATION
Niue is the largest uplifted coral island in the world. Distance from Auckland, New Zealand, 2,161 km; from Rarotonga, 933 km. Area, 261 sq. km; height above sea level, 67 metres. The population has been declining steadily, from around 6,000 in the 1960s to 1,789 recorded in the 2001 census, giving a population density of 7 per sq. km. Migration to New Zealand is the main factor in population change. The capital is Alofi.

SOCIAL STATISTICS
Annual growth rate, 1992–2002, –1·2%. In the period 1997–2001 average number of births registered was 29 per year; average number of deaths, 16. Fertility rate, 2001, 2·6 births per woman.

CLIMATE
Oceanic, warm and humid, tempered by trade winds. May to Oct. are cooler months. Temperatures range from 20°C to 28°C.

CONSTITUTION AND GOVERNMENT
There is a Legislative Assembly (*Fono*) of 20 members, 14 elected from 14 constituencies and six elected by all constituencies.

RECENT ELECTIONS
Parliamentary elections were held on 30 April 2005. Seven of parliament's 20 seats, including that of Prime Minister Young Vivian, were uncontested. A total of 17 incumbent candidates were re-elected.

CURRENT ADMINISTRATION
High Commissioner: Anton Ojala.

Prime Minister: Young Vivian (Niue People's Party; took office in May 2002 and re-elected in May 2005).

ECONOMY

Budget

Financial aid from New Zealand, 1995–96, totalled NZ$8·4m.

ENERGY AND NATURAL RESOURCES

Electricity

Production in 2000 was about 3m. kWh; installed capacity was 1,000 kW in 2000.

Agriculture

In 2001 there were approximately 4,000 ha. of arable land and 3,000 ha. of permanent crops. The main commercial crops of the island are coconuts, taro and yams.

In 2002 there were 2,000 pigs.

Fisheries

In 2001 the total catch was approximately 200 tonnes, exclusively from marine waters.

INTERNATIONAL TRADE

Imports and Exports

Imports, 2002, NZ$3·25m.; exports, NZ$0·14m.

COMMUNICATIONS

Civil Aviation

Weekly commercial air services link Niue with New Zealand, Sydney and Samoa.

Telecommunications

There is a wireless station at Alofi, the port of the island. Telephone main lines (2002) 1,100. There were 900 Internet users in 2002 and 400 mobile phone subscribers in 2001.

SOCIAL INSTITUTIONS

Justice

There is a High Court under a Chief Justice, with a right of appeal to the New Zealand Supreme Court.

Education

In 2002 there was one primary school with 17 teachers and 251 pupils, and one secondary school with 29 teachers and 240 pupils. There is also the University of the South Pacific.

Health

In 2003 there were four doctors, two dentists, three midwives and 14 nursing personnel. The 24-bed hospital at Alofi was destroyed by Cyclone Heta in Jan. 2004.

RELIGION

At the 1991 census, 1,487 people belonged to the Congregational (Ekalesia Niue); Latter-day Saints (213), Roman Catholics (90), Jehovah's Witness (47), Seventh Day Adventists (27), other (63), no religion (34), not stated (1).

CULTURE

Broadcasting

There were 1,000 radio receivers in 1997. Cable television is available.

Press

A weekly newspaper is published in English and Niuean; circulation about 400.

Tourism

In 2002 there were 3,155 visitors (1,158 on vacation).

NICARAGUA

HONDURAS

NICARAGUA

• Matagalpa

León • □ MANAGUA

Granada • Lake Nicaragua

PACIFIC OCEAN

Caribbean Sea

© Research Machines plc 2006   COSTA RICA

0   50 mi
0   75 km

República de Nicaragua

Capital: Managua
Population projection, 2010: 6·07m.
GDP per capita, 2003: (PPP$) 3,262
HDI/world rank: 0·690/112

KEY HISTORICAL EVENTS

Colonization of the Nicaraguan Pacific coast was undertaken by Spaniards from Panama, beginning in 1523. France and Britain, however, and later the USA, all tried to play a colonial or semi-colonial role in Nicaragua. Nicaragua became an independent republic in 1838 but its independence was often threatened by US intervention. Between 1910 and 1930 the country was under almost continuous US military occupation.

In 1914 the Bryan-Chamarro Treaty entitled the USA to a permanent option for a canal route through Nicaragua, a 99-year option for a naval base in the Bay of Fonseca on the Pacific coast and occupation of the Corn Islands on the Atlantic coast. The Bryan-Chamarro Treaty was not abrogated until 14 July 1970 when the Corn Islands returned to Nicaragua.

The Somoza family dominated Nicaragua from 1933 to 1979. Imposing a brutal dictatorship, they secured for themselves a large share of the national wealth. In 1962 the radical Sandinista National Liberation Front was formed with the object of overthrowing the Somozas. After 17 years of civil war the Sandinistas triumphed. On 17 July 1979 President Somoza fled into exile. The USA made efforts to unseat the revolutionary government by supporting the Contras (counter-revolutionary forces). It was not until 1988 that the state of emergency was lifted as part of the Central American peace process. Rebel anti-Sandinista activities had ceased by 1990; the last organized insurgent group negotiated an agreement with the government in April 1994.

In Oct. 1998 Hurricane Mitch devastated the country causing 3,800 deaths.

TERRITORY AND POPULATION

Nicaragua is bounded in the north by Honduras, east by the Caribbean, south by Costa Rica and west by the Pacific. Area, 131,812 sq. km (121,428 sq. km dry land). The coastline runs 450 km on the Atlantic and 305 km on the Pacific. The census population in April 1995 was 4,357,099 (density, 33·3 per sq. km). 2005 estimate: 5,487,000. In 2003, 57·3% of the population were urban.

The UN gives a projected population for 2010 of 6·07m.

15 administrative departments and two autonomous regions are grouped in three zones. Areas (in sq. km), populations at the 1995 census and chief towns:

	Area	Population	Chief town
Pacific Zone	18,429	2,467,742	
Carazo	1,050	149,407	Jinotepe
Chinandega	4,926	350,212	Chinandega
Granada	929	155,683	Granada
León	5,107	336,894	León
Managua	3,672	1,093,760	Managua
Masaya	590	241,354	Masaya
Rivas	2,155	140,432	Rivas
Central-North Zone	35,960	1,354,246	
Boaco	4,244	136,949	Boaco
Chontales	6,378	144,635	Juigalpa
Estelí	2,335	174,894	Estelí
Jinotega	9,755	257,933	Jinotega
Madriz	1,602	107,567	Somoto
Matagalpa	8,523	383,776	Matagalpa
Nueva Segovia	3,123	148,492	Ocotal
Atlantic Zone	67,039	535,111	
Atlántico Norte[1]	32,159	192,716	Puerto Cabezas
Atlántico Sur[1]	27,407	272,252	Bluefields
Río San Juan	7,473	70,143	San Carlos

[1]Autonomous region.

The capital is Managua with (1999 estimate) 930,000 inhabitants. Other cities (1995 populations): León, 123,865; Chinandega, 97,387; Masaya, 88,971; Granada, 71,783; Estelí, 71,550; Tipitapa, 67,925; Matagalpa, 59,397; Juigalpa, 36,999.

The population is of Spanish and Amerindian origins with an admixture of Afro-Americans on the Caribbean coast. Ethnic groups in 2000: Mestizo (mixed Amerindian and White), 63%; White, 14%; Black, 8%; Amerindian, 5%. The official language is Spanish.

SOCIAL STATISTICS

2002 estimates: births, 175,000; deaths, 28,000. Estimated rates (per 1,000 population), 2002: births, 32·8; deaths, 5·2. Annual population growth rate, 1992–2002, 2·8%. 2003 life expectancy: male 67·3 years, female 72·1. Infant mortality, 2001, 36 per 1,000 live births; fertility rate, 2001, 4·0 births per woman.

CLIMATE

The climate is tropical, with a wet season from May to Jan. Temperatures vary with altitude. Managua, Jan. 81°F (27°C), July 81°F (27°C). Annual rainfall 38" (976 mm).

CONSTITUTION AND GOVERNMENT

A new Constitution was promulgated on 9 Jan. 1987 and underwent reforms in 1995 and 2000. It provides for a unicameral 92-seat *National Assembly* comprising 90 members directly elected by proportional representation, together with one seat for the previous president and one seat for the runner-up in the previous presidential election.

The *President* and *Vice-President* are directly elected for a five-year term commencing on the 10 Jan. following their date of election. The President may stand for a second term, but not consecutively.

National Anthem
'Salve a ti Nicaragua' ('Hail to thee, Nicaragua'); words by S. Ibarra Mayorga, tune by L. A. Delgadillo.

RECENT ELECTIONS
Presidential and parliamentary elections took place on 4 Nov. 2001. In the presidential elections Enrique Bolaños Geyer was elected with 56·3% of votes cast, defeating José Daniel Ortega Saavedra (42·3%) and Alberto Saborío (1·4%). At the parliamentary elections the Constitutional Liberal Party gained 47 seats with 53·2% of votes cast; the Sandinista National Liberation Front, 43 (42·1%); and the Conservative Party of Nicaragua, 2 (2·1%).

Presidential and parliamentary elections are scheduled to take place on 5 Nov. 2006.

CURRENT ADMINISTRATION
President: Enrique Bolaños Geyer; b. 1928 (Constitutional Liberal Party; in office since 10 Jan. 2002).

Vice President: Alfredo Gómez Urcuyo.

In March 2006 the government comprised:

Minister of Agriculture and Forestry: Mario Salvo Horvilleur. *Defence:* Avil Ramírez Valdivia. *Development, Industry and Commerce:* Alejandro Arguello. *Education, Sports and Culture:* Miguel Ángel García. *Environment and Natural Resources:* Cristóbal Sequeira González. *Family:* Ivania del Socorro Toruño Padilla. *Finance and Public Credit:* Mario Arana Sevilla. *Foreign Affairs:* Norman José Caldera Cardenal. *Government:* Dr Julio Vega Pasquier. *Health:* Margarita Gurdián López. *Labour:* Virgilio Gurdián Castellón. *Transportation and Infrastructure:* Ricardo Vega Jackson.

Office of the President (Spanish only):
http://www.presidencia.gob.ni/

CURRENT LEADERS
Enrique Bolaños

Position
President

Introduction
Enrique Bolaños, leader of the Constitutional Liberal Party, won the presidential elections of Nov. 2001. He assumed office in Jan. 2002, tasked with rejuvenating Nicaragua's ailing economy, but has since been hampered by congressional opposition.

Early Life
Bolaños was born in 1928 near Managua. Having graduated from Saint Louis University in Missouri, USA, he embarked on a career in business. During the Sandinista revolution he was jailed for his criticism of the government, and his business interests were nationalized. In 1996 he was appointed vice-president in the corruption-tainted government of Arnoldo Aleman. With strong backing from the US government, and especially the governor of Florida, he stood successfully for the presidency at the elections of Nov. 2001, winning with 56·3% of the vote.

Career in Office
Among Bolaños' chief election promises was the elimination of government corruption, with offenders facing prison. Former president Aleman was subsequently convicted and jailed for fraud and money laundering. However, this move cost Bolaños the support of his party's Aleman loyalists who allied with the opposition Sandinistas to secure control of the National Assembly, leaving Bolaños politically isolated. In 2005 the Assembly sought to amend the constitution and weaken the president's powers, leading to court action and political stalemate.

Economically, advocating a free market with low unemployment and a redeveloped infrastructure, Bolaños negotiated with the World Bank, International Monetary Fund and Inter-American Development Bank in April 2002 to secure increased long-term financing of development projects, debt relief and structural support loans. In Jan. 2004 the World Bank agreed to cancel 80% of Nicaragua's debt, and later in that year Russia wrote off the country's debts incurred during the Soviet era.

Keen to develop relations with the USA, Bolaños vowed on election to combat drug smuggling and he supported the Bush regime in the aftermath of the 11 Sept. 2001 attacks. He has since signed trade agreements with the USA and other Central American countries, reducing tariffs on major exports.

DEFENCE
In 2003 defence expenditure totalled US$31m. (US$6 per capita), representing 1·2% of GDP.

Army
There are six regional commands. Strength (2002) 12,000.

Navy
The Nicaraguan Navy was some 800 strong in 2002.

Air Force
The Air Force has been semi-independent since 1947. Personnel (2002) 1,200, with no combat aircraft and 15 armed helicopters.

INTERNATIONAL RELATIONS
Nicaragua is a member of the UN, WTO, OAS, Inter-American Development Bank, ACS, IOM, SELA and the Central American Common Market.

ECONOMY
In 2002 agriculture accounted for 18·0% of GDP, industry 25·0% and services 57·0%.

Overview
Nicaragua, one of Latin America's poorest countries, suffers from low productivity, high current account deficit, high unemployment and a severe external debt burden. As a result the economy is dependent on foreign aid, amounting to 20% of GDP. Coffee and meat account for around 40% of exports. The collapse of coffee prices has had serious impact on rural living standards. The country's leading trading partners are the USA, the members of the Central American Common Market and the EU. Corruption is a problem. Structural reforms are focused on government procurement, the reform of social security and privatization. The unemployment rate is 8–10%. Half the population lives in poverty and about 17% fall below the extreme poverty line.

Currency
The monetary unit is the *córdoba* (NIO), of 100 *centavos*, which replaced the córdoba oro in 1991 at par. Inflation was 6·6% in 2003 and 9·3% in 2004. In May 2002 foreign exchange reserves were US$402m. In March 2002 total money supply was 4,754m. córdobas.

Budget
In 2002 budgetary central government revenue was 11,142m. córdobas (9,357m. córdobas in 2001) and expenditure 9,493m. córdobas (10,316m. córdobas in 2001). Principal sources of revenue in 2002: taxes on goods and services, 5,473m. córdobas; grants, 2,579m. córdobas; taxes on income, profits and capital gains, 1,610m. córdobas. Main items of expenditure by economic type in 2002: compensation of employees, 3,444m. córdobas; grants, 2,504m. córdobas; interest, 1,694m. córdobas.

Performance

Real GDP growth was 2·3% in 2003 and 5·1% in 2004. Total GDP in 2004 was US$4·4bn.

Banking and Finance

The Central Bank of Nicaragua came into operation on 1 Jan. 1961 as an autonomous bank of issue, absorbing the issue department of the National Bank. The *President* is Dr Mario Alonso Icabalceta. There were seven private commercial banks in 2000.

There is a stock exchange in Managua.

ENERGY AND NATURAL RESOURCES

Environment

Nicaragua's carbon dioxide emissions from the consumption and flaring of fossil fuels in 2002 were the equivalent of 0·7 tonnes per capita.

Electricity

Installed capacity in 2000 was 0·6m. kW. In 2000, 2·29bn. kWh were produced; consumption per capita in 2000 was 474 kWh.

Minerals

Production of gold in 2001 was 3,745 kg; silver (2001), 2,498 kg; limestone (2001), 580,000 tonnes.

Agriculture

In 2001 there were 1·94m. ha. arable land and 236,000 ha. permanent cropland. 95,000 ha. were irrigated in 2001. Production (in 1,000 tonnes) in 2000: sugarcane, 4,000; maize, 364; rice, 285; dry beans, 114; sorghum, 102; bananas, 92; coffee, 82; oranges, 71; groundnuts, 67; cassava, 52; pineapples, 47; plantains, 40; soybeans, 23.

In 2000 there were 1·66m. cattle, 400,000 pigs, 245,000 horses and 10m. chickens. Animal products (in 1,000 tonnes), 2000: beef and veal, 49; pork, bacon and ham, 6; poultry, 39; milk, 231; eggs, 30.

Forestry

The forest area in 2000 was 3·28m. ha., or 27·0% of the land area. Timber production was 5·88m. cu. metres in 2001.

Fisheries

In 2001 the catch was 22,799 tonnes (21,748 tonnes from sea fishing), up from 4,582 tonnes in 1989.

INDUSTRY

Industry contributed 26·0% of GDP in 2001, with manufacturing accounting for 14·4%. Important industries include chemicals, textiles, metal products, oil refining and food processing. Production in 2000 (in 1,000 tonnes): cement, 568; residual fuel oil, 411; raw sugar, 398; distillate fuel oil, 205; petrol, 102; wheat flour (2001), 60; vegetable oil (2001), 21; rum (1998), 7·7m. litres; sawnwood (2002), 45,000 cu. metres.

Labour

The workforce in 2001 was 1,900,400 (1,315,000 males). In 2001, 1,701,700 persons were in employment, of whom 739,000 were engaged in agriculture, hunting, forestry and fishing; 294,300 in community, social and personal services; 279,800 in wholesale and retail trade, and restaurants and hotels; and 131,600 in manufacturing. There were 178,000 unemployed in 2000, a rate of 9·8%.

INTERNATIONAL TRADE

Foreign debt was US$6,485m. in 2002.

Imports and Exports

Imports and exports in US$1m.:

	1998	1999	2000	2001	2002
Imports f.o.b.	1,397·1	1,698·2	1,653·1	1,620·4	1,636·4
Exports f.o.b.	580·1	552·4	649·9	614·6	605·1

Main imports in 1999 were: machinery and transport equipment, 29·8%; chemicals, 15·2%; foodstuffs, 14·7%; petroleum and related products, 7·7%. Principal exports were: coffee, 27·8%; seafood, 13·5%; meat, 8·8%; gold, 5·9%.

Main import suppliers, 1999: USA, 33·2%; Costa Rica, 12·1%; Guatemala, 7·8%; Panama, 7·1%; El Salvador, 5·8%; Japan, 5·3%. Main export markets, 1999: USA, 36·3%; El Salvador, 13·4%; Germany, 10·5%; Honduras, 6·8%; Costa Rica, 5·4%; Belgium, 4·0%.

COMMUNICATIONS

Roads

Road length in 2002 was 18,712 km, of which 11·4% were asphalted. In 2002 there were 83,168 passenger cars (15·6 per 1,000 inhabitants), 6,947 buses and coaches, 106,115 trucks and vans and 28,973 motorcycles and mopeds.

Civil Aviation

In 1999 scheduled airline traffic of Nicaragua-based carriers flew 0·8m. km, carrying 59,000 passengers (all on international flights). The Augusto Sandino international airport at Managua handled 754,000 passengers in 2001 (608,000 on international flights) and 20,000 tonnes of freight.

Shipping

The merchant marine totalled 4,000 GRT in 2002. The Pacific ports are Corinto (the largest), San Juan del Sur and Puerto Sandino through which pass most of the external trade. The chief eastern ports are El Bluff (for Bluefields) and Puerto Cabezas.

Telecommunications

In 2002 there were 411,600 telephone subscribers, or 76·6 per 1,000 population, and 150,000 PCs in use (27·9 for every 1,000 persons). Mobile phone subscribers numbered 202,800 in 2002. Nicaragua had 90,000 Internet users in 2002.

Postal Services

In 2002 there were 215 post offices.

SOCIAL INSTITUTIONS

Justice

The judicial power is vested in a Supreme Court of Justice at Managua, five chambers of second instance and 153 judges of lower courts.

The population in penal institutions in Oct. 2004 was 5,610 (100 per 100,000 of national population).

Education

Adult literacy rate in 2003 was 76·7% (male, 76·8%; female, 76·6%). In 2002 there were 8,251 primary schools with 923,391 pupils, 364,012 secondary school pupils and (2001) 70,925 students at university level.

In 1994–95 there were two universities and three specialized universities (agriculture; engineering; polytechnic) with 1,260 academic staff.

In 2000–01 total expenditure on education came to 13·8% of total government expenditure. A 15-year National Plan for Education is under way which aims to transform education by means of expanding provision in rural areas, providing greater access to pre-school and adult education, improving the quality of teacher training, modernizing the curriculum and investing in materials and infrastructure.

Health

In 2003 there were 32 hospitals, with a provision of nine beds per 10,000 population. There were 8,986 physicians, 1,585 dentists and 5,862 nurses in 2003.

RELIGION

The prevailing form of religion is Roman Catholicism (3·59m. adherents in 2001), but religious liberty is guaranteed by the Constitution. There were also 810,000 Protestants in 2001. There is one arch-bishopric, seven bishoprics and one cardinal.

CULTURE

World Heritage Sites

Nicaragua has one site on the UNESCO World Heritage List: the Ruins of León Viejo (inscribed on the list in 2000), a 16th century Spanish settlement.

Broadcasting

Broadcasting is administered by the Instituto Nicaraguense de Telecomunicaciones y Correos (Telcor). There were 640,000 television sets (colour by NTSC) in 2001 and 1·37m. radio receivers in 2000.

Press

In 1996 there were four daily newspapers in Managua, with a total circulation of 135,000.

Tourism

In 2002 there were 472,000 foreign tourists, spending US$116m.

DIPLOMATIC REPRESENTATIVES

Of Nicaragua in the United Kingdom (Suite 31, Vicarage House, 58–60 Kensington Church St., London, W8 4DP)
Ambassador: Piero P. Coen Ubilla.

Of the United Kingdom in Nicaragua (embassy in Managua closed in March 2004)
Ambassador: Georgina Butler (resides in San José, Costa Rica).

Of Nicaragua in the USA (1627 New Hampshire Ave., NW, Washington, D.C., 20009)
Ambassador: Salvador Stadthagen.

Of the USA in Nicaragua (Km. 4½ Carretera Sur, Managua)
Ambassador: Paul Trivelli.

Of Nicaragua to the United Nations
Ambassador: Eduardo J. Sevilla Somoza.

Of Nicaragua to the European Union
Ambassador: Vacant.
Chargé d'Affaires a.i.: Ricardo Paúl Lira.

FURTHER READING

Dematteis, L. and Vail, C., *Nicaragua: a Decade of Revolution.* New York, 1991
Dijkstra, G., *Industrialization in Sandinista Nicaragua: Policy and Party in a Mixed Economy.* Boulder (CO), 1992
Jones, Adam, *Beyond the Barricades: Nicaragua and the Struggle for the Sandinista Press, 1979–1998.* Ohio Univ. Press, Athens (OH), 2002
Walker, T. W., *Nicaragua: the Land of Sandino.* 2nd ed. Boulder (CO), 1991
Woodward, R. L., *Nicaragua.* [Bibliography] 2nd ed. ABC-Clio, Oxford and Santa Barbara (CA), 1994

National Statistical Office: Dirección General de Estadística y Censos, Managua.
Website (Spanish only): http://www.inec.gob.ni/

NIGER

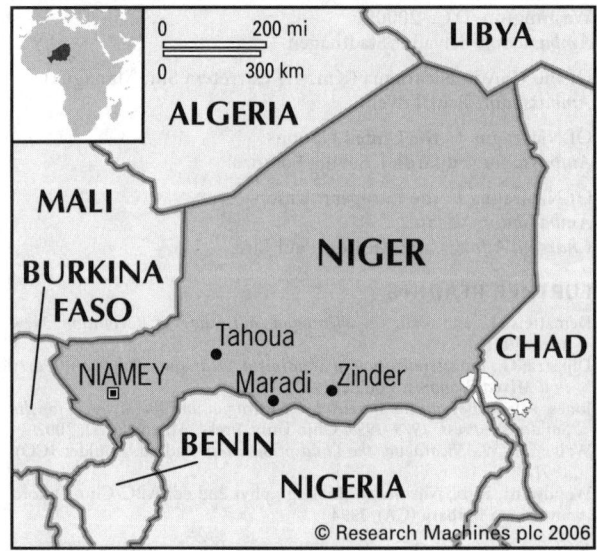

République du Niger

Capital: Niamey
Population projection, 2010: 16·43m.
GDP per capita, 2003: (PPP$) 835
HDI/world rank: 0·281/177

KEY HISTORICAL EVENTS

Niger was occupied by France after 1883. It achieved full independence on 3 Aug. 1960. Guerrilla activity by Tuaregs of the Armed Resistance Organization (ORA) seeking local autonomy in the north continued into 1995. On 27 Jan. 1996 the army chief of staff Gen. (then Col.) Barré Maïnassara deposed President Mahamane Ousmane and dissolved parliament. In April 1999 President Maïnassara was assassinated by bodyguards at Niamey airport. A week after the President's assassination, Daouda Mallam Wanké, leader of the presidential guard and the officer widely suspected of being behind the killing, was named as Maïnassara's successor. In Aug. 2005 severe food shortages led to more than 2·5m. people facing starvation.

TERRITORY AND POPULATION

Niger is bounded in the north by Algeria and Libya, east by Chad, south by Nigeria, southwest by Benin and Burkina Faso, and west by Mali. Area, 1,186,408 sq. km, with a population at the 2001 census (provisional) of 10,790,352; density, 9 per sq. km. The estimated population in 2005 was 13,957,000. In 2003, 77·8% of the population were rural.

The UN gives a projected population for 2010 of 16·43m.

The country is divided into the capital, Niamey, an autonomous district, and seven departments. Area, population and chief towns at the 2001 census (provisional):

Department	Sq. km	Population	Chief town	Population
Agadez	634,209	313,274	Agadez	76,957
Diffa	140,216	329,658	Diffa	23,233
Dosso	31,002	1,479,095	Dosso	43,293
Maradi	38,581	2,202,035	Maradi	147,038
Niamey	670	674,950	Niamey	674,950
Tahoua	106,677	1,908,100	Tahoua	72,446
Tillabéry	89,623	1,858,342	Tillabéry	16,181
Zinder	145,430	2,024,898	Zinder	170,574

The population is composed chiefly of Hausa (53%), Songhai and Djerma (21%), Fulani (10%), Tuareg (10%) and Kanuri-Manga (4%). The official language is French. Hausa, Djerma and Fulani are national languages.

SOCIAL STATISTICS

Estimates, 2000: births, 593,000; deaths, 205,000. Estimated birth rate in 2000 was 55·2 per 1,000 population (the highest in the world); estimated death rate, 19·1. Niger has one of the youngest populations of any country, with 49% of the population under the age of 15. Infant mortality, 2001, 156 per 1,000 live births. Annual population growth rate, 1992–2002, 3·5%. Expectation of life at birth, 2003, 44·3 years for males and 44·4 for females. Fertility rate, 2001, 8·0 children per woman (the highest anywhere in the world).

CLIMATE

Precipitation determines the geographical division into a southern zone of agriculture, a central zone of pasturage and a desert-like northern zone. The country lacks water, with the exception of the southwestern districts, which are watered by the Niger and its tributaries, and the southern zone, where there are a number of wells. Niamey, 95°F (35°C). Annual rainfall varies from 22" (560 mm) in the south to 7" (180 mm) in the Sahara zone. The rainy season lasts from May until Sept., but there are periodic droughts.

CONSTITUTION AND GOVERNMENT

Theoretically, Niger is a unitary multi-party democracy. The *President* is directly elected for a five-year term renewable once. There is 113-member *National Assembly* elected for a five-year term by proportional representation.

At a referendum on 12 May 1996, 90% of votes cast were in favour of a new constitution; turnout was 33%. The new constitution was promulgated on 18 July 1999.

National Anthem

'Auprès du grand Niger puissant' ('By the banks of the mighty great Niger'); words by M. Thiriet, tune by R. Jacquet and N. Frionnet.

RECENT ELECTIONS

In the first round of presidential elections held on 16 Nov. 2004 incumbent Tandja Mamadou won 40·7% of the votes followed by former prime minister Mahamadou Issoufou with 24·6%; former president Mahamane Ousmane with 17·4%; a second former prime minister, Amadou Cheiffou, with 6·4%; former foreign minister Moumouni Adamou Djermakoye with 6·1%; and a third former prime minister, Hamid Algabid, with 4·9%. Turnout was 48·3%. In the run-off on 4 Dec. 2004 Tandja Mamadou won 65·5% of the vote with Mahamadou Issoufou taking 34·5%. Turnout was 45·0%.

Parliamentary elections were held on 4 Dec. 2004. The National Movement for the Development Society (MNSD) won 38 seats; the Democratic and Social Convention, 22; the Nigerien Party for Democracy and Socialism, 17; the Social Democratic Rally, 7; the Rally for Democracy and Progress, 6; the Alliance for Democracy and Progress, 5; and the Party for Socialism and Democracy in Niger, 1. Turnout was 44·7%.

CURRENT ADMINISTRATION

President: Tandja Mamadou; b. 1938 (MNSD; sworn in 22 Dec. 1999 and re-elected in Dec. 2004).

In March 2006 the government comprised:

Prime Minister: Hama Amadou; b. 1950 (MNSD; sworn in 3 Jan. 2000, having previously held office Feb. 1995–Jan. 1996).

Minister of Animal Resources: Abdoulaye Jina. *Defence:* Hassane Souley 'Bonto'. *Basic Education and Literacy:* Hamani Arouna. *Finance and Economy:* Ali Lamine Zène. *Foreign Affairs and Co-operation:* Aïchatou Mindaoudou. *Health and Disease Control:* Ary Ibrahim. *Secondary and Higher Education, Research and Technology:* Ousmane Galidama. *Interior and Decentralization:* Mounkaïla Mody. *Justice and Keeper of the Seals:* Matty Elhadji Salissou. *Mines and Energy:* Mohamed Abdoulahi. *Privatization and Restructuring of Enterprises:* Gazoli Laouali Rahamou. *Civil Service and Labour:* Kanda Siptey. *Transport:* Souleymane Kane. *Agricultural Development:* Labo Moussa. *Youth, Sports and Francophonie:* Abdouramane Seydou. *Promotion of Women and Protection of Children:* Ousmane Zeinalou Mouley. *Territorial and Community Development:* Mahamane Moussa. *Commerce, Industry and Promotion of Private Sector:* Sala Habi Mahamadou Salissou. *Urban Development, Housing and Public Property:* Diallo Aissa Abdoulaye. *Culture, Arts and Communication:* Oumarou Adari. *Population and Social Work:* Boukari Zila Mohamadou. *Tourism and Handicrafts:* Amadou Nouhou. *Professional and Technical Training, Responsible for Youth Employment:* Abdou Daouda. *Minister of State Responsible for Water Resources, Environment and Desertification Control:* Abdou Labo. *Minister of State Responsible for Equipment:* Seyni Oumarou. *Minister Responsible for Institutions and Government Spokesman:* Mohamed Ben Omar.

CURRENT LEADERS

Tandja Mamadou

Position
President

Introduction
Both head of state and of government, Tandja Mamadou became president in Dec. 1999 and was re-elected for a second and final term in Dec. 2004. He is also leader of the National Movement for the Development Society (MNSD).

Early Life
Tandja Mamadou was born in 1938. A former lieutenant-colonel, he began his career in politics after taking part in a coup to overthrow Niger's first elected president, Diori Hamani. As minister of the interior, he was responsible for policing, national security and immigration.

In 1993 Mamadou ran for president but lost to Mahamane Ousmane. He ran again in 1996 but lost after a coup put Ibrahim Barré Maïnassara in power. In 1999 Maïnassara was assassinated, signalling a return to military government. Democracy was restored within the year and elections were held in Oct.–Nov. Mamadou was sworn in on 22 Dec. 1999, having defeated former prime minister Mahamadou Issoufou in the presidential poll. Shortly afterwards, Mamadou made Hama Amadou prime minister.

Career in Office
When Tandja Mamadou took office Niger was heavily in debt, foreign aid having been cut following the Maïnassara coup. His priorities have since been to promote economic development, secure foreign investment and reduce government spending.

After drawing attention to environmental threats including soil erosion, deforestation and poaching, hunting was banned. In Oct. 2000 Mamadou gave support to the ECOWAS public health initiative aiming to immunize 70m. children against polio. In 2001 students of the University of Niamey staged violent protests against reductions in their government grants. Aug. 2002 saw soldiers mutiny in the east of the country and in the capital in protest at non-payment of wages and poor conditions.

In Jan. 2003 US President George W. Bush claimed to have documentary evidence that Iraq had attempted to buy uranium from Niger to use in the production of nuclear weapons. However, in March the IAEA (International Atomic Energy Agency) declared the documents forgeries and an apology was issued. Also in 2003 the government banned slavery in Niger, although it is likely that the practice continues.

In Nov.–Dec. 2004 Mamadou again beat Issoufou for the presidency, receiving almost two-thirds of the vote in the second round, and his party won the largest number of parliamentary seats. Earlier in the year Niger held its first municipal elections, with parties backing the president winning the most seats.

Niger remains one of the poorest countries in the world, with high levels of unemployment and large foreign debt. Although Mamadou has been praised for restoring stability, he continues to face internal hostility. This intensified in 2005 after the government cancelled a ceremony to release 7,000 slaves, claiming that slavery had ceased to exist since 2003. During 2005 there were widespread protests at tax increases, and in Aug. Mamadou was criticized for denying that the country was gripped by famine, despite a UN warning that drought had dramatically increased malnutrition. However, he has won favour for his support for the UNICEF campaign to introduce free pre-natal care.

DEFENCE

Selective conscription for two years operates. Defence expenditure totalled US$25m. in 2003 (US$2 per capita), representing 1·0% of GDP.

Army

There are three military districts. Strength (2002) 5,200. There are additional paramilitary forces of some 5,400.

Air Force

In 2002 the Air Force had 100 personnel. There are no combat aircraft.

INTERNATIONAL RELATIONS

Niger is a member of the UN, WTO, the African Union, African Development Bank, ECOWAS, the Lake Chad Basin Commission, OIC, Islamic Development Bank, IOM, International Organization of the Francophonie, and is an ACP member state of the ACP-EU relationship.

ECONOMY

Agriculture accounted for 39·6% of GDP in 2002, industry 17·0% and services 43·4%.

Currency

The unit of currency is the *franc CFA* (XOF) with a parity of 655·957 francs CFA to one euro. In May 2002 total money supply was 84,319m. francs CFA and foreign exchange reserves were US$85m. Gold reserves were 11,000 troy oz in June 2000. Inflation in 2004 was 0·4%.

Budget

In 2000 revenue (in 1,000m. francs CFA) was 162·2 and expenditure 204·8. Taxes accounted for 63·4% of revenues, and external aids and gifts 32·1%. Current expenditures accounted for 67·6% of expenditure.

Performance

Real GDP growth was 5·3% in 2003 and 0·9% in 2004; total GDP in 2004 was US$3·1bn.

Banking and Finance

The regional Central Bank of West African States (BCEAO)—*Acting Governor,* Justin Baro Damo—functions as the bank of issue. There were six commercial banks in 2002, three development banks and a savings bank.

There is a stock exchange in Niamey.

ENERGY AND NATURAL RESOURCES

Environment
In 2002 Niger's carbon dioxide emissions from the consumption and flaring of fossil fuels were the equivalent of 0·1 tonnes per capita.

Electricity
Installed capacity was 0·1m. kW in 2000. Production in 2000 amounted to about 238m. kWh, with consumption per capita an estimated 42 kWh.

Minerals
Large uranium deposits are mined at Arlit and Akouta. Uranium production (2002), 3,075 tonnes. Niger's uranium production is exceeded only by those of Canada and Australia. Phosphates are mined in the Niger valley, and coal reserves are being exploited by open-cast mining (production of hard coal in 2000 was an estimated 175,000 tonnes). Salt production in 1997 was 3,000 tonnes.

Agriculture
Production is dependent upon adequate rainfall. There were 4·49m. ha. of arable land in 2001 and 11,000 ha. of permanent crops. 66,000 ha. were irrigated in 2001. There were 128 tractors in 2001. Production estimates in 2000 (in 1,000 tonnes): millet, 2,250; sorghum, 400; onions, 180; sugarcane, 140; cassava, 120; groundnuts, 110; rice, 73; tomatoes, 65; sweet potatoes, 35.

Livestock (2000): cattle, 2·22m.; goats, 6·60m.; sheep, 4·30m.; asses, 530,000; camels, 410,000; chickens, 20m. Livestock products (in 1,000 tonnes), 2000: milk, 168; meat, 125; cheese, 14; eggs, 9.

Forestry
There is a government programme of afforestation as a protection from desert encroachment. There were 1·33m. ha. of forests in 2000 (1·0% of the land area). Timber production in 2001 was 3·27m. cu. metres, mainly for fuel.

Fisheries
There are fisheries on the River Niger and along the shores of Lake Chad. In 2001 the catch was 20,800 tonnes, exclusively from inland waters.

INDUSTRY
Some small manufacturing industries, mainly in Niamey, produce textiles, food products, furniture and chemicals. Output of cement in 2000 (estimate), 30,000 tonnes.

Labour
The labour force in 1996 totalled 4,497,000 (56% males). Nearly 90% of the economically active population in 1994 were engaged in agriculture, fisheries and forestry.

Trade Unions
The national confederation is the *Union Syndicale des Travailleurs du Niger,* which has 15,000 members in 31 unions.

INTERNATIONAL TRADE
Foreign debt was US$1,797m. in 2002.

Imports and Exports
In 2003 imports were valued at US$488·5m. (US$371·2m. in 2002) and exports at US$351·8m. (US$279·4m. in 2002). In 1998 the main imports were (in US$1m.): foodstuffs, 120·6; refined petroleum, 56·4; machinery and transport equipment, 55·5; manufactured goods, 52·8; and chemicals, 41·0. The main exports in 1998 were: uranium, 133·0; road vehicles, 37·2; cigarettes, 34·6;

vegetables (especially onions), 29·7; textiles, 27·2; and livestock, 26·2.

The main import suppliers in 1999 were France (22·4%), Côte d'Ivoire (15·1%), China (8·3%) and Nigeria (8·0%). The main export destinations in 1999 were France (44·5%), Nigeria (27·0%), Japan (17·9%) and Spain (4·2%).

COMMUNICATIONS

Roads
In 2002 there were approximately 10,100 km of roads including 800 km of paved roads. Niamey and Zinder are the termini of two trans-Sahara motor routes; the Hoggar–Aïr–Zinder road extends to Kano and the Tanezrouft–Gao–Niamey road to Benin. A 648-km 'uranium road' runs from Arlit to Tahoua. There were, in 2002, 16,200 passenger cars (1·4 per 1,000 inhabitants) and 18,200 trucks and vans.

Civil Aviation
There is an international airport at Niamey (Diori Hamani Airport), which handled 87,000 passengers in 2001 (85,000 on international flights). In 2003 there were international flights to Abidjan, Bamako, Casablanca, Dakar, Khartoum, Libreville, Ouagadougou, Paris and Tripoli. In 1999 scheduled airline traffic of Niger-based carriers flew 3·0m. km, carrying 84,000 passengers (all on international flights).

Shipping
Sea-going vessels can reach Niamey (300 km inside the country) between Sept. and March.

Telecommunications
Niger had 23,800 telephone subscribers in 2001 (2·1 per 1,000 population)—the lowest penetration rate of any country in the world. In 2002 there were 7,000 PCs in use (0·6 per 1,000 persons) and 16,600 mobile phone subscribers. Internet users numbered 15,000 in 2002.

Postal Services
In 2003 there were 52 post offices, or one for every 230,000 persons.

SOCIAL INSTITUTIONS

Justice
There are Magistrates' and Assize Courts at Niamey, Zinder and Maradi, and justices of the peace in smaller centres. The Court of Appeal is at Niamey.

The population in penal institutions in 2002 was approximately 6,000 (52 per 100,000 of national population).

Education
In 2000–01 there were 578 teachers for 12,300 children in pre-primary schools and 15,668 teachers for 656,589 pupils in primary schools. During the period 1990–95 only 18% of females of primary school age were enrolled in school. In 2001–02 there were 112,033 pupils in secondary schools. There were 13,400 students in tertiary education (806 academic staff) in 2000–01. There is a university and an Islamic university.

Adult literacy in 2003 was 14·4% (male, 19·6%; female, 9·4%), among the lowest in the world.

In 2000–01 total expenditure on education came to 2·8% of GNP.

Health
In 1998 there were 1·2 hospital beds per 10,000 inhabitants. There were 386 physicians, 21 dentists, 2,668 nurses, 461 midwives and 63 pharmacists in 2002.

RELIGION
In 2001 there were 9·39m. Sunni Muslims. There are some Roman Catholics, and traditional animist beliefs are widespread.

CULTURE

World Heritage Sites

Niger has three sites on the UNESCO World Heritage List: the Aïr and Ténéré Natural Reserves (inscribed on the list in 1991), part of the largest protected area in Africa (7·7m. ha.); and the 'W' National Park of Niger (1996), a savannah and forested area of biodiversity.

Broadcasting

La Voix du Sahel and Télé-Sahel under the government's Office de Radiodiffusion Télévision du Niger are responsible for radio and TV broadcasting (colour by PAL). In 2000 there were 1·27m. radio sets and in 2001 there were 110,000 TV sets.

Press

In 1998 there were two daily newspapers with a combined circulation of 4,000.

Tourism

In 2002 there were 60,000 foreign tourists; spending by tourists totalled US$19m.

DIPLOMATIC REPRESENTATIVES

Of Niger in the United Kingdom
Ambassador: Adamou Seydou (resides in Paris).

Of the United Kingdom in Niger
Ambassador: Gordon Wetherell (resides in Accra, Ghana).

Of Niger in the USA (2204 R. St., NW, Washington, D.C., 20008)
Ambassador: Vacant.
Chargé d'Affaires a.i.: Fatima Djibo Sidikou.

Of the USA in Niger (BP 11201, Rue des Ambassades, Niamey)
Ambassador: Vacant.
Chargé d'Affaires a.i.: John Davison.

Of Niger to the United Nations
Ambassador: Aboubacar Ibrahim Abani.

Of Niger to the European Union
Ambassador: Abdou Agbarry.

FURTHER READING

Miles, W. F. S., *Hausaland Divided: Colonialism and Independence in Nigeria and Niger.* Cornell Univ. Press, 1994
Zamponi, Lynda F., *Niger.* [Bibliography] ABC-Clio, Oxford and Santa Barbara (CA), 1994

National Statistical Office: Direction de la Statistique et de l'Informatique, Ministère du Plan, Niamey.

NIGERIA

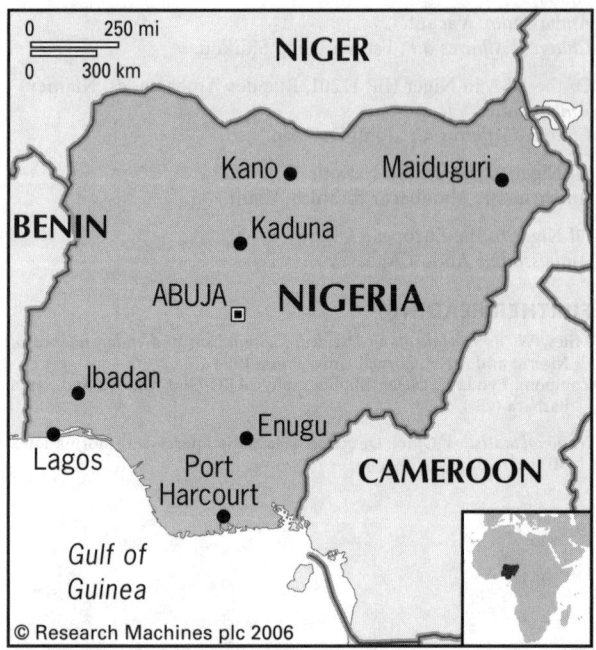

0 250 mi
0 300 km

NIGER

Kano • Maiduguri •

BENIN

Kaduna •

ABUJA □ NIGERIA

Ibadan •

Enugu •

Lagos • Port Harcourt

CAMEROON

Gulf of Guinea

© Research Machines plc 2006

Federal Republic of Nigeria

Capital: Abuja
Population projection, 2010: 145·99m.
GDP per capita, 2003: (PPP$) 1,050
HDI/world rank: 0·453/158

KEY HISTORICAL EVENTS

The earliest evidence of human settlement in Nigeria dates from 9000 BC and by 2000 BC its inhabitants were cultivating crops and domestic animals. However, the first organized society was of the Nok people, from around 800 BC to AD 200. Traces of Nok influence are visible in Nigerian art today, particularly in areas such as Igbo, Ukwe, Esie and Benin City. By AD 1000, Nok had given way to the Kanem, thanks to the trans-Saharan trade route that ran from West Africa to the Mediterranean.

In the 11th century northern Nigeria split into seven independent Hausa city-states, Biram, Daura, Gobir, Kano, Katsina, Rano and Zaria. By the 14th century, two states had developed in the south, Oyo and Benin, with the Igbo people of the southeast living in small village communities. South of the Hausa states and west of the Niger, the Ife flourished between the 11th and 15th centuries. The importance of the Ife civilization is evident today; all Yoruba states claim that their leaders are descended from the Ife as a way of establishing legitimacy, and its ritual is imitated in their modern public ceremonies.

Most of the north was held by the Songhai empire by the early 16th century, only to be taken later in the century by Kanem-Bornu, allowing the Hausa states to retain their autonomy. At the end of the 18th century, Fulani religious groups waged war in the north, merging states to create the single Islamic state of the Sokoto Caliphate.

In the late 15th century Portuguese navigators, following the demise of the spice trade, began to purchase slaves from middlemen in the region. They were followed by British, French and Dutch traders. Wealthy traders established towns such as Bonny, Owome and Okrika. Slave trading had a profound effect on Nigeria. From the 1650s until the 1860s, it caused a forced migration of around 3·5m. people. Within Nigeria itself, the defensive measures adopted to avoid enslavement led to the reinforcement of ethnic distinctions and of the north-south divide.

After the abolition of the slave trade in Britain in 1807, attempts to find a lucrative alternative and to discourage the predominance of slavery in Nigeria (other countries continued to trade in slaves until 1875) led to a large-scale campaign to encourage the production of palm oil for export. This itself caused the development of an internal slave trade, involving slaves in the collection and manufacture of palm fruits, as well as the transportation of the oil. The British also took over the mines at Jos at the expense of the livelihoods of independent tin producers. When heavy reliance on mining exports resulted in the neglect of agricultural work, Nigeria experienced its first food shortage.

Religious missions were active at this time, with Presbyterians, Methodists, Baptists and the Church Missionary Society (CMS) operating in Lagos, Abeokuta, Ibadan, Oyo and Ogbomoso. The CMS pioneered trade on the Niger by encouraging merchants to run steamboats, partially as a means of travel for the missionaries but also to ship goods.

In 1804 Usuman dan Fodio began a 'Holy war' to reform the practice of Islam in the north, conquering the Hausa city-states, though Kanem-Bornu retained its independence. However, by the late 19th century Kanem-Bornu's power was in decline. Usuman's son, Muhammed Bello, established a state centred at Sokoto, controlling most of northern Nigeria for the rest of the century. In the south, the Oyo region was troubled by civil wars, only brought to a close when the British intervened and the Oyo Empire collapsed. Britain took Lagos as its colony in 1861.

In 1879 Sir George Goldie gained all British firms trading on the Niger, and in the 1880s took over French companies trading there, signing treaties with African leaders and enabling Britain's domination of southern Nigeria in 1884–85. In 1887, Jaja, an African trader based in the Niger Delta, was deported following his fierce opposition to European competition. Goldie's firm received a British Royal Charter as the Royal Niger Company to administer the Niger River and north Nigeria, and this monopoly of trade on the river angered Africans and Europeans alike. The Royal Niger Company also lacked sufficient power to control north Nigeria. In 1900 its charter was revoked and British forces moved in, taking Sokoto in 1903. By 1906 Britain controlled Nigeria as the Colony (Lagos), the Protectorate of Southern Nigeria and the Protectorate of Northern Nigeria, amalgamating the regions in 1914 to establish the Colony and Protectorate of Nigeria. The administration was based on existing leadership systems. Yet the appointment of African officials failed to gain wide acceptance from Nigeria's people. The British governor made all major decisions, and the traditional authority of African rulers was weakened irreparably.

British dominance met with major resistance from the Nigerian people. In the south, the tribal Yoruba group, the Ijebu, fought against colonial rule in 1892, as did the Aro in the east and the Aniocha (both Igbo groups) in the west. There were also rebellions in the north. The British forces responded with brutality, destroying the homes of many Nigerians in order to secure their capitulation.

British colonial rule brought development in the transportation and communications systems and a shift towards cash crops. Western and Christian influences prevailed, including widespread use of the English language. This influence spread far more rapidly in the south, where British control had been secure over a longer period, and this added to the growing disparity between north and south. Nigerian forces helped defeat the German army in Cameroon during the First World War, involved in an arduous campaign until 1916.

Growing unrest and widespread anticolonialism became focused in the 1920s as demands for African representation increased. In 1923 Herbert Macaulay, grandson of the first Nigerian to be ordained, established the first Nigerian political party, the Nigerian National Democratic Party. In 1944 he united the party with several others to form the National Council of Nigeria and the Cameroon (NCNC). In response to this activity, the British attempted to quell demands for an end to colonial rule by granting some political reforms. In 1947 they announced a new constitution that they claimed would give traditional authorities a greater voice. This met with great resistance, and in 1951 the British agreed to form a new constitution that would provide for elected representation on a regional basis.

Three political parties developed, the National Council of Nigeria and the Cameroons (later the National Convention of Nigerian Citizens), largely supported by the Igbo, the Action Group, with mostly Yoruba membership, and the Northern People's Congress. When the constitution failed in 1952, a new one divided Nigeria into three regions, Eastern, Western and Northern, plus the federal territory of Lagos. In 1956 the Western and Eastern regions became self-governing, as did the Northern region in 1959.

In 1960 Nigeria declared independence. Elections failed to elect any one party by a majority, and the NPC and the NCNC formed a coalition government, with Abukar Tafawa Balewa (NPC) as prime minister. Nnamdi Azikiwe, who had helped Herbert Macaulay to establish the NCNC in 1944, was governor-general. When Nigeria became a republic in 1963 Azikiwe became president.

Continuing conflict between north and south undermined the new republic. In 1966 fighting culminated in a military coup that installed Maj.-Gen. Aguiyi-Ironsi, an Igbo, as head of a military government. Another coup later in the year placed Lieut.-Col. Yakubu Gowon in power and saw many northern Igbo massacred. In May 1967 the Igbo people of the south declared their region independent from the rest of the country, naming the breakaway republic Biafra. Civil war raged for three years until federal Nigeria triumphed at the price of 1m. dead and widespread famine and destruction.

This was followed by a period of relative prosperity as oil prices rose. Foreign interest and investment flourished but government overspending and high levels of corruption and crime led to social chaos. In the 1980s recession sent oil prices down, and Nigeria found itself struggling with major debt, rising inflation and mass unemployment.

Gowon's regime was overthrown in 1975 by Gen. Murtala Muhammed whose plans for a new capital to be built at Abuja drained the economy. He was assassinated in 1976, to be succeeded by Gen. Olusegun Obasanjo who oversaw the transition to civilian rule, while juggling the need for Western aid with his support for African nationalist movements.

In 1979 elections brought Alhaji Shehu Shagari to power. Shagari's government came under popular attack for alleged corruption but he was re-elected in 1983, amidst rumours of voting irregularities. Under Shagari relations with the USA improved, heralded by a visit from President Jimmy Carter. However, dogged by worsening economic problems, Shagari was ousted in a military coup in 1983 and replaced by Gen. Muhammadu Buhari. Buhari's regime quickly fell out of favour with the public when it arrested not only the politicians blamed for the country's social and economic problems, but also journalists and other civilians.

A bloodless coup in 1985 brought to power Maj.-Gen. Ibrahim Babangida, who promulgated a new constitution with the aim of returning to civilian government. Babangida, however, clung to power and refused to accept electoral defeat in 1990, 1992 and 1993. Unrest eventually forced his resignation, but after just three months of rule by an interim leader, one of Babangida's long-term allies, Gen. Sani Abacha, became president and closed down all unions and political institutions. He extended his military rule for a further three years in 1995, proposing a return to civilian rule after this period. To this end five political parties were formed in 1996. However, the Abacha regime attracted international controversy when it executed writer Ken Saro-Wiwa and eight other human rights activists for alleged seditious political activity. Nigeria was suspended from the Commonwealth as a result. Further outrage followed with the arrest of former leader Obasanjo and the murder of the wife of leading political dissident, Chief Moshood Abiola, who had claimed victory at the presidential elections of 1993. Rioting and civil unrest broke out across Nigeria and Abacha's family was accused of siphoning off US$4bn. of national assets.

Abacha died in office in 1998. Maj.-Gen. Abdusalam Abubakar came to power and brought about a return to civilian rule, scrapping plans that would have extended Abacha's rule and releasing political prisoners. Abiola was scheduled to be freed as part of this process but died the day before his scheduled release. In Feb. 1999 Nigeria chose Obasanjo, the 62-year-old retired general and previous military leader, to be president.

This transition of power greatly improved Nigeria's international standing and the country was readmitted to the Commonwealth. However, tribal and religious conflict continued and fighting between the Igbo Christians and Hausa Muslims over the implementation of Islamic law has left thousands dead. The country's infrastructure remains fragile and Obasanjo's re-election in 2003 was accompanied by violence and rumours of ballot-rigging and bribery.

TERRITORY AND POPULATION

Nigeria is bounded in the north by Niger, east by Chad and Cameroon, south by the Gulf of Guinea and west by Benin. It has an area of 923,768 sq. km (356,667 sq. miles). For sovereignty over the Bakassi Peninsula see CAMEROON: Territory and Population. Census population, 1991, 88,244,581 (43,969,970 females; urban, 36%); population density, 95·8 per sq. km. Estimate, 2005, 131,530,000; density, 142 per sq. km. In 2003, 53·4% of the population were rural.

The UN gives a projected population for 2010 of 145·99m.

There were 30 states and a Federal Capital Territory (Abuja) in 1991.

Area, population and capitals of these states:

State	Area (in sq. km)	Population (1991 census)	Capital
Adamawa	36,917	2,124,049	Yola
Bauchi	64,605	4,294,413	Bauchi
Benue	34,059	2,780,398	Makurdi
Borno	70,898	2,596,589	Maiduguri
Jigawa	23,154	2,829,929	Dutse
Kaduna	46,053	3,969,252	Kaduna
Kano	20,131	5,362,040	Kano
Katsina	24,192	3,878,344	Katsina
Kebbi	36,800	2,062,226	Birnin-Kebbi
Kogi	29,833	2,099,046	Lokoja
Kwara	36,825	1,566,469	Ilorin
Niger	76,363	2,482,367	Minna
Plateau	58,030	3,283,784	Jos
Sokoto	65,735	4,392,391	Sokoto
Taraba	54,473	1,480,590	Jalingo
Yobe	45,502	1,411,481	Damaturu
Federal Capital Territory	7,315	378,671	Abuja
Total North	730,885	46,992,039	

State	Area (in sq. km)	Population (1991 census)	Capital
Abia	6,320	2,297,978	Umuahia
Akwa Ibom	7,081	2,359,736	Uyo
Anambra	4,844	2,767,903	Awka
Cross River	20,156	1,865,604	Calabar
Delta	17,698	2,570,181	Asaba
Edo	17,802	2,159,848	Benin City
Enugu	12,831	3,161,295	Enugu
Imo	5,530	2,485,499	Owerri
Lagos	3,345	5,685,781	Ikeja
Ogun	16,762	2,338,570	Abeokuta
Ondo	20,959	3,884,485	Akure
Osun	9,251	2,203,016	Oshogbo
Oyo	28,454	3,488,789	Ibadan
Rivers	21,850	3,983,857	Port-Harcourt
Total South	192,883	41,252,542	

Six new states were created in 1996, three in the north and three in the south. In the north, Zamfara State was created from Sokoto, with its headquarters at Gusau; Nassarawa State was created from Plateau, with its headquarters at Lafia; and Gombe State was created from Bauchi, with its headquarters at Gombe. In the south, Ekiti State was created from Ondo, with its capital at Ado-Ekiti; Bayelsa State was created from Rivers, with its headquarters at Yenagoa; and Ebonyi State was created by merging Abia and Enugu, with its headquarters at Abakaliki.

Abuja replaced Lagos as the federal capital and seat of government in Dec. 1991.

Estimated population of the largest cities, 1995:

Lagos	1,484,000[1]	Ikorodu	180,300
Ibadan	1,365,000	Ilawe-Ekiti	179,900
Ogbomosho	711,900	Owo	178,900
Kano	657,300	Ikirun	177,000
Oshogbo	465,000	Calabar	170,000
Ilorin	464,000	Shaki	169,700
Abeokuta	416,800	Ondo	165,400
Port Harcourt	399,700	Akure	158,200
Zaria	369,800	Gusau	154,000
Ilesha	369,000	Ijebu-Ode	152,500
Onitsha	362,700	Effon-Alaiye	149,300
Iwo	353,000	Kumo	144,400
Ado-Ekiti	350,500	Shomolu	144,100
Abuja (capital)	339,100	Oka	139,600
Kaduna	333,600	Ikare	137,300
Mushin	324,900	Sapele	135,800
Maiduguri	312,100	Deba Habe	135,400
Enugu	308,200	Minna	133,600
Ede	299,500	Warri	122,900
Aba	291,600	Bida	122,500
Ife	289,500	Ikire	120,200
Ila	257,400	Makurdi	120,100
Oyo	250,100	Lafia	119,500
Ikerre	238,500	Inisa	116,800
Benin City	223,900	Shagamu	114,300
Iseyin	211,800	Awka	108,400
Katsina	201,500	Gombe	105,200
Jos	201,200	Ejigbo	103,300
Sokoto	199,900	Igboho	103,300
Ilobu	194,400	Agege	100,300
Offa	192,300	Ugep	100,000

[1]Greater Lagos had a population of 12,763,000 in 1999.

There are about 250 ethnic groups. The largest linguistic groups are the Yoruba (17·5% of the total) and the Hausa (17·2%), followed by Igbo (13·3%), Fulani (10·7%), Ibibio (4·1%), Kanuri (3·6%), Egba (2·9%), Tiv (2·6%), Bura (1·1%), Edo (1·0%) and Nupe (1·0%). The official languages are English and (since 1997) French, but 50% of the population speak Hausa as a *lingua franca*.

SOCIAL STATISTICS

2000 estimates: births, 4,530,000; deaths, 1,530,000. Rates, 2000 estimates (per 1,000 population): births, 39·5; deaths, 13·3. Infant

mortality, 2001, 110 (per 1,000 live births). Annual population growth rate, 1992–2002, 2·8%. Life expectancy at birth, 2003, was 43·1 years for males and 43·6 years for females. Fertility rate, 2001, 5·6 children per woman.

CLIMATE

Lying wholly within the tropics, temperatures everywhere are high. Rainfall varies greatly, but decreases from the coast to the interior. The main rains occur from April to Oct. Lagos, Jan. 81°F (27·2°C), July 78°F (25·6°C). Annual rainfall 72" (1,836 mm). Ibadan, Jan. 80°F (26·7°C), July 76°F (24·4°C). Annual rainfall 45" (1,120 mm). Kano, Jan. 70°F (21·1°C), July 79°F (26·1°C). Annual rainfall 35" (869 mm). Port Harcourt, Jan. 79°F (26·1°C), July 77°F (25°C). Annual rainfall 100" (2,497 mm).

CONSTITUTION AND GOVERNMENT

The constitution was promulgated on 5 May 1999, and entered into force on 29 May. Nigeria is a federation, comprising 36 states and a federal capital territory. The constitution includes provisions for the creation of new states and for boundary adjustments of existing states. The legislative powers are vested in a *National Assembly*, comprising a *Senate* and a *House of Representatives*. The 109-member Senate consists of three senators from each state and one from the federal capital territory, who are elected for a term of four years. The House of Representatives comprises 360 members, representing constituencies of nearly equal population as far as possible, who are elected for a four-year term. The president is elected for a term of four years and must receive not less than one-quarter of the votes cast at the federal capital territory.

National Anthem

'Arise, O compatriots, Nigeria's call obey'; words by a collective, tune by B. Odiase.

GOVERNMENT CHRONOLOGY

(NCNC = National Council of Nigeria and the Cameroons; NPN = National Party of Nigeria; PDP = People's Democratic Party; n/p = non-partisan)

Heads of State

President of the Republic

1963–66	NCNC	Benjamin Nnamdi Azikiwe

Heads of the Military Government

1966	military	Johnson Aguiyi-Ironsi
1966–75	military	Yakubu Gowon
1975–76	military	Murtala Ramat Muhammed
1976–79	military	Olusegun Obasanjo

President of the Republic

1979–83	NPN	Shehu Shagari

Head of the Federal Military Government

1983–85	military	Muhammadu Buhari

Chairman of the Armed Forces Ruling Council, then Chairman of the National Defence and Security Council

1985–93	military	Ibrahim Babangida

Head of the Interim National Government

1993	n/p	Ernest Shonekan

Chairmen of the Provisional Ruling Council

1993–98	military	Sani Abacha
1998–99	military	Abdulalam Abubakar

President of the Republic

1999–	PDP	Olusegun Obasanjo

RECENT ELECTIONS

In elections to the House of Representatives on 12 April 2003 the People's Democratic Party (PDP) won 223 seats with 54·5% of the vote, the All Nigeria People's Party (ANPP) 96 seats (27·4%), the Alliance for Democracy (AD) 34 seats (8·8%), the United Nigeria

People's Party (UNPP) 2 seats (2·8%), the All Progressives Grand Alliance (APGA) 2 seats (1·4%), the National Democratic Party (NDP) 1 seat (1·9%) and the People's Redemption Party (PRP) 1 seat (0·8%). Turnout was 50·0%.

In the Senate elections on the same day 76 seats went to the PDP, 27 to the ANPP and 6 to the AD. Turnout was 49·2%.

Presidential elections were held on 19 April 2003. President Olusegun Obasanjo (PDP) won against 19 opponents with 61·9% of the votes cast. His main opponent, Muhammadu Buhari (ANPP), received 32·2%, and Chukwuemeka Ojukwu (APGA) 3·3%. Buhari refused to accept the result, claiming serious irregularities. International observers witnessed evidence of widespread fraud. Turnout was 69%.

CURRENT ADMINISTRATION

President: Olusegun Obasanjo; b. 1937 (PDP; inaugurated 29 May 1999 and re-elected 19 April 2003).

Vice President: Atiku Abubakar.

In March 2006 the government comprised:

Minister of Agriculture: Malam Adamu Bello. *Aviation:* Prof. Babalola Borishade. *Commerce:* Idris Waziri. *Communications:* Chief Cornelius Adebayo. *Co-operation and Integration:* Lawan Gana Guba. *Culture and Tourism:* Chief Franklin Ogbuewu. *Defence:* Dr Rabiu Kwankaso. *Education:* Chinwe Nora Obaji. *Environment:* Helen Esuene. *Federal Capital Territory:* Mallam Nasir El-Rufai. *Finance:* Ngozi Okonjo-Iweala. *Foreign Affairs:* Oluyemi Adeniji. *Health:* Prof. Eyitayo Lambo. *Housing and Urban Development:* Rahman Mimiko. *Industries:* Fidelis Tapgun. *Information and National Orientation:* Frank Nweke, Jr. *Intergovernmental Affairs, Special Duties and Youth Development:* Musa Mohamed. *Internal Affairs:* Magaji Mohamed. *Justice:* Chief Bayo Ojo. *Labour and Productivity:* Dr Hassan Lawal. *Police Affairs:* Broderick Bozimo. *Power and Steel:* Liyel Imoke. *Science and Technology:* Prof. Turner Isoun. *Solid Minerals:* Obiageli Ezekwesili. *Sports and Social Development:* Samaila Sambawa. *Transport:* Dr Abiye Sekibo. *Water Resources:* Muktar Shagari. *Women's Affairs:* Mariam Ciroma. *Works:* Vacant.

Nigerian Parliament: http://www.nigeriacongress.org

CURRENT LEADERS

Olusegun Obasanjo

Position
President

Introduction
Olusegun Obasanjo became president again in 1999, having previously held the office from 1976–79. During his first tenure he guided the country through the transition from military dictatorship to civilian government.

Having opposed the reimposition of army rule in the 1990s, he stood successfully for the presidency in 1999. However, his attempts to reform several national institutions have been hampered by racial and religious unrest and widespread corruption.

Early Life
Olusegun Obasanjo was born on 5 March 1937 in Abeokuta, in southwest Nigeria. He joined the army in 1958 and received military training both in Nigeria and abroad. During his military career, he served with UN peacekeeping forces and led an army commando division in the 1967–70 Biafran civil war. Obasanjo became chief of staff to Gen. Muhammed who led a military coup in June 1975, deposing Yakubu Gowon and promising to return Nigeria to civilian rule by Oct. 1979.

Career in Office
When Muhammed was assassinated in 1976, Obasanjo took over as head of state, paving the way for democratic elections

and civilian rule, as well as tightening links with the USA. He adhered scrupulously to the political schedule set by Gen. Muhammed and used oil revenues to develop and diversify the country's economy.

During Obasanjo's first presidential term and Abuja was made the new capital. A new constitution, published in 1978, lifted the ban on political activity and the formation of political parties. In line with his determination to return to civilian government, elections were held in 1979. Obasanjo, who chose not to stand, handed power to Alhaji Shehu Shagari, a northerner from the National Party of Nigeria (NPN).

Obasanjo founded the African Leadership Forum in 1988 to help African leaders to further their national interests. He was a vocal opponent of Gen. Sani Abacha, who reimposed military rule after a coup in 1993, and in 1995 was imprisoned for allegedly attempting a coup. Released after Abacha's death in 1998, Obasanjo joined the People's Democratic Party (PDP). In Feb. 1999 he was elected president in free elections with almost two-thirds of the vote. He proposed democratic reforms and promised to reorganize the police and the military and to stamp out government corruption. However, continuing ethnic disputes, often spilling into violence, have hindered his tenure.

In Oct. 2002 Obasanjo was at the centre of a territorial dispute when the International Court of Justice (ICJ) awarded Cameroon ownership of the Bakassi Peninsula in the Gulf of Guinea and ordered Nigeria to withdraw from the oil-rich area. The decision was based on a 1917 agreement between Britain and Germany, then the colonial powers. Obasanjo denied the validity of territorial treaties made before independence but was later reported to have accepted the court's decision.

In Nov. 2002 Nigeria's religious tensions were highlighted by rioting between Muslims and Christians in the northern city of Kaduna. Over 200 people died in the fighting sparked by the hosting of an international beauty pageant in Abuja and a newspaper article considered offensive by Muslims. The violence followed international concern over the sentencing, under Sharia law, to death by stoning of a woman accused of adultery. Obasanjo subsequently stated that no stonings would be carried out in Nigeria.

The build-up to the presidential elections of April 2003, when 19 candidates stood, was marked by rising tensions. Obasanjo claimed victory with 62% of the vote, with Muhammadu Buhari, candidate for the All Nigeria People's Party (ANPP), winning 32%. However, Buhari rejected the result and international monitors reported voting irregularities. Nevertheless, Obasanjo received international recognition. More violent clashes between Muslims and Christians in May 2004 left hundreds dead, and a state of emergency was declared in the central state of Plateau.

On the world stage, Obasanjo has helped to further the New Partnership for Africa's Development (NEPAD), a common plan for the continent's economic recovery.

DEFENCE

In 2003 defence expenditure totalled US$853m., equivalent to US$6 per capita and representing 1·8% of GDP.

Nigeria's armed forces have over 3,000 personnel in peacekeeping missions in other African countries, notably Liberia and Sierra Leone.

Army

Strength (2002) 62,000.

Navy

The Navy includes one frigate with a helicopter and two corvettes. The Navy has a small aviation element. Naval personnel in 2002 totalled 7,000, including Coastguard. The main bases are at Apapa (Lagos) and Calabar.

Air Force

The Air Force has been built up with the aid of a German mission; much first-line equipment was received from the former Soviet Union. Personnel (2002) total about 9,500, with about 86 combat aircraft including MiG-21s, Jaguars and Alpha Jets. In addition there were about 16 armed helicopters. Serviceability of both combat aircraft and helicopters is about 50%.

INTERNATIONAL RELATIONS

Nigeria is a member of the UN, WTO, the African Union, African Development Bank, ECOWAS, the Lake Chad Basin Commission, OIC, OPEC, IOM, Islamic Development Bank and is an ACP member state of the ACP-EU relationship.

ECONOMY

Agriculture accounted for 31·2% of GDP in 2002, industry 43·8% and services 25·0%.

Overview

Nigeria's economy is highly dependent on oil, which accounts for 33% of GDP, 76% of government revenues and 95% of export revenues. Since independence in 1960 weak and corrupt government has damaged the economy. GDP per capita, at approximately US$350, is below the level at independence and the Sub-Saharan average of US$450. Approximately 66% of the population live in poverty, compared to 43% in 1985. The black market economy constitutes 77% of the country's official GDP, one of the highest percentages in the world.

Inequality is rife. The middle-income oil-producing economy (encompassing around 5m. people) has a per capita income of approximately US$2,200 whilst the non-oil producing economy (115m. people) has an average per capita income of US$200. A ten-year rift with the IMF ended with an agreement in Jan. 1999 on a Fund-monitored economic reform programme, which includes provisions for abolishing the dual exchange rate, ending the subsidy on local fuel and increasing privatization. Quarterly monitoring commenced in 2004, although a formal programme with the IMF has yet to be announced. Since the establishment of a democratically elected government in 1999 a series of reforms have been put in place to fight endemic corruption. In 2004 the National Economic Empowerment and Development Strategy was launched, focusing on poverty reduction, wealth creation and human development.

Currency

The unit of currency is the *naira* (NGN) of 100 *kobo*. Foreign exchange reserves were US$9,226m. in May 2002 (US$1,443m. in 1995). A dual exchange rate, abolished in Oct. 1999, allowed the government to purchase US dollars for 25% of the market price. Gold reserves were 687,000 troy oz in May 2002. Inflation rates (based on IMF statistics):

1995	1996	1997	1998	1999	2000	2001	2002	2003	2004
72·9%	29·3%	8·5%	10·0%	6·6%	6·9%	18·0%	13·7%	14·0%	15·0%

In March 2002 total money supply was ₦835,923m.

Budget

The financial year is the calendar year. 2000 revenue, ₦1,927,087m. (tax revenue 33·1%; non-tax revenue 66·9%); expenditure, ₦1,834,305m. In 1999 recurrent expenditure accounted for 75·6% of total expenditures and capital expenditure 24·4%.

Performance

Real GDP growth rates (based on IMF statistics):

1997	1998	1999	2000	2001	2002	2003	2004
3·2%	0·3%	1·5%	5·4%	3·1%	1·5%	10·7%	6·0%

Before the discovery of oil in the early 1970s Nigeria's GDP per head was around US$200. By the early 1980s it had reached around US$800, but has now declined to some US$300. Total GDP in 2004 was US$72·1bn.

Banking and Finance

The Central Bank of Nigeria (CBN) is the bank of issue (*Governor*, Prof. Charles C. Soludo).

A banking crisis resulted in a decline in the number of banks to 74 at March 1999. In 2004 a major banking reform was announced. However, despite attempts to strengthen the banking sector, the financial condition of the banks deteriorated. Subsequently the CBN requested technical assistance from the IMF to strengthen the banking system. There are three main banks—Union Bank of Nigeria, First Bank of Nigeria and United Bank for Africa. In Jan. 2005 United Bank for Africa and Standard Trust Bank, Nigeria's fifth-biggest bank, agreed to merge and create the largest bank in west Africa. In 2002 there were 12 merchant banks and two development banks. In 2004 bank reserves at the CBN totalled ₦187bn. and CBN net foreign assets amounted to ₦2,250bn.

Nigeria was one of three countries and territories named in a report in June 2005 as failing to co-operate in the fight against international money laundering. The Financial Action Task Force on Money Laundering was set up by the G7 group of major industrialized nations.

The Nigerian Stock Exchange is in Lagos.

ENERGY AND NATURAL RESOURCES

Environment

Nigeria's carbon dioxide emissions from the consumption and flaring of fossil fuels were the equivalent of 0·8 tonnes per capita in 2002.

Electricity

Installed capacity, 2002, 5·9m. kW. Production, 2001, 18·11bn. kWh (38% kWh hydro-electric); consumption per capita was 152 kWh in 2001.

Oil and Gas

Oil accounts for around 97% of Nigeria's exports. The cumulative income from oil over more than 30 years exceeds US$330,000m. Nigeria's oil production amounted to 98·6m. tonnes in 2002. Reserves in 2002 totalled 24·0bn. bbls. There are four refineries. Oil income in 1998 was around US$1bn. a month, representing more than 75% of government revenue, but unrest which threatened to escalate into civil war caused production to be cut by around a third. Most of Nigeria's oil wealth comes from onshore wells, but there are also large untapped offshore deposits.

Natural gas reserves, 2002, were 3,510bn. cu. metres; production, 2002, 17·7bn. cu. metres. Nigeria has signed an agreement for a US$430m., 600-km pipeline to supply natural gas to Benin, Ghana and Togo. It is expected to come into operation in late 2006 moving around 1,415,000 cu. metres per day in the first instance, in the process helping to reduce Nigeria's dependence on oil for government revenue. In Dec. 2002 the African Development Bank, six Nigerian banks and 19 international banks announced plans to invest US$1bn. in the Nigeria Liquefied Natural Gas company (NLNG) to exploit exports to the USA and Europe. Ownership of the NLNG is shared between the Nigerian National Petroleum Corporation, Total Fina Elf, Royal Dutch/Shell and AGIP.

Minerals

Production, 1998 (in tonnes): limestone, 3·66m.; coal (2000), 61,000; marble, 22,460. There are large deposits of iron ore, coal (reserves estimate 245m. tonnes), lead and zinc. There are small quantities of gold and uranium. Lead production was 5,000 tonnes in 2002. Tin is also mined.

Agriculture

Of the total land mass, 75% is suitable for agriculture, including arable farming, forestry, livestock husbandry and fisheries. In

2001, 28·5m. ha. were arable and 2·7m. ha. permanent cropland. 0·23m. ha. were irrigated in 2001. 90% of production was by smallholders with less than 3 ha. in 2000, and less than 1% of farmers had access to mechanized tractors. Main food crops are millet and sorghum in the north, plantains and oil palms in the south, and maize, yams, cassava and rice in much of the country. The north is, however, the main food producing area. Cocoa is the crop that contributes most to foreign exchange earnings. Output, 2000 (in 1,000 tonnes): cassava, 32,697; yams, 25,873; sorghum, 7,520; millet, 5,960; maize, 5,476; taro, 3,835; rice, 3,277; groundnuts, 2,783; plantains, 1,902; sweet potatoes, 1,662; palm oil, 896; pineapples, 881; tomatoes, 879. Nigeria is the biggest producer of yams, accounting for more than two-thirds of the annual world output. It is also the leading cassava and taro producer and the second largest millet producer.

Livestock, 2000: cattle, 19·83m.; sheep, 20·50m.; goats, 24·30m.; pigs, 4·86m.; chickens, 126m. Products (in 1,000 tonnes), 2000: beef and veal, 298; goat meat, 154; mutton and lamb, 91; pork, bacon and ham, 78; poultry meat, 172; milk, 386; eggs, 435.

Forestry
There were 13·52m. ha. of forests in 2000, or 14·8% of the land area. Timber production in 2003 was 69·87m. cu. metres.

Fisheries
The total catch in 2003 was 475,162 tonnes, of which 300,194 tonnes came from sea fishing.

INDUSTRY
In 2001 industry contributed for 35·5% of GDP, with manufacturing accounting for 4·2%. 2002 production (in 1,000 tonnes) included: cement (2001), 3,000; petrol, 2,603; residual fuel oil, 2,578; distillate fuel oil, 2,516; kerosene, 1,177; palm oil (2001), 903; paper and products (1998), 57; cigarettes (1995), 256m. units. Also plywood (2001), 55,000 cu. metres.

Labour
The labour force in 2004 totalled an estimated 55·67m. There were 33 work stoppages in 2003–04 with 407,000 working days lost (233·5m. working days lost in 1994–95).

Trade Unions
All trade unions are affiliated to the Nigerian Labour Congress.

INTERNATIONAL TRADE
Nigeria's external debt was US$30,476m. in 2002. President Obasanjo failed to settle with the IMF in March 2002, preventing rescheduling and debt relief.

Imports and Exports
Imports (f.o.b.) in 2004 totalled US$11,096m.; exports (f.o.b.) US$23,657m. Principal imports in 1999 were: machinery and transport equipment, 27·7%; foodstuffs, 26·1%; manufactured goods, 19·9%; chemicals, 15·7%. In 1999 crude oil amounted to 98·9% of exports by value. Other exports included ships and boats, and cocoa.

In 2000 the main import suppliers were: UK, 10·9%; USA, 9·2%; France, 8·9%; Germany, 7·4%; China, 6·3%. Main export markets: USA, 46·1%; Spain, 10·7%; India, 6·1%; France, 5·2%; Portugal, 3·6%.

COMMUNICATIONS
Roads
The road network covered 194,394 km in 2002, including 1,194 km of motorways. In 2002 there were 941,100 motor cars and 668,600 trucks and vans. There were 16,793 road accidents with 6,364 fatalities in 1996.

Rail
In 1999 there were 3,557 route-km of track (3,505 km of 1,067 mm gauge). Passenger-km travelled in 1999 came to 479m. and freight tonne-km to 47m.

Civil Aviation
Lagos (Murtala Muhammed) is the major airport, and there are also international airports at Port Harcourt and Kano (Mallam Aminu Kano Airport). The national carrier is Nigeria Airways. The government sold a 49% stake to a UK leasing company, Airwing Aerospace, in 2002. In 2001 Lagos handled 2,735,000 passengers (1,485,000 on domestic flights) and, in 1998, 15,100 tonnes of freight. Nigeria Airways flew 2·7m. km in 1999, carrying 109,200 passengers (30,300 on international flights).

Shipping
In 2002 the merchant marine totalled 411,000 GRT, including oil tankers 285,000 GRT. In 1997 vessels totalling 2,464,000 NRT entered ports and vessels totalling 2,510,000 NRT cleared. The principal ports are Lagos and Port Harcourt. There is an extensive network of inland waterways.

Telecommunications
In 2002 there were 2,335,100 telephone subscribers (19·4 per 1,000 persons) and 853,000 PCs in use (7·1 per 1,000 persons). Mobile phone subscribers numbered 1,633,000 in 2002. The largest mobile phone company is MTN Nigeria Communications. Nigeria had 420,000 Internet users in 2002.

Postal Services
In 2003 there were 4,228 post offices. A total of 62m. pieces of mail were processed in 2003.

SOCIAL INSTITUTIONS
Justice
The highest court is the Federal Supreme Court, which consists of the Chief Justice of the Republic, and up to 15 Justices appointed by the government. It has original jurisdiction in any dispute between the Federal Republic and any State or between States; and to hear and determine appeals from the Federal Court of Appeal, which acts as an intermediate appellate Court to consider appeals from the High Court.

High Courts, presided over by a Chief Justice, are established in each state. All judges are appointed by the government. Magistrates' courts are established throughout the Republic, and customary law courts in southern Nigeria. In each of the northern States of Nigeria there are the Sharia Court of Appeal and the Court of Resolution. Muslim Law has been codified in a Penal Code and is applied through Alkali courts. In Oct. 1999 *sharia*, or Islamic law, was introduced in the northern province of Zamfara. The death penalty is in force and was last used in Jan. 2002.

The population in penal institutions in March 2002 was 39,368 (33 per 100,000 of national population).

Education
The adult literacy rate was 66·8% in 2002 (74·4% among males and 59·4% among females). Under the new Universal Basic Education scheme it was hoped that this would rise to 70% by 2003. Free, compulsory education is to be provided for all children aged between six and 15 under the terms of the scheme. In 2002 there were 49,343 primary schools with 29·58m. pupils and 537,741 teachers; 10,000 secondary schools with 7·49m. pupils and 187,126 teachers; and 1·25m. students at 158 tertiary education institutions.

In 1995 there were 13 universities, two agricultural and five technological universities, 21 polytechnics, seven colleges and two institutes. There were 150,072 university students and 10,742 academic staff.

Health
Health personnel, 2000: 30,885 doctors, 2,180 dentists and 8,642 pharmacists.

Nigeria has made significant progress in the reduction of undernourishment in the past 25 years. By 2000 only 9% of the population was undernourished, one of the lowest rates in sub-Saharan Africa.

RELIGION

Muslims and Christians both constitute about 45% of the population; traditional animist beliefs are also widespread. Northern Nigeria is mainly Muslim; southern Nigeria is predominantly Christian and western Nigeria is evenly divided between Christians, Muslims and animists. In May 2005 the Roman Catholic church had two cardinals.

CULTURE

World Heritage Sites

The Sukur Cultural Landscape, a hilly area in Adamawa State (northeastern Nigeria), was entered on the UNESCO World Heritage list in 1999. Osun Sacred Grove is one of the last remnants of primary high forest in southern Nigeria and was inscribed in 2005.

Broadcasting

In 2003 the Federal Radio Corporation of Nigeria, a statutory body, was broadcasting from five national radio stations in English, Yoruba, Hausa and Igbo, and an international service, Voice of Nigeria (eight languages in 2003). In 2001 there were six private radio stations in operation. The government-owned Nigerian Television Authority transmits a national service (colour by PAL, in English only), and over 30 states have their own stations. In 2001 there were nine private stations and two private satellite stations. In 2000 there were 23m. radio sets and in 2001 there were 12m. TV sets.

Press

In 1998 there were 25 daily newspapers with a combined circulation of 2,760,000.

Tourism

In 2002 there were 831,000 foreign visitors; spending by tourists totalled US$156m.

DIPLOMATIC REPRESENTATIVES

Of Nigeria in the United Kingdom (Nigeria House, 9 Northumberland Ave., London, WC2N 5BX)
High Commissioner: Dr Christopher Kolade.

Of the United Kingdom in Nigeria (Dangote House, Aguyi Ironsi St., Wuse, Abuja)
High Commissioner: Richard Gozney, CMG.

Of Nigeria in the USA (3519 International Court, NW, Washington, D.C., 20008)
Ambassador: George A. Obiozor.

Of the USA in Nigeria (Plot 1075, Diplomatic Drive, Central District Area, Abuja)
Ambassador: John Campbell.

Of Nigeria to the United Nations
Ambassador: Aminu Wali.

Of Nigeria to the European Union
Ambassador: Vacant.
Chargé d'Affaires a.i.: V. A. Okoedion.

FURTHER READING

Forrest, T., *Politics and Economic Development in Nigeria.* Boulder (CO), 1993

Maier, K., *This House Has Fallen: Midnight in Nigeria.* Penguin Press, London and PublicAffairs, New York, 2000

Miles, W. F. S., *Hausaland Divided: Colonialism and Independence in Nigeria and Niger.* Cornell Univ. Press, 1994

National Statistical Office: Federal Office of Statistics, Plot 205, Bacita Close, Gakki, Area 2, P.M.B. 127, Abuja.

Website: http://www.nigeriabusinessinfo.com/fos.htm

NORWAY

Tromsø

Norwegian Sea

0   150 mi

0   200 km

SWEDEN

Trondheim

FINLAND

NORWAY

Bergen   Hamar

OSLO

Stavanger

Baltic
Sea   ESTONIA

© Research Machines plc 2006

Kongeriket Norge
(Kingdom of Norway)

Capital: Oslo
Population projection, 2010: 4·73m.
GDP per capita, 2003: (PPP$) 37,670
HDI/world rank: 0·963/1

KEY HISTORICAL EVENTS

The first settlers arrived at the end of the Ice Age, as the glaciers retreated north. Archaeological remains in Finnmark in the north and in Rogaland in the southwest of Norway date from between 9500 to 8000 BC and suggest coastal, hunting-fishing communities. By 2500 BC a new influx of settlers brought cattle and crop farming and gradually replaced the earlier hunting-fishing communities. Although there is little evidence of the impact of the bronze and iron ages on Norway as its people had not yet found ways to exploit their natural resources for trade, links with Roman-occupied Gaul in the first four centuries AD were strong. By the time of the collapse of the Roman Empire, tribal groups had started to develop and by 800 AD had each established their own legislative and adjudicatory assemblies, known as *things*.

In the ninth century communities from the Vik, an area between the south coasts of Norway and Sweden, gave their name to the people collectively known as Vikings. The Norwegian Vikings sailed to the Atlantic islands, England, France, Scotland and Ireland, and also colonized Iceland. One of the many whose exploits were faithfully recorded by the saga writers was Eric the Red, who discovered Greenland. His son, Leif Erikson, voyaged across the Davis Strait, to America, becoming possibly the first European to do so.

The first steps towards centralized rule were taken by Harold Fairhair who extended his rule along the coastal region of Norway. Battles with rival chieftains culminated in about 900 when Harold was proclaimed king of the Norwegians. His successors were less assertive and by the mid-tenth century the country was effectively under the suzerainty of Harold Bluetooth, king of Denmark and Skåne. Bluetooth's grandson, Canute the Great, fought successfully to incorporate England into his North Sea Empire before setting his sights on Sweden. But the limitations of royal authority were shown on the death of Canute when the English, unchallenged, simply chose their own king while the Danish and Norwegian nobles decided that whichever of their own monarchs lived longest should take power in both countries, an agreement which for a time resulted in a Norwegian ruler for Denmark.

Viking Strength

The Viking's territorial expansion came to an end with the Norwegian King Harald Hardrada's defeat at the battle of Stamford Bridge in England in 1066. Supported by the English church, the Norwegian monarchy gained strength. By the 12th century the balance of power between the church and monarchy had become a source of civil conflict which was only resolved when Håkon IV became King in 1217. Thus began Norway's 'Golden Age' in which the unity of the kingdom was solidly established. Blood feuds were prohibited, a royal council was created, and primogeniture was introduced to secure the continuity of the monarchic line. Under Håkon's rule, both Greenland and Iceland ceded control to Norway. It was Håkon's son, Magnus VI, known as the Lawmender, who oversaw the codification of a national law system between 1274–76, elements of which have survived to this day. Under Erik II, Magnus' son, much of the royal power was divested to wealthy magnates. His succession by his brother Håkon V in 1299 marked a renewed effort to strengthen the monarchy and also a movement of political power to Oslo.

Union with Sweden came in 1319 with the coronation of Magnus VII, the son of Håkon's daughter and Duke Erik of Sweden. This was to last until 1355, when the Swedish crown passed to Magnus' son. Between 1349–50 Norway fell victim to the Black Death which killed around two-thirds of its population. The effects of this were to dramatically reduce the strength of the nobility and to undermine the cohesion of the government, as many official positions were taken up by Danes and Swedes. Newly vulnerable to the threat of encroachment by the Germans, the incentive for all three Scandinavian kingdoms to unite was strong. When the Danish king died in 1375 his widow, Margaret, claimed the throne on behalf of her five-year-old son, Olav. Acting for her son, Margaret became regent of Denmark and, on the death of Håkon, regent of Norway. Confirmed as regent of Denmark and Norway, Margaret defeated Albrecht, the German claimant to the Swedish throne, thus clearing the way to a Nordic union. With the death of her son in 1387 and unable to take the triple crown for herself, she nominated her five-year-old nephew, Erik of Pomerania, as king of all three countries. His election was formalized at Kalmar in 1397.

From 1450 the Norwegian government was based in Copenhagen and many administrative positions were taken by Germans and Danes. An attempt by the Norwegian council to gain independence in 1523 led to civil war between 1534–36 and the council's subsequent abolition. Norway was then to remain a province of Denmark, with limited control over internal affairs, until the 19th century.

In the Napoleonic Wars, Denmark and Norway were allied with Napoleon I. Napoleon's defeat at the battle of Leipzig in 1813 was followed by a successful attack on Denmark from Sweden which resulted in the Treaty of Kiel (Jan. 1814). With the signing of the treaty Norway was conceded to the Swedish throne and, despite Denmark's continued resistance, its newly written constitution came into force in Nov. 1814. Although the arrangement meant the regency and foreign policy were to be shared with Sweden, the new constitution gave Norway control over internal affairs, with a newly established political base at Christiana.

The economic damage of the Napoleonic Wars was remedied by the rapid expansion of the fishing industry and, from the 1850s onwards, agriculture. In the latter half of the century, the merchant navy grew to become the third largest in the world after the United States and Great Britain.

Independence

From the 1880s, successive steps towards self-government within the union culminated in a referendum in which the overwhelming majority of Norwegians voted for separation. In Oct. 1905 Oscar II renounced his title to the western provinces and a month later a Danish prince was confirmed as Håkon VII of free Norway. Reigning for 52 years, he was succeeded by his son.

At the outset of the First World War Norway declared its neutrality. This did not prevent the loss of almost half of its merchant navy and damage to the economy as a result of trade embargos. But despite the hardships of the 1930s' depression, industrial expansion continued.

From 1940 to 1944, during the Second World War, Norway was occupied by the Germans who set up a pro-German government under Vidkun Quisling. Apart from this wartime episode, the social democrats held office, and the majority in the *Storting* (parliament), from 1935 to 1965. Norway's first post-war prime minister, Einar Gerhardsen, had spent four years in a concentration camp. He had been vice-chairman of Oslo city council until he became leader of the underground anti-Nazi movement in the early days of the occupation. As recently elected social democrat leader he was the natural choice to head the 1945 caretaker government.

The action needed to restore Norway's prosperity was self evident: to make good the heavy losses in the merchant fleet; to increase the output of hydro-electricity; and to develop new industries. The chief worry for the social democrats was the likely impact of communists who had gained credit for leading the resistance. Talks on a possible merger of the parties were as unproductive as parallel negotiations in Denmark, but the electoral results of each party's going its own way were markedly different in the two countries. More confident of their purpose, the Norwegian social democrats took the electorate by storm, increasing their share of the popular vote in the 1945 election by close on 10%. Their advance gave them the one prize that eluded their colleagues everywhere else in Scandinavia—an absolute majority and the freedom to govern without always looking over their shoulder.

The government was supported wholeheartedly by the trade unions. In return for price controls and food subsidies which stabilized the cost of living for almost five years, and the guarantee of full employment, the unions accepted compulsory arbitration for all wage disputes and virtually forswore the use of the strike weapon. Returned in 1949 with an increased majority, the social democrats were able to point to a rise in productivity and living standards well beyond that achieved by most other Western countries. But the general increase in world prices triggered by the Korean War meant that Norway had to pay much more for essential imports. The use of subsidies to counteract price increases reached its limit when they became the largest item in the national budget. In 1950 food prices were allowed to get closer to their market level and the cost of living

started on an upward curve, leading to a 30% increase over three years. Industrial investment suffered a sharp cutback.

The social democrats held on to power until the mid-sixties when a centre right coalition took over led by Per Borten. By 1969 the social democrats had recovered much of their lost ground. The centre right coalition government struggled on with a majority of two until the EEC issue broke through the normally placid surface of Norwegian politics.

Although Norway's application for membership in the EEC in 1969 was successful, a referendum held in 1972 found more than 53% of voters opposed to joining. Norway had been a member of EFTA since that organization's foundation, and continued to sign up to a series of bilateral free-trade treaties with members of the EEC, but opposition to joining the EEC remained strong. On the inception of the EU in 1992, Norway, like its Scandinavian neighbours, applied for membership. But, again, a referendum was won by the anti-European lobby.

Norway's continued reluctance to join the EU hinges on its dependence on the export of petroleum and natural gas. Since the 1960s and the discovery of vast off-shore deposits, the oil and gas export industry has contributed to making Norway one of the world's richest economies.

TERRITORY AND POPULATION

Norway is bounded in the north by the Arctic Ocean, east by Russia, Finland and Sweden, south by the Skagerrak Straits and west by the Norwegian Sea. The total area of mainland Norway is 323,802 sq. km, including 19,522 sq. km of fresh water. Total coastline, including fjords, 25,148 km. There are more than 50,000 islands along the coastline. Exposed mountain (either bare rock or thin vegetation) makes up over 70% of the country. 25% of the land area is woodland and 4% tilled land.

Population (2001 census) was 4,520,947 (2,240,281 males; 2,280,666 females); population density per sq. km, 14·8. Estimated population, 1 Jan. 2005, 4,606,363; population density, 15·1. With the exception of Iceland, Norway is the most sparsely populated country in Europe.

The UN gives a projected population for 2010 of 4·73m.

There are 19 counties (*fylke*). Land area, population and densities:

	Land area (sq. km)	Population (2001 census)	Population (2005 estimate)	Density per sq. km 2005
Østfold	3,887	252,520	258,542	67
Akershus	4,579	476,440	494,218	108
Oslo (City)	426	512,093	529,846	1,243
Hedmark	26,082	187,878	188,376	7
Oppland	23,787	183,302	183,174	8
Buskerud	13,797	239,591	243,491	18
Vestfold	2,147	216,333	220,736	103
Telemark	13,854	165,732	166,289	12
Aust-Agder	8,312	102,848	103,596	12
Vest-Agder	6,677	157,697	161,276	24
Rogaland	8,590	377,579	393,104	46
Hordaland	14,551	411,100	448,343	31
Sogn og Fjordane	17,680	107,261	107,032	6
Møre og Romsdal	14,590	243,888	244,689	17
Sør-Trøndelag	17,830	266,098	272,567	15
Nord-Trøndelag	20,777	127,444	128,444	6
Nordland	36,074	237,561	236,825	7
Troms	24,884	151,646	152,741	6
Finnmark	45,757	73,936	73,074	2
Mainland total	304,280[1]	4,520,947	4,606,363	15

[1]117,485 sq. miles.

The Arctic territories of Svalbard and Jan Mayen have an area of 61,397 sq. km. Persons staying on Svalbard and Jan Mayen are registered as residents of their home Norwegian municipality.

At Jan. 2004, 77·3% of the population lived in urban areas. Population of the principal urban settlements on 1 Jan. 2004:

Oslo	794,356	Ålesund	43,655
Bergen	211,326	Haugesund	39,987
Stavanger/Sandnes	169,455	Sandefjord	39,069
Trondheim	144,434	Moss	34,323
Frederikstad/Sarpsborg	95,994	Bodø	33,134
Drammen	89,500	Arendal	30,860
Porsgrunn/Skien	84,657	Hamar	28,296
Kristiansand	63,020	Larvik	22,845
Tromsø	51,352	Halden	21,921
Tønsberg	44,343		

The official language is Norwegian, which has two versions: Bokmål (or Riksmål) and Nynorsk (or Landsmål).

The Sami, the indigenous people of the far north, number some 40,000 and form a distinct ethnic minority with their own culture and language.

SOCIAL STATISTICS

Statistics for calendar years:

	Marriages	Divorces	Births	Still-born	Outside marriage[1]	Deaths
1999	23,456	9,124	59,298	241	30,198	45,170
2000	25,356	10,053	59,234	225	29,368	44,002
2001	19,722	10,308	56,696	241	28,194	43,981
2002	24,069	10,450	55,434	197	27,890	44,465
2003	22,361	10,750	56,458	213	28,218	42,478

[1]Excluding still-born.

Rates per 1,000 population, 2003, birth, 2·4; death, 9·3; marriage, 4·9; divorce, 2·4. Average annual population growth rate, 1992–2002, 0·54% (2002, 0·62%). In 2003 there were 502 suicides, giving a rate of 11·0 per 100,000 population (men, 16·5 per 100,000; women, 5·6).

Expectation of life at birth, 2004, was 77·5 years for males and 82·3 years for females. Infant mortality, 2003, 3·5 per 1,000 live births; fertility rate, 2004, 1·83 births per woman. 51% of births are to unmarried mothers. In 2003 the average age at marriage was 35·8 years for males and 32·4 years for females (32·5 years and 29·7 years respectively for first marriages).

At 1 Jan. 2005 the immigrant population totalled 364,981, including 26,950 from Pakistan, 22,859 from Sweden, 19,197 from Denmark and 18,369 from Iraq. In 2004 Norway received 7,950 asylum applications. Most were from Afghanistan (1,059), Somalia (957), Russia (938), and Serbia and Montenegro (860).

A UNICEF report published in 2005 showed that 3·4% of children in Norway live in poverty (in households with income below 50% of the national median), the third lowest percentage of any country behind Denmark and Finland.

In the Human Development Index, or HDI (measuring progress in countries in longevity, knowledge and standard of living), Norway ranked first in the world in the list published in the Human Development Report for both 2001 and 2002, having been second behind Canada for the previous two years.

CLIMATE

There is considerable variation in the climate because of the extent of latitude, the topography and the varying effectiveness of prevailing westerly winds and the Gulf Stream. Winters along the whole west coast are exceptionally mild but precipitation is considerable. Oslo, Jan. 24·3°F (−4·3°C), July 61·5°F (16·4°C). Annual rainfall 30·0" (763 mm). Bergen, Jan. 34·7°F (1·5°C), July 58·1°F (14·5°C). Annual rainfall 88·6" (2,250 mm). Trondheim, Jan. 26°F (−3·5°C), July 57°F (14°C). Annual rainfall 32·1" (870 mm). Bergen has one of the highest rainfall figures of any European city. The sun never fully sets in the northern area of the country in the summer and even in the south, the sun rises at around 3 a.m. and sets at around 11 p.m.

CONSTITUTION AND GOVERNMENT

Norway is a constitutional and hereditary monarchy.

The reigning King is **Harald V**, born 21 Feb. 1937, married on 29 Aug. 1968 to Sonja Haraldsen. He succeeded on the death of his father, King Olav V, on 21 Jan. 1991. *Offspring*: Princess Märtha Louise, born 22 Sept. 1971 (married Ari Behn, b. 30 Sept. 1972, on 24 May 2002; *offspring*, Maud Angelica, b. 29 April 2003; Leah Isadora, b. 8 April 2005); Crown Prince Haakon Magnus, born 20 July 1973 (married Mette-Marit Tjessem Høiby, b. 19 Aug. 1973, on 25 Aug. 2001; *offspring*, Ingrid Alexandra, b. 21 Jan. 2004; Sverre Magnus, b. 3 Dec. 2005; *offspring* of Crown Princess Mette-Marit from previous relationship, Marius, b. 13 Jan. 1997). The king and queen together receive an annual personal allowance of 7·0m. kroner from the civil list, and the Crown Prince and Crown Princess together 4·7m. kroner. Princess Märtha Louise relinquished her allowance in 2002. Women have been eligible to succeed to the throne since 1990. There is no coronation ceremony. The royal succession is in direct male line in the order of primogeniture. In default of male heirs the King may propose a successor to the *Storting*, but this assembly has the right to nominate another, if it does not agree with the proposal.

The Constitution, voted by a constituent assembly on 17 May 1814 and modified at various times, vests the legislative power of the realm in the *Storting* (Parliament). The royal veto may be exercised; but if the same Bill passes two Stortings formed by separate and subsequent elections it becomes the law of the land without the assent of the sovereign. The King has the command of the land, sea and air forces, and makes all appointments.

The 169-member Storting (increased from 165 for the 2005 election) is directly elected by proportional representation. The country is divided into 19 districts, each electing from 4 to 15 representatives.

The Storting, when assembled, divides itself by election into the *Lagting* and the *Odelsting*. The former is composed of one-fourth of the members of the Storting, and the other of the remaining three-fourths. Each Ting (the Storting, the Odelsting and the Lagting) nominates its own president. Most questions are decided by the Storting, but questions relating to legislation must be considered and decided by the Odelsting and the Lagting separately. Only when the Odelsting and the Lagting disagree, the Bill has to be considered by the Storting in plenary sitting, and a new law can then only be decided by a majority of two-thirds of the voters. The same majority is required for alterations of the Constitution, which can only be decided by the Storting in plenary sitting. The Storting elects five delegates, whose duty it is to revise the public accounts. The Lagting and the ordinary members of the Supreme Court of Justice (the *Høyesterett*) form a High Court of the Realm (the *Riksrett*) for the trial of ministers, members of the *Høyesterett* and members of the Storting. The impeachment before the *Riksrett* can only be decided by the Odelsting.

The executive is represented by the King, who exercises his authority through the Cabinet. Cabinet ministers are entitled to be present in the Storting and to take part in the discussions, but without a vote.

National Anthem

'Ja, vi elsker dette landet' ('Yes, we love this land'); words by B. Bjørnson, tune by R. Nordraak.

GOVERNMENT CHRONOLOGY

Prime Ministers since 1945. (DNA = Labour Party; H = Conservative Party; KrF = Christian People's Party; Sp = Center Party)

1945–51	DNA	Einar Henry Gerhardsen
1951–55	DNA	Oscar Fredrik Torp
1955–63	DNA	Einar Henry Gerhardsen
1963	H	John Fyrstenberg Lyng

1963–65	DNA	Einar Henry Gerhardsen
1965–71	Sp	Per Borten
1971–72	DNA	Trygve Martin Bratteli
1972–73	KrF	Lars Korvald
1973–76	DNA	Trygve Martin Bratteli
1976–81	DNA	Odvar Nordli
1981	DNA	Gro Harlem Brundtland
1981–86	H	Kåre Isaachsen Willoch
1986–89	DNA	Gro Harlem Brundtland
1989–90	H	Jan Peder Syse
1990–96	DNA	Gro Harlem Brundtland
1996–97	DNA	Thorbjørn Jagland
1997–2000	KrF	Kjell Magne Bondevik
2000–01	DNA	Jens Stoltenberg
2001–05	KrF	Kjell Magne Bondevik
2005–	DNA	Jens Stoltenberg

RECENT ELECTIONS

At the elections for the Storting held on 12 Sept. 2005 the following parties were elected: Labour Party (DNA), winning 61 out of 169 seats (with 32·7% of the vote); Progress Party (FrP), 38 (22·1%); Conservative Party (H), 23 (14·1%); Socialist Left Party (SV), 15 (8·8%); Christian People's Party (KrF), 11 (6·8%); Centre Party (Sp), 11 (6·5%); Liberal Party (V), 10 (5·9%). Turnout was 77·1%. The opposition Labour Party formed a coalition government with the Socialist Left Party and the Centre Party to give Norway its first majority government in two decades.

CURRENT ADMINISTRATION

In March 2006 the coalition government comprised:

Prime Minister: Jens Stoltenberg; b. 1959 (Labour Party/DNA; sworn in 17 Oct. 2005, having previously held office from March 2000 to Oct. 2001).

Minister of Agriculture and Food: Terje Riis-Johansen (Sp). *Culture and Church Affairs:* Trond Giske (DNA). *Defence:* Anne-Grete Strøm-Erichsen (DNA). *Development Co-operation:* Erik Solheim (SV). *Education:* Øystein Kåre Djupedal (SV). *Environment:* Helen Oddveig Bjørnøy (SV). *Equality and Consumer Affairs:* Karita Bekkemellem (DNA). *Finance:* Kristin Halvorsen (SV). *Fisheries and Coastal Affairs:* Helga Pedersen (DNA). *Foreign Affairs:* Jonas Gahr Støre (DNA). *Health and Care Services:* Sylvia Kristin Brustad (DNA). *Justice:* Knut Storberget (DNA). *Labour and Social Affairs:* Bjarne Håkon Hanssen (DNA). *Local Government and Regional Development:* Åslaug Marie Haga (Sp). *Petroleum and Energy:* Odd Roger Enoksen (Sp). *Renewal:* Heidi Grande Røys (SV). *Trade and Industry:* Odd Eriksen (DNA). *Transport and Communication:* Liv Signe Navarsete (Sp).

Office of the Prime Minister: http://odin.dep.no

CURRENT LEADERS

Jens Stoltenberg

Position
Prime Minister

Introduction
Jens Stoltenberg became prime minister of Norway for a second time on 17 Oct. 2005, following the victory of his centre-left coalition in parliamentary elections a month earlier. He had previously held the office from 2000–01. He has pledged to use Norway's oil wealth to improve education, health and care for the elderly.

Early Life
Jens Stoltenberg was born in Oslo on 16 March 1959, the son of Thorvald Stoltenberg, a former foreign minister, and Karin Stoltenberg, also a politician. Having attended a Steiner school in Oslo, he studied economics at Oslo University. Here he became an active member of the Norwegian Labour Party (Det Norske Arbeiderpartiet, DNA) and was appointed leader of the Labour Youth League in 1985, having served on its central board for six years. Between 1985–89 he was vice president of the International Union of Socialist Youth. He worked for a brief spell at the national statistics office and was an economics lecturer at the University of Oslo before serving for two years as leader of the Oslo Labour Party (1990–92). He was also a junior minister in the department of the environment at this time.

Elected a member of the Storting (parliament) for Oslo in the Sept. 2003 general election, Stoltenberg served as minister of trade and energy in Gro Harlem Brundtland's administration and oversaw Norway's accession to the European Economic Area in 1994. The government had applied for full EU membership in 1992 but the Norwegian electorate rejected the treaty in a referendum in Nov. 1994.

When Brundtland resigned in Oct. 1996 her successor, Thorbjørn Jagland, made Stoltenberg minister of finance, a post he held for a year until the DNA lost power to the conservative Christian People's Party, led by Kjell Magne Bondevik. Bondevik, who attempted to govern with a coalition which held a slim majority, resigned in March 2000 and Stoltenberg (by now deputy leader of the DNA) was asked to form a government. On 17 March 2000 he was sworn in to become the youngest prime minister in Norway's history.

Career in Office
Stoltenberg kept up Norway's reputation as an international peace-broker by mediating between Tamil separatists and the government of Sri Lanka. More controversially, Stoltenberg ushered in reforms to the welfare state that included the part-privatization of several state-owned services. In the parliamentary elections of Sept. 2001 the party suffered a heavy defeat, gaining only 24% of the vote. Bondevik returned as prime minister of a centre-right coalition. A DNA party leadership battle between Stoltenberg and Jagland (leader since 1992) ensued with Stoltenberg emerging victorious.

Thanks to burgeoning oil and gas exports and high international prices, the economy prospered under Bondevik but Stoltenberg tapped into people's dissatisfaction with the welfare system. The DNA's campaign in the run-up to the Sept. 2005 parliamentary elections centred on increased funding for education, health and care of the elderly. In partnership with the Socialist Left Party and the Centre Party, the DNA took 87 of 169 seats. Stoltenberg was sworn in to office on 17 Oct. 2005.

Soltenberg vowed to reform the welfare system while creating conditions for Norway to develop as a knowledge-based economy. He also pledged sustainable management of the country's fish and energy resources.

DEFENCE

Conscription is for 12 months, with four to five refresher training periods.

In 2003 defence spending totalled US$4,387m. (US$962 per capita), representing 2·0% of GDP. Expenditure per capita was the highest of any European country in 2003.

Army

There are a Northern and a Southern command, and within these the Army is organized in two joint commands, four land commands and 14 territorial regiments.

Strength (2002) 14,700 (including 8,700 conscripts). The fast mobilization reserve numbers 89,000.

Navy

The Royal Norwegian Navy has three components: the Navy, Coast Guard and Coastal Artillery. Main naval combatants include six new German-built Ula class submarines and three frigates.

The personnel of the Navy totalled 6,100 in 2002, of whom 3,300 were conscripts. 160 served in Coastal Defence and 270 in the Coast Guard. The main naval base is at Bergen (Håkonsvern), with subsidiary bases at Horten and Tromsø.

The naval elements of the Home Guard on mobilization can muster some 4,900 personnel.

Air Force

The Royal Norwegian Air Force comprises the Air Force and the Anti-air Artillery.

Total strength (2002) is about 5,000 personnel, including 3,200 conscripts. There were 61 combat aircraft in operation including F-16A/Bs.

Home Guard

The Home Guard is organized in small units equipped and trained for special tasks. Service after basic training is one week a year. The Home Guard consists of the Land Home Guard (strength, 2002, 73,000), Sea Home Guard and Anti-Air Home Guard. *See under* Navy *above.*

INTERNATIONAL RELATIONS

Norway is a member of the UN, WTO, BIS, NATO, EFTA, OECD, Council of Europe, OSCE, CERN, Council of the Baltic Sea States, Nordic Council, Inter-American Development Bank, Asian Development Bank, IOM and the Antarctic Treaty, and an Associate Member of the WEU. Norway has acceded to the Schengen accord abolishing border controls between Norway, Austria, Belgium, Denmark, Finland, France, Germany, Greece, Iceland, Italy, Luxembourg, the Netherlands, Portugal, Spain and Sweden.

In a referendum on 27–28 Nov. 1994, 52·2% of votes cast were against joining the EU. The electorate was 3,266,182; turn-out was 88·88%.

Norway gave US$2·2bn. in international aid in 2004, which at 0·87% of GNI made it the world's most generous country as a percentage of its gross national income.

ECONOMY

Services accounted for 59·9% of GDP in 2002, industry 38·3% and agriculture 1·8%.

Transparency International, the anti-corruption organization, ranked Norway 8th in the world in a survey of the countries with the least corruption in business and government in 2005. It received 8·9 out of 10 in the annual index.

Overview

Norway has one of the world's highest levels of GDP per capita and one of the lowest levels of income inequality. The UN Human Development Index, which measures quality of life based on longevity, education levels and GNP, rated Norway number one in the world in 2005. The country is the world's third largest oil exporter after Saudi Arabia and Russia, which distinguishes it from its Western European neighbours. The state-controlled oil sector accounted for over a third of the country's exports and roughly one-sixth of GDP in 2005. The country is also well endowed with other natural resources such as hydropower, fish, forests and minerals.

Norway's economic system is a combination of free market capitalism and an advanced welfare state. It was transformed in the mid-1970s when it emerged as a major oil and gas exporter. Since then the country has enjoyed solid growth, significantly linked to global oil prices. In 2002 and 2003 the economy grew at below average rates as a result of the drop in oil prices but has since recovered and is thought to have entered a cyclical upswing in mid-2003. Unemployment in the country is low, averaging 4% in the first half of the 2000s. Public-sector consumption as a share of GDP is slightly above the West European average but below that of neighbours Denmark and Sweden. Gross fixed investment's share of GDP is also slightly above the West

European average as a result of the large amount of capital absorbed by the country's offshore oil sector. However, private consumption as a share of GDP is one of the smallest in Western Europe, accounting for 44·5% in 2004 compared to 60·2% in the European Big Four countries.

The two main threats to the Norwegian economy are the risks of economic overheating and the loss of competitiveness in non-oil sectors, both of which are closely related to Norway's oil sector. The heavy investment that pours into the oil sector when prices are high and the private consumption that this stimulates can combine with upwards pressure on wages resulting from Norway's tight labour market to overheat the economy from the demand side. High oil prices also put pressure on the Norwegian krone to appreciate, which hurts the competitiveness of the country's non-oil export sectors. Fiscal and monetary policy must therefore seek to contain these risks. Another significant policy issue is how to finance future pensions for an ageing population. Oil revenues allow Norway to run large fiscal surpluses, which averaged 11·5% of GDP per year from 2000–04, and the country has been saving a large portion of its fiscal surpluses in a government petroleum fund but the OECD warns that oil revenues will only supply a small part of Norway's future pension liabilities.

Currency

The unit of currency is the *Norwegian krone* (NOK) of 100 øre. After Oct. 1990 the krone was fixed to the ecu in the EMS of the EU in the narrow band of 2·25%, but it was freed in Dec. 1992. Inflation rates (based on OECD statistics):

1995	1996	1997	1998	1999	2000	2001	2002	2003	2004
2·4%	1·2%	2·6%	2·3%	2·3%	3·1%	3·0%	1·3%	2·5%	0·5%

Foreign exchange reserves were US$16,048m. and gold reserves 1·18m. troy oz in June 2002. In May 2002 total money supply was 658,812m. kroner.

Budget

Central government current revenue and expenditure (in 1m. kroner) for years ending 31 Dec.:

	2001	2002	2003[1]	2004[1]
Revenue	710,627	699,383	723,168	776,166
Expenditure	485,744	564,021	581,500	605,465

[1]Provisional.

The standard rate of VAT is 25·0%.

Performance

Real GDP growth rates (based on OECD statistics):

1995	1996	1997	1998	1999	2000	2001	2002	2003	2004
4·4%	5·3%	5·2%	2·6%	2·1%	2·8%	2·7%	1·1%	0·4%	2·9%

The strong performance of the Norwegian economy in 1993–98 lifted mainland GDP by 20%, but there was a significant slowdown in 1998 when the oil price collapsed at a time when the labour market was overheated. Norway's total GDP in 2004 was US$250·2bn.

The OECD reported in Sept. 2002 that 'Strong growth through the five years to 1998 was induced by a strong expansion in the private sector due to the improvement in competitiveness in the early 1990s, a significant fall in interest rates in 1993 and higher oil investments. It necessitated a fiscal and monetary policy tightening, which, together with a drop in oil investment, has damped activity since then. Despite moderate output growth in recent years, the labour market has remained tight, causing a sharp deterioration in competitiveness. Furthermore, as Norway is the world's third largest oil exporter…, the high oil price since 2000 has led to very large current account and government surpluses.'

Banking and Finance

Norges Bank is the central bank and bank of issue. Supreme authority is vested in the Executive Board consisting of seven members appointed by the King and the Supervisory Council consisting of 15 members elected by the Storting. The *Governor* is Svein Gjedrem. Total assets and liabilities at 31 Dec. 2001 were 987,693m. kroner. This was estimated to have risen to 1,078,787m. kroner by 31 Dec. 2002.

There are three major commercial banks: Nordea Bank Norge ASA, DNB Holding ASA and Fokus. Total assets and liabilities of the 22 commercial banks at 31 Dec. 2001 were 826,250m. kroner. The number of savings banks at 31 Dec. 2001 was 130; total assets and liabilities on 31 Dec. 2001 were 625,183m. kroner.

There is a stock exchange in Oslo.

ENERGY AND NATURAL RESOURCES

Environment

Norway's carbon dioxide emissions from the consumption and flaring of fossil fuels in 2002 were the equivalent of 10·1 tonnes per capita. An *Environmental Sustainability Index* compiled for the World Economic Forum meeting in Jan. 2005 ranked Norway second in the world behind Finland, with 73·4%. The index measured the ability of countries to maintain favourable environmental conditions and examined various factors including pollution levels and the use or abuse of natural resources.

In 2004 there were 24 national parks (total area, 2,165,000 ha.), 1,701 nature reserves (341,800 ha.), 153 landscape protected areas (1,407,100 ha.) and 98 other areas with protected flora and fauna (12,500 ha.).

Norway is one of the world leaders in recycling. In 2003, 46% of all household waste was recycled.

Electricity

Norway is the sixth largest producer of hydropower in the world and the largest in Europe. The potential total hydro-electric power was estimated at 205,067m. kWh in 2004. Installed electrical capacity in 2002 was 28·0m. kW, nearly 99% of it hydro-electric. Production, 2003, was 107,273m. kWh (99% hydro-electric). Consumption per capita in 2002, at 26,640 kWh, was one of the highest in the world. In 1991 Norway became the first country in Europe to deregulate its energy market. Norway is a net importer of electricity.

Oil and Gas

There are enormous oil reserves in the Norwegian continental shelf. In 1966 the first exploration well was drilled. Production of crude oil, 2004, 151,690,000 tonnes. Norway is the world's third biggest oil exporter after Saudi Arabia and Russia, with net oil exports of around 2·9m. bbls. a day in 2004. It had proven reserves of 10·3bn. bbls. in 2002. In March 1998 Norway announced that it would reduce its output for the year by 100,000 bbls. per day as part of a plan to cut global crude production. In June 2001 the Norwegian government sold a 17·5% stake in Statoil, the last major state-owned oil company in western Europe. The privatization was the largest in Norway's history.

Output of natural gas, 2004, 80·3bn. cu. metres with proven reserves of 2,380bn. cu. metres.

Minerals

Production (in tonnes), 2004: coal, 2,904,000; aluminium, 1,321,700; ilmenite concentrate, 860,000; iron ore, 408,000; zinc, 128,500; nickel, 71,400; refined copper, 35,600.

Agriculture

Norway is barren and mountainous. The arable area is in strips in valleys and around fjords and lakes.

In 2004 the agricultural area was 1,036,200 ha., of which 654,300 ha. were meadow and pasture, 147,800 ha. were sown to barley, 86,200 ha. to oats, 84,900 ha. to wheat and 14,100 ha. to

potatoes. Production (in 1,000 tonnes) in 2004: hay (2003), 2,684; barley, 626; wheat, 420; potatoes (2003), 372; oats, 368.

Livestock, 2003, 941,824 cattle (324,081 milch cows), 968,245 sheep (one year and over), 45,010 dairy goats, 100,382 pigs for breeding, 3,468,242 hens, 100,000 silver and platinum fox, 320,000 blue fox, 440,000 mink and 203,200 reindeer.

Forestry

In 2003 the total area under forests was 8·87m. ha., or 27·4% of the total land area. Productive forest area, 2000, approximately 7·45m. ha. About 80% of the productive area consists of conifers and 20% of broadleaves. In 2003, 7·70m. cu. metres of roundwood were cut.

Fisheries

The total number of fishermen in 2004 was 15,586, of whom 2,909 had another chief occupation. In 2004 the number of registered fishing vessels (all with motor) was 6,739, and of these 1,445 were open boats.

The catch in 2004 totalled 2,519,674 tonnes, almost entirely from sea fishing. The catch of herring in 2004 totalled 616,221 tonnes, cod 231,081 tonnes and saithe 210,625. 14,746 seals were caught in 2004 (of which 9,895 harp and 4,851 hooded seals). Commercial whaling was prohibited in 1988, but recommenced in 1993: 671 whales were caught in 2002. Norway is the third largest exporter of fishery commodities, after Thailand and China. In 2001 exports were valued at US$3·64bn.

INDUSTRY

The leading companies by market capitalization in Norway in Nov. 2005 were: Den Norske Stats Oljeselskap AS (Statoil), US$47·3bn.; Norsk Hydro ASA (US$25·2bn.), an oil, metals and chemicals producer; and Telenor ASA (US$16·3bn.), a telecommunications company.

Industry is chiefly based on raw materials. Paper and paper products, industrial chemicals and basic metals are important export manufactures. In the following table figures are given for industrial establishments in 2002. The values are given in 1m. kroner.

Industries	Establish-ments	Number of employees	Gross value of production	Value added
Coal and peat	6	252	739	220
Metal ores	6	392	663	335
Other mining and quarrying	350	3,299	5,792	2,445
Food products	1,521	47,687	115,817	28,990
Beverages and tobacco	44	5,353	12,995	7,739
Textiles	293	4,171	3,869	1,480
Clothing, etc.	98	1,114	1,144	426
Leather and leather products	25	381	411	128
Wood and wood products	956	14,320	17,798	5,630
Pulp, paper and paper products	88	8,402	17,008	4,876
Printing and publishing	1,768	31,061	35,176	14,790
Refined petroleum products and basic chemicals	80	7,712	44,821	6,375
Other chemical products	101	5,808	14,441	5,296
Rubber and plastic products	331	5,774	7,236	2,568
Other non-metallic mineral products	581	9,797	14,783	5,296
Basic metals	127	12,412	39,477	8,615
Metal products, except machinery/equipment	1,286	20,664	22,181	9,267
Machinery and equipment	1,188	22,690	35,619	12,886

Industries	Establish-ments	Number of employees	Gross value of production	Value added
Office machinery and computers	16	389	831	100
Electrical machinery and apparatus	322	7,797	11,478	3,936
Radio, television, communication equipment	85	5,573	9,222	2,769
Medical, precision and optical instruments	303	6,408	10,758	4,028
Oil platforms	110	19,242	29,420	10,280
Motor vehicles and trailers	127	5,659	7,188	2,522
Other transport equipment	534	14,627	25,884	6,548
Other manufacturing industries	788	12,052	13,569	4,964
Total	11,134	273,036	498,319	152,510

Labour

Norway has a tradition of centralized wage bargaining. Since the early 1960s the contract period has been for two years with intermediate bargaining after 12 months, to take into consideration such changes as the rate of inflation.

The labour force averaged 2,382,000 in 2004 (1,119,000 females). The total number of employed persons in 2004 averaged 2,276,000 (1,074,000 females), of whom 2,105,000 were salaried employees and wage earners, 161,000 self-employed and 7,000 family workers. Distribution of employed persons by occupation in 2002 showed 440,000 in health and social work; 401,000 in trade; 293,000 in manufacturing and mining; 272,000 in finance; 161,000 in transport and communications; 157,000 in construction; 145,000 in public administration, services and defence; 86,000 in agriculture; 31,000 in oil and gas extraction; 14,000 in public utilities.

There were 106,000 registered unemployed in 2004, giving a rate of 4·5%.

There were 12 work stoppages in 2005 (five in 2003): 141,179 working days were lost (962 in 2003).

Trade Unions

There were 1,510,633 union members at the end of 2004.

INTERNATIONAL TRADE

Imports and Exports

Total imports and exports in calendar years (in 1m. kroner):

	2000	2001	2002	2003	2004
Imports	302,842	296,111	276,433	283,269	325,994
Exports	529,812	532,262	472,953	482,933	553,263

Major import suppliers in 2004 (value in 1m. kroner): Sweden, 51,100·8; Germany, 44,265·5; Denmark, 23,915·5; UK, 21,291·3; China, 16,180·6; USA, 15,815·3; Netherlands, 14,296·0; France, 13,659·9; Finland, 12,991·4; Italy, 11,483·8. Imports from economic areas: EU, 230,285·9; Nordic countries, 88,961·9; OECD, 270,488·0.

Major export markets in 2004 (value in 1m. kroner): UK, 125,081·3; Germany, 72,784·5; Netherlands, 56,192·2; France, 48,522·2; USA, 42,326·0; Sweden, 37,259·2; Canada, 21,123·5; Denmark, 20,382·6; Italy, 16,035·8; Spain, 15,356·3. Exports to economic areas: EU, 437,234·4; Nordic countries, 68,593·1; OECD, 519,217·8.

Principal imports in 2004 (in 1m. kroner): motor vehicles, 34,365·8 (including passenger cars and station wagons, 19,258·3); electrical machinery, 17,279·1; office machines and computers, 15,458·1 (including automatic data processing machines, 9,543·8); general industrial machinery and equipment, 15,305·8; metalliferous ores and metal scrap, 14,833·7; telecommunications

and sound apparatus and equipment, 13,846·1; manufactures of metals, 13,499·2; iron and steel, 12,054·5; specialized machinery for particular industries, 11,825·9.

Principal exports in 2004 (in 1m. kroner): petroleum, petroleum products and related materials, 266,830·2 (including crude petroleum, 247,421·1); natural and manufactured gas, 83,905·8 (including natural gas, 74,016·8); non-ferrous metals, 35,280·3 (including aluminium, 23,770·5); fish, crustaceans and molluscs, and preparations thereof, 27,281·3; iron and steel, 11,740·9; transport equipment excluding road vehicles, 10,359·4; general industrial machinery and equipment, 9,332·0; paper, paperboard and products, 8,873·5; electrical machinery, apparatus and appliances, 7,300·4.

COMMUNICATIONS

Roads

In 2004 the length of public roads (including roads in towns) totalled 92,513 km. Total road length in 2004 included: national roads, 27,252 km; provincial roads, 27,027 km; local roads, 38,234 km. Number of registered motor vehicles, 2004, included: 1,977,922 passenger cars (including station wagons and ambulances), 284,029 vans, 237,812 tractors and special purpose vehicles, 144,855 mopeds, 103,716 motorcycles, 85,149 combined vehicles, 80,623 goods vehicles (including lorries) and 30,592 buses. In 2004 there were 8,425 road accidents with 227 fatalities.

Rail

The length of state railways in 2003 was 4,077 km (2,518 km electrified). In 2004 passenger-km travelled came to 2,290m. and freight tonne-km to 2,199m. Sales and other operating income totalled 6,296m. kroner in 2004.

There is a metro (104 km) and a tram network (146 km) in Oslo.

Civil Aviation

The main international airports are at Oslo (Gardermoen), Bergen (Flesland), Trondheim (Værnes) and Stavanger (Sola). Kristiansand (Kjevik) and Torp also have a few international flights. The Scandinavian Airlines System (SAS) resulted from the 1950 merger of the three former Scandinavian airlines. SAS Norge ASA is the Norwegian partner (SAS Denmark A/S and SAS Sverige AB being the other two). Norway and Denmark each hold two-sevenths of the capital of SAS and Sweden three-sevenths. Braathens is the major airline after SAS, carrying 5,936,600 passengers in 1999 (648,700 on international flights).

In 2001 Oslo (Gardermoen) handled 13,930,774 passengers (7,221,998 on domestic flights) and 50,068 tonnes of freight. Bergen is the second busiest airport for passenger traffic, with 3,472,226 in 2001 (2,744,835 on domestic flights), and Stavanger second busiest for freight, with 7,486 tonnes (and 2,672,055 passengers) in 2001.

Shipping

The Norwegian International Ship Register was set up in 1987. At 31 Dec. 2004, 651 ships were registered (383 Norwegian) totalling 16,017,000 GRT. 161 tankers accounted for 4,859,000 GRT. There were also 749 ships totalling 2,700,000 GRT on the Norwegian Ordinary Register. These figures do not include fishing boats, tugs, salvage vessels, icebreakers and similar special types of vessels. In 2002 Norway's merchant fleet represented 4·3% of total world tonnage. In 2001, 49,557,000 passengers were carried by coastwise shipping on long distance, local and ferry services. The warm Gulf Stream ensures ice-free harbours throughout the year.

Telecommunications

There were 7,167,000 telephone subscribers in 2002 (1,573·1 per 1,000 inhabitants) and 2,405,000 PCs (527·9 for every 1,000 persons). Norway had 3,840,400 mobile phone subscribers in 2002 and 332,000 fax machines. Internet users numbered 2·68m.

in July 2002, approximately 59% of the population. Since 2000 the government has been reducing its interest in Telenor, the country's largest telecommunications operator, and in March 2004 lowered its stake to 54·0%.

Postal Services

In 2001 post offices began to be converted to Post in Shops. 452 post offices were replaced by 519 Post in Shops. In addition, 29 post offices were upgraded to Post Shops and five Business Centres and five Call Centres were established. The final target is a minimum of 1,150 Post in Shops, 300 Post Shops and 20 Business Centres. In 2003 a total of 2,750m. items of mail were processed, or 603 per person.

SOCIAL INSTITUTIONS

Justice

The judicature is common to civil and criminal cases; the same professional judges preside over both. These judges are state officials. The participation of lay judges and jurors, both summoned for the individual case, varies according to the kind of court and kind of case.

The 96 city or district courts of first instance are in criminal cases composed of one professional judge and two lay judges, chosen by ballot from a panel elected by the local authority. In civil cases two lay judges may participate. These courts are competent in all cases except criminal cases where the maximum penalty exceeds six years imprisonment. In every community there is a Conciliation Board composed of three lay persons elected by the district council. A civil lawsuit usually begins with mediation by the Board which can pronounce judgement in certain cases.

The five high courts, or courts of second instance, are composed of three professional judges. Additionally, in civil cases two or four lay judges may be summoned. In serious criminal cases, which are brought before high courts in the first instance, a jury of ten lay persons is summoned to determine whether the defendant is guilty according to the charge. In less serious criminal cases the court is composed of two professional and three lay judges. In civil cases, the court of second instance is an ordinary court of appeal. In criminal cases in which the lower court does not have judicial authority, it is itself the court of first instance. In other criminal cases it is an appeal court as far as the appeal is based on an attack against the lower court's assessment of the facts when determining the guilt of the defendant. An appeal based on any other alleged mistakes is brought directly before the Supreme Court.

The Supreme Court (Høyesterett) is the court of last resort. There are 18 Supreme Court judges. Each individual case is heard by five judges. Some major cases are determined in plenary session. The Supreme Court may in general examine every aspect of the case and the handling of it by the lower courts. However, in criminal cases the Court may not overrule the lower court's assessment of the facts as far as the guilt of the defendant is concerned.

The Court of Impeachment (Riksretten) is composed of five judges of the Supreme Court and ten members of Parliament.

The population in penal institutions in Sept. 2002 was 2,662 (59 per 100,000 of national population).

Education

Free compulsory schooling in primary and lower secondary schools was extended to 10 years from 9, and the starting age lowered to 6 from 7, in July 1997. All young people between the ages of 16 and 19 have the statutory right to three years of upper secondary education. In 2003 there were 5,924 kindergartens (children up to six years old) with 205,172 children and 58,422 staff. In 2003–04 there were 3,209 primary and lower secondary schools with 617,577 pupils and 65,376 teachers; 235,160 pupils and 25,024 teachers at 685 (2001–02) upper secondary schools; and (2001–02) 60 colleges, with 116,356 students and 4,946 teachers.

There are four universities: Oslo (founded 1811), with 31,426 students in Oct. 2001; Bergen (1946), with 16,579 students; Tromsø (1968), with 6,171 students; and the Norwegian University of Science and Technology (1996, formerly the University of Trondheim and the Norwegian Institute of Technology), with 19,403 students. There are also six university colleges and 26 state colleges. In 2001–02 the universities and university colleges had 81,358 students, and the state colleges 116,256 students. The University of Tromsø is responsible for Sami language and studies.

In 2000–01 total expenditure on education came to 6·9% of GNP and 16·2% of total government spending. The adult literacy rate is at least 99%.

Health

The health care system, which is predominantly publicly financed (mainly by a national insurance tax), is run on both county and municipal levels. Persons who fall ill are guaranteed medical treatment, and health services are distributed according to need. In 2003 there were the equivalent of 7,676 full-time doctors, 23,439 nurses and 5,413 auxiliary nursing personnel. In 2003 there were 17,141 hospital beds (excluding those in psychiatric institutions). In 2003 Norway spent 10·3% of its GDP on health. In 2003–04, 27% of men and 25% of women smoked. The rate among women is one of the highest in the world.

Welfare

In 2002 there were 624,054 old age pensioners who received a total of 72,685m. kroner, 292,224 disability pensioners who received 35,662m. kroner, 25,914 widows and widowers who received 1,935m. kroner and 25,470 single parents who received 2,078m. kroner. In 2002, 1,061,460 children received family allowances. Maternity leave is for one year on 80% of previous salary; unused portions may pass to a husband. In 2002 sickness benefits totalling 46,659·1m. kroner were paid: 26,117·0m. kroner in sickness allowances and 20,542·1m. kroner in medical benefits. Expenditure on benefits at childbirth and adoption totalled 8,511·4m. kroner to 125,177 recipients in 2002.

RELIGION

There is freedom of religion, the Church of Norway (Evangelical Lutheran), however, being the national church, endowed by the State. Its clergy are nominated by the King. Ecclesiastically Norway is divided into 11 dioceses, 100 deaneries and 1,298 parishes. About 86% of Norwegians belong to the Church of Norway and approximately 77% of infants were baptised in the Church in 2004. There were 328,400 members of registered and unregistered religious communities outside the Church of Norway, subsidized by central government and local authorities in 2004. There were also 92 Muslim congregations with 80,838 members. The Roman Catholics are under a Bishop at Oslo, a Vicar Apostolic at Trondheim and a Vicar Apostolic at Tromsø.

CULTURE

World Heritage Sites

Norway's UNESCO heritage sites (with year listed) are: the 12–13th century wooden church in Sogn og Fjordane on the west coast, the Urnes Stave Church (1979); the 58 wooden buildings in Bergen's wharf of Bryggen (1979); the wooden houses of the copper mining village of Røros (1980), active between the 17–20th centuries; the pre-historic Rock Drawings of Alta (1995) in the Alta Fjord; Vegaøyan—the Vega Archipelago (2004), a cluster of dozens of islands centred on Vega, just south of the Arctic Circle; the West Norwegian Fjords—Geirangerfjord and Naerøyfjord (2005); and the Struve Geodetic Arc (2005). The Arc is a chain of survey triangulations spanning from Norway to the Black Sea that helped establish the exact shape and size of the earth and is shared with nine other countries.

Broadcasting

The Norwegian Broadcasting Corporation is a non-commercial enterprise operated by an independent state organization and broadcasts one programme (P1) on long, medium, and short-waves and on FM and one programme (P2) on FM. Local programmes are also broadcast. It broadcasts one TV programme from 2,259 transmitters. Colour programmes are broadcast by the PAL system. In 2000 there were 4·1m. radio and 3·0m. television receivers.

Cinema

There were 401 cinemas in 2003, with a seating capacity of 84,290. Attendances totalled 13·0m.

Press

There were 65 daily newspapers with a combined average net circulation of 2·17m. in 2004, and 91 weeklies and semi-weeklies with 689,000 in 2002. Norway has one of the highest circulation rates of daily newspapers in Europe, at 596 per 1,000 inhabitants in 2000. In 1999 a total of 4,985 book titles were published.

Tourism

In 2000 there were 4,348,000 foreign tourists. In 2004 there were 1,079 hotels and 794 camping sites. Receipts from foreign tourism totalled US$2·74bn. in 2002.

Libraries

In 2003 there were 892 public libraries, 3,431 school libraries and 336 special and research libraries (three national).

Theatre and Opera

There were 7,522 theatre and opera performances attended by 1,549,064 people at 22 theatres in 2003.

Museums and Galleries

There were 263 museums in 2003 (27 art, 196 social history, eight natural history and 32 mixed social and natural history), with 8,523,048 visitors.

DIPLOMATIC REPRESENTATIVES

Of Norway in the United Kingdom (25 Belgrave Sq., London, SW1X 8QD)
Ambassador: Bjarne Lindstrøm.

Of the United Kingdom in Norway (Thomas Heftyesgate 8, 0244 Oslo)
Ambassador: Mariot Leslie.

Of Norway in the USA (2720 34th St., NW, Washington, D.C., 20008)
Ambassador: Knut Vollebaek.

Of the USA in Norway (Drammensveien 18, 0244 Oslo)
Ambassador: Benson K. Whitney.

Of Norway to the United Nations
Ambassador: Johan L. Løvald.

Of Norway to the European Union
Ambassador: Bjørn T. Grydeland.

FURTHER READING

Statistics Norway (formerly Central Bureau of Statistics). *Statistisk Årbok; Statistical Yearbook of Norway.—Economic survey* (annual, from 1935; with English summary from 1952, now published in *Økonomiske Analyser,* annual).—*Historisk Statistikk; Historical Statistics.—Statistisk Månedshefte* (with English index)
Norges Statskalender. From 1816; annual from 1877

Petersson, O., *The Government and Politics of the Nordic Countries.* Stockholm, 1994
Turner, Barry, (ed.) *Scandinavia Profiled.* Macmillan, London, 2000

National library: The National Library of Norway, Drammensveien 42b, 0255 Oslo.
National Statistical Office: Statistics Norway, PB 8131 Dep., N-0033 Oslo.
Website: http://www.ssb.no/

Svalbard

An archipelago situated between 10° and 35° E. long. and between 74° and 81° N. lat. Total area, 61,020 sq. km (23,560 sq. miles). The main islands are Spitsbergen, Nordaustlandet, Edgeøya, Barentsøya, Prins Karls Forland, Bjørnøya, Hopen, Kong Karls Land and Kvitøya. The Arctic climate is tempered by mild winds from the Atlantic.

The archipelago was probably discovered by Norsemen in 1194 and rediscovered by the Dutch navigator Barents in 1596. In the 17th century whale-hunting gave rise to rival Dutch, British and Danish-Norwegian claims to sovereignty; but when in the 18th century the whale-hunting ended, the question of the sovereignty of Svalbard lost its significance. It was again raised in the 20th century, owing to the discovery and exploitation of coalfields. By a treaty, signed on 9 Feb. 1920 in Paris, Norway's sovereignty over the archipelago was recognized. On 14 Aug. 1925 the archipelago was officially incorporated in Norway.

Total population on 1 Jan. 2005 was 2,400, of whom 1,645 were Norwegians, 747 Russians and eight Poles. Coal is the principal product. There are two Norwegian and two Russian mining camps. 2,904,301 tonnes of coal were produced from Norwegian mines in 2004 valued at 1,304m. kroner.

There were 2,413 motor vehicles and trailers registered at 31 Dec. 1999, including 1,145 snow scooters. There are research and radio stations, and an airport near Longyearbyen (Svalbard Lufthavn) opened in 1975.

Greve, T., *Svalbard: Norway in the Arctic.* Oslo, 1975
Hisdal, V., *Geography of Svalbard.* Norsk Polarinstitutt, Oslo, rev. ed., 1984

Jan Mayen

This bleak, desolate and mountainous island of volcanic origin and partly covered by glaciers is situated at 71° N. lat. and 8° 30' W. long., 300 miles north-northeast of Iceland. The total area is 377 sq. km (146 sq. miles). Beerenberg, its highest peak, reaches a height of 2,277 metres. Volcanic activity, which had been dormant, reactivated in Sept. 1970.

The island was possibly discovered by Henry Hudson in 1608, and it was first named Hudson's Tutches (Touches). It was again and again rediscovered and renamed. Its present name derives from the Dutch whaling captain Jan Jacobsz May, who indisputably discovered the island in 1614. It was uninhabited, but occasionally visited by seal hunters and trappers, until 1921 when Norway established a radio and meteorological station. On 8 May 1929 Jan Mayen was officially proclaimed as incorporated into the Kingdom of Norway. Its relation to Norway was finally settled by law of 27 Feb. 1930. A LORAN station (1959) and a CONSOL station (1968) have been established.

Bouvet Island

Bouvetøya

This uninhabited volcanic island, mostly covered by glaciers and situated at 54° 25' S. lat. and 3° 21' E. long., was discovered in 1739 by a French naval officer, Jean Baptiste Loziert Bouvet, but no flag was hoisted until, in 1825, Capt. Norris raised the Union Jack. In 1928 Great Britain waived its claim to the island in favour of Norway, which in Dec. 1927 had occupied it. A law of 27 Feb. 1930 declared Bouvetøya a Norwegian dependency. The area is 49 sq. km (19 sq. miles). Since 1977 Norway has had an automatic meteorological station on the island.

Peter I Island

Peter I Øy

This uninhabited island, situated at 68° 48' S. lat. and 90° 35' W. long., was sighted in 1821 by the Russian explorer, Admiral von Bellingshausen. The first landing was made in 1929 by a Norwegian expedition which hoisted the Norwegian flag. On 1 May 1931 Peter I Island was placed under Norwegian sovereignty,

and on 24 March 1933 it was incorporated as a dependency. The area is 156 sq. km (60 sq. miles).

Queen Maud Land

Dronning Maud Land

On 14 Jan. 1939 the Norwegian Cabinet placed that part of the Antarctic Continent from the border of Falkland Islands dependencies in the west to the border of the Australian Antarctic Dependency in the east (between 20° W. and 45° E.) under Norwegian sovereignty. The territory had been explored only by Norwegians and hitherto been ownerless. In 1957 it was given the status of a dependency.

OMAN

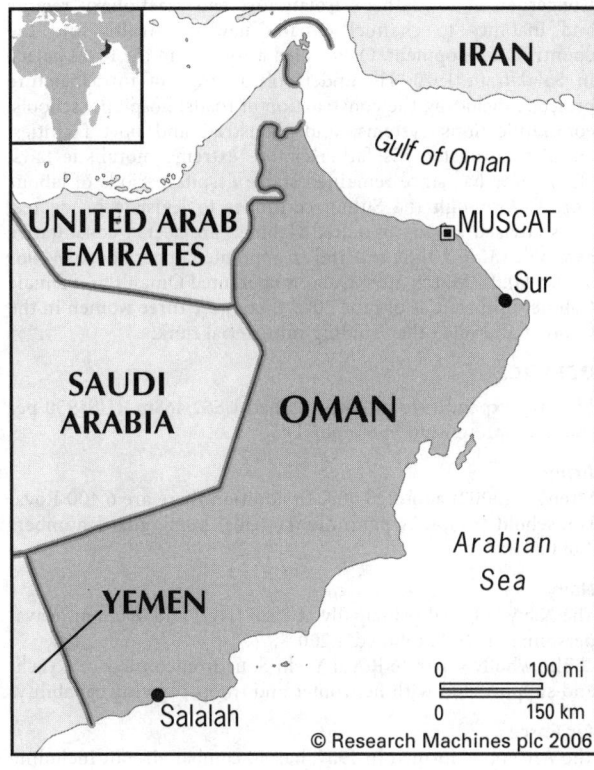

IRAN

Gulf of Oman

UNITED ARAB EMIRATES

☐ MUSCAT

Sur

SAUDI ARABIA

OMAN

Arabian Sea

YEMEN

Salalah

0 — 100 mi
0 — 150 km

© Research Machines plc 2006

Saltanat 'Uman
(Sultanate of Oman)

Capital: Muscat
Population projection, 2010: 2·86m.
GDP per capita, 2002: (PPP$) 13,340
HDI/world rank: 0·781/71

KEY HISTORICAL EVENTS

The ancestors of present day Oman are believed to have arrived in two waves of migration, the first from the Yemen and the second from northern Arabia. In the 9th century maritime trade flourished and Sohar became the greatest sea port in the Islamic world. In the early 16th century the Portuguese occupied Muscat. The Ya'aruba dynasty introduced a period of renaissance in Omani fortunes both at home and abroad, uniting the country and bringing prosperity; but, on the death in 1718 of Sultan bin Saif II, civil war broke out over the election of his successor. Persian troops occupied Muttrah and Muscat but failed to take Sohar which was defended by Ahmad bin Said, who expelled the Persians from Oman after the civil war had ended. In 1744 the Al bu Said family assumed power and has ruled to the present day. Oman remained largely isolated from the rest of the world until 1970 when Said bin Taimur was deposed by his son Qaboos in a bloodless coup.

TERRITORY AND POPULATION

Situated at the southeast corner of the Arabian peninsula, Oman is bounded in the northeast by the Gulf of Oman and southeast by the Arabian Sea, southwest by Yemen and northwest by Saudi Arabia and the United Arab Emirates. There is an enclave at the northern tip of the Musandam Peninsula. An agreement of April 1992 completed the demarcation of the border with Yemen, and an agreement of March 1990 finalized the border with Saudi Arabia.

With a coastline of 1,700 sq. km from the Strait of Hormuz in the north to the borders of the Republic of Yemen, the Sultanate is strategically located overlooking ancient maritime trade routes linking the Far East and Africa with the Mediterranean.

The Sultanate of Oman occupies a total area of 309,500 sq. km and includes different terrains that vary from plain to highlands and mountains. The coastal plain overlooking the Gulf of Oman and the Arabian Sea forms the most important and fertile plain in Oman.

The **Kuria Muria** islands were ceded to the UK in 1854 by the Sultan of Muscat and Oman. On 30 Nov. 1967 the islands were retroceded to the Sultan of Muscat and Oman, in accordance with the wishes of the population. They are now known as the **Halaniyat Islands**.

In 2003 the census population was 2,340,815 (density 7·6 per sq. km.), chiefly Arabs, and including 0·6m. foreign workers.

The UN gives a projected population for 2010 of 2·86m.

In 2003, 77·6% of the population lived in urban areas. The census population of the capital, Muscat, in 2003 was 632,073.

The official language is Arabic; English is in commercial use.

SOCIAL STATISTICS

2002 estimates: births, 71,000; deaths, 10,000. Estimated rates, 2002 (per 1,000 population): births, 25·7; deaths, 3·5. Consequently Oman has a very young population, with approximately 41% of the population under the age of 15. Expectation of life at birth, 2003, was 72·8 years for males and 75·7 years for females. Average annual population growth rate, 1992–2002, 3·3%. Fertility rate, 2001, 5·6 births per woman, down from 7·8 in 1988. Oman has achieved some of the most rapid advances ever recorded. Infant mortality declined from 200 per 1,000 live births in 1960 to 12 per 1,000 live births in 2001, and as recently as 1970 life expectancy was just 40.

CLIMATE

Oman has a desert climate, with exceptionally hot and humid months from April to Oct., when temperatures may reach 47°C. Light monsoon rains fall in the south from June to Sept., with highest amounts in the western highland region. Muscat, Jan. 28°C, July 46°C. Annual rainfall 101 mm. Salalah, Jan. 29°C, July 32°C. Annual rainfall 98 mm.

CONSTITUTION AND GOVERNMENT

Oman is a hereditary absolute monarchy. The Sultan legislates by decree and appoints a Cabinet to assist him. The Basic Statute of the State was promulgated on 6 Nov. 1996.

The present Sultan is **Qaboos bin Said Al Said** (b. Nov. 1940).

In 1991 a new consultative assembly, the *Majlis al-Shura*, replaced the former State Consultative Chamber. The Majlis consists of 83 elected members. It debates domestic issues, but has no legislative or veto powers. There is also an upper house, the *Majlis al Dawla*, which consists of 58 appointed members; it too has advisory powers only.

In Dec. 2002 the Sultan of Oman extended voting rights to all citizens over the age of 21.

National Anthem

'Ya Rabbana elifidh lana jalalat al Saltan' ('O Lord, protect for us his majesty the Sultan'); words by Rashid bin Aziz, tune by Rodney Bashford.

GOVERNMENT CHRONOLOGY

Sultans since 1932.
1932–70   Said bin Taimur Al Said
1970–   Qaboos bin Said Al Said

RECENT ELECTIONS

The last elections to the *Majlis al-Shura* were on 4 Oct. 2003. No parties are allowed. 83 legislators were chosen for three-year terms from among 506 candidates (including 15 women). Two women were elected.

CURRENT ADMINISTRATION

The Sultan is nominally Prime Minister and Minister of Foreign Affairs, Defence and Finance.

In March 2006 the other Ministers were:

Special Representative of the Sultan: Thuwayni bin Shihab Al Said.

Deputy Prime Minister for Cabinet Affairs: Fahd bin Mahmud Al Said. *Minister Responsible for Foreign Affairs:* Yusuf bin Alawi bin Abdallah. *Agriculture and Fisheries:* Salim bin Hilal bin Ali al-Khalili. *Civil Service:* Hilal bin Khalid al-Ma'awali. *Commerce and Industry:* Maqbul bin Ali bin Sultan. *Defence Affairs:* Badr bin Saud bin Harib Al Busaidi. *Transportation and Communications:* Mohammed bin Abdullah bin Isa Al Harthi. *Education:* Yahya bin Saud bin Mansour Al Suleimi. *Housing, Electricity and Water:* Khamis bin Mubarak bin Issa Al Alawi. *Regional Municipalities, Environment and Water Resources:* Abdullah bin Salem bin Amer Al Rawas. *National Economy:* Ahmad bin Abd al-Nabi al-Makki. *Health:* Dr Ali bin Muhammad bin Musa. *Information:* Hamad bin Mohammed bin Mohsin al Rashdi. *Interior:* Saud bin Ibrahim bin Saud Al Busaidi. *Justice:* Muhammad bin Abdallah bin Zahir al-Hinai. *National Heritage and Culture:* Sayyid Haitham bin Tariq Al Said. *Oil and Gas:* Muhammad bin Hamad bin Seif al-Rumhi. *Social Development:* Sharifa bint Khalfan bin Nasser Al-Yahyaeyah. *Awqaf and Religious Affairs:* Abdallah bin Muhammad bin Abdallah al-Salimi. *Sport:* Ali bin Masoud bin Ali Al-Sunaidi. *Diwan of the Royal Court:* Said Ali bin Hamoud al-Busaidi. *Royal Office:* Gen. Ali bin Majid al-Mamari. *Higher Education:* Rawya bint Saud Al-Bussaidi. *Legal Affairs:* Muhammad bin Ali bin Nasir al-Alawi. *Labour:* Jama bin Ali bin Juma. *Tourism:* Rajiha bint Abdul Amir ibn Ali. *Minister of State and Governor of the Capital:* Sayyid Al-Mutassim bin Hamoud al-Busaidi. *Minister of State and Governor of Dhofar:* Muhammad bin Ali al-Qutaybi.

CURRENT LEADERS

Qaboos bin Said

Position
Sultan

Introduction
Qaboos has been the Sultan since 23 July 1970 when he deposed his father, Said bin Taimur. He has carried out an ambitious social and economic modernization programme, opening Oman to the outside world through accession to the League of Arab States, Gulf Co-operation Council and United Nations and pursuing a moderate regional foreign policy while preserving a longstanding political and military relationship with the United Kingdom.

Qaboos is currently prime minister, minister of defence, minister of foreign affairs, minister of finance and chairman of the central bank.

Early Life
Born in Salalah on 18 Nov. 1940, Qaboos was taught locally before attending a private school in England from the age of 16. In 1960 he went to the British Royal Military Academy at Sandhurst as an officer cadet. He subsequently served in the British army on operational duty and then studied local government in England before returning to Oman.

Career in Office
Concerned at his father's isolationist and reactionary regime and inability to channel Oman's new oil wealth into the country's development, Qaboos led a coup from the royal palace in Salalah in 1970. He undertook a range of infrastructure projects, including the construction of roads, hospitals, schools, communications systems, and industrial and port facilities. He also abrogated his father's more extreme moralistic laws. His regime has since remained stable despite periods of labour unrest. Although the Sultan continues to legislate by decree, he is advised by an appointed Cabinet, an elected consultative assembly (*Majlis al-Shura*) and an appointed upper house (*Majlis al Dawla*). In March 2004 Qaboos appointed Oman's first female Cabinet minister; as of June 2005 there were three women in the Cabinet and one other holding ministerial rank.

DEFENCE

Military expenditure in 2003 totalled US$2,468m. (US$950 per capita), representing 11·6% of GDP.

Army

Strength (2002) about 25,000. In addition there are 6,400 Royal Household troops. A paramilitary tribal home guard numbers 4,000.

Navy

The Navy is based principally at Seeb (HQ) and Wudam. Naval personnel in 2002 totalled 4,200.

The wholly separate Royal Yacht Squadron consists of a yacht and support ship with helicopter and troop-carrying capability.

Air Force

The Air Force, formed in 1959, has 40 combat aircraft including in 2002 two strike/interceptor squadrons of Jaguars and a ground attack squadron of Hawks.

Personnel (2002) about 4,100.

INTERNATIONAL RELATIONS

A 1982 Memorandum of Understanding with the UK provided for regular consultations on international and bilateral issues.

Oman is a member of the UN, WTO, the League of Arab States, the Organization of the Islamic Conference, Islamic Development Bank and the Gulf Co-operation Council.

ECONOMY

Industry accounted for 53·2% of GDP in 2002, services 44·7% and agriculture 2·1%.

Currency

The unit of currency is the *Rial Omani* (OMR). It is divided into 1,000 *baiza*. The rial is pegged to the US dollar. In June 2002 foreign exchange reserves were US$3,133m., total money supply was RO 813m. and gold reserves totalled 1,000 troy oz (291,000 troy oz in April 2002). Following three years of deflation there was inflation of 0·2% in 2003 and 0·8% in 2004.

In 2001 the six Gulf Arab states—Oman, along with Bahrain, Kuwait, Qatar, Saudi Arabia and the United Arab Emirates—signed an agreement to establish a single currency by 2010.

Budget

Budget revenue and expenditure (in RO 1m.):

	1997	1998	1999	2000	2001
Revenue	1,867·4	1,426·6	1,401·8	1,831·2	2,077·2
Expenditure	1,848·0	1,820·1	1,859·4	2,179·5	2,295·1

In 1999 approximately 70% of total revenue came from oil.

Performance

Real GDP growth was 1·9% in 2003 and 4·5% in 2004. Total GDP in 2002 was US$20·1bn.

Banking and Finance

The bank of issue is the Central Bank of Oman, which commenced operations in 1975 (*President*, Hamood Sangour Al Zadjali). All banks must comply with BIS capital adequacy ratios and have a minimum capital of RO 20m. (minimum capital requirement for foreign banks established in Oman is RO 3m.). In 2002 there were 15 commercial banks (of which nine were foreign) and three specialized banks. The largest bank is BankMuscat SAOG, with assets of RO 1·3bn. It was created in 2000 following a merger between BankMuscat and the Commercial Bank of Oman.

There is a stock exchange in Muscat, which is linked with those in Bahrain and Kuwait.

ENERGY AND NATURAL RESOURCES

Environment

Oman's carbon dioxide emissions from the consumption and flaring of fossil fuels in 2002 were the equivalent of 8·2 tonnes per capita.

Electricity

Installed capacity was 2·4m. kW in 2000. Production in 2000 was 12·06bn. kWh, with consumption per capita 5,021 kWh (2000).

Oil and Gas

The economy is dominated by the oil industry. Oil in commercial quantities was discovered in 1964 and production began in 1967. Production in 2003 was 40·7m. tonnes. In 2000 exports of oil stood at 29·5m. tonnes. Total proven reserves were estimated in 2002 to be 5·5bn. bbls. It was announced in Aug. 2000 that two new oilfields in the south of the country had been discovered, with a potential combined daily production capacity of 12,200 bbls. a day. Earlier in 2000 oil began to be pumped from two further recently-discovered oilfields.

Gas is likely to become the second major source of income for the country. Oman's proven gas reserves were 864bn. cu. metres in 2002. The discovery in 2000 of two new fields could yield a daily production of 1·78m. cu. metres. Natural gas production was 14·8bn. cu. metres in 2002.

Water

Oman relies on a combination of aquifers and desalination plants for its water, augmented by a construction programme of some 60 recharge dams. Desalination plants at Ghubriah and Wadi Adai provide most of the water needs of the capital area. In 1999 water production was 20,136m. gallons.

Minerals

Production in 1998 (in 1,000 tonnes): limestone, 1,902; marble, 166; gypsum, 165; chromite, 30; salt, 14; silver (2001), 3 tonnes; gold (2000), 1,029 kg. The mountains of the Sultanate of Oman are rich in mineral deposits; these include chromite, coal, asbestos, manganese, gypsum, limestone and marble. The government is studying the exploitation of gold, platinum and sulphide.

Agriculture

Agriculture and fisheries are the traditional occupations of Omanis and remain important to the people and economy of Oman to this day. The country now produces a wide variety of fresh fruit, vegetables and field crops. The country is rapidly moving towards its goal of self-sufficiency in agriculture with the total area under cultivation standing at over 70,000 ha. and total output more than 1m. tonnes. This has not been achieved without effort. In a country where water is a scarce commodity it has meant educating farmers on efficient methods of irrigation and building recharge dams to make the most of infrequent rainfall. In 2001 there were 38,000 ha. of arable land and 43,000 ha. of permanent crops. 62,000 ha. were irrigated in 2001. According to a census of 1992–93, about 103,000 people were employed in agriculture of whom a third were women.

The coastal plain (Batinah) northwest of Muscat is fertile, as are the Dhofar highlands in the south. In the valleys of the interior, as well as on the Batinah coastal plain, date cultivation has reached a high level, and there are possibilities of agricultural development.

Agricultural products, 2000 estimates (in 1,000 tonnes): dates, 135; tomatoes, 34; watermelons, 32; lemons and limes, 31; bananas, 28. Vegetable and fruit production are also important, and livestock are raised in the south where there are monsoon rains. Camels (98,000 in 2000) are bred by the inland tribes. Other livestock, 2000: sheep, 180,000; cattle, 213,000; goats, 729,000; chickens, 3m.

Fisheries

The catch was 126,531 tonnes in 2001, exclusively sea fish. More than 80% is taken by some 85,000 self-employed fishermen.

INDUSTRY

Apart from oil production, copper smelting and cement production, there are light industries, mainly food processing and chemical products. The government gives priority to import substitute industries.

Labour

Males constituted 84% of the labour force in 1999. In 1995 there were 619,351 employees in the private sector and 110,529 persons in government service. The employment of foreign labour is being discouraged following 'Omanization' regulations of 1994.

INTERNATIONAL TRADE

Total foreign debt was US$4,639m. in 2002. A royal decree of 1994 permits up to 65% foreign ownership of Omani companies with a five-year tax and customs duties exemption.

Oman, along with Bahrain, Kuwait, Qatar, Saudi Arabia and the United Arab Emirates began the implementation of a customs union in Jan. 2003.

Imports and Exports

Imports and exports in US$1m.:

	2000	2001	2002	2003	2004
Imports f.o.b.	4,593	5,310	5,636	6,086	7,873
Exports f.o.b.	11,318	11,073	11,172	11,670	13,345

Main import suppliers, 2000: United Arab Emirates, 29·5%; Japan, 18·1%; UK, 5·8%; USA, 5·4%; Germany, 3·7%; South Korea, 3·4%.

In 1999 crude oil exports made up approximately 74% of total exports. Main export markets in 2000 were: United Arab Emirates, 40·1%; Saudi Arabia, 8·4%; Iran, 7·8%; Yemen, 7·8%; USA, 5·5%; UK, 3·8%.

In 2000 the value of Oman's exports rose 56·4% compared to 1999. Over the same period oil exports rose by 61·1%.

COMMUNICATIONS

Roads

A network of adequate graded roads links all the main sectors of population, and only a few mountain villages are not accessible by motor vehicles. In 2002 there were about 32,800 km of roads including 550 km of motorways and 2,160 km of main roads. In 2002 there were 301,500 passenger cars and 114,200 vans and lorries. In 1999 there were 8,947 road accidents and 473 deaths.

Civil Aviation

Oman has a 25% share in Gulf Air with Bahrain, Qatar and the UAE. In 2003 Gulf Air ran services in and out of Seeb International Airport (20 miles from Muscat) to Abu Dhabi,

Amman, Bahrain, Bangkok, Bombay, Cairo, Dar es Salaam, Delhi, Dubai, Frankfurt, Kuwait, London, Madras, Manila, Nairobi, Riyadh and Thiruvananthapuram. Oman Air also flies on some international routes. In 2001 Seeb International Airport (Muscat) handled 2,612,916 passengers and 70,337 tonnes of freight.

There are plans to expand Oman's two major airports, Seeb International and Salalah (mainly domestic flights).

Shipping
In Mutrah a deep-water port (named Mina Qaboos) was completed in 1974. The annual handling capacity is 1·5m. tonnes. Mina Salalah, the port of Salalah, has a capacity of 1m. tonnes per year. Sea-going shipping totalled 19,000 GRT in 2002.

Telecommunications
The General Telecommunications Organization maintains a telegraph office at Muscat and an automatic telephone exchange. In 2002 there were 692,500 telephone subscribers (255·4 per 1,000 persons) and 95,000 PCs in use (35·0 for every 1,000 persons). Mobile phone subscribers numbered 464,900 in 2002 and there were 9,700 fax machines. In 2002 there were 18,000 Internet users.

Postal Services
In 2003 there were 610 post offices. 32m. items of mail were processed in 2003.

SOCIAL INSTITUTIONS

Justice
The population in penal institutions in 2000 was 2,020 (81 per 100,000 of national population).

Education
Adult literacy was 74·4% in 2002 (male, 82·0%; female, 65·4%). In 2003–04 there were 1,022 schools. The total number of pupils in state education in 2003–04 was 576,472 (139,082 in basic education and 437,390 in general education) with 32,345 teachers (13,939 in basic education and 18,406 in general education). Oman's first university, the Sultan Qaboos University, opened in 1986 and in 2003–04 there were 12,437 students.

In 2001–02 total expenditure on education came to 4·4% of GNP.

Health
In 2003 there were 49 hospitals with 4,501 beds. There were also 129 health centres. In 2002 there were 3,478 doctors, 297 dentists, 594 pharmacists and 8,004 nursing staff.

RELIGION
In 2001, 83·5% of the population were Muslim. There were also Hindu and Christian minorities.

CULTURE

World Heritage Sites
The four sites under Omani jurisdiction are (with the year entered on the list): Bahla Fort (1987); the archaeological sites of Bat, Al-Khutm and Al-Ayn, a collection of settlements and necropolises of the 3rd millennium BC (1988); the Arabian Oryx Sanctuary, a protected area for endangered species (1994); and the Frankincense Trail, a group of archaeological sites representing the production and distribution of frankincense (2000).

Broadcasting
The government-owned Radio Oman broadcasts in Arabic and English. A colour (PAL) television service, the government-owned Oman Television, covering Muscat and the surrounding area, started transmission in 1974. A television service for Dhofar opened in 1975. In 1991 there were seven television stations. Total number of radios (2000), 1·49m.; and televisions (2000), 1·35m. (563 per 1,000 inhabitants). Television usage has increased dramatically since 1980, when there were just 35,000 TV receivers in Oman (31 per 1,000 inhabitants). Oman had both the greatest percentage increase in the number of TV receivers of any country in the world between 1980 and 2000 and the greatest numerical increase in the number of receivers per 1,000 inhabitants.

Press
In 1998 there were five daily newspapers with a combined circulation (1996) of 63,000.

Tourism
Foreign visitors numbered 602,000 in 2002; spending by tourists totalled US$116m. In 1999 there were 102 hotels with a total of over 5,100 rooms. Tourism accounts for 1% of GDP.

Festivals
National Day (18 Nov.); Spring Festival in Salalah (July–Aug.); Ramadan (Dec.).

Libraries
Three public libraries are run by the Royal Court of Diwan, the Islamic Institute and the Ministry of National Heritage.

Theatre and Opera
There is one national theatre.

Museums and Galleries
The main attractions are the Omani Museum (est. 1974) at Medinat al-Alam; the Omani-French Museum, Children's Museum and Bait al-Zubair (a historic house) at Muscat; the Natural History Museum at the Ministry of National Heritage and Culture; the National Museum; Salalah Museum; the Sultan's Armed Forces museum at Bait al-Falaj; the Oil & Gas Exhibition at Mina al-Fahal. There is also a museum in the historic fort at Sohar.

In 1998 total museum attendance was 96,000.

DIPLOMATIC REPRESENTATIVES

Of Oman in the United Kingdom (167 Queen's Gate, London, SW7 5HE)
Ambassador: Hussain bin Ali bin Abdullatif.

Of the United Kingdom in Oman (PO Box 185, Mina Al Fahal, Postal Code 116, Muscat)
Ambassador: Stuart Laing.

Of Oman in the USA (2535 Belmont Rd, NW, Washington, D.C., 20008)
Ambassador: Hunaina Sultan Ahmed Al-Mughairi.

Of the USA in Oman (PO Box 202, Medinat Qaboos, Muscat)
Ambassador: Richard L. Baltimore.

Of Oman to the United Nations
Ambassador: Fuad Mubarak Al-Hinai.

Of Oman to the European Union
Ambassador: Khadija bint Hassan Salman Al-Lawati.

FURTHER READING

Clements, F. A., *Oman.* [Bibliography] 2nd ed. ABC-Clio, Oxford and Santa Barbara (CA), 1994
Owtram, Francis, *A Modern History of Oman: Formation of the State since 1920.* I. B. Tauris, London, 2002
Skeet, I., *Oman: Politics and Development.* London, 1992

National Statistical Office: Ministry of National Economy, Information and Documentation Centre, POB 881, Muscat 113.
Website: http://www.moneoman.gov.om

PAKISTAN

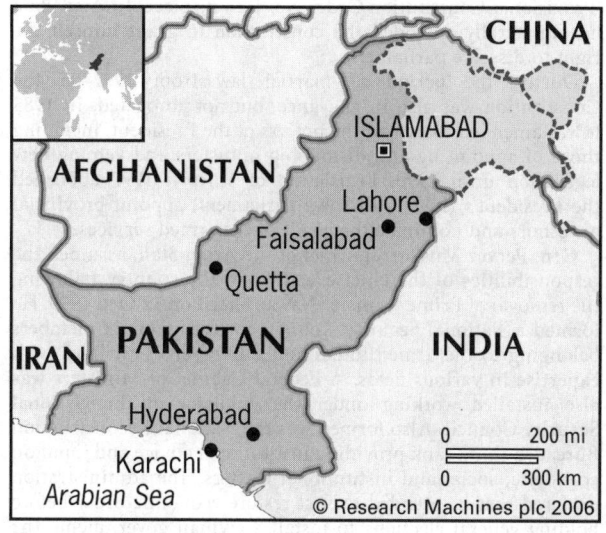

© Research Machines plc 2006

Islami Jamhuriya e Pakistan
(Islamic Republic of Pakistan)

Capital: Islamabad
Population projection, 2010: 175·18m.
GDP per capita, 2003: (PPP$) 2,097
HDI/world rank: 0·527/135

KEY HISTORICAL EVENTS

The State of Pakistan was created on 14 Aug. 1947 to provide Indian Muslims with their own state. Partition was marked by widespread communal violence in which hundreds of thousands died and millions were made homeless. The first governor general, and the man considered Pakistan's founding father, Mohammad Ali Jinnah, died in 1948. The first war with India over the disputed territory of Kashmir occurred in the same year. In 1951 Pakistan's first prime minister, Liaquat Ali Kahn, was assassinated. As the popularity of the ruling Muslim League declined, Pakistan's government worked in increasingly unstable conditions.

Pakistan's status was that of a Dominion within the Commonwealth; it became a republic in 1956 and left the Commonwealth in 1972. Efforts to rejoin were opposed by India until 1989 when Pakistan once more became a full member of the Commonwealth.

The first of several periods of martial law began in 1958, followed by the rule of Field Marshal Mohammad Ayub Khan (until 1969) and Gen. Agha Mohammad Yahya Khan (until 1971). During the latter's term, differences between East and West Pakistan came to a head. Civil war broke out in March 1971 and ended in Dec. 1971 with the creation of Bangladesh. A new constitution came into force on 14 Aug. 1973, providing a federal parliamentary government with a president as head of state and a prime minister as head of the government. Zulfiquar Ali Bhutto became prime minister. His government was thought by traditionalists to be not sufficiently Islamic. There was an army coup led by Gen. Mohammad Zia ul-Haq in July 1977. Zulfiquar Ali Bhutto was hanged for conspiring to murder. His daughter, Benazir, held power twice in the 1990s but was eventually overthrown in 1996 when the President,

Farooq Leghari, dismissed the government for corruption and mismanaging the economy.

Kashmir

Relations between Pakistan and India have foundered on the issue of Kashmir, a disputed territory divided by a ceasefire line negotiated by the UN in 1949. On 28 May 1998 Pakistan carried out five nuclear tests in the deserts of Balochistan in response to India's tests earlier in the month. US President Bill Clinton invoked sanctions but Pakistan subsequently carried out a sixth test. With first steps towards a nuclear agreement, the USA lifted most sanctions. On 11 June, following India's example, Pakistan announced a unilateral moratorium on nuclear tests. On 12 Oct. 1999 the military chief, Gen. Pervez Musharraf, seized power in a coup, overthrowing the democratically-elected government of prime minister Nawaz Sharif. The coup, which lasted less than three hours, was launched after the prime minister had tried to dismiss Gen. Musharraf from his position as army chief of staff. The former prime minister and his senior allies were placed under house arrest and subsequently put on trial. Nawaz Sharif was found guilty of corruption and sentenced to life imprisonment. The coup marked the first time in history that a military regime had taken over an affirmed nuclear power.

There have been some 35,000 deaths since the outbreak of the Kashmir insurgency in 1988. Negotiations with India over the future of the disputed territory of Kashmir began in July 1999. In May 2001 India ended its six-month long ceasefire. It then invited Pakistan's government to enter talks about the dispute, which ended with hopes of avoiding further violence. Following the attacks on New York and Washington of 11 Sept. 2001 Pakistan found itself in a central role in the war against terrorism. With neighbouring Afghanistan believed to be sheltering Osama bin Laden, the USA persuaded President Musharraf to allow American forces access to Pakistani air bases. In return the USA lifted the remaining sanctions imposed on Pakistan after it carried out a series of nuclear tests in 1998. In Dec. 2001 an attack was made on the Indian parliament by suicide bombers. Although no group claimed responsibility, the Indian authorities suspected Kashmiri separatists, leading to increasing tension between Pakistan and India. However, President Musharraf's subsequent crackdown on militants helped to bring the two countries back from the brink of war. Tension between Pakistan and India increased following an attack on an Indian army base in Indian-occupied Kashmir on 14 May 2002. The attack, which killed 31 people, was linked to Islamic terrorists infiltrating into the Kashmir valley from Pakistan. It drew widespread criticism of President Musharraf for failing to combat terrorism in the disputed region. Between 25 and 28 May Pakistan carried out three tests of short-range ballistic missiles. In Nov. 2003 Pakistan and India agreed to another attempt at a ceasefire along the Line of Control in Kashmir.

In Oct. 2005 Pakistan-administered Kashmir was struck by the most destructive earthquake in nearly 30 years. The death toll was put at 73,000, with more than 69,000 injured and 3m. left homeless.

TERRITORY AND POPULATION

Pakistan is bounded in the west by Iran, northwest by Afghanistan, north by China, east by India and south by the Arabian Sea. The area (excluding the disputed area of Kashmir) is 796,095 sq. km (307,374 sq. miles); population (1998 census, excluding Azad, Kashmir, Baltistan, Diamir and Gilgit), 130,579,571 (females, 62,739,434). 2005 estimate: 157,935,000. In 2003, 65·9% lived in rural areas. There were 1·1m. refugees in 2003, mostly from

Afghanistan, the highest number in any country in the world (although the number of Afghan refugees in Pakistan by the end of 2003 was nearly half the 2001 total).

The UN gives a projected population for 2010 of 175·18m.

The population of the principal cities is as follows:

		1998 census			
Karachi	9,339,023	Multan	1,197,384	Peshawar	982,816
Lahore	5,143,495	Hyderabad	1,166,894	Quetta	565,137
Faisalabad	2,008,861	Gujranwala	1,132,509	Islamabad	529,180
Rawalpindi	1,409,768				

Population of the provinces (census of 1998):

	Area (sq. km)	1998 census population (in 1,000) Total	Male	Female	Urban	1998 density per sq. km
North-West Frontier Province	74,521	17,555	8,963	8,592	2,973	236
Federally administered Tribal Areas	27,219	3,138	1,635	1,503	83	115
Federal Capital Territory Islamabad	907	799	430	369	524	881
Punjab	205,344	72,585	37,509	35,076	22,699	353
Sind	140,914	29,991	15,823	14,168	14,662	213
Balochistan	347,190	6,511	3,481	3,030	1,516	19

Urdu is the national language and the *lingua franca*, although only spoken by about 8% of the population; English is used in business, higher education and in central government. Around 48% of the population speak Punjabi.

SOCIAL STATISTICS

Estimates, 2002: births, 4,310,000; deaths, 1,230,000. Estimated birth rate in 2002 was 28·7 per 1,000 population; estimated death rate, 8·2. Infant mortality (per 1,000 live births), 84 (2001). Formal registration of marriages and divorces has not been required since 1992. Expectation of life in 2003 was 62·8 years for men and 63·2 years for women. Annual population growth rate, 1992–2002, 2·5%. Fertility rate, 2001, 5·2 births per woman.

CLIMATE

A weak form of tropical monsoon climate occurs over much of the country, with arid conditions in the north and west, where the wet season is only from Dec. to March. Elsewhere, rain comes mainly in the summer. Summer temperatures are high everywhere, but winters can be cold in the mountainous north. Islamabad, Jan. 50°F (10°C), July 90°F (32·2°C). Annual rainfall 36" (900 mm). Karachi, Jan. 61°F (16·1°C), July 86°F (30°C). Annual rainfall 8" (196 mm). Lahore, Jan. 53°F (11·7°C), July 89°F (31·7°C). Annual rainfall 18" (452 mm). Multan, Jan. 51°F (10·6°C), July 93°F (33·9°C). Annual rainfall 7" (170 mm). Quetta, Jan. 38°F (3·3°C), July 80°F (26·7°C). Annual rainfall 10" (239 mm).

CONSTITUTION AND GOVERNMENT

Under the 1973 Constitution, the *President* was elected for a five-year term by a college of parliamentary deputies, senators and members of the Provincial Assemblies. Parliament is bicameral, comprising a *Senate* of 100 members and a *National Assembly* of 342. In the *Senate*, each of the four provinces is allocated 14 seats, while the federally administered tribal areas and the federal capital are assigned eight and two seats respectively. In addition, each province is conferred four seats for technocrats and four for women. Two seats, one for technocrats and another for women, are reserved for the federal capital. The *National Assembly* is directly elected for five-year terms. 272 members are

elected in single-seat constituencies, there are ten seats for non-Muslim minorities and 60 seats for women.

Following the 1999 coup Gen. Musharraf announced that the Constitution was to be held 'in abeyance' and issued a 'Provisional Constitution Order No. 1' in its place. In Aug. 2002 he unilaterally amended the constitution to grant himself the right to dissolve parliament.

During the period of martial law from 1977–85 the Constitution was also in abeyance, but not abrogated. In 1985 it was amended to extend the powers of the President, including those of appointing and dismissing ministers and vetoing new legislation until 1990. Legislation of 1 April 1997 abolished the President's right to dissolve parliament, appoint provincial governors and nominate the heads of the armed services.

Gen. Pervez Musharraf, Chief of the Army Staff, assumed the responsibilities of the chief executive of the country following the removal of Prime Minister Nawaz Sharif on 12 Oct. 1999. He formed a National Security Council consisting of six members belonging to the armed forces and a number of civilians with expertise in various fields. A Federal Cabinet of Ministers was also installed working under the guidance of the National Security Council. Also formed was the National Reconstruction Bureau, a think tank providing institutional advice and input on economic, social and institutional matters. The administration declared that it intended to first restore economic order before holding general elections to install a civilian government. The Supreme Court of Pakistan allowed the administration a three-year period, which expired on 12 Oct. 2002, to accomplish this task. Elections were held on 10 Oct. 2002. On 30 April 2002 a referendum was held in which 97·7% voted in favour of extending Musharraf's rule by a further five years. Turnout was around 50%. He amended the constitution in Aug. 2002 to formally extend his mandate by five years. The constitution was further amended in Dec. 2003 to enhance Musharraf's power and allow a vote of confidence in his presidency.

The Constitution obliges the government to enable the people to order their lives in accordance with Islam.

National Anthem

'Pak sarzamin shadbad' ('Blessed be the sacred land'); words by Abul Asr Hafeez Jaulandhari, tune by Ahmad G. Chaagla.

GOVERNMENT CHRONOLOGY

Heads of State since 1947. (ML = Muslim League; n/p = non partisan; PML-N = Pakistan Muslim League-Nawaz Sharif; PPP = Pakistan People's Party; RP = Republican Party)

Governors-General

1947–48	ML	Mohammad Ali Jinnah
1948–51	ML	Khwaja Nazimaddin
1951–55	ML	Ghulam Mohammad
1955–56	military	Iskander Ali Mirza

Presidents of the Republic

1956–58	RP	Iskander Ali Mirza
1958–69	military	Mohammad Ayub Khan
1969–71	military	Agha Mohammad Yahya Khan
1971–73	PPP	Zulfiqar Ali Bhutto
1973–78	PPP	Fazal Elahi Chaudhry
1978–88	military	Mohammad Zia ul-Haq
1988–93	n/p	Ghulam Ishaq Khan
1993–97	PPP	Farooq Ahmed Khan Leghari
1998–2001	PML-N	Mohammad Rafiq Tarar
2001–	military	Pervez Musharraf

RECENT ELECTIONS

Pakistan's first general elections since the military coup in 1999 took place on 10 Oct. 2002. The former prime minister Benazir Bhutto's Pakistan People's Party won 71 of 272 seats with 25·8% of votes cast; pro-Musharraf Pakistan Muslim League

(Quaid-e-Azam) took 69 with 25·7%; while a coalition of six hardline Islamic parties, Muttahida Majlis-e-Amal, won 53 with 11·3%. Despite winning 9·4% of the vote, the Pakistan Muslim League (Nawaz Sharif) of exiled former prime minister Nawaz Sharif took only 19 seats. The remaining seats went to smaller parties and non-partisans. After the election, allocation of seats to women and minority representatives was carried out in accordance with the constitution resulting in the Pakistan Muslim League (Quaid-e-Azam) having 117 seats, the Pakistan People's Party 81, the Muttahida Majlis-e-Amal 60 and Pakistan Muslim League (Nawaz Sharif) 19. Turnout was 42%.

CURRENT ADMINISTRATION

President: Gen. Pervez Musharraf; b. 1943 (since 20 June 2001).

Following the overthrow of prime minister Nawaz Sharif in Oct. 1999, Gen. Pervez Musharraf assumed power. He appointed a National Security Council to function as the country's supreme governing body and subsequently a full cabinet of ministers. In June 2001 he declared himself president. Following the elections of Oct. 2002 a coalition government was formed. In March 2006 it comprised:

Prime Minister and Minister of Finance: Shaukat Aziz; b. 1949 (PML-Q; sworn in 28 Aug. 2004).

Senior Federal Minister for Defence: Rao Sikandar Iqbal. *Minister for Commerce:* Humayoon Akhtar Khan. *Communication:* Muhammad Shamim Siddiqui. *Culture, Sports and Youth Affairs:* Muhammad Ajmal Khan. *Defence Production:* Habibullah Khan Warriach. *Education:* Javed Ashraf Qazi. *Environment:* Tahir Iqbal. *Food, Agriculture and Livestock:* Sikandar Hayat Khan Bosan. *Foreign Affairs:* Mian Khursheed Mehmood Kasuri. *Frontier Affairs:* Sardar Yar Muhammad Rind. *Health:* Mohammad Nasir Khan. *Housing and Works:* Safwanullah Syed. *Industries and Production:* Jehangir Khan Tareen. *Information and Broadcasting:* Sheikh Rashid Ahmad. *Information Technology:* Awais Ahmad Khan Leghari. *Interior:* Aftab Ahmed Khan Sherpao. *Kashmir Affairs and Northern Areas:* Makhdoom Faisal Saleh Hayat. *Labour, Manpower and Overseas Pakistanis:* Ghulam Sarwar Khan. *Law, Justice and Human Rights:* Muhammad Wasi Zafar. *Local Government and Rural Development:* Abdul Razzaq Thahim. *Narcotics Control:* Ghaus Bux Khan Maher. *Parliamentary Affairs:* Sher Afghan Khan Niazi. *Petroleum and Natural Resources:* Amanullah Khan Jadoon. *Population Welfare:* Chaudhry Shahbaz Hussain. *Ports and Shipping:* Babar Khan Ghauri. *Privatization and Investment:* Abdul Hafeez Shaikh. *Railways:* Mian Shamim Haider. *Religious Affairs:* Muhammad Ijaz-ul-Haq. *Science and Technology:* Nouraiz Shakoor. *Social Welfare and Special Education:* Zobaida Jalal. *Textiles Industry:* Mushtaq Ali Cheema. *Tourism:* Syed Ghazi Ghulb Jamal. *Water and Power:* Liaquat Ali Jatoi.

Government Website: http://www.pakistan.gov.pk

CURRENT LEADERS

Gen. Pervez Musharraf

Position
President

Introduction
Gen. Pervez Musharraf, the self-declared president of Pakistan, took power in a bloodless coup in 1999, ousting the democratically-elected prime minister, Nawaz Sharif. It was the first time that a military leader had taken control of a nuclear power. Musharraf styled himself as a caretaker leader, responsible for safeguarding the country while corruption was dealt with, the economy revitalized and 'true' democratic elections held. His leadership was not recognized by the international community and drew sanctions from the USA. The US war in Afghanistan, however, allowed Musharraf to exploit Pakistan's strategic importance to the US military effort and to re-establish political ties with Washington.

As a military commander, Musharraf has a history of involvement in the struggle over Kashmir and since coming to power his relations with India have been dominated by the issue. Tension between the two countries increased in the aftermath of the war in Afghanistan but was eased in late 2003 by a series of reciprocated offers to re-establish bilateral links.

Early Life
Born in Delhi on 11 Aug. 1943, Pervez Musharraf's family migrated to newly-formed Pakistan in 1947. Between the ages of six and 13 he was brought up in Turkey where his father was a secretary of foreign affairs for the Pakistani government. He has frequently cited as his hero the Turkish leader Mustafa Kemal Atatürk, a secular modernizer who fought for Turkish independence. On military service Musharraf settled in Gujranwala in north-east Pakistan.

Following training in the command and staff college, Quetta, and in the UK, Musharraf was commissioned in the Pakistani artillery in 1964. He saw active service in the India-Pakistan war of 1965 when, as a Lieut.-Col., he had command of two artillery regiments. Following promotion to brigadier, he commanded an armoured division, and an artillery and an infantry brigade. In the second armed conflict with India he was in charge of a commando battalion of the Special Services Group. Further promotions in 1991 and 1995 took him to the ranks of Maj.-Gen. and Lieut.-Gen.

On 7 Oct. 1998 Nawaz Sharif, then prime minister of Pakistan, appointed Musharraf as Chief of Army Staff. At the time Musharraf was in command of the 1st Strike Corps based at Mangla, a key military element in Pakistani strategy in Kashmir. The appointment was widely interpreted as a move by Sharif to appoint a figure who would not pose a threat to his leadership. Musharraf's ethnic background (he was not a member of the Punjabi officer class) was seen as a block to his advancement. The former Chief of Army Staff, Gen. Jehangir Karamat, had resigned after calling for the army to have a greater political role. Musharraf took the opposite view, stating that 'the Pakistani army is not involved in politics.' In Jan. 1999, however, he took responsibility for the water and power development authority, previously a civilian administration.

In early 1999 the Joint Chief of Staff Committee (JCSC) was reorganized, giving it increased power in nuclear command and the promise that the chairman would always be from the military. Musharraf took on this additional role in April 1999, becoming the strategic commander of Pakistan's nuclear forces. During armed conflict in Kargil in 1999 between Indian and Pakistani forces, a growing gap between the increasingly powerful chief of army staff and the prime minister became obvious. As Sharif withdrew support, senior army officers became incensed at what they saw as a betrayal. Musharraf, meanwhile, raised his profile, frequently appearing on television to comment on the conflict.

The schism reached a head on 12 Oct. 1999. While Musharraf was on a diplomatic trip to Sri Lanka, Sharif replaced him with Gen. Ziauddin. He then refused permission for Musharraf's plane to land at Karachi airport despite the plane being low on fuel. In a dramatic turn of events the army took power and placed Sharif under arrest. Musharraf declared himself Pakistan's Chief Executive.

Career in Office
The coup attracted international censure and invoked sanctions from the USA. Within Pakistan itself, however, the response was ambivalent. To many, a determined military government appeared the last ditch solution to Pakistan's crippling economic and social problems.

Having announced a National Security Council to take over the administration of the country, Musharraf instituted a series of reforms. He created a juvenile justice ordinance protecting children's rights and a national commission on the status of women. His most highly publicized initiative was a National Accountability Bureau (NAB) to target defaulters on government loans. In its first few months repayments were estimated at US$152m. (although this was only 6% of the total target revenue). While the measure won him popularity for combating corruption, he exempted the judiciary and the military from prosecutions relating to the NAB. The Bureau was given wide-ranging authority to investigate the legitimacy of private wealth when it went beyond 'visible means of income'. After the deadline was reached for the repayment of loans, a list of outstanding defaulters was published and 21 arrests made on charges of corruption. Both Nawaz Sharif and the husband of former prime minister Benazir Bhutto were included in the list.

Despite Musharraf's insistence that he would make efforts to restore democracy, Pakistan was suspended from the Commonwealth in mid-Nov. 1999. Later that month Nawaz Sharif was formally 'charged with hijacking, kidnapping and conspiracy to murder. He was sentenced to 14 years' imprisonment, subsequently leaving for exile in Saudi Arabia. Tough economic measures, avoided by Sharif's administration, were adopted by Musharraf. A 15% sales tax implemented in early 2000 provoked the longest strike in Pakistan's history.

On 12 May 2000 Pakistan's Supreme Court unanimously validated the Oct. 1999 coup and granted Musharraf executive and legislative authority for three years from the date of the coup. The security of his leadership was further strengthened in June 2001 when he unexpectedly declared himself president, dissolving the provisional and national assemblies and dismissing former head of state, Rafiq Tarar. Guaranteeing himself a future place in Pakistan's administration, regardless of the outcome of democratic elections, the move was also an attempt to strengthen the legitimacy of his leadership before the Agra summit with India, which took place one month later. This first meeting between Musharraf and the then Indian prime minister, Atal Bihari Vajpayee, was hailed as an important step for bilateral relations, but failed to produce significant agreement, most notably over Kashmir. Musharraf's insistence on Kashmir as the core issue was met with an equal degree of insistence from India that Pakistani-funded cross-border terrorism was the central obstacle to improved relations.

The attacks of 11 Sept. 2001 in the USA brought Musharraf's leadership to greater prominence at the international level. As a neighbour of Afghanistan—home to the al-Qaeda terrorist organization blamed for the attack—and sharing strong political links with the Taliban (Afghanistan's *de facto* government), Pakistan became central to attempts to put diplomatic pressure on the regime to secure the surrender of chief suspect Osama bin Laden. Despite intense pressure from Muslims within his own country, Musharraf committed Pakistan to the international anti-terror coalition. Rioting in Quetta and Peshawar, on the Afghan border, followed the first US military strike on Afghanistan. Musharraf downplayed the public sentiment against the US campaign and gave his support for 'short... targeted' military action, stating that 'Pakistan [had taken] the decision of being part of the world, of the world community and a part of a coalition to fight terrorism'. Soon after, Musharraf ejected three senior ministers (all linked to the 1999 coup) who were seen to support hardline Islamic sentiment.

Musharraf's role as a key ally of the USA led to a deterioration in relations with India, which held him responsible for terrorism in Kashmir. He denied giving financial backing to terrorists, admitting only to 'moral, diplomatic and political support' for the Kashmiri 'freedom-fighters'. However, a suicide attack on 1 Oct. 2001 in Srinagar (the administrative centre of Indian-controlled Kashmir) resulting in the death of 38 people, and then a further terrorist attack on the Indian parliament building in New Delhi

on 13 Dec. 2001, forced the Pakistani president into action. Musharraf banned the two militant Islamic organizations linked to the attacks, the Jaish-e-Mohammed and the Lashkar-e-Taiba.

Military tension across the Line of Control (the border between the Indian-occupied and Pakistani-occupied areas of Kashmir) increased throughout Dec. 2001 with a mass mobilization of troops on both sides. India produced a list of Pakistani terrorist suspects, demanding that they be handed over for trial. Although not meeting this demand, Musharraf ordered a series of arrests as part of a domestic clamp-down and gave a ground-breaking address in Jan. 2002 denouncing extremism and condemning terrorist actions related to Kashmir. Well received by the USA, the speech made less impact in India. An attack on an Indian army base in Indian-controlled Kashmir in May, killing 31 people, undermined the confidence which Musharraf sought to build. This and other terrorist activity increased border tension. Although Musharraf gave a second speech denouncing terrorism, he went ahead with a series of missile tests between 25–28 May, provoking international criticism.

In a referendum held on 30 April 2002, 97·7% of the votes cast were in favour of extending Musharraf's presidential rule for a further five years. Following the referendum, Musharraf reconstituted a National Security Council giving him, as chairman, power to override prime ministerial decisions once a new, democratically-elected government had been installed. Following parliamentary elections held in Oct. 2002, the pro-Musharraf Pakistan Muslim League (Quaid-e-Azam) emerged as the largest party with 117 seats.

In March 2003 Pakistan and India both held tests of short-range nuclear-capable missiles. The tests followed soon after India had blamed Pakistan for a massacre of 24 Hindus in Kashmir. In the same month the USA granted US$250m. of aid to Pakistan, ending the last of its sanctions against the country implemented after Musharraf's seizure of power in 1999. The aid was perceived as key to Pakistan's further co-operation in the US-led war against terrorism. Relations with India showed signs of improving from early May 2003. Indian Prime Minister Vajpayee declared his intention of restoring full diplomatic links, which Musharraf welcomed and promised to reciprocate. By late 2003 relations had improved greatly; both sides declared a ceasefire across the Kashmir Line of Control, transport and sporting links were restored, and from Jan. 2004 direct flights were resumed. Pakistan hosted a meeting of the South Asian Association for Regional Co-operation (SAARC) in Jan. 2004, at which Musharraf met with Vajpayee and agreed to open direct talks on Kashmir. Musharraf's offer to drop demands for a Kashmiri referendum was welcomed by the international community and India. Since the election of a new Congress-led Indian government in May 2004, the two countries have continued to engage in regular dialogue, and in April 2005 Musharraf visited New Delhi for informal talks with Prime Minister Manmohan Singh. Also in April, a bus service between Pakistani- and Indian-administered Kashmir (Muzaffarabad–Srinagar) began for the first time in nearly 60 years.

In Dec. 2003 Musharraf survived an assassination attempt in Islamabad, an attack he blamed on Islamic extremists. Despite internal opposition, he nevertheless consolidated his hold on political power during 2004. In April parliament approved the new military-led National Security Council, thereby institutionalizing the role of the armed forces in civilian affairs. The following month, Pakistan was readmitted to the Commonwealth. Then in Dec. 2004, despite having promised to relinquish the role, Musharraf announced that he would continue as head of the Army.

In Oct. 2005, following a co-ordinated terrorist attack in the Indian capital of New Delhi by suspected Islamic militants, Musharraf condemned the atrocity and called for the demilitarization of Kashmir.

DEFENCE

A *Council for Defence and National Security* was set up in Jan. 1997, comprising the President, the Prime Minister, the Ministers of Defence, Foreign Affairs, Interior, Finance and the military chiefs of staff. The Council advised the government on the determination of national strategy and security priorities, but was disbanded in Feb. 1997. The Council was revived in Oct. 1999 following the change of government but was to have a wider scope and not restrict itself to defence matters.

Defence expenditure in 2003 totalled US$3,129m. (US$21 per capita), representing 4·5% of GDP.

Nuclear Weapons

Pakistan began a secret weapons programme in 1972 to reach parity with India, but was restricted for some years by US sanctions. The Stockholm International Peace Research Institute estimates that Pakistan has manufactured between 30 and 50 nuclear weapons. In May 1998 Pakistan carried out six nuclear tests in response to India's tests earlier in the month. Pakistan, known to have a nuclear weapons programme, has not signed the Comprehensive Nuclear-Test-Ban-Treaty, which is intended to bring about a ban on any nuclear explosions. According to *Deadly Arsenals*, published by the Carnegie Endowment for International Peace, Pakistan has both chemical and biological weapon research programmes.

Army

Strength (2004) 550,000. There were also about 292,000 personnel in paramilitary units: National Guard, Frontier Corps and Pakistan Rangers. Army reserves number around 500,000. In April 2004 the army announced a cut-back of 50,000 soldiers.

Most armoured equipment is of Chinese origin including over 2,400 main battle tanks. There is an air wing with fixed-wing aircraft and 21 attack helicopters.

Navy

The combatant fleet includes seven French-built diesel submarines, three midget submarines for swimmer delivery and eight ex-British frigates. The Naval Air wing operates six combat aircraft and nine armed helicopters.

The principal naval base and dockyard are at Karachi. Naval personnel in 2004 totalled 24,000. There is a marine force estimated at 1,400 personnel and naval reserves of 5,000.

Air Force

The Pakistan Air Force came into being on 14 Aug. 1947. It has its headquarters at Peshawar and is organized within three air defence sectors, in the northern, central and southern areas of the country. There is a flying college at Risalpur and an aeronautical engineering college at Korangi Creek.

Total strength in 2004 was 415 combat aircraft and 45,000 personnel. Equipment included Mirage IIIs, Mirage 5s, F-16s, Q-5s and J-7s. There were 8,000 Air Force reservists.

INTERNATIONAL RELATIONS

Pakistan is a member of the UN, WTO, the Commonwealth (not 1972–89), Asian Development Bank, Economic Co-operation Organisation (ECO), South Asian Association for Regional Co-operation (SAARC), IOM, Organisation of Islamic Conference (OIC), Islamic Development Bank, Non-Aligned Movement (NAM), Inter-Parliamentary Union (IPU), IMCO, International Atomic Energy Agency (IAEA), D-8, Conference on Disarmament, United Nations Commission on Human Rights, International Narcotics Control Board, United Nations Environment Programme and the Colombo Plan. Following Gen. Musharraf's coup in Oct. 1999, Pakistan was suspended from the Commonwealth's councils. The suspension was ended in May 2004.

ECONOMY

Agriculture accounted for 23·6% of GDP in 2002, industry 22·9% and services 53·4%. In Jan. 1999 the IMF approved a loan of US$575m. to Pakistan.

Overview

Agriculture contributes just under a quarter of GDP. Pakistan is one of the world's largest producers of raw cotton but historically the country's textile exports have added little value. Chiefly grown in Punjab province, cotton production is crucial to the success of the yarn-spinning industry concentrated around Karachi. In recent years Pakistan has enjoyed increased US quotas for higher added value textile products, largely as a result of Pakistan's support for US military action in Afghanistan.

The economy grew strongly in 2004 and 2005. The agricultural sector posted above-average output results during the period and broad-based growth was supported by sound macroeconomic management and progress in implementing structural reforms, particularly in privatization. Financial sector health has improved and all but one of Pakistan's public-sector banks have been privatized. Inflation picked up in 2004 as a result of fast economic growth. The State Bank of Pakistan reacted to price pressure by raising key rates in 2005. The size of fiscal deficits in the first half of the 2000s, averaging 3·6% of GDP, compares favourably with the 7–8% levels seen throughout the previous two decades. Public debt was also reduced from 75·1% of GDP in 2001 to under 60% in 2004.

In Oct. 2005 a devastating earthquake struck northern Pakistan but was not expected to cut into economic growth as the affected areas account for little of Pakistan's total production. However, the cost of reconstruction will strain Pakistan's public finances and the country's current-account balance is likely to be adversely affected.

Currency

The monetary unit is the *Pakistan rupee* (PKR) of 100 *paisas*. Gold reserves in June 2002 were 2·09m. troy oz; foreign exchange reserves, US$4,822m. Inflation rates (based on IMF statistics):

1997	1998	1999	2000	2001	2002	2003	2004
11·4%	6·5%	4·1%	4·4%	3·1%	3·2%	2·9%	7·4%

The rupee was devalued by 3·65% in Sept. 1996, 8·5% in Oct. 1996 and 8·7% in Oct. 1997, and by 4·2% in June 1998 in response to the financial problems in Asia. In May 2002 total money supply was Rs978,848m.

Budget

The financial year ends on 30 June. Revenue and expenditure (in Rs1m.):

	1997–98	1998–99	1999–2000	2000–01	2001–02[1]
Revenue	433,636	464,372	531,300	535,091	632,799
Expenditure	584,624	627,147	725,642	739,662	843,081

[1]Provisional.

Performance

Real GDP growth rates (based on IMF statistics):

1995	1996	1997	1998	1999	2000	2001	2002	2003	2004
4·9%	2·9%	1·8%	3·1%	4·0%	3·0%	2·5%	4·1%	5·7%	7·1%

Pakistan's total GDP in 2004 was US$96·1bn.

Banking and Finance

The State Bank of Pakistan is the central bank (*Governor*, Dr Shamshad Akhtar); it came into operation as the Central Bank on 1 July 1948 and was nationalized in 1974 with other banks. Private commercial bank licences were re-introduced in 1991.

The State Bank of Pakistan is the issuing authority of domestic currency, custodian of foreign exchange reserves and bankers for the federal and provincial governments and for scheduled banks. It also manages the rupee public debt of the federal and provincial governments. The National Bank of Pakistan acts as an agent of the State Bank where the State Bank has no offices of its own.

In Feb. 1994 the State Bank of Pakistan was granted more autonomy to regulate the monetary sector of the economy.

In Dec. 1999 the Supreme Court ruled that Islamic banking methods, whereby interest is not permitted, had to be used from 1 July 2001. However, the decision was rescinded in June 2002. The State Bank offered three options for the implementation of Islamic banking practices: i) banks to establish an independent Islamic bank; ii) the opening of subsidiaries of existing commercial banks; iii) the establishment of new branches to execute Islamic banking procedures.

In Sept. 2003 total assets of public sector commercial banks amounted to Rs980,300m., total assets of local private banks to Rs1,122,400m., total assets of foreign banks to Rs276,900m. and total assets of all commercial banks amounted to Rs2,379,600m. In Dec. 2005 total deposits of scheduled banks (stocks) equalled Rs2,661,697m. and net foreign assets amounted to Rs523,044m.

There were 37 commercial banks in Sept. 2003 (five state-owned and 15 foreign) with assets Rs2,380bn. In 2002 there were 45 leasing banks, operating in accordance with Sharia demands. There is a Federal Bank for Co-operatives.

Foreign direct investment was a record high US$1,405m. in 2003, up from US$823m. in 2002 and US$385m. in 2001.

There are stock exchanges in Islamabad, Karachi and Lahore.

ENERGY AND NATURAL RESOURCES

Environment
Pakistan's carbon dioxide emissions from the consumption and flaring of fossil fuels were the equivalent of 0·7 tonnes per capita in 2002.

Electricity
Installed capacity of the State Power System in 2001 was 17·46m. kW, of which 4·83m. kW was hydro-electric, 12·17m. kW was thermal and 0·46m. kW was nuclear. In 2003 there were two nuclear reactors in use. Production in 2002 was an estimated 69·30bn. kWh, of which 71% was thermal and 26% was hydro-electric. Consumption per capita in 2002 was about 469 kWh. By 1999, 10·55m. consumers had access to electric power including 66,949 villages (of a total of 125,083).

Oil and Gas
Crude petroleum production in 2000 was 2·7m. tonnes. Reserves in 2002 were 298m. bbls. Exploitation is mainly through government incentives and concessions to foreign private sector companies. Natural gas production in 2002 was 20·9bn. cu. metres with 750bn. cu. metres of proven reserves (2002). The French oil company Total agreed a US$3bn. deal with the government in July 2003 for exploration in the Arabian Sea.

Water
Pakistan's Indus Basin irrigation system is the largest and oldest in the world. It includes a network of 43 independent canal systems and two storage reservoirs. Total length of main canals is 58,000 km which serve 35m. acres of cultivatable land.

Currently three major surface water projects are under way, as are flood control schemes and programmes to check the problems of waterlogging and salinity.

Minerals
Production (tonnes, 1998–99): limestone, 8·72m.; coal (2000), 3·17m.; rock salt, 870,000; gypsum (2000), 377,000; dolomite, 102,859; china clay, 66,000; fire clay, 61,000; chromite, 22,000; barytes, 20,000; fullers earth, 11,000; bauxite (2001), 4,000. Other minerals of which useful deposits have been found are magnesite, sulphur, marble, antimony ore, bentonite, celestite, fluorite, phosphate rock, silica sand and soapstone.

Agriculture
The north and west are covered by mountain ranges. The rest of the country consists of a fertile plain watered by five big rivers and their tributaries. Agriculture is dependent almost entirely on the irrigation system based on these rivers. Area irrigated, 2001, 17·82m. ha. Agriculture employs around half of the workforce. In 1998–99 it provided 24·5% of GDP. In 2001 there were 21·49m. ha. of arable land and 672,000 ha. of permanent crops.

Pakistan is self-sufficient in wheat, rice and sugar. Areas harvested, 2000: wheat, 8·46m. ha.; seed cotton, 2·95m. ha.; rice, 2·31m. ha.; sugarcane, 1·01m. ha.; chick-peas, 0·97m. ha.; maize, 0·89m. ha. Production, 2000 (1,000 tonnes): sugarcane, 46,333; wheat, 21,079; rice, 7,000; seed cotton, 5,735; cottonseed, 3,824; cotton lint, 1,912; potatoes, 1,868; onions, 1,648; maize, 1,351; oranges, 1,310; mangoes, 938; apples, 600; dates, 580; chick-peas, 565.

A Land Reforms Act of 1977 reduced the upper limit of land holding to 100 irrigated or 200 non-irrigated acres. A new agricultural income tax was introduced in 1995, from which holders of up to 25 irrigated or 50 unirrigated acres are exempt. Of about 5m. farms, 12% are of less than 10 ha.

Livestock, 2000 (in 1m.): goats, 47·4; sheep, 24·1; buffaloes, 22·7; cattle, 22·0; asses, 4·5; camels, 1·2; poultry, 148·0.

Livestock products, 2000 (in 1,000 tonnes): beef and veal, 357; poultry, 327; goat, 323; mutton and lamb, 190; buffalo milk, 16,910; cow milk, 8,039; goat milk, 586; eggs, 331; wool, 62.

Forestry
The area under forests in 2000 was 2·36m. ha., some 3·1% of the total land area. Timber production in 2003 totalled 27·98m. cu. metres.

Fisheries
In 2003 the catch totalled 564,743 tonnes, approximately 70% from marine waters and the rest from inland waters.

INDUSTRY

Industry is based largely on agricultural processing, with engineering and electronics. Government policy is to encourage private industry, particularly small businesses. The public sector, however, is still dominant in large industries. Steel, cement, fertilizer and vegetable ghee are the most valuable public sector industries.

Production in tonnes (in 1998–99 unless otherwise stated): cement (2000–01), 9,674,000; sugar (2002), 3,334,000; residual fuel oil (2001), 3,005,000; distillate fuel oil (2002), 2,215,000; petrol (2002), 1,250,000; cotton yarn, 895,000; pig iron, 735,000; vegetable ghee, 615,000; coke, 443,000; paper and board, 256,000; steel billets, 212,000; soda ash, 186,000; caustic soda, 82,000; jute textiles, 63,000; sulphuric acid (2001), 57,000; cotton cloth, 443m. sq. metres; bicycles, 409,000 items; jeeps and cars, 28,815 items.

Labour
Out of 36·85m. people in employment in 1999–2000, 31·69m. were males. A total of 17·84m. persons were engaged in agriculture, hunting, forestry and fishing, 5·23m. in community, social and personal services, 4·98m. in wholesale and retail trade, restaurants and hotels, and 4·23m. in manufacturing.

In 2001 there were four industrial disputes and 7,078 working days were lost.

Trade Unions
In 1997 there were 7,355 trade unions with a membership of 1,022,275.

INTERNATIONAL TRADE

Foreign debt was US$33,672m. in 2002. Most foreign exchange controls were removed in Feb. 1991. Foreign investors may repatriate both capital and profits, and tax exemptions are available for companies set up before 30 June 1995.

Imports and Exports

Trade in US$1m.:

	1998	1999	2000	2001	2002
Imports f.o.b.	9,834	9,520	9,896	9,741	10,406
Exports f.o.b.	7,850	7,673	8,739	9,131	9,792

Major imports in 1998–99 (in Rs1m.): machinery, 52,759; petroleum and petroleum products, 44,867; chemicals, 40,329; edible oils, 31,892; transport equipment, 18,247; grains, pulses and flour, 14,948; dyes and colours, 4,770. Major exports in 1998–99 (in Rs1m.): cotton cloth, 40,295; cotton yarns, 33,928; rice, 19,439; carpets, 6,723; leather, 6,346.

Major import suppliers in 1998–99 (in Rs1m.): USA, 26,737; Japan, 26,597; Saudi Arabia, 21,825; Kuwait, 17,478; UK, 14,395; Germany, 13,413. Major export markets in 1998–99 (in Rs1m.): USA, 60,890; Hong Kong, 20,654; Germany, 18,929; UK, 18,537; UAE, 14,421; Japan, 9,696.

COMMUNICATIONS

Roads

In 2000–01 there were 249,972 km of roads. There are ten motorways providing links between Pakistan's major cities. These include the M-1 from Islamabad to Peshawar, the M-2 from Islamabad to Lahore, the M-4 from Faisalabad to Multan and the M-9 from Karachi to Hyderabad. In 2002 there were 1,008,927 passenger cars, 111,931 trucks, 72,819 buses and 1,545,133 motorcycles. There were 12,440 road accidents involving injury in 1998, with 5,290 fatalities.

All traffic in Pakistan drives on the left. All cars must be insured and registered. Minimum age for driving: 18 years.

Rail

In 2000 Pakistan Railways had a route length of 7,791 km (of which 293 km electrified) mainly on 1,676 mm gauge, with some metre gauge line. Passenger-km travelled in 2002–03 came to 19·8bn. and freight tonne-km to 4·6bn.

Civil Aviation

There are international airports at Karachi, Islamabad, Lahore, Peshawar and Quetta.

The national carrier is the state-owned Pakistan International Airlines, or PIA. It covers 55 international and 37 domestic stations. During 1998–99, 59,097,000 revenue km were flown, compared with 78,796,000 during 1996–97. The revenue passengers carried totalled 3·86m. during 1998–99 and revenue tonne km came to 1,001m. Operating revenues of the corporation stood at Rs16,745bn. and operating expenditure at Rs19,603bn. during 1997–98. PIA resumed flights to Delhi in Jan. 2004.

Shipping

In 2002 ocean-going shipping totalled 247,000 GRT, including oil tankers 50,000 GRT. The busiest port is Karachi. In 2001–02 cargo traffic totalled 25,852,000 tonnes (6,244,000 tonnes loaded and 19,608,000 tonnes discharged). In 1998–99, 1,262 international vessels were handled at the port of Karachi. There is also a port at Port Qasim.

Telecommunications

The telegraph and telephone system is government-owned. Telephone subscribers numbered 4,893,600 in 2002, or 33·5 per 1,000 inhabitants, and in 2001 there were 600,000 PCs in use (4·2 for every 1,000 persons). In March 1999 there were 401 telegraph offices and 155 customer service centres working in the country. There were 1,238,600 mobile phone subscribers in 2002 and 456,000 fax machines in use. Pakistan had 1·5m. Internet users in 2002.

Postal Services

In 2003 there were 15,035 post offices.

SOCIAL INSTITUTIONS

Justice

The Federal Judiciary consists of the Supreme Court of Pakistan, which is a court of record and has three-fold jurisdiction; original, appellate and advisory. There are four High Courts in Lahore, Peshawar, Quetta and Karachi. Under the Constitution, each has power to issue directions of writs of *Habeas Corpus, Mandamus, Certiorari* and others. Under them are district and sessions courts of first instance in each district; they have also some appellate jurisdiction. Criminal cases not being sessions cases are tried by judicial magistrates. There are subordinate civil courts also.

The Constitution provides for an independent judiciary, as the greatest safeguard of citizens' rights. There is an Attorney-General, appointed by the President, who has right of audience in all courts and the Parliament, and a Federal Ombudsman.

A Federal Shariat Court at the High Court level has been established to decide whether any law is wholly or partially un-Islamic. In Aug. 1990 a presidential ordinance decreed that the criminal code must conform to Islamic law (Shariah), and in May 1991 parliament passed a law incorporating it into the legal system.

378,301 crimes were reported in 2001. Execution of the death penalty for murder, in abeyance since 1986, was resumed in 1992. In 2005 there were 33 confirmed executions. There were 9,528 murders in 2001. The population in penal institutions in 2002 was 87,000 (59 per 100,000 of national population).

Education

The National Education Policy (1998–2010) was launched in March 1998. The major aim was the eradication of illiteracy and the spread of a basic education. The policy stresses vocational and technical education, disseminating a common culture based on Islamic ideology. The principle of free and compulsory primary education has been accepted as the responsibility of the state. The adult literacy rate in 2003 was 48·7% (61·7% among males and 35·2% among females). Pakistan has the lowest literacy rate among males outside of Africa. Adult literacy programmes are being strengthened.

About 77% of children aged 5–9 are enrolled at school. Figures for 2000–01:

	Students (in 1,000)	Teachers (in 1,000)	Institutions
Primary	17,135	408·9	147,700
Middle	3,759	209·6	25,500
Secondary	1,565	260·2	14,800
Secondary vocational	83	9·4	630
Arts and Science Colleges	763	27·5	916
Professional Colleges	159	9·1	352
Universities	125	6·0	26

There are also more than 4,000 seminary schools. In 2000–01 total expenditure on education came to 1·8% of GNP and 7·8% of total government spending.

Health

In 2002 there were 906 hospitals and 4,590 dispensaries (with a total of 98,264 beds) and 862 maternity and child welfare centres. There were 102,541 doctors, 44,520 nurses, 23,084 midwives, 5,057 dentists and 45,390 pharmacists (2001).

Welfare

The official retirement age is 60 (men) or 55 (women and miners). To qualify for a pension, 15 years of contributions are needed.

The minimum old age and survivor pension is Rs700 per month (as of Nov. 2001).

Medical services, provided mainly through social security facilities, cover cash and medical benefits such as general medical care, specialist care, medicines, hospitalization, maternity care and transportation.

RELIGION

Pakistan was created as a Muslim state. The Muslims are mainly Sunni, with an admixture of 15–20% Shia. Religious groups: Muslims, 93%; Christians, 2%; Hindus, Parsees, Buddhists, Qadianis and others. Pakistan has the second highest number of Muslims, after Indonesia. There is a Minorities Wing at the Religious Affairs Ministry to safeguard the constitutional rights of religious minorities.

CULTURE

There is a Pakistan National Council of the Arts, a cultural organization to promote art and culture in Pakistan and abroad.

World Heritage Sites
There are six sites under Pakistani jurisdiction which appear on the UNESCO World Heritage List. They are (with year entered on list): the archaeological ruins at Moenjodaro (1980), Taxila (1980), the Buddhist ruins at Tahkt-i-Bahi and the neighbouring city remains at Sahr-i-Bahlol (1980), Thatta (1981), the Fort and Shalamar Gardens in Lahore (1981) and Rohtas Fort (1997). The Fort and Shalamar Gardens in Lahore are among the 34 sites included in the World Heritage in Danger List.

Broadcasting
The Pakistan Broadcasting Corporation is an autonomous body operating 24 stations for 19 regional languages and 16 foreign languages. Five of its major stations have three channels (two AM and one FM). The second AM is generally reserved for sports, educational and entertainment broadcasting whilst FM channels cater mostly for music lovers. There is a school channel broadcasting on FM.

The network of PBC transmitters consists of 28 medium wave transmitters with a radiating power of 2,261 kW, 13 short wave transmitters of 1,131 kW and 5 FM transmitters of 12 kW. It covers 95% of the population and 80% of the total area of the country. A separate government authority, Azad Kashmir Radio, broadcasts in Kashmir.

The commercial Pakistan Television Corporation transmits on 13 VHF/UHF channels (colour by PAL). PTV's signal is also uplinked through Asiasat Transponder. There are six PTV centres in the major cities—Islamabad, Lahore, Karachi, Peshawar and Quetta—and 36 rebroadcast centres. Its headquarters is in Islamabad. Its transmissions reach 88% of the population. Number of sets in use: TV (2001), 21·4m.; radio (2000), 14·7m.

Cinema
There were 600 screens in 1999. 49 full-length films were made in 1999 in Urdu, Punjabi, Pushto and Sindhi. There were seven film studios.

Press
In 2003 there were 204 dailies and 741 non-daily newspapers. Average combined circulation of all dailies in 2003 was 6,245,775. The most popular daily paper in 2001 was *Jang* with a circulation of 775,000.

Tourism
In 2002 there were 498,000 foreign tourists. More than half of foreign tourist arrivals in 1997 were for the purpose of visiting friends and relatives, followed by business (18·3%), holidays and recreation (13·4%) and religion (2·5%). Tourist revenue in 2002 was US$105m.

Festivals
Pakistan is rich in culture. Famous festivals include the Eid Festival, Eid-e-Milad un Nabi (Birthday of Prophet Muhammad), the Basnat Festival, Shab-e-Baraat Festival and the Independence Day Festival.

Libraries
The Liaqat National Library is in Karachi, and the library of the National Archives is in Islamabad. Baitul Quran at Lahore is exclusively devoted to the manuscripts of the Holy Koran. The libraries of the Punjab University, Karachi University and the Quaid-i-Azam library in Lahore hold a combined 700,000 volumes. The Islamic Research Institute Library at Islamabad has an important collection on Islam.

Theatre and Opera
There are regular theatrical productions in the major cities. There are 15 fully equipped theatre halls in Rawalpindi, Lahore, Karachi and Peshawar, and traditional street theatre is still prominent.

Museums and Galleries
There are dozens of galleries and museums in Islamabad, Lahore, Karachi, Peshawar and Quetta. Amongst the most famous are the National Art Gallery, Shakir Ali Museum, Choukandi Art Gallery, Karachi Art Council, Tasneen Art Gallery, the Lahore Art Museum, the National Heritage Museum and the National Archives. There are also dozens of archaeological sites in Pakistan dating back to 3,000 BC including Moenjodaro, Harppa, Taxila, Kot Diji and Dir.

DIPLOMATIC REPRESENTATIVES

Of Pakistan in the United Kingdom (35–36 Lowndes Sq., London, SW1X 9JN)
High Commissioner: Maleeha Lodhi.

Of the United Kingdom in Pakistan (Diplomatic Enclave, Ramna 5, Islamabad)
High Commissioner: Mark J. Lyall Grant, CMG.

Of Pakistan in the USA (3517 International Court, NW, Washington, D.C., 20008)
Ambassador: Jehangir Karamat.

Of the USA in Pakistan (Diplomatic Enclave, Ramna, 5, Islamabad)
Ambassador: Ryan C. Crocker.

Of Pakistan to the United Nations
Ambassador: Munir Akram.

Of Pakistan to the European Union
Ambassador: Tariq Fatemi.

FURTHER READING

Government Planning Commission. *Ninth Five Year Plan, 1998–2003*. Karachi, 1998

Federal Bureau of Statistics.—*Pakistan Statistical Yearbook.—Statistical Pocket Book of Pakistan*. (Annual)

Ahmed, A. S., *Jinnah, Pakistan and Islamic Identity: The Search for Saladin*. London, 1997

Ahsan, A., *The Indus Saga and the Making of Pakistan*. Oxford, 1997

Akhtar, R., *Pakistan Year Book*. Karachi/Lahore

Bhutto, B., *Daughter of the East*. London, 1988

Burki, S. J., *Pakistan: the Continuing Search for Nationhood*. 2nd ed. Boulder (Colo.), 1992

James, W. E. and Roy, S. (eds.) *The Foundations of Pakistan's Political Economy: Towards an Agenda for the 1990s*. London, 1992

Joshi, V. T., *Pakistan: Zia to Benazir*. Delhi, 1995

Malik, I. H., *State and Civil Society in Pakistan: the Politics of Authority, Ideology and Ethnicity*. London, 1996

National library: National Library of Pakistan, Islamabad.

National Statistical Office: Federal Bureau of Statistics, Statistics Division, Islamabad.

Website: http://www.statpak.gov.pk/

PALAU

Republic of Palau

Capital: Koror
Population, 2000: 19,000
GDP per capita: not available

KEY HISTORICAL EVENTS

Spain acquired sovereignty over the Palau Islands in 1886 but sold the archipelago to Germany in 1899. Japan occupied the islands in 1914 and in 1921 they were mandated to Japan by the League of Nations. Captured by Allied Forces in 1944, the islands became part of the UN Trust Territory of the Pacific Islands created on 18 July 1947 and administered by the USA. Following a referendum in July 1978 in which Palauans voted against joining the new Federated States of Micronesia, the islands became autonomous from 1 Jan. 1981. A referendum in Nov. 1993 favoured a Compact of Free Association with the USA. Palau became an independent republic on 1 Oct. 1994.

TERRITORY AND POPULATION

The archipelago lies in the western Pacific and has a total land area of 490 sq. km (189 sq. miles). It comprises 26 islands and over 300 islets. Only nine of the islands are inhabited, the largest being Babelthuap (396 sq. km), but most inhabitants live on the small island of Koror (18 sq. km) to the south, containing the present headquarters (a new capital is being built at Melekeok in eastern Babelthuap). The total population of Palau at the time of the 2000 census was 19,129, giving a density of 37·7 per sq. km. Koror's population according to the 2000 census was 13,303. In 2000 approximately 70% of the population were Palauans.

In 2000 an estimated 69·5% of the population lived in urban areas. Some 6,000 Palauans live abroad. The local language is Palauan; both Palauan and English are official.

SOCIAL STATISTICS

2001 births, 300; deaths, 138. Rates, 2001 (per 1,000 population): births, 15·3; deaths, 7·0; infant mortality, 17 per 1,000 live births. Annual population growth rate, 1992–2002, 2·3%. Expectation of life: males, 69 years; females, 73. Fertility rate, 2001, 2·8 births per woman.

CLIMATE

Palau has a pleasantly warm climate throughout the year with temperatures averaging 81°F (27°C). The heaviest rainfall is between July and Oct.

CONSTITUTION AND GOVERNMENT

The Constitution was adopted on 2 April 1979 and took effect from 1 Jan. 1981. The Republic has a bicameral legislature, the *Olbiil Era Kelulau* (National Congress), comprising a 9-member *Senate* and a 16-member *House of Delegates* (one from each of the Republic's 16 states), both elected for a term of four years as are the *President* and *Vice-President*. Customary social roles and land and sea rights are allocated by a matriarchal 16-clan system.

National Anthem

'Belau loba klisiich er a kelulul' ('Palau is coming forth with strength and power'); words anonymous, tune Y. O. Ezekiel.

RECENT ELECTIONS

At the elections on 2 Nov. 2004 Tommy Remengesau, Jr was re-elected president with 66·5% of votes cast against 33·5% for Polycarp Basilius. At the legislative elections which were also held on 2 Nov. 2004 only non-partisans were elected.

CURRENT ADMINISTRATION

President: Tommy Remengesau, Jr; b. 1956 (in office since 1 Jan. 2001).

Vice-President and Minister of Justice: Elias Camsek Chin.
In March 2006 the cabinet consisted of:
Minister of Commerce and Trade: Otoichi Besebes. *Community and Cultural Affairs:* Alexander Merep. *Education:* Mario Katosang. *Finance:* Elbuchel Sadang. *Health:* Victor Yano. *Resources and Development:* Fritz Koshiba. *State:* Temmy Shmull.

CURRENT LEADERS

Tommy Remengesau Jr.

Position
President

Introduction
Tommy Remengesau, Jr was sworn in as president on 1 Jan. 2001 and re-elected in Nov. 2004. The US-educated career politician has prioritized the development of information technology and the Internet for the remote Pacific archipelago.

Early Life
Tommy Esang Remengesau, Jr was born on 28 Feb. 1956 on the island of Koror, Palau in the US-administered Trust Territory of the Pacific Islands (TTPI). The eldest son of Thomas O. Remengesau, Sr, president in 1988–89, he graduated in criminal justice from Grand Valley State College in Michigan, USA in 1978. On his return to Palau, Remengesau began work at the *Olbiil Era Kelulau* (OEK), Palau's national congress. In 1984 he became the youngest Palauan to be elected a senator in the OEK. Re-elected in 1988, he served on the committee on ways and means, playing a key role in reducing Palau's budget deficit and securing financial stability.

In 1992 Remengesau was elected vice-president and the following year Palauan voters approved a Compact of

Free Association with the USA. With responsibility for the administration (finance) portfolio, Remengesau was credited with reforming the financial system and preparing the new sovereign state (established in 1994) for membership of the IMF and the World Bank Group. He won the 2000 presidential elections, claiming 52% of the vote against Peter Sugiyama.

Career in Office

Remengesau pledged to reduce his country's dependence on the USA and announced plans to increase revenue from tourism, while preserving the country's natural environment. He began a new four-year term following the election of Nov. 2004, having claimed 66·5% of the vote against Polycarp Basilius.

INTERNATIONAL RELATIONS

Palau is a member of the UN, IMF, Asian Development Bank, the Pacific Islands Forum and the Pacific Community.

ECONOMY

Currency

US currency is used.

Budget

Central government revenues for fiscal year 2001 were US$44·0m. and expenditures US$78·0m.

Performance

Real GDP growth was 1·1% in 2001, following negative growth in 2000, of –0·7%. Total GDP in 2004 was US$0·1bn.

Banking and Finance

The National Development Bank of Palau is situated in Koror. Other banks include the Bank of Guam, the Bank of Hawaii, Bank Pacific, Melekeok Government Bank and the Pacific Savings Bank.

ENERGY AND NATURAL RESOURCES

Environment

Palau's carbon dioxide emissions in 1999 were the equivalent of 12·9 tonnes per capita.

Electricity

Electricity production was about 210m. kWh in 2000; installed capacity was 62,000 kW in 2000.

Agriculture

The main agricultural products are bananas, coconuts, copra, cassava and sweet potatoes. In 1997 agriculture contributed 7% of GDP. In 2001 there were 4,000 ha. of arable land and 2,000 ha. of permanent crop land.

Forestry

Forests covered 35,000 ha. in 2000, or 76·1% of the land area.

Fisheries

In 2001 the catch totalled approximately 2,000 tonnes, mainly tuna.

INDUSTRY

There is little industry, but the principal activities are food-processing and boat-building.

Labour

The economically active population totalled 10,686 in 1995, of whom 2,630 worked in government services, 1,896 in agriculture and 1,005 in tourism.

INTERNATIONAL TRADE

Imports and Exports

Imports (2001) US$105·3m.; exports (2001) US$23·4m. The main trading partner is Japan for exports and the USA for imports.

COMMUNICATIONS

Roads

There were 61 km of roads in 1996 of which 36 km are paved.

Civil Aviation

The main airport is on Koror (Airai). In 2003 there were scheduled flights to Guam, Manila, Yap (Micronesia) and Taipei.

Shipping

There is a port at Malakal. In 1995 over 280 vessels called there, delivering cargo totalling in excess of 70,000 tonnes.

Telecommunications

In 2001 there were 6,600 telephone access lines.

SOCIAL INSTITUTIONS

Justice

There is a Supreme Court and various subsidiary courts. The population in penal institutions in Feb. 2003 was 103 (523 per 100,000 national population).

Education

In 2002–03 there were 3,048 pupils at primary schools and 1,231 at secondary schools. In 2004 there were 23 primary schools and six secondary schools. There were 727 students at Palau Community College in 2002–03. The adult literacy rate is 92%.

In 1999–2000 total expenditure on education came to 20·0% of total government spending.

Health

In 1998 there was one hospital, 20 physicians, two dentists, 26 nurses and one midwife.

RELIGION

The majority of the population is Roman Catholic.

CULTURE

Broadcasting

There is a radio station (WSZB) which broadcasts daily on AM and FM, and ICTV Cable TV presents 12 channels with CNN. In 1997 there were an estimated 11,000 televisions and 12,000 radios.

Press

The local newspaper *Tia Belau* is published bi-weekly.

Tourism

Tourism is a major industry, particularly marine-based. There were 59,000 foreign tourists in 2002, bringing in US$59m. in revenue.

DIPLOMATIC REPRESENTATIVES

Of the United Kingdom in Palau
Ambassador: Peter Beckingham (resides in Manila, Philippines).

Of Palau in the USA (1700 Pennsylvania Ave., NW, Suite 400, Washington, D.C., 20006)
Ambassador: Hersey Kyota.

Of the USA in Palau (PO Box 6028, PW 96940, Koror)
Ambassador: Vacant.
Chargé d'Affaires a.i.: Deborah L. Kingsland.

Of Palau to the United Nations
Ambassador: Stuart Beck.

PANAMA

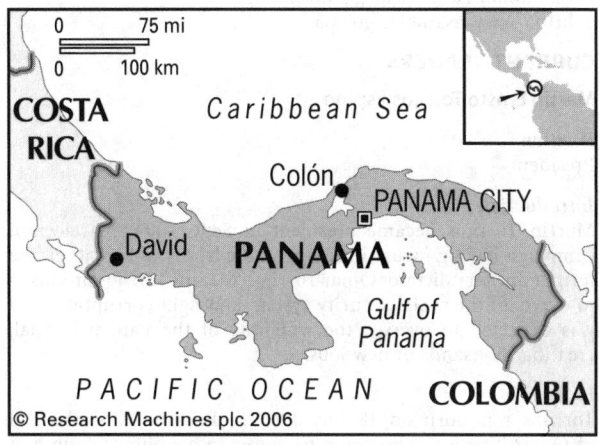

República de Panamá

Capital: Panama City
Population projection, 2010: 3·51m.
GDP per capita, 2003: (PPP$) 6,854
HDI/world rank: 0·804/56

KEY HISTORICAL EVENTS

A revolution, inspired by the USA, led to the separation of Panama from the United States of Colombia and the declaration of its independence on 3 Nov. 1903. This was followed by an agreement making it possible for the USA to build and operate a canal connecting the Atlantic and Pacific oceans through the Isthmus of Panama. The treaty granted the USA in perpetuity the use, occupation and control of a Canal Zone, in which the USA would possess full sovereign rights. In return the USA guaranteed the independence of the republic. The Canal was opened on 15 Aug. 1914.

The US domination of Panama provoked frequent anti-American protests. In 1968 Col. Omar Torrijos Herrera took power in a coup and attempted to negotiate a more advantageous treaty with the USA. Two new treaties between Panama and the USA were agreed on 10 Aug. and signed on 7 Sept. 1977. One dealt with the operation and defence of the Canal until the end of 1999 and the other guarantees permanent neutrality.

Torrijos vacated his position as chief of government in 1978 but maintained his power as head of the National Guard until his death in an air crash in 1981. Subsequently, Gen. Manuel Noriega, Torrijos' successor as head of the National Guard, became the strong man of the regime. His position was threatened by some internal political opposition and economic pressure applied by the USA but in Oct. 1989 a US-backed coup attempt failed. On 15 Dec. Gen. Noriega declared a 'state of war' with the USA. On 20 Dec. the USA invaded. Gen. Noriega surrendered on 3 Jan. 1990. Accused of drug dealing he was convicted by a court in Miami and is now serving a 40-year jail sentence. All remaining US troops left the country when the Panama Canal was handed back to Panama at the end of 1999.

TERRITORY AND POPULATION

Panama is bounded in the north by the Caribbean Sea, east by Colombia, south by the Pacific Ocean and west by Costa Rica. The area is 75,001 sq. km. Population at the census of 2000 was 2,839,177 (1,432,566 males); density, 37·6 per sq. km. The estimated population in 2005 was 3,232,000. The population was 57·2% urban in 2003.

The UN gives a projected population for 2010 of 3·51m.

The largest towns (2000) are Panama City, the capital, on the Pacific coast (469,307); its suburb San Miguelito (293,745); Tocumen (82,419); and David (77,057).

The areas and populations of the nine provinces and the five indigenous districts were:

Province	Sq. km	Census 2000	Capital
Bocas del Toro	4,601	89,269	Bocas del Toro
Chiriquí	6,477	368,790	David
Coclé	4,927	202,461	Penonomé
Colón	4,891	204,208	Colón
Darién	11,091	39,151	La Palma
Emberá[1]	4,398	8,246	Cirilo Guainora
Herrera	2,341	102,465	Chitré
Kuna de Madungandí[1]	2,319	3,305	—
Kuna de Wargandí[1]	775	1,133	—
Kuna Yala[1]	2,393	32,446	El Porvenir
Los Santos	3,805	83,495	Las Tablas
Ngöbe-Buglé[1]	6,673	110,080	Chichica
Panamá	9,633	1,385,052	Panama City
Veraguas	10,677	209,076	Santiago

[1]Indigenous district.

The population is a mix of African, American, Arab, Chinese, European and Indian immigrants. The official language is Spanish.

SOCIAL STATISTICS

2003 births, 61,753; deaths, 13,248; marriages, 10,310; divorces, 2,732. Birth rate, 2003 (per 1,000 population), 19·8; death rate, 4·3. Annual population growth rate, 1992–2002, 2·0%. Expectation of life at birth, 2003, was 72·3 years for males and 77·4 years for females. In 1999 the most popular age range for marrying was 25–29 for both males and females. Infant mortality, 2003, 15 per 1,000 live births; fertility rate, 2001, 2·5 births per woman.

CLIMATE

Panama has a tropical climate, unvaryingly with high temperatures and only a short dry season from Jan. to April. Rainfall amounts are much higher on the north side of the isthmus. Panama City, Jan. 79°F (26·1°C), July 81°F (27·2°C). Annual rainfall 70" (1,770 mm). Colón, Jan. 80°F (26·7°C), July 80°F (26·7°C). Annual rainfall 127" (3,175 mm). Balboa Heights, Jan. 80°F (26·7°C), July 81°F (27·2°C). Annual rainfall 70" (1,759 mm). Cristóbal, Jan. 80°F (26·7°C), July 81°F (27·2°C). Annual rainfall 130" (3,255 mm).

CONSTITUTION AND GOVERNMENT

The 1972 Constitution, as amended in 1978, 1983, 1994 and 2004, provides for a *President*, elected for five years, two *Vice-Presidents* and a 72-seat *Legislative Assembly* (since increased to 78 seats) to be elected for five-year terms by a direct vote. As a result of the amendment of 2004 there will be only one *Vice-President* and only 71 seats from 2009. To remain registered, parties must have attained at least 50,000 votes at the last election. A referendum held on 15 Nov. 1992 rejected constitutional reforms by 64% of votes cast. Turnout was 40%. In a referendum on 30 Aug. 1998 voters rejected proposed changes to the constitution which would allow for a President to serve a second consecutive term.

National Anthem

'Alcanzamos por fin la victoria' ('We achieve victory in the end'); words by J. de la Ossa, tune by Santos Jorge.

GOVERNMENT CHRONOLOGY

(CNP = National Patriotic Coalition; PA = Arnulfista Party; PL = Liberal Party; PLN = National Liberal Party; PP = Panamenista Party; PR = Republican Party; PRA = Authentic Revolutionary Party; PRD = Revolutionary Democratic Party; n/p = non-partisan)

Heads of State since 1941.

Presidents of the Republic

1941–45	n/p	Ricardo Adolfo de la Guardia Arango
1945–48	PL	Enrique Adolfo Jiménez Brin
1948–49	PL	Domingo Díaz Arosemena
1949	PL	Daniel Chanis Pinzón
1949–51	PRA	Arnulfo Arias Madrid
1951–52	PRA	Alcibíades Arosemena Quinzada
1952–55	CNP	José Antonio Remón Cantera
1955–56	CNP	Ricardo Manuel Arias Espinosa
1956–60	CNP	Ernesto de la Guardia Navarro
1960–64	PLN	Roberto Francisco Chiari Remón
1964–68	PLN	Marco Aurelio Robles Méndez
1968	PP	Arnulfo Arias Madrid

Chairmen of the Provisional Junta of Government

1968–69	military	José María Pinilla Fábrega
1969–72	n/p	Demetrio Basilio Lakas Bahas

Presidents of the Republic

1972–78	n/p	Demetrio Basilio Lakas Bahas
1978–82	n/p	Arístides Royo Sánchez
1982–84	n/p	Ricardo de la Espriella Toral
1984	n/p	Jorge Enrique Illueca Sibauste
1984–85	PRD	Nicolás Ardito Barletta Vallarino
1985–88	PR	Eric Arturo Delvalle Cohen-Henríquez
1989–94	PA	Guillermo David Endara Galimany
1994–99	PRD	Ernesto Pérez Balladares González
1999–2004	PA	Mireya Elisa Moscoso de Arias
2004–	PRD	Martín Erasto Torrijos Espino

De facto rulers from 1968–89.

1968–81	military	Omar Efraín Torrijos Herrera
1982–83	military	Rubén Darío Paredes del Río
1983–89	military	Manuel Antonio Noriega Moreno

RECENT ELECTIONS

In the presidential election on 2 May 2004 Martín Torrijos Espino of the Revolutionary Democratic Party (PRD) won 47·5% of the vote. Guillermo Endara Galimany (Solidarity Party) won 30·6%, José Miguel Alemán (Arnulfist Party; PA) 17·0% and Ricardo Martinelli (Democratic Change; CD) 4·9%.

In the Legislative Assembly elections, also held on 2 May 2004, the PRD won 41 seats, with 37·8% of the vote. The PA won 17 seats with 19·2%; Solidarity Party, 9, with 15·7%; the Nationalist Republican Liberal Movement (Molirena), 4, with 8·6%; CD, 3, with 7·4%; the National Liberal Party, 3, with 5·2%; the People's Party, 1, with 6·0%. Turnout for both elections was 76·9%.

CURRENT ADMINISTRATION

President: Martín Torrijos Espino; b. 1963 (Revolutionary Democratic Party; sworn in 1 Sept. 2004). His father, Omar Torrijos Herrera, was the military ruler of Panama from 1968 to 1981.

First Vice-President and Minister of Foreign Affairs: Samuel Lewis Navarro. *Second Vice-President:* Rubén Arosemana Valdés.

In March 2006 the government comprised:

Minister of Government and Justice: Héctor Alemán. *Public Works:* Carlos Vallarino. *Economy and Finance:* Ricaurte Vásquez. *Agricultural Development:* Guillermo Salazar. *Commerce and Industry:* Alejandro Ferrer. *Health:* Camilo Alleyne. *Labour and Work Development:* Reynaldo Rivera. *Education:* Juan Bosco

Bernal. *Housing:* Balbina Herrera. *Youth, Women, Childhood and Family:* Leonor Calderón. *Minister of the Presidency:* Ubaldino Real.

Panamanian Parliament (Spanish only):
   http://www.asamblea.gob.pa

CURRENT LEADERS

Martín Erasto Torrijos Espino

Position
President

Introduction
Martín Torrijos became president in Sept. 2004, his election campaign having focused heavily on the legacy of his father, the former military dictator Omar Torrijos. Martín Torrijos promised to overhaul the social security system and fight corruption, and was expected to oversee the widening of the Panama Canal, creating thousands of new jobs.

Early Life
Torrijos was born on 18 July 1963 in Panama City, the son of Omar Torrijos, who came to power in a military coup and served as *de facto* president from 1968–81. Omar Torrijos won popularity by negotiating a deal with US President Jimmy Carter in 1977, guaranteeing the transfer of the Panama Canal from US to Panamanian control in 1999.

In 1977 Martín Torrijos attended the St John's Military Academy in Wisconsin, USA. During the summer of 1979 he participated in the anti-Somoza movement in Nicaragua. He graduated in economics and political science from the Texas A&M University in 1988. On returning to Panama he became heavily involved in the Revolutionary Democratic Party (PRD), taking on the leadership of the youth wing.

A successful businessman, in 1994 he was appointed deputy minister for justice and the interior in the government of Ernesto Pérez Balladares. At the 1999 presidential election Torrijos stood as the PRD candidate, but was defeated by the Arnulfist Party candidate Mireya Moscoso, the wife of Arnulfo Arias who had been deposed by Omar Torrijos in 1968. Moscoso's government was beset by allegations of corruption and ineptitude and soon lost public backing.

Meanwhile, Torrijos was acting as economic advisor to numerous international companies while overseeing a restructuring of the PRD. Standing as the PRD candidate at the 2004 elections, he campaigned on a platform of fighting corruption and unemployment while improving the social security system, and regularly evoked the memory of his father, popularly regarded as the liberator of the Panama Canal. Martín Torrijos was elected to the presidency with 47·5% of the vote on 2 May 2004 and was sworn in on 1 Sept.

Career in Office
In the weeks before Torrijos took office, Moscoso pardoned four Cuban exiles who had been accused of attempting to assassinate Cuban president Fidel Castro. Havana immediately cut diplomatic ties, as did Venezuela. On taking office Torrijos set about normalizing relations and ties were restored in Nov. 2004.

In May 2005 Torrijos began his social security reforms by announcing plans to raise pension contributions and increase the retirement age. Several weeks of popular protest ensued. He also promised that proposals to modernize the Panama Canal, including a US$5bn. canal-widening project, would be put to popular referendum. Internationally, he is aiming to negotiate a free trade pact with the USA. In a bid to distance himself from the excesses of his father's rule, he promised an investigation into alleged human rights abuses during Omar Torrijos' time in office.

DEFENCE

The armed forces were disbanded in 1990 and constitutionally abolished in 1994. Divided between both coasts, the National Maritime Service, a coast guard rather than a navy, numbered around 400 personnel in 2002. In addition there is a paramilitary police force of 11,000 and a paramilitary air force of 400 with no combat aircraft. In 2003 defence expenditure totalled US$100m. (US$34 per capita), representing 0·9% of GDP. For Police *see* JUSTICE *below*.

INTERNATIONAL RELATIONS

Panama is a member of the UN, WTO, OAS, Inter-American Development Bank, ACS, IOM and Non-aligned Movement.

ECONOMY

Agriculture accounted for 5·7% of GDP in 2002, industry 13·8% and services 80·5%.

Currency

The monetary unit is the *balboa* (PAB) of 100 *centésimos*, at parity with the US dollar. The only paper currency used is that of the USA. US coinage is also legal tender. Inflation was 1·4% in 2003 and 2·3% in 2004. In June 2002 foreign exchange reserves were US$1,055m. In March 2002 total money supply was 1,121m. balboas.

Budget

Budgetary central government revenue and expenditure (in 1m. balboas), year ending 31 Dec.:

	1999	2000	2001
Revenue	1,907·7	1,935·6	1,964·0
Expenditure	1,486·6	1,529·0	1,620·3

Performance

Real GDP growth was 4·3% in 2003 and 6·0% in 2004. Total GDP in 2004 was US$13·8bn.

Banking and Finance

There is no statutory central bank. Banking is supervised and promoted by the Superintendency of Banks (formerly the National Banking Commission); the *Superintendente* is Delia Cárdenas. Government accounts are handled through the state-owned *Banco Nacional de Panama*. In 2002 there were two other state banks, 47 banks operating under general licence, 29 under international licence and six as representative offices. Total assets of commercial banks, June 1996, US$33,400m., total deposits, US$25,000m. (including offshore, US$15,900m.).

There is a stock exchange in Panama City.

Weights and Measures

The US and metric system are used.

ENERGY AND NATURAL RESOURCES

Environment

Panama's carbon dioxide emissions from the consumption and flaring of fossil fuels in 2002 were the equivalent of 4·5 tonnes per capita.

Electricity

In 2000 capacity was 1·3m. kW. Production was 5·00bn. kWh in 2002, with consumption per capita 1,734 kWh (2000).

Minerals

Limestone, clay and salt are produced. There are known to be copper deposits.

Agriculture

In 2001 there were 548,000 ha. of arable land and 147,000 ha. of permanent crops. Production in 2000 (in 1,000 tonnes): sugarcane, 2,000; bananas, 807; rice, 319; plantains, 111; melons and watermelons, 102; oranges, 85; maize, 80; cassava, 32; pineapples, 29; potatoes, 22; yams, 20. Livestock (2000): 1,360,000 cattle, 280,000 pigs, 166,000 horses and 12m. chickens.

Forestry

Forests covered 2·88m. ha. in 2000 (38·6% of the land area). There are great timber resources, notably mahogany. Production in 2001 totalled 1·34m. cu. metres.

Fisheries

In 2001 the catch totalled approximately 235,000 tonnes (mainly shrimp), almost entirely from sea fishing.

INDUSTRY

The main industry is agricultural produce processing. Other areas include oil refining, chemicals and paper-making. Residual fuel oil production (2000), 1,194,000 tonnes; cement (2001), 760,000 tonnes; distillate fuel oil (2000), 516,000 tonnes; petrol (2000), 274,000 tonnes; sugar (2002), 152,000 tonnes.

Labour

In Aug. 2003 a total of 1,145,982 persons were in employment, with principal areas of activity as follows: agriculture, hunting and forestry, 228,305; wholesale and retail trade/repair of motor vehicles, motorcycles and personal and household goods, 196,418; manufacturing, 105,830; transport, storage and communications, 85,883. In Aug. 2003 the unemployment rate was 13·1%.

Trade Unions

77,500 workers belonged to trade unions in 1994, of whom 27,000 were members of the *Confederación de Trabajadores de la República de Panamá*.

INTERNATIONAL TRADE

The Colón Free Zone is an autonomous institution set up in 1953. 1,556 companies were operating there in 1997. Factories in export zones are granted tax exemption on profits for 10–20 years and exemption from the provisions of the labour code. Foreign debt was US$8,298m. in 2002.

Imports and Exports

Imports and exports in US$1m.:

	1998	1999	2000	2001	2002
Imports f.o.b.	7,714·6	6,689·4	6,981·4	6,671·7	6,460·2
Exports f.o.b.	6,350·1	5,303·3	5,838·5	5,996·4	5,283·8

Main imports: machinery and apparatus, transport equipment, mineral fuels. Main exports: bananas, shellfish, sugar. Chief import suppliers, 1999: USA, 36%; Japan, 7%; Ecuador, 5%; Mexico, 5%. Chief export markets, 1999: USA, 45%; Germany, 11%; Costa Rica, 5%; Belgium, 4%.

COMMUNICATIONS

Roads

In 2002 there were 11,978 km of roads, of which 35·9% were paved. The road from Panama City westward to the cities of David and Concepción and to the Costa Rican frontier, with several branches, is part of the Pan-American Highway. The Trans-Isthmian Highway connects Panama City and Colón. In 2003 there were 251,500 passenger cars, 77,400 lorries and vans and 17,000 buses and coaches. There were 401 road accident fatalities in 2002.

Rail

The 1,524 mm gauge *Ferrocarril de Panama*, which connects Ancón on the Pacific with Cristóbal on the Atlantic along the bank of the Panama Canal, is the principal railway. The United Brands Company runs 376 km of railway, and the Chiriquí National Railroad 171 km.

Civil Aviation

There is an international airport at Panama City (Tocumén International). The national carrier is COPA, which flew to 15 different countries in 2003. In 1999 it flew 23·9m. km and carried 932,500 passengers. In 2002 Tocumén International handled 1,938,933 passengers and 84,362 tonnes of freight.

Shipping

Panama, a nation with a transcendental maritime career and a strategic geographic position, is the shipping world's preferred flag for ship registry. The Ship Registry System equally accepts vessels of local or international ownership, as long as they comply with all legal parameters. Ship owners also favour Panamanian registry because fees are low. Today, the Panamanian fleet is the largest in the world with 6,222 ships registered and 103,581,459 net tons in 2001.

All the international maritime traffic for Colón and Panama runs through the Canal ports of Cristóbal, Balboa and Manzanillo International.

Panama Canal

The Panama Canal Commission is concerned primarily with the operation of the Canal. In Oct. 2002 a new toll structure was adopted based on ship size and type.

At present some 90% of the world's shipping fleet can use the Canal, but this is set to drop as many new ships are too wide for the Canal. Feasibility studies for an additional set of locks that could take today's largest ships are under way.

Administrator of the Panama Canal Authority. Alberto Alemán Zubieta.

Particulars of the ocean-going commercial traffic through the Canal are given as follows:

Fiscal year ending 30 Sept.	No. of vessels transiting	Cargo in long tons	Tolls revenue (in US$1)
2002	11,790	187,815,000	587,567,000
2003	11,634	188,273,000	664,667,000

Most numerous transits by flag (2003): Panama, 2,740; Liberia, 1,347; Bahamas, 922; Cyprus, 697; Malta, 565.

Statistical Information: The Panama Canal Authority Corporate Communications Division

Annual Reports on the Panama Canal, by the Administrator of the Panama Canal

Rules and Regulations Governing Navigation of the Panama Canal. The Panama Canal Authority

Major, J., *Prize Possession: the United States and the Panama Canal, 1903–1979.* CUP, 1994

Telecommunications

Panama had 936,400 telephone subscribers in 2002, or 311·5 per 1,000 persons, and there were 115,000 PCs in use (38·3 for every 1,000 persons). There were 525,800 mobile phone subscribers in 2002 and 268,000 fax machines in 1999. There were 120,000 Internet users in 2001.

Postal Services

In 2003 there were 125 post and telegraph offices.

SOCIAL INSTITUTIONS

Justice

The Supreme Court consists of nine justices appointed by the executive. There is no death penalty. The police force numbered 13,000 in 1999, and includes a Presidential Guard.

The population in penal institutions in March 2003 was 10,630 (354 per 100,000 of national population).

Education

Adult literacy was 91·9% in 2003 (male, 92·5%; female, 91·2%). Elementary education is compulsory for all children from seven to 15 years of age. In 2002 there were 408,249 pupils at 3,116 primary schools and 244,097 pupils with 15,181 teachers at secondary schools. There were four universities and twenty specialist institutions with 117,624 students and 8,444 academic staff. There were also a nautical school, a business school and institutes of teacher training and tourism.

In 2000–01 total expenditure on education came to 6·2% of GNP.

Health

In 2002 there were 61 hospitals with a provision of 25 beds per 10,000 persons. There were 4,203 physicians, 897 dentists, 3,451 nurses and 612 pharmacists.

RELIGION

80% of the population is Roman Catholic, 14% Protestant. The remainder of the population follow other religions (notably Islam). There is freedom of religious worship and separation of Church and State. Clergymen may teach in the schools but may not hold public office.

CULTURE

World Heritage Sites

Panama has four sites on the UNESCO World Heritage List: the Fortifications on the Caribbean side of Panama: Portobelo-San Lorenzo (inscribed on the list in 1980); Darien National Park (1981); the Archaeological Site of Panamá Viejo and the Historic District of Panamá (1997, 2003); and the Coiba National Park (2005).

Broadcasting

There are about 60 broadcasting stations, mostly commercial, grouped in the Asociación Panameña de Radiodifusión. There are four television channels (colour by NTSC) and an educational channel. In 2000 there were 884,000 radio sets and in 2001 there were 560,000 TV sets in use.

Press

In 1996 there were seven dailies with a combined circulation of 166,000, equivalent to 62 per 1,000 inhabitants.

Tourism

In 2002 there were 534,000 foreign tourists, bringing revenue of US$679m.

DIPLOMATIC REPRESENTATIVES

Of Panama in the United Kingdom (40 Hertford St., London, W1J 7SH)
Ambassador: Liliana Fernándes.

Of the United Kingdom in Panama (Torre Swiss Bank, Calle 53, Apartado 889, Panama City 1)
Ambassador: Jim Malcolm, OBE.

Of Panama in the USA (2862 McGill Terr., NW, Washington, D.C., 20008)
Ambassador: Federico Antonio Humbert Arias.

Of the USA in Panama (Apartado 0816-02561, Panama City 5)
Ambassador: William Eaton.

Of Panama to the United Nations
Ambassador: Ricardo Alberto Arias.

Of Panama to the European Union
Ambassador: Rolando A. Guevara Alvarado.

FURTHER READING

Statistical Information: The Controller-General of the Republic (Contraloria General de la República, Calle 35 y Avenida 6, Panama City) publishes an annual report and other statistical publications.

McCullough, D. G., *The Path Between the Seas: The Creation of the Panama Canal, 1870–1914.* Simon and Schuster, New York, 1999

Sahota, G. S., *Poverty Theory and Policy: a Study of Panama.* Johns Hopkins Univ. Press, 1990

Other titles are listed under Panama Canal, *above.*

National library: Biblioteca Nacional, Departamento de Información, Av. Balboa y Federico Boyd, Ciudad de Panama.

Website (Spanish only): http://www.contraloria.gob.pa

PAPUA NEW GUINEA

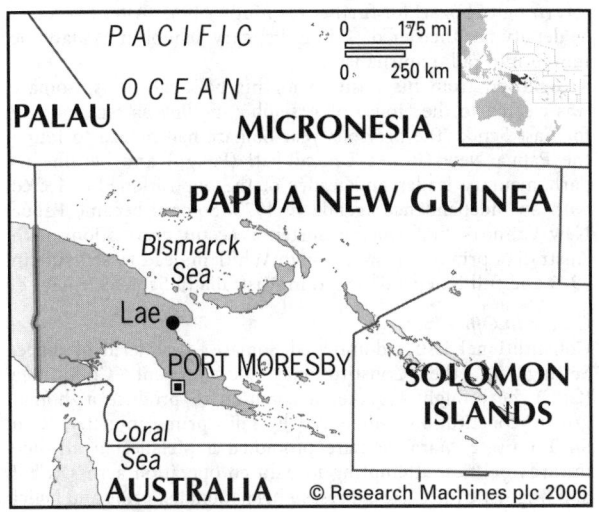

Capital: Port Moresby
Population projection, 2010: 6·45m.
GDP per capita, 2003: (PPP$) 2,619
HDI/world rank: 0·523/137

KEY HISTORICAL EVENTS

The Spanish first claimed the island in 1545 but the first attempt at colonization was made in 1793 by the British. In 1828 the Dutch claimed the west half of the island as part of the Dutch East Indies. On 6 Nov. 1884 a British Protectorate was proclaimed over the southern portion of the eastern half of New Guinea and in 1888 the territory was annexed. On 1 Sept. 1906 the Governor-General of Australia declared that British New Guinea was to be known henceforth as the Territory of Papua. The northern portion of New Guinea was a German colony until 1914 when Australian armed forces occupied it. For the next seven years it remained under their administration until becoming a League of Nations mandated territory in 1921, administered by Australia, and later a UN Trust Territory (of New Guinea). Australia granted Papua New Guinea self-government on 1 Dec. 1973, and on 16 Sept. 1975 Papua New Guinea became a fully independent state.

What began in 1988 as an armed campaign by tribes claiming traditional land rights against the Australian owner of the massive Panguna copper field soon escalated into a civil war for the secession of the island of Bougainville. Fighting between the government and the Bougainville Revolutionary Army (BRA) continued until 3 Sept. 1994 when a peace agreement set up a provisional Bougainville government. The ceasefire was broken by the rebels in mid-1995. In April 1998 the government of Papua New Guinea signed a 'permanent' truce with the secessionists. The nine-year rebellion claimed 20,000 lives. In Jan. 2001 the government and Bougainville signed a peace agreement that set Bougainville on course to an autonomous government and a referendum on independence. Following elections in May and early June 2005 the new autonomous Bougainville government was sworn into office on 15 June 2005.

TERRITORY AND POPULATION

Papua New Guinea extends from the equator to Cape Baganowa in the Louisiade Archipelago to 11° 40' S. lat. and from the border of West Irian to 160° E. long. with a total area of 462,840 sq. km. According to the 2000 census the population was 5,190,786 (2,691,744 males); density, 11·2 per sq. km. The estimated population in 2005 was 5,887,000.

The UN gives a projected population for 2010 of 6·45m.

In 2003, 86·8% of the population lived in rural areas. In 1999 population of Port Moresby (National Capital District) was 293,000. Population of other main towns (1990 census): Lae, 80,655; Madang, 27,057; Wewak, 23,224; Goroka, 17,855; Mount Hagen, 17,392; Rabaul, 17,022. Area and population of the provinces:

Provinces	Sq. km	Census 2000	Capital
Bougainville	9,300	175,160	Arawa
Central	29,500	183,983	Port Moresby
Chimbu	6,100	259,703	Kundiawa
East New Britain	15,500	220,133	Rabaul
East Sepik	42,800	343,181	Wewak
Eastern Highlands	11,200	432,972	Goroka
Enga	12,800	295,031	Wabag
Gulf	34,500	106,898	Kerema
Madang	29,000	365,106	Madang
Manus	2,100	43,387	Lorengau
Milne Bay	14,000	210,412	Alotau
Morobe	34,500	539,404	Lae
National Capital District	240	254,158	—
New Ireland	9,600	118,350	Kavieng
Oro	22,800	133,065	Popondetta
Sandaun	36,300	185,741	Vanimo
Southern Highlands	23,800	546,265	Mendi
West New Britain	21,000	184,508	Kimbe
Western	99,300	153,304	Daru
Western Highlands	8,500	440,025	Mount Hagen

The principal local languages are Neo-Melanesian (or Pidgin, a creole of English) and Hiri Motu. English is in official use.

SOCIAL STATISTICS

Estimates, 2003: births, 177,000; deaths, 53,000. Rates, 2003 estimates (per 1,000 population): births, 31·2; deaths, 9·3. Expectation of life at birth in 2003 was 54·9 years for males and 56·0 years for females. Annual population growth rate, 1992–2002, 2·6%. Infant mortality, 2001, 70 per 1,000 live births; fertility rate, 2001, 4·4 births per woman.

CLIMATE

There is a monsoon climate, with high temperatures and humidity the year round. Port Moresby is in a rain shadow and is not typical of the rest of Papua New Guinea. Jan. 82°F (27·8°C), July 78°F (25·6°C). Annual rainfall 40" (1,011 mm).

CONSTITUTION AND GOVERNMENT

The constitution took effect on 16 Sept. 1975. The head of state is the British sovereign, who is represented by a *Governor-General*, nominated by parliament for six-year terms. A single legislative house, known as the *National Parliament*, is made up of 109 members: 89 district representatives and 20 provincial representatives (MPs). The members are elected by universal suffrage; elections are held every five years. All citizens over the age of 18 are eligible to vote and stand for election. Voting is by secret ballot and follows the limited preferential system. The *Prime Minister*, nominated by parliament and appointed by the Governor-General, selects ministers for the National Executive Council. The government cannot be subjected to a vote of no confidence in the first 18 months of office. The 20 provincial assemblies, comprising elected national MPs, appointed members and elected local government representatives, are headed by a Governor, normally the provincial representative in the National Parliament.

National Anthem

'Arise, all you sons of this land'; words and tune by T. Shacklady.

RECENT ELECTIONS

Parliamentary elections were scheduled to take place between 15 June and 29 July 2002 but a troubled electoral process meant that results in some areas were left undeclared. Sir Michael Somare's National Alliance Party won 19 out of 109 seats; Sir Mekere Morautu's People's Democratic Movement, 12 seats; the People's Progress Party, 8; the Papua and Niugini Union Pati, 6; the People's Action Party, 5; the People's Labour Party, 4; ind., 17.

Sir Paulias Matane was elected governor-general by parliament on 27 May 2004.

CURRENT ADMINISTRATION

Governor-General: Sir Paulias Matane; b. 1931 (took office on 29 June 2004).

In April 2006 the government comprised:

Prime Minister: Sir Michael Somare, GCMG, CH; b. 1936 (National Alliance Party; sworn in on 5 Aug. 2002 for the third time, having previously been prime minister from 1975 to 1980 and from 1982 to 1985).

Deputy Prime Minister and Minister of Oil and Energy: Sir Moi Avei.

Minister of Agriculture and Livestock: Matthew Siune. *Correctional Institutional Services:* Posi Menai. *Culture and Tourism:* David Basua. *Defence:* Matthew Gubag. *Education:* Michael Laimo. *Environment and Conservation:* William Duma. *Finance, Forestry, National Planning and Monitoring:* Patrick Pruaitch. *Fisheries:* Ben Semri. *Foreign Affairs:* Sir Rabbie Namaliu. *Health and Bougainville Affairs:* Sir Peter Barter. *Higher Education, Research, Science and Technology:* Brian Pulayasi. *Housing:* Mark Maipakai. *Inter-Governmental Relations:* Melchior Pep. *Internal Security:* Alphonse Willie. *Justice:* Bire Kimisopa. *Labour and Industrial Relations:* Roy Biyama. *Lands:* Petrus Thomas. *Mining:* Sam Akoitai. *Public Services:* Sinai Brown. *State Enterprises and Information:* Puka Temu. *Trade and Industry:* Paul Tiensten. *Transport and Civil Aviation:* Don Poyle. *Treasury:* Bart Philemon. *Welfare and Social Development:* Lady Carol Kidu. *Works:* Gabriel Kapris.

Speaker of Parliament: Jeffery Nape.

Government Website: http://www.pngonline.gov.pg

CURRENT LEADERS

Sir Michael Somare

Position
Prime Minister

Introduction
Sir Michael Somare GCMG, CH was the first prime minister of independent Papua New Guinea, having negotiated its independence from Australia. His reputation for surrounding himself with able ministers did not prevent him from being twice toppled by close associates, a common occurrence in Papua New Guinean politics. Returning in 2002 to serve his third term 17 years after his second, Somare faced a depressed economy and the ramifications of the Bougainville peace agreement. Relations with his country's most important neighbour, Australia, have been strained and Somare has pressed for closer ties with East Asia and the Pacific. He was knighted by Queen Elizabeth II of the UK in 1990 and was honoured with a pontifical knighthood by Pope John Paul II in 1992.

Early Life
Michael Somare was born on 9 April 1936 in Rabaul, East New Britain, the eldest child of Kambe Somare and Ludwig Somare

Sana, a policeman from East Sepik province. During the Second World War Somare received his early education at a Japanese-run school in Karau, the family village in East Sepik, where he learnt Japanese. He left Sogari High School in 1957 to teach until returning to Sogari for further training in 1962. After two years as deputy headmaster of Talidig Primary School in Madang he moved into radio journalism.

Removed from his position for his political views, Somare was elected to the House of Assembly in 1968 as regional MP for East Sepik. The previous year Somare had helped to found the Papua New Guinea United Pati (Pangu) and became its parliamentary leader and leader of the opposition. Re-elected with an independence agenda in 1972, Somare became Papua New Guinea's first chief minister. Peaceful negotiations with Australia's prime minister, Gough Whitlam, lead to self-rule in 1973 and full independence from Australia in Sept. 1975.

Career in Office
Constitutional issues dominated Somare's first term of office. Setting up the Constitutional Development Committee (CPC), he brought together a coalition to produce a 'home-grown' constitution. Influenced by Fiji's prime minister, Ratu Sir Kamisese Mara, Somare promoted a Melanesian attitude towards politics, attempting to gain co-operation across tribal and linguistic lines. He expressed his nationalist pride and belief in traditional practices by training to succeed his father as *sana* (peacemaker) of his village.

Negotiations with Australia, although mostly cordial, were complicated by territorial uncertainties, finally settled by the Torres Strait Treaty of Dec. 1978. The treaty established a Protected Zone for the coastal peoples of southern Papua and the Torres Strait Islanders, allowing them free movement across the new sea border for traditional practices.

Having won the 1977 elections, Somare's coalition with the People's Progress Party collapsed when its leader, Julius Chan, toppled him with a vote of no confidence in 1980. After two years of Chan's premiership, Somare returned as prime minister with an electoral mandate. In Nov. 1985 he was again forced from office by a vote of no confidence, this time led by his successor, Paias Wingti. Somare stepped down as Pangu leader in May 1988 and was succeeded by Rabbie Namaliu, who formed a government in July 1988. Serving as Namaliu's foreign minister, Somare courted the Association of South East Asian Nations (ASEAN), to which Papua New Guinea held observer status, signing a Treaty of Amity and Co-operation in 1989. Urging less dependence on Australia, Papua New Guinea's largest aid donor and importer, Somare persuaded Namaliu's government to reduce foreign control of the mining industry, causing a dent in exports.

The 1990s saw deteriorating relations between Somare and his party. In 1992 he regained the Pangu leadership but resigned in 1993. Somare again left Pangu only to rejoin in 1994. His attention turned to regional politics between 1995–99 when he served as governor of East Sepik after the passing of the Organic Law on Provincial and Local-level Governments, which gave more power to national MPs in their constituencies. His relationship with Pangu ended in 1997 when he was ejected by the Pangu MPs. Forming his own party, the National Alliance—drawing support in the Islands and Momase, his home region—he was re-elected to parliament in 1997. Despite initial support from Bill Skate of the People's National Congress and his coalition partners, Somare lost to Skate in the vote for prime minister. Following the early termination of Skate's premiership in 1999, Somare was appointed to Sir Mekere Morauta's government and given the foreign affairs and Bougainville portfolios. As foreign minister Somare implemented the rejection of Skate's diplomatic recognition of Taiwan, restoring good relations with the People's Republic of China, a major aid donor. Instead, Somare proposed reciprocal investment and trading relations with Taiwan while adhering to the 'One China' principle. Morauta dismissed him in Dec. 2000, accusing him of disloyalty, whereupon Somare became leader of the opposition. In Aug. 2001 Somare accompanied former US president Jimmy Carter to observe East Timor's first parliamentary elections.

The elections of 2002 were the country's most violent and unpredictable. About 70% of MPs were ousted, irregularities were rife and over 30 people died. Somare managed to install Skate as speaker, strengthening his own chances of being elected prime minister. Surrounded by a police cordon, Parliament unanimously voted for Somare. Changes in the electoral system, pushed through by Morauta, tightened up party rules, ensuring MPs remained loyal, thus giving Somare better prospects for stable government. Somare pleased MPs by adopting his old approach of inclusive government, appointing ministers regardless of political affiliations, including former prime minister Sir Rabbie Namaliu.

The success of the National Alliance was partly attributed to the perilous state of the economy, then in its third year of recession. Somare accused Morauta's government of reckless spending, leading to high inflation and a deficit of US$50m. in the first half of 2002, compared to a US$3.5m. surplus for the first six months of 2001. Spending cuts stabilized the currency, the *kina*, which had fallen dramatically during the previous three administrations from a value of US$1.25 in June 1995 to US$0.25 by Aug. 2002.

Australian Prime Minister John Howard's belief that Morauta had been Papua New Guinea's last hope promised difficult relations with the new government. Despite threats to turn away from Australia, in Sept. 2003 Somare agreed to a deal involving operational duties for Australian policemen and professionals within Papua New Guinea's administration, a step beyond the advisory roles previously agreed. This caused unrest in Somare's coalition, with Sir Julius Chan warning against confrontation with Australia. Following a Supreme Court ruling in May 2005 that the Australian deployment violated the country's constitution, the policemen left Papua New Guinea. However, a further agreement was reached in Aug. 2005 whereby a reduced Australian contingent would return to help train the Papuan police and tackle corruption.

During the state visit of Malaysia's outgoing prime minister, Dr Mahathir Mohamad, in Oct. 2003, Somare pressed for full membership of ASEAN, as part of a shift towards Asia for aid and investment.

DEFENCE

The Papua New Guinea Defence Force had a total strength of 3,100 in 2002 consisting of land, maritime and air elements. The Navy is based at Port Moresby and Manus. Personnel numbered 400 in 2002. There is an air force, 250 strong in 2002, but it does not possess any combat aircraft.

Defence expenditure in 2003 totalled US$19m. (US$3 per capita), representing 0.5% of GDP.

INTERNATIONAL RELATIONS

Papua New Guinea is a member of the UN, WTO, the Commonwealth, Asian Development Bank, Colombo Plan, APEC, Antarctic Treaty, the South Pacific Commission and the Pacific Community and is an observer at ASEAN and an ACP member state of the ACP-EU relationship.

ECONOMY

Agriculture accounted for 27.2% of GDP in 2002, industry 39.4% and services 33.4%.

Currency

The unit of currency is the *kina* (PGK) of 100 *toea*. The kina was floated in Oct. 1994. Foreign exchange reserves were US$457m. and gold reserves 63,000 troy oz in April 2002. Inflation was 14.7% in 2003 but fell to 2.1% in 2004. In March 2002 total money supply was K1,663m.

Budget

In 2001 budgetary central government revenue was K2,835.4m. (K2,764.2m. in 2000) and expenditure K2,799.0m. (K2,925.3m. in 2000). Principal sources of revenue in 2001: taxes on income, profits and capital gains, K1,567.9m.; taxes on international trade and transactions, K592.1m.; taxes on goods and services, K342.5m. Main items of expenditure by economic type in 2001: use of goods and services, K1,025.1m.; compensation of employees, K736.0m.; grants, K576.3m.

Performance

Papua New Guinea experienced a three-year recession, with the economy shrinking by 1.2% in 2000, 2.3% in 2001 and 0.8% in 2002. Since then there has been a recovery, with growth of 2.7% in 2003 and 2.5% in 2004. Total GDP in 2004 was US$3.9bn.

Banking and Finance

The Bank of Papua New Guinea (*Governor*, L. Wilson Kamit, CBE) assumed the central banking functions formerly undertaken by the Reserve Bank of Australia on 1 Nov. 1973. A national banking institution, the Papua New Guinea Banking Corporation, has been established. This bank has assumed the Papua New Guinea business of the Commonwealth Trading Bank of Australia.

In 2002 there were seven commercial banks (Australia and New Zealand Banking Group; Bank of Hawaii; Bank of South Pacific; Maybank; MBf Finance; Papua New Guinea Banking Corporation; Westpac Bank) and a Rural Development Bank.

Total commercial bank deposits, 1992, K1,318.2m. Total savings account deposits, 1992, K226.8m. In addition, the Agriculture Bank of Papua New Guinea had assets of K82.6m. in 1992, and finance companies and merchant banks had total assets of K198.4m.

There is a stock exchange in Port Moresby.

ENERGY AND NATURAL RESOURCES

Environment

Carbon dioxide emissions from the consumption and flaring of fossil fuels in 2002 were the equivalent of 0.5 tonnes per capita.

Electricity

Installed capacity was 0.5m. kW in 2000. Production in 2000 was 2.18bn. kWh, around 51% of it hydro-electric. Consumption per capita was 453 kWh.

Oil and Gas

Natural gas reserves in 2002 were 350bn. cu. metres; output in 1998 was 83m. cu. metres. Crude oil production (1999), 29m. bbls. Oil predominantly comes from the Iagifu field in the Southern Highlands. There were 238m. bbls. of proven oil reserves in 2002.

Minerals

In 2001 mining produced 15.5% of GDP. Copper is the main mineral product. Gold, copper and silver are the only minerals produced in quantity. The Misima open-pit gold mine was opened in 1989 but its resources were depleted by the end of 2001. The Porgera gold mine opened in 1990 with an expected life of 20 years. Major copper deposits in Bougainville have proven reserves of about 800m. tonnes; mining was halted by secessionist rebel activity. Copper and gold deposits in the Star Mountains of the Western Province are being developed by Ok Tedi Mining Ltd at the Mt Fubilan mine. Production of gold commenced in 1984 and of copper concentrates in 1987. In 2005 Ok Tedi Mining Ltd produced 192,978 tonnes of copper and 16 tonnes of gold. Gold mining also began at Lihir in 1997. In 2002 total gold production was 63 tonnes; silver production in 2002 was 64 tonnes.

Agriculture

In 2002 agriculture employed 73% of the economically active population. In 2001 there were 210,000 ha. of arable land and 650,000 ha. of permanent cropland. Minor commercial crops include pyrethrum, tea, peanuts and spices. Locally consumed food crops include sweet potatoes, maize, taro, bananas, rice and sago. Tropical fruits grow abundantly. There is extensive grassland. The sugar industry has made the country self-sufficient in this commodity while a beef-cattle industry is being developed.

Production (2000, in 1,000 tonnes): coconuts, 826; bananas, 700; sweet potatoes, 480; sugarcane, 430; palm oil, 299; yams, 220; copra, 170; taro, 170; cassava, 120; coffee, 83.

Livestock (2000): pigs, 1·55m.; cattle, 87,000; chickens, 4m.

Forestry

The forest area totalled 30·60m. ha. in 2000 (67·6% of the land area). In 1995 about 15m. ha. of high quality tropical hardwoods were considered suitable for development. Timber production is important for both local consumption and export. Timber production was 8·60m. cu. metres in 2001.

Fisheries

Tuna is the major resource. In 2001 the fish catch was an estimated 122,419 tonnes (89% sea fish).

INDUSTRY

Secondary and service industries are expanding for the local market. The main industries are food processing, beverages, tobacco, timber products, wood and fabricated metal products. Industry accounted for 42·7% of GDP in 2001, with manufacturing contributing 8·1%. Production (2002): palm oil, 370,000 tonnes; copra, 110,000 tonnes; wood-based panels, 79,000 cu. metres; sawnwood, 70,000 cu. metres.

Labour

The labour force in 1996 totalled 2,160,000 (58% males). In 1996 formal employment in the building and construction industries rose by 27·5%, but around 85% of the population is dependent on non-monetarized agriculture.

INTERNATIONAL TRADE

Australian aid amounts to an annual $A300m. The 'Pactra II' agreement of 1991 established a free trade zone with Australia and protects Australian investments. Foreign debt was US$2,485m. in 2002.

Imports and Exports

Imports in 2001 were US$932·4m. (US$998·8m. in 2000); exports, US$1,812·9m. (US$2,094·1m. in 2000). The main imports in terms of value are machinery and transport equipment, manufactured goods, and food and live animals; and the main exports crude petroleum, gold and logs.

Of imports in 1999, Australia furnished 53·5%; Singapore, 12·9%; Japan, 5·6%; New Zealand, 4·1%; USA, 3·6%; of exports, Australia took 38·1%; Japan, 16·9%; Germany, 9·6%; USA, 6·6%; South Korea, 5·8%.

COMMUNICATIONS

Roads

In 2002 there were 19,600 km of roads, only about 690 km of which were paved. There were 36,000 passenger cars and 60,000 trucks and vans in 2002.

Civil Aviation

Jacksons International Airport is at Port Moresby. The state-owned national carrier is Air Niugini. In 2003 there were scheduled international flights to Brisbane, Cairns, Honiara, Manila, Singapore, Sydney and Tokyo. There are a total of 177 airports and airstrips with scheduled services.

Shipping

There are 12 entry and four other main ports served by five major shipping lines; the Papua New Guinea Shipping Corporation is state-owned. Sea-going shipping totalled 72,000 GRT in 2002, including oil tankers 2,000 GRT.

Telecommunications

In 2001 there were 72,700 telephone subscribers, or 13·7 for every 1,000 inhabitants. In 2002, 321,000 PCs were in use (58·7 for every 1,000 persons). There were 15,000 mobile phone subscribers in 2002 and 800 fax machines in 1995. Internet users numbered 75,000 in 2002. In Dec. 2004 the government rejected a bid by a South African joint venture to acquire a 51% stake in the state-owned telecommunications company Telikom PNG.

Postal Services

The 1996 Postal Service Act created the government-owned Post PNG Limited. In 2004 its network consisted of 31 post offices, 26 agency post offices and two international mail exchange centres.

SOCIAL INSTITUTIONS

Justice

The judicial system consists of a Supreme Court, a National Court, and district and local courts. The Supreme Court sittings are usually held with three or five judges. In 2004 there were 64,709 court cases registered of which 16,459 were civil cases. The discretionary use of the death penalty for murder and rape was introduced in 1991.

The population in penal institutions in 2002 was 3,302 (66 per 100,000 of national population).

Education

Obligatory universal primary education is a government objective. In 1990 about two-thirds of eligible children were attending school. In 2001 there were 3,055 elementary and primary schools with 395,129 pupils and 11,307 teachers, 77,451 pupils in secondary schools (2,187 teachers) and 14,333 students in institutes of higher education. There are six universities: the University of Papua New Guinea (UPNG), Port Moresby; the Papua New Guinea University of Technology, Lae; Divine Word University, Madang; Pacific Adventist University, Boroko; the University of Goroka; and the University of Vudal, Rabaul. UPNG, founded in 1965, has two campuses in the capital, five provincial open campuses and 13 study centres. In 2002 there were also ten colleges, eight nursing schools and three academic institutes.

Adult literacy rate was 57·3% in 2003 (63·4% among males and 50·9% among females).

In 2000–01 total expenditure on education came to 2·4% of GNP and 17·5% of total government spending.

Health

In 2000 there were 275 physicians, 90 dentists and 2,841 nurses. Provision of hospital beds in 1993 was 34 per 10,000 persons.

RELIGION

At the 2000 census there were 4·93m. Christians: Roman Catholics made up 27·0%; Lutherans, 19·5%; United Church, 11·5%; Anglicans, 3·2%. In 1998 the Catholic Church had four archdioceses (Madang, Mount Hagen, Port Moresby and Rabaul), 14 dioceses, 340 parishes and 540 priests.

CULTURE

Broadcasting

The National Broadcasting Commission operates three networks: national, provincial and commercial. A national service is relayed throughout the country. Each province has a broadcasting service, while the larger urban centres are also covered by a commercial network relayed from Port Moresby. Two commercial television stations broadcast from Port Moresby (colour by PAL). In 2001 there were 110,000 television receivers and in 2000 there were 446,000 radio receivers.

Press
In 2004 there were two daily newspapers (the *Post-Courier* and the *National*) and a number of weeklies and monthlies. The *Post-Courier* is the oldest (1969) and most widely read, with a daily circulation of 29,000.

Tourism
In 2002 there were 54,000 (58,000 in 2000) visitors; spending by tourists totalled US$101m. in 2001.

Festivals
Alongside the major Christian festivals several cultural shows are held, in Enga (late July), at Mount Hagen (Western Highlands; late Aug.) and at Goroka (Eastern Highlands; mid-Sept.). Independence Day is celebrated on 16 Sept.

DIPLOMATIC REPRESENTATIVES

Of Papua New Guinea in the United Kingdom (3rd Floor, 14 Waterloo Pl., London, SW1Y 4AR)
High Commissioner: Jean Kekedo, OBE.

Of the United Kingdom in Papua New Guinea (PO Box 212, Waigani NCD 131)
High Commissioner: David Gordon-Macleod.

Of Papua New Guinea in the USA (1779 Massachusetts Ave., NW, Washington, D.C., 20036)
Ambassador: Evan Paki.

Of the USA in Papua New Guinea (Douglas St., Port Moresby)
Ambassador: Robert W. Fitts.

Of Papua New Guinea to the United Nations
Ambassador: Robert Aisi.

Of Papua New Guinea to the European Union
Ambassador: Vacant.
Chargé d'Affaires a.i.: Kapi Maro.

FURTHER READING

National Statistical Office. *Summary of Statistics.* Annual.—*Abstract of Statistics.* Quarterly.
Bank of Papua New Guinea. *Quarterly Economic Bulletin.*
Turner, A., *Historical Dictionary of Papua New Guinea.* Metuchen (NJ), 1995

National Statistical Office: National Statistical Office, PO Box 337, Waigani, National Capital District, Port Moresby.
Website: http://www.nso.gov.pg

PARAGUAY

BOLIVIA
Bahía Negra
BRAZIL
PARAGUAY
Pedro Juan Caballero
ARGENTINA
ASUNCIÓN
Ciudad del Este
0   100 mi
0   200 km
© Research Machines plc 2006

República del Paraguay

Capital: Asunción
Population projection, 2010: 6·88m.
GDP per capita, 2003: (PPP$) 4,684
HDI/world rank: 0·755/88

KEY HISTORICAL EVENTS

Paraguay was occupied by the Spanish in 1537 and became a Spanish colony as part of the viceroyalty of Peru. The area gained its independence, as the Republic of Paraguay, on 14 May 1811. Paraguay was then ruled by a succession of dictators. A devastating war fought from 1865 to 1870 between Paraguay and a coalition of Argentina, Brazil and Uruguay reduced Paraguay's population from about 600,000 to 233,000. Further severe losses were incurred during the war with Bolivia (1932–35) over territorial claims in the Chaco inspired by the unfounded belief that minerals existed in the territory. A peace treaty by which Paraguay obtained most of the area her troops had conquered was signed in July 1938.

A new constitution took effect in Feb. 1968 under which executive power is discharged by an executive president. Gen. Alfredo Stroessner Mattiauda was re-elected seven times between 1958 and 1988. Since then, Paraguay has been under more or less democratic government. On 23 March 1999 Paraguay's vice-president Luis Maria Argaña was assassinated. The following day, Congress voted to impeach President Raúl Cubas who was said to be implicated in the murder. He then resigned.

TERRITORY AND POPULATION

Paraguay is bounded in the northwest by Bolivia, northeast and east by Brazil and southeast, south and southwest by Argentina. The area is 406,752 sq. km (157,042 sq. miles).

The 2002 census population was 5,163,198 (2,603,242 males), giving a density of 12·7 per sq. km. In 2003, 57·2% lived in urban areas.

The UN gives a projected population for 2010 of 6·88m.

In 2002 the capital, Asunción, had a population of 512,112. Other major cities (2002 census populations) are: Ciudad del Este, 222,274; San Lorenzo, 204,356; Luque, 185,127.

There are 17 departments and the capital city. Area and population at the 2002 census:

Department	Area in sq. km	Population
Asunción (city)	117	512,112
Central	2,465	1,362,893
Alto Paraná	14,895	558,672
Itapúa	16,525	453,692
Caaguazú	11,474	435,357
San Pedro	20,002	318,698
Cordillera	4,948	233,854
Paraguari	8,705	221,932
Concepción	18,051	179,450
Guairá	3,846	178,650
Canendiyú	14,667	140,137
Caazapá	9,496	139,517
Amambay	12,933	114,917
Misiones	9,556	101,783
Neembucú	12,147	76,348
Oriental	*159,827*	*5,028,012*
Presidente Hayes	72,907	82,493
Boquerón[1]	91,669	41,106
Alto Paraguay[2]	82,349	11,587
Occidental	*246,925*	*135,186*

[1]Incorporates former department of Nueva Asunción.
[2]Incorporates former department of Chaco.

The population is mixed Spanish and Guaraní Indian. There are 89,000 unassimilated Indians of other tribal origin, in the Chaco and the forests of eastern Paraguay. 24·8% of the population speak only Guaraní; 51·5% are bilingual (Spanish/Guaraní); and 7·6% speak only Spanish.

Mennonites, who arrived in three groups (1927, 1930 and 1947), are settled in the Chaco and eastern Paraguay. There are also Korean and Japanese settlers.

SOCIAL STATISTICS

2002 births, 123,674; deaths, 19,416. Rates, 2002 (per 1,000 population): birth, 24·0; death, 3·8. Annual population growth rate, 1990–2002, 2·2%. Expectation of life, 2003: 68·7 years for males and 73·2 for females. Infant mortality, 2001, 26 per 1,000 live births; fertility rate, 2001, 3·9 births per woman.

CLIMATE

A tropical climate, with abundant rainfall and only a short dry season from July to Sept., when temperatures are lowest. Asunción, Jan. 81°F (27°C), July 64°F (17·8°C). Annual rainfall 53" (1,316 mm).

CONSTITUTION AND GOVERNMENT

On 18 June 1992 a Constituent Assembly approved a new constitution. The head of state is the *President,* elected for a non-renewable five-year term. Parliament consists of an 80-member *Chamber of Deputies,* elected from departmental constituencies, and a 45-member *Senate,* elected from a single national constituency.

National Anthem

'Paraguayos, república o muerte!' ('Paraguayans, republic or death!'); words by F. Acuña de Figueroa, tune by F. Dupuy.

RECENT ELECTIONS

Parliamentary and presidential elections were held on 27 April 2003. Nicanor Duarte Frutos of the ruling Republican National Alliance–Colorado Party (ANR) was elected president with 37·1% of votes cast. Julio César Franco Gómez of the Authentic Radical Liberal Party (PLRA) won 24·0%, Pedro Fadul Niella of the Movement Fatherland of the Best (MPQ) 21·3% and Guillermo Sánchez Guffanti of the National Union of Ethical Citizens (UNACE) 13·5%. Turnout was 64·2%. As a result of the election the Colorado Party maintained its status as the longest-ruling party in the world.

In the Chamber of Deputies the ANR won 37 seats with 35·3% of votes cast, the PLRA won 21 seats (25·7%), the MPQ won 10 seats (15·3%), the UNACE won 10 seats (14·7%) and the Party for a Country of Solidarity (PPS) won 2 seats (3·3%). Turnout was 64%. In the Senate the ANR won 16 seats, the PLRA won 12, the MPQ won 8, the UNACE won 7 and the PPS won 2. Turnout was 58·8%.

CURRENT ADMINISTRATION

President: Nicanor Duarte Frutos; b. 1956 (ANR; sworn in 15 Aug. 2003).

Vice-President: Luis Alberto Castiglioni.

In March 2006 the cabinet comprised:

Minister of Agriculture and Livestock: Nelson Gustavo Ruiz Díaz Roa. *Education and Culture:* Blanca Ovelar de Duarte. *Finance:* Ernst Bergen. *Foreign Affairs:* Leila Rachid Lichi de Cowles. *Industry and Commerce:* Raúl José Vera Bogado. *Interior:* Rogelio Benítez Vargas. *Justice and Labour:* Derlis Alcides Céspedes Aguilera. *National Defence:* Roberto González. *Public Health and Social Welfare:* María Teresa León. *Public Works and Communications:* José Alberto Alderete.

CURRENT LEADERS

Nicanor Duarte Frutos

Position
President

Introduction
Nicanor Duarte Frutos was elected in April 2003, extending the power of the Republican National Alliance–Colorado Party (ANR) which has ruled Paraguay continuously since 1947. Duarte won power despite a struggling economy and accusations of party corruption. He represents the party's traditionalist faction.

Early Life
Óscar Nicanor Duarte Frutos was born on 11 Oct. 1956 and brought up in Coronel Oviedo, an agricultural town in Paraguay. He joined the Colorado Party at the age of 14, and went on to study law and political science before pursuing a career in journalism.

Having served as education minister in the 1990s, Duarte took 37% of the vote at the 2003 elections, defeating three other candidates. Elected in April, he took up his position as leader in Aug. that year.

Career in Office
Upon his election as president, Duarte announced plans to fight corruption, reinvigorate the economy and improve the nation's standing in the international community. He aimed to create jobs through public work programmes and, in a bid to improved efficiency in government, promised to reform the customs and internal revenue services. Despite his stated desire to reduce crime, his opponents have accused Duarte of protecting corrupt officials.

DEFENCE

The army, navy and air forces are separate services under a single command. The President of the Republic is the active C.-in-C. Conscription is for 12 months (two years in the navy).

In 2003 defence expenditure totalled US$44m. (US$8 per capita), representing 0·8% of GDP.

Army
Strength (2002) 14,900 (10,400 conscripts). In addition there is a paramilitary Special Police Force numbering 14,800.

Navy
Personnel in 2002 totalled 2,000 including 900 marines (of which 200 conscripts) and 100 naval aviation.

Air Force
The air force had a strength of 1,700 in 2002 (600 conscripts). There are 28 combat aircraft including F-5E/Fs.

INTERNATIONAL RELATIONS

Paraguay is a member of the UN, WTO, OAS, Inter-American Development Bank, MERCOSUR, LAIA and IOM.

ECONOMY

In 2002 agriculture accounted for 22·0% of GDP, industry 28·4% and services 49·6%.

Currency
The unit of currency is the *guaraní* (PYG), notionally divided into 100 *céntimos*. In May 2002 total money supply was 2,373·85bn. guaranís. Foreign exchange reserves were US$450m. in June 2002 and gold reserves 35,000 troy oz. Inflation was 4·3% in 2004.

Budget
Budgetary central government revenue and expenditure in 1bn. guaranís:

	2001	2002	2003
Revenue	4,972·0	5,078·1	6,065·6
Expenditure	4,530·1	4,918·7	5,215·1

Principal sources of revenue in 2003: taxes on goods and services, 2,278·4bn. guaranís; taxes on international trade and transactions, 665·1bn. guaranís; taxes on income, profits and capital gains, 623·9bn. guaranís. Main items of expenditure by economic type in 2003: compensation of employees, 2,724·0bn. guaranís; social benefits, 991·0bn. guaranís; grants, 593·4bn. guaranís.

Performance
Real GDP growth was 3·8% in 2003 and 4·0% in 2004. GDP per capita fell from US$1,930 in 1996 to approximately US$1,125 in 2000. Total GDP in 2004 was US$7·1bn.

Banking and Finance
The Central Bank is a state-owned autonomous agency with the sole right of note issue, control over foreign exchange and the supervision of commercial banks (*Governor*, Mónica Pérez dos Santos). There is a Superintendencia de Bancos under Rodrigo Fernando Ortiz Frutos. In 2002 there were five commercial banks and 11 foreign banks.

There is a stock exchange in Asunción.

ENERGY AND NATURAL RESOURCES

Environment
Paraguay's carbon dioxide emissions from the consumption and flaring of fossil fuels were the equivalent of 0·6 tonnes per capita in 2002.

Electricity
Installed capacity was 8·1m. kW in 2000. Output (2000), 53·52bn. kWh (almost exclusively hydro-electric); consumption per capita in 2000 was 1,116 kWh.

Minerals

The country is poor in minerals. Limestone, gypsum, kaolin and salt are extracted. Deposits of bauxite, iron ore, copper, manganese and uranium exist. 2001 output: limestone, 16,320 tonnes; kaolin, 66,500 tonnes.

Agriculture

In 1999 agriculture employed 35% of the workforce and produced 90% of the country's exports. In 2001 there were approximately 3·02m. ha. of arable land and 90,000 ha. of permanent crops.

At the agrarian census of 1991 there were 307,221 farms working 23,799,737 ha. 122,750 farms had fewer than 5 ha.; 884 had over 5,000 ha.

Output (in 1,000 tonnes), 2000: cassava, 3,500; sugarcane, 2,850; soybeans, 2,750; maize, 900; wheat, 250; oranges, 209; seed cotton, 205; cottonseed, 123; watermelons, 110; rice, 93. *Yerba maté*, or strongly flavoured Paraguayan tea, continues to be produced but is declining in importance.

Livestock (2000): 9·91m. cattle, 2·70m. pigs, 413,000 sheep, 400,000 horses and 25m. chickens.

Forestry

The area under forests in 2000 was 23·37m. ha., or 58·8% of the total land area. Timber production was 9·69m. cu. metres in 2001.

Fisheries

In 2001 the catch totalled approximately 25,000 tonnes, exclusively from inland waters.

INDUSTRY

Paraguay is one of the least industrialized countries in Latin America. Industries include meat packing, sugar processing, cement, textiles, brewing, wood products and consumer goods. In 2001 industry accounted for 27·5% of GDP, with manufacturing contributing 14·1%.

Labour

The labour force in 2002 totalled 1,980,492 (67·9% males). In 2002, 27% of the economically active population were engaged in agriculture, fisheries, hunting and forestry.

Trade Unions

Trade unionists number about 30,000 (*Confederación Paraguaya de Trabajadores* and *Confederación Cristiana de Trabajadores*).

INTERNATIONAL TRADE

Foreign debt was US$2,967m. in 2002.

Imports and Exports

Trade in US$1m.:

	1998	1999	2000	2001	2002
Imports f.o.b.	3,941·5	2,752·9	2,904·0	2,507·0	2,390·9
Exports f.o.b.	3,548·6	2,312·4	2,225·8	1,951·8	2,319·3

Main imports in 1999: machinery, 36·0%; chemicals, 11·9%; manufactured goods, 11·9%; petroleum and related products, 11·0%; tobacco, 8·7%. Main exports: soybeans, 41·5%; cotton, 8·4%; soy oilcake, 7·1%; timber, 5·0%; soybean oil, 4·9%.

Main import suppliers in 1999: Brazil, 28·6%; Argentina, 17·8%; USA, 13·7%; Japan, 6·1%; Germany, 3·8%; Spain, 3·1%. Main export markets, 1999: Brazil, 31·7%; Netherlands, 18·5%; UK, 12·9%; USA, 7·8%; Argentina, 7·2%; Chile, 3·1%.

COMMUNICATIONS

Roads

In 2002 there were around 29,500 km of roads, of which 53·9% were paved. Passenger cars numbered 294,700 in 2002, there were 148,800 trucks and vans and (1999) 9,000 buses and coaches. There were 1,949 road accidents in 1999 resulting in 160 fatalities.

Rail

The President Carlos Antonio López (formerly Paraguay Central) Railway runs from Asunción to Encarnación, on the Río Alto Paraná, with a length of 441 km (1,435 mm gauge), and connects with Argentine Railways over the Encarnación-Posadas bridge opened in 1989. In 1994 traffic amounted to 182,000 tonnes and 24,000 passengers.

Civil Aviation

There is an international airport at Asunción (Silvio Pettirossi). The main Paraguay-based carrier is Transportes Aereos del Mercosur, which flew 4·3m. km and carried 195,000 passengers (all on international flights) in 1999. In 2000 Asunción handled 466,000 passengers (422,000 on international flights) and 6,600 tonnes of freight.

Shipping

Asunción, the chief port, is 1,500 km from the sea. In 2002 ocean-going shipping totalled 47,000 GRT, including oil tankers 4,000 GRT.

Telecommunications

In 2002 telephone subscribers numbered 1,940,200 (335·6 per 1,000 population) and 200,000 PCs were in use (34·6 for every 1,000 persons). There were 1,667,000 mobile phone subscribers in 2002 and 1,700 fax machines in 1995. Paraguay had approximately 100,000 Internet users in 2002.

Postal Services

In 2003 there were 258 post offices.

SOCIAL INSTITUTIONS

Justice

The 1992 constitution confers a large measure of judicial autonomy. The highest court is the Supreme Court with nine members. Nominations for membership must be backed by six of the eight members of the Magistracy Council, which appoints all judges, magistrates and the electoral tribunal. The Council comprises elected representatives of the Presidency, Congress and the bar. There are special Chambers of Appeal for civil and commercial cases, and criminal cases. Judges of first instance deal with civil, commercial and criminal cases in six departments. Minor cases are dealt with by Justices of the Peace.

The Attorney-General represents the State in all jurisdictions, with representatives in each judicial department and in every jurisdiction.

The population in penal institutions in 1999 was 4,088 (75 per 100,000 of national population). The death penalty was abolished for all crimes in 1992.

Education

Adult literacy was 91·6% in 2003 (male, 93·1%; female, 90·2%). Education is free and nominally compulsory. In 2000–01 there were 966,476 pupils at primary schools and 459,260 at secondary level. In 2001 there were 14 universities (one Roman Catholic) and one institute. There were 83,041 students in tertiary education in 2000–01.

In 2000–01 total public expenditure on education came to 5·0% of GNP and 11·2% of total government spending.

Health

In 2003 there were 1,117 health establishments (including 84 hospitals) with 7,167 beds. There were 6,400 physicians, 1,947 dentists and 1,089 nurses in 2000.

RELIGION

Religious liberty was guaranteed by the 1967 constitution. Article 6 recognized Roman Catholicism as the official religion of the country. It had 3·5m. adherents in 2002. There are Mennonite, Anglican and other communities as well. In 2002 followers of other religions (mostly Protestants) totalled 322,000.

CULTURE

World Heritage Sites

Paraguay has one site on the UNESCO World Heritage List: the Jesuit Missions of La Santísima Trinidad de Paraná and Jesús de Tavarangue (inscribed on the list in 1993).

Broadcasting

In 1993 there were 30 commercial radio stations and in 1999 there were four TV stations (colour by PAL M) and two cable TV stations. In 2000 there were 1·2m. television receivers and 961,000 radio receivers.

Cinema

There are 15 cinemas in Asunción.

Press

In 1996 there were five daily newspapers with a combined circulation of 213,000, at a rate of 43 per 1,000 inhabitants.

Tourism

In 2002 there were 250,000 foreign tourists, bringing revenue of US$62m.

DIPLOMATIC REPRESENTATIVES

Of Paraguay in the United Kingdom (3rd Floor, 344 High St. Kensington, London, W14 8NS)
Ambassador: Vacant.
Chargé d'Affaires a.i.: María Cristina Acosta.

Of the United Kingdom in Paraguay
Ambassador: John Hughes (resides in Buenos Aires, Argentina).

Of Paraguay in the USA (2400 Massachusetts Ave., NW, Washington, D.C., 20008)
Ambassador: James Spalding Hellmers.

Of the USA in Paraguay (1776 Mariscal López Ave., Asunción)
Ambassador: James C. Cason.

Of Paraguay to the United Nations
Ambassador: Eladio Loizaga.

Of Paraguay to the European Union
Ambassador: Emilio Gimenez Franco.

FURTHER READING

Gaceta Official, published by Imprenta Nacional, Estrella y Estero Bellaco, Asunción
Anuario Daumas. Asunción
Anuario Estadístico de la República del Paraguay. Asunción. Annual

Nickson, R. A. and Lambert, P. (eds.) *The Transition to Democracy in Paraguay.* Macmillan, London and St Martin's Press, New York, 1997

National library: Biblioteca Nacional, Calle de la Residenta, 820 c/ Perú, Asunción.
National Statistical Office: Dirección General de Estadísticas, Enuestas y Censos.
Website (Spanish only): http://www.dgeec.gov.py

PERU

República del Perú

Capital: Lima
Population projection, 2010: 30·06m.
GDP per capita, 2003: (PPP$) 5,260
HDI/world rank: 0·762/79

KEY HISTORICAL EVENTS

The Incas of Peru were conquered by the Spanish in the 16th century and subsequent Spanish colonial settlement made Peru the most important of the Spanish viceroyalties in South America. On 28 July 1821 Peru declared its independence, but it was not until after a war which ended in 1824 that the country gained its freedom. In a war with Chile (1879–83) Peru's capital, Lima, was captured and she lost some of her southern territory. Tacna, in the far south of the country, remained in Chilean control from 1880 until 1929. In 1924 Dr Victor Raúl Haya de la Torre founded the *Alianza Popular Revolucionaria Americana* to oppose the dictatorial government then in power. The party was banned between 1931 and 1945, and between 1948 and 1956 its leader failed regularly in the presidential elections although it was at times the largest party in Congress. The closeness of the 1962 elections led Gen. Ricardo Pérez Godoy, Chairman of the Joint Chiefs-of-Staff, to seize power. A coup led by Gen. Nicolás Lindley López deposed him in 1963. There followed, after elections, a period of civilian rule but the military staged yet another coup in 1968. In 1978–79 a constituent assembly drew up a new constitution, after which a civilian government was installed. However, Peru was plagued by political violence for nearly 20 years between the early 1980s and the late 1990s with 69,000 people killed by Maoist Shining Path insurgents, the smaller Tupac Amaru Revolutionary Movement and government forces. On 5 April 1992 President Alberto Fujimori suspended the constitution and dissolved the parliament. A new constitution was promulgated on 29 Dec. 1993. But while Peru has enjoyed stability and economic growth, there was still rule by autocracy which put some politicians above the law. Embroiled in a bribery and corruption scandal, President Fujimori's discredited administration came to an end in Nov. 2000 with his resignation while out of the country.

TERRITORY AND POPULATION

Peru is bounded in the north by Ecuador and Colombia, east by Brazil and Bolivia, south by Chile and west by the Pacific Ocean. Area, 1,285,216 sq. km (including the area of the Peruvian part of Lake Titicaca).

For an account of the border dispute with Ecuador, *see* ECUADOR: Territory and Population.

Census population (provisional), 2005, 26,152,265 (73·9% urban in 2003); density, 20·3 per sq. km.

The UN gives a projected population for 2010 of 30·06m.

Area and population estimate of the 24 departments and the constitutional province of Callao, together with their capitals:

Department	Area (in sq. km)	Population 2004	Capital	Population 2002
Amazonas	39,249	443,025	Chachapoyas	19,128
Ancash	35,915	1,139,083	Huaraz	82,321
Apurímac	20,896	478,315	Abancay	64,655
Arequipa	63,345	1,126,636	Arequipa	760,329
Ayacucho	43,815	571,563	Ayacucho	132,498
Cajamarca	33,318	1,532,878	Cajamarca	118,699
Callao[1]	147	811,874	Callao	786,500
Cusco	71,987	1,237,802	Cusco	301,342
Huancavelica	22,131	459,988	Huancavelica	39,029
Huánuco	36,849	833,640	Huánuco	157,024
Ica	21,328	709,556	Ica	217,696
Junín	44,197	1,274,781	Huancayo	321,390
La Libertad	25,500	1,550,796	Trujillo	611,007
Lambayeque	14,231	1,141,228	Chiclayo	491,292
Lima	34,802	8,011,820	Lima	6,953,203
Loreto	368,852	931,444	Iquitos	362,531
Madre de Dios	85,301	104,891	Puerto Maldonado	35,627
Moquegua	15,734	163,757	Moquegua	49,053
Pasco	25,320	277,475	Cerro de Pasco	67,959
Piura	35,892	1,685,972	Piura	346,041
Puno	71,999	1,297,103	Puno	107,050
San Martín	51,253	777,694	Moyobamba	35,489
Tacna	16,076	309,765	Tacna	243,600
Tumbes	4,669	211,089	Tumbes	96,810
Ucayali	102,411	464,399	Pucallpa	231,059

[1]Constitutional province.

In 1991 there were some 100,000 Peruvians of Japanese origin. Indigenous peoples account for 47% of the population.

The official languages are Spanish (spoken by 79·8% of the population in 2003), Quechua (16·4%) and Aymara (2·3%).

SOCIAL STATISTICS

2004 estimates: births, 621,000; deaths, 168,000; infant deaths (under 1 year), 20,000. Rates per 1,000 population (2004 estimates): birth, 22·5; death, 6·1. Annual population growth rate, 2000–04, 1·5%; infant mortality, 2001, 30 per 1,000 live births. Life expectancy, 2003: males, 67·5 years; females, 72·6. Fertility rate, 2004, 2·8 births per woman.

CLIMATE

There is a very wide variety of climates, ranging from tropical in the east to desert in the west, with perpetual snow in the Andes. In coastal areas, temperatures vary very little, either daily or annually, though humidity and cloudiness show considerable variation, with highest humidity from May to Sept. Little rain is experienced in that period. In the Sierra, temperatures remain fairly constant over the year, but the daily range is considerable. There the dry season is from April to Nov. Desert conditions occur in the extreme south, where the climate is uniformly dry, with a few heavy showers falling between Jan. and March. Lima, Jan. 74°F (23·3°C), July 62°F (16·7°C). Annual rainfall 2" (48 mm). Cusco, Jan. 56°F (13·3°C), July 50°F (10°C). Annual rainfall 32" (804 mm). El Niño is the annual warm Pacific current which moves to the coasts of Peru and Ecuador. El Niño in 1982–83 resulted in agricultural production down by 8·5% and fishing output down by 40%. El Niño in 1991–94 was unusually long. El Niño in 1997–98 resulted in a sudden rise in the surface temperature of the Pacific by 9°F (5°C) and caused widespread damage and loss of life.

CONSTITUTION AND GOVERNMENT

The 1980 Constitution provided for a legislative *Congress* consisting of a *Senate* and a *Chamber of Deputies*, and an Executive formed of the President and a Council of Ministers appointed by him. Elections were to be every five years with the President and Congress elected, at the same time, by separate ballots.

On 5 April 1992 President Fujimori suspended the 1980 constitution and dissolved Congress.

A referendum was held on 31 Oct. 1993 to approve the twelfth constitution, including a provision for the president to serve a consecutive second term. 52·24% of votes cast were in favour. The constitution was promulgated on 29 Dec. 1993. In Aug. 1996 Congress voted for the eligibility of the President to serve a third consecutive term of office.

Congress has 120 members, elected for a five-year term by proportional representation. In March 2003 it voted to re-establish the Senate, which had been dissolved by former president Alberto Fujimori in 1992.

All citizens over the age of 18 are eligible to vote. Voting is compulsory.

National Anthem

'Somos libres, seámoslo siempre' ('We are free, let us always be so'); words by J. De La Torre Ugarte, tune by J. B. Alcedo.

GOVERNMENT CHRONOLOGY

Heads of State since 1945. (AP = Popular Action; APRA = American Popular Revolutionary Alliance; FDN = National Democratic Front; MDP = Pradista Democratic Movement/Peruvian Democratic Movement; NM-C90 = New Majority/Change 90; PP = Peru Possible; PR = Restorer Party)

President of the Republic
1945–48	FDN	José Luis Bustamante y Rivero

Chairmen of the Military Junta of Government
1948–50	military	Manuel Apolinario Odría Amoretti
1950	military	Zenón Noriega Agüero

Presidents of the Republic
1950–56	PR	Manuel Apolinario Odría Amoretti
1956–62	MDP	Manuel Prado y Ugarteche

Junta of Government/Joint Command of the Armed Forces
1962–63	military	Ricardo Pío Pérez Godoy, Nicolás Lindley López, Juan Francisco Torres Matos, Pedro Vargas Prada Peirano

Presidents of the Republic
1963–68	AP	Fernando Belaúnde Terry
1968–75	military	Juan Francisco Velasco Alvarado
1975–80	military	Francisco Morales Bermúdez
1980–85	AP	Fernando Belaúnde Terry
1985–90	APRA	Alan Gabriel Ludwig García Pérez
1990–2000	NM-C90	Alberto Keinya Fujimori Fujimori
2000–01	AP	Valentín Paniagua Corazao
2001–	PP	Alejandro Celestino Toledo Manrique

RECENT ELECTIONS

The first round of presidential elections were held on 9 April 2006. Ollanta Humala Tasso of the Union for Peru won 29·7% of the votes, followed by Alan García Pérez of the Peruvian Aprista Party (formerly the American Popular Revolutionary Alliance) with 25·0%, Lourdes Flores Nano of the National Unity Party with 24·6% and Martha Chávez Cossio of Alliance for the Future with 6·9%. There were 15 other candidates. A run-off was set to be held on 4 June 2006.

In the congressional elections of 8 April 2001 the Peru Possible party gained 45 seats with 26·3% of votes cast. The American Popular Revolutionary Alliance gained 28 seats (19·7%), the National Unity Party 17 (13·8%), the Moralizing Independent Front 11 (11·0%), Union for Peru 6 (4·0%) and We Are Peru 4 (4·9%). Other parties won three seats or fewer.

CURRENT ADMINISTRATION

President: Alejandro Toledo Manrique; b. 1946 (Peru Possible; sworn in on 28 July 2001).

First Vice-President: Vacant. *Second Vice-President:* David Waisman.

In March 2006 the government comprised:

President of the Council of Ministers (Prime Minister): Pedro Pablo Kuczynski; b. 1938 (sworn in 16 Aug. 2005).

Minister of Foreign Affairs: Óscar Maúrtua de Romaña. *Defence:* Marciano Rengifo Ruiz. *Economy and Finance:* Fernando Zavala Lombardi. *Interior:* Rómulo Pizarro Tomasio. *Justice:* Alejandro Ignacio Tudela Chopitea. *Education and Culture:* Javier Sota Nadal. *Health:* Pilar Mazzetti Soler. *Agriculture:* Manuel Manrique. *Labour:* Carlos Almerí. *Foreign Trade and Tourism:* Alfredo Ferrero Diez Canseco. *Energy and Mines:* Glodomiro Sánchez Mejía. *Transport and Communications:* José Ortiz Rivera. *Production:* David Lemor. *Housing, Construction and Sanitation:* Rudecindo Vega Carreazo. *Women's Affairs and Social Development:* Ana María Romero-Lozada.

President of the Council of Ministers (Spanish only):
http://www.pcm.gob.pe

CURRENT LEADERS

Alejandro Toledo

Position
President

Introduction
A former economist for the World Bank, President Alejandro Toledo represents the Peru Possible party. Elected in July 2001, Toledo took over from interim president Valentín Paniagua. This was after former president Alberto Fujimori had resigned in Nov. 2000 amid corruption allegations following ten years in power. The first elected president of indigenous origin, Toledo pledged to combat widespread poverty, invigorate the economy and eradicate government corruption.

Early Life
Toledo was born on 28 March 1946 in Cabana, a small Andean village. From a large, poor family, he grew up in the coastal town of Chimbote where his parents had moved to find work in the fishing business. The young Toledo worked at odd jobs including shoeshining. While studying in San Pedro, he took to politics while writing for *La Prensa* newspaper. On winning a

scholarship, he studied economics at San Francisco University and completed a doctorate in human resources at Stanford University in the USA. He then worked as an economics advisor for international organizations including the UN, the World Bank and the International Labour Organization in Geneva.

On his return to Peru, he became actively involved in politics. Representing Peru Possible, a mix of left and centre politicians, he fought his first presidential campaign in 1995 when he received 4% of the vote. In his second attempt in 2000 he competed against Fujimori, who was running for a third consecutive term. Gaining only 23% of votes, Toledo withdrew from the presidential race accusing the Fujimori camp of vote rigging. Fujimori's third term was short-lived and the autocratic leader resigned a few months later. Having gone into exile in Japan, he was subsequently charged in Peru with treason.

Toledo fought his third election against the former president, Alan García, who represented the American Popular Revolutionary Alliance. During Toledo's electoral campaign he exploited his indigenous roots, aiming to attract those Peruvians who had suffered discrimination by the European elite. Toledo's wife, the Belgian anthropologist Elaine Karp, delivered campaign speeches in Quechua (the main indigenous language). Toledo claimed that during García's 1985–90 rule Peruvians had been subjected to food rationing caused by hyperinflation, corruption, terrorism and army brutality and that human rights had suffered. García fought back accusing Toledo of financing his campaign with laundered money. Videotapes collected by Fujimori's former spy chief Vladimiro Montesinos, imprisoned from 2002 for abuse of power, reveal that corruption, bribery and blackmail were endemic in the previous government.

After the first round of voting in April 2001, Toledo was ahead of García, but without a clear majority. In the run-off García conceded to Toledo. International observers agreed the election had been free and democratic.

Career in Office

Following his inauguration, Toledo attended a religious ceremony in his honour at the ancient Inca citadel Machu Picchu. He pledged to combat the country's endemic poverty by boosting industry and agriculture and kick-starting the flagging economy. He aimed to continue the free-market policies of Fujimori in order to attract foreign investors, and hoped to create 1m. jobs over five years. Owing to Lima's overwhelming economic and political domination, Toledo also promised decentralization. During his presidency, his government has achieved economic growth, but his efforts to reduce poverty have not made a significant impact and he has encountered difficulties in implementing institutional reforms.

Corruption and other scandals have meanwhile dampened Toledo's personal popularity, and in Jan. 2005 a former army officer, Ollanta Humala, and his nationalist followers staged a brief but unsuccessful rebellion in the south of the country, calling on Toledo to resign. In May 2005 a commission found the president guilty of electoral fraud, although Congress later voted not to impeach him.

In 2005–06 Toledo's reputation was further damaged through professional and personal scandal. In Aug. 2005 his approval fell to just 7% and in Feb. 2006 his nephew was given a suspended prison sentence after being found guilty of rape. Toledo subsequently decided not to run in the 2006 presidential elections.

DEFENCE

There is selective conscription for two years. In 2003 defence expenditure totalled US$893m. (US$33 per capita), representing 1·4% of GDP.

Army

There are four military regions. In 2002 the Army comprised approximately 50,300 personnel (32,900 conscripts) and 188,000 reserves. In addition there is a paramilitary national police force of 90,000 personnel.

Navy

The principal ship of the Navy is the former Netherlands cruiser *Almirante Grau*, built in 1953. Other combatants include six diesel submarines (two in refit) and four Italian-built frigates.

The Naval Aviation branch operates nine armed helicopters.

Callao is the main base, where the dockyard is located and most training takes place. Smaller bases exist at Iquitos, Paita, San Lorenzo Island and Talara.

Naval personnel in 2002 totalled 25,000 (10,000 conscripts) including 800 Naval Air Arm and 4,000 Marines.

Air Force

The operational force consists of five combat groups. There are military airfields at Talara, Chiclayo, Piura, Pisco, Lima (two), Iquitos and La Joya, and a floatplane base at Iquitos.

In 2002 there were some 15,000 personnel (2,000 conscripts) and 116 combat aircraft (including Su-22s, Su-25s, Mirage 2000s, Mirage 5s and MiG-29s) and 19 armed helicopters.

INTERNATIONAL RELATIONS

Peru is a member of the UN, WTO, OAS, Inter-American Development Bank, the Andean Group, LAIA, APEC, IOM and Antarctic Treaty.

ECONOMY

Agriculture produced 10·1% of GDP in 2003, industry 30·1% and services 59·8%.

Overview

The Peruvian economy has undergone a significant transformation since 1990—the authorities ended hyperinflation and a debt crisis, implemented tax and pension reforms, and liberalized and privatized the economy. Inflation fell steadily through to 2000 and has since been kept low under the central bank's inflation targeting framework, permitting a gradual reduction of interest rates. In 2004 real per capita GDP was 30% higher than in 1990. The economy suffered a prolonged recession between 1997 and 2001 owing to spillover from crises in emerging markets but has since responded favourably to a policy of fiscal responsibility, targeted social programmes to provide assistance to the poor and job creation programmes. Private investment has been concentrated in the natural resource sector, leading to limited employment creation. According to the IMF the Peruvian investment climate is relatively hostile. Despite positive overall macroeconomic performance the percentage of Peruvians living in poverty reached 54·8% in 2001 owing to increasingly unequal income distribution. The authorities have undertaken structural reforms to open the economy, reduce labour costs in the formal sector and to improve the climate for private investment; however, according to the IMF these reforms are being undertaken with uneven progress.

Currency

The monetary unit is the *nuevo sol* (PES), of 100 *céntimos*, which replaced the *inti* in 1990 at a rate of 1m. intis = 1 nuevo sol. Inflation, which had been over 7,000% in 1990, was just 3·7% in 2004. Foreign exchange reserves were US$8,053m. in June 2002, gold reserves totalled 1·10m. troy oz and total money supply was 21,506m. sols.

Budget

Central government revenue and expenditure (in 1m. sols), year ending 31 Dec.:

	2001	2002	2003
Revenue	30,327	31,785	34,742
Expenditure	31,913	33,133	35,416

In Dec. 2005 the World Bank approved a US$150m. loan to assist with the government decentralization process and enhance competitiveness.

Performance

Real GDP growth was 4·0% in 2003 and 4·8% in 2004. Total GDP in 2004 was US$68·4bn.

Banking and Finance

The bank of issue is the Banco Central de Reserva (*President*, Oscar Dancourt Masias), which was established in 1922. The government's fiscal agent is the Banco de la Nación. In 2002 there were three other government banks (Banco Central Hipotecario del Perú; Banco de la Nación; Corporación Financiera de Desarrollo), ten commercial banks, one regional bank and three foreign banks. Legislation of April 1991 permitted financial institutions to fix their own interest rates and reopened the country to foreign banks. The Central Reserve Bank sets the upper limit.

There are stock exchanges in Lima and Arequipa.

ENERGY AND NATURAL RESOURCES

Peru lays claim to 84 of the world's 114 ecosystems; 28 of its climate types; 19% of all bird species; 20% of all plant species; and 25 conservation areas (seven national parks, eight national reserves, seven national sanctuaries and three historic sanctuaries).

Environment

Peru's carbon dioxide emissions from the consumption and flaring of fossil fuels in 2002 were the equivalent of 1·1 tonnes per capita.

Electricity

In 2001 output was 20·6bn. kWh. Total generating capacity was 6·1m. kW in 2003. 66·1% of the population were supplied with electricity in 1996. Consumption per capita in 2000 was 776 kWh. Peru's reliance on hydro-generated electricity means that electricity production was affected by the drought brought on by the 1997–98 El Niño.

Oil and Gas

Proven oil reserves in Jan. 2003 amounted to 323m. bbls. Output, 2003, 4·5m. tonnes. Natural gas reserves in 2003 were 246bn. cu. metres; output in 2001 was 370m. cu. metres. Commercial development of the huge Camisea gas field began in late 2004.

Minerals

Mining accounted for some 8·4% of GDP in 1996. Lead, copper, iron, silver, zinc and petroleum are the chief minerals exploited. Mineral production (in 1,000 tonnes): iron (1996), 2,876; zinc (2001), 1,057; copper (2001), 722; lead (1996), 249; silver (2001), 2·4; gold (2001), 0·14. 12,000 tonnes of coal were produced in 2000. Early in 1998 Southern Peru Copper, the country's largest mining company, estimated that 3,000 tonnes of copper production had been lost as a result of flooding caused by El Niño.

Agriculture

There are four natural zones: the Coast strip, with an average width of 80 km; the Sierra or Uplands, formed by the coast range of mountains and the Andes proper; the Montaña or high wooded region which lies on the eastern slopes of the Andes; and the jungle in the Amazon Basin, known as the Selva. Legislation of 1991 permits the unrestricted sale of agricultural land. Workers in co-operatives may elect to form limited liability companies and become shareholders.

Production in 2000 (in 1,000 tonnes): sugarcane, 7,750; potatoes, 3,187; rice, 1,665; plantains, 1,415; maize, 1,271; cassava, 986; onions, 367; oranges, 318; lemons and limes, 310; sweet potatoes, 230; tomatoes, 197; mangoes, 180; barley, 175; seed cotton, 175.

Livestock, 2000: sheep, 14·4m.; cattle, 4·9m.; alpacas, 3·0m.; pigs, 2·8m.; poultry, 81m. Livestock products (in 1,000 tonnes), 2000: poultry meat, 580; beef and veal, 136; pork, bacon and ham, 95; mutton and lamb, 31; milk, 1,048.

In 2001 there were 3·70m. ha. of arable land and 0·51m. ha. of permanent crops. 1·2m. ha. were irrigated in 2001.

Coca was cultivated in 2000 on approximately 34,000 ha., down from 115,000 ha. in 1995.

Forestry

In 2000 the area covered by forests was 65·22m. ha., or 50·9% of the total land area. The forests contain valuable hardwoods; oak and cedar account for about 40%. In 2001 roundwood removals totalled 8·37m. cu. metres.

Fisheries

Sardines and anchovies are caught offshore to be processed into fishmeal, of which Peru is a major producer. Fishing in deeper waters is being developed, subject to government conservation by the imposition of quotas and fishing bans. Total catch in 2001 was 7,986,103 tonnes, almost entirely from sea fishing. In 1999 the catch had a value of US$801·5m. Peru's annual catch is the second largest in the world after that of China. In the first nine months of 1997, 1·3m. tonnes of fishmeal was produced, up 3·4% over the same period for 1996.

INDUSTRY

About 70% of industries are located in the Lima/Callao metropolitan area. Industry accounted for 29·7% of GDP in 2001, with manufacturing contributing 15·3%. Production, 2000 (in 1,000 tonnes): cement, 3,265; residual fuel oil, 2,915; distillate fuel oil, 1,700; prepared animal feeds (2001), 1,508; petrol, 1,411; kerosene, 1,099; sugar (2001), 755; soft drinks, 1,110·8m. litres; beer, 570·6m. litres; cigarettes, 3·6bn. units.

Labour

The labour force in 1996 totalled 8,652,000 (71% males). In 1993, 1,852,800 people worked in agriculture, 1,167,000 in commerce, 783,900 in manufacturing, 599,700 in services, 347,500 in transport, 255,000 in building, 72,200 in mining and 18,700 in electricity production. In 2002 an estimated 8·4% of the workforce was unemployed, up from 5·9% in 1991.

Trade Unions

Trade unions have about 2m. members (approximately 1·5m. in peasant organizations and 500,000 in industrial). The major trade union organization is the *Confederación de Trabajadores del Perú*, which was reconstituted in 1959 after being in abeyance for some years. The other labour organizations recognized by the government are the *Confederación General de Trabajadores del Perú*, the *Confederación Nacional de Trabajadores* and the *Central de Trabajadores de la Revolución Peruana*.

INTERNATIONAL TRADE

An agreement of 1992 gives Bolivia duty-free transit for imports and exports through a corridor leading to the Peruvian Pacific port of Ilo from the Bolivian frontier town of Desaguadero, in return for Peruvian access to the Atlantic via Bolivia's roads and railways. Foreign debt was US$29,958m. in 2004.

Imports and Exports

Trade in US$1m.:

	1999	2000	2001	2002	2003
Imports f.o.b.	6,184	6,777	6,645	6,893	7,818
Exports f.o.b.	6,040	6,857	6,937	7,665	8,940

Main import suppliers in 2001 were: USA, 23·1%; Argentina, 6·2%; Chile, 5·9%; Japan 5·9%. Main export markets, 2001: USA, 24·8%; UK, 13·5%; China, 6·2%; Japan, 5·6%. Leading imports in 1998 were raw and intermediate materials (41·3%), machinery

(24·9%) and consumer goods (23·0%). Leading exports in 1998 were gold (16·2%), copper and copper products (13·6%) and zinc products (7·8%).

COMMUNICATIONS

Roads
In 2003 there were 78,398 km of roads, of which 12·8% were paved. By the end of March 1998, 700 km of road had been affected by the 1997–98 El Niño. In 2002 there were 791,862 cars, 400,015 lorries and vans and 45,089 buses and coaches. There were 74,221 road accidents involving injury in 2002 with 2,929 fatalities.

Rail
Total length (2002), 2,121 km on 1,435- and 914-mm gauges. Passenger-km travelled in 2002 came to 98m. and freight tonne-km to 1,008m.

Civil Aviation
There is an international airport at Lima (Jorge Chávez International). In 1996 there were 32 airports. The main Peruvian airlines are Lan Perú and Nuevo Continente. In 2003 services were also provided by the domestic airlines Aero Cóndor, AVIANDINA and Transportes Aereos Nacionales de Selva, and by more than 20 international carriers. In 1999 scheduled airline traffic of Peruvian-based carriers flew 27·2m. km, carrying 1,900,000 passengers (150,000 on international flights). In 2001 Jorge Chávez International handled 4,089,914 passengers (2,128,872 on international flights) and 112,709 tonnes of freight.

Shipping
In 2004 there were 46 sea-going vessels and 651 lake and river craft. In 2002 sea-going shipping totalled 240,000 GRT (including oil tankers 15,000 GRT). In 2002 vessels totalling 8,260,000 net registered tons entered ports and vessels totalling 6,112,000 NRT cleared. Callao is the busiest port, handling 11,609,000 tonnes of cargo in 2002. There are also ports at Chimbote, Paita and Talara.

Telecommunications
Peru had 4,073,100 telephone subscribers in 2002, or 152·3 per 1,000 population, and there were 1,488,000 PCs in use (55·6 for every 1,000 persons). There were 2,306,900 mobile phone subscribers in 2002 and 55,000 fax machines. In 2002 there were 2,500,000 Internet users.

Postal Services
In 2003 there were 1,771 post offices.

SOCIAL INSTITUTIONS

Justice
The judicial system is a pyramid at the base of which are the justices of the peace who decide minor criminal cases and civil cases involving small sums of money. The apex is the Supreme Court with a president and 12 members; in between are the judges of first instance, who usually sit in the provincial capitals, and the superior courts.

The police had some 85,000 personnel in 1991. The population in penal institutions in Oct. 2004 was 32,129 (114 per 100,000 of national population).

Education
Adult literacy was 87·7% in 2003 (male, 93·5%; female, 82·1%). Elementary education is compulsory and free between the ages of 7 and 16; secondary education is also free. In 2003 there were 1,095,665 children in pre-school education, 4,237,378 pupils in primary and 2,567,896 in secondary schools. In 2002 the student numbers in the 31 state and 40 private universities were 273,326 and 189,326 respectively. There were 286,149 students in other forms of further education.

In 1999–2000 total expenditure on education came to 3·5% of GNP and 21·1% of total government spending.

Health
There were 483 hospitals with 43,074 beds (provision of 16 beds per 10,000 inhabitants) in 2002. There were 29,138 physicians, 3,190 dentists and 21,351 nurses in 2002.

Peru made the greatest progress of any country in the reduction of undernourishment during the 1990s. Between 1990–92 and 2000–02 the proportion of undernourished people declined from 42% of the population to 13%.

Welfare
An option to transfer from state social security (IPSS) to privately-managed funds was introduced in 1993.

RELIGION
Religious liberty exists, but the Roman Catholic religion is protected by the State, and since 1929 only Roman Catholic religious instruction is permitted in schools, state or private. There were 23·17m. Catholics in 2001 as well as 1·73m. Protestants and 1·19m. with other beliefs (mostly non-religious). In May 2005 there was one cardinal.

CULTURE

World Heritage Sites
There are ten sites in Peru appearing on the UNESCO World Heritage List. They are (with year entered on list) the City of Cusco (1983), the Historic Sanctuary of Machu Picchu (1983), Chavin (Archaeological site) (1985), Huascaran National Park (1985), Chan Chan Archaeological Zone (1986), Manu National Park (1987), Historic Centre of Lima (1988), Rio Abiseo National Park (1990), Lines and Geoglyphs of Nasca and Pampas de Jumana (1994) and the Historical Centre of the City of Arequipa (2000).

Broadcasting
Radio broadcasting is conducted by hundreds of national, provincial and local stations grouped in the Asociación de Radiodifusores del Perú and the Unión de Radioemisores de Provincias del Perú. There are 59 TV companies (colour by NTSC). There were 3·9m. TV sets in use in 2001 and 7·1m. radio receivers in 2000.

Press
There were 57 dailies in 1998 with a combined circulation of 570,000. A total of 2,286 book titles were published in 2002.

Tourism
There were 976,000 foreign visitors in 2003 (591,000 in 1996), bringing foreign exchange earnings of US$923m.

DIPLOMATIC REPRESENTATIVES

Of Peru in the United Kingdom (52 Sloane St., London, SW1X 9SP)
Ambassador: Luis Solari Tudela.

Of the United Kingdom in Peru (Torre Parque Mar, Piso 22, Avenida Jose Larco 1301, Miraflores, Lima)
Ambassador: Richard Ralph, CVO, CMG.

Of Peru in the USA (1700 Massachusetts Ave., NW, Washington, D.C., 20036)
Ambassador: Eduardo Ferrero Costa.

Of the USA in Peru (Avenida La Encalada Cdra 17-Monterrico, Lima)
Ambassador: J. Curtis Struble.

Of Peru to the United Nations
Ambassador: Oswaldo de Rivero Barreto.

Of Peru to the European Union
Ambassador: José Urrutia Ceruti.

FURTHER READING

Instituto Nacional de Estadística e Informática.—*Anuario Estadistico del Perú.—Perú: Compendio Estadístico.* Annual.—*Boletin de Estadistica Peruana.* Quarterly

Banco Central de Reserva. Monthly Bulletin.—*Renta Nacional del Perú.* Annual, Lima

Cameron, M. A., *Democracy and Authoritarianism in Peru: Political Coalitions and Social Change.* London, 1995

Daeschner, J., *The War of the End of Democracy: Mario Vargas Llosa vs. Alberto Fujimori.* Lima, 1993

Gorriti, Gustavo, (trans. Robin Kirk) *The Shining Path: A History of the Millenarian War in Peru.* Univ. of North Carolina Press, 1999

Stokes, S. C., *Cultures in Conflict: Social Movements and the State in Peru.* California Univ. Press, 1995

Strong, S., *Shining Path.* London, 1993

Vargas Llosa, A., *The Madness of Things Peruvian: Democracy under Siege.* Brunswick (NJ), 1994

National Statistical Office: Instituto Nacional de Estadística e Informática, Av. Gral. Garzón 654–658, Jesús María, Lima.

Website (Spanish only): http://www.inei.gob.pe

PHILIPPINES

Republika ng Pilipinas

Capital: Manila
Population projection, 2010: 90·05m.
GDP per capita, 2003: (PPP$) 4,321
HDI/world rank 0·758/84

KEY HISTORICAL EVENTS

Discovered by Magellan in 1521, the Philippine islands were conquered by Spain in 1565 and named after the Spanish king, Philip. In Dec. 1898, following the Spanish-American War, the Philippines were ceded to the USA. The Philippines acquired self-government as a Commonwealth of the USA in March 1934. The islands were occupied by the Japanese from 1942 to 1945. Independence was achieved in July 1946. From independence until 1972 the Philippines were governed under a constitution based largely on the US pattern. In Sept. 1972 President Ferdinand Marcos declared martial law. In May 1980 Benigno Aquino, Jr, the leading opponent of Marcos, was released from prison to go to the USA for medical treatment. While abroad he was exiled. He was killed shortly after returning to the Philippines in 1983. At the presidential elections of Feb. 1986 Ferdinand Marcos was opposed by Aquino's widow, Corazón.

Aquino became president, Marcos fled the country and a new constitution limiting the president to a single, six-year term in office was ratified in Feb. 1987. Insurgent activities carried out since 1972 by the Moro National Liberation Front (Muslims) were ended by a peace agreement of 2 Sept. 1996 which provides for a Muslim autonomous region in an area of Mindanao island in southern Philippines. The rebellion left more than 120,000 people dead. In Oct. 2000 impeachment proceedings began against President Estrada who was alleged to have received more than US$10·8m. from gambling kickbacks. His impeachment trial collapsed in Jan. 2001 when he was forced from office by mass protests. Subsequently Estrada's supporters tried to overthrow his successor, Gloria Macapagal-Arroyo. In Nov. 2001 the fragile peace between the government and Islamic militants was shattered. Since then violence has frequently erupted, notably in early 2005 when fighting on the southern island of Jolo left 90 dead on both sides and caused 12,000 people to flee. On 14 Feb. 2005 three bombs were detonated killing nine and injuring 130. In Feb. 2006 President Arroyo declared a week-long state of emergency after the military declared it had discovered a coup plot.

TERRITORY AND POPULATION

The Philippines is situated between 21° 25' and 4° 23' N. lat. and between 116° and 127° E. long. It is composed of 7,100 islands and islets, 3,144 of which are named. Approximate land area, 300,076 sq. km (115,859 sq. miles). The largest islands (in sq. km) are Luzon (104,688), Mindanao (94,630), Samar (13,080), Negros (12,710), Palawan (11,785), Panay (11,515), Mindoro (9,735), Leyte (7,214), Cebu (4,422), Bohol (3,865) and Masbate (3,269).

The census population in May 2000 was 76,498,735; density, 255·0 per sq. km. The estimated population in 2005 was 83,054,000. In 2003, 61·0% of the population lived in urban areas.

The UN gives a projected population for 2010 of 90·05m.

The area (in 1,000) and population of the 16 regions (from north to south):

Region	Sq. km	2000
Ilocos	12,840	4,200,478
Cordillera[1]	18,294	1,365,220
Cagayan Valley	26,838	2,813,159
Central Luzon	18,231	8,030,945
National Capital	636	9,932,560
Southern Tagalog	46,924	11,793,655
Bicol	17,633	4,674,855
Western Visayas	20,223	6,208,733
Central Visayas	14,951	5,701,064
Eastern Visayas	21,432	3,610,355
Northern Mindanao	14,033	2,747,585
Southern Mindanao	27,141	5,189,335
Central Mindanao	14,373	2,598,210
Western Mindanao	16,042	3,091,208
Muslim Mindanao[2]	11,638	2,412,159
Caraga	18,847	2,095,367

[1]Administrative region. [2]Autonomous region.

Since the 2000 census Southern Tagalog has been divided into two new regions, Calabarzon and Mimaropa. Southern Mindanao has become Davao, Central Mindanao is now Soccsksargen and Western Mindanao is Zamboanga.

City populations (2000 census, in 1,000) are as follows; all on Luzon unless indicated in parenthesis.

Quezon City[1]	2,160	Davao (Mindanao)	1,147
Manila (the capital)[1]	1,673	Cebu (Cebu)	662
Caloocan[1]	1,233	Zamboanga (Mindanao)	600

Pasig[1]	582	Mandaluyong[1]	304
Makati[1]	524	Iligan (Mindanao)	285
Valenzuela[2]	521	Butuan (Mindanao)	267
Taguig[2]	510	Mandaue (Cebu)	256
Las Piñas[2]	499	Navotas[2]	254
Parañaque[2]	489	Baguio[1]	250
Cagayan de Oro (Mindanao)	462	Batangas	245
Marikina[2]	437	Angeles	243
Bacolod (Negros)	429	Lipa City	219
General Santos (Mindanao)	412	Cabanatuan	218
Muntilupa[1]	393	San Pablo	205
Iloilo (Panay)	366	Lapu-Lapu (Cebu)	200
Pasay[1]	363	Lucena City	196
Malabon[2]	356	Olongapo	194

[1]City within Metropolitan Manila. Population of Metro Manila in 1999, 10,546,000.
[2]Municipality within Metropolitan Manila.

Filipino (based on Tagalog) is spoken as a mother tongue by only 29·3%; among the 76 other indigenous languages spoken, Cebuano is spoken as a mother tongue by 23·3% and Ilocano by 9·3%. English, which along with Filipino is one of the official languages, is widely spoken. In 2000 some 5·5m. Filipinos were living and working abroad, including 2m. in the USA, 850,000 in Saudi Arabia and 620,000 in Malaysia.

SOCIAL STATISTICS

Registered births, 2002, 1,640,698; deaths, 396,176; marriages (2001), 559,162. Divorce is illegal. Birth rate per 1,000 population (2000), 26·8; death rate, 5·9. Expectation of life at birth, 2003, was 68·3 years for males and 72·5 years for females. Annual population growth rate, 1992–2002, 2·1%. Infant mortality, 2001, 29 per 1,000 live births; fertility rate, 2001, 3·4 births per woman.

CLIMATE

Some areas have an equatorial climate while others experience tropical monsoon conditions, with a wet season extending from June to Nov. Mean temperatures are high all year, with very little variation. Manila, Jan. 77°F (25°C), July 82°F (27·8°C). Annual rainfall 83·3" (2,115·9 mm).

CONSTITUTION AND GOVERNMENT

A new Constitution was ratified by referendum in Feb. 1987 with the approval of 78·5% of voters. The head of state is the *President*, directly elected for a non-renewable six-year term.

Congress consists of a 24-member upper house, the *Senate* (elected for a six-year term by proportional representation, half of them renewed every three years), and a *House of Representatives* of not more than 250 members (214 directly elected and the rest from party and minority-group lists, for a three-year term).

A campaign led by the president at the time, Fidel Ramos, to amend the constitution to allow him to stand for a second term was voted down by the Senate by 23 to one in Dec. 1996.

National Anthem

'Land of the Morning', lyric in English by M. A. Sane and C. Osias, tune by Julian Felipe; 'Lupang Hinirang', Tagalog lyric by the Institute of National Language.

GOVERNMENT CHRONOLOGY

Presidents since 1946. (KBL = New Society Movement; Lakas-CMD = Lakas-Christian Muslim Democrats; LE-NUCD = People's Power-National Union of Christian Democrats; LMP = Struggle of the Philippine Masses; PL = Liberal Party; PN = Nationalist Party; UNIDO = Nationalist Democratic Organization)

1946–48	PL	Manuel Roxas y Acuña
1948–53	PL	Elpidio Quirino y Rivera
1953–57	PN	Ramon Magsaysay y del Fierro
1957–61	PN	Carlos Polestico García
1961–65	PL	Diosdado Pañgan Macapagal
1965–86	PN, KBL	Ferdinand Emmanuel Edralin Marcos
1986–92	UNIDO	Corazón Cojuangco Aquino
1992–98	LE-NUCD	Fidel Valdez Ramos
1998–2001	LMP	Joseph Marcelo Ejercito Estrada
2001–	Lakas-CMD	Gloria Macapagal-Arroyo

RECENT ELECTIONS

The presidential elections of 10 May 2004 were won by President Gloria Macapagal-Arroyo (Lakas-Christian Muslim Democrats) with 40·0% of the votes cast, ahead of Fernando Poe, Jr (Coalition of United Filipinos) with 36·5% of the vote and Panfilo Morena Lacson (Struggle of Democratic Filipinos) with 10·9%. There were two other candidates.

Elections to the House of Representatives were also held on 10 May 2004. Out of a total of 211 seats, 93 went to Lakas-Christian Muslim Democrats, 53 to the National People's Coalition, 34 to the Liberal Party and 11 to the Laban ng Demokratikong Pilipino (Philippine Democratic Party). The remaining seats were shared among party list representatives, non-partisans and others or were vacant.

Senate elections were also most recently held on 10 May 2004, following which Lakas-Christian Muslim Democrats had 7 seats, Coalition of United Filipinos 3, the Liberal Party 3 and non-partisans and others 10 with 1 vacant.

CURRENT ADMINISTRATION

President: Gloria Macapagal-Arroyo; b. 1947 (Lakas-Christian Muslim Democrats; sworn in 20 Jan. 2001 and elected on 10 May 2004). Her father, Diosdado Macapagal, had been president from 1961–65.

Vice-President: Noli de Castro (elected on 10 May 2004).

In March 2006 the government comprised:

Minister of Justice: Raul Gonzalez. *Trade and Industry:* Peter Favila. *Finance:* Margarito Teves. *National Defence:* Avelino Cruz, Jr. *Agriculture:* Domingo Panganiban. *Foreign Affairs:* Alberto Romulo. *Public Works and Highways:* Hermogenes Ebdane, Jr. *Energy:* Raphael Perpetuo Lotilla. *Education, Culture and Sports (acting):* Fe Hidalgo. *Labour and Employment:* Patricia Santo Thomas. *Health:* Francisco Duque III. *Agrarian Reform (acting):* Nasser Pangandaman. *Tourism:* Joseph Durano. *Budget and Management:* Rolando Andaya, Jr. *Transport and Communications:* Leandro Mendoza. *Science and Technology:* Estrella Alabastro. *Environment and Natural Resources:* Angelo Reyes. *Social Welfare and Development:* Dr Esperanza Cabral. *Socio-Economic Planning:* Augusto Santos. *Interior and Local Government:* Ronaldo Puno.

Executive Secretary: Eduardo Ermita.

Speaker of the House of Representatives: Jose de Venecia.

Government Website: http://www.gov.ph

CURRENT LEADERS

Gloria Macapagal-Arroyo

Position
President

Introduction
Gloria Macapagal-Arroyo was swept to power in Jan. 2001 when her predecessor was forced from office by mass street protests. She is the daughter of Diosdado Macapagal, the president of the Philippines from 1961–65.

Early Life
Gloria Macapagal was born on 5 April 1947 into a prominent Filipino political family. After education at a convent high school in the Philippines, she took a degree in commerce at Georgetown University in Washington, D.C., where the future US president Bill Clinton was one of her classmates. Returning

to the Philippines, she studied for a master's degree and a PhD at Filipino universities. Macapagal began a career in teaching, first at her old high school and later as a university lecturer. During this time, she married, becoming Mrs Arroyo, but in her subsequent political career she has used both her maiden and married names.

Prominent as an economist as well as a member of a political dynasty, Arroyo was appointed to the government of President Corazón Aquino in 1986 as assistant secretary of the department of trade and industry, rising to become under-secretary. She also held the post of executive director of the garments and textile export board. During her tenure the Filipino textile industry grew to become the country's top foreign-currency earner.

When Aquino's presidency ended in 1992, Arroyo stood for the Senate and was elected at her first attempt. Although she had held office in the outgoing government, Arroyo was still something of a political unknown, and her initial appeal to many voters was the memory of her popular father. However, when she stood for re-election in 1995 her own reputation won her nearly 16m. votes, the greatest number ever received by an individual in Philippine elections. As a senator, Arroyo drafted and introduced 55 bills on economic and social reform.

In 1998, Arroyo stood as a candidate for the vice-presidency. The presidency was won by Joseph Estrada, a former cinema actor, but in her electoral race, Arroyo received more votes than Estrada—12·7m., the largest number ever received by anyone in a Philippine presidential or vice-presidential contest.

President Estrada appointed her vice-president and secretary of social welfare and development. She resigned from the Cabinet in Oct. 2000, but retained her role as vice-president. By that time the Estrada government was in trouble, the president having been accused of cronyism and taking bribes from illegal gambling syndicates. Impeachment proceedings began. Arroyo led the calls for Estrada to resign. Mass street protests forced Estrada to flee the presidential palace and the Supreme Court declared the presidency to be vacant. On 20 Jan. 2001, Arroyo was sworn in as the president of the Philippines.

Career in Office

The immediate challenge facing President Arroyo was reconciliation. Many supporters of President Estrada initially refused to recognize the transfer of power. She took office at a difficult time for the country, politically and economically. Arroyo set economic recovery, including a privatization programme, and economic and social reform as her priorities. However, one of her main problems has been Islamic terrorism and the continued guerrilla activity by separatists in the south of the country and by communist insurgents. Arroyo negotiated a cessation of hostilities with the separatists in 2003, pending formal peace talks, although clashes with government troops have still taken place, notably in Jan.–Feb. 2005. She has vowed to wipe out the Abu Sayyaf, an Islamic terrorist organization responsible for bombings and the kidnapping and murder of foreign tourists and others, which has been linked to al-Qaeda by the US government.

In July 2003 Ramon Cardenas, a former junior minister to ex-President Joseph Estrada, was arrested after leading a military uprising in Manila. Several hundred troops took possession of a shopping and residential complex but withdrew after accusing Arroyo's government of corruption. Standing for Lakas-Christian Muslim Democrats, Arroyo was returned to power in the presidential elections of May 2004, ahead of Fernando Poe, Jr of the Coalition of United Filipinos. Despite coming under intense pressure to resign in July 2005 over allegations of electoral vote-rigging, she survived an opposition attempt to impeach her in Sept. Arroyo declared a week-long state of emergency in Feb. 2006 after the military reported a plot to oust her in a coup.

DEFENCE

An extension of the 1947 agreement granting the USA the use of several Army, Navy and Air Force bases was rejected by the Senate in Sept. 1991. An agreement of Dec. 1994 authorizes US naval vessels to be repaired in Philippine ports. The Philippines is a signatory of the South-East Asia Collective Defence Treaty.

Defence expenditure in 2003 totalled US$783m. (US$10 per capita), representing 1·0% of GDP.

Army

The Army is organized into five area joint-service commands.

Strength (2002) 66,000, with reserves totalling 100,000. The paramilitary Philippines National Police numbered 40,500 in 2002 with a further 62,000 auxiliaries.

Navy

The Navy consists principally of ex-US ships completed in 1944 and 1945, and serviceability and spares are a problem. The modernization programme in progress has been revised and delayed, but the first 30 inshore patrol craft of US and Korean design have been delivered. The present fleet includes one ex-US frigate.

Navy personnel in 2002 was estimated at 24,000 including 7,500 marines.

Air Force

The Air Force had a strength of 16,000 in 2002, with 49 combat aircraft and about 67 armed helicopters. Its fighter-bomber wing is equipped with one squadron of F-5As (only three or four operational).

INTERNATIONAL RELATIONS

The Philippines is a member of the UN, WTO, Asian Development Bank, ASEAN, APEC, the Colombo Plan and IOM.

ECONOMY

Agriculture accounted for 14·7% of GDP in 2002, industry 32·5% and services 52·8%.

Overview

Market-oriented reforms have been implemented in the Philippines over the last two decades. Foreign investment and trade barriers have been dismantled and many industries deregulated. Most state industrial assets were privatized between 1992–95 and monopolies were dismantled in the telecommunications, oil, civil aviation, shipping, water and power industries. However, privatization is incomplete and loss-making public enterprises, notably in the energy sector, continue to burden the country's finances.

High public debt remains a significant problem. Despite strong growth and a reduction in the budget deficit from 4·7% to 3·9%, public debt rose from 78% of GDP in 2003 to 79% in 2004. President Arroyo was re-elected in 2004 on a platform of public debt reduction and has focused on addressing low government revenues, which equalled 14·5% of GDP in 2004. Tax collection has become more aggressive and a VAT increase was passed in Nov. 2005. Further fiscal restructuring measures are on the table but it is feared that reform momentum could slow for the government's fear of losing public support. While budget deficits have not been alarmingly high in recent years, 37% of government revenues went to debt interest payments in 2004, thereby limiting the amount spent on infrastructure, education and health and lowering the country's future growth potential.

Healthy demand for semiconductors in 2004 and 2005 helped raise nominal exports and drive growth. Despite achieving solid growth over the years, per capita GDP was lower in 2004 than it was in 1995 and sustained high growth is required to reduce unemployment and poverty rates.

Currency

The unit of currency is the *peso* (PHP) of 100 *centavos*. Inflation rates (based on IMF statistics):

1997	1998	1999	2000	2001	2002	2003	2004
5·9%	9·7%	6·5%	4·3%	6·8%	3·0%	3·5%	6·0%

Foreign exchange reserves were US$14,163m. in June 2002 and gold reserves 8·22m. troy oz (3·58m. troy oz in 1995). Total money supply in April 2002 was 410,581m. pesos.

Budget

Total government revenue and expenditure (in 1m. pesos), year ending 31 Dec.:

	1996	1997	1998	1999	2000	2001
Revenue	409,880	470,105	462,119	478,210	513,386	561,741
Expenditure	401,017	467,319	511,398	585,435	645,804	706,327

Expenditure (2001) included (in 1,000m. pesos): education, 121·4; economic affairs and services, 90·8; transport and communications, 53·1; public order and safety, 47·7.

Total internal public debt was 1,293,900m. pesos in 2001.

VAT was introduced in 1988. The standard rate was raised from 10·0% to 12·0% in Feb. 2006.

Performance

Real GDP growth rates (based on IMF statistics):

1995	1996	1997	1998	1999	2000	2001	2002	2003	2004
4·7%	5·8%	5·2%	−0·6%	3·4%	4·4%	1·8%	4·4%	4·5%	6·0%

Total GDP in 2004 was US$86·4bn.

Banking and Finance

The Central Bank (*Chairman*, Amando Tetangco, Jr) issues the currency, manages foreign exchange reserves and supervises the banking system. At 30 June 2003 there were 42 commercial banks (24 regular commercial banks and 18 universal banks), 93 thrift banks and 771 rural and co-operative banks. In June 2003 the total number of banking institutions was 6,414, with total assets of 3,529,128m. pesos.

There is a stock exchange in Manila.

The financial crisis that struck southeast Asia in 1997 led to the floating of the peso in July. It subsequently lost 36% of its value against the dollar.

Weights and Measures

The metric system is used but with some local units, including the *picul* (63·25 kg) for sugar and fibres, and the *cavan* (16·5 gallons) for cereals.

ENERGY AND NATURAL RESOURCES

Environment

Carbon dioxide emissions from the consumption and flaring of fossil fuels in 2002 were the equivalent of 0·8 tonnes per capita.

Electricity

Total installed capacity was 14·7m. kW in 2002. Production was estimated at 48·47bn. kWh in 2002. Consumption per capita was about 610 kWh in 2002.

Oil and Gas

The largest natural gas field is the Camago-Malampaya gas field, discovered off the island of Palawan in 1992, with reserves initially put at 76bn. cu. metres but now increased to 85bn. cu. metres. The Philippines' total natural gas reserves in 2002 were 105bn. cu. metres.

Crude petroleum reserves were 178m. bbls. in 2002.

Water

Water production in 1997 was 997m. cu. metres and water consumption 230m. cu. metres. Breakdown of water consumption: industrial, 89m. cu. metres; residential, 82m. cu. metres; and commercial, 59m. cu. metres.

Minerals

Mineral production in 2003 (in tonnes): coal, 2,029,000; salt, 429,160; silica sand, 372,200; copper, 80,920; chromite refractory ore (chromium content), 13,220; nickel bearing ore (2002), 26,532 (nickel content); gold, 37,840 kg; silver, 9,530 kg. Other minerals include rock asphalt, sand and gravel. Total value of mineral production, 2003, 139,597m. pesos.

Agriculture

Agriculture is a mainstay of the economy, contributing up to 30% of national output. In 2001 there were 5·65m. ha. of arable land and 5·0m. ha. of permanent crops. In 2001, 37·4% of the working population was employed in agriculture. In 2002 agricultural production grew by 2·6% (7·4% in 2001).

Output (in 1,000 tonnes) in 2002: sugarcane, 21,417; rice, 13,271; coconuts (2000), 5,761; bananas, 5,275; maize (2000), 4,486; copra (2000), 2,000; pineapples, 1,639; cassava, 1,626. The output of copra is the highest of any country in the world. Minor crops are fruits, nuts, vegetables, coffee, cacao, peanuts, ramie, rubber, maguey, kapok, abaca and tobacco.

Livestock, 2003: buffaloes, 3·18m.; cattle, 2·56m.; pigs, 12·36m.; goats, 3·27m.; chickens, 128·51m.; ducks, 9·81m.

Forestry

Forests covered 5·79m. ha. (19·4% of the land area) in 2000. Approximately two-thirds of the total forest area was timberland in 2000. Timber production was 15·99m. cu. metres in 2003.

Fisheries

The catch in 2003 was 2,169,164 tonnes (94% from marine waters).

INDUSTRY

Leading sectors are foodstuffs, oil refining and chemicals. Production, 2002 (in 1,000 tonnes): cement (2001), 11,378; residual fuel oil, 5,169; distillate fuel oil, 4,008; petrol, 2,072; sugar, 1,988; paper and paperboard, 1,056; plywood, 409,000 cu. metres.

Labour

In 2003 the total workforce was 34,635,000, of whom 30,418,000 were employed (19,263,000 in non-agricultural work). Employees by sector, 2003: 14·4m. in services; 11·2m. in agriculture, hunting, forestry and fisheries; 4·9m. in industry. 3·9m. persons were registered unemployed in 2004. 868,000 persons worked overseas in 2003 (652,000 land-based).

The unemployment rate in Oct. 2001 was 9·8%.

Trade Unions

In the third quarter of 2000 there were 10,217 unions with a total membership of 3,778,000.

INTERNATIONAL TRADE

Foreign debt totalled US$59,342m. in 2002. A law of June 1991 gave foreign nationals the right to full ownership of export and other firms considered strategic for the economy.

Imports and Exports

Values of imports and exports in US$1m.:

	1998	1999	2000	2001	2002
Imports f.o.b.	29,524	29,252	33,481	31,986	33,975
Exports f.o.b.	29,496	34,211	37,295	31,243	34,383

Main imports: electronics and components, mineral fuels, lubricants and related materials, industrial machinery and equipment, telecommunications equipment, transport equipment.

Principal exports: electronics, garments, machinery, transport equipment and apparatus, and processed foods. In 2001 electronics exports were worth US$21·6bn. and constituted 67% of all exports. In 1992 they had been worth just US$3bn.

Main sources of import in 2001: Japan, 20·3%; USA, 18·5%; Singapore, 6·6%; South Korea, 6·3%. Main export markets, 2001: USA, 27·5%; Japan, 15·7%; the Netherlands, 9·2%; Singapore, 7·2%.

COMMUNICATIONS

Roads
In 2002 roads totalled 202,124 km; of these, 30,329 km were national roads and 49,805 km were regional roads. In 2002, 4,163,939 motor vehicles were registered, including 749,553 passenger cars, 1,686,229 buses and coaches, and 1,470,383 motorcycles. In 2000 there were 859 fatalities in road accidents (645 in 1996).

Rail
In 1995 the National Railways totalled 429 km (1,067 mm gauge). In 2003 passenger-km totalled 83·1m. There is a light metro railway in Manila.

Civil Aviation
There are international airports at Manila (Ninoy Aquino) and Cebu (Mactan International). In Sept. 1998 the Asian economic crisis that had started more than a year earlier forced the closure of the national carrier, Philippine Airlines, after it had suffered huge losses. However, it has since resumed its operations both internally and externally. In 1999 scheduled airline traffic of Philippine-based carriers flew 53·0m. km, carrying 5,004,000 passengers (1,922,000 on international flights). In 2001 Manila handled 12,545,000 passengers (7,144,000 on international flights) and 356,700 tonnes of freight.

Shipping
The main ports are Cagayan de Oro, Cebu, Davao, Iloilo, Manila and Zamboanga. Manila, the leading port, handled 43,820,000 tonnes of cargo in 2002. In 2002 merchant shipping totalled 5,320,000 GRT, including oil tankers 146,000 GRT.

Telecommunications
Telephone subscribers numbered 18,511,900 in 2002, or 232·9 per 1,000 inhabitants, and there were 2·2m. PCs in use (equivalent to 27·7 for every 1,000 persons). Mobile phone subscribers numbered 15,201,000 in 2002 and there were 132,000 fax machines. In 2002 there were approximately 3·5m. Internet users.

Postal Services
In 2003 there were 2,476 post offices.

SOCIAL INSTITUTIONS

Justice
There is a Supreme Court which is composed of a chief justice and 14 associate justices; it can declare a law or treaty unconstitutional by the concurrent votes of the majority sitting. There is a Court of Appeals, which consists of a presiding justice and 50 associate justices. There are 15 regional trial courts, one for each judicial region, with a presiding regional trial judge in each of its 720 branches. Municipal trial courts and municipal circuit trial courts are found in the municipalities of the Philippines. If the court covers one municipality it is a municipal trial court; if it covers two or more municipalities it is a municipal circuit trial court. In Metropolitan Manila the equivalents are metropolitan trial courts, and in the cities outside Metropolitan Manila the courts are known as municipal trial courts in cities.

The Supreme Court may designate certain branches of the regional trial courts to handle exclusively criminal cases, juvenile and domestic relations cases, agrarian cases, urban land reform cases which do not fall under the jurisdiction of quasijudicial

bodies and agencies and/or such other special cases as the Supreme Court may determine. The death penalty, abolished in 1987, was officially restored in Dec. 1993 as punishment for 'heinous crimes'. In Feb. 1999 a rapist was executed, the first incident of capital punishment in the Philippines since 1976. In Dec. 2003 President Arroyo lifted a moratorium on executions imposed in Jan. 2000.

In 2003 there were 116,000 police. Local police forces are supplemented by the Philippine Constabulary, which is part of the armed forces.

In 2003 the prison population was 24,381.

Constabulary
Since 1990 public order has been maintained completely by the Philippine National Police. Qualified Philippine Constabulary personnel were absorbed by the PNP or were transferred to branches or services of the Armed Forces of the Philippines.

Education
Public elementary education is free and schools are established in virtually all parts of the country. The majority of secondary and post-secondary schools are private. Formal education consists of an optional one to two years of pre-school education; six years of elementary education; four years of secondary education; and four to five years of tertiary or college education leading to academic degrees. Three-year post-secondary non-degree technical/vocational education is also considered formal education. In 2002–03 there were 14,033 pre-school institutions (5,534 private) with (2000–01) 19,678 teachers; 41,288 elementary schools (4,529 private) with (2001–02) 331,448 teachers; 7,890 secondary schools (3,261 private) with (2001–02) 112,210 teachers. In 2002–03 there were 1,626 tertiary schools (1,235 private). In 2000–01 there were 592,289 children in pre-school; in 2001–02 there were 12,826,218 pupils in elementary schools, 5,813,879 in secondary schools and 2,466,056 students in tertiary education.

Non-formal education consists of adult literacy classes, agricultural and farming training programmes, occupation skills training, youth clubs, and community programmes of instructions in health, nutrition, family planning and co-operatives.

In 1994–95 in the public sector there were 20 universities, one technological university, one polytechnic and one technological institute, and 123 other institutions of higher education. In the private sector there were 49 universities, four specialized universities (one Christian; one Roman Catholic; one medical; one for women) and 405 other institutions of higher education.

The adult literacy rate in 2003 was 92·6% (92·5% among males and 92·7% among females).

Total expenditure on education in 2001–02 came to 3·1% of GNP and was equivalent to 14·0% of total government spending.

Health
In 2003 there were 1,723 hospitals (1,061 private) with 85,040 beds (1·1 beds per 1,000 inhabitants). In 2002 there were 91,408 physicians, 44,129 dentists, 347,349 nurses, 140,675 midwives and 47,463 pharmacists.

Welfare
The Social Security System (SSS) is a contributory scheme for employees. Disbursements in 2001 (in 1m. pesos): social security, 37,813 (1,775,996 recipients); employees' compensation, 1,201 (90,356 recipients).

RELIGION
82% of the population are Roman Catholics, 5% Protestants, 5% Muslims and 7% Buddhists or other religions. There were 181,500 Latter-day Saints (Mormons) in 2000.

The Roman Catholic Church has three cardinals, 23 archbishoprics, 91 bishoprics, 79 dioceses, 2,328 parishes and some 20,873 chapels or missions.

CULTURE

World Heritage Sites
The Philippines has five sites on the UNESCO World Heritage List: Tubbataha Reef Marine Park (inscribed on the list in 1993); the Baroque Churches of the Philippines (1993); the Rice Terraces of the Philippine Cordilleras (1995); the Historic Town of Vigan (1999); and Puerto-Princesa Subterranean River National Park (1999).

Broadcasting
In 2002 there were 952 AM and FM radio stations and 225 television stations (colour by NTSC). There were 13·5m. TV sets in use in 2001 and 12·4m. radio receivers in 2000.

Cinema
In 2002 there were 690 cinemas with a seating capacity of 450,605. 103 feature films were produced in 2000.

Press
There were 31 daily newspapers in 2003, with a combined circulation of 5,497,000. In 2002 a total of 1,510 book titles were published.

Tourism
In 2003, 1,907,000 foreign visitors brought foreign exchange receipts of US$1,740m.

DIPLOMATIC REPRESENTATIVES

Of the Philippines in the United Kingdom (9A Palace Green, London, W8 4QE)
Ambassador: Edgardo B. Espiritu.

Of the United Kingdom in the Philippines (Floors 15–17, LV Locsin Building, 6752 Ayala Ave., Makati, Metro Manila)
Ambassador: Peter Beckingham.

Of the Philippines in the USA (1600 Massachusetts Ave., NW, Washington, D.C., 20036)
Ambassador: Albert F. del Rosario.

Of the USA in the Philippines (1201 Roxas Blvd, Manila)
Ambassador: Kristie A. Kennedy.

Of the Philippines to the United Nations
Ambassador: Lauro L. Baja, Jr.

Of the Philippines to the European Union
Ambassador: Clemencio Montesa.

FURTHER READING

National Statistics Office. *Philippine Statistical Yearbook.*

Boyce, J. K., *The Political Economy of Growth and Impoverishment in the Marcos Era.* London, 1993

Hamilton-Paterson, J., *America's Boy: The Marcoses and the Philippines.* Granta, London, 1998

Kerkvliet, B. J. and Mojares, R. B. (eds.) *From Marcos to Aquino: Local Perspectives on Political Transition in the Philippines.* Hawaii Univ. Press, 1992

Larkin, J. A., *Sugar and the Origins of Modern Philippine Society.* California Univ. Press, 1993

Vob, R. and Yap, J. T., *The Philippine Economy: East Asia's Stray Cat? Structure, Finance and Adjustment.* London and The Hague, 1996

National Statistical Office: National Statistics Office, POB 779, Manila. *Website:* http://www.census.gov.ph

POLAND

© Research Machines plc 2006

Rzeczpospolita Polska
(Polish Republic)

Capital: Warsaw
Population projection, 2010: 38·36m.
GDP per capita, 2003: (PPP$) 11,379
HDI/world rank: 0·858/36

KEY HISTORICAL EVENTS

In the 7th and 8th centuries Slavic peoples first settled on the forest covered plains between the Odra and Vistula rivers. Poland takes its name from the Polanie ('plain dwellers'), whose ruler Mieszko I, first in line of the Piast dynasty, founded the Polish state in 966. Christianity came via Bohemia and Moravia to the Kraków region, and in 991 Mieszko I placed Poland under the Holy Roman See. His son and heir, Bolesław I the Brave (ruled 992–1025) continued his father's territorial expansionism until Poland's boundaries were much as they are today. He established an independent Polish Catholic Church in the year 1000 and was officially crowned the first king of Poland in 1024 with the support of Holy Roman Emperor Otto III. The growing power of the church stimulated economic activity ranging from the manufacture of parchment and glass to building and painting.

In the twelfth century, under the rule of Bolesław III, German infiltration and internecine struggles led to Bolesław's 1138 Testament which divided the kingdom between his three sons. Around this time, many Jewish immigrants from Western Europe were attracted by the offer of asylum. The General Charter of Jewish Liberties was published in 1264 by Bolesław V, the Duke of Kraków.

A series of Mongol invasions in 1241–42 laid waste much of Poland, and in 1308 the crusades of the Teutonic Knights captured Gdańsk, cutting off Poland's access to the sea. In 1320 Władysław I Łokietek (the Short) of Kraków reunited the majority of the Polish lands that had been divided in 1138 and was crowned king of a united Poland. His son Casimir III the Great (Kasimierz, ruled 1333–70) continued this work, and his reign brought prosperity and administrative efficiency. He negotiated a truce with the Teutonic Knights and fostered closer diplomatic relations with the neighbouring kingdoms of Bohemia and Hungary.

Casimir III was the last monarch in the Piast line, and when he died his nephew Louis of Anjou, simultaneously King Lajos I of Hungary, donned the Polish crown. His death led to a disjointed succession. After a brief civil war his eleven-year-old daughter Jadwiga married Jagiełło, the pagan Grand Duke of Lithuania, who converted to Catholicism. Their marital union in 1386 signalled the beginning of the Jagiełłonian dynasty which ruled over Lithuania and Poland, at the time the largest state in Europe. The Jagiełłonian period to 1572 is regarded as an economic and cultural 'golden age'. This joint, multi-ethnic power managed to quell opposition on its eastern and western fronts. Poland–Lithuania crushed the Tatars and in 1410 defeated an army of 27,000 Teutonic Knights at the Battle of Tannenberg. In 1454 the Polish–Teutonic war broke out. King Casimir IV (1427–92) led a successful campaign, taking control of Western Prussia. At the Peace of Toruń in 1466 Gdańsk was returned to the Polish crown. The city, granted autonomy in exchange for its efforts in the war, thrived on shipping trade with the Netherlands, Spain and England among others while the population outgrew that of Warsaw.

The link between Poland and Lithuania was further strengthened by the Union of Lublin in 1569, which was primarily signed to protect both parties from expansionist threats on the Eastern front from Russia's Tsar Ivan IV (the Terrible). Warsaw became the capital of the two kingdoms which were henceforth known as the Commonwealth of Poland-Lithuania.

The last Jagiełłonian, Zygmunt II, died in 1572, after which the nobility introduced an elective monarchy with powers limited by the Acta Henriciana, so called because the first elected king to whom it applied was Henri III de Valois. He was obliged to swear his allegiance to maintaining the elective monarchy, which consulted the nobles on tax and warfare, respected religious tolerance and held a bi-annual meeting of the Sejm, the bicameral assembly dating from 1493. In contrast to many other countries in Europe, the Commonwealth was sufficiently broadminded on religious issues to abide by the Statute of Toleration (1573), although Catholicism was still the official religion.

Polish Wars

During this period, many foreign leaders were elected, partly to neutralize external interests. In 1573 Catherine de Médicis of France organized the elections of her third son, Henry, duke of Anjou, to the Polish crown. When he returned to France as king on his brother's death, he was succeeded by a Transylvanian, Prince István Bathory. He increased Poland-Lithuania's force—a necessity given Ivan the Terrible's bellicose claims. In campaigns throughout 1578–81 the latter was beaten with a huge loss of Russian lives, and the territories he had encroached upon were restored.

1587 marked the beginning of Vasa rule, with Swedish-born Sigismund III taking the throne. But his succession led to territorial claims from his native land. Disapproving of Sigismund's Catholic persuasion, Calvinist Sweden occupied Livonia and Pomerania. In alliance with Russia, King Karl X of Sweden mounted a full invasion of Poland-Lithuania, devastating Warsaw and Kraków. During the ensuing Polish–Swedish war of 1655–60, support for Poland-Lithuania came from the Netherlands and Denmark. The Poles fought back against the invaders, winning a major battle at Częstochowa. King Jan Kazimiercz (John Casimir), the last in line of the Vasa dynasty, went into exile.

Hopes of salvation for the Commonwealth came with Jan III Sobieski's election to the throne in 1674. He fought off the Ottomans who were advancing onto Polish territory. But further invasions and wars weakened Poland. The Great Northern War of 1700–21 had Poland as the battleground for fierce fighting between Russia, Denmark-Norway and Saxony-Poland (also Prussia from 1715) on one side against Sweden on the other. Each of the warring factions occupied parts of Poland, which was also subject to internecine fighting. Russia played the dominant role in Polish affairs until Frederick II, king of an increasingly powerful Prussia, proposed the division of Poland between Russia, Prussia and Austria. The outcome was the first Partition of Poland, in 1772. Austria was awarded the Kingdom of Galicia-Lodomeria, with 2·5m. inhabitants. Russia took over an area with a population of over 1m. Prussia contented itself with 0·5m. new citizens, and the long-desired connection between Western Pomerania and East Prussia.

In 1791 Stanisław II, the last king of the remaining Poland–Lithuania, introduced a constitution which amounted to a bid for independence. The three surrounding superpowers nonetheless engaged in a second partition in 1793. A peasant uprising against Russian rule, led by Tadeusz Kościuszko, was crushed, along with Poland itself which lost control of all its territory to Austria, Prussia and Russia in the third partition (1795).

The territory remained a battleground, particularly during the Napoleonic wars. Napoleon established the Grand Duchy of Warsaw in 1807, which had a French-style constitution, but came under Saxon, and later Russian, administration. Polish legions, which fought on the French side against Prussia, incurred heavy losses. In 1815, when the victorious Allies redistributed the territory Napoleon had won, the 'Congress' Kingdom of Poland reappeared, this time under Russian rule, with the Tsar as its hereditary king.

Thereafter the inhabitants suffered attempts by their colonizers to assimilate their cultures. A series of uprisings against the Russians took place throughout the century. In the November Revolution of 1830 inexperienced military cadets were suppressed by Tsar Nicholas, who led a campaign of bloody reprisals. Around 8,000 Poles emigrated after this defeat—many of them intellectuals, and most headed for France. During the peasants' revolt in Galicia in 1846 up to 2,000 nobles were murdered and their land ravaged. There was a strong insurgent movement among the peasants, but in 1848 they failed once more to topple their oppressors, this time the Prussians.

The January Uprising against the Russians which began in 1863–64 and ended in the spring of 1865 again led to defeat. Wide-scale Russianization followed, though the abolition of serfdom marked a significant concession. As part of Bismarck's 'Kulturkampf'—the Germanization of the Prussian zones—German was introduced as the official language and Polish began to be taught in schools as a foreign language. Anti-Semitism became rife, and pogroms were not unusual. Many Jewish and Gentile Poles fled.

The Habsburg-dominated part of Poland, Galicia, was more tolerant of Polish nationalism which centred on Kraków. At one point the Austrian prime minister, finance minister and foreign minister were all Polish. Newly-formed parties began to gain significance, with the National Democrats under Roman Dmowski campaigning for autonomy and Józef Piłsudski's Socialists engaging in an underground struggle for independence. Piłsudski led an anti-Russian uprising in 1905, and was to take up arms against Russia in the First World War when Poland's territory again bore the brunt of much of the fighting between its three partitioners.

In 1917 a Polish National Committee, formed by Roman Dmowski in Paris, was recognized by the Allies. One of its members and US representative was the pianist Ignacy Jan Paderewski, who urged the Americans to support the cause for Polish independence. President Woodrow Wilson's 'Fourteen Points' for peace addressed the Polish issue, guaranteeing independence and access to the sea under point thirteen. A Polish army was formed in France in 1918. In Poland, Piłsudski set up the Polish legions and a rival government. Poland regained its independence under Piłsudski's leadership on 11 Nov. 1918.

But while the Paris Peace Conference recognized the republic, the question of its borders was highly contentious. Poland challenged Lithuania over Vilnius, the city changing hands more than once before the Second World War. Fighting also took place against Ukraine over the issue of Galicia. A war with Russia followed over the next two years, which Poland narrowly managed to win before signing the Soviet–Polish Peace Treaty in Riga in 1921. The Treaty established the borders between Russia, Ukraine and Belarus, the last two being swallowed up by the USSR the following year. Gdańsk was awarded the status of a free city, and the Polish Corridor was formed between German West and East Prussia and the rest of Germany.

Between the wars there were 16 palatinates, all centrally governed from Warsaw. The new republic was first headed by President Narutowicz, the representative of the left and centre parties, who served for only days before being assassinated by a right-wing fanatic, and replaced in 1922 by Stanisław Wojciechowski. A series of intra-party disputes and factionalisms led the way for Józef Piłsudski to mount a coup in May 1926, seizing the power he maintained under a dictatorship until his death in 1935.

Second World War
In foreign affairs Poland managed to maintain a balance between its two most intimidating neighbours, Germany and the USSR, signing a non-aggression pact with Germany in 1934. However, the Molotov–Ribbentrop non-aggression pact of Aug. 1939 secretly agreed to partition Poland between Germany and the Soviet Union in the event of war. British and French guarantees of Polish independence that had been agreed in April of the same year obliged them to declare war on Nazi Germany two days after Hitler's troops marched into Poland on 1 Sept. 1939.

The response of Britain and France signalled the start of the Second World War. The German army invaded Poland along the entire front from the Baltic Sea to Slovakia, annexing over half of the country within three weeks. Stalin's troops marched into Poland from the Eastern Front on 17 Sept., leaving the country occupied for most of the duration of the war. The Nazis undertook a policy of liquidation—not only of Jews and ethnic 'undesirables' but also of the intelligentsia, so as to avoid any possibility of a Polish leadership class. Many Polish children seen as racially pure were taken away from their parents to be brought up as Germans, while others were deported. A total of over 6m. Polish nationals, or 17% of the population, were killed in the war, half of them Jewish. Not all of the murders were attributable to the Nazis, however. In 1989 Soviet authorities finally admitted to having murdered 15,000 Polish officers who went missing in May 1940. The Soviet secret service had been equally keen to obliterate potential opposition leaders.

Polish forces regrouped on Allied soil under a government-in-exile headed by Gen. Władysław Sikorski, first in Paris and then, after 1940, in London. In Poland an underground national army, the AK, was formed under Gen. Komorowski to fight against the occupiers and to organize resistance. After Germany's invasion of the USSR in 1941, Poland was occupied solely by Nazi forces. Many of the largest concentration camps were built on Polish soil, including Auschwitz near Kraków.

In 1943 the exiled prime minister Gen. Sikorski was killed in a plane crash. He was replaced by Stanisław Mikołajczyk of the Polish Peasants' Party. The same year saw a Jewish uprising in the Warsaw ghetto, and in 1944 there was a second rebellion against the Nazi occupation in the capital which lasted for two months. The Red Army was on the threshold of Warsaw throughout the two month revolt, but did not intervene. 150,000 civilians and 18,000 members of the AK lost their lives with virtually the whole of the remaining urban population deported and 85% of the city destroyed. By the time of Warsaw's liberation in Jan. 1945, the Jewish population numbered 200. The decimated underground movement was forced to seek assistance from Moscow, and after a number of compromises the Soviets recognized the Polish Committee of National Liberation, or the 'Lublin Committee', which proclaimed itself the sole legal government when Lublin was liberated in July 1944.

Poland's postwar fate was decided by the Allies at the Yalta and Potsdam conferences. At Yalta, Stalin agreed that the Lublin government should be extended to include non-Communists from the exile government, a promise that he failed to keep. Stanisław Mikołajczyk and three other members joined the provisional cabinet in July 1945. Nonetheless, many Polish politicians left the country. The Potsdam conference set Poland's Western border along the Oder–Neisse line, with all former German territories east of these rivers handed to Poland. As a result, Poles and Germans had to be resettled.

The first postwar elections were held in Jan. 1947. The Stalinist Polish Workers' Party (PPR) managed to crush both official and underground opposition and a Communist-dominated coalition under the leadership of Władysław Gomułka, the 'Democratic Bloc', won over three-quarters of the votes. Bolesław Bierut, leader of the USSR-backed Polish Communist Party, was named president. Defeated, Stanisław Mikołajczyk fled the country. An independently minded politician, Gomułka entered into conflict with Stalin by opposing agricultural collectivization and by speaking out against the formation of Cominform (Communist Information Bureau) in 1947. As a result he was removed as Secretary General of the PPR in Sept. 1948. Removed from the party altogether in late 1949, he was ultimately put under house arrest in July 1951. In 1948 the Polish United Workers' Party (PZPR) was formed, with Bierut as first party secretary. The nationalization of industry, land expropriation and the restructuring of the economy to favour heavy industry, including arms production, were accompanied in 1952 by a Soviet-style constitution and the renaming of the country as the People's Republic of Poland. This 'Stalinization' also included political and religious suppression and persecution, which targeted the Catholic church in particular.

Postwar Reform

In 1955 Poland joined other Eastern bloc countries in signing the Warsaw Pact military treaty. Meanwhile, the planned economy was failing, leading to widespread public unrest as food prices spiralled. Workers' strikes and riots in Poznań in 1956 were brutally suppressed by the authorities resulting in the death of 53 people. At this time Gomułka, the opponent of Stalinism, gained in popularity. Re-admitted to the party in 1956, Gomułka was reinstated as first secretary of the Party.

He attempted to introduce reforms, gaining public support for his pledges of a 'Polish way' to socialism. Gomułka cut the power of the secret police, halted agricultural collectivization and brought an end to attacks on the Catholic Church. However, the suppression of freedom of expression continued and the economy did not improve. Gomułka's popular appeal began

to falter. Student riots sprang up throughout the 1960s. In the 'March events' of 1968, the campaign for intellectual freedom led to widespread student riots and a reactive Party campaign against intellectuals and Jews, many of whom were forced to flee abroad.

The sense of unrest and dissatisfaction with the party remained. Increased food prices in Dec. 1970 resulted in riots and strikes in the shipyards of Gdańsk, Szczecin and Gdynia. These were met with armed opposition, the authorities firing into the masses and killing several demonstrators. Gomułka and other leaders subsequently resigned, although Gomułka at least had the satisfaction of procuring West Germany's recognition of the Oder–Neisse line as the official Western border of Poland in Dec. 1970.

Solidarity

Edward Gierek succeeded Gomułka as first secretary, and in the following years launched a reform programme which was chiefly financed by loans from Western banks. He was hoping for a Polish economic miracle, but lacked the will to push through the necessary reforms. Short term rewards were not enough to overcome the problems of a failing infrastructure, economic mismanagement of successive governments and a faltering world economy following the 1973 world oil crisis. Further demonstrations took place in several cities in 1976 to protest at more food price increases, and in Radom a Workers' Defence Committee was founded. While the government expressed disapproval, it did not act against the Committee.

In 1978 the election of Karol Wojtyła, Cardinal of Kraków, as Pope John Paul II boosted Poland's national self-esteem, celebrated in his trip to his native country the following year. Nonetheless, increased meat prices in July 1980 led to more waves of strikes, rippling out from the Ursus tractor plant near Warsaw across the country, and culminating in the Lenin shipyards in Gdańsk, where the Solidarity movement was born. The first independent trade union to be established in a communist country soon boasted a membership of 10m. Its leader, Lech Wałęsa, was a shipyard electrician. He set up a strike committee, the first of a succession across the country, and drew up a 21-point accord, demanding the right to strike and to form independent trade unions, the abolition of censorship, freedom of expression, the release of political prisoners and access to the media. Soviet and Polish communist efforts to curb Solidarity's popularity failed and the group was officially recognized after some government resistance.

The social unrest, coupled with failing health, led to Gierek's resignation in Sept. 1980. In Feb. 1981 Gen. Wojciech Jaruzelski, the defence minister, became prime minister. This brought the military into the political front line and in Dec. 1981 Jaruzelski imposed martial law. A Military Council of National Salvation was established and Solidarity was proscribed. Wałęsa was among the thousands of members who were arrested and imprisoned. Demonstrations and strikes provoked the government into even stricter controls with the banning of all independent trade unions, although martial law was dropped a year later.

New hope was given to Poland in 1983, by the Pope's second visit, and by the award of the Nobel Peace Prize to Lech Wałęsa. Economic difficulties continued throughout the 1980s, and when the government proposed unpopular economic reforms in 1987, support for Solidarity led to nationwide strikes during 1988. Jaruzelski was forced to embark on negotiations with Wałęsa and the Catholic Church. Agreement was reached in April 1989 and Solidarity was given legal status and freedom to fight the up-coming elections, whilst the previously ceremonial post of Presidency was vested with new legislative powers. In return, Solidarity agreed to compete for only 35% of the seats in the Sejm.

At the July 1989 elections Solidarity won virtually all the seats they contested but because of the 35% rule Jaruzelski was voted in as president. However, Solidarity refused to join the communists in a grand coalition and Jaruzelski had to appoint Tadeusz Mazowiecki, an official of Solidarity, to be Poland's first non-communist premier in over 40 years. Jaruzelski subsequently resigned.

The first round of presidential elections in Nov. 1990 pitted Lech Wałęsa against Tadeusz Mazowiecki. Wałęsa won 43% of the votes in the first round and 74% in the second round in Dec., when he was inaugurated. Mazowiecki resigned his premiership and was replaced by Jan Bielcki, whose government held office until Aug. 1991. Genuinely free parliamentary elections did not take place until Oct. 1991, when there was a surprisingly low electoral turnout. In the absence of a clear-cut winner, several parties combined to form a centre-right coalition headed by Jan Olszewski. Owing to disputes both within the party and with President Wałęsa, however, the government lasted only seven months. This factionalism and inability to make compromises was typical of Poland's early post-Communist years. The government formed under Hanna Suchocka, Poland's first female prime minister, fared no better.

As in other post-Communist states, the economic measures necessary for the transition to a profitable market economy were highly unpopular with the electorate, not least when industrial modernization led to unemployment. In 1990 the finance minister, Leszek Balcerowicz, had introduced a range of tight austerity measures, including price rises and currency devaluation in an attempt to stabilize the economy before opening it to market forces. The Polish economy prospered but Wałęsa's popular appeal diminished as his tenure progressed. His skills as Solidarity's leader revolved around his ability to speak for the common people, but in government his tone was often regarded as aggressive and his style of leadership autocratic. Solidarity's loyalties as a trade union were often incompatible with its responsibilities as a political party. The elections of 1993 saw the return of the left under Waldemar Pawlak of the Polish Peasants' Party. After a series of intra-party quarrels and accusations of corruption, Pawlak's premiership ended in Feb. 1995.

Pawlak was replaced by the Communist Józef Oleksy of the Democratic Left Alliance. The left gained further political clout when Wałęsa was ousted in the presidential elections of 1995 by Aleksander Kwaśniewski. Redundancies in the Gdańsk shipyards in 1997 saw a renewed outbreak of nationwide strikes. Revising its political agenda, Solidarity forged a coalition of 25 centre-right parties to create Solidarity Election Action. This party emerged as the strongest in the 1997 general election when Jerzy Buzek, a member of Solidarity since its inception, became prime minister. A new constitution came into effect, reducing the powers of the president and committing the country to a social market economy.

Kwaśniewski's communist heritage caused concern among many Western leaders, but he confirmed his intention to press for EU and NATO membership. Market reforms and privatization continued apace. In 1999, at a joint ceremony with Czech president Vaclav Havel, Kwaśniewski signed Poland into NATO. The following year Kwaśniewski secured a second term and in 2001 Buzek was succeeded by Leszek Miller. A former communist turned social democrat, Miller's key aim was to prepare Poland for entry into the EU. Facing a deteriorating economy, he bid to cut the national debt by increases in taxation and spending cuts. On 1 May 2004 Poland became a member of the EU.

TERRITORY AND POPULATION

Poland is bounded in the north by the Baltic Sea and Russia, east by Lithuania, Belarus and Ukraine, south by the Czech Republic and Slovakia and west by Germany. Poland comprises an area of 312,685 sq. km (120,728 sq. miles).

At the census of 20 May 2002 the population was 38,230,080 (18·52m. males; 61·8% urban), giving a density of 122·3 per sq. km.

The UN gives a projected population for 2010 of 38·36m.

The country is divided into 16 regions or voivodships (*wojewodztwo*), created from the previous 49 on 1 Jan. 1999 following administrative reform. Area (in sq. km) and population (in 1,000) in 2002 (density per sq. km in brackets).

Voivodship	Area	Population	
Dolnośląskie	19,948	2,907	(146)
Kujawsko-Pomorskie	17,970	2,069	(115)
Lubelskie	25,121	2,199	(88)
Lubuskie	13,981	1,009	(72)
Łódzkie	18,219	2,613	(143)
Małopolskie	15,190	3,232	(213)
Mazowieckie	35,559	5,124	(144)
Opolskie	9,412	1,065	(113)
Podkarpackie	17,844	2,104	(117)
Podlaskie	20,187	1,209	(60)
Pomorskie	18,293	2,180	(119)
Śląskie	12,331	4,743	(386)
Świętokrzyskie	11,708	1,297	(111)
Warmińsko-Mazurskie	24,192	1,428	(59)
Wielkopolskie	29,826	3,352	(112)
Zachodniopomorskie	22,896	1,698	(74)

Population (in 1,000) of the largest towns and cities (2002):

Warszawa (Warsaw)	1,671·7	Częstochowa	251·4
Łódź	789·3	Sosnowiec	232·6
Kraków (Cracow)	758·5	Radom	229·7
Wrocław (Breslau)	640·4	Kielce	212·4
Poznań	578·9	Toruń	211·2
Gdańsk (Danzig)	461·3	Gliwice	203·8
Szczecin (Stettin)	415·4	Zabrze	195·3
Bydgoszcz	373·8	Bytom	193·5
Lublin	357·1	Bielsko-Biała	178·0
Katowice	327·2	Olsztyn	173·1
Białystok	291·4	Rzeszów	160·4
Gdynia	253·5	Ruda Śląska	150·6

The population is 96·7% Polish. Minorities at the 2002 census included 173,153 Silesians, 152,987 Germans, 48,737 Belarusians and 30,957 Ukrainians. There are an estimated 300,000 people in Poland of Kashubian ethnicity (direct descendants of an early Slavic tribe of Pomeranians). They generally declare Polish nationality and consider themselves both Poles and Kashubians.

A movement for Silesian autonomy has attracted sufficient support to suggest that further moves towards decentralization may soon be considered. A Council of National Minorities was set up in March 1991. There is a large Polish diaspora, some 65% in the USA.

The national language is Polish.

SOCIAL STATISTICS

2003 (in 1,000): births, 351·1; deaths, 365·2; marriages, 195·4; divorces, 48·6; infant deaths, 2·5. Rates (per 1,000 population): birth, 9·2; death, 9·6; marriage, 5·1; divorce, 1·2; infant mortality (per 1,000 live births), 7·0. A law prohibiting abortion was passed in 1993, but an amendment of Aug. 1996 permits it in cases of hardship or difficult personal situation. The most popular age range for marrying in 1999 was 20–24 for both males and females. Expectation of life at birth, 2003, was 70·3 years for males and 78·4 years for females. In 1998 there were 22,200 emigrants (including 16,100 to Germany) and 8,900 immigrants. 71% of Polish emigrants between 1990 and 1998 settled in Germany. Number of suicides, 2001, 5,855; the suicide rate per 100,000 population was 26·7 among males and 4·3 among females in 2001. Annual population growth rate, 1992–2002, 0·1%; fertility rate, 2001, 1·3 births per woman.

CLIMATE

Climate is continental, marked by long and severe winters. Rainfall amounts are moderate, with a marked summer maximum. Warsaw, Jan. 24°F (−4·3°C), July 64°F (17·9°C). Annual rainfall 18·3" (465 mm). Gdańsk, Jan. 29°F (−1·7°C), July 63°F (17·2°C). Annual rainfall 22·0" (559 mm). Kraków, Jan. 27°F (−2·8°C), July 67°F (19·4°C). Annual rainfall 28·7" (729 mm). Poznań, Jan. 26°F (−3·3°C), July 64°F (17·9°C). Annual rainfall 21·0" (534 mm). Szczecin, Jan. 27°F (−3·0°C), July 64°F (17·7°C). Annual rainfall 18·4" (467 mm). Wrocław, Jan. 24°F (−4·3°C), July 64°F (17·9°C). Annual rainfall 20·7" (525 mm).

CONSTITUTION AND GOVERNMENT

The present Constitution was passed by national referendum on 25 May 1997 and became effective on 17 Oct. 1997. The head of state is the *President*, who is directly elected for a five-year term (renewable once). The President may appoint, but may not dismiss, cabinets.

The authority of the republic is vested in the *Sejm* (Parliament of 460 members), elected by proportional representation for four years by all citizens over 18. There is a 5% threshold for parties and 8% for coalitions, but seats are reserved for representatives of ethnic minorities even if their vote falls below 5%. 69 of the Sejm seats are awarded from the national lists of parties polling more than 7% of the vote. The Sejm elects a *Council of State* and a *Council of Ministers*. There is also an elected 100-member upper house, the *Senate*. The President and the Senate each has a power of veto which only a two-thirds majority of the Sejm can override. The President does not, however, have a veto over the annual budget. The *Prime Minister* is chosen by the President with the approval of the Sejm.

A *Political Council* consultative to the presidency consisting of representatives of all the major political tendencies was set up in Jan. 1991.

National Anthem

'Jeszcze Polska nie zginęła' ('Poland has not yet perished'); words by J. Wybicki, tune by M. Ogiński.

GOVERNMENT CHRONOLOGY

First Secretaries of the Polish United Workers' Party (1943–90) and Presidents of the Republic (since 1990). (PiS = Law and Justice Party; PZPR = Polish United Workers' Party; SdRP = Social Democracy of the Republic of Poland; SLD = Democratic Left Alliance; n/p = non-partisan)

First Secretaries of PZPR

1943–48	Władysław Gomułka
1948–52	Bolesław Bierut
1952–54	Hilary Minc
1954–56	Bolesław Bierut
1956	Edward Ochab
1956–70	Władysław Gomułka
1970–80	Edward Gierek
1980–81	Stanisław Kania
1981–89	Wojciech Jaruzelski (military)
1989–90	Mieczysław F. Rakowski

Presidents

1989–90	n/p	Wojciech Jaruzelski
1990–95	Solidarność	Lech Wałęsa
1995–2005	SdRP/SLD	Aleksander Kwaśniewski
2005–	PiS	Lech Kaczyński

Prime Ministers since 1945. (AWS = Solidarity Electoral Action; KLD = Liberal Democratic Congress; PC = Centre Alliance; PiS = Law and Justice Party; PPR = Polish Workers' Party; PPS = Polish Socialist Party; PSL = Polish Peasants' Party; PZPR = Polish United Workers' Party; RS AWS = Social Movement-Solidarity Electoral Action; SdRP = Social Democracy of the Republic of Poland; SLD = Democratic Left Alliance; UD = Democratic Union)

1945–47	PPS	Edward Osóbka-Morawski
1947–52	PPR, PZPR	Józef A. Z. Cyrankiewicz
1952–54	PZPR	Bolesław Bierut
1954–70	PZPR	Józef A. Z. Cyrankiewicz
1970–80	PZPR	Piotr Jaroszewicz
1980	PZPR	Edward Babiuch
1980–81	PZPR	Józef Pińkowski
1981–85	PZPR/military	Wojciech Jaruzelski
1985–88	PZPR	Zbigniew Messner
1988–89	PZPR	Mieczysław F. Rakowski
1989	PZPR	Czesław Kiszczak
1989–91	Solidarność, UD	Tadeusz Mazowiecki
1991	KLD	Jan Krzysztof Bielecki
1991–92	PC	Jan Olszewski
1992	PSL	Waldemar Pawlak
1992–93	UD	Hanna Suchocka
1993–95	PSL	Waldemar Pawlak
1995–96	SdRP/SLD	Józef Oleksy
1996–97	SdRP/SLD	Włodzimierz Cimoszewicz
1997–2001	RS AWS/AWS	Jerzy Karol Buzek
2001–04	SLD	Leszek Miller
2004–05	SLD	Marek Belka
2005–	PiS	Kazimierz Marcinkiewicz

RECENT ELECTIONS

Parliamentary elections were held on 25 Sept. 2005. The Law and Justice Party (PiS) won 155 of 460 seats with 27·0% of the votes, ahead of the Citizen's Platform (PO), with 133 seats (24·1%); Self-Defence of the Polish Republic (SRP) won 56 seats (11·4%); Democratic Left Alliance (SLD) won 55 (11·3%); League of Polish Families (LPR), 34 (8·0%); Polish Peasants' Party (PSL), 25 (7·0%); German Minority (MN), 2 (0·3%). In the Senate, the Law and Justice Party won 49 seats, with the Citizen's Platform winning 34 and League of Polish Families 7. The remaining ten seats were taken by other parties and independents. Turnout was 40·6%.

Presidential elections were held in two rounds on 9 and 23 Oct. 2005. In the first round 12 candidates stood; turnout was 49·7%. Donald Tusk of the Citizen's Platform (PO) gained 36·3% of votes cast, Lech Kaczyński of the the Law and Justice Party (PiS) 33·1%, Andrzej Lepper of Self-Defence of the Polish Republic (SRP) 15·1% and Marek Borowski of the Democratic Party (PD) 10·3%. Other candidates obtained 2% or less. In the second round run-off Lech Kaczyński was elected president with 54·0% of the vote against 46·0% for Donald Tusk.

European Parliament

Poland has 54 representatives. At the June 2004 elections turnout was 20·4%. The PO won 15 seats with 24·1% of votes cast (political affiliation in European Parliament: European People's Party–European Democrats); the LPR, 10 with 15·9% (Independence and Democracy Group); the PiS, 7 with 12·7% (Union for a Europe of Nations); the SRP, 6 with 10·8% (non-attached); the Democratic Left Alliance–Union of Labour, 5 with 9·3% (Party of European Socialists); the Freedom Union, 4 with 7·3% (Alliance of Liberals and Democrats for Europe); the PSL, 4 with 6·3% (European People's Party–European Democrats); the Social Democratic Poland Party, 3 with 5·3% (Party of European Socialists).

CURRENT ADMINISTRATION

President: Lech Kaczyński; b. 1949 (PiS; sworn in 23 Dec. 2005).

In March 2006 the minority PiS government consisted of:

Prime Minister: Kazimierz Marcinkiewicz; b. 1959 (PiS; sworn in 31 Oct. 2005).

Deputy Prime Ministers: Ludwik Dorn (also *Minister of Interior and Administration*); Zyta Gilowska (also *Minister of Finance*).

Minister of Agriculture and Rural Development: Krzysztof Jurgiel. *Economy:* Piotr Grzegorz Woźniak. *Labour and Social*

Policy: Krzysztof Michałkiewicz. *Foreign Affairs:* Stefan Meller. *Culture and National Heritage:* Kazimierz Michał Ujazdowski. *Sport:* Tomasz Lipiec. *Regional Development:* Grażyna Gęsicka. *Health:* Zbigniew Religa. *Justice:* Zbigniew Ziobro. *Education and Science:* Michał Seweryński. *Treasury:* Wojciech Jasiński. *National Defence:* Radosław Sikorski. *Transport and Construction:* Jerzy Polaczek. *Environment:* Jan Szyszko. *Minister and Member of Council of Ministers:* Zbigniew Wassermann.

Speaker of the Sejm: Marek Jurek (PiS).

Office of the Prime Minister: http://www.kprm.gov.pl

CURRENT LEADERS

Lech Kaczyński

Position
President

Introduction
Lech Kaczyński beat Donald Tusk in a run-off for the presidency in Oct. 2005. The conservative former mayor of Warsaw campaigned on a nationalist platform and garnered most votes in the country's poorer eastern provinces. His victory confirmed Poland's shift to the political right—the parliamentary elections in Sept. 2005 were won by the conservative Law and Justice Party, led by Lech Kaczyński's identical twin brother, Jarosław.

Early Life
Lech Alexander Kaczyński was born on 18 June 1949 in Warsaw, the son of an engineer and a philologist. As a child, Lech Kaczyński and his brother, Jarosław, appeared in a popular film comedy, *The Two That Stole The Moon*. Lech studied law and administration at Warsaw University. Having received a PhD from Gdańsk University in 1976, he embarked on an academic career, lecturing at both Gdańsk University and Cardinal Stefan Wyszynski University in Warsaw.

An activist in the democratic anti-Communist movement, in Aug. 1980 Kaczyński became a legal advisor to the strike committee in the Gdańsk shipyard and the Solidarność (Solidarity) movement. However, Kaczyński was one of many Solidarity activists to be arrested and interned after Gen. Jaruzelski, the first secretary of the Polish United Workers' Party (PZPR), declared martial law in Dec. 1981. From the mid-1980s Kaczyński was an advisor to Solidarity's leader, Lech Wałęsa, and helped establish the Citizens Committee Solidarity (OKP) in Dec. 1988. Kaczyński was present at the 'round table' negotiations that paved the way for multi-party elections in June 1989, at which he was elected a member of the Sejm.

In May 1990 Lech and his brother split the OKP and established the Centre Agreement Party (PC) to support Wałęsa's successful presidential campaign. Kaczyński was appointed minister of state for national security in the presidential office, but disagreements led to him leaving office in late 1991. Appointed chairman of the Supreme Control Chamber in Feb. 1992, Kaczyński became a leading critic of Wałęsa until the president was ousted by Aleksander Kwaśniewski in elections of Nov. 1995.

Kaczyński returned to the Sejm in 1997 as a representative of the Solidarity Electoral Action (AWS) grouping of nationalist, conservative, centrist and Catholic parties. He served as attorney general and minister of justice in Jerzy Buzek's government between June 2000 and July 2001, gaining popularity for his hard-line approach to law and order until dismissed by Buzek over a controversial criminal investigation. In 2001, shortly before parliamentary elections in Sept., the Kaczyński brothers established the right-wing Law and Justice Party (PiS). The Democratic Left Alliance (SLD) emerged victorious but the PiS took 44 seats in the 460-seat Sejm.

Lech Kaczyński was elected mayor of Warsaw in Nov. 2002 and supported the construction of the Museum of the Warsaw Rising. More controversially, he banned gay movement parades in 2004 and 2005. In March 2005 he declared his intention to run for president in the Oct. elections and campaigned on a nationalist platform, arguing the case for a Fourth Republic. He beat Donald Tusk (of the reformist Citizen's Platform) with 54% of the vote in a run-off on 23 Oct. 2005.

Career in Office
Kaczyński has said he will work to achieve a 'moral renewal' in Poland, campaigning for justice for victims of communist crimes, fighting corruption, providing economic security and combining modernization with tradition. He pledged to strengthen ties with the USA and improve relations with France, Ukraine and the Baltic States. However, relations with Russia and Germany look set to remain difficult. Within the EU, Kaczyński is expected to speak out against a common foreign policy. Regarding Polish membership of the euro zone, Kaczyński has said the issue will be decided by referendum, possibly in 2010.

Kazimierz Marcinkiewicz

Position
Prime Minister

Introduction
Kazimierz Marcinkiewicz was elected Poland's prime minister in Oct. 2005. The teacher-turned-economist has conservative and nationalist views and is a close ally of President Lech Kaczyński.

Early Life
Kazimierz Marcinkiewicz was born on 20 Dec. 1959 in Gorzów Wielkopolski, northwest Poland. He graduated in physics from Wrocław University before completing a post-graduate course in administration at the Adam Mickiewicz University in Poznań. Returning to Gorzów Wielkopolski, he worked as a teacher and in 1983 he joined Solidarność (Solidarity), the self-governing trade union. He edited and published an independent educational periodical, *Pokolenie*, and the Catholic magazine, *Aspekty*. In Sept. 1989, amid the death throes of the ruling Polish United Workers' Party (PZPR) and the creation of a multi-party system, Marcinkiewicz became a founder-member of the Christian–National Union party (ZChN).

A conservative and nationalist party, ZChN performed well in the Oct. 1991 elections and its representative, Jan Olszewski, became prime minister. Marcinkiewicz, who had been head of the board of education in Gorzów Wielkopolski, was appointed deputy minister of national education in 1992 in the short-lived government of Hanna Suchoka. From 1994 he was a member of both the ZChN's main board and its regional administration in Gorzów Wielkopolski. The party was excluded from the Sejm from 1993–97 and was wracked by infighting but was nevertheless one of the key groupings within Solidarity Electoral Action (AWS). Marcinkiewicz served as deputy chairman of the Sejm education, science and youth commission and from 1999–2000 was head of the political cabinet under Prime Minister Jerzy Buzek (AWS). The AWS–UW (Freedom Union) coalition government was credited with implementing reforms to local government, health, pensions and education.

In Feb. 2001 Marcinkiewicz founded the Right-Wing Alliance party, which later became part of the Law and Justice party (PiS), founded by the twins Lech and Jarosław Kaczyński. He subsequently served as chairman of the Sejm state treasury commission and gained plaudits for his economic competence. Following the PiS' victory in the parliamentary elections of 25 Sept. 2005, Marcinkiewicz was nominated as their candidate for the premiership, with the blessing of PiS leader Jarosław Kaczynski. Marcinkiewicz was expected to form a coalition with the Citizen's Platform (PO), the pro-market party which came second in the elections, but talks collapsed and the PiS formed a minority government supported by the populist Samoobrona, the right-wing League of Polish Families (LPR) and the Polish Peasants' Party (PSL).

Career in Office

The PiS has campaigned to defend traditionalist Catholic values by maintaining state benefits for the poor, cracking down on crime and corruption and overhauling security structures. Marcinkiewicz has also pledged to tackle high unemployment, bring down the budget deficit and place the economy on a sounder footing.

DEFENCE

Poland is divided into four military districts: Warsaw, Pomerania, Kraków and Silesia. In 2003 military expenditure totalled US$4,095m. (US$107 per capita), representing 2·0% of GDP.

Three-year civilian duty as a conscientious alternative to conscription of 12 months was introduced in 1988.

Army

Strength (2002) 104,050 (including 58,700 conscripts). In accordance with a programme of modernization of the armed forces, the strength has been gradually declining, from 230,000 in the socialist era in 1988 to 186,000 in 1995 and further to the current figure of just over 104,000. In addition there were 188,000 Army reservists in 2002 and 14,100 border guards.

Navy

The fleet comprises three ex-Soviet and one ex-Norwegian diesel submarines, one ex-Soviet destroyer, three frigates and four corvettes. Naval Aviation operated 26 combat aircraft (including MiG-21s) and 12 armed helicopters.

Personnel in 2002 totalled 14,300 including 7,500 conscripts and 2,000 in Naval Aviation. Bases are at Gdynia, Hel, Świnoujście and Kolobrzeg.

Air Force

The Air Force had a strength (2002) of 36,450 (14,800 conscripts). There are two air defence corps (North and South) with 201 combat aircraft (including MiG-21/29s and Su-22s).

INTERNATIONAL RELATIONS

A treaty of friendship with Germany signed on 17 June 1991 renounced the use of force, recognized Poland's western border as laid down at the Potsdam conference of 1945 (the 'Oder–Neisse line') and guaranteed minority rights in both countries.

Poland is a member of the UN, WTO, NATO, BIS, EU, the Council of Europe, OECD, OSCE, CEFTA, CERN, CEI, Council of the Baltic Sea States, IOM, the Antarctic Treaty and is an associate partner of the WEU. A referendum held on 8 June 2003 approved accession to the EU, with 77·4% of votes cast for membership and 22·6% against. Poland became a member of the EU on 1 May 2004.

ECONOMY

Agriculture accounted for 3·1% of GDP in 2002, industry 30·5% and services 66·4%.

Overview

During the years of communist rule the Polish economy was heavily skewed towards heavy industry to the neglect of services. At the beginning of 1990 Poland became the first country in Central and Eastern Europe to embrace economic change. As a result the industrial sector declined from 35% of GDP in 1992 to 27·8% in 1999 and the service sector expanded to 60% of GDP in 2000. In spite of slow privatization in the manufacturing sector, the private sector accounted for 72% of GDP in 2001, up from 18% in 1989. Most of the banking sector has been privatized, as have many large industries. In 1990 and 1991 the economy shrank 11·5% and 7% respectively but economic restructuring has since helped to achieve productivity gains. The Economist

Intelligence Unit estimates that from 1994–2003 total factor productivity grew at an annual average of over 3%. Transition policies included liberalizing prices, making the Polish złoty convertible, fixing the exchange rate and lowering import barriers. Such policy changes could have induced economic crises had it not been for sound macroeconomic management of the country over the years. An unspectacular yet solid growth performance since the initial transition shock has helped raise living standards in Poland. Per capita income levels began to grow robustly in 1994 after a decade and a half of stagnation and by 2004 had grown to over two and a half times 1993 levels, reaching US$6,265 per annum.

The economic environment is friendly with transparent rules for investment and equal treatment for domestic and foreign firms. However, despite a successful transition there are many areas where further progress is needed. According to the World Bank, the main impediment to stronger growth is the public sector. Weak public finances, high fiscal deficits, administrative inefficiencies, weakness in the judicial system, low investment in public infrastructure and non-competitive state-led sectors are all highlighted for reform. The privatization push that began in the 1990s has slowed significantly. The health care sector, which has proved more difficult than expected to reform, is an area of particular concern and a significant fiscal liability. Unemployment appeared to peak at 19·8% in 2002 but remains high, at nearly 18% in 2005.

Lowering the tax burden on labour, which is high in Poland compared to other EU members, would benefit employment. Unemployment is highest in areas once dominated by state farms, primarily in the northeast, whereas former industrial areas have proven dynamic. Agriculture in Poland has resisted structural change and continues to be dominated by small and inefficient farms. Though counting for only 3·3% of GDP in 2000, agriculture accounts for a large share of total employment and is a powerful influence on politics. EU funding should help with the restructuring of agriculture and increase investment in the rural infrastructure. Polish exporters have benefited from EU market integration.

Currency

The currency unit is the *złoty* (PLN) of 100 *groszy*. A new złoty was introduced on 1 Jan. 1995 at 1 new złoty = 10,000 old złotys. Inflation rates (based on OECD statistics):

1995	1996	1997	1998	1999	2000	2001	2002	2003	2004
28·0%	19·8%	14·9%	11·6%	7·2%	9·9%	5·4%	1·9%	0·7%	3·4%

Inflation, in single figures since 1999, had been nearly 250% in 1990. The złoty became convertible on 1 Jan. 1990. In 1995 the złoty was subject to a creeping devaluation of 1·2% per month; it was allowed to float in a 14% (+/–7%) band from 16 May 1995. In April 2000 Poland introduced a floating exchange rate. Foreign exchange reserves were US$26,557m. and gold reserves 3·31m. troy oz in June 2002 (0·47m. troy oz in 1996). In Feb. 2002 total money supply was 88,109m. złotys.

Budget

Budget revenue and expenditure (in 1m. złotys):

	1997	1998	1999	2000	2001
Revenue	172,507	196,952	201,131	213,865	223,758
Expenditure	185,431	207,370	216,912	236,865	263,580

VAT is 22·0% (reduced rates, 7% and 3%). Taxes accounted for 87·9% of state revenues in 2001. Social security and welfare accounted for 51·5% of expenditures.

Performance

Real GDP growth rates (based on OECD statistics):

1995	1996	1997	1998	1999	2000	2001	2002	2003	2004
7·0%	6·0%	6·8%	4·8%	4·1%	4·0%	1·0%	1·4%	3·8%	5·4%

Poland was the fastest growing economy in the EU in 2004. Total GDP in 2004 was US$241·8bn. Real GDP in 2002 was 30% higher than in 1989. No other ex-communist country has seen such consistent progress since 1989. The private sector accounts for more than 70% of GDP.

Banking and Finance

The National Bank of Poland (established 1945) is the central bank and bank of issue (*Governor*, Dr Leszek Balcerowicz). There were 73 banks operating at the end of 2000, of which only seven were controlled—directly or indirectly—by the Polish government through its state treasury. PKO Bank Polski, Poland's major savings bank, had assets in 2002 of US$21·4bn. Other leading banks are Bank Pekao and BPH PBK.

In 2003 Poland received US$4,225m. of foreign direct investment, down from US$9,341m. in 2000 although up from just US$89m. in 1990. It receives the most foreign direct investment of any of the former socialist countries of central and eastern Europe. The total stock of FDI at the end of 2002 was US$47·9bn.

There is a stock exchange in Warsaw.

ENERGY AND NATURAL RESOURCES

Environment

Poland's carbon dioxide emissions from the consumption and flaring of fossil fuels in 2002 were the equivalent of 7·0 tonnes per capita.

Electricity

Installed capacity was 30·6m. kW in 2002. Production (2003) 149·16bn. kWh; consumption per capita was 3,549 kWh in 2002.

Oil and Gas

Total oil reserves (2002) amount to some 115m. bbls.; natural gas reserves (2002), 170bn. cu. metres. Crude oil production was 767,000 tonnes in 2001; natural gas (2003), 5·2m. cu. metres. The largest oil distributor is Polski Koncern Naftowy ORLEN SA, created by the merger of Petrochemia Płock and Centrala Produktów Naftowych.

Minerals

Poland is a major producer of coal (reserves of some 120,000m. tonnes), copper (56m. tonnes) and sulphur. Production (in tonnes): coal (2003), 102·3m.; brown coal (2003), 60·9m.; salt (2002), 4·2m.; copper (2001), 474,000; silver (2001), 1,193.

Agriculture

Poland's agriculture sector employed 18·8% of the working population in 2000. In 2001 there were 13·97m. ha. of arable land and 0·34m. ha. of permanent crops. In 2001 private farms accounted for 84·5% of the total area of agricultural land, state-owned farms for 12·5% and collective farms 3·0%. There were 2m. farms in 2000. In 2001 agriculture, hunting and forestry contributed 3·8% of GDP.

Output in 2000 (in 1,000 tonnes): potatoes, 24,232; sugarbeets, 13,134; wheat, 8,503; rye, 4,003; barley, 2,783; cabbages, 1,899; apples, 1,450; oats, 1,070.

Livestock, 2003: cattle, 5·49m. (including cows, 2·90m.); pigs, 18·61m.; sheep (2001), 340,000; horses (2001), 550,000; chickens (2001), 48m. Milk production (2001) was 7,025m. litres; meat (2000), 2·85m. tonnes; eggs (2000), 425,000 tonnes.

In 2001 there were 1,308,500 tractors and 97,000 harvester-threshers in use.

Forestry

In 2000 forest area was 9·05m. ha. (predominantly coniferous), or 29·7% of the land area. State-owned forests account for 82%

of Poland's forests, with the balance being private or municipal. Timber production in 2003 was 27·14m. cu. metres.

Fisheries

The catch was 180,254 tonnes in 2003; 160,260 tonnes were sea fish. In 2001 there were 7,100 people employed in the fishing industry.

INDUSTRY

The leading companies by market capitalization in Poland in May 2004 were: Bank Pekao (US$5·4bn.); and Telekomunikacja Polska (US$5·4bn.).

In 2001 there were 2,054 state firms, 161,049 limited liability companies, 252,608 other companies and 18,812 co-operatives. Production in 2001 unless otherwise indicated (in 1,000 tonnes): cement (2003), 11,312; crude steel (2003), 9,107; pig iron (2002), 5,300; petrol (2002), 3,932; residual fuel oil (2002), 3,325; distillate fuel oil (2002), 3,314; fertilizers, 2,280; paper and paperboard (2002), 2,230; ammonia, 2,070; nitrogenous acid, 2,060; sulphuric acid, 1,945; sugar (2003), 1,899; soda ash, 1,130; sulphur, 1,066; paints and lacquers, 696; plastics in primary forms, 656; vodka, 575; beer, 2,516·3m. litres; soft drinks, 2,185·2m. litres; mineral water, 1,392·5m. litres; cigarettes, 81·7bn. units; bricks, 779m. units; television receivers (2003), 6,792,000 units; tractors (2003), 4,708,000 units; refrigerators and freezers (2003), 1,001,000 units; washing machines (2003), 881,000 units; telephone sets (2003), 742,000 units; cars (2003), 338,000 units; buses (2003), 1,837 units.

Output of light industry: cotton woven fabrics (2001), 285·0m. sq. metres; silk fabrics (2001), 25·0m. sq. metres; woollen woven fabrics (2001), 10·0m. sq. metres; synthetic fibres (1999), 74,100 tonnes; shoes (2003), 37·4m. pairs.

Since 1993 employment in the Polish mining industry has fallen by 40% and 23 mines have closed. The Polish government aims to reduce employment even further, to 100,000 by the end of 2006. Around 125,000 jobs have been lost in the steel industry since the early 1990s; by 2003 it employed just 23,000 people. In 2002 the four largest state-owned steel enterprises were regrouped into one company, Polskie Huty Stali SA, which was privatized in 2003.

Labour

In 2003 a total of 13,617,000 persons were in employment. In Dec. 2002, 2,441,000 persons worked in industry, 1,998,000 in trade and repairs, 897,000 in property, renting and business activities, 895,000 in education, 852,000 in health and social services, 725,000 in transport, storage and communications, and 676,000 in construction. The unemployment rate increased steadily for several years peaking at 19·8% in 2002, compared to the EU average of 7·7%. It has declined slightly since then, and in Dec. 2005 stood at 17·4%. Unemployment among the under 25s is in excess of 40%. Workers made redundant are entitled to one month's wages after one year's service, two months after two years' service and three months after three or more years' service. A five-day working week was introduced in May 2001. The number of hours worked was reduced to 40 in 2003. Retirement age is 60 for women and 65 for men.

Trade Unions

In 1980 under Lech Wałęsa, Solidarity was an engine of political reform. Dissolved in 1982 it was re-legalized in 1989 and successfully contested the parliamentary elections, but was defeated in 1993. It had 2·3m. members in 1991 and 1·2m. in 1998. The official union in the 1980s, OPZZ, had 5m. members in 1990; there were also about 4,000 small unions not affiliated to it. In 1998 OPZZ had 3m. members, and there were some 340 registered unions nationwide. As 22% of members of parliament belong to the two leading unions, they constitute a significant political influence.

INTERNATIONAL TRADE

There were over 30,000 joint ventures in Dec. 1998. Legislation of 1991 removed limits on the repatriation of profits, reduced the number of cases needing licences and ended a 10% ceiling on share purchases. Licenses are required for investment in ports, airports, arms manufacture, estate agency and legal services. Foreign debt was US$69,521m. in 2002.

Imports and Exports

Trade in US$1m.:

	1998	1999	2000	2001	2002
Imports f.o.b.	45,303	45,132	48,210	49,324	53,991
Exports f.o.b.	32,467	30,060	35,902	41,664	46,742

The main imports in 2001 were machinery and apparatus (26·1%); chemicals and chemical products (13·9%); road vehicles (7·8%); crude petroleum (5·7%); food (5·3%). Leading exports were machinery and apparatus (20·4%); road vehicles (8·9%); food (7·1%); furniture and furniture parts (6·9%); chemicals and chemical products (5·9%).

Main import suppliers, 2001: Germany, 24·0%; Russia, 8·8%; Italy, 8·3%; France, 6·8%; UK, 4·2%. Main export markets, 2001: Germany, 34·4%; France, 5·4%; Italy, 5·4%; United Kingdom, 5·0%; Netherlands, 4·7%. In 2000 trade with the European Union accounted for 61·2% of Polish imports and 70·0% of Polish exports.

COMMUNICATIONS

Roads

In 2001 there were 364,697 km of roads, including 399 km of motorways. In 2000 there were 9,991,260 passenger cars, 1,783,008 lorries and vans, 82,356 buses and 802,618 motorcycles and mopeds. In 2000 public transport totalled 31,735m. passenger-km and freight 72,843m. tonne-km. There were 5,534 road accident fatalities in 2001.

Rail

In 1999 Poland had 22,891 km of railways in use (11,614 km electrified). Over 95% is standard 1,435 mm gauge with the rest narrow gauge. By 2000 PKP, the country's train operator, was 6bn. złotys (US$1·3bn.) in debt. In 2002 railways carried 304·0m. passengers and 222·9m. tonnes of freight. Passenger-km travelled in 2001 came to 22·5bn. and freight tonne-km to 47·9bn. Some regional railways are operated by local authorities. An 11 km metro opened in Warsaw in 1995, and there are tram/light rail networks in 14 cities.

Civil Aviation

The main international airport is at Warsaw (Frederic Chopin), with some international flights from Kraków (John Paul II Balice International), Gdańsk, Katowice, Poznań, Szczecin and Wrocław. The national carrier is LOT-Polish Airlines (68% state-owned). It flew 49·0m. km in 1999, carrying 2,140,700 passengers (1,791,100 on international flights). In 2001 Warsaw handled 4,713,655 passengers (4,053,949 on international flights) and 38,983 tonnes of freight.

Shipping

The principal ports are Gdańsk, Szczecin, Świnoujście and Gdynia. 51·75m. tonnes of cargo were handled in 2003. Ocean-going services are grouped into Polish Ocean Lines based on Gdynia and operating regular liner services, and the Polish Shipping Company based on Szczecin and operating cargo services. Poland also has a share in the Gdynia America Line. In 2001, 22·43m. tonnes of freight and 581,000 passengers were carried. In 2002 the merchant marine totalled 586,000 GRT. Ships with a capacity of 524,000 GRT were built in 1995. In 2001 vessels totalling 26,568,000 NRT entered ports and vessels totalling 31,730,000 NRT cleared. In 1999 there were 3,813 km

of navigable inland waterways. In 2001 inland barges carried 10·3m. tonnes of freight (including coastal traffic).

Telecommunications

There were 21,404,700 telephone subscribers in 2001, or 554·1 per 1,000 persons. There were 14·0m. mobile phone subscribers in 2002. The privatization of *Telekomunikacja Polska* (TP SA), the former state telecom operator, was completed in 2001. France Télécom, the biggest foreign investor in Poland, now owns a 47·5% stake in the company. In 2002 there were 4,079,000 PCs (105·6 per 1,000 persons) and 174,000 fax machines. The number of Internet users in 2002 was 8·8m.

Postal Services

In 2003 there were 8,304 post offices. A total of 2,553m. pieces of mail were handled in 2003, or 66 items per person.

SOCIAL INSTITUTIONS

Justice

The penal code was adopted in 1969. Espionage and treason carry the severest penalties. For minor crimes there is provision for probation sentences and fines. In 1995 the death penalty was suspended for five years; it had not been applied since 1988. A new penal code abolishing the death penalty was adopted in June 1997.

There exist the following courts: one Supreme Court, one high administrative court, 10 appeal courts, 44 voivodship courts, 288 district courts, 66 family consultative centres and 34 juvenile courts. Judges and lay assessors are appointed. Judges for higher courts are appointed by the President of the Republic from candidatures proposed by the National Council of the Judiciary. Assessors are nominated by the Minister of Justice. Judges have life tenure. An ombudsman's office was established in 1987.

Family consultative centres were established in 1977 for cases involving divorce and domestic relations, but divorce suits were transferred to ordinary courts in 1990. 238,391 criminal sentences were passed in 1997. There were 1,093 convictions for murder in 1997. The population in penal institutions in March 2003 was 83,113 (218 per 100,000 of national population).

Education

Basic education from seven to 16 is free and compulsory. Free secondary education is then optional in general or vocational schools. Primary schools are organized in complexes based on wards under one director ('ward collective schools'). In 2000–01 there were: pre-primary schools, 18,003 with 885,400 pupils and 73,700 teachers; primary schools, 16,766 with 3,220,600 pupils and 226,400 teachers; lower secondary schools, 6,295 with 1,189,900 pupils and 70,100 teachers; upper secondary schools, 10,573 with 2,452,100 pupils and 135,300 teachers; tertiary institutions, 310 with 1,584,800 students and 79,900 academic staff. In 1997–98 institutions of higher education included 13 universities, 30 polytechnics, 14 agricultural schools, 93 schools of economics, 19 teachers' training colleges, 16 theological colleges and 11 medical schools. In the 15 years from 1980 to 1995 the number of university students in Poland more than trebled. During the 1990s there was a boom in private higher education—by 1998 a quarter of all students in higher education were at private colleges.

The adult literacy rate in 2001 was 99·7%.

Religious (Catholic) instruction was introduced in all schools in 1990; for children of dissenting parents there are classes in ethics.

In 2000–01 total expenditure on education came to 5·3% of GNP and 12·2% of total government spending.

Health

Medical treatment is free and funded from the state budget. Medical care is also available in private clinics. In 2000 there were 767 hospitals with a total of 214,680 beds. There were 85,031 physicians, 11,758 dentists, 189,632 nurses, 22,161 pharmacists and 21,997 midwives in 2000. In Jan. 1999 reform of the health care system was inaugurated. All citizens can now choose their own doctor, who is paid by one of the health-maintenance organizations which are financed directly from the state budget. The share of income tax paid by employers, equalling 7·5% of the amount earned by them, is assigned for the financing of the health care system. In 2001 Poland spent 6·3% of its GDP on health.

Welfare

Social security benefits are administered by the State Insurance Office and funded 45% by a payroll tax and 55% from the state budget. Pensions, disability payments, child allowances, survivor benefits, maternity benefits, funeral subsidies, sickness compensation and alimony supplements are provided. In 2003 social benefits totalling 133,064·5m. złotys were paid (including 112,980·2m. złotys in retirement pay and pensions). There were a total of 9,206,000 pensioners in 2003. Unemployment benefits are paid from a fund financed by a 3% payroll tax. It is indexed in various categories to the average wage and payable for 12 months.

RELIGION

Church-State relations are regulated by laws of 1989 which guarantee religious freedom, grant the Church radio and TV programmes and permit it to run schools, hospitals and old age homes. The Church has a university (Lublin), an Academy of Catholic Theology and seminaries. The archbishop of Warsaw is the primate of Poland (since 1981, Cardinal Józef Glemp; b. 1929). The religious capital is Gniezno, whose archbishop will be the future primate. In Oct. 1978 Cardinal Karol Wojtyła, archbishop of Kraków, was elected Pope as John Paul II. In May 2005 there were seven cardinals.

Statistics of major churches as at Dec. 1997:

Church	Congregations	Places of Worship[1]	Clergy	Adherents
Roman Catholic	9,941	17,188	26,911	34,841,893
Uniate	63	101	72	110,380
Old Catholics	149	148	145	50,918
Polish Orthodox	249	3250	292	555,765
Protestant (30 sects)	1,189	865	1,882	159,906
Muslim	10	12	10	5,227
Jewish	24	17	3	1,402
Jehovah's Witnesses	1,692	—	—	122,982

[1]Dec. 1994.

CULTURE

World Heritage Sites

The ten sites under Polish jurisdiction included on the UNESCO world heritage list (with year entered) are: Kraków's Historic Centre (1978), Poland's former capital; Wieliczka Salt Mine (1978), a mine since the 13th century; Auschwitz Concentration Camp (1979), the German concentration camp and nearby Birkenau death camp; Historic Centre of Warsaw (1980), celebrating the 20th century reconstruction of the city's 18th century heart decimated during World War II; Old City of Zamosc (1992), a 16th century town; Medieval Town of Toruń (1997); Castle of the Teutonic Order in Malbork (1997), a medieval brick castle; Kalwaria Zebrzydowska: the Mannerist Architectural and Park Landscape Complex and Pilgrimage Park (1999); Churches of Peace in Jawor and Świdnica (2001), Europe's biggest timber-framed religious buildings; Wooden Churches of Southern Little Poland (2003).

In addition, Poland and Belarus are jointly responsible for Belovezhskaya Pushcha/Bialowieza Forest (1979), in the Baltic/Black Sea region; and Poland and Germany are jointly responsible for Muzkauer Park/Park Muzakowski (2004), a landscaped park astride the Neisse river.

Broadcasting

The public *Polskie Radio i Telewizja* broadcasts three radio programmes and two TV programmes. There are also four commercial TV channels: *Polsat, TVN, RTL7* and *Nasza TV*. Colour programmes are transmitted by the PAL system. A direct-to-home satellite pay television service was launched in 1998. A digital TV platform *Wizja TV* started broadcasting in Sept. 1998, followed by *Canal Plus'* digital platform. Links with the West are provided through the Eutelstat satellite. Some cable programmes are broadcast in Polish from abroad. In 1992 independent radio and TV broadcasting were introduced under the aegis of a nine-member National Council of Broadcasting and Television. Radio sets in use in 2000, 20·2m.; TV sets in 2001, 15·5m.

Cinema

In 2002 there were 854 cinema screens; admissions (2003), 23·8m. 27 full-length films were made in 2002.

Press

In 2002 there were 46 daily newspapers with a combined daily circulation of 3,598,000 (93 per 1,000 inhabitants). The most popular newspapers are *Gazeta Wyborcza, Rzeczpospolita* and the tabloid *Super Express*. 19,192 book titles were published in 1999 (including 4,176 literature, 3,829 social sciences and 3,304 applied sciences).

Tourism

There were 14·0m. foreign visitors in 2002, bringing in revenue of US$4·5bn. Germans account for about 60% of all tourists to Poland.

Festivals

The most significant festivals are the International Chopin Festival at Duszniki Zdrój, held in Aug., and the Warsaw Autumn Festival, held in Sept.

Libraries

In 1997, 9,230 libraries housed 135·87m. books.

Theatre and Opera

The audience in 156 theatres in 2000 was 6·96m.; in 1997 the 21 opera houses had a total audience for the year of 1·49m.

Museums and Galleries

There were 608 museums in 1998, with 17·69m. visitors. In 2000 there were 253 art galleries, with 2·64m. visitors.

DIPLOMATIC REPRESENTATIVES

Of Poland in the United Kingdom (47 Portland Pl., London, W1B 1JH)
Ambassador: Zbigniew Matuszewski.

Of the United Kingdom in Poland (Aleje Róż 1, 00-556 Warsaw)
Ambassador: Charles Crawford, CMG.

Of Poland in the USA (2640 16th St., NW, Washington, D.C., 20009)
Ambassador: Janusz Reiter.

Of the USA in Poland (Aleje Ujazdowskie 29/31, 00-540 Warsaw)
Ambassador: Victor Ashe.

Of Poland to the United Nations
Ambassador: Andrzej Towpik.

Of Poland to the European Union
Ambassador: Marek Grela.

FURTHER READING

Central Statistical Office, *Rocznik Statystyczny*. Annual.—*Concise Statistical Yearbook of Poland.—Statistical Bulletin*. Monthly.

Lukowski, Jerzy and Zawadzki, Hubert, *A Concise History of Poland*. CUP, 2001

Mitchell, K. D. (ed.) *Political Pluralism in Hungary and Poland: Perspectives on the Reforms*. New York, 1992

Prazmowska, Anita J., *History of Poland*. Palgrave Macmillan, Basingstoke, 2004

Sanford, G. and Gozdecka-Sanford, A., *Poland*. [Bibliography] 2nd ed. ABC-Clio, Oxford and Santa Barbara (CA), 1993

Sikorski, R., *The Polish House: An Intimate History of Poland*. London, 1997; US title: *Full Circle*. New York, 1997

Slay, B., *The Polish Economy: Crisis, Reform and Transformation*. Princeton Univ. Press, 1994

Staar, R. F. (ed.) *Transition to Democracy in Poland*. New York, 1993

Turner, Barry, (ed.) *Central Europe Profiled*. Macmillan, London, 2000

Wedel, J., *The Unplanned Society: Poland During and After Communism*. Columbia Univ. Press, 1992

National library: Biblioteka Narodowa, Rakowiecka 6, Warsaw.

National Statistical Office: Central Statistical Office, Aleje Niepodległości 208, 00-925 Warsaw.

Website: http://www.stat.gov.pl

PORTUGAL

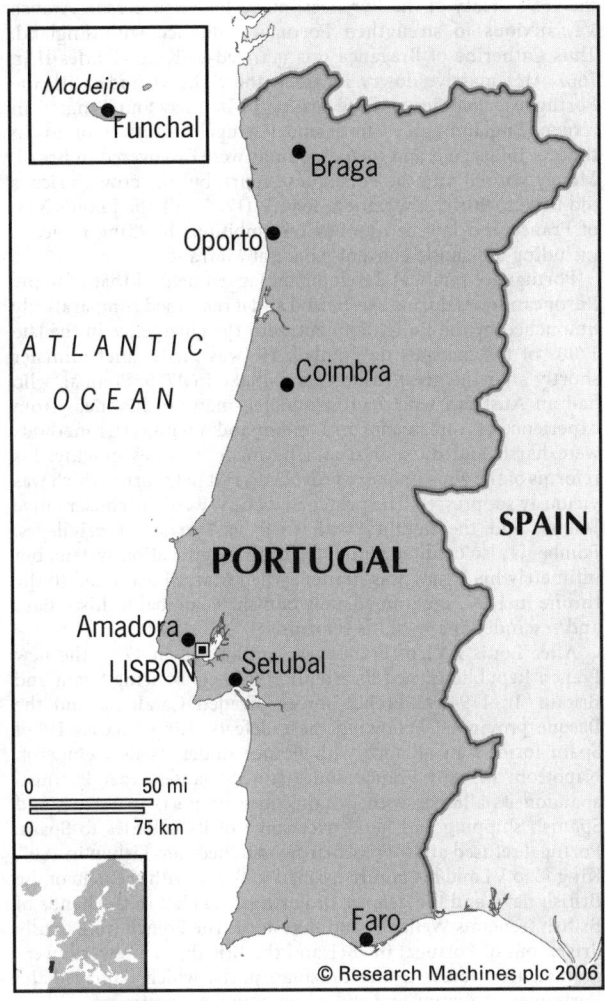

República Portuguesa

Capital: Lisbon
Population projection, 2010: 10·71m.
GDP per capita, 2003: (PPP$) 18,126
HDI/world rank: 0·904/27

KEY HISTORICAL EVENTS

The western fringe of the Iberian peninsula was inhabited from at least 8000 BC by Neolithic peoples known as Iberians. Archaeological evidence points to the arrival of Celtic tribes in the north and west of the peninsula in the first millennium BC and the establishment of Phoenician settlements in the southwest around Cádiz from around 800 BC. From 241 BC the Iberian peninsula came under the influence of Carthage, and then Rome after 206 BC. The Romans made their way north to what is now central Portugal and clashed with a Celtic federation, the Lusitanians. They resisted the Roman advance under their leader Viriathus until he was killed in 140 BC, after which the Romans were able to move north across the Douro river. In 25 BC Augustus founded Augustus Emirita (now Mérida) as the capital of Lusitania.

From AD 409, with the Roman Empire in decline, the Iberian Peninsula was invaded by Germanic tribes from central Europe, including the Suevi and Visigoths, who established Christian kingdoms. Southern Galicia was settled by the Suevi, who were converted to Christianity by St Martin of Braga in around AD 550. Following the arrival of Muslim armies in Iberia in 711, the southern part of what is now Portugal became part of the Muslim dominion of al-Andalus and absorbed its influences for five centuries. The northern and western fringes of Iberia remained largely agrarian, poor and Christian.

From 850 the Christians began to push southward: the region between the rivers Minho and Douro became known as Territorium Portugualense and was ruled by Mumadona Dias after 931. Fernando I, King of Castile, drove the Muslims from the city of Viseu in 1058 and reconquered Coimbra in 1064. Fernando's successor, Afonso VI of Leon, set up his power base in the town of Braga. His daughter, Teresa, who was married to Henry of Burgundy, then governed Portugal as regent for their son, Afonso Henriques. Teresa eventually lost the support of many of the powerful local barons, who united behind Afonso and made him the first king of Portugal in 1139.

Muslim chroniclers refer to Afonso I as 'the cursed of Allah'. He crusaded southwards through the Muslim strongholds, capturing Lisbon in 1147. However, the Portuguese reconquest was not completed for 150 years, when Afonso III finally took Algarve in the far south. Afonso III established the first Cortes (government) at Leiria in 1254. Large swathes of the newly conquered lands were given over to the army and monastic orders to ensure their protection. Afonso's son, Dinis (1279–1325), became one of the most celebrated of the Burgundian dynasty. He established trade links with other European powers and in 1317 worked with a Genoese admiral to establish a formal navy. Dinis made the vernacular, rather than Latin, the official language and founded the first university in Lisbon in 1290.

The later kings of the House of Burgundy were entangled in various marriage alliances with neighbouring Castile. Fernando I (1367–83) inherited the Portuguese crown as a battle raged in Castile between King Pedro 'the Cruel' and his half-brother Enrique de Trastámara. Both sides attempted to garner support from outside the kingdom, with the English supporting Pedro (Peter) and his heirs and the French backing Enrique (Henry) and his supporters. Enrique eventually prevailed, being crowned Enrique II of Castile in 1369. The new king offered his support to Fernando, who accepted, and Castilian rule was duly established in Portugal.

King Fernando ensured that his heiress, Beatriz, married Juan I of Castile but, though the entrenched nobility broadly supported Castilian rule, commoners in Portugal's coastal towns wanted independence and rebelled. Their choice for ruler was João of Avis, half brother of Fernando, and he was declared King João I in 1384. A year later, assisted by English archers, the Portuguese won a famous victory over Juan I and his Castilian army at the battle of Aljbarrota. This military success marked the beginning of a 200-year era of independence for Portugal, and the Anglo-Portuguese alliance was cemented by King João's marriage in 1387 to Philippa of Lancaster, sister of England's future King Henry IV.

Empire Building

Having made peace with Spain, João turned his attention overseas. The capture of the town of Ceuta on the north African coast in 1415 was the beginning of a remarkable era of discovery by Portuguese mariners, spearheaded by João's third son Henry who became known as Henry the Navigator. He founded a school of navigation at Sagres and organized numerous expeditions along the west coast of Africa. Madeira and the Azores were also discovered and settled during this period.

Relations with Castile deteriorated sharply during the reign of Afonso V (1438–81). Afonso married Juana, daughter of Enrique IV of Castile, and laid claim to the Castilian throne. Following the marriage of Fernando II and Isabella I of Castile and the merging of the powerful kingdoms of Aragon and Castile, Afonso's claim began to look increasingly untenable. There were lengthy battles for land in the Zamora and Toro regions, which Afonso eventually lost in 1476. Peace was established three years later by Afonso's heir, João II. During his reign overseas explorations were resumed, and Portugal became a haven for tens of thousands of Jews fleeing persecution in Spain.

In 1487 Bartolomeu Dias rounded the southern cape of Africa, but the Portuguese crown rejected Christopher Columbus' proposal for finding a new westward route to the Indies. He was backed instead by Fernando II and Isabella I of Castile and reached the New World in 1492. The two countries, with their fleets of sailing ships and entrepreneurial merchants, now had a stake in much of the rest of the world, and needed to divide their discoveries. The 1493 Treaty of Tordesillas gave the newly-unified Spain all lands west of a vertical line drawn 370 degrees west of the Cape Verde Islands. Land to the east was to be the property of Portugal, which happened to include Brazil, prompting speculation that Portuguese mariners already knew of its existence. In 1497, with backing from King Manuel I, Vasco da Gama set out from Lisbon in a fleet of purpose-built cargo ships known as *naus*. Two years later he returned, having mapped out a sea route to India. Indian spices were especially prized in Europe: they were used for preserving food, in the preparation of medicines and in glues, perfumes, dyes and varnishes. The Portuguese built an administrative capital at Goa, after seizing it in 1510, and by 1550 it was considered the nation's second city.

Fortified trading posts were later established along the coast of East Africa and India, and commercial centres set up with the consent of native rulers further east. The vast profits generated by the spice trade made Manuel I 'the Fortunate' one of the wealthiest rulers in Europe. But such rapid expansion came at a price: Portugal suffered from a 'brain drain'—many of the nation's entrepreneurs had moved overseas, leaving the domestic economy weakened. The king was no longer dependent on taxes from the people, who then lost political influence. The Cortes did not meet for 23 years between 1502–25 and the expulsion of many of Manuel's Jewish subjects in 1496 (a condition of his marriage to Princess Isabella of Castile—daughter of Isabella I) dealt a heavy blow to the economy, depriving it of much of its financial expertise.

When King Sebastião inherited the throne in 1557, he was keen to establish Portuguese authority closer to home, and in 1568 he launched a disastrous crusade to eradicate Islam in the Maghreb. More than 10,000 Portuguese troops were killed, including Sebastião himself by superior Moroccan forces. The throne passed to the elderly and childless Cardinal Henrique, who soon died. The line of succession passed to the cardinal's nephew, Felipe II of Spain.

Spanish Rule

Felipe II saw his opportunity and annexed Portugal in 1580. The Spanish empire was at its height and Portuguese merchants saw the commercial advantages in forming an alliance with Spain. To begin with, Portugal was granted considerable autonomy but it was gradually eroded. The Inquisition was established in Portugal and the ports of Lisbon and Oporto were closed to English and Dutch ships, which then made their own way to the east and snatched control of the spice trade. The 'Spanish domination' of Portugal lasted for 60 years, though after 1621 Spain was considerably weakened by the cost of defending its empire against France and England. A rebellion in Catalonia spurred the Portuguese to stage

their own revolution: they rallied around the duke of Bragança, who was duly crowned King João IV in 1640.

João IV was anxious to formalize new alliances with the other European powers. Spain's peace with France, set out in the 1659 Treaty of the Pyrenees, made João's successor, Afonso VI, anxious to strengthen Portugal's alliance with England. Thus Catherine of Bragança was married to King Charles II in 1662. Her massive dowry included the right to trade with the Portuguese colonies and the cession of Bombay and Tangier. In return, England agreed to defend Portugal and its colonies. In the late 1600s gold and then diamonds were discovered in Brazil. Money poured into the Portuguese court, but the crown's riches did little to enrich the nation. João V (1706–50) aped Louis XIV of France and lavished money on ambitious building projects, including a gigantic convent-palace at Mafra.

Portuguese political development lagged behind that of many European states during this period and it remained comparatively untouched by the Enlightenment until the emergence in the late 1700s of the marquis de Pombal. He was made chief minister shortly after the great Lisbon earthquake in 1755. Pombal, who had an Austrian wife, had formulated many of his ideas from experience as ambassador in London and Vienna. His methods were harsh and dictatorial and he made enemies quickly: his reforms of the wine industry provoked a riot in Oporto, which was viciously suppressed. His principal victims were the conservative Jesuits, and the nobility with their vast array of privileges. Pombal is also credited with reforming the education system, but ultimately his legacy was limited; when Maria I ascended to the throne in 1777, she immediately banished Pombal to his estates and rescinded many of his reforms.

After Louis XVI of France was guillotined in 1793, the new French Republic turned its attention to neighbouring Spain and Britain. In 1794–95 French forces invaded Catalonia and the Basque provinces. Following these defeats, King Charles IV of Spain formed an alliance with France under its new emperor, Napoleon. In 1801 France and Spain demanded that Portugal abandon its alliance with Britain, open its ports to French and Spanish shipping and hand over some of its colonies to Spain. Portugal refused and a French army marched into Lisbon in 1807. King João VI and his family escaped to Brazil with the help of the British navy and the defence of Portugal was left in the hands of British Generals Wellesley and Beresford. The French were finally driven out of Portugal in 1811 and the British, as a reward, were granted free access to the Brazilian ports, which damaged the Portuguese economy and stoked-up popular resentment.

An army-backed revolution flared up in Oporto in 1820, after which an unofficial Cortes was set up to devise a new liberal constitution. The Cortes would be a single chamber parliament elected by universal male suffrage, and feudal and clerical rights would be abolished. João VI returned from Brazil the following year and accepted the new constitution. Brazil declared its independence, with Pedro IV (João's elder son) as emperor.

Following João's death in 1826, Pedro also became king of Portugal but abdicated in favour of his daughter, Maria II, on condition that she accept a new charter limiting royal authority and marry Miguel, his brother. But Miguel seized the throne and defeated the liberals. Pedro IV returned to Portugal in 1832 to lead the liberals in the Miguelist Wars. Maria was eventually restored to the throne. As governments came and went, little was done to address the parlous state of the economy until 1852, when the duke of Saldanha introduced reforms. The late 1850s saw improvements in the nation's infrastructure under the new ministry of public works but by the start of the reign of Carlos I in 1889, Portugal was burdened with high unemployment, leading to strikes and public demonstrations. Explorations in Africa strengthened Portugal's hold on Angola and Mozambique but the British refused to give up territory which would have linked the two colonies. Carlos attempted to end inefficiency and corruption, establishing a dictatorship in 1906 under the conservative João Franco. Amidst growing public discontent, Carlos and his eldest son Prince Luís Filipe were assassinated in 1908. Manuel II succeeded to the throne but in 1910 a republican revolution forced his abdication and flight to Britain.

The first republican leader was Teófilo Braga but the change of rule did not cure Portugal's chronic economic problems. In the First World War Portugal was at first neutral, then joined the Allies in 1916. The economy deteriorated and insurrections of both the right and the left made conditions worse. In 1926 a military coup overthrew the government, and Gen. Carmona became president. António de Oliveira Salazar was made finance minister in 1928 and reorganized the national accounts.

Dictatorship to Democracy

Salazar became prime minister in 1932. His *Estado Novo* (New State) had a strongly nationalist and dictatorial flavour. Political parties, unions and strikes were abolished and dissent was crushed by the notorious PIDE (Polícia Internacional e de Defesa do Estado) secret police force. Portugal was neutral in the Second World War but allowed the Allies to establish naval and air bases. Although the colony of Goa was seized by India in 1961, Salazar was determined to cling on to the African territories. Despite growing independence movements in Angola, Guinea-Bissau and Mozambique in the 1960s, by 1968 over 100,000 Portuguese were fighting in Africa. On the domestic front, censorship of the press and of cultural activities grew especially severe in the mid-1960s and student demonstrations were sternly repressed.

In 1968 Salazar suffered a stroke and was replaced by Marcello Caetano as premier. Under Caetano repression was eased but the unpopular wars in Africa continued. In 1974, amid mounting public discontent, a group of officers formed the Movement of Armed Forces and toppled the government in a bloodless coup known as 'the Revolution of the Carnations'. Gen. António de Spínola was appointed head of the ruling military junta. The secret police force was abolished. All political prisoners were released; full civil liberties, including freedom of the press and of all political parties, were restored, and in 1975, Angola, Mozambique, São Tomé e Príncipe and Cape Verde were granted independence. East Timor was forcibly taken over by Indonesia. Following an attempted revolt in late 1975, the military junta was dissolved and a Supreme Revolutionary Council ruled until a new constitutional government resumed in the following year. During the late 1970s several moderate, Socialist-dominated governments tried unsuccessfully to stabilize the country politically and economically. In 1982 a centre-right coalition revised the constitution, reducing presidential power and the right of the military to intervene in politics. From 1983 to 1985 a coalition government under Socialist leader Mário Soares began to make some tangible improvements to the chaos and poverty that were the legacy of Salazar's long dictatorship.

In 1985 the centrist Social Democratic party under Aníbal Cavaco Silva won an undisputed majority in parliament. In 1986 Soares was elected to the presidency, and Portugal was admitted to the European Community. Political stability and economic reforms created a favourable business climate, especially for renewed foreign investment, and Portugal became one of the fastest growing economies in Europe. The Socialists returned to power as a minority government after the 1995 parliamentary elections. Macao, Portugal's colony on the south coast of China, was handed back to China in 1999. Portugal joined the single European currency in 2001. In Jan. 2006 the centre-right candidate Aníbal Cavaco Silva was elected president, beginning a period of political 'cohabitation' alongside the Socialist prime minister, Jóse Sócrates.

TERRITORY AND POPULATION

Mainland Portugal is bounded in the north and east by Spain and south and west by the Atlantic Ocean. The Atlantic archipelagoes of the Azores and of Madeira form autonomous but integral parts of the republic, which has a total area of 91,947 sq. km. Population (2001 census), 10,356,117 (5,355,976 females).

Mainland Portugal is divided into five regions. At the time of the 2001 census the regions, with their populations, were: North (3,687,293); Central (1,783,596); Lisbon and Tagus Valley (3,467,483); Alentejo (535,753); Algarve (395,218). Population of the Azores, 241,763; Madeira, 245,011. Density (2001), 113 per sq. km (North, 173; Central, 75; Lisbon and Tagus Valley, 291; Alentejo, 20; Algarve, 79; Azores, 104; Madeira, 315). In 2002 Lisbon and Tagus Valley became a smaller Lisbon province, with Central and Alentejo increasing in size. The United Nations population estimate for 2005 was 10,495,000.

The UN gives a projected population for 2010 of 10·71m.

In 2003, 54·6% of the population lived in urban areas. The populations of the districts and Autonomous Regions (2001 census):

Areas	Population	Areas	Population
North	*3,687,293*	Pinhal Interior Norte	138,535
Alto Trás os Montes	223,333	Pinhal Interior Sul	44,803
Ave	509,968	Pinhal Litoral	250,990
Cávado	393,063	Serra da Estrela	49,895
Douro	221,853	*Lisbon and Tagus Valley*[1]	*3,467,483*
Entre Douro e Vouga	276,812	Grande Lisboa	1,947,261
Grande Porto	1,260,680	Lezíria do Tejo[2]	240,832
Minho-Lima	250,275	Médio Tejo[3]	226,090
Tâmega	551,309	Oeste[3]	338,711
Central	*1,783,596*	Península de Setúbal	714,589
Baixo Mondego	340,309	*Alentejo*	*535,753*
Baixo Vouga	385,724	Alentejo Central	173,646
Beira Interior Norte	115,325	Alentejo Litoral	99,976
Beira Interior Sul	78,123	Alto Alentejo	127,026
Cova da Beira	93,579	Baixo Alentejo	135,105
Dão Lafões	286,313	*Algarve*	*395,218*

[1]Lisbon since 2002. [2]Now part of Alentejo. [3]Now part of Central.

In 2002, 239,113 foreigners were legally registered: 108,132 African; 24,806 Brazilian; 15,906 British; 14,617 Spanish; 11,877 German. 200,000 immigrants have come to Portugal from eastern Europe since 1999, mainly from Ukraine.

The chief cities are Lisbon (the capital; 2001 metropolitan area population, 2,683,000), Oporto (2001 metropolitan area population, 1,261,000), Amadora, Braga, Coimbra, Funchal (in Madeira) and Setúbal.

The national language is Portuguese.

The Azores islands lie in the mid-Atlantic Ocean, between 1,200 and 1,600 km west of Lisbon. They are divided into three widely separated groups with clear channels between, São Miguel (759 sq. km) together with Santa Maria (97 sq. km) being the most easterly; about 160 km northwest of them lies the central cluster of Terceira (382 sq. km), Graciosa (62 sq. km), São Jorge (246 sq. km), Pico (446 sq. km) and Faial (173 sq. km); still another 240 km to the northwest are Flores (143 sq. km) and Corvo (17 sq. km), the latter being the most isolated and undeveloped of the islands. São Miguel contains over half the total population of the archipelago.

Madeira comprises the island of Madeira (745 sq. km), containing the capital, Funchal; the smaller island of Porto Santo (40 sq. km), lying 46 km to the northeast of Madeira; and two groups of uninhabited islets, Ilhas Desertas (15 sq. km), being 20 km southeast of Funchal, and Ilhas Selvagens (4 sq. km), near the Canaries.

SOCIAL STATISTICS

Statistics for calendar years:

	Marriages	Live births	Still births	Deaths	Divorces
1999	68,710	116,038	437	108,268	17,881
2000	63,752	120,071	445	105,813	19,302
2001	58,390	112,825	390	105,582	19,044

	Marriages	Live births	Still births	Deaths	Divorces
2002	56,457	114,456	388	106,690	27,960
2003	53,735	112,589	—	109,148	22,818

Vital statistics rates, 2002 (per 1,000 population): birth, 11·0; death, 10·2. Annual population growth rate, 1992–2002, 0·2%. In 2001 the most popular age range for marrying was 25–29 for both males and females. Expectation of life at birth, 2003, was 73·9 years for males and 80·6 years for females. Infant mortality in 2001 was five per 1,000 live births, down from 77 per 1,000 live births in 1960, representing the greatest reduction in infant mortality rates in Europe over the past 40 years. Around one in five babies are born outside marriage, up from one in 14 in 1970. Fertility rate, 2001, 1·5 births per woman.

In 2002 Portugal received 245 asylum applications.

CLIMATE

Because of westerly winds and the effect of the Gulf Stream, the climate ranges from the cool, damp Atlantic type in the north to a warmer and drier Mediterranean type in the south. July and Aug. are virtually rainless everywhere. Inland areas in the north have greater temperature variation, with continental winds blowing from the interior. Lisbon, Jan. 52°F (11°C), July 72°F (22°C). Annual rainfall 27·4" (686 mm). Oporto, Jan. 48°F (8·9°C), July 67°F (19·4°C). Annual rainfall 46" (1,151 mm).

CONSTITUTION AND GOVERNMENT

Portugal is governed under the constitution of April 1976, amended in 1982, 1989, 1992, 1997, 2001, 2004 and 2005. The 1982 revision abolished the (military) Council of the Revolution and reduced the role of the President under it. Portugal is a sovereign, unitary republic. Executive power is vested in the *President*, directly elected for a five-year term (for a maximum of two consecutive terms). Political parties may support a candidate in presidential elections but not actually field a candidate. The President appoints a Prime Minister and, upon the latter's nomination, other members of the Council of Ministers. The 230-member *National Assembly* is a unicameral legislature elected for four-year terms by universal adult suffrage under a system of proportional representation. Women did not have the vote until 1976.

Portugal's first referendum, on whether to ease abortion restrictions, was held on 28 June 1998. 51% of voters favoured keeping most abortions a crime, against 49% in favour of permitting the procedure on demand. Turnout was just 32%. However, the result would have had legal force only if the turnout had exceeded 50%.

National Anthem

'Herois do mar, nobre povo' ('Heroes of the sea, noble breed'); words by Lopes de Mendonça, tune by Alfredo Keil.

GOVERNMENT CHRONOLOGY

(PS = Socialist Party; PSD = Social Democratic Party; UN = National Union; n/p = non-partisan)

Presidents since 1926.

1926–51	UN/military	António (Óscar de) Fragoso Carmona
1951–58	UN/military	Francisco (Higino de) Craveiro Lopes
1958–74	UN/military	Américo (de Deus Rodrigues) Thomaz
1974	National Salvation Junta (all military)	
1974	military	António (Sebastião Ribeiro) de Spínola
1974–76	military	Francisco da Costa Gomes
1976–86	military, n/p	(António dos Santos) Ramalho Eanes
1986–96	PS	Mário (Alberto Nobre Lopes) Soares
1996–2006	PS	Jorge (Fernando Branco de) Sampáio
2006–	PSD	Aníbal (António) Cavaco Silva

Prime Ministers since 1932.

1932–68	UN	António de Oliveira Salazar
1968–74	UN	Marcello (das Neves Alves) Caetano
1974	n/p	Adelino da Palma Carlos
1974–75	military	Vasco (dos Santos) Gonçalves
1975–76	military	José (Batista) Pinheiro de Azevedo
1976–78	PS	Mário (Alberto Nobre Lopes) Soares
1978	n/p	Alfredo (Jorge) Nobre da Costa
1978–79	n/p	Carlos (Alberto) da Mota Pinto
1980	PSD	Francisco (Manuel Lumbrales de) Sá Carneiro
1981–83	PSD	Francisco (José Pereira) Pinto Balsemão
1983–85	PS	Mário (Alberto Nobre Lopes) Soares
1985–95	PSD	Aníbal (António) Cavaco Silva
1995–2002	PS	António (Manuel de Oliveira) Guterres
2002–04	PSD	José Manuel Durão Barroso
2004–05	PSD	Pedro (Miguel de) Santana Lopes
2005–	PS	José Sócrates (Carvalho Pinto de Sousa)

RECENT ELECTIONS

At the presidential elections of 22 Jan. 2006, the centre-right former prime minister Aníbal Cavaco Silva won 50·5% of the vote, Manuel Alegre (ind.) 20·7%, former president Mário Soares 14·3%, Jerónimo de Sousa 8·6%, Francisco Louçã 5·3% and António Garcia Pereira 0·4%. Turnout was 62·6%.

At the parliamentary elections of 20 Feb. 2005 the Socialist Party (PS) won 121 seats (45·1% of votes cast); the Social Democratic Party (PSD), 75 (28·7%); the Communist Party/Green Party coalition (Unitarian Democratic Coalition; UDC), 14 (7·6%); the Popular Party (PP), 12 (7·3%); and the Left Bloc (BE), 8 (6·4%). Turnout was 65·0%.

European Parliament

Portugal has 24 (25 in 1999) representatives. At the June 2004 elections turnout was 38·7% (40·4% in 1999). The PS won 12 seats with 45·0% of votes cast (political affiliation in European Parliament: Party of European Socialists); the PSD 7 and the PP 2, with a combined vote of 34·0% (European People's Party–European Democrats); the UDC, 2 with 9·0% (European Unitary Left/Nordic Green Left); the BE, 1 with 5·0% (European Unitary Left/Nordic Green Left).

CURRENT ADMINISTRATION

President: Aníbal Cavaco Silva; b. 1939 (ind.; sworn in 9 March 2006).

In March 2006 the Socialist Party government was composed as follows:

Prime Minister: José Sócrates; b. 1957 (PS; sworn in 12 March 2005).

Ministers of State: Fernando Teixeira dos Santos (also *Minister of Finance*); Diogo Freitas do Amaral (also *Minister of Foreign Affairs*); António Costa (also *Minister of Internal Affairs*).

Minister of Agriculture, Rural Development and Fisheries: Jaime Silva. *Culture:* Isabel Pires de Lima. *Economy and Innovation:* Manuel Pinho. *Education:* Maria de Lurdes Rodrigues. *Environment, Territorial Planning and Regional Development:* Francisco Nunes Correia. *Health:* António Correia de Campos. *Justice:* Alberto Costa. *Labour and Social Security:* José Vieira da Silva. *National Defence:* Luís Amado. *Parliamentary Affairs:* Augusto Santos Silva. *Public Works, Transportation and Communications:* Mário Lino. *Science, Technology and Higher Education:* Mariano Gago. *Minister for the Presidency:* Pedro Silva Pereira.

Government Website: http://www.portugal.gov.pt

CURRENT LEADERS

Aníbal Cavaco Silva

Position
President

Introduction
When Aníbal Cavaco Silva was elected president on 22 Jan. 2006 he became the first centre-right politician to fill the largely ceremonial post since the country's 1974 revolution. The free-market economist played a key role in preparing Portugal's entry to the EEC in 1986 and served as prime minister from 1985–95.

Early Life
Aníbal António Cavaco Silva was born in Boliqueime, Algarve, southern Portugal on 15 July 1939. Educated in Faro and Lisbon, he graduated in finance from the Technical University of Lisbon in 1964. He worked as a researcher for the Calouste Gulbenkian Foundation in Lisbon from 1967 to 1971 before studying for a PhD in economics at the University of York, UK.

Returning to Portugal in 1974, the year of the 'Revolution of Carnations' when the socialist Armed Forces Movement toppled Dr Marcello Caetano's dictatorship, Cavaco Silva taught economics at the Catholic University of Lisbon. He also joined the newly formed centre-right Popular Democratic Party (PPD), which became the Social Democratic Party (PSD) in 1976. From 1977 he worked as director of the research and statistics department of the Bank of Portugal. Elected to parliament for the PSD in Oct. 1980, Cavaco Silva served as minister of finance and planning, initially under PSD leader and prime minister, Francisco Sá Carneiro, and then under Francisco Balsemão.

A powerful advocate of free-market economics, Cavaco Silva's reforms, combined with a constitutional reduction in presidential power, paved the way for Portugal's entry into the EEC (later EU) in 1986. Elected head of the PSD on 2 June 1985, he led the party to victory in elections in Oct. 1985. He retained the position for ten years, the longest tenure of any democratically elected prime minister in Portuguese history. The PSD won a clear majority of seats in legislative elections in both 1987 and 1991, with analysts attributing Cavaco Silva's success to economic liberalization, tax cuts and the flow of funds from the EEC.

Cavaco Silva stepped down as leader of the PSD prior to the 1995 elections, which were won by the Socialist Party. He stood in the 1996 presidential election but after losing to the Socialist candidate, Jorge Sampaio, he retired from politics, serving as an advisor to the board of the Bank of Portugal and teaching economics at the Catholic University of Portugal. In Oct. 2005 Cavaco Silva returned to the political fray and announced his candidacy for the forthcoming presidential election. He received 50·5% of the votes cast on 22 Jan. 2006, narrowly avoiding the need for a second round, and was sworn in on 9 March 2006.

Career in Office
Cavaco Silva's victory over the two Socialist candidates, Manuel Alegre and Mário Soares, was a setback for the Socialist prime minister, Jóse Sócrates, who had presided over a period of economic stagnation. The result ushers in a new era of 'cohabitation' in Portuguese politics, but analysts predict that the two leaders will find common ground to implement economic reform.

José Sócrates

Position
Prime Minister

Introduction
José Sócrates was swept into power as Portugal's prime minister following a resounding victory for his Socialist Party (PS) in a snap parliamentary election on 20 Feb. 2005. The former civil engineer is a modernizer who describes himself as a 'market-oriented socialist'. Previously an environment minister, he is committed to sustainable development and sees educational reform and the development of high-tech industries as a way of reviving the country's flagging economy.

Early Life
José Sócrates Carvalho Pinto de Sousa was born in Vilar de Macada, Alijó, near the northern city of Oporto, on 6 Sept. 1957. He attended secondary school in Covilhã in the district of Castelo Branco and went on to study at the Institute of Engineering in Coimbra, before completing a masters degree in medical engineering at the National School of Public Health. Sócrates then worked as a medical engineer for Castelo Branco's municipal authority. He joined the PS in 1981 and was first elected as a member of the Portuguese assembly in 1987, the year after the government—a Social Democratic Party (PSD)-led coalition—had taken the country into the European Community. In 1991 Sócrates became a member of the National Secretariat of the PS, and was spokesman for the environment.

Following the victory of the Socialists over the centre-right PSD in the 1995 general election, Sócrates held a range of portfolios under Prime Minister António Guterres. He served as secretary of state in the ministry of the environment and territorial planning for two years from 1995, before being made deputy minister to Guterres. In Oct. 1999, after Guterres had led the PS to another election win, Sócrates was promoted to minister for the environment, a post he held until the parliamentary elections of March 2002. He gained a reputation for boldness and determination, and is widely regarded as the man who brought the Euro 2004 football tournament to Portugal.

When the Socialists lost power to the PSD, led by José Manuel Durão Barroso, in March 2002, Sócrates remained in the spotlight by taking part in a weekly television debate against Pedro Santana Lopes, then the Social Democratic mayor of Lisbon. Following the resignation of Ferro Rodrigues as leader of the PS in 2004, Sócrates bid for the post of secretary-general, and won the vote of almost 80% of party members in Sept. 2004. Sócrates was again in direct opposition to Santana Lopes, who had taken over as prime minister and leader of the PSD in July 2004 when Barroso resigned to become head of the European Commission. Already unpopular at the time of Barroso's resignation, the PSD-led coalition struggled to improve Portugal's moribund economy. There was also a month-long delay to the start of the school year and disunity over Santana Lopes' plan to introduce tax cuts and public-sector pay rises. By Nov. loss of confidence in Santana Lopes' administration had reached the point where the president, Jorge Sampãio, felt obliged to dissolve parliament and call a snap general election, two years ahead of schedule.

Sócrates focused the PS' campaign on the promise to provide disciplined and transparent leadership and pledged to reform the country's education system, alleviate poverty and boost employment. The strategy proved successful—the PS gained 45% of the vote in the elections on 20 Feb. 2005, up from 38% in 2002. With 121 seats in Portugal's 230-seat parliament, it was the first time since the end of the Salazar-Caetano dictatorship in 1974 that the PS had received an outright majority. On 24 Feb. Sócrates was called on by President Sampãio to form a new government, which took office on 12 March 2005.

Career in Office
In his inaugural address as Portugal's prime minister, Sócrates pledged to restore confidence in the country and its institutions. He also vowed to increase the economy's competitiveness while cutting the budget deficit and fulfilling the requirements of the European Stability and Growth Pact. Sócrates said his model for the country was a 'Nordic social democracy'—a society combining efficient capitalist enterprise with generous social services.

However, critics described Sócrates' vision as unobtainable, pointing out that his economic reforms would lead to further job losses and suggesting that improvements to the education system to provide a labour force adapted to high-tech industries would take many years.

DEFENCE

Conscription was abolished in Nov. 2004. Portugal now has a purely professional army.

In 2003 defence expenditure totalled US$3,173m. (US$311 per capita), representing 2·1% of GDP.

Army

Strength (2002) 25,400. There are Army reserves totalling 210,000. Paramilitary forces include the National Republican Guard (25,600) and the Public Security Police (20,800).

Navy

The combatant fleet comprises two French-built diesel submarines and six frigates. Naval personnel in 2002 totalled 10,800 (360 conscripts) including 1,580 marines. There were 930 naval reserves.

Air Force

The Air Force in 2002 had a strength of about 7,000. There were 50 combat aircraft plus 15 in store.

INTERNATIONAL RELATIONS

Portugal is a member of the UN, WTO, BIS, EU, OECD, NATO, WEU, the Council of Europe, OSCE, CERN, Inter-American Development Bank and IOM. Portugal is a signatory to the Schengen accord abolishing border controls between Portugal, Austria, Belgium, Denmark, Finland, France, Germany, Greece, Iceland, Italy, Luxembourg, the Netherlands, Norway, Spain and Sweden.

The Community of Portuguese-speaking Countries (CPLP, comprising Angola, Brazil, Cape Verde, Guinea-Bissau, Mozambique, Portugal and São Tomé e Príncipe) was founded in July 1996 with headquarters in Lisbon, primarily as a cultural and linguistic organization.

ECONOMY

Services account for about 68% of GDP, industry 28% and agriculture 4%.

Overview

The economy has become increasingly service-based since the 1980s. The agriculture and fishing sectors accounted for 3·8% of GDP in 2000, compared to 24% in 1960. The primary sector accounted for 12·1% of total employment in 2001 owing, according to the Economist Intelligence Unit, to inefficient land tenure rights and the sluggish adoption of productivity-enhancing farming methods. Since joining the EC in 1986 Portugal has attracted significant amounts of foreign direct investment and income levels have approached the EU average. Convergence has stalled, however, and Eastern Europe has become a rival for foreign investment. Though its labour costs are the lowest in Western Europe, the liberalization of Eastern Europe means Portugal can no longer rely on labour costs alone for competitiveness.

Privatization and liberalization have proceeded steadily over the years. Export industries, such as clothing and textiles, have been modernized but industrial restructuring has been slow and the industrial base lacks economies of scale. Productivity remains well below the EU average, primarily because of poor management skills and a weak education system. Portugal has been among the most serious violators of the euro zone's 3% deficit ceiling. The country has also been running structural trade and current-account deficits. Trade is strongly oriented towards Europe, with other EU countries accounting for over three-quarters of both exports and imports.

Currency

On 1 Jan. 1999 the euro (EUR) became the legal currency in Portugal; irrevocable conversion rate 200·482 escudos to 1 euro. The euro, which consists of 100 cents, has been in circulation since 1 Jan. 2002. There are seven euro notes in different colours and sizes denominated in 500, 200, 100, 50, 20, 10 and 5 euros, and eight coins denominated in 2 and 1 euros, then 50, 20, 10, 5, 2 and 1 cents. On the introduction of the euro there was a 'dual circulation' period before the escudo ceased to be legal tender on 28 Feb. 2002. Euro banknotes in circulation on 1 Jan. 2002 had a total value of €10·6bn.

Inflation rates (based on OECD statistics):

1995	1996	1997	1998	1999	2000	2001	2002	2003	2004
4·0%	2·9%	1·9%	2·2%	2·2%	2·8%	4·4%	3·7%	3·3%	2·5%

Gold reserves were 19·51m. troy oz in June 2002 and foreign exchange reserves US$10,125m. Total money supply was €7,091m. in June 2002.

Budget

In 2001 budgetary central government revenue was €33,913m. (€32,942m. in 2000) and expenditure €37,748m. (€35,397m. in 2000). Principal sources of revenue in 2001: taxes on goods and services, €14,343m.; taxes on income, profits and capital gains, €11,153m.; grants, €1,818m. Main items of expenditure by economic type in 2001: compensation of employees, €15,763m.; grants, €5,784m.; interest, €3,840m.

The standard rate of VAT is 21·0% (reduced rates, 12% and 5%).

Performance

Real GDP growth rates (based on OECD statistics):

1995	1996	1997	1998	1999	2000	2001	2002	2003	2004
4·3%	3·6%	4·2%	4·7%	3·9%	3·8%	2·0%	0·5%	−1·2%	1·2%

In the years since Portugal joined the European Union its GDP per head has risen from being 53% of the EU average to being 71% in 2002. Portugal's total GDP in 2004 was US$168·3bn.

Banking and Finance

The central bank and bank of issue is the Bank of Portugal, founded in 1846 and nationalized in 1974. Its *Governor* is Vítor Manuel Ribeiro Constâncio.

On 31 Dec. 1998 there were 81 banks, six savings institutions and 160 mutual agricultural credit institutions. The largest Portuguese bank is the state-owned Caixa Geral de Depósitos, which held 21% of all deposits at the end of 1998. There were 19 branches of foreign credit institutions operating in Portugal in 1998.

There are stock exchanges in Lisbon and Oporto.

ENERGY AND NATURAL RESOURCES

Environment

Portugal's carbon dioxide emissions from the consumption and flaring of fossil fuels in 2002 were the equivalent of 6·7 tonnes per capita.

Electricity

Installed capacity was 11·2m. kW in 2002. Production in 2002 was 46·10bn. kWh; consumption per capita was 4,647 kWh. Portugal's electricity market is in the process of being fully liberalized.

Minerals

Portugal possesses considerable mineral wealth. Production in tonnes (2001): limestone, marl and calcite, 37,654,000; granite, 30,155,000; marble, 835,000; salt, 625,785; kaolin, 146,436; copper, 82,965; tin, 1,174; tungsten, 698.

Agriculture

There were 416,000 farms in 2000. The agricultural sector employs 11·5% of the workforce. In 2001 there were 1·99m. ha. of arable land and 715,000 ha. of permanent crops.

The following figures show the production (in 1,000 tonnes) of the chief crops:

Crop	2000	2001	2002	Crop	2000	2001	2002
Cabbages[1]	155	141	140	Olive oil[2]	249	350	310
Carrots[1]	150	150	150	Olives[1]	260	271	240
Fruits				Onions[1]	110	110	110
oranges	255	222	277	Potatoes	743	694	781
apples	227	265	300	Rice	143	146	146
grapes	892	895	1,039	Sugarbeets	462	281	644
pears	142	142	125	Tomatoes	891	912	867
Maize	875	907	797	Wheat	355	154	413
Oats	112	39	61	Wine[2]	6,452	7,525	6,421

[1]Estimates. [2]In hectolitres.

Livestock (1,000 head):

	2000	2001	2002
Cattle	1,414	1,404	1,395
Pigs	2,338	2,389	2,344
Sheep	3,578	3,459	3,457
Goats	623	561	538
Poultry[1]	43,000	42,000	42,000

[1]Estimates.

Animal products in 2001 (1,000 tonnes): meat, 805·9; milk, 2,052·9; eggs, 124·5; cheese, 76·5.

Forestry

Forests covered 3·67m. ha. (40·1% of the land area) in 2000. Portugal is a major producer of cork. Estimated production, 2001, 158,000 tonnes; production of resin, 15,000 tonnes. Timber production was 9·67m. cu. metres in 2003.

Fisheries

The fishing industry is important, although much less so than in the past, and the Portuguese eat more fish per person than in any other European Union member country (more than twice the EU average). In 2002 there were 10,548 registered fishing vessels (8,284 with motors) and 21,554 registered fishermen. The catch was 148,246 tonnes in 2002 (almost exclusively from marine waters).

The 2002 fishing catch consisted of:

Species	Tonnes	Value (in €1m.)
Sardine	63,731	38,128
Mackerel	22,255	26,407
Shellfish	18,975	75,149
Other	43,285	127,404
Total	148,246	267,088

INDUSTRY

The leading companies by market capitalization in Portugal in Nov. 2005 were: EDP—Electricidade de Portugal (US$10·7bn.); Portugal Telecom SGPS SA (US$10·7bn.); and BCP—Banco Comercial Português (US$8·1bn.).

Output of major industrial products (in tonnes unless otherwise specified):

Product	2001	2002
Ready-mix concrete	25,658,038	25,567,852
Portland cement	10,162,310	9,760,964
Refined sugar	381,626	399,621
Preparation of animal food feeds	3,933,649	3,905,501
Beer (hectolitres)	6,829,719	7,124,710
Woven fabrics of synthetic staple fibres[1]	60,624	56,251
Footwear with leather uppers (1,000 pairs)	72,373	68,757
Wood pulp	1,784,347	1,806,403

Product	2001	2002
Petrol	2,619,805	2,484,639
Glass bottles (1,000)	3,663,323	3,890,782

[1]In 1,000 sq. metres.

Labour

The maximum working week was reduced from 44 hours to 40 in 1997. A minimum wage is fixed by the government. In 2004 the minimum wage was €365·60 a month. Retirement is at 65 years for men and 62 for women. In 2003, out of a working population of 5,460,300 (2,947,900 male), 5,118,000 (2,787,100 male) were employed. Unemployment has been gradually increasing, from 4·1% in 2001 to 5·0% in 2002, 6·2% in 2003 and 6·7% in 2004. In June 2005 it stood at 7·1% (still less than the EU average), down slightly from an eight-year high of 7·3% in Feb. 2005. Employment (in 1,000) by sector, 2003 (males in parentheses): services, 2,823·1 (1,283·6); industry, construction, energy and water, 1,652·8 (1,174·7); agriculture, forestry and fishing, 642·1 (328·7). The immigrant population makes up 10% of the labour force.

Trade Unions

There are two major trade union confederations in Portugal: the Confederação Geral dos Trabalhadores Portugueses—Intersindical Nacional (CGTP) and the União Geral de Trabalhadores (UGT). In 2002 there were 388 unions.

INTERNATIONAL TRADE

Imports and Exports

In 2003 imports (c.i.f.) totalled US$43·71bn. (US$36·94bn. in 2002); exports (f.o.b.), US$30·49bn. (US$24·96bn. in 2002).

In 2003 chemicals, manufactured goods classified chiefly by material and miscellaneous manufactured articles accounted for 40·6% of Portugal's imports and 50·2% of exports; machinery and transport equipment 33·9% of imports and 36·7% of exports; food, live animals, beverages and tobacco 11·3% of imports and 6·8% of exports; mineral fuels, lubricants and related materials 10·4% of imports and 2·5% of exports; and crude materials, inedible, animal and vegetable oil and fats 3·8% of imports and 3·8% of exports.

Imports and exports to main trading partners, 2002 and 2003 (in US$1m.):

From or to	Imports		Exports	
	2002	2003	2002	2003
Spain	10,266·4	12,505·4	5,058·1	6,782·0
Germany	5,515·4	6,429·2	4,650·8	4,668·4
France	3,755·9	4,307·6	3,045·7	3,884·4
UK	1,917·5	2,131·4	2,628·0	3,322·2
Italy	2,346·0	2,765·5	1,179·8	1,472·8
Netherlands	1,697·9	1,963·6	944·2	1,151·2
Belgium/Luxembourg	1,202·0	1,418·5	1,159·3	1,434·6
USA	853·4	874·3	1,445·0	1,800·8

In 2003 fellow European Union members accounted for 76·0% of Portugal's imports and 78·5% of exports.

COMMUNICATIONS

Roads

In 2001 there were 1,659 km of motorways, 7,510 km of national roads and 4,500 km of secondary roads. In 2001 the number of vehicles registered included 4,416,557 passenger cars, 572,082 motorcycles and mopeds, 334,379 vans and lorries and 18,280 buses and coaches. In 2002 there were 1,655 deaths in road accidents. With 16·0 deaths per 100,000 population in 2002, Portugal has among the highest death rates in road accidents of any industrialized country.

Rail

In 2002 total railway length was 3,600 km. Passenger-km travelled in 2002 came to 3·93bn. and freight tonne-km to 2·58bn. There is a metro (19 km) and tramway (94 km) in Lisbon. A new metro was opened in Oporto in 2002.

Civil Aviation

There are international airports at Portela (Lisbon), Pedras Rubras (Oporto), Faro (Algarve) and Funchal (Madeira). The national carrier is the state-owned TAP-Air Portugal, with some domestic and international flights being provided by Portugália. In 1998 TAP flew 77·7m. km, carrying 4,680,900 passengers; Portugália flew 18·4m. km, carrying 841,600 passengers (472,300 international). In 2001 Lisbon handled 9,212,000 passengers (6,927,000 on international flights) and 82,900 tonnes of freight. Faro was the second busiest in terms of passenger traffic, with 4,579,000 passengers, and Oporto was the second busiest for freight, with 36,200 tonnes.

Shipping

In 2002, 10,476 vessels of 111·31m. tonnes entered the mainland ports. 251,093 passengers embarked and 250,658 disembarked at all Portuguese ports during 2002; 12·84m. tonnes of cargo were loaded and 42·76m. tonnes unloaded. In 2002 merchant ships totalled 1,100,000 GRT, including oil tankers 424,000 GRT.

Telecommunications

Portugal Telecom (PT) was formed from a merger of three state-owned utilities in 1994. It is now fully privatized. Telephone subscribers numbered 12,889,900 in 2002 (1,238·3 per 1,000 population) and there were 1,394,000 PCs in use (133·9 per 1,000 persons). There were 8,528,900 mobile phone subscribers in 2002 and 108,000 fax machines. Portugal had 4·4m. Internet users in June 2002.

Postal Services

The number of post offices was 3,537 in 2003; a total of 1,082m. pieces of mail were processed during 2003.

SOCIAL INSTITUTIONS

Justice

There are four judicial districts (Lisbon, Oporto, Coimbra and Evora) divided into 55 circuits. In 2002 there were 371 courts, including 327 common courts of first instance. There are also 29 administration and fiscal courts.

There are four courts of appeal in each district, and a Supreme Court in Lisbon.

Capital punishment was abolished completely in the Constitution of 1976.

In 2002 there were 55 prisons with an inmate capacity of 11,465. The population in penal institutions in May 2003 was 14,300 (137 per 100,000 of national population).

Education

Adult literacy rate was 92·5% in 2001 (male 95·0%; female 90·3%). Compulsory education has been in force since 1911, but only 9·8% of the population goes on to further education, compared to the EU average of 21·2%. In 2001 only 21·2% of the population aged 25–64 had undergone secondary education compared to an EU average of 65·7%.

In 2000–01 there were 6,233 pre-school establishments (3–6 years) with 224,575 pupils, and 13,859 compulsory basic school establishments (6–10 years) with 1,139,402 pupils. There were 378,691 pupils in secondary schools in 2000–01. There were 35,949 teachers on the mainland in the 1st cycle of basic school, and 113,267 in the 2nd and 3rd cycles of basic school and in secondary schools.

The higher education system consists of 14 state universities and 14 private universities, plus one non-integrated university institution, 15 state polytechnic institutions, 17 non-integrated polytechnic institutions, one Catholic university and 105 private higher education institutions; plus four military university institutions and one military polytechnic institution.

In 2000–01 there were a total of 310 higher education institutes altogether with a total of 387,703 students. Females account for 64% of Portugal's university graduates.

Total expenditure on education came to 6·1% of GNP in 2001–02 (12·7% of total government expenditure).

Health

There were 391 clinics in 2002; and 221 hospitals and 512 medical centres in 1999. In 2002 there were 33,751 doctors, 4,134 dentists, 7,962 pharmacists and 41,799 nurses. In 2003 Portugal spent 9·6% of its GDP on health.

Welfare

In 2001, €25,817m. were paid in social security benefits. Cash payments in euros (and types) were: 9,984m. (old age), 8,070m. (sickness), 3,186m. (disability), 1,846m. (survivors), 1,458m. (family), 940m. (unemployment), 328m. (social exclusion), 6m. (housing).

RELIGION

There is freedom of worship, both in public and private, with the exception of creeds incompatible with morals and the life and physical integrity of the people. There were 9·52m. Roman Catholics in 2001. In May 2005 there were two cardinals.

CULTURE

World Heritage Sites

(With year entered on list). In the Central Zone of the Town of Angra do Heroísmo in the Azores (1983) are the fortresses of San Sebastião and San Filipe, the latter built around 1590 on the orders of King Phillip II of Spain. The Monastery of the Hieronymites was built at the turn of the 16th century in Belém, Lisbon, while the capital's Tower of Belém was constructed as a monument to Vasco da Gama's explorations (both 1983). The Monastery of Batalha (1983) near Leiria was built from 1388. The Convent of Christ in Tomar (1983) was originally built in 1160 as the centre of the Templar order. It was taken over by the Order of Christ in 1360 of which Henry the Navigator was made governor in 1418, and was greatly enriched in the 16th century. Other sites are the medieval walled Historic Centre of Evora (1988), the Gothic Cistercian 12th century Monastery of Alcobaça, north of Lisbon (1989), the Cultural Landscape of Sintra (1995), the Historic Centre of Oporto (1996), the Upper Palaeolitic Rock-Art Sites in the Côa Valley (1998) and the Laurisilva of Madeira (1999), an area of biodiverse laurel forest. In 2001 two more sites were added: the Alto Douro Wine Region, famous for its port wine since the 18th century, and the Historic Centre of Guimarães, a town closely associated with the formation of Portuguese identity. The Landscape of the Pico Island Vineyard Culture followed in 2004.

Broadcasting

Radiodifusão Portuguesa broadcasts three programmes on medium wave and on FM as well as three regional services and an external service, Radio Portugal (English, French, Italian). There are two state-owned TV channels (Canal 1 and Radiotelevisão Portuguesa 2) and two independent channels, including one religious (colour by PAL). Radio Trans Europe is a high-powered short-wave station, retransmitting programmes of different broadcasting organizations. Number of receivers: TV (2001), 4·27m.; radio (2000), 3·08m. In 2001 there were 1·12m. cable TV subscribers.

Press

In 2002 there were 30 daily newspapers (morning and evening editions) including six in the Azores and three in Madeira, with a combined annual circulation of 489,366,999. In addition there were 1,077 periodicals in 2002 with a combined circulation of 196,072,944. In 2002 a total of 11,331 book titles were published.

Tourism

In 2002 tourist revenue increased to US$5,919m. In 2002 there were (in 1,000) 27,194 foreign visitors (28,150 in 2001), including from Spain, 20,706; UK, 1,973; Germany, 906; France, 867; the Netherlands, 508; Italy, 321. There were 1,898 hotel establishments with 239,903 accommodation capacity in 2002.

DIPLOMATIC REPRESENTATIVES

Of Portugal in the United Kingdom (11 Belgrave Sq., London, SW1X 8PP)
Ambassador: Fernando Andresen Guimarães.

Of the United Kingdom in Portugal (Rua de São Bernardo 33, 1200 Lisbon)
Ambassador: Dame Glynne Evans, DBE, CMG.

Of Portugal in the USA (2012 Massachusetts Ave., NW, Washington, D.C., 20036)
Ambassador: Pedro Manuel Dos Reis Alves Catarino.

Of the USA in Portugal (Ave. das Forcas Armadas, 1600 Lisbon)
Ambassador: Alfred Hoffman, Jr.

Of Portugal to the United Nations
Ambassador: João Manuel Guerra Salgueiro.

FURTHER READING

Instituto Nacional de Estatística. *Anuário Estatístico de Portugal/Statistics Year-Book.— Estatísticas do Comércio Externo.* 2 vols. Annual from 1967

Birmingham, David, *A Concise History of Portugal.* CUP, 1993
Laidlar, John, *Lisbon.* [Bibliography] ABC-Clio, Oxford and Santa Barbara (CA), 1997
Maxwell, K., *The Making of Portuguese Democracy.* CUP, 1995
Page, Martin, *The First Global Village: How Portugal Changed the World.* Editorial Notícias, Lisbon, 2002
Saraiva, J. H., *Portugal: A Companion History.* Manchester, 1997
Wheeler, D. L., *Historical Dictionary of Portugal.* Metuchen (NJ), 1994

National library: Biblioteca Nacional de Lisboa, Campo Grande, Lisbon.
National Statistical Office: Instituto Nacional de Estatística (INE), Avenida António José de Almeida, 1000–043 Lisbon.
Website: http://www.ine.pt

QATAR

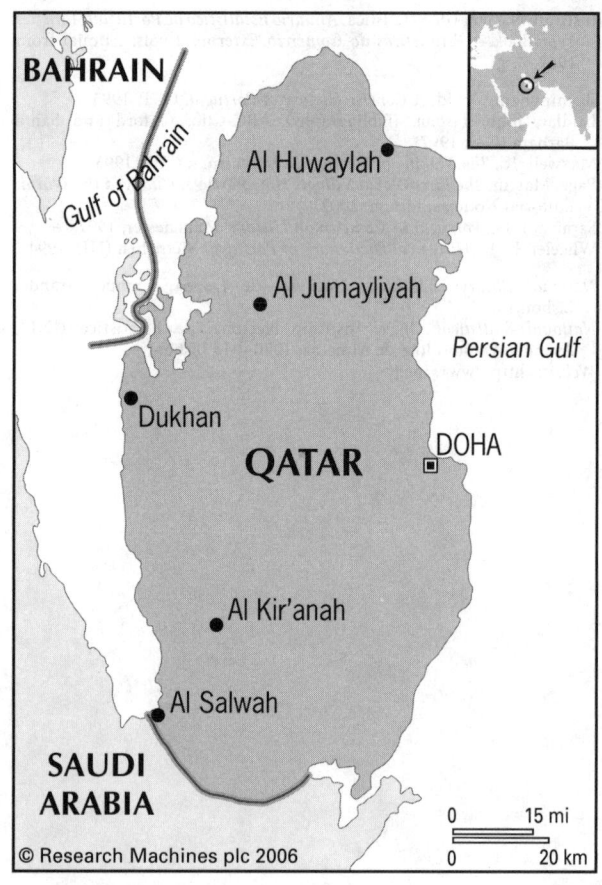

BAHRAIN

Gulf of Bahrain

Al Huwaylah

Al Jumayliyah

Persian Gulf

Dukhan

QATAR

DOHA

Al Kir'anah

Al Salwah

SAUDI ARABIA

0   15 mi
0   20 km

© Research Machines plc 2006

the most important of which is Halul, the storage and export terminal for the offshore oilfields. The area of Qatar is 11,493 sq. km. Population at the 2004 census, 744,029 (496,382 males); density 64·7 per sq. km. In 2003, 92·0% of the population lived in urban areas.

The UN gives a projected population for 2010 of 894,000.

In 2004 there were ten municipalities:

	2004 census population		2004 census population
Doha	339,847	Al Jumayliyah	10,303
Al Rayyan	272,860	Al Shamal	4,915
Al Wakra	31,441	Jarian Al Batnah	6,678
Umm Salal	31,605	Al Ghwayriyah	2,159
Al Khour	31,547	Mesaieed	12,674

The capital is Doha, which is the main port, and had a census population in 2004 of 339,847. Other towns are Dukhan (the centre of oil production), Umm Said (the oil-terminal of Qatar), Ruwais, Wakra, Al-Khour, Umm Salal Mohammad and Umm-Bab.

About 40% of the population are Arabs, 18% Indian, 18% Pakistani and 10% Iranian. Other nationalities make up the remaining 14%.

The official language is Arabic.

SOCIAL STATISTICS

Births, 2002, 12,200; deaths, 1,220; marriages, 2,351; divorces, 732. 2002 rates per 1,000 population: births, 20·3; deaths, 2·0. Qatar's 2002 death rate was the second lowest in the world (only Kuwait's was lower). Infant mortality, 2001 (per 1,000 live births), 11. Expectation of life in 2003 was 71·2 years for males and 76·0 for females. Annual population growth rate, 1992–2002, 2·0%. Fertility rate, 2001, 3·4 births per woman.

CLIMATE

The climate is hot and humid. Doha, Jan. 62°F (16·7°C), July 98°F (36·7°C). Annual rainfall 2·5" (62 mm).

CONSTITUTION AND GOVERNMENT

Qatar is ruled by an *Amir*. HH Sheikh Hamad bin Khalifa Al Thani, KCMG (b. 1952) assumed power after deposing his father on 27 June 1995. The heir apparent was Sheikh Hamad's third son, Sheikh Jasim bin Hamad Al Thani (b. 1978), but in Aug. 2003 he named his fourth son, Sheikh Tamim bin Hamad Al Thani (b. 1979), as heir apparent instead.

Qatar's first written constitution was approved in June 2004 and came into force on 9 June 2005. It allows for a 45-member *Consultative Council* or *Majlis al-Shura*, with 30 members directly elected and 15 appointed by the Amir.

A *Council of Ministers* is assisted by a 35-member nominated Advisory Council.

National Anthem

'As-Salam Al-Amiri' ('Peace for the Amir'); words by Sheikh Mubarak bin Saïf al-Thani, tune by Abdul Aziz Nasser Obaidan.

GOVERNMENT CHRONOLOGY

Amirs since 1971.
1971–72   Sheikh Ahmad bin Ali Al Thani
1972–95   Sheikh Khalifa bin Hamad Al Thani
1995–   Sheikh Hamad bin Khalifa Al Thani

RECENT ELECTIONS

It was decided in 1998 that the Central Municipal Council should be an elected Assembly.

Dawlat Qatar
(State of Qatar)

Capital: Doha
Population projection, 2010: 894,000
GDP per capita, 2002: (PPP$) 19,844
HDI/world rank: 0·849/40

KEY HISTORICAL EVENTS

Qatar embraced Islam in the 7th century AD. As with the rest of the Middle East, Qatar came under Turkish rule for several centuries. Ottoman power was nominal, with real power being in the hands of local sheikhs and tribal leaders. In 1915 the Turks withdrew, and on 3 Nov. 1916 Qatar signed a protection treaty with Britain. The dominant economic activity had traditionally been pearl diving, but around 1930 the pearl market collapsed. In 1939 oil was discovered. Although the Second World War delayed progress, exporting began in 1949. This was to change Qatar dramatically. Qatar declared its independence from Britain on 3 Sept. 1971, ending the Treaty of 1916 which was replaced by a treaty of friendship between the two countries.

TERRITORY AND POPULATION

Qatar is a peninsula running north into the Persian Gulf. It is bounded in the south by Saudi Arabia. The territory includes a number of islands in the coastal waters of the peninsula,

CURRENT ADMINISTRATION

In March 2006 the government comprised:

Amir, Minister of Defence and C.-in-C. of the Armed Forces: HH Sheikh Hamad bin Khalifa Al Thani; b. 1952.

Prime Minister: Sheikh Abdallah bin Khalifa Al Thani; b. 1959 (in office since 29 Oct. 1996).

First Deputy Prime Minister and Minister of Foreign Affairs: Sheikh Hamad bin Jasim bin Jabir Al Thani. *Second Deputy Prime Minister and Minister of Energy and Industry:* Abdallah bin Hamad Al Attiyah. *Deputy Prime Minister:* Muhammad bin Khalifa Al Thani. *Economy and Commerce:* Sheikh Mohammed bin Ahmed bin Jassim Al Thani. *Finance:* Yusif Husayn Al Kamal. *Education:* Sheikha Ahmad Al Mahmoud. *Justice:* Hasan bin Abdallah Al Ghanim. *Endowments and Islamic Affairs:* Faisal bin Abdullah Al Mahmoud. *Municipal Affairs and Agriculture:* Hassan Dhabit Al Dousari. *Public Health:* Dr Hajar bin Ahmad Al Hajar. *Housing and Civil Service Affairs:* Sheikh Falah bin Jasim bin Jabir Al Thani. *Interior:* Abdullah bin Khalid Al Thani.

CURRENT LEADERS

Sheikh Hamad bin Khalifa Al Thani

Position
Amir

Introduction
Sheikh Hamad is the eighth member of the Al Thani family to rule Qatar, having seized power from his father, Sheikh Khalifa, on 27 June 1995.

Early Life
Born in Doha in 1952, Hamad graduated from the Royal Military Academy, Sandhurst in 1971. He then joined the Qatari military with the rank of major. In 1975 he was promoted to major-gen. and commander-in-chief of the armed forces. On his appointment as Crown Prince and heir apparent in May 1977, he also became minister of defence.

Career in Office
Having ousted his father in 1995, Hamad appointed himself prime minister. However, in Oct. 1996 he relinquished the premiership to his younger brother Sheikh Abdallah. The Amir is credited with initiating plans for an elected consultative council (through the new constitution which he approved in 2004 and which took effect in June 2005), giving women the right to vote in municipal elections (from 1999) and ending official media censorship. He has also encouraged foreign investment in Qatar's oil and natural gas industries. In foreign relations he has overseen the resolution of longstanding border disputes with Bahrain and Saudi Arabia. In Aug. 2003 he named his fourth son as his heir apparent.

DEFENCE

Defence expenditure in 2003 totalled US$1,923m. (US$3,082 per capita), representing 10·0% of GDP. The expenditure per capita in 2003 was the highest in the world.

Army
Personnel (2002) 8,500.

Navy
Personnel in 2002 totalled 1,800; the base is at Doha.

Air Force
The Air Force operates 18 combat aircraft including Mirage 2000 fighters and 19 armed helicopters. Personnel (2002) 2,100.

INTERNATIONAL RELATIONS

Qatar is a member of the UN, WTO, the League of Arab States, OPEC, the Gulf Co-operation Council, OIC and Islamic Development Bank.

In March 2001 the International Court of Justice ruled on a long-standing dispute between Bahrain and Qatar over the boundary between the two countries and ownership of certain islands. Both countries accepted the decision.

ECONOMY

Industry accounted for 70·7% of GDP in 2002, services 28·9% and agriculture 0·4%.

Currency
The unit of currency is the *Qatari riyal* (QAR) of 100 *dirhams*, introduced in 1973. Foreign exchange reserves were US$1,184m. in April 2002 and gold reserves 169,000 troy oz. Total money supply in April 2002 was 5,685m. riyals. There was inflation of 6·8% in 2004.

In 2001 the six Gulf Arab states—Qatar, along with Bahrain, Kuwait, Oman, Saudi Arabia and the United Arab Emirates—signed an agreement to establish a single currency by 2010.

Budget
Revenue (2001–02) 22,754m. riyals; expenditure, 20,504m. riyals. Crude oil accounts for about 90% of revenues.

Performance
Real GDP growth was 7·3% 2002, 8·6% in 2003 and 9·3% in 2004. Qatar's total GDP in 2001 was US$16·5bn.

Banking and Finance
The Qatar Monetary Agency, which functioned as a bank of issue, became the Central Bank in 1995 (*Governor*, Abdullah Atiyya). In 2003 there were eight commercial domestic banks and seven foreign banks. The largest bank is the Qatar National Bank, with assets in 2003 of 34·8bn. riyals.

A stock exchange was established in Doha by the Amir's decree in 1995, initially to trade only in Qatari stocks.

Heavy investment in energy development increased foreign debt from US$1,300bn. in 1991 to US$10,400bn. in 1997.

ENERGY AND NATURAL RESOURCES

Environment
Qatar's carbon dioxide emissions from the consumption and flaring of fossil fuels in 2002 were the equivalent of 46·1 tonnes per capita, the highest of any sovereign country.

Electricity
Installed capacity was 1·9m. kW in 2000. Production was 9·17bn. kWh in 2000; consumption per capita was 16,227 kWh.

Oil and Gas
Proven reserves of oil (2002) 15·2bn. bbls. Output, 2002, 34·7m. tonnes. Oil accounted for 59% of GDP in 2002.

The North Field, the world's biggest single reservoir of gas and containing 12% of the known world gas reserves, is half the size of Qatar itself. Development cost is estimated at US$25bn. In 2002 natural gas reserves were 14,400bn. cu. metres (the third largest after Russia and Iran); output in 2002 was 29·3bn. cu. metres.

Water
Two main desalination stations have a daily capacity of 167·6m. gallons of drinkable water. A third station is planned, with a capacity of 40m. gallons a day.

Agriculture
10% of the working population is engaged in agriculture. Percentage of total agricultural area under various crops in 1993: vegetables, 28%; green fodder, 23%; cereals, 22%; palm dates, 20%; fruits, 7%. Government policy aims at ensuring self-sufficiency in agricultural products. In 2001, 13,000 ha. were irrigated. There were 18,000 ha. of arable land in 2001 and 3,000 ha. of permanent crops. Production (2000) in 1,000 tonnes:

dates, 17; tomatoes, 11; pumpkins and squash, 9; aubergines, 5; barley, 5; cucumbers and gherkins, 5; melons and watermelons, 5; onions, 4.

Livestock (2000): sheep, 215,000; goats, 179,000; camels, 50,000; cattle, 14,000; chickens, 4m. Livestock products, 2000 (in 1,000 tonnes): meat, 13; milk, 11; eggs, 4.

Fisheries
The catch in 2001 totalled 8,606 tonnes, entirely from sea fishing. The state-owned Qatar National Fishing Company has three trawlers and its refrigeration unit processes 10 tonnes of shrimp a day.

INDUSTRY
According to the Financial Times Survey (FT 500), the largest companies in Qatar by market capitalization on 4 Jan. 2001 were Qatar Telecom Company (US$1,642·7m.) and Qatar National Bank (US$1,283·4m.).

2001 output (in 1,000 tonnes): ammonia, 1,408; cement, 1,209; residual fuel oil (2000), 940; steel billets, 891; urea (1998), 875; propane (2002), 743; steel bars, 714; butane (2002), 618; distillate fuel oil (2000), 602; ethylene, 535; polyethylene (2002), 379. There is an industrial zone at Umm Said.

Labour
In 1998 the labour force totalled 293,000. In 1999 males constituted 85% of the labour force—only the United Arab Emirates had a lower percentage of females in its workforce.

INTERNATIONAL TRADE
Qatar, along with Bahrain, Kuwait, Oman, Saudi Arabia and the United Arab Emirates began the implementation of a customs union in Jan. 2003.

Imports and Exports
Total imports and exports in calendar years (in 1m. riyals):

	1999	2000	2001	2002
Imports	8,196	10,664	12,323	13,287
Exports	26,258	42,202	39,571	39,960

The main imports are machinery and equipment, consumer goods, food and chemicals. Main exports are petroleum products (75%), steel and fertilizers. Principal import suppliers in 2002: USA, 14·5%; Japan, 11·7%; Italy, 10·0%; UK, 8·5%; United Arab Emirates, 7·8%. Leading export markets, 2002: Japan, 46·7%; South Korea, 15·8%; Singapore, 9·3%; United Arab Emirates, 4·0%; Thailand, 3·4%.

COMMUNICATIONS

Roads
In 2002 there were about 1,230 km of roads, of which 1,100 km were paved. Passenger cars in 2002 numbered 230,155 (374 per 1,000 inhabitants); there were 14,344 trucks and vans and 104,341 buses and coaches. In 2002 there were 68,550 road traffic accidents resulting in 148 fatalities.

Civil Aviation
Gulf Air is owned equally by Qatar, Bahrain, Oman and the UAE. In 2003 it operated services from Doha International to Abu Dhabi and Bahrain. A Qatari airline, Qatar Airways, operates on the same routes, and in 2003 additionally flew to Amman, Bangkok, Beirut, Bombay, Cairo, Casablanca, Colombo, Damascus, Damman, Dhaka, Dubai, Frankfurt, Hyderabad, Islamabad, Jakarta, Jeddah, Karachi, Kathmandu, Khartoum, Kochi, Kuala Lumpur, Kuwait, Lahore, London, Malé, Manchester, Manila, Milan, Munich, Muscat, Paris, Peshawar, Riyadh, Salalah, Sana'a, Sharjah and Thiruvananthapuram. In June 2003 Qatar Airways commissioned 32 aircraft worth US$5·1bn. from Airbus SAS. Doha handled 2,759,000 passengers (all on international flights) and 64,000 tonnes of freight in 2001.

Shipping
In 2002 sea-going vessels totalled 623,000 GRT, including oil tankers 210,000 GRT. In 1993, 1,383 vessels with a total tonnage of 66,255,841 GRT and 2,697,629 tonnage of cargo was discharged.

Telecommunications
Qatar had 443,200 telephone subscribers in 2002, or 726·6 per 1,000 persons, and there were 110,000 PCs in use. There were 267,200 mobile phone subscribers in 2002 and 13,800 fax machines. In 2002 there were approximately 70,000 Internet users.

Postal Services
There were 53 post offices in 2003.

SOCIAL INSTITUTIONS

Justice
The Judiciary System is administered by the Ministry of Justice which comprises three main departments: legal affairs, courts of justice and land and real estate register. There are five Courts of Justice proclaiming sentences in the name of HH the Amir: the Court of Appeal, the Labour Court, the Higher Criminal Court, the Civil Court and the Lower Criminal Court. The death penalty is in force. There was one execution in 2003, but none in 2004 or 2005. The population in penal institutions in 2000 was 570 (95 per 100,000 of national population).

All issues related to personal affairs of Muslims under Islamic Law embodied in the Holy Koran and Sunna are decided by Sharia Courts.

Education
Adult literacy rate was 81·7% in 2001 (80·8% among males and 83·7% among females). There were, in 2002–03, 56,821 pupils and 5,460 teachers at 162 primary schools, 15,825 pupils and 1,784 teachers at secondary schools and, in 2000–01, 7,808 students and 595 teachers at higher education institutions. There were 265 Arab and foreign private schools with 56,183 pupils and 4,092 teachers in 2002–03. The University of Qatar had 7,867 students and 676 academic staff in 2003–04.

Students abroad (2003–04) numbered 374. In 2002–03, 2,009 men and 940 women attended night schools and literacy centres.

Health
There were three government and two private hospitals in 2002. In 2002 there were 1,204 government-employed doctors, 145 government-employed dentists, 279 government-employed pharmacists and 3,139 government-employed nurses.

RELIGION
The population is almost entirely Muslim.

CULTURE

Broadcasting
The government ministry of information operates the Qatar Broadcasting Service and the Qatar Television Service. The Qatar Television Service transmits in Arabic (Qatar Television One, on channels 9 and 11) and in English (Qatar Television Two, on channel 37). Transmissions are received from Bahrain, the United Arab Emirates or Saudi Arabia. There are also satellite and cable broadcasters (Al-Jazeera Satellite Channel and Qatar Cable Vision). Al-Jazeera has a reputation for outspoken, independent reporting and has become increasingly high-profile since the attacks on the USA on 11 Sept. 2001. There were 530,000 television receivers in use (colour by PAL) in 2001 and 256,000 radios in 1997.

Press

There are three Arabic language daily newspapers—*Al-Rayah*, *Al-Sharq* and *Al-Watan*. The *Gulf Times* and *Al-Jazeera* (The Peninsula) are English dailies. In 1996 the combined circulation was 90,000.

Tourism

In 2002 there were 693,000 foreign tourists.

DIPLOMATIC REPRESENTATIVES

Of Qatar in the United Kingdom (1 South Audley St., London, WIK 1NB)
Ambassador: Khalid Rashid Salem Al-Homoudi Al-Mansouri.

Of the United Kingdom in Qatar (PO Box 3, Doha, Qatar)
Ambassador: Simon Collis.

Of Qatar in the USA (2555 M St., NW, Washington, D.C., 20037)
Ambassador: Nasser Bin Hamad Bin Mubarak Al Khalifa.

Of the USA in Qatar (22 February St., Doha)
Ambassador: Chase Untermeyer.

Of Qatar to the United Nations
Ambassador: Nassir Abdulaziz Al-Nasser.

Of Qatar to the European Union
Ambassador: Vacant.
Chargé d'Affaires a.i.: Khamis B. Al-Sahoti.

FURTHER READING

Central Statistical Organization. *Annual Statistical Abstract.*

El-Nawawy, Mohammed and Iskandar, Adel, *Al-Jazeera: How the Free Arab News Network Scooped the World and Changed the Middle East.* Westview Press, Boulder (CO), 2002
Unwin, P. T. H., *Qatar.* [Bibliography] ABC-Clio, Oxford and Santa Barbara (CA), 1982

National Statistical Office: Central Statistical Organization, Presidency of the Council of Ministers, Doha.

ROMANIA

```
                    0        75 mi
UKRAINE         ─────────────────
                    0       100 km

        MOLDOVA

HUNGARY              Iași•

    •Cluj-Napoca

        ROMANIA

  •Timișoara      •Brașov

        BUCHAREST▣  Constanța•

SERBIA
AND                           Black
MONT.    BULGARIA             Sea

                    © Research Machines plc 2006
```

România

Capital: Bucharest
Population projection, 2010: 21·29m.
GDP per capita, 2003: (PPP$) 7,277
HDI/world rank: 0·792/64

KEY HISTORICAL EVENTS

The foundation of the feudal 'Danubian Principalities' of Wallachia and Moldavia in the late 13th and early 14th centuries marks the beginning of modern Romania. The nobility acted as the Turks' agents until 1711 when, suspected of pro-Russian sentiments, they were replaced by Greek merchant adventurers, the Phanariots. The Phanariot period of ruthless extortion and corruption was ameliorated by Russian influence. Between 1829 and 1834 the foundations of the modern state were laid but Russian interference soon became repressive. The Moldavian and Wallachian assemblies were fused in 1862. In 1866 Carol of Hohenzollern came to the throne and a constitution adopted based on that of Belgium of 1831. Romania was formally declared independent by the Treaty of Berlin of 1878.

This was a period of expansion for an economy controlled by land-owners and nascent industrialists. The condition of the peasantry remained miserable and the rebellion of 1907 was an expression of their discontent. Romania joined the First World War on the allied side in 1916. The spoils of victory brought Transylvania (with large Hungarian and German populations), Bessarabia, Bukovina and Dobrudja into the union with the 'Old Kingdom'. Hit by the world recession, Romania was drawn into Germany's economic orbit. Against this background the fascist Iron Guard assassinated the Liberal leader in 1934. Carol II adopted an increasingly totalitarian rule. Following Nazi and Soviet annexations of Romanian territory in 1940, he abdicated in favour of his son Mihai. The government of the fascist Ion Antonescu declared war on the USSR on 22 June 1941. On 23 Aug. 1944 Mihai, with the backing of a bloc of opposition parties, deposed Antonescu and switched sides.

The armistice of Sept. 1944 gave the Soviet army control of Romania's territory. This, and the 'spheres of influence' diplomacy of the Allies, predetermined the establishment of communism in Romania. Transylvania was restored to Romania (although it lost Bessarabia and Southern Dobrudja), and large estates were broken up for the benefit of the peasantry. Elections in Nov. 1946 were held in an atmosphere of intimidation and fraudulence. Mihai was forced to abdicate and a people's republic was proclaimed. The communist leader, Gheorghe Gheorghiu-Dej, purged himself of his fellow leaders in the early 1950s. Under Nicolae Ceauşescu, who became the effective centre of power in 1965, Romania took a relatively independent stand in foreign affairs while becoming increasingly repressive and impoverished domestically.

An attempt by the authorities on 16 Dec. 1989 to evict a Protestant pastor, László Tökés, from his home in Timişoara provoked a popular protest which escalated into a mass demonstration against the government. A state of emergency was declared but the Army went over to the rebels and Nicolae and Elena Ceauşescu fled the capital. A dissident group which had been active before the uprising, the National Salvation Front (FSN), proclaimed itself the provisional government. The Ceauşescus were captured and after a secret two hour trial by military tribunal, summarily executed on 25 Dec. The following day Ion Iliescu, leader of the FSN, was sworn in as President. But the Iliescu-led administration, while committed to reform, was inhibited by its communist origins. The economy stalled and the debts piled up. Iliescu was voted out of office and his government replaced by a four-party coalition led by President Emil Constantinescu. Iliescu returned as president in 2000. The economy continued to struggle but in 2004 Romania joined NATO and was given a target date of 2007 for EU membership.

TERRITORY AND POPULATION

Romania is bounded in the north by Ukraine, in the east by Moldova, Ukraine and the Black Sea, south by Bulgaria, southwest by Serbia and Montenegro and northwest by Hungary. The area is 238,391 sq. km. Population (2002 census), 21,680,974; density, 90·9 per sq. km. In 2003, 54·6% of the population lived in urban areas. Romania's population has been falling at such a steady rate since 1990 that its population at the time of the 2002 census was the same as that in the late 1970s.

The UN gives a projected population for 2010 of 21·29m.

Romania is divided into 41 counties (*judeţ*) and the municipality of Bucharest (Bucuresti).

County	Area in sq. km	Population (2002 census)	Capital	Population (in 1,000) (2002)
Bucharest[1]	228	1,926,334		
Alba	6,242	382,747	Alba Iulia	66
Arad	7,754	461,791	Arad	173
Argeş	6,826	652,625	Piteşti	168
Bacău	6,621	706,623	Bacău	176
Bihor	7,544	600,246	Oradea	207
Bistriţa-Năsăud	5,355	311,657	Bistriţa	81
Botoşani	4,986	452,834	Botoşani	115
Brăila	4,766	373,174	Brăila	216
Braşov	5,363	589,028	Braşov	285
Buzău	6,103	496,214	Buzău	134
Călăraşi	5,088	324,617	Călăraşi	70
Caraş-Severin	8,520	333,219	Reşiţa	84
Cluj	6,674	702,755	Cluj-Napoca	318
Constanţa	7,071	715,151	Constanţa	310

County	Area in sq. km	Population (2002 census)	Capital	Population (in 1,000) (2002)
Covasna	3,710	222,449	Sf. Gheorghe	62
Dâmboviţa	4,054	541,763	Tîrgovişte	90
Dolj	7,414	734,231	Craiova	303
Galaţi	4,466	619,556	Galaţi	299
Giurgiu	3,526	297,859	Giurgiu	69
Gorj	5,602	387,308	Tîrgu Jiu	97
Harghita	6,639	326,222	Miercurea-Ciuc	42
Hunedoara	7,063	485,712	Deva	69
Ialomiţa	4,453	296,572	Slobozia	53
Iaşi	5,476	816,910	Iaşi	321
Ilfov[1]	1,593	300,123	—	—
Maramureş	6,304	510,110	Baia Mare	138
Mehedinţi	4,933	306,732	Drobeta-Turnu Severin	105
Mureş	6,714	580,851	Tîrgu Mureş	150
Neamţ	5,896	554,516	Piatra-Neamţ	105
Olt	5,498	489,274	Slatina	79
Prahova	4,716	829,945	Ploieşti	233
Sălaj	3,864	248,015	Zalău	63
Satu Mare	4,418	367,281	Satu Mare	115
Sibiu	5,432	421,724	Sibiu	155
Suceava	8,553	688,435	Suceava	106
Teleorman	5,790	436,025	Alexandria	50
Timiş	8,697	677,926	Timişoara	318
Tulcea	8,499	256,492	Tulcea	92
Vâlcea	5,765	413,247	Râmnicu Vâlcea	108
Vaslui	5,318	455,049	Vaslui	71
Vrancea	4,857	387,632	Focşani	102

[1]Bucharest municipality and surrounding localities of Ilfov cover 1,821 sq. km.

At the 2002 census the following ethnic minorities numbered over 50,000: Hungarians, 1,431,807 (mainly in Transylvania); Roma (Gypsies), 535,140; Ukrainians, 61,098; Germans, 59,764. A *Council of National Minorities* made up of representatives of the government and ethnic groups was set up in 1993. The actual number of Roma is estimated to be nearer 2m. Romania has the largest Roma population of any country.

The official language is Romanian.

SOCIAL STATISTICS

2001: births, 220,368; deaths, 259,603; infant deaths, 4,057; marriages, 129,930; divorces, 31,135. Rates, 2001 (per 1,000 population): live births, 9·8; deaths, 11·6; marriages, 5·8; divorces, 1·4. Infant mortality, 2001 (per 1,000 live births), 19. Expectation of life at birth, 2003, was 67·8 years for males and 75·0 years for females. In 2001 the most popular age range for marrying was 25–29 for males and 20–24 for females. Measures designed to raise the birth rate were abolished in 1990, and abortion and contraception legalized. The annual abortion rate, at nearly 80 per 1,000 women aged 15–44, ranks among the highest in the world. Annual population growth rate, 1992–2002, −0·3%; fertility rate, 2001, 1·3 births per woman.

CLIMATE

A continental climate with an annual average temperature varying between 8°C in the north and 11°C in the south. Bucharest, Jan. 27°F (−2·7°C), July 74°F (23·5°C). Annual rainfall 23·1" (579 mm). Constanţa, Jan. 31°F (−0·6°C), July 71°F (21·7°C). Annual rainfall 15" (371 mm).

CONSTITUTION AND GOVERNMENT

A new Constitution was approved by a referendum on 18–19 Oct. 2003. Turnout was 55·7%, and 89·7% of votes cast were in favour. The Constitution, which replaces the previous one from 1991, defines Romania as a republic where the rule of law prevails in a social and democratic state. Private property rights and a market economy are guaranteed. The new pro-European constitution is aimed at helping Romania achieve EU membership.

The head of state is the *President*, elected by direct vote for a maximum of two five-year terms. The president is not allowed to be affiliated with any political party while in office. The President appoints the *Prime Minister*, who then has to be approved by a vote in parliament. The President is empowered to veto legislation unless it is upheld by a two-thirds parliamentary majority. The National Assembly consists of a 332-member *Chamber of Deputies* and a 137-member *Senate*; both are elected for four-year terms from 42 constituencies by modified proportional representation, the number of seats won in each constituency being determined by the proportion of the total vote. 18 seats in the Chamber of Deputies are reserved for ethnic minorities. There is a 3% threshold for admission to either house. Votes for parties not reaching this threshold are redistributed.

There is a *Constitutional Court*.

National Anthem

'Deşteaptăte, Române, din somnul cel de moarte' ('Wake up, Romanians, from your deadly slumber'); words by A. Muresianu, tune by A. Pann.

GOVERNMENT CHRONOLOGY

(FDSN = Democratic National Salvation Front; FSN = National Salvation Front; PCR = Romanian Communist Party; PD = Democratic Party; PDSR = Party of Social Democracy in Romania; PNL = National Liberal Party; PNTCD = National Peasant Party Christian Democratic; PSD = Social Democratic Party)

Heads of State since 1940.

King
1940–47		Mihai I

Presidents of the Presidium of the Grand National Assembly
1947–52	PCR	Constantin Ion Parhon
1958	PCR	Anton Moisescu
1958–61	PCR	Ion Gheorghe Maurer

Chairmen of the Council of State
1961–65	PCR	Gheorghe Gheorghiu-Dej
1965–67	PCR	Chivu Stoica
1967–74	PCR	Nicolae Ceauşescu

Presidents
1974–89	PCR	Nicolae Ceauşescu
1989–96	PCR, n/p, FSN, FDSN, PDSR	Ion Iliescu
1996–2000	PNTCD	Emil Constantinescu
2000–04	PDSR, PSD	Ion Iliescu
2004–	PD	Traian Băsescu

Heads of Government since 1945.

Chairmen of the Council of Ministers
1945–52	PCR	Petru Groza
1952–55	PCR	Gheorghe Gheorghiu-Dej
1955–61	PCR	Chivu Stoica
1961–74	PCR	Ion Gheorghe Maurer
1974–79	PCR	Manea Mănescu
1979–82	PCR	Ilie Verdeţ
1982–89	PCR	Constantin Dăscalescu

Prime Ministers
1989–91	FSN	Petre Roman
1991–92	n/p	Teodor Stolojan
1992–96	n/p, PDSR	Nicolae Văcaroiu
1996–98	PNTCD	Victor Ciorbea
1998–99	PNTCD	Radu Vasile
1999–2000	n/p	Mugur Isărescu
2000–04	PDSR/PSD	Adrian Năstase
2004–	PNL	Călin Popescu-Tăriceanu

RECENT ELECTIONS

Presidential elections were held in two rounds on 28 Nov. and 12 Dec. 2004. In the first round Prime Minister Adrian Năstase of the National Union (alliance of Social Democratic Party and Humanist Party) received 40·9% of votes cast, Traian Băsescu of the Justice and Truth Alliance (alliance of Democratic Party and National Liberal Party) 33·9%, Corneliu Vadim Tudor of the Greater Romania Party 12·6% and Markó Béla of the Hungarian Democratic Federation of Romania 5·1%. There were eight other candidates. In the second round run-off Traian Băsescu was elected president with 51·2% of the vote against 48·8% for Adrian Năstase.

In parliamentary elections held on 28 Nov. 2004 the National Union took 132 seats (36·8% of the vote) in the lower house and 57 seats (37·2% of the vote) in the Senate, the Justice and Truth Alliance 113 seats (31·5%) in the lower house and 49 (31·8%) in the Senate, the Greater Romania Party 47 seats (13·0%) and 21 (13·6%) and the Hungarian Democratic Federation of Romania 22 seats (6·2%) and 10 (6·2%).

CURRENT ADMINISTRATION

President: Traian Băsescu; b. 1951 (Justice and Truth Alliance; sworn in 20 Dec. 2004).

In March 2006 the coalition government of the Justice and Truth Alliance, Hungarian Democratic Federation of Romania and the Conservative Party (formerly Humanist Party) comprised:

Prime Minister: Călin Popescu-Tăriceanu; b. 1952 (Justice and Truth Alliance; sworn in 29 Dec. 2004).

Minister of Defence: Teodor Athanasiu. *Foreign Affairs:* Mihai-Răzvan Ungureanu. *Public Finance:* Sebastian Vlădescu. *Administration and Interior:* Vasile Blaga. *Justice:* Monica Luisa Macovei. *Labour, Social Solidarity and the Family:* Gheorghe Barbu. *Economy and Commerce:* Ioan-Codruţ Şereş. *Agriculture, Forests and Rural Development:* Gheorghe Flutur. *Transport, Construction and Tourism:* Gheorghe Dobre. *Education and Research:* Mihail Hărdău. *European Integration:* Anca Daniela Boaglu. *Health:* Eugen Nicolăescu. *Culture and Religious Affairs:* Adrian Iorgulescu. *Communications and Information Technology:* Zsolt Nagy. *Environment and Water Resources:* Sulfina Barbu.

Government Website: http://www.gov.ro

CURRENT LEADERS

Traian Băsescu

Position
President

Introduction
Traian Băsescu, a former ship's captain and the charismatic mayor of Bucharest, fought the country's 2004 presidential elections on a tough anti-corruption platform, and emerged victorious. He took over from Ion Iliescu, who had served as president for much of the post-Communist period.

Early life
Băsescu was born in the village of Basarabi near the Romanian port of Constanţa on 4 Nov. 1951. He studied at the Marine Institute in Constanţa, graduating in 1976 from the commercial section of the faculty of navigation. He then joined the merchant navy, controlled in Romania's Communist era by NAVROM, and worked his way through the ranks, becoming a captain in 1981. He went on to captain some of the country's largest merchant ships and was promoted to Admiral of Romania's merchant fleet by the mid-1980s. In 1987 Băsescu travelled to Antwerp, Belgium to work as head of the NAVROM Agency. Two years later he returned to Bucharest and entered the political scene as general director of the State Inspectorate of Civic Navigation

in the Ministry of Transport, in what turned out to be the final months of Nicolae Ceauşescu's 24-year grip on power. After the dramatic collapse of Ceauşescu's regime in Dec. 1989, Băsescu was promoted to deputy minister in the Ministry of Transport. He became minister of transport in 1991 in the government dominated by the National Salvation Front (FSN), which had received mass support in the first post-Communist elections on 20 May 1990.

Following a split in the FSN in 1992, Băsescu joined Petre Roman in the newly-established centre-left Democratic Party and, in 1996, he co-ordinated Roman's unsuccessful presidential campaign—the victor was Emil Constantinescu, a former rector of Bucharest University. Băsescu was re-elected as a Democratic Party MP in 1996 and served as minister of transport until 2000, when he stood as the Democratic Party candidate in the Bucharest mayoral election. He won and began co-ordinating the regeneration of large areas of the city, gaining praise for his direct approach—from cracking down on the notorious packs of stray dogs to improving traffic flow. When the government blocked his plans for a new bypass and improved municipal central heating systems, Băsescu asked citizens to sign a petition, and eventually managed to convince the officials to back down.

Following disagreements with Petre Roman, Băsescu replaced him as leader of the (opposition) Democratic Party in 2001. Two years later, in Sept. 2003, Băsescu became a co-chairman of the centre-right Justice and Truth Alliance (DA), forged between his Democratic Party and the National Liberal Party (PNL). Băsescu's energetic rule as mayor of Bucharest proved popular, and he was re-elected to the post in June 2004, easily beating his rival, Mircea Geoana.

Three months later Băsescu decided to contest the presidential election as the candidate for the Justice and Truth Alliance, following the withdrawal of the group's first choice, Theodor Stolojan, on grounds of ill health. Băsescu campaigned on a strong anti-corruption and pro-Western ticket, although he had to fend off accusations from the ruling Social Democratic Party (PSD) that he had been an informer for the Communist-era *Securitate* (secret police). A court ruled that the allegations could not be proved, and Băsescu went on to win 33·9% of the vote in the first round of the election on 28 Nov., forcing a run-off against the PSD candidate, Adrian Năstase. When all the ballots were counted from the presidential run-off on 12 Dec. 2004, Băsescu emerged victorious with 51·2% of the vote.

Career in Office
Băsescu's first task as president was the formation of a new government, which became possible for his Justice and Truth Alliance when the small Humanist Party (since renamed the Conservative Party) pledged their support, in addition to the backing of the ethnic Hungarian Democratic Federation of Romania. Băsescu appointed the PNL leader and former minister of the economy Călin Popescu-Tăriceanu to the post of prime minister. In his inaugural address Băsescu said that fighting corruption would remain his priority and that he intended to steer Romania on a course to enter the European Union by Jan. 2007. He also stressed the need to strengthen strategic partnerships with the USA and the UK, as well as to improve relations with Russia and the former Soviet states.

Călin Popescu-Tăriceanu

Position
Prime Minister

Introduction
Călin Popescu-Tăriceanu entered Romanian politics in early 1990 following the collapse of Nicolae Ceauşescu's Communist regime. He was appointed prime minister in Dec. 2004 by President Traian Băsescu, his fellow member of the centre-right Justice and Truth Alliance.

Early Life

Born in Bucharest on 14 Jan. 1952, Popescu-Tăriceanu was educated at the Sf. Sava High School and then at the Hydro-engineering faculty of the Bucharest Construction Institute. A masters degree in science, research methods and mathematics followed at Bucharest University. In 1976 Popescu-Tăriceanu served as an engineer at the National Water Administration in Argeş county division and at a construction company in Bucharest. Returning to the Bucharest Construction Institute in 1980, he worked as a tutor in hydro-engineering, a position he held for the next ten years. Following the collapse of Nicolae Ceauşescu's regime in Dec. 1989, Popescu-Tăriceanu entered politics, helping to re-establish the National Liberal Party (PNL). He was a member of the provisional Council of National Unity, an unelected parliament that governed Romania in the spring of 1990. After the first post-Communist elections on 20 May 1990, Popescu-Tăriceanu represented the PNL in a government that was dominated by the National Salvation Front (FSN). At this time he also founded Romania's first private radio station. In Dec. 1990 the PNL, together with other right-of-centre opposition groups, formed the Democratic Convention of Romania (CDR), which served in the government of Teodor Stolojan from Oct. 1991. After withdrawing from the Democratic Convention in April 1992, the PNL suffered a disastrous defeat in the elections held on 27 Sept. 1992. This led to serious splits in the party, and Popescu-Tăriceanu concentrated on his business interests, becoming Director General of Radio Contact Romania and establishing the Association of Automobile Producers and Importers (APIA).

Popescu-Tăriceanu returned to parliament in 1996 when he was elected as a deputy representing the CDR. He served in the cabinet headed by Prime Minister Victor Ciorbea and held the portfolio of trade and industry in 1996–97, where he became unpopular with trade unions for his decision to close unprofitable mines. He also led attempts to restructure Romania's oil sector and the National Electric Company. Following the crushing defeat of the CDR by the Social Democratic Party (PSD), led by Ion Iliescu, in the Nov. 2000 general election, Popescu-Tăriceanu and others led the PNL out of the CDR, and later (in early 2002) joined forces with the reformist Democratic Party to form the Justice and Truth Alliance (DA). It was intended to be a vehicle for co-ordinating opposition efforts against the ruling, and allegedly corrupt, PSD.

In March 2004 Popescu-Tăriceanu was made manager of the DA's campaign for the local elections in June. In late Oct. 2004 the alliance endorsed Popescu-Tăriceanu as its prime ministerial candidate in the Romanian legislative elections, which took place alongside the presidential election on 28 Nov. Both Popescu-Tăriceanu and the DA's presidential candidate, Traian Băsescu, campaigned on fighting corruption, creating jobs, alleviating poverty and establishing a non-political judiciary. The DA performed strongly at the polls, coming within a few percentage points of the PSD and eliminating the government's majority. When Băsescu triumphed over Adrian Năstase in the presidential run-off on 12 Dec., he invited Popescu-Tăriceanu to form the next government. Alliances were forged with both the Hungarian Democratic Federation of Romania and the Humanist Party (renamed the Conservative Party in May 2005) in a centre-right coalition that was approved by parliament on 28 Dec. The following day, Popescu-Tăriceanu was sworn in as Romania's prime minister.

Career in Office

Presenting his government's programme to parliament, Popescu-Tăriceanu pledged to fight corruption and poverty and carry out reforms needed for his country's entry into the European Union in 2007. His first step was to lower income and corporate profit taxes to a 16% flat rate, in a bid to reduce the size of the country's black market economy and encourage foreign investment. On 25 April 2005 he participated in the signing ceremony of Romania's EU Accession Treaty in Luxembourg.

DEFENCE

Military service is compulsory for 12 months.

In 2003 military expenditure totalled US$1,313m. (US$59 per capita), representing 2·3% of GDP.

Army

Strength (2002) 66,000 (21,000 conscripts) and 130,000 reservists. The Ministry of the Interior operates a paramilitary Frontier Guard (22,900 strong) and a Gendarmerie (57,000).

Navy

The fleet includes one destroyer and six frigates. There is also a naval infantry force.

The headquarters of the Navy is at Mangalia with the main base at Constanţa. The Danube flotilla is based at Brăila. Personnel in 2002 totalled 6,200.

Air Force

The Air Force numbered some 17,000 in 2002, with 202 combat aircraft and 21 attack helicopters. These included MiG-21, MiG-23 and MiG-29 fighters.

INTERNATIONAL RELATIONS

Romania is a member of the UN, WTO, BIS, NATO, the Council of Europe, the Central European Initiative, OSCE, BSEC, Danube Commission, IOM, Antarctic Treaty, the International Organization of the Francophonie and is an Associate Partner of the WEU and an Associate Member of the EU. At the European Union's Helsinki Summit in Dec. 1999 Romania, along with five other countries, was invited to begin full negotiations for membership in Feb. 2000, but entry into the EU is likely to be in 2007 at the earliest. Romania became a member of NATO on 29 March 2004.

ECONOMY

Agriculture accounted for 13·1% of GDP in 2002, industry 38·1% and services 48·8%.

Overview

The fall of the Ceauşescu government in Dec. 1989 brought economic turbulence. After 1993 the economy grew in line with the recovery of the rest of Eastern Europe but fell back into recession in the final third of the 1990s, reversing earlier gains and causing it to fall behind other Eastern European nations. Successive governments failed to introduce structural reforms and the result was macroeconomic instability, with growth often followed by inflationary flare-ups and macroeconomic imbalance. Reform was finally embraced in 2000. Structural change and a tight monetary policy were implemented to discipline business. In the early 2000s the economy grew every year, averaging over 5% annually. Industry and agriculture have been overtaken by the service sector since the transition from socialism, though to a lesser extent than in other Eastern European countries. Privatization has extended to the telecommunications, motor, steel and banking industries. But Romania has been relatively slow in transforming its economy and there is uncertainty as to the political will for continued reform. Annual inflation, averaging around 50% in the 1990s, was brought down to 11·9% in 2004. Business is hampered by bureaucratic barriers and corruption is endemic. A quarter of the population still lives in poverty.

Currency

The monetary unit has since 1 July 2005 been the *new leu*, pl. *new lei* (RON) notionally of 100 *bani*, which replaced the *leu* (ROL) at a rate of one new leu = 10,000 lei. Foreign exchange reserves were US$6,352m. and gold reserves 3·38m. troy oz in May 2002. Inflation rates (based on IMF statistics):

1995	1996	1997	1998	1999	2000	2001	2002	2003	2004
32·3%	38·8%	154·8%	59·1%	45·8%	45·7%	34·5%	22·5%	15·3%	11·9%

Total money supply was 57,213·9bn. lei in May 2002.

Budget
Total revenue and expenditure (in 1bn. lei) for calendar years:

	1997	1998	1999	2000	2001
Revenue	68,394	107,051	171,135	237,161	311,320
Expenditure	79,734	124,595	191,341	273,990	354,837

VAT, introduced in July 1993, is 19%.

Performance
Real GDP growth rates (based on IMF statistics):

1995	1996	1997	1998	1999	2000	2001	2002	2003	2004
8·0%	3·9%	−6·1%	−4·8%	−1·2%	2·1%	5·7%	5·1%	5·2%	8·3%

Total GDP in 2004 was US$73·2bn.

Banking and Finance
The National Bank of Romania (founded 1880; nationalized 1946) is the central bank and bank of issue under the Minister of Finance. Its *Governor* is Dr Mugur Isărescu. In 2002 there were 31 banks, plus eight branches of foreign banks. Only three banks remain state-owned. The largest bank is Romanian Commercial Bank (Banca Comerciala Romana), with a market share of 31% and assets in 2002 of US$4·5bn.; the government sold a 61·9% stake to Austria's Erste Bank AG in Dec. 2005. The size of the government's share in the banking sector fell from over 80% in the mid-1990s to just over 40% in 2002.

A stock exchange re-opened in Bucharest in 1995.

ENERGY AND NATURAL RESOURCES

Environment
Romania's carbon dioxide emissions from the consumption and flaring of fossil fuels were the equivalent of 4·5 tonnes per capita in 2002.

Electricity
Installed electric power 2002: 21·9m. kW; output, 2002, 54·94bn. kWh (29% hydro-electric). Consumption per capita in 2002 was 2,385 kWh. A nuclear power plant at Cernavoda began working in 1996.

Oil and Gas
Oil production in 2002 was 6·1m. tonnes, but with annual consumption of nearly twice as much a large amount has to be imported. There were 1·0bn. bbls. of proven oil reserves in 2002. Romania was the first country to start oil exploration, and in the late 1850s was the world's leading oil producer, with an output of 200 tonnes a year. Natural gas production in 2002 totalled 10·8bn. cu. metres with 100bn. cu. metres in proven reserves (2002).

The oil company Petrom, Romania's largest company, was privatized in 2004 when the government sold a 51% stake to the Austrian oil and gas group ÖMV.

Minerals
The principal minerals are oil and natural gas, salt, lignite, iron and copper ores, bauxite, chromium, manganese and uranium. Output (in 1,000 tonnes): lignite (2002), 30,401; salt (2001), 2,224; iron ore (1999), 131; zinc (2000), 27.

Agriculture
Romania has the biggest agricultural area in eastern Europe after Poland. In 2000, 42·8% of the workforce was employed in agriculture. There were 13·94m. ha. of agricultural land in 2002 including 8·96m. ha. of arable land and 4·63m. ha. of permanent pasture. There were 3,081,000 ha. of irrigated land in 2001. There were 164,221 tractors and 27,051 harvester-threshers in 2001.

Production (2000, in 1,000 tonnes): wheat, 4,320; maize, 4,200; potatoes, 3,650; sugarbeets, 1,500; cabbages, 1,000; grapes, 981; sunflower seeds, 900; melons and watermelons, 900; tomatoes, 758; barley, 750.

Livestock, 2002 (in 1,000): cattle, 2,865; sheep, 7,221; pigs, 8,229; horses, 909; goats, 737; poultry, 82,000.

A law of Feb. 1991 provided for the restitution of collectivized land to its former owners or their heirs up to a limit of 10 ha. Land could be resold, but there was a limit of 100 ha. on total holdings. In 2000 a law was passed allowing the restitution of state farm land for the first time (up to 50 ha. of farmland and 10 ha. of forest land per family).

Forestry
Total forest area was 6·45m. ha. in 2000 (28·0% of the land area); natural forest covered 6·36m. ha. and forest plantations 0·09m. ha. Timber production in 2003 was 13·96m. cu. metres.

Fisheries
The catch in 2003 totalled 10,050 tonnes (216,938 tonnes in 1988), of which 8,438 tonnes were from inland waters.

INDUSTRY

In 2001 industry accounted for 37·0% of GDP. Industrial output grew by 7·5% in 2001.

Output of main products (in 1,000 tonnes): cement (2001), 5,668; crude steel (2002), 5,500; distillate fuel oil (2002), 4,689; rolled steel (2000), 3,685; petrol (2002), 3,569; pig iron (2002), 2,500; residual fuel oil (2002), 2,050; fertilizers (2000), 1,931; lime (2001), 1,790; wheat flour (2001), 1,597; ammonia (2001), 1,155; steel tubes (2001), 665; caustic soda (2001), 661; soda ash (2001), 451; paper and paperboard (2002), 370.

Labour
The labour force in 2002 totalled 10·08m.; the employed population was 9·23m., of whom 3·36m. worked in agriculture and 2·38m. in manufacturing and construction. In 2002, 41% of the total workforce were women. The average retirement ages of 50 for women and 54 for men are among the lowest in the world. A minimum monthly wage was set in 1993; it is 2·8m. lei for full-time adult employees from 1 Jan. 2004. The average monthly wage was 5,498,528 lei in Nov. 2002. Unemployment was 8·4% in 2002 (6·7% in 2001).

Trade Unions
In 2002 the National Confederation of Free Trade Unions-Fratia had 44 professional federations, 41 regional branches and 800,000 members; the other major confederations were the National Trade Union Bloc (375,000), Democratic Trade Union Confederation of Romania (345,000), Alfa Cartel (325,000 members) and Meridien (170,000).

INTERNATIONAL TRADE

Foreign debt was US$14,683m. in 2002. In Nov. 1993 the USA granted Romania most-favoured-nation status.

Foreign investors may establish joint ventures or 100%-owned domestic companies in all but a few strategic industries. After an initial two-year exemption, profits are taxed at 30%, dividends at 10%. The 1991 constitution prohibits foreign nationals from owning real estate.

Imports and Exports
Trade in US$1m.:

	1998	1999	2000	2001	2002
Imports f.o.b.	10,927	9,595	12,050	14,354	16,487
Exports f.o.b.	8,302	8,503	10,366	11,385	13,876

Principal imports are mineral fuels, machinery and transport equipment, and textiles; main export commodities are textiles, mineral products and chemicals.

Romania's main import sources in 2001 were: Italy (20·0%); Germany (15·2%); Russia (7·6%); France (6·3%). In 2001 Romania's main export markets were: Italy (25·1%); Germany (15·6%); France (8·1%); UK (5·2%). The EU accounts for approximately 59% of Romanian imports and 65% of exports.

COMMUNICATIONS

Roads

There were 78,492 km of roads in 2001: 113 km of motorways, 14,822 km of national roads, 35,853 km of country roads and 27,817 km of communal roads. In addition there were 119,988 km of urban roads in 2000. At least two-thirds of the main roads are in urgent need of repair. Passenger cars in 2001 numbered 3,225,512 (144 per 1,000 inhabitants). In 2002 there were 7,047 road accidents involving injury resulting in 2,398 deaths.

Rail

Length of standard-gauge route in 2001 was 10,958 km, of which 3,950 km were electrified; there were 378 km of narrow-gauge lines and 57 km of 1,524 mm gauge. Freight carried in 2001, 72·6m. tonnes; passengers, 113·7m. There is a metro (62·4 km) and tram/light rail network (338 km) in Bucharest, and tramways in 14 other cities.

Civil Aviation

Tarom (*Transporturi Aeriene Române*) is the 92·6%-state-owned airline. In 2002 it provided domestic services and international flights to Amman, Amsterdam, Ancona, Athens, Beijing, Beirut, Berlin, Bologna, Brussels, Budapest, Cairo, Chişinău, Copenhagen, Damascus, Dubai, Düsseldorf, Frankfurt, İstanbul, Larnaca, London, Luxembourg, Madrid, Milan, Moscow, Munich, New York, Paris, Prague, Rome, Sofia, Stuttgart, Tel Aviv, Thessaloniki, Treviso, Verona, Vienna, Warsaw and Zürich. In 1999 it flew 23·7m. km, carrying 978,600 passengers (842,700 on international flights). Other Romanian airlines which operated international flights in 2001 were Romavia, Jaro International, Grivco Air, Acvila Air, Carpat Air and Tiriac Air.

Bucharest's airports are at Baneasa (mainly domestic flights) and Otopeni (international flights). Constanţa, Cluj-Napoca, Oradea, Arad, Sibiu and Timişoara also have some international flights. Otopeni handled 1,981,508 passengers in 2001 and 11,410 tonnes of freight; Timişoara handled 161,000 passengers in 2001 and Banaesa 74,000.

Shipping

In 2001 the merchant marine comprised 163 vessels totalling 1·45m. DWT. The total GRT was 403,974, including oil tankers and container ships, in 2000. In 2001 vessels totalling 12,646,000 NRT entered ports and vessels totalling 13,817,000 NRT cleared. The main ports are Constanţa and Constanţa South Agigea on the Black Sea and Galaţi, Brăila and Tulcea on the Danube. In 2001 sea-going transport carried 0·38m. tonnes of freight. In 2001 the length of navigable inland waterways was 1,779 km including: Danube River, 1,075 km; Black Sea Canal, 64 km; Poarta Alba–Midia Navodari Canal, 28 km. The Romanian inland waterway fleet comprised 169 tugs and pushers and 1,695 dumb and pushed vessels with a carrying capacity of 2·23m. tonnes. The freight carried by Romanian vessels was 383,700 tonnes. The traffic of goods in the Romanian inland ports amounted to 18·7m. tonnes.

Telecommunications

Telephone subscribers numbered 7,961,100 in 2001, or 355·6 per 1,000 population, and there were 898,000 PCs in use (40·2 per 1,000 persons). The telecommunications sector was fully liberalized on 1 Jan. 2003, ending the monopoly of the Greek-controlled operator Romtelecom. OTE, the major shareholder, increased its stake in Romtelecom to 54% in Jan. 2003, with the government retaining 46% of shares. There were 5,110,600 mobile phone subscribers in 2002 and 40,000 fax machines. The number of Internet users in 2002 was 1·8m.

Postal Services

There were 6,840 post offices in 2003.

SOCIAL INSTITUTIONS

Justice

Justice is administered by the Supreme Court, the 41 county courts, 81 courts of first instance and 15 courts of appeal. Lay assessors (elected for four years) participate in most court trials, collaborating with the judges. In 1994 there were 2,471 judges. The *Procurator-General* exercises 'supreme supervisory power to ensure the observance of the law'. The Procurator's Office and its organs are independent of any organs of justice or administration, and only responsible to the Grand National Assembly, which appoints the Procurator-General for four years. The death penalty was abolished in Jan. 1990 and is forbidden by the 1991 constitution. The population in penal institutions in Nov. 2003 was 43,489 (200 per 100,000 of national population).

Education

Education is free and compulsory from the age of six. There is compulsory school attendance for ten years. Primary education comprises four years of study, secondary education comprises lower secondary education (organized in two cycles: grades 5th–8th in elementary schools and grades 9th–10th in high schools or vocational schools) and upper secondary education includes further education in high schools. Further secondary education is also available at *lycées*, professional schools or advanced technical schools.

In 2002–03 there were 9,547 kindergartens with 34,300 teachers and 630,000 children; 12,456 primary and secondary schools with 154,000 teachers and 2,198,000 pupils; 1,388 *lycées* (upper secondary schools) with 61,000 teachers and 740,000 pupils; in post-secondary vocational schools there were 6,100 teachers and 270,000 pupils. In 2002–03 primary and secondary education in Hungarian was given to 106,515 pupils, in German to 10,019 pupils and in other national minority languages to 1,536 pupils.

In 2002–03 there were 125 higher education institutions with 742 faculties, 30,000 teaching staff and 596,297 students (545,405 for long-term studies and 50,892 for short-term studies). The distribution of pupils and subjects studied was as follows: pedagogy, 30·3%; economics, 26·5%; technical subjects, 25·6%; law, 10·6%; medicine and pharmacy, 5·4%; arts, 1·5%.

Adult literacy rate in 2003 was 97·3% (male 98·4%; female 96·3%).

In 2000 total expenditure on education came to 3·6% of GNP and represented 12·2% of total government expenditure.

Health

In 2000 there were 439 hospitals, 166,817 hospital beds and 47,354 doctors (including 4,983 dentists).

Welfare

In Dec. 2004 pensioners comprised 3,050,500 old age and retirement, 1,441,800 retired farmers, 798,200 disability, 639,500 survivor allowance and 418,000 social assistance. These drew average monthly pensions ranging from 792,698 lei to 3,504,205 lei. The social security spending in 2002 was 10·4% of GDP.

RELIGION

The government officially recognizes 17 religions (which receive various forms of state support); the predominant one is the Romanian Orthodox Church. It is autocephalous, but retains dogmatic unity with the Eastern Orthodox Church. It is made up of five metropolitan sees, with 10 archdioceses and 13 dioceses,

158 deaneries and 10,987 parishes. There were 12,320 priests and deacons in 2003.

Religious affiliation at the 2002 census included: Romanian Orthodox, 18,817,975 (about 87% of the population); Roman Catholic, 1,026,429; Protestant Reformed Church, 701,077; Pentecostal, 324,462; Greek Catholics or Uniates, 191,556; Baptist, 126,639; Seventh Day Adventist, 93,670; Muslim, 67,257.

CULTURE

Sibiu will be one of two European Capitals of Culture for 2007. The title attracts large European Union grants.

World Heritage Sites

Romania has seven sites on the UNESCO World Heritage List: the Danube Delta (inscribed on the list in 1991); the Villages with Fortified Churches in Transylvania (1993); the Monastery of Horezu (1993); the Churches of Moldavia (1993); the Historic Centre of Sighisoara (1999); the Dacian Fortresses of the Orastie Mountains (1999); and the Wooden Churches of Maramures (1999).

Broadcasting

A National Audiovisual Council was established in 1992, and is the only authority which is permitted to grant broadcasting audiovisual licences to private stations. By 2003 it had granted 3,318 cable licences, 260 television broadcasting licences, 422 radio broadcasting licences, 62 licences for satellite television stations and 15 licences for satellite radio stations. The public radio and TV stations have broadcasts in Romanian, and in Hungarian and German as well as other minority languages in Romania. The public television station also broadcasts by satellite in its programme *TVR International*. The public radio stations broadcast three radio programmes on medium wave and FM. Radio receivers, 2000, 7·3m.; TV (colour by SECAM H), 2001, 8·5m.

Cinema

In 1999 there were 306 cinemas (excluding private ones), with 109,000 seats.

Press

There were, in 1999, 100 daily papers and 2,200 periodicals, including 200 periodicals in minority languages. 8,000 book titles were published in 1999.

Tourism

In 2002 there were 3,204,000 foreign tourists, bringing revenue of US$612m.

Libraries

In 1997 there were 3,246 public libraries, 48 National libraries and 339 Higher Education libraries; they held a combined 92,382,000 volumes. There were 1,994,000 registered public library users in 1997.

DIPLOMATIC REPRESENTATIVES

Of Romania in the United Kingdom (Arundel House, 4 Palace Green, London, W8 4QD)
Ambassador: Dan Ghibernea.

Of the United Kingdom in Romania (24 Strada Jules Michelet, 70154 Bucharest)
Ambassador: Quinton Quayle.

Of Romania in the USA (1607 23rd St., NW, Washington, D.C., 20008)
Ambassador: Sorin Dumitru Ducaru.

Of the USA in Romania (7–9 Strada Tudor Arghezi, Bucharest)
Ambassador: Nicholas Taubman.

Of Romania to the United Nations
Ambassador: Mihnea Ioan Motoc.

Of Romania to the European Union
Ambassador: Lazar Comanescu.

FURTHER READING

Comisia Nationala pentru Statistica. *Anuarul Statistic al României/ Romanian Statistical Yearbook.* Bucharest, annual.—*Revista de Statistica.* Monthly

Gallagher, T., *Romania after Ceauşescu; the Politics of Intolerance.* Edinburgh Univ. Press, 1995

Rady, M., *Romania in Turmoil: a Contemporary History.* London, 1992

Siani-Davies, M. and P., *Romania.* [Bibliography] 2nd ed. ABC-Clio, Oxford and Santa Barbara (CA), (rev. ed.) 1998

National Statistical Office: Comisia Nationala pentru Statistica, 16 Libertatii Ave., sector 5, Bucharest.

Website: http://www.insse.ro

RUSSIA

1. KARACHAI-CHERKESSIA	5. CHUVASHIA	10. INGUSHETIA
2. ADYGEYA	6. TARTARSTAN	11. NORTH OSSETIA
3. KALMYKIA	7. UDMURTIA	12. KABARDINO-BALKARIA
4. MORDOVIA	8. MARI-EL	13. DAGESTAN
	9. CHECHNYA	

A. ESTONIA
B. LATVIA
C. BELARUS
D. TURKEY

Rossiiskaya Federatsiya

Capital: Moscow
Population projection, 2010: 140·03m.
GDP per capita, 2003: (PPP$) 9,230
HDI/world rank: 0·795/62

KEY HISTORICAL EVENTS

Archaeological evidence points to the influence of Arabic and Turkic cultures prior to the 4th century AD. Avar, Goth, Hun and Magyar invasions punctuated the development of the East Slavs over the next five centuries, while trade with Germanic, Scandinavian and Middle Eastern regions began in the 8th century.

In 882 the Varangian prince Oleg of Novgorod took Kyiv and made it the capital of Kievan Rus, the first unified state of the East Slavs, uniting Finnish and Slavic tribes. During the 10th century, trade was extended between the Baltic and Black Seas, forming Kyiv's main economy. The Varangians, led by Rurik of Jutland, led attacks on Baghdad and Constantinople, subsequently establishing a trade link with the latter.

During the 13th century the area was invaded from the west by Teutonic Knights, Lithuanians and Swedes, and from the south by Mongol and Tatar tribes. In 1223 Genghis Khan's grandson, Batu Khan, conquered Kievan Rus. Despite the ruthless reign of the Mongols, trade flourished during the period and many cities were reinvigorated. The Mongols and Tatars created an ascendency known as the 'Golden Horde' around most of Western Russia and Central Asia and made Itil (near modern Astrakhan) the capital. Its dominance lasted until the 15th century when internal struggles finally forced the break-up of the empire.

Co-operation between Moscow's leader Ivan and the Mongol Öz Beg (ruled 1312–41), in addition to geographical advantages and natural resources, allowed Moscow to develop and prosper. The city was first consolidated under the Muscovite Grand Duke Ivan III (ruled 1462–1505), who adopted the Roman title of tsar and Byzantine ritual after marrying into Byzantine royalty. Ivan annexed the East Slavic regions, as well as Belarus and the Ukraine, conquered Novgorod in 1478 and opened up contacts with Western Europe.

The empire was strengthened and further expanded by his son Vasily III and reformed by Vasily's successor Ivan IV, a sickly and volatile ruler known as Ivan the Terrible (or 'Awesome', *Grozny*) who came to the throne at the age of 16 in 1547. Ivan's divisive and suppressive administration, *oprichnina*, led a reign of terror from 1566–72 in which thousands were executed (although it is believed that initially the Russian nobles, or boyars, had strong control over the throne and its direction, including local government reforms, a new law code and restrictions of hereditary rights). Ivan bolstered the military and led campaigns against the khanates of Kazan (1552), Astrakhan (1556) and the Crimea, extending Russia's territory towards Siberia and down to the Caspian Sea. But the costly war with Livonia (1558–82) drained Russia's resources. Ivan murdered his son in 1581 leaving a hereditary gap and a struggle for succession.

Russia was ruled nominally by Ivan's mentally subnormal brother Fyodor I—in actuality by Fyodor's brother-in-law Boris

Godunov, who succeeded Fyodor in 1598. But in 1601 False Dmitri claimed to be Ivan IV's son (Dmitri had died in 1591) and challenged Boris for the throne. With the backing of the boyars, the Cossacks and the Polish nobility, Dmitri succeeded Boris as tsar on the latter's death in 1605. There followed a chaotic period of instability as differing sides fought for control of the realm. The following year Dmitri was assassinated and the boyars crowned the rebel leader Vasily Shuysky in return for privileges. But soon a subgroup of boyars led by the Romanovs gave support to a second False Dmitri in 1608, establishing a shadow government just outside Moscow. Shuysky turned to Sweden for help, bargaining away territory and triggering Poland's invasion of Muscovy and the siege of Smolensk (1609). Both governments collapsed in disunity and a coalition government was formed. A peace treaty signed with Sweden in 1617 lost Russia Novgorod in exchange for Baltic control, while an armistice with Poland began the following year.

Romanovs

With the Polish occupiers ejected from Moscow, Mikhail Fyodorovich Romanov, the first of a dynasty that would rule until 1917, became tsar of a country ruined by war and with regions occupied by Swedish, Polish or rebel forces. But by avoiding involvement in the Thirty Years' War, in which Sweden and Poland were embroiled, he managed to restore some stability to Russia and strengthen its holdings in the southern regions. His son Aleksey inherited the throne as a child. Unpopular measures implemented by Aleksey's advisor, Boris Ivanovich Morozov, including a crippling salt tax, led to a riot in 1648 and rebellion in Novgorod and Pskov. Eastern Ukraine was annexed, while the support of a Cossack rebellion against Polish rule in the Ukraine degenerated into a costly war with Sweden and Poland over Ukrainian, Baltic and Belorussian territory. Russia consequently lost the Baltic coast to Sweden in 1661 and later Belarus and parts of the Ukraine to Poland. Sophia succeeded Aleksey to the disputed throne in 1682, followed seven years later by her half brother Peter the Great.

The reign of Peter I (1689–1725) signalled a new era for Russia that broke so far with Muscovy tradition as to be seen as the birth of modern Russia. The empire was expanded and strengthened, and there was increased trade with Western Europe. His modest upbringing and travels to the West gave Peter a novel pro-European stance. The capital was transferred from Moscow to the newly built St Petersburg (1712), as part of a Europeanization programme. Peter introduced radical structural changes to the Russian body politic, converting it into the Western European mould. The tsardom of Muscovy became the Empire of All Russias and Peter became head of state as opposed to ruling patriarch. Administrative reforms divided Russia into eight main provinces, put the church under state control and introduced compulsory secular education for the nobility, although the rights of the peasantry were abolished and they were forced into serfdom. Peter expanded industry, created the navy, introduced army conscription and strengthened the southern border against the Crimean Tatars. He formed an alliance with Denmark, Poland and Saxony against Sweden, resulting in the Great Northern War (1700–21), which ended with Russia claiming Livonia in the Treaty of Nystad (1721). The expanded empire made Russia the leading Baltic power.

Catherine the Great

Despite Peter's rejection of hereditary rule in favour of appointing a successor, his choice was never named before his sudden death. The rest of the 18th century was marked by disputed succession. After Peter's death, his widow Catherine I was declared empress, though Peter's collaborator Prince Menshikov ruled in her name. A supreme privy council was established to distribute power; Peter's grandson, Peter II, ruled briefly before dying of smallpox. He was succeeded by Peter I's

niece, Anna, the duchess of Courland (1730), then by her niece Anna Leopoldovna, before Peter I's daughter, Elizabeth, came to power in 1741 in a bloodless coup. During her 21-year reign, her father's reforms were consolidated and Western culture and literature flourished. She founded the University of Moscow and established the St Petersburg Academy of Arts. At the end of her reign Russia was involved in the Seven Years' War, occupying Berlin for a short time before Elizabeth's death in 1762. Russia's subsequent withdrawal saved Frederick the Great's Prussia from destruction.

The childless Elizabeth's nephew came to power; but Peter III proved an unpopular ruler. His politically ambitious wife, Catherine the Great, plotted to depose him, claiming the throne for herself soon after. Influenced by the Enlightenment, she attempted to implement legislative, educative and administrative reforms. But many of these, as well as the emancipation of the serfs, were blocked by the nobility. The imposed Russification of the Ukrainian, Polish and Baltic regions proved unpopular, while civil unrest led to the Pugachev Revolt (1773–75), in which peasants, Cossacks and workers rebelled against the aristocracy. Catherine's foreign policy was an aggressive expansion plan to the south and east to make Russia the leading European power at the expense of the Turks and Tatars. She forged a path through to the Mediterranean Sea to maximize maritime trade routes and developed close relations with Prussia and Austria with whom Poland was shared. But despite two wars with Turkey she never succeeded in taking Constantinople, as much an emotional as a political prize.

After Catherine's death in 1796, her son Paul's tyrannical rule led to his murder in 1801. His son Alexander I adopted more liberal policies in administration, science and education. War with France in 1805 led to a crushing defeat at Austerlitz, but when Napoleon invaded Russia in 1812 his army fell victim to the Russian winter. Alexander's death in 1825 provoked instability and uprisings which were quashed by military force. Russia was defeated by Britain, France and Turkey in the Crimean War (1853–56). During the war, Alexander II came to power (ruled 1855–81), following the death of Nicholas I (ruled 1825–55). He implemented progressive reforms, the most important of which was the partial emancipation of the serfs in 1861. Major judicial reform followed three years later and universal military service in 1874. But towards the end of his reign Alexander's increasingly conservative measures exacerbated the revolutionary mood of socialist-influenced university students and the peasantry. He was assassinated in 1881 and was succeeded by Alexander III (1881–94). Labour reforms introduced by Alexander III were harsh and restrictive and the peasants' lot failed to improve. The government's neglect of agricultural policy resulted in crop failure and widespread famine in 1891.

The Russian empire had expanded to the far reaches of Asia, to Afghanistan and into Central Europe. By the end of Alexander III's reign, only half the population spoke Russian or were members of the Orthodox Church.

Revolution

Nicholas II's reign (1894–1917) marked the end of Tsarist Russia. Like his father, he did little to improve social conditions for the masses, concentrating instead on military power. Industrial growth produced an unskilled urban working class whose living conditions fuelled revolutionary feeling. Socialism and Liberalism were also taking hold of the educated middle classes—doctors, teachers and engineers—as well as disaffected civil servants. In 1904 Nicholas embarked on an unpopular war with Japan. The middle classes campaigned for a legislative assembly. In Jan. 1905 the priest, Georgy Gapon, led a protest of factory workers to St Petersburg's Winter Palace. Tsarist troops opened fire on the crowds killing over 100 people. Public outrage to 'Bloody Sunday' soon spread throughout the country. A general strike, paralysing most of Russia, led to violence between monarchists and insurgents well into 1907, while factions in the armed forces rebelled. Yielding to the pressure of the 1905 revolution, the tsar permitted the establishment of the first *Duma* (parliament), which convened in St Petersburg in 1906. But it lasted little more the 70 days and would have a further three incarnations in the following six years alone. Violence continued into 1907.

In 1912 the two strands of the Social Democratic Workers' Party—the Bolsheviks (or majority) led by Vladimir Ilyich Ulianov (Lenin), and the Mensheviks (or minority)—split, the Bolsheviks pursuing revolution, the Mensheviks evolutionary change. The outbreak of the First World War in 1914 temporarily unified Russians in the war effort. The tsar took command of the armed forces in 1915, leaving an authoritarian vacuum that allowed the tsarina and the influential advisor Grigori Rasputin to implement various unpopular ministerial changes. Rasputin was assassinated by disgruntled nobles in 1916. Depleting military resources and social unrest caused by hardship forced the end of the tsar's reign. A succession of anti-tsar demonstrations culminated in a mass protest in St Petersburg. Soldiers deserted, allying themselves with the workers, a pattern repeated throughout the country. A provisional government comprising Menshevik and Bolshevik elements was established and Tsar Nicholas abdicated on 2 March 1917. The Royal Family was executed in July 1918.

Tension between moderate Mensheviks and radical Bolsheviks intensified and in Oct. 1917 the Bolsheviks led by Lenin, newly returned from exile, seized control. The new government headed by Lenin, the Council of People's Commissars, created the Soviet constitution the following year. Russia was declared the Soviet Republic of Workers, Soldiers and Peasants and the capital was moved back to Moscow. But this did not stabilize the political situation. Russia eventually withdrew from the First World War in 1918 but its forced acceptance of the unfavourable Brest-Livotsk treaty led many to abandon the government. Between 1918–21 a civil war raged between the Bolshevik Red Army, led by Lenin's ally Leon Trotsky, and the White Army, formed by former imperial officers, Cossacks, anti-communists and anarchists. The government imposed 'war communism'—forced labour and expropriation of business and food supplies—to support its cause, and eventually overcame the White Army. Lenin instituted the New Economic Policy (NEP) in 1921 to replace War Communism, reintroducing a monetary system and private ownership of small-scale industry and agriculture. In 1922 the Union of Soviet Socialist Republics was established comprising Russia, the Ukraine, Belarus and Transcaucasia. The Turkmen and Uzbek republics were added two years later, and the Tadzhik republic joined in 1929.

Stalin
On Lenin's death in 1924, Joseph Stalin (Ioseb Dzhugashvili) became general secretary of the Communist Party. Stalin rejected the 'state capitalism' of the NEP, which had failed to provide enough food for the urban workforce. From 1928 Stalin pursued a programme of industrialization and from 1933 agricultural collectivization, which cost the lives of 10m. peasants through famine or persecution. Constructing a personality cult for Lenin and himself, Stalin reasserted his absolute authority in massive purges; in 1934 and 1937 the NKVD (political police) eliminated millions of political dissidents.

Despite a non-aggression pact signed with Germany in Aug. 1939, the USSR was forced into the Second World War (termed the Great Patriotic War) in 1941 when the Nazi's Plan Barbarossa targeted Kyiv, Moscow and Leningrad for invasion. Up to 20m. Soviet lives were lost, almost 1m. in the battle of Stalingrad alone (1942–43). Expansion before and during the war created 15 aligned republics. Transcaucasia was divided into Armenia, Georgia and Azerbaijan, Kazakh and Kirghiz Soviet Socialist Republics were formed, and, along with Latvia, Lithuania, Estonia and Moldavia, were incorporated into the USSR. Following the

war, Stalin managed to gain Western acceptance of a Soviet sphere of influence in Eastern Europe. The Baltic States and large tracts of land from neighbouring countries were annexed, while puppet regimes established Poland, Czechoslovakia, East Germany, Hungary, Bulgaria and Romania as satellites of Moscow.

The blockade of West Berlin (1948–49) and the Soviet detonation of an atomic bomb in Aug. 1949 were major factors in the escalation of the Cold War, waged indirectly in the Korean War (1950–53). On Stalin's death his successor, Nikita Khrushchev, reversed many of Stalin's policies and condemned his predecessor. In reaction to the famine in his native Ukraine, he developed the vast wheatfields in Kazakhstan. Relaxing control in the Eastern Bloc allowed for some liberalization although the Hungarian Uprising and the Poznań Riots in Poland (both 1956) were brutally suppressed and the Berlin Wall built in 1961. Relations with the Soviet Union's great ideological ally, China, collapsed over differences in interpretation of Marxist doctrine and Chinese opposition to Khrushchev's attempts at détente with the West (which came to be known as 'peaceful co-existence'). The Cuban Missile Crisis of 1962 intensified hostilities with the West and led the world to the brink of nuclear war. Khrushchev's perceived failure in the crisis, coupled with food shortages, led to widespread discontent. He was forced out of office in a 1964 coup led by Leonid Brezhnev, who ruled until 1982.

Soviet Reform
By the 1970s, Russia's international status had reached its zenith. Along with the USA, it was perceived as one of two global superpowers, despite relative economic stagnation. But Brezhnev kept a tight grip on the Eastern Bloc, introducing his 'Brezhnev Doctrine' which permitted the Soviet Union to intervene in the Eastern Bloc countries if Communist rule was ever threatened. In Aug. 1968 the USSR invaded Czechoslovakia to suppress an increasingly liberal regime. Relations with the West were further strained when the Soviets invaded Afghanistan in 1979. By the end of his tenure Brezhnev's failing health mirrored the country's economic decline. The domestic price of Brezhnev's obsessive pursuit of prominence in the space race was the failure of the agricultural and consumer-goods sectors and the decline of living standards. From his death in 1982, the country was led by his aides Yuri Andropov, a short-lived reformer, then Konstantin Chernenko.

When the latter died in 1985, Mikhail Gorbachev became general secretary of the Communist Party. He launched *perestroika*, a policy of economic and structural reform. *Glasnost* ('openness') extended civil liberties, including freedom of the press, and led to official rejection of Stalinist-style totalitarianism. The political system was overhauled, with electoral processes made more democratic and some free-market principles introduced. Gorbachev sought warmer relations with both Communist and Western governments and withdrew troops from Afghanistan in 1989. In a rejection of the 'Brezhnev Doctrine', throughout 1989 and 1990 Gorbachev refused to intervene as one Communist regime after another fell in the Eastern Bloc. Within the USSR, the republics demanded independence. Initially rejected, ethnic tensions arose between and within the republics, with heavy fighting in the Caucasus. Suppressed for so long, the newfound freedom also brought chaos and Gorbachev was blamed. Nonetheless, he won the first USSR presidential elections. Opposition parties were legalized soon after, although he was reluctant to open up the economy to privatization. An attempted coup led to Gorbachev's house arrest for three days and though the coup failed, largely owing to Russian president Boris Yeltsin's intervention (elected June 1991), Gorbachev's leadership was existing on borrowed time. In quick succession Gorbachev resigned his party membership, dismantled the central committee and took KGB and military control away from the Communists. On Christmas Day 1991

Gorbachev resigned as Soviet president and the Soviet Union was dissolved.

Yeltsin

A period of confrontation in 1992–93 between President Yeltsin and parliament climaxed when thousands of armed anti-Yeltsin demonstrators assembled on 3 Oct. 1993 and were urged to seize the Kremlin and television centre. On 4 Oct. troops took the parliament building by storm after a 10-hour assault in which 140 people died. Vice-President Rutskoi and Speaker Khasbulatov were arrested.

Boris Yeltsin was re-elected president in 1996. Many took this as a signal of confidence in the new, democratic Russia. But the reality was a state in which democratic institutions were weakened to the point of impotence by racketeering and bureaucratic dead-weight. Russia defaulted on its debt, the rouble halved in value, imports fell by 45% and oil revenues slumped. On 17 Aug. 1998 the government freed the rouble, in effect devaluing it, imposed currency controls and froze the domestic debt market.

In Aug. 1999 Boris Yeltsin appointed as prime minister Vladimir Putin, a former KGB colonel and director of the KGB's successor organization, the FSB. On 31 Dec. 1999 Yeltsin resigned the presidency, nominating Putin as his interim successor, a job he retained after a clear-cut victory in the presidential election of March 2000. Under Putin, Russia continued war with separatist Chechnya that began in Dec. 1994. One of his primary aims has been to reduce the power of the business oligarchs and to fight corruption. Tax cuts have been introduced, and in 2000 a programme of regional reform divided Russia's 89 regions into seven new districts run by Kremlin representatives.

Following the attacks on the USA in Sept. 2001, Putin made clear his support for the war on terrorism. In Oct. 2002 a group of Chechen rebels took control of a Moscow theatre and held hostage 800 people for three days, before Russian troops stormed the building. An anaesthetic gas, used to combat the rebels, also killed many of the hostages. The rebels had been demanding that Russia end the war in Chechnya. The new relationship with the USA faltered as a result of the war with Iraq, which Russia opposed. Russia's vulnerability to terrorism was highlighted in Sept. 2004 when hostage takers seized a school in Beslan, in the Russian republic of North Ossetia. A three-day standoff ended with more than 350 people killed, nearly half of them children. Chechen rebels claimed responsibility for the siege.

TERRITORY AND POPULATION

Russia is bounded in the north by various seas (Barents, Kara, Laptev, East Siberian) which join the Arctic Ocean, and in which is a fringe of islands, some of them large. In the east Russia is separated from the USA (Alaska) by the Bering Strait; the Kamchatka peninsula separates the coastal Bering and Okhotsk Seas. Sakhalin Island, north of Japan, is Russian territory. Russia is bounded in the south by North Korea, China, Mongolia, Kazakhstan, the Caspian Sea, Azerbaijan, Georgia, the Black Sea and Ukraine, and in the west by Belarus, Latvia, Estonia, the Baltic Sea and Finland. Kaliningrad (the former East Prussia) is an exclave on the Baltic Sea between Lithuania and Poland in the west. Russia's area is 17,075,400 sq. km and it has 11 time zones. The 2002 census population was 145,166,731 (53·5% females); density, 8·6 per sq. km. Population estimate, 1 Jan. 2005: 143,474,200. Ethnicity in 2002 showed 79·8% were Russians, 3·8% Tatars, 2·0% Ukrainians, 1·1% Bashkir and 1·1% Chuvash. There are also small numbers of Armenians, Avars, Belarusians, Chechens, Germans, Jews, Kazakhs, Mari, Mordovians and Udmurts.

In 2003, 73·3% of the population lived in urban areas.

The UN gives a projected population for 2010 of 140·03m.

Russia's population has been declining since the break-up of the Soviet Union and will continue to do so in the future. By 2050 its population is projected to be the same as it was in the early 1950s.

The two principal cities are Moscow, the capital, with a 2002 census population of 10·13m. and St Petersburg (formerly Leningrad), with 4·16m. Other major cities (with 2002 populations) are: Novosibirsk (1·43m.), Nizhny Novgorod (1·31m.), Yekaterinburg (1·29m.), Samara (1·16m.) and Omsk (1·13m.). In May 2000 President Putin signed a decree dividing Russia into seven federal districts, in the process creating a layer above the various administrative units (see CONSTITUTION AND GOVERNMENT below). The new districts, with their administrative centres and 2002 populations in brackets, are: Central (Moscow, 38·00m.), North-Western (St Petersburg, 13·97m.), Southern (Rostov-on-Don, 22·91m.), Volga (Nizhny Novgorod, 31·15m.), Ural (Yekaterinburg, 12·37m.), Siberian (Novosibirsk, 20·06m.) and Far-Eastern (Khaborovsk, 6·69m.).

The national language is Russian.

SOCIAL STATISTICS

2003 births, 1,477,301; deaths, 2,365,826; marriages, 1,091,778; divorces, 798,824. Rates, 2003 (per 1,000 population): birth, 10·2; death, 16·4; marriage, 7·6; divorce, 5·5. At the beginning of the 1970s the death rate had been just 9·4 per 1,000 population. Infant mortality, 2001 (per 1,000 live births), 18. There were 2,014,710 legal abortions in 2001. The annual abortion rate, at approximately 70 per 1,000 women aged 15–44, ranks among the highest in the world. The divorce rate is also among the highest in the world. The most popular age range for marrying in 1999 was 18–24 for both males and females. Expectation of life at birth, 2003, was 59·0 years for males and 72·1 years for females. With a difference of 13·1 years, no other country has a life expectancy for females so high compared to that for males. The low life expectancy (down from 64·6 years for males and 74·0 years for females in the USSR as a whole in 1989) and the low birth rate (down from 17·6 per 1,000 population in the USSR in 1989) is causing a demographic crisis, with the population declining by approximately 750,000 a year. If current trends continue, the population could fall by nearly 40m. in the first half of the 21st century. Disease, pollution, poor health care and alcoholism are all contributing to the dramatic decline in the population. More than 40,000 Russians died of alcohol poisoning in 2002. In 2000, 35% of Russians were living below the poverty line, up from 21% in 1997. Annual population growth rate, 1992–2002, −0·3%; fertility rate, 2001, 1·2 births per woman. The suicide rate, at 38·7 per 100,000 population in 2002, is one of the highest in the world. Among males it was 69·3 per 100,000 population in 2002.

CLIMATE

Moscow, Jan. −9·4°C, July 18·3°C. Annual rainfall 630 mm. Arkhangelsk, Jan. −15°C, July 13·9°C. Annual rainfall 503 mm. St Petersburg, Jan. −8·3°C, July 17·8°C. Annual rainfall 488 mm. Vladivostok, Jan. −14·4°C, July 18·3°C. Annual rainfall 599 mm.

CONSTITUTION AND GOVERNMENT

The Russian Soviet Federative Socialist Republic (RSFSR) adopted a declaration of republican sovereignty by 544 votes to 271 in June 1990. It became a founding member of the Commonwealth of Independent States (CIS) in Dec. 1991, and adopted the name 'Russian Federation'. A law of Nov. 1991 extended citizenship to all who lived in Russia at the time of its adoption and to those in other Soviet republics who requested it.

According to the 1993 Constitution the Russian Federation is a 'democratic federal legally-based state with a republican form of government'. The Federation consists of 88 subjects (administrative units), of which 21 are republics, one autonomous region, nine autonomous areas, seven territories, 48 regions and two federal cities. The state is secular. Individuals have freedom of movement within or across the boundaries of the Federation; there is freedom of assembly and association, and freedom to engage in any entrepreneurial activity not forbidden by law. The state itself is based upon a separation of powers and upon federal principles, including a Constitutional Court. The most important matters of state are reserved for the federal government, including socio-economic policy, the budget, taxation, energy, foreign affairs and defence. Other matters, including the use of land and water, education and culture, health and social security, are for the joint management of the federal and local governments, which also have the right to legislate within their spheres of competence. A central role is accorded to the *President*, who defines the 'basic directions of domestic and foreign policy' and represents the state internationally. The President is directly elected for a four-year term, and for not more than two consecutive terms; he must be at least 35 years old, a Russian citizen, and a resident in Russia for the previous ten years. 2m. signatures are needed to validate a presidential candidate not affiliated to a party represented in the State Duma, no more than 2·5% of which may come from any one region or republic. The President has the right to appoint the prime minister, and (on his nomination) to appoint and dismiss deputy prime ministers and ministers, and may dismiss the government as a whole. In the event of the death or incapacity of the President, the Prime Minister becomes head of state.

Parliament is known as the *Federal Assembly* (Federalnoe Sobranie). The 'representative and legislative organ of the Russian Federation', it consists of two chambers: the *Federation Council* (Sovet Federatsii) and the *State Duma* (Gosudarstvennaya Duma). The Federation Council, or upper house, consists of 178 deputies. The State Duma, or lower house, consists of 450 deputies elected for a four-year term. From 2007 all deputies to the State Duma will be elected from party lists by proportional representation. There is a 7% threshold for the party-list seats. To qualify for candidacy an individual must be nominated by a registered political party. Incumbent parties are automatically included in the ballot; others must obtain a minimum of 200,000 supporting signatures of which no more than 5% may come from any one region. Alternatively, non-incumbent parties may put forward a deposit of 60m. roubles, which is returned if the party manages to win at least 4% of the popular vote. Parties which gain at least 35 seats may register as a faction, which gives them the right to join the Duma Council and chair committees. Any citizen aged over 21 may be elected to the State Duma, but may not at the same time be a member of the upper house or of other representative bodies. The Federation Council considers all matters that apply to the Federation as a whole, including state boundaries, martial law, and the deployment of Russian forces elsewhere. The Duma approves nominations for Prime Minister, and adopts federal laws (they are also considered by the Federation Council but any objection may be overridden by a two-thirds majority; objections on the part of the President may be overridden by both houses on the same basis). The Duma can reject nominations for Prime Minister but after the third rejection it is automatically dissolved. It is also dissolved if it twice votes a lack of confidence in the government, or if it refuses to express confidence in the government when the matter is raised by the Prime Minister.

A law was approved in June 2001 to reduce the proliferation of political parties (numbering some 200 in 2001). It took effect in July 2003. The new law introduced stricter registration criteria and obliging existing parties to re-register within two years. In order to register, political parties are required to have at least 50,000 members, with no fewer than 100 members in more than half of Russia's 88 territorial entities. Multiple party membership is banned.

There is a 19-member *Constitutional Court*, whose functions under the 1993 Constitution include making decisions on the constitutionality of federal laws, presidential and government decrees, and the constitutions and laws of the subjects of the Federation. It is governed by a Law on the Constitutional Court, adopted in July 1994. Judges are elected for non-renewable 12-year terms.

National Anthem

In Dec. 2000 the Russian parliament, on President Putin's initiative, decided that the tune of the anthem of the former Soviet Union should be reintroduced as the Russian national anthem. Written by Alexander Alexandrov in 1943, the anthem was composed for Stalin. New words were written by Sergei Mikhalkov, who had written the original words for the Soviet anthem in 1943. The new anthem is 'Rossiya—svyashennaya nasha derzhava, Rossiya—lyubimaya nasha strana' ('Russia—our holy country, Russia—our beloved country'). Boris Yeltsin had introduced a new anthem during his presidency—'Patriotic Song', from an opera by Mikhail Glinka and arranged by Andrei Petrov.

GOVERNMENT CHRONOLOGY

General/First Secretaries of the Central Committee of the USSR (1922–91) and Presidents of Russia (1991–)

1922–53	Joseph Stalin
1953–64	Nikita Sergeyevich Khrushchev
1964–82	Leonid Ilyich Brezhnev
1982–84	Yuriy Vladimirovich Andropov
1984–85	Konstantin Ustinovich Chernenko
1985–91	Mikhail Sergeyevich Gorbachev
1991–99	Boris Nikolayevich Yeltsin
1999–	Vladimir Vladimirovich Putin

RECENT ELECTIONS

Vladimir Putin was re-elected for a four-year term in presidential elections on 14 March 2004, gaining 71·2% of the votes cast. Nikolai Kharitonov (Communist Party of the Russian Federation; KPRF) won 13·7% of the vote; Sergei Glazyev (Rodina) 4·1%; Irina Khakamada 3·9%; Oleg Malyshkin (Liberal Democratic Party; LDPR) 2·0%; and Sergei Mironov 0·8%. Turnout was 64·3%.

Elections for the State Duma were held on 7 Dec. 2003: United Russia won 222 seats (with 37·6% of the votes); the KPRF 51 seats (12·6%); Rodina (Motherland)–National Patriotic Union 37 seats (9·0%); the LDPR 36 seats (11·5%); the People's Party of the Russian Federation 16 seats (1·2%); Jabloko (Apple)–Russian Democratic Party 4 seats (4·3%); and the Agrarian Party of Russia 3 seats (3·6%). 67 other party representatives were elected and 11 non-partisans. Turnout was 55·8%.

CURRENT ADMINISTRATION

President: Vladimir Putin; b. 1952 (sworn in 7 May 2000 having been acting president since 31 Dec. 1999).

In March 2006 the government comprised:

Prime Minister: Mikhail Fradkov; b. 1950 (sworn in 5 March 2004).

First Deputy Prime Minister: Dmitry Medvedev.

Deputy Prime Ministers: Alexander Zhukov; Sergei Ivanov (also *Minister of Defence*).

Minister of Agriculture and Food: Alexei Gordeyev. *Civil Defence, Emergencies and Natural Disasters:* Sergei Shoigu. *Communications:* Leonid Reiman. *Culture and Information:* Alexander Sokolov. *Economic Development and Trade:* German Gref. *Education and Science:* Andrei Fursenko. *Finance:* Alexei Kudrin. *Foreign Affairs:* Sergei Lavrov. *Health and Social Development:* Mikhail Zurabov. *Industry and Energy:* Viktor Khristenko. *Internal Affairs (MVD):* Rashid Nurgaliev. *Justice:* Yuri Chaika. *Nationalities Affairs:* Vladimir Yakovlev. *Natural*

Resources: Yuri Trutnev. *Transportation and Communications:* Igor Levitin. *Head of the Ministerial Apparatus:* Dimitri Kozak. *Chairman of the State Duma*: Guennadi N. Seleznev.

Government Website: http://www.gov.ru

CURRENT LEADERS

Vladimir Vladimirovitch Putin

Position
President

Introduction
Vladimir Putin became acting president on 31 Dec. 1999 and was confirmed in the position following elections in March 2000. His appointment was the culmination of a rapid political rise in the post-Communist era. Little known internationally, his KGB past aroused early concerns but he quickly gained respect within Russia as a modernizer and efficient administrator. He has made a determined effort to establish a new international role for his country. His handling of the Chechen war has led to criticism at home and abroad. His opposition to the US-led attack on Iraq in 2003 strained what had been improving relations with Washington.

Early Life
Vladimir Putin was born in Leningrad on 7 Oct. 1952, the son of a war veteran who, with his wife, had survived the siege of Leningrad. Baptized into Russian Orthodoxy, he was an accomplished athlete, excelling at wrestling and martial arts. After graduating from law school in 1975, he began a 15-year career with the KGB's foreign intelligence arm, stationed in Leningrad and East Germany. When collapse threatened the Soviet Union, he retired as a colonel and embarked on a political career.

In the early 1990s Putin worked in local government in St Petersburg as an advisor to the city mayor, himself becoming deputy mayor in 1994, and chairman of the committee on external relationships. In 1996 President Yeltsin brought Putin to Moscow and appointed him deputy chief Kremlin administrator. He became the Kremlin's official in charge of relations with Russia's diverse regions and in 1998 head of the Federal Security Service (successor of the KGB) and secretary of the presidential Security Council. Putin was named acting prime minister in Aug. 1999 when Yeltsin sacked Russia's government for the fourth time in 17 months. His hardline campaign to suppress rebels in Chechnya brought him much popular support. In addition, he expressed a desire to reinvigorate Russia's intelligence and security bodies which had been in decline since the Communist collapse.

Career in Office
Putin became the acting president of Russia after Yeltsin's resignation on 31 Dec. 1999 and was officially elected president on 26 March 2000, taking 53% of the vote. His election programme prioritized a 'dictatorship of law' to combat high crime rates, as well as pledging to vanquish poverty and promote family values, patriotism and fair business conditions. One of his first public addresses as acting president underlined his support for 'freedom of speech, conscience and the press', which he propagated along with private property rights as tenets of a 'civilized society'.

He quickly set about exercising firm control over local government and the economy, with a stated aim of reducing corruption. In a bid to centralize power in Moscow, he restructured 89 legislative regions into seven districts, each with a government-approved leader (the majority of whom had military or security backgrounds). He reversed tax concessions that Yeltsin had brought in to assist the regions and reserved the right to dismiss any democratically-elected politician found to have broken the law.

Putin also removed several high-profile business and media figures from official positions. Yeltsin's daughter was dismissed as a Kremlin adviser but immunity was granted to Yeltsin himself, one of the more controversial moves of the then acting president. Putin appointed former finance minister and Yeltsin ally Mikhail Kasyanov as prime minister while placing other supporters in key Kremlin positions. Putin's economic policy has been influenced by his allegiance to Anatoly Chubais, who led the wave of privatization in Russia in the early 1990s. He is also an admirer of Margaret Thatcher and her 1980s privatization programme in the UK.

In April 2001 Putin's Unity party merged with the opposition Fatherland bloc, led by the mayor of Moscow, Yury Luzhkov. To pass legislation the president needed a simple majority of 226, with the merger giving him at least 132. In the summer of 2001 new laws on land, labour and pensions were proposed. These were opposed by the Communists whose leader Gennady Zyuganov called for a national demonstration against the land reforms.

After Oct. 2001 Russians were free to buy residential and commercial land for the first time since the Bolsheviks took power in 1917. Farm land, making up 98% of the total, was not covered by the law. Critics feared that a privileged few would buy up the land much as they bought privatized businesses in the 1990s. Supporters maintained that it would attract foreign investment, speed up economic reform and stop the illegal sale of land.

Putin's image was dented by the sinking of the Kursk nuclear submarine in Aug. 2000 when all 118 Russian sailors on board died. He was widely condemned for inaction, refusing to return from his holiday and turning down offers of help from Norway and the UK. He was subsequently dogged by allegations of an official cover-up. The same summer saw a fire at the Ostankino TV tower in Moscow and various terrorist bomb attacks on Russian civilians. The Kursk was finally raised in Aug. 2001, a salvage operation costing US$65m.

Putin has come under international scrutiny for heavy-handed treatment of the Russian media. He has been blamed for persecution of Andrey Babitsky, a Radio Liberty journalist who broadcast unfavourable reports on the Chechen war, and for the closure of the TV station TV6. While the Kremlin insisted the station's problems were financial, others believed they stemmed from the outspoken criticism by its head, Boris Berezovsky.

Putin has aimed at re-establishing Russia as a major international power after a decade of diminishing stature. He has sought ties with NATO following strained relations during the Kosovo conflict and disapproval of former socialist allies Poland, Hungary and the Czech Republic joining the alliance.

Putin has used the war with Chechnya to establish his 'strong man' credentials, but heavy Russian losses lost him support. Alleged human rights abuses have led to a suspension of Russia's voting rights in the Council of Europe. In Oct. 2002 Chechen rebels took 800 people hostage inside a Moscow theatre, demanding the immediate withdrawal of Russian troops from Chechnya. The siege lasted three days before the Russian military stormed the building using an anaesthetic gas which killed the rebels and over 100 hostages. Soon after, a Chechen politician, Ahmed Zakayev, was arrested in Copenhagen at the request of the Russian government on suspicion of being involved. Despite Moscow's calls for his extradition, he was released by the Danish authorities.

In March 2003 Putin promised greater autonomy for Chechnya. This followed a referendum in the republic supporting a new constitution which would keep Chechnya within Russia but provide for a president and parliament. Moscow claimed 96% support for the proposals although no international observers were present and the referendum was opposed by separatist groups. In May 2003, following two suicide bomb attacks, Putin reaffirmed his determination to defeat Chechnya's rebel forces. He offered an amnesty for rebels who handed over their weapons by 1 Aug. 2003 and for Russian troops accused of human rights violations.

Some observers anticipated that Putin's foreign policy would strive for a reversion to pro- and anti-Western blocs but many others believed Russia was realigning itself as a mediating force between the West and developing nations. Following the 11 Sept. attacks on New York and Washington, D.C. there was a rapprochement between Russia and the USA. In 2001 Putin gave unprecedented support for UN military action in Afghanistan. His offers of military assistance to the Afghan Northern Alliance, the use of Russian airspace for humanitarian aid and his role in persuading Tajikistan and Uzbekistan to support the campaign were well received in the West where leaders were quick to downplay Russia's role in Chechnya. In May 2002 Putin and US President George W. Bush signed an anti-nuclear deal agreeing to reduce their respective strategic nuclear warheads by two-thirds over the next ten years.

However, tension between the two countries increased over the question of Iraq in late 2002. While President Bush attempted to garner support for military action in Iraq—with Russia holding a power of veto within the UN Security Council—he warned Putin at the same time that he would not support Russian military incursions into Georgia. Putin had criticized Georgian president Eduard Shevardnadze for tolerating Chechen activity in the Pankisi Gorge. In Oct. 2002 Russia and Georgia agreed to joint patrols on the shared border. Furthermore, Putin's political dealings with 'rogue' nations, including North Korea and Cuba, received mixed responses from political observers, as did Russia's trading of nuclear fuel and weapons with India, Iran, Iraq and Syria.

By late 2002-early 2003 Russia was among those UN Security Council members opposed to a US/UK-championed resolution specifically permitting military action against Saddam Hussein's regime in Iraq. When US-led forces began attacking in 2003 Russia condemned the action and delayed ratifying the US-Russian strategic arms control treaty (see above) until the war was over. Putin refuted accusations by the USA that it had breached UN sanctions by selling armaments, including anti-tank missiles and jamming equipment, to Iraq. When the UN agreed in principle to reinstate Iraq's oil-for-food programme, halted at the outbreak of war, Russia was one of several UN Security Council members to emphasize that resumption of the programme did not signify UN backing for the invasion. In early April 2003 the US House of Representatives approved a package including finance for reconstruction contracts in post-war Iraq. The House specified that companies from Russia, as well as France, Germany and Syria, should not be entitled to benefit from the fund. In May 2003 Russia voted to accept a UN resolution on Iraq's future jointly proposed by the USA, UK and Spain. In return for the immediate ending of sanctions, the UN was to co-operate with the occupying forces to form a new government. In addition Russia would be able to complete longstanding contracts with Iraq.

In April 2003 Putin announced plans to increase Russia's military presence in Tajikistan. The proposals, which he said had the backing of the Tajik president Emomali Rakhmonov, followed intelligence reports of increased activity by the Taliban and al-Qaeda in neighbouring Afghanistan.

In his state-of-the-nation address in May 2003 Putin urged his listeners to work towards bringing Russia into the 'league of progressive nations'. He argued that European and global economic integration would allow free movement of Russians and enable them to interact with the world's top businesses. Despite tension in Russia's relationship with the UK as a result of differences over Iraq, Putin made an official state visit to Britain, the first by a Russian leader for over a century.

Chechen violence continued in 2003 with a suicide bombing at a rock music festival in July. Following a referendum in which Chechens agreed to a Moscow-approved constitution, Putin announced that a presidential vote would go ahead. In Oct. 2003, with a turnout of 85%, the pro-Moscow leader Akhmad Kadyrov was elected.

Putin publicly endorsed a pro-government party—United Russia—that was competing in the Dec. 2003 parliamentary elections. Hitherto he had avoided party politics. Leading up to the March 2004 presidential elections, Putin was criticized by the international press over his use of the Russian media to influence voting. While there was little or no coverage of the mysterious kidnapping of Ivan Rybkin, a presidential candidate who subsequently fled the country, the media were dominated by Putin's campaign. On Feb. 2004 Putin dismissed the entire Russian cabinet, including Prime Minister Mikhail Kasyanov. On 1 March Mikhail Fradkov was appointed Russia's new prime minister.

In the March 2004 poll Putin was re-elected, claiming 71% of the vote and leaving his closest rival, the Communist Nikolai Kharitonov with less than 14%. However, OSCE election monitors were critical of what they considered to be unbalanced media coverage heavily slanted in his favour. In May 2004 Putin set out his goals for his second term—modernizing Russia and raising living standards while aiming for a more stable democracy able to pursue strategic interests abroad. The cutting of state benefits led to worker protests across Russia as many demanded further action against poverty.

Following the killing of Akhmad Kadyrov in a bomb attack in Chechnya's capital in May 2004, Putin pledged to send extra troops to deal with the conflict. Alu Alkhanov was elected president of Chechnya on 29 Aug. 2004, and in Chechen parliamentary elections in Nov. 2005 the pro-Moscow United Russia party claimed about 60% of the popular vote.

In the aftermath of the bloodbath which ended the Beslan school siege in Sept. 2004, Putin controversially took control of the appointment of regional governors who had been directly elected for the previous decade. Critics saw the move as undermining democracy.

In May 2005 Mikhail Khodorkovsky, a billionaire former head of oil-exporting company Yukos, was sentenced to nine years' imprisonment for tax evasion and fraud. His conviction was widely viewed as politically motivated, owing to his criticism of Putin's regime.

Under the current constitution, Putin's second term of presidential office (which expires in 2008) must also be his last.

DEFENCE

The President of the Republic is C.-in-C. of the armed forces. Conscription was raised from 18 months to two years in April 1995, but is scheduled to be reduced to one year from 2008.

The START 2 nuclear arms cutting treaty was ratified by the Duma in April 2000, seven years after it had been signed. This obliged both Russia and the USA to reduce their stocks of strategic weapons from some 6,000 nuclear warheads to 3,500. At the height of the Cold War each side had possessed over 10,000.

A presidential decree of Feb. 1997 ordered a cut in the armed forces of 200,000 men, reducing them to an authorized strength of 1,004,100 in 1999. This figure included 200,000 staff at the Ministry of Defence and 478,000 paramilitary troops (including 196,000 border troops).

Military expenditure totalled US$65,200m. in 2003 (US$455 per capita), representing 4·9% of GDP. Only the USA spent more on defence in 2003.

Nuclear Weapons

Russia's strategic warhead count is now shrinking and stood at 3,980 in Jan. 2005 according to the Stockholm International

Peace Research Institute. Shortfalls in planned investments to replace current systems as they reach the end of their service lives means the number of strategic warheads will decline rapidly over the next decade. Current plans are to cut stockpiles to between 2,000 and 2,500, but President Putin has proposed that the target for both Russia and the USA should be 1,500, with even further reductions to follow. On 24 May 2002 the USA and Russia signed an arms control treaty to reduce the number of US and Russian warheads, from between 6,000 and 7,000 each to between 1,700 and 2,200 each, over the next ten years. Russia has pledged to dismantle its biological and chemical weapons programme and to destroy its stockpiles of such weapons, believed to be the largest in the world.

Arms Trade. Russia was the world's third largest exporter after the USA and the UK in 2003, with sales worth US$3,400m., or 11·8% of the world total.

Army
A Russian Army was created by presidential decree in March 1992. In 2004 forces numbered around 360,000 (190,000 conscripts). There were estimated to be around 20,000,000 reserves (all armed forces) of whom 2,400,000 had seen service within the previous five years. There were around 17,000 Russian troops stationed outside Russia (including 7,800 in Tajikistan and 3,000 in Georgia) in 2004, the majority in various states of the former USSR. In April 2003 plans were announced to increase military presence in Tajikistan following intelligence reports of increased activity by the Taliban and the al-Qaeda terrorist network in neighbouring Afghanistan.

The Army is deployed in six military districts and one Operational Strategic Group. Equipment includes some 22,800 main battle tanks (including T-55s, T-62s, T-64A/-Bs, T-72L/-Ms, T-80/-U/UD/UMs and T-90s) plus 150 light tanks (PT-76).

The Military Transport Aviation Command has some 1,700 attack helicopters in the inventory (of which 600 in store) including Mi-24s and Ka-50s. Funding shortages have reduced serviceability drastically.

Strategic Nuclear Ground Forces
In 2004 there were three rocket armies, each with launcher groups, ten silos and one control centre. Inter-continental ballistic missiles numbered 635. Personnel, 100,000 (50,000 conscripts).

Navy
The Russian Navy continues to reduce steadily and levels of sea-going activity remain very low with activity concentrated on a few operational units in each fleet. The safe deployment and protection of the reduced force of strategic missile-firing sub-marines remains its first priority; and the defence of the Russian homeland its second. The strategic missile submarine force operates under command of the Strategic Nuclear Force commander whilst the remainder come under the Main Naval Staff in Moscow, through the Commanders of the fleets.

The Northern and Pacific fleets count the entirety of the ballistic missile submarine force, all nuclear-powered sub-marines, the sole operational aircraft carrier and most major surface warships. The Baltic Fleet organization is based in the St Petersburg area and in the Kaliningrad exclave. Some minor war vessels have been ceded to the Baltic republics. The Black Sea Fleet was for some years the object of wrangling between Russia and Ukraine. Russia eventually received four-fifths of the Black Sea Fleet's warships, with Ukraine receiving about half of the facilities. It was agreed that Russia would rent three harbours for warships and two airfields for a period of 20 years, for a payment of approximately US$100m. annually. The small Caspian Sea flotilla, formerly a sub-unit of the Black Sea Fleet, has been divided between Azerbaijan (25%), and Russia, Kazakhstan and

Turkmenistan, the littoral republics (75%). In May 2003 Russia held joint exercises with the Indian fleet in the Arabian Sea for the first time since the collapse of the USSR.

The material state of all the fleets is suffering from continued inactivity and lack of spares and fuel. The nuclear submarine refitting and refuelling operations in the Northern and Pacific Fleets remain in disarray, given the large numbers of nuclear submarines awaiting defuelling and disposal. The strength of the submarine force has now essentially stabilized, but there are still large numbers of decommissioned vessels awaiting their turn for scrapping in a steadily deteriorating state. In Jan. 2003 it was announced that up to a fifth of the fleet was to be scrapped.

The aircraft carrier *Admiral Kuznetsov* is now operational, albeit with a limited aviation capability, and she deployed to the Mediterranean in Dec. 1995.

In 2004 there were 14 operational nuclear-fuelled ballistic-missile submarines, constituted as follows:

Class	No.	Missiles	Total no of missiles
Delta-IV	6	16 SS-N-23	96
Delta-III	6	16 SS-N-18	96
Typhoon	2	20 SS-N-20	40
			——
			232

The attack submarine fleet comprises a wide range of classes, from the enormous 16,250 tonne 'Oscar' nuclear-powered missile submarine to diesel boats of around 2,000 tonnes. The inventory of tactical nuclear-fuelled submarines comprises seven 'Oscar II', one former strategic 'Yankee'-class, eight 'Akula'-class, one 'Sierra'-class and five 'Victor III'-class submarines.

The diesel-powered 'Kilo' class, of which the Navy operates 15, is still building at a reduced rate mostly for export.

Cruisers are divided into two categories; those optimized for anti-submarine warfare (ASW) are classified as 'Large Anti-Submarine Ships' and those primarily configured for anti-surface ship operations are classified 'Rocket Cruisers'. The principal surface ships of the Russian Navy include the following classes:

Aircraft Carrier. The *Admiral Kuznetsov* of 67,500 tonnes was completed in 1989. It is capable of embarking 20 aircraft and 15–17 helicopters. All other aircraft carriers have been decommissioned or scrapped.

Cruisers. The ships of this classification are headed by the two ships of the Kirov-class, the largest combatant warships, apart from aircraft carriers, to be built since the Second World War. There are, in addition, three Slava-class and one of the Nikolaev ('Kara') class in operation.

Destroyers. There are seven Udaloy-class, the first of which entered service in 1981, one Udaloy II-class and five Sovremenny-class guided missile destroyers in operation. In addition there is a single remaining 'modified Kashin'-class ship in operation.

Frigates. There are six frigates in operation including the first of a new class, the 'Neustrashimy', three Krivak I-class and two Krivak II-class ships.

The Russian Naval Air Force operates some 266 combat aircraft including 58 Tu-22M bombers and 58 Su-24, 10 Su-25 and 49 Su-27 fighters. There were an additional 161 armed helicopters in operation.

Total Naval personnel in 2004 numbered 155,000, of whom an estimated 16,000 were conscripts. Some 11,000 serve in the strategic submarine force, 35,000 in naval aviation, 9,500 naval infantry/coastal defence troops.

Air Force
The Air Force (VVS) and Air Defence Troops (PVO) amalgamated in March 1998 under one Air Force command. Personnel is

estimated at 184,600 and comprises some 1,736 combat aircraft and an estimated 700 armed helicopters.

The Air Force is organized into three main Commands: Long-Range Aviation, Tactical Aviation and Military Transport Aviation. An air force base opened in Kyrgyzstan in Oct. 2003.

Long-Range Aviation comprised in 2004 (numbers in brackets) Tu-160 (15), Tu-22M (116) and Tu-95 (63) bombers, some equipped to carry nuclear weapons.

Tactical Aviation comprised in 2004 (numbers in brackets) Su-24 (371) and Su-25 (235) fighter-bombers and MiG-29 (255), MiG-31 (256) and Su-27 (392) fighters. In addition MiG-25 and Su-24s are used for reconnaissance missions.

INTERNATIONAL RELATIONS

Russia is a member of the UN (Security Council), BIS, the NATO Partnership for Peace, CIS, the Council of Europe, OSCE, Council of the Baltic Sea States, BSEC, Danube Commission, APEC and the Antarctic Treaty. On 16 May 1997 NATO ratified a 'Fundamental Act on Relations, Co-operation and Mutual Security' with Russia.

Although not a member of the World Trade Organization, President Putin has made it a stated goal and membership may be achieved before the end of 2006.

ECONOMY

Agriculture accounted for 5·7% of GDP in 2002, industry 34·0% and services 60·3%.

In Oct. 1991 a programme was launched to create a 'healthy mixed economy with a powerful private sector'. The prices of most commodities were freed on 2 Jan. 1992.

Privatization, which is overseen by the State Committee on the Management of State Property, began with small and medium-sized enterprises. A state programme of privatization of state and municipal enterprises was approved by parliament in June 1992, and vouchers worth 10,000 roubles each began to be distributed to all citizens in Oct. 1992. These could be sold or exchanged for shares. Employees had the right to purchase 51% of the equity of their enterprises. 25 categories of industry (including raw materials and arms) remained in state ownership. The voucher phase of privatization ended on 30 June 1994. A post-voucher stage authorized by presidential decree of 22 July 1994 provides for firms to be auctioned for cash following the completion of the sale of up to 70% of manufacturing industry for vouchers. The Ministry of Property Relations was established in 2000 with the mandate of overall federal policies on property issues and the management of state property, and in Dec. 2001 a new Federal Law on Privatization of State and Municipal Property was adopted. By that time a total of 129,811 enterprises had been sold. In 2004 only 36% of total employment was still in the public sector.

Overview

Russia has experienced robust economic growth since the sharp depreciation that occurred in the wake of the 1998 economic crisis, with real growth averaging 6·8% between 1999–2004 (just below the target rate of 7·25% to double GDP in a decade). The gains in total factor productivity and rises in real wages and consumption have been surprising given that Russia has a relatively low investment-to-GDP ratio compared to other market economies and a concentration of investments in primary commodity sectors. Growth has been driven by export-orientated industries, particularly the oil industry which has reacted to higher oil prices by increasing output and investment. High investment in other sectors has spurred growth in total factor productivity and real wages, allowing consumption to increase. Large gains in terms-of-trade have seen the export sector flourish and helped reduce unemployment from over 13% at the time of the crisis to 8% in the mid-2000s.

Though still vibrant, the economy has slackened since 2004 owing to lower oil investment. The 2003 Yukos oil company tax scandal triggered concerns about the progress of government reforms, state intervention and the severity of the reaction of the tax authorities. Additionally, a sharp rise in the marginal tax rate on oil to nearly 90% for prices above $25 per barrel has taken a toll on oil investment.

Concerns about government commitment to structural reforms were reinforced after the parliamentary elections of late 2003. In the early 2000s progress on structural reform was limited, with reforms to pensions and the electricity sector scaled down, while reforms of the public administration, social and military sectors stalled. The government has, however, stepped up the pace of private sector reform since 2003. Social benefits reform in 2005 was an important advance towards reshaping the Soviet-era entitlement programmes though strong opposition to the legislation has had negative consequences for other areas in the reform agenda, notably health and education.

The government has gained recognition for its reform efforts at the international level. In 2002 both the EU and the USA granted market status to the Russian economy. Russia hopes to achieve membership of the WTO but, in order to complete the accession process, the government must reform the financial and banking sector, provide a non-discriminatory environment for foreign businesses and ensure the protection of intellectual property rights.

The federal budget has been in surplus since 2000, mainly as a result of spending restraint. Since 2000 federal budgets have been drafted to aim for surpluses based on conservative oil price assumptions. Many tax rates have been significantly reduced and tax bases have been broadened, diminishing the incentives and opportunities for tax evasion. General government expenditures in 2004 were approximately 10% below pre-crisis levels without any significant impact on public service provision.

Currency

The unit of currency is the *rouble* (RUR), of 100 *kopeks*. In Jan. 1998 the rouble was redenominated by a factor of a thousand. Foreign exchange reserves were US$60,710m. in July 2003 and gold reserves 12·44m. troy oz in June 2002. In Feb. 2005 Russia abandoned its *de facto* dollar peg and switched to a euro-dollar basket. Inflation rates (based on IMF statistics):

1997	1998	1999	2000	2001	2002	2003	2004
14·8%	27·7%	85·7%	20·8%	21·5%	15·8%	13·7%	10·9%

Inflation had been 2,510% in 1992. Total money supply in June 2003 was 2,604·5bn. roubles. In Nov. 2000 President Putin and President Lukashenka of Belarus agreed the introduction of a single currency. The Russian rouble is scheduled to be introduced into Belarus in Jan. 2008.

Budget

Budgetary central government revenue totalled 2,579·9bn. roubles in 2003 (2,220·9bn. roubles in 2002) and expenditure 2,102·9bn. roubles (1,339·3bn. roubles in 2002). Principal sources of revenue in 2003: taxes on goods and services, 1,137·3bn. roubles; taxes on international trade and transactions, 452·8bn. roubles; social security contributions, 365·5bn. roubles. Main items of expenditure by economic type in 2003: grants, 701·3bn. roubles; use of goods and services, 460·9bn. roubles; compensation of employees, 419·5bn. roubles.

VAT is 18% (reduced rate, 10%).

Performance

Real GDP growth rates (based on IMF statistics):

1995	1996	1997	1998	1999	2000	2001	2002	2003	2004
−4·1%	−3·6%	1·4%	−5·3%	6·3%	10·0%	5·1%	4·7%	7·3%	7·2%

GDP grew by 1·4% in 1997, the first expansion since the Soviet Union's collapse in 1991; but many economists believed that the booming informal economy added over 25% to the value of GDP. With oil revenues well down and a collapse of the rouble in 1998, Russia defaulted on its debt. In 1998 real GDP growth was −5·3%. There was then a highly impressive turnaround, with growth of 6·3% in 1999 and a record 10·0% in 2000. In 2001 there was growth of 5·1%, in spite of the world economic slowdown and the effects of the attacks on the USA of 11 Sept. 2001, followed by 4·7% in 2002, 7·3% in 2003 and 7·2% in 2004. Total GDP was US$582·4bn. in 2004. In May 2003 President Vladimir Putin announced a target of doubling GDP by 2010. In June 2002 Russia was acknowledged as a market economy under United States trade law, symbolically underscoring the country's transformation from a state-planned economy.

In Sept. 2004 the OECD observed: 'The major economic challenge facing Russia is the achievement of long-term, sustainable growth...Resource dependency makes the Russian economy vulnerable to external shocks....especially volatile energy prices....Structural reforms should focus on improving the quality of institutions and the efficiency of resource allocation.'

Banking and Finance

The central bank and bank of issue is the State Bank of Russia (*Governor*, Sergey Mikhailovich Ignatiev). The Russian Bank for Reconstruction and Development and the State Investment Company were created in 1993 to channel foreign and domestic investment. Foreign bank branches have been operating since Nov. 1992.

By 1995 the number of registered commercial banks had increased to around 5,000 but following the Aug. 1997 liquidity crisis, owing to the ensuing bankruptcies, mergers and the Central Bank's revoking of licences, the number fell to 2,500. This has since fallen to 1,300. Approximately 80% of the commercial banks were state-owned through ministries or state enterprises. In 2001 the leading banks were Sberbank (assets of 771·5bn. roubles), Vneshtorgbank (146·5bn. roubles) and Gazprombank (104·3bn. roubles). In 2001 there were around 1,300 credit institutions.

In the wake of one of the worst financial crises which Russia's market economy had experienced, the central bank tripled interest rates to 150% in May 1998 in an effort to restore stability to the financial system. In 2002 the banking sector in Russia was healthier than at any time since the collapse of the former Soviet Union.

There are stock exchanges in Moscow, Novosibirsk, St Petersburg and Vladivostok.

ENERGY AND NATURAL RESOURCES

Environment

Russia's carbon dioxide emissions from the consumption and flaring of fossil fuels in 2002 accounted for 6·2% of the world total (the third highest after the USA and China), and were equivalent to 10·6 tonnes per capita. An *Environmental Sustainability Index* compiled for the World Economic Forum meeting in Jan. 2005 ranked Russia 33rd in the world, with 56·1%. The index measured the ability of countries to maintain favourable environmental conditions and examined various factors including pollution levels and the use or abuse of natural resources.

Electricity

In 2002 installed capacity was 214·5m. kW and electricity production 889·6bn. kWh. Consumption per capita was 4,181 kWh in 2001. The dominant electricity company is Unified Energy System of Russia (52·7% state-owned). It generated 617·4bn. kWh in 2002 (69% of all electricity produced in Russia). It is set to be broken up and its generating capacity sold off in the course of 2006. There were 30 nuclear reactors in use in 2003.

Oil and Gas

Russia is the second largest oil producer (after Saudi Arabia) and the second largest exporter (again, after Saudi Arabia). Oil and gas account for 50% of Russia's export revenues. In 2002 there were proven crude petroleum reserves of 60·0bn. bbls. 2002 production of crude petroleum was 379·6m. tonnes (10·7% of the world total and the second highest after Saudi Arabia). There is an extensive domestic oil pipeline system. The main export pipeline to Europe is the Druzhba pipeline (crossing Belarus before splitting into northern and southern routes). The main export terminal is at Novorossiisk on the Black Sea. Other export pipeline developments include the Baltic Pipeline System (the first stage of which became operational in Dec. 2001 with the opening of a new terminal at Primorsk) and the Caspian Pipeline Consortium's pipeline from Tengiz (Kazakhstan) to Novorossiisk, which was commissioned in March 2001.

Output of natural gas in 2002 was 554·9bn. cu. metres, making Russia the world's largest producer. It also has the largest reserves of natural gas—in 2002 it had proven reserves of 47,570bn. cu. metres. There is a comprehensive domestic distribution system (run by state-owned Gazprom, in which the government has a 50%-plus-one stake), as well as gas pipelines linking Russia with former Soviet republics. In Russia's biggest-ever takeover Gazprom agreed in Sept. 2005 to buy a 72·7% stake in Sibneft, a leading oil company. The main export pipelines run from western Siberia through Ukraine and Belarus to European markets. Russia is seeking to diversify its gas export routes and a number of pipeline projects are under development. Russia is also looking to export its natural gas to Asian markets.

Minerals

Russia contains great mineral resources: iron ore, coal, gold, platinum, copper, zinc, lead, tin and rare metals. Output (in tonnes): coal (2002), 163·5m.; iron ore (2001), 83m.; lignite (2002), 77·4m.; bauxite (2001), 4m.; aluminium (2000), 3·25m.; copper (2001), 620,000; nickel (2002), 310,000; zinc (2000), 136,000; chrome ore (2000), 100,000; tin (2000), 5,000; molybdenum (2000), 2,400; gold (2001), 152. Salt production, 1999 estimate: 2m. tonnes. Diamond production, 2002: 23·0m. carats. Only Australia and Botswana produce more diamonds. Annual uranium production is nearly 3,000 tonnes.

Agriculture

A presidential decree of Dec. 1991 authorized the private ownership of land on a general basis, but excluded farmland. Nevertheless, large state and collective farms, inherited from the Soviet era, were forced officially to reorganize, with most becoming joint-stock companies. Farm workers could branch off as private farmers by obtaining a grant of land from their parent farm, although they lacked full ownership rights. In 2002 over 90% of Russia's 400m. ha. of farmland remained under the control of the state or former collectives. In Jan. 2003 a new law came into force regulating the possession, use and disposal of land plots designated as agricultural land. The law provides that: the authorities may confiscate farmland if its owners are using it for non-agricultural purposes; regional authorities will have the first option to purchase farmland from its owners; and farmland can only be sold to third parties if authorities refuse their option to buy. The law also deprives foreigners of the right to own agricultural land, although they may lease it for up to 49 years. In 2001 there were 123·86m. ha. of arable land and 1·86m. ha. of permanent crops. There were 4·6m. ha. of irrigated land in 2001.

Output in 2000 (in 1,000 tonnes) included: wheat, 36,000; potatoes, 35,297; sugarbeets, 14,041; barley, 13,266; oats, 5,500;

rye, 5,300; cabbages, 4,500; sunflower seeds, 3,900; tomatoes, 1,985; maize, 1,800; carrots, 1,605; onions, 1,320; apples, 1,200. Russia is the world's largest producer of oats and the second largest producer of potatoes and sunflower seeds.

Livestock, 2000: cattle, 27·5m.; pigs, 18·3m; sheep, 14·0m.; poultry, 342m. Livestock products in 2000 (in tonnes): meat, 4·3m.; milk, 31·8m.; eggs, 1·9m.; cheese, 364,000.

Forestry

Russia has the largest area covered by forests of any country in the world, with 851·39m. ha. in 2000 (50·4% of the land area). In 2003 timber production was 168·50m. cu. metres, down from 228·52m. in 1992. In 2003 Russia was the world's largest exporter of roundwood with 31·8% of the world total.

Fisheries

Total catch in 2003 was 3,281,248 tonnes (down from 8,211,516 tonnes in 1989). Approximately 94% of the fish caught are from marine waters.

INDUSTRY

As a result of Soviet central planning, Russian industry remains dominated by heavy industries, such as energy and metals. In 2001 fuels and energy production accounted for almost 20% of industrial output and metallurgy for 17%. Machine building and metalworking remained the largest processing industry, accounting for almost 20% of industrial production, followed by chemical manufacture. Light industry accounted for less than 2% of industrial output in 2001. Russia had fewer than 1m. small- and medium-sized enterprises at the end of 2001. Small- and medium-sized enterprises account for only 10–15% of GDP.

The leading companies by market capitalization in Russia in May 2004 were: Gazprom (US$70·8bn.), a gas company; Surgutneftegas (US$25·9bn.), an oil and gas field construction company; and Lukoil Holding (US$23·7bn.), an oil production company.

Output (in tonnes) includes: crude steel (2002), 59·8m.; residual fuel oil (2002), 58·9m.; distillate fuel oil (2002), 52·7m.; rolled steel (2000), 46·7m.; pig iron (2002), 46·2m.; cement (2001), 35·3m.; petrol (2002), 29·0m.; jet fuels (2002), 9·3m.; bread (2001), 8·6m.; sulphuric acid (2001), 8·2m.; paper and paperboard (2002), 5·9m.; steel pipe (2001), 5·4m.; cellulose (2000), 5·0m.; sugar (2002), 1·8m.; caustic soda (2000), 1·2m.; biscuits, pastry and cakes (2001), 1·0m.; soap, washing powder and detergents (2000), 436,000; synthetic fibre (2000), 164,000; (in sq. metres) glass (2001), 33·8m.; (in units) bricks (2000), 10,700m.; motor vehicles (1999), 1·2m.; tractors (1999), 15,417; combine harvesters (2001), 9,063; watches (2000), 6·5m.; refrigerators (2001), 1·5m.; televisions (2001), 1·0m.; washing machines (2001), 1·0m.; cigarettes (2001), 355·6bn.; beer (2001), 6,370m. litres; soft drinks (2001), 2,730·0m. litres; vodka and liquors (2000), 1,230m. litres; mineral water (2001), 1,220m. litres.

Labour

In 2004 the economically active population numbered 72·9m., of whom 67·1m. were in employment (7·9% unemployed). Average monthly wages were 6,831·8 roubles in 2004 (compared to 5,498·5 roubles in 2003 and 4,360·3 in 2002); the minimum wage from Oct. 2003 was 600 roubles (compared to 250 roubles in 2001 and 107·8 in 2000). In 2004, 25·5m. people, or 17·8% of the population, had an average per capita money income lower than the subsistence minimum. The state Federal Employment Service was set up in 1992. Unemployment benefits are paid by the Service for 12 months, payable at: 75% of the average monthly wage during the last two months preceding unemployment for the first three months; 60% for the next four months; and 45% for the last five months. Annual paid leave is 24 working days. The workforce was 65·90m. in 2004, of which 14·13m. worked in industry, 11·34m. in wholesale and retail trade and

catering, 6·79m. in agriculture, 6·06m. in education, 5·14m. in construction, 4·78m. in public health, physical culture and social security, and 4·22m. in transport. In 2001, 47,100 working days were lost through strikes (6,000,500 in 1996). Retirement age is 55 years for women, 60 for men.

Trade Unions

The Federation of Independent Trade Unions (founded 1990) is the successor to the former Communist official union organization. In 2002 it comprised 78 regional and 48 sectoral trade unions, with a total membership of 40m. There are also free trade unions.

INTERNATIONAL TRADE

Foreign debt was US$147,541m. in 2002 (much of it inherited from the Soviet Union). Most CIS republics have given up claims on Soviet assets in return for Russia assuming their portion of foreign debt. A Foreign Investment Agency was set up in Dec. 1992. The level of foreign direct investment in Russia is very low relative to other transition economies; the cumulative investment figure from 1991–2001 was US$18,200m. The largest investors in Russia are the USA, Germany, Netherlands and Cyprus. The main areas of investment are pipeline transport, trade and fuel industry. Following an agreement to supply oil to the US West Coast in 2002, Russia is looking to secure American investment in its oil industry.

Imports and Exports

Trade in US$1m.:

	2000	2001	2002	2003	2004
Imports f.o.b.	44,862	53,764	60,966	76,070	96,307
Exports f.o.b.	105,034	101,884	107,301	135,929	183,452

Germany provided 14·3% of imports in 2002, Belarus 8·8%, Ukraine 7·0%, the USA 6·4%, China 5·2% and Italy 4·8%. In 2002 Germany accounted for 7·6% of exports, Italy 7·0%, the Netherlands 6·8%, China 6·4%, Belarus 5·5% and Ukraine 5·5%. In 2001, of imports, 21·8% by value was machinery and apparatus, 16·1% food and live animals, 12·1% chemicals and chemical products, 4·5% road vehicles and 3·5% iron and steel. Of exports, 24·8% by value was crude petroleum, 18·0% natural gas, 9·5% refined petroleum, 6·8% non-ferrous metals and 5·6% iron and steel.

COMMUNICATIONS

Roads

In 2002 there were 952,000 km of roads, of which 752,000 were hard surfaced. In 2002, 23,269m. passengers were carried by automotive services, 8,176m. by trolleybuses and 6,987m. by trams. There were 20,353,000 passenger cars in use in 2000 plus 4,400,600 trucks and vans and 640,100 buses and coaches. There were 30,916 road deaths in 2001.

Rail

Length of railways in 2002 was 86,200 km of 1,520 mm gauge (of which 40,300 km electrified), and 957 km of 1,067 mm gauge on Sakhalin island. In 2002, 1,270·9m. passengers and 1,084·2m. tonnes of freight were carried by rail; passenger-km travelled came to 153bn. and freight tonne-km to 1,508bn. There are metro services in Moscow (265 km), St Petersburg (110 km), Nizhny Novgorod (17 km), Novosibirsk (13 km), Samara (9 km) and Yekaterinburg (8 km).

Civil Aviation

The main international airports are at Moscow (Sheremetevo) and St Petersburg (Pulkovo). The national carrier is Aeroflot International Russian Airlines (51·2% state-owned). Pulkovo, Siberia and Transaero also operate internationally.

In 1999 Aeroflot carried 4,438,900 passengers (3,275,800 on international flights) and flew 164·2m. km; Pulkovo Airlines carried 1,337,800 passengers (464,900 on international flights) and flew 29·1m. km. Moscow Sheremetevo handled 11,513,739 passengers in 2001 (8,405,378 on international flights) and 100,203 tonnes of freight. Moscow Vnukovo is mainly used for internal flights and was the second busiest airport in 2001, handling 3,666,304 passengers (2,956,135 on domestic flights) and 56,583 tonnes of freight. St Petersburg was the third busiest in 2001 for passengers (2,866,471) and for freight (20,014 tonnes).

Shipping
At the end of 2001 the merchant fleet comprised 4,727 vessels totalling 10,247,803 GRT. In Jan. 2005, 128 vessels (51% of tonnage) were registered under foreign flags. Vessels totalling 117,306,000 NRT entered ports in 2002 and vessels totalling 100,620,000 NRT cleared. In 2002, 31·1m. passengers and 115·7m. tonnes of freight were carried on 95,900 km of inland waterways. The busiest ports are Novorossiisk (which handled 63,291,000 tonnes in 2002) and St Petersburg (42,680,000 tonnes in 2002).

Telecommunications
Russia had 53,168,100 telephone subscribers in 2002, or 362·7 for every 1,000 persons, but in 2001 there were 5·81m. people on the waiting list for a line—the largest number of any country in the world. In 2002 there were 17,608,800 mobile phone subscribers, 13·0m. PCs in use (88·7 per 1,000 persons) and 55,000 fax machines. Internet users numbered 18·0m. in Dec. 2001.

Postal Services
In 2003 there were 40,314 post offices (one for every 3,550 persons).

SOCIAL INSTITUTIONS

Justice
The Supreme Court is the highest judicial body on civil, criminal and administrative law. The Supreme Arbitration Court deals with economic cases. The KGB, and the Federal Security Bureau which succeeded it, were replaced in Dec. 1992 by the Federal Counter-Intelligence Service. The legal system is, however, crippled by corruption.

A new civil code was introduced in 1993 to replace the former Soviet code. It guarantees the inviolability of private property and includes provisions for the freedom of movement of capital and goods.

12-member juries were introduced in a number of courts after Nov. 1993, but in the years that followed jury trials were not widely used. However, on 1 Jan. 2003 jury trials began to be phased in nationwide. A new criminal code came into force on 1 Jan. 1997, based on respect for the rights and freedoms of the individual and the sanctity of private property. A further new code that entered force on 1 July 2002 introduced new levels of protection for defendants and restrictions on law enforcement officials. The death penalty is retained for five crimes against the person. It is not applied to minors, women or men over 65.

In 2000, 2,952,400 crimes were recorded, including 28,904 murders, 132,393 robberies and 6,978 rapes. Russia's murder rate, at 19·9 per 100,000 population in 2000, ranks among the highest in the world. In 1996 there were 140 executions (86 in 1995; 1 in 1992). President Yeltsin placed a moratorium on capital punishment in 1996 when Russia joined the Council of Europe, but parliament has refused to abolish the death penalty. The prison population in Aug. 2003 was 865,000. Russia's prison population rate (606 per 100,000 population in Aug. 2003) is the second highest in the world after the USA. In 2003 there were 1,010 prison establishments and institutions.

Education
Adult literacy rate in 2003 was 99·4% (male, 99·7%; female, 99·2%). In 2004 there were 4·42m. children in 47,200 pre-school

institutions, 16·17m. pupils in 63,182 primary and secondary day schools; 6·88m. students in 1,071 higher educational establishments (including correspondence students). In addition there were 708 private schools with 70,000 pupils.

The Russian Academy of Sciences, founded in 1724 and reorganized in 1925 as the Academy of Sciences of the Union of Soviet Socialist Republics, was restored under its present name in 1991. It is the highest scientific self-governing institution in Russia and has 18 divisions on particular areas of science. The Academy also has three regional branches: the Urals Branch, the Siberian Branch and the Far East Branch.

Health
Doctors in 2001 numbered 604,365, and hospital beds (2000) 1·67m. There were 47 doctors per 10,000 people in 2000 and 116 hospital beds per 10,000 persons. There were 46,209 dentists, 1,140,048 nurses, 10,215 pharmacists and 67,825 midwives in 2001. Expenditure on health in 2000 was 5·3% of GDP. In 1999 and 2000 Russia experienced the highest rate of growth of HIV cases in the world; by March 2003 there were 237,000 registered cases. In 2001 there were 93 cases of tuberculosis per 100,000 people. In 2004, 35·8% of Russians aged 18 and over smoked (males, 61·3%; females, 15·0%). The annual average cigarette consumption per adult between 1992–2000 was 2,691.

Welfare
Russia is in the process of implementing a reform of its pensions system, the focus of which is to move away from a distributive system to an accumulating (funded) scheme. Instead of citizens paying 28% of their monthly salary into the state pension fund, since 2004 it has been possible to pay between 2% and 6% to private asset managers.

State welfare provision in 1999 included: old age, disability and survivor pensions; sickness and maternity benefits; work injury payments; unemployment benefits; and family allowances. In the period April–June 2002 the average monthly pension was 1,337 roubles. The subsistence level for pensioners was 1,383 roubles a month.

RELIGION
The Russian Orthodox Church is the largest religious association in the country. In early 2003 it had 128 dioceses (compared with 67 in 1989), over 19,000 parishes (6,893 in 1988) and about 480 monasteries (18 in 1980). There are also five theological academies, 26 seminaries, 29 pre-seminaries, two Orthodox universities, a theological institute, a women's pre-seminary and 28 icon-painting schools. In 2001 there were 23·6m. adherents. The total number of theological students is around 6,000. There are still many Old Believers, whose schism from the Orthodox Church dates from the 17th century. The Russian Church is headed by the Patriarch of Moscow and All Russia (Patriarch Alexius II of St Petersburg and Novgorod, b. 1929; elected June 1990), assisted by the Holy Synod, which has seven members—the Patriarch himself and the Metropolitans of Krutitsy and Kolomna (Moscow), St Petersburg and Kyiv *ex officio*, and three bishops alternating for six months in order of seniority from the three regions forming the Moscow Patriarchate. The Patriarchate of Moscow maintains jurisdiction over 119 eparchies, of which 59 are in Russia; there are parishes of Russian Orthodox abroad, in Belarus, Ukraine, Kazakhstan, Moldova, Uzbekistan, the Baltic states, and in Damascus, Geneva, Prague, New York and Japan. There is a spiritual mission in Jerusalem, and a monastery at Mt Athos in Greece. A Russian Orthodox church was consecrated in Dublin in Ireland in Feb. 2003. Muslims represent the second largest religious community in Russia, numbering 19m. There are an estimated 2m. Protestants, and Jewish communities, primarily in Moscow and St Petersburg, numbered 590,000 in 2001. The *Grand Mufti* is Talgat Tadzhuddin.

CULTURE

World Heritage Sites

Russia's heritage sites as classified by UNESCO (with year entered on list) are: the Historic Centre of St Petersburg (1990); the Kremlin and Red Square in Moscow (1990); Khizi Pogost (1990); the Historic Monuments of Novgorod and surroundings (1992); Cultural and Historic Ensemble of the Solovetsky Islands (1992); the White Monuments of Vladimir and Suzdal (1992); Architectural Ensemble of the Trinity Sergius Lavra in Sergiev Posad (1993); the Church of the Ascension, Kolomenskoye (1994); Virgin Komi Forests (1995); Lake Baikal (1996); Volcanoes of Kamchatka (1996, 2001); Golden Mountains of Altai (1998); Western Caucasus (1999); the Ensemble of Ferapontov Monastery (2000); Historic and Architectural Complex of the Kazan Kremlin (2000); Central Sikhote-Alin (2001); the Citadel, Ancient City and Fortress Buildings of Derbent (2003); Ensemble of the Novodevichy Convent in southwest Moscow (2004); Natural System of Wrangel Island Reserve (2004); the historical centre of the city of Yaroslavl (2005).

The Russian Federation also shares three UNESCO sites, with Lithuania (Curonian Spit) and Mongolia (Uvs Nuur Basin). The Struve Geodetic Arc (2005) is a chain of survey triangulations spanning from Norway to the Black Sea that helped establish the exact shape and size of the earth and is shared with nine other countries.

Broadcasting

In 2000 there were 79·0m. television receivers. Television broadcasting is still largely state-controlled. In Nov. 2001 a court ordered that the parent company of TV6, the last independent station, be liquidated. It was closed down in Jan. 2002. There are two major channels, ORT (Russian Public Television) and RTR (Russian Television). Colour is by SECAM H. In 2003, 99% of the population could receive TV broadcasts. There are also local city channels. Access to cable TV varies with locality. 96% of the population in 2002 could receive radio broadcasts. In 2000 there were 61·1m. radio receivers.

Cinema

There were approximately 1,450 cinema screens in urban areas in 2003; admissions in 2002 totalled an estimated 65m. with box office receipts of US$112m. In 2000, 50 feature films were produced in Russia.

Press

In 2002 there were 436 daily newspapers with combined annual sales of 7,850m. There were 10,188 non-daily newspapers in 2000. The most popular daily newspaper in 2002 was *Komsomolskaya Pravda* with a circulation of 674,000. A presidential decree of 22 Dec. 1993 brought the press agencies ITAR-TASS and RIA-Novosti under state control. In 2000, 56,180 titles were published. Russia's media is becoming relatively independent, but press freedom has suffered setbacks since Vladimir Putin became president.

Tourism

There were 7,943,000 foreign visitors in 2002; revenue from foreign tourists amounted to US$4·19bn.

DIPLOMATIC REPRESENTATIVES

Of Russia in the United Kingdom (13 Kensington Palace Gdns, London, W8 4QX)
Ambassador: Yury V. Fedotov.

Of the United Kingdom in Russia (Smolenskaya Naberezhnaya 10, 121099 Moscow)
Ambassador: Anthony Brenton, CMG.

Of Russia in the USA (2650 Wisconsin Ave., NW, Washington, D.C., 20007)
Ambassador: Yury Ushakov.

Of the USA in Russia (8 Bolshoy Devyatinskiy Pereuulok, 121099 Moscow)
Ambassador: William J. Burns.

Of Russia to the United Nations
Ambassador: Andrey I. Denisov.

Of Russia to the European Union
Ambassador: Vacant.

FURTHER READING

Rossiiskii Statisticheskii Ezhegodnik. Moscow, annual (title varies)

Acton, E., *et al., Critical Companion to the Russian Revolution.* Indiana Univ. Press, 1997
Aron, Leon, *Boris Yeltsin: A Revolutionary Life.* HarperCollins, London, 2000
Aslund, Anders (ed.) *Economic Transformation in Russia.* New York, 1994.—*Building Capitalism: the Transformation of the Former Soviet Bloc.* CUP, 2002
Brady, Rose, *Kapitalizm: Russia's Struggle to Free its Economy.* Yale Univ. Press, 2000
Cambridge Encyclopedia of Russia and the Former Soviet Union. CUP, 1995
Dunlop, J., *Russia Confronts Chechnya: Roots of a Separatist Conflict, Vol. 1.* CUP, 1998
Fowkes, B. (ed.) *Russia and Chechnia: The Permanent Crisis, Essays on Russo-Chechen Relations.* St Martin's Press, New York, 1998
Freeze, G. (ed.) *Russia: A History.* OUP, 1997
Gall, C. and de Waal, T., *Chechnya: Calamity in the Caucasus.* New York, 1998
Gorbachev, Mikhail, *On My Country and the World*; translated from Russian. Columbia Univ. Press, New York, 2000
Granville, Brigitte and Oppenheimer, Peter (eds.) *Russia's Post-Community Economy.* OUP, 2001
Gustafson, Thane, *Capitalism Russian-Style.* Cambridge Univ. Press, 2000
Hollander, Paul, *Political Will and Personal Belief: The Decline and Fall of Soviet Communism.* Yale Univ. Press, 2000
Hosking, Geoffrey, *Russia and the Russians, A History from Rus to the Russian Federation.* Allen Lane/The Penguin Press, London, 2001
Kochan, L., *The Making of Modern Russia.* 2nd ed., revised by R. Abraham. London, 1994
Kotkin, Stephen, *Armageddon Averted: the Soviet Collapse 1970–2000.* OUP, 2001
Lieven, A., *Chechnya: Tombstone of Russian Power.* Yale Univ. Press, 1998
Lloyd, J., *Rebirth of a Nation.* London, 1998
Marks, Steven, *How Russia Shaped the Modern World: From Art to Anti-Semitism, Ballet to Bolshevism.* Princeton Univ. Press, 2002
Paxton, J., *Encyclopedia of Russian History.* Denver (CO), 1993.—*Leaders of Russia and the Soviet Union.* Fitzroy Dearborn, London, 2004
Pitman, L., *Russia/USSR.* [Bibliography] 2nd ed. ABC-Clio, Oxford and Santa Barbara (CA), 1994
Putin, Vladimir, *First Person*; interviews, translated from Russian. Hutchinson, London, 2000
Remnick, D., *Resurrection: The Struggle for a New Russia.* Picador, London, 1998
Riasanovsky, N. V., *A History of Russia.* 5th ed. OUP, 1993
Sakwa, R., *Russian Politics and Society.* 2nd ed. London, 1996
Service, Robert, *A History of Twentieth-Century Russia.* Harvard Univ. Press, 1997.—*Lenin: A Biography.* Macmillan, London, 2000.—*Russia: Experiment with a People.* Pan Macmillan, London, 2002
Shevtsova, Lilia, *Putin's Russia.* Carnegie Endowment for International Peace, Washington, D.C., 2003
Shriver, G. (ed. and transl.) *Post-Soviet Russia, A Journey Through the Yeltsin Era.* Columbia Univ. Press, 2000
Westwood, J. N., *Endurance and Endeavour: Russian History, 1812–1992.* 4th ed. OUP, 1993
White, Stephen, *et al., How Russia Votes.* Chatham House (NJ), 1997
White, Stephen, Sakwa, Richard and Gitelman, Zvi, (eds.) *Developments in Russian Politics 6.* Palgrave Macmillan, Basingstoke, 2005
Woodruff, David, *Money Unmade: Barter and the Fate of Russian Capitalism.* Cornell Univ. Press, 2000
Yeltsin, B., *The View from the Kremlin* (in USA *The Struggle for Russia*). London and New York, 1994

National Statistical Office: Gosudarstvennyi Komitet po Statistike (*Goskomstat*), Moscow.
Website: http://www.gks.ru

THE REPUBLICS

Status

The 21 republics that with Russia itself constitute the Russian Federation were part of the RSFSR in the Soviet period. On 31 March 1992 the federal government concluded treaties with the then 20 republics, except Checheno-Ingushetia and Tatarstan, defining their mutual responsibilities. The *Council of the Heads of the Republics* is chaired by the Russian President and includes the Russian Prime Minister. Its function is to provide an interaction between the federal government and the republican authorities.

Adygeya

Part of Krasnodar Territory. Area, 7,600 sq. km (2,950 sq. miles); population (2002 census), 477,109. Estimated population, 1 Jan. 2005, 444,400. Capital, Maikop (2002 census, 156,931). Established 27 July 1922; granted republican status in 1991.

President: Hazret Sovmen, b. 1937 (took office on 8 Feb. 2002).

Prime Minister: Asfar Khagur (took office on 30 Dec. 2004).

Chief industries are timber, woodworking, food processing and there is some engineering and gas production. Agriculture consists primarily of crops (beets, wheat, maize), on partly irrigated land. Industry accounted for 15·2% of gross regional product in 2003 and agriculture 13·6%.

In 2004 there were 12,400 pupils in 126 pre-school institutions and 50,700 pupils in 175 primary and secondary day schools. There were 20,000 students at the two institutions of higher education, Adygeya State University and Maikop State Technological Institute.

In 2004 the rates of doctors and hospital beds per 10,000 population were 37·2 and 110 respectively.

Altai

Part of Altai Territory. Area, 92,600 sq. km (35,750 sq. miles); population (2002 census), 202,947. Estimated population, 1 Jan. 2005, 203,900. Capital, Gorno-Altaisk (2002 census, 53,538). Established 1 June 1922 as Oirot Autonomous Region; renamed 7 Jan. 1948; granted republican status in 1991 and renamed in 1992.

Chairman of the Government: Aleksandr Berdnikov (since 20 Jan. 2006).

Cattle breeding predominates. Chief industries are clothing and footwear, foodstuffs, gold mining, timber, chemicals and dairying. Industrial output was valued at 838m. roubles in 2004 and agricultural output at 2,972m. roubles. In 2000, 91,200 people were economically active, of whom 72,000 were in employment.

In 2004 there were 6,600 pupils in 130 pre-school institutions and 32,300 pupils in 202 primary and secondary day schools. There were 6,000 students at Gorno-Altaysk State University.

The rates of doctors and hospital beds per 10,000 population in 2004 were 38·0 and 123 respectively.

Bashkortostan

Area 143,600 sq. km (55,450 sq. miles), population (2002 census), 4,104,336. Estimated population, 1 Jan. 2005, 4,078,800. Capital,

Ufa (2002 census population, 1,042,437). Bashkiria was annexed to Russia in 1557. It was constituted as an Autonomous Soviet Republic on 23 March 1919. A declaration of republican sovereignty was adopted in 1990, and a declaration of independence on 28 March 1992. A treaty of Aug. 1994 with Russia preserves the common legislative framework of the Russian Federation while defining mutual areas of competence. The main ethnic groups are Russians, Tatars and Bashkirs. There are also Chuvash and Mari minorities.

A constitution was adopted on 24 Dec. 1993. It states that Bashkiria conducts its own domestic and foreign policy, that its laws take precedence in Bashkiria, and that it forms part of the Russian Federation on a voluntary and equal basis.

President: Murtaza Gubaidullovich Rakhimov (since 7 April 1990).

Prime Minister: Rafael Baidavletov (since 12 Jan. 1999).

Industrial production was valued at 354,000m. roubles in 2004 and agricultural output at 57,160m. roubles. The most important industries are oil and oil products; there are also engineering, glass and building materials enterprises. Agriculture specializes in wheat, barley, oats and livestock.

In 2004 there were 144,600 pupils in 1,904 pre-school institutions and 583,300 pupils in 3,187 primary and secondary day schools. There were 150,200 students in 17 institutions of higher education. There is a state university and a branch of the Academy of Sciences with eight learned institutions.

In 2004 the rates of doctors and hospital beds per 10,000 population were 41·9 and 104 respectively.

Buryatia

Area is 351,300 sq. km (135,650 sq. miles). The Buryat Republic, situated to the south of Sakha, adopted the Soviet system on 1 March 1920. This area was penetrated by the Russians in the 17th century and finally annexed from China by the treaties of Nerchinsk (1689) and Kyakhta (1727). Population (2002 census), 981,238. Estimated population, 1 Jan. 2005, 969,200. Capital, Ulan-Ude (2002 census population, 359,391). The main ethnic groups are Russians, followed by Buryats. There are also Ukrainian, Tatar and Belarusian minorities.

There is a 65-member parliament, the *People's Hural.*

President: Leonid Potapov (in power since 21 Oct. 1991).

The main industries are engineering, brown coal and graphite, timber, building materials, sheep and cattle farming. Industrial production was valued at 32,161m. roubles in 2004 and agricultural output at 8,352m. roubles.

In 2004 there were 30,100 pupils in 423 pre-school institutions and 139,000 pupils in 572 primary and secondary day schools. There were 31,900 pupils in five institutions of higher education.

In 2004 the rates of doctors and hospital beds per 10,000 population were 38·3 and 109 respectively. The level of poverty in Buryatia was 38·2% in 2003.

Chechnya

The area of the Republic of Chechnya is 15,000 sq. km (5,800 sq. miles). The population at the 2002 census was 1,103,686. The estimated population at 1 Jan. 2005 was 1,141,300. Capital,

Dzhohar (since March 1998; previously known as Grozny; 2002 census population, 210,720). The Chechens and Ingushes were conquered by Russia in the late 1850s. In 1920 each nationality were constituted areas within the Soviet Mountain Republic and the Chechens became an Autonomous Region on 30 Nov. 1922. In Jan. 1934 the two regions were united, and on 5 Dec. 1936 constituted as the Checheno-Ingush Autonomous Republic. This was dissolved in 1944 and the population was deported en masse, allegedly for collaboration with the German occupation forces. It was reconstituted on 9 Jan. 1957: 232,000 Chechens and Ingushes returned to their homes in the next two years.

In 1991 rebel leader Jokhar Dudayev seized control of Chechnya and won elections. In Nov. he declared an independent Chechen Republic. Ingush desire to separate from Chechnya led to fighting along the Chechen-Ingush border and a deployment of Russian troops. An agreement to withdraw was reached between Russia and Chechnya on 15 Nov. 1992. The separation of Chechnya and Ingushetia was formalized in Dec. 1992. In April 1993 President Dudayev dissolved parliament. Hostilities continued throughout 1994 between the government and forces loosely grouped under the 'Provisional Chechen Council'. The Russian government, which had never recognized the Chechen declaration of independence of Nov. 1991, moved troops and armour into Chechnya on 11 Dec. 1994. Grozny was bombed and attacked by Russian ground forces at the end of Dec. 1994 and the presidential palace was captured on 19 Jan. 1995, but fighting continued. On 30 July 1995 the Russian and Chechen authorities signed a ceasefire. However, hostilities, raids and hostage-taking continued; Dudayev was killed in April 1996 and a ceasefire was agreed on 30 Aug. 1996.

Fighting broke out again, however, in Sept. 1999 as Russian forces launched attacks on 'rebel bases'. Fighting intensified and more than 200,000 civilians were forced to flee, mostly to neighbouring Ingushetia. By Feb. 2000 much of Grozny had been destroyed and was closed by the Russians. In June 2000 Vladimir Putin declared direct rule. The war continues, with estimates of the number of deaths varying from 6,500 to 15,000. Over 4,000 Russian soldiers have been killed. However, on 18 Nov. 2001 the first official meeting between negotiators for the Russian government and Chechen separatists took place. In Oct. 2002 a group of Chechen rebels took control of a Moscow theatre and held hostage 800 people for three days, before Russian troops stormed the building. An anaesthetic gas, used to combat the rebels, also killed many of the hostages.

On 23 March 2003 a referendum was held on a new constitution that would keep Chechnya within Russia but give it greater autonomy, and provide a new president and parliament for the republic. Although 96% of votes cast were in favour of the new constitution there was criticism of the conduct of the referendum. Presidential elections held on 5 Oct. 2003 were won by the Kremlin-backed candidate Akhmad Kadyrov, with 80·8% of the vote, but there was widespread condemnation of the electoral process. President Kadyrov was assassinated on 9 May 2004. Presidential elections held on 29 Aug. 2004, widely seen as rigged, were won by the Kremlin-backed Alu Alkhanov with 73·5% of the vote, against 5·9% for Movsur Khamidov, head of the Chechen department of the Federal Security Service. There were five other candidates. Turnout was 85·2%. On 27 Nov. 2005 the first parliamentary elections took place since Russian troops restored Moscow's control over Chechnya in 1999. In the elections to the People's Assembly (lower chamber) the United Russia party won 19 of 38 seats with 60·7% of the vote, the Communist Party 3 with 12·2%, the Union of Rightist Forces 1 with 12·4%, the Eurasian Union 1 with 3·9%; independents won 14 seats. In the Council of the Republic (upper chamber), United Russia won 14 of 20 seats, the Communist Party 3 and the Union of Rightist Forces 3.

Separatist President Aslan Maskhadov was killed by Russian troops on 8 March 2005.

Moscow-backed President: Alu Alkhanov; b. 1957.
Prime Minister: Ramzan Kadyrov; b. 1976.
Separatist President: Abdul-Khalim Sadulayev; b. 1967.

Checheno-Ingushetia had a major oilfield, and a number of engineering works, chemical factories, building materials works and food canneries. There was a timber, woodworking and furniture industry. In 2003 oil production was 1·8m. tonnes. Chechnya's oil reserves are estimated at some 220m. bbls. Industrial output in the two republics was valued at 213,000m. roubles in 1993, agricultural output at 79,000m. roubles.

In 2004 there were 212,300 pupils in 460 primary and secondary day schools. There were 23,500 students in three institutions of higher education. In 1995 the rates of doctors and hospital beds per 10,000 population were 21·1 and 91 respectively.

FURTHER READING

Lieven, A. and Bradner, H., *Chechnya: Tombstone of Russian Power.* Yale Univ. Press, 1999

Chuvashia

Area, 18,300 sq. km (7,050 sq. miles); population (2002 census), 1,313,754. Estimated population, 1 Jan. 2005, 1,229,300. Capital, Cheboksary (2002 census population, 440,621). The territory was annexed by Russia in the middle of the 16th century. On 24 June 1920 it was constituted as an Autonomous Region, and on 21 April 1925 as an Autonomous Republic. The main ethnic groups are Chuvash, followed by Russians. There are also Tatar and Mordovian minorities. Republican sovereignty was declared in Sept. 1990.

President: Nikolai Fedorov (took office on 21 Jan. 1994).

The timber industry antedates the Soviet period. Other industries include railway repair works, electrical and other engineering industries, building materials, chemicals, textiles and food industries. Grain crops account for nearly two-thirds of all sowings and fodder crops for nearly a quarter. Chuvashia is Russia's main producer of hops and the republic has a significant brewing industry. Industrial output was valued at 49,826m. roubles in 2004 and agricultural output at 12,722m. roubles.

In 2004 there were 47,100 pupils at 433 pre-school institutions and 166,200 pupils in 619 primary and secondary day schools. There were 63,900 students in seven higher educational establishments.

In 2004 the rates of doctors and hospital beds per 10,000 population were 46·8 and 116 respectively.

Dagestan

Area, 50,300 sq. km (19,400 sq. miles); population (2002 census), 2,576,531. Estimated population, 1 Jan. 2005, 2,621,800. Capital, Makhachkala (2002 census population, 462,412). Over 30 nationalities inhabit this republic apart from Russians; the most numerous are Dagestanis and there are also Azerbaijani, Chechen and Jewish minorities. Annexed from Persia in 1723, Dagestan was constituted an Autonomous Republic on 20 Jan. 1921. In 1991 the Supreme Soviet declared the area of republican, rather than autonomous republican, status. Many of the nationalities who live in Dagestan have organized armed militias, and in May 1998 rebels stormed the government building in Makhachkala. In Aug. 1999 Dagestan faced attacks from Islamic militants who invaded from Chechnya. Although Russian troops tried to restore order and discipline, the guerrilla campaign has continued with a series of bombings targeting Russian military personnel.

President: Mukhu Aliyev (in office since 20 Feb. 2006).

Prime Minister: Shamil Zaynalov (in office since 6 March 2006).

There are engineering, oil, chemical, woodworking, textile, food and other light industries. Agriculture is varied, ranging from wheat to grapes, with sheep farming and cattle breeding. Industrial output was valued at 6,568m. roubles in 2001 and agricultural output at 13,162m. roubles.

In 2004 there were 55,900 pupils in 593 pre-schools and 443,300 pupils in 1,683 primary and secondary day schools. There were 105,500 students in 15 institutions of higher education. There is a branch of the Russian Academy of Sciences with ten learned institutions.

In 2004 the rates of doctors and hospital beds per 10,000 population were 38·2 and 70 respectively.

Ingushetia

The history of Ingushetia is interwoven with that of Chechnya (*see above*). Ingush desire to separate from Chechnya led to fighting along the Chechen-Ingush border and a deployment of Russian troops. The separation of Ingushetia from Chechnya was formalized by an amendment of Dec. 1992 to the Russian Constitution. On 15 May 1993 an extraordinary congress of the peoples of Ingushetia adopted a declaration of state sovereignty within the Russian Federation. Skirmishes between Ingush refugees and local police broke out in Aug. 1999 and tensions remained high with the danger of further outbreaks of fighting. The Russian attacks on neighbouring Chechnya in Sept. 1999 led to thousands of Chechen refugees fleeing to Ingushetia.

In April 2004 President Murat Zyazikov survived an assassination attempt, as did Prime Minister Ibragim Malsagov in Aug. 2005.

The capital is Magas (since 1999; formerly Nazran; 2002 census population, 125,066).

Area, 4,300 sq. km (1,700 sq. miles); population (2002 census), 467,294. Estimated population, 1 Jan. 2005, 481,600.

There is a 27-member parliament. On 27 Feb. 1994 presidential elections and a constitutional referendum were held. Turnout was 70%. At the referendum 97% of votes cast approved a new constitution stating that Ingushetia is a democratic law-based secular republic forming part of the Russian Federation on a treaty basis.

President: Murat Zyazikov.

Prime Minister: Ibragim Malsagov.

Industry accounted for 14·6% of gross regional product in 2003 and agriculture 14·1%. A special economic zone for Russian residents was set up in 1994, and an 'offshore' banking tax haven in 1996.

In 2004 there were 2,500 pupils in 20 pre-school institutions and 64,600 pupils in 113 primary and secondary day schools. There were 9,400 students in five institutions of higher education.

In 2004 the rates of doctors and hospital beds per 10,000 population were 22·8 and 41 respectively.

Kabardino-Balkaria

Area, 12,500 sq. km (4,850 sq. miles); population (2002 census), 901,494. Estimated population, 1 Jan. 2005, 896,900. Capital, Nalchik (2002 census population, 274,974). Kabarda was annexed to Russia in 1557. The republic was constituted on 5 Dec. 1936. The main ethnic groups are Kabardinians, followed by Russians and Balkars. There are also Ukrainian, Ossetian and German minorities.

A treaty with Russia of 1 July 1994 defines their mutual areas of competence within the legislative framework of the Russian Federation. The recent history of Kabardino-Balkaria has been marked by the instability that has plagued the whole of the north Caucasus. In Oct. 2005 militants staged a large-scale assault on government buildings in Nalchik, an act for which Chechen rebel leader Shamil Besayev claimed responsibility. All mosques in the capital have been closed.

President: Arsen Kanokov (took office on 28 Sept. 2005).

Main industries are ore-mining, timber, engineering, coal, food processing, timber and light industries, building materials. Grain, livestock breeding, dairy farming and wine-growing are the principal branches of agriculture. Agriculture accounted for 31·9% of gross regional product in 2003 and industry 14·2%.

In 2004 there were 26,100 pupils in 102 pre-school institutions and 123,400 pupils in 371 primary and secondary day schools. There were 28,500 students in four institutions of higher education. There is a branch of the Academy of Sciences with five learned institutions.

In 2004 the rates of doctors and hospital beds per 10,000 population were 41·3 and 101 respectively.

Kalmykia

Area, 76,100 sq. km (29,400 sq. miles); population (2002 census), 292,410. Estimated population, 1 Jan. 2005, 289,900. Capital, Elista (2002 census population, 104,254). The population is mainly Kalmyk and Russian, with small Chechen, Kazakh and German minorities.

The Kalmyks migrated from western China to Russia (Nogai Steppe) in the early 17th century. The territory was constituted an Autonomous Region on 4 Nov. 1920, and an Autonomous Republic on 22 Oct. 1935; this was dissolved in 1943. On 9 Jan. 1957 it was reconstituted as an Autonomous Region and on 29 July 1958 as an Autonomous Republic once more. In Oct. 1990 the republic was renamed the Kalmyk Soviet Socialist Republic; it was given its present name in Feb. 1992.

President: Kirsan Nikolaevich Ilyumzhinov (since April 1993).

In April 1993 the Supreme Soviet was dissolved and replaced by a professional parliament consisting of 25 of the former deputies. On 5 April 1994 a specially-constituted 300-member constituent assembly adopted a 'Steppe Code' as Kalmykia's basic law. This is not a constitution and renounces the declaration of republican sovereignty of 18 Oct. 1990. It provides for a *President* elected for five-year terms with the power to dissolve parliament, and a 27-member parliament, the *People's Hural,* elected every four years. It stipulates that Kalmykia is an equal member and integral part of the Russian Federation, functioning in accordance with the Russian constitution.

Main industries are oil and gas production, canning and building materials. Cattle breeding and irrigated farming (mainly fodder crops) are the principal branches of agriculture. Overgrazing during the Soviet period has led to the desertification of Kalmykia's pastures and agricultural output has declined substantially in recent years. Agriculture accounted for 10·4% of gross regional product in 2003 and industry 6·4%.

In 2004 there were 9,500 pupils in 119 pre-school institutions and 44,900 pupils in 213 primary and secondary day schools. There were 10,000 students in two institutions of higher education. Chess forms part of the general school curriculum; President Kirsan Ilyumzhinov has been president of FIDE, the international chess federation, since Nov. 1995. In 2004 the rates of doctors and hospital beds per 10,000 population were 51·0 and 136 respectively. The main religion is Buddhism.

Karachai-Cherkessia

Area, 14,300 sq. km (5,500 sq. miles); population (2002 census), 439,470. Estimated population, 1 Jan. 2005, 434,500. Capital, Cherkessk (2002 census population, 116,244). A Karachai Autonomous Region was established on 26 April 1926 (out of a previously united Karachaevo-Cherkess Autonomous Region created in 1922), and dissolved in 1943. A Cherkess Autonomous Region was established on 30 April 1928. The present Autonomous Region was re-established on 9 Jan. 1957. The Region declared itself a Soviet Socialist Republic in Dec. 1990. Tension between the two ethnic groups increased after the first free presidential election in April 1999 was won by Vladimir Semyonov, an ethnic Karchayev. Despite numerous allegations of fraud the result was upheld by the Supreme Court. There were subsequently fears that the ethnic Cherkess opposition would attempt to set up breakaway government bodies.

President: Mustafa Batdyev, b. 1950 (took office on 4 Sept. 2003).

There are ore-mining, engineering, chemical and woodworking industries. The Kuban-Kalaussi irrigation scheme irrigates 200,000 ha. Livestock breeding and grain growing predominate in agriculture. Conflict in the north Caucasus has had a serious impact on the economy and the agricultural sector is supported by central government. Agriculture accounted for 19·4% of gross regional product in 2003 and industry 18·7%.

In 2004 there were 10,900 pupils in 99 pre-school institutions and 60,000 pupils in 190 primary and secondary day schools. There were 16,200 students in two institutions of higher education.

In 2004 the rates of doctors and hospital beds per 10,000 population were 33·9 and 101 respectively.

Karelia

The Karelian Republic, capital Petrozavodsk (2002 census population, 266,160), covers an area of 172,400 sq. km, with a 2002 census population of 716,281. Estimated population, 1 Jan. 2005, 703,100. Russians constitute the majority of the population, with some Karelians, Belarusians and Ukrainians.

Karelia (formerly Olonets Province) became part of the RSFSR after 1917. In June 1920 a Karelian Labour Commune was formed and in July 1923 this was transformed into the Karelian Autonomous Soviet Socialist Republic (one of the autonomous republics of the RSFSR). On 31 March 1940, after the Soviet-Finnish war, practically all the territory (with the exception of a small section in the neighbourhood of the Leningrad area) which had been ceded by Finland to the USSR was added to Karelia, and the Karelian Autonomous Republic was transformed into the Karelo-Finnish Soviet Socialist Republic as the 12th republic of the USSR. In 1946, however, the southern part of the republic, including its whole seaboard and the towns of Viipuri (Vyborg) and Keksholm, was attached to the RSFSR, reverting in 1956 to autonomous republican status within the RSFSR. In Nov. 1991 it declared itself the 'Republic of Karelia'.

Head of the Republic: Sergei Katanandov (in power since May 1998).

Karelia has a wealth of timber, some 70% of its territory being forest land. It is also rich in other natural resources, having large deposits of mica, diabase, spar, quartz, marble, granite, zinc, lead, silver, copper, molybdenum, tin, baryta and iron ore. Its lakes and rivers are rich in fish.

There are timber mills, paper-cellulose works, mica, chemical plants, power stations and furniture factories. Industrial output was valued at 512,000m. roubles in 2004. Over half of Karelia's production output is exported annually, principally to EU countries. Exports totalled US$842m. in 2004.

In 2004 there were 28,800 pupils in 496 pre-schools and 81,100 pupils in 293 primary and secondary day schools. There were 21,900 students in three institutions of higher education. There is a branch of the Russian Academy of Sciences with seven learned institutions.

In 2004 the rates of doctors and hospital beds per 10,000 population were 49·4 and 123 respectively.

Khakassia

Area, 61,900 sq. km (23,900 sq. miles); population (2002 census), 546,072. Estimated population, 1 Jan. 2005, 541,000. Capital, Abakan (2002 census population, 165,197). Established 20 Oct. 1930; granted republican status in 1991.

Chairman of the Government: Aleksei Lebed (since 9 Jan. 1997).

There are coal- and ore-mining, timber and woodworking industries. The region is linked by rail with the Trans-Siberian line. Industrial output was valued at 25,651m. roubles in 2004 and agricultural output at 3,807m. roubles.

In 2004 there were 16,500 pupils in 157 pre-school institutions and 69,200 pupils in 289 primary and secondary day schools. There were 20,400 students in three higher education institutions.

In 2004 the rates of doctors and hospital beds per 10,000 population were 37·3 and 110 respectively.

Komi

Area, 415,900 sq. km (160,550 sq. miles); population (2002 census), 1,018,674. Estimated population, 1 Jan. 2005, 996,400. Capital, Syktyvkar (2002 census population, 230,011). Annexed by the princes of Moscow in the 14th century, the territory was constituted as an Autonomous Region on 22 Aug. 1921 and as an Autonomous Republic on 5 Dec. 1936. The largest ethnic group are Russians, followed by Komis, with Ukrainian and Belarusian minorities.

A declaration of sovereignty was adopted by the republican parliament in Sept. 1990, and the designation 'Autonomous' dropped from the republic's official name.

Head of the Republic: Vladimir Torlopov (since 15 Jan. 2002).

There are coal, oil, timber, gas, asphalt and building materials industries, and light industry is expanding. Livestock breeding (including dairy farming) is the main branch of agriculture. Industrial output was valued at 87·5bn. roubles in 2004 and agricultural output at 4·3bn. roubles.

In 2004 there were 47,700 pupils in 412 pre-schools and 128,300 pupils in 531 primary and secondary day schools. There were 35,400 students in seven institutions of higher education.

In 2004 the rates of doctors and hospital beds per 10,000 population were 43·9 and 116 respectively.

Mari-El

Area, 23,200 sq. km (8,950 sq. miles); population (2002 census), 727,979. Estimated population, 1 Jan. 2005, 716,900. Capital, Yoshkar-Ola (2002 census population, 256,719). The Mari people were annexed to Russia, with other peoples of the Kazan Tatar Khanate, when the latter was overthrown in 1552. On 4 Nov. 1920 the territory was constituted as an Autonomous Region, and on 5 Dec. 1936 as an Autonomous Republic. The republic renamed itself the Mari Soviet Socialist Republic in Oct. 1990, and adopted a new constitution in June 1995. In Dec. 1991 Vladislav Zotin was elected the first president. The main ethnic groups are Russians, followed by Maris, with some Tatars.

President: Leonid Markelov (since 14 Jan. 2001).

Coal is mined. The main industries are metalworking, timber, paper, woodworking and food processing. Crops include grain, flax, potatoes, fruit and vegetables. Industry accounted for 24·4% of gross regional product in 2003 and agriculture 16·5%.

In 2004 there were 25,700 pupils in 265 pre-school institutions and 88,600 pupils in 382 primary and secondary day schools. There were 28,500 students in five institutions of higher education.

In 2004 the rates of doctors and hospital beds per 10,000 population were 35·2 and 125 respectively.

Mordovia

Area, 26,200 sq. km (10,100 sq. miles); population (2002 census), 888,766. Estimated population, 1 Jan. 2005, 866,600. Capital, Saransk (2002 census population, 304,866). By the 13th century the Mordovian tribes had been subjugated by Russian princes. In 1928 the territory was constituted as a Mordovian Area within the Middle-Volga Territory, on 10 Jan. 1930 as an Autonomous Region and on 20 Dec. 1934 as an Autonomous Republic. The main ethnic groups are Russians, followed by Mordovians, with some Tatars.

President: Nikolai Merkushkin (in power since Jan. 1995).

Industries include wood-processing and the production of building materials, furniture, textiles and leather goods. Agriculture is devoted chiefly to grain, sugarbeet, sheep and dairy farming. Industrial output was valued at 29,117m. roubles in 2002.

In 2004 there were 23,900 pupils in 241 pre-school institutions and 97,300 students in 713 primary and secondary day schools. There were 42,900 students in four institutions of higher education.

In 2004 the rates of doctors and hospital beds per 10,000 population were 51·4 and 134 respectively.

North Ossetia (Alania)

Area, 8,000 sq. km (3,100 sq. miles); population (2002 census), 710,275. Estimated population, 1 Jan. 2005, 704,400. Capital, Vladikavkaz (2002 census population, 315,608). North Ossetia was annexed by Russia from Turkey and named the Terek region in 1861. On 4 March 1918 it was proclaimed an Autonomous Soviet Republic, and on 20 Jan. 1921 set up with others as the Mountain Autonomous Republic, with North Ossetia as the Ossetian (Vladikavkaz) Area within it. On 7 July 1924 the latter was constituted as an Autonomous Region and on 5 Dec. 1936 as an Autonomous Republic. In the early 1990s there was

a conflict with neighbouring Ingushetia to the east, and to the south the decision of the Georgian government to disband the republic of South Ossetia led to ethnic war, with North Ossetia supporting the South Ossetians. Pressure for Ossetian reunification continues. In Sept. 2004 hostage takers seized a school in the town of Beslan. A three-day standoff ended with more than 350 people killed, nearly half of them children. Chechen rebels claimed responsibility for the siege.

A new Constitution was adopted on 12 Nov. 1994 under which the republic reverted to its former name, Alania. Ossetians are the largest ethnic group, followed by Russians, with some Chechens, Armenians and Ukrainians.

President: Taimuraz Mamsurov.

Prime Minister: Aleksandr Merkulov.

The main industries are non-ferrous metals (mining and metallurgy), maize processing, timber and woodworking, textiles, building materials, distilleries and food processing. There is also a varied agriculture. Agriculture accounted for 16·8% of gross regional product in 2003 and industry 13·0%.

In 2004 there were 22,000 pupils in 216 pre-school institutions and 95,200 pupils in 218 primary and secondary day schools. There were 32,200 students in nine institutions of higher education.

In 2004 the rates of doctors and hospital beds per 10,000 population were 68·0 and 115 respectively.

Sakha

The area is 3,103,200 sq. km (1,197,750 sq. miles), making Sakha the largest republic in the Russian Federation; population (2002 census), 949,280. Estimated population, 1 Jan. 2005, 950,700. Capital, Yakutsk (2002 census population, 210,642). The Yakuts were subjugated by the Russians in the 17th century. The territory was constituted an Autonomous Republic on 27 April 1922. The largest ethnic group are Russians, followed by Yakuts, with Ukrainian and Tatar minorities.

President: Vyacheslav Shtyrov (since 27 Jan. 2002).

The principal industries are mining (gold, tin, mica, coal) and livestock-breeding. Silver- and lead-bearing ores and coal are worked. Large diamond fields have been opened up; Sakha produces most of the Russian Federation's output. Timber and food industries are developing. Trapping and breeding of fur-bearing animals (sable, squirrel, silver fox) are an important source of income. Industry accounted for 41·1% of gross regional product in 2003 and agriculture 3·6%.

In 2004 there were 51,900 pupils in 697 pre-school institutions and 168,400 pupils in 692 primary and secondary day schools. There were 43,700 students in eight institutions of higher education.

In 2004 the rates of doctors and hospital beds per 10,000 population were 49·5 and 147 respectively.

Tatarstan

Area, 68,000 sq. km (26,250 sq. miles); population (2002 census), 3,779,265. Estimated population, 1 Jan. 2005, 3,768,500. Capital, Kazan (2002 census population, 1,105,289). From the 10th to the 13th centuries this was the territory of the Volga-Kama Bulgar State; conquered by the Mongols, it became the seat of the Kazan (Tatar) Khans when the Mongol Empire broke up in the 15th century, and in 1552 was conquered again by Russia. On 27 May 1920 it was constituted as an Autonomous Republic. The main ethnic groups are Tatars and Russians, with Chuvash, Ukrainian and Mordovian minorities.

In Oct. 1991 the Supreme Soviet adopted a declaration of independence. At a referendum in March 1992, 61·4% of votes cast were in favour of increased autonomy. A Constitution was adopted in April 1992, which proclaims Tatarstan a sovereign state which conducts its relations with the Russian Federation on an equal basis. On 15 Feb. 1994 the Russian and Tatar presidents signed a treaty defining Tatarstan as a state united with Russia on the basis of the constitutions of both, but the Russian parliament has not ratified it.

President: Mintimer Sharipovich Shaimiyev (since June 1991).

The republic has engineering, oil and chemical, timber, building materials, textiles, clothing and food industries. Industrial production was valued at 252,037m. roubles in 2003 and agricultural output at 43,639m. roubles.

In 2004 there were 149,900 pupils in 1,982 pre-school institutions and 472,900 pupils in 2,448 primary and secondary day schools. There were 207,100 students in 35 institutions of higher education. There is a branch of the Russian Academy of Sciences with four learned institutions. In 2004 the rates of doctors and hospital beds per 10,000 population were 44·9 and 109 respectively.

Tuva

Area, 170,500 sq. km (65,800 sq. miles); population (2002 census), 305,510. Estimated population, 1 Jan. 2005, 307,600. Capital, Kyzyl (2002 census population, 104,105). Tuva was incorporated in the USSR as an autonomous region on 11 Oct. 1944 and elevated to an Autonomous Republic on 10 Oct. 1961. The largest ethnic group are Tuvans, followed by Russians. Tuva renamed itself the 'Republic of Tuva' in Oct. 1991.

A new constitution was promulgated on 22 Oct. 1993 which adopts the name 'Tyva' for the republic. This constitution provides for a 32-member parliament (*Supreme Hural*), and a *Grand Hural* alone empowered to change the constitution, asserts the precedence of Tuvan law and adopts powers to conduct foreign policy. It was approved by 62·2% of votes cast at a referendum on 12 Dec. 1993.

Chairman of the Government: Sherig-ool Dizizhikovich Oorzhak.

Tuva is well-watered and hydro-electric resources are important. The Tuvans are mainly herdsmen and cattle farmers and there is much good pastoral land. There are deposits of gold, cobalt and asbestos. The main exports are hair, hides and wool. There are mining, woodworking, garment, leather, food and other industries. Industrial production was valued at 1,700m. roubles in 2003 and agricultural output at 1,994m. roubles.

In 2004 there were 14,700 pupils in 217 pre-school institutions and 64,400 pupils in 176 primary and secondary day schools. There were 5,800 students at Tuva State University.

In 2004 the rates of doctors and hospital beds per 10,000 population were 42·7 and 178 respectively.

Udmurtia

Area, 42,100 sq. km (16,250 sq. miles); population (2002 census), 1,570,316. Estimated population, 1 Jan. 2005, 1,552,800. Capital,

Izhevsk (2002 census population, 632,140). The Udmurts (formerly known as 'Votyaks') were annexed by the Russians in the 15th and 16th centuries. On 4 Nov. 1920 the Votyak Autonomous Region was constituted (the name was changed to Udmurt in 1932), and on 28 Dec. 1934 was raised to the status of an Autonomous Republic. The main ethnic group are Russians, followed by Udmurts, with Tatar, Ukrainian and Mari minorities. A declaration of sovereignty and the present state title were adopted in Sept. 1990.

A new parliament was established in Dec. 1993 consisting of a 50-member upper house, the *Council of Representatives*, and a full-time 35-member lower house.

President: Alexander Alexandrovich Volkov (in power since April 1995).

Heavy industry includes the manufacture of locomotives, machine tools and other engineering products, most of them for the defence industries, as well as timber and building materials. There are also light industries: clothing, leather, furniture and food. Industrial production was valued at 82,405m. roubles in 2004 and agricultural output at 16,662m. roubles.

In 2004 there were 73,900 pupils in 806 pre-school institutions and 185,400 pupils in 849 primary and secondary day schools. There were 73,300 students in eight institutions of higher education.

In 2004 the rates of doctors and hospital beds per 10,000 population were 56·4 and 131 respectively.

Autonomous Districts and Provinces

Agin-Buryat
Situated in Chita region (Eastern Siberia); area, 19,000 sq. km, population (2002 census), 72,213. Estimated population, 1 Jan. 2005, 73,500. Capital, Aginskoe. Formed 1937, its economy is basically pastoral.

Chukot
Situated in Magadan region (Far East); area, 737,700 sq. km, population (2002 census), 53,824. Estimated population, 1 Jan. 2005, 50,700. Capital, Anadyr. Formed 1930. Population chiefly Russian, also Chukchi, Koryak, Yakut, Even. Minerals are extracted in the north, including gold, tin, mercury and tungsten.

Evenki
Situated in Krasnoyarsk territory (Eastern Siberia); area, 767,600 sq. km, population, (2002 census) 17,697. Estimated population, 1 Jan. 2005, 17,400, chiefly Evenks. Capital, Tura. Formed 1930.

Khanty-Mansi
Situated in Tyumen region (western Siberia); area, 523,100 sq. km, population (2002 census), 1,432,817. Estimated population, 1 Jan. 2005, 1,469,000, chiefly Russians but also Khants and Mansi. Capital, Khanty-Mansiisk. Formed 1930.

Koryak
Situated in Kamchatka; area, 301,500 sq. km, population (2002 census), 25,157. Estimated population, 1 Jan, 2005, 23,800. Capital, Palana. Formed 1930.

Nenets
Situated in Archangel region (Northern Russia); area, 176,700 sq. km, population (2002 census), 41,546. Estimated population, 1 Jan. 2005, 42,000. Capital, Naryan-Mar. Formed 1929.

Taimyr

Situated in Krasnoyarsk territory, this most northerly part of Siberia comprises the Taimyr peninsula and the Arctic islands of Severnaya Zemlya. Area, 862,100 sq. km, population (2002 census), 39,786. Estimated population, 1 Jan. 2005, 39,400, excluding the mining city of Norilsk which is separately administered. Capital, Dudinka. Formed 1930.

Ust-Ordyn-Buryat

Situated in Irkutsk region (Eastern Siberia); area, 22,400 sq. km, population (2002 census), 135,327. Estimated population, 1 Jan. 2005, 134,100. Capital, Ust-Ordynsk. Formed 1937.

Yamalo-Nenets

Situated in Tyumen region (western Siberia); area, 750,300 sq. km, population (2002 census), 507,006. Estimated population, 1 Jan. 2005, 523,400. Capital, Salekhard. Formed 1930.

Yevreyskaya (Jewish) Autonomous Oblast (Province)

Part of Khabarovsk Territory. Area, 36,000 sq. km (13,895 sq. miles); population (2002 census), 190,915. Estimated population, 1 Jan. 2005, 188,800, chiefly Russians, but also Ukrainians and Jews. Capital, Birobijan (2002 census population, 77,250). Established as Jewish National District in 1928. There is a Yiddish national theatre, newspaper and broadcasting service.

RWANDA

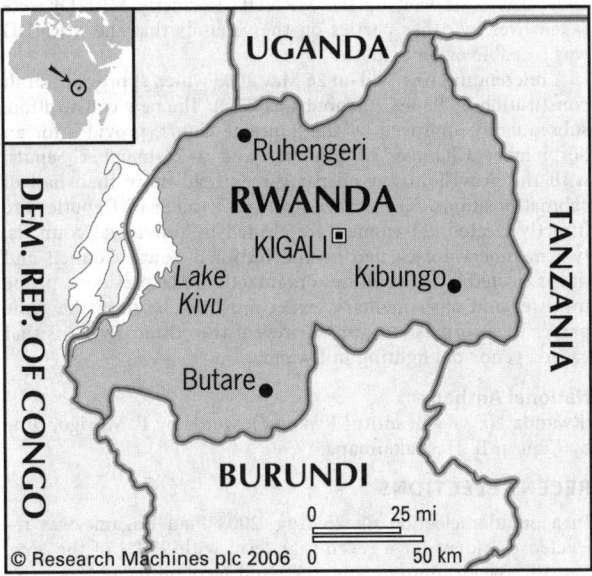

Republika y'u Rwanda

Capital: Kigali
Population projection, 2010: 10·12m.
GDP per capita, 2003: (PPP$) 1,268
HDI/world rank: 0·450/159

KEY HISTORICAL EVENTS

The Twa—hunter-gatherer pygmies—were the first people to inhabit Rwanda. They now comprise 1% of the population. The Hutu were the next group to settle in Rwanda. They arrived at some point between AD 500 and 1100. They were small-scale agriculturalists, led by a king who ruled over clan groups. The final group to migrate to Rwanda was the Tutsi around 1400. Their ownership of cattle and their combat skills gained for them the economic and political control of the country. A feudalistic system developed where the Tutsi lent cows to the Hutu in return for labour and military service. At the apex was the Tutsi king, the *mwami* (pl., *abami*), who was believed to be of divine origin. The *abami* consolidated their power by centralizing the monarchy and reducing the power of neighbouring chiefs. Mwami Kigeri IV (reigned 1853–95) established the borders of Rwanda in the 19th century.

The Conference of Berlin in 1885 placed Rwanda under German control. However, no German actually reached the area until 1894 when Count von Götzen arrived and became the governor of German East Africa. The Belgians and British also wanted control of the area owing to its strategic position at the juncture of their separate empires. However, by 1910 German ownership was accepted.

A consequence of German control of Rwanda was the arrival of the Catholic Church through the mission of the White Fathers, who established schools and missions from 1899. Germany did not change the political structure of the country but made use of the mwami, Yuhi V (reigned 1896–1931), who accepted German overlordship. The First World War disrupted this relationship by stripping Germany of all her colonies. Rwanda was occupied by Belgian forces in 1916 and was declared a Belgian mandate

in Aug. 1923 by the League of Nations. The Belgians ruled more directly than the Germans, curtailing the mwami's power and favouring the Tutsi minority on more explicitly racial grounds. From 1952 the UN ordered Belgium to integrate Rwandans into the political system. The Belgians continued their policy of favouring the fairer skinned Tutsi and placed them in a position of domination over the Hutu majority. Increasing civil unrest erupted into a civil war by 1959. A state of Ruanda-Urundi was established in 1960, under Belgian trusteeship, following an election. In 1961, while abroad, Mwami Kigeli V was exiled by the Belgians, who refused to allow him to return despite pressure from the UN. On 27 June 1962 the parliament voted to terminate the trusteeship and on 1 July 1962 Rwanda became independent.

Independence

The independent state of Rwanda was first governed by the Parmehutu party (a Hutu party representing the 85% Hutu population), led by Grégoire Kayibanda, but this was not accepted by some Tutsis. An attempted invasion in 1963 by Tutsis who had fled to Uganda and Burundi was repelled. In retaliation over 12,000 Tutsis in Rwanda were massacred by the Hutu. The next massacre in 1972–73 was partly in response to massacres of Hutus in neighbouring Tutsi-dominated Burundi. This massacre was also an attempt by Kayibanda to revive his waning popularity. Instead it gave an opportunity for Maj.-Gen. Juvénal Habyarimana, a senior army commander, to launch a bloodless coup and take over government. In 1975 Habyarimana formed *le Mouvement Révolutionaire National pour le Développement* (MRND), and turned Rwanda into a one-party and tightly controlled police state, discriminating against the Tutsi in favour of the Hutu.

In 1990 the Rwandan Patriotic Front (RPF), of between 5,000 and 10,000 Tutsis, invaded Rwanda from Uganda, starting a civil war. A ceasefire was agreed on 29 March 1991 and on 14 July 1992 the Arusha Accords were signed. These allowed other political parties to stand for election and share power.

Many Hutus opposed Arusha. Multi-partyism led to the rise of far-right Hutu power groups, who believed that the only solution to Hutu-Tutsi problems was the extermination of the Tutsi. The assassination of the first legitimately elected Hutu president of Burundi, on 21 Oct. 1993, by Tutsi army officers and the following massacre of over 150,000 Hutus in Burundi served to further destabilize the situation in Rwanda. The assassination of Habyarimana in a plane crash on 6 April 1994, probably shot down by Hutu extremists, was the first step in a carefully premeditated genocide which killed around 1m. Rwandans in three months and forced over 2m. to flee to neighbouring countries.

Among the victims was the moderate Hutu prime minister, Agathe Uwilingiyimana. Gangs of *interahamwe* (civilian death squads) roamed the capital, Kigali, killing, looting and raping Tutsis and politically-moderate Hutus. When the RPF, led by Paul Kagame, reached Kigali the killings spread to other parts of the county.

France dispatched 2,000 troops on a humanitarian mission on 22 June 1994 to maintain a 'safe zone'. Owing to France's greater affinity with the French-speaking Hutu former government, this zone served as an escape route for killers to flee to Zaïre.

The RPF declared the war over on 17 July 1994 and was quickly recognized as the new government. Genocide trials began in Arusha, Tanzania in Dec. 1996. In Sept. 1998 Jean Kambanda, the former prime minister (April–July 1994), was sentenced to life imprisonment.

Rwanda was destabilized by the presence of Hutu refugee camps on the Zaïre borders. Amongst the 1·1m. refugees were *interahamwe* who used the camps as bases for attacks on Rwanda. These were broken up by Laurent Kabila in May 1997, before he assumed power in Zaïre (later renamed the Democratic Republic of the Congo).

In April 2000 Paul Kagame (the Tutsi vice-president and defence minister) was elected president by parliament, replacing Pasteur Bizimungu, a Hutu who had been appointed by the RPF, in July 1994. Kagame was re-elected president in Aug. 2003 in Rwanda's first democratic elections since the atrocities.

TERRITORY AND POPULATION

Rwanda is bounded south by Burundi, west by the Democratic Republic of the Congo, north by Uganda and east by Tanzania. A mountainous state of 25,314 sq. km (9,774 sq. miles), its western third drains to Lake Kivu on the border with the Democratic Republic of the Congo and thence to the Congo river, while the rest is drained by the Kagera river into the Nile system.

The population was 7,164,994 at the 1991 census, of whom over 90% were Hutu, 9% Tutsi and 1% Twa (pygmy). 2002 census population, 8,128,553; density, 321·1 per sq. km.

The UN gives a projected population for 2010 of 10·12m.

In 2003 the population was 81·5% rural, but urbanization is increasing rapidly.

The areas and populations of the 12 administrative divisions (11 provinces and Kigali City) are:

Province	Area (in sq. km)	Population (2002 census)
Butare	1,872	725,914
Byumba	1,694	707,786
Cyangugu	1,894	607,495
Gikongoro	1,974	489,729
Gisenyi	2,047	864,377
Gitarama	2,141	856,488
Kibungo	2,964	702,248
Kibuye	1,748	469,016
Kigali City	313	603,049
Kigali-Ngali	2,780	789,330
Ruhengeri	1,657	891,498
Umutara	4,230	421,623

Kigali, the capital, had 603,049 inhabitants in 2002; other towns are Butare, Gisenyi, Gitarama and Ruhengeri.

Kinyarwanda, the language of the entire population, French and English (since 1996) are the official languages. Swahili is spoken in the commercial centres.

SOCIAL STATISTICS

2000 estimates: births, 325,000; deaths, 159,000. Estimated birth rate in 2000 was 42·1 per 1,000 population; estimated death rate, 20·6. Annual population growth rate, 1992–2002, 3·2%. Life expectancy at birth in 2003 was 45·6 years for females and 42·1 for males, up from 23·1 years for females and 22·1 years for males during the period 1990–95 (at the height of the civil war). Infant mortality, 2001, 96 per 1,000 live births; fertility rate, 2001, 5·9 births per woman.

CLIMATE

Despite the equatorial situation, there is a highland tropical climate. The wet seasons are from Oct. to Dec. and March to May. Highest rainfall occurs in the west, at around 70" (1,770 mm), decreasing to 40–55" (1,020–1,400 mm) in the central uplands and to 30" (760 mm) in the north and east. Kigali, Jan. 67°F (19·4°C), July 70°F (21·1°C). Annual rainfall 40" (1,000 mm).

CONSTITUTION AND GOVERNMENT

Under the 1978 Constitution the MRND was the sole political organization.

A new Constitution was promulgated in June 1991 permitting multi-party democracy.

The Arusha Agreement of Aug. 1994 provided for a transitional 70-member National Assembly, which began functioning in Nov. 1994. The seats won by the MRNDD (formerly MRND) were taken over by other parties on the grounds that the MRNDD was culpable of genocide.

A referendum was held on 26 May 2003 which approved a draft constitution by 93·4% (turnout was 87%). The new constitution, subsequently approved by the Supreme Court, provides for an 80-member *Chamber of Deputies* and a 26-member *Senate*, with the provision that no party may hold more than half of cabinet positions. 53 members of the Chamber of Deputies are directly elected, 24 women are elected by provincial councils, two members are elected by the National Youth Council and one is elected by a disabilities organization. The president, prime minister and parliamentary leader must not be from the same party. These provisions aim to prevent the ethnic divisions that caused genocidal fighting in Rwanda.

National Anthem

'Rwanda Nziza' ('Beautiful Rwanda'); words by F. Murigo, tune by Capt. J.-B. Hashakaimana.

RECENT ELECTIONS

In a popular election on 25 Aug. 2003 Paul Kagame was re-elected president for a seven-year term with 95·1% of the vote. Faustin Twagiramungu won 3·6% and Népomuscène Nayinzira won 1·3%. Turnout was 96·6%.

In the first democratic parliamentary elections since the 1994 genocide, held on 30 Sept. 2003, President Kagame's Rwandan Patriotic Front (RPF) and its coalition won 73·8% of the vote. The RPF took 33 seats, the Christian-Democratic Party 3 seats and the Islamic Democratic Party 2 seats; the Rwandese Socialist Party and the Democratic Union of the Rwandese People took one seat each. The Social Democratic Party (SDP) won 12·3% (7 seats), the Liberal Party, 10·6% (6 seats). The Party for Progress and Concord won 2·2% but no seats. Turnout was 96·5%. Following the Sept. 2003 election, of the 80 Members of Parliament there were 41 men (51·2%) and 39 women (48·8%), the highest percentage of women in a parliament of any country in the world.

CURRENT ADMINISTRATION

President: Paul Kagame; b. 1957 (RPF—Tutsis; sworn in 22 April 2000 having been acting president since 24 March 2000 and re-elected in Aug. 2003).

In March 2006 the government comprised:

Prime Minister: Bernard Makuza; b. 1961 (MDR/Republican Democratic Movement—Hutus; sworn in 8 March 2000).

Minister of Agriculture and Livestock: Anastase Murekezi. *Defence:* Maj. Gen. Marcel Gatsinzi. *Lands, Environment, Forestry, Water and Natural Resources:* Christophe Bazivamo. *Commerce, Industry, Investment Promotion, Tourism and Co-operatives:* Protais Kabanda Mitali. *Education:* Jeanne d'Arc Mujawamariya. *Gender and Family Promotion:* Valérie Nyirahabineza. *Finance and Planning:* James Musoni. *Foreign Affairs and Regional Co-operation:* Charles Murigande. *Health:* Jean Ntawukuriryayo Damascène. *Justice:* Edda Mukabagwiza. *Internal Affairs:* Musa Fazili Harelimana. *Youth, Culture and Sports:* Joseph Habineza. *Local Government, Good Governance, Rural Development and Social Affairs:* Protais Musoni. *Infrastructure:* Stanislas Kamanzi. *Public Service and Labour:* Manasseh Nshuti. *Information:* Laurent Nkusi. *Minister at the President's Office in Charge of Science, Technology and Research:* Romain Murenzi. *Minister at the President's Office:* Solina Nyirahabimana.

Government Website: http://www.gov.rw

CURRENT LEADERS

Paul Kagame

Position
President

Introduction
Paul Kagame has long played a dominant role in Rwandan politics. He was elected president by the transitional National Assembly in April 2000, replacing Pasteur Bizimungu. Kagame, who is leader of the ruling Rwandan Patriotic Front (RPF), is the first member of the Tutsi minority to be president of Rwanda. Although a leading force in the country, he is a low-key public figure. He has openly criticized the United Nations, arguing it could have done more to avoid the genocide of 1994 when around 1m. Rwandans were killed. Since joining the government in 1994 Kagame has been heavily involved in military intervention in the Democratic Republic of the Congo. Democratic elections in 2003 cemented his mandate as president.

Early Life
Kagame was born in Oct. 1957 in the Gitarama prefecture of central Rwanda. Following violence in Rwanda, his family fled to Uganda in 1960 where he grew up in a refugee camp. He received primary and secondary schooling in Uganda and then studied at Makerere University in Kampala. In 1979 Kagame joined the National Salvation Front (FRONASA), led by Yoweri Museveni, which took part in the Tanzanian removal of Idi Amin's regime in 1979. In 1980 he became a founding member of Museveni's National Resistance Army (NRA) and fought against the dictatorship of Milton Obote in Uganda. He became head of intelligence of the NRA in 1986 and the following year, together with Fred Rwigyema, established the Rwandan Patriotic Front (RPF) with support from Museveni.

The RPF first invaded Rwanda in 1990 when Kagame was on military training in Kansas, USA. After Rwigyema's death, Kagame returned and took over as military leader, leading the guerrilla war against Juvénal Habyarimana and his Hutu government. In 1993 a peace agreement was signed, but following the death of President Habyarimana in 1994 violence recurred with the Hutu massacres of the Tutsi. The RPF resumed the civil war and soon gained control over the country. The new government of national unity, formed in July 1994, was led by Pasteur Bizimungu, a Hutu, with Kagame as vice president and defence minister.

Career in Office
Rwanda's involvement in the Democratic Republic of the Congo (DRC; known as Zaïre until 1997) began covertly in 1996 with an agreement with Uganda to oust the Zaïrean president Mobutu Sese Seko. Kagame and Museveni sent troops back into the east of the DRC in 1998 to assist rebel groups against President Laurent Kabila and to eliminate the *interahamwe* (death squads from the 1994 genocide in Rwanda). In Nov. 1998 Kagame publicly admitted that Rwandese forces were active in the DRC for reasons of national security. Divisions appeared between the allied forces leading to support for different rebel groups and three confrontations in Kisangani, a major northern city. Kisangani's mineral wealth prompted allegations, categorically denied, that Uganda and Rwanda clashed over the allocation of spoils. Relations between Kagame and Museveni continued to sour, owing to the movement of dissidents taking refuge in each other's countries. The massive enlargement and reorganization of the Rwandese forces was interpreted as a direct threat by Museveni, who appealed to the British government in Aug. 2001 for financial support for increases in defence spending. The UK international development minister chaired talks between the two presidents in London in Nov. 2001, where once again they pledged not to support dissident groups.

In March 2000 President Bizimungu resigned, leaving Kagame as interim president. Bizimungu claimed that he and the prime minister, Pierre-Celéstin Rwigema, were hounded from office for being Hutus. Elected president by the transitional National Assembly in April 2000, Kagame relinquished the defence ministry to Col. Emmanuel Habyarimana, a Hutu, and promoted Nyamuasa Kayumba, the army chief, to maj.-gen., a rank only Kagame himself had held previously. Kagame has attempted to portray himself as a civilian and neutral president, calling for ethnic peace and reconciliation as a Rwandan rather than a Tutsi.

Following the assassination of Laurent Kabila in Jan. 2001, his son and successor, Joseph Kabila, met Kagame in Washington, D.C., ending the impasse. During the African Union summit in Durban in July 2002, Kagame again met with Kabila. Kagame accused the DRC of harbouring Hutu militias and was not willing to withdraw his troops until they were disarmed. Kabila blamed Rwanda for killing more than 3·5m. inhabitants of the DRC and refused to co-operate until Rwandan troops were withdrawn. However, on 30 July 2002 in Pretoria, South Africa, the two nations signed a peace deal under which the DRC agreed to disarm and arrest Hutu rebels and Rwanda withdrew its troops from the DRC in Oct. 2002.

Kagame was elected president by a popular democratic vote on 25 Aug. 2003. His massive win—with 95% of the vote—prompted allegations of irregularities from his main rival, Faustin Twagiramungu, although he accepted the win in Sept. Museveni's attendance at Kagame's inauguration ceremony demonstrated the easing of tensions between the two men.

Bernard Makuza

Position
Prime Minister

Introduction
Bernard Makuza became prime minister of Rwanda in March 2000, nine days after the former prime minister, Pierre-Celéstin Rwigema, resigned amidst corruption allegations.

Early Life
Bernard Makuza was born in 1961. The former ambassador to Germany, Makuza returned to Rwanda to take up the post of prime minister. He is head of the predominately Hutu Republican Democratic Movement (MDR).

Career in Office
While the power of government resides with the president, the prime minister has a strong public image. In Jan. 2003 Makuza headed a national ceremony to mark the opening of rehabilitation centres for those who admitted taking part in the 1994 genocide. In Sept. 2004, alongside UN Secretary-General Kofi Annan and the Democratic Republic of the Congo's president, Joseph Kabila, Makuza was part of a UN-backed body created to resolve the civil unrest on the border between Rwanda and the DRC. In Oct. 2005 he opened the 6th African Congress on Savings and Credit Co-operatives; a two-day conference held in Kigali, it discussed the reduction of poverty in Africa via the management of co-operatives. Makuza has aimed to improve political, economic and trade relations with foreign countries and has forged a strong partnership with China.

DEFENCE

In 2003 defence expenditure totalled US$69m. (US$8 per capita), representing 4·1% of GDP.

Army

Strength (2003) about 40,000. There was a national police of some 10,000 in 2002.

INTERNATIONAL RELATIONS

Rwanda is a member of the UN, WTO, the African Union, African Development Bank, COMESA, IOM, the International Organization of the Francophonie and is an ACP member state of the ACP-EU relationship.

ECONOMY

Agriculture accounted for 41·9% of GDP in 2002, industry 21·5% and services 36·6%.

Currency

The unit of currency is the *Rwanda franc* (RWF) notionally of 100 *centimes*. On 3 Jan. 1995, 500-, 1,000- and 5,000-Rwanda franc notes were replaced by new issues, demonetarizing the currency taken abroad by exiles. The currency is not convertible. Foreign exchange reserves were US$180m. in June 2002. Gold reserves are negligible. Inflation was 7·4% in 2003 and 12·0% in 2004. Total money supply in Dec. 2001 was 63,606m. Rwanda francs.

Budget

In 2000 revenues were 132·4bn. Rwanda francs and expenditures 131·7bn. Rwanda francs.

Performance

Real GDP growth was 35·2% in 1995, following five years of negative growth peaking in a rate of –50·2% in 1994 at the height of the civil war. By 2000 the growth had slowed, but was still 6·0%. In 2003 growth was only 0·9%, rising in 2004 to 4·0%. Total GDP in 2004 was US$1·8bn.

Banking and Finance

The central bank is the National Bank of Rwanda (founded 1960; *Governor*, François Kanimba), the bank of issue since 1964. There are seven commercial banks (Banque de Kigali, Banque de Commerce et de Développement Industriel, Banque Continentale Africaine au Rwanda, Banque à la Confiance d'Or, Banque Commerciale du Rwanda, Caisse Hypothécaire du Rwanda and Compagnie Générale de Banque), one development bank (Rwandan Development Bank) and one credit union system (Rwandan Union of Popular Banks).

ENERGY AND NATURAL RESOURCES

Environment

Carbon dioxide emissions from the consumption and flaring of fossil fuels in 2002 were the equivalent of 0·1 tonnes per capita.

Electricity

Installed capacity was 43,000 kW in 2000. Production was estimated at 169m. kWh in 2000 and consumption per capita an estimated 24 kWh.

Oil and Gas

In 2002 proven natural gas reserves were 57bn. cu. metres.

Minerals

Production (2002): cassiterite, 197 tonnes; wolfram, 153 tonnes.

Agriculture

There were 1·0m. ha. of arable land in 2001 and 300,000 ha. of permanent crops. Production (2000 estimates, in 1,000 tonnes): plantains, 2,212; sweet potatoes, 1,033; cassava, 821; dry beans, 215; pumpkins and squash, 206; potatoes, 175; sorghum, 155; taro, 91; maize, 63; sugarcane, 40; coffee, 15; dry peas, 15; tea, 14; rice, 12.

Long-horned Ankole cattle play an important traditional role. Efforts are being made to improve their present negligible economic value. There were, in 2000, 725,000 cattle, 700,000 goats, 320,000 sheep, 160,000 pigs and 1m. chickens.

Forestry

Forests covered 307,000 ha. (12·4% of the land area) in 2000. Timber production in 2001 was 7·84m. cu. metres.

Fisheries

The catch in 2001 totalled 6,828 tonnes, entirely from inland waters.

INDUSTRY

There are about 100 small-sized modern manufacturing enterprises in the country. Food manufacturing is the dominant industrial activity (64%) followed by construction (15·3%) and mining (9%). There is a large modern brewery.

Labour

The labour force in 1996 totalled 3,021,000 (51% males). Over 90% of the economically active population in 1995 were engaged in agriculture, fisheries and forestry.

INTERNATIONAL TRADE

Rwanda, Burundi and the Democratic Republic of the Congo make up the Economic Community of the Great Lakes. Foreign debt was US$1,435m. in 2002.

Imports and Exports

In 2002 imports (f.o.b.) amounted to US$233·3m. (US$245·2m. in 2001); exports (f.o.b.) US$67·2m. (US$93·3m. in 2001). Leading imports are capital goods, food and energy products; major exports are coffee, tea and tin. Main import suppliers, 1999: Japan, 13·1%; Belgium, 12·8%; Kenya, 12·5%; Saudi Arabia, 8·0%. Main export markets, 1999: Kenya, 62·4%; Tanzania, 13·9%; Germany, 7·9%; Belgium, 6·5%.

COMMUNICATIONS

Roads

There were an estimated 9,497 km of roads in 2002, of which 8·1% were paved. There are road links with Burundi, Uganda, Tanzania and the Democratic Republic of the Congo. In 2002 there were 8,900 passenger cars and 6,300 trucks and vans.

Civil Aviation

There is an international airport at Kigali (Gregoire Kayibanda), which handled 103,000 passengers (100,000 on international flights) in 2001. In 2003 there were scheduled flights to Addis Ababa, Brussels, Bujumbura, Douala, Entebbe, Johannesburg and Nairobi. A national carrier, Rwandair Express, began operations in 2003 flying to Entebbe and Johannesburg.

Telecommunications

Rwanda had 134,000 telephone subscribers in 2002 (equivalent to 16·4 per 1,000 persons) including 110,800 mobile phone subscribers. Internet users numbered 25,000 in 2002. In 1995 there were 500 fax machines.

Postal Services

In 2003 there were 25 post offices, or one for every 335,000 persons.

SOCIAL INSTITUTIONS

Justice

A system of Courts of First Instance and provincial courts refer appeals to Courts of Appeal and a Court of Cassation situated in Kigali. In 1998 a number of people were executed for genocide in the civil war in 1994, including 22 at five different locations throughout the country on 24 April 1998.

The population in penal institutions in 2002 was approximately 112,000, of which 103,000 were being held on suspicion of genocide.

Education

In 2003–04 there were 2,262 primary schools with 28,254 teachers for 1·8m. pupils; 230,909 secondary pupils with 7,750 teachers; and 15,353 (2001–02) students at university level. Adult literacy rate in 2003 was 64·0% (male, 70·5%; female, 58·8%).

In 2000–01 total expenditure on education came to 2·8% of GNP.

Health

In 2002 there were 155 doctors, four dentists, 11 pharmacists, 1,735 nursing personnel and ten midwives. Hospital bed provision in 1990 was one per 588 people.

In 2003 an estimated 250,000 people were living with HIV. There were 1·38m. reported cases of malaria in 1992.

RELIGION

In 2001 approximately 47% of the population were Roman Catholics, 19% Protestants and 7% Muslims. Some of the population follow traditional animist religions. Before the civil war there were nine Roman Catholic bishops and 370 priests. By the end of 1994, three bishops had been killed and three reached retiring age; 106 priests had been killed and 130 had sought refuge abroad.

CULTURE

Broadcasting

The state-controlled *Radiodiffusion de la République Rwandaise* is responsible for broadcasting. Colour transmission is on the SECAM V system. There were about 587,000 radio sets in 2000 and 600 television receivers in 1997.

Press

In 1998 there was one daily newspaper with a circulation of 600, equivalent to a rate of one per 9,000 population.

Tourism

In 2001 there were 113,000 foreign tourists; spending by tourists totalled US$25m.

DIPLOMATIC REPRESENTATIVES

Of Rwanda in the United Kingdom (120–122 Seymour Place, London, W1H 1NR)
Ambassador: Claver Gatete.

Of the United Kingdom in Rwanda (Parcelle No. 1131, Blvd de l'Umuganda, Kacyira-Sud, POB 576, Kigali)
Ambassador: Jeremy Macadie.

Of Rwanda in the USA (1714 New Hampshire Ave., NW, Washington, D.C., 20009)
Ambassador: Dr Zac Nsenga.

Of the USA in Rwanda (Blvd de la Révolution, POB 28, Kigali)
Ambassador: Michael R. Arietti.

Of Rwanda to the United Nations
Ambassador: Stanislas Kamanzi.

Of Rwanda to the European Union
Ambassador: Emmanuel Kayitana Imanzi.

FURTHER READING

Braeckman, C., *Rwanda: Histoire d'un Génocide.* Paris, 1994
Dorsey, L., *Historical Dictionary of Rwanda.* Metuchen (NJ), 1995
Fegley, Randall, *Rwanda.* [Bibliography] ABC-Clio, Oxford and Santa Barbara (CA), 1993
Gourevitch, P., *We Wish to Inform You That Tomorrow We Will Be Killed With Our Families.* Picador, London, 1998
Prunier, G., *The Rwanda Crisis: History of a Genocide.* Farnborough, 1995

ST KITTS AND NEVIS

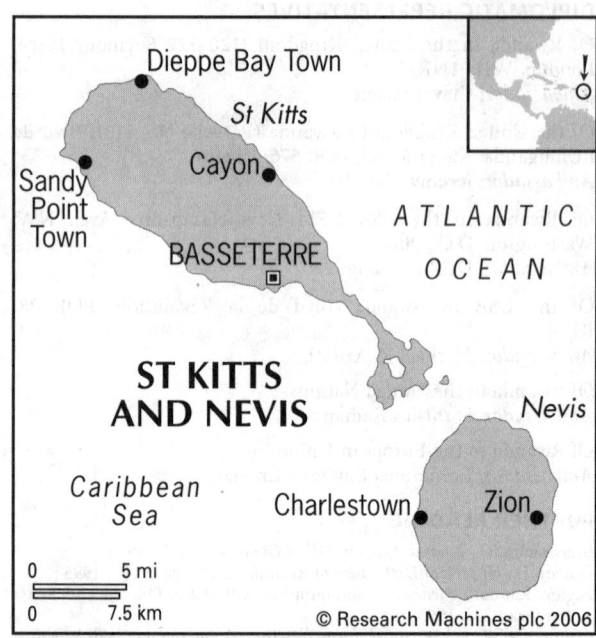

Federation of St Kitts and Nevis

Capital: Basseterre
Population, 2001: 46,000
GDP per capita, 2003: (PPP$) 12,404
HDI/world rank: 0·834/49

KEY HISTORICAL EVENTS

The islands of St Kitts (formerly St Christopher) and Nevis were discovered and named by Columbus in 1493. They were settled by Britain in 1623 and 1628, but ownership was disputed with France until 1783. In Feb. 1967 colonial status was replaced by an 'association' with Britain, giving the islands full internal self-government. St Kitts and Nevis became fully independent on 19 Sept. 1983. In Oct. 1997 the five-person Nevis legislature voted to end the federation with St Kitts. However, in a referendum held on 10 Aug. 1998 voters rejected independence, only 62% voting for secession when a two-thirds vote in favour was needed. In Sept. 1998 Hurricane Georges caused devastation, leaving 25,000 people homeless, with some 80% of the houses in the islands damaged.

TERRITORY AND POPULATION

The two islands of St Kitts and Nevis are situated at the northern end of the Leeward Islands in the eastern Caribbean. Nevis lies 3 km to the southeast of St Kitts. Population, 2001 census (provisional), 46,111. In 2003, 67·8% of the population were rural.

	Sq. km	Census 1991	Census 2001 (provisional)	Chief town	Census 2001 (provisional)
St Kitts	176·1	31,824	34,930	Basseterre	13,220
Nevis	93·3	8,794	11,181	Charlestown	1,820
	269·4	40,618	46,111		

In 2000, 90·4% of the population were Black. English is the official and spoken language.

SOCIAL STATISTICS

Births, 2001, 803; deaths, 352. Rates, 2001 (per 1,000 population): births, 17·4; deaths, 7·6. Infant mortality, 2001 (per 1,000 live births), 20. Expectation of life in 1999 was 68·0 years for males and 71·8 for females. Annual population growth rate, 1991–2001, 1·4%; fertility rate, 2001, 2·4 births per woman.

CLIMATE

Temperature varies between 21·4–30·7°C, with a sea breeze throughout the year and low humidity. Rainfall in 1999 was 1,706·9 mm.

CONSTITUTION AND GOVERNMENT

The British sovereign is the head of state, represented by a Governor-General. The 1983 Constitution described the country as 'a sovereign democratic federal state'. It allowed for a unicameral Parliament consisting of 11 elected Members (eight from St Kitts and three from Nevis), three appointed Senators and one *ex officio* member. Nevis was given its own Island Assembly and the right to secession from St Kitts.

National Anthem

'O Land of beauty! Our country where peace abounds'; words and tune by K. A. Georges.

RECENT ELECTIONS

At the National Assembly elections on 25 Oct. 2004 the Labour Party gained 7 seats, the Concerned Citizens Movement 2, the People's Action Movement 1 and the Nevis Reformation Party 1. Turnout was just over 67%.

CURRENT ADMINISTRATION

Governor-General: Sir Cuthbert Montraville Sebastian, GCMG, OBE; b. 1921 (appointed 1 Jan. 1996).

In March 2006 the government comprised:

Prime Minister, Minister of Finance, Sustainable Development, Information and Technology, Tourism, Culture and Sports: Dr Denzil L. Douglas; b. 1936 (Labour Party; sworn in 7 July 1995 and re-elected in 2000 and 2004).

Deputy Prime Minister, Minister of Education, Youth, Social and Community Development, and Gender Affairs: Sam Condor.

Minister of Housing, Agriculture, Fisheries and Consumer Affairs: Cedric Liburd. *Foreign Affairs, International Trade, Industry and Commerce:* Timothy Harris. *Attorney General and Legal Affairs:* Delano Bart. *Public Works, Utilities, Transport and Posts:* Dr Earl Asim Martin. *National Security, Justice, Immigration and Labour:* G. A. Dwyer Astaphan. *Health:* Rupert Herbert.

The *Nevis Island* legislature comprises an Assembly of three nominated members and elected members from each electoral district on the Island, and an Administration consisting of the Premier and two other persons appointed by the Deputy Governor-General.

The Premier of *Nevis* is Vance Amory.

Government Website: http://www.stkittsnevis.net

CURRENT LEADERS

Dr Denzil L. Douglas

Position
Prime Minister

Introduction
Denzil Douglas has been prime minister of St Kitts and Nevis since 1995. In Oct. 2004 he was re-elected for his third consecutive term after securing seven out of a possible eleven seats.

Early Life

Born in 1953, Denzil Llewellyn Douglas is a graduate of the University of the West Indies. He worked as a family physician before embarking on a career in politics. Douglas was a Labour party activist from an early age and became leader of the St Kitts and Nevis Labour Party in 1989.

The 1995 election was called following drug smuggling allegations brought against the prime minister at the time, Kennedy Simmonds. Douglas was elected and also took over the foreign affairs portfolio, which he retained until 2000.

Career in Office

Since becoming prime minister, Douglas has worked hard to try and mend relations between the islands of St Kitts and Nevis. In 1998 a referendum on secession was held after occupants of Nevis complained that the federal government in St Kitts was ignoring their needs. Although they failed to gain the two-thirds vote needed to break away, unrest remains. Douglas wants to tackle the differences between Kitts and Nevis via constitutional reform rather than secession.

In Nov. 2004 Douglas chaired a CARICOM–UK conference aimed at reducing stigma and discrimination against those living with HIV and aids in the Caribbean. Douglas has campaigned strongly for the reduction of poverty, exacerbated in St Kitts and Nevis when Hurricane Georges devastated the Caribbean in 1998. In May 2005, he chaired the first Caribbean Forum of Development, aimed at transforming the regional economy, and achieving international competitiveness and sustainable growth. He has called for the cancellation of international debt, which has been crippling many Caribbean Islands.

While he has been widely praised for his work promoting tourism and combating crime in Kitts and Nevis, he has been criticized for not reviving the islands' ailing sugar industry. In March 2005 the government effectively closed the 300 year-old industry after another loss-making harvest.

Douglas holds several ministerial posts including that of minister of finance.

INTERNATIONAL RELATIONS

St Kitts and Nevis is a member of the UN, WTO, the Commonwealth, OAS, ACS, CARICOM, OECS and is an ACP member state of the ACP-EU relationship.

ECONOMY

Agriculture accounted for 3·2% of GDP in 2002, industry 29·7% and services 67·1%.

Currency

The East Caribbean *dollar* (XCD) (of 100 *cents*) is in use. Inflation was 2·3% in 2003 and 2·1% in 2004. In May 2002 foreign exchange reserves were US$65m. Total money supply was EC$106m. in May 2002.

Budget

In 1999 recurrent revenues were EC$191·4m. (US$70·9m.) and recurrent expenditures EC$236·8m. (US$87·7m.). In 2000 revenues were estimated to be EC$237·8m. (US$88·1m.) and expenditures EC$243·7m. (US$90·3m.). Estimates for 2001 were: revenues, EC$231·4m. (US$85·7m.); expenditure, EC$268·8m. (US$99·6m.).

Performance

Real GDP growth was 0·6% in 2003, rising to 4·0% in 2004. Total GDP was US$0·4bn. in 2004.

Banking and Finance

The East Caribbean Central Bank (*Governor*, Sir Dwight Venner) is located in St Kitts. It is a regional bank that serves the OECS countries. In 2002 there were four domestic commercial banks (Bank of Nevis, Caribbean Banking Corporation, Nevis Co-operative Bank and St Kitts-Nevis-Anguilla National Bank), three foreign banks and one development bank. Nevis has some 9,000 offshore businesses registered.

St Kitts and Nevis is a member of the Eastern Caribbean Securities Exchange, based in Basseterre.

ENERGY AND NATURAL RESOURCES

Environment

Carbon dioxide emissions from the consumption and flaring of fossil fuels in 2002 were the equivalent of 2·6 tonnes per capita.

Electricity

Installed capacity was 20,000 kW in 2000. Production in 2000 was about 100m. kWh.

Agriculture

Main crops are coconuts, cotton, bananas, yams and molasses, and until 2005 sugarcane. The sugar industry was closed down following the 2005 harvest after years of losses at the state-run sugar company. In 2001 there were 7,000 ha. of arable land and 1,000 ha. of permanent crops. Most of the farms are small-holdings and there are a number of coconut estates amounting to some 400 ha. under public and private ownership. Production, 2000 (in 1,000 tonnes): sugarcane, 188; coconuts, 1.

Livestock (2000): goats, 15,000; sheep, 7,000; cattle, 4,000; pigs, 3,000.

Forestry

The area under forests in 2000 was 4,000 ha., or 11·1% of the total land area.

Fisheries

The catch in 2001 was 591 tonnes.

INDUSTRY

There are three industrial estates on St Kitts and one on Nevis. Export products include electronics and data processing equipment, and garments for the US market. Other small enterprises include food and drink processing, particularly sugar and cane spirit, and construction. Production of raw sugar (2001), 20,000 tonnes; molasses (1994), 6,000 tonnes.

Labour

In 1994 the economically active population numbered 16,608, of which 22·3% worked in services, finance and real estate, 20·3% in trade and restaurants, 16·5% in public administration and defence, and 10·5% in construction.

INTERNATIONAL TRADE

Foreign debt in 2002 amounted to US$255m.

Imports and Exports

Imports, 2002, US$177·59m.; exports, US$64·42m. Main trading partners are the USA, the UK and other CARICOM members. In 2002, 41·5% of imports were from the USA and 66·6% of exports went to the USA. Trinidad and Tobago is the second largest import supplier and the United Kingdom the second largest export destination. Main imports include machinery, manufactures, food and fuels. Major exports are sugar, machinery, food, electronics, beverages and tobacco.

COMMUNICATIONS

Roads

In 2002 there were about 383 km of roads, of which 42·5% were paved; and 6,900 passenger cars and 2,500 commercial vehicles.

Rail

There are 58 km of railway, formerly operated by the sugar industry but now used for tourist purposes.

Civil Aviation

The main airport is the Robert Llewelyn Bradshaw International Airport (just over 3 km from Basseterre). In 2003 there were flights to Anguilla, Antigua, Barbados, British Virgin Islands, Dominica, Grenada, Jamaica, Netherlands Antilles, Nevis (Newcastle), Philadelphia, Puerto Rico, St Lucia, St Vincent, Trinidad and the US Virgin Islands.

Shipping

There is a deep-water port at Bird Rock (Basseterre). 202,000 tons of cargo were unloaded in 1999 and 24,000 tons loaded. The government maintains a commercial motor boat service between the islands.

Telecommunications

In 2002 there were 28,500 telephone subscribers, or 606·4 per 1,000 inhabitants, and 9,000 PCs in use (191·5 for every 1,000 persons). Mobile phone subscribers numbered 5,000 in 2002. In 2002 there were 10,000 Internet users.

Postal Services

In 2003 there were seven post offices.

SOCIAL INSTITUTIONS

Justice

Justice is administered by the Supreme Court and by Magistrates' Courts. They have both civil and criminal jurisdiction. St Kitts and Nevis was one of ten countries to sign an agreement in Feb. 2001 establishing a Caribbean Court of Justice to replace the British Privy Council as the highest civil and criminal court. In the meantime the number of signatories has risen to twelve. The court was inaugurated at Port-of-Spain, Trinidad on 16 April 2005.

The population in penal institutions in Sept. 2003 was 195 (equivalent to 415 per 100,000 of national population).

Education

Adult literacy was 98% in 1998–99. Education is compulsory between the ages of 5 and 17. In 1998–99 there were 2,490 pupils in 71 pre-primary schools and 28 nurseries with 196 pre-primary teachers. In 1998–99 there were 5,947 pupils (3,556 male) and 293 teachers (57 male) in 23 primary schools, 4,528 pupils and 345 teachers in seven secondary schools, and 1,153 pupils (555 male) and 70 teachers (13 male) in nine private schools. There is an Extra-Mural Department of the University of the West Indies, a Non-formal Youth Skills Training Centre (with 55 students) and a Teachers' Training College. Clarence Fitzroy Bryant College has a Sixth Form Division (with 234 students), a Nursing Division (34 students), a Teaching Education Division (61 students), a Division of Technical and Vocational Studies (145 students) and an Adult Education Division (500 students).

In 2000–01 total expenditure on education came to 3·3% of GNP and 16·0% of total government spending.

Health

In 1999 there were 46 doctors, 14 dentists, 184 nurses and 17 pharmacists; and four hospitals, with a provision of 49 beds per 10,000 population.

RELIGION

In 2001, 25·6% of the population were Anglican, 25·6% Methodist and 17·9% Pentecostal. There are also followers of other beliefs, including Roman Catholics, Baptists and Church of God.

CULTURE

World Heritage Sites

There is one site on the UNESCO World Heritage List: Brimstone Hill Fortress National Park (inscribed on the list in 1999), a well-preserved example of 17th and 18th century British military architecture.

Broadcasting

There are three AM radio stations and two TV stations. Cable television is also available. There were 12,000 television sets (colour by NTSC) in 2000 and 28,000 radio receivers in 1997.

Press

In 2000 there were two weekly and one twice-weekly newspapers.

Tourism

In 1999 an estimated 84,000 tourists visited out of a total of 224,397 arrivals including 137,389 by yacht. In 1999, 40·9% of visitors came from the USA and 15·5% from the UK. There were 30 hotels in 1999 (20 on St Kitts and 10 on Nevis) with 1,508 rooms. Receipts from tourism in 2002 totalled US$57m.

DIPLOMATIC REPRESENTATIVES

Of St Kitts and Nevis in the United Kingdom (2nd Floor, 10 Kensington Ct, London, W8 5DL)
High Commissioner: James Williams.

Of the United Kingdom in St Kitts and Nevis
High Commissioner: Duncan Taylor (resides in Bridgetown, Barbados).

Of St Kitts and Nevis in the USA (OECS Building, 3216 New Mexico Ave., NW, 3rd Floor, Washington, D.C., 20016)
Ambassador: Izben Cordinal Williams.

Of the USA in St Kitts and Nevis
Ambassador: Mary E. Kramer (resides in Bridgetown, Barbados).

Of St Kitts and Nevis to the United Nations
Ambassador: Joseph Christmas.

Of St Kitts and Nevis to the European Union
Ambassador: George Bullen.

FURTHER READING

Statistics Division. *National Accounts.* Annual.—*St Kitts and Nevis Quarterly.*

Moll, Verna Penn, *St Kitts and Nevis.* [Bibliography] ABC-Clio, Oxford and Santa Barbara (CA), 1995

National library: Public Library, Burdon St., Basseterre.
National Statistical Office: Statistics Division, Ministry of Finance, Planning and Development, Church St., Basseterre.

ST LUCIA

Capital: Castries
Population projection, 2010: 168,000
GDP per capita, 2003: (PPP$) 5,709
HDI/world rank: 0·772/76

KEY HISTORICAL EVENTS

The island was probably discovered by Columbus in 1502. An unsuccessful attempt to colonize by the British took place in 1605 and again in 1638 when settlers were soon murdered by the Caribs who inhabited the island. France claimed the right of sovereignty and ceded it to the French West India Company in 1642. St Lucia regularly and constantly changed hands between Britain and France, until it was finally ceded to Britain in 1814 by the Treaty of Paris. Since 1924 the island has had representative government. In March 1967 St Lucia gained full control of its internal affairs while Britain remained responsible for foreign affairs and defence. On 22 Feb. 1979 St Lucia achieved independence, opting to remain in the British Commonwealth.

TERRITORY AND POPULATION

St Lucia is an island of the Lesser Antilles in the eastern Caribbean between Martinique and St Vincent, with an area of 617 sq. km (238 sq. miles). Population (2001 census) 158,076 (51% females); density, 255·7 per sq. km. The estimated population in 2005 was 161,000. In 2003 the population was 69·5% rural.

Area and populations of the ten administrative districts at the 2001 census were:

Districts	Sq. km	Population
Anse-la-Raye	} 47	6,495
Canaries		1,906
Castries	79	61,341
Choiseul	31	6,372
Dennery	70	12,773
Gros Inlet	101	19,816

Districts	Sq. km	Population
Laborie	38	7,978
Micoud	78	17,153
Soufrière	51	7,328
Vieux Fort	44	16,329

The UN gives a projected population for 2010 of 168,000.

The official language is English, but 80% of the population speak a French Creole.

In 2000, 50% of the population was Black, 44% were of mixed race and 3% of south Asian ethnic origin.

The capital is Castries (population, 1999, 57,000).

SOCIAL STATISTICS

2001 births, 2,919; deaths, 960. Rates, 2001 (per 1,000 population): births, 18·5; deaths, 6·1. Infant mortality, 2001 (per 1,000 live births), 17. Expectation of life in 2003 was 70·9 years for males and 73·9 for females. Annual population growth rate, 1992–2002, 0·9%; fertility rate, 2001, 2·6 births per woman.

CLIMATE

The climate is tropical, with a dry season from Jan. to April. Most rain falls in Nov.–Dec.; annual amount varies from 60" (1,500 mm) to 138" (3,450 mm). The average annual temperature is about 80°F (26·7°C).

CONSTITUTION AND GOVERNMENT

The head of state is the British sovereign, represented by an appointed Governor-General. There is a 17-seat *House of Assembly* elected for five years and an 11-seat *Senate* appointed by the Governor-General.

National Anthem

'Sons and daughters of St Lucia'; words by C. Jesse, tune by L. F. Thomas.

RECENT ELECTIONS

At the elections of 3 Dec. 2001 the St Lucia Labour Party gained 14 seats and the United Workers' Party 3.

CURRENT ADMINISTRATION

Governor-General: Dame Perlette Louisy; b. 1946 (appointed 17 Sept. 1997).

In March 2006 the government comprised:

Prime Minister and Minister of Finance, Economic Affairs, International Financial Services and Information: Dr Kenny Anthony; b. 1951 (appointed 24 May 1997 and re-elected in 2001).

Deputy Prime Minister and Minister of Education, Human Resource Development, Youth and Sports: Mario Michel.

Minister of Agriculture, Forestry and Fisheries: Ignatius Jean. *Home Affairs and Internal Security:* Calixte George. *Commerce, Tourism, Investment and Consumer Affairs:* Philip Pierre. *Communications, Works, Transport and Public Utilities:* Felix Finisterre. *Foreign Affairs, International Trade and Civil Aviation:* Petrus Compton. *Health, Human Services, Family Affair and Gender Relations:* Damian Greaves. *Physical Development, Environment and Housing:* Ferguson John. *Labour, Public Service and Co-operatives:* Velon John. *Justice and Attorney General:* Victor La Corbiniere. *Social Transformation, Culture and Local Government:* Menissa Rambally.

Government Website: http://www.stlucia.gov.lc

CURRENT LEADERS

Dr Kenny Anthony

Position
Prime Minister

Introduction
Dr Kenny Anthony became prime minister in 1997 when his St Lucia Labour Party (SLP) won 16 out of 17 seats in the biggest electoral landslide in St Lucian history. It marked a return to power for the SLP after an absence of over a decade. Anthony secured a second term in a general election of Dec. 2001 when the SLP won 14 of 17 seats.

Early Life
Kenny Davis Anthony was born on 8 Jan. 1951. He studied law at the University of the West Indies before undertaking PhD studies at the University of Birmingham in the UK.

Anthony joined the SLP on his return to St Lucia and became its leader in 1996. He served as minister of education from 1980–81. A former consultant for the UN development programme, Anthony was also a member of the CARICOM secretariat from 1995–97. He has served as chairman of the Organisation of Eastern Caribbean States (OECS). He was sworn in as prime minister in May 1997.

Career in Office
Anthony has been at the centre of a dispute with the WTO over preferential treatment for Latin American banana suppliers within the EU. Bananas are St Lucia's chief export and Anthony has claimed that the WTO policy has severely damaged the national economy and increased unemployment. In Sept. 2002 tropical storm Lili hit the island, devastating the banana crop and exacerbating economic problems. The government has attempted to diversify the economy, increasing investment in tourism. In July 2004 the Pitons Management Area was made a World Heritage Site. In Jan. 2005 Anthony signed a memorandum of understanding with the UNDP and the Poverty Reduction Fund.

In July 2003 parliament amended the constitution to replace the oath of allegiance to the English monarch with a pledge of loyalty to the St Lucian people (although Elizabeth II remains head of state). In Nov. 2003 St Lucia voted to join the Caribbean Court of Justice and passed a new criminal code. Conservatives and Catholics led protests against provisions for legalizing abortions in special cases and for imprisonment for spreading 'false news'. In Jan. 2004 Anthony fired minister of gender relations Sarah Flood-Beaubrun after she attacked the government as 'child killers'. In Dec. 2004 a further criminal code contained new provisions against kidnapping, stalking, sexual harassment at work and sexual crimes against men. It also sought to address the high levels of money laundering in the Caribbean islands.

Internationally, Anthony has continued to promote close ties with China. In Feb. 2005 the government launched an HIV/AIDS prevention and control project, funded in part by the Global Fund and the World Bank. Anthony has overseen extensive domestic infrastructure development, including construction of new roads and a stadium to host the 2007 cricket world cup. Education spending has also risen significantly. However, Anthony has received criticism for St Lucia's high levels of borrowing, with the debt to GDP ratio standing at around 63% in 2005.

INTERNATIONAL RELATIONS

St Lucia is a member of the UN, WTO, OAS, ACS, CARICOM, OECS, the Commonwealth, the International Organization of the Francophonie and is an ACP member state of the ACP-EU relationship.

ECONOMY

In 2002 agriculture contributed 6·4% of GDP, industry 18·5% and services 75·1%.

Currency

The East Caribbean *dollar* (XCD) (of 100 *cents*) is in use. US dollars are also normally accepted. Inflation was 1·0% in 2003 and 1·5% in 2004. Foreign exchange reserves were US$90m. in May 2002. Total money supply was EC$320m. in May 2002.

Budget

The fiscal year ends on 31 March. Revenues were EC$469·9m. in the fiscal year 1998–99 and expenditures EC$496·6m.

Performance

There was real GDP growth of 2·9% in 2003 and 4·0% in 2004. Total GDP in 2004 was US$0·7bn.

Banking and Finance

The East Caribbean Central Bank based in St Kitts and Nevis functions as a central bank. The *Governor* is Sir Dwight Venner. There are three domestic banks (Caribbean Banking Corporation, St Lucia Co-operative Bank, East Caribbean Financial Holding Company) and three foreign banks.

St Lucia is a member of the Eastern Caribbean Securities Exchange, based in Basseterre.

ENERGY AND NATURAL RESOURCES

Environment

Carbon dioxide emissions from the consumption and flaring of fossil fuels in 2002 were the equivalent of 2·4 tonnes per capita.

Electricity

Installed capacity in 2000 was 66,000 kW. Production in 2000 was 275m. kWh; consumption per capita in 2000 was 1,858 kWh.

Agriculture

In 2001 St Lucia had 4,000 ha. of arable land and 14,000 ha. of permanent crops. Bananas, cocoa, breadfruit and mango are the principal crops, but changes in the world's trading rules and changes in taste are combining to depress the banana trade. Farmers are experimenting with okra, tomatoes and avocados to help make up for the loss. Production, 2000 (in 1,000 tonnes): bananas, 92; mangoes, 28; coconuts, 12; yams, 5; copra, 2.

Livestock (2000): pigs, 15,000; sheep, 13,000; cattle, 12,000; goats, 10,000.

Forestry

In 2000 the area under forests was 9,000 ha. (14·8% of the total land area).

Fisheries

In 2001 the total catch was 1,983 tonnes.

INDUSTRY

The main areas of activity are clothing, assembly of electronic components, beverages, corrugated cardboard boxes, tourism, lime processing and coconut processing.

Labour

In 1993 the economically active population totalled 81,000, around a quarter of whom were engaged in agriculture, fisheries and forestry.

INTERNATIONAL TRADE

Foreign debt in 2002 amounted to US$415m.

Imports and Exports

Imports and exports for calendar years in US$1m.:

	1998	1999	2000	2001	2002
Imports	295·1	312·0	312·5	272·1	277·0
Exports	70·4	60·9	63·1	54·4	70·0

Main imports in 2001: food products, 23·0%; machinery and apparatus, 14·9%; refined petroleum, 9·8%. Main exports, 2001: bananas, 46·9%; beer, 18·1%; clothing, 7·1%. Main import suppliers, 2001: USA, 41·8%; Trinidad and Tobago, 15·8%; UK, 9·0%; Japan, 4·2%. Main export markets, 2001: UK, 47·3%; USA, 17·6%; Barbados, 13·4%; Antigua and Barbuda, 3·1%.

COMMUNICATIONS

Roads
The island had about 1,210 km of roads in 2002, of which 150 km were main roads and a further 150 km secondary roads. Passenger cars numbered 13,100 in 2002.

Civil Aviation
There are international airports at Hewanorra (near Vieux-Fort) and Vigie (near Castries). In 2001 Vigie handled 378,000 (373,000 on international flights) and Hewanorra 301,000 passengers (291,000 on international flights).

Shipping
There are two ports, Castries and Vieux Fort. Merchant shipping in 1995 totalled 1,000 GRT. In 1997 vessels totalling 6,803,000 net registered tons entered the ports.

Telecommunications
Main telephone lines numbered 48,900 in 2000 (313·5 per 1,000 persons), and there were 22,000 PCs (141 for every 1,000 persons). There were 14,300 mobile phone subscribers in 2002. Internet users numbered 13,000 in 2001. In 1994 there were 560 fax machines.

Postal Services
There were 27 post offices in 2003.

SOCIAL INSTITUTIONS

Justice
The island is divided into two judicial districts, and there are nine magistrates' courts. Appeals lie to the Eastern Caribbean Supreme Court of Appeal. St Lucia was one of ten countries to sign an agreement in Feb. 2001 establishing a Caribbean Court of Justice to replace the British Privy Council as the highest civil and criminal court. In the meantime the number of signatories has risen to twelve. The court was inaugurated at Port-of-Spain, Trinidad on 16 April 2005.

The population in penal institutions in Aug. 2003 was 460 (287 per 100,000 of national population).

Education
Primary education is free and compulsory. In 2002–03 there were 81 primary schools with 1,057 teachers for 27,175 pupils; and (1999–2000) 12,817 pupils and 645 teachers at secondary level. There is a community college. The adult literacy rate was 90·1% in 2003 (89·5% among males and 90·6% among females).

In 2000–01 total expenditure on education came to 6·1% of GNP and 16·9% of total government spending.

Health
In 2002 there were five hospitals (with 305 beds) and 35 health centres. There were 70 physicians, seven dentists and 302 nurses.

RELIGION
In 2001, 79% of the population was Roman Catholic.

CULTURE

World Heritage Sites
There is one UNESCO site in St Lucia: Pitons Management Area (inscribed on the list in 2004). The site near the town of Soufrière includes the Pitons, two volcanic spires rising side by side from the sea, linked by the Piton Mitan ridge.

Broadcasting
There were 32,000 TV (colour by PAL) and 111,000 radio receivers in 1997. In 2003 there were three television stations broadcasting locally and on satellite and a satellite network, Cablevision. The government-owned Radio St Lucia broadcasts in English and Creole. There were two other radio stations in 2003.

Press
In 2003 there were seven newspapers. The weekly *One Caribbean* had the highest circulation (7,500). *The Voice*, founded in 1885, has a thrice-weekly combined circulation of 15,000.

Tourism
The number of tourists in 2002 was 253,463, plus 387,180 cruise arrivals. Receipts in 2002 totalled US$256m.

DIPLOMATIC REPRESENTATIVES
Of St Lucia in the United Kingdom (1 Collingham Gdns, Earls Court, London, SW5 0HW)
High Commissioner: Emmanuel H. Cotter, MBE.

Of the United Kingdom in St Lucia (NIS Waterfront Building, 2nd Floor, Castries)
High Commissioner: Duncan Taylor (resides in Bridgetown, Barbados).

Of St Lucia in the USA (3216 New Mexico Ave., NW, Washington, D.C., 20016)
Ambassador: Sonia Merlyn Johnny.

Of the USA in St Lucia
Ambassador: Mary E. Kramer (resides in Bridgetown, Barbados).

Of St Lucia to the United Nations
Ambassador: Julian Hunte.

Of St Lucia to the European Union
Ambassador: George Bullen.

FURTHER READING
Momsen, Janet Henshall, *St Lucia.* [Bibliography] ABC-Clio, Oxford and Santa Barbara (CA), 1996

National Statistical Office: Central Statistical Office, Chreiki Building, Micoud Street, Castries.
Website: http://www.stats.gov.lc/

ST VINCENT AND THE GRENADINES

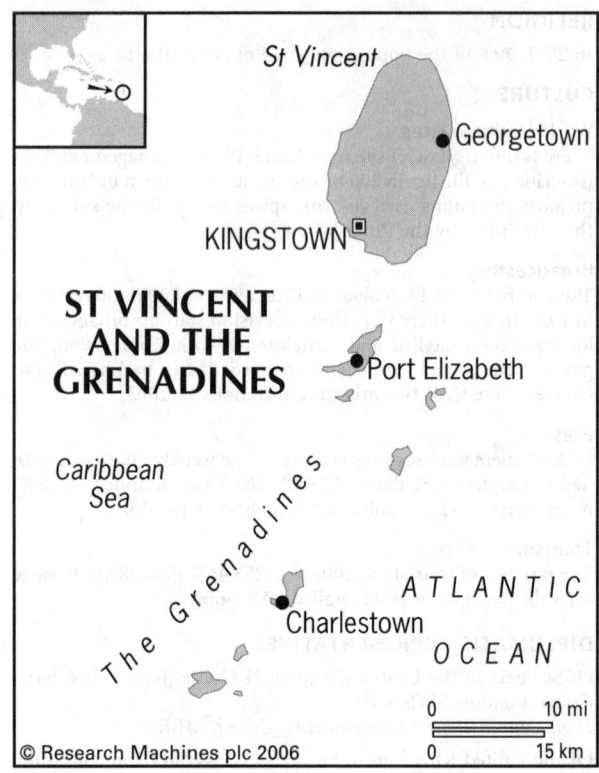

St Vincent

Georgetown

KINGSTOWN

ST VINCENT
AND THE
GRENADINES

Port Elizabeth

Caribbean
Sea

The Grenadines

ATLANTIC

Charlestown

OCEAN

0   10 mi

0   15 km

© Research Machines plc 2006

Capital: Kingstown
Population projection, 2010: 122,000
GDP per capita, 2003: (PPP$) 6,123
HDI/world rank: 0·755/87

KEY HISTORICAL EVENTS

St Vincent was discovered by Columbus on 22 Jan. (St Vincent's Day) 1498. British and French settlers occupied parts of the islands after 1627. In 1773 the Caribs recognized British sovereignty and agreed to a division of territory between themselves and the British. Resentful of British rule, the Caribs rebelled in 1795, aided by the French, but the revolt was subdued within a year. On 27 Oct. 1969 St Vincent became an Associated State with the UK responsible only for foreign policy and defence, while the islands were given full internal self-government. On 27 Oct. 1979 the colony gained full independence as St Vincent and the Grenadines.

TERRITORY AND POPULATION

St Vincent is an island of the Lesser Antilles, situated in the eastern Caribbean between St Lucia and Grenada, from which latter it is separated by a chain of small islands known as the Grenadines. The total area of 389 sq. km (150 sq. miles) comprises the island of St Vincent itself (345 sq. km) and those of the Grenadines attached to it, of which the largest are Bequia, Mustique, Canouan, Mayreau and Union.

The population at the 1991 census was 106,499, of whom 8,367 lived in the St Vincent Grenadines. 2003 official estimate, 116,812 (58·2% urban); density 300 per sq. km.

The UN gives a projected population for 2010 of 122,000.

The capital, Kingstown, had 28,000 inhabitants in 1999 (including suburbs). The population is mainly of Black (65·5%) and mixed (23·5%) origin, with small White, Asian and American minorities.

English and French patois are spoken.

SOCIAL STATISTICS

Births, 2001, 1,967; deaths, 720. 2001 birth rate, 18·0 per 1,000 population; death rate, 6·6. Infant mortality, 2001, 22 per 1,000 live births. Life expectancy, 2003, was 68·3 years for males and 73·9 years for females. Annual population growth rate, 1992–2002, 0·6%; fertility rate, 2001, 1·9 births per woman.

CLIMATE

The climate is tropical marine, with northeast trades predominating and rainfall ranging from 150" (3,750 mm) a year in the mountains to 60" (1,500 mm) on the southeast coast. The rainy season is from June to Dec., and temperatures are equable throughout the year.

CONSTITUTION AND GOVERNMENT

The head of state is Queen Elizabeth II, represented by a Governor-General. Parliament is unicameral and consists of a 21-member *House of Assembly,* 15 of which are directly elected for a five-year term from single-member constituencies. The remaining six are senators appointed by the Governor-General (four on the advice of the Prime Minister and two on the advice of the Leader of the Opposition).

National Anthem
'St Vincent, land so beautiful'; words by Phyllis Punnett, tune by J. B. Miguel.

RECENT ELECTIONS

At the elections to the House of Assembly on 7 Dec. 2005 the ruling Unity Labour Party (ULP, social-democratic) won 12 of the 15 elected seats with 55·3% of the vote, against 3 (44·7%) for the opposition New Democratic Party (NDP, conservative).

CURRENT ADMINISTRATION

Governor-General: Sir Frederick Ballantyne (since 2 Sept. 2002).

In March 2006 the government comprised:
Prime Minister, Minister of Finance, Economic Planning, National Security, Legal Affairs and Grenadine Affairs: Dr Ralph E. Gonsalves; b. 1946 (ULP; sworn in 29 March 2001 and re-elected in Dec. 2005).

Deputy Prime Minister and Minister of Foreign Affairs, Commerce and Trade: Louis Straker.

Minister of National Mobilization, Social Development, Relations with Non-Governmental Organizations, Family, Gender Affairs and Persons with Disabilities: Mike Browne. *Education:* Girlyn Miguel. *Rural Transformation, Information, Public Service and Ecclesiastical Affairs:* Selmon Walters. *Health and Environment:* Dr Douglas Slater. *Urban Development, Labour, Culture and Electoral Matters:* René Baptiste. *Transportation and Works:* Clayton Burgin. *Agriculture, Forestry and Fisheries:* Montgomery Daniel. *Telecommunications, Science, Technology and Industry:* Dr Jerrol Thompson. *Tourism, Youth and Sports:* Glen Beache. *Housing, Informal Human Settlements, Physical Planning, and Lands and Surveys:* Julian Francis. *Minister of State in the Prime Minister's Office:* Conrad Sayers.

CURRENT LEADERS

Dr Ralph E. Gonsalves

Position
Prime Minister

Introduction
Dr Ralph E. Gonsalves became prime minister of St Vincent and the Grenadines in 2001 after his Unity Labour Party (ULP) won 12 of 15 seats in an election brought forward from 2003 after anti-government protests in 2000. He won a second term in Dec. 2005.

Early Life
'Comrade Ralph' was born in 1945. He studied at the University of the West Indies in Jamaica, gaining a PhD in political science. He later graduated in law from the University of the West Indies in Barbados, before returning to St Vincent and Grenadines to practise law. In 1968, while president of the Guild of Undergraduates, Gonsalves led a student protest to ban radical historian Walter Rodney from the Island.

The ULP is an amalgamation of the St Vincent Labour Party and the Movement for National Unity. After coming close to winning the 1998 elections, Gonsalves led the party to victory in 2001, signalling the end of 15 years of New Democrat rule.

Career in Office
Gonsalves began a campaign to tackle the problems of money laundering, gun crime and drug-related crime. In June 2003 St Vincent and Grenadines was removed from a list of uncooperative countries in the fight against money laundering throughout the Caribbean islands. In Jan. 2005 death row prisoners were told they would face hanging once their appeals were exhausted. Gonsalves is the chairman of the Regional Security System council of ministers, put together to tackle security threats throughout the islands.

The St Vincent and Grenadines economy is reliant on the banana trade but a decline in price and demand has led to diversification. In June 2004 Gonsalves announced the launch of National Investments Promotions Incorporated, an organization aiming to attract investment and boost exports. The tourism sector has seen significant growth, with a new airport in the planning stages. However, the government continues to pay large subsidies to banana farmers.

Gonsalves is committed to maintaining close ties with Taiwan and Cuba. Taiwan has pledged to invest in the 2007 cricket world cup and in May 2005 made a gift of computer equipment to the St Vincent and Grenadines government to enhance efficiency. In Jan. 2005 Gonsalves met with Fidel Castro to announce that a Cuban Embassy would be established in St Vincent and Grenadines and a St Vincent and Grenadines consulate would open in Cuba. In Jan. 2005 Castro promised Cuban assistance to Gonsalves' campaign to increase national literacy rates.

Gonsalves is chairman of the national HIV/AIDS council and Feb. 2005 saw the launch of the World Bank-assisted HIV/AIDS prevention and control project, with the government expected to invest at least US$1·7m. over five years. Gonsalves has aligned himself with the fight against climate change. In April 2005 he signed agreements with St Lucia and Dominica to introduce measures to combat climate change in the coastal areas of the three Windward Islands (with substantial funding from the USA and Japan). In May 2005 his government ratified the Kyoto protocol.

In parliamentary elections in Dec. 2005 Gonsalves and the ULP retained their 12 seats. Gonsalves was sworn in for a new term and assumed responsibility for the national security portfolio.

He has announced plans to allow everyone in St Vincent and Grenadines access to secondary school education. The number receiving secondary school education increased by 2,700 in the period 2001–05.

INTERNATIONAL RELATIONS

St Vincent and the Grenadines is a member of UN, WTO, OAS, ACS, CARICOM, OECS, the Commonwealth and is an ACP member state of the ACP-EU relationship.

ECONOMY

Agriculture accounted for 10·5% of GDP in 2002, industry 25·2% and services 64·3%.

Currency

The currency in use is the *East Caribbean dollar* (XCD). Inflation was 0·2% in 2003 and 3·0% in 2004. Foreign exchange reserves were US$60m. in May 2002, and total money supply was EC$272m.

Budget

Total revenue and expenditure in EC$1m. for calendar years:

	1997	1998	1999	2000	2001
Revenue	240·5	260·3	276·1	278·9	294·0
Expenditure	337·0	320·9	315·1	309·0	353·2

Performance

Real GDP growth was 4·0% in 2004 (3·9% in 2003). In 2004 total GDP was US$0·4bn.

Banking and Finance

The East Caribbean Central Bank is the bank of issue. The *Governor* is Sir Dwight Venner. There are branches of Barclays Bank PLC, the Caribbean Banking Corporation, FirstCaribbean International, the Canadian Imperial Bank of Commerce and the Bank of Nova Scotia. Locally-owned banks: First St Vincent Bank, Owens Bank, New Bank, the National Commercial Bank and St Vincent Co-operative Bank. The 'offshore' sector numbered over 11,000 organizations in 2001.

St Vincent and the Grenadines is a member of the Eastern Caribbean Securities Exchange, based in Basseterre.

ENERGY AND NATURAL RESOURCES

Environment

Carbon dioxide emissions from the consumption and flaring of fossil fuels were the equivalent of 1·5 tonnes per capita in 2002.

Electricity

Installed capacity was 16,000 kW in 2000. Production in 2000 was estimated at 85m. kWh; consumption per capita in 2000 was about 752 kWh.

Agriculture

According to the 1985–86 census of agriculture, 29,649 acres of the total acreage of 85,120 were classified as agricultural lands; 5,500 acres were under forest and woodland and all other lands accounted for 1,030 acres. The total arable land was about 8,932 acres, of which 4,016 acres were under temporary crops, 2,256 acres under temporary pasture, 2,289 acres under temporary fallow and other arable land covering 371 acres. 16,062 acres were under permanent crops, of which approximately 5,500 acres were under coconuts and 7,224 acres under bananas; the remainder produce cocoa, citrus, mangoes, avocado pears, guavas and miscellaneous crops. In 2001 there were 7,000 ha. of arable land and 7,000 ha. of permanent crops. The sugar industry was closed down in 1985 although some sugarcane is grown for rum production. Production (2000, in 1,000 tonnes): bananas, 43; coconuts, 24; sugarcane, 20; copra, 2; maize, 2; sweet potatoes, 2.

Livestock (2000, in 1,000): sheep, 13; pigs, 10; cattle, 6; goats, 6.

Forestry

Forests covered 6,000 ha. in 2000, or 15·4% of the land area.

Fisheries

Total catch, 2001, 45,778 tonnes (all from sea fishing).

INDUSTRY

Industries include assembly of electronic equipment, manufacture of garments, electrical products, animal feeds and flour, corrugated galvanized sheets, exhaust systems, industrial gases, concrete blocks, plastics, soft drinks, beer and rum, wood products and furniture, and processing of milk, fruit juices and food items. Rum production, 1994, 0·4m. litres.

Labour

The Department of Labour is charged with looking after the interest and welfare of all categories of workers, including providing advice and guidance to employers and employees and their organizations and enforcing the labour laws. In 1991 the total labour force was 41,682, of whom 33,355 (11,699 females) were employed.

INTERNATIONAL TRADE

Foreign debt was US$206m. in 2002.

Imports and Exports

Imports and exports for calendar years in US$1m.:

	1998	1999	2000	2001	2002
Imports	170·0	177·0	144·4	152·0	157·2
Exports	50·1	49·6	51·7	42·8	40·4

Principal imports are basic manufactures, machinery and transport equipment, and food products. Principal exports are bananas, packaged flour and packaged rice.

Main import suppliers, 2001: USA, 34·5%; CARICOM countries (in particular Trinidad and Tobago), 31·2%; UK, 12·0%. Main export markets, 2001: CARICOM countries (in particular Trinidad and Tobago), 53·7%; UK, 36·8%.

COMMUNICATIONS

Roads

In 2002 there were 829 km of roads, of which 70% were paved. Vehicles in use (2002): 10,504 passenger cars; 3,019 commercial vehicles.

Civil Aviation

There is an airport (E. T. Joshua) on mainland St Vincent at Arnos Vale. An airport on Union also has regular scheduled services. In 1995 E. T. Joshua handled 185,000 passengers and 1,200 tonnes of freight.

Shipping

In 2000 the merchant navy had 1,366 vessels. Merchant shipping in 2002 totalled 6,584,000 GRT, including oil tankers 313,000 GRT.

In 2001 vessels totalling 1,790,000 net registered tons entered and cleared ports.

Telecommunications

There is a fully digital automatic telephone system with 37,300 telephone subscribers in 2002, equivalent to 318·8 for every 1,000 inhabitants. In 2000 there were 17,500 stations and digital radio provide links to Bequia, Mustique, Union, Petit St Vincent and Palm Island. The telephone network has almost 100% geographical coverage. There were 10,000 mobile phone subscribers in 2002 and 14,000 PCs in use (119·7 for every 1,000 persons). In 2002 there were 7,000 Internet users.

Postal Services

There were 41 post offices in 1997.

SOCIAL INSTITUTIONS

Justice

Law is based on UK common law as exercised by the Eastern Caribbean Supreme Court on St Lucia. Final appeal lies to the UK Privy Council. In 1995 there were 4,700 criminal matters disposed of in the three magisterial districts which comprise 11 courts. 62 cases were dealt with in the Criminal Assizes in the High Court. St Vincent and the Grenadines was one of twelve countries to sign an agreement establishing a Caribbean Court of Justice to replace the British Privy Council as the highest civil and criminal court. The court was inaugurated at Port-of-Spain, Trinidad on 16 April 2005. Strength of police force (1995), 663 (including 19 gazetted officers).

The population in penal institutions in Oct. 2001 was 302 (270 per 100,000 of national population).

Education

In 2000–01 there were 162 teachers for 2,537 children in pre-primary schools, 761 teachers for 18,200 pupils in primary schools and 405 teachers for 9,756 pupils in secondary schools. In 1989 there were 677 students at university level. Adult literacy in 1998 was 82%.

In 2000–01 total expenditure on education came to 9·9% of GNP and 13·4% of total government spending.

Health

In 1997 there were 11 hospitals with a provision of 19 beds per 10,000 persons. In 1998 there were 59 physicians, six dentists and 267 nurses, and in 1991 there were 27 pharmacists.

RELIGION

In 2001 there were estimated to be 20,000 Anglicans, 17,000 Pentecostalists, 12,000 Methodists, 12,000 Roman Catholics and 52,000 followers of other religions.

CULTURE

Broadcasting

The National Broadcasting Corporation (NBC) is part government-owned and part commercial. In 2003 NBC Radio was broadcasting on three FM frequencies. There were 77,000 radio sets in 1997 and 26,000 TV sets (colour by NTSC) in 2000.

Press

In 1996 there was one daily newspaper, *The Herald*, with a circulation of 1,000, at a rate of 9 per 1,000 inhabitants.

Tourism

In 2003 there were 78,535 staying visitors and 64,965 cruise ship arrivals. Tourism receipts in 2002 totalled US$81m.

Libraries

The St Vincent Public Library is in Kingstown.

DIPLOMATIC REPRESENTATIVES

Of St Vincent and the Grenadines in the United Kingdom (10 Kensington Ct, London, W8 5DL)
High Commissioner: Cenio Elwin Lewis.

Of the United Kingdom in St Vincent and the Grenadines (POB 132, Granby St., Kingstown)
High Commissioner: Duncan Taylor (resides in Bridgetown, Barbados).

Of St Vincent and the Grenadines in the USA (3216 New Mexico Ave., NW, Washington, D.C., 20016)
Ambassador: Ellsworth I. A. John.

Of the USA in St Vincent and the Grenadines
Ambassador: Mary E. Kramer (resides in Bridgetown, Barbados).

Of St Vincent and the Grenadines to the United Nations
Ambassador: Margaret Hughes Ferrari.

Of St Vincent and the Grenadines to the European Union
Ambassador: George Bullen.

FURTHER READING

Potter, Robert B., *St Vincent and the Grenadines*. [Bibliography] ABC-Clio, Oxford and Santa Barbara (CA), 1992
Sutty, L., *St Vincent and the Grenadines*. London, 1993

SAMOA

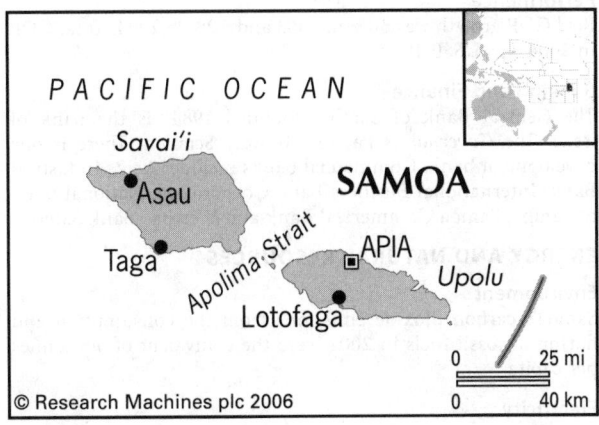

O le Malo Tutoatasi o Samoa
(Independent State of Samoa)

Capital: Apia
Population projection, 2010: 189,000
GDP per capita, 2003: (PPP$) 5,854
HDI/world rank: 0·776/74

KEY HISTORICAL EVENTS

Polynesians settled in the Samoan group of islands in the southern Pacific from about 1000 BC. Although probably sighted by the Dutch in 1722, the first European visitor was French in 1768. Treaties were signed between the Chiefs and European nations in 1838–39. Continuing strife among the chiefs was compounded by British, German and US rivalry for influence. In the Treaty of Berlin 1889 the three powers agreed to Western Samoa's independence and neutrality. When unrest continued, the treaty was annulled and Western Samoa became a German protectorate until in 1914 it was occupied by a New Zealand expeditionary force. The island was administered by New Zealand from 1920 to 1961. On 1 Jan. 1962 Western Samoa gained independence. In July 1997 the country renamed itself the Independent State of Samoa.

TERRITORY AND POPULATION

Samoa lies between 13° and 15° S. lat. and 171° and 173° W. long. It comprises the two large islands of Savai'i and Upolu, the small islands of Manono and Apolima, and several uninhabited islets lying off the coast. The total land area is 2,830·8 sq. km (1,093·0 sq. miles), of which 1,707·8 sq. km (659·4 sq. miles) are in Savai'i, and 1,117·6 sq. km (431·5 sq. miles) in Upolu; other islands, 5·4 sq. km (2·1 sq. miles). The islands are of volcanic origin, and the coasts are surrounded by coral reefs. Rugged mountain ranges form the core of both main islands. The large area laid waste by lava-flows in Savai'i is a primary cause of that island supporting less than one-third of the population of the islands despite its greater size than Upolu.

Population at the 2001 census, 176,848. The population at the 2001 census was 134,024 in Upolu (including Manono and Apolima) and 42,824 in Savai'i. The capital and chief port is Apia in Upolu (population 38,836 in 2001). The estimated population in 2005 was 185,000. In 2003, 77·7% of the population lived in rural areas.

The UN gives a projected population for 2010 of 189,000.

The official languages are Samoan and English.

SOCIAL STATISTICS

2003 estimates: births, 5,100; deaths, 1,000. Rates, 2003 estimates (per 1,000 population): births, 28·6; deaths, 5·5. Expectation of life in 2003 was 67·2 years for males and 73·7 for females. Annual population growth rate, 1992–2002, was 0·8%. Infant mortality, 2001, 20 per 1,000 live births; fertility rate, 2001, 4·3 births per woman.

CLIMATE

A tropical marine climate, with cooler conditions from May to Nov. and a rainy season from Dec. to April. The rainfall is unevenly distributed, with south and east coasts having the greater quantities. Average annual rainfall is about 100" (2,500 mm) in the drier areas. Apia, Jan. 80°F (26·7°C), July 78°F (25·6°C). Annual rainfall 112" (2,800 mm).

CONSTITUTION AND GOVERNMENT

HH Malietoa Tanumafili II is the sole Head of State for life. Future Heads of State will be elected by the Legislative Assembly and hold office for five-year terms.

The executive power is vested in the *Head of State*, who swears in the *Prime Minister* (who is elected by the Legislative Assembly) and, on the Prime Minister's advice, the Ministers to form the Cabinet. The Constitution also provides for a *Council of Deputies* of three members, of whom the chairman is the Deputy Head of State.

The *Legislative Assembly* contains 49 members serving five-year terms. 47 are elected exclusively by *matai* (customary family heads) and the other two by non-Samoans on separate electoral rolls.

National Anthem

'Samoa, tula'i ma sisi ia laufu'a ('Samoa, Arise and Raise your Banner'); words and tune by S. I. Kuresa.

RECENT ELECTIONS

At the most recent elections, on 31 March 2006, the Human Rights Protection Party (HRPP) won 29 seats; the Samoan National Development Party, 12; and non-partisans, 8.

CURRENT ADMINISTRATION

Head of State: HH Malietoa Tanumafili II, GCMG, CBE; b. 1913.

In April 2006 the cabinet was composed as follows:

Prime Minister and Minister of Foreign Affairs and Trade: Tuila'epa Sailele Malielegaoi; b. 1945 (HRPP; sworn in 23 Nov. 1998, and re-elected in March 2001 and March 2006).

Deputy Prime Minister and Minister of Commerce, Industry and Labour: Misa Telefoni Retzlaff. *Agriculture:* Taua Tavaga Kitiona Seuala. *Education, Sports and Culture:* Toomata Alapati Poese Toomata. *Health:* Gatoloaifaana Amataga Alesana Gidlow. *Natural Resources and Environment:* Faumuina Tiatia Liuga. *Justice and Courts Administration:* Unasa Mesi Galo. *Women's Affairs, Community and Social Development:* Fiame Naomi Mataafa. *Communication and Information Technology:* Mulitalo Sealiimalietoa Siafausa Vui. *Finance:* Niko Lee Hang. *Police:* Toleafoa Apulu Faafisi. *Revenue:* Tuuu Anasii Leota. *Works, Transportation and Infrastructure:* Tuisugaletaua Sofara Aveau.

Government Website: http://www.govt.ws

CURRENT LEADERS

Tuila'epa Sailele Malielegaoi

Position
Prime Minister

Introduction
Tuila'epa Sailele Malielegaoi became prime minister in Nov. 1998 and won further terms in March 2001 and March 2006. He is leader of the Human Rights Protection Party (HRPP), the traditional ruling party of Samoa since 1982.

Early Life
Tuila'epa Sailele Malielegaoi was born on 14 April 1945 in Lepa, Samoa. He was educated in Samoa and at New Zealand's Auckland University, graduating with a masters degree in commerce in 1969. He was the first Samoan to gain a masters degree.

In 1978 he moved to Brussels to work for the European Economic Community. He entered Samoa's parliament two years later while working as a partner in the accounting firm Coopers and Lybrand. He was elected to the premiership after former prime minister Tofilau Eti Alesana retired in 1998.

Career in Office
Malielegaoi wants Samoa to diversify its economy, which is dependent on fishing and agriculture and susceptible to natural disasters. He has focused on developing the tourism industry. In Aug. 2004 the government introduced Internet access to assist economic development.

Malielegaoi is keen to promote education in Samoa and there is a scholarship scheme offering study opportunities in New Zealand, Australia and Fiji. In Jan. 2003 a new inter-denominational Christian secondary school was opened. The police and health sectors have also received increased funding. In Jan. 2004 parliament voted to abolish the death penalty and in the same year Australia provided $A7m. to fund training of Samoan security forces.

Malielegaoi has pursued close relations with China. In Jan. 2003 China agreed to help build an aquatic centre at the Tuanaimato Sports Complex in Samoa for the 2007 South Pacific Games. Japan has also invested in Samoa, providing funding for education and vocational training and for development of a 100-acre waste disposal site. In Feb. 2004 Samoa and New Zealand met for mutual assistance talks and to reconfirm their 1962 treaty of friendship.

Samoa hosted the 35th Pacific Forum in 2004. Its agenda included regional economic and political co-operation and the Pacific-wide campaign to tackle HIV and AIDS.

Malielegaoi was re-elected for a third term when his Human Rights Protection Party won the March 2006 election.

INTERNATIONAL RELATIONS

Samoa, as an independent state, deals directly with other governments and international organizations. It has diplomatic relations with a number of countries.

Samoa is a member of the UN, the Commonwealth, Asian Development Bank, the Pacific Community, the Pacific Islands Forum and is an ACP member state of the ACP-EU relationship.

ECONOMY

Agriculture accounts for approximately 40% of GDP, industry 25% and services 35%.

Currency

The unit of currency is the *tala* (WST) of 100 *sene*. Inflation was 4·2% in 2003 and 2·4% in 2004. Foreign exchange reserves were US$61m. in June 2002. Total money supply was 92m. tala in June 2002.

Budget

For 2000–01 revenue was SA$262·4m. (tax revenue, 66·6%); expenditure, SA$281·7m. (current expenditure, 58·4%).

Performance

Real GDP growth was 3·1% in 2003 and 3·2% in 2004. Total GDP in 2004 was US$0·4bn.

Banking and Finance

The Central Bank of Samoa (founded 1984) is the bank of issue. The *Governor* is Papali'i Tommy Scanlan. There is one development bank. Commercial banks include: ANZ, Industrial Bank, International Business Bank Corporation, National Bank of Samoa, Samoa Commercial Bank and Westpac Bank Samoa.

ENERGY AND NATURAL RESOURCES

Environment

Samoa's carbon dioxide emissions from the consumption and flaring of fossil fuels in 2002 were the equivalent of 0·8 tonnes per capita.

Electricity

Installed capacity in 2000 was 20,000 kW. Production was about 66m. kWh. in 2000 and consumption per capita an estimated 386 kWh.

Agriculture

In 2001 there were 60,000 ha. of arable land and 69,000 ha. of permanent cropland. The main products (2000 estimates, in 1,000 tonnes) are coconuts (130), taro (37), copra (11), bananas (10), papayas (10), pineapples (6) and mangoes (5).

Livestock (2000): cattle, 26,000; pigs, 179,000; asses, 7,000.

Forestry

Forests covered 105,000 ha. (37·2% of the land area) in 2000. Timber production was 131,000 cu. metres in 2001.

Fisheries

Fish landings in 2001 totalled approximately 12,966 tonnes.

INDUSTRY

Some industrial activity is being developed associated with agricultural products and forestry.

Labour

In 1991 the total labour force numbered 57,142 (39,839 males).

INTERNATIONAL TRADE

Total external debt was US$234m. in 2002.

Imports and Exports

In 1999 imports (f.o.b.) were valued at US$115·66m. (US$96·91m. in 1998) and exports (f.o.b.) at US$18·15m. (US$20·40m. in 1998). Main imports are machinery and transport equipment, foodstuffs and basic manufactures. Principal exports are coconuts, palm oil, taro and taamu, coffee and beer. New Zealand is the principal trading partner, in 1997 accounting for 37·9% of imports and 48·1% of exports. Australia is the second biggest supplier of imports and American Samoa the second biggest export market.

COMMUNICATIONS

Roads

In 2002 the road network covered 790 km, of which 235 km were main roads. In 1998 there were 3,400 passenger cars and 3,200 trucks and vans.

Civil Aviation

There is an international airport at Apia (Faleolo), which handled 156,000 passengers (155,000 on international flights) in 2001. The national carrier is Polynesian Airlines. In 2003 it operated domestic services and international flights to American Samoa, Auckland, the Fiji Islands, Honolulu, Los Angeles, Niue, Sydney and Tonga.

Shipping
Sea-going shipping totalled 10,000 GRT in 2002. Samoa is linked to Japan, USA, Europe, the Fiji Islands, Australia and New Zealand by regular shipping services.

Telecommunications
There are three radio communication stations at Apia. Radio telephone service connects Samoa with American Samoa, the Fiji Islands, New Zealand, Australia, Canada, USA and UK. Telephone subscribers numbered 13,000 in 2002 (72·0 per 1,000 population) and there were 1,000 PCs in use (6·7 per 1,000 persons). There were 2,700 mobile phone subscribers in 2002 and 600 fax machines. Samoa had 4,000 Internet users in 2002.

Postal Services
In 2003 there were 36 post offices.

SOCIAL INSTITUTIONS

Justice
The population in penal institutions in Nov. 2003 was 281 (158 per 100,000 of national population). The death penalty, not used in more than 50 years, was abolished in 2004.

Education
In 2002 there were 38,946 pupils at primary schools with 1,446 teachers, and 14,159 pupils and 749 teachers at secondary schools. The University of the South Pacific has a School of Agriculture in Samoa, at Apia. A National University was established in 1984. In 1994–95 it had 614 students and 30 academic staff. There is also a Polytechnic Institute which provides mainly vocational and training courses.

The adult literacy in 2002 was 98·7% (98·9% among males and 98·4% among females).

In 1999–2000 total expenditure on education came to 3·9% of GNP and 13·3% of total government spending.

Health
In 2002 there were 33 general hospitals (with 320 beds), one private hospital, 11 district hospitals and 12 primary health care centres. In 2002 there were 43 physicians, six dentists, 333 nurses and 13 midwives.

RELIGION
In 2001 there were 46,200 Latter-day Saints (Mormons), 44,000 Congregationalists, 38,100 Roman Catholics, 21,800 Methodists, and the remainder of the population follow other beliefs. In May 2005 the Roman Catholic church had one cardinal.

CULTURE

Broadcasting
Samoa has a state-run commercial TV station, *Televise Samoa* and, since 2001, *Pro-Com Sky Cable TV*. There are four radio stations, three on FM and one on AM. In 2001 there were 26,000 television sets (colour by NTSC) and in 1997 there were 178,000 radio receivers.

Press
There are two dailies, plus a weekly, a fortnightly and a monthly. The most widely read newspaper is the independent *Samoa Observer*.

Tourism
In 2002 there were 89,000 foreign tourists, bringing revenue of US$45m.

DIPLOMATIC REPRESENTATIVES
Of Samoa in the United Kingdom and to the European Union
Acting High Commissioner: Francella Strickland (resides in Brussels).
Honorary Consul: Prunella Scarlett, LVO (Church Cottage, Pedlinge, Nr Hythe, Kent, CT21 4JL).

Of the United Kingdom in Samoa
High Commissioner: Richard Fell, CVO (resides in Wellington).
Honorary Consul: c/o Kruse Enari and Barlow, 2nd Floor, NPF Building, Beach Rd, PO Box 2029, Apia.

Of the USA in Samoa
Ambassador: William P. McCormick (resides in Wellington).

Of Samoa in the USA and to the United Nations (800 Second Ave., Suite 400D, New York, NY, 10017)
Ambassador: Ali'ioaiga Feturi Elisaia.

Of Samoa to the European Union
Ambassador: Tauiliili Uili Meredith.

FURTHER READING
Hughes, H. G. A., *American Samoa, Western Samoa, Samoans Abroad.* [Bibliography] ABC-Clio, Oxford and Santa Barbara (CA), 1997

SAN MARINO

ITALY

Serravalle

SAN MARINO

☐ SAN MARINO   Faetano

Fiorentino   ITALY

0   1 mi
0   1.5 km

© Research Machines plc 2006

Repubblica di San Marino

Capital: San Marino
Population, 2000: 27,000
GDP per capita: not available

KEY HISTORICAL EVENTS

San Marino is a small republic situated on the Adriatic side of central Italy. According to tradition, St Marinus and a group of Christians settled there to escape persecution. By the 12th century San Marino had developed into a commune ruled by its own statutes and consul. Unsuccessful attempts were made to annex the republic to the papal states in the 18th century and when Napoleon invaded Italy in 1797 he respected the rights of the republic and even offered to extend its territories. In 1815 the Congress of Vienna recognized the independence of the republic. On 22 March 1862 San Marino concluded a treaty of friendship and co-operation, including a *de facto* customs union, with Italy, thus preserving its independence although completely surrounded by Italian territory.

TERRITORY AND POPULATION

San Marino is a land-locked state in central Italy, 20 km from the Adriatic. Area is 61·19 sq. km (23·6 sq. miles) and the population (2002), 28,753; at Dec. 1999 some 13,104 citizens lived abroad.

In 2002 an estimated 89% of the population were urban. Population density, 440·5 per sq. km. The capital, San Marino, has 4,429 inhabitants (2000); the largest town is Serravalle (8,547 in 2000), an industrial centre in the north.

SOCIAL STATISTICS

Births, 2000, 290; deaths, 188; marriages, 193; divorces, 38. Birth rate, 2000 (per 1,000 population), 10·8; death rate, 7·0. Annual population growth rate, 1992–2002, 1·4%; fertility rate, 2001, 1·3 births per woman. The World Health Organization's 2004 World Health Report put citizens of San Marino in second place in a

'healthy life expectancy' list behind Japan, with an expected 73·4 years of healthy life for babies born in 2002.

CLIMATE

Temperate climate with cold, dry winters and warm summers.

CONSTITUTION AND GOVERNMENT

The legislative power is vested in the *Great and General Council* of 60 members elected every five years by popular vote, two of whom are appointed every six months to act as *Captains Regent*, who are the heads of state.

Executive power is exercised by the ten-member *Congress of State*, presided over by the Captains Regent. The *Council of Twelve*, also presided over by the Captains Regent, is appointed by the Great and General Council to perform administrative functions and is a court of third instance.

National Anthem

No words, tune monastic, transcribed by F. Consolo.

RECENT ELECTIONS

In parliamentary elections on 10 June 2001 the Christian Democratic Party won 25 of 60 seats, with 41·4% of the vote; the Socialist Party 15 with 24·2%; the Progressive Democratic Party 12 with 20·8%; the Popular Democratic Alliance 5 with 8·2%; the Communist Refoundation 2 with 3·4%; and the National Alliance 1 with 1·9%.

CURRENT ADMINISTRATION

Captains Regent: Loris Francini (since 1 April 2006); Gian Franco Terenzi (since 1 April 2006).

In March 2006 the Congress of State comprised:

Minister of Foreign and Political Affairs, Economic Planning and Justice: Fabio Berardi. *Internal Affairs and Civil Protection:* Loris Francini. *Finance, Budget and Transport:* Pier Marino Mularoni. *Industry, Craftsmanship, Commerce, Telecommunications and Economic Co-operation:* Claudio Felici. *Public Education, Universities, Cultural Institutions and Information:* Rosa Zafferani. *Territory, Agriculture and Environment:* Gian Carlo Venturini. *Health, Social Security and Social Affairs:* Massimo Roberto Rossini. *Labour and Co-operation, Tourism, Sport and Post:* Paride Andreoli.

CURRENT LEADERS

Loris Francini

Position
Captain Regent

Introduction
Loris Francini is serving his second six-month term as captain regent. His current term began in April 2006.

Early Life
Loris Francini was born in San Marino on 12 Aug. 1962. He studied at the Scientific Lyceum Serpieri in Rimini before graduating in economics from the University of Bologna in 1988. He then spent a year as private secretary to the minister of commerce and relations with the township councils, before serving as director of the motor vehicle registry office from 1990 until 1992. He was then private secretary to the minister of finance and budget until 1993. A member of the Christian Democratic Party (PDCS) since 1982, he was elected one of the party's representatives in the Great and General Council in 1993. He served on the parliamentary commissions for institutional

reforms, domestic and constitutional affairs, town planning, health and territory and had several spells as a member of the Council of Twelve.

Career in Office

Francini was first elected captain regent on 1 April 1998, and served the six-month term with Alberto Cecchetti. From Dec. 2002 until Dec. 2004 he served as secretary of state for internal affairs, institutional affairs, civil protection and relations with the township councils. His second term of office as captain regent began on 1 April 2006, alongside Gian Franco Terenzi. He is also vice-secretary of the PDCS.

Gian Franco Terenzi

Position

Captain Regent

Introduction

Gian Franco Terenzi began his third term of office as captain regent in April 2006, having previously held the post in 1987–88 and 2000–01.

Early Life

Gian Franco Terenzi was born in San Marino on 2 Jan. 1941. A graduate in social sciences, he entered politics in 1978, sitting as a representative of the Christian Democratic Party (PDCS) in the Great and General Council. He served his first term as captain regent from Oct. 1987 until April 1988 alongside Rossano Zafferani.

Career in Office

An entrepreneur and businessman since the early 1960s, Terenzi is president of the National Union of Craftsmen (UNAS) and the San Marino-China Association. He has variously been a member of the parliamentary commissions for foreign affairs, information, transport, telecommunications, security and public order, finance, industry and labour. He has also had several spells on the Council of Twelve. On the international stage, he is a prominent figure within the World Association of Small and Medium Enterprises.

He was captain regent for a second time, in partnership with Enzo Colombini, from Oct. 2000 until April 2001 and was elected for a third time on 1 April 2006 to serve a six-month term with Loris Francini.

DEFENCE

Military service is not obligatory, but all citizens between the ages of 16 and 55 can be called upon to defend the State. They may also serve as volunteers in the Military Corps. There is a military Gendarmerie.

INTERNATIONAL RELATIONS

San Marino maintains a traditional neutrality, and remained so in the First and Second World Wars. It has diplomatic and consular relations with over 70 countries.

San Marino is a member of the UN, the Council of Europe, the OSCE and various UN specialized agencies.

ECONOMY

Currency

Since 1 Jan. 2002 San Marino has been using the euro. Italy has agreed that San Marino may mint a small part of the total Italian euro coin contingent with their own motifs. Inflation in 2001 was 3·3%.

Budget

Budgetary central government revenue for 2002 totalled €274·7m.; expenditure, €281·5m.

Performance

Real GDP growth was 7·5% in 2001.

Banking and Finance

The Instituto di Credito Sammarinese (*President*, Antonio Valentini), the central bank and bank of issue, was set up in 1986 with public and private resources. Commercial banks include: Banca di San Marino, Credito Industriale Sammarinese, Cassa di Risparmio della Repubblica di San Marino and the Banca Agricola Commerciale della Repubblica di San Marino.

ENERGY AND NATURAL RESOURCES

Electricity

Electricity is supplied by Italy.

Agriculture

There were 1,000 ha. of arable land in 2001. Wheat, barley, maize and vines are grown.

INDUSTRY

Labour

Out of 18,077 people in employment in 2000, 5,867 worked in manufacturing and 3,509 in wholesale and retail trade. In Dec. 2000 there were 428 registered unemployed persons.

Trade Unions

There are two Confederations of Trade Unions: the Democratic Confederation of Sammarinese Workers and the Sammarinese Confederation of Labour.

INTERNATIONAL TRADE

Imports and Exports

Import commodities are a wide range of consumer manufactures and foodstuffs. Export commodities are building stone, lime, wine, baked goods, textiles, varnishes and ceramics. San Marino maintains a customs union with Italy.

COMMUNICATIONS

Roads

A bus service connects San Marino with Rimini. There are 252 km of public roads and 40 km of private roads, and (1999) 26,320 passenger cars and 2,763 commercial vehicles.

Civil Aviation

The nearest airport is Rimini, 10 km to the east, which had scheduled flights in 2003 to Berlin, Düsseldorf, Frankfurt, Hamburg, Helsinki, Munich, Naples and Rome.

Telecommunications

San Marino had 20,600 main telephone lines in 2002 and 16,800 mobile phone subscribers. Internet users numbered 14,300 in 2002.

Postal Services

In 2001 there were 11 post offices.

SOCIAL INSTITUTIONS

Justice

Judges are appointed permanently by the Great and General Council; they may not be San Marino citizens. Petty civil cases are dealt with by a justice of the peace; legal commissioners deal with more serious civil cases, and all criminal cases and appeals lie to them from the justice of the peace. Appeals against the legal commissioners lie to an appeals judge, and the Council of the Twelve functions as a court of third instance.

Education

Education is compulsory up to 16 years of age. In 2000 there were 15 nursery schools with 991 pupils and 119 teachers, 14 elementary schools with 1,894 pupils and 240 teachers, 3 junior high schools with 729 pupils and 140 teachers, and one high school with 1,348 pupils and 87 teachers. The University of San Marino began operating in 1988.

Health

In 2000 there were 141 hospital beds and 117 doctors. A survey published by the World Health Organization in June 2000 to measure health systems in all of the sovereign countries and find which country has the best overall health care ranked San Marino in third place.

RELIGION

The great majority of the population are Roman Catholic.

CULTURE

Broadcasting

San Marino RTV (colour by PAL) is the state broadcasting company.

In 1999 there were 8,932 television receivers. There were 16,000 radio receivers in 1998.

Press

San Marino had three daily newspapers in 1999 with a combined daily circulation of 1,800.

Tourism

By the end of Nov. 2000, 3·07m. tourists had visited San Marino during the year.

DIPLOMATIC REPRESENTATIVES

Of the United Kingdom to San Marino
Ambassador: Sir Ivor Roberts, KCMG (resides in Rome).

Of San Marino to the United Nations
Ambassador: Daniele Bodini.

Of San Marino to the European Union
Ambassador: Savina Zafferani.

FURTHER READING

Edwards, Adrian and Michaelides, Chris, *San Marino.* [Bibliography] ABC-Clio, Oxford and Santa Barbara (CA), 1996

Information: Office of Cultural Affairs and Information of the Department of Foreign Affairs.

SÃO TOMÉ E PRÍNCIPE

ATLANTIC OCEAN

Gulf of Guinea

Santo António • Príncipe

SÃO TOMÉ E PRÍNCIPE

Santa Catarina • SÃO TOMÉ
São Tomé

0   25 mi
0   40 km

© Research Machines plc 2005

República Democrática de São Tomé e Príncipe

Capital: São Tomé
Population projection, 2010: 174,000
GDP per capita, 2002: (PPP$) 1,231
HDI/world rank: 0·604/126

KEY HISTORICAL EVENTS

The islands of São Tomé and Príncipe off the west coast of Africa were colonized by Portugal in the fifteenth century. There may have been a few African inhabitants or visitors earlier but most of the population arrived during the centuries when the islands served as an important slave-trading depot for South America. In the 19th century the islands became the first parts of Africa to grow cocoa. In 1876 Portugal officially abolished slavery but in practice it continued thereafter with many Angolans, Mozambicans and Cape Verdians being transported to work on the cocoa plantations. Because the slave-descended population was cut off from African culture, São Tomé had a higher proportion than other Portuguese colonies of *assimilados* (Africans acquiring full Portuguese culture and certain rights). São Tomé saw serious riots against Portuguese rule in 1953. From 1960 a Movement for the Liberation of São Tomé e Príncipe operated from neighbouring African territories. In 1970 Portugal formed a 16-member legislative council and a provincial consultative council. Following the Portuguese revolution of 1974 a transitional government was formed. Independence came on 12 July 1975. Independent São Tomé e Príncipe officially proclaimed Marxist-Leninist policies but maintained a non-aligned foreign policy and has received aid from Portugal.

The government was surprised by a coup on 16 July 2003 while President Fradique de Menezes and his foreign minister were abroad. The coup leader, Major Fernando Pereira, installed a junta but accepted a general amnesty from parliament on 24 July after agreeing to allow the ousted president to form a government of national unity.

TERRITORY AND POPULATION

The republic, which lies about 200 km off the west coast of Gabon, in the Gulf of Guinea, comprises the main islands of São Tomé (845 sq. km) and Príncipe and several smaller islets including Pedras Tinhosas and Rolas. It has a total area of 1,001 sq. km (387 sq. miles). Population (census, 2001) 137,599; density, 163 per sq. km. The estimated population in 2005 was 157,000. In 2003, 62·2% of the population were rural.

The UN gives a projected population for 2010 of 174,000.

Areas and populations of the two provinces:

Province	Sq. km	Census 2001	Chief town	Census 2001
São Tomé	859	131,633	São Tomé	51,886
Príncipe	142	5,966	São António	1,040

The official language is Portuguese. Lungwa São Tomé, a Portuguese Creole, and Fang, a Bantu language, are the spoken languages.

SOCIAL STATISTICS

2004 estimates: births, 5,200; deaths, 1,400. Rates, 2004 estimates (per 1,000 population): birth, 34; death, 9; infant mortality, 57 per 1,000 live births (2001). Expectation of life, 2003, 62·0 years for males and 64·0 years for females. Annual population growth rate, 1992–2002, 2·6%; fertility rate, 2001, 6·0 births per woman.

CLIMATE

The tropical climate is modified by altitude and the effect of the cool Benguela current. The wet season is generally from Oct. to May, but rainfall varies considerably, from 40" (1,000 mm) in the hot and humid northeast to 150–200" (3,800–5,000 mm) on the plateau. São Tomé, Jan. 79°F (26·1°C), July 75°F (23·9°C). Annual rainfall 38" (951 mm).

CONSTITUTION AND GOVERNMENT

The 1990 constitution was approved by 72% of votes at a referendum of March 1990 and became effective in Sept. 1990. It abolished the monopoly of the Movement for the Liberation of São Tomé e Príncipe (MLSTP). The *President* must be over 34 years old, and is elected by universal suffrage for one or two (maximum) five-year terms. He or she is also head of government and appoints a Council of Ministers. The 55-member *National Assembly* is elected for four years.

Since April 1995 **Príncipe** has enjoyed internal self-government, with a five-member regional government and an elected assembly.

National Anthem

'Independência total, glorioso canto do povo' ('Total independence, glorious song of the people'); words by A. N. do Espírito Santo, tune by M. de Sousa e Almeida.

RECENT ELECTIONS

At the presidential election on 29 July 2001 Fradique de Menezes (Independent Democratic Action) was elected by 56·3% of votes cast against Manuel Pinto da Costa (Liberation Movement of São Tomé e Príncipe) with 38·4% and three other opponents. Turnout was 62·4%.

At the National Assembly elections on 26 March 2006 the Force for Change Democratic Movement (MDFM) won 23 seats with 36·8% of votes cast, the Liberation Movement of São Tomé e Príncipe (MLSTP) 20 (29·5%), Independent Democratic Action (ADI) 11 (20·0%), and the New Way Movement (MNR) 1 (4·7%).

CURRENT ADMINISTRATION

President, C.-in-C: Fradique Bandeira Melo de Menezes; b. 1942 (Independent Democratic Action; sworn in 23 July 2003, having previously held office from 3 Sept. 2001 to 16 July 2003).

In April 2006 the coalition government comprised:

Prime Minister and Minister of Social Communication and Regional Integration: Tomé Soares da Vera Cruz; b. 1955 (MDFM; in office since 26 March 2006).

Deputy Prime Minister and Minister of Planning and Finances: Maria dos Santos Tebus Torres.

Minister of Economy: Cristina Maria Fernandes Dias. *Education, Culture, Youth and Sports:* Maria de Fátima Leite de Sousa Almeida. *Foreign Affairs, Co-operation and Communities:* Carlos Gustavo dos Anjos. *Defence and Internal Order:* Óscar Sacramento e Sousa. *Public Works and Infrastructures:* Delfim Santioago das Neves. *Health:* Arlindo de Assunção Carvalho. *Justice and Relations with Parliament:* Justino Tavares Veiga. *Labour, Solidarity, Family and Women's Affairs:* Maria de Cristo Hilário dos Santos Raposo de Carvalho. *Public Administration, State Reform and Territorial Administration:* Armindo Vaz Rodrigues Aguiar. *Natural Resources and the Environment:* Manuel de Deus Lima.

CURRENT LEADERS

Fradique Bandeira Melo de Menezes

Position
President

Introduction
President since Sept. 2001, Fradique de Menezes has weathered numerous political storms. Tensions have mounted since the discovery of large offshore oil reserves, revenue from which looks set to transform the archipelago.

Early Life
Fradique Bandeira Melo de Menezes was born in Madalena on the island of São Tomé in 1942, the son of a Portuguese father and a São Toméan mother. He attended school in both São Tomé and Portugal, before studying education and psychology at the Free University of Brussels, Belgium. De Menezes then completed post-graduate studies in international trade in the USA. In 1967 he took up work at Marconi Radio in Lisbon, before working for various US companies in Brussels.

He returned to São Tomé e Príncipe following the country's independence from Portugal in July 1975 and taught at the National High School. In the late 1970s he worked at the ministry of agriculture, under the Marxist-inspired Liberation Movement of São Tomé e Príncipe (MLSTP). De Menezes relocated to London in 1981, where he was director of São Tomé e Príncipe's Commercial Center. From 1983–86 he served as his country's ambassador to the European Community. When de Menezes returned to São Tomé in 1986 the MLSTP had begun to embrace economic and political reforms. He was appointed minister of foreign affairs but left politics to pursue business interests, establishing companies involved in shipping, agriculture (cocoa) and investment.

Following constitutional reform in 1990 and the country's first multi-party elections in Jan. 1991, de Menezes was elected to parliament. He ran against the former president, Manuel Pinto da Costa, in the July 2001 presidential election to win in the first round, with 56·3% of the vote. He was sworn in as president on 3 Sept. 2001.

Career in Office
De Menezes promised to reverse the country's crippling economic crisis but progress has been slow. The discovery of substantial oil deposits offshore brought optimism but also raised the political temperature. While de Menezes was visiting Nigeria in July 2003 his government was toppled in a military coup. International intervention led to agreement with the coup leaders and de Menezes was restored on 23 July 2003. As political infighting continued, de Menezes dismissed the prime minister and appointed a new cabinet after a corruption scandal in Sept. 2004. There were further reshuffles in June 2005 and again in April 2006 following the resignation of the prime minister.

INTERNATIONAL RELATIONS

São Tomé e Príncipe is a member of the UN, the African Union, African Development Bank, the International Organization of the Francophonie and is an ACP member state of the ACP-EU relationship.

ECONOMY

In 2002 agriculture accounted for 20·0% of GDP, industry 17·0% and services 63·0%.

Overview

Most branches of the economy were nationalized after independence, but economic liberalization began in 1985 and accelerated in the 1990s.

Currency

The unit of currency is the *dobra* (STD) of 100 *centimos*. From a rate of 69·0% in 1997 inflation had fallen to 9·2% in 2002 before rising 12·8% by 2004. In Dec. 1997 foreign exchange reserves were US$12m. Total money supply in April 2002 was 98,789m. dobras (up from 23,683m. dobras in Dec. 1996).

Budget

In 2000 revenues totalled 183·4bn. dobras and expenditures 244·4bn. dobras.

Performance

Real GDP growth was 3·8% in 2004 (4·0% in 2003). In 2004 total GDP was US$62m.

Banking and Finance

In 1991 the Banco Central de São Tomé e Príncipe (*Governor,* Vacant) replaced the Banco Nacional as the central bank and bank of issue. A private commercial bank, the Banco Internacional de São Tomé e Príncipe, began operations in 1993.

ENERGY AND NATURAL RESOURCES

Environment

In 2002 carbon dioxide emissions from the consumption and flaring of fossil fuels were the equivalent of 0·7 tonnes per capita.

Electricity

Installed capacity, 2000, 6,000 kW. Production was about 18m. kWh in 2000, with consumption per capita being an estimated 130 kWh.

Oil and Gas

There are large oil reserves around São Tomé e Príncipe that could greatly add to the country's wealth; the Joint Development Zone was set up with Nigeria to administer the exploitation because the reserves are located in shared waters. The first license to begin exploration was granted in April 2004.

Agriculture

After independence all landholdings over 200 ha. were nationalized into 15 state farms. These were partially privatized in 1985 by granting management contracts to foreign companies, and distributing some state land as small private plots. There were 6,000 ha. of arable land in 2001 and 47,000 ha. of permanent crops. Production (2000 in 1,000 tonnes): coconuts, 29; bananas, 19; cassava, 5; palm kernels, 4; cocoa beans, 3; maize, 2. There were 4,000 cattle, 3,000 sheep, 2,000 pigs and 5,000 goats in 2000.

Forestry
In 2000 forests covered 27,000 ha., or 31·9% of the land area. In 2001, 9,000 cu. metres of timber were cut.

Fisheries
There are rich tuna shoals. The total catch in 2001 came to approximately 3,500 tonnes.

INDUSTRY
Manufacturing contributed 4·2% of GDP in 2001. There are a few small factories in agricultural processing (including beer and palm oil production), timber processing, bricks, ceramics, printing, textiles and soap-making.

Labour
In 1994 the economically active population was 54,000. There were 15,000 registered unemployed.

INTERNATIONAL TRADE
Foreign debt was US$333m. in 2002. In 1999 São Tomé e Príncipe was the most heavily indebted country in the world in relation to the GNP, owing 615% of its GNP.

Imports and Exports
Trade figures for 2002: imports, US$28·0m.; exports, US$5·1m. Cocoa accounts for two-thirds of all exports.

In 2000 the main import suppliers were Portugal (41·7%), Angola (13·0%) and Japan (10·8%); main export markets were the Netherlands (57·7%) and Portugal (10·9%).

COMMUNICATIONS
Roads
There were 384 km of roads in 2002, 273 km of which were asphalted. Approximately 4,000 passenger cars were in use in 1996 (30 per 1,000 inhabitants), plus 1,540 trucks and vans.

Civil Aviation
São Tomé airport had flights in 2003 to Cape Verde, Libreville, Lisbon and Luanda. In 1999 São Tomé handled 32,298 passengers and 1,877 tonnes of freight. There is a light aircraft service to Príncipe.

Shipping
São Tomé is the main port, but it lacks a deep water harbour. Neves handles oil imports and is the main fishing port. Portuguese shipping lines run routes to Lisbon, Oporto, Rotterdam and Antwerp. In 2002 merchant shipping totalled 86,000 GRT.

Telecommunications
There were 8,200 telephone subscribers in 2002, or 54·4 per 1,000 population, including 2,000 mobile phone subscribers. Internet users numbered 11,000 in 2002 and there were 300 fax machines in use.

Postal Services
In 2003 there were ten post offices.

SOCIAL INSTITUTIONS
Justice
Members of the Supreme Court are appointed by the National Assembly. There is no death penalty. The population in penal institutions in April 2002 was 130 (79 per 100,000 of national population).

Education
Adult literacy was 57·0% in 1998. Education is free and compulsory. In 1999–2000 there were 71 primary schools and 20,258 pupils, and 10 secondary schools and 10,672 pupils; more than 90% of primary age children were attending school in 1995. There is a vocational centre, a school of agriculture and a pre-university *lycée*.

Health
In 1996 there were 61 physicians, seven dentists, 167 nurses and 39 midwives.

RELIGION
In 2001, 81% of the population were Roman Catholic. There is a small Protestant church and a Seventh Day Adventist school.

CULTURE
Broadcasting
Radio broadcasting is conducted by the government-controlled Rádio Nacional. There is a Voice of America radio station, a religious station and a private German station. There were 38,000 radio receivers in 1997 and 34,000 TV receivers in 2000.

Press
There are four weekly newspapers.

Tourism
In 2001 there were 8,000 foreign tourists, bringing revenue of US$10m.

DIPLOMATIC REPRESENTATIVES
Of São Tomé e Príncipe in the United Kingdom (resides in Brussels)
Ambassador: Vacant.
Chargé d'Affaires a.i.: Armindo de Brito Fernandes.

Of the United Kingdom in São Tomé e Príncipe
Ambassador: Ralph Publicover (resides in Luanda, Angola).

Of São Tomé e Príncipe in the USA
Ambassador: Vacant.

Of the USA in São Tomé e Príncipe
Ambassador: Barrie R. Walkley (resides in Libreville, Gabon).

Of São Tomé e Príncipe to the United Nations
Ambassador: Vacant.
Chargé d'Affaires a.i.: Domingos Augusto Ferreira.

Of São Tomé e Príncipe to the European Union
Ambassador: Vacant.
Chargé d'Affaires a.i.: António de Lima Viegas.

FURTHER READING
Shaw, Caroline S., *São Tomé e Príncipe*. [Bibliography] ABC-Clio, Oxford and Santa Barbara (CA), 1994

SAUDI ARABIA

Al-Mamlaka al-Arabiya as-Saudiya
(Kingdom of Saudi Arabia)

Capital: Riyadh
Population projection, 2010: 27·66m.
GDP per capita, 2003: (PPP$) 13,226
HDI/world rank: 0·772/77

KEY HISTORICAL EVENTS

Nomadic tribes have existed across the Arabian peninsula for thousands of years. The pre-Islamic period saw the development of civilizations based on trade in frankincense and spices, notably the Minaeans from about the 12th century BC in the southwest of what is now Saudi Arabia and Yemen. The Sabaean and Himyarite kingdoms flourished from around 650 BC and 115 BC respectively, their loose federations of city states lasting until the 6th century AD. Although increased involvement in trade brought these civilizations into contact with the Roman and Persian empires—the two great regional powers before the advent of Islam—they remained politically independent for the most part. The Nabataeans, an Aramaic people whose capital was at Petra, modern-day Jordan, spread their influence into northern Arabia over a period covering the 1st century BC and the 1st AD before annexation of their territory by Rome. Persian influence was meanwhile prevalent along Arabia's eastern coast, centred on Dilmun which covered parts of the mainland and the island of Bahrain.

By the 6th century AD the Hejaz region in northwestern Arabia was becoming increasingly powerful and an important link in the overland trade route from Egypt and the Byzantine Empire to the wider East. One of the principal cities of Hejaz was Makkah (Mecca), a centre on the camel train routes and site of pilgrimage to numerous pre-Islamic religious shrines. The leading tribe in the city was the Quraysh, into which the Prophet Muhammad was born in 570. Muhammad and his followers (known as Muslims) took control of Makkah in 630. He had earlier declared himself a prophetic reformer, destroying the city's pagan idols and declaring it a centre of Muslim pilgrimage dedicated to the worship of Allah (God) alone. Muhammad died in AD 632, by then commanding the loyalty of almost all of Arabia.

The leaders who succeeded Muhammad, known as caliphs, spread the Islamic faith throughout and beyond the Arab world.

However, Arabia itself began to fragment and by the latter part of the 7th century it had become a province of the Islamic realm, although the holy cities of Makkah and Madinah retained their spiritual focus. Meanwhile, increasingly remote from the main centres of Islamic authority under the Umayyad and Abbasid caliphate dynasties, Arabia became an arena for sectarian divisions—Shia, Sunni and Kharijite—which developed within the Islamic faith.

After 1269 most of the Hejaz region came under the suzerainty of the Egyptian Mameluks. The Ottoman Turks conquered Egypt in 1517 and, to counter the influence of the Christian Portuguese presence in the Gulf region, extended their nominal control over the whole Arabian Peninsula. Portuguese traders were followed by British, Dutch and French merchants during the 17th and 18th centuries, the British gradually securing political and commercial supremacy in the Gulf and southern Arabia through a system of protectorates and local treaties.

Saudi Arabia's origins as a political entity lay in the rise of the puritanical Wahhabi movement of the 18th century, which called for a return to the original principles of Islam and gained the allegiance of the powerful Al-Saud dynasty (founded in the 15th century) in the Nejd region of central Arabia. The Al-Saud/Wahhabi armies brought most of the peninsula under their control by 1811, attracting the suspicion of the Ottoman Turkish government. The Sultan whereupon called on his viceroy in Egypt, Mehmet Ali, to suppress the Wahhabis, who were defeated between 1811 and 1818. Nevertheless, the house of Al-Saud continued to hold sway over the interior of Arabia until 1891 when, after a long period of tribal warfare, the rival Al-Rashid family seized control of the city of Riyadh with Ottoman support.

The Al-Saud family was exiled to Kuwait but Abdulaziz Ibn Abdul Rahman (known to Europeans as Ibn Saud) restored Wahhabi fortunes as he recaptured Riyadh in 1902 and reasserted Al-Saud control over Nejd by 1906. On the eve of the First World War Abdulaziz conquered the al Hasa region east of Nejd on the Gulf from the Ottoman Turks. In 1920 he captured the Asir region and in 1921 added the Jebel Shammar territory (northwest of Nejd) of the Al-Rashid family. In 1925 Abdulaziz completed his conquest of Hejaz, overthrowing Hussein, Sharif of Makkah and a member of the Hashimi family. Abdulaziz became both Sultan of Nejd and King of the Hejaz. Britain recognized Abdulaziz as an independent ruler by the Treaty of Jeddah on 20 May 1927, and in 1932 Nejd and Hejaz were unified as the Kingdom of Saudi Arabia, ruled as an absolute monarchy under Islamic law.

Abdulaziz ruled until his death on 9 Nov. 1953, concentrating during his reign on the political consolidation and modernization of the country. Oil was discovered in 1938 and its commercial exploitation was developed with the support of the USA after the Second World War.

Crown Prince Saud succeeded his father and ruled until Nov. 1964, when he was effectively deposed by his brother Faisal. During his reign Saudi relations with the pan-Arabist Nasser regime in Egypt deteriorated, most notably over the 1962 revolution in Yemen.

As king and prime minister, Faisal instituted a programme of economic expansion using the kingdom's increasing oil production revenues. In 1970 he initiated the first of the five-year economic development programmes. Over that same period, financial support was given to other Arab states in their conflict with Israel. The Oct. 1973 Arab-Israeli war heralded an oil crisis in which Arab producers, including Saudi Arabia, cut supplies to the USA and other Western countries leading to a fourfold increase in oil prices. However, Faisal subsequently adopted a more conciliatory stance than more radical members of the Organization of Petroleum Exporting Countries (OPEC, founded in 1960) and the close Saudi economic relationship with the USA was reinforced with a co-operation agreement in 1974. In March 1975 Faisal was assassinated by a nephew, believed to be mentally unstable, and his half-brother Khalid became king.

Khalid continued Faisal's policies promoting Islamic solidarity and Arab unity in the wake of hostilities with Israel. In practice his moderate stance was in marked contrast to the militancy of many other Arab states, particularly over oil pricing by OPEC and opposition to Egypt's 1978 peace treaty with Israel. Khalid was also involved in early efforts to stop the civil war in Lebanon, and inaugurated the Gulf Co-operation Council (GCC) in 1981. Domestically he maintained the royal family's absolute political control and the conservative Islamic character of the country. However, opposition to his regime was demonstrated in Nov. 1979 when Sunni Muslim fundamentalists occupied the Grand Mosque at Makkah. A two-week siege ensued with over 200 deaths. The second and third five-year development plans (1975–79 and 1980–84), both launched by Khalid, set in train much of the country's current economic infrastructure. Owing to Khalid's poor health throughout his reign much of his executive responsibility was assumed by his younger half-brother, Crown Prince Fahd.

Fahd succeeded to the throne on 13 June 1982. Like his predecessors he maintained absolute power but broadened the process of political consultation and decision-making by setting up the Consultative Council (*Majlis Al-Shura*) of royal appointees from 1993. In 1986 he assumed the title of 'Custodian of the Two Holy Mosques' but the Saudi role in protecting religious pilgrims incurred international criticism in 1987 when 400 Iranian worshippers were killed in clashes in Makkah with security forces and again in 1994 when 270 pilgrims died in a stampede. Internationally, Fahd adopted a moderate policy on regional problems and closely allied the kingdom with the USA. Fahd was a key participant in diplomatic efforts to end the Iran-Iraq war in 1988 and in the 1989 Taif reconciliation accord bringing the 14-year Lebanese civil war to a close. His pro-Western stance and co-operation in the 1990–91 Gulf crisis were crucial to the deployment and successful military operations of the US-led multinational force raised against Iraq following its invasion of Kuwait.

However, anti-Western disaffection among Saudi nationals has become more overt in recent years. In 1996 a bomb exploded at a US military complex at Dhahran, killing 19 and wounding over 300. A series of bomb blasts in the country in 2000, blamed by Saudi officials on British nationals engaged in criminal activity, was widely believed abroad to be the work of Saudi dissidents. Up to 15 Saudi nationals were involved in the attacks on New York and Washington, D.C. on 11 Sept. 2001, co-ordinated by Saudi dissident Osama bin Laden. In Nov. 2002, the Saudi government refused permission for the US to use its military facilities to attack Iraq, even if sanctioned by the United Nations. In May 2003 suicide bombers killed ten US citizens and many others at housing compounds for Western expatriate workers in Riyadh. In April 2003 the US agreed to pull out most of its troops from the kingdom, while stressing that the two countries would remain allies.

As King Fahd's health declined, his half brother, Crown Prince Abdullah Ibn Abdulaziz Al-Saud, assumed responsibility for government in 1996. When King Fahd died on 1 Aug. 2005, Crown Prince Abdullah was appointed his successor.

TERRITORY AND POPULATION

Saudi Arabia, which occupies nearly 80% of the Arabian peninsula, is bounded in the west by the Red Sea, east by the Persian Gulf, Qatar and the United Arab Emirates, north by Jordan, Iraq and Kuwait and south by Yemen and Oman. For the border dispute with Yemen *see* YEMEN: Territory and Population. The total area is 2,149,690 sq. km (829,995 sq. miles). Riyadh is the political, and Makkah (Mecca) the religious, capital.

The total population (provisional) at the 2004 census was 22,673,538; density, 10·5 per sq. km. Approximately 76% of the population are Saudi nationals. In 2003, 87·6% of the population lived in urban areas.

The UN gives a projected population for 2010 of 27·66m.

Principal cities with 2004 population estimates (in 1m.): Riyadh, 4·09; Jeddah, 2·80; Makkah, 1·29; Madinah, 0·92; Dammam, 0·74; Taif, 0·52.

The Neutral Zone (5,700 sq. km, 3,560 sq. miles), jointly owned and administered by Kuwait and Saudi Arabia from 1922 to 1966, was partitioned between the two countries in 1966, but the exploitation of the oil and other natural resources continues to be shared.

The official language is Arabic.

SOCIAL STATISTICS

2001 estimates: births, 715,000; deaths, 84,000. Birth rate (2001) was approximately 34 per 1,000 population; death rate, 4. 75% of the population is under the age of 30. Expectation of life at birth, 2003, was 70·1 years for males and 73·9 years for females. Annual population growth rate, 1992–2002, 3·0%. Infant mortality, 2001, was 23 per 1,000 live births, down from 58 in the years 1980–85. Fertility rate, 2001, 5·7 births per woman.

CLIMATE

A desert climate, with very little rain and none at all from June to Dec. The months May to Sept. are very hot and humid, but winter temperatures are quite pleasant. Riyadh, Jan. 58°F (14·4°C), July 108°F (42°C). Annual rainfall 4" (100 mm). Jeddah, Jan. 73°F (22·8°C), July 87°F (30·6°C). Annual rainfall 3" (81 mm).

CONSTITUTION AND GOVERNMENT

The reigning King, **Abdullah Ibn Abdulaziz Al-Saud** (b. 1924), Custodian of the two Holy Mosques, succeeded in Aug. 2005, after King Fahd's death. *Crown Prince:* Prince Sultan Ibn Abdulaziz Al-Saud (b. 1928). The Saudi royal family is around 8,000-strong.

Constitutional practice derives from Sharia law. There is no formal Constitution, but three royal decrees of 1 March 1992 established a Basic Law which defines the systems of central and municipal government, and set up a 60-man Consultative Council (*Majlis Al-Shura*) of royal nominees in Aug. 1993. The *Chairman* is Ekramul Haque. In July 1997 the King decreed an increase of the Consultative Council to a chairman plus 90 members, selected from men of science and experience; and in May 2001 it was increased again to a chairman plus 120 members. The Council does not have legislative powers.

Saudi Arabia is an absolute monarchy; executive power is discharged through a *Council of Ministers,* consisting of the King, Deputy Prime Minister, Second Deputy Prime Minister and Cabinet Ministers.

The King has the post of *Prime Minister* and can veto any decision of the Council of Ministers within 30 days.

In Oct. 2003 the government announced that municipal elections would be held in 2004 for the first time, followed by city elections and partial elections to the *Majlis Al-Shura* in the following years.

National Anthem

'Sarei lil majd walaya' ('Onward towards the glory and the heights'); words by Ibrahim Khafaji, tune by Abdul Rahman al Katib.

GOVERNMENT CHRONOLOGY

Kings since 1932.

1932–53	Abdulaziz Ibn Abdul Rahman Al-Saud
1953–64	Saud Ibn Abdulaziz Al-Saud
1964–75	Faisal Ibn Abdulaziz Al-Saud
1975–82	Khalid Ibn Abdulaziz Al-Saud
1982–2005	Fahd Ibn Abdulaziz Al-Saud
2005–	Abdullah Ibn Abdulaziz Al-Saud

RECENT ELECTIONS

Saudi Arabia's first ever elections were held in three phases between Feb.–April 2005 to create 178 local municipal councils. Half of the 1,184 seats were elected by the people and the other half appointed. Women were not permitted to stand for election or to vote. There are no political parties, but most seats were won by candidates backed by conservative Muslim clerics.

CURRENT ADMINISTRATION

In March 2006 the Council of Ministers comprised:

Prime Minister: King Abdullah Ibn Abdulaziz Al-Saud; b. 1924.

First Deputy Prime Minister, Minister of Defence and Aviation and Inspector-General: Crown Prince Sultan Ibn Abdulaziz Al-Saud.

Minister of Municipal and Rural Affairs: Prince Meta'ab Ibn Abdul Aziz Al-Saud. *Interior:* Prince Nayef Ibn Abdulaziz Al-Saud. *Foreign Affairs:* Prince Saud Al-Faisal Ibn Abdulaziz Al-Saud. *Agriculture:* Dr Fahd Ibn Abdulrahman Balghanaim. *Water and Electricity:* Abdul Rahman Al-Hussayen. *Civil Service:* Muhammad Ibn Ali Al-Fayez. *Education:* Abdullah Ibn Saleh Al-Obeid. *Finance:* Dr Ibrahim Ibn Abdulaziz Al-Assaf. *Health:* Dr Hamad Ibn Abdullah Al-Manie. *Higher Education:* Dr Khalid Ibn Mohammed Al-Angary. *Commerce and Industry:* Dr Hashim Ibn Abdullah Al-Yamani. *Culture and Information:* Iyad Ibn Amin Madani. *Islamic Affairs, Endowments, Call and Guidance:* Sheikh Saleh Ibn Abdulaziz Al-Ashaikh. *Justice:* Dr Abdullah Ibn Mohammed Ibn Ibrahim Al-Ashaikh. *Labour:* Dr Ghazi Ibn Abdulrahman Al-Qusaibi. *Social Affairs:* Abdulmohsen Al-Akkas. *Petroleum and Mineral Resources:* Ali Ibn Ibrahim Al-Naimi. *Pilgrimage:* Fouad Ibn Abdul-Salam Al-Farsi. *National Economy and Planning:* Khalid Ibn Muhammad Al-Qusaibi. *Communications and Information Technology:* Muhammad Ibn Jameel Mulla. *Transport:* Dr Jubarah Ibn Eid Al-Suraiseri.

Majlis Website: http://www.shura.gov.sa

CURRENT LEADERS

King Abdullah Ibn Abdulaziz Al-Saud

Position
King

Introduction
King Abdullah administered Saudi Arabia on behalf of his half-brother, King Fahd, between 1996 and King Fahd's death on 1 Aug. 2005, following which he was named King Fahd's successor. Abdullah has maintained the strict Islamic code of governance associated with the Wahhabi Saudis while attempting to rein in the excesses of the princely class. He has gained respect internationally for his efforts in the Middle East peace process, but at times relations with the USA administration have been strained.

Early Life
Prince Abdullah Ibn Abdulaziz was born in Riyadh in 1924, the only son of Fahda bint Asi bin Shurayim Shammar, the eighth wife of Abdulaziz Ibn Abdul Rahman Al-Saud, then Sultan of Nejd, who founded the Kingdom of Saudi Arabia in 1932. Abdulaziz, known as Ibn Saud by Europeans, reared his massive family in the Bedouin tradition, educating his sons at court and instilling them with Islamic and Arab virtues.

Abdullah's career began in 1952 when he was given the command of the Saudi National Guard by his half-brother, King Saud, the first son to succeed Abdulaziz. The National Guard comprised descendants of Abdulaziz's Bedouin warriors who took part in the expansion of Saudi power. Abdullah has maintained control of the National Guard, modernizing it and establishing military schools to supply its officers.

King Khalid Ibn Abdulaziz appointed Abdullah second deputy prime minister on his accession in 1975. In this post Abdullah became involved in foreign policy, visiting the USA in 1976 to meet President Gerald Ford. On the accession of King Fahd Ibn Abdulaziz in 1982, Abdullah was designated crown prince and first deputy prime minister.

Career in Office
The succession in Saudi Arabia is decided by the Saudi princes, who number over 4,000 (some sources claim an estimated 8,000). A crown prince is traditionally selected by seniority and ability. Since the death of the kingdom's founder, Abdulaziz, in 1953, only his sons have been considered suitable for the succession. Abdullah, who has only two full sisters and no full brothers, lacks a fraternal support base and relies on alliances forged with other factions within the family, most notably the sons of King Faisal, Prince Saud (foreign minister since 1975) and Prince Turki (head of Saudi intelligence).

Known as a devout Muslim, Abdullah has 14 sons and 20 daughters by six wives. His reputation for piety has earned him support from religious leaders. He gained prominence abroad in Jan. 1996 when King Fahd fell ill. Although regent for less than two months, Abdullah was soon considered the *de facto* ruler of Saudi Arabia on account of the King's recurrent illnesses and absences from the country. It was likely that Abdullah consulted and, to some extent, ruled with Fahd's Sudairi brothers, Sultan and Salman, the second deputy prime minister and the governor of Riyadh respectively.

Hopes for political reform under Abdullah have been disappointed. However, he has attacked the corruption and profligacy of the princes. His insistence on budgetary accountability has been met with resistance by many of his extended family. In 1999 Prince Talal Ibn Abdulaziz, another half-brother, made a call for more openness in Saudi governance.

The late 1990s saw a drop in Saudi earnings from oil. By Jan. 1999 a barrel of oil was priced at around US$10. In July 1999, Abdullah set up a Higher Economic Council to provide a technical policy for the Saudi oil industry. By the end of 1999 OPEC cutbacks on production and high levels of world demand had increased the price of oil dramatically. By Aug. 2005 oil prices were at record levels amid ongoing geopolitical concerns and problems with a number of refineries in the USA, exacerbated by Hurricane Katrina, which struck the southeastern coast of the USA that month.

Abdullah's foreign policy has concentrated on improving relations within the Arab world and the Gulf region and encouraging the peace process in the Middle East. He has shown support for militant Islamic groups such as Hizbollah and has condemned Israeli aggression in Lebanon. In early 2002 he proposed a peace plan for the Palestinian situation. In essence, the proposal was a restatement of the UN resolution for the Oslo peace process, which demanded the withdrawal of Israeli authority to the 1967 boundaries. However, his offer of normalization of relations with the Arab world in addition to recognition was seen as a greater incentive for Israeli compromise. Abdullah's subsequent retraction was explained as a reaction to Israeli Prime Minister Ariel Sharon's move to an 'unprecedented level' of violence against the Palestinians.

Abdullah is seen as less pro-Western than King Fahd. The attacks on New York, USA, in Sept. 2001, although condemned by

Abdullah, created serious tensions owing to the high proportion of Saudi nationals among the perpetrators. Abdullah also declined a visit to the USA on two occasions before the attacks, complaining of US one-sidedness in the Palestinian issue. His relations with President George W. Bush, whom he met in Texas in April 2002, have been mixed. Abdullah stated that Bush was 'uninformed' about the Middle East and the plight of the Palestinians yet maintained that the USA would remain a firm ally.

Internal reforms have been slow under Abdullah, but some key issues have been addressed. Female education, previously the preserve of the *ulema* (religious leaders), was placed under the jurisdiction of the ministry of education in 2002 and Abdullah has supported the increase of female employment. His visit to a Riyadh slum in Nov. 2002, wholly out of character for the Saudi royal family, heralded the establishment of a committee for the eradication of poverty in Saudi Arabia.

The issue of human rights has complicated external relations and provoked civil unrest in Saudi Arabia. Abdullah has rejected Western calls for the abolition of sharia law and the emancipation of women, stating that it is 'absurd to impose on an individual or a society rights that are alien to its beliefs or principles'. However, in Aug. 2002 the justice ministry announced the licensing of lawyers in an attempt to moderate the sharia system.

Saudi Arabia was gripped by widespread demonstrations against the regime's pro-US stance in 2002, causing open rifts in the Saudi family, particularly between the factions of Abdullah and Prince Sultan. Abdullah appointed a personal representative to Washington to balance the influence of the Saudi ambassador, Prince Bandar, son of Prince Sultan. These developments have been explained as an attempt by Abdullah to bypass Sultan, seen by many Saudis as corrupt.

Abdullah has been forced to focus on the issue of Islamic fundamentalism since the suicide bombings in Riyadh in May 2003. The attacks, which caused the death of 34 people including many foreign nationals, were blamed by the US administration and by the crown prince on a resurgent al-Qaeda. Further attacks by suspected al-Qaeda terrorists were recorded in Riyadh in April 2004, Yanbu and Khobar in May 2004, Jeddah in Dec. 2004 and to the northwest of Riyadh in April 2005.

The long-proposed reintroduction of foreign investment in the Saudi gas industry was rejected in June 2003. Despite support from the crown prince, US oil conglomerate Exxon Mobil's bid for the US$15bn. project in the South Ghawar gasfield was blocked by the petroleum and mineral resources minister, Ali Al-Naimi.

DEFENCE

Defence expenditure in 2003 totalled US$18,747m. (US$832 per capita), representing 8·9% of GDP.

5,000 US troops were stationed in Saudi Arabia after the 1991 Gulf War and were joined by a further 20,000 during the 2003 conflict. However, virtually all US troops have now been withdrawn. The Peninsular Shield Force of about 7,000 comprises units from all Gulf Co-operation Council countries.

Army

Strength (2002) was approximately 75,000. There is a paramilitary Frontier Force (approximately 10,500) and a National Guard (see below).

Navy

The Royal Saudi Naval Forces fleet includes four frigates and four corvettes. Naval Aviation forces operate 21 armed helicopters, both ship and shore based.

The main naval bases are at Riyadh (HQ Naval Forces), Jeddah (Western Fleet) and Jubail (Eastern Fleet). Naval personnel in 2002 totalled 15,500, including 3,000 marines.

Air Force

Current combat units include F-15s, F-5Bs, F-5Fs, Tornado strike aircraft and Tornado interceptors. The Air Force operates 432 combat aircraft in all and numbered about 18,000 personnel in 2002.

Air Defence Force

This separate Command was formerly part of the Army. In 2002 it operated surface-to-air missile batteries and had a strength of 16,000.

National Guard

The total strength of the National Guard amounted to approximately 100,000 (75,000 active, 25,000 tribal levies) in 2002. The National Guard's primary role is the protection of the Royal Family and vital points in the Kingdom. It is directly under royal command. The UK provides small advisory teams to the National Guard in the fields of general training and communications.

INTERNATIONAL RELATIONS

Saudi Arabia is a member of the UN, BIS, the League of Arab States, the Gulf Co-operation Council, OPEC, OIC and Islamic Development Bank. It became a member of the World Trade Organization in Dec. 2005.

In April 2001 Saudi Arabia and Iran signed a security pact to fight drug trafficking and terrorism, 13 years after the two countries had broken off relations.

ECONOMY

The oil sector accounts for 45% of GDP. Agriculture accounted for 5·2% of GDP in 2002, industry 52·0% and services 42·8%.

Overview

Saudi Arabia is the world's leading oil exporter and producer. The Saudi economy is dominated by the oil sector, which the Economist Intelligence Unit estimates has accounted for roughly 35% of GDP, 75% of government revenue and 85% of exports since the end of the Gulf war in 1991. In 1998 American and European oil companies were allowed to invest in the energy sector for the first time. The industrial sector, influenced by the oil sector, is based on hydrocarbon resources. In 2003 petroleum refining accounted for 25·8% of manufacturing GDP. The country also has deposits of iron ore, phosphates, bauxite and copper. Steps have been taken to combat money laundering. Structural reforms were introduced in 1999 to attract foreign investment. The stock market was opened to foreign investors and tax and customs administrations were reformed. A tourism authority has also been established.

After a poor economic performance in the 1980s the Saudi economy did relatively well in the 1990s. In the 1980s the country's economy posted negative annual growth rates over five years. Only in 1999 was growth negative in the 1990s, when growth was −0·7% on the year. However, at 3·1% the average annual growth rate over the 1990s was not impressive relative to other developing countries, particularly countries in the Asia Pacific region. In 2001 and 2002 the Saudi economy barely grew at all. Rising oil prices lifted the economy in 2003 when growth accelerated to 7·7% on the year. Following the trend in real GDP, per capita GDP fell dramatically in the 1980s before stabilizing in the latter part of the decade. Though still below pre-1983 levels, per capita GDP levels in the 1990s made a modest recovery before growing more robustly with the rise of oil prices in 2003.

In 2004 and 2005 economic conditions were favourable thanks to record oil revenues and prudent macroeconomic management. As a result of high oil prices, the economy's current account surplus and the government's fiscal surplus both grew strongly. Recent fiscal surpluses have been used to reduce central government debt. Over half of the 2004 fiscal surplus was used to this end, reducing government debt by 16% to 66% of GDP, while the rest was put into a fund to finance investment in priority areas over a five-year period. The recent boom has also seen strong growth in the private sector and in non-oil segments of the economy. Private sector growth was supported by a liberalized financial sector. In 2005 the country's financial sector continued to perform well and the Saudi stock market was among the world's best performing. The weakness of the dollar in much of the first half of the 2000s caused the *rial* to depreciate, enhancing the competitiveness of non-oil exports. Further structural reforms, less corruption, more privatization and vigilant macroeconomic management will be necessary in order for the Saudi economy to remain buoyant.

Currency
The unit of currency is the *rial* (SAR) of 100 *halalah*. Foreign exchange reserves totalled US$14,859m. in June 2002 and gold reserves were 4·60m. troy oz. Total money supply in June 2002 was SAR193,002m. Inflation rates (based on IMF statistics):

1995	1996	1997	1998	1999	2000	2001	2002	2003	2004
5·0%	0·9%	−0·4%	−0·2%	−1·3%	−0·6%	−0·8%	0·2%	0·6%	0·3%

In 2001 the six Gulf Arab states—Saudi Arabia, along with Bahrain, Kuwait, Oman, Qatar and the United Arab Emirates—signed an agreement to establish a single currency by 2010.

Budget
In 1986 the financial year became the calendar year. 2002 budget: revenue, SAR157bn.; expenditure, SAR202bn.

Oil sales account for 80% of state income. Expenditure in 2002: defence and security, SAR69bn.; human resource development, SAR47bn.; public administration, SAR45bn.; health and social development, SAR19bn.

Performance
Real GDP growth rates (based on IMF statistics):

1997	1998	1999	2000	2001	2002	2003	2004
2·5%	2·8%	−0·7%	4·9%	0·5%	0·1%	7·7%	5·2%

Following sluggish growth in 2001 and 2002 high economic growth since then has been largely as a consequence of a surge in oil prices. Total GDP in 2004 was US$250·6bn. Per capita GDP is now around half the level of 1980.

Banking and Finance
The Saudi Arabian Monetary Agency (*Governor*, Hamad Saud Al-Sayari, appointed 1983), established in 1953, functions as the central bank and the government's fiscal agent. In 2002 there were three national banks (the National Commercial Bank, the Al-Rajhi Banking and Investment Corporation and the Riyad Bank), five specialist banks, eight foreign banks and three government specialized credit institutions. The leading banks are National Commercial Bank (assets in 1999 of US$22,895m.), Saudi-American (US$20,520m.) and Riyad Bank (US$17,167m.). Sharia (the religious law of Islam) forbids the charging of interest; Islamic banking is based on sharing clients' profits and losses and imposing service charges. In 1999 total assets of commercial banks were 415,227m. rials.

A number of industry sectors are closed to foreign investors, including petroleum exploration, defence-related activities and financial services.

There is a stock exchange.

ENERGY AND NATURAL RESOURCES

Environment
Saudi Arabia's carbon dioxide emissions from the consumption and flaring of fossil fuels in 2002 were the equivalent of 14·0 tonnes per capita.

Electricity
By 1995 over 100 electricity producers had been amalgamated into four companies. Installed capacity was 24·1m. kW in 2002. All electricity is thermally generated. Production was an estimated 145·6bn. kWh in 2002; consumption per capita in 2002 was about 6,620 kWh.

Oil and Gas
Proven oil reserves (2003) 262·7bn. bbls. (the highest of any country and around 23% of world resources). Oil production began in 1938 by Aramco, which is now 100% state-owned and accounts for about 99% of total crude oil production. Saudi crude output in 2002 totalled 418·1m. tonnes (434·1m. tonnes in 2001) and accounted for 11·7% of the world total oil output. In 1998 oil export revenues were US$33bn., rising to US$41bn. in 1999 and US$70bn. in 2000, before falling to US$56bn. in 2001.

Production comes from 14 major oilfields, mostly in the Eastern Province and offshore, and including production from the Neutral Zone. The Ghawar oilfield, located between Riyadh and the Persian gulf, is the largest in the world, with estimated reserves of 70bn. bbls. Oil reserves are expected to run out in approximately 2085.

In 2002 natural gas reserves were 6,360bn. cu. metres; output in 2002 was 56·4bn. cu. metres. The gas sector has been opened up to foreign investment.

Water
Efforts are under way to provide adequate supplies of water for urban, industrial, rural and agricultural use. Most investment has gone into sea-water desalination. In 1996, 33 plants produced 1·9m. cu. metres a day, meeting 70% of drinking water needs. Total annual consumption was 18,200m. cu. metres in 1995. Irrigation for agriculture consumes the largest amount, from fossil reserves (the country's principal water source), and from surface water collected during seasonal floods. In 1996 there were 183 dams with a holding capacity of 450m. cu. metres. Treated urban waste water is an increasing resource for domestic purposes; in 1996 there were two recycling plants in operation.

Minerals
Production began in 1988 at Mahd Al-Dahab gold mine, the largest in the country. In 1999 total gold production was 4,570 kg. Deposits of iron, phosphate, bauxite, uranium, silver, tin, tungsten, nickel, chrome, zinc, lead, potassium ore and copper have also been found.

Agriculture
Land ownership is under the jurisdiction of the Ministry of Municipal and Rural Affairs.

Since 1970 the government has spent substantially on desert reclamation, irrigation schemes, drainage and control of surface water and of moving sands. Undeveloped land has been distributed to farmers and there are research and extension programmes. Large scale private investment has concentrated on wheat, poultry and dairy production.

In 2001 there were 3·60m. ha. of arable land and 194,000 ha. of permanent cropland. Approximately 1·62m. ha. were irrigated in 2001. In 2002, 8·5% of the economically active population were engaged in agriculture (19·1% in 1990).

About 200,000 tonnes of barley are produced annually as animal fodder. Production of other crops, 2000 (in 1,000 tonnes): wheat, 2,046; dates, 712; melons and watermelons, 426; potatoes, 394; tomatoes, 277; sorghum, 204; cucumbers and gherkins, 125; grapes, 116; onions, 95.

Livestock (2000): 297,000 cattle, 7,576,000 sheep, 4,305,000 goats, 400,000 camels and 130m. chickens. Livestock products (2000, in 1,000 tonnes): milk, 747; meat, 579; eggs, 136.

Forestry
The area under forests was 1·5m. ha. (0·7% of the land area) in 2000.

Fisheries

In 2003 the total catch was 52,929 tonnes, entirely from sea fishing.

INDUSTRY

According to the Financial Times Survey (FT 500), the largest companies in Saudi Arabia by market capitalization on 25 March 2004 were Saudi Telecom (US$37·5bn.), SABIC (Saudi Basic Industries), at US$35·1bn., and Saudi Electricity (US$23·1bn.).

In 2001 industry accounted for 51·8% of GDP, with manufacturing contributing 10·2%. The government encourages the establishment of manufacturing industries. Its policy focuses on establishing industries that use petroleum products, petrochemicals and minerals. Petrochemical and oil-based industries have been concentrated at eight new industrial cities, with the two principal cities at Jubail and Yanbu. Products include chemicals, plastics, industrial gases, steel and other metals. In 2004 there were 3,657 factories employing 340,000 workers.

Labour

The labour force in 2001 totalled 6,338,000. In 1999 females constituted 15% of the labour force—only the United Arab Emirates had a lower percentage of females in its workforce. In 2001, 35·7% of the economically active population were engaged in wholesale and retail trade, 18·7% in manufacturing, 15·7% in construction, 6·7% in research, consultancy and recruitment. In 1995 less than 1% worked in the oil sector. There are 6m. foreign workers, including over 1m. Egyptians and over 1m. Indians. Unemployment, which was less than 8% in 1999, reached 12% in 2002. Young people in particular are affected by unemployment.

INTERNATIONAL TRADE

In 1999 foreign debt totalled US$9bn.

Saudi Arabia, along with Bahrain, Kuwait, Oman, Qatar and the United Arab Emirates began the implementation of a customs union in Jan. 2003.

Imports and Exports

Trade in SAR1m.:

	1998	1999	2000	2001	2002
Imports f.o.b.	103,117	96,312	103,890	107,276	111,009
Exports f.o.b.	145,023	189,579	289,756	254,225	267,716

The principal export is crude oil; refined oil, petro-chemicals, fertilizers, plastic products and wheat are other major exports. Saudi Arabia is the world's largest exporter of oil, accounting for over 87% of all the country's exports in 2002. Major import suppliers, 1999: USA, 20·8%; Japan, 9·1%; UK, 7·4%; South Korea, 3·5%. Main export destinations, 1999: USA, 18·8%; Japan, 17·5%; South Korea, 9·2%; Singapore, 5·9%.

COMMUNICATIONS

Roads

In 2000 there was a total road network of 152,044 km. The total length of all asphalted roads was 45,461 km. A causeway links Saudi Arabia with Bahrain. Passenger cars in use in 2002 numbered 3,414,000 (150 per 1,000 inhabitants) and there were 4,866,000 trucks and vans. Women are not allowed to drive. In 1998 there were 153,727 road accidents resulting in 3,474 deaths.

Rail

1,435 mm gauge lines of 1,392 km link Riyadh and Dammam with stops at Hofuf and Abqaiq. The network is to be extended by 2,000 km at an estimated cost of US$2·6bn., in four phases, consisting of links to Jeddah, the Jordanian border, Jubail, and Makkah and Madinah. In 1999 railways carried 770,400 passengers and 1·8m. tonnes of freight.

Civil Aviation

The national carrier is the state-owned Saudia. In 1999 Saudia carried 12·7m. passengers, 260,300 tonnes of air cargo and operated 115,300 flights. At the end of 1999 Saudia owned 125 aircraft. There are four major international airports, at Jeddah (King Abdulaziz), Dhahran, Riyadh (King Khaled), and the newly constructed King Fahd International Airport at Dammam. There are also 22 domestic airports. In 2001 Jeddah handled 10,237,161 passengers (5,413,841 on international flights) and 188,386 tonnes of freight. Riyadh was the second busiest airport in 2001, handling 8,702,697 passengers (5,428,429 on domestic flights) and 155,245 tonnes of freight. In 1999, 26·1m. passengers travelled through the country's airports. The volume of air cargo carried was 463,000 tonnes.

Shipping

The ports of Dammam and Jubail are on the Persian Gulf and Jeddah, Yanbu and Jizan on the Red Sea. There is a deepwater oil terminal at Ras Tanura, and 16 minor ports. In 2002 the ports handled 104·2m. tonnes of cargo. In 1995 the merchant marine comprised 110 vessels totalling 8·2m. DWT. In 2002 shipping totalled 1·47m. GRT, including oil tankers 664,000 GRT.

Telecommunications

Saudi Arabia had 8,325,500 telephone subscribers in 2002 or 361·0 per 1,000 inhabitants, and there were 3·0m. PCs in use (130·2 per 1,000 population). There were 5,008,000 mobile phone subscribers in 2002 and 540,000 fax machines. The number of Internet users in 2002 was 1,418,900. The government sold a 30% stake in Saudi Telecom Company in Dec. 2002.

Postal Services

In 2003 there were 1,517 main post offices. A total of 636m. pieces of mail were processed in 2003.

SOCIAL INSTITUTIONS

Justice

The religious law of Islam (Sharia) is the common law of the land, and is administered by religious courts, at the head of which is a chief judge, who is responsible for the Department of Sharia Affairs. Sharia courts are concerned primarily with family inheritance and property matters. The Committee for the Settlement of Commercial Disputes is the commercial court. Other specialized courts or committees include one dealing exclusively with labour and employment matters; the Negotiable Instruments Committee, which deals with cases relating to cheques, bills of exchange and promissory notes; and the Board of Grievances, whose preserve is disputes with the government or its agencies and which also has jurisdiction in trademark-infringement cases and is the authority for enforcing foreign court judgments.

The death penalty is in force for murder, rape, sodomy, armed robbery, sabotage, drug trafficking, adultery and apostasy; executions may be held in public. There were 90 confirmed executions in 2005. The population in penal institutions in 2000 was 23,720 (110 per 100,000 of national population).

Education

The educational system provides students with free education, books and health services. General education consists of kindergarten, six years of primary school and three years each of intermediate and high school. In 1996–97 there were 893 pre-primary schools with 7,703 teachers and 85,484 pupils. In 1998–99 there were 12,234 primary schools with 189,008 teachers and 2,259,849 pupils; 5,901 intermediate schools with 86,630 teachers and 1,035,363 pupils; 3,117 secondary schools with 53,618 teachers and 704,566 pupils. At teacher training colleges there were 1,438 teachers and 21,366 students and at vocational schools 2,536 teachers and 21,551 students. Students can attend either high schools offering programmes in arts and sciences, or vocational schools. Girls' education is administered separately. In 1996 there were more than 30 special schools for the handicapped with about 4,550 students. The adult literacy rate in 2003 was 79·4% (87·1% among males and 69·3% among females). Although Saudi girls were not even allowed to attend school until 1964 women now make up 55% of Saudi Arabia's university students.

In 1996 there were 2,343 adult education centres. In 1997–98 there were seven universities, two Islamic universities and one university of petroleum and minerals. In 1999 there were 120,666 students in higher education institutions with 18,925 teachers. In 1998–99 total expenditure on education came to 9·3% of GNP.

Health
In 1999 there were 1,756 health care centres and clinics, 706 private dispensaries; and, in 2001, 324 hospitals with 46,622 beds. 31,983 doctors, 67,421 nursing and (1999) 37,077 technical staff were employed at these facilities. At Jeddah there is a quarantine centre for pilgrims.

Welfare
The retirement age is 60 (men) or 55 (women), with eligibility based on 120 months of contributions. The minimum monthly old-age pension is SAR1,500, calculated as 2·5% of the average monthly wage during the previous two years multiplied by the number of years of contributions. A 1969 law requires employers with more than 20 employees to pay 100% of wages for the first 30 days of sick leave and 75% of wages for the next 60 days.

Workers' medical benefits include medical, dental and diagnostic treatment, hospitalization, medicines, appliances, transportation and rehabilitation.

RELIGION
In 2001, 90% of the total population were Sunni Muslims, 4% Shias, 4% Christians and 1% Hindus. The *Grand Mufti*, Sheikh Abdul Aziz bin Abdullah bin Mohammed Al-Sheikh, has cabinet rank. A special police force, the Mutaween, exists to enforce religious norms.

The annual *Hajj*, the pilgrimage to Makkah, takes place from the 8th to the 13th day of Dhu al Hijjah, the last month of the Islamic year. It attracts more than 1·8m. pilgrims annually. In the current Islamic year, 1427, the *Hajj* will begin on 29 Dec. 2006 in the Gregorian calendar.

CULTURE

Broadcasting
The government-controlled Broadcasting Service of the Kingdom of Saudi Arabia and Saudi Arabian Television are responsible for broadcasting. Radio programmes include two home services, two religious services, services in English and French and an external service. Aramco Oil has a private station. There are TV programmes in Arabic and English; Channel 3 TV is a non-commercial independent. Colour is by SECAM H. In 2000 there were 7·2m. radio sets and in 2001 there were 5·9m. TV sets.

Press
In 1996 there were 13 daily newspapers with a combined circulation of 1,105,000, equivalent to 59 per 1,000 inhabitants. In 1995 there were 168 non-daily newspapers with a combined circulation of 2,150,000 (or 117 per 1,000). The most widely read newspaper is *Asharq Al-Awsat* ('Middle East'), with an average daily circulation of 248,482 in Jan.–June 1998. In 1997 a total of 3,780 book titles were published.

Tourism
There were 6,727,000 foreign tourists in 2001; spending by tourists totalled US$3·42bn.

Calendar
Saudi Arabia follows the Islamic *hegira* (AD 622, when Mohammed left Makkah for Madinah), which is based upon the lunar year of 354 days. The Islamic year 1427 corresponds to 31 Jan. 2006–19 Jan. 2007, and is the current lunar year.

Libraries
There was one National library in 1999 and 80 public libraries, with 1,883,120 volumes.

DIPLOMATIC REPRESENTATIVES

Of Saudi Arabia in the United Kingdom (30 Charles St., London, W1J 5DZ)
Ambassador: Prince Mohammed Bin Nawaf Bin Abdulaziz Al-Saud.

Of the United Kingdom in Saudi Arabia (PO Box 94351, Riyadh 11693)
Ambassador: Sherard Cowper-Coles, CMG, LVO.

Of Saudi Arabia in the USA (601 New Hampshire Ave., NW, Washington, D.C., 20037)
Ambassador: Prince Turki Al-Faisal.

Of the USA in Saudi Arabia (PO Box 94309, Riyadh)
Ambassador: James C. Oberwetter.

Of Saudi Arabia to the United Nations
Ambassador: Fawzi Bin Abdul Majeed Shobokshi.

Of Saudi Arabia to the European Union
Ambassador: Nassir Alassaf.

FURTHER READING

Al-Rasheed, Madawi, *A History of Saudi Arabia*. CUP, 2002
Azzam, H., *Saudi Arabia: Economic Trends, Business Environment and Investment Opportunities*. London, 1993
Kostiner, J., *The Making of Saudi Arabia: from Chieftaincy to Monarchical State*. OUP, 1994
Mackey, Sandra, *The Saudis: Inside the Desert Kingdom*. Revised ed. W. W. Norton, New York, 2003
Peterson, J. E., *Historical Dictionary of Saudi Arabia*. Metuchen (NJ), 1994
Wright, J. W. (ed.) *Business and Economic Development in Saudi Arabia: Essays with Saudi Scholars*. London, 1996

National Statistical Office: Ministry of Finance and National Economy, Department of Statistics, Riyadh.
Website: http://www.planning.gov.sa/statistic/sindexe.htm

SENEGAL

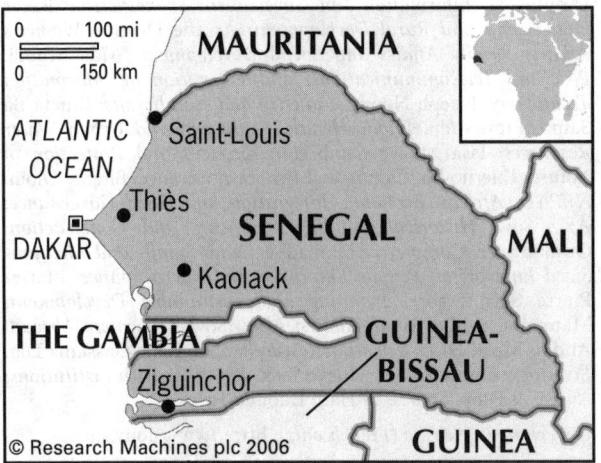

© Research Machines plc 2006

République du Sénégal

Capital: Dakar
Population projection, 2010: 13·08m.
GDP per capita, 2003: (PPP$) 1,648
HDI/world rank: 0·458/157

KEY HISTORICAL EVENTS

For much of the 1st millennium AD Senegal was under the influence of the gold-rich Ghana Empire of the Soninke people. In western Senegal the Takrur state was established in the 9th century. Islam was brought in the 11th century by the Zenega Berbers of southern Mauritania, who gave their name to the region, and the Moroccan Almoravids embarked on a proselytizing campaign. The power of the Malinke (Madingo) in present-day Mali expanded in the 13th and 14th centuries, especially under Mansa Musa, who subjugated Takrur and the Tukulor in Senegal. The west was dominated by the Jolof empire, which fragmented into four kingdoms in the 16th century.

Portuguese trading colonies were established on Gorée Island and at Rufisque in around 1444, encouraging the growth of the slave trade. The Dutch took control of Senegalese trade in the 17th century, only to be evicted in 1677 by the French, based at Saint-Louis at the mouth of the Sénégal River. Inland, the Tukolor created a Muslim theocracy in Fouta Toro, usurping the Denianké Dynasty in 1776. Tukolor power grew in the 1850s under al-Hajj Umar Tal, whose *jihad* was contained by treaty with the French in 1857. Britain accepted French hegemony in the region in 1814 after half a century of colonial rivalry, while retaining the Gambia River. Railway construction in 1879 cemented French control over western Senegal and Dakar became the capital of French West Africa in 1904. Casamance and eastern Senegal were conquered in the 1890s.

Senegalese service in the French army in the First World War secured representation in Paris and French citizenship for Africans in certain communes. The colonial administration followed a moderate liberalization programme, including the right to form political parties and trade unions. However, the decline in the groundnut trade in the 1930s increased poverty in Senegal. The expansion of the vote after the Second World War gave support to the Democratic Bloc (BDS), which joined the Socialist Party to become the Progressive Union (UPS), dominating the 1959 elections in the newly-autonomous Senegal. Membership of the French Community lasted until independence on 20 June 1960 as part of the Federation of Mali with French Soudan (Mali); the Federation was dissolved on 20 Aug. 1960.

Leopold Sédar Senghor, the BDS founder and leader of the UPS, was elected president on 5 Sept. 1960. Relations with his prime minister, Mamadou Dia, deteriorated and Senghor had him arrested in Dec. 1962 after an attempted coup. Presidential power was augmented by referendum in 1963, allowing Senghor to ban all other parties in 1966. Senghor appointed Abdou Diouf prime minister in 1973 and began relaxing political restrictions. Abdoulaye Wade founded the Democratic Party (PDS) and a Marxist-Leninist party was formed. Recession and political agitation forced Senghor's resignation in Dec. 1980; Diouf succeeded him and was confirmed by elections in 1983, 1988 and 1993.

Diouf pursued a vigorous foreign policy via the Organization of African Unity and the Economic Community of West African States. He reinstated the Gambian president, Sir Dawda Jawara, in 1981, creating the Senegambian confederation, which lasted until 1989. Unrest in the southern Casamance region escalated into secessionist civil war in the early 1990s. A skirmish on the Mauritanian border in 1989 resulted in the death of Senegalese and Mauritanians expatriates and the closing of the border, a dispute not resolved until 1994. The deterioration of the economy and the Casamance crisis led to electoral defeat in 2000. He conceded peacefully, handing power to his long-term rival, PDS leader Abdoulaye Wade. The coalition with Moustapha Niasse, his prime minister and key electoral ally, broke down in March 2001.

TERRITORY AND POPULATION

Senegal is bounded by Mauritania to the north and northeast, Mali to the east, Guinea and Guinea-Bissau to the south and the Atlantic to the west with The Gambia forming an enclave along that shore. Area, 196,722 sq. km. Population (2002 census, provisional), 9,956,202. The United Nations population estimate for 2005 was 11·66m., giving a density of 59·3 per sq. km. In 2003 the population was 50·4% rural.

The UN gives a projected population for 2010 of 13·08m.

The areas, populations and capitals of the eleven regions:

Region	Area (in sq. km)	2002 estimate (in 1,000)	Capital
Dakar	550	2,267	Dakar
Diourbel	4,359	1,050	Diourbel
Fatick	7,935	613	Fatick
Kaolack	16,010	1,066	Kaolack
Kolda	21,011	836	Kolda
Louga	29,188	678	Louga
Matam	25,083	423	Matam
Saint-Louis	19,044	689	Saint-Louis
Tambacounda	59,602	606	Tambacounda
Thiès	6,601	1,290	Thiès
Ziguinchor	7,339	438	Ziguinchor

Dakar, the capital, had a provisional census population in 2002 of 1,983,093. Other large cities (with 2002 provisional census population) are: Thiès (237,849), Rufisque (179,797), Kaolack (172,305), Saint-Louis (154,555), Mbour (153,503) and Ziguinchor (153,269).

Ethnic groups are the Wolof (36% of the population), Fulani (16%), Serer (16%), Diola (9%), Tukulor (9%), Bambara (6%), Malinké (6%) and Sarakole (2%).

The official language is French; Wolof is widely spoken.

SOCIAL STATISTICS

2000 estimates: births, 352,000; deaths, 109,000. Rates, 2000 estimates (per 1,000 population): births, 37·6; deaths, 11·6. Annual population growth rate, 1992–2002, 2·4%; infant mortality, 2001, 79 per 1,000 live births. Life expectancy in 2003 was 54·5 years for men and 56·9 for women. Fertility rate, 2001, 5·2 births per woman.

CLIMATE

A tropical climate with wet and dry seasons. The rains fall almost exclusively in the hot season, from June to Oct., with high humidity. Dakar, Jan. 72°F (22·2°C), July 82°F (27·8°C). Annual rainfall 22" (541 mm).

CONSTITUTION AND GOVERNMENT

A new constitution was approved by a referendum held on 7 Jan. 2001. The head of state is the *President*, elected by universal suffrage for not more than two five-year terms (previously two seven-year terms). The *President* has the power to dissolve the National Assembly, without the agreement, as had been the case, of a two-thirds majority. The new constitution also abolished the upper house (the Senate), confirmed the status of the prime minister and for the first time gave women the right to own land. For the unicameral, 120-member *National Assembly*, 65 members are elected by simple majority vote in single or multi-member constituencies with 55 elected by a system of party-list proportional representation.

National Anthem

'Pincez tous vos koras, frappez les balafos' ('All pluck the koras, strike the balafos'); words by Léopold Sédar Senghor, tune by Herbert Pepper.

RECENT ELECTIONS

Presidential elections took place on 27 Feb. and 19 March 2000. In the first round of voting, incumbent Abdou Diouf won 41·3% of the vote, Abdoulaye Wade of the Senegalese Democratic Party received 31·0%, Moustapha Niasse 16·8% and Djibo Ka 7·1%. In the run-off between Diouf and Wade, Wade won, in his fifth attempt to become President, with 58·5% of the vote, ending 40 years of uninterrupted rule by the Socialist Party. Wade is the last president to be elected to a seven-year term. 'Some commentators seized upon the peaceful transition as evidence of Africa's maturing democratic tradition. But while Senegal's success story is worth celebrating it remains an exception'. (*Time*, 10 July 2000).

Parliamentary elections were held on 27 April 2001. Turnout was 67·4%. Coalition 'Sopi', a coalition led by President Abdoulaye Wade's Senegalese Democratic Party, took 89 seats with 49·6% of votes cast, the Alliance of Progressive Forces 11 with 16·1%, the Socialists 10 with 17·4% and the Union for Democratic Renewal 3 with 3·7%. Six other parties claimed two seats or fewer.

CURRENT ADMINISTRATION

President: Abdoulaye Wade; b. 1926 (PDS; sworn in 1 April 2000).

In March 2006 the government was composed as follows:

Prime Minister: Macky Sall; b. 1961 (PDS; sworn in 21 April 2004).

Minister of State, Infrastructure, Equipment and Transport: Habib Sy. *Minister of State, Minister of Foreign Affairs:* Cheikh Tidiane Gadio. *Minister of State, Minister of Economy and Finance:* Abdoulaye Diop. *Minister of State, Minister of Justice:* Cheikh Tidiane Sy. *Minister of State, Minister of Maritime Economy:* Djibo Leïty Kâ.

Minister of Armed Forces: Bécaye Diop. *Interior and Local Communities:* Ousmane Ngom. *Education:* Moustapha Sourang. *Technical Education and Professional Training:* Georges Tendeng. *Tourism and Civil Aviation:* Ousmane Masseck Ndiaye. *Energy and Mines:* Madické Niang. *Agriculture, Rural Water Resources and Food Security:* Farba Senghor. *Civil Service, Labour and Employment:* Adama Sall. *Health and Medical Prevention:* Abdou Fall. *International Co-operation and Decentralized Co-operation:* Lamine Bâ. *Information and Government Spokesperson:* Bacar Dia. *Urban and Rural Development:* Assane Diagne. *Women's Affairs, Family Affairs and Social Development:* Aïda Mbodj. *Post and Telecommunications, and Promotion of Information Technology:* Joseph Ndong. *Industry and Handicrafts:* Bineta Bâ Samb. *Prevention, Public Health, Sanitation and Urban Water Resources:* Issa Mbaye Samb. *Environment and Protection of Nature:* Thierno Lô. *Culture and Historical Heritage:* Birame Diouf. *NEPAD, African Economic Integration and Good Governance:* Aziz Sow. *Historical Buildings, Housing and Construction:* Oumar Sarr. *Commerce:* Mamadou Diop. *Small- and Medium-Sized Enterprises, Female Enterprise and Micro-finance:* Marie-Pierre Sarr Traoré. *Planning and Sustainable Development:* Mamadou Sidibé. *Youth Affairs:* Aliou Sow. *Senegalese Abroad:* Abdou Malal Diop. *Scientific Research:* Yaye Kene Gassama Dia. *Livestock:* Oumy Khairy Gueye Seck. *Relations with Institutions:* Awa Fall Diop. *Sports:* El Hadj Daouda Faye.

Government Website (French only): http://www.gouv.sn

CURRENT LEADERS

Abdoulaye Wade

Position
President

Introduction
A barrister, writer and newspaper editor, Abdoulaye Wade spent nearly 40 years in opposition before becoming president at his fifth attempt in 2000. His election marked the end of Senegal's socialist era.

Early Life
Wade was born on 29 May 1926, in Kébémer. He was educated in Senegal and at the Sorbonne in Paris, France, where he studied law and economics. After practising as a barrister in France for some years, he returned to Senegal to take up an academic post at the University of Dakar.

In 1974 he created the liberal Parti Démocratique Sénégalais (PDS; Senegalese Democratic Party), one of the three parties allowed under the 1976 constitution. He unsuccessfully stood as a presidential candidate in the 1978 elections against Léopold Sédar Senghor. In the same year he entered the National Assembly.

He lost the 1988 presidential race against Abdou Diouf. The latter accused Wade of inflaming riots with his claims of election fraud and Wade was arrested. He spent several months in prison while Diouf declared a state of emergency. However, following his release Wade was appointed a minister in Diouf's government in 1991. He resigned the following year and in 1993 once more stood unsuccessfully for the presidency. He joined Diouf's government again in March 1995, resigning three years later.

By 2000 public dissatisfaction with Diouf's leadership was running high, yet he emerged with most votes after the first round of a presidential poll against Wade and six other candidates. Diouf and Wade went into a run-off, and Wade, benefiting from the absence of the other candidates (particularly Moustapha Niasse), won 58·5% of the vote. He was sworn in as the new president on 1 April 2000 and formed a coalition government with Niasse as prime minister.

Career in Office
Wade's election promises included boosting the economy and confronting growing poverty, while raising literacy and health levels. But attempts to implement necessary reforms have been hampered by Senegal's crippling levels of international debt. In addition, Wade's popular standing was soon diminished by the

resignation of Niasse in 2001, on whom he had relied for electoral victory. Nevertheless, his coalition won almost 75% of National Assembly seats in the 2001 elections. In Oct. 2002 the transport and armed forces ministers resigned following the death of around 1,000 people in the sinking of a state-operated ferry. The following month Wade dismissed Prime Minister Madior Boye (who on appointment was Africa's only female leader) and her entire cabinet, replacing her with Idrissa Seck. He in turn was replaced in April 2004 by Macky Sall of the PDS. In April 2005, 14 PDS deputies in the National Assembly defected, protesting an increasing lack of democracy and transparency.

Negotiations between the government and the Casamance separatist movement culminated in a ceasefire in Dec. 2004 and the signing of a peace agreement in early 2005.

DEFENCE

There is selective conscription for two years. Defence expenditure totalled US$86m. in 2003 (US$9 per capita), representing 1·4% of GDP.

Army

There are four military zones. The Army had a strength of 8,000 (3,500 conscripts) in 2002. There is also a paramilitary force of gendarmerie and customs of about 5,800.

Navy

Personnel (2002) totalled 600, and bases are at Dakar and Casamance.

Air Force

The Air Force, formed with French assistance, has eight combat aircraft but serviceability is low. Personnel (2002) 800.

INTERNATIONAL RELATIONS

Senegal is a member of the UN, WTO, the African Union, African Development Bank, ECOWAS, OIC, Islamic Development Bank, IOM, International Organization of the Francophonie and is an ACP member state of the ACP-EU relationship.

A short section of the boundary with The Gambia is indefinite.

ECONOMY

Agriculture accounted for 15·0% of GDP in 2002, industry 21·6% and services 63·4%.

Currency

Senegal is a member of the Union Economique et Monétaire Ouest-Africaine (UEMOA). The unit of currency is the *franc CFA* (XOF) with a parity of 655·957 francs CFA to one euro. In May 2002 total money supply was 567,374m. francs CFA and foreign exchange reserves totalled US$507m. In June 2000 gold reserves were 29,000 troy oz. Inflation was 0·5% in 2004.

Budget

In 2001 the government's total revenue was 602·1bn. francs CFA and total expenditure was 737·6bn. francs CFA.

Performance

Real GDP growth was 6·5% in 2003, falling slightly to 6·2% in 2004. Senegal's total GDP in 2004 was US$7·7bn.

Banking and Finance

The Banque Centrale des États de l'Afrique de l'Ouest is the bank of issue of the franc CFA for all the countries of the West African Economic and Monetary Union (Benin, Burkina Faso, Côte d'Ivoire, Mali, Niger, Senegal and Togo) but has had its headquarters in Dakar, the Senegalese capital, since 1973. Its *Acting Governor* is Justin Baro Damo. There are eight commercial banks, the largest including Banque Internationale pour le Commerce et l'Industrie and Banque de l'Habitat (25% state-owned). There are also four development banks and an Islamic bank.

Senegal is affiliated to the regional BRVM stock exchange (serving the member states of the West African Economic and Monetary Union), based in Abidjan, Côte d'Ivoire.

ENERGY AND NATURAL RESOURCES

Environment

Senegal's carbon dioxide emissions from the consumption and flaring of fossil fuels in 2002 were the equivalent of 0·5 tonnes per capita.

Electricity

In 2000 installed capacity was 0·2m. kW. Production in 2000 was 1·47bn. kWh and consumption per capita 155 kWh.

Minerals

In 2002, 2m. tonnes of calcium phosphate were produced. Limestone production in 2002 totalled 1,461,000 tonnes. In 2002 the Sabodala mine in eastern Senegal had proven gold ore reserves of 2·6m. tonnes; annual gold production is approximately 600 kg. Exploration of further gold reserves increased greatly throughout the 1990s. While only three research permits were issued in 1994 this figure had risen to 35 by 1998, with South African, British, American, Canadian and Australian companies all active in the country.

Agriculture

Because of erratic rainfall 25% of agricultural land needs irrigation. Most land is owned under customary rights and holdings tend to be small. In 2001, 2·46m. ha. were used as arable land and 40,000 ha. for permanent crops. 71,000 ha. were irrigated in 2001. There were 700 tractors in 2001 and 155 harvester-threshers. Production, 2000 (in 1,000 tonnes): sugarcane, 889; groundnuts, 828; millet, 506; watermelons, 260; rice, 240; sorghum, 147; mangoes, 75; maize, 66; onions, 65.

Livestock (2000): 4·30m. sheep, 3·59m. goats, 2·96m. cattle, 510,000 horses, 384,000 asses, 330,000 pigs. Animal products (2000, in 1,000 tonnes): meat, 162; milk, 135.

Forestry

Forests covered 6·21m. ha. in 2000 (32·2% of the land area). Roundwood production in 2001 amounted to 5·94m. cu. metres.

Fisheries

The fishing fleet comprises 167 vessels totalling 40,600 GRT. In 2001 the total catch was 405,409 tonnes (385,409 tonnes from sea fishing).

INDUSTRY

Predominantly agricultural and fish processing, phosphate mining, petroleum refining and construction materials.

Labour

The workforce (10 years and over) in 1996 was 2,509,000, of whom 77% were engaged in subsistence farming; 60% of the workforce is in the public sector.

Trade Unions

There are two major unions, the *Union Nationale des Travailleurs Sénégalais* (government-controlled) and the *Confédération Nationale des Travailleurs Sénégalais* (independent) which broke away from the former in 1969 and in 1994 comprised 75% of salaried workers.

INTERNATIONAL TRADE

Foreign debt was US$3,918m. in 2002.

Imports and Exports

In 2003 imports (f.o.b.) totalled US$2,065m. and exports (f.o.b.) US$1,257m. Chief imports: food and beverages, capital goods. Chief exports: fish, groundnuts, petroleum products, phosphates and cotton. Main import suppliers, 2001: France, 27·8%; Nigeria, 9·8%; Thailand, 7·7%; Germany, 4·8%; USA, 4·2%. Main export markets, 2001: France, 16·7%; India, 12·4%; Greece, 7·3%; Mali, 6·9%; Italy, 6·0%.

COMMUNICATIONS

Roads
The length of roads in 2002 was estimated to be 14,583 km, of which 4,270 km were paved. In 2002 there were 112,700 passenger cars (11 per 1,000 inhabitants), 57,100 trucks and vans and (1999) 10,500 buses and coaches. There were 646 deaths as a result of road accidents in 1999.

Rail
There are four railway lines: Dakar-Kidira (continuing in Mali), Thiès-Saint-Louis (193 km), Diourbel-Touba (46 km) and Guinguinéo-Kaolack (22 km). Total length (2000), 906 km (metre gauge). In 2000 railways carried 4·3m. passengers and 1·7m. tonnes of freight, much of which was for export.

Civil Aviation
The international airport is at Dakar/Yoff (Léopold Sédar Senghor), which handled 1,138,000 passengers (1,106,000 on international flights) and 23,200 tonnes of freight in 2001. Air Sénégal is 50% state-owned; in 2003 it flew to Abidjan, Bamako, Banjul, Bissau, Casablanca, Conakry, Cotonou, Las Palmas, Lomé, Lyon, Marseille, Niamey, Nouakchott, Ouagadougou, Paris and Praia in addition to operating on domestic routes. Trans African Airlines flew to Abidjan, Bamako, Brazzaville, Cotonou, Lomé and Pointe-Noire. In 1999 scheduled airline traffic of Senegal-based carriers flew 3·3m. km, carrying 103,000 passengers (84,000 on international flights).

Shipping
In 2002 the merchant marine totalled 47,000 GRT. 5·5m. tonnes of freight were handled in the port of Dakar in 1995. There is a river service on the Senegal from Saint-Louis to Podor (363 km) open throughout the year, and to Kayes (924 km) open from July to Oct. The Senegal River is closed to foreign flags. The Saloum River is navigable as far as Kaolack, the Casamance River as far as Ziguinchor.

Telecommunications
In 2002 telephone subscribers numbered 778,000 (79·4 for every 1,000 persons) and there were 200,000 PCs in use (20·4 per 1,000 persons). Senegal had 553,400 mobile phone subscribers in 2002. Internet users numbered 105,000 in 2002.

Postal Services
There were 137 post offices in 2003.

SOCIAL INSTITUTIONS

Justice
There are *juges de paix* in each *département* and a court of first instance in each region. Assize courts are situated in Dakar, Kaolack, Saint-Louis and Ziguinchor, while the Court of Appeal resides in Dakar. The death penalty, last used in 1967, was abolished in Dec. 2004.

The population in penal institutions in Sept. 2002 was 5,360 (54 per 100,000 of national population).

Education
The adult literacy rate in 2003 was 39·3% (51·1% among males and 29·2% among females). In 2003–04 there were 1,382,749 pupils and 32,010 teachers in 6,060 primary schools; 355,732 pupils in secondary schools; and (1998–99), 29,303 students in tertiary education. There are four universities (Cheikh Anta Diop, Gaston Berger, Dakar Bourguiba and Sahel). In 1995–96 there were a further 19 institutions of higher education.

In 2000–01 total expenditure on education came to 3·2% of GNP.

Health
In 2001 there were 22 hospitals, 411 rural maternity homes (2000), 58 health centres and 888 health posts. There were 649 doctors (266 in government service), 93 dentists, 588 midwives (547 government) and 1,876 other medical personnel (1,630 government) in 1996. There were 322 pharmacists (16 in government service). Senegal has been one of the most successful countries in Africa in the prevention of AIDS. Levels of infection have remained low, with the anti-AIDS programme having started as far back as 1986. The infection rate has been kept below 2%.

RELIGION
The population was 93% Sunni Muslim in 2001, the remainder being Christian (mainly Roman Catholic) or animist.

CULTURE

World Heritage Sites
Gorée Island, off the coast of Senegal, was added to the UNESCO World Heritage List in 1978. It was formerly the largest slave trading centre on the African coast. The Djoudj Sanctuary in the Senegal River delta (added in 1981), protects 1·5m. birds. Niokolo-Koba National Park, along the banks of the Gambia River (added in 1981), is home to the Derby eland (largest of the antelopes). The Island of Saint-Louis joined the UNESCO list in 2000, as a reminder of its status as capital between 1872 to 1957.

Broadcasting
The government-owned *Office de Radio-Télévision du Sénégal* broadcasts a national and an international radio service from ten main transmitters. There are also regional services. There is also a TV service (colour by SECAM V). In 2000 there were 1·32m. radio receivers (141 per 1,000 inhabitants) and 376,000 TV receivers (40 per 1,000 inhabitants). As recently as 1980 there had been just 8,000 TV receivers, or only 1·4 per 1,000. The percentage rise in the proportion of the population having TV receivers, at more than 2,700%, was the highest anywhere in the world over the same period.

Press
In 1996 there was one daily newspaper with a circulation of 45,000, equivalent to 5·3 per 1,000 inhabitants.

Tourism
446,000 foreign tourists visited in 2002. Revenue amounted to US$156m.

DIPLOMATIC REPRESENTATIVES
Of Senegal in the United Kingdom (39 Marloes Rd, London, W8 6LA)
Ambassador: Mamadou Niang.

Of the United Kingdom in Senegal (20 Rue du Docteur Guillet, Dakar)
Ambassador: Peter Newall.

Of Senegal in the USA (2112 Wyoming Ave., NW, Washington, D.C., 20008)
Ambassador: Amadou Lamine Ba.

Of the USA in Senegal (Ave. Jean XXIII, Dakar)
Ambassador: Robert Jackson.

Of Senegal to the United Nations
Ambassador: Paul Badji.

Of Senegal to the European Union
Ambassador: Saliou Cisse.

FURTHER READING

Centre Français du Commerce Extérieur. *Sénégal: un Marché.* Paris, 1993

Adams, A. and So, J., *A Claim in Senegal, 1720–1994.* Paris, 1996
Dilley, Roy M. and Eades, Jerry S., *Senegal.* [Bibliography] ABC-Clio, Oxford and Santa Barbara (CA), 1994
Phillips, L. C., *Historical Dictionary of Senegal.* 2nd ed, revised by A. F. Clark. Metuchen (NJ), 1995

National Statistical Office: Direction de la Prévision et de la Statistique, BP 116, Dakar.
Website (French only): http://www.ansd.org

SERBIA AND MONTENEGRO

Državna Zajednica Srbija i Crna Gora
(State Union of Serbia and Montenegro)

Capital: Belgrade (Administrative and Legislative),
Podgorica (Judicial)
Population projection, 2010: 10·48m.
GDP per capita: not available
GNI per capita: $930

KEY HISTORICAL EVENTS

The assassination of Archduke Franz Ferdinand of Austria in Sarajevo on 28 June 1914 precipitated the First World War. In the winter of 1915–16 the Serbian army was forced to retreat to Corfu, where the government aimed at a centralized, Serb-run state. But exiles from Croatia and Slovenia wanted a South Slav federation. This was accepted by the victorious Allies as the basis for the new state. The Croats were forced by the pressure of events to join Serbia and Montenegro on 1 Dec. 1918. From 1918–29 the country was known as the Kingdom of the Serbs, Croats and Slovenes.

A constitution of 1921 established an assembly but the trappings of parliamentarianism could not bridge the gulf between Serbs and Croats. The Croat peasant leader Radić was assassinated in 1928; his successor, Vlatko Maček, set up a separatist assembly in Zagreb. On 6 Jan. 1929 the king suspended the constitution and established a royal dictatorship. In Oct. 1934 he was murdered by a Croat extremist while on an official visit to France.

During the regency of Prince Paul, the government pursued a pro-fascist line. On 25 March 1941 Paul was persuaded to adhere to the Axis Tripartite Pact. On 27 March he was overthrown by military officers in favour of the boy king Peter. Germany invaded on 6 April. Within ten days Yugoslavia surrendered; king and government fled to London. Resistance was led by a royalist group and the communist-dominated partisans of Josip Broz, nicknamed Tito.

Having succeeded in liberating Yugoslavia, Tito set up a Soviet-type constitution. But he was too independent for Stalin, who sought to topple him. However, Tito made a *rapprochement* with the west and it was the Soviet Union under Khrushchev which had to extend the olive branch in 1956. Yugoslavia evolved its 'own road to socialism'. Collectivization of agriculture was abandoned; and Yugoslavia became a champion of international 'non-alignment'. A collective presidency came into being with the death of Tito in 1980.

Dissensions in Kosovo between Albanians and Serbs, and in parts of Croatia between Serbs and Croats, reached crisis point after 1988. On 25 June 1991 Croatia and Slovenia declared independence. Fighting began in Croatia between Croatian forces and Serb irregulars from Serb-majority areas of Croatia. On 25 Sept. the UN Security Council imposed a mandatory arms embargo on Yugoslavia. A three-month moratorium agreed at EU peace talks on 30 June having expired, both Slovenia and Croatia declared their complete independence from the Yugoslav federation on 8 Oct. After 13 ceasefires had failed, a fourteenth was signed on 23 Nov. under UN auspices. A Security Council resolution of 27 Nov. proposed the deployment of a UN peacekeeping force if the ceasefire was kept. Fighting, however, continued. On 15 Jan. 1992 the EU recognized Croatia and Slovenia as independent states. Bosnia-Herzegovina was recognized on 7 April 1992 and Macedonia on 8 April 1993. A UN delegation began monitoring the ceasefire on 17 Jan. and the UN Security Council on 21 Feb. voted to send a 14,000-strong peacekeeping force to Croatia and Yugoslavia. On 27 April 1992 Serbia and Montenegro created a new federal republic of Yugoslavia.

On 30 May, responding to further Serbian military activities in Bosnia and Croatia, the UN Security Council voted to impose sanctions. In mid-1992 NATO committed air, sea and eventually land forces to enforce sanctions and protect humanitarian relief operations in Bosnia. At a joint UN-EC peace conference on Yugoslavia held in London on 26–27 Aug. some 30 countries and all the former republics of Yugoslavia endorsed a plan to end the fighting in Croatia and Bosnia, install UN supervision of heavy weapons, recognize the borders of Bosnia-Herzegovina and return refugees. At a further conference at Geneva on 30 Sept. the Croatian and Yugoslav presidents agreed to make efforts to bring about a peaceful solution in Bosnia, but fighting continued. Following the Bosnian-Croatian-Yugoslav (Dayton) agreement all UN sanctions were lifted in Nov. 1995.

In July 1997 Slobodan Milošević switched his power base to become president of federal Yugoslavia. The former Yugoslav foreign minister, Milan Milutinović, succeeded Milošević as Serbian President. Meanwhile, in Montenegro, the pro-western Milo Djukanović succeeded a pro-Milošević president.

Kosovo

In 1998 unrest in Kosovo, with its largely Albanian population, led to a bid for outright independence. Violence flared resulting in what a US official described as 'horrendous human rights violations', including massive shelling of civilians and destruction of villages. A US-mediated agreement to allow negotiations to proceed during an interim period of autonomy allowed for food and medicine to be delivered to refugees and American support for a degree of autonomy (short of independence), accepted in principle by President Milošević, lifted the immediate threat of NATO air strikes. Further outbreaks of violence in early 1999 were followed by the departure of the 800-strong team of international 'verifiers' of the fragile peace. Peace talks in Paris broke down without a settlement though subsequently Albanian freedom fighters accepted terms allowing them broad autonomy. The sticking point on the Serbian side was the international insistence on having 28,000 NATO-led peacemakers in Kosovo to keep apart the warring factions. Meanwhile, the scale of Serbian repression in Kosovo persuaded the NATO allies to take direct action. On the night of 24 March 1999 NATO aircraft began a bombing campaign against Yugoslavian military targets. Further Serbian provocation in Kosovo caused hundreds of thousands of ethnic Albanians to seek refuge in neighbouring countries. On 9 June NATO and Yugoslavia signed an accord on the Serb withdrawal from Kosovo, and on 11 June NATO's peacekeeping force, KFOR, entered Kosovo.

When the general election held on 24 Sept. 2000 resulted in a victory for the opposition democratic leader Vojislav Koštunica, President Milošević demanded a second round of voting. A strike by miners at the Kolubara coal mine on 29 Sept. was followed by a mass demonstration in Belgrade on 5 Oct. when the parliament building was set on fire and on 6 Oct. Slobodan Milošević accepted defeat. He was arrested on 1 April 2001 after a 30-hour confrontation with the authorities. On 28 June he was handed over to the United Nations War Crimes Tribunal in The Hague to face charges of crimes against humanity. Prime Minister Zoran Žižić resigned the next day. On 12 Feb. 2002 the trial of Slobodan Milošević, on charges of genocide and war crimes in the Balkans over a period of nearly ten years, began at the International Criminal Tribunal in The Hague.

On 14 March 2002 Serbia and Montenegro agreed to remain part of a single entity called Serbia and Montenegro, thus relegating the name Yugoslavia to history. The agreement was ratified in principle by the federal parliament and the republican parliaments of Serbia and Montenegro on 9 April 2002. The new union came into force on 4 Feb. 2003. Most powers in this loose confederation are divided between the two republics. After 4 Feb. 2006 Serbia and Montenegro were to have the right to vote for independence. Montenegro was scheduled to hold a referendum on 21 May 2006. For details, *see* Addenda, page xxxi. The final status of Kosovo, which is legally part of Serbia, remains unresolved.

For the early history of Serbia and Montenegro *see* MONTENEGRO: Key Historical Events and SERBIA: Key Historical Events.

TERRITORY AND POPULATION

Serbia and Montenegro is bounded in the north by Hungary, northeast by Romania, east by Bulgaria, south by Macedonia and Albania, and west by the Adriatic Sea, Bosnia-Herzegovina and Croatia. Area, 102,173 sq. km. Population (2002 census, without data for Kosovo and Metohija), 8,116,552 (4,166,165 females). Population density (2002), 88·9 per sq. km. The estimated population in 2005 (with Kosovo and Metohija) was 10,503,000. In 2002 an estimated 56·8% of the population lived in urban areas.

The UN gives a projected population for 2010 of 10·48m.

In Feb. 2003 the new confederation of Serbia and Montenegro came into being: this comprised the two republics of Montenegro and Serbia, and the two provinces of Kosovo and Metohija, and Vojvodina within Serbia. The confederal capital is Belgrade (Beograd); some capital functions, including the Supreme Court, are sited in Podgorica. Populations (2001 estimates) of principal towns:

Belgrade	1,581,129	Subotica	142,166
Novi Sad	266,176	Zrenjanin	130,070
Niš	248,561	Pančevo	122,435
Kragujevac	180,192	Smederevo	116,592
Podgorica	168,069	Čačak	114,794

The 1991 census was not carried out in Kosovo and Metohija. 1991 estimated population: Priština, 155,499; Prizren, 92,303; Peć, 68,163; Kosovska Mitrovica, 64,323.

Main ethnic groups: Serbs, 62·1%; Albanians, 17·1%; Hungarians, 4·3%; Montenegrins, 4·3%; Croats, 3·1%; Gypsies, 1·4%; Slovaks, 0·9%; Romanians, 0·8%. At the 1991 census, 361,452 nationals worked abroad.

Refugees and internally displaced persons are estimated at about 600,000.

The official language is Serbian, the eastern variant (Croatian is the western) of Serbo-Croat. Serbian is written in the Cyrillic alphabet.

SOCIAL STATISTICS

2003 (excluding Kosovo and Metohija): live births, 87,370; deaths, 109,650; marriages, 45,964; divorces, 8,432. 2003 rates (per 1,000 population): birth, 10·7; death, 13·5; marriage, 5·6; infant mortality, 9·2 (per 1,000 live births). In 2001 the most popular age for marrying was 24 for males and 20 for females. Expectation of life in 2003: males, 70·0 years; females, 75·2. Annual population growth rate, 1992–2002, 0·2%. Fertility rate, 2001, 1·71 births per woman.

CLIMATE

Most parts have a central European type of climate, with cold winters and hot summers. 2000, Belgrade, Jan. −1·0°C, July 23·5°C. Annual rainfall 367·7 mm. Podgorica, Jan. 2·8°C, July 26·5°C. Annual rainfall 1,499 mm.

CONSTITUTION AND GOVERNMENT

The head of state is the *President*, elected by the members of the federal parliament for a non-renewable four-year term.

The union parliament, the *Assembly of Serbia and Montenegro*, has 126 members, 91 elected from the assembly of Serbia and 35 elected from the assembly of Montenegro for a term of four years. Its assent is necessary to all legislation. The Assembly elects the President and the five-member Cabinet, which has responsibility for foreign affairs, defence, human and minority rights, international economic relations and internal economic affairs.

National Anthem

'Hej, Slaveni, jošte živi reč naših dedova' ('O Slavs, our ancestors' words will live'), with words by S. Tomašik and tune anonymous, is the provisional anthem of Serbia and Montenegro.

GOVERNMENT CHRONOLOGY

Federal Presidents since 1992. (DPS = Democratic Party of Socialist; DSS = Serb Democratic Party; SPS = Socialist Party of Serbia; n/p = non-partisan)

1992–93	n/p	Dobrica Cosić
1993–97	SPS	Zoran Lilić
1997–2000	SPS	Slobodan Milošević
2000–03	DSS	Vojislav Koštunica
2003–	DPS	Svetozar Marović

RECENT ELECTIONS

Svetozar Marović, a Montenegrin and deputy leader of the Democratic Party of Socialists, was elected president by the members of the Union Assembly on 7 March 2003, receiving 65 votes, with 47 against.

On 25 Feb. 2003 the assemblies of Serbia and Montenegro elected deputies from their own number to serve concurrently as members of the Union Assembly. In these elections the Democratic Opposition of Serbia (DOS) gained 37 seats, the Democratic List for European Montenegro (DLECG) (including the Democratic Party of Socialists/DPS) 19, the Democratic Party of Serbia (DSS) 17, (Montenegrin) Together for Changes (ZP) 14, the Serb Socialist Party (SPS) 12, the Serb Radical Party (SRS) 8, the Social Democratic Party (SDP) 5, the Party of Serb Unity (SSJ) 5, the Christian Democratic Party of Serbia (DHSS) 2, the (Serb) Democratic Alternative (DA) 2, others 5.

CURRENT ADMINISTRATION

In March 2006 the government comprised the following:
Union President: Svetozar Marović; b. 1955 (Democratic Party of Socialists/DPS; sworn in 7 March 2003).
Minister for Defence: Zoran Stanković. *Foreign Affairs:* Vuk Drašković. *Human and Minority Rights:* Rasim Ljajić. *Internal Economic Affairs:* Amir Nurković. *International Economic Relations:* Prof. Predrag Ivanović.

Government Website: http://www.gov.yu

CURRENT LEADERS

Svetozar Marović

Position
President

Introduction
Svetozar Marović became the first president of the newly-constituted nation of Serbia and Montenegro in March 2003. A Montenegrin, he is deputy leader of the Democratic Party of Socialists (DPS) which advocates Montenegrin independence. On his election by the federal parliament, Marović was expected to push for increased integration into Europe and the European Union and promised greater co-operation with the UN War Crimes Tribunal in The Hague investigating atrocities in the Balkan wars of the 1990s.

Early Life
Marović was born on 31 March 1955 in Kotor on Montenegro's Adriatic coast. He graduated in law from the University of Podgorica and entered Montenegro's parliament in 1990 as a representative of the DPS. He later became a member of the Montenegrin presidency, parliamentary speaker, chairman of the foreign policy and international relations committee and member of the federal parliament. He was voted DPS vice-president, deputy to Montenegro's Prime Minister Milo Djukanović. He was also the founder of Budva's annual summer theatre festival.

In March 2002 the parliaments of Yugoslavia, Serbia and Montenegro agreed to replace the federation of Yugoslavia with the more loosely affiliated Serbia and Montenegro. Vojislav Koštunica gave up his position as head of state to stand for the Serbian presidency. Serbia and Montenegro officially came into being in Feb. 2003. It was agreed that the new entity's first president would be from Montenegro and Marović was the only candidate. He was approved by parliament in March 2003.

Career in Office
Marović's term of office was scheduled to last at least three years, at which point either republic could call a referendum on full independence. He was expected to pursue closer ties with the EU and NATO and promised to work with the War Crimes Tribunal in The Hague. Towards this aim he stated his ambition to place the army and police under more transparent civilian control. Within days of Marović's selection by parliament, Serbia and Montenegro faced political unrest following the assassination of Serbian Prime Minister Zoran Djindjić.

Marović promised to improve living standards throughout the country. He also suggested that he could favour a change in the status of Kosovo—the Albanian-dominated province which saw some of the heaviest fighting during the break-up of Yugoslavia during the 1990s—paving the way for eventual Albanian self-determination but with safeguards for the rights of Serbian and other minorities in the province. In June 2003 the government agreed to talks with the authorities in Kosovo, the first since 1999, to discuss practical issues including infrastructure and communications.

In Oct. 2005 Serbia and Montenegro began talks on a Stabilization and Association Agreement with the EU.

DEFENCE

Military service is for nine months. Military expenditure totalled US$642m. in 2003 (US$79 per capita), representing 3·0% of GDP. In 1985 expenditure had been US$2,904m.

Army

Personnel (2002) were about 60,000 (37,000 conscripts). In addition there are Ministry of Interior troops numbering about 40,000.

Navy

The Navy comprises four diesel submarines and three frigates. A Marine force of 900 is divided into two 'brigades'.

Personnel in 2002 totalled 3,500 including Marines. The force is based at Kotor.

Air Force

Personnel (2002) 11,000 (3,000 conscripts), with 103 combat aircraft and 442 armed helicopters.

INTERNATIONAL RELATIONS

The former Yugoslavia (SFRY) was a member of the UN and its self-proclaimed successor state (Federal Republic of Yugoslavia) was excluded during the Milošević era from the General Assembly and related bodies such as the IMF and World Bank. However, after Vojislav Koštunica became president in Oct. 2000 Yugoslavia was admitted both to the UN and the IMF. Serbia and Montenegro has succeeded the former Yugoslavia in membership of the UN. It is also a member of the Council of Europe, BSEC, Danube Commission, BIS and IOM.

ECONOMY

Overview

Serbia and Montenegro's economic performance has been turbulent since 1990. In the early 1990s the economy suffered from the consequences of years of socialist mismanagement and from the splintering of a previously integrated Yugoslav market. In 1991–93 the economy shrunk 23·4% per year on average. From 1994–98 the economy stabilized, averaging 5·5% annual GDP growth, but the US bombardment of the country in 1999 caused the economy to shrink by 24·4%. The economy suffered particularly from damaged infrastructure and economic sanctions. Much of the US$1·28bn. pledged by the USA, EU and World Bank to rebuild the country following the arrest of Slobodan Milošević went to the repayment of international debt.

A reform programme has been implemented to create a market economy but foreign investors have been reluctant to enter the market and the country's institutions remain weak. In the first half of the 2000s the economy grew at an annual average of 4·5%. The energy and light manufacturing industries have seen output growth while heavy industry has declined. Inflation remains high but is down from the hyperinflation of 2001. Unemployment has grown steadily since 1990, stabilizing at over 30% in recent years. Economic expansion in 2005 was driven principally by growth in the financial services and transport and communications sectors. The EU's decision to begin stabilization and association negotiations with Serbia and Montenegro has boosted investor interest in the country and in response the Serbian government is looking to step up the privatization of state assets.

Currency

The unit of currency of Serbia is the *dinar* (YUD) of 100 *paras*. On 1 Jan. 2001 Yugoslavia adopted a managed float regime. The National Bank of Yugoslavia began setting the exchange rate of the dinar daily in the foreign exchange market on the previous day. Montenegro adopted the euro as its sole legal currency on 1 Jan. 2002, having made the Deutsche Mark legal tender alongside the dinar on 2 Nov. 1999. In the new Serbia and Montenegro there is a National Bank of Serbia and a Central Bank of Montenegro. In Kosovo both the dinar and the euro are legal tender. Inflation declined from 91·1% in 2001 to 21·2% in 2002, and further to 11·3% in 2003 and 9·5% in 2004. In Dec. 2000 total foreign exchange reserves were US$890m. and in Dec. 2001 foreign exchange reserves reached US$1,808m. Total money supply was 111·2bn. dinars in Dec. 2004.

Budget

The federal budget for 2001 was set at US$4·3bn.

Performance

There was real GDP growth of 2·7% in 2003 and 7·2% in 2004 growth, but economic activity is recovering from a very low base. Total GDP in 2004 was US$24·0bn. (excluding Kosovo).

Banking and Finance

The banking system of Serbia and Montenegro consists of the central bank, commercial banks and other financial organizations, such as the Post Office Savings Bank, savings and credit organizations and savings and loan associations. The National Bank is the bank of issue responsible for monetary policy, stability of the currency of Serbia, the dinar, control of the money supply and prescribing the method of maintaining internal and external liquidity. The dinar became fully convertible in May 2002. The present *Governor* of the National Bank of Serbia is Radovan Jelašić. The National Bank of Montenegro is also recognized under the constitution.

There is a stock exchange in Belgrade.

ENERGY AND NATURAL RESOURCES

Environment

Serbia and Montenegro's carbon dioxide emissions from the consumption and flaring of fossil fuels were the equivalent of 4·2 tonnes per capita in 2002.

Electricity

Installed capacity in 2000 was 11·8m. kW. Output in 2004 (without Kosovo and Metohija), was 37,152m. kWh, of which 23,788m. kWh were thermal and 13,364m. kWh hydro-electric. Consumption per capita was 1,942 kWh in 2000 (without Kosovo and Metohija).

Oil and Gas

Crude oil production (2004, without Kosovo and Metohija), 652,000 tonnes; natural gas, 318m. cu. metres.

Minerals

Lignite production (2004, without Kosovo and Metohija), 35,267,000 tonnes; copper ore, 5,495,000 tonnes; bauxite, 610,000 tonnes.

Agriculture

In 2004 (without Kosovo and Metohija) there were 5,631,000 ha. of agricultural land, of which 4,441,000 ha. were arable (2,026,000 ha. cereals; 390,000 ha. fodder crops), 726,000 ha. meadow and 1,150,000 ha. pasture. In 2004, 3,840,000 ha. were in private farms and 601,000 ha. in agricultural organizations. In 2002 there were 1,047,000 ha. of permanent crops. The economically active agricultural population was 542,000 in 2002.

Crop production, 2004 (without Kosovo and Metohija, in 1,000 tonnes): maize, 6,579; sugarbeets, 2,814; wheat, 2,761; potatoes, 1,108; plums, 567; grapes, 467; soybeans, 318.

Livestock, 2005 (without Kosovo and Metohija, in 1,000): pigs, 3,189; sheep, 1,828; cattle, 1,254; goats (2004), 195; horses, 34; poultry, 17,521.

Livestock products, 2004 (without Kosovo and Metohija): meat, 462,000 tonnes; milk, 1,771,000 litres; eggs, 1,640m. In 2004, 157,835,000 litres of wine were produced.

Forestry

The forest area is 2,858,000 ha., of which 1,341,000 ha. are in private hands. Timber production in 2003 (without Kosovo and Metohija) was 3·05m. cu. metres.

Fisheries

In 2001 total catch was 1,088 tonnes (672 tonnes from inland waters).

INDUSTRY

In Dec. 2000 there were 211,195 enterprises and institutions, including 122,789 private enterprises, 439 public enterprises, 166 co-operatives and 1,983 social enterprises. In 2000 industrial production was only 39% of the 1989 total.

Industrial output (in 1,000 tonnes) in 2004 (without data for Kosovo and Metohija): cement, 2,240; crude steel, 1,175; pig iron, 959; residual fuel oil (2000), 461; sugar, 353; artificial fertilizers (2003), 293; distillate fuel oil (2000), 253; petrol (2000), 158; plastics (2001), 157; sulphuric acid, 62; passenger cars, 14,549 units; refrigerators (2002), 10,109 units; tractors, 4,245 units; TV sets (2003), 1,590 units; trucks, 647 units.

Labour

In 2004 there were 2,194,155 workers employed, including 510,000 in manufacturing, 232,000 in trade, 144,000 in education, 133,000 in transport and communications, 80,000 in public administration and social insurance, 72,000 in agriculture, forestry and water works supply and 37,000 in hotels and restaurants. In Oct. 2004 there were 690,753 self-employed people. Average monthly wage in 2004 (without Kosovo and Metohija) was 14,113 dinars. Unemployment in 2003 was officially 27·5%.

INTERNATIONAL TRADE

According to the law on foreign investments that was in force in 2000, foreign investors were allowed to make investments in all activities except those in the field of production and turnover of armaments, public information and communications systems, and restricted zones, where they could own up to 49% of capital. In 2000 there were 373 contracts on foreign investments registered. UN sanctions against Yugoslavia were lifted in Nov. 1995 following the Bosnian-Croatian-Yugoslav (Dayton) agreement on Bosnia. External debt was US$12,688m. in 2002.

Imports and Exports

Foreign trade, in US$1m., for calendar year:

	2001	2002	2003	2004
Imports	4,837	6,320	7,952	11,366
Exports	1,903	2,275	2,650	3,801

Breakdown by Standard International Trade Classification categories (value in US$1m.):

	Imports		Exports	
	2003	2004	2003	2004
0. Food and live animals	568	722	498	646
1. Beverages and tobacco	140	173	39	66
2. Crude materials	227	341	141	210
3. Fuels and lubricants	1,210	1,703	59	91
4. Animal and vegetable oils	17	18	17	62
5. Chemicals	1,066	1,469	246	392
6. Manufactured goods	1,598	2,218	839	1,376
7. Machinery and transport equipment	2,270	3,572	310	424

	Imports		Exports	
	2003	2004	2003	2004
8. Miscellaneous manufactured items	766	1,086	457	510
9. Other	90	64	44	24

Main trading partners, 2003 (imports and exports in US$1m.): Germany, 1,081 and 288; Russia, 1,033 and 127; Italy, 806 and 358; Bosnia-Herzegovina, 224 and 397; France, 289 and 115; Macedonia, 140 and 220.

COMMUNICATIONS

Roads

In 2004 (without data for Kosovo and Metohija) there were 45,818 km of roads comprising 5,916 km of main roads, 11,311 km of regional roads and 28,591 km of other roads. In 2004 there were 1,554,080 passenger cars, 147,385 trucks and vans, and 9,817 buses and coaches. Passenger-km in 2004, without Kosovo and Metohija, were 3,777m. (public transport); tonne-km of freight carried, 342m. There were 1,048 deaths in road accidents in 2000.

Rail

In 2004 there were 4,059 km of railway, of which 1,415 km were electrified. 8,753,000 passengers and 6,478,000 tonnes of freight were carried.

Civil Aviation

There are five airports, the chief ones being at Belgrade and Tivat. The national carrier is JAT (Jugoslovenski Aero Transport) which operates internal flights and in 2003 flew to most major centres in Europe and the Middle East. In March 2003 the airline stated it would retain its name despite the change of name of the country.

Shipping

In 2004 Serbia and Montenegro possessed two sea-going passenger vessels and one cargo vessel. Length of navigable waterways (2001), 1,419 km. In 2004 there were 468 cargo vessels and 3,295,000 tonnes of freight were transported.

Telecommunications

Telephone subscribers numbered 5,243,400 in 2002 (489·1 for every 1,000 persons) and there were 290,000 PCs in use (27·1 per 1,000 persons). There were 2,750,400 mobile phone subscribers in 2002 and 20,000 fax machines in 1999. In 2002 there were 640,000 Internet users.

Postal Services

There were 1,706 post offices in 2004.

SOCIAL INSTITUTIONS

Justice

In 2002 there were two supreme courts, 32 district courts and 153 communal courts, with 2,390 judges and 8,080 lay assessors (without data for Montenegro). There were also 19 economic courts with 262 judges.

In 2002, 35,548 criminal sentences were passed.

The death penalty was abolished for all crimes in 2001.

Education

Compulsory primary education lasts eight years, secondary 3–4 years. In 2004 (without data for Kosovo and Metohija) there were 1,922 nursery schools with 174,017 pupils and 19,164 employees of which 9,680 were teachers. In 2003–04 there were 4,051 primary schools with 737,575 pupils and 49,897 teachers, and 536 secondary schools with 334,502 pupils and 29,061 teachers. In 2000–01 there were 51 institutions of tertiary education with 50,901 students and 1,612 teachers, and 87 institutions of higher education with 151,568 full-time students and 10,027 academic staff.

Adult literacy rate, 1995, 97·9% (male, 98·6%; female, 97·3%).

In 1999–2000 total expenditure on education came to 5·1% of GNP.

Health

In 2002 there were 21,455 doctors, 3,663 dentists, 1,945 pharmacists and 50,702 hospital beds.

Welfare

In 2000 there were 1,349,252 pensioners, of whom 557,754 were old age, 431,527 disability and 339,971 survivors' pensioners. 7,229,004 working days were lost through sickness. In 1999 pensions and disability insurance totalled 25,534,514,000 dinars; old age pension, 8,511,079,000 dinars; and disability, 4,866,896,000 dinars. In 1999, 1,353m. dinars were paid in child allowances.

RELIGION

Religious communities are separate from the State and are free to perform religious affairs. All religious communities recognized by law enjoy the same rights. Religious breakdown, 2001: Serbian Orthodox, 6·7m.; Muslims, 2·0m.; Roman Catholics, 0·6m.

Serbia has been traditionally Orthodox. Muslims are found in the south as a result of the Turkish occupation. The Serbian Orthodox Church with its seat in Belgrade has 27 bishoprics within the boundaries of former Yugoslavia and 12 abroad (five in the USA and Canada, five in Europe and two in Australia). The Serbian Orthodox Church numbers about 2,000 priests. Its *Patriarch* is Pavle (enthroned 2 Dec. 1990).

As well as in Serbia, the Serbian Orthodox Church is the official church in Montenegro. The Montenegrin church was banned in 1922, but in Oct. 1993 a breakaway Montenegrin church was set up under its own patriarch.

Relations with the Vatican are regulated by a 'Protocol' of 1966.

The Jewish religion has nine communities making up a common league of Jewish Communities with its seat in Belgrade.

CULTURE

World Heritage Sites

There are five sites on the UNESCO World Heritage List: the Natural and Culturo-Historical Region of Kotor (inscribed on the list in 1979); Stari Ras and Sopoćani (1979); Durmitor National Park (1980); Studenica Monastery (1986); Dečani Monastery (2004).

Broadcasting

In 2001 (without data for Kosovo and Metohija) there were 70 TV centres (24 private) with 291,324 hours of programme, of which information and documentary 66,990 hours; and 184 broadcasting radio stations (80 private) with 1,004,000 hours of programme, of which 150,000 information and documentary. There were 2,282,000 TV (colour by PAL) and 1,143,000 radio receivers in use in 2001.

Cinema

In 2001 (without data for Kosovo and Metohija) there were 167 cinemas. Cinema attendances were 4,017,000; in 2000, three full-length films were made.

Press

In 2001 there were 27 dailies, 580 other newspapers and 491 periodicals. 4,643 book titles (840 by foreign authors) were published in 2001 in a total of 6,189,000 copies.

Tourism

There were 2,075,000 foreign tourists in 2004 (excluding Kosovo and Metohija). Tourist receipts totalled US$77m in 2002.

Libraries

In 1998 (without data for Kosovo and Metohija) there were three National, 689 public, 143 Higher Education and eleven non-specialized libraries with a combined 33,681,000 volumes and 8,332,811 registered users.

Museums and Galleries

In 2000 (without data for Kosovo and Metohija) there were 32 art galleries with 1,055 exhibitions and 142 museums with 1,361,000 visitors.

DIPLOMATIC REPRESENTATIVES

Of Serbia and Montenegro in the United Kingdom (28 Belgrave Sq., London, SW1X 8QB)
Ambassador: Dragiša Burzan.

Of the United Kingdom in Serbia and Montenegro (Resavska 46, 11000 Belgrade)
Ambassador: David Gowan.

Of Serbia and Montenegro in the USA (2134 Kalorama Rd, NW, Washington, D.C., 20008)
Ambassador: Ivan Vujacić.

Of the USA in Serbia and Montenegro (Kneza Miloša, 50, 11000 Belgrade)
Ambassador: Michael C. Polt.

Of Serbia and Montenegro to the United Nations
Ambassador: Nebojša Kaludjerović.

Of Serbia and Montenegro to the European Union
Ambassador: Pavle Jevremović.

FURTHER READING

Federal Statistical Office. *Statistical Yearbook.*

Allcock, J. B., *Explaining Yugoslavia.* Columbia Univ. Press, 2000
Anzulovic, Branimir, *Heavenly Serbia: From Myth to Genocide.* C. Hurst, London, 1999
Bennett, C., *Yugoslavia's Bloody Collapse: Causes, Course and Consequences.* Farnborough, 1995
Bokovoy, M. K., *et al.,* (eds.) *State-Society Relations in Yugoslavia 1945–1992.* London, 1997
Carpenter, Ted Galen, (ed.) *Nato's Empty Victory.* Cato Institute, Washington, D.C., 2000
Cohen, L. J., *Broken Bonds: the Disintegration of Yugoslavia.* Boulder (CO), 1993
Dijlas, A., *The Contested Country: Yugoslav Unity and the Communist Revolution, 1919–1953.* Harvard Univ. Press, 1991
Dyker, D. and Vejvoda, I. (eds.) *Yugoslavia and After: a Study in Fragmentation, Despair and Rebirth.* Harlow, 1996
Friedman, F. (ed.) *Yugoslavia: a Comprehensive English-Language Bibliography.* London, 1993
Glenny, M., *The Fall of Yugoslavia.* London, 1992
Gow, J., *Triumph of the Lack of Will: International Diplomacy and the Yugoslav War.* London and Columbia Univ. Press, 1997
Judah, Tim, *The Serbs: History, Myth and the Destruction of Yugoslavia.* Yale Univ. Press, 1997.—*Kosovo: War and Revenge.* Yale Univ. Press, 2000
Magaš, B., *The Destruction of Yugoslavia: Tracking the Break-up, 1980–92.* London, 1993
Thomas, Robert, *Serbia Under Milosevic: Politics in the 1990s.* C. Hurst, London, 1999
Udovicki, J., and Ridgeway, J. (eds.) *Burn This House: The Making and Unmaking of Yugoslavia.* Duke, 1997
Woodward, S. L., *Balkan Tragedy: Chaos and Dissolution after the Cold War.* Brookings Institution (Washington), 1995

National Statistical Office: Federal Statistical Office, Kneza Miloša 20, 11000 Belgrade. *Director:* Dr Ranko Nedeljković.
Website: http://www.szs.sv.gov.yu

REPUBLICS AND PROVINCES

In Feb. 2003 the new Union of Serbia and Montenegro comprised the two republics of Montenegro and Serbia, and the two provinces of Kosovo and Metohija, and Vojvodina within Serbia.

Montenegro

KEY HISTORICAL EVENTS

Montenegro emerged as a separate entity on the break-up of the Serbian Empire in 1355. Owing to its mountainous terrain, it was never effectively subdued by Turkey. It was ruled by Bishop Princes until 1851, when a royal house was founded. The Treaty of Berlin (1828) recognized the independence of Montenegro and doubled the size of the territory. The remains of King Nicholas I, who was deposed in 1918, were returned to Montenegro for reburial in Oct. 1989. Though part of the Yugoslav federation, Montenegro holds jealously to its independence and tries to keep its political distance from Serbia.

On 14 March 2002 Montenegro and Serbia agreed to a new structure for the Yugoslav federation. Following European Union-brokered talks it was agreed that they would remain part of a single entity called Serbia and Montenegro, thus relegating the name Yugoslavia to history. On 9 April 2002 the parliaments of Serbia and Montenegro ratified the agreement on the redefinition of relations between the two republics, and on 31 May 2002 the Yugoslav federal parliament also adopted the proposals. A Constitutional Commission completed the drafting of a Constitutional Charter in Dec. 2002. A referendum was scheduled to be held on 21 May 2006 to decide whether to break away from Serbia. For details, *see* Addenda, page xxxi.

TERRITORY AND POPULATION

Montenegro is a mountainous region which opens to the Adriatic in the southwest. It is bounded in the west by Croatia, northwest by Bosnia-Herzegovina, in the northeast by Serbia and in the southeast by Albania. The capital is Podgorica (population, 2003, 136,473), although some capital functions have been transferred to Cetinje, the historic capital of the former kingdom of Montenegro. Its area is 13,812 sq. km. Population at the 2003 census was 620,145 (314,920 females), of which the predominating ethnic groups were Montenegrins (267,669), Serbs (198,414) and Albanians (31,163). Population density per sq. km (2003), 44·9.

SOCIAL STATISTICS

Statistics for calendar years:

	Live births	Deaths	Marriages	Divorces
2001	8,839	5,431	3,893	492
2002	8,499	5,513	3,794	506
2003	8,344	5,704	4,050	494
2004	7,849	5,707	3,440	505

CONSTITUTION AND GOVERNMENT

There is a 75-member single-chamber National Assembly.

A referendum was held on 29 Feb.–1 March 1992 to determine whether Montenegro should remain within a common state, Yugoslavia, as a sovereign republic. The electorate was 412,000, of whom 66% were in favour. President Milo Djukanović had pledged a referendum on independence in May 2002, but this was postponed with the announcement of the creation of the new entity of Serbia and Montenegro, which came into being on 4 Feb. 2003. Montenegro was scheduled to hold a referendum on independence on 21 May 2006. For details, *see* Addenda, page xxxi.

RECENT ELECTIONS

Parliamentary elections were held on 20–21 Oct. 2002. President Milo Djukanović's pro-independence Democratic List for a European Montenegro (including the Democratic Socialist Party) won 39 out of 75 seats with 44·8% of votes cast; the 'Together for Changes' coalition won 30 with 35·9%; the Liberal Alliance, 4 with 5·4%; and the 'Albanians Together' Democratic Coalition, 2 with 2·3%. Turnout was 77·5%.

In presidential elections held on 22 Dec. 2002 acting president Filip Vujanović won 83·9% of the vote but the result was not valid because the turnout was less than the required 50%. A follow-up election on 9 Feb. 2003 also failed with a turnout of 47·7%. Parliament's subsequent amendment of the law on turnout allowed Vujanović to claim victory on 11 May 2003 with 63·3% against Miodrag Zivković with 30·8% and Dragan Hajduković with 3·9%. Turnout was 48·5%.

CURRENT ADMINISTRATION

President: Filip Vujanović; b. 1954 (sworn in on 22 May 2003).

Prime Minister: Milo Djukanović; b. 1962 (sworn in on 8 Jan. 2003).

Government Website: http://www.montenegro.yu

ECONOMY

Currency
On 2 Nov. 1999 the pro-Western government decided to make the Deutsche Mark legal tender alongside the dinar. Subsequently it was made the sole official currency, and consequently the euro became the currency of Montenegro on 1 Jan. 2002.

Budget
In 2004 total revenue was €77,568m. and total expenditure was €75,839m.

Banking and Finance
The Central Bank of Montenegro (*President of the Council,* Ljubisa Krgović) was established in Nov. 2000. Montenegro has 11 commercial banks.

ENERGY AND NATURAL RESOURCES

Electricity
Electricity production in 2004 was 3·31m. kWh.

Minerals
Lignite production in 2004 totalled 1,514,264 tonnes; bauxite production was 610,000 tonnes.

Agriculture
In 2004 the cultivated area was 188,766 ha. Yields (2004, in 1,000 tonnes): potatoes, 117; grapes, 43; maize, 10; oranges and tangerines, 7; plums, 6; wheat, 3. Livestock (15 Jan. 2005, 1,000 head): poultry, 800; sheep, 254; cattle, 169; pigs, 27.

Forestry
Timber cut in 2004: 527,165 cu. metres.

INDUSTRY

Production (1997): heavy semi-manufactures, 24,807 tonnes; cotton carded yarn, 166 tonnes.

Labour
In 2004 there were 143,485 people employed, including 26,277 in manufacturing; 24,105 in wholesale and retail trade, repair of vehicles, personal and household goods; 14,146 in transport, storage and communications; 13,098 in education; 11,606 in health and social work; 9,563 in hotels and restaurants; and 9,337 in public administration and compulsory social security. In Oct. 2004 there were 49,266 employees and 31,328 self-employed persons. Average monthly salary in 2004 was €302·81. Unemployment was running at 27·7% in Oct. 2004.

COMMUNICATIONS

Roads
In 2004 there were 7,314 km of roads. Passenger-km in 2004 were 100·6m.; tonne-km of freight carried, 64·5m.

Rail
In 2004 there were 250 km of railway. 1,066,000 passengers and 1,006,000 tonnes of freight were carried in 2004.

SOCIAL INSTITUTIONS

Justice
In 1997 there were two District Courts, 15 Communal Courts and two Economic courts of law with 222 judges.

Education
In 2004–05 there were: 82 pre-schools with 11,761 pupils and 673 teachers; 457 primary schools with 74,205 pupils and 4,796 teachers; and 47 secondary schools with 32,078 pupils and 2,245 teachers. A total of 11,011 students were enrolled at the University of Montenegro at the beginning of the 2004–05 academic year.

CULTURE

Broadcasting
In 2004 Montenegro had 31 radio stations and 13 television centres and studios.

Tourism
There were 703,484 tourist arrivals in 2004, staying for a total of 4,561,094 nights.

FURTHER READING

Treadway, J. D., *The Falcon and the Eagle: Montenegro and Austria-Hungary, 1908–1914.* Purdue University Press, 1998

Serbia

KEY HISTORICAL EVENTS

The Serbs received Orthodox Christianity from the Byzantines in 891, but shook off the latter's suzerainty to form a prosperous state, firmly established under Stevan Nemanja (1167–96). A Serbian Patriarchate was established at Peć during the reign of Stevan Dušan (1331–55). Dušan planned the conquest of Constantinople, but he was forestalled by incursions of Turks. After he died many Serbian nobles accepted Turkish vassalage; the reduced Serbian state under Prince Lazar received the coup de grace at Kosovo on St Vitus day, 1389. Turkish preoccupations with a Mongol invasion and wars with Hungary, however, postponed the total incorporation of Serbia into the Ottoman Empire until 1459.

The Turks permitted the Orthodox church to practise, though the Patriarchate was abolished in 1776. The native aristocracy was eliminated and replaced by a system of fiefdoms held in return for military or civil service. Local self-government based on rural extended family units (*zadruga*) continued. In its heyday the Ottoman system probably bore no harder on the peasantry than the Christian feudalism it had replaced, but with the gradual decline of Ottoman power, corruption, oppression and reprisals led to economic deterioration and social unrest.

In 1804 murders carried out by mutinous Turkish infantry provoked a Serbian rising under Djordje Karadjordje. The

Sultan's army disciplined the mutineers, but was then defeated by the intransigent Serbs. By the Treaty of Bucharest (1812), however, Russia agreed that Serbia, known as Servia until 1918, should remain Turkish. The Turks reoccupied Serbia with ferocious reprisals. A new rebellion broke out in 1815 under Miloš Obrenović which, this time with Russian support, won autonomy for Serbia within the Ottoman empire. Obrenović had Karadjordje murdered in 1817. In 1838 he was forced to grant a constitution establishing an appointed state council, and abdicated in 1839. In 1842 a coup overthrew the Obrenovićs and Alexander Karadjordjević was elected as ruler. He was deposed in 1858.

During the reign of the western-educated Michael Obrenović (1860 until his assassination in 1868) the foundations of a modern centralized and militarized state were laid, and the idea of a 'Great Serbia', first enunciated in Prime Minister Garašanin's *Draft Programme* of 1844, took root. Milan Obrenović, adopting the title of king, proclaimed formal independence in 1882. He suffered defeats against Turkey (1876) and Bulgaria (1885) and abdicated in 1889. Alexander Obrenović was assassinated in 1903, and replaced by Peter Karadjordjević, who brought in a period of stable constitutional rule.

In its foreign policy, Serbia's striving for an outlet to the sea was consistently thwarted by Austria. Annexing Bosnia in 1908, Austria forced the Serbs to withdraw from the Adriatic after the first Balkan war (1912).

Following the break-up of Yugoslavia, in March 1998 a coalition government was formed between the Socialist Party of Slobodan Milošević and the ultra-nationalist Radical Party.

On 14 March 2002 Serbia and Montenegro agreed to a new structure for the Yugoslav federation. Following European Union-brokered talks it was agreed that they would remain part of a single entity called Serbia and Montenegro, thus relegating the name Yugoslavia to history. On 9 April 2002 the parliaments of Serbia and Montenegro ratified the agreement on the redefinition of relations between the two republics, and on 31 May 2002 the Yugoslav federal parliament also adopted the proposals. A Constitutional Commission completed the drafting of a Constitutional Charter in Dec. 2002, which was ratified by both republics in Jan. 2003, reviewable after three years.

TERRITORY AND POPULATION

Serbia is bounded in the northwest by Croatia, in the north by Hungary, in the northeast by Romania, in the east by Bulgaria, in the south by Macedonia and in the west by Albania, Montenegro and Bosnia-Herzegovina. It includes the two provinces (formerly autonomous) of Kosovo and Metohija in the south and Vojvodina in the north. With these Serbia's area is 88,361 sq. km; without, 55,968 sq. km. The capital is Belgrade (2002 census population, 1,120,092). Population at the 2002 census was (with Vojvodina) 7,498,001, of which the predominating ethnic group was Serbs (6,212,838); population density per sq. km, 97·7. 2002 census population (without Kosovo and Vojvodina), 5,466,009, of which the predominating ethnic group was Serbs (4,891,031); population density per sq. km, 96·8.

SOCIAL STATISTICS

In 2003 there were a total of 58,644 live births in Serbia (without Kosovo and Vojvodina), a rate of 10·7 per 1,000 inhabitants. There were 74,205 deaths (13·6 per 1,000) and 30,787 marriages (5·6 per 1,000). Rate of natural increase in 2003: –2·9 per 1,000 population.

CONSTITUTION AND GOVERNMENT

There is a 250-member single-chamber National Assembly. The *President* is elected by universal suffrage for not more than two five-year terms.

In Sept. 1990 a new constitution was adopted by the National Assembly. It defined Serbia as a 'democratic' instead of a 'socialist' republic, laid down a framework for multi-party elections, and described Serbia as 'united and sovereign on all its territory', thus stripping Kosovo and Vojvodina of the attributes of autonomy granted by the 1974 federal constitution.

RECENT ELECTIONS

Elections to the Serbian National Assembly were held on 28 Dec. 2003. The Srpska Radikalna Stranka (SRS; Serb Radical Party) won 82 seats (27·7% of the vote); the Demokratska Stranka Srbije (DSS; Democratic Party of Serbia), 53 (18·0%); the Demokratska Stranka (DS; Democratic Party), 37 (12·6%); G17 Plus, 34 (11·7%); SPO-NS, 23 (7·7%); and the Socijalisticka Partija Srbije (SPS; Serb Socialist Party), 21 (7·7%). Five other parties or coalitions failed to win seats. Turnout was 59·3%. Following the election a coalition government was formed between DSS, G17 Plus and SPO-NS.

In the first round of presidential elections held on 29 Sept. 2002 Yugoslav President Vojislav Koštunica won 30·9% of votes cast, with 27·4% of the vote going to Miroljub Labus and 23·2% for Vojislav Seselj, the favoured candidate of former premier Slobodan Milošević. Turnout was 55·5%. A run-off between Koštunica and Labus took place on 13 Oct. 2002 but was declared invalid owing to a turnout of 45·5%—less than the legally-required 50%. A further attempt to hold a new election on 8 Dec. 2002 again failed when fewer than 50% of the electorate voted. A third attempt on 16 Nov. 2003 also failed for the same reason. In Feb. 2004 parliament abolished the 50% turnout requirement. Another round of elections was held in June 2004. In the first round, on 13 June, Tomislav Nikolić (SRS) took 30·4% of the vote, followed by Boris Tadić (DS) with 27·6%, Bogoljub Karić with 18·2% and Dragan Maršićanin (DSS) with 13·3%. Turnout was 47·6%. In the run-off on 27 June Tadić took 53·7%, defeating Nikolić with 45·0%. Turnout was 48·7%.

CURRENT ADMINISTRATION

President: Boris Tadić; b. 1958 (DS; took office on 11 July 2004).

Prime Minister: Vojislav Koštunica; b. 1944 (DSS; took office on 3 March 2004).

Government Website: http://www.serbia.sr.gov.yu

ECONOMY

Budget
In 2003 total revenue was 366,504m. dinars; total expenditure was 353,329m. dinars. VAT at 18% (reduced rate 8%) was introduced on 1 Jan. 2005.

ENERGY AND NATURAL RESOURCES

Electricity
Electricity production in 2004 was 33·87m. kWh.

Minerals
(Excluding Kosovo and Vojvodina, in 1,000 tonnes). 2004: lignite, 33,753; copper ore, 5,495 tonnes.

Agriculture
(Excluding Kosovo and Vojvodina). In 2004 the cultivated area was an estimated 2,604,000 ha. Yields in 2004 (in 1,000 tonnes): maize, 2,843; wheat, 1,195; potatoes, 692; plums, 515; grapes, 343; cabbage and kale, 273; tomatoes, 128; sugarbeets, 125. Livestock estimates (in 1,000): cattle, 867; pigs, 1,975; sheep, 1,381; poultry, 10,808.

Forestry
Timber cut in 2004: 2,691,000 cu. metres.

INDUSTRY

(Excluding Kosovo and Vojvodina). 2004: rolled steel, 1,543,453 tonnes; cement, 1,332,000 tonnes; pig iron, 959,019 tonnes;

cotton fabrics, 5,852,000 sq. metres; woollen fabrics, 144,000 sq. metres; cars, 13,516 units; lorries, 647 units.

Labour

In Oct. 2004 there were 2,930,846 workers employed (without Kosovo and Metohija), including 700,681 in agriculture, forestry and water supply; 551,429 in manufacturing; 441,800 in wholesale and retail trade and repair; 170,861 in public administration and social insurance; 166,619 in health and social work; and 163,628 in transport, storage and communications. In Oct. 2004 there were 2,059,417 employees and 659,427 self-employed persons. Average annual salary in Sept. 2004 (without Kosovo and Metohija) was 21,085 dinars. Unemployment was running at 18·5% with Vojvodina in Oct. 2004 and 18·4% without.

SOCIAL INSTITUTIONS

Justice

In 2002 there was one Supreme Court, 30 District Courts and 138 Communal Courts with 2,180 judges and 17 Economic Courts of Law with 237 judges.

Education

In 2003–04 there were: 1,804 kindergartens and pre-schools with 161,938 pupils; 3,592 primary schools with 664,577 pupils; 491 secondary schools with 303,596 pupils; and 223 high and higher schools with 218,368 students.

FURTHER READING

Judah, T., *The Serbs: History, Myth and the Destruction of Yugoslavia.* Yale Univ. Press, 1997

Kosovo and Metohija

KEY HISTORICAL EVENTS

Kosovo has a large ethnic Albanian majority. Following Albanian-Serb conflicts, the Kosovo and Serbian parliaments adopted constitutional amendments in March 1989 surrendering much of Kosovo's autonomy to Serbia. Renewed Albanian rioting broke out in 1990. The Prime Minister and six other ministers resigned in April 1990 over ethnic conflicts. In July 1990, 114 of the 130 Albanian members of the National Assembly voted for full republican status for Kosovo but the Serbian National Assembly declared this vote invalid and unanimously voted to dissolve the Kosovo Assembly. Direct Serbian rule was imposed causing widespread violence. Western demands for negotiations in granting Kosovo some kind of special status were rejected. Ibrahim Rugova, the leader of the main Albanian party, the Democratic League of Kosovo (LDK), declared himself 'president' demanding talks on independence. In 1998 armed conflict between Yugoslavia and the Kosovo Liberation Army led to 200,000 people, or a tenth of the population of the whole province, fleeing the fighting. Further repression by Serbian forces led to the threat of NATO direct action. Air strikes against Yugoslavian military targets began on 24 March 1999. Retaliation against Albanian Kosovars led to a massive exodus of refugees. On 9 June after 78 days of air attacks NATO and Yugoslavia signed an accord on the Serb withdrawal from Kosovo, and on 11 June NATO's peacekeeping force, KFOR, entered Kosovo. In Nov. 2001 the Organization for Security and Co-operation in Europe mounted elections for a provincial assembly that were deemed fair and democratic.

TERRITORY AND POPULATION

Area: 10,887 sq. km. The capital is Priština. The 1991 census was not taken. Population estimate of Kosovo and Metohija, 1991, 1,956,196 (1,596,072 Albanians, 194,190 Serbs); density, 179·7 per sq. km. In 2002 the estimated population was 1,970,000, made up of 88% Albanians, 7% Serbs and 5% others. Population estimate of Priština, 1997, 242,000.

SOCIAL STATISTICS

Statistics for 2004: live births, 33,897; deaths, 6,255; marriages, 16,938; divorces, 1,329.

CONSTITUTION AND GOVERNMENT

Kosovo is presently under interim international administration, sanctioned by the UN Security Council resolution 1244 of 10 June 1999. The United Nations Interim Administration Mission in Kosovo (UNMIK) has administered Kosovo since the arrival of KFOR (NATO-led peacekeeping force).

There is a 120-member multi-ethnic parliamentary assembly, which first convened on 10 Dec. 2001. The new assembly brought together representatives of Kosovo's ethnic Albanian majority and its Serbian minority for the first time in more than a decade.

RECENT ELECTIONS

Parliamentary elections held on 23 Oct. 2004; turnout was 51%. The Democratic League of Kosovo won 49 seats with 45·3% of the vote, the Democratic Party of Kosovo 31 with 28·7%, the Alliance for the Future of Kosovo 9 with 8·3%, the Ora Party 9 with 6·3%, the Albanian Christian Democratic Party of Kosovo 2 with 1·8%, the Turkish Democratic Party of Kosovo 2 with 1·4% and the Justice Party 2 with 1·0%. Following the election the Democratic League of Kosovo formed a coalition government with the Alliance for the Future of Kosovo.

Ibrahim Rugova was re-elected president by parliament on 3 Dec. 2004. He received 64 votes with 32 against. On the same day parliament elected Ramush Haradinaj prime minister by 72 votes to 3 against.

CURRENT ADMINISTRATION

President: Dr Fatmir Sejdiu; b. 1951 (Democratic League of Kosovo; since 10 Feb. 2006).

Prime Minister: Agim Çeku; b. 1960 (Alliance for the Future of Kosovo; since 10 March 2006).

Special Representative and Head of the United Nations Interim Administration in Kosovo (UNMIK): Søren Jessen-Petersen (Denmark; took office on 16 Aug. 2004).

UNMIK Website: http://www.unmikonline.org

ECONOMY

Budget

Total revenue in 2003 was €835·3m., including €184·6m. in international aid. Total expenditure was €791·6m.

Banking and Finance

In Aug. 1999 the Deutsche Mark became legal tender alongside the Yugoslav dinar, and on 1 Jan. 2002 the euro became the official currency of Kosovo. The Serb dinar is also legal tender in Kosovo but is used only by ethnic Serbs.

ENERGY AND NATURAL RESOURCES

Electricity

Electricity production in 1997 was 4·87m. kWh.

Minerals

Production (1997): lignite, 8,421,991 tonnes.

Agriculture

The cultivated area in 2004 was 264,340 ha. Yields in 2004 (in 1,000 tonnes): wheat, 197; maize, 92; potatoes, 56; peppers, 40; plums, 16. Livestock (in 1,000): cattle, 241; milch cows, 129; sheep, 124; pigs, 47; chickens, 1,617.

Forestry

Timber cut in 1997: 130,000 cu. metres.

INDUSTRY

Production (1997): cement, 89,528 tonnes; sulphuric acid, 26,900 tonnes.

Labour

In 1997 there were 120,763 workers in the public sector, including 54,223 in industry, 10,471 in education and culture, 9,245 in trade, catering and tourism, 8,933 in transport and communications, 7,880 in communities and organizations and 1,526 in commercial services. In Oct. 1997 in the private sector there were 35,869 self-employed and employed, including 15,113 in trade, 5,023 in catering and tourism, 4,364 in arts and crafts and 2,006 in transport and communications. Average monthly salary in Dec. 1998 was 1,066 dinars.

COMMUNICATIONS

Roads

In 2004 there were 1,925 km of main and regional roads in Kosovo. Total vehicle registrations in April 2003 were 234,297.

Rail

Total length of railways in 2004 was 333 km.

Civil Aviation

There is an international airport at Priština, which handled 884,098 passengers in 2002.

Telecommunications

In 2003 there were 101,059 main telephone lines and 315,000 mobile phones.

SOCIAL INSTITUTIONS

Justice

In 2004 there were five district courts and 23 municipal courts.

Education

In 2002–03 there were: 465 pre-schools and nurseries with 1,018 teachers and 20,365 pupils; 992 primary schools with 15,733 teachers and 299,934 pupils; and 128 secondary schools with 5,439 teachers and 89,387 pupils. In 2001–02, 21,216 students attended the University of Priština.

FURTHER READING

Malcolm, N., *Kosovo: a Short History.* New York Univ. Press, 1998
Vickers, M., *Between Serb and Albanian: A History of Kosovo.* C. Hurst, London, 1998

Vojvodina

KEY HISTORICAL EVENTS

After the Battle of Kosovo in 1389 Turkish attacks on the Balkans led to mass migrations of Serbian people to Vojvodina. Turkish rule ended after their 1716–18 war with Austria and the Požarevac peace agreement. In exchange for acting as frontier protectors, the Austrians granted the people of Vojvodina freedom of confession and religious autonomy. However, by 1848 discontent had brewed and a short-lived revolution occurred, in which the Serbs formed an alliance with the Croats, and Vojvodina was briefly declared as an independent dukedom. After the First World War Vojvodina became part of the first Yugoslav state. In 1974 President Tito granted autonomy to Vojvodina, but this status was brought into question after Vojvodina's largely anti-Milošević provincial assembly resigned their positions in 1988. In 1989 the Serbian government, led by Slobodan Milošević, stripped Vojvodina of most of its autonomous rights and secured Serbian control. Since the fall of Milošević in Oct. 2000 there

have again been demands for increased autonomy. However, the Assembly of Vojvodina has now only very limited powers.

TERRITORY AND POPULATION

Area: 21,506 sq. km. The capital is Novi Sad. Population of Vojvodina at the 2002 census, 2,031,992 (1,321,807 Serbs, 290,207 Hungarians); density, 94·5 per sq. km. Population of Novi Sad, 2002, 191,405.

SOCIAL STATISTICS

In 2003 there were a total of 20,381 live births in Vojvodina, a rate of 9·9 per 1,000 inhabitants. There were 29,741 deaths (14·4 per 1,000) and 11,127 marriages (5·4 per 1,000). Rate of natural increase in 2003: –4·5 per 1,000.

CONSTITUTION AND GOVERNMENT

The 1990 Serbian constitution deprived Vojvodina of its autonomy. Serbo-Croat was declared the only official language in 1991.

RECENT ELECTIONS

In March 2003 the Assembly of Vojvodina comprised 120 deputies, of which the Democratic Opposition of Serbia had 117 seats and the coalition of the Socialist Party of Serbia and Yugoslav Left two.

CURRENT ADMINISTRATION

President of the Assembly: Bojan Kostreš; b. 1974 (in office since 30 Oct. 2004).

Chairman of the Executive Council: Bojan Pajtić; b. 1970 (in office since 30 Oct. 2004).

Government Website: http://www.vojvodina.sr.gov.yu

ECONOMY

Budget

In 2003 total revenue was 66,538m. dinars; total expenditure was 59,234m. dinars.

ENERGY AND NATURAL RESOURCES

Electricity

Electricity production in 2004 was 526m. kWh.

Agriculture

The cultivated area in 2004 was an estimated 1,648,000 ha. Yields (in 1,000 tonnes): maize, 3,726; sugarbeets, 2,689; wheat, 1,563; potatoes, 283. Livestock estimates (in 1,000): cattle, 212; sheep, 195; pigs, 1,190; poultry, 5,823.

Forestry

Timber cut in 2004: 699,000 cu. metres.

INDUSTRY

Production (2004): cement, 908,000 tonnes; fertilizers, 651,166 tonnes; crude petroleum, 640,000 tonnes; plastics, 179,000 tonnes.

Labour

In Oct. 2004 there were 748,809 persons employed, including 175,673 in manufacturing; 163,738 in agriculture, forestry and water works supply; 114,868 in wholesale and retail trade and repair; 42,170 in construction; 40,979 in health and social work; and 38,176 in transport, storage and communications. In Oct. 2004 there were 569,488 employees and 154,801 self-employed persons. Unemployment was 18·8% in Oct. 2004.

SOCIAL INSTITUTIONS

Education

In 2003–04 there were: 620 kindergartens and pre-schools with 46,696 pupils; 535 primary schools with 178,905 pupils; 124 secondary schools with 78,008 pupils; and 50 high and higher schools with 46,273 students.

SEYCHELLES

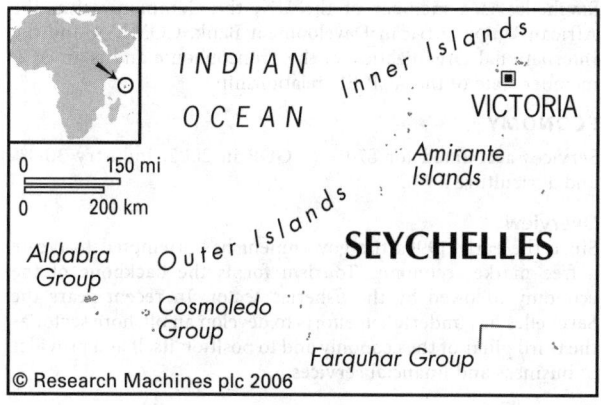

© Research Machines plc 2006

Republic of Seychelles

Capital: Victoria
Population, 2001: 81,000
GDP per capita, 2002: (PPP$) 10,232
HDI/world rank: 0·821/51

KEY HISTORICAL EVENTS

The Seychelles were colonized by the French in 1756 to establish spice plantations to compete with the Dutch monopoly. The islands were captured by the English in 1794. Subsequently, Britain offered to return Mauritius and its dependencies, which included the Seychelles, to France if that country would renounce all claims to her possessions in India. France refused and the Seychelles were formally ceded to Britain as a dependency of Mauritius. In Nov. 1903 the Seychelles archipelago became a separate British Crown Colony. Internal self-government was achieved on 1 Oct. 1975 and independence as a republic within the British Commonwealth on 29 June 1976.

The first president, James Mancham, was deposed in a coup on 5 June 1977. Under the new constitution, the Seychelles People's Progressive Front became the sole legal party. There were several attempts to overthrow the regime, but in 1979 and 1984 Albert René was the only candidate in the presidential elections. Under the new constitution approved in June 1993, President René was re-elected against two opponents. He stood down in 2004.

TERRITORY AND POPULATION

The Seychelles consists of 115 islands in the Indian Ocean, north of Madagascar, with a combined area of 455 sq. km (175 sq. miles) in two distinct groups and a population (2002 census, provisional) of 81,177. The Granitic group of 40 islands cover 232 sq. km (90 sq. miles); the principal island is Mahé, with 153 sq. km (59 sq. miles) and 70,828 inhabitants at the 2002 census, the other inhabited islands of the group being Praslin, La Digue, Silhouette, Fregate and North, which together had 8,538 inhabitants in 1997.

The Outer or Coralline group comprises 75 islands spread over a wide area of ocean between the Mahé group and Madagascar, with a total land area of 223 sq. km (86 sq. miles). The main islands are the Amirante Isles (including Desroches, Poivre, Daros and Alphonse), Coetivy Island and Platte Island, all lying south of the Mahé group; the Farquhar, St Pierre and Providence Islands, north of Madagascar; and Aldabra, Astove, Assumption and the Cosmoledo Islands, about 1,000 km southwest of the Mahé group. Aldabra (whose lagoon covers 142 sq. km), Farquhar

and Desroches were transferred to the new British Indian Ocean Territory in 1965, but were returned by Britain to the Seychelles on the latter's independence in 1976.

Victoria, the chief town, had a census population of 24,970 in 2002. In 2003, 50·0% of the population was urban.

The official languages are Creole, English and French but 91% of the population speak Creole.

SOCIAL STATISTICS

2001 births, 1,440; deaths, 554. 2001 rates per 1,000 population, birth, 17·7; death, 6·8; infant mortality (2001), 13 per 1,000 births. Annual population growth rate, 1992–2002, 1·0%. Life expectancy at birth in 2003 was estimated to be 72 years (67 for males and 77 for females). Fertility rate, 2001, 1·8 births per woman.

CLIMATE

Though close to the equator, the climate is tropical. The hot, wet season is from Dec. to May, when conditions are humid, but southeast trades bring cooler conditions from June to Nov. Temperatures are high throughout the year, but the islands lie outside the cyclone belt. Victoria, Jan. 80°F (26·7°C), July 78°F (25·6°C). Annual rainfall 95" (2,287 mm).

CONSTITUTION AND GOVERNMENT

Under the 1979 Constitution the Seychelles People's Progressive Front (SPPF) was the sole legal Party. There is a unicameral People's Assembly consisting of 34 seats, of which 25 are directly elected and nine are allocated on a proportional basis, and an executive president directly elected for a five-year term. A constitutional amendment of Dec. 1991 legalized other parties. A commission was elected in July 1992 to draft a new constitution. The electorate was some 50,000; turnout was 90%. The SPPF gained 14 seats on the commission, the Democratic Party, eight; the latter, however, eventually withdrew. At a referendum in Nov. 1992 the new draft constitution failed to obtain the necessary 60% approval votes. The commission was reconvened in Jan. 1993. At a further referendum on 18 June 1993 the constitution was approved by 73·6% of votes cast.

National Anthem

'Koste Seselwa' ('Come Together Seychellois'); words and tune by D. F. M. André and G. C. R. Payet.

RECENT ELECTIONS

In parliamentary elections held on 4–6 Dec. 2002 President France-Albert René's Seychelles People's Progressive Front won 23 of the 34 seats with 54·3% of the vote, against 11 for the Seychelles National Party (42·6%). Turnout was 87%. In presidential elections held between 31 Aug.–2 Sept. 2001 France-Albert René was re-elected for a sixth term, obtaining 54·2% of the votes, with his nearest rival, Wavel Ramkalawan of the Seychelles National Party, polling 44·9%.

CURRENT ADMINISTRATION

On 14 April 2004 France-Albert René stepped down as president, a post he had held since 1977.

President: James Alix Michel; b. 1944 (SPPF; took office on 14 April 2004). The President is *Minister of Internal Affairs, Defence, Police, Finance and Legal Affairs.*

Vice-President, Minister of Tourism and Transport, Public Administration, Information Technology and Communications: Joseph Belmont.

In March 2006 the government comprised:

Minister of Economic Planning and Employment: Jacqueline Dugasse. *Education and Youth:* Danny Faure. *Environment and Natural Resources:* Ronny Jumeau. *Foreign Affairs:* Patrick Pillay. *Health and Social Services:* Vincent Meriton. *Land Use and Habitat:* Joel Morgan. *Local Government, Sports and Culture:* Sylvette Pool.

CURRENT LEADERS

James Alix Michel

Position
President

Introduction
Former Vice-President James Michel came to power in April 2004, handpicked by then president France-Albert René to succeed to the presidency on René's retirement after 27 years in power. Michel had been vice-president since 1996 and had previously held a variety of ministerial positions.

Early Life
James Alix Michel was born in the Seychelles on 18 Aug. 1944. He was a teacher before deciding to pursue a career in politics. His profile rose in the mid-1970s because of his involvement in the country's booming tourism industry.

In 1976, just before independence, he joined René's left-of-centre Seychelles People's United Party (SPUP)—renamed the Seychelles People's Progressive Front (SPPF) in 1978. He was a member of the SPUP's central committee when the party staged a bloodless coup in 1977, overthrowing the country's first president, James Mancham, and replacing him with René. There followed a 16-year one-party socialist dictatorship, during which time Michel held a series of important ruling party and ministerial positions. For several periods he was in charge of the highly-regulated Seychellois economy. On René's retirement in April 2004, Michel was sworn in as president.

Career in Office
Despite his allegiance to René, Michel was under pressure to speed up the country's democratization process, which had begun with multi-party elections in 1993. He also pledged to introduce more open political dialogue, particularly over matters concerning the Seychellois economy, and to develop the private sector. In Jan. 2005 Michel granted the Emirates Group the rights to operate non-stop flights three times a week between the Seychelles and Dubai in order to enhance the tourism industry and to increase trade for the business and cargo communities.

In March 2005 Michel detailed his foreign policy, underpinned by a desire to cement stronger regional ties in the Indian Ocean region—particularly in light of the Seychelles' exit in July 2004 from the Southern African Development Community, ostensibly because of high membership fees. He has particularly focused on strengthening relations with Mauritius, working alongside the then Mauritian prime minister, Paul Bérenger, to strengthen the Indian Ocean Commission. Michel favours increased promotion of the Seychelles as a high-quality and safe tourist resort, and is seeking to make the country a leader in environmental issues.

In June 2005 Michel announced plans for a new national pension fund and a scheme to set-up a savings account of R1,000 for every Seychellois child, both of which came into effect in Jan. 2006.

DEFENCE

The Defence Force comprises all services. Personnel (2002) Army, 200; Paramilitary, 250; Coastguard-naval, 200; Air Wing, 20.

Defence expenditure totalled US$12m. in 2003 (US$141 per capita), representing 1·6% of GDP.

Coastguard

There is no longer a navy or air force in the Seychelles. Instead, the Seychelles Coast Guard has superseded these former forces.

Based at Port Victoria it includes a small air wing with no combat aircraft.

INTERNATIONAL RELATIONS

Seychelles is a member of the UN, the Commonwealth, the African Union, African Development Bank, COMESA and the International Organization of the Francophonie and is an ACP member state of the ACP-EU relationship.

ECONOMY

Services accounted for 67·1% of GDP in 2002, industry 30·0% and agriculture 2·9%.

Overview

Since the early 1990s the government has attempted to create a free market economy. Tourism forms the backbone of the economy followed by the fisheries sector. In recent years the Seychelles has undertaken efforts to develop an offshore sector as the third pillar of the economy and to position itself as a provider of business and financial services.

Currency

The unit of currency is the *Seychelles rupee* (SCR) divided into 100 *cents*. In June 2002 foreign exchange reserves were US$39m. In April 2002 total money supply was 1,384m. rupees. Inflation was 3·2% in 2003 and 3·9% in 2004.

Budget

Fiscal budget in 1m. rupees, for calendar years:

	1996	1997	1998	1999	2000
Total revenue	1,151·1	1,273·5	1,372·9	1,491·9	1,377·1
Total expenditure	1,495·2	1,680·9	1,879·7	1,905·0	1,969·8

Performance

There was a recession in both 2003 and 2004, with the economy contracting by 6·3% and 2·0% respectively. Total GDP was US$0·7bn. in 2004.

Banking and Finance

The Central Bank of Seychelles (established in 1983; *Governor*, Francis Chang Leng), which is the bank of issue, and the Development Bank of Seychelles provide long-term lending for development purposes. There are also six commercial banks, including two local banks (the Seychelles Savings Bank and the Seychelles International Mercantile Banking Co-operation or NOUVOBANQ), and four branches of foreign banks (Barclays Bank, Banque Française Commerciale, Habib Bank and Bank of Baroda).

ENERGY AND NATURAL RESOURCES

Environment

Carbon dioxide emissions from the consumption and flaring of fossil fuels were the equivalent of 7·6 tonnes per capita in 2002.

Electricity

Installed capacity on Mahé and Praslin combined was 28,000 kW in 2000. Production in 2000 was 164m. kWh and consumption per capita 2,025 kWh.

Water

There are two raw water reservoirs, the Rochon Dam and La Gogue Dam, which have a combined holding capacity of 1·05bn. litres.

Treated water consumption in 1998 was 5·5bn. litres.

Agriculture

The main cash crop in 1998 was cinnamon bark, of which 289 tonnes were exported, followed by tea production with exports of 250 tonnes (green leaf). Crops grown for local consumption include bananas, oranges, cassava, sweet potatoes, paw-paw, yams and vegetables. The staple food crop, rice, is imported from Asia. Livestock, 2000: 18,000 pigs, 5,000 goats, 1,000 cattle and 1m. chickens. In 2001 there were 1,000 ha. of arable land and 6,000 ha. of permanent crop land.

Forestry
In 2000 forests covered 30,000 ha., or 66·7% of the total land area. The Ministry of Environment has a number of ongoing forestry projects which aim at preserving and upgrading the local system. There are also a number of terrestrial nature reserves including three national parks, four special reserves and an 'area of outstanding natural beauty'.

Fisheries
The fisheries sector is the Seychelles' second largest foreign exchange earner. In 1998 it accounted for at least 93% of export revenue. Total catch in 2001 was 47,550 tonnes, exclusively from sea fishing. 1998 fisheries exports amounted to 457·7m. rupees, of which: canned tuna, 412·2m.; fresh/frozen fish, 11·9m.; frozen prawns, 33·6m. Total 1998 fish production (in tonnes) was as follows: canned tuna, 18,939; fresh/frozen fish, 3,334; frozen prawns, 642.

INDUSTRY
Local industry is expanding, the major development in recent years being in tuna canning; in 2000 output totalled 28,781 tonnes, up from 7,500 tonnes in 1995. This is followed by brewing, with 7·1m. litres in 2003. Other main activities include production of cigarettes (40m. in 2000), dairy production, prawn production, paints and processing of cinnamon barks.

Labour
Some 71% of the workforce is employed in services. In 1999, 3,791 people worked in hotels and restaurants and 1,217 in other tourism related jobs. 15,700 are formally employed in the private sector, 6,800 in the public sector and 4,200 in the parastatal sector.

Trade Unions
There are two major trade unions, the National Workers' Union and the Forum for Progress.

INTERNATIONAL TRADE
Foreign debt totalled US$253m. in 2002.

Imports and Exports
Total trade, in US$1m., for calendar years:

	1998	1999	2000	2001	2002
Imports (f.o.b.)	334·6	369·8	311·6	421·9	376·3
Exports (f.o.b.)	122·8	145·7	194·8	216·4	236·7

Principal imports: machinery and transport equipment; manufactured goods; food, beverages and tobacco; mineral fuel; chemicals. Principal origins of import, 2000: South Africa (13·6%), France (11·5%), Italy (10·6%), UK (10·6%). Principal exports: canned tuna; frozen prawns; fresh and frozen fish; cinnamon bark. Main export markets, 1998: UK (23·1%), Yemen (21·2%), Germany (19·4%), France (13·2%), Italy (12·9%).

COMMUNICATIONS

Roads
In 2002 there were 463 km of roads, of which 87·9% were surfaced. There were 6,700 passenger cars in 2002 (86 per 1,000 inhabitants) and 2,600 commercial vehicles.

Rail
There are no railways in the Seychelles.

Civil Aviation
Seychelles International airport is on Mahé. In 2003 Air Seychelles flew on domestic routes and to Bombay, Comoros, Dubai, Frankfurt, Johannesburg, London, Malé, Mauritius, Munich, Paris, Réunion, Rome, Singapore and Zürich. In 1999 it flew 8·8m. km, carrying 347,200 passengers (109,500 on international flights). In 2001 Seychelles International handled 598,133 passengers (330,726 on international flights) and 5,607 tonnes of freight.

Shipping
The main port is Victoria, which is also a tuna-fishing and fuel and services supply centre. In 2002 merchant shipping totalled 65,000 GRT. In 1999 vessels totalling 1,139,000 net registered tons entered ports. Sea freight (1998) included: imports, 636,000 tonnes; exports, 47,000 tonnes; transhipments (fish), 39,000 tonnes.

Telecommunications
There were 65,500 telephone subscribers in 2001, or 799·7 per 1,000 population, and 13,000 PCs were in use in 2002 (156·6 per 1,000 persons). Mobile phone subscribers numbered 44,700 in 2002 and there were 600 fax machines. Internet users numbered 11,700 in 2002.

Postal Services
In 2003 there were five post offices. The central post office is in Victoria.

SOCIAL INSTITUTIONS

Justice
In 1998, 3,951 criminal and other offences were recorded by the police. The death penalty was abolished for all crimes in 1993. The population in penal institutions in 2003 was 149 (186 per 100,000 of national population).

Education
Adult literacy was 91·9% in 2003 (91·4% among males and 92·3% among females). Education is free from five to 12 years in primary schools, and 13 to 17 in secondary schools. There are three private schools providing primary and secondary education and one dealing only with secondary learning. Education beyond 18 years of age is funded jointly by the government and parents. In 2003 there were 9,477 pupils and 675 teachers in primary schools, 7,551 pupils and 552 teachers in secondary schools and 1,652 students and 193 teachers at polytechnic level.

Public expenditure on education came to 5·7% of GNP in 2002–03.

Health
In 2003 there were 107 doctors, 16 dentists and 422 nurses. In 2003 there were seven hospitals with 419 beds. The health service is free.

Welfare
Social security is provided for people of 63 years and over, for the disabled and for families needing financial assistance. There is also assistance via means testing for those medically unfit to work and for mothers who remain out of work for longer than their designated maternity leave. Orphanages are also subsidized by the government.

RELIGION
87% of the inhabitants are Roman Catholic, the remainder of the population being followers of other religions (mainly Anglicans, with some 7th Day Adventists, Bahais, Muslims, Hindus, Pentecostalists, Jehovah's Witnesses, Buddhists and followers of the Grace and Peace church).

CULTURE

World Heritage Sites
Entered on the UNESCO World Heritage List in 1982, the four coral islands of Aldabra Atoll protect a shallow lagoon. A

heritage site since 1983, the Vallée de Mai Nature Reserve is a natural palm forest on the small island of Praslin.

Broadcasting

Broadcasting is under the auspices of the Seychelles Broadcasting Corporation (SBC), an independent body. The SBC owns two radio stations; the AM station which hosts most programmes in Creole with frequent use of English and French; and Paradise FM which broadcasts mainly in English. There is also a religious station, FEBA. The RFI and BBC also transmit programmes locally.

There is only one local TV station directed by the SBC. International TV channels can be reached through Cable TV. TV colour is by PAL. There were 42,000 radio receivers in 1997 and 16,550 TV sets in 2001.

Cinema

There is one cinema, based in Victoria.

Press

There are one daily and two weekly newspapers, as well as two monthly magazines.

Tourism

Tourism is the main foreign exchange earner. Visitor numbers were 132,000 in 2002, spending US$130m.

Festivals

There are numerous religious festivals including Kavadi, an annual procession organized by the Hindu Association of Seychelles. Secular festivals include the annual Youth Festival, Jazz Festival, Creole Festival, Kite Festival and the Subios Festival, a celebration of the underwater world.

Libraries

There is a national library in Victoria with branches on Praslin and La Digue Islands. It also provides a mobile service, and there are libraries in all educational institutions.

Theatre and Opera

There are three national theatres, all located on Mahé. The Mont Fleuri Theatre and the International Conference Centre serve central Mahé while the Anse Royale Theatre caters for the southern region of the island.

Museums and Galleries

There are four museums: the Historical Museum, the Natural History Museum, the National Heritage Museum and the Eco Musée, a museum of the country's economic activities. There is also a National Art Gallery, located in the National Library, and a number of smaller galleries exhibiting mostly local artists.

DIPLOMATIC REPRESENTATIVES

Of Seychelles in the United Kingdom (Box 4PE, 2nd Floor, Eros House, 111 Baker St., London, W1M 1FE)
High Commissioner: Callixte d'Offay (resides in Paris).

Of the United Kingdom in Seychelles (3rd Floor, Oliaji Trade Centre, Francis Rachel St., PO Box 161, Victoria, Mahé)
High Commissioner: Diana Skingle.

Of Seychelles in the USA (800 2nd Ave., Suite 400C, New York, NY 10017)
Ambassador: Emile Patrick Jérémie Bonnelame.

Of the USA in Seychelles
Ambassador: Vacant (resides in Port Louis, Mauritius).
Chargé d'Affaires a.i.: Stephen Schwartz.

Of Seychelles to the United Nations
Ambassador: Emile Patrick Jérémie Bonnelame.

Of Seychelles to the European Union
Ambassador: Callixte d'Offay.

FURTHER READING

Bennett, G. and Bennett, P. R., *Seychelles.* [Bibliography] ABC-Clio, Oxford and Santa Barbara (CA), 1993
Scarr, D., *Seychelles Since 1970: History of a Slave and Post-Slavery Society.* Africa World Press, Lawrenceville (NJ), 2000

National Statistical Office: Statistics and Database Administration Section (MISD), P. O. Box 206, Victoria, Mahé. *Seychelles in Figures*
Website: http://www.seychelles.net/misdstat/

SIERRA LEONE

© Research Machines plc 2006

Republic of Sierra Leone

Capital: Freetown
Population projection, 2010: 6·13m.
GDP per capita, 2003: (PPP$) 548
HDI/world rank: 0·298/176

KEY HISTORICAL EVENTS

The Colony of Sierra Leone originated in 1787 when English settlers bought a piece of land intended as a home for natives of Africa who were waifs in London. The land was later used as a settlement for Africans rescued from slave-ships. The hinterland was declared a British protectorate on 21 Aug. 1896. Sierra Leone became independent as a member state of the British Commonwealth on 27 April 1961. In a general election in March 1967, Dr Siaka Stevens' All People's Congress came to power and was installed despite a military coup to prevent his taking office. Sierra Leone became a republic on 19 April 1971 with Dr Siaka Stevens as executive president. Following a referendum in June 1978, a new constitution was instituted under which the ruling All People's Congress became the sole legal party.

A military coup on 29 April 1992 deposed the president and set up a National Provisional Ruling Council whose chairman was in turn deposed in a military coup on 16 Jan. 1996. Presidential and parliamentary elections in Feb.–March 1996 resulted in a new government led by President Ahmad Tejan Kabbah. He was ousted in May 1997 by a group of junior officers. In Feb. 1998 a Nigerian-led intervention force launched an air and artillery offensive against the military junta. For the first time a group of African states joined together to restore a democratically-elected president. On 10 March President Kabbah returned from exile in Guinea, promising a 'new beginning'. But in Jan. 1999 the country again erupted into civil war. Nigeria sent troops to support President Kabbah but having lost control of the diamond fields and with no other resources, the government was powerless. The war, which continued for nearly ten years, has reduced Sierra Leone to one of the poorest countries in the world.

The government reached an agreement with the rebel movement in July 1999 to bring the civil war to an end. Under the terms of the accord the Revolutionary United Front (RUF) was to gain four key government posts along with effective control of the country's mineral resources. In return the RUF was to surrender its weapons. However, civil war broke out again in early 2000. Responding to a government appeal British forces were sent to back up the UN peacekeeping force (UNMASIL). Foday Sankoh, rebel leader of the RUF, was captured and handed over to UN forces in May 2000. In July 2001 the RUF announced that it was formally recognizing the civil government under President Ahmad Tejan Kabbah. By Sept. 2001 there were signs that the civil war might be at an end, and in Jan. 2002 President Kabbah declared the war over. He was re-elected in a presidential election in May 2002 and has been at the forefront of the fight against corruption. Both the UN and the International Monetary Fund have praised the 'remarkable progress' made in Sierra Leone.

TERRITORY AND POPULATION

Sierra Leone is bounded on the northwest, north and northeast by Guinea, on the southeast by Liberia and on the southwest by the Atlantic Ocean. The area is 71,740 sq. km (27,699 sq. miles). Population (census 2004, provisional), 4,963,298; density, 69·2 per sq. km. In 2003, 61·2% of the population were rural.

The UN gives a projected population for 2010 of 6·13m.

The capital is Freetown, with 822,000 inhabitants in 1999.

Sierra Leone is divided into four provinces:

	Sq. km	Census 2004 (provisional)	Capital	Census 2004 (provisional)
Eastern Province	15,553	1,187,532	Kenema	137,696
Northern Province	35,936	1,718,240	Makeni	85,017
Southern Province	19,694	1,106,602	Bo	167,144
Western Province	557	950,924	Freetown	786,900

The provinces are divided into districts as follows: Bo, Bonthe, Moyamba, Pujehun (Southern Province); Kailahun, Kenema, Kono (Eastern Province); Bombali, Kambia, Koinaduga, Port Loko, Toukolili (Northern Province).

The principal peoples are the Mendes (26% of the total) in the south, the Temnes (25%) in the north and centre, the Konos, Fulanis, Bulloms, Korankos, Limbas and Kissis. English is the official language; a Creole (Krio) is spoken.

SOCIAL STATISTICS

2000 estimates: births, 217,000; deaths, 103,000. Estimated birth rate in 2000 was 49·1 per 1,000 population; estimated death rate, 23·3. Annual population growth rate, 1992–2002, 1·5%. Expectation of life at birth in 2003 was 42·1 years for females and 39·4 years for males. The World Health Organization's 2004 World Health Report ranked Sierra Leone in last place in a 'healthy life expectancy' list, with an expected 28·6 years of healthy life for babies born in 2002. Infant mortality was 182 per 1,000 live births in 2001 (the highest in the world). Fertility rate, 2001, 6·5 births per woman.

CLIMATE

A tropical climate, with marked wet and dry seasons and high temperatures throughout the year. The rainy season lasts from about April to Nov., when humidity can be very high. Thunderstorms are common from April to June and in Sept. and

Oct. Rainfall is particularly heavy in Freetown because of the effect of neighbouring relief. Freetown, Jan. 80°F (26·7°C), July 78°F (25·6°C). Annual rainfall 135" (3,434 mm).

CONSTITUTION AND GOVERNMENT

In a referendum in Sept. 1991 some 60% of the 2·5m. electorate voted for the introduction of a new constitution instituting multi-party democracy. The constitution has been amended several times since. There is a 124-seat *National Assembly* (112 members elected by popular vote and 12 filled by paramount chiefs).

There is a *Supreme Council of State (SCS)*, and a *Council of State Secretaries*.

National Anthem

'High We Exalt Thee, Realm of the Free'; words by C. Nelson Fyle, tune by J. J. Akar.

RECENT ELECTIONS

Presidential and parliamentary elections were held on 14 May 2002. In the presidential election, incumbent Ahmad Tejan Kabbah won with 70·6% of the vote ahead of Ernest Koroma with 22·4% and Alimany Paolo Bangura with 1·7%. There were six other candidates. In parliamentary elections, Kabbah's Sierra Leone People's Party (SLPP) won 83 of the 112 seats with Koroma's All People's Congress taking 27 seats.

CURRENT ADMINISTRATION

President and Minister of Defence: Ahmad Tejan Kabbah; b. 1932 (SLPP; elected 17 March 1996 and re-elected in May 2002).

Vice-President: Solomon Berewa.

In March 2006 the government comprised:

Minister of Agriculture and Food Security: Sama Sahr Mondeh. *Country Planning, Forestry, Environment and Social Welfare:* Alfred Bobson Sesay. *Development and Economic Planning:* Mohamed Daramy. *Education, Science and Technology:* Alpha Wurie. *Energy and Power:* Lloyd During. *Finance:* John Benjamin. *Foreign Affairs and International Co-operation:* Momodu Koroma. *Health and Sanitation:* Abator Thomas. *Information and Broadcasting:* Septimus Kaikai. *Internal Affairs:* Pascal Egbenda. *Justice:* Frederick Carew. *Labour, Industrial Relations and Social Security:* Alpha Timbo. *Local Government and Community Development:* Sidikie Brima. *Marine Resources:* Chernor Jalloh. *Mineral Resources:* Mohamed Swarray Alhaji Deen. *Political and Parliamentary Affairs:* Eya Mbayo. *Social Welfare, Gender and Children's Affairs:* Shirley Yema Gbujama. *Tourism and Culture:* Okere Adams. *Trade and Industry:* Kadi Sesay. *Transport and Communications:* Prince Harding. *Works, Housing and Technical Maintenance:* Caiser Boima. *Youth and Sport:* Dennis Bright.

Government Website: http://www.sierra-leone.org/govt.html

CURRENT LEADERS

Ahmad Tejan Kabbah

Position
President

Introduction
Ahmad Tejan Kabbah, leader of the Sierra Leone People's Party, has been president since 1996. His aim is to build a lasting peace as the country emerges from a long civil war and to strengthen a devastated economy.

Early Life
Kabbah was born in 1932 and was educated in Sierra Leone and the UK. He entered the civil service in 1959, becoming a permanent secretary in the late 1960s. He subsequently spent over 20 years working for the UN Development Programme, travelling throughout the world.

He returned to Sierra Leone in 1992, shortly after the military had seized power. They invited him to chair the National Advisory Council. He was elected president at elections in 1996.

Career in Office
In May 1997 Kabbah was removed in a military coup and fled to Guinea. However, with the support of a West African intervention force and the British military, Kabbah re-established his government nine months later. Backed by the UN, he opened negotiations with the Revolutionary United Front (RUF) which resulted in several accords. By late 2001 the RUF acknowledged the legitimacy of the Kabbah government and in Jan. 2002 he declared the war at an end. In May 2002 he won re-election for a further five-year term.

Despite lingering concerns in the international community over his authoritarian rule, he has been promised significant international aid in a bid to rebuild the country. In July 2002 Kabbah inaugurated Sierra Leone's Truth and Reconciliation Commission, aiming to heal the rifts caused by the country's bloody conflicts. However, unlike the South African model, the commission did not have the power to grant an amnesty. Having heard around 9,000 testimonies, the Commission submitted its report in 2005.

Corruption remains a problem under Kabbah's government, deterring prospective donor and creditor countries, and the security situation has necessitated the retention of UN peacekeeping forces.

DEFENCE

In 2003 military expenditure totalled US$17m. (US$3 per capita), representing 2·2% of GDP.

The UN peacekeeping force (UNAMSIL) numbered 11,278 troops and 241 military observers in Nov. 2003, making it one of the largest peacekeeping operation in the world at the time.

Army

Following the civil war, the Army has disbanded and a new National Army has been formed with a strength of some 13,000.

Navy

Based in Freetown there is a small naval force of 200 operating five patrol and coastal combatants.

INTERNATIONAL RELATIONS

Sierra Leone is a member of the UN, WTO, the African Union, African Development Bank, ECOWAS, IOM, OIC, Islamic Development Bank and the Commonwealth and is an ACP member state of the ACP-EU relationship.

ECONOMY

Agriculture accounted for 52·6% of GDP in 2002, industry 31·6% and services 15·7%.

Currency

The unit of currency is the *leone* (SLL) of 100 *cents*. Foreign exchange reserves were US$28m. in June 2002. Inflation was 7·5% in 2003 and 14·2% in 2004. Exchange controls were liberalized in 1993. Total money supply in June 2002 was 191,105m. leones.

Budget

In 2002 the government's total revenue was 239,425m. leones (64·0% customs duties and excise taxes) and total expenditure was 701,834m. leones (65·1% recurrent expenditures).

Performance

GNP per capita was US$200 in 1996 compared to US$390 in 1982. Real GDP growth was –0·8% in 1998, but the civil war resulted in the economy shrinking by 8·1% in 1999. There was positive growth in 2000 for the first time since 1994, with a rate of 3·8%, rising to 18·2% in 2001 and further to 27·5% in 2002. Real GDP growth was 9·3% in 2003 and 7·4% in 2004. Total GDP in 2004 was US$1·1bn. Sierra Leone is among the world's bottom five countries in income and life expectancy.

Banking and Finance

The bank of issue is the Bank of Sierra Leone which was established 1964 (*Governor*, Dr James Rogers). There are four commercial banks (two foreign).

ENERGY AND NATURAL RESOURCES

Environment

Carbon dioxide emissions from the consumption and flaring of fossil fuels in 2002 were the equivalent of 0·2 tonnes per capita.

Electricity

Installed capacity was 0·1m. kW in 2000. Production in 2000 was around 246m. kWh; consumption per capita in 2000 was an estimated 56 kWh.

Minerals

The chief minerals mined are diamonds (352,000 carats in 2002) and rutile (203,000 tonnes in 1994–95). There are also deposits of gold, iron ore and bauxite. The presence of rich diamond deposits partly explains the close interest of neighbouring countries in the politics of Sierra Leone.

Agriculture

Agriculture engaged 61% of the workforce in 2002, mainly in small-scale peasant production. Cattle production is important in the north. Production (2000 estimates, in 1,000 tonnes): cassava, 241; rice, 199; palm oil, 36; plantains, 28; sweet potatoes, 28; sugarcane, 21. In 2001 there were 500,000 ha. of arable land and 64,000 ha. of permanent crops.

Livestock (2000): cattle, 420,000; goats, 200,000; sheep, 365,000; pigs, 52,000; chickens, 6m.

Forestry

In 2000 forests covered 1,055,000 ha., or 14·7% of the total land area. Timber production in 2001 was 5·49m. cu. metres.

Fisheries

In 2001, 75,210 tonnes of fish were caught (61,210 tonnes from marine waters).

INDUSTRY

There are palm oil and rice mills; sawn timber, joinery products and furniture are produced.

Labour

The workforce was 1,610,000 in 1996 (64% males). In 1995 around two-thirds of the economically active population were engaged in agriculture, fisheries and forestry. 14,800 persons were registered unemployed in 1992.

INTERNATIONAL TRADE

Foreign debt was US$1,448m. in 2002.

Imports and Exports

Total trade for 2002: imports, 554·8bn. leones; exports, 102·0bn. leones. Main exports are bauxite, diamonds, gold, coffee and cocoa. A UN-mandated diamond export certification scheme is in force. The Security Council has commended Sierra Leone's government for its efforts in monitoring trade to prevent diamonds from becoming a future source of conflict.

The main import suppliers in 2001 were UK (25·3%), Netherlands (10·1%), USA (7·9%), Germany (6·3%). Principal export markets in 2001 were Belgium (40·6%), USA (9·1%), UK (8·5%), Germany (7·8%).

COMMUNICATIONS

Roads

There were 11,300 km of roads in 2002, of which 8·0% were surfaced. In 2002 there were 11,353 passenger cars and 3,565 vans and trucks. There were 66 deaths as a result of road accidents in 1999.

Civil Aviation

Freetown Airport (Lungi) is the international airport. In 2003 Sierra National Airlines flew to Banjul and London. Other international carriers operated flights to Abidjan, Accra, Brussels, Conakry, Dakar, Lagos and Monrovia. In 1999 scheduled airline traffic of Sierra Leone-based carriers flew 0·3m. km, carrying 19,000 passengers (all on international flights).

Shipping

The port of Freetown has a very large natural harbour. Iron ore is exported through Pepel, and there is a small port at Bonthe. In 2002 the merchant fleet totalled 23,000 GRT. 2·31m. tonnes of cargo were loaded in 1993 and 0·59m. tonnes discharged.

Telecommunications

In 2001 Sierra Leone had 49,600 telephone subscribers (10·1 per 1,000 population) and in 2002 there were 4,500 fax machines. The country's telecommunications network was virtually destroyed during the civil war, and reconstruction and modernization is regarded as a matter of extreme urgency. In 2002 Sierra Leone had 8,000 Internet users. In 2002 there were 66,300 mobile phone subscribers.

Postal Services

In 2002 there were 45 post offices.

SOCIAL INSTITUTIONS

Justice

The High Court has jurisdiction in civil and criminal matters. Subordinate courts are held by magistrates in the various districts. Native Courts, headed by court Chairmen, apply native law and custom under a criminal and civil jurisdiction. Appeals from the decisions of magistrates' courts are heard by the High Court. Appeals from the decisions of the High Court are heard by the Sierra Leone Court of Appeal. Appeal lies from the Sierra Leone Court of Appeal to the Supreme Court which is the highest court.

The death penalty is in force, and 24 soldiers were executed on 19 Oct. 1998 for their part in the May 1997 coup.

Education

The adult literacy rate in 2003 was 29·6% (39·8% among males and 20·5% among females). Primary education is partially free but not compulsory. In 2001–02 there were 2,704 primary schools with 554,308 pupils and 14,932 teachers. In 2000–01 there were 246 secondary schools with 107,776 pupils and 5,264 teachers, and 9,660 students and 1,321 staff at teacher training institutions. There were also 174 technical/vocational establishments with 49,488 pupils and 2,514 staff. There were five institutes of higher education in 1992–93 with 4,742 students and 600 teachers. Fourah Bay College and Njala University College are the two constituent colleges of the University of Sierra Leone. They had 2,571 students and 257 academic staff in 1990–91.

In 2000–01 total expenditure on education came to 3·8% of GNP.

Health

In 2000 there were 145 general practitioners, 1,331 nurses and five dentists. In 2000 there were 64 hospitals with 692 beds.

RELIGION

There were 2·49m. Muslims in 2001. Traditional animist beliefs persist; there is also a Christian minority.

CULTURE

Broadcasting
Broadcasting is under the auspices of the government-controlled Sierra Leone Broadcasting Service and Sierra Leone Television, which is part commercial. There were 65,000 TV sets (colour by PAL) in 2001 and 1·14m. radio sets in 2000.

Press
In Jan. 2001 there were two daily newspapers (*Concord Times* and *For di People*), 13 weekly papers, 11 twice weekly newspapers and six other newspapers. Several papers are published irregularly. The state-owned *Sierra News* had the highest circulation in 2001 (5,000), followed by *For di People* (4,500). Most newspapers in Sierra Leone were founded in the 1990s.

Tourism
In 2000 there were 10,000 foreign tourists, bringing revenue of US$12m.

DIPLOMATIC REPRESENTATIVES

Of Sierra Leone in the United Kingdom (Oxford Circus House, 245 Oxford St., London, W1R 1LF)
High Commissioner: Sulaiman Tejan-Jalloh.

Of the United Kingdom in Sierra Leone (Spur Rd, Freetown)
High Commissioner: Dr John Mitchiner.

Of Sierra Leone in the USA (1701 19th St., NW, Washington, D.C., 20009)
Ambassador: Ibrahim M. Kamara.

Of the USA in Sierra Leone (Corner Walpole and Siaka Stevens St., Freetown)
Ambassador: Thomas N. Hull.

Of Sierra Leone to the United Nations
Ambassador: Joe Robert Pemagbi.

Of Sierra Leone to the European Union
Ambassador: Fode Maclean Dabor.

FURTHER READING

Binns, Margaret and J. Anthony, *Sierra Leone.* [Bibliography] ABC-Clio, Oxford and Santa Barbara (CA), 1992
Conteh-Morgan, E. and Dixon-Fyle, M., *Sierra Leone at the End of the Twentieth Century: History, Politics, and Society.* Peter Lang Publishing, Berne, 1999
Ferme, M., *The Underneath of Things: Violence, History, and the Everyday in Sierra Leone.* Univ. of California Press, 2001

National Statistical Office: Statistics Sierra Leone, A. J. Momoh Street, Tower Hill, P.M.B. 595, Freetown.
Website: http://www.statistics-sierra-leone.org

SINGAPORE

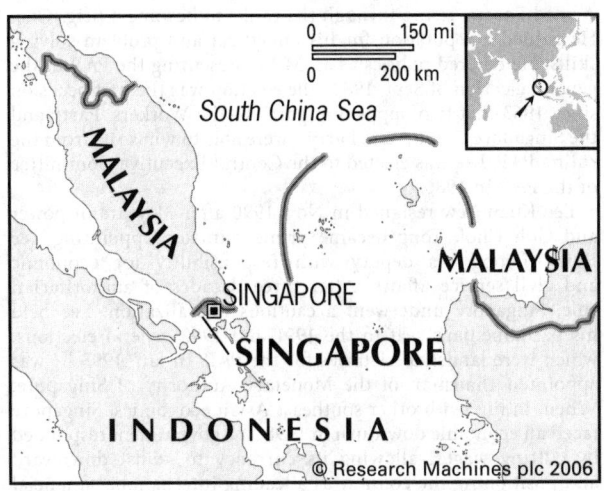

Republic of Singapore

Population projection, 2010: 4·59m.
GDP per capita, 2003: (PPP$) 24,481
HDI/world rank: 0·907/25

KEY HISTORICAL EVENTS

Singapore Island became part of the Javanese Majapahit Empire in the 14th century. The Portuguese took control of the area in the 16th century, followed by the Dutch a hundred years later. In 1819 Sir Thomas Stamford Raffles, the British East India Administrator, established a trading settlement. The lease to the British East India Company by the Sultan of Johore was followed by the treaty of 2 Aug. 1824 ceding the entire island in perpetuity to the company. In 1826 Penang, Melaka and Singapore were combined as the Straits Settlements. With the opening of the Suez Canal in 1869 and the advent of the steamship, an era of prosperity began for Singapore. Growth continued with the export of tin and rubber from the Malay peninsula.

Singapore fell to the Japanese in 1942, whose occupation continued until the end of the Second World War. In 1945 Singapore became a Crown Colony, being separated from Penang and Melaka. In June 1959 the state was granted internal self-government. When the Federation of Malaysia was formed in Sept. 1963, Singapore became one of the 14 states of the newly created country.

On 7 Aug. 1965, by agreement with the Malaysian government, Singapore left the Federation of Malaysia and became an independent sovereign state.

TERRITORY AND POPULATION

The Republic of Singapore consists of Singapore Island and some 63 smaller islands. Singapore Island is situated off the southern extremity of the Malay peninsula, to which it is joined by a 1·1 km causeway carrying a road, railway and water pipeline across the Strait of Johor and by a 1·9 km bridge at Tuas, opened on 2 Jan. 1998. The Straits of Johor between the island and the mainland are 914 metres wide. The island is 682·3 sq. km in area, including the offshore islands.

Census of population (2000): Chinese residents 2,505,379 (76·8%), Malays 453,633 (13·9%), Indians 257,791 (7·9%) and others 46,406 (1·4%); resident population, 3,263,209. Total population in June 2001 was 4,131,200. The population is 100% urban. Population density, 6,055 per sq. km. The estimated population in 2005 was 4,326,000.

The UN gives a projected resident population for 2010 of 4·59m.

Malay, Chinese (Mandarin), Tamil and English are the official languages; Malay is the national language and English is the language of administration.

SOCIAL STATISTICS

2002 births, 40,864; deaths, 15,815. Birth rate per 1,000 population, 2002, 11·4; death rate, 4·4. Annual population growth rate, 1992–2002, 2·8%; infant mortality, 2000, 3·3 per 1,000 live births (one of the lowest in the world); life expectancy, 2003, 76·7 years for males and 80·6 years for females. Fertility rate, 2001, 1·5 births per woman. In 2003 the mean age of bridegrooms at first marriage was 30·2 years and of brides 27·2 years.

Source: Singapore Department of Statistics

CLIMATE

The climate is equatorial, with relatively uniform temperature, abundant rainfall and high humidity. Rain falls throughout the year but tends to be heaviest from Nov. to Jan. Average daily temperature is 26·8°C with a maximum daily average of 30·9°C and a minimum daily average of 23·9°C. Mean annual rainfall is 2,345 mm.

CONSTITUTION AND GOVERNMENT

Singapore is a republic with a parliamentary system of government. The organs of state—the executive, the legislature and the judiciary—are provided for by a written constitution. The Constitution is the supreme law of Singapore and any law enacted after the date of its commencement, which is inconsistent with its provisions, is void. The present constitution came into force on 3 June 1959 and was amended in 1965.

The Head of State is the *President*. The administration of the government is vested in the Cabinet headed by the *Prime Minister*. The Prime Minister and the other Cabinet Members are appointed by the President from among the Members of Parliament (MPs). The Cabinet is collectively responsible to Parliament.

Parliament is unicameral consisting of 84 elected members and one Non-Constituency MP (NCMP), elected by secret ballot from single-member and group representation constituencies as well as nine Nominated Members of Parliament (NMPs) who are appointed for a two-year term on the recommendation of a Special Select Committee of Parliament. With the customary exception of those serving criminal sentences, all citizens over 21 are eligible to vote. Voting in an election is compulsory. Group representation constituencies may return up to six Members of Parliament (four before 1996), one of whom must be from the Malay community, the Indian or other minority communities. To ensure representation of parties not in the government, provision is made for the appointment of three (or up to a maximum of six) NCMPs. The number of NCMPs is reduced by one for each opposition candidate returned. There is a common roll without communal electorates.

A Presidential Council to consider and report on minorities' rights was established in 1970. The particular function of this council is to draw attention to any Bill or to any subsidiary legislation which, in its opinion, discriminates against any racial or religious community.

National Anthem

'Majulah Singapura' ('Onward Singapore'); words and tune by Zubir Said.

GOVERNMENT CHRONOLOGY

Prime Ministers since 1959. (PAP = People's Action Party)

1959–90	PAP	Lee Kuan Yew
1990–2004	PAP	Goh Chok Tong
2004–	PAP	Lee Hsien Loong

RECENT ELECTIONS

In parliamentary elections held on 6 May 2006 the ruling People's Action Party (PAP) won 82 of 84 seats (with 66·6% of votes cast), including 37 seats won automatically before the election because the opposition did not contest them. The Workers' Party and the Singapore Democratic Alliance both took one seat each.

Presidential elections were scheduled for 27 Aug. 2005. However, these were cancelled after the incumbent president S. R. Nathan emerged as the only candidate who satisfied the requirements of the certificate of eligibility. He thus gained the presidency unopposed.

CURRENT ADMINISTRATION

President: S. R. Nathan; b. 1924 (sworn in 1 Sept. 1999; re-elected unopposed in Aug. 2005).

In March 2006 the cabinet comprised:

Prime Minister and Minister of Finance: Lee Hsien Loong; b. 1952 (PAP; sworn in 12 Aug. 2004).

Senior Minister, Prime Minister's Office: Goh Chok Tong. *Minister Mentor, Prime Minister's Office:* Lee Kuan Yew, GCMG, CH. *Deputy Prime Ministers:* Prof. Shunmugam Jayakumar (*Minister of Law and Co-ordinating Minister for National Security*); Wong Kan Seng (*Minister of Home Affairs*).

Minister of Health: Khaw Boon Wan. *Information, Communications and the Arts:* Dr Lee Boon Yang. *Education:* Tharman Shanmugaratnam. *Foreign Affairs:* BG (NS) George Yong-Boon Yeo. *Defence:* RAdm (NS) Teo Chee Hean. *Manpower:* Dr Ng Eng Hen (also *Second Minister for Defence*). *Community Development and Sports:* Vivian Balakrishnan. *Environment and Water Resources:* Dr Yaacob Ibrahim (also *in Charge of Muslim Affairs*). *Transport:* Yeo Cheow Tong. *National Development:* Mah Bow Tan. *Trade and Industry:* Lim Hng Kiang. *Ministers in Prime Minister's Office:* Lim Boon Heng; Lim Swee Say; Raymond Lim Siang Keat (also *Second Minister for Foreign Affairs and Second Minister for Finance*).

Government Website: http://www.gov.sg

CURRENT LEADERS

Lee Hsien Loong

Position
Prime Minister

Introduction
When Lee Hsien Loong was sworn in as prime minister of Singapore on 12 Aug. 2004, it was only the second time the southeast Asian city-state had changed its leader since independence in the 1960s. His father, Lee Kuan Yew, was the country's charismatic leader for 31 years and oversaw a transformation from a third-world colony to a prosperous export-driven economy. Lee Hsien Loong, a former military strategist turned politician, has pledged a vibrant economy while maintaining a cohesive society.

Early Life
Lee Hsien Loong was born in Singapore on 10 Feb. 1952, the eldest son of a wealthy and well-connected Hakka-Chinese family. His father, Lee Kuan Yew, was Singapore's first prime minister, and led the former British colony as head of the People's Action Party (PAP) from its first period of self-governance in 1959, through independence in 1965, until 1990. Lee Hsien Loong attended state primary and secondary schools in Singapore, and was awarded a president's scholarship to study mathematics and computer science at Cambridge University, UK. He graduated in 1974 with first class honours and returned to serve in the Singapore Armed Forces, rising through the ranks to become a Brig.-Gen. He gained a reputation for his analytical and problem-solving skills. He entered politics as an MP representing the PAP in the general election of Sept. 1984. The election was the first occasion since 1963 that two opposition parties—the Workers' Party and the Singapore Democratic Party—were able to win seats from the ruling PAP. Lee was elected to the Central Executive Committee of the PAP in 1986.

Lee Kuan Yew resigned in Nov. 1990 after 31 years in power and Goh Chok Tong became prime minister, appointing Lee Hsien Loong his deputy with responsibility for economic and civil service affairs. After three decades of authoritarian rule, Singapore underwent a cautious liberalization. Lee held his parliamentary seat in the 1991 and 1997 general elections, which were landslide victories for the PAP. In Jan. 1998 he was appointed chairman of the Monetary Authority of Singapore. When, in line with other southeast Asian economies, Singapore faced an economic downturn in 1998, the government responded by cutting wages, allowing its currency to adjust downward and positioning the country as a leading international financial centre. Despite continued economic pressures, the PAP won the 2001 general election by a large majority. Lee was re-elected, and was appointed minister of finance on 23 Nov. 2001. He pursued a tax-cutting agenda and brought in pensions reforms and policies to liberalize the financial sector.

Career in Office
On 12 Aug. 2004 Lee was sworn in as prime minister. He remains the minister for finance but handed the chairmanship of the Monetary Authority to Goh Chok Tong, who became senior minister in the cabinet. In his opening address as Singapore's third prime minister, Lee said his goal was to 'build a vibrant and competitive economy ... and improve the lives of all Singaporeans.' He pledged to maintain the open, consultative style of the Goh Chok Tong era and signalled that social liberalization would continue: '... our people should feel free to express diverse views, pursue unconventional ideas ... we should have the confidence to engage in robust debate, so as to understand our problems, conceive fresh solutions, and open up new spaces.' This reflected the demands of a highly-educated population that is less tractable than before, and the government's realization that Singapore must move beyond manufacturing, where it is often outperformed by China, and into 'knowledge-based' industries that depend more on individual creativity and entrepreneurship.

In April 2005 Lee announced his government's controversial decision to legalize gambling, paving the way for the building of two large casino resorts and, more generally, hinting at a more permissive atmosphere within the country.

Singapore's usually fraught relations with neighbouring Malaysia improved in Jan. 2005 when the two countries settled a dispute over land reclamation work in their border waters.

DEFENCE

Compulsory military service in peacetime for all male citizens and permanent residents was introduced in 1967. The period of service for officers and non-commissioned officers is 30 months, other ranks 24 months. Reserve liability continues to age 50 for officers, 40 for other ranks. In 2000 the SAF (Singapore Armed Forces) comprised 350,000 Operationally Ready National Servicemen and an estimated 60,000 regulars and full-time National Servicemen.

An agreement with the USA in Nov. 1990 provided for an increase in US use of naval and air force facilities.

Singapore is a member of the Five Powers Defence Arrangement, with Australia, New Zealand, Malaysia and the UK.

In 2003 defence expenditure totalled US$4,741m. (US$1,116 per capita), representing 5·2% of GDP.

Army

Strength (2000) 50,000 (including 35,000 conscripts) plus 260,000 reserves. In addition there is a Civil Defence Force totalling over 87,000 including 3,720 conscripts, 23,000 Operationally Ready National Servicemen and 55,146 civil defence volunteers.

Navy

The Republic of Singapore Navy comprises four commands: Fleet, Coastal Command (COSCOM), Naval Logistics Command and Training Command. The fleet includes four diesel submarines. The Navy numbers an estimated 9,600 personnel including approximately 6,000 conscripts and 3,600 regulars. There are two naval bases: Tuas Naval Base and Changi Naval Base, the first phase of which was completed in 2000 and replaces Brani Naval Base.

Air Force

The Republic of Singapore Air Force (RSAF) has fighter squadrons comprising the F16 Falcon and the F5S/F Tiger.

Personnel strength (2000) about 13,500 (3,000 conscripts), with 165 combat aircraft and 20 armed helicopters.

INTERNATIONAL RELATIONS

Singapore is a member of the UN, BIS, WTO, the Commonwealth, Asian Development Bank, Colombo Plan and ASEAN and has ratified the Convention on the Prohibition of the Development, Production, Stockpiling and Use of Chemical Weapons and on their Destruction (CWC), and the UN Framework Convention on Climate Change (UNFCCC).

ECONOMY

Manufacturing (14%), transport and communications (7%), and wholesale and trade (7%) were the main engines for growth in 1999. Services accounted for 64% of GDP in 2000, goods producing industries 33% and owner-occupied dwellings 3·2%.

According to the anti-corruption organization *Transparency International*, Singapore ranked 5th in the world in a 2005 survey of the countries with the least corruption in business and government. It received 9·4 out of 10 in the annual index.

Overview

Singapore is estimated by the Economist Intelligence Unit to have the highest per capita GDP at purchasing power parity in Asia. It is credited with one of the least corrupt, most competitive and most open economies in the world. In the decade prior to the 1997 Asian financial crisis, the economy grew at an average annual rate of 9·2%. In 1998 the economy shrunk 0·8%, much less than its neighbours, and growth resumed in 1999–2000. Manufacturing, particularly electronics, has been the country's main engine of growth.

The country has received significant amounts of foreign investment for decades and inflows remain strong. The country is a secure destination for foreign investment, with political stability, high defence spending and a close relationship with the USA. Industry is dominated by foreign multinationals and a few large domestic enterprises with government links. While exports have driven Singapore's growth, the economy's openness leaves it vulnerable to external demand shocks. In 2001 the global economic slowdown caused Singapore's economy to shrink by 2%. The continued slump in the technology sector and the impact of SARS kept growth below average in 2002–03 but in 2004 a rebound in global electronics demand helped the economy grow by 8·4%. The government is seeking to shift the economy away from manufacturing, where other Asian countries are seen as rising competitors, into knowledge-driven industries. Singapore has become an increasingly important offshore banking centre and liberal rules on stem cell research have helped attract foreign

scientists, advancing the country's goal of becoming a leading biomedical innovation centre.

Currency

The unit of currency is the *Singapore dollar* (SGD) of 100 *cents*. Total money supply in June 2002 was S$34,888m. There was inflation of 0·5% in 2003 and 1·7% in 2004. Total foreign reserves at June 2002 were S$79,668m.

Budget

The fiscal year begins on 1 April. Budgetary central government revenue and expenditure for financial years (in S$1m.):

	1998	1999	2000	2001
Revenue	42,137	43,046	47,427	41,694
Expenditure	24,562	25,203	26,610	30,183

Singapore has the largest current account surplus of any country in relation to the size of its economy, standing at S$36·4bn. in 1999, representing 24% of GNP.

Performance

Real GDP growth rates (based on IMF statistics):

1997	1998	1999	2000	2001	2002	2003	2004
8·6%	−0·8%	6·8%	9·6%	−1·9%	3·2%	1·4%	8·4%

Total GDP was US$106·8bn. in 2004. Singapore was placed sixth in the world in the Growth Competitiveness Index in the World Economic Forum's *Global Competitiveness Report 2005–2006*. It had been first in 1999. In the 2005 *World Competitiveness Yearbook*, compiled by the International Institute for Management Development, Singapore came third in the world ranking, down from second in 2004.

Banking and Finance

The Monetary Authority of Singapore (*Governor*, Goh Chok Tong) performs the functions of a central bank, except the issuing of currency which is the responsibility of the Board of the Commissioners of Currency.

The Development Bank of Singapore and the Post Office Savings Bank were merged in 1998 to become the largest bank in southeast Asia and one of the leading banks in Asia, with a customer base of more than 3·3m. and a total deposit base of about S$71bn. Together, their total asset value is approximately S$94·5bn.

In April 2004 there were 115 commercial banks in Singapore, of which five were local. There were 49 representative offices, 23 foreign banks with full licences, 37 with 'wholesale' licences and 50 with 'offshore' licences. The total assets/liabilities amounted to S$384,600m. in Dec. 2001. Total deposits of non-bank customers in Dec. 1999 amounted to S$174,454·1m. and advances including bills financing totalled S$147,185·5m. in 1999. There were 66 merchant banks as at 31 Dec. 1999.

The Singapore Exchange (SGX), a merger of the Stock Exchange of Singapore and the Singapore International Monetary Exchange, was officially launched on 1 Dec. 1999.

ENERGY AND NATURAL RESOURCES

Environment

Singapore's carbon dioxide emissions from the consumption and flaring of fossil fuels in 2002 were the equivalent of 27·2 tonnes per capita.

Electricity

In 1995 Singapore Power Pte. Ltd. took over from the Public Utilities Board the responsibility for the provision of electricity and gas. Electrical power is generated by five gas and oil-fired power stations, with a total generating capacity of 7,657m. kW (2001). Production (2001) 33,061m. kWh. Consumption per capita (2000) 8,800 kWh.

Oil and Gas

Replacing the Kallang Gasworks, the Senoko Gasworks started operations in Oct. 1996. It had a total gas production capacity of 1·6m. cu. metres per day. In Jan. 2001 a 640-km gas pipeline linking Indonesia's West Natuna field with Singapore came on stream. It is expected to provide Singapore with US$8bn. worth of natural gas over a 20-year period.

Water

Singapore uses an average of 1·25m. cu. metres of water per day. Singapore's water supply comes from local sources and sources in Johor, Malaysia. The total water supply system comprises 19 raw water reservoirs, nine treatment works, 15 storage or service reservoirs and 5,150 km of pipelines.

Agriculture

Only about 1·49% of the total area is used for farming. Local farms provide only about 35% of hen eggs, 1·6% of chickens and 2·4% of ducks. 18,928 tonnes of vegetables and fruits were produced for domestic consumption in 1999. In 2001 alone Singapore imported 44·1m. chickens, 7m. ducks, 722m. hen eggs, 210,077 tonnes of meat and meat products, 226,126 tonnes of fish and fish products, 352,919 tonnes of vegetables and 358,595 tonnes of fruits for local consumption.

Agro-technology parks house large-scale intensive farms to improve production of fresh food. As of the end of 2000, a total of 1,465 ha. of land in Murai, Sungei Tengah, Nee Soon, Loyang, Mandai and Lim Chu Kang had been developed into Agro-technology Parks. Through open tenders, auctions and direct allocations, 247 farms have been allocated 777 ha. of land for the production of livestock, eggs, milk, aquarium fish, food fish (fish for consumption), fruits, vegetables, orchids and ornamental and aquatic plants, as well as for the breeding of birds and dogs. When the Agro-technology Parks are fully developed, their output is expected to reach S$450m.

Forestry

In 2000 forests covered 2,000 ha., or 3·3% of the total land area.

Fisheries

The total local supply of fish in 2003 was 2,085 tonnes. Singapore imported 528,000 tonnes of fish and fish products. There are 93 fish processing establishments supplying products for the domestic market, nine establishments for the EU export market and 88 licensed marine farms.

INDUSTRY

The leading companies by market capitalization in Singapore in Nov. 2005 were: Singapore Telecommunications (US$24·7bn.); DBS Group Holdings (US$14·5bn.), a banking group; and the United Overseas Bank (US$13·2bn.).

The largest industrial area is at Jurong, with 35 modern industrial estates housing over 4,036 establishments (engaging ten people or more) in 1999, and 340,907 workers.

Production, 1999 (in S$1m.), totalled 134,533: including electronic products, 70,140·4; chemicals and chemical products, 13,684·1; petroleum, 13,621·6; fabricated metal products, 6,253·9; transport equipment, 5,772·8; food, beverages and tobacco, 3,407·2; publishing, printing and reproduction of recorded media, 2,997·0.

Labour

In June 2004 Singapore's labour force comprised 2,183,300 people, of whom 2,066,900 were employed and 116,400 were unemployed. The principal areas of employment in June 2004 were manufacturing (356,700 people), wholesale and retail trade (319,700), business services (254,000), transport, storage and communications (212,500) and hotels and restaurants (129,300). The unemployment rate averaged 3·4% throughout 2004 (4·0% in 2003). The average worker put in 46·3 hours a week in 2004; average monthly earnings in 2004 were S$3,329.

Legislation regulates the principal terms and conditions of employment such as hours of work, sick leave and other fringe benefits. Young people of 14–16 years may work in industrial establishments, and children of 12–14 years may be employed in approved apprenticeship schemes. A trade dispute may be referred to the Industrial Arbitration Court.

The Ministry of Manpower operates an employment service and provides the handicapped with specialized on-the-job training. The Central Provident Fund was established in 1955 to make provision for employees in their old age. At the end of 2004 there were 3,018,000 members with S$111,874m. standing to their credit in the fund. The legal retirement age is 62.

Source: Singapore Department of Statistics

Trade Unions

In 2001 there were 71 registered employee trade unions, three employer unions and one federation of trade unions—the National Trades Union Congress (NTUC). The total membership of the trade unions increased from 272,769 in 1998 to 338,311 in 2001. The vast majority (99%) of the total union membership belonged to the 69 NTUC-affiliated unions. The largest union, the United Workers of Electronic Industries (UWEEI), had 39,508 members in 2000.

INTERNATIONAL TRADE

Foreign investment of up to 40% of the equity of domestic banks is permitted. Total external trade in 2001 was S$425·7bn.

Imports and Exports

Total imports were S$222,811m. in 2003; and total exports S$251,096m. in 2003.

Imports and exports (in S$1m.), by country, 1999:

	Imports (c.i.f.)	Exports (f.o.b.)
Australia	2,464	5,373
China	9,649	6,643
France	4,397	3,709
Germany	6,111	5,522
Hong Kong	5,400	14,915
Italy	2,026	734
Japan	31,325	14,421
Korea (South)	7,063	6,027
Malaysia	29,283	32,164
Saudi Arabia	5,536	547
Taiwan	7,540	9,477
Thailand	8,889	8,536
UK	4,623	7,247
USA	32,044	37,215

The major import sources in 2003 were Malaysia (17%), USA (14%), Japan (12%) and China (9%); the leading export markets in 2003 were Malaysia (16%), USA (13%), Hong Kong (10%) and China (7%).

Imports (1999, in S$1m.): machinery and transport equipment, 113,365; mineral fuels, 17,075; manufactured goods, 14,973; chemicals and chemical products, 11,212; food, beverages and tobacco, 6,948; crude materials, 1,471; animal and vegetable oils, 504; miscellaneous manufactured articles, 19,575; miscellaneous transactions necessary, 3,019.

Exports (1999, in S$1m.): machinery and transport equipment, 128,807; mineral fuels, 15,335; chemicals and chemical products, 15,326; manufactured goods, 8,445; food, beverages and tobacco, 4,934; crude materials, 1,562; animal and vegetable oils, 483; miscellaneous manufactured articles, 16,414; miscellaneous transactions necessary, 2,984.

In May 2003 the US and Singapore signed a free trade agreement removing tariffs on trade worth an estimated US$33bn. per annum.

Trade Fairs

Singapore ranked as the world's 5th most important convention city in 2002, and the leading convention city in Asia, according to the Union des Associations Internationales (UAI). In 1999 Singapore hosted 140 meetings recognized by UAI, 2,314 incentive groups, 880 conventions and CommunicAsia, Asia Pacific's largest communications and IT event.

COMMUNICATIONS

Roads

In 2002 there were 3,130 km of public roads (100% asphalt-paved). Singapore has one of the densest road networks in the world.

In 2002 there were 404,274 private cars, 12,707 buses and 131,437 motorcycles and scooters.

Rail

A 25·8-km main line runs through Singapore, connecting with the States of Malaysia and as far as Bangkok. Branch lines serve the port of Singapore and the industrial estates at Jurong. The total rail length of the Mass Rapid Transit (SMRT) metro is 89·4 km. The 20 km North-East Line (operated by SBS Transit), the world's first fully automated heavy metro, became operational in 2003. In late 1999 the Light Rapid Transit System (LRT) began operations, linking the Bukit Panjang Estate with Choa Chu Kang in the North West region.

Civil Aviation

As of Dec. 2001 Singapore Changi Airport was served by 61 airlines with more than 3,200 weekly flights to and from 138 cities in 50 countries. The national airline is Singapore Airlines, which in 1999 carried 14,527,200 passengers and flew 313·6m. km. Its subsidiary, Silk Air, serves Asian destinations. A total of 28,093,759 passengers were handled in 2001, and 1,507,062 tonnes of freight.

Shipping

Singapore has a large container port, the world's busiest in terms of shipping tonnage in 2001 and second only to Hong Kong in terms of containers handled. The economy is dependent on shipping and entrepôt trade.

A total of 146,265 vessels of 960m. gross tonnes (GT) entered Singapore during 2001. In 2001, 3,353 vessels with a total of 23·2m. GT were registered in Singapore. The Singapore merchant fleet ranked 7th among the principal merchant fleets of the world in 2001. Total cargo handled in 2000 was 326·11m. tonnes, and total container throughput in 2001 was 15,570,000 TEUs (twenty-foot equivalent units), ranking Singapore second behind Hong Kong on container traffic.

Telecommunications

In Dec. 2001 there were 1,948,500 telephone lines (penetration rate of 485 per 1,000 population), 2,858,800 mobile phone subscribers and 481,600 pager subscribers. In 1997 Singapore Telecom, one of the largest companies in Asia, lost its monopoly with the entry of a new mobile phone operator and three new paging operators. Singapore had three mobile phone operators, six Internet service providers, and three paging operators as of Feb. 2001. In April 2002 there were 2·31m. Internet users, or 51·84% of the population. In Aug. 2000, 42% of households were Internet subscribers. The Telecommunication Authority of Singapore (TAS) is the national regulator and promoter of the telecommunication and postal industries. As of Nov. 1999 PC penetration in homes had reached 59% of the population. In 2001 there were 2·1m. PCs or 508·3 per 1,000 inhabitants.

According to the World Economic Forum's *Global Information Technology Report 2004–2005* Singapore is the world's leading country in exploiting global information technology developments.

Postal Services

In 1999 there were various postal outlets in operation, comprising 62 main branches and 90 smaller branches. Various services included stamp vendors, postage label vending machines and Self-Service Automated Machines (SAM). A total of 1,487m. postal articles were handled in 1999. During the late 1990s mail volume increased by about 30m. items per year.

SOCIAL INSTITUTIONS

Justice

There is a Supreme Court in Singapore which consists of the High Court and the Court of Appeal. The Supreme Court is composed of a Chief Justice and 11 Judges. The High Court has unlimited original jurisdiction in both civil and criminal cases. The Court of Appeal is the final appellate court. It hears appeals from any judgement or order of the High Court in any civil matter. The Subordinate Courts consist of a total of 47 District and Magistrates' Courts, the Civil, the Family and Crime Registries, the Primary Dispute Resolution Centre, and the Small Claims Tribunal. The right of appeal to the UK Privy Council was abolished in 1994.

Penalties for drug trafficking and abuse are severe, including a mandatory death penalty. In 1994 there were 76 executions, although since then the average annual number has generally been declining—there were two confirmed executions in 2005.

The Technology Court was introduced in 1995 where documents were filed electronically. This process was implemented in Aug. 1998 in the Magistrates appeal and the Court of Appeal.

The population in penal institutions in 2002 (excluding those in drug rehabilitation centres) was 16,310 (388 per 100,000 of national population).

Education

The general literacy rate rose from 84% in 1980 to 92·5% in 2003 (male 96·6%; female 88·6%). Kindergartens are private and fee-paying. Compulsory primary state education starts at six years and culminates at 11 or 12 years with an examination which influences choice of secondary schooling. There are 17 autonomous and eight private fee-paying secondary schools. Tertiary education at 16 years is divided into three branches: junior colleges leading to university; four polytechnics; and ten technical institutes.

Statistics of schools in 2001.

	Schools	Pupils	Teachers
Primary schools	194	302,733	12,011
Secondary schools	162	187,858	9,491
Junior colleges and Centralized institutes	17	24,582	1,869

There are three universities: the National University of Singapore (established 1905) with 32,028 students in 2001–02, the Nanyang Technological University (established 1991) with 23,025 in 2001–02, and the Singapore Management University (established in 2000).

In 2000–01 total expenditure on education came to 3·5% of GNP and accounted for 23·6% of total government expenditure.

Health

There are 27 hospitals (five general hospitals, one community hospital, seven specialist hospitals/centres and 14 private), with 11,897 beds in 2001. In 2001 there were 5,747 doctors, 1,087 dentists, 17,398 registered nurses and midwives and 1,141 pharmacists.

The leading causes of death are cancer (4,238 deaths in 2000), heart disease (3,940) and pneumonia (1,794).

Welfare

The Central Provident Fund (CPF) was set up in 1955 to provide financial security for workers upon retirement or when they are no longer able to work. In 2001 there were 2,922,673 members with S$92,221m. standing to their credit in the Fund.

RELIGION

In 2001, 41·0% of the population were Buddhists and Taoists, 12·0% Muslims, 11·7% Christians and 3·2% Hindus; 0·5% belonged to other religions.

CULTURE

The National Arts Council (NAC) was established in 1991 to spearhead the development of the arts.

Broadcasting

The Television Corporation of Singapore broadcasts mainly English and Chinese programmes. Malay and Tamil programmes are offered on Suria and Central, two channels launched in Jan. 2000. A sports-only channel, Sportscity, was also launched in Jan. 2000. Colour is by PAL. There were 816,000 TV licences in 2001 and 2·70m. radio receivers in 2000. Cable subscribers numbered 302,000 in 2001.

Press

In 2001 there were ten daily newspapers, in four languages, with a total daily circulation of about 1·59m. copies. In 2000 a new newspaper, *Project Eyeball*, and two free commuter tabloids, *Streats* and *Today,* were launched. *Project Eyeball* was suspended in June 2001.

Tourism

There were 7,522,200 visitors in 2001. Most came from Indonesia, Japan, Malaysia, Australia, the UK, China, the USA and Taiwan. The total tourism receipts for 2001 came to S$9·16bn. The total number of gazetted hotels increased from 94 in 1997 to 101 in 2000, providing 30,700 rooms.

Festivals

Every Jan. or Feb. the Lunar New Year is celebrated. Other Chinese festivals include Qing Ming (a time for the remembrance of ancestors), Yu Lan Jie (Feast of the Hungry Ghosts) and the Mid-Autumn Festival (Mooncake or Lantern festival).

Muslims in Singapore celebrate Hari Raya Puasa (to celebrate the end of a month-long fast) and Hari Raya Haji (a day of prayer and commemoration of the annual Mecca pilgrimage). There are also Muharram (a New Year celebration) and Maulud (Prophet Muhammad's birthday).

Hindus celebrate the Tamil New Year in mid-April. Thaipusam is a penitential Hindu festival popular with Tamils; and Diwali, the Festival of Lights, is celebrated by Hindus and Sikhs.

Other festivals include Thimithi (a fire-walking ceremony) and Navarathiri (nine nights' prayer).

Buddhists observe Vesak Day, which commemorates the birth, enlightenment and Nirvana of the Buddha, and falls on the full moon day in May.

Christmas, Good Friday and Easter Sunday are also recognized.

DIPLOMATIC REPRESENTATIVES

Of Singapore in the United Kingdom (9 Wilton Crescent, London, SW1X 8SP)
High Commissioner: Michael Eng Cheng Teo.

Of the United Kingdom in Singapore (100 Tanglin Rd, Singapore 247919)
High Commissioner: Alan Collins, CMG.

Of Singapore in the USA (3501 International Pl., NW, Washington, D.C., 20008)
Ambassador: Chan Heng Chee.

Of the USA in Singapore (27 Napier Rd, Singapore 258508)
Ambassador: Patricia L. Herbold.

Of Singapore to the United Nations
Ambassador: Vanu Gopala Menon.

Of Singapore to the European Union
Ambassador: Walter Woon.

FURTHER READING

Department of Statistics. *Monthly Digest of Statistics.—Yearbook of Statistics.*
The Constitution of Singapore. Singapore, 1992
Information Division, Ministry of Information and the Arts. *Singapore* [*year*]: a Review of [*the previous year*].
Ministry of Trade and Industry, *Economic Survey of Singapore.* (Quarterly and Annual)

Chew, E. C. T., *A History of Singapore.* Singapore, 1992
Huff, W. G., *Economic Growth of Singapore: Trade and Development in the Twentieth Century.* CUP, 1994
Myint, S., *The Principles of Singapore Law.* 2nd ed. Singapore, 1992
Tan, C. H., *Financial Markets and Institutions in Singapore.* 7th ed. Singapore, 1992
Vasil, R. K., *Governing Singapore.* Singapore, 1992

National library: National Library, Stamford Rd, Singapore 178896.
National Statistical Office: Department of Statistics, Minister of Trade and Industry, Singapore 179434.
Website: http://www.singstat.gov.sg

SLOVAKIA

© Research Machines plc 2006

Slovenská Republika

Capital: Bratislava
Population projection, 2010: 5·40m.
GDP per capita, 2003: (PPP$) 13,494
HDI/world rank: 0·849/42

KEY HISTORICAL EVENTS

The Czechoslovak State came into existence on 28 Oct. 1918 after the dissolution of Austria-Hungary. Two days later the Slovak National Council declared its wish to unite with the Czechs. The Treaty of St Germain-en-Laye (1919) recognized the Czechoslovak Republic, consisting of the Czech lands (Bohemia, Moravia, part of Silesia) and Slovakia. In March 1939 the German-sponsored Slovak government proclaimed Slovakia independent and Germany incorporated the Czech lands into the Reich as the 'Protectorate of Bohemia and Moravia'. A government-in-exile, headed by Dr Edvard Beneš, was set up in London. Liberation by the Soviet Army and US Forces was completed by May 1945. Territories taken by the Germans, Poles and Hungarians were restored to Czechoslovak sovereignty. Elections were held in May 1946 following which a coalition government under a Communist prime minister, Klement Gottwald, remained in power until 20 Feb. 1948, when 12 of the non-Communist ministers resigned in protest against infiltration of Communists into the police. In Feb. a predominantly Communist government was formed by Gottwald. In May 1948 elections resulted in an 89% majority for the government and President Beneš resigned.

In 1968 pressure for liberalization culminated in the overthrow of the Stalinist leader, Antonín Novotný, and his associates. Under Alexander Dubček's leadership the 'Prague Spring' began to take shape and the outlines of a new political system described as 'socialism with a human face' began to appear as the Communist Party introduced an 'Action Programme' of far-reaching reforms. Soviet pressure to abandon this programme was exerted between May and Aug. 1968 and finally Warsaw Pact forces occupied Czechoslovakia on 21 Aug. The Czechoslovak government was compelled to accept a policy of 'normalization' (*i.e.*, abandonment of most reforms) and the stationing of Soviet forces.

Mass demonstrations demanding political reform began in Nov. 1989. After the authorities' use of violence to break up a demonstration on 17 Nov., the Communist leader resigned. On 30 Nov. the Federal Assembly abolished the Communist Party's sole right to govern, and a new Government was formed on 3 Dec. The protest movement continued to grow and on 10 Dec. another Government was formed. Gustáv Husák resigned as President and was replaced by Václav Havel on the unanimous vote of 323 members of the Federal Assembly on 29 Dec.

At the June 1992 elections the Movement for Democratic Slovakia, led by Vladimír Mečiar, campaigned on the issue of Slovak independence, and on 17 July the Slovak National Council adopted a declaration of sovereignty by 113 to 24 votes. President Havel resigned as federal president on 20 July. On 1 Sept. 1992 the Slovak National Council adopted, by 114 votes to 16 with 4 abstentions (and a boycott by the Hungarian deputies), a Constitution for an independent Slovakia to come into being on 1 Jan. 1993. Economic property was divided between Slovakia and the Czech Republic in accordance with a Czechoslovakian law of 13 Nov. 1992. Government real estate became the property of the republic in which it was located. Other property was divided by specially-constituted commissions in the proportion of two (Czech Republic) to one (Slovakia) on the basis of population size. Military material was divided on the two:one principle. Regular military personnel were invited to choose which armed force they would serve in.

Slovakia became a member of NATO in March 2004 and the European Union in May 2004.

TERRITORY AND POPULATION

Slovakia is bounded in the northwest by the Czech Republic, north by Poland, east by Ukraine, south by Hungary and southwest by Austria. Its area is 49,034 sq. km (18,932 sq. miles). Census population in 2001 was 5,379,455 (2,612,515 male; 2,766,940 female); density, 109·7 per sq. km. The estimated population in 2005 was 5,401,000.

The UN gives a projected population for 2010 of 5·40m.

In 2003, 57·5% of the population lived in urban areas. There are eight administrative regions (*Kraj*), one of which is the capital, Bratislava. They have the same name as the main city of the region.

Region	Area in sq. km	2001 population
Banská Bystrica	9,455	662,121
Bratislava	2,053	599,015
Košice	6,753	766,012
Nitra	6,343	713,422
Prešov	8,993	789,968
Trenčin	4,501	605,582
Trnava	4,148	551,003
Žilina	6,788	692,332

The capital, Bratislava, had a population in 2001 of 428,700. The population of other principal towns (2001, in 1,000): Košice, 236; Prešov, 93; Nitra, 87; Žilina, 85; Banská Bystrica, 83; Trnava, 70; Martin, 60; Trenčin, 58.

The population is 85·8% Slovak, 9·7% Hungarian, 1·6% Roma and 0·8% Czech, with some Ruthenians, Ukrainians, Germans and Poles.

A law of Nov. 1995 makes Slovak the sole official language.

SOCIAL STATISTICS

Births, 2001, 51,136; deaths, 51,980; marriages, 23,795; divorces, 9,817. Rates (per 1,000 population), 2000: birth, 10·2; death, 9·8; marriage, 4·8; divorce, 1·7. Expectation of life, 2003, was 70·1 years for males and 77·9 for females. In 2001 the most popular age range for marrying was 25–29 for males and 20–24 for females. Annual population growth rate, 1992–2002, 0·2%. Infant mortality, 2001 (per 1,000 live births), 8. Fertility rate, 2001, 1·3 births per woman.

CLIMATE

A humid continental climate, with warm summers and cold winters. Precipitation is generally greater in summer, with thunderstorms. Autumn, with dry, clear weather and spring, which is damp, are each of short duration. Bratislava, Jan. –0·7°C. June 19·1°C. Annual rainfall 649 mm.

CONSTITUTION AND GOVERNMENT

The constitution became effective on 1 Jan. 1993, creating a parliamentary democracy with universal suffrage from the age of 18. Parliament is the unicameral *National Council*. It has 150 members elected by proportional representation to serve four-year terms. The constitution was amended in Sept. 1998 to allow for the direct election of the *President*, who serves for a five-year term. The President may serve a maximum of two consecutive terms.

The Judicial Branch consists of a *Supreme Court*, whose judges are elected by the National Council, and a *Constitutional Court*, whose judges are appointed by the President from a group of nominees approved by the National Council.

Citizenship belongs to all citizens of the former federal Slovak Republic; other residents of five years standing may apply for citizenship. Slovakia grants dual citizenship.

National Anthem

'Nad Tatrou sa blýska' ('Storm over the Tatras'); words by J. Matúška, tune anonymous.

GOVERNMENT CHRONOLOGY

(DU = Democratic Union; HZD = Movement for Democracy; HZDS = Movement for a Democratic Slovakia; KDH = Christian Democratic Movement; SDK = Slovak Democratic Coalition; SDKÚ = Slovak Democratic and Christian Union; SOP = Party of Civic Understanding; n/p = non-partisan)

Presidents since 1993.

1993–98	n/p	Michal Kováč
1999–2004	SOP, n/p	Rudolf Schuster
2004–	HZD, n/p	Ivan Gašparovič

Prime Ministers since 1993.

1993–94	HZDS	Vladimír Mečiar
1994	DU	Jozef Moravčík
1994–98	HZDS	Vladimír Mečiar
1998–	KDH/SDK, SDKÚ	Mikuláš Dzurinda

RECENT ELECTIONS

Elections to the National Council were held on 20 and 21 Sept. 2002. Former prime minister Vladimír Mečiar's Movement for a Democratic Slovakia (HZDS) won 36 seats with 19·5% of votes cast—the HZDS became the LS-HZDS when it added the prefix 'The People's Party' in June 2003. The Slovak Democratic and Christian Union (SDKÚ) won 28 seats with 15·1%; the Direction Party (Smer), 25 with 13·5%; the Party of the Hungarian Coalition (SMK), 20 with 11·2%; the Christian Democratic Movement (KDH), 15 with 8·3%; the New Civic Alliance (ANO), 15 with 8·0%; and the Slovak Communist Party (KSS), 11 with 6·3%. Turnout was 70·0%.

In the first round of presidential elections on 3 April 2004, former prime minister Vladimír Mečiar of the LS-HZDS won 32·7% of the vote, against 22·3% for Ivan Gašparovič (Movement for Democracy; HZD) and 22·1% for Eduard Kukan (SDKÚ). There were three other candidates. Turnout was 47·9%. In the run-off held on 17 April Gašparovič won 59·9% against 40·1% for Mečiar.

European Parliament

Slovakia has 14 representatives. At the June 2004 elections turnout was 16·7% (the lowest in the EU). The SDKÚ won 3 seats with 17·1% of votes cast (political affiliation in European Parliament: European People's Party–European Democrats); the LS-HZDS, 3 with 17·1% (non-attached); the Smer, 3 with 16·9% (Party of European Socialists); the KDH, 3 with 16·2% (European People's Party–European Democrats); the SMK, 2 with 13·2% (European People's Party–European Democrats).

Parliamentary elections were scheduled to take place on 17 June 2006.

CURRENT ADMINISTRATION

President: Ivan Gašparovič; b. 1941 (HZD; sworn in on 15 June 2004).

A coalition government was appointed on 15 Oct. 2002 composed of members of the Slovak Democratic and Christian Union (SDKÚ), the Party of the Hungarian Coalition (SMK), the Christian Democratic Movement (KDH) and the New Civic Alliance (ANO). In Feb. 2006 the Christian Democratic Movement left the coalition. In March 2006 the cabinet was composed as follows:

Prime Minister: Mikuláš Dzurinda; b. 1955 (SDKÚ; sworn in on 30 Oct. 1998; re-appointed 15 Oct. 2002).

Deputy Prime Ministers: Ivan Mikloš (SDKÚ; also *Minister of Finance*); Jirko Malchárek (ANO; also *Minister of Economy*); Pál Csáky (SMK; *Responsible for European Integration, Human Rights and Minorities*).

Minister of Foreign Affairs: Eduard Kukan (SDKÚ). *Interior:* Martin Pado (SDKÚ). *Defence:* Martin Fedor (SDKÚ). *Justice:* Lucia Žitňanská (ind.). *Culture:* František Tóth (ANO). *Healthcare:* Rudolf Zajac (ANO). *Education:* László Szigeti (SMK). *Labour, Social Affairs and Family Affairs:* Iveta Radičová (SDKÚ). *Environment:* László Miklós (SMK). *Agriculture:* Zsolt Simon (SMK). *Transport, Post and Telecommunications:* Pavol Prokopovič (SDKÚ). *Construction and Public Works:* László Gyurovszky (SMK).

The *Speaker* is Jozef Migas.

Office of the Prime Minister: http://www.government.gov.sk

CURRENT LEADERS

Ivan Gašparovič

Position
President

Introduction
Shortly before Slovakia became a member of the European Union on 1 May 2004, a 63-year old lawyer, Ivan Gašparovič, was elected as the country's president. Instrumental in drawing up Slovakia's constitution prior to the dissolution of Czechoslovakia in 1993, Gašparovič was also a close ally of the controversial nationalist former prime minister, Vladimír Mečiar, the man he beat in the second round of the presidential election.

Early Life
Ivan Gašparovič was born in Poltár, near Lučenec in southern Slovakia on 27 March 1941. His father, Vladimir Gašparović, had migrated to the region from Rijeka, Croatia at the end of the First World War. The family moved to Bratislava, where Vladimir worked as a teacher in a secondary school. Having studied at the Law Faculty of the Komenský University in Bratislava from 1959–64, Ivan Gašparovič worked in the district prosecutor's office of Bratislava's Martin district (1965–66), and then became a prosecutor at the municipal prosecutor's office. In early 1968 he joined the Communist Party of Czechoslovakia and actively supported the reforms of Alexander Dubček, the party's Slovak

first secretary. Under Dubček, in what became known as the Prague Spring, democratization went further than in any other Communist state—press censorship was reduced and Slovakia was granted political autonomy. However, opposition grew swiftly in the USSR and in other Warsaw Pact states which invaded Czechoslovakia on the night of 20 Aug. 1968. The following year Dubček was replaced by Gustáv Husák, who spearheaded a 'normalization' policy that turned Czechoslovakia into one of Central Europe's most repressive states.

Gašparovič left the Communist Party after the events of 1968 and began work as a teacher at the Department of Criminal Law, Criminology and Criminological Practice at the Komenský University. He remained there until 1990 when he became the vice chancellor in Feb. of that year, two months after the 'Velvet Revolution' had swept aside the Communists. Václav Havel, the playwright and former dissident who was elected federal president in Dec. 1989, nominated Gašparovič as prosecutor-general of Czechoslovakia. He moved to Prague and took up the post in July 1990, as the new government began to tackle the legacy of Communism—a moribund economy, high unemployment and widespread social discontent. Under the 1968 constitution Czechoslovakia was a federal republic—each republic had a council and an assembly, but the federal government dealt with defence and foreign affairs. Arguments over the nature of the federation broke out and in 1991 Vladimír Mečiar formed the Movement for a Democratic Slovakia (HZDS). Gašparovič returned to Bratislava to teach at the Komenský University and joined the HZDS in 1992. Mečiar led the party to victory in the June 1992 elections, and Gašparovič became an HZDS member of the Slovak parliament. In late 1992 he was one of the authors of the constitution of Slovakia, which came into effect on 1 Jan. 1993 when the republic formally declared its independence.

Gašparovič was speaker of the Slovak parliament until Oct. 1998 and a close ally of Prime Minister Mečiar, whose controversial policies in the mid-1990s included stripping away the rights of the country's large Hungarian community and clamping down on the media. Slovakia became increasingly isolated from Western Europe until Mečiar's nationalist government was defeated in Sept. 1998 by an alliance of liberals, centrists, left-wingers and ethnic Hungarians. Mikuláš Dzurinda became prime minister and steered Slovakia through various reforms required for EU and NATO membership. From Oct. 1998–July 2002, when the HZDS was in opposition, Gašparovič was a member of the parliamentary committee for the supervision of the SIS (the Slovak equivalent of the US Central Intelligence Agency—CIA).

In July 2002 Gašparovič and some other members stormed out of the HZDS after being struck off the list of candidates for the parliamentary elections in Sept. 2002. The HZDS went on to poll only 3·3% of the vote, not enough to win seats in the parliament. Gašparovič returned to the Law Faculty of the Komenský University, but also established a new political party called the Movement for Democracy (HZD). In April 2004 he ran for president against Mečiar, who was attempting to make a comeback after losing the 2002 legislative elections. Although Mečiar won more votes than Gašparovič in the first round, he failed to win a majority. In the second round, Gašparovič secured nearly 60% of the vote after receiving the support of the eliminated candidates.

Career in Office

Ivan Gašparovič succeeded Rudolf Schuster as president of the Slovak Republic on 15 June 2004 and began a five-year term of office. Although he was expected to be more acceptable than Mečiar to Slovakia's new EU partners, his nationalist-populist leanings are at odds politically with the minority centre-right administration led by Mikuláš Dzurinda.

Mikuláš Dzurinda

Position
Prime Minister

Introduction
Mikuláš Dzurinda was appointed prime minister in 1998 as leader of the Slovak Democratic Coalition (SDK). Two years later he founded the Slovak Democratic and Christian Union (SDKÚ) and won a second term of office in 2002. He has been credited with establishing good relations with NATO and the EU and for improving Slovakia's economic and political structure.

Early Life
Mikuláš Dzurinda was born on 4 Feb. 1955 in Spišský Štvrtok, a village in the east of Slovakia. He graduated from the University of Transport and Communication in Žilina in 1979 and went on to gain a Candidate of Sciences post-graduate degree in 1988. He worked as an economic analyst for the transport research institute and in the Bratislava division of Czechoslovak Railways before founding the Christian Democratic Movement (KDH).

The party was officially constituted in 1990 and Dzurinda became deputy minister of transportation and posts after the Czechoslovak elections of 1991. In 1992 he entered the Slovak national council, sitting on the committee for budget and finance. In 1993, after the establishment of the Slovak Republic, Dzurinda was appointed chairman of the KDH and in 1994 he became Slovak minister of transportation, posts and public works. Dzurinda returned to the opposition benches after the 1994 election. In 1997 he became spokesman for the SDK (comprising the KDH, the Democratic Party, the Democratic Union, the Social Democratic Party of Slovakia and the Green Party of Slovakia). The following year he was appointed its chairman. He led them to victory at that year's elections and was sworn in as prime minister on 30 Oct. 1998.

Career in Office
In Jan. 2000 Dzurinda founded the Slovak Democratic and Christian Union (SDKÚ), made up of the KDH, the Party of Hungarian Coalition (SMK) and the Alliance of the New Citizen. As leader of the coalition, he was elected prime minister again in Oct. 2002.

In Sept. 2000 Slovakia gained entry into the OECD. In Feb. 2001 Dzurinda approved changes to the constitution to facilitate Slovakia's entry into NATO and the EU. He de-centralized power while increasing the authority of the state audit office. There was greater recognition of minority rights, building on a law introduced in July 1999 to improve the status of minority languages. In Jan. 2002 eight regional parliaments were created in keeping with EU membership requirements. Accession talks were completed at the Copenhagen summit in Dec. 2002. In May 2003 a referendum gave backing to accession and in May 2004 Slovakia was one of ten new countries to join the EU. Parliament ratified the EU constitution the following year. Slovakia was invited to join NATO in Nov. 2002 and admitted in March 2004. Dzurinda has worked hard to encourage foreign investment. During his first term the US steel industry pledged to invest around US$1bn. and Korea's Hyundai company are also significant investors. In 2003 Slovakia recorded a 4·5% growth rate, with growth predicted to continue steadily.

Domestically, Dzurinda has overhauled the pensions and benefits system. There have been cuts in benefits for those not actively seeking employment and healthcare costs have risen. The tax system has been simplified with the introduction of a 19% flat rate. However, while Dzurinda's economic overhaul of Slovakia has been applauded by the international community, he has faced some hostility at home. The average hourly wage remains low and there is little job security. In Feb. 2004 there were riots in eastern Slovakia in protest at benefits cuts. In 2005 several deputies quit in protest at Dzurinda's leadership and in

Sept. 2005 the opposition boycotted parliament in an attempt to force early elections.

DEFENCE

Conscription is for 12 months. In 2003 military expenditure totalled US$627m. (US$117 per capita), representing 1·9% of GDP.

Army

Personnel (2002), 13,000 (including 10,400 conscripts). In addition there are a border police of 1,700, 1,350 civil defence troops and 250 guard troops.

Air Force

There are 60 combat aircraft, including Su-22, Su-25, MiG-21 and MiG-29 fighters and 19 attack helicopters. Personnel (2002), 10,200.

INTERNATIONAL RELATIONS

Slovakia is a member of the UN, WTO, BIS, NATO, EU, Council of Europe, OSCE, OECD, CEFTA, CERN, CEI, Danube Commission, IOM and an associate partner of the WEU. A referendum held on 16–17 May 2003 approved accession to the EU, with 92·5% of votes cast for membership and 7·5% against. Turn-out was 52·2%. Slovakia became a member of NATO on 29 March 2004 and the EU on 1 May 2004. On 11 May 2005 Slovakia became the sixth country to ratify the proposed EU constitution. The parliament approved the treaty by 116 votes to 27, with four abstentions.

Slovakia has had a long-standing dispute with Hungary over the Gabčíkovo-Nagymaros Project, involving the building of dam structures in both countries for the production of electric power, flood control and improvement of navigation on the Danube as agreed in a treaty signed in 1977 between Czechoslovakia and Hungary. In late 1998 Slovakia and Hungary signed a protocol easing tensions between the two nations and settling differences over the dam.

ECONOMY

Agriculture accounted for 4·0% of GDP in 2002, industry 28·6% and services 67·4%.

Overview

The economy has experienced high growth rates since 1998, driven by growing exports and foreign direct investment, particularly in the car industry. Real GDP has been growing at approximately 4% per annum, private demand is strong and the export sector is expanding steadily. Membership of the EU since May 2004 has reinforced this trend with demand slowly shifting from external to domestic sources. However, the unemployment rate ran at nearly 18% in 2005, of which two-thirds is long-term. Fiscal deficit has been lowered since the early 2000s by structural reforms, including expenditure reduction in social benefits and health, and the termination of some government guarantees on unrecoverable loans. The fiscal deficit stood at 3·8% in 2004, down from 7·2% in 2002. The declining fiscal deficit makes the attainment of the Maastricht ceiling of 3% in 2007 increasingly credible, in preparation for the planned adoption of the euro in 2009. Structural reforms earmarked for coming years to strengthen economic transition include the reformation of the education system, the promotion of labour mobility, the development of infrastructure and the reduction of taxes on labour.

The economy has been undergoing constant restructuring since 1998, when economic policy shifted from state intervention towards pro-market reforms. In the first years after independence in 1993 economic policy was misdirected—structural reforms were postponed and expansionary fiscal policies supported domestic consumption and employment. Following economic transition the heavy industry and agriculture sectors shrank

while the service sector increased its share of GDP to 65% in 2004.

Currency

The unit of currency is the *Slovak koruna* or crown (SKK) of 100 *haliers*, introduced on 8 Feb. 1993. The koruna was devalued by 10% in July 1993. Since Oct. 1998 the koruna has operated in a managed float. Foreign exchange reserves were US$4,420m. and gold reserves 1·13m. troy oz in June 2002. Inflation rates (based on OECD statistics):

1995	1996	1997	1998	1999	2000	2001	2002	2003	2004
9·8%	5·8%	6·1%	6·7%	10·6%	12·0%	7·3%	3·1%	8·6%	7·5%

Total money supply in Dec. 2001 was 225,566m. koruny.

Budget

Government revenue and expenditure (in 1m. koruny):

	1997	1998	1999	2000	2001
Revenue	265,146	274,677	315,436	325,402	331,649
Expenditure	290,026	303,952	317,447	368,407	386,901

VAT, personal and company income tax, real estate taxes and inheritance taxes came into force in Jan. 1993. VAT is 19% (since 1 Jan. 2004).

Performance

Real GDP growth rates (based on OECD statistics):

1995	1996	1997	1998	1999	2000	2001	2002	2003	2004
5·8%	6·1%	4·6%	4·2%	1·5%	2·0%	3·8%	4·6%	4·5%	5·5%

Slovakia's total GDP in 2004 was US$41·1bn.

Banking and Finance

The central bank and bank of issue is the Slovak National Bank, founded in 1993 (*Governor*, Ivan Šramko). It has an autonomous statute modelled on the German Bundesbank, with the duties of maintaining control over monetary policy and inflation, ensuring the stability of the currency, and supervising commercial banks. However, it is now proposed to amend the central bank law to allow the government to appoint half the members of the board and force the bank to increase its financing of the budget deficit.

In Oct. 1998 the Slovak National Bank abandoned its fixed exchange rate system, whereby the crown's value was fixed within a fluctuation band against a number of currencies, and chose to float the currency.

Decentralization of the banking system began in 1991, and private banks began to operate. The two largest Slovak banks were both privatized in 2001. The Austrian bank Erste Bank bought an 87·18% stake in Slovenská Sporiteľňa (Slovak Savings Bank) and the Italian bank IntesaBci bought a 94·47% stake in Všeobecná úverová banka (General Credit Bank). In 2000 Slovenská Sporiteľňa had assets of US$3·3bn. and Všeobecná úverová banka US$2·8bn. In 2003 there were 13 commercial banks and two savings banks.

Foreign direct investment in Slovakia in 2000 totalled US$1,986·9m., more than the total amount in the previous seven years of the country's existence.

There is a stock exchange in Bratislava.

ENERGY AND NATURAL RESOURCES

Environment

Slovakia's carbon dioxide emissions from the consumption and flaring of fossil fuels in 2002 were the equivalent of 7·2 tonnes per capita.

Electricity

Installed capacity in 2002 was 7·4m. kW, of which 2·3m. kW is hydro-electric and 2·2m. kW nuclear. Production in 2000 was

31·99bn. kWh, with consumption per capita 5,425 kWh. There were six nuclear reactors in use in 2003. In 2002 about 65% of electricity was nuclear-generated, a percentage exceeded only in Lithuania and France.

Oil and Gas

In 2002 natural gas reserves were 14bn. cu. metres and oil reserves 9m. bbls. Natural gas production in 2000 amounted to 163m. cu. metres. Slovakia is a net energy importer, relying heavily on Russia for its oil and gas.

Minerals

In 2000, 3·65m. tonnes of lignite were produced. 477,000 tonnes of iron ore were extracted in 2000. There are also reserves of copper, lead, zinc, limestone, dolomite, rock salt and others.

Agriculture

In 2001 there were 1·45m. ha. of arable land and 126,000 ha. of permanent crops. In 2002 agriculture employed 8·5% of the economically active population.

A federal law of May 1991 returned land seized by the Communist regime to its original owners, to a maximum of 150 ha. of arable to a single owner.

Production, 2000 (in 1,000 tonnes): wheat, 1,254; sugarbeets, 961; maize, 440; potatoes, 419; barley, 397; rapeseed, 134; sunflower seeds, 117; cabbages, 99; apples, 81; tomatoes, 73; rye, 64; grapes, 61.

Livestock, 2000: cattle, 665,000; pigs, 1·56m.; sheep, 340,000; chickens, 12m. Livestock products, 2000 (in 1,000 tonnes): meat, 303; milk, 1,116; eggs, 65; cheese, 54.

Forestry

The area under forests in 2000 was 2·18m. ha., or 45·3% of the total land area. In 2001 timber production was 5·24m. cu. metres.

Fisheries

In 2001 the total catch was 1,531 tonnes, exclusively freshwater fish.

INDUSTRY

The main industries in Slovakia are chemical products, machinery, electrical apparatus, textiles, clothing and footwear, metal and metal products, food and beverages, paper, earthenware and ceramics. Industry accounted for 31·8% of GDP in 2001, with manufacturing contributing 23·3%. 2002 output included (in 1m. tonnes): crude steel, 4·3; pig iron, 3·5; cement (2001), 3·1; distillate fuel oil (2000), 2·1; coke (1999), 1·6; residual fuel oil (2000), 0·5. Motor vehicle production (2002), 226,000 units. The car-manufacturing sector accounts for a quarter of Slovakia's economy.

Labour

Out of 2,123,700 people in employment in 2001, 553,600 were in manufacturing, 255,700 in wholesale and retail trade/repair of motor vehicles, motorcycles and personal and household goods, 169,500 in construction and 168,900 in education. Workers in Slovakia put in among the longest hours of any country in the industrialized world. In 2002 the average worker put in 1,979 hours. The average monthly salary in 2001 was 12,365 koruny. Slovakia has the cheapest labour force in the EU. In Oct. 2003 the monthly minimum wage was increased to 6,080 koruny. Unemployment is among the highest in Europe, but has been declining slightly in recent years. It stood at 19·4% in 2001, but then declined to 18·7% in 2002 and still further to 16·9% in Dec. 2004. Youth unemployment is particularly high—in 2001 it was in excess of 39%. In 2004 part-time work accounted for less than 3% of all employment in Slovakia—the lowest percentage in the EU.

INTERNATIONAL TRADE

Foreign debt was US$13,013m. in 2002.

Imports and Exports

In 2004 imports (f.o.b.) totalled US$29·26bn. (US$22·00bn. in 2003); exports (f.o.b.), US$27·78bn. (US$21·96bn. in 2003). Main import sources in 2004 were: Germany, 23·8%; Czech Republic, 13·2%; Russia, 9·4%; Italy, 5·6%; Austria, 4·3%. The leading export markets in 2004 were: Germany, 28·6%; Czech Republic, 13·3%; Austria, 7·8%; Italy, 6·4%; Poland, 5·5%. In 2004 machinery and transport equipment accounted for 39·6% of Slovakia's imports and 45·9% of exports; chemicals, manufactured goods classified chiefly by material and miscellaneous manufactured articles 39·3% of imports and 41·4% of exports; mineral fuels, lubricants and related materials 12·5% of imports and 6·7% of exports; food, live animals, beverages and tobacco 4·7% of imports and 3·2% of exports; and crude materials, inedible, animal and vegetable oil and fats 3·9% of imports and 2·8% of exports.

COMMUNICATIONS

Roads

In 2002 there were 42,970 km of roads, including 302 km of motorways. In 2002 there were 1,326,891 passenger cars, 164,484 trucks and lorries, 10,589 buses and coaches and 47,900 motorcycles and mopeds. In 2002 there were 7,866 road accidents resulting in 626 fatalities.

Rail

In 2000 the length of railway routes was 3,665 km. Most of the network is 1,435 mm gauge with short sections on three other gauges. Passenger-km travelled in 2000 came to 2,870m. and freight tonne-km to 11,234m. There are tram/light rail networks in Bratislava and Košice.

Civil Aviation

The main international airport is at Bratislava (M. R. Stefánik), with some international flights from Košice. There are three Slovakia-based airlines. In 2003 Air Slovakia had flights to Kuwait, Larnaca and Tel Aviv; Slovak Airlines operated domestic services and also flew to Moscow; SkyEurope (central Europe's first low-cost airline) operated domestic services and also flew to Berlin, Dubrovnik, Mahé, Milan, Munich, Split, Stuttgart and Zürich. In 2001 Bratislava handled 288,422 passengers (279,028 on international flights) and 2,880 tonnes of freight.

Shipping

Merchant shipping in 2002 totalled 7,000 GRT. In 1999 vessels totalling 336,000 NRT entered ports.

Telecommunications

There were 4,326,100 telephone subscribers in 2002, or 804·4 per 1,000 persons, and 970,000 PCs in use (180·4 per 1,000 persons). In 2000 Deutsche Telekom bought a 51% stake in the state-owned Slovakia Telecom. There were 2,923,400 mobile phone subscribers in 2002 and 59,000 fax machines. Slovakia had 862,800 Internet users in 2002.

Postal Services

In 2003 there were 1,617 post offices.

SOCIAL INSTITUTIONS

Justice

The post-Communist judicial system was established by a federal law of July 1991. This provided for a unified system of four types of court: civil, criminal, commercial and administrative. Commercial courts arbitrate in disputes arising from business activities. Administrative courts examine the legality of the decisions of state institutions when appealed by citizens. In addition, there are military courts which operate under the jurisdiction of the Ministry of Defence. There is a Supreme

Court, and a hierarchy of courts under the Ministry of Justice at republic, region and district level. District courts are courts of first instance. Cases are usually decided by senates comprising a judge and two associate judges, although occasionally by a single judge. (Associate judges are citizens in good standing over the age of 25 who are elected for four-year terms). Regional courts are courts of first instance in more serious cases and also courts of appeal for district courts. Cases are usually decided by a senate of two judges and three associate judges, although again occasionally by a single judge. The Supreme Court interprets law as a guide to other courts and functions also as a court of appeal. Decisions are made by senates of three judges. The judges of the Supreme Court are nominated by the President; other judges are appointed by the National Council.

The population in penal institutions in Sept. 2003 was 8,829 (164 per 100,000 of national population).

Education

In 1996–97 there were 3,396 pre-school institutions with 170,138 children and 15,633 teachers. In 1995–96 there were 2,485 primary schools with 661,082 pupils and 39,224 teachers, 190 grammar schools with 76,380 students and 5,457 teachers, and 364 vocational schools with 119,853 pupils and 9,558 teachers. There were 357 secondary vocational apprentice training centres with 139,688 pupils and 6,056 teachers; and 400 special schools with 29,914 children and 3,862 teachers. There were 14 universities or university-type institutions with 74,322 students.

In 2000–01 expenditure on education came to 4·2% of GNP. In 1999–2000 total education expenditure was 13·8% of total government spending.

The adult literacy rate in 2003 was 99·6% (99·7% among males and 99·6% among females).

Health

In 2001 there were 17,556 physicians, 2,378 dentists, 39,428 nurses and 2,605 pharmacists. In 2003 there were 52,363 beds in health establishments in total, of which 33,055 were in hospitals. In 2001 Slovakia spent 5·7% of its GDP on health.

Welfare

The age of retirement is 62 for both men and women. To qualify for an old-age pension an employment period of 25 years, for both men and women, is mandatory. The social insurance system has set the minimum pension (with full career) at 550 koruny a month and the maximum pension at 8,282 koruny a month for all pensions. State unemployment benefit is 50% of previous earnings during the first three months, thereafter 45% of previous earnings.

RELIGION

A federal Czechoslovakian law of July 1991 provides the basis for church-state relations and guarantees the religious and civic rights of citizens and churches. Churches must register to become legal entities but operate independently of the state. A law of 1993 restored confiscated property to churches and religious communities unless it had passed into private hands, co-operative farms or trading companies. In 2001, 68·9% of the population were Roman Catholic, 6·9% members of the Evangelical Church of the Augsburg Confession, 4·1% Greek Catholic and 2·0% Calvinist. In May 2005 there were two cardinals.

CULTURE

World Heritage Sites

Slovakia has four sites on the UNESCO World Heritage List: Vlkolínec (inscribed on the list in 1993), a group of 45 traditional log houses; Banská Štiavnica (1993), a medieval mining town;

Spišský Hrad and its Associated Cultural Monuments (1993)—13th century Spiš Castle is one of the largest castle complexes in central Europe; Bardejov Town Conservation Reserve (2000), a medieval fortified town. Slovakia also shares a UNESCO site with Hungary: the Caves of Aggtelek and Slovak Karst.

Broadcasting

Broadcasting is the responsibility of the government-controlled Slovak Broadcasting Council. The state-run Slovak Radio broadcasts on four wavelengths, and there are 12 private regional stations. Slovak Television is a public corporation. It transmits on two channels (colour by PAL), the second being shared with a commercial station. There are several independent local TV stations, and two cable networks. Number of sets: TV (2001), 2·2m.; radio (2000), 5·2m.

Cinema

In 2002 there were 283 cinema screens; total admissions in 2002 were 2·9m.

Press

Slovakia had 19 daily newspapers in 2002 with a combined average daily circulation of 511,000. In 1999 a total of 3,153 book titles were published.

Tourism

In 2002 there were 1,399,000 foreign tourists, spending US$724m.

Festivals

The Bratislava Rock Festival takes place in June and the Bratislava Music Festival and Interpodium is in Oct. The Myjava Folklore Festival is held each June, the Zvolen Castle Games in June–July, Theatrical Nitra is in Sept., and there is an annual Spring Music Festival in Košice.

DIPLOMATIC REPRESENTATIVES

Of Slovakia in the United Kingdom (25 Kensington Palace Gdns, London, W8 4QY)
Ambassador: Vacant.
Chargé d'Affaires a.i.: Radovan Javorčik.

Of the United Kingdom in Slovakia (Panska 16, 81101 Bratislava)
Ambassador: Judith Macgregor.

Of Slovakia in the USA (3523 International Court, NW, Washington, D.C., 20008)
Ambassador: Rastislav Kacer.

Of the USA in Slovakia (4 Hviezdoslavovo Namestie, 81102 Bratislava)
Ambassador: Rodolphe Vallee.

Of Slovakia to the United Nations
Ambassador: Peter Burian.

Of Slovakia to the European Union
Ambassador: Miroslav Adamis.

FURTHER READING

Kirschbaum, S. J., *A History of Slovakia: the Struggle for Survival.* London and New York, 1995
Krejcí, Jaroslav and Machonin, Pavel, *Czechoslovakia 1918–1992: A Laboratory for Social Change.* Macmillan, London, 1996
Wheaton, B. and Kavan, Z., *Velvet Revolution: Czechoslovakia 1988–91.* Boulder (CO), 1992

National Statistical Office: Statistical Office of the Slovak Republic, Miletičova 3, 82467 Bratislava.
Website: http://www.statistics.sk/

SLOVENIA

Map labels: HUNGARY, AUSTRIA, Maribor, Jesenice, Škofja Loka, LJUBLJANA, ITALY, SLOVENIA, Kroper, Gulf of Venice, CROATIA. Scale: 0 25 mi, 0 25 km. © Research Machines plc 2006

Republika Slovenija

Capital: Ljubljana
Population projection, 2010: 1·96m.
GDP per capita, 2003: 19,150 (PPP$)
HDI/world rank: 0·904/26

KEY HISTORICAL EVENTS

The lands originally settled by Slovenes in the 6th century were steadily encroached upon by Germans. Slovenia developed as part of Austria-Hungary, after the defeat of the latter in the First World War becoming part of the Kingdom of the Serbs, Croats and Slovenes (Yugoslavia) on 1 Dec. 1918.

In Oct. 1989 the Slovene Assembly voted a constitutional amendment giving it the right to secede from Yugoslavia. On 2 July 1990 the Assembly adopted a 'declaration of sovereignty' and a referendum was held on 23 Dec. 1990 in which 88·5% of participants voted for independence. On 25 June 1991 Slovenia declared independence but agreed to suspend this for three months at peace talks sponsored by the EU. Federal troops moved into Slovenia on 27 June to secure Yugoslavia's external borders, but after some fighting withdrew by the end of July. After the agreed three-month moratorium Slovenia (and Croatia) declared their independence from the Yugoslav Federation on 8 Oct. 1991. Slovenia became a member of NATO in March 2004 and the European Union in May 2004.

TERRITORY AND POPULATION

Slovenia is bounded in the north by Austria, in the northeast by Hungary, in the southeast and south by Croatia and in the west by Italy. The length of coastline is 47 km. Its area is 20,273 sq. km. The capital is Ljubljana: Dec. 2004 population, 251,716. Maribor (population of 93,371 in 2004) is the other major city. In 2002 the census population was 1,964,036. Population (31 March 2005), 1,998,079 (females, 1,020,522); density per sq. km, 98·6. In 2003, 50·8% of the population lived in urban areas.

The UN gives a projected population for 2010 of 1·96m.

The official language is Slovene.

In April 2004 voters rejected plans to restore the civil rights of Slovenia's ethnic minorities, mainly nationals of other former Yugoslav republics, which were 'erased' in 1992.

SOCIAL STATISTICS

Statistics for calendar years:

	Live births	Deaths	Growth rate per 1,000	Marriages	Divorces
2000	18,180	18,588	−0·2	7,201	2,125
2001	17,477	18,508	−0·5	6,935	2,274
2002	17,501	18,701	−0·6	7,064	2,457
2003	17,321	19,451	−1·1	6,756	2,461
2004	17,961	18,523	−0·3	6,558	2,411

Rates, 2003 (per 1,000 population): birth, 8·7; death, 9·7. Infant mortality, 2003: 4·0 (per 1,000 live births). There were 540 suicides in 2002 (29 suicides per 1,000 deaths).

In 2002 the most popular age range for marrying was 25–29 years for both males and females. Expectation of life, 2003, was 72·7 years for males and 80·0 for females. Annual population growth rate, 1991–2002, 0·3%. Fertility rate, 2003, 1·2 births per woman.

CLIMATE

Summers are warm, winters are cold with frequent snow. Ljubljana, Jan. −4°C, July 22°C. Annual rainfall 1,383 mm.

CONSTITUTION AND GOVERNMENT

The constitution became effective on 23 Dec. 1991. Slovenia is a parliamentary democratic republic with an executive that consists of a directly-elected president, aided by a council of ministers, and a prime minister. It has a bicameral parliament (*Skupščina Slovenije*), consisting of a 90-member *National Assembly* (*Državni Zbor*), 88 members elected for four-year terms by proportional representation with a 4% threshold and two members elected by ethnic minorities; and a 40-member, advisory *State Council* (*Državni Svet*), elected for five-year terms by interest groups and regions. It has veto powers over the National Assembly. Administratively the country is divided into 136 municipalities and 11 urban municipalities.

The Judicial branch consists of a *Supreme Court*, whose judges are elected by the National Assembly, and a *Constitutional Court*, whose judges are elected for nine-year terms by the National Assembly and nominated by the president.

National Anthem

'Zdravljica' ('A Toast'); words by Dr France Prešeren, tune by Stanko Premrl.

GOVERNMENT CHRONOLOGY

(LDS = Liberal Democracy of Slovenia; NSi = New Slovenia Christian People's Party; SDS = Slovenian Democratic Party; SKD = Slovenian Christian Democrats; SLS+SKD = Slovenian People's Party; n/p = non-partisan)

Presidents since 1990.
1990–2002	n/p	Milan Kučan
2002–	LDS	Janez Drnovšek

Prime Ministers since 1990.
1990–92	SKD	Lojze Peterle
1992–2000	LDS	Janez Drnovšek
2000	SLS+SKD, NSi	Andrej Bajuk
2000–02	LDS	Janez Drnovšek
2002–04	LDS	Anton (Tone) Rop
2004–	SDS	Janez Janša

RECENT ELECTIONS

Elections were held for the National Assembly on 3 Oct. 2004; turnout was 60·7%. The centre-right Slovenian Democratic Party

(SDS) won 29 seats with 29·1% of votes cast; the ruling Liberal Democracy of Slovenia (LDS), 23 with 22·8%; United List of Social Democrats of Slovenia (ZLSD; former Communists), 10 with 10·2%; New Slovenia Christian People's Party (NSi), 9 with 9·0%; Slovene People's Party (SLS), 7 with 6·8%; Slovenian National Party (SNS), 6 with 6·3%; Democratic Party of Retired People of Slovenia (DeSUS), 4 with 4·0%.

Presidential elections were held on 10 Nov. and 1 Dec. 2002. The turnout in the first round was 70·8%. Prime Minister Janez Drnovšek (LDS) received 44·4% of votes cast against 30·8% for Barbara Brezigar, his nearest rival. There were seven other candidates. In the run-off held on 1 Dec. 2002 Janez Drnovšek received 56·6% of votes cast against 43·4% for Barbara Brezigar.

European Parliament

Slovenia has seven representatives. At the June 2004 elections turnout was 28·3%. The NSi won 2 seats with 23·6% of votes cast (political affiliation in European Parliament: European People's Party–European Democrats); the LDS-DeSUS, 2 with 21·9% (Alliance of Liberals and Democrats for Europe); the SDS, 2 with 17·7% (European People's Party–European Democrats); the ZLSD, 1 with 14·2% (Party of European Socialists).

CURRENT ADMINISTRATION

President: Janez Drnovšek; b. 1950 (LDS; sworn in 22 Dec. 2002).

In March 2006 the coalition government of the Slovenian Democratic Party (SDS), New Slovenia Christian People's Party (NSi), Slovene People's Party (SLS) and Democratic Party of Retired People of Slovenia (DeSUS) comprised:

Prime Minister: Janez Janša; b. 1958 (SDS; sworn in 6 Dec. 2004).

Minister of Agriculture, Food and Forestry: Marija Lukačič (SDS). *Culture:* Vasko Simoniti (SDS). *Defence:* Karl Erjavec (DeSUS). *Economy:* Andrej Vizjak (SDS). *Education and Sport:* Milan Zver (SDS). *Environment and Spatial Planning:* Janez Podobnik (SLS). *Finance:* Andrej Bajuk (NSi). *Foreign Affairs:* Dimitrij Rupel (SDS). *Health:* Andrej Bručan (SDS). *Higher Education, Science and Technology:* Jure Zupan (NSi). *Interior:* Dragutin Mate (SDS). *Justice:* Lovro Šturm (NSi). *Labour, Family and Social Affairs:* Janez Drobnič (NSi). *Public Administration:* Gregor Virant (SDS). *Transport:* Janez Božič (SLS). *Minister without Portfolio Responsible for Local Self-Government and Regional Development:* Ivan Žagar (SLS). *Minister without Portfolio Responsible for* Structural *Reforms:* Joe Damijan (ind.).

Office of the Prime Minister: http://www.sigov.si

CURRENT LEADERS

Janez Drnovšek

Position
President

Introduction
Janez Drnovšek became Slovenia's president in Dec. 2002. He was independent Slovenia's first prime minister from 1992–2002, except for a brief period in opposition in 2000. Along with his presidential predecessor, Milan Kučan, he has overseen political and economic reforms resulting in entry into NATO and the European Union in 2004.

Early Life
Drnovšek was born on 17 May 1950 in Celje. He studied monetary policy at the University of Maribor and worked in the banking sector before entering politics in the 1980s. Following Slovenia's democratic elections of 1989, Drnovšek was appointed Slovenian representative to the rotating presidency of Federal Yugoslavia. He was president of the collective presidency for a year until May 1990, during which time he headed the Non-Alignment Movement, which rejected association with either the USA or the USSR. He pressed for Yugoslav entry into the European Community (later the EU), economic reform, multi-party elections and the release of political prisoners held within federal Yugoslavia.

As Yugoslavia began to disintegrate, Drnovšek sought a diplomatic solution. A declaration of Slovenian independence won majority backing in a referendum during 1990 and the country announced its split with Yugoslavia in 1991. Yugoslav troops entered the country and a short war ensued. Drnovšek acted as a chief negotiator in the Brioni agreement that brought the conflict to an end. In April 1992 Slovenia held its first elections as an independent state, Drnovšek winning the premiership and Milan Kučan the presidency.

Career in Office
Drnovšek and Kučan retained their positions for ten years, except for seven months in 2000 when Drnovšek was out of office. Their long tenures provided Slovenia with political and economic stability that few other former Yugoslav states enjoyed. The two worked closely to ensure Slovenia's acceptance on the international stage and forged closer ties with the West. Slovenia joined the IMF in 1993 and became a member of NATO's Partnership for Peace Programme. In 1999 it granted airspace to NATO for its bombing raids on Kosovo and Serbia. In 1996 Slovenia signed an associate agreement with the EU and opened full membership talks the following year. In Oct. 2002 the EU included Slovenia in its plans for enlargement scheduled for 2004.

Domestically, Drnovšek oversaw the implementation of major economic reforms, including privatization programmes and restructuring of the banking and commercial sectors. Unable to rely on markets in the former Yugoslavia, increased trade was established with the USA and the EU. Slovenia was one of the founding members of the WTO.

Drnovšek was re-elected in 1996 but in 2000 his coalition was destabilized by party mergers among the centre-right. He called a vote of confidence in April 2000 but was defeated and replaced as prime minister by Andrej Bajuk of the Social Democrats. The new coalition split over plans to reform the electoral system and at the elections of Oct. 2000 Drnovšek was returned as prime minister, heading a government consisting of his centre-left Liberal Democrats, United List, the Slovene People's Party, the Slovene Young People's Party and the DeSUS party.

The Slovenian constitution barred Kučan from standing for a third term as president in Nov. 2002. Drnovšek ran against Barbara Brezigar, an independent backed by the centre-right, and won with 57% of the vote. As president, he oversaw Slovenia's integration into NATO and the EU in 2004.

Janez Janša

Position
Prime Minister

Introduction
A key figure in Slovenia's independence movement in the late 1980s, former defence minister Janez Janša was elected prime minister by parliament on 9 Nov. 2004. He has been the head of the Slovenian Democratic Party (SDS) since 1995.

Early Life
Janez Janša was born on 17 Sept. 1958 in Ljubljana. In 1982 he graduated in defence studies from the Faculty of Sociology, Journalism and Political Science of the University of Ljubljana, after which he became an intern at the Republican Secretariat for Defence. In the same year he was appointed president of a wing of the youth organization Alliance of the Socialist Youth of Slovenia—ZSMS. He assisted with the publication of a report that criticized conditions within the Yugoslav People's Army

(JNA), which led to a strong condemnation by the Bureau for State Authority. In late 1986 he became the secretary of a journal published by the students' union of the University of Ljubljana which touched on highly sensitive subjects such as the use of the Slovene language in the JNA.

In early 1987 Janša and Igor Omerza founded MikroAda, which soon became a technical service for the emerging political and social movements. A working paper for the constitution of Slovenia written by Slovene novelists, lawyers and sociologists was published by MikroAda in early 1988. It was strongly condemned by the Central Committee of the League of Communists and Janša was arrested and detained in a military prison. He, along with three journalists, later faced trial for betraying military secrets. The trial of the 'Ljubljana Four' provoked mass demonstrations in the capital which became known as the Slovene Spring. Janša was found guilty and sentenced to 18 months imprisonment at a maximum-security prison but was relocated to an open prison near Ljubljana following a public outcry.

The Slovene Assembly subsequently passed constitutional amendments increasing the Republic's autonomy and nullifying federal laws. Janša was released in the summer of 1989 and he became editor of the weekly *Demokracija* magazine which became the unofficial voice of the opposition (Demos). Also in 1989 he assisted in the foundation of the centre-right Slovene Democratic Alliance (SDZ) and was elected as its vice-president. The Slovene Communists left the Yugoslav League of Communists, and the first multi-party elections were held in April 1990. Janša was elected to parliament on an SDZ party ticket and became the minister for defence in the new Demos coalition government which, by Dec. 1990, had enabled a successful plebiscite on Slovenian independence. As minister for defence (until 1994) Janša oversaw the transformation of the Territorial Defence force into the first Slovene army. This army fought the JNA in the ten-day war that followed Slovenia's declaration of independence on 25 June 1991 until a truce—the Brioni agreement—was brokered by the European Community.

In the autumn of 1991 the Slovene Democratic Alliance disintegrated and Janša joined the Social Democratic Party of Slovenia (SDS—which was to become the Slovenian Democratic Party in 2003) the following year. In the 1992 elections Janša was returned to parliament and in May 1993 he became president of the party (and was subsequently re-elected to the post in 1995, 1999 and 2001). In March 1994 the National Assembly impeached Janša for 'transgression of the civilian sphere by the military' and removed him from office, which led to demonstrations against corruption in the civil service outside parliament buildings. He was re-elected to the National Assembly in 1996 when the SDS increased its representation in parliament and became the main opposition party. Between 1997 and 1998 Janša was the head of the Slovene parliamentary delegation to the North Atlantic Assembly (NAA). He was again defence minister from June–Oct. 2000 in the short-lived government of Andrej Bajuk. In the Oct. 2000 elections, Janša was again re-elected and the SDS became the second largest political party in Slovenia.

In the run-up to the general election in Oct. 2004 the SDS campaigned on a promise to cut the costs of state administration and press ahead with privatization in anticipation of Slovenia adopting the euro. The strategy was successful and the SDS won, almost doubling its vote and ending nearly 12 years of centre-left Liberal Democrat-led governments.

Career in Office

Janez Janša was elected Slovenia's prime minister on 9 Nov. 2004. His SDS party forged a coalition with three other parties— New Slovenia Christian People's Party, the Slovene People's Party (both centre-right) and the centre-left Democratic Party of Retired People of Slovenia. Parliament approved the new government in Dec. Janša promised to reduce taxes, work on increasing the efficiency of the privatization process and reform

the labour market. Relations with neighbouring Croatia remain difficult, although Janša suggested in his opening address that the problems could be solved through co-operation and strategic partnership. 'Croatia will soon join us in the EU and NATO. It would make sense for our countries to help each other before and after this. However, we must not be naive: Slovenia has no new demands, but we do intend to keep what belongs to us.'

DEFENCE

Compulsory military service for seven months ended in Sept. 2003. The Army is expected to be fully professional by 2010.

In 2003 military expenditure totalled US$378m. (US$192 per capita), representing 1·4% of GDP.

Army

There are six military districts. Personnel (2002), 9,000 (4,000 conscripts) and an army reserve of 20,000. There is a paramilitary police force of 4,500 with 5,000 reserves.

Navy

There is an Army Maritime element numbering 100 personnel.

Air Force

The Army Air element numbers 250 with eight armed helicopters.

INTERNATIONAL RELATIONS

Slovenia is a member of the UN, WTO, BIS, NATO, EU, Council of Europe, OSCE, CEFTA, CEI, the Inter-American Development Bank and IOM, and is an Associate Partner of the WEU. Slovenia held a referendum on EU membership on 23 March 2003, in which 89·6% of votes cast were in favour of accession. It became a member of NATO on 29 March 2004 and the EU on 1 May 2004. On 1 Feb. 2005 Slovenia became the third European Union member to ratify the proposed EU constitution. The parliament approved the treaty by 79 votes to four, with seven abstentions.

ECONOMY

Agriculture accounted for 2·3% of GDP in 2003, industry 31·9% and services 65·8%.

Overview

Slovenia ranks amongst the most developed of the ten EU accession members that joined in May 2004. Slovenia has a GDP per capita in purchasing power standards of 70% of current EU members, higher than that of Greece and Portugal. The country has achieved an average growth rate of 4% since 1996. Tight monetary and fiscal policies have contributed to macroeconomic stability, balanced fiscal budgets and open foreign trade. The country attracts low levels of foreign direct investment (FDI), partly owing to a reluctance to allow foreign participation in key industries. The authorities aim to adopt the euro in Jan. 2007; by 2004 Slovenia had already met the Maastricht criteria for long-term interest rates and the fiscal deficit and debt ratios. According to the IMF, Slovenia must still allow for policy challenges before the successful adoption of the euro; these challenges include reducing the inflation rate, making wage-setting mechanisms more flexible and enhancing the flexibility of fiscal policy. Since 1996 Slovenia has had single-digit inflation. The inflation rate has declined from 8·9% in 2000 to 3·2% in 2004. The pace of privatization has been slower than in most other Central and Eastern European countries, with enterprises in key sectors remaining under state ownership. The authorities are currently preparing for the liberalization of the natural gas sector, road transport and railways.

Currency

The unit of currency is the *tolar* (SLT) of 100 *stotinas*, which replaced the Yugoslav dinar. Since 28 June 2004 the tolar has been pegged to the euro at a rate of 239·640 tolars = one euro.

Slovenia is aiming to adopt the euro as its currency on 1 Jan. 2007. Inflation was 4·6% in 2003 and 3·2% in 2004. Foreign exchange reserves were US$5,268m. and gold reserves 243,000 troy oz in June 2002. Total money supply in June 2002 was 495,309m. tolars.

Budget

In 2001 total revenues were 1,772·1bn. tolars (1,559·9bn. tolars in 2000) and expenditures 1,843·5bn. tolars (1,621·7bn. tolars in 2000).

Tax revenues in 2001 totalled 1,659·7bn. tolars (including: domestic taxes on goods and services, 659·3bn. tolars; social security contributions, 627·4bn. tolars; tax on income, profits and capital gains, 256·7bn. tolars). Items of expenditure in 2001 included: social security and welfare, 802·4bn. tolars; health, 267·1bn. tolars; education, 197·9bn. tolars.

VAT is 20·0% (reduced rate, 8·5%).

Performance

The GDP growth rate was 3·5% in 2002, 2·7% in 2003 and 4·2% in 2004. Of all the central and eastern European countries that joined the European Union in May 2004, Slovenia has the highest per capita GDP. Real GDP in 2002 was 21% higher than in 1989—only Poland among the ex-socialist countries has seen greater progress since 1989. Total GDP in 2004 was US$32·2bn.

Banking and Finance

The central bank and bank of issue, the Bank of Slovenia, was founded on 25 June 1991 upon independence. Its current *Governor* is Mitja Gaspari, appointed on 1 April 2001 for a term of six years. In 2003 there were 20 commercial banks (five subsidiaries of foreign banks and one branch office of a foreign bank) and two savings banks. The largest bank is Nova Ljubljanska banka (NLB), which has a market share of around one third and had assets in 2003 of US$9·1bn. Other large banks are Nova Kreditna Banka Maribor (NKBM) and Abanka Vipa. In 2002 Slovenia received a record US$1·64bn. of foreign direct investment.

There is a stock exchange in Ljubljana (LSE).

ENERGY AND NATURAL RESOURCES

Environment

Slovenia's carbon dioxide emissions from the consumption and flaring of fossil fuels were the equivalent of 8·4 tonnes per capita in 2002.

Electricity

Installed capacity was 3·0m. kW in 2003. There was one nuclear power station in operation. In 2003, 5,207m. kWh were nuclear-produced, 5,657m. kWh thermal and 3,155m. kWh hydro-electric. The total amount of electricity produced in 2003 was 14,019m. kWh. Consumption per capita in 2003 was 6,455 kWh.

Minerals

Brown coal production was 617,000 tonnes in 2003.

Agriculture

Only around 1·4% of the population work in agriculture. Output (in 1,000 tonnes) in 2003: maize, 224; sugarbeets, 202; wheat, 123; potatoes, 108; grapes, 104.

Livestock in 2003: pigs, 620,506; cattle, 450,226; sheep, 105,660; poultry, 4,533,674. Livestock products, 2003: meat, 177,200 tonnes; milk, 64·24m. litres.

In 2003 there were 172,753 ha. of arable land and 28,608 ha. of permanent crops.

Forestry

In 2003 the area under forests was 1·16m. ha., or 57·2% of the total land area. Timber production in 2003 was 2·59m. cu. metres.

Fisheries

Total marine fish catch in 2003 was 1,087 tonnes. Freshwater farming produced 1,148 tonnes.

INDUSTRY

Industry contributed 30·0% of GDP in 2003. Traditional industries are metallurgy, furniture-making and textiles. The manufacture of electric goods and transport equipment is being developed.

Production (in 1,000 tonnes): ready mixed concrete (2003), 1,874; cement (2000), 1,252; paper and paperboard (2003), 598; crude steel (2000), 519; passenger cars (2001), 118,979 units; refrigerators for household use (2000), 841,000 units; washing machines (2000), 488,000 units.

Labour

Registered labour force was 874,921 in 2003. In 2003, 433,098 people worked in services, 308,059 in industry, and 36,092 in agriculture and forestry. In 2003 there were 97,674 registered unemployed; in 2003 the registered unemployment rate was 11·2%. In 2003 the average monthly gross wage per employee was 253,200 tolars.

INTERNATIONAL TRADE

Foreign debt amounted to US$8,799m. in 2002. In 1997 Slovenia accepted 18% of the US$4,400m. commercial bank debt of the former Yugoslavia.

Imports and Exports

Imports (f.o.b.) in 2003 were worth US$13,854m. (US$10,932m. in 2002) and exports (f.o.b.) US$12,767m. (US$10,357m. in 2002). Exports accounted for 56·5% of GDP in 2003.

Major imports are road vehicles, electrical machinery, industrial machinery, petroleum and petroleum products, and iron and steel. Major exports are electrical machinery, apparatus and appliances (11·6%), road vehicles and parts (11·4%), and furniture (6·9%).

Share of imports from principal markets in 2003: Germany, 19·3%; Italy, 18·3%; France, 10·1%; Austria, 8·6%; Croatia, 3·6%. Exports: Germany, 23·1%; Italy, 13·1%; Croatia, 8·9%; Austria, 7·3%; France, 5·7%. About 63% of trade is with EU countries.

COMMUNICATIONS

Roads

In 2003 there were 20,155 km of road including 477 km of motorways. There were in 2003: 889,580 passenger cars; 2,188 buses; 48,926 trucks; and 42,549 motorcycles and mopeds. 54·5m. passengers and 62m. tonnes of freight were carried by road in 2003. There were 11,676 traffic accidents in 2003 in which 242 persons were killed.

Rail

In 2003 there were 1,229 km of 1,435 mm gauge, of which 504 km were electrified. In 2003, 15·1m. passengers and 17·3m. tonnes of freight were carried.

Civil Aviation

There is an international airport at Ljubljana (Brnik), which handled 927,440 passengers (all on international flights) and 6,239 tonnes of freight in 2003. The national carrier, Adria Airways, has flights to most major European cities and Tel Aviv. In 1999 scheduled airline traffic of Slovenia-based carriers flew 9·1m. km, carrying 556,000 passengers.

Shipping

The biggest port is at Koper. Sea-going shipping totalled 9,146 GRT in 2001. In 2002 vessels totalling 6,825,000 NRT entered ports and vessels totalling 4,430,000 NRT cleared.

Telecommunications

In 2002 Slovenia had 2,677,400 telephone subscribers (1,341·4 per 1,000 inhabitants), including 1,667,200 mobile phone subscribers. The leading telecommunications operator is the state-owned Telekom Slovenije. In 2001 there were 11,072 fax machines in use. The number of Internet users in 2002 was 750,000. There were 600,000 PCs in use (300·6 per 1,000 persons) in 2002.

Postal Services

In 2003 there were 554 post offices.

SOCIAL INSTITUTIONS

Justice

There are 44 district courts, 11 regional courts, four higher courts, an administrative court and a supreme court. There are also four labour and social courts, and a higher labour and social court. The population in penal institutions in Sept. 2002 was 1,120 (56 per 100,000 of national population).

Education

Adult literacy rate in 2002 was 99·7% (99·7% male; 99·6% female). In 2002–03 there were 809 primary schools with 177,535 pupils and 15,625 teachers; and 143 secondary schools with 103,538 pupils and 8,482 teachers. In 2003–04 there were 49 institutions of higher education with 87,205 students and 6,894 (2000–01) teaching staff. There are three universities, at Koper, Ljubljana and Maribor.

In 2003 total government expenditure on education came to 5·9% of GNP.

Health

In 2001 there were 4,361 doctors and 28 hospitals with 10,286 beds. In 2001 there were 1,178 dentists, 14,245 nurses and 776 pharmacists.

Welfare

There were 485,895 people receiving pensions in 2001, of which 296,160 were old-age pensioners. Disability and pension insurance expenses were 655,233m. tolar in 2001.

RELIGION

57·8% of the population were Roman Catholic according to the 2002 census.

CULTURE

World Heritage Sites

Slovenia has one site on the UNESCO World Heritage List: Škocjan Caves (inscribed on the list in 1988), consisting of limestone caves, passages and waterfalls more than 200 metres deep.

Broadcasting

The government-controlled Radiotelevizija Slovenija broadcasts three national radio programmes, and also programmes in Hungarian and Italian. There are six nationwide radio networks as well as regional and local stations. Public television transmission is carried out by the two stations of Televizija Slovenija (colour by PAL). There are also national independent TV networks, a network serving Ljubljana and district and several local stations.

There were 730,000 TV receivers in 2001 and 792,000 radio sets in 2000.

Cinema

There were 76 cinemas with a total of 20,738 seats in 2002, and an annual attendance of 2·7m. Four full-length films were made in 2002.

Press

In 2003 there were five national daily newspapers, 47 weeklies and four published twice a week. In 2003 a total of 3,965 book titles were published.

Tourism

1,373,000 foreign tourists came to Slovenia in 2003; receipts from tourism in 2004 totalled US$1,625m. Tourism accounted for 5% of GDP in 2000.

Libraries

In 2002 there were one national library, 54 higher education libraries, 125 special libraries, 60 public libraries and 648 school libraries; they held a combined 26,820,000 volumes.

Theatre and Opera

In 2002 there were nine professional theatres and two operas.

Museums and Galleries

Museums totalled 111 in 2000, with 1·5m. visitors that year.

DIPLOMATIC REPRESENTATIVES

Of Slovenia in the United Kingdom (10 Little College St., London, SW1P 3SH)
Ambassador: Iztok Mirošič.

Of the United Kingdom in Slovenia (4th Floor, 3 Trg Republike, 1000 Ljubljana)
Ambassador: Hugh Mortimer, LVO.

Of Slovenia in the USA (1525 New Hampshire Ave., NW, Washington, D.C., 20036)
Ambassador: Samuel Žbogar.

Of the USA in Slovenia (Presernova 31, 1000 Ljubljana)
Ambassador: Thomas B. Robertson.

Of Slovenia to the United Nations
Ambassador: Roman Kirn.

Of Slovenia to the European Union
Ambassador: Ciril Stokelj.

FURTHER READING

Benderly, J. and Kraft, E. (eds.) *Independent Slovenia: Origins, Movements, Prospects.* London, 1995

Carmichael, Cathie, *Slovenia.* [Bibliography] ABC-Clio, Oxford and Santa Barbara (CA), 1996

National Statistical Office: National Statistical Office, Vožarski Pot 12, 1000 Ljubljana.
Website: http://www.stat.si

SOLOMON ISLANDS

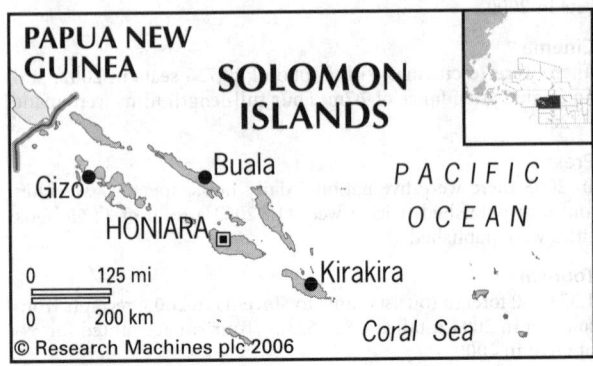

© Research Machines plc 2006

Capital: Honiara
Population projection, 2010: 537,000
GDP per capita, 2003: (PPP$) 1,753
HDI/world rank: 0·594/128

KEY HISTORICAL EVENTS

The Solomon Islands were discovered by Europeans in 1568 but 200 years passed before contact was made again. The southern Solomon Islands were placed under British protection in 1893; the eastern and southern outliers were added in 1898 and 1899. Santa Isabel and the other islands to the north were ceded by Germany in 1900. Full internal self-government was achieved on 2 Jan. 1976 and independence on 7 July 1978.

In June 2000 there was a coup by rebels from the island of Malaita. Prime Minister Bartholomew Ulufa'alu was held at gunpoint for two days. As conflict between the so-called Malaita Eagles and the Isatabu Freedom Movement escalated during 2003, an Australian-led peacekeeping force landed to restore order.

TERRITORY AND POPULATION

The Solomon Islands lie within the area 5° to 12° 30' S. lat. and 155° 30' to 169° 45' E. long. The group includes the main islands of Guadalcanal, Malaita, New Georgia, San Cristobal (now Makira), Santa Isabel and Choiseul; the smaller Florida and Russell groups; the Shortland, Mono (or Treasury), Vella La Vella, Kolombangara, Ranongga, Gizo and Rendova Islands; to the east, Santa Cruz, Tikopia, the Reef and Duff groups; Rennell and Bellona in the south; Ontong Java or Lord Howe to the north; and many smaller islands. The land area is estimated at 28,370 sq. km (10,954 sq. miles). The larger islands are mountainous and forest clad, with flood-prone rivers of considerable energy potential. Guadalcanal has the largest land area and the greatest amount of flat coastal plain. Population (1999 census), 409,042; density, 14·4 per sq. km. 2005 population estimate: 478,000. In 2003, 83·5% of the population lived in rural areas.

The UN gives a projected population for 2010 of 537,000.

The islands are administratively divided into a Capital Territory and nine provinces. Area and population:

Province	Sq. km	Census 1999	Capital
Central Islands	615	21,577	Tulagi
Rennell and Bellona	671	2,377	Tigoa
Guadalcanal	5,336	60,275	Honiara
Isabel	4,136	20,421	Buala
Makira and Ulawa	3,188	31,006	Kirakira
Malaita	4,225	122,620	Auki
Temotu	895	18,912	Lata (Santa Cruz)

Province	Sq. km	Census 1999	Capital
Western	5,475	62,739	Gizo
Choiseul	3,837	20,008	Taro
Capital Territory	22	49,107	—

The capital, Honiara, on Guadalcanal, is the largest urban area, with an estimated population in 1999 of 68,000. 93% of the population are Melanesian; other ethnic groups include Polynesian, Micronesian, European and Chinese.

English is the official language, and is spoken by 1–2% of the population. In all 120 indigenous languages are spoken; Melanesian languages are spoken by 85% of the population.

SOCIAL STATISTICS

2002 estimates: births, 15,300; deaths, 2,100. Estimated birth rate in 2002 was 33·0 per 1,000 population; estimated death rate, 4·6. Life expectancy, 2003, 63·0 years for women and 61·6 for men. Annual population growth rate, 1992–2002, 3·2%. Infant mortality, 2001, 20 per 1,000 live births; fertility rate, 2001, 5·4 births per woman.

CLIMATE

An equatorial climate with only small seasonal variations. Southeast winds cause cooler conditions from April to Nov., but northwest winds for the rest of the year bring higher temperatures and greater rainfall, with annual totals ranging between 80" (2,000 mm) and 120" (3,000 mm).

CONSTITUTION AND GOVERNMENT

The Solomon Islands are a constitutional monarchy with the British Sovereign (represented locally by a Governor-General, who must be a Solomon Island citizen) as Head of State. Legislative power is vested in the single-chamber *National Parliament* composed of 50 members, elected by universal adult suffrage for five years. Parliamentary democracy is based on a multi-party system. Executive authority is effectively held by the Cabinet, led by the Prime Minister.

The Governor-General is appointed for up to five years, on the advice of Parliament, and acts in almost all matters on the advice of the Cabinet. The Prime Minister is elected by and from members of Parliament. Other Ministers are appointed by the Governor-General on the Prime Minister's recommendation, from members of Parliament. The Cabinet is responsible to Parliament. Emphasis is laid on the devolution of power to provincial governments, and traditional chiefs and leaders have a special role within the arrangement.

National Anthem

'God save our Solomon Islands from shore to shore'; words and tune by P. Balekana.

RECENT ELECTIONS

National elections were held on 5 April 2006. The National Party won 4 seats, the Rural Advancement Party 4, the People's Alliance Party 3, the Democratic Party 3, ind. 30 and three other parties won 2 seats each.

Deputy Prime Minister Synder Rini succeeded in gaining the support of enough independent members of parliament to form a government, which led to rioting in Honiara. Rini resigned shortly before a motion of no-confidence was due to take place, and was succeeded by Manasseh Sogavare, a former prime minister.

Nathaniel Waena was elected governor-general by parliament on 15 June 2004. He defeated Sir Peter Kenilorea and the incumbent, Sir John Lapli.

CURRENT ADMINISTRATION

Governor-General: Nathaniel Waena (since 7 July 2004).

In May 2006 the government comprised:

Prime Minister: Manasseh Sogavare; b. 1954 (sworn in 4 May 2006, having previously been prime minister from June 2000–Dec. 2001).

Deputy Prime Minister and Minister of Forests, Environment and Conservation: Job Dudley Tausinga.

Minister of Public Service: Joses Wawari Sanga. *National Reform and Aid Co-ordination:* Gordon Darcy Lilo. *Finance and Treasury:* Bartholomew Ulufa'alu. *Police and National Security:* Charles Dausabea. *Justice and Legal Affairs:* Samuel Manetoali. *Education and Human Resources Development:* Derek Sikua. *Health and Medical Services:* Clay Forau Soalaoi. *Foreign Affairs:* Patteson Oti. *Commerce, Industries and Employment:* Francis Billy Hilly. *Culture and Tourism:* Nelson Ne'e. *Agriculture and Livestock:* Trevor Olavae. *Lands and Surveys:* Leslie Boseto. *Infrastructure and Development:* Stanley Festus Sofu. *Communication, Aviation and Meteorology:* Patrick Vahoe. *Fisheries and Marine Resources:* Nollen Leni. *Mines and Energy:* Toswell Kaua. *Provincial Government and Constituency Development:* Japhet Waipora. *Home Affairs:* Bernard Ghiro. *National Reconciliation and Peace:* Sam S. Iduri.

Government Website: http://www.pmc.gov.sb

CURRENT LEADERS

Manasseh Sogavare

Position

Prime Minister

Introduction

Manasseh Sogavare's first premiership (2000–01) began in the wake of a coup and ended after a controversial attempt to postpone elections. He took office for the second time in May 2006 after the brief tenure of Snyder Rini, when the capital, Honiara, suffered rioting and attacks on the Chinese community.

Early Life

Manasseh Damukana Sogavare was born in 1954 at Gauraisa, northern Papua New Guinea, the son of Seventh Day Adventist missionaries from the island of Choiseul in the western Solomons. He was educated in Madang Province (PNG) before moving to Honiara in 1965, where he attended the Betikama SDA high school. He later graduated from the University of the South Pacific at Suva and from New Zealand's Waikato University.

Sogavare pursued a civil service career, becoming chief tax collector. In 1997 he became MP for East Choiseul. Prime Minister Bartholomew Ulufa'alu appointed him finance minister after the Aug. 1997 election but dismissed him in July 1998. Tensions grew in 1998 between the indigenous peoples of Guadacanal island (site of the capital) and long-term residents from Malaita island, who were seen to dominate the civil service. In 2000 Sogavare became leader of the People's Progressive Party (PPP). Ulufa'alu resigned after the Malaita Eagles seized parliament, and Sogavare was chosen to succeed him by MPs.

Career in Office

Sogavare took office on 30 June 2000, forming the Coalition for National Unity, Reconciliation and Peace. Snyder Rini, leader of the Association of Independents, was finance minister. In Oct. 2000 a peace treaty was signed with militias, followed by a further treaty in Feb. 2001. Parliament was dissolved in Aug. 2001 ahead of scheduled elections but the government attempted to push through a constitutional amendment to extend its mandate by another year. Amid corruption allegations, widespread unrest and pressure from the National Union of Workers for a general strike, Sogavare called elections for 5 Dec. 2001. The PPP won

only three seats and Sogavare was succeeded by Sir Allan Kemakeza.

The Social Credit Party, a new party led by Sogavare, ran in the elections of 5 April 2006 on a platform of monetary and financial reform (based on New Zealand's Social Credit Party). Sogavare and his allies attempted to oust Kemakeza's successor, Rini, on 18 April 2006 but, having come third in a parliamentary vote for premier, he switched his allegiance to Rini, in exchange for control of the commerce ministry. Rioting broke out in Honiara in protest at perceived Taiwanese and local Chinese political interference, and much of the city's Chinatown area was destroyed. Following a no-confidence motion, Rini resigned on 26 April and Sogavare was elected prime minister on 4 May, defeating Deputy Prime Minister Fred Fono by 28 votes to 22.

Sogavare has suggested cutting ties with Taiwan in return for diplomatic relations with the People's Republic of China. Despite previous opposition to Australian intervention, he has expressed support for the continuing presence of the Australian-led Regional Assistance Mission to the Solomon Islands force. On 5 May Sogavare appointed a five-party unity cabinet, including two former premiers, Ulufa'alu and Francis Hilly Billy. Australia promptly criticized the appointments of Charles Dausebea and Nelson Ne'e, two MPs arrested for inciting the Honiara riots.

DEFENCE

The marine wing of the Royal Solomon Islands Police operates three patrol boats and a number of fast crafts for surveillance of fisheries and maritime boundaries. There is also an RSI Police Field Force stationed at the border with Papua New Guinea.

In July 2003 an Australian-led peacekeeping force landed to restore stability after years of ethnic fighting and high-level corruption. The force included troops from Fiji Islands, New Zealand, Papua New Guinea and Tonga.

INTERNATIONAL RELATIONS

The Solomon Islands are a member of the UN, WTO, the Commonwealth, the Asian Development Bank, the Pacific Community, the Pacific Islands Forum and is an ACP member state of the ACP-EU relationship. The Solomon Islands are also a member of the World Trade Organization and other organizations for regional technical co-operation.

ECONOMY

Overview

The Solomon Islands Alliance for Change (SIAC) coalition embarked on a reform programme in 1997 to encourage private enterprise, including a reduction of the civil service and a tightening of government revenue collection.

Currency

The *Solomon Island dollar* (SBD) of 100 *cents* was introduced in 1977. It was devalued by 20% in Dec. 1997 and 25% in March 2002. Inflation was 10·1% in 2003 and 6·9% in 2004. In Jan. 2002 foreign exchange reserves were US$28m. Total money supply was SI$243m. in Sept. 2000.

Budget

In 2003 revenues totalled SI$681·3m. and expenditures SI$670·9m. Tax revenue accounted for 48·9% of revenues in 2003 and grants 45·4%; current expenditure accounted for 60·2% of expenditures.

Performance

Real GDP growth was 5·6% in 2003 and 5·5% in 2004. Total GDP in 2004 was US$0·2bn.

Banking and Finance

The Central Bank of Solomon Islands is the bank of issue; its *Governor* is Rick N. Houenipwela ('Hou'). There are three commercial banks and a development bank.

ENERGY AND NATURAL RESOURCES

Environment
Carbon dioxide emissions from the consumption and flaring of fossil fuels in 2002 were the equivalent of 0·4 tonnes per capita.

Electricity
Installed capacity in 2000 was 12,000 kW. Production in 2000 was about 33m. kWh and consumption per capita an estimated 74 kWh. The Solomon Islands Electricity Authority is undertaking projects to increase power generation capacity including the construction of a major hydro-electricity power plant.

Oil and Gas
The potential for oil, petroleum and gas production has yet to be tapped.

Minerals
In 1999 gold output from mining totalled 3,456 kg and silver output 2,138 kg. The only mine in the Solomon Islands closed in 2000 owing to the civil unrest, but it is hoped that production will resume in the future. The value of gold exports in 1999 was SI$113·7m.

Agriculture
Land is held either as customary land (88% of holdings) or registered land. Customary land rights depend on clan membership or kinship. Only Solomon Islanders own customary land; only Islanders or government members may hold perpetual estates of registered land. Coconuts, cocoa, rice and other minor crops are grown. Production, 2000 (in 1,000 tonnes): coconuts, 318; sweet potatoes, 75; taro, 32; palm oil, 28; yams, 25; copra, 23; palm kernels, 7. Agricultural produce earned SI$104·7m. in exports in 1997. In 2000 there were 42,000 ha. of arable land and 18,000 ha. of permanent crops.

Livestock (2000): pigs, 59,000; cattle, 12,000.

Forestry
Forests covered 2·54m. ha. in 2000 (88·8% of the land area). Earnings from forest resources increased from SI$266·6m. in 1994 to SI$309·9m. in 1995 and SI$349·3m. in 1996 but then slumped in 1997 to SI$309·4m. owing to a fall in prices and a government moratorium on the issue of new logging licences. Timber production was 692,000 cu. metres in 2001.

Fisheries
Solomon Islands' waters are among the richest in tuna. Catches have remained well below the maximum sustainable catch limits. Previously closed areas within its territorial waters have been opened to American fishing interests but sustainable harvest rates will not be at risk. The total catch in 2001 was an estimated 30,075 tonnes.

INDUSTRY
Industries include palm oil manufacture (35,000 tonnes in 2002), processed fish production (13,700 tonnes in 2000), rice milling, fish canning, fish freezing, saw milling, food, tobacco and soft drinks. Other products include wood and rattan furniture, fibreglass articles, boats, clothing and spices.

Labour
The Labour Division of the Ministry of Commerce, Employment and Tourism monitors and regulates the domestic labour market. The labour force in 1996 totalled 202,000 (54% males). Around 38% of the economically active population in 1993 were engaged in community, social and personal services and 27% in agriculture, fisheries and forestry.

Trade Unions
Trade Unions exist by virtue of the Trade Unions Act of 1976. The Solomon Islands Council of Trade Unions (SICTU) is the central body. Affiliated members of the SICTU are Solomon Islands National Union of Workers and the Solomon Islands Public Employees Union (SIPEU). SIPEU, which represents employees of the public sector, is the largest single trade union.

INTERNATIONAL TRADE
The Solomon Islands are a member of the World Trade Organization. The government recognizes the private sector as an engine for growth. Through encouraging the private sector the government hopes that the base for a broad diversification of tradeable goods and services can be established.

Total foreign debt in 2002 was US$180m.

Imports and Exports
Imports 2002, SI$436·3m.; exports, SI$390·0m. Main imports, 2002: food and live animals, 24·9%; mineral fuels and lubricants, 17·3%; machinery and transport equipment, 13·2%. Main exports: timber, 65·2%; fish products, 18·1%; cocoa beans, 7·1%. Principal import suppliers (2002): Australia, 31·5%; Singapore, 19·8%; New Zealand, 5·2%. Principal export markets (2002): Japan, 17·1%; South Korea, 16·7%; Philippines, 6·8%.

Trade Fairs
An annual National Cultural and Trade Show/Fair is held in July to coincide with the anniversary of independence.

COMMUNICATIONS

Roads
In 2002 there was estimated to be a total of 1,360 km of roads, of which 34 km were paved. The unpaved roads included 800 km of private plantation roads.

Civil Aviation
A new terminal has been opened at Henderson International Airport in Honiara. The national carrier is Solomon Airlines. In 1999 scheduled airline traffic of Solomon Islands-based carriers flew 4·1m. km, carrying 98,000 passengers (23,000 on international flights).

Shipping
There are international ports at Honiara, Yandina in the Russell Islands and Noro in New Georgia, Western Province. In 2002 the merchant marine totalled 8,000 GRT.

Telecommunications
Telecommunications are operated by Solomon Telekom, a joint venture between the government of Solomon Islands and Cable & Wireless (UK). Telecommunications between Honiara and provincial centres are facilitated by modern satellite communication systems. Telephone subscribers numbered 7,600 in 2002 (17·1 per 1,000 inhabitants) and there were 18,000 PCs in use (40·5 per 1,000 inhabitants). There were approximately 1,000 mobile phone subscribers in 2002 and 900 fax machines. Internet users numbered 2,200 in 2002.

Postal Services
The Solomon Islands Postal Corporation, a statutory company established in 1996, administers postal services. In 2003 there were 27 post offices.

SOCIAL INSTITUTIONS

Justice
Civil and criminal jurisdiction is exercised by the High Court of Solomon Islands, constituted 1975. A Solomon Islands Court of Appeal was established in 1982. Jurisdiction is based on the principles of English law (as applying on 1 Jan. 1981). Magistrates' courts can try civil cases on claims not exceeding SI$2,000, and criminal cases with penalties not exceeding 14 years' imprisonment. Certain crimes, such as burglary and arson, where the maximum sentence is for life, may also be tried by magistrates. There are also local courts, which decide matters concerning customary titles to land; decisions may be

put to the Customary Land Appeal Court. There is no capital punishment.

The population in penal institutions in 2004 was 275 (56 per 100,000 of national population).

Education

In 2002 there were 82,330 pupils at primary and 21,700 pupils at secondary level. The adult literacy rate in 1998 was 62·0%.

Training of teachers and trade and vocational training is carried out at the College of Higher Education. The University of the South Pacific Centre is at Honiara. Other rural training centres run by churches are also involved in vocational training.

In 2000–01 total expenditure on education came to 3·6% of GNP and in 1999–2000 accounted for 15·4% of total government spending.

Health

A free medical service is supplemented by the private sector. An international standard immunization programme is conducted in conjunction with the WHO for infants. Tuberculosis has been eradicated but malaria remains a problem. In 1997 there were 11 hospitals, 31 doctors and 464 registered nurses and 283 nursing aides.

RELIGION

92% of the population were Christians in 2001.

CULTURE

Broadcasting

The Solomon Islands Broadcasting Corporation (SIBC) operates a national service and an FM service for Honiara. The other FM station—FM100—is privately operated and broadcasts news and entertainment on a 24-hour basis. There were 12,000 TV receivers in 2001 and 57,000 radio receivers in 1997.

Cinema

Private interests operate three cinemas in the capital. There are small cinemas in the provincial centres.

Press

There are two main newspapers in circulation. *The Solomon Star* is daily and the *Solomon Voice* is weekly. The Government Information Service publishes a monthly issue of the *Solomon Nius* which exclusively disseminates news of government activities. Non-government organizations such as the Solomon Islands Development Trust (SIDT) also publish monthly papers on environmental issues.

Tourism

Tourism in the Solomon Islands is still in a development stage. The emphasis is on establishing major hotels in the capital and provincial centres, to be supplemented by satellite Eco-tourism projects in the rural areas. The Solomon Islands Visitors Bureau is the statutory institution for domestic co-ordination and international marketing. In 2002 there were 37,000 foreign tourists, bringing revenue of US$7m.

Festivals

Festivities and parades in the capital and provincial centres normally mark the National Day of Independence. The highlight is the annual National Trade and Cultural Show.

Libraries

There is a National Library operated by the government in Honiara. The other library facilities are those of the Solomon Islands College of Higher Education and the University of the South Pacific (SI) Centre.

Museums and Galleries

There is a National Museum which has a display of traditional artefacts. Early government and public records are kept at the National Archives and a National Art Gallery displays a number of fine arts and works by Solomon Islands artists.

DIPLOMATIC REPRESENTATIVES

Of the Solomon Islands in the United Kingdom (resides in Brussels)
High Commissioner: Robert Sisilo.

Of the United Kingdom in the Solomon Islands (Telekom House, Mendana Ave., Honiara)
High Commissioner: Richard Lyne.

Of the USA in the Solomon Islands
Ambassador: Robert W. Fitts (resides in Port Moresby, Papua New Guinea).

Of the Solomon Islands in the USA and to the United Nations (800 2nd Ave, Suite 400L, New York, NY 10017)
Ambassador: Collin Beck.

Of the Solomon Islands to the European Union
Ambassador: Robert Sisilo.

FURTHER READING

Bennett, J. A., *Wealth of the Solomons: A History of a Pacific Archipelago, 1800–1978.* Univ. of Hawaii Press, 1987

National Statistical Office: Solomon Islands National Statistical Office, PO Box G6, Department of Finance, Honiara.

SOMALIA

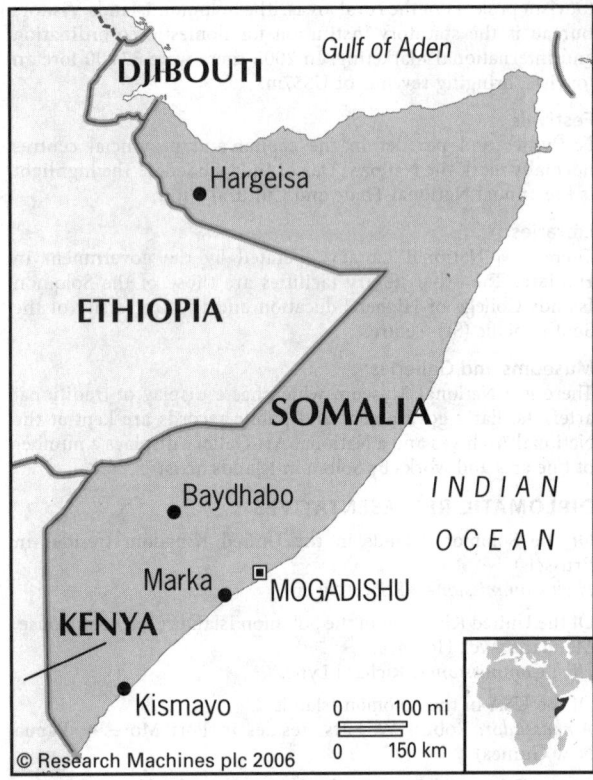

Gulf of Aden

DJIBOUTI

Hargeisa

ETHIOPIA

SOMALIA

Baydhabo

INDIAN

OCEAN

Marka ▣ MOGADISHU

KENYA

Kismayo

0   100 mi

0   150 km

© Research Machines plc 2006

Jamhuriyadda Dimugradiga ee Soomaaliya
(Somali Democratic Republic)

Capital: Mogadishu
Population projection, 2010: 9·59m.
GDP per capita: not available

KEY HISTORICAL EVENTS

The origins of the Somali people can be traced back 2,000 years when they displaced an earlier Arabic people. They converted to Islam in the 10th century and were organized in loose Islamic states by the 19th century. The northern part of Somaliland was created a British protectorate in 1884. The southern part belonged to two local rulers who, in 1889, accepted Italian protection for their lands. The Italian invasion of Ethiopia in 1935 was launched from Somaliland and in 1936 Somaliland was incorporated with Eritrea and Ethiopia to become Italian East Africa. In 1940 Italian forces invaded British Somaliland but in 1941 the British, with South African and Indian troops, recaptured this territory as well as occupying Italian Somaliland. After the Second World War British Somaliland reverted to its colonial status and ex-Italian Somaliland became the UN Trust Territory of Somaliland, administered by Italy.

The independent Somali Republic came into being on 1 July 1960 as a result of the merger of the British Somaliland Protectorate, which first became independent on 26 June 1960, and the Italian Trusteeship Territory of Somaliland. On 21 Oct. 1969 Maj.-Gen. Mohammed Siyad Barre took power in a coup. Various insurgent forces combined to oppose the Barre regime in a bloody civil war. Barre fled on 27 Jan. 1991 but interfactional fighting continued. In Aug. 1992 a new coalition government agreed a UN military presence to back up relief efforts to help the estimated 1·5–2m. victims of famine. On 11 Dec. 1992 the leaders of the two most prominent of the warring factions, Ali Mahdi Muhammad and Muhammad Farah Aidid, agreed to a peace plan under the aegis of the UN and a pact was signed on 15 Jan. 1993. At the end of March, the warring factions agreed to disarm and form a 74-member National Transitional Council. On 4 Nov. 1994 the UN Security Council unanimously decided to withdraw UN forces; the last of these left on 2 March 1995.

The principal insurgent group in the north of the country, the Somali National Movement, declared the secession of an independent **'Somaliland Republic'** on 17 May 1991. The Somalian government rejected the secession and Muhammad Aidid's forces launched a campaign to reoccupy the 'Republic' in Jan. 1996. Muhammad Farah Aidid was assassinated in July 1996 and succeeded by his son Hussein Aidid. In July 1998 leaders in the northeast of Somalia proclaimed an 'autonomous state' named **Puntland.**

Peace efforts in neighbouring Djibouti culminated in July 2000 in the establishment of a power-sharing agreement and a national constitution to see Somalia through a three-year transitional period. The election of members of parliament and a civilian government followed in Aug. 2000, and in Oct. the new government moved from Djibouti back to Somalia.

In April 2002 **'Southwestern Somalia'** broke away from Mogadishu, thereby creating a third autonomous Somali state.

TERRITORY AND POPULATION

Somalia is bounded north by the Gulf of Aden, east and south by the Indian ocean, and west by Kenya, Ethiopia and Djibouti. Total area 637,657 sq. km (246,201 sq. miles). At the last census, in 1987, the population was 7,114,431. Estimated population (2005): 8,228,000; density, 13 per sq. km. Population counting is complicated owing to large numbers of nomads and refugee movements as a result of famine and clan warfare.

The UN gives a projected population for 2010 of 9·59m.

In 2000 an estimated 66·7% of the population were rural.

The country is administratively divided into 18 regions (with chief cities): Awdal (Saylac), Bakol (Xuddur), Bay (Baydhabo), Benadir (Mogadishu), Bari (Boosaso), Galgudug (Duusa Marreeb), Gedo (Garbahaarrey), Hiran (Beledweyne), Jubbada Dexe (Jilib), Jubbada Hoose (Kismayo), Mudug (Gaalkacyo), Nogal (Garowe), Woqooyi Galbeed (Hargeisa), Sanaag (Ceerigabo), Shabeellaha Dhexe (Jawhar), Shabeellaha Hoose (Marka), Sol (Las Anod), Togder (Burao). Somaliland comprises the regions of Awdal, Woqooyi Galbeed, Togder, Sanaag and Sol. Puntland consists of Bari, Nogal and northern Mudug. Southwestern Somalia consists of Bay, Bakol, Gedo, Jubbada Hoose and Shabeellaha Dhexe.

The capital is Mogadishu (1999 population, 1,162,000). Other large towns are (with 1990 estimates) Hargeisa (90,000), Kismayo (90,000), Berbera (70,000) and Marka (62,000).

The national language is Somali. Arabic is also an official language and English and Italian are spoken extensively.

SOCIAL STATISTICS

Births, 1997 estimate, 300,000; deaths, 121,000. Rates, 1997 estimate (per 1,000 population): birth, 45·5; death, 18·3. Infant mortality, 1997, 126 per 1,000 live births. Annual population growth rate, 1992–2002, 2·8%. Life expectancy in 1997, 46·2 years. Fertility rate, 2001, 7·3 births per woman.

CLIMATE

Much of the country is arid, although rainfall is more adequate towards the south. Temperatures are very high on the northern coasts. Mogadishu, Jan. 79°F (26·1°C), July 78°F (25·6°C). Annual rainfall 17" (429 mm). Berbera, Jan. 76°F (24·4°C), July 97°F (36·1°C). Annual rainfall 2" (51 mm).

CONSTITUTION AND GOVERNMENT

The constitution of 1979 authorized a sole legal party, the Somali Revolutionary Socialist Party. There was an elected President and People's Assembly. The constitution was amended in 1984.

A conference of national reconciliation in July 1991 and again in March 1993 allowed for the setting up of a transitional government charged with reorganizing free elections, but inter-factional fighting and anarchy have replaced settled government.

In Aug. 2000 a transitional parliament with a three-year mandate was inaugurated, at the time in neighbouring Djibouti but subsequently in Mogadishu. There was a 245-member *Transitional National Assembly* appointed by clan chiefs.

Under an agreed charter the transitional assembly was to elect a president who in turn was to form a government. However, ongoing wrangling between Somalia's rival factions continues. In Nov. 2002 leaders of the Somali factions met in order to begin the process of drawing up a new federal constitution. In Jan. 2004 the country's leaders signed an agreement to form a new government based along clan lines. In Aug. 2004 a new 275-member Somali Transitional Federal Parliament was inaugurated in Nairobi, Kenya. The newly-formed government began the process of returning from Kenya to Somalia in June 2005. Amid concern over security in Mogadishu, parliament met for the first time in Feb. 2006 in Baidoa.

Puntland. Puntland, in the northeast region of Somalia, declared itself an 'autonomous state' in July 1998 under the leadership of Abdullahi Yusuf. Since its creation, Puntland has been locked in dispute with Somaliland over control of the Sanaag and Sol areas.

Puntland covers 300,000 sq. km and had a population in 2000 of 2m. The capital is Garowe. Somali is the official language and the Somali shilling is the official currency. Puntland has not received international recognition.

Somaliland. An independent 'Somaliland Republic', based on the territory of the former British protectorate which ran from 1884 until Somali independence in 1960, was established on 17 May 1991 by the principal insurgent group in the north of the country, the Somali National Movement. The Somali government rejected the secession and Muhammad Aidid's forces launched an unsuccessful campaign to reoccupy Somaliland in Jan. 1996. Somaliland is also engaged in a long-running dispute with Puntland over control of the Sanaag and Sol regions. The Republic has failed to secure international recognition although it has in effect seceded from Somalia but has developed close relations with Ethiopia.

Somaliland covers 137,600 sq. km. The capital is Hargeisa and there is a port at Berbera. There is a population of around 3·5m. Somali is the official language and Arabic and English are also widely used.

There is a bicameral government with a house of representatives and one of elected elders. Dahir Riyale Kahin became *President* in May 2002 and was re-elected in April 2004. The judiciary is independent. The official currency is the Somaliland shilling. The Bank of Somaliland, the central bank, was founded in 1994. The economy is reliant on livestock farming.

Southwestern Somalia. In April 2002 Southwestern Somalia broke away from Mogadishu and was declared an autonomous state by the Rahanwein Resistance Army. Hassan Muhammad Nur 'Shatigadud' was named president but fighting between

Shatigadud and several of his deputies ensued, notably around the capital, Baydhabo.

National Anthem

'Somaliyaay toosoo' ('Somalia wake up'); words and tune anonymous.

RECENT ELECTIONS

Somalia's Transitional Federal Parliament elected Abdullahi Yusuf Ahmed president on 10 Oct. 2004 in Nairobi, Kenya. In the first round Abdullahi Yusuf Ahmed won 80 votes, followed by Abdullahi Ahmed Addou with 35 and Mohamed Qanyare Afrah with 33. There were 23 other candidates. In the second round Ahmed won 147 votes, Addou 83 and Afrah 38, ahead of three other candidates. A third round run-off was required in which Ahmed won 189 against 79 for Addou.

CURRENT ADMINISTRATION

President: Abdullahi Yusuf Ahmed; b. 1934 (sworn in 14 Oct. 2004).

In March 2006 the Transitional Federal Government comprised:

Prime Minister: Ali Muhammad Ghedi; b. 1952 (in office since 3 Nov. 2004).

Vice-Prime Minister, Minister of Finance: Salim Aliyow Ibroow. *Vice-Prime Minister, Minister of Information:* Mohamuud Abdullahi 'Sifir' Jama. *Vice-Prime Minister, Minister of Internal Affairs:* Hussein M. Farah Aidid.

Minister of Agriculture: Hassan Muhammad Nur 'Shatigadud'. *Commerce:* Musse Suddi Yalahow. *Constitutional Affairs:* Abdalla Derow Isaaq. *Culture and Heritage:* Abdi Hashi Abdullahi. *Defence:* Gen. Abdirahman Mohamud Ali. *Development of Co-operatives:* Mohamed Abdullahl Kaamil. *Disabled and Orphanages:* Hussein Elaabe Fahiye. *Education:* Ali Abdullahi Osoble. *Energy:* Mohamednuraani Bakar. *Environment and Disaster Management:* Mohamed Osman Maye. *Family and Women's Affairs:* Fowsiiya Mohamed Sheikh Hussein. *Fisheries and Marine Resources:* Hassan Abshir Farah. *Foreign Affairs:* Abdullahi Sheikh Ismail. *Health:* Abdiaziz Sheikh Yussuf. *Higher Education:* Hussein M. Shiekh Hussein. *Industry:* Abdi Mohamed Tarah. *Justice:* Sheikh Adan Mohamed 'Madobe' Nur. *Labour and Human Resources:* Saalah Ali Saalah. *Lands and Settlements:* Moulid Ma'ane Mohamud. *Livestock and Forest Management:* Ibrahim Mohamed Isaaq. *Military Training and Reintegration:* Botaan Isse Alim. *Monetary Affairs:* Abdikanin Ahmed Ali. *National Security:* Mohamed Qanyare Afrah. *Oil:* Yussuf Mohamed Ali. *Planning and International Co-operation:* Abdirisaaq Osman Hassan. *Ports and Marine Affairs:* Ali Ismail Abdi. *Public Works and Housing:* Osman Hassan Ali Ato. *Regional Co-operation:* Ismail Hure Buubaa. *Reconciliation and Diaspora Affairs:* Sheikh Adan Sheikh Mohamed. *Reconstruction and Resettlement:* Barre Adan Shire. *Religious Affairs:* Omar M. Mohamud Filish. *Rural Development:* Mohamed Mohamuud 'Gamadhere' Guleed. *Science and Technology:* Ismail Hassan Jama. *Sports and Youth Affairs:* Ahmed Abdullahl Jama Daakir. *State Goods and Public Markets:* Mohamuud Sayid Adaan. *Surface and Air Transport:* Ibrahim Adan Hassan. *Transport, Post and Telecommunications:* Ali Ahmed Jama. *Tourism and Wildlife:* Mohamed Mohamud Heyd. *Water and Natural Resources:* Mohamud Salaad Nuur.

CURRENT LEADERS

Abdullahi Yusuf Ahmed

Position
Transitional President

Introduction
Abdullahi Yusuf Ahmed was elected transitional president of Somalia in Oct. 2004. The transitional government began

its return from exile in Kenya in June 2005, a step towards establishing the country's first functioning government since the overthrow of President Siad Barre in 1991. Somalia's fourteenth leader since Barre, Abdullahi has held power longer than any of his thirteen predecessors.

Early Life

Abdullahi Yusuf Ahmed was born on 15 Dec. 1934 in Galcacyo in the Mudug province of Italian Somalia. He studied in Italy and the Soviet Union and, following the country's independence in June 1960, joined the Somali National Army (SNA). He achieved the rank of colonel but refused to take part in the coup led by Siad Barre which followed the assassination of President Abdirashid Ali Shermarke in Oct. 1969. Abdullahi was jailed but released in the early 1970s and appointed manager of a state agency. He was reinstated as a commander in 1977 when the SNA attempted to 'liberate' the ethnically-Somali region of Ogaden in Ethiopia.

The following year, with the support of several members of his Majerteen clan, Abdullahi staged an unsuccessful coup and fled to Kenya. Moving to Ethiopia in 1979, he formed the Somali Salvation Democratic Front (SSDF) to oppose Siad Barre. Abdullahi became embroiled in arguments with the Ethiopian leader, Haile Mengistu, and was jailed, released only in 1991 when the dictator's regime fell.

Siad Barre was driven out of Mogadishu, the Somali capital, on 27 Jan. 1991 by the United Somali Congress militia. Somalia slid into anarchy, divided into a dozen regions controlled by warlords. Abdullahi focused his political ambitions in Puntland and was elected president of the relatively peaceful province in July 1998. Having failed to extend his term of office, which expired on 1 July 2001, he fought for control of the country. In the election for the transitional presidency of Somalia, held in the Kenyan capital, Nairobi, on 10 Oct. 2004, he received 189 out of 268 votes.

Career in Office

Abdullahi has promised to rebuild his war-ravaged country and has asked for international assistance. The transitional government began returning to Somalia in June 2005 but arguments broke out over its location, with Abdullahi favouring Jowhar while other members supported a return to Mogadishu. The parliament met for the first time in Feb. 2006 at a compromise location, Baidoa in central Somalia.

DEFENCE

With the breakdown of government following the 1991 revolution armed forces broke up into clan groupings, four of them in the north and six in the south.

Defence expenditure totalled US$38m. in 2002 (US$4 per capita), representing 4·0% of GDP.

Army

Following the 1991 revolution there are no national armed forces. In Northern Somalia the Somali National Movement controls an armed clan of 5–6,000 out of a total of 7,000 armed forces in the area. In the rest of the country several local groups control forces of which the Ali Mahdi Faction controls the largest, an armed clan of 10,000.

INTERNATIONAL RELATIONS

Somalia is a member of the UN, the African Union, African Development Bank, OIC, Islamic Development Bank, the League of Arab States and the Intergovernmental Authority on Development and is an ACP member state of the ACP-EU relationship.

ECONOMY

Agriculture accounts for approximately 59% of GDP, industry 10% and services 31%.

Overview

'Scientific Socialism' was implemented by the military government of Muhammad Siad Barre in the 1970s. In the 1980s exports and manufacturing declined rapidly. In 1983 Saudi Arabia banned the import of Somali livestock, which earned about 80% of foreign currency. An IMF-backed Five Year Plan was instituted in 1987, which included privatization schemes and the reduction of the budget deficit. Civil war from 1988 precipitated the collapse of the national economy, government and banking system. Somalis became dependent on remittances, estimated at US$800m. annually, from the overseas diaspora in the 1990s.

Currency

The unit of currency is the *Somali shilling* (SOS) of 100 *cents*.

Budget

Budget for 1991: revenue, Som.Sh. 151,453m.; expenditure, Som. Sh. 141,141m.

Performance

Real GDP growth was 0·0% in both 1997 and 1998. Total GDP in 1998 was estimated to be US$4bn.

Banking and Finance

Prior to the collapse of central government in 1990, the bank of issue, now inactive, was the Central Bank of Somalia (*Governor*, Dr Mahmamud Mohamed Ulusow). The separatist Somaliland Republic has its own functioning central bank in Hargeisa, the Bank of Somaliland (*Governor*, Abdourahman Dualeh Mohamoud). Remittance companies (*hawala*) took the place of banks in the 1990s, channelling approximately US$800m. a year. Al-Barakaat, the largest *hawala*, was shut down in Nov. 2001. All national banks were bankrupted by 1990. The Universal Bank of Somalia, the first commercial bank in Mogadishu since 1990, opened with European backing in Jan. 2002.

ENERGY AND NATURAL RESOURCES

Environment

Carbon dioxide emissions from the consumption and flaring of fossil fuels in 2002 were the equivalent of 0·1 tonnes per capita.

Electricity

In 2000 installed capacity was 80,000 kW. Production (2000, estimate): 282m. kWh.

Oil and Gas

Natural gas reserves were 5·7bn. cu. metres in 2002.

Minerals

There are deposits of chromium, coal, copper, gold, gypsum, lead, limestone, manganese, nickel, sepiolite, silver, titanium, tungsten, uranium and zinc.

Agriculture

Somalia is essentially a pastoral country, and about 80% of the inhabitants depend on livestock-rearing (cattle, sheep, goats and camels). Half the population is nomadic. In 2001 there were 1·05m. ha. of arable land and 26,000 ha. of permanent cropland. 200,000 ha. were irrigated in 2001. There were 1,700 tractors in 2001. Estimated production, 2000 (in 1,000 tonnes): sugarcane, 220; maize, 210; sorghum, 100; cassava, 70; bananas, 55.

Livestock (2000): 13·1m. sheep; 12·3m. goats; 6·1m. camels; 5·1m. cattle. Somalia has the greatest number of camels of any country in the world.

Forestry

In 2000 the area under forests was 7·52m. ha., or 12·0% of the total land area. In 2001, 9·63m. cu. metres of roundwood were cut. Wood and charcoal are the main energy sources. Frankincense and myrrh are produced.

Fisheries

Approximately 20,000 tonnes of fish were caught in 2001, almost entirely from marine waters.

INDUSTRY

A few small industries exist including sugar refining (production was 20,000 tonnes in 2001), food processing and textiles.

Labour

The labour force totalled 4,291,000 in 1996 (57% males). Approximately 74% of the economically active population in 1995 were engaged in agriculture, fisheries and forestry.

INTERNATIONAL TRADE

Foreign debt was US$2,688m. in 2002.

Imports and Exports

Imports in 1999 were estimated at US$180m. and exports at US$150m.

Principal exports: livestock, hides and skins, bananas. Main import suppliers, 1999: Djibouti, 27%; Kenya, 12%; India, 9%; Thailand, 5%. Main export markets, 1999: Yemen, 29%; Saudi Arabia, 28%; United Arab Emirates, 28%; Oman, 6%.

COMMUNICATIONS

Roads

In 2002 there were an estimated 22,100 km of roads, of which 2,600 km were paved. Passenger cars numbered 12,700 in 2002, and there were 10,400 trucks and vans.

Civil Aviation

There are international airports at Mogadishu and Hargeisa. In 2003 there were flights to Addis Ababa, Dire Dawa, Djibouti, Jeddah and Nairobi in addition to internal services.

Shipping

There are deep-water harbours at Kismayo, Berbera, Marka and Mogadishu. The merchant fleet (2002) totalled 6,000 GRT.

Telecommunications

Somalia had 100,000 main telephone lines in 2002, equivalent to ten for every 1,000 persons. There were 35,000 mobile phone subscribers in 2002. In 2002 there were 89,000 Internet users. In the absence of a government-controlled telecommunications monopoly three companies—Telcom, Nationlink and Hormuud—compete for both landline and mobile customers.

SOCIAL INSTITUTIONS

Justice

There are 84 district courts, each with a civil and a criminal section. There are eight regional courts and two Courts of Appeal (at Mogadishu and Hargeisa), each with a general section and an assize section. The Supreme Court is in Mogadishu. The death penalty is in force and was used in 2000.

Education

The nomadic life of a large percentage of the population inhibits education progress. In 1990 adult literacy was estimated at 24%. In 1985 (latest data available) there were 194,335 pupils and 9,676 teachers in primary schools, and 37,181 pupils and 2,320 teachers in secondary schools; and in 1984 (latest data available), 613 students with 30 teachers at teacher-training establishments. The National University of Somalia in Mogadishu (founded 1959) had 4,650 students and 550 academic staff in 1994–95.

Health

In 1997 Somalia had 265 physicians, 13 dentists, 1,327 nurses and 70 pharmacists. In 1988 there were seven hospital beds per 10,000 inhabitants.

Somalia has among the highest percentages of undernourished people of any country—73% in 1996, up from fewer than 60% in the early 1980s.

RELIGION

The population is almost entirely Sunni Muslims.

CULTURE

Broadcasting

The state television station was destroyed in fighting in 1991. Mogadishu-based HornAfrik was launched in 1999 as the first independent radio and television broadcaster. The National Transitional Government runs Radio Mogadishu–Voice of the Somali Republic. The Somali Broadcasting Corporation, based in Boosaaso, was shut down by the government of Puntland in May 2002. The Somaliland government banned all private radio stations in June 2002, giving Radio Hargeisa a monopoly. In 2000 there were 435,000 radio and 102,000 TV receivers (colour by PAL).

Press

The Somali press collapsed in 1991, with most of its facilities destroyed. Since 2000 several independent newspapers have emerged, including the daily *Wartire* in Hargeisa (Somaliland) and the weeklies *Yamayska* and *Bulsho* in Puntland. There were six daily newspapers in Mogadishu in Oct. 2002. In 1996 average daily circulation of newspapers totalled 10,000.

Tourism

In 1998 there were 10,000 foreign tourists.

DIPLOMATIC REPRESENTATIVES

The Embassy of Somalia in the United Kingdom closed on 2 Jan. 1992.

Of the United Kingdom in Somalia (Waddada Xasan Geedd Abtoow 7–8, Mogadishu)
Staff temporarily withdrawn.

The Embassy of Somalia in the USA closed on 8 May 1991. A liaison office opened in March 1994, and withdrew to Nairobi in Sept. 1994.

Of Somalia to the United Nations
Ambassador: Elmi Ahmed Duale.

Of Somalia to the European Union
Ambassador: Vacant.

FURTHER READING

Abdisalam, M. I.-S., *The Collapse of the Somali State*. London, 1995

Ghalib, J. M., *The Cost of Dictatorship: the Somali Experience*. New York, 1995

Lewis, I. M., *Blood and Bone: the Call of Kinship in Somali Society*. Lawrenceville (NJ), 1995.—*Understanding Somalia: a Guide to Culture, History and Social Institutions*. 2nd ed. London, 1995

Omar, M. O., *The Road to Zero: Somalia's Self-Destruction*. London, 1995

Samatar, A. I. (ed.) *The Somali Challenge: from Catastrophe to Renewal?* Boulder (CO), 1994

National Statistical Office: Central Statistical Department, State Planning Commission, Mogadishu.

SOUTH AFRICA

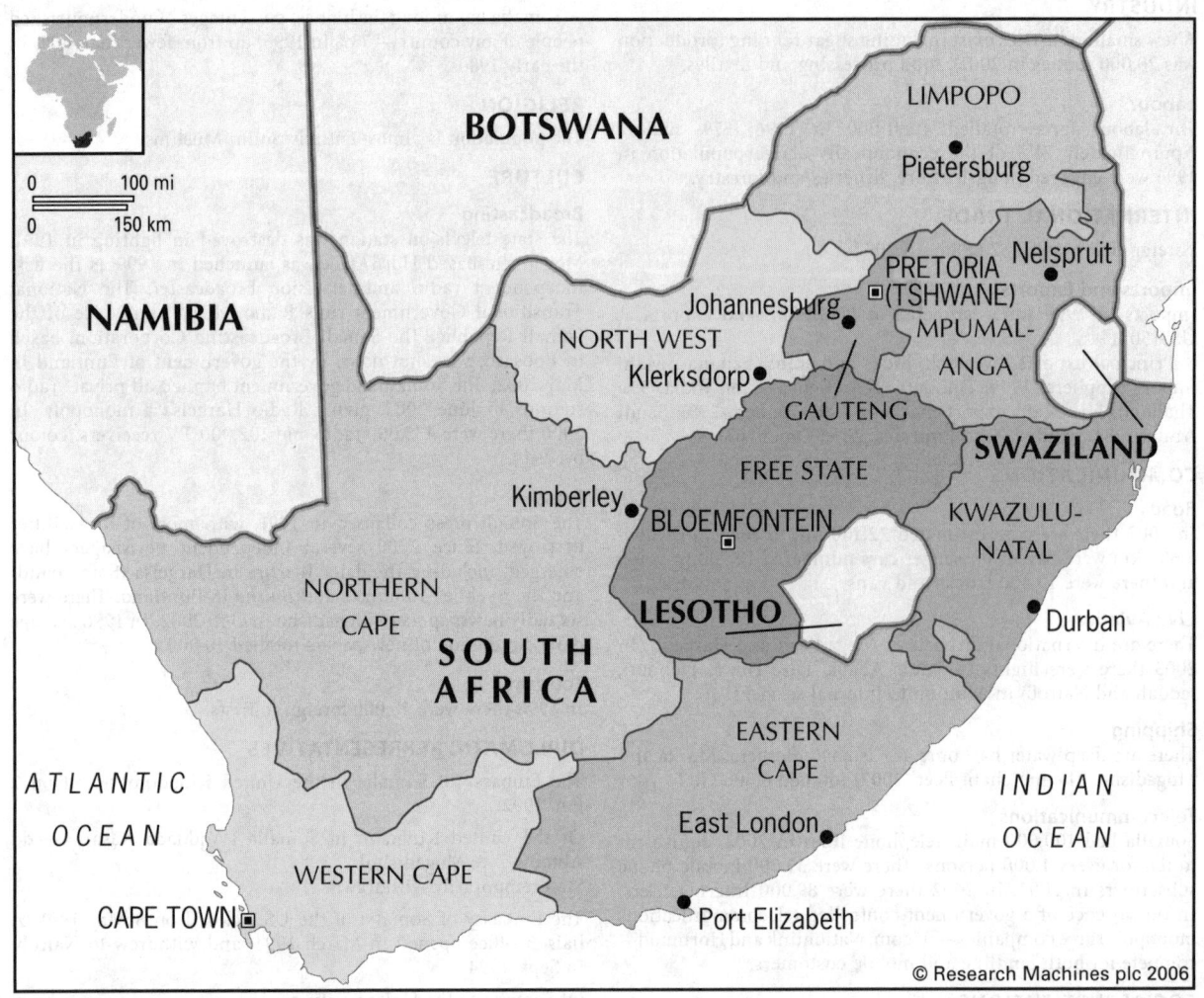

© Research Machines plc 2006

Republic of South Africa

Capital: Pretoria/Tshwane (Administrative), Cape Town
(Legislative), Bloemfontein (Judicial)
Seat of Parliament: Cape Town
Seats of Government: Cape Town, Pretoria
Population projection, 2010: 47·82m.
GDP per capita, 2003: (PPP$) 10,346
HDI/world rank: 0·658/120

KEY HISTORICAL EVENTS

The San and the Khoikhoi were the indigenous peoples of
southern Africa. The San were nomadic hunter-gatherers who
had lived from the land at the edge of the Kalahari desert for
thousands of years. The Khoikhoi shared customs with the San
and spoke related languages but also herded cattle and lived
in more settled communities. The Khoikhoi settlements were
most numerous in the Orange River valley and around the
Cape. From the fourth century AD the eastern part of southern
Africa was settled by Bantu-speaking groups, moving south
from the continent's drier interior. They were mixed farmers:
herding sheep and cattle, hunting game, cultivating sorghum
and making tools and weapons from iron.

The hunting and herding communities of southern Africa
came into contact with the wider world at the end of the
fifteenth century. Portuguese mariners first rounded the Cape
peninsula in 1487 and opened a trade route into the Indian
Ocean. A century later the route was used by Spanish, English,
Dutch and French seafarers. They landed occasionally on the
Cape peninsula and bartered sheep and cattle with Khoikhoi
pastoralists in return for iron and copper goods. In 1649 the
Dutch East India Company, the world's most powerful trading
corporation, established a trading post at the Cape. Three years
later Jan van Riebeeck arrived with orders to establish a fort
at Table Bay and supply passing ships with meat, fruit and
vegetables. Within a decade slaves were brought in to work on
building and maintaining the infrastructure, and settlers began
to arrive from the Netherlands. Relations between the Dutch and
the Khoikhoi soon deteriorated: quarrels over rights to graze
cattle escalated into warfare as early as 1659.

Over the next century the population of the Cape Colony
reached 10,000. It was a diverse community, where traders from
Europe and Asia converged and exchanged goods and news.

Large farms, cultivating vines and grain, were established in the fertile valleys to the east of Cape Town. Devastated by smallpox in 1713, the Khoikhoi population was unable to prevent *trekboers* (Dutch pastoral farmers) from moving to the north and east of the Cape colony. By 1770 trekboers were grazing their cattle as far east as the Fish river, where they came into contact with Xhosa farmers. More numerous and powerful than the Khoikhoi, and with greater resistance to European diseases, the Xhosa fought the Dutch settlers in a series of 'Frontier Wars'.

By the late 18th century Dutch sea power was on the wane. Vying with France for control of the main trade routes to Asia and the Americas, the British first seized Cape Town in 1795. Following the peace treaties of 1814, which ended the Napoleonic Wars, British sovereignty over the colony was confirmed. For the British, the main purpose of their acquisition was to provide a stepping-stone to their increasingly important colonies in Asia.

In the first two decades of the 19th century the Zulu people of the northeastern region (Natal) strengthened their power-base under their leader, Shaka. In response to a prolonged drought the Zulus conquered lands from rival Nguni groups, which culminated in widespread havoc and destruction, known as the *Mfecane*. From the chaos new kingdoms emerged, notably Gaza and Swaziland, while the Sotho, under King Moshoeshoe, formed the mountain territory now known as Lesotho.

The *Mfecane* led to the migration of thousands of Basotho and Batswana from the High veld and Xhosa from the coastal plains into the Cape Colony. In the 1830s Boer settlers, increasingly dissatisfied with British rule and, realising that the *Mfecane* had caused the depopulation of land to the north and east, began to move there. In the 'Great Trek' that began in 1836, the Afrikaners were seeking a free and independent state which they achieved in the establishment of the Orange Free State and Transvaal in 1854.

Meanwhile, the British strengthened their hold over the Cape Colony and Natal by bringing in new settlers. Between 1860 and 1866, 6,000 Indians arrived in Natal from Madras and Calcutta to work as indentured labourers on the new sugar plantations. The population of the Cape Colony included many Afrikaners as well as the 'coloured' community (descendants of Khoikhoi, white settlers and Malay slaves). Most coloureds spoke Afrikaans, an offshoot of Dutch.

Britain annexed the Transvaal in 1877, and in 1879 fought the Zulus. Under King Ketshwayo the Zulus were victorious at Isandhlwana but were then defeated at Ulundi. Britain restored independence to the Transvaal (the South African Republic) in 1884 and annexed Zululand in 1887. Both the British and the Boers fought African resistance for many years, the last major rising being in Natal in 1906. However, the British and Boers continued to be rivals, especially after the discovery of diamonds at Kimberley in 1867 and of gold in the Transvaal in 1884. This led to an economic boom. Cecil Rhodes, owner of the De Beers company and for a time prime minister of the Cape, was the dominant entrepreneurial figure.

Boer War

In the 1890s the British, under Rhodes, sought control over the Transvaal goldfields. Despite being thwarted in their attempts to spark off rebellion amongst the Afrikaners of the South African Republic, the British continued to press for control. The Afrikaners, led by Paul Kruger, decided they would have to fight to keep their independence and declared war on Britain in late 1899. The contest appeared unequal, with the might of the British army against only 35,000 Boer soldiers. The Boers suffered a heavy defeat at Paardeberg in 1900, but then switched to guerrilla warfare. The British army, led by Gen. Kitchener, responded by setting up concentration camps and destroying crops and farmsteads. The 'scorched earth' policy was strongly criticized in Europe, but had the desired effect—in 1902 the Boer republics signed the Treaty of Vereeniging and came under

British rule. They were given self-government in 1907 and on 31 May 1910 the Cape Colony, Natal, the Transvaal and the Orange Free State combined to form the Union of South Africa, a self-governing dominion under the British Crown.

The first general election in 1910 demonstrated the power of the Afrikaners within the new union—the South African party won 67 seats compared with 39 seats for the mainly English-speaking Unionist Party. Louis Botha became prime minister and Jan Smuts was made Minister of the Interior, Mines and Defence. The Union's economy was based on gold and diamond mining, for which there was organized recruitment of migrant African labourers from Union territory and other parts of Africa. Pass Laws were in operation, controlling Africans' movements in the towns and industrial areas, where they were regarded officially as temporary residents and segregated in 'townships'. Following the Land Act of 1913, 87% of the land was reserved for white ownership while Africans farmed as tenants or squatters. White miners' annual earnings were 12 times those of their black counterparts in 1911. African protests at segregation and absence of political rights were led by the South African Native National Congress (SANNC), founded in 1912 and renamed the African National Congress (ANC) in 1923.

African rights were further suppressed after the coming to power in 1924 of the Afrikaner Nationalist Party, led by J. B. Hertzog. The government secured recognition of full independence for South Africa by the Statute of Westminster on 11 Dec. 1931. It also promoted the status of the Afrikaans language and introduced new segregation measures such as the Native Laws Amendment Act of 1937, which set limits on the numbers of blacks who could live in urban areas. Jan Smuts came to power in 1939 heading a coalition government broadly in favour of the war against Nazi Germany.

Apartheid

In 1948 Smuts' Unionist Party was sensationally defeated by the right-wing National Party which had campaigned for *apartheid*, a new policy for dealing with the 'racial problem'. After 1948 the term apartheid soon developed from a political slogan into a systematic programme of social engineering championed by Hendrik Verwoerd, who became prime minister in 1958. A plethora of new laws from the Group Areas Act to the Prohibition of Mixed Marriages Act strengthened existing segregation and increased racial inequality. Blacks were divided into one of ten tribal groups, and forced to move to so-called Homelands, which were intended to become self-sufficient, self-governing states. Chief Buthelezi was pivotal in the Inkatha movement which attempted, but ultimately failed, to unite Homeland leaders. The massacre by police of 69 protesters against the Pass Laws at Sharpeville on 21 March 1960 led to a major crisis from which, however, the government emerged even stronger. The ANC and the Pan African Congress were banned and the leaders, including Nelson Mandela, were jailed in 1964. After withdrawing from the British Commonwealth in 1961, South Africa became increasingly isolated. To the north, former European colonies were becoming independent, often socialist, republics.

On 16 June 1976 thousands of students demonstrated in Soweto, an African township outside Johannesburg, against mandatory schooling in Afrikaans. Many died when police broke up the demonstration and rioting spread throughout the country. When P. W. Botha became prime minister in 1978, elements of the apartheid system were modified. Africans were allowed to form legal trade unions and the acts banning marriage and sexual relations between people of different races were repealed.

A new constitution, approved in a referendum of white voters on 2 Nov. 1983 and in force from 3 Sept. 1984, created a new three-part parliament, with a House of Assembly for the Whites, a House of Representatives for the Coloureds and a House of Delegates for the Indians; Africans remained without representation. From late 1984 Blacks in the cities and industrial areas staged large-scale protests. In June 1986 a state of emergency was imposed. Foreign condemnation led to the first economic sanctions against South Africa, imposed by a number of countries including the USA and Britain.

By 1989 a start had been made on dismantling apartheid and the government, led by F. W. de Klerk, announced its willingness to consider the extension of black South Africans' political rights. In Feb. 1990 a 30-year ban on the ANC was lifted and Nelson Mandela was released from prison on 11 Feb. 1990. At the Whites-only referendum on 17 March 1992, on the granting of constitutional equality to all races, 1,924,186 (68·7%) votes were in favour; 875,619 against.

On 22 Dec. 1993 parliament approved (by 237 votes to 45) a Transitional Constitution paving the way for a new multi-racial parliament which was elected on 29 April 1994. There was a decisive victory for the ANC and on 9 May 1994 Nelson Mandela was elected president. The new government included six ministers from the National Party and three from the Inkatha Freedom Party.

In 1997 the Truth and Reconciliation Commission, chaired by Archbishop Desmond Tutu, began hearings regarding human rights violations between 1960 and 1993. The commission promised amnesty to those who confessed their crimes under the apartheid system. Nelson Mandela, whose term as president cemented his reputation as one of the world's great statesmen, retired in 1999. His deputy, Thabo Mbeki, was elected president in a landslide vote, having already assumed many of Mandela's governing responsibilities. Mbeki has since wrestled with a developing economy, continuing inequality and a high crime rate. The nation remains in the grip of an AIDS epidemic and Mbeki has been criticized by the international community for lack of leadership on the issue.

TERRITORY AND POPULATION

South Africa is bounded in the north by Namibia, Botswana and Zimbabwe, northeast by Mozambique and Swaziland, east by the Indian Ocean, and south and west by the South Atlantic, with Lesotho forming an enclave. Area: 1,219,090 sq. km. This area includes the uninhabited Prince Edward Island (41 sq. km) and Marion Island (388 sq. km), lying 1,900 km southeast of Cape Town. The islands were handed over to South Africa in Dec. 1947 to prevent their falling into hostile hands. In 1994 Walvis Bay was ceded to Namibia, and Transkei, Bophuthatswana, Venda and Ciskei were re-integrated into South Africa.

At the census of 2001 the population was 44,819,782 (23,385,739 females), consisting of: Black African, 35,416,167 (79·0% of total population); White, 4,293,641 (9·6%); Coloured, 3,994,506 (8·9%); Indian, 1,115,468 (2·5%). Estimated population at 30 June 2003 was 46,429,823 (24,279,515 females), consisting of: Black African, 36,914,284; White, 4,244,346; Coloured, 4,131,096; Indian, 1,140,097.

The UN gives a projected population for 2010 of 47·82m.

56·9% of the population was urban in 2003. In 1999 cities with the largest populations were (estimate in 1,000): Johannesburg (Gauteng), 4,074·6; Durban (KwaZulu-Natal), 2,554·4; Cape Town (Western Cape), 2,522·5; Port Elizabeth (Eastern Cape), 1,327·7; Pretoria—renamed Tshwane in 2005 (Gauteng), 1,411·9; Bloemfontein (Free State), 584; East London (Eastern Cape), 332.

There were 6,545 immigrants in 2002 (4,835 in 2001) and 10,890 emigrants (12,260 in 2001).

Population by province, according to the 2001 census:

Province	Total (including unspecified)	African	White	Coloured	Indian/ Asian
Eastern Cape	6,436,764	5,635,079	304,506	478,807	18,372
Free State	2,706,776	2,381,073	238,791	83,193	3,719
Gauteng	8,837,179	6,522,792	1,758,398	337,974	218,015
KwaZulu-Natal	9,426,017	8,002,407	483,448	141,887	798,275
Mpumalanga	3,122,991	2,886,345	203,244	22,158	11,244
Northern Cape	822,727	293,976	102,042	424,389	2,320
Northern Province[1]	5,273,642	5,128,616	126,276	10,163	8,587
North-West	3,669,350	3,358,450	244,035	56,959	9,906
Western Cape	4,524,336	1,207,429	832,901	2,438,976	45,030

[1]Now Limpopo.

There are 11 official languages. Numbers of home speakers at the 2001 census: IsiZulu, 10,677,305 (23·8% of population); IsiXhosa, 7,907,153 (17·6%); Afrikaans, 5,983,426 (13·3%); Sepedi, 4,208,980 (9·4%); English, 3,673,203 (8·6%); Setswana, 3,677,016 (8·2%); Sesotho, 3,555,186 (8·2%); Xitsonga, 1,992,207 (4·4%); Siswati, 1,194,430 (2·75%); Tshivenda, 1,021,757 (2·3%); IsiNdebele, 711,821 (1·6%). The use of any of these languages is a constitutional right 'wherever practicable'. Each province may adopt any of these as its official language. English is the sole language of command and instruction in the armed forces.

SOCIAL STATISTICS

Births: total number of registered live births in 2004 was 1,475,809 (1,677,415 in 2003).

Officially recorded marriages: the following statistics reflect marriages contracted and divorces granted during 2003, as registered by the civil registration system. (From 1998, under a new bill, customary and traditional marriages are recognized in law.) The total number of marriages officially recorded in 2003 was 178,689 (177,202 in 2002). Western Cape had the highest marriage rate (595 per 100,000 in 2003), Gauteng the second highest (560 per 100,000) followed by Free State (457 per 100,000). Limpopo had the lowest rate (216 per 100,000). Of the total marriages officially recorded in 2003, 99,286 (54·9%) were solemnized by civil rites and 51,242 in religious ceremonies. 28,161 were classed under 'unspecified'. In 2003 the average age for marrying was 34 years for men and 29 years for women. Divorces granted in 2003 totalled 28,587 (31,370 in 2002). Gauteng had the highest divorce rate (797 per 100,000 married couples); Western Cape (726). Eastern Cape had the lowest rate (135 per 100,000).

Deaths: the number of deaths increased from 318,287 in 1997 to 454,603 in 2003. Deaths from AIDS are likely to result in life expectancy being just 38 by 2010. A Statistics South Africa report published in Feb. 2005 concluded that the average number of deaths rose from 870 a day in 1997 to 1,370 a day in 2002, with AIDS as the factor underlying much of the increase in mortality. The annual number of deaths in South Africa has increased by 57% since 1997. According to the State of SA's Population Report 2000 the annual population growth rate 1996–2001 was 2·2% and the fertility rate 2·9 births per woman. Life expectancy at birth, 2003, was 46·8 years for males and 50·2 for females. Infant mortality, 2001, 56 per 1,000 live births.

CLIMATE

There is abundant sunshine and relatively low rainfall. The southwest has a Mediterranean climate, with rain mainly in winter, but most of the country has a summer maximum, although quantities show a decrease from east to west. Pretoria, Jan. 73·4°F (23·0°C), July 53·6°F (12·0°C). Annual rainfall 26·5" (674 mm). Bloemfontein, Jan. 73·4°F (23·0°C), July 45·9°F (7·7°C). Annual rainfall 22" (559 mm). Cape Town, Jan. 69·6°F (20·9°C), July 54·0°F (12·2°C). Annual rainfall 20·3" (515 mm). Johannesburg, Jan. 68·2°F (20·1°C), July 50·7°F (10·4°C). Annual rainfall 28·1" (713 mm).

CONSTITUTION AND GOVERNMENT

An Interim *Constitution* came into effect on 27 April 1994 and was in force until 3 Feb. 1997. Under it, the National Assembly and Senate formed a Constitutional Assembly, which had the task of drafting a definitive Constitution. This was signed into law in Dec. 1996 and took effect on 4 Feb. 1997. The 1996 Constitution defines the powers of the President, Parliament (consisting of the National Assembly and the National Council of Provinces—NCOP), the national executive, the judiciary, public administration, the security services and the relationship between the three spheres of government. It incorporates a Bill of Rights pertaining to, *inter alia*, education, housing, food and water supply, and security, in addition to political rights. All legislation must conform to the Constitution and the Bill of Rights. The Constitution was amended in 2001 to provide that Constitutional Court judges are appointed for a non-renewable 12-year term of office, or until they reach the age of 70 years, except where an Act of Parliament extends the term of office of a Constitutional Court judge. This Constitution Amendment Act also made the head of the Constitutional Court the Chief Justice. The head of the Supreme Court of Appeal is now the President of that Court.

A *Constitutional Court*, consisting of a president, a deputy president and nine other judges, was inaugurated in Feb. 1995. The Court's judges are appointed by the President of the Republic from a list provided by the Judicial Service Commission, after consulting the President of the Constitutional Court (now the Chief Justice) and the leaders of parties represented in the National Assembly.

Parliament is the legislative authority and has the power to make laws for the country in accordance with the Constitution. It consists of the National Assembly and the NCOP. Parliamentary sittings are open to the public.

The *National Assembly* consists of no fewer than 350 and no more than 400 members directly elected for five years, 200 from a national list and 200 from provincial lists in the following proportions: Eastern Cape, 28; Free State, 14; Gauteng, 44; KwaZulu-Natal, 42; Limpopo, 25; Mpumalanga, 11; Northern Cape, 4; North-West, 12; Western Cape, 20. In terms of the 1993 Constitution, which still regulated the 1999 elections, the nine provincial legislatures are elected at the same time and candidates may stand for both. If elected to both, they have to choose between sitting in the national or provincial assembly. In the former case, the runner-up is elected to the Provincial Assembly.

From 21 March 2003, for a period of two weeks, members of the National Assembly and provincial legislatures were allowed to defect to other political parties without losing their seats in both houses, in accordance with a constitutional amendment of 2003. The Act provided for three 'window' periods. The first one was a transitional arrangement consisting of a 15-day period starting on 21 March 2003. The second and third periods were to be for 15 days each, from 1 to 15 Sept. in the second and fourth years following the date of a national and provincial election.

The *National Council of Provinces* (NCOP) consists of 54 permanent members and 36 special delegates and aims to represent provincial interests in the national sphere of government. Delegations from each province consist of ten representatives. Bills (except finance bills) may be introduced in either house but must be passed by both. A finance bill may only be introduced in the National Assembly. If a bill is rejected by one house it is referred back to both after consideration by a joint National Assembly-NCOP committee called the Mediation Committee. Bills relating to the provinces must be passed by the NCOP. By Aug. 2003 more than 780 pieces of legislation had been passed since 1994.

The Constitution mandates the establishment of *Traditional Leaders* by means of either provincial or national legislation. The National House of Traditional Leaders was established in April 1997. Each provincial House of Traditional Leaders nominated three members to be represented in the National House. The National House advises national government on the role of traditional leaders and on customary law.

National Anthem

A combination of shortened forms of 'Die Stem van Suid-Afrika'/ 'The Call of South Africa' (words by C. J. Langenhoven; tune by M. L. de Villiers) and the ANC anthem 'Nkosi sikelel' iAfrika'/ 'God bless Africa' (words and tune by Enos Santonga).

GOVERNMENT CHRONOLOGY

Presidents from 1961. (ANC = African National Congress; NP = National Party; UP = United Party)

1961–67	NP	Charles Robberts Swart
1968–75	NP	Jacobus Johannes Fouché
1975–78	NP	Nicolaas Johannes Diederichs
1978–79	NP	Balthazar Johannes Vorster
1979–84	NP	Marais Viljoen
1984–89	NP	Pieter Willem Botha
1989–94	NP	Frederik Willem de Klerk
1994–99	ANC	Nelson Rolihlahla Mandela
1999–	ANC	Thabo Mvuyelwa Mbeki

Prime Ministers since 1939.

1939–48	military/UP	Jan Christiaan Smuts
1948–54	NP	Daniël François Malan
1954–58	NP	Johannes Gerhardus Strijdom
1958–66	NP	Hendrik Frensch Verwoerd
1966–78	NP	Balthazar Johannes Vorster
1978–84	NP	Pieter Willem Botha

RECENT ELECTIONS

Parliamentary elections were held on 14 April 2004. Turnout was 89·3%. The African National Congress (ANC) won 279 seats in Parliament's National Assembly with 69·7% of votes cast, the Democratic Alliance (DA) 50 with 12·4%, the Inkatha Freedom Party (IFP) 28 with 7·0%, the United Democratic Movement (UDM) 9 with 2·3%, the New National Party (NNP) 7 with 1·7%, the Independent Democrats (ID) 7 with 1·7%, the African Christian Democratic Party (ACDP) 6 with 1·6%, Freedom Front Plus (VF+) 4 with 0·9%, United Christian-Democratic Party (UCDP) 3 with 0·8%, Pan African Congress of Azania (PAC) 3 with 0·7%, Minority Front (MF) 2 with 0·4% and the Azanian People's Organisation (AZAPO) 2 with 0·3%.

CURRENT ADMINISTRATION

President: Thabo M. Mbeki; b. 1942 (ANC; sworn in 16 June 1999; re-elected 23 April 2004).

In March 2006 the government comprised:

Deputy President: Phumzile Mlambo-Ngcuka.

Minister of Agriculture and Land Affairs: Angela Thoko Didiza. *Arts and Culture:* Zweledinga Pallo Jordan. *Communications:* Dr Ivy F. Matsepe-Cassaburri. *Correctional Services:* Ngconde Balfour. *Defence:* M. G. Patrick Lekota. *Education:* Naledi Pandor. *Environmental Affairs and Tourism:* Marthinus van Schalkwyk. *Finance:* Trevor A. Manuel. *Foreign Affairs:* Dr Nkosazana C. Dlamini-Zuma. *Health:* Dr Manto E. Tshabalala-Msimang. *Home Affairs:* Nosiviwe Mapisa-Nqakula. *Housing:* Dr Lindiwe N. Sisulu. *Intelligence:* Ronald Kasrils. *Justice and Constitutional Development:* Brigitte Sylvia Mabandla. *Labour:* Membathisi M. S. Mdladlana. *Minerals and Energy:* Lindiwe Hendricks. *Provincial and Local Government:* F. Sydney Mufamadi. *Public Enterprises:* Alexander Erwin. *Public Service and Administration:* Geraldine J. Fraser-Moleketi. *Public Works:* Stella N. Sigcau. *Safety and Security:* Charles Nqakula. *Science and Technology:* Mosibudi Mangena. *Social Development and Welfare:* Zola S. T. Skweyiya. *Sport and Recreation:* Mankenkisi Stofile. *Trade and Industry:* Mandisi Bongani Mabuto Mpahlwa. *Transport:* Jeffrey Thamsanqa Radebe. *Water Affairs and Forestry:* Buyelwa Patience Sonjica. *Minister in the Presidency:* Essop G. Pahad.

Government Website: http://www.gov.za

CURRENT LEADERS

Thabo Mbeki

Position
President

Introduction
A leading anti-apartheid campaigner and prominent member of the ANC, Thabo Mbeki was chosen in 1997 to replace Nelson Mandela as party leader. Two years later he led the ANC to electoral victory and succeeded Mandela as president. He is credited with improving South Africa's economy, but has been criticized for doubting the link between HIV and AIDS (which has reached epidemic proportions in South Africa) and for his ambivalence towards the extremist rule of Zimbabwe's Robert Mugabe.

Early Life
Thabo Mvuyelwa Mbeki was born in Idutywa, Transkei on 24 June 1942. Both his parents were teachers and anti-apartheid activists. Mbeki became politically active at the age of 14 when he enlisted in the ANC Youth League. Whilst studying for his A-levels he was elected secretary of the African Students' Association.

In 1962 his father was arrested and sentenced to life imprisonment. Mbeki went to the UK where he studied economics at Sussex University. He was employed in the ANC's London office by Oliver Tambo and in 1970 was sent to the USSR for military training. He then moved to Lusaka in Zambia where he was appointed assistant secretary of the Revolutionary Council. For the next five years Mbeki worked for the ANC in Swaziland, Botswana, Zambia and Nigeria. In 1978 he served as a political secretary to Tambo and subsequently became director of information and publicity. This role allowed him to increase international awareness of the plight of black South Africans and to enlist the support of many white South Africans who opposed apartheid. In 1989 Mbeki was chosen to head the ANC's department of international affairs, a position which involved him in the negotiations that ended apartheid. In 1993 he was appointed as the party's national chairman.

After the elections of April 1994 Mbeki was made deputy president of the government of national unity. He was chosen to succeed Mandela in Dec. 1997. In the June 1999 election his party won 66% votes and Mbeki replaced Mandela as president.

Career in Office
Mbeki's first months in office were dogged by speculation that he was introducing a more autocratic, less democratic style of government. This was largely brought on by his decision to replace several provincial premiers with nominees of his choosing. He made clear his intentions to change the segregated 'two nations' character of South Africa and in order to achieve this he acknowledged that his government would have to reduce crime, corruption and unemployment. His international reputation suffered when, despite overwhelming evidence, he refused to admit that a link between the HIV virus and full-blown AIDS, claiming instead that the primary cause of the disease was poverty. This view attracted sharp criticism not just from his political opponents but from allies within the trade union movement, nurses, doctors, gay rights groups and even Mandela himself. He was further criticized for failing to condemn the extremist rule of Zimbabwe's Robert Mugabe.

Within the party Mbeki's biggest problem has been to secure agreement with ANC's leftwing partners—the Congress of South African Trade Unions (COSATU) and the Communist Party—on remaining social and racial inequalities, while privatizing some state industries. A two-day strike was mounted by COSATU in Oct. 2002. In the same month white right-wing extremists began a terrorist bombing campaign in an attempt to overthrow the government. Nonetheless, Mbeki and the ANC retained a strong powerbase. At the 2002 ANC conference, as the sole candidate Mbeki was re-elected party chairman for a further five years, thus making him ANC candidate for the 2004 presidential elections.

Mbeki was one of the first leaders to respond to the USA's action against Iraq. Although he was not overtly critical, he made clear his wish for greater involvement by the United Nations.

Following the defection of two MPs in March 2003 the ANC gained control of the Western Cape province. South Africa's main opposition party, the Democratic Alliance, and the Inkatha Freedom Party formed a coalition in Nov. 2003 to strengthen their chances against the ANC in forthcoming elections.

The ANC were successful in the parliamentary elections of 14 April 2004, winning 279 of the 400 seats in the National Assembly with 69·7% of votes cast. The Democratic Alliance won 50 seats and Inkatha 28. Mbeki was unanimously voted president for another five-year term. In June 2005 Mbeki sacked his vice-president, Jacob Zuma—previously a top contender to succeed to the presidency—after he was linked with a corruption scandal. He was replaced by Phumzile Mlambo-Ngcuka, formerly the minister for minerals and energy.

DEFENCE

The South African National Defence Force (SANDF) comprises four services, namely the SA Army, the SA Air Force, the SA Navy and the SA Military Health Service (SAMHS). SAMHS personnel at the end of 2000 totalled 7,328 (3,900 women). South Africa ended conscription in 1994. In July 2002 the SANDF consisted of 76,000 members.

Defence expenditure totalled US$2,633m. in 2003 (equivalent to US$58 per capita), and represented 1·6% of GDP. Defence expenditure in 1985 was US$3,252m. (US$97 per capita and 3·8% of GDP).

Army

Personnel of the South African National Defence Force totalled 60,000 in 2002 (excluding 16,716 civilian employees). Regular army reserves numbered 14,615 in 2002, and the territorial army had a strength of 56,334.

Navy

Navy personnel in 2002 totalled 5,000, with 1,330 reserves. The fleet is based at the naval bases at Simon's Town on the west coast and Durban on the east and includes four *Warrior* class fast attack craft (missile) and two *Daphné* class submarines. Over the three-year period 2005–07 the German Submarine Consortium is supplying three additional submarines. The *SAS Amatola*, the first of four corvettes from Germany, arrived in Nov. 2003.

Air Force

Strength (2002) 9,250, with 434 reserves. The Air Force has 84 combat aircraft (*Cheetah* Cs, *Cheetah* Ds, *Impala* Mk1s and *Impala* Mk2s) and 12 attack helicopters.

INTERNATIONAL RELATIONS

South Africa is a member of the UN, BIS, WTO, the Commonwealth (except during 1961–94), the African Union, the Southern African Development Community, the Non-Aligned Movement, the African Development Bank, the Antarctic Treaty and is an ACP member state of the ACP-EU relationship.

ECONOMY

Agriculture accounted for 4·1% of GDP in 2002, industry 32·2% and services 63·7%.

Overview

Until recently South Africa's economy was dominated by agriculture and the mining of precious metals. Mining remains an important source of foreign-exchange earnings while agriculture, which has become increasingly diversified away from maize, continues to be an important source of employment. However, manufacturing and financial services have grown to contribute a greater share of GDP than these two traditional sectors. An advanced financial sector and growing tourism help make services the largest contributor to the country's total output. Manufacturing, accounting for roughly one-fifth of total output, principally involves metals and engineering, especially steel-related products.

In the early 1990s the removal of international sanctions following the end of apartheid and the adoption of structural reforms opened the economy to international competition, leading to productivity gains and greater penetration of international markets. These structural reforms have contributed to a sustained increase in growth rates. In the decade from 1994 the economy grew at an average annual rate of 2·9% and exhibited much less volatility than during the previous decade, when average annual growth was 1%. The growth performance of the economy during the post-apartheid period was fostered by trade liberalization and increased private sector participation in the economy. The country's growth performance has been supported by sound macroeconomic management. Strong public finances sustained a competitive exchange rate and low interest rates for much of the post-apartheid period while monetary policy contained inflationary pressures. The medium-term outlook for the economy is favourable.

South Africa is one of only a few African countries to have reached the upper middle-income group. Its economy is the largest in the Sub-Saharan region and heavily influences trade and investment flows on the continent. However, the country remains among the most unequal in the world. Despite a rising black middle-class, the World Bank estimates that 13% of the population, mostly white, was living in 'first world' conditions in 2004, whereas just over half of the population lived in 'third world' conditions. The IMF urges the South African government to reform its labour policies. The country has one of highest HIV/AIDS infection rates in the world, which, in addition to human costs, threatens much of the economic and social progress achieved to date. There are likely to be demographic changes as a result of the HIV/AIDS pandemic, with far-reaching economic and social consequences such as increased poverty and diminished economic growth resulting from the loss of skilled labour.

Currency

The unit of currency is the rand (ZAR) of 100 cents. A single free-floating exchange rate replaced the former two-tier system on 13 March 1995. Inflation rates (based on IMF statistics):

1995	1996	1997	1998	1999	2000	2001	2002	2003	2004
8·7%	7·3%	8·6%	6·9%	5·2%	5·4%	5·7%	9·2%	5·8%	1·4%

Foreign exchange reserves were US$5,673m. and gold reserves 5·72m. troy oz in June 2002. Total money supply was R339,233m. in June 2002.

Budget

The central government's State Revenue Account in R1bn.:

	1998–99	1999–2000	2000–01	2001–02	2002–03
Revenue	184·0	198·2	215·6	248·1	265·2
Expenditure	201·4	214·8	233·9	262·6	287·9

The 2002 budget provided for expenditure of 26·6% of GDP; revenue, 24·5% of GDP. South Africa's deficit was revised to 2·1% in 2002–03. About R47·5bn. or 4·4% of GDP, is spent on debt servicing.

Income tax is the Government's main source of income. As of 2001, South Africa's source-based income tax system was replaced with a residence-based system. With effect from the years of assessment commencing on or after 1 Jan. 2001, residents are (subject to certain exclusions) taxed on their worldwide income, irrespective of where their income is earned. Foreign taxes are credited against South African tax payable on foreign income. Foreign income and taxes are translated into the South African monetary unit, the Rand.

Value-added Tax (VAT) has remained at 14% since 1993. Corporate taxes were reduced to 30% in 1999. A tiered corporate tax was introduced in 2000 with taxes for small businesses reduced by half. R9·9bn. was returned to taxpayers in reduced personal income tax for all income groups but particularly for lower and middle income groups. The marginal tax rate for high-income earners was cut to 42% from 45%. A capital gains tax was introduced from 1 April 2001 and became effective on 1 Oct. 2001.

Performance

Real GDP growth rates (based on IMF statistics):

1997	1998	1999	2000	2001	2002	2003	2004
2·6%	0·5%	2·4%	4·2%	2·7%	3·6%	2·8%	3·7%

Gross international reserves were about US$7·9bn. in Dec. 2002. Total GDP in 2004 was US$212·8bn.

Banking and Finance

The central bank and bank of issue is the South African Reserve Bank (SARB; established 1920), which functions independently. Its *Governor* is Tito Mboweni. The Banks Act, 1990 governs the operations and prudential requirements of banks.

At the end of Dec. 2002, 42 banks, including 14 branches of foreign banks and two mutual banks, were registered with the Office of the Registrar of Banks. Furthermore, 52 foreign banks had authorized representative offices in South Africa. The banking institutions collectively employed 115,734 workers at 8,438 branches and agencies; their combined assets amounted to R970·9bn. (31 Oct. 2001). Banking in South Africa is dominated by five banks: Standard Bank, FirstRand, Absa and Nedcor, which are commercial banks, and Investec, an investment bank.

The stock exchange, the JSE Securities Exchange, is based in Johannesburg. Foreign nationals have been eligible for membership since Nov. 1995.

ENERGY AND NATURAL RESOURCES

Environment

In 1998 the Committee for Environmental Co-ordination was established to harmonize the work of government departments on environmental issues, and to co-ordinate environmental implementation and national management plans at provincial level.

SANParks manages a system of 20 national parks and there are some 9,000 privately owned game ranches in South Africa, expanding at a rate of 300,000 ha. per annum.

South Africa's carbon dioxide emissions from the consumption and flaring of fossil fuels in 2002 were the equivalent of 8·4 tonnes per capita.

Electricity

South African households use over 25% of the country's energy. Coal supplies 75% of primary energy requirements, followed by oil (20·7%), nuclear (3·0%) and natural gas (1·3%). There is one nuclear power station (Koeberg) with two reactors, two gas turbine generators, two conventional hydroelectric plants and two pumped storage stations. Nuclear energy is being investigated as a future potential energy source and alternative to coal. Eskom, a public utility, generates 95% of the country's electricity (as well as two-thirds of the electricity for the African continent) and owns and operates the national transmission system.

During 2002 Eskom electrified 211,628 homes against the government target of 205,371. Between 1994 and 2003 a total of 3·8m. households were connected to the extended national electricity grid. According to the census of 2001 the percentage of households using electricity had increased from 57·6% to 69·7%. An estimated 7·12m. of South Africa's 10·77m. households had electricity at the end of 2001. In 2003, 196,357 GWh of electricity were consumed.

The energy sector contributes about 15% to GDP and employs about 250,000 people. Because of South Africa's large coal deposits, the country is one of the four cheapest electricity suppliers in the world. Residential use is characterized by poor access to facilities and inefficient or hazardous energy sources, such as fuel wood and paraffin.

The first wind-energy farm in Africa was opened at Klipheuwel in the Western Cape on 21 Feb. 2003.

Oil and Gas

South Africa has limited oil reserves and relies on coal for much of its oil production. It has a highly developed synthetic fuels industry. Sasol Oil and Petro SA are the two major players in the synthetic fuel market. Synfuels meet approximately 40% of local demand. Natural gas production in 2000 amounted to 1·7bn. cu. metres; however, the prospects for natural gas production have increased by the discovery of offshore reserves close to the Namibian border in 2000. Production is scheduled to commence during 2006 and will be channelled to regulate electricity production.

Petro SA is responsible for exploration of both offshore natural gas and onshore coal-bed methane. The EM gas-field complex off Mossel Bay in the Western Cape started production in the third quarter of 2000, and will ensure sufficient feedstock to PetroSA to maintain current liquid fuel production levels at 36,000 bbls. of petroleum products a day until 2009. The oilfield, Sable, situated about 150 km south off the coast of Mossel Bay, is expected to produce 17% of South Africa's oil needs. Coming into operation in Aug. 2003, it was initially projected to produce 30,000 to 40,000 bbls. of crude oil a day. PetroSA's gas-to-liquid plant supplies about 7% of South Africa's liquid fuel needs.

South Africa is one of the major oil refining nations in Africa with a crude refining capacity of 543,000 bbls. per day.

Minerals

The value of total primary minerals output increased by 17·1% to R115·2m. in 2002; total sales of all minerals, including gold, was R137·5m.

Preliminary 2002 figures indicated that mining contributed R30·6bn. or 8·5% of gross value added, an improvement of R13·86bn. on 2001. The preliminary figures also indicated a 1·5% rise in employment in the mining sector from 407,154 in 2001 to 413,087 in 2002. There were 749 mines and quarries. Sales of primary mineral products accounted for 34·3% of South Africa's total export revenue during 2001.

Preliminary figures for mineral production (in tonnes), 2002: coal, 221·5m.; iron ore, 36m.; limestone, 18·8m.; chrome ore, 6·4m.; manganese, 3·3m.; aluminium, 707,000; copper, 130,000; zinc, 64,000; nickel, 38,500; gold, 399; platinum-group metals, 243; silver, 113; diamonds (2001), 11,162,630 carats. In 2002 gold production increased for the first time since 1993 while revenue rose by 22·4% to £3·94bn. South Africa is the world's leading producer of both gold and platinum.

Agriculture

South Africa has a dual agricultural economy, comprising a well-developed commercial sector and a predominantly subsistence-orientated sector. Much of the land suitable for mechanized farming has unreliable rainfall. Of the total farming area, natural pasture occupies 81% (69·6m. ha.) and planted pasture 2% (2m.

ha.). About 13% of South Africa's surface area can be used for crop production. High potential arable land comprises only 22% of the total arable land. Annual crops and orchards are cultivated on 9·9m. ha. of dry land and 1·5m. ha. under irrigation. In 2002 there were 45,818 commercial farming units with a gross farming income of R53·3m. The agricultural sector grew by 4% in 2002, following a decline of 1·7% in 2001. The net income of the farming sector increased from R10,591m. in 2001 to R20,277m. in 2002. Primary agriculture contributes about 2·9% to GDP and almost 9% of formal employment. In 2002 there were 940,820 paid farm workers.

Production (2002, in 1,000 tonnes):

(*Field crops*): maize 13,906; wheat 4,213; sugarcane 3,284; sunflower seeds 2,160; hay 1,778; tobacco 529; grain sorghum 382; ground-nuts 322; cotton 155; other 1,237. Total 27,966. South Africa is the main maize producer in the SADC.

(*Horticulture*): deciduous and other fruit 4,396; vegetables 3,522; citrus 2,915; potatoes 2,438; viticulture 2,088; subtropical fruit 941; other 1,124. Total 17,424.

(*Animal products*): poultry and poultry products 10,767; cattle and cattle slaughtered 5,289; sheep and goats slaughtered 1,413; pigs slaughtered 1,090; fresh milk 2,794; milk for dairy products 1,391; wool 1,269.

Total value of field crops in 2002 (R1,000), 16,476,933; horticulture, 14,228,909; animal and animal products, 21,222,618; other products, 1,400,592.

The value of agricultural imports increased by 13·9% and the value of exports increased by 37·6% for 2001 compared to 2000. In 2002 agricultural exports contributed 8·3% of total exports. Based on 2001 export values, sugar (R2,703m.), wine (R1,963m.), citrus fruit (R1,799m.), grapes (R1,327m.) and preserved fruit and nuts (R990m.) were the most important export products. Rice (R954m.), oil-cake (R762m.), undenatured ethyl alcohol (R602m.), tobacco (R456m.) and palm oil (R455m.) were the most important import products. During 2001 the UK, the Netherlands, Japan and Mozambique were the largest export destinations.

South Africa is one of the largest exporters in the world of avocados, grapes, sugar, citrus and deciduous fruit. According to the South African Wine and Spirits Export Association, the export of white wine increased from 20m. litres in 1992 to 218m. litres in 2002.

Forestry

Africa has developed one of the largest man-made forestry resources in the world. Production from these plantations approached 15·1m. cu. metres, valued at almost R11·86m. in 2001. Together with processed products, the total industry turnover was approximately R2·7bn. in 2001, including R2·0bn. worth of wood-pulp. More than 11·8m. tons (pulpwood, mining timber, matchwood and charcoal) and 3·2m. cu. metres (sawlogs, veneer and poles) were sold in this period. Collectively, the forestry sector employs about 151,000 people. An equivalent of about 60,000 full-time staff are employed in the primary sector (growing and harvesting), while the balance are employed in the processing industries (sawmilling, pulp and paper, mining timber and poles, and board products). In 2001 the forestry industry contributed 1·2% to the entire South African GDP.

Indigenous high forest covers only about 534,000 ha. or 0·4% of the country's surface. The private sector owns 971,098 ha. (or 72%) of the total plantation area of 1,351,176 ha. as well as 161 of the 167 processing plants in the country. The remaining 28% (380,663 ha.) is under public ownership. The department of water affairs and forestry is pursuing a reform programme in the forestry sector which will eventually see the government leasing all State-owned forest land to private-sector operators. In 2000–01 there were 1,280 registered private timber growers and more than 14,000 unregistered growers.

The industry was a net exporter to the value of over R5·7bn. in 2002, more than 97% of which was in the form of converted value-added products. The forest-products industry contributed 3·58% of total exports and 1·99% of total imports in 2002. In 2002 paper exports were the most important (R4·25bn. or 38% of the total), followed by solid wood products (R3·78bn. or 34% of the total), pulp (R2·89bn. or 26% of the total), and other products (R0·28bn. or 2% of the total). Woodchip exports, mainly to Japan, accounted for 52% (R1·96bn.) of the total solid wood products exports.

Fisheries

The commercial marine fishing industry is valued at more than R3bn. annually and employs 28,000 people directly. It is an important employer because it pays a relatively high average wage (approximately R36,000) to its employees, of whom the majority are semi-skilled. In 2000 the commercial fishing fleet consisted of 4,477 vessels licensed by the department of environmental affairs and tourism.

The total number of fishing rights allocated stands at 2,200, 1,700 of which are small, medium and micro enterprises. The total catch in 2003 was 822,854 tonnes, over 99% of which came from marine fishing. Deep sea hake amounts to over half of the total catch and an estimated 35% of fish is exported.

INDUSTRY

The leading companies by market capitalization in South Africa, excluding banking and finance, in May 2004 were: Anglo American Platinum Corp. Ltd (US$31·3bn.), the world's primary platinum group metals producer; Sasol Ltd (US$10·4bn.), a coal, oil and gas producer; and AngloGold Ashanti Ltd (US$9·3bn.), the world's leading gold producer.

Actual value of sales of the principal groups of industries (in R1m.) in 2003: basic iron and steel, non-ferrous metal products and machinery, 152·4; petroleum, chemical products, rubber and plastic products, 144·1; food and beverages, 137·5; motor vehicles, parts and accessories and other transport equipment, 107·0; wood and wood products, paper, publishing and printing, 67·9; textiles, clothing, leather and footwear, 40·1. Total actual value including other groups, R731·7m. Manufacturing contributed R108,470m. towards GDP of R544,654m. in 1999, and thus accounted for 20% of the total.

Labour

The Employment Equity Act, 1998 signalled the beginning of the final phase of transformation in the job market, which began with the implementation of the Labour Relations Act. It aims to avoid all discrimination in employment. The Basic Conditions of Employment Act, 1997 applies to all workers except for the South African National Defence Force (SANDF), the South African Secret Service (SASS) and the National Intelligence Agency (NIA). The new provisions include a reduction in the maximum hours of work from 46 to 45 hours per week (however, the Act allows for the progressive reduction of working hours to 40 per week).

The number of those who are economically active—both the employed and the unemployed—was 16·8m. in March 2003. The number of unemployed rose from 2·2m. in 1996 to 5·2m. in March 2003. In March 2003 the unemployment rate was 31·2% (29·4% in Feb. 2002).

The Unemployment Insurance Fund (UIF), providing benefits to unemployed workers, increased its income from R2·1bn. in 2001 to R3·8bn. in 2002–03. By June 2003 more than 530,000 employers had registered their employees with the UIF, while the number of employer declarations stood at 413,111, with a total of R8·2m. received in contributions. This translates to more than 67% of employers having registered.

Trade Unions

By mid-2003 there were 362 trade unions and 240 registered employer organizations operating in South Africa. In 2000 there were 3·6m. members of trade unions. The most important trade union groups or federations are Federation of Trade Unions of South Africa (FEDUSA), National Council of Trade Unions (NACTU) and Congress of South African Trade Unions (COSATU). The three largest trade unions are the National Union of Mineworkers (NUM), the National Union of Metalworkers of South Africa (NUMSA), both COSATU affiliates, and the Public Servants Association, an affiliate of FEDUSA. Employers also have the right to form associations and to register them with the Department of Labour. The Labour Court has been operating since Nov. 1996.

INTERNATIONAL TRADE

Since 1994 the (rand) value of both exports and imports in manufactured goods has more than doubled. South Africa's four main trading partners in 1999 were the UK, USA, Germany and Japan. In 1999 merchandise exports represented 86% (R148·9bn.) of total exports (merchandise plus net gold exports and excluding receipts for services). The balance of payments on current account reverted from a deficit of R2·9bn. in 2001 to a surplus of R3·3bn. in 2002. This was the first time since 1994 that a surplus was recorded for a full calendar year. Total foreign debt in 2002 was US$25,041m. Total net gold exports in 1999 amounted to R24·2bn. During 1999 the value of merchandise imports was R150·3bn.

The USA is South Africa's number one trading partner in terms of total trade (the sum of exports and imports) recorded in 2002 and the first six months of 2003. Exports to the USA rose in nominal terms from R30bn. in 2001 to R35bn. in 2002. Imports from the USA increased in nominal terms from R25bn. to R31bn. from 2001 to 2002.

Europe accounts for almost half of South Africa's total foreign trade. Seven of South Africa's top ten trading partners are European countries. In 2001–02 South African manufactured exports to Europe grew by 19·8%. A trade, co-operation and development agreement was provisionally implemented on 1 Jan. 2000, under the terms of which South Africa will grant duty-free access to 86% of EU imports over a period of 12 years, while the EU will liberalize 95% of South Africa's imports over a ten-year period. The Agreement provides for ongoing EU financial assistance in grants and loans for development co-operation, which amounts to some R900m. per annum.

In 2002 approximately 16% of South Africa's exports were destined for Africa while imports accounted for only 4% of South Africa's total imports. Within the Southern African Development Community (SADC), a smaller group of countries including South Africa, Botswana, Lesotho, Namibia and Swaziland have organized themselves into the Southern African Customs Union (SACU), sharing a common tariff regime without any internal barriers. Trade with SADC countries increased from R16bn. to approximately R32bn. during the period 1998 to 2002. However, in 2002, there was a significant increase in the amount of imports from the region, to approximately R4·2bn.

Japan is South Africa's largest trading partner in Asia. It became South Africa's third-largest export destination during 2002. At the end of 2002 total trade between the two countries stood at R43·9bn.

Imports and Exports

Trade in US$1m.:

	1998	1999	2000	2001	2002
Imports f.o.b.	27,208	24,554	27,320	25,856	26,713
Exports f.o.b.	29,264	28,627	31,636	30,716	31,085

Main imports (in R1bn.):

	1997	1998	1999
Machinery and mechanical appliances	40,555	52,057	45,629
Mineral products	16,782	12,943	15,507

	1997	1998	1999
Chemicals or allied industries	13,836	15,667	16,959
Vehicles, aircraft, vessels and			
associated transport equipment	7,116	8,914	10,689
Plastics and articles thereof	5,349	5,871	6,100

Main exports (in R1bn.):

	1997	1998	1999
Natural or cultured pearls	32,345	33,538	35,173
Base metals and articles thereof	20,859	22,461	24,619
Mineral products	18,418	19,037	21,512
Products of chemicals or allied industries	8,908	9,218	9,987
Vehicles, aircraft, vessels and			
associated transport equipment	6,604	7,933	12,217
Machinery and mechanical appliances	8,278	9,916	12,008

In Oct. 1998 a transshipment facility for containers opened at Kidatu, southwest of Dar es Salaam, Tanzania, providing a link between the 1,067 mm gauge railways of the southern part of Africa and the 1,000 mm gauge lines of the north. With the opening up of new markets for South Africa elsewhere in the continent, it will help to boost trade and facilitate the shipment of cargo to countries to the north.

COMMUNICATIONS

The public company Transnet Limited was established on 1 April 1990. It handles 176m. tonnes of rail freight per year, 2·8m. tonnes road freight and 194m. tonnes of freight through the harbours, while 13·8m. litres are pumped through its petrol pipelines annually. For the financial year ended 31 March 2001 Transnet reported a profit of R3,287m. (compared to a net loss of R779m. for 2000).

The company, through South African Airways (SAA), flies 6·1m. domestic, regional and international passengers per year. In total, Transnet is worth R72bn. in fixed assets and has a workforce of some 80,000 employees.

Transnet Limited consists of nine main divisions, a number of subsidiaries and related businesses—Spoornet, the National Ports Authority (NPA), South African Port Operations (SAPO), Petronet, Freightdynamics, Propnet, Metrorail, Transtel and Transwerk.

Roads

In 2003 the South African road network comprised some 534,076 km of roads and streets. There is a primary roads network of 9,400 km, with plans to extend it to 20,000 km. Toll roads, which are serviced by 31 mainline toll plazas, cover about 2,200 km. The network includes 1,437 km of dual-carriage freeway, 440 km of single-carriage freeway and 56,967 km of single-carriage main road with unlimited access. South Africa has the longest road network in Africa. As at 31 Dec. 2002 there were 6·99m. registered motor vehicles, more than 4m. of which were motor cars. In 1999 there were 452,915 road accidents with 10,523 fatalities.

Rail

The South African Rail Commuter Corporation Limited (SARCC), an agency of the department of transport, is responsible for commuter rail services. It owns all commuter rail assets and property worth R5bn. SARCC contracts Metrorail (a division of Transnet) to provide services on its behalf. Metrorail carries more than 2·2m. passengers daily, serves 473 stations and operates tracks covering 2,400 km through five metropolitan areas. Metrorail is responsible for some 17% of all public transport in South Africa.

Spoornet provides freight transport and some long-distance passenger transport, including the luxurious Blue Train. Total route length (SARCC and Spoornet) was 22,657 km in 2000.

Civil Aviation

Responsibility for civil aviation safety and security lies with the South African Civil Aviation Authority (SACAA). The Airports Company South Africa (ACSA) owns and operates South Africa's principal airports. The main international airports are: Johannesburg, Cape Town, Durban, Bloemfontein, Port Elizabeth, Pilanesberg, Lanseria and Upington. In April 2003 the Cabinet approved the status of the Kruger Mpumalanga Airport, near Nelspruit, as an international airport. ACSA also has a 35-year concession to operate Pilanesberg International Airport near Sun City in North-West Province.

South African Airways (SAA), Comair, SA Express and SA Airlink operate scheduled international air services. 13 independent operators provide internal flights which link up with the internal network of SAA, Comair and SA Express.

In 2001 Johannesburg handled 11,245,322 passengers (5,898,227 on domestic flights) and 253,212 tonnes of freight. Cape Town handled 4,613,488 passengers (3,639,636 on domestic flights). Durban handled 2,405,726 passengers (2,355,576 on domestic flights) and 8,191 tonnes of freight.

The new R750m. domestic terminal at Johannesburg International Airport (JIA) was opened in March 2003. It is the largest terminal in Africa and will increase the airport's total capacity to more than 18m. passengers annually.

Shipping

The South African Maritime Safety Authority (SAMSA) was established on 1 April 1998 as the authority responsible for ensuring the safety of life at sea and the prevention of sea pollution from ships. Approximately 98% of South Africa's exports are conveyed by sea.

The National Ports Authority supervises 16 of South Africa's ports. The largest ports include the deep water ports of Richards Bay, with its multi-product dry bulk handling facilities, multi-purpose terminal and the world's largest bulk coal terminal, and Saldanah featuring a bulk ore terminal adjacent to a bulk oil jetty with extensive storage facilities. Durban, Cape Town and Port Elizabeth provide large container terminals for deep-sea and coastal container traffic. The Port of Durban handles 1·2m. containers per annum. East London, the only river port, has a multi-purpose terminal and dry dock facilities. Mossel Bay is a specialized port serving the south coast fishing industry and offshore gas fields. Trade at the sea ports increased by 74% between 1994–2004, with container throughput more than doubling.

In 2002 the merchant fleet totalled 144,000 GRT, including oil tankers 3,000 GRT. During 1998 the major ports handled a total of 187,008,889 tonnes of cargo, and a total of 13,559 ships' calls were registered.

Telecommunications

According to a study by World Wide Worx, 2·89m. South Africans (one out of every 15) had access to the Internet by the end of 2001. The number was estimated to be 3·1m. by the end of 2002. In 2002 there were 271,000 fax machines. South Africa has approximately 5·3m. installed telephones and 4·3m. installed exchange lines, representing 39% of total lines installed in Africa.

Telkom SA, the national operator, was awarded a five-year licence in May 1997 giving the company the exclusive right to provide telecommunications services. It was required to install 2·8m. new lines, including 120,000 payphones in the five years to March 2002. Over the same period it was required to provide first-time telephone services for over 3,000 villages, install more than 20,000 new lines for priority customers such as schools and hospitals and replace around 1,200m. analogue lines with digital technology. The transmission network is almost wholly digital. The initial public offering of Telkom on the Johannesburg Securities Exchange and the New York Stock Exchange in March 2003 realized R3·9bn. on the first day.

South Africa, with the operators Vodacom and MTN, is the fourth fastest-growing GSM (Global Systems for Mobile

Communications) market in the world. By Oct. 2003 there were 15m. cellular users in the country. The sector was predicted to be worth R20bn. by 2004.

Postal Services

The South African Post Office handles an average of 6m. letters a day, 70% of which are prepaid mass-mailed letters sent by companies using franking machines. SAPO services over 40m. South Africans and numerous public and private institutions. It delivers mail items to over 7·5m. delivery points. SAPO has 2,760 postal outlets countrywide and 30 mail processing centres.

Public Information Terminals (PiTs) offer government information and an e-mail service, Internet browsing, business sections and educational services. By Sept. 2001, 100 kiosks had been installed in post offices.

SOCIAL INSTITUTIONS

Justice

All law must be consistent with the Constitution and its Bill of Rights. Judgments of courts declaring legislation, executive action, or conduct to be invalid are binding on all organs of state and all persons. The common law of the Republic is based on Roman-Dutch law—that is the uncodified law of Holland as it was at the date of the cession of the Cape to the United Kingdom in 1806. South African law has, however, developed its own unique characteristics.

Judges hold office until they attain the age of 70 or, if they have not served for 15 years, until they have completed 15 years of service or have reached the age of 75, when they are discharged from active service. A judge discharged from active service must be ready to perform service for an aggregate of three months a year until the age of 75. The Chief Justice of South Africa, the Deputy Chief Justice, the President of the Supreme Court of Appeal and the Deputy President of the Supreme Court of Appeal are appointed by the President after consulting the Judicial Service Commission. In the case of the Chief Justice and Deputy Chief Justice, the President must also consult the leaders of parties represented in the National Assembly. The President on the advice of the Judicial Service Commission (JSC) appoints all other judges. No judge may be removed from office unless the JSC finds that the judge suffers from incapacity, is grossly incompetent or is guilty of gross misconduct, and the National Assembly calls for that judge to be removed by a resolution supported by at least two thirds of its members.

The higher courts include: 1) *The Constitutional Court* (CC), which consists of the Chief Justice of South Africa, the Deputy Chief Justice of South Africa and nine other judges. It is the highest court in all matters in which the interpretation of the Constitution or its application to any law, including the common law, is relevant; 2) *The Supreme Court of Appeal*, consisting of a President, a Deputy President and the number of judges of appeal determined by an Act of Parliament. It is the highest court of appeal in all other matters; 3) *The High Courts*, which may decide constitutional matters other than those which are within the exclusive jurisdiction of the Constitutional Court, and any other matter other than one assigned by Parliament to a court of a status similar to that of a High Court. Each High Court is presided over by a Judge President who may divide the area under his jurisdiction into circuit districts. In each such district there shall be held at least twice in every year and at such times and places determined by the Judge President, a court which shall be presided over by a judge of the High Court. Such a court is known as the circuit court for the district in question; 4) *The Land Claims Court*, established under the Restitution of Land Rights Act of 1994 deals with claims for restitution of rights in land to persons or communities dispossessed of such rights after 1913 as a result of past racially discriminatory laws or practices. It has jurisdiction throughout the Republic and the power to determine such claims and related matters such as compensation

and rights of occupation; 5) *The Labour Court*, established under the Labour Relations Act, 1995 deals with labour disputes. It is a superior court that has authority, inherent powers and standing in relation to matters under its jurisdiction, equal to that the High Court has in relation to matters under its jurisdiction. Appeals from decisions of the Labour Court lie to the Labour Appeal Court which has authority in labour matters equivalent to that of the Supreme Court of Appeal in other matters.

The lower courts are called Magistrates' Courts. Magisterial districts have been grouped into 13 clusters headed by chief magistrates. From the magistrates court there is an appeal to the High Court having jurisdiction in that area, and then to the Supreme Court of Appeal. In cases involving constitutional matters there is a further appeal to the Constitutional Court. Sentences imposed by district magistrates above a prescribed limit are in most cases subject to automatic review by a judge.

The death penalty was abolished in June 1995 and no executions have taken place since 1989. In 1999 there were 24,210 murders, a rate of 56·2 per 100,000 persons (1994: 26,832 murders, representing a rate of 69·5 per 100,000 persons). South Africa has one of the highest murder rates in the world. Spending on police, prisons and justice services amounted to R23·5bn. in 1999. The population in penal institutions in Oct. 2003 was 180,952 (402 per 100,000 of national population).

Education

The South African Schools Act, 1996 became effective on 1 Jan. 1997 and provides for: compulsory education for students between the ages of seven and 15 years of age, or students reaching the ninth grade, whichever occurs first. Pupils normally enrol for Grade 1 education at the beginning of the year in which they turn seven years of age although earlier entry at the age of six is allowed if the child meets specified criteria indicating that they have reached a stage of school readiness.

In 2003 the South African public education system accommodated 11·7m. school pupils, 448,868 university students, 216,499 technikon students and over 356,000 further education and training college students. There were 27,458 primary, secondary, combined and intermediate schools with 354,201 educators.

In the 2003–04 financial year R69,063m. was allocated to education. In 1999–2000 total expenditure on education came to 5·8% of GNP and 18·1% of total government spending.

There were 22 universities in 2002, two of which are mainly non-residential institutions offering distance tuition; and 15 technikons. The University of South Africa (UNISA) is the oldest and largest university in South Africa and one of the largest distance education institutions in the world. There were 130,347 students and 1,168 teaching and research staff in 2001. In 2000 Vista University (eight campuses) had 26,063 students, the University of Pretoria 25,865, the University of Port Elizabeth 22,366, Rand Afrikaans University (Johannesburg) 20,798 and the University of Stellenbosch 17,532.

According to the *State of South Africa's Population Report 2000*, 18·3% of the population over 20 years of age has had no schooling. The adult literacy rate in 2002 was 86·0% (86·7% for males and 85·3% for females).

Health

Some 40% of South Africans live in poverty and 75% of these live in rural areas where they are deprived of access to health services. By April 2003 free public health services were provided at about 3,500 public health clinics nationwide. There is also a network of mobile clinics run by the government to provide primary and preventive health care.

30,153 doctors were registered with the Health Profession Council of South Africa (HPCSA) at the end of 2002. These include doctors working for the state, doctors in private practice and specialists. Doctors train at the medical schools of eight universities and the majority go on to practise privately. At the end of 2002, 4,499 dentists and 172,869 registered and enrolled nurses and enrolled nursing auxiliaries were registered with the HPCSA. At the end of 2001, 849 oral hygienists and 347 dental therapists were registered. In Dec. 2001, 10,782 pharmacists were registered with the South African Pharmacy Council. Chris Hani Baragwanath Hospital, situated to the southwest of Johannesburg, with its 2,964 beds, is the largest hospital in the world.

In Oct. 1998 the first traditional hospital was opened in Mpumalanga—the Samuel Traditional Hospital. There are about 350,000 traditional healers in South Africa providing services to between 60% and 80% of their communities.

Approximately 4·7m. South Africans are HIV-infected, the highest number in the world (equivalent to nearly 11% of the population of South Africa and nearly 12% of all the people believed to be infected worldwide). In Aug. 2003 the government announced plans to roll out the provision of anti-retrovirals (ARVs) in the public health sector. Under plans to enhance comprehensive care for HIV/AIDS patients in the public sector, it is hoped a universal provision of the drugs will see 1·2m. people on treatment by 2008. It is also envisaged that there will be at least one service point in every local municipality across the country by 2008 for the treatment and care of HIV and AIDS sufferers.

Welfare
At Sept. 2003 the department of social development was disbursing grants through its provincial offices to 6·5m. beneficiaries at a monthly cost of R2·5bn. Recipients are means-tested to determine their eligibility. 3·8m. people received the child support grant (CSG) of R160 per month and 2m. (women aged 60 and above, men aged 65 and above) received old-age grants of R700 per month. The age of children eligible for the CSG will be progressively increased to include children up to the age of 14 years.

Other benefits paid are the disability, foster child, care dependency and war veterans' grants as well as institutional grants and grants in aid.

The total budget allocation for the payment of social assistance by the provincial departments of social development was R18,798bn. in 2000–01.

RELIGION

South Africa is a secular state and freedom of worship is guaranteed by the Constitution. Almost 80% of the population professes the Christian faith. Other major religious groups are Hindus, Muslims and Jews. A sizeable minority of the population subscribe to traditional African faiths. In 1992 the Anglican Church of Southern Africa voted by 79% of votes cast for the ordination of women. In May 2005 there was one cardinal.

CULTURE

World Heritage Sites
UNESCO world heritage sites under South African jurisdiction (with year entered on list) are: Greater St Lucia Wetland Park (1999), encompassing marine, wetland and savannah environments; Robben Island (1999), used since the 17th century as a prison, hospital and military base—it was the location for Nelson Mandela's incarceration; fossil hominid sites of Sterkfontein, Swartkrans, Kromdraai and environs (1999), offering evidence of human evolution over 3·5m. years; uKhahlamba/Drakensberg Park (2000), including caves with 4,000-year old paintings; Mapungubwe Cultural Landscape (2003), a savannah landscape at the confluence of the Limpopo and Shashe rivers and the site of the largest kingdom in Africa in the 14th century; Cape Floral Region Protected Areas (2004); Vredefort Dome (2005), part of a meteorite impact structure.

Broadcasting
Television and radio are regulated by an independent authority, ICASA. The South African Broadcasting Corporation (SABC), the country's public broadcaster, comprises four full-spectrum free-to-air channels, two satellite pay-TV channels aimed at audiences in Africa, and Bop-TV, which the SABC runs on behalf of the State. Combined, the free-to-air channels are licensed to broadcast in 11 languages and reach a daily adult audience of almost 17m. via the terrestrial signal distribution network and a satellite signal.

M-Net, South Africa's first private subscription television service, was launched in 1986. Today, it has over 1·23m. subscribers in 49 countries across the African continent. In March 1998 the consortium Midi Television was awarded the first privately owned free-to-air television licence.

The SABC's national radio network comprises 20 stations which, combined, reach an average daily adult audience of 20m. Between 1994 and 2003, 94 community radio broadcasting and 10 commercial licences were awarded by ICASA.

In Sept. 1999, 85% of the population was able to receive a television signal (colour by PAL). There are more than 4m. licensed television households. About 50% of all programmes transmitted are produced in South Africa. It is estimated that 88% of the rural population listens to the radio in a seven-day period, compared to 79% in 1994.

Press
The major press groups are Independent Newspapers (Pty) Ltd, Media24 Ltd, CTP/Caxton Publishers and Printers Ltd, and Johnnic Publishing Ltd.

Other important media players include Primedia, Nail (New Africa Investments Limited) and Kagiso Media. Nail has unbundled into a commercial company (New Africa Capital) and a media company (New Africa Media).

The only truly national newspapers are: *Sunday Times* (circulation, July–Dec. 2002, 504,295), *Rapport* (338,702), *The Sunday Independent* (40,151) and the weekly newspaper *City Press*. *Die Burger Saterdag* (Cape Town) is the largest Afrikaans daily (116,370). In 2003 there were 17 dailies, seven Sunday newspapers and 24 weekly newspapers.

Tourism
South Africa has one of the fastest-growing tourist industries, contributing R25bn. to the economy in 2000. It contributed 7·1% of gross domestic product in 2002. 6·4m. tourists travelled to the country in 2002. Tourism employs an estimated 3% of South Africa's workforce. It is projected that by 2010 the tourism economy will employ more than 1·2m. people (directly and indirectly). Tourism is the fourth-largest industry in South Africa, supporting some 6,500 accommodation establishments.

Festivals
Best-known arts festivals: the Klein Karoo Festival (Oudtshoorn, Western Cape), which has a strong Afrikaans component, is held in April; the Grahamstown Arts Festival in the Eastern Cape is held in June/July; the Mangaung African Cultural Festival (Macufe) is held in Sept. in Bloemfontein; and the Aardklop Arts Festival, in Potchefstroom in the North-West province, is held in Sept. The Encounters South African International Documentary Festival has been held since 1999.

DIPLOMATIC REPRESENTATIVES

Of South Africa in the United Kingdom (South Africa House, Trafalgar Square, London, WC2N 5DP)
High Commissioner: Lindiwe Mabuza.

Of the United Kingdom in South Africa (255 Hill St., Arcadia, Pretoria 0001)
High Commissioner: Rt Hon. Paul Boateng.

Of South Africa in the USA (3051 Massachusetts Ave., NW, Washington, D.C., 20008)
Ambassador: Barbara Joyce Mosima Masekela.

Of the USA in South Africa (877 Pretorius St., Arcadia, Pretoria 0083)
Ambassador: Jendayi Frazer.

Of South Africa to the United Nations
Ambassador: Dumisana Shadrack Kumalo.

Of South Africa to the European Union
Ambassador: Jeremy Matthews Matjila.

FURTHER READING

Government Communication and Information System (GCIS), including extracts from the *South Africa Yearbook 2004/05*, compiled and published by GCIS.

Beinart, W., *Twentieth Century South Africa*. OUP, 1994
Brewer, J. (ed.) *Restructuring South Africa*. London, 1994
Butler, Anthony, *Contemporary South Africa*. Palgrave Macmillan, Basingstoke, 2003
Davenport, T. R. H., *South Africa: a Modern History*. 5th ed. Macmillan, Basingstoke, 2000
Davis, G. V., *South Africa*. [Bibliography] 2nd ed. ABC-Clio, Oxford and Santa Barbara (CA), 1994
De Klerk, F. W., *The Last Trek—A New Beginning*. Macmillan, London, 1999

Fine, B and Rustomjee Z., *The Political Economy of South Africa*. London, 1996
Giliomee, Hermann, *The Afrikaners: Biography of a People*. Univ. of Virginia Press, Charlottesville, 2003
Guelke, Adrian, *Rethinking the Rise of Apartheid*. Palgrave Macmillan, Basingstoke, 2004
Hough, M. and Du Plessis, A. (eds.) *Selected Documents and Commentaries on Negotiations and Constitutional Development in the RSA, 1989–1994*. Pretoria Univ., 1994
Johnson, R. W. and Schlemmer, L. (eds.) *Launching Democracy in South Africa: the First Open Election, 1994*. Yale Univ. Press, 1996
Mandela, N., *Long Walk to Freedom: the Autobiography of Nelson Mandela*. Abacus, London, 1994
Meredith, M., *South Africa's New Era: the 1994 Election*. London, 1994
Mostert, N., *Frontiers: the Epic of South Africa's Creation and the Tragedy of the Xhosa People*. London, 1992
Nattrass, N. and Ardington, E. (eds.) *The Political Economy of South Africa*. Cape Town and OUP, 1990
Thompson, L., *A History of South Africa*. 2nd ed. Yale Univ. Press, 1996
The Truth and Reconciliation Commission of South Africa Report, 5 vols. Macmillan, London, 1999
Turner, Barry, (ed.) *Southern Africa Profiled*. Macmillan, London, 2000
Waldmeir, P., *Anatomy of a Miracle: the End of Apartheid and the Birth of the New South Africa*. London, 1997
Who's Who in South African Politics. 5th ed. London, 1995

National Statistical Office: Statistics South Africa, Private Bag X44, Pretoria 0001.
Website: http://www.statssa.gov.za/

SOUTH AFRICAN PROVINCES

In 1994 the former provinces of the Cape of Good Hope, Natal, the Orange Free State and the Transvaal, together with the former 'homelands' or 'TBVC countries' of Transkei, Bophuthatswana, Venda and Ciskei, were replaced by nine new provinces. Transkei and Ciskei were integrated into Eastern Cape, Venda into Northern Province (now Limpopo), and Bophuthatswana into Free State, Mpumalanga and North-West.

The administrative powers of the provincial governments in relation to the central government are set out in the 1999 Constitution after a revision of the original text, demanded by the Constitutional Court in 1996.

Eastern Cape

TERRITORY AND POPULATION

The area is 169,580 sq. km and the population at the 2001 census was 6,436,764, the third largest population in South Africa. Of that number: female, 3,461,251; African/Black, 5,635,079 (87% of the population); Coloured, 478,807 (7%); White, 304,506 (5%); Indian/Asian, 18,372 (0·3%). 37% of the population lived in urban areas in 1996. Density (2001), 38 per sq. km. Estimated population as at 30 June 2003, 6,503,201. Life expectancy at birth, 1996, was 60·4 years. At the 2001 census 83·2% spoke IsiXhosa as their home language, 9·3% Afrikaans, 3·6% English and 2·4% Sesotho.

Eastern Cape comprises 77 administrative districts (including Umzimkulu district, an enclave within KwaZulu-Natal).

SOCIAL STATISTICS

Registered live births in 2002 totalled 288,180; deaths, 73,072. Total number of marriages officially recorded in 2002 was 19,278 and divorces granted 1,761.

CONSTITUTION AND GOVERNMENT

The provincial capital is Bisho. There is a 63-seat provincial legislature.

RECENT ELECTIONS

At the provincial elections held on 14 April 2004, 51 seats were won by the ANC, 6 by the UDM, 5 by the DA and 1 by the PAC.

CURRENT ADMINISTRATION

In Feb. 2006 the ANC Executive Council comprised:
Premier: Nosimo Balindlela; b. 1949 (took office on 26 April 2004).

Minister of Agriculture: Gugile Nkwinti. *Economic Affairs, Environment and Tourism:* Andre de Wet. *Education:* Mkhangeli Matomela. *Finance and Provincial Expenditure:* Billy Nel. *Health:* Dr M. Bevan Goqwana. *Housing, Local Government and Traditional Affairs:* Sam Kwelita. *Provincial Safety and Liaison, Roads and Transport:* Thobile Mhlahlo. *Public Works:* Christian Martin. *Social Development:* Tokozile Xasa. *Sports, Recreation, Arts and Culture:* Nomsa Lizzie Jajula.

Speaker: Noxolo Kiviet. *Director-General:* Dr M. E. Tom (ANC).

Government Website: http://www.ecprov.gov.za

ENERGY AND NATURAL RESOURCES

Electricity

In 2003, 7,136 GWh of electricity were consumed. Approximately 42% of households have electricity.

Water

According to the 2001 census, 62·4% of households had access to piped water.

Minerals

Total output of mining and quarrying in 1999 was valued at R57m. with 7,154 persons employed.

Agriculture

There are around 6,000 commercial farms with an average area of 1,500 ha. Of this area only 7% is arable land with 45% not farmed at present owing to land ownership disputes in the former homelands (Transkei and Ciskei). Livestock accounts for 77% of commercial agricultural production; 18% comprises horticulture. Gross farming income for 2002 was R3·2m.; total value of field crops (R1,000), 184,361; horticulture, 833,403; animal and animal products, 2,160,350. The total number of paid farm workers in 2002 was 64,654.

Forestry

Forestry activities are found in the northeast area of the former Transkei, in Stutterheim and in the northwest of the province. In 1999 there were 169,484 ha. of plantation forests.

Fisheries

There is a relatively small sea-fishing industry based on squid, sardines, hake, kingklip and crayfish. Aquaculture produces abalone for export to the Far East.

INDUSTRY

Manufacturing is based mainly in Port Elizabeth and East London with motor manufacturing as the prime industry. Wool, mohair and hides are an important area of the province's agro-industry. Value of manufacturing output in 1999 totalled R14,783m. with 97,035 persons employed.

Labour

As at Sept. 2003 the economically active population numbered 1,636,000, of whom 520,000 were unemployed (31·8%), the highest unemployment rate of all the provinces. Eastern Cape is the centre of South Africa's motor manufacturing industry with the main production centres based at Port Elizabeth and East London.

COMMUNICATIONS

Roads

Total road network at Dec. 2000 was 38,000 km. Between Dec. 1999 and April 2000 the province's roads were severely damaged by floods. A R40m. reconstruction programme commenced in Oct. 2000. There were 911 fatalities as a result of road traffic accidents in 1998.

Civil Aviation

The province has four airports (Port Elizabeth, East London, Umtata and Bulembu).

Shipping

There are two deep-water ports—Port Elizabeth and East London—with a third planned at Coega.

Telecommunications

According to the 2001 census, 29·0% of households had a telephone or mobile phone.

SOCIAL INSTITUTIONS

Education

In 1998 there were 2,301,930 enrolled in schools and a total of 68,033 teaching staff. In that year a total of 37,349 students attended the Province's four universities and three technikons. At the 2001 census more than 22·8% of people aged 20 years and above had no schooling at all, while 6·3% had completed higher education.

Health

In 1999 there were 105 hospitals (including 21 private and semi-private hospitals) and 20,736 hospital beds. In the 1997–98

financial year a total of R112m. was allocated to the Primary School Nutrition Programme.

Welfare

The budget allocated for welfare in 2000–01 was R3,950,911, an increase of 7·5% on 1999–2000.

CULTURE

Broadcasting

In 1996 there were 243,662 TV licence holders.

Free State

TERRITORY AND POPULATION

The Free State lies in the centre of South Africa and is situated between the Vaal River in the north and the Orange River in the south. It borders on the Northern Cape, Eastern Cape, North-West, Mpumalanga, KwaZulu-Natal and Gauteng Province and shares a border with Lesotho. The area is 129,480 sq. km, 10·62% of South Africa's total surface area. The province is the third largest in South Africa but has the second smallest population and the second lowest population density. The population at the 2001 census was 2,706,776. Of that number: female, 1,409,171; African/Black, 2,381,073 (88% of the population); White, 238,791 (9%); Coloured, 83,193 (3%); Indian/Asian, 3,719 (0·1%). Estimated population as at 30 June 2003, 2,738,231. 63% of the population were between 15 and 64 and at least 69% of the population lived in urban areas in 1996 (in 1911, 80% lived in rural areas). Annual population growth rate: 1–2%. Density (2001), 21 per sq. km. Life expectancy at birth, 1996, was 52·8 years. At the 2001 census, 64·3% (1,742,939) of the population spoke Sesotho as their home language, 11·9% (323,082) Afrikaans, 9·1% (246,192) IsiXhosa, 6·8% (185,389) Setswana, 5·1% (138,091) IsiZulu and 1·2% (31,246) English.

Free State comprises 52 administrative districts. The provincial capital is Bloemfontein (meaning 'fountain of flowers'). Bloemfontein's indigenous name is Mangaung, which means 'place of the big cats'.

SOCIAL STATISTICS

Registered live births in 2002 totalled 65,566; deaths, 40,715. The total number of marriages officially recorded in 2002 was 13,359 and divorces granted 1,063.

CLIMATE

Temperatures are mild with averages ranging from 19·5°C in the west to 15°C in the east. Maximum temperatures in the west can reach 36°C in summer. Winter temperatures in the high-lying areas of the eastern Free State can drop as low as –15°C. The western and southern areas are semi-desert.

CONSTITUTION AND GOVERNMENT

There is a 30-seat provincial legislature. The Free State Executive Council, headed by the *Premier*, administers the province through ten Departments.

The Free State House of Traditional Leaders advises the Legislature on matters pertaining to traditional authorities and tribal matters.

RECENT ELECTIONS

In the election held on 14 April 2004 the ANC retained its majority and won 25 of the 30 seats; the DA three; the ACDP one; and VF+ one.

CURRENT ADMINISTRATION

In Feb. 2006 the ANC Executive Council comprised:

Premier: Beatrice Marshoff; b. 1957 (took office on 26 April 2004).

Minister of Agriculture: Caska Mokitlane. *Education:* Mantsheng Tsopo. *Finance:* Pule Makgoe. *Health:* Sakhiwo Belot. *Local Government and Housing:* Malefetsane Mafereka. *Public Safety, Security and Liaison:* France Morule. *Public Works, Roads and Transport:* Seiso Mohai. *Social Development:* Zanele Dlungwana. *Sports, Arts, Culture, Science and Technology:* Suzan Mnumzana. *Tourism, Environment and Economic Affairs:* Neo Masithela.

Speaker: Mxolisi Dukwane. *Director-General:* Khotso de Wee.

Government Website: http://www.fs.gov.za

ENERGY AND NATURAL RESOURCES

Electricity

In the Free State, Eskom distributes electricity through 3,000 km of distribution lines, 9,000 km of reticulation (network) lines; and has an installed capacity of 1,200,740 MVA. Mining (60% of sales) and local governments (30% of sales) are Eskom's biggest Free State's customers.

In 2003, 9,648 GWh of electricity were consumed.

Water

The largest storage dams are the Gariep and Vanderkloof dams, both of which have hydro-electric stations.

According to the 2001 census, 95·7% of households had access to piped water.

Minerals

The province contributes about 16·5% of South Africa's total mineral output. Apart from rich gold and diamond deposits, the Free State is the source of numerous other minerals and is the founding home of South Africa's famous oil-from-coal industry centred on Sasolburg. Bentonite clays, gypsum, salt and phosphates are to be found while large concentrates of thorium-ilminite-zircon also occur. Mining is the province's biggest source of employment: 69,547 employees in 1999.

Agriculture

Good agricultural conditions allow for a wide variety of farming industries. Of the total 12·7m. ha., 90% (11·5m. ha.) is utilized as farmland. Of this, 63·9% is natural grazing; 2·1% is for nature conservation; and 1·1% is used for other purposes. Dryland cultivation is practised on 97% of the arable land, while the remaining 3% is under irrigation.

Free State has the highest number of commercial farming units of all the provinces: 8,531 in 2002 with a gross farming income of R9·1m. Paid farm workers in 2002 numbered 115,478. Total value of field crops in 2002 (R1,000), 5,067,205; horticulture, 620,318; animal and animal products, 3,410,581. The eastern region is the major producer of small grains; the northern region, maize and beef; and the southern region, mutton and wool. The province produces about 40% of total maize and 50% of total wheat production in South Africa.

INDUSTRY

Labour

As at Sept. 2003 the economically active population numbered 1,046,000, of whom 300,000 were unemployed (28·6%).

COMMUNICATIONS

Roads

The Free State Department of Public Works, Roads and Transport is responsible for maintenance of a rural network, which consists of 20,452 km tertiary gravel roads, 21,470 km secondary gravel roads, 6,965 km primary paved roads, and 910 km national roads, of which 25 km are not tarred. There were 817 fatalities as a result of road traffic accidents in 1998.

Rail

Spoornet is one of the biggest companies in the Free State with 4,217 employees. Spoornet transports most of the province's maize, wheat, gold ore, petroleum and fertilizer. The Spoornet infrastructure consists of approximately 4,000 km of tracks, of which 1,300 km are electrified.

Telecommunications

According to the 2001 census, 35·3% of households had a telephone or mobile phone.

Postal Services

In 2005 there were 105 post offices, 15 Postpoints (situated in locations such as chainstores, etc.) and 40 retail postal agencies.

SOCIAL INSTITUTIONS

Justice

Small claims courts operate in 11 centres, providing informal forums where citizens appear in person before a commissioner. The decision of the commissioner is final and the parties cannot appeal to a higher court. Civil claims can be instituted in the magistrates' court, there being 67 magistrate's offices in the province. The Free State provincial division of the Supreme Court is in Bloemfontein. The Circuit Court is a local division of the provincial division of the Supreme Court which visits certain areas. The Circuit Court tries criminal cases only. In 1998, 523 attorneys and 42 advocates practised in the province.

Education

In 1998 there were 810,000 pupils and 24,078 teachers. More than 2,000 farm schools cater for 95,000 pupils. Nine technical colleges provide vocational training for school leavers. Technikon Free State has 8,000 students on the main campus in Bloemfontein and four campuses for distance education situated in Welkom, Kimberley, Kroonstad and Qwaqwa. There are eight teacher training colleges with 4,600 students. The University of the Orange Free State is the only fully fledged residential university and, in 1998, had a student population of 9,787. 1998 literacy rate: 84·42%. According to the 1996 census, 16% of those aged 20 and over had no schooling; 33% had some secondary education.

Health

In 1999 there were 43 hospitals (including 9 private and semi-private hospitals) and 8,722 hospital beds.

CULTURE

Broadcasting

Apart from the national broadcaster, SABC, several private and community radio stations exist, catering for the three primary language groups in the province. In 1996 there were 164,092 TV licence holders.

Press

There is one daily newspaper, *Di Volksblad*, which is published in Afrikaans. Several 'knockanddrop'-type weekly newspapers are produced on a regional basis.

FURTHER READING

Free State: The Winning Province. Chris van Rensburg Publications, Johannesburg, 1997

Gauteng

TERRITORY AND POPULATION

Gauteng is the smallest province in South Africa, covering an area of 18,810 sq. km (approximately 1·4% of the total land surface of South Africa). The population at the 2001 census was 8,837,179. Of that number: female, 4,392,500; African/Black, 6,522,792 (74%); White, 1,758,398 (20%); Coloured, 337,974 (3·8%); Indian/Asian, 218,015 (2·5%). Estimated population as at 30 June 2003, 9,415,231. 97% of the population lived in urban areas in 1996. Density (2001), 470 per sq. km. Life expectancy at birth, 1996, was 59·6 years. At the 2001 census, 21·5% spoke IsiZulu as their home language, 14·3% Afrikaans, 13·1% Sesotho, 12·4% English, 10·7% Sepedi, 8·4% Setswana, 7·6% IsiXhosa, 5·7% Xitsonga, 1·9% IsiNdebele, 1·7% Tshivenda and 1·4% SiSwati.

The province of Gauteng, at first called Pretoria-Witwatersrand-Vereeniging (PWV), comprises 23 administrative districts. The provincial capital is Johannesburg. In the Sesotho language, Gauteng means 'Place of Gold'.

SOCIAL STATISTICS

Registered live births in 2002 totalled 203,864; deaths, 95,186. The total number of marriages officially recorded in 2002 was 45,400 and divorces granted 11,666.

CONSTITUTION AND GOVERNMENT

There is a 73-seat provincial legislature.

RECENT ELECTIONS

At the provincial elections held on 14 April 2004, 51 seats were won by the ANC, 15 by the DA, two by the IFP and one each by ACDP, ID, UDM, VF+ and the PAC.

CURRENT ADMINISTRATION

In Feb. 2006 the ANC Executive Council comprised:

Premier: Mbhazima Sam Shilowa; b. 1958 (took office on 15 June 1999, reinaugurated on 29 April 2004).

Minister of Agriculture, Conservation and the Environment: Khabisi Mosunkutu. *Community Safety:* Firoz Cachalia. *Education:* Angelina Motshekga. *Finance and Economic Affairs:* Paul Mashatile. *Health, and Social Development (acting):* Gwendoline M. Ramokgopa. *Housing:* Nomvula Mokonyane. *Local Government:* Dorothy Mahlangu. *Public Transport, Roads and Works:* Ignatius Jacobs. *Sport, Arts, Culture and Recreation:* Barbara Creecy.

Speaker: Richard Mdakane. *Director-General:* Mogopodi Mokoena.

Government Website: http://www.gpg.gov.za

ENERGY AND NATURAL RESOURCES

Electricity

In 2003, 52,531 GWh of electricity were consumed.

Water

The largest storage dam on the southern edge of the province is the Vaal Dam. According to the 2001 census, 97·5% of households had access to piped water.

Minerals

In 1999, 104,017 people were employed in mining.

Agriculture

There were 2,206 commercial farming units in 2002 with a gross farming income of R4·0m. Paid farm workers in the same year numbered 29,537. Total value of field crops in 2002 (R1,000), 384,056; horticulture, 811,240; animal and animal products, 2,695,978.

INDUSTRY

Labour

As at Sept. 2003 the economically active population numbered 4,499,000, of whom 1,269,000 were unemployed (28·2%). About 38,000 workers are employed by the motor manufacturing industry which contributes an estimated 4·3% of the province's GDP. The aluminium industry is worth about US$20m.

COMMUNICATIONS

Roads

There were 2,010 fatalities as a result of road traffic accidents in 1998.

Civil Aviation

Johannesburg International Airport is the main airport in the province.

Telecommunications

According to the 2001 census, 56·1% of households had a telephone or mobile phone; only 1·6% had no access at all to a telephone.

SOCIAL INSTITUTIONS

Education

In 1998 there were 1·6m. children enrolled in schools with a total of 44,324 teaching staff. In that year a total of 336,004 students attended the Province's six universities and five technikons. According to the 1996 census, 40% of the population had some secondary education—the highest rate in any of South Africa's provinces.

Health

In 1999 there were 105 hospitals (including 78 private and semi-private hospitals) and 29,322 hospital beds.

CULTURE

Broadcasting

There were 978,762 TV licence holders in 1996.

Kwazulu-Natal

TERRITORY AND POPULATION

The area is 92,180 sq. km and the population at the 2001 census was 9,426,017. Of that number: female, 5,016,926; African/Black, 8,002,407 (84·8% of the population); Indian/Asian, 798,275 (8·5%); White, 483,448 (5·1%); Coloured, 141,887 (1·5%). Estimated population as at 30 June 2003, 9,761,032. 43% lived in urban areas in 1996. Density (2001), 102 per sq. km. Life expectancy at birth, 1996, was 53·0 years. At the 2001 census, 80·8% spoke IsiZulu as their home language, 13·6% English, 2·3% IsiXhosa and 1·5% Afrikaans.

KwaZulu-Natal comprises 66 administrative districts. The provincial capital is Pietermaritzburg, chosen by referendum in 1995.

SOCIAL STATISTICS

Registered live births in 2002 totalled 395,450; deaths, 116,982. The total number of marriages officially recorded in 2002 was 24,472 and divorces granted 3,515.

CONSTITUTION AND GOVERNMENT

There is an 80-seat provincial legislature.

RECENT ELECTIONS

At the provincial elections held on 14 April 2004, 38 seats were won by the ANC, 30 by the IFP, seven by DA, two by ACDP, two by the Minority Front and one by UDM.

CURRENT ADMINISTRATION

In Feb. 2006 the ANC-led coalition government comprised:

Premier: J. S. 'S'bu' Ndebele; b. 1948 (ANC; took office on 23 April 2004).

Minister of Agriculture and Environmental Affairs: Prof. Gabriel Ndabandaba (ANC). *Arts, Culture and Tourism:* Narend Singh (IFP). *Education:* Ina Cronjé (ANC). *Finance and Economic Development:* Dr Zweli Mkhize (ANC). *Health:* Peggy Nkonyeni (ANC). *Housing, Local Government and Traditional Affairs:* Mike Mabuyakhulu (ANC). *Public Works:* Blessed Gwala (IFP). *Social Welfare and Population Development:* Inkosi Nyanga Ngubane (IFP). *Sports and Recreation:* Amichand Rajbansi (Minority Front). *Transport, Community Safety and Liaison:* Bheki Cele (ANC).

Speaker: Willis Mchunu (ANC). *Director-General:* Prof. Mandla Mchunu.

Government Website: http://www.kwazulunatal.gov.za

ENERGY AND NATURAL RESOURCES

Electricity
In 2003, 39,231 GWh of electricity were consumed.

Water
According to the 2001 census, 73·2% of households had access to piped water.

Minerals
Coal is mined in the north of the province and Richards Bay is the centre for South Africa's aluminium industry. In 1999, 6,888 people were employed in mining.

Agriculture
There were 4,038 commercial farming units in 2002 with a gross farming income of R6·4m. Paid farm workers in the same year numbered 113,401. Total value of field crops in 2002 (R1,000), 2,773,151; horticulture, 614,458; animal and animal products, 2,615,346. Sugarcane production is the main agricultural activity with (in 2002) 156,075 ha. under planting on dry land and 45,961 ha. on irrigated land.

INDUSTRY

Labour
As at Sept. 2003 the economically active population numbered 3,182,000, of whom 996,000 were unemployed (31·3%).

COMMUNICATIONS

Roads
In 2000 the road network totalled 42,000 km. There were 1,432 fatalities as a result of road traffic accidents in 1998.

Civil Aviation
Durban International Airport is the main airport in the province.

Shipping
Durban harbour is the busiest in South Africa and one of the ten largest harbours in the world. Coal is exported from Richards Bay.

Telecommunications
According to the 2001 census, 39·0% of households had a telephone or mobile phone.

SOCIAL INSTITUTIONS

Education
Since 1995 education has been provided by a unified KwaZulu-Natal Education Department (KZNED). In 1998 there were 2,725,371 children enrolled in schools with a total of 74,834 teaching staff. In that year a total of 30,684 students attended the Province's three universities and three technikons. According to the 1996 census, 23% of the population aged 20 and above had no schooling; 32% had some secondary education.

Health
In 1999 there were 100 hospitals (including 41 private and semi-private hospitals) and 31,266 hospital beds.

CULTURE

Broadcasting
There were 392,573 TV licence holders in 1996.

Tourism
In 2000 the revenue from KwaZulu-Natal's foreign holiday market was estimated at R3·6bn.

Limpopo

TERRITORY AND POPULATION

The area is 123,280 sq. km and the population at the 2001 census was 5,273,642. Of that number: female, 2,878,858; African/Black, 5,128,616 (97% of the population); White, 126,276 (2·4%); Coloured, 10,163 (0·2%); Indian/Asian, 8,587 (0·2%). Estimated population as at 30 June 2003, 5,413,586. 11% lived in urban areas in 1996. Density (2001), 43 per sq. km. Life expectancy at birth, 1996, was 60·1 years. At the 2001 census 52·0% spoke Sepedi as their home language, 22·3% Xitsonga, 15·9% Tshivenda, 2·3% Afrikaans and 1·5% IsiNdebele.

Limpopo (Northern Province until March 2003) comprises 32 administrative districts. The provincial capital is Pietersburg.

SOCIAL STATISTICS

Registered live births in 2002 totalled 215,287; deaths, 38,639. The total number of marriages officially recorded in 2002 was 14,970 and divorces granted 1,149.

CONSTITUTION AND GOVERNMENT

There is a 49-seat provincial legislature.

RECENT ELECTIONS

At the provincial elections held on 14 April 2004, 45 seats were won by the ANC, two by the DA and one each by ACDP and UDM.

CURRENT ADMINISTRATION

In Feb. 2006 the ANC Executive Council comprised:

Premier: Sello Moloto; b. 1965 (sworn in on 26 April 2004).

Minister of Agriculture: Dikeledi Magadzi. *Economic Development, Environment and Tourism:* Collins Chabane. *Education:* Dr P. Aaron Motsoaledi. *Health and Social Development:* Charles Sekoati. *Local Government and Housing:* Maite Nkoana-Mashabane. *Provincial Treasury:* Happy Joyce Mashamba. *Public Works:* Thumba Mufamadi. *Roads and Transport:* Stan Motimele. *Safety, Security and Liaison:* Machwene Semenya. *Sports, Recreation, Arts and Culture:* Joe Maswanganyi.

Speaker: Tshenwani Farasani. *Director-General:* Dr Nelly Manzini.

Government Website: http://www.limpopo.gov.za

ENERGY AND NATURAL RESOURCES

Electricity
In 2003, 9,442 GWh of electricity were consumed.

Water
According to the 2001 census, 78·0% of households had access to piped water.

Minerals

Mining is an important industry in the province with, in 2002, 49,000 people employed.

Agriculture

There were 2,915 commercial farming units in 2002 with a gross farming income of R4·6m. Paid farm workers in the same year numbered 101,249. Total value of field crops in 2002 (R1,000), 785,982; horticulture, 2,319,058; animal and animal products, 1,368,681.

INDUSTRY

Labour

As at Sept. 2003 the economically active population numbered 1,139,000, of whom 349,000 were unemployed (30·6%).

COMMUNICATIONS

Roads

There were 547 fatalities as a result of road traffic accidents in 1998.

Telecommunications

According to the 2001 census, 28·0% of households had a telephone or mobile phone, the lowest number of all the provinces.

SOCIAL INSTITUTIONS

Education

In 1998 there were 1,810,603 children enrolled in schools with a total of 57,155 teaching staff. 17,933 students attended the Province's two universities in the same year. According to the 1996 census, almost 37% of the population aged 20 years and over had no schooling.

Health

In 1999 there were 45 hospitals (including two private and semi-private hospitals) and 12,358 hospital beds.

CULTURE

Broadcasting

There were 99,362 TV licence holders in 1996.

Mpumalanga

TERRITORY AND POPULATION

The area is 78,370 sq. km and the population at the 2001 census was 3,122,991. Of that number: female, 1,625,658; African/Black, 2,886,345 (92·4% of the population); White, 203,244 (6·5%); Coloured, 22,158 (0·7%); Indian/Asian, 11,244 (0·4%). Estimated population as at 30 June 2003, 3,246,729. 39·1% lived in urban areas in 1996. Density (2001), 40 per sq. km. Life expectancy at birth, 1996, was 53·5 years. At the 2001 census, 30·8% spoke SiSwati as their home language, 26·3% IsiZulu, 12·1% IsiNdebele, 10·8% Sepedi, 6·1% Afrikaans, 3·8% Xitsonga, 3·7% Sesotho, 2·7% Setswana, 1·7% English and 1·5% IsiXhosa.

Mpumalanga comprises 28 administrative districts. The provincial capital is Nelspruit.

SOCIAL STATISTICS

Registered live births in 2002 totalled 113,505; deaths, 35,277. The total number of marriages officially recorded in 2002 was 10,139 and divorces granted 1,255.

CONSTITUTION AND GOVERNMENT

There is a 30-seat provincial legislature.

RECENT ELECTIONS

At the provincial elections held on 14 April 2004, 27 seats were won by the ANC, two by the DA and one by VF+.

CURRENT ADMINISTRATION

In Feb. 2006 the ANC government comprised:

Premier: Thabang Makwetla; b. 1957 (took office on 30 April 2004).

Minister of Agriculture and Land Administration: Madala Masuku. *Culture, Sports and Recreation:* Nomsa Mtsweni. *Economic Development and Planning:* S. William Lubisi. *Education:* Siphosezwe Masango. *Finance:* Mmathulare Coleman. *Health and Social Services:* Pogisho Phasha. *Local Government and Housing:* Jabu Mahlangu. *Public Works:* K. Candith Mashego-Dlamini. *Roads and Transport:* Fish Mahlalela. *Safety and Security:* Dinah Pule.

Speaker: Yvonne 'Pinky' Phosa. *Director-General:* Khaya Ngema.

Government Website: http://www.mpumalanga.gov.za

ENERGY AND NATURAL RESOURCES

Electricity

In 2003, 25,279 GWh of electricity were consumed.

Water

According to the 2001 census, 86·7% of households had access to piped water.

Minerals

In 1999, 61,826 people were employed in mining. The province is rich in coal reserves and produces about 80% of the country's supplies.

Agriculture

There were 5,104 commercial farming units in 2002 with a gross farming income of R6·2m. Paid farm workers in the same year numbered 108,083. Total value of field crops in 2002 (R1,000), 2,566,165; horticulture, 1,624,945; animal and animal products, 1,853,552.

INDUSTRY

Labour

As at Sept. 2003 the economically active population numbered 1,040,000, of whom 260,000 were unemployed (25·0%).

COMMUNICATIONS

Roads

There were 1,074 fatalities as a result of road traffic accidents in 1998.

Telecommunications

According to the 2001 census, 37·9% of households had a telephone or mobile phone.

SOCIAL INSTITUTIONS

Education

In 1998 there were 935,528 children enrolled in schools with a total of 1,967 teaching staff. According to the 1996 census, 28% of those aged 20 years and over had no schooling; 38% had some secondary education.

Health

In 1999 there were 35 hospitals (including ten private and semi-private hospitals) and 5,048 hospital beds. In Oct. 1998 the first traditional hospital was opened in Mpumalanga—the Samuel Traditional Hospital.

CULTURE

Broadcasting

There were 138,085 TV licence holders in 1996.

Tourism

The number of international visitors increased from 14% to 21% between Jan. 2000 and Aug. 2001.

Northern Cape

TERRITORY AND POPULATION

The area is 361,800 sq. km and the population at the 2001 census was 822,727. Of that number: female, 421,559; Coloured, 424,389 (51·6% of the population); African/Black, 293,976 (35·7%); White, 102,042 (12·4%); Indian/Asian, 2,320 (0·3%). Estimated population as at 30 June 2003, 818,848. At least 70% lived in urban areas in 1996. Density (2001), 2 per sq. km. Life expectancy at birth, 1996, was 55·6 years. At the 2001 census, 68·0% spoke Afrikaans as their home language, 20·8% Setswana, 6·2% IsiXhosa and 2·5% English.

Northern Cape comprises six administrative districts: Diamond Fields with Kimberley as the provincial and economic capital; Kalahari, which is the second richest and densely populated area in the province and includes the magisterial districts of Kuruman and Postmasburg; Hantam (North-West) with the towns of Calvinia, Sutherland, Williston, Fraserburg and Carnavon; Benede-Orange with Upington as the agricultural, economic and cultural capital of the region; Bo-Karoo with De Aar as the capital of the area; and Namaqualand which is strong in mining.

SOCIAL STATISTICS

Registered live births in 2002 totalled 20,998; deaths, 11,267. The total number of marriages officially recorded in 2002 was 3,790 and divorces granted 536.

CONSTITUTION AND GOVERNMENT

There is a 30-seat provincial legislature.

RECENT ELECTIONS

At the provincial elections held on 14 April 2004, 21 seats were won by the ANC, three by the DA, two by ID, two by the NNP and one each by VF+ and ACDP.

CURRENT ADMINISTRATION

In Feb. 2006 the ANC Executive Council comprised:

Premier: E. Dipuo Peters (took office on 30 April 2004).

Minister of Agriculture and Land Reform: Tina M. Joemat-Petterson. *Education:* Gomolelo Lucas. *Environmental Affairs and Tourism:* Pieter Saaiman. *Finance and Economic Affairs:* Penene Pakes Dikgetsi. *Health:* Kagisho Molusi. *Local Government and Housing:* Eunice Silao. *Safety and Liaison:* Boeboe van Wyk. *Social Services and Population Development:* Goolam H. Akharawaray. *Sport, Arts and Culture:* Themsi Madikane. *Transport, Roads and Public Works:* Fred Wyngaardt.

Speaker: Connie Seoposengwe. *Director-General:* M. Hendry Hendricks (ANC).

ENERGY AND NATURAL RESOURCES

Electricity

In 2003, 4,401 GWh of electricity were consumed.

Water

According to the 2001 census, 96·6% of households had access to piped water.

Minerals

The province is well endowed with a variety of mineral deposits. Diamonds are found in shallow water at Port Nolloth,

Hondeklipbaai and Lamberts Bay, and also mined inland along the entire coastal strip from the Orange river mouth in the north to Lamberts Bay in the south. Copper is mined in Namaqualand. Iron and manganese occur in two parallel north-south belts from Postmasburg in the south to Sishen/Kathu/Hotazel in the north. Limestone, asbestos and gypsum salt are also mined. In 1999, 19,235 people were employed in mining.

Agriculture

Intensive irrigation takes place along the Orange River which supports vineyards and agribusiness. Stock farming predominates in the Bo-Karoo and Hantam areas. There were 6,114 commercial farming units in 2002 with a gross farming income of R3·6m. Paid farm workers in the same year numbered 99,251. Total value of field crops in 2002 (R1,000), 971,869; horticulture, 1,065,784; animal and animal products, 1,517,207.

INDUSTRY

Labour

As at Sept. 2003 the economically active population numbered 288,000, of whom 79,000 were unemployed (27·5%).

COMMUNICATIONS

Roads

At 31 Jan. 2001 there were 158,326 vehicles registered of which 1,241 were government-owned. There were 306 fatalities as a result of road traffic accidents in 1998.

Rail

The main rail link is between Cape Town and Johannesburg, via Kimberley. Other main lines link the Northern Cape with Port Elizabeth via De Aar while another links Upington with Namibia.

Civil Aviation

Five airports are used for scheduled flights—Kimberley, Upington, Aggeneys, Springbok and Alexander Bay.

Telecommunications

According to the 2001 census, 41·8% of households had a telephone or mobile phone.

SOCIAL INSTITUTIONS

Education

In 1999 there were 184,910 children enrolled in schools with a total of 6,070 teaching staff. There is no university in the province but there are some technical colleges and a nursing college in Kimberley. According to the 1996 census, almost 21% of those aged 20 years and over had no schooling; 31% had some secondary education.

Health

In 2000 there were 38 hospitals and 90 clinics (including some that are privately-run). In 2001 there were 176 doctors, 1,539 nurses and ten dentists.

CULTURE

Broadcasting

There were 85,140 TV licence holders in 1996.

Tourism

Parks are a major tourism asset with the total area under protection being 1,080,200 ha. Provincial nature reserves occupy 50,240 ha. Hunting is a growing activity in the province.

North-West

TERRITORY AND POPULATION

The area is 116,190 sq. km and the population at the 2001 census was 3,669,350. Of that number: female, 1,847,802; African/Black, 3,358,450 (91·3% of the total population); White, 244,035 (6·6%); Coloured, 56,959 (1·5%); Indian/Asian, 9,906 (0·3%). Estimated population as at 30 June 2003, 3,791,984. Density (2001), 32 per sq. km. Life expectancy at birth, 1996, was 53·3 years. At the 2001 census 65·2% spoke Setswana as their home language, 7·5% Afrikaans, 5·8% IsiXhosa, 5·7% Sesotho, 4·7% Xitsonga, 4·2% Sepedi, 2·5% IsiZulu, 1·3% IsiNdebele, 1·2% English and 0·6% SiSwati.

North-West Province comprises 32 administrative districts. The provincial capital is Mmabatho.

SOCIAL STATISTICS

Registered live births in 2002 totalled 104,696; deaths, 44,269. The total number of marriages officially recorded in 2002 was 13,483 and divorces granted 2,065.

CONSTITUTION AND GOVERNMENT

There is a 33-seat provincial legislature.

RECENT ELECTIONS

At the provincial elections held on 14 April 2004 the ANC won 27 seats, UCDP three, DA two and VF+ one.

CURRENT ADMINISTRATION

In Feb. 2006 the ANC Executive Council comprised:

Premier: Ednah Molewa; b. 1957 (took office on 30 April 2004).

Minister of Agriculture, Conservation and Environment: Mandlenkosi Eliot Mayisela. *Economic Development and Tourism:* Darkey Afrika. *Education:* Rev. Johannes Tselapedi. *Finance:* Maureen Modiselle. *Health:* R. Nomende Rasmeni. *Local Government and Housing:* Frans Vilakazi. *Public Works:* Howard D. Yawa. *Safety, Transport and Roads:* Jerry D. Thibedi. *Social Development:* Nikiwe Num. *Sports, Arts and Culture:* Ndleleni Duma.

Speaker: Thandi Modise. *Director-General:* Dr M. A. Bakane-Tuoane.

Government Website: http://www.nwpg.gov.za

ENERGY AND NATURAL RESOURCES

Electricity
In 2003, 28,101 GWh of electricity were consumed.

Water
According to the 2001 census, 86·2% of households had access to piped water.

Minerals
In 1999, 132,499 people were employed in mining. Gold is mined at Orkney and Klerksdorp, and diamonds at Lichtenburg, Koster, Christiana and Bloemhof.

Agriculture
There were 5,349 commercial farming units in 2002 with a gross farming income of R5·1m. Paid farm workers in the same year numbered 85,992. Total value of field crops in 2002 (R1,000), 2,448,308; horticulture, 363,358; animal and animal products, 2,305,785.

INDUSTRY

Labour
As at Sept. 2003 the economically active population numbered 1,184,000, of whom 348,000 were unemployed (29·4%).

Manufacturing contributes 7% of the province's GDP and is mainly dependent on the production of fabricated metals (51%), non-metallic metals (21%) and the food sector (18%).

COMMUNICATIONS

According to the 2001 census, 34·5% of households had a telephone or mobile phone.

Roads
There were 685 fatalities as a result of road traffic accidents in 1998.

Telecommunications
Around 34·5% of the population had telephones or mobile phones in 2001; 6·7% had no access at all to a telephone.

SOCIAL INSTITUTIONS

Education
In 1998 there were 953,737 children enrolled in schools with a total of 31,962 teaching staff. In the same year, 24,296 students attended the Province's two universities and one technikon. According to the 1996 census, almost 22% of those aged 20 or over had no schooling.

Health
In 1999 there were 32 hospitals (including ten private hospitals) and 6,389 hospital beds.

CULTURE

Broadcasting
In 1996 there were 116,680 TV licence holders.

Tourism
In 1999 there was a total of 343,915 international visitors (5·5% of total international visitors to South Africa) with 114,639 jobs created as a result.

Western Cape

TERRITORY AND POPULATION

The area is 129,386 sq. km. Population, 2001 census, 4,524,336. Of that number: females, 2,332,014; Coloured, 2,438,976 (53·9%); African/Black, 1,207,429 (26·7%); White, 832,901 (18·4%); Indian/Asian, 45,030 (1·0%). Density (2001), 35 per sq. km. Estimated population as at 30 June 2003, 4,740,981. Life expectancy at birth, 1996, was 60·8 years. At the 2001 census, 55·3% spoke Afrikaans as their home language, 23·7% IsiXhosa and 19·3% English. In 1996, 3·5m. (85% of total population) lived in urban areas.

There are 41 administrative districts. The capital is Cape Town.

SOCIAL STATISTICS

Registered live births in 2002 totalled 102,482; deaths, 43,667. The total number of marriages officially recorded in 2002 was 26,852 and divorces granted 5,846.

CONSTITUTION AND GOVERNMENT

There is a 42-seat provincial parliament.

RECENT ELECTIONS

At the provincial elections held on 14 April 2004, 19 seats were won by the ANC, 12 by the DA, five by the NNP, three by ID, two by ACDP and one by the UDM.

CURRENT ADMINISTRATION

In Feb. 2006 the ANC/NNP provincial cabinet comprised:

Premier: Ebrahim Rasool; b. 1962 (ANC; took office on 30 April 2004).

Minister of Agriculture: Kobus Dowry (NNP). *Community Safety:* Leonard Ramatlakane (ANC). *Cultural Affairs, Sport and Recreation:* Whitey Jacobs (ANC). *Education:* Cameron Dugmore (ANC). *Environment, Planning and Economic Development:* Tasneem Essop (ANC). *Finance and Tourism:* Lynne Brown (ANC). *Health:* Pierre Uys (NNP). *Local Government and Housing:* Richard Dyantyi (ANC). *Public Works and Transport:* Marius Fransman (ANC). *Social Services and Poverty Alleviation:* Kholeka Mqulwana (ANC).

Speaker: Shaun Byneveldt (ANC). *Director-General:* Dr Gilbert Lawrence.

Government Website: http://www.westerncape.gov.za

ENERGY AND NATURAL RESOURCES

Electricity

In 2003, 20,581 GWh of electricity were consumed.

Water

Many small rural towns and farming communities rely on groundwater for domestic water supplies. In comparison with the rest of the country relatively few people in the province do not have access to adequate water supplies.

Minerals

In 1999, 2,561 people were employed in mining.

Agriculture

There were 7,185 commercial farming units in 2002 with a gross farming income of R11·1m. Paid farm workers in the same year numbered 223,175. Total value of field crops in 2002 (R1,000), 1,295,835; horticulture, 5,976,340; animal and animal products, 3,295,138. The province is one of the world's finest grape-growing regions as well as producing other fruits such as apples, peaches and oranges. The Klein Karoo region is the centre of the ostrich-farming industry in South Africa with leatherware, feathers and meat exported worldwide.

INDUSTRY

Labour

As at Sept. 2003 the economically active population numbered 2,179,000, of whom 448,000 were unemployed (20·6%), the lowest unemployment rate of all the provinces.

COMMUNICATIONS

Roads

Motor vehicles registered (1996) totalled 1,102,226, including 679,977 passenger cars, 238,087 light commercial vehicles, 35,478 heavy commercial vehicles and 28,153 motorcycles. There were 1,286 fatalities as a result of road traffic accidents in 1998.

Civil Aviation

Cape Town International Airport is the main airport in the province.

Telecommunications

According to the 2001 census, 63·1% of households had a telephone or mobile phone; only 1·6% had no access at all to a telephone.

SOCIAL INSTITUTIONS

Education

In 1998 there were 902,879 children enrolled in schools with a total of 25,393 teaching staff. In that year, 60,330 students attended the Province's three universities and two technikons. The Western Cape has the highest adult-education level in South Africa with only 5·7% of the population aged 20 years and over with no schooling. According to the 1996 census, 10·6% of people aged 20 years and over had higher education qualifications.

Health

In 1999 there were 86 hospitals (including 32 private and semi-private hospitals) and 14,641 hospital beds. Of the nine provinces Western Cape has the lowest prevalence of HIV.

CULTURE

Broadcasting

There were 681,644 TV licence holders in 1996.

Tourism

Overseas visitors to the province in 2002 totalled 976,000 (excluding Africa); domestic visitor trips, 4,326,000.

SPANE

© Research Machines plc 2006

Reino de España
(Kingdom of Spain)

Capital: Madrid
Population projection, 2010: 43·99m.
GDP per capita, 2003: (PPP$) 22,391
HDI/world rank: 0·928/21

KEY HISTORICAL EVENTS

A bridge between Europe and Africa, the Iberian peninsula has absorbed influences from both regions. The original inhabitants were Iberians, who spoke a non Indo-European language, and Celtic peoples, who were mainly to the north and west of the peninsula. From the 8th century BC the Phoenicians established trading colonies such as Gades (Cádiz), importing metalworking skills, music and literacy in the form of a semi-syllabic script. The Greeks established a trading settlement in Catalonia named Empirion (now Ampurias) around 575 BC, and there is evidence of other Greek and Phoenician settlements along the Mediterranean coast.

From 241 BC the Iberian peninsula came under the influence of Carthage in North Africa. The Carthaginians, led by Hamilcar Barca, landed at Cádiz and moved north and east. They eventually founded a new capital at Cartagena: the city grew rapidly and had a population of around 30,000 by 215 BC. A Roman presence began at this time, further north in Catalonia. The first legionnaires established their base at Tarragona, from where they waged war on the Carthaginians. Fighting between the two powers ebbed and flowed for years, until the Carthaginians were forced off the peninsula in 206 BC. Roman laws and customs were gradually adopted over the following six centuries, but there were frequent rebellions among the native peoples.

Roman rule was on the wane throughout Europe by AD 400, and Roman Hispania was no exception. In 409 Visigoths, Suevi and Vandals crossed the Pyrenees and began to establish themselves as the new rulers. By 470 most of the leading families were of Germanic origin. Toledo became the capital and seat of successive Visigothic monarchs until the early 700s. At this time, the Romans were defeated in North Africa by Muslim armies,

who began to turn their attention to the Iberian peninsula. Toledo fell to Arab and Berber forces and the death of King Roderic in 711 marked the end of Visigothic hegemony.

The Muslim conquerors brought a new language, religion and culture, which dominated large parts of the Iberian peninsula for the next five hundred years, though there were sizeable Jewish communities in the southern and eastern towns and there were some Christian principalities in the north. The Umayyad dynasty used Córdoba as the administrative centre of al-Andalus ('Land of the Vandals') until 1031. New trade links were established, connecting Córdoba with Egypt and Persia and most of the Islamic world. People and ideas flooded in and the great cities of Córdoba and Sevilla (Seville) became beacons of modernity and creativity in fields ranging from architecture to botany, medicine, poetry and techniques for irrigation.

While al-Andalus prospered, the Christian principalities to the north in places such as Asturia, the Basque territories and northern Catalonia remained relatively poor and agrarian. However, from about 900 there was a gradual expansion southwards towards al-Andalus, described as the start of the *Reconquista*, or reconquest of Spain by the Christians. By 1000 there was considerable contact between the Christian principalities and France: Norman knights fought in Catalonia and French settlers arrived in towns along the pilgrimage route to Santiago de Compostela, bringing with them new ideas and skills.

From the 1120s the Muslim governors of al-Andalus found themselves under threat from both northern Christian rulers and native Andalusi. Alfonso VII of Leon-Castile eventually conquered Córdoba in 1146 and the strategically important Almería, on the Mediterranean coast, in 1147. Following these victories, the three most powerful Christian kingdoms of Aragon, Castile and Portugal pushed south and east and by 1300 the last remaining Islamic dominion was the amirate of Granada. Muslim inhabitants were expelled from many towns and cities, though in rural areas the Islamic faith and the Arabic language survived for centuries. While Córdoba declined, Barcelona blossomed: it emerged as a great economic success story on a par with Genoa and Venice.

Castile and Aragon were the dominant kingdoms by the early 1300s, but they were both characterized by infighting and rebellion. King Pedro the Cruel of Castile was challenged by a coalition of nobles led by his half brother Enrique de Trastámara. The English supported Pedro (Peter) and his heirs and the French backed Enrique (Henry) and his supporters. Enrique eventually prevailed, and was crowned Enrique II in 1369.

The Modern State

The Spanish monarchy was founded in 1469 following the marriage of Isabel (Isabella), princess of Castile and Fernando (Ferdinand), heir to the throne of Aragon. Under their joint reign, they laid the foundations for a unified Spain. In 1478 they established the notorious Spanish Inquisition, expelling and executing tens of thousands of Jews and other non-Christians. Four years later the last Islamic territory of Granada was besieged. It surrendered in 1492, the year in which Christopher Columbus reached the New World.

When Fernando and Isabel's son Juan died in 1497, the succession to the Spanish crowns passed to his sister, Juana *la loca* (the Mad). Juana married Philip (Felipe) the Handsome, heir through his father, Emperor Maximilian I, to the Habsburg domains in Germany and Flanders. When Fernando died in 1516, Juana and Felipe's son, Charles of Ghent, inherited Spain, its colonies in the New World, Naples and, following the death of Maximilian I in 1519, the Habsburg territories. Shortly afterwards he was elected Holy Roman Emperor, a title he held as Charles V (Carlos I of Spain). Charles, in the space of only a few years, commanded one of the most extensive empires since Rome.

Columbus paved the way for the Spanish colonies in the new world but for 30 years after his discoveries attention focused on the Caribbean. It was only in 1521 that Hernando Cortés overthrew the Aztecs, with help from native Indian allies. After 1540 gold and silver began pouring into Spanish coffers from mines in Peru and Mexico. Sugar plantations were established in the Caribbean and the indigenous populations were gradually wiped out. Maintaining control of the new empire was a serious challenge and Charles V relied heavily on co-operation from Italians, Flemings and Germans. The rise of Spain as a military power began in the 1560s in the reign of Felipe II. He built a powerful navy and annexed Portugal in 1580. The new fleet patrolled the American supply routes, fended off attacks from the English and set up new colonies in the Philippines and at Buenos Aires.

Spain's Golden Age began to lose its lustre in the late 16th century, following a popular uprising in the Netherlands under William of Orange. The Dutch were beginning to establish their own colonies in Asia and started making inroads in Brazil. Spain was weakened by the cost of defending its empire against France and England and in 1640 the unity of the Iberian peninsula itself came under threat by rebellions in Catalonia and Portugal. The crowning of Carlos II, a disabled child, in 1665 symbolized Spain's growing vulnerability and isolation from the rest of Europe.

Carlos II died without issue in 1700 and left the throne to Philippe, duke of Anjou and grandson of King Louis XIV of France. Felipe (Philippe) V was the first in a line of five Bourbon monarchs, who reigned in Spain until 1833. Under Felipe V, and his successor Fernando VI, Spain restored some of its influence in Europe, particularly in Italy, where Naples and Sicily were recovered from Austria in 1734. Educational reforms led to a period of Enlightenment in the 1760s, with many universities replacing conservative Jesuit doctrines with modern physics, astronomy and political theory. The 1780s, when Spain was ruled by Carlos III, were a period of both stability and prosperity. Catalonia became a centre of the early industrial revolution with its booming textile trade and Madrid saw a flowering of artistic expression encapsulated by the work of Goya.

When Louis XVI was guillotined in 1793 the new French Republic turned its attention to neighbouring Spain and Britain, and declared war on them. In 1794–95 French forces invaded Catalonia and the Basque provinces. Following these defeats, King Carlos IV of Spain formed an alliance with France under its new emperor, Napoleon. Hostilities with Britain were resumed, though defeat for the Franco-Spanish naval forces at the Battle of Trafalgar further undermined links with the Spanish colonies and damaged the economy.

In 1808 the weak and unpopular Carlos IV abdicated and the Spanish crown passed to Fernando VII, though his right to the throne was ceded to Napoleon later that year. However, Napoleon misjudged the mood of the Spanish public who rioted in Madrid and began a five-year war of independence. In 1813 the French forces were finally expelled but ideas from revolutionary France were beginning to take root. The medieval Cortes (parliament) was revived and a reformist group known as the Liberals ushered in Spain's first constitution. The following year, Fernando VII was restored to the Spanish throne, which was broadly welcomed by a war-ravaged public. Fernando's first act was to declare the new constitution null and void, and his 20 year reign was characterized by a return to the old regime: the Inquisition was re-established, the Liberals were persecuted, free speech was repressed and Spain entered a severe economic recession.

End of Empire

Queen Isabel II inherited the Spanish throne in 1833 as a child. During her reign there were various attempts to reinstate a constitution by the Liberals and progressives to reinstate a constitution. Her support for neo-catholic reactionaries in her governments of the 1860s fanned the flames of revolution. In 1868 Isabel was deposed and the Cortes brought in a new constitution at last. Amadeo I of Savoy was chosen as the new monarch, but he was unable to adapt to Spanish politics and abdicated in 1873. The Cortes immediately proclaimed a republic but it was marked by great instability and less than a year later a coup restored the Bourbon monarchy, with Alfonso XII, the son of exiled Isabel II, as king.

The disastrous Spanish-American War of 1898 marked the end of the Spanish Empire. Spain was defeated by the USA in a series of one-sided naval battles, resulting in the loss of Cuba, Puerto Rico, Guam and the Philippines. Spain was neutral during the First World War, which led to a boom in trade and industry. Barcelona's Hispano-Suiza factories produced aircraft engines for the French air force and some of Europe's most luxurious cars. However, this prosperity did not filter through society and workers demonstrated against high food prices. In 1923 Gen. Miguel Primo de Rivera, marquis of Estella, led a coup, abolished the 1876 constitution and closed down the Cortes. Primo de Rivera was determined to clear out what he saw as corrupt, self-serving politicians. His alternative to the constitutional monarchy was the National Political Union but it attracted only opportunists and right-wing enthusiasts. There were improvements in the nation's infrastructure, but de Rivera's public works programmes were hit by financial difficulties in 1929, and the dictator resigned the following year.

1931 marked the beginning of a new genuinely democratic era for Spain. Municipal elections were held and won by a republican-socialist coalition. King Alfonso XIII exiled himself and the Second Republic was declared. The 1936 elections saw the country split in two, with the Republican government and its supporters on one side (an uneasy alliance of communists, socialists and anarchists) and the Nationalists (the army, the Catholic church, monarchists and the fascist-style Falange Party) on the other.

Civil War

The assassination of the opposition leader José Calvo Sotelo by Republican police officers in July 1936 gave the army, led by Gen. Francisco Franco, an excuse to stage a coup. It was the failure of the military coup to overthrow the government that led to a protracted civil war. The Nationalists received extensive military and financial support from Nazi Germany and fascist Italy, while the Republican government received support from the Soviet Union and, to a lesser degree, from the International Brigades, made up of foreign idealists.

By 1939 the Nationalists, led by Franco, had prevailed. More than 350,000 Spaniards had died in the fighting, but more bloodletting ensued. An estimated 100,000 Republicans were executed or died in prison after the civil war. Franco's cure for Spain's 'sick' economy was withdrawal from world markets and the establishment of a self-sufficient autarky, but by the late 1940s inflation was rising steeply and Spain was losing ground to other European countries. Franco allowed a gradual liberalization of the economy, but despite this and the readmission of Spain to the UN in 1955 the economy remained in deep trouble. The desperate conditions endured by hundreds of thousands of workers led to nationwide strikes and there was growing opposition to the Franco regime among university students and intellectuals. During the 1960s the regime also faced passionate demands for independence in Catalonia and the Basque Country.

Franco died in 1975, having earlier named Juan Carlos, the grandson of Alfonso XIII, his successor. Under King Juan Carlos, Spain made the transition back to democracy. The first elections were held in 1977 and a new constitution was approved by referendum in 1978. In Feb. 1981 there was an attempted fascist coup, when for 18 hours the deputies of the lower house of parliament and the Cabinet were held hostage. However, order was restored and the episode is now seen as the final, futile attempt to turn back the clock. The following year saw a spectacular victory for the socialist party which presided over a rapid expansion in the economy during its 14 years in power. In 1986 Spain joined the European Economic Community, which cemented the nation's status as a popular location for foreign investors and tourists, though its international reputation has suffered from the ongoing violent campaign waged by ETA, the separatist terrorist group that is attempting to secure an independent Basque homeland.

In 1996 Spaniards voted in a conservative party under the leadership of José María Aznar. In March 2000 he was re-elected with an absolute majority; his success was attributed to the buoyant state of the Spanish economy, which averaged in excess of 4% annual growth during Aznar's first term of office.

Madrid suffered Spain's worst terrorist attack on 11 March 2004 when four commuter trains were bombed, killing 191 and injuring over 1,800 people. The government initially blamed ETA but suspicion quickly moved to al-Qaeda and North African operatives. On 14 March the Socialists, led by José Luis Rodríguez Zapatero, defeated the People's Party in general elections. The last Spanish troops left Iraq in May 2004.

TERRITORY AND POPULATION

Spain is bounded in the north by the Bay of Biscay, France and Andorra, east and south by the Mediterranean and the Straits of Gibraltar, southwest by the Atlantic and west by Portugal and the Atlantic. Continental Spain has an area of 492,592 sq. km, and including the Balearic and Canary Islands and the towns of Ceuta and Melilla on the northern coast of Africa, 506,030 sq. km (195,378 sq. miles). Population (census, 2001), 40,847,371 (20,825,521 females). In 2003, 76·5% of the population lived in urban areas; population density in 2001 was 83 per sq. km. The estimated population in 2005 was 43,064,000. In 2002 foreigners resident in Spain numbered 1,977,944, including 307,458 from Morocco, 259,522 from Ecuador, 191,018 from Colombia, 128,121 from the UK and 113,308 from Germany. Foreigners constitute 4·7% of the population.

The UN gives a projected population for 2010 of 43·99m.

The growth of the population has been as follows:

Census year	Population	Rate of annual increase	Census year	Population	Rate of annual increase
1860	15,655,467	0·34	1960	30,903,137	1·05
1910	19,927,150	0·72	1970	33,823,918	0·95
1920	21,303,162	0·69	1981	37,746,260	1·05
1930	23,563,867	1·06	1991	38,872,268	0·30
1940	25,877,971	0·98	2001	40,847,371	0·51
1950	27,976,755	0·81			

Area and population of the autonomous communities (in italics) and provinces at the 2001 census:

Autonomous community/ Province	Area (sq. km)	Population	Per sq. km
Andalusia	*87,595*	*7,357,558*	*84*
Almería	8,775	536,731	61
Cádiz	7,436	1,116,491	150
Córdoba	13,771	761,657	55
Granada	12,647	821,660	65
Huelva	10,128	462,579	45
Jaén	13,496	643,820	46
Málaga	7,306	1,287,017	176
Sevilla	14,036	1,727,603	123
Aragón	*47,720*	*1,204,215*	*25*
Huesca	15,636	206,502	13
Teruel	14,810	135,858	9
Zaragoza	17,274	861,855	50

Autonomous community/ Province	Area (sq. km)	Population	Per sq. km
Asturias	*10,604*	*1,062,998*	*100*
Baleares	*4,992*	*841,669*	*169*
Basque Country	*7,234*	*2,082,587*	*288*
Álava	3,037	286,387	94
Guipúzcoa	1,980	673,563	340
Vizcaya	2,217	1,122,637	506
Canary Islands	*7,492*	*1,694,477*	*226*
Palmas, Las	4,111	887,676	216
Santa Cruz de Tenerife	3,381	806,801	239
Cantabria	*5,321*	*535,131*	*101*
Castilla-La Mancha	*79,461*	*1,760,516*	*22*
Albacete	14,924	364,835	24
Ciudad Real	19,813	478,957	24
Cuenca	17,140	200,346	12
Guadalajara	12,214	174,999	14
Toledo	15,370	541,379	35
Castilla y León	*94,224*	*2,456,474*	*26*
Ávila	8,050	163,442	20
Burgos	14,292	348,934	24
León	15,581	488,751	31
Palencia	8,052	174,143	22
Salamanca	12,350	345,609	28
Segovia	6,921	147,694	21
Soria	10,306	90,717	9
Valladolid	8,111	498,094	61
Zamora	10,561	199,090	19
Catalonia	*32,113*	*6,343,110*	*198*
Barcelona	7,728	4,805,927	622
Gerona	5,910	565,304	96
Lérida	12,172	362,206	30
Tarragona	6,303	609,673	97
Extremadura	*41,634*	*1,058,503*	*25*
Badajoz	21,766	654,882	30
Cáceres	19,868	403,621	20
Galicia	*29,575*	*2,695,880*	*91*
Coruña, La	7,951	1,096,027	138
Lugo	9,856	357,648	36
Orense	7,273	338,446	47
Pontevedra	4,495	903,759	201
Madrid	*8,028*	*5,423,384*	*676*
Murcia	*11,314*	*1,197,646*	*106*
Navarra	*10,391*	*555,829*	*53*
Rioja, La	*5,045*	*276,702*	*55*
Valencian Community	*23,255*	*4,162,776*	*175*
Alicante	5,817	1,461,925	251
Castellón	6,632	484,566	73
Valencia	10,806	2,216,285	205
Ceuta[1]	*20*	*71,505*	*3,575*
Melilla[1]	*12*	*66,411*	*5,534*
Total	506,030	40,847,371	81

[1]Ceuta and Melilla gained limited autonomous status in 1994.

The capitals of the autonomous communities are: *Andalusia:* Sevilla (Seville); *Aragón:* Zaragoza (Saragossa); *Asturias:* Oviedo; *Baleares:* Palma de Mallorca; *Basque Country:* Vitoria; *Canary Islands:* dual capitals, Las Palmas and Santa Cruz de Tenerife; *Cantabria:* Santander; *Castilla-La Mancha:* Toledo; *Castilla y León:* Valladolid; *Catalonia:* Barcelona; *Extremadura:* Mérida; *Galicia:* Santiago de Compostela; *Madrid:* Madrid; *Murcia:* Murcia (but regional parliament in Cartagena); *Navarra:* Pamplona; *La Rioja:* Logroño; *Valencian Community:* Valencia.

The capitals of the provinces are the towns from which they take the name, except in the cases of Álava (capital, Vitoria), Guipúzcoa (San Sebastián) and Vizcaya (Bilbao).

The islands which form the Balearics include Majorca, Minorca, Ibiza and Formentera. Those which form the Canary Archipelago are divided into two provinces, under the name of their respective capitals: Santa Cruz de Tenerife and Las Palmas de Gran Canaria. The province of Santa Cruz de Tenerife is constituted by the islands of Tenerife, La Palma, Gomera and Hierro; that of Las Palmas by Gran Canaria, Lanzarote and Fuerteventura, with the small barren islands of Alegranza, Roque del Este, Roque del Oeste, Graciosa, Montaña Clara and Lobos.

Places under Spanish sovereignty in Africa (Alhucemas, Ceuta, Chafarinas, Melilla and Peñón de Vélez) constitute the two provinces of Ceuta and Melilla.

Populations of principal towns in 2001:

Town	Population	Town	Population
Albacete	152,155	Logroño	136,841
Alcalá de Henares	179,602	Lorca	79,481
Alcobendas	95,104	Lugo	89,509
Alcorcón	149,594	Madrid	3,016,788
Algeciras	106,710	Málaga	535,686
Alicante	293,629	Marbella	115,871
Almería	173,338	Mataró	109,298
Avilés	83,511	Móstoles	198,819
Badajoz	136,851	Murcia	377,888
Badalona	210,370	Orense	109,011
Baracaldo	95,515	Oviedo	202,938
Barcelona	1,527,190	Palencia	80,801
Bilbao	353,950	Palma de Mallorca	358,462
Burgos	167,962	Palmas, Las	370,649
Cáceres	84,439	Pamplona	189,364
Cádiz	136,236	Parla	80,545
Cartagena	188,003	Reus	91,616
Castellón de la Plana	153,225	Sabadell	187,201
Córdoba	314,805	Salamanca	156,006
Cornellá de Llobregat	81,881	San Baudilio de	
Coruña, La	242,458	Llobregat	80,041
Coslada	79,862	San Fernando	84,014
Elche	201,731	San Sebastián	181,700
Ferrol, El	79,520	Santa Coloma de	
Fuenlabrada	179,735	Grammanet	115,568
Getafe	153,868	Santa Cruz de Tenerife	217,415
Gijón	270,211	Santander	184,661
Granada	240,522	Santiago de Compostela	93,273
Guecho	84,024	Sevilla	704,114
Hermanas, Dos	103,282	Tarragona	117,184
Hospitalet	244,323	Tarrasa	179,300
Huelva	140,862	Telde	91,160
Jaén	112,921	Torrejón de Ardoz	101,056
Jerez de la Frontera	187,087	Valencia	761,871
Laguna, La	135,004	Valladolid	318,576
Leganés	173,163	Vigo	288,324
León	135,794	Vitoria	221,270
Lérida	115,000	Zaragoza	620,419

Languages

The Constitution states that 'Castilian is the Spanish official language of the State', but also that 'All other Spanish languages will also be official in the corresponding Autonomous Communities'. At the last linguistic census (2001) Catalan (an official EU language since 1990) was spoken in Catalonia by 74·5% of people and understood by 94·5%. It is also spoken in Baleares, Valencian Community (where it is frequently called Valencian), and in Aragón, a narrow strip close to the Catalonian and Valencian Community boundaries. Galician, a language very close to Portuguese, was understood in 1998 by 98·4% of people in Galicia and spoken by 89·2%; Basque by a significant and increasing minority in the Basque Country, and by a small minority in northwest Navarra. It is estimated that one-third of all Spaniards speaks one of the other three official languages as well as standard Castilian. In bilingual communities, both Castilian and the regional language are taught in schools and universities.

SOCIAL STATISTICS

Statistics for calendar years:

	Marriages	Divorces	Births	Deaths
1999	208,129	36,900	380,130	371,102
2000	216,451	38,973	397,632	360,391
2001	208,057	37,586	406,380	360,131
2002	211,522	42,017	418,846	368,618
2003[1]	210,155	—	439,863	383,729

[1]Provisional.

Rate per 1,000 population, 2002: births, 10·1; deaths, 8·9; marriages, 5·1. In 2002 the most popular age range for marrying was 25–29 for both males and females. Annual population growth rate, 1992–2002, 0·4%. Suicide rate (per 100,000 population), 2000: 8·4. Expectation of life, 2003, was 75·9 years for males and 83·2 for females. Infant mortality, 2001, four per 1,000 live births; fertility rate, 2001, 1·1 births per woman (one of the lowest rates in the world). In 2002 Spain received 6,179 asylum applications, equivalent to 0·2 per 1,000 inhabitants.

CLIMATE

Most of Spain has a form of Mediterranean climate with mild, moist winters and hot, dry summers, but the northern coastal region has a moist, equable climate, with rainfall well distributed throughout the year, mild winters and warm summers, and less sunshine than the rest of Spain. The south, in particular Andalusia, is dry and prone to drought.

Madrid, Jan. 41°F (5°C), July 77°F (25°C). Annual rainfall 16·8" (419 mm). Barcelona, Jan. 46°F (8°C), July 74°F (23·5°C). Annual rainfall 21" (525 mm). Cartagena, Jan. 51°F (10·5°C), July 75°F (24°C). Annual rainfall 14·9" (373 mm). La Coruña, Jan. 51°F (10·5°C), July 66°F (19°C). Annual rainfall 32" (800 mm). Sevilla, Jan. 51°F (10·5°C), July 85°F (29·5°C). Annual rainfall 19·5" (486 mm). Palma de Mallorca, Jan. 51°F (11°C), July 77°F (25°C). Annual rainfall 13·6" (347 mm). Santa Cruz de Tenerife, Jan. 64°F (17·9°C), July 76°F (24·4°C). Annual rainfall 7·72" (196 mm).

CONSTITUTION AND GOVERNMENT

Following the death of General Franco in 1975 and the transition to a democracy, the first democratic elections were held on 15 June 1977. A new Constitution was approved by referendum on 6 Dec. 1978, and came into force 29 Dec. 1978. It established a parliamentary monarchy.

The reigning king is **Juan Carlos I**, born 5 Jan. 1938. The eldest son of Don Juan, Conde de Barcelona, Juan Carlos was given precedence over his father as pretender to the Spanish throne in an agreement in 1954 between Don Juan and General Franco. Don Juan, who resigned his claims to the throne in May 1977, died on 1 April 1993. King (then Prince) Juan Carlos married, in 1962, Princess Sophia of Greece, daughter of the late King Paul of the Hellenes and Queen Frederika. *Offspring:* Elena, born 20 Dec. 1963, married 18 March 1995 Jaime de Marichalar (*Offspring:* Felipe, b. 17 July 1998; Victoria, b. 9 Sept. 2000); Cristina, born 13 June 1965, married 4 Oct. 1997 Iñaki Urdangarín (*Offspring:* Juan, b. 29 Sept. 1999; Pablo, b. 6 Dec. 2000; Miguel, b. 30 Apr. 2002; Irene, b. 5 June 2005); Felipe, Prince of Asturias, heir to the throne, born 30 Jan. 1968, married 22 May 2004 Letizia Ortiz Rocasolano (*Offspring:* Leonor, b. 8 Nov. 2005).

The King receives an allowance, part of which is taxable, approved by parliament each year. In 2005 this was €7·8m. There is no formal court; the (private) *Diputación de la Grandeza* represents the interests of the aristocracy.

Legislative power is vested in the *Cortes Generales*, a bicameral parliament composed of the Congress of Deputies (lower house) and the Senate (upper house). The *Congress of Deputies* has not less than 300 nor more than 400 members (350 in the general election of 2004) elected in a proportional system under which electors choose between party lists of candidates in multi-member constituencies.

The *Senate* has 259 members of whom 208 are elected by a majority system: the 47 mainland provinces elect four senators each, regardless of population; the larger islands (Gran Canaria, Mallorca and Tenerife) elect three senators and each of the smaller islands or groups of islands (Ibiza-Formentera, Minorca, Fuerteventura, Gomera, Hierro, Lanzarote and La Palma) elect one senator. To these each self-governing community appoints one senator, and an additional senator for every million inhabitants in their respective territories. Currently 51 senators are appointed by the self-governing communities. Deputies and senators are elected by universal secret suffrage for four-year terms. The Prime Minister is elected by the Congress of Deputies.

The *Constitutional Court* is empowered to solve conflicts between the State and the Autonomous Communities; to determine if legislation passed by the Cortes is contrary to the Constitution; and to protect the constitutional rights of individuals violated by any authority. Its 12 members are appointed by the monarch. It has a nine-year term, with a third of the membership being renewed every three years.

National Anthem
'Marcha Real' ('Royal March'); no words, tune anonymous.

GOVERNMENT CHRONOLOGY

Heads of government since 1939. (PP = Popular Party; PSOE = Spanish Socialist Workers' Party; UCD = Central Democratic Union)

1939–73	military	Francisco Franco
1973	military	Luis Carrero
1973–76	civilian	Carlos Arias Navarro
1976	military	Fernando de Santiago
1976–81	UCD	Adolfo Suárez
1981–82	UCD	Leopoldo Calvo-Sotelo
1982–96	PSOE	Felipe González
1996–2004	PP	José María Aznar
2004–	PSOE	José Luis Rodríguez Zapatero

RECENT ELECTIONS

A general election took place on 14 March 2004. Turnout was 77·2%. In the *Congress of Deputies* the Spanish Socialist Workers' Party (PSOE) won 164 seats with 42·6% of votes cast; the Popular Party (PP), 148 with 37·6%; Convergence and Union (CiU; Catalan nationalists), 10 with 3·2%; the Catalan separatist Republican Left of Catalunya (ERC), 8 with 2·5%; Basque Nationalist Party (PNV), 7 with 1·6%; the Communist-led United Left Coalition (IU), 5 with 5·0%; Canarian Coalition (CC), 3 with 0·9%; Galician Nationalist Bloc (BNG), 2 with 0·8%; the Aragonese Junta, 1 with 0·4%; the non-radical separatist Basque Solidarity Party (EA), 1 with 0·3%; Navarra Yes, 1 with 0·2%. The Andalusian Party (PA) won no seats with 0·7%. In the *Senate*, the PP won 102 seats; PSOE, 81; Entesa Catalana de Progrés, 12; CiU, 4; PNV, 4; CC, 3.

European Parliament
Spain has 54 (64 in 1999) representatives. At the June 2004 elections turnout was 45·9% (64·3% in 1999). The PSOE (political affiliation in European Parliament: Party of European Socialists) won 24 seats and the Greens (Greens/European Free Alliance) 1 seat, with a combined 43·3% of votes cast; the PP, 23 with 41·3% (European People's Party–European Democrats); Galeuzca (a coalition of the PNV, BNG and the Democratic Convergence of Catalunya), 3 with 5·2% (PNV and the Democratic Convergence of Catalunya have affiliated themselves with the Alliance of Liberals and Democrats for Europe and BNG with Greens/European Free Alliance); the IU (a coalition of United Left Coalition and Initiative for Catalonia-Greens, 2 with 4·2% (one European Unitary Left/Nordic Green Left; one Greens/European Free Alliance); Europa de los Pueblos, 1 with 2·5% (Greens/European Free Alliance).

CURRENT ADMINISTRATION

In April 2006 the government comprised:
President of the Council and Prime Minister: José Luis Rodríguez Zapatero; b. 1960 (PSOE; elected 14 March 2004 and sworn in 17 April 2004).
First Vice-President and Minister for the Presidency: María Teresa Fernandez de la Vega. *Second Vice-President and Minister*

for the Economy: Pedro Solbes. *Foreign Affairs and Co-operation:* Miguel Ángel Moratinos. *Justice:* Juan Fernando López Aguilar. *Interior:* Alfredo Pérez Rubalcaba. *Defence:* José Antonio Alonso. *Education and Science:* Mercedes Cabrera. *Labour, Social Affairs and Immigration:* Jesús Caldera. *Agriculture and Fisheries:* Elena Espinosa. *Public Administration:* Jordi Sevilla. *Health and Consumer Affairs:* Elena Salgado. *Environment:* Cristina Narbona. *Development:* Magdalena Álvarez. *Industry, Commerce and Tourism:* José Montilla. *Culture:* Carmen Calvo. *Housing:* María Antonia Trujillo.

Government Website: http://www.la-moncloa.es

CURRENT LEADERS

José Luis Rodríguez Zapatero

Position
Prime Minister

Introduction
José Luis Rodríguez Zapatero, leader of the Spanish Socialist Workers' Party (PSOE; Partido Socialista Obrero Español), became prime minister in March 2004 when his party unexpectedly defeated the Popular Party (PP) in the aftermath of the terrorist attack that month on Madrid. Since taking office, he has announced the withdrawal of Spanish troops from Iraq and called for greater international co-operation against terrorism.

Early Life
Rodríguez Zapatero (known as Zapatero) was born on 4 Aug. 1960 in Valladolid. He studied law at the Universidad de León before embarking on a career in politics. From a traditionally left-wing family, Zapatero was strongly influenced by his grandfather, a republican captain executed by nationalists in 1936 at the beginning of the Spanish Civil War. In 1977, before the first post-Franco democratic elections, Zapatero attended a socialist political rally in Gijón. He was inspired by former PSOE leader Felipe González Márquez and in 1978 he joined the PSOE as a youth member. Four years later he became the PSOE youth leader in his home region of León. In 1986 he was elected to parliament representing León, becoming the youngest member of the *Cortes* at that time. His party standing was further enhanced in 1988 when he became the regional leader of the León PSOE.

In 1996 the PSOE's 14-year domination ended with the election of José María Aznar. The following year González resigned as PSOE leader amid corruption charges and the revelation of his government's brutal treatment of captured Basque terrorists, for which two of his former ministers were imprisoned. During the following three years the party floundered under the leadership of Joaquín Almunia, who resigned in March 2000 following a humiliating election defeat. Zapatero then became one of four candidates for the party leadership, along with the better-known members José Bono, Matilde Fernández and Rosa Diez. At the 35th PSOE party conference, Zapatero won a surprise victory with 41·8%, narrowly defeating Bono's 40·8%.

On election Zapatero set out his plans for the rejuvenation of the flagging PSOE. He changed the party's executive committee, installing many young politicians in a bid to revitalize the party's image. Zapatero's ambition was to create an effective opposition to Aznar and present himself as a strong candidate for prime minister. His *Nueva Vía* (New Way) represented a shift from the traditions of socialism to more centrist politics, with echoes of Tony Blair's New Labour ideology in British politics. This move reduced the ideological distance between the ruling and opposition leaders, Aznar having abandoned traditional right-wing politics for a more moderate, centrist stance.

On 11 March 2004 Madrid's rail network was hit by terrorist bombings that killed 191 people. Aznar's government blamed

ETA in the immediate aftermath, but evidence soon pointed to a link with North Africa. At the general election three days later, the PP suffered a backlash of voter hostility and were unexpectedly defeated by the PSOE. Zapatero was sworn in as prime minister on 17 April 2004.

Career in Office
Although lacking an absolute majority, Zapatero declined to form a coalition, saying that he would govern through consensus with other groups. Reiterating his opposition to the war in Iraq and criticizing the failure of US-led forces to install a workable post-war structure, he announced that Spanish troops would be withdrawn from Iraq by the end of May 2004. At the same time, he increased Spain's military commitment to the UN-led force in Afghanistan and called for increased international co-operation to counter terrorism. His domestic agenda included an expected increase in welfare spending and promised reform of the tax system. Observers believed he would be more sympathetic than his predecessor to regions with large nationalist movements.

In Feb. 2005 a car bomb exploded in Madrid, injuring about 40 people. Although ETA was thought to be responsible, the Zapatero government offered peace talks the following May if the organization would disarm. Also in Feb. the Spanish electorate endorsed the European Union's proposed new constitution treaty in a referendum. In June 2005 parliament defied the Roman Catholic Church by legalizing gay marriage and granting homosexual couples adoption and inheritance rights.

DEFENCE
Conscription was abolished in 2001. The government had begun the phased abolition of conscription in 1996. In 2002 the armed forces became fully professional. However, a shortfall in recruitment in Spain has meant that descendants of Spanish migrants, many of whom have never been to Europe, are now joining. Since 1989 women have been accepted in all sections of the armed forces.

In 2003 defence expenditure totalled US$9,944m. (US$242 per capita), representing 1·2% of GDP.

Army
A Rapid Reaction Force is formed from the Spanish Legion and the airborne and air-portable brigades. There is also an Army Aviation Brigade consisting of 153 helicopters (28 attack).

Strength (2004) 95,600. In 2002, 4,450 were stationed on the Balearic Islands, 8,600 on the Canary Islands and 8,100 in Ceuta and Melilla. There were 265,000 army reservists in 2004.

Guardia Civil
The paramilitary *Guardia Civil* numbers 72,600.

Navy
The principal ship of the Navy is the *Príncipe de Asturias*, a light vertical/short take-off and landing aircraft carrier. Her air group includes AV-8S Matador (Harrier) combat aircraft. There are also eight French-designed submarines and 16 frigates.

The Naval Air Service operates 17 combat aircraft and 37 armed helicopters. Personnel numbered 700 in 2004. There are 5,600 marines.

Main naval bases are at Ferrol, Rota, Cádiz, Cartagena, Palma de Mallorca, Mahón and Las Palmas (Canary Islands).

In 2004 personnel totalled 22,900 including the marines and naval air arm. There were 18,500 naval reservists in 2004.

Air Force
The Air Force is organized as an independent service, dating from 1939. It is administered through four operational commands. These are geographically oriented following a reorganization in 1991 and comprise Central Air Command, Strait Air Command, Eastern Air Command and Air Command of the Canaries.

There were 177 combat aircraft in 2004 including 91 EF/A-18s, 23 F-5Bs and 52 Mirage F-1s.

Strength (2004) 22,750. There were 45,000 air force reservists in 2004.

INTERNATIONAL RELATIONS
Spain is a member of the UN, WTO, BIS, the Council of Europe, NATO, OECD, WEU, the EU, OSCE, CERN, Inter-American Development Bank, Asian Development Bank and the Antarctic Treaty, and is a signatory to the Schengen accord, which abolishes border controls between Spain, Austria, Belgium, Denmark, Finland, France, Germany, Greece, Iceland, Italy, Luxembourg, the Netherlands, Norway, Portugal and Sweden.

On 20 Feb. 2005 Spain became the first European Union member to approve the proposed EU constitution through a referendum, with 76·7% of votes cast in favour and 17·2% against, although turn-out was only 42·3%. The constitution was ratified by Parliament on 28 April 2005 with 311 votes to 19 and by the Senate on 18 May 2005 with 225 votes to six.

ECONOMY
Agriculture accounted for 3·4% of GDP in 2002, industry 30·1% and services 66·5%.

Overview
Spain made significant economic strides in the 1980s when productivity growth was at its highest. After difficulties during the Europe-wide recession of the early 1990s Spain's macroeconomic performance has been strong. Structural reforms and sound macroeconomic policies have helped to encourage growth and employment creation since the late 1990s. Fiscal policy was tightened over the years bringing annual budget deficits down from over 6% of GDP in the mid 1990s to near balance since 2001. Despite a global economic slowdown, growth in 2002 was more than one percent greater than the euro zone average. Average incomes in Spain remain below the Western European average but have converged significantly.

The service sector share of total Spanish GDP has grown significantly over the years largely at the expense of the agriculture, forestry and fishery sector. Banking, retailing, telecommunications and tourism are the main components of the service sector. Strong demand for tourist-related buildings, foreign demand for property and high levels of investment in infrastructure have combined to make the construction sector a large part of total GDP (9·1% in 2001). Agriculture is concentrated on wine, olive oil, fruit and vegetables. Thanks to its climate the southeast region is one of the most competitive suppliers of fresh produce to European markets. Spain's fishing fleet and related industry are highly developed as a result of the country's maritime location and high domestic consumption of fish. Vehicle production for export is Spain's most prominent manufacturing industry, accounting for roughly 5% of GDP. The country has become a leading car manufacturer in Europe, exporting roughly four out of five vehicles produced. Several Spanish companies have been actively expanding abroad via acquisitions. Spanish banks are particularly competitive on the international scene.

Despite solid recent growth, there are areas of concern. The Spanish real-estate market is widely held to be over-valued, creating the risk of macroeconomic instability. Unemployment has been reduced from over 20% in 1997 to below 10% but remains above the EU average and female participation is low. Inflation has also remained roughly 1% above the euro zone average. The OECD warns that the continuation of this inflation trend could undermine Spanish competitiveness. Productivity growth has been negative since 1999 according to the Economist Intelligence Unit, averaging –0·7% annually. In order to raise productivity, lower inflation and cut unemployment, the OECD recommends reforming the education system, enhancing competition in several sheltered sectors and removing rigidities in labour, goods and services markets. Despite progress, research and development (R&D) activities are low by Western European standards. The OECD suggests fostering private R&D spending by improving framework conditions and sharpening incentives in the education system by giving schools greater autonomy, linking university financing to performance and raising university fees.

Currency

On 1 Jan. 1999 the euro (EUR) became the legal currency in Spain; irrevocable conversion rate 166·386 pesetas to 1 euro. The euro, which consists of 100 cents, has been in circulation since 1 Jan. 2002. There are seven euro notes in different colours and sizes denominated in 500, 200, 100, 50, 20, 10 and 5 euros, and eight coins denominated in 2 and 1 euros, then 50, 20, 10, 5, 2 and 1 cents. On the introduction of the euro there was a 'dual circulation' period before the peseta ceased to be legal tender on 28 Feb. 2002. Euro banknotes in circulation on 1 Jan. 2002 had a total value of €68·6bn.

Foreign exchange reserves were US$28,939m. in June 2002 (US$65,773m. in Feb. 1998) and gold reserves 16·83m. troy oz. Inflation rates (based on OECD statistics):

1995	1996	1997	1998	1999	2000	2001	2002	2003	2004
4·6%	3·6%	1·9%	1·8%	2·2%	3·5%	2·8%	3·6%	3·1%	3·1%

The inflation rate in 2005 according to the Bank of Spain was 3·4%. Total money supply was €34,255m. in June 2002.

Budget

In 2001 revenues totalled €212,571m. (€197,510m. in 2000) and expenditures €209,402m. (€199,791m. in 2000). Principal sources of revenue in 2001: social security contributions, €81,985m.; taxes on income, profits and capital gains, €54,829m.; taxes on goods and services, €49,737m. Main items of expenditure in 2001: social protection, €83,052m.; general public services, €60,492m.; health, €32,308m.

VAT is normally 16%, with a rate of 7% on certain services (catering and hospitality), and 4% on basic foodstuffs.

Performance

Real GDP growth rates (based on OECD statistics):

1995	1996	1997	1998	1999	2000	2001	2002	2003	2004
2·8%	2·4%	3·9%	4·5%	4·7%	5·0%	3·5%	2·7%	3·0%	3·1%

The real GDP growth rate in 2005 according to the Bank of Spain was 3·4%. Total GDP (2004): US$991·4bn.

The OECD reported in April 2005: 'For a decade now, Spain's performance has been remarkable.…Fiscal consolidation, the fall in interest rates due to the introduction of the single currency, structural reforms pursued since the mid-1990s and a surge in immigration have created a virtuous circle of rapidly rising activity sustained by strong job creation.…[However] unemployment is still widespread; productivity gains remain meagre; inflation is relatively high, eroding international competitiveness; and the surge in house prices is a cause for concern. Against this background, it will be important to tackle the impediments to the continued dynamism of the Spanish economy by accelerating the pace of structural reform.'

Banking and Finance

The central bank is the Bank of Spain (*Governor*, Jaime Caruana) which gained autonomy under an ordinance of 1994. Its Governor is appointed for a six-year term. The Banking Corporation of Spain, *Argentaria*, groups together the shares of all state-owned banks, and competes in the financial market with private banks. In 1993 the government sold 49·9% of the capital of Argentaria; the remainder in two flotations ending on 13 Feb. 1998.

Spanish banking is dominated by two main banks—BSCH (Banco Santander Central Hispano) and BBVA (Banco Bilbao Vizcaya Argentaria). BSCH had assets of €335·5bn in Sept. 2002 and BBVA assets of €309·2bn. in March 2003.

There are stock exchanges in Madrid, Barcelona, Bilbao and Valencia.

ENERGY AND NATURAL RESOURCES

Environment

In 2002 Spain's carbon dioxide emissions from the consumption and flaring of fossil fuels were the equivalent of 8·3 tonnes per capita.

Electricity

Installed capacity was 60·4m. kW in 2002. The total electricity output in 2002 amounted to an estimated 246·05bn. kWh, of which 26% was nuclear, 11% hydro-electric and 63% other (carbon, natural gas, petroleum). Consumption per capita in 2001 was 5,970 kWh.

In Oct. 2000 Endesa SA and Iberdrola SA, the country's two largest electricity companies, announced merger plans. The new company would have been in charge of 80% of Spain's electricity output. However, in Feb. 2001 the two companies shelved the proposed merger. In 2003 there were nine nuclear reactors in operation.

Oil and Gas

Spain is heavily dependent on imported oil; Mexico is its largest supplier. Crude oil production (2000), 227,000 tonnes.

The government sold its remaining stake in the oil, gas and chemicals group Repsol in 1997. Natural gas production (2001) totalled 509m. cu. metres. Ever increasing consumption means that Spain has to import large quantities of natural gas, primarily from Algeria.

Wind

Spain is one of the world's largest wind-power producers, with 7,814 turbines and an installed capacity of 4,635 MW at the end of 2002.

Minerals

Coal production (2000), 11·32m. tonnes; other principal minerals (in 1,000 tonnes): lignite (2002), 12,282; gypsum and anhydrite (2001), 7,500; anthracite (2001), 4,694; salt (2000), 3,869; potash (2001), 570; aluminium (2001), 376; zinc (2001), 184; pyrites (2001), 152; fluorspar (2001), 134; lead (2001), 49. In 1995 a large mercury deposit was found in southern Spain which could raise mercury levels to within a quarter of proven world reserves. Gold production, 2001, 3,300 kg; silver production, 2000, 66,000 kg.

Agriculture

There were 1,287,000 farms in Spain in 2000. Agriculture employed about 5·9% of the workforce in 2002. It accounts for 15·8% of exports and 15·6% of imports.

There were 13·02m. ha. of arable land in 2001 and 4·93m. ha. of permanent crops. In 2002 there were 914,000 tractors and 52,000 harvester-threshers; in 2001 there were 132,000 milking machines in use.

Principal crops	Area (in 1,000 ha.)			Yield (in 1,000 tonnes)		
	2000	2001	2002	2000	2001	2002
Barley	3,278	2,992	3,100	11,063	6,249	8,333
Sugarbeets	125	107	115	7,930	6,755	8,040
Wheat	2,353	2,177	2,402	7,294	5,008	6,783
Maize	433	513	463	3,992	4,982	4,463
Potatoes	119	115	114	3,078	2,992	3,104
Oats	432	446	473	954	665	916
Rice	117	116	113	827	876	815
Sunflower seeds	839	858	754	919	871	757

Spain has more land dedicated to the grape than any other country in the world and is ranked third among wine producers (behind Italy and France). Production of wine (2001), 30,951,000 hectolitres; of grapes, 5,272,000 tonnes.

The area planted with tomatoes in 2002 was 60,000 ha., yielding 3,878,000 tonnes; with onions, 23,000 ha., yielding 992,000 tonnes; peppers, 23,000 ha., yielding 980,000 tonnes.

Fruit production (2002, in tonnes): oranges, 2,867,000; tangerines, 1,952,000; peaches, 1,247,000; lemons, 920,000; apples, 653,000; pears, 603,000.

Production of olives, 2001–02, 6,983,000 tonnes; olive oil, 1,422,000 tonnes. Spain is the world's leading producer both of olives and olive oil.

Livestock (2000): cattle, 6·20m.; sheep, 23·70m.; goats, 2·87m.; pigs, 23·68m.; chickens, 128·0m.; asses and mules, 0·26m.; horses, 0·25m. Livestock products (2000, in 1,000 tonnes): pork, bacon and ham, 2,962; beef and veal, 697; mutton and lamb, 222; poultry meat, 891; milk, 6,526; cheese, 175; eggs, 522.

Forestry

In 2000 the area under forests was 14·37m. ha., or 28·8% of the total land area. In 2003 timber production was 16·11m. cu. metres.

Fisheries

Spain is the second largest fishing country in the EU after Denmark; it is also the EU's leading importer of fishery commodities. Fishing vessels had a total tonnage of 519,867 tonnes in 2002, the highest in the EU (596,441 GRT in 1994); fleets have been gradually reduced from 20,558 boats in 1991 to 14,887 in 2002. Total catch in 2003 amounted to 896,317 tonnes, almost exclusively sea fish.

INDUSTRY

The leading companies by market capitalization in Spain in Nov. 2005 were: Banco Santander Central Hispano (BSCH), US$79·6bn.; Telefónica SA (US$76·3bn.); Banco Bilbao Vizcaya Argentaria S.A. (BBVA), US$60·0bn.

Industrial products, 2002 (in tonnes): cement (2000), 38·2m.; distillate fuel oil, 20·8m.; crude steel, 16·4m.; residual fuel oil, 12·1m.; petrol, 8·9m.; paper and paperboard, 5·4m.; plastics (1999), 4·1m.; pig iron, 4·0m.; jet fuels, 3·6m.; sulphuric acid (1999), 3·3m.; nitrogenous fertilizers (2000), 951,000; cigarettes (2001), 74·8bn. units.

The number of vehicles manufactured in 2002 was 2,855,000. 2·15m. refrigerators were manufactured in 2000, 2·7m. washing machines in 2002 and 4·2m. TV sets in 2002. In 2001, 4,730·5m. litres of soft drinks, 4,072·3m. litres of mineral water and 2,680·2m. litres of beer were produced.

Labour

The economically active population numbered 15,945,600 in 2001, with the principal areas of activity as follows: manufacturing, 3,005,600; wholesale and retail trade/repair of motor vehicles, motorcycles and personal and household goods, 2,555,900; construction, 1,850,200; real estate, renting and business activities, 1,238,300; public administration and defence/ compulsory social security, 1,008,100. The monthly minimum wage for adults (2004) was €460·50. The average working week in 2003 was 35·4 hours. The retirement age is 65 years. In 2004 part-time work accounted for less than 9% of all employment in Spain—the lowest percentage in western Europe.

Spain's unemployment rate reached a peak of nearly 25% in 1994 but has been steadily declining in recent years and in Dec. 2005 was 8·5%. The unemployment rate among women is double that among men. Between 1996 and early 2000 Spain created as many new jobs as were created in the rest of the EU put together. In spite of the high unemployment rate, by 2000 there were labour shortages in agriculture and construction, as a result of which the government reached an agreement with Morocco to import temporary contract labour.

Between 1993 and 2002 strikes cost Spain an average of 248 days per 1,000 employees a year, compared to the EU average of 64 per 1,000. Spain's figure was the highest in the EU.

Trade Unions

The Constitution guarantees the establishment and activities of trade unions provided they have a democratic structure. The most important trade unions are *Comisiones Obreras* (CO), with 790,000 members in 1997, and *Unión General de Trabajadores* (UGT), which had 775,000 members in 1997.

INTERNATIONAL TRADE

Imports and Exports
Trade in US$1m.:

	2000	2001	2002	2003	2004
Imports f.o.b.	152,856	152,039	161,794	203,203	249,984
Exports f.o.b.	115,769	117,522	127,161	158,047	184,154

In 2004 chemicals, manufactured goods classified chiefly by material and miscellaneous manufactured articles accounted for 41·7% of imports and 43·4% of exports; machinery and transport equipment 37·7% of imports and 40·3% of exports; food, live animals, beverages and tobacco 8·4% of imports and 12·2% of exports; mineral fuels, lubricants and related materials 8·8% of imports and 1·1% of exports; and crude materials, inedible, animal and vegetable oil and fats 3·4% of imports and 3·0% of exports.

Leading import sources in 2004 were Germany (16·1%), France (15·2%), Italy (9·1%), United Kingdom (6·1%), the Netherlands (4·1%); leading export markets in 2004 were: France (19·3%), Germany (11·7%), Portugal (9·4%), Italy (9·0%), United Kingdom (9·0%). In 2004 the EU accounted for 62·2% of Spain's imports and 70·0% of exports.

COMMUNICATIONS

Roads
In 2001 the total length of roads was 664,852 km; the network included 11,152 km of motorways, 24,458 km of highways/national roads and 139,341 km of secondary roads. 99% of all roads in Spain were paved in 2001. In 2001 private road transport totalled 359,667m. passenger-km and public road transport 51,712m. passenger-km; freight transport totalled 114,011m. tonne-km in 2001. Number of cars (2001), 18,150,880; trucks and vans, 3,949,001; buses, 56,146; motorcycles and mopeds, 3,291,200. In 2002, 5,347 persons were killed in road accidents.

Rail
The total length of the state railways in 2000 was 13,868 km, mostly broad (1,668-mm) gauge (7,525 km electrified). State railways are run by the National Spanish Railway Network (RENFE). There is a high-speed standard-gauge (1,435-mm) railway from Madrid to Sevilla, opened in 1992. The line has been extended northwards from Madrid to Lérida, with passenger services beginning in Oct. 2003. Passenger-km travelled in 2000 came to 19·9bn. and freight tonne-km to 12·1bn. There are metros in Madrid (228 km), Valencia (118 km), Barcelona (102 km) and Bilbao (36 km). In 2003 the construction of two 40 km-long rail tunnels under the Straits of Gibraltar was agreed with Morocco with an estimated cost of US$30m.

Civil Aviation
There are international airports at Madrid (Barajas), Barcelona (Prat del Llobregat), Alicante, Almería, Bilbao, Gerona, Las Palmas de Gran Canaria, Ibiza, Lanzarote, Málaga, Palma de Mallorca, Santiago de Compostela, Sevilla, Tenerife (Los Rodeos and Reina Sofía), Valencia, Valladolid and Zaragoza. There are 43 airports open to civil traffic. A small airport in Seo de Urgel operates in Andorra. The national carrier is Iberia Airlines. Iberia Airlines, which was 99·8% state-owned, went through the first stage of privatization in 1999 before the second phase was indefinitely postponed in Nov. 1999. Of other airlines, the largest are Air Europa and Spanair. Services are also provided by about

70 foreign airlines. In 1999 Iberia flew 258·8m. km, carrying 22,203,700 passengers (8,447,600 on international flights). Madrid was the busiest airport in 2001, handling 33,777,862 passengers (16,718,209 on domestic flights) and 294,692 tonnes of freight. Barcelona was the second busiest in 2001, with 20,545,680 (10,075,536 on domestic flights) and 76,966 tonnes of freight. Palma de Mallorca was the third busiest for passengers, with 19,122,832 (14,317,984 on international flights). Las Palmas was the third busiest for freight, with 40,615 tonnes in 2001.

Shipping
In 2000 the merchant fleet comprised 1,554 vessels (of 100 gross tons or more) totalling 2·03m. GRT (including oil tankers 600,000 GRT); shipyards launched 363,910 CGT in 2001. In 2001 vessels totalling 198,696,000 NRT entered ports and vessels totalling 59,267,000 NRT cleared. The leading ports are Algeciras-La Linea (51,251,000 tonnes of cargo in 2002), Barcelona, Bilbao, Ceuta, Las Palmas, Santa Cruz de Tenerife, Tarragona and Valencia.

Telecommunications
In 2002 there were 52,180,600 telephone subscribers (1,282·6 per 1,000 persons) and 7,972,000 PCs were in use (196·0 per 1,000 persons). The government disposed of its remaining 21% stake in Telefónica in Feb. 1997, bringing 1·4m. shareholders into the company's equity base. A second operator, Retevisión, accounts for 3% of the domestic market, which was wholly deregulated in 1998. The mobile phone business was deregulated in 1995; the market is shared by Telefónica (with a 56% share of the market), Airtel and Amena (Retevisión).

Spain had 33,531,000 mobile phone subscribers in 2002 (824 for every 1,000 persons). There were 7·89m. Internet users in May 2002. In 2002 fax machines numbered 1·18m.

Postal Services
In 2003 there were 3,343 post offices; a total of 5,630m. pieces of mail were processed during the year, or 137 items per person.

SOCIAL INSTITUTIONS

Justice
Justice is administered by Tribunals and Courts, which jointly form the Judicial Power. Judges and magistrates cannot be removed, suspended or transferred except as set forth by law. The Constitution of 1978 established the *General Council of the Judicial Power*, consisting of a President and 20 magistrates, judges, attorneys and lawyers, governing the Judicial Power in full independence from the state's legislative and executive organs. Its members are appointed by the *Cortes Generales*. Its President is that of the Supreme Court (*Tribunal Supremo*), who is appointed by the monarch on the proposal of the General Council of the Judicial.

The Judicature is composed of the Supreme Court; 17 Higher Courts of Justice, one for each autonomous community; 52 Provincial High Courts; Courts of First Instance; Courts of Judicial Proceedings, not passing sentences; and Penal Courts, passing sentences.

The Supreme Court consists of a President, and various judges distributed among seven chambers: one for civil matters, three for administrative purposes, one for criminal trials, one for social matters and one for military cases. The Supreme Court has disciplinary faculties; is court of appeal in all criminal trials; for administrative purposes decides in first and second instance disputes arising between private individuals and the State; and in social matters makes final decisions.

A new penal code came into force in May 1996, replacing the code of 1848. It provides for a maximum of 30 years imprisonment in specified exceptional cases, with a normal maximum of 20 years. Sanctions with a rehabilitative intent include fines adjusted to means, community service and weekend imprisonment. The death penalty was abolished by the 1978 Constitution. The prison

population in Nov. 2003 was 56,140 (138 per 100,000 of national population); 102,031 criminal sentences were passed in 2002. A jury system commenced operating in Nov. 1995 in criminal cases (first trials in May 1996). Juries consist of nine members.

A juvenile criminal law of 1995 lays emphasis on rehabilitation. It raised the age of responsibility from 12 to 14 years. Criminal conduct on the part of children under 14 is a matter for legal protection and custody. 14- and 15-year-olds are classified as 'minors'; 16- and 17-year-olds as 'young persons'; and the legal majority for criminal offences is set at 18 years. Persons up to the age of 21 may, at the courts' discretion, be dealt with as juveniles.

The *Audiencia Nacional* deals with terrorism, monetary offences and drug-trafficking where more than one province is involved. Its president is appointed by the General Council of the Judicial Power.

There is an Ombudsman (*Defensor del Pueblo*), who is elected for a five-year term (currently Enrique Múgica Herzog; b. 1932).

Education
In 1991 the General Regulation of the Educational System Act came into force. This Act gradually extends the school-leaving age to 16 years and determines the following levels of education: infants (3–5 years of age), primary (6–11), secondary (12–15) and baccalaureate or vocational and technical (16–17). Primary and secondary levels of education are now compulsory and free. Religious instruction is optional.

In Sept. 1997 a joint declaration with trade unions, parents' and schools' associations was signed in support of a new finance law guaranteeing that spending on education will reach 6% of GDP within five years, thus protecting it from changes in the political sphere. In 2004 total expenditure on education came to 5·4% of GNP.

A new compulsory secondary education programme has replaced the Basic General Education programme which was in force since 1970. In addition, university entrance exams underwent reform in 1997, resulting in greater emphasis now being placed on the teaching of Humanities at secondary level.

In 2004–05 pre-primary education (under six years) was undertaken by 1,419,307 pupils; primary or basic education (6–14 years): 2,494,598 pupils. In 200–01 there were 75,040 teachers in pre-primary and 175,135 teachers in primary schools. Secondary education (14–17 years), including high schools and technical schools, was conducted at 6,276 schools, with 3,054,263 pupils and 167,182 teachers in 2004–05.

In 2003 there were 71 universities: 50 public state universities and 21 private universities (including Catholic establishments). In 2004–05 there were 1,330,574 students at state universities; 132,197 at private universities.

The adult literacy rate is at least 99%.

Health
In 2003 there were 190,665 doctors, 56,501 pharmacists and 220,769 nurses (including 6,764 midwives). There were 17,538 dentists in 2000. Number of hospitals (2001), 767, with 146,367 beds. In 2003 Spain spent 7·7% of its GDP on health.

Welfare
The social security budget was €82,425,871,000 in 2004, including €66·1bn. for pensions, €5·3bn. for temporary incapacity, €1·4bn. for health and €620m. for social services. The minimum pension in 2001 was the equivalent of just over €5,000 per year, made in 14 payments.

In 2003 the system of contributions to the social security and employment scheme was: for pensions, sickness, invalidity, maternity and children, a contribution of 28·3% of the basic wage (23·6% paid by the employer, 4·7% by the employee); for unemployment benefit, a contribution of 7·55% (6·0% paid by the employer, 1·55% by the employee). There are also minor contributions for a Fund of Guaranteed Salaries, working accidents and professional sicknesses, and for vocational training.

RELIGION

There is no official religion. Roman Catholicism is the religion of the majority. In May 2005 there were eight cardinals. There are 11 metropolitan sees and 52 suffragan sees, the chief being Toledo, where the Primate resides. The archdioceses of Madrid-Alcalá and Barcelona depend directly from the Vatican. There are about 0·25m. other Christians, including several Protestant denominations, about 60,000 Jehovah's Witnesses and 29,000 Latter-day Saints (Mormons), and 0·45m. Muslims, including Spanish Muslims in Ceuta and Melilla. The first synagogue since the expulsion of the Jews in 1492 was opened in Madrid on 2 Oct. 1959. The number of people of Judaist faith is estimated at about 15,000.

CULTURE

World Heritage Sites

There are 37 sites under Spanish jurisdiction that appear on the UNESCO World Heritage List. They are (with year entered on list): Parque Güell, Palacio Güell and Casa Mila in Barcelona (1984), Burgos Cathedral (1984), Historic Centre of Córdoba (1984), Alhambra, Generalife and Albayzin, Granada (1984), Monastery and site of the Escurial, Madrid (1984), Altamira Cave (1985), Old Town of Segovia and its Aqueduct (1985), Monuments of Oviedo and the Kingdom of the Asturias (1985), Santiago de Compostela (Old Town) (1985), Old Town of Ávila, with its Extra-Muros churches (1985), Mudejar Architecture of Teruel (1986), Historic City of Toledo (1986), Garajonay National Park (1986), Old Town of Cáceres (1986), Cathedral, Alcazar and Archivo de Indias in Sevilla (1987), Old City of Salamanca (1988), Poblet Monastery (1991), Archaeological Ensemble of Mérida (1993), Royal Monastery of Santa Maria de Guadalupe (1993), Route of Santiago de Compostela (1993), Doñana National Park (1994), Historic Walled Town of Cuenca (1996), La Lonja de la Seda de Valencia (1996), Las Médulas (1997), the Palau de la Música Catalana and the Hospital de Sant Pau, Barcelona (1997), San Millán Yuso and Suso Monasteries (1997), University and Historic Precinct of Alcalá de Henares (1998), Rock-Art of the Mediterranean Basin on the Iberian Peninsula (1998), Ibiza, Biodiversity and Culture (1999), San Cristóbal de La Laguna (1999), the Archaeological Ensemble of Tarraco (2000), The Palmeral of Elche (2000), the Roman Walls of Lugo (2000), Catalan Romanesque Churches of the Vall de Boí (2000), Archaeological Site of Atapuerca (2000), Ubeda-Baeza: Urban duality, cultural unity (2003), and for France and Spain: Pyrénées—Mount Perdu (1997).

Broadcasting

Radio Nacional de España broadcasts five programmes on medium-wave and FM, as well as many regional programmes; it has one commercial programme.

The most successful domestic network is that of an independent, Cadena SER (*Sociedad Española de Radiodifusión*); *Cadena de Ondas Populares Españolas* (COPE) is owned by the Roman Catholic church. Two independent radio networks cover the whole of Spain. They are *Antena 3* and *Radio 80* (taken over by SER in 1992). *Radio Exterior* broadcasts abroad.

Televisión Española broadcasts two channels (TVE1 and TVE2) and also has an international channel. There are three nationwide commercial TV networks: *Antena 3*, *Tele 5* and the pay-TV channel *Canal Plus*, which had 1·4m. subscribers in 1997. There were in 1999 the following regional TV networks: *TV3* (launched in 1983) and *Canal 33* (1989), both broadcasting in Catalan; *ETB1* (1983) and *ETB2* (1987), both broadcasting in

Basque—*ETB1* exclusively so and *ETB2* partly so, but additionally with much output in Castilian; *Televisión de Galicia* (1985), in Galician; *TM3* (1989), in Castilian, for the area of Madrid; *Canal 9* (1989), mostly in Valencian (Catalan); and *Tele-Sur* (1989), in Castilian, for Andalusia. There are two digital TV channels, *Vía Digital* and *Canal Satélite Digital*, both launched in 1997. Colour transmissions are carried by PAL.

Number of receivers: radios (2000), 13·5m.; TV (2001), 22·8m.

Cinema

There were 1,112 cinemas (4,348 screens) in 2004 with an audience of 141·5m. (18·8m. for Spanish films and 122·6m. for foreign films). In Nov. 1997 the Madrid School of Cinema was established. In 2004 gross box office receipts came to €680m.

Press

In 2003–04 there were 91 daily newspapers with a total daily circulation of 4·10m. copies. Eight publishing groups controlled around 80% of the daily press, with another 100 or so independents accounting for the other 20%. The main titles are: *El País* (average daily circulation 462,000), *El Mundo* (300,000) and *ABC* (276,000), along with the dedicated sports paper, *Marca* (386,000).

In 2003, 72,048 book titles were published of which 21,661 were categorized as literature, history and literary criticism.

Tourism

In 2003 Spain was behind only France in the number of foreign visitor arrivals, and behind only the USA for tourism receipts. In 2003 tourism accounted for 11·4% of GDP; receipts for 2003 amounted to US$41·8m. In 2003, 51,830,000 tourists visited Spain. Overnight stays in hotels in 2004 (provisional) totalled 235m. of which 48·8% were between June and Sept.; there were 1·1m. places available in hotels. Average occupancy rate was 53·6% in 2004.

Festivals

Religious Festivals: Epiphany (6 Jan.), the Feast of the Assumption (15 Aug.), All Saints Day (1 Nov.) and Immaculate Conception (8 Dec.) are all public holidays. Cultural Festivals: Day of Andalusia (28 Feb.), the Feast of San José in Valencia (19 March) is the culmination of a 13-day festival; the Festival of the Sardine in Murcia is an end of Easter parade in which a huge papier mâché sardine is burned; Feria de Abril is a huge festival in Sevilla at the end of April which features flamenco dancing and bull-fighting; the San Fermines Festival, which takes place in mid-July, is most famous for the running of the bulls in the streets of Pamplona; La Tomatina, a battle of revellers armed with 50 tonnes of tomatoes, takes place on the last Wednesday in Aug. and is the highlight of the annual fiesta in Buñol, Valencia; National Day of Catalonia (11 Sept.); Spanish National Day (12 Oct.).

The next World Expo will be held in Zaragoza from 14 June–14 Sept. 2008.

Libraries

In 2002 there were 3,832 public libraries, one National library, 1,762 specialized libraries, 410 for specific user groups, 355 Higher Education libraries and 11 central libraries of Autonomous Communities; they held a combined 117·6m. volumes. There were 153m. visits to libraries by more than 12·6m. users in 2002. 62·7% of libraries had Internet access in 2002.

Museums and Galleries

Spain had 1,438 museums in 2000 with 3·7m. visitors. The Museu del Prado in Madrid received 1·8m. visitors in 2000.

DIPLOMATIC REPRESENTATIVES

Of Spain in the United Kingdom (39 Chesham Pl., London, SW1X 8SB)
Ambassador: Carlos Miranda.

Of the United Kingdom in Spain (Calle de Fernando el Santo, 16, 28010 Madrid)

Ambassador: Stephen J. L. Wright, CMG.

Of Spain in the USA (2375 Pennsylvania Ave., NW, Washington, D.C., 20037)

Ambassador: Carlos Westendorp y Cabeza.

Of the USA in Spain (Serrano 75, 28006 Madrid)

Ambassador: Eduardo Aguirre, Jr.

Of Spain to the United Nations

Ambassador: Juan Antonio Yáñez-Barnuevo.

FURTHER READING

Barton, Simon, *A History of Spain.* Palgrave Macmillan, Basingstoke, 2004

Carr, Raymond (ed.) *Spain: A History.* OUP, 2000

Closa, Carlos and Heywood, Paul, *Spain and the European Union.* Palgrave Macmillan, Basingstoke, 2004

Conversi, D., *The Basques, The Catalans and Spain.* C. Hurst, London, 1997

Harrison, Joseph and Corkhill, David, *Spain: A Modern European Economy.* Ashgate Publishing, Aldershot, 2004

Heywood, P., *The Government and Politics of Spain.* London, 1995

Hooper, J., *The New Spaniards.* 2nd ed. [of *The Spaniards*] London, 1995

Powell, C., *Juan Carlos of Spain: Self-Made Monarch.* London and New York, 1996

Shields, Graham J., *Spain.* [Bibliography] 2nd ed. ABC-Clio, Oxford and Santa Barbara (CA), 1994.—*Madrid.* [Bibliography] ABC-Clio, Oxford and Santa Barbara (CA), 1996

National library: Biblioteca Nacional, Madrid.

National Statistical Office: Instituto Nacional de Estadística (INE), Paseo de la Castellana, 183, Madrid.

Website: http://www.ine.es

SRI LANKA

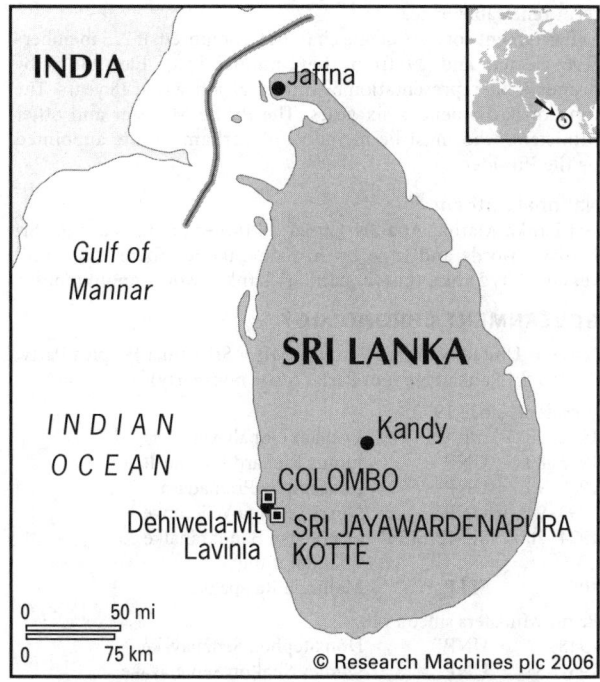

Sri Lanka Prajathanthrika Samajavadi Janarajaya
(Democratic Socialist Republic of Sri Lanka)

Capital: Sri Jayewardenepura Kotte (Administrative
and Legislative), Colombo (Commercial)
Population projection, 2010: 21·56m.
GDP per capita, 2003: (PPP$) 3,778
HDI/world rank: 0·751/93

KEY HISTORICAL EVENTS

In the 18th century the central kingdom, Kandy, was the only
surviving independent state on the island of Ceylon. The Dutch,
who had obtained their first coastal possessions in 1636, had
driven out the Portuguese to become the dominant power in
the island. In 1796 the British East India Company sent a
naval force to Ceylon (as the British then called it). The Dutch
surrendered their possessions, which left the British in control of
the maritime areas surrounding Kandy. These areas were at first
attached to the Madras Presidency of India but in 1802 they were
constituted a separate colony under the Crown. Once the British
began to develop their new territory they came to see Kandy as
a threat. The Kandyan Convention of 1815 annexed Kandy to
British Ceylon while recognizing most of the traditional rights
of the chiefs. However, in 1817 the chiefs rebelled. The rebellion
was suppressed and the rights established by the Convention
were abolished.

Ceylon was then united for the first time since the 12th century.
The British built up a plantation economy. Coffee was dominant
until an outbreak of *Hoemilia vastatrix* fungus destroyed the
plants in 1870. Spices, cocoa and rice all followed but tea became
the main cash crop after successful experiments in the 1880s.
Foreign rule served to subdue the traditional hostility between
northern Tamils and southern Sinhalese. The Ceylon National
Congress, formed in 1919, contained both Sinhalese and Ceylon

Tamil groups. (The Indian Tamils brought in as a labour force
for the tea estates were a separate community.) Tamil national
feeling, however, was expressed over the issue of the use of Tamil
languages in schools. As early as 1931 a general election took
place under universal suffrage, just two years after the first one
in the UK. On 4 Feb. 1948 Ceylon became a Dominion of the
Commonwealth. In 1956 Solomon Bandaranaike became prime
minister at the head of the People's United Front, advocating
neutral foreign policy and the promotion of Sinhalese national
culture at home. In Sept. 1959 he was murdered; his widow
Sirimavo Bandaranaike succeeded him in July 1960 at the head
of an increasingly socialist government. In May 1972 Ceylon
became a republic and adopted the name Sri Lanka. In July
1977 the United National Party (dominant until 1956) returned
to power and in 1978 a new constitution set up a presidential
system. The problem of communal unrest remained unsolved
and Tamil separatists were active. In 1983 the Tamil United
Liberation Front members of parliament were asked to renounce
their objective for a separate Tamil state in the north and the
east of the country. They refused and withdrew from parliament.
Militant Tamils then began armed action which developed into
civil war. A state of emergency ended on 11 Jan. 1989, but
violence continued.

President Ranasinghe Premadasa was assassinated on 1 May
1993. A ceasefire was signed on 3 Jan. 1995, but fighting broke
out again in April. The 'Liberation Tigers of Tamil Eelam'
stronghold of Jaffna in the far north of the country was captured
by government forces in Dec. 1995 and by mid-1997 was under
government control. In April 2000 the Tamil Tigers captured
a military garrison at Elephant Pass, the isthmus that links
Jaffna to the rest of Sri Lanka, increasing the possibility that
they might re-take the Jaffna peninsula. A month-long ceasefire
began in Dec. 2001 amid signs that the Tigers might be willing
to engage in peace talks, and on 22 Feb. 2002 the government
and Tamil Tiger leaders agreed to an internationally-monitored
ceasefire, paving the way to the first full-scale peace talks for
seven years. An estimated 61,000 people died during the 19-
year long conflict. In late 2002 the Tamil Tigers abandoned
their ambitions for a separate state, settling instead for regional
autonomy. However, in Nov. 2003 President Kumaratunga
declared a state of emergency after dismissing three ministers,
suspending parliament and sending troops on to the streets. She
had accused the government of making too many concessions to
Tamil Tiger rebels.

On 26 Dec. 2004 Sri Lanka, along with a number of other south
Asian countries, was hit by a devastating tsunami following an
undersea earthquake. The death toll in Sri Lanka alone was put
at 31,000.

TERRITORY AND POPULATION

Sri Lanka is an island in the Indian Ocean, south of the Indian
peninsula from which it is separated by the Palk Strait. On
28 June 1974 the frontier between India and Sri Lanka in the
Palk Strait was redefined, giving to Sri Lanka the island of
Kachchativu.

Area (in sq. km) and population (2001 census, provisional):

District	Area	Population
Amparai	4,415	589,344
Anuradhapura	7,179	746,466
Badulla	2,861	774,555
Batticaloa	2,854	486,447[1]
Colombo	669	2,234,289
Galle	1,652	990,539
Gampaha	1,387	2,066,096

District	Area	Population
Hambantota	2,609	525,370
Jaffna	1,025	490,621[1]
Kalutara	1,598	1,060,800
Kandy	1,940	1,272,463
Kegalla	1,693	779,774
Kilinochchi	1,279	127,263[1]
Kurunegala	4,816	1,452,369
Mannar	1,996	151,577[1]
Matale	1,993	442,427
Matara	1,283	761,236
Moneragala	5,639	396,173
Mullaitivu	2,617	121,667[1]
Nuwara Eliya	1,741	700,083
Polonnaruwa	3,293	359,197
Puttalam	3,072	705,342
Ratnapura	3,275	1,008,164
Trincomalee	2,727	340,158[1]
Vavuniya	1,967	149,835[1]
Total	65,610	18,732,255

[1]Estimates.

Population (in 1,000) according to ethnic group and nationality at the 2001 census included: 13,815 Sinhalese, 1,351 Sri Lanka Moors, 856 Indian Tamils, 730 Sri Lanka Tamils, 48 Malays, 35 Burghers.

Population, 2001 (census, provisional), 18,732,255 (in some areas experiencing civil war estimates were used and combined with actual totals for other districts); density, 286 per sq. km. The estimated population in 2005 was 20,743,000. In 2003, 78·9% of the population lived in rural areas.

The UN gives a projected population for 2010 of 21·56m.

Between the mid-1980s and the mid-1990s approximately 0·3m. Tamils left the country, one-third as refugees to India and two-thirds to seek political asylum in the West.

Colombo (the largest city) had 642,163 inhabitants in 2001. Other major towns and their populations (2001 census, provisional) are: Dehiwela-Mt Lavinia, 209,800; Moratuwa, 177,200; Jaffna, 145,600; Negombo, 121,900; Sri Jayewardenepura Kotte (now the administrative and legislative capital), 115,800; Kandy, 110,000; Kalmunai, 94,500; Galle, 90,900.

Sinhala and Tamil are the official languages; English is in use.

SOCIAL STATISTICS

Births, 1999, 329,121; deaths, 114,392. 1999 birth rate (per 1,000 population), 17·3; death rate, 6·0; infant mortality rate, 1999 (per 1,000 live births), 17. Life expectancy, 2003, 76·8 years for females and 71·5 for males. Annual population growth rate, 1992–2002, 0·9%. Infant mortality, 2001, 17 per 1,000 live births; fertility rate, 2001, 2·1 births per woman. Sri Lanka has the third oldest population in Asia, after Japan and Singapore, thanks largely to relatively good health and a low fertility rate.

CLIMATE

Sri Lanka, which has an equatorial climate, is affected by the North-east Monsoon (Dec. to Feb.), the South-west Monsoon (May to July) and two inter-monsoons (March to April and Aug. to Nov.). Rainfall is heaviest in the southwest highlands while the northwest and southeast are relatively dry. Colombo, Jan. 79·9°F (26·6°C), July 81·7°F (27·6°C). Annual rainfall 95·4" (2,424 mm). Trincomalee, Jan. 78·8°F (26°C), July 86·2°F (30·1°C). Annual rainfall 62·2" (1,580 mm). Kandy, Jan. 73·9°F (23·3°C), July 76·1°F (24·5°C). Annual rainfall 72·4" (1,840 mm). Nuwara Eliya, Jan. 58·5°F (14·7°C), July 60·3°F (15·7°C). Annual rainfall 75" (1,905 mm).

On 26 Dec. 2004 an undersea earthquake centred off the Indonesian island of Sumatra caused a huge tsunami that flooded large areas along the southern and eastern coasts of Sri Lanka resulting in 31,000 deaths. In total there were 290,000 deaths in twelve countries.

CONSTITUTION AND GOVERNMENT

A new constitution for the Democratic Socialist Republic of Sri Lanka was promulgated on 7 Sept. 1978.

The Executive *President* is directly elected for a seven-year term renewable once.

Parliament consists of one chamber, composed of 225 members (196 elected and 29 from the National List). Election is by proportional representation by universal suffrage at 18 years. The term of Parliament is six years. The Prime Minister and other Ministers, who must be members of Parliament, are appointed by the President.

National Anthem

'Sri Lanka Matha, Apa Sri Lanka' ('Mother Sri Lanka, thee Sri Lanka'); words and tune by A. Samarakone. There is a Tamil version, 'Sri Lanka thaaya, nam Sri Lanka'; words anonymous.

GOVERNMENT CHRONOLOGY

(UNP = United National Party; SLMP = Sri Lanka People's Party; SLFP = Sri Lanka Freedom Party; n/p = non-party)

Presidents since 1972.

1972–78	n/p	William Gopallawa
1978–89	UNP	Junius Richard Jayewardene
1989–93	UNP	Ranasinghe Premadasa
1993–94	UNP	Dingiri Banda Wijetunge
1994–2005	SLMP/SLFP	Chandrika Bandaranaike Kumaratunga
2005–	SLFP	Mahinda Rajapaksa

Prime Ministers since 1948.

1948–52	UNP	Don Stephen Senanayake
1952–53	UNP	Dudley Shelton Senanayake
1953–56	UNP	John Lionel Kotalawela
1956–59	SLFP	Solomon Ridgeway Dias Bandaranaike
1959–60	SLFP	Vijayananda Dahanayake
1960	UNP	Dudley Shelton Senanayake
1960–65	SLFP	Sirimavo Ratwatte Dias Bandaranaike
1965–70	UNP	Dudley Shelton Senanayake
1970–77	SLFP	Sirimavo Ratwatte Dias Bandaranaike
1977–78	UNP	Junius Richard Jayewardene
1978–89	UNP	Ranasinghe Premadasa
1989–93	UNP	Dingiri Banda Wijetunge
1993–94	UNP	Ranil Wickremasinghe
1994	SLMP/SLFP	Chandrika Bandaranaike Kumaratunga
1994–2000	SLFP	Sirimavo Ratwatte Dias Bandaranaike
2000–01	SLFP	Ratnasiri Wickremanayake
2001–04	UNP	Ranil Wickremesinghe
2004–05	SLFP	Mahinda Rajapaksa
2005–	SLFP	Ratnasiri Wickremanayake

RECENT ELECTIONS

Presidential elections were held on 17 Nov. 2005. Prime Minister Mahinda Rajapaksa of the United People's Freedom Alliance (made up of six parties including the Sri Lanka Freedom Party) was elected with 50·3% of the vote, ahead of Ranil Wickremesinghe, a former prime minister, of the United National Party with 48·4%. There were 11 other candidates. Turnout was 73·7%.

In Feb. 2004 President Kumaratunga dissolved parliament, dismissed the cabinet of Prime Minister Ranil Wickremesinghe and called for new elections. At the election of 2 April 2004 the United People's Freedom Alliance gained 105 seats with 45·6% of the vote; the United National Party 82 with 37·8%; the Sri Lanka Tamil Government Party/Tamil National Alliance 22 with 6·8%; the National Heritage Party 9 with 6·0%; and the Sri Lanka Muslim Congress 5 with 2·0%. Other parties received less than 1% of votes cast. Turnout was 76·0%.

CURRENT ADMINISTRATION

In March 2006 the cabinet comprised:

President and Minister of Finance and Defence: Mahinda Rajapaksa; b. 1945 (Sri Lanka Freedom Party; sworn in 19 Nov. 2005).

Prime Minister, Minister of Internal Administration: Ratnasiri Wickremanayake; b. 1933 (Sri Lanka Freedom Party; sworn in 21 Nov. 2005 for a second time, having previously been prime minister from Aug. 2000 to Dec. 2001).

Minister of Agriculture, Environment, Irrigation and Mahaweli Development: Maithripala Sirisena. *Child Development and Women's Empowerment:* Sumedha Jayasena. *Constitutional Affairs and National Integration:* D. E. W. Gunasekera. *Disaster Management and Human Rights:* Mahinda Samarasinghe. *Education:* Susil Premajayantha. *Enterprise Development and Investment Promotion:* Rohitha Bogollagama. *Foreign Affairs, Ports and Aviation:* Mangala Samaraweera. *Healthcare and Nutrition:* Nimal Siripala de Silva. *Housing and Construction:* Ferial Ashraff. *Infrastructure Development and Fisheries:* Athaullah Ahamed Lebbe Marikkar. *Justice and Judicial Reforms:* Amarasiri Gardiye Dodangoda. *Labour Relations and Foreign Employment:* Athauda Seneviratne. *Mass Media and Information:* Anura Priyadharshana Yapa. *Post and Telecommunications and Upcountry Development:* D. M. Jayaratne. *Power and Energy:* John Seneviratne. *Provincial Councils and Local Government:* Janaka Bandara Tennakoon. *Public Administration and Home Affairs:* Sarath Amunugama. *Railways, Transport, Petroleum and Petroleum Resources Development:* A. H. M. Fowzie. *Rural Industries and Self-Employment Promotion:* R. M. S. B. Navinne. *Science and Technology:* Tissa Vitharana. *Social Services and Social Welfare:* Douglas Devananda. *Tourism:* Anura Bandaranaike. *Trade, Commerce, Consumer Affairs and Marketing Development, and Highways:* Jeyaraj Fernandopulle. *Urban Development and Water Supply:* Dinesh Gunawardene. *Vocational and Technical Education:* Piyasena Gamage.

Government Website: http://www.priu.gov.lk

CURRENT LEADERS

Mahinda Rajapaksa

Position
President

Introduction
Mahinda Rajapaksa succeeded Chandrika Kumaratunga as the executive president of Sri Lanka in Nov. 2005. The human rights lawyer and former prime minister has promised to boost reconstruction work in the coastal provinces destroyed in the Indian Ocean tsunami of 2004. He has ruled out widespread devolution for minority Tamils and has rejected outright the demands of the Liberation Tigers of Tamil Eelam (LTTE) for an ethnic homeland.

Early Life
Mahinda Rajapaksa was born on 18 Nov. 1945 in Weeraketiya in the southern district of Hambantota, Ceylon. He was educated at Richmond College, Galle, followed by Nalanda and Thurston Colleges in Colombo. While studying law at Vidyodaya University he joined the centre-left Sri Lanka Freedom Party (SLFP) and in 1970 was elected as the party's parliamentary representative for Beliatta, Hambantota. His father, D. A. Rajapaksa, an SLFP member from its inception in 1951, had held the same seat from Sri Lanka's independence in 1948 until 1965. Having graduated in 1974 Rajapaksa practised as a lawyer in the southern town of Tangalle. He specialized in labour law and human rights, and received plaudits for his work on behalf of the underprivileged.

Rajapaksa lost his parliamentary seat in the landslide defeat of the SLFP to the United National Party (UNP) in the general election of 1977. He continued his legal work, combining it with projects to improve education and training for young people in the south. The UNP administration, led by President J. R. Jayewardene, liberalized the economy and reduced unemployment but was unable to stem violence. The parliamentary elections in Feb. 1989 (in which Rajapaksa regained his seat) were preceded by terror campaigns by both the LTTE and the banned People's Liberation Front (JVP) in the south. Rajapaksa joined Mangala Samaraweera's 'Mother's Front', a group representing the mothers of those who 'disappeared' in the violence of 1988–89. He served on the central committee of the SLFP from the early 1990s and became an increasingly vocal critic of president Ranasinghe Premadasa and his UNP government.

Following narrow victory for the SLFP (as part of the People's Alliance coalition) in the parliamentary elections of 1994, Rajapaksa was appointed minister for labour by President Chandrika Kumaratunga. His attempts to reform labour laws and introduce a workers' charter met with resistance. He was moved to the fisheries ministry, where he was praised for improving living conditions for fishermen, establishing a coastal guard service and a university of oceanography. Following defeat for the People's Alliance in legislative elections in Dec. 2001, Rajapaksa became leader of the parliamentary opposition. He forged alliances including, controversially, the Sinhala-nationalist JVP to form the United People's Freedom Alliance (UPFA). The Alliance won the parliamentary elections that followed Kumaratunga's sacking of the UNP government in Feb. 2004. Kumaratunga then appointed Rajapaksa as prime minister and he was sworn in on 6 April 2004.

Career in Office
The UPFA did not win sufficient seats in the 225-seat parliament to command a majority and Rajapaksa's government struggled to implement its promises to halt privatization, increase wages and create 125,000 jobs within three months. The government was also criticized for its handling of the aftermath of the Indian Ocean tsunami on 26 Dec. 2004, which killed more than 30,000 Sri Lankans and displaced nearly half a million people.

Rajapaksa was chosen as the SLFP's presidential candidate for the election of Nov. 2005 and narrowly defeated the UNP's Ranil Wickremesinghe. He took office on 19 Nov. 2005 and vowed a tougher approach to dealings with the LTTE, arguing that the four-year ceasefire agreement had not brought peace. He appointed Ratnasiri Wickremanayake, known for his hardline approach to the LTTE, as prime minister. Some of the business community are reportedly concerned that Rajapaksa's left-leaning policies might lead to reversals of previous reforms.

Ratnasiri Wickremanayake

Position
Prime Minister

Introduction
Ratnasiri Wickremanayake was unexpectedly returned to the largely ceremonial office of prime minister in Nov. 2005 by the new executive president, Mahinda Rajapaksa. Wickremanayake, a law graduate and long-term member of the leftist Sri Lanka Freedom Party (SLFP), is known as a hardliner. He has previously advocated that the Tamil Tiger rebels (LTTE), who have waged a separatist insurgency since 1972, should be militarily defeated.

Early Life
Ratnasiri Wickremanayake was born in southern Ceylon on 5 May 1933. He was educated at Ananda College, Colombo and studied law in London during the mid- and late-1950s. He intended to become a barrister but chose instead to enter politics. Following his return to Sri Lanka, he was elected at the July 1960 legislative elections to represent the Kalutara district, Horana for the People's United Front alliance. Sirimavo Bandaranaike led

the leftist Sri Lanka Freedom Party (SLFP) to victory and became the world's first female prime minister.

Wickremanayake joined the SLFP in 1962 and became deputy minister for justice following the parliamentary elections of May 1970. The government increased state involvement in the economy, including social welfare programmes and rice subsidies, but anger at the slow pace of reforms triggered an armed rebellion by the Marxist People's Liberation Front (JVP) in April 1971. The uprising was crushed but spiralling inflation (partly caused by rapidly rising oil prices), high unemployment and a growing trade deficit followed and the SLFP suffered a humiliating defeat to the United National Party (UNP) in the parliamentary elections of July 1977.

Wickremanayake was promoted to general secretary of the SLFP in 1977, although Bandaranaike remained party leader. The SLFP was returned to power in Aug. 1994 as the principal party of the People's Alliance (PA) and Wickremanayake was appointed minister of public administration, home affairs and plantation industries. He also served as leader of the house in the cabinet of the new president, Chandrika Kumaratunga, the daughter of Bandaranaike. The government attempted to broker peace with the LTTE but the ethnic war intensified after April 1995 and by the late 1990s over 50,000 people had been killed in the conflict.

Wickremanayake became prime minister in Aug. 2000 after the resignation of Bandaranaike and headed a minority SLFP government supported by the JVP until Oct. 2001, when it became apparent that the government was about to lose a no-confidence motion. While prime minister, Wickremanayake spurned suggestions of compromise with the LTTE. He was then leader of the opposition until he made way for Mahinda Rajapaksa in April 2002. Following the victory of the United People's Freedom Alliance (UPFA—which included the SLFP and the JVP) in elections that followed Kumaratunga's sacking of the UNP government in Feb. 2004, Wickremanayake was appointed minister of Buddhist affairs, public security, and law and order, and deputy minister for defence. He held these posts until the new president (and former prime minister), Rajapaksa, appointed him prime minister. Wickremanayake was sworn in on 21 Nov. 2005.

Career in Office
Wickremanayake's appointment appeared to reinforce President Rajapaksa's hardline stance on any future peace negotiations with the LTTE. The government, criticized for its response to the devastating Indian Ocean tsunami in Dec. 2004, is struggling to implement its promises to halt privatization, increase wages and create 125,000 jobs within three months.

DEFENCE
Defence expenditure in 2003 totalled US$515m. (US$27 per capita), representing 2·8% of GDP.

Army
Strength (2002), 118,000. In addition there were 1,100 reserves. Paramilitary forces consist of the Ministry of Defence Police (60,600, including 1,000 women and a 3,000-strong anti-guerrilla force), the Home Guard (13,000) and the National Guard (some 15,000).

Navy
The main naval base is at Trincomalee. Personnel in 2002 numbered 20,600, including a reserve of about 2,400.

Air Force
Air Force bases are at Anuradhapura, Katunayake, Ratmalana, Vavuniya and China Bay, Trincomalee. Total strength (2002) about 19,300 with 22 combat aircraft and 24 armed helicopters. Main attack aircraft types included Kfirs and MiG-27s.

INTERNATIONAL RELATIONS
Sri Lanka is a member of the UN, WTO, the Commonwealth, the Asian Development Bank, the Colombo Plan, SAARC and IOM.

ECONOMY
Agriculture accounted for 20·5% of GDP in 2002, industry 26·3% and services 53·2%.

The conflict with the minority separatists, the Tamil Tigers, is estimated to have cost the country between 1 and 1·5% in growth per year.

Overview
20 years of civil war and conflict have disrupted inter-regional commerce, deepened poverty, damaged infrastructure and weakened public finances. Since the commencement of the peace process in Feb. 2002, the government has embarked upon reforms to invigorate and revive the economy. Reforms that have played a key role in economic development include the floatation of the exchange rate, privatization, the introduction of a VAT system, the amendment of banking laws and the restructuring of financial markets. In June 2003 the international community promised aid worth US$4·5bn. over the following four years conditional on the continuation of the peace process. In 2002 the main sources of growth were consumption and tourism and in 2003 exports and private investment added further impetus to growth. In 2003 heightened political instability had adverse implications for financial markets and foreign private investment. The tsunami of Dec. 2004 has had an adverse effect on the economy, particularly in relation to tourism.

Currency
The unit of currency is the *Sri Lankan rupee* (LKR) of 100 *cents*. Foreign exchange reserves were US$884m. and gold reserves 626,000 troy oz in Dec. 2001. Inflation was 7·6% in 2004, up from 6·3% in 2003. Total money supply in March 2002 was Rs 125,695m.

Budget
Revenue and expenditure of central government in Rs 1m. for financial years ending 31 Dec.:

	1996	1997	1998	1999	2000	2001[1]
Revenue	146,280	165,036	175,032	195,905	211,282	231,463
Expenditure	212,787	228,732	253,808	267,611	322,048	367,966

[1]Provisional.

The principal sources of revenue in 2001 were: general sales tax, 21%; excise taxes, 19%; national security levy, 18%; import duties, 13%; income tax, 13%; non-tax revenue, 11%.

The principal items of recurrent expenditure in 2001 were: public debt interest, 32%; defence, 22%; public service, 15%; provincial councils, 10%; pensions, 9%; welfare, 8%.

Performance
The economy contracted by 1·5% in 2001, but recovered in 2002, with growth of 4·0%. Real GDP growth was 6·0% in 2003 and 5·4% in 2004. Total GDP in 2004 was US$20·1bn.

Banking and Finance
The Central Bank of Sri Lanka is the bank of issue (*Governor*, Sunil Mendis). Two state-owned commercial banks, the Bank of Ceylon and the People's Bank, account for about 70% of bank lending. There are also 21 private banks (17 foreign). There are four development banks and two merchant banks. Total assets of commercial banks at 31 Dec. 2003, Rs 899,492m. Assets of the Sri Lanka National Savings Bank at 31 Dec. 1999 were Rs 100,813m. In the five years to Sept. 2000 Sri Lanka attracted US$715m. in foreign direct investment, including more than US$200m. in 1999.

There is a stock exchange in Colombo.

ENERGY AND NATURAL RESOURCES

Environment
Carbon dioxide emissions from the consumption and flaring of fossil fuels in 2002 were the equivalent of 0·6 tonnes per capita.

Electricity
Installed capacity (2000), 2·1m. kW. Production, 2000, 6·84bn. kWh (47% hydro-electric). Consumption per capita in 2000 was 354 kWh.

Oil and Gas
Construction of a US$1·6bn. oil refinery at Hambantota in the south of the island began in 1999.

Water
The Mahaweli Authority scheme, which began in 1978, had led to the irrigation of 354,000 ha. of land by 2001.

Minerals
Gems are among the chief minerals mined and exported. Graphite is also important; production in 2001 was 4,895 tonnes. Production of ilmenite, 1998, 34,118 tonnes. Some rutile is also produced (1,930 tonnes in 1998). Salt extraction is the oldest industry. The method is solar evaporation of sea-water. Production, 2001, 130,272 tonnes.

Agriculture
There were 896,000 ha. of arable land in 2001 and 1·02m. ha. of permanent crops. Agriculture engages 47·5% of the labour force. Main crops in 2000 (in 1,000 tonnes): rice, 2,767; coconuts, 1,950; sugarcane, 1,114; plantains, 600; tea, 285; cassava, 260; rubber, 99; mangoes, 86. Tea plantations are being returned to the private sector after nationalization in 1975. Sri Lanka ranks third in the world for tea production, behind India and China.

Livestock in 2000: 1,617,000 cattle; 728,000 buffaloes; 514,000 goats; 10m. chickens.

Forestry
The area under forests in 2000 was 1·94m. ha., or 30·0% of the land area. In 2001, 6·52m. cu. metres of roundwood were cut.

Fisheries
Total catch in 2001 was 279,640 tonnes (89% from sea fishing).

INDUSTRY
The main industries are the processing of rubber, tea, coconuts and other agricultural commodities, tobacco, textiles, clothing and leather goods, chemicals, plastics, cement and petroleum refining. Industrial production fell by 2·1% in 2001.

Labour
The labour force in 2003 totalled 7,653,716 (67% males). In 2003 the economically active workforce numbered 7,012,755, of which 2,384,397 worked in agriculture, forestry and fishing, 1,156,682 in manufacturing and 867,131 in wholesale and retail trade, repair of motor vehicles and household goods. In 2003 the unemployment rate was 8·4%.

Trade Unions
In 2002 there were 1,513 functioning trade unions with 640,673 members.

INTERNATIONAL TRADE
Foreign debt in 2002 was US$9,611m.

Imports and Exports
Trade in US$1m.:

	1999	2000	2001	2002	2003
Imports f.o.b.	5,365·5	6,483·6	5,376·9	5,495·0	6,004·8
Exports f.o.b.	4,596·2	5,439·6	4,816·9	4,699·2	5,133·2

Principal imports in 1999: manufactured goods, 39·2%; machinery and transport equipment, 23·2%; foodstuffs, 12·7%; chemicals, 8·4%; petroleum, 5·1%. Principal exports: clothing, 51·3%; tea, 13·7%; yarn and fabrics, 4·6%.

In 1999 the main import suppliers were Japan (10·4%), India (9·5%), Singapore (8·4%) and UK (4·7%). The main export markets were the USA (39·6%), the UK (13·3%), Germany (4·8%) and Japan (3·5%).

COMMUNICATIONS

Roads
In 2000 the road network totalled 74,828 km in length, including 11,462 km of national roads and 10,404 of secondary roads. Number of motor vehicles, 2002, 1,573,529, comprising 253,447 passenger cars, 67,702 buses and coaches, 328,913 trucks and vans and 923,467 motorcycles and mopeds. There were 2,029 fatalities in road accidents in 2002.

Rail
In 2003 there were 1,449 km of railway (1,676 mm gauge). Passenger-km travelled in 2001–02 came to 4,079m. and freight tonne-km to 131m.

Civil Aviation
There is an international airport at Colombo (Bandaranaike). The national carrier is SriLankan Airlines (formerly Air Lanka), which has been part-owned and managed by Emirates since 1998. In 1999 SriLankan Airlines flew 28·1m. km and carried 1,421,500 passengers (all on international flights). Colombo handled 2,646,033 passengers and 100,471 tonnes of freight in 2001.

Shipping
In 2002 the merchant marine totalled 81,000 GRT, including oil tankers 6,000 GRT. Colombo is a modern container port; Trincomalee and Galle are natural harbours. In 2003, 4,032 merchant vessels totalling 88m. GRT entered the ports: 19,959,000 tonnes of goods were unloaded and 10,541,000 tonnes loaded. In 2002 vessels totalling 39,336,000 NRT entered ports.

Telecommunications
Sri Lanka had 1,814,700 telephone subscribers in 2002 (95·8 per 1,000 population) and there were 250,000 PCs in use (13·2 for every 1,000 persons). There were 931,600 mobile phone subscribers in 2002 and 24,000 fax machines. There were approximately 200,000 Internet users in 2002.

Postal Services
In 2003 there were 4,680 post offices, or one for every 4,070 persons.

SOCIAL INSTITUTIONS

Justice
The systems of law which are valid are Roman-Dutch, English, Tesawalamai, Islamic and Kandyan.

Kandyan law applies in matters relating to inheritance, matrimonial rights and donations; Tesawalamai law applies in Jaffna as above and in sales of land. Islamic law is applied to all Muslims in respect of succession, donations, marriage, divorce and maintenance. These customary and religious laws have been modified by local enactments.

The courts of original jurisdiction are the High Court, Provincial Courts, District Courts, Magistrates' Courts and Primary Courts. District Courts have unlimited civil jurisdiction. The Magistrates' Courts exercise criminal jurisdiction. The Primary Courts exercise civil jurisdiction in petty disputes and criminal jurisdiction in respect of certain offences.

The Constitution of 1978 provided for the establishment of two superior courts, the Supreme Court and the Court of Appeal.

The Supreme Court is the highest and final superior court of record and exercises jurisdiction in respect of constitutional matters, jurisdiction for the protection of fundamental rights, final appellate jurisdiction in election petitions and jurisdiction in respect of any breach of the privileges of Parliament. The Court of Appeal has appellate jurisdiction to correct all errors in fact or law committed by any court, tribunal or institution.

The population in penal institutions in 2002 was 17,485 (91 per 100,000 of national population). The death penalty, last used in 1976, was reactivated in Nov. 2004 after a 28-year moratorium.

Police
The strength of the police service in 2003 was 39,242.

Education
Education is free and is compulsory from age five to 14 years. The literacy rate in 2001 was 91·9% (male, 94·5%; female, 89·3%). Sri Lanka's rate compares very favourably with the rates of 58·0% in India and 44·0% in Pakistan.

In 1995 there were 9,657 primary schools with 70,537 teachers for 1·9m. pupils. There were 2·3m. secondary pupils with 103,572 teachers and 63,660 students in higher education with 2,636 staff. There are nine universities, one open (distance) university and one Buddhist and Pali university.

In 1998–99 total expenditure on education came to 3·1% of GNP.

Health
In 2002 there were 576 hospitals and 411 central dispensaries. The hospitals had 59,144 beds. There were 7,963 physicians and 14,716 nurses in 2000; and 471 dentists, 848 pharmacists and 7,725 midwives in 1999. Total state budget expenditure on health, 2002, Rs 25,691m.

Welfare
To qualify for an old-age pension an individual must be above the age of 55 for men or 50 for women. However, a grant is payable at any age if the person is emigrating permanently. Old-age benefits are made up of a lump sum equal to total employee and employer contributions, plus interest.

The family allowances programme is being implemented in stages. Families earning below Rs1,000 a month are entitled to Rs500 a month benefit.

RELIGION
In 2001 the population was 71% Buddhist, 12% Hindu, 9% Muslim and 7% Roman Catholic.

CULTURE
World Heritage Sites
Sri Lanka has seven sites on the UNESCO World Heritage List: Sacred City of Anuradhapura (inscribed on the list in 1982); Ancient City of Polonnaruwa (1982); Ancient City of Sigiriya (1982); Sinharaja Forest Reserve (1988); Sacred City of Kandy (1988); Old Town of Galle and its Fortifications (1988); and the Golden Temple of Dambulla (1991).

Broadcasting
Broadcasting is provided by the Sri Lanka Broadcasting Corporation. There were 2·2m. TV sets (colour by PAL) in 2001 and 3·9m. radio receivers in 2000.

Press
In 2002 there were 13 daily newspapers with a combined circulation of 493,000, at a rate of 26 per 1,000 inhabitants.

Tourism
In 2001 there were 337,000 foreign tourists, bringing revenue of US$211m.

DIPLOMATIC REPRESENTATIVES
Of Sri Lanka in the United Kingdom (13 Hyde Park Gdns, London, W2 2LU)
High Commissioner: Kshenuka Senewiratne.

Of the United Kingdom in Sri Lanka (190 Galle Rd, Kollupitiya, Colombo 3)
High Commissioner: Stephen Evans, CMG, OBE.

Of Sri Lanka in the USA (2148 Wyoming Ave., NW, Washington, D.C., 20008)
Ambassador: Bernard Goonetilleke.

Of the USA in Sri Lanka (210 Galle Rd, Kollupitiya, Colombo 3)
Ambassador: Jeffrey J. Lunstead.

Of Sri Lanka to the United Nations
Ambassador: Prasad Kariyawasam.

Of Sri Lanka to the European Union
Ambassador: Chrysantha Romesh Jayasinghe.

FURTHER READING
De Silva, C. R., *Sri Lanka: a History.* Delhi, 1991
McGowan, W., *Only Man is Vile: the Tragedy of Sri Lanka.* New York, 1992

National Statistical Office: Department of Census and Statistics, POB 563, Colombo 7.
Website: http://www.statistics.gov.lk

SUDAN

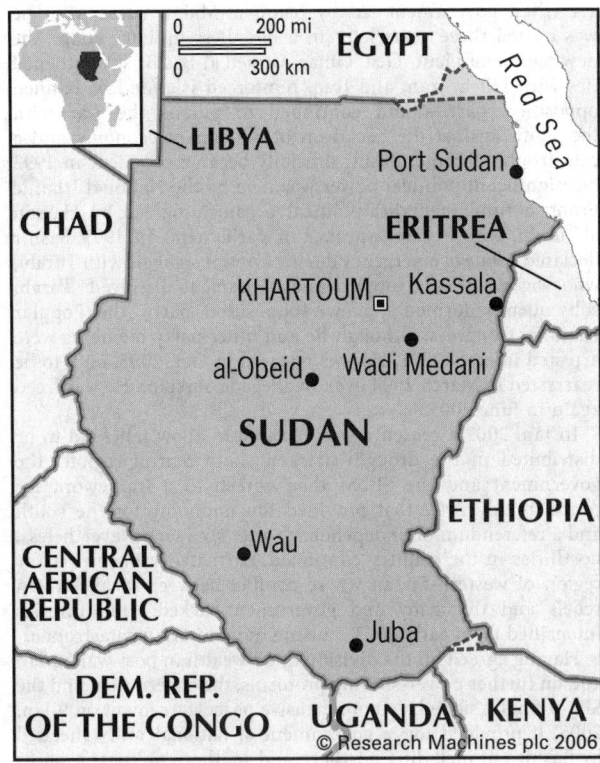

Jamhuryat es-Sudan
(The Republic of The Sudan)

Capital: Khartoum
Population projection, 2010: 40·25m.
GDP per capita, 2003: (PPP$) 1,910
HDI/world rank: 0·512/141

KEY HISTORICAL EVENTS

The earliest inhabitants of Sudan were Mesolithic hunter-gatherers, who lived and travelled in the region around Khartoum from as early as 30,000 BC. They had domesticated animals by 4,000 BC. Cultural influences from Egypt rippled through to Nubia in north-eastern Sudan from around 3,000 BC, when Egypt's first dynasty moved south along the river Nile in search of construction materials and slaves. By 2,000 BC it had reached as far south as the river Nile's fourth cataract, more than 700 km beyond Aswan. Egyptian-controlled Nubia was divided into Wawat in the north—centred on Aswan—and Kush in the south—based at Nepata (modern Marawi). When Egypt's power waned in the 11th century BC (the end of the New Kingdom) Kush, with its Egyptian and African influences, mineral resources and its position on trade routes linking the Nile to the Red Sea, became a powerful kingdom. At its height, under King Piantkhi in 750 BC, the whole of Egypt was brought under Kushite control. However, it proved to be short-lived: the invasion of Egypt by Assyrian forces in 671 BC forced a retreat to Nepata. From there, the kingdom of Kush continued to exert control over the middle Nile for much of the next millennium, developing a distinctive culture and language. By AD 200 Kush

was in decline, and was finally overthrown in 350 by the king of Aksum from the Ethiopian highlands.

Sudan was brought back into contact with the Mediterranean world in the 6th century by the arrival of Coptic Christian missionaries. They travelled south along the Nile and established churches in the three middle-Nile kingdoms that had superseded Kush: Nobatia in the north and Maqurrah and 'Alwah in the south, near modern Khartoum. Egypt was invaded by Arabs in 639 and came under Muslim rule. Raiding parties moved up the Nile and absorbed Nobatia. The king of Maqurrah engineered a truce at Dunqulah with an Arab military expedition, commanded by 'Abd Allah ibn Sa'd, preserving the kingdom for a further six centuries.

In 1250 Egypt came under the control of Mamluk sultans, supported by a caste of warrior slaves. They pushed south into Nubia, bringing chaos and devastation to Maqurrah and opening it up to waves of Arab immigrants, particularly the Juhaynah people. They intermarried with the Nubians and introduced Arab Muslim culture. Alwah, to the south, retained its Christian traditions until 1500, when, weakened by Bedouin raids, it collapsed under an Arab confederation led by Abd Allah Jamma. The Arabs themselves came under attack in the region around modern Khartoum from warriors of the Funj dynasty, a kingdom that had its origins in the Blue Nile's upper reaches. The Funj established their supremacy in the Al Jazirah region by 1607 and expanded northwards under Badi II Abu Daqn later in the 17th century. It was a relatively peaceful and stable period and the teaching of Islam flourished in schools and mosques along the Nile. The Funj themselves adopted Islam but retained a number of traditional African customs and beliefs.

Egyptian Ascendency
In 1820 Muhammad Ali, viceroy of Egypt under the Ottoman Turks, sent an army southward to conquer Sudan. The Funj kingdom collapsed and within a year Ali's forces had taken control of the Nile valley from Nubia to the Ethiopian foothills. There was initial resistance but the appointment of Ali Kurshid Agha as governor general in 1826 led to the establishment of Khartoum as the administrative capital, improvements to agriculture and the development of the trade in slaves and ivory. Ismail Pasha became viceroy of Egypt in 1863 and announced a grand scheme to modernize and control the entire Nile river system from the Mediterranean to the Great Lakes of East Africa. Ismail needed the financial help of the European powers, who in return demanded an end to the slave trade. The British had a particular interest in Egyptian affairs following the opening of the Suez Canal in 1869. Ismail commissioned the Englishmen Samuel Baker and then Charles Gordon to establish Egyptian control in southern Sudan and Central Africa and to crush slavery. The controllers of the slave trade were powerful and proved hard to defeat, especially away from the Nile. In addition, there was unease among Muslims about the crusading style of both (Christian) men. In 1879, amid rising discontent, Ismail's financial backing dramatically collapsed and his grand project was suddenly curtailed. Ismail was exiled and Gordon resigned.

Rise of the Mahdi
The power vacuum was filled by Muhammad Ahmad in 1881; he declared himself the Mahdi ('divinely guided one') and led a movement that sought an end to Egyptian (Ottoman) influence and a return to the simplicity of early Islam. By 1882 the Mahdi had garnered the support of a least 30,000 armed followers (the Ansar). They captured the town of Al Abayyid, which led to a British order for the evacuation of Egyptians and foreigners

from Khartoum, overseen by Charles Gordon. The campaign failed disastrously: Gordon was killed by Mahdists at Khartoum in early 1885. The Mahdi died in the same year, but his successor, the Khalifa Abdallahi, continued to build up the Mahdist state.

In the 1890s the European powers were vying for control of Africa and the British made plans for the control of the Nile valley and the reconquest of Sudan. In a series of attacks between 1896 and 1898, an Anglo-Egyptian force of 25,800 men under Herbert (later Lord) Kitchener destroyed the Mahdist state. Anglo-Egyptian agreements in 1899 established a joint (condominium) government of Sudan: in theory it was administered by a governor-general, appointed by Egypt with the consent of Great Britain. In practice the governor-general, Sir Reginald Wingate, controlled the condominium government from Khartoum. Sudanese resentment over colonial rule erupted in various Mahdist uprisings but they never attracted sufficient support to pose a threat to the government. In 1911 the Sudan Plantations syndicate launched a scheme to irrigate the Al Jazirah region and establish a large cotton plantation for Britain's textile industry. The cotton crop became the mainstay of the economy.

Sudanese nationalist sentiment grew in the early 1920s when 'Ali 'Abd al Latif, inspired by Egyptian nationalists, founded the White Flag League. When Governor-General Sir Lee Stack was assassinated in 1924 in Cairo (capital of newly-independent Egypt), the British ordered all Egyptian troops out of Sudan and British rule continued unchallenged until after the Second World War. The British saw the south of Sudan as a separate region and attempted to divorce it from Islamic influences in the north and centre of the country—the grander plan was to integrate the southern provinces and their largely Christian and animist peoples with British East Africa. In 1948 a predominantly elective legislative assembly was convened for the whole territory. In the 1948 elections the Independence Front, which favoured the creation of an independent republic, gained a majority over the National Front, which aimed for union with Egypt.

Independence
Following the 1952 revolution in Egypt, Britain and Egypt agreed to prepare Sudan for independence. It duly became a parliamentary republic in 1956.

Sudan's democracy proved to be short-lived; the liberalism that had largely been imported via the British administration was a weak force and the political parties became mired in internecine fighting. At the same time, a revolt raged in the south over Islamic domination. In 1958 Gen. Ibrahim Abboud led a military coup that ended the parliamentary system. In 1964, unable to improve Sudan's poor economic performance or to end the southern revolt, Abboud agreed to the re-establishment of civilian government. A coalition, headed by Muhammad Ahmad Mahjub, soon descended into the factional disputes and little progress was made in solving the country's economic and social problems.

In 1969 Col. Muhammad Gaafur al-Nimeiry staged a successful coup. He banned all political parties and nationalized banks and numerous industries. The civil war was finally ended by an agreement between the government and the Southern Sudan Liberation Front signed in 1972 at Addis Ababa. In the same year the Sudanese Socialist Union, the country's only political organization, elected a 'people's assembly' to draw up a new constitution, adopted in 1973. Nimeiry's regime became the target of criticism at home because of worsening economic conditions and for its support of Egypt's part in the Camp David Accords with Israel; in the late 1970s Nimeiry dismissed his cabinet and closed universities in an attempt to quell opposition.

Accelerating Violence
From the early 1980s political instability in southern Sudan increased. Nimeiry responded by imposing Sharia law in 1983,

inflaming a renewed civil war with the largely Christian and animist Sudan People's Liberation Movement (SPLM) led by John Garang. Having survived numerous earlier coup attempts, Nimeiry was overthrown in 1985. Following elections in 1986 a civilian government led by Sadiq al-Mahdi ruled until he was ousted three years later in a bloodless military coup. The new regime of Lieut.-Gen. Omar Ahmed al-Bashir strengthened ties with Libya, Iran, and Iraq, reinforced Islamic law, banned opposition parties and continued to pursue the war with the south against the backdrop of a stagnant economy and a catastrophic famine. Bashir officially became president in 1993 but significant political power was held by the National Islamic Front, a fundamentalist political organization led by Hassan al-Turabi, who became speaker of parliament. In 1999 Bashir declared a state of emergency during a power struggle with Turabi, who was eventually toppled and parliament dissolved. Turabi subsequently formed his own opposition party, the Popular National Congress, although he and other party members were arrested in early 2001. He was released in Oct. 2003, only to be rearrested in March 2004 over an alleged coup plot. He was freed again in June 2005.

In Jan. 2002 a ceasefire was declared to allow relief aid to be distributed in the drought-stricken south-central region. The government and the SPLM then agreed to a framework for peace in July 2002 that provided for autonomy for the south and a referendum on independence after six years. Nevertheless, hostilities in the country continued, particularly in the Darfur region of western Sudan where conflict between local African rebels and the army and government-backed Arab militias intensified from early 2003, causing humanitarian catastrophe.

Having agreed on the division of oil wealth in post-war Sudan and on further power-sharing protocols, the government and the SPLM finally signed a comprehensive peace agreement on 9 Jan. 2005. It provided for: a government of national unity (headed by Bashir but including northern and southern political groups) during a six-year transition period; self-determination for the South, with a referendum on secession at the end of the transition period; a permanent ceasefire; and the disengagement of forces. In more than 20 years of civil war, over 2m. people were thought to have died and more than 4m. made refugees. The agreement was briefly undermined in July 2005 when John Garang, SPLM leader and first vice-president in the power-sharing government, was killed in an air crash, provoking clashes between southern Sudanese and northern Arabs in Khartoum. His SPLM deputy, Salva Kiir Mayardit, took over as first vice-president in Aug. The power-sharing government was formed officially in Sept. 2005 and a devolved government of southern Sudan was established in Oct.

Although the comprehensive peace agreement focused mainly on the north-south civil war, some of its provisions for power-sharing and decentralization are applicable to Darfur. However, despite ongoing peace talks and UN and other international intervention to stop the violence, the conflict has continued. The government and Arab militias have been accused of systematic abuses of human rights, and the UN Security Council referred such crimes to the International Criminal Court in March 2005. The targeting of civilians in the conflict has led to the displacement of some 2m. people.

TERRITORY AND POPULATION

Sudan is bounded in the north by Egypt, northeast by the Red Sea, east by Eritrea and Ethiopia, south by Kenya, Uganda and the Democratic Republic of the Congo, west by the Central African Republic and Chad, and northwest by Libya. Its area, including inland waters, is 2,505,810 sq. km. In 1993 the census population was 25·6m. Population estimate (2005), 36·23m., giving a density of 14·4 per sq. km. In 2003, 61·1% of the population were rural. The UN gives a projected population for 2010 of 40·25m.

In Feb. 1994 the former nine regions were subdivided to form 26 federal states as follows:

Former region	New states
Khartoum	Khartoum
Bahr al-Ghazal	Western Bahr al-Ghazal; Northern Bahr al-Ghazal; Warab
Central	Gezira; White Nile; Sinnar; Blue Nile
Darfur	Northern Darfur; Southern Darfur; Western Darfur
Eastern	Red Sea; Gedaref; Kassala
Equatoria	Eastern Equatoria; Western Equatoria; Bahr al-Jabal
Kurdufan	Northern Kurdufan; Southern Kurdufan; Western Kurdufan
Northern	Nile; Northern State
Upper Nile	Upper Nile; Unity State; Jonglei; Buheyrat

The capital, Khartoum, had a population of 2,628,000 in 1999. Other major cities, with 1993 populations, are Port Sudan (305,385), Kassala (234,270), Nyala (228,778), al-Obeid (228,096), Wadi Medani (218,714) and al-Qadarif (189,384).

The northern and central thirds of the country are populated by Arab and Nubian peoples, while the southern third is inhabited by Nilotic and Bantu peoples. Sudan has more internally displaced people (4m. in 2000) than any other country.

Arabic, the official language, is spoken by 49% of inhabitants. English is the second language.

SOCIAL STATISTICS

2004 estimates: births, 1,172,000; deaths, 391,000. Rates, 2004 estimates (per 1,000 population): birth, 33; death, 11. Infant mortality, 2001 (per 1,000 live births), 65. Expectation of life in 2003 was 57·9 years for females and 54·9 for males. Annual population growth rate, 1992–2002, 2·3%. Fertility rate, 2001, 4·6 births per woman.

CLIMATE

Lying wholly within the tropics, the country has a continental climate and only the Red Sea coast experiences maritime influences. Temperatures are generally high for most of the year, with May and June the hottest months. Winters are virtually cloudless and night temperatures are consequently cool. Summer is the rainy season inland, with amounts increasing from north to south, but the northern areas are virtually a desert region. On the Red Sea coast, most rain falls in winter. Khartoum, Jan. 64°F (18·0°C), July 89°F (31·7°C). Annual rainfall 6" (157 mm). Juba, Jan. 83°F (28·3°C), July 78°F (25·6°C). Annual rainfall 39" (968 mm). Port Sudan, Jan. 74°F (23·3°C), July 94°F (34·4°C). Annual rainfall 4" (94 mm). Wadi Halfa, Jan. 50°F (10·0°C), July 90°F (32·2°C). Annual rainfall 0·1" (2·5 mm).

CONSTITUTION AND GOVERNMENT

The constitution was suspended after the 1989 coup and a 12-member Revolutionary Council then ruled. A 300-member Provisional National Assembly was appointed in Feb. 1992 as a transitional legislature pending elections. These were held in March 1996. On 26 May 1998 President Omar Hassan Ahmed al-Bashir approved a new constitution. Notably this lifted the ban on opposition political parties, although the government continued to monitor and control criticism until the constitution came legally into effect. The constitution was partially suspended in Dec. 1999.

In accordance with the peace deal agreed in Dec. 2004 to bring an end to the civil war and signed in Jan. 2005 there is a lower house, the 450-seat interim National Assembly, with members appointed by decree by the president, and an upper house, the Council of States, also with members appointed. The peace deal specified that 52% of National Assembly seats should go to the ruling National Congress Party, 28% to the former southern rebel Sudan People's Liberation Movement (the political wing of the Sudan People's Liberation Army), 14% to the northern

opposition parties and 6% to their counterparts in the south. A new interim power-sharing constitution was adopted on 6 July 2005 giving the south some autonomy and allowing former rebels to take up seats in the country's government.

National Anthem
'Nahnu Jundullah, Jundu Al-Watlan' ('We are the Army of God and of Our Land'); words by A. M. Salih, tune by A. Murjan.

GOVERNMENT CHRONOLOGY

(DUP = Democratic Unionist Party; NCP = National Congress party; NUP = National Unionist Party; SSU = Sudan Socialist Union; Umma = 'Community of the Believers' Party)

Heads of State since 1956.

Commission of Sovereignty
1956–58   Abd al-Fattah Mohammad al-Mughrabi; Mohammad Uthman ad-Dardiri; Ahmad Mohammad Yasin; Ahmad Mohammad Salih; Siricio Iro Wani

Chairman of the Supreme Council of the Armed Forces
Ibrahim Abboud 17 Nov 1958–16 Nov 1964 (+1983) military (1)

Commission of Sovereignty (I)
1964–65   Abd al-Halim Mohammad; Tijani al-Mahi; Mubarak Shaddad; Ibrahim Yusuf Sulayman; Luigi Adwok Bong Gicomeho.

Commission of Sovereignty (II)
1965   Ismail al-Azhari; Abd Allah al-Fadil al-Mahdi, Luigi Adwok Bong Gicomeho; Abd al-Halim Mohammad; Khidr Hamad

Chairman of the Council of Sovereignty
1965–69   NUP   Ismail al-Azhari

Chairmen of the Revolutionary Command Council
1969–71   military, SSU   Gaafur Muhammad al-Nimeiry
1971   military, SSU   Abu Bakr an-Nur Uthman
1971   military, SSU   Gaafur Muhammad al-Nimeiry

President
1971–85   military, SSU   Gaafur Muhammad al-Nimeiry

Chairman of the Transitional Military Council
1985–86   military   Abd ar-Rahman Siwar ad-Dhahab

Chairman of the Council of Sovereignty
1986–89   DUP   Ahmad Ali al-Mirghani

Chairman of the Revolutionary Command Council of National Salvation
1989–93   military   Omar Hassan Ahmed al-Bashir

President
1993–   military, NCP   Omar Hassan Ahmed al-Bashir

Heads of Government since 1952.

Chief Ministers
1952–53   Umma   Abd ar-Rahman al-Mahdi
1954–56   NUP   Ismail al-Azhari

Prime Ministers
1954–56   NUP   Ismail al-Azhari
1956–58   Umma   Abd Allah Khalil
1958–64   military (de facto)   Ibrahim Abboud
1964–65   n/p   Sirr al-Khatim al-Khalifah
1965–66   Umma   Muhammad Ahmad Mahgoub
1966–67   Umma   Sadiq al-Mahdi
1967–69   Umma   Muhammad Ahmad Mahgoub
1969   n/p   Babiker Awadalla
1969–76   military, SSU   Gaafur Muhammad al-Nimeiry
1976–77   SSU   Rashid Bakr
1977–85   military, SSU   Gaafur Muhammad al-Nimeiry
1985–86   n/p   al-Jazuli Dafallah
1986–89   Umma   Sadiq al-Mahdi

RECENT ELECTIONS

Presidential elections were held from 13–22 Dec. 2000. President Omar Hassan Ahmed al-Bashir was re-elected by 86·5% of votes cast, with his nearest rival, former president Gaafur Muhammad al-Nimeiry, gaining 9·6%. The main opposition groups and most of the electorate boycotted the polls. At the National Assembly elections held at the same time the ruling National Congress Party (NCP) won 355 of the 360 seats. In accordance with the peace deal that brought an end to the civil war, when parliament re-opened in Aug. 2005 the National Congress Party had 52% of the seats, the Sudan People's Liberation Movement 28%, the northern opposition 14% and dissident southern groups 6%.

CURRENT ADMINISTRATION

President: Lieut.-Gen. Omar Hassan Ahmed al-Bashir; b. 1944 (NCP; appointed 1989, re-elected March 1996 and Dec. 2000).

First Vice-President: Salva Kiir Mayardit. *Second Vice-President:* Ali Uthman Muhammad Taha.

In Sept. 2005 a government of national unity was formed as part of the agreement to end the civil war. In March 2006 it comprised:

Minister of Agriculture and Forestry: Mohamed Alamin Isa Alaghbash. *Animal and Fish Resources:* Galwak Deng. *Culture, Youth and Sports:* Mohamed Yusif Abdella. *Defence:* Lieut.-Gen. Abdel Rahim Mohamed Hussein. *Education:* Hamid Mohamed Ibrahim. *Energy and Mining:* Awad Ahmed al-Jaz. *Environment and Physical Development:* Dr Ahmed Babiker Nahar. *External Trade:* George Boreng Nyami. *Federal Government:* Abdel Basit Salih Sebdarat. *Finance and National Economy:* Al-Zobeir Ahmed Hassan. *Foreign Affairs:* Dr Lam Akol. *General Education:* Hamid Mohamed Ibrahim. *Guidance and Awqaf:* Dr Azhari Altijani. *Health:* Dr Tabitha Shokaya. *Higher Education and Scientific Research:* Dr Peter Newot Kok. *Humanitarian Affairs:* Kosti Manyebi. *Industry:* Jalal Yousif el Degair. *Information and Communication:* Alzahawi Ibrahim Malik. *International Co-operation:* Dr Altijani Salih Fidail. *Interior:* Alzubeir Beshir Taha. *Investment:* Malik Agar Ayar. *Irrigation and Water Resources:* Kamal Ali Mohamed. *Justice:* Mohamed Ali Almardi. *Labour, Public Service and Development of Human Resources:* Alison Manani Magaya. *Parliamentary Affairs:* Joseph Okello. *Presidency:* Bakri Hassan Salih. *Science and Technology:* Lieut.-Gen. Abdelrahman Saeed. *Tourism and Wildlife:* Joseph Malwal. *Transports, Roads and Bridges:* Kol Manyang Jok. *Welfare and Social Planning:* Samya Ahmed Mohammed. *Minister of the Cabinet:* Deng Alor Kuwal.

CURRENT LEADERS

Lieut.-Gen. Omar Hassan Ahmed al-Bashir

Position
President

Introduction
Omar al-Bashir is one of Africa's longest serving presidents, having seized power in 1989. He has since been re-elected twice, in 1996 and 2000, although both polls were boycotted by the main opposition groups. His rule has been characterized by civil war and genocide, although he signed a significant peace agreement in Jan. 2005 to end the long-running insurrection in southern Sudan.

Early Life
Bashir was born to a family of Sudanese peasants in 1944. He went to primary school in his home village before his family moved to Khartoum, where he completed secondary education. Having joined the Sudanese air force as a teenager, he soon made the grade as an officer and was sent to a military college in Egypt. He later served with a Sudanese unit that fought against Israel alongside Egyptian forces in the 1973 war. Promotions followed

quickly and by the early 1980s he was a general. His political life began with the military coup of 1989 when, together with a group of middle-ranking officers, he overthrew the elected government of Sadiq al-Mahdi and installed a Revolutionary Command Council.

Career in Office
The National Islamic Front (later renamed the National Congress Party), led by Hassan al-Turabi, gave support to Bashir's new military regime. Influenced by Turabi, and by the long campaigns fought in southern Sudan against animist and Christian secessionist rebels, Bashir began the Islamization of Sudan and introduced Sharia law, policies that further alienated the South. He moved Sudan into the radical Arab camp, allying his country with Libya and Syria. Political and economic isolation followed, aggravating the distress caused by instability and civil war.

In 1993 Bashir declared himself president. Long-promised elections were held in March 1996, when Bashir was elected head of state against obscure candidates in a poll that was regarded internationally as deeply flawed. For a time Sudan provided a haven for radical Islamic refugees who had been forced to quit their own states. These fundamentalists included al-Qaeda's Osama bin Laden. In 1992 and 1994 Bashir stepped up the campaign against the southern rebel Sudan People's Liberation Movement (SPLM), but the latter gained back most of their losses in 1995. By 1998 Sudan was regarded as a pariah state by the USA. In that year, US missiles destroyed a pharmaceutical factory in Khartoum that was suspected, wrongly as it turned out, of producing chemical weapons.

In 1999 Bashir declared a state of emergency during a power struggle with Turabi, then the speaker of the Sudanese parliament, who had moved to reduce the president's powers. Turabi, who had previously been regarded as Bashir's mentor, was toppled and parliament dissolved. In Dec. 2000 Bashir was re-elected as president, although the main opposition parties again boycotted the poll and disputed the result.

In the wake of the 11 Sept. 2001 attacks in the USA, Bashir made an effort to gain international acceptability. However, despite relaxations in the Sharia law, Sudan continued to be regarded by many in the West as a rogue state, crippled by poverty and conflict. Sudan was also cited by the UN for gross human rights violations, including forced labour, slavery and terrorism. Meanwhile, the civil war in the South continued, by this time having claimed over 2m. lives and displaced more than 4m. refugees.

On 9 Jan. 2005, after three years of talks, Bashir's government and the SPLM finally signed a comprehensive peace agreement. It provided for a government of national unity (headed by Bashir but also comprising members of the National Congress Party, the SPLM and other northern and southern political forces), self-determination for the South, a permanent ceasefire and the disengagement of forces. In July 2005 the agreement was briefly threatened when John Garang, the leader of the SPLM and first vice-president in the power-sharing government, was killed in a helicopter accident, provoking clashes between southern Sudanese and Arab northerners. Garang was replaced as first vice-president by his SPLM deputy, Salva Kiir Mayardit, in Aug. The formation of the national unity government was announced on 20 Sept. 2005 and a devolved government of southern Sudan was established on 22 Oct.

In addition to the civil war in the South, Bashir's regime has also overseen fierce fighting in the western province of Darfur between government-backed Arab militias and local black rebel forces. Since 2003 the conflict has reached new heights despite international attempts to stop the violence, the targeting of civilians having led to the displacement of some 2m. people and a humanitarian catastrophe.

DEFENCE

There is conscription for three years. Defence expenditure totalled US$426m. in 2003 (US$13 per capita), representing 2·7% of GDP. According to *Deadly Arsenals*, published by the Carnegie Endowment for International Peace, Sudan has both biological and chemical weapons research programmes.

Army

Strength (2002) 112,500 (20,000 conscripts). There is a para-military People's Defence Force of about 7,000 and additional army reserves of 85,000.

Navy

The navy operates in the Red Sea and also on the River Nile. The flotilla suffers from lack of maintenance and spares. Personnel in 2002 were believed to number 1,500. Major bases are at Port Sudan (HQ), Flamingo Bay and Khartoum.

Air Force

Personnel totalled (2002) about 3,000, with over 40 combat aircraft including F-5s, J-6s (Chinese-built versions of MiG-19s), F-7s (Chinese-built versions of MiG-21s) and MiG-23s.

INTERNATIONAL RELATIONS

Sudan is a member of the UN, the African Union, African Development Bank, COMESA, the Intergovernmental Authority on Development, IOM, OIC, Islamic Development Bank, the League of Arab States and is an ACP member state of the ACP-EU relationship.

Following the attacks on New York and Washington on 11 Sept. 2001 Sudan sought to distance itself from fundamentalism and international terrorism.

ECONOMY

Agriculture accounted for 39·2% of GDP, industry 18·3% and services 42·5% in 2002.

Overview

Since 1997 the Sudanese authorities have undertaken economic reforms that have contributed to broad based growth. In 1997 Sudan began implementing IMF macroeconomic reforms that have successfully stabilized inflation. Sudan began exporting crude oil in 1999 and recorded its first trade surplus in 1999. Current oil production stands at 220,000 bbls. per day, of which 70% is exported. In 2002 and 2003 Sudan adopted a further economic reform programme in which the authorities switched to indirect monetary management and broad money targeting, introduced a managed float exchange rate regime and began strengthening the fiscal regime. Sudan's primary resources are agricultural, but oil production and exports have been increasing in importance since Oct. 2000. Sudan's trade regime is considered by the IMF to be fairly open, with few non-tariff trade barriers and a simple average tariff rate of 22·7%. However, exports other than oil are stagnant owing to foreign currency constraints, inadequate infrastructure and a small industrial sector.

Currency

Until 1992 the monetary unit was the *Sudanese pound* (SDP) of 100 *piastres* and 1,000 *milliemes*. This was replaced in May 1992 by the *dinar* at a rate of 1 dinar = £S10. Sudanese pounds remain legal tender. Inflation was 7·7% in 2003 and 8·4% in 2004. Foreign exchange reserves were US$224m. in June 2002 and total money supply was 307,763m. dinars.

Budget

In 2001 revenues totalled 365·2bn. dinars and expenditures 418·8bn. dinars. Tax revenue accounted for 51·5% of revenues in 2001; current expenditure accounted for 81·9% of expenditures.

Performance

Real GDP growth was 4·6% in 2003 and 6·9% in 2004. Sudan's total GDP in 2004 was US$19·6bn.

Banking and Finance

The Bank of Sudan (*Governor*, Sabir Mohammed Hassan) opened in Feb. 1960 with an authorized capital of £S1·5m. as the central bank and bank of issue. Banks were nationalized in 1970 but in 1974 foreign banks were allowed to open branches. The application of Islamic law from 1 Jan. 1991 put an end to the charging of interest in official banking transactions, and seven banks are run on Islamic principles. Mergers of seven local banks in 1993 resulted in the formation of the Khartoum Bank, the Industrial Development Bank and the Savings Bank. In 2000 there were 25 commercial and private banks. In May 2000 the government announced plans for the banks to merge into six groups to consolidate the national economy but the restructure was yet to be implemented by 2006.

A stock exchange opened in Khartoum in 1995.

ENERGY AND NATURAL RESOURCES

Environment

Sudan's carbon dioxide emissions from the consumption and flaring of fossil fuels in 2002 were the equivalent of 0·3 tonnes per capita. An *Environmental Sustainability Index* compiled for the World Economic Forum meeting in Jan. 2005 ranked Sudan 140th in the world out of 146 countries analysed, with 35·9%. The index measured the ability of countries to maintain favourable environmental conditions and examined various factors including pollution levels and the use or abuse of natural resources.

Electricity

Installed capacity was 0·8m. kW in 2000. Production in 2000 was 2·26bn. kWh, with consumption per capita 73 kWh.

Oil and Gas

In 2002 oil reserves totalled 563m. bbls. In June 1998 Sudan began exploiting its reserves and on 31 Aug. 1999 it officially became an oil producing country; production in 2000 totalled 9·3m. tonnes. An oil refinery at Al-Jayli, with a capacity of 2·5m. tonnes, opened in 2000. Natural gas reserves in 2002 were 113bn. cu. metres.

Minerals

Mineral deposits include graphite, sulphur, chromium, iron, manganese, copper, zinc, fluorspar, natron, gypsum and anhydrite, magnesite, asbestos, talc, halite, kaolin, white mica, coal, diatomite (kieselguhr), limestone and dolomite, pumice, lead, wollastonite, black sands and vermiculite pyrites. Chromite and gold are mined. Production of salt, 2001: 77,783 tonnes; chromium ore (metal content), 2002: 14,000 tonnes; gold, 2001: 5,417 kg.

Agriculture

80% of the population depends on agriculture. Land tenure is based on customary rights; land is ultimately owned by the government. There were 16·23m. ha. of arable land in 2001 and 420,000 ha. of permanent crops. 1·95m. ha. were irrigated in 2001. There were 11,856 tractors in 2001 and 1,590 harvester-threshers.

Production (2000 estimates) in 1,000 tonnes: sugarcane, 4,982; sorghum, 2,521; groundnuts, 990; millet, 496; sesame seed, 305; seed cotton, 245; tomatoes, 242; wheat, 214; mangoes, 192; dates, 176; melons and watermelons, 169; cottonseed, 157. Livestock (2000): cattle, 37·09m.; sheep, 42·80m.; goats, 37·80m.; chickens, 42m.; camels, 3·8m.

Forestry

Forests covered 61·63m. ha. in 2000, or 25·9% of the total land area. The annual loss of 959,000 ha. of forests between 1990 and 2000 was exceeded only in Brazil and Indonesia. In 2001, 19·04m. cu. metres of roundwood were cut.

Fisheries
In 2001 the total catch was 58,000 tonnes, of which 53,000 tonnes were freshwater fish.

INDUSTRY
Production figures (in 1,000 tonnes): distillate fuel oil (2000), 835; sugar (2002), 744; wheat flour (1999), 532; residual fuel oil (2000), 305; cement (2001), 146; vegetable oils (2001), 32. In 2000 an industrial complex assembling 12,000 vehicles a year opened.

Labour
The total workforce in 1996 was 10,652,000 (71% males). 68% of the economically active population in 1995 were engaged in agriculture, fisheries and forestry.

INTERNATIONAL TRADE
Foreign debt was US$16,389m. in 2002.

Imports and Exports
In 2002 imports (f.o.b.) amounted to US$2,152·8m. (US$1,395·1m. in 2001); exports (f.o.b.) US$1,949·1m. (US$1,698·7m. in 2001). The main imports are petroleum products, machinery and equipment, foodstuffs, manufactured goods, medicines and chemicals. Main exports are oil, cotton, gum arabic, oil seeds, sorghum, livestock, sesame, gold and sugar. The main import sources in 2000 were Saudi Arabia (11·8%), France (8·6%), Italy (6·3%), United Arab Emirates (5·5%) and Germany (5·4%). Principal export markets in 2000 were Saudi Arabia (18·1%), Japan (15·7%), UK (9·2%), South Korea (7·9%) and Italy (7·1%).

COMMUNICATIONS

Roads
In 2002 there were estimated to be 11,900 km of roads, of which 4,320 km were paved. There were an estimated 87,400 passenger cars and 57,400 trucks and vans in 2002.

Rail
The total length of the railways is 4,599 km. In 2000 the railways carried 0·4m. passengers and 1·4m. tonnes of freight.

Civil Aviation
There is an international airport at Khartoum. The national carrier is the government-owned Sudan Airways, which operates domestic and international services. In 1999 scheduled airline traffic of Sudan-based carriers flew 6·7m. km, carrying 390,000 passengers (245,000 on international flights).

Shipping
Supplementing the railways are regular steamer services of the Sudan Railways. Port Sudan is the major seaport; Suakin port opened in 1991. Sea-going shipping totalled 33,000 GRT in 2002, including oil tankers 1,000 GRT.

Telecommunications
In 2002 Sudan had 862,600 telephone subscribers (26·5 per 1,000 persons) and 200,000 PCs were in use (6·1 per 1,000 persons). There were 45,000 fax machines and 190,800 mobile phone subscribers in 2002. The number of Internet users in 2002 was 84,000.

Postal Services
In 2003 there were 218 post offices.

SOCIAL INSTITUTIONS

Justice
The judiciary is a separate independent department of state, directly and solely responsible to the President of the Republic.

The general administrative supervision and control of the judiciary is vested in the High Judicial Council.

Civil Justice is administered by the courts constituted under the Civil Justice Ordinance, namely the High Court of Justice—consisting of the Court of Appeal and Judges of the High Court, sitting as courts of original jurisdiction—and Province Courts—consisting of the Courts of Province and District Judges. The law administered is 'justice, equity and good conscience' in all cases where there is no special enactment. Procedure is governed by the Civil Justice Ordinance.

Justice for the Muslim population is administered by the Islamic law courts, which form the Sharia Divisions of the Court of Appeal, High Courts and Kadis Courts; President of the Sharia Division is the Grand Kadi. In Dec. 1990 the government announced that Sharia would be applied in the non-Muslim southern parts of the country as well.

Criminal Justice is administered by the courts constituted under the Code of Criminal Procedure, namely major courts, minor courts and magistrates' courts. Serious crimes are tried by major courts, which are composed of a President and two members and have the power to pass the death sentence. Major Courts are, as a rule, presided over by a Judge of the High Court appointed to a Provincial Circuit or a Province Judge. There is a right of appeal to the Chief Justice against any decision or order of a Major Court, and all its findings and sentences are subject to confirmation by him.

Lesser crimes are tried by Minor Courts consisting of three Magistrates and presided over by a Second Class Magistrate, and by Magistrates' Courts.

The population in penal institutions in March 2003 was approximately 12,000 (36 per 100,000 of national population).

Education
In 2000–01 there were 12,985 teachers for 349,306 pupils at pre-primary schools; 96,050 teachers (1999–2000) for 2·8m. pupils at primary schools; and (1999–2000) 42,513 secondary school teachers for 979,514 pupils. In 1996 there were 17 universities, two Islamic universities, one university of science and technology, and an institute of advanced banking. There were also 14 other higher education institutions. Adult literacy rate in 2001 was 58·8% (male, 70·0%; female, 47·7%).

Health
In 2000 there were 4,973 physicians, 218 dentists, 26,730 nurses and 311 pharmacists. Hospital bed provision in 2004 was 74 per 100,000 population.

RELIGION
Islam is the state religion. In 2001, 70% of the population were Sunni Muslims, concentrated in the north; Christians (17%) and traditional animists (12%) are concentrated in the south. In May 2005 the Roman Catholic church had one cardinal.

CULTURE

World Heritage Sites
Sudan has one site on the UNESCO World Heritage List: Gebel Barkal and the Sites of the Napatan Region (inscribed on the list in 2003), a collection of tombs, pyramids and palaces of the Second Kingdom of Kush (900 BC to AD 350).

Broadcasting
Broadcasting is controlled by the Sudan National Broadcasting Corporation and Sudan Television (colour by PAL). There are also two regional TV stations, in the centre and in the north of the country. There were 12·27m. TV sets in 2001 and 16·30m. radio receivers in 2000.

Press
In 1999 there were around 20 daily newspapers. Opposition newspapers are permitted although they are vetted by an official censor.

Tourism

In 2001 there were 50,000 foreign tourists, spending a total of US$56m. There were seven National Parks and ten protected areas in 2000.

DIPLOMATIC REPRESENTATIVES

Of Sudan in the United Kingdom (3 Cleveland Row, London, SW1A 1DD)
Ambassador: Dr Hassan Abdin Mohammad Osman.

Of the United Kingdom in Sudan (off Sharia Al Baladia, Khartoum East)
Ambassador: Ian Cliff, OBE.

Of Sudan in the USA (2210 Massachusetts Ave., NW, Washington, D.C., 20008)
Ambassador: Vacant.
Chargé d'Affaires a.i.: Khidir Haroun Ahmed.

Of the USA in Sudan (Sharia Ali Abdul Latif, POB 699, Khartoum)
Ambassador: Vacant.
Chargé d'Affaires a.i.: Cameron Hume.

Of Sudan to the United Nations
Ambassador: Elfatih Mohamed Ahmed Erwa.

Of Sudan to the European Union
Ambassador: Ali Youssif Ahmed.

FURTHER READING

Daly, M. W., *Sudan.* [Bibliography] 2nd ed. ABC-Clio, Oxford and Santa Barbara (CA), 1992
Daly, M. W. and Sikainga, A. A. (eds.) *Civil War in the Sudan.* I. B. Tauris, London, 1993
Deng, F. M., *War of Visions: Conflict of Identities in the Sudan.* The Brookings Institution, Washington, D.C., 1995

SURINAME

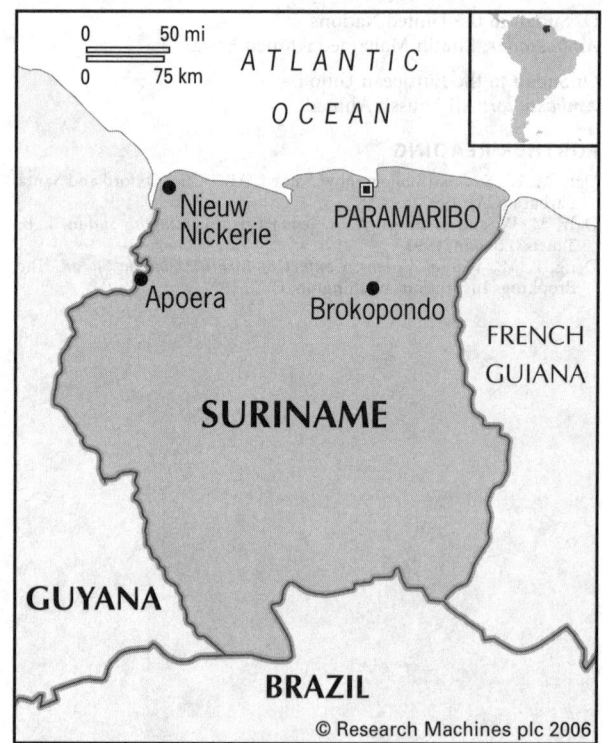

Republic of Suriname

Capital: Paramaribo
Population projection, 2010: 462,000
GDP per capita, 2002: (PPP$) 6,590
HDI/world rank: 0·755/86

KEY HISTORICAL EVENTS

The first Europeans to reach the area were the Spanish in 1499 but it was the British who established a colony in 1650. At the peace of Breda (1667), Suriname was assigned to the Netherlands in exchange for the colony of New Netherland in North America. Suriname was twice in British possession during the Napoleonic Wars, in 1799–1802 and 1804–16, when it was returned to the Netherlands.

On 25 Nov. 1975 Suriname gained full independence. On 25 Feb. 1980 the government was ousted in a coup and a National Military Council (NMC) established. A further coup on 13 Aug. replaced several members of the NMC and the State President. Other attempted coups took place in 1981 and 1982, with the NMC retaining control. In Oct. 1987 a new constitution was approved by referendum. Following elections in Nov. Suriname returned to democracy in Jan. 1988 but on 24 Dec. 1990 a further military coup deposed the government. There was a peace agreement with rebel groups in Aug. 1992 and elections were held in May 1996.

TERRITORY AND POPULATION

Suriname is located on the northern coast of South America between 2–6° North latitude and 54–59° West longitude. It is bounded in the north by the Atlantic Ocean, east by French Guiana, west by Guyana, and south by Brazil. Area, 163,820 sq. km. Census population, 2004, 492,829; density, 3·0 per sq. km. The United Nations population estimate for 2004 was 446,000.

The UN gives a projected population for 2010 of 462,000.

The capital, Paramaribo, had (2004 census) 242,946 inhabitants.

Suriname is divided into ten districts. They are (with 2004 census population and chief town): Brokopondo, population 14,215 (Brokopondo); Commewijne, 24,649 (Nieuw Amsterdam); Coronie, 2,887 (Totness); Marowijne, 16,642 (Albina); Nickerie, 36,639 (Nieuw Nickerie); Para, 18,749 (Onverwacht); Paramaribo, 242,946—representing 49% of Suriname's total population (Paramaribo); Saramacca, 15,980 (Groningen); Sipaliwini, 34,136 (local authority in Paramaribo); Wanica, 85,986 (Lelydorp).

Major ethnic groups in percentages of the population in 2004: Indo-Pakistani, 26%; Creole, 18%; Javanese, 15%; Bushnegroes (Blacks), 15%; Amerindian, 4%. 66·7% of the population lived in urban areas in 2004.

The official language is Dutch. English is widely spoken next to Hindi, Javanese and Chinese as inter-group communication. A vernacular, called 'Sranan' or 'Surinamese', is used as a *lingua franca*. In 1976 it was decided that Spanish was to become the nation's principal working language.

SOCIAL STATISTICS

Births, 2003, 9,634; deaths, 3,154. 2003 rates per 1,000 population: birth rate, 20·0; death rate, 6·6. Expectation of life, 2003, was 65·9 years for males and 72·6 for females. Annual population growth rate, 1992–2004, 1·4%. Infant mortality, 2002, 21·1 per 1,000 live births; fertility rate, 2003, 2·4 births per woman. Abortion is illegal.

CLIMATE

The climate is equatorial, with uniformly high temperatures and rainfall. The temperature is an average of 27°C throughout the year; there are two rainy seasons (May–July and Nov.–Jan.) and two dry seasons (Aug.–Oct. and Feb.–April). Paramaribo, Jan. 21°C, July 32·4°C. Average rainfall 182·3 mm.

CONSTITUTION AND GOVERNMENT

The current constitution was ratified on 30 Sept. 1987. Parliament is a 51-member *National Assembly*. The head of state is the *President*, elected for a five-year term by a two-thirds majority by the National Assembly, or, failing that, by an electoral college, the United People's Assembly, enlarged by the inclusion of regional and local councillors, by a simple majority.

National Anthem

'God zij met ons Suriname' ('God be with our Suriname'); words by C. A. Hoekstra, tune by J. C. de Puy. There is a Sranan version, 'Opo kondreman oen opo'; words by H. de Ziel.

RECENT ELECTIONS

Parliamentary elections were held on 25 May 2005. The New Front for Democracy (NF) won 23 of the available 51 seats (41·5% of the vote). The NF alliance comprises the National Party of Suriname (8 seats), the Progressive Reform Party (7), Pertjajah Luhur (6) and the Suriname Labour Party (2). The National Democratic Party won 15 seats (22·8%), People's Alliance for Progress took 5 (14·6%), A-Com took 5 (7·0%) and Alternative-1 took 3 (6·3%).

On 3 Aug. 2005 Runaldo Ronald Venetiaan was re-elected *President* by the United People's Assembly, claiming 560 out of 879 votes, after no candidate had won the necessary two-thirds majority in two earlier elections in the National Assembly. Ram Sardjoe was elected *Vice-President* and *Prime Minister*.

CURRENT ADMINISTRATION

President: Runaldo Ronald Venetiaan; b. 1936 (National Party of Suriname; sworn in 12 Aug. 2000 for a second time, having previously held office from Sept. 1991 to Sept. 1996).

Vice-President and Prime Minister: Ram Sardjoe; b. 1935 (Progressive Reform Party; sworn in 12 Aug. 2005).

In March 2006 the government comprised:

Minister of Agriculture and Fisheries: Kermechend Raghoebarsingh. *Defence:* Ivan Fernald. *Education and Human Development:* Edwin Wolf. *Finance:* Humphrey Hildenberg. *Foreign Affairs:* Lygia Kraag-Keteldijk. *Health:* Celsius Waterberg. *Interior:* Maurits Hassankhan. *Justice and Police:* Chandrikapersad Santokhi. *Labour:* Clifford Marica. *Natural Resources:* Gregory Rusland. *Physical* Planning, Land and Forestry Management: Michael Jong Tjien Fa. *Planning and Development Co-operation:* Rick Van Ravenswaay. *Public Works:* Ganeshkoemar Kandhai. *Regional Development:* Michel Felisie. *Social Affairs:* Hendrik Setrowidjojo. *Trade and Industry:* Vacant. *Transport, Communication and Tourism:* Alice Amafo.

CURRENT LEADERS

Runaldo Ronald Venetiaan

Position
President

Introduction
Runaldo Ronald Venetiaan has been president of Suriname since 2000, having previously held the office between 1991 and 1996. He was re-elected in 2005. Dedicated to free market principles, he has implemented a series of measures to bring the struggling economy that he inherited under control. His first term in office was also characterized by a programme of austerity measures.

Early Life
Venetiaan was born on 18 June 1936 in Paramaribo. He later moved to the Netherlands, where he studied mathematics and physics at Leiden University. Returning to Suriname, he undertook a teaching career before being appointed minister of education in 1973 in the government of Henck Arron, holding office until a military coup in 1980. After civilian government was re-established, Venetiaan resumed his role in the education ministry in 1988. In 1991 the New Front for Democracy won parliamentary elections and elected Venetiaan to the presidency.

Career in Office
In 1992 Venetiaan signed a peace accord with the rebel Surinamese Liberation Army, which had been operational since the mid-1980s. Among the primary aims of Venetiaan's first term was to secure economic stability after the years of coups and counter-coups. Despite stabilizing the currency and achieving a budget surplus, his austerity measures were widely unpopular and he lost the 1996 election to Jules Wijdenbosch, an ally of former military dictator Desi Bouterse, who instigated increased public spending.

With Wijdenbosch increasingly under attack for economic mismanagement, elections were called for May 2000 and Venetiaan led the New Front to victory. He took over a faltering economy burdened by bureaucracy, high inflation, a devalued currency, overwhelming international debt and a collapsing healthcare system. In response, he cut public spending, replaced the guilder (in Jan. 2004) with the Suriname dollar and restructured the economically significant banana industry.

Internationally, his term was dominated by a longstanding disagreement with Guyana over maritime boundaries. The

UN established a tribunal to mediate in June 2004. At the parliamentary elections of May 2005 Venetiaan's New Front for Democracy coalition returned the largest number of MPs, with the National Democratic Party of Bouterse second. However, the New Front failed to obtain the two-thirds majority required to elect the president. In Aug. 2005 Venetiaan won a second term of office when he polled 560 votes against 315 for his opponent, Rabin Parmessar, in a vote by the United People's Conference, consisting of MPs and elected local and district representatives.

DEFENCE

In 2004 defence expenditure totalled US$19·6m. (US$40 per capita), representing 1·2% of GDP.

Army
Total strength was estimated at 1,400 in 2002.

Navy
In 2002 personnel, based at Paramaribo, totalled 240.

Air Force
Personnel (2002): 200. There were seven combat aircraft.

INTERNATIONAL RELATIONS

In June 2000 a maritime dispute arose between Suriname and Guyana over offshore oil exploration.

Suriname is a member of the UN, WTO, OAS, Inter-American Development Bank, ACS, CARICOM, OIC, Islamic Development Bank and is an ACP member state of the ACP-EU relationship.

ECONOMY

In 2002 agriculture contributed 11·1% of GDP, industry 19·6% and services 69·3%.

Currency
The unit of currency is the *Suriname dollar* (SRD) of 100 *cents*, introduced on 1 Jan. 2004 to replace the *Suriname guilder* (SRG) at a rate of one Suriname dollar = 1,000 Suriname guilders. Foreign exchange reserves totalled US$114m. and gold reserves were 263,000 troy oz in June 2002. Total money supply in April 2002 was 417,896m. Sf. Inflation was 9·0% in 2004, down from 23·1% in 2003. In 1999 it had been 98·7%.

Budget
2004 revenue (in 1m. Suriname dollars) was 1,175·8 made up of: direct taxes, 368·4; indirect taxes, 431·1; bauxite levy and other revenues, 103·1; aid, 273·2.

Total expenditure in 2004 (in 1m. Suriname dollars) was 1,545·7, made up of: wages and salaries, 380·3; grants and contributions, 291·3; other current expenditures, 645·1; capital expenditure, 229·0.

Performance
After two years of recession in 1999 and 2000 real GDP growth was 4·5% in 2001, 3·0% in 2002, 5·3% in 2003 and 4·6% in 2004. In 2004 total GDP was US$1·1bn.

Banking and Finance
The Central Bank of Suriname (*Governor,* Andre Telting) is a bankers' bank and also the bank of issue. There are three commercial banks; the Suriname People's Credit Bank operates under the auspices of the government. There is a post office savings bank, a mortgage bank, an investment bank, a long-term investments agency, a National Development Bank and an Agrarian Bank.

ENERGY AND NATURAL RESOURCES

Environment
Suriname's carbon dioxide emissions from the consumption and flaring of fossil fuels in 2002 were the equivalent of 4·0 tonnes per capita.

Electricity

Installed capacity in 1999 was 0·4m. kW. Production (1999) 1·64bn. kWh; consumption per capita in 1999 was 3,814 kWh.

Oil and Gas

Crude oil production (2004), 4,098,463 bbls. Reserves in 2002 were 74m. bbls.

Minerals

Bauxite is the most important mineral. Suriname is the seventh largest bauxite producer in the world. Production (2004), 4,217,000 tonnes.

Agriculture

Agriculture is restricted to the alluvial coastal zone; in 2001 there were 57,000 ha. of arable land and 10,000 ha. of permanent crops. The staple food crop is rice: production, 164,000 tonnes in 2000. Other crops (2000 in 1,000 tonnes): sugarcane, 90; bananas, 49; plantains, 11; oranges, 10; coconuts, 9; groundnuts, 9; cassava, 3. Livestock in 2000: cattle, 128,727; sheep, 7,360; goats, 6,930; pigs, 22,280; poultry, 2·0m.

Forestry

Forests covered 14·11m. ha. in 2000, or 90·5% of the land area. In terms of percentage coverage, Suriname was the world's most heavily forested sovereign country in 2000. Production of roundwood in 2003 was 150,765 cu. metres.

Fisheries

The catch in 2004 amounted to an estimated 20,177 tonnes, almost entirely from marine waters.

INDUSTRY

There is no longer any aluminium smelting, but there are food-processing and wood-using industries. Production: alumina (2001), 1,900,000 tonnes; residual fuel oil (2000), 258,000 tonnes; cement (2001), 60,000 tonnes; prepared animal feeds (1996), 14,000 tonnes; wheat flour (1996), 14,000 tonnes; sawnwood (2003), 56,000 cu. metres.

Labour

Out of 156,705 people in employment in 2004, 27,995 were in public administration and defence; 25,012 in wholesale and retail trade; 14,031 in construction; 12,593 in agriculture, fishing, hunting and forestry; and 10,971 in manufacturing. In 2004 there were 16,425 unemployed persons, or 9·5% of the workforce.

INTERNATIONAL TRADE

Imports and Exports

In 2004 imports (f.o.b.) amounted to US$740·0m. (US$703·9m. in 2003); exports (f.o.b.) US$782·2m. (US$590·3m. in 2003).

Principal imports, 2004: nonelectrical machinery, 14·4%; food products, 11·9%; road vehicles, 9·5%. Principal exports, 2004: alumina, 40·8%; gold, 29·3%; crustaceans and molluscs, 3·6%.

In 2004 imports (in US$1m.) were mainly from the USA (165·2), Netherlands (147·8), Trinidad and Tobago (131·4), Japan (96·6) and Netherlands Antilles (20·8); exports were mainly to Norway (173·0), USA (138·0), Canada (73·3), France (60·0) and Netherlands (14·5).

COMMUNICATIONS

Roads

The road network covered 4,492 km in 2000, of which 26·0% were paved. In 2004 there were 76,466 passenger cars, 25,364 trucks and vans, 4,166 buses and coaches and 39,693 motorcycles and mopeds. There were 69 fatalities in road accidents in 2004.

Rail

There are two single-track railways.

Civil Aviation

There is an international airport at Paramaribo (Johan Adolf Pengel). The national carrier is Surinam Airways, which in 2003 had flights to Amsterdam, Belem, Cayenne, Curaçao, Georgetown, Haiti, Miami and Port of Spain. In 1999 scheduled airline traffic of Suriname-based carriers flew 5·6m. km, carrying 194,000 passengers (190,000 on international flights). In 2004 there were 149,589 passenger arrivals and 148,353 departures.

Shipping

The Royal Netherlands Steamship Co. operates services to the Netherlands, the USA, and regionally. The Suriname Navigation Co. maintains services from Paramaribo to Georgetown, Cayenne and the Caribbean area. Merchant shipping in 2002 totalled 5,000 GRT. In 2000 vessels totalling 1,120,000 NRT entered ports and vessels totalling 2,186,000 NRT cleared.

Telecommunications

Telephone subscribers numbered 164,400 in 2001, equivalent to 373·6 for every 1,000 persons, and 20,000 PCs were in use (45·5 per 1,000 inhabitants). There were 108,400 mobile phone subscribers in 2002 and 1,300 fax machines. In 2002 there were 20,000 Internet users.

Postal Services

In 2002 there were 38 post offices.

SOCIAL INSTITUTIONS

Justice

Members of the court of justice are nominated by the President. There are three cantonal courts. Suriname was one of ten countries to sign an agreement in Feb. 2001 establishing a Caribbean Court of Justice to replace the British Privy Council as the highest civil and criminal court. In the meantime the number of signatories has risen to twelve. The court was inaugurated at Port-of-Spain, Trinidad on 16 April 2005.

The population in penal institutions in June 1999 was 1,933 (437 per 100,000 of national population).

Education

Adult literacy was 88·0% in 2003 (92·3% among males and 84·1% among females). In 2003–04, 298 primary schools out of a total of 312 had 3,096 teachers and 62,086 pupils; 124 secondary schools had 41,904 pupils. In 2000–01 the university had 2,745 students. There is a teacher training college with (2000–01) 1,942 students.

Health

In 2004 there were 1,611 general hospital beds. In 2003 there were 295 physicians.

RELIGION

At the 2004 census there were 200,744 Christians of varying denominations, 98,240 Hindus and 66,307 Muslims.

CULTURE

World Heritage Sites

Suriname has two sites on the UNESCO World Heritage List: Central Suriname Nature Reserve (inscribed on the list in 2000); and the Historic Inner City of Paramaribo (2002).

Broadcasting

The government controls the partly commercial Stichting Radio Omroep Suriname and Radio Suriname Internationaal, and Surinaamse Televisie Stichting. There were 115,000 TV sets (colour by NTSC) in 2001 and 300,000 radio receivers in 1997. There were 27 radio and 16 television stations in 2005.

Cinema

There were two cinemas in Paramaribo in 1999.

Press

There were four daily newspapers in 2005.

Tourism

In 2002 there were 85,000 foreign tourist arrivals; tourist receipts totalled US$62m.

Festivals

The people of Suriname celebrate Chinese New Year (Jan.); Phagwa, a Hindu celebration (March–April); Id-Ul-Fitre, the sugar feast at the end of Ramadan (May); Avondvierdaagse, a carnival (during the Easter holidays); Suriflora, a celebration of plants and flowers (April–May); Keti koti, an Afro-Surinamese holiday to commemorate the abolition of slavery (1 July); Suri-pop, a popular music festival (July); Nationale Kunstbeurs, arts and crafts (Oct.–Nov.); Divali, the Hindu ceremony of light (Nov.); Djaran Kepang, a Javanese dance held on feast days; Winti-prey, a ceremony for the Winti gods.

Museums and Galleries

The main museums (1998) were: Surinaams Museum and Fort Zeelandia in Paramaribo; the Open Air Museum at Nieuw Amsterdam. Art Galleries include: Suriname Art 2000; the Academy for Higher Arts and Cultural Education; and the Ready Tex Art Boutique, all in Paramaribo; and Nola Hatterman Instituut at Fort Zeelandia.

DIPLOMATIC REPRESENTATIVES

Of Suriname in the United Kingdom
Ambassador: Edgar S. R. Amanh (resides in The Hague).

Of the United Kingdom in Suriname
Ambassador: Stephen Hiscock (resides in Georgetown, Guyana).

Of Suriname in the USA (4301 Connecticut Ave., NW, Washington, D.C., 20008)
Ambassador: Henry Lothar Illes.

Of the USA in Suriname (Dr Sophie Redmondstraat 129, Paramaribo)
Ambassador: Marsha E. Barnes.

Of Suriname to the United Nations
Ambassador: Ewald Wensley Limon.

Of Suriname to the European Union
Ambassador: Gerhard Otmar Hiwat.

FURTHER READING

Dew, E. M., *Trouble in Suriname, 1975–1993.* New York, 1995

National Statistical Office: Algemeen Bureau voor de Statistiek, POB 244, Paramaribo.

SWAZILAND

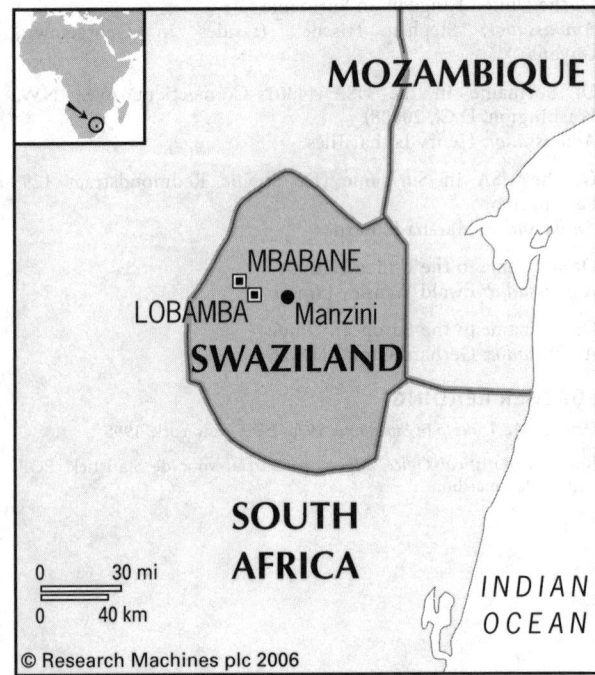

Umbuso weSwatini
(Kingdom of Swaziland)

Capital: Mbabane (Administrative), Lobamba (Legislative)
Population projection, 2010: 1·01m.
GDP per capita, 2003: (PPP$) 4,726
HDI/world rank: 0·498/147

KEY HISTORICAL EVENTS

The Swazi migrated into the country to which they have given their name in the last half of the 18th century. The independence of the Swazis was guaranteed in the conventions of 1881 and 1884 between the British Government and the Government of the South African Republic. In 1894 the South African Republic was given powers of protection and administration. In 1902, after the conclusion of the Boer War, a special commissioner took charge, and under an order-in-council in 1903 the Governor of the Transvaal administered the territory. Swaziland became independent on 6 Sept. 1968. A state of emergency imposed in 1973 is still in force. On 25 April 1986 King Mswati III was installed as King of Swaziland.

TERRITORY AND POPULATION

Swaziland is bounded in the north, west and south by South Africa, and in the east by Mozambique. The area is 17,363 sq. km (6,704 sq. miles). *De facto* population (census 1997), 929,718 (489,564 females); density, 53·5 per sq. km. 2005 population estimate: 1,032,000. In 2003, 76·4% of the population were rural. More than 50% of the population is under 18 years of age.

The UN gives a projected population for 2010 of 1·01m.

The country is divided into four districts: Hhohho, Lubombo, Manzini and Shiselweni.

Main urban areas: Mbabane, the administrative capital (73,000 inhabitants in 1999); Manzini; Big Bend; Mhlume; Nhlangano.

The population is 84% Swazi and 10% Zulu. The official languages are Swazi and English.

SOCIAL STATISTICS

2000 estimates: births, 35,000; deaths, 23,000. Estimated rates, 2000 (per 1,000 population): births, 33·4; deaths, 22·0. As a result of the impact of AIDS, expectation of life has gradually been declining. It was 58 years in 1995, but by 2003 was down to 32·9 years for females and 32·1 years for males, the lowest in the world overall. In 2002, 38·6% of all adults were infected with HIV. In Sept. 2001 King Mswati III told the teenage girls of the country to stop having sex for five years as part of the country's drive to reduce the spread of HIV. Annual population growth rate, 1992–2002, 1·9%. Infant mortality, 2001, 106 per 1,000 live births; fertility rate, 2001, 4·5 births per woman.

CLIMATE

A temperate climate with two seasons. Nov. to March is the wet season, when temperatures range from mild to hot, with frequent thunderstorms. The cool, dry season from May to Sept. is characterized by clear, bright sunny days. Mbabane, Jan. 68°F (20°C), July 54°F (12·2°C). Annual rainfall 56" (1,402 mm).

CONSTITUTION AND GOVERNMENT

The reigning King is **Mswati III** (b. 1968; crowned 25 April 1986), who succeeded his father, King Sobhuza II (reigned 1921–82). The King rules in conjunction with the Queen Mother (his mother, or a senior wife). Critics of the King or his mother run the risk of arrest.

A new constitution was signed into law on 26 July 2005 and came into force in Jan. 2006. There is a *House of Assembly* of 65 members, 55 of whom are elected each from one constituency (*inkhundla*), and ten appointed by the King; and a *House of Senators* of 30 members, ten of whom are elected by the House of Assembly and 20 appointed by the King. Elections are held in two rounds, the second being a run-off between the five candidates who come first in each constituency.

There is also a traditional *Swazi National Council* headed by the King and Queen Mother at which all Swazi men are entitled to be heard.

National Anthem

'Nkulunkulu mnikati wetibusiso temaSwati' ('O Lord our God bestower of blessings upon the Swazi'); words by A. E. Simelane, tune by D. K. Rycroft.

RECENT ELECTIONS

At the elections of 18 Oct. 2003 only non-partisans were elected. Political parties are illegal and advocates of multi-party politics are considered to be troublemakers.

CURRENT ADMINISTRATION

In March 2006 the cabinet comprised:
Prime Minister: Absalom Themba Dlamini (sworn in on 26 Nov. 2003).
Deputy Prime Minister: Albert H. Shabangu.
Minister for Agriculture and Co-operatives: Mtiti Fakudze. *Economic Planning and Development:* Rev. Absalom Muntu Dlamini. *Education:* Constance Simelane. *Enterprise and Employment:* Lutfo Dlamini. *Finance:* Majozi Sithole. *Foreign Affairs and Commerce:* Moses Mathendele Dlamini. *Health and Social Welfare:* Mfomfo Nkambule. *Housing and Urban Development:* Mabili Dlamini. *Interior:* Prince Gabheni

Dlamini. *Justice:* Prince David Dlamini. *Natural Resources and Energy:* Dumsile Sukati. *Public Service and Information:* Themba Msibi. *Public Works and Transport:* Elijah Shongwe. *Regional Development and Youth Affairs:* Sipho Shongwe. *Tourism, Environment and Communication:* Thandie Shongwe.

Government Website: http://www.gov.sz

CURRENT LEADERS

Mswati III

Position
King

Introduction
Mswati came to the throne in 1986. Effectively an absolute monarchy, he has received domestic and international criticism for his suppression of political opposition. Among the greatest challenges of Mswati's reign has been the rapid increase in cases of HIV and AIDS in Swaziland.

Early Life
Mswati was born on 19 April 1968 in Manzini to one of the wives of King Sobhuza II and given the name Makhosetive (King of All Nations). Sobhuza's death in 1982 left a power vacuum that led to several years of infighting between various queens regent, crown princes and members of Liqoqo (the traditional advisory body which wielded significant power over the crown). In Oct. 1985 Makhosetive's mother dismissed several leading Liqoqo figures and recalled her son from his schooling in England. Makhosetive was crowned as Mswati III in April 1986.

Career in Office
Among Mswati's first acts as King was to dissolve the Liqoqo. Popular discontent grew at the prohibition on opposition political parties and Mswati's increasingly autocratic rule, leading to the establishment of the illegal People's United Democratic Movement (Pudemo). In 1990 Mswati agreed to open dialogue on the nation's political future. The national assembly was directly elected for the first time in 1993 and Mswati announced plans for a new constitution the following year.

With little progress having been made by 1996, Mswati established a constitutional commission. Pudemo continued to co-ordinate opposition, criticizing the King for filling the commission with his conservative supporters and boycotting the national assembly elections of Oct. 1998. In 2000 Pudemo leader Mario Masuku demanded an end to the state of emergency called 27 years earlier and was arrested for sedition. He was imprisoned pending his trial which collapsed in 2002. On his release he stated his belief that government could only be reformed when the monarchy was 'wiped out'. In 2001 the constitutional commission reported back, providing the framework for the writing of a new constitution but asserting that the majority of the population did not favour the formation of new parties. In Dec. 2002, amid declining relations with the judiciary, six court of appeal judges resigned in protest at the King's use of rule by decree. The judges claimed that Mswati's repeal of several court decisions was unconstitutional. The crisis gave renewed impetus to the opposition alliance who called for a series of mass strikes. A new draft constitution was presented to the King in 2003, introducing a bill of rights but maintaining the executive role of the monarchy and the ban on political parties. Having been adopted by parliament and signed by the King in 2005, the constitution came into force in Jan. 2006.

Swaziland has one of the highest AIDS rates in the world. In Oct. 2001 Mswati ordered that all virgins should abstain from sex for five years or face a fine. The following month Mswati paid a cow in recompense for taking an 18 year-old bride, Zena Mahlangu. Mahlangu's mother accused aides of the King of kidnapping her daughter and undertook legal proceedings to secure her return. Although the case collapsed, it received international attention and highlighted the growing challenges to Mswati's autocratic style.

Swaziland's economy is reliant on neighbouring South Africa. By early 2003 up to 25% of the population were at risk from food shortages. Mswati's decision to spend US$45m. on a royal jet was criticized by the IMF who suggested that such use of limited foreign exchange reserves could put off potential international donors.

DEFENCE

Army Air Wing
There are two Israeli-built Arava transports with weapon attachments for light attack duties.

INTERNATIONAL RELATIONS

Swaziland is a member of the UN, WTO, the African Union, African Development Bank, COMESA, SADC, the Commonwealth and is an ACP member state of the ACP-EU relationship.

ECONOMY

Agriculture accounted for 15·7% of GDP in 2002, industry 49·8% and services 34·5%.

Currency
The unit of currency is the *lilangeni* (plural *emalangeni*) (SZL) of 100 *cents* but Swaziland remains in the Common Monetary Area and the South African rand is legal tender. In 2004 inflation was 3·5%. In June 2002 foreign exchange reserves were US$253m. and total money supply was 832m. emalangeni.

Budget
The fiscal year begins on 1 April. Total revenue in financial year 2000 totalled 2,708·2m. emalangeni and total expenditure 2,899·7m. emalangeni.

Performance
Real GDP growth was 2·1% in 2004 (2·7% in 2003). Total GDP in 2004 was US$2·4bn.

Banking and Finance
The central bank and bank of issue is the Central Bank of Swaziland (*Governor,* Martin Dlamini), established in 1974. In 2004 there were four banking institutions, three foreign (South African-owned) private banks, Swazibank (state-owned) and a housing bank. In 2003 there were 178 credit and saving unions.

In 1990 Swaziland Stock Brokers was established to trade in stocks and shares for institutional and private clients.

ENERGY AND NATURAL RESOURCES

Environment
Swaziland's carbon dioxide emissions from the consumption and flaring of fossil fuels were the equivalent of 0·8 tonnes per capita in 2002.

Electricity
Installed capacity was 50,000 kW in 1993. Production was about 348m. kWh in 2001; total consumption was an estimated 963m. kWh. Swaziland imports about two-thirds of its electricity needs from South Africa.

Minerals
Output (in tonnes) in 2002: coal, 313,272; asbestos (2000), 12,690; quarry stone (2001), 350,000 cu. metres. Diamond production was 64,000 carats in 1994. The diamond mine closed down in 1996 and the asbestos mine in 2000.

The oldest known mine (iron ore) in the world, dating back to 41,000 BC, was located at the Lion Cavern Site on Ngwenya Mountain.

Agriculture

In 2001 there were 178,000 ha. of arable land and 12,000 ha. of permanent cropland. Production (2000, in 1,000 tonnes): sugarcane, 4,436; maize, 72; grapefruit and pomelos, 47; oranges, 36; seed cotton, 23; cottonseed, 15; pineapples, 11; groundnuts, 8; cotton lint, 7.

Livestock (2000): cattle, 610,000; goats, 440,000; pigs, 33,000; chickens, 3m.

Forestry

Forests covered 522,000 ha. in 2000, or 30·3% of the land area. In 2001 timber production was 890,000 cu. metres.

Fisheries

Estimated total catch, 2001, approximately 70 tonnes, exclusively from inland waters.

INDUSTRY

Most industries are based on processing agricultural products and timber. Footwear and textiles are also manufactured, and some engineering products.

Labour

In June 1996, 89,860 persons were in formal employment; 15,892 Swazis worked in gold mines in South Africa in 1994. Unemployment rose to 30% in 1999.

Trade Unions

In 1998 there were 21 affiliated trade unions grouped in the Swaziland Federation of Trade Unions with a combined membership of 83,000, and four unions grouped in the Swaziland Federation of Labour.

INTERNATIONAL TRADE

Swaziland has a customs union with South Africa and receives a pro rata share of the dues collected. External debt was US$342m. in 2002.

Imports and Exports

In 2002 imports (f.o.b.) amounted to US$1,034·6m. (US$1,116·4m. in 2001); exports (f.o.b.) US$955·2m. (US$1,039·7m. in 2001). Main import products are motor vehicles, machinery, transport equipment, foodstuffs, petroleum products and chemicals; main export commodities are soft drink concentrates, sugar, wood pulp and cotton yarn.

By far the most significant trading partner is South Africa. In 2001, 94·5% of imports came from South Africa; 78·0% of exports went to South Africa in 2001.

COMMUNICATIONS

Roads

The total length of roads in 2000 was 3,107 km, of which 1,420 km were main roads. There were 40,544 passenger cars in 2001 plus 38,090 trucks and vans and 5,737 buses and coaches. There were 5,352 road accidents involving injury in 2001 with 255 fatalities.

Rail

In 1997 the system comprised 301 km of route (1,067 mm gauge). Freight tonne-km in 2000 came to 875m.

Civil Aviation

There is an international airport at Manzini (Matsapha). Swazi Express Airways had flights in 2003 to Durban and Maputo. In 1999 scheduled airline traffic of Swaziland-based carriers flew 0·6m. km, carrying 12,000 passengers (all on international flights).

Telecommunications

Swaziland had 98,100 telephone subscribers in 2002, or 95·0 for every 1,000 persons, and 25,000 PCs were in use. In 2002 there were 1,700 fax machines. There were around 20,000 Internet users and 63,000 mobile phone subscribers in 2002.

Postal Services

There were 58 post offices in 2003, or one for every 18,600 persons.

SOCIAL INSTITUTIONS

Justice

The constitutional courts practice Roman-Dutch law. The judiciary is headed by the Chief Justice. There is a High Court and various Magistrates and Courts. A Court of Appeal with a President and three Judges deals with appeals from the High Court. There are 16 courts of first instance. There are also traditional Swazi National Courts.

The population in penal institutions in Aug. 2002 was 3,400 (359 per 100,000 of national population).

Education

In 2001 there were 541 primary schools with 212,064 children and 6,594 teachers. The teacher/pupil ratio has decreased from 40/1 in the 1970s to 32/1. About half the children of secondary school age attend school. There are also private schools. In 2001 there were 61,335 children (3,647 teachers) in secondary and high school classes. Many secondary and high schools teach agricultural activities.

The University of Swaziland, at Matsapha, had 3,692 students in 2000. There are three teacher training colleges (total enrolment in 1994–95, 857) and eight vocational institutions (1,150 students and 147 teachers in 1991). There is also an institute of management.

Rural education centres offer formal education for children and adult education geared towards vocational training. The adult literacy rate in 2003 was 79·2% (80·4% among males and 78·1% among females).

In 1999–2000 total expenditure on education came to 6·0% of GNP.

Health

In 2005 there were 400 health institutions, of which nine were hospitals and 19 were health centres. There were 184 physicians, 3,345 nurses, 20 dentists and 46 pharmacists in 2000.

RELIGION

In 2001 there were 480,000 African Christians, 160,000 Protestants and the remainder of the population followed other religions (including traditional beliefs).

CULTURE

Broadcasting

The Broadcasting Corporation and Swaziland Television Authority are government-owned. Swaziland Broadcasting Services run on a semi-commercial basis. In 2000 there were 169,000 radio receivers and in 2001 there were 32,000 television receivers (colour by PAL).

Press

In 2003 there were three daily newspapers: *The Swazi Observer* (English-language with a circulation of 3,000 in 1999), *The Times of Swaziland* (English, 15,000), founded in 1897, and *Tikhatsi* (siSwati, 7,500).

Tourism

There were 256,000 foreign tourists in 2002, bringing revenue of US$26m.

Festivals

The annual Umhlanga (Reed Dance) takes place in Aug. or early Sept. in honour of the Queen Mother.

Libraries

There is a government-subsidized National Library Service with 250,000 volumes, which comprises two libraries at Mbabane and Manzini with 11 branches throughout the country.

DIPLOMATIC REPRESENTATIVES

Of Swaziland in the United Kingdom (20 Buckingham Gate, London, SW1E 6LB)
High Commissioner: Mary M. Kanya.

Of the United Kingdom in Swaziland
High Commissioner: Rt Hon. Paul Boateng (resides in Pretoria, South Africa).

Of Swaziland in the USA (1712 New Hampshire Ave., NW, Washington, D.C., 20009)
Ambassador: Ephraim M. Hlophe.

Of the USA in Swaziland (2350 Mbabane Place, Dulles, Mbabane)
Ambassador: Lewis W. Lucke.

Of Swaziland to the United Nations
Ambassador: Phesheya Mbongeni Dlamini.

Of Swaziland to the European Union
Ambassador: Thembayena Annastasia Dlamini.

FURTHER READING

Matsebula, J. S. M., *A History of Swaziland*. 3rd ed. London, 1992
Nyeko, B., *Swaziland*. [Bibliography] 2nd ed. ABC-Clio, Oxford and Santa Barbara (CA), 1994

National Statistical Office: Central Statistical Office, POB 456, Mbabane.

SWEDEN

Konungariket Sverige
(Kingdom of Sweden)

Capital: Stockholm
Population projection, 2010: 9·17m.
GDP per capita, 2003: (PPP$) 26,750
HDI/world rank: 0·949/6

KEY HISTORICAL EVENTS

Sweden was covered by a thick ice cap until 14,000 years ago, when the ice began to retreat. The first human traces, in southern Sweden, date from 10,000 BC. Between 8000 and 6000 BC the country was populated by hunters and fishermen, using simple stone tools. Artefacts found in graves show that the Bronze Age was marked by a relatively advanced culture. From 500 BC to 800 AD agriculture became the basis for society and the economy. The Viking Age (800–1050) took expansion eastwards. Swedish Vikings reached into today's Russia, where they set up trading stations and principalities, such as Novgorod and Rurik. The Vikings also travelled to the Black and Caspian Seas and developed trading links with the Byzantine Empire and the Arabs.

In 830 the Frankish monk Ansgar introduced Christianity to Sweden with little success. In the 11th century, English missionaries had greater success. However, paganism was dominant until the end of the 11th century when the country was fully Christianized. Olof Skötkonung, who proclaimed himself ruler of Sweden, supported the new religion. But many pagans refused to abandon their old faith and civil wars continued. Following the Viking era the country remained a federation of provinces, which became united in the 12th century.

By 1200 Sweden had developed into a kingdom with largely the same borders as it has today, except that Skåne, Halland and Blekinge in the south of Sweden formed part of Denmark, and Jämtland, Härjedalen and Bohuslän in the west belonged to Norway. There was a struggle for power between the Sverker and Erik families, who ruled alternately in 1160–1250. However, by the middle of the 13th century with the building of royal castles and introduction of provincial administration, the crown was able to assert the authority of the central government and impose laws valid for the whole kingdom. Among the most important figures of the 13th century was Birger Jarl, who promoted the newly founded city of Stockholm. At a time when Hanseatic merchants traded in Sweden, Stockholm contained a large German population, and on the southeast coast of Sweden, Kalmar and Gotland were controlled by German immigrants. The Hanseatic trading posts to the east included Finland, which was brought into the Swedish kingdom. A new law code, valid for the entire country, was introduced in 1350 by King Magnus Eriksson. In 1340 Valdemar Atterdag became king of Denmark and entered into conflict with Sweden over the southern provinces of Skåne, Halland and Blekinge. He attacked Gotland in 1361 in one of the bloodiest battles in Nordic history, to secure a base for further assaults on Sweden and to overthrow the Hanseatic League.

In the 14th century trade increased and until the mid-16th century the Hanseatic League dominated Sweden's trade. In 1350 the Black Death decimated the population. Inheritance and marriage ties united the crowns of Denmark, Norway and Sweden in 1389, under the rule of Queen Margaret of Denmark. In 1397 the loose association known as the Union of Kalmar confirmed her five-year old nephew, Erik of Pomerania, as king of the three countries. The Swedish nationalist Sten Sture, who was made king of Sweden in 1470, defeated the Danes at the Battle of Brunkeberg in Stockholm. Following this success, Sten Sture promoted nationalistic sentiment by the public display of a great wood carving of St George slaying the dragon (now placed in Stockholm cathedral) and the setting up of the first Swedish university at Uppsala. The union period (1397–1521) was characterized by conflicts between central government (represented by the king), the high nobility and the rebellious burghers and peasants. These conflicts culminated in the Stockholm Bloodbath in 1520, when eighty leading men in Sweden were executed at the incentive of the Danish king, Christian II. This provoked rebellions, and in 1521 Christian II was overthrown by Gustav Vasa, a Swedish nobleman, who was elected king in 1523.

Empire Building

During the reign of Gustav Vasa (1523–60) the foundations of the Swedish national state were laid. With the Reformation, Sweden was converted into a Lutheran country and the church was turned into a national institution. At the same time power was concentrated in the hands of the king and in 1544 a hereditary monarchy was established. By the 16th century Scandinavia was divided into two states, Sweden-Finland and Denmark-Norway. Since the dissolution of the union with Denmark and Norway, Swedish foreign policy focused on dominating the Baltic Sea, and this led to wars with Denmark from the 1560s.

In 1611 Gustavus Adolphus (Gustaf II Adolf) consolidated Sweden's position on the Russian side of the Baltic Sea. Sweden defeated Denmark in two wars (1643 and 1657) to take control of the previously Danish provinces of Skåne, Halland, Blekinge and Gotland and the Norwegian provinces of Bohuslän, Jämtland and Härjedalen. Gustavus Adolphus also took his troops into northern Europe to play a role in pushing back the Catholic forces in the Thirty Years War. This cost him his life, but gave Sweden large possessions in the north of Germany. Finland and the present-day Baltic republics also belonged to Sweden making it a great power in northern Europe.

Following the death of King Karl XII in 1718 the Swedish Parliament (Riksdag) established a new constitution that abolished royal absolutism and placed power in the hands of Parliament. But royal authority was soon reasserted. After defeat in the Great Northern War (1700–21) against Denmark, Poland and Russia, Sweden lost most of its Baltic territories, including a part of Finland and all its north-German possessions except west Pomerania. During the Napoleonic Wars, Sweden lost Finland to Russia and withdrew from its remaining German provinces. In 1810 Napoleon's marshal Jean-Baptiste Bernadotte assumed power as Karl XIV Johan. He tried to win back Finland from Russia, but had to make do with a union of Sweden and Norway, confirmed by the treaty of Kiel in 1814.

The short war against Norway in 1814 was Sweden's last military adventure. Since then Sweden has favoured neutrality. For this reason, there was no early application to join the EEC (European Economic Community). But in line with a commitment to liberalize trade, Sweden was a founder member of EFTA (European Free Trade Agreement) in 1959. After the Cold War and the collapse of the Soviet Union, the policy of neutrality was seen by many as obsolete. Sweden became a member of the EU (European Union) in 1995.

Following constitutional reforms in 1974 the remaining powers of the king were reduced to purely ceremonial functions. Carl XVI Gustaf, who succeeded the throne in 1973, is the first Swedish king to be bound by the new constitution. In 1980 the order of succession was amended to allow for male/female equal right of inheritance to the crown. Hence, Princess Victoria is the heir apparent rather than her younger brother Prince Carl Philip.

Modern Economy

After the Napoleonic Wars, Sweden suffered economic stagnation. The country was poor with 90% of the population living off the land. Out of a population of five million, over one million emigrated between 1866 and 1914, mostly to North America. Industry did not start to grow until the 1890s. However, it then developed rapidly and after the Second World War Sweden was transformed into one of the leading industrial nations in Europe. In the six years to 1951 the country's GNP rose by 20%. Economic success was partly thanks to the early utilization of hydro-electric power which supported the pulp and paper industries of the northern forests. Sweden invented the ball-bearing, the adjustable spanner, the primus stove and the cream separator, as well as the safety match and dynamite. By 1956 the economy was booming, poverty had almost disappeared and unemployment was at a minimum. Sweden was one of the richest countries in Europe.

Social democracy began as the political offshoot of the trade unions. The working class was supported by intellectuals, such as the scientist Hjalmar Branting, who was the first Scandinavian socialist prime minister. The first representative of social democracy entered the government in 1917. Universal suffrage was introduced for men in 1909 and for women in 1921. In the 1930s, when the Social Democrats had become the governing party, plans for the welfare society were laid. Reforms included restrictions on child and female labour, free elementary education and old-age pensions. A four-party coalition for the duration of the Second World War was succeeded by a Social Democrat government with Per Albin Hansson as prime minister. Following his death in 1946, Tage Erlander became prime minister and stayed in office until 1969. He was succeeded by Olof Palme who was prime minister between 1969 and 1976. Owing to the rise in oil prices in 1973, unemployment increased. From the mid-1970s the improvements in living standards slowed and in the late 1980s it almost halted completely. The economic crisis drove the Social Democrats out of government and in 1976 a non-socialist coalition was formed under Centre Party chairman Thorbjörn Fälldin. Conflicts over the expansion of nuclear power led to several government reshuffles. In 1982 the Social Democrats resumed office with Olof Palme as prime minister. The assassination of Palme in 1986 shook the country, which had been spared political violence for nearly 200 years. Ingvar Carlsson took over as head of government. In the 1990s industrial production fell and unemployment rose, which led to a high budget deficit and increased national debt. Popular dissatisfaction showed in the 1991 election, when a non-socialist coalition government was formed with Carl Bildt as prime minister. Launching a programme of deregulation and privatization, Bildt did much to prepare the economy for closer involvement with Europe. Capital gains taxes were reduced, as too were social benefits. But in spite of all efforts, the government did not manage to reduce unemployment, the budget deficit or the national debt. Hence, the 1994 election put the Social Democrats back in power, with Ingvar Carlsson as prime minister. In 1996 he stepped down to be replaced by Göran Persson. Despite economic problems, the country still boasts one of the highest standards of living and one of the most advanced welfare systems.

TERRITORY AND POPULATION

Sweden is bounded in the west and northwest by Norway, east by Finland and the Gulf of Bothnia, southeast by the Baltic Sea and southwest by the Kattegat. The area is 450,295 sq. km, including water (96,000 lakes) totalling 39,960 sq. km. At the 1990 census the population was 8,587,353. Estimate, Dec. 2004, 9,011,392; density 20·0 per sq. km. In 2003, 83·4% of the population lived in urban areas.

The UN gives a projected population for 2010 of 9·17m.

Area, population and population density of the counties (län):

	Land area (in sq. km)	Population (1990 census)	Population (31 Dec. 2004)	Density per sq. km (31 Dec. 2004)
Stockholm	6,519	1,640,389	1,872,900	287
Uppsala	7,037	268,503	302,564	43
Södermanland	6,103	255,546	261,070	43
Östergötland	10,605	402,849	415,990	39
Jönköping	10,495	308,294	329,297	31
Kronoberg	8,467	177,880	178,285	21
Kalmar	11,219	241,149	234,496	21
Gotland	3,151	57,132	57,661	18
Blekinge	2,947	150,615	150,335	51
Skåne	11,035	1,068,587	1,160,919	105
Halland	5,462	254,568	283,788	52
Västra Götaland	23,956	1,458,166	1,521,895	64
Värmland	17,591	283,148	273,547	16
Örebro	8,546	272,474	273,920	32
Västmanland	6,318	258,544	261,005	41
Dalarna	28,196	288,919	276,042	10
Gävleborg	18,200	289,346	276,599	15
Västernorrland	21,684	261,099	244,195	11
Jämtland	49,343	135,724	127,424	3
Västerbotten	55,190	251,846	256,875	5
Norrbotten	98,249	263,546	252,585	3

There are some 17,000 Sami (Lapps).

On 31 Dec. 2004 foreign-born persons in Sweden numbered 1,100,262. Of these, 277,103 were from Nordic countries; 392,637 from the rest of Europe; 65,249 from Africa; 26,515 from North America; 55,488 from South America; 272,279 from Asian countries; 6,954 from the former USSR; 3,517 from Oceania; and 520 country unknown. Of the total 186,589 were born in Finland. More than 12% of the population of Sweden is foreign-born, the highest proportion in any of the Nordic countries.

Immigration: 2002, 64,087; 2003, 63,795; 2004, 62,028. Emigration: 2002, 33,009; 2003, 35,023; 2004, 36,586.

Population of the 50 largest communities, 1 Jan. 2005:

Stockholm	765,044	Skellefteå	71,786
Göteborg	481,410	Haninge	71,355
Malmö	269,142	Kungsbacka	68,696
Uppsala	182,076	Järfälla	61,564
Linköping	136,912	Karlskrona	61,137
Västerås	131,014	Kalmar	60,649
Örebro	126,982	Täby	60,422
Norrköping	124,410	Solna	59,098
Helsingborg	121,179	Sollentuna	58,897
Jönköping	119,927	Östersund	58,459
Umeå	109,390	Mölndal	57,752
Lund	101,423	Gotland	57,661
Borås	98,886	Falun	54,994
Sundsvall	93,707	Örnsköldsvik	54,945
Gävle	92,081	Norrtälje	54,366
Eskilstuna	91,168	Varberg	54,338
Halmstad	87,929	Trollhättan	53,154
Huddinge	87,681	Uddevalla	50,068
Karlstad	81,768	Skövde	49,856
Södertälje	80,405	Nyköping	49,575
Nacka	78,715	Hässleholm	48,945
Växjö	76,755	Borlänge	46,988
Botkyrka	75,830	Motala	42,062
Kristianstad	75,592	Lidingö	41,407
Luleå	72,565	Piteå	40,830

A 16-km long fixed link with Denmark was opened in July 2000 when the Öresund motorway and railway bridge between Malmö and Copenhagen was completed.

The official language is Swedish.

SOCIAL STATISTICS

Statistics for calendar years:

	Total living births	To mothers single, divorced or widowed	Stillborn	Marriages	Divorces	Deaths exclusive of still-born
2000	90,441	50,037	355	39,895	21,502	93,461
2001	91,466	50,756	349	35,778	21,022	93,752
2002	95,815	53,678	352	38,012	21,322	95,009
2003	99,157	55,532	359	39,041	21,130	92,961
2004	100,928	55,991	333	43,088	20,106	90,532

Rates, 2004, per 1,000 population: births, 11·2; deaths, 10·1; marriages, 4·8; divorces, 2·2. Sweden has one of the highest rate of births outside marriage in Europe, at 55% in 2004. In 2004 the most popular age range for marrying was 30–34 for both men and women. Expectation of life in 2003: males, 77·9 years; females, 82·4. The World Health Organization's 2004 World Health Report put the Swedes in third place in a 'healthy life expectancy' list behind Japan and San Marino, with an expected 73·3 years of healthy life for babies born in 2002. Annual population growth rate, 1993–2002, 0·2%. Infant mortality, 2004, 3·1 per 1,000 live births (one of the lowest rates in the world). Fertility rate, 2004, 1·8 births per woman. In 2004 Sweden received 23,161 asylum applications (33,016 in 2002), equivalent to 2·6 per 1,000 inhabitants.

A UNICEF report published in 2005 showed that 4·2% of children in Sweden live in poverty (in households with income below 50% of the national median). A similar report from 2000 had shown that the poverty rate of children in lone-parent families in Sweden was 6·7%, compared to 1·5% in two-parent families.

CLIMATE

The north has severe winters, with snow lying for 4–7 months. Summers are fine but cool, with long daylight hours. Further south, winters are less cold, summers are warm and rainfall well distributed throughout the year, although slightly higher in the summer. Stockholm, Jan. 0·4°C, July 17·2°C. Annual rainfall 385 mm.

CONSTITUTION AND GOVERNMENT

The reigning King is **Carl XVI Gustaf**, b. 30 April 1946, succeeded on the death of his grandfather Gustaf VI Adolf, 15 Sept. 1973, married 19 June 1976 to Silvia Renate Sommerlath, b. 23 Dec. 1943 (Queen of Sweden). *Daughter* and *Heir Apparent:* Crown Princess Victoria Ingrid Alice Désirée, Duchess of Västergötland, b. 14 July 1977; *son:* Prince Carl Philip Edmund Bertil, Duke of Värmland, b. 13 May 1979; *daughter:* Princess Madeleine Thérèse Amelie Josephine, Duchess of Hälsingland and Gästrikland, b. 10 June 1982. *Sisters of the King.* Princess Margaretha, b. 31 Oct. 1934, married 30 June 1964 to John Ambler; Princess Birgitta (Princess of Sweden), b. 19 Jan. 1937, married 25 May 1961 (civil marriage) and 30 May 1961 (religious ceremony) to Johann Georg, Prince of Hohenzollern; Princess Désirée, b. 2 June 1938, married 5 June 1964 to Baron Niclas Silfverschiöld; Princess Christina, b. 3 Aug. 1943, married 15 June 1974 to Tord Magnuson. *Uncles of the King.* Count Sigvard Bernadotte of Wisborg, b. 7 June 1907, died 4 Feb. 2002; Count Carl Johan Bernadotte of Wisborg, b. 31 Oct. 1916.

Under the 1975 Constitution Sweden is a representative and parliamentary democracy. The King is Head of State, but does not participate in government. Parliament is the single-chamber *Riksdag* of 349 members elected for a period of four years in direct, general elections.

The manner of election to the *Riksdag* is proportional. The country is divided into 29 constituencies. In these constituencies 310 members are elected. The remaining 39 seats constitute a nationwide pool intended to give absolute proportionality to parties that receive at least 4% of the votes. A party receiving less than 4% of the votes in the country is, however, entitled to participate in the distribution of seats in a constituency, if it has obtained at least 12% of the votes cast there.

A parliament, the *Sameting*, was instituted for the Sami (Lapps) in 1993.

National Anthem

'Du gamla, du fria' ('Thou ancient, thou free'); words by R. Dybeck; folk-tune.

GOVERNMENT CHRONOLOGY

Prime Ministers since 1936. (C = Centre Party; FpL = People's Party-Liberals; M = Moderate Party; SAP = Swedish Social Democratic Labour Party)

1936–46	SAP	Per Albin Hansson
1946–69	SAP	Tage Fritiof Erlander
1969–76	SAP	Sven Olof Joachim Palme
1976–78	C	Thorbjörn Fälldin
1978–79	FpL	Ola Ullsten
1979–82	C	Thorbjörn Fälldin
1982–86	SAP	Sven Olof Joachim Palme
1986–91	SAP	Ingvar Gösta Carlsson
1991–94	M	Carl Bildt
1994–96	SAP	Ingvar Gösta Carlsson
1996–	SAP	Göran Persson

RECENT ELECTIONS

In parliamentary elections held on 15 Sept. 2002 Prime Minister Göran Persson's Swedish Social Democratic Labour Party (SAP) won 144 seats with 39·8% of votes cast (131 with 36·4% in 1998), the Moderate Alliance Party 55 with 15·2% (82 with 22·9%), the Liberal Party 48 with 13·3% (17 with 4·7%), the Christian Democratic Party 33 with 9·1% (42 with 11·8%), the Left Party 30 with 8·3% (43 with 12·0%), the Centre Party 22 with 6·1% (18 with 5·1%) and the Green Party 17 with 4·6% (16 with 4·5%). Turnout was 80·1%. Following the 2002 election, of the 349 Members of Parliament there were 191 men (54·7%) and 158 women (45·3%). Only Rwanda has a higher percentage of women in its parliament.

Parliamentary elections are scheduled to take place on 17 Sept. 2006.

European Parliament

Sweden has 19 (22 in 1999) representatives. At the June 2004 elections turnout was 37·2% (38·3% in 1999). The SAP won 5 seats with 24·8% of votes cast (political affiliation in European Parliament: Party of European Socialists); the Moderate Party, 4 with 18·2% (European People's Party–European Democrats); June List, 3 with 14·4% (Independence and Democracy Group); Vänsterpartiet (Far Left), 2 with 9·8% (European Unitary Left/ Nordic Green Left); the Liberal Party, 2 with 9·8% (Alliance of Liberals and Democrats for Europe); the Centre Party, 1 with 6·3% (Alliance of Liberals and Democrats for Europe); the Green Party, 1 with 5·9% (Greens/European Free Alliance); the Christian Democratic Party, 1 with 5·7% (European People's Party–European Democrats).

CURRENT ADMINISTRATION

A minority Social Democratic government was formed in Oct. 1998. Following parliamentary elections in Sept. 2002 a new Social Democratic government was formed. In April 2006 the government comprised:

Prime Minister: Göran Persson; b. 1949 (SAP; sworn in 21 March 1996).

Deputy Prime Minister: Bosse Ringholm.

Minister of Agriculture, Food and Consumer Affairs: Ann-Christin Nykvist. *Communications and Regional Policy:* Ulrica Messing. *Defence:* Leni Björklund. *Education and Culture:* Leif Pagrotsky. *Foreign Affairs:* Jan Eliasson. *Employment:* Hans Karlsson. *Environment:* Lena Sommestad. *Finance:* Pär Nuder. *Health and Elderly Care:* Ylva Johansson. *Housing:* Mona Sahlin. *Industry and Trade:* Thomas Östros. *Integration, Metropolitan and Gender Equality Issues:* Jens Orback. *International Development Co-operation:* Carin Jämtin. *Justice:* Thomas Bodström. *Local Government Finances and Financial Market Issues:* Sven-Erik Österberg. *Migration and Asylum Policy:* Barbro Holmberg. *Pre-School Education, Youth Affairs and Adult Learning:* Lena Hallengren. *Public Health and Social Services:* Morgan Johansson. *Schools:* Ibrahim Baylan. *Social Affairs:* Berit Andnor.

The *Speaker* is Björn von Sydow.

Office of the Prime Minister: http://www.sweden.gov.se

CURRENT LEADERS

Göran Persson

Position
Prime Minister

Introduction
Göran Persson was elected leader of the Swedish Social Democratic Labour Party (SAP) in 1996 following Ingvar Carlsson's retirement. The general election held in spring that year returned the Social Democrats to government, and Persson became prime minister on 21 March. He was re-elected, albeit on a reduced share of the vote, on 21 Sept. 1998. He led the SAP to re-election in Sept. 2002 to form a minority government reliant on the support of either the Greens or the Left Party.

Early Life
Persson was born in Vingåker on 29 Jan. 1949. He was educated at the University College of Örebro and began his political career in 1971 as a secretary for the Swedish Social Democratic Youth League. He became a board member of the League the following year. From 1974–76 he was the secretary of the Worker's Educational Association in Sörmland. For a decade Persson pursued a career in finance as the vice-chairman of the board of Oppunda Savings Bank, but continued to participate in municipal politics and was elected as a member of parliament in 1979. During the 1980s he continued to balance his political career with participation in various local and private projects. In 1984 he abandoned his parliamentary seat, and the following year he became a municipal commissioner for Katrineholm. In 1989 Persson received his first ministerial portfolio, that of a minister in the department of education. He was re-elected to parliament in 1991, and in the same year became the chairman of the standing committee on agriculture. In 1992 he became a party spokesman on industrial policy. In 1993 he was chosen as a deputy member of the SAP executive committee, and in 1994 he was appointed minister of finance. This latter role groomed Persson for the party leadership, which he was awarded in 1996. In March that year he became prime minister.

Career in Office
In his first term Persson was preoccupied with Sweden's entry into the EU and its political and economic consequences. On the domestic front he remained committed to imposing a high level tax on top earners to finance the welfare state. A gradual disenchantment with social democratic policies meant that in 1998 Persson led the SAP to their worst general election performance in 40 years. As a result he rapidly came under pressure to cut taxes, liberalize Sweden's labour market and shift the welfare budget from direct transfers to spending on health care and education. A growing mood of scepticism about Sweden's role in the EU in the wake of the Danish rejection of monetary union also hindered the pro-Europe Persson. In 2001 Persson was further immersed in European politics as the union presidency passed to Sweden. During this period he argued tirelessly for the enlargement of the EU to take in Central European applicants.

Persson again led the SAP at the Sept. 2002 elections, winning almost 40% of the vote. Unable to form a majority government, he survived a vote of confidence in early Oct. when he secured the support of the Green Party. His minority administration has since relied on the backing of the Greens or the Left Party to stay in office. In return for Green support, Persson agreed to implement a green tax, cut defence expenditure and reduce greenhouse gas emissions by 2010. In Sept. 2003 Swedish voters rejected a proposal to adopt the EU single currency by 56% to 42% in a referendum, despite the ruling SAP's support for the euro. Although the Swedish economy remains robust compared with most other European countries, Persson's government has lost popular support over continuing high levels of unemployment and is facing a resurgent opposition in the approach to the 2006 parliamentary elections.

DEFENCE

The Supreme Commander is, under the government, in command of the three services. The Supreme Commander is assisted by the Swedish Armed Forces HQ. There is also a Swedish Armed Forces Logistics Organization.

The conscription system consists of 7½–18 months of military service for males. Females have the possibility to serve on a voluntary basis.

In 2003 military expenditure totalled US$5,532m. (US$618 per capita), representing 1·8% of GDP. Sweden's national security policy is currently undergoing a shift in emphasis. Beginning with the decommissioning of obsolete units and structures, the main thrust of policy is the creation of contingency forces adaptable to a variety of situations.

The government stressed that Sweden's membership of the EU (in 1995) did not imply any change in Sweden's traditional policy of non-participation in military alliances, with the option of staying neutral in the event of war in its vicinity.

Sweden has modern air raid shelters with capacity for some 7m. people. Since this falls short of providing protection for the whole population, evacuation and relocation operations would be necessary in the event of war.

The National Board of Psychological Defence, whose main task is to safeguard the free and undisrupted transmission of news, has also made preparations for 'psychological defence' in wartime. This is regarded as the best possible antidote against enemy propaganda, disinformation and rumour-mongering of the kind that can be expected in times of war.

Army

The Army consists of one division HQ and divisional units, six army brigade command and control elements, and 54 battalions. Army strength, Jan. 2003, 20,000 (10,769 conscripts). The Army can mobilize a reserve of approximately 200,000 of whom 85,000 are Home Guard and 11,100 reservists.

The Home Guard is part of the Army. Its main task is to protect important local installations against sabotage.

Navy

The Navy has two surface warfare flotillas, one mine warfare flotilla, one submarine flotilla and one amphibious brigade.

The personnel of the Navy in Jan. 2003 totalled 5,600 (active manpower, including 2,600 conscripts). Strength available for mobilization, 20,000 (includes 2,500 reservists).

Air Force

The Air Force consists of three fighter control and air surveillance battalions, eight air-base battalions, eight fighter squadrons, two air transport squadrons (central) and two air transport squadrons (regional).

Strength (Jan. 2003) 6,500 (2,000 conscripts), plus 16,000 available for mobilization (including 1,670 reservists).

During peacetime all the helicopters of the Swedish Armed Forces are organized into a detached organization directly under the Swedish Armed Forces Headquarters.

INTERNATIONAL RELATIONS

Sweden is a member of the UN, WTO, BIS, NATO Partnership for Peace, BIS, OECD, EU, Council of Europe, OSCE, CERN, Nordic Council, Council of the Baltic Sea States, Inter-American Development Bank, Asian Development Bank, IOM and the Antarctic Treaty. Sweden is a signatory to the Schengen accord, which abolishes border controls between Sweden, Austria, Belgium, Denmark, Finland, France, Germany, Greece, Iceland, Italy, Luxembourg, the Netherlands, Norway, Portugal and Spain.

Sweden gave US$2·7bn. in international aid in 2004, which at 0·78% of GNI made it the world's fourth most generous country as a percentage of its gross national income.

In a referendum held on 14 Sept. 2003 Swedish voters rejected their country's entry into the common European currency, 56·1% opposing membership of the euro against 41·8% voting in favour. Turn-out was 81·2%.

ECONOMY

Services accounted for 70·0% of GDP in 2002, industry 28·2% and agriculture 1·8%.

According to the anti-corruption organization *Transparency International*, in 2005 Sweden ranked 6th in the world in a survey of the countries with the least corruption in business and government. It received 9·2 out of 10 in the annual index.

Overview

Sweden has performed well since the 2001 global technology crash which severely impacted Ericsson, Sweden's largest exporter. After being crippled by a long period of slower than average growth, Sweden is experiencing higher per capita GDP growth than the euro area average, sustained by productivity gains and underpinned by well-designed monetary and fiscal policy. A strong recovery in the telecommunications and

automobile sectors has fuelled export growth since 2003; strong export growth combined with rising capacity utilization and low interest rates has led to a revival in business investment.

Sweden combines an extensive welfare state with a market economy. The trend of higher public spending and an all-encompassing welfare state has stalled the long-overdue process of lowering the high tax burden. Expenditure ceilings and a target for the cyclically adjusted budget surplus have governed fiscal policy since 1997 but the general government balance has been moving away from the 2% structural surplus target. Monetary policy has targeted a 2% inflation rate since 1993 and the IMF have praised the design and operation of the inflation-targeting framework implemented by the Riksbank. In Sept. 2003 a referendum rejected adopting the euro.

The employment rate is high by international standards but below the government target of 80%. Effective employment is lower than that portrayed by employment statistics because of large numbers of employees benefiting from sick leave, social assistance, labour market programmes and mid-life sabbaticals. Sick leave, in particular, has become a major policy concern; on an average day approximately 18% of the labour force is on sick leave or disability benefit. Effective labour supply is being squeezed at both ends of the age spectrum. In 2004 total disability pensions increased by 12%, with almost 30% of the increase comprising pensioners below 40. The younger generation is also taking longer to complete tertiary education; since 1987 the age at which a young person attains full-time employment has increased by five years. The working age population in Sweden will start to diminish by 2010 unless bolstered by net immigration. Raising productivity and enhancing effective labour supply is a key strategy in the management of demographic trends and in the maintenance of living standards.

The authorities have deregulated a number of sectors, including electricity, telecommunications and parts of transport. Sweden is facing further pressure from the EU to privatize its state monopolies in line with internal markets regulations, particularly in the pharmaceuticals, construction and alcoholic beverages sectors.

Currency

The unit of currency is the *krona* (SEK), of 100 *öre*. Inflation rates (based on OECD statistics):

1995	1996	1997	1998	1999	2000	2001	2002	2003	2004
2·5%	0·5%	0·7%	−0·3%	0·5%	0·9%	2·4%	2·2%	1·9%	0·4%

The inflation rate in 2005 according to Statistics Sweden was 0·5%. Foreign exchange reserves were US$14,967m. and gold reserves 5·96m. troy oz in June 2002.

Budget

Revenue of 718·2bn. kr. and expenditure of 751·0bn. kr. was estimated for the total budget (Current and Capital) for financial year 2005.

Revenue and expenditure for 2004 (1m. kr.):

Revenue	
Tax revenues	637,001
—Taxes on income	45,706
—Social security contribution	266,040
—Taxes on property	37,126
—Taxes on goods and services	308,876
—Reallocation fee	−5,776
—Cash difference account	−5,458
—Tax reductions	−9,513
From government activities	35,082
From sale of property	136
Loans repaid	2,391
Computed revenues	8,252
Contributions, etc., from the EU	11,555
Total revenue	694,418

Expenditure	
The Swedish political system	7,539
Economy and fiscal administration	9,221
Tax administration and collection	8,569
Justice	26,318
Foreign policy administration and international co-operation	1,267
Total defence	42,846
International development assistance	19,907
Immigrants and refugees	7,466
Health care, medical care, social services	36,809
Financial security in the event of illness and disability	122,916
Financial security in old age	51,229
Financial security for families and children	53,925
The labour market	67,481
Working life	1,091
Study support	20,833
Education and university research	43,981
Culture, the media, religious organizations and leisure	8,739
Community planning, housing supply and construction	8,723
Regional balance and development	3,301
General environment and conservation	3,330
Energy	2,069
Communications	29,139
Agriculture and forestry, fisheries, etc.	12,219
Business sector	3,690
General grants to municipalities	69,834
Interest on central government debt, etc.	52,718
Contribution to the European Community	25,563
Other expenditure	7,037
Total expenditure	747,761

VAT is 25% (reduced rates, 12% and 6%). In 2002 tax revenues were 50·6% of GDP (the highest percentage of any developed country).

Performance

Real GDP growth rates (based on OECD statistics):

1995	1996	1997	1998	1999	2000	2001	2002	2003	2004
4·2%	1·3%	2·6%	3·6%	4·3%	4·4%	1·2%	2·0%	1·6%	3·1%

The real GDP growth rates in 2004 and 2005 according to Sweden's National Institute of Economic Research were 3·7% and 2·7% respectively. Sweden's total GDP in 2004 was US$346·4bn.

Sweden was ranked third in the Growth Competitiveness Index behind Finland and the USA in the World Economic Forum's *Global Competitiveness Report 2005–2006*.

In 2004 the state debt amounted to 1,257bn. kr.

Banking and Finance

The central bank and bank of issue is the *Sveriges Riksbank*. The bank has 11 trustees, elected by parliament, and is managed by a directorate, including the governor, appointed by the trustees. The *Governor* is Stefan Ingves, appointed for a six-year term. In 2004 there were 50 commercial banks. Their total deposits in 2000 amounted to 1,104,570m. kr.; advances to the public in 2000 amounted to 975,212m. kr. In April 2003 there were 77 savings banks and 20 branches of foreign banks. The largest banks are Nordea Bank AB (previously MeritaNorbanken, formed in 1997 when Nordbanken of Sweden merged with Merita of Finland), Svenska Handelsbanken, Skandinavska Enskilda Banken and FöreningsSparbanken. In April 2000 MeritaNordbanken acquired Denmark's Unidanmark, thereby becoming the Nordic region's biggest bank in terms of assets. It became Nordea Bank AB in Dec. 2001. By Oct. 2000 approximately 27% of the Swedish population were using e-banking.

There is a stock exchange in Stockholm.

ENERGY AND NATURAL RESOURCES

Environment

Sweden's carbon dioxide emissions from the consumption and flaring of fossil fuels in 2002 were the equivalent of 6·2 tonnes per capita. An *Environmental Sustainability Index* compiled for the World Economic Forum meeting in Jan. 2005 ranked Sweden fourth in the world, with 71·7%. The index measured the ability of countries to maintain favourable environmental conditions and examined various factors including pollution levels and the use or abuse of natural resources.

Electricity

Sweden is rich in hydro-power resources. Installed capacity was 32,504 MW in 2002, of which 16,232 MW was in hydro-electric plants, 9,453 MW in nuclear plants and 6,462 MW in thermal plants. Electricity production in 2002 was 146,733m. kWh; consumption was 163,344 kWh. In 2002 consumption per capita was 16,996 kWh. A referendum of 1980 called for the phasing out of nuclear power by 2010. In Feb. 1997 the government began denuclearization by designating one of the 12 reactors for decommissioning. The state corporation Vattenfall was given the responsibility of financing and overseeing the transition to the use of non-fossil fuel alternatives. In 2003 there were 11 nuclear reactors in operation.

Minerals

Sweden is a leading producer of iron ore with around 2% of the world's total output. It is the largest iron ore exporter in Europe. There are also deposits of copper, gold, lead, zinc and alum shale containing oil and uranium. Iron ore produced, 2001, 19·5m. tonnes; zinc (mine output, zinc content), 156,334 tonnes; copper (mine output, copper content), 74,269 tonnes.

The mining industry accounts for 1·0% of the market value of Sweden's total industrial production and employs 0·5% of the total industrial labour force.

Agriculture

In 2000 agricultural land totalled 3,466,562 ha. In 2003 there were 2,668,586 ha. of arable land and 494,414 ha. of natural pasture on agricultural holdings of more than 2 ha. Of the land used for arable farming in 2003, 2–5 ha. holdings covered a total area of 33,984 ha.; 5·1–10 ha. holdings covered 83,816 ha.; 10·1–20 ha., 190,616; 20·1–30 ha., 187,153; 30·1–50 ha., 361,728; 50·1–100 ha., 708,726 and holdings larger than 100 ha. covered 1,102,564 ha. There were 66,780 agricultural enterprises in 2003 compared to 150,014 in 1971 and 282,187 in 1951. Around 37% of the enterprises were between 5 and 20 ha. Figures compiled by the Soil Association, a British organization, show that in 1999 Sweden set aside 268,000 ha. (11·2% of its agricultural land—one of the highest proportions in the world) for the growth of organic crops.

Agriculture accounts for 5·8% of exports and 7·9% of imports. The agricultural sector employs 3% of the workforce.

Chief crops	Area (1,000 ha.)			Production (1,000 tonnes)		
	2002	2003	2004	2002	2003	2004
Ley	941·0	933·3	934·8	2,737·0	2,530·8	2,481·3
Wheat	339·6	411·3	403·4	2,088·1	2,256·2	2,412·3
Sugarbeet	54·8	50·1	47·6	2,664·3	2,484·4	2,287·1
Barley	416·8	368·5	397·3	1,757·2	1,528·4	1,691·9
Potatoes	31·7	30·5	31·7	913·6	857·1	979·1
Oats	295·0	279·8	229·7	1,167·0	1,089·5	925·3
Rye	24·4	24·4	24·4	126·7	116·7	133·4

Milk production (in 1,000 tonnes) 2003, 3,253; meat, 433; cheese, 125; butter, 49.

Livestock, 2004: cattle, 1,628,464; sheep and lambs, 465,561; pigs, 1,818,037; poultry, 6,619,962. There were 139,070 reindeer in Sami villages in 2003. Harvest of moose during open season 2004: 96,563.

Forestry

Forests form one of the country's greatest natural assets. The growing stock includes 43% spruce, 39% pine and 16% broad-leaved. In 2000 forests covered 27·13m. ha. (65·9% of the land area). The state owns only 5% of productive forest lands. During 1993 most government-owned timberland was transferred to a forest production corporation (AssiDomän) in which the state owns 51% of shares, and the remaining 49% are quoted on the stock exchange. Public ownership accounts for 8% of the forests, limited companies own 37%, the state 5% and the remaining 50% is in private hands. Of the 67·3m. cu. metres of wood felled in 2003, 34·5m. cu. metres were sawlogs, 26·3m. cu. metres pulpwood, 5·9m. cu. metres fuelwood and 0·5m. cu. metres other.

Fisheries
In 2004 the total catch was 262,272 tonnes, worth 870·7m. kr. In 2002 the fishing fleet comprised 1,820 vessels of 45,371 gross tonnes.

INDUSTRY
The leading companies by market capitalization in Sweden in Nov. 2005 were: Telefonaktiebolaget LM Ericsson (US$51·8bn.); Nordea (US$26·7bn.), a financial services group; and TeliaSonera (US$23·8bn.), a telecommunications company.

Manufacturing is mainly based on metals and forest resources. Chemicals (especially petro-chemicals), building materials and decorative glass and china are also important.

Industry groups	Sales value of production (gross) in 1m. kr. 2003
Manufacturing industry	*1,255,805*
Food products, beverages and tobacco	114,749
Textiles and textile products, leather and leather products	12,681
Wood and wood products	67,145
Pulp, paper and paper products, publishers and printers	164,991
Coke, refined petroleum products and nuclear fuel	8,576
Chemicals, chemical products and man-made fibres	103,332
Rubber and plastic products	33,279
Other non-metallic mineral products	22,168
Basic metals	83,510
Fabricated metal products, machinery and equipment	608,606
Other manufacturing industries	36,768
Mines and quarries	*14,621*

In 2001 industry accounted for 27·4% of GDP, with industrial production growing by 0·3%.

Labour
In 2004 there were 4,213,000 persons in the labour force, employed as follows: 795,000 in trade and communication; 711,000 in manufacturing, mining, quarrying, electricity and water services; 683,000 in health and social work; 589,000 in financial services and business activities; 515,000 in education, research and development; 338,000 in personal services and cultural activities, and sanitation; 246,000 in public administration; 242,000 in construction; 90,000 in agriculture, forestry and fishing. The unemployment rate in March 2005 was 6·3%. In 2004, 75·0% of men and 71·8% of women between the ages of 15 and 64 were in employment. No other major industrialized nation has such a small gap between the employment rates of the sexes. The average monthly salary in 2003 was 22,800 kr. (24,800 kr. for men and 20,700 kr. for women).

In 2004 a total of 15,282 working days were lost through strikes, compared to 733,284 in 1995.

Trade Unions
At 31 Dec. 2004 the Swedish Trade Union Confederation (LO) had 16 member unions with a total membership of 1,861,321; the Central Government Organization of Salaried Employees (TCO) had 19, with 1,274,522; the Swedish Confederation of Professional Associations (SACO) had 26, with 569,308; the Central Organization of Swedish Workers (SAC) had 7,267 members.

INTERNATIONAL TRADE

Imports and Exports
Imports and exports (in 1m. kr.):

	2000	2001	2002[1]	2003[1]	2004[1]
Imports	672,412	662,746	656,664	679,329	736,510
Exports	804,056	806,466	805,696	825,850	903,866

[1]Provisional.

Breakdown by Standard International Trade Classification (SITC, revision 3) categories (value in 1bn. kr.):

	Imports		Exports	
	2003	2004	2003	2004
0. Food and live animals	43·6	46·6	20·7	23·2
1. Beverages and tobacco	7·6	7·6	5·3	5·5
2. Crude materials	21·9	25·9	45·5	48·4
3. Fuels and lubricants	65·2	71·7	28·1	37·6
4. Animal and vegetable oils	2·1	2·2	1·8	2·0
5. Chemicals	74·1	79·1	99·0	103·5
6. Manufactured goods	99·2	111·6	171·2	185·5
7. Machinery and transport equipment	274·4	297·3	375·4	415·3
8. Miscellaneous manufactured items	91·0	94·2	76·9	80·8
9. Other	0·2	0·1	1·8	2·1

Principal exports in 2004 (in 1bn. kr.): road vehicles, 129·0; telecommunications, sound recording and similar appliances, 84·5; paper, paperboard and manufactures thereof, 66·7; medical and pharmaceutical preparations, 52·9; iron and steel, 51·6. Machinery and transport equipment accounts for some 46% of Swedish exports. This includes mobile telephony, which is the largest product group in the Swedish export market. The telecommunications company Ericsson is now the leading export company, ahead of Volvo.

Imports and exports by countries (value in 1bn. kr.):

	Imports from		Exports to	
	2003	2004	2003	2004
Denmark	62·9	67·6	52·8	60·3
Finland	40·0	47·2	47·1	51·6
France	37·6	40·2	40·0	43·3
Germany	126·2	138·1	82·2	91·9
Netherlands	45·5	49·7	40·5	43·2
Norway	52·0	56·1	71·2	78·1
UK	54·3	54·9	64·0	70·6
USA	27·2	25·7	94·8	96·6

In 2004 other EU member countries accounted for 72·8% of imports and 58·6% of exports. Exports were equivalent to 44% of Sweden's GDP in 1999.

COMMUNICATIONS

Roads
In 2005 there were 213,700 km of roads open to the public of which 98,312 km were state-administered roads (main roads, 15,353 km; secondary roads, 82,952 km). There were also 1,684 km of motorway. 79% of all roads in 2005 were surfaced. Motor vehicles in 2004 included 4,113,000 passenger cars, 440,000 lorries, 13,000 buses and 391,000 motorcycles and mopeds. There were 985,000 Volvos, 408,000 Volkswagens, 371,000 Saabs and 322,000 Fords registered in 2004. Sweden has the lowest death rate in road accidents of any industrialized country, at 5·9 deaths per 100,000 people in 2003. 480 people were killed in traffic accidents in 2004.

Rail

Total length of railways at 31 Dec. 2004 was 11,050 km (7,745 km electrified). In 2003, 148m. passengers and 58m. tonnes of freight were carried. There is a metro in Stockholm (110 km), and tram/light rail networks in Stockholm (8 km), Göteborg (118 km) and Norrköping (13 km).

Civil Aviation

The main international airports are at Stockholm (Arlanda), Göteborg (Landvetter) and Malmö (Sturup). The principal carrier is Scandinavian Airlines System (SAS), which resulted from the 1950 merger of the three former Scandinavian airlines. SAS Sverige AB is the Swedish partner (SAS Denmark A/S and SAS Norge ASA being the other two). Sweden holds three-sevenths of the capital of SAS and Denmark and Norway each two-sevenths. SAS has a joint paid-up capital of 14,241m. Sw. kr. Capitalization of SAS Sverige AB, 5,560m. Sw. kr., of which 50% is owned by the government and 50% by private enterprises.

Malmö Aviation and Skyways AB, both Sweden-based carriers, operate some international as well as domestic flights.

In 2004 Stockholm (Arlanda) handled 16,253,872 passengers (10,694,071 on international flights) and (2001) 112,775 tonnes of freight. Göteborg (Landvetter) was the second busiest airport, handling 3,897,296 passengers (2,633,412 on international flights) and (2001) 51,814 tonnes of freight. Malmö handled 1,719,055 passengers in 2004 (1,064,346 on domestic flights).

Shipping

The mercantile marine consisted on 31 Dec. 2004 of 435 vessels of 3·58m. GRT. Cargo vessels entering Swedish ports in 2004 numbered 19,753 (106·69m. GRT) while passenger ferries numbered 73,269 (928·47m. GRT). The number of cargo vessels leaving Swedish ports in 2004 totalled 19,812 (102·31m. GRT) and the number of passenger ferries leaving was 73,484 (931·29m. GRT).

The busiest port is Göteborg. In 2004 a total of 36·40m. tonnes of goods were loaded and unloaded there (33·06m. tonnes unloaded from and loaded to foreign ports). Other major ports are Brofjorden, Trelleborg, Malmö and Luleå.

Telecommunications

There were 14,528,000 telephone subscribers in 2002, or 1,624·5 per 1,000 population. In June 2000 the state sold off a 30% stake in the Swedish telecommunications operator Telia. In Dec. 2002 Telia and the Finnish telecommunications operator Sonera merged to become TeliaSonera. The Swedish state owns 45% and the Finnish state 14%. In 2002 there were 7,949,000 mobile phone subscribers in use. More than 88% of Swedes are mobile phone subscribers—among the highest penetration rates in the world. There were 5,556,000 PCs in 2002, equivalent to 621·3 per 1,000 population—the second highest rate in the world behind the USA. In 2002 there were 698,000 fax machines in use. In Sept. 2002 there were 6·02m. Internet users, or 67·81% of the total population (the second highest percentage in the world, after Iceland).

Sweden has been one of the most active countries in the adoption of information technology. Kista Science Park, in the northwest of Stockholm, was ranked second equal in the world by *Wired Magazine* in 2000 in a listing of the most significant locations for IT research and development. Silicon Valley was ranked second.

Postal Services

There were 1,740 post offices at the end of 2001. In the meantime many traditional post offices have closed down and have been replaced by up to 3,000 new postal service outlets in locations such as shops and petrol stations. A total of 5,555m. pieces of mail were processed in 1999, equivalent to 627 per person.

SOCIAL INSTITUTIONS

Justice

Sweden has two parallel types of courts—general courts that deal with criminal and civil cases and general administrative courts that deal with cases related to public administration. The general courts have three instances: district courts, courts of appeal and the Supreme Court. There are 60 district courts, of which 23 also serve as real estate courts and four courts of appeal. The administrative courts also have three instances: 23 county administrative courts, four administrative courts of appeal and the Supreme Administrative Court. In addition, a number of special courts and tribunals have been established to hear specific kinds of cases and matters.

Every district court, court of appeal, county administrative court and administrative court of appeal has a number of lay judges. These take part in the adjudication of both specific concrete issues and matters of law; each has the right to vote.

Criminal cases are normally tried by one judge and three lay judges. Civil disputes are normally heard by a single judge or three judges. In the courts of appeal, criminal cases are determined by three judges and two lay judges. Civil cases are tried by three or four judges. In the settlement of family cases, lay judges take part in the proceedings in both the district court and in the court of appeal. Proceedings in the general administrative courts are in writing; i.e. the court determines the case on the basis of correspondences between the parties. Nevertheless, it is also possible to hold a hearing. The cases are determined by a single judge or one judge and three lay judges. In the administrative court of appeal, cases are normally heard by three judges or three judges and two lay judges.

Those who lack the means to take advantage of their rights are entitled to legal aid. Everyone suspected of a serious crime or taken into custody has the right to a public counsel (advocate). The title advocate can only be used by accredited members of the Swedish Bar Association. Qualifying as an advocate requires extensive theoretical and practical training. All advocates in Sweden are employed in the private sector.

The control over the way in which public authorities fulfil their commitments is exercised by the Parliamentary Ombudsmen and the Chancellor of Justice. In 2003–04 the Ombudsmen received 5,174 cases altogether, of which 100 were instituted on their own initiative. Sweden has no constitutional court. However, in each particular case the courts do have a certain right to ascertain whether a statute meets the standards set out by superordinate provisions.

The population in penal institutions in Oct. 2004 was 7,332 (81 per 100,000 of national population). There are 56 prisons spread throughout the country.

There were 209 reported murders in 2004 (121 in 1990 and 175 in 2000).

In June 2003 Sweden agreed to accommodate the prison term of Biljana Plavšić, the ex-president of the Republika Srpska in Bosnia-Herzegovina, who was sentenced to 11 years for crimes against humanity by the International War Crimes Tribunal at the Hague.

Education

In 2004–05 there were 650,432 pupils in primary education (grades 1–6 in compulsory comprehensive schools); secondary education at the lower stage (grades 7–9 in compulsory comprehensive schools) comprised 373,292 pupils. In secondary education at the higher stage (the integrated upper secondary school) there were 347,713 pupils in Oct. 2004 (excluding pupils in the fourth year of the technical course regarded as third-level education). The folk high schools, 'people's colleges', had 27,476 pupils on courses of more than 15 weeks in the autumn of 2004.

In municipal adult education there were 226,851 students in 2003–04.

There are also special schools for pupils with visual and hearing handicaps (667 pupils in 2004) and for those who are intellectually disabled (21,856 pupils).

In 2003–04 there were 397,679 students enrolled for undergraduate studies in integrated institutions for higher education. The number of students enrolled for postgraduate studies in 2004 was 19,260.

In 2001–02 total expenditure on education came to 7·3% of GNP and accounted for 12·8% of total government expenditure. The adult literacy rate is at least 99%. In an OECD literacy survey carried out between 1994 and 1999, analysing prose literacy, document literacy and quantitative literacy, Sweden led the world, ahead of Denmark and Norway.

Health
In 2004 there were 27,000 doctors, 4,300 dentists, 81,900 nurses and midwives and 27,088 hospital beds. In 2002 Sweden spent 9·2% of its GDP on health.

In 2002–03, 17·5% of Swedes were smokers (males, 16%; females, 19%).

Welfare
Social insurance benefits are granted mainly according to uniform statutory principles. All persons resident in Sweden are covered, regardless of citizenship. All schemes are compulsory, except for unemployment insurance. Benefits are usually income-related. Most social security schemes are at present undergoing extensive discussion and changes.

Type of social insurance scheme	Payments 2004 (in 1m. kr.)
Old-age pension	188,536
Sickness insurance	108,748
Unemployment insurance	32,614
Parental insurance	23,029
Child allowance	20,873
Survivor's pension	16,987
Attendance allowance	12,748
Housing supplement	10,964
Work injury insurance	6,487

Under a Pension Reform Plan Sweden is one of the world's leaders in the shift to private pension systems. In the new system each worker's future pension will be based on the amount of money accumulated in two separate individual accounts. The bulk of retirement income will come from a notional account maintained by the government on behalf of the individual, but a significant portion of retirement income will come from a completely private individual account. There are two types of pension—the income pension and the premium pension. The income pension comes under a pay-as-you-go system, with the premium pension being a scheme where contributions are invested in a fund chosen by the insured person.

RELIGION
The Swedish Lutheran Church was disestablished in 2000. It is headed by Archbishop Karl Gustav Hammar (b. 1943) and has its metropolitan see at Uppsala. In 1996 there were 13 bishoprics and 2,544 parishes. The clergy are chiefly supported from the parishes and the proceeds of the church lands. Around 87% of the population, equivalent to 7·7m. people, belong to the Church of Sweden. Other denominations, in 2001: Pentecostal Movement, 89,482 members; The Mission Covenant Church of Sweden, 65,299; InterAct, 28,955; Salvation Army, 19,745; Örebro Missionary Society (1996), 22,801; The Baptist Union of Sweden, 18,003; Swedish Evangelical Mission, 17,283; Swedish Alliance Missionary Society, 12,868; Holiness Mission (1996), 6,393. There were also 95,000 Roman Catholics (under a Bishop resident at Stockholm). The Orthodox and Oriental churches number around 98,500 members.

There were around 250,000 Muslims and 18,000 Jews in Sweden in 1998, making Islam Sweden's second largest religion.

CULTURE

World Heritage Sites
Sweden has 14 sites on the UNESCO World Heritage List, as follows: the royal palace of Drottningholm (1991); the Viking settlements of Birka and Hovgården (1993); the Engelsberg ironworks (1993); the Bronze Age rock carvings in Tanum (1994); Skogskyrkogården cemetery (1994); the Hanseatic town of Visby (1995); the Lapponian area (home of the Sami people in the Arctic circle) (1996); the church town of Gammelstad in Luleå (1996); the naval port of Karlskrona (1998); the High Coast (located on the west coast of the southern Gulf of Bothnia) (2000); the agricultural landscape of Southern Öland (2000); the Mining Area of the Great Copper Mountain in Falun (2001); the Varberg Radio Station (2004) at Grimeton in southern Sweden; and the Struve Geodetic Arc (2005). The Arc is a chain of survey triangulations spanning from Norway to the Black Sea that helped establish the exact shape and size of the earth and is shared with nine other countries.

Broadcasting
3,404,000 combined radio and TV reception fees were paid in 2004. There were 8·3m. radio receivers and 5·1m. television sets in 2000. There were 2·0m. cable TV subscribers in 2001. *Sveriges Radio AB* is a non-commercial semi-governmental corporation, transmitting three national programmes and regional programmes. It also broadcasts two TV programmes (colour by PAL). One channel, TV4, is commercial but semi public service, and there are five fully commercial satellite channels, TV3, Kanal 5, TV6, ZTV and TV8.

Cinema
In 2004 there were 1,178 cinemas. Total attendance was 17m. A total of 218 new foreign films and 36 new Swedish films were shown during 2004. In 2004 gross box office receipts came to 1,274m. kr.

Press
In 2004 there were 165 daily newspapers with an average weekday net circulation of 4·0m. More than 80% of people in Sweden read a daily newspaper. The leading papers in terms of circulation in 2004 were the tabloid Social Democratic *Aftonbladet*, with average daily sales of 452,300; the independent *Dagens Nyheter*, with average daily sales of 368,200; the liberal tabloid *Expressen*, with average daily sales of 363,000; and the liberal *Göteborgs-Posten*, with average daily sales of 248,800. In 2004 a total of 17,683 book titles were published.

Tourism
There were 7,458,000 foreign tourists in 2002, bringing revenue of US$5·50bn. In 2001 foreign visitors stayed 4,926,857 nights in hotels and 964,052 in holiday villages and youth hostels. In 2001 there were 2,618 accommodation establishments with 261,160 beds.

Libraries
In 2004 there were one national library, 329 public libraries, 39 university libraries and 31 special libraries.

Theatre and Opera
State-subsidized theatres gave 13,989 performances for audiences totalling 2,734,533 during 2003. The National Theatre (Kungliga Dramatiska Teatern) and the National Opera (Operan) are both located in Stockholm.

Museums and Galleries

Sweden had 237 public museums and art galleries in 2003 with a combined total of 16,331,000 visits.

DIPLOMATIC REPRESENTATIVES

Of Sweden in the United Kingdom (11 Montagu Pl., London, W1H 2AL)
Ambassador: Staffan Carlsson.

Of the United Kingdom in Sweden (Skarpögatan 6–8, S-115 93 Stockholm)
Ambassador: Anthony Cary, CMG.

Of Sweden in the USA (1501 M St., NW, Suite 900, Washington, D.C., 20005-1702)
Ambassador: Gunnar Lund.

Of the USA in Sweden (Dag Hammarskjölds Väg 31, S-115 89 Stockholm)
Ambassador: Teel Bivins.

Of Sweden to the United Nations
Ambassador: Anders Lidén.

FURTHER READING

Statistics Sweden. *Statistik Årsbok/Statistical Yearbook of Sweden.— Historisk statistik för Sverige* (Historical Statistics of Sweden). 1955 ff.—*Allmän månadsstatistik* (Monthly Digest of Swedish Statistics).— *Statistiska meddelanden* (Statistical Reports). From 1963

Henrekson, M., *An Economic Analysis of Swedish Government Expenditure.* Aldershot, 1992
Petersson, O., *Swedish Government and Politics.* Stockholm, 1994
Sveriges statskalender. Published by Vetenskapsakademien. Annual, from 1813
Turner, Barry, (ed.) *Scandinavia Profiled.* Macmillan, London, 2000

National library: Kungliga Biblioteket, Stockholm.
National Statistical Office: Statistics Sweden, PO Box 24300, SE–104 51 Stockholm.
Website: http://www.scb.se/
Swedish Institute Website: http://www.si.se

SWITZERLAND

Schweizerische Eidtgenossenschaft—
Confédération Suisse—
Confederazione Svizzera[1]

Capital: Berne
Population projection, 2010: 7·30m.
GDP per capita, 2003: (PPP$) 30,552
HDI/world rank: 0·947/7

KEY HISTORICAL EVENTS

The history of Switzerland can be traced back to Aug. 1291 when the Uri, Schwyz and Unterwalden entered into a defensive league. In 1353 the league included eight members and in 1515, 13. In 1648 the league became formally independent of the Holy Roman Empire. No addition was made to the number of cantons until 1798 in which year, under the influence of France, the unified Helvetic Republic was formed. This failed to satisfy the Swiss and in 1803 Napoleon granted a new constitution and increased the number of cantons to 19. In 1815 the perpetual neutrality of Switzerland and the inviolability of her territory were guaranteed by Austria, France, Great Britain, Portugal, Prussia, Spain and Sweden, and the Federal Pact, which included three new cantons, was accepted by the Congress of Vienna. In 1848 a new constitution was approved. The 22 cantons set up a federal government (consisting of a federal parliament and a federal council) and a federal tribunal. This constitution, in turn, was on 29 May 1874 superseded by the present constitution, which also combines the federal principle with a national and local use of referendums. Female franchise dates only from Feb. 1971. In a national referendum held in Sept. 1978, 69·9% voted in favour of the establishment of a new canton, Jura, which was established on 1 Jan. 1979.

Switzerland was neutral in both world wars. After the First World War, it joined the League of Nations, which was based in Geneva. But after the Second World War neutrality was thought to conflict with membership of the UN, though Switzerland participated in its agencies, and since 1948 has been a contracting party to the Statute of the International Court of Justice. In March 2001 a referendum on whether to begin immediate talks on joining the European Union was rejected.

But in a referendum in March 2002 Switzerland did vote to join the UN, with 54·6% of voters in favour of membership.

TERRITORY AND POPULATION

Switzerland is bounded in the west and northwest by France, north by Germany, east by Austria and Liechtenstein and south by Italy. Area and population by canton (with date of establishment):

Canton	Area (sq. km) (31 Dec. 1997)	Census Population (1 Dec. 2000)	Population Estimate (31 Dec. 2004)
Uri (1291)	1,077	34,777	35,083
Schwyz (1291)	908	128,704	135,989
Obwalden (1291)	491	32,427	33,162
Nidwalden (1291)	276	37,235	39,497
Lucerne (1332)	1,494	350,504	354,731
Zürich (1351)	1,729	1,247,906	1,261,810
Glarus (Glaris) (1352)	685	38,183	38,317
Zug (1352)	239	100,052	105,244
Fribourg (Freiburg) (1481)	1,671	241,706	250,377
Solothurn (Soleure) (1481)	791	244,341	247,379
Basel-Town (Bâle-V.) (1501)	37	188,079	186,753
Basel-Country (Bâle-C.) (1501)	518	259,374	266,305
Schaffhausen (Schaffhouse) (1501)	298	73,392	73,788
Appenzell-Outer Rhoden (1513)	243	53,504	52,841
Appenzell-Inner Rhoden (1513)	173	14,618	15,029
Berne (1553)	5,959	957,197	955,378
St Gallen (St Gall) (1803)	2,026	452,837	458,821
Graubünden (Grisons) (1803)	7,105	187,058	187,812
Aargau (Argovie) (1803)	1,404	547,493	565,122
Thurgau (Thurgovie) (1803)	991	228,875	232,978
Ticino (Tessin) (1803)	2,812	396,846	319,931
Vaud (Waadt) (1803)	3,212	640,657	647,382
Valais (Wallis) (1815)	5,224	272,399	287,976
Neuchâtel (Neuenburg) (1815)	803	167,949	167,910
Geneva (1815)	282	413,673	427,396
Jura (1979)	838	68,224	69,091
Total	41,284	7,228,010	7,415,102

In 2004 there were 3,786,400 females and 1,524,700 resident foreign nationals. In 2000 foreign nationals made up 20·6% of the population, one of the highest proportions in western Europe. In 2003, 67·6% of the population lived in urban areas. Population density in 2003 was 178·4 per sq. km. The population at the 2000 census was 7,288,010. The United Nations population estimate for 2000 was 7,167,000.

The UN gives a projected population for 2010 of 7·30m.

German, French and Italian and Romansch (spoken mostly in Graubünden) are the official languages. German is spoken by the majority of inhabitants in 19 of the 26 cantons, French in Fribourg, Vaud, Valais, Neuchâtel, Jura and Geneva, and Italian in Ticino. At the 2000 census 63·7% of the population gave German as their mother tongue, 20·4% French, 6·5% Italian, 0·5% Romansch and 9·0% other languages.

At the beginning of 2004 the five largest cities were Zürich (342,853); Geneva (178,500); Basle (164,802); Berne (122,299); Lausanne (116,811). In 2003 the population figures of conurbations were: Zürich, 1,081,700; Geneva, 484,500; Basle,

[1]The Latin 'Confoederatio Helvetica' is also in use.

484,100; Berne, 342,900; Lausanne, 304,800; other towns, 2004 (and their conurbations, 2003), Winterthur, 91,159 (125,900); St Gallen, 70,628 (145,500); Lucerne, 57,271 (197,500); Biel, 48,524 (89,400).

SOCIAL STATISTICS

Statistics for calendar years:

	Live births	Marriages	Divorces	Deaths
2000	78,458	39,758	10,511	62,528
2001	73,509	35,987	15,778	61,287
2002	72,372	40,213	16,363	61,768
2003	71,848	40,056	16,799	63,070
2004	73,082	39,460	17,949	60,180

Rates (2004, per 1,000 population): birth, 9·9; death, 8·1; marriage, 5·3; divorce, 2·4. In 2003 the most popular age range for marrying was 30–34 for males and 25–29 for females. Expectation of life, 2004: males, 78·6 years; females, 83·7. In 2002 the suicide rate per 100,000 population was 19·8 (males, 27·5; females, 10·5). Annual population growth rate, 2003–04, 0·7%. Infant mortality, 2003, 4·3 per 1,000 live births; fertility rate, 2003, 1·4 births per woman. In 2004 Switzerland received 14,217 asylum applications, equivalent to 1·9 per 1,000 inhabitants.

CLIMATE

The climate is largely dictated by relief and altitude, and includes continental and mountain types. Summers are generally warm, with quite considerable rainfall; winters are fine, with clear, cold air. Berne, Jan. 32°F (0°C), July, 65°F (18·5°C). Annual rainfall 39·4" (986 mm).

CONSTITUTION AND GOVERNMENT

A new Constitution was accepted on 18 April 1999 in a popular vote and came into effect on 1 Jan. 2000, replacing the constitution dating from 1874. Switzerland is a republic. The highest authority is vested in the electorate, i.e., all Swiss citizens over 18. This electorate, besides electing its representatives to the Parliament, has the voting power on amendments to, or on the revision of, the Constitution as well as on Switzerland joining international organizations for collective security or supranational communities (mandatory referendum). It also takes decisions on laws and certain international treaties if requested by 50,000 voters or eight cantons (facultative referendum), and it has the right of initiating constitutional amendments, the support required for such demands being 100,000 voters (popular initiative). The Swiss vote in more referendums—three or four a year—than any other nation. A mandatory referendum and a Constitutional amendment demanded by popular initiative require a double majority (a majority of the voters and a majority of the cantons voting in favour of the proposal) to be accepted while a facultative referendum is accepted if a majority of the voters vote in favour of the proposal. Between 1971 and 2004, 106 initiatives were put to the vote but only seven were adopted. Turnout dropped from a peak of 64·0% in the 1930s to a low of 40·6% in the 1980s.

The Federal government is responsible for legislating matters of foreign relations, defence (within the framework of its powers), professional education and technical universities, protection of the environment, water, public works, road traffic, nuclear energy, foreign trade, social security, residence and domicile of foreigners, civil law, banking and insurance, monetary policy and economic development. It is also responsible for formulating policy concerning statistics gathering, sport, forests, fishery and hunting, post and telecommunications, radio and television, private economic activity, competition policy, alcohol and gambling.

The legislative authority is vested in a parliament of two chambers: the Council of States (*Ständerat/Conseil des États*)

and the National Council (*Nationalrat/Conseil National*). The Council of States is composed of 46 members, chosen and paid by the 23 cantons of the Confederation, two for each canton. The mode of their election and the term of membership depend on the canton. Three of the cantons are politically divided—Basle into Town and Country, Appenzell into Outer-Rhoden and Inner-Rhoden, and Unterwalden into Obwalden and Nidwalden. Each of these 'half-cantons' sends one member to the State Council. The Swiss parliament is a militia/semi-professional parliament.

The National Council has 200 members directly elected for four years, in proportion to the population of the cantons, with the proviso that each canton or half-canton is represented by at least one member. The members are paid from federal funds. The parliament sits for at least four ordinary three-week sessions annually. Extraordinary sessions can be held if necessary and if demanded by the Federal Council, 25% of the National Council or five cantons.

The 200 seats are distributed among the cantons according to population size:

Zürich	34	Basel-Town (Bâle-V.)	5
Berne	26	Graubünden (Grisons)	5
Vaud (Waadt)	18	Neuchâtel (Neuenburg)	5
Aargau (Argovie)	15	Schwyz	4
St Gallen (St Gall)	12	Zug	3
Geneva	11	Jura	2
Lucerne	10	Schaffhausen (Schaffhouse)	2
Ticino (Tessin)	8	Appenzell Inner-Rhoden	1
Basel-Country (Bâle-C.)	7	Appenzell Outer-Rhoden	1
Fribourg (Freiburg)	7	Glarus	1
Solothurn (Soleure)	7	Nidwalden	1
Valais (Wallis)	7	Obwalden	1
Thurgau (Thurgovie)	6	Uri	1

A general election takes place by ballot every four years. Every citizen of the republic who has entered on his 18th year is entitled to a vote, and any voter may be elected a deputy. Laws passed by both chambers may be submitted to direct popular vote, when 50,000 citizens or eight cantons demand it; the vote can be only 'Yes' or 'No'. This principle, called the *referendum*, is frequently acted on.

The chief executive authority is deputed to the *Bundesrat*, or Federal Council, consisting of seven members, elected for four years by the *United Federal Assembly*, i.e., joint sessions of both chambers, such as to represent both the different geographical regions and language communities. The members of this council must not hold any other office in the Confederation or cantons, nor engage in any calling or business. In the Federal Parliament legislation may be introduced either by a member, or by either chamber, or by the Federal Council (but not by the people). Every citizen who has a vote for the National Council is eligible to become a member of the executive.

The *President* of the Federal Council (called President of the Confederation) and the Vice-President are the first magistrates of the Confederation. Both are elected by the United Federal Assembly for one calendar year from among the Federal Councillors, and are not immediately re-eligible to the same offices. The Vice-President, however, may be, and usually is, elected to succeed the outgoing President.

The seven members of the Federal Council act as ministers, or chiefs of the seven administrative departments of the republic. The city of Berne is the seat of the Federal Council and the central administrative authorities.

National Anthem

'Trittst im Morgenrot daher'/'Sur nos monts quand le soleil'/ 'Quando il ciel di porpora' ('When the morning skies grow red'); German words by Leonard Widmer, French by C. Chatelanat, Italian by C. Valsangiacomo, tune by Alberik Zwyssig.

GOVERNMENT CHRONOLOGY

Presidents since 1945. (CVP/PDC = Christian Democratic People's Party; FDP/PRD = Free Democratic Party/Radical Democratic Party; SPS/PSD = Social Democratic Party of Switzerland; SVP/UDC = Swiss People's Party/Centre Democratic Union)

1945	SVP/UDC	Adolf Eduard von Steiger
1946	FDP/PRD	Karl Kobelt
1947	CVP/PDC	Philipp Etter
1948	CVP/PDC	Enrico Celio
1949	SPS/PSD	Ernst Nobs
1950	FDP/PRD	Max-Édouard Petitpierre
1951	SVP/UDC	Adolf Eduard von Steiger
1952	FDP/PRD	Karl Kobelt
1953	CVP/PDC	Philipp Etter
1954	FDP/PRD	Rodolphe Rubattel
1955	FDP/PRD	Max-Édouard Petitpierre
1956	SVP/UDC	Markus Feldmann
1957	FDP/PRD	Hans Streuli
1958	CVP/PDC	Thomas Emil Leo Holenstein
1959	FDP/PRD	Paul Chaudet
1960	FDP/PRD	Max-Édouard Petitpierre
1961	SVP/UDC	Friedrich Traugott Wahlen
1962	FDP/PRD	Paul Chaudet
1963	SPS/PSD	Willy Spühler
1964	CVP/PDC	Ludwig von Moos
1965	SPS/PSD	Hans-Peter Tschudi
1966	FDP/PRD	Hans Schaffner
1967	CVP/PDC	Roger Bonvin
1968	SPS/PSD	Willy Spühler
1969	CVP/PDC	Ludwig von Moos
1970	SPS/PSD	Hans-Peter Tschudi
1971	SVP/UDC	Rudolf Gnägi
1972	FDP/PRD	Nello Celio
1973	CVP/PDC	Roger Bonvin
1974	FDP/PRD	Ernst Brugger
1975	SPS/PSD	Pierre Graber
1976	SVP/UDC	Rudolf Gnägi
1977	CVP/PDC	Kurt Furgler
1978	SPS/PSD	Willi Ritschard
1979	CVP/PDC	Hans Hürlimann
1980	FDP/PRD	Georges-André Chevallaz
1981	CVP/PDC	Kurt Furgler
1982	FDP/PRD	Fritz Honegger
1983	SPS/PSD	Pierre Aubert
1984	SVP/UDC	Leon Schlumpf
1985	CVP/PDC	Kurt Furgler
1986	CVP/PDC	Alphons Egli
1987	SPS/PSD	Pierre Aubert
1988	SPS/PSD	Otto Stich
1989	FDP/PRD	Jean-Pascal Delamuraz
1990	CVP/PDC	Arnold Koller
1991	CVP/PDC	Flavio Cotti
1992	SPS/PSD	René Felber
1993	SVP/UDC	Adolf Ogi
1994	SPS/PSD	Otto Stich
1995	FDP/PRD	Kaspar Villiger
1996	FDP/PRD	Jean-Pascal Delamuraz
1997	CVP/PDC	Arnold Koller
1998	CVP/PDC	Flavio Cotti
1999	SPS/PSD	Ruth Dreifuss
2000	SVP/UDC	Adolf Ogi
2001	SPS/PSD	Moritz Leuenberger
2002	FDP/PRD	Kaspar Villiger
2003	FDP/PRD	Pascal Couchepin
2004	CVP/PDC	Joseph Deiss
2005	SVP/UDC	Samuel Schmid
2006	SPS/PSD	Moritz Leuenberger

RECENT ELECTIONS

In elections to the *National Council* on 19 Oct. 2003 the Swiss People's Party/Centre Democratic Union (SVP) took 26·6% of the vote (55 seats), the Social Democratic Party of Switzerland (SPS) took 23·4% (52), the Free Democratic Party/Radical Democratic Party (FDP) took 17·3% (36), the Christian Democratic People's Party (CVP) took 14·4% (28), the Greens took 7·4% (13), the Protestant People's Party took 2·3% (3), the Liberal Party took 2·2% (4), the Federal Democratic Union took 1·3% (2) and the Swiss Labour Party took 0·7% (2 seats). The following parties won one seat each: the Swiss Democrats, the League of Ticinesians, Solidarities, the Christian Social Party and the Socialist Green Alternative of Zug. Turnout was 45·6%.

In the Council of States the CVP hold 15 seats, the FDP 14, the SPS 9 and the SVP 8.

At an election held in the United Federal Assembly on 7 Dec. 2005 Moritz Leuenberger was elected president for 2006 and Micheline Calmy-Rey was elected vice-president.

CURRENT ADMINISTRATION

In March 2006 the Federal Council comprised:

President of the Confederation and Chief of the Department of Environment, Transport, Communications and Energy: Moritz Leuenberger; b. 1946 (SPS; sworn in 1 Jan. 2006).

Vice President and Chief of the Department of Foreign Affairs: Micheline Calmy-Rey; b. 1945 (SPS; sworn in 1 Jan. 2006).

Minister of Defence, Civil Protection and Sports: Samuel Schmid (SVP). *Economic Affairs:* Joseph Deiss (CVP). *Finance:* Hans-Rudolf Merz (FDP). *Home Affairs:* Pascal Couchepin (FDP). *Justice and Police:* Christoph Blocher (SVP).

Federal Authorities Website: http://www.admin.ch

CURRENT LEADERS

Moritz Leuenberger

Position
President

Introduction
The Swiss president is not a traditional head of state and has no powers above the other members of the federal council. The president serves a one year term and is elected at the beginning of each year by the federal assembly. Though banned from immediate re-election, the presidential candidate can take the post again at a later date. Moritz Leuenberger first served as president in 2001, and was re-elected in Dec. 2005.

Early Life
Moritz Leuenberger was born on 21 Sept. 1946 in Biel, Switzerland. He trained as a lawyer and ran a practice in Zürich until 1991. Whilst working as a lawyer, Leuenberger began his political career and became president of the Social Democratic Party of Switzerland (SPS/PSD) in 1972, a post he held until 1980. From 1973–83 he was a member of the city parliament and in 1979 was elected to the national council. From 1991–95 he was a member of the cantonal council of the Zürich government and was elected to Swiss government on 27 Sept. 1995. He is head of the federal department of environment, transport, energy and communications. Leuenberger is the author of several publications dealing with transport issues in Switzerland and he received an honorary doctorate from the University of Udine in 2001.

Career in Office
Leuenberger first held office in 2001 and in March of that year oversaw a national referendum on Swiss membership of the European Union. 77% of votes were against opening talks and Leuenberger declared any move towards membership as 'politically premature'. He called for membership plans to be put on hold until the 2003–07 legislative period.

In Sept. 2001 parliament voted in favour of joining the United Nations. In Oct. 2001 Swiss Air declared itself bankrupt after payment problems to fuel suppliers. In Dec. 2001 citizens voted against a proposal to scrap the Swiss army.

After serving his year as president Leuenberger became transport minister in 2002 and focused on traffic transfer policy including the construction of two trans-Alpine rail tunnels.

In Dec. 2005 Leuenberger was elected for a second term, as president for 2006. He is expected to be succeeded by vice-president Micheline Calmy-Rey in 2007.

DEFENCE

There are fortifications in all entrances to the Alps and on the important passes crossing the Alps and the Jura. Large-scale destruction of bridges, tunnels and defiles are prepared for an emergency.

In 2004 military expenditure totalled 4·53m. Swiss francs, the equivalent of US$3,577m. (US$484 per capita), representing 1·0% of GDP.

Army

There are about 4,000 regular soldiers, but some 220,000 conscripts undergo training annually (18 or 21 weeks recruit training at 20; six or seven refresher courses of 19 days every year between 21 and 30). Proposals ('Army XXI') implemented in 2004 envisaged an Armed Forces based on the three areas of promoting peace, defence and general civil affairs support. Troop levels were cut to 220,000 (120,000 conscripts, 20,000 recruits, 80,000 reservists).

Since 2004 Switzerland has a Chief of the Armed Forces in the rank of a lieutenant-general. In peacetime the Army has no general; in time of war the Federal Assembly in joint session of both Houses appoints a general.

In 1999 for the first time a small Swiss contingent was deployed outside the country, in Kosovo.

Navy

There is no Navy in the Swiss Armed Forces but the Land Forces include a small Marine component with patrol boats.

Air Force

The Air Force has five air base commands. The fighter squadrons are equipped with Swiss-built F-5E Tiger IIs and F/A-18s. Personnel (2005), 19,000 on mobilization, with 85 combat aircraft.

INTERNATIONAL RELATIONS

Switzerland is a member of the UN, WTO, BIS, OECD, the Council of Europe and the NATO Partnership for Peace, OSCE, EFTA, CERN, Inter-American Development Bank, Asian Development Bank, IOM, Antarctic Treaty and the International Organization of the Francophonie. In a referendum in 1986 the electorate voted against UN membership, but in a further referendum on 4 March 2002, 54·6% of votes cast were in favour of joining. Switzerland officially became a member at the UN's General Assembly in Sept. 2002. An official application for membership of the EU was made in May 1992, but in Dec. 1992 the electorate voted against joining the European Economic Area. At a referendum in March 2001, 76·7% of voters rejected membership talks with the EU, with just 23·3% in favour; turn-out was 55·1%. However, the government reaffirmed plans to begin entry talks by 2007. Switzerland ratified membership of the Schengen accord, which abolishes border controls between the member countries, in a referendum on 5 June 2005, although the treaty is unlikely to be implemented until 2007.

ECONOMY

Services accounted for about 72·3% of GDP in 2003, industry 26·5% and agriculture 1·2%.

According to the anti-corruption organization *Transparency International*, Switzerland ranked 7th in the world in a 2005 survey of the countries with the least corruption in business and government. It received 9·1 out of 10 in the annual index.

Overview

Switzerland is a small but open economy with one of the highest living standards in the world. Owing to a lack of raw materials, prosperity is built on labour skills, a business-friendly environment and technological expertise. Major service sectors include tourism and banking. Switzerland experienced a downturn in growth during the global economic slowdown in 2001 but has witnessed moderate recovery since late 2003. However, the return to growth has not improved labour market conditions, with employment declining in manufacturing in 2004 and unemployment rising above 4%. While Switzerland is still one of Europe's wealthiest countries, per capita GDP growth has been below that of the OECD average for several years. High labour costs and product market rigidities in the sheltered economy pose problems of competitiveness. In 2004 the Swiss authorities launched a reform agenda to open sheltered sectors, to reduce the role of the state, to intensify external economic relations and to improve the education system in a bid to boost competition and growth.

Sub-national governments have substantial autonomy. The central government carries the responsibility for foreign policy, defence, pensions, postal services, telecommunications, railway services and currency. All other responsibilities are dealt with at the canton level, notably economic regulation, education, healthcare and the judiciary. This system has led to large income disparities across cantons, with tax revenue per capita differing by a factor of two across cantons. Federal transfers, through 34 different subsidy schemes, aimed to diminish regional disparities but the system has created incentives to overstate the number of eligible projects and has not achieved its goals. In 2004 a referendum approved the New Financial Equalization System which will replace subsidies with grants and provide a clearer division between federal and sub-national responsibilities.

In 2000 the National Bank introduced a monetary policy framework aimed at keeping inflation below 2%. Inflation has remained stable despite pressures imposed by global oil price increases. Monetary independence is crucial to Switzerland as it permits lower interest rates than those prevailing in the euro zone, giving Swiss companies a competitive advantage.

Strains are building in the pension and healthcare systems, which generated a combined deficit of 5% of GDP in 2004. Public finances are likely to come under increasing pressure with the projected 16% increase in the old-age dependency ratio by 2035. Switzerland is the world's second most expensive country for health care, which accounted for 11·5% of GDP in 2003. The health care system, mostly financed by the private sector, suffers from regional fragmentation, financial fragmentation, supply-pushed demand and insufficient competition. Since there is little cost control in the health care sector, the share of subsidized households is likely to grow rapidly. A lack of public consensus on the solution to long-term fiscal challenges has led to the rejection by referendum of recent proposals to raise the retirement age and increase the VAT rate to finance social security.

Currency

The unit of currency is the *Swiss franc* (CHF) of 100 *centimes* or *Rappen*. Foreign exchange reserves were US$56,006m. in 2004; gold reserves were 66·24m. troy oz in June 2002 (83·28m. troy oz in March 2000). Inflation rates (based on OECD statistics):

1995	1996	1997	1998	1999	2000	2001	2002	2003	2004
1·8%	0·8%	0·5%	0·0%	0·8%	1·6%	1·0%	0·6%	0·6%	0·8%

The inflation rate in 2005 according to the Swiss National Bank was 1·2%. Total money supply in June 2002 was 171,584m. Swiss francs.

Budget
Revenue and expenditure of the Confederation, in 1m. Swiss francs, for calendar years:

	2000	2001	2002	2003	2004
Revenue	51,683	48,908	47,405	47,161	48,629
Expenditure	47,131	50,215	50,722	49,962	50,285

VAT is 7·6%, with reduced rates of 3·6% and 2·4%.

Performance
Real GDP growth rates (based on OECD statistics):

1995	1996	1997	1998	1999	2000	2001	2002	2003	2004
0·4%	0·5%	1·9%	2·8%	1·3%	3·6%	1·0%	0·3%	−0·3%	2·1%

Total GDP was US$359·5bn. in 2004.

Banking and Finance
The National Bank, with headquarters divided between Berne and Zürich, opened on 20 June 1907. It has the exclusive right to issue banknotes. The *Chairman* is Jean-Pierre Roth.

On 31 Dec. 2004 there were 338 banks with total assets of 2,490,768m. Swiss francs. They included 24 cantonal banks, three big banks, 83 regional and saving banks, one *Raiffeisen* (consisting of around 420 member banks) and 277 other banks. The number of banks has come down from over 495 in 1990. In 2004 the largest banks in order of market capitalization were UBS (US$79·2bn.) and Crédit Suisse Groupe (US$37·2bn.). UBS ranks third in Europe by market capitalization. Banking, insurance and other finance activities is one of Switzerland's most successful industries, and contributes 14·5% of the country's GDP. Switzerland is the capital of the offshore private banking industry. It is reckoned that a third of the internationally invested private assets worldwide are managed by Swiss banks.

Money laundering was made a criminal offence in Aug. 1990. Complete secrecy about clients' accounts remains intact, but anonymity is lifted in cases of criminal offences such as money laundering, corruption and terrorism.

The stock exchange system has been reformed under federal legislation of 1990 on securities trading and capital market services. The four smaller exchanges have been closed and activity concentrated on the major exchanges of Zürich, Basle and Geneva, which harmonized their operations with the introduction of the Swiss Electronic Exchange (EBS) in Dec. 1995. Zürich is a major international insurance centre.

In Aug. 1998 Crédit Suisse and UBS AG agreed a deal to pay US$1·25bn. (£750m.) to Holocaust survivors over a three-year-period in an out-of-court settlement. The deal brought to an end the issue of money left in Holocaust victims' Swiss Bank accounts which were allowed to remain dormant after the war.

ENERGY AND NATURAL RESOURCES

Environment
In 2002 carbon dioxide emissions from the consumption and flaring of fossil fuels were the equivalent of 5·9 tonnes per capita. An *Environmental Sustainability Index* compiled for the World Economic Forum meeting in Jan. 2005 ranked Switzerland seventh in the world, with 63·7%. The index measured the ability of countries to maintain favourable environmental conditions and examined various factors including pollution levels and the use or abuse of natural resources.

Switzerland is the world leader in recycling. In 1998, 52% of all household waste was recycled, including 91% of glass and 89% of aluminium cans (in both cases the highest percentage of any country).

Electricity
The Swiss Energy programme aims to stabilize consumption, by limiting increases to a maximum of 5% by 2010 (from a base of 2000). Installed capacity was 17·4m. kW in 2004. Domestic production was 63·5bn. kWh in 2004. 30·0% of energy produced in 2004 was hydro-electric from storage power stations, 40·0% nuclear, 25·3% hydro-electric from turbine power stations and 4·7% from conventional thermal. In Sept. 1990, 54% of citizens voted for a ten-year moratorium on the construction of new nuclear plants. There are currently five nuclear reactors in use. Consumption per capita in 2004 was 7,534 kWh.

Minerals
In 2001 approximately 5,200 people were employed in mining and quarrying. Production in 2002 (in 1,000 tonnes): gypsum, 300; lime, 60; salt, 43.

Agriculture
The country is self-sufficient in milk. Agriculture is protected by subsidies, price guarantees and import controls. Farmers are guaranteed an income equal to industrial workers. Agriculture occupied 3·8% of the total workforce in 2004. In 1999 there were 293,949 ha. of open arable land, 115,933 ha. of cultivated grassland and 608,798 ha. of natural grassland and pastures. In 1999 there were 12,921 ha. of vineyards. In 1999 there were 73,591 farms (41% in mountain or hill regions), of which 5,258 were under 1 ha., 18,154 over 20 ha., and 23,300 in part-time use (1996). In 2004 there were 406,000 ha. of arable land and 23,000 ha. of permanent crops. Approximately 11·0% of all agricultural land is used for organic farming—one of the highest proportions in the world.

Area harvested, 2004 (in 1,000 ha.): cereals, 162; coarse grains, 74; sugarbeets, 19; potatoes, 13. Production, 2000 (in 1,000 tonnes): sugarbeets, 1,449; wheat, 539; potatoes, 526; barley, 258; maize, 181; carrots, 56; rapeseed, 53. Fruit production (in 1,000 tonnes) in 2003 was: apples, 208; grapes, 152; pears, 90. Wine is produced in 25 of the cantons. In 2004 vineyards produced 109,000 tonnes of wine.

Livestock, 2004 (in 1,000): cattle, 1,545; pigs, 1,538; sheep, 441; goats, 71; horses, 54; chickens, 8,000. Livestock products, 2004 (in 1,000 tonnes): meat, 445; milk, 3,917; cheese, 162.

Forestry
The forest area was 1·20m. ha. in 2003 (30·3% of the land area). In 2004, 5·2m. cu. metres of roundwood were cut.

Fisheries
Total catch, 2003, 1,814 tonnes, exclusively freshwater fish.

INDUSTRY

The leading companies by market capitalization in Switzerland, excluding banking and finance, in Sept. 2005 were: Novartis AG (US$127·5bn.), a pharmaceuticals company; Nestlé SA (US$118·2bn.), a world leader in food and beverages; and Roche AG (US$97·6bn.), a healthcare company.

The chief food producing industries, based on Swiss agriculture, are the manufacture of cheese, butter, sugar and meat. Among the other industries, the manufacture of textiles, clothing and footwear, chemicals and pharmaceutical products, the production of machinery (including electrical machinery and scientific and optical instruments) and watch and clock making are the most important. The leading industries in 2003 in terms of value added (in 1m. Swiss francs) were: construction, 23,914 (5·5% of GDP); chemicals and chemical products, 14,649 (3·3%); machinery, 11,655 (2·7%); medical and optical instruments and watches, 10,967 (2·5%); electricity and water production, transmission and supply, 10,253 (2·3%).

Labour
In the second quarter of 2005 the total working population was 3,974,000, of whom 645,000 people were in manufacturing,

565,000 in trade, 481,000 in health and social services, and 454,000 in property, renting and business activities. In June 2005 the unemployment rate stood at 4·5%. In 2005, 83·9% of men and 70·4% of women between the ages of 15 and 64 were in employment. The percentage of men in employment is one of the highest among the major industrialized nations.

The foreign labour force was 829,000 in 2005 (335,000 women). Of these 167,000 were Italian, 162,000 from the West Balkan countries, 96,000 Portuguese, 93,000 German and 40,000 French. In 2005 approximately 522,000 EU citizens worked in Switzerland.

Trade Unions

The Swiss Federation of Trade Unions had about 540,000 members in 2005.

INTERNATIONAL TRADE

Legislation of 1991 increased the possibilities of foreign ownership of domestic companies.

Imports and Exports

Imports and exports, excluding gold (bullion and coins) and silver (coins), were (in 1m. Swiss francs):

	2000	2001	2002	2003	2004
Imports	139,402	141,889	130,193	129,743	138,778
Exports	136,015	138,492	136,523	135,405	147,388

In 2004 the EU accounted for 81·4% of imports (112·9bn. Swiss francs) and 61·9% of exports (91·3bn. Swiss francs). Main import suppliers in 2004 (share of total trade): Germany, 32·8%; Italy, 11·3%; France, 9·9%; Netherlands, 5·0%; USA, 4·7%. Main export markets: Germany, 20·2%; USA, 10·4%; France, 8·7%; Italy, 8·3%; UK, 5·1%.

Main imports in 2004 (in 1m. Swiss francs): consumer goods, 55,318; raw materials and semi-manufactures, 35,680; equipment goods, 34,946.

Main exports in 2004 (in 1m. Swiss francs): chemicals, 49,445; machinery and electronics, 33,479; precision instruments, clocks and watches and jewellery, 24,195.

COMMUNICATIONS

Roads

In 2003 there were 71,293 km of roads, comprising 1,795 km of motorways, 18,088 km of cantonal roads and 51,446 km of local roads. Motor vehicles in 2004 (in 1,000): passenger cars, 3,811; commercial vehicles, 298; buses, 17; motorcycles and mopeds, 745. Goods transport by road, 2001, totalled 23,500m. tonne-km. There were 67,680 road accidents (22,891 accidents involving personal injury) in 2004 with 478 fatalities. In 1990 there had been 954 fatalities.

Rail

In 2002 the length of the general traffic railways was 5,021 km, of which the Swiss Federal Railways (SBB) 3,003 km. In 2002 the Federal Railway carried 319m. passengers and 59m. tonnes of freight. In 2000 work began on what is set to be the world's longest rail tunnel—the 58-km long tunnel under the Gotthard mountain range in the Alps linking Erstfeld and Bodio. The tunnel is scheduled to open in 2015. There are a number of tram/light rail networks, notably in Basle, Berne, Geneva, Lausanne, Neuchâtel and Zürich. There are many other lines, the most important of which are the Berne–Lötschberg–Simplon (114 km from Berne to Brig) and Rhaetian (397 km) networks.

Civil Aviation

Switzerland owns seven airports with international scheduled and charter traffic: Basle (the binational Euroairport, which also serves Mulhouse in France), Berne (Belp), Geneva (Cointrin), Lugano (Agno), Sion, St Gallen (Altenrhein) and Zürich (Kloten).

In 2004 these airports handled almost 29m. passengers and around 326,000 tonnes of freight and mail. Swissair, the former national carrier, faced collapse and grounded flights in Oct. 2001. In April 2002 a successor airline, swiss, took over as the national carrier. Services were also provided in 2003 by over 80 foreign airlines. Zürich is the busiest airport, handling 20,814,000 passengers in 2001 (19,698,000 on international flights) and 352,600 tonnes of freight. Geneva handled 7,431,000 passengers and 29,000 tonnes of freight in 2001. Together these two airports accounted for over 90% of Swiss air traffic in 2004.

Shipping

In 2002 there were 1,244 km of navigable waterways. 12·3m. tonnes of freight were transported on the Rhine and Swiss lakes in 1997. A merchant marine was created in 1941, the place of registry of its vessels being Basle. In 2002 it totalled 559,000 GRT.

Telecommunications

Switzerland had 11,525,000 telephone subscribers in 2004 (1,554·3 per 1,000 persons) and there were 6,105,000 PCs in use, equivalent to 823·3 per 1,000 population—the highest rate in the world. Mobile phone subscribers numbered 6,275,000 in 2004. In 2002 there were 283,000 fax machines; in 2003, 20·8% of all private households had a fax machine. There were 3·5m. Internet users in 2004.

Postal Services

In Jan. 2005 there were 2,585 post offices, or one for every 2,869 persons.

SOCIAL INSTITUTIONS

Justice

The Federal Court, which sits at Lausanne, consists of 30 judges and 30 supplementary judges, elected by the Federal Assembly for six years and eligible for re-election; the President and Vice-President serve for two years and re-election is not practised. The Tribunal has original and final jurisdiction in suits between the Confederation and cantons; between different cantons; between the Confederation or cantons and corporations or individuals; between parties who refer their case to it; or in suits which the constitution or legislation of cantons places within its authority. It is a court of appeal against decisions of other federal authorities, and of cantonal authorities applying federal laws. The Tribunal comprises two courts of public law, two civil courts, a chamber of bankruptcy, a chamber of prosecution, a court of criminal appeal, a court of extraordinary appeal and a federal criminal court.

A Federal Insurance Court sits in Lucerne, and comprises 11 judges and 11 supplementary judges elected for six years by the Federal Assembly.

A federal penal code replaced cantonal codes in 1942. It abolished capital punishment except for offences in wartime; this latter proviso was abolished in 1992.

The population in penal institutions in Sept. 2002 was 4,987 (68 per 100,000 of national population).

Education

Education is administered by the confederation, cantons and communes and is free and compulsory for nine years. Compulsory education consists of four years (Basel-Town and Vaud), five years (Aargau, Basel-Country, Neuchâtel and Ticino) or six years (other cantons) of primary education, and the balance in Stage I secondary education. This is followed by three to five years of Stage II secondary education in general or vocational schools. Tertiary education is at universities, universities of applied science, higher vocational schools and advanced vocational training institutes.

In 2003 there were 153,780 children in pre-primary schools. There were 813,448 pupils in compulsory education (465,777 at primary, 297,240 at lower secondary and 50,431 at special schools), 91,796 in Stage II general secondary education and 218,846 in Stage II vocational education, and 160,165 students in higher education, including 111,100 students at universities and 43,525 at universities of applied sciences.

There are ten universities (date of foundation and students in 2004–05): Basle (1460, 9,222); Berne (1528, 13,274); Fribourg (1889, 9,913); Geneva (1559, 14,652); Lausanne (1537, 10,231); Lucerne (16th century, 1,500); Neuchâtel (1866, 3,296); St Gallen (1899, 4,556); Ticino (1996, 1,856); Zürich (1523, 23,395); and three institutions of equivalent status: St Gallen PHS (1867, 324), Federal Institute of Technology Lausanne (1853, 6,493), Federal Institute of Technology Zürich (1854, 12,388). The seven universities of applied sciences were founded in 1997. Enrolment figures for 2003 were: Espace Mittelland, 7,001; Western Switzerland, 4,689; Northwestern Switzerland, 5,547; Central Switzerland, 4,827; Ticino, 1,111; Eastern Switzerland, 2,496; Zürich, 17,854. About 17% of university students are foreign, a proportion exceeded only in Australia.

In 2002 total public expenditure on education came to 25,009m. Swiss francs, the equivalent of 6·2% of GNP, and accounted for 12·9% of total government expenditure. The adult literacy rate is at least 99%.

Health

In 2004 there were 27,742 doctors, 59,833 nurses (2000), 3,679 dentists and 4,284 pharmacists. There were 354 hospitals with 42,742 beds in 2003. In 2002 the Swiss smoked an average 1,940 cigarettes per person. In 2003 Switzerland spent 11·5% of its GDP on health—the highest percentage of any European country. Although active euthanasia is illegal in Switzerland, doctors may help patients die if they have given specific consent.

Welfare

The Federal Insurance Law against accident and illness, of 13 June 1911, entitled all citizens to insurance against illness; foreigners could also be admitted to the benefits. Major reform of the law was ratified in 1994 and came into effect in 1996, making it compulsory for all citizens. Subsidies are paid by the Confederation and the Cantons only for insured persons with low incomes. Also compulsory are the Old-Age and Survivors' Insurance (OASI, since 1948), Invalidity Insurance (II, since 1960) and Accident Insurance (1984/1996). Unemployment Insurance (1984) and Occupational benefit plans (Second Pillar, 1985) are compulsory for employees only.

The following amounts (in 1m. Swiss francs) were paid in social security benefits:

	2001	2002	2003
Old-age and survivors' insurance	28,624	28,710	29,695
Occupational pension plans	27,596	27,321	27,628
Sickness insurance	14,059	14,642	15,635
Disability insurance	8,751	9,287	10,014
Health system subsidies	6,442	7,255	7,669
Unemployment insurance	2,283	3,593	5,195
Family allowances	4,163	4,385	4,493
Accident insurance for employees	4,321	4,438	4,610
Wage continuation	3,761	4,063	3,460
Supplementary benefits (OASI/II)	2,351	2,528	2,671
Total (including other benefits)	108,194	112,345	117,663

RELIGION

There is liberty of conscience and of creed. At the 2000 census 41·8% of the population were Roman Catholic, 35·3% Protestant and 11·1% without religion. In 2000 the figures were estimated to be: Roman Catholics, 3,048,000; Protestants, 2,569,000; other, 1,671,000. In May 2005 the Roman Catholic church had three cardinals with Swiss nationality.

CULTURE

World Heritage Sites

There are six sites in Switzerland that appear on the UNESCO World Heritage List. They are (with the year entered on list): the Abbey-Cathedral of St Gallen (1983), the 9th-century Benedictine convent of St John at Müstair (1983), the Old City of Berne (1983), the three castles and city walls of Bellinzona (2000), the Jungfrau-Aletsch-Bietschhorn mountain region (2001) and Monte San Giorgio (2003).

Broadcasting

Schweizerische Radio- und Fernsehgesellschaft/Société Suisse de Radiodiffusion et Télévision/Società Svizzera di Radiotelevisione is a non-profit-making company responsible for radio and television services. It has seven television channels and 16 radio stations broadcasting in the four national languages. There are German, French and Italian radio and TV networks (colour by PAL). The German radio service has three programmes, local programmes and also broadcasts in Romansch; the French service ('Suisse Romande') has three programmes, as does the Italian. There is an external service, Swiss Radio International (Arabic, English, Spanish). In 2005 there were 48 local radio and 19 local television stations. The UN and the Red Cross have radio stations. There were 4·0m. TV sets in use in 2001 and 7·2m. radio receivers in 2000. More than 90% of households have cable TV—in 1999 there were 2·62m. TV licences altogether and 2·39m. cable TV subscribers.

Cinema

There were 326 cinemas in 2004; total attendance for the year was 17·2m. 47 films were produced in 2004.

Press

There were 86 daily newspapers in 2004 and 134 non-daily papers; their combined circulation was 3,837,648 in 2004. Over 11,000 book titles were published in 2004; more than half of these were in German, 2,428 in French and 383 in Italian.

Tourism

Tourism is an important industry. In 2003 there were 11,400,000 foreign tourists staying in hotels and health establishments, bringing revenue of 5,178m. Swiss francs. In 1999 overnight stays by tourists totalled 67,772,000. 12·01m. Swiss citizens travelled abroad in 1999.

Festivals

The Lucerne Festival is one of Europe's leading cultural events and since 2001 has been split into three festivals: Ostern during Lent, Sommer in Aug.–Sept. and Piano in Nov. The 2002 festivals were attended by a total of 102,800 people. The Montreux Jazz Festival is held annually in July. The 2003 festival attracted 230,000 people.

Libraries

In 2003 there were three National libraries with a total of 4,048,693 volumes and at least 600 users; there were fourteen university main libraries with 30,632,979 volumes and at least 238,000 users; 66 general public libraries with 11,036,983 volumes and at least 493,000 users. There were 28 specialist libraries with 3,891,626 volumes and at least 163,000 users.

Museums and Galleries

In 2003 there were 982 museums.

DIPLOMATIC REPRESENTATIVES

Of Switzerland in the United Kingdom (16–18 Montagu Pl., London, W1H 2BQ)
Ambassador: Alexis P. Lautenberg.

Of the United Kingdom in Switzerland (Thunstrasse 50, 3005 Berne)
Ambassador: Simon Featherstone.

Of Switzerland in the USA (2900 Cathedral Ave., NW, Washington, D.C., 20008)
Ambassador: Christian Blickenstorfer.

Of the USA in Switzerland (Jubilaeumstrasse 93, 3005, Berne)
Ambassador: Pamela P. Willeford.

Of Switzerland to the United Nations
Ambassador: Peter Maurer.

Of Switzerland to the European Union
Ambassador: Bernhard Marfurt.

FURTHER READING

Office Fédéral de la Statistique. *Annuaire Statistique de la Suisse.*

Butler, Michael, Pender, Malcolm and Charnley, Joy, *Making of Modern Switzerland, 1848–1998.* Macmillan, Basingstoke, 2000

Church, Clive, *Politics and Government of Switzerland.* Palgrave Macmillan, Basingstoke, 2003

Kriesi, Hanspeter, Farago, Peter, Kohli, Martin and Zarin-Nejadan, Milad, *Contemporary Switzerland.* Palgrave Macmillan, Basingstoke, 2005

New, M., *Switzerland Unwrapped: Exposing the Myths.* London, 1997

National library: Bibliothèque Nationale Suisse, Hallwylstr. 15, 3003 Berne.

National Statistical Office: Office Fédéral de la Statistique, Espace de l'Europe 10, 2010 Neuchâtel.

SFSO Information Service e-mail: *information@bfs.admin.ch*

Website: http://www.statistik.admin.ch

SYRIA

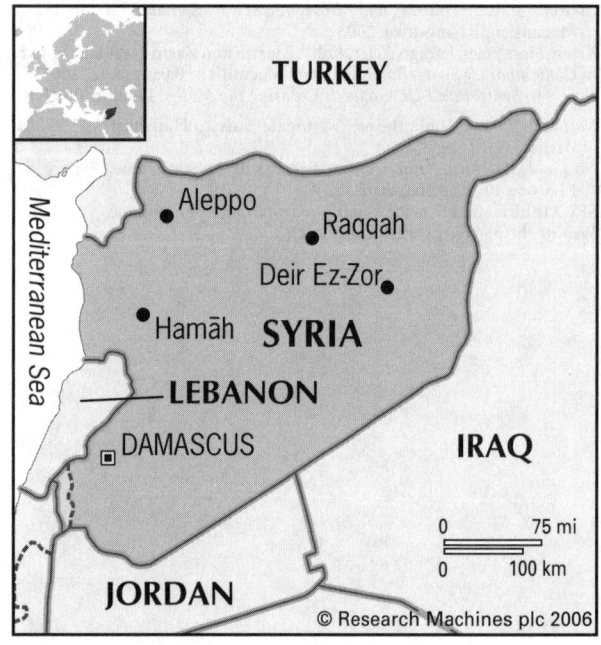

© Research Machines plc 2006

Jumhuriya al-Arabya as-Suriya
(Syrian Arab Republic)

Capital: Damascus
Population projection, 2010: 21·43m.
GDP per capita, 2003: (PPP$) 3,576
HDI/world rank: 0·721/106

KEY HISTORICAL EVENTS

Ancient Syria, an area including modern Israel, Lebanon and Jordan, witnessed some of the world's earliest civilizations, such as Semitic Ebla, which flourished in the 25th century BC near Aleppo. Subsequent centuries brought Mesopotamian influences and empires, including the Akkadians and Ur. The Amorite cities were overrun by the Hittites in the mid-2nd millennium BC before the establishment of the Hurrian kingdom of Mitanni, destroyed by Hittite and Egyptian conflict over the Fertile Crescent. Aramaean kingdoms were harried by warfare with Assyria, which extended its empire from the northeast in the 9th century BC. Immigration of Cimmerians and Scythians in the 7th century broke Assyrian hegemony, which was followed by Babylonian rule.

The Persian King Cyrus defeated Babylon in 539 BC, returning the enslaved Israelites to Jerusalem. Persian rule in turn fell to the onslaught of Alexander the Great in the 4th century BC. His Greek successors—Seleucids and Ptolemies—ruled Syria until the expansion of Rome in the early 2nd century BC. Syria became a Roman province in 64 BC. The Greek cities of the interior (the Decapolis) were rebuilt, including Damascus. Palmyra (Tadmur), an important city on the trade routes to the Euphrates, rose against Rome under Queen Zenobia but was defeated in 272 AD. Syria became an important frontier zone under Diocletian, who established lines of defences (*limes*) against eastern invaders. Syria's cities, such as Edessa, contained the earliest Christian communities; Antioch, where St Peter preached, was made a patriarchate in 451.

Syria continued to prosper under Byzantium until the Persian invasions of the 6th century. Emperor Heraclius' victory over the Persians in the 620s was short-lived as Muslim Arab forces triumphed at the Battle of the Yarmuk River in 636. Damascus became the capital of the Umayyad Caliphate in 661, though Christians and Jews were tolerated. The collapse of the Umayyads led to the establishment of the Abbasid Caliphate in Baghdad in 750. The Abbasids' successors were defeated by a resurgent Byzantium in 969 and the Seljuk Turks in 1085. However, in 1098 Edessa and Antioch were taken by Christian crusaders, followed by Jerusalem in 1099. Zengi of Mosul recovered much of Syria in the 12th century, paving the way for the empire-building of Saladin. Mongol invasions from 1260 were repelled by the Egyptian Mamluks, who removed the last crusaders from the Holy Land in 1302. The Mamluk state survived until defeat at the hands of the Ottoman Turks in 1516 and Syria became part of a Levantine empire.

An Egyptian insurrection in Syria was defeated in 1840 with European intervention. Turko-Arab relations deteriorated in the early 20th century until the British and French defeated the Ottomans in 1918. Faisal ibn Husayn of Mecca became king of Syria in March 1920 but was evicted by France, who took control of the Syrian mandate. The separation of Lebanon, Palestine and Transjordan reduced Syria to its modern borders. During the Second World War the French Vichy government's forces were defeated by the British and Free French and elections were held in 1943. The nationalist Shukri al-Kuwatli was elected president and European forces withdrew in 1946.

A series of military coups between 1949–54 interrupted civilian government. A pact with the USSR in 1956 took second place to the Pan-Arabism that led to union with Egypt in Feb. 1958. However, Syrian discontent led to secession in Sept. 1961. The 1963 coup brought the Ba'athists (Arab Renaissance Party) to power. The Syrian Ba'athists split from the Iraqi Ba'athists, creating serious tensions between the two countries and Syrian support for Iran. War with Israel in 1967 resulted in the loss of the Golan Heights. Lieut.-Gen. Hafez al-Assad seized power in 1970. He was elected president in 1971 and embarked on a 'corrective movement' to crack down on corruption. Domestic opposition to the Alawite (Shia sect) regime was suppressed; the Sunni fundamentalist Muslim Brotherhood was brutally destroyed along with the city of Hamah in 1982. Syrian forces invaded Lebanon in 1976 to prevent a Palestinian victory over the Maronite Christians. Syrian influence remained strong in Lebanon despite Israeli victories in the country.

Assad joined the international coalition against the Iraqi occupation of Kuwait in 1991 and engaged in unsuccessful direct talks with Israel in the 1990s. He was succeeded on his death in 2000 by his son, Bashar, who refused to back the US-led invasion of Iraq in 2003.

TERRITORY AND POPULATION

Syria is bounded by the Mediterranean and Lebanon in the west, by Israel and Jordan in the south, by Iraq in the east and by Turkey in the north. The frontier between Syria and Turkey was settled by the Franco-Turkish agreement of 22 June 1929. The area is 185,180 sq. km (71,498 sq. miles). The census of 1994 gave a population of 13,782,000. Estimate (2005), 19,043,000 (50·2% urban, 2003); density, 103 per sq. km.

The UN gives a projected population for 2010 of 21·43m.

Area and population (1996 estimate, in 1,000) of the 14 districts (*mohafaza*):

	Sq. km	Population
Aleppo (Halab)	18,500	3,694
Damascus City	105	1,347
Damascus District	18,032	1,237
Dará	3,730	689
Deir Ez-Zor	33,060	994
Hamah	8,883	1,415
Hasakah	23,334	1,013
Homs (Hims)	42,223	1,471
Idlib	6,097	1,270
Lattakia (Ladhiqiyah)	2,297	936
Qunaytirah	1,861	330
Raqqah	19,616	592
Suwaydá	5,550	380
Tartous	1,892	730

The capital is Damascus (Dimashq), with a 1999 population of 2,270,000. Other principal towns (population, 1994 in 1,000): Aleppo, 1,840 (1995); Homs, 558; Lattakia, 303; Hamah, 273; Al-Kamishli, 165; Raqqah, 138; Deir Ez-Zor, 133.

Arabic is the official language, spoken by 90% of the population, while 9% speak Kurdish (chiefly Hasakah governorate) and 1% other languages.

SOCIAL STATISTICS

2001 births, estimate, 524,000; deaths, 88,000. Rates, 2001 estimate (per 1,000 population): birth, 30·9; death, 5·2. Infant mortality, 2001 (per 1,000 live births), 23. Expectation of life, 2003, was 71·6 years for males and 75·1 for females. Annual population growth rate, 1992–2002, 2·6%. Fertility rate, 2001, 3·8 births per woman.

CLIMATE

The climate is Mediterranean in type, with mild wet winters and dry, hot summers, though there are variations in temperatures and rainfall between the coastal regions and the interior, which even includes desert conditions. The more mountainous parts are subject to snowfall. Damascus, Jan. 38·1°F (3·4°C), July 77·4°F (25·2°C). Annual rainfall 8·8" (217 mm). Aleppo, Jan. 36·7°F (2·6°C), July 80·4°F (26·9°C). Annual rainfall 10·2" (258 mm). Homs, Jan. 38·7°F (3·7°C), July 82·4°F (28°C). Annual rainfall 3·4" (86·7 mm).

CONSTITUTION AND GOVERNMENT

A new Constitution was approved by plebiscite on 12 March 1973 and promulgated on 14 March. It confirmed the Arab Socialist Renaissance *(Ba'ath)* Party, in power since 1963, as the 'leading party in the State and society'. Legislative power is held by a 250-member People's Assembly *(Majlis al-Sha'ab)*, renewed every four years in 15 multi-seat constituencies, in which 167 seats are guaranteed for the Al Jabha al Watniyah at Wahdwamiyah (JWW/National Progressive Front) alliance of parties (i.e. the Ba'ath party and partners). The government is formed by the Ba'ath. The president is appointed by the Parliament and is confirmed for a seven-year term in a referendum. At a referendum on 10 July 2000 Bashar al-Assad (b. 1965) was confirmed as *President* following the death of his father, who had been president since 1971.

National Anthem

'Humata al Diyari al aykum salaam' ('Defenders of the Realm, on you be peace'); words by Khalil Mardam Bey, tune by M. S. and A. S. Flayfel.

GOVERNMENT CHRONOLOGY

Heads of State since 1943. (HS = People's Party; HSQ = Syrian National Party; KW = National Bloc)

President
1943–49	KW	Shukri al-Kuwatli

Chairmen of Supreme Military Council
1949	military	Husni al-Zaim
1949	military	Muhammad Sami Hilmi al-Hinnawi

President
1949–51	KW	Hashim Bay Khalid al-Atassi

Chairman of Supreme Military Council
1951	military	Adib ash-Shishakli

Presidents
1951–53	military	Fawzi Silu
1953–54	military	Adib ash-Shishakli
1954–55	KW	Hashim Bay Khalid al-Atassi
1955–58	HSQ	Shukri al-Kuwatli

United Arab Republic
1958–61

President
1961–63	HS	Nazim al-Qudsi

Chairmen of National Revolutionary Command Council
1963	military/Ba'ath	Lu'ayy al-Atassi
1963–64	military/Ba'ath	Muhammad Amin al-Hafez

Chairman of Presidential Council
1964–66	military	Muhammad Amin al-Hafez

Heads of State
1966–70	Ba'ath	Nur ad-Din Mustafa al-Atassi
1970–71	Ba'ath	Ahmad al-Hasan al-Khatib
1971	military/Ba'ath	Abu Sulayman Hafez al-Assad

Presidents
1971–2000	Ba'ath	Abu Sulayman Hafez al-Assad
2000–	Ba'ath	Bashar al-Assad

RECENT ELECTIONS

Elections were held on 5 March 2003. The ruling National Progressive Front (led by the Ba'ath Party) won 167 of 250 seats and non-partisan candidates the remaining 83. Turnout was 63%.

CURRENT ADMINISTRATION

Following the death of Lieut.-Gen. Hafez al-Assad on 10 June 2000, a presidential referendum was held on 10 July 2000. The former president's son Bashar al-Assad won 97·3% of the vote.

President: Bashar al-Assad; b. 1965 (Ba'ath; sworn in 17 July 2000).

Vice-Presidents: Farouk al-Shara; Najah al-Attar.

In March 2006 the government comprised:

Prime Minister: Mohammed Naji al-Otari; b. 1944 (Ba'ath; sworn in 10 Sept. 2003).

Deputy Prime Minister for Economic Affairs: Abdullah Dardari.

Minister of Agriculture: Adel Safar. *Awqaf:* Muhammad Ziyad Al-Ayyoubi. *Communications and Technology:* Amr Nazir Salem. *Culture:* Riyad Naasan Agha. *Defence:* Gen. Hassan Turkmani. *Economy and Trade:* Amer Hassan Loutfi. *Education:* Ali Saad. *Electricity:* Ahmad Khaled Ali. *Expatriates:* Butheina Shaaban. *Finance:* Mohammed al-Hussein. *Foreign Affairs:* Walid Muallem. *Health:* Maher Houssami. *Higher Education:* Ghiath Barakat. *Housing and Building:* Hammoud al-Hussein. *Industry:* Fouad Issa Jony. *Information:* Mohsen Bilal. *Interior:* Bassam Abdelmajid. *Irrigation:* Nader al-Boni. *Justice:* Mohammed Al-Ghafari. *Local Administration and Environment:* Helal al-Atrash. *Petroleum and Mineral Resources:* Sufian Allaw. *Presidential Affairs:* Ghassan al-Laham. *Social Affairs and Labour:* Diala Al-Hajj Aref. *Tourism:* Saadallah Agha al-Qalaa. *Transport:* Yarob Souleiman Badr.

CURRENT LEADERS

Bashar al-Assad

Position
President

Introduction
Bashar al-Assad was confirmed as president in a national referendum in July 2000 following the death of his father the previous month. He had not been groomed for a political career, pursuing instead a medical education in England. However, on the death of his elder brother Basil—their father's chosen successor—in an accident in 1994, Assad was recalled to Damascus. Thereafter he rose through the senior ranks of the armed forces, consolidating his influence and authority within his father's regime to achieve the first-ever father-to-son succession to the highest office in an Arab republic.

Early Life
Assad was born in Damascus on 11 Sept. 1965. After attending high school in the capital, he went to London, England, to study ophthalmology. Having returned to Syria upon the death of his brother, he became commander of the Syrian army's armoured division. Assad reportedly used this position to install his own supporters and remove ageing senior figures and potential rivals from the army and security services. He was appointed to the rank of Colonel in 1999.

When President Hafez al-Assad died suddenly on 10 June 2000, Syria's political establishment was quick to demonstrate support for his son. The People's Assembly voted to change the constitution to lower the minimum age for a president from 40 to 34—Assad's age at that time. The Assembly and the dominant Ba'ath Party approved his nomination for the presidency (as the only candidate) and the party elected him as its secretary-general. He was also declared commander-in-chief of the armed forces, his military rank having been elevated to Lieutenant-General. In a national referendum held on 10 July 2000, Assad was endorsed as president with 97·3% of the votes cast.

Career in Office
In his inaugural address to the People's Assembly, Assad spoke of the need for economic reform. He called for the restructuring of the state-dominated economy and improved competitiveness, the dismantling of bureaucracy and the ending of corruption. Private investment has since been encouraged. However, initial signs of political liberalization—a partial lifting of censorship, the release of some political prisoners, tolerance of criticism of the government and party, and the limited introduction of the Internet—faded in 2001 and dissidents were again arrested and detained. On the international stage, peace with Israel remained a priority, although with the stipulation that the Israelis give up the whole of the Golan Heights seized in the Six-Day War of 1967. However, the renewed Palestinian *intifada* against Israeli occupation polarized the already volatile politics of the Middle East and a Syrian-Israeli accord became increasingly unlikely.

In 2002–03 Syria opposed US military threats against Iraq, fearing the consequences of another war in the Middle East. Syria claimed that UN Security Council Resolution 1441 did not support an invasion without further UN approval. US-led forces invaded Iraq in March 2003 and Saddam Hussein was toppled the following month. The USA subsequently threatened Assad with economic, diplomatic or other undefined sanctions, suggesting that Syria was harbouring members of Saddam Hussein's regime and had been involved in the development of chemical weapons.

In Sept. 2003 the president appointed a new prime minister, Mohammed Naji al-Otari, in response to criticism of the pace of reform. Al-Otari, the parliamentary speaker, was selected as a compromise candidate committed to modernization of Syria.

In Jan. 2004 Assad visited Turkey, the first Syrian leader to do so, improving several decades of cool relations between the two countries. The following May the USA imposed economic sanctions on Syria for alleged support for terrorism and failure to stop militants entering Iraq. A UN Security Council resolution adopted in Sept. 2004 and the subsequent assassination of former Lebanese prime minister Rafiq al-Hariri in Beirut in Feb. 2005 (allegedly with Syrian involvement) increased the international pressure on Assad to remove Syria's forces from Lebanon completely. Although the withdrawal was completed in April, the UN continued through 2005 to probe al-Hariri's murder, implicating senior Syrian officials and chiding Assad's government for its perceived lack of co-operation with UN investigators.

DEFENCE

Military service is compulsory for a period of 30 months. Defence expenditure in 2003 totalled US$1,522m. (US$88 per capita), representing 7·0% of GDP. According to *Deadly Arsenals*, published by the Carnegie Endowment for International Peace, Syria has a chemical weapons programme and a biological weapons research programme. Syria had 14,000 troops based in Lebanon in early 2005, but in March 2005 the two countries agreed that Syria would begin to redeploy the troops to the Bekaa Valley in the east of the country. They were subsequently all withdrawn from Lebanon.

Army

Strength (2002) about 215,000 (including conscripts) with an additional 280,000 available reservists. In addition there is a gendarmerie of 8,000 and a Workers Militia of approximately 100,000.

Navy

The Navy includes three diesel submarines and two small frigates. A small naval aviation branch of the Air Force operates anti-submarine helicopters. Personnel in 2002 numbered approximately 4,000. The main base is at Tartous.

Air Force

The Air Force, including Air Defence Command, had (2002) about 40,000 personnel, 611 combat aircraft and 90 armed helicopters, including 170 MiG-21, 134 MiG-23, 30 MiG-25 and 22 MiG-29 supersonic interceptors. In addition there were 90 Su-22 and 20 Su-24 fighter-bombers, as well as some MiG-25 reconnaissance aircraft.

INTERNATIONAL RELATIONS

A Treaty of Brotherhood, Co-operation and Co-ordination with Lebanon of May 1991 provides for close relations in the fields of foreign policy, the economy, military affairs and security. By the treaty the Lebanese government's decisions are subject to review by six joint Syrian-Lebanese bodies.

Syria is a member of the UN, the League of Arab States, OIC and Islamic Development Bank.

ECONOMY

In 2002 agriculture accounted for 23·5% of GDP, industry 29·3% and services 47·1%.

Overview

Between 1990–95 economic growth was strong at 5–7%, owing to reform measures taken in the early 1990s and a major oil discovery. Since 1995 economic growth has slowed significantly. Since 2000 growth rates have been low, between 1·5 and 3·5%, which are relatively low given Syria's rate of population growth of 2·6% per annum. The agricultural sector generates 30% of GDP and over half of Syria's export earnings come from crude petroleum. The weak performance of the economy is attributed to an inefficient state-owned banking system and other state-owned enterprises, multiple exchange rates and exchange controls, restrictions on private sector activity, large agricultural subsidies and the pressures of rapid population growth.

Currency

The monetary unit is the *Syrian pound* (SYP) of 100 *piastres*. Inflation was 5·0% in 2003 and 4·6% in 2004. Gold reserves were 833,000 troy oz in April 2002. Total money supply in Dec. 2001 was £Syr.419,916m.

Budget

Budget revenue and expenditure (in £Syr.1m.):

	1995	1996	1997	1998	1999
Revenue	131,002	152,231	179,202	180,437	196,127
Expenditure	141,957	155,596	181,723	185,973	190,300

Performance

There was real GDP growth of 2·6% in 2003 and 3·4% in 2004; total GDP in 2004 was US$23·1bn.

Banking and Finance

The Central Bank is the bank of issue. Commercial banks were nationalized in 1963. The *Governor* of the Central Bank is Adib Mayaleh. In Aug. 2000 it was announced that private banks were to be established for the first time in nearly 40 years and that a stock exchange would be set up for the first time ever. It is expected to open in 2007. In 2004 there were six foreign private banks.

ENERGY AND NATURAL RESOURCES

Environment

Syria's carbon dioxide emissions from the consumption and flaring of fossil fuels in 2002 were the equivalent of 2·9 tonnes per capita.

Electricity

Installed capacity was 6·0m. kW in 2000. Production in 2000 was approximately 22·63bn. kWh, with consumption per capita an estimated 1,386 kWh.

Oil and Gas

Crude oil production (2003), 29·5m. tonnes. Reserves in 2002 were 2,500m. bbls. Gas reserves (2002), 240bn. cu. metres. Natural gas production (2002), 4·1bn. cu. metres.

Water

In 1992 there were five main dams and 127 surface dams. Production of drinking water, 1995, 608·86m. cu. metres.

Minerals

Phosphate deposits have been discovered. Production, 2001, 2,043,000 tonnes; other minerals are gypsum (345,000 tonnes in 2001) and salt (106,000 tonnes in 2001). There are indications of lead, copper, antimony, nickel, chrome and other minerals widely distributed. Sodium chloride and bitumen deposits are being worked.

Agriculture

The arable area in 2001 was 4·64m. ha. and there were 815,000 ha. of permanent cropland. 1·27m. ha. were irrigated in 2001. In 2001 there were 100,347 tractors and 4,500 harvester-threshers in use.

Production of principal crops, 2001 (in 1,000 tonnes): wheat, 4,745; sugarbeets, 1,175; seed cotton, 1,010; olives, 866; tomatoes, 732; cottonseed, 656; potatoes, 480; oranges, 465; grapes, 389; apples, 263; watermelons, 218; maize, 216; barley, 196.

Production of animal products, 2000 (in 1,000 tonnes): milk, 1,696; meat, 350; eggs, 120; cheese, 89.

Livestock (2000, in 1,000): sheep, 14,500; goats, 1,100; cattle, 920; asses, 198; chickens, 22,000.

Forestry

In 2000 there were 461,000 ha. of forest (2·5% of the land area). Timber production in 2001 was 50,000 cu. metres.

Fisheries

The total catch in 2001 was 8,291 tonnes (72% freshwater fish).

INDUSTRY

Public-sector industrial production in 2001 included (in tonnes): cement, 5,428,000; residual fuel oil (2000), 4,906,000; distillate fuel oil (2000), 4,307,000; petrol (2000), 1,294,000; fertilizers (2000), 330,000; vegetable oil, 89,000; cotton yarn, 83,000; refrigerators (2000), 96,000 units; washing machines (2000), 66,000 units; cigarettes, 12·0bn. units; woollen carpets (2000), 1·7m. sq. metres.

Labour

In 1996 the labour force totalled 4,396,000 (74% males). Unemployment was nearly 20% in 2000.

Trade Unions

In 1995 there were 199 trade unions with 460,967 members.

INTERNATIONAL TRADE

Foreign debt was US$21,504m. in 2002.

Imports and Exports

Trade in US$1m.:

	2000	2001	2002	2003	2004
Imports f.o.b.	3,723	4,282	4,458	4,430	5,935
Exports f.o.b.	5,146	5,706	6,668	5,762	5,561

Main imports, 1999 included: machinery and transport equipment, 19·7%; foodstuffs, 17·8%; iron and steel, 11·5%; chemicals, 9·9%; textile yarn, 9·1%. Main exports included: petroleum and products, 68·4%; vegetables and fruit, 11·0%; cotton, 4·1%.

In 2000 imports came mainly from Germany (6·8%), USA (6·8%), Italy (6·2%), Ukraine (6·2%) and China (5·3%). Exports in 2000 went mainly to Italy (32·0%), France (22·5%), Turkey (10·4%), Saudi Arabia (5·9%) and Lebanon (4·1%).

COMMUNICATIONS

Roads

In 2002 there were 46,698 km of roads, including 6,807 km of main roads and 27,073 km of secondary roads. There were in 2002 a total of 181,017 passenger cars, 46,560 buses and coaches and 367,048 vans and lorries. In 2002 there were 7,154 road accidents involving injury resulting in 1,653 deaths.

Rail

In 1995 the network totalled 2,423 km of 1,435 mm gauge (Syrian Railways) and 327 km of 1,050 mm gauge (Hedjaz-Syrian Railway). Passenger-km travelled in 2000 came to 196m. and freight tonne-km to 1,568m.

Civil Aviation

The main international airport is at Damascus, with some international traffic at Aleppo and Lattakia. The national carrier is the state-owned Syrian Arab Airlines. In 1998 it flew 12·8m. km, carrying 665,300 passengers (642,800 on international flights). Damascus handled an estimated 1,747,000 passengers in 2000 (1,660,000 on international flights) and 25,000 tonnes of freight. Aleppo was the second busiest airport in 2000, handling an estimated 227,000 passengers (156,000 on international flights) and 2,000 tonnes of freight.

Shipping

In 2002 the merchant marine totalled 472,000 GRT. Vessels totalling 2,827,000 NRT entered ports in 2001 and vessels totalling 2,794,000 NRT cleared.

Telecommunications

There were 2,499,300 telephone subscribers in 2002 (146·7 per 1,000 inhabitants), but in 2000 a total of 3·03m. people had been on the waiting list for a line. Mobile phone subscribers numbered 400,000 in 2002. There were 330,000 PCs in use (19·4 for every 1,000 persons) in 2002 and 25,000 fax machines. The number of Internet users in 2002 was 220,000.

Postal Services

There were 600 post offices in 2003.

SOCIAL INSTITUTIONS

Justice

Syrian law is based on both Islamic and French jurisprudence. There are two courts of first instance in each district, one for civil and one for criminal cases. There is also a Summary Court in each sub-district, under Justices of the Peace. There is a Court of Appeal in the capital of each governorate, with a Court of Cassation in Damascus. The death penalty is in force, and executions may be held in public.

The population in penal institutions in 1997 was 14,000 (93 per 100,000 of national population).

Education

In 1995 there were 1,037 kindergartens with 90,681 children; 10,420 primary schools with 113,384 teachers and 2,651,247 pupils; 2,526 intermediate and secondary schools with 50,779 teachers and 841,964 pupils. In 1995, 14 teacher colleges had 766 teachers and 4,989 students; 292 schools for technical education had 10,105 teachers and 72,859 students. Adult literacy in 2003 was 82·9% (male, 91·0%; female, 74·2%).

In 1995–96 there were four universities and one higher institution of political science, with 161,185 students and 4,806 academic staff.

In 2000–01 total expenditure on education came to 4·4% of GNP and accounted for 11·1% of total government expenditure.

Health

In 1995 there were 17,623 beds in 294 hospitals, and 795 health centres. There were 23,742 physicians, 12,206 dentists, 32,938 nurses and 8,862 pharmacists in 2001 and 6,063 midwives in 1995.

RELIGION

In 2001 there were an estimated 14·39m. Muslims (namely Sunni with some Shias and Ismailis). There are also Druzes and Alawites. Christians (920,000 in 2001) include Greek Orthodox, Greek Catholics, Armenian Orthodox, Syrian Orthodox, Armenian Catholics, Protestants, Maronites, Syrian Catholics, Latins, Nestorians and Assyrians. There are also Jews and Yezides. In May 2005 the Roman Catholic church had one cardinal.

CULTURE

World Heritage Sites

There are four sites under Syrian jurisdiction that appear in the UNESCO World Heritage List. They are (with year entered on the list): the old city of Damascus, dating from the 3rd millennium BC (1979); the old city of Bosra, once the capital of the Roman province of Arabia (1980); Palmyra (Tadmur), a desert oasis northeast of Damascus (1980); and the old city of Aleppo, located at the crossroads of various trade routes since the 2nd millennium BC (1986).

Broadcasting

Broadcasting is controlled by the government-owned Syrian Broadcasting and Television Organization. There are two national radio programmes and an external service and two TV programmes (colour by SECAM H). In 2000 there were 4·50m. radio sets and in 2001 there were 2·86m. TV sets.

Press

In 1996 there were eight national daily newspapers with a combined circulation of 287,000.

Tourism

In 2002 there were 1,658,000 foreign tourists; revenue totalled US$1·37bn.

DIPLOMATIC REPRESENTATIVES

Of Syria in the United Kingdom (8 Belgrave Sq., London, SW1X 8PH)
Ambassador: Sami M. Khiyami.

Of the United Kingdom in Syria (Kotob Building, 11 Mohammad Kurd Ali St., Malki, Damascus POB 37)
Ambassador: Peter Ford.

Of Syria in the USA (2215 Wyoming Ave., NW, Washington, D.C., 20008)
Ambassador: Imad Mustafa.

Of the USA in Syria (Abu Rumaneh, Al Mansur St. No. 2, Damascus)
Ambassador: Margaret Scobey.

Of Syria to the United Nations
Ambassador: Fayssal Mekdad.

Of Syria to the European Union
Ambassador: Toufic Salloum.

FURTHER READING

Choueiri, Y., *State and Society in Syria and Lebanon.* Exeter Univ. Press, 1994

George, Alan, *Syria: Neither Bread nor Freedom.* Zed Books, London, 2003

Kienle, Eberhard, *Contemporary Syria: Liberalization Between Cold War and Peace.* I. B. Tauris, London, 1997

National Statistical Office: Central Bureau of Statistics, Office of the Prime Minister, Damascus.

TAJIKISTAN

© Research Machines plc 2006

Jumkhurii Tojikiston

Capital: Dushanbe
Population projection, 2010: 6·99m.
GDP per capita, 2003: (PPP$) 1,106
HDI/world rank: 0·652/122

KEY HISTORICAL EVENTS

The Tajik Soviet Socialist Republic was formed from those regions of Bokhara and Turkestan where the population consisted mainly of Tajiks. It was admitted as a constituent republic of the Soviet Union on 5 Dec. 1929. In Aug. 1990 the Tajik Supreme Soviet adopted a declaration of republican sovereignty and in Sept. 1991 Tajikistan declared independence. In Dec. 1991 the republic became a member of the CIS. After demonstrations and fighting, the Communist government was replaced by a Revolutionary Coalition Council on 7 May 1992. Following further demonstrations, President Nabiev was ousted on 7 Sept. Civil war broke out, and the government resigned on 10 Nov. On 30 Nov. it was announced that a CIS peacekeeping force would be sent to Tajikistan. A state of emergency was imposed in Jan. 1993. On 23 Dec. 1996 a ceasefire was signed. A further agreement on 8 March 1997 provided for the disarmament of the Islamic-led insurgents, the United Tajik Opposition, and their eventual integration into the regular armed forces. A peace agreement brokered by Iran and Russia was signed in Moscow on 27 June 1997 stipulating that the opposition should have 30% of ministerial posts in a Commission of National Reconciliation. President Rakhmonov, first elected in 1994, won a second term in 1999. The country's first multi-party parliamentary election was held in Feb. 2000, although it was criticized by observers for failing to meet democratic standards.

Ethnic conflict and terrorist attacks continue to plague Tajikistan, with Russia offering military support. Fighting in the Fergana Valley, particularly by the Islamist Movement of Uzbekistan, is a cause for concern for all Central Asian governments.

TERRITORY AND POPULATION

Tajikistan is bordered in the north and west by Uzbekistan and Kyrgyzstan, in the east by China and in the south by Afghanistan. Area, 143,100 sq. km (55,240 sq. miles). It includes two regions (Sughd and Khatlon), one autonomous region (Gorno-Badakhshan Autonomous Region), the city of Dushanbe and regions of republican subordination. 2000 census population, 6,127,000 (3,082,000 males); density, 42·8 per sq. km. 80% of the population in 2000 were Tajiks, 15% Uzbeks and 1% Russians. The estimated population in 2005 was 6,507,000.

The UN gives a projected population for 2010 of 6·99m.

In 2003, 75·2% of the population lived in rural areas, making it the most rural of the former Soviet republics.

The capital is Dushanbe (2000 population, 562,000). Other large towns are Khujand (formerly Leninabad), Kulyab and Kurgan-Tyube.

The official language is Tajik, written in Arabic script until 1930 and after 1992 (the Roman alphabet was used 1930–40; the Cyrillic, 1940–92).

SOCIAL STATISTICS

Estimates, 2000: births, 165,400; deaths, 28,800. Rates, 2000 estimate (per 1,000 population): births, 27·0; deaths, 4·7. Life expectancy, 2003, 61·0 years for men and 66·3 for women. Annual growth, 1992–2002, 1·2%. Infant mortality, 2001, 53 per 1,000 live births; fertility rate, 2001, 3·1 births per woman.

CLIMATE

Considering its altitude, Tajikistan is a comparatively dry country. July to Sept. are particularly dry months. Winters are cold but spring comes earlier than farther north. Dushanbe, Jan. –10°C, July 25°C. Annual rainfall 375 mm.

CONSTITUTION AND GOVERNMENT

In Nov. 1994 a new Constitution was approved by a 90% favourable vote by the electorate, which enhanced the President's powers. The head of state is the *President*, elected by universal suffrage. When the 1994 Constitution took effect the term of office was five years. However, an amendment to the Constitution prior to the 1999 election extended the presidential term to seven years, although a president could only serve one term. A further referendum approved in June 2003 allows President Rakhmonov to serve two additional terms after his current one expires in Nov. 2006, theoretically enabling him to remain in office until 2020. The Organization for Security and Co-operation in Europe and the USA expressed concerns at the result. Tajikistan has a bicameral legislature. The lower chamber is the 63-seat *Majlisi Namoyandagon* (*Assembly of Representatives*), with 41 members elected in single-seat constituencies and 22 by proportional representation for five-year terms. The upper chamber is the 33-seat *Majlisi Milliy* (*National Assembly*), with 25 members chosen for five-year terms by local deputies and eight appointed by the president.

National Anthem

'Zinda bosh, ey Vatan, Tochikistoni ozodi man' ('Live long, O Nation, my free Tajikistan'); words by Gulnazar Keldi, tune by Suleiman Yudakov.

RECENT ELECTIONS

At presidential elections on 6 Nov. 1999 President Rakhmonov was re-elected with around 97% of votes cast. His opponent, Davlat Ismonov, received around 2%. Turnout was 98%.

In parliamentary elections held on 27 Feb. 2005 the People's Democratic Party of Tajikistan (PDPT) won 52 of 63 seats (74% of the vote), the Communist Party (CP) 4 (13%), the Islamic Renaissance Party of Tajikistan (IRP) 2 (8%), and ind. 5. Turnout was 92·6%. With one party having secured more than two-thirds support, a second round of voting scheduled for 13 March was cancelled. Elections to the National Assembly were held on 12 March 2000. 25 of the 33 seats were voted for by local majlisi deputies and 8 were appointed by the president.

CURRENT ADMINISTRATION

President: Emomali Rakhmonov; b. 1952 (PDPT; as Speaker elected by the former Supreme Soviet 19 Nov. 1992, re-elected 6 Nov. 1994 and 6 Nov. 1999).

In March 2006 the government comprised:

Prime Minister: Akil Akilov; b. 1944 (PDPT; sworn in 20 Dec. 1999).

First Deputy Prime Minister: Hajji Akbar Turajonzoda. *Deputy Prime Ministers:* Asadullo Gulomov; Khayrinisso Mavlonova.

Minister of Agriculture: Voris Madaminov. *Communications:* Saidmahmad Zubaidov. *Culture:* Radjabmat Amirov. *Defence:* Col.-Gen. Sherali Khairullaev. *Economy and Trade:* Hakim Soliyev. *Education:* Abdujabbor Rahmonov. *Emergency Situations:* Mirzo Ziyoyev. *Energy:* Jurabek Nurmahmadov. *Finance:* Safarali Najmuddinov. *Foreign Affairs:* Talbak Nasarov. *Grain Products:* Bekmurod Urokov. *Health:* Nusratullo Faizulloev. *Industry:* Zayd Saidov. *Internal Affairs:* Khomiddin Sharipov. *Justice:* Halifabobo Hamidov. *Labour and Social Services:* Zokir Vazirov. *Land Improvement and Water Resources:* Abduqohir Nazirov. *Security:* Khayriddin Abdurahimov. *State Revenue:* Ghulomjon Babaev. *Transport:* Abdurahim Ashurov.

CURRENT LEADERS

Emomali Rakhmonov

Position
President

Introduction
Emomali Rakhmonov, a former cotton-farm administrator, became Tajikistan's head of state in Nov. 1992, after the country's first post-Soviet leader, Rahmon Nabiev, was forced to resign. Rakhmonov has survived civil war and an assassination attempt but reforming institutions and raising living standards in one of the region's poorest countries has proved a hard challenge.

Early Life
Emomali Sharipovich Rakhmonov was born on 5 Oct. 1952 in the Danghara district of the Kulob province of the Tajik Soviet Socialist Republic (SSR). He studied electronics and from 1969 worked at a vegetable-oil extraction factory in Qurghonteppa. After three years in the Soviet Navy, Rakhmonov became an administrator at Lenin *Kholkov* (collective farm) in Danghara, constructing a power base as chairman of the farm's trade union committee.

He studied economics by correspondence and in 1982 graduated from the Tajik State University. He was elected people's deputy of the supreme council of the Tajik SSR in 1990. Tajikistan declared independence in Sept. 1991 but hopes of an economically viable state were undermined by civil war. On 19 Nov. 1992, following Nabiev's forced resignation and the annulment of the office of president, Rakhmonov was elected chairman of the supreme council and head of state. On 6 Nov. 1994, following Inter-Tajik peace talks, Rakhmonov won presidential elections, claiming 58·3% of the vote.

Career in Office
Civil war continued through the early years of Rakhmonov's presidency and by the time hostilities between the Islamist-led opposition and his Moscow-backed administration ended in June 1997, at least 50,000 people had died. In March 1998 Rakhmonov joined the centrist People's Democratic Party of Tajikistan (PDPT). He was re-elected president on 6 Nov. 1999

with 97% of the vote. On 22 June 2003 he won a referendum to allow him to run for two further seven-year terms. Rakhmonov's grip on power was underlined in the general elections of Feb. 2005 when his PDPT won 52 of the 63 seats in the lower house of parliament. The opposition Islamic and communist parties alleged fraud and observers said the vote failed to meet international standards.

DEFENCE

In 2002 the Army had a strength of 6,000. There is a paramilitary Border Guard of 1,200. An estimated 12,000 Russian Federal Border Guards, 7,800 Russian Army personnel and some Air Force units are stationed in the country.

Defence expenditure in 2003 totalled US$150m. (US$24 per capita), representing 2·1% of GDP.

In April 2003 Russia announced plans to increase its military presence in Tajikistan in response to intelligence reports of increased activity by the Taliban and al-Qaeda in neighbouring Afghanistan.

Army

Personnel strength approximately 6,000.

INTERNATIONAL RELATIONS

Tajikistan is a member of the UN, the NATO Partnership for Peace, CIS, OSCE, ECO, IOM, OIC and Islamic Development Bank.

ECONOMY

In 2002 agriculture accounted for 24·3% of GDP, industry 24·0% and services 51·7%.

Overview

The economy is mainly agrarian; the sector employs two-thirds of the labour force and contributes 11% to export revenues, despite under 10% of land being arable. Economic growth averaged 7·5% between 1999–2001 and improved inflation management has aided the implementation of macroeconomic policies. Civil war and repeated changes of political leadership in the 1990s prevented the government from establishing a coherent economic policy to address the challenges of independence from the Soviet Union. As a result, the economy deteriorated more rapidly than in other ex-Soviet countries. In 1995 GDP per capita had been reduced to 40% of the 1991 level; during this period the economy reverted to subsistence agriculture as food and labour markets collapsed. In 1996 a reform programme began, supported by the IMF and the World Bank. Despite a slow start and the Russian financial crisis in 1998, the focus on economic reconstruction has enabled the economy to make significant progress in the transition toward a market economy. Reforms have included small-scale privatization, land reform, the restructuring of the banking system and the legal system and the development of market-based institutions.

Currency

The unit of currency is the *somoni* (TJS) of 100 *dirams*, which replaced the Tajik rouble on 30 Oct. 2000 at 1 somoni = 1,000 Tajik roubles. The introduction of the new currency was intended to strengthen the national banking system. The IMF voiced their support for the new currency, which it believes will contribute to macroeconomic stability and expedite the transition to a market economy. Inflation in 1993 was 2,195%, declining to 418% in 1996 and still further to 32·9% in 2000, the reduction being helped by a US$22m. IMF loan in 1996 and maintenance of a tighter monetary regime. By 2004 the rate had fallen to 7·1%.

Budget

Total revenue in 2001 was 288·7m. somoni and total expenditure was 292·5m. somoni.

Performance

Annual real GDP growth was negative for four consecutive years in the mid-1990s. However, the economy slowly recovered and in 2003 growth was 10·2%, rising to 10·6% in 2004. Total GDP in 2004 was US$2·1bn.

Banking and Finance

The central bank and bank of issue is the National Bank (*Chairman*, Murotali Alimardonov). In 1998 there were 27 commercial and private banks but the number had fallen to 14 by 2002 after a process of consolidation.

ENERGY AND NATURAL RESOURCES

Environment

In 2002 Tajikistan's carbon dioxide emissions from the consumption and flaring of fossil fuels were the equivalent of 0·8 tonnes per capita.

Electricity

Installed capacity in 2000 was 4·4m. kW. Production was 14·2bn. kWh in 2000 and consumption per capita 2,517 kWh.

Oil and Gas

In 2000 oil production was 18,000 tonnes; natural gas output in 2000 was 40m. cu. metres.

Minerals

There are deposits of brown coal, lead, zinc, iron ore, antimony, mercury, gold, silver, tungsten and uranium. Lignite production, 2000, 20,000 tonnes. Aluminium production, 2001, 289,000 tonnes.

Agriculture

Area under cultivation in 1997 was 9·6m. ha., mainly in the hands of state and collective farms. In 2001 there were 930,000 ha. of arable land and 130,000 ha. of permanent crops. Cotton is the major cash crop, with various fruits, sugarcane, jute, silk, rice and millet also being grown.

Output of main agricultural products (in 1,000 tonnes) in 2000: wheat, 358; seed cotton, 294; potatoes, 250; cottonseed, 210; tomatoes, 185; onions, 128. Livestock, 2000: 1·59m. sheep; 1·04m. cattle; 590,000 goats; 1m. chickens. Livestock products, 2000 (in 1,000 tonnes): meat, 31; milk, 331.

Forestry

Forests covered 400,000 ha. in 2000, or 2·8% of the land area.

Fisheries

Total catch in 2001 was 137 tonnes, exclusively from inland waters.

INDUSTRY

Major industries: aluminium, electro-chemical plants, textile machinery, carpet weaving, silk mills, refrigerators, hydro-electric power. Output: cement (2001), 69,000 tonnes; mineral nitrogenous fertilizer (2000), 4,000 tonnes; cotton woven fabrics (2001), 14m. sq. metres; carpets and rugs (1999), 1m. sq. metres; silk fabrics (2001), 248,000 sq. metres; footwear (2001), 100,000 pairs.

Labour

The economically active force in 1997 totalled 1,143,000. The principal areas of activity were: agriculture, hunting and forestry, 528,000; education, 160,000; manufacturing, 137,000; and health and social work, 82,000. In 2000 the unemployment rate was 3·0%.

INTERNATIONAL TRADE

Total external debt was US$1,153m. in 2002.

Imports and Exports

In 2002 imports were valued at US$822·9m. and exports at US$699·1m. Main imports: petroleum products, grain, manufactured consumer goods; main exports: cotton and aluminium. Principal import suppliers, 2000: Uzbekistan, 28·8%; Russia, 16·1%; Ukraine, 13·1%; Kazakhstan, 12·8%. Principal export markets in 2000: Russia, 37·4%; Netherlands, 25·7%; Uzbekistan, 14·1%; Switzerland, 10·4%.

COMMUNICATIONS

Roads

In 2000 there were 27,767 km of roads. There were an estimated 8,820 passenger cars, buses, lorries and vans in 1996. In 2000 there were 1,333 road accidents, resulting in 406 fatalities.

Rail

Length of railways, 2000, 533 km. Passenger-km travelled in 2000 came to 83m. and freight tonne-km to 1·33bn.

Civil Aviation

There are international airports at Dushanbe and Khujand. The national carrier is Tajikistan Airlines, which in 2003 flew to İstanbul, Moscow, Munich and a variety of Asian cities. In 2003 there were flights with other airlines to Bishkek, Ekaterinburg, Samara and St Petersburg. In 1999 scheduled airline traffic of Tajikistan-based carriers flew 4·1m. km, carrying 156,000 passengers (79,000 on international flights).

Telecommunications

Tajikistan had 250,800 telephone subscribers in 2002, or 39·3 for every 1,000 persons. In 2002 mobile phone subscribers numbered 13,200 and there were 3,500 Internet users. There were 2,500 fax machines in 2002.

Postal Services

In 2003 there were 593 post offices.

SOCIAL INSTITUTIONS

Justice

In 1994, 14,279 crimes were reported, including 636 murders or attempted murders. The population in penal institutions in Sept. 2003 was approximately 10,000 (159 per 100,000 of national population). The death penalty is in force.

Education

The adult literacy rate in 2003 was 99·5% (99·7% among males and 99·3% among females). In 2000–01 there were 680,100 pupils and 31,216 teachers at primary schools; 847,445 pupils and 54,593 teachers at secondary schools; and 78,540 students at higher education institutions.

There is one university, which had 7,220 students in 1994–95.

In 2001–02 total expenditure on education came to 2·5% of GNP.

Health

There were 449 hospitals in 1994. In 2001 there were 13,393 physicians, 1,051 dentists, 26,887 nurses, 680 pharmacists and 3,932 midwives.

Welfare

In Jan. 1994 there were 0·41m. old age pensioners and 0·2m. other pensioners.

RELIGION

The Tajiks are predominantly Sunni Muslims (80%); Shia Muslims, 5%.

CULTURE

Broadcasting

Broadcasting is controlled by the State Teleradio Broadcasting Company. Tajik Radio broadcasts three national programmes, a Radio Moscow relay and a foreign service (Dari, Iranian). In 2000 there were 870,000 radio receivers and in 2001 there were 2·2m. TV receivers.

Press
There were two daily newspapers in 1996 with a combined circulation of 120,000, equivalent to 21 per 1,000 inhabitants.

Tourism
In 2001, 4,000 foreign tourists visited Tajikistan.

DIPLOMATIC REPRESENTATIVES

Of Tajikistan in the United Kingdom
Honorary Consul: Benjamin Brahms (33 Ovington Square, London, SW3 1LJ).

Of the United Kingdom in Tajikistan (65 Mirzo Tursunzade St., Dushanbe)
Ambassador: Graeme Loten.

Of Tajikistan in the USA (1005 New Hampshire Ave., NW, Washington, D.C., 20037)
Ambassador: Khamrokhon Zaripov.

Of the USA in Tajikistan (10 Pavlov St., Dushanbe)
Ambassador: Richard E. Hoagland.

Of Tajikistan to the United Nations
Ambassador: Sirodjidin Aslov.

Of Tajikistan to the European Union
Ambassador: Sharif Rahimov.

FURTHER READING

Abdullaev, K. and Akbarzadeh, S., *Historical Dictionary of Tajikistan.* Rowman and Littlefield Publishing, Lanham, Maryland, 2002

Akiner, S., *Tajikistan: Disintegration or Reconciliation?* Royal Institute of International Affairs, London, 2001
Djalili, M. R. (ed.) *Tajikistan: The Trials of Independence.* Macmillan, Basingstoke, 1998

Gorno-Badakhshan Autonomous Region

Comprising the Pamir massif along the borders of Afghanistan and China, the province was set up on 2 Jan. 1925, initially as the Special Pamir Province. Area, 63,700 sq. km (24,590 sq. miles). The population in 2004 was 217,900 (mainly Tajiks with a Kirghiz minority). Capital, Khorog (2000: 30,000). The inhabitants are predominantly Ismaili Muslims.

Mining industries are developed (gold, rock-crystal, mica, coal, salt). Wheat, fruit and fodder crops are grown, and cattle and sheep are bred in the western parts. In 1990 there were 74,200 cattle and 329,500 sheep and goats. Total area under cultivation, 16,236 ha. In 2004 the region was 69% self-sufficient in food; humanitarian aid had comprised 85% of all food consumed in 1993.

The area is the most impoverished in Tajikistan, with 84% of the population falling below the poverty line in 2003, compared to a national average of 64%. Around 20% of the population of working age is employed abroad, mainly in the Russian Federation. Unemployment is approximately 70%.

In 1990–91 there were 47,600 students at all levels of education. One of the three campuses of the new Central Asian University is scheduled to open in Khorog in late 2006. There were 140 doctors in 1991 and 1,400 paramedics in 2004.

TANZANIA

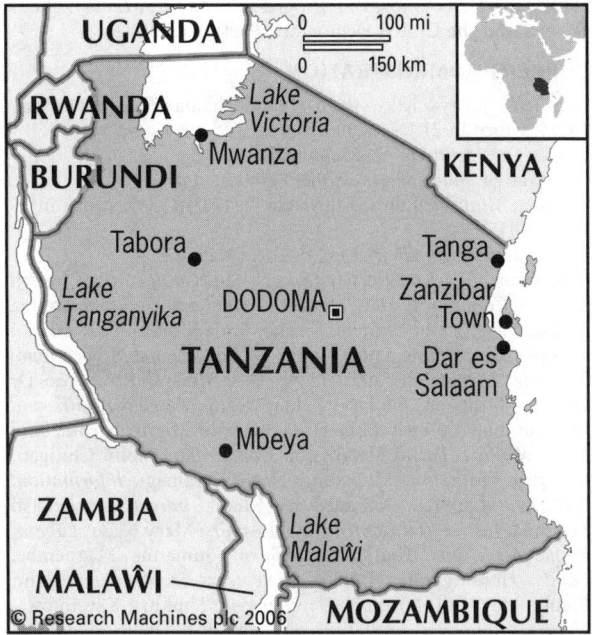

Jamhuri ya Muungano wa Tanzania
(United Republic of Tanzania)

Capital: Dodoma
Population projection, 2010: 41·84m.
GDP per capita, 2003: (PPP$) 621
HDI/world rank: 0·418/164

KEY HISTORICAL EVENTS

Archaeological evidence suggests that present-day Tanzania was inhabited by Khoisan-speaking hunter-gatherers from at least 10,000 BC. The Sandawe and Hadze of north-central Tanzania are descendents of these groups. Cushitic-speaking cattle herders migrated south from Ethiopia and Sudan from around 1,000 BC. Beginning in the first millennium AD, Tanzania was settled by Bantu-speaking iron-working farmers, whose origins are considered to be in the borderlands of present-day Nigeria and Cameroon.

Seafarers from Arabia established a trading settlement on the coast at Kilwa around 800 AD, and Persian merchants settled on the islands of Zanzibar and Pemba. Nilotic-speaking pastoralists (including the Maasai and Luo) moved south into Tanzania between 900 AD and 1700 AD. Sultan Hassan bin Sulaiman I established control of Kilwa around 1270. Islam spread and a thriving Afro-Arab 'Swahili' culture took hold in coastal areas.

Portuguese explorers arrived off Kilwa in July 1500, heralding two centuries of Portuguese control over various East African trading ports. Zanzibar came under Omani control in the 1650s and prospered as a centre of the slave trade, extending its influence over the coastal hinterland and into the mainland interior. Britain attempted to end the slave trade by signing the Treaty of Moresby with the Sultan of Zanzibar in 1822. During the 1880s the German imperialist, Dr Carl Peters, founded German East Africa by signing agreements with several local rulers. A series of agreements between Britain and Germany and the Sultan of Zanzibar saw Germany become the dominant influence over most of mainland Tanzania, while the Sultan of Zanzibar retained control of a strip of coastal territories and Britain ruled Zanzibar as a protectorate.

German East Africa was conquered by the Allies in the First World War and subsequently divided between the Belgians, the Portuguese and the British. The country was administered as a League of Nations mandate until 1946, and then as a UN trusteeship territory until 9 Dec. 1961. Tanganyika achieved responsible government in Sept. 1960 and full self-government on 1 May 1961. On 9 Dec. 1961 Tanganyika became a sovereign independent member state of the Commonwealth of Nations. On 9 Dec 1962 the country adopted a republican form of government (still within the British Commonwealth) and Dr Nyerere was elected as the first president.

Zanzibar gained internal self-government on 24 June 1963, followed by full independence on 9 Dec. 1963. On 12 Jan. 1964 the sultanate was overthrown by a revolt of the Afro-Shirazi Party leaders who established the People's Republic of Zanzibar. Also in Jan. 1964 there was an attempted coup against Nyerere who had to seek British military help. On 26 April 1964 Tanganyika, Zanzibar and Pemba combined to form the United Republic of Tanzania. The first multi-party elections were held in 1995.

'In a continent where the search is always on for success stories, Tanzania has come to be regarded as one of the clearer successes. As international donors prepare to increase their aid to Africa in keeping with the promises made at last month's Group of Eight summit, it will be near the front of the line, a test case of a country that is seen as doing most things right.' (*Financial Times*, 2 Aug. 2005).

TERRITORY AND POPULATION

Tanzania is bounded in the northeast by Kenya, north by Lake Victoria and Uganda, northwest by Rwanda and Burundi, west by Lake Tanganyika, southwest by Zambia and Malaŵi, and south by Mozambique. Total area 942,799 sq. km (364,881 sq. miles), including the offshore islands of Zanzibar (1,554 sq. km) and Pemba (906 sq. km) and inland water surfaces (59,050 sq. km). 2002 census population, 34,443,603 (17,613,742 females), giving a density of 36·5 per sq. km. The United Nations population estimate for 2002 was 36,205,000.

The UN gives a projected population for 2010 of 41·84m.

In 2003, 64·6% of the population lived in rural areas. 0·5m. Hutu refugees were forcibly repatriated to Rwanda in Dec. 1996. Tanzania has the highest refugee population in Africa, with 650,000 at the end of 2003.

The chief towns (2002 census populations) are Dar es Salaam, the chief port and former capital (2,336,055), Arusha (270,485), Mbeya (230,318) and Mwanza (209,806). Dodoma, the capital, had a population of 149,180 in 2002.

The United Republic is divided into 26 administrative regions of which 21 are in mainland Tanzania, three in Zanzibar and two in Pemba. Areas and 2002 populations of the regions:

Region	Sq. km	Population
Arusha	36,486	1,288,088
Dar es Salaam	1,393	2,487,288
Dodoma	41,311	1,692,025
Iringa	56,864	1,490,892
Kagera	28,388	2,028,157
Kigoma	37,037	1,674,047
Kilimanjaro	13,309	1,376,702
Lindi	66,046	787,624
Manyara	45,820	1,037,605
Mara	19,566	1,363,397

Region	Sq. km	Population
Mbeya	60,350	2,063,328
Morogoro	70,799	1,753,362
Mtwara	16,707	1,124,481
Mwanza	19,592	2,929,644
Pwani (Coast)	32,407	885,017
Rukwa	68,635	1,136,354
Ruvuma	63,498	1,113,715
Shinyanga	50,781	2,796,630
Singida	49,341	1,086,748
Tabora	76,151	1,710,465
Tanga	26,808	1,636,280
Zanzibar and Pemba	2,460	981,754
Pemba North	574	185,326
Pemba South	332	175,471
Zanzibar North	470	136,639
Zanzibar South	854	94,244
Zanzibar West	230	390,074

The official languages are English and Swahili (spoken as a mother tongue by only 8·8% of the population, but used as a lingua franca by 91%).

SOCIAL STATISTICS

2000 estimates: births, 1,320,000; deaths, 460,000. Rates, 2000 estimates (per 1,000 population): births, 37·9; deaths, 13·1. Annual population growth rate, 1992–2002, 2·6%. Life expectancy in 2003 was 45·5 years for men and 46·3 for women. 45% of the population was below 15 years old in 2002. Infant mortality, 2001, 104 per 1,000 live births; fertility rate, 2001, 5·2 births per woman.

CLIMATE

The climate is very varied and is controlled largely by altitude and distance from the sea. There are three climatic zones: the hot and humid coast, the drier central plateau with seasonal variations of temperature, and the semi-temperate mountains. Dodoma, Jan. 75°F (23·9°C), July 67°F (19·4°C). Annual rainfall 23" (572 mm). Dar es Salaam, Jan. 82°F (27·8°C), July 74°F (23·3°C). Annual rainfall 43" (1,064 mm).

CONSTITUTION AND GOVERNMENT

The current constitution dates from 25 April 1977 but underwent major revisions in Oct. 1984. The *President* is head of state, chairman of the party and commander-in-chief of the armed forces. The *Prime Minister* is also the leader of government business in the National Assembly.

The 324-member *Bunge (National Assembly)* is composed of 232 constituency representatives, 75 appointed women, ten Union presidential nominees, five representatives of the Zanzibar House of Representatives and two *ex officio* members (one of whom is the Attorney General). In Dec. 1979 a separate Constitution for Zanzibar was approved. Although at present under the same Constitution as Tanzania, Zanzibar has, in fact, been ruled by decree since 1964.

National Anthem

'God Bless Africa/Mungu ibariki Afrika'; words collective, tune by M. E. Sontonga and V. E. Webster.

GOVERNMENT CHRONOLOGY

Presidents since 1964. (TANU = Tanganyika African National Union; CCM = Chama Cha Mapinduzi (Revolutionary State Party))

1964–85	TANU/CCM	Julius Kambarage Nyerere
1985–95	CCM	Ali Hassan Mwinyi
1995–2005	CCM	Benjamin William Mkapa
2005–	CCM	Jakaya Mrisho Kikwete

RECENT ELECTIONS

Presidential and parliamentary elections were held on 14 Dec. 2005. Jakaya Kikwete of Chama Cha Mapinduzi (Revolutionary

State Party) was elected president with 80·3% of votes cast against nine other candidates. Turnout was 72·4%. In the parliamentary elections Chama Cha Mapinduzi gained 206 of 232 seats, the Civic United Front 19, Chama Cha Democracia na Maendeleo (Party for Democracy and Progress) 5, the Tanzania Labour Party 1 and the United Democratic Party 1.

CURRENT ADMINISTRATION

President: Jakaya Kikwete; b. 1950 (Chama Cha Mapinduzi/CCM; sworn in 21 Dec. 2005).

　　Vice-President: Dr Ali Mohamed Sheni.

　　In March 2006 the government consisted of:

　　Prime Minister: Edward Lowassa; b. 1953 (CCM; sworn in 30 Dec. 2005).

　　President of Zanzibar: Amani Abeid Karume.

　　Minister of Agriculture, Food Security and Co-operatives: Joseph Mungai. *Community Development, Gender and Children:* Sophia Simba. *Defence and National Service:* Juma Kapuya. *East African Co-operation Affairs:* Andrew Chenge. *Education and Vocational Training:* Margareth Sitta. *Energy and Mineral Resources:* Dr Ibrahim Msabaha. *Finance:* Zakia Meghji. *Foreign Affairs and International Co-operation:* Dr Asha-Rose Migiro. *Health and Social Welfare:* David Mwakyusa. *Home Affairs:* John Chiligati. *Industry, Trade and Marketing:* Nazir Karamagi. *Information, Culture and Sports:* Mohamed Seif Khatib. *Infrastructure:* Basil Mramba. *Justice and Constitutional Affairs:* Mary Nagu. *Labour, Employment and Youth Development:* Jumanne Maghembe. *Lands, Housing and Human Settlements Development:* John Pombe Magufuli. *Livestock Development:* Shukuru Kawambwa. *Natural Resources and Tourism:* Anthony Diallo. *Planning, Economy and Empowerment:* Dr Juma Ngasongwa. *Public Security and Safety:* Harithi Bakari Mwapachu. *Science, Technology and Higher Education:* Peter Msolla. *Water:* Stephen Wassira.

Government Website: http://www.tanzania.go.tz

CURRENT LEADERS

Jakaya Kikwete

Position
President

Introduction
Jakaya Kikwete became president of Tanzania on 14 Dec. 2005, winning an overwhelming majority in national elections that were generally considered free and fair. A Muslim from the coastal district of Bagamoyo, Kikwete was a military leader in the 1970s and 1980s and served as foreign minister for ten years from 1995.

Early Life
Jakaya Mrisho Kikwete was born on 7 Oct. 1950 in Msoga, Bagamoyo District on the coast of Tanganyika. He attended schools in Msoga and Kibaha, before studying economics at the University of Dar es Salaam. In 1975, while at university, Kikwete joined the ruling Tanganyika African National Union, which later became the Chama Cha Mapinduzi (CCM, Revolutionary State Party). Following his graduation in 1978, Kikwete joined the Tanzania People's Defence Force (TPDF), where he served as lieutenant from 1972–79 and subsequently as captain.

In 1984, having spent a year at the Monduli military officers college in Arusha, Kikwete became chief political instructor of the TPDF. In 1988 he was elected to represent Bagamoyo parliamentary constituency, a post he held for three consecutive terms. He was deputy minister of energy, water and minerals from 1988–90 before being promoted to minister and serving under President Ali Hassan Mwinyi for four years. Following constitutional reform that legalized opposition parties in 1992, Kikwete retired from the army.

In 1995, having served as finance minister for a year, Kikwete became one of fourteen challengers for the CCM leadership. He lost to Benjamin Mkapa, who led the party to victory in national elections in Oct. 1995 amid widespread allegations of voting irregularities. Kikwete was appointed foreign minister, a post he held until 2005, winning praise for his mediation work in war-torn Burundi and the Democratic Republic of the Congo. His department was credited with advancing regional integration within the East African Community and in the Southern African Development Community. Kikwete won the right to lead his party into the 2005 national elections and emerged victorious from the poll on 14 Dec. He received 80% of the vote and replaced Mkapa as president. The CCM retained its overwhelming majority in parliament, with 206 out of 232 seats.

Career in Office

In his inauguration speech, Kikwete vowed to continue the free-market policies of Mkapa and prioritized the improvement of relations with the semi-autonomous islands of Zanzibar. Kikwete inherits a country in which poverty is widespread but whose economy is growing at a rate of 6% a year. He is expected to maintain political stability and the country should benefit from rising gold production and donor-supported investment.

DEFENCE

Conscription is for two years, which may include civilian service. Defence expenditure totalled US$301m. in 2003 (US$8 per capita), representing 3·1% of GDP.

Army

Strength (2002), 23,000. There is also a Citizen's Militia of 80,000 and a paramilitary Police Field Force of 1,400.

Navy

Personnel in 2002 totalled about 1,000. The principal bases are at Dar es Salaam, Zanzibar and Mwanza.

Air Force

The Tanzanian People's Defence Force Air Wing was built up initially with the help of Canada, but combat equipment has been acquired from China. Personnel totalled 3,000 in 2002 (including some 2,000 air defence troops), with J-7 (MiG-21), J-6 (MiG-19) and J-5 (MiG-17) combat aircraft, mostly in store.

INTERNATIONAL RELATIONS

Tanzania is a member of the UN, WTO, the African Union, the Commonwealth, African Development Bank, COMESA, SADC, EAC, IOM and is an ACP member state of the ACP-EU relationship.

In Nov. 1999 a treaty was signed between Tanzania, Kenya and Uganda to create a new East African Community as a means of developing East African trade, tourism and industry and laying the foundations for a future common market and political federation.

ECONOMY

Agriculture accounted for 44·7% of GDP in 2002, industry 16·1% and services 39·2%.

Overview

Since the mid-1990s Tanzania has undertaken IMF structural reforms and has made major progress towards restoring macro-economic stability and promoting private sector-led growth. Between 1993 and 2002, 66% of all state-owned enterprises were privatized. The majority of companies privatized were small and medium sized companies; the privatization of the larger more strategic enterprises is continuing.

Currency

The monetary unit is the *Tanzanian shilling* (TZS) of 100 *cents*. Foreign exchange reserves were US$1,199m. in June 2002.

Inflation, which was 26·5% in 1995, had fallen to 4·3% in 2004, the lowest rate for more than 20 years. Total money supply in May 2002 was Sh. 792,213m.

Budget

The fiscal year ends 30 June. Total revenues in 2001–02 were an estimated US$764m. and government expenditure totalled US$989m. Tax revenues accounted for 91% of total revenues.

Performance

Real GDP growth was 7·1% in 2003 and 6·7% in 2004. Total GDP in 2004 was US$10·9bn. (mainland Tanzania only).

Banking and Finance

The central bank is the Bank of Tanzania (*Governor*, Daudi Ballali).

On 6 Feb. 1967 all commercial banks with the exception of National Co-operative Banks were nationalized, and their interests vested in the National Bank of Commerce on the mainland (fully privatized in March 2000) and the Peoples' Bank in Zanzibar. However, in 1993 private-sector commercial banks were allowed to open. In 1997 the National Bank of Commerce, which controls 70% of the country's banking and has 34 branches, was split into a trade bank, a regional rural bank and a micro-finance bank. It was privatized in 2000, with the South African concern Absa Group Limited purchasing a 55% stake. The government retained 30% with the International Finance Corporation holding 15%. In 2000 there were 17 banks operating in Tanzania.

Foreign direct investment totalled US$224·2m. in 2001.

A stock exchange opened in Dar es Salaam in 1996.

ENERGY AND NATURAL RESOURCES

Environment

Tanzania's carbon dioxide emissions from the consumption and flaring of fossil fuels in 2002 were the equivalent of 0·1 tonnes per capita.

Electricity

Installed capacity was 0·5m. kW in 2000. Production in 2000 was 2·55bn. kWh, with consumption per capita estimated at 74 kWh. In 1998 only 10% of the population had access to electricity. By 2015 the government aims to have increased this to 40% under a new structure principally managed by the private sector.

Oil and Gas

A number of international companies are exploring for both gas and oil. In 2002 natural gas reserves were 28bn. cu. metres.

Minerals

Tanzania's mineral resources include gold, nickel, cobalt, silver and diamonds. International funds injected to improve Tanzania's economy have resulted in notable increases, particularly in gold production. The first commercial gold mine began operating in Mwanza in 1998. By 2000 production revenue had reached US$184m., up from US$3·3m. in 1998. Gold production in 2001 totalled 30,088 kg. Large deposits of coal and tin exist but mining is on a small scale. Diamond production in 2001 totalled 191,000 carats, worth US$27·7m.

Agriculture

About 80% of the workforce are engaged in agriculture, chiefly in subsistence farming. Agricultural produce contributes around 85% of exports. There were 4·0m. ha. of arable land in 2001 and 950,000 ha. of permanent crops. 170,000 ha. were irrigated in 2001. There were 7,600 tractors in 2001. Production of main agricultural crops in 2000 (in 1,000 tonnes) was: cassava, 5,758; maize, 2,551; sugarcane, 1,355; bananas and plantains, 1,304; sweet potatoes, 480; rice, 379; coconuts, 350; sorghum, 335; dry beans, 260; potatoes, 250. Zanzibar is a major producer of cloves.

Livestock (2000): 14·38m. cattle; 4·20m. sheep; 9·95m. goats; 28m. chickens. Livestock products (2000, in 1,000 tonnes): milk, 781; meat, 326; eggs, 58; honey, 25.

Forestry
Forests covered 38·81m. ha. in 2000 (43·9% of the total land area). In 2001, 23·26m. cu. metres of roundwood were cut.

Fisheries
Catch (2001) 335,900 tonnes, of which 283,000 tonnes were from inland waters.

INDUSTRY

Industry is limited, and is mainly textiles, petroleum and chemical products, food processing, tobacco, brewing and paper manufacturing.

INTERNATIONAL TRADE

Foreign debt was US$7,244m. in 2002.

Imports and Exports
In 2002 imports (f.o.b.) amounted to US$1,511·3m. (US$1,560·3m. in 2001); exports (f.o.b.) US$902·5m. (US$776·4m. in 2001). Principal imports, 2002: consumer goods, 31·0%; machinery and apparatus, 22·2%; transport equipment, 13·2%; crude and refined petroleum, 11·8%. Principal exports, 2002: minerals (notably gold), 42·4%; cashew nuts, 5·8%; tobacco, 5·6%; coffee, 4·0%; tea, 3·4%. Main import suppliers, 2002: South Africa, 11·4%; Japan, 8·4%; India, 6·5%; Russia, 6·1%; UAE, 5·9%. Main export markets, 2002: UK, 18·5%; France, 17·4%; Japan, 11·0%; India, 7·3%; Netherlands, 6·2%.

COMMUNICATIONS

Roads
In 2002 there were about 88,200 km of roads, of which 3,700 km were paved. Passenger cars in use in 2002 numbered 73,500, there were 63,000 trucks and vans and (1996) 86,000 buses and coaches.

Rail
In 1977 the independent Tanzanian Railway Corporation was formed. The network totals 2,722 km (metre-gauge), excluding the joint Tanzanian Zambian (Tazara) railway's 969 km in Tanzania (1,067 mm gauge) operated by a separate administration. In 2000 the state railway carried 0·6m. passengers and 1·2m. tonnes of freight, and in 1994 the Tazara carried 1·8m. passengers and 0·6m. tonnes of freight.

In Oct. 1998 a transhipment facility for containers opened at Kidatu, southwest of Dar es Salaam, providing a link between the 1,067 mm gauge railways of the southern part of Africa and the 1,000 mm gauge lines of the north.

Civil Aviation
There are three international airports: Dar es Salaam, Zanzibar and Kilimanjaro (Moshi/Arusha). Air Tanzania, the national carrier, provides domestic services and in 2003 had flights to Abu Dhabi, Blantyre, Johannesburg, Lilongwe, Mombasa, Muscat and Nairobi. In 1999 Air Tanzania Corporation flew 3·1m. km, carrying 190,000 passengers (75,400 on international flights). Dar es Salaam is the busiest airport, handling 602,834 passengers in 2001 (359,772 on international flights) and 10,786 tonnes of freight.

Shipping
In 2002 the merchant marine totalled 47,000 GRT, including oil tankers 8,000 GRT. The main seaports are Dar es Salaam, Mtwara, Tanga and Zanzibar. There are also ports on the lakes. In 1991, 1m. tonnes of freight were loaded, and 2·9m. unloaded.

Telecommunications
Tanzania had 831,600 telephone subscribers in 2002 (24·1 per 1,000 inhabitants) and there were 144,000 PCs in use (4·2 per 1,000 inhabitants). There were 670,000 mobile phone subscribers in 2002 and 100 fax machines in 1995. Tanzania had 80,000 Internet users in 2002.

Postal Services
In 2003 there were 422 post offices.

SOCIAL INSTITUTIONS

Justice
The Judiciary is independent in both judicial and administrative matters and is composed of a four-tier system of Courts: Primary Courts; District and Resident Magistrates' Courts; the High Court and the Court of Appeal. The Chief Justice is head of the Court of Appeal and the Judiciary Department. The Court's main registry is at Dar es Salaam; its jurisdiction includes Zanzibar. The Principal Judge is head of the High Court, also headquartered at Dar es Salaam, which has resident judges at seven regional centres.

The population in penal institutions in June 2002 was 44,063 (120 per 100,000 of national population).

Education
In 1999–2000 there were 11,409 primary schools with 103,731 teachers for 4·19m. pupils. At secondary level there were 247,579 pupils with 12,496 (1997) teachers in 826 schools, and at university level in 2000–01 there were 21,960 students with 2,192 academic staff. Primary school fees were abolished in Jan. 2002.

Technical and vocational education is provided at several secondary and technical schools, and at the Dar es Salaam Technical College. There are 42 teacher training colleges, including the college at Chang'ombe for secondary-school teachers.

There is one university, one university of agriculture and one open university. There are also nine other institutions of higher education.

Adult literacy rate in 2003 was 69·4% (male, 77·5%; female, 62·2%). In 1998–99 total expenditure on education came to 2·2% of GNP.

Health
In 2002 there were 822 physicians, 218 dentists (1995), 13,292 nurses, 13,953 midwives (1995) and 365 pharmacists. In 1991 there were 173 hospitals with 24,130 beds.

RELIGION

In 2001 there were 18·3m. Christians (including Roman Catholics, Anglicans and Lutherans) and 11·5m. Muslims. Muslims are concentrated in the coastal towns; Zanzibar is 99% Muslim. The remainder of the population follow traditional religions. In May 2005 the Roman Catholic church had one cardinal.

CULTURE

World Heritage Sites
Tanzania has six sites on the UNESCO World Heritage List: Ngorongoro Conservation Area (inscribed on the list in 1979); the Ruins of Kilwa Kisiwani and of Songo Mnara (1981); Serengeti National Park (1981); Selous Game Reserve (1982); Kilimanjaro National Park (1987); and the Stone Town of Zanzibar (2000).

Broadcasting
The government-controlled Radio Tanzania and Sauti ya Tanzania Zanzibar are responsible for radio broadcasting on the mainland and on Zanzibar respectively. On the mainland there is a national service and a commercial programme in Swahili and an external service in English. There is television only on Zanzibar provided by the government-run Television Zanzibar (colour by PAL). There were 1·5m. TV sets in 2001 and 9·1m. radio receivers in 2000.

Press
In 2002 there were seven dailies with a combined circulation of 102,000.

Tourism

Tourism contributes approximately 16% of GDP. There were, in 2001, 12 national parks in Tanzania. In 2000 there were 459,000 foreign tourists, bringing revenue of US$739m.

DIPLOMATIC REPRESENTATIVES

Of Tanzania in the United Kingdom (3 Stratford Pl., London, W1C 1AS)
High Commissioner: Hassan Omar Gumbo Kibelloh.

Of the United Kingdom in Tanzania (Umoja House, Garden Ave., PO Box 9200 Dar es Salaam)
High Commissioner: Dr Andrew Pocock.

Of Tanzania in the USA (2139 R. St., NW, Washington, D.C., 20008)
Ambassador: Andrew Mhando Daraja.

Of the USA in Tanzania (686 Old Bagamoyo Rd, Msasani, PO Box 9123, Dar es Salaam)
Ambassador: Michael Retzer.

Of Tanzania to the United Nations
Ambassador: Augustine Philip Mahiga.

Of Tanzania to the European Union
Ambassador: Ali Abeid Aman Karume.

FURTHER READING

Darch, C., *Tanzania*. [Bibliography] 2nd ed. ABC-Clio, Oxford and Santa Barbara (CA), 1996

National Statistical Office: National Bureau of Statistics, Box 796, Dar es Salaam.
Website: http://www.tanzania.go.tz/statistics.html

THAILAND

© Research Machines plc 2006

Prathet Thai
(Kingdom of Thailand)

Capital: Bangkok
Population projection, 2010: 66·78m.
GDP per capita, 2003: (PPP$) 7,595
HDI/world rank: 0·778/73

KEY HISTORICAL EVENTS

The Thais migrated to the present territory from Nan Chao in the Yunnan area of China in the 8th and 9th centuries. Thailand's leading general, Chao Phraya Chakkri, assumed the throne in 1782, thus establishing the dynasty which still heads the Thai state. Siam, as Thailand was called until 1939, remained an independent state ruled by an absolute monarchy until 24 June 1932. Discontented with the social, political and economic stagnation of the country, a group of rebels calling themselves the People's Party precipitated a bloodless coup. The rebels seized control of the army and persuaded the king to accept the introduction of constitutional monarchy. When, the following year, the king tried to dissolve the newly appointed

General Assembly, the army moved to prevent him, thus becoming the dominant force behind the government, which they have remained ever since. Nationalism dominated political life through the 1930s. In 1939 Field Marshal Pibul Songgram became premier and embarked on a pro-Japanese policy that brought Thailand into the Second World War on Japan's side.

After 1945 political life was characterized by periods of military rule interspersed with short attempts at democratic, civilian government. Democratic government was reintroduced for a short time after 1963 and again from 1969 to 1971 when another successful military coup was staged, aimed at checking the high crime rate and the growth of Communist insurgence. A new, moderately democratic constitution was introduced in 1978.

On 23 Feb. 1991 a military junta seized power in the most recent of 17 coups since 1932. Following the appointment of Gen. Suchinda Kraprayoon as prime minister on 17 April 1992 there were massive anti-government demonstrations over several weeks in the course of which many demonstrators were killed. Gen. Suchinda resigned and in May the legislative assembly voted that future prime ministers should be elected by its members rather than appointed by the military. The 1995 election was fought against a background of political and financial corruption. After the 1996 election a new constitution was drafted allowing for the separation of the executive, legislative and judicial branches of government.

On 26 Dec. 2004 Thailand, along with a number of other south Asian countries, was hit by a devastating tsunami following an undersea earthquake. The death toll in Thailand was put at 5,000.

TERRITORY AND POPULATION

Thailand is bounded in the west by Myanmar, north and east by Laos and southeast by Cambodia. In the south it becomes a peninsula bounded in the west by the Indian Ocean, south by Malaysia and east by the Gulf of Thailand. The area is 513,115 sq. km (198,114 sq. miles).

At the 2000 census the population was 60,916,441 (30,901,208 females); density, 118·7 per sq. km. 20,825,262 lived in the Northeastern region, 11,433,061 in the Northern region, 14,215,503 in the Central region, 8,087,471 in the Southern region and 6,355,144 in Bangkok. The estimated population in 2005 was 64,233,000. In 2003, 68·0% of the population lived in rural areas.

The UN gives a projected population for 2010 of 66·78m.

Thailand is divided into four regions, 76 provinces and Bangkok, the capital. Population of Bangkok (2000 census figure), 6,355,144. Other towns (2000 census figures): Samut Prakan (378,741), Nonthaburi (291,555), Udon Thani (222,425), Nakhon Ratchasima (204,641), Hat Yai (187,920).

Thai is the official language, spoken by 53% of the population as their mother tongue. 27% speak Lao (mainly in the northeast), 12% Chinese (mainly in urban areas), 3·7% Malay (mainly in the south) and 2·7% Khmer (along the Cambodian border).

SOCIAL STATISTICS

2000 births, 773,009; deaths, 365,741. 2000 birth rate per 1,000 population, 12·5; death rate, 5·9. Annual population growth rate, 1992–2002, 1·1%. Of the total population in 2002, 22% were under 15 years, 72% between 15 and 64 years, and 6% aged 65 and over. Expectation of life (2003): 66·3 years for men; 73·8 years for women. Infant mortality, 2001, 24 per 1,000 live births; fertility rate, 2001, 2·0 births per woman.

CLIMATE

The climate is tropical, with high temperatures and humidity. Over most of the country, three seasons may be recognized. The rainy season is June to Oct., the cool season from Nov. to Feb. and the hot season is March to May. Rainfall is generally heaviest in the south and lightest in the northeast. Bangkok, Jan. 78°F (25·6°C), July 83°F (28·3°C). Annual rainfall 56" (1,400 mm).

On 26 Dec. 2004 an undersea earthquake centred off the Indonesian island of Sumatra caused a huge tsunami that flooded coastal areas in western Thailand resulting in 5,000 deaths. In total there were 290,000 deaths in twelve countries.

CONSTITUTION AND GOVERNMENT

The reigning King is **Bhumibol Adulyadej**, born 5 Dec. 1927. King Bhumibol married on 28 April 1950 Princess Sirikit, and was crowned 5 May 1950 (making him currently the world's longest-reigning monarch). *Offspring:* Princess Ubol Ratana (born 5 April 1951, married Aug. 1972 Peter Ladd Jensen); Crown Prince Vajiralongkorn (born 28 July 1952, married 3 Jan. 1977 Soamsawali Kitiyakra); Princess Maha Chakri Sirindhorn (born 2 April 1955); Princess Chulabhorn (born 4 July 1957, married 7 Jan. 1982 Virayudth Didyasarin).

Parliament consists of a 200-member *Senate,* fully elected for the first time in 2000, and a 500-member *House of Representatives,* elected for four-year terms by universal suffrage of citizens over 17 years, with 400 constituency MPs and 100 from party lists. The current constitution dates from 1997. It is Thailand's 16th since 1932 and the first to emerge from public consultation rather than a military coup. It particularly tries to eradicate vote-buying. It introduced proportional representation for some seats, established an independent election commission and required that votes be counted away from the polling stations. The constitution further required all cabinet members to resign their parliamentary seats.

The *Prime Minister* is elected by the House of Representatives.

National Anthem

'Prathet Thai ruam nua chat chua Thai' ('Thailand, cradle of Thais wherever they may be'); words by Luang Saranuprapan, tune by Phrachen Duriyang.

GOVERNMENT CHRONOLOGY

Heads of Government since 1944. (PCT = Thai Nation Party; PKS = Social Action Party; PKWM = New Aspiration Party; PP = Democratic Party; SP = United Thai People's Party; ST = Free Thai Movement; TRT = Thai Rak Thai; n/p = non-partisan)

Prime Ministers

1944–45	military	Khuang Aphaiwong
1945	n/p	Tawee Boonyaket
1945–46	ST	Seni Pramoj
1946	military	Khuang Aphaiwong
1946	n/p	Pridi Phanomyong
1946–47	military	Thamrong Nawasawat
1948–57	military	Plaek Pibulsongkram
1957	n/p	Pote Sarasin
1958	military	Thanom Kittikachorn
1959–63	military	Sarit Thanarat
1963–73	military, SP	Thanom Kittikachorn
1973–75	n/p	Sanya Thammasak
1975	PP	Seni Pramoj
1975–76	PKS	Kukrit Pramoj
1976	PP	Seni Pramoj

Chairman of the National Administrative Reform Council

1976–80	military (de facto ruler)	Sangad Chaloryu

Prime Ministers

1976–77	n/p	Thanin Kraivichien
1977–80	military	Kriangsak Chomanan
1980–88	military	Prem Tinsulanonda
1988–91	PCT	Chatichai Choonhavan

Chairman of the National Peacekeeping Council

1991	military	Sunthorn Kongsompong

Prime Ministers

1991–92	n/p	Anand Panyarachun
1992	military	Suchinda Kraprayoon
1992	n/p	Anand Panyarachun
1992–95	PP	Chuan Leekpai
1995–96	PCT	Banharn Silpa-Archa
1996–97	PKWM	Chavalit Yongchaiyudh
1997–2001	PP	Chuan Leekpai
2001–06	TRT	Thaksin Shinawatra
2006–	TRT	Chidchai Vanasatidya

RECENT ELECTIONS

At the elections to the House of Representatives of 2 April 2006 the Thai Rak Thai Party (TRT) gained 460 seats. The election had been boycotted by the three opposition parties after Thaksin Shinawatra reportedly refused to sign a pledge to implement constitutional reforms. Thaksin subsequently stepped down.

There were elections to the Senate on 4 March, 29 April, 4 June and 9 July 2000. 200 members were elected in single-seat constituencies. Only non-partisans were allowed to stand. A number of members were disqualified amid allegations of vote fraud.

CURRENT ADMINISTRATION

Following the 2001 election a coalition was formed between the TRT, PCT and PKWM. It was renewed following the Feb. 2005 election and in April 2006 comprised:

Prime Minister (acting) and Minister of Justice: Chidchai Vanasatidya; b. 1946 (TRT; since 5 April 2006).

Deputy Prime Ministers: Suchai Charoenratanakul; Somkid Jatusripitak (also *Minister of Commerce*); Suriya Jungrungreangkit (also *Minister of Industry*); Wissanu Krea-Ngam; Suwat Liptapanlop; Surakiart Sathirathai.

Minister of Agriculture and Co-operatives: Sudarat Keyuraphan. *Culture:* Uraiwan Thienthong. *Defence:* Gen. Thammarak Isarangura Na Ayutthaya. *Education:* Chaturon Chaisang. *Energy:* Wiset Jupibal. *Finance:* Thanong Bidaya. *Foreign Affairs:* Kantathi Suphamongkhon. *Information and Communications Technology:* Sora-at Klinpratoom. *Interior:* Kongsak Wanthana. *Labour:* Somsak Thepsutin. *Natural Resources and Environment:* Yongyut Tiyapairat. *Public Health:* Phinij Jarusombat. *Science and Technology:* Pravich Rattanapian. *Social Development and Human Security:* Watana Muangsook. *Tourism and Sports:* Pracha Maleenont. *Transport:* Pongsak Ruktapongpisal.

Office of the Prime Minister: http://www.thaigov.go.th

CURRENT LEADERS

Chidchai Vanasatidya

Position
Acting Prime Minister

Introduction
Chidchai Vanasatidya was appointed acting prime minister by outgoing premier Thaksin Shinawatra in April 2005. As an unelected official, Chidchai—a long-term ally of Thaksin—is constitutionally barred from leading the next government.

Early Life
Chidchai Vanasatidya was born on 13 Aug. 1946 in Ubon Ratchathani, northeast Thailand. In 1970 he graduated in public administration from the Police Cadet Academy. He gained a Master's in police administration from Eastern Kentucky

University (USA) in 1973, and a PhD in justice administration from the University of Louisville, Kentucky in 1976. Joining the Thai police, he became secretary-general of the narcotics board (2003) and deputy commissioner-general (2004).

Appointed interior minister in March 2005, Chidchai waged war on illegal drugs and faced a Muslim insurgency in the south. In Aug. 2005 he moved to the justice ministry but kept control of security in the south. In Jan. 2006 he criticized the intelligence services for failing to stop a night of 101 linked arson attacks.

From Feb. 2006 the People's Alliance for Democracy, a group of non-governmental organizations, called for Thaksin's resignation and reforms to counter the influence of corrupt businesses over state institutions. In March 2006 Thaksin made Chidchai his deputy. In elections on 2 April the Thai Rak Thai party (TRT) won 56% of votes but 33% were 'no votes' in recognition of the opposition boycott. On 5 April Thaksin resigned, citing fatigue, and appointed Chidchai as his successor.

Career in Office

Without a parliamentary seat, the legality of Chidchai's role has been questioned amid claims that Thaksin continues to run the country. In May 2006 Chidchai complained that Myanmarese government attacks against the Karen National Union had spilled into Thailand, home to a large population of Karen hill people.

DEFENCE

Conscription is for two years. In 2003 defence expenditure totalled US$1,931m. (US$31 per capita), representing 1·3% of GDP.

Army

Strength (2002) 190,000. In addition there were 50,000 National Security Volunteer Corps, 20,000 *Thahan Phran* (a volunteer irregular force), 40,000 Border Police and a 50,000 strong paramilitary provincial police force.

Navy

The Royal Thai Navy is, next to the Chinese, the most significant naval force in the South China Sea. The fleet includes a small Spanish-built vertical/short-take-off-and-land carrier *Chakrinaruebet*, which entered service in 1997 and operates 13 ex-Spanish AV-8A Harrier aircraft and helicopters, and 12 frigates. Manpower was 68,000 (2002) including 18,000 marines and a naval air wing of 1,700.

The main bases are at Bangkok, Sattahip, Songkla and Phang Nga, with the riverine forces based at Nakhon Phanom.

Air Force

The Royal Thai Air Force had a strength (2002) of 48,000 personnel and 194 combat aircraft, including F-16s and F-5Es. The RTAF is made up of a headquarters and Combat, Logistics Support, Training and Special Services Groups.

INTERNATIONAL RELATIONS

Thailand is a member of the UN, WTO, BIS, Asian Development Bank, ASEAN, the Colombo Plan, APEC, the Mekong Group and IOM.

In 2001 tension between Thailand and neighbouring Myanmar escalated amid a series of border skirmishes, in part over the cross-border trade in drugs. In May 2002 the border between the two countries was closed following a diplomatic row. It was re-opened in Oct. 2002.

ECONOMY

In 2002 agriculture accounted for 9·3% of GDP, industry 42·7% and services 48·0%.

Thailand's 'shadow' (black market) economy is estimated to constitute approximately 70% of the country's official GDP, one of the highest percentages of any country in the world.

Overview

Thailand has transformed into a diverse, industrialized economy in the last thirty years. In 1999 the agricultural sector accounted for less than 50% of total employment for the first time in the country's history. An export-oriented, labour-intensive manufacturing sector has developed through the promotion of foreign investment. During the 1990s the fastest growth was seen in the high technology goods sector, such as computer accessories and motor vehicle parts.

The Asian financial crisis of the late-1990s damaged the Thai economy, with GDP contracting by 10·5% in 1998 as high inflation, rising unemployment and poverty took grip. Following the crisis, Thailand implemented reforms to the financial sector, corporate governance and competition policy. The economy recovered quickly and since 1999 has grown at over 4% every year except for 2001, when it grew by 2·1% despite a global slowdown. GDP growth averaged 6·65% in 2003–04, boosted by export growth and increased consumption and investment spending. Economic growth slowed in 2005 but remained healthy in spite of several recent misfortunes (the tsunami, bird flu and drought) which have been detrimental to the vital tourism sector. In July 2005 the government responded to high energy prices by abandoning fuel subsidies, aiming to limit consumption and reign in energy imports.

Currency

The unit of currency is the *baht* (THB) of 100 *satang*. After being pegged to the US dollar, the baht was devalued and allowed to float on 2 July 1997. It was the devaluation of the baht that sparked the financial turmoil that spread throughout the world over the next year. Foreign exchange reserves were US$35,985m. and gold reserves 2·50m. troy oz in June 2002. Total money supply in May 2002 was 598,378m. baht. Inflation rates (based on IMF statistics):

1997	1998	1999	2000	2001	2002	2003	2004
5·6%	8·1%	0·3%	1·6%	1·7%	0·6%	1·8%	2·7%

The inflation rate in 2005 according to the Bank of Thailand was 4·5%.

Budget

In 2002–03 budgetary central government revenue was 1,045·6bn. baht (871·7bn. baht in 2001–02) and expenditure 921·1bn. baht (1,155·0bn. baht in 2001–02). Principal sources of revenue in 2002–03: taxes on goods and services, 449·3bn. baht; taxes on income, profits and capital gains, 332·6bn. baht; taxes on international trade and transactions, 110·0bn. baht. Main items of expenditure by economic type in 2002–03: compensation of employees, 325·8bn. baht; use of goods and services, 213·3bn. baht; grants, 177·9bn. baht.

Performance

Real GDP growth rates (based on IMF statistics):

1997	1998	1999	2000	2001	2002	2003	2004
−1·4%	−10·5%	4·4%	4·8%	2·2%	5·3%	6·9%	6·1%

Thailand's total GDP in 2004 was US$163·5bn.

Banking and Finance

The Bank of Thailand (founded in 1942) is the central bank and bank of issue, an independent body although its capital is government-owned. Its assets and liabilities in 2002 were 2,853,897m. baht. Its *Governor* is Pridiyathorn Devakula. In 2002 there were 30 commercial banks, 13 domestic banks and 21 foreign banks. In addition the Thai government controlled four banks in 2002: the Bank of Agriculture and Agricultural Co-operatives, the Government Housing Bank, the Government Savings Bank and the Export-Import Bank of Thailand. Total assets of commercial banks, 2002, 6,900,947m. baht. Deposits, 2001, 5,109,973m. baht.

There is a stock exchange (SET) in Bangkok.

Weights and Measures
The metric system is official but traditional units are still employed: one *catty* = 600 grams; one *picul* = 100 catty; one *wah* = 2 metres; one *sen* = 20 wah; one *rai* = 1 sq. sen.

ENERGY AND NATURAL RESOURCES

Environment
Thailand's carbon dioxide emissions from the consumption and flaring of fossil fuels were the equivalent of 3·0 tonnes per capita in 2002.

Electricity
Installed capacity, 2002, was 29·5m. kW. Output, 2002, 115·51bn. kWh, with consumption per capita 1,860 kWh.

Oil and Gas
Proven crude petroleum reserves in 2002 were 600m. bbls. Production of crude petroleum (2003), 9·0m. tonnes. Thailand and Vietnam settled an offshore dispute in 1997 which stretched back to 1973. Demarcation allowed for petroleum exploration in the Gulf of Thailand, with each side required to give the other some revenue if an underground reservoir is discovered which straddles the border.

Production of natural gas (2002), 18·9bn. cu. metres. Estimated reserves, 2002, 380bn. cu. metres. In April 1998 Thailand and Malaysia agreed to share equally the natural gas jointly produced in an offshore area which both countries claim as their own territory.

Minerals
The mineral resources include antimony, cassiterite (tin ore), copper, gold, lignite, manganese, molybdenum, rubies, sapphires, scheelite, silver, wolfram, zinc and zircons. Production, 2002 (in tonnes): limestone, 53·67m.; lignite, 19·60m.; gypsum, 6·33m.; salt (2001), 952,265; feldspar, 710,543; zinc ore, 151,575; kaolin clay, 127,182; fluorite, 2,270.

Agriculture
In 2001 there were 15·0m. ha. of arable land and 3·3m. ha. of permanent cropland. 4·92m. ha. were irrigated in 2001. The chief produce is rice, a staple of the national diet. Output of the major crops in 2000 was (in 1,000 tonnes): sugarcane, 51,210; rice, 23,403; cassava, 18,509; maize, 4,571; pineapples, 2,281; natural rubber, 2,236; bananas, 1,720; coconuts, 1,373; mangoes, 1,350; tangerines, mandarins and satsumas, 640; palm oil, 520; watermelons, 400; soybeans, 346; oranges, 320; onions, 300; sorghum, 250. Thailand is the world's leading producer of both natural rubber and pineapples.

Livestock, 2000: cattle, 6,100,000; pigs, 7,682,000; buffaloes, 2,100,000; goats, 130,000; sheep, 42,000; chickens, 172m.; ducks, 22m.

Forestry
Forests covered 14·76m. ha. in 2000, or 28·9% of the land area. Teak and other hardwoods grow in the deciduous forests of the north; elsewhere tropical evergreen forests are found, with the timber yang the main crop (a source of yang oil). In 2003, 27·91m. cu. metres of roundwood were cut.

Fisheries
In 2003 the total catch came to 2,817,482 tonnes with marine fishing accounting for 93% of all fish caught. Thailand is the leading exporter of fishery commodities in the world, with exports in 2001 totalling US$4·04bn.

INDUSTRY

The leading companies by market capitalization in Thailand in May 2004 were: PTT, a petroleum exploration and production company (US$10·9bn.); Advanced Info Service (AIS), a mobile phone provider (US$6·5bn.); and the Siam Cement Group (US$6·4bn.).

Production of manufactured goods in 2002 included 31·68m. tonnes of cement, 14·47m. tonnes of distillate fuel oil, 5·95m. tonnes of sugar, 5·87m. tonnes of residual fuel oil, 5·75m. tonnes of petrol, 2·5m. tonnes of crude steel, 768,098 tonnes of synthetic fibre, 519,006 tonnes of galvanized iron sheets, 208,000 tonnes of tin plate (2001), 1,636·0m. litres of soft drinks (2001), 1,238·0m. litres of beer (2001), 30·8bn. cigarettes, 169,304 automobiles and 415,593 commercial vehicles, and 6,096,000 televisions.

Labour
In the period Sept.–Dec. 2003 the total labour force was 35·5m.; 14·2m. persons were employed in agriculture, hunting and forestry, 5·3m. in manufacturing, 5·2m. in wholesale and retail trade and 2·1m. in hotels and restaurants. The unemployment rate was 2·4% in June 2002. A minimum wage is set by the National Wages Committee. It varied between 140 baht and 184 baht per day in Jan. 2006.

INTERNATIONAL TRADE

Foreign debt was US$59,211m. in 2002.

Imports and Exports
Trade in US$1m.:

	1998	1999	2000	2001	2002
Imports f.o.b.	36,515	42,762	56,193	54,620	57,020
Exports f.o.b.	52,753	56,775	67,894	63,202	66,795

In 1999 main imports by category: machinery and transport equipment, 43·1%; chemicals, 10·8%; petroleum, 9·5%; iron and steel, 5·4%. Exports: machinery and transport equipment, 41·9%; manufactured goods, 11·8%; fish and seafood, 7·0%; clothing, 6·0%; chemicals, 5·0%; rice, 3·3%.

In 1999 the main import sources were Japan (24·4%), USA (12·8%), Singapore (5·9%), China (5·0%), Malaysia (5·0%) and South Korea (3·5%). Principal export destinations were USA (21·7%), Japan (14·1%), Singapore (8·7%), Hong Kong (5·1%), Netherlands (3·8%), Malaysia (3·6%) and the UK (3·6%).

COMMUNICATIONS

Roads
In 2000 there were 57,403 km of roads, of which 98·5% were paved. Vehicles in use in 2002 included: 2·66m. passenger cars, 3·54m. commercial vehicles and 16·58m. motorcycles.

Rail
The State Railway totals 3,500 km. Passenger-km travelled in 2002 came to 8·9bn. and freight tonne-km to 2·4bn. A metro ('Skytrain'), or elevated transit system, was opened in Bangkok in 1999. A second (underground) mass transit system in Bangkok, the Bangkok Subway, was opened in 2004.

Civil Aviation
There are international airports at Bangkok (Don Muang), Chiangmai, Phuket and Hat Yai. The national carrier, Thai Airways International, is 53·98% state-owned. In 1999 it flew 163·4m. km, carrying 15,950,500 passengers (10,100,400 on international flights). Bangkok handled 28,808,422 passengers in 2001 (21,395,311 on international flights) and 840,033 tonnes of freight. Phuket is the second busiest airport for passenger traffic, with 3,557,319 passengers in 2001 (2,225,031 on domestic flights), and Chiangmai the second busiest for freight, with 23,786 tonnes in 2001. A new Bangkok airport (Suvarnabhumi) was scheduled to open in mid-2006.

Shipping

In 2002 merchant shipping totalled 1,880,000 GRT, including oil tankers 209,000 GRT. Vessels totalling 68,079,000 NRT entered ports in 2000 and vessels totalling 33,154,000 NRT cleared.

Telecommunications

In 2002 telephone subscribers numbered 22,616,800 (365·5 per 1,000 population) and 2,461,000 PCs were in use (39·8 for every 1,000 inhabitants). There were 16,117,000 mobile phone subscribers in 2002 and 283,000 fax machines. Thailand had 4·8m. Internet users in 2002.

Postal Services

There were 4,453 post offices in 2003, or one for every 14,100 persons.

SOCIAL INSTITUTIONS

Justice

The judicial power is exercised in the name of the King, by *(a)* courts of first instance, *(b)* the court of appeal *(Uthorn)* and *(c)* the Supreme Court *(Dika)*. The King appoints, transfers and dismisses judges, who are independent in conducting trials and giving judgment in accordance with the law.

Courts of first instance are subdivided into 20 magistrates' courts *(Kwaeng)* with limited civil and minor criminal jurisdiction; 85 provincial courts *(Changwad)* with unlimited civil and criminal jurisdiction; the criminal and civil courts with exclusive jurisdiction in Bangkok; the central juvenile courts for persons under 18 years of age in Bangkok.

The court of appeal exercises appellate jurisdiction in civil and criminal cases from all courts of first instance. From it appeals lie to Dika Court on any point of law and, in certain cases, on questions of fact.

The Supreme Court is the supreme tribunal of the land. Besides its normal appellate jurisdiction in civil and criminal matters, it has semi-original jurisdiction over general election petitions. The decisions of Dika Court are final. Every person has the right to present a petition to the government who will deal with all matters of grievance.

The death penalty is still in force and there were four executions in 2003. The population in penal institutions in mid-2002 was 258,076 (401 per 100,000 of national population).

Education

Education is compulsory for children for nine years and is free in local municipal schools. In 2002 there were 6,096,208 pupils with (in 1999) 293,391 teachers. There were 4,068,188 secondary school pupils in 2002 with (in 1999) 242,892 teachers. There were 946,187 students in vocational education in 2001. In higher education there were 1,984,843 students in 2002. In 1996 there were 13 universities, two open (distance) universities, four institutes of technology and one institute of development administration in the public sector, and nine universities and one institute of technology in the private sector.

The adult literacy rate in 2003 was 92·6% (94·9% among males and 90·5% among females).

In 2000–01 total expenditure on education came to 5·5% of GNP.

Health

In 2002 there were 3,658 hospitals, with a provision of 69 beds per 10,000 population. In 2000 there were 18,025 doctors, 4,141 dentists, 6,384 pharmacists, 70,978 nurses and (in 1997) 2,677 midwives. Thailand has been one of the most successful countries in the developing world in the fight against AIDS. By the mid-1990s the government was spending US$80m. a year on AIDS education, and the number of sexually transmitted diseases reported from government clinics fell from some 400,000 in 1986 to below 50,000 in 1995. However, since 1996 AIDS expenditure has been declining rapidly. As a result, HIV infections are now increasing among several risk groups after a period of overall decline.

RELIGION

At the 2000 census 94·6% of the population were Buddhists and 4·6% Muslims. In May 2005 the Roman Catholic church had one cardinal.

CULTURE

World Heritage Sites

There are five sites in Thailand that appear on the UNESCO World Heritage List. They are (with the year entered on list): the Thung Yai-Huai Kha Khaeng wildlife sanctuaries (1991); the palace, temples, Buddhas, etc. of the historic town of Sukhothai (1991); the 15th–18th century historic town of Ayutthaya (1991); the Bronze Age Ba Chiang archaeological site (1992); and the mountainous Dong Phayayen-Khao Yai forest complex (2005).

Broadcasting

The Radio and Television Executive Committee controls the administrative, legal, technical and programming aspects of broadcasting, and consists of representatives of various government bodies. All radio stations are operated by, or under the supervision of, government agencies. Radio Thailand broadcasts three national programmes, provincial programmes, an educational service and an external service (nine languages), and the Voice of Free Asia. Television of Thailand is the state service (colour by PAL). There are three commercial channels and an Army service. At the 2000 census 91·5% of households had televisions and 77·2% had radios. In 2001 there were 18·4m. TV receivers.

Press

In 1998 there were 34 daily newspapers, with a combined circulation of about 11·8m. 9,068 book titles were published in 2002.

Tourism

In 2002, 10·87m. foreign tourists visited Thailand. Tourist revenue in 2002 was US$7·90bn.

DIPLOMATIC REPRESENTATIVES

Of Thailand in the United Kingdom (29–30 Queen's Gate, London, SW7 5JB)
Ambassador: Vikrom Koompirochana.

Of the United Kingdom in Thailand (Wireless Rd, Bangkok 10330)
Ambassador: David Fall.

Of Thailand in the USA (1024 Wisconsin Ave., NW, Washington, D.C., 20007)
Ambassador: Kasit Piromya.

Of the USA in Thailand (120 Wireless Rd, Bangkok 10330)
Ambassador: Ralph Boyce.

Of Thailand to the United Nations
Ambassador: Laxanachantorn Laohaphan.

Of Thailand to the European Union
Ambassador: Vacant.

FURTHER READING

National Statistical Office *Thailand Statistical Yearbook*.

Krongkaew, M. (ed.) *Thailand's Industrialization and its Consequences.* London, 1995

Kulick, E. and Wilson, D., *Thailand's Turn: Profile of a New Dragon.* London and New York, 1993 (NY, 1994)

Smyth, David, *Thailand.* [Bibliography] 2nd ed. ABC-Clio, Oxford and Santa Barbara (CA), 1998

National Statistical Office: National Statistical Office, Thanon Lan Luang, Bangkok 10100.
Website: http://www.nso.go.th

TOGO

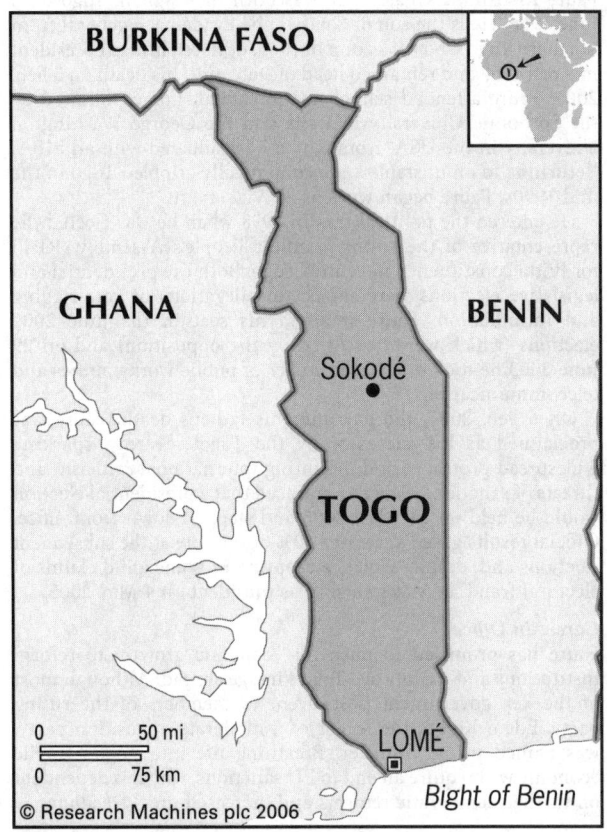

República Togolaise

Capital: Lomé
Population projection, 2010: 6·98m.
GDP per capita, 2003: (PPP$) 1,696
HDI/world rank: 0·512/143

KEY HISTORICAL EVENTS

Europeans, beginning with the Portuguese who first visited the area in 1471–72, traded on the coast for centuries, especially in slaves. In the 19th century palm oil exports flourished at Anecho, Agoue and Porto Seguro, where British, French and German traders operated. Several prominent Togolese families of partly Brazilian or Portuguese origin, still important among the coastal African élite, arose at that time. Despite the important rival influences of Britain and France in the area, it was Germany that established colonial rule on the coast in 1884. German control was then extended inland but only in 1912 was the colony fully subdued.

German Togo was overrun by the Allies in 1914. It was partitioned in 1919 into British and French Mandated Territories under the League of Nations. After the Second World War French Togo and British Togoland became Trust Territories under the United Nations. In British Togoland a referendum was held on 9 May 1956, in which a majority voted for union with Gold Coast, although most people in the south voted for union with French Togo. The whole territory was merged with what soon afterwards became independent Ghana, but many Togolese

objected. In French Togo partial self-government was granted in 1956. On 27 April 1960 the country became independent.

On 13 Jan. 1963 President Olympio was murdered by soldiers. His successor was deposed in a bloodless military coup in Jan. 1967 and on 14 April 1967 Gen. (then Col.) Gnassingbé Eyadéma assumed the Presidency. A new constitution was approved in 1992. On Gnassingbé Eyadéma's death on 5 Feb. 2005 the military installed his son, Faure Gnassingbé, as his successor. The next day parliament changed the constitution to legalize his succession. Under international pressure he stepped down on 25 Feb. 2005, with parliament speaker Abass Bonfoh becoming interim president. Faure Gnassingbé won presidential elections held in April 2005 but the result was greeted by allegations of vote rigging and riots which claimed 400–500 lives.

TERRITORY AND POPULATION

Togo is bounded in the west by Ghana, north by Burkina Faso, east by Benin and south by the Gulf of Guinea. The area is 56,785 sq. km. At the last census, in 1981, the population was 2,700,982. 2005 estimate, 6·14m.; density, 108 per sq. km.

The UN gives a projected population for 2010 of 6·98m.

In 2003, 64·8% of the population lived in rural areas. In 2000, 45% were below the age of 15. The capital is Lomé (population in 1999, 790,000), other towns being Sokodé (51,000), Lama-Kara (35,000), Atakpamé (30,000), Kpalimé (30,000), Bassar (22,000), Dapaong (22,000) and Mango (20,000).

Area, population and chief town of the five regions:

Region	Area in sq. km	Population (1998 estimate)	Chief town
Centrale	13,182	449,000	Sokodé
De La Kara	11,630	580,500	Lama-Kara
Des Plateaux	16,975	1,007,000	Atakpamé
Des Savanes	8,602	542,000	Dapaong
Maritime	6,396	1,828,000	Lomé

There are 37 ethnic groups. The south is largely populated by Ewe-speaking peoples (forming 23% of the population), Watyi (10%) and other related groups, while the north is mainly inhabited by Hamitic groups speaking Kabre (14%), Tem (6%) and Gurma (3%). The official language is French but Ewe and Kabre are also taught in schools.

SOCIAL STATISTICS

2000 estimates: births, 177,000; deaths, 60,000. Estimated rates, 2000 (per 1,000 population): births, 38·7; deaths, 13·2. Expectation of life (2003) was 52·4 years for males and 56·3 for females. Annual population growth rate, 1992–2002, 2·9%. Infant mortality, 2001, 79 per 1,000 live births; fertility rate, 2001, 5·5 births per woman.

CLIMATE

The tropical climate produces wet seasons from March to July and from Oct. to Nov. in the south. The north has one wet season, from April to July. The heaviest rainfall occurs in the mountains of the west, southwest and centre. Lomé, Jan. 81°F (27·2°C), July 76°F (24·4°C). Annual rainfall 35" (875 mm).

CONSTITUTION AND GOVERNMENT

A referendum on 27 Sept. 1992 approved a new constitution by 98·11% of votes cast. Under this the *President* and the *National Assembly* were directly elected for five-year terms. Initially the president was allowed to be re-elected only once. However, on 30 Dec. 2002 parliament approved an amendment to the constitution lifting the restriction on the number of times that the president may be re-elected. The National Assembly has 81 seats and is elected for a five-year term in single-seat constituencies.

National Anthem

'Terre de nos aïeux' ('Land of our forefathers').

RECENT ELECTIONS

In presidential elections held on 24 April 2005 Faure Gnassingbé (son of former president Gnassingbé Eyadéma) of the Togolese People's Assembly (Rassemblement du Peuple Togolais; RPT) won with 60·2% of the vote. Emmanuel Bob Akitani of the Union des Forces de Changement (UFC) took 38·2%. Nicolas Lawson of the Renewal and Redemption Party won 1·0% and Harry Olympio of the Rally for Support of Democracy 0·6%. Turnout was 63·6%. The UFC claimed the results were rigged and there were widespread protests in Lomé. Gnassingbé was confirmed as president by the constitutional court on 3 May 2005.

At the parliamentary elections on 27 Oct. 2002 the main opposition parties to the RPT, the former sole party, boycotted the election, protesting a lack of transparency in the voting process. The RPT won 72 of the available 81 seats, down seven on its 1999 showing. Turnout was 67%.

CURRENT ADMINISTRATION

President: Faure Gnassingbé; b. 1966 (RPT; sworn in 4 May 2005).

In March 2006 the government comprised:

Prime Minister: Edem Kodjo; b. 1938 (Patriotic Pan-African Convergence; sworn in 9 June 2005, having previously been prime minister from April 1994 to Aug. 1996).

Minister of State, Minister of Foreign Affairs and African Integration: Zarifou Ayéva. *Minister of State, Minister of Agriculture, Animal Breeding and Fisheries:* Charles Kondi Agba. *Minister of Commerce, Industry and Handicrafts:* Jean-Lucien Savi de Tové. *Communication and Civic Education:* Kokou Tozoun. *Culture, Tourism and Leisure:* Gabriel Sassouvi Dossey-Anyroh. *Defence:* Kpatcha Gnassingbé. *Development and Land Management:* Yendja Yentchabré. *Economy, Finance and Privatization:* Payadowa Boukpessi. *Environment and Forest Resources:* Issifou Okoulou-Kantchati. *Equipment, Transportation, Posts and Telecommunications:* Kokouvi Dogbé. *Health:* Suzanne Aho Assouma. *Higher Education and Research:* Fidèl Comlan Mensah Nouboukpo. *Human Rights, Democracy and Reconciliation:* Loreta Mensah Akuété. *Justice and Keeper of the Seals:* Tchessa Abi. *Labour, Employment and Civil Service:* Yves Mado Nagou. *Mines, Energy and Water Resources:* Kokou Solété Agbémadon. *Population, Social Affairs and Advancement of Women:* Kangni Sokpo Diallo. *Primary and Secondary Education:* Komi Klassou. *Relations with Institutions of the Republic:* Comlangan Mawutoè d'Almeida. *Security:* Col. Pitalouna-Ani Laokpessi. *Technical Education and Professional Training:* Antoine Agbéwanou Edoh. *Territorial Administration and Decentralization:* Katari Foli-Bazi. *Urban Communities:* Marc Aklessou Akitèm. *Youth and Sports:* Agouta Ouyenga.

Government Website (French only):
  http://www.republicoftogo.com/

CURRENT LEADERS

Faure Gnassingbé

Position
President

Introduction
Faure Gnassingbé was installed as president after the death of his father, who had been one of Africa's longest-serving leaders. The appointment led to violent protests and international condemnation. Forced to step down, he contested a presidential

election and emerged victorious in April 2005 with just over 60% of the vote.

Early Life
Faure Essozimna Gnassingbé was born in Afagnan, Togo on 6 June 1966. He is the son of Gnassingbé Eyadéma, a general from northern Togo who led a coup in 1963, declared himself president in April 1967 and remained head of state until his death on 5 Feb. 2005. Faure attended school in the capital, Lomé, followed by the Sorbonne University in Paris and the George Washington University in the USA, from which he graduated with an MBA. Returning to an unstable and economically crippled Togo in the mid-1990s, Faure began work as a civil servant.

He entered the political fray in 1998 when he was elected the representative of the ruling Togolese People's Assembly (RPT) for Blitta constituency in central Togo. Both the presidential and legislative elections were subject to allegations of vote-rigging and intimidation. Faure retained his seat in the June 2002 elections (which were boycotted by the opposition) and on 29 June 2003 he took office as minister of public works, mines and telecommunications.

On 6 Feb. 2005, the day after his father's death, Faure was proclaimed as his successor by the Togolese army, sparking widespread protest. Amid mounting international criticism and threats of sanctions, Faure announced that a presidential election would be held on 24 April 2005 and stepped down from office. Official results gave Faure over 60% of the vote at the subsequent elections and, despite violence erupting in Lomé amid claims of electoral fraud, he was sworn in as president on 4 May 2005.

Career in Office
Faure has promised to push for economic growth, to reform institutions and to improve Togo's image abroad. Although most of the key government posts went to members of the ruling party, Edem Kodjo, the leader of a moderate opposition party, was named prime minister. Breathing life into Togo's fragile economy will require an end to EU sanctions, which is dependent on further democratic reforms and increased press freedom.

DEFENCE

There is selective conscription which lasts for two years. Defence expenditure totalled US$31m. in 2003 (US$6 per capita), representing 1·7% of GDP.

Army

Strength (2002) 9,000, with a further 750 in a paramilitary gendarmerie.

Navy

In 2002 the Naval wing of the armed forces numbered 200 and was based at Lomé.

Air Force

The Air Force—established with French assistance—numbered (2002) 250, with 16 combat aircraft.

INTERNATIONAL RELATIONS

Togo is a member of the UN, WTO, the African Union, African Development Bank, ECOWAS, the International Organization of the Francophonie, OIC, IOM and the Islamic Development Bank, and is an ACP member state of the ACP-EU relationship.

ECONOMY

Agriculture contributed 38·1% of GDP in 2002, industry 18·5% and services 43·3%.

Overview

After civil and economic turmoil in the early 1990s, a structural redevelopment programme, launched in 1994, resulted in positive growth. Privatization began in the 1980s and resumed in 1996 with World Bank support.

Currency

The unit of currency is the *franc CFA* (XOF) with a parity of 655·957 francs CFA to one euro. Foreign exchange reserves were US$201m. in May 2002 and total money supply was 173,247m. francs CFA. Gold reserves were 13,000 troy oz in June 2000. Inflation in 2004 was 1·2%.

Budget

In 1999 revenues were 140·4bn. francs CFA and expenditures 173·7bn. francs CFA.

Performance

Real GDP growth was 4·4% in 2003, falling to 2·9% in 2004. Total GDP in 2004 was US$2·1bn.

Banking and Finance

The bank of issue is the Central Bank of West African States (BCEAO). The *Acting Governor* is Justin Baro Damo. In 2003 there were six commercial banks, three development banks, a savings bank and a credit institution.

ENERGY AND NATURAL RESOURCES

Environment

Togo's carbon dioxide emissions from the consumption and flaring of fossil fuels in 2002 were the equivalent of 0·2 tonnes per capita.

Electricity

Installed capacity in 2000 was 38,000 kW. In 2000 production totalled around 68m. kWh. Additional electricity is imported from Ghana. Consumption per capita in 2000 was 128 kWh.

Minerals

Output of phosphate rock in 2002 was 1·1m. tonnes. Other minerals are limestone, iron ore and marble.

Agriculture

Agriculture supports about 80% of the population. Most food production comes from individual holdings under 3 ha. Inland, the country is hilly; dry plains alternate with arable land. There were 2·51m. ha. of arable land in 2001 and 0·12m. ha. of permanent crops. There are considerable plantations of oil and cocoa palms, coffee, cacao, kola, cassava and cotton. Production, 2000 (in 1,000 tonnes): cassava, 694; yams, 666; maize, 494; seed cotton, 162; sorghum, 142; cottonseed, 91; rice, 81; cotton lint, 65; dry beans, 45; millet, 39; groundnuts, 35.

Livestock (2000, in 1,000): cattle, 215; sheep, 740; pigs, 850; goats, 1,110; chickens, 8,000.

Forestry

Forests covered 510,000 ha. in 2000, or 9·4% of the land area. Teak plantations covered 8,600 ha. In 2001, 5·78m. cu. metres of roundwood were cut.

Fisheries

The catch in 2001 totalled 23,163 tonnes (78% from marine waters).

INDUSTRY

Industry is small-scale. Cement and textiles are produced and food processed. In 2001 industry accounted for 21·1% of GDP, with manufacturing contributing 9·7%.

Labour

In 1996 the workforce was 1,739,000 (60% males). Around 62% of the economically active population in 1995 were engaged in agriculture, fisheries and forestry. In 2002 the statutory minimum wage was 125·16 francs CFA per hour.

Trade Unions

With the abandonment of single-party politics, the former monolithic Togo National Workers Confederation (CNTT) has split into several federations and independent trade unions.

INTERNATIONAL TRADE

A free trade zone was established in 1990. Foreign debt was US$1,581m. in 2002.

Imports and Exports

In 2003 imports (f.o.b.) amounted to US$754·5m. (US$575·6m. in 2002); exports (f.o.b.) US$597·7m. (US$424·2m. in 2002). The main import suppliers in 2001 were France (19·1%), Canada (6·5%), Italy (6·1%), Côte d'Ivoire (5·7%) and Germany (4·5%). Principal export destinations in 2001 were Ghana (22·4%), Benin (16·9%), Burkina Faso (10·4%), Philippines (6·3%) and Niger (4·5%). Leading imports are food, refined petroleum, and chemicals and chemical products; main exports are cement, phosphates and cotton.

COMMUNICATIONS

Roads

There were an estimated 7,520 km of roads in 2002, of which 2,380 km were paved. In 2002 there were 16,400 passenger cars, 16,100 commercial vehicles and (1996) 59,000 motorcycles.

Rail

There are four metre-gauge railways connecting Lomé, with Aného (continuing to Cotonou in Benin), Kpalimé, Tabligbo and (via Atakpamé) Blitta; total length 525 km. In 1994 the railways carried 5·7 tonne-km and 0·6m. passengers.

Civil Aviation

In 2003 Trans African Airlines flew from Tokoin airport, near Lomé, to Abidjan, Bamako, Brazzaville, Cotonou, Dakar and Pointe-Noire. There were also international flights with other airlines to Addis Ababa, Brussels, Douala, Kinshasa, Lagos, Libreville, Ouagadougou and Paris. In 2001 Tokoin handled 151,000 passengers (all on international flights) and 5,100 tonnes of freight. In 1999 scheduled airline traffic of Togo-based carriers flew 3·0m. km, carrying 84,000 passengers (all on international flights).

Shipping

In 2002 merchant shipping totalled 13,000 GRT.

Telecommunications

Togo had 221,200 telephone subscribers in 2002 (44·1 per 1,000 population) and there were 150,000 PCs in use (29·9 per 1,000 persons). Togo had 200,000 Internet users and 170,000 mobile phone subscribers in 2002. There were 19,000 fax machines in 2002.

Postal Services

In 2003 there were 54 post offices.

SOCIAL INSTITUTIONS

Justice

The Supreme Court and two Appeal Courts are in Lomé, one for criminal cases and one for civil and commercial cases. Each receives appeal from a series of local tribunals.

The population in penal institutions in Aug. 2003 was 3,200 (65 per 100,000 of national population).

Education

The adult literacy rate in 2003 was 53·0% (68·5% among males and 38·3% among females). In 2000–01 there were 945,103 pupils and 27,523 teachers in primary schools, and 288,764 pupils in secondary schools; in 1999–2000 there were 15,171 students in higher education institutions. In 1990 about 50% of children of school age were attending school. The University of Benin at Lomé (founded in 1970) had 9,139 students and 134 academic staff in 1994–95.

In 2000–01 total expenditure on education came to 4·9% of GNP and accounted for 23·2% of total government expenditure.

Health

In 1990 hospital bed provision was 16 per 10,000 population. In 2001 there were 265 physicians, 25 dentists, 782 nurses, 346 midwives and 141 pharmacists. Government expenditure on health in 1995 was estimated at 5,900m. francs CFA.

RELIGION

In 2001, 38% of the population followed traditional animist religions; 35% were Christian and 19% Muslim.

CULTURE

World Heritage Sites

There is one UNESCO site in Togo: Koutammakou, the land of the Batammariba (inscribed on the list in 2004).

Broadcasting

Broadcasting is provided by the government-controlled Radiodiffusion-Télévision Togolaise. There were 170,000 TV receivers (colour by SECAM V) in 2001 and 1·33m. radio sets in 2000.

Press

There is one government-controlled daily newspaper (circulation 10,000).

Tourism

In 2001 there were 57,000 foreign tourists; spending by tourists totalled US$11m.

DIPLOMATIC REPRESENTATIVES

Of Togo in the United Kingdom (resides in Paris)
Ambassador: Tchao Sotou Bere.

Of the United Kingdom in Togo
Ambassador: Gordon Wetherell (resides in Accra, Ghana).

Of Togo in the USA (2208 Massachusetts Ave., NW, Washington, D.C., 20008)
Ambassador: Akoussouleou Bodjona.

Of the USA in Togo (Rue Kouenou and Beniglato 15, BP 852, Lomé)
Ambassador: David B. Dunn.

Of Togo to the United Nations
Ambassador: Vacant.

Of Togo to the European Union
Ambassador: Ohara Kati Korga.

FURTHER READING

Decalo, Samuel, *Togo.* [Bibliography] ABC-Clio, Oxford and Santa Barbara (CA), 1995

TONGA

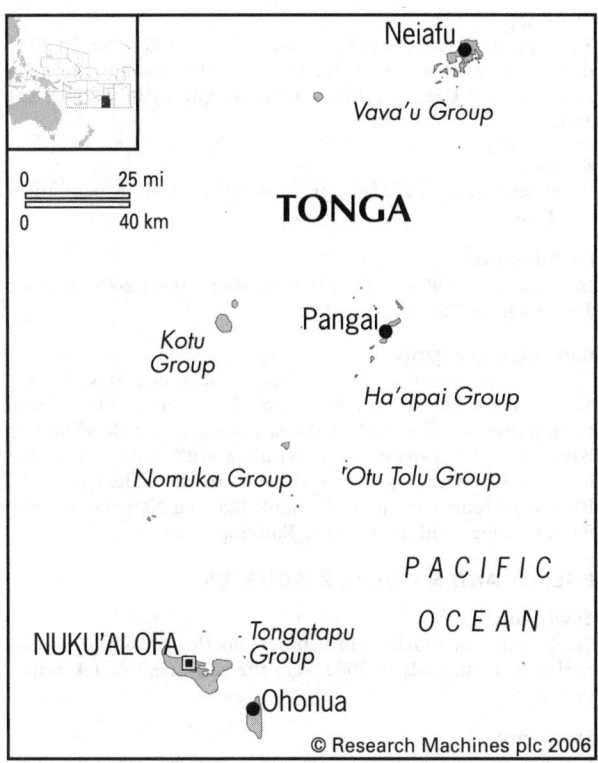

Kingdom of Tonga

Capital: Nuku'alofa
Population projection, 2010: 103,000
GDP per capita, 2003: (PPP$) 6,992
HDI/world rank: 0·810/54

KEY HISTORICAL EVENTS

The Tongatapu group of islands in the south western Pacific Ocean were discovered by Tasman in 1643. The Kingdom of Tonga attained unity under Taufa'ahau Tupou (George I) who became ruler of his native Ha'apai in 1820, of Vava'u in 1833 and of Tongatapu in 1845. By 1860 the kingdom had become converted to Christianity. In 1862 the king granted freedom to the people from arbitrary rule of minor chiefs and gave them the right to the allocation of land for their own needs. These institutional changes, together with the establishment of a parliament of chiefs, paved the way towards a democratic constitution. By the Anglo-German Agreement of 14 Nov. 1899, the Tonga Islands became a British protectorate. The protectorate was dissolved on 4 June 1970 when Tonga, the only ancient kingdom surviving from the pre-European period in Polynesia, achieved independence within the Commonwealth.

TERRITORY AND POPULATION

The Kingdom consists of some 169 islands and islets with a total area, including inland waters and uninhabited islands, of 748 sq. km (289 sq. miles), and lies between 15° and 23° 30′ S. lat and 173° and 177° W. long, its western boundary being the eastern boundary of the Fiji Islands. The islands are split up into the following groups (reading from north to south): the Niuas, Vava'u, Ha'apai, Tongatapu and 'Eua. The three main groups, both from historical and administrative significance, are Tongatapu in the south, Ha'apai in the centre and Vava'u in the north. Census population (1996) 97,784; density, 131 per sq. km. 2005 population estimate: 102,000. In 2003, 66·5% of the population lived in rural areas.

The UN gives a projected population for 2010 of 103,000.

The capital is Nuku'alofa on Tongatapu, population (1999) 37,000.

There are five divisions comprising 23 districts:

Division	Sq. km	Census 1996	Capital
Niuas	72	2,018	Hihifo
Vava'u	119	15,715	Neiafu
Ha'apai	110	8,138	Pangai
Tongatapu	261	66,979	Nuku'alofa
'Eua	87	4,934	Ohonua

Tongan and English are both spoken.

SOCIAL STATISTICS

Births, 2000, 2,471; deaths, 653; marriages, 747; divorces, 75. Expectation of life, 2003: males, 71·0 years; females, 73·5. Annual population growth rate, 1992–2002, 0·3%. Infant mortality, 1999 estimate, 38 per 1,000 live births. Fertility rate, 2001, 3·8 births per woman.

CLIMATE

Generally a healthy climate, although Jan. to March hot and humid, with temperatures of 90°F (32·2°C). Rainfall amounts are comparatively high, being greatest from Dec. to March. Nuku'alofa, Jan. 25·8°C, July 21·3°C. Annual rainfall 1,643 mm. Vava'u, Jan. 27·3°C, July 23·4°C. Annual rainfall 2,034 mm.

CONSTITUTION AND GOVERNMENT

The reigning King is **Taufa'ahau Tupou IV**, GCVO, GCMG, KBE, born 4 July 1918, succeeded on 16 Dec. 1965 on the death of his mother, Queen Salote Tupou III.

The current Constitution, last revised on 1 Jan. 1967, is almost identical with that originally granted in 1875 by King George Tupou I. There is a Privy Council, Cabinet, Legislative Assembly and Judiciary. The 30-member *Legislative Assembly*, which meets annually, is composed of the King, nine nobles elected by their peers, nine elected representatives of the people and the Privy Councillors (numbering 11); the King appoints one of the nine nobles to be the Speaker. The elections are held triennially.

National Anthem

'E 'Otua, Mafimafi, ko ho mau 'eiki Koe' ('Oh Almighty God above, thou art our Lord and sure defence'); words by Prince Uelingtoni Ngu Tupoumalohi, tune by K. G. Schmitt.

RECENT ELECTIONS

Elections were held on 16 March 2005 for the nine elected seats. Seven seats were won by the Human Rights and Democracy Movement in Tonga.

CURRENT ADMINISTRATION

In March 2006 the government comprised:

Prime Minister, Minister of Labour, Commerce and Industry, Communications, Civil Aviation, Marine Affairs and Ports: Fred Sevele (in office since 11 Feb. 2006—acting until 30 March 2006).

Deputy Prime Minister, Minister of Environment and Tourism: Cecil James Cocker.

Minister of Agriculture, Fisheries and Food: Siosaia Ma'Ulupekotofa Tuita. *Education:* Tevita Hala Palefau. *Finance:* Siosiua Utoikamanu. *Foreign Affairs, and Defence (acting):* Sonatane Tu'a Taumoepeau Tupou. *Forestry:* Peauafi Haukinima. *Health:* Dr Viliami Tangi. *Justice and Attorney General:* Siaosi Taimani 'Aho. *Lands, Surveys and Natural Resources:* Fielakepa. *Police, Fire Services and Prisons:* Nuku. *Works and Disaster Relief Activities:* Tu'Ivakano.

Government Website: http://www.pmo.gov.to

CURRENT LEADERS

Fred Sevele

Position
Prime Minister

Introduction
Fred Sevele was appointed Tonga's first 'citizen' prime minister in March 2006 by King Taufa'ahau Tupou IV. With a background in business, Sevele supports greater democracy and aims to boost the economy by developing the fishing and tourism sectors.

Early Life
Feleti 'Fred' Vaka'uta Sevele was born in 1945 in the Kingdom of Tonga and educated at Apifo'ou College, Tonga, followed by St John's College on Ovalau, Fiji Islands and the Marist Brothers High School on Suva, Fiji Islands. He later studied economic geography at the University of Canterbury, New Zealand, receiving his PhD in 1972. He went on to establish numerous businesses in Tonga, becoming one of the archipelago's most successful entrepreneurs. By the late 1990s he was a prominent supporter of the pro-democracy movement.

In March 1999 Sevele was elected as one of nine people's representatives to the legislative assembly, winning re-election in 2002 and 2005. In March 2005 King Taufa'ahau Tupou IV named Sevele as minister of labour, commerce and industries, in line with new guidelines requiring four cabinet ministers to be appointed from the elected members. Sevele won plaudits for negotiating Tonga's entry into the World Trade Organization in Dec. 2005.

When the prime minister, HRH Prince 'Ulukalala Lavaka Ata, unexpectedly resigned on 11 Feb. 2006 after six years in the post, the king appointed Sevele as acting prime minister. No official reason was given for 'Ulukalala's departure but it followed three years of political upheaval that saw the collapse of Royal Tongan Airlines, a strike by civil servants and budgetary shortfalls. On 30 March 2006 the king announced that Sevele had been appointed Tonga's first non-aristocratic prime minister.

Career in Office
Sevele has stated his determination to make better use of local resources and rely less on overseas aid and assistance programmes. He is expected to push for greater democracy, raising the prospect of parliament becoming a fully elected body.

DEFENCE

Navy
A naval force, some 125-strong in 1999, was based at Touliki, Nuku'alofa.

Air Force
An Air Force was created in 1996 and operates three Beech 18s for maritime patrol.

INTERNATIONAL RELATIONS
Tonga is a member of the UN, WTO, the Commonwealth, the Asian Development Bank, the Pacific Community and the Pacific Islands Forum, and is an ACP member state of the ACP-EU relationship.

ECONOMY
In 2002 agriculture accounted for 28·5% of GDP, industry 15·1% and services 56·3%.

Currency
The unit of currency is the *pa'anga* (TOP) of 100 *seniti*. In 2004 there was inflation of 11·8%. In June 2002 foreign exchange reserves were US$22m. Total money supply in June 2002 was T$42m.

Budget
Revenues were T$77·5m. in 2000–01, with expenditures T$84·7m.

Performance
In 2004 real GDP growth was 1·5%, down from 2·9% in 2003. Total GDP in 2004 was US$0·2bn.

Banking and Finance
The National Reserve Bank of Tonga (*Governor,* Siosi Cocker Mafi) was established in 1989 as a bank of issue and to manage foreign reserves. The Bank of Tonga and the Tonga Development Bank are both situated in Nuku'alofa with branches in the main islands. Other commercial banks in Nuku'alofa are ANZ Banking Group Ltd, the MBF Bank Ltd, the National Reserve Bank of Tonga and the Westpac Banking Corp.

ENERGY AND NATURAL RESOURCES

Environment
Tonga's carbon dioxide emissions from the consumption and flaring of fossil fuels in 2002 were the equivalent of 1·4 tonnes per capita.

Electricity
Production (2000 estimate) 35m. kWh. Installed capacity (2000) 8,000 kW.

Agriculture
In 2001 there were 17,000 ha. of arable land and 31,000 ha. of permanent crops. Production (2000 estimates, in 1,000 tonnes): yams, 31; cassava, 28; taro, 27; coconuts, 25; sweet potatoes, 5; plantains, 4; lemons and limes, 3; oranges, 3.

Livestock (2000): pigs, 81,000; goats, 14,000; horses, 11,000; cattle, 9,000.

Forestry
Timber production in 2001 was 2,000 cu. metres.

Fisheries
In 2001 the catch totalled 4,673 tonnes.

INDUSTRY
The main industries produce food and beverages, paper, chemicals, metals and textiles.

INTERNATIONAL TRADE
Foreign debt in 2002 amounted to US$74m.

Imports and Exports
In 2002 imports were valued at US$73·4m. and exports at US$18·1m. Main imports are food and live animals, basic manufactures, machinery and transport equipment, and mineral fuels and lubricants; main exports are coconut oil, vanilla beans, root crops, desiccated coconut and watermelons. The leading import suppliers in 1999–2000 were USA (35·2%), Australia (23·0%), New Zealand (12·3%) and Fiji Islands (10·3%). Principal export markets were Japan (57·5%), USA (18·5%), New Zealand (7·6%) and Australia (2·6%).

COMMUNICATIONS

Roads

In 2002 there were 680 km of roads (184 km paved). Vehicles in use in 2000 numbered approximately 8,400 passenger cars, 8,700 trucks and vans, and (1996) 40 buses and coaches.

Civil Aviation

There is an international airport at Nuku'alofa on Tongatapu. The national carrier was the state-owned Royal Tongan Airlines, but it ceased operations in May 2004 owing to financial difficulties. Two carriers, Peau Vava'u and Airlines Tonga, now provide inter-island services. In 1998 Nuku'alofa (Fua'Amotu International) handled 129,000 passengers (88,000 on international flights) and 1,100 tonnes of freight.

Shipping

In 2002 sea-going shipping totalled 291,000 GRT, including oil tankers 41,000 GRT. Two shipping lanes provide monthly services to American Samoa, Australia, the Fiji Islands, Kiribati, New Caledonia, New Zealand, Samoa and Tuvalu.

Telecommunications

The operation and development of the National Telcommunication Network and Services are the responsibilities of the Tonga Telecommunication Commission (TCC). There were 14,600 telephone subscribers in 2002, or 147·0 per 1,000 population. In 2002 mobile phone subscribers numbered 3,400 and there were 2,000 PCs in use. There were approximately 400 fax machines and 2,900 Internet users in 2002. Ucall mobile GSM digital has been in operation in Tonga since Dec. 2001.

Postal Services

In 2001 there were eight post offices.

SOCIAL INSTITUTIONS

Justice

The judiciary is presided over by the Chief Justice. The enforcement of justice is the responsibility of the Attorney-General and the Minister of Police. In 1994 the UK ceased appointing Tongan judges and subsidizing their salaries.

The population in penal institutions in 2004 was 116 (105 per 100,000 of national population).

Education

In 2002 there were a total of 17,105 pupils with 773 teachers in primary schools and 14,567 pupils with 1,012 teachers in secondary schools. There is an extension centre of the University of the South Pacific at Nuku'alofa, a teacher training college and three technical institutes.

Adult literacy in 1996 was estimated at 98·5%. In 2000–01 total expenditure on education came to 5·3% of GNP and accounted for 17·8% of total government expenditure.

Health

There were four hospitals in 1993 with a provision of 28 beds per 10,000 inhabitants. In 2001 there were 35 physicians, 33 dentists, 322 nurses, 19 midwives and 17 pharmacists.

RELIGION

In 2001 there were 44,000 adherents of the Free Wesleyan Church and 16,000 Roman Catholics, with the remainder of the population being followers of other religions (notably Latter-day Saints).

CULTURE

Broadcasting

The Tonga Broadcasting Commission is an independent statutory board which operates two programmes. There is also a religious service. There were 61,000 radio sets in 1997. There are two television channels, and in 1997 an estimated 2,000 TV receivers.

Press

In 1996 there was one daily newspaper with a circulation of 7,000.

Tourism

There were 37,000 visitors in 2002. Receipts totalled US$9m.

DIPLOMATIC REPRESENTATIVES

Of Tonga in the United Kingdom (36 Molyneux St., London, W1H 5BQ)
Acting High Commissioner: Dr Sione Ngongo Kioa.

Of the United Kingdom in Tonga
High Commissioner: Charles Mochan (resides in Suva, Fiji).

Of Tonga in the USA (250 E. 51st St., New York, NY 10022)
Ambassador: Fekitamoeloa 'Utoikamanu.

Of the USA in Tonga
Ambassador: Larry M. Dinger (resides in Suva, Fiji Islands).

Of Tonga to the United Nations
Ambassador: Fekitamoeloa 'Utoikamanu.

Of Tonga to the European Union
Ambassador: Col. Fetu'utolu Tupou.

FURTHER READING

Campbell, I. C., *Island Kingdom: Tonga, Ancient and Modern.* Canterbury (NZ) Univ. Press, 1994
Wood-Ellem, E., *Queen Salote of Tonga, The Story of an Era 1900–1965.* Auckland Univ. Press, 2000

TRINIDAD AND TOBAGO

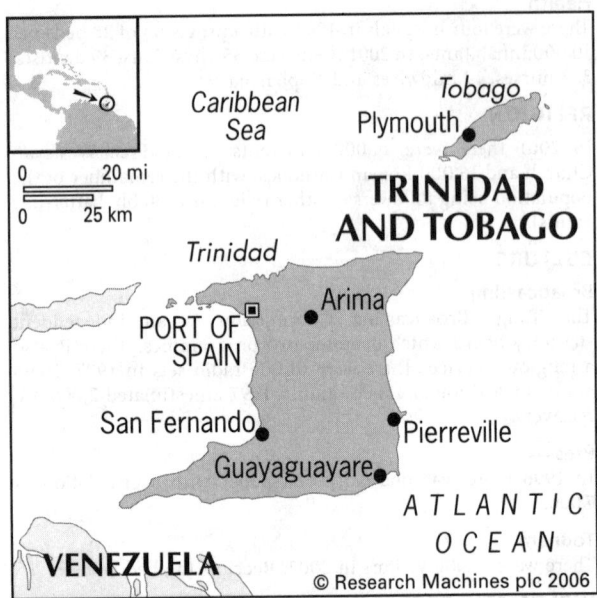

Republic of Trinidad and Tobago

Capital: Port-of-Spain
Population projection, 2010: 1·32m.
GDP per capita, 2003: (PPP$) 10,766
HDI/world rank: 0·801/57

KEY HISTORICAL EVENTS

When Columbus visited Trinidad in 1498 the island was inhabited by Arawak Indians. Tobago was occupied by the Caribs. Trinidad remained a neglected Spanish possession for almost 300 years until it was surrendered to a British naval expedition in 1797. The British first attempted to settle Tobago in 1721 but the French captured the island in 1781 and transformed it into a sugar-producing colony. In 1802 the British acquired Tobago and in 1899 it was administratively combined with Trinidad. When slavery was abolished in the late 1830s, the British subsidized immigration from India to replace plantation labourers. Sugar and cocoa declined towards the end of the 19th century. Oil and asphalt became the dominant sources of income. On 31 Aug. 1962 Trinidad and Tobago became an independent member of the Commonwealth. A Republican Constitution was adopted on 1 Aug. 1976.

TERRITORY AND POPULATION

The island of Trinidad is situated in the Caribbean Sea, about 12 km off the northeast coast of Venezuela; several islets, the largest being Chacachacare, Huevos, Monos and Gaspar Grande, lie in the Gulf of Paria which separates Trinidad from Venezuela. The smaller island of Tobago lies 30·7 km further to the northeast. Altogether, the islands cover 5,128 sq. km (1,980 sq. miles), of which Trinidad (including the islets) has 4,828 sq. km (1,864 sq. miles) and Tobago 300 sq. km (116 sq. miles). In 2000 the census population was 1,262,366 (Trinidad, 1,208,282; Tobago, 54,084); density, 246 per sq. km. The estimated population in 2005 was 1,305,000.

The UN gives a projected population for 2010 of 1·32m.

In 2003, 75·4% of the population were urban. Capital, Port-of-Spain (2000 census, 49,031); other important towns, San Fernando (55,419), Arima (32,278) and Point Fortin (19,056). The main towns on Tobago are Scarborough and Plymouth. Those of African descent are (2000) 39·2% of the population; East Indians, 38·6%; mixed races, 16·3%; European, Chinese and others, 5·9%.

English is generally spoken.

SOCIAL STATISTICS

Births, 1999, 18,600; deaths, 9,400. 1999 birth rate (per 1,000 population), 14·5; death rate, 7·3; growth rate, 0·6%. Expectation of life, 2003, was 66·9 years for males and 73·0 for females. Annual population growth rate, 1992–2002, 0·5%. Infant mortality, 2001, 17 per 1,000 live births; fertility rate, 2001, 1·6 births per woman.

CLIMATE

A tropical climate cooled by the northeast trade winds. The dry season runs from Jan. to June, with a wet season for the rest of the year. Temperatures are uniformly high the year round. Port-of-Spain, Jan. 76·3°F (24·6°C), July 79·2°F (26·2°C). Annual rainfall 1,869·8 mm.

CONSTITUTION AND GOVERNMENT

The 1976 Constitution provides for a bicameral legislature of a *Senate* and a *House of Representatives*, who elect the *President*, who is head of state. The *Senate* consists of 31 members, 16 being appointed by the President on the advice of the Prime Minister, six on the advice of the Leader of the Opposition and nine at the discretion of the President.

The *House of Representatives* consists of 36 (34 for Trinidad and two for Tobago) elected members and a Speaker elected from within or outside the House.

Executive power is vested in the Prime Minister, who is appointed by the President, and the Cabinet.

National Anthem

'Forged from the love of liberty'; words and music by P. Castagne.

GOVERNMENT CHRONOLOGY

Presidents since 1976.
1976–87	Ellis Emmanuel Innocent Clarke
1987–97	Noor Mohammed Hassanali
1997–2003	Arthur Napoleon Raymond Robinson
2003–	George Maxwell Richards

Prime Ministers since independence. (PNM = People's National Movement; NAR = National Alliance for Reconstruction; UNC = United National Congress)
1962–81	PNM	Eric Eustace Williams
1981–86	PNM	George Michael Chambers
1986–91	NAR	Arthur Napoleon Raymond Robinson
1991–95	PNM	Patrick Augustus Mervyn Manning
1995–2001	UNC	Basdeo Panday
2001–	PNM	Patrick Augustus Mervyn Manning

RECENT ELECTIONS

In parliamentary elections held on 7 Oct. 2002 the People's National Movement (PNM) won 20 out of 36 seats with 50·7% of votes cast, against 16 seats with 46·5% for the United National Congress (UNC). Turnout was 69·8%. As a result Patrick Manning of the People's National Movement was returned to power. The elections ended a year-long deadlock between Manning and opposition leader, Basdeo Panday. Panday, who previously served as the country's first prime minister of East Indian descent between 1995–2001, refused to accept Manning's appointment as prime minister following the election of Dec. 2001, in which both parties had taken 18 seats.

CURRENT ADMINISTRATION

President: Maxwell Richards; b. 1931 (PNM; sworn in 17 March 2003).

In March 2006 the cabinet comprised:

Prime Minister, Minister for Finance: Patrick Manning; b. 1946 (PNM; sworn in 24 Dec. 2001).

Minister for Agriculture, Land and Marine Resources: Jarrette Narine. *Community Development and Culture:* Joan Yuille-Williams. *Education:* Hazel Manning. *Foreign Affairs:* Knowlson Gift. *Health:* John Rahael. *Housing:* Dr Keith Rowley. *Labour, and Small and Micro Enterprise Development:* Danny Montano. *Legal Affairs:* Christine Kangaloo. *Local Government:* Rennie Dumas. *National Security:* Martin Joseph. *Planning and Development:* Camille Robinson-Regis. *Public Administration and Information, and Energy and Energy Industries:* Lenny Saith. *Public Utilities:* Penelope Beckles. *Science, Technology and Tertiary Education:* Mustapha Abdul-Hamid. *Social Development:* Anthony Roberts. *Sports and Youth Affairs:* Roger Boynes. *Tourism:* Howard Chin Lee. *Trade, Industry and Consumer Affairs:* Ken Valley. *Works and Transport:* Colm Imbert. *Attorney General:* John Jeremie.

Government Website: http://www.gov.tt/

CURRENT LEADERS

George Maxwell Richards

Position
President

Introduction
George Maxwell Richards became president of Trinidad and Tobago in March 2003. A chemical engineer by training, he is a non-partisan and it was hoped that his mixed-race background might defuse some of the ethnic tension in the country's political life.

Early Life
Richards was born in San Fernando, Trinidad in 1931. He graduated from the Queen's Royal College in the capital, Port-of-Spain, in 1955 and took a masters degree in chemical engineering at Manchester University in the UK. In 1963 he obtained his PhD from Cambridge University.

Richards began his working life as a trainee with a Trinidadian oil company in 1950. From 1957–65 he worked for Shell Trinidad before taking a lectureship in chemical engineering at the University of the West Indies. Five years later he became professor of chemical engineering. In 1980 he was appointed deputy principal and pro-vice chancellor of the university and was promoted to principal in 1985, a post he held until late-1986. Richards was also active on the boards of several commercial companies and between 1977 and 2003 he chaired the government salaries review commission.

Following tied parliamentary elections in 2001, Arthur Robinson, then president, was forced to choose between Patrick Manning and Basdeo Panday for the premiership. When Robinson selected Manning he was accused of bias and the non-partisan nature of the presidency came under scrutiny. When Manning nominated Richards for the presidency, he cited Richards' lack of a party political background as a key reason.

Ganace Ramdial opposed Richards for the presidency, but in a secret ballot in Feb. 2003 parliament elected Richards by 43 votes to 25. He was sworn in on 17 March 2003.

Career in Office
The presidency is primarily a ceremonial role and, following the unavoidable politicizing of the position after the 2001 elections, Richards emphasized on assuming office that he was 'completely apolitical'. Richards' mixed race (including black, Chinese and white roots) was expected to diffuse some of the tensions resulting from Trinidad and Tobago's racially divided political structure. He has been outspoken in his criticism of the rising crime rate in the country.

Patrick Manning

Position
Prime Minister

Introduction
Patrick Augustus Mervyn Manning became prime minister for the second time in Dec. 2001, having previously held the post from 1991–95. The elections of Dec. 2001 returned a hung parliament but Manning's People's National Movement (PNM) gained a majority at elections held in Oct. 2002. Manning has aimed to develop the country's oil, gas and tourism sectors.

Early Life
Patrick Manning was born on 17 Aug. 1946 in San Fernando, Trinidad. He graduated from the town's Presentation College in 1965 and worked for a year as an oil refinery operator before studying geology at the University of the West Indies (Jamaica) from 1966–69. He was then employed as a geologist for the Texaco oil company until 1971.

In that year Manning joined parliament as the member for San Fernando East and was appointed parliamentary secretary at the ministry of petroleum and mines. Between 1973–78 he served as parliamentary secretary at the prime minister's office and at the ministries of planning and development, industry and commerce, and works, transport and communications. In 1978 he joined the finance ministry with responsibility for the maintenance portfolio and later the public service portfolio. He was then appointed minister of information in the prime minister's office. In 1981 he was named minister of information and minister of industry and commerce, and from 1981–86 served as minister of energy and natural resources.

In 1986 the PNM lost its first general election since independence in 1962. Manning succeeded George Chambers as party leader on an interim basis in Dec. 1986. He was confirmed in the job the following year and led the party to victory at the elections of Dec. 1991.

Career in Office
During his first tenure Manning set about making the economy more competitive. His government floated the Trinidad and Tobago dollar in a bid to encourage investment. In 1995 he attempted to dismiss the speaker of the House of Representatives, Occah Seapaul, over a scandal regarding testimony Seapaul had given in a court trial. She refused to leave and suspended several government members. The PNM, already suffering a weakened majority after by-election losses the previous year, was thrown into crisis. Manning called a state of emergency and put Seapaul under house arrest. He called early elections for Nov. 1995, hoping to take advantage of an improved economic outlook to bolster his government. The PNM lost to the United National Congress (UNC) and Manning was succeeded as prime minister by Basdeo Panday.

Panday won a second term in Dec. 2000 but at new elections 12 months later, following a split in the government, the UNC and PNM tied with 18 seats each. The two parties agreed a deal by which President Robinson would elect the prime minister. Panday withdrew from the pact when Manning was selected and demanded new elections. Without cross party co-operation Manning was unable to form a workable government. Parliament was suspended in April 2002, and at elections held in Oct. the PNM won a majority, claiming 20 of the 36 available seats.

To reform the economy, Manning has proposed reductions in income and corporation tax. He has also aimed to exploit the country's tourism sector while continuing to develop the long-established oil and gas industries. In foreign policy, he has sought a more prominent role for Trinidad and Tobago within CARICOM. In April 2005 the Caribbean Court of Justice, a final court of appeal intended to replace the British Privy Council, was inaugurated in Trinidad. Manning has been criticized for failing to bring the growing crime problem under control. In Oct. 2005 at least 10,000 people took part in a protest, named the Death March, against the level of violent crime.

DEFENCE

The Defence Force has one infantry battalion, one engineer and one service battalion. The small air element is under the control of the Coast Guard. Personnel in 2002 totalled 2,700.

The police force has 4,294 personnel.

In 2003 defence expenditure totalled US$29m. (US$22 per capita), representing 0·3% of GDP. In the 1999–2000 budget the Ministry of National Security received a total allocation of $1,154m.

Navy

In 2002 there was a coastguard of 700 including an air wing of 50.

INTERNATIONAL RELATIONS

Trinidad and Tobago is a member of the UN and many of its specialized agencies including WIPO, IMF, the World Bank, IDA, IFC, IOB and ILO; and of WTO, the Commonwealth, OAS, Inter-American Development Bank, CARICOM, Association of Caribbean States (ACS), Caribbean Development Bank, Andean Development Bank and is an ACP member state of the ACP-EU relationship.

ECONOMY

Services accounted for 53·0% of GDP in 2002, industry 45·7% and agriculture 1·3%.

Currency

The unit of currency is the *Trinidad and Tobago dollar* (TTD) of 100 *cents*. Inflation was 3·8% in 2003 and 3·7% in 2004. In April 1994 the TT dollar was floated and managed by the Central Bank at TT$6·06 to US$1·00. Foreign exchange reserves in April 2002 were US$1,875m. and gold reserves 61,000 troy oz. Total money supply in March 2002 was TT$6,697m.

Budget

The fiscal year for the budget is 1 Oct. to 30 Sept. In 1999–2000 total government revenue was TT$12,028·5m. (TT$10,263·6m. in 1998–99) and total expenditure was TT$12,308·5m. (TT$10,526·3m. in 1998–99). The 2000–01 budget envisaged total recurrent revenue of TT$12,539·0m. (TT$9,998·2m. in 1998–99) and total capital expenditure of TT$1,027·0m. (TT$1,033·8m. in 1999–2000).

Performance

Real GDP growth was 13·2% in 2003 and 6·2% in 2004. Total GDP in 2004 was US$12·5bn.

Banking and Finance

The Central Bank of Trinidad and Tobago began operations in 1964 (*Governor*, Ewart Williams). Its net reserves were US$1,281·1m. in Aug. 2000. There are seven commercial banks. Government savings banks are established in 69 offices, with a head office in Port-of-Spain. The stock exchange in Port-of-Spain participates in the regional Caribbean exchange.

ENERGY AND NATURAL RESOURCES

Environment

Carbon dioxide emissions from the consumption and flaring of fossil fuels were the equivalent of 23·7 tonnes per capita in 2002. An *Environmental Sustainability Index* compiled for the World Economic Forum meeting in Jan. 2005 ranked Trinidad and Tobago 139th in the world out of 146 countries analysed, with 36·3%. The index measured the ability of countries to maintain favourable environmental conditions and examined various factors including pollution levels and the use or abuse of natural resources.

Electricity

In 2000 installed capacity was 1·47m. kW, electricity production was 5·46bn. kWh and consumption per capita 4,233 kWh.

Oil and Gas

Oil production is one of Trinidad's leading industries. Commercial production began in 1908; production of crude oil in 2003 was 7·9m. tonnes. Reserves in 2002 totalled 700m. bbls. Crude oil is also imported for refining. Oil accounted for 30% of GDP and 75% of revenues in 1996, but dependence on the oil industry is declining.

In 2002 production of natural gas was 16·8bn. cu. metres. Proven reserves of natural gas were 660bn. cu. metres in 2002. A major discovery of approximately 50bn. cu. metres was made by BP in 2000, followed by a further discovery of approximately 30bn. cu. metres in 2002.

Agriculture

Production of main crops (2000 estimates, in 1,000 tonnes): sugarcane, 1,500; coconuts, 23; oranges, 20; grapefruit and pomelos, 8; pumpkins and squash, 8; rice, 7; bananas, 6; maize, 5; plantains, 4. There were 75,000 ha. of arable land and 47,000 ha. of permanent cropland in 2001, and 11,000 ha. of pasture in 1999.

Livestock (2000): goats, 59,000; pigs, 41,000; cattle, 35,000; sheep, 12,000; chickens, 10m. Livestock products, 2000 estimates: meat, 30,000 tonnes (including poultry, 26,000 tonnes); milk, 10,000 tonnes.

Forestry

Forests covered 259,000 ha. in 2000, or 50·5% of the land area. Timber production for 2001 was 92,000 cu. metres.

Fisheries

The catch in 2001 totalled 11,408 tonnes.

INDUSTRY

Industrial production includes: ammonia and urea (production, 1998, 3,946,700 tonnes), iron and steel (2001, 3,550,800 tonnes), residual fuel oil (2000, 3,294,000 tonnes), methanol (1999, 2,149,800 tonnes), distillate fuel oil (2000, 1,697,000 tonnes), petrol (2000, 1,345,000 tonnes), cement (2001, 697,000 tonnes), sugar (2002, 104,000 tonnes), rum (1998, 3,916,000 proof gallons), beer (2000, 62·5m. litres), cigarettes (2000, 2,050,000 units). Trinidad and Tobago ranks among the world's largest producers of ammonia and methanol.

Labour

The working population in the first quarter of 2003 was 588,300. The number of unemployed was 65,000. 77,300 people worked in construction (including electricity and water); 55,500 in manufacturing (including other mining and quarrying); 38,600 in transport storage and communication; 37,800 in agriculture; 17,500 in petroleum and gas; other services, 295,300. Total employment: 523,300. The unemployment rate in the first quarter of 2003 was 11·0%.

Trade Unions

About 30% of the labour force belong to unions, which are grouped under the National Trade Union Centre.

INTERNATIONAL TRADE

The Foreign Investment Act of 1990 permits foreign investors to acquire land and shares in local companies, and to form companies. External debt was US$2,672m. in 2002.

Imports and Exports

In 2003 imports totalled US$3,911·7m. and exports US$5,204·9m. Crude petroleum accounts for 19% of imports, and refined petroleum 29% of exports. The principal import sources in 2001 were USA (34·4%), Venezuela (11·1%), Brazil (5·1%), United Kingdom (4·9%) and Panama (4·6%). The main export markets in 2001 were USA (42·3%), Mexico (7·4%), Jamaica (7·0%), Barbados (5·5%) and France (3·9%).

COMMUNICATIONS

Roads

In 2002 there were about 8,320 km of roads, of which 51·1% were paved. There were 177,900 passenger cars and 38,700 commercial vehicles in 2002.

Civil Aviation

There is an international airport at Port-of-Spain (Piarco) and in Tobago (Crown Point). In 2001 Piarco handled 1,725,111 passengers (1,317,811 on international flights) and 29,673 tonnes of freight. The national carrier is BWIA West Indies Airways, which was privatized in March 1995 by the Acker group of companies. In 2003 it flew to Antigua, Barbados, Caracas, Georgetown, Grenada, Kingston, London, Manchester, Miami, Nassau, New York, Paramaribo, St Kitts, St Maarten, San Jose, Santo Domingo, Toronto and Washington. In 1999 it carried 1,111,700 passengers (1,045,900 on international flights).

Shipping

Sea-going shipping totalled 27,000 GRT in 2002; 3,687,328 tonnes of cargo were handled at Port-of-Spain in 1999. There is a deep-water harbour at Scarborough (Tobago). The other main harbour is Point Lisas.

Telecommunications

International and domestic communications are provided by Telecommunications Services of Trinidad and Tobago (TSTT) by means of a satellite earth station and various high-quality radio circuits. The marine radio service is also maintained by TSTT. There were 687,000 telephone subscribers in 2002, or 527·8 per 1,000 inhabitants, and 104,000 PCs (79·5 for every 1,000 persons). There were 361,900 mobile phone subscribers in 2002 and 8,500 fax machines. Internet users numbered 138,000 in 2002.

Postal Services

In 2003 there were 135 post offices.

SOCIAL INSTITUTIONS

Justice

The High Court consists of the Chief Justice and 11 puisne judges. In criminal cases a judge of the High Court sits with a jury of 12 in cases of treason and murder, and with nine jurors in other cases. The Court of Appeal consists of the Chief Justice and seven Justices of Appeal. In hearing appeals, the Court is comprised of three judges sitting together except when the appeal is from a Summary Court or from a decision of a High Court judge in chambers. In such cases two judges would comprise the Court. There is a limited right of appeal from it to the Privy Council. There are three High Courts and 12 magistrates' courts. There is an *Ombudsman*. Trinidad and Tobago was one of ten countries to sign an agreement in Feb. 2001 establishing a Caribbean

Court of Justice to replace the British Privy Council as the highest civil and criminal court. In the meantime the number of signatories has risen to twelve. The court was inaugurated at Port-of-Spain on 16 April 2005.

The death penalty is authorized and still used. There were ten executions in 1999.

The population in penal institutions in Oct. 2003 was 3,991 (307 per 100,000 of national population).

Education

In 1999–2000 there were 162,736 pupils enrolled in 481 primary schools, 17,715 in government secondary schools, 21,068 in assisted secondary schools, 33,053 in junior secondary schools, 21,930 in senior comprehensive schools, 3,057 in senior secondary schools, 8,677 in composite schools and 3,935 in technical and vocational schools. There were 4,121 pupils enrolled in the three Technical and Vocational schools for the period 1998–99. The University of the West Indies campus in St Augustine (1999–2000) had 7,585 students and 477 academic staff. 1,307 of the students were from other countries.

Adult literacy was 98·5% in 2002 (male, 99·0%; female, 97·9%).

In 2000–01 total expenditure on education came to 4·3% of GNP and accounted for 16·7% of total government expenditure.

Health

In 1999 there were 1,171 physicians, 189 dentists, 500 pharmacists and 71 hospitals and nursing homes with 4,384 beds. There were 1,936 nurses and midwives and 1,486 nursing assistants in government institutions.

RELIGION

In 2001, 29·9% of the population were Roman Catholics (under the Archbishop of Port-of-Spain), 24·2% Hindus, 19·2% Protestants, 11·2% Anglicans (under the Bishop of Trinidad and Tobago) and 6·0% Muslims.

CULTURE

Broadcasting

Radio programmes are overseen by the Telecommunications Authority. There are 16 commercial stations. There are three TV stations, as well as community and cable services. There were 449,000 television receivers (colour by NTSC) in 2001 and 672,000 radio sets in 2000.

Press

There are three daily newspapers (*Trinidad Express, Trinidad Guardian* and *Newsday*), with a total daily circulation of 195,692 in Dec. 1999, and three Sunday newspapers, with a total circulation of 165,646. Weekly newspapers include *Punch, The Catholic News, The Probe, The Bomb, Show Time, The Independent* and *The Chutney Star. The Mirror* is published three times a week.

Tourism

There were 409,007 tourist arrivals in 2003, plus 55,532 cruise ship visitors. Revenue from tourism in 2002 was US$224m.

Festivals

Religious festivals: the Feast of La Divina Pastora, or Sipari Mai, a Catholic and Hindu celebration of the Holy Mother Mary; Saint Peter's Day Celebration, the Patron Saint of Fishermen; Hosein, or Hosay, a Shia Muslim festival; Phagwah, a Hindu spring festival; Santa Rosa, a Caribbean Amerindian festival; Eid-ul-Fitr, the Muslim festival at the end of Ramadan; Divali, the Hindu festival of light; Christmas. Cultural festivals: Carnival (on 19 and 20 Feb. in 2007); Spiritual Baptist Shouter Liberation Day, a recognition of the Baptist religion; Indian Arrival Day, commemorating the arrival of the first East Indian labourers; Sugar and Energy Festival; Pan Ramajay, a music festival of all types; Emancipation, a recognition of the period of slavery;

Tobago Heritage Festival, celebrating Tobago's traditions and customs; Parang Festival, traditional folk music of Christmas; Pan Jazz Festival; Music Festival, predominantly classical music but Indian and Calypso are included.

When a public holiday falls on a Sunday, the holiday is celebrated on the Monday immediately following.

DIPLOMATIC REPRESENTATIVES

Of Trinidad and Tobago in the United Kingdom (42 Belgrave Sq., London, SW1X 8NT)
High Commissioner: Glenda Morean-Phillip.

Of the United Kingdom in Trinidad and Tobago (19 St Clair Ave., Port-of-Spain)
High Commissioner: Ronald Nash, CMG, LVO.

Of Trinidad and Tobago in the USA (1708 Massachusetts Ave., NW, Washington, D.C., 20036)
Ambassador: Marina Annette Valere.

Of the USA in Trinidad and Tobago (15 Queen's Park West, Port-of-Spain)
Ambassador: Roy L. Austin.

Of Trinidad and Tobago to the United Nations
Ambassador: Philip Sealy.

Of Trinidad and Tobago to the European Union
Ambassador: Learie Edgar Rousseau.

FURTHER READING

Chambers, F., *Trinidad and Tobago.* [Bibliography] ABC-Clio, Oxford and Santa Barbara (CA), 1986
Williams, E., *History of the People of Trinidad and Tobago.* Africa World Press, Lawrenceville (NJ), 1993

Central library: The Central Library of Trinidad and Tobago, Queen's Park East, Port-of-Spain.
National Statistical Office: Central Statistical Office, 80 Independence Square, Port-of-Spain.
Website: http://cso.gov.tt

TUNISIA

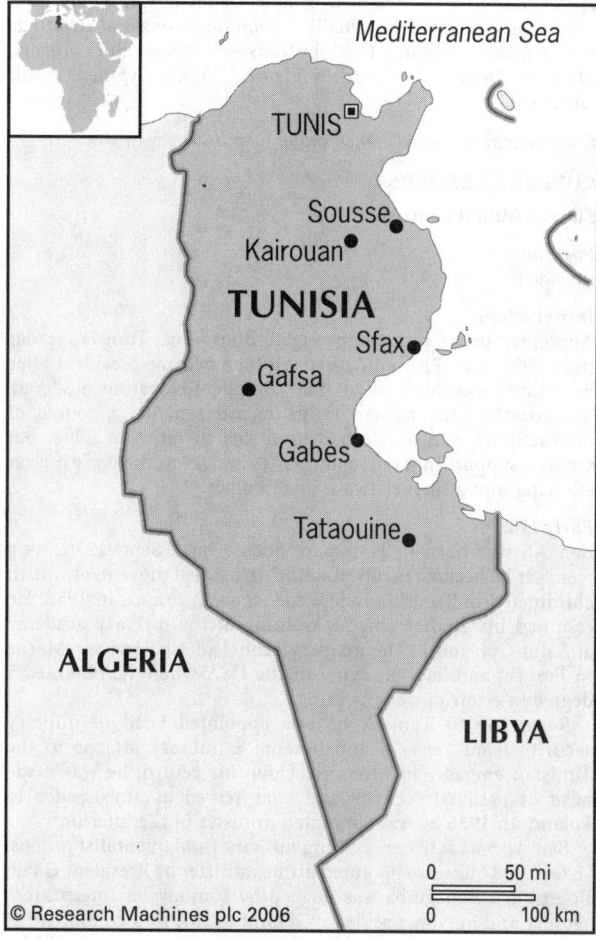

Mediterranean Sea

TUNIS □

Sousse ●
Kairouan ●

TUNISIA

Sfax ●
Gafsa ●

Gabès ●

Tataouine ●

ALGERIA

LIBYA

0 — 50 mi
0 — 100 km

© Research Machines plc 2006

**Jumhuriya at-Tunisiya
(Republic of Tunisia)**

Capital: Tunis
Population projection, 2010: 10·64m.
GDP per capita, 2003: (PPP$) 7,161
HDI/world rank: 0·753/89

KEY HISTORICAL EVENTS

Settled by the Phoenicians, the area became a powerful state under the dynasty of the Berber Hafsids (1207–1574). Tunisia was nominally a part of the Ottoman Empire from the end of the 17th century and descendants of the original Ottoman ruler remained Beys of Tunis until the modern state of Tunisia was established. A French protectorate since 1883, Tunisia saw anti-French activity in the late 1930s. However, Tunisia supported the Allies in the Second World War and was the scene of heavy fighting. France granted internal self-government in 1955 and Tunisia became fully independent on 20 March 1956. A constitutional assembly was established and Habib Bourguiba became prime minister. A republic was established in 1957, the Bey deposed and the monarchy was abolished; Bourguiba became president. In 1975 the constitution was changed so

that Bourguiba could be made President-for-life. Bourguiba was overthrown in a bloodless coup in 1987. His successor, Zine El Abidine Ben Ali, introduced democratic reforms but a long running struggle with Islamic fundamentalists has been marked by sporadic violence and the suspension of political rights.

TERRITORY AND POPULATION

Tunisia is bounded in the north and east by the Mediterranean Sea, west by Algeria and south by Libya. The area is 164,150 sq. km, including inland waters. In 2004 the census population was 9,910,872; density, 60 per sq. km. In 2003, 63·7% of the population were urban.

The UN gives a projected population for 2010 of 10·64m.

The areas and populations (2004 census) of the 24 governorates:

	Land area in sq. km	Population
Aryanah (Ariana)	498	422,246
Bajah (Béja)	3,558	304,501
Banzart (Bizerta)	3,685	524,128
Bin Arus (Bin Arous)	761	505,773
Jundubah (Jendouba)	3,102	416,608
Kaf (Le Kef)	4,965	258,790
Madaniyin (Médénine)	8,588	432,503
Mahdiyah (Mahdia)	2,966	377,853
Manubah (Manouba)	1,060	335,912
Munastir (Monastir)	1,019	455,590
Nabul (Nabeul)	2,788	693,890
Qabis (Gabès)	7,175	342,630
Qafsah (Gafsa)	8,990	323,709
Qasrayn (Kassérine)	8,066	412,278
Qayrawan (Kairouan)	6,712	546,209
Qibili (Kebili)	22,084	143,218
Safaqis (Sfax)	7,545	855,256
Sidi Bu Zayd (Sidi Bouzid)	6,994	395,506
Silyanah (Siliana)	4,631	233,985
Susah (Sousse)	2,621	544,413
Tatawin (Tataouine)	38,889	143,524
Tawzar (Tozeur)	4,719	97,526
Tunis	346	983,861
Zaghwan (Zaghouan)	2,768	160,963

Tunis, the capital, had (2004 census in 1,000) 728·5 inhabitants. Other main cities (2004 census in 1,000): Sfax, 265·1; Ariana, 240·7; Sousse, 173·0; Ettadhamen, 118·5; Kairouan, a holy city of the Muslims, 117·9; Gabès, 116·3; Bizerta, 114·4.

The official language is Arabic but French is the main language in the media, commercial enterprise and government departments. Berber-speaking people form less than 1% of the population.

SOCIAL STATISTICS

Births, 2002 estimate, 163,000; deaths, 2002 estimate, 57,000; marriages (2001), 61,800. Rates (2002): birth, 16·7 per 1,000 population; death, 5·8. Annual population growth rate, 1992–2002, 1·3%. In 1998 the most popular age range for marrying was 30–34 for males and 20–24 for females. Expectation of life, 2003, was 71·2 years for males and 75·4 for females. Infant mortality, 2002, 22 per 1,000 live births; fertility rate, 2001, 2·2 births per woman.

CLIMATE

The climate ranges from warm temperate in the north, where winters are mild and wet and the summers hot and dry, to desert in the south. Tunis, Jan. 48°F (8·9°C), July 78°F (25·6°C). Annual rainfall 16" (400 mm). Bizerta, Jan. 52°F (11·1°C), July 77°F

(25°C). Annual rainfall 25" (622 mm). Sfax, Jan. 52°F (11·1°C), July 78°F (25·6°C). Annual rainfall 8" (196 mm).

CONSTITUTION AND GOVERNMENT

The Constitution was promulgated on 1 June 1959 and reformed in 1988. The office of President-for-life was abolished and Presidential elections were to be held every five years. The *President* and the *National Assembly* are elected simultaneously by direct universal suffrage for a period of five years. On 27 May 2002 a referendum was held in which 99% of votes cast were in favour of abolishing the three-term limit on the presidency and of raising the age limit for incumbent presidents from 70 to 75 years. The results were viewed with scepticism by human rights groups and opposition figures, who saw the referendum as an attempt by President Zine El Abidine Ben Ali to retain power. Ben Ali was scheduled to retire in 2004 after his third presidential term.

The *Majlis al-Nuwaab* (*National Assembly*) has 189 seats, with members elected from single-seat constituencies.

National Anthem

'Humata al Hima' ('Defenders of the Homeland'); words by Mustapha al Rafi and Abdoul Kacem Chabbi, tune by M. A. Wahab.

GOVERNMENT CHRONOLOGY

Presidents since 1957. (ND = Neo-Destur Party; PSD = Socialist Destourian Party; RCD = Constitutional Democratic Assembly)
1957–87   ND, PSD   Habib Ali Bourguiba
1987–   PSD, RCD   Zine El Abidine Ben Ali

RECENT ELECTIONS

Presidential and parliamentary elections were held on 24 Oct. 2004; turnout was 91·5%. President Zine El Abidine Ben Ali (Constitutional Democratic Assembly) was re-elected by 94·4% of votes cast against 3·8% for Mohamed Bouchiha (Popular Unity Party), 0·9% for Mohamed Ali Halouani (Ettajdid Movement) and 0·8% for Mounir Béji (Social Liberal Party). In the parliamentary elections the ruling Constitutional Democratic Assembly (CDA) won 152 of 189 available National Assembly seats with 87·6% of votes cast, the Movement of Social Democrats 14 with 4·6%, the Popular Unity Party 11 with 3·6%, the Unionist Democratic Union 7 with 2·2%, the Democratic Initiative Movement 3 with 1·0% and the Social Liberal Party 2 with 0·6%. The main opposition party, the Progressive Democratic Party, boycotted the elections, claiming that they were rigged.

CURRENT ADMINISTRATION

President: Zine El Abidine Ben Ali; b. 1936 (CDA; sworn in 7 Nov. 1987, re-elected March 1994, Oct. 1999 and Oct. 2004).

In March 2006 the cabinet comprised:

Prime Minister: Mohamed Ghannouchi; b. 1941 (CDA; sworn in on 17 Nov. 1999).

Special Adviser to the President and Spokesman for the President: Abdelaziz Ben Dhia. *Minister of Defence:* Kamel Morjane. *State Property and Land Affairs:* Ridha Grira. *Justice and Human Rights:* Béchir Tekkari. *Foreign Affairs:* Abdelwahab Abdallah. *Interior and Local Development:* Rafik Belhaj Kacem. *Development and International Co-operation:* Mohamed Nouri Jouini. *Environment and Sustainable Development:* Nadhir Hamada. *Equipment, Housing and Land Development:* Samira Khayach Belhaj. *Social Affairs, Solidarity and Tunisians Abroad:* Ali Chaouch. *Finance:* Mohamed Rachid Kechiche. *Trade and Handicrafts:* Mondher Zenaïdi. *Tourism:* Tijani Haddad. *Education and Training:* Sadok Korbi. *Higher Education:* Lazhar Bououni. *Scientific Research, Technology and Expertise Development:* Taieb Hadhri. *Employment and Vocational Integration of Youth:* Chadli Laroussi. *Public Health:* Kechrid Ridha. *Culture and Protection of National Heritage:* Mohamed Aziz Ben Achour. *Religious*

Affairs: Boubaker El Akhzouri. *Industry, Energy and Small and Medium-Sized Enterprises:* Afif Chelbi. *Family, Children, Seniors' and Women's Affairs:* Saloua Ayachi Labben. *Youth, Sport and Physical Education:* Abdallah Kaâbi. *Agriculture and Water Resources:* Mohamed Habib Haddad. *Communication Technologies:* Montassar Ouaili. *Communications and Relations with Parliament:* Rafaa Dekhil. *Transport:* Abderrahim Zouari. *Minister Director of the Presidential Office:* Ahmed Iyadh Ouederni.

Government Website (French only): http://www.ministeres.tn

CURRENT LEADERS

Zine-Al Abidine Ben Ali

Position
President

Introduction
Appointed prime minister by Habib Bourguiba, Tunisia's leader from 1957, Zine El Abidine Ben Ali then became president after Bourguiba was deposed in 1987. Despite advocating moderate liberalization, his human rights record remains a source of international unease. He had been due to retire in 2004, but secured support in a referendum for changes to the constitution allowing him a further two terms in office.

Early Life
Ben Ali was born in Hammam Sousse on 3 Sept. 1936. As a teenager he became involved in the nationalist movement, which culminated in Tunisia's independence from France in 1956. He resumed his studies abroad, training at the military academy at Saint-Cyr and at the artillery school of Châlons-sur-Marne in France, and later studying in the USA where he obtained a degree in electronic engineering.

Returning to Tunisia, he was appointed head of military security from 1964–74 and became a military attaché to the Tunisian embassy in Morocco. Upon his return, he was made head of national security and later served as ambassador to Poland. In 1986 he was appointed minister of the interior.

Ben Ali was active in fighting militant fundamentalist groups. In Oct. 1987 he was appointed prime minister by President Habib Bourguiba. Bourguiba was dogged by rumours of intermittent senility and in Nov. was declared unfit to rule by a committee of doctors and deposed in a bloodless coup. Ben Ali replaced him as president.

Career in Office
As leader of the Constitutional Democratic Assembly, Ben Ali has been overwhelmingly re-elected in March 1994, Oct. 1999 and most recently in Oct. 2004. The cancellation of the 1992 election at a point when the opposition seemed likely to win prompted international criticism. Due to retire in 2004, he initiated changes to the constitution in 2002 to allow him to govern for another two terms. In the Oct. 2004 elections the main opposition group, the Progressive Democratic Party, withdrew its candidates two days before polling, arguing that the vote would be worthless.

Ben Ali inherited an economically stable country and has overseen a reduction in the poverty rate and improving literacy levels. He has expressed his commitment to furthering women's rights and has authorized the release of some political prisoners, but human rights groups remain critical of his regime. He has maintained tight control of the media and the treatment of journalists and political opponents critical of his rule has caused international concern.

DEFENCE

Selective conscription is for one year. Defence expenditure in 2003 totalled US$494m. (US$50 per capita), representing 2·0% of GDP.

Army

Strength (2002) 27,000 (22,000 conscripts). There is also a National Guard numbering 12,000.

Navy

In 1999 naval personnel totalled 4,500. Forces are based at Bizerta, Sfax and Kelibia.

Air Force

The Air Force operated 29 combat aircraft in 2002, including 15 F-5E/F Tiger II fighters, and 15 armed helicopters. Personnel (2002) about 3,500 (700 conscripts).

INTERNATIONAL RELATIONS

Tunisia is a member of the UN, WTO, the African Union, the Islamic Conference, the League of Arab States, Arab Maghreb Union, African Development Bank, IOM, Islamic Development Bank and the International Organization of the Francophonie.

ECONOMY

In 2002 agriculture accounted for 10·3% of GDP, industry 29·3% and services 60·4%.

Overview

Tunisia's economic record compares favourably with many developing countries, particularly on the African continent. After a balance of payments crisis in the mid-1980s, the government introduced reforms to stabilize the economy. Steps were taken to improve macroeconomic policy, foster the non-public sector and liberalize prices and controls. The annual growth rate has been positive every year since 1987. In the 1990s the economy grew steadily at an average annual rate of 5%. Inflation and annual budget deficits have been brought down from previous high levels and poverty has been reduced significantly.

In 1995 Tunisia signed an association agreement with the EU (the first by the EU with a Mediterranean neighbour), which was scheduled to phase out tariffs on both sides over 12 years. Tunisia's trade is highly oriented towards the EU, with France, Italy, Germany and Spain the country's most important trading partners in descending order. Tunisia's economy is diversified relative to many of its non-European neighbours, with significant mining, tourism, energy, manufacturing and agricultural sectors. In the first half of the 2000s growth was strong, except in 2002 when a drought hit the agricultural sector and growth slowed to 1·7%. The initial phase of the Iraq war also had a detrimental impact on tourism. Tunisia's textile exporters will continue to lose EU market share to Asia as a result of the end of the Multi-Fibre Agreement quota system in Jan. 2005 but the recovery of the agriculture and tourism sectors should allow the economy to continue growing at a healthy rate.

Currency

The unit of currency is the *Tunisian dinar* (TND) of 1,000 *millimes*. The currency was made convertible on 6 Jan. 1993. Foreign exchange reserves were US$2,195m. and gold reserves 218,000 troy oz in June 2002. Inflation was 2·8% in 2003 and 3·6% in 2004. Total money supply was 6,687m. dinars in April 2002.

Budget

The fiscal year is the calendar year. Budgetary central government revenue totalled 7,611m. dinars in 2003 (7,342m. dinars in 2002) and expenditure 6,976m. dinars (6,624m. dinars in 2002). Taxes accounted for 87·1% of total revenues in 2003.

Performance

Real GDP growth was 5·8% in 2004 (5·6% in 2003). Tunisia's total GDP in 2004 was US$28·2bn.

Banking and Finance

The Central Bank of Tunisia (*Governor*, Taoufik Baccar) is the bank of issue. In 2003 there were 12 commercial banks, six development banks, two merchant banks and five 'offshore' banks.

There is a small stock exchange (42 companies trading in 2002).

ENERGY AND NATURAL RESOURCES

Environment

Tunisia's carbon dioxide emissions from the consumption and flaring of fossil fuels in 2002 were the equivalent of 2·2 tonnes per capita.

Electricity

Installed capacity was 2·3m. kW in 2000. Production in 2000 was about 10·07bn. kWh; consumption per capita was an estimated 1,040 kWh.

Oil and Gas

Crude petroleum production (2003) was 3·1m. tonnes with 0·3m. bbls. in proven reserves (2002). Natural gas production (2000), 2·1bn. cu. metres with 76bn. cu metres in proven reserves (2002).

Water

In 1993 there were 20 large dams, 250 hillside dams and some 1,000 artificial lakes.

Minerals

Mineral production (in 1,000 tonnes) in 2001: phosphate rock, 8,144; salt, 654; iron ore, 294; zinc ore (concentrated), 73; lead ore (concentrated), 7 (2000).

Agriculture

There are five agricultural regions: the *north*, mountainous with large fertile valleys; the *northeast*, with the peninsula of Cap Bon, suited for the cultivation of oranges, lemons and tangerines; the *Sahel*, where olive trees abound; the *centre*, a region of high tablelands and pastures; and the *desert* of the south, where dates are grown.

Some 23% of the population are employed in agriculture. Large estates predominate; smallholdings are tending to fragment, partly owing to inheritance laws. There are some 0·4m. farms in 1990 (0·32m. in 1960). Of the total area of 15,583,000 ha., about 9m. ha. are productive, including 2m. under cereals, 3·6m. used as pasturage, 0·9m. forests and 1·3m. uncultivated. In 2001, 381,000 ha. were irrigated. There were 2·77m. ha. of arable land in 2001 and 2·13m. ha. of permanent crops. There were 35,100 tractors in 2001 and 2,850 harvester-threshers. The main crops are cereals, citrus fruits, tomatoes, melons, olives, dates, grapes and olive oil. Production, 2000 (in 1,000 tonnes): olives, 1,000; tomatoes, 905; wheat, 842; melons, including watermelons, 475; potatoes, 290; barley, 242; chillies and green peppers, 190; grapes, 150; onions, 133; oranges, 115; apples, 108; dates, 103; sugarbeets, 76; peaches and nectarines, 73; tree nuts, 61; almonds, 60.

Livestock, 2000 (in 1,000): sheep, 6,600; goats, 1,400; cattle, 790; camels, 231; asses, 230; mules, 81; horses, 56. Livestock products, 2000 (in 1,000 tonnes): meat, 219; milk, 919; eggs, 80.

Forestry

In 2000 there were 510,000 ha. of forests (3·1% of the land area). Timber production in 2001 was 2·32m. cu. metres.

Fisheries

In 2001 the catch amounted to 98,482 tonnes, almost exclusively from marine waters.

INDUSTRY

Production (in 1,000 tonnes): cement (2000), 5,647; sulphuric acid (1999), 4,858; residual fuel oil (2000), 653; phosphoric acid (2000), 607; distillate fuel oil (2000), 537; lime (2001), 467; crude steel (2002), 220. Industry accounted for 28·8% of GDP in 2001, with manufacturing contributing 18·5%.

Labour

The labour force in 2002 totalled 3,375,700 (71·8% males), of which 2,852,000 were employed. Unemployment was 14·9% in 2002.

Trade Unions

The Union Générale des Travailleurs Tunisiens won 27 seats in the parliamentary elections of 1 Nov. 1981. There are also the Union Tunisienne de l'Industrie, du Commerce et de l'Artisanat (UTICA, the employers' union) and the Union National des Agriculteurs (UNA, farmers' union).

INTERNATIONAL TRADE

In Feb. 1989 Tunisia signed a treaty of economic co-operation with the other countries of Maghreb: Algeria, Libya, Mauritania and Morocco. Foreign debt was US$12,625m. in 2002.

Tunisia was the first country to sign a partnership agreement with the European Union. The agreement aims at creating a non-agricultural free trade zone by 2008.

Imports and Exports

Trade in US$1m.:

	1998	1999	2000	2001	2002
Imports f.o.b.	7,875	8,014	8,093	8,997	8,981
Exports f.o.b.	5,724	5,873	5,840	6,606	6,857

Main imports in 1999: machinery and transport equipment, 34·2%; textile yarn and fabrics, 16·0%; chemicals and related products, 8·1%; foodstuffs, 6·1%; clothing, 5·7%; petroleum, 5·3%; iron and steel, 3·2%. Main exports in 1999: clothing and accessories, 41·0%; manufactured goods, 10·1%; electric machinery, 9·5%; petroleum, 7·2%; olive oil, 5·5%; fertilizers, 5·0%; phosphorous pentoxide and phosphoric acids, 4·0%.

The main import suppliers in 2000 were France (26·3%), Italy (19·1%) and Germany (9·6%). Main export markets in 2000 were France (26·8%), Italy (23·0%) and Germany (12·5%).

COMMUNICATIONS

Roads

In 2001 there were 18,997 km of roads, including 142 km of motorways and 4,750 km of national roads. 65·4% of all roads in 2001 were paved. Vehicles in 2002 numbered 869,931 (585,194 passenger cars, 266,499 trucks and vans, 12,181 buses and coaches and 6,057 motorcycles). In 2000 there were 12,652 road accidents which resulted in 1,499 fatalities.

Rail

In 2002 there were 2,197 km of railways on metre and 1,435 mm gauge track. Passenger-km travelled in 2002 came to 1,274m. and freight tonne-km to 2,341m. There is a tramway in Tunis (32 km).

Civil Aviation

The national carrier, Tunis Air, is 64·86% state-owned. It carried 1,922,600 passengers in 1999 (all on international flights) and flew 27·3m. km. There are six international airports. In 2001 Monastir (Habib Bourguiba) handled 3,894,000 passengers (3,885,000 on international flights) and 800 tonnes of freight. Tunis-Carthage handled 3,315,000 (3,061,000 on international flights) and 21,800 tonnes of freight. Djerba handled 2,161,000 passengers (1,945,000 on international flights) and 700 tonnes of freight.

Shipping

There are ports at Tunis, its outer port Tunis-Goulette, Sfax, Sousse and Bizerta, all of which are directly accessible to ocean-going vessels. The ports of La Skhirra and Gabès are used for the shipping of Algerian and Tunisian oil. In 2002 sea-going shipping totalled 186,000 GRT, including oil tankers 20,000

GRT. In 2001 vessels totalling 58,610,000 GRT entered ports and vessels totalling 58,595,000 GRT cleared.

Telecommunications

There were 1,651,900 telephone subscribers (168·3 per 1,000 persons) in 2002, and 300,000 PCs in use (30·6 per 1,000 persons). Tunisia had 503,900 mobile phone subscribers and 58,000 fax machines in 2002. Internet users numbered 505,500 in 2002.

Postal Services

In 2003 there were 1,221 post offices. A total of 123m. pieces of mail were processed in 2003.

SOCIAL INSTITUTIONS

Justice

There are 51 magistrates' courts, 13 courts of first instance, three courts of appeal (in Tunis, Sfax and Sousse) and the High Court in Tunis.

A Personal Status Code was promulgated on 13 Aug. 1956 and applied to Tunisians from 1 Jan. 1957. This raised the status of women, made divorce subject to a court decision, abolished polygamy and decreed a minimum marriage age.

The population in penal institutions in Dec. 1996 was 23,165 (252 per 100,000 of national population).

Education

The adult literacy rate in 2003 was 74·3% (83·4% among males and 65·3% among females). All education is free from primary schools to university. In 2002–03 there were 4,486 state primary schools with 59,245 teachers and 1,265,462 pupils; and 51,738 teachers and 1,057,233 pupils at 1,117 state secondary schools.

Higher education includes six universities, three of them being specialized by faculty, a teacher training college, a school of law, two centres of economic studies, two schools of engineering, two medical schools, a faculty of agriculture, two institutes of business administration and one school of dentistry.

In 2000–01 total expenditure on education came to 7·2% of GNP and accounted for 17·4% of total government expenditure.

Health

There were 167 hospitals and specialized institutes and centres in 2002; provision of beds was 18 per 10,000 population. In 2000 there were 7,339 doctors, 1,319 dentists, 26,409 nurses (1997) and 1,841 pharmacists.

Welfare

A system of social security was set up in 1950 (amended 1963, 1964 and 1970).

RELIGION

The constitution recognizes Islam as the state religion. In 2001 there were 9·72m. Sunni Muslims. The remainder of the population follow other religions, including Roman Catholicism.

CULTURE

World Heritage Sites

Tunisia has eight sites on the UNESCO World Heritage List: the Amphitheatre of El Jem (inscribed on the list in 1979); the Site of Carthage (1979); the Medina of Tunis (1979); Ichkeul National Park (1980); the Punic Town of Kerkuane and its Necropolis (1985); the Medina of Sousse (1988); Kairouan (1988); and Dougga/Thugga (1997).

Broadcasting

The government-owned Radiodiffusion-Télévision Tunisienne provides a national radio programme, an international service—Radio Tunisie Internationale (French and Italian)—and two regional programmes. There are Arabic and French TV networks (colour by SECAM V). Number of sets: TV (2001), 2·00m.; radio (2000), 1·51m.

Press

In 2000 there were seven daily newspapers with a total average circulation of 179,963, giving a rate of 19 per 1,000 inhabitants. Press freedom is severely limited.

Tourism

In 2002 there were 5,064,000 foreign tourists, bringing revenue of US$1·4bn.

DIPLOMATIC REPRESENTATIVES

Of Tunisia in the United Kingdom (29 Prince's Gate, London, SW7 1QG)
Ambassador: Mohamed Ghariani.

Of the United Kingdom in Tunisia (Rue du Lac Windermere, Les Berges du Lac, 1053, Tunis)
Ambassador: Alan Goulty, CMG.

Of Tunisia in the USA (1515 Massachusetts Ave., NW, Washington, D.C., 20005)
Ambassador: Nejib Hachana.

Of the USA in Tunisia (Les Berges du Lac, 1053 Tunis)
Ambassador: William J. Hudson.

Of Tunisia to the United Nations
Ambassador: Ali Hachani.

Of Tunisia to the European Union
Ambassador: Tahar Sioud.

FURTHER READING

Pazzanita, A. G., *The Maghreb.* [Bibliography] ABC-Clio, Oxford and Santa Barbara (CA), 1998

National Statistical Office: Institut National de la Statistique, 27 Rue de Liban, Tunis.
Website (French only): http://www.ins.nat.tn

TURKEY

Türkiye Cumhuriyeti
(Republic of Turkey)

Capital: Ankara
Population projection, 2010: 78·08m.
GDP per capita, 2003: (PPP$) 6,772
HDI/world rank: 0·750/94

KEY HISTORICAL EVENTS

The area of modern Turkey equates to the ancient region of Anatolia (Asia Minor). There is evidence of human habitation in Anatolia around 7500 BC. Between 1900 and 1600 BC the area came under Hittite rule, vying for power with Egypt and eventually extending into Syria. Anatolia was regularly invaded by forces from the Greek islands and was overrun by invading Persians in the 6th century BC.

Alexander the Great defeated the Persians around 330 BC. After his death there was a long civil war between the Seleucids and the Ptolemies, while the kingdoms of Galatia, Armenia, Pergamum, Cappadocia, Bithynia and Pontus all established footholds in the region. Rome gained dominance around the 2nd century BC and brought stability and prosperity. Turkey was home to some of the earliest centres of Christianity, such as Antioch (modern Antakya) and Ephesus. In AD 324 the Emperor Constantine began the construction of a new capital, Constantinople, at Byzantium. Constantinople became the centre of the Byzantine (Eastern Roman) Empire, which reached its pinnacle under Justinian in the mid-6th century.

Islamic troops attacked Constantinople in the 670s initiating centuries of warfare and rivalry between Islamic forces and Byzantium. The Great Seljuk Empire established dominance over an area that encompassed modern Turkey during the 11th century. They came under threat during the Crusades and from the Mongols but fell to the Ottomans (an alliance of Turkish warriors who emerged in the 13th century). The Ottomans, under Mehmet, seized Constantinople in 1453. Under the rule of Suleiman the Magnificent (1494–1566) the empire expanded to its fullest extent (including an area from Morocco to Persia and westwards into the Balkans) and Constantinople developed into a centre of cultural and intellectual excellence.

From the late 16th century, however, the Empire began to decline, its power weakening rapidly in the 19th century. The Kingdom of Greece broke away from Ottoman rule in 1832, with Serbs, Romanians, Armenians, Albanians, Bulgarians and Arabs demanding independence soon afterwards. Attempts by Turkey to re-define itself were further hindered in the 20th century by World War I, during which it sided with Germany. In fighting with Greece over disputed territory from 1920–22, the Turkish National Movement was led by Mustafa Kemal (Atatürk: 'Father of the Turks'), who wanted a republic based on a modern secular society. Turkey became a republic on 29 Oct. 1923. Islam ceased to be the official state religion in 1928 and women were given the franchise.

On 27 May 1960 the Turkish Army overthrew the government and party activities were suspended. A new constitution was approved in a referendum held on 9 July 1961 and general elections held the same year. On 12 Sept. 1980 the Turkish armed forces again drove the government from office. A new constitution was enforced after a national referendum on 7 Nov. 1982. In the face of mounting Islamicization of government policy, the Supreme National Security Council reaffirmed its commitment to the secularity of the state. On 6 March 1997 Prime Minister Necmettin Erbakan, leader of the pro-Islamist Welfare Party, promised to combat Muslim fundamentalism but in June he was forced to resign by a campaign led by the Army.

There are quarrels with Greece over the division of Cyprus, oil rights under the Aegean and ownership of uninhabited islands close to the Turkish coast. Kurdish rebels have for many years been active in the southeast, occupying a large part of the Turkish army. However, in Feb. 2000 the Kurdish Workers' party (PKK) formally abandoned its 15-year rebellion and adopted the democratic programme urged by its imprisoned leader, Abdullah Öçalan. The conflict has cost 40,000 lives.

TERRITORY AND POPULATION

Turkey is bounded in the west by the Aegean Sea and Greece, north by Bulgaria and the Black Sea, east by Georgia, Armenia and Iran, and south by Iraq, Syria and the Mediterranean. The area (including lakes) is 780,580 sq. km (301,382 sq. miles). At the 1990 census the population was 56,473,035. The most recent census took place in Oct. 2000, by when the population had increased to 67,844,903. The estimated population in 2005 was 73,193,000. In 2003, 66·3% of the population lived in urban areas.

The UN gives a projected population for 2010 of 78·08m.

Turkish is the official language. Kurdish and Arabic are also spoken.

Some 12m. Kurds live in Turkey. In Feb. 1991 limited use of the Kurdish language was sanctioned, and in Aug. 2002 parliament legalized Kurdish radio and television broadcasts.

Area and population of the 81 provinces at the 2000 census:

	Area in sq. km	Population		Area in sq. km	Population
Adana	12,788	1,854,270	Bilecik	4,307	194,326
Adıyaman	7,614	623,811	Bingöl	8,125	255,395
Afyon	14,230	812,416	Bitlis	6,707	388,678
Ağrı	11,376	528,744	Bolu	10,037	270,654
Aksaray	7,626	400,145	Burdur	6,887	256,803
Amasya	5,520	365,231	Bursa	10,963	2,106,687
Ankara	25,706	4,007,860	Çanakkale	9,737	464,975
Antalya	20,591	1,726,205	Çankırı	7,388	269,529
Ardahan	5,576	133,756	Çorum	12,820	597,065
Artvin	7,436	191,934	Denizli	11,868	843,122
Aydın	8,007	953,006	Diyarbakır	15,355	1,364,209
Balıkesir	14,292	1,076,347	Düzce	1,014	314,266
Bartın	2,140	184,178	Edirne	6,276	402,606
Batman	4,694	446,719	Elazığ	9,153	572,933
Bayburt	3,652	97,358	Erzincan	11,903	315,806

	Area in sq. km	Population		Area in sq. km	Population
Erzurum	25,066	942,340	Manisa	13,810	1,260,169
Eskişehir	13,652	706,009	Mardin	8,891	705,098
Gaziantep	6,207	1,293,849	Mersin	15,853	1,668,007
Giresun	6,934	524,010	Muğla	13,338	717,384
Gümüşhane	6,575	186,953	Muş	8,196	453,654
Hakkâri	7,121	235,841	Nevşehir	5,467	309,914
Hatay	5,403	1,232,910	Niğde	7,312	348,081
Iğdir	3,539	168,634	Ordu	6,001	887,765
Isparta	8,933	514,379	Osmaniye	3,320	463,196
İstanbul	5,220	10,033,478	Rize	3,920	365,938
İzmir	11,973	3,387,908	Sakarya	4,817	746,060
Kahraman-			Samsun	9,579	1,203,681
maraş	14,327	1,008,069	Şanlıurfa	18,584	1,436,956
Karabük	4,074	225,102	Siirt	5,406	264,778
Karaman	9,163	243,399	Sinop	5,862	225,574
Kars	9,442	327,056	Şırnak	7,172	354,061
Kastamonu	13,108	376,725	Sivas	28,488	752,828
Kayseri	16,917	1,049,659	Tekirdağ	6,218	626,549
Kilis	1,338	114,724	Tokat	9,958	828,027
Kırıkkale	4,365	383,508	Trabzon	4,685	979,295
Kırklareli	6,550	328,461	Tunceli	7,774	93,584
Kırşehir	6,570	253,239	Uşak	5,341	322,654
Kocaeli	3,626	1,203,335	Van	19,069	877,524
Konya	38,157	2,217,969	Yalova	674	168,593
Kütahya	11,875	656,716	Yozgat	14,123	682,919
Malatya	12,313	853,658	Zonguldak	3,481	615,599

Population of cities of over 200,000 inhabitants in 2000:

İstanbul	9,119,315	Samsun	633,118
Ankara	3,540,522	Balikesir	577,595
İzmir	2,750,273	Erzurum	565,516
Bursa	1,616,649	Eskişehir	557,028
Adana	1,400,523	Malatya	499,713
Konya	1,314,146	Trabzon	485,081
Mersin	1,021,086	Sakarya	450,146
Gaziantep	1,018,700	Van	446,976
Antalya	933,847	Sivas	419,897
Urfa	839,817	Denizli	410,776
Diyarbakır	818,396	Elazığ	366,839
Kayseri	721,211	Batman	305,475
Manisa	714,760	Kırıkkale	285,294

SOCIAL STATISTICS

Births, 2001, 1,507,000; deaths, 463,000. 2001 birth rate per 1,000 population, 21·8; death rate, 6·7. 2001 marriages, 453,213 (rate of 6·5 per 1,000 population); divorces (2000), 34,862 (rate of 0·5 per 1,000 population). Annual population growth rate, 1990–2002, 1·6%. Expectation of life, 2003, was 66·5 years for males and 71·1 for females. Infant mortality, 2001, 36 per 1,000 live births. Fertility rate, 2001, 2·4 births per woman. In 1999 the most popular age for marrying was 25–29 for males and 20–24 for females.

CLIMATE

Coastal regions have a Mediterranean climate, with mild, moist winters and hot, dry summers. The interior plateau has more extreme conditions, with low and irregular rainfall, cold and snowy winters, and hot, almost rainless summers. Ankara, Jan. 32·5°F (0·3°C), July 73°F (23°C). Annual rainfall 14·7" (367 mm). İstanbul, Jan. 41°F (5°C), July 73°F (23°C). Annual rainfall 28·9" (723 mm). İzmir, Jan. 46°F (8°C), July 81°F (27°C). Annual rainfall 28" (700 mm).

CONSTITUTION AND GOVERNMENT

On 7 Nov. 1982 a referendum established that 98% of the electorate were in favour of a new Constitution. The *President* is elected for seven-year terms. The Presidency is not an executive position, and the President may not be linked to a political party. There is a 550-member *Turkish Grand National Assembly*, elected by universal suffrage (at 18 years and over) for five-year terms by proportional representation. There is a *Constitutional Court* consisting of 15 regular and five alternating members.

National Anthem

'Korkma! Sönmez bu şafaklarda yüzen al sancak' ('Be not afraid! Our flag will never fade'); words by Mehmed Akif Ersoy, tune by Zeki Üngör.

GOVERNMENT CHRONOLOGY

(AKP = Justice and Development Party; ANAP = Motherland Party; AP = Justice Party; CGP = Republican Reliance Party; CHP = Republican People's Party; DP = Democrat Party; DSP = Democratic Left Party; DYP = True Path Party; RP = Welfare Party; n/p = non-partisan)

Heads of State since 1938.

Presidents of the Republic

1938–50	CHP	Mustafa İsmet İnönü
1950–60	DP	Mahmut Celal Bayar

Chairman of the Committee of National Unity (MBK) and Head of State

1950–61	military	Cemal Gürsel

Presidents of the Republic

1961–66	n/p (ex-military)	Cemal Gürsel
1966–73	n/p (ex-military)	Cevdet Sunay
1973–80	n/p (ex-military)	Fahri Korutürk

Chairman of the National Security Council (MGK) and Head of State

1980–82	military	Kenan Evren

Presidents of the Republic

1982–89	n/p (ex-military)	Kenan Evren
1989–93	ANAP	Turgut Özal
1993–2000	DYP	Süleyman Demirel
2000–	n/p	Ahmet Necdet Sezer

Prime Ministers since 1942.

1921–22	military	Mustafa Fevzı Çakmak
1922–23	n/p	Hüseyin Rauf Bey
1923–23	CHP	Ali Fehti Okyar
1923–24	CHP	Mustafa İsmet İnönü
1924–25	CHP	Ali Fethi Okyar
1925–37	CHP	Mustafa İsmet İnönü
1937–39	CHP	Mahmut Celal Bayar
1939–42	CHP	Refik İbrahım Saydam
1942–46	CHP	Mehmet Şükrü Saraçoğlu
1946–47	CHP	Mehmet Recep Peker
1947–49	CHP	Hasan Saka
1949–50	CHP	Mehmet Şemsettin Günaltay
1950–60	DP	Adnan Menderes
1960–61	military	Cemal Gürsel
1961–65	CHP	Mustafa İsmet İnönü
1965	n/p	Suat Hayri Ürgüplü
1965–71	AP	Süleyman Demirel
1971–72	n/p	İsmaıl Nıhat Erım
1972–73	CGP	Ferit Melen
1973–74	n/p	Mehmet Naim Talu
1974–74	CHP	Mustafa Bülent Ecevıt
1975–77	AP	Süleyman Demirel
1977–77	CHP	Mustafa Bülent Ecevıt
1977–78	AP	Süleyman Demirel
1978–79	CHP	Mustafa Bülent Ecevıt
1979–80	AP	Süleyman Demirel
1980–83	n/p	Saim Bülent Ulusu
1983–89	ANAP	Turgut Özal
1989–91	ANAP	Yıldırım Akbulut
1991	ANAP	Ahmet Mesut Yılmaz
1991–93	DYP	Süleyman Demirel
1993–96	DYP	Tansu Çıller
1996	ANAP	Ahmet Mesut Yılmaz
1996–97	RP	Necmettin Erbakan
1997–99	ANAP	Ahmet Mesut Yılmaz

1999–2002	DSP	Mustafa Bülent Ecevıt
2002–03	AKP	Abdullah Gül
2003–	AKP	Recep Tayyip Erdoğan

RECENT ELECTIONS

Parliamentary elections were held on 3 Nov. 2002. The Justice and Development Party (AKP)—former Islamists—won 363 of the 550 seats with 34·3% of votes cast, against 178 seats and 19·4% for the Republican People's Party (CHP). Remaining seats went to independents. Parties which failed to secure the 10% of votes needed to gain parliamentary representation included the True Path Party (DYP) with 9·6%; the Nationalist Action Party (MHP), 8·3%; the Youth Party (GP), 7·2%; the Democratic People's Party (DEHAP), 6·2%; the Motherland Party (ANAP), 5·1%; the Saadet Party (SP), 2·5%; the Democratic Left Party (DSP) of outgoing Prime Minister Bülent Ecevit, 1·2%; the Grand Unity Party (BBP), 1·1%; and the New Turkey Party (YTP), 1·0%. Turnout was 78·9%. An absolute majority was achieved in a Turkish parliamentary election for the first time in 15 years.

Voting for president took place on 1 May 2000 in parliament. Ahmet Necdet Sezer failed to obtain the required two-thirds majority in the first two rounds. However, in the third round only a simple majority is required, which he received gaining 330 of the 550 available votes.

CURRENT ADMINISTRATION

President: Ahmet Necdet Sezer; b. 1941 (sworn in 16 May 2000).

In March 2006 the government comprised:

Prime Minister: Recep Tayyip Erdoğan; b. 1954 (AKP; sworn in 14 March 2003).

Deputy Prime Ministers: Abdullah Gül (also *Foreign Minister*); Abdüllatif Şener (also *Minister of State*); Mehmet Ali Şahin (also *Minister of State*).

Minister of Defence: Vecdi Gönül. *Development and Public Works:* Faruk Nafiz Özak. *Interior:* Abdülkadir Aksu. *Justice:* Cemil Çiçek. *Finance:* Kemal Unakıtan. *Education:* Hüseyin Çelik. *Health:* Recep Akdağ. *Transport:* Binalı Yıldırım. *Agriculture:* Mehmet Mehdi Eker. *Labour:* Murat Başesgioğlu. *Trade and Industry:* Ali Coşkun. *Energy:* Hilmi Güler. *Culture and Tourism:* Atilla Koç. *Environment and Forestry:* Osman Pepe. *Ministers of State:* Nimet Çubukçu; Mehmet Aydın; Beşir Atalay; Ali Babacan; Kürşad Tüzmen.

The *Speaker* is Bülent Arınç.

Office of the Prime Minister (Turkish only):
http://www.basbakanlik.gov.tr

CURRENT LEADERS

Ahmet Necdet Sezer

Position
President

Introduction
In April 2000 the Turkish Grand National Assembly rejected a constitutional amendment allowing Süleyman Demirel a second term of office as president. Sezer, at the time the president of the Constitutional Court, was sworn in as the tenth president of the republic on 16 May 2000. A staunch secularist and supporter of freedom of expression, he is the first president in modern Turkish history to have been neither an active politician nor a military commander.

Early Life
Ahmet Necdet Sezer was born in Afyon on 13 Sept. 1941. He attended Afyon High School and read law at the University of Ankara. After completion of military service he returned to his legal career and became a supervisory judge at the court

of appeals in Ankara. In 1978 he received a masters degree in civil law. Five years later he was elected to the High Court. His political influence increased in 1988 when President Kenan Evren appointed him to the Constitutional Court. Sezer became Chief Justice of the Constitutional Court in Jan. 1998. He won the presidential election after a third ballot in May 2000.

Career in Office
Despite winning Bülent Ecevit's backing for the presidency, Sezer came into conflict with the prime minister after he vetoed two bills, one allowing for the dismissal of public employees deemed to have been subversive and the second privatizing several state-owned banks. His first official foreign engagement came on 23 June 2000 when he made a controversial visit to the Turkish Republic of Northern Cyprus (recognized only by Turkey), underlining Turkey's support for the Turkish Cypriots. During his first few months in office, Sezer also made clear his commitment to maintaining the country's secular status and ensuring Turkish entry to the EU. However, the failure in March 2003 of the leaders of the Greek and Turkish sectors of Cyprus to agree on UN proposals for the island's reunification put Turkey's own ambitions to join the EU at risk, since it would not be able to recognize one of the member states (Greek Cyprus).

Turkey underwent a constitutional crisis in 2002 when the Justice and Development Party (AKP) won the Nov. general elections but its leader, Recep Tayyip Erdoğan, was ineligible for a parliamentary seat (and therefore the premiership) because of a conviction received under a defunct religious law. The AKP's deputy leader, Abdullah Gül, was named prime minister. In Dec. 2002, after pressure to call a referendum which he was likely to lose, Sezer agreed to constitutional changes which would allow Erdoğan to stand for a parliamentary seat and so become eligible for the premiership. Erdoğan returned to parliament in a by-election in March 2003 and was subsequently appointed prime minister.

In March 2003 Turkey authorized limited assistance to the USA during the war with Iraq and was rewarded with substantial aid. However, Turkey's deployment of troops in Kurdish-held northern Iraq to block any attempts to establish a Kurdish separatist state caused international unease. In April 2005 Sezer made an official visit to Syria, despite objections from the US government regarding the presence of Syrian troops in Lebanon. He stated that the purpose of the visit was to strengthen bilateral ties and contribute to peace and stability in the region.

In mid-2005 he came into conflict with parliament by blocking amendments to a new penal code which eased restrictions on Islamic teaching. His presidential veto was subsequently overturned.

Reçep Tayyip Erdoğan

Position:
Prime Minister

Introduction
Recep Tayyip Erdoğan became prime minister in March 2003. He led the Justice and Development Party (AKP) to victory at the general elections of Nov. 2002 but, because of a previous criminal conviction, was banned from standing for a parliamentary seat thus making him ineligible for the premiership. A constitutional amendment allowed him to stand for election in early 2003 and he subsequently replaced his party deputy, Abdullah Gül, as prime minister. For many years a prominent Islamist spokesman, Erdoğan has remoulded himself as a pro-European moderate conservative, although he continues to cause unease among many of Turkey's secularists. He has identified Turkey's admission to the European Union as his government's top priority and introduced reforms that paved the way for the opening of membership talks from Oct. 2005.

Early Life

Erdoğan was born in 1954 in the Black Sea coastal city of Rize and his family later moved to İstanbul. He used income from his work as a streetseller to attend Koranic college before graduating in economics from Marmara University in İstanbul. While a student, Erdoğan became active in Islamist politics and was introduced to Necmettin Erbakan, who would become Turkey's first Islamist premier.

After a career as a professional soccer player, Erdoğan took a job with İstanbul's transport division but was forced to leave in 1980 for refusing to shave off his moustache. Increasingly prominent within municipal politics, he was made mayor of İstanbul in 1994 and won a reputation for running an effective and transparent administration free of corruption.

Erdoğan was a member of the pro-Islamist Welfare Party, until it was outlawed in 1998 for contravening Turkey's secularist constitution. In the same year he was imprisoned for inciting racial hatred when he read a pro-Islamist poem at a political rally. He served four months of a ten-month sentence. Following the banning of the Virtue Party (the successor party to Welfare) in June 2001, Erdoğan established the AKP, espousing pro-Western and democratic policies. Amid widespread discontent with the administration of incumbent Bülent Ecevit, the AKP won outright victory at the general elections of Nov. 2002. Erdoğan remained as the party's figurehead while Abdullah Gül, his deputy and a former foreign minister, was named prime minister.

President Ahmet Necdet Sezer approved constitutional changes in Dec. 2002, as a result of which Erdoğan was able to successfully contest a by-election in Feb. 2003. Gül stood down to be replaced by Erdoğan the following month.

Career in Office

Despite the AKP's Islamic roots, Erdoğan's long-term goal is to prove that Turkey can operate as both a Muslim and democratic state within Europe. He has voiced his commitment to democratization, including liberalizing laws on the freedom of expression and human rights that were partly responsible for Turkey's omission from the EU expansion plans advanced in 2002. When Gül took office, the party confirmed its support for further privatization.

The early weeks of Erdoğan's tenure were dominated by the US-led invasion of neighbouring Iraq. With Turkish popular opinion against the USA, the government refused to allow the deployment of tens of thousands of US troops on its territory, endangering US$30bn. worth of aid and loans from the USA as well as a US$16bn. IMF loan. The decision followed shortly after NATO's defence planning committee had authorized US proposals for military aid to Turkey, which included surveillance planes, anti-missile systems and chemical and biological protection units.

Negotiations between the USA and Turkey continued after US-led troops attacked Iraq in March 2003. The Turkish parliament agreed to the use of its airspace by the US air force but still would not allow troops on the ground. Turkey's deployment of troops in Kurdish-held northern Iraq to block any attempts to establish a Kurdish separatist state caused international concern. However, the USA agreed aid for Turkey in excess of US$1bn. in its emergency wartime spending plans and Turkey permitted the USA to transport food, fuel and medical provisions into Iraq over the Turkish border.

Turkey's wish for early entry into the EU was undermined by the failure in March 2003 of the leaders of the Greek and Turkish sectors of Cyprus to agree on UN proposals for the island's reunification. A revised UN reunification plan was put to both sides in twin referenda in April 2004. which was endorsed by Turkish Cypriots, but rejected by Greek Cypriots. Because both sides had to approve the proposals, the island remained divided as it joined the EU the following month. To fulfil the political criteria for EU membership, Erdoğan had pushed through parliament a series of reform packages in 2003 to bring Turkey in line with EU legislation. Human rights were addressed with guarantees of freedom of speech for the Kurdish minority, and the influence of the military in the political system—seen as unacceptable by EU countries—was curbed. In 2004 a protocol abolishing the death penalty was signed and penal reforms introduced tougher measures to prevent torture and violence against women (although a controversial proposal to criminalize adultery was dropped). Once Erdoğan's government had introduced the necessary legislative and constitutional reforms, and made a deal to recognize Cyprus as an EU member, the European Council agreed in Dec. 2004 to open accession negotiations with Turkey in Oct. 2005. In May 2005 the parliament approved amendments to the penal code after complaints that the previous version was too restrictive of media freedom. On 3 Oct. 2005 EU accession talks began.

DEFENCE

The *National Security Council*, chaired by the Prime Minister and comprising military leaders and the ministers of defence and the economy, also functions as a *de facto* constitutional watchdog. Reforms passed in July 2003 in preparation for EU membership aimed to reduce the influence of the military in the political system. In Oct. 2003 the Turkish parliament voted to send 10,000 troops to Iraq, which would have made it the third largest force in the country after the USA and the UK, but the Iraqi Governing Council rejected the plan.

Conscription is 18 months.

In 2003 defence expenditure totalled US$11,649m., up from US$3,489m. in 1985. Spending per capita in 2003 was US$165, up from US$69 per capita in 1985. The 2003 expenditure represented 4·9% of GDP.

Army

Strength (2002) 402,000 (325,000 conscripts) with a potential reserve of 258,700. There is also a paramilitary gendarmerie-cum-national guard of 150,000. In addition 36,000 Turkish troops are stationed in Northern Cyprus.

Navy

The fleet includes 13 diesel submarines and 19 frigates. The main naval base is at Gölcük in the Gulf of İzmit. There are five others, at Aksaz-Karaağaç, Eregli, İskenderun, İzmir and Mersin. There are three naval shipyards: Gölcük, İzmir and Taşkizak.

The naval air component operates 16 armed helicopters. There is a Marine Regiment some 3,100-strong.

Personnel in 2002 totalled 52,750 (34,500 conscripts) including marines.

Air Force

The Air Force is organized as two tactical air forces, with headquarters at Eskisehir and Diyarbakır. There were 485 combat aircraft in operation in 2002 including F-5A/Bs, F-4E Phantoms and F-16C/Ds.

Personnel strength (2002), 60,100 (31,500 conscripts).

INTERNATIONAL RELATIONS

In Oct. 1998 Turkish troops mobilized on the border with Syria in protest against Syrian support for Kurdish rebels operating from its territory.

Following the terror attacks on New York and Washington of 11 Sept. 2001 Turkey expressed support for the USA, later becoming the first Muslim country to send soldiers to Afghanistan, to help train anti-Taliban fighters and to administer aid.

Turkey is a member of the UN, WTO, BIS, OECD, NATO, Council of Europe, OSCE, BSEC, Asian Development Bank, ECO, OIC, Islamic Development Bank, IOM and an Associate Member of the WEU, and has applied to join the EU. At the European Union's Helsinki Summit in Dec. 1999 Turkey was awarded candidate status. Talks on membership began in Oct. 2005 but Turkey is unlikely to join the EU before 2015 at the earliest.

ECONOMY

Agriculture accounted for 13·4% of GDP in 2002, industry 29·1% and services 57·5%.

Overview

Long-term macroeconomic mismanagement has made the country vulnerable to financial crises. In recent years strong growth has been interrupted by sharp recessions in 1994, 1999 and 2001. In 2000 Turkey committed to a programme of wide-ranging structural reforms, strong fiscal adjustment and a pre-announced exchange rate crawl. However, the financial and currency crisis in 2001 caused the collapse of the three-year exchange rate-based stabilization programme and brought the country to the brink of debt default. A strengthened programme was introduced in May 2001 with additional IMF support. Key structural reforms emphasized public sector reform, liberalizing markets and building a strong banking sector. The crisis led to Turkey's central bank becoming independent. Privatization and liberalization have progressed, notably in the telecommunications sector, but infrastructure, utilities, many basic industries, some food-processing industries and just under a third of the banking sector are still state-owned. However, IMF and World Bank pressure is helping push through privatization and liberalization initiatives in most of these areas.

Tight fiscal policies, IMF-inspired reforms and the independence of the central bank have brought Turkey improved macroeconomic health. Debt ratios have been reduced significantly, interest rates slashed and inflation brought under control in spite of high crude oil prices. In 2004 GDP growth was nearly 9% and inflation was at its lowest level in more than a quarter of a century. In 2005 inflation fell slightly further and growth, though down significantly from 2004 levels, remained robust. Over the course of the year the central bank repeatedly cut interest rates without causing inflationary pressures. External debt has also been reduced, from 77·8% in 2001 to 53·4% in 2004 and further still in 2005. Much of the public revenues have been absorbed by debt repayment over the years but budget deficits have also been reduced significantly, falling to below 4% in 2005 from over 14% in 2002. Confidence in Turkey's economic prospects was reflected in the record performance of its stock market in 2004 and 2005.

Agriculture's share of GDP declined steadily from the 1960s to the 1980s before stabilizing at around 13% in recent years, a share significantly higher than the norm for developed countries. Agriculture still accounts for roughly a third of total employment. In Jan. 1996 a customs union was established with the EU. Turkey's largest industrial sector, textiles and clothing, accounts for close to a third of industrial employment but is expected to shrink in the face of stiff Asian competition following the end of the global textile quota system in 2005. However, Turkey's economy displays dynamism as its automotive, auto parts and electronics industries have grown. Significant amounts of foreign direct investment in vehicle manufacturing has raised productivity and helped the industry become Turkey's third biggest after food and textiles and its second largest export sector, after textiles. The country also has one of the most successful tourism sectors in the region.

Currency

The unit of currency is the *new Turkish lira* (YTL) of 100 *kuruş*. It was introduced on 1 Jan. 2005, replacing the Turkish lira (TRL) at 1 new Turkish lira = 1m. Turkish lira. Gold reserves were 3·73m. troy oz in June 2002 and foreign exchange reserves US$22,238m. Inflation rates (based on OECD statistics):

1995	1996	1997	1998	1999	2000	2001	2002	2003	2004
89·1%	80·4%	85·7%	84·6%	64·9%	54·9%	54·4%	45·0%	25·3%	10·6%

The inflation rate in 2005 according to the Turkish Statistical Institute was 8·2%. Total money supply in Dec. 2001 was TRL5,188,070bn.

Budget

The fiscal year is the calendar year. Revenue and expenditure in TRL1trn.:

	1999	2000	2001	2002
Revenue	19,798·3	35,425·8	51,090·0	73,569·0
Expenditure	29,467·3	49,134·2	79,856·0	111,512·0

Tax revenues were TRL66,105trn. in 2002. VAT is 18%, with reduced rates of 8% and 1%.

Performance

Real GDP growth rates (based on OECD statistics):

1995	1996	1997	1998	1999	2000	2001	2002	2003	2004
7·2%	7·0%	7·5%	3·1%	−4·7%	7·4%	−7·5%	7·9%	5·8%	8·9%

When the economy shrank by 7·5% in 2001 it represented Turkey's worst economic performance since the Second World War. Total GDP was US$302·0bn. in 2004.

Banking and Finance

The Central Bank (Merkez Bankası; *Governor*, Süreyya Serdengeçti) is the bank of issue. In 2003 there were 36 commercial banks (three state-owned, two under the Deposit Insurance Fund, 18 private, 13 foreign), and 14 development and investment banks. The Central Bank's assets were US$51·66bn. in 2003. The assets and liabilities of deposit money banks were US$25·8bn. Turkey's two state-owned banks, Ziraat Bankası (the Agricultural Bank, with a public mission to lend to farmers) and Halk Bankası (with a public mission to lend to small and medium sized enterprises), together accounted for 27% of total assets in the Turkish banking sector in Dec. 2002. Ziraat Bankası is Turkey's largest bank, with 18·1% of total assets as of March 2003. A comprehensive restructuring plan for Ziraat has been developed with the assistance of international consultants and the IMF in preparation for privatization. Ziraat Bankası and Halk Bankası have been put under joint professional management and privatization plans are being developed.

Foreign direct investment in 2003 was US$575m. In Sept. 2000 a Banking Regulation and Supervision Board was established to serve as an independent banking regulator. In Dec. 2000 the IMF gave Turkey an emergency loan of US$7·5bn. as the country experienced a financial crisis after ten banks were placed in receivership. The economic crisis continued as the *lira* was floated on the international market and lost 30% of its value against the US dollar in the space of 12 hours in Feb. 2001. Within a week the lira had been devalued by approximately 40%. In April 2001 Turkey secured a further US$10bn. loan from the IMF and the World Bank. This was followed in Feb. 2002 with a three-year US$16bn. loan from the IMF, taking total loans paid or pledged to USS$31bn.

There is a stock exchange in İstanbul (ISE).

ENERGY AND NATURAL RESOURCES

Environment

In 2002 Turkey's carbon dioxide emissions from the consumption and flaring of fossil fuels were the equivalent of 2·7 tonnes per capita.

Electricity

In 2003 installed capacity was 31·28m. kW (10·6m. kW hydro-electric); gross production in 2002 was 129·4bn. kWh and consumption per capita 1,904 kWh.

Oil and Gas

Crude oil production (2002) was 2,541,000 tonnes. Reserves in 2002 were 296m. bbls. Refinery distillation output in 2000 amounted to 23·7m. tonnes. In 2000, 21,583,000 tonnes of crude petroleum were imported. Natural gas output was 370m. cu. metres in 2002.

Accords for the construction of an oil pipeline from Azerbaijan through Georgia to the Mediterranean port of Ceyhan in southern Turkey were signed in Nov. 1999. Work on the pipeline began in Sept. 2002 and it was officially opened in May 2005.

Minerals

Turkey is rich in minerals, and is a major producer of chrome.

Production of principal minerals (in 1,000 tonnes) in 2002 was: lignite, 49,627; iron, 3,433; coal, 3,313; magnesite, 3,044; copper (gross weight), 2,940; boron, 2,214; salt, 2,197; chrome, 327.

Agriculture

In 2002 there were 6,745,000 households engaged in farming, of which 148,190 were engaged purely in animal farming. Holdings are increasingly fragmented by the custom of dividing land equally amongst sons. Agriculture accounts for 46% of the workforce but only 13·4% of GDP. In 2001 Turkey had 23·81m. ha. of arable land and 2·55m. ha. of permanent crops. Approximately 4·5m. ha. were irrigated in 2001. Vineyards, orchards and olive groves occupied 2,530,000 ha. in 1998.

Production (2000, in 1,000 tonnes) of principal crops: sugarbeets, 16,854; wheat, 16,500; barley, 6,800; tomatoes, 6,800; melons and watermelons, 5,800; potatoes, 5,475; grapes, 3,400; apples, 2,500; maize, 2,500; onions, 2,300; seed cotton, 2,151; cucumbers and gherkins, 1,550; chillies and green peppers, 1,400; cottonseed, 1,360; oranges, 1,100; aubergines, 850; tree nuts, 831; sunflower seeds, 800; cotton lint, 791; cabbages, 732; olives, 600; hazelnuts, 550; lemons and limes, 520; apricots, 500; chick-peas, 500; tangerines and mandarins, 500. Turkey is the largest producer of apricots and hazelnuts.

Livestock, 2000 (in 1,000): sheep, 29,435; cattle, 11,031; goats, 8,057; asses, 603; horses, 330; buffaloes, 176; mules, 133; chickens, 27,000. Livestock products, 2000 (in 1,000 tonnes): milk, 9,876; meat, 1,386; eggs, 660; cheese, 131; honey, 71.

Forestry

There were 20·7m. ha. of forests in 2000. Timber production was 15·81m. cu. metres in 2003.

Fisheries

The catch in 2003 totalled 507,772 tonnes (463,074 tonnes from marine waters). Aquaculture production, 1995, 21,607 tonnes (mainly carp and trout).

INDUSTRY

Production in 2001 (in 1,000 tonnes unless otherwise stated): cement, 30,125; crude steel (2002), 16,500; residual fuel oil (2002), 7,970; distillate fuel oil (2002), 7,720; petrol (2002), 3,718; coke (1999), 2,802; sugar (2002), 2,128; paper and paperboard (2002), 1,643; iron and steel bars (1997), 1,193; nitrogenous fertilizers, 748; cotton yarn, 557; ethylene, 400; polyethylene, 263; sulphuric acid, 234; olive oil (2002), 206; pig iron, 158; PVC, 147; cotton woven fabrics (2000), 567m. sq. metres; woollen woven fabrics (2000), 91m. sq. metres; carpets, 12,974,000 sq. metres; TV sets, 8,025,000 units; refrigerators, 2,245,000 units; motor cars, 277,000 units; lorries, 30,112 assembled units; tractors, 15,020 units; cigarettes, 77·2bn. units.

Labour

In 2001 there were 20,367,000 people in employment (5,463,000 women): 7,184,000 were engaged in agriculture, hunting and forestry, 3,548,000 in manufacturing, 2,883,000 in wholesale and retail trade/repair of motor vehicles, motorcycles and personal and household goods and 1,118,000 in public administration and defence/compulsory social security. In 2002 the unemployment rate stood at 9·9%. In 1996, 93% of male workers and 80% of female workers worked more than 40 hours a week. The proportion of adults between the ages of 15 and 64 in employment has gradually fallen, from 69% in 1975 to only 50% in 1997. Although the population of working age has been growing at an average of 3% a year, total employment has grown at only 1·5% a year. The monthly minimum wage has been YTL489 since 1 Jan. 2005.

Trade Unions

There are four national confederations (including Türk-İş and Disk) and six federations. There are 35 unions affiliated to Türk-İş and 17 employers' federations affiliated to Disk, whose activities were banned on 12 Sept. 1980. In 2001 labour unions totalled 104 and employers' unions 49. Some 2·75m. workers belonged to unions in 2003. Membership is forbidden to civil servants (including schoolteachers). There were 52 strikes in 2000 involving 18,705 workers, with 368,475 working days lost.

INTERNATIONAL TRADE

Total foreign debt in June 2002 was US$125,700m. A customs union with the EU came into force on 1 Jan. 1996.

Imports and Exports

Trade in US$1m.:

	1998	1999	2000	2001	2002
Imports f.o.b.	45,440	39,768	54,041	41,399	51,203
Exports f.o.b.	31,220	29,325	31,664	31,334	35,761

Chief imports (2002) in US$1m.: machinery and automotive industry products, 15,539; minerals and oil, 9,026; chemicals, 7,873; food and agricultural raw materials, 3,981; iron and steel, 2,162. Chief exports: machinery and automotive industry products, 8,587; ready-made garments, 8,057; textile products, 4,244; food products, 3,627; iron and steel, 1,824.

The main import suppliers in 2002 (in US$1m.) were: Germany, 6,967; Italy, 4,102; Russia, 3,863; USA, 3,050; France, 3,007; UK, 2,416; Japan, 1,445. Main export markets: Germany, 5,811; USA, 3,229; UK, 2,987; Italy, 2,237; France, 2,108; Russia, 1,168. The EU accounts for 46·7% of imports and 54·6% of exports.

COMMUNICATIONS

Roads

In 2002 there were 354,421 km of roads, including 1,851 km of motorway. In 2002 the total number of road vehicles was 7,283,250 (4,600,140 cars, 1,274,406 trucks and vans, 361,797 buses and coaches and 1,046,907 motorcycles and mopeds). There were 2,954 fatalities from road accidents in 2001.

Rail

Total length of railway lines in 2000 was 8,671 km (1,435 mm gauge), of which 1,752 km were electrified. Passenger-km travelled in 2000 came to 5·81bn. and freight tonne-km to 9·73bn. There are metro systems operating in Ankara, Bursa, İstanbul and İzmir.

Civil Aviation

There are international airports at İstanbul (Atatürk), Dalaman (Muğla), Ankara (Esenboga), İzmir (Adnan Menderes), Adana and Antalya. The national carrier is Turkish Airlines, which is 75·2% state-owned. In 2000 it flew 144·1m. km and carried 11,951,493 passengers (5,514,007 on international flights). In 2001 İstanbul handled 12,601,431 passengers (8,827,732 on international flights) and 161,359 tonnes of freight. Antalya was the second busiest airport for passenger traffic, with 9,170,469 passengers (8,638,634 on international flights) and Ankara third with 3,159,315 passengers (2,107,013 on domestic flights).

Shipping

In 2000 the merchant shipping fleet consisted of 1,153 vessels totalling 5,833,000 GRT, including oil tankers 625,000 GRT. The main ports are: İskenderun, İstanbul, İzmir, Mersin, Samsun and Trabzon.

In 2001 vessels totalling 125,997,000 GRT entered ports and vessels totalling 96,867,000 GRT cleared.

Telecommunications

In 2002 telephone subscribers numbered 42,289,200 (628·6 for every 1,000 persons) and there were 3·0m. PCs in use (44·6 per 1,000 persons). In 2002 there were 151,000 fax machines. Turkey had 4·9m. Internet users in 2002 and 23,374,400 mobile phone subscribers. In Nov. 2005 the government sold a 55% stake in Türk Telecom to a consortium led by Saudi Arabia's Oger Telecom and Telecom Italia.

Postal Services

In 2003 there were 4,421 post offices. A total of 990m. pieces of mail were processed in 2003.

SOCIAL INSTITUTIONS

Justice

The unified legal system consists of: (1) justices of the peace (single judges with limited but summary penal and civil jurisdiction); (2) courts of first instance (single judges, dealing with cases outside the jurisdiction of (3) and (4)); (3) central criminal courts (a president and two judges, dealing with cases where the crime is punishable by imprisonment over five years); (4) commercial courts (three judges); (5) state security courts, to prosecute offences against the integrity of the state (a president and two judges).

The civil and military High Courts of Appeal sit at Ankara. The Council of State is the highest administrative tribunal; it consists of five chambers. Its 31 judges are nominated from among high-ranking personalities in politics, economy, law, the army, etc. The Military Administrative Court deals with the judicial control of administrative acts and deeds concerning military personnel. The Court of Jurisdictional Disputes is empowered to resolve disputes between civil, administrative and military courts. The Supreme Council of Judges and Public Prosecutors appoints judges and prosecutors to the profession and has disciplinary powers.

The Civil Code and the Code of Obligations have been adapted from the corresponding Swiss codes. The Penal Code is largely based upon the Italian Penal Code, and the Code of Civil Procedure closely resembles that of the Canton of Neuchâtel. The Commercial Code is based on the German.

The population in penal institutions in Sept. 2003 was 64,051 (92 per 100,000 of national population).

The death penalty, not used since 1984, was abolished in peacetime in Aug. 2002. The government signed a European Convention protocol abolishing the death penalty entirely in Jan. 2004.

Education

Adult literacy in 2003 was 88·3% (male, 95·7%; female, 81·1%). The Basic Education Law of 1997 extended the duration of compulsory schooling from five to eight years. Primary education is compulsory and co-educational from the age of six to 14 and, in state schools, free. There are plans to raise the duration of compulsory schooling to 12 years. Religious instruction (Sunni Muslim) in state schools is now compulsory. In Aug. 2002 parliament legalized education in Kurdish. In 1991 there were 5,197 religious secondary schools with 0·29m. pupils up to 14 years.

Statistics for 2001–02	Number	Teachers	Students
Pre-school institutions	10,554	14,520	256,392
Primary schools	34,993	375,511	10,310,844
High schools	2,637	72,609	1,490,376
Vocational and technical high schools	3,428	66,176	821,893

In 2003 there were 76 universities. In 2002–03 a total of 1,894,000 students enrolled at 1,379 establishments of higher education (including the universities); teaching staff numbered 74,134. In 2001, 41,867 students were studying abroad.

In 2000–01 total expenditure on education came to 3·4% of GNP. Only 18% of Turkey's workforce has completed secondary education and only 8% has higher education qualifications.

Health

In 2002 there were 95,190 physicians, 17,108 dentists, 79,059 nurses, 22,322 pharmacists and 41,513 midwives. There were 1,172 hospitals with 180,797 beds in 2003 and 114 health centres. In 1998, 39% of the population aged 15 and over smoked—a rate only exceeded in Russia and the Fiji Islands.

Welfare

In 2000, 1,349,151 beneficiaries received TRL2,273,278,239m. from the Government Employees Retirement Fund. Of these, 820,167 persons were retired and 376,131 were widows, widowers or orphans of retired persons. There were 3,339,327 beneficiaries from the Social Insurance Institution in 2000 (3,216,445 through disability, old age and death insurance).

RELIGION

Islam ceased to be the official religion in 1928. The Constitution guarantees freedom of religion but forbids its political exploitation or any impairment of the secular character of the republic.

In 2001 there were 64·36m. Muslims, two-thirds Sunni and one-third Shia (Alevis). The Greek Orthodox, Gregorian Armenian, Armenian Apostolic and Roman Catholic Churches are represented in İstanbul, and there are small Uniate, Protestant and Jewish communities.

CULTURE

World Heritage Sites

UNESCO world heritage sites under Turkish jurisdiction (with year entered on list) are: Historic Areas of İstanbul (1985), including the ancient Hippodrome of Constantine, the 6th-century Hagia Sophia and the 16th-century Suleymaniye Mosque; Göreme National Park and the Rock Sites of Cappadocia (1985); Great Mosque and Hospital of Divriği (1985), founded in the early 13th century; Hattusha (1986), the former capital of the Hittite Empire; Nemrut Dag (1987), including the 1st century BC mausoleum of Antiochus I; Xanthos-Letoon (1988), the capital of Lycia; Hierapolis-Pamukkale (1988), including mineral forests, petrified waterfalls and the ruins of ancient baths, temples and other Greek monuments; City of Safranbolu (1994), a caravan station from the 13th century; Archaeological Site of Troy (1998).

Broadcasting

Broadcasting is regulated by the nine-member Radio and Television Supreme Council. The government monopoly of broadcasting was abolished in 1994 and in 2002 there were 36 national, 108 regional and 1043 local radio stations; and 15 national, 16 regional and 229 local TV stations (colour by PAL). The Turkish Radio Television Corporation (TRT) broadcasts tourist radio programmes and a foreign service, Voice of Turkey. Number of receivers in use: TV (2001), 21·2m.; radio (2000), 38·6m.

Cinema

In 2002 there were 951 cinema screens; total admissions in 2002 were 23·6m.

Press

In 2002 there were 26 daily newspapers with a combined average daily circulation of 3·5m. In 2002, 3,450 periodicals were published. The most widely read newspapers are *Hürriyet* and *Sabah*, with average daily circulations of 640,000 and 470,000 respectively. In 1999, 2,920 book titles were published.

Tourism

In 2002 there were 13,247,000 foreign visitors. Revenue totalled US$9·01bn. in 2002. Tourism accounts for 4·9% of the country's GDP.

DIPLOMATIC REPRESENTATIVES

Of Turkey in the United Kingdom (43 Belgrave Sq., London, SW1X 8PA)
Ambassador: Akin Alptuna.

Of the United Kingdom in Turkey (Sehit Ersan Caddesi 46/A, Cankaya, Ankara)
Ambassador: Sir Peter Westmacott, KCMG, LVO.

Of Turkey in the USA (2525 Massachusetts Ave., NW, Washington, D.C., 20008)
Ambassador: Nabi Şensoy.

Of the USA in Turkey (110 Atatürk Blvd, Ankara)
Ambassador: Ross Wilson.

Of Turkey to the United Nations
Ambassador: Baki İlkin.

Of Turkey to the European Union
Ambassador: Oğuz Demiralp.

FURTHER READING

State Institute of Statistics. *Türkiye İstatistik Yilliği/Statistical Yearbook of Turkey.—Diş Ticaret İstatistikleri/Foreign Trade Statistics* (Annual).—*Aylik İstatistik Bülten* (Monthly).

Abramowitz, Morton, (ed.) *Turkey's Transformation and American Policy.* Century Foundation, New York, 2000

Ahmad, F., *The Making of Modern Turkey.* London, 1993

Barkey, Henri J. and Fuller, Graham E., *Turkey's Kurdish Question.* Rowman and Littlefield, Lanham (MD), 1999

Goodwin, Jason, *Lords of the Horizons: a History of the Ottoman Empire.* Henry Holt, New York, USA, 1999

Howe, Marvin, *Turkey Today: A Nation Divided over Islam's Revival.* Westview, Oxford, 2000

İnalcık, H., Faroqhi, S., McGowan, B., Quataert, D. and Pamuk, Ş., *An Economic and Social History of the Ottoman Empire.* Cambridge Univ. Press, 1994

Kedourie, S., *Turkey: Identity, Democracy, Politics.* London, 1996

Mango, Andrew, *Ataturk.* John Murray, London and Overlook, New York, 1999

McDowall, David, *A Modern History of the Kurds.* I. B. Tauris, London, 1996

Pettifer, J., *The Turkish Labyrinth: Atatürk and the New Islam.* London, 1997

Pope, N. and Pope, H., *Turkey Unveiled: Atatürk and After.* London, 1997

Zürcher, E. J., *Turkey: a Modern History.* London and New York, 1993 (NY, 1994)

National Statistical Office: State Institute of Statistics Prime Ministry, Necatibey Caddesi no. 114, 06100 Ankara.
Website: http://www.die.gov.tr/ENGLISH/index.html

TURKMENISTAN

KAZAKHSTAN
UZBEKISTAN
Turkmenbashi
Balkanabad
Caspian
Sea
TURKMENISTAN
ASHGABAT
Mary
IRAN
0 100 mi
0 150 km
AFGHANISTAN
© Research Machines plc 2006

Capital: Ashgabat
Population projection, 2010: 5·16m.
GDP per capita, 2003: (PPP$) 5,938
HDI/world rank: 0·738/97

KEY HISTORICAL EVENTS

Until 1917 Russian Central Asia was divided politically into the Khanate of Khiva, the Emirate of Bokhara and the Governor-Generalship of Turkestan. The Khan of Khiva was deposed in Feb. 1920 and a People's Soviet Republic was set up. In Aug. 1920 the Amir of Bokhara suffered the same fate. The former Governor-Generalship of Turkestan was constituted an Autonomous Soviet Socialist Republic within the RSFSR on 11 April 1921. In the autumn of 1924 the Soviets of the Turkestan, Bokhara and Khiva Republics decided to redistribute their territories on a nationality basis. The redistribution was completed in May 1925 when the new states of Uzbekistan, Turkmenistan and Tadzhikistan were accepted into the USSR as Union Republics. Following the break-up of the Soviet Union, Turkmenistan declared independence in Oct. 1991. Saparmurad Niyazov was elected president and founded the Democratic Party of Turkmenistan, the country's only legal party. Also prime minister and Supreme Commander of the armed forces, parliament proclaimed him head of state for life in Dec. 1999. He holds the official title of 'Turkmenbashi', leader of all Turkmen. In July 2000 President Niyazov introduced a law requiring all officials to speak Turkmen.

TERRITORY AND POPULATION

Turkmenistan is bounded in the north by Kazakhstan, in the north and northeast by Uzbekistan, in the southeast by Afghanistan, in the southwest by Iran and in the west by the Caspian Sea. Area, 448,100 sq. km (186,400 sq. miles). The 1995 census population was 4,483,251; density 10·0 per sq. km. In 1999, 85% of the population were Turkmen, 7% Russian, 5% Uzbek and 3% other. Since then the Russian population has declined dramatically as the rights of Russians living in Turkmenistan deteriorated considerably. A dual-citizenship treaty between Turkmenistan and Russia has been rescinded. 2005 population estimate: 4,833,000. In 2003, 54·6% of the population lived in rural areas.

The UN gives a projected population for 2010 of 5·16m.

There are five administrative regions (*velayaty*): Ahal, Balkan, Dashoguz, Lebap and Mary, comprising 42 rural districts,

15 towns and 74 urban settlements. The capital is Ashgabat (formerly Ashkhabad; 1999 population, 525,000); other large towns are Turkmenabat (formerly Chardzhou), Mary (Merv), Balkanabad (Nebit-Dag) and Dashoguz.

Languages spoken include Turkmen, 77%; Uzbek, 9%; Russian, 7%; other, 7%.

SOCIAL STATISTICS

2002 estimates: births, 105,000; deaths, 31,000. Estimated rates, 2002 (per 1,000 population): births, 22·0; deaths, 6·4. Annual population growth rate, 1992–2002, 2·1%. Life expectancy, 2003: 58·3 years for males and 66·8 for females. Infant mortality, 2001, 76 per 1,000 live births; fertility rate, 2001, 3·3 births per woman.

CLIMATE

The summers are warm to hot but the humidity is relatively low. The winters are cold but generally dry and sunny over most of the country. Ashgabat, Jan. –1°C, July 25°C. Annual rainfall 375 mm.

CONSTITUTION AND GOVERNMENT

A new constitution was adopted on 18 May 1992. It provides for an executive head of state. The 50-member *Majlis* (Assembly) serves as the main legislative body. The 2,507-member *Khalk Maslakhaty* (People's Council) is the highest representative body. It is composed of the 50 Majlis members, ten appointees, 50 directly elected representatives, the Council of Ministers, the Supreme Court chairman, the Procurator General and the heads of local councils. It is charged with constitutional and legislative review and may pass a motion of no-confidence in the president.

At a referendum on 16 Jan. 1994, 99·99% of votes cast were in favour of prolonging President Niyazov's term of office to 2002. In 1999 the *Khalk Maslakhaty* declared him president for life.

National Anthem

'Turkmenbasyn guran beyik binasy' ('The country which Turkmenbashi has built'); composed by Veli Muhatov.

RECENT ELECTIONS

At the presidential elections of June 1992, the electorate was 1·86m. Saparmurad Niyazov was re-elected unopposed by 99·5% of votes cast.

Majlis elections were held on 19 Dec. 2004 and 9 Jan. 2005. The only party standing was the Democratic Party (DP; former Communists). All 50 seats were filled; turnout was 76·9%. Elections to the *Khalk Maslakhaty* took place on 7 April 2003 under the same system.

CURRENT ADMINISTRATION

In March 2006 the government comprised:

President and Prime Minister: Saparmurad Niyazov (Saparmurad Turkmenbashi since 1993); b. 1940 (DP; sworn in 27 Oct. 1990).

Deputy Prime Ministers: Gurbanguly Berdimukhamedov (also *Minister of Health and Medical Industry*); Dortguly Aydogdiyev (also *Minister of Textile Industry*).

Minister of Agriculture: Esenmyrat Orazgeldiev. *Communications:* Resulberdi Khozhagurbanov. *Culture, Television and Radio Broadcasting:* Maral Byashimova. *Defence:* Maj.-Gen. Agageldy Mamedgeldiev. *Economy and Finance:* Atamyrat Berdiyev. *Education:* Shemshat Annagylyjova. *Environmental Protection:* Magtymguly Akmuradov. *Foreign Affairs:* Rashid

Meredov. *Construction and Construction Materials:* Batyr Gaipov. *Internal Affairs:* Akmamet Rakhmanov. *Justice:* Asyrgeldi Gulgaraev. *Motor Transport and Roads:* Baymuhammet Kelov. *National Security:* Geldymukhamet Ashirmukhamedov. *Oil and Gas:* Gurbanmyrat Atayev. *Power Engineering and Industry:* Yusup Davudov. *Railways:* Orazberdy Hudayberdiev. *Social Security:* Orazmurat Begmuradov. *Trade and Foreign Economic Relations:* Gurbangeldi Melekeyev. *Water Resources:* Tekebay Altayev.

Chairman, Supreme Council (Majlis): Ovezgeldi Atayev.

CURRENT LEADERS

Saparmurad Niyazov

Position
President

Introduction
Saparmurad Niyazov was chairman of the Turkmenistan Supreme Soviet and became effective head of state when Turkmenistan claimed sovereignty in 1990. He oversaw the nation's declaration of independence in 1991 and has been head of state and government ever since. Styling himself 'Turkmenbashi', he has been constitutionally promised his position for life. His autocratic rule has been characterized by eccentric lawmaking and overspending on public projects. He has also been severely criticized internationally for human rights abuses and the absence of an organized political opposition.

Early Life
Saparmurad Niyazov was born on 18 Feb 1940 in Ashgabat. According to official biographies, his father died during World War II and the rest of his family perished in the 1948 Ashgabat earthquake. In 1962 Niyazov joined the Communist Party and four years later graduated in engineering from the Leningrad Polytechnical Institute. He worked in the mining and energy industries and rose through the Communist ranks. In 1985 he was appointed president of the Council of Ministers of the Soviet Socialist Republic of Turkmenistan and, later, first secretary of the central committee of the Communist Party of Turkmenistan. In early 1990 he became chairman of the Republic's Supreme Soviet. In Oct. 1990 the Supreme Soviet proclaimed its political and economic sovereignty, Niyazov therefore becoming its effective head of state. He supported the unsuccessful coup attempt against the president of the USSR, Mikhail Gorbachev, in 1991. Shortly before the collapse of the USSR at the end of that year, he declared Turkmenistan's independence and took the country into the Russian-led Commonwealth of Independent States.

Career in Office
In 1992 Niyazov was elected unopposed as president, heading a new Democratic Party (DP) the policies of which did not differ greatly from those of the Communist Party he had earlier banned. Also in 1992 a new constitution was promulgated, enhancing Niyazov's position as both head of state and government, as well as supreme commander of the armed forces.

In a referendum in Jan. 1994 his period of office was extended to 2002, and in Dec. 1999 the parliament, made up exclusively of DP members, proclaimed him head of state for life. In 2001 he announced he would step down by 2010. His time in office has been dominated by the construction of a personality cult. Modelling himself as 'Turkmenbashi' (leader of all Turkmen), his drive for the 'complete and universal' introduction of the national language in public life compelled officials to speak Turkmen or lose their positions, while foreign languages were removed from the school curriculum. He also introduced a development programme which was to produce a fully democratic society by 2010 but which would require the continuation of the one-party state in the interim.

In Aug. 2002 Niyazov revised the calendar, naming the months after himself, his mother and Rukhname, a spiritual guide written by him which was added to the school curriculum in Sept. 2002. He also redefined the ages of man, stating that adolescence lasts until 25 years of age and old age begins at 85. He had earlier banned smoking in public as a result of himself suffering a smoking-related heart complaint. Niyazov's government exercises firm control over the Turkmen media, and in 2000 Niyazov launched a television station named 'The Epoch of Turkmenbashi'.

His attempts to boost the economy have included the legalization of private landownership and the encouragement of foreign investment, particularly in the country's oil- and gas-rich regions. However, he has received international criticism for his lavish spending on projects such as the Palace of Congress and a fountain complex in Ashgabat while poverty remains widespread. In 2000 he set out plans for a 2,000 sq. km man-made lake in the Karakum desert to ensure year-round availability of water, but environmentalists believe any such construction would devastate the region's ecosystem. In 2004 he ordered the construction of a giant ice palace in Turkmen desert.

In mid-2002 an opposition alliance-in-exile, the Turkmen Democratic Opposition, was formed in Vienna, consisting of members of banned parties and social movements. In Nov. 2002 there was a coup attempt against Niyazov. He blamed exiled opponents who in turn accused him of fabricating the attempt in order to crack down further on domestic opposition. A new wave of repression and imprisonment followed the incident, including the detention of a former foreign minister Boris Shikhmuradov who was considered to be the leader of the exiled activists. Surveillance cameras were installed on main streets in Ashgabat after the failed coup. Parliamentary elections in Dec. 2004 and Jan. 2005 returned presidential supporters to all seats.

Turkmenistan has an uneasy relationship with its neighbours, preferring to avoid regional co-operation. In 2003 Niyazov issued a decree cancelling the 1993 dual citizenship agreement with Russia. Those holding dual citizenship were given two months in which to decide which passport to retain, causing a diplomatic row with Moscow. Russians were reported to fear being trapped in a country widely criticized for human rights abuses and with severe restrictions on foreign travel for its citizens. Relations with Uzbekistan worsened after Niyazov's government accused the Uzbek government in 2002 of shielding opposition leaders. However, the two presidents later signed a friendship declaration and an agreement on water resources in 2004.

DEFENCE

Defence expenditure in 2003 totalled US$350m. (US$72 per capita), representing 1·2% of GDP.

Army
In 2002 the Army was 14,500-strong.

Navy
The government has announced its intention to form a Navy/Coast Guard. The Caspian Sea Flotilla is operating as a joint Russian, Kazakhstani and Turkmenistani flotilla under Russian command. It is based at Astrakhan.

Air Force
The Air Force, with 3,000 personnel, had 89 combat aircraft in 2002 (with an additional 200 in store) including Su-17s and MiG-29s.

INTERNATIONAL RELATIONS

Turkmenistan is a member of the UN, the NATO Partnership for Peace, OSCE, CIS, Asian Development Bank, ECO, OIC and Islamic Development Bank.

ECONOMY

In 2002 agriculture accounted for 21·3% of GDP, industry 41·0% and services 37·7%. In 1999 an estimated 25% of economic output was being produced by the private sector.

Overview

The economy is dependent on the gas and cotton industries. Export of Turkmenistan's large gas reserves has been hindered by reliance on Russian pipelines. A privatization programme was launched on 1 June 1994.

Currency

The unit of currency is the *manat* (TMM) of 100 *tenesi*. Foreign exchange reserves were US$300m. in 1993. Inflation was 5·6% in 2003 and 5·9% in 2004. The manat was devalued in 1994 to an official rate of US$1 = 230 manat.

Budget

Revenues were 3,693bn. manat in 1999 and expenditures 3,894bn. manat.

Performance

Total GDP in 2004 was US$6·2bn. Annual real GDP growth averaged −10·6% between 1994 and 1997. However, a revival in the economy led to growth of 6·7% in 1998, followed by a spectacular 16·4% in 1999, 18·6% in 2000, 20·4% in 2001, 15·8% in 2002, 17·1% in 2003 and 17·2% in 2004. The rapid growth of recent years is largely down to large-scale gas exports to Russia.

Banking and Finance

There are two types of bank in Turkmenistan—state commercial banks and joint stock open-end commercial banks. The central bank is the State Central Bank of Turkmenistan (*Chairman,* Jumaniyaz Annaorazov). A government-led restructuring of the banking sector in 1999 saw the total number of banks reduced from 67 to 12 by 2002.

ENERGY AND NATURAL RESOURCES

Environment

Carbon dioxide emissions from the consumption and flaring of fossil fuels in 2002 were the equivalent of 7·4 tonnes per capita. An *Environmental Sustainability Index* compiled for the World Economic Forum meeting in Jan. 2005 ranked Turkmenistan 144th in the world out of 146 countries analysed, with 33·1%. The index measured the ability of countries to maintain favourable environmental conditions and examined various factors including pollution levels and the use or abuse of natural resources.

Electricity

Installed capacity in 2000 was 3·9m. kW. Production was 9·85bn. kWh in 2000, with consumption per capita 1,853 kWh in 2000.

Oil and Gas

Turkmenistan possesses the world's fifth largest reserves of natural gas and substantial oil resources, but disputes with Russia have held up development. Expansion and development of the Garashsyzlyk area could lead to oil production approaching 500,000 bbls. a day by 2007. Oil production in 2003 was 10·4m. tonnes.

In 2002 gas reserves were estimated at 2,010bn. cu. metres and oil reserves at 500m. bbls. In 2003 crude petroleum production was 10·0m. tonnes and natural gas 59·1bn. cu. metres.

Minerals

There are reserves of coal, sulphur, magnesium, potassium, lead, barite, viterite, bromine, iodine and salt.

Agriculture

Cotton and wheat account for two-thirds of agricultural production. Barley, maize, corn, rice, wool, silk and fruit are also produced. 2000 produced a bumper wheat harvest. Production of main crops (2000, in 1,000 tonnes): wheat, 1,700; seed cotton, 1,040; cottonseed, 625; cotton lint, 187; grapes, 152; tomatoes, 145; watermelons, 65. There were 1·75m. ha. of arable land in 2001 and 65,000 ha. of permanent crops.

Livestock, 2000: sheep, 5·60m.; cattle, 850,000; goats, 368,000; pigs, 46,000; chickens, 4m.

Forestry

There were 3·76m. ha. of forests (8·0% of the land area) in 2000.

Fisheries

There are fisheries in the Caspian Sea. The total catch in 2001 was 12,749 tonnes, exclusively freshwater fish.

INDUSTRY

Main industries: oil refining, gas extraction, chemicals, manufacture of machinery, fertilizers, textiles and clothing. Output, 2000 (in tonnes): residual fuel oil, 2,365,000; distillate fuel oil, 2,247,000; petrol, 1,132,000; cement (2001), 448,000; cotton woven fabrics (2001), 61·0m. sq. metres; footwear (2001), 375,000 pairs.

Labour

The labour force in 1996 totalled 1,750,000 (55% males). Of the total workforce, 44% were engaged in agriculture, 21% in services and 10% in mining, manufacturing and public utilities. Average monthly wage in 1994 was 1,000 manat.

INTERNATIONAL TRADE

External debt was US$1,771m. in 2001.

Imports and Exports

Imports, 2000, US$1,785m.; exports, US$2,506m. Main imports: light manufactured goods, processed food, metalwork, machinery and parts. Main exports: gas, oil and cotton. The main import suppliers in 1998 were Ukraine (16·1%), Turkey (13·1%), Russia (11·6%), Germany (6·9%) and USA (6·4%). The leading export markets were Iran (24·1%), Turkey (18·3%), Azerbaijan (6·9%), UK (4·9%) and Russia (4·7%).

COMMUNICATIONS

Roads

Length of roads in 2002, 58,592 km (of which 81·2% were paved). In 1998 there were 492 fatalities as a result of road accidents.

Rail

Length of railways in 2000, 2,521 km of 1,520 mm gauge. A rail link to Iran was opened in May 1996, and there are plans to build a further 2,000 km of rail network. In 2000, 3·5m. passengers and 18·0m. tonnes of freight were carried.

Civil Aviation

In 2003 Avia Company Turkmenistan operated flights from Ashgabat to Abu Dhabi, Almaty, Amritsar, Bangkok, Birmingham, Delhi, Dubai, Frankfurt, İstanbul, Kyiv, London, Moscow and Tashkent. In 1999 scheduled airline traffic of Turkmenistan-based carriers flew 8·6m. km, carrying 220,000 passengers (all on international flights).

Shipping

In 2002 sea-going shipping totalled 46,000 GRT (including oil tankers, 6,000 GRT). In 1993, 1·1m. tonnes of freight were carried by inland waterways.

Telecommunications

Telephone subscribers numbered 382,200 in 2002 (78·8 per 1,000 population), including 8,200 mobile phone subscribers. There were 8,000 Internet users in 2001.

Postal Services

There were 195 post offices in 2003.

SOCIAL INSTITUTIONS

Justice
In 1994, 14,824 crimes were reported, including 308 murders and attempted murders. The death penalty was abolished in 1999 (there were over 100 executions in 1996). The population in penal institutions in Oct. 2000 was approximately 22,000 (489 per 100,000 of national population).

Education
There is compulsory education until the age of 14. In 1994–95 there were 1,900 primary and secondary schools with 940,600 pupils; and in 1993–94 there were 11 higher educational institutions with 38,900 students, 41 technical colleges with 29,000 students, and 11 music and art schools.

In Jan. 1994, 0·2m. children (29·5% of those eligible) were attending pre-school institutions. In 1999 adult literacy was over 98%.

Health
There were 270 hospitals in 2002 with 32,000 beds. In 1997 there were 14,022 physicians, 1,010 dentists, 21,436 nurses, 1,566 pharmacists and 3,664 midwives.

Welfare
In Jan. 1994 there were 0·3m. old-age, and 0·16m. other, pensioners.

RELIGION

Around 87% of the population in 2001 were Muslims (mostly Sunni).

CULTURE

World Heritage Sites
Turkmenistan has two sites on the UNESCO World Heritage List: the State Historical and Cultural Park 'Ancient Merv' (inscribed on the list in 1999), the oldest and best-preserved Central Asian Silk Route city, dominated by Seljuk architecture; and Kunya-Urgench (2005), the ancient capital of the Khorezem region.

Broadcasting
Turkmen Radio is government-controlled. It broadcasts two national programmes and one regional, a Moscow Radio relay and a foreign service, Voice of Turkmen. There is one state-run TV station broadcasting on three channels. In 2000 there were 1·2m. radio receivers and in 2001 there were 880,000 television sets.

Press
In 2000 there were two daily newspapers with a combined average circulation of 31,512.

Tourism
In 2002 there were 481,000 foreign tourists. Receipts totalled US$120m.

Calendar
In Aug. 2002 President Saparmurad Niyazov renamed the days of the week and the months, for example with Jan. becoming 'Turkmenbashi' after the president's official name, meaning 'head of all the Turkmen'. April has been renamed in honour of the president's mother. Tuesday is now 'Young Day' and Saturday 'Spiritual Day'.

DIPLOMATIC REPRESENTATIVES

Of Turkmenistan in the United Kingdom (2nd Floor, St George's House, 14–17 Wells St., London, W1T 3PD)
Ambassador: Yazmurad N. Seryaev.

Of the United Kingdom in Turkmenistan (3rd Floor, Office Building, Ak Atin Plaza Hotel, Ashgabat)
Ambassador: Peter Butcher.

Of Turkmenistan in the USA (2207 Massachusetts Ave., NW, Washington, D.C., 20008)
Ambassador: Meret Bairamovich Orazov.

Of the USA in Turkmenistan (9 Puskin St., Ashgabat)
Ambassador: Tracey Jacobson.

Of Turkmenistan to the United Nations
Ambassador: Aksoltan T. Ataeva.

Of Turkmenistan to the European Union
Ambassador: Niyazklych Nurklychev.

FURTHER READING

Abazov, Rafis, *Historical Dictionary of Turkmenistan.* Scarecrow Press, Lanham, Maryland, 2005

TUVALU

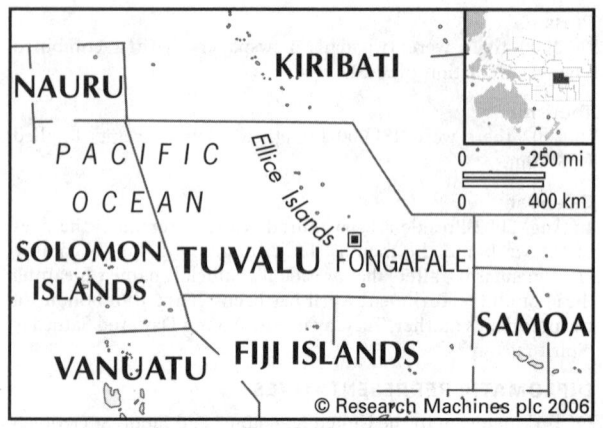

Capital: Fongafale
Population, 2000: 11,000
GDP per capita: not available

KEY HISTORICAL EVENTS

Formerly known as the Ellice Islands, Tuvalu is a group of nine islands in the western central Pacific. Joining the British controlled Gilbert Islands Protectorate in 1916, they became the Gilbert and Ellice Islands colony.

After the Japanese occupied the Gilbert Islands in 1942, US forces occupied the Ellice Islands. A referendum held in 1974 produced a large majority in favour of separation from the Ellice Islands. Independence was achieved on 1 Oct. 1978. Early in 1979 the USA signed a treaty of friendship with Tuvalu and relinquished its claim to the four southern islands in return for the right to veto any other nation's request to use any of Tuvalu's islands for military purposes.

TERRITORY AND POPULATION

Tuvalu lies between 5° 30' and 11° S. lat. and 176° and 180° E. long. and comprises Nanumea, Nanumaga, Niutao, Nui, Vaitupu, Nukufetau, Funafuti (administrative centre; 2002 estimated population, 4,492), Nukulaelae and Niulakita. Population (census 2002) 9,561, excluding an estimated 1,500 who were working abroad, mainly in Nauru and Kiribati. Area approximately 26 sq. km (10 sq. miles). Density, 2002, 373 per sq. km.

In 2002 an estimated 52·9% of the population lived in rural areas. The population is of a Polynesian race.

Both Tuvaluan and English are spoken.

SOCIAL STATISTICS

2000 births, 229; deaths, 109. Rates (per 1,000 population): births, 21; deaths, 10; infant mortality (per 1,000 live births), 35. Expectation of life: males, 64 years; females, 71. Annual population growth rate, 1992–2002, 1·4%; fertility rate, 2000, 2·9 births per woman.

CLIMATE

A pleasant but monotonous climate with temperatures averaging 86°F (30°C), though trade winds from the east moderate conditions for much of the year. Rainfall ranges from 120" (3,000 mm) to over 160" (4,000 mm). Funafuti, Jan. 84°F (28·9°C), July 81°F (27·2°C). Annual rainfall 160" (4,003 mm). Although the islands are north of the recognized hurricane belt they were badly hit by hurricanes in the 1990s, raising fears for the long-term future of Tuvalu as the sea level continues to rise.

CONSTITUTION AND GOVERNMENT

The Head of State is the British sovereign, represented by an appointed Governor-General. The Constitution provides for a Prime Minister and the cabinet ministers to be elected from among the 15 members of the *Fale I Fono (Parliament).*

National Anthem

'Tuvalu mote Atua' ('Tuvalu for the Almighty'); words and tune by A. Manoa.

RECENT ELECTIONS

Elections were held on 2 Aug. 2002. Only non-partisans were elected as there are no political parties. Maatia Toafa was elected prime minister by parliament on 11 Oct. 2004 by eight votes to seven against Elisala Pita.

Parliamentary elections were scheduled to take place on 3 Aug. 2006.

CURRENT ADMINISTRATION

Governor-General: Filoimea Telito (sworn in 15 April 2005).

In March 2006 the cabinet comprised:

Prime Minister and Minister of Foreign Affairs and Labour: Maatia Toafa (sworn in 11 Oct. 2004; acting prime minister from 27 Aug. 2004 to 10 Oct. 2004).

Deputy Prime Minister and Minister of Works and Energy, Communications and Transport: Saufatu Sopoanga. *Finance, Economic Planning and Industries:* Bikenibeu Paeniu. *Natural Resources:* Samuelu P. Teo. *Home Affairs, Rural and Urban Development:* Leti Pelesala. *Health, Education and Sport:* Alesana Seluka.

Speaker: Otinielu Tausi.

CURRENT LEADERS

Maatia Toafa

Position
Prime Minister

Introduction
Maatia Toafa became prime minister in 2004, succeeding Saufatu Sopanga. The threat posed by global warming to low-lying Tuvalu is among the most pressing issues he faces.

Early Life
Toafa was born on 1 May 1954. He was schooled in Kiribati and in 1978 graduated in business studies from the Co-operative Education Centre based at Suva in the Fiji Islands. He later studied at the International Co-operative College at Loughborough in the UK and gained an MBA in 1997 from Suva's University of the South Pacific.

From 1976–96 he worked for the Tuvalu Co-operative Society, eventually holding the post of general manager. In 1997 he became a project officer with the Pacific Islands forum secretariat, based in the Fiji Islands, a post he held for five years.

In Aug. 2003 he was named deputy prime minister with responsibility for works, communications and transport. In Aug. 2004 the government of Prime Minister Saufatu Sopanga lost a parliamentary vote of confidence and Toafa was appointed acting prime minister. The appointment was confirmed by parliamentary vote and he was sworn in on 11 Oct. 2004. As prime minister, he automatically assumed responsibility for the foreign relations portfolio.

Career in Office
Climate change is of ongoing concern for the Tuvalu administration. At only four metres above sea level at its highest point, there are fears that Tuvalu could become the first nation

state to be submerged by rising sea levels caused by global warming. In Oct. 2005 Toafa voiced his support for a UN proposal to designate those fleeing environmental catastrophes as refugees. In June 2005 Toafa had protested that Australia and New Zealand should not pressurize Tuvalu into ending its support of sustainable whale hunting.

Toafa has overseen an extensive review of the constitution which may result in a referendum on Queen Elizabeth II's continuing role as head of state.

INTERNATIONAL RELATIONS

Tuvalu is a member of the UN, the Commonwealth, Asian Development Bank, the Pacific Community and the Pacific Islands Forum, and is an ACP member state of the ACP-EU relationship.

ECONOMY

Currency

The unit of currency is the Australian *dollar* although Tuvaluan coins up to $A1 are in local circulation.

Budget

In 2001 the budget envisaged revenue of $A26·7m. and expenditure of $A35·3m.

Performance

Real GDP growth was 5·2% in 2001.

Banking and Finance

The Tuvalu National Bank was established at Funafuti in 1980, and is a joint venture between the Tuvalu government and Wespac International. There is also a development bank.

ENERGY AND NATURAL RESOURCES

Electricity

Installed capacity was 2·6 MW in 2002; production was 4,355 MWh.

Agriculture

Coconut palms are the main crop. Production of coconuts (2000 estimate), 2,000 tonnes. Fruit and vegetables are grown for local consumption. Livestock, 2000: pigs, 13,000.

Fisheries

Sea fishing is excellent, particularly for tuna. Total catch, 2001, approximately 500 tonnes. A seamount was discovered in Tuvaluan waters in 1991 and is a good location for deep-sea fish. The sale of fishing licences to American and Japanese fleets provides a significant source of income.

INDUSTRY

Small amounts of copra, handicrafts and garments are produced.

INTERNATIONAL TRADE

Imports and Exports

Commerce is dominated by co-operative societies, the Tuvalu Co-operative Wholesale Society being the main importer. Main sources of income are copra, stamps, handicrafts and remittances from Tuvaluans abroad. 1999 imports, US$10·7m.; 1999 exports, US$1·4m. The leading import suppliers are Australia, the Fiji Islands, New Zealand and Japan. The main export destination is Australia.

COMMUNICATIONS

Roads

In 2002 there were 20 km of roads.

Civil Aviation

In 2002 Air Kiribati operated four flights a week from Funafuti International to Suva.

Shipping

Funafuti is the only port and a deep-water wharf was opened in 1980. In 2002 merchant shipping totalled 49,000 GRT.

Telecommunications

In 2002 there were approximately 700 main telephone lines in operation. There were 1,300 Internet users in 2002.

SOCIAL INSTITUTIONS

Justice

There is a High Court presided over by the Chief Justice of the Fiji Islands. A Court of Appeal is constituted if required. There are also eight Island Courts with limited jurisdiction.

Education

There were 1,798 pupils at nine primary schools in 2001, and 558 pupils at Motufoua Secondary School in 2001. The Fetuvalu High School reopened in 2002 with Form 3 only. Education is free and compulsory from the ages of six to 13. There is a Maritime Training School at Funafuti, and the University of the South Pacific, based in the Fiji Islands, has an extension centre at Funafuti.

In 1999–2000 total expenditure on education came to 16·8% of total government expenditure.

Health

In 2002 there was one central hospital situated at Funafuti and clinics on each of the other eight islands; there were seven doctors and 34 nurses.

RELIGION

The majority of the population are Christians, mainly Protestant, but with small groups of Roman Catholics, Seventh Day Adventists, Jehovah's Witnesses and Bahais. There are some Muslims and Latter-day Saints (Mormons).

CULTURE

Broadcasting

The Tuvalu Broadcasting Service transmits daily, and all islands have daily radio communication with Funafuti. There were about 4,000 radio receivers in 1997 and 100 TV sets in 1996.

Press

The Government Broadcasting and Information Division produces *Tuvalu Echoes*, a fortnightly publication, and *Te Lama*, a monthly religious publication.

Tourism

There were 1,304 visitor arrivals in 2002 (639 in 1995).

DIPLOMATIC REPRESENTATIVES

Of Tuvalu in the United Kingdom (Tuvalu House, 230 Worple Road, London, SW20 8RH)
Honorary Consul: Dr Iftikhar A. Ayaz.

Of the United Kingdom in Tuvalu
High Commissioner: Charles Mochan (resides in Suva, Fiji Islands).

Of Tuvalu in the USA
Ambassador: Vacant.

Of the USA in Tuvalu
Ambassador: Larry M. Dinger (resides in Suva, Fiji Islands).

Of Tuvalu to the United Nations
Ambassador: Enele S. Sopoaga.

FURTHER READING

Bennetts, P. and Wheeler, T., *Time and Tide: The Islands of Tuvalu.* Lonely Planet Publications, Melbourne, 2001

National Statistical Office: Ministry of Finance, Economic Planning and Industries, Private Bag, Vaiaku, Funafuti.

UGANDA

Republic of Uganda

Capital: Kampala
Population projection, 2010: 34·57m.
GDP per capita, 2003: (PPP$) 1,457
HDI/world rank: 0·508/144

KEY HISTORICAL EVENTS

Bantu-speaking mixed farmers first migrated into southwest Uganda from the west around 500 BC. There is evidence that they smelted iron for tools and weapons. In the following centuries Nilotic-speaking pastoralists entered northern Uganda from the upper Nile valley (now southern Sudan). By AD 1300 several kingdoms (the Chwezi states) had been established in southern Uganda. In 1500 Nilotic-speaking Luo people invaded the Chwezi states and established the kingdoms of Buganda, Bunyoro and Ankole. At this time, northern Uganda became home to the Alur and Acholi ethnic groups. During the 17th century Bunyoro was southern Uganda's most powerful state, controlling an area that stretched into present-day Rwanda and Tanzania. From about 1700 the kingdom of Buganda expanded (largely at the expense of Bunyoro), and a century later it dominated a large territory bordering Lake Victoria from the Victoria Nile to the Kagera River. The *kabaka* (king) maintained a large court and a powerful army and traded in cattle, ivory and slaves.

Arab traders from Zanzibar on Africa's east coast reached Lake Victoria by 1844. Ahmad bin Ibrahim introduced the kabaka to foreign trade; imported cloth and firearms were exchanged for ivory and slaves. Ibrahim also introduced Islam to the region. In 1862 John Speke, a British explorer attempting to find the source of the Nile, became the first European to visit Buganda, by then a highly developed state supported by an army numbering more than 150,000 and a significant navy. He met with Kabaka Mutesa I; as did Henry Stanley, who reached Buganda in 1875. Mutesa, fearful of attacks from Egypt, agreed to Stanley's proposal to allow Christian missionaries to enter his realm. Members of the British Protestant Church Missionary Society arrived in 1877 and were followed two years later by representatives of the French Roman Catholic White Fathers. Both were successful in recruiting converts and by the 1880s they had become fiercely antagonistic. Trade with the Indian Ocean ports continued, bringing with it greater Islamic influence.

Mutesa was succeeded by Mwanga in 1884. He was wary of the new foreign ideologies and attempted to halt their spread but was deposed by Christian and Muslim converts in 1888. He was later reinstated but with considerably reduced power and influence. In 1889 Mwanga was visited by Carl Peters, a German doctor, and the kabaka subsequently signed a treaty of friendship with Germany. Britain was concerned by the growth of German influence and the potential threat to its position on the Nile. In 1890 the two European powers signed a treaty giving Britain rights to what was to become Uganda and giving Germany control over land to the southeast (now Tanzania). Frederick Lugard, acting as an agent of the Imperial British East Africa Company (IBEA), arrived in Buganda with a detachment of troops and in 1892 he backed Protestant converts in an attack on the French Catholic mission.

British Rule

In 1894 Britain made Uganda a protectorate. Allying with the Protestant Baganda chiefs, the British set about conquering the rest of the country, assisted by Nubian mercenary troops, formerly in the service of the khedive of Egypt. The British deposed Mwanga and replaced him with his infant son Daudi Chwa. Bunyoro had been spared the religious civil wars of Buganda and was firmly united by its king, Kabarega. Following five years of conflict, the British occupied Bunyoro and conquered Acholi and the northern region. Other African chiefdoms, such as Ankole in the southwest, signed treaties with the British, as did the chiefdoms of Busoga. In 1900 an agreement was signed between the British administration under Sir Harry Johnston and Buganda, giving the kingdom considerable autonomy and transforming it into a constitutional monarchy controlled largely by Protestant chiefs. Half of Bunyoro's conquered territory was also awarded to Buganda, including the historic heartland of the kingdom containing several royal tombs. Buganda doubled in size from ten to twenty counties (*sazas*), but the 'lost counties' of Bunyoro remained a grievance.

Economic Development

In 1901 a railway from Mombasa on the Indian Ocean reached Kisumu, on Lake Victoria, connected by boat with Uganda. The railway was later extended to Kampala. The railway had cost far more than was anticipated and the British, anxious for a return on their investment, turned to cotton to provide raw materials for British mills. Buganda, with its strategic location on the north shore of Lake Victoria, reaped the benefits of cotton growing; it soon became the major export crop and made the Buganda kingdom relatively prosperous. Coffee and sugar production accelerated in the 1920s. The country attracted few permanent European settlers and the cash crops were mostly produced by African smallholders, rather than the plantation system used in other colonies. Many South Asians were encouraged to settle in Uganda, where they played a leading role in the country's commerce. In 1921 a legislative council for the protectorate was established (although its first African member was admitted only in 1945).

The colonial government regulated the buying and processing of cash crops, setting prices and reserving the role of intermediary for Asians, who were thought to be more efficient. The British and Asians repelled African attempts to break into cotton ginning, leading to resentment among the Baganda. In addition, on the Asian-owned sugar plantations established in the 1920s, labour for sugarcane and other cash crops was increasingly provided by migrants from the fringes of Uganda and beyond. In 1949 discontented Baganda rioted and burned down the houses of pro-government chiefs in Kampala. The rioters had three demands: the right to bypass government price controls on the sales of cotton, the removal of the Asian monopoly over cotton ginning, and the right to have their own representatives in local government. They were also critical of the young kabaka, Frederick Walugembe Mutesa II. The British governor, Sir John Hall, regarded the riots as the work of communist-inspired agitators such as the Uganda African Farmers Union (UAFU), founded by I. K. Musazi in 1947. The UAFU was banned and none of the requested reforms were implemented. Musazi's Uganda National Congress replaced the UAFU in 1952 but remained a discussion group rather than an organized political party.

Meanwhile, the British began to prepare for an independent Uganda. Britain's post-war withdrawal from India, nationalism in West Africa and a more liberal philosophy in the Colonial Office all had an effect. Sir Andrew Cohen was installed as governor in 1952 and pursued economic and political reforms: removing obstacles to African cotton ginning, encouraging co-operatives, establishing the Uganda Development Corporation and reorganizing the Legislative Council to include Africans elected from districts across the country for the first time. There was also talk of a future federation of east African territories (Kenya, Uganda and Tanganyika). However, there was resistance among the Baganda, who feared the erosion of their power-base. Mutesa II refused to co-operate with Cohen's plan for an integrated Buganda. Cohen deported him to exile in London, setting off a storm of protest. Two year later Mutesa II was reinstated, officially as a constitutional monarch, but in reality having considerable political clout. In 1960 a political organizer from Lango, Milton Obote, formed a new party, the Uganda People's Congress (UPC), as a coalition of all those who opposed Buganda dominance (apart from the Catholic-dominated Democratic Party (DP)).

Independence

On 9 Oct. 1962 Uganda became independent, with Obote as prime minister and the kabaka as head of state. Buganda was given considerable autonomy. In 1963 Uganda became a republic and Mutesa II was elected president. The first years of independence were dominated by a struggle between the central government and Buganda. In 1966 Obote introduced a new constitution that ended Buganda's autonomy and restored the 'lost counties' to the Bunyoro. Obote then captured the kabaka's palace at Mengo and forced the kabaka to flee the country. In 1967 a new constitution was introduced giving the central government—especially the president—power and dividing Buganda into four districts. The traditional kingships were also abolished. The 1960s saw a steady build-up of military power in Uganda, under Major Gen. Idi Amin Dada.

In Jan. 1971 Obote was deposed in a coup by Idi Amin. Amin was faced with opposition within the army by officers and troops loyal to Obote but by the end of 1971 he was in firm control. In 1972 he ordered Asians who were not citizens of Uganda to leave the country and within three months all 60,000 had left, most of them for Britain. Their expulsion hit the Ugandan economy hard. Amin's rule became increasingly dictatorial and brutal; it is estimated that over 300,000 Ugandans were killed during the 1970s. His corrupt administration led to divisions in the military and a number of coup attempts. Israel conducted a successful raid on the Entebbe airport in 1976 to rescue passengers on a plane hijacked by Palestinian terrorists. Amin's expulsion of Israeli technicians won him the support of Arab nations such as Libya.

In 1976 Amin declared himself president for life and two years later he invaded Tanzania in an attempt to annex the Kagera region. The following year Tanzania launched a successful counter-invasion, unifying anti-Amin forces under the Uganda National Liberation Front (UNLF). Amin's forces were driven out and he fled to exile in Saudi Arabia. Tanzania left an occupation force in Uganda. Yusufu Lule was installed as president but was quickly replaced by Godfrey Binaisa, who was then overthrown in a military coup on 10 May 1980 headed by Paulo Muwanga. Shortly after the Muwanga 1980 coup, Obote made a triumphant return from Tanzania and rallied his former UPC supporters. His main opponents were the DP, led by Paul Kawanga Ssemogerere. The DP were announced as winners on 10 Dec. 1980 but Muwanga seized control of the Electoral Commission and announced a UPC victory 18 hours later, verified by the Commonwealth Observer Group.

In Feb. 1981, shortly after the new Obote government took office, with Paulo Muwanga as vice-president and minister of defence, a former Military Commission member, Yoweri Museveni, and his armed supporters declared themselves the National Resistance Army (NRA). Museveni vowed to overthrow Obote by means of a popular rebellion, and what became known as 'the war in the bush' began. Approximately 200,000 Ugandans sought refuge in neighbouring Rwanda, Zaïre and Sudan. In 1985 a military coup deposed Obote and Lieut.-Gen. Tito Okello became head of state. When it was not given a role in the new regime, the NRA continued its guerrilla campaign. It took Kampala in 1986 and Museveni became the new president. He concentrated on rebuilding the ruined economy by cutting back the army and civil service and reforming agriculture and industry. In 1993 Museveni permitted the restoration of traditional kings, including Ronald Muwenda Mutebi II as kabaka. In May 1996 Museveni was returned to office in the country's first direct presidential elections.

Museveni was re-elected in March 2001, following a period of relative stability and economic growth. However, his popularity was diminished by discontent with Uganda's intervention in the Democratic Republic of the Congo's (formerly Zaïre) civil war and signs of corruption in the government. Uganda's forces were largely withdrawn from the Democratic Republic of the Congo by the end of 2002. Fighting continues with the Lord's Resistance Army, a fanatically religious group led by Joseph Kony that has terrorized northern Uganda.

TERRITORY AND POPULATION

Uganda is bounded in the north by Sudan, in the east by Kenya, in the south by Tanzania and Rwanda, and the west by the Democratic Republic of the Congo. Total area 241,548 sq. km, including inland waters.

The 2002 census population was 24,748,977 (12,124,761 males, 12,624,216 females); density, 102 per sq. km. The largest city is Kampala, the capital (population of 1,208,544 in 2002). Other major towns are Jinja, Mbale, Masaka, Gulu, Entebbe, Soroti and Mbarara. In 2003, 87·7% of the population lived in rural areas.

The projected population for 2010 is 34·57m.

The country is administratively divided into 56 districts, which are grouped in four geographical regions (which do not have administrative status). Area and estimated population of the regions in 2002:

Region	Area in sq. km	Population in 1,000
Central Region	61,352	6,683·9
Eastern Region	39,525	6,301·7
Northern Region	85,392	5,346·0
Western Region	55,278	6,417·4

The official language is English, but Kiswahili is used as a *lingua franca*. About 70% of the population speak Bantu languages; Nilotic languages are spoken in the north and east.

Uganda is host to around 500,000 refugees from a number of neighbouring countries, and internally displaced people. Probably in excess of 100,000 southern Sudanese fled to Uganda during 1996.

SOCIAL STATISTICS

2000 estimates: births, 1,188,000; deaths, 404,000. Rates, 2000 estimates (per 1,000 population): births, 50·6; deaths, 17·2. Uganda has one of the youngest populations of any country, with half of the population under the age of 15. Uganda's life expectancy at birth in 2003 was 46·9 years for males and 47·6 years for females. Life expectancy declined dramatically until the late 1990s, largely owing to the huge number of people in the country with HIV. However, for both males and females expectation of life is now starting to rise again. Annual population growth rate, 1992–2002, 3·0%. Infant mortality, 2001, 79 per 1,000 live births; fertility rate, 2001, 7·1 births per woman.

CLIMATE

Although in equatorial latitudes, the climate is more tropical because of its elevation, and is characterized by two distinct rainy seasons, March–May and Sept.–Nov. In comparison, June–Aug. and Dec.–Feb. are comparatively dry. Temperatures vary little over the year. Kampala, Jan. 74°F (23·3°C), July 70°F (21·1°C). Annual rainfall 46·5" (1,180 mm). Entebbe, Jan. 72°F (22·2°C), July 69°F (20·6°C). Annual rainfall 63·9" (1,624 mm).

CONSTITUTION AND GOVERNMENT

The *President* is head of state and head of government, and is elected for a five-year term by adult suffrage. In Aug. 2005 Parliament amended the constitution to allow an incumbent to hold office for more than two terms, thus enabling President Museveni to serve another term in office. Having lapsed in 1966, the kabakaship was revived as a ceremonial office in 1993. Ronald Muwenda Mutebi (b. 13 April 1955) was crowned Mutebi II, 36th Kabaka, on 31 July 1993.

Until 1994 the national legislature was the 278-member National Resistance Council, but this was replaced by a 284-member *Constituent Assembly* in March 1994. A new constitution was adopted on 8 Oct. 1995 and the Constituent Assembly dissolved. Since 1996 Uganda's parliament has been the 303-seat *National Assembly*.

A referendum on the return of multiparty democracy was held on 29 June 2000, but 88% of voters supported President Museveni's 'no-party' Movement system of government. Turnout was 51%. In Feb. 2003 President Museveni pledged to lift the ban on political parties. In a referendum held on 28 July 2005, 92·4% of voters backed the restoration of a multiparty political system, although the opposition called for a boycott.

National Anthem

'Oh, Uganda, may God uphold thee'; words and tune by G. W. Kakoma.

RECENT ELECTIONS

Presidential elections were held on 23 Feb. 2006. President Museveni was re-elected by 59·3% of votes cast, with his main rival, Kizza Besigye, receiving 37·4% of the vote. Turnout was 68·6%.

Parliamentary elections were held on 26 June 2001. 214 non-partisan members were directly elected in single-seat constituencies. 78 other members had been elected earlier in the month from special interest groups (53 District Women Representatives, ten army representatives, and five each to represent the disabled, the trade unions and youth). Turnout was 70·3%.

CURRENT ADMINISTRATION

President: Yoweri K. Museveni; b. 1945 (sworn in 27 Jan. 1986; re-elected 1996, 2001 and 2006).

In March 2006 the government comprised:

Vice-President: Prof. Gilbert Bukenya (sworn in 6 June 2003).

Prime Minister: Apollo Nsibambi; b. 1938 (sworn in 5 April 1999).

First Deputy Prime Minister and Minister of Disaster Preparedness and Refugees: Brig.-Gen. Moses Ali. *Deputy Prime Minister and Minister of Public Service:* Henry Muganwa Kajura.

Minister of Defence: Amama Mbabazi. *Education and Sports:* Namirembe Bitamazire. *Foreign Affairs:* Sam Kutesa. *Trade, Industry, Tourism, Wildlife and Antiquities:* Daudi Migereko. *Energy and Mineral Development:* Syda Bbumba. *Health:* Jim Katugugu Muhwezi. *Gender, Labour and Social Development:* Zoe Bakoko Bakoru. *Justice, Constitutional Affairs and Attorney General:* Kiddu Makubuya. *Local Government:* Prof. Tarsis Barana Kabwegyere. *Internal Affairs:* Ruhakana Ruganda. *Water, Lands and Environment:* Col. Kahinda Otafiire. *Public Works, Transport, Housing and Communications:* John Nasasira. *Finance, Planning and Economic Development:* Ezra Suruma. *Agriculture, Animal Industry and Fisheries:* Janat Mukwaya. *Security:* Betty Akech. *Minister without Portfolio:* Crispus Kiyonga. *Office of the President:* Beatrice Wabudeya. *Office of the Prime Minister:* Mondo George Kagonyera.

Speaker of Parliament: Edward Ssekandi.

Ugandan Parliament: http://www.parliament.go.ug

CURRENT LEADERS

Yoweri Museveni

Position
President

Introduction
Yoweri Museveni became president of Uganda in 1986 and has been largely credited with transforming the country's economy after the years of misrule by Idi Amin Dada and Milton Obote. He won the first direct presidential elections in 1996 and was re-elected in 2001. In July 2005 a national referendum approved the lifting of restrictions on multi-party politics (in force since Museveni came to power) and the National Assembly abolished a constitutional limit on presidential terms. He won a further term in Feb. 2006.

Early Life
Yoweri Kaguta Museveni was born in 1944 in Ankole, western Uganda, where he attended Mbarara High School and Ntare School. He studied economics and political science at the University of Dar es Salaam, Tanzania, graduating in 1970. While at university Museveni was politically active and became the chairman of a leftist student group linked to African liberation movements. In 1971 Idi Amin Dada came to power in Uganda and Museveni went back to Tanzania. He was a founder of the Front for National Salvation, one of the rebel groups that overthrew Amin in 1979. Museveni held various ministerial posts before running for president in 1980. Defeated by Milton Obote, he formed the National Resistance Army, which took power on 26 Jan. 1986 when Museveni declared himself president and minister of defence. His movement was supported by Col. Qadhafi of Libya.

Career in Office
For much of his presidency, Museveni has been favoured by Western nations and foreign aid donors for opening up the Ugandan economy and reducing poverty. Primary school education increased markedly and, thanks to anti-AIDS campaigns, he succeeded in reducing HIV levels. But Museveni's image has been tarnished internationally since Ugandan troops invaded eastern Democratic Republic of the Congo in 1998 in support of rebel forces. In Sept. 2002 a peace agreement was signed, committing Uganda to withdraw its troops.

After coming to power, Museveni claimed that political parties divided poor countries like Uganda into ethnic, religious and tribal groups. His preferred system therefore had individuals competing for political office on individual merit. However, after 2001 calls for a return to multiparty democracy in Uganda became more persistent, and this was approved in a national referendum in July 2005, although the turnout was low. Museveni's government nevertheless supported the restoration. Parliament meanwhile voted to lift the constitutional two-term limit on the office of president. Museveni stood for re-election in Feb. 2006 and won a further term with almost 60% of the vote.

In Oct. 2005 Kizza Besigye—Museveni's main opposition rival in the 2001 presidential poll which was tainted by violence—returned to Uganda from exile in South Africa to contest the 2006 elections. His subsequent arrest for treason provoked violent street protests before his release on bail in early Jan. 2006. Concern over alleged human rights abuses by Museveni's government led the UK and other European countries to suspend direct development aid in Dec. 2005.

Despites Uganda's own reliance on foreign aid, Museveni has urged African leaders to focus on developing trade in favour of dependence on aid.

DEFENCE

In 2003 defence expenditure totalled US$154m. (US$6 per capita), representing 2·4% of GDP.

Army
The Uganda People's Defence Forces had a strength estimated at 50–60,000 in 2002. There is a Border Defence Unit about 600-strong and local defence units estimated at 15,000.

Navy
There is a Marine unit of the police (400-strong in 2002).

Air Force
The Army's aviation wing operated 16 combat aircraft and two armed helicopters in 2002.

INTERNATIONAL RELATIONS

Uganda is a member of UN, WTO, the African Union, African Development Bank, COMESA, EAC, IOM, Islamic Conference Organization, Islamic Development Bank, the Commonwealth, the Intergovernmental Authority on Development and is an ACP member state of the ACP-EU relationship.

In Nov. 1999 Uganda, Tanzania and Kenya created a new East African Community to develop East African trade, tourism and industry and to lay the foundations for a future common market and political federation.

ECONOMY

In 2002 agriculture accounted for 31·0% of GDP, industry 21·5% and services 47·5%.

Overview
In the early 1990s the economy achieved high GDP growth rates, annual inflation was reduced to under 10% and the incidence of poverty fell considerably. However, since the late 1990s growth has decreased, partly owing to the collapse in coffee prices. The economy grew at 6% per year between 1998 and 2003, while average underlying inflation stayed fairly constant at approximately 5%. The political climate in Uganda stabilized in the early 1980s, allowing ambitious economic reforms. Under the Poverty Eradication Action Plan (PEAP), launched in 1997, the authorities pursued a strategy to reduce poverty to less than 10% of the population by 2017. Whilst the long term growth rate has fallen short of achieving this target, the incidence of poverty has been greatly reduced from 44% of the population in 1997 to 35% in 2000. Uganda's fiscal and external stability indicators have worsened in recent years; the government has set out a plan to achieve fiscal consolidation to improve stability which includes increasing revenue collection and decreasing public administration expenditure.

Currency
The monetary unit is the *Uganda shilling* (UGS) notionally divided into 100 *cents*. In 1987 the currency was devalued by 77% and a new 'heavy' shilling was introduced worth 100 old shillings. Inflation was 5·7% in 2003 and 5·0% in 2004. Foreign exchange reserves in May 2002 were US$893m. Total money supply in April 2002 was Shs 966,075m.

Budget
The provisional total expenditure for the financial year 2001 (year ending 30 June) was Shs 1,516bn. In 2000 total revenue (provisional) was Shs 1,105bn. Expenditures (in Shs) in 2000–01 included: education, 401bn.; defence, 212bn.; roads, 138bn.; health, 111bn.; agriculture, 22bn.

Performance
Real GDP growth was 4·5% in 2003, rising to 5·8% in 2004. In recent times Uganda has consistently been among Africa's best performers. In spite of growth rates which averaged 6·4% over ten years to 1998, per capita income is only just around the level of 1971, when Gen. Idi Amin came to power. Uganda's total GDP in 2004 was US$6·8bn.

Banking and Finance
The Bank of Uganda (*Governor,* Emmanuel Tumusiime Mutebile) was established in 1966 and is the central bank and bank of issue. In addition there are five foreign, six commercial and two development banks. There is also the state-owned Uganda Development Bank, which is scheduled for eventual privatization.

In 2003 foreign direct investment totalled a record high US$283m.

ENERGY AND NATURAL RESOURCES

Environment
Uganda's carbon dioxide emissions from the consumption and flaring of fossil fuels were the equivalent of 0·1 tonnes per capita in 2002.

Electricity
Installed capacity in 2000 was 0·3m. kW, about 95% of which was provided by the Owen Falls Extension Project (a hydro-electric scheme). Production (2000) 1·57bn. kWh. Per capita consumption (2000) 64 kWh. Only 5% of the population has access to electricity and less than 1% of the rural population.

Oil and Gas
Oil was discovered in northwest Uganda in 1999. A Canadian company Heritage Oil Corporation and Energy Africa is exploring the potential for commercial exploitation.

Minerals
In Nov. 1997 extraction started on the first of an estimated US$400m. worth of cobalt from pyrites. Tungsten and tin concentrates are also mined. There are also significant quantities of clay and gypsum.

Agriculture
80% of the workforce is involved with agriculture. In 2001 the agricultural area included 5·10m. ha. of arable land and 2·10m. ha. of permanent crops. Agriculture is one of the priority areas for increased production, with many projects funded both locally and externally. It contributes 90% of exports. Production (2000 estimates) in 1,000 tonnes: plantains, 9,533; cassava, 4,966; sweet potatoes, 2,398; sugarcane, 1,550; maize, 1,096; bananas, 610; millet, 534; potatoes, 478; dry beans, 420; sorghum, 361; coffee, 205. Coffee is the mainstay of the economy, accounting for more

than 50% of the annual commodity export revenue. Uganda is the world's leading producer of plantains.

Livestock (2000): cattle, 5·97m.; goats, 3·70m.; sheep, 1·98m.; pigs, 0·97m.; chickens, 25m. Livestock products, 2000 (in 1,000 tonnes): milk, 511; meat, 234.

Forestry

In 2000 the area under forests was 4·19m. ha., or 21·0% of the total land area. Exploitable forests consist almost entirely of hardwoods. Timber production in 2001 totalled 37·79m. cu. metres. Uganda has great potential for timber-processing for export, manufacture of high-quality furniture and wood products, and various packaging materials.

Fisheries

In 2001 fish landings totalled 220,726 tonnes, entirely from inland waters. Fish farming (especially carp and tilapia) is a growing industry. Uganda's fish-processing industry has greatly expanded in recent years, and fisheries exports, valued at US$87m. in 2002, now rival coffee and tourism as the major foreign currency earners.

INDUSTRY

Production (in 1,000 tonnes): cement (2001), 416; sugar (2002), 160; soap (1999), 84; beer (1999), 117·8m. litres. In 2001 industry accounted for 20·9% of GDP, with manufacturing contributing 9·8%. Industrial production grew by 5·4% in 2001.

Labour

The labour force in 1996 totalled 10,084,000 (52% males). Around 80% of the workforce are involved in the coffee business.

INTERNATIONAL TRADE

Foreign debt was US$4,100m. in 2002.

Imports and Exports

In 2002 imports (f.o.b.) amounted to US$1,113·5m. (US$1,026·6m. in 2001); exports (f.o.b.) US$480·7m. (US$451·6m. in 2001). Coffee, cotton, tea and tobacco are the principal exports. Coffee accounts for nearly 70% of exports—in 1998–99 coffee exports were worth US$282·2m. Timber, tea and fish exports are increasingly important. The main import suppliers in 2001 were Kenya (41·0%), UK (7·6%) and India (6·8%). In 2001 the main export markets were Germany (12·0%), Netherlands (10·2%) and the USA (8·7%). During the 1990s exports grew by an average of 30% every year.

COMMUNICATIONS

Roads

In 1999 there were an estimated 27,000 km of roads, of which 6·7% were paved. There were 53,800 passenger cars in 2002, 44,000 lorries and vans and (1998) 15,800 buses and coaches. In 1999 there were 4,986 road accidents resulting in 1,527 deaths.

In 1997 the government embarked upon a ten-year road-improvement programme, costing US$1·5bn., funded by inter-national loans.

Rail

The Uganda Railways network totals 1,241 km (metre gauge). In 1996 passenger services were suspended and have not been reinstated in the meantime. Freight tonne-km in 2000 came to 210m.

A US$20m. project is under way to establish a direct rail link between Kampala and Johannesburg, South Africa.

Civil Aviation

There is an international airport at Entebbe, 40 km from Kampala. The main Ugandan carrier is East African Airlines, which in 2003 flew to Bujumbura, Johannesburg and Nairobi. In 1999 scheduled airline traffic of Uganda-based carriers flew 4·6m. km, carrying 179,000 passengers (36,000 on international flights). In 2001 Entebbe handled 370,063 passengers (343,722 on international flights) and 37,195 tonnes of freight.

Telecommunications

There were 448,300 telephone subscribers in 2002 (18·1 per 1,000 persons) and 82,000 PCs in use (3·3 per 1,000 persons). Mobile phone subscribers numbered 393,300 in 2002 and there were 100,000 Internet users. In 2002 there were 5,000 fax machines.

Postal Services

In 2000 there were 316 post offices.

SOCIAL INSTITUTIONS

Justice

The Supreme Court of Uganda, presided over by the Chief Justice, is the highest court. There is a Court of Appeal and a High Court below that. Subordinate courts, presided over by Chief Magistrates and Magistrates of the first, second and third grade, are established in all areas: jurisdiction varies with the grade of Magistrate. Chief and first-grade Magistrates are professionally qualified; second- and third-grade Magistrates are trained to diploma level at the Law Development Centre, Kampala. Chief Magistrates exercise supervision over and hear appeals from second- and third-grade courts, and village courts.

The population in penal institutions in May 2002 was approximately 21,900 (89 per 100,000 of national population). The death penalty is still in force. In 2003 there were three executions.

Education

In 2003 there were 7,633,314 pupils and 145,587 teachers at 13,353 primary schools. In 1995, 93·9% of primary schools were government-aided and 6·1% private. There were 683,609 students and 38,549 teachers at 2,055 secondary schools in 2003. In 1995 there were 13,174 students in 94 primary teacher training colleges; 13,360 students in 24 technical institutes and colleges; 22,703 students in 10 national teachers' colleges; 1,628 students in 5 colleges of commerce; 504 students in the Uganda Polytechnic, Kyambogo; 800 students in the National College of Business Studies, Nakawa. In 1995–96 there was one university and one university of science and technology in the public sector, and one Christian, one Roman Catholic and one Islamic university in the private sector. In 1995–96 there were 30,266 students in tertiary education. The adult literacy rate was 68·9% in 2002 (78·8% among males and 59·2% among females).

School attendance has trebled since Yoweri Museveni became president in 1986. In 1997 free primary education was introduced, initially for four children in every family but from 2003 for all children. In 1999–2000 total expenditure on education came to 2·3% of GNP.

Health

In 2001 there were 946 health centres (189 private) and 104 hospitals (49 private). In 2002 there were 1,175 physicians, 75 dentists, 1,350 nurses and 850 midwives. Uganda has been one of the most successful African countries in the fight against AIDS. A climate of free debate, with President Museveni recognizing the threat as early as 1986 and making every government department take the problem seriously, resulted in HIV prevalence among adults declining from approximately 30% in 1992 to 11% in 2000.

RELIGION

In 2001 there were 10·05m. Roman Catholics, 9·45m. Anglicans and 1·25m. Muslims. In May 2005 there was one Roman Catholic cardinal. Traditional beliefs are also widespread.

CULTURE

World Heritage Sites

Uganda has three sites on the UNESCO World Heritage List: Bwindi Impenetrable National Park (inscribed on the list in

1994); Rwenzori Mountains National Park (1994); and the Tombs of the Buganda Kings at Kasubi (2001).

Broadcasting

The government runs Radio Uganda, which has ten stations and transmits three regional programmes, and Uganda Television with nine stations and one programme. Colour is by PAL. There are three private television operators.

There were about 2·9m. radio receivers and 620,000 television sets in 2000.

Press

There were four daily newspapers in 2001 with a combined circulation of 69,000, and six non-daily newspapers and periodicals.

Tourism

In 2002 there were 254,000 foreign tourists; spending by tourists totalled US$185m.

Festivals

The main festivals are for Islamic holidays (March and June), Martyrs' Day (3 June), Heroes' Day (9 June) and Independence Day (9 Oct.).

Theatre and Opera

There is a National Theatre at Kampala.

Museums and Galleries

The Nommo Gallery houses famous works of art, and is involved in educational and other cultural programmes.

DIPLOMATIC REPRESENTATIVES

Of Uganda in the United Kingdom (Uganda House, 58/59 Trafalgar Square, London, WC2N 5DX)
High Commissioner: Vacant.
Chargé d'Affaires a.i: Elizabeth Kanyogonya.

Of the United Kingdom in Uganda (4 Windsor Loop, PO Box 7070, Kampala)
High Commissioner: Francois Gordon, CMG.

Of Uganda in the USA (5911 16th St., NW, Washington, D.C., 20011)
Ambassador: Edith Ssempala.

Of the USA in Uganda (1577 Ggaba Rd, Kampala)
Ambassador: Vacant.
Chargé d'Affaires a.i.: William E. Fitzgerald.

Of Uganda to the United Nations
Ambassador: Francis Butagira.

Of Uganda to the European Union
Ambassador: Vacant.
Chargé d'Affaires a.i.: Lewis Balinda.

FURTHER READING

Museveni, Y., *What is Africa's Problem?* London, 1993.—*The Mustard Seed.* London, 1997
Mutibwa, P., *Uganda since Independence: a Story of Unfulfilled Hopes.* London, 1992
Nyeko, B., *Uganda.* [Bibliography] 2nd ed. ABC-Clio, Oxford and Santa Barbara (CA), 1996

National Statistical Office: Uganda Bureau of Statistics, P. O. Box 13, Entebbe.

UKRAINE

Ukraina

Capital: Kyiv (formerly Kiev)
Population projection, 2010: 44·13m.
GDP per capita, 2003: (PPP$) 5,491
HDI/world rank 0·766/78

KEY HISTORICAL EVENTS

Kyiv (formerly Kiev) was the centre of the Rus principality in the 11th and 12th centuries and is still known as the Mother of Russian cities. The western Ukraine principality of Galicia was annexed by Poland in the 14th century. At about the same time, Kyiv and the Ukrainian principality of Volhynia were conquered by Lithuania before being absorbed by Poland. Poland, however, could not subjugate the Ukrainian cossacks, who allied themselves with Russia. Ukraine, except for Galicia (part of the Austrian Empire, 1772–1919), was incorporated into the Russian Empire after the second partition of Poland in 1793.

In 1917, following the Bolshevik revolution, the Ukrainians in Russia established an independent republic. Austrian Ukraine proclaimed itself a republic in 1918 and was federated with its Russian counterpart. The Allies ignored Ukrainian claims to Galicia, however, and in 1918 awarded that area to Poland. From 1922 to 1932, drastic efforts were made by the USSR to suppress Ukrainian nationalism. Ukraine suffered from the forced collectivization of agriculture and the expropriation of foodstuffs; the result was the famine of 1932–33 when more than 7m. people died. Following the Soviet seizure of eastern Poland in Sept. 1939, Polish Galicia was incorporated into the Ukrainian SSR. When the Germans invaded Ukraine in 1941 hopes that an autonomous or independent Ukrainian republic would be set up under German protection were disappointed. Ukraine was re-taken by the USSR in 1944. The Crimean region was joined to Ukraine in 1954.

On 5 Dec. 1991 the Supreme Soviet declared Ukraine's independence. Ukraine was one of the founder members of the Commonwealth of Independent States in Dec. 1991. After independence Crimea, which was part of Russia until 1954, became a source of contention between Moscow and Kyiv. The Russian Supreme Soviet laid claim to the Crimean port city of Sevastopol, the home port of the 350-ship Black Sea Fleet, despite an agreement to divide the fleet. There was also conflict between Ukraine and Russia over possession and transfer of nuclear weapons, delivery of Russian fuel to Ukraine and military and political integration within the CIS. Leonid Kuchma was elected president in 1994 and re-elected in 1999. Support for him fell after public demonstrations against maladministration including the accusation that he was responsible for the murder of a radical journalist. Conflicts between the presidential administration and government led to the sacking of reform-minded prime minister Viktor Yushchenko in April 2001, who was replaced by Kuchma loyalist Anatolii Kinakh at the end of May. The Pope's historic visit to Ukraine in June 2001 was accompanied by disturbances, particularly in the capital. Presidential elections in Oct. and Nov. 2004 were won by Kuchma's chosen successor, Viktor Yanukovich, who defeated Viktor Yushchenko in the second round run-off. But observers claimed the election failed to meet democratic standards. Widespread protests followed in Kyiv. After the poll was declared invalid Yushchenko was elected president in the repeat of the run-off.

TERRITORY AND POPULATION

Ukraine is bounded in the east by the Russian Federation, north by Belarus, west by Poland, Slovakia, Hungary, Romania and Moldova, and south by the Black Sea and Sea of Azov. Area, 603,700 sq. km (233,090 sq. miles). In 2001 the census population was 48,416,000, of whom 25,941,000 were female (67·3% urban in 2003); density, 80 per sq. km. 78% of the population were Ukrainians, 17% Russians and 5% others—Belarusians, Moldovans, Hungarians, Bulgarians, Poles and Crimean Tatars (most of the Tatars were forcibly transported to Central Asia in 1944 for anti-Soviet activities during the Second World War). The estimated population in 2005 was 46,481,000.

The UN gives a projected population for 2010 of 44·13m.

Ukraine is divided into 24 provinces, two municipalities (Kyiv and Simferopol) and the Autonomous Republic of Crimea. Area and populations (2001 census):

	Area (sq. km)	Population (in 1,000)
Cherkaska	20,900	1,402
Chernihivska	31,900	1,236
Chernivetska	8,100	923
Crimea	26,100	2,031
Dnipropetrovska	31,900	3,560
Donetska	26,500	4,843
Ivano-Frankivska	13,900	1,409
Kharkivska	31,400	2,910
Khersonska	28,500	1,174
Khmelnitska	20,600	1,431
Kirovohradska	24,600	1,129
Kyiv	800	2,607
Kyivska	28,100	1,828
Luhanska	26,700	2,546
Lvivska	21,800	2,626
Mykolaïvska	24,600	1,264
Odeska	33,300	2,468
Poltavska	28,800	1,630
Rivnenska	20,100	1,173
Sevastopol	900	378
Sumska	23,800	1,300
Ternopilska	13,800	1,142
Vinnytska	26,500	1,772
Volynska	20,200	1,061

	Area (sq. km)	Population (in 1,000)
Zakarpatska	12,800	1,258
Zaporizhska	27,200	1,926
Zhytomyrska	29,900	1,389

The capital is Kyiv (population 2,602,000 in 2001). Other towns with 2001 populations over 0·2m. are:

	Population (in 1,000)		Population (in 1,000)
Kharkiv	1,470	Chernihiv	301
Dnipropetrovsk	1,064	Cherkasy	295
Odesa	1,029	Sumy	293
Donetsk	1,016	Horlivka	292
Zaporizhzhya	814	Zhytomyr	284
Lviv	732	Dniprodzerzhynsk	256
Kryvy Rih	667	Khmelnitsky	254
Mykolaïv	514	Kirovohrad	253
Mariupol	492	Rivne	249
Luhansk	463	Chernivtsi	240
Makiïvka	390	Kremenchuk	234
Vinnytsya	357	Ternopil	228
Simferopol	343	Ivano-Frankivsk	218
Sevastopol	341	Lutsk	209
Kherson	328	Bila Tserkva	200
Poltava	318		

The 1996 Constitution made Ukrainian the sole official language. Russian (the language of 33% of the population), Romanian, Polish and Hungarian are also spoken. Additionally, the 1996 Constitution abolished dual citizenship, previously available if there was a treaty with the other country (there was no such treaty with Russia). Anyone resident in Ukraine since 1991 may be naturalized.

SOCIAL STATISTICS

2001 births, 376,478; deaths, 745,952; marriages, 309,602; divorces, 181,334. Rates (per 1,000 population), 2000: births, 7·8; deaths, 15·4. Annual population growth rate, 1992–2002, −0·6%. Life expectancy, 2003: males, 60·1 years, females, 72·5. In 2001 the most popular age range for marrying was 20–24 for both males and females. Infant mortality, 2001, 17 per 1,000 live births; fertility rate, 2001, 1·1 births per woman (one of the lowest rates in the world).

CLIMATE

Temperate continental with a subtropical Mediterranean climate prevalent on the southern portions of the Crimean Peninsula. The average monthly temperature in winter ranges from 17·6°F to 35·6°F (−8°C to 2°C), while summer temperatures average 62·6°F to 77°F (17°C to 25°C). The Black Sea coast is subject to freezing, and no Ukrainian port is permanently ice-free. Precipitation generally decreases from north to south; it is greatest in the Carpathians where it exceeds more than 58·5" (1,500 mm) per year, and least in the coastal lowlands of the Black Sea where it averages less than 11·7" (300 mm) per year.

CONSTITUTION AND GOVERNMENT

In a referendum on 1 Dec. 1991, 90·3% of votes cast were in favour of independence. Turnout was 83·7%.

A new Constitution was adopted on 28 June 1996. It defines Ukraine as a sovereign, democratic, unitary state governed by the rule of law and guaranteeing civil rights. The head of state is the *President*, elected directly by the people for a five-year term. An amendment to the constitution that came into effect on 1 Jan. 2006 gives increased powers to parliament, including the right to appoint and dismiss the prime minister. However, after parliament dismissed the prime minister and the cabinet on 10 Jan. 2006 President Yushchenko stated that only the new parliament that was to be elected in March 2006 would have such powers.

Parliament is the 450-member unicameral *Supreme Council*, elected for four-year terms. Prior to the March 2006 election half of the members were chosen from party lists by proportional vote and half from individual constituencies, but in accordance with a constitutional amendment for the 2006 election all 450 members were chosen from party lists.

There is an 18-member *Constitutional Court*, six members being appointed by the President, six by parliament and six by a panel of judges. Constitutional amendments may be initiated at the President's request to parliament, or by at least one third of parliamentary deputies. The Communist Party was officially banned in the country in 1991, but was renamed the Socialist Party of Ukraine. Hard-line Communists protested against the ban, which was rescinded by the Supreme Council in May 1993.

National Anthem

'Shche ne vmerla, Ukraïny i slava, i volya' ('Ukraine's freedom and glory has not yet perished'); words by P. Chubynsky, tune by M. Verbytsky.

GOVERNMENT CHRONOLOGY

Presidents since 1991.

1991–94	Leonid Makarovich Kravchuk
1994–2005	Leonid Danylovich Kuchma
2005–	Viktor Andriyovich Yushchenko

Prime Ministers since 1990.

1990–92	Vitold Pavlovich Fokin
1992	Valentyn Kostyantynovich Symonenko
1992–93	Leonid Danylovich Kuchma
1994–95	Vitaliy Anriyovich Masol
1995–96	Yevhen Kyrylovich Marchuk
1996–97	Pavlo Ivanovich Lazarenko
1997–99	Valeriy Pavlovich Pustovoytenko
1999–01	Viktor Andriyovich Yushchenko
2001–02	Anatolii Kyrylovich Kinakh
2002–05	Viktor Fedorovich Yanukovich
2005	Yuliya Volodymyrivna Tymoshenko
2005–	Yuriy Ivanovich Yekhanurov

RECENT ELECTIONS

Parliamentary elections were held on 26 March 2006. The Party of Regions of Ukraine won 186 of 450 seats with 32·1% of votes cast, the Yuliya Tymoshenko Election Bloc 129 (22·3%), the Our Ukraine Party 81 (13·9%), the Socialist Party 33 (5·7%) and the Communist Party 21 (3·7%). Turnout was 67·1%.

Presidential elections were held in two rounds on 31 Oct. and 21 Nov. 2004. In the first round former prime minister Viktor Yushchenko won 39·9% of the vote against 39·3% for Prime Minister Viktor Yanukovich, 5·8% for Oleksandr Moroz and 5·0% for Petro Symonenko. Western observers claimed the election failed to meet democratic standards. In the second round Viktor Yanukovich won 51·5% of the vote and Viktor Yushchenko 48·5%. Again the election was deemed to be flawed, leading to widespread protests in the capital, Kyiv. On 27 Nov. 2004 parliament passed a resolution declaring the poll invalid. On 1 Dec. parliament dismissed Prime Minister Viktor Yanukovich's government in a no-confidence vote and on 3 Dec. the Supreme Court annulled the second round of the election. When it was held again on 26 Dec. Viktor Yushchenko received 54·1% of the vote and Viktor Yanukovich 45·9%.

CURRENT ADMINISTRATION

President: Viktor Yushchenko; b. 1954 (sworn in 23 Jan. 2005).

In March 2006 the government comprised:

Prime Minister (acting): Yuriy Yekhanurov; b. 1948 (sworn in 22 Sept. 2005 having previously been acting prime minister since 8 Sept. 2005; again acting prime minister since parliament dismissed the government on 10 Jan. 2006).

First Deputy Prime Minister: Stanislas Stachevskyi. *Deputy Prime Ministers:* Roman Bezsmertny (also *Minister of Regional Policy*); Yuri Melnyk (also *Minister of Agricultural Affairs*); Viatcheslav Kyrylenko (also *Minister of Humanitarian and Social Affairs*).

Minister of Agrarian Policy: Oleksandr Baranivsky. *Coal Industry:* Viktor Topolov. *Construction, Architecture and Housing:* Pavlo Kachur. *Culture and Tourism:* Ihor Lykhovy. *Defence:* Anatoliy Hrytsenko. *Economy:* Arsenii Yatseniouk. *Education and Science:* Stanislav Nikolayenko. *Emergency Situations:* Viktor Baloha. *Environmental Protection:* Pavlo Ihnatenko. *Family, Youth Affairs and Sports:* Yuriy Pavlenko. *Finance:* Victor Pynzenyk. *Foreign Affairs:* Borys Tarasyuk. *Fuel and Energy:* Ivan Plachkov. *Health:* Yurii Polyatchenko. *Industrial Policy:* Volodymyr Shandra. *Interior:* Yurii Lutsenko. *Justice:* Serhii Holovatyi. *Labour and Social Policy:* Ivan Sakhan. *Transport and Communications:* Viktor Bondar. *Minister of the Cabinet:* Bohdan Butsa.

Government Website: http://www.kmu.gov.ua

CURRENT LEADERS

Viktor Yushchenko

Position
President

Introduction
After a drawn-out and bitter contest for the presidency of Ukraine, the pro-EU and reformist former banker, Viktor Yushchenko, emerged as the winner in Jan. 2005. Following allegations of vote-rigging in the Nov. 2004 election, tens of thousands of Yushchenko's orange-clad supporters protested and forced a rerun.

Early Life
Viktor Andriyevich Yushchenko was born on 23 Feb. 1954 in the town of Khoruzhivka, Sumy Oblast in northeastern Ukraine. He attended the Finance and Economics Institute in Ternopil, western Ukraine and graduated in 1975, after which he undertook a year's service in the Soviet Army. Returning to Sumy in 1976, Yushchenko worked as an economist and department chief at the Ulyanivka branch of the USSR's central bank. In 1984 he obtained a postgraduate degree in finance and credit from the Ukrainian Institute of Economics and Agricultural Management. Shortly afterwards he moved to Kyiv and was appointed Deputy Director for Agricultural Credit at the Ukrainian office of the USSR's central bank, a position he held until 1987. He then took up the post of Department Director at the Kyiv office of the USSR's Agro-Industrial bank. In 1991, the year in which the nascent Ukrainian parliament declared the country's independence, Yushchenko was promoted to Deputy Chairman of the Board of Directors at the Agro-Industrial bank.

He was a key figure in the establishment of the National Bank of Ukraine, becoming its governor in 1993 and developing the institution's monetary, fiscal and credit policies against a backdrop of hyperinflation, plunging agricultural and industrial output, and falling living standards. He oversaw the introduction of Ukraine's new currency, the hryvnia, in 1996 and was credited with bringing in policies that diminished the impact of the Russian rouble crash on Ukraine's economy in 1997. His astute leadership led to him winning the Global Finance Award as the one of the world's top five central bankers. Yushchenko then survived a corruption scandal that engulfed the central bank and in Dec. 1999 was appointed prime minister by the president, Leonid Kuchma. Yushchenko's free-market approach, his decision to pay off Ukraine's debts to Russia and his enhancement of conditions for foreign and domestic investment brought some improvement to the economy. But his government came into conflict with oligarchs from eastern Ukraine who controlled the oil and gas sectors and were linked to Kuchma (and Moscow).

In 2001 Yushchenko's government was ousted by a no-confidence vote, with Kuchma preferring to back the powerful clans from the Russian-speaking east of the country. Yushchenko began talks with liberal and nationalist opposition forces and, in Jan. 2002, created 'Our Ukraine'—a coalition of centre-right groups. In the parliamentary elections in March 2002 Our Ukraine reduced the Communist Party's dominance in parliament, but failed to secure the necessary majority needed to form a new government. Instead, pro-Kuchma forces, led by the For United Ukraine party, received enough support to hold the balance of power.

When Kuchma's term ended in 2004, Yushchenko ran against the prime minister, Viktor Yanukovich (backed by the powerful clans in eastern Ukraine and Moscow) for the presidency. It was an acrimonious campaign, and Yushchenko became ill after dining with the head of a Russian intelligence agency, developing a condition that left his face disfigured. There were accusations of poisoning, which further increased tensions. Neither candidate reached the 50% margin required for victory in the election on 31 Oct. 2004. A run-off was held on 21 Nov. and the final vote showed a victory for Yanukovich, which contrasted sharply with the results of the exit polls. International observers reported electoral irregularities and there were huge public protests in Kyiv and elsewhere, which led to the Supreme Court invalidating the results and rerunning the election on 26 Dec. The next day Yushchenko was declared the victor by 8 percentage points, although this time Yanukovich claimed to have been the victim of electoral fraud. Despite resigning as prime minister on 31 Dec., Yanukovich continued to protest about the conduct of the election. On 11 Jan. 2005 the electoral commission reaffirmed Yushchenko as the official winner of the rerun presidential election, with 54·1% of the vote. Following the Supreme Court's rejection of Yanukovich's final appeal on 20 Jan., Yushchenko was inaugurated as president on 23 Jan.

Career in Office
Addressing a crowd estimated at more than 100,000 in Kyiv's Independence Square, Yushchenko described his inauguration as a victory of freedom over tyranny. 'We will create new jobs. Whoever wants to work will have the opportunity to work and get an appropriate salary,' Yushchenko promised. 'We will fight corruption in Ukraine. Taxes will be enforced, business will be transparent ... we will become an honest nation ... Our road to the future is the one that the European Union is proceeding along ... My goal is Ukraine in a united Europe.'

On 4 Feb. 2005 the Ukrainian parliament approved President Yushchenko's nomination of Yuliya Tymoshenko as the new prime minister. She was one of his key supporters, but a controversial figure—Russian authorities having accused her of bribery when she ran a Ukrainian gas trading company in the mid-1990s. The new government's programme had the goal of bringing Ukraine closer to the EU and also confronting a number of domestic problems within Ukraine, particularly corruption. However, the optimism that followed the 'orange revolution' soon faded and, following public disagreements within the government and further corruption allegations, Yushchenko sacked his entire cabinet on 8 Sept. 2005, including Tymoshenko. He appointed Yuriy Yekhanurov, an economist and technocrat, as the new prime minister.

In Jan. 2006, after the signing of an agreement with Russia ending a damaging dispute over prices for Russian gas supplies, the Ukraine parliament passed a vote of no confidence in the Yekhanurov government. President Yushchenko questioned the legal validity of the move ahead of the March 2006 parliamentary elections.

Yuriy Yekhanurov

Position
Prime Minister (acting)

Introduction
Yuriy Yekhanurov, an experienced technocrat, economist and long-time ally of President Yushchenko, was appointed as Ukraine's prime minister in Sept. 2005. Ahead of the March 2006 parliamentary elections, he was charged with stabilizing government and the economy after the first post-'orange revolution' administration had become mired in infighting and allegations of corruption.

Early Life
Yuriy Ivanovich Yekhanurov was born on 23 Aug. 1948 in Belkachi, Yakutia, in Soviet Russia. He was at school in Bichursk, Buryatia (Siberia) until 1963. When his family moved to Kyiv in the Ukrainian Soviet Socialist Republic, he attended the Technical School for Construction. Having begun work as an apprentice in a concrete manufacturing plant in 1967, Yekhanurov rose to become the complex's executive director in 1978, a position he held for seven years. During this period he undertook advanced studies in economics at the Kyiv Institute of Economics, graduating in 1983 with a 'candidate degree' (equivalent to a PhD). In Aug. 1988 he was nominated deputy director of Glavkievstroy (the municipal department for construction).

Following the break-up of the USSR and Ukraine's declaration of independence in Aug. 1991, Yekhanurov was involved in economic policy as an advocate of sweeping liberalization and privatization. In 1992 he joined the department for economic reform in Kyiv's municipal administration and a year later entered the government as deputy minister of the economy. Between 1994 and early 1997 he oversaw the initial stage of privatization in Ukraine as head of the State Property Fund. Subsequently he served as minister of the economy in the government of Pavlo Lazarenko, before being nominated as head of the state committee for business development. He became a member of the Popular Democratic Party in 1998 (providing political support to President Leonid Kuchma) and was elected as the parliamentary member for Zhytomyr district. In Dec. 1999 he was appointed first vice-prime minister of Ukraine in the new government of Viktor Yushchenko, the former head of the National Bank of Ukraine.

After the government was ousted by President Leonid Kuchma in May 2001, Yekhanurov became first deputy head of the presidential administration, working on issues of administrative reform. He joined Yushchenko's 'Our Ukraine' centre-right opposition and represented the bloc in parliament in 2002. He then served as chairman of the committee for industrial policy and entrepreneurship and took up a professorship at the Taras Shevchenko National University. On 3 April 2005, following the 'orange revolution', the newly-elected President Yushchenko appointed Yekhanurov as governor of the city of Dnipropetrovsk.

Career in Office
On 8 Sept. 2005 Yekhanurov was appointed acting prime minister by Yushchenko. The president's action came in the wake of his decision to sack his entire cabinet, including Prime Minister Tymoshenko, because of infighting and allegations of corruption. Parliamentary approval for Yekhanurov's appointment required two rounds of voting and on 22 Sept. 2005 he secured the support of 289 out of 339 deputies. Yekhanurov set out his plans to improve the country's business climate by lifting state controls and to achieve Ukraine's membership of the World Trade Organization.

In Jan. 2006, following an agreement with Russia ending a dispute over Russian gas prices, Ukraine's parliament dismissed Yekhanurov's government. However, President Yushchenko questioned the legal basis of the action ahead of the March 2006 parliamentary elections. Yekhanurov continued to perform his duties but in an acting capacity.

DEFENCE

The 1996 Constitution bans the stationing of foreign troops on Ukrainian soil, but permits Russia to retain naval bases. Conscription is for 18 months (army and air force) or two years (navy). On 31 May 1997 the presidents of Ukraine and Russia signed a Treaty of Friendship and Co-operation which provided *inter alia* for the division of the former Soviet Black Sea Fleet and shore installations. There were around 1m. armed forces reserves in 1999.

Military expenditure in 2003 totalled US$5,500m. (US$114 per capita), representing 2·1% of GDP.

Army

In 2002 ground forces numbered about 150,700. There were three Operational Commands (North, South and West). Equipment included 3,905 main battle tanks (T-55s, T-64s, T-72s, T-80s and T-84s) and 205 attack helicopters.

In addition there were 44,000 Ministry of Internal Affairs troops, 45,000 Border Guards and 9,500 civil defence troops.

Navy

In 2002 the Ukrainian elements of the former Soviet Black Sea Fleet numbered 13,500, including 2,500 Naval Aviation and an estimated 3,000 naval infantry, with fleet units based at Sevastopol and Odesa. The operational forces include two frigates and one cruiser (*Ukraina*) in refit.

The aviation forces of the former Soviet Black Sea Fleet under Ukrainian command include anti-submarine and maritime reconnaissance aircraft. The personnel of the Ukrainian Naval Aviation Force numbered (2002) about 2,500.

Air Force

Ukraine is limited to 1,090 combat aircraft and 330 armed helicopters under the Conventional Forces in Europe Agreement, and will have to dispose of some material.

Equipment includes 449 combat aircraft. Active aircraft type include Tu-22Ms, MiG-29s, Su-24s, Su-25s and Su-27s.

Personnel (including Air Defence), 2002, 49,100.

INTERNATIONAL RELATIONS

Ukraine is a member of the UN, CIS, the Council of Europe, OSCE, CEI, BSEC, Danube Commission, the NATO Partnership for Peace and IOM. It aims to become a member of the WTO during 2006.

Ukraine has received over US$2bn. in US assistance, more than any other former Soviet republic.

ECONOMY

In 2002 agriculture accounted for 15·3% of GDP, industry 38·2% and services 46·5%.

Overview

The Ukrainian economy has experienced a sharp slowdown since the political upheaval of the 2004 presidential elections. Economic growth averaged 8·4% between 2000 and 2004, peaking at 12·1% in 2004, the highest rate in Europe. Industrial production played a leading role in generating growth, with industrial production growing 87% between 1999 and 2004. In 2005 growth slowed progressively owing to a combination of a slowing global economy, an appreciating exchange rate, loose monetary policy and increased taxes. Nominal public wages were increased by more than 50%, further fuelling inflationary pressures.

The Yushchenko government has set a new political agenda, focusing on institutional reform and increasing integration with the EU and NATO. The National Strategy for EU Integration comprises a long-term agenda to reform the economy across all spheres in line with the EU Acquis Communautaire. However, with the exception of trade policy, institutional change has been limited. The crux of Ukraine's growth problem is low efficiency caused by market unfriendly institutions, weak governance and weak administration. Foreign direct investment flows have been limited by weak property rights, complex regulations and high levels of corruption and bureaucracy.

Currency
The unit of currency is the *hryvnia* of 100 *kopiykas*, which replaced karbovanets on 2 Sept. 1996 at 100,000 karbovanets = 1 hryvnia. 2000 saw the introduction of a floating exchange rate for the hryvnia. Inflation had been as high as 4,735% in 1993 but declined to just 0·8% in 2002, before rising in 2003 to 5·2% and further in 2004 to 9·0%. Foreign exchange reserves in June 2002 were US$3,105m.; gold reserves were 494,000 troy oz (negligible in 1992). Total money supply in June 2002 was 32,530m. hryvnias.

Budget
2001 budget (in 1m. hryvnias): revenue, 54,569·3; expenditure, 58,973·6.

Tax revenue in 2001 (in 1m. hryvnias) totalled 44,265·8 (including social security contributions, 19,637·7; and domestic taxes on goods and services, 15,871·6). Expenditure included (in 1m. hryvnias): social security and welfare, 25,466·9; general public services, 4,327·8; and education, 3,651·0.

Performance
Ukraine's economy has seen some progress in the last few years. Between 1994 and 1998 average annual real GDP growth was –10·0%, and it was still negative in 1999, at –0·2%. In 2000, however, the economy expanded by 5·9% and in 2001 real GDP growth was 9·2%. 2002 saw growth of 5·2%. In 2003 and 2004 there was growth of 9·6% and 12·1% respectively. In 2004 total GDP was US$65·1bn.

Banking and Finance
A National Bank was founded in March 1991. It operates under government control, its Governor being appointed by the President with the approval of parliament. The *Governor* is Volodymyr Stelmakh. There were 176 banks in all in 2003, with assets totalling 85,232m. hryvnias. The largest banks are PrivatBank, Aval and PromInvestBank.

There is a stock exchange in Kyiv.

ENERGY AND NATURAL RESOURCES

Environment
Carbon dioxide emissions from the consumption and flaring of fossil fuels in 2002 were the equivalent of 7·9 tonnes per capita.

Electricity
Installed capacity was 53·9m. kW in 2000. In 2000 production was 171·45bn. kWh; consumption per capita was 3,381 kWh. A Soviet programme to greatly expand nuclear power-generating capacity in the country was abandoned in the wake of the 1986 accident at Chernobyl. Chernobyl was closed down on 15 Dec. 2000. It is planned that two new reactors will be built to replace it. In 2003 there were 13 nuclear reactors in use; in 2002 they supplied 46% of output.

Oil and Gas
In 2000 output of crude petroleum was 3·8m. tonnes; in 2002 production of natural gas was 17·2bn. cu. metres with 1,120bn. cu. metres of proven gas reserves.

Water
In 2004 water consumption totalled 9,973m. cu. metres.

Minerals
Ukraine's industrial economy, accounting for more than a quarter of total employment, is based largely on the republic's vast mineral resources. The Donetsk Basin contains huge reserves of coal, and the nearby iron-ore reserves of Kryvy Rih are equally rich. Among Ukraine's other mineral resources are manganese, bauxite, nickel, titanium and salt. Coal accounts for roughly 30% of the country's energy production. Coal production, 2000, 79·92m. tonnes; iron ore production, 2001, 54·7m. tonnes; manganese ore production, 2000, 2·7m. tonnes; salt production, 2000, 2·3m. tonnes.

Agriculture
Ukraine has extremely fertile black-earth soils in the central and southern portions, totalling nearly two-thirds of the territory. The original vegetation of the area formed three broad belts that crossed the territory of Ukraine latitudinally. Mixed forest vegetation occupied the northern third of the country, forest-steppe the middle portion and steppe the southern third of the country. Now, however, much of the original vegetation has been cleared and replaced by cultivated crops. In 2001 there were 32·56m. ha. of arable land and 0·93m. ha. of permanent crops.

Output (in 1,000 tonnes) in 2000: sugarbeets, 13,185; potatoes, 13,037; wheat, 10,159; barley, 6,873; maize, 3,840; sunflower seeds, 3,460; apples, 1,325; tomatoes, 1,320; pumpkins and squash, 1,100; cabbages, 1,070. Livestock, 2000: 10,627,000 cattle, 10,073,000 pigs, 10,060,000 sheep, 825,000 goats, 698,000 horses, 94m. chickens, 22m. ducks. Livestock products, 2000 (in 1,000 tonnes): meat, 1,720; milk, 12,562; eggs, 477.

Forestry
The area under forests in Ukraine in 2000 was 9·58m. ha. (16·5% of the total land area). In 2001, 9·86m. cu. metres of timber were produced.

Fisheries
In 2001 the catch totalled 351,260 tonnes, of which 346,917 tonnes were from sea fishing. The total catch in 1988 had been 1,048,157 tonnes.

INDUSTRY

In 2001 industry accounted for 39·0% of GDP, with manufacturing contributing 23·3%. Industrial production grew by 8·6% in 2001. Output, 2002 (in tonnes unless otherwise stated): crude steel, 33·4m.; pig iron, 27·1m.; rolled ferrous metals, 26·4m.; cement (2001), 5·8m.; residual fuel oil (2000), 3·2m.; distillate fuel oil (2000), 2·7m.; mineral fertilizer, 2·3m.; petrol (2000), 2·1m.; sugar (2001), 1·8m.; sulphuric acid (2001), 1·0m.; milk products (2004), 724,000; processed meats (1997), 558,400; paper and paperboard, 532,000; butter, 131,000; fabrics, 90m. sq. metres; footwear (2001), 14·6m. pairs; refrigerators, 583,000 units; washing machines (2001), 166,000 units; cigarettes (2001), 69·7bn. units.

Labour
In 2000 a total of 18,063,000 persons were in employment. The principal areas of activity were (in 1,000): agriculture, hunting, forestry and fishing, 4,977; manufacturing, 2,914; wholesale and retail trade, and restaurants and hotels, 1,406; transport, storage and communication, 1,228. In April 2001 there were 1,149,200 unemployed and the registered level of unemployment was 4·2%.

Trade Unions
There are 13 trade unions grouped in a Federation of Ukrainian Trade Unions (*Chair*, Oleksandr Stoyan).

INTERNATIONAL TRADE

In 2002 total foreign debt was US$13,555m.

Imports and Exports

Trade in US$1m.:

	1998	1999	2000	2001	2002
Imports f.o.b.	16,283	12,945	14,943	16,893	17,959
Exports f.o.b.	13,699	13,189	15,722	17,091	18,669

Main import suppliers in 1999: Russia, 47·9%; Germany, 7·3%; Turkmenistan, 3·7%; USA, 3·1%. Main exports markets in 1999: Russia, 19·2%; China, 5·9%; Turkey, 5·4%; Germany, 4·5%.

Main imports, 2002: fuel and energy products, 41·0%; machinery, 22·4%; chemicals and chemical products, 13·1%. Main exports: ferrous and nonferrous metals, 39·3%; wood and wood products, 14·5%; food and raw materials, 13·2%.

COMMUNICATIONS

Roads

In 2002 there were 169,679 km of roads, including 12,202 km of national roads. There were 5,399,967 passenger cars in 2002 and 1,744,359 motorcycles and mopeds. There were 34,488 road accidents involving injury in 2002 (5,982 fatalities).

Rail

Total length was 22,302 km in 2000, of which 9,170 km were electrified. Passenger-km travelled in 2000 came to 51·8bn. and freight tonne-km to 172·8bn. There are metros in Kyiv, Kharkiv, Kryvy Rih and Dnipropetrovsk.

Civil Aviation

The main international airport is Kyiv (Boryspil), and there are international flights from seven other airports. There are two major Ukrainian carriers. Ukraine International Airlines operated international flights in 2005 to Amsterdam, Barcelona, Berlin, Brussels, Dubai, Düsseldorf, Helsinki, Kuwait, Lisbon, London, Madrid, Paris, Rome, Vienna and Zürich. Aerosvit had international flights in 2005 to Ashgabat, Athens, Baku, Bangkok, Beijing, Belgrade, Birmingham, Budapest, Cairo, Delhi, Dubai, Hamburg, İstanbul, Lanarca, Moscow, New York, Prague, St Petersburg, Sofia, Stockholm, Tel Aviv, Toronto and Warsaw.

In 2001 Kyiv handled 1,517,130 passengers (1,458,524 on international flights) and 11,875 tonnes of freight. Simferopol was the second busiest airport for passenger traffic, with 325,323 passengers (248,574 on international flights), and Odesa the second busiest for freight, with 3,588 tonnes.

Shipping

In 2003, 2m. passengers and 10m. tonnes of freight were carried by inland waterways. In 1995 there were 649 ocean-going vessels, totalling 5·83m. DWT. 38 vessels (5·09% of total tonnage) were registered under foreign flags. In 2002 GRT totalled 1,350,000, including oil tankers 39,000 GRT. The main seaports are Mariupol, Odesa, Kherson and Mykolaïv. Odesa is the leading port, and takes 30m. tonnes of cargo annually. In 2001 vessels totalling 7,404,000 NRT entered ports and vessels totalling 49,310,000 NRT cleared.

Telecommunications

In 2001 telephone subscribers numbered 12,894,200 (256·4 per 1,000 persons), but a total of 2·34m. people were on the waiting list for a line. There were 4,200,000 mobile phone subscribers in 2002, 951,000 PCs in use (19·0 per 1,000 persons) and 900,000 Internet users. There were 62,000 fax machines in 2002.

Postal Services

In 2003 there were 15,252 post offices. In 2003, 340m. pieces of mail were processed.

SOCIAL INSTITUTIONS

Justice

A new civil code was voted into law in June 1997. Justice is administered by the Constitutional Court of Ukraine and by courts of general jurisdiction. The Supreme Court of Ukraine is the highest judicial organ of general jurisdiction. The death penalty was abolished in 1999. Over the period 1991–95, 642 death sentences were awarded and 442 carried out; there were 169 executions in 1996. In March 1997 death penalties were still being awarded but not carried out. 553,994 crimes were reported in 2000.

The population in penal institutions in April 2003 was 198,858 (415 per 100,000 of national population).

Education

In 2003–04 the number of pupils in 21,900 primary and secondary schools was 5·9m.; 339 further education establishments had 1,843,800 students, and 670 technical colleges, 592,900 students; 977,000 children were attending pre-school institutions.

In 2005–06 there were 16 universities including an international university of information systems, management and business.

Adult literacy rate in 2003 was 99·4% (male, 99·7%; female, 99·2%).

In 2000–01 total expenditure on education came to 4·4% of GNP.

Health

In 2001 there were 146,582 physicians, 19,275 dentists, 377,376 nurses, 26,066 midwives and 23,488 pharmacists (1998). There were 451,000 beds in 2,900 hospitals in 2004.

Welfare

There were 10·3m. old-age pensioners in 2002 and 3·5m. other pensioners. The total included 821,000 Chernobyl victims. In 2002 social insurance and pension security programmes totalled 27·4bn. hryvnias, representing 12·4% of GDP.

RELIGION

The majority faith is the Orthodox Church, which is split into three factions. The largest is the Ukrainian Orthodox Church, Moscow Patriarchate (the former exarchate of the Russian Orthodox Church), headed by Metropolitan Volodymyr (Sabodan), Metropolitan of Kyiv and All Ukraine, which recognizes Aleksi II (Aleksey Mikhailovich Ridiger) as Patriarch of Moscow and All Russia and insists that all Ukrainian churches should be under Moscow's jurisdiction. There were 9·5m. adherents in 2001. The second largest is the Ukrainian Orthodox Church, Kyivan Patriarchate, headed by Metropolitan Filaret (Denysenko), Patriarch of Kyiv and All Rus-Ukraine, which was created in June 1992. It had 4·8m. adherents in 2001. Metropolitan Filaret was excommunicated by the Ukrainian Orthodox Church, Moscow Patriarchate in Feb. 1997. The third faction is the Ukrainian Autocephalous Orthodox Church, headed by Metropolitan Mefodiy (Kudryakov) of Ternopil, which favours the unification of the three bodies. Only the Ukrainian Orthodox Church, Moscow Patriarchate is in communion with world Orthodoxy.

The hierarchy of the Roman Catholic Church (*Primate*, Cardinal Marian Jaworski, Archbishop Metropolitan of Lviv) was restored by the Pope's confirmation of ten bishops in Jan. 1991. In May 2005 there were two cardinals. The Ukrainian Greek Catholic Church (*Head*, Cardinal Lubomyr Husar, Major Archbishop, Metropolitan of Lviv and Galicia) is a Church of the Byzantine rite, which is in full communion with the Roman Church. Catholicism is strong in the western half of the country.

CULTURE

World Heritage Sites

Ukraine has three sites on the UNESCO World Heritage List: Kyiv—Saint Sophia Cathedral and Related Monastic Buildings, Kyiv—Pechersk Lavra (inscribed on the list in 1990); Lviv—the Ensemble of the Historic Centre (1998); and the Struve Geodetic

Arc (2005). The Arc is a chain of survey triangulations spanning from Norway to the Black Sea that helped establish the exact shape and size of the earth and is shared with nine other countries.

Broadcasting

Broadcasting is administered by the government State Teleradio Company of Ukraine. The state-controlled Ukrainian Radio broadcasts three national and various regional programmes, a shared relay with Radio Moscow, and a foreign service (Ukrainian, English, German and Romanian). There were four independent stations in 1993 and 44m. radio receivers in 2000. The state-controlled Ukrainian Television broadcasts on two channels (colour by SECAM H). In 2001 there were 23m. television receivers.

Cinema

In 1999 there were 7,795 cinemas with a total attendance of 5,138,000. Three full-length films were made in 1999.

Press

In 2000 there were 61 daily newspapers with an average combined circulation of 8,683,100 (175 per 1,000 inhabitants). In 1999 a total of 6,282 book titles were published.

Tourism

There were 6,326,000 foreign tourists in 2002; total receipts were US$2,992m.

Libraries

In 1999 there were 19,079 libraries with 301·8m. volumes of books and 17·3 m. registered users.

DIPLOMATIC REPRESENTATIVES

Of Ukraine in the United Kingdom (60 Holland Park, London, W11 3SJ)
Ambassador: Ihor Kharchenko.

Of the United Kingdom in Ukraine (01025 Kyiv, Desyatinna 9)
Ambassador: Robert Brinkley.

Of Ukraine in the USA (3350 M St., NW, Washington, D.C., 20007)
Ambassador: Oleh Shamshur.

Of the USA in Ukraine (10 Yurii Kotsiubynskyi St., Kyiv 01901)
Ambassador: John Herbst.

Of Ukraine to the United Nations
Ambassador: Valeriy P. Kuchynsky.

Of Ukraine to the European Union
Ambassador: Roman Shpek.

FURTHER READING

Encyclopedia of Ukraine, 5 vols. Toronto, 1984–93

D'Anieri, Paul, *Economic Interdependence in Ukrainian–Russian Relations*. State Univ. of New York Press, 2000
Koropeckyj, I. S., *The Ukrainian Economy: Achievements, Problems, Challenges*. Harvard Univ. Press, 1993
Kuzio, Taras, *Ukraine under Kuchma: Political Reform, Economic Transformation and Security Policy in Independent Ukraine*. London, 1997
Kuzio, Taras, Kravchuk, Robert and D'Anieri, Paul, *State and Institution Building in Ukraine*. St Martin's Press, New York, 2000
Kuzio, T. and Wilson, A., *Ukraine: Perestroika to Independence*. London, 1994
Lieven, Anatol, *Ukraine and Russia: A Fraternal Rivalry*. United States Institute of Peace Press, 2000

Magocsi, P. R., *A History of Ukraine*. Toronto Univ. Press, 1997
Motyl, A. J., *Dilemmas of Independence: Ukraine after Totalitarianism*. New York, 1993
Nahaylo, B., *Ukrainian Resurgence*. 2nd ed. Univ. of Toronto Press, 2000
Reid, A., *Borderland: A Journey Through the History of Ukraine*. Weidenfeld & Nicolson, London, 1997
Wilson, Andrew, *The Ukrainians: Unexpected Nation*. Yale University Press, 2000.—*Ukraine's Orange Revolution*. Yale University Press, 2006

National Statistical Office: State Committee of Statistics of Ukraine.
Website: http://www.ukrstat.gov.ua/

Crimea

The Crimea is a peninsula extending southwards into the Black Sea with an area of 26,100 sq. km. Population (Oct. 2005), 1,990,000 (ethnic groups, 2001 census: Russians, 58·3%; Ukrainians, 24·3%; Tatars, 12·0%). The capital is Simferopol (2001 census, 363,000).

It was occupied by Tatars in 1239, conquered by Ottoman Turks in 1475 and retaken by Russia in 1783. In 1921 after the Communist revolution it became an autonomous republic, but was transformed into a province (*oblast*) of the Russian Federation in 1945, after the deportation of the Tatar population in 1944 for alleged collaboration with the German invaders in the Second World War. 46% of the total Tatar population perished during the deportation. Crimea was transferred to Ukraine in 1954 and became an autonomous republic in 1991. About half the surviving Tatar population of 0·5m. had returned from exile by 2000. The Tatar population is disproportionately disadvantaged within Crimea, with an unemployment rate of over 60% in 2000.

At elections held in two rounds on 16 and 30 Jan. 1994 Yuri Meshkov was elected *President*. The post of president was abolished by Ukraine after calls for a referendum on Crimean independence.

Parliamentary elections were held on 31 March 2002. Turnout was around 63%. The Serhii Kunitsyn Block obtained 39 seats, the Leonid Hrach Block 28, Crimean Tatars 5, the Russian Block 5, SDPUo 3 and ind. 20. The *Prime Minister* is Anatolii Fedorovych Burdyugov and the *Chairman of Parliament* Boris Deich.

On 2 Nov. 1995 parliament adopted a new constitution which defines the Crimea as 'an autonomous republic forming an integral part of Ukraine'. The status of 'autonomous republic' was confirmed by the 1996 Ukrainian Constitution, which provides for Crimea to have its own constitution as approved by its parliament. The Prime Minister is appointed by the Crimean parliament with the approval of the Ukrainian parliament.

The Tatar National Kuriltay (Parliament) elects an executive board (*Mejlis*). The *Chairman* is Mustafa Jemilev. A power-sharing agreement of 12 May 2005 guarantees the Crimean Tatars two ministry portfolios and the post of deputy prime minister in the Crimean local government.

In 2004 there were 624 pre-school institutions with 38,000 pupils and 638 primary and secondary schools with 241,000 students and 20,396 teachers. There were 68,000 students studying at 35 institutes of higher education in 2004.

UNITED ARAB EMIRATES

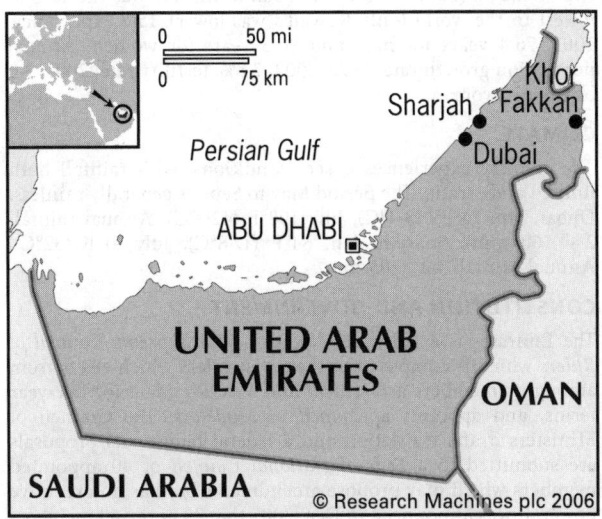

Imarat al-Arabiya al-Muttahida

Capital: Abu Dhabi
Population projection, 2010: 5·03m.
GDP per capita: not available
GNI per capita: $25,300
HDI/world rank: 0·849/41

KEY HISTORICAL EVENTS

Archaeological evidence indicates that in the 3rd millennium BC a culture known as Umm al-Nar developed in modern-day Abu Dhabi, its influence spreading inland and along the coast of Oman to the south. There was trade with both the Mesopotamian civilization and the Indus culture, particularly the export of copper (then the most valuable natural resource) from the Hajar mountains. Later settlements, with Hellenistic features and dating from between the 3rd century BC and the 3rd century AD, have been discovered at Meleiha, near the Sharjah coast, and at Al-Dur in the emirate of Umm al Qaiwain. There are indications that the coastal areas of the United Arab Emirates (UAE) and Oman came under Sassanian (Persian) influence from the 4th century AD until the early 7th century when the Islamic era began. After the death of the Prophet Muhammad, tribes in the Dibba region along the eastern coast rebelled before Islamic forces won a decisive battle in AD 632.

During the Middle Ages much of the region was part of the Persian Kingdom of Hormuz (from 1300), which controlled the approach to the Gulf and most of the trade. European intervention in the Gulf began in the early 16th century when the Portuguese established a commercial monopoly, building a number of forts including Julfar (in modern-day Ras al-Khaimah), a major medieval trading centre. Portuguese ascendancy was later challenged by the Dutch and then by the British, who wielded their naval power in the Gulf in the 18th century to protect trade with India.

By that time two major tribal confederations had grown powerful along the coast of the lower Gulf. The largest tribal grouping, the Bani Yas, was established on the coast by the late 16th century. A large Bani Yas settlement was founded in Abu Dhabi in the 1760s, following the discovery of water on Abu Dhabi island, and in 1793 it became the seat of government of the

al-Nahyan branch of the tribal confederation. There is further evidence of elements of the Bani Yas population extending from Qatar in the west to Dubai in the east and inland to the Liwa oasis belt. The Qawasim, a branch of the Huwalah tribe, were a maritime people (largely operating from Ras al-Khaimah) who emerged as an important group once the Omani empire of the late 17th and early 18th centuries was destroyed at the end of the Omani-Persian war in 1720. They established control over other strands of the Huwalah between Sharjah and Musandam and with a large fleet, posed a serious challenge to British shipping.

Piracy was rife until the early 19th century when the British sent several naval expeditions to the Gulf ports to suppress the raiders. In 1820 Britain signed the General Treaty of Peace against piracy and the slave trade with the principal Arab sheikhdoms. From this and later agreements the area became known as the Trucial Coast from the 1850s (the term Trucial referring to the fact that the component sheikhdoms were bound by the truces concluded with Britain). Britain assumed responsibility for the defence of the territory under the maritime treaty of 1853 and, under the exclusive treaties of 1892, for external relations of each of the Trucial sheikhdoms. The sheikhdoms were otherwise autonomous and followed the traditional form of Arab monarchy, with each ruler having virtually absolute power over his subjects.

The collapse of the pearl market, which was believed to have originated in the Gulf in the late Stone Age, and the world economic depression of the early 20th century seriously undermined the economies of the Trucial States. Their subsequent economic transformation began with the discovery of oil off the coast of Abu Dhabi.

Sheikh Shakhbut bin Sultan al-Nahyan, the ruler of Abu Dhabi from 1928–66, granted the first of several oil exploration concessions to foreign companies in 1939. However, the Second World War delayed exploration. The first commercial discovery was made in the late 1950s and the first exports began in 1962. Sheikh Shakhbut, who was seen as an obstacle to the development of the oil industry, was deposed in 1966 in favour of his younger brother Sheikh Zayed bin Sultan al-Nahyan. The president of the UAE for more than 30 years until his death in 2004, he was re-elected by the rulers of the other emirates at five-year intervals. In the late 1960s oil was discovered in Dubai and in Sharjah, and then in Ras al-Khaimah in the 1980s.

In Jan. 1968 Britain announced the withdrawal of its military forces from the area by 1971. In March the Trucial States joined Bahrain and Qatar (which were also under British protection) in what was named the Federation of Arab Emirates. It was intended that the Federation should become fully independent but the interests of Bahrain and Qatar proved to be incompatible with those of the other sheikhdoms and both seceded from the Federation in 1971 to become separate independent entities. Six of the Trucial States (Abu Dhabi, Dubai, Sharjah, Umm al Qaiwain, Ajman and Fujairah) had agreed a federal constitution for achieving independence as the United Arab Emirates. The British accordingly terminated its special treaty relationship, and the UAE became independent on 2 Dec. 1971. The remaining sheikhdom, Ras al-Khaimah, joined the UAE in Feb. 1972. At independence Sheikh Zayed of Abu Dhabi took office as the first President of the loose federation. Sheikh Rashid bin Said al-Maktoum, the ruler of Dubai for over 30 years from 1958, became Vice-President. The al-Maktoum family, like the al-Nahyan rulers of Abu Dhabi, are a dynastic line of the Bani Yas tribe. The UAE instituted the Federal National Council, a 40-member consultative body appointed by the seven rulers. After the oil price increases of 1973–74—the UAE having given support to the Arab cause in the 1973 war with Israel—the economy and wealth of the new federation developed rapidly.

An attempted coup took place in Sharjah in 1987. Sheikh Sultan Bin Mohammad al-Qassimi abdicated in favour of his brother after admitting mismanagement of the emirate's economy but was restored to power by the Supreme Council of Rulers. In 1991 the UAE became involved in a major international financial scandal when the Bank of Credit and Commerce International (BCCI), in which the Abu Dhabi ruling family held a controlling 77% interest, collapsed. Abu Dhabi sued BCCI for damages in 1993 and several executives were convicted for fraud, given prison sentences and ordered to pay compensation.

Sheikh Rashid bin Said al-Maktoum died in 1990 and was succeeded by his son Sheikh Maktoum bin Rashid al-Maktoum as ruler of Dubai and UAE vice-president. In June 1996 the Federal National Council approved a permanent constitution replacing the provisional document that had been renewed every five years since 1971. At the same time, Abu Dhabi City was designated as the UAE's permanent capital.

In foreign relations the UAE has adopted a largely pro-Western and anti-Iranian stance. Following the fall of the Shah of Iran in 1979 and the outbreak of the Iran–Iraq war in 1980, the stability of the entire region was threatened. Partly in response to Iranian threats to close the Strait of Hormuz to shipping carrying oil exports from Gulf countries, the UAE joined with five other states to form the Gulf Co-operation Council (GCC) in 1981 to work towards political and economic integration. There has been further tension with Iran relating to territorial claims over the island of Abu Musa and the Greater and Lesser Tunb islands, strategically located in the Strait of Hormuz. Iran claimed sovereignty over the islands in the early 1990s and rejected a proposal by the GCC for the claim to be resolved by the International Court of Justice. In 1996 Iran opened an airport on Abu Musa and a power station on Greater Tunb, further damaging relations. Following UAE criticism of a rapprochement between Saudi Arabia and Iran, the GCC reiterated its support for the Emirates in the dispute in 2001. Iran rejected what it claimed was a biased and unconsultative decision. An agreement demarcating the joint border between the UAE and Oman was ratified in 2003.

UAE forces joined the US-led international coalition against Iraq after the invasion of Kuwait in 1990. Following the Sept. 2001 attacks in the USA, the UAE's banking sector was subject to international scrutiny, and the government consequently ordered financial institutions to freeze the assets of 62 organizations and individuals suspected of funding terrorist movements. The USA stationed forces in the UAE during the invasion of Iraq in March 2003.

TERRITORY AND POPULATION

The Emirates are bounded in the north by the Persian Gulf, northeast by Oman, east by the Gulf of Oman and Oman, south and west by Saudi Arabia. Their area is approximately 83,600 sq. km (32,300 sq. miles), excluding over 100 offshore islands. The total population at the 1995 census was 2,377,453 (797,710 females). 2005 population estimate, 4,496,000; density, 54 per sq. km. About one-tenth are nomads. In 2003, 85·1% of the population lived in urban areas. Approximately 78% of the population are foreigners, the highest percentage of any country.

The UN gives a projected population for 2010 of 5·03m.

Populations of the seven Emirates, 2003 estimates (in 1,000): Abu Dhabi, 1,591; Ajman, 235; Dubai, 1,204; Fujairah, 118; Ras al-Khaimah, 195; Sharjah, 636; Umm al Qaiwain, 62. The chief cities are Abu Dhabi, the federal capital (population of 904,000 in 1999), Dubai, Sharjah and Ras al-Khaimah. In addition to being the most populous Emirate, Abu Dhabi is also the wealthiest, ahead of Dubai.

The official language is Arabic; English is widely spoken.

SOCIAL STATISTICS

2002 births, 58,070; deaths, 5,994. 2002 birth rate (per 1,000 population), 19·8; death rate, 2·0; infant mortality rate (per 1,000 live births), 8 (2001). The UAE's 2002 death rate was the second lowest in the world (only Kuwait's was lower). Life expectancy, 2003, 76·4 years for men and 80·8 years for women. Annual population growth rate, 1992–2002, 2·8%; fertility rate, 2001, 3·0 births per woman.

CLIMATE

The country experiences desert conditions, with rainfall both limited and erratic. The period May to Sept. is generally rainless. Dubai, Jan. 74°F (23·4°C), July 108°F (42·3°C). Annual rainfall 2·4" (60 mm). Sharjah, Jan. 64°F (17·8°C), July 91°F (32°C). Annual rainfall 4·2" (105 mm).

CONSTITUTION AND GOVERNMENT

The Emirates is a federation, headed by a *Supreme Council of Rulers* which is composed of the seven rulers which elects from among its members a *President* and *Vice-President* for five-year terms, and appoints a *Council of Ministers*. The Council of Ministers drafts legislation and a federal budget; its proposals are submitted to a *Federal National Council* of 40 appointed members which may propose amendments but has no executive power. It was announced in Dec. 2005 that 20 of the 40 members would in future be elected through councils for each of the seven Emirates. There is a *National Consultative Council* made up of citizens.

The current constitution came into force on 2 Dec. 1971 and was made permanent in 1996.

National Anthem

'Ishy Biladi' (Long live my Homeland); words by Abdullah Al Hassan, tune by Mohamed Abdel Wahab.

GOVERNMENT CHRONOLOGY

Presidents since 1971.
1971–2004　　Sheikh Zayed bin Sultan al-Nahyan
2004–　　　　Sheikh Khalifa bin Zayed al-Nahyan

CURRENT ADMINISTRATION

President: HH Sheikh Khalifa bin Zayed al-Nahyan, Ruler of Abu Dhabi (b. 1948; appointed 3 Nov. 2004).

Members of the Supreme Council of Rulers:

President: HH Sheikh Khalifa bin Zayed al-Nahyan.

Vice-President and Prime Minister: HH Sheikh Muhammad bin Rashid al-Maktoum, Ruler of Dubai (b. 1949).

HH Dr Sheikh Sultan bin Mohammed al-Qassimi, Ruler of Sharjah.

HH Sheikh Saqr bin Mohammed al-Qassimi, Ruler of Ras al-Khaimah.

HH Sheikh Hamad bin Mohammed al-Sharqi, Ruler of Fujairah.

HH Sheikh Humaid bin Rashid al-Nuaimi, Ruler of Ajman.

HH Sheikh Rashid bin Ahmed al-Mualla, Ruler of Umm al Qaiwain.

In March 2006 the cabinet comprised:

Prime Minister and Minister of Defence: HH Sheikh Muhammad bin Rashid al-Maktoum; b. 1949 (sworn in 5 Jan. 2006).

Deputy Prime Ministers: HH Sheikh Sultan bin Zayed al-Nahyan; HH Sheikh Hamdan bin Zayed al-Nahyan.

Minister of the Interior: Maj.-Gen. Sheikh Saif bin Zayed al-Nahyan. *Finance and Industry:* HH Sheikh Hamdan bin Rashid al-Maktoum. *Economy:* Sheikha Lubna al-Qasimi. *Culture, Youth and Community Development:* Abdul Rahman Mohammed Al Owais. *Education:* Hanif Hassan Ali. *Higher Education and Scientific Research:* Sheikh Nahyan bin Mubarak Al Nahyan. *Energy:* Mohammed bin Dha'en Al Hamili. *Labour:* Ali bin

Abdullah Al Ka'abi. *Justice:* Mohammed bin Nakhira al-Dhahiri. *Foreign Affairs:* Sheikh Abdullah bin Zayed al-Nahyan. *Health:* Humaid Mohammed Obeid Al-Qattami. *Public Works:* Sheikh Hamdan bin Mubarak al-Nahyan. *Social Affairs:* Mohammed Khalfan Al Roumi. *Environment and Water:* Mohammed Saeed Al-Kindi. *Presidential Affairs:* Sheikh Mansour bin Zayed Al Nahyan.

Government Website: http://www.uae.gov.ae

CURRENT LEADERS

Sheikh Khalifa bin Zayed al-Nahyan

Position
President

Introduction
Sheikh Khalifa bin Zayed al-Nahyan was appointed president of the United Arab Emirates on 3 Nov. 2004, the day after the death of his father, Sheikh Zayed, who helped establish the country in 1971 and presided over it for 33 years. Sheikh Khalifa has continued his father's policies of co-operation with neighbouring Arab countries and with the USA, and reducing the UAE's economy's dependence on oil and gas extraction.

Early Life
Sheikh Khalifa bin Zayed al-Nahyan, the eldest son of his father, was born in 1948 in the oasis-town of Al Ain in the east of the emirate of Abu Dhabi. In 1966, following his father's promotion to the post of Ruler of Abu Dhabi, he was appointed Ruler's Representative in the Emirate's eastern province. Three years later Sheikh Khalifa was nominated as Crown Prince and head of Abu Dhabi's new Department of Defence.

When, in July 1971, Sheikh Zayed took the initiative to bring together the rulers of the Trucial States to form the United Arab Emirates (becoming the federation's president later in 1971), he appointed Sheikh Khalifa as prime minister of Abu Dhabi. Following the dissolution of Abu Dhabi's cabinet in late 1973 (it became the Abu Dhabi Executive Council) as part of the strengthening of the UAE's new institutions, Sheikh Khalifa assumed two posts—deputy prime minister in the UAE's federal cabinet and chairman of the Abu Dhabi Executive Council. He oversaw the implementation of a massive development programme in Abu Dhabi, funded by revenue from the Emirate's vast oil reserves, which included the construction of housing, water mains, roads and general infrastructure. In May 1976, following the unification of the armed forces of the seven Emirates, Sheikh Khalifa was nominated as Deputy Supreme Commander of the UAE Armed Forces. He went on to establish numerous military training institutions and was responsible for the procurement of equipment and weapons.

To advance the development of Abu Dhabi and ensure that citizens benefited from the country's growing wealth, Sheikh Khalifa established the Abu Dhabi Department of Social Services and Commercial Buildings in 1981 to offer low-interest loans for house building. The scheme was extended in 1991 and 2000, in line with the rapid increase in the country's population. From the late 1980s, Sheikh Khalifa was Chairman of the Supreme Petroleum Council, where he worked to develop the UAE's petrochemicals and industrial complex at Ruwais in an attempt to diversify the economy. He also served as chairman of the Abu Dhabi Fund for Development (responsible for the country's overseas aid programme), chairman of the Abu Dhabi Investment Authority and head of the Environmental Research and Wildlife Development Agency.

In late 1991 and early 1992 Sheikh Khalifa and his father were mired in the scandal surrounding the collapse of the BCCI bank, 77% of which was owned by the Abu Dhabi government. This followed a fraud in which its founder, Agha Hassan Abedi, and other officers stole billions of dollars. Sheikh Khalifa's scheme to compensate creditors resulted in a payout of US$1·8bn.

When Sheikh Zayed's health began to decline in the late 1990s, Sheikh Khalifa became the public face of the UAE, along with Sheikh Maktoum, Ruler of Dubai. On 3 Nov. 2004, the day after the death of Sheikh Zayed, Sheikh Khalifa was appointed president of the UAE.

Career in Office
Speaking after the swearing-in ceremony for new cabinet ministers on 21 Nov. 2004, Sheikh Khalifa said his key objective as president was to continue on the path laid down by his father. A strong supporter of the six-member Gulf Co-operation Council, Sheikh Khalifa was expected to follow his father's example of promoting solidarity between Arab states, supporting the Palestinian people and helping to restore stability in Iraq. In Dec. 2005 he announced plans for the UAE's first elections, in which half of the members of the consultative Federal National Council would be elected by a limited number of citizens.

DEFENCE

In 2003 defence expenditure totalled US$1,642m. (US$406 per capita), representing 2·1% of GDP.

Army
The strength was (2002) 35,000.

Navy
The combined naval flotilla of the Emirates includes two frigates. Personnel in 2002 numbered 2,500. The main base is at Abu Dhabi, with minor bases in the other Emirates.

Air Force
Personnel (2002) 4,000, with 101 combat aircraft (including Mirage 2000s and *Hawks*), and 49 armed helicopters.

The USA maintains 1,300 Air Force personnel in the UAE.

INTERNATIONAL RELATIONS

The UAE is a member of the UN, WTO, OPEC, the Gulf Co-operation Council, the League of Arab States and Islamic Development Bank.

ECONOMY

In 2002 agriculture accounted for 3·5% of GDP, industry 51·0% and services 45·5%.

Overview
The UAE has a strong record of market-oriented economic reform and prudent macroeconomic management. The economy has been liberalized and the private sector has grown in importance. Reforms to open the country to foreign investment and widen the tax base are in prospect.

The UAE is the sixth largest oil exporter in the world and the oil and gas sector accounts for around a third of GDP. There has been economic diversification into manufacturing, tourism, media, shipping and financial and commercial services. Growth is expected to remain strong, buoyed by persistently high oil prices and industrial growth. The economy has been running significant current account surpluses (US$12·7bn. in 2004), primarily from oil although non-oil exports in manufacturing, agriculture and services have also grown. Domestic demand has been strong as a result of favourable economic conditions and population growth driven by the influx of expatriate workers.

Demand strength has raised inflation, particularly in real estate and some services. Inflation is particularly high in Dubai. Abu Dhabi remains the UAE's dominant economy but Dubai's growth makes it an increasingly important economic region. Tourism and investor confidence have been resilient in the face of unfavourable geopolitical conditions but regional instability is a potential threat to the economy. A trade and investment framework agreement (TIFA) was signed with the USA in 2004 and a free trade agreement is under negotiation.

Currency

The unit of currency is the *dirham* (AED) of 100 *fils*. Gold reserves were 397,000 troy oz in May 2002 and foreign exchange reserves US$13,428m. Inflation was 3·1% in 2003 and 4·6% in 2004. Total money supply in May 2002 was DH 44,564m.

In 2001 the six Gulf Arab states—the United Arab Emirates, along with Bahrain, Kuwait, Oman, Qatar and Saudi Arabia—signed an agreement to establish a single currency by 2010.

Budget

The fiscal year is the calendar year. Revenue in 2001 totalled DH 82,480m. and expenditure DH 96,083m.

Revenue is principally derived from oil-concession payments. Defence, education, and public order and safety are the main items of expenditure.

Performance

In 2000 total GDP was US$70·3bn. There was real GDP growth of 11·3% in 2003 and 8·5% in 2004.

Banking and Finance

The UAE Central Bank was established in 1980 (*Governor*, Sultan bin Nasser Al-Suweidi). The largest banks are National Bank of Abu Dhabi, National Bank of Dubai, Emirates Bank International, Mashreqbank and Abu Dhabi Commercial Bank. Foreign banks are restricted to eight branches each.

There are stock exchanges in Abu Dhabi and Dubai.

ENERGY AND NATURAL RESOURCES

Environment

In 2002 carbon dioxide emissions from the consumption and flaring of fossil fuels were the equivalent of 43·5 tonnes per capita, among the highest in the world.

Electricity

Installed capacity was 5·8m. kW in 2000. Production in 2000 was approximately 31·89bn. kWh, with consumption per capita an estimated 12,237 kWh.

Oil and Gas

Oil and gas provided about 33·7% of GDP in 2002. Oil production, 2002, 105·6m. tonnes. The UAE produced 3·0% of the world total oil output in 2002, and had reserves in 2003 amounting to 97·8bn. bbls. Only Saudi Arabia, Iran and Iraq have greater reserves. Oil production in Abu Dhabi is 85% of the UAE's total.

Abu Dhabi has reserves of natural gas, nationalized in 1976. There is a gas liquefaction plant on Das Island. Gas proven reserves (2002) were 6,010bn. cu. metres. Natural gas production, 2002, 46·0bn. cu. metres.

Water

Production of drinking water by desalination of sea water (1994) was 117,000m. gallons.

Minerals

Sulphur, gypsum, chromite and lime are mined.

Agriculture

The fertile Buraimi Oasis, known as Al Ain, is largely in Abu Dhabi territory. By 1994, 21,194 farms had been set up on land reclaimed from sand dunes. A lack of water and good soil means few natural opportunities for agriculture but there is a programme of fostering agriculture by desalination, dam-building and tree-planting; strawberries, flowers and dates are now cultivated for export. 72,370 ha. were under cultivation in 1994. In 2001 there were 50,000 ha. of arable land and 188,000 ha. of permanent cropland. Output, 2000 (estimates, in 1,000 tonnes): tomatoes, 780; dates, 318; melons and watermelons, 78; cabbages, 58; pumpkins and squash, 31; aubergines, 28; lemons

and limes, 18. Livestock products, 2000 (in 1,000 tonnes): meat, 89; milk, 45; eggs, 13.

Livestock (2000): goats, 1·2m.; sheep, 467,000; camels, 200,000; cattle, 110,000; chickens, 15m.

Forestry

321,000 ha. were under forests in 2000 (3·8% of the total land area).

Fisheries

Catch, 2001, approximately 110,000 tonnes (exclusively marine fish).

INDUSTRY

According to the Financial Times Survey (FT 500), the largest companies in the United Arab Emirates by market capitalization on 4 Jan. 2001 were Etisalat (market capitalization of US$6,164·2m.), National Bank of Dubai (market capitalization of US$1,689·3m.) and Emaar Properties (market capitalization of US$1,594·5m.).

In 2001 industry accounted for 52·4% of GDP, with manufacturing contributing 13·8%. Products include aluminium, cable, cement, chemicals, fertilizers (Abu Dhabi), rolled steel and plastics (Dubai, Sharjah), and tools and clothing (Dubai). The diamond business is becoming increasingly important in Dubai.

Labour

Males constituted 87% of the economically active labour force in 2000 (the highest percentage of any country in the world). A total of 1,779,000 persons were in employment in 2000, with the leading areas of activity as follows: construction, 340,100; wholesale and retail trade/repair of motor vehicles, motorcycles and personal and household goods, 246,700; public administration and defence/compulsory social security, 235,400; manufacturing, 195,000. In 2000 the unemployment rate was 2·3%.

INTERNATIONAL TRADE

There are free trade zones at Jebel Ali (administered by Dubai), Sharjah and Fujairah. Foreign companies may set up wholly owned subsidiaries. In 1994 there were 650 companies in the Jebel Ali zone.

The United Arab Emirates, along with Bahrain, Kuwait, Oman, Qatar and Saudi Arabia began the implementation of a customs union in Jan. 2003.

Imports and Exports

Imports in 2001 totalled DH 120·6bn.; exports DH 176·9bn. Principal imports: machinery and transport equipment, food and textiles. Crude petroleum and natural gas are the main exports.

Main import suppliers, 2001: Japan (10·2%), USA (9·6%), UK (8·8%), China (8·6%), Germany (6·7%), India (6·7%). Main export markets: Japan (36·4%), India (7·5%), South Korea (7·1%), Singapore (6·3%), Iran (3·8%), Oman (3·4%).

COMMUNICATIONS

Roads

In 2002 there were 1,145 km of roads. There were 379,500 passenger cars (116 per 1,000 inhabitants) and 199,200 trucks and vans in 2002.

Civil Aviation

There are international airports at Abu Dhabi, Al Ain, Dubai, Fujairah, Ras al-Khaimah and Sharjah. Dubai is the busiest airport, handling 12,401,000 passengers and 611,900 tonnes of freight in 2001. In 2000 Abu Dhabi handled 2,894,000 passengers and Sharjah 196,200 tonnes of freight. Gulf Air is owned equally by Abu Dhabi, Bahrain, Oman and Qatar. Dubai set up its own airline, Emirates, in 1985. It now operates internationally, and in 1997 carried 3,555,700 passengers (all on international flights). In 2003 two budget airlines inaugurated scheduled services out of the UAE—Gulf Traveller, the low cost branch of Gulf Air, and Air Arabia. Etihad Airways, the national airline of the United Arab Emirates, began operations in March 2004.

Shipping
There are 15 commercial seaports, of which five major ports are on the Persian Gulf (Zayed in Abu Dhabi, Rashid and Jebel Ali in Dubai, Khalid in Sharjah, and Saqr in Ras al-Khaimah) and two on the Gulf of Oman: Fujairah and Khor Fakkan. Rashid and Fujairah are important container terminals. In 2002 the merchant marine totalled 703,000 GRT, including oil tankers 221,000 GRT.

Telecommunications
Telephone subscribers numbered 3,521,700 in 2002 (1,100·5 per 1,000 persons) and there were 450,000 PCs in use (140·6 for every 1,000 persons). There were 2,428,100 mobile phone subscribers in 2002 and 1,175,600 Internet users. There were 15,700 fax machines in use in 2002.

Postal Services
In 2003 there were 279 post offices.

SOCIAL INSTITUTIONS

Justice
The basic principles of the law are Islamic. Legislation seeks to promote the harmonious functioning of society's multi-national components while protecting the interests of the indigenous population. Each Emirate has its own penal code. A federal code takes precedence and ensures compatibility. There are federal courts with appellate powers, which function under federal laws. Emirates have the option to merge their courts with the federal judiciary.

The death penalty for drug smuggling was introduced in April 1995.

Education
In 2000–01 there were 67,749 pre-primary pupils with 3,691 teachers, 280,248 primary pupils with 17,573 teachers, and 220,134 secondary pupils with 16,950 teachers. In 2002–03 there were 16,128 students at the Emirates University and 14,265 students in higher colleges. There were 2,245 students at the four faculties of Zayed University in 2002–03. The adult literacy rate in 2002 was 77·3% (75·6% among males and 80·7% among females). In 1998–99 total expenditure on education came to 1·8% of GNP.

Health
In 2003 there were 38 government hospitals with 5,722 beds. In 2003 there were 27 private hospitals, 131 government health centres and 1,281 private clinics. There were 5,825 physicians in 2001 and 954 dentists, 12,045 nurses and 1,086 pharmacists.

RELIGION
Most inhabitants are Sunni Muslims, with a small Shia minority.

CULTURE

Broadcasting
There are several government authorities providing broadcasting nationally (Voice of the United Arab Emirates, Capital Radio, which is partly commercial, and United Arab Emirates Television Service), and regionally (UAE Radio and Television-Dubai, Ras al-Khaimah Broadcasting, Umm al Qaiwain Broadcasting and Sharjah TV). The major satellite news channels are Al-Arabiya, based in Dubai, and Abu Dhabi TV. Both came to prominence at the time of the war in Iraq in March–April 2003. There were 780,000 TV sets (colour by PAL) in 2001 and 1·03m. radio receivers in 2000.

Press
In 1996 there were nine daily newspapers (five Arabic and four English) with a combined circulation of 0·3m.

Tourism
In 2002 there were 3,920,000 foreign tourists; spending by tourists totalled US$1,328m.

DIPLOMATIC REPRESENTATIVES
Of the UAE in the United Kingdom (30 Prince's Gate, London, SW7 1PT)
Ambassador: Easa Saleh Al Gurg, CBE.

Of the United Kingdom in the UAE (POB 248, Abu Dhabi)
Ambassador: Richard Makepeace.

Of the UAE in the USA (3522 International Court, NW, Washington, D.C., 20008)
Ambassador: Alasari Saeed Aldhahri.

Of the USA in the UAE (POB 4009, Abu Dhabi)
Ambassador: Michele J. Sison.

Of the UAE to the United Nations
Ambassador: Abdulaziz Nasser Al-Shamsi.

Of the UAE to the European Union
Ambassador: Abdel Hadi Abdel Wahid Al-Khajah.

FURTHER READING
Clements, F. A., *United Arab Emirates.* [Bibliography] ABC-Clio, Oxford and Santa Barbara (CA), (rev. ed.) 1998
Vine, P. and Al Abed, I., *United Arab Emirates: A New Perspective.* Trident Press, Naples, Florida, 2001

UNITED KINGDOM OF GREAT BRITAIN AND NORTHERN IRELAND

© Research Machines plc 2006

Capital: London
Population projection, 2010: 61·18m.
GDP per capita, 2003: (PPP$) 27,147
HDI/world rank: 0·939/15

KEY HISTORICAL EVENTS

Remains of Stone Age settlements of hunters and fishermen suggest that the first inhabitants crossed from the low countries of Continental Europe on one or more wide causeways. By the time their successors had turned to subsistence farming, the land links to the continent had disappeared under the sea. These offshore islands created at the ending of the Ice Age shared, with nearside Europe, a slowly evolving agricultural economy using bronze and iron tools. The Ancient Britons were Celts, whose ancestors had migrated from the valleys of the Rhine, the Rhône and the Danube. Having asserted their command of northern Italy and France (Gaul), the Celts established a bridgehead to Ireland and thence to Britain. By 600 BC they were the undisputed dominant force of Western Europe and were to remain so until challenged by the Romans.

The Romans were dominant from AD 78. From the 3rd century they were increasingly harried by tribes of Celts from Scotland and Ireland and by Angles and Saxons from northern Germany. Celtic tradition, presided over by druids (religious leaders) and bards (storytellers), survived most successfully in Ireland and Wales where Roman influence was barely visible. Scotland resisted the Roman legions; Hadrian's Wall was built as a northern frontier between the Tyne and Solway Firth in the early 2nd century AD. Roman authority was challenged, notably by Boadicea, queen of the Iceni tribe of East Anglia. The rebellion and the brutal repression that followed led to a long period of peaceful settlement, during which the Romans established a road network linking new towns such as Londinium (London) and Eboracum (York). But by the 5th century Roman Britain had disintegrated into a collection of warring kingdoms. The English and Welsh economies thrived on the export of silver, lead, gold, iron and other minerals. With the spread of Christianity, chiefly by Irish missionaries, came the beginnings of an education and legal system.

After the withdrawal of the Roman legions in the early 5th century, the Romano-British were pushed back to higher land in the west by waves of invading Saxons, Angles and Jutes. Danish invasions in 865 established the Danelaw in northern England. Alfred the Great of Wessex resisted Danish expansion, strengthening Anglo-Saxon unity.

Norman Conquest
William, duke of Normandy led the Norman Conquest and was crowned king in 1066. When William died in 1087 he left Normandy to his eldest son Robert, thus separating it from England. The French dialect known as Anglo-Norman was spoken by the ruling class in England for two centuries after the Conquest. The Norman heritage was preserved also in the overlap between French and English feudal lords. Henry II, the founder of the Plantagenet dynasty, was feudatory lord of half of France. But most of the French possessions were lost by Henry's son John. Thereafter, the Norman baronage came to regard themselves as English. The ambitions of Edward III began and those of Henry V renewed the Hundred Years War (1338–1453) with France, which ended with the loss of all the remaining French possessions except Calais.

The dynastic struggle between the rival houses of York and Lancaster was concluded by the invasion of Henry (VII) Tudor in 1485. His son, Henry VIII, asserted royal authority over the church and rejected papal authority. Tudor power reached its zenith with Elizabeth I, under whom Protestantism became firmly established in England. The Spanish Armada—an attempt by Catholic Spain to return England to the papal fold—was repelled in 1588.

The accession of James VI of Scotland to the English throne in 1603 brought the two countries into dynastic union. A struggle for supremacy between Crown and Parliament culminated in the Civil War, begun in 1642. Charles I was executed by Parliament in 1649, beginning the rule of Protector Oliver Cromwell. The Stuart monarchy was restored in 1660, on terms which conceded financial authority and thus decision-making power to Parliament. The attempt of James II, a Catholic, to restore the royal prerogative led to the intervention of William of Orange. James fled the country and the crown was taken by William (III) and his wife Mary as queen regnant. The accession of William involved England in a protracted war against France.

The parliaments of England and Scotland were united in 1707 under Queen Anne, the first British monarch. With the accession of the Hanoverian George I in 1714, the system of Parliamentary party government took hold. By the mid-18th century London had taken over from Amsterdam as the leading financial centre. With easy access to capital, entrepreneurs were able to invest in new, improved methods of production. With the harnessing of steam power made possible by the engineering genius of Thomas Newcomen and James Watt, economic enterprise shifted away from the southeast to the north of England, Scotland and South Wales where there were large reserves of coal. The demand for raw materials and the pursuit of markets for finished goods opened up trade throughout the civilized world and extended British influence.

American Colonies

Britain's first successful colonies in North America were established in the reign of James I of England (1603–25) and, soon afterwards, Bermuda, St Kitts, Barbados and Nevis were colonized. By the mid-17th century, Britain controlled the American east coast and had strong bases in India and in the West Indies, where the sugar economy was dependent on slave labour imported from West Africa. Critical to imperial expansion was Britain's rivalry with France. Britain emerged much strengthened from the War of the League of Augsburg (1689–97) and the War of Spanish Succession (1702–13) while French ambitions in Europe and beyond were severely curtailed. But it was the Seven Years' War (1756–63), in which France and Prussia were the chief contenders, that deprived France of her remaining territorial claims in North America and India and confirmed Britain as the world's leading maritime power.

Relations between Parliament and Crown went through an unsettled period in the reign of George III, who was blamed for the loss of the American colonies. The War of Independence ended with Britain's recognition of American right to self-government in 1783. In 1793 revolutionary France declared war and was not finally defeated until 1815. The demands of war further stimulated the new, steam-powered industries. Despite Britain finding itself the pre-eminent world power, after 1815 there was frequent unrest as an increasingly urban and industrial society found its interests poorly represented by a parliament composed chiefly of landowners. The Reform Act of 1832 extended representation in Parliament and further acts (1867, 1884, 1918 and 1928) led gradually to universal adult suffrage.

Ireland was brought under direct rule from Westminster in 1801, creating the United Kingdom of Great Britain and Ireland. The accession of Victoria in 1837 was the beginning of an era of unprecedented material progress. Early industrial development produced great national wealth but its distribution was uneven and the condition of the poor improved slowly. Whereas early Victorian reforms were responses to obvious distress, governments after 1868 were more inclined towards preventive state action.

The Victorian empire included India, Canada, Australasia and vast territories in Africa and Eastern Asia. There was war with Russia in the Crimea (1854–56); most wars, however, were fought to conquer or pacify colonies. After 1870 the Suez Canal enabled Britain to control the empire more efficiently; Britain became a 40% shareholder in 1875 and the controlling power in Egypt in 1882. The most serious imperial wars were the Boer Wars of 1881 and 1899–1902 against the Dutch settlers in South Africa. After a less than glorious victory, Britain negotiated a Union of South Africa, by which South Africa enjoyed the same autonomy agreed for Canada (1867), Australia (1901) and later New Zealand (1907). The 'dominion status' of these countries was clarified by the Statute of Westminster (1931).

With the spread of trade unionism and the emergence of the Labour Party, the gap between right- and left-wing politics widened after 1900. Labour had to wait until 1924 to form its first government but the Liberal landslide of 1906 carried forward the programme of social reform. David Lloyd George's People's Budget led to the abolition of the Lords' right to override the House of Commons while a contributory insurance scheme to cover basic health care, a modest benefit for the unemployed,

free school meals and non-contributory old age pensions were all introduced.

On 3 Aug. 1914 Germany invaded Belgium. Britain was obliged by treaty to retaliate by declaring war. Four years of bloody trench warfare ensued in northern France and Belgium, with American intervention in 1917 helping to break the stalemate. The United Kingdom alone lost 715,000 soldiers and another 200,000 from the empire. Rebellions broke out in Ireland, born of the failure of successive attempts to agree a formula for Irish Home Rule. The issue was complicated by factional disagreement in southern Ireland and the wish of northern Ireland (Ulster) to remain in the United Kingdom. In 1920, after four years' conflict, the Government of Ireland Act partitioned the country. The northern six counties remained British, a parliament was created and a Unionist government took office. The southern 26 counties moved by stages to complete independence as the Irish Free State in 1922.

Second World War

A post-war boom was followed by a lengthy recession and heavy unemployment, exacerbated by the reluctance of politicians to adopt Keynesian economics. Germany revived as a military power in the 1930s, unchecked by reluctant neighbours after the punitive Treaty of Versailles. British Prime Minister Neville Chamberlain agreed to the German acquisition of parts of Czechoslovakia at the Munich Agreement in 1938. His policy of appeasement was much criticized, though it is arguable that Britain was in no position to go to war in 1938. Germany invaded Poland on 1 Sept. 1939. Britain, bound once more by treaty, declared war. In May 1940 Chamberlain was replaced as prime minister by Winston Churchill, who formed a national unity government. Although British military casualties were less than in the 1914–18 war, the civilian population was hit much worse during the Second World War; over 90,000 died, many as a result of German bombing in the Battle of Britain in 1940.

The war ended with German and Japanese defeat in 1945, by which stage the United Kingdom was virtually bankrupt. In 1939 the country had had assets of around £3,000m. By the end of the war, it owed about the same amount. A pre-war balance of payments deficit averaging £43m. a year had jumped to £750m. It was a time of great social upheaval. In the 1945 election a Labour government under Clement Attlee was returned with a large majority and a socialist programme, which emphasized wealth distribution above wealth creation, was implemented. It undertook to establish a free National Health Service, an ambitious housing programme and the state control of major industries. Subsequent governments modified but generally accepted the changes.

With Britain bankrupted, the United States stepped into the breach as the now undisputed free world leader. Fearing a European breakdown and a Communist takeover, the Marshall Plan was implemented by the USA, providing massive investment to rebuild Europe. An essential condition of the Marshall Plan was a joint effort of the participating nations to put their economies in order. But when continental leaders made the first tentative moves towards European unity, the UK was unwilling to be closely involved. With the independence of India (and Pakistan), the centrepiece of the British Empire, in 1947, decolonization took root, reaching its climax in the 1960s. Rather than to Europe, Britain now looked instead to a Commonwealth of freely associated states, recognizing the British monarch as symbolic Commonwealth head (some states chose to retain the monarch as head of state), and to the 'special relationship' with the United States.

In March 1957 France, Germany, Italy, Belgium, the Netherlands and Luxembourg signed the Treaty of Rome, which laid down terms for the European Economic Community. Two years later seven of the European countries outside the Common Market— Austria, Denmark, Norway, Portugal, Sweden, Switzerland and the UK—formed the European Free Trade Association. When the United Kingdom moved to join the EEC in 1962, five of the six members of the Community were willing to support the application but France vetoed it. A second application, in 1967, also failed but admission was achieved in 1973 under the Conservative government of Edward Heath. Membership of the Community was endorsed by referendum in 1975.

On the wider international scene, the limits of independent military action were made clear by the Suez crisis of 1956 when the UK, in collusion with France and Israel, used force to stop President Nasser of Egypt nationalizing the Suez Canal. Assumed American support was not forthcoming and the enterprise collapsed when the UK was left alone to cope with a potentially disastrous run on sterling. In the 1960s and 1970s the UK began to come to terms with advanced technology. Old-established industries such as textiles, shipbuilding, iron and steel and coal mining, the leaders of the first industrial revolution, gave way to manufacturing that relied on the microchip. Service industries, particularly in the financial sector, occupied an increasing share of the economy and trade restrictions were dismantled throughout the world.

In 1979 a Conservative government led by Margaret Thatcher came to power, committed to a free market economy. State industry was returned to private enterprise, the trade unions (blamed for the crippling 1978–79 Winter of Discontent) lost much of their power to direct government policy, and high earners were to benefit from lower taxation. A period of readjustment climaxed with a coal miners' strike during 1984–85 that turned into a trial of strength between the government and organized labour. The Labour Party and allied unions, themselves in the process of modernization, distanced themselves from the socialist rhetoric of the miners' leaders and the strike collapsed.

Despite rising living standards, there was concern about the quality of essential services such as education and health and disillusionment with a Conservative administration unable to construct a coherent European policy. In 1997 a Labour government, led by Tony Blair, was returned with a large Commons majority. Like Thatcher, he believed in the free market. In addition he introduced reforms in the system of government including the abolition of voting rights of hereditary peers in the House of Lords and the setting up of directly elected assemblies for Scotland, Wales and Northern Ireland. Prime Minister Blair has shown far greater enthusiasm for involvement in Europe, arguing for entry into the single currency, should certain economic criteria be met. Conversely, the war in Iraq has gone some way to re-cementing the 'special' relationship with the USA. Fears of terrorist reprisals for British involvement in the Iraq war were realised on 7 July 2005 when bombs planted on three London underground trains and a bus killed 52 people.

TERRITORY AND POPULATION

Area (in sq. km) and population at the census taken on 29 April 2001:

Divisions	Area	Population
England	130,281	49,138,831
Wales	20,732	2,903,085
Scotland	77,925	5,062,011
Northern Ireland	14,135	1,685,267
	243,073	58,789,194

Population of the United Kingdom (present on census night) at the four previous decennial censuses:

Divisions	1961	1971	1981	1991
England[1]	43,460,525	46,018,371	46,226,100[2]	46,382,050
Wales	2,644,023	2,731,204	2,790,500[2]	2,811,865
Scotland	5,179,344	5,228,963	5,130,700	4,998,567
Northern Ireland	1,425,042	1,536,065	1,532,196[3]	1,577,836
United Kingdom	52,708,934	55,514,603	55,679,496[2]	55,770,318

[1]Areas now included in Wales formed the English county of Monmouthshire until 1974.
[2]The final counts for England and Wales are believed to be over-stated as a result of an error in processing. The preliminary counts presented here rounded to the nearest hundred are thought to be more accurate.
[3]There was a high level of non-enumeration in Northern Ireland during the 1981 census mainly as a result of protests in Catholic areas about the Republican hunger strikes.

UK population estimate, mid-2004, 59,787,000 (30,544,000 females and 29,243,000 males); density, 246 per sq. km. In 2003, 89·1% of the population lived in urban areas.

The projected population for 2010 is 61·18m.

Population of the United Kingdom by sex at census day 2001:

Divisions	Males	Females
England	23,923,390	25,215,441
Wales	1,403,900	1,499,185
Scotland	2,432,494	2,629,517
Northern Ireland	821,449	863,818
United Kingdom	28,581,233	30,207,961

Households in the United Kingdom at the 2001 census: England, 21,262,000; Wales, 1,276,000; Scotland, 2,192,000; Northern Ireland, 627,000.

The age distribution in the United Kingdom at census day in 2001 was as follows (in 1,000):

Age-group	England and Wales	Scotland	Northern Ireland	United Kingdom
Under 5	3,094	277	115	3,486
5 and under 10	3,308	307	123	3,738
10 ,, 15	3,425	323	133	3,881
15 ,, 20	3,217	317	129	3,663
20 ,, 25	3,122	314	109	3,545
25 ,, 35	7,419	699	242	8,360
35 ,, 45	7,749	781	247	8,777
45 ,, 55	6,887	689	199	7,775
55 ,, 65	5,507	550	162	6,219
65 ,, 70	2,292	239	65	2,596
70 ,, 75	2,074	207	58	2,339
75 ,, 85	2,933	271	77	3,281
85 and upwards	1,012	88	23	1,123

In 2001, 18·85% of the population of the UK were under the age of 14, 60·35% between 15 and 59, 13·29% between 60 and 74, and 7·51% aged 75 and over. In 1951 only 3·54% of the population had been 75 and over.

England and Wales. The census population (present on census night) of England and Wales 1801 to 2001:

Date of enumeration	Population	Pop. per sq. mile	Date of enumeration	Population	Pop. per sq. mile[1]
1801	8,892,536	152	1901	32,527,843	558
1811	10,164,256	174	1911	36,070,492	618
1821	12,000,236	206	1921	37,886,699	649
1831	13,896,797	238	1931	39,952,377	685
1841	15,914,148	273	1951	43,757,888	750
1851	17,927,609	307	1961	46,104,548	791
1861	20,066,224	344	1971	48,749,575	323
1871	22,712,266	389	1981	49,016,600	325
1881	25,974,439	445	1991	49,193,915	330
1891	29,002,525	497	2001	52,041,916	345

[1]Per sq. km from 1971.

Estimated population of England and Wales, mid-2004, 53,017,000 (27,046,000 females and 25,971,000 males).

The birthplaces of the population of Great Britain at census day 2001 were: England, 43,967,372; Wales, 2,815,088; Scotland,

5,229,366; Northern Ireland, 256,503; Ireland, 494,154; other European Union countries, 763,171; elsewhere, 3,578,273.

Ethnic Groups. The 1991 census was the first to include a question on ethnic status.

Percentage figures from the 2001 census relating to ethnicity in England and Wales:

	England and Wales (%)	England (%)	Wales (%)
White			
British	87·5	87·0	96·0
Irish	1·2	1·3	0·6
Other	2·6	2·7	1·3
Mixed			
White and Black Caribbean	0·5	0·5	0·2
White and Black African	0·2	0·2	0·1
White and Asian	0·4	0·4	0·2
Other Mixed	0·3	0·3	0·1
Asian or Asian British			
Indian	2·0	2·1	0·3
Pakistani	1·4	1·4	0·3
Bangladeshi	0·5	0·6	0·2
Other Asian	0·5	0·5	0·1
Black or Black British			
Caribbean	1·1	1·1	0·1
African	0·9	1·0	0·1
Other Black	0·2	0·2	0·0
Chinese	0·4	0·4	0·2
Other ethnic groups	0·4	0·4	0·2

In Scotland about 2% of the population in 2001 were from a minority (non-White) ethnic group, compared with 1·3% in 1991. Pakistanis formed the largest such group, constituting 0·3%.

11 'Standard Regions' (also classified as 'level 1 regions' for EU purposes) are identified in the UK as economic planning regions. They have no administrative significance. They are: Northern Ireland, Scotland, Wales and eight regions of England (East Anglia, East Midlands, North, North West, South East, South West, West Midlands, Yorkshire and Humberside).

The following table shows the distribution of the urban and rural population of England and Wales (persons present) in 1951, 1961, 1971 and 1981:

	England and Wales	Population Urban districts[1]	Rural districts[1]	Percentage Urban	Rural
1951	43,757,888	35,335,721	8,422,167	80·8	19·2
1961	46,071,604	36,838,442	9,233,162	80·0	20·0
1971	48,755,000	38,151,000	10,598,000	78·2	21·5
1981	49,011,417	37,686,863	11,324,554	76·9	23·1

[1]As existing at each census.

Urban and rural areas were re-defined for the 1981 and 1991 censuses on a land use basis. In Scotland 'localities' correspond to urban areas. The 1981 census gave the usually resident population of England and Wales as 48,521,596, of which 43,599,431 were in urban areas; and of Scotland as 5,035,315, of which 4,486,140 were in localities.

British Citizenship. Under the British Nationality Act 1981 there are three main forms of citizenship: citizenship for persons closely connected with the UK; British Dependent Territories citizenship; British Overseas citizenship. British citizenship is acquired automatically at birth by a child born in the UK if his or her mother or father is a British citizen or is settled in the UK. A child born abroad to a British citizen is a British citizen by descent. British citizenship may be acquired by registration for stateless persons, and for children not automatically acquiring such citizenship or born abroad to parents who are citizens by descent; and, for other adults, by naturalization. Requirements for the latter include five years' residence (three years for applicants married to a British citizen). The Hong Kong (British Nationality) Order 1986 created the status of British National (Overseas) for

citizens connected with Hong Kong before 1997, and the British Nationality (Hong Kong) Act 1990 made provision for up to 50,000 selected persons to register as British citizens.

Emigration and Immigration. Immigration is mainly governed by the Immigration Act 1970 and Immigration Rules made under it. British and Commonwealth citizens with the right of abode before 1983 are not subject to immigration control, nor are citizens of European Economic Area countries. Other persons seeking to work or settle in the UK must obtain a visa or entry clearance.

Total international migration estimates for recent years are as follows.

Inflows:

	Total	British	Non-British
2000	483,400	104,100	379,300
2001	479,600	106,300	373,300
2002	512,800	94,600	418,200
2003	512,600	105,800	406,800

Outflows:

	Total	British	Non-British
2000	320,700	161,100	159,600
2001	307,700	159,200	148,500
2002	359,400	185,700	173,700
2003	361,500	190,900	170,600

The number of emigrants from the UK in 2003, at 361,500, was the highest on record for a calendar year.

In 2003 there were 141,490 acceptances for settlement in the UK (115,965 in 2002), including from: Asia, 55,190; Africa, 45,835; Europe, 15,390. Main individual countries were: Pakistan, 13,120; India, 11,460; South Africa, 8,930; Nigeria, 7,695; Somalia, 6,820; USA, 5,695; Bangladesh, 5,610; Jamaica, 4,500; Turkey, 4,340; Australia, 4,160.

Asylum. In 2004 there were 33,960 applications for asylum (compared to 49,405 in 2003, a record 84,130 in 2002, 71,025 in 2001, 29,640 in 1996 and 2,905 in 1984). The main countries of origin in 2004 were Iran, Somalia, China and Zimbabwe. Applications, including dependants, were 40,625 in 2004. While respecting its obligations to political refugees under the UN Convention and Protocol relating to the status of Refugees, the government has powers under the Asylum and Immigration Act 1996 to weed out applicants seeking entry for non-political reasons and to designate certain countries as not giving risk of persecution. In the period 1999–2003 the UK received 356,035 applications for asylum and granted asylum to 46,455 persons.

Coleman, D. and Salt, J., *The British Population: Patterns, Trends and Processes.* OUP, 1992

See also ENGLAND, SCOTLAND, WALES *and* NORTHERN IRELAND: Territory and Population

SOCIAL STATISTICS

UK statistics, 2003: births, 695,525 (288,500 outside marriage); deaths, 612,033; marriages, 306,214; divorces, 166,737; abortions (2002), 197,119. Great Britain statistics, 2003: births, 673,877; deaths, 597,571; marriages, 298,457; divorces, 164,418. The number of births in 2003 was the highest since 1999, but prior to that the lowest since 1975. In 1976, uniquely in British history, deaths in the UK (680,800) exceeded births (675,500). In 2002 cancer caused 159,000 deaths (23% of all deaths in the UK, making it the biggest killer, ahead of coronary heart disease, at 114,000 (16%) and respiratory diseases, at 79,000 (12%)). UK life expectancy, 2003: males, 76·0 years; females, 80·6. The World Health Organization's 2004 World Health Report put the UK in 24th place in a 'healthy life expectancy' list, with an expected 70·6 years of healthy life for babies born in 2002 (down from 71·7 years in 1999). Annual population growth rate, 1992–2002,

0·3%. In 2002 there were 5,882 suicides (4,354 among men and 1,468 among women), giving a suicide rate of 10 per 100,000 population. Infant mortality, 2003, 5·3 per 1,000 live births. Fertility rate, 2001, 1·6 births per woman. Of the 695,525 live births in the UK in 2003, 41·5% were to unmarried women, up from 6% in 1961 and 20% in 1986. In 1999 for the first time there were more births to women in the 30–34 age group than in the 25–29 bracket. UK birth rate (per 1,000 population), 2003, 11·7; death rate, 2003, 10·3. The average age of first marriage in England and Wales in 2001 was 30·6 years for men and 28·4 years for women, up from 24·6 years for men and 22·6 years for women in 1971. 40% of marriages in 1999 were religious and 60% civil, compared to 52% religious and 48% civil in 1981. Same-sex civil partnerships were legalized in Dec. 2005.

In 2003, 16·0% of the total population was over 65, up from 11·7% in 1960. As the ageing population continues to grow, it has been estimated that by 2010 there will be 350,000 more people over the age of 80 than there were at the end of the 20th century. The first decade of the new century is also expected to see a rise of 1·4m., or 23%, in the number of people between 55 and 64. By 2000 the number of centenarians had surpassed 8,000.

In 2000 the average household in Great Britain consisted of 2·4 people, down from 3·1 in 1961. There were more than 1·5m. single parents in 2001, comprising 6·5% of all households.

England and Wales statistics (in 1,000), 2003 (and 2002): births, 621 (596); deaths, 539 (535); marriages, 268 (256); divorces, 153 (148). In 2002 there was a rise in the number of births for the first time since 1996.

Britain has one of the highest rates of drug usage in Europe. Figures released in Nov. 1999 showed that approaching 40% of schoolchildren aged 15 and 16 have tried cannabis, and 9% of adults did so in the previous 12 months. Use of ecstasy, amphetamines and LSD in England and Wales was the highest in the European Union. Drug-related deaths increased by 70% between 1992 and 1999.

A UNICEF report published in 2005 showed that 15·4% of children in Great Britain live in poverty (in households with income below 50% of the national median), compared to just 2·4% in Denmark. A similar report from 2000 had shown that the poverty rate of children in lone-parent families in the UK was 45·6%, compared to 13·3% in two-parent families.

See also NORTHERN IRELAND: Social Statistics

CLIMATE

The climate is cool temperate oceanic, with mild conditions and rainfall evenly distributed over the year, though the weather is very changeable because of cyclonic influences. In general, temperatures are higher in the west and lower in the east in winter and rather the reverse in summer. Rainfall amounts are greatest in the west, where most of the high ground occurs.

London, Jan. 39°F (3·9°C), July 64°F (17·8°C). Annual rainfall 25" (635 mm). Aberdeen, Jan. 38°F (3·3°C), July 57°F (13·9°C). Annual rainfall 32" (813 mm). Belfast, Jan. 40°F (4·5°C), July 59°F (15·0°C). Annual rainfall 37·4" (950 mm). Birmingham, Jan. 38°F (3·3°C), July 61°F (16·1°C). Annual rainfall 30" (749 mm). Cardiff, Jan. 40°F (4·4°C), July 61°F (16·1°C). Annual rainfall 42·6" (1,065 mm). Edinburgh, Jan. 38°F (3·3°C), July 58°F (14·5°C). Annual rainfall 27" (686 mm). Glasgow, Jan. 39°F (3·9°C), July 59°F (15·0°C). Annual rainfall 38" (965 mm). Manchester, Jan. 39°F (3·9°C), July 61°F (16·1°C). Annual rainfall 34·5" (876 mm).

CONSTITUTION AND GOVERNMENT

The reigning Queen, Head of the Commonwealth, is **Elizabeth II** Alexandra Mary, b. 21 April 1926, daughter of King George VI and Queen Elizabeth; married on 20 Nov. 1947 Lieut. Philip Mountbatten (formerly Prince Philip of Greece), created Duke of Edinburgh, Earl of Merioneth and Baron Greenwich on the same day and created Prince Philip, Duke of Edinburgh, 22 Feb.

1957; succeeded to the crown on the death of her father, on 6 Feb. 1952.

Offspring. Prince Charles Philip Arthur George, Prince of Wales (Heir Apparent), b. 14 Nov. 1948; married Lady Diana Frances Spencer on 29 July 1981; after divorce, 28 Aug. 1996, Diana, Princess of Wales. She died in Paris in a road accident on 31 Aug. 1997; married Camilla Parker Bowles on 9 April 2005. *Offspring of first marriage:* William Arthur Philip Louis, b. 21 June 1982; Henry Charles Albert David, b. 15 Sept. 1984. Princess Anne Elizabeth Alice Louise, the Princess Royal, b. 15 Aug. 1950; married Mark Anthony Peter Phillips on 14 Nov. 1973; divorced, 1992; married Cdr Timothy Laurence on 12 Dec. 1992. *Offspring of first marriage:* Peter Mark Andrew, b. 15 Nov. 1977; Zara Anne Elizabeth, b. 15 May 1981. Prince Andrew Albert Christian Edward, created Duke of York, 23 July 1986, b. 19 Feb. 1960; married Sarah Margaret Ferguson on 23 July 1986; after divorce, 30 May 1996, Sarah, Duchess of York. *Offspring:* Princess Beatrice Mary, b. 8 Aug. 1988; Princess Eugenie Victoria Helena, b. 23 March 1990. Prince Edward Antony Richard Louis, created Earl of Wessex and Viscount Severn, 19 June 1999, b. 10 March 1964; married Sophie Rhys-Jones, Countess of Wessex, on 19 June 1999. *Offspring:* Lady Louise Alice Elizabeth Mary, b. 8 Nov. 2003.

Sister of the Queen. Princess Margaret Rose, Countess of Snowdon, b. 12 Aug. 1930; married Antony Armstrong-Jones (created Earl of Snowdon, 3 Oct. 1961) on 6 May 1960; divorced, 1978; died 9 Feb. 2002. *Offspring:* David Albert Charles (Viscount Linley), b. 3 Nov. 1961, married Serena Alleyne Stanhope on 8 Oct. 1993. *Offspring:* Charles Patrick Inigo Armstrong Jones, b. 1 July 1999. Lady Sarah Frances Elizabeth Chatto, b. 1 May 1964; married Daniel Chatto on 14 July 1994. *Offspring:* Samuel David Benedict Chatto, b. 28 July 1996; Arthur Robert Nathaniel Chatto, b. 5 Feb. 1999.

The Queen's legal title rests on the statute of 12 and 13 Will. III, ch. 3, by which the succession to the Crown of Great Britain and Ireland was settled on the Princess Sophia of Hanover and the 'heirs of her body being Protestants'. By proclamation of 17 July 1917 the royal family became known as the House and Family of Windsor. On 8 Feb. 1960 the Queen issued a declaration varying her confirmatory declaration of 9 April 1952 to the effect that while the Queen and her children should continue to be known as the House of Windsor, her descendants, other than descendants entitled to the style of Royal Highness and the title of Prince or Princess, and female descendants who marry and their descendants should bear the name of Mountbatten-Windsor.

Lineage to the throne. 1) Prince of Wales. 2) Prince William of Wales. 3) Prince Henry of Wales. 4) Duke of York. 5) Princess Beatrice of York. 6) Princess Eugenie of York.

By letters patent of 30 Nov. 1917 the titles of Royal Highness and Prince or Princess are restricted to the Sovereign's children, the children of the Sovereign's sons and the eldest living son of the eldest son of the Prince of Wales.

Provision is made for the support of the royal household, after the surrender of hereditary revenues, by the settlement of the Civil List soon after the beginning of each reign. The Civil List Act of 1 Jan. 1972 provided for a decennial, and the Civil List (Increase of Financial Provision) Order 1975 for an annual review of the List, but in July 1990 it was again fixed for one decade.

The Civil List of 2001–10 provides for an annuity of £7,900,000 to the Queen; and £359,000 to Prince Philip. These amounts are the same as for the period 1991–2000. The income of the Prince of Wales derives from the Duchy of Cornwall. The Civil List was exempted from taxation in 1910. The Queen has paid income tax on her private income since April 1993.

The supreme legislative power is vested in Parliament, which consists of the Crown, the House of Lords and the House of Commons, and dates in its present form from the middle of the 14th century. A Bill which is passed by both Houses and receives Royal Assent becomes an Act of Parliament and part of statute law.

Parliament is summoned, and a General Election is called, by the sovereign on the advice of the Prime Minister. A Parliament may last up to five years, normally divided into annual sessions. A session is ended by prorogation, and most Public Bills which have not been passed by both Houses then lapse, unless they are subject to a carry over motion. A Parliament ends by dissolution, either by will of the sovereign or by lapse of the five-year period.

Under the Parliament Acts 1911 and 1949, all Money Bills (so certified by the Speaker of the House of Commons), if not passed by the Lords without amendment, may become law without their concurrence within one month of introduction in the Lords. Public Bills, other than Money Bills or a Bill extending the maximum duration of Parliament, if passed by the Commons in two successive sessions and rejected each time by the Lords, may become law without being passed by the Lords provided that one year has elapsed between Commons second reading in the first session and third reading in the second session, and that the Bill reaches the Lords at least one month before the end of the second session. The Parliament Acts have been used three times since 1949: in 1991 for the War Crimes Act, in 1999 for the European Parliamentary Elections Act and for the Sexual Offences (Amendment) Act in 2000.

Peerages are created by the sovereign, on the advice of the prime minister, with no limits on their number. The following are the main categories of membership (composition at 1 Dec. 2005, excluding 12 peers who were on leave of absence):

Party	Life Peers	Hereditary: Elected by Party	Hereditary: Elected Office Holders	Hereditary: Royal Office Holders	Bishops	Total
Conservative	158	40	9	...	...	207
Labour	206	2	2	...	...	210
Liberal Democrat	69	3	2	...	...	74
Crossbench	161	28	2	2	...	193
Archbishops and Bishops	...	...	...	...	26	26
Other	9	2	...	...	...	11
Total	603	75	15	2[1]	26	721

[1]The Duke of Norfolk, Earl Marshal and the Marquess of Cholmondeley, Lord Great Chamberlain.

Composition by type:

Archbishops and bishops	26	
Life Peers under the Appellate Jurisdiction Act 1876	28	(1 woman)
Life Peers under the Life Peerages Act 1958	587	(131 women)
Peers under the House of Lords Act 1999	92	(3 women)
Total	733	

The House of Commons consists of members (of both sexes) representing constituencies determined by the Boundary Commissions. Persons under 21 years of age, Clergy of the Church of England and of the Scottish Episcopal Church, Ministers of the Church of Scotland, Roman Catholic clergymen, civil servants, members of the regular armed forces, policemen, most judicial officers and other office-holders named in the House of Commons (Disqualification) Act are disqualified from sitting in the House of Commons. No peer eligible to sit in the House of Lords can be elected to the House of Commons unless he has disclaimed his title, but Irish peers and holders of courtesy titles, who are not members of the House of Lords, are eligible.

The Representation of the People Act 1948 abolished the business premises and University franchises, and the only persons entitled to vote at Parliamentary elections are those registered as residents or as service voters. No person may vote in more than one constituency at a general election. All persons may apply to vote by post if they are unable to vote in person, or if they fulfil certain legal requirements they may also be entitled to vote by proxy. Elections are held on the first-past-the-post system, in which the candidate who receives the most votes is elected.

All persons over 18 years old and not subject to any legal incapacity to vote and who are either British subjects or citizens of Ireland are entitled to be included in the register of electors for the constituency containing the address at which they were residing on the qualifying date for the register, and are entitled to vote at elections held during the period for which the register remains in force.

Members of the armed forces, Crown servants employed abroad and the wives accompanying their husbands, are entitled, if otherwise qualified, to be registered as 'service voters' provided they make a 'service declaration'. To be effective for a particular register, the declaration must be made on or before the qualifying date for that register. In certain circumstances, British subjects living abroad may also vote.

The Parliamentary Constituencies Act 1986, as amended by the Boundary Commissions Act 1992, provided for the setting up of Boundary Commissions for England, Wales, Scotland and Northern Ireland. The Commissions' last reports were made in 1995, and thereafter reports are due at intervals of not less than eight and not more than 12 years; and may be submitted from time to time with respect to the area comprised in any particular constituency or constituencies where some change appears necessary. Any changes giving effect to reports of the Commissions are to be made by Orders in Council laid before Parliament for approval by resolution of each House. The Parliamentary electorate of the United Kingdom and Northern Ireland in the register in Dec. 2004 numbered 44,180,243 (37,043,608 in England, 2,233,467 in Wales, 3,857,631 in Scotland and 1,045,537 in Northern Ireland).

At the UK general election held on 5 May 2005, 645 out of 646 members were returned, 528 from England, 59 from Scotland, 40 from Wales and 18 from Northern Ireland. Every constituency returns a single member. Voting was postponed in Staffordshire South owing to the death of a candidate shortly before the election. This constituency was previously a Conservative seat.

One of the main aspects of the Labour government's programme of constitutional reform is Scottish and Welsh devolution. In the referendum on Scottish devolution on 11 Sept. 1997, 1,775,045 votes (74·3%) were cast in favour of a Scottish parliament and 614,400 against (25·7%). The turnout was 60·4%, so around 44·8% of the total electorate voted in favour. For the second question, on the Parliament's tax-raising powers, 1,512,889 votes were cast in favour (63·5%) and 870,263 against (36·5%). This represented 38·4% of the total electorate.

On 18 Sept. 1997 in Wales there were 559,419 votes cast in favour of a Welsh assembly (50·3%) and 552,698 against (49·7%). The turnout was 51·3%.

For current MPs' salaries see below. Members of the House of Lords are unsalaried but may recover expenses incurred in attending sittings of the House within maxima for each day's attendance of £64·00 for day subsistence, £128·00 for night subsistence and £53·50 for secretarial and research assistance and office expenses. Additionally, Members of the House who are disabled may recover the extra cost of attending the House incurred by reason of their disablement. In connection with attendance at the House and parliamentary duties within the UK, Lords may also recover the cost of travelling to and from home.

The executive government is vested nominally in the Crown, but practically in a committee of Ministers, called the Cabinet, which is dependent on the support of a majority in the House of Commons. The head of the Cabinet is the *Prime Minister*, a position first constitutionally recognized in 1905. The Prime Minister's colleagues in the Cabinet are appointed on his recommendation.

Salaries. Members of Parliament received an annual salary of £59,095 in 2005–06. Ministers who are MPs also receive a ministerial salary. Total salaries accepted for 2005–06 (including parliamentary salaries where applicable): Prime Minister, £183,932 (£124,837 ministerial salary); Cabinet Ministers, £74,902 or £133,997 if also members of the House of Commons (Cabinet Ministers in the House of Lords, £101,668); Ministers of State, £97,949 (in the Lords £79,382); Parliamentary Under-Secretaries, £88,586 (in the Lords, £69,138); Government Chief Whip, £133,997 (in the Lords, £79,382); Leader of the Opposition, £127,757 (in the Lords, £69,138); Speaker, £133,997; Attorney-General, £106,358; Lord Advocate, £99,682 (2004–05); Solicitor-General for Scotland, £86,007 (2004–05). Cabinet Ministers in the Commons (but not the Lords) receive the parliamentary salary. MPs are also entitled to Office Costs, Supplementary London, Additional Costs, Mileage, Temporary Assistance and Winding Up Allowances, reimbursement of costs owing to recall during a recess and a Resettlement Grant. Ministers receive a severance payment of three months' salary. In 2006–07 the salary of an MP is rising to £60,277, of a Cabinet Minister to £136,677 and of the Prime Minister to £187,610.

The Privy Council. Before the development of the Cabinet System, the Privy Council was the chief source of executive power, but now its functions are largely formal. It advises the monarch to approve Orders in Council and on the issue of royal proclamations, and has some independent powers such as the supervision of the registration of the medical profession. It consists of all Cabinet members, the Archbishops of Canterbury and York, the Speaker of the House of Commons and senior British and Commonwealth statesmen. The Judicial Committee is the final court of appeal from courts of the UK dependencies, the Channel Islands and the Isle of Man, and some Commonwealth countries.

Freedom of Information Act. The Freedom of Information Act 2000 was implemented gradually between Nov. 2002 and Jan. 2005 when the General Right of Access to all information became law. Not to be confused with the Data Protection Act of 1998, the FOIA allows individuals to gain access to information held by public authorities in England, Wales and Northern Ireland. A separate Act applies in Scotland. Some information is exempted from release, for example security-related documents. An independent Commissioner for Information oversees the process.

Bogdanor, V., *Devolution in the United Kingdom.* OPUS, 1999

Bruce, A., *et al. The House of Lords: 1,000 Years of British Tradition.* London, 1994

Butler, D. and Butler, G., *British Political Facts, 1900–1994.* London, 1994

Dod's Parliamentary Companion. London [published after elections]

Harrison, B., *The Transformation of British Politics, 1860–1995.* OUP, 1996

Norris, P., *Electoral Change in Britain since 1945.* Oxford, 1996

Shell, D., *The House of Lords.* 2nd ed. Hemel Hempstead, 1992

The Times Guide to the House of Commons. London, [published after elections]

Waller, R. and Criddle, B., *The Almanac of British Politics.* 7th ed. London, 2002

See also NORTHERN IRELAND.

Local Government

Administration is carried out by four types of bodies: (i) local branches of some central ministries, such as the Departments of Health and Social Security; (ii) local sub-managements of nationalized industries; (iii) specialist authorities such as the National Rivers Authority; and (iv) the system of local

government described below. The phrase 'local government' has come to mean that part of the local administration conducted by elected councils. There are separate systems for England, Wales and Scotland.

The Local Government Act 1992 provided for the establishment of new unitary councils (authorities) in England, responsible for all services in their areas, though the two-tier structure of district and county councils remained for much of the country. In 1996 all of Wales and Scotland was given unitary local government systems.

Local authorities have statutory powers and claims on public funds. Relations with central government are maintained through the Department for Communities and Local Government in England, and through the Welsh and Scottish Executives. In England the Home Office and the Department for Education and Skills are also concerned with some local government functions. (These are performed by departments within the Welsh and Scottish Offices.) Ministers have powers of intervention to protect individuals' rights and safeguard public health, and the government has power to cap (i.e. limit) local authority budgets.

The chair of the council is one of the councillors elected by the rest. In boroughs and cities his or her title is Mayor. Mayors of cities may have the title of Lord Mayor conferred on them. 53 towns in England and Wales and five in Scotland have the status of city. Brighton and Hove, Wolverhampton and Inverness were awarded city status in 2000. In 2002 Preston, Newport, Stirling, Lisburn and Newry were given city status to mark Queen Elizabeth II's golden jubilee. In Scotland, the chair of city councils is deemed Lord Provost, and is elsewhere known as Convenor or Provost. In Wales, the chair is called Chairman in counties and Mayor in county boroughs. Any parish or community council can by simple resolution adopt the style 'town council' and the status of town for the parish or community. Basic and other allowances are payable to councillors (except Scottish community councillors).

Functions. Legislation in the 1980s initiated a trend for local authorities to provide services by, or in collaboration with, commercial or voluntary bodies rather than provide them directly. Savings are encouraged by compulsory competitive tendering. In England, county councils are responsible for strategic planning, transport planning, non-trunk roads and regulation of traffic, personal social services, consumer protection, disposal of waste, the fire and library services and, partially, for education. District councils are responsible for environmental health, housing, local planning applications (in the first instance) and refuse collection. Unitary authorities combine the functions of both levels.

Finance. Revenue is derived from the Council Tax, which supports about one-fifth of current expenditure, the remainder being funded by central government grants and by the redistribution of revenue from the national non-domestic rate (property tax). Capital expenditure is financed by borrowing within government-set limits and sales of real estate.

Elections. England: The 36 metropolitan districts are divided into wards, each represented by three councillors. One-third of the councillors are elected each year for three years out of four. All metropolitan districts had an election on 4 May 2006. The 238 district councils and the 47 English unitary authorities are divided into wards. Each chooses either to follow the metropolitan district system, or to have all seats contested once every four years, or to elect by halves every two years. 88 district councils had an election on 4 May 2006. The 34 county councils have one councillor for each electoral division, elected every four years, with elections next scheduled for 2009.

In London there are 33 councils (including the City of London), the whole of which are elected every four years. London borough elections took place on 4 May 2006. The Greater London Authority has a 25-member Assembly, elected using AMS (Additional

Member System), and a directly elected mayor, elected by the SV (Supplementary Vote) system. For the election of London Assembly members London is divided into 14 constituencies. Each constituency elects one member, in addition to which there are 11 'London Member' seats. Elections take place every four years. Ken Livingstone (ind.) was elected mayor on 4 May 2000, and re-elected as the Labour candidate on 10 June 2004.

Wales: The 22 unitary authorities are split between single and multi-member wards, elected every four years. Elections were last held on 10 June 2004.

Scotland: The 32 unitary authorities hold elections every four years. The last elections were held on 1 May 2003.

Resident citizens of the UK, Ireland, a Commonwealth country or an EU country may (at age 18) vote and (at age 21) stand for election.

Election Results. Local government elections for 37 county and unitary authority councils on 5 May 2005 resulted in the Conservative control of 24 councils, Labour 6, the Liberal Democrats 3, with no overall control in 4. The Conservatives gained 152 seats (bringing their total to 1,193), Labour lost 114 (total 612), the Liberal Democrats gained 40 (total 493), the Greens gained 6 (total 8), Residents' Associations gained 3 (total 8) and others lost 35 (total 78).

Local government elections for 176 councils on 4 May 2006 resulted in the Conservative control of 68 councils, Labour 29 and the Liberal Democrats 13, with no overall control in 66. The Conservatives gained 316 seats (bringing their total to 1,830), Labour lost 319 (total 1,439), the Liberal Democrats gained 2 (total 909), Residents' Associations lost 13 (total 35) and others gained 11 (total 205).

The election to provide London with an elected Mayor and a 25-member London Assembly took place on 10 June 2004. Ken Livingstone (Lab.) won with 55·39% of the vote after counting second preferences. He gained 828,380 first and second votes (685,541 as first votes), beating Steve Norris (Conservative) into second place.

National Anthem
'God Save the Queen' (King) (words and tune anonymous; earliest known printed source, 1744).

GOVERNMENT CHRONOLOGY
Governments and Prime Ministers since the Second World War (Con = Conservative Party; Lab = Labour Party):

1945–51	Lab	Clement Attlee
1951–55	Con	Winston Churchill
1955–57	Con	Sir Anthony Eden
1957–63	Con	Harold Macmillan
1963–64	Con	Sir Alec Douglas-Home
1964–70	Lab	Harold Wilson
1970–74	Con	Edward Heath
1974–76	Lab	Harold Wilson
1976–79	Lab	James Callaghan
1979–90	Con	Margaret Thatcher
1990–97	Con	John Major
1997–	Lab	Tony Blair

RECENT ELECTIONS
At the general election of 5 May 2005, 27,132,327 votes were cast. The Labour Party won 356 seats with 35·2% of votes cast (413 seats with 42·0% in 2001); the Conservative Party 197 with 32·3% (166 with 32·7%); the Liberal Democratic Party 62 with 22·1% (52 with 18·8%); others 3 (1). Regional parties (Scotland): the Scottish National Party won 6 seats (5 in 2001); (Wales): Plaid Cymru 3 (4); (Northern Ireland): the Democratic Unionist Party 9 (5); Sinn Féin 5 (4); the Social and Democratic Labour Party 3 (3); the Ulster Unionist Party 1 (6). Labour gained no seats and lost 47; the Conservatives gained 36 seats and lost 3; the Liberal Democrats gained 16 seats and lost 5. Turnout was 61·3%.

Following the general election of May 2005, 128 of 646 seats were held by women, approximately 19·8%; Rwanda has the highest proportion of women MPs, with 48·8% following the election of Sept. 2003.

At the 2005 general election, an estimated 75% of the electorate aged over 65 voted, compared to only 37% of those between 18–24.

European Parliament
The United Kingdom has 78 (87 in 1999) representatives. At the June 2004 elections turnout was 38·9% (24·0% in 1999—the lowest in any of the EU member countries). The Conservative Party won 27 seats with 27·4% of votes cast (political affiliation in European Parliament: European People's Party–European Democrats); the Labour Party, 19 with 22·3% (Party of European Socialists); UK Independence Party, 12 with 16·8% (11 Independence and Democracy Group, one non-attached); the Liberal Democrats, 12 with 15·1% (Alliance of Liberals and Democrats for Europe); the Green Party, 2 with 6·2% (Greens/European Free Alliance); the Scottish National Party, 2 with 3·0% (Greens/European Free Alliance); Plaid Cymru, 1 with 1·1% (Greens/European Free Alliance). Voting for these parties was on a proportional system, used for the first time in Britain in 1999. Voting in Northern Ireland was by the transferable vote system: the Democratic Unionist Party (non-attached), the Ulster Unionist Party (European People's Party–European Democrats) and Sinn Féin (European Unitary Left/Nordic Green Left) gained 1 seat each.

CURRENT ADMINISTRATION
In May 2006 the government consisted of the following:

(a) 23 MEMBERS OF THE CABINET
Prime Minister, First Lord of the Treasury and Minister for the Civil Service: Tony Blair, b. 1953.
Deputy Prime Minister and First Secretary of State: John Prescott, b. 1938.
Chancellor of the Exchequer: Gordon Brown, b. 1951.
Secretary of State for Foreign and Commonwealth Affairs: Margaret Beckett, b. 1943.
Secretary of State for the Home Department: Dr John Reid, b. 1947.
Secretary of State for the Environment, Food and Rural Affairs: David Miliband, b. 1965.
Secretary of State for Transport and for Scotland: Douglas Alexander, b. 1967.
Secretary of State for Health: Patricia Hewitt, b. 1948.
Chancellor of the Duchy of Lancaster and Minister for the Cabinet Office and for Social Exclusion: Hilary Armstrong, b. 1945.
Secretary of State for Northern Ireland and for Wales: Peter Hain, b. 1950.
Secretary of State for Defence: Des Browne, b. 1952.
Secretary of State for Culture, Media and Sport: Tessa Jowell, b. 1947.
Parliamentary Secretary to the Treasury and Chief Whip: Jacqui Smith, b. 1962.
Secretary of State for Education and Skills: Alan Johnson, b. 1950.
Chief Secretary to the Treasury: Stephen Timms, b. 1955.
Lord Privy Seal and Leader of the House of Commons: Jack Straw, b. 1946.
Minister without Portfolio: Hazel Blears, b. 1956.
Leader of the House of Lords and Lord President of the Council: Baroness Amos, b. 1954.
Secretary of State for Constitutional Affairs and Lord Chancellor: Lord Falconer of Thoroton, QC, b. 1951.
Secretary of State for International Development: Hilary Benn, b. 1953.

Secretary of State for Work and Pensions: John Hutton, b. 1955.

Secretary of State for Trade and Industry: Alistair Darling, b. 1953.

Secretary of State for Communities and Local Government and Minister for Women: Ruth Kelly, b. 1968.

(Non-cabinet member but attends cabinet meetings): Lord Grocott, b. 1940, *Lords Chief Whip and Captain of the Honourable Corps of Gentlemen at Arms.*

(b) LAW OFFICERS
Attorney General: Lord Goldsmith, QC, b. 1950.
Solicitor General: Mike O'Brien, b. 1954
Advocate General for Scotland: Lord Davidson of Glen Clova, QC, b. 1950.

(c) MINISTERS OF STATE (BY DEPARTMENT)
Department for Communities and Local Government: Yvette Cooper, b. 1969; Phil Woolas, b. 1959.

Department for Constitutional Affairs: Harriet Harman, b. 1950.

Department of Culture, Media and Sport: Richard Caborn, b. 1943, *Minister for Sport.*

Ministry of Defence: Adam Ingram, b. 1947, *Minister for Armed Forces.*

Department for Education and Skills: Beverley Hughes, b. 1950, *Minister for Children and Families;* Bill Rammell, b. 1959, *Minister for Higher Education and Lifelong Learning;* Jim Knight, b. 1965, *Minister for Schools.*

Department of the Environment, Food and Rural Affairs: Ian Pearson, b. 1959; Lord Rooker, b. 1941 *(also Northern Ireland Office).*

Foreign and Commonwealth Office: Geoff Hoon, b. 1953, *Minister for Europe;* Ian McCartney, b. 1951, *Minister for Trade (also Department of Trade and Industry);* Dr Kim Howells, b. 1946.

Department of Health: Rosie Winterton, b. 1958; Andy Burnham, b. 1970; Lord Warner of Brockley, b. 1940; Caroline Flint, b. 1961.

Home Office: Liam Byrne, b. 1970, *Minister for Immigration;* Baroness Scotland of Asthal, QC, b. 1965, *Minister for Justice;* Tony McNulty, b. 1958, *Minister for Police and Security.*

Northern Ireland Office: Lord Rooker, b. 1941 *(also Department of the Environment, Food and Rural Affairs);* David Hanson, b. 1957.

Department for Trade and Industry: Ian McCartney, b. 1951, *Minister for Trade (also Foreign and Commonwealth Office);* Malcolm Wicks, b. 1947, *Minister for* Energy; Margaret Hodge, MBE, b. 1944, *Minister for Industry and the Regions.*

Department of Transport: Dr Stephen Ladyman, b. 1952.

Treasury: John Healey, b. 1960, *Financial Secretary;* Ed Balls, b. 1967, *Economic Secretary;* Dawn Primarolo, b. 1954, *Paymaster-General.*

Department for Work and Pensions: Jim Murphy, b. 1967, *Minister for Employment and Welfare Reform;* James Purnell, b. 1970, *Minister for Pensions Reform.*

(d) PARLIAMENTARY SECRETARIES AND UNDER-SECRETARIES (BY DEPARTMENT)
Cabinet Office: Pat McFadden, b. 1965; Ed Miliband, b. 1969.

Department for Communities and Local Government: Baroness Andrews, OBE, b. 1943; Angela Smith, b. 1959; Meg Munn, b. 1959.

Department for Constitutional Affairs: Baroness Ashton of Upholland, b. 1956; Bridget Prentice, b. 1952; Vera Baird, QC, b. 1951.

Department of Culture, Media and Sport: David Lammy, b. 1972; Shaun Woodward, b. 1958.

Ministry of Defence: Tom Watson, b. 1967; Lord Drayson, b. 1960.

Department for Education and Skills: Phil Hope, b. 1955; Lord Adonis, b. 1963; Parmjit Dhanda, b. 1971.

Department for the Environment, Food and Rural Affairs: Ben Bradshaw, b. 1960; Barry Gardiner, b. 1957.

Foreign and Commonwealth Office: Lord Triesman, b. 1943.

Department of Health: Ivan Lewis, b. 1967.

Home Office: Joan Ryan, b. 1955; Vernon Coaker, b. 1953; Gerry Sutcliffe, b. 1953.

Department for International Development: Gareth Thomas, b. 1967.

Northern Ireland Office: Paul Goggins, b. 1953; Maria Eagle, b. 1961; David Cairns, b. 1966 (also Scotland Office).

Scotland Office: David Cairns, b. 1966 (also Northern Ireland Office).

Department for Trade and Industry: Lord Sainsbury of Turville, b. 1940; Jim Fitzpatrick, b. 1952.

Department for Transport: Derek Twigg, b. 1959; Gillian Merron, b. 1959.

Wales Office: Nick Ainger, b. 1949.

Department for Work and Pensions: Lord Hunt of Kings Heath, OBE, b. 1949; Anne McGuire, b. 1949; James Plaskitt, b. 1954.

Leader of the House of Commons: Nigel Griffiths, b. 1953, *Deputy Leader of the House of Commons.*

(e) OPPOSITION FRONT BENCH
Leader of the Opposition: David Cameron, b. 1966.

Shadow leader of the House of Lords: Lord Strathclyde, b. 1960.

The *Speaker* of the House of Commons is Michael Martin (Labour), elected on 23 Oct. 2000.

Government Website: http://www.direct.gov.uk

CURRENT LEADERS

Tony Blair

Position
Prime Minister

Introduction
Tony Blair led a rejuvenated Labour Party to a landslide victory in the 1997 general election, ending 18 years of Conservative rule, and was returned to power convincingly in 2001 and again in 2005. Espousing 'Third Way' centrist policies, Prime Minister Blair has instigated major constitutional and public service reforms, pursued peace in Northern Ireland and sought closer integration with Europe. He has been criticized on the left for his perceived attachment to Thatcherite economic policies, the tight control he exerts over his government's image, and his close alignment of UK foreign policy with that of the USA. In the aftermath of the 11 Sept. 2001 attacks on the USA, Blair has been President Bush's closest international ally in the war on terrorism. He has also fully supported US policy in Iraq since the invasion in 2003 which deposed Saddam Hussein, despite widespread opposition both domestically and from EU and UN partners. In Aug. 2003 Blair became the longest continuously-serving Labour prime minister and in May 2005, despite a significant drop in Labour's parliamentary majority at the general election, he won an unprecedented third term.

Early Life
Anthony Charles Lynton Blair was born in Edinburgh on 6 May 1953. His mother was a teacher and his father a lawyer who, in 1963, was about to stand as a Conservative parliamentary candidate when he was disabled by a stroke. Blair was brought up in Durham, and educated at Fettes College in Edinburgh. He graduated in law from St John's College, Oxford, in 1975 and was called to the bar a year later, joining the chambers of Derry Irvine (later to become Blair's Lord Chancellor).

Blair joined the Labour Party in 1976 and in 1982 contested unsuccessfully a by-election in Beaconsfield before winning the seat of Sedgefield at the 1983 general election. Under Neil Kinnock's leadership of the party, he became assistant spokesman on treasury affairs from 1984 and then deputy spokesman on trade and industry. He joined the shadow cabinet in Oct. 1988 as shadow secretary for energy, moving to employment in 1989. Following the Labour defeat at the 1992 elections, Kinnock was replaced by John Smith who made Blair shadow home secretary. When Smith suffered a fatal heart attack in 1994, Blair was elected to succeed him as leader. He continued to modernize the party, carrying on the work begun by Kinnock and consolidated by Smith. In 1995 Blair won a significant victory in abolishing Clause IV of the party constitution which had committed Labour to public ownership of leading industries.

Promoting free-market economics, tough action on crime and a more positive European policy than the Conservatives, Labour made major gains in the 1995 local elections. John Major's Conservative government was undermined by scandal while Blair, backing up his personal charisma with a team of skilled 'spin doctors', convinced voters previously fearful of Labour's left-wing heritage that the party was capable of ruling.

At the general election of May 1997 Labour inflicted a crushing defeat on the Conservatives, virtually removing them as a force in Scotland and Wales and making major gains throughout England.

Career in Office
Once in office, Blair quickly instigated major constitutional reforms. Following national referendums on devolution, Scotland gained its own parliament with tax-raising powers while Wales got an assembly with more limited authority. The make-up of the House of Lords was revolutionized when the majority of hereditary peers were removed. London was granted the right to elect its own mayor.

The UK economy has generally prospered under Blair and Chancellor Gordon Brown, with steady growth and declining unemployment. One of the first manifesto pledges of 1997 to be implemented was independence for the Bank of England. The newly-formed Monetary Policy Committee (MPC) was given the power to set interest rates; the maintenance for five years of the Treasury's inflation target of 2·5% was seen as a success for the MPC.

In foreign policy Blair has tried to strike a balance between preserving the close relationship with the USA, built up through the Thatcher and Major years, while promoting closer ties with the EU. Labour's victory in 1997 was welcomed by many EU governments; the then German Chancellor Helmut Kohl described it as repudiation of Euroscepticism. This view was bolstered by Blair's commitment to sign up to the EU Social Chapter, rejected by the UK in the Maastricht Treaty negotiations in the early 1990s. But the UK has still to decide on joining the European single currency. In June 2003 Chancellor Gordon Brown ruled out the UK's imminent entry to the eurozone after the economy was judged to have failed four out of five key tests for entry.

Since the 11 Sept. 2001 attacks on the USA, Blair has been President George W. Bush's staunchest ally in the military campaigns in Afghanistan and Iraq. When in Sept. 2002 Bush challenged the UN to act on Iraq, Blair was the only leader with the power of veto within the UN Security Council to unequivocally support the USA, although he maintained his commitment to securing a UN resolution. Blair ordered 35,000 troops to the Gulf region—more than a quarter of the total standing army. Following the report of the UN weapons inspecting team in Jan. 2003, Blair and Bush pushed for a second UN resolution to disarm Iraq in the face of perceived Iraqi non-cooperation. Despite opposition from several members of the UN Security

Council, Blair continued to back Bush and did not rule out going to war even without the backing of an explicit UN resolution. In Feb. 2003 over 1m. people marched in London to protest against his stand over Iraq. The USA and UK sought to obtain a further resolution sanctioning action against Iraq unless it disarmed, but deep divisions within the Security Council remained—with the USA, UK and Spain favouring military action, and France, Germany, Russia and China opposing any military intervention. With Bush emphasizing his right to act independently of the UN, attempts to draft a second resolution acceptable to all parties were abandoned. In March 2003 parliament granted Blair permission to send UK forces to Iraq, although 139 Labour MPs voted against war. This was the strongest revolt by his own party since Blair took office. Several ministers resigned over the issue, including the former foreign secretary and leader of the House of Commons Robin Cook.

US-led forces launched an invasion of Iraq in March 2003. By early April 2003 they were in control of the majority of the country including Baghdad and Saddam Hussein's regime had been effectively removed. In May 2003 the UN ratified a resolution, co-sponsored by the USA, UK and Spain, on Iraq's future. Under its terms UN special representatives were to co-operate with the occupying forces to form a new government and the occupying forces were to remain until an internationally acceptable government was in place. Blair's international standing was confirmed by his address to both houses of the US Congress in July 2003. In his speech he defended the war in Iraq, arguing that even in the absence of weapons of mass destruction (WMD), 'we will have destroyed a threat that at its least is responsible for inhuman carnage and suffering. That is something I am confident history will forgive'.

After victory in Iraq, the failure to discover any persuasive evidence of WMD raised doubts over the legitimacy of the war. Blair came under increasing pressure after the disclosure that a senior government science adviser, Dr David Kelly, had been exposed as the source of a media report that had criticized the government's search for such weapons. Kelly's suicide in July 2003 led to a public enquiry headed by Lord Hutton. His report, delivered in Jan. 2004, controversially exonerated the Blair government over allegations of exaggerated intelligence about Iraq's WMD as a justification for going to war. A further investigation, chaired by Lord Butler and delivered in July 2004, criticized the flawed quality of the WMD intelligence but found no deliberate attempt by the Blair government to mislead. Nevertheless, the intense scrutiny of the government's actions and its self-presentation heightened opposition and media attacks on the government's perceived dependence on 'spin'. While British troops remain in Iraq helping to quell an ongoing and violent insurgency, Blair has supported political moves to introduce democratic and representative government, most recently through national elections to a new parliament which were held in Dec. 2005.

In Northern Ireland, Blair continued the political initiatives started by the Major administration, and in 1998 secured the Good Friday Agreement. Establishing a power-sharing scheme centred on a Northern Ireland Assembly, it seemed to offer the first realistic chance of peace in the territory in 30 years. However, in Oct. 2002 the Assembly executive was suspended for the fourth time in its three-year history over allegations of IRA spying at the Northern Ireland Office. The peace process received a further jolt later the same month when the IRA broke off communications with the weapons decommissioning body. Elections for the Northern Ireland Assembly took place in Nov. 2003 despite the continuing suspension of the devolved administration. Reflecting further sectarian polarization in the province, hardline Unionists and Sinn Féin nationalists made gains at the expense of more moderate parties. Political progress has since been slow, although Blair's government welcomed the

IRA's formal declaration in July 2005 that it was ending its armed campaign to pursue peaceful political dialogue.

Within the EU, Blair has supported efforts to introduce a new constitution to reflect the considerable enlargement of the Union from May 2004. However, the rejection of the proposed constitution signed by EU leaders in Oct. 2004 by French and Dutch voters in referendums in mid-2005 has stalled further progress. He has also championed accession negotiations with Turkey, which began in Oct. 2005. At the EU summit in Dec. 2005, as leaders of the 25 member states finally agreed a deal on the budget for the enlarged Union for 2007–13, Blair was forced to concede a reduction in the UK's annual budget rebate (dating from 1984) but failed to secure cuts in spending on the controversial common agricultural policy.

In the public services, Blair has put emphasis on improving the overstretched health and education systems (claiming 'education is the best economic policy there is'), although progress in these areas has been less discernible. In April 2003 he guided through parliament national health service reforms which included the establishment of self-governing hospitals that would be financially rewarded for strong performance. However, there were Labour fears that the reforms would lead to a growing divide between high- and low-performing institutions and Blair suffered a significant revolt from his own party. Radical government proposals for school reform (announced in late 2005) have also attracted considerable opposition among Labour MPs, and in Nov. 2005 Blair suffered his first parliamentary defeat since coming to power in 1997 in a Labour rebellion over controversial anti-terrorism legislation.

Blair's influence over the party's image has led to allegations that he is a 'control freak'. In elections for the leader of the Welsh assembly and the London mayor, his attempt to control the nomination of candidates led to intra-party discord. The Millennium Dome construction project was an embarrassingly expensive failure, and the government was accused of mishandling the agricultural crisis brought on by an outbreak of foot-and-mouth disease in 2001.

Blair's aim to avoid allegations of sleaze that so damaged the previous Conservative government has been tested by several scandals, most significantly involving his close allies Peter Mandelson and David Blunkett, who have both twice to date had to resign cabinet posts.

Blair has twice suffered brief health scares in Oct. 2003 and Oct. 2004 over a heart abnormality. Political speculation meanwhile continues about when, or if, he will step down during his third term as prime minister and make way for Chancellor Gordon Brown.

DEFENCE

The Defence Council was established on 1 April 1964 under the chairmanship of the Secretary of State for Defence, who is responsible to the Sovereign and Parliament for the defence of the realm. Vested in the Defence Council are the functions of commanding and administering the Armed Forces. The Secretary of State heads the Department of Defence.

Defence policy decision-making is a collective governmental responsibility. Important matters of policy are considered by the full Cabinet or, more frequently, by the Defence and Overseas Policy Committee under the chairmanship of the Prime Minister.

Total full-time trained strength in 2004 numbered 190,200, untrained regulars 22,500 and reserve personnel 246,700. In 2004 UK armed forces abroad included 22,000 personnel based in Germany, about 9,200 in Iraq, 3,275 based in Cyprus, about 3,000 in Kuwait, 1,200 based in the Falkland Islands, 1,120 based in Brunei, 1,100 serving as part of SFOR II in Bosnia-Herzegovina and 575 based in Gibraltar.

The ban on homosexuals serving in the armed forces, which had been upheld by a House of Commons vote in May 1996, was suspended in Sept. 1999 after the European Court of Human Rights ruled that the current ban was unlawful.

Defence Budget. It was announced in July 2002 that the defence budget would rise by £3·5bn. (US$5·4bn.) over three years, the largest sustained increase in planned defence spending in 20 years. The defence budget for 2004–05 was £29,710m. (US$57,239m.), rising to £30,888m. (US$59,509m.) for 2005–06.

Defence spending in 2003 represented 2·4% of GDP, down from 5·2% in 1985. Per capita defence expenditure in 2003 totalled £438 (US$722).

Nuclear Weapons. Having carried out its first test in 1952, there have been 45 tests in all. The nuclear arsenal consisted of approximately 185 warheads in Jan. 2005 according to the Stockholm International Peace Research Institute.

Arms Trade. The UK is a net-exporter of arms and in 2003 was the world's second largest exporter after the USA (with sales worth US$4·7bn., or 16·3% of the world total).

In 2003 BAE SYSTEMS was the UK's largest arms producing company and the 4th largest in the OECD. It accounted for US$15·8bn. of arms sales. Rolls Royce was the 15th largest producer, accounting for US$3·0bn. of sales.

The UK was the 9th largest recipient of major conventional weapons in the world during the period 1998–2002, spending US$575m. in 2002 (US$1,217m. in 2001).

Army

The Chief of the General Staff (CGS) is the professional head of the Army and is responsible for its overall fighting effectiveness. Day-to-day management is the responsibility of the Army Board, comprising 12 individuals from the Government and the Army. Operational command rests with the MOD via the tri-service Permanent Joint Headquarters (PJHQ) at Northwood, north London. The Field Army's Headquarters—Headquarters Land Command—is at Wilton, near Salisbury.

The established strength of the Regular Army in 2004 was 116,760 which includes soldiers under training and Gurkhas. In addition there were some 3,390 Royal Irish Home Service soldiers. There were 3,700 Gurkhas in 2004. The strength of the Regular Reserves was 160,800. There were 10,700 soldiers based in Northern Ireland in 2004 in addition to the 3,390 Royal Irish Home Service soldiers.

The review of the Future Army Structure (FAS) was announced in Dec. 2004. FAS is a re-balancing of the Army to ensure that it is better able to meet the challenges and threats of the 21st century. It will complement the existing heavy and lightweight capabilities with medium weight forces and ensure that the Army is equipped, trained and organized to meet the demands of multiple, concurrent and expeditionary operations across the full spectrum of military tasks.

The role of the Territorial Army (TA) is to act as a general Reserve for the Army by reinforcing it as required, and by providing the framework and basis for regeneration and reconstruction to cater for the unforeseen in times of national emergency. The TA also provides a nationwide link between the military and civil communities. Strength, 2004, 40,350. In addition, men who have completed service in the Regular Army normally have some liability to serve in the Regular Reserve. Closer and better integration of the TA and Regular Reserves has been central to FAS. The future structure involves rebalancing to reflect the changes in the Regular Army's structure and enhance the TA's ability to provide specialist support.

Equipment includes 386 Challenger 2 tanks, the Army's main battle tank. The Challenger 2, which entered service in June 1998, superseded the Challenger 1. The Warrior Infantry Fighting Vehicle is a highly successful fighting vehicle that can be fitted with Enhanced Armour. The Combat Vehicle Reconnaissance (Tracked) series is a group of fast and agile armoured vehicles. Their exceptionally low ground pressure and small size makes them useful where the terrain is hostile and movement difficult.

Women serve throughout the Army in the same regiments and corps as men. There are only a few roles in which they are not employed such as the Infantry and Royal Armoured Corps.

The Oxford Illustrated History of the British Army. OUP, 1995

Navy

Control of the Royal Navy is vested in the Defence Council and is exercised through the Admiralty Board, chaired by the Secretary of State for Defence.

The C.-in-C. Fleet, headquartered at Northwood, is responsible for the command of the fleet, while command of naval establishments in the UK is exercised by the C.-in-C. Naval Home Command from Portsmouth. Main naval bases are at Devonport, Portsmouth and Faslane, with a minor base overseas at Gibraltar.

The Royal Naval Reserve (RNR) and the Royal Marines Reserve (RMR) are volunteer forces which together in 2004 numbered 3,500. The RNR provides trained personnel in war to supplement regular forces.

The roles of the Royal Navy are first, to deploy the national strategic nuclear deterrent, second to provide maritime defence of the UK and its dependent territories, third to contribute to the maritime elements of NATO's force structure and fourth to meet national maritime objectives outside the NATO area. Personnel strength was about 40,950 (including Royal Marines) in 2004.

The strategic deterrent is borne by four Trident submarines—*Vanguard, Victorious, Vigilant* and *Vengeance.* They are each capable of deploying 16 US-built Trident II D5 missiles.

The strength of the fleet's major units in the respective years:

	1999	2000	2001	2002	2003	2004
Strategic Submarines	3	4	4	4	4	4
Nuclear Submarines	11	11	11	11	11	11
Diesel Submarines	nil	nil	nil	nil	nil	nil
Aircraft Carriers	2[1]	2[1]	2[1]	2[1]	2[1]	2[1]
Destroyers	11	11	11	11	11	11
Frigates	20	20	20	21	20	20

[1]Following government policy, of the three Carriers held, only two are kept in operational status.

The principal surface ships are the Light vertical/short take-off and landing Aircraft Carriers of the Invincible class (*Invincible, Illustrious* and *Ark Royal*) completed 1980–85, embarking an air group including Sea Harrier vertical/short take-off and landing fighters. Two of these ships are maintained in the operational fleet, with the third (currently *Ark Royal*) either in refit or reserve. These ships are to be replaced with a new class of two large aircraft carriers due in service in 2012 and 2015. A Helicopter Carrier, specifically designed for amphibious operations, HMS *Ocean*, entered service in 1998 and was joined by two amphibious Landing Platform Docks (LPD), HMS *Albion* and HMS *Bulwark*, in 2003 and 2004 respectively.

The Fleet Air Arm (6,200-strong in 2004) had 188 aircraft in 2004, of which 26 were combat aircraft (Sea Harrier vertical/short take-off and landing fighter aircraft) and 162 were armed helicopters.

The Royal Marines Command, 7,000-strong in 2004, provides a commando brigade comprising three commando groups. The Special Boat Squadron and specialist defence units complete the operational strength.

The total number of trained naval service personnel was 36,300 in April 2004 (down from 45,600 in April 1996).

Jane's Fighting Ships. London, annual
The Oxford Illustrated History of the Royal Navy. OUP, 1996

Air Force

The Royal Flying Corps was established in May 1912, with military and naval wings, of which the latter became the independent Royal Navy Air Service in July 1914. On 2 Jan. 1918 an Air Ministry was formed, and on 1 April 1918 the Royal Flying Corps and the Royal Navy Air Service were amalgamated, under the Air Ministry, as the Royal Air Force (RAF).

In 1937 the units based on aircraft carriers and naval shore stations again passed to the operational and administrative control of the Admiralty, as the Fleet Air Arm. In 1964 control of the RAF became a responsibility of the Ministry of Defence.

The RAF is administered by the Air Force Board, of which the Secretary of State for Defence is Chairman. Following recommendations in the 1998 Strategic Defence Review, which placed increased emphasis on Joint and Expeditionary operations, the RAF has been significantly restructured. The creation of the tri-service Defence Logistics Organisation (DLO) resulted in the closure of Logistics Command on 31 Oct. 1999 with most of the logistics support functions previously carried out by the Command now subsumed into the new organization. However, those former Logistics Command Units responsible for tasks falling to the RAF rather than DLO have now been incorporated within the two remaining RAF Commands: Strike Command and Personnel and Training Command.

Headquarters Strike Command is based at RAF High Wycombe. Strike Command's mission is 'to generate agile Air Power and develop capabilities to achieve precise effects across the spectrum whenever and wherever they are required'. It is responsible for all of the RAF's frontline forces. It operates a fleet of some 396 aircraft, which includes a highly capable combat aircraft fleet comprising Tornado GR4 and F3, Harrier GR7/9, Jaguar and Typhoon aircraft. The Typhoon is currently entering frontline service, while the Jaguar will retire from service in 2007.

As an expeditionary force, the RAF, on an increasing basis, exercises and operates overseas. Current and recent basing/deployments include the Falklands, Cyprus, Italy and the Balkans, Scandinavia, North America, the Middle East and the Far East.

Personnel and Training Command was established in 1994 with its Headquarters at RAF Innsworth, Gloucester, and has two main components—the RAF Personnel Management Agency (RAF PMA), which handles the career management of RAF Regular and Reserve Forces, and the Training Group Defence Agency (TGDA), which is responsible for recruitment and training. As a result of an RAF Process and Organisation Review, both Command Headquarters are set to be combined into an integrated Headquarters at RAF High Wycombe during 2006. Personnel and Training Command will still exercise responsibility for the RAF PMA and TGDA.

RAF personnel, 1 Oct. 2005, 50,010 (including 6,125 women); total trained personnel, 47,800. Since Dec. 1991 women have been eligible to fly combat aircraft. There were also 8,440 Air Force reserves in 2005 including 1,480 volunteers. In addition there were 26,720 ex-RAF personnel with a recall liability, having left the RAF with a service pension.

INTERNATIONAL RELATIONS

The UK is a member of the UN, WTO, NATO, BIS, OECD, EU, the Council of Europe, WEU, OSCE, CERN, the Commonwealth, Inter-American Development Bank, Asian Development Bank, IOM and the Antarctic Treaty.

In 2004 the UK gave US$7·9bn. in international aid, representing 0·36% of its GDP. In actual terms this made the UK the 4th most generous country in the world, but as a percentage of GDP only the 11th most generous.

ECONOMY

In 2003 services accounted for 72·4% of GDP, industry 26·6% and agriculture 1·0%.

According to the anti-corruption organization *Transparency International*, in 2005 the United Kingdom ranked equal 11th in the world in a survey of the countries with the least corruption in business and government. It received 8·6 out of 10 in the annual index.

Overview

The UK ranks among the world's top five largest economies. Economic growth has been relatively immune to global conditions in recent years, attributable to the flexible labour and product markets, which are among the most flexible in the OECD. Unemployment ran at approximately 4·7%–4·8% through 2004 and the first half of 2005, its lowest level since the 1970s, but was up to 5·1% by the end of 2005. From 1993–2004 the UK enjoyed sustained non-inflationary output growth, the longest period of expansion in 30 years. A slowdown in 2005 reflected earlier monetary tightening, sharp increases in energy prices and a rise in tax revenues. Inflation has been stabilized close to its target of 2·5%, falling as low at 1% at the end of 2004.

Strong performance has been driven by a healthy services sector and strong domestic demand, although weaknesses in the manufacturing sector and erratic export performance remain hindrances. Although high oil prices have led to decreased export demand, the terms of trade impact has been negligible as oil imports and exports are balanced. House price inflation, which peaked at 23% in 2002, had been reigned in to 4% by 2005. House prices are subject to a relatively large measure of estimated overvaluation in the UK, acting as both a sign of confidence in economic developments and a reminder of past booms.

Domestic demand is the key driver of growth, supported by strong growth in real labour earnings and house prices, and healthy corporate profitability. Private consumption accounts for nearly 70% of GDP. Despite almost closing the GDP per capita gap with other European countries, the disparity with the most successful OECD countries (Canada, USA and Australia) remains, partly owing to weaker productivity levels in the UK. Average labour productivity growth was estimated at 2% per annum in the decade to 2003, close to the OECD median. Nonetheless, poor productivity performance is a recurring problem which the OECD suggests has four main causes: a low level of general skills in the workforce; poor innovation performance; underinvestment in public infrastructure; and excessive planning restrictions. In addition, low levels of gross fixed investment (approximately 17% of GDP) have constrained potential productivity growth.

The service sector accounts for over two-thirds of GDP. The financial services sector represents 20% of GDP thanks to the strength of the City of London and the rapid growth in business services. The strong growth performance over the last decade is partly attributable to the high share of value added produced in high growth sectors, especially knowledge intensive services. High technology industries, such as pharmaceuticals, aircraft, information communications technology equipment and precision instruments, accounted for almost 35% of manufacturing exports in 2005. Knowledge intensive services, such as telecommunications, insurance, finance and business services accounted for 23% of value added in 2005.

Monetary policy has been conducted by the Bank of England since 1997. Between 1997–2004 average RPIX inflation was stable at around the 2·5% target, despite high housing appreciation. Low goods price inflation, resulting from falling import prices and increases in distribution sector productivity, offset house price inflation. However, British interest rates during this period were higher than in other higher-inflation G7 countries, partly attributable to large fiscal deficits since 2000.

In 2002 the UK accounted for 4% of total value added in manufacturing, making it the sixth-largest manufacturing nation in the world. However, the manufacturing sector, accounting for 20% of GDP, has declined more than in other industrialized countries. This trend, whilst common to other OECD countries, has been more severe in the UK in part as a result of the

strong currency and low productivity. As imports have outpaced exports, the trade deficit has widened.

From 1979–97 the Conservative government introduced reforms making the UK one of Europe's freest economies. The subsequent Labour government continued with privatization, deregulation and competition reforms. In 2005 the OECD declared the UK to be among the leading countries in the OECD in terms of liberal product market regulation and of labour market flexibility. Low product market regulation, low barriers to foreign investment and labour market flexibility have prompted higher levels of foreign direct investment than in most other EU countries. The UK has exceptionally high numbers of non-EU businesses when compared with its European neighbours.

The Code for Fiscal Stability, introduced in 1998, stipulates that the government may borrow only to invest and not to support current spending. The 'sustainable investment' or 'golden' rule aims at maintaining the public sector net debt below 40% of GDP over the economic cycle. The UK fiscal position has deteriorated significantly since 2000. An expansionary fiscal policy has helped to thwart the global downturn but the cyclically adjusted balance declined by 4·5% of GDP from 2000–04. The general government deficit decreased from a surplus of 3·75% in 2000 to a deficit of just over 3% in 2005. This runs contrary to the attainment of the golden rule and the overall deficit needs to be reduced to ensure new government debt lies below the 40% ceiling. Net government debt (37% in 2005) is the second lowest amongst the G7 and the lowest in the EU. Although the debt burden is low, a persistent deficit challenges the credibility of the government's fiscal commitments.

Spending on health care and education are low compared to other OECD and EU countries and public services are over-stretched. Nonetheless, public expenditure on health, education and infrastructure as a share of GDP rose by nearly 5% in the period 2000–05, to a level of nearly 45%. Pension reform is currently at the forefront of public debate, with half the working age population over 35 having inadequate savings to supplement the state pension.

Currency

The unit of currency is the *pound sterling* (£; GBP) of 100 *pence* (p.). Before decimalization on 15 Feb. 1971 £1 = 20 shillings (*s*) of 12 pence (*d*). A gold standard was adopted in 1816, the sovereign, a £1, or twenty-shilling gold coin, weighing 7·98805 grams. It is eleven-twelfths pure gold and one-twelfth alloy. Currency notes for £1 and 10*s*. were first issued by the Treasury in 1914, replacing the circulation of sovereigns. The issue of £1 and 10*s*. notes was taken over by the Bank of England in 1928. 10*s*. notes ceased to be legal tender in 1970 and £1 notes (in England and Wales) in 1988. Sterling was a member of the exchange rate mechanism of the European Monetary System from 8 Oct. 1990 until 16 Sept. 1992 ('Black Wednesday').

Inflation. Consumer Price Index (CPI) inflation rates (based on OECD statistics):

1995	1996	1997	1998	1999	2000	2001	2002	2003	2004
2·7%	2·5%	1·8%	1·6%	1·3%	0·8%	1·2%	1·3%	1·4%	1·3%

The inflation rate in 2005 according to the Office of National Statistics was 2·1%.

Coinage. Estimated number of coins in circulation at 31 Dec. 2004: £2, 249m.; £1, 1,410m.; 50p, 738m.; 20p, 2,128m.; 10p, 1,567m.; 5p, 3,578m.; 2p, 6,339m.; 1p, 10,360m.

Banknotes. The Bank of England issues notes in denominations of £5, £10, £20 and £50 up to the amount of the fiduciary issue. Under the provisions of the Currency Act 1983 the amount of the fiduciary issue is limited, but can be altered by direction of HM Treasury on the advice of the Bank of England. Since Nov.

1998 the limit has been £34,300m., although this was temporarily raised to £50,000m. over the millennium period.

All current series Bank of England notes are legal tender in England and Wales. Some banks in Scotland (Bank of Scotland, Clydesdale Bank and the Royal Bank of Scotland) and Northern Ireland (Bank of Ireland, First Trust Bank, Northern Bank and Ulster Bank) have note-issuing powers.

The total amount of Bank of England notes in circulation at 29 Dec. 2004 was £39,130m., of which £39,125m. represented notes with other banks and the public, and £5m. notes in the Banking Department of the Bank of England.

Foreign exchange reserves were US$34,583m. and gold reserves 10·10m. troy oz in June 2002 (22·98m. troy oz in April 1999).

Budget

The March 2006 budget forecast public sector borrowing for 2005–06 at £37·1bn., falling to £36bn. in 2006–07, £30bn. in 2007–08, £25bn. in 2008–09, £24bn. in 2009–10 and £23bn. in 2010–11. Public sector net debt as a proportion of GDP is put at 36·4% for 2005–06, rising to 38·4% by 2010–11.

Current spending for 2005–06 is set at £481·9bn., increasing to £612bn. by 2010–11. Net investment is to rise from £25·7bn. in 2005–06 to £36bn. by 2010–11.

Among the budget's provisions is an increase in the inheritance tax threshold to £325,000. Investment in schools is to increase from £5·6bn. per year to £8bn. over a five-year period, towards a long-term goal of achieving annual per pupil expenditure parity between state and private schools (with respective per pupil expenditure standing at £5,000 and £8,000). Following the award of the 2012 Olympic Games to London, £600m. is to be made available to fund world-class athletes. Other measures include a boost for child trust accounts with a further payment of £250 (or £500 for children from low-income families) on the child reaching seven years of age, while car tax is cut to zero for vehicles with the lowest rates of emissions and raised to £210 for the most polluting. There are also new measures to tackle tax fraud and avoidance and the number of community support officers is increased from 6,000 to 16,000.

'This was in fact a holding Budget, delivered by a chancellor boxed in by tricky public finances and from a government unwilling yet to take the big decisions during this parliament. In a nutshell, Mr Brown's Budget amounted to a small redistribution of resources from VAT fraudsters to the nation's schools… While, by no means in bad shape, the economy left the chancellor with no room for big gestures.' (*Financial Times*, 23 March 2006).

Current Budget (in £1bn.)	2004–05 Outturn	2005–06 Estimate	2006–07 Projection
Current Receipts	451·3	486·1	516·4
Current Expenditure	455·4	481·9	506·7
Surplus on Current Budget (in £1bn.)	2004–05 Outturn	2005–06 Estimate	2006–07 Projection
	−19·0	−11·4	−7
Current Receipts (in £1bn.)	2004–05 Outturn	2005–06 Estimate	2006–07 Projection
Total HM Revenue and Customs	371·1	399·8	424·4
Net Taxes and National Insurance Contributions	426·5	458·7	486·5
Current Receipts	451·3	486·1	516·4
Departmental Expenditure Limits (Resource Budget, in £1bn.)	2004–05 Outturn	2005–06 Estimate	2006–07 Planned
Education and Skills	23·0	24·6	53·4
Health	69·2	76·9	82·0
of which: NHS	66·9	74·7	80·0
Transport	5·3	5·7	6·9
Office of the Deputy Prime Minister	3·5	3·3	3·5

Departmental Expenditure Limits (Resource Budget, in £1bn.)	2004–05 Outturn	2005–06 Estimate	2006–07 Planned
Local Government	43·3	46·1	22·5
Home Office	12·0	12·7	13·1
Departments for Constitutional Affairs	3·3	3·7	3·9
Law Officer's Departments	0·6	0·6	0·7
Defence	31·3	33·3	32·6
Foreign and Commonwealth Office	1·7	2·0	1·8
International Development	3·8	4·4	5·0
Trade and Industry	4·3	5·5	5·6
Environment, Food and Rural Affairs	2·8	3·0	3·0
Culture, Media and Sport	1·3	1·4	1·5
Work and Pensions	7·8	7·9	7·8
Scotland[1]	19·3	20·8	22·2
Wales[1]	10·3	11·5	11·7
Northern Ireland Executive[1]	6·3	6·8	7·1
Northern Ireland Office	1·2	1·0	1·2
Chancellor's Departments	4·9	5·0	5·1
Cabinet Office	2·0	2·1	2·0

[1]For Scotland, Wales and Northern Ireland, the split between current and capital budgets is decided by the respective executives.

VAT, introduced on 1 April 1973, is 17·5% (reduced rate, 5·0%). In 2005–06 tax revenues were estimated at 37·5% of GDP (36·2% in 2004–05).

Performance

In 2004 total GDP was US$2,140·9bn. (£1,184·8bn).

Real GDP growth rates (based on OECD statistics):

1995	1996	1997	1998	1999	2000	2001	2002	2003	2004
2·9%	2·7%	3·2%	3·2%	3·0%	4·0%	2·2%	2·0%	2·5%	3·2%

The real GDP growth rate in 2005 according to the Office of National Statistics was 1·8% (the lowest in more than a decade).

The March 2004 *OECD Economic Survey* reported: 'The performance of the UK economy has been impressive in recent years, underpinned by wide-ranging structural reforms and sound macroeconomic policy frameworks. The OECD projects growth above potential in 2004 and 2005, with unemployment remaining low, but instability stemming from the housing market is a risk. … Ensuring macroeconomic stability, while addressing the remaining weaknesses through further structural reforms offers the prospect of continuing strong economic performance.'

In the 2006 budget the estimated growth rate for the year was put at 2·0–2·5%. Growth for 2007 is forecast to be 2·75–3·25%.

In the World Economic Forum's *Global Competitiveness Report 2005–2006* the UK was placed 13th in the world in the Growth Competitiveness Index (11th in the 2004–2005 index) and 6th in the Business Competitiveness Index (also 6th in the 2004–2005 index).

Banking and Finance

The Bank of England is the government's banker and the 'banker's bank'. It has the sole right of note issue in England and Wales. It was founded by Royal Charter in 1694 and nationalized in 1946. The capital stock has, since 1 March 1946, been held by HM Treasury. The *Governor* (appointed for five-year terms) is Mervyn King (b. 1948; took office 2003).

The statutory Bank Return is published weekly. End-Dec. figures are as follows (in £1m.):

	Notes in circulation	Notes and coins in Banking Department	Public deposits (government)	Other deposits[1]
2000	30,690	10	382	10,062
2001	32,895	5	452	11,317

	Notes in circulation	Notes and coins in Banking Department	Public deposits (government)	Other deposits[1]
2002	33,897	3	690	14,049
2003	36,606	4	918	16,586
2004	39,125	5	803	19,633

[1]Including Special Deposits.

Major British Banking Groups' statistics at end Dec. 2004: total deposits (sterling and currency), £1,692,458m.; sterling market loans, £358,206m.; market loans (sterling and currency), £529,088m.; advances (sterling and currency), £1,363,908m.; sterling investments, £126,423m.

Britain's largest bank is HSBC, both in terms of assets and market capitalization. It had assets in Dec. 2003 totalling US1,034bn. The Royal Bank of Scotland is the second largest bank, both by assets and market capitalization. By Oct. 2000

approximately 5% of the British population were using e-banking.

In May 1997 the power to set base interest rates was transferred from the Treasury to the Bank of England. The government continues to set the inflation target but the Bank has responsibility for setting interest rates to meet the target. Base rates are now set by a nine-member Monetary Policy Committee at the Bank; members include the Governor. Membership of the Court (the governing body) was widened. The 1998 Act provides for Court to consist of the Governor, two Deputy Governors and 16 Directors. The Act also established the MPC as a Committee of the Bank and sets a framework for its operations. Responsibility for supervising banks was transferred from the Bank to the Financial Services Authority (FSA). The base rate was lowered from 4·75% to 4·50% on 4 Aug. 2005.

National Savings Bank. Statistics for 2003–04 and 2004–05:

	Ordinary accounts		Investment accounts		Premium bonds	
	2003–04 in £1,000	2004–05 in £1,000	2003–04 in £1,000	2004–05 in £1,000	2003–04 in £1,000	2004–05 in £1,000
Amounts—						
Received	626,189	124,841	822,832	801,870	7,496,842	5,755,325
Interest credited	838,385	4,285	1,342,621	218,764	—	—
Paid	(4,313)	(909,819)	(178,707)	(1,550,895)	2,956,794	3,397,462
Due to depositors at 31 March	1,338,849	358,156	6,885,441	6,355,180	24,251,384	26,609,147

There are stock exchanges in Belfast, Birmingham, Glasgow and Manchester which function mainly as representative offices for the London Stock Exchange (called International Stock Exchange until May 1991). In July 1991 the 91 share-holders voted unanimously for a new memorandum and articles of association which devolves power to a wider range of participants in the securities industry, and replaces the Stock Exchange Council with a 14-member board. The Financial Times Stock Exchange 100 (FTSE 100) ended 2005 at 5,618·8, up from 4,814·4 at the end of 2004 (gaining 16·7% during the year—the best performance since 1999 and the third consecutive annual rise).

The UK received US$20·30bn. worth of foreign direct investment in 2003 and US$78·40bn. in 2004. By the end of 2002 the UK had attracted foreign direct investment totalling US$568bn.—a figure exceeded only by the USA.

Roberts, R. and Kynaston, D. (eds.) *The Bank of England: Money, Power and Influence, 1694–1994*. OUP, 1995

Weights and Measures
Conversion to the metric system, which replaced the imperial system, became obligatory on 1 Oct. 1995. The use of the pint for milk deliveries and bar sales, and use of miles and yards in road signs, is exempt indefinitely, and the use of the pound (weight) in selling greengrocery was exempt until 1999.

ENERGY AND NATURAL RESOURCES

Environment
The UK's carbon dioxide emissions from the consumption and flaring of fossil fuels in 2002 were the equivalent of 9·4 tonnes per capita. The UK's total emission of greenhouse gases is estimated to have fallen from 777m. tonnes in 1990 to 696m. tonnes in 2002. An *Environmental Sustainability Index* compiled for the World Economic Forum meeting in Jan. 2005 ranked the UK 65th in the world out of 146 countries analysed, with 50·2%. The index measured the ability of countries to maintain favourable environmental conditions and examined various factors including pollution levels and the use or abuse of natural resources.

In England and Wales 14·5% of household waste was recycled in 2002–03; in Scotland 7% was recycled in 2001–02.

Electricity
The Electricity Act of 1989 implemented the restructuring and transfer to the private sector of the electricity supply industry.

(England and Wales)

Generators. Under the 1989 Act, National Power and Powergen took over the fossil fuel and hydro-electric power stations previously owned by the Central Electricity Generating Board, and were privatized in 1991. National Power was split into two companies in 2000, International Power plc and Innogy plc. Nuclear Electric, responsible for operating the 12 nuclear power stations, and Scottish Nuclear were merged as a single holding company in 1996 with two new operating subsidiaries, Magnox Electric and British Energy. Both were privatized in 1996. Under licence, generating companies may also be involved in electricity supply. There were a total of 31 nuclear reactors in use in the UK at 15 nuclear power stations in the UK in Sept. 2002. The UK generation market is now very diverse, with 42 major power producers compared to seven in 1990.

Transmission. The privatized National Grid Transco is responsible for operating the transmission system and for co-ordinating the operation of power stations connected to it. The company also operates the Cross-Channel link with France and the interconnection with the Scottish power system.

Distribution and Supply. The 12 Area Boards were replaced under the 1989 Act by 12 successor companies, which were privatized in 1990. These were: East Midlands Electricity (now Powergen Energy); Eastern Electricity (now part of Powergen); London Electricity (now LE Group); Manweb (now part of ScottishPower); Midlands Electricity (now Aquila Networks Services); Northern Electric (supply business now owned by Innogy); Norweb (now part TXU Europe, part United Utilities); SEEBOARD (now part of LE Group); Southern Electric (now part of Scottish and Southern Energy); SWALEC (renamed Hyder, and now part of Western Power Distribution); South Western Electricity (now part of Western Power Distribution); and Yorkshire Electricity (supply business owned by Innogy, distribution business owned by Northern Electric). The companies are in the main responsible for maintaining their local distribution networks, and have a statutory duty to supply electricity to their tariff customers.

However, following a number of mergers and takeovers in the industry, some companies are now responsible only for distribution or supply in their areas. Some of the companies are also involved in the retailing of electrical goods and electrical contracting, and some have diversified into other business activities.

See also SCOTLAND.

The Electricity Association. The Electricity Association is the trade association of the UK electricity companies, providing a forum for members to discuss matters of common interest, a collective voice for the electricity industry when needed, and specialist research and professional services. It publishes an annual *Electricity Industry Review*, which contains detailed information on the development of the industry during the previous year.

Regulation. The Office of Electricity Regulation (*'Offer'*) was set up under the 1989 Act to protect consumer interests following privatization. In 1999 it was merged with the Office of Gas Supply (*'Ofgas'*) to form the Office of Gas and Electricity Markets (*'Ofgem'*), reflecting the opening up of all markets for electricity and gas supply to full competition from May that year, with many suppliers now offering both gas and electricity to customers.

Statistics. The electricity industry contributes about 1·3% of the UK's Gross Domestic Product. The installed capacity of all UK power stations in 2001 was 67,965 MW. In 2000 the fuel generation mix was: coal-fired 34%, nuclear 25%, gas 38%, hydro and renewables 2%, and oil 1%. 314,586 GWh were supplied to 28m. customers, of which domestic users took 29%, industrial users 29% and commercial and other users the remaining 42%. The average domestic consumption per capita in 2002 was 6,614 kWh.

Electricity Association. *Electricity Industry Review.* Annual
Surrey, J. (ed.) *The British Electricity Experience: Privatization—the Record, the Issues, the Lessons.* London, 1996

Oil and Gas

Production in 1,000 tonnes, in 2003: throughput of crude and process oils, 84,515; refinery use, 5,390. Refinery output: gas/diesel oil, 27,579; motor spirit, 22,627; fuel oil, 9,513; aviation turbine fuel, 5,277; burning oil, 3,521; naphtha, 3,516; propane, butane and other petroleum gases, 2,976; bitumen, 1,925; lubricating oils, 576. Total output of petroleum products, 79,139. Crude oil production (2003), 106·1m. tonnes. The UK's oil production is the second highest in Europe after that of Norway, and is the eleventh highest in the world, greater than that of either Kuwait or Libya. The UK had proven oil reserves of 4·5bn. bbls. at the end of 2003 and is a net exporter of oil.

In 2003 the total income from sales of oil produced was £14·5bn., with the value of net exports of oil and oil products £4·5bn.

The first significant offshore gas discovery was made in 1965 in the North Sea, followed in 1969 by the first commercial oil offshore. Offshore production of gas began in 1967 and oil in 1975.

Oil and gas have played an important part in providing the UK's energy needs. In 2003, either through direct use or as a source of energy to produce electricity, oil and gas accounted for some 74% of total UK energy consumption, with UK-based production supplying some 92% of the gas consumed.

Oil products also provide important contributions to other industries, such as feedstocks for the petro-chemical industry and lubricants for various uses. While the importance of oil as a source of energy for electrical generation and use by industry and commercial operations has declined with the increasing use of gas, oil still makes up around 20% of total industrial uses of energy. Its prime importance is in the transport sector, where it provides 99% of the total energy used.

The United Kingdom usually exports around two-thirds of the oil it produces, with the key export markets being the USA and other EU countries.

The reform of the old nationalized gas industry began with the Gas Act of 1986, which paved the way for the privatization later that year of the British Gas Corporation, and established the Director General of Gas Supply (DGSS) as the independent regulator. This had a limited effect on competition, as British Gas retained a monopoly on tariff (domestic) supply. Competition progressively developed in the industrial and commercial (non-tariff) market.

The Gas Act 1995 amended the 1986 Act to prepare the way for full competition, including the domestic market. It created three separate licences—for Public Gas Transporters who operate pipelines, for Shippers (wholesalers) who contract for gas to be transported through the pipelines, and for Suppliers (retailers) who then market gas to consumers. It also placed the DGSS under a statutory duty to secure effective competition.

The domestic market was progressively opened to full competition from 1996 until May 1998.

In 1997 British Gas took a commercial decision to de-merge its trading business. Centrica plc (a new company) was formed to handle the gas sales, gas trading, services and retail businesses of BG, together with the gas production businesses of the North and South Morecambe Field. The remaining parts of the business, including transportation and storage and the international downstream activities, were contained in BG plc. As a result of subsequent changes, Transco (owner and operator of the UK's National Gas Transmission System) is now owned by National Grid Transco (NGT). NGT is also the owner and operator of the National Electricity Grid.

The regulator for Britain's gas and electricity industries is *Ofgem* (Office of the Gas and Electricity Markets), created in 1999 through the merger of *Ofgas* (Office of Gas Supply) and *Offer* (Office of Electricity Regulation). Its role is to protect and advance the interests of consumers by promoting competition where possible.

A second European Directive was published in June 2003 with rules for the internal market in natural gas. Member states were allowed one year to execute its provisions; the UK implemented the directive in July 2004.

The UK became a net importer of gas in 2004. In preparation for increasing import dependency, several gas infrastructure projects are scheduled to come on stream over the next few years, supplying the UK with gas from a number of sources, including Norway, Continental Europe, Qatar and Algeria. There is already a pipeline (the Interconnector) linking the UK and European gas grids. This link to Continental Europe opened in Oct. 1998 and has an export capacity of 20bn. cu. metres a year and an import capacity of 8·5bn. cu. metres a year.

Proven gas reserves in 2003 were some 630bn. cu. metres. Production was 102·7bn. cu. metres in 2003. In 2003, 35% of gas produced was used by domestic users and 29% by electricity generators.

Wind

In 2003 there were 84 wind farms and 1,043 turbines with a capacity of 649·4 MW for electricity generation.

Minerals

Legislation to privatize the coal industry was introduced in 1994 and established the Coal Authority to take over from British Coal Corporation. The Coal Authority is the owner of almost all the UK's coal reserves; it licenses private coal-mining, deals with subsidence claims in former mining areas and disposes of property not required for operational purposes. In 2004 there were nine former British Coal collieries, six additional deep mines and 45 opencast mines, employing some 7,630 mineworkers.

Total production from deep mines was 15·6m. tonnes in 2003 (83·8m. tonnes in 1988). Output from opencast sites, 2003, 12·1m. tonnes (1988, 17·9m. tonnes). In 2003 inland coal consumption was 62·4m. tonnes (113·3m. tonnes in 1988).

Output of non-fuel minerals in Great Britain, 2003 (in 1,000 tonnes): limestone, 84,445; sand and gravel, 80,221; igneous rock, 45,305; dolomite (2002), 12,946; sandstone, 11,665; clay and shale, 10,680; chalk, 8,066; salt, 5,800; industrial sand, 4,073; china clay, 2,378.

Steel and metals

Steel production in recent years (in 1m. tonnes):

2000	15·2
2001	13·5
2002	11·7
2003	13·1
2004	13·8

Deliveries of finished steel products from UK mills in 2004 were worth £5bn. in product sales and comprised 7·1m. tonnes to the UK domestic market and 6·3m. tonnes for export. About 60% of UK steel exports went to other EU countries. UK steel imports in 2004 were about 7·2m. tonnes. The UK steel industry's main markets are construction (24%), engineering (23%), automotive (18%) and metal goods (13%). Corus Group (formerly British Steel) is the UK's largest steel producer and makes about 85% of UK crude steel. The UK steel industry has improved productivity nearly five-fold over the past 20 years.

Agriculture

Land use in 2003: agriculture, 70%; urban, 14%; forests, 12%; other, 4%. In 2003 agricultural land in the UK totalled (in 1,000 ha.) 18,438, comprising agricultural holdings, 17,202; and common grazing, 1,236. Land use of the former (in 1,000 ha.): all grasses, 6,884; crops, 4,478; rough grazing, 4,329; bare fallow, 33; other, 1,478. Area sown to crops (in 1,000 ha.): cereals, 3,059; other arable crops, 1,098; horticultural crops, 175; fruit, 34.

In 2001 there were 5·70m. ha. of arable land and 51,000 ha. of permanent crops.

Figures compiled by the Soil Association show that in April 2003 the area of fully organic farmland in the UK was 534,300 ha. Including land in conversion, 4·3% of the agricultural land was managed organically in April 2002. Organic food sales for the UK in 2003–04 totalled £1·12bn., up from £805m. in 2000–01.

Farmers receiving financial support under the EU's Common Agricultural Policy are obliged to 'set-aside' land in order to control production. In 2002 such set-aside totalled 611,000 ha.

There were 500,000 tractors and 47,000 harvester-threshers in 2001.

The number of workers employed in agriculture was, in 2003, 170,900 (44,800 female) of whom 62,600 were seasonal or casual workers. Of the 108,400 regular workers, 38,000 were part-time. In 1990 the number of workers employed in agriculture had been 273,800. There were some 303,100 farm holdings in 2003. Average size of holdings, 56·6 ha.

Total farm incomes dropped from £5·3bn. to £1·7bn. between 1995 and 2000, before rising to £2·4bn. in 2002. Food and live animals accounted for 3·0% of exports and 6·4% of imports in 2002, down from 4·5% of exports and 8·6% of imports in 1991.

Area given over to principal crops in the UK:

	Wheat	Sugarbeets	Barley	Potatoes	Oilseed rape	Oats
			Area (1,000 ha.)			
1999	1,847	183	1,179	178	417	92
2000	2,086	173	1,128	166	332	109
2001	1,635	177	1,245	165	404	112
2002	1,996	169	1,101	158	357	126
2003	1,837	162	1,078	145	460	122

Production of principal crops in the UK:

	Wheat	Sugarbeets	Barley	Potatoes	Oilseed rape	Oats
			Total product (1,000 tonnes)			
1999	14,867	10,584	6,581	7,131	1,737	541
2000	16,704	9,079	6,492	6,636	1,129	640
2001	11,580	8,335	6,660	6,649	1,157	621
2002	15,973	9,557	6,126	6,966	1,468	753
2003	14,288	9,296	6,370	5,918	1,771	749

Horticultural crops. 2002–03 output (in 1,000 tonnes): carrots, 561; onions, 350; cabbage, 255; peas, 177; apples, 140; cauliflowers, 117; lettuce, 111; turnips and swedes, 106.

Livestock in the UK as at June in each year (in 1,000):

	1999	2000	2001	2002	2003
Cattle	11,423	11,135	10,602	10,345	10,517
(dairy)	(2,440)	(2,336)	(2,251)	(2,227)	(2,192)
(beef)	(1,924)	(1,842)	(1,708)	(1,657)	(1,700)
Sheep	44,656	42,264	36,716	35,834	35,846
Pigs	7,284	6,482	5,845	5,588	5,047
Poultry	153,506	157,138	166,881	156,290	167,097

Livestock products, 2003 (1,000 tonnes): beef and veal, 699; pork, bacon and ham, 687; lamb and mutton, 306; poultry meat, 1,515; cheese, 363; hens' eggs, 8,136m. (units). Milk production in 2003 totalled 14,354m. litres.

In March 1996 the government acknowledged the possibility that bovine spongiform encephalopathy (BSE) might be transmitted to humans as a form of Creutzfeldt-Jakob disease via the food chain. Confirmed cases of BSE in cattle in the UK: 1988, 2,180; 1989, 7,133; 1990, 14,181; 1991, 25,026; 1992, 36,680; 1993, 34,370; 1994, 23,943; 1995, 14,301; 1996, 8,013; 1997, 4,310; 1998, 3,179; 1999, 2,256; 2000, 1,311; 2001, 781; 2002, 445; 2003, 173; 2004, 82; 2005, 39. Confirmed deaths attributed to nvCJD (new variant Creutzfeldt-Jakob Disease, the form of the disease thought to be linked to BSE): 1995, 3; 1996, 10; 1997, 10; 1998, 18; 1999, 15; 2000, 28; 2001, 20; 2002, 17; 2003, 18; 2004, 9; 2005, 5.

British beef was widely banned overseas and in March 1996 the European Commission introduced a ban on the export of bovine animals, semen and embryos, beef and beef products and mammalian meat and bonemeal from the UK. The government introduced a number of preventive measures including bans on sales of older meat and the use of meat in animal feed and fertilizer, and compensation schemes. Following inspections, the European Commission allowed for the export of deboned beef and beef products beginning 1 Aug. 1999. In March 2006 the ban was also lifted on exporting live animals born after 1 Aug. 1996 and exporting beef and beef products made from cattle slaughtered after 15 June 2005.

In Feb. 2001 the UK was hit by a major foot-and-mouth disease epidemic for the first time since 1967–68, with 2,030 confirmed cases and 4,050,000 animals being slaughtered during the months which followed. The last confirmed case was on 30 Sept. 2001. In the 1967–68 epidemic there had been 2,364 cases with approximately 434,000 animals slaughtered.

Forestry

In March 2003 the area of woodland in Britain was 2,722,000 ha., of which the Forestry Commission managed 787,000 ha. There were approximately 29,500 full-time equivalent jobs in the forestry industry and wood-processing industries in 1998–99, of which 11,200 were in wood processing, 5,900 in forest establishment and maintenance, 5,800 in harvesting and haulage, 4,600 in other non-forest activities such as office work research, and 2,000 in other forest activities such as nurseries and road construction. In 2003 a total of 7·84m. cu. metres of roundwood was produced.

New planting (2002–03), 12,950 ha. (816 ha., Forestry Commission; 12,134 ha., private woodlands).

Forestry Commission (*Website:* http://www.forestry.gov.uk). *Forestry Facts and Figures.* Annual

Fisheries

Quantity (in 1,000 tonnes) and value (in £1,000) of fish of British taking, landed in Great Britain (excluding salmon and sea-trout):

Quantity	1999	2000	2001	2002	2003
Wet fish	389·8	337·6	322·2	334·9	315·3
Shell fish	116·7	127·0	136·2	130·7	129·3
	506·5	464·7	458·3	465·6	444·6
Value					
Wet fish	297,831	268,816	256,364	250,845	221,091
Shell fish	166,299	153,247	167,323	163,844	170,508
	464,131	422,063	423,687	414,689	391,599

In Dec. 2003 the fishing fleet comprised 6,735 registered vessels (11,108 in 1993). Major fishing ports: (England) Brixham, Newlyn, Plymouth; (Scotland) Aberdeen, Fraserburgh, Kinlochbervie, Lerwick, Mallaig, Peterhead, Scrabster, Ullapool.

In the period 1999–2001 the average person in the UK consumed 20 kg of fish and fishery products a year, compared to the European Union average of 24 kg.

INDUSTRY

The largest companies by market capitalization in the UK on 12 March 2006 were: BP, at £130,862m. (US$225,950m.), compared to £123,329m. (US$237,199m.) in March 2005; HSBC, at £112,924m. (US$194,978m.), compared to £96,049m. (US$184,731m.); and GlaxoSmithKline, at £91,781m. (US$158,472m.), compared to £75,574m. (US$145,351m.).

In 2004 there were 157,510 manufacturing firms, of which 185 employed 1,000 or over persons, and 110,620 employed nine or fewer.

Chemicals and chemical products. Manufacturers' sales, (in £1m.) in 2002: primary plastics and other plastic products (2001), 17,023; pharmaceutical preparations and basic pharmaceutical products, 9,154; organic basic chemicals, 5,454; paints, etc., 2,729; rubber products, 2,395; perfumes and toilet products, 2,377; soap, polish and detergents, 1,891; inorganic basic chemicals, 1,109; dyes, 1,022, fertilizers, etc., 699.

Construction. Total value (in £1m.) of constructional work in Great Britain in 2003 was 93,284, including new work, 50,353 (of which housing, 15,362). Cement production, 2003, 11,215,000 tonnes; brick production, 2003, 2,772m. units.

Electrical Goods. Manufacturers' sales (in £1m.) for 2002: computers, etc., 5,815; radio and electronic capital goods (2000), 3,595; electronic valves and tubes and other electronic components, 3,412; television and radio receivers, sound or video recording, 2,693; telephone and telegraph equipment, 2,214.

Engineering, machinery and instruments. Manufacturers' sales (in £1m.) for 2002: motor vehicles, 20,491; aircraft and spacecraft, 11,509; parts and accessories for motor vehicles and engines, 8,775; appliances for measuring, checking and testing, 5,194; non-domestic cooling and ventilation equipment (2001), 3,280; lifting and handling equipment, 2,708; medical and surgical equipment and orthopaedic appliances, 2,145. Car production, 2003, 1,657,558 units.

Foodstuffs, etc. Manufacturers' sales (in £1m.) for 2002: operation of dairies, 5,371; bread, fresh pastry goods and cakes, 4,015; beer, 3,472; cocoa, chocolate and sugar confectionery, 3,470; meat production and preservation, 3,435; biscuits, rusks, preserved pastry goods and cakes, 3,005; mineral water and soft drinks (2001), 2,973; grain mill products, 2,816; fruit and vegetable processing and preservation, 2,472; prepared feeds for farm animals, 2,252; distilled alcoholic beverages, 2,109; poultry production and preservation (2001), 1,996; tobacco products,

1,825. Alcoholic beverage production, 2003: beer, 5,801·4m. litres (5,955·2m. litres in 1991); wine, 1,158·4m. litres (658·3m. litres in 1991); spirits, 455·3m. litres (447·6m. litres in 1991).

Metals. Manufacturers' sales (in £1m.) for 2002: metal structures and parts of structures, 4,959; general mechanical engineering, 2,892; forging, pressing, stamping and roll forming of metal, 1,778; light metal packaging, 1,091; treatment and coating of metals, 1,020; steel tubes, 1,015.

Textiles and clothing. Manufacturers' sales (in £1m.) in 2002: women's outerwear and underwear, 1,426; carpets and rugs, 841; household textiles, 783; textile weaving, 737; preparation and spinning of textile fibres, 556; men's outerwear and underwear, 521.

Wood products, furniture, paper and printing. Manufacturers' sales (in £1m.) in 2002: furniture of whatever construction, 7,041; journals and periodicals, 7,028; wood products except furniture, 4,961; newspapers, 4,110; paper and paperboard, 3,384; publishing of books, 3,236; cartons, boxes and cases, 3,054.

Labour

In 2004 the UK's total economically active population (i.e. all persons in employment plus the claimant unemployed) was (in 1,000) 29,821 (13,642 females), of whom 28,382 (13,032 females) were in employment, including 24,526 (11,957 females) as employees and 3,628 (963 females) as self-employed. In 1994 only 25,451,000 people had been in employment, representing an increase of 2,931,000 in ten years. UK employees by form of employment in 2004 (in 1,000): wholesale and retail trade, repair of motor vehicles, motorcycles and household goods, 4,562; real estate renting and business activities, 4,072; manufacturing industry, 3,281; health and social work, 2,951; education, 2,313; hotels and restaurants, 1,828; transport, storage and communications, 1,561; public administration and defence, compulsory social security, 1,518; construction, 1,268; financial intermediation, 1,095; agriculture, hunting, forestry and fishing, 226. Between 1999 and 2004 employment in service industries increased by 1,901,000 while employment in manufacturing declined by 770,000 over the same period.

Registered unemployed in UK as at spring (in 1,000; figures seasonally adjusted): 1999, 1,759 (6·1%); 2000, 1,638 (5·6%); 2001, 1,431 (4·9%); 2002, 1,542 (5·2%); 2003, 1,489 (5·0%); 2004, 1,438 (4·8%)—the lowest rate in more than 20 years. Of the 1,438,000 unemployed people, 829,000 were men and 609,000 women. The number of unemployed people on benefits was 904,200 in Jan. 2006 (giving a rate of 2·9%, up from 2·6% in Jan. 2005). The unemployment rate on the International Labour Organization (ILO) definition, which includes all those who are looking for work whether or not claiming unemployment benefits, was 5·1% in Oct.–Dec. 2005.

In 2001 there were 3·7m. businesses in the UK of which 1·6m. were registered at Companies House. Approximately 99% of UK businesses have fewer than 50 employees. There were an estimated 342,000 business start-ups in 2001, with business closures numbering 410,000.

Workers (in 1,000) involved in industrial stoppages (and working days lost): 1999, 141 (0·24m.); 2000, 183 (0·50m.); 2001, 180 (0·52m.); 2002, 943 (1·32m.); 2003, 151 (0·49m.). In 1975, 6m. working days had been lost through stoppages. Between 1994 and 2003 strikes cost Britain an average of 23 working days per 1,000 employees a year.

The Wages Councils set up in 1909 to establish minimum rates of pay (in 1992 of 2·5m. workers) were abolished in 1993. The Labour government, elected in May 1997, was committed to the introduction of a National Minimum Wage and established a Low Pay Commission to advise on its implementation. It is currently £5·05 an hour for adults and £4·25 for 18–21 year olds. In April 2005 the average gross salary in Britain for full-time employees was £28,258 (£31,515 for men; £22,975 for women). Average hourly pay for full-time employees excluding overtime in April 2004 in Britain was £12·80 (£13·73 for males and £11·521 for females). Average weekly earnings were highest in London, at £590·30, and lowest in the northeast, at £355·20.

Britons in full-time employment worked an average of 43·1 hours a week in 2003, compared to the EU average of 40·0 hours. Men in full-time employment put in longer hours than in any other European country.

Trade Unions

In 2003 there were 71 unions affiliated to the Trades Union Congress (TUC) with a total membership of 6·7m. (2·7m. of them women), down from a peak of 12·2m. in 1980. The unions affiliated to the TUC in 2003 ranged in size from UNISON with 1·29m. members to the Sheffield Wool Shear Workers' Union with 15 members. The four largest unions, however, account for more than half the total membership. In 2004, 59% of public-sector employees and 18% of private-sector employees were unionized.

The TUC's executive body, the General Council, is elected at the annual Congress. Congress consists of representatives of all unions according to the size of the organization, and is the principal policy-making body.

The General Secretary (Brendan Barber, b. 1951) is elected from nominations submitted by the unions. The TUC draws up policies and promotes and publicizes them. It makes representations to government, employers and international bodies. The TUC also carries out research and campaigns, and provides a range of services to unions including courses for union representatives.

The TUC is affiliated to the International Confederation of Free Trade Unions, the Trade Union Advisory Committee of OECD, the Commonwealth Trade Union Council and the European Trade Union Confederation. The TUC provides a service of trade union education. It provides members to serve, with representatives of employers, on the managing boards of such bodies as the Health and Safety Commission and the Advisory, Conciliation and Arbitration Service.

Clegg, H. A., *A History of British Trade Unions since 1889* [until 1951]. 3 vols. Oxford, 1994

Pelling, H., *A History of British Trade Unionism.* 5th ed. London, 1992.

Taylor, R., *The TUC From the General Strike to New Unionism.* Palgrave, Basingstoke, 2000

Willman, P. *et al., Union Business: Trade Union Organization and Financial Reform in the Thatcher Years.* CUP, 1993

INTERNATIONAL TRADE

Imports and Exports

Value of the imports and exports of merchandise, excluding bullion and specie (in US$1m.):

	Total imports	Total exports
2004	457,131·6	346,546·8
2005	488,235·6	379,032·0

Until 1992 all overseas trade statistics were compiled from Customs declarations. With the inception of the Single Market on 1 Jan. 1993, however, the requirement for Customs declarations in intra-EU trade was removed.

In 2004 the UK's trade with non-EU-15 countries was: imports, US$217,678·8m.; exports, US$155,084·4m. (2003 figures were imports US$178,982·4m. and exports US$136,588·8m.).

In 2004 other EU-15 members accounted for 53·6% of the UK's foreign trade, compared with 25·2% in 1956. The USA accounted for 11·8%, up from 9·1% in 1956, and the rest of the world 34·6%, down from 65·7% in 1956.

Figures for trade by countries and groups of countries (in US$1m.):

EU-15 countries	Imports from 2003	Imports from 2004	Exports to 2003	Exports to 2004
EU	203,230·8	239,452·8	168,080·4	191,462·4
Austria	4,317·6	4,194·0	2,011·2	1,964·4
Belgium and Luxembourg	20,535·6	24,588·0	17,840·4	18,985·2
Denmark	4,768·8	5,505·6	3,504·2	3,648·0
Finland	4,306·8	4,268·4	2,400·0	2,449·2
France and Monaco	31,670·4	35,760·0	29,641·2	33,476·4
Germany	53,124·0	62,854·8	32,814·0	39,172·8
Greece	1,008·0	1,186·8	2,004·0	2,526·0
Ireland	15,753·6	18,410·4	20,416·8	25,239·6
Italy	18,660·0	21,592·8	13,610·4	15,156·0
Netherlands	25,042·8	32,558·4	21,424·8	21,730·8
Portugal, Azores and Madeira	3,126·0	3,477·6	2,335·2	2,838·0
Spain	13,490·4	15,835·2	13,964·4	16,429·2
Sweden	7,425·6	9,222·0	6,112·8	7,846·8
Other foreign countries				
Europe—				
Baltic States	1,742·4	2,379·6	646·8	614·4
Czech Republic	2,343·6	2,352·0	1,635·6	1,762·8
Hungary	1,863·6	2,866·8	1,393·2	1,692·0
Iceland	507·6	674·4	238·8	314·4
Norway	10,768·8	16,130·4	3,183·6	3,663·6
Poland	2,566·8	3,303·6	2,379·6	2,562·0
Romania	1,130·4	1,446·0	831·6	1,118·4
Russia	4,059·6	6,501·6	2,318·4	2,691·6
Slovakia	428·4	474·0	387·6	402·0
Switzerland and Liechtenstein	6,446·4	6,576·0	4,758·0	5,415·6
Turkey	4,471·2	6,174·0	2,786·4	3,619·2
Other in Europe	2,101·2	2,236·8	3,116·4	3,788·4
Africa—				
Algeria	427·2	686·4	310·8	307·2
Egypt	723·6	932·4	756·0	1,227·6
Morocco	745·2	954·0	584·4	625·2
Nigeria	145·2	207·6	1,227·6	1,420·8
South Africa and Namibia	5,122·8	6,540·0	2,925·6	3,483·6
Tunisia	230·4	352·8	238·8	277·2
Other in Africa	4,209·6	4,957·2	2,643·6	2,874·0
Asia and Oceania—				
Australia	2,984·4	3,480·0	3,754·8	4,407·6
China	14,023·2	19,471·2	3,162·0	4,359·6
Hong Kong	9,235·2	10,794·0	4,087·2	4,846·8
India	3,508·8	4,286·4	3,740·4	4,116·0
Indonesia	1,568·4	1,761·6	736·8	729·6
Japan	13,479·6	15,081·6	6,109·2	6,943·2
Korea (South)	4,282·8	5,732·4	2,389·2	2,661·6
Malaysia	3,134·4	3,783·6	1,696·8	1,826·4
New Zealand	922·8	1,084·8	612·0	766·8
Pakistan	870·0	1,035·6	480·0	634·8
Philippines	1,196·4	1,230·0	628·8	579·6
Singapore	4,489·2	6,331·2	2,598·0	3,148·8
Taiwan	3,686·4	4,383·6	1,478·4	1,746·0
Thailand	2,760·0	3,297·6	937·2	1,173·6
Other in Asia and Oceania	3,292·8	4,178·4	846·0	872·4
Middle East—				
Iran	50·4	80·4	778·8	816·0
Israel	1,440·0	1,726·8	2,248·8	2,558·4
Kuwait	558·0	764·4	620·4	654·0
Saudi Arabia	1,280·4	2,223·6	3,007·2	2,961·6
United Arab Emirates	1,567·2	1,569·6	2,827·2	4,189·2
Other Middle East	529·2	685·2	2,317·2	2,647·2
America—				
Argentina	421·2	499·2	222·0	327·6
Brazil	2,476·8	2,895·6	1,356·0	1,452·0
Canada	6,217·2	7,832·4	5,365·2	6,116·4
Chile	692·4	885·6	200·4	248·4
Colombia	373·2	518·4	174·0	213·6
Mexico	830·4	771·6	1,135·2	1,148·4

America—	Imports from		Exports to	
	2003	2004	2003	2004
USA	39,453·6	42,068·4	47,936·4	52,494·0
Venezuela	190·8	390·0	237·6	344·4
Other in America	2,139·6	2,620·8	1,442·4	1,464·0
Total, foreign countries (including some not specified above)	382,213·2	457,131·6	304,669·2	346,546·8

In 2004 chemicals, manufactured goods classified chiefly by material and miscellaneous manufactured articles accounted for 41·4% of imports and 42·3% of exports; machinery and transport equipment 40·7% of the UK's imports and 41·3% of exports; mineral fuels, lubricants and related materials 6·5% of imports and 8·8% of exports; food, live animals, beverages and tobacco 8·6% of imports and 5·6% of exports; and crude materials, inedible, animal and vegetable oil and fats 2·8% of imports and 2·0% of exports.

Trade Fairs

London ranks as the third most popular convention city behind Paris and Brussels according to the Union des Associations Internationales (UAI), hosting 1·9% of all international meetings held in 2002.

COMMUNICATIONS

Roads

Responsibility for the construction and maintenance of trunk roads belongs to central government. Roads not classified as trunk roads are the responsibility of county or unitary councils.

In 2003 there were 392,321 km of public roads, classified as: motorways, 3,477 km; trunk roads, 9,341 km; other major roads, 37,292 km; minor roads, 342,212 km.

In 2003 journeys by car, vans and taxis totalled 678bn. passenger km (less than 60bn. in the early 1950s). Even in the early 1950s passenger km in cars, vans and taxis exceeded the annual total at the end of the 20th century by rail. Motor vehicles in 2003 included 24,985,000 passenger cars, 1,005,000 mopeds, scooters and motorcycles, 96,000 public transport vehicles and 2,730,000 other private and light goods vehicles. In 2002, 74% of households had regular use of a car with 29% of households having use of two or more cars. New vehicle registrations in 2003, 3,231,900. Driving tests, 2003–04 (in 1,000): applications, 1,526; tests held, 1,399; tests passed, 598; pass rate, 42%. The driving test was extended in 1996 to include a written examination.

Road casualties in Great Britain in 2004, 280,840 including 3,221 killed. Britain has one of the lowest death rates in road accidents of any industrialized country, at 6·1 deaths per 100,000 people in 2003.

Inter- and intra-urban bus and coach journeys average 47bn. passenger-km annually. Passenger journeys by local bus services, 2002–03, 4,452m. For London buses *see* Transport for London *under* Rail, *below*.

Rail

In 1994 the nationalized railway network was restructured to allow for privatization. Ownership of the track, stations and infrastructure was vested in a government-owned company, Railtrack, which was privatized in May 1996.

Passenger operations were reorganized into 25 train-operating companies, which were transferred to the private sector by Feb. 1997. By March 1997 all freight operations were also privatized. On 3 Oct. 2002 a new private sector not-for-dividend company limited by guarantee, Network Rail, took over from Railtrack plc as network owner and operator. The train-operating companies pay Network Rail for access to the rail network, and lease the rolling stock from three private-sector companies.

The rail network comprises around 16,100 route km (a third electrified). Annual passenger-km have increased from 32·1bn.

in 1996–97 to 42·4bn. in 2004–05, an increase of 32%. Passenger journeys have increased by 35% from 801m. in 1996–97 to 1,083m. in 2004–05. The amount of freight moved declined gradually over many years to 13·0bn. tonne-km in 1994–95 but has since risen to 20·6bn. tonne-km in 2004–05. In 2003–04 a total of 39 people (excluding trespassers and suicides) were fatally injured on the railways (compared to 3,221 deaths in road accidents in 2004).

Eurotunnel PLC holds a concession from the government to operate the Channel Tunnel (49·4 km), through which vehicle-carrying and Eurostar passenger trains are run in conjunction with French and Belgian railways. A new dedicated high-speed line is planned to connect the Channel Tunnel to London St Pancras. This line will be used by both international and domestic trains. Construction is being undertaken in two sections with the first section having opened in Sept. 2003. The entire line should open in 2007.

Transport *for* London (T*f*L) is accountable to the Mayor of London and is responsible for implementing his Transport Strategy as well as planning and delivering a range of transport facilities. T*f*L's remit covers London Underground (since July 2003), London Buses, the Docklands Light Railway and Croydon Tramlink. It is also responsible for London River Services, Victoria Coach Station and London's Transport Museum, and provides transport for users with reduced mobility via Dial-a-Ride. As well as running the central London congestion charging scheme, T*f*L manages a 580 km network of London's main roads, all 4,600 traffic lights and the private hire trade. It also provides grants to London Boroughs to fund local transport improvements.

Every weekday in Greater London, 5·4m. journeys are made on London's buses, 3m. on the underground, 7m. on foot, 0·3m. by bicycle, 0·2m. by taxi, 160,000 on the Docklands Light Railway and 60,000 on Croydon Tramlink.

The privately franchised Docklands Light Railway is operated in east inner London.

There are metros in Glasgow and Newcastle, and light rail systems in Birmingham/Wolverhampton, Blackpool, Manchester, Nottingham and Sheffield.

Civil Aviation

All UK airports handled a total of 216·6m. passengers in 2004. Of those, 128·9m. were handled by London area airports (Heathrow, Gatwick, London City, Luton and Stansted).

Busiest airports in 2004:

	Passengers	International		Freight (tonnes)
Heathrow	67,342,743	60,184,174	Heathrow	1,325,173
Gatwick	31,466,770	27,473,591	Nottingham	
Manchester	21,249,841	17,698,750	East Midlands	253,053
Stansted	20,910,842	18,172,660	Stansted	225,772
Birmingham	8,862,388	7,460,468	Gatwick	218,204
			Manchester	149,181

Heathrow is Europe's busiest airport for passenger traffic, ahead of Paris Charles de Gaulle, Frankfurt, Amsterdam, Madrid and Gatwick, the sixth busiest. More international passengers use Heathrow than any other airport in the world.

Following the Civil Aviation Act 1971, the Civil Aviation Authority (CAA) was established as an independent public body responsible for the economic and safety regulation of British civil aviation. A CAA wholly owned subsidiary, National Air Traffic Services, operates air traffic control. Highlands and Islands Airports Ltd is owned by the Scottish Office and operates ten airports.

There were 17,587 civil aircraft registered in the UK at 1 Jan. 2005.

British Airways is the largest UK airline, with a total of 228 aircraft in service at 31 Dec. 2004. British airways operates long- and short-haul international services, as well as an extensive domestic network. British Airways also has franchise agreements with other UK operators: British Mediterranean Airways, Comair, GB Airways, Loganair, Regional Air and Sun-Air of Scandinavia. Other major airlines in 2004 (with numbers of aircraft): BMI British Midland (31); Britannia Airways (37), since renamed Thomsonfly; British Airways Citiexpress Ltd (63); easyJet (94); First Choice Airways (30), formerly Air 2000; Flybe British European (35); My Travel Airways UK (31); Virgin Atlantic (35). According to CAA airline statistics, in 2003 British Airways flew 565·0m. km and carried 30,133,666 passengers (25,202,807 on international flights). Virgin Atlantic ranked second on the basis of aircraft-km flown (102·8m. km) and easyJet second on the basis of passengers carried (18,122,036). In April 2003 British Airways announced that Concorde, the world's first supersonic jet which began commercial service in 1976, would be permanently grounded from Oct. 2003. In recent years low-cost airlines such as Ryanair and easyJet have become increasingly popular. Serving only domestic and European destinations, they recovered quickly from the slump of the airline business following the attacks on New York and Washington on 11 Sept. 2001.

The most frequently flown route into and out of the UK in 2004 was Heathrow–New York John F. Kennedy and vice-versa (2,965,793 passengers), followed by Heathrow–Dublin and vice-versa (2,097,036) and Heathrow–Amsterdam and vice-versa (2,005,551).

Shipping

The UK-owned merchant fleet (trading vessels over 100 GT) in Sept. 2005 totalled 680 ships of 16·6m. DWT and 13·3m. GT. The UK-owned and registered fleet totalled 384 ships of 5·1m. DWT.

The average age (DWT) of the UK-owned fleet was 9·0 years, while that of the world fleet was 12·0 years. Total gross international revenue in 2004 was £10,113m. The net direct contribution to the UK balance of payments was £3,817m.; there were import savings of £1,799m., giving a total contribution of £5,616m.

The principal ports are (with 1m. tonnes of cargo handled in 2004): Grimsby and Immingham (57·6), Tees and Hartlepool (53·8), London (53·3), Milford Haven (38·5), Southampton (38·4). Total traffic in 2004 was 573·1m. tonnes.

Inland Waterways

There are approximately 3,500 miles (5,630 km) of navigable canals and river navigations in Great Britain. Of these, the publicly-owned British Waterways (BW) is responsible for some 385 miles (620 km) of commercial waterways (maintained for freight traffic) and some 1,160 miles (1,868 km) of cruising waterways (maintained for pleasure cruising, fishing and amenity). BW is also responsible for a further 450 miles (732 km) of canals, some of which are not navigable. BW's trading income for the year to 31 March 2003 was £81·7m. Third party-funding principally for restoration schemes contributed £27·9m. Additionally, British Waterways was in receipt of Government grants of £82·0m.

River navigations and canals managed by other authorities include the Thames, Great Ouse and Nene, Norfolk Broads and Manchester Ship Canal.

The Association of Inland Navigation Authorities (AINA) represents some 30 navigation authorities providing an almost complete UK coverage.

Telecommunications

In 2004 there were around 120 operators offering fixed telecommunication services, including six mobile phone operators. Fixed-link telephone services were offered by BT, Mercury Communications, Kingston Communications (Hull), most of the cable operators and the public telecommunications

operators. BT (then British Telecom) was established in 1981 to take over the management of telecommunications from the Post Office. In 1984 it was privatized as British Telecommunications plc, changing its trading name from British Telecom to BT in 1991.

By 1998 all of the BT system was served by digital exchanges. There are almost 3·5m. km of optical fibre in place. In 2002 there were 85,066,000 telephone subscribers (equivalent to 1,439·6 per 1,000 population). 91% of UK households had a fixed telephone in 2004, a fall from a peak of 94% in 2000 as increasingly UK consumers began using mobile telephones as their main form of telecommunication. In March 2002, 70% of the lines were residential and 30% business. There were 146,300 public payphones in 2002. BT handles a daily average of 103m. telephone calls a day and 22m. calls to emergency fire, police or ambulance services a year. Total estimated UK retail telecommunications expenditure in the year to Sept. 2004 was £37·7bn., an increase of 4% on the previous year.

In 2002 there were 3·50m. fax receivers. Electronic services include electronic mail ('e-mail') and a complete corporate global messaging network. BT telephone, television and business services are carried by 15–20 satellites. In 2002 BT employed 108,600 persons worldwide.

In 2004 there were 61,091,000 mobile telephone subscribers in the UK (1,021·6 per 1,000 persons), up from 8,841,000 in 1997. The leading operators are T-Mobile, including Virgin Mobile (with an estimated 26·3% share of the market); O2, including Tesco Mobile (24·1%); Orange (23·2%); Vodafone (22·4%); and 3 (4·1%). 3 was launched by Hutchison on 3 March 2003 and is the UK's first mainland third generation mobile network.

Telecommunications services are regulated by the Office of Communications ('Ofcom') in the interests of consumers.

Internet

In Sept. 2002 there were 34·3m. Internet users in the UK (more than in any other country in Europe), just over 57% of the total population. According to a survey published in Dec. 1999, 3·6m. children between the ages of seven and 16 used the Internet, with 52% of users being boys, compared to 61% in March 1999. In 2002, 55% of households had a home computer; there were 24·0m. PCs in total in 2002 (405·7 per 1,000 inhabitants). In 2002, 45% of households had Internet access. By the end of 2004 around 30% of fixed lines were either ISDN or broadband enabled and there were over 6m. UK broadband subscribers (38% of all Internet connections).

Postal Services

Royal Mail Group plc operates three distinct businesses: Royal Mail (letter delivery), Parcelforce Worldwide (parcel delivery) and Post Office Ltd (retailing and agency services). Every area of the country is served by regional offices for each of the businesses. Royal Mail collects and delivers 82m. letters a day to the 27m. UK addresses. Other services include electronic mail, guaranteed mail deliveries (same-day and overnight to UK addresses), and Swiftair deliveries to 140 other countries and territories. The British Postal Consultancy Service provides advice to administrations abroad.

In 2002 there were almost 17,500 post offices, around 600 operated directly by Post Office Ltd, the remainder (sub-post offices) on a franchise or agency basis, and 120,000 posting points. Staff numbered 200,000 in 2001–02.

SOCIAL INSTITUTIONS

Justice

England and Wales. The legal system of England and Wales, divided into civil and criminal courts, has at the head of the superior courts, as the ultimate court of appeal, the House of Lords, which hears each year appeals in civil matters, including a certain number from Scotland and Northern Ireland, as well as some appeals in criminal cases. In order that civil cases may go from the Court of Appeal to the House of Lords, it is necessary to obtain the leave of either the Court of Appeal or the House itself, although in certain cases an appeal may lie direct to the House of Lords from the decision of the High Court. An appeal can be brought from a decision of the Court of Appeal or the Divisional Court of the Queen's Bench Division of the High Court in a criminal case, provided that the Court is satisfied that a point of law 'of general public importance' is involved, and either the Court or the House of Lords is of the opinion that it is in the public interest that a further appeal should be brought. As a judicial body, the House of Lords consists of the Lord Chancellor (although the present Lord Chancellor, Lord Falconer of Thoroton, has chosen not to sit judicially), the Lords of Appeal in Ordinary, commonly called Law Lords, and such other members of the House as hold or have held high judicial office. The final court of appeal for certain of the Commonwealth countries is the Judicial Committee of the Privy Council which, in addition to Privy Counsellors who are or have held high judicial office in the UK, includes others who are or have been Chief Justices or Judges of the Superior Courts of Commonwealth countries.

The Government published proposals in 2003 to set up a new Supreme Court, separate from the House of Lords, which would take over responsibility for the cases heard by the House of Lords and the devolution cases presently heard by the Judicial Committee of the Privy Council. Provisions to give effect to this were included in the Constitutional Reform Bill introduced in 2004, which received royal assent on 24 March 2005.

Civil Law. The main courts of original civil jurisdiction are the High Court and county courts.

The High Court has exclusive jurisdiction to deal with specialist classes of case e.g. judicial review. It has concurrent jurisdiction with county courts in cases involving contract and tort although it will only hear those cases where the issues are complex or important. The High Court also has appellate jurisdiction to hear appeals from lower tribunals.

The judges of the High Court are attached to one of its three divisions: Chancery, Queen's Bench and Family; each with its separate field of jurisdiction. The Heads of the three divisions are the Lord Chief Justice (Queen's Bench), the Vice-Chancellor (Chancery) and the President of the Family Division. In addition there are 107 High Court judges (100 men and seven women). For the hearing of cases at first instance, High Court judges sit singly. Appellate jurisdiction is usually exercised by Divisional Courts consisting of two (sometimes three) judges, though in certain circumstances a judge sitting alone may hear the appeal. High Court business is dealt with in the Royal Courts of Justice and by over 130 District Registries outside London.

County courts can deal with all contract and tort cases, and recovery of land actions, regardless of value. They have upper financial limits to deal with specialist classes of business such as equity and Admiralty cases. Certain county courts have been designated to deal with family, bankruptcy, patents and discrimination cases.

There are about 220 county courts located throughout the country, each with its own district. A case may be heard by a circuit judge or by a district judge. Defended claims are allocated to one of three tracks—the small claims track, the fast track and the multi-track. The small claims track provides a simple and informal procedure for resolving disputes, mainly in claims for debt, where the value of the claim is no more than £5,000. Parties should be able to do this without the need for a solicitor. Other claims valued between £5,000 and £15,000 will generally be allocated to the fast track, and higher valued claims which could not be dealt with justly in the fast track may be allocated to the multi-track.

Specialist courts include the Patents Court, which deals only with matters concerning patents, registered designs and appeals against the decision of the Comptroller General of Patents. Cases suitable to be heard by a county court are dealt with at Central London County Court.

The Court of Appeal (Civil Division) hears appeals in civil actions from the High Court and county courts, and tribunals. Its President is the Master of the Rolls, aided by up to 37 Lords Justices of Appeal (as at 1 Jan. 2004) sitting in six or seven divisions of two or three judges each.

Civil proceedings are instituted by the aggrieved person, but as they are a private matter, they are frequently settled by the parties through their lawyers before the matter comes to trial. In very limited classes of dispute (e.g. libel and slander), a party may request a jury to sit to decide questions of fact and the award of damages.

Criminal Law. At the base of the system of criminal courts in England and Wales are the magistrates' courts which deal with over 96% of criminal cases. In general, in exercising their summary jurisdiction, they have power to pass a sentence of up to six months imprisonment and to impose a fine of up to £5,000 on any one offence. They also deal with the preliminary hearing of cases triable at the Crown Court. In addition to dealing summarily with over 2·0m. cases, which include thefts, assaults, drug abuse, etc., they also have a limited civil and family jurisdiction.

Magistrates' courts normally sit with a bench of three lay justices. Although unpaid they are entitled to loss of earnings and travel and subsistence allowance. They undergo training after appointment and they are advised by a professional legal adviser. In central London and in some provincial areas full-time District Judges (formerly known as stipendiary magistrates) have been appointed. Generally they possess the same powers as the lay bench, but they sit alone. On 31 March 2004 the total strength of the lay magistracy was 28,029 including 13,846 women. Justices are appointed on behalf of the Queen by the Lord Chancellor.

Justices are selected and trained specially to sit in Youth and Family Proceedings Courts. Youth Courts deal with cases involving children and young persons up to and including the age of 17 charged with criminal offences (other than homicide and other grave offences). These courts normally sit with three justices, including at least one man and one woman, and are accommodated separately from other courts.

Family Proceedings Courts deal with matrimonial applications and Children Act matters, including care, residence and contact and adoption. These courts normally sit with three justices including at least one man and one woman.

Above the magistrates' courts is the Crown Court. This was set up by the Courts Act 1971 to replace quarter sessions and assizes. Unlike quarter sessions and assizes, which were individual courts, the Crown Court is a single court which is capable of sitting anywhere in England and Wales. It has power to deal with all trials on indictment and has inherited the jurisdiction of quarter sessions to hear appeals, proceedings on committal of persons from the magistrates' courts for sentence, and certain original proceedings on civil matters under individual statutes.

The jurisdiction of the Crown Court is exercisable by a High Court judge, a Circuit judge or a Recorder or Assistant Recorder (part-time judges) sitting alone, or, in specified circumstances, with justices of the peace. The Lord Chief Justice has given directions as to the types of case to be allocated to High Court judges (the more serious cases) and to Circuit judges or Recorders respectively.

Appeals from magistrates' courts go either to a Divisional Court of the High Court (when a point of law alone is involved) or to the Crown Court where there is a complete re-hearing on appeals against conviction and/or sentence. Appeals from the Crown Court in cases tried on indictment lie to the Court of Appeal (Criminal Division). Appeals on questions of law go by right, and appeals on other matters by leave. The Lord Chief

Justice or a Lord Justice sits with judges of the High Court to constitute this court. Thereafter, appeals in England and Wales can be made to the House of Lords.

There remains as a last resort the invocation of the royal prerogative exercised on the advice of the Home Secretary. In 1965 the death penalty was abolished for murder and in 1998 abolished for all crimes.

All contested criminal trials, except those which come before the magistrates' courts, are tried by a judge and a jury consisting of 12 members. The prosecution or defence may challenge any potential juror for cause. The jury decides whether the accused is guilty or not. The judge is responsible for summing up on the facts and directing the jury on the relevant law. He sentences offenders who have been convicted by the jury (or who have pleaded guilty). If, after at least two hours and ten minutes of deliberation, a jury is unable to reach a unanimous verdict it may, on the judge's direction, provided that in a full jury of 12 at least ten of its members are agreed, bring in a majority verdict. The failure of a jury to agree on a unanimous verdict or to bring in a majority verdict may involve the retrial of the case before a new jury.

The Employment Appeal Tribunal. The Employment Appeal Tribunal, which is a superior Court of Record with the like powers, rights, privileges and authority of the High Court, was set up in 1976 to hear appeals on questions of law against decisions of employment tribunals and of the Certification Officer. The appeals are heard by a judge sitting alone or with two members (in exceptional cases four) appointed for their special knowledge or experience of industrial relations either on the employer or the trade union side, with always an equal number on each side. The great bulk of their work is concerned with the problems which can arise between employees and their employers.

Military Courts. Offences committed by persons subject to service law under the Army Act 1955, the Air Force Act 1955 or the Naval Discipline Act 1957 may be dealt with either summarily or by courts-martial.

The Personnel of the Law. All judicial officers are independent of Parliament and the Executive. They are appointed by the Crown on the advice of the Prime Minister or the Lord Chancellor, or directly by the Lord Chancellor himself, and hold office until retiring age. Under the Judicial Pensions and Retirement Act 1993 judges normally retire by age 70 years.

The legal profession is divided; barristers, who advise on legal problems and can conduct cases before all courts, usually act for the public only through solicitors, who deal directly with the legal business brought to them by the public and have rights to present cases before certain courts. The distinction between the two branches of the profession has been weakened since the passing of the Courts and Legal Services Act 1990, which has enabled solicitors to obtain the right to appear as advocates before all courts. Long-standing members of both professions are eligible for appointment to most judicial offices.

For all judicial appointments up to and including the level of Circuit Judge (except for Recordership, which is achieved on promotion from assistant Recordership), it is necessary to apply in writing to be considered for appointment. Vacancies are advertised. A panel consisting of a judge, an official and a lay member decide whom to invite for interview and also interview the shortlisted applicants. They make recommendations to the Lord Chancellor, who retains the right of final recommendation to the Sovereign or appointment, as appropriate.

Legal Services. The system of legal aid in England and Wales was established after the Second World War under the Legal Aid and Advice Act 1949. The Legal Aid Board was then set up under the Legal Aid Act 1988, and took over the administration of legal aid from the Law Society in 1989. The Legal Services Commission (LSC) was set up under the Access to Justice Act 1999 and replaced the Legal Aid Board on 1 April 2000. The LSC is an executive non-departmental public body. It comprises a Chair and 11 Commissioners, all appointed by the Lord Chancellor. It is responsible for the development and administration of two schemes in England and Wales: the *Community Legal Service*, which from 1 April 2000 replaced the old civil scheme of legal aid, bringing together networks of funders and suppliers into partnerships to provide the widest possible access to information and advice; and the *Criminal Defence Service*, which from 2 April 2001 replaced the old system of criminal legal aid and provides criminal services to people accused of crimes. Only organizations with a contract with the LSC are able to provide advice or representation funded by the LSC.

Under the Community Legal Service, which improves access to justice for those most in need, the LSC directly funds legal services for eligible clients. Some solicitors are prepared to give a free or low-cost initial interview whether or not the client qualifies for funding. The different levels of service in civil matters are *Legal Help, Help at Court, Family Mediation, Help with Mediation, General Family Help* and *Legal Representation*. *Legal Representation* is available in two forms *(Investigative Help* and *Full Representation)*.

The purpose of the Criminal Defence Service is to ensure that people suspected or accused of a crime have access to advice, assistance and representation, as the interests of justice require. The different levels of service are: *Police Station Advice and Assistance* (covers support for individuals questioned by police about an offence, whether or not they have been arrested); *Advice and Assistance* (covers help from a solicitor with general advice, writing letters, negotiating, obtaining a barrister's opinion and preparing a written case); *Advocacy Assistance* (covers the cost of a solicitor to prepare a client's case and initial representation in certain proceedings in both the magistrates' and the crown court); *Representation* (covers the cost of a solicitor to prepare a client's defence before a court appearance and to represent the client there, plus dealing with issues such as bail).

In 2004–05 the Commission received funding of £2·0bn. with which to fund the provision of services and spent £96·4m. on administration costs. Community Legal Services payments in 2004–05 came to £845·9m. (856,100 acts of assistance) and net Criminal Defence Services payments to £509·7m. (1,463,700 acts of assistance), giving net Legal Services Commission payments of £1,355·6m. and a total of 2,319,800 acts of assistance.

See also SCOTLAND.

CIVIL JUDICIAL STATISTICS

ENGLAND AND WALES	2004
Appellate Courts	
Judicial Committee of the Privy Council	68
House of Lords	52
Court of Appeal	1,059
High Court of Justice (appeals and special cases from inferior courts)	4,207
Courts of First Instance (excluding Magistrates' Courts and Tribunals)	
High Court of Justice:	
Chancery Division	35,457
Queen's Bench Division	14,830
County courts: Matrimonial suits	167,193
County courts: Other	1,597,123
Restrictive Practices Court	—

CRIMINAL STATISTICS

ENGLAND AND WALES

	Total number of offenders[1]		Indictable offences[1]	
	2003	2004	2003	2004
Aged 10 and over				
Proceeded against in magistrates' courts	2,000,822	2,022,604	509,179	453,325
Found guilty at magistrates' courts	1,431,520	1,488,036	278,089	260,185

	Total number of offenders[1]		Indictable offences[1]	
	2003	2004	2003	2004
Aged 10 and over				
Found guilty at the				
Crown Court	59,690	60,464	56,998	57,651
Cautioned	241,803	255,768	150,749	156,271
Aged 10 and under 18				
Proceeded against in				
magistrates' courts	140,790	136,662	74,671	69,873
Found guilty at				
magistrates' courts	89,658	93,179	43,166	44,112
Found guilty at the				
Crown Court	2,883	3,011	2,790	2,904
Cautioned[2]	91,933	105,058	58,676	42,517

[1]On the principal offence basis. [2]From 1 June 2000 the Crime and Disorder Act 1998 came into force nationally and removed the use of cautions for persons under 18 and replaced them with reprimands and final warnings.

British Crime Survey (BCS) interviews in 2004–05 estimate that there were approximately 10·8m. crimes against adults living in private households in England and Wales. This represents a reduction of 7% compared with the estimate based on interviews for 2003–04. In the year to March 2005 crimes recorded by the police in England and Wales totalled 5·6m., a fall of 6% compared with 2003–04. 75% of all recorded crimes were against property.

In Sept. 2003 the prison population in England and Wales was 73,741 (72,097 in Sept. 2002). In 2001 the incarceration rate of 137 people per 100,000 inhabitants was the highest in western Europe. The annual average prison population rose 58% between 1992 and 2002, but the recorded crime level went up by only 18%. During this time the female prison population rose by 175%, from 1,562 to 4,299, but the male prison population only rose by 54%. These figures do not include prisoners held in police cells.

See also SCOTLAND and NORTHERN IRELAND.

Police

In England and Wales there are 43 police forces, each maintained by a police authority typically comprising nine local councillors, three magistrates and five independent members. London is policed by the Metropolitan Police Service (responsible for the 23-member Metropolitan Police Authority, 12 of whom are members of the Greater London Assembly) and the City of London Police (whose police authority is the City of London Corporation). A tripartite arrangement (Secretary of State for Scotland, Chief Constable and Police Authority) exists for the accountability of the police service in Scotland.

Figures show that the total strength of the police service in England and Wales at 31 March 2005 was 141,230 (including 29,119 women). Police officers are supported by police staff and at the end of March 2005 there were 70,827 police staff (approximately 37,000 female). There were 11,918 special constables in March 2005 (including 3,844 women). In addition there are around 6,300 community support officers and 1,133 designated officers (investigation officers, detention officers and escort officers). Total provision for policing in England and Wales to be supported by grant in 2005–06 was £11·8bn. This is a cash increase of £746m. over 2004–05, or 6·7%, and builds on substantial government investment in the Police Service over the past three years.

Education

Adult Literacy and Numeracy. The government published the *Skills for Life Strategy* in 2001 in response to the recommendations in the 1999 Moser report (*A Fresh Start. Improving Literacy and Numeracy*). The strategy covers adults aged 16 and above at skills levels of pre-entry up to and including Level 2. The results of the 2003 *Skills for Life Needs and Impact Survey* showed that in England 5·2m. adults aged 16–65 have literacy levels below Level 1 (equivalent to the level expected of an average 11 year old) and 15m. have numeracy skills below Level 1. By July 2003, 470,000 adults had achieved a first literacy, language or numeracy

qualification. Ultimately, the strategy aims to help 2·25m. adults improve their literacy, language and numeracy skills by 2010, with an interim target of 1·5m. adults by 2007.

The Publicly Maintained System of Education. Compulsory schooling begins at the age of five (four in Northern Ireland) and the minimum leaving age for all pupils is 16. No tuition fees are payable in any publicly maintained school (but it is open to parents, if they choose, to pay for their children to attend independent schools run by individuals, companies or charitable institutions). The post-school or tertiary stage, which is voluntary, includes universities, further education establishments and other higher education establishments (including those which provide courses for the training of teachers), as well as adult education and the youth service. Financial assistance (grants and loans) is generally available to students in higher education and to some students on other courses in further education.

National Curriculum. The National Curriculum was introduced in 1988 and revised in 1999. It determines the content of what will be taught, sets attainment targets for learning and determines how performance will be assessed and reported.

The National Curriculum comprises the core subjects of English, maths and science; and foundation subjects of information communication technology, design and technology, history, geography, modern foreign languages, art and design, music, PE and citizenship.

At key stage 4 (ages 14–16) schools must provide access for each pupil to a minimum of one course in the arts (art and design, music, dance, drama and media arts), one course in the humanities (history and geography), at least one modern foreign language, and design and technology. However, since Sept. 2004 these subject areas are no longer compulsory for key stage 4 pupils.

In addition, pupils must be taught religious education, sex education (though parents have the right to withdraw their children from either) and, for pupils aged over 14, careers education. Every school must also provide a form of daily collective worship, but with the right to withdraw.

Early Years Education. Early years education services include: state nursery schools, nursery classes in primary schools and reception classes; private, voluntary and independent sector nursery schools; and childminder networks. There are 35,000 settings in the state private and voluntary sectors delivering the government's early education curriculum. Since March 2004 all three and four year-olds have been provided with a free, part-time, early education place available at any of these settings.

Primary Schools. These provide compulsory education for pupils from the age of five up to the age of 11 (12 in Scotland). Most public sector primary schools take boys and girls in mixed classes. Some pre-compulsory age pupils attend nursery classes within primary schools, however, and in England some middle schools cater for pupils at either side of the secondary education transition age. There are 22,509 public sector mainstream primary schools with an average of 22 pupils per teacher.

Middle Schools. A number of local education authorities operate a middle school system. These provide for pupils from the age of 8, 9 or 10 up to the age of 12, 13 or 14, and are deemed either primary or secondary according to the age range of the pupils.

Secondary Schools. There are 4,225 secondary schools in Great Britain providing for pupils from the age of 11 upwards. Some local authorities have retained selection at age 11 for entry to grammar schools, of which there are 234. There are 130 secondary modern schools providing a general education up to the minimum school leaving age of 16, although exceptionally some pupils stay on beyond that age. In public sector mainstream secondary schools in Great Britain there are an average 16 pupils per teacher.

Almost all local education authorities operate a system of comprehensive schools to which pupils are admitted without reference to ability or aptitude. There are 3,420 such schools in Great Britain with over 3·4m. pupils. With the development of comprehensive education, various patterns of secondary schools have come into operation. Principally these are: 1) All-through schools with pupils aged 11 to 18 or 11 to 16; pupils over 16 being able to transfer to an 11 to 18 school or a sixth form college providing for pupils aged 16 to 19. (Since 1 April 1993, sixth form colleges have been part of the further education sector—there are 102 sixth form colleges). 2) Local education authorities operating a three-tier system involving middle schools where transfer to secondary school is at ages 12, 13 or 14. These correspond to 12 to 18, 13 to 18 and 14 to 18 comprehensive schools respectively. 3) In areas where there are no middle schools a two-tier system of junior and senior comprehensive schools for pupils aged 11 to 18, with optional transfer to these schools at age 13 or 14.

Specialist Schools. These include Business and Enterprise Colleges, Mathematics and Computing Colleges, Science Colleges, Engineering Colleges, Technology Colleges, Language Colleges, Art Colleges, Music Colleges, Humanities Colleges and Sports Colleges. There is a programme to help existing maintained secondary schools to specialize in a particular area of the curriculum, while continuing to cover the full National Curriculum. To be included in the programme, schools must raise sponsorship and then prepare development plans, in competition with other schools, to seek extra government funding. They must also demonstrate how they will share their resources and expertise with local schools and the wider community. The first Technology Colleges operated from Sept. 1994. By Sept. 2001 there were 685 Specialist Schools in England. In 2004 there were 1,956 Specialist Schools.

City Technology Colleges. Established in partnership between government and business sponsors under the Education Reform Act 1988, there are 14 independent all-ability secondary schools. They teach the full National Curriculum but give special emphasis to technology, science and mathematics. Government meets all recurrent costs. Sponsors are required to provide a 20% contribution towards the cost of all capital projects.

Music and Dance Scheme (formerly the Music and Ballet Scheme). The 'Aided Pupil Scheme' for boys and girls with outstanding talent in music or dance (principally ballet) helps parents with the fees and boarding costs at eight specialist private schools in England. Since Sept. 2004 a national grants scheme has been piloted.

Special Education. It is estimated that, nationally, some 20% of the school population will have special educational needs at some time during their school career. In just over 2% of cases the Local Education Authority will need to make a statutory assessment of special educational needs under the Education Act 1996. (In Scotland pupils are assessed for a Record of Needs.)

Maintained schools must use their best endeavours to make provision for such pupils. The Special Educational Needs Code of Practice, a revised version of which came into force on 1 Jan. 2002, gives practical guidance.

Further Education (Non-University). In April 2001 the Learning and Skills Council (LSC) took over the responsibility for funding the Further Education (FE) sector in England. The LSC is primarily responsible for funding full- and part-time education and training provision for people aged 16 to 19 in FE colleges, sixth form colleges, work-based and LEA maintained institutions. It also funds some higher education in FE sector colleges and since April 2002 has had responsibility for school sixth form funding. It also makes provision for learning basic skills and adult and community learning for those aged 19 and over.

Further education is the largest sector providing educational opportunities for the over 16s. There are 415 FE colleges in England, with 3·9m. students. Of the students on Council funded provision, 18% were under 19 and 82% were adults.

In Wales, the National Council for Education and Training (CETW) funds FE provision. The Scottish FEFC (SFEFC) funds FE colleges in Scotland, while the Department for Employment and Learning funds FE colleges in Northern Ireland.

The Youth Service. The priority age group for the service is 13–19 year olds, but the target age group may extend to 11–25 year olds. Provision is usually in the form of youth clubs and centres, or through 'detached' or outreach work aimed at young people at risk from alcohol or drug misuse, or of drifting into crime. There is an increasing emphasis on youth workers working with disaffected, and socially excluded, young people.

The Learning and Skills Act, 2000 gives the Secretary of State power to secure the provision of support for all 13–19 year olds for the purpose of encouraging and enabling young people to stay on and to participate in education and training.

Local Authority youth services are required to provide adequate facilities for further education including social, physical and recreational training and organized leisure time. The Youth Service provides a key contribution to the Connexions Service (a free information, guidance, advice and job placement service to all young people under the age of 21 years), which began operating in England in April 2001. In 2004–05, £460m. was invested. There are currently 88 national voluntary youth organizations running a total of 98 projects. This includes nine joint projects involving two or more organizations.

Independent/State School Partnerships Grant Scheme. The aim is to promote collaborative working between the independent and state school sectors to raise standards in education. A total of 47 one-, two-, and three-year projects are receiving £1·6m. of funding which commenced in 2003.

Higher Education (HE) Student Support. Students are expected to make a contribution towards their tuition fees. The maximum that a student was expected to pay towards their tuition in 2004–05 was £1,150. The annual income threshold at which fees start to be payable is set at £21,475. It is expected that about 60% of all students will not have to pay fees. Students on teacher training courses (other than first degrees), in the fifth or later years of medical and dental courses, and on NHS-funded courses in professions allied to medicine, pay no fees.

Loans are available to help with students' living costs. All students are entitled to 75% of the maximum loan, with the remaining quarter subject to income assessment. The maximum loans available in 2002–03 were: £5,050 (living away from home and studying in London); £4,095 (living away from home and studying outside London); and £3,240 (living at home). These loans do not have to be repaid until the student has left university or college and is earning over £10,000 a year. They are repaid on an income contingent basis, set at 9% of gross income over £10,000 a year.

In 2004–05 part-time students were eligible for a fee grant of up to £575 and a course grant of up to £250 for help with other costs.

Applications for support in HE are made through Local Education Authorities. Students' loan accounts are managed by the Student Loans Company (SLC).

Extra, non-repayable, help is targeted at: those with disabilities; those with dependants; and those entering HE from low-income families in inner city areas. Help is also available from universities and colleges for students who get into financial difficulties. In 2004–05 the amount available to be distributed by universities and colleges to students in financial difficulties was £70m.

Postgraduate studentships and research grants are available from the Research Councils and the Arts and Humanities Research Board (AHRB). There are six grant-awarding Research Councils which each report to the Office of Science and Technology in the Department for Trade and Industry. They offer awards to students studying within the broad spectrum of economics, engineering, astronomy, and medical, biological and physical sciences. There are three types of funding: advanced course studentships which are for masters level taught courses, usually of one year's duration, research masters training awards and standard research studentships, which are for PhD or MPhil students on programmes of up to three years full-time or five years part-time.

The AHRB also makes awards for postgraduate study and research. It funds studentships in the humanities for Masters and Doctoral programmes, as well as awards for students undertaking a range of professional or vocational training in these subject areas. Both Research Council and AHRB funding is awarded on a competitive basis. In 2002–03 the six Research Councils granted 6,538 awards, while in the same year the AHRB made 1,809 awards. The British Academy complements the work of the AHRB and the Economic and Social Research Council by supporting individual scholars with personal research grants, for amounts up to £5,000; postdoctoral fellowships; research readerships and professorships; grants with international programmes, including overseas exchange schemes; and support for conferences.

Career Development Loans (CDLs). Introduced in 1988, CDLs are specifically designed to help individuals acquire and improve vocational skills, and are aimed at those who would otherwise not have reasonable or adequate access to the funds. Loans of between £300 and £8,000 can be applied for to support up to two years of education or learning (plus up to one year's practical work experience where it forms part of the course). The Department for Education and Skills operates the programme in partnership with three high street banks (Barclays, The Co-operative and the Royal Bank of Scotland). The Department for Education and Skills pays the interest on the loan for the period of supported learning and for up to one month afterwards. The individual then repays the loan to the bank in accordance with their loan agreement. Subject to certain conditions it may be possible for individuals to defer their loan re-payments for up to 17 months.

By Oct. 2004 over £750m. had been advanced to over 208,000 applicants.

Teachers. Qualified teacher status (QTS) is linked to an undergraduate or postgraduate course of teacher training. Computerized skills tests in numeracy and literacy now form part of the requirements for QTS. Newly qualified teachers are then required to complete an induction programme during their first year of teaching.

Those who are recognized as qualified teachers in Scotland or Northern Ireland are also entitled to apply to the General Teaching Council for England or the General Teaching Council for Wales for qualified teacher status. Teachers who are nationals of participating member states of the European Economic Area who are recognized as qualified in their own countries may also be entitled to apply for qualified teacher status if they meet the requirements on the mutual recognition of qualifications.

Those who have trained overseas in a country outside of the European Economic Area with at least two years' teaching experience may be eligible for assessment against the induction and qualified teacher status standards without further training. Those who are successful are exempted from serving an induction period.

From Sept. 2000 a new, flexible, modular postgraduate route was introduced to allow trainees to receive more individualized teacher training. This takes account of any prior learning and experience, and is broken up into flexible modules which trainees can undertake when convenient to them.

In 2003–04 there were about 33,930 new entrants to conventional initial teacher training courses.

In Jan. 2004, 472,500 (provisional) full-time equivalent teachers were employed in maintained schools in the UK.

Finance. Total managed education and training expenditure by central and local government in the UK for 2004–05 was £52·0bn. (£49·4bn. in 2001–02 and £35·4bn. in 1994–95). This equates to 5·4% of GDP (4·9% in 2001–02 and 5·1% in 1994–95).

Independent Schools. Independent schools which belong to an association affiliated to the Independent Schools Council (accounting for 80% of pupils) are subject to an inspection regime agreed between the government and the ISC. Non-association schools are inspected by HM inspectors from OFSTED on a five-six year cycle.

The earliest of the independent schools were founded by medieval churches. Many were founded as 'grammar' (classical) schools in the 16th century, receiving charters from the reigning sovereign. Reformed mainly in the middle of the 19th century, among the best-known are Eton College, founded in 1440 by Henry VI; Winchester College (1394), founded by William of Wykeham, Bishop of Winchester; Harrow School, founded in 1560 as a grammar school by John Lyon, a yeoman; and Charterhouse (1611). Among the earliest foundations are King's School, Canterbury, founded 600; King's School, Rochester (604) and St Peter's, York (627).

Higher Education. In 2003–04 there were almost 2·1m. higher education students in the UK at some 90 universities, 60 higher education colleges or on higher education courses in further education colleges. The number of male and female students is roughly equal, although female students do now outnumber males. 25% of the UK population between the ages of 25 and 64 have been through tertiary education, compared to an OECD average of 22%.

Total funding for higher education institutions in England was around £12·7bn. in 2002–03. Approximately 60% of this comes from UK or European Union governments in the form of grants via the funding councils, public contributions to standard tuition fees and research grants and contracts. Higher education institutions are funded by four UK bodies, one each for England, Scotland, Wales and Northern Ireland. Their roles include: allocating funds for teaching and research; promoting high-quality education and research; advising government on the needs of higher education; informing students about the quality of higher education available; and ensuring the proper use of public funds.

Open University. The Open University received its Royal Charter on 1 June 1969 and is an independent, self-governing institution, awarding its own degrees at undergraduate and postgraduate level. It is financed by the government through the Higher Education Funding Council for England for all its students in England, Wales and Northern Ireland and through the Scottish HEFC for the teaching of its students in Scotland, and by the receipt of students' fees. At the heart of most courses is a series of specially produced textbooks or 'course units' (which are also widely used in the rest of the HE sector). They are closely integrated with a varying mix of set books, recommended reading, television programmes, audio and video tapes, home experiment kits, computer-based learning programmes, multimedia resources and network services. There are also 339 local tutorial centres where face-to-face tutorials may be offered. No formal qualifications are required for entry to undergraduate courses. Residents from most countries of Western Europe aged 18 or over may apply (though some courses are not available outside the UK). There are over 200 undergraduate courses; many are available on a one-off basis. In

2003–04 there were over 149,700 undergraduates and over 20,700 postgraduate level students. The university has 4,784 full-time staff working at Milton Keynes and in 13 Regional Centres throughout the country. There are almost 8,000 part-time associate lecturers.

The only university independent of the state system is the *University of Buckingham*, which opened in 1976 and received a Royal charter in 1983. It offers two-year honours degrees, the academic year commencing in Jan., July or Oct., and consisting of four ten-week terms. There are four areas of study: Business; Humanities; Law; and Sciences. In 2003 there were 578 full-time and 43 part-time undergraduate students and 105 postgraduate students. There were 58 teachers (seven part-time).

All universities charge fees, but financial help is available to students from several sources, and the majority of students receive some form of financial assistance.

See also SCOTLAND *and* NORTHERN IRELAND.

British Council
The purpose of the British Council is to build mutually beneficial relationships between people in the UK and other countries, and to increase appreciation of the UK's creative ideas and achievements. Established in 1934 and incorporated by Royal Charter in 1940, it is the UK's international organization for educational and cultural relations. Its headquarters are in London and Manchester, with further centres in Belfast, Cardiff and Edinburgh. Independent and non-political, it is represented in 110 countries, running a mix of offices, libraries, information centres, Knowledge and Learning Centres and English-teaching operations. Its main areas of activity are in education and training, examination administration, English language teaching, learning and capacity building, the arts and sciences, sport, governance and civil society. The British Council's total income in 2003–04 was £473m. This was made up of government grants (£171m.), revenues from English-language teaching and client-funded education services (£199m.) and development programmes, principally in education and training, which are managed on behalf of the British government and other clients (£103m.).

Chair: Lord Kinnock.

Director-General: David Green, KCMG.

Headquarters: 10 Spring Gdns, London, SW1A 2BN.

Website: http://www.britishcouncil.org

Health
The National Health Service (NHS) in England and Wales started on 5 July 1948. There is a separate Act for Scotland.

The NHS is a charge on the national income in the same way, for example, as the armed forces. Every person normally resident in the UK is entitled to use any part of the service, and no insurance qualification is necessary.

Since its inception, the NHS has been funded from general taxation and national insurance (NI) contributions, and the present government has maintained the original principle that the NHS should be a service provided to all those who need it, regardless of their ability to pay or where they live. In 2004–05 the NHS in England was funded 20·2% by NI contributions, 73·9% by general taxation and 2·5% by charges for drugs and dental treatment, and the rest from other receipts. Health authorities may raise funds from voluntary sources; hospitals may take private, paying patients.

The NHS is the second largest government spending programme. In 2004–05 the planned total expenditure on health as a percentage of GDP in the UK was 8·3%; the planned UK net NHS expenditure for 2004–05 was £88·6bn.

Organization. The National Health Service and Community Care Act, 1990, provided for a major restructuring of the NHS. From 1 April 1991 health authorities became the purchasers of health care, concentrating on their responsibilities to plan and obtain services for their local residents by the placement of health service contracts with the appropriate units. Day-to-day management tasks became the responsibility of hospitals and other units, with whom the contracts are placed, in their capacity as providers of care.

The 28 Strategic Health Authorities (SHAs), created in 2002, control local health care and are the key link between the Department of Health and the NHS. They monitor performance and standards of local NHS organizations (apart from NHS Foundation Trusts).

Primary Care Trusts (PCTs), introduced in 2000, control local health care and are financed directly by the Department of Health (75% of the NHS budget). They hold to account provider organizations (including NHS Foundation Trusts) for delivery of services which they have commissioned. At 30 Sept. 2003 there were 302 PCTs. Revenue allocation in Dec. 2002 for the financial years 2003–04, 2004–05 and 2005–06 totalled £148bn. (£135bn. for 2006–07 and 2007–08 was allocated in Feb. 2005). These allocations cover Hospital and Community Health Services (HCHS), prescription of drugs, HIV/AIDS and GP infrastructure (staff, premises and IT).

Services. The NHS broadly consists of hospital and specialist services, general medical, dental and ophthalmic services, pharmaceutical services, community health services and school health services. In general these services are free of charge; the main exceptions are prescriptions, spectacles, dental and optical examination, dentures and dental treatment, amenity beds in hospitals, and some community services, for which contributory charges are made with certain exemptions.

As at 30 Sept. 2003 there were 28,568 Unrestricted Principals and Equivalents (UPEs) in England each with an average of 1,802 patients. There were 1,783 in Wales with an average of 1,695 patients each and 3,876 in Scotland with an average of 1,380. There were 18,400 general dental practitioners including their assistants in England, 1,015 in Wales and 2,123 in Scotland. In Great Britain in 2003 there were 80,537 hospital medical staff and 349,701 qualified nursing and midwifery staff, excluding agency staff. As at 31 March 2005 there were 32,194 General Medical Practitioners, excluding retainers and registrars (an increase of 1·2% since Dec. 2004); 31,210 consultants (increase of 1·1%) and 2,435 GP Registrars (increase of 2·1%). In 2002–03 provision of beds in England was 38 per 10,000 population. There were 186,290 hospital beds in England in 2002–03 (232,201 in 1992–93).

Private. In recent years increasing numbers of people have turned to private medical insurance. This covers the costs of private medical treatment (PMI) for curable short-term medical conditions. PMI includes the costs of surgery, specialists, nursing and accommodation at a private hospital or in a private ward of an NHS hospital. Approximately 11% of the UK population have private medical insurance. The leading companies are BUPA Healthcare, AXA PPP healthcare and Norwich Union Healthcare Ltd.

In 2001, 27% of the population of the UK aged 15 and over smoked. In 1974 the percentage had been 45%, with 51% of males and 41% of females smoking. Over the years the difference between the percentage of men and of women who smoke has been declining; in 2001, 28% of men and 26% of women smoked. Among 11- to 15-year-olds 12% of girls but only 9% of boys smoked in 2000. The overall percentage of the UK population who are smokers is similar to the average for the EU as a whole, but among men the percentage of smokers in the UK is lower than in the EU as a whole whereas among women it is higher. Alcohol consumption has increased in recent years. Whereas in 1961 the average Briton consumed the equivalent of 4·5 litres of pure alcohol a year, by 2003 this figure had risen to 9·1 litres. By 2000, 22·0% of the population were considered obese (having a body mass index over 30), compared to 14·0% in 1991 and 7·0% in 1980.

The UK's AIDS rate stands at 24·1 cases per 100,000 population.

A survey published by the World Health Organization in June 2000 to measure health systems in all of the sovereign countries and find which country has the best overall health care ranked the UK in 18th place.

See also NORTHERN IRELAND.

Personal Social Services

Under the Local Authority Social Services Act, 1970, and in Scotland the Social Work (Scotland) Act, 1968, the welfare and social work services provided by local authorities were made the responsibility of a new local authority department—the Social Services Department in England and Wales, and Social Work Departments in Scotland headed by a Director of Social Work, responsibility in Scotland passing in 1975 to the local authorities. The social services thus administered include: the fostering, care and adoption of children, welfare services and social workers for people with learning difficulties and the mentally ill, the disabled and the aged, and accommodation for those needing residential care services. Legislation of 1996 permits local authorities to make cash payments as an alternative to community care. In Scotland the Social Work Departments' functions also include the supervision of persons on probation, of adult offenders and of persons released from penal institutions or subject to fine supervision orders.

Personal Social Services staff numbered 213,300 at 30 Sept. 2004. The total revenue resources for PSS was £13,814.97m. for 2004–05. Expenditure is reviewed by the Social Services Inspectorate and the Audit Commission (in Scotland by the Social Work Services Inspectorate and the Accounts Commission).

Welfare

The National Insurance Act 1965 now operates under the Social Security Contributions and Benefits Act 1992 and the Social Security Administration Act 1992.

Since 1975 Class 1 contributions have been related to the employee's earnings and are collected with PAYE income tax. Class 2 and Class 3 contributions remain flat-rate, but, in addition to Class 2 contributions, those who are self-employed may be liable to pay Class 4 contributions, which for the year 2006–07 are at the rate of 8% on profits or gains between £5,035 and £33,540 (with a further 1% contribution on any profit exceeding the upper limit), which are assessable for income tax under Schedule D. The non-employed and others whose contribution record is not sufficient to give entitlement to benefits are able to pay a Class 3 contribution of £7.55 per week in 2006–07 voluntarily, to qualify for a limited range of benefits. Class 2 weekly contributions for 2006–07 for men and women are £2.10. Class 1A contributions are paid by employers who provide employees with a car and fuel for their private use.

The Social Security Pensions Act 1975 introduced earnings-related retirement, invalidity and widows' pensions. Members of occupational pension schemes may be contracted out of the earnings-related part of the state scheme relating to retirement and widows' benefits. Employee's national insurance contribution liability depends on whether he/she is in contracted-out or not contracted-out employment.

Full-rate contributions for non-contracted-out employment in 2006–07:

Weekly Earnings (in £1)	Employee pays	Employer pays
Below 84 (Lower Earnings Limit)	Nil	Nil
84–97 (Primary Threshold/Secondary Threshold)	Nil	Nil
97–645 (Upper Earnings Limit)	11%	12.8%
Over 645 (Upper Earnings Limit)	See footnote[1]	12.8%
[1]£60.28 plus 1% on earnings over £645 per week.		

For contracted-out employment, the contracted-out rebate for primary contributions (employee's contribution) is 1.6% of earnings between the lower earnings limit and the upper earnings limit for all forms of contracting-out; the contracted-out rebate for secondary contributions (employer's contributions) is 3.5% of earnings between the lower earnings limit and the upper earnings limit.

Contributions together with interest on investments form the income of the *National Insurance Fund* from which benefits are paid. 28,660,000 persons (12,800,000 women) paid contributions in 2002–03, including 25,810,000 employees at standard rate.

Receipts, 2002–03 (in £1m.), 86,716, including: contributions, 59,658; investment income, 1,457; compensation from Consolidated Fund for recoveries, 775. Disbursements (in £1m.), 59,449, including: Retirement Pensions, 45,240; Incapacity Benefit, 7,104; Personal Pensions, 3,366; administration, 1,280; Widow's Pensions, 1,142; Jobseekers' Allowance (Contributory), 519; transfers to Northern Ireland, 350; Redundancy Payments, 255; Pensioners' Lump Sums, 124; Maternity Allowances, 70.

Statutory Sick Pay (SSP). Employers are responsible for paying statutory sick pay (SSP) to their employees who are absent from work through illness or injury for up to 28 weeks in any three-year period. All employees aged between 16 and 65 (60 for women) with earnings above the Lower Earnings Limit are covered by the scheme whenever they are sick for four or more days consecutively. The weekly rate is £70.05. For most employees SSP completely replaces their entitlement to state incapacity benefit which is not payable as long as any employer's responsibility for SSP remains.

Contributory benefits. Qualification for these depends upon fulfilment of the appropriate contribution conditions, except that persons who are incapable of work as the result of an industrial accident may receive incapacity benefit followed by invalidity benefit without having to satisfy the contributions conditions.

Jobseekers' Allowance. Unemployed persons claiming the allowance must sign a 'Jobseekers' Agreement' setting out a plan of action to find work. The allowance is not payable to persons who left their job voluntarily or through misconduct. Claimants with sufficient National Insurance contributions are entitled to the allowance for six months regardless of their means; otherwise, recipients qualify through a means test and the allowance is fixed according to family circumstances, at a rate corresponding to Income Support for an indefinite period. In May 2004 there were 755,200 people receiving the Jobseekers' Allowance (569,200 males). Payments start at £34.60 per week.

Incapacity benefit. Entitlement begins when entitlement to SSP (if any) ends. There are three rates: a lower rate for the first 28 weeks; a higher rate between the 29th and 52nd week; and a long-term rate from the 53rd week of incapacity. It also comprises certain age additions and increases for adult and child dependants. A more objective medical test of incapacity for work was introduced for incapacity benefit as well as for other social security benefits paid on the basis of incapacity for work. This test applies after 28 weeks' incapacity for work and assesses ability to perform a range of work-related activities rather than the ability to perform a specific job. Benefit is taxable after 28 weeks. Some 1,486,600 claims were being made in Feb. 2004.

Statutory Maternity Pay. Pregnant working women may be eligible to receive statutory maternity pay directly from their employer for a maximum of 26 weeks if average gross earnings are £84 a week or more (2006–07). There are two rates: a higher rate (90% of average earnings for the first six weeks), and a lower rate of £108.85 or 90% of earnings (whichever is less) for up to 20 weeks. For women who do not qualify for Statutory Maternity Pay, including self-employed women, there is a Maternity Allowance.

A payment of £500 from the Social Fund (Sure Start Maternity Grant) may be available if the mother or her partner are receiving income support, income-based Jobseeker's Allowance, Working

Families' Tax Credit or Disabled Person's Tax Credit. It is also available if a woman adopts a baby.

Statutory Paternity Pay. From 6 April 2003 working fathers have the right to two weeks paid paternity leave providing average gross earnings are £84 a week or more (2006–07). This will be paid at the same rate as the lower rate of Statutory Maternity Pay (£108·85 a week or 90% of average weekly earnings if this is less than £108·85).

Bereavement Benefits. Available to both men and women, Bereavement Benefits were introduced from 9 April 2001 to replace the former Widows' Benefit scheme. There are three main types of Bereavement Benefits available to men and women widowed on or after 9 April 2001: bereavement payment, widowed parent's allowance and bereavement allowance. *Bereavement Payment* is a single tax-free lump sum of £2,000 payable immediately on bereavement. A widower/widow may be able to get this benefit if their late spouse has paid enough National Insurance Contributions (NIC) and was under 60 at death; or was not getting a Category A State Retirement Pension at death. *Widowed Parent's Allowance* is a weekly benefit payable when the widower/widow is receiving Child Benefit. The amount of Widowed Parent's Allowance is based on the late spouse's NIC record. He/she may also get benefit for the eldest dependent child and further higher benefit for each subsequent child; also an additional pension based on their late spouse's earnings. If the late spouse was a member of a contracted-out occupational scheme or a personal pension scheme, that scheme is responsible for paying the whole or part of the additional pensions. Widowed Parent's Allowance is taxable. *Bereavement Allowance* is a weekly benefit payable to widows and widowers without dependent children and is payable between age 45 and State Pension age. The amount of Bereavement Allowance payable to a widower/widower between 45 and 54 is related to their age at the date of entitlement. Their weekly rate is reduced by 7% for each year they are aged under 55 so that they get 93% rate at age 54, falling to 30% at age 45. Those aged 55 or over at the date of entitlement will get the full rate of Bereavement Allowance. The amount of Bereavement Allowance is based on the late spouse's NIC record and is payable for a maximum of 52 weeks from the date of bereavement. A widower/widow cannot get a Bereavement Allowance at the same time as a Widowed Parent's Allowance. Women widowed before 9 April 2001 continue to receive their Widows' Benefit entitlement on the arrangements that existed before that date so long as they continue to satisfy the qualifying conditions. There were some 167,500 recipients of Widows' Benefits and 46,400 recipients of Bereavement Benefits in March 2004.

Retirement Pension. The state retirement ('old-age') pension scheme has two components: a basic pension and an earnings-related pension (State Earnings Related Pension—SERPS). The amount of the first is subject to National Insurance contributions made; SERPS is 1·25% of average earnings between the lower weekly earnings limit for Class I contribution liability and the upper earnings limit for each year of such earnings, building up to 25% in 20 years. For individuals reaching pensionable age after 6 April 1999, changes in the way pensions are calculated will be phased in over ten years to include a lifetime's earnings with an accrual rate of 20%. Pensions are payable to women at 60 years of age and men at 65, but the age differential will be progressively phased out starting in April 2010. There are standard rates for single persons and for married couples, the latter being 159% of two single-person rates. Proportionately reduced pensions are payable where contribution records are deficient. Proposals were announced in Nov. 2005 for the state-pension age to be increased to 66 by 2030, 67 by 2040 and 68 by 2050.

Employees in an occupational scheme may contract out of SERPS provided that the occupational scheme provides a pension not less than the 'guaranteed minimum pension'. Self-employed persons, and also employees, may substitute personal pension schemes for SERPS.

Self- and non-employed persons may contribute voluntarily for retirement pension.

Persons who defer claiming their pension during the five years following retirement age are paid an increased amount, as do men and women who had paid graduated contributions. In March 2004 some 11,368,800 persons were receiving National Insurance retirement pensions (7,107,800 women and 4,261,000 men). The full basic state pension in 2006–07 is £84·25 per week for a single person and £134·75 per week for a married couple. Since 1 Oct. 1989 the pension for which a person has qualified may be paid in full whether a person continues in work or not irrespective of the amount of earnings. Although for males the official retirement age is 65, in 2004 the average actual retirement age among males was 63·8 years.

At the age of 80 a small age addition is payable. In addition non-contributory pensions are now payable, subject to residence conditions, to persons aged 80 and over who do not qualify for a retirement pension or qualify for one at a low rate.

Pensioners whose pension is insufficient to live on may qualify for Income Support.

Non-Contributory Benefits

Child Benefit. Child benefit is a tax-free cash allowance normally paid to the mother. The weekly rates are highest for the eldest qualifying child (£17·45 weekly in 2006–07) and less for each other child (£11·70 weekly in 2006–07). Child benefit is payable for children under 16, for 16- and 17-year-olds registered for work or training, and for those under 19 receiving full-time non-advanced education. Some 7,353,000 families received benefit in Aug. 2004.

Child Support Agency. The Child Support Agency is responsible for calculating, collecting and enforcing child maintenance payments. The non-resident parent pays 15% of their net income if they have one child, 20% for two and 30% for three or more children. The agency currently deals with around 1·5m. child support cases. In Feb. 2006 an Operational Improvement Plan was announced that is aimed at providing more money for a larger number of cases, a more efficient and effective system and a reduction in child poverty.

Working Tax Credit. This tackles poor work incentives and persistent poverty among working people. For families with children, credit is available for those with incomes up to a maximum of around £14,000. It also extends support to low-income working people without children aged 25 or over working 30 hours or more a week. The Working Tax Credit is not just restricted to those with children; the amount of the award varies considerably depending on the prevailing circumstances. Both single persons and couples may be eligible.

Child Tax Credit. The Child Tax Credit aims at creating a single system of support for families with children, payable irrespective of the work status of the adults in the household. This means that the Child Tax Credit forms a stable and secure income bridge as families move off welfare and into work. It also provides a common framework of assessment, so that all families are part of the same inclusive system. The Child Tax Credit provides a family element of up to £545 per year and a child element of up to £1,765 per child per year in addition to Child Benefit. The amount paid varies depending on the number of children and the gross annual joint income.

Guardian's Allowance. A person responsible for an orphan child may be entitled to a guardian's allowance in addition to child benefit. Normally, both the child's parents must be dead but when they never married or were divorced, or one is missing, or serving a long sentence of imprisonment, the allowance may be paid on the death of one parent only. Some 2,900 families received benefit in Aug. 2004.

Attendance Allowance. This is a tax-free Social Security benefit for disabled people over 65 who need help with personal care. The rates are increased for the terminally ill. There were some 1,391,900 recipients in May 2004.

Carers' Allowance. This is a taxable benefit which may be paid to those who forgo the opportunity of full-time work to care for a person who is receiving attendance allowance, constant attendance allowance or the highest or middle-core component of Disability Living Allowance. There is a weekly rate, with increases for dependants. In March 2002 there were 387,000 recipients.

Disability Living Allowance. This is a non-taxable benefit available to people disabled before the age of 65, who need help with getting around or with personal care for at least three months. The mobility component has two weekly rates, the care component has three. There were some 2,606,700 recipients in May 2004.

Industrial Injuries Disablement and Death Benefits. The scheme provides a system of insurance against 'personal injury by accident arising out of and in the course of employment' and against certain prescribed diseases and injuries owing to the nature of the employment. There are no contribution conditions for the payment of benefit. There were 266,500 recipients in March 2004. Two types of benefit are provided:

—*Disablement benefit.* This is payable where, as the result of an industrial accident or prescribed disease, there is a loss of physical or mental faculty. The loss of faculty will be assessed as a percentage by comparison with a person of the same age and sex whose condition is normal. If the assessment is between 14–100% benefit will be paid as weekly pension. The rates vary from 20% disabled to 100% disablement. Assessments of less than 14% do not normally attract basic benefit except for certain progressive chest diseases. Pensions for persons under 18 are at a reduced rate. When injury benefit was abolished for industrial accidents occurring and prescribed diseases commencing on or after 6 April 1983, a common start date was introduced for the payment of disablement benefit 90 days (excluding Sundays) after the date of the relevant accident or onset of the disease.

—*Death Benefit.* This is payable to the widow of a person who died before 11 April 1988 as the result of an industrial accident or a prescribed disease. For deaths which occurred on or after 11 April 1988, a widow is entitled to full widow's benefits. Allowances may be paid to people who are suffering from pneumoconiosis or byssinosis or certain other slowly developing diseases due to employment before 5 July 1948. They must not at any time have been entitled to benefit under the Industrial Injuries provision of the Social Security Act, or compensation under Workmen's Compensation Acts, or have received damages through the courts.

War Pensions. Pensions are payable for disablement or death as a result of service in the armed forces. Similar schemes exist for other groups such as merchant seamen injured as a result of war or for civilians injured by enemy action in the Second World War. The amount depends on the degree of disablement. There were some 247,500 recipients in March 2004.

Housing Benefit. The housing benefit scheme assists persons who need help to pay their rent, using general assessment rules and benefit levels similar to those for the income support scheme. The scheme sets a limit of £16,000 on the amount of capital a person may have and still remain entitled. Restrictions on the granting of benefit to persons under 25 were introduced in 1995. In 2004 some 1,808,000 claims for rent rebate and 2,071,400 for rent allowance were being made at any one time.

Income Support. Income Support is a non-contributory benefit for people aged 16 or over, not working 16 hours or more a week or with a partner not working more than 24 hours or more per week, and not required to be available for employment. These include single parents, long-term sick or disabled persons, and those caring for them who qualify for Invalid Care Allowance. Income Support is not payable if the claimant (or claimant and partner together) has capital assets that total more than £16,000. These include savings, investments or property other than their home. Savings/capital assets worth under £6,000 are ignored. Savings between £6,000 and £16,000 are treated as if each £250 or part of £250 brings in an income of £1 per week. Income Support claimants whose partners are of pensionable age may have up to £12,000 and still be entitled to Income Support. Claimants in residential care and nursing homes are allowed to have up to £16,000 and still be entitled to Income Support. From 6 Oct. 2003 a new Pension Credit replaced Minimum Income Guarantee (Income Support for people aged 60 and over). In 2004 there were 2,171,500 Income Support claimants at any one time and 2,492,600 Pension Credit claimants. The average weekly award was £91·82 in May 2004.

Council Tax Benefit. Subject to rules broadly similar to those governing the provision of income support and housing benefit, people may receive rebates of up to 100% of their council tax. In 2004 some 4,800,200 households received such help. A person who is liable for the council tax may also claim benefit (called 'second adult rebate') for a second adult who is not liable to pay the council tax and who is living in the home on a non-commercial basis.

The Social Fund. This comprises: *Sure Start Maternity Grant* (a payment of up to £500 for each baby expected, born or adopted, payable to persons receiving Income Support, Income-based Jobseekers' Allowance, Child Tax Credit, Working Tax Credit or Pension Credit); *Funeral Payments* (a payment of fees levied by the burial authorities and crematoria, plus up to £700 for other funeral expenses, to persons receiving Income Support, Income-based Jobseekers' Allowance, Housing Benefit, Child Tax Credit, Working Tax Credit or Pension Credit); *Cold Weather Payments* (a payment of £8·50 for any consecutive seven days when the temperature is below freezing to persons receiving income support who are pensioners, disabled or have a child under five); *Winter Fuel Payments* (a payment of £200 to every household with a person aged 60 or over providing they do not live permanently in a hospital, residential care or nursing home, or £300 if the household has someone aged 80 years old or over). The Discretionary Social Fund comprises: *Community Care Grants* (payments to help persons receiving income support to move into the community or avoid institutional care); *Budgeting Loans* (interest-free loans to persons receiving income support for expenses difficult to budget for); *Crisis Loans* (interest-free loans to anyone without resources in an emergency where there is no other means of preventing serious risk to health or safety). Savings over £500 (£1,000 for persons aged 60 or over) are taken into account before payments are made.

Hill, M., *The Welfare State in Britain: a Political History since 1945.* Aldershot, 1993
Timmins, N., *The Five Giants: a Biography of the Welfare State.* London, 1995

RELIGION

The Anglican Communion has originated from the Church of England and parallels in its fellowship of autonomous churches the evolution of British influence beyond the seas from colonies to dominions and independent nations. The Archbishop of Canterbury presides as *primus inter pares* at the decennial meetings of the bishops of the Anglican Communion at the Lambeth Conference and at the biennial meetings of the Primates and the Anglican Consultative Council. The last Conference was held in Canterbury in 1998 and was attended by 743 bishops. Average attendance at Sunday worship in 2001 numbered 1·6m., compared to 3·5m. in 1950.

The Anglican Communion consists of 38 self-governing Churches. These are: The Anglican Church of Aotearoa, New Zealand and Polynesia; The Anglican Church of Australia; The Church of Bangladesh; The Episcopal Anglican Church of Brazil; The Church of the Province of Burundi; The Anglican Church of Canada; The Church of the Province of Central Africa; The Anglican Church of the Central America Region; The Province of the Anglican Church of the Congo; The Church of England; Hong Kong Sheng Kung Hui; The Church of the Province of the Indian Ocean; The Church of Ireland; Nippon Sei Ko Kai; The Episcopal Church in Jerusalem and the Middle East; The Church of the Province of Kenya; The Anglican Church of Korea; The Church of the Province of Melanesia; The Anglican Church of Mexico; The Church of the Province of Myanmar (Burma); The Church of the Province of Nigeria; The Church of North India; The Church of Pakistan; The Anglican Church of Papua New Guinea; The Philippine Episcopal Church; The Province of the Episcopal Church of Rwanda; The Scottish Episcopal Church; The Church of the Province of South East Asia; The Church of the Province of Southern Africa; The Anglican Church of the Southern Cone of America; The Church of South India; The Episcopal Church of the Sudan; The Church of the Province of Tanzania; The Church of the Province of Uganda; The Episcopal Church in the United States of America; The Church in Wales; The Church of the Province of West Africa; and The Church in the Province of the West Indies. There are Extra Provincial Dioceses of Bermuda, Cuba, Portugal, Puerto Rico, Spain, Sri Lanka and Venezuela, and new provinces are also currently in formation. Churches in Communion include the Mar Thoma Syrian Church, the Philippine Independent Church, and some Lutheran and Old Catholic Churches in Europe. The Church in China is known as a 'post denominational' Church whose formation included Anglicans in the Holy Catholic Church in China.

England and Wales. The established Church of England, which baptizes about 20% of the children born in England (i.e. excluding Wales but including the Isle of Man and the Channel Islands), is Anglican. Civil disabilities on account of religion do not attach to any class of British subject. Under the Welsh Church Acts, 1914 and 1919, the Church in Wales and Monmouthshire was disestablished as from 1 April 1920, and Wales was formed into a separate Province.

The Queen is, under God, the supreme governor of the Church of England, with the right, regulated by statute, to nominate to the vacant archbishoprics and bishoprics. The Queen, on the advice of the First Lord of the Treasury, also appoints to such deaneries, prebendaries and canonries as are in the gift of the Crown, while a large number of livings and also some canonries are in the gift of the Lord Chancellor.

There are two archbishops (at the head of the two Provinces of Canterbury and York), and 42 diocesan bishops including the bishop of the diocese in Europe, which is part of the Province of Canterbury. Dr Rowan Williams was enthroned as *Archbishop of Canterbury* in Feb. 2003. Each archbishop has also his own particular diocese, wherein he exercises episcopal, as in his Province he exercises metropolitan, jurisdiction. In Dec. 2002 there were 62 suffragan and assistant bishops, 41 deans and provosts of cathedrals and 114 archdeacons. The *General Synod*, which replaced the Church Assembly in 1970 in England, consists of a House of Bishops, a House of Clergy and a House of Laity, and has power to frame legislation regarding Church matters. The first two Houses consist of the members of the Convocations of Canterbury and York, each of which consists of the diocesan bishops and elected representatives of the suffragan bishops, six

for Canterbury province and three for York (forming an Upper House); deans and archdeacons, and a certain number of proctors elected as the representatives of the priests and deacons in each diocese, together with, in the case of Canterbury Convocation, four representatives of the Universities of Oxford, Cambridge, London and the Southern Universities, and in the case of York two representatives of the Universities of Durham and Newcastle and the other Northern Universities, and three archdeacons to the Armed Forces, the Chaplain General of Prisons and two representatives of the Religious Communities (forming the Lower House). The House of Laity is elected by the lay members of the Deanery Synods but also includes three representatives of the Religious Communities. The Houses of Clergy and Laity also include a small number of *ex officio* members. Every Measure passed by the General Synod must be submitted to the Ecclesiastical Committee, consisting of 15 members of the House of Lords nominated by the Lord Chancellor and 15 members of the House of Commons nominated by the Speaker. This committee reports on each Measure to Parliament, and the Measure receives the Royal Assent and becomes law if each House of Parliament resolves that the Measure be presented to the Queen.

Parochial affairs are managed by annual parochial church meetings and parochial church councils. In 2002 there were 12,900 ecclesiastical parishes, inclusive of the Isle of Man and the Channel Islands. These parishes do not, in many cases, coincide with civil parishes. Although most parishes have their own churches, not every parish nowadays can have its own incumbent or priest. About 2,000 non-stipendiary clergy hold a bishop's licence to officiate at services.

In 2002 there were 5,060 incumbents excluding dignitaries, 1,935 other clergy of incumbent status and 1,502 assistant curates working in the parishes.

Women have been admitted to Holy Orders (but not the Episcopate) as deacons since 1987 and as priests since 1994. At 31 Dec. 2002 there were 1,247 full-time stipendiary women clergy, 1,197 of whom were in the parochial ministry. Between 1993 and 2002, 495 clergymen resigned because they disagreed with the ordination of women. 67 clergymen subsequently re-entered the Church of England ministry and of the 495 who resigned, 258 are known to have joined the Roman Catholic Church and 29 the Orthodox Church.

Private persons possess the right of presentation to over 2,000 benefices; the patronage of the others belongs mainly to the Queen, the bishops and cathedrals, the Lord Chancellor, and the colleges of the universities of Oxford and Cambridge. In addition to the dignitaries and parochial clergy already identified there were, in 2002, 112 cathedral and 309 full-time non-parochial clergy working within the diocesan framework, giving a total of 9,182 full-time stipendiary clergy working within the diocesan framework as at Dec. 2002. In addition there were 249 part-time stipendiary clergy. Although these figures account for the majority of active clergy in England, there are many others serving in parishes and institutions who cannot be quantified with any certainty. They include 1,159 full-time hospital, Forces, prison, industrial, and school and college chaplains.

Of the 40,609 buildings registered for the solemnization of marriages at 30 June 2000 (statistics from the Office of National Statistics), 16,481 belonged to the Church of England and the Church in Wales, and 24,128 to other religious denominations (Methodist, 6,641; Roman Catholic, 3,342; Baptist, 3,109; United Reformed, 1,675; Congregational, 1,257; Calvinistic Methodist, 1,084; Jehovah's Witnesses, 817; Salvation Army, 751; Brethren, 742; Unitarians, 165; other Christian, 4,095; Sikhs, 147; Muslims, 127; other non-Christian, 176). Of the 249,227 marriages celebrated in 2001 (331,150 in 1990), 60,878 were in the Established Church and the Church in Wales (115,328 in 1990), 28,111 in other denominations (43,837 in 1990) and 160,238 were civil marriages in Register Offices (156,875 in 1990).

Roman Catholics in England and Wales were estimated at 4,105,635 in 2004. There are 22 dioceses in five provinces and one Bishopric of the Forces (also covers Scotland). Cormac Murphy O'Connor was installed as *Archbishop of Westminster* in March 2000. He was created a cardinal in Feb. 2001. In May 2005 there were two Roman Catholic cardinals, one of whom is in Scotland. There are five archbishops, 17 other diocesan bishops and seven auxiliary or assistant bishops. There are 5,128 priests in active ministry and 2,799 parish churches. There are 1,250 convents of female religious, who number 8,450.

Membership of other denominations in the UK in 1991 (and 1975): Presbyterians, 1,291,672 (1·65m.); Methodists, 483,387 (0·61m.); Baptists, 241,842 (0·27m.); other Protestants, 123,677; independent churches, 408,999; Orthodox, 265,258 (0·2m.); Afro-Caribbean churches, 69,658; Latter-day Saints (Mormons) (1998), 173,800; Jehovah's Witnesses, 0·12m.; Spiritualists, 60,000; Muslims, 0·99m. (0·4m.); Sikhs, 0·39m. (0·12m.); Hindus, 0·14m. (0·1m.); Jews, 108,400 (0·11m.).

In 2001 for the first time the census asked an optional question about religion. In England and Wales 37·3m. people described themselves as Christian. In England, 3·1% of the population stated their religion as Muslim, 1·1% Hindu, 0·7% Sikh, 0·5% Jewish and 0·3% Buddhist. In Wales, 0·7% of the population stated their religion as Muslim, 0·2% Buddhist, 0·2% Hindu, 0·1% Jewish and 0·1% Sikh. In England and Wales 7·7m. people said they had no religion (14·6% in England and 18·5% in Wales). Just over 4m. people chose not to answer the religion question.

In Scotland the 2001 census asked two questions on religion—religion of upbringing and current religion. For religion of upbringing, the largest groups were Church of Scotland (47%), no religion (18%) and Roman Catholic (17%). The equivalent percentages for current religion were 42%, 28% and 16%.

Across all denominations, adult church attendance in the UK was less than 8% of the population in 2000.

The Salvation Army is an international Christian church working in 109 countries. In 2004 in the UK it had 821 local church centres and 92 social service centres with 4,545 employees and 1,507 active Salvation Army officers (ministers).

There is a 400-member Board of Deputies of British Jews.

In 2002 there were approximately 1·57m. visits to York Minster, 1·11m. to Canterbury Cathedral, 1·06m. to Westminster Abbey, London and 781,000 to St Paul's Cathedral, London.

See also SCOTLAND *and* NORTHERN IRELAND.

Bradley, I., *Marching to the Promised Land: Has the Church a Future?* London, 1992.
De La Noy, M., *The Church of England: a Portrait.* London, 1993.

CULTURE

World Heritage Sites

Sites under UK jurisdiction which appear on UNESCO's world heritage list are (with year entered on list): Giant's Causeway and Causeway Coast (1986), rock formations on the Antrim Plateau in Northern Ireland; Durham Castle and Cathedral (1986), the largest example of a Norman cathedral; Ironbridge Gorge (1986), built in the 18th century and considered the emblem of the industrial revolution; Studley Royal Park, including the Ruins of Fountains Abbey (1986), developed from the 18th century on the site of a former Cistercian abbey in Yorkshire; Stonehenge, Avebury and Associated Sites (1986), among the world's most famous pre-historic monoliths; Castles and Town Walls of King Edward in Gwynedd (1986), a testament to the early period of English colonization in the late 13th century; St Kilda (1986), a volcanic archipelago on the coast of the Hebrides; Blenheim Palace (1987), seat of the Dukes of Marlborough near Oxford and birthplace of Sir Winston Churchill; City of Bath (1987), with remains from its time as a Roman spa town, and home to many examples of neo-classical Georgian architecture; Frontiers of the Roman Empire sites (1987 and 2005) is shared with Germany and contain the border line of the Roman Empire at its greatest extent in the 2nd century AD, specifically Hadrian's Wall; Westminster Palace, Westminster Abbey and Saint Margaret's Church (1987)—the palace is the medieval seat of parliament re-built in the 19th century, the abbey the site of all coronations since the 11th century and Saint Margaret's is a small medieval gothic church; Henderson Island (1988), a South Pacific atoll; Tower of London (1988), a Norman fortress built to guard London; Canterbury Cathedral, St Augustine's Abbey and St Martin's Church (1988), the spiritual seat of the Church of England; Old and New Towns of Edinburgh (1995), the Scottish capital; Gough Island Wildlife Reserve (1995), one of the least disturbed island and marine eco-systems in the region; Maritime Greenwich (1997), including Britain's first Palladian building, designed by Inigo Jones, Christopher Wren's Royal Naval College and the Royal Observatory; Heart of Neolithic Orkney (1999), comprising several important neolithic monuments; Historic Town of St George's and Related Fortifications, Bermuda (2000), an example of early English New World colonialism; Blaenavon Industrial Landscape (2000), a symbol of South Wales' role as a coal and iron provider in the 19th century; Dorset and East Devon Coast (2001), which demonstrate rock formations and fossil remains from the Mesozoic Era; Derwent Valley Mills (2001), 18th-century cotton mills at the forefront of the Industrial Revolution; New Lanark (2001), Robert Owen's model industrial community and cotton mills of the early 19th century; Saltaire (2001), a mid-19th century planned industrial community for the textile industry; Royal Botanical Gardens, Kew (2003), containing important botanical collections in a historic landscape; Liverpool—Maritime Mercantile City (2004).

Broadcasting

Radio and television services are provided by the British Broadcasting Corporation (BBC), by licensees of the Office of Communications ('Ofcom') and by the Welsh-language Sianel Pedwar Cymru (S4C, Channel 4 Wales). The BBC, constituted by Royal Charter, has responsibility for providing domestic and external broadcast services, the former financed from the television licence revenue, the latter by government grant. The domestic services provided by the BBC include eight national television services, ten national radio network services and a network of local radio stations. Government proposals for the future of the BBC after 2006 were published in March 2005.

Ofcom is responsible for licensing and regulating all non-BBC TV services (except S4C), provided in and from the UK whether analogue or digital. These include ITV1 (regional and breakfast-time licensees), Channel 4, Channel 5, cable and satellite and additional services, such as teletext. Ofcom is also responsible for licensing and regulating independent and national, local and community radio services. S4C is transmitted in Wales, and is funded by the government. The Welsh Authority is the regulator and board of management of S4C.

The BBC's domestic radio services are available on Long Wave, Medium Wave and VHF/FM; those licensed by Ofcom on Medium Wave and VHF/FM. Television services other than those only on cable and satellite are broadcast at UHF in 625-line definition and in colour (by PAL). The BBC World Service, which started life in 1932 as the Empire Service, broadcast in 43 languages to an audience estimated at 150m. in 2002–03. As the self-financed BBC Worldwide TV, the BBC is also involved in commercial joint ventures to provide international television services.

The broadcasting authorities are independent of government and are publicly accountable to Parliament for the discharge of their responsibilities. Their duties and powers are laid down in the BBC Royal Charter and the Communications Act 2003.

All independent (non-BBC) radio and television services other than S4C are financed by the sale of broadcasting advertising time, commercial sponsorship, subscription (in the case of cable and satellite services) and ancillary services, such as sales of goods and products, interactive services and pay-per-view revenues.

Ofcom became the new communications sector regulator at the end of 2003, taking over from the Broadcasting Standards Commission (BSC), the Independent Television Commission (ITC), Oftel, the Radio Authority and the Radiocommunications Agency. The aims of Ofcom are: to balance the promotion of choice and competition with the duty to foster plurality, informed citizenship, protect viewers, listeners and customers and promote cultural diversity; serve the interests of the citizen-consumer as the communications industry enters the digital age; support the need for innovators, creators and investors to flourish within markets driven by full and fair competition between all providers; and to encourage the evolution of electronic media and communications networks to the greater benefit of all who live in the UK.

The number of television receiving licences in force on 31 March 2004 was 23,899,000, of which 23,824,000 were for colour. There were 10·5m. satellite and cable TV subscribers in late 2004 (7·1m. with BSkyB, 2·1m. with NTL and 1·3m. with Telewest). In 2000 there were 84·5m. radio receivers, or 1,432 per 1,000 inhabitants—a figure only exceeded in the USA, with 2,118 per 1,000 inhabitants.

Cinema

In 2003 there were 776 cinemas in the UK with 3,433 screens. Admissions were 171·3m. in 2004. Admissions had totalled 500m. in 1960, but had fallen as low as 54m. in 1984. Gross box office takings in 2004 amounted to £770m. In 2004, 451 films were released in the UK, of which 93 were UK films (including USA/UK films and UK co-productions).

Press

In 2006 there were ten national dailies with a combined average daily circulation in Jan. 2006 of 11,508,670, and ten national Sunday newspapers (12,608,127). There were also about 100 morning, evening and Sunday regional newspapers and 2,000 weeklies (about 1,000 of these for free distribution). There were about 6,500 other commercial periodicals and 4,000 professional and business journals. In 2000 the number of daily newspapers sold per annum was 4bn., down 20% from 5bn. in 1962. The most widely read daily is the tabloid *The Sun*, with an average daily circulation of 3,319,237 in Jan. 2006. The most widely read Sunday paper is the tabloid *News of the World*, which had an average circulation of 3,789,076 in Jan. 2006.

In Jan. 1991 the Press Complaints Commission replaced the former Press Council. It has 15 members and a chair (Sir Christopher Meyer), including seven editors. It is funded by the newspaper industry.

In 2002 a record 125,390 book titles were published (119,001 in 2001), including 11,810 fiction and 10,519 children's books.

Tourism

In 2004 UK residents made 126·6m. trips within the UK, passing 408·9m. nights in accommodation and spending £24,357m. Of these, 57·2m. were holiday-makers spending £12,813m. Visits from foreign tourists to the UK totalled 27·8m. in 2004, a 12% increase compared with 2003. Spending increased by 10% in 2004 to £13bn. In 2004 the UK ranked sixth in the international tourism earnings league behind the USA, Spain, France, Italy and Germany. The main countries of origin for foreign visitors in 2004 were: USA (3·6m.), France (3·3m.), Germany (2·9m.), Ireland (2·6m.) and the Netherlands (1·6m.).

The leading free admission attraction in 2004 was Blackpool Pleasure Beach, Lancs, with an estimated 6·2m. visits. The leading tourist attractions charging admission in 2004 were: the British Airways London Eye, with 3·7m. visits; the Tower of London, with 2·1m.; Flamingo Land Theme Park in Malton, North Yorkshire, with 2·1m.; Pleasureland Theme Park in Southport, with 2·1m.; and Pleasure Beach in Great Yarmouth, with 1·5m.

In Sept. 2004 there were 1·4m. (not seasonally adjusted) people working in tourism-related industries.

UK residents made 61·4m. trips abroad in 2003. Spain is the most popular destination for Britons travelling abroad for leisure (29·8% of holidays taken abroad by UK residents in 2003), followed by France (18·1%), Greece (6·6%) and the USA (5·5%). There were 58·3m. trips abroad made by British residents in 2001, up from 13·4m. in 1978.

Festivals

Among the most famous music festivals are the Promenade Concerts or 'Proms', which take place at the Royal Albert Hall in London every year from July to Sept; the Glyndebourne season in Sussex (May to Aug.); the Aldeburgh Festival in Suffolk (June); the Glastonbury Festival in Somerset (June); and the Buxton Festival in Derbyshire (July). The annual London Film Festival takes place in Nov. Literary festivals include the Hay Festival in Herefordshire (late May/early June) and Cheltenham Festival of Literature in Gloucestershire (Oct.). The Edinburgh Festival and the Fringe Festival both take place in Aug./early Sept. and are major international festivals of culture. The Brighton Festival in May is England's largest arts festival. The multicultural Notting Hill Carnival in London takes place at the end of Aug. Other major events in the annual calendar are the New Year's Day Parade in London, the Crufts Dog Show at the Birmingham National Exhibition Centre (March), the Ideal Home Exhibition in London (March–April), the London Marathon (April), the Chelsea Flower Show (May), Royal Ascot (horse racing, in June), Wimbledon (tennis, in June–July), Henley Royal Regatta (July), Cowes (yachting, in Aug.) and the Lord Mayor's Show in London (Nov.).

Libraries

In 2001–02 there were 4,614 public libraries, six National libraries and 875 Higher Education libraries; they held a combined 284,900,000 volumes. There were 36,111,642 registered library users in 2001–02.

Museums and Galleries

The museums with the highest number of visitors are all in London. In 2004 there were 4,959,946 visits to the National Gallery, 4,868,127 to the British Museum, 4,441,225 to the Tate Modern, 3,240,344 to the Natural History Museum and 2,010,825 to the Victoria and Albert Museum.

DIPLOMATIC REPRESENTATIVES

Of the USA in Great Britain (24/31 Grosvenor Sq., London, W1A 1AE)
Ambassador: Robert H. Tuttle.

Of Great Britain in the USA (3100 Massachusetts Ave., NW, Washington, D.C., 20008)
Ambassador: Sir David Manning, KCMG.

Of Great Britain to the United Nations
Ambassador: Sir Emyr Jones Parry, KCMG.

Great Britain's permanent representative to the European Union
Ambassador: John Grant, CMG.

FURTHER READING

Office for National Statistics titles are published by Palgrave Macmillan. The Stationery Office (TSO) publishes most other government publications.
Palgrave Macmillan, Basingstoke. *UK 20xx*. Palgrave Macmillan.—*Annual Abstract of Statistics*. Palgrave Macmillan.—*Monthly Digest of Statistics*. Palgrave Macmillan.—*Social Trends*. Palgrave Macmillan.—*Regional Trends*. Palgrave Macmillan
Central Office of Information. *The Monarchy*. 1992
Directory of British Associations. Beckenham, annual

Beloff, M., *Britain and the European Union: Dialogue of the Deaf*. London, 1997

Black, Jeremy, *A History of the British Isles*. 2nd ed. Palgrave Macmillan, Basingstoke, 2002

Bogdanor, Vernon, *Devolution in the United Kingdom*. OUP, 1999

Bourke, Richard, *Peace in Ireland: The War of Ideas*. Random House, London, 2003

Cairncross, A., *The British Economy Since 1945: Economic Policy and Performance, 1945–1995*. 2nd ed. London, 1995

Creaton, Heather, *London*. [Bibliography] ABC-Clio, Oxford and Santa Barbara (CA), 1996

Davies, Norman, *The Isles: A History*. Macmillan, London, 1999

Dunleavy, Patrick, Gamble, Andrew, Heffernan, Richard and Peele, Gillian (eds.) *Developments in British Politics 7*. Palgrave Macmillan, Basingstoke, 2003

Gascoigne, B. (ed.) *Encyclopedia of Britain*. London, 1994

Harbury, C. D. and Lipsey, R. G., *Introduction to the UK Economy*. 4th ed. Oxford, 1993

Irwin, J. L., *Modern Britain: an Introduction*. 3rd ed. London, 1994

Leventhal, F. M. (ed.) *20th-Century Britain: an Encyclopedia*. New York, 1995

Marr, A., *Ruling Britannia: the Failure and Future of British Democracy*. London, 1995

McCormick, John, *Contemporary Britain*. Palgrave Macmillan, Basingstoke, 2003

Neumann, Peter R., *Britain's Long War: British Strategy in the Northern Ireland Conflict, 1969–98*. Palgrave Macmillan, Basingstoke, 2003

Oakland, J., *British Civilization: an Introduction*. 3rd ed. London, 1995

Oxford History of the British Empire. 2 vols. OUP, Oxford, 1999

Palmer, A. and Palmer, V., *The Chronology of British History*. London, 1995

Penguin History of Britain. 9 vols. London, 1996

Sked, A. and Cook, C., *Post-War Britain: a Political History*. 4th ed. London, 1993

Speck, W. A., *A Concise History of Britain, 1707–1975*. CUP, 1993

Strong, R., *The Story of Britain*. London, 1996

Other more specialized titles are listed under TERRITORY AND POPULATION; CONSTITUTION AND GOVERNMENT; ARMY; NAVY; BANKING AND FINANCE; ELECTRICITY; TRADE UNIONS; RELIGION; *and* WELFARE, *above. See also Further Reading in Scotland, Wales and Northern Ireland.*

National Statistical Office: National Statistics, 1 Drummond Gate, London, SW1V 2QQ.

Website: http://www.statistics.gov.uk/

ENGLAND

KEY HISTORICAL EVENTS

Emperor Claudius' invasion in AD 43 established Roman rule in southern England. After the failed rebellions in AD 60 of Queen Boudicca of the Iceni and the suppression of Wales by AD 78, there was a long period of peaceful settlement, during which the Romans established new towns such as Londinium (London) and Eboracum (York). After the withdrawal of the Roman legions in the early 5th century, Pictish and Saxon raiders harassed the British towns. Defensive Saxon settlements were at first encouraged by the authorities but their rebellion soon threatened the Roman way of life. The Romano-British were pushed back to higher land in the west by waves of invading Saxons, Angles and Jutes. After a period of Mercian supremacy under Offa in the 8th century, the West Saxons (Wessex) dominated southern England. Danish invasions in 865 established the Danelaw in northern England. Alfred the Great of Wessex and his son Edward resisted Danish expansion, strengthening Anglo-Saxon unity under Alfred's successors—Athelstan became the first king of all England in 927.

Danish rule over England was reasserted by Sweyn in 994 and his son, Canute. The Anglo-Saxon restoration was short-lived; William, duke of Normandy led the Norman Conquest in 1066, defeating Harold II at the Battle of Hastings. When William died in 1087, he left Normandy to his eldest son Robert, thus separating it from England. Henry II, the founder of the Plantagenet dynasty, was feudatory lord of half of France but Henry's son John lost most of the French possessions. The barons forced John to sign the Magna Carta in 1215, later interpreted as the source of English civil liberties. Thereafter, the Norman baronage came to regard themselves as English.

The Hundred Years War (1338–1453) with France ended with the loss of all remaining French possessions except Calais. In 1387 and in later outbreaks, the Black Death reduced the population by over a third. A dynastic struggle between the rival houses of York and Lancaster was concluded by the invasion of Henry Tudor in 1485. His son, Henry VIII, asserted royal authority over the church, breaking with Rome. Tudor power reached its zenith with Elizabeth I. Philip II's Spanish Armada, destroyed in 1588, was sent to turn back the Protestant tide in England and to counter English ambitions in the New World.

The accession of James VI of Scotland to the English throne in 1603 brought the two countries into personal union. Charles I's defeat in the Civil War resulted in a republican Commonwealth but the Stuart monarchy was restored in 1660. England and Scotland were united in 1707 under Anne, queen of Great Britain.

TERRITORY AND POPULATION

At the census taken on 29 April 2001 the area of England was 130,281 sq. km and the population 49,138,831, giving a density of 377 per sq. km. England covers 53·7% of the total area of the United Kingdom. Households at the 2001 census: 21,262,000. Estimated population of England, mid-2004, 50,065,000.

Population (present on census night) at the four previous decennial censuses:

1961	1971	1981	1991
43,460,525[1]	46,018,371[1]	46,226,100[2]	46,382,050

[1]Area now included in Wales formed the English county of Monmouthshire until 1974. [2]The final count is believed to be over-stated as a result of an error in processing. The preliminary counts presented here rounded to the nearest hundred are thought to be more accurate.

Population at census day 2001:

Males	Females	Total
23,923,390	25,215,441	49,138,831

For further statistical information, see under Territory and Population, United Kingdom.

Eight 'Standard Regions' (also classified as 'level 1 regions' for EU purposes) are identified in England as economic planning regions. They have no administrative significance. Estimated population of the regions of England (in 1,000), 2003, East Anglia, 2,219; East Midlands, 4,252; West Midlands, 5,320; North, 3,029; North West, 6,315; South East, 18,712 (including Greater London, 7,388); South West, 4,999; Yorkshire and Humberside, 5,009. Although the populations of most of the regions increased during the 1990s, the North and the North West saw their populations decline, by 45,000 and 72,000 respectively between 1991 and 2001. The population on census day in 2001 in the nine English Government Office regions was as follows: East, 5,388,154; East Midlands, 4,172,179; London, 7,172,036; North East, 2,515,479; North West, 6,730,800; South East, 8,000,550;

South West, 4,928,458; West Midlands, 5,267,337; Yorkshire and the Humber, 4,965,838.

Following the local government reorganization in the mid-1990s, there is a mixed pattern to local government in England. Apart from Greater London, England is divided into 34 counties with two tiers of administration; a county council and district councils. There are six metropolitan county areas containing 36 single-tier metropolitan districts.

In addition, there are 46 single-tier unitary authorities which, with the exception of the Isle of Wight, were formerly district councils in the shire counties of England. The Isle of Wight is a unitary county council.

As a consequence of the establishment of the 46 unitary authorities, a number of county areas were abolished. These were Avon, Cleveland and Humberside. Berkshire County Council was also abolished but the county itself is retained for ceremonial purposes. Greater London comprises 32 boroughs and the City of London.

Area in sq. km of English counties and unitary authorities, and population at census day 2001:

	Area (sq. km)	Population		Area (sq. km)	Population
Metropolitan counties			*Non-metropolitan counties*		
Greater			Somerset (Som)	3,451	498,093
Manchester	1,276	2,482,352	Staffordshire		
Merseyside	645	1,362,034	(Staffs)	2,620	806,737
South Yorkshire	1,552	1,266,337	Suffolk	3,801	668,548
Tyne and Wear	540	1,075,979	Surrey	1,663	1,059,015
West Midlands	902	2,555,596	Warwickshire	1,975	505,885
West Yorkshire	2,029	2,079,217	West Sussex	1,991	753,612
			Wiltshire		
Non-metropolitan counties			(Wilts)	3,255	432,973
Bedfordshire			Worcestershire	1,741	542,107
(Beds)	1,192	381,571			
Buckingham-			*Unitary Authorities*		
shire (Bucks)	1,565	479,028	Bath and North		
Cambridge-			East Somerset	346	169,045
shire (Camb)	3,046	552,655	Blackburn with		
Cheshire	2,083	673,777	Darwen	137	137,471
Cornwall and			Blackpool	35	142,284
Isles of Scilly	3,563	501,267	Bournemouth	46	163,441
Cumbria	6,768	487,607	Bracknell Forest	109	109,606
Derbyshire	2,547	734,581	Brighton and Hove	83	247,820
Devon	6,564	704,499	Bristol, City of	110	380,615
Dorset	2,542	390,986	Darlington	197	97,822
Durham	2,226	493,470	Derby	78	221,716
East Sussex	1,709	492,324	East Riding of		
Essex	3,465	1,310,922	Yorkshire	2,408	314,076
Gloucestershire			Halton	79	118,215
(Gloucs)	2,653	564,559	Hartlepool	94	88,629
Hampshire			Herefordshire,		
(Hants)	3,679	1,240,032	County of	2,180	174,844
Hertfordshire			Isle of Wight	380	132,719
(Herts)	1,643	1,033,977	Kingston upon		
Kent	3,544	1,329,653	Hull, City of	71	243,595
Lancashire			Leicester	73	279,923
(Lancs)	2,903	1,134,976	Luton	43	184,390
Leicestershire			Medway	192	249,502
(Leics)	2,083	609,579	Middlesbrough	54	134,847
Lincolnshire			Milton Keynes	309	207,063
(Lincs)	5,921	646,646	North East		
Norfolk	5,371	796,733	Lincolnshire	192	157,983
Northampton-			North Lincoln-		
shire			shire	846	152,839
(Northants)	2,364	629,676	North Somerset	374	188,556
Northumber-			Nottingham	75	266,995
land	5,013	307,186	Peterborough	343	156,060
North Yorkshire			Plymouth	80	240,718
(N. Yorks)	8,038	569,660	Poole	65	138,299
Nottingham-			Portsmouth	40	186,704
shire (Notts)	2,085	748,503	Reading	40	143,214
Oxfordshire			Redcar and		
(Oxon)	2,605	605,492	Cleveland	245	139,141
Shropshire			Rutland	382	34,560
(Salop)	3,197	283,240	Slough	33	119,070

	Area (sq. km)	Population		Area (sq. km)	Population
Unitary Authorities			*Unitary Authorities*		
Southampton	50	217,478	Thurrock	163	143,042
Southend-on-Sea	42	160,256	Torbay	63	129,702
South			Warrington	181	191,084
Gloucestershire	497	245,644	West Berkshire	704	144,445
Stockton-on-Tees	204	178,405	Windsor and		
Stoke-on-Trent	93	240,643	Maidenhead	197	133,606
Swindon	230	180,061	Wokingham	179	150,257
Telford and			York	272	181,131
Wrekin	290	158,285			

Source: Office of National Statistics

In 2003 London had a population of 7,388,000. Populations of next largest cities were: Birmingham (2003), 992,000; Leeds (2003), 715,000; Sheffield (2003), 513,000; Bradford (2001), 468,000; Liverpool (2003), 442,000; Manchester (2003), 432,000; Bristol (2003), 392,000.

Greater London Boroughs. Total area 1,572 sq. km. Population at census day 2001: 7,172,036 (inner London, 2,765,975). Population by borough (census day 2001):

Barking and		Islington[1]	175,787
Dagenham	163,944	Kensington and	
Barnet	314,561	Chelsea[1]	158,922
Bexley	218,307	Kingston	
Brent	263,463	upon Thames	147,295
Bromley	295,530	Lambeth[1]	266,170
Camden[1]	198,027	Lewisham[1]	248,924
Croydon	330,688	Merton	187,908
Ealing	300,947	Newham[1]	243,737
Enfield	273,563	Redbridge	238,628
Greenwich	214,540	Richmond	
Hackney[1]	202,819	upon Thames	172,327
Hammersmith		Southwark[1]	244,867
and Fulham[1]	165,243	Sutton	179,667
Haringey[1]	216,510	Tower Hamlets[1]	196,121
Harrow	207,389	Waltham Forest	218,277
Havering	224,248	Wandsworth[1]	260,383
Hillingdon	242,435	Westminster,	
Hounslow	212,344	City of[1]	181,279

[1]Inner London borough.

Source: Office of National Statistics

The City of London (677 acres) is administered by its Corporation which retains some independent powers. Population at census day 2001: 7,186.

CLIMATE

For more detailed information, see under Climate, United Kingdom.

London, Jan. 39°F (3·9°C), July 64°F (17·8°C). Annual rainfall 25" (635 mm). Birmingham, Jan. 38°F (3·3°C), July 61°F (16·1°C). Annual rainfall 30" (749 mm). Manchester, Jan. 39°F (3·9°C), July 61°F (16·1°C). Annual rainfall 34·5" (876 mm).

RECENT ELECTIONS

At the UK general election held in May 2005, 528 members were returned from England. Voting in Staffordshire South was postponed owing to the death of a candidate shortly before the election.

See also Constitution and Government, Recent Elections and Current Administration in United Kingdom.

DEFENCE

For information on defence, see United Kingdom.

ECONOMY

For information on the economy, see United Kingdom.

ENERGY AND NATURAL RESOURCES

For information on energy and natural resources, see United Kingdom.

Water

The Water Act of Sept. 1989 privatized the nine water and sewerage authorities in England: Anglian; North West (now United Utilities Water plc); Northumbrian; Severn Trent; South West; Southern; Thames; Wessex; Yorkshire. There are also 16 water only companies in England and Wales. The Act also inaugurated the National Rivers Authority, with environmental and resource management responsibilities, and the 'regulator' *Office of Water Services (Ofwat)*, charged with protecting consumer interests.

INDUSTRY

Labour

The unemployment rate in the spring of 2005 was 4·6%, compared to 4·7% for the UK as a whole. Unemployment was lowest in the southwest (3·5%) and highest in London (6·7%).

INTERNATIONAL TRADE

For information on international trade, see United Kingdom.

COMMUNICATIONS

For information on communications, see United Kingdom.

Shipping

Total cargo handled in 2004 was 379·2m. tonnes.

SOCIAL INSTITUTIONS

Education

For details on the nature and types of school, see under Education, United Kingdom.

In 2004–05 education and skills expenditure by Central and Local government in England was expected to top £52bn. In Jan. 2001 there were 506 public-sector nursery and primary schools with nursery classes in England; in addition, there were 2,300 independent schools with provision for children under five (including direct grant nurseries). In 2001 there were 44,990 pupils under five attending nursery schools and pupils under five in nursery and infant classes in primary schools. Some of these children were attending part-time.

In Jan. 2001 there were 4,406,215 pupils at 18,069 primary schools in England, of which 2,070 were infant schools providing for pupils up to the age of about seven, the remainder mainly taking pupils from age five through to 11. Nearly all primary schools take both boys and girls. 15% of primary schools had 100 full-time pupils or fewer.

In Jan. 2001 there were 463 middle schools in England deemed either primary or secondary according to the age range of the school concerned.

In Jan. 2001 there were 3,481 secondary schools in England. Some local authorities have retained selection at age 11 for entry to grammar schools, of which there were 159 in 2001. There were a small number of technical schools in 2001 which specialize in technical studies. There were 145 secondary modern schools in 2001, providing a general education up to the minimum school leaving age of 16, although exceptionally some pupils stay on beyond that age.

Almost all local education authorities operate a system of comprehensive schools to which pupils are admitted without reference to ability or aptitude. In Jan. 2004 there were 2,807 such schools in England with over 2·9m. pupils. With the development of comprehensive education, various patterns of secondary schools have come into operation. Principally these are: 1) All-through schools with pupils aged 11 to 18 or 11 to 16; pupils over 16 being able to transfer to an 11 to 18 school or a sixth form college providing for pupils aged 16 to 19. (There are currently 102 sixth form colleges in England). 2) Local education authorities operating a three-tier system involving middle schools where transfer to secondary school is at ages 12, 13 or 14. These correspond to 12 to 18, 13 to 18 and 14 to 18 comprehensive schools respectively; or 3) In areas where there are no middle schools a two-tier system of junior and senior comprehensive schools for pupils aged 11 to 18 with optional transfer to these schools at age 13 or 14.

Under the Education Act 1996 children have special educational needs if they have a learning difficulty which calls for special educational provision to be made for them. In some cases the Local Education Authority will need to make a statutory assessment of special educational needs under the Education Act 1996, which may ultimately lead to a 'statement'. In England the total number of pupils with statements in 2004 was 261,100. In 2004 there were 1,078 maintained special schools and 70 non-maintained special schools.

Outside the state system of education there were in England about 2,302 independent schools in Jan. 2004, ranging from large prestigious schools to small local ones. Some provide boarding facilities but the majority include non-resident day pupils. There are about 586,940 pupils in these schools, which represent about 7% of the total pupil population in England.

Further Education (Non-University). In 2002–03, 3·9m. students were enrolled at FE colleges in England. Those on Learning and Skills Council funded provision were studying for 6·6m. qualifications. Total funding for the FE sector in 2001–02 was £4,029m.

Higher Education. In 2004–05 there were 130 higher education institutions in England funded by the Higher Education Funding Council for England (HEFCE), of which 76 were universities, 14 general higher education colleges and 40 specialist higher education colleges. HEFCE distributes public money for teaching and research to universities and colleges. It works in partnership with the higher education sector and advises government on higher education policy. In 2004–05 HEFCE distributed a total of £6bn., including £4·28bn. for teaching and £1·38bn. for research.

a) *Universities, 2003–04*		
Name (Location)	No. of students (2003–04)	No. of academic staff (2003–04)
Anglia Polytechnic University (Chelmsford)[1]	24,315	765
Aston University (Birmingham)	7,940	725
University of Bath	13,855	785
University of Birmingham	32,110	2,445
Bournemouth University (Poole)	15,880	730
University of Bradford	12,395	1,365
University of Brighton	19,635	1,525
University of Bristol	22,705	2,220
Brunel University (Uxbridge)	15,130	1,060
University of Cambridge[2]	25,470	3,955
University of Central England in Birmingham	25,160	1,590
University of Central Lancashire (Preston)	32,610	975
City University (London)	22,365	745
Coventry University	18,580	995
De Montfort University (Leicester)	23,665	1,450
University of Derby	23,755	940
University of Durham	16,185	1,135
University of East Anglia (Norwich)	15,255	1,165
University of East London (London)	15,385	635
University of Essex (Colchester)	11,340	835
University of Exeter	14,130	1,050
University of Gloucestershire (Cheltenham)	9,955	540
University of Greenwich (London)	20,305	855
University of Hertfordshire (Hatfield)	23,520	1,295
University of Huddersfield	19,070	855
University of Hull	21,240	990

a) *Universities, 2003–04*

Name (Location)	No. of students (2003–04)	No. of academic staff (2003–04)
Keele University (Newcastle-under-Lyme)	11,815	535
University of Kent (Canterbury)	14,600	1,065
Kingston University (Kingston-upon-Thames)	19,880	1,115
Lancaster University	17,670	890
University of Leeds	35,170	2,655
Leeds Metropolitan University	51,455	1,530
University of Leicester	16,220	1,320
University of Lincoln	17,145	595
University of Liverpool	21,660	1,910
Liverpool John Moores University	22,830	1,185
University of London[2]	126,496	15,355
London Metropolitan University	32,450	1,950
London South Bank University	22,250	825
Loughborough University of Technology	16,860	1,365
University of Luton	12,155	350
University of Manchester[3]	31,495	2,955
University of Manchester Institute of Science and Technology[3]	7,615	1,390
Manchester Metropolitan University	33,500	1,870
Middlesex University (London)	22,415	855
University of Newcastle upon Tyne	18,335	1,865
University of Northumbria at Newcastle	25,605	1,170
University of Nottingham	32,695	2,470
Nottingham Trent University	27,595	1,570
Open University[4]	169,220	1,090
University of Oxford[2]	22,180	3,850
Oxford Brookes University	18,345	1,165
University of Plymouth	28,420	1,050
University of Portsmouth	20,920	1,070
University of Reading	14,550	1,445
Roehampton University	8,045	480
University of Salford	19,405	1,465
University of Sheffield	26,095	2,435
Sheffield Hallam University	27,655	1,210
University of Southampton	23,365	2,280
Staffordshire University (Stoke-on-Trent)	14,865	775
University of Sunderland	18,720	855
University of Surrey (Guildford)	17,235	1,060
University of Sussex (Brighton)	11,995	1,390
University of Teesside (Middlesbrough)	21,650	705
Thames Valley University (London)	25,710	655
University of Warwick (Coventry)	29,150	1,535
University of the West of England, Bristol	26,650	1,535
University of Westminster (London)	26,610	1,560
University of Wolverhampton	23,990	890
University of York	12,385	1,155

[1]Renamed Anglia Ruskin University in Oct. 2005.
[2]See listing of colleges below. [3]In Oct. 2004 University of Manchester and University of Manchester Institute of Science and Technology merged to form University of Manchester. [4]Entirely distance learning —see page 1287.

b) *University of Cambridge; University of London; University of Oxford*
   University of Cambridge Colleges:
Christ's College; Churchill College; Clare College; Corpus Christi College; Darwin College; Downing College; Emmanuel College; Fitzwilliam College; Girton College; Gonville and Caius College; Homerton College; Hughes Hall; Jesus College; King's College; Lucy Cavendish; Magdalene College; New Hall; Newnham College; Pembroke College; Peterhouse; Queen's College; Robinson College; St Catharine's College; St Edmund's College; St John's College; Selwyn College; Sidney Sussex College; Trinity College; Trinity Hall; Wolfson College.

   University of London Colleges (no. of students/academic staff 2003–04):
Birkbeck (16,645/1,700); Courtauld Institute of Art (390/35); Goldsmiths College (7,695/355); Heythrop College (671/NA); Imperial College London (12,045/3,180); Institute of Cancer Research (155/470); Institute of Education (6,685/310); King's College London (21,315/2,835); London

Business School (1,650/115); London School of Economics and Political Science (8,570/1,305); London School of Hygiene and Tropical Medicine (940/455); Queen Mary, University of London (10,370/1,435); Royal Academy of Music (705/395); Royal Holloway, University of London (7,600/970); Royal Veterinary College (1,250/165); St George's Hospital Medical School (3,430/660); School of Oriental and African Studies (4,335/760); School of Pharmacy (1,345/105); University College London (1,345/105). The University of London also had 34,000 external programme students in 2003–04.

   University of Oxford Colleges:
All Souls College; Balliol College; Brasenose College; Christ Church; Corpus Christi College; Exeter College; Green College; Harris Manchester College; Hertford College; Jesus College; Keble College; Kellogg College; Lady Margaret Hall; Linacre College; Lincoln College; Magdalen College; Mansfield College; Merton College; New College; Nuffield College; Oriel College; Pembroke College; The Queen's College; St Anne's College; St Antony's College; St Catherine College; St Cross College; St Edmund Hall; St Hilda's College; St Hugh's College; St John's College; St Peter's College; Somerville College; Templeton College; Trinity College; University College; Wadham College; Wolfson College; Worcester College. *Permanent Private Halls:* Blackfriars; Campion Hall; Greyfriars; Regent's Park College; St Benet's Hall; St Stephen's House; Wycliffe Hall.

c) *Colleges of Art, Dance, Drama and Music*
Arts Institute at Bournemouth; Central School of Speech and Drama (London); Conservatoire for Dance and Drama (London)[1]; Cumbria Institute of the Arts; Dartington College of Arts (Totnes); Falmouth College of Arts[2]; Kent Institute of Art and Design (Maidstone)[3]; Leeds College of Music; University of the Arts, London; Norwich School of Art and Design; Ravensbourne College of Design and Communication (Bromley); Rose Bruford College of Speech and Drama (Sidcup); Royal College of Art (London); Royal College of Music (London); Royal Northern College of Music (Manchester); The Surrey Institute of Art and Design, University College (Farnham)[4]; Trinity College of Music (London)[5]; Wimbledon School of Art.

[1]Affiliate schools: Bristol Old Vic Theatre School; Central School of Ballet; The Circus Space; London Academy of Music and Dramatic Art; London Contemporary Dance School; Northern School of Contemporary Dance; The Royal Academy of Dramatic Art. [2]Since renamed University College Falmouth. [3]Since merged with the Surrey Institute of Art and Design, University College to become University College for the Creative Arts at Canterbury, Epsom, Farnham, Maidstone and Rochester. [4]Since merged with Kent Institute of Art and Design to become University College for the Creative Arts at Canterbury, Epsom, Farnham, Maidstone and Rochester. [5]Since renamed Trinity Laban.

d) *Other Institutions*
Bath Spa University College[1]; Birmingham College of Food, Tourism and Creative Studies; Bishop Grosseteste College (Lincoln); Bolton Institute of Higher Education[2]; Buckinghamshire Chilterns University College (High Wycombe); Canterbury Christ Church University College[3]; University College Chester[4]; University College Chichester; Cranfield University; Edge Hill College of Higher Education (Ormskirk); Harper Adams University College (Newport); Homerton College, Cambridge; Liverpool Hope University College[5]; University of London (Institutes and Activities); Newman College of Higher Education (Birmingham); University College Northampton[6]; Royal Agricultural College (Cirencester); Royal College of Nursing (London); College of St Mark and St John (Plymouth); St Martin's College (Lancaster); St Mary's College (Twickenham); Southampton Institute[7]; Trinity and All Saints College (Leeds); University College Winchester[8]; University College Worcester[9]; Writtle College (Chelmsford); York St John College.

[1]Since renamed Bath Spa University. [2]Since renamed University of Bolton. [3]Since renamed Canterbury Christ Church University. [4]Since renamed University of Chester. [5]Since renamed Liverpool Hope University. [6]Since renamed University of Northampton. [7]Since renamed Southampton Solent University. [8]Since renamed University of Winchester. [9]Since renamed University of Worcester.

Health

As at 30 Sept. 2004 there were around 1·3m. employees in the National Health Service including 117,036 doctors, 397,515 qualified nursing, midwifery and health visiting staff (including practice nurses) and 17,272 qualified ambulance staff.

CULTURE
Tourism
The leading free admission attraction in 2004 was Blackpool Pleasure Beach, Lancs, with an estimated 6·2m. visits. The leading tourist attractions charging admission in 2004 were: the British Airways London Eye, with 3·7m. visits; the Tower of London, with 2·1m.; Flamingo Land Theme Park in Malton, North Yorkshire, with 2·1m.; Pleasureland Theme Park in Southport, with 2·1m.; and Pleasure Beach in Great Yarmouth, with 1·5m.

FURTHER READING
See Further Reading in United Kingdom.

SCOTLAND

KEY HISTORICAL EVENTS

Earliest evidence of human settlement in Scotland dates from the Middle Stone Age. Hunters and fishermen on the west coast were succeeded by farming communities as far north as Shetland. The Romans, who were active in the first century AD, built Hadrian's Wall between the Tyne and Solway Firth as their northern frontier. At this time, the Picts formed two kingdoms north of the Firth of Clyde. From the 6th century, the Celtic Scots from Dalriada, northern Ireland, fought with Angles and Britons for control of southern Scotland.

In 843 Kenneth MacAlpine united the Scots and the Picts to found the kingdom of Scotland. A legal and administrative uniformity was established by David I (reigned 1124–53). William the Lion abandoned claims to Northumbria in 1209 but began the alliance with France. In 1286 Edward I of England asserted his claim as overlord of Scotland and appointed his son to succeed to the crown. Resistance to English rule was led by William Wallace and later by Robert Bruce, who defeated the English at Bannockburn in 1314. His grandson, Robert II, became the first Stewart (Stuart) king in 1371.

Royal minorities undermined the authority of the crown in the 15th century until the accession of James IV in 1488. Relations with England improved after his marriage to Margaret Tudor in 1503 but when Henry VIII invaded France, James attacked England and was killed at the Battle of Flodden in 1513. The young James V was assailed by conflicting pressures from pro-French and pro-English factions but having secured his personal rule, he entered into two successive French marriages. His daughter, Mary Queen of Scots, married the French Dauphin in 1558. Protestant opposition to French influence was bolstered by Elizabeth I of England, who sent troops. Mary was in France when the Scottish parliament renounced papal authority, bolstering the reformist movement, led by John Knox. Returning to Scotland after her husband's death in 1561, Mary was forced to take refuge in England. Her son, James VI, survived the animosity between his own and his mother's followers to make an alliance with England. Deemed a threat because of her claim to the English throne, Mary was executed on Elizabeth's orders in 1587.

Elizabeth died without issue in 1603 and was succeeded by James. Although he styled himself 'king of Great Britain', England and Scotland remained independent. Charles I alienated much of the Scottish nobility and was defeated in the Bishops' Wars by the Covenanters, who rejected English interference in the Scottish church. Scottish armies fought for both sides in the English Civil War, which led to the execution of Charles I in 1649. However, the Scots soon united to accept Charles II as their king. Having established dominance in England, Cromwell moved against Scotland forcing Charles II into exile. His restoration in 1660 was welcomed in both kingdoms. His successor, James VII (James II of England), was less astute in managing religious and political differences. The collapse of his regime in 1688 and the arrival of William of Orange confirmed the Protestant ascendancy in Scotland and England.

The union of parliament in 1707 brought Scotland more directly under English authority. However, Scotland retained its own legal and ecclesiastical systems. The remaining supporters of James VII, the Jacobites, led two abortive risings on behalf of James' son and grandson (the old and new Pretenders) but were defeated decisively at Culloden in 1746.

TERRITORY AND POPULATION

The total area of Scotland is 77,925 sq. km (2001), including its islands, 186 in number, and inland water 1,580 sq. km. Scotland covers 32·1% of the total area of the United Kingdom.

Population (including military in the barracks and seamen on board vessels in the harbours) at the dates of each census:

Date of enumeration	Population	Pop. per sq. mile[1]
1801	1,608,420	53
1811	1,805,864	60
1821	2,091,521	70
1831	2,364,386	79
1841	2,620,184	88
1851	2,888,742	97
1861	3,062,294	100
1871	3,360,018	113
1881	3,735,573	125
1891	4,025,647	135
1901	4,472,103	150
1911	4,760,904	160
1921	4,882,497	164
1931	4,842,980	163
1951	5,096,415	171
1961	5,179,344	174
1971	5,228,963	67
1981	5,130,735	66
1991	4,998,567	60
2001	5,062,011	65

[1]Per sq. km from 1971.

Population at census day 2001:

Males	Females	Total
2,432,494	2,629,517	5,062,011

In 2001, 58,652 people aged three and over spoke Gaelic (65,978 in 1991). Households at the 2001 census: 2,192,000.

The age distribution in Scotland at census day on 2001 was as follows (in 1,000):

Age-group		
Under 5		277
5 and under 10		307
10 ,, 15		323
15 ,, 20		317
20 ,, 25		314
25 ,, 35		699
35 ,, 45		781
45 ,, 55		689
55 ,, 65		550
65 ,, 70		239
70 ,, 75		207
75 ,, 85		271
85 and upwards		88

Land area and population by administrative area (30 June 2004):

Council Area	Area (sq. km)	Population
Aberdeen City	186	203,450
Aberdeenshire	6,313	232,850
Angus	2,182	108,560
Argyll and Bute	6,909	91,190
Clackmannanshire	159	48,240
Dumfries and Galloway	6,426	147,930
Dundee City	60	141,870
East Ayrshire	1,262	119,720
East Dunbartonshire	175	106,550
East Lothian	679	91,580
East Renfrewshire	174	89,610
Edinburgh, City of	264	453,670
Eilean Siar[1]	3,071	26,260
Falkirk	297	147,460
Fife	1,325	354,600
Glasgow City	175	577,670
Highland	25,659	211,340
Inverclyde	160	82,430
Midlothian	354	79,610
Moray	2,238	87,720
North Ayrshire	885	136,020
North Lanarkshire	470	322,790
Orkney Islands	990	19,500
Perth and Kinross	5,286	137,520
Renfrewshire	261	170,610
Scottish Borders	4,732	109,270
Shetland Islands	1,466	21,940
South Ayrshire	1,222	111,850
South Lanarkshire	1,772	305,410
Stirling	2,187	86,370
West Dunbartonshire	159	91,970
West Lothian	427	162,840
Total	77,925	5,078,400

[1]Formerly Western Isles.

Estimated population of Scotland, mid-2004, 5,078,400 (2,632,200 females and 2,446,200 males), giving a density of 65 per sq. km.

Glasgow is Scotland's largest city, with an estimated population of 577,090 in 2003, followed by Edinburgh, the capital (estimated 2003 population, 448,370), and Aberdeen, with 206,600.

The birthplaces of the 2001 census day population in Scotland were: Scotland, 4,410,400; England, 408,948; Wales, 16,623; Northern Ireland, 33,528; Ireland 21,774; other European Union countries, 44,432; elsewhere, 126,306.

SOCIAL STATISTICS

	Estimated resident population at 30 June[1]	Total births	Live births outside marriage	Deaths	Marriages	Divorces, annulments and dissolutions
1999	5,119,200	55,147	22,722	60,281	29,940	11,864
2000	5,114,600	53,076	22,625	57,799	30,367	11,143
2001	5,064,200	52,527	22,760	57,382	29,621	10,631
2002	5,054,800	51,270	22,534	58,103	29,826	10,826
2003	5,057,400	52,432	23,864	58,472	30,757	10,928
2004	5,078,400	53,957	25,202	56,187	32,154	11,227

[1]Includes merchant navy at home and forces stationed in Scotland.

Birth rate, 2004, per 1,000 population, 10·6; death rate, 11·1; marriage, 6·3; infant mortality per 1,000 live births, 4·9; sex ratio, 1,060 male births to 1,000 female. Average age of marriage in 2004: males, 35·9, females, 33·4. Expectation of life, 2004: males, 73·8 years, females, 79·1.

CLIMATE

For more detailed information, see under Climate, United Kingdom.

Aberdeen, Jan. 38°F (3·3°C), July 57°F (13·9°C). Annual rainfall 32" (813 mm). Edinburgh, Jan. 38°F (3·3°C), July 58°F (14·5°C). Annual rainfall 27" (686 mm). Glasgow, Jan. 39°F (3·9°C), July 59°F (15°C). Annual rainfall 38" (965 mm).

CONSTITUTION AND GOVERNMENT

In a referendum on devolution on 11 Sept. 1997, Scotland's voters opted for devolved government, calling for the reinstatement of a separate parliament in Scotland, the first since union with England in 1707. 1,775,045 votes (74·3%) were cast in favour of a Scottish parliament and 614,400 against (25·7%). On a turnout of 60·4%, around 44·8% of the total electorate voted in favour. For the second question, on the Parliament's tax-raising powers, 1,512,889 votes were cast in favour (63·5%) and 870,263 against (36·5%). This represented 38·4% of the total electorate.

The Scottish Parliament is made up of 129 members and managed a budget of £27·4bn. in 2005–06. The parliament may pass laws and has limited tax raising powers; it is also responsible for devolved issues, including health, education, police and fire services; however, 'reserved issues' (foreign policy, constitutional matters, and many domestic areas including social security, trade and industry, and employment legislation) remain the responsibility of the British Parliament in Westminster.

RECENT ELECTIONS

At the UK general election held in May 2005, 59 members were returned from Scotland. Labour won 41 seats; the Liberal Democrats, 11; the Scottish National Party, 6; Conservative, 1. At the June 2004 European Parliament elections Labour won 2 seats, the Scottish National Party 2, the Conservatives 2 and Liberal Democrats 1.

In elections to the Scottish Parliament on 1 May 2003, Labour won 50 seats (4 by regional list), against 27 (18 by regional list) for the Scottish National Party, 18 (15 by regional list) for the Conservatives, 17 (4 by regional list) for the Liberal Democrats, 7 (all by regional list) for the Greens, 6 (all by regional list) for the Scottish Socialist Party (SSP) and 4 ind. Of the 129 seats, 73 were won on a first-past-the-post basis and 56 through proportional representation (regional list). Turnout was 49%. Donald Dewar was elected as *First Minister* on 13 May 1999. He died on 11 Oct. 2000. Jim Wallace was acting first minister until the election of Henry McLeish on 26 Oct. 2000. McLeish resigned on 8 Nov. 2001 and Wallace again assumed the post temporarily. Jack McConnell was elected first minister on 23 Nov. 2001 and re-elected on 15 May 2003.

See also Constitution and Government, Recent Elections and Current Administration in United Kingdom.

CURRENT ADMINISTRATION

First Minister: Jack McConnell; b. 1960 (Labour).
   Presiding Officer: George Reid.

Scottish Executive: http://www.scotland.gov.uk

DEFENCE

For information on defence, see United Kingdom.

ECONOMY

Currency

The Bank of Scotland, Clydesdale Bank and the Royal Bank of Scotland have note-issuing powers.

Budget

Government expenditure in Scotland came to £38·6bn. in 2002–03 (including social security £13·4bn., health £6·4bn. and education £5·2bn.). Revenues totalled £31·6bn. (including income tax £7·9bn., social security receipts £5·2bn. and VAT £5·2bn.).

Performance
GDP rose by 0·9% in the third quarter of 2004 and 1·8% in the year ending the third quarter of 2004.

Banking and Finance
There is a stock exchange in Glasgow.

ENERGY AND NATURAL RESOURCES

Electricity
The Electricity Act 1989 created three new companies in Scotland. ScottishPower and Scottish Hydro-Electric (now renamed Scottish and Southern Energy) are vertically integrated companies carrying out generation, transmission, distribution and supply of electricity within their areas. They were privatized in 1990. Scottish Nuclear, responsible for operating the two Scottish nuclear power stations, was merged with Nuclear Electric in 1996. ScottishPower now owns Manweb in England, and Scottish Hydro-Electric has merged with Southern Electric under its new group name.

Water
Water supply is the responsibility of the Regional and Island local authorities. Seven river purification boards are responsible for environmental management.

Agriculture
In 2000 total agricultural area was 5,492,000 ha., of which 3,392,000 ha. were used for rough grazing and 1,839,000 ha. for crops and grass.

Selected crop production, 2000 (1,000 tonnes): barley, 1,729; potatoes, 1,114; wheat, 829; oats, 116.

Livestock, 2000 (in 1,000): cattle, 2,028; sheep, 9,184; pigs, 558; poultry, 14,296.

Forestry
Total forest area in 2003 was 1,327,000 ha., of which 470,000 ha. was owned by the Forestry Commission.

Fisheries
The major fishing ports are Aberdeen, Mallaig, Lerwick and Peterhead. In 2001 there were 2,595 fishing vessels that landed 289,700 tonnes of fish worth £256·7m.

INDUSTRY

Labour
In 2002 the economically active population numbered 2,549,000 (1,181,000 females), of whom 173,000 (66,000 females) were unemployed. This equates to an unemployment rate of 6·8% (7·8% for men and 5·6% for women). By Sept. 2001 employment in Scotland was at its highest in 40 years. In June 2002, 26·9% of the active workforce were in public administration, education and health, 23·7% in distribution, hotels and catering and repairs, 17·0% in banking, finance and insurance, and 12·6% in manufacturing.

COMMUNICATIONS

Roads
Responsibility for the construction and maintenance of trunk roads belongs to the Scottish Office. Roads not classified as trunk roads are the responsibility of county or unitary councils. In 2003 there were 54,500 km of public roads, of which 383 km were motorways. There were 2,104,000 licensed private and light goods vehicles.

Rail
Total railway length in 2003 was 2,698 km. In 2002–2003 a total of 62·2m. passengers travelled by rail and 8·9m. tonnes of freight were carried. There is a metro in Glasgow.

Civil Aviation
There are major airports at Aberdeen, Edinburgh, Glasgow and Prestwick. In 2002 Glasgow was the sixth busiest for passenger traffic in the UK, with 7,768,590 passengers (4,297,116 on domestic flights). Prestwick was the sixth busiest UK airport for freight in 2002, handling 39,500 tonnes. In 2002, 19,783,479 passengers and 68,516 tonnes of freight were carried by Scottish airports.

Shipping
The principal Scottish port is Forth, which handled 34·9m. tonnes of cargo in 2004.

SOCIAL INSTITUTIONS

Justice
The High Court of Justiciary is the supreme criminal court in Scotland and has jurisdiction in all cases of crime committed in any part of Scotland, unless expressly excluded by statute. It consists of the Lord Justice General, the Lord Justice Clerk and 30 other Judges, who are the same Judges who preside in the Court of Session, the Scottish Supreme Civil Court. One Judge is seconded to the Scottish Law Commission. The Court is presided over by the Lord Justice General, whom failing, by the Lord Justice Clerk, and exercises an appellate jurisdiction as well as being a court of first instance. The home of the High Court is Edinburgh, but the court visits other towns and cities in Scotland on circuit and indeed the busiest High Court sitting is in Glasgow. The court sits in Edinburgh both as a Court of Appeal (the *quorum* being two judges if the appeal is against sentence or other disposals, and three in all other cases) and on circuit as a court of first instance. Although the decisions of the High Court are not subject to review by the House of Lords, with the Scotland Act 1998 coming into force on 20 May 1999, there is a limited right of appeal against the termination of a devolution issue to the Judicial Committee of the Privy Council. One Judge sitting with a Jury of 15 persons can, and usually does, try cases, but two or more Judges (with a Jury) may do so in important or complex cases. The court has a privative jurisdiction over cases of treason, murder, rape, breach of duty by Magistrates and certain statutory offences under the Official Secrets Act 1911 and the Geneva Conventions Act 1957. It also tries the most serious crimes against person or property and those cases in which a sentence greater than imprisonment for three years is likely to be imposed.

The appellate jurisdiction of the High Court of Justiciary extends to all cases tried on indictment, whether in the High Court or the Sheriff Court, and persons so convicted may appeal to the court against conviction or sentence, or both, except where the sentence is fixed by law. In such an appeal, a person may bring under review any alleged miscarriage of justice including an alleged miscarriage of justice based on the existence and significance of evidence not heard at the original proceedings provided there is reasonable explanation of why it was not heard and an alleged miscarriage of justice where the Jury returned a verdict which no reasonable Jury, properly directed, could have returned. It is also a court of review from courts of summary jurisdiction, and on the final termination of any summary prosecution the convicted person may appeal to the court by way of stated case on questions of law, but not on questions of fact, except in relation to a miscarriage of justice alleged by the person accused on the basis of the existence and significance of additional evidence not heard at the original proceedings provided that there is a reasonable explanation of why it was not heard. Before cases proceed to a full hearing, leave of appeal must first be granted. Grounds of appeal and any relevant reports are sifted by a Judge sitting alone in chambers, who will decide if there are arguable grounds of appeal. Should leave of appeal be refused, this decision may be appealed to the High Court within 14 days, when the matter will be reviewed by three Judges. The

Lord Advocate is entitled to appeal to the High Court against any sentence passed on indictment on the ground that it is unduly lenient, or on a point of law. Both the prosecution and defence, at any time in solemn and summary proceedings, may appeal by way of Bill of Advocation in order to correct irregularities in the preliminary stages of a case. In summary proceedings the accused may appeal by Bill of Suspension, where he desires to bring under review a warrant, conviction or judgement issued by an inferior Judge. In summary proceedings the accused can also appeal against sentence alone by way of Stated Case. In summary proceedings the Crown can appeal against a sentence on the grounds that it is unduly lenient. The court also hears appeals under the Courts-Martial (Appeals) Act 1951.

The Sheriff Court has an inherent universal criminal jurisdiction (as well as an extensive civil one), limited in general to crimes and offences committed within a sheriffdom (a specifically defined region), which has, however, been curtailed by statute or practice under which the High Court of Justiciary has exclusive jurisdiction in relation to the crimes mentioned above. The Sheriff Court is presided over by a Sheriff Principal or a Sheriff, who when trying cases on indictment sits with a Jury of 15 people. His powers of awarding punishment involving imprisonment are restricted to a maximum of three years, but he may under certain statutory powers remit the prisoner to the High Court for sentence if this is felt to be insufficient. The Sheriff also exercises a wide summary criminal jurisdiction and when doing so sits without a Jury; and he has concurrent jurisdiction with every other court within his Sheriff Court district in regard to all offences competent for trial in summary courts. The great majority of offences which come before courts are of a more minor nature and as such are disposed of in the Sheriff Summary Courts or in the District Courts (see below). Where a case is to be tried on indictment either in the High Court of Justiciary or in the Sheriff Court, the Judge may, before the trial, hold a preliminary or first diet to decide questions of a preliminary nature, whether relating to the competency or relevancy of proceedings or otherwise. Any decision at a preliminary diet (other than a decision to adjourn the first or preliminary diet or discharge trial diet) can be the subject of an appeal to the High Court of Justiciary prior to the trial. The High Court also has the exclusive power to provide a remedy for all extraordinary occurrences in the course of criminal business where there is no other mode of appeal available. This is known as the Nobile Officium powers of the High Court and all petitions to the High Court as the Nobile Officium must be heard before at least three judges.

In cases to be tried on indictment in the Sheriff Court a first diet is mandatory before the trial diet to decide questions of a preliminary nature and to identify cases which are unlikely to go to trial on the date programmed. Likewise in summary proceedings, an intermediate diet is again mandatory before trial. In High Court cases such matters may be dealt with at a preliminary diet.

District Courts have jurisdiction in more minor offences occurring within a district which before recent local government reorganization corresponded to district council boundaries. These courts are presided over by Lay Magistrates, known as Justices, who have limited powers for fine and imprisonment. In Glasgow District there are also Stipendiary Magistrates, who are legally qualified, and who have the same sentencing powers as Sheriffs.

The Court of Session, presided over by the Lord President (the Lord Justice General in criminal cases), is divided into an inner-house comprising two divisions of five judges each with a mainly appellate function, and an outer-house comprising 22 single Judges sitting individually at first instance; it exercises the highest civil jurisdiction in Scotland, with the House of Lords as a Court of Appeal.

CIVIL JUDICIAL STATISTICS

	2001	2002
House of Lords (Appeals from Court of Session)	2	7
Court of Session—		
General Department	4,187	3,563
Petition Department	1,119	1,292
Sheriff Courts—Ordinary Cause	49,001	46,605
Sheriff Courts—Summary Cause	40,931	36,465
Small Claims	39,193	32,256

CRIMINAL STATISTICS
(Persons proceeded against in Scottish courts)

All Crimes and Offences	2000	2001	2002
Persons proceeded against	137,169	139,823	142,900[1]
Persons with a charge proved			
Total	118,147	120,289	124,950
Crimes	39,950	41,853	42,046
Persons aged 8–15[2]	64	81	128

[1]Estimate. [2]Except for serious offences which qualify for solemn proceedings, children aged 8–15 are not proceeded against in Scottish courts. Children within this age group that commit crime are generally referred to the reporter of the children's panel or are given a police warning.

In 2002 there were 427,000 crimes reported, of which 16,000 were violent. The average prison population in Scotland in Nov. 2003 was 6,569.

Police

In Scotland, the unitary councils have the role of police authorities. Establishment levels were abolished in Scotland on 1 April 1996. The actual strength at 31 March 2002 was 12,513 men and 2,738 women. There were 1,119 special constables. The total police net expenditure in Scotland for 2003–04 was £888·8m.

Education

In Sept. 2002 there were 2,833 publicly funded (local authority, grant-aided and self-governing) primary, secondary and special schools. All teachers employed in these schools require to be qualified.

Pre-school Education. In Jan. 2003 there were 2,782 pre-school centres that were in partnership with their local authority and 105,078 pupils enrolled in these centres.

Primary Education. In Sept. 2002 there were 2,258 publicly funded primary schools with 413,713 pupils and 22,980 full-time equivalent teachers.

Secondary Education. In Sept. 2002 there were 386 publicly funded secondary schools with 316,903 pupils and 578 adults. All but 21 schools provided a full range of Scottish Certificate of Education courses and non-certificate courses. Pupils who start their secondary education in schools which do not cater for a full range of courses may be transferred at the end of their second or fourth year to schools where a full range of courses is provided. There were 25,040 full-time equivalent teachers in secondary schools.

Independent schools. There were 151 independent schools in Sept. 2002, with a total of 30,370 pupils. A small number of the Scottish independent schools are of the 'public school' type, but they are not known as 'public schools' since in Scotland this term is used to denote education authority (i.e., state) schools.

Special Education. In Sept. 2002 there were 189 publicly funded special schools with 7,981 pupils.

Further Education. Under the Further and Higher Education (Scotland) Act 1992 funding of the Further Education colleges was transferred to central government in 1993. With effect from 1 July 1999 Scotland's FE colleges are funded by the Scottish Further Education Funding Council, a new executive Non Departmental Public Body established by the Secretary of State for Scotland on 1 Jan. 1999.

There are 42 incorporated FE colleges as well as the FE colleges in Orkney and Shetland, which are run by the local education authorities, and two privately managed colleges, Sabhal Mor Ostaig and Newbattle Abbey College. The colleges offer training in a wide range of vocational areas and co-operate with the Scottish Qualifications Authority, the Enterprise, Transport and Lifelong Learning Department and the Education Department of the Scottish Executive in the development of new courses. The qualifications offered by colleges aim to improve the skills of the nation's workforce and increase the country's competitiveness. The colleges benefit from co-operation with industry, through involvement with Industry Lead Bodies and National Training Organizations whose responsibility it is to identify education, training and skills needs at sectoral level. Industry is also represented on college boards of management. Colleges and schools in Scotland are directly involved in providing the new national qualifications introduced in 1999 as a result of the Higher Still development programme.

In 2001–02 there were 453,933 enrolments on vocational courses at Scotland's 46 further education institutions; the full-time equivalent staff number in the colleges was 12,500.

Full-time students resident in Scotland (and EU students) undertaking non-advanced (further education) courses are mainly supported through discretionary further education bursaries which are administered locally by further education colleges within National Policy Guidelines issued by the Scottish Further Education Funding Council. The Colleges have delegated discretionary powers for some aspects of the bursary support award.

In May 2000 the Scottish Executive announced the abolition of tuition fees for all eligible Scottish (and EU) full-time further education students from autumn 2000. The Executive also made a commitment to take steps to align, from autumn 2001, the levels of support available on a weekly basis for FE students with those that will apply for HE students and to begin to align the systems of assessment of parental/family contributions.

Higher Education. In Scotland in 2002 there were 21 institutions of higher education funded by the Scottish Higher Education Funding Council (SHEFC), with the exception of the Scottish Agricultural College which is funded by the Scottish Executive Rural Affairs Department. Included in this total is the Open University. SHEFC took over the responsibility for funding the Open University in Scotland at the start of the 2000–01 academic session. University education in Scotland has a long history. Four universities—St Andrews, Glasgow, Aberdeen and Edinburgh, known collectively as the 'ancient Scottish universities'—were founded in the 15th and 16th centuries. Four further universities—Strathclyde, Heriot-Watt, Stirling and Dundee—were formally established as independent universities between 1964 and 1967, and four others—Napier, Paisley, Robert Gordon and Glasgow Caledonian—were granted the title of university in 1992, with a fifth, the University of Abertay, Dundee, being added in 1994.

Of the remaining higher education institutions, which all offer courses at degree level (although not themselves universities), five were formerly Central Institutions: Edinburgh College of Art, Glasgow School of Art, Queen Margaret University College (Edinburgh), Royal Scottish Academy of Music and Drama (Glasgow) and Scottish Agricultural College (Perth).

Two additional higher education institutions were established in 2001. UHI Millennium Institute was designated as a higher education institution on 1 April when it took over from the local colleges of further education and other non-SHEFC funded institutions responsibility for all HE provision and all students on courses of HE in the Academic Partner institutions. Bell College of Technology became a higher education institution on 1 Aug. when its transfer from the further to the higher education sector was completed.

Further education colleges may also provide higher education courses.

University and HE student and staff figures:

Name (and Location)	Full-time and sandwich students (2001–02)	Full-time academic staff (2001–02)
Aberdeen Univ.	10,816	1,307
Abertay Dundee Univ.	3,898	250
Bell College of Technology (Hamilton)	2,619	176
Dundee Univ.	9,362	1,310
Edinburgh College of Art	1,623	81
Edinburgh Univ.	19,278	2,723
Glasgow School of Art	1,387	69
Glasgow Caledonian Univ.	11,699	730
Glasgow Univ.	16,651	2,368
Heriot-Watt Univ. (Edinburgh)	5,729	684
Napier Univ. (Edinburgh)	9,550	622
Paisley Univ.	6,532	460
Queen Margaret University College (Edinburgh)	3,241	196
Robert Gordon Univ. (Aberdeen)	7,501	507
Royal Scottish Academy of Music and Drama (Glasgow)	650	28
St Andrews Univ.	6,975	723
Scottish Agricultural College (Perth)	691	257
Stirling Univ.	6,853	563
Strathclyde Univ. (Glasgow)	14,892	1,361
UHI Millennium Institute (Inverness)	2,763	—

In 2001–02 there were 72,809 full-time students in further education colleges (27,610 studying at higher education level and 45,199 studying at further education level) of which 37,672 were female (14,687 HE and 22,985 FE).

All the higher education institutions are independent and self-governing. In addition to funding through the higher education funding councils, they receive tuition fees from the Students Awards Agency for Scotland for students domiciled in Scotland, and through local education authorities for students domiciled in England and Wales. Institutions which carry out research may also receive funding through the five Research Councils administered by the Office of Science and Technology.

Health

In 2002 there were 3,765 GPs with average patient list size of 1,392, and 1,891 dental practitioners.

Welfare

In Feb. 2004 there were 941,800 retirement pensioners, 290,000 beneficiaries of incapacity benefit, 285,800 recipients of disability living allowance, 239,400 claimants of income support, 235,200 of pension credit, 134,600 recipients of attendance allowance and 106,900 claimants of Jobseekers' Allowance. A total of 438,200 households were receiving housing benefit in Feb. 2004 and 528,200 council tax benefit. There were 0·5m. families with child tax credit or working tax credit awards, or with children and receiving out-of-work benefits in Jan. 2004.

RELIGION

The Church of Scotland, which was reformed in 1560, subsequently developed a presbyterian system of church government which was established in 1690 and has continued to the present day.

The supreme court is the General Assembly, which now consists of some 800 members, ministers and elders in equal numbers, together with members of the diaconate commissioned by presbyteries. It meets annually in May, under the presidency of a Moderator appointed by the Assembly. The Queen is normally represented by a Lord High Commissioner, but has occasionally attended in person. The royal presence in a special throne gallery in the hall but outside the Assembly symbolizes the independence from state control of what is nevertheless recognized as the national Church in Scotland.

There are also 46 presbyteries in Scotland, together with one presbytery of England, one presbytery of Europe, and one presbytery of Jerusalem. At the base of this conciliar structure of Church courts are the kirk sessions, of which there were 1,497 on 31 Dec. 2004. The total communicant membership of the Church at that date was 535,834.

The Episcopal Church of Scotland is a province of the Anglican Church and is one of the historic Scottish churches. It consists of seven dioceses. As at 31 Dec. 2002 it had 304 churches and missions, 483 clergy and 45,077 members, of whom 29,831 were communicants.

There are in Scotland some small outstanding Presbyterian bodies and also Baptists, Congregationalists, Methodists and Unitarians.

The Roman Catholic Church which celebrated the centenary of the restoration of the Hierarchy in 1978, had in Scotland (2005) one cardinal archbishop, one archbishop, six bishops, two bishops emeriti, 29 permanent deacons, 822 clergy, 472 parishes and 750,000 adherents.

The proportion of marriages in Scotland according to the rites of the various Churches in 2004 was: Church of Scotland, 29·6%; Roman Catholic, 6·1%; Baptist Union of Scotland, 1·2%; United Free Church of Scotland, 0·9%; others, 12·7%; civil, 49·5%.

CULTURE

Press

Average daily circulation in Jan. 2005 for the daily *Scotsman* was 69,771 and the *Daily Record* 471,708; and for *Scotland on Sunday* 81,475 and the *Sunday Mail* 585,657.

Tourism

There were 1,589,000 overseas visitors to Scotland in 2001, spending £757m. Overall tourism receipts totalled £4·17bn. The tourist attraction receiving the most visitors is Edinburgh Castle, with 1,127,000 visits in 2001. In 2001 around 9% of the workforce was employed in the tourism industry.

Festivals

The Edinburgh Festival and the Fringe Festival both take place in Aug./early Sept. and are major international festivals of culture.

Museums and Galleries

The most visited museum is Kelvingrove Art Gallery and Museum in Glasgow, with 1,031,138 visits in 2001.

FURTHER READING

Scottish Executive. Scottish Economic Report. TSO (twice yearly).— *Scottish Abstract of Statistics.* TSO (annual)

Brown, A., *et al., Politics and Society in Scotland.* London, 1996
Bruce, D., *The Mark of the Scots.* Birch Lane Press, 1997
Dennistoun, R. and Linklater, M. (eds.) *Anatomy of Scotland.* Edinburgh, 1992
Devine, T. M. and Finlay, R. J. (eds.) *Scotland in the 20th Century.* Edinburgh Univ. Press, 1996
Harvie, C., *Scotland and Nationalism: Scottish Society and Politics, 1707–1994.* 2nd ed. London, 1994
Hunter, J., *A Dance Called America.* Edinburgh, 1997
Keay, J. and J., *Collins Encyclopedia of Scotland: The Story of a Nation.* London, 2000
Macleod, J., *Highlanders: A History of the Gaels.* London, 1997
Magnusson, M., *Scotland: The Story of a Nation.* London, 2000
McCaffrey, J. F., *Scotland in the Nineteenth Century.* London, 1998
Mitchell, James, *Governing Scotland.* Palgrave Macmillan, Basingstoke, 2003

WALES

KEY HISTORICAL EVENTS

After the Roman evacuation, Wales divided into tribal kingdoms. Cunedda Wledig, a prince from southern Scotland, founded a dynasty in the northwest region of Gwynedd—to become the focus for Welsh unity—while the Irish exerted an influence in the kingdom of Dyfed. Offa's Dyke, a defensive earthwork, was the dividing line between England and Wales. In the late 9th century the kings of southern Wales swore fealty to Alfred of Wessex, a relationship assumed by the English crown. Gruffudd ap Llywelyn of Gwynedd briefly united Wales from 1055–63. His death was followed by Norman expansion into southern Wales, where the Marcher lordships were created.

With the accession of Llywelyn the Great (1194–1240), the house of Gwynedd overcame rival claims from Powys and Deheubarth to forge a stable political state under English suzerainty. His grandson, Llywelyn ap Gruffydd (1246–82), was recognized as prince of Wales by Henry III but Llywelyn intrigued against Edward I, who reduced Gwynedd's hegemony. Wales was annexed and subdued by a network of castles. Edward's infant son, born at Caernarvon, was made prince of Wales.

Loyalty to Henry VIII, who was of Welsh descent, was rewarded with political influence. The Act of Union in 1536 made English law general, admitted Welsh representatives to Parliament and established the Council of Wales and the Marches.

TERRITORY AND POPULATION

At the census taken on 29 April 2001 the population was 2,903,085. The area of Wales is 20,732 sq. km. Population density, 2001 census: 140 per sq. km. Wales covers 8·5% of the total area of the United Kingdom.

Population at census day 2001:

Males	Females	Total
1,403,900	1,499,185	2,903,085

Population (present on census night) at the four previous decennial censuses:

1961	1971	1981	1991
2,644,023[1]	2,731,204[1]	2,790,500[2]	2,811,865

[1] Areas now recognized as Monmouthshire and small sections of various other counties formed the county of Monmouthshire in England until 1974. [2] The final count is believed to be over-stated as a result of an error in processing. The preliminary counts presented here rounded to the nearest hundred are thought to be more accurate.

Estimated population, mid-2004, 2,952,000. Cardiff, the capital and largest city, had a population in 2001 of 305,340; Swansea, the second largest city, had a population of 223,293 in 2001.

In 2001, 457,950 people aged three and over were able to speak, read and write Welsh. Households at the 2001 census: 1,276,000.

For further statistical information, see under Territory and Population, United Kingdom.

Wales is divided into 22 unitary authorities (cities and counties, counties and county boroughs).

Designations, areas and populations of the unitary authority areas at census day 2001:

Unitary Authority	Designation	Area (sq. km)	Population
Blaenau Gwent	County Borough	109	70,058
Bridgend	County Borough	251	128,650

Unitary Authority	Designation	Area (sq. km)	Population
Caerphilly	County Borough	278	169,521
Cardiff	City and County	139	305,340
Carmarthenshire	County	2,394	173,635
Ceredigion	County	1,792	75,384
Conwy	County Borough	1,126	109,597
Denbighshire	County	837	93,092
Flintshire	County	438	148,565
Gwynedd	County	2,535	116,838
Isle of Anglesey	County	711	66,828
Merthyr Tydfil	County Borough	111	55,983
Monmouthshire	County	849	84,879
Neath and Port Talbot	County Borough	441	134,471
Newport	County Borough	190	137,017
Pembrokeshire	County	1,589	112,901
Powys	County	5,181	126,344
Rhondda Cynon Taff	County Borough	424	231,952
Swansea	City and County	378	223,293
The Vale of Glamorgan	County Borough	331	119,500
Torfaen	County Borough	126	90,967
Wrexham	County Borough	504	128,477

SOCIAL STATISTICS

2002: births, 30,205 (10·4 per 1,000 population); deaths, 33,172 (11·4 per 1,000 population); marriages (2000), 14,125 (4·9 per 1,000 population); divorces (2000), 7,704; still births, 164 (5 per 1,000 births); infant mortality, 142 (5 per 1,000 live births).

CLIMATE

For more detailed information, see under Climate, United Kingdom.

Cardiff, Jan. 40°F (4·4°C), July 61°F (16·1°C). Annual rainfall 42·6" (1,065 mm).

CONSTITUTION AND GOVERNMENT

One of the main aspects of the British Labour government's programme of constitutional reform is devolution. On 18 Sept. 1997 in the referendum there were 559,419 votes cast in favour of a Welsh assembly (50·3%) and 552,698 against (49·7%). The turnout was 51·3%.

RECENT ELECTIONS

At the UK general election in May 2005, 40 members were returned from Wales. Labour won 29 seats (34 in 2001), Liberal Democrats 4 seats (2), Plaid Cymru 3 seats (4), Conservatives 3 seats (0), others 1 seat.

At the 2004 European Parliamentary elections, 2 Labour candidates were elected, 1 Conservative and 1 Plaid Cymru.

In the elections to the Welsh Assembly on 1 May 2003, Labour won 30 seats (all constituencies), followed by Plaid Cymru with 12 (7 by regional list), the Conservatives with 11 (10 by regional list), the Liberal Democrats with 6 (3 by regional list) and 1 independent constituency. Of the 60 seats, 40 seats were won on a first-past-the-post basis and 20 through proportional representation (regional list). 30 seats were won by women. Turnout was 38%.

See also Constitution and Government, Recent Elections and Current Administration in United Kingdom.

CURRENT ADMINISTRATION

First Secretary: Rhodri Morgan; b. 1939 (Labour).
Presiding Officer: Dafydd Elis-Thomas.

National Assembly for Wales: http://www.wales.gov.uk

DEFENCE

For information on defence, see United Kingdom.

ECONOMY

For information on the economy, see United Kingdom.

ENERGY AND NATURAL RESOURCES

For information on energy and natural resources, see United Kingdom.

Water

The Water Act of Sept. 1989 privatized Welsh Water (Dŵr Cymru Cyfyngedig), along with the nine water authorities in England.

Agriculture

In 2002 there were 36,743 agricultural holdings. Of these, 4,584 were under 2 ha., 11,448 were between 2 and 19 ha., 4,254 were between 20 and 39 ha. and 10,527 were over 40 ha. In total, 5,660 were rough-grazing holdings.

The area of tillage in 2002 was 64,800 ha. (64,100 ha. for crops and 700 ha. bare fallow). Major crops, 2001 provisional (1,000 tonnes): barley, 152; wheat, 80; potatoes, 73; oats, 19.

Livestock, 2002: sheep and lambs, 10,050,100; cattle, 1,195,100; pigs, 44,300; poultry, 6,072,000.

Forestry

In 2003 there were 110,000 ha. of Forestry Commission woodland and 176,000 ha. of non-Forestry Commission woodland.

Fisheries

The major fishing port is Milford Haven. In 2002, in all ports, 17,395 tonnes of fish worth £11,479,000 were landed. There were 500 fishing vessels registered in Wales in 2002.

INDUSTRY

Selected industrial production (gross value added), 2000, provisional (£1m.): textiles and textile products, 1,819; basic metals and fabricated metal products, 1,358; electrical and optical equipment, 1,308; chemicals, chemical products and man-made fibres, 819; food products, beverages and tobacco, 791; transport equipment, 786.

Labour

At Dec. 2002 the workforce numbered 1,291,100. There were 45,500 people claiming unemployment benefit and 162,000 people were self-employed. The largest employment sectors in 2001 were: public administration, education and health, 341,800; distribution, hotels and restaurants, 259,400; manufacturing, 189,000. As a proportion of total employees, 75·9% of the active workforce were in service industries. The unemployment rate in 2002 was 5·6%, compared to 5·1% for the UK as a whole. In 2002, 80,100 working days were lost due to industrial disputes.

INTERNATIONAL TRADE

For information on international trade, see United Kingdom.

COMMUNICATIONS

Roads

Responsibility for the construction and maintenance of trunk roads belongs to the Welsh Office. Roads not classified as trunk roads are the responsibility of county or unitary councils. In 2003 there were 133 km of motorway, 1,576 km of trunk roads and 2,711 km of principal roads. 1,433,300 vehicles were registered in 2001, including 1,288,000 private and light goods vehicles. In 2002 there were 9,700 reported accidents which led to 14,336 casualties and 147 deaths.

Civil Aviation

Cardiff Airport handled 1,524,332 passengers in 2001 (1,410,974 on international flights) and 1,137 tonnes of freight.

Shipping

The principal ports are (with 1m. tonnes of cargo handled in 2004): Milford Haven (38·5) and Port Talbot (8·6).

Postal Services

Royal Mail employs 6,500 people in Wales and delivers to 1·5m. addresses. In 2000–01 the Post Office handled 490·8m. letters and 0·7m. parcels.

SOCIAL INSTITUTIONS

Justice

In March 2002 police strength amounted to 7,194. During the financial year 2000–01 there were 238,445 notable offences, including 38,230 violent and 1,698 sexual offences. The clear-up rate was 40·8%. 17,643 people were found guilty of indictable offences in Magistrates' Courts in 2001 and 4,106 in Crown Courts.

Education

There were 34 maintained nursery schools in Jan. 2004, and 63,712 pupils under five years provided for in nursery schools and in nursery or infants classes in primary schools.

In Jan. 2004 there were 273,961 pupils at 1,588 primary schools. Within these figures, 448 primary schools use Welsh as the sole or main medium of instruction. Such schools are to be found in all parts of Wales but are mainly concentrated in the predominantly Welsh-speaking areas of west and northwest Wales. Generally, children transfer from primary to secondary schools at 11 years of age.

In Jan. 2004 there were 227 secondary schools. All maintained secondary schools are classified as comprehensive; there are no middle schools in Wales. In 2003–04, 54 of the secondary schools were classed as Welsh-speaking as defined in section 354(b) of the Education Act 1996.

Since Sept. 1999, in accordance with the Schools Standards and Framework Act 1998, all maintained schools, including grant maintained schools, in Wales had to change category to one of the following: Community, Community Special, Foundation, Voluntary Controlled, Voluntary Aided. These categories continue to remain in place with the introduction of the Education Act 2002.

Under the Education Act 1996, children have special educational needs if they have a learning difficulty which calls for special educational provision to be made for them. In a minority of cases the local education authority will need to make a statutory assessment of special educational needs under the Education Act 1996, which may ultimately lead to a 'statement of Special Educational Needs'. The total number of pupils with statements in Jan. 2004 was 16,959. From April 2002 Special Educational Needs (SEN) guidance for Wales is set out in the SEN Code of Practice for Wales.

In Jan. 2004, 9,616 full-time pupils attended 60 independent schools.

Post-16 Learning. The National Council for Education and Training Wales (ELWa) was formed from the merger of the four TECs (training and enterprise councils), the Council of Welsh TECs and Further Education Funding Council for Wales (FEFCW) and has been operational since April 2001. It is responsible for the planning and promoting of further, adult and continuing education, work-based training and school sixth forms. The cash grant in aid allocation for 2002–03 was £488·9m. In 2001–02 the FEFCW supported 42,923 full-time and sandwich students and 217,036 students studying part-time in the further education sector at 26 further education institutions and ten higher education institutions. In addition, in 2001–02 ELWa supported 35,520 starts in work-based training or with training to return to the workplace. In 2001, 12% of 16- to 18-year-olds did not have a qualification; five percentage points lower than in 1996. The percentage of adults with no qualification fell from 23% in 1996 to 21% in 2001; and 40% of adults had an NVQ level three or equivalent, up from 35% in 1996. Between 1996 and 1999 it was estimated that around seven in ten adults had functional basis skills in either literacy or numeracy. In 2004 approximately 75% of adults had functional basic skills in literacy and 47% in numeracy.

Higher Education. In 2002–03 there were 13 institutions of higher education funded directly by the Higher Education Funding Council for Wales (HEFCW), including the University of Glamorgan and the colleges of the University of Wales. In 2002–03 the total budget was £327·44m. There were 126,209 students in the higher education sector in 2002–03, excluding those registered with the Open University, of which 71,893 were full-time and 54,316 part-time students, excluding those enrolled on higher education provision at further education colleges.

Higher Education Institutes (HEIs)	Full-time/sandwich HE students at HEIs (2002–03)	No. of academic staff (2002–03)[1]
Univ. of Glamorgan (Pontypridd)	10,247	758
Univ. of Wales, Aberystwyth	6,991	573
Univ. of Wales, Bangor	7,229	719
Cardiff University[2]	16,980	1,835
Univ. of Wales, Lampeter	1,064	102
Univ. of Wales College, Newport	2,925	261
Univ. of Wales, Swansea	8,912	881
Univ. of Wales College of Medicine	2,404	796
Univ. of Wales Institute, Cardiff	6,797	387
North East Wales Institute of Higher Education (Wrexham)	2,636	191
Royal Welsh College of Music and Drama	552	66
Swansea Institute of Higher Education	3,459	200
Trinity College Carmarthen	1,310	81

[1]Staff who meet the 25% full-time equivalent threshold.
[2]The public name of the University of Wales, Cardiff.

Health

In 2000–01 there were 1,903 GPs, 1,015 dentists and 24,314 nurses, midwives and health visitors. The average daily number of hospital beds available in 2000–01 was 14,600, of which 11,700 were occupied. 514,700 in-patient cases were reported, with stays lasting an average 8·3 days. 61,100 people were on hospital waiting lists.

Welfare

In 2001, 569,000 people received retirement pensions and contributory old-age pensions; 359,000 families received child benefit; and 236,000 people received some form of income support.

RELIGION

Under the Welsh Church Acts, 1914 and 1919, the Church in Wales and Monmouthshire was disestablished as from 1 April 1920, and Wales was formed into a separate Province.

CULTURE

Broadcasting

Radio and television services are provided by the Welsh-language Sianel Pedwar Cymru (S4C, Channel 4 Wales). S4C is funded by the government. It acts as both broadcaster and regulator. In 2000–01 there were 1,150,100 television licenses, of which 1,143,500 were colour.

Tourism

In 2004 there were some 9m. domestic trips (from elsewhere in the UK) into Wales. Visitors stayed 31·5m. nights and spent £1·5bn.

Festivals

Every year there are local and national *eisteddfods* (festivals for musical competitions, etc.). The National Eisteddfod of Wales takes place every Aug. alternating between north and south Wales. In 2007 it will be held at Mold.

Libraries

In 2001–02 there were 913 libraries with 5,068,000 books. 1,161,000 items were borrowed. The National Library is in Aberystwyth.

Theatre and Opera

There is a Welsh National Opera and the BBC National Orchestra of Wales.

Museums and Galleries

The leading museum is the National History Museum, St Fagans, Cardiff, which received 631,731 visits in 2004.

FURTHER READING

National Assembly. Digest of Welsh Statistics. National Statistics. Great Britain (annual)

Andrews, Leighton, *Wales Says Yes. The Inside Story of the Yes for Wales Referendum Campaign.* Seren, Bridgend, 1999

Davies, J., *History of Wales.* London, 1993

History of Wales. vols. 3, 4 (1415–1780). 2nd ed. OUP, 1993

Jenkins, G. H., *The Foundations of Modern Wales 1642–1780.* Oxford, 1988.—*The Welsh Language and its Social Domains 1801–1911: A Social History of the Welsh Language.* Univ. of Wales Press, 2000

Jones, G. E., *Modern Wales: a Concise History.* 2nd ed. CUP, 1994

May, J. (ed.) *Reference Wales.* Wales Univ. Press, 1994

Morgan, K. and Mungham, G., *Redesigning Democracy. The Making of the Welsh Assembly.* Seren, Bridgend, 2000

NORTHERN IRELAND

KEY HISTORICAL EVENTS

The Government of Ireland Act 1920 granted Northern Ireland its own bicameral parliament (Stormont). The rejection of home rule by the rest of Ireland (which pursued independence) forced a separation along primarily religious lines, with a large Catholic minority in the six northern counties. Between 1921–72 Stormont had full responsibility for local affairs except for taxation and customs; Northern Ireland was on the whole neglected by Westminster, allowing the virtual exclusion of Catholics from political office. The (predominantly Protestant) Unionist government ignored demands from London and the Catholic community to end communal discrimination.

In the late 1960s a Civil Rights campaign and reactions to it escalated into serious rioting and sectarian violence involving the Irish Republican Army (IRA, a terrorist organization aiming to unify Northern Ireland with the Republic of Ireland) and loyalist paramilitary organizations, such as the Ulster Defence Association. The British Army was deployed to protect civilians and was at first welcomed by the Catholic community. However, British soldiers shot dead 13 Catholic civil rights protesters in (London)Derry on 30 Jan. 1972—'Bloody Sunday'—prompting the Republic of Ireland's foreign minister to demand United Nations intervention. 467 people died in 1972, on account of 'the Troubles', and nearly 1,800 between 1971–77. The Northern Ireland government resigned and direct rule from Westminster was imposed.

Attempts have been made by successive governments to find a means of restoring greater power to Northern Ireland's political representatives on a widely acceptable basis, including a Constitutional Convention (1975–76), a Constitutional Conference (1979–80) and 78-member Northern Ireland Assembly elected by proportional representation in 1982. This was dissolved in 1986, partly in response to Unionist reaction to the Anglo-Irish Agreement signed on 15 Nov. 1985, which established an Intergovernmental Conference of British and Irish ministers to monitor issues of concern to the nationalist community. The Provisional IRA bombing of a Remembrance Day service in Enniskillen in 1987 killed 11. Universally condemned, it galvanized the anti-violence campaign.

On 15 Dec. 1993 the British and Irish prime ministers, John Major and Albert Reynolds, issued a joint declaration as a basis for all-party talks to achieve a political settlement. They invited Sinn Féin, the political wing of the IRA, to join the talks in an All-Ireland Forum after the cessation of terrorist violence. The IRA announced 'a complete cessation of military operations' on 31 Aug. 1994. On 13 Oct. 1994 the anti-IRA Combined Loyalist Military Command also announced a ceasefire 'dependent upon the continued cessation of all nationalist republican violence'.

Elections were held on 30 May 1996 to constitute a 110-member forum to take part in talks with the British and Irish

governments. The Ulster Unionist Party won 30 seats, the Social Democratic and Labour Party 21 seats, the Democratic Unionist Party 24 seats and Sinn Féin 17 seats. Opening plenary talks, excluding Sinn Féin, began under the chairmanship of US Senator George Mitchell on 12 June 1996. A marathon negotiating struggle on 9–10 April 1998 led to agreement on a framework for sharing power designed to satisfy Protestant demands for a reaffirmation of their national identity as British, Catholic desires for a closer relationship with the Republic of Ireland and Britain's wish to return to Northern Ireland the powers London assumed in 1972.

Under the Good Friday Agreement, there was to be a democratically elected legislature in Belfast, a ministerial council giving the governments of Northern Ireland and Ireland joint responsibilities in areas like tourism, transportation and the environment, and a consultative council meeting twice a year to bring together ministers from the British and Irish parliaments, and the three assemblies being created in Northern Ireland and in Scotland and Wales. The Irish government eliminated from its constitution its territorial claim on Northern Ireland.

In the referendum on 22 May 1998, 71·1% of votes in Northern Ireland were cast in favour of the Good Friday peace agreement and 94·4% in the Republic of Ireland. As a consequence, in June, Northern Ireland's 1·2m. voters elected the first power-sharing administration since the collapse of the Sunningdale Agreement in 1974.

On 15 Aug. 1998 a 200 kg bomb exploded in the centre of Omagh. The dissident republican group the 'Real IRA' claimed responsibility. 29 people died and over 200 were injured, making it the single bloodiest incident of the Troubles—about 3,300 deaths had been recorded since the Troubles began by the end of 1998.

In Nov. 1999 the Mitchell talks finally produced an agreement between the Ulster Unionists and Sinn Féin, paving the way for devolved government. The new Northern Ireland Assembly met on 29 Nov. 1999 and on 2 Dec. legislative powers were fully devolved from London to Belfast. However, on 11 Feb. 2000 the Assembly was suspended following a breakdown in negotiations on the decommissioning of IRA weapons. Direct rule from London was restored. Devolved government resumed on 30 May after the IRA agreed to open their arms dumps to independent inspection.

First Minister David Trimble resigned on 30 June 2001 to pressure republicans over decommissioning but on 22 Oct. Sinn Féin president Gerry Adams announced that he had recommended a 'ground-breaking' step on the arms issue. The IRA made a start on decommissioning arms, ammunition and explosives. David Trimble was re-elected first minister on 6 Nov. 2001.

On 15 Oct. 2002 the Assembly executive was again suspended over allegations of IRA spying at the Northern Ireland Office. Direct rule from London was re-imposed and on 30 Oct. the IRA cut off its links with the weapons decommissioning body. The Ulster Volunteer Force followed suit on 17 Jan. 2003. Elections for the Northern Ireland Assembly took place on 26 Nov. 2003. The theft of £26·5m. from the Northern Bank in Belfast in Dec. 2004 suggested closer than acknowledged associations between Sinn Féin and the IRA. Controversy surrounding the raid put the peace process on hold. In July 2005 the IRA formally announced an end to its armed campaign. In Sept. 2005 it claimed to have destroyed its arsenal of weapons.

TERRITORY AND POPULATION

Area (revised by Ordnance Survey of Northern Ireland) and population were as follows:

District	Mid-year population estimates 2002	Area in ha. (including inland water)
Antrim	48,877	57,686
Ards	74,079	37,619
Armagh	54,958	67,060
Ballymena	58,953	63,202
Ballymoney	27,478	41,820
Banbridge	42,356	45,263
Belfast	274,114	11,488
Carrickfergus	38,109	8,184
Castlereagh	66,329	8,514
Coleraine	56,181	48,551
Cookstown	33,039	62,244
Craigavon	81,500	37,842
Derry (Londonderry)	106,193	38,731
Down	64,836	64,670
Dungannon	48,232	78,360
Fermanagh	58,148	187,582
Larne	30,944	33,567
Limavady	33,210	58,558
Lisburn	109,384	44,684
Magherafelt	40,400	57,280
Moyle	16,244	47,976
Newry and Mourne	88,549	90,243
Newtownabbey	80,218	15,056
North Down	76,984	8,149
Omagh	48,919	113,045
Strabane	38,407	86,165
Northern Ireland	*1,696,641*	*1,413,540*

Northern Ireland's area of 14,135 sq. km represents 5·8% of the total area of the United Kingdom. Chief town (mid-year estimate, 2002): Belfast, 274,114.

Population by gender at the 2002 mid-year estimate was: females, 51·26%; males, 48·74%.

SOCIAL STATISTICS

In 2002 there were 21,385 births, 14,586 deaths, 7,599 marriages and 2,165 divorces.

CLIMATE

For more detailed information, see under Climate, United Kingdom.

Belfast, Jan. 40°F (4·5°C), July 59°F (15·0°C). Annual rainfall 37·4" (950 mm).

CONSTITUTION AND GOVERNMENT

Under the Northern Ireland Act 1998 power that was previously exercised by the NI Departments was devolved to the Northern Ireland Assembly and its Executive Committee of Ministers. The Secretary of State remains responsible for those matters specified in Schedules 2 and 3 of the Act. These broadly equate to policing, security policing, criminal justice, and international relations.

The Parliamentary electorate of Northern Ireland in the register in Dec. 2004 numbered 1,045,537.

Secretary of State for Northern Ireland. Peter Hain.

RECENT ELECTIONS

At the general election of 5 May 2005, 18 members were returned from Northern Ireland. The Democratic Unionist Party won 9 seats (5 in 2001); Sinn Féin 5 (4); the Social and Democratic Labour Party 3 (3); the Ulster Unionist Party 1 (6).

In the Northern Ireland Assembly elections on 26 Nov. 2003 the Democratic Unionist Party won 30 of the 108 seats, the Ulster Unionist Party 27, Sinn Féin 24, the Social Democratic and Labour Party 18, Alliance Party of Northern Ireland 6, Progressive Unionist Party 1, United Kingdom Unionist Party 1, ind. 1. Turnout was 63·1%.

At the June 2004 European Parliament elections, voting was by the single transferable vote system: the Democratic Ulster Unionist Party (32·0%), Sinn Féin (26·3%) and the Ulster Unionist Party (Popular European Party) (16·6%) gained 1 seat each. Turnout was 51·2%.

CURRENT ADMINISTRATION

David Trimble (Ulster Unionist Party) was elected as the Northern Ireland Assembly's 'First Minister' on 6 Nov. 2001 at a special meeting of the Assembly, having resigned from the post on 30 June 2001. Mark Durkan (Social Democratic and Labour Party) was elected deputy first minister. They were joint leaders of the administration. The Assembly has been suspended since Oct. 2002.

Northern Ireland Executive: http://www.nics.gov.uk

ECONOMY

Overview

The Northern Ireland government Department of Enterprise, Trade and Investment (DETI) is responsible for economic policy development, energy, tourism, mineral development, health and safety at work, Companies Registry, Insolvency Service, consumer affairs, and labour market and economic statistics services. DETI has four agencies: Invest Northern Ireland (Invest NI), the Northern Ireland Tourist Board (NITB), the Health and Safety Executive for Northern Ireland (HSENI) and the General Consumer Council for Northern Ireland (GCCNI).

Currency

Banknotes are issued by Allied Irish Banks, Bank of Ireland, First Trust Bank, Northern Bank and Ulster Bank.

Banking and Finance

The Department of Finance and Personnel is responsible for control of the expenditure of Northern Ireland departments, involving liaison with HM Treasury, the European Commission and the Northern Ireland Office on financial matters, economic and social research and analysis; to review and develop rating policy and legislation; procurement for the Northern Ireland public sector; formulation of policy for central personnel management, and legal services, including law reform. The Department's Agencies are: Business Development Service; Land Registers NI; Northern Ireland Statistics and Research Agency; Rate Collection Agency and Valuation and Lands Agency.

Income of the Northern Ireland Consolidated Fund (in £1,000 sterling):

	2000–01	2001–02	2002–03
Attributed share of UK taxes			
Grant in Aid from UK government	7,405,400[1]	7,998,998[1]	7,799,000[1]
Regional and district rates	544,600	568,184	609,163
Other receipts	547,028	404,257	385,400
Total	8,497,028	8,971,439	8,793,563

[1]In 2000–01 the funding mechanism was changed to replace the 'Grant in Aid' and 'Attributed share of UK taxation' with a 'Block Grant'.

The public debt at 31 March 2003 was as follows: Ulster Savings Certificates, £13,926,000; Ulster Development Bonds, £12,239,000; borrowing from UK government, £1,380,424,832; borrowing from Northern Ireland government funds, £206,410,359. Excess of public income over public expenditure at 31 March 2003: £453,391,609. Net assets available for debt repayment: £517,176,241.

The above amount of public debt is offset by equal assets in the form of loans from government to public and local bodies, and of cash balances.

ENERGY AND NATURAL RESOURCES

Electricity

There are three power stations with an installed capacity of some 2,100 MW.

In addition, electricity is also supplied through a 500 MW interconnector linking the Northern Ireland Electricity (NIE) and Scottish Power networks and a number of interconnectors linking the NIE network with the Electricity Supply Board (ESB) network in the Republic of Ireland.

Oil and Gas

In Sept. 2001 the Northern Ireland executive approved grant support for the development of the gas network outside the Greater Belfast area, to the North/North West region and for the construction of a South/North pipeline. The North West gas pipeline supplies gas for the Combined Cycle Turbine power station at Coolkeeragh outside Londonderry, which opened in June 2005. The South/North pipeline is scheduled to be completed by the end of 2006. Negotiations are ongoing to grant a license to supply gas to the major towns along the route of both these.

Minerals

Output of minerals (in 1,000 tonnes), 2002: basalt and igneous rock (other than granite), 6,681; sandstone, 6,574; sand and gravel, 5,512; limestone, 4,514; other minerals (rocksalt, fireclay, diatomite, granite, chalk, clay and shale), 242. There are lignite deposits of 1,000m. tonnes which have not yet been developed.

Agriculture

Provisional gross output in 2001:

	Quantity	Value (£1m.)
Cattle and calves	547,500	371·4
Sheep and lambs	864,000	59·3
Pigs	940,500	58·7
Poultry (1,000 tonnes)	184·3	115·4
Eggs (m. dozen)	64·9	24·2
Milk (1m. litres)	1,780·0	292·3
Other livestock products	—	8·0
Cereals (1,000 tonnes)	181·9	20·7
Potatoes (1,000 tonnes)	254·4	23·9
Fruit (1,000 tonnes)	37·1	3·0
Vegetables (1,000 tonnes)	49·0	14·9
Mushrooms (1,000 tonnes)	24·0	27·6
Other crops	—	6·9
Flowers, ornamentals and nursery stock	—	13·1
Capital formation	—	48·8
Contract work	—	35·8
Other items	—	18·0
Gross output	—	1,141·9

Area (in 1,000 ha.) on farms:

	2001	2002	2003
Cereals	40	38	38
Potatoes	7	7	6
Horticulture	3	3	3
Other crops	5	5	6
Grass	840	844	848
Rough grazing	154	152	153
Other land	20	19	20
Total area	1,068	1,067	1,074

Livestock (in 1,000 heads) on farms at June census:

	2001	2002	2003
Dairy cows	295	298	290
Beef cows	312	307	295
Other cattle	1,072	1,080	1,100
Ewes	1,232	1,129	1,106
Sows	41	39	43
Laying hens	2,143	2,099	2,203
Broilers	8,864	11,273	12,811

INDUSTRY

Labour

The main sources of employment statistics are the Census of Employment, conducted every two years, and the Quarterly Employment Survey. In Dec. 1999 there were 625,030 employees, of whom 309,010 were males. Employment in manufacturing and construction amounted to 137,340, 22% of the total employees in employment. 19,400 of these jobs were in the food, drink and tobacco industries, 9,360 in the manufacture of wearing apparel, 9,100 in textiles, 30,840 in construction and 68,640 in other sectors of manufacturing. Unemployment in the spring of 2003, at 5·2%, was the lowest in more than 25 years.

COMMUNICATIONS

Roads

In April 2003 the total length of public roads was 24,825 km, graded for administrative purposes as follows: motorway, 133 km (including 19 km slip roads); Class '1' dual carriageway, 150 km; Class '1' single carriageway, 2,113 km; Class '2', 2,869 km; Class '3', 4,705 km; unclassified, 14,874 km.

The Northern Ireland Transport Holding Company (NITHC) oversees the provision of public transport services in Northern Ireland. Its subsidiary companies, Ulsterbus, Citybus and Northern Ireland Railways, are responsible for the delivery of most bus and rail services under the brand name of Translink.

At 31 March 2000 there were 1,963 professional hauliers and 5,322 vehicles licensed to engage in road haulage.

The number of motor vehicles licensed at 31 Dec. 2002 was 794,477, including private light goods, 666,731; goods vehicles, 20,244; motorcycles, scooters and mopeds, 17,598.

Rail

Northern Ireland Railways, a subsidiary of the Northern Ireland Transport Holding Company, provides rail services within Northern Ireland and cross-border services to Dublin, jointly with Irish Rail. The number of track km operated is 340. In 2002–03 railways carried 6·3m. passengers, generating passenger receipts of £15·4m.

Civil Aviation

There are scheduled air services to three airports in Northern Ireland: Belfast International, George Best (Belfast City) and City of Derry. Scheduled services are provided by easyJet, bmibaby (British Midland), British Airways' franchise partners and British European (Flybe), Eastern Airways, My Travel Lite, Cityexpress and Flykeen. In 2002–03 the airports collectively handled approximately 6m. passengers. Belfast International, the busiest airport, is Northern Ireland's main charter airport with holiday flights operated direct to European destinations by a wide range of local and UK tour operators. Belfast International handled 3·7m. passengers in 2003.

Belfast City Airport offers commuter services to 16 regional airports in Great Britain including services to London Heathrow.

The City of Derry Airport is situated 14 km from Londonderry and provides services from the northwest of Ireland to Dublin and to two United Kingdom destinations (Glasgow and London Stansted). There are two other licensed airfields at St Angelo and Newtownards. They are used principally by flying clubs, private owners and air taxi businesses.

Shipping

There are five commercial ports in Northern Ireland. Belfast is the largest port, competing with Larne for the majority of the passenger and Roll-on Roll-off services that operate to and from Northern Ireland. Passenger services are currently available to Liverpool, Stranraer, Cairnryan and Troon. In addition, Belfast, Londonderry and Warrenpoint ports offer bulk cargo services mostly for British and European markets. They also occasionally service other international destinations direct.

Total tonnage of goods through the principal ports in Northern Ireland in 2004 was 23·4m. tonnes. Belfast handled 13·6m. tonnes of cargo in 2004.

SOCIAL INSTITUTIONS

Justice

The Lord Chancellor has responsibility for the administration of all courts through the Northern Ireland Court Service and for the appointment of judges and magistrates. The court structure has three tiers: the Supreme Court of Judicature of Northern Ireland (comprising the Court of Appeal, the High Court and the Crown Court), the County Courts and the Magistrates' Courts. There are 20 Petty Sessions districts which when grouped together for administration purposes form seven County Court Divisions and four Crown Court Circuits.

The County Court has general civil jurisdiction subject to an upper monetary limit. Appeals from the Magistrates' Courts lie to the County Court, or to the Court of Appeal on a point of law, while appeals from the County Court lie to the High Court or, on a point of law, to the Court of Appeal.

Police

Following legislation introduced in the House of Commons in May 2000, the Royal Ulster Constabulary has been replaced by the Police Service of Northern Ireland (PSNI). The Police Authority for Northern Ireland has been replaced by the newly formed Northern Ireland Policing Board. The Police Service continues to undergo significant changes arising from the recommendations of the Commission into the future of policing in Northern Ireland published in 1999. In 2003 the PSNI comprised 7,336 regular officers including those student officers undergoing training, 1,645 full-time reserve officers and 888 part-time reserves. The proportion of Catholic regular officers, which was around 8% in Sept. 1999, had increased to 13·9% by Dec. 2003.

The population in penal institutions in Nov. 2003 was 1,220 (70 per 100,000 population).

Education

Public education, other than university education, is presently administered by the Department of Education, the Department of Employment and Learning, and locally by five Education and Library Boards. The Department of Education is concerned with the range of education from nursery education through to secondary, youth services and for the development of community relations within and between schools. The Department of Employment and Learning is responsible for higher education, further education, student support, postgraduate awards, and the funding of teacher training.

Each Education and Library Board is the local education authority for its area. Boards were first appointed in 1973, the year of local government reorganization, and are normally reappointed every four years following the District Council elections. The membership of each Board consists of District councillors, representatives of transferors of schools, representatives of trustees of maintained schools and other persons who are interested in the service for which the Board is responsible. Boards have a duty, amongst other things, to ensure that there are sufficient schools of all kinds to meet the needs of their areas. The Boards are responsible for costs associated with capital works at controlled schools. Voluntary schools, including maintained and voluntary grammar schools, can receive grant-aid from the Department of Education toward capital works of up to 85%, or 100% if they have opted to change their management structures so that no single interest group has a majority of nominees. Most voluntary grammar schools can receive the same rate of grant on the purchase of equipment. The Boards award university and other scholarships; they provide school milk and meals; free books and assisted transport for certain pupils; they enforce school attendance; provide a curriculum advisory and support service to all schools in their area; regulate the employment of children and young people; and secure the provision of youth and recreational facilities. They are also required to develop a comprehensive and efficient library service for their area. Board expenditure is funded at 100% by the Department of Education. Integrated schools receive 100% funding for recurrent costs from the Department of Education, and, where long-term viability has been established, for capital works.

The Education Reform (NI) Order 1989 made provision for the setting up of a Council for Catholic Maintained Schools with effect from April 1990. The Council has responsibility for all maintained schools under Roman Catholic Management which are under the auspices of the diocesan authorities and of religious orders. The main objective of the Council is to promote high standards of education in the schools for which it is responsible. Its functions include providing advice on matters relating to its schools, the employment of teaching staff and administration of appointment procedures, the promotion of effective management, and the promotion and co-ordination of effective planning and rationalization of school provision in the Catholic Maintained sector. The membership of the Council consists of trustee representatives appointed by the Northern Roman Catholic Bishops, parents, teachers, and persons appointed by the Head of the Department of Education in consultation with the Bishops.

There is a Council for the Curriculum, Examinations and Assessment which conducts public examinations and oversees the selection procedure and arrangements for pupil assessment. There is also the Northern Ireland Council for Integrated Education, both of which are grant-aided by the Department of Education.

Integrated Schools. The Department of Education has a statutory duty to encourage and facilitate the development of integrated education. It does not seek to impose integration but responds to parental demand for new integrated schools where this does not involve unreasonable public expenditure. The emphasis for future development of the integrated sector has increasingly been on the transformation of existing schools to integrated status. In Dec. 2003 there were 50 grant-aided integrated schools, with a total enrolment of 16,494 pupils, about 5% of all pupils.

Irish Medium Education. Following a commitment in the Belfast Agreement, the 1998 Education Order placed a statutory duty on the Department to encourage and facilitate the development of Irish-medium education. It also provided for the funding of an Irish-medium promotional body, and funding of Irish-medium schools on the same basis as integrated schools. In Dec. 2003 there were 14 Irish-medium primary schools, one post-primary and twelve units, two of which are post-primary catering for 2,455 pupils.

Pre-school Education. Pre-school Education is provided in nursery schools or nursery classes in primary schools, reception classes and in funded places in voluntary and private settings.

There were 100 nursery schools in 2002–03 with 6,269 pupils, and 7,823 nursery pupils in primary schools. A further 1,180 reception pupils were enrolled in primary schools. In addition there were 5,804 children in funded places in voluntary and private pre-school centres.

Primary Education. Primary Education is from four to 11 years. In 2002–03 there were 897 primary schools with 165,179 pupils. There were also 20 preparatory departments of grammar schools with 2,620 pupils. In 2002–03 there were 8,753 FTE primary school teachers and 154 FTE preparatory department teachers.

Secondary Education. Secondary Education is from 11 to 18 years. In 2002–03 there were 71 grammar schools with 63,102 pupils and 164 secondary schools with 92,645 pupils. In 2002–03 there were 6,722 FTE secondary school teachers and 4,118 FTE grammar school teachers.

Further Education. There are 16 institutions of further education. In 2001–02 there were 1,815 full-time and 3,113 part-time teachers, approximately 25,000 full-time enrolments, approximately 36,000 part-time enrolments and approximately 31,000 evening students on vocational courses. There were about 75,000 students on non-vocational (mostly evening) courses.

Special Education. The Education and Library Boards provide for children with special educational needs up to the age of 19. This provision may be made in ordinary classes in primary or secondary schools or in special units attached to those schools, or in special schools. In 1999–2000 there were 53 special schools with 4,861 pupils. This includes three hospital schools.

Universities. There are two universities: the Queen's University of Belfast (founded in 1849 as a college of the Queen's University of Ireland and reconstituted as a separate university in 1908) had 20,912 students, 1,514 full-time and 113 part-time academic staff in 2001–02. The University of Ulster, formed on 1 Oct. 1984, has campuses in Belfast, Coleraine, Jordanstown and Londonderry. In the 2001–02 academic year it had 21,223 students, 1,309 full-time and 93 part-time academic staff.

Full-Time Initial Teacher Education takes place at both universities and at two university colleges of education—Stranmillis and St Mary's—the latter mainly for the primary school sector, in respect of which four-year (Hons) BEd courses are available. The training of teachers for secondary schools is provided, in the main, in the education departments of the two universities, but four-year (Hons) BEd courses are also available in the colleges for intending secondary teachers of religious education, business studies and craft, design and technology. There were a total of 1,840 students (1,479 women) in training at the two university colleges and the two universities during 2001–02.

Health

The Department of Health and Social Services is responsible for the provision of integrated health and personal social services. Four Health and Social Services Boards are responsible for assessing the requirements of their resident populations and for purchasing appropriate services. Since 1 April 1996 services have been delivered exclusively by HSS Trusts (similar to NHS Trusts in the rest of the UK) established under the Health and Personal Social Services (NI) Order 1991.

A total of 19 HSS Trusts are fully operational. Seven HSS Trusts based on acute hospitals and the regional Northern Ireland Ambulance Service are identical in structure and management to NHS Trusts in Great Britain. Of the remaining 12, five provide community-based health and personal social services and six provide both hospital and community-based health and personal social services, reflecting the integrated nature of these services in Northern Ireland. In 2003 there were 1,083 doctors (principals), with an average of 1,647 patients each.

Welfare

The Social Security Agency's remit is now part of the Department for Social Development, and social security schemes are similar to those in Great Britain.

National Insurance. During the year ended 31 March 1999 the expenditure of the National Insurance Fund at £1,251·1m. exceeded contributions by £163·7m. The shortfall in income was made up by a Treasury Grant, investment income and a transfer from the Great Britain Fund. Total benefit expenditure was £1,177·9m., excluding £4·1m. which was subsequently recovered from damages paid to recipients of National Insurance Fund Benefits. Employers received £1m. reimbursement in respect of Statutory Sick Pay paid to their employees. £14·6m. was paid in Jobseekers' Allowance contributions. Widows Benefit amounted to £33·2m. and Retirement Pensions to £802·2m. Incapacity Benefits totalled £323·7m. Maternity Allowance of £1·1m. was paid and employers were reimbursed £17·6m. in respect of Statutory Maternity Pay. £39·3m. was given to personal pension plan providers.

Child Benefit. During the year ended 31 March 1999, £261·4m. was paid. *Income Support:* In 1998–99, £513·6m. was paid. *Family Credit:* In 1998–99, £98·0m. was paid.

RELIGION

According to the 2001 census there were: Roman Catholics, 678,462; Presbyterians, 348,742; Church of Ireland, 257,788; Methodists, 59,173; other Christian, 102,221; other religions and philosophies, 5,028. There were also 233,853 persons with no religion or religion was not stated.

CULTURE

Tourism

There were an estimated 1·74m. visits to Northern Ireland in 2002, contributing £274m. to the economy. Domestic holiday makers contributed a further £12m. The Northern Ireland Tourist Board is responsible for encouraging tourism. Nine Areas of Outstanding Natural Beauty and 47 Statutory Nature Reserves have been declared, and there are many country and regional parks.

FURTHER READING

Aughey, A. and Morrow, D. (eds.) *Northern Ireland Politics.* Harlow, 1996

Bloomfield, D., *Peacemaking Strategies in Northern Ireland.* London, 1998

Bourke, Richard, *Peace in Ireland: The War of Ideas.* Random House, London, 2003

Bow, P. and Gillespie, G., *Northern Ireland: a Chronology of the Troubles, 1968–1993.* Dublin, 1993

Dixon, Paul, *Northern Ireland: The Politics of War and Peace.* Palgrave, Basingstoke, 2001

Fay, Marie-Thérèse, Morrisey, Mike and Smyth, Marie, *Northern Ireland's Troubles.* Pluto Press, London, 1999

Fletcher, Martin, *Silver Linings: Travels Around Northern Ireland.* Little, Brown, London, 2000

Hennessey, T., *A History of Northern Ireland 1920–96.* London, 1998

Kennedy-Pipe, C., *The Origins of the Present Troubles in Northern Ireland.* Harlow, 1997

Loughlin, James, *The Ulster Question Since 1945.* Macmillan, London, 1998

McDonald, Henry, *Trimble.* Bloomsbury, London, 2000

McGarry, J. and O'Leary, B. (eds.) *Explaining Northern Ireland: Broken Images.* Oxford, 1995

Neumann, Peter R., *Britain's Long War: British Strategy in the Northern Ireland Conflict, 1969–98.* Palgrave Macmillan, Basingstoke, 2003

Rose, Peter, *How the Troubles Came to Northern Ireland.* Macmillan, London, 1999

Ruane, J. and Todd, J., *The Dynamics of Conflict in Northern Ireland: Power, Conflict and Emancipation.* CUP, 1997

Statistical office: Northern Ireland Statistics and Research Agency (NISRA).

Website: http://www.nisra.gov.uk

ISLE OF MAN

KEY HISTORICAL EVENTS

The Isle of Man was first inhabited approximately 10,000 years ago and the island became attached to Norway in the 9th century. In 1266 it was ceded to Scotland, but it came under English control in 1333.

The Isle of Man has been a British Crown dependency since 1765, with the British government responsible for its defence and foreign policy. Otherwise it has extensive right of self-government.

A special relationship exists between the Isle of Man and the European Union providing for free trade, and adoption by the Isle of Man of the EU's external trade policies with third countries. The island remains free to levy its own system of taxes.

TERRITORY AND POPULATION

Area, 572 sq. km (221 sq. miles); resident population census April 2001, 76,315, giving a density of 134 per sq. km. In 2001 an estimated 73% of the population lived in urban areas. The principal towns are Douglas (population, 25,308), Onchan (adjoining Douglas; 8,706), Ramsey (7,626), Peel (3,779) and Castletown (3,082). The island is divided into six sheadings— Ayre, Garff, Glenfaba, Michael, Middle and Rushen. Garff is further subdivided into two parishes and the others each have three parishes.

SOCIAL STATISTICS

2003: births, 860; deaths, 852; marriages (2002), 430. Annual growth rate, 1996–2001, 1·3%.

CLIMATE

Lying in the Irish Sea, the island's climate is temperate and lacking in extremes. Thunderstorms, snow and frost are infrequent, although the island tends to be windy. July and Aug. are the warmest months with an average daily maximum temperature of around 17·6°C (63°F).

CONSTITUTION AND GOVERNMENT

As a result of Revestment in 1765, the Isle of Man became a dependency of the British Crown. The UK government is responsible for the external relations of the island, including its defence and international affairs, and the island makes a financial contribution to the cost of these services. The Isle of Man has a special relationship with the European Union. It neither contributes funds to, nor receives money from, the EU. The Isle of Man is not represented in either the UK or European Parliaments.

The island is administered in accordance with its own laws by the High Court of *Tynwald*, consisting of the President of Tynwald, the *Legislative Council* and the *House of Keys*. The Legislative Council is composed of the Lord Bishop of Sodor and Man, eight members selected by the House of Keys and the Attorney General, who has no vote. The House of Keys is an assembly of 24 members chosen by adult suffrage. The President of Tynwald is chosen by the Legislative Council and the House of Keys, sitting together as Tynwald. An open-air Tynwald ceremony is held in early July each year at St Johns. Until 1990 the Lieut.-Governor, appointed by the UK government, presided over Tynwald.

A Council of Ministers was instituted in 1990, replacing the Executive Council which had acted as an advisory body to the Lieut.-Governor. The Council of Ministers consists of the Chief Minister (elected for a five-year term) and the ministers of the nine major departments, being the Treasury; Agriculture, Fisheries and Forestry; Education; Health and Social Security; Home Affairs; Local Government and the Environment; Tourism and Leisure; Trade and Industry; and Transport.

RECENT ELECTIONS

Elections to the House of Keys were held on 22 Nov. 2001. The Alliance for Progressive Government won 3 seats with 14·6% of the vote; the Manx Labour Party 2 seats (17·3% of the vote); while non-partisans won 17 seats. The Manx Nationalist Party boycotted the elections. Turnout was 57·6%.

CURRENT ADMINISTRATION

Lieut.-Governor: Sir Paul Haddacks.
  President: Noel Cringle (elected April 2000).
  In March 2006 the *Chief Minister* was Donald Gelling. *Finance Minister:* Allan Bell.

Website: http://www.gov.im

ECONOMY

Currency

The Isle of Man government issues its own notes and coins on a par with £ sterling. Various commemorative coins have been minted. Inflation was around 3% at the end of 2003.

Budget

The Isle of Man is statutorily required to budget for a surplus of revenue over expenditure. Revenue is raised from income tax, taxes on expenditure, health and social security contributions, and fees and charges for services.

The standard rate of tax is 10% for personal income, and there is a higher rate of 18%. Companies are liable at 10% on their first £100m. of taxable income and 18% on the balance.

There is a Customs and Excise Agreement with the UK, and rates of tax on expenditure are the same as those in the UK with very few exceptions. In addition, there is a reciprocal agreement on social security with the UK, and the rates of health and social security (National Insurance) contributions are the same as in the UK.

In 2003–04 the Isle of Man government budgeted for expenditure of £700m. and revenue of £705m.

Performance

In 2001–02 GNP was £1,179m. and GDP was £1,128m. Real GDP growth in 2001–02 was 5·4%. Just over 80% of national income is generated from services with the finance sector being the single largest contributor (37%).

Banking and Finance

The banking sector is regulated by the Financial Supervision Commission which is responsible for the licensing and supervision of banks, deposit-takers and financial intermediaries giving financial advice, and receiving client monies for investment and management. A compensation fund to protect investors was set up in 1991 under the Commission.

In Sept. 2003 the deposit base was £29bn., and there were 57 licensed banks, 86 investment businesses and two building societies with Isle of Man licences.

The insurance industry is regulated by the Insurance and Pensions Authority. In June 2003 there were 188 insurance companies.

ENERGY AND NATURAL RESOURCES

Electricity

The Manx Electricity Authority generates most of the island's electricity by oil-fired power stations although there is a small hydro-electric plant. A cable link with the UK power grid came into operation in Nov. 2000. In 2002, 345m. kWh were sold.

Oil and Gas

All oil and gas needs are met from imports, with gas being imported via a link to the Scotland–Eire gas pipeline. The island's gas suppliers and distributors are in the private sector.

Minerals

Although lead and tin mining industries were major employers in the past, they have long since shut down and the only mining activity in the island is now for aggregates. The Lady Isabella, built in 1854 to drain the mines above Laxey, is one of the largest waterwheels in Europe.

Agriculture

The area farmed is about 113,000 acres, being 80% of a total land area of around 141,500 acres. 66,000 acres are grassland with a further 35,000 acres for rough grazing. There are approximately 171,000 sheep, 34,000 cattle, 11,000 poultry and 3,000 pigs on the island's 726 farms. Agriculture now contributes less than 2% of the island's GDP.

Forestry

The Department of Agriculture, Fisheries and Forestry has a forestry estate of some 6,800 acres. Commercial forestry is directed towards softwood production. The Manx National Glens and other amenity areas are maintained for public use by the Department, which owns some 18,000 acres of the island's hills and uplands open for public use.

Fisheries

The Isle of Man is noted for the Manx kipper, a gutted smoked herring. Scallops and the related queen scallops (queenies) are the economic mainstay of the Manx fishing fleet. In 2002 the total catch was 2,923 tonnes.

INDUSTRY

Labour

The economically active population in 2001 was 39,685, of whom 5,703 were self-employed and 635 were unemployed. Employment by sector: finance, 23%; professional services, 20%; distributive services, 11%; manufacturing, 8%; construction, 6%.

At the end of 2003 there were 334 persons on the unemployment register, giving an unemployment rate of 0·8%.

Trade Unions

There were 49 registered trade unions in 2003.

INTERNATIONAL TRADE

The Isle of Man forms part of the customs union of the European Union, although the island is not part of the EU itself. The relationship with the EU provides for free trade and the adoption of the EU's external trade policies and tariffs with non-EU countries.

Imports and Exports

The Isle of Man is in customs and excise union with the United Kingdom, which is also its main trading partner.

COMMUNICATIONS

Roads

There are 800 km of good roads. At the end of March 2003 there were 63,233 licensed vehicles, with 50,596 of these being private cars. Omnibus services operate to all parts of the island. The TT (Tourist Trophy) motorcycle races take place annually on the 60·75-km Mountain Circuit.

Rail

Several novel transport systems operate on the island during the summer season from May to Sept. Horse-drawn trams run along Douglas promenade, and the Manx Electric Railway links Douglas, Laxey, Ramsey and Snaefell Mountain (621 metres) in the north. The Isle of Man Steam Railway also operates between Douglas and Port Erin in the south.

Civil Aviation

Ronaldsway Airport in the south handles scheduled services linking the island with Belfast, Birmingham, Blackpool, Bristol, Brussels, Dublin, East Midlands, Edinburgh, Glasgow, Jersey, Leeds, Liverpool, London, Manchester, Prestwick and Southampton. Air taxi services also operate.

Shipping

Car ferries run between Douglas and the UK and the Irish Republic. In 2003 there were 272 merchant vessels on the island's shipping register.

Telecommunications

Manx Telecom Limited, a wholly owned subsidiary of O2, holds the telecommunications licence issued by the Communications Commission for the Isle of Man.

Postal Services

The Isle of Man Post Office Authority operates the island's mail system and issues various commemorative stamps.

SOCIAL INSTITUTIONS

Justice

The First Deemster is the head of the Isle of Man's judiciary. The Isle of Man Constabulary numbered 246 all ranks in 2003.

The average size of the prison population during 2003 was 69·5, equivalent to 104 per 100,000 of national population. A further 13 persons are serving their sentences in the United Kingdom.

Education

Education is compulsory between the ages of five and 16. In 2003 there were 6,744 pupils in the 35 primary schools and 5,566 pupils in the five secondary schools operated by the Department of Education. The Department also runs a college of further education and a special school. Government expenditure on education totalled £78m. in 2003–04. The island has a private primary school, a private secondary school and an international business school.

Health

The island has had its own National Health Service since 1948, providing medical, dental and ophthalmic services. In 2003–04 government expenditure on the NHS was £108m. There are two hospitals, one of which opened in 2003. In 2004 there were 112 full-time equivalent physicians, 41 full-time and five part-time general practitioners, 39 full-time and two part-time dentists, and 24 pharmacies.

Welfare

Numbers receiving certain benefits at Dec. 2003: Retirement Pension, 15,702; Child Benefit, 9,313; Sick and Disablement Benefits, 5,680; Income Support, 2,589; Jobseekers' Allowance, 163. Total government expenditure on the social security system in 2003–04 was £155·4m.

RELIGION

The island has a rich heritage of Christian associations, and the Diocese of Sodor and Man, one of the oldest in the British Isles, has existed since 476.

CULTURE

Broadcasting

Manx Radio is a commercial broadcaster operated by the government from Douglas.

Press

In 2003 there were three weekly newspapers, one bi-weekly newspaper and one monthly newspaper. There are also various magazines concentrating on Manx issues.

Tourism

During the late 19th century through to the middle of the 20th century, tourism was one of the island's main sources of income and employment. Tourism now contributes around 5% of the island's GDP. There were 239,000 visitors during 2002.

FURTHER READING

Additional information is available from: Economic Affairs Division, Illiam Dhone House, 2 Circular Rd, Douglas, Isle of Man, IM1 1PQ. *e-mail: economics@gov.im*

Isle of Man Digest of Economic and Social Statistics, Isle of Man Government, annual

Belchem, J. (ed.) *A New History of the Isle of Man, Volume V—The Modern Period 1830–1999.* Liverpool Univ. Press, 2000

Kermode, D. G., *Offshore Island Politics: The Constitutional and Political Development of the Isle of Man in the Twentieth Century.* Liverpool Univ. Press, 2001

Moore, A. W., *A History of the Isle of Man.* London, 1900; reprinted Manx National Heritage, 1992

Solly, M., *Government and Law in the Isle of Man.* London, 1994

Manx National Heritage publishes a series of booklets including *Early Maps of the Isle of Man, The Art of the Manx Crosses, The Ancient & Historic Monuments of the Isle of Man, Pre-historic Sites of the Isle of Man.*

CHANNEL ISLANDS

KEY HISTORICAL EVENTS

The Channel Islands consist of Jersey, Guernsey and the following dependencies of Guernsey: Alderney, Brechou, Great Sark, Little Sark, Herm, Jethou and Lihou. They were an integral part of the Duchy of Normandy at the time of the Norman Conquest of England in 1066. Since then they have belonged to the British Crown and are not part of the UK. The islands have created their own form of self-government, with the British government at Westminster being responsible for defence and foreign policy. The Lieut.-Governors of Jersey and Guernsey, appointed by the Crown, are the personal representatives of the Sovereign as well as being the commanders of the armed forces. The legislature of Jersey is 'The States of Jersey', and that of Guernsey is 'The States of Deliberation'.

Left undefended from 1940 to 1945 the islands were the only British territory to fall to Germany.

TERRITORY AND POPULATION

The Channel Islands cover a total of 194 sq. km (75 sq. miles), and in 2001 had a population of approximately 150,000.

The official languages are French and English, but English is now the main language.

CLIMATE

The climate is mild, with an average temperature for the year of 11·5°C. Average yearly rainfall totals: Jersey, 862·9 mm; Guernsey, 858·9 mm. The wettest months are in the winter. Highest temperatures recorded: Jersey (St Helier), 36·0°C; Guernsey (airport), 33·7°C. Maximum temperatures usually occur in July and Aug. (daily maximum 20·8°C in Jersey, slightly lower in Guernsey). Lowest temperatures recorded: Jersey, –10·3°C; Guernsey, –7·4°C. Jan. and Feb. are the coldest months (mean temperature approximately 6°C).

CONSTITUTION AND GOVERNMENT

The Lieut.-Governors and Cs.-in-C. of Jersey and Guernsey are the personal representatives of the Sovereign, the Commanders of the Armed Forces of the Crown, and the channel of communication between the Crown and the insular governments. They are appointed by the Crown and have a voice but no vote in the islands' legislatures. The Secretaries to the Lieut.-Governors are their staff officers.

ENERGY AND NATURAL RESOURCES

Fisheries

Total catch in 2001 was 3,927 tonnes, exclusively from sea fishing.

EXTERNAL ECONOMIC RELATIONS

The Channel Islands are not members of the EU, but participate in ERM through their monetary union with the UK. Trade with the UK is classed as domestic.

COMMUNICATIONS

Civil Aviation

Scheduled air services are maintained by Aer Lingus, Aurigny Air Services, bmibaby, British Airways, British Midland, Cathay Pacific Airways, Flybe British European, Scot Airways, Twin Jet and VLM Airlines.

Shipping

Passenger and cargo services between Jersey, Guernsey and England (Poole) are maintained by Condor Ltd hydrofoil; between Guernsey, Jersey and England and St Malo by the Commodore Shipping Co. Emeraude Ferries connect Jersey and Guernsey with St Malo; local companies run between Guernsey, Alderney and England, and between Guernsey and Sark. In 1998 the merchant marine totalled 2,000 GRT.

SOCIAL INSTITUTIONS

Justice

Justice is administered by the Royal Courts of Jersey and Guernsey, each of which consists of the Bailiff and 12 Jurats, the latter being elected by an electoral college. There is an appeal from the Royal Courts to the Courts of Appeal of Jersey and of Guernsey. A final appeal lies to the Privy Council in certain cases. A stipendiary magistrate in each, Jersey and Guernsey, deals with minor civil and criminal cases.

RELIGION

Jersey and Guernsey each constitutes a deanery under the jurisdiction of the Bishop of Winchester. The rectories (12 in Jersey; 10 in Guernsey) are in the gift of the Crown. The Roman Catholic and various Nonconformist Churches are represented.

FURTHER READING

Lemprière, R., *History of the Channel Islands.* Rev. ed. London, 1980

Jersey

TERRITORY AND POPULATION

The area is 116·2 sq. km (44·9 sq. miles). Resident population (2001 census), 87,186 (44,701 females); density, 750 per sq. km. The chief town is St Helier on the south coast. It had a population of 28,310 in 2001. The official language is English (French until 1960). The island has its own language, known as Jersey French, or Jérriaise. French and Portuguese are also spoken.

SOCIAL STATISTICS

In 2002 there were 1,023 births and 841 deaths. Infant mortality rate, 1995 (per 1,000 live births), 6·5. In 2002 there were 641 marriages and 309 division petitions for divorce. Life expectancy, 1999: males, 75 years; females, 81 years.

CONSTITUTION AND GOVERNMENT

The island parliament is the *States of Jersey*. The States comprises the Bailiff, the Lieut.-Governor, the Dean of Jersey, the Attorney-General and the Solicitor-General, and 53 members elected by universal suffrage: 12 Senators (elected for six years, six retiring every third year), the Constables of the 12 parishes (every third year) and 29 Deputies (every third year). They all have the right to speak in the Assembly, but only the 53 elected members have the right to vote; the Bailiff has a casting vote. Except in specific instances, enactments passed by the States require the sanction of The Queen-in-Council. The Lieut.-Governor has the power of veto on certain forms of legislation.

A new post of chief minister was inaugurated in 2005. The chief minister, who is elected by the States, presides over a nine-member Council of Ministers responsible for government policy.

CURRENT ADMINISTRATION

Lieut.-Governor and C.-in-C. of Jersey: Air Chief Marshal Sir John Cheshire, KBE, CBE.

Secretary and Aide-de-Camp to the Lieut.-Governor: Lieut.-Col. C. Woodrow, OBE, MC, QGM.

Bailiff of Jersey and President of the States: Sir Philip Bailhache.

Chief Minister: Frank Walker.

Government Website: http://www.gov.je

ECONOMY

Currency

The States issue banknotes in denominations of £50, £20, £10, £5 and £1. Coinage from 1p to 50p is struck in the same denominations as the UK. There were £61,016,580 worth of States of Jersey banknotes in 2003 and £4,997,000 worth of coinage in circulation in 2002. Inflation in Sept. 2003 was 3·8%.

Budget

2003 forecast: revenue, £440m.; expenditure, £394m. Income from taxation was forecast to be £375m.

Parochial rates are payable by owners and occupiers.

Performance

From 1999–2001 GDP grew by 3·35%.

Banking and Finance

In 2002 there were 59 banks; combined deposits were £139·3bn. There were 2,829 registered companies in 2002.

The rate of company tax is currently 20%, but a 0% rate of tax is to be introduced by 2009.

ENERGY AND NATURAL RESOURCES

Agriculture

2002 total agricultural exports, £34,031,576. Jersey Royal New Potatoes account for 68% of the agricultural exports to the UK. 49·6% of the island's land area was farmed commercially in 2002. In 2001 there were 352 commercial farms. In 2002 there were 6,350 cattle (3,970 milch cows).

Fisheries

There were 212 fishing vessels in 2002. The total catch in 2000 was 1,851 tonnes. The value of the fishing industry in 2002 was estimated at £8,707,335.

INDUSTRY

Principal activities: light industry, mainly electrical goods, textiles and clothing.

Labour

At the 2001 census 46,590 persons were economically active, and 150 persons were registered unemployed. Financial services was the largest employment sector, followed by distributive trades, construction, and then hotels and restaurants. Nearly a quarter of all jobs are in the financial and legal sector. By Oct. 2001 there was full employment and over 3,310 unfilled vacancies.

EXTERNAL ECONOMIC RELATIONS

Imports and Exports

Since 1980 the Customs have ceased recording imports and exports. Principal imports: machinery and transport equipment, manufactured goods, food, mineral fuels, and chemicals. Principal exports: machinery and transport equipment, food, and manufactured goods.

COMMUNICATIONS

Roads

In 2002 there were 74,007 private cars, 3,599 hire cars, 7,899 vans, 4,211 lorries, 847 buses and coaches, and 8,505 motorcycles and scooters.

Civil Aviation

Jersey airport is situated at St Peter. It covers approximately 375 acres. In 2002 the airport handled 1,534,808 passengers.

Shipping

All vessels arriving in Jersey from outside Jersey waters report at St Helier or Gorey on first arrival. There is a harbour of minor importance at St Aubin. Number of commercial vessels entering St Helier in 2002, 3,346; number of visiting yachts, 6,741. There were 459,594 passenger arrivals and 459,348 passenger departures in 2002.

Telecommunications

Postal, and overseas telephone and telegraph services, are maintained by the Postal Administration of Jersey. The local telephone service is maintained by the Insular Authority. In 2002 main telephone lines numbered 74,273. There were 71,500 mobile phone subscribers.

Postal Services

In 2003 there were 21 post offices; a total of 72·5m. letters were processed.

SOCIAL INSTITUTIONS

Justice

Justice is administered by the Royal Court, consisting of the Bailiff and 12 Jurats (magistrates). There is a final appeal in certain cases to the Sovereign in Council. There is also a Court of Appeal, consisting of the Bailiff and two judges. Minor civil and criminal cases are dealt with by a stipendiary magistrate.

In 2002 there were 15,201 telephone calls requiring operational response; there were 5,427 crime offences, 1,134 disorder offences and 716 road traffic accidents. In Dec. 2003 the daily average prison population was 170.

Education

In 2002 there were seven States secondary schools, one high school and three special needs secondary schools. There were 25 States primary schools. 4,936 pupils attended secondary schools and 7,386 attended primary schools. There were 613 full-time students at the further education college. Expenditure on public education amounted to £81m. in 2001.

Health

Expenditure on public health in 1999 was £79,829,619. In 2000 there were five hospitals with 651 beds. In 2001 there were 94 doctors (general practitioners).

Welfare

A contributory Health Insurance Scheme is administered by the Social Security Department. In 2002 state expenditure for supplementation on the Social Security Fund was £48,136,000. £4,925,000 was paid out in Family Allowance, £5,823,000 on Disability Transport Allowance, £2,910,000 on Non-native Welfare, £3,094,000 on Attendance Allowance and £1,151,000 on the administration of community benefits.

CULTURE

Tourism

In 2002 there were 872,000 visitors to the island, spending £238m.

FURTHER READING

Balleine, G. R., *A History of the Island of Jersey.* Rev. ed. Chichester, 1981

States of Jersey Library: Halkett Place, St Helier.

Guernsey

TERRITORY AND POPULATION

The area is 63·1 sq. km. Census population (2001) 59,807. The main town is St Peter Port (2001 population of 16,488).

English is spoken, as is a Norman-French dialect in country areas.

SOCIAL STATISTICS

Births during 2001 were 593; deaths, 564.

CONSTITUTION AND GOVERNMENT

The States of Deliberation, the Parliament of Guernsey, is composed of the following members: the Bailiff, who is President *ex officio*; H.M. Procureur and H.M. Comptroller (Law Officers of the Crown), who have a voice but no vote; 45 People's Deputies elected by popular franchise; ten Douzaine Representatives elected by their Parochial Douzaines; two representatives of the States of Alderney. Since May 2004 there has been a slimmed-down States of Deliberation, and an executive form of government has been introduced. For the first time a chief minister has been appointed. There are also ministers, a deputy chief minister, members of departmental committees, chairmen and members of committees.

The States of Election, an electoral college, elects the Jurats. It is composed of the following members: the Bailiff (President *ex officio*); the 12 Jurats or 'Jurés-Justiciers'; H.M. Procureur and H.M. Comptroller; the 45 People's Deputies and 34 representatives from the 10 Parochial Douzaines.

Since Jan. 1949 all legislative powers and functions (with minor exceptions) formerly exercised by the Royal Court have been vested in the States of Deliberation. Projets de Loi (Bills) require the sanction of The Queen-in-Council.

RECENT ELECTIONS

Elections for People's Deputies were held on 21 April 2004.

CURRENT ADMINISTRATION

Lieut.-Governor and C.-in-C. of Guernsey and its Dependencies: Vice Adm. Sir Fabian Malbon, KBE.

Secretary and Aide-de-Camp to the Lieut.-Governor: Colonel R. H. Graham, MBE.

Bailiff of Guernsey and President of the States: Geoffrey Rowland.

Chief Minister: Laurie Morgan.

Government Website: http://www.gov.gg

ECONOMY

Budget

Year ended 31 Dec. 2001: revenue, including Alderney, £280,165,000; expenditure, including Alderney, £222,901,000. The standard rate of income tax is 20p in the pound. States and parochial rates are very moderate. No super-tax or death duties are levied.

Banking and Finance

There were 67 banks in 2002. Financial services account for about 66% of the export economy.

The general rate of income tax payable by Guernsey companies, currently 20%, is to be reduced to 0% for the tax year 2008.

INDUSTRY

Trade Unions

There is a Transport & General Workers' Union.

EXTERNAL ECONOMIC RELATIONS

Imports and Exports

In 2002, 74,066,580 litres of petrol and oils were imported. Horticulture exports (2001) in £1m.: plant production, 20·28; cut flowers, 11·68; postal flowers, 6·10; food, 3·65; seeds, 0·26.

Trade Fairs

There are several trade fairs each year.

COMMUNICATIONS

Civil Aviation

The airport is situated at La Villiaze. There were direct flights in 2003 to Alderney, Belfast, Birmingham, Bristol, Brussels, Dinard, Dublin, East Midlands, Edinburgh, Exeter, Geneva, Glasgow, Jersey, London (Gatwick and Stansted), Manchester, Milan, Rotterdam, Southampton and Toulouse. In 2002 passenger movements totalled 837,916.

Shipping

The principal port is St Peter Port. There is also a harbour at St Sampson's (mainly for commercial shipping). In 2002 passenger movements totalled 463,530. Ships registered at 31 Dec. 2002 numbered 2,223 and 250 fishing vessels. In 2002, 9,644 yachts visited Guernsey.

Telecommunications

There were 55,000 main telephone lines in 2002, or 874 per 1,000 population. Mobile phone subscribers numbered 37,000 in 2002 and there were 700 fax machines in 1999. Guernsey Telecom was sold to Cable and Wireless in May 2002 and now trades as C & W Guernsey.

SOCIAL INSTITUTIONS

Justice

The population in penal institutions in Nov. 2003 was 83 (equivalent to 128 per 100,000 population).

Education

There are two public schools, one grammar school, a number of modern secondary and primary schools, and a College of Further Education. The total number of schoolchildren in Sept. 2002 was 8,993. Facilities are available for the study of art, domestic science and many other subjects of a technical nature.

Health

Guernsey is not covered by the UK National Health Service. Public health is overseen by the States of Guernsey Insurance Authority and Department of Health. A private medical insurance scheme to provide specialist cover for all residents was implemented by the States on 1 Jan. 1996. In 2005 there was one hospital and 112 general practitioners and consultants.

CULTURE

Broadcasting

Guernsey is served by BBC Radio Guernsey, Island FM and Channel Television.

Press

The *Guernsey Evening Press* is published daily except Sundays.

Tourism

There were 405,000 visitors in 2001; tourism contributed 12% of the economy.

FURTHER READING

Marr, L. J., *A History of Guernsey*. Chichester, 1982

Statistical office: Policy and Research Unit, P. O. Box 43, Sir Charles Frossard House, La Charroterie, St. Peter Port, GY4 6EF.
Website: http://www.gov.gg/esu

Alderney

GENERAL DETAILS

Population (2001 estimate, 2,400). The main town is St Anne's. The island has an airport.

The Constitution of the island (reformed 1987) provides for its own popularly elected President and States (10 members), and its own Court. Elections were held for the five members of the States in Dec. 2004. Alderney levies its taxes at Guernsey rates and passes the revenue to Guernsey, which charges for the services it provides.

President of the States. Sir Norman Browse.
Chief Executive. David Jeremiah, OBE.
Greffier. Sarah Kelly.

FURTHER READING

Coysh, V., *Alderney*. Newton Abbot, 1974

Sark

GENERAL DETAILS

2001 population estimate, 580. The Constitution is a mixture of feudal and popular government with its Chief Pleas (parliament), consisting of 40 tenants and 12 popularly elected deputies, presided over by the Seneschal. The head of the island is the Seigneur. Sark has no income tax. Motor vehicles, except tractors, are not allowed.

Seigneur. J. M. Beaumont.
Seneschal. R. J. Guille.

FURTHER READING

Hathaway, S., *Dame of Sark: An Autobiography*. London, 1961

UNITED KINGDOM OVERSEAS TERRITORIES

There are 14 British Overseas Territories: Anguilla, Bermuda, British Antarctic Territory, British Indian Ocean Territory, British Virgin Islands, Cayman Islands, Falkland Islands, Gibraltar, Montserrat, Pitcairn Islands, St Helena and its Dependencies (Ascension Island and Tristan da Cunha), South Georgia and the South Sandwich Islands, the Sovereign Base Areas of Akrotiri and Dhekelia in Cyprus, and the Turks and Caicos Islands. Three (British Antarctic Territory, British Indian Ocean Territory and South Georgia and the South Sandwich Islands) have no resident populations and are administered by a commissioner instead of a governor.

Gibraltar is a peninsula bordering the south coast of Spain; the Sovereign Base Areas are in Cyprus and the remainder are islands in the Caribbean, Pacific, Indian Ocean and South Atlantic. Gibraltar and the Falkland Islands are the subjects of territorial claims by Spain and Argentina respectively.

The Overseas Territories are constitutionally not part of the United Kingdom. They have separate constitutions, and most of them have elected governments with varying degrees of responsibilities for domestic matters. The Governor, who is appointed by, and represents, HM the Queen, retains responsibility for external affairs, internal security, defence, and in most cases the public service.

At the launch of the White Paper 'Partnership for Progress and Prosperity', in March 1999, the Foreign Secretary of the time, Robin Cook, outlined four underlying principles for the relationship between Britain and the Overseas Territories: self-determination for the Territories; mutual obligations and responsibilities; freedom for the Territories to run their own affairs to the greatest degree possible; and Britain's firm commitment to help the territories develop economically and to assist them in emergencies. He also offered British citizenship, with the right of abode in the UK, to those citizens of the Overseas Territories who did not already enjoy it. The Overseas Territories Consultative Council was established in 1999. The Council, which meets annually, is a forum for discussion of key policy issues between British government ministers and heads of territory governments. On 21 May 2002 the citizenship provisions of the British Overseas Territories Act came into force. It granted British citizenship to the citizens of all Britain's Overseas Territories (except those who derived their British nationality by virtue only of a connection with the Sovereign Base Areas of Akrotiri and Dhekelia in Cyprus).

Anguilla

KEY HISTORICAL EVENTS

Anguilla was probably given its name by the Spaniards or the French because of its eel-like shape. It was inhabited by Arawaks for several centuries before the arrival of Europeans. Anguilla was colonized in 1650 by English settlers from neighbouring St Kitts. In 1688 the island was attacked by a party of Irishmen who then settled. Anguilla was subsequently administered as part of the Leeward Islands, and from 1825 became even more closely associated with St Kitts. In 1875 a petition sent to London requesting separate status and direct rule from Britain met with a negative response. Again in 1958 the islanders formally petitioned the Governor requesting a dissolution of the political and administrative association with St Kitts, but this too failed. From 1958 to 1962 Anguilla was part of the Federation of the West Indies.

Opposition to rule from St Kitts erupted on 30 May 1967 when St Kitts policemen were evicted from the island and Anguilla refused to recognize the authority of the State government any longer. During 1968–69 the British government maintained a 'Senior British Official' to advise the local Anguilla Council and devise some solution to the problem. In March 1969, following the ejection from the island of a high-ranking British civil servant, British security forces occupied Anguilla. A Commissioner was installed, and in 1969 Anguilla became *de facto* a separate dependency of Britain, a situation rendered *de jure* on 19 Dec. 1980 under the Anguilla Act 1980 when Anguilla formally separated from the state of St Kitts, Anguilla-Nevis. A new constitution came into effect in 1982 providing for a large measure of autonomy under the Crown.

TERRITORY AND POPULATION

Anguilla is the most northerly of the Leeward Islands, some 112 km (70 miles) to the northwest of St Kitts and 8 km (5 miles) to the north of St Martin/Sint Maarten. The territory also comprises the island of Sombrero and several other off-shore islets or cays. The total area of the territory is about 155 sq. km (60 sq. miles). *De jure* census population (2001) was 11,561; density of 74·6 per sq. km. Average annual population increase between 1992 and 2001 was 3·2%. People of African descent make up 90% of the population, mixed origins 5% and white 4%. The capital is The Valley. In 1995 an estimated 89% of the population lived in rural areas.

The official language is English.

SOCIAL STATISTICS

Births, 2001, 183; deaths, 66. In 2001 life expectancy at birth for females was 78·0 years and for males 77·9 years. Households numbered 3,788 in 2001.

CLIMATE

Tropical oceanic climate with rain throughout the year, particularly between May and Dec. Tropical storms and hurricanes may occur between July and Nov. Generally summers are hotter than winters although there is little variation in temperatures.

CONSTITUTION AND GOVERNMENT

A set of amendments to the constitution came into effect in 1990, providing for a Deputy Governor, a Parliamentary Secretary and an Opposition Leader. The *House of Assembly* consists of a Speaker, Deputy Speaker, seven directly elected members for five-year terms, two nominated members and two *ex officio* members: the Deputy Governor and the Attorney-General. The Governor discharges his executive powers on the advice of an Executive Council comprising a Chief Minister, three Ministers and two *ex officio* members: the Deputy Governor, Attorney-General and the Secretary to the Executive Council.

RECENT ELECTIONS

In parliamentary elections held on 21 Feb. 2005 the United Front (Anguilla National Alliance and Anguilla Democratic Party) won four of seven seats, the Anguilla National Strategic Alliance two and the Anguilla United Movement one. Turnout was 74·6%. A coalition of Anguilla National Alliance and Anguilla Democratic Party was formed following the election to serve a second term.

CURRENT ADMINISTRATION

Governor: Alan Huckle; b. 1948 (took office on 28 May 2004).

Chief Minister: Osbourne Fleming; b. 1940 (Anguilla National Alliance; sworn in 6 March 2000).

Government Website: http://www.gov.ai

ECONOMY

Currency

The *Eastern Caribbean dollar* (*see* ANTIGUA AND BARBUDA).

Budget

In 1998 government revenue was EC$72·3m. and expenditure EC$71·0m. The main sources of revenue are custom duties, tourism and bank licence fees. There is little taxation. A 'Policy Plan' with the UK provided for £10·5m. of aid in 1994–97.

Performance

Real GDP growth was –4·3% in 1995 and 7·0% in 1994.

Banking and Finance

The East Caribbean Central Bank based in St Kitts-Nevis functions as a central bank. The *Governor* is Sir Dwight Venner. There is a small offshore banking sector. In 1996 there were two domestic and two foreign commercial banks.

ENERGY AND NATURAL RESOURCES

Electricity

Production (2000) 45·8m. kWh.

Agriculture

Because of low rainfall, agriculture potential is limited. About 1,200 ha. are cultivable. Main crops are pigeon peas, maize and sweet potatoes. Livestock consists of sheep, goats, pigs and poultry. The island relies on imports for food.

Fisheries

Fishing is a thriving industry (mainly lobster). The estimated total catch in 2001 was 250 tonnes.

INDUSTRY

Labour

The unemployment rate was 7·8% in July 2002.

EXTERNAL ECONOMIC RELATIONS

Imports and Exports

Merchandise imports in 2002 (and 2001) were US$61·5m. (US$68·5m.); exports in 2002 (and 2001) were US$4·8m. (US$3·6m.)

COMMUNICATIONS

Roads

There are about 40 miles of tarred roads and 25 miles of secondary roads. In 1991 there were 2,450 passenger cars and 733 commercial vehicles.

Civil Aviation

Wallblake is the airport for The Valley. Anguilla is linked to neighbouring islands by services operated by American Airlines, Caribbean Star Airlines, Coastal Air Transport, LIAT and WINAIR.

Shipping

The main seaports are Sandy Ground and Blowing Point, the latter serving passenger and cargo traffic to and from St Martin. In 2002 merchant shipping totalled 1,000 GRT.

Telecommunications

There is a modern internal telephone service with (2002) 5,796 main lines in operation; and fax and Internet services. In 2002 there were 3,402 mobile phone subscribers.

SOCIAL INSTITUTIONS

Justice

Justice is based on UK common law as exercised by the Eastern Caribbean Supreme Court on St Lucia. Final appeal lies to the UK Privy Council.

Education

Adult literacy was 80% in 1995. Education is free and compulsory between the ages of five and 17 years. There are six government primary schools with (1996) 1,540 pupils and one comprehensive school with (1996) 1,060 pupils. Higher education is provided at regional universities and similar institutions.

In 1998–99 expenditure on education came to 14·4% of total expenditure.

Health

In 2003 there was one hospital with a total of 36 beds; there were also four health centres and a government dental clinic. There were nine government-employed and five private doctors, two dentists and 32 nurses in 2003.

Welfare

A social security system was instituted in 1982 to provide age and disability pensions, and sickness and maternity benefits.

RELIGION

There were in 2001 Anglicans (29%), Methodists (24%), plus Seventh Day Adventists, Pentecostalists, Church of God, Baptists and Roman Catholics as significant minorities.

CULTURE

Broadcasting

There is one government (Radio Anguilla) and two other radio broadcasters. TV is privately owned; there are two channels and a cable system. In 1997 there were 3,000 radio and 1,000 television receivers.

Press

In 1995 there were one daily, two weeklies and a quarterly periodical.

Tourism

Tourism accounts for 50% of GDP. In 2000 there were 44,000 visitor arrivals (around two-thirds from the USA); revenue totalled US$55m.

FURTHER READING

Petty, C. L., *Anguilla: Where there's a Will, there's a Way.* Anguilla, 1984.—*A Handbook History of Anguilla.* Anguilla, 1991.

Statistical office: Anguilla Statistics Department, PO Box 60, The Valley, Anguilla.
Website: http://www.gov.ai/statistics

Bermuda

KEY HISTORICAL EVENTS

The islands were discovered by Juan Bermúdez, probably in 1503, but were uninhabited until British colonists were wrecked there in 1609. A plantation company was formed; in 1684 the Crown took over the government. A referendum in Aug. 1995 rejected independence from the UK.

TERRITORY AND POPULATION

Bermuda consists of a group of 138 islands and islets (about 20 inhabited), situated in the western Atlantic (32° 18' N. lat., 64° 46' W. long.); the nearest point of the mainland, 940 km distant, is Cape Hatteras (North Carolina). The area is 53·3 sq. km (20·6 sq. miles). In June 1995 the USA surrendered its lease on land used since 1941 for naval and air force bases. At the 2000 census the population numbered 62,059; density, 1,164 per sq. km. Capital, Hamilton; population, 2000, 969. Population of St George's, 2000, 1,752.

Ethnic composition, 2000: Black, 54·8%; White, 34·0%.

The official language is English.

SOCIAL STATISTICS

In 2001 there were 831 live births, 923 marriages and 442 deaths. Average annual growth rate, 1991–2000, 0·7%. Life expectancy at birth, 2001: 70 years (male); 78 years (female).

CLIMATE

A pleasantly warm and humid climate, with up to 60" (1,500 mm) of rain spread evenly throughout the year. Hamilton, Jan. 63°F (17·2°C), July 79°F (26·1°C). Annual rainfall 58" (1,463 mm).

CONSTITUTION AND GOVERNMENT

Under the 1968 constitution the *Governor*, appointed by the Crown, is normally bound to accept the advice of the Cabinet in matters other than external affairs, defence, internal security and the police, for which he retains special responsibility. The legislature consists of a Senate of 11 members, five appointed by the Governor on the recommendation of the Premier, three by the Governor on the recommendation of the Opposition Leader and three by the Governor in his own discretion. The members of the *House of Assembly* are elected, one from each of 36 constituencies (as of 2003) by universal suffrage.

At a referendum on 17 Aug. 1995, 16,369 votes were cast against the option of independence, and 5,714 were in favour. The electorate was 38,000; turnout was 58%.

RECENT ELECTIONS

A general election was held on 24 July 2003. Turnout was 74·9%. The Progressive Labour Party (PLP) won 22 of the 36 seats in parliament, with 51·6% of votes cast. The United Bermuda Party (UBP), which had been in government for 35 years until 1998, won 14 seats, with 48·0%. The PLP is largely representative of the black population, while the UBP membership is mostly white.

CURRENT ADMINISTRATION

Governor: Sir John Vereker; b. 1944 (took office on 11 April 2002).

Premier: Alex Scott; b. 1940 (took office on 29 July 2003).

Government Website: http://www.gov.bm

DEFENCE

The Bermuda Regiment numbers 600 personnel, mostly part-time. There are 29 professional staff.

ECONOMY

Bermuda is the world's third largest insurance market after London and New York. Reserves of insurance companies total BD$39bn.

Currency

The unit of currency is the *Bermuda dollar* (BMD) of 100 *cents* at parity with the US dollar. Inflation was 2·9% in 2001, up from 2·7% in 2000.

Budget

The fiscal year ends on 31 March. The 2002–03 budget envisaged revenue of BD$609m. and current expenditure of BD$571m. Estimated chief sources of revenue (in BD$1m.) in 2002–03: customs duties, 177; companies fees, 48; land tax, 37; passenger tax, 22; vehicle licences, 22.

Performance

Real GDP growth was 1·5% in 2002. GDP in 2001 was $2·2bn.

Banking and Finance

Bermuda is an offshore financial centre with tax exemption facilities. In 2002 there were 13,318 international companies registered in Bermuda, with insurers the most important category. There are three commercial banks, with total assets of BD$17,974m. in 2001. HSBC bought the Bank of Bermuda in 2003 for US$1·3bn. At the end of 2001 there were 12,101 exempted companies, 578 exempted partnership companies, 639 non-resident companies and 14 non-resident insurance companies on the Bermuda register. Bermuda is now the world's third largest insurance market after London and New York. The Bermuda Monetary Authority (*Chairman,* Cheryl-Ann Lister) acts as a central bank. There is a stock exchange, the BSX.

Weights and Measures

Metric, except that US and Imperial (British) measures are used in certain fields.

ENERGY AND NATURAL RESOURCES

Environment

Bermuda's carbon dioxide emissions from the consumption and flaring of fossil fuels in 2002 were the equivalent of 8·9 tonnes per capita.

Electricity

Installed capacity was 0·1m. kW in 2000. Production in 2000 was 603m. kWh, with consumption per capita 9,571 kWh.

Minerals

Bermuda is rich in limestone.

Agriculture

The chief products are fresh vegetables, bananas and citrus fruit. In 1995, 839 acres were being used for production of vegetables, fruit and flowers as well as for pasture, forage and fallow. In 2001, 613 persons were employed in agriculture. In 2001 the total value of agricultural products was BD$354,000. Livestock, 2002: 1,000 cattle, 1,000 horses, 1,000 pigs.

Forestry

Approximately 20% of land is woodland.

Fisheries

In 2003 there were 361 registered commercial fishing vessels and 381 registered fishermen. The total catch in 2001 was 315 tonnes. Fishing is centred on reef-dwelling species such as groupers and lobsters.

INDUSTRY

Bermuda's leading industry is tourism, with annual revenue in excess of US$350m.

Labour

The labour force numbered 37,597 in 2001.

Trade Unions

There are nine trade unions with a total membership (1995) of 8,728.

EXTERNAL ECONOMIC RELATIONS

Foreign firms conducting business overseas only are not subject to a 60% Bermuda ownership requirement. In 2002, 10,328 international companies had a physical presence in Bermuda.

Imports and Exports

The visible adverse balance of trade is more than compensated for by invisible exports, including tourism and off-shore insurance business.

Merchandise imports in 2001 (and 2000) were US$750m. (US$719m.); exports in 2001 (and 2000) were US$45m. (US$51m.). In 1999 the USA accounted for 17·8% of imports and 9·8% of exports, and the UK 15·4% of imports and 6·9% of exports. The EU (excluding the UK) accounted for 35·4% of imports and 77·9% of exports.

Principal imports are food, beverages and tobacco, machinery, chemicals, clothing, fuels and transport equipment. The bulk of exports comprise sales of fuel to aircraft and ships, and re-exports of pharmaceuticals.

COMMUNICATIONS

Roads

There are 225 km of public highway and 222 km of private roads. In 2001 there were a total of 45,342 vehicles including: 20,334 private cars; 856 buses, taxis and limousines; 3,676 trucks; 7,724 auxiliary cycles; and 11,918 motorcycles and scooters. There are heavy fines for breaking the speed limit of 35 km/h (22 mph). Bermuda limits cars to one per household and bans hire vehicles.

Civil Aviation

The Bermuda International Airport is 19 km from Hamilton. It handled 833,511 passengers and 5,771 tonnes of freight in 2001. Air Canada, American Airlines, British Airways, Continental Airlines, Delta Airlines and US Airways serve Bermuda with regular scheduled services.

Shipping

There are three ports: Hamilton, St George's and Dockyard. There is an open shipping registry. In 2002 ships registered totalled 4·80m. GRT, including oil tankers 898,000 GRT. In 2001, 1,566 overseas ships called in Bermuda.

Telecommunications

Telephone subscribers numbered 86,000 in 2002, equivalent to 1,323·1 for every 1,000 inhabitants, and there were 34,000 PCs in use (523·1 per 1,000 inhabitants). In 2002 there were 30,000 mobile phone subscribers. Bermuda had 25,000 Internet users in April 2000.

Postal Services

There were 15 post offices in 2001.

SOCIAL INSTITUTIONS

Justice

There are four magistrates' courts, three Supreme Courts and a Court of Appeal. The police had a strength of about 433 men and women in 2003.

Bermuda is the only country in the world where McDonald's restaurants are banned by law.

Education

Education is compulsory between the ages of five and 16, and government assistance is given by the payment of grants and, where necessary, school fees. In 2001 there were 6,284 pupils in government schools and 3,606 in private schools. There were 714 full-time students attending the Bermuda College in 2001. A restructuring of secondary school education has resulted in the construction of two new state-of-the-art secondary schools, Cedarbridge Academy and the Berkeley Institute.

In 2002 the adult literacy rate was 98%. In 1998–99 total expenditure on education came to 17·0% of total government spending.

Health

In 2001 there were two hospitals, 120 physicians and surgeons, 62 dentists and hygienists, eight optometrists, 36 pharmacists, 14 dieticians and 528 nurses.

RELIGION

Many religions are represented, but the larger number of worshippers are attracted to the Anglican, Methodist, Roman Catholic, Seventh Day Adventist, African Methodist Episcopal and Baptist faiths.

CULTURE

Broadcasting

Radio and television broadcasting are commercial; there are two broadcasting companies which offer a choice of five AM and three FM radio stations, and three TV channels. A cable

TV service also offers some 40 channels (colour by NTSC). In 2000 there were 82,000 radio and, in 1998, 66,000 TV receivers, or 1,031 TVs per 1,000 inhabitants—more than anywhere else in the world.

Press

In 2003 there was one daily newspaper with a circulation of about 17,000 and two weeklies with a combined circulation of about 15,000.

Tourism

In 2002, 283,967 tourists visited Bermuda by air and sea. Visitor expenditure in 2002 was US$274·2m.

FURTHER READING

Government Department of Statistics. *Bermuda Facts and Figures.* Annual.

Ministry of Finance. *Economic Review.* Annual.

Boultbee, P. and Raine, D., *Bermuda.* [Bibliography] ABC-Clio, Oxford and Santa Barbara (CA), 1998

Zuill, W. S., *The Story of Bermuda and Her People.* 2nd ed. London, 1992

National library: The Bermuda National Library, Hamilton.

Statistical office: Government Department of Statistics, Hamilton.

British Antarctic Territory

KEY HISTORICAL EVENTS

The British Antarctic Territory was established on 3 March 1962, as a consequence of the entry into force of the Antarctic Treaty, to separate those areas of the then Falkland Islands Dependencies which lay within the Treaty area from those which did not (i.e. South Georgia and the South Sandwich Islands).

TERRITORY AND POPULATION

The territory encompasses the lands and islands within the area south of 60°S latitude lying between 20°W and 80°W longitude (approximately due south of the Falkland Islands and the Dependencies). It covers an area of some 1,700,000 sq. km, and its principal components are the South Orkney and South Shetland Islands, the Antarctic Peninsula (Palmer Land and Graham Land), the Filchner and Ronne Ice Shelves and Coats Land.

There is no indigenous or permanently resident population. There is, however, an itinerant population of scientists and logistics staff of about 300, manning a number of research stations.

CURRENT ADMINISTRATION

Commissioner: Tony Crombie (non-resident).

Administrator: Dr Michael Richardson.

British Indian Ocean Territory

KEY HISTORICAL EVENTS

This territory was established to meet UK and US defence requirements by an Order in Council on 8 Nov. 1965, consisting then of the Chagos Archipelago (formerly administered from Mauritius) and the islands of Aldabra, Desroches and Farquhar (all formerly administered from Seychelles). The latter islands became part of Seychelles when that country achieved independence on 29 June 1976. In Nov. 2000 the High Court ruled that the 2,000 Ilois people deported between 1967 and 1973 had been removed unlawfully. However, Chagos islanders lost a UK High Court case for compensation and the right to return in 2003.

TERRITORY AND POPULATION

The group, with a total land area of 60 sq. km (23 sq. miles), comprises five coral atolls (Diego Garcia, Peros Banhos, Salomon, Eagle and Egmont), of which the largest and southernmost, Diego Garcia, covers 44 sq. km (17 sq. miles) and lies 725 km (450 miles) south of the Maldives. A US Navy support facility has been established on Diego Garcia. There is no permanent population.

CURRENT ADMINISTRATION

Commissioner: Tony Crombie (non-resident).

Administrator: Tony Humphries.

Commissioner's Representative: Cdr Adam Peters.

British Virgin Islands

KEY HISTORICAL EVENTS

Discovered by Columbus on his second voyage in 1493, British Virgin Islands were first settled by the Dutch in 1648 and taken over in 1666 by a group of English planters. The islands were annexed to the British Crown in 1672. Constitutional government was granted in 1773, but was later surrendered in 1867. A Legislative Council formed in that year was abolished in 1902. In 1950 a partly nominated and partly elected Legislative Council was restored. A ministerial system of government was introduced in 1967.

TERRITORY AND POPULATION

The Islands form the eastern extremity of the Greater Antilles and number 60, of which 16 are inhabited. The largest, with estimated populations (2000), are Tortola, 16,630; Virgin Gorda, 3,063; Anegada, 204; and Jost Van Dyke, 176. Other islands had a total population (estimate 2000) of 181; marine population (estimate 1989), 124. Total area 151 sq. km (58 sq. miles); total population (1991 census), 16,749. The most recent estimate of the population of the British Virgin Islands was 20,254 in 2000. In 1995 an estimated 56% of the population were urban. The capital, Road Town, on the southeast of Tortola, is a port of entry; population (estimate 2000), 7,974.

The official language is English. Spanish and Creole are also spoken.

SOCIAL STATISTICS

Birth rate, 2001, was 15·4 per 1,000 population; death rate, 4·9 per 1,000. Life expectancy in 2001 was an estimated 75·5 years. Annual growth rate, 1·96% in 2000.

CLIMATE

A pleasant healthy sub-tropical climate with summer temperatures lowered by sea breezes and cool nights. Road Town (1999), Jan. 21°C, July 27°C; rainfall (1998), 1471 mm.

CONSTITUTION AND GOVERNMENT

The Constitution dates from 1967 but was amended in 1977 and 1994. The Executive Council consists of the Governor, the Chief Minister, the Attorney-General *ex officio* and four ministers. The ministers are appointed by the Governor from among the elected members of the Legislative Council. The *Legislative Council* consists of the five ministers, five directly elected members from constituencies and four members from 'at large' seats covering the territory as a whole. The Speaker is elected from outside the Council.

RECENT ELECTIONS

In parliamentary elections on 16 June 2003 the National Democratic Party (NDP) won eight of the 13 seats, ahead of the governing Virgin Islands Party (VIP) with five seats. Turnout was 72%.

CURRENT ADMINISTRATION

Governor: David Pearey.

  Chief Minister: Dr Orlando Smith (NDP; sworn in 17 June 2003).

INTERNATIONAL RELATIONS

The Islands are an associate member of CARICOM, OECS, UNESCO and ECLAC.

  The UK government is responsible for the international relations of the Territory. Through this link, the Territory is party to a large number of treaties and international covenants.

ECONOMY

The economy is based on tourism and international financial services.

Currency

The official unit of currency is the US dollar.

Budget

In 2000 revenue was US$183·1m. and expenditure US$134·6m. (goods and services, US$63·7m.; wages and salaries, US$50·1m.; subsidies and transfers, US$19·7m.; interest payments, US$1·2m.) Outstanding debt, in 2000, US$37·1m.

Performance

Real GDP growth was 8·7% in 2001 following growth of 4·4% in 2000. In 2001 the GDP per capita was US$35,954.

Banking and Finance

In 2003 there were 13 banks and in 1999 there were 189 trust companies. As of Sept. 2001 total deposits were US$1,143·8m. Financial Services has surpassed the performance of the tourism industry to become the largest contributor to the GDP. As of 30 June 2001, 448,767 International Business Companies were registered in the British Virgin Islands.

ENERGY AND NATURAL RESOURCES

Electricity

Production, 2000, 260·1m. kWh. In 2000 installed capacity was 13,000 kW.

Agriculture

The value of agricultural production in 1997 was US$1·52m. despite three destructive hurricanes in the course of the year. In 1994: total land suitable for agriculture, 5,324 acres; crops, 1,767 acres; and pastures, 3,557 acres. Agricultural production is limited, with the chief products being livestock (including poultry), fish, fruit and vegetables.

  Livestock (2002): cattle, 2,000; pigs, 2,000; sheep, 6,000; goats, 10,000.

Forestry

The area under forests in 2000 was 3,000 ha., or 20·0% of the total land area.

Fisheries

The total catch was approximately 50 tonnes in 2001.

INDUSTRY

The construction industry is a significant employer. There are ice-making plants, cottage industries producing tourist items and a rum distillery.

Labour

In 1997, of the 11,996 strong labour force, 21·4% were employed in the public sector, 3·6% in industry, 0·2% in agriculture and 74·8% in other areas. In 1991 the unemployment rate was 3·6%.

EXTERNAL ECONOMIC RELATIONS

Imports and Exports

In 2000 imports were US$237·6m. and exports US$26·6m. There is a very small export trade, almost entirely with the Virgin Islands of the USA.

COMMUNICATIONS

Roads

In 2000 there were 362·09 km of paved roads and 10,631 registered vehicles.

Civil Aviation

Beef Island Airport, about 16 km from Road Town, is capable of receiving 80-seat short-take-off-and-landing jet aircraft. Several airlines serve the British Virgin Islands, notably LIAT and Caribbean Star Airlines. There are scheduled flights to Puerto Rico and a number of islands in the Eastern Caribbean.

Shipping

There are two deep-water harbours: Port Purcell and Road Town. There are services to the Netherlands, UK, USA and other Caribbean islands. Merchant shipping totalled 23,000 GRT in 2002.

Telecommunications

In 2002 there were 11,700 main telephone lines and 8,000 mobile phone subscribers. Internet users numbered 4,000 in 2002. An external telephone service links Tortola with Bermuda and the rest of the world.

SOCIAL INSTITUTIONS

Justice

Law is based on UK common law. There are courts of first instance. The appeal court is in the UK.

Education

In 1997 adult literacy was 98·2%. Primary education is provided in 15 government schools, three secondary divisions, 16 private schools and one school for children with special needs. Total number of pupils in primary schools (1997) 2,633.

  Secondary education to GCSE level and Caribbean Examination Council level is provided by the BVI High School, and the secondary divisions of the schools on Virgin Gorda and Anegada. Total number of secondary level pupils (1997), 1,424. In 1996 the total number of classroom teachers in all government schools was 116.

  In 1986 a branch of the Hull University (England) School of Education was established.

  Government expenditure, 1995 (estimate), US$4·3m.

Health

As of 31 Dec. 2000 there were 19 doctors, 74 nurses, 44 public hospital beds and one private hospital with ten beds. Expenditure, 2000 (estimate) was US$7·6m.

RELIGION

There are Anglican, Methodist, Seventh-Day Adventist, Roman Catholic, Baptist, Pentecostal and other Christian churches in the Territory. There are also Jehovah's Witness and Hindu congregations.

CULTURE

Broadcasting

Radio ZBVI transmits 10,000 watts; and British Virgin Islands Cable TV operates a cable system of 43 television channels and one pay-per-view channel (colour by NTSC). In 2000 there were 9,000 radio sets and 6,200 TV receivers.

Press
In 2000 there were three weekly newspapers.

Tourism
Tourism is the most important industry and in 2000 accounted for some 14·1% of economic activity. There were 519,409 foreign tourists in 2000 of which 281,119 were overnight visitors, 188,522 were cruise ship arrivals and 49,768 day-trippers. Total tourist expenditure for 2000 was US$315m. In 1999 the tourism industry employed 12,509 people.

FURTHER READING
Moll, V. P., *Virgin Islands*. [Bibliography] ABC-Clio, Oxford and Santa Barbara (CA), 1991

Cayman Islands

KEY HISTORICAL EVENTS
The islands were discovered by Columbus on 10 May 1503 and (with Jamaica) were recognized as British possessions by the Treaty of Madrid in 1670. Grand Cayman was settled in 1734 and the other islands in 1833. They were administered by Jamaica from 1863, but remained under British sovereignty when Jamaica became independent on 6 Aug. 1962.

TERRITORY AND POPULATION
The Islands consist of Grand Cayman, Cayman Brac and Little Cayman. They are located in the Caribbean Sea, about 305 km (190 miles) northwest of Jamaica; area, 260 sq. km (100 sq. miles). Census population of 1999, 39,410 (52·5% Caymanians by birth). Estimated density, 1999, 152 per sq. km. Estimated population 2001, 41,400. The spoken language is English. The chief town is George Town with a population of 20,626.

The areas and populations of the islands are:

	Sq. km	1989	1999
Grand Cayman	197	23,881	37,473
Cayman Brac	39	1,441	1,822
Little Cayman	26	33	115

SOCIAL STATISTICS
2001: births, 622; deaths, 133. 2000: resident marriages, 397. Annual growth rate, 1989–99, 4·5%.

CLIMATE
The climate is tropical maritime, with a cool season from Nov. to March. The average yearly temperature is 27°C, and rainfall averages 57" (1,400 mm) a year at George Town. Hurricanes may be experienced between July and Nov.

CONSTITUTION AND GOVERNMENT
The 1972 Constitution provides for a *Legislative Assembly* consisting of the Speaker (who may be an elected member), three official members (the Chief Secretary, the Attorney General and the Financial Secretary) and 15 elected members. The *Executive Council* consists of the Governor (as Chairman), the three official members and five ministers elected by the elected members of the Legislative Assembly. The Islands are a self-governing overseas territory of the United Kingdom.

RECENT ELECTIONS
At the Legislative Assembly elections on 11 May 2005 the People's Progressive Movement won 9 of the 15 available seats, the United Democratic Party 5 and ind. 1. Turnout was 78%.

CURRENT ADMINISTRATION
Governor: Stuart Jack.

Government Website: http://www.gov.ky

ECONOMY

Currency
The unit of currency is the *Cayman Island dollar* (KYD/CI$) of 100 *cents*.

Budget
31 Dec. 2001: revenue, CI$273·2m.; expenditure, CI$288·8m. Public debt, CI$92·5m.; total reserves, CI$10·2m.

Performance
Real GDP growth in 2002 was an estimated 1·9%; in 2000 growth slowed to an estimated 3·2%, down from a five-year average of 5%.

Banking and Finance
Financial services, the Island's chief industry, are monitored by the Cayman Islands Monetary Authority (*Chairman,* Timothy Ridley). At Dec. 2001, 545 commercial banks and trust companies held licenses that permit the holders to offer services to the public, 31 domestically. Most of the world's leading banks have branches or subsidiaries in the Cayman Islands. At the end of 2001, 64,495 companies, almost all offshore, were registered as well as 2,937 mutual funds and 542 insurance companies. Assets of Cayman-registered banks exceeded US$1trn. in 2004. The financial services industry contributes 25% of the Cayman Islands' GDP.

ENERGY AND NATURAL RESOURCES

Electricity
Installed capacity was 115 MW in 2000, and an all-time peak demand of 70·18 MW occurred in Oct. 2000. Production in 2000 was about 330m. kWh; consumption per capita was an estimated 8,684 kWh.

Agriculture
Mangoes, bananas, citrus fruits, yams, cassava, breadfruit, tomatoes, honey, beef, pork and goatmeat are produced for local consumption.

Fisheries
In 2001 the total catch was 125 tonnes.

INDUSTRY

Labour
Unemployment rate: 7·5% of workforce in Oct. 2002 (10% Oct. 2001).

EXTERNAL ECONOMIC RELATIONS

Imports and Exports
Imports, 1998, totalled US$505·56m.; exports, US$1·44m.

COMMUNICATIONS

Roads
There were (2000) about 461 miles of road on Grand Cayman; 25 miles on Cayman Brac and on the three islands 25,061 licensed motor vehicles.

Civil Aviation
George Town (Owen Roberts) on Grand Cayman and Cayman Brac have international airports. George Town handled 918,000 passengers (837,000 on international flights) and 3,400 tonnes of freight in 2001. Cayman Airways and Island Air provide a regular inter-island service. Cayman Airways also flies to Miami, Houston, Tampa, Cuba and Jamaica. Eight additional international airlines provide services to London, Toronto,

Jamaica, the Bahamas, Honduras and five US cities, including New York and Atlanta.

Shipping
Motor vessels ply regularly between the Cayman Islands, Jamaica, Cuba and Florida. In 2001, 192,303 tonnes of cargo were offloaded at the port on Grand Cayman, 13,552 on Cayman Brac and, in 2000, 1,845 at Little Cayman.

Telecommunications
At the end of 2001 there were 31,926 direct telephone lines and over 17,000 mobile customers.

SOCIAL INSTITUTIONS
Justice
There is a Grand Court, sitting six times a year for criminal sessions at George Town under a Chief Justice and two puisne judges. There are three Magistrates presiding over the Summary Court.

The population in penal institutions in Nov. 2003 was 210 (equivalent to 501 per 100,000 population, one of the highest rates in the world).

Education
In 2002 there were ten government primary schools with 2,212 pupils, and 1,913 pupils attended the three government high schools. In 2001 about 2,240 students were enrolled in ten private schools. There are two government facilities for special educational needs: a school for children and a training centre for adults. Four institutions—a private four-year college, a private medical college, the government community college and law school—provide tertiary education.

Health
The government's health services complex in George Town includes a 124-bed hospital, a dental clinic and an eye clinic. On Grand Cayman there are four district health centres. There is a hospital on Cayman Brac (18 beds) and a health centre on Little Cayman. In 2001 there were 38 doctors in government service (including four on Cayman Brac) and 37 in private practice.

RELIGION
The residents are primarily Christian (85%) and over 12 denominations meet regularly; Church of God, Presbyterian/United, Roman Catholic, Baptist and Seventh-Day Adventists are the largest. Other religions, including Ba'hai, Buddhism, Hinduism, Islam and Judaism, have representation in the community.

CULTURE
Broadcasting
There are seven radio stations (one Christian), four broadcast television channels (two Christian) and a 38-channel microwave relay cable system.

Press
There are two newspapers, both printed on weekdays. News and opinion are also available on at least seven Internet sites.

Tourism
Tourism is the chief industry after financial services, and in 2000 there were 3,756 beds in hotels and 2,341 rooms in apartments, guest houses and cottages. There were 334,071 tourist arrivals by air and 1,214,757 cruise ship arrivals. Tourism receipts in 1999 totalled US$439m.

FURTHER READING
Compendium of Statistics of the Cayman Islands, 2003. Cayman Islands Government Statistics Office, 2004

Cayman Islands Annual Report 2003. Cayman Islands Government Information Services, 2004

Boultbee, Paul G., *Cayman Islands.* [Bibliography] ABC-Clio, Oxford and Santa Barbara (CA), 1996

Falkland Islands

KEY HISTORICAL EVENTS
France established a settlement in 1764 and Britain a second settlement in 1765. In 1770 Spain bought out the French and drove off the British. This action on the part of Spain brought that country and Britain to the verge of war. The Spanish restored the settlement to the British in 1771, but the settlement was withdrawn on economic grounds in 1774. In 1806 Spanish rule was overthrown in Argentina, and the Argentine claimed to succeed Spain in the French and British settlements in 1820. The British objected and reclaimed their settlement in 1832 as a Crown Colony.

On 2 April 1982 Argentine forces occupied the Falkland Islands. On 3 April the UN Security Council called, by 10 votes to 1, for Argentina's withdrawal. After a military campaign, but without a formal declaration of war, the UK regained possession on 14–15 June when Argentina surrendered. In April 1990 Argentina's Congress declared the Falkland and other British-held South Atlantic islands part of the new Argentine province of Tierra del Fuego though the threat of hostilities has been lifted.

TERRITORY AND POPULATION
The Territory comprises numerous islands situated in the South Atlantic Ocean about 480 miles northeast of Cape Horn covering 12,200 sq. km. The main East Falkland Island, 6,760 sq. km; the West Falkland, 5,410 sq. km, including the adjacent small islands. The population at the census of 2001 was 2,379. The only town is Stanley, in East Falkland, with a 2001 population of 1,989. The population is nearly all of British descent, with 1,326 born in the Islands (2001 census figures) and 925 in the UK. In 1995, 84·1% lived in urban areas. A British garrison of about 2,000 servicemen, stationed in East Falkland in 1991, is not included in the 2001 census figures, but the 534 civilians employed there are.

The official language is English.

SOCIAL STATISTICS
In 2000 there were 27 births and 11 deaths on the islands.

CLIMATE
A cool temperate climate, much affected by strong winds, particularly in spring. Stanley, Jan. 49°F (9·4°C), July 35°F (1·7°C). Annual rainfall 24" (625 mm).

CONSTITUTION AND GOVERNMENT
A new Constitution came into force in 1997, updating the previous constitution of 1985 which incorporated a chapter protecting fundamental human rights, and in the preamble recalled the provisions on the right of self-determination contained in international covenants.

Executive power is vested in the Governor who must consult the Executive Council except on urgent or trivial matters. He must consult the Commander British Forces on matters relating to defence and internal security (except police).

There is a *Legislative Council* consisting of eight members (five from Stanley and three from Camp, elected every four years) and two *ex officio* members, the Chief Executive and Financial Secretary. Only elected members have a vote.

British citizenship was withdrawn by the British Nationality Act 1981, but restored after the Argentine invasion of 1982.

RECENT ELECTIONS
Elections to the Legislative Assembly were held on 17 Nov. 2005. Only non-partisans were elected.

CURRENT ADMINISTRATION

Governor: Howard Pearce, CVO.
   Chief Executive: Chris Simpkins.

Government Website: http://www.falklands.gov.fk

DEFENCE

Since 1982 the Islands have been defended by a 2,000-strong garrison of British servicemen. In addition there is a local volunteer defence force.

ECONOMY

The GNP of the Islands is estimated to have tripled from 1985–87 as a result of the expansion of the fishing industry. In 1998–99 the GNP was estimated at £53m.

Overview

In 2001 the Falklands Islands government published the Islands Plan, a three-year rolling programme aimed at achieving sustainable economic growth whilst preserving the natural environment. Policy-making is also influenced by the Falkland Islands Development Corporation (FIDC), established in 1984.

Currency

The unit of currency is the *Falkland Islands pound* (FKP) of 100 *pence*, at parity with £1 sterling.

Budget

Revenue and expenditure (in £ sterling) for fiscal year ending 30 June 2000 was: revenue, 52·3m.; expenditure, 40·4m.

Banking and Finance

The only bank is Standard Chartered Bank, which had assets of £31m. in 1997.

ENERGY AND NATURAL RESOURCES

Electricity

Electricity production in 2000 totalled about 15m. kWh. Installed capacity in 2000 was 9,000 kW.

Oil and Gas

In 1996 the Falkland Islands government awarded production licences to Shell, Amerada Hess, Desire Petroleum and International Petroleum Corporation (Sodra), allowing them to begin oil exploration. The licensed areas are situated 150 km north of the Islands over the North Falkland Basin. Six exploration wells were drilled in 1998 and analysis of the findings suggested that in excess of 60bn. bbls. of oil have been generated in the basin.

Agriculture

The economy was formerly based solely on agriculture, principally sheep farming. Following a programme of sub-division, much of the land is divided into family-size units. There were 100 farms in 1997, averaging 33,600 acres and 8,200 sheep. Wool is the principal product; 1,870,000 tonnes worth £2,292,000 was exported to the UK in 1998.

   Livestock: in April 2000 there were over 700,000 sheep. 2002 estimates: cattle, 4,000; horses, 1,000.

Fisheries

Since the establishment of a 150-mile interim conservation and management zone around the Islands in 1986 and the consequent introduction, on 1 Feb. 1987, of a licensing regime for vessels fishing within the zone, income from the associated fishing activities is now the largest source of revenue. Licences raised £25m. in 1992 but this figure had fallen to £20m. by 1998–99. In 2000 the fish catch (1,000 tonnes) was: illex, 190; loligo, 64; blue whiting, 23; hoki, 20; hake, 3; others, 19. The growth in the annual fish catch since the mid 1980s has been one of the fastest in the world.

On 26 Dec. 1990 the Falklands outer conservation zone was introduced which extends beyond the 150-mile zone out to 200 miles from baselines. In Nov. 1992 commercial fishing in the outer zone was banned, the zone was reopened to fishing in 1994. A UK-Argentine South Atlantic Fisheries Commission was set up in 1990; it meets at least twice a year. In 2001 there were 27 registered fishing vessels.

INDUSTRY

Labour

In 2001 there were 2,025 people employed full-time, including 358 in construction and 326 in agriculture, hunting and fishing. The growth of the fishing industry has ensured practically zero unemployment.

EXTERNAL ECONOMIC RELATIONS

Around 85% of trade is with the UK, the rest with Latin America, mainly Chile. In 1998 imports totalled £23·5m.; exports (mainly wool), £3·5m. (1995).

COMMUNICATIONS

Roads

There are over 50 km of surfaced roads and another 400 km of unsurfaced road. This includes the 80 km between Stanley and Mount Pleasant Airport. Other settlements outside Stanley are linked by tracks. There were about 1,100 private cars in 1996.

Civil Aviation

Air communication is currently via Ascension Island. An airport, completed in 1986, is sited at Mount Pleasant on East Falkland. RAF Tristar aircraft operate a twice-weekly service between the Falklands and the UK. A Chilean airline, LAN Airlines, runs a weekly service to Puerto Montt, Punta Arenas, Rio Gallegos and Santiago. Aircraft movements at Stanley Airport in 1998 amounted to 4,264 with 7,715 passengers moving through the airport.

Shipping

A charter vessel calls four or five times a year to and from the UK. Vessels of the Royal Fleet Auxiliary run regularly to South Georgia. Sea links with Chile and Uruguay began in 1989. In 2002 merchant shipping totalled 54,000 GRT.

Telecommunications

Number of telephone main lines in 2002 was 2,400. International direct dialling is available, as are international facsimile links. In 2002 there were 1,900 Internet users.

Postal Services

In 2003 there were two post offices and 900 post boxes. Airmail is generally received and dispatched twice weekly and surface post is airlifted out about once every two weeks. Surface mail is received approximately once every three weeks.

SOCIAL INSTITUTIONS

Justice

There is a Supreme Court, and a Court of Appeal sits in the UK; appeals may go from that court to the judicial committee of the Privy Council. The senior resident judicial officer is the Senior Magistrate. There is an Attorney General and a Senior Crown Counsel.

Education

Education is compulsory between the ages of five and 16 years. In Stanley in 2002 there were 30 pre-school pupils, 190 primary pupils (18 teachers) and 160 pupils in the 11–16 age range (18 teachers). In rural areas students attend small settlement schools or are visited by one of seven travelling teachers. Lessons may also be carried out over the radio or telephone.

Health

The Government Medical Department is responsible for all medical services to civilians. Primary and secondary health care facilities are based at the King Edward VII Memorial Hospital, the only hospital on the islands. It has 28 beds. It is staffed by five doctors, six sisters (including four midwives), eight staff nurses, a health visitor, counsellor, physiotherapist, social worker and an auxiliary nursing staff. The Royal Army Medical Corps staff the surgical facilities. There are two dentists on the island. Estimated expenditure (1994–95), £2,092,490.

Welfare

In 1998 total amount spent on old age pension payments was £504,075. Total amount spent on family allowance payments was £336,365.

CULTURE

Broadcasting

The Falkland Islands Broadcasting Station (FIBS), in conjunction with British Forces Broadcasting Service (BFBS), broadcasts 24 hours a day on FM and MW. Some BBC World Service programmes are also available.

BFBS also provides a single channel TV service (UKPAL) to Stanley, Mount Pleasant and most outlying camp settlements and a cable TV service is also in operation. In 1997 there were 1,000 TV and 1,000 radio sets.

Tourism

In the 1999–2000 season there were estimated to be 30,000 cruise ship visitors, representing a 400% increase over three seasons. There are tourist lodges at Port Howard, San Carlos, Sea Lion Island and Pebble Island. Stanley has two hotels.

FURTHER READING

Day, Alan, *The Falkland Islands, South Georgia and the South Sandwich Islands.* [Bibliography] ABC-Clio, Oxford and Santa Barbara (CA), 1996

Gough, B., *The Falkland Islands/Malvinas: the Contest for Empire in the South Atlantic.* London, 1992

Gibraltar

KEY HISTORICAL EVENTS

The Rock of Gibraltar was settled by Moors in 711. In 1462 it was taken by the Spaniards, from Granada. It was captured by Admiral Sir George Rooke on 24 July 1704, and ceded to Great Britain by the Treaty of Utrecht, 1713. The cession was confirmed by the treaties of Paris (1763) and Versailles (1783). In 1830 Gibraltar became a British crown colony.

On 10 Sept. 1967 a UN resolution on the decolonization of Gibraltar led to a referendum to ascertain whether the people of Gibraltar wished to retain their link with the UK. Out of an electorate of 12,762, an overwhelming majority voted to retain the British connection.

The border was closed by Spain in 1969, opened to pedestrians in 1982 and fully opened in 1985. In 1973 Gibraltar joined the European Community as a dependent territory of the United Kingdom. In 2001 talks were held between Britain and Spain over the colony's sovereignty. In a joint statement, the British and Spanish foreign ministers said they would work towards a comprehensive agreement by the summer of 2002. Gibraltar's government held an unofficial referendum on sharing sovereignty with Spain on 7 Nov. 2002 in which 98·97% of votes cast were against joint sovereignty. While Britain sees the principle of shared sovereignty as the definitive solution, Spain maintains its historic claim to outright control.

TERRITORY AND POPULATION

Gibraltar is situated in latitude 36°07' N and longitude 05°21' W. Area, 6·5 sq. km (2½ sq. miles) including port and harbour. Total population, (2003), 28,605 (of whom 23,069 were British Gibraltarian, 3,270 Other British and 2,266 Non-British); density, 4,400 per sq. km. The population is mostly of Genoese, Portuguese and Maltese and Spanish descent.

The official language is English. Spanish, Italian and Portuguese are also spoken.

SOCIAL STATISTICS

Statistics (2003): births, 363; deaths, 234; marriages, 829. Rates per 1,000 population, 2000: birth, 15·1; death, 9·7; marriage, 26·7 (the highest in Europe and one of the highest in the world).

CLIMATE

The climate is warm temperate, with westerly winds in winter bringing rain. Summers are pleasantly warm and rainfall is low. Mean maximum temperatures: Jan. 16°C, July 28°C. Annual rainfall 722 mm.

CONSTITUTION AND GOVERNMENT

A new Constitution was introduced in 1969. The Legislative and City Councils were merged to produce an enlarged legislature known as the *Gibraltar House of Assembly.* Executive authority is exercised by the Governor, who is also Commander-in-Chief. The Governor retains direct responsibility for matters relating to defence, external affairs and internal security. However, he is normally required to act in accordance with the advice of the Gibraltar Council, which consists of four *ex officio* members (the Deputy Governor, the Deputy Fortress Commander, the Attorney-General and the Financial and Development Secretary) together with five elected members of the House of Assembly appointed by the Governor after consultation with the Chief Minister. There is a Council of Ministers presided over by the Chief Minister.

The House of Assembly consists of a Speaker appointed by the Governor, 15 elected and two *ex officio* members (the Attorney-General and the Financial and Development Secretary).

Gibraltarians have full UK citizenship.

RECENT ELECTIONS

At the elections of 27 Nov. 2003 the electorate was 10,317 and turnout was 57·73%. The ruling Gibraltar Social Democratic Party (GSD) gained eight seats with 51% of votes cast. The opposition alliance of the Gibraltar Socialist Labour Party and the Liberal Party took 40% of the vote, gaining five and two seats respectively.

CURRENT ADMINISTRATION

Governor and C.-in-C: Sir Francis Richards, KCMG, CVO, b. 1945 (sworn in on 27 May 2003).

Chief Minister: Peter Caruana; b. 1956 (GSD; elected in 1996, re-elected in 2000 and 2003).

Deputy Chief Minister and Minister for Trade and Industry and Communications: Joe Holliday. *Education:* Dr Bernard Linares. *Health:* Lieut. Col. Ernest Britto. *Housing:* Clive Beltran. *Social Affairs:* Yvette Del Agua. *Heritage, Culture, Youth and Sport:* Fabian Vinet. *Environment:* Jaime Netto.

Speaker (House of Assembly): Haresh Budhrani, QC.

Government Website: http://www.gibraltar.gov.gi

DEFENCE

The Ministry of Defence presence consists of a tri-service garrison numbering approximately 900 uniformed personnel. Supporting the garrison are approximately 1,100 locally-employed civilian personnel. The garrison supports a NATO Headquarters.

ECONOMY

Overview

The economy is primarily dependent on service industries and port facilities, with income derived from tourism, transhipment and, perhaps most importantly in terms of growth, the provision of financial services.

Currency

The legal tender currency is UK sterling. Also legal tender are Government of Gibraltar Currency notes and coins. The *Gibraltar pound* (GIP) of 100 *pence* is at parity with the UK £1 sterling. The total of Government of Gibraltar notes in circulation at 31 March 2004 was £14·3m. The annual rate of inflation was 2·5% in 2003.

Budget

Departmental revenue credited to the Consolidated Fund for the year ending 31 March 2003 totalled £166·3m. whilst expenditure amounted to £135·3m. The main sources of Consolidated Fund revenues were Income Tax (£65·5m.), import duties (£29·2m.), Corporation Tax (£16·9m.) and General Rates (£12m.). Main items of Consolidation Fund expenditure: Education, Culture and Training (£19·8m.); Social Affairs (£13·3m.); Electricity (£12·5m.); Technical Services (£12·2m.); contributions to the Gibraltar Health Authority (£11·9m.); Police (£8m.); Housing (£7·5m.); Tourism and Transport (£7·2m.).

Performance

In 2002–03 Gibraltar's GDP was £507·2m., equivalent to £17,770 per head.

Banking and Finance

At March 2004 there were 17 authorized banks. The majority of these are either subsidiaries or branches of major UK or other European Economic Area (EEA) banks. In 1989 the Financial Services Commission was established to regulate financial activities. The banking sector provides services to both local and non-resident customers. Many of these banks specialize in providing private banking to high net worth individuals who are not resident in Gibraltar.

ENERGY AND NATURAL RESOURCES

Environment

Gibraltar's carbon dioxide emissions from the consumption and flaring of fossil fuels in 2002 were the equivalent of 144·1 tonnes per capita, the highest in the world.

Electricity

Production in 2004 amounted to 136m. kWh.

Oil and Gas

Gibraltar is dependent on imported petroleum for its energy supplies.

Agriculture

Gibraltar lacks agricultural land and natural resources; the territory is dependent on imports of foodstuffs and fuels.

INDUSTRY

The industrial sector (including manufacturing, construction and power) employed around 16% of the working population in 2004.

Labour

The total number of employee jobs at Oct. 2004 was 15,994. Principal areas of employment (Oct. 2004): community, social and personal services, 4,073; trade, restaurants and hotels, 3,671; construction, 1,788; manufacturing, 453; electricity and water, 275; other, 5,734. (Figures cover only non-agricultural activities, excluding mining and quarrying). An estimated 2% of the labour force were unemployed in 2002.

Trade Unions

In 1991 there were eight registered trade unions.

EXTERNAL ECONOMIC RELATIONS

Gibraltar has a special status within the EU which exempts it from the latter's fiscal policy.

Imports and Exports

Imports in 2003 totalled £286·1m. and exports £90·1m (excluding petroleum products).

Britain provided 28% of imports in 2003 and is the largest source. Other major trade partners include the Netherlands, Spain and Japan. Foodstuffs accounted for 7% of total imports in 2003. Value of non-fuel imports, 2003, £286·1m. Mineral fuels comprised about 60% of the value of total imports in 2003. Exports are mainly re-exports of petroleum and petroleum products supplied to shipping, and include manufactured goods, wines, spirits, malt and tobacco. Gibraltar depends largely on tourism, offshore banking and other financial sector activity, the entrepôt trade and the provision of supplies to visiting ships. In 2003 Gibraltar recorded a visible trade deficit of £196·0m.

COMMUNICATIONS

Roads

There are 56 km of roads including 6·8 km of pedestrian way. In 2004 there were 12,395 private vehicles, 5,358 motorcycles, 1,065 goods vehicles and 98 omnibuses and 103 taxis.

Civil Aviation

There is an international airport, Gibraltar North Front. Scheduled flights were operated in 2003 by British Airways to London (Gatwick), and by Monarch Airlines to London (Luton) and Manchester. In 2003, 133,005 passengers arrived by air and 132,852 departed; 66 tonnes of freight were loaded and 325 tonnes were unloaded (figures exclude military freight). The airport was designed to accommodate 1m. passengers a year, but is underutilized owing to Spain's exclusion of Gibraltar as a European regional airport.

Shipping

The Strait of Gibraltar is a principal ocean route between the Mediterranean and Black Sea areas and the rest of the world. A total of 6,751 merchant ships of 147·7m. GRT entered port during 2003, including 5,758 deep-sea ships of 146·1m. GRT. In 2003, 4,387 calls were made by yachts of 147,510 GRT. 167 cruise liners called during 2003 involving 137,979 passengers.

Telecommunications

Gibtelecom and its two wholly owned subsidiaries Gibraltar Telecommunications International Limited (Gibtel) and Gibconnect are responsible for the provision of most of the telecommunications and internet services and the supply of communications equipment in Gibraltar.

As at 31 Dec. 2003 the Group's fixed exchange lines stood at 25,657. By the end of 2003 there were 15,709 mobile GSM phone customers.

Postal Services

Airmail is dispatched to London, and via London to destinations worldwide, six times a week in direct flights. Surface letter mail and parcel mail to and from the United Kingdom is dispatched and received via the land frontier five times a week.

SOCIAL INSTITUTIONS

Justice

The judicial system is based on the English system. There is a Court of Appeal, a Supreme Court, presided over by the Chief Justice, a Court of First Instance and a Magistrates' Court.

The population in penal institutions in Nov. 2003 was 31 (equivalent to 112 per 100,000 population).

Education

Free compulsory education is provided between ages four and 15 years. The medium of instruction is English. The comprehensive system was introduced in Sept. 1972 and all schools currently follow a locally adapted version of the National Curriculum for England and Wales. In the 2003–04 academic year there were 11 primary and two secondary schools. Primary schools are divided into first schools for children aged 4–8 years and middle schools for children aged 8–12 years. All primary schools are mixed though secondary schools are single-sex.

Vocational education and training is available at the Gibraltar College (a post-15 institution), the Construction Training Centre and the Cammell Laird Training Centre; the former two are managed by the Gibraltar government and the latter by Cammell Laird (and part-funded by the Government). In Sept. 2003 there were 3,082 pupils at government primary schools, 305 at private primary schools and 198 at the Services school. 970 pupils were enrolled at the boys' comprehensive school and 954 at the girls' comprehensive. There were 309 students in the Gibraltar College. Government expenditure on education in the year ended 31 March 2004 was £19m.

Health

The Gibraltar Health Authority is the organization responsible for providing health care in Gibraltar. The Authority operates a Group Practice Medical Scheme which is a contributory scheme and enables registered persons to access free medical treatment. In 2002 there were two hospitals with 226 beds. Total expenditure on medical and health services during year ended 31 March 2002 was £31·4m.

Welfare

The social security system consists of: the Social Security (Employment Injuries Insurance) Scheme which only applies to employed persons; the Social Security (Short-Term Benefits) Scheme which provides for payments of maternity grants. maternity allowance, death grants and unemployment benefit; and the Social Security (Open Long-Term Benefits) Scheme which provides for pensions and widows' allowances.

RELIGION

According to the 2001 census 78·1% of the population were Roman Catholic, 7·0% Church of England, 4·0% Muslim, 2·1% Jewish and 1·8% Hindu. In 2004 there were seven Roman Catholic and three Anglican churches (including one Catholic and one Anglican cathedral), one Presbyterian and one Methodist church, four synagogues and two mosques.

CULTURE

Broadcasting

Radio Gibraltar broadcasts for 24 hours daily, 22 hours in English and two hours in Spanish; and GBC Television operates for 24 hours daily in English (colour by PAL). At 31 Dec. 2003 there were 7,500 TV licences.

Press

In 2003 there were two daily papers and one weekly.

Tourism

In 2004 more than 7·6m. tourists visited Gibraltar (including day-visitors) bringing in revenue of £229m. There are around 900 hotel beds in Gibraltar. Tourism accounts for an estimated 35% of GDP.

FURTHER READING

Gibraltar Year Book. Gibraltar (Annual)

Morris, D. S. and Haigh, R. H., *Britain, Spain and Gibraltar, 1940–90: the Eternal Triangle.* London, 1992

Montserrat

KEY HISTORICAL EVENTS

Montserrat was discovered by Columbus in 1493 and colonized by Britain in 1632, who brought Irish settlers to the island. Montserrat formed part of the federal colony of the Leeward Islands from 1871 until 1958, when it became a separate colony following the dissolution of the Federation.

On 18 July 1995 the Soufriere Hills volcano erupted for the first time in recorded history, which led to over half the inhabitants being evacuated to the north of the island, and the relocation of the chief town, Plymouth. Another major eruption on 25 June 1997 caused a number of deaths and led to further evacuation.

TERRITORY AND POPULATION

Montserrat is situated in the Caribbean Sea, 43 km southwest of Antigua. The area is 102·3 sq. km (39·5 sq. miles). Census population, 2001, 4,482. What was previously the capital, Plymouth, is now deserted as a result of the continuing activity of the Soufriere Hills volcano. The safe area is in the north of the island.

The official language is English.

CLIMATE

A tropical climate with an average annual rainfall of 60" (1,500 mm) the wettest months being Sept.–Dec., with a hurricane season June–Nov. Plymouth, Jan. 76°F (24·4°C), July 81°F (27·2°C).

CONSTITUTION AND GOVERNMENT

Montserrat is a British Overseas Territory. The Constitution dates from the 1989 Montserrat Constitutional Order. The head of state is Queen Elizabeth II, represented by a *Governor* who heads an Executive Council, comprising also the Chief Minister, the Financial Secretary, the Attorney-General and three other ministers. The *Legislative Council* consists of seven elected members, two civil service officials (the Attorney-General and Financial Secretary) and two nominated members; it sits for five-year terms.

RECENT ELECTIONS

In elections to the Legislative Council on 2 April 2001 the New People's Liberation Movement won seven of the nine seats against two for the National Progressive Party.

CURRENT ADMINISTRATION

Governor: Deborah Barnes Jones; b. 1956 (since 10 May 2004).

Chief Minister: John Osborne; b. 1936 (since 5 April 2001, having previously been in office from 1978 to 1991).

INTERNATIONAL RELATIONS

Montserrat is a member of CARICOM and the OECS.

ECONOMY

Currency

Montserrat's currency is the *Eastern Caribbean dollar* (*see* ANTIGUA AND BARBUDA: Currency).

Budget

In 1998 the estimated expenditure was EC$60·6m. compared with actual expenditure of EC$63·5m. in 1997, a reduction of 5%.

Performance

Real GDP growth was −2·9% in 1995 and 0·8% in 1994.

Banking and Finance

The East Caribbean Central Bank based in St Kitts and Nevis functions as a central bank. The *Governor* is Sir Dwight Venner. In 2003 there were four commercial banks and in 1996 there were 21 offshore banks. Responsibility for overseeing offshore banking rests with the Governor.

ENERGY AND NATURAL RESOURCES

Electricity

Production (2000) 12m. kWh. Installed capacity (2000): 4,000 kW.

Agriculture

The volcanic eruptions in 1997 dramatically reduced the area of land under cultivation. Agriculture, now concentrated in the north, is showing signs of recovering. In 2002 there were 2,000 ha. of arable and permanent crop land. The main products have traditionally been potatoes, tomatoes, onions, mangoes and limes. Meat production began in 1994 and the island soon became self-sufficient in chicken, mutton and beef.

Livestock (2002); cattle, 10,000; pigs, 1,000; sheep, 5,000; goats, 7,000.

Forestry

The area under forests in 2000 was 3,000 ha., or 27·3% of the total land area.

Fisheries

The total catch in 2001 was estimated at 50 tonnes.

INDUSTRY

Manufacturing has in recent years contributed about 6% to GDP and accounted for 10% of employment, but has been responsible for about 80% of exports. It has been limited to rice milling and the production of light consumer goods such as electronic components, light fittings, plastic bags and leather goods. The volcanic activity has put a halt to the milling of rice in the exclusion zone and curtailed the production of light consumer goods.

Trade Unions

There is one trade union, the Montserrat Allied Workers Union (MAWU).

EXTERNAL ECONOMIC RELATIONS

Imports and Exports

Imports in 2002 totalled US$25·4m.; exports, US$1·5m. The USA was the main trading partner.

COMMUNICATIONS

Roads

In 1995 there were 205 km of paved roads, 25 km of unsurfaced roads and 50 km of tracks. In 1995 there were 2,700 cars and 400 commercial vehicles registered. These figures changed as a result of the volcanic eruptions of 1995 and 1997 but since then the government, through the Ministry of Communications and Works, has been focusing its road developments in the north of the island, and a number of road work projects are under way.

Civil Aviation

At the W. H. Bramble airport LIAT used to provide services to Antigua with onward connections to the rest of the eastern Caribbean, but it was closed in June 1997 as volcanic activity increased. A new airport opened in Feb. 2005.

Shipping

Plymouth is the port of entry, but alternative anchorage was provided at Old Bay Road during the volcanic crisis.

Telecommunications

Number of telephone main lines, 2000, 2,811. With the migration of people to the north and overseas, and the subsequent destruction of the southern part of the island, the number of telephones has since shrunk to 2,100. There were 489 mobile phone subscribers in 2000.

SOCIAL INSTITUTIONS

Justice

Law is based on UK common law as exercised by the Eastern Caribbean Supreme Court. Final appeal lies to the UK Privy Council. Law is administered by the West Indies Associated States Court, a Court of Summary Jurisdiction and Magistrate's Courts.

Education

In 1996–97 there were 11 primary schools (only four open), a comprehensive secondary school with three campuses, and a technical college. Schools are run by the government, the churches and the private sector. There is a medical school, the American University of the Caribbean.

In 2000–01 total expenditure on education came to 7·9% of total government spending.

Health

In 1996 there were four medical officers, one surgeon, one dentist and one hospital with 69 beds.

RELIGION

In 1997, 25% of the population were Anglican, 20% Methodist, 15% Pentecostal, 10% Adventist and 10% Roman Catholic.

CULTURE

Broadcasting

There is a government-owned radio station (ZJB) and two commercial stations (Radio Antilles and GEM Radio). There is a commercial cable TV company (colour by NTSC).

Press

In 1996 there was one weekly newspaper.

Tourism

Tourism at one time contributed about 30% of GDP. There were 36,077 visitors including 11,636 cruise ship arrivals in 1994. However, after the volcanic eruptions the tourist industry declined dramatically; over half the island is closed. There were 8,375 visitors in 2003.

FURTHER READING

Fergus, H. A., *Montserrat: History of a Caribbean Colony*. London, 1994

Pitcairn Island

KEY HISTORICAL EVENTS

Pitcairn was discovered by Carteret in 1767, but remained uninhabited until 1790, when it was occupied by nine mutineers of HMS *Bounty*, with 12 women and six men from Tahiti. Nothing was known of their existence until the island was visited in 1808.

TERRITORY AND POPULATION

Pitcairn Island (4·6 sq. km; 1·75 sq. miles) is situated in the Pacific Ocean, nearly equidistant from New Zealand and Panama (25° 04' S. lat., 130° 06' W. long.). Adamstown is the only settlement. The population in 2003 was 48. The uninhabited islands of Henderson (31 sq. km), Ducie (3·9 sq. km) and Oeno (5·2 sq. km) were annexed in 1902. Henderson is a World Heritage Site.

CLIMATE

An equable climate, with average annual rainfall of 80" (2,000 mm) spread evenly throughout the year. Mean monthly temperatures range from 75°F (24°C) in Jan. to 66°F (19°C) in July.

CONSTITUTION AND GOVERNMENT

The Local Government Ordinance of 1964 constitutes a *Council* of ten members, of whom six are elected annually, three are nominated (one by the six elected members and two by the Governor), and the Island Secretary is an *ex officio* member. No political parties exist. The Island Magistrate, who is elected triennially, presides over the Council; other members hold office for only one year. Liaison between Governor and Council is through a Commissioner in the Auckland, New Zealand, office of the British Consulate-General.

CURRENT ADMINISTRATION

Governor: Richard Fell.
 Mayor: Jay Warren.

Government Website: http://www.government.pn

ECONOMY

Currency
New Zealand currency is used.

Budget
For the year to 31 March 1997 revenue was NZ$604,234 and expenditure NZ$601,665.

ENERGY AND NATURAL RESOURCES

Fisheries
The catch in 2001 was approximately eight tonnes.

COMMUNICATIONS

Roads
There were (1997) 6 km of roads. In 1997 there were 29 motorcycles.

SOCIAL INSTITUTIONS

Justice
The Island Court consists of the Island Magistrate and two assessors.

Education
In 2004 there was one teacher and nine pupils.

FURTHER READING

Murray, S., *Pitcairn Island: the First 200 Years.* La Canada (CA), 1992

St Helena

KEY HISTORICAL EVENTS

The island was uninhabited when discovered by the Portuguese in 1502. It was administered by the East India Company from 1659 and became a British colony in 1834. Napoleon died there in exile in 1821.

Public demonstrations took place in April 1997 against government spending cuts and the Governor's imposition of his own head of social services.

TERRITORY AND POPULATION

St Helena, of volcanic origin, is 3,100 km from the west coast of Africa. Area, 122 sq. km (47 sq. miles), with a cultivable area of 243 ha. The population at the 1998 census was 5,157. In 1995 an estimated 62·6% of the population were urban. The capital and port is Jamestown, population (1998) 1,300.

The official language is English.

Ascension is a small island of volcanic origin, of 88 sq. km (34 sq. miles), 700 miles northwest of St Helena. There are 120 ha. providing fresh meat, vegetables and fruit. The estimated population in 1999 was 1,050.

The island is the resort of sea turtles, rabbits, the sooty tern or 'wideawake', and feral donkeys.

A cable station connects the island with St Helena, Sierra Leone, St Vincent, Rio de Janeiro and Buenos Aires. There is an airstrip (Miracle Mile) near the settlement of Georgetown; the Royal Air Force maintains an air link with the Falkland Islands.

Administrator: Michael Hill.

Tristan da Cunha is the largest of a small group of islands in the South Atlantic, lying 2,124 km (1,320 miles) southwest of St Helena, of which they became dependencies on 12 Jan. 1938. Tristan da Cunha has an area of 98 sq. km and a population (2002) of 284, all living in the settlement of Edinburgh. Inaccessible Island (10 sq. km) lies 20 miles west, and the three Nightingale Islands (2 sq. km) lie 20 miles south of Tristan da Cunha; they are uninhabited. Gough Island (90 sq. km) is 220 miles south of Tristan and has a meteorological station.

Tristan consists of a volcano rising to a height of 2,060 metres, with a circumference at its base of 34 km. The volcano, believed to be extinct, erupted unexpectedly early in Oct. 1961. The whole population was evacuated without loss and settled temporarily in the UK; in 1963 they returned to Tristan. Potatoes remain the chief crop. Cattle, sheep and pigs are now reared, and fish are plentiful.

Population in 1996, 292. The original inhabitants were shipwrecked sailors and soldiers who remained behind when the garrison from St Helena was withdrawn in 1817.

At the end of April 1942 Tristan da Cunha was commissioned as HMS *Atlantic Isle*, and became an important meteorological and radio station. In Jan. 1949 a South African company commenced crawfishing operations. An Administrator was appointed at the end of 1948 and a body of basic law brought into operation. The Island Council, which was set up in 1932, consists of a Chief Islander, three nominated and eight elected members (including one woman), under the chairmanship of the Administrator.

Administrator: Mike Hentley.

SOCIAL STATISTICS

2001 figures for St Helena: births, 36; deaths, 41; marriages, 20; divorces (2000), 9. Annual growth rate, 1990–95, 0·6%.

CLIMATE

A mild climate, with little variation. Temperatures range from 75–85°F (24–29°C) in summer to 65–75°F (18–24°C) in winter. Rainfall varies between 13" (325 mm) and 37" (925 mm) according to altitude and situation.

CONSTITUTION AND GOVERNMENT

The St Helena Constitution Order of 1988 entered into force on 1 Jan. 1989. The *Legislative Council* consists of the Governor, two *ex officio* members (the Government Secretary and the Treasurer) and 12 elected members. The Governor is assisted by an *Executive Council* consisting of the two *ex officio* members and the chairs of the six Council Committees.

RECENT ELECTIONS

The last Legislative Council elections were on 31 Aug. 2005. Only non-partisans were elected.

CURRENT ADMINISTRATION

Governor and C.-in-C: Michael Clancy.

Government Website: http://www.sainthelena.gov.sh

ENERGY AND NATURAL RESOURCES

Electricity
Production in 2000 totalled 7m. kWh. Installed capacity in 2000 was 4,000 kW.

Agriculture
In 2001 there were 4,000 ha. of arable land.

Fisheries
The total catch in 2001 was 866 tonnes.

INDUSTRY

Labour
In 2000 there were 270 registered unemployed persons.

COMMUNICATIONS

Roads
There were (2003) 94 km of all-weather motor roads. There were 1,931 vehicles in 2002.

Shipping
There is a service from Cardiff (UK) six times a year, and links with South Africa and neighbouring islands. In 1995 vessels entered totalling 55,000 net registered tons.

Telecommunications
In 2002 there were 2,200 main telephone lines in operation. There were 500 Internet users in 2002.

SOCIAL INSTITUTIONS

Justice
Police force, 32; cases are dealt with by a police magistrate.

Education
In 2002–03 there were eight schools with, in 1999–2000, 87 teachers and 860 pupils. The Prince Andrew School (opened in 1989) offers vocational courses leading to British qualifications.

Health
There were four doctors, one dentist and one hospital in 2001.

RELIGION

There are ten Anglican churches, four Baptist chapels, three Salvation Army halls, one Seventh Day Adventist church and one Roman Catholic church.

CULTURE

Broadcasting
The Cable & Wireless Ltd cable connects St Helena with Cape Town and Ascension Island. The government-run Radio St Helena broadcasts daily and relays BBC programmes. Number of radio receivers (1997), approximately 3,000. Television reception was introduced in 1996 from the BBC World Service, South African M-Net and a US Satellite channel. There were some 2,000 TV receivers in 1997.

FURTHER READING

Day, A., *St. Helena, Ascension and Tristan da Cunha.* [Bibliography] ABC-Clio, Oxford and Santa Barbara (CA), 1997

South Georgia and the South Sandwich Islands

KEY HISTORICAL EVENTS

The first landing and exploration was undertaken by Capt. James Cook, who formally took possession in the name of George III on 17 Jan. 1775. British sealers arrived in 1788 and American sealers in 1791. Sealing reached its peak in 1800. A German team was the first to carry out scientific studies there in 1882–83. Whaling began in 1904 and ceased in 1966, and the civil administration was withdrawn. Argentine forces invaded South Georgia on 3 April 1982. A British naval task force recovered the Island on 25 April 1982.

TERRITORY AND POPULATION

South Georgia lies 1,300 km southeast of the Falkland Islands and has an area of 3,760 sq. km. The South Sandwich Islands are 760 km southeast of South Georgia and have an area of 340 sq. km. In 1993 crown sovereignty and jurisdiction were extended from 19 km (12 miles) to 322 km (200 miles) around the islands. There is no permanent population. The British Antarctic Survey operate a fisheries science facility at King Edward Point and a biological station on Bird Island. The South Sandwich Islands are uninhabited.

CLIMATE

The climate is wet and cold, with strong winds and little seasonal variation. 15°C is occasionally reached on a windless day. Temperatures below −15°C at sea level are unusual.

CONSTITUTION AND GOVERNMENT

Under the new Constitution which came into force on 3 Oct. 1985 the Territories ceased to be dependencies of the Falkland Islands. The Government of South Georgia and the South Sandwich Islands (GSGSSI) administers the island. The local administration is the responsibility of the Government Officer based at King Edward Point. Executive power is vested in a Commissioner, who is also the Governor of the Falkland Islands. On matters relating to defence, the Commissioner consults the officer commanding Her Majesty's British Forces in the South Atlantic. The Commissioner, whenever practicable, consults the Executive Council of the Falkland Islands on the exercise of functions that in his opinion might affect the Falkland Islands. There is no Legislative Council. Laws are made by the Commissioner (Howard Pearce, CVO, resident in the Falkland Islands).

ECONOMY

Budget
The total projected revenue of the Territories (2006) was £4,037,700, of which 85% from fishing licenses, 8% landing fees, 3% philatelic sales and 2% harbour dues. Expenditure (projected), £4,265,900, includes 50% fisheries research and protection, 12% King Edward Point running costs, 11% observer fees and 6% Grytviken remediation and maintenance projects.

COMMUNICATIONS

The bases at King Edward Point and Bird Island have modern satellite communication systems. King Edward Point is regularly visited by the GSGSSI Fishery Patrol Vessel. Other visiting vessels include cruise ships, BAS research ships, warships and auxiliaries, fishing vessels and yachts.

SOCIAL INSTITUTIONS

Justice
There is a Supreme Court for the Territories and a Court of Appeal in the United Kingdom. Appeals may go from that court to the Judicial Committee of the Privy Council. The British Antarctic Survey base commander at King Edward Point is usually appointed a magistrate.

CULTURE

Tourism
In the region of 4,000 tourists visit the island annually.

FURTHER READING

Day, Alan, *The Falkland Islands, South Georgia and the South Sandwich Islands.* [Bibliography] ABC-Clio, Oxford and Santa Barbara (CA), 1996

Headland, R.K., *The Island of South Georgia.* CUP, 1984

Sovereign Base Areas of Akrotiri and Dhekelia in Cyprus

KEY HISTORICAL EVENTS

The Sovereign Base Areas (SBAs) are those parts of the island of Cyprus that stayed under British jurisdiction and remained British sovereign territory when the 1960 Treaty of Establishment created the independent Republic of Cyprus. The Akrotiri facility formed a strategic part of the West's nuclear capacity during the Cold War. The SBAs were used for the deployment of troops in the Gulf War in 1991. Military intelligence is now the key role of the SBAs. The construction of massive antennae at the RAF communications base at Akrotiri sparked violent riots in 2001 and 2002, led by a Greek Cypriot MP. In Feb. 2003 the British Government offered to surrender approximately half the area of the SBAs as an incentive for a settlement between the Greek and Turkish administrations in Cyprus.

TERRITORY AND POPULATION

The Sovereign Base Areas (SBAs), with a total land area of 254 sq. km (98 sq. miles), comprise the Western SBA (123 sq. km), including Episkopi Garrison and RAF Akrotiri (opened 1956), and the Eastern SBA (131 sq. km), including Dhekelia Garrison. The SBAs cover 3% of the land area of the island of Cyprus. There are approximately 3,000 military personnel and approximately 5,000 civilians. The British Government has declared that it will not develop the SBAs other than for military purposes. Citizens and residents of the Republic of Cyprus are guaranteed freedom of access and communications to and through the SBAs.

The SBAs are administered as military bases reporting to the Ministry of Defence in London. The Administrator is the Commander, British Forces Cyprus. The joint force headquarters are at Episkopi. Greek and English are spoken.

CURRENT ADMINISTRATION

Administrator: Maj.-Gen. Peter Thomas Clayton Pearson (appointed Sept. 2003).

The Turks and Caicos Islands

KEY HISTORICAL EVENTS

After a long period of rival French and Spanish claims the islands were eventually secured to the British Crown in 1766, and became a separate colony in 1973 after association at various times with the colonies of the Bahamas and Jamaica.

TERRITORY AND POPULATION

The Islands are situated between 21° and 22°N. lat. and 71° and 72°W. long., about 80 km east of the Bahamas, of which they are geographically an extension. There are over 40 islands, covering an estimated area of 500 sq. km (193 sq. miles). Only seven are inhabited: Grand Caicos, the largest, is 48 km long by 3 to 5 km broad; Grand Turk, the capital and main political and administrative centre, is 11 km long by 2 km broad. Population, 2001 census, 19,886; Grand Turk, 3,976; Middle Caicos, 301;

North Caicos, 1,347; Parrot Cay, 58; Providenciales, 13,021; Salt Cay, 120; South Caicos, 1,063. The estimated population for 2004 was 26,023. An estimated 56·4% of the population were rural in 1995.

The official language is English.

SOCIAL STATISTICS

2004: births, 300; deaths, 218. Annual growth rate, 1995–99, 3·3%.

CLIMATE

An equable and healthy climate as a result of regular trade winds, though hurricanes are sometimes experienced. Grand Turk, Jan. 76°F (24·4°C), July 83°F (28·3°C). Annual rainfall 21".

CONSTITUTION AND GOVERNMENT

A new Constitution was introduced in 1988 and amended in 1992. The Executive Council comprises two official members: the Chief Secretary and the Attorney-General; a Chief Minister and five other ministers from among the elected members of the Legislative Council; and is presided over by the Governor. The Legislative Council consists of a Speaker, the two official members of the Executive Council, 13 elected members and three appointed members.

RECENT ELECTIONS

At general elections held on 24 April 2003 for the 13 elective seats on the Legislative Council, the People's Democratic Movement (PDM) won seven seats and the People's National Party (PNP) won six. By-elections on 7 Aug. 2003 gave the PNP a majority and a total of eight seats on the Council.

CURRENT ADMINISTRATION

Governor: Richard Tauwhare; b. 1959 (took office on 11 July 2005).

Chief Minister: Michael Misick; b. 1966 (PNP; took office on 15 Aug. 2003).

INTERNATIONAL RELATIONS

The Islands are a member of CARICOM.

ECONOMY

Overview

The economy is based on free-market private sector-led development. The focus is on the service sector, but tourism and finance are still the dominant industries.

Currency

The US dollar is the official currency. Inflation was 3·3% in 2004.

Budget

In 2004–05 current revenues were US$118m. and current expenditures US$122m.

Performance

GDP growth was 2·0% in 2002 (1·6% in 2001).

Banking and Finance

There were six commercial banks in 2004. Offshore finance is a major industry.

Weights and Measures

The Imperial system is generally in use.

ENERGY AND NATURAL RESOURCES

Electricity

Electrical services are provided to all of the inhabited islands. Total electricity production for 2000 was about 5m. kWh. Installed capacity in 2000 was 4,000 kW. Total electrical power consumption in 2003 was 102m. kWh. For all US appliances, 110 volts, 60 cycles, are suitable.

Oil and Gas
Both oil and gas are imported.

Agriculture
Farming is done on a small scale mainly for subsistence.

Fisheries
In 2003 the total catch was 998 tonnes. Conch and lobster are the traditional catches.

INDUSTRY

Labour
In 2001, out of a total population of 13,436 aged 15 or over, 10,181 were working, 1,094 unemployed and 2,161 economically inactive.

EXTERNAL ECONOMIC RELATIONS

Imports and Exports
Imports, 2004, US$220·6m.; exports, US$12·2m. The main export is dried, frozen and processed fish.

COMMUNICATIONS

Civil Aviation
The international airports are on Grand Turk and Providenciales. International services are provided by Air Canada, Air Jamaica, American Airlines, Bahamasair, British Airways, Delta Airlines, TCI Skyking, Tropical Airways d'Haiti and US Airways. An internal air service provides regular daily flights between the inhabited islands.

Shipping
The main ports are at Grand Turk, Cockburn Harbour and Providenciales. There is a service to Miami. In 2002 the merchant fleet totalled 1,000 GRT.

Telecommunications
There are internal and international cable, telephone, telegraph and fax services.

Postal Services
Postal services are provided on all of the inhabited islands by the government. Postal agencies such as UPS, DHL and Federal Express also exist. There were six post offices in 2003.

SOCIAL INSTITUTIONS

Justice
Laws are a mixture of Statute and Common Law. There is a Magistrates Court and a Supreme Court. Appeals lie from the Supreme Court to the Court of Appeal which sits in Nassau, Bahamas. There is a further appeal in certain cases to the Privy Council in London.

Education
The adult literacy rate is 98%. Education is free between the ages of five and 14 in the ten government primary schools; there are also four private primary schools. Total school enrolment in 2004–05 was 1,931 in government primary schools and 1,282 in government secondary schools. There were 1,670 pupils enrolled in the private schools.

In 2000–01 total expenditure on education came to 16·8% of total government expenditure.

Health
In 2004 there were 17 doctors, two dentists and 43 hospital beds.

RELIGION

There are Anglican, Catholic, Methodist, Baptist and Evangelist groups.

CULTURE

Broadcasting
The government operates the semi-commercial Radio Turks and Caicos. There are also two commercial stations and one religious. In 1997 there were about 8,000 radio sets. There is cable and satellite TV.

Press
There is one weekly and one bi-weekly newspaper.

Tourism
Number of visitors, 2004, 171,500. Tourism receipts totalled US$285m. in 2000. In 2002 tourism accounted for 33·9% of GDP.

FURTHER READING

Boultbee, P. G., *Turks & Caicos Islands*. [Bibliography] ABC-Clio, Oxford and Santa Barbara (CA), 1991

UNITED STATES OF AMERICA

© Research Machines plc 2006

CANADA

0 — 400 mi
0 — 600 km

Seattle
WASHINGTON

MONTANA

NORTH DAKOTA

MINNESOTA

MICHIGAN

VT MAINE
NH
Boston

IDAHO

SOUTH DAKOTA

WISCONSIN

NEW YORK
MA

OREGON

WYOMING

Detroit

Chicago

RI
CT

San Francisco

NEVADA

UTAH

NEBRASKA

IOWA

ILLINOIS

OHIO

New York

Philadelphia

PV
NJ

MD DE

WASHINGTON D.C.

INDIANA

WV

CALIFORNIA

Las Vegas

COLORADO

KANSAS

MISSOURI

KENTUCKY

VIRGINIA

ARIZONA

NEW MEXICO

OKLAHOMA

TENNESSEE

NORTH CAROLINA

Los Angeles

San Diego

Phoenix

ARKANSAS

Atlanta

SOUTH CAROLINA

UNITED STATES

Dallas

TEXAS

MISSISSIPPI

ALABAMA

GEORGIA

ATLANTIC OCEAN

PACIFIC OCEAN

San Antonio

LOUISIANA

Houston

New Orleans

FLORIDA

Miami

THE BAHAMAS

MEXICO

Gulf of Mexico

CUBA

ALASKA

Anchorage

Bering Sea

Gulf of Alaska

0 — 600 mi
0 — 800 km

0 — 200 mi
0 — 300 km

Honolulu

PACIFIC OCEAN

HAWAII

CT	CONNECTICUT	NJ	NEW JERSEY
DE	DELAWARE	PV	PENNSYLVANIA
MA	MASSACHUSETTS	RI	RHODE ISLAND
MD	MARYLAND	VT	VERMONT
NH	NEW HAMPSHIRE	WV	WEST VIRGINIA

Capital: Washington, D.C.
Population projection, 2010: 312·25m.
GDP per capita, 2003: (PPP$) 37,562
HDI/world rank: 0·944/10

KEY HISTORICAL EVENTS

The earliest inhabitants of the north American continent can be traced back to Palaeolithic times. The Pueblo culture in modern-day Colorado and New Mexico flourished from the 11th to the 14th century AD. In the 12th century permanent settlements appeared in the east where cultivation and fishing supported major fortified towns. The first Europeans to make their presence felt were the Spanish, who based themselves in Florida before venturing north and west. Santa Fe in New Mexico was founded in 1610. But by the mid-17th century there was competition from the French centred on Quebec who colonized the banks of the St Lawrence River.

Elizabethan adventurers were eager to exploit the New World but it was not until 1607 that an English colony was established.

This was at Jamestown in what is now southern Virginia. After a perilous start when disease and malnutrition carried off most of the settlers, Virginia's population grew rapidly to meet the European demand for tobacco. Maryland, originally a refuge for persecuted Catholics, also thrived on the tobacco trade. To make up for the shortage of labour, slaves were imported from Africa.

In 1620 a hundred pilgrims landed at Plymouth Rock to found a Puritan enclave, which became the colony of Massachusetts. Other settlements soon followed, accommodating a broad range of Christian radicals fleeing persecution. Not all were tolerant of beliefs that differed from their own. Pennsylvania, the colony named after the Quaker William Penn, was exceptional in offering freedom of worship to 'all persons who confess and acknowledge the one almighty and eternal God'. In 1664 the British took control of neighbouring Dutch colonies. New Amsterdam became New York. Almost all of the eastern seaboard was now claimed by British settlers who were also venturing inland.

Their main European rivals were the French who claimed a vast area around and to the southwest of the Great Lakes. With

American Indian tribes allied to both sides, there was heavy fighting in 1744 and 1748. But within a decade British forces had captured most of the French strongholds. After the Treaty of Paris in 1763, Britain commanded the whole of North America east of the Mississippi while Spain, having surrendered Florida, gained Louisiana from France. For a brief period colonization was restricted to the area east of the Appalachians, the rest of the territory being reserved for Indian tribes. This soon became a point of issue between the settlers who were intent on expansion and the government in London, which wanted a settled, self-supporting community benefiting British trade. Having disposed of the French threat, the colonists felt confident enough to defy orders that ignored their interests. In particular, they objected to the Navigation Acts which required goods to be carried in British vessels and to various taxes imposed without consultation. 'No taxation without representation' became a rallying cry for disaffected colonists. The centre of opposition was Boston, scene of the infamous 'tea party' when, in 1773, militants destroyed a cargo of East India tea. In 1775 the arrest of rebel ringleaders served only to provoke the 13 colonies to co-operate in further acts of rebellion, including the setting up of a *de facto* government which appointed George Washington commander of American forces.

Independence

The War of Independence was by no means a clear-cut affair. British forces, never more than 50,000 strong, were supported by a powerful body of colonists who remained loyal to the Crown. The war lasted for seven years from 1776 with both sides often getting close to a conclusive victory. The decisive moment came at last with the surrender of Gen. Burgoyne and his 8,000 troops in upper New York state in Oct. 1777, a defeat that persuaded a cautious France to enter the war. Under the peace terms secured in 1783 Britain kept Canada leaving the new United States with territory stretching from the Atlantic to the Mississippi. A constitution based on democratic principles buttressed by inalienable rights including the ownership of property came into force in 1789. It allowed for a federal government headed by a president and executive, a legislature with a House of Representatives and a Senate, and a judiciary with ultimate authority on constitutional matters exercised by a Supreme Court. The first president was George Washington, who was elected in 1789. In 1800 Washington, D.C. was declared the national capital.

Hostilities with Britain resumed in 1812 amidst accusations that Britain was using the excuse of the Napoleonic wars to harass American shipping and to encourage Indian resistance to expansion into the Midwest. Most of the fighting took place on the Canadian border where an attempted invasion was decisively repulsed. But Louisiana, having reverted to French rule and subsequently sold to the USA, was secured for the Union. With the exception of Louisiana, other American territories that had once been part of the Spanish empire fell to Mexico. But not for long. In 1836 Texas broke away from Mexico, surviving as an independent republic until 1845 when it was annexed by the USA. This provoked war with Mexico which ended in 1848 with the USA taking over what are now the states of California, Arizona, Colorado, Utah, Nevada and New Mexico. Any temptation there might have been for European involvement in the struggle was removed by the Monroe Doctrine, a declaration by President Monroe that interference from the Old World in matters concerning the western hemisphere would not be tolerated. It was a measure of the growing military and economic self confidence of the USA that such a warning, delivered in 1823, was taken seriously.

The westward expansion began soon after independence but accelerated with the destruction of Indian power and the removal of the native population to designated reservations. In 1846 a long-running dispute with Britain confirming US title to Oregon acted as a spur to migration as did the Californian gold rush of 1848. By the 1850s the railway network was bringing people and economic prosperity to the mid-west. Population quadrupled between 1815 to 1860, from 8m. to almost 31m. In 1862 the Homestead Act allocated 160 acres to anyone who was ready to farm it. By 1890 the west was won.

Civil War

The transition from a rural society to an industrial power of world importance created tensions, not least between the slave-owning southern states and the rest of the Union which favoured the abolition of slavery. Economic as well as humanitarian factors were in play since the North resented the advantage cheap labour gave to the South. The opposing view held that the South, by now the world's largest cotton producer, depended on slavery for its commercial survival. Mutual antagonism came to a head with the secession of the southern states from the Union in 1860–61 and their formation as a Confederacy. Despite sporadic outbreaks of violence, civil war was not in prospect until Confederate troops fired on the US flag at Fort Sumter. Lincoln ordered a blockade of the South. The recruitment of rival armies followed within weeks. The war turned out to be much bloodier than anyone had expected. More American lives were lost in the Civil War than in the two world wars combined. The military balance was maintained until 1863 when the North secured a crushing victory at the Battle of Gettysburg. However, the war continued until April 1865 when Robert E. Lee surrendered to Ulysses S. Grant at Appomattox Courthouse in Virginia. A few days later Lincoln was assassinated, a loss that the southern states had subsequent cause to regret. Contrary to Lincoln's hopes, a generous settlement was now out of the question. Instead of a gradual transition to a new society, the South was rushed into a social revolution. This in turn led to terrorist violence and acts of vengeance against freed slaves. From this carnage emerged the notorious Ku Klux Klan as the standard bearer of lynch law. While the 13th amendment prohibited slavery, political freedom was denied to the black community by state-imposed literacy tests and discriminatory property taxes.

That America had interests beyond its own borders was made evident by the Spanish war of 1898 which resulted in the USA becoming the dominant power in the Caribbean though the effort to take over in the Philippines came up against Filipino resistance and led to a heavy death toll.

By 1900 the USA rivalled Britain and Germany as the world's dominant power. With vast natural resources and a manufacturing capacity that secured 11% of world trade, it was clear that Europe was soon to lose its grip on world affairs. Ironically, though, it was Europe as the chief supplier of labour that gave the USA the impetus it needed to fulfil its promise. Between 1881 and 1920, 23m. immigrants entered the USA, the largest population movement ever recorded.

Given the nationalistic mix that constituted early 20th century America it is scarcely surprising that popular opinion was against involvement in the First World War. But events, including German U-boat harassment of American shipping, soon proved that isolationism was not an option. It was not until 1917 that America joined the hostilities but the resurgence of energy created by the arrival of the American Expeditionary Force was critical to the Allied breakthrough.

Post-war America, relatively unscathed by the European conflict, was unquestionably the most powerful nation and as such was able to dictate terms at the Versailles peace conference. But President Wilson's 'fourteen points' which set out a plan for collective security policed by a League of Nations failed to win support in the one country that was critical to its success. The Treaty was rejected by the Senate in 1920 and America retreated once again into isolationism.

A resumption of economic growth was accompanied by a struggle to impose a common set of values, chiefly white and

Protestant, on a diverse population. To outsiders the most extraordinary experiment in social engineering was Prohibition, a federal imposed attempt to outlaw all alcoholic drinks. Whatever gain there was to the health of the nation, the chief beneficiaries were the bosses of organized crime.

New Deal

Dreams of everlasting prosperity were shattered by the 1929 Stock Market Crash. A succession of bank failures was followed by widespread bankruptcies and mass unemployment which sent the economy into a further downward spin. The beginning of the end to the agony came with the election to the presidency of Franklin D. Roosevelt, who pushed through Congress a series of radical measures known collectively as the New Deal, aimed at revitalizing the nation. With the abandonment of the gold standard, cheap loans to restart factories and farms and huge investment in public works proved to be the key to recovery though unemployment remained high until production was boosted by the demands of another world war. In 1935 Roosevelt's social security act provided the bare bones of an American welfare state.

Roosevelt was well aware of the dangers to the USA if the fascist dictators were allowed to triumph, but as in 1914, there was formidable opposition to direct involvement. Roosevelt compromised by supplying Britain with much needed armaments on favourable terms. But it was events in Asia rather than in Europe that eventually persuaded America of the need for direct action. Opposition to Japanese expansion into China and southeast Asia, including an oil embargo and a freezing of Japanese assets in the USA, brought a savage retaliation at Pearl Harbor, when much of the US fleet was destroyed. America declared war on Japan while Germany declared war on America. The US military effort focused initially on the Pacific but after 1942 American forces were also committed to the campaign in north Africa and Europe. With the D-Day landings in June 1944, US troops led the attack on Germany and in May 1945, within a month of Roosevelt's death, Germany surrendered. By then Vice President Harry Truman had been confirmed as Roosevelt's successor and forced a Japanese surrender by sacrificing Hiroshima and Nagasaki to the atomic bomb.

This time, in the aftermath of war, the USA needed no encouragement to assume the leadership of the free world. The threat of a Soviet takeover in Europe was countered by the formation of NATO in 1949 and the provision of dollar aid under the 1947 Marshall Plan to kick-start European economic recovery. In addition, the Truman doctrine provided a $400m. aid package for the Turkish and Greek governments. The risk of a return to isolationism receded still further when China fell to communism. In 1950 American troops went to the aid of South Korea when it was invaded by the communist North. Though technically under the aegis of the UN, the campaign was an almost entirely American affair led by General Douglas MacArthur. When Chinese forces became involved, MacArthur spoke openly of extending the war to the Chinese mainland, a threat countered strongly by President Truman who forced MacArthur's resignation to establish undisputed political control over the military.

A ceasefire was negotiated after Dwight Eisenhower was elected president in 1953. The USA took the lead in setting up the South East Asia Treaty Organization on the same lines as NATO. Eisenhower had a decisive influence on the Suez crisis in 1956 when he refused to support the invasion of Egypt by British, French and Israeli forces. Domestically he made little headway against a powerful Democratic opposition in both Houses of Congress. His attempts to thaw the Cold War also met with frustration. He handed over the Republican presidential candidacy to his vice-president Richard Nixon, who lost the 1960 election by a slim margin to John F. Kennedy.

Civil Rights

In the early 1960s civil rights were high on the political agenda. The thuggish tactics of Senator Joe McCarthy and the House Committee on Un-American Activities during the previous decade brought into focus basic democratic freedoms guaranteed by the Constitution while growing protests against racial discrimination led to legislation to enforce equality of opportunity in education and employment. The civil rights movement peaked in the early 1960s when the imposition of federal law in the South led to acts of violence against liberal protesters. Foremost among the campaigners for racial equality was Martin Luther King, Jr. who was awarded the Nobel Peace Prize in 1964 and who was assassinated four years later.

Social tensions were exacerbated by the Cold War confrontation. In his first year of office Kennedy was embarrassed by the failed Bay of Pigs invasion when anti-Castro Cubans, trained and supported by the CIA, attempted to overthrow the country's communist regime. The building of the Berlin Wall in Aug. 1961 symbolized a hardening of the Cold War. In 1962 Kennedy had to confront the prospect of the Soviets placing missiles in Cuba. The prospect of world war was only too real until an agreement between the two nations allowed for a withdrawal of the missiles on the condition of a US promise not to invade Cuba. The incident prompted a thawing in East–West relations and in 1963 the USA, UK and USSR signed the Nuclear Test Ban Treaty which, for the first time, put a brake on the spread of nuclear weapons. Less hopeful was the acceleration of the conflict in Vietnam. Kennedy increased the American military presence in South Vietnam from 700 at the beginning of his term in office to 15,000 to counter the threat of communist domination by the North. Domestically, Kennedy's government pledged $1·2bn. for social and housing programmes.

Kennedy was assassinated in Dallas in Nov. 1963 and his vice president, Lyndon Johnson, was inaugurated as his successor. Johnson oversaw the implementation of civil rights legislation initiated by the Kennedy administration, epitomized by the Voting Rights Act, and also introduced Medicare (health insurance for the elderly). By 1966 over 350,000 American troops were in Vietnam and by the following year almost 80,000 Americans had been killed or wounded. The public turned against involvement in southeast Asia, not least because increased military expenditure led to a delay in domestic reforms.

Watergate

Johnson decided not to contest the 1968 presidential election. His likely successor for the Democrat nomination was John Kennedy's brother, Bobby, but he was assassinated in June of that year. The Republican nominee, Richard Nixon, won the presidency. With falling support for US involvement in Vietnam, he reduced the number of troops stationed there from 550,000 in 1969 to 30,000 three years later but authorized military operations in North Vietnam, Laos and Cambodia in the hope of forcing North Vietnam to the negotiating table. Elsewhere, he signed the Strategic Arms Limitation Treaty (SALT) with Moscow in 1972 and relaxed trade restrictions against China.

Nixon was re-elected as president in 1973 and shortly afterwards agreed a ceasefire with North Vietnam. However, his second term of office was cut short by the Watergate scandal. The charges against him centred on White House-released taped transcripts of discussions in which Nixon authorized a cover-up of a break-in at the Democratic party headquarters in the Watergate complex, Washington, D.C. in 1972. Threatened with Congressional impeachment, Nixon announced his resignation in Aug. 1974.

Gerald Ford, who replaced Nixon, granted his predecessor a controversial 'full, free and absolute pardon'. Ford lost the 1976 presidential election to Democrat Jimmy Carter. Perceived as a Washington outsider, Carter's often strained relations with Congress and the Senate obstructed his domestic agenda. The economy suffered and by 1980 inflation and unemployment were both running high. Internationally, he secured the neutrality of the Panama Canal and brokered the influential Camp David talks between Egypt and Israel. He also re-established diplomatic ties with China. Henry Kissinger, who was secretary of state for part of Nixon's and all of Carter's years in office, oversaw America's withdrawal from southeast Asia, winning the Nobel Peace Prize jointly with his North Vietnamese counterpart Le Duc Tho in 1974. Attempts at further improving US–Soviet relations were scuppered when the signing of the Strategic Arms Limitation Treaty (SALT II) was postponed because of the Soviet invasion of Afghanistan in 1979. The incursion also led to a US boycott of the 1980 Moscow Olympics. Radical Iranian students stormed the US embassy in Tehran in late 1979 and seized over 50 US hostages. After a year of negotiations, a secret US military rescue mission failed and contributed to Republican Ronald Reagan's landslide victory at the 1980 presidential polls.

Reagan's economic policies, known as 'Reaganomics', re-defined American society in the 1980s. In his first year of office he introduced a 25% tax cut for individuals and corporations. He slashed welfare but increased military expenditure. In terms of governmental structure, he was intent on delegating many federal programmes to state and local levels. A recession in 1982 prompted tax increases and set the pattern of boom and bust that characterized his tenure. In 1986 he reduced the number of tax rates, abolishing tax altogether for many low-income earners. In Oct. 1987 the stock market collapsed, losing a third of its value over two months, and by the end of his presidency, Reagan had seen the national debt more than triple to $2·5trn.

End to the Cold War

Relations between the USA and USSR deteriorated in the early 1980s. The shooting down of a South Korean airliner carrying American citizens in 1983 led to a further deployment of US missiles in Western Europe while US proposals for the Strategic Defense Initiative (known as 'Star Wars') added to tensions. In 1983 the USA invaded Grenada, scene of a coup, in a bid to curb Soviet–Cuban influence in the Caribbean. However, relations between the two superpowers improved in the mid-eighties after successful negotiations on nuclear arms limitations. Reagan met Soviet leader Mikhail Gorbachev in 1985 and in 1987 the two leaders signed a treaty in Washington, D.C. agreeing to destroy a range of intermediate-range nuclear weapons.

Reagan's foreign policy elsewhere was unstinting in its protection of US interests. In 1986 he bombed Tripoli after Libya was accused of involvement in the bombing of a nightclub in West Berlin which killed two American servicemen. The following year he became embroiled in the Iran-Contra affair. The CIA was found to have sold arms to Iran to fund anti-communist guerrillas in Nicaragua. Reagan and his deputy, George Bush, were cleared of direct involvement but Reagan was censured for allowing the affair to develop.

Bush took over the presidency in 1989 and continued an active foreign policy. At the end of 1989 he authorized the invasion of Panama to remove Gen. Manuel Antonio Noriega from power. The collapse of the Soviet empire in 1990 extended US economic aid to Eastern Europe and Bush signed a non-aggression pact with Soviet leader Mikhail Gorbachev which effectively ended the Cold War. In 1990–91 Bush led a coalition of European and Arab states to counter the Iraqi invasion of Kuwait. Around 500,000 US troops were stationed in the Persian Gulf and when trade embargoes and diplomacy failed to persuade Iraq to withdraw, Bush authorized a military offensive in Jan. 1991. By the end of Feb. Kuwaiti independence had been restored. Domestically, Bush was badly damaged when he was forced to raise taxes despite his election promise of 'no new taxes'.

The Democrats regained control of the White House with the election of Bill Clinton in 1992. Clinton combined economic recovery at home with an active foreign policy which underlined America's role as the only superpower. He secured the passage of the North American Free Trade Agreement, which created a free-trade zone between the United States, Canada and Mexico, cut the United States budget deficit by 50% in his first term and in his second term authorized America's first tax cut since 1981. Unemployment reached its lowest levels since the late-1960s and in 1998 there was a federal budget surplus for the first time in almost 30 years. His social legislation included anti-crime provisions, the Family and Medical Leave Act, a welfare reform bill and an increase in the minimum wage. He also appointed Madeleine Albright as the first-ever female secretary of state.

On the international scene Clinton brokered talks between the Palestinian leader Yasser Arafat and Israeli Prime Minister Yitzhak Rabin which resulted in limited Palestinian self-rule. He sent peacekeeping troops to Bosnia-Herzegovina and Haiti and in 1995 was instrumental in securing the Dayton accords that offered peace between Yugoslavia, Croatia and Bosnia-Herzegovina. Relations with Vietnam were normalized and diplomatic and trade links with China much improved. He was also an important figure in the formulation of the 1998 Good Friday agreement which sought to reach a peace settlement in Northern Ireland.

Clinton retained a hard-line stance against Iraq, sending forces against Saddam Hussein in 1994, 1996 and 1998. Sudan and Afghanistan were attacked in 1998 having been linked with the al-Qaeda terrorist network held responsible for the bombing of US embassies in Tanzania and Kenya. In 1999 there was a Clinton-led NATO campaign of air strikes against Yugoslavia when the country's leaders refused to end a campaign of violence against ethnic Albanians in Kosovo. Yugoslav president Slobodan Milošević was forced to withdraw his troops and allow an international peacekeeping force in Kosovo.

However, Clinton's second term of office was dominated by scandal. He reached an out-of-court agreement with Paula Jones, a state government employee who had accused him of sexual harassment. Clinton and his wife, Hilary, were also accused of criminal wrongdoing over a land deal in Arkansas, known as Whitewater, though they were both eventually cleared of the charges. Most damagingly, Clinton had an affair with Monica Lewinsky, a White House intern. Having denied the sexual nature of the affair under oath, Clinton was impeached for perjury and obstruction of justice although the senate trial ended when neither motion gained a simple majority.

In 2000 Clinton's vice president, Al Gore, lost the presidential election to George W. Bush, son of the earlier President George Bush. Gore was defeated despite winning the popular vote. In 2001 Bush's first budget included a $1·25trn. tax cut. He attracted international criticism in his early months in office for refusing to ratify the Kyoto Agreement on global warming and climate change and for his bid to replace the 1972 Anti-Ballistic Missile Treaty with a new accord allowing for a missile defence system in the United States. Following talks with Russian President Vladimir Putin in June 2001 the two leaders signed an anti-nuclear deal to reduce their respective strategic nuclear warheads by two-thirds over the next ten years.

War on Terrorism

On 11 Sept. 2001 the heart of New York City was devastated after hijackers flew two jet airliners into the World Trade Center. A plane also crashed into the Pentagon, in Washington, D.C., and a fourth hijacked plane crashed near the town of Shanksville, Pennsylvania. The death toll, initially put at 6,700, was eventually lowered to 2,752, with 67 countries reporting dead or missing citizens. Osama bin Laden, the Saudi dissident leader of the al-Qaeda terrorist network and believed to be living in Afghanistan at the invitation of the ruling Taliban, immediately became the chief suspect and military action against Afghanistan followed, with air strikes beginning on 7 Oct. 2001. Despite the UN establishing a fragile multi-party government in Afghanistan, the USA continues to carry out special missions against Taliban and al-Qaeda targets.

In early 2002 Bush declared North Korea, Iran and Iraq 'an axis of evil' and by Sept. 2002 was pressing the UN to act against Iraq. Bush's foreign policy has been played out against a background of domestic recession. On 20 March 2003 US forces, supported by the UK, launched attacks on Iraq, and initiated a war aimed at 'liberating Iraq'. On 9 April 2003 American forces took control of central Baghdad, effectively bringing an end to Saddam Hussein's rule. Bush won a second term as president in Nov. 2004.

TERRITORY AND POPULATION

The United States is bounded in the north by Canada, east by the North Atlantic, south by the Gulf of Mexico and Mexico, and west by the North Pacific Ocean. The area of the USA is 3,794,083 sq. miles (9,826,630 sq. km), of which 3,537,439 sq. miles (9,161,923 sq. km) are land and 256,645 sq. miles (664,707 sq. km) are water (comprising Great Lakes, inland and coastal water).

Population at each census from 1790 to 2000 (including Alaska and Hawaii from 1960). Figures do not include Puerto Rico, Guam, American Samoa or other Pacific islands, or the US population abroad. Residents of Indian reservations not included before 1890.

	White	Black	Other races	Total
1790	3,172,464	757,208	—	3,929,672
1800	4,306,446	1,002,037	—	5,308,483
1810	5,862,073	1,377,808	—	7,239,881
1820	7,866,797	1,771,562	—	9,638,359
1830	10,537,378	2,328,642	—	12,866,020
1840	14,195,805	2,873,648	—	17,069,453
1850	19,553,068	3,638,808	—	23,191,876
1860	26,922,537	4,441,830	78,954	31,443,321
1870	34,337,292	5,392,172	88,985	39,818,449
1880	43,402,970	6,580,793	172,020	50,155,783
1890	55,101,258	7,488,676	357,780	62,947,714
1900	66,868,508	8,834,395	509,265	76,212,168
1910	81,812,405	9,828,667	587,459	92,228,531
1920	94,903,540	10,463,607	654,421	106,021,568
1930	110,395,753	11,891,842	915,065	123,202,660
1940	118,357,831	12,865,914	941,384	132,165,129
1950	135,149,629	15,044,937	1,131,232	151,325,798
1960	158,831,732	18,871,831	1,619,612	179,323,175
1970	177,748,975	22,580,289	2,882,662	203,211,926
1980	188,371,622	26,495,025	11,679,158	226,545,805
1990	199,686,070	29,986,060	19,037,743	248,709,873
2000	211,460,626	34,658,190	35,303,090	281,421,906

The mid-year population estimate for 2005 was 296,410,404. The UN gives a projected population for 2010 of 312·25m.

2000 density, 30·7 per sq. km (79·6 per sq. mile). Urban population (persons living in places with at least 2,500 inhabitants) at the 2000 census was 222,358,309 (79·0%); rural, 59,063,597. In 1990 it was 75·2%; in 1980, 73·7%; in 1970, 73·6%.

Sex distribution by race of the population at the 2000 census:

	Males	Females
White	103,773,194	107,687,432
Black or African American	16,465,185	18,193,005
American Indian and Alaska Native	1,233,982	1,241,974
Asian	4,948,741	5,294,257
Native Hawaiian and Other Pacific Islander	202,629	196,206
Other Race	8,009,214	7,349,859
Two or More Races	3,420,618	3,405,610
Total	138,053,563	143,368,343

Alongside these racial groups, and applicable to all of them, a category of 'Hispanic origin' comprised 35,305,818 persons (including 20,640,711 of Mexican ancestry), up 12,927,277

from 22,378,541 in 1990. Hispanics are now the largest ethnic minority in the USA.

Among ten-year age groups the 35–44 age group contained most people according to the 2000 census, with a total of 45,148,527 (16·0% of the population).

At the 2000 census there were 104,705,000 households, up from 93,347,000 in 1990.

At the 2000 census there were 50,454 people aged 100 or over, compared to 36,000 in 1990. Of the 50,454 centenarians in 2000, 40,397 were female, and of the 36,000 in 1990, 28,000 were female.

The 2000 census showed that 47·0m. persons five years and over spoke a language other than English in the home, including Spanish or Spanish Creole by 28·1m.; French or French Creole by 2·1m.; Chinese by 2·0m.; German by 1·4m.; Tagalog by 1·2m.; Italian by 1·0m.; Vietnamese by 1·0m.

The following table includes population statistics, the year in which each of the original 13 states (Connecticut, Delaware, Georgia, Maryland, Massachusetts, New Hampshire, New Jersey, New York, North Carolina, Pennsylvania, Rhode Island, South Carolina, Virginia) ratified the constitution, and the year when each of the other states was admitted into the Union. Traditional abbreviations for the names of the states are shown in brackets with postal codes for use in addresses.

The USA is divided into four geographic regions comprised of nine divisions. These are, with their 2000 census populations: Northeast (comprised of the New England and Middle Atlantic divisions), 53,594,378; Midwest (East North Central, West North Central), 64,392,776; South (South Atlantic, East South Central, West South Central), 100,236,820; West (Mountain, Pacific), 63,197,932.

Geographic divisions and states		Land area: sq. miles, 2000	Census population 1 April 2000	Pop. per sq. mile, 2000
United States		3,537,439	281,421,906	79·6
New England		62,810	13,922,517	221·7
Connecticut (1788)	(Conn./CT)	4,845	3,405,565	702·9
Maine (1820)	(Me./ME)	30,862	1,274,923	41·3
Massachusetts (1788)	(Mass./MA)	7,840	6,349,097	809·8
New Hampshire (1788)	(N.H./NH)	8,968	1,235,786	137·8
Rhode Island (1790)	(R.I./RI)	1,045	1,048,319	1,003·2
Vermont (1791)	(Vt./VT)	9,250	608,827	65·8
Middle Atlantic		99,448	39,671,861	398·9
New Jersey (1787)	(N.J./NJ)	7,417	8,414,350	1,134·4
New York (1788)	(N.Y./NY)	47,214	18,976,457	401·9
Pennsylvania (1787)	(Pa./PA)	44,817	12,281,054	274·0
East North Central		243,513	45,155,037	185·4
Illinois (1818)	(Ill./IL)	55,584	12,419,293	223·4
Indiana (1816)	(Ind./IN)	35,867	6,080,485	169·5
Michigan (1837)	(Mich./MI)	56,804	9,938,444	175·0
Ohio (1803)	(Oh./OH)	40,948	11,353,140	277·3
Wisconsin (1848)	(Wis./WI)	54,310	5,363,675	98·8
West North Central		507,913	19,237,739	37·9
Iowa (1846)	(Ia./IA)	55,869	2,926,324	52·4
Kansas (1861)	(Kans./KS)	81,815	2,688,418	32·9
Minnesota (1858)	(Minn./MN)	79,610	4,919,479	61·8
Missouri (1821)	(Mo./MO)	68,886	5,595,211	81·2
Nebraska (1867)	(Nebr./NE)	76,872	1,711,263	22·3
North Dakota (1889)	(N.D./ND)	68,976	642,200	9·3
South Dakota (1889)	(S.D./SD)	75,885	754,844	9·9

Geographic divisions and states		Land area: sq. miles, 2000	Census population 1 April 2000	Pop. per sq. mile, 2000
South Atlantic		266,115	51,769,160	194·5
Delaware (1787)	(Del./DE)	1,954	783,600	401·0
Dist. of Columbia (1791)	(D.C./DC)	61	572,059	9,378·0
Florida (1845)	(Fla./FL)	53,927	15,982,378	296·4
Georgia (1788)	(Ga./GA)	57,906	8,186,453	141·4
Maryland (1788)	(Md./MD)	9,774	5,296,486	541·9
North Carolina (1789)	(N.C./NC)	48,711	8,049,313	165·2
South Carolina (1788)	(S.C./SC)	30,110	4,012,012	133·2
Virginia (1788)	(Va./VA)	39,594	7,078,515	178·8
West Virginia (1863)	(W. Va./WV)	24,078	1,808,344	75·1
East South Central		178,596	17,022,810	95·3
Alabama (1819)	(Al./AL)	50,744	4,447,100	87·6
Kentucky (1792)	(Ky./KY)	39,728	4,041,769	101·7
Mississippi (1817)	(Miss./MS)	46,907	2,844,658	60·6
Tennessee (1796)	(Tenn./TN)	41,217	5,689,283	138·0
West South Central		426,094	31,444,850	73·8
Arkansas (1836)	(Ark./AR)	52,068	2,673,400	51·3
Louisiana (1812)	(La./LA)	43,562	4,468,976	102·6
Oklahoma (1907)	(Okla./OK)	68,667	3,450,654	50·3
Texas (1845)	(Tex./TX)	261,797	20,851,820	79·7
Mountain		856,078	18,172,295	21·2
Arizona (1912)	(Ariz./AZ)	113,635	5,130,632	45·2
Colorado (1876)	(Colo./CO)	103,718	4,301,261	41·5
Idaho (1890)	(Id./ID)	82,747	1,293,953	15·6
Montana (1889)	(Mont./MT)	145,552	902,195	6·2
Nevada (1864)	(Nev./NV)	109,826	1,998,257	18·2
New Mexico (1912)	(N. Mex./NM)	121,356	1,819,046	15·0
Utah (1896)	(Ut./UT)	82,144	2,233,169	27·2
Wyoming (1890)	(Wyo./WY)	97,100	493,782	5·1
Pacific		896,874	45,025,637	50·2
Alaska (1959)	(Ak./AK)	571,951	626,932	1·1
California (1850)	(Calif./CA)	155,959	33,871,648	217·2
Hawaii (1960)	(Hi./HI)	6,423	1,211,537	188·6
Oregon (1859)	(Oreg./OR)	95,997	3,421,399	35·6
Washington (1889)	(Wash./WA)	66,544	5,894,121	88·6
Outlying Territories, total		4,033	4,199,913[1]	1,041·4[1]
American Samoa (1900)		77	57,291	744
Guam (1898)		212	154,805	737
Johnston Atoll (1858)		1	1,100[2]	1,100[2]
Midway Islands (1867)		2	150[2]	75[2]
Northern Marianas (1947)		179	69,221	387
Puerto Rico (1898)		3,425	3,808,610	1,112
Virgin Islands (1917)		134	108,612	811
Wake Island (1898)		3	124[2]	41[2]

[1]Based on a combination of 2000 census figures and estimates for the minor outlying islands as indicated. [2]2000 estimate.

The 2000 census showed 31,107,889 foreign-born persons. The ten countries contributing the largest numbers who were foreign-born were: Mexico, 9,177,487; Philippines, 1,369,070; India, 1,022,552; China, 988,857; Vietnam, 988,174; Cuba, 872,716; Korea, 864,125; Canada, 820,771; El Salvador, 817,336; Germany, 706,704; Dominican Republic, 687,677. A total of 849,807 immigrants were admitted in 2000 (1,536,483 in 1990).

Population of cities with over 100,000 inhabitants at the censuses of 1990 and 2000:

Cities	Census 1990	Census 2000	Cities	Census 1990	Census 2000
New York, NY	7,322,564	8,008,278	St Paul, MN	272,235	287,151
Los Angeles, CA	3,485,398	3,694,820	Corpus Christi, TX	257,453	277,454
Chicago, IL	2,783,726	2,896,016	Aurora, CO	222,103	276,393
Houston, TX	1,630,553	1,953,631	Raleigh, NC	207,951	276,093
Philadelphia, PA	1,585,577	1,517,550	Newark, NJ	275,221	273,546
Phoenix, AZ	983,403	1,321,045	Lexington-Fayette, KY	225,366	260,512
San Diego, CA	1,110,549	1,223,400	Anchorage, AK	226,338	260,283
Dallas, TX	1,006,877	1,188,580	Louisville, KY	269,063	256,231
San Antonio, TX	935,933	1,144,646	Riverside, CA	226,505	255,166
Detroit, MI	1,027,974	951,270	St Petersburg, FL	238,629	248,232
San Jose, CA	782,248	894,943	Bakersfield, CA	174,280	247,057
Indianapolis, IN	741,952	791,926	Stockton, CA	210,943	243,771
San Francisco, CA	723,959	776,733	Birmingham, AL	265,968	242,820
Jacksonville, FL	635,230	735,617	Jersey City, NJ	228,537	240,055
Columbus, OH	632,910	711,470	Norfolk, VA	261,229	234,403
Austin, TX	465,622	656,562	Baton Rouge, LA	219,531	227,818
Baltimore, MD	736,014	651,154	Hialeah, FL	188,004	226,419
Memphis, TN	610,337	650,100	Lincoln, NE	191,972	225,581
Milwaukee, WI	628,088	596,974	Greensboro, NC	183,521	223,891
Boston, MA	574,283	589,141	Plano, TX	128,713	222,030
Washington, DC	606,900	572,059	Rochester, NY	231,636	219,773
Nashville-Davidson, TN	510,784	569,891	Glendale, AZ	148,134	218,812
El Paso, TX	515,342	563,662	Garland, TX	180,650	215,768
Seattle, WA	516,259	563,374	Madison, WI	191,262	208,054
Denver, CO	467,610	554,636	Fort Wayne, IN	173,072	205,727
Charlotte, NC	395,934	540,828	Fremont, CA	173,339	203,413
Fort Worth, TX	447,619	534,694	Scottsdale, AZ	130,069	202,705
Portland, OR	437,319	529,121	Montgomery, AL	187,106	201,568
Oklahoma City, OK	444,719	506,132	Shreveport, LA	198,525	200,145
Tucson, AZ	405,390	486,699	Augusta-Richmond County, GA	44,639	199,775
New Orleans, LA	496,938	484,674	Lubbock, TX	186,206	199,564
Las Vegas, NV	258,295	478,434	Chesapeake, VA	151,976	199,184
Cleveland, OH	505,616	478,403	Mobile, AL	196,278	198,915
Long Beach, CA	429,433	461,522	Des Moines, IA	193,187	198,682
Albuquerque, NM	384,736	448,607	Grand Rapids, MI	189,126	197,800
Kansas City, MO	435,146	441,545	Richmond, VA	203,056	197,790
Fresno, CA	354,202	427,652	Yonkers, NY	188,082	196,086
Virginia Beach, VA	393,069	425,257	Spokane, WA	177,196	195,629
Atlanta, GA	394,017	416,474	Glendale, CA	180,038	194,973
Sacramento, CA	369,365	407,018	Tacoma, WA	176,664	193,556
Oakland, CA	372,242	399,484	Irving, TX	155,037	191,615
Mesa, AZ	288,091	396,375	Huntington Beach, CA	181,519	189,594
Tulsa, OK	367,302	393,049	Arlington, VA[1]	170,897	189,453
Omaha, NE	335,795	390,007	Modesto, CA	164,730	188,856
Minneapolis, MN	368,383	382,618	Durham, NC	136,611	187,035
Honolulu, HI	365,272	371,657	Columbus, GA	179,278	186,291
Miami, FL	358,548	362,470	Orlando, FL	164,693	185,951
Colorado Springs, CO	281,140	360,890	Boise City, ID	125,738	185,787
St Louis, MO	396,685	348,189	Winston-Salem, NC	143,485	185,776
Wichita, KS	304,011	344,284	San Bernardino, CA	164,164	185,401
Santa Ana, CA	293,742	337,977	Jackson, MS	196,637	184,256
Pittsburgh, PA	369,879	334,563	Little Rock, AR	175,795	183,133
Arlington, TX	261,721	332,969	Salt Lake City, UT	159,936	181,743
Cincinnati, OH	364,040	331,285	Reno, NV	133,850	180,480
Anaheim, CA	266,406	328,014	Newport News, VA	170,045	180,150
Toledo, OH	332,943	313,619	Chandler, AZ	90,533	176,581
Tampa, FL	280,015	303,447	Laredo, TX	122,899	176,576
Buffalo, NY	328,123	292,648	Henderson, NV	64,942	175,381

Cities	Census 1990	Census 2000
Knoxville, TN	165,121	173,890
Amarillo, TX	157,615	173,627
Providence, RI	160,728	173,618
Chula Vista, CA	135,163	173,556
Worcester, MA	169,759	172,648
Oxnard, CA	142,216	170,358
Dayton, OH	182,044	166,179
Garden Grove, CA	143,050	165,196
Oceanside, CA	128,398	161,029
Tempe, AZ	141,865	158,625
Huntsville, AL	159,789	158,216
Ontario, CA	133,179	158,007
Chattanooga, TN	152,466	155,554
Fort Lauderdale, FL	149,377	152,397
Springfield, MA	156,983	152,082
Springfield, MO	140,494	151,580
Santa Clarita, CA	110,642	151,088
Salinas, CA	108,777	151,060
Tallahassee, FL	124,773	150,624
Rockford, IL	139,426	150,115
Pomona, CA	131,723	149,473
Paterson, NJ	140,891	149,222
Overland Park, KS	111,790	149,080
Santa Rosa, CA	113,313	147,595
Syracuse, NY	163,860	147,306
Kansas City, KS	149,767	146,866
Hampton, VA	133,793	146,437
Lakewood, CO	126,481	144,126
Vancouver, WA	46,380	143,560
Irvine, CA	110,330	143,072
Aurora, IL	99,581	142,990
Moreno Valley, CA	118,779	142,381
Pasadena, TX	119,363	141,674
Hayward, CA	111,498	140,030
Brownsville, TX	98,962	139,722
Bridgeport, CT	141,686	139,529
Hollywood, FL	121,697	139,357
Warren, MI	144,864	138,247
Torrance, CA	133,107	137,946
Eugene, OR	112,669	137,893
Pembroke Pines, FL	65,452	137,427
Salem, OR	107,786	136,924
Pasadena, CA	131,591	133,936
Escondido, CA	108,635	133,559
Sunnyvale, CA	117,229	131,760
Savannah, GA	137,560	131,510
Fontana, CA	87,535	128,929
Orange, CA	110,658	128,821
Naperville, IL	85,351	128,358
Alexandria, VA	111,183	128,283
Rancho Cucamonga, CA	101,409	127,743
Grand Prairie, TX	99,616	127,427
Fullerton, CA	114,144	126,003
Corona, CA	76,095	124,966
Flint, MI	140,761	124,943
Mesquite, TX	101,484	124,523
Sterling Heights, MI	117,810	124,471
Sioux Falls, SD	100,814	123,975
New Haven, CT	130,474	123,626
Topeka, KS	119,883	122,377
Concord, CA	111,348	121,780

Cities	Census 1990	Census 2000
Evansville, IN	126,272	121,582
Hartford, CT	139,739	121,578
Fayetteville, NC	75,695	121,015
Cedar Rapids, IA	108,751	120,758
Elizabeth, NJ	110,002	120,568
Lansing, MI	127,321	119,128
Lancaster, CA	97,291	118,718
Fort Collins, CO	87,758	118,652
Coral Springs, FL	79,443	117,549
Stamford, CT	108,056	117,083
Thousand Oaks, CA	104,352	117,005
Vallejo, CA	109,199	116,760
Palmdale, CA	68,842	116,670
Columbia, SC	98,052	116,278
El Monte, CA	106,209	115,965
Abilene, TX	106,654	115,930
North Las Vegas, NV	47,707	115,488
Beaumont, TX	114,323	113,866
Waco, TX	103,590	113,726
Independence, MO	112,301	113,288
Peoria, IL	113,504	112,936
Inglewood, CA	109,602	112,580
Springfield, IL	105,227	111,454
Simi Valley, CA	100,217	111,351
Lafayette, LA	94,440	110,257
Gilbert, AZ	29,188	109,697
Carrollton, TX	82,169	109,576
Bellevue, WA	86,874	109,569
West Valley City, UT	86,976	108,896
Clearwater, FL	98,784	108,787
Costa Mesa, CA	96,357	108,724
Peoria, AZ	50,618	108,364
South Bend, IN	105,511	107,789
Downey, CA	91,444	107,323
Waterbury, CT	108,961	107,271
Manchester, NH	99,567	107,006
Allentown, PA	105,090	106,632
McAllen, TX	84,021	106,414
Joliet, IL	76,836	106,221
Lowell, MA	103,439	105,167
Provo, UT	86,835	105,166
West Covina, CA	96,086	105,080
Wichita Falls, TX	96,259	104,197
Erie, PA	108,718	103,717
Daly City, CA	92,311	103,621
Clarksville, TN	75,494	103,445
Norwalk, CA	94,279	103,298
Gary, IN	116,646	102,746
Berkeley, CA	102,724	102,743
Santa Clara, CA	93,613	102,361
Green Bay, WI	96,466	102,313
Cape Coral, FL	74,991	102,286
Arvada, CO	89,235	102,153
Pueblo, CO	98,640	102,121
Athens-Clarke County, GA	45,734	101,489
Cambridge, MA	95,802	101,355
Westminster, CO	74,625	100,940
San Buenaventura (Ventura), CA	92,575	100,916
Portsmouth, VA	103,907	100,565
Livonia, MI	100,850	100,545
Burbank, CA	93,643	100,316

[1] Arlington CDP (census designated place) is not incorporated as a city.

Immigration and naturalization. The Immigration and Nationality Act, as amended, provides for the numerical limitation of most immigration. The Immigration Act of 1990 established major revisions in the numerical limits and preference system regulating legal immigration. The numerical limits are imposed on visas issued and not admissions. The maximum number of visas allowed to be issued under the preference categories in 2003 was 397,532: 226,000 for family-sponsored immigrants and 171,532 for employment-based immigrants. Within the overall limitations the per-country limit for independent countries is set to 7% of the total family and employment limits, while dependent areas are limited to 2% of the total.

Immigrant aliens admitted to the USA for permanent residence, by country or region of birth, for fiscal years:

Country or region of birth	Immigrants admitted			
	2000	2001	2002	2003
All countries	849,807	1,064,318	1,063,732	705,827
Europe	132,480	175,371	174,209	100,769
Bosnia-Herzegovina	11,828	23,640	25,373	6,168
Germany	7,638	9,886	8,961	5,101
Poland	10,114	11,818	12,746	10,526
Russia	17,110	20,413	20,833	13,951
Ukraine	15,810	20,975	12,217	11,666
UK	13,385	18,436	16,421	9,601
Other Europe	56,595	70,203	68,658	43,759
Asia	265,400	349,776	342,099	244,759
China and Taiwan	54,692	68,597	71,118	47,606
Hong Kong	5,419	8,321	6,090	3,582
India	42,046	70,290	71,105	50,372
Japan	7,094	9,619	8,301	5,993
Korea (North and South)	15,830	20,742	21,021	12,512
Philippines	42,474	53,154	51,308	45,397
Thailand	3,785	4,291	4,175	3,158
Vietnam	26,747	35,531	33,627	22,133
Other Asia	67,313	79,231	75,354	54,006
North and Central America	344,805	407,888	404,437	250,726
Canada	16,210	21,933	19,519	11,446
Mexico	173,919	206,426	219,380	115,864
Cuba	20,831	27,703	28,272	9,304
Dominican Republic	17,536	21,313	22,604	26,205
El Salvador	14,606	31,272	31,168	28,296
Haiti	22,364	27,120	20,268	12,314
Jamaica	16,000	15,393	14,898	13,384
Trinidad and Tobago	6,660	6,665	5,771	4,153
Other Caribbean	4,807	5,352	4,676	3,455
Other Central America	51,837	44,642	37,811	26,269
Other North America	35	69	70	36
South America	56,074	68,888	74,506	55,247
Colombia	14,498	16,730	18,845	14,777
Ecuador	7,685	9,706	10,602	7,083
Other South America	33,891	42,452	45,059	33,387
Africa	44,731	53,948	60,269	48,738
Australia and New Zealand	3,031	4,044	3,705	2,731
Other countries	3,286	4,403	4,507	2,857

The total number of immigrants admitted from 1820 up to 30 Sept. 2003 was 68,923,308; this included 7,227,324 from Germany, 6,675,296 from Mexico and 5,443,948 from Italy.

The number of immigrants admitted for legal permanent residence in the United States in the fiscal year 2003 was 705,827. Included in this total were 358,411 aliens previously living abroad who obtained immigrant visas through the US Department of State and became legal permanent residents upon entry into the United States. The remaining 347,416 legal immigrants, including former undocumented immigrants, refugees and asylees, had adjusted status through the Citizenship and Immigration Services (USCIS).

A total of 463,204 persons were naturalized in fiscal year 2003 (including 56,093 persons born in Mexico).

The refugee admissions ceiling for the fiscal year 2003 was fixed at 70,000, including 20,000 from Africa and 16,500 from Europe.

SOCIAL STATISTICS

Figures include Alaska beginning with 1959 and Hawaii beginning with 1960.

	Live births	Deaths	Marriages	Divorces	Deaths under 1 year
1900	—	343,217	709,000	56,000	—
1910	2,777,000	696,856	948,000	83,000	—
1920	2,950,000	1,118,070	1,274,476	170,505	170,911
1930	2,618,000	1,327,240	1,126,856	195,961	143,201
1940	2,559,000	1,417,269	1,595,879	264,000	110,984
1950	3,632,000	1,452,454	1,667,231	385,144	103,825
1960	4,257,850	1,711,982	1,523,000	393,000	110,873
1970	3,731,386	1,921,031	2,158,802	708,000	74,667
1980	3,612,258	1,989,841	2,390,252	1,189,000	45,526
1990	4,158,212	2,148,463	2,448,000	1,182,000	38,351
1994	3,952,767	2,278,994	2,362,000	1,191,000	31,000
1995	3,899,589	2,312,132	2,336,000	1,169,000	30,000
1996	3,891,494	2,314,690	2,344,000	1,150,000	28,000
1997	3,880,894	2,314,245	2,384,000	1,163,000	28,000
1998	3,941,553	2,337,256	2,244,000	—	28,000
1999	3,959,417	2,391,399	2,358,000	—	28,000
2000	4,058,814	2,403,351	2,329,000	—	27,000
2001	4,025,933	2,416,425	2,345,000	—	28,000
2002	4,021,726	2,443,387	2,254,000	—	28,000
2003	4,089,950	2,448,288	2,187,000[1]	—	—

[1]Preliminary.

Rates (per 1,000 population):

	Birth	Death	Marriage	Divorce
1994	15·0	8·7	9·1	4·6
1995	14·6	8·7	8·9	4·4
1996	14·4	8·6	8·8	4·3
1997	14·2	8·5	8·9	4·3
1998	14·3	8·5	8·4	—
1999	14·2	8·6	8·6	—
2000	14·4	8·5	8·2	—
2001	14·1	8·5	8·2	—
2002	13·9	8·5	7·8	—
2003	14·1	8·4	7·5[1]	—

[1]Preliminary.

Rate of natural increase per 1,000 population: 5·4 in 2002; 5·7 in 2003. Annual population growth rate, 1990–2000, 1·3%.

Even though the marriage rate shows a gradual decline, it remains much higher than in most other industrial countries. The most popular age range for marrying is 25–29 for males and 20–24 for females. The number of births to unmarried women in 2003 was 1,415,995 (34·6% of all births), compared to 666,000 in 1980. The rate of births to teenage women was 41·6 per 1,000 women in 2003. Between 1970 and 2003 the annual number of births rose by 9·6%. The number of births within marriage declined by 19·8% in the same period whereas the number outside of marriage rose by 255·1%. Whereas in 1970 as many as 83·4% of children lived with both biological parents, by 2000 only 60·4% were living with married biological parents and 2·1% with unmarried biological parents.

Infant mortality rates, per 1,000 live births: 29·2 in 1950; 12·9 in 1980; 7·0 in 2002. Fertility rate, 2003, 2·1 births per woman (3·6 in 1960).

There were an estimated 1·29m. abortions in 2002 (1·61m. in 1990), giving a rate of 20·9 for every 1,000 women aged 15–44, compared to a high of 29·3 per 1,000 in 1980 and 1981.

Expectation of life, 1970: males, 67·1 years; females, 74·7 years. 2003: males, 74·6 years; females, 80·0 years.

Numbers of deaths by principal causes, 2002 (and as a percentage of all deaths): heart disease, 696,947 (28·5%); cancer, 557,271 (22·8%); stroke, 162,672 (6·7%); chronic lower respiratory disease, 124,816 (5·1%); accidents, 106,742 (4·4%); diabetes mellitus, 73,249 (3·0%); pneumonia and influenza, 65,681 (2·7%); Alzheimer's disease, 58,866 (2·4%); kidney diseases, 40,974 (1·7%); septicemia, 33,865 (1·4%); suicide, 31,655 (1·3%); liver diseases, 27,257 (1·1%).

The number of Americans living in poverty in 2003 was 35·9m. or 12·5% of the total population, down from 15·1% in 1993.

A UNICEF report published in 2005 showed that 21·9% of children in the USA live in poverty (in households with income below 50% of the national median), compared to just 2·4% in Denmark. A similar report from 2000 had shown that the poverty rate of children in lone-parent families in the USA was 55·4%, compared to 15·8% in two-parent families.

CLIMATE

For temperature and rainfall figures, see entries on individual states as indicated by regions, below, of mainland USA.

Pacific Coast. The climate varies with latitude, distance from the sea and the effect of relief, ranging from polar conditions in North Alaska through cool to warm temperate climates further south. The extreme south is temperate desert. Rainfall everywhere is moderate. See Alaska, California, Oregon, Washington.

Mountain States. Very varied, with relief exerting the main control; very cold in the north in winter, with considerable snowfall. In the south, much higher temperatures and aridity produce desert conditions. Rainfall everywhere is very variable as a result of rain-shadow influences. See Arizona, Colorado, Idaho, Montana, Nevada, New Mexico, Utah, Wyoming.

High Plains. A continental climate with a large annual range of temperature and moderate rainfall, mainly in summer, although unreliable. Dust storms are common in summer and blizzards in winter. See Nebraska, North Dakota, South Dakota.

Central Plains. A temperate continental climate, with hot summers and cold winters, except in the extreme south. Rainfall is plentiful and comes at all seasons, but there is a summer maximum in western parts. See Mississippi, Missouri, Oklahoma, Texas.

Mid-West. Continental, with hot summers and cold winters. Rainfall is moderate, with a summer maximum in most parts. See Indiana, Iowa, Kansas.

Great Lakes. Continental, resembling that of the Central Plains, with hot summers but very cold winters because of the freezing of the lakes. Rainfall is moderate with a slight summer maximum. See Illinois, Michigan, Minnesota, Ohio, Wisconsin.

Appalachian Mountains. The north is cool temperate with cold winters, the south warm temperate with milder winters. Precipitation is heavy, increasing to the south but evenly distributed over the year. See Kentucky, Pennsylvania, Tennessee, West Virginia.

Gulf Coast. Conditions vary from warm temperate to subtropical, with plentiful rainfall, decreasing towards the west but evenly distributed over the year. See Alabama, Arkansas, Florida, Louisiana.

Atlantic Coast. Temperate maritime climate but with great differences in temperature according to latitude. Rainfall is ample at all seasons; snowfall in the north can be heavy. See Delaware, District of Columbia, Georgia, Maryland, New Jersey, New York State, North Carolina, South Carolina, Virginia.

New England. Cool temperate, with severe winters and warm summers. Precipitation is well distributed with a slight winter maximum. Snowfall is heavy in winter. See Connecticut, Maine, Massachusetts, New Hampshire, Rhode Island, Vermont. See also Hawaii and Outlying Territories.

CONSTITUTION AND GOVERNMENT

The form of government of the USA is based on the constitution adopted on 17 Sept. 1787 and effective from 4 March 1789.

By the constitution the government of the nation is composed of three co-ordinate branches, the executive, the legislative and the judicial.

The Federal government has authority in matters of general taxation, treaties and other dealings with foreign countries, foreign and inter-state commerce, bankruptcy, postal service, coinage, weights and measures, patents and copyright, the armed forces (including, to a certain extent, the militia), and crimes against the USA; it has sole legislative authority over the District of Columbia and the possessions of the USA.

The 5th article of the constitution provides that Congress may, on a two-thirds vote of both houses, propose amendments to the constitution, or, on the application of the legislatures of two-thirds of all the states, call a convention for proposing amendments, which in either case shall be valid as part of the constitution when ratified by the legislatures of three-fourths of the several states, or by conventions in three-fourths thereof, whichever mode of ratification may be proposed by Congress. Ten amendments (called collectively 'the Bill of Rights') to the constitution were added 15 Dec. 1791; two in 1795 and 1804; a 13th amendment, 6 Dec. 1865, abolishing slavery; a 14th in 1868, including the important 'due process' clause; a 15th, 3 Feb. 1870, establishing equal voting rights for white and black; a 16th, 3 Feb. 1913, authorizing the income tax; a 17th, 8 April 1913, providing for popular election of senators; an 18th, 16 Jan. 1919, prohibiting alcoholic liquors; a 19th, 18 Aug. 1920, establishing woman suffrage; a 20th, 23 Jan. 1933, advancing the date of the President's and Vice-President's inauguration and abolishing the 'lameduck' sessions of Congress; a 21st, 5 Dec. 1933, repealing the 18th amendment; a 22nd, 27 Feb. 1951, limiting a President's tenure of office to two terms, or two full terms in the case of a Vice-President who has succeeded to the office of President and has served two years or less of another President's term, or one full term in the case of a Vice-President who has succeeded to the office of President and has served more than two years of another President's term; a 23rd, 30 March 1961, granting citizens of the District of Columbia the right to vote in national elections; a 24th, 4 Feb. 1964, banning the use of the poll-tax in federal elections; a 25th, 10 Feb. 1967, dealing with Presidential disability and succession; a 26th, 22 June 1970, establishing the right of citizens who are 18 years of age and older to vote; a 27th, 7 May 1992, providing that no law varying the compensation of Senators or Representatives shall take effect until an election has taken place.

National motto. 'In God we trust'; formally adopted by Congress 30 July 1956.

Presidency

The executive power is vested in a president, who holds office for four years, and is elected, together with a vice-president chosen for the same term, by electors from each state, equal to the whole number of senators and representatives to which the state may be entitled in the Congress. The President must be a natural-born citizen, resident in the country for 14 years, and at least 35 years old.

The presidential election is held every fourth (leap) year on the Tuesday after the first Monday in Nov. Technically, this is an election of presidential electors, not of a president directly; the electors thus chosen meet and give their votes (for the candidate to whom they are pledged, in some states by law, but in most states by custom and prudent politics) at their respective state capitals on the first Monday after the second Wednesday in Dec. next following their election; and the votes of the electors of all the states are opened and counted in the presence of both Houses of Congress on the sixth day of Jan. The total electorate vote is one for each senator and representative. Electors may not be a member of Congress or hold federal office. If no candidate secures the minimum 270 college votes needed for outright victory, the 12th Amendment to the Constitution applies, and the House of Representatives chooses a president from among the first three finishers in the electoral college. (This last happened in 1824). If the successful candidate for President dies before taking office the Vice-President-elect becomes President; if no candidate has a majority or if the successful candidate fails to qualify, then, by the 20th amendment, the Vice-President acts as President until a president qualifies. The duties of the Presidency, in absence of the President and Vice-President by reason of death, resignation, removal, inability or failure to qualify, devolve upon the Speaker of the House under legislation enacted on 18 July 1947. In case of absence of a Speaker for like reason, the presidential duties devolve upon the President *pro tem.* of the Senate and successively upon those members of the cabinet in order of precedence, who have the constitutional qualifications for President.

The presidential term, by the 20th amendment to the constitution, begins at noon on 20 Jan. of the inaugural year. This amendment also installs the newly elected Congress in office on 3 Jan. instead of—as formerly—in the following Dec. The President's salary is $400,000 per year (taxable), with an additional $50,000 to assist in defraying expenses resulting from official duties. Also he may spend up to $100,000 non-taxable for travel and $19,000 for official entertainment. In 1999 the presidential salary was increased for the president taking office in Jan. 2001, having remained at $200,000 a year since 1969. The office of Vice-President carries a salary of $212,100 and $10,000 allowance for expenses, all taxable. The Vice-President is *ex officio* President of the Senate, and in the case of 'the removal of the President, or of his death, resignation, or inability to discharge the powers and duties of his office', he becomes the President for the remainder of the term.

Cabinet. The administrative business of the nation has been traditionally vested in several executive departments, the heads of which, unofficially and *ex officio*, formed the President's cabinet. Beginning with the Interstate Commerce Commission in 1887, however, an increasing amount of executive business has been entrusted to some 60 so-called independent agencies, such as the Housing and Home Finance Agency, Tariff Commission, etc.

All heads of departments and of the 60 or more administrative agencies are appointed by the President, but must be confirmed by the Senate.

Congress. The legislative power is vested by the Constitution in a Congress, consisting of a Senate and House of Representatives.

Electorate. By amendments of the constitution, disqualification of voters on the ground of race, colour or sex is forbidden. The electorate consists of all citizens over 18 years of age. Literacy tests have been banned since 1970. In 1972 durational residency requirements were held to violate the constitution. In 1973 US citizens abroad were enfranchised.

With limitations imposed by the constitution, it is the states which determine voter eligibility. In general states exclude from voting: persons who have not established residency in the jurisdiction in which they wish to vote; persons who have been convicted of felonies whose civil rights have not been restored; persons declared mentally incompetent by a court.

Illiterate voters are entitled to receive assistance in marking their ballots. Minority-language voters in jurisdictions with statutorily prescribed minority concentrations are entitled to have elections conducted in the minority language as well as English. Disabled voters are entitled to accessible polling places. Voters absent on election days or unable to go to the polls are generally entitled under state law to vote by absentee ballot.

The Constitution guarantees citizens that their votes will be of equal value under the 'one person, one vote' rule.

Senate. The Senate consists of two members from each state (but not from the District of Columbia), chosen by popular vote for six years, approximately one-third retiring or seeking re-election every two years. Senators must be no less than 30 years of age; must have been citizens of the USA for nine years, and be residents in the states for which they are chosen. The Senate has complete freedom to initiate legislation, except revenue bills (which must originate in the House of Representatives); it may, however, amend or reject any legislation originating in the lower house. The Senate is also entrusted with the power of giving or withholding its 'advice and consent' to the ratification of all treaties initiated by the President with foreign powers, a two-thirds majority of senators present being required for approval. (However, it has no control over 'international executive agreements' made by the President with foreign governments; such 'agreements' cover a wide range and are more numerous than formal treaties.) The Senate has 21 Standing Committees to which all bills are referred for study, revision or rejection. The House of Representatives has 20 such committees. In both Houses each Standing Committee has a chairman and a majority representing the majority party of the whole House; each has numerous sub-committees. The jurisdictions of these Committees correspond largely to those of the appropriate executive departments and agencies. Both Houses also have a few select or special Committees with limited duration.

House of Representatives. The House of Representatives consists of 435 members elected every second year. The number of each state's representatives is determined by the decennial census, in the absence of specific Congressional legislation affecting the basis. The number of representatives for each state in the 109th congress, which began in Jan. 2005 (based on the 2000 census), is given below:

Alabama	7	Louisiana	7	Ohio	18
Alaska	1	Maine	2	Oklahoma	5
Arizona	8	Maryland	8	Oregon	5
Arkansas	4	Massachusetts	10	Pennsylvania	19
California	53	Michigan	15	Rhode Island	2
Colorado	7	Minnesota	8	South Carolina	6
Connecticut	5	Mississippi	4	South Dakota	1
Delaware	1	Missouri	9	Tennessee	9
Florida	25	Montana	1	Texas	32
Georgia	13	Nebraska	3	Utah	3
Hawaii	2	Nevada	3	Vermont	1
Idaho	2	New Hampshire	2	Virginia	11
Illinois	19	New Jersey	13	Washington	9
Indiana	9	New Mexico	3	West Virginia	3
Iowa	5	New York	29	Wisconsin	8
Kansas	4	North Carolina	13	Wyoming	1
Kentucky	6	North Dakota	1		

The constitution requires congressional districts within each state to be substantially equal in population. Final decisions on congressional district boundaries are taken by the state legislatures and governors. By custom the representative lives in the district from which he is elected. Representatives must be not less than 25 years of age, citizens of the USA for seven years and residents in the state from which they are chosen.

In addition, five delegates (one each from the District of Columbia, American Samoa, Guam, the US Virgin Islands and Puerto Rico) are also members of Congress. They have a voice but no vote, except in committees. The delegate from Puerto Rico is the resident commissioner. Puerto Ricans vote at primaries, but not at national elections. Each of the two Houses of Congress is sole 'judge of the elections, returns and qualifications of its own members'; and each of the Houses may, with the concurrence of two-thirds, expel a member. The period

usually termed 'a Congress' in legislative language continues for two years, terminating at noon on 3 Jan.

The salary of a senator is $165,200 per annum, with tax-free expense allowance and allowances for travelling expenses and for clerical hire. The salary of the Speaker of the House of Representatives is $212,100 per annum, with a taxable allowance. The salary of a Member of the House is $165,200 ($183,500 for the Majority Leader and Minority Leader).

No senator or representative can, during the time for which he is elected, be appointed to any *civil* office under authority of the USA which shall have been created or the emoluments of which shall have been increased during such time; and no person holding *any* office under the USA can be a member of either House during his continuance in office. No religious text may be required as a qualification to any office or public trust under the USA or in any state.

Indians. By an Act passed on 2 June 1924 full citizenship was granted to all Indians born in the USA, though those remaining in tribal units were still under special federal jurisdiction. The Indian Reorganization Act of 1934 gave the tribal Indians, at their own option, substantial opportunities of self-government and the establishment of self-controlled corporate enterprises empowered to borrow money and buy land, machinery and equipment; these corporations are controlled by democratically elected tribal councils. Recently a trend towards releasing Indians from federal supervision has resulted in legislation terminating supervision over specific tribes. In 1988 the federal government recognized that it had a special relationship with, and a trust responsibility for, federally recognized Indian entities in continental USA and tribal entities in Alaska. In 2003 the Bureau of Indian Affairs listed 562 'Indian Entities Recognized and Eligible to Receive Services'. Indian lands (1991) amounted to 52,092,247 acres, of which 41,868,582 was tribally owned and 10,233,665 in trust allotments. Indian lands are held free of taxes. Total Indian population at the 2000 census was 2,475,956, of which California (333,346), Oklahoma (273,230), Arizona (255,879) and New Mexico (173,483) accounted for more than 40%.

The **District of Columbia,** ceded by the State of Maryland for the purposes of government in 1791, is the seat of the US government. It includes the city of Washington, and embraces a land area of 61 sq. miles. The Reorganization Plan No. 3 of 1967 instituted a Mayor Council form of government with appointed officers. In 1973 an elected Mayor and elected councillors were introduced; in 1974 they received power to legislate in local matters. Congress retains power to enact legislation and to veto or supersede the Council's acts. Since 1961 citizens have had the right to vote in national elections. On 23 Aug. 1978 the Senate approved a constitutional amendment giving the District full voting representation in Congress. This has still to be ratified.

The Commonwealth of Puerto Rico, American Samoa, Guam and the Virgin Islands each have a local legislature, whose acts may be modified or annulled by Congress, though in practice this has seldom been done. Puerto Rico, since its attainment of commonwealth status on 25 July 1952, enjoys practically complete self-government, including the election of its governor and other officials. The conduct of foreign relations, however, is still a federal function and federal bureaux and agencies still operate in the island.

General supervision of territorial administration is exercised by the Office of Territories in the Department of Interior.

Local Government

The Union comprises 13 original states, seven states which were admitted without having been previously organized as territories, and 30 states which had been territories—50 states in all. Each state has its own constitution (which the USA guarantees shall be republican in form), deriving its authority, not from Congress, but from the people of the state. Admission of states into the Union has been granted by special Acts of Congress, either (1) in the form of 'enabling Acts' providing for the drafting and ratification of a state constitution by the people, in which case the territory becomes a state as soon as the conditions are fulfilled, or (2) accepting a constitution already framed, and at once granting admission.

Each state is provided with a legislature of two Houses (except Nebraska, which since 1937 has had a single-chamber legislature), a governor and other executive officials, and a judicial system. Both Houses of the legislature are elective, but the senators (having larger electoral districts usually covering two or three counties compared with the single county or, in some states, the town, which sends one representative to the Lower House) are less numerous than the representatives, while in 38 states their terms are four years; in 12 states the term is two years. Of the four-year senates, Illinois, Montana and New Jersey provide for two four-year terms and one two-year term in each decade. Terms of the lower houses are usually shorter; in 45 states, two years. The trend is towards annual sessions of state legislatures; most meet annually now whereas in 1939 only four did.

The Governor is elected by direct vote of the people over the whole state for a term of office ranging in the various states from two to four years, and with a salary ranging from $70,000 (Maine) to $179,000 (New York). His duty is to see to the faithful administration of the law, and he has command of the military forces of the state. He may recommend measures but does not present bills to the legislature. In some states he presents estimates. In all but one of the states (North Carolina) the Governor has a veto upon legislation, which may, however, be overridden by the two Houses, in some states by a simple majority, in others by a three-fifths or two-thirds majority. In some states the Governor, on his death or resignation, is succeeded by a Lieut.-Governor who was elected at the same time and has been presiding over the state Senate. In several states the Speaker of the Lower House succeeds the Governor.

National Anthem

The Star-spangled Banner, 'Oh say, can you see by the dawn's early light'; words by F. S. Key, 1814, tune by J. S. Smith; formally adopted by Congress 3 March 1931.

GOVERNMENT CHRONOLOGY

PRESIDENTS OF THE USA

Name	Party[1]	From state	Term of service	Born	Died
George Washington	(F.)	Virginia	1789–97	1732	1799
John Adams	(F.)	Massachusetts	1797–1801	1735	1826
Thomas Jefferson	(D.)	Virginia	1801–09	1743	1826
James Madison	(D.)	Virginia	1809–17	1751	1836
James Monroe	(D.)	Virginia	1817–25	1759	1831
John Quincy Adams	(n.p.)	Massachusetts	1825–29	1767	1848
Andrew Jackson	(D.)	Tennessee	1829–37	1767	1845
Martin Van Buren	(D.)	New York	1837–41	1782	1862
William H. Harrison	(W.)	Ohio	Mar.–Apr. 1841	1773	1841
John Tyler	(W.)	Virginia	1841–45	1790	1862
James K. Polk	(D.)	Tennessee	1845–49	1795	1849
Zachary Taylor	(W.)	Louisiana	1849–July 1850	1784	1850
Millard Fillmore	(W.)	New York	1850–53	1800	1874
Franklin Pierce	(D.)	New Hampshire	1853–57	1804	1869
James Buchanan	(D.)	Pennsylvania	1857–61	1791	1868
Abraham Lincoln	(R.)	Illinois	1861–Apr. 1865	1809	1865
Andrew Johnson	(D.)	Tennessee	1865–69	1808	1875
Ulysses S. Grant	(R.)	Illinois	1869–77	1822	1885
Rutherford B. Hayes	(R.)	Ohio	1877–81	1822	1893
James A. Garfield	(R.)	Ohio	Mar.–Sept. 1881	1831	1881
Chester A. Arthur	(R.)	New York	1881–85	1830	1886
Grover Cleveland	(D.)	New York	1885–89	1837	1908
Benjamin Harrison	(R.)	Indiana	1889–93	1833	1901
Grover Cleveland	(D.)	New York	1893–97	1837	1908
William McKinley	(R.)	Ohio	1897–Sept. 1901	1843	1901
Theodore Roosevelt	(R.)	New York	1901–09	1858	1919
William H. Taft	(R.)	Ohio	1909–13	1857	1930
Woodrow Wilson	(D.)	New Jersey	1913–21	1856	1924
Warren Gamaliel Harding	(R.)	Ohio	1921–Aug. 1923	1865	1923
Calvin Coolidge	(R.)	Massachusetts	1923–29	1872	1933
Herbert C. Hoover	(R.)	California	1929–33	1874	1964
Franklin D. Roosevelt	(D.)	New York	1933–Apr. 1945	1882	1945
Harry S Truman	(D.)	Missouri	1945–53	1884	1972
Dwight D. Eisenhower	(R.)	New York	1953–61	1890	1969
John F. Kennedy	(D.)	Massachusetts	1961–Nov. 1963	1917	1963
Lyndon B. Johnson	(D.)	Texas	1963–69	1908	1973
Richard M. Nixon	(R.)	California	1969–74	1913	1994
Gerald R. Ford	(R.)	Michigan	1974–77	1913	—
James Earl Carter	(D.)	Georgia	1977–81	1924	—
Ronald W. Reagan	(R.)	California	1981–89	1911	2004
George H. Bush	(R.)	Texas	1989–93	1924	—
Bill (William J.) Clinton	(D.)	Arkansas	1993–2001	1946	—
George W. Bush	(R.)	Texas	2001–	1946	—

[1]F. = Federalist; D. = Democrat; n.p. = no party; W. = Whig; R. = Republican.

VICE-PRESIDENTS OF THE USA

Name	Party[1]	From state	Term of service	Born	Died
John Adams	(F.)	Massachusetts	1789–97	1735	1826
Thomas Jefferson	(R.)	Virginia	1797–1801	1743	1826
Aaron Burr	(R.)	New York	1801–05	1756	1836
George Clinton	(R.)	New York	1805–12[2]	1739	1812
Elbridge Gerry	(R.)	Massachusetts	1813–14[2]	1744	1814
Daniel D. Tompkins	(R.)	New York	1817–25	1774	1825
John C. Calhoun	(NR./D.)	South Carolina	1825–32[2]	1782	1850
Martin Van Buren	(D.)	New York	1833–37	1782	1862
Richard M. Johnson	(D.)	Kentucky	1837–41	1780	1850
John Tyler	(D.)	Virginia	Mar.–Apr.1841[2]	1790	1862
George M. Dallas	(D.)	Pennsylvania	1845–49	1792	1864
Millard Fillmore	(W.)	New York	1849–50[2]	1800	1874
William R. King	(D.)	Alabama	Mar.–Apr. 1853[2]	1786	1853
John C. Breckinridge	(D.)	Kentucky	1857–61	1821	1875
Hannibal Hamlin	(R.)	Maine	1861–65	1809	1891
Andrew Johnson	(D.)	Tennessee	Mar.–Apr. 1865[2]	1808	1875
Schuyler Colfax	(R.)	Indiana	1869–73	1823	1885
Henry Wilson	(R.)	Massachusetts	1873–75[2]	1812	1875
William A. Wheeler	(R.)	New York	1877–81	1819	1887
Chester A. Arthur	(R.)	New York	Mar.–Sept. 1881[2]	1830	1886
Thomas A. Hendricks	(D.)	Indiana	Mar.–Nov. 1885[2]	1819	1885
Levi P. Morton	(R.)	New York	1889–93	1824	1920
Adlai Stevenson	(D.)	Illinois	1893–97	1835	1914
Garret A. Hobart	(R.)	New Jersey	1897–99[2]	1844	1899
Theodore Roosevelt	(R.)	New York	Mar.–Sept. 1901[2]	1858	1919
Charles W. Fairbanks	(R.)	Indiana	1905–09	1855	1920
James S. Sherman	(R.)	New York	1909–12[2]	1855	1912
Thomas R. Marshall	(D.)	Indiana	1913–21	1854	1925
Calvin Coolidge	(R.)	Massachusetts	1921–Aug. 1923[2]	1872	1933
Charles G. Dawes	(R.)	Illinois	1925–29	1865	1951
Charles Curtis	(R.)	Kansas	1929–33	1860	1935
John N. Garner	(D.)	Texas	1933–41	1868	1967
Henry A. Wallace	(D.)	Iowa	1941–45	1888	1965
Harry S. Truman	(D.)	Missouri	1945–Apr. 1945[2]	1884	1972
Alben W. Barkley	(D.)	Kentucky	1949–53	1877	1956
Richard M. Nixon	(R.)	California	1953–61	1913	1994
Lyndon B. Johnson	(D.)	Texas	1961–Nov. 1963[2]	1908	1973
Hubert H. Humphrey	(D.)	Minnesota	1965–69	1911	1978
Spiro T. Agnew	(R.)	Maryland	1969–73	1918	1996
Gerald R. Ford	(R.)	Michigan	1973–74	1913	—
Nelson Rockefeller	(R.)	New York	1974–77	1908	1979
Walter Mondale	(D.)	Minnesota	1977–81	1928	—
George H. Bush	(R.)	Texas	1981–89	1924	—
Danforth Quayle	(R.)	Indiana	1989–93	1947	—
Albert Gore	(D.)	Tennessee	1993–2001	1948	—
Richard B. Cheney	(R.)	Wyoming	2001–	1941	—

[1]F. = Federalist; R. = Republican; NR. = National Republican; D. = Democrat; W. = Whig. [2]Position vacant thereafter until commencement of the next presidential term.

RECENT ELECTIONS

At the presidential election on 2 Nov. 2004 turnout was 53·6% (51·2% in 2000). Certified results gave George W. Bush (R.) 62,028,285 votes (50·73%), John Kerry (D.) 59,028,109 (48·27%), Ralph Nader (ind.) 463,647 (0·38%), Michael Badnarik (Libertarian Party) 397,234 (0·32%), Michael Peroutka (Constitution Party) 143,609 (0·12%), David Cobb (Green Party) 119,862 (0·10%). Electoral college votes: Bush, 286; Kerry, 251; John Edwards, 1.

Voting percentages and electoral college votes by state in 2004:

a) Majority for Bush

State	Bush (%)	Kerry (%)	3rd Place (%)	Electoral College (votes)
Alabama	62·5	36·8	0·4[1]	9
Alaska	61·1	35·5	1·6[1]	3
Arizona	54·9	44·4	0·6[2]	10
Arkansas	54·3	44·5	0·6[1]	6
Colorado	51·7	47·0	0·6[1]	9
Florida	52·1	47·1	0·4[1]	27
Georgia	58·0	41·4	0·6[2]	15
Idaho	68·4	30·3	0·6[2]	4
Indiana	59·9	39·3	0·7[2]	11
Iowa	49·9	49·2	0·4[1]	7
Kansas	62·0	36·6	0·8[1]	6
Kentucky	59·6	39·7	0·5[1]	8
Louisiana	56·7	42·2	0·4[1]	9
Mississippi	59·0	40·2	0·3[1]	6
Missouri	53·3	46·1	0·4[2]	11
Montana	59·1	38·6	1·4[1]	3
Nebraska	65·9	32·7	0·7[1]	5
Nevada	50·5	47·9	0·6[1]	5
New Mexico	49·8	49·0	0·5[1]	5
North Carolina	56·0	43·6	0·3[2]	15
North Dakota	62·9	35·5	1·2[1]	3
Ohio	50·8	48·7	0·3[2]	20
Oklahoma	65·6	34·4	—	7
South Carolina	58·0	40·9	0·3[1]	8
South Dakota	59·9	38·4	1·1[1]	3
Tennessee	56·8	42·5	0·4[1]	11
Texas	61·1	38·2	0·5[2]	34
Utah	71·5	26·0	1·2[1]	5
Virginia	53·7	45·5	0·3[2]	13
West Virginia	56·1	43·2	0·5[1]	5
Wyoming	68·9	29·1	1·1[1]	3

[1]Nader. [2]Badnarik.

b) Majority for Kerry

State	Kerry	Bush	3rd Place	
California	54·3	44·4	0·4[2]	55
Connecticut	54·3	43·9	0·8[1]	7
Delaware	53·3	45·8	0·6[1]	3
D.C.	89·2	9·3	0·7[1]	3
Hawaii	54·0	45·3	0·4[3]	4
Illinois	54·8	44·5	0·6[2]	21
Maine	53·6	44·6	1·1[1]	4
Maryland	55·9	42·9	0·5[1]	10
Massachusetts	61·9	36·8	0·5[2]	12
Michigan	51·2	47·8	0·5[1]	17
Minnesota	51·1	47·6	0·7[1]	9
New Hampshire	50·2	48·9	0·7[1]	4
New Jersey	52·9	46·2	0·5[1]	15
New York	58·4	40·1	1·4[1]	31
Oregon	51·3	47·2	0·4[2]	7
Pennsylvania	50·9	48·4	0·4[2]	21
Rhode Island	59·4	38·7	1·1[1]	4
Vermont	58·9	38·8	1·4[1]	3
Washington	52·8	45·6	0·8[1]	11
Wisconsin	49·7	49·3	0·5[1]	10

[1]Nader. [2]Badnarik. [3]Cobb.

Following the elections of 2 Nov. 2004 the 109th Congress (2005–06) is constituted as follows: Senate—55 Republicans,

44 Democrats and 1 ind. (51 Democrats, 48 Republicans and 1 ind. for the 108th Congress); House of Representatives—232 Republicans, 202 Democrats, 1 ind. (229 Republicans, 204 Democrats, 1 ind. and 1 vacancy for the 108th Congress).

The Speaker of the House of Representatives is Dennis Hastert (R.). The Majority Leader of the Senate is Bill Frist (R.).

CURRENT ADMINISTRATION

President of the United States: George W. Bush, of Texas; b. 1946. Majored in History at Yale (1968); MA in Business Administration (1975); unsuccessfully ran for Congress (1977); became shareholder in Texas Rangers baseball team (1988); governor of Texas (1994–2000).

Vice President: Richard 'Dick' Cheney, b. Wyoming, 1941. Deputy White House counselor in Nixon administration (1970); assistant to the president and White House chief of staff during the Ford administration (1974); House of Representatives (1979–89); Secretary of Defense (1989–93). Vice President since 2001.

In May 2006 the cabinet consisted of the following:

1. *Secretary of State* (created 1789). Condoleezza Rice, b. Alabama, 1954. Fellow of Stanford University Center for International Security and Arms Control (1981–89); Soviet affairs adviser to George H. Bush (1989–91); Provost of Stanford University (1993–99); National security adviser (2001–05).

2. *Secretary of the Treasury* (1789). John Snow, b. Ohio, 1939. PhD in Economics (1965) and LLB (1967). Entered Department of Transportation in 1972; Deputy Undersecretary of Transportation in Ford administration (1975–76). Joined Chessie System Inc. in 1977; President and CEO (1989) of CSX Corp. and Chairman (1991); Secretary of the Treasury since 2003.

3. *Secretary of Defense* (1947). Donald Rumsfeld, b. Illinois, 1932. Elected to the House of Representatives (1962–69); Ambassador to the North Atlantic Treaty Organisation (1973–74); Secretary of Defense to President Ford (1975–77); Special US negotiator for Middle Eastern problems (1983–84); Secretary of Defense since 2001.

4. *Attorney General* (Department of Justice, 1870). Alberto 'Al' Gonzales, b. Texas, 1955. Joined Vinson & Elkins law firm in Houston in 1982; Legal adviser to Governor Bush in Texas (1994–97); Texas Secretary of State (1997–99); Judge of Supreme Court of Texas (1999–2000); White House counsel (2001–05).

5. *Secretary of the Interior* (1849). Lynn Scarlett (Acting Secretary).

6. *Secretary of Agriculture* (1889). Michael Johanns, b. Iowa, 1950. Lancaster county board of commissioners (1982–86); Lincoln city council (1989–91); Mayor of Lincoln (1991–99); Governor of Nebraska (1999–2005).

7. *Secretary of Commerce* (1903). Carlos Gutierrez, b. Cuba, 1954. Career with Kellogg Company began in 1975 in Mexico City; General Manager Kellogg operations in Mexico (1985); Chairman of the board and Chief Executive Officer of the Kellogg Company (1999–2005).

8. *Secretary of Labor* (1913). Elaine Chao, b. Taiwan, 1953. White House Fellow (1983–84); Deputy Secretary of the US Department of Transportation in Washington (1989–91); Director of the Peace Corps (1992); President of United Way of America (1992–96); Chairman of Heritage Foundation's Asian Studies Center Advisory Council (1998); Secretary of Labor since 2001.

9. *Secretary of Health and Human Services* (1953). Michael O. Leavitt, b. Utah, 1951. Former president and chief executive of the Leavitt Group; Governor of Utah for three terms (1992–2003); Chief of the Environmental Protection Agency (2003–05).

10. *Secretary of Housing and Urban Development* (1966). Alphonso Jackson, b. Texas. Director of Public Safety, St Louis (1977); President and CEO of the Texas Housing Authority (1989–96); President of American Electric Power-TEXAS (1996–

2001); deputy secretary and chief operating officer of Housing and Urban Development (2001–04). Secretary of Housing and Urban Development since 2004.

11. *Secretary of Transportation* (1967). Norman Mineta, b. California, 1931. Congressman for Silicon Valley (1974–95); Chairman, US House of Representatives Committee on Public Works and Transportation (1993); Chairman, Federal Aviation Administration's National Civil Aviation Review Commission (1997). He is the only Democrat in the cabinet. Secretary of Transportation since 2001.

12. *Secretary of Energy* (1977). Samuel W. Bodman, b. Chicago, 1938. Member of the American Academy of Arts and Sciences; Chairman, CEO, and Director (variously) of Cabot Corporation (1987–2001); Deputy commerce secretary (2001–03); Deputy treasury secretary (2003–05).

13. *Secretary of Education* (1979). Margaret Spellings, b. Michigan, 1958. Political director of George W. Bush's first gubernatorial campaign (1994); Senior adviser to Governor Bush on Education in Texas (1994–2000); Assistant to president for domestic policy (2000–05).

14. *Secretary of Veterans' Affairs* (1989). R. James 'Jim' Nicholson, b. Iowa, 1938. Westpoint Graduate (1961); 30 years service in Army; retired as a Colonel (1991); Chair of Republican National Committee (1997–2001); US Ambassador to the Vatican (2001–05).

15. *Secretary of Homeland Security* (2002). Michael Chertoff, b. New Jersey, 1953. Special counsel US Senate Whitewater Commission (1994–96); Director of the Justice Department's criminal division (2001–03); Federal judge on the 3rd US Circuit Court of Appeals (2003–05).

Each of the above cabinet officers receives an annual salary of $183,500 and holds office during the pleasure of the President.

A number of administrators also have honorary cabinet status.

Key White House Posts: White House Chief of Staff: Joshua Bolten; National Security Adviser: Stephen Hadley; White House Counsel: Harriet Miers; Press Secretary: Tony Snow; Assistant for Economic Affairs: Allan Hubbard; Office of Management and Budget: Vacant; Council of Economic Advisors: Edward Lazear; Office of the US Trade Representative: Vacant.

Office of the President: http://www.whitehouse.gov

CURRENT LEADERS

George W. Bush

Position
President

Introduction
The 43rd president of the USA, George Walker Bush took office in 2001 after one of the most controversial presidential elections in history. He is the first president since 1888 to reach the White House despite losing the popular vote. Within nine months of taking office, Bush was plunged into one of the most challenging periods of any presidency after the USA was subjected to unprecedented attacks by Islamic militants on 11 Sept. 2001. In Feb. 2003, following a clash with the UN, Bush authorized US-led forces to attack Iraq and remove Saddam Hussein from power. He was re-elected in Nov. 2004 for a second term with 51% of the popular vote and inaugurated in Jan. 2005.

Early Life
Bush was born in New Haven, Connecticut on 6 July 1946 and grew up in Midland and Houston, Texas. He attended Phillips Academy, Yale University and the Harvard Business School, and was awarded a degree in history and an MBA. Bush served as a pilot in the Texas National Guard in the 1960s and set up his own oil and gas business in the mid-1970s.

Bush failed to get elected as a Republican Party candidate to the House of Representatives in 1978. He returned to his oil business until 1986, when he sold his interests to help his father George H. W. Bush in his successful campaign to become US president in the 1988 elections. In 1989 Bush headed a group of investors who bought the Texas Rangers baseball team and acted as managing general partner of the team for five years. In 1994 he challenged Ann Richards, the Democratic governor of Texas and, despite beginning the election campaign as the underdog, won with 53·5% of the vote.

During his spell as governor, Bush's tough stance on drugs and crime, allied with large tax cuts, a welfare reform programme and increased spending on education, proved popular and he was re-elected in 1998. In 1999 Bush announced that he would try for the Republican presidential nomination. His campaign fund raised around $100m., a figure that persuaded many of his opponents to withdraw from the race. Despite losing the New Hampshire primary, Bush recovered to secure the nomination and picked former defence secretary Richard Cheney as his running mate.

Bush's campaign focused on promises of tax cuts and 'compassionate conservative' social policies. Despite taking an early lead in the polls, the gap between Bush and his Democratic opponent Al Gore narrowed as the election approached. Bush lost the popular vote by 500,000 votes, but the outcome of the election ultimately hinged on Florida's 25 electoral college votes. Bush narrowly led Gore in Florida after machine counts, but Gore sought a manual recount of several counties and the final result of the election remained uncertain for five weeks as the courts debated legal challenges and counter-challenges. The Florida Supreme Court ordered a manual recount in two counties, but the US Supreme Court reversed this decision, handing Bush the election by 271 electoral college votes to 266.

Career in Office
Bush was inaugurated as the 43rd president of the USA on 20 Jan. 2001, becoming only the second son of a former president to also reach the White House. With much controversy still surrounding his election he immediately struck a conciliatory stance, declaring: 'I was not elected to serve one party, but to serve one nation.'

In April 2001 Bush presented his first detailed budget proposals, including a $1·6trn. tax cut. He was forced to trim this figure to $1·25trn. in May after bowing to pressure from Congress. The same month, the Republicans lost control of the Senate for the first time in seven years when Senator James Jeffords left the party to serve as an independent. Nevertheless, Bush still won approval from the House and the Senate for millions of tax refund cheques, reductions in most tax rates, and tax relief measures for married couples and the parents of young children.

In March 2001 Bush refused to ratify the environmental measures recommended by the Kyoto Agreement on global warming and climate change, attracting criticism from European nations. In Aug. Congress approved his plan to stimulate energy production, involving billions of dollars in tax breaks and exploration incentives for energy producers.

Bush also initiated a highly controversial plan to replace the 1972 Anti-Ballistic Missile Treaty with a new accord so that he could introduce a US missile defence system. Having discussed this proposal with the Russian president Vladimir Putin, the two leaders agreed in May 2002 to reduce their respective strategic nuclear warheads by two-thirds over the next ten years.

Bush's presidency and the US' relationship with the rest of the world were transformed by the events of 11 Sept. 2001 when the country suffered devastating attacks. Two hijacked passenger airliners were crashed into the World Trade Center towers in New York City, another hit the Pentagon in Washington, D.C., while a fourth came down in a Pennsylvania field before reaching its intended target, which may have been the White House. Both World Trade Center towers collapsed and part of the Pentagon was destroyed. The total number of people killed was around 3,000, including many rescue workers.

The attacks had international political and economic ramifications. Bush announced a war against terrorism. With evidence pointing to the involvement of Osama bin Laden and his al-Qaeda organization, the president threatened military action against Afghanistan's Taliban regime which had been sheltering the terrorist network. Bush sought to establish a global alliance to put pressure on Afghanistan, receiving support from Europe as well as co-operation from Pakistan and Uzbekistan and the acquiescence of Iran. In Oct. 2001 mainly US and British forces attacked Taliban and al-Qaeda forces in Afghanistan and the following month the Northern Alliance, an Afghan group opposed to the Taliban, retook the capital, Kabul. Meetings of various Afghan leaders were organized by the UN to produce a new interim government (headed by Hamid Karzai) and to ratify an agreement allowing a UN peacekeeping force to enter Afghanistan.

As well as maintaining his war on terror, Bush also sought to counter the economic effects of the Sept. 11 attacks as the USA entered recession. He announced an economic revitalization package, including an extra $18bn. for emergency military spending, and sent the US budget into deficit for the first time in five years. Defence remained Bush's priority into 2002. In Nov. he announced the creation of a department of homeland security, an amalgamation of 22 agencies with a budget of $40bn. He also set up a commission to investigate the failure of intelligence agencies to prevent the 11 Sept. 2001 attacks. In Jan 2003 Bush announced a further stimulus for the US economy, including tax cuts and extended unemployment aid.

In Jan. 2002, in his state of the union address, Bush referred to North Korea, Iran and Iraq as 'an axis of evil'. From the following Sept. he began to focus on Saddam Hussein's regime in Iraq, which he accused of stockpiling weapons of mass destruction (WMD). He successfully campaigned for a UN resolution demanding a renewal of weapons inspections. UN inspectors began their investigation in Nov. 2002 and were scheduled to make their final report back in Jan. 2003. The resolution required Iraq's full co-operation, and in Dec. 2002 the government provided a dossier detailing Iraq's chemical, biological and nuclear capabilities. The document was sent to UN experts for analysis to decide if it complied with the resolution's demands. The USA increased its military presence in the Middle East throughout Dec. 2002 and Jan. 2003.

In his report to the Security Council on 27 Jan. 2003, the head of the UN weapons inspectors criticized Iraq's insufficient co-operation but concluded that the investigations neither proved nor disproved that Iraq had a nuclear weapons programme. Bush responded that he still believed Iraq had no intention of disarming. Following talks with UK Prime Minister Tony Blair in early Feb. Bush agreed to work with the UN towards a further resolution sanctioning action against Iraq unless it disarmed. Deep divisions within the Security Council emerged, notably between the USA, UK and Spain who favoured a military threat and France, Germany, Russia and China who opposed any military intervention. With Bush emphasizing his right to act independently of the UN, attempts to draught a second resolution acceptable to all parties were abandoned.

US-led forces launched an invasion of Iraq in March 2003. By early April 2003 troops were in control of the country and Saddam Hussein's regime had collapsed. Bush also threatened Syria with economic, diplomatic or other unspecified sanctions after suggesting that the Syrian government was harbouring members of Saddam Hussein's regime and had been involved in the development of chemical weapons. In May 2003 the UN ratified a resolution, co-sponsored by the USA, UK and Spain, on

Iraq's future. Under its terms UN special representatives were to co-operate with the occupying forces to form a new government and the occupying forces were to remain until an internationally-acceptable government was in place. In July 2004 a critical US Senate report said that the USA and its allies had gone to war in Iraq on flawed intelligence. While substantial US forces remain in Iraq helping to quell an ongoing and violent Islamic insurgency, Bush has supported political moves to introduce democratic and representative government, most recently through national elections to a new parliament which were held in Dec. 2005. However, there has been much negative publicity surrounding the reported abuse of Iraqi prisoners in US military custody (and similarly of terrorist suspects detained since the Afghanistan campaign at the US naval base at Guantánamo Bay in Cuba).

Developments elsewhere in the Middle East have remained volatile during Bush's presidency, particularly those connected with the Israeli-Palestinian conflict. In April 2003 the 'roadmap to peace', jointly produced by the USA, UN, EU and Russia, was published. The document called for an immediate ceasefire and paved the way for the establishment of a Palestinian state. Then in April 2004, in a major shift of US policy, Bush announced his endorsement of Israeli prime minister Ariel Sharon's plan to remove all Jewish settlements in Gaza while holding on to larger settlement blocs in the occupied West Bank, and accepted that Israel would not make a full and complete return to its pre-1967 borders.

Relations with North Korea worsened from late 2002/early 2003 when Pyongyang reactivated a nuclear plant unused since a treaty was signed in 1994, and demanded the withdrawal of UN International Atomic Energy Agency (IAEA) inspectors. Kim Jong Il then withdrew from the nuclear Non-Proliferation Treaty, accusing the USA of posing a nuclear threat and planning to remove its government. Bush outlined a 'tailored containment' strategy, involving economic sanctions, but the proposals faced opposition from the South Korean government. Over the next two years there followed several rounds of inconclusive negotiations between North Korea and the USA, together with South Korea, Japan, China and Russia. During this period Kim's regime admitted publicly in Feb. 2005 that it had built nuclear weapons for self-defence before agreeing in principle in Sept. 2005 to give up its development programme in return for aid and security guarantees. However, that accord was almost immediately undermined when North Korea then demanded the delivery of civil nuclear equipment. Furthermore, tensions with Iran increased in late 2005 when Tehran re-commenced its uranium enrichment research programme. Iran's claims that the research was for peaceful purposes were received with scepticism and Iran was reported to the UN security council by the IAEA in Feb. 2006.

In his 'State of the Union' address in Jan. 2006 Bush reasserted that the USA was 'committed to an historic, long-term goal—we seek the end of tyranny in our world...the future security of America depends on it'.

DEFENCE

The President is C.-in-C. of the Army, Navy and Air Force.

The National Security Act of 1947 provides for the unification of the Army, Navy and Air Forces under a single Secretary of Defense with cabinet rank. The President is also advised by a National Security Council and the Office of Civil and Defense Mobilization.

Defence expenditure in 2003 totalled US$404,920m. (US$1,391 per capita), representing 3·7% of GDP (down from 6·1% of GDP in 1985). The USA spent more on defence in 2003 than the next thirteen biggest spenders combined. US expenditure was 41% of the world total. In 1997 the Quadrennial Defense Review (QDR) was implemented—a plan to transform US defence strategy and military forces.

The estimated number of active military personnel in 2004 was 1,433,600.

The USA is the world's largest exporter of arms, with sales in 2003 worth $13·6bn., or 47·5% of the world total. In 2003 Lockheed Martin and Boeing were the two largest arms producing companies in the USA, accounting for $24·9bn. and $24·4bn. worth of sales respectively.

The USA's last nuclear test was in 1993. In accordance with START I—the treaty signed by the US and USSR in 1991 to reduce strategic offensive nuclear capability—the number of nuclear warheads (intercontinental ballistic missiles, submarine-launched ballistic missiles and bombers) in Jan. 2005 was approximately 4,216. In 1990 the number of warheads had been 12,718. Strategic nuclear delivery vehicles were made up as follows:

Intercontinental ballistic missiles: 500 Minuteman III; 10 Peacekeeper (MX).

Submarine-launched ballistic missiles: 48 Trident I (C-4); 288 Trident II (D-5).

Bombers: 93 B-52H; 21 B-2.

In May 2001 President Bush called for the development of an anti-missile shield to move beyond the constraints of the Anti-Ballistic Missile Treaty. In Dec. 2001 he announced that the USA was unilaterally abandoning the Treaty. As the relationship with Russian president Vladimir Putin strengthened following the events of 11 Sept. 2001 he proposed a reduction of operational nuclear warheads to between 1,700 and 2,200 by 2010. On 24 May 2002 the USA and Russia signed an arms control treaty to reduce the number of US and Russian warheads, from between 6,000 and 7,000 each to between 1,700 and 2,200 each, over the next ten years.

Army

Secretary of the Army. Francis J. Harvey.

The Secretary of the Army is the head of the Department of the Army. Subject to the authority of the President as C.-in-C. and of the Secretary of Defense, he is responsible for all affairs of the Department.

The Army consists of the Active Army, the Army National Guard of the US, the Army Reserve and civilian workforce; and all persons appointed to or enlisted into the Army without component; and all persons serving under call or conscription, including members of the National Guard of the States, etc., when in the service of the US. The strength of the Active Army was (2003) 485,000 (including 71,400 women).

The Army budget for fiscal years 2005–07 is as follows: 2005, $98,376m.; 2006, $99,251m.; 2007, $110,435m.

The US Army Forces Command, with headquarters at Fort McPherson, Georgia, commands the Third US Army; four continental US Armies, and all assigned Active Army and US Army Reserve troop units in the continental US, the Commonwealth of Puerto Rico, and the Virgin Islands of the USA. The headquarters of the continental US Armies are: First US Army, Fort George G. Meade, Maryland; Second US Army, Fort Gillem, Georgia; Fifth US Army, Fort Sam Houston, Texas; Sixth US Army, Presidio of San Francisco, California. The US Army Space Command, with headquarters in Colorado Springs (CO), is the Army component to the US Space Command.

Approximately 32% of the Active Army is deployed outside the continental USA. Several divisions, which are located in the USA, keep equipment in Germany and can be flown there in 48–72 hours. Headquarters of US Seventh and Eighth Armies are in Europe and Korea respectively.

Combat vehicles of the US Army are the tank, armoured personnel carrier, infantry fighting vehicle, and the armoured command vehicle. The first-line tanks are the M1A1 Abrams tank, and the M1 Abrams. The standard armoured infantry personnel carrier is the M2 Bradley Fighting Vehicle (BFV), which is replacing the older M113.

The Army has nearly 4,900 aircraft, all but about 300 of them helicopters, including AH-1 Cobra and AH-64 Apache attack helicopters.

Over 95% of recruits enlisting in the Army have a high-school education and over 50% of the Army is married. Women serve in both combat support and combat service support units.

The National Guard is a reserve military component with both a state and a federal role. Enlistment is voluntary. The members are recruited by each state, but are equipped and paid by the federal government (except when performing state missions). As the organized militia of the several states, the District of Columbia, Puerto Rico and the Territories of the Virgin Islands and Guam, the Guard may be called into service for local emergencies by the chief executives in those jurisdictions; and may be called into federal service by the President to thwart invasion or rebellion or to enforce federal law. In its role as a reserve component of the Army, the Guard is subject to the order of the President in the event of national emergency. In 2004 it numbered 460,050 (Army, 351,350; Air Force, 108,700).

The Army Reserve is designed to supply qualified and experienced units and individuals in an emergency. Members of units are assigned to the Ready Reserve, which is subject to call by the President in case of national emergency without declaration of war by Congress. The Standby Reserve and the Retired Reserve may be called only after declaration of war or national emergency by Congress. In 2004 the Army Reserve numbered 324,100.

Navy

Secretary of the Navy. Donald C. Winter.

The Navy's Operating Forces include the Atlantic Fleet, divided between the 2nd fleet (home waters) and 6th fleet (Mediterranean) and the Pacific Fleet, similarly divided between the 3rd fleet (home waters), the 7th fleet (West Pacific) and the 5th fleet (Indian Ocean), which was formally activated in 1995 and maintained by units from both Pacific and Atlantic.

The authorized budget for the Department of the Navy (which includes funding both for the Navy and Marine Corps) for fiscal years 2005–07 is as follows: 2005, $122,598m.; 2006, $125,702m.; 2007, $129,012m.

Personnel and fleet strength declined during the mid-1990s but are now stabilizing. The '600-ship battle force' planned in the late 1980s has reduced to a current figure of 317. The Navy personnel total in 2004 was 376,750.

The operational strength of the Navy in the year indicated:

Category	1992	1997	2003	2004
Strategic Submarines	23	18	16	16
Nuclear Attack Submarines	87	67	56	56
Aircraft Carriers	12	11[1]	12[1]	12[1]
Amphibious Carriers	13	11	11	11
Cruisers	46	30	27	27
Destroyers	51	56	49	49
Frigates	90	31	30	30

[1]Includes the USS *John F. Kennedy* as 'operational and training reserve carrier' in the Naval Reserve Force.

Ships in the inactive reserve are not included in the table, but those serving as Naval Reserve Force training ships are.

Submarine Forces. A principal part of the US naval task is to deploy the seaborne strategic deterrent from nuclear-powered ballistic missile-carrying submarines (SSBN), of which there were 16 in 2004, all of the Ohio class. The listed total of 56 nuclear-powered attack submarines includes two of three new Seawolf class and 51 of the Los Angeles class. There is also one of the Sturgeon class and two converted submarines of the Ohio class.

Surface Combatant Forces. The surface combatant forces are comprised of modern cruisers, destroyers and frigates. These ships provide multi-mission capabilities to achieve maritime dominance in the crowded and complex littoral warfare environment.

The cruiser force consists of 27 Ticonderoga class ships. There are 39 guided-missile Arleigh Burke Aegis class destroyers, ten Spruance class destroyers and 30 (22 active and eight in the reserve force) Oliver Hazard Perry class guided missile frigates.

Aircraft carriers. There are eight nuclear-powered Nimitz class carriers. The USS *Enterprise,* completed in 1961, was the prototype nuclear-powered carrier. The two ships of the Kitty Hawk and one of the John F. Kennedy classes were completed between 1961 and 1968, and represent the last oil-fuelled carriers built by the US Navy. All carriers deploy an air group which comprises on average two squadrons each of F-14 Tomcat fighters and three squadrons each of F/A-18 Hornet fighter/ground attack aircraft.

Naval Aviation. The principal function of the naval aviation organization (strength in 2004 of 98,588) is to train and provide combat ready aviation forces. The main carrier-borne combat aircraft in the current inventory are 877 F/A-18 Hornet dual-purpose fighter/attack aircraft out of a total of 1,705 combat aircraft.

The Marine Corps

While administratively part of the Department of the Navy, the Corps ranks as a separate armed service, with the Commandant serving in his own right as a member of the Joint Chiefs of Staff, and responsible directly to the Secretary of the Navy. Its strength had stabilized at 175,350 by 2004.

The role of the Marine Corps is to provide specially trained and equipped amphibious expeditionary forces. The Corps includes an autonomous aviation element numbering 34,686 in 2004.

The US Coast Guard

The Coast Guard operates under the Department of Transportation in time of peace and as part of the Navy in time of war or when directed by the President. The act of establishment stated the Coast Guard 'shall be a military service and branch of the armed forces of the United States at all times'.

The Coast Guard is the country's oldest continuous sea-going service and its missions include maintenance of aids to navigation, icebreaking, environmental response (oil spills), maritime law enforcement, marine licensing, port security, search and rescue and waterways management.

The workforce in 2004 was made up of approximately 40,360 military personnel augmented by 6,750 civilians. On an average Coast Guard day, the service saves 14 lives, conducts 120 law enforcement boardings, seizes 209 pounds of marijuana and 170 pounds of cocaine, boards 90 large vessels for port safety checks, processes 120 seaman's documents, investigates 17 marine accidents, inspects 64 commercial vessels, assists 328 people in distress, saves $2,490,000 in property, services 150 aids to navigation and interdicts 176 illegal immigrants.

Air Force

Secretary of the Air Force. Michael W. Wynne.

The Department of the Air Force was activated within the Department of Defense on 18 Sept. 1947, under the terms of the National Security Act of 1947.

The USAF has the mission to defend the USA through control and exploitation of air and space. For operational purposes the service is divided into eight major commands, 37 field operating agencies and three direct-reporting units.

The bulk of the combat forces are grouped under the Air Combat Command, which controls strategic bombing, tactical strike, air defence and reconnaissance assets in the USA.

Air Force bombers include the B-1B Lancer, the B-2A and the B-52G/H Stratofortress, which has been the primary manned strategic bomber for 50 years. In the fighter category are the F-15 Eagle, the F-16 Fighting Falcon and the F-117A, the world's first operational aircraft to exploit low-observable stealth technology.

The Air Force budget for fiscal years 2005–07 is as follows: 2005, $119,639m.; 2006, $127,533m.; 2007, $133,347m.

In 2004 the Air Force had approximately 379,500 military personnel. Since 1991 women have been authorized to fly combat aircraft, but not until 1993 were they allowed to fly fighters.

INTERNATIONAL RELATIONS

The USA is a member of the UN, WTO, NATO, BIS, OECD, OSCE, OAS, Inter-American Development Bank, Asian Development Bank, Pacific Community, Colombo Plan, IOM and the Antarctic Treaty.

In 2004 the USA gave US$19·7bn. in international aid, the highest figure of any country. In terms of a percentage of GNI, however, the USA was one of the least generous major industrialized countries, giving just 0·17% (compared to more than 0·6% in the early 1960s).

ECONOMY

Services accounted for approximately 72% of GDP in 2003, industry 26% and agriculture 2%.

According to the anti-corruption organization *Transparency International,* in 2005 the USA ranked 17th in the world in a survey of the countries with the least corruption in business and government. It received 7·6 out of 10 in the annual index.

Per capita income in 2004 was $33,041, up from $19,572 in 1990.

Overview

The United States of America is the world's largest economy. At purchasing power parity it is roughly three times that of Japan and its volume of trade is the largest in the world, although the value of the external sector as a percentage of GDP is relatively low. The USA is self-sufficient in most raw materials, with the notable exception of oil. Core industries include motor vehicles, steel, aerospace, chemicals, telecommunications, electronics and computers. Since 1992 the economy has grown at higher rates than the OECD and G7 averages in every year except 2001 and per capita GDP is higher than in other G7 countries. US workers tend to work long hours and the country has outperformed other developed nations in terms of productivity growth.

In 1995 labour productivity in advanced European countries had reached US levels but since then US labour and total factor productivity growth has outpaced that of Europe and Japan. The principal sectors in which the USA outperforms its rivals are retail, wholesale and finance. It has also been able to extract greater efficiency gains from IT related investments. US firms enjoy greater flexibility than counterparts in Western Europe and Japan in decisions to lay off workers and increase capital equipment expenditure, facilitating higher IT-related productivity gains. The USA does, however, have higher income inequality than other advanced economies and the gap between skilled and unskilled labour incomes has been growing over the last three decades. Most income gains have accrued to the richest 20% of Americans.

The attacks of 11 Sept. 2001 posed serious challenges to the dollar payment system and the stock exchange in New York. The stock market closed for a week and trading in corporate bonds virtually stopped. However, by 17 Sept. 2001 the stock exchanges had reopened and saw the largest volume of trading in a single day in New York stock exchange history. The day ended with the market down about 5%. Share prices tumbled and in June 2002 the NASDAQ 100 was at its lowest level since 1998 and over 60% below its level of March 2000.

Business fixed investment relative to GDP plummeted in 2001–02 after reaching record highs in 2000–01. Confidence in the corporate market declined after the collapse of energy giant Enron in Dec. 2002 was followed by several other accounting scandals. With investor confidence low, the dollar fell to near parity with the euro for the first time since the introduction of the euro in Jan. 2002. In 2002 Congress passed the Sarbanes-Oxley legislation, which reformed accounting procedures and introduced stronger supervision of publicly traded companies.

In the third quarter of 2003 the economy recorded an annualized growth rate of 7·2%, the highest in 19 years, fuelled by tax cuts, low interest rates and increased consumer and business spending. Interest rates began rising from historic lows in 2003 with the federal funds rate reaching 4·5% by the end of 2005. Growth remained strong through 2005 despite the impact of Hurricane Katrina and high oil prices. The OECD noted that the Federal Bank's monetary tightening was 'blunted by surprisingly low long-term interest rates'. In the fourth quarter of 2005 business investment slowed.

Despite the economy proving remarkably resilient following the sluggish growth of the early 2000s, there remain significant challenges. After four years of budgetary surpluses from 1998–2001 the federal government's accounts fell into deficit owing to lower tax receipts following the two quarters of negative growth in 2001, tax cuts, the termination of the stock market bubble and an expansion of defence and homeland security expenditure. In 2003 and 2004 the US budget deficit fell below 3% of GDP. In 2005 accounts improved, primarily because of growth-generated increased tax receipts, but were not expected to improve significantly until spending is curtailed.

Further fiscal pressures will emerge from the retirement of the baby-boom generation and the rise in life expectancy, increasing strain on entitlement programmes. Spending on social security, Medicare and Medicaid is projected to rise from 8% of GDP to 18% by 2050. The programmes' unfunded liability is estimated by the IMF to be 180% of GDP if measured over a 75-year horizon. The USA also faces a large current account deficit. Between Jan. 2002 and Feb. 2004 the dollar fell by more than 12% on a trade weighted average basis against the currencies of its major trading partners. The depreciation of the dollar was conducive to restraining the large and growing current account deficit. Nonetheless large trade deficits, low national savings and the absorption of global savings contributed to bringing the US current account deficit to over 6% of GDP in 2005. Despite the depreciation of the dollar since 2002, the IMF believes that the real exchange rate still remains high given the country's massive current account deficit. The size of the deficit, and the possibility of a sharp dollar depreciation, is considered to be one of the biggest threats to the global economy.

Another threat to the USA and global economy is the possibility of a sharp correction in the US house price boom seen in recent years, impacting on US consumer spending and global growth. The OECD also argues that the low national savings rate in the USA and the resulting under-investment in domestically-owned capital could hinder growth in the long run.

Currency

The unit of currency is the *dollar* (USD) of 100 *cents*. Notes are issued by the 12 Federal Reserve Banks, which are denoted by a branch letter (A = Boston, MA; B = New York, NY; C = Philadelphia, PA; D = Cleveland, OH; E = Richmond, VA; F = Atlanta, GA; G = Chicago, IL; H = St Louis, MO; I = Minneapolis, MN; J = Kansas City, MO; K = Dallas, TX; L = San Francisco, CA).

Inflation rates (based on OECD statistics):

1995	1996	1997	1998	1999	2000	2001	2002	2003	2004
2·8%	2·9%	2·3%	1·5%	2·2%	3·4%	2·8%	1·6%	2·3%	2·7%

The inflation rates in 2004 and 2005 according to the Bureau of Economic Analysis were 3·3% and 3·4% respectively. Foreign exchange reserves in June 2002 were US$32,166m. Gold reserves in June 2002 were 262·0m. troy oz. The USA has the most gold reserves of any country, and more than the combined reserves

of the next two (Germany and France). Total money supply in March 2002 was $1,552bn.

Budget

The budget covers virtually all the programmes of federal government, including those financed through trust funds, such as for social security, Medicare and highway construction. Receipts of the government include all income from its sovereign or compulsory powers; income from business-type or market-orientated activities of the government is offset against outlays. The fiscal year ends on 30 Sept. (before 1977 on 30 June). Budget receipts and outlays, including off-budget receipts and outlays (in $1m.):

Fiscal year ending in	Receipts	Outlays	Surplus (+) or deficit (−)
1950	39,443	42,562	−3,119
1960	92,492	92,191	+301
1970	192,807	195,649	−2,842
1980	517,112	590,941	−73,829
1990	1,032,094	1,253,130	−221,036
2000	2,025,457	1,789,216	+236,241
2003	1,782,532	2,160,117	−377,585
2004	1,880,279	2,293,006	−412,727
2005	2,153,859	2,472,205	−318,346
2006[1]	2,285,491	2,708,677	−423,186
2007[1]	2,415,852	2,770,097	−354,245

[1]Estimates.

President George W. Bush unveiled his newest budget proposals in Feb. 2006. The budget submitted to Congress involves cutting spending in 141 programmes (notably in the area of health), but spending on defence was set to increase by 6·9% and homeland security by 3·3%.

Budget and off-budget receipts, by source, for fiscal years (in $1m.):

Source	2005	2006[1]	2007[1]
Individual income taxes	927,222	997,599	1,096,366
Corporation income taxes	278,282	277,122	260,567
Social insurance and retirement receipts	794,125	841,087	884,126
Excise taxes	73,094	73,511	74,608
Other	81,136	96,172	100,185
Total	2,153,859	2,285,491	2,415,852

[1]Estimates.

Budget and off-budget outlays, by function, for fiscal years (in $1m.):

Function	2005	2006[1]	2007[1]
National defence	495,335	535,943	527,428
Education, training, employment and social service	97,526	109,651	87,576
Health	250,612	268,789	280,941
Medicare	298,638	342,987	392,000
Income security	345,847	360,632	367,206
Social security	523,305	554,740	585,940
Veterans' benefits and services	70,151	70,410	73,946
Energy	429	2,621	972
Natural resources and environment	28,023	32,731	31,049
Commerce and housing credit	7,574	9,087	11,177
Transportation	67,894	71,637	76,294
Community and regional development	26,264	52,025	28,159
Net interest	183,986	220,053	247,315
International affairs	34,592	34,750	33,274
General science, space and technology	23,674	23,996	25,445
Agriculture	26,566	26,846	25,733
Administration of justice	40,019	41,342	44,344
General government	16,994	19,085	20,170
Allowances	—	3,726	5,464
Undistributed offsetting receipts	−65,224	−72,374	−94,336
Total	2,472,205	2,708,677	2,770,097

[1]Estimates.

Budget and off-budget outlays, by agency, for fiscal years (in $1m.):

Agency	2005	2006[1]	2007[1]
Legislative Branch	4,000	4,427	4,438
The Judiciary	5,566	6,088	6,386
Agriculture	85,284	95,712	92,783
Commerce	6,168	6,462	6,603
Defence—Military	474,434	512,079	504,863
Education	72,945	83,984	64,484
Energy	21,347	21,703	21,419
Health and Human Services	581,527	641,464	699,580
Homeland Security	39,302	66,753	43,553
Housing and Urban Development	42,518	46,807	44,668
Interior	9,101	9,112	9,432
Justice	22,723	22,294	24,682
Labor	46,965	51,434	53,357
State	12,817	13,620	14,487
Transportation	56,931	61,253	65,651
Treasury	408,742	452,125	494,293
Veterans Affairs	69,995	70,410	73,844
Corps of Engineers	4,766	7,413	5,879
Defence—Civil	43,483	45,668	47,299
Environmental Protection Agency	7,920	7,930	7,904
Executive Office of the President	7,723	7,362	2,391
General Services Administration	55	407	898
International Assistance Programmes	14,954	16,302	16,843
National Aeronautics and Space Administration	15,613	15,554	16,356
National Science Foundation	5,435	5,760	5,838
Office of Personnel Management	59,511	63,459	67,265
Small Business Administration	2,502	1,188	605

Agency	2005	2006[1]	2007[1]
Social Security Administration	561,326	592,450	622,709
Other independent agencies	14,765	17,304	21,626
Allowances	—	3,726	5,464
Undistributed Offsetting Receipts	−226,213	−241,573	−275,503
Total	2,472,205	2,708,677	2,770,097

[1]Estimates.

National Debt. Federal debt held by the public (in $1m.), and per capita debt (in $1) on 30 June to 1976 and on 30 Sept. since then:

	Public debt	Per capita		Public debt	Per capita
1920	24,299	229	1990	2,411,558	9,696
1930	16,185	132	2000	3,409,804	12,083
1940	42,772	324	2001	3,319,615	11,643
1950	219,023	1,447	2002	3,540,427	12,294
1960	236,840	1,321	2003	3,913,443	13,456
1970	283,198	1,394	2004	4,295,544	14,628
1980	711,923	3,143	2005	4,592,229	15,493

National Income

The Bureau of Economic Analysis of the Department of Commerce prepares detailed estimates on the national income and product. In Dec. 2003 the Bureau revised these accounts back to 1929. The principal tables are published monthly in *Survey of Current Business;* the complete set of national income and product tables are published in the *Survey* normally each Aug., showing data for recent years.

Gross Domestic Product
(in $1,000m.)

	2000	2001	2002	2003	2004
Gross Domestic Product	9,817·0	10,128·0	10,469·6	10,971·2	11,734·3
Personal consumption expenditures	6,739·4	7,055·0	7,350·7	7,709·9	8,214·3
Durable goods	863·3	883·7	923·9	950·1	987·8
Nondurable goods	1,947·2	2,017·1	2,079·6	2,189·0	2,368·3
Services	3,928·8	4,154·3	4,347·2	4,570·8	4,858·2
Gross private domestic investment	1,735·5	1,614·3	1,582·1	1,670·4	1,928·1
Fixed investment	1,679·0	1,646·1	1,570·2	1,654·9	1,872·6
Nonresidential	1,232·1	1,176·8	1,066·3	1,082·4	1,198·8
Structures	313·2	322·6	279·2	276·9	298·4
Equipment and software	918·9	854·2	787·1	805·6	900·4
Residential	446·9	469·3	503·9	572·5	673·8
Change in private inventories	56·5	−31·7	11·9	15·4	55·4
Net exports of goods and services	−379·5	−367·0	−424·4	−500·9	−624·0
Exports	1,096·3	1,032·8	1,005·9	1,045·6	1,173·8
Goods	784·3	731·2	697·6	724·3	818·1
Services	311·9	301·6	308·4	321·3	355·7
Imports	1,475·8	1,399·8	1,430·3	1,546·5	1,797·8
Goods	1,243·5	1,167·9	1,189·3	1,283·9	1,495·9
Services	232·3	231·9	241·0	262·6	301·9
Government consumption expenditures and gross investment	1,721·6	1,825·6	1,961·1	2,091·9	2,215·9
Federal	578·8	612·9	679·7	754·8	827·6
National defence	370·3	392·6	437·1	496·7	552·7
Nondefence	208·5	220·3	242·5	258·2	274·9
State and local	1,142·8	1,212·8	1,281·5	1,337·1	1,388·3

Relation of Gross Domestic Product, Gross National Product, Net National Product, National Income and Personal Income
(in $1,000m.)

	2000	2001	2002	2003	2004
Gross domestic product	9,817·0	10,128·0	10,469·6	10,971·2	11,734·3
Plus: Income receipts from the rest of the world	382·7	322·4	305·7	343·7	415·4
Less: Income payments to the rest of the world	343·7	278·8	275·0	275·6	361·7
Equals: Gross national product	9,855·9	10,171·6	10,500·2	11,039·3	11,788·0
Less: Consumption of fixed capital	1,187·8	1,281·5	1,292·0	1,331·3	1,435·3
Private	990·8	1,075·5	1,080·3	1,112·8	1,206·2
Domestic business	836·1	903·7	893·6	911·5	973·3
Capital consumption allowances	943·9	1,028·7	1,109·3	1,127·6	1,228·6
Less: Capital consumption adjustment	107·8	124·9	215·7	216·2	255·3

Relation of Gross Domestic Product, Gross National Product,
Net National Product, National Income and Personal Income

(in $1,000m.)

	2000	2001	2002	2003	2004
Households and institutions	154·8	171·7	186·8	201·3	232·8
Government	197·0	206·0	211·6	218·5	229·1
General government	166·4	172·7	178·3	183·5	192·0
Government enterprises	30·6	33·3	33·4	35·1	37·2
Equals: Net national product	8,668·1	8,890·2	9,208·3	9,708·0	10,352·8
Less: Statistical discrepancy	−127·2	−89·6	−21·0	47·1	76·8
Equals: National income	8,795·2	8,979·8	9,229·3	9,660·9	10,275·9
Less: Corporate profits with inventory valuation and capital consumption adjustment	817·9	767·3	886·3	1,031·8	1,161·5
Taxes on production and imports less subsidies	664·6	673·3	724·4	754·8	809·4
Contributions for government social insurance	702·7	731·1	750·0	776·6	822·2
Net interest and miscellaneous payment on assets	559·0	566·3	520·9	528·5	505·5
Business current transfer payments (net)	87·1	92·8	84·3	81·6	91·1
Current surplus of government enterprises	5·3	−1·4	0·9	1·3	−3·0
Plus: Personal income receipts on assets	1,387·0	1,380·0	1,333·2	1,338·7	1,396·5
Personal current transfer receipts	1,084·0	1,193·9	1,286·2	1,344·0	1,427·5
Equals: Personal income	8,429·7	8,724·1	8,881·9	9,169·1	9,713·3
Addenda:					
Gross domestic income	9,944·1	10,217·6	10,490·6	10,924·2	11,657·5
Gross national income	9,983·1	10,261·3	10,521·2	10,992·3	11,711·2
Gross national factor income	9,226·1	9,496·5	9,711·7	10,154·6	10,813·7
Net domestic product	8,629·1	8,846·5	9,177·6	9,639·9	10,299·0
Net domestic income	8,756·3	8,936·2	9,198·6	9,592·9	10,222·2
Net national factor income	8,038·3	8,215·0	8,419·8	8,823·3	9,378·4

National Income by Type of Income

(in $1,000m.)

	2000	2001	2002	2003	2004
National income	8,795·2	8,979·8	9,229·3	9,660·9	10,275·9
Compensation of employees	5,782·7	5,942·1	6,091·2	6,321·1	6,687·6
Wage and salary accruals	4,829·2	4,942·8	4,980·9	5,111·1	5,389·4
Government	774·7	815·9	865·9	903·3	939·5
Other	4,054·5	4,126·9	4,115·0	4,207·8	4,450·0
Supplements to wages and salaries	953·4	999·3	1,110·3	1,210·0	1,298·1
Employer contributions for employee pension and insurance funds	609·9	642·7	745·1	830·0	895·5
Employer contributions for government social insurance	343·5	356·6	365·2	380·0	402·7
Proprietors' income with inventory valuation and capital consumption adjustment	728·4	771·9	768·4	810·2	889·6
Farm	22·7	19·7	10·6	27·7	35·8
Nonfarm	705·7	752·2	757·8	782·4	853·8
Rental income of persons with capital consumption adjustment	150·3	167·4	152·9	131·7	134·2
Corporate profits with inventory valuation and capital consumption adjustment	817·9	767·3	886·3	1,031·8	1,161·5
Taxes on corporate income	265·2	204·1	192·6	232·1	271·1
Profits after tax with inventory valuation and capital consumption adjustment	552·7	563·2	693·7	799·7	890·3
Net dividends	377·9	370·9	399·2	423·2	493·0
Undistributed profits with inventory valuation and capital consumption adjustment	174·8	192·3	294·5	376·5	397·3
Net interest and miscellaneous payments	559·0	566·3	520·9	528·5	505·5
Taxes on production and imports	708·9	728·6	762·8	801·4	852·8
Less: Subsidies	44·3	55·3	38·4	46·7	43·5
Business current transfer payments (net)	87·1	92·8	84·3	81·6	91·1
To persons (net)	42·4	50·0	37·3	30·5	33·0
To government (net)	43·7	47·5	46·6	48·9	51·5
To the rest of the world (net)	1·0	−4·7	0·3	2·3	6·6
Current surplus of government enterprises	5·3	−1·4	0·9	1·3	−3·0
Cash flow:					
Net cash flow with inventory valuation and capital consumption adjustment	864·8	944·8	1,036·6	1,130·8	1,196·9
Undistributed profits with inventory valuation and capital consumption adjustment	174·8	192·3	294·5	376·5	397·3
Consumption of fixed capital	690·0	752·5	742·1	754·4	799·6
Less: Inventory valuation adjustment	−14·1	11·3	−2·2	−13·3	−39·6
Equals: Net cash flow	878·9	933·5	1,038·9	1,144·1	1,236·6
Addenda:					
Proprietors' income with inventory valuation and capital consumption adjustment	728·4	771·9	768·4	810·2	889·6

National Income by Type of Income

(in $1,000m.)

	2000	2001	2002	2003	2004
Farm	22·7	19·7	10·6	27·7	35·8
Proprietors' income with inventory valuation adjustment	28·5	25·5	15·8	33·0	41·7
Capital consumption adjustment	−5·8	−5·9	−5·2	−5·3	−5·9
Nonfarm	705·7	752·2	757·8	782·4	853·8
Proprietors' income (without inventory valuation and capital consumption adjustment)	641·8	657·0	646·3	658·5	723·9
Inventory valuation adjustment	−1·6	1·4	−0·7	−1·7	−4·7
Capital consumption adjustment	65·5	93·8	112·2	125·6	134·6
Rental income of persons with capital consumption adjustment	150·3	167·4	152·9	131·7	134·2
Rental income of persons (without capital consumption adjustment)	160·8	178·5	164·4	143·7	149·5
Capital consumption adjustment	−10·5	−11·1	−11·4	−12·1	−15·3
Corporate profits with inventory valuation and capital consumption adjustment	817·9	767·3	886·3	1,031·8	1,161·5
Corporate profits with inventory valuation adjustment	759·3	719·2	766·2	923·9	1,019·7
Profits before tax (without inventory valuation and capital consumption adjustment)	773·4	707·9	768·4	937·2	1,059·3
Taxes on corporate income	265·2	204·1	192·6	232·1	271·1
Profits after tax (without inventory valuation and capital consumption adjustment)	508·2	503·8	575·8	705·1	788·2
Net dividends	377·9	370·9	399·2	423·2	493·0
Undistributed profits (without inventory valuation and capital consumption adjustment)	130·3	132·9	176·6	281·9	295·2
Inventory valuation adjustment	−14·1	11·3	−2·2	−13·3	−39·6
Capital consumption adjustment	58·6	48·1	120·1	107·9	141·8

Real Gross Domestic Product

(in 1,000m. chained [2000] dollars[1])

	2000	2001	2002	2003	2004
Gross domestic product	9,817·0	9,890·7	10,048·8	10,320·6	10,755·7
Personal consumption expenditures	6,739·4	6,910·4	7,099·3	7,306·6	7,588·6
Durable goods	863·3	900·7	964·8	1,028·5	1,089·9
Nondurable goods	1,947·2	1,986·7	2,037·1	2,101·8	2,200·4
Services	3,928·8	4,023·2	4,100·4	4,183·9	4,310·9
Gross private domestic investment	1,735·5	1,598·4	1,557·1	1,617·4	1,809·8
Fixed investment	1,679·0	1,629·4	1,544·6	1,600·0	1,755·1
Nonresidential	1,232·1	1,180·5	1,071·5	1,085·0	1,186·7
Structures	313·2	306·1	253·8	243·1	248·4
Equipment and software	918·9	874·2	820·2	846·8	947·6
Residential	446·9	448·5	469·9	509·4	561·8
Change in private inventories	56·5	−31·7	12·5	15·5	52·0
Net exports of goods and services	−379·5	−399·1	−471·3	−521·4	−601·3
Exports	1,096·3	1,036·7	1,013·3	1,031·2	1,117·9
Goods	784·3	736·3	707·0	719·7	783·6
Services	311·9	300·4	306·0	311·2	334·1
Imports	1,475·8	1,435·8	1,484·6	1,552·6	1,719·2
Goods	1,243·5	1,204·1	1,248·2	1,309·2	1,452·7
Services	232·3	231·6	236·5	243·7	267·1
Government consumption expenditures and gross investment	1,721·6	1,780·3	1,858·8	1,911·1	1,952·3
Federal	578·8	601·4	643·4	687·8	723·7
National defence	370·3	384·9	413·2	449·7	481·3
Non-defence	208·5	216·5	230·2	238·0	242·2
State and local	1,142·8	1,179·0	1,215·4	1,223·3	1,228·4
Residual	0·2	1·6	3·0	2·6	−5·1

[1]In 1996 the chain-weighted method of estimating GDP replaced that of constant base-year prices. In chain-weighting the weights used to value different sectors of the economy are continually updated to reflect changes in relative prices.

Performance

Total GDP in 2004 was US$11,667·5bn., representing approximately 30% of the world's total GDP. Real GDP growth rates (based on OECD statistics):

1995	1996	1997	1998	1999	2000	2001	2002	2003	2004
2·5%	3·7%	4·5%	4·2%	4·4%	3·7%	0·8%	1·6%	2·7%	4·2%

The economy contracted in the first and third quarters of 2001, but recovery in the final quarter was sufficient to give an overall growth rate of 0·8% in 2001. The real GDP growth rate in 2005 according to the Bureau of Economic Analysis was 3·5%. In the 2005 *World Competitiveness Yearbook*, compiled by the International Institute for Management Development, the USA came top in the world ranking. The USA was first in the Business Competitiveness Index and second behind Finland in the Growth Competitiveness Index in the World Economic Forum's *Global Competitiveness Report 2005–2006*. In both the Business Competitiveness Index and the Growth Competitiveness Index it had been in the same positions in 2004–2005.

According to the May 2004 *OECD Economic Survey* 'Economic performance over the past two decades has been impressive. Underpinned by an increased reliance on competitive forces, which have been stronger than in most other Member countries for some time, productivity and output have accelerated significantly. In recent years, helped by timely macroeconomic policy responses, the economy has demonstrated its capacity to adjust to adverse shocks, so that the per capita growth gap against other countries has widened further. The outlook is for this to continue in the next few years, with real GDP expanding by around 4 per cent per annum. Nonetheless, there are a number of challenges that need to be addressed….By far the top priority is to confront the current and projected federal budget deficits.'

Banking and Finance

The Federal Reserve System, established under The Federal Reserve Act of 1913, comprises the Board of seven Governors, the 12 regional Federal Reserve Banks with their 25 branches, and the Federal Open Market Committee. The seven members of the Board of Governors are appointed by the President with the consent of the Senate. Each Governor is appointed to a full term of 14 years or an unexpired portion of a term, one term expiring every two years. The Board exercises broad supervisory authority over the operations of the 12 Federal Reserve Banks, including approval of their budgets and of the appointments of their presidents and first vice presidents; it designates three of the nine directors of each Reserve Bank including the Chairman and Deputy Chairman. The Chairman of the Federal Reserve Board is appointed by the President for four-year terms. The *Chairman* is Ben Bernanke. The Board has supervisory and regulatory responsibilities over banks that are members of the Federal Reserve System, bank holding companies, bank mergers, Edge Act and agreement corporations, foreign activities of member banks, international banking facilities in the USA, and activities of the US branches and agencies of foreign banks. Legislation of 1991 requires foreign banks to prove that they are subject to comprehensive consolidated supervision by a regulator at home, and have the Board's approval to establish branches, agencies and representative offices. The Board also assures the smooth functioning and continued development of the nation's vast payments system. Another area of the Board's responsibilities involves the implementation by regulation of major federal laws governing consumer credit.

In 2004, three of the four largest banks in the world in terms of market value were US banks. Citigroup was the largest ($240·9bn.). The second and fourth largest were Bank of America ($183·4bn.) and J. P. Morgan Chase ($141·0bn.). Citigroup had assets in March 2004 of $1·26trn. (ranking it second in the world behind Japan's Mizuho Financial Group). Bank of America's market capitalization figure reflects its merger in April 2004 with FleetBoston Financial; J. P. Morgan Chase's market capitalization figure reflects its merger in July 2004 with Bank One.

The key stock exchanges are the New York Stock Exchange (NYSE), the Nasdaq Stock Exchange (NASDAQ) and the American Stock Exchange (ASE). There are several other stock exchanges, in Philadelphia, Boston, San Francisco (Pacific Stock Exchange) and Chicago, although trading is very limited in them.

The USA received $56·83bn. worth of foreign direct investment in 2003 and $95·86bn. in 2004 (the most of any country). By the end of 2002 it had attracted foreign direct investment totalling $1,505bn.—more than twice as much as any other country.

By Oct. 2000 approximately 18% of the population were using e-banking.

Weights and Measures

The US Customary System derives from the British Imperial System. It differs in respect of the *gallon* (= 0·83268 Imperial gallon); *bushel* (= 0·969 Imperial bushel); *hundredweight* (= 100 lb); and the *short* or *net ton* (= 2,000 lb).

ENERGY AND NATURAL RESOURCES

Environment

The USA's carbon dioxide emissions from the consumption and flaring of fossil fuels in 2002 accounted for 23·4% of the world total, higher than any other country, and were equivalent to 20·0 tonnes per capita. The population of the USA is only 4·6% of the world total. An *Environmental Sustainability Index* compiled for the World Economic Forum meeting in Jan. 2005 ranked the USA 45th in the world, with 52·9%. The index measured the ability of countries to maintain favourable environmental conditions and examined various factors including pollution levels and the use or abuse of natural resources.

In March 2001 President Bush rejected the 1997 Kyoto Protocol, which aims to combat the rise in the earth's temperature through the reduction of industrialized nations' carbon dioxide emissions from the consumption and flaring of fossil fuels by an average 5·2% below 1990 levels by 2012. In Feb. 2002 he unveiled an alternative climate-change plan to the Kyoto Protocol, calling for voluntary measures to reduce the rate of increase of US carbon dioxide emissions from the consumption and flaring of fossil fuels.

The USA recycled 26·7% of its household waste in 2002.

Electricity

Net capacity in 2003 was 948·4m. kW. Fossil fuel accounts for approximately 70% of electricity generation. In 2003, 20% of electricity was produced by nuclear reactors. (The last one to begin commercial operation was in 1996.) The USA has more nuclear reactors in use than any other country in the world. In 2005 the USA had a nuclear generating capacity of 97,838 MW, with 103 nuclear reactors at 64 sites. Electricity production in 2003 was the highest in the world, at 3,883,185m. kWh. Consumption per capita in 2002 was 13,456 kWh.

Oil and Gas

Crude oil production (2002), 2,097m. bbls. Production has been gradually declining since the mid-1980s, when annual production was 3,274m. bbls. Only Saudi Arabia and Russia produce more crude oil. Proven reserves were 30·4bn. bbls. in 2002, but they are expected to be exhausted by 2011. Output (2002) was valued at $47·21bn. Imported supplies account for approximately half of US oil consumption, with Saudi Arabia supplying a sixth of US oil imports. In Oct. 2002 the USA took its first delivery of Russian oil for its Strategic Petroleum Reserve as a consequence of an energy dialogue declared by Presidents George W. Bush and Vladimir Putin at their summit in May 2002.

The USA is by far the largest single consumer of natural gas, and the second largest producer after Russia. Natural gas production, 2002, was 19·34trn. cu. ft. Proven gas reserves in 2002 totalled 184trn. cu. ft.

Wind

The USA is one of the largest producers of wind-power. By the end of 2003 total installed capacity amounted to 6,374 MW.

Water

The total area covered by water is 256,645 sq. miles. Americans' average annual water usage is nearly 67,000 cu. ft per person—more than twice the average for an industrialized nation.

Non-Fuel Minerals

The USA is wholly dependent upon imports for columbium, bauxite, mica sheet, manganese, strontium and graphite, and imports over 80% of its requirements of industrial diamonds, fluorspar, platinum, tantalum, tungsten, chromium and tin.

Total value of non-fuel minerals produced in 2003 was $38,000m. ($33,445m. in 1990). Details of some of the main minerals produced are given in the following tables.

Production of metals:

	Unit	Quantity 2003	Value ($1m.) 2003
Copper	1,000 tonnes	1,120	2,100
Gold	tonnes	277	3,250
Iron ore	1m. tonnes	44	1,200

	Unit	Quantity 2003	Value ($1m.) 2003
Lead	1,000 tonnes	449	433
Silver	tonnes	1,240	196
Zinc	1,000 tonnes	738	661
Total metals (including others)			7,840

Precious metals are mined mainly in California and Utah (gold); and Nevada, Arizona and Idaho (silver).

Production of non-metals:

	Unit	Quantity 2003	Value ($1m.) 2003
Barite	1,000 tonnes	468	14
Boron	1,000 tonnes	1,150	591
Bromine	1,000 tonnes	216	155
Cement	1m. short tons	88	6,460
Clays	1,000 tonnes	40,030	1,645
Diatomite	1,000 tonnes	620	160
Feldspar	1,000 tonnes	800	43
Garnet (industrial)	1,000 tonnes	29	3
Gypsum	1m. tonnes	17	114
Lime	1m. tonnes	18[1]	1,120[1]
Phosphate rock	1m. tonnes	35	946
Pumice	1,000 tonnes	870	22
Salt	1m. tonnes	41	1,130
Sand and gravel	1m. tonnes	1,187	6,599
Stone (crushed)	1m. tonnes	1,530	9,160

[1]2002.

Aluminium production for 2002, 2·71m. tonnes; uranium production for 2002, 919 tonnes. The USA is the world's leading producer of salt.

Coal

Proven recoverable coal reserves were 271,878m. short tons in 2004, more than a quarter of the world total. Output in 2002 (in 1m. short tons): 1,094·3 including bituminous coal, 565·7; sub-bituminous coal, 444·7; lignite, 82·1; anthracite, 1·3. 2002 output from opencast workings, 736m. short tons; underground mines, 357m. short tons. Value of total output, 2002, $19·48bn.

Agriculture

Agriculture in the USA is characterized by its ability to adapt to widely varying conditions, and still produce an abundance and variety of agricultural products. From colonial times to about 1920 the major increases in farm production were brought about by adding to the number of farms and the amount of land under cultivation. During this period nearly 320m. acres of virgin forest were converted to crop land or pasture, and extensive areas of grasslands were ploughed.

During the next 20 years the number of farms reached a plateau of about 6·5m., and the acreage planted to crops held relatively stable around 330m. acres. The major source of increase in farm output arose from the substitution of power-driven machines for horses and mules. Greater emphasis was placed on development and improvement of land, and the need for conservation of basic agricultural resources was recognized. A successful conservation programme, highly co-ordinated and on a national scale—to prevent further erosion, to restore the native fertility of damaged land and to adjust land uses to production capabilities and needs—has been in operation since early in the 1930s.

Since the Second World War the uptrend in farm output has been greatly accelerated by increased production per acre and per farm animal. These increases are associated with a higher degree of mechanization; greater use of lime and fertilizer; improved varieties, including hybrid maize and grain sorghums; more effective control of insects and disease; improved strains of livestock and poultry; and wider use of good husbandry practices, such as nutritionally balanced feeds, use of superior sites and better housing. During this period land included in

farms decreased slowly, crop land harvested declined somewhat more rapidly, but the number of farms declined sharply.

All land in farms totalled less than 500m. acres in 1870, rose to a peak of over 1,200m. acres in the 1950s and declined to 938m. acres in 2002, even with the addition of the new States of Alaska and Hawaii in 1960. The number of farms declined from 6·35m. in 1940 to 2·13m. in 2003, as the average size of farms doubled. The average size of farms in 2003 was 441 acres, but ranged from a few acres to many thousand acres. In 2002 the total value of land and buildings was $1,144,906m. The average value of land and buildings per acre in 2002 was $1,213.

At the 2000 census 59,063,597 persons (21·0% of the population) were rural, of whom 2,987,531 (just over 1% of the total population) lived on farms. In 2002 there were 1,909,598 farms managed by families or individuals (89·7% of all farms); 1,428,136 farms (67·1% of all farms) were managed by full owners (farmers who own all the land they operate). Hired farmworkers numbered 793,000 in 2002. There were 4·8m. tractors in 2002 and 662,000 harvester-threshers. In 2002 there were 176·02m. ha. of arable land and 2·05m. ha. of permanent crops. 22·5m. ha. were irrigated in 2002.

Cash receipts from farm marketings and government payments (in $1bn.):

	Crops	Livestock and livestock products	Total
2000	92·4	99·5	192·0
2001	93·4	106·4	199·8
2002	99·5	93·5	192·9

Net farm income was $35·3bn. in 2002.

The harvest area and production of the principal crops for 2002 and 2003 were:

	2002 Harvested 1m. acres	2002 Production 1m.	2002 Yield per acre	2003 Harvested 1m. acres	2003 Production 1m.	2003 Yield per acre
Corn for grain (bu.)	69·3	8,967	129	71·1	10,114	142
Soybeans (bu.)	72·5	2,756	38·0	72·3	2,418	33·4
Wheat (bu.)	45·8	1,606	35·0	52·8	2,337	44·2
Cotton (bales)[1]	12·4	17·2	665	12·1	18·2	725
Potatoes (cwt.)	1·3	458	362	1·3	459	367
Hay (sh. tons)	63·9	149	2·34	63·3	157	2·48

[1]Yield in lb.

The USA is the world's leading producer of maize, soybeans, sorghum and tree nuts and the second largest producer of tomatoes, carrots, seed cotton, cottonseed, sugarbeets and apples.

Fruit. Utilized production, in 1,000 tons:

	2001	2002	2003
Apples	4,607	4,203	4,449
Grapefruit	2,462	2,424	2,063
Grapes	6,568	7,362	6,324
Oranges	12,221	12,374	11,526
Peaches	1,168	1,236	1,207

The farm value of the above crops in 2003 was: apples, $1,730m.; grapefruit, $258m.; grapes, $2,534m.; oranges, $1,612m.; peaches, $467m.

In 2003 the USA set aside 950,000 acres (0·2% of its agricultural land) for the growth of organic crops. Organic food sales for the USA in 2003 totalled $10·4bn. (the highest in the world).

Dairy produce. In 2003 production of milk was 170,300m. lb; cheese, 8,598m. lb; butter, 1,242m. lb; ice cream, 1,015m. gallons; non-fat dry milk, 1,589m. lb; yoghurt, 2,388m. lb. The USA is the world's largest producer of both cheese and milk.

Livestock. In 2003 there were 8,493m. broilers and 274m. turkeys. Eggs produced, 2003, 87·2bn.

Value of production (in $1m.) was:

	2001	2002	2003
Cattle and calves	29,403	27,098	32,168
Hogs and pigs	11,416	8,691	9,729
Broilers	16,696	13,437	15,215
Turkeys	2,797	2,732	2,720
Eggs	4,446	4,281	5,315

Livestock numbered, in 2004 (1m.): cattle and calves (including milch cows), 94·9; sheep and lambs, 6·1; hogs and pigs, 60·4. Approximate value of livestock (in $1bn.), 2004: cattle, 77·7; hogs and pigs, 4·0; sheep and lambs (in $1m.), 721.

Forestry
Forests covered a total area of 749m. acres (303m. ha.) in 2002, or 33% of the land area. Between 1990 and 2000 new planting resulted in the total area under forests increasing by an average of 959,000 acres annually (388,000 ha.), a total exceeded only in China. The national forests had an area of 148,456,000 acres in 2002. In 1997 there were 504m. acres of timberland (109m. acres federally owned or managed, 37m. acres state, county or municipality owned, 358m. acres private). Timber production was 15,823m. cu. ft in 2003. The USA is the world's largest producer of roundwood (13·4% of the world total in 2003). It is also the highest consumer of roundwood; timber consumption in 2003 totalled 15·55bn. cu. ft.

There are 677 designated wilderness areas throughout the USA, covering a total of 106·4m. acres (43·1m. ha.). More than half of the areas are in Alaska (54%), followed by California (13%), Arizona, Washington and Idaho.

Fisheries
In 2002 the domestic catch was 9,397·2m. lb, valued at $3,092·3m. (including 1,178·6m. lb of shellfish valued at $1,706·4m.). Main species landed in terms of value ($1m.): shrimp, 460·9; crab, 397·7; American lobster, 293·3; Alaska pollock, 203·7; sea scallops, 203·7. Disposition of the domestic catch in 2002 (1m. lb): fresh or frozen, 6,826; tinned, 652; cured, 117; reduced to meal or oil, 1,802. The USA's imports of fishery commodities in 2001 ($10·29bn.) were exceeded only by those of Japan.

In the period 1999–2001 the average American citizen consumed 47·0 lb (21·3 kg) of fish and fishery products a year, compared to an average 35·5 lb (16·1 kg) for the world as a whole.

Tennessee Valley Authority
Established by Act of Congress, 1933, the TVA is a multiple-purpose federal agency which carries out its duties in an area embracing some 41,000 sq. miles in the seven Tennessee River Valley states: Tennessee, Kentucky, Mississippi, Alabama, North Carolina, Georgia and Virginia. In addition, 76 counties outside the Valley are served by TVA power distributors. It is the largest public power company in the USA. Its three directors are appointed by the President, with the consent of the Senate; headquarters are in Knoxville (TN).

INDUSTRY
The largest companies in the USA—and the world—by market capitalization in Feb. 2006 were: The Exxon Mobil Corporation (US$374·1bn.), the world's largest integrated oil company; The General Electric Company (US$340·6bn.); and The Microsoft Corporation (US$277·8bn.), the world's leading software company. According to a survey published by the New York-based Interbrand in July 2005, Coca-Cola is the most valuable brand, worth US$67·5bn.

The following table presents industry statistics of manufactures as reported at various censuses from 1909 to 1980 and from the Annual Survey of Manufactures for years in which no census was taken.

The annual Surveys of Manufactures carry forward the key measures of manufacturing activity which are covered in detail by the Census of Manufactures. The large plants in the surveys account for approximately two-thirds of the total employment in operating manufacturing establishments in the USA.

	Production workers (average for year)	Production workers' wages total ($1,000)	Value added by manufacture ($1,000)
1909	3,261,736	3,205,213	8,160,075
1919	9,464,916	9,664,009	23,841,624
1929	8,369,705	10,884,919	30,591,435
1933	5,787,611	4,940,146	14,007,540
1939	7,808,205	8,997,515	24,487,304
1950	11,778,803	34,600,025	89,749,765
1960	12,209,514	55,555,452	163,998,531
1970	13,528,000	91,609,000	300,227,600
1980	13,900,100	198,164,000	773,831,300
1990	12,232,700	275,208,400	1,346,970,100
2000	11,943,646	363,380,819	1,973,622,421
2001	11,212,063	342,268,242	1,851,693,858
2002	10,352,516	337,118,875	1,892,790,646
2003	9,794,517	329,715,154	1,912,124,316

The total number of employees in the manufacturing industry in 2003 was approximately 13,876,000; there were 350,815 manufacturing establishments in 2002. Manufacturing employment has been steadily declining since the turn of the millennium. Much of the decline reflects the recession that began in 2001 and the relatively weak recovery in demand that followed. In 2000 manufacturing contributed 17% of GDP and provided 14% of jobs, down from 27% of GDP and 31% of jobs in 1960. Industrial production grew far faster during the 1990s than in any other major economy, output expanding by 46·5% during the period 1990–2000. The leading industries in 2003 in terms of value added by manufacture (in $1m.) were: chemicals and allied products, 259,689; transportation equipment, 258,638; food, 210,688; computer and electronic products, 203,599; fabricated metal products, 137,195. In 2002 a total of 12,272,000 motor vehicles were made in the USA, making it the world's leading vehicle producer.

In 2003 principal commodities produced (by value of shipments, in $1m.) were: transportation equipment, 653,411; food, 481,684; chemicals and allied products, 447,441; computer and electronic products, 353,767; machinery, 252,984.

Net profits (2003) for manufacturing corporations were $307bn. before tax ($234bn. after tax).

The USA is the second largest beer producer after China, with 6,163m. gallons in 2004; and second after China for cigarette production, with 565bn. units in 2002.

Iron and Steel. Output of the iron and steel industries (in 1m. net tons of 2,000 lb) in recent years was:

	Pig iron (including ferro-alloys)	Raw steel	Steel by method of production[1]	
			Electric	Basic Oxygen
1999	51·0	107·4	49·7	57·7
2000	52·8	112·4	52·8	59·6
2001	46·4	99·3	47·1	52·2
2002	44·3	101·0	50·9	50·1
2003	44·8	103·3	52·7	50·6

[1]The sum of these two items should equal the total in the preceding column; any difference is due to rounding.

In 2002 iron and steel mills and ferroalloy manufacturing employed 119,900 persons (93,800 production workers). The total payroll amounted to $6,296·3m. (average of $51,421 per employee). Hourly earnings in 2002 ranged from $14·76 to a maximum of $24·96.

Labour

The Bureau of Labor Statistics estimated that in 2004 the civilian labour force was 147,401,000 (66·0% of those 16 years and over), of whom 139,252,000 were employed and 8,149,000 (5·5%) were unemployed. The unemployment rate has declined from its recent high of 6·3% in June 2003; it was 4·7% in Jan. 2006. Total non-farm payroll employment rose by 2,172,000 in the 12 months ending Dec. 2004. Employment by industry in 2004:

Industry Group	Male	Female	Total	Percentage distribution
Employed (1,000 persons):	74,524	64,728	139,252	100·0
Agriculture, forestry, fisheries, and hunting	1,687	546	2,232	1·6
Mining	483	55	539	0·4
Construction	9,727	1,041	10,768	7·7
Manufacturing: Durable goods	7,600	2,728	10,329	7·4
Manufacturing: Non-durable	3,885	2,270	6,155	4·4
Wholesale and retail trade	11,580	9,289	20,869	15·0
Transportation and utilities	5,342	1,671	7,013	5·0
Information	1,962	1,501	3,463	2·5
Finance activities	4,396	5,572	9,969	7·2
Professional and business services	8,068	6,039	14,108	10·1
Education and health services	7,222	21,497	28,719	20·6
Leisure and hospitality	5,783	6,037	11,820	8·5
Other services	3,330	3,573	6,903	5·0
Public administration	3,458	2,908	6,365	4·6

A total of 14 strikes and lockouts of 1,000 workers or more occurred in 2003, involving 129,200 workers and 4,091,200 idle days; the number of idle days was about one out of every 10,000 available workdays.

On 1 Sept. 1997 the federal hourly minimum wage was raised from $4·75 to $5·15 an hour. On 1 Oct. 1996 it had been raised from $4·25 to $4·75 an hour, the first time it had been raised since 1991. Americans work among the longest hours in the industrialized world, averaging 1,815 hours in 2002. Median weekly earnings were $620 in 2003.

Labour relations are legally regulated by the National Labor Relations Act, amended by the Labor–Management Relations (Taft–Hartley) Act, 1947 as amended by the Labor–Management Reporting and Disclosure Act, 1959, again amended in 1974, and the Railway Labor Act of 1926, as amended in 1934 and 1936.

Trade Unions

The labour movement comprises 78 national and international labour organizations plus a large number of small independent local or single-firm labour organizations. The American Federation of Labor and the Congress of Industrial Organizations merged into one organization, the AFL–CIO, in 1955, with 9m. members in 2005. Its president is John Sweeney, elected 1995. There were 15,776,000 union members in total in 2003.

Unaffiliated or independent labour organizations, inter-state in scope, had an estimated total membership excluding all foreign members (1993) of about 3m.

Labour organizations represented 13·8% (17·1m.) of wage and salary workers in 2004; a newly developing 'associative unionism' is not based on the workplace, but provides representation for employees which is portable throughout their work history; 12·5% (15·5m.) were actual members of unions. 36·4% of employees in the public sector, and 7·9% in the private sector, were members of unions in 2004. Strongholds of organized labour are, industry-wise, iron and steel, railways, coal mining and car building; region-wise, East coast cities and the mid-West industrial belt.

INTERNATIONAL TRADE

The North American Free Trade Agreement (NAFTA) between the USA, Canada and Mexico was signed on 7 Oct. 1992 and came into effect on 1 Jan. 1994. The UK has had 'most-favoured-nation' status since 1815.

Imports and Exports

Total value of imports and exports of goods (in $1bn.):

	Imports	Exports
2001	1,141·0	729·1
2002	1,164·7	693·1
2003	1,257·1	724·8
2004	1,469·7	818·8

The USA is both the world's leading importer and the leading trading nation, although only the second largest exporter after Germany. In 2003 its trade accounted for 16·8% of the world's imports and 9·6% of exports.

Principal imports and exports (in $1m.), 2003:

	Imports	Exports
Agricultural commodities		
Animal feeds	635	3,885
Coffee	1,612	5
Corn	151	4,963
Cotton, raw and linters	27	3,219
Hides and skins	74	1,653
Meat and preparations	4,403	7,261
Soybeans	47	7,935
Sugar	535	6
Tobacco, unmanufactured	690	1,035
Vegetables and fruits	11,454	8,123
Wheat	141	3,955
Manufactured goods		
ADP equipment, office machinery	80,826	28,852
Airplane parts	4,474	14,524
Airplanes	12,327	23,418
Alcoholic beverages	3,693	551
Aluminium	7,238	2,941
Artwork/antiques	4,398	1,157
Basketware, etc.	7,854	4,692
Chemicals – cosmetics	5,611	6,557
Chemicals – dyeing	2,480	4,137
Chemicals – fertilizers	2,130	2,341
Chemicals – inorganic	7,419	5,577
Chemicals – medicinal	31,516	18,775
Chemicals – organic	32,876	20,105
Chemicals – plastics	12,161	21,069
Chemicals – other	6,857	12,986
Clothing	68,162	4,960
Cork, wood, lumber	7,276	3,387
Electrical machinery	82,433	69,772
Fish and preparations	10,930	3,084
Footwear	15,603	495
Furniture and parts	24,356	3,608
Gem diamonds	12,931	338
General industrial machinery	38,467	30,115
Gold, non-monetary	2,932	4,820
Iron and steel mill products	11,112	6,268
Lighting, plumbing	6,003	1,347
Metal manufactures, misc.	17,985	11,218
Metal ores; scrap	3,142	5,646
Metalworking machinery	5,335	4,108
Optical goods	2,992	2,249
Paper and paperboard	14,849	9,814
Photographic equipment	5,046	3,330
Plastic articles	10,216	6,778
Platinum	2,624	481
Power generating machinery	32,485	31,495
Printed materials	4,148	4,607
Pulp and waste paper	2,597	4,096
Records/magnetic media	5,852	4,473
Rubber articles	2,358	1,412
Rubber tyres and tubes	5,258	2,200
Scientific instruments	23,661	27,998
Specialized industrial machinery	20,841	23,371
Television, VCR, etc.	71,137	16,851
Textile yarn, fabric	17,257	10,457
Toys/games/sporting goods	21,566	3,155
Travel goods	4,842	291
Vehicles	172,578	60,521
Watches/clocks/parts	3,600	242
Wood manufactures	9,289	1,578
Mineral fuel		
Coal	1,176	1,621

	Imports	Exports
Crude oil	101,722	155
Petroleum preparations	26,735	7,057
Natural gas	20,621	1,300

Imports and exports by selected countries for the calendar years 2002 and 2003 (in $1m.):

Country	General imports 2002	General imports 2003	Exports incl. re-exports 2002	Exports incl. re-exports 2003
Belgium	9,807	10,141	13,326	15,218
Brazil	15,781	17,884	12,376	11,218
Canada	209,088	224,166	160,923	169,770
China	125,192	152,379	22,128	28,418
France	28,240	29,221	19,016	17,068
Germany	62,506	68,047	26,630	28,848
Hong Kong	9,328	8,850	12,594	13,542
Ireland	22,438	25,841	6,745	7,698
Italy	24,220	25,437	10,057	10,570
Japan	121,429	118,029	51,449	52,064
South Korea	35,572	36,963	22,576	24,099
Malaysia	24,009	25,438	10,344	10,921
Mexico	134,616	138,073	97,470	97,457
Netherlands	9,848	10,972	18,311	20,703
Saudi Arabia	13,150	18,069	4,781	4,596
Singapore	14,802	15,158	16,218	16,576
Taiwan	32,148	31,600	18,382	17,488
Thailand	14,793	15,181	4,860	5,842
UK	40,745	42,667	33,205	33,895
Venezuela	15,093	17,144	4,430	2,839

COMMUNICATIONS

Roads

On 31 Dec. 2003 the total public road mileage was 3,974,103 miles (urban, 940,970; rural, 3,033,133). Of the urban roads, 12% were state controlled and 87% under local control. 22% of rural roads were controlled by the states, 75% of rural roads were under local control and the remainder were federal park and forest roads. State highway funds were $104,919m. in 2002.

Motor vehicles registered in 2002: 229,620,000, of which 135,921,000 automobiles, 92,939,000 trucks and 761,000 buses. There were 194,296,000 licensed drivers in 2002 and 4,963,000 motorcycle registrations. The average distance travelled by a passenger car in the year 2001 was 11,800 miles. There were 43,220 fatalities in road accidents in 2003.

Rail

Freight service is provided by 12 major independent railroad companies and several hundred smaller operators. Long-distance passenger trains are run by the National Railroad Passenger Corporation (Amtrak), which is federally assisted. Amtrak was set up in 1971 to maintain a basic network of long-distance passenger trains, and is responsible for almost all non-commuter services over some 38,000 route-km, of which it owns only 1,256 km (555 km electrified). Outside the major conurbations, there are almost no regular passenger services other than those of Amtrak, which carried 23,269,000 passengers in 2002. Passenger revenue for Amtrak (2002) was $1,304·3m.; revenue passenger miles, 5,314m.

Civil Aviation

The busiest airport in 2002 was Atlanta (Hartsfield International), which handled 37,720,556 passenger enplanements (34,610,400 on domestic flights). The second busiest was Chicago (O'Hare) with 31,706,328 passenger enplanements (27,347,895 on domestic flights), followed by Los Angeles International, with 26,911,570 passenger enplanements (19,814,818 on domestic flights). As well as being the three busiest airports in the USA for passenger traffic in 2002, they are also three of the five busiest in the world. The five busiest in the world in 2002 were Atlanta, Chicago O'Hare, London Heathrow, Tokyo Haneda and Los Angeles. New York (John F. Kennedy) was the busiest airport in the

USA for international passenger enplanements in 2002, with 7,278,793, ahead of Los Angeles International, with 7,096,752.

The leading airports in 2002 on the basis of aircraft departures completed were Chicago, O'Hare (461,394); Atlanta, Hartsfield International (445,461); Dallas/Fort Worth (388,643).

There were 42 airports with more than 100,000 international enplanements in 2002. These were, in descending order: New York (John F. Kennedy); Los Angeles; Miami; Chicago (O'Hare); New York (Newark); San Francisco; Atlanta (Hartsfield); Houston (George Bush); Honolulu; Dallas/Fort Worth; Washington, D.C. (Dulles International); Boston; Detroit (Metropolitan-Wayne County); Philadelphia; Guam; Minneapolis/St Paul; Seattle; San Juan (Luis Muñoz Marin International); Orlando International; New York (LaGuardia); Denver; Phoenix; Charlotte; Cincinnati (Northern Kentucky International); Fort Lauderdale (Hollywood International); Las Vegas (McCarran); Orlando (Sanfort); Saipan; Pittsburgh; Baltimore; St Louis (Lambert); Tampa; San Diego (Lindbergh Field); Memphis; Cleveland-Hopkins; San Jose; Oakland; San Antonio; Portland; Raleigh-Durham; Washington, D.C. (Ronald Reagan Washington National); Chicago (Midway).

In 2002 Delta Air Lines carried the most passengers of any airline in the world with 86,854,120 (around 4% on international flights), ahead of American Airlines, with 85,710,781 (around 10% on international flights), and the low-cost carrier Southwest Airlines, with 72,517,787 (all on domestic flights). American Airlines carried the most international passengers of any US carrier, ahead of United Airlines, with 8% of their passengers on international flights. United Airlines filed for bankruptcy in Dec. 2002, as did Delta Air Lines in Sept. 2005. United Airlines emerged from bankruptcy protection in Feb. 2006.

In 2003 US flag carriers in scheduled service enplaned 646·5m. revenue passengers.

Shipping

In July 2002 the cargo-carrying US flag fleet consisted of 36,098 vessels, of which 3,869 were of 1,000 GRT and over (2,196 liquid carriers, 759 dry bulk carriers, 123 containerships and 791 other freighters). Of 32,229 vessels of less than 1,000 GRT, 2,214 were liquid carriers, 23,010 dry bulk carriers, four containerships and 7,001 other freighters. Shipping capacity in July 2002 was 76,876,000 GRT, of which the vessels of 1,000 GRT and over totalled 30,495,000 GRT while those of less than 1,000 GRT totalled 46,381,000 GRT. On 1 Jan. 2003 the US merchant marine included 416 ocean-going self-propelled merchant vessels of 1,000 gross tons or over, with an aggregate 13·3m. DWT. This included 110 tankers of 5·8m. DWT.

In 2001 vessels totalling 451,929,000 NRT entered, and 310,973,000 NRT cleared, all US ports. The busiest port is South Louisiana, which handled 235,053,000 tonnes of cargo in 2002 and ranks fourth in the world. Other major ports are Houston, Los Angeles, Long Beach, Corpus Christi, New York-New Jersey and Philadelphia.

Telecommunications

Regional private companies formed from the American Telephone and Telegraph Co. after its dissolution in 1995 ('Baby Bells') operate the telephone, telegraph, telex and electronic transmission services system at the national and local levels. In 2004 telephone subscribers numbered 359,052,100 (or 1,208·8 per 1,000 persons). There were 181,105,100 cellphone subscribers in 2004 (609·7 per 1,000 persons). The leading cellphone operators are Cingular (with more than 49m. subscribers), Verizon, Sprint-Nexel and T-Mobile. There were 190m. PCs in 2002 (658·9 for every 1,000 persons—the highest rate in the world) and 34m. fax machines. The number of Internet users in 2004 was estimated to be 185·0m., or 62·3% of the population. Internet commerce, or e-commerce, amounted to $1,679bn. in 2003, the highest in the world.

Legislation on the media and telecommunications of 1996 coming into force on 31 March 1999 aimed at deregulating the market while preserving safeguards against over-concentration of individual ownership: a single company may not control a network reaching more than 35% of TV viewers, or produce a newspaper and a television service in the same market. Local companies are now permitted to operate long-distance telephone services and also cable TV services.

Postal Services

The US Postal Service superseded the Post Office Department on 1 July 1971.

Postal business for the years ended in Sept. included the following items:

	2000	2001	2002	2003
Number of post offices, stations and branches	38,060	38,123	37,683	37,579
Operating revenue ($1m.)	64,540	65,834	66,463	68,529
Operating expenditures ($1m.)	62,992	65,640	65,234	63,902

SOCIAL INSTITUTIONS

Justice

Legal controversies may be decided in two systems of courts: the federal courts, with jurisdiction confined to certain matters enumerated in Article III of the Constitution, and the state courts, with jurisdiction in all other proceedings. The federal courts have jurisdiction exclusive of the state courts in criminal prosecutions for the violation of federal statutes, in civil cases involving the government, in bankruptcy cases and in admiralty proceedings, and have jurisdiction concurrent with the state courts over suits between parties from different states, and certain suits involving questions of federal law.

The highest court is the Supreme Court of the US, which reviews cases from the lower federal courts and certain cases originating in state courts involving questions of federal law. It is the final arbiter of all questions involving federal statutes and the Constitution; and it has the power to invalidate any federal or state law or executive action which it finds repugnant to the Constitution. This court, consisting of nine justices appointed by the President who receive salaries of $203,000 a year (the Chief Justice, $212,100), meets from Oct. until June every year. For the term ended Sept. 2003 it disposed of 9,406 cases, deciding 84 on their merits. In the remainder of cases it either summarily affirms lower court decisions or declines to review. A few suits, usually brought by state governments, originate in the Supreme Court, but issues of fact are mostly referred to a master.

The US courts of appeals number 13 (in 11 circuits composed of three or more states and one circuit for the District of Columbia and one Court of Appeals for the Federal Circuit); the 179 circuit judges receive salaries of $175,100 a year. Any party to a suit in a lower federal court usually has a right of appeal to one of these courts. In addition, there are direct appeals to these courts from many federal administrative agencies. In the year ending 30 Sept. 2003, 62,390 appeals were filed in the courts of appeals, including 1,543 in the Federal Circuit.

The trial courts in the federal system are the US district courts, of which there are 94 in the 50 states, one in the District of Columbia and one each in the Commonwealth of Puerto Rico and the Territories of the Virgin Islands, Guam and the Northern Marianas. Each state has at least one US district court, and three states have four apiece. Each district court has from one to 28 judgeships. There are 663 US district judges ($165,200 a year), who received 252,962 civil cases in 2002-03.

In addition to these courts of general jurisdiction, there are special federal courts of limited jurisdiction. The US Court of Federal Claims (16 judges at $165,200 a year) decides claims for money damages against the federal government in a wide variety of matters; the Court of International Trade (13 judges at $165,200) determines controversies concerning the classification and valuation of imported merchandise.

The judges of all these courts are appointed by the President with the approval of the Senate; to assure their independence, they hold office during good behaviour and cannot have their salaries reduced. This does not apply to judges in the Territories, who hold their offices for a term of ten years or to judges of the US Court of Federal Claims. The judges may retire with full pay at the age of 70 years if they have served a period of ten years, or at 65 if they have 15 years of service, but they are subject to call for such judicial duties as they are willing to undertake.

In 2002-03, of the 254,499 civil cases filed in the district courts, 168,332 arose under various federal statutes (such as labour, social security, tax, patent, securities, antitrust and civil rights laws); 46,295 involved personal injury or property damage claims; 32,356 dealt with contracts; and 7,503 were actions concerning real property.

In 2000 the number of lawyers in the USA passed the 1m. mark, equivalent to 363 per 100,000 people.

Among the 68,533 offenders convicted in 2001 in the district courts, 25,088 persons were charged with alleged infractions of drug laws, 12,349 with property offences, 4,347 with public order offences and 2,604 with violent offences. All other people convicted were charged with miscellaneous general offences.

Persons convicted of federal crimes may be fined, released on probation under the supervision of the probation officers of the federal courts, confined in prison, or confined in prison with a period of supervised release to follow, also under the supervision of probation officers of the federal courts. Federal prisoners are confined in 87 institutions incorporating various security levels that are operated by the Bureau of Prisons. On 31 Dec. 2002 the total number of prisoners under the jurisdiction of Federal or State adult correctional authorities was 1,440,655. A record 2,033,331 inmates were held in Federal or State prisons or local jails at the end of 2002, giving a rate of 701 per 100,000 population (the highest of any country).

The state courts have jurisdiction over all civil and criminal cases arising under state laws, but decisions of the state courts of last resort as to the validity of treaties or of laws of the USA, or on other questions arising under the Constitution, are subject to review by the Supreme Court of the US. The state court systems are generally similar to the federal system, to the extent that they generally have a number of trial courts and intermediate appellate courts, and a single court of last resort. The highest court in each state is usually called the Supreme Court or Court of Appeals with a Chief Justice and Associate Justices, usually elected but sometimes appointed by the Governor with the advice and consent of the State Senate or other advisory body; they usually hold office for a term of years, but in some instances for life or during good behaviour. The lowest tribunals are usually those of Justices of the Peace; many towns and cities have municipal and police courts, with power to commit for trial in criminal matters and to determine misdemeanours for violation of the municipal ordinances.

There were no executions from 1968 to 1976. The US Supreme Court had held the death penalty, as applied in general criminal statutes, to contravene the eighth and fourteenth amendments of the US constitution, as a cruel and unusual punishment when used so irregularly and rarely as to destroy its deterrent value. The death penalty was reinstated by the Supreme Court in 1976, but has not been authorized in Alaska, the District of Columbia, Hawaii, Iowa, Kansas, Maine, Massachusetts, Michigan, Minnesota, New York, North Dakota, Rhode Island, Vermont, West Virginia and Wisconsin. There were, in Oct. 2004, 3,471 (including 50 women) prisoners under sentence of death. In 2005 there were 60 executions (59 in 2004 but only 14 in 1991). From 1977-2005 there were 1,004 executions of which 355 were in Texas and 95 in Virginia. The death penalty for offenders under the age of 18 was abolished in March 2005. For the first time since 1963, there were two executions under federal jurisdiction in 2001. In Sept. 2003 the federal Court of Appeals in San Francisco overturned over 100 death sentences in Arizona, Idaho and Montana on the grounds that judges, not juries, had passed sentence, contravening a Supreme Court ruling of 2002.

There were 16,137 murders in 2004, reversing the upward trend of the previous four years. The murder rate in 2003 was 5·5 per 100,000 persons, down from 10·5 per 100,000 in 1980 and the lowest rate in forty years. 70·3% of all murders in 2004 were carried out with firearms.

Education
The adult literacy rate is at least 99%.

Elementary and secondary education is mainly a state responsibility. Each state and the District of Columbia has a system of free public schools, established by law, with courses covering 12 years plus kindergarten. There are three structural patterns in common use; the K8-4 plan, meaning kindergarten plus eight elementary grades followed by four high school grades; the K6-3-3 plan, or kindergarten plus six elementary grades followed by a three-year junior high school and a three-year senior high school; and the K5-3-4 plan, kindergarten plus five elementary grades followed by a three-year middle school and a four-year high school. All plans lead to high-school graduation, usually at age 17 or 18. Vocational education is an integral part of secondary education. Many states also have two-year colleges in which education is provided at a nominal cost. Each state has delegated a large degree of control of the educational programme to local school districts (numbering 14,559 in school year 2001–02), each with a board of education (usually three to nine members) selected locally and serving mostly without pay. The school policies of the local school districts must be in accord with the laws and the regulations of their state Departments of Education. While regulations differ from one jurisdiction to another, in general it may be said that school attendance is compulsory from age seven to 16.

'Charter schools' are legal entities outside the school boards administration. They retain the basics of public school education, but may offer unconventional curricula and hours of attendance. Founders may be parents, teachers, public bodies or commercial firms. Organization and conditions depend upon individual states' legislation. The first charter schools were set up in Minnesota in 1991. By Oct. 2001, 2,348 charter schools were operating in 36 states and Washington, D.C.

In 1940 a new category was established—the 'functionally illiterate', meaning those who had completed fewer than five years of elementary schooling; for persons 25 years of age or over this percentage was 1·6 in March 2002 (for the Black population as a whole it was 1·6%); it was 0·5% for white and 0·6% for Blacks in the 25–29-year-old group. It was reported in March 2002 that 84·1% of all persons 25 years old and over had completed four years of high school or more, and that 26·7% had completed a bachelor's degree or more. In the age group 25 to 29, 86·4% had completed four years of high school or more, and 29·3% had completed a bachelor's degree or more. However, according to a report published in 2003 about a third of American fourth graders (aged 9–10) are unable to read at a basic level.

In the autumn of 2002, 16,611,711 students (9,946,359 full-time and 9,409,595 women) were enrolled in 4,168 colleges and universities; 2,571,000 were first-time students. It is projected that in 2010 the student population will number 17,490,000.

In 2002–03 expenditure for public elementary and secondary education totalled $438,808m., comprising $376,262m. for current operating expenses, $42,992m. for capital outlay and $11,746m. for interest on school debt. The current expenditure per pupil in average daily attendance was $7,875.

In 2003–04 total expenditure on education came to 7·9% of GNP.

Estimated total expenditures for private elementary and secondary schools in 2003–04 were about $35,600m. In 2003–04 college and university spending totalled about $351,200m., of which about $223,200m. was spent by institutions under public control. In 2000–01 the federal government contributed about 11% of total current-fund revenue; state governments, 36%; student tuition and fees, 18%; and all other sources, 35%. Federal support for vocational education in fiscal year 2002 amounted to about $1,806m.

Summary of statistics of regular schools (public and private), teachers and pupils for 2002–03 (compiled by the US National Center for Education Statistics):

Schools by level	Number of schools	Teachers (in 1,000)[1]	Enrolment (in 1,000)
Elementary schools:			
Public	65,718	1,619	34,135
Private	17,427[1]	229	5,042
Secondary schools:			
Public	22,599	1,415	14,067
Private	2,704[1]	165	1,359
Higher education:			
Public	1,712	792	12,752
Private	2,456	365	3,860
Total	129,056[2]	4,585	71,215

[1]Data from 2001–02. [2]Includes combined elementary and secondary school, and special education, alternative, and other schools not classified by grade span.

In the autumn of 2003 there were 15·9 pupils per teacher in public elementary schools in the USA and 16·2 pupils per teacher in public secondary schools.

Most of the private elementary and secondary schools are affiliated with religious denominations. In the autumn of 2001 there were 6,763 Catholic elementary schools with 1,793,593 pupils and 103,897 teachers, and 1,110 secondary schools with 615,711 pupils and 42,671 teachers.

During the school year 2002–03 high-school graduates numbered about 2,986,000 (of whom about 2,685,000 were from public schools). Institutions of higher education conferred about 1,291,000 bachelor's degrees during the year 2001–02; 595,000 associate's degrees; 482,000 master's degrees; 44,000 doctorates; and 81,000 first professional degrees. In the fiscal year 2002 the US Department of Education provided $15,525m. in grants, loans, work-study programmes and other financial assistance to post-secondary students.

During the academic year 2002–03, 586,000 foreign students were enrolled in American colleges and universities. The countries with the largest numbers of students in American colleges were: India, 74,600; China, 64,800; South Korea, 51,500; Japan, 46,000; Taiwan, 28,000; Canada, 26,500.

In 2002–03, 174,600 US students were enrolled at colleges and universities abroad. The country attracting the most students from the USA was the United Kingdom, with 31,700.

School enrolment, Oct. 2002, embraced 95·2% of the children who were 5 and 6 years old; 98·3% of the children aged 7–13 years; 96·4% of those aged 14–17; 63·3% of those aged 18–19; and 34·4% of those aged 20–24.

The US National Center for Education Statistics estimates the total enrolment in the autumn of 2003 at all of the country's elementary, secondary and higher educational institutions (public and private) at 70·7m. (68·5m. in the autumn of 2000).

The number of teachers in regular public and private elementary and secondary schools in 2001 increased slightly to about 3,388,000. The estimated average annual salary of public school teachers was $45,800 in spring 2003.

Health
Admission to the practice of medicine (for both doctors of medicine and doctors of osteopathic medicine) is controlled

in each state by examining boards directly representing the profession and acting with authority conferred by state law. Although there are a number of variations, the usual time now required to complete training is eight years beyond the secondary school with up to three or more years of additional graduate training. Certification as a specialist may require between three and five more years of graduate training plus experience in practice. In Jan. 2002 the estimated number of physicians (MD and DO—in all forms of practice) in the USA, Puerto Rico and outlying US areas was 853,200 (615,400 in 1990 and 467,700 in 1980).

Dental employment in 2002 numbered 153,000.

Number of hospitals listed by the American Hospital Association in 2002 was 5,794, with 976,000 beds (equivalent to 3·4 beds per 1,000 population). Of the total, 240 hospitals with 50,000 beds were operated by the federal government; 1,136 with 124,000 beds by state and local government; 3,025 with 582,000 beds by non-profit organizations (including church groups); 766 with 108,000 beds were investor-owned. The categories of non-federal hospitals were (2002): 4,927 short-term general and special hospitals with 821,000 beds; 124 non-federal long-term general and special hospitals with 18,000 beds; 477 psychiatric hospitals with 85,000 beds; four tuberculosis hospitals with fewer than 500 beds.

Patient admissions to community hospitals (2002) was 34,478,000; average daily census was 538,900. There were 556·4m. outpatient visits.

Personal health care costs in 2002 totalled $1,340,200m., distributed as follows: hospital care, $486,500m.; physicians and clinical services, $339,500m.; prescription drugs, $162,400m.; nursing-home care, $103,200m.; dentists, $70,300m.; home health care, $36,100m.; medical durables, $18,800m.; other personal health care, $123,400m. Total national health expenditure in 2002 amounted to $1,553·0bn. In 2003 the USA spent 15·0% of its GDP on health—4% more than any other leading industrialized nation. Public spending on health amounted to 44·9% of total health spending in 2002 (the lowest percentage of any major industrialized nation). A survey published by the World Health Organization in June 2000 to measure health systems in all of the sovereign countries and find which country has the best overall health care ranked the USA in 37th place.

In 2002, 22·4% of Americans (24·8% of males and 20·1% of females) were smokers, down from a peak of over 40% in 1964. In the period 1999–2002, 31·1% of the adult population were considered obese (having a body mass index over 30), compared to 14·6% in 1971–74.

Welfare

Social welfare legislation was chiefly the province of the various states until the adoption of the Social Security Act of 14 Aug. 1935. This as amended provides for a federal system of old-age, survivors and disability insurance; health insurance for the aged and disabled; supplemental security income for the aged, blind and disabled; federal state unemployment insurance; and federal grants to states for public assistance (medical assistance for the aged and aid to families with dependent children generally and for maternal and child health and child welfare services).

Legislation of Aug. 1996 began the transfer of aid administration back to the states, restricted the provision of aid to a maximum period of five years, and abolished benefits to immigrants (both legal and illegal) for the first five years of their residence in the USA. The Social Security Administration (formerly part of the Department of Health and Human Services but an independent agency since March 1995) has responsibility for a number of programmes covering retirement, disability, Medicare, Supplemental Security Income and survivors. The Administration for Children and Families (ACF), an agency of the Department of Health and Human Services, is responsible for federal programmes which promote the economic and social wellbeing of families, children, individuals and communities. ACF has federal responsibility for the following programmes: Temporary Assistance for Needy Families; low income energy assistance; Head Start; child care; child protective services; and a community services block grant. The ACF also has federal responsibility for social service programmes for children, youth, native Americans and persons with developmental disabilities.

The Administration on Aging (AoA), an agency in the US Department of Health and Human Services, is one of the nation's largest providers of home- and community-based care for older persons and their caregivers. Created in 1965 with the passage of the Older Americans Act (OAA), AoA is part of a federal, state, tribal and local partnership called the National Network on Aging. It serves about 7m. older persons and their caregivers, and consists of 56 State Units on Aging, 655 Area Agencies on Aging, 236 Tribal and Native organizations, two organizations that serve Native Hawaiians, 29,000 service providers and thousands of volunteers. These organizations provide assistance and services to older individuals and their families in urban, suburban, and rural areas throughout the USA.

The Health Care Financing Administration, an agency of the Health and Human Services Department, has federal responsibility for health insurance for the aged and disabled. Unemployment insurance is the responsibility of the Department of Labor.

In 2003 an average of 2,025,000 families (4,932,000 recipients) were receiving payments under Temporary Assistance for Needy Families. Total payments under Temporary Assistance for Needy Families were $25,414m. in 2002. The role of Child Support Enforcement is to ensure that children are supported by their parents. Money collected is for children who live with only one parent because of divorce, separation or out-of-wedlock birth. In 2002, $20,137m. was collected on behalf of these children.

The Social Security Act provides for protection against the cost of medical care through Medicare, a two-part programme of health insurance for people age 65 and over, people of any age with permanent kidney failure, and for certain disabled people under age 65 who receive Social Security disability benefits. In 2002 payments totalling $148,031m. were made under the hospital portion of Medicare. During the same period, $108,825m. was paid under the voluntary medical insurance portion of Medicare. Medicare enrolment in July 2003 totalled 41·0m.

In 2003 about 46·4m. beneficiaries were on the rolls; the average paid to a retired worker (not counting any benefits paid to his/her dependants) in 2003 was $922 per month. Full retirement benefits are now payable at age 65, with reduced benefits available as early as age 62. The age for full retirement benefits is gradually increasing until it reaches 67 in 2027. In 1995 the average actual retirement age for males was 63.

Medicaid is a jointly-funded, Federal-State health insurance programme for certain low-income and needy people. It covers 50m. individuals including children, the aged, blind, and/or disabled, and people who are eligible to receive federally-assisted income maintenance payments.

In Dec. 2002, 6·79m. persons were receiving Supplementary Security Income payments. 1,251,000 old-age persons received $4,803m. in benefits; 77,000 blind people received $416m.; and 5,459,000 disabled people received $28,499m. Payments, including supplemental amounts from various states, totalled $33,718m. in 2002.

In 2002 a total of $522,156m. was spent on cash and non-cash benefits (such as food stamps) for persons with limited incomes. In 2003 the food stamp programme helped 21,262,000 persons at a cost of $21,407m.; and 28·4m. persons received help from the national school lunch programme at a cost of $6,339m.

RELIGION

The Yearbook of American and Canadian Churches, published by the National Council of the Churches of Christ in the USA,

New York, gave the following figures available from official statisticians of church bodies: the principal religions (numerically or historically) or groups of religious bodies (in 2002 unless otherwise stated) are shown below:

	No. of churches	Membership (in 1,000)
Baptist bodies		
Southern Baptist Convention	42,775	16,248
National Baptist Convention, USA (not available)	9,000	5,000
National Baptist Convention of America, Inc. (2000)	2,500[1]	3,500
American Baptist Churches in the USA	5,836	1,484
American Baptist Association (1998)	1,760	275
Conservative Baptist Association of America (2000)	1,191	224
Baptist Missionary Association of America (2000)	1,322	295
Christian Church (Disciples of Christ)	3,691	786
Christian Churches and Churches of Christ (2000)	5,471	1,439
Church of the Nazarene (2000)	5,070	637
Churches of Christ (2000)	13,027	1,646
Progressive National Baptist Convention, Inc. (1995)	2,000	2,500
The Episcopal Church (2001)	7,344	2,334
Jehovah's Witnesses	11,876	1,022
Latter-day Saints		
Church of Jesus Christ of Latter-day Saints (Mormons)	11,879	5,411
Reorganized Church of Jesus Christ of Latter-day Saints (1999)	1,236	137
Lutheran bodies		
Evangelical Lutheran Church in America	10,721	5,038
The Lutheran Church–Missouri Synod	6,142	2,513
Wisconsin Evangelical Lutheran Synod (2000)	1,241	722
Mennonite churches		
Mennonite Church (2000)	1,063	120
Old Order Amish Church (2000)	1,290	97
Methodist bodies		
United Methodist Church	35,102	8,251
African Methodist Episcopal Church (2000)	6,200	2,500
African Methodist Episcopal Zion Church	3,226	1,431
Wesleyan Church (USA) (2000)	1,602	123
Pentecostal bodies		
The Church of God in Christ (1991)	15,300	5,500
Assemblies of God	12,133	2,687
Church of God (Cleveland, Tenn.)	6,623	945
Pentecostal Assemblies of the World, Inc. (1998)	1,750	1,500
Presbyterian bodies		
Presbyterian Church (USA)	11,097	3,407
Presbyterian Church in America (2000)	1,458	306
Reformed Churches		
Reformed Church in America (2000)	898	289
Christian Reformed Church in North America (1999)	739	197
The Salvation Army (2000)	1,332	415
United Church of Christ	5,850	1,331
Seventh-day Adventist Church	4,619	919
Roman Catholic Church[2]	19,484	66,407
Orthodox Churches		
Greek Orthodox Archdiocese of America (2000)	508	1,500
Orthodox Church in America	725	900
Oriental Orthodox Churches		
Armenian Apostolic Church of America (2000)	36	360
Armenian Apostolic Church, Diocese of America (1991)	72	414
Coptic Orthodox Church (2000)	100	300
Non-Christian Religions		
Hindus (2001)	—	766
Islam (2001)	—	1,104
Jews (2001)	—	2,831
Buddhist (2001)	—	1,082

[1]1987. [2]In May 2005 there were 14 cardinals.

CULTURE

World Heritage Sites

There are 23 sites under American jurisdiction that appear on the UNESCO World Heritage List. They are (with year entered on list): Mesa Verde National Park, Colorado (1978); Yellowstone National Park, Wyoming/Idaho/Montana (1978); Wrangell-St Elias National Park and Preserve, Alaska (1979); Everglades National Park, Florida (1979); Grand Canyon National Park, Arizona (1979); Independence Hall, Pennsylvania (1979); Redwood National Park, California (1980); Mammoth Cave National Park, Kentucky (1981); Olympic National Park, Washington State (1981); Cahokia Mounds State Historic Site, Illinois (1982); Great Smoky Mountains National Park, North Carolina/Tennessee (1983); San Juan National Historic Site and La Fortaleza, Puerto Rico (1983); the Statue of Liberty, New York (1984); Yosemite National Park, California (1984); Monticello and the University of Virginia, Charlottesville, Virginia (1987); Chaco Culture National Historic Park, New Mexico (1987); Aztec Ruins National Monument, New Mexico (1987); Hawaii Volcanoes National Park, including Mauna Loa, Hawaii (1987); Glacier Bay National Park and Preserve, Alaska (1992); Pueblo de Taos, New Mexico (1992); Carlsbad Caverns National Park, New Mexico (1995); Waterton-Glacier International Peace Park, Montana (1995).

Broadcasting

The licensing agency for broadcasting stations is the Federal Communications Commission, an independent federal body composed of five Commissioners appointed by the President. Its regulatory activities comprise: allocation of spectrum space; consideration of applications to operate individual stations; and regulation of their operations. In 2002 there were 10,965 commercial radio stations, 1,333 commercial TV stations, 381 non-commercial TV stations and 9,339 cable TV systems. Programming is targeted to appeal to a given segment of the population or audience taste. There are five national TV networks (three commercial; colour by NTSC) with 46 national cable networks. All major cities have network affiliates and additional commercial stations.

Legislation on the media and telecommunications of 1996 came into force on 31 March 1999 deregulating the market while preserving safeguards against over-concentration of individual ownership: a single company may not control a network reaching more than 35% of TV viewers, or produce a newspaper and a television service in the same market. Local companies are now permitted to operate long-distance telephone services and also cable TV services.

Broadcasting to countries abroad is conducted by The Voice of America, which functions under a seven-member council nominated by the President and reviewed by Congress. Voice of America has an annual audience of 94m. and broadcasts in over 50 languages.

In 2000 there were 598m. radio receivers in use, equivalent to 2,118 per 1,000 inhabitants. No other country averaged more than 1,500 radios per 1,000 inhabitants. There were 267m. TV receivers in use in 2001, equivalent to 938 per 1,000 inhabitants (a rate exceeded only in Bermuda). In 2003 there were 70·5m. cable TV subscribers.

Cinema

In 2003 there were 35,995 screens, including 634 drive-ins. Attendance in 2003 totalled 1,574m.; gross box office receipts came to $9·49bn. 459 new films were released in 2003.

Press

In 2003 there were 1,456 daily newspapers with a combined daily circulation of 55·2m., the second highest in the world behind Japan. There were 787 morning papers and 680 evening papers, plus 917 Sunday papers (circulation, 58·8m.). Unlike

Japan, where circulation is rising, in the USA it has fallen since 1985, when daily circulation was 62·8m. The most widely read newspapers are *USA Today* (average daily circulation in 2003 of 2·6m.), followed by the *Wall Street Journal* (1·8m.) and the *New York Times* (1·7m.).

Books published in 2003 totalled a record high 171,061, of which 20,187 were juvenile, 18,701 sociology and economics, 17,599 fiction and 10,824 history. In 2003 US book sales totalled a record $23,421m.

Tourism

In 2002 the USA received 41,892,000 foreign visitors (50,945,000 in 2000), of whom 12,968,000 were from Canada and 9,807,000 from Mexico. 21% of all tourists were from Europe. Only France and Spain received more tourists than the USA in 2002.

In 2002 visitors to the USA spent approximately $66,547m. (excluding transportation paid to US international carriers). The USA has the highest annual revenue from tourists of any country (nearly twice as much as Spain, which received the second most in 2002). Expenditure by US travellers in foreign countries for 2002 was an estimated $58,044m. (excluding transportation paid to foreign flag international carriers).

Festivals

There are major opera festivals at Cooperstown (Glimmerglass), New York State (July–Aug.); Santa Fe, New Mexico (June–Aug.); and Seattle, Washington (Aug.). Among the many famous film festivals are the Sundance Film Festival in Jan. and the New York Film Festival in late Sept./early Oct.

Museums and Galleries

Among the most famous museums are the National Gallery in Washington, D.C., the Museum of Fine Arts in Boston, the Metropolitan Museum, the Guggenheim Museum, and the Museum of Modern Art, all in New York, and the Museum of Art in Philadelphia. In 2002, 27% of US adults visited an art museum at least once.

DIPLOMATIC REPRESENTATIVES

Of the USA in the United Kingdom (24 Grosvenor Sq., London, W1A 1AE)
Ambassador: Robert H. Tuttle.

Of the United Kingdom in the USA (3100 Massachusetts Ave., NW, Washington, D.C., 20008)
Ambassador: Sir David Manning.

Of the United States to the United Nations
Ambassador: John Bolton.

Of the United States to the European Union
Ambassador: Rockwell A. Schnabel.

FURTHER READING

OFFICIAL STATISTICAL INFORMATION

The Office of Management and Budget, Washington, D.C., 20503 is part of the Executive Office of the President; it is responsible for co-ordinating all the statistical work of the different Federal government agencies. The Office does not collect or publish data itself. The main statistical agencies are as follows:

(1) Data User Services Division, Bureau of the Census, Department of Commerce, Washington, D.C., 20233. Responsible for decennial censuses of population and housing, quinquennial census of agriculture, manufactures and business; current statistics on population and the labour force, manufacturing activity and commodity production, trade and services, foreign trade, state and local government finances and operations. (*Statistical Abstract of the United States*, annual, and others).

(2) Bureau of Labor Statistics, Department of Labor, 441 G Street NW, Washington, D.C., 20212. (*Monthly Labor Review* and others).

(3) Information Division, Economic Research Service, Department of Agriculture, Washington, D.C., 20250. (*Agricultural Statistics*, annual, and others).

(4) National Center for Health Statistics, Department of Health and Human Services, 3700 East-West Highway, Hyattsville, MD 20782. (*Vital Statistics of the United States*, monthly and annual, and others).

(5) Bureau of Mines Office of Technical Information, Department of the Interior, Washington, D.C., 20241. (*Minerals Yearbook*, annual, and others).

(6) Office of Energy Information Services, Energy Information Administration, Department of Energy, Washington, D.C., 20461.

(7) Statistical Publications, Department of Commerce, Room 5062 Main Commerce, 14th St and Constitution Avenue NW, Washington, D.C., 20230; the Department's Bureau of Economic Analysis and its Office of Industry and Trade Information are the main collectors of data.

(8) Center for Education Statistics, Department of Education, 555 New Jersey Avenue NW, Washington, D.C., 20208.

(9) Public Correspondence Division, Office of the Assistant Secretary of Defense (Public Affairs P.C.), The Pentagon, Washington, D.C., 20301-1400.

(10) Bureau of Justice Statistics, Department of Justice, 633 Indiana Avenue NW, Washington, D.C., 20531.

(11) Public Inquiry, APA 200, Federal Aviation Administration, Department of Transportation, 800 Independence Avenue SW, Washington, D.C., 20591.

(12) Office of Public Affairs, Federal Highway Administration, Department of Transportation, 400 7th St. SW, Washington, D.C., 20590.

(13) Statistics Division, Internal Revenue Service, Department of the Treasury, 1201 E St. NW, Washington, D.C., 20224.

Statistics on the economy are also published by the Division of Research and Statistics, Federal Reserve Board, Washington, D.C., 20551; the Congressional Joint Committee on the Economy, Capitol; the Office of the Secretary, Department of the Treasury, 1500 Pennsylvania Avenue NW, Washington, D.C., 20220.

OTHER OFFICIAL PUBLICATIONS

Economic Report of the President. Annual. Bureau of the Census. *Statistical Abstract of the United States.* Annual. *Historical Statistics of the United States, Colonial Times to 1970.*

United States Government Manual. Washington. Annual.

The official publications of the USA are issued by the US Government Printing Office and are distributed by the Superintendent of Documents, who issued in 1940 a cumulative *Catalogue of Public Documents of the Congress and of All Departments of the Government of the United States.* This *Catalog* is kept up to date by *United States Government Publications, Monthly Catalog* with annual index and supplemented by *Price Lists.* Each *Price List* is devoted to a special subject or type of material.

Treaties and other International Acts of the United States of America (Edited by Hunter Miller), 8 vols. Washington, 1929–48. This edition stops in 1863. It may be supplemented by *Treaties, Conventions, International Acts, Protocols and Agreements Between the US and Other Powers, 1776–1937* (Edited by William M. Malloy and others). 4 vols. 1909–38. A new Treaty Series, *US Treaties and Other International Agreements,* was started in 1950.

Writings on American History. Washington, annual from 1902 (except 1904–5 and 1941–47).

NON-OFFICIAL PUBLICATIONS

The Cambridge Economic History of the United States. vol. 1. CUP, 1996; vol. 2. CUP, 2000; vol. 3. CUP, 2000

Bacevich, Andrew J., *American Empire: The Realities and Consequences of US Diplomacy.* Harvard Univ. Press, 2002

Brogan, H., *The Longman History of the United States of America.* 2nd ed. Longman, London and New York, 1999

Daalder, Ivo H. and Lindsay, James M., *America Unbound: the Bush Revolution in Foreign Policy.* Brookings Institution Press, Washington (D.C.), 2003

Duncan, Russell and Goddard, Joe, *Contemporary America.* 2nd ed. Palgrave Macmillan, Basingstoke, 2005

Fawcett, E. and Thomas, T., *America and the Americans.* London, 1983

Foner, E. and Garraty, J. A. (eds.) *The Reader's Companion to American History.* New York, 1992

Haass, Richard, *The Reluctant Sheriff: The United States After the Cold War.* New York, 1998

Herstein, S. R. and Robbins, N., *United States of America.* [Bibliography] ABC-Clio, Oxford and Santa Barbara (CA), 1982

Jenkins, Philip, *A History of the United States.* 2nd ed. Palgrave Macmillan, Basingstoke, 2002

Jennings, F., *The Creation of America.* CUP, 2000

Jentleson, B. W. and Paterson, T. G. (eds.) *Encyclopedia of US Foreign Relations.* 4 vols. OUP, 1997

Little, Douglas, *American Orientalism: The United States and the Middle East since 1945.* Univ. of North Carolina Press, 2002

Lord, C. L. and E. H., *Historical Atlas of the US.* Rev. ed. New York, 1969

Merriam, L. A. and Oberly, J. (eds.) *United States History: an Annotated Bibliography.* Manchester Univ. Press, 1995

Morison, S. E. with Commager, H. S., *The Growth of the American Republic.* 2 vols. 5th ed. OUP, 1962–63

Norton, M. B., *People and Nation: the History of the United States.* 4th ed. 2 vols. New York, 1994

Peele, Gillian, Bailey, Christopher, J., Cain, Bruce and Peters, B. Guy (eds.) *Developments in American Politics 4.* Palgrave Macmillan, Basingstoke, 2002

Pfucha, F. P., *Handbook for Research in American History: a Guide to Bibliographies and Other Reference Works.* 2nd ed. Nebraska Univ. Press, 1994

Prestowitz, Clyde, *Rogue Nation: American Unilateralism and the Failure of Good Intentions.* Basic Books, New York, 2003

Who's Who in America. Annual

Zunz, Oliver, *Why the American Century?* Univ. of Chicago Press, 1999

National library: The Library of Congress, Independence Ave. SE, Washington, D.C., 20540. *Librarian:* James H. Billington.

National statistical office: Bureau of the Census, Washington, D.C., 20233. *Director:* Louis Kincannon.

Website: http://www.census.gov

STATES AND TERRITORIES

GENERAL DETAILS

Against the names of the Governors, Lieut.-Governors and the Secretaries of State, (D.) stands for Democrat and (R.) for Republican.

See also Local Government on page 1343.

FURTHER READING

Official publications of the various states and insular possessions are listed in the *Monthly Check-List of State Publications,* issued by the Library of Congress since 1910.

The Book of the States. Biennial. Council of State Governments, Lexington, 1953 ff.

State Government Finances. Annual. Dept. of Commerce, 1966 ff.

Bureau of the Census. *State and Metropolitan Area Data Book.* Irregular.—*County and City Data Book.* Irregular.

Hill, K. Q., *Democracy in the 50 States.* Nebraska Univ. Press, 1995

Alabama

KEY HISTORICAL EVENTS

The early European explorers were Spanish, but the first permanent European settlement was French, as part of French Louisiana after 1699. During the 17th and 18th centuries the British, Spanish and French all fought for control of the territory; it passed to Britain in 1763 and thence to the USA in 1783, except for a Spanish enclave on Mobile Bay, which lasted until 1813. Alabama was organized as a Territory in 1817 and was admitted to the Union as a state on 14 Dec. 1819.

The economy was then based on cotton, grown in white-owned plantations by black slave labour imported since 1719. Alabama seceded from the Union at the beginning of the Civil War (1861) and joined the Confederate States of America; its capital Montgomery became the Confederate capital. After the defeat of the Confederacy the state was re-admitted to the Union in 1878. Attempts made during the reconstruction period to find a role for the newly freed black slaves—who made up about 50% of the population—largely failed, and when whites regained political control in the 1870s a strict policy of segregation came into force. At the same time Birmingham began to develop as an important centre of iron- and steel-making. Most of the state was still rural. In 1915 a boll-weevil epidemic attacked the cotton and forced diversification into other farm produce. More industries developed from the power schemes of the Tennessee Valley Authority in the 1930s. The black population remained mainly rural, poor and without political power, until the 1960s when confrontations on the issue of civil rights produced reforms.

TERRITORY AND POPULATION

Alabama is bounded in the north by Tennessee, east by Georgia, south by Florida and the Gulf of Mexico and west by Mississippi. Land area, 50,744 sq. miles (131,426 sq. km). Census population, 1 April 2000, 4,447,100 (55·4% urban), an increase of 10·1% since 1990; July 2005 estimate, 4,557,808.

Population in five census years was:

	White	Black	Indian	Asiatic	Total	Per sq. mile
1930	1,700,844	944,834	465	105	2,646,248	51·3
			All others			
1970	2,533,831	903,467	6,867		3,444,165	66·7
1980	2,872,621	996,335	24,932		3,893,888	74·9
1990	2,975,797	1,020,705	44,085		4,040,587	79·6
2000	3,162,808	1,155,930	128,362		4,447,100	87·6

Of the total population in 2000, 2,300,596 were female, 3,323,678 were 18 years old or older and 2,462,673 were urban. In 2000 the Hispanic population was 75,830, up from 24,629 in 1990 (an increase of 207·9%).

The large cities (2000 census) were: Birmingham, 242,820 (metropolitan area, 921,106); Montgomery (the capital), 201,568 (333,055); Mobile, 198,905 (540,258); Huntsville, 158,216 (342,376); Tuscaloosa, 77,906 (164,875).

SOCIAL STATISTICS

Births, 2003, 59,552 (13·2 per 1,000 population); deaths (2002), 46,069 (10·3 per 1,000 population). 2002 infant deaths, 9·1 per 1,000 live births. 2001: marriages, 44,158 (9·8); divorces, 24,059 (5·3).

CLIMATE

Birmingham, Jan. 46°F (7·8°C), July 80°F (26·7°C). Annual rainfall 54" (1,372 mm). Mobile, Jan. 52°F (11·1°C), July 82°F (27·8°C). Annual rainfall 62" (1,575 mm). Montgomery, Jan. 49°F (9·4°C), July 81°F (27·2°C). Annual rainfall 52" (1,321 mm). The growing season ranges from 190 days (north) to 270 days (south). Alabama belongs to the Gulf Coast climate zone (*see* UNITED STATES: Climate).

CONSTITUTION AND GOVERNMENT

The current constitution dates from 1901; it has had 742 amendments (as at April 2005). The legislature consists of a Senate of 35 members and a House of Representatives of 105 members, all elected for four years. The Governor and Lieut.-Governor are elected for four years.

For the 109th Congress, which convened in Jan. 2005, Alabama sends seven members to the House of Representatives. It is represented in the Senate by Richard Shelby (D. 1987–94; R. 1994–2011) and Jeff Sessions (R. 1997–2009).

Applicants for registration must take an oath of allegiance to the United States and fill out an application showing evidence that they meet State voter registration requirements.

Montgomery is the capital.

RECENT ELECTIONS

In the 2004 presidential election Bush polled 1,176,394 votes; Kerry, 693,933; Nader, 6,701.

CURRENT ADMINISTRATION

Governor: Bob Riley (R.), 2003–07 (salary: $96,361).
  Lieut.-Governor: Lucy Baxley (D.), 2003–07 ($48,870).
  Secretary of State: Nancy Worley (D.), 2003–07 ($71,500).

Government Website: http://www.alabama.gov

ECONOMY

Per capita personal income (2004) was $27,630.

Budget

In 2003 total state revenue was $19,099m. Total expenditure was $18,471m. (education, $7,054m.; public welfare, $4,532m.; hospitals, $1,211m.; highways, $1,164m.; health, $762m.) Outstanding debt, in 2003, $6,285m.

Performance

Gross State Product was $139,840m. in 2004, ranking Alabama 25th in the United States.

ENERGY AND NATURAL RESOURCES

Oil and Gas

In 2001 Alabama produced 9·3m. bbls. of crude petroleum.

Water

The total area covered by water is approximately 1,675 sq. miles.

Minerals

Principal minerals, 1999–2000 (in net 1,000 tons): limestone, 41,766; coal, 20,317; sand and gravel, 7,846. Value of non-fuel mineral production in 2003 was $863m.

Agriculture

The number of farms in 2002 was 47,000, covering 8·9m. acres; the average farm had 189 acres and was valued at $1,698 per acre.

Cash receipts from farm marketings, 2002: crops, $584m.; livestock and poultry products, $2,378m.; total, $2,962m. The net farm income in 2002 was $1,200m. Principal sources: broilers, cattle and calves, eggs, hogs, dairy products, greenhouses and nursery products, peanuts, soybeans, cotton and vegetables. In 2002 broilers accounted for the largest percentage of cash receipts from farm marketings; cattle and calves were second, eggs third, cotton fourth.

Forestry

Alabama had 22·99m. acres of forested land in 2002 of which 647,000 acres were national forest. Area of commercial timberland, 2002, 22,325,022 acres, of which 629,022 acres were public forests and 21,696,000 acres private forests. Harvest volumes in 1995, 294·12m. cu. ft softwood saw timber, 78·63m. cu. ft hardwood saw timber, 744·47m. cu. ft paper fibre and 11·74m. cu. ft poles. Total harvest, 1994, was 1,128·9m. cu. ft. The estimated delivered timber value of forest products in 1994 was $1,359m.

INDUSTRY

In 2001 the state's 5,200 manufacturing establishments had 312,000 employees, earning $10,202m. Alabama is both an industrial and service-oriented state. The chief industries are lumber and wood products, food and kindred products, textiles and apparel, non-electrical machinery, transportation equipment and primary metals.

Labour

In 2003, 1,875,000 were employed in non-agricultural sectors, of whom 371,000 were in in trade, transportation and utilities; 359,000 in government; 294,000 in manufacturing; 187,000 in education and health services; 186,000 in professional and business services. In 2003 the total labour force numbered 2,147,400, of whom 5·8% (124,700) were unemployed. A seasonally adjusted calculation for Dec. 2003 numbered the labour force at 2,163,000, with 126,100 (5·8%) unemployed. Average weekly earnings were $547·69 in Dec. 2002.

COMMUNICATIONS

Roads

Total road length in 2003 was 94,434 miles, comprising 73,476 miles of rural road and 20,958 miles of urban road. Registered motor vehicles numbered 4,329,245.

Rail

In 2001 the railways had a length of 4,728 miles including side and yard tracks.

Civil Aviation

In 2005 there were 97 public-use airports. There were 2,473,731 passenger enplanements in 2003.

Shipping

There are 1,600 miles of navigable inland water and 50 miles of Gulf Coast. The only deep-water port is Mobile, with a large ocean-going trade; total tonnage (1997), 36·3m. tons. The Alabama State Docks also operates a system of ten inland docks; there are several privately run inland docks.

SOCIAL INSTITUTIONS

Justice

In 2003 there were 385 law enforcement agencies and six state agencies employing 10,414 sworn and 5,306 civilian people. There were 194,334 offences reported in 2003 of which 18% were cleared by arrest. Total property value stolen in 2003 was $251,864,387 of which 18% was recovered. In total, for past and present felony and misdemeanour crimes, there were 27,156 people arrested for Part I offences, 183,012 for Part II offences, 16,524 for drug violations and 30,905 for alcohol violations. There were 297 homicides in 2003. As of 30 Sept. 2003 there were 27,727 people in prison or community-based facilities of which 190 were on death row awaiting execution. There were also 39,265 people on probation and/or parole. Following the reinstatement of the death penalty by the US Supreme Court in 1976 death sentences have been awarded since 1983. There were two executions in 2004 and four in 2005.

In 41 counties the sale of alcoholic beverages is permitted, and in 26 counties it is prohibited; but it is permitted in eight cities within those 26 counties. Draught beverages are permitted in 22 counties.

Education

In the school year 1996–97 the 1,333 public elementary and high schools required 44,942 teachers to teach 717,284 students enrolled in grades K-12. In 1995–96 there were 16 public senior institutions with 127,465 students and 4,887 faculty members. As of autumn 1998–99 the 19 community colleges had 73,432 students and 4,811 faculty members; two public junior colleges had 3,465 students and 257 faculty members; nine public technical colleges had 8,686 students and 652 faculty members.

Health
In 2002 there were 106 community hospitals with 15,900 beds. A total of 676,000 patients were admitted during the year.

Welfare
Medicare enrolment in July 2003 totalled 719,246. In 2002 a total of 765,328 people in Alabama received Medicaid. In Dec. 2004 there were 881,978 Old-Age, Survivors, and Disability Insurance (OASDI) beneficiaries. A total of 47,109 people were receiving payments under Temporary Assistance for Needy Families (TANF) in Sept. 2004.

RELIGION

Membership in selected religious bodies (in 2000): Southern Baptist Convention (1,380,121), United Methodist Church (327,734), Roman Catholic (150,647), Churches of Christ (119,049), Church of God (68,766), Assemblies of God (59,970). There are also large numbers of Black Baptists and members of the African Methodist Episcopal Zion Church.

CULTURE

Tourism
In 2001 tourists spent approximately $6·1bn. in Alabama, representing an increase of 1% over 2000 spending.

FURTHER READING

Alabama Official and Statistical Register. Montgomery. Quadrennial
Alabama County Data Book. Alabama Dept. of Economic and Community Affairs. Annual
Directory of Health Care Facilities. Alabama State Board of Health
Economic Abstract of Alabama. Center for Business and Economic Research, Univ. of Alabama, 2000

Alaska

KEY HISTORICAL EVENTS

Discovered in 1741 by Vitus Bering, Alaska's first settlement, on Kodiak Island, was in 1784. The area known as Russian America with its capital (1806) at Sitka was ruled by a Russo-American fur company and vaguely claimed as a Russian colony. Alaska was purchased by the United States from Russia under the treaty of 30 March 1867 for $7·2m. Settlement was boosted by gold workers in the 1880s. In 1884 Alaska became a 'district' governed by the code of the state of Oregon. By Act of Congress approved 24 Aug. 1912 Alaska became an incorporated Territory; its first legislature in 1913 granted votes to women, seven years in advance of the Constitutional Amendment.

During the Second World War the Federal government acquired large areas for defence purposes and for the construction of the strategic Alaska Highway. In the 1950s oil was found. Alaska became the 49th state of the Union on 3 Jan. 1959. In the 1970s new oilfields were discovered and the Trans-Alaska pipeline was opened in 1977. The state obtained most of its income from petroleum by 1985.

Questions of land-use predominate; there are large areas with valuable mineral resources, other large areas held for the native peoples and some still held by the Federal government. The population increased by over 400% between 1940 and 1980.

TERRITORY AND POPULATION

Alaska is bounded north by the Beaufort Sea, west and south by the Pacific and east by Canada. The total area is 663,267 sq. miles (1,717,854 sq. km), making it the largest state of the USA; 571,951 sq. miles (1,481,346 sq. km) are land and 91,316 sq. miles (236,507 sq. km) are water. It is also the least densely populated state. Census population, 1 April 2000, was 626,932, an increase of 14·0% over 1990; July 2005 estimate, 663,661.

Population in five census years was:

	White	Black	All Others	Total	Per sq. mile
1950	92,808	—	35,835	128,643	0·23
1970	236,767	8,911	54,704	300,382	0·53
1980	309,728	13,643	78,480	401,851	1·00
1990	415,492	22,451	112,100	550,043	1·00
2000	434,534	21,787	170,611	626,932	1·10

Of the total population in 2000, 324,112 were male, 436,215 were 18 years old or older and 411,257 were urban. Alaska's Hispanic population was 24,795 in 2000, up from 17,803 in 1990. As of July 2003, 19% of Alaska's population was identified as Alaska Native or American Indian.

The largest county equivalent and city is in the borough of Anchorage, which had a 2000 census population of 260,283. Census populations of the other 14 county equivalents, 2000: Fairbanks North Star, 82,840; Matanuska-Susitna, 59,322; Kenai Peninsula, 49,691; Juneau, 30,711; Bethel, 16,006; Ketchikan Gateway, 14,070; Kodiak Island, 13,913; Valdez-Cordova, 10,195; Nome, 9,196; Sitka, 8,835; North Slope, 7,385; Northwest Arctic, 7,208; Wade Hampton, 7,028; Wrangell-Petersburg, 6,684. Largest incorporated places in 2000 were: Anchorage, 260,683; Juneau, 30,711; Fairbanks, 30,224; Sitka, 8,335; Ketchikan, 7,922; Kenai, 6,942; Kodiak, 6,334; Bethel, 5,471; Wasilla, 5,469; Barrow, 4,581.

SOCIAL STATISTICS

Births, 2003, 10,086 (15·5 per 1,000 population); deaths (2002), 3,030 (4·7—the lowest rate in any US state). 2002 infant mortality (per 1,000 live births), 5·5. 2001: marriages, 5,100; divorces, 2,600.

CLIMATE

Anchorage, Jan. 12°F (–11·1°C), July 57°F (13·9°C). Annual rainfall 15" (371 mm). Fairbanks, Jan. –11°F (–23·9°C), July 60°F (15·6°C). Annual rainfall 12" (300 mm). Sitka, Jan. 33°F (0·6°C), July 55°F (12·8°C). Annual rainfall 87" (2,175 mm). Alaska belongs to the Pacific Coast climate zone (*see* UNITED STATES: Climate).

CONSTITUTION AND GOVERNMENT

The state has the right to select 103·55m. acres of vacant and unappropriated public lands in order to establish 'a tax basis'; it can open these lands to prospectors for minerals, and the state is to derive the principal advantage in all gains resulting from the discovery of minerals. In addition, certain federally administered lands reserved for conservation of fisheries and wild life have been transferred to the state. Special provision is made for federal control of land for defence in areas of high strategic importance.

The constitution of Alaska was adopted by public vote, 24 April 1956. The state legislature consists of a Senate of 20 members (elected for four years) and a House of Representatives of 40 members (elected for two years).

For the 109th Congress, which convened in Jan. 2005, Alaska sends one member to the House of Representatives. It is represented in the Senate by Ted Stevens (R. 1968–2009) and Lisa Murkowski (R. 2002–11). The franchise may be exercised by all citizens over 18.

The capital is Juneau.

RECENT ELECTIONS

In the 2004 presidential election Bush polled 190,889 votes; Kerry, 111,025; Nader, 5,069.

CURRENT ADMINISTRATION

Governor: Frank Murkowski (R.), Dec. 2002–Dec. 2006 (salary: $85,776).

Lieut.-Governor: Loren Leman (R.), Dec. 2002–Dec. 2006 ($80,040).

Government Website: http://www.state.ak.us

ECONOMY

Per capita personal income (2004) was $34,085.

Budget

In 2003 total state revenue was $6,924m. Total expenditure was $8,122m. (education, $1,694m.; public welfare, $1,313m.; highways, $811m.; government administration, $378m.; natural resources, $256m.) Outstanding debt, in 2003, $5,830m.

Performance

2004 Gross State Product was $34,023m., ranking Alaska 45th in the United States.

ENERGY AND NATURAL RESOURCES

Oil and Gas

Alaska ranks second behind Texas among the leading oil producers in the USA, with 18% of the national total. Commercial production of crude petroleum began in 1959 and by 1961 had become the most important mineral by value. Production: 2001, 351m. bbls. Proven reserves in 2000 were 4,861m. bbls. Oil comes mainly from Prudhoe Bay, the Kuparuk River field and several Cook Inlet fields. Revenue to the state from petroleum in 2003 was $1,947·6m. (84% of general fund revenues). General fund unrestricted oil revenue collections in 2003: royalty and bonus, $840·3m.; severance tax, $599·0m.; corporate income tax, $151·1m.; property tax, $48·7m. In 2001, 471bn. cu. ft of natural gas was produced. Natural gas (liquid) production, 1997, 35m. bbls. Proven reserves as at 31 Dec. 1997, 631m. bbls.

Oil from the Prudhoe Bay Arctic field is now carried by the Trans-Alaska pipeline to Prince William Sound on the south coast, where a tanker terminal has been built at Valdez.

Water

The total area covered by water is approximately 91,316 sq. miles.

Minerals

Estimated value of production, 2003, in $1,000: zinc, 486,916; gold, 191,986; industrial minerals (including sand, gravel and building stone), 100,000; silver, 90,773; lead, 70,094; coal, 37,975; peat, 175. Total 2003 value, $980·3m. Value of non-fuel mineral production in 2003 was $1,060m.

Agriculture

In some parts of the state the climate during the brief spring and summer (about 100 days in major areas and 152 days in the southeastern coastal area) is suitable for agricultural operations, thanks to the long hours of sunlight, but Alaska is a food-importing area. In 2002 there were 590 farms covering a total of 920,000 acres. The average farm had 1,559 acres in 2002 and was valued at $367 per acre.

Farm income, 2002: crops, $23m.; livestock and products, $28m. The net farm income in 2002 was $20m. Principal sources: greenhouse products, dairy products, hay and potatoes.

In 2002 there were 12,609 cattle and calves, 530 sheep and lambs, 1,200 hogs and pigs, and 2,900 poultry. There were about 15,000 reindeer in Alaska in 2002. Sales of reindeer meat and by-products in 2002 were valued at $453,000.

Forestry

Of the 126·87m. forested acres of Alaska, 10·46m. acres are national forest land. The interior forest covers 115m. acres;
more than 13m. acres are considered commercial forest, of which 3·4m. acres are in designated parks or wilderness and unavailable for harvest. The coastal rain forests provide the bulk of commercial timber volume; of their 13·6m. acres, 7·6m. acres support commercial stands, of which 1·9m. acres are in parks or wilderness and unavailable for harvest. In 1992, 590m. bd ft of timber were harvested from private land for a total value of $548·9m., and in 1993, 9·38m. bd ft from state land for $342·6m.

There are 677 designated wilderness areas throughout the USA, covering a total of 106·4m. acres (43·1m. ha.). Nearly 54% of the system is in Alaska (57·5m. acres or 23·3m. ha.).

Fisheries

In 2002 commercial fishing landed 5,066m. lb of fish and shellfish at a value of $811·5m. The most important species are salmon, crab, herring, halibut and pollock.

INDUSTRY

In 2003 the state's 549 manufacturing establishments had 11,000 employees, earning $339m. The largest manufacturing sectors are wood processing, seafood products and printing and publishing.

Labour

Total non-agricultural employment, 2003: 300,000. Employees by branch, 2003: government, 82,000; trade, transportation and utilities, 61,000; education and health services, 33,000; leisure and hospitality, 30,000; professional and business services, 23,000. The unemployment rate in 2003 was 8·0%.

COMMUNICATIONS

Roads

Alaska's highway and road system, 2003, totalled 14,229 miles comprising 2,069 miles of urban road and 12,160 miles of rural road. Registered motor vehicles numbered 636,783.

The Alaska Highway extends 1,523 miles from Dawson Creek, British Columbia, to Fairbanks, Alaska. It was built by the US Army in 1942, at a cost of $138m. The greater portion of it, because it lies in Canada, is maintained by Canada.

Rail

There is a railway from Skagway to the town of Whitehorse, the White Pass and Yukon route, in the Canadian Yukon region (this service operates seasonally, although only the section between Skagway and Carcross is in service). The government-owned Alaska Railroad runs from Seward to Fairbanks. This is a freight service with only occasional passenger use. In 2003 there were 466 miles of main line and 59 miles of branch line.

Civil Aviation

Alaska's largest international airports are Anchorage and Fairbanks. In 1999 Alaska Airlines flew 209·2m. km, carrying 13,604,000 passengers (1,530,300 on international flights). There were 4,432,447 passenger enplanements statewide in 2003. General aviation aircraft in the state per 1,000 population is about ten times the US average.

Shipping

Regular shipping services to and from the USA are furnished by two steamship and several barge lines operating out of Seattle and other Pacific coast ports. A Canadian company also furnishes a regular service from Vancouver, BC. Anchorage is the main port.

A 1,435 nautical-mile ferry system for motor cars and passengers (the 'Alaska Marine Highway') operates from Bellingham, Washington and Prince Rupert (British Columbia) to Juneau, Haines (for access to the Alaska Highway) and Skagway. A second system extends throughout the south-central region of Alaska linking the Cook Inlet area with Kodiak Island and Prince William Sound.

SOCIAL INSTITUTIONS

Justice
The death penalty was abolished in Alaska in 1957. In Oct. 2004 the prison population totalled 4,886.

Education
Total expenditure on public schools in 2003 was $1·4bn. In 2003 there were 8,100 public school teachers; average salary, 2002–03, $49,694. In 2003 there were 133,000 pupils enrolled at public schools. The University of Alaska (founded in 1922) main campuses had (autumn 1993) 33,087 students. Other colleges had 2,718 students in autumn 1993.

Health
In 2002 there were 19 community hospitals with 1,400 beds. A total of 48,000 patients were admitted during the year.

Welfare
Medicare enrolment in July 2003 totalled 47,749. In 2002 a total of 109,641 people in Alaska received Medicaid. In Dec. 2004 there were 62,781 Old-Age, Survivors, and Disability Insurance (OASDI) beneficiaries. A total of 12,708 people were receiving payments under Temporary Assistance for Needy Families (TANF) in Sept. 2004.

RELIGION

Many religions are represented, including Roman Catholic, Southern Baptist, Mormon, Lutheran and other denominations.

CULTURE

Tourism
About 2·7m. people visited the state in 2003–04; visitors spent $1,839m. in 2000–01.

FURTHER READING

Statistical Information: Department of Commerce and Economic Development, Economic Analysis Section, POB 110804, Juneau 99811. Publishes *The Alaska Economy Performance Report.*

Alaska Industry-Occupation Outlook to 1995. Department of Labor, Juneau, 1992.
Annual Financial Report. Department of Administration, Juneau.
Falk, Marvin W., *Alaska.* [Bibliography] ABC-Clio, Oxford and Santa Barbara (CA), 1995
Naske, C.-M. and Slotnick, H. E., *Alaska: a History of the 49th State.* 2nd ed. Univ. of Oklahoma Press, 1995

State library: POB 110571, Juneau, Alaska 99811-0571.

Arizona

KEY HISTORICAL EVENTS

Spaniards looking for sources of gold or silver entered Arizona in the 16th century, finding there people from several Native American groups, including Tohono O'odham, Navajo, Hopi and Apache. The first Spanish Catholic mission was founded in the early 1690s by Father Eusebio Kino, settlements were made in 1752 and a Spanish army headquarters was set up at Tucson in 1776. The area was governed by Mexico after the collapse of Spanish colonial power. Mexico ceded it to the USA in the Treaty of Guadelupe Hidalgo after the Mexican-American war (1848). Arizona was then part of New Mexico; the Gadsden Purchase (of land south of the Gila River) was added to it in 1853. The whole was organized as the Arizona Territory on 24 Feb. 1863.

Miners and ranchers began settling in the 1850s. Conflicts between Indian and immigrant populations intensified when troops were withdrawn to serve in the Civil War. The Navajo surrendered in 1865, but the Apache continued to fight, under Geronimo and other leaders, until 1886. Arizona was admitted to the Union as the 48th state in 1912.

Large areas of the state have been retained as Indian reservations and as parks to protect the exceptional desert and mountain landscape. In recent years this landscape and the Indian traditions have been used to attract tourist income.

TERRITORY AND POPULATION

Arizona is bounded north by Utah, east by New Mexico, south by Mexico, west by California and Nevada. Land area, 113,634 sq. miles (294,313 sq. km). Of the total area in 2001, 27% was Indian Reservation, 17% was in individual or corporate ownership, 20% was held by the US Bureau of Land Management, 16% by the US Forest Service, 13% by the State and 7% by others. Census population on 1 April 2000 was 5,130,632, an increase of 40·0% over 1990. July 2005 estimate, 5,939,292. The rate of Arizona's population increase during the 1990s was the second fastest in the USA, at 40%. Nevada is the only state to have had faster growth.

Population in six census years:

	White	Black	American Indian	Chinese	Japanese	Total	Per sq. mile
1910	171,468	2,009	29,201	1,305	371	204,354	1·8
1930	378,551	10,749	43,726	1,110	879	435,573	3·8
1960	1,169,517	43,403	83,387	2,937	1,501	1,302,161	11·3
			All others				
1980	2,260,288	74,159	162,854	383,768		2,718,215	23·9
1990	2,963,186	110,524	203,527	387,991		3,665,228	32·3
2000	3,873,611	158,873	255,879	842,269		5,130,632	45·2

Of the total population in 2000, 2,561,057 were female, 3,763,685 were 18 years old or older and 4,523,535 were urban. Arizona's Hispanic population was 1,295,617 in 2000 (25·3%) up from 739,861 in 1990 (an increase of 88·2%).

In 2004 the estimated population of Phoenix was 1,416,055; Tucson, 521,605; Mesa, 447,130; Glendale, 233,330; Scottsdale, 221,130; Chandler, 220,705; Tempe, 160,820; Gilbert, 164,685; Peoria, 132,300; Yuma, 86,070. The Phoenix–Mesa metropolitan area had a 2000 census population of 3,251,876.

SOCIAL STATISTICS

In 2003: births, 90,783 (16·1 per 1,000); deaths, 42,830 (7·8 per 1,000). In 2004: marriages, 37,882; dissolutions of marriages, 24,403. Infant mortality, 2004, 6·7 per 1,000 live births.

CLIMATE

Phoenix, Jan. 53·6°F (12°C), July 93·5°F (34°C). Annual rainfall 7·66" (194 mm). Yuma, Jan. 56·5°F (13·6°C), July 93·7°F (34·3°C). Annual rainfall 3·17" (80 mm). Flagstaff, Jan. 28·7°F (−1·8°C), July 66·3°F (19·1°C). Annual rainfall 22·8" (579 mm). Arizona belongs to the Mountain States climate zone (*see* UNITED STATES: Climate).

CONSTITUTION AND GOVERNMENT

The state constitution (1911, with 129 amendments) placed the government under direct control of the people through the initiative, referendum and the recall provisions. The state Senate consists of 30 members, and the House of Representatives consists of 60, all elected for two years.

For the 109th Congress, which convened in Jan. 2005, Arizona sends eight members to the House of Representatives. It is represented in the Senate by John McCain (R. 1987–2011) and Jon Kyl (R. 1995–2007).

The state capital is Phoenix. The state is divided into 15 counties.

RECENT ELECTIONS

In the 2004 presidential election Bush polled 1,104,294 votes; Kerry, 893,524; Badnarik, 11,856.

CURRENT ADMINISTRATION

Governor: Janet Napolitano (D.), 2003–07 (salary: $95,000).
   Secretary of State: Janice K. Brewer (R.), 2003–07 ($70,000).

Government Website: http://www.az.gov

ECONOMY

Per capita personal income in 2004 was $28,609.

Budget

In 2003 total state revenue was $17,927m. Total expenditure was $19,606m. (education, $6,419m.; public welfare, $4,482m.; highways, $1,840m.; health, $845m.; hospitals, $54m.) Outstanding debt, in 2003, $5,554m.

Performance

Gross State Product was $199,953m. in 2004, ranking Arizona 22nd in the United States.

ENERGY AND NATURAL RESOURCES

Primary energy sources are coal (35·2%), nuclear (24·5%), gas (19·5%) and hydroelectric (18·9%).

Electricity

As of 2002, 52 power generating plants were located in Arizona.

Oil and Gas

In 2004 oil production totalled 51,972 bbls. from 18 producing wells. Gas totalled 331m. cu. ft from nine producing wells.

Water

The total area covered by water is approximately 364 sq. miles.

Minerals

The mining industry historically has been and continues to be a significant part of the economy. By value the most important mineral produced is copper. Production in 2003 was 834,426 short tons. Most of the state's silver and gold are recovered from copper ore. Other minerals include sand and gravel, molybdenum, coal and gemstones. Value of non-fuel mineral production in 2003 was $2,100m.

Agriculture

Arizona, despite its dry climate, is well suited for agriculture along the water-courses and where irrigation is practised on a large scale from great reservoirs constructed by the USA as well as by the state government and private interests. Irrigated area in 2002 was 931,735 acres. The wide pasture lands are favourable for the rearing of cattle and sheep, but numbers are either stationary or declining compared with 1920.

In 2002 Arizona contained 7,300 farms and ranches and the total farm and pastoral area was 26·5m. acres; in 2002 there were 1,261,894 acres of crop land. In 2002 the average farm was 3,645 acres (the second largest average size in the USA after Wyoming) and was valued at $398 per acre. Farming is highly commercialized and mechanized and concentrated largely on cotton picked by machines.

Area under cotton in 2004: upland cotton, 240,000 acres (723,000 bales harvested); American Pima cotton, 3,000 acres (5,600 bales harvested).

In 2003 the cash income from crops was $1,385m., and from livestock and products $1,260m. The net farm income in 2004 was $1,399m. Most important cereals are wheat, corn and barley; most important crops include lettuce, cotton, citrus fruit, broccoli, spinach, cauliflower, melons, onions, potatoes and carrots. In 2004 there were 860,000 cattle, 114,000 sheep, 127,000 hogs and 30,000 goats.

Forestry

The state had a forested area of 25,900,000 acres in 2005, of which 11,430,000 acres were national forest.

INDUSTRY

In 2003 the state's 4,792 manufacturing establishments had 165,057 employees, earning $7,138m. Total value added by manufacturing in 2003 was $29,016m.

Labour

In the first quarter of 2004 (preliminary data) the state had 128,632 employers with an average of 2,324,920 employees earning an average quarterly wage of $8,853. Employees by branch, 2003 (in 1,000): trade, transportation and utilities, 445; government, 394; professional and business services, 320; education and health services, 246; leisure and hospitality, 232. The unemployment rate in 2004 was 5·0%.

COMMUNICATIONS

Roads

In 2003 there were 57,529 miles of roads comprising 21,900 miles of urban road and 35,629 miles of rural road. There were 3,573,994 registered vehicles.

Civil Aviation

In 2005 there were 6,487 registered aircraft and 323 landing facilities of which 217 were airports (including 81 for public use) and 106 were heliports. There were 20,534,545 passenger enplanements statewide in 2003.

SOCIAL INSTITUTIONS

Justice

A 'right-to-work' amendment to the constitution, adopted 5 Nov. 1946, makes illegal any concessions to trade-union demands for a 'closed shop'.

At 30 June 2005 the Arizona state prison held 29,912 male and 2,798 female prisoners. Chain gangs were reintroduced into prisons in 1995. The death penalty is authorized. There were three executions in 2000 but none since then.

Education

School attendance is compulsory between the ages of six and 16. In 2003–04, K-12 enrolment numbered 1,012,068 students. There are 234 school districts containing 1,199 elementary schools, 305 high schools and 72 combined schools. Charter schools first opened their doors in 1995. There are 694 charter schools providing parents and students with expanded educational choices. In 2003–04 the total funds appropriated by the state legislature for all education, including the Board of Regents and community colleges, was $4,181,833,300. The state maintains three universities: the University of Arizona (Tucson) with an enrolment of 33,070 in 2004; Arizona State University (three campuses) with 49,495; Northern Arizona University (Flagstaff) with 17,221.

Health

In 2005 there were 89 licensed hospitals; capacity 12,650 beds; more than 17,000 licensed physicians; 4,005 dentists; and 46,681 registered nurses.

Welfare

Medicare enrolment in July 2003 totalled 728,885. In 2002 a total of 878,362 people in Arizona received Medicaid. Old-age assistance (maximum depending on the programme) is given to needy citizens 65 years of age or older through the federal supplemental security income (SSI) programme. In Dec. 2003 SSI payments went to 13,211 aged, and 78,444 disabled and blind (average of $391·29 each.) In Sept. 2001, 100,618 individuals received Cash Assistance for an average $100·03 each. Cash Assistance cases numbering 39,059 received an average of $283·45 each. A total of 107,443 people were receiving payments under Temporary Assistance for Needy Families (TANF) in Sept. 2004.

RELIGION

The leading religious bodies are Roman Catholics and Latter-day Saints (Mormons); others include United Methodists, Presbyterians, Baptists, Lutherans, Episcopalians, Eastern Orthodox, Jews and Muslims.

CULTURE

Tourism

In 2004 Arizona had 28·4m. visitors (27·8m. domestic visitors and 0·6m. overseas visitors) and 434,635 tourism-related jobs. In 2004 domestic visitors spent $13·07bn.

FURTHER READING

Statistical information: College of Business and Public Administration, Univ. of Arizona, Tucson 85721. Publishes *Arizona Statistical Abstract.*

Alexander, David V., *Arizona Frontier Military Place Names: 1846–1912.* Las Cruces, NM, 1998

Arizona Commission of Indian Affairs. *Resource Directory, 1997/98.* Phoenix, 1998

Arizona Department of Commerce. *Community Profiles.* Phoenix, 1999

Arizona Department of Health Services, Center for Health Statistics. *Arizona Health Status and Vital Statistics, 1998.* Phoenix, 2000

Arizona Historical Society. *1999/2000 Official Directory, Arizona Historical Museums and Related Support Organizations.* Tucson, 1999

August, Jack L., *Vision in the Desert: Carl Hayden and the Hydropolitics in the American Southwest.* Texas Christian Univ. Press, Fort Worth, 1999

Leavengood, Betty, *Lives Shaped by Landscape: Grand Canyon Women.* Pruett Co., Boulder, 1999

Office of the Secretary of State. *Arizona Blue Book, 1997–98.* 1998

Shillingberg, William B., *Tombstone, A. T.: A History of Early Mining, Milling and Mayhem.* Arthur H. Clark Co., Spokane, 1999

State Government Website: http://www.az.gov/webapp/portal/

Arizona State Library, Archives & Public Records (ASLAPR) Website: http://www.lib.az.us

---

Arkansas

KEY HISTORICAL EVENTS

In the 16th and 17th centuries French and Spanish explorers entered Arkansas, finding there tribes of Chaddo, Osage and Quapaw. The first European settlement was French, at Arkansas Post in 1686, and the area became part of French Louisiana. The USA bought Arkansas from France as part of the Louisiana Purchase in 1803, it was organized as a Territory in 1819 and entered the Union on 15 June 1836 as the 25th state.

The eastern plains by the Mississippi were settled by white plantation-owners who grew cotton with black slave labour. The rest of the state attracted a scattered population of small farmers. The plantations were the centre of political power. Arkansas seceded from the Union in 1861 and joined the Confederate States of America. At that time the slave population was about 25% of the total.

In 1868 the state was re-admitted to the Union. Attempts to integrate the black population into state life achieved little, and a policy of segregation was rigidly adhered to until the 1950s.

In 1957 federal authorities ordered that high school segregation must end. The state governor called on the state militia to prevent desegregation; there was rioting, and federal troops entered Little Rock, the capital, to restore order. It was another ten years before school segregation finally ended.

The main industrial development followed the discovery of large reserves of bauxite.

TERRITORY AND POPULATION

Arkansas is bounded north by Missouri, east by Tennessee and Mississippi, south by Louisiana, southwest by Texas and west by Oklahoma. Land area, 52,068 sq. miles (134,855 sq. km). Census population on 1 April 2000 was 2,673,400, an increase of 13·7% from that of 1990. July 2005 estimate, 2,779,154.

Population in five census years was:

	White	Black	Indian	Asiatic	Total	Per sq. mile
1910	1,131,026	442,891	460	472	1,574,449	30·0
1960	1,395,703	388,787	580	1,202	1,786,272	34·0
			All others			
1980	1,890,332	373,768		22,335	2,286,435	43·9
1990	1,944,744	373,912		32,069	2,350,725	45·1
2000	2,138,598	418,950		115,852	2,673,400	51·3

Of the total population in 2000, 1,368,707 were female, 1,993,031 were 18 years old or older and 1,404,179 were urban. In 2000 the Hispanic population of Arkansas was 86,866, up from 19,876 in 1990. The increase of 337% was the second largest increase in the USA over the same period.

Little Rock (capital) had a population of 183,183 in 2000; Fort Smith, 80,268; North Little Rock, 60,433; Fayetteville, 58,047; Jonesboro, 55,515; Pine Bluff, 55,085; Springdale, 45,798; Conway, 43,167. The population of the largest metropolitan statistical areas in 2000 was: Little Rock–North Little Rock, 583,845; Fayetteville–Springdale–Rogers, 311,121; Fort Smith, 207,290; Texarkana, 129,749; Pine Bluff, 84,278.

SOCIAL STATISTICS

Births, 2003, were 37,784 (13·9 per 1,000); deaths (2002), 28,513 (10·5 per 1,000). 2002 infant mortality (per 1,000 live births), 8·3. 2001: marriages, 38,400; divorces, 17,100.

CLIMATE

Little Rock, Jan. 39·9°F, July 84°F. Annual rainfall 52·4". Arkansas belongs to the Gulf Coast climate zone (*see* UNITED STATES: Climate).

CONSTITUTION AND GOVERNMENT

The General Assembly consists of a Senate of 35 members elected for four years, partially renewed every two years, and a House of Representatives of 100 members elected for two years. The sessions are biennial and usually limited to 60 days. The Governor and Lieut.-Governor are elected for four years.

For the 109th Congress, which convened in Jan. 2005, Arkansas sends four members to the House of Representatives. It is represented in the Senate by Blanche Lincoln (D. 1999–2011) and Mark Pryor (D. 2003–09).

The state is divided into 75 counties; the capital is Little Rock.

RECENT ELECTIONS

In the 2004 presidential election Bush polled 572,898 votes; Kerry, 469,953; Nader, 6,171.

CURRENT ADMINISTRATION

Governor: Mike Huckabee (R.), 2003–07 (salary 2006–07: $80,848).

Lieut.-Governor: Winthrop Rockefeller (R.), 2003–07 ($39,075).

Secretary of State: Charlie Daniels (D.), 2003–07 ($50,529).

Government Website: http://www.state.ar.us

ECONOMY

Per capita personal income (2004) was $25,724.

Budget

In 2003 total revenue was $11,805m. Total expenditure was $12,085m. (education, $4,529m.; public welfare, $2,705m.; highways, $1,098m.; hospitals, $543m.; government administration, $443m.) Outstanding debt, in 2003, $3,295m.

Performance

2004 Gross State Product was $80,902m., ranking Arkansas 34th in the United States.

Banking and Finance

At 30 June 2005 total bank deposits were $41,354m.

ENERGY AND NATURAL RESOURCES

Oil and Gas

2001 production of crude oil was 8m. bbls.; natural gas, 467bn. cu. ft.

Water

The total area covered by water is approximately 1,110 sq. miles.

Minerals

The US Bureau of Mines estimated Arkansas' mineral value in 1992 at $287m. Mining employment totalled 3,600 in Oct. 1992. Crushed stone was the leading mineral commodity produced, in terms of value, followed by bromine. Value of domestic non-fuel mineral production in 2003 was $445m.

Agriculture

In 2002, 48,500 farms had a total area of 14·6m. acres; average farm was 301 acres and was valued at $1,469 per acre. 7·46m. acres were harvested cropland. Arkansas ranked first in the production of broilers in 2002 (1,182m. birds) and in the acreage and production of rice (46·2% of US total production) and third in turkeys (28·5m. birds).

Farm income, 2002: crops, $1,575m.; livestock and products, $2,952m. The net farm income in 2002 was $816m.

Forestry

In 2002 the state had a forested area of 18,771,000 acres, of which 2,483,000 acres were national forest.

INDUSTRY

In 2001 the state's 3,226 manufacturing establishments had 229,000 employees, earning $6,462m. Total value added by manufacturing in 2001 was $19,868m.

Labour

Total non-agricultural employment, 2003: 1,144,000. Employees by branch, 2003 (in 1,000): trade, transportation and utilities, 240; manufacturing, 206; government, 198; education and health services, 140; professional and business services, 103. The unemployment rate in 2003 was 6·2%.

COMMUNICATIONS

Roads

Total road mileage (2003), 98,539 miles—urban, 10,807; rural, 87,732. There were 1,888,555 registered motor vehicles.

Rail

In 2003 there were in the state 2,750 miles of commercial railway. In 2002 rail service was provided by three Class I (1,893 miles) and 23 short-line (Class III) railways (857 miles).

Civil Aviation

In 2005 there were 241 airports (100 public-use and 141 private). There were 1,617,841 passenger enplanements statewide in 2003.

Shipping

There are about 1,000 miles of navigable rivers, including the Mississippi, Arkansas, Red, White and Ouachita Rivers. The Arkansas River/Kerr-McClellan Channel flows diagonally eastward across the state and gives access to the sea via the Mississippi River.

SOCIAL INSTITUTIONS

Justice

In June 2003 there were 12,378 federal and state prisoners. In 1996, 524,000 violent crimes were committed and a total of 4,175,000 property crimes. The death penalty is authorized. There was one execution in 2004 and one in 2005.

Education

In the school year 1992–93 public elementary and secondary schools had 440,682 enrolled pupils and 25,771 classroom teachers. Average salary of teachers in elementary schools was $25,771, junior high $27,492 and high $27,760.

Higher education is provided at 34 institutions: nine state universities, one medical college, 12 private or church colleges, 12 community or two-year branch colleges and 12 technical colleges. Total enrolment in institutions of higher education in the autumn of 1993 was 99,344.

In the autumn of 1993 there were two vocational-training schools and nine technical institutes with 28,261 students.

Health

In 2002 there were 87 community hospitals with 9,900 beds. A total of 384,000 patients were admitted during the year.

Welfare

Medicare enrolment in July 2003 totalled 452,676. In 2002 a total of 579,278 people in Arkansas received Medicaid. In Dec. 2004 there were 553,533 Old-Age, Survivors, and Disability Insurance (OASDI) beneficiaries. A total of 21,095 people were receiving payments under Temporary Assistance for Needy Families (TANF) in Sept. 2004.

RELIGION

There were (2000) 665,307 Southern Baptists, 179,383 United Methodists, 115,967 Roman Catholics, 87,244 Baptist Missionary Association members and 86,342 adherents of the Church of Christ.

CULTURE

Broadcasting

An educational TV network provides 24-hour a day telecasting; it had five transmitters in 2000.

FURTHER READING

Statistical information: Arkansas Institute for Economic Advancement, Univ. of Arkansas at Little Rock, Little Rock 72204. Publishes *Arkansas State and County Economic Data.*

Agricultural Statistics for Arkansas. Arkansas Agricultural Statistics Service, Little Rock. Annual

Current Employment Developments. Dept. of Labor, Little Rock. Monthly

Statistical Summary for the Public Schools of Arkansas. Dept. of Education, Little Rock. Annual

California

KEY HISTORICAL EVENTS

There were many small Indian tribes, but no central power, when the area was discovered in 1542 by the Spanish navigator Juan Cabrillo. The Spaniards did not begin to establish missions until the 18th century, when the Franciscan friar Junipero Serra settled at San Diego in 1769. The missions became farming and ranching villages with large Indian populations. When the Spanish empire collapsed in 1821, the area was governed from newly independent Mexico.

The first wagon-train of American settlers arrived from Missouri in 1841. In 1846, during the war between Mexico and the USA, Americans in California proclaimed it to be part of the USA. The territory was ceded by Mexico on 2 Feb. 1848 and became the 31st state of the Union on 9 Sept. 1850.

Gold was discovered in 1848–49 and there was an immediate influx of population. The state remained isolated, however, until the development of railways in the 1860s. From then on the population doubled on average every 20 years. The sunny climate attracted fruit-growers, market-gardeners and wine producers. In the early 20th century the bright lights and cheap labour attracted film-makers to Hollywood, Los Angeles.

Southern California remained mainly agricultural with an Indian or Spanish-speaking labour force until after the Second World War. Now more than 90% of the population is urban, with the main manufacture being hi-technology equipment, much of it for the aerospace, computer and office equipment industries.

TERRITORY AND POPULATION

Land area, 155,959 sq. miles (403,932 sq. km). Census population, 1 April 2000, 33,871,648, an increase of 4,111,627, or 13·8%, over 1990. July 2005 estimate, 36,132,147. The growth rate reflects continued high though somewhat reduced natural increase (excess of births over deaths) as well as substantial net immigration.

Population in five census years was:

	White	Black	Japanese	Chinese	Total (incl. all others)	Per sq. mile
1910	2,259,672	21,645	41,356	36,248	2,377,549	15·2
1930	5,408,260	81,048	97,456	37,361	5,677,251	36·4
1960	14,455,230	883,861	157,317	95,600	15,717,204	100·8

	White	Black	Asian/other	Hispanic	Total	Per sq mile
1990	20,524,327	2,208,801	7,026,893	7,687,938	29,760,021	190·8
2000	20,170,059	2,263,882	11,437,707	10,966,556	33,871,648	217·2

Of the total population in 2000, 16,996,756 (50·2%) were female, 24,621,819 were 18 years old or older and 31,989,663 were urban (94·44%, the highest of the states).

In addition to having the highest population of any state in the USA, California has the largest Hispanic population of any state in terms of numbers and the second largest in terms of percentage of population. In 2000 there were 10,966,556 Hispanics living in California (32·4% of the overall population), representing a rise of 3,278,618 since 1990, the largest numeric rise of any state over the same period. By 2020 Hispanics are projected to form a majority.

The 50 largest cities with 2004 population estimates are:

Los Angeles	3,912,200	Santa Ana	349,100
San Diego	1,294,000	Anaheim	343,000
San Jose	926,200	Bakersfield	279,700
San Francisco	792,700	Riverside	277,000
Long Beach	487,100	Stockton	269,100
Fresno	456,100	Chula Vista	209,100
Sacramento	441,000	Fremont	209,100
Oakland	411,600	Modesto	206,200
Glendale	205,300	Pasadena	144,000
Huntington Beach	198,800	Corona	141,800
San Bernardino	196,300	Escondido	140,500
Oxnard	186,100	Orange	136,700
Oceanside	173,300	Fullerton	134,200
Irvine	171,800	Sunnyvale	131,700
Garden Grove	171,000	Palmdale	131,300
Ontario	167,900	Lancaster	129,200
Santa Clarita	164,900	Thousand Oaks	126,100
Pomona	158,400	Concord	124,900
Moreno Valley	155,100	El Monte	123,500
Fontana	154,800	Vallejo	121,100
Rancho Cucamonga	154,800	Simi Valley	118,800
Santa Rosa	154,400	Inglewood	117,600
Salinas	152,200	Costa Mesa	113,000
Torrance	146,200	Downey	112,800
Hayward	144,600	West Covina	111,400

Metropolitan areas (2000 census): Los Angeles–Riverside–Orange County, 16,373,645; San Francisco–Oakland–San Jose, 7,039,362; San Diego, 2,813,833; Sacramento–Yolo, 1,796,857; Fresno, 922,516.

SOCIAL STATISTICS

Births in 2003, 540,997 (15·2 per 1,000 population); deaths in 2002, 234,565 (6·7 per 1,000 population); marriages (2003), 194,914. Infant deaths, 2002, 5·5 per 1,000 live births.

CLIMATE

Los Angeles, Jan. 58°F (14·4°C), July 74°F (23·3°C). Annual rainfall 15" (381 mm). Sacramento, Jan. 45°F (7·2°C), July 76°F (24·4°C). Annual rainfall 18" (457 mm). San Diego, Jan. 57°F (13·9°C), July 71°F (21·7°C). Annual rainfall 10" (259 mm). San Francisco, Jan. 51°F (10·6°C), July 59°F (15°C). Annual rainfall 20" (508 mm). Death Valley, Jan. 52°F (11°C), July 100°F (38°C). Annual rainfall 1·6" (40 mm). California belongs to the Pacific Coast climate zone (see UNITED STATES: Climate).

CONSTITUTION AND GOVERNMENT

The present constitution became effective from 4 July 1879; it has had numerous amendments since 1962. The Senate is composed of 40 members elected for four years—half being elected every two years—and the Assembly, of 80 members, elected for two years. Two-year regular sessions convene in Dec. of each even numbered year. The Governor and Lieut.-Governor are elected for four years.

For the 109th Congress, which convened in Jan. 2005, California sends 53 members to the House of Representatives. It is represented in the Senate by Dianne Feinstein (D. 1993–2007) and Barbara Boxer (D. 1993–2011).

The capital is Sacramento. The state is divided into 58 counties.

RECENT ELECTIONS

In the 2004 presidential election Kerry polled 6,745,485 votes and Bush 5,509,826 votes. Badnarik came third with 50,165.

In the 2003 special election Arnold Schwarzenegger polled 4,206,284 votes and Cruz Bustamante polled 2,724,874.

Governor Gray Davis was the first statewide officeholder to be recalled in California. In the Statewide Special Election held on 7 Oct. 2003, 55·4% of Californians voted to remove Davis from the office, while 44·6% voted against the recall. With this outcome, Davis became only the second governor in United States history to be recalled from office. Republican Arnold Schwarzenegger won the replacement vote by a wide margin. The election results were certified on 14 Nov. 2003 and Governor Schwarzenegger was sworn into office on 17 Nov.

CURRENT ADMINISTRATION

Governor: Arnold Schwarzenegger (R.), Nov. 2003–Jan. 2007 (salary: $175,000).

Lieut.-Governor: Cruz Bustamante (D.), 2003–07 ($131,250).
Secretary of State: Bruce McPherson (R.), 2005–07 ($131,250).
Attorney General: Bill Lockyer (D.), 2003–07 ($148,750).

Government Website: http://www.ca.gov

ECONOMY

Per capita personal income (2004) was $35,172.

Budget

For the year ending 30 June 2004, total state revenues were $96·2bn. Total expenditures were $97·2bn. (education, $39·2bn.; health and human services, $26·8bn.; youth and adult corrections, $5·4bn.) Debt outstanding (2004) $33·0bn.

Performance

California's economy, the largest among the 50 states and one of the largest in the world, has major components in high technology, trade, entertainment, agriculture, manufacturing, tourism, construction and services. California experienced an economic recession in 2001 and a sluggish recovery in 2002, with greatest impacts in the high technology sector. The economic recovery, however, broadened and strengthened in 2003 and improved considerably in 2004. Personal income was up 5·4% from a year earlier in the first half of 2004. Made-in-California merchandise exports began to turn around in the fourth quarter of 2003 after falling by 26% in the preceding three years. In the first three quarters of 2004 exports were 20% higher than a year earlier. If California were a country in its own right it would be the world's eighth largest economy, after the USA, Japan, Germany, the United Kingdom, France, Italy and China. 2004 Gross State Product was $1,550,753m., the highest in the United States and representing more than 13% of the USA's total GDP. Taxable sales in 2003 totalled $460,097m.

Banking and Finance

In 2002 there were 9,510 establishments of depository institutions which included 5,807 commercial banks, 2,225 savings institutions and 1,378 credit unions.

In 2003 savings and loan associations had deposits of $231,071m. Total mortgage loans were $340,861m. On 31 Dec. 2003 all insured commercial banks had demand deposits of $37,844m. and time and savings deposits of $302,404m. Total loans reached $344,729m., of which real-estate loans were $248,152m. Credit unions had assets totalling $95,935m. and total loans outstanding were $58,066m.

ENERGY AND NATURAL RESOURCES

Electricity

Californians spent $20bn. on electricity in 1999. Total consumption amounted to 260,936m. kWh. 75% of electricity is derived from in-state resources. In Jan. 2001 Governor Gray Davis announced a state of emergency after power shortages led to a series of blackouts.

Oil and Gas

California is the nation's third largest oil producing state. Total onshore and offshore production was 257m. bbls. in 2002. California ranks tenth out of US states for the production of natural gas. Net natural gas production in 2002 was 322bn. cu. ft.

Water

The total area covered by water is approximately 7,736 sq. miles. Water quality is judged to be good along 83% of the 960 miles of assessed coastal shoreline.

Minerals

Gold output was 5,284 kg in 2003. Asbestos, boron minerals, diatomite, sand and gravel, lime, salt, magnesium compounds, clays, cement, silver, gypsum and iron ore are also produced.

In 2003 California ranked first among the states in non-fuel mineral production, accounting for more than 9% of the US total. The value of non-fuel minerals produced (2003) was $3·2bn.; the mining industry employed around 22,000 persons in 2003 (compared to 48,000 in the early 1980s).

Agriculture

California is the most diversified agricultural economy in the world, producing more than 350 agricultural commodities. It is by far the largest agricultural producer and exporter in the United States. The state grows more than half of the nation's total of fruits, nuts and vegetables. Many of these commodities are specialty crops and almost solely produced in California. There were, in 2003, 78,500 farms, comprising 27·1m. acres; average farm, 345 acres, valued at $3,526 per acre (2002). The net farm income in 2002 was $5,197m. (the largest of any state). In 2003 income from marketings reached $27·8bn. Fruit and nut cash receipts, at $7·84bn., were 1% above the previous year and comprised 27% of the total. Vegetable receipts increased 6% from $6·58bn. in 2002 to $6·96bn. in 2003 and comprised 24% of the total. Livestock and poultry receipts jumped 12% and also comprised 24% of the total. California's three leading commodities in cash receipts are milk with $4·03bn., nursery products with $2·44bn. and grapes with $2·30bn.

Production of cotton lint, 2000, was 578,200 short tons; other field and seed crops included (in 1m. short tons): hay and alfalfa, 9; sugarbeets, 2; rice, 2; wheat, 1. Principal fruit, nut and vegetable crops in 2001 (in 1,000 short tons): tomatoes, 9,183; wine, table and raisin grapes, 5,962; lettuce, 3,623; oranges, 2,044; lemons, 859; almonds, 415; grapefruit, 211.

In 2001 there were 1·6m. milch cows; 5·2m. all cattle and calves; 0·84m. sheep and lambs; and 0·15m. hogs and pigs.

Forestry

In 2002 California had 40·23m. acres of forested land, of which 18,515,000 acres were national forest. There are about 16·6m. acres of productive forest land, from which about 2,900m. bd ft are harvested annually. Total value of timber harvest, 2002, $452m. ($576m. in 2001). Lumber production, 2002, 1,690m. bd ft.

Fisheries

The catch in 2003 was 274m. lb; leading species in landings were squid, sardine, crab, urchin, mackerel, sole, salmon, tuna, herring and whiting.

INDUSTRY

In 2003 the fastest-growing industries were in public and private education, retail trade, health services, social services, management consulting and engineering. California achieved better employment levels in 2004. The improvement was primarily as a result of better job growth in construction, trade, transportation and utilities, and information. Limiting the improvement in job growth in 2004 were larger declines in government employment and smaller gains in employment in the financial sector.

Labour

In 2003 the civilian labour force was 17·5m., of whom 16·3m. were employed. A total of 47,600 jobs were lost during 2003, led by computer and electronic product manufacturing, information and management of companies and enterprises. The unemployment rate held steady at 6·7% in 2003.

INTERNATIONAL TRADE

Imports and Exports

Estimated foreign trade through Californian ports totalled $350bn. in 2003. Exports of made-in-California goods increased in 2003 after falling by 23% in the preceding two years. High technology goods dominate, comprising almost three-quarters of all made-in-California exports. Electronic components and computers account for almost half of total exports.

Total agricultural exports for 2002 were $6·5bn. California's top markets are Canada, European Union, Japan, Hong Kong, Mexico, South Korea, Taiwan, Indonesia, India and Malaysia.

COMMUNICATIONS

Roads
In 2003 California had 71,260 miles of roads inside cities and 98,320 miles outside. There were about 20·5m. registered cars and about 6·8m. commercial vehicles. Motor vehicle collision fatalities in 2003 were 5,714.

Rail
In addition to Amtrak's long-distance trains, local and medium-distance passenger trains run in the San Francisco Bay area sponsored by the California Department of Transportation, and a network of commuter trains around Los Angeles opened in 1992.

There are metro and light rail systems in San Francisco and Los Angeles, and light rail lines in Sacramento, San Diego and San Jose.

Civil Aviation
In 2003 there were a total of 939 public and private airports, heliports, stolports and seaplane bases.

A total of 54,970,030 passengers (14,623,903 international; 40,346,127 domestic) embarked/disembarked at Los Angeles airport in 2003. It handled approximately 2,022,076 tonnes of freight (987,864 international; 1,034,212 domestic). At San Francisco airport, in 2003, 28,786,385 passengers (6,695,151 international; 22,091,234 domestic) embarked/disembarked, and 483,413 tonnes of freight (282,574 tonnes international; 200,839 tonnes domestic) were handled. There were 77,512,512 passenger enplanements in 2003.

Shipping
The chief ports are San Francisco and Los Angeles.

SOCIAL INSTITUTIONS

Justice
A 'three strikes law', making 25-years-to-life sentences mandatory for third felony offences, was adopted in 1994 after an initiative (i.e. referendum) was 72% in favour. However, the state's Supreme Court ruled in June 1996 that judges may disregard previous convictions in awarding sentences. In 2004 there were 32 adult prisons. State prisons, 30 June 2004, had 152,859 male and 10,641 female inmates. In June 2004 there were some 3,932 juveniles in custody. As of 30 Nov. 2004 there were 7,527 adults serving 'three strikes' sentences. The death penalty has been authorized following its reinstatement by the US Supreme Court in 1976. Death sentences have been passed since 1980. The first execution since 2002 was carried out in Jan. 2005. In total there were two executions in 2005.

Education
Full-time attendance at school is compulsory for children from six to 18 years of age for a minimum of 175 days per annum. In autumn 2003 there were 6·9m. pupils enrolled in both public and private elementary and secondary schools. Total state expenditure on public education, 2002–03, was $39·2bn.

Community colleges had 1,631,629 students in autumn 2003. California has two publicly-supported higher education systems: the University of California (1868) and the California State University and Colleges. In autumn 2003 the University of California, with campuses for resident instruction and research at Berkeley, Los Angeles (UCLA), San Francisco and six other centres, had 208,391 students. California State University and Colleges with campuses at Sacramento, Long Beach, Los Angeles, San Francisco and 15 other cities had 407,530 students. In addition to the 28 publicly-supported institutions for higher education there are 117 private colleges and universities which had a total estimated enrolment of 322,018 in the autumn of 2003.

Health
In 2002 there were 383 community hospitals; capacity, 74,300 beds. A total of 3,430,000 patients were admitted in 2002. On 30 June 2001 state hospitals for the mentally disabled had 4,814 patients.

Welfare
Medicare enrolment in July 2003 totalled 4,078,426. In 2002 a total of 9,301,001 people in California received Medicaid.

On 1 Jan. 1974 the federal government (Social Security Administration) assumed responsibility for the Supplemental Security Income/State Supplemental Program which replaced the State Old-Age Security. The SSI/SSP provides financial assistance for needy aged (65 years or older), blind or disabled persons. An individual recipient may own assets up to $2,000; a couple up to $3,000, subject to specific exclusions. In 2002–03 fiscal year an average of 95,477 cases per month were receiving an average of $230 in assistance in the general relief programme. A total of 1,105,392 people were receiving payments under Temporary Assistance for Needy Families (TANF) in Sept. 2004.

RELIGION
There is a strong Roman Catholic presence. There were an estimated 994,000 Jews and 529,575 Latter-day Saints (Mormons) in 2000.

CULTURE

Tourism
The travel and tourism industry provides 5·4% of the state's $1·4trn. economy. Visitors in 2003 spent $78·2bn. generating $3·2bn. in state and local tax revenues. California was the state most visited by overseas travellers in 2003, with 3·9m. overseas visitors—25% of the market share. In 2002 there were 316m. person trips, 309m. from within the United States and 8m. from abroad.

FURTHER READING
California Government and Politics. Hoeber, T. R., *et al*, (eds.) Sacramento, Annual

California Statistical Abstract. 46th ed. Dept. of Finance, Sacramento, 2006

Economic Report of the Governor. Dept. of Finance, Sacramento, Annual

Bean, W. and Rawls, J. J., *California: an Interpretive History.* 6th ed. New York, 1993

Gerston, L. N. and Christensen, T., *California Politics and Government: a Practical Approach.* 3rd ed. New York, 1995

State Library: The California State Library, Library-Courts Bldg, Sacramento 95814.

Colorado

KEY HISTORICAL EVENTS
Spanish explorers claimed the area for Spain in 1706; it was then the territory of the Arapaho, Cheyenne, Ute and other Plains and Great Basin Indians. Eastern Colorado, the hot, dry plains, passed to France in 1802 and then to the USA as part of the Louisiana Purchase in 1803. The rest remained Spanish, becoming Mexican when Spanish power in the Americas ended. In 1848, after war between Mexico and the USA, Mexican

Colorado was ceded to the USA. A gold rush in 1859 brought a great influx of population, and in 1861 Colorado was organized as a Territory. The Territory officially supported the Union in the Civil War of 1861–65, but its settlers were divided and served on both sides.

Colorado became a state in 1876. Mining and ranching were the mainstays of the economy. In the 1920s the first large projects were undertaken to exploit the Colorado River. The Colorado River Compact was agreed in 1922, and the Boulder Dam (now Hoover Dam) was authorized in 1928. Since then irrigated agriculture has overtaken mining as an industry and is as important as ranching. In 1945 the Colorado-Big Thompson project diverted water by tunnel beneath the Rocky Mountains to irrigate 700,000 acres (284,000 ha.) of northern Colorado. Now more than 80% of the population is urban, with the majority engaged in telecommunications, aerospace and computer technology.

TERRITORY AND POPULATION

Colorado is bounded north by Wyoming, northeast by Nebraska, east by Kansas, southeast by Oklahoma, south by New Mexico and west by Utah. Land area, 103,718 sq. miles (268,628 sq. km).

Census population, 1 April 2000, 4,301,261, an increase of 30·6% over 1990. In July 2005 the Census Bureau estimate was 4,665,177.

Population in five census years was:

	White	Black	Indian	Asiatic	Total	Per sq. mile
1910	783,415	11,453	1,482	2,674	799,024	7·7
1950	1,296,653	20,177	1,567	5,870	1,325,089	12·7
			All others			
1980	2,571,498	101,703		216,763	2,889,964	27·9
1990	2,905,474	133,146		255,774	3,294,394	31·8
2000	3,560,005	165,063		576,193	4,301,261	41·5

Of the total population in 2000, 2,165,983 were male, 3,200,466 were 18 years old or older and 3,633,185 were urban. The Hispanic population in 2000 was 735,601, up from 424,302 in 1990 (an increase of 73·4%). Large cities, with 2001 populations: Denver City, 560,365; Colorado Springs, 369,853; Aurora, 283,650; Lakewood, 144,426; Fort Collins, 122,521; Pueblo, 103,030; Westminster, 102,905; Arvada, 102,470.

Main metropolitan areas (2001): Denver–Boulder–Greeley, 2,660,666; Colorado Springs, 533,526; Fort Collins–Loveland, 259,707; Pueblo, 144,383.

SOCIAL STATISTICS

Births, 2003, were 69,339 (15·2 per 1,000 population); deaths (2002), 29,210 (6·5 per 1,000 population). Infant mortality, 2002, 6·1 per 1,000 live births. Marriages, 2000, 36,104 (8·4 per 1,000 population); divorces, 20,063.

CLIMATE

Denver, Jan. 31°F (–0·6°C), July 73°F (22·8°C). Annual rainfall 14″ (358 mm). Pueblo, Jan. 30°F (–1·1°C), July 83°F (28·3°C). Annual rainfall 12″ (312 mm). Colorado belongs to the Mountain States climate zone (see UNITED STATES: Climate).

CONSTITUTION AND GOVERNMENT

The constitution adopted in 1876 is still in effect with (1989) 115 amendments. The General Assembly consists of a Senate of 35 members elected for four years, one-half retiring every two years, and of a House of Representatives of 65 members elected for two years. Sessions are annual, beginning 1951. Qualified as electors are all citizens, male and female (except convicted, incarcerated criminals), 18 years of age, who have resided in the state and the

precinct for 32 days immediately preceding the election. There is a seven-member State Supreme Court.

For the 109th Congress, which convened in Jan. 2005, Colorado sends seven members to the House of Representatives. It is represented in the Senate by Wayne Allard (R. 1997–2009) and Ken Salazar (D. 2005–11).

The capital is Denver. There are 64 counties.

RECENT ELECTIONS

In the 2004 presidential election Bush polled 1,101,255 votes; Kerry, 1,001,732; Nader, 12,718.

CURRENT ADMINISTRATION

Governor: Bill Owens (R.), 2003–07 (salary: $90,000).
  Lieut.-Governor: Jane Norton (R.), 2003–07 ($68,500).
  Secretary of State: Gigi Dennis (R.), 2005–07 ($68,500).

Government Website: http://www.colorado.gov

ECONOMY

Per capita personal income (2004) was $36,109.

Budget

In 2003 total revenue was $13,806m. and total expenditure $17,691m. Major areas of expenditure were: education, $6,134m.; public welfare, $3,443m.; highways, $1,378m.; correction, $724m.; health, $709m. Debt outstanding, in 2003, was $8,921m.

Performance

2004 Gross State Product was $199,969m., ranking Colorado 21st in the United States.

Banking and Finance

There are 180 commercial banks insured with the Federal Deposit Insurance Corporation, with $47,631m. in total assets.

ENERGY AND NATURAL RESOURCES

Oil and Gas

In 2001 Colorado produced 803bn. cu. ft of natural gas and 19·2m. bbls. of crude oil. It ranked sixth in the USA for daily gas production, and eleventh in crude oil production. Total production value of all hydrocarbons was $3·05bn.

Water

The Rocky Mountains of Colorado form the headwaters for four major American rivers: the Colorado, Rio Grande, Arkansas and Platte. The total area covered by water is approximately 376 sq. miles.

Minerals

Coal (2003): 35·8m. short tons were produced. In 2001 there were 14,000 people employed in mining, including 8,300 in extracting oil and natural gas. Value of domestic non-fuel mineral production in 2003 was $672m.

Agriculture

In 2002 farms and ranches numbered 30,000, with a total of 31·3m. acres of agricultural land. 5,748,610 acres were harvested crop land; average farm, 1,043 acres. Average value of farmland and buildings per acre in 2002 was $756. Farm income 2002: from crops, $1,379m.; from livestock and products, $3,502m. The net farm income in 2002 was $711m.

Production of principal crops in 2001: corn for grain, 149·8m. bu.; wheat for grain, 69·2m. bu.; barley for grain, 8·6m. bu.; hay, 4,780,000 tons; dry beans, 1,785,000 cwt; oats and sorghum, 11·4m. bu.; sugarbeets, 824,000 tons; potatoes, 23,274,000 cwt; vegetables, 9,523 tons; fruits, 21,900 tons.

In 2001 the number of farm animals was: 3,050,000 cattle, 91,000 milch cows, 780,000 swine and 370,000 sheep.

Forestry

The state had a forested area of 21,637,000 acres in 2002, of which 10,561,000 acres were national forest.

INDUSTRY

In 2001, 2,233,400 were employed in non-agricultural sectors, of which 692,400 were in services; 527,300 in trade; 346,800 in government; 198,500 in manufacturing; 145,800 in construction; 144,500 in finance and insurance; 144,000 in transportation and communications; 14,000 in mining. In manufacturing in 2002 the biggest sub-sectors were: non-electrical machinery, 28,800; food products, 25,400; printing and publishing, 24,900; instruments, 20,500; and electrical machinery, 16,700.

Labour

In 2002 the total labour force was estimated at 2,369,600 of which 2,243,400 were employed. Employees by branch, 2003 (in 1,000): trade, transportation and utilities, 404; government, 357; professional and business services, 287; leisure and hospitality, 246; education and health services, 214. The unemployment rate in 2003 was 6·0%.

Trade Unions

In 2000, 9% of all wage and salary workers were members of unions, compared to a national average of 13·5%. Among manufacturing workers, only 6·6% belonged to labour unions.

INTERNATIONAL TRADE

Imports and Exports

In 2001 Colorado exported $6·1bn. in goods. The largest trading partners were Canada, Japan, Germany, United Kingdom, China (including Hong Kong), Mexico and France. Largest export categories are electronic integrated circuits and microassemblies, automatic data processing machines, components for office machines, measuring instruments and medical devices.

Trade Fairs

The National Western Stock Show and Rodeo is the largest event of its kind in the USA, drawing over 600,000 visitors.

COMMUNICATIONS

Roads

In 2003 there were 86,821 miles of road (9,113 miles state highway agency), of which 18,128 miles were urban roads and 68,693 miles rural roads. There were 2,027,397 motor vehicle registrations.

Rail

There were 2,747 miles of railway in 2002.

Civil Aviation

In 2000 there were 79 airports open to the public; 17 with commercial service, 62 public non-commercial (general aviation) and 14 private non-commercial. There were 19,803,868 passenger enplanements statewide in 2003.

Telecommunications

Colorado is headquarters to Qwest Communications and AT&T Broadband and Internet Services. Other major communications employers are Level 3 Communications, Avaya and MCIWorldCom.

SOCIAL INSTITUTIONS

Justice

In June 2003 there were 19,085 federal and state prisoners. The death penalty is authorized but has not been used since 1997.

Education

In 2001 the public elementary and secondary schools had 742,145 pupils, 41,104 teachers (1999); teachers' salaries averaged $36,291. Enrolments in four-year state universities and colleges in 2000 were: University of Colorado at Boulder, 25,458 students; University of Colorado at Denver, 11,328; University of Colorado at Colorado Springs, 6,581; University of Colorado Health Sciences Centre, 2,358; Colorado State University (Fort Collins), 22,939; University of Northern Colorado (Greeley), 10,926; Colorado School of Mines (Golden), 3,287; Metropolitan State College of Denver, 16,773; Colorado State University-Pueblo (was University of Southern Colorado), 4,085; Mesa State College (Grand Junction), 4,893; Fort Lewis College (Durango), 4,260; Adams State College (Alamosa), 2,511; Western State College of Colorado (Gunnison), 2,456.

2000 total enrolments: private four-year universities and colleges, 23,000; two-year colleges, 80,168; all universities and colleges, 221,023.

Health

In 2002 there were 68 community hospitals with 9,600 beds. A total of 427,000 patients were admitted during the year.

Welfare

Medicare enrolment in July 2003 totalled 493,454. In 2002 a total of 425,878 people in Colorado received Medicaid. In Dec. 2004 there were 569,257 Old-Age, Survivors, and Disability Insurance (OASDI) beneficiaries. A total of 34,147 people were receiving payments under Temporary Assistance for Needy Families (TANF) in Sept. 2004.

RELIGION

The leading religious denominations (2000) in the state are: 752,505 Roman Catholics; 92,326 Latter-day Saints (Mormons); 85,083 Southern Baptists; 77,286 United Methodists; 72,000 Jews.

CULTURE

Broadcasting

There are 97 commercial and public radio stations, broadcasting on both AM and FM frequencies. There are also 14 commercial and four public television stations.

Press

There are 27 daily newspapers. In addition there are 41 weekly newspapers including seven regional business journals.

Tourism

Skiing is a major tourist attraction. Colorado is particularly renowned for the Rocky Mountain National Park and the Mesa Verde National Park, a World Heritage Site.

FURTHER READING

Statistical information: Business Research Division, Univ. of Colorado, Boulder 80309. Publishes *Statistical Abstract of Colorado.*
Griffiths, M. and Rubright, L., *Colorado: a Geography.* Boulder, 1983

State Government Website: http://www.colorado.gov
State Library: Colorado State Library, 201 E. Colfax, Rm. 314, Denver 80203.

Connecticut

KEY HISTORICAL EVENTS

Formerly territory of Algonquian-speaking Indians, Connecticut was first colonized by Europeans during the 1630s, when English Puritans moved there from Massachusetts Bay. Settlements were founded in the Connecticut River Valley at Hartford, Saybrook, Wethersfield and Windsor in 1635. They formed an organized commonwealth in 1637. A further settlement was made at New

Haven in 1638 and was united to the commonwealth under a royal charter in 1662. The charter confirmed the commonwealth constitution, drawn up by mutual agreement in 1639 and called the Fundamental Orders of Connecticut.

The area was agricultural and its population of largely English descent until the early 19th century. After the War of Independence Connecticut was one of the original 13 states of the Union. Its state constitution came into force in 1818 and survived with amendment until 1965 when a new one was adopted.

In the early 1800s a textile industry was established using local water power. By 1850 the state had more employment in industry than in agriculture, and immigration from the continent of Europe (and especially from southern and eastern Europe) grew rapidly throughout the 19th century. Some immigrants worked in whaling and iron-mining, but most sought industrial employment. Settlement was spread over a large number of small towns, with no single dominant culture.

Yale University was founded at New Haven in 1701. The US Coastguard Academy was founded in 1876 at New London, a former whaling port.

TERRITORY AND POPULATION

Connecticut is bounded in the north by Massachusetts, east by Rhode Island, south by the Atlantic and west by New York. Land area, 4,845 sq. miles (12,548 sq. km).

Census population, 1 April 2000, 3,405,565, an increase of 3·6% since 1990. July 2005 estimate, 3,510,297.

Population in five census years was:

	White	Black	Indian	Asian	Total	Per sq. mile
1910	1,098,897	15,174	152	533	1,114,756	231·3
1930	1,576,700	29,354	162	687	1,606,903	333·4
1980	2,799,420	217,433	4,533	18,970	3,107,576	634·3

	White	Black	Indian	Asian	Others	Total	Per sq. mile
1990	2,859,353	274,269	6,654	50,078	96,762	3,287,116	678·6
2000	2,780,355	309,843	9,639	82,313	148,567	3,405,565	702·9

Of the total population in 2000, there were 320,323 persons of Hispanic origin, up from 213,116 in 1990 (an increase of 50·3%). Of the total population in 2000, 1,756,246 were female, 2,563,877 were 18 years old or older and 2,988,057 were urban. There were 183 residents in five Indian Reservations.

The chief cities and towns are (2000 census populations):

Bridgeport	139,529	Danbury	74,848
New Haven	123,626	New Britain	71,538
Hartford	121,578	West Hartford	63,589
Stamford	117,083	Greenwich	61,101
Waterbury	107,271	Bristol	60,062
Norwalk	82,951	Meriden	58,244

SOCIAL STATISTICS

Births (2003) were 42,873 (12·3 per 1,000 population); deaths (2002), 30,122 (8·7 per 1,000 population). 2002 infant mortality rate (per 1,000 live births), 6·5. 2001: marriages, 18,600; divorces, 9,700.

CLIMATE

New Haven: Jan. 25°F (–3·8°C), July 74°F (23·4°C). Annual rainfall 45" (1,143 mm). Connecticut belongs to the New England climate zone (see UNITED STATES: Climate).

CONSTITUTION AND GOVERNMENT

The 1818 Constitution was revised in 1955. On 30 Dec. 1965 a new constitution went into effect, having been framed by a constitutional convention in the summer of 1965 and approved by the voters in Dec. 1965.

The General Assembly consists of a Senate of 36 members and a House of Representatives of 151 members. Members of each House are elected for the term of two years. Legislative sessions are annual.

For the 109th Congress, which convened in Jan. 2005, Connecticut sends five members to the House of Representatives. It is represented in the Senate by Christopher Dodd (D. 1981–2011) and Joseph Lieberman (D. 1989–2007).

There are eight counties. The state capital is Hartford.

RECENT ELECTIONS

In the 2004 presidential election Kerry polled 857,488 votes; Bush, 693,826; Nader, 12,969.

CURRENT ADMINISTRATION

Governor: M. Jodi Rell (R.), July 2004–Jan. 2007 (salary: $150,000).

Lieut.-Governor: Kevin Sullivan (D.), July 2004–Jan. 2007 ($110,000).

Secretary of State: Susan Bysiewicz (D.), 2003–07 ($110,000).

Government Website: http://www.ct.gov

ECONOMY

Per capita personal income (2004) was $45,506, the second highest in the country.

Budget

In 2003 total state revenue was $18,241m. Total expenditure was $20,721m. (education, $4,794m.; public welfare, $3,785m.; hospitals, $1,432m.; government administration, $1,011m.; highways, $694m.) Outstanding debt, in 2003, $22,490m.

Performance

Gross State Product in 2004 was $185,802m., ranking Connecticut 23rd in the United States.

ENERGY AND NATURAL RESOURCES

Water

The total area covered by water is approximately 699 sq. miles.

Minerals

The state has some mineral resources: crushed stone, sand, gravel, clay, dimension stone, feldspar and quartz. Total non-fuel mineral production in 2003 was valued at $142m.

Agriculture

In 2002 the state had 3,900 farms with a total area of 360,000 acres; the average farm size was 92 acres, valued at $9,491 per acre in 2002 (the highest of any state). Farm income (2002): crops $314m., and livestock and products $154m. The net farm income in 2002 was $100m. Principal crops are greenhouse and nursery products, grains, hay, tobacco, vegetables, maize, melons, fruit, nuts and berries.

Livestock (2002): 61,000 all cattle (value $59·8m.), 5,580 sheep, 3,232 swine and 3·8m. poultry ($8·7m.).

Forestry

Total forested area was 1,859,000 acres in 2002.

INDUSTRY

In 2002 the state's 5,384 manufacturing establishments had 214,910 employees, earning $9,878m. Total value added by manufacturing in 2002 was $27,673m.

Labour

Total non-agricultural employment, 2005, 1,674,800. Employees by branch, 2003 (in 1,000): trade, transportation and utilities, 305; education and health services, 263; government, 246; manufacturing, 200; professional and business services, 196. The unemployment rate in 2003 was 5·5%.

COMMUNICATIONS

Roads

The total length of highways in 2003 was 21,089 miles comprising 14,969 miles of urban road and 6,120 miles of rural road. Motor vehicles registered in 2003 numbered 2,963,540.

Rail

In 2003 there were 597 miles of railway route miles.

Civil Aviation

In 2005 there were 54 airports (44 private), 92 heliports and six seaplane bases. There were 3,120,676 passenger enplanements statewide in 2003.

SOCIAL INSTITUTIONS

Justice

In June 2004 there were 19,497 federal and state prisoners. The death penalty for murder is authorized, and was used in May 2005 for the first time since 1960.

Education

Instruction is free for all children and young people between the ages of four and 21 years, and compulsory for all children between the ages of seven and 16 years. In 2000 there were 1,135 public local schools, three academies, 17 state vocational-technical schools, 24 state or state-aided schools, 17 regional educational service centres and 375 non-public schools. In 2003 there were 553,204 public school pupils and in 1998–99 there were 36,012 full-time, professional public teachers. Expenditure of the state on public schools, 1999–2000, $5,300m. Average salary of teachers in public schools, 1999, $51,000 (the highest in the United States). In 1999–2000 expenditure per pupil (public elementary and secondary) was $9,365. There were an estimated 28,200 public high-school graduates in 1999.

In 2002 Connecticut had 46 colleges, of which one state university, one external degree college, four state colleges, 12 community-technical colleges and a US Coast Guard Academy were state funded. The University of Connecticut at Storrs, founded 1881, had 26,629 students in 2003. Yale University, New Haven, founded in 1701, had 11,032 students in 1998; Wesleyan University, Middletown, founded 1831, 3,204 students in 1998; Trinity College, Hartford, founded 1823, 2,258 students in 1998; Connecticut College, New London, founded 1915, 1,800 students in 1998; The University of Hartford, founded 1877, 6,892 students in 1998. The state colleges had 35,448 students in 2003. The US Coast Guard Academy had 795 students in 1998. There were 19 independent (four-year course) colleges and four independent (two-year course) colleges as well as two seminaries, a College of Hospitality Management and a Learning Collaborative.

Health

In 2003 there were 31 community hospitals with 7,108 beds. A total of 293,000 patients were admitted during 2002.

Welfare

Medicare enrolment in July 2003 totalled 522,403. In 2003 a total of 318,000 people in Connecticut received Medicaid. In Dec. 2004 there were 583,427 Old-Age, Survivors, and Disability Insurance (OASDI) beneficiaries. A total of 42,063 people were receiving payments under Temporary Assistance for Needy Families (TANF) in Sept. 2004.

RELIGION

The leading religious denominations (2000) in the state are Roman Catholic (1,372,562 members), United Churches of Christ (124,770), Jewish (108,280), Protestant Episcopal (73,550) and United Methodist (51,183). There are also large numbers of Black Baptists.

CULTURE

Broadcasting

In 2003 there were 71 broadcasting stations and 12 television stations.

Press

In 1994 there were 141 newspapers.

FURTHER READING

State Register and Manual. Secretary of State. Hartford (CT). Annual
Halliburton, W. J., *The People of Connecticut*. Norwalk, 1985

State Library: Connecticut State Library, 231 Capitol Avenue, Hartford (CT) 06105.
State Book Store: Dept. of Environmental Protection, 79 Elm St., Hartford (CT) 06106.
Business Incentives: Connecticut Economic Resource Center, 805 Brook St., Rocky Hill (CT) 06067.
Connecticut Tourism: Dept. of Economic and Community Development, 865 Brook St., Rocky Hill (CT) 06067.

Delaware

KEY HISTORICAL EVENTS

Delaware was the territory of Algonquian-speaking Indians who were displaced by European settlement in the 17th century. The first settlers were Swedes who came in 1638 to build Fort Christina (now Wilmington), and colonize what they called New Sweden. Their colony was taken by the Dutch from New Amsterdam in 1655. In 1664 the British took the whole New Amsterdam colony, including Delaware, and called it New York.

In 1682 Delaware was granted to William Penn, who wanted access to the coast for his Pennsylvania colony. Union of the two colonies was unpopular, and Delaware gained its own government in 1704, although it continued to share a royal governor with Pennsylvania until the War of Independence. Delaware then became one of the 13 original states of the Union and the first to ratify the federal constitution (on 7 Dec. 1787).

The population was of Swedish, Finnish, British and Irish extraction. The land was low-lying and fertile, and the use of slave labour was legal. There was a significant number of black slaves, but Delaware was a border state during the Civil War (1861–65) and did not leave the Union.

19th-century immigrants were mostly European Jews, Poles, Germans and Italians. The north became industrial and densely populated, more so after the Second World War with the rise of the petrochemical industry. Industry in general profited from the opening of the Chesapeake and Delaware Canal in 1829; it was converted to a toll-free deep channel for ocean-going ships in 1919.

TERRITORY AND POPULATION

Delaware is bounded in the north by Pennsylvania, northeast by New Jersey, east by Delaware Bay, south and west by Maryland. Land area 1,954 sq. miles (5,061 sq. km). Census population, 1 April 2000, was 783,600, an increase of 17·6% since 1990. July 2005 estimate, 843,524.

Population in five census years was:

	White	Black	Indian	Asiatic	Total	Per sq. mile
1910	171,102	31,181	5	34	202,322	103·0
1960	384,327	60,688	597	410	446,292	224·0
			All others			
1980	488,002	96,157	10,179		594,338	290·8
1990	535,094	112,460	18,614		666,168	325·9
2000	584,773	150,666	48,161		783,600	401·0

Of the total population in 2000, 403,059 were female, 589,013 were 18 years old or older and 627,758 were urban. The Hispanic population in 2000 was 37,277, up from 15,824 in 1990 (an increase of 135·6%).

The 2000 census figures show Wilmington with a population of 72,664; Dover, 32,135; Newark, 28,547; Milford City, 6,732; Seaford City, 6,699; Middletown, 6,161.

SOCIAL STATISTICS

Births in 2003, 11,329 (13·9 per 1,000 population); deaths (2002), 6,861 (8·5 per 1,000 population). 2002 infant mortality (per 1,000 live births), 8·7. 2001: marriages, 5,200 (6·7 per 1,000 population); divorces, 3,100 (4·0).

CLIMATE

Wilmington, Jan. 31°F (−0·6°C), July 76°F (24·4°C). Annual rainfall 43" (1,076 mm). Delaware belongs to the Atlantic Coast climate zone (see UNITED STATES: Climate).

CONSTITUTION AND GOVERNMENT

The present constitution (the fourth) dates from 1897, and has had 51 amendments; it was not ratified by the electorate but promulgated by the Constitutional Convention. The General Assembly consists of a Senate of 21 members elected for four years and a House of Representatives of 41 members elected for two years.

For the 109th Congress, which convened in Jan. 2005, Delaware sends one member to the House of Representatives. It is represented in the Senate by Joseph Biden (D. 1973–2009) and Thomas Carper (D. 2001–07).

The state capital is Dover. Delaware is divided into three counties.

RECENT ELECTIONS

In the 2004 presidential election Kerry polled 200,152 votes; Bush, 171,660; Nader, 2,153.

CURRENT ADMINISTRATION

Governor: Ruth Ann Minner (D.), 2005–09 (salary: $132,500).
   Lieut.-Governor: John C. Carney, Jr (D.), 2005–09 ($73,027).
   Secretary of State: Dr Harriet Smith Windsor (D.), appointed 2001 ($119,682).

Government Website: http://www.delaware.gov

ECONOMY

Per capita personal income (2004) was $35,559.

Budget

In 2003 total revenue was $5,041m. Total expenditure was $4,858m. (education, $1,594m.; public welfare, $748m.; highways, $346m.; government administration, $309m.; health, $283m.) Debt outstanding, in 2003, $4,358m.

Performance

2004 Gross State Product was $54,274m., ranking Delaware 38th in the United States.

Banking and Finance

Delaware National Bank has branches statewide. Also based in Delaware, MBNA is the world's largest independent credit card issuer, with managed loans of $97·5bn.

ENERGY AND NATURAL RESOURCES

Electricity

Net generation of electric energy, 2001, 1·9bn. kWh.

Water

The total area covered by water is approximately 536 sq. miles.

Minerals

The mineral resources of Delaware are not extensive, consisting chiefly of clay products, stone, sand and gravel and magnesium compounds. Total non-fuel mineral production in 2003 was valued at $16m. (includes production for District of Columbia).

Agriculture

Delaware is mainly an industrial state, with agriculture as its principal industry. There were 560,000 acres in 2,400 farms in 2002. The average farm was 233 acres and was valued (land and buildings) at $4,054 per acre in 2002. Farm income (2002): crops $177m., and livestock and products $546m. The net farm income in 2002 was $82m. The major product is broilers, accounting for $494·2m. in cash receipts, out of total farm cash receipts of $727·7m. in 2002.

The chief crops are greenhouse products, corn for feed and soybeans.

Forestry

Total forested area was 383,000 acres in 2002.

INDUSTRY

In 2001 the state's 694 manufacturing establishments had 42,000 employees, earning $1,745m. Total value added by manufacturing in 2001 was $6,621m. Main manufactures are chemicals, transport equipment and food.

Labour

Total non-agricultural employment, 2003, 414,000. Employees by branch, 2003 (in 1,000): trade, transportation and utilities, 78; professional and business services, 59; government, 57; education and health services, 50; financial activities, 46. The unemployment rate in 2003 was 4·4%.

COMMUNICATIONS

Roads

In 2003 there were 5,893 miles of roads comprising 2,028 miles of urban road and 3,865 miles of rural road. In 2003 total vehicles registered numbered 686,817.

Rail

In 1999 the state had 271 miles of active rail line, 23 miles of which is part of Amtrak's high-speed Northeast corridor. In 1999 there were 710,245 passenger trips beginning or ending in Delaware—645,808 of which were commuter trips. An important component of Delaware's freight infrastructure is the rail access to the Port of Wilmington.

Civil Aviation

In 2005 Delaware had 15 public use airports and one helistop. There were 2,381 passenger enplanements statewide in 2003.

SOCIAL INSTITUTIONS

Justice

In June 2003 there were 6,879 federal and state prisoners. The death penalty is authorized. There were two executions in 2001, none in 2002, 2003 or 2004, and one in 2005.

Education

The state has free public schools and compulsory school attendance. In Sept. 1999 the elementary and secondary public schools had 113,598 enrolled pupils and 7,023 classroom teachers. Another 26,584 children were enrolled in private and parochial schools. State appropriation for public schools (financial year 1998–99) was about $615m. Average salary of classroom teachers (financial year 1998–99), $43,164. The state supports the University of Delaware at Newark (1834) which had 930 full-time faculty members and 21,346 students in Sept. 1998, Delaware State University, Dover (1892), with 177 full-time faculty members and 3,155 students, and the four campuses of Delaware Technical and Community College (Wilmington, Stanton, Dover and Georgetown) with 301 full-time faculty members and 45,535 students.

Health

In 2002 there were six community hospitals with 2,000 beds. A total of 93,000 patients were admitted during the year.

Welfare

Medicare enrolment in July 2003 totalled 119,302. In 2002 a total of 167,162 people in Delaware received Medicaid. In Dec. 2004 there were 145,825 Old-Age, Survivors, and Disability Insurance (OASDI) beneficiaries. A total of 12,757 people were receiving payments under Temporary Assistance for Needy Families (TANF) in Sept. 2004.

RELIGION

The leading religious denominations are Roman Catholics, Methodists, Episcopalians and Lutherans.

FURTHER READING

Statistical information: Delaware Economic Development Office, Dover, DE 19901. Publishes *Delaware Statistical Overview.*
State Manual, Containing Official List of Officers, Commissions and County Officers. Secretary of State, Dover. Annual
Smeal, L., *Delaware Historical and Biographical Index.* New York, 1984

District of Columbia

KEY HISTORICAL EVENTS

The District of Columbia, organized in 1790, is the seat of the government of the USA, for which the land was ceded by the states of Maryland and Virginia to the USA as a site for the national capital. It was established under Acts of Congress in 1790 and 1791. Congress first met in it in 1800 and federal authority over it became vested in 1801. In 1846 the land ceded by Virginia (about 33 sq. miles) was given back.

TERRITORY AND POPULATION

The District forms an enclave on the Potomac River, where the river forms the southwest boundary of Maryland. The land area of the District of Columbia is 61 sq. miles (159 sq. km).

Census population, 1 April 2000, was 572,059 (100% urban), a decrease of 5·72% from that of 1990. July 2005 estimate, 550,521. Metropolitan area of Washington, D.C.–Baltimore (2000), 7,608,070. The Hispanic population in 2000 was 44,953, up from 32,710 in 1990 (an increase of 37·4%). Of the total population in 2000, 302,693 were female and 457,067 were 18 years old or older.

Population in five census years was:

	White	Black	Indian	Chinese and Japanese	Total	Per sq. mile
1910	236,128	94,446	68	427	331,069	5,517·8
1960	345,263	411,737	587	3,532	763,956	12,523·9
				All others		
1980	171,768	448,906		17,659	638,333	10,464·4
1990	179,667	339,604		87,629	606,900	9,949·2
2000	176,101	343,312		52,646	572,059	9,378·0

SOCIAL STATISTICS

Births, 2003, were 7,619 (13·5 per 1,000 population); deaths (2002), 5,851 (10·2). 2002 infant mortality rate (per 1,000 live births), 11·3. 2001: marriages, 3,500 (6·8 per 1,000 population); divorces, 1,200 (2·3). The abortion rate, at 68·1 for every 1,000 women in 2000, is the highest of any US state.

CLIMATE

Washington, Jan. 34°F (1·1°C), July 77°F (25°C). Annual rainfall 43" (1,064 mm). The District of Columbia belongs to the Atlantic Coast climate zone (*see* UNITED STATES: Climate).

CONSTITUTION AND GOVERNMENT

Local government, from 1 July 1878 until Aug. 1967, was that of a municipal corporation administered by a board of three commissioners, of whom two were appointed from civil life by the President, and confirmed by the Senate, for a term of three years each. The other commissioner was detailed by the President from the Engineer Corps of the Army. The Commission form of government was abolished in 1967 and a new Mayor Council instituted with officers appointed by the President with the advice and consent of the Senate. On 24 Dec. 1973 the appointed officers were replaced by an elected Mayor and councillors, with full legislative powers in local matters as from 1974. Congress retains the right to legislate, to veto or supersede the Council's acts. The 23rd amendment to the federal constitution (1961) conferred the right to vote in national elections. The District has one delegate and one shadow delegate to the House of Representatives and two shadow senators. The Congressman may participate but not vote on the House floor.

RECENT ELECTIONS

In the 2004 presidential election Kerry polled 202,970 votes (89·2% of the vote—Kerry's best result); Bush, 21,256; Nader, 1,485.

CURRENT ADMINISTRATION

Mayor: Anthony A. Williams (D.), 2003–07 (salary: $145,600).
  Secretary of the District (acting): Patricia Elwood (D.), appointed May 2005 (salary: $128,619).

Government Website: http://www.dc.gov

ECONOMY

Per capita personal income (2004) was $52,101, the highest in the country.

Budget

The District's revenues are derived from a tax on real and personal property, sales taxes, taxes on corporations and companies, licences for conducting various businesses and from federal payments. The District of Columbia has no bonded debt not covered by its accumulated sinking fund.

Performance

Gross State Product was $76,685m. in 2004.

ENERGY AND NATURAL RESOURCES

Water

The total area covered by water is approximately 7 sq. miles.

Minerals

Non-fuel mineral production is included in figures for Delaware.

INDUSTRY

In 2001 the state's 162 manufacturing establishments had 3,000 employees, earning $92m. Total value added by manufacturing in 2001 was $93m. The main industries are government service, service, wholesale and retail trade, finance, real estate, insurance, communications, transport and utilities.

Labour

Total non-agricultural employment, 2003, 665,000. Employees by branch, 2003 (in 1,000): government, 231; professional and business services, 141; education and health services, 88; leisure and hospitality, 49; financial activities, 31. The unemployment rate in 2003 was 7·0%.

COMMUNICATIONS

Roads
In 2003 there were 1,535 miles of roads (1,428 miles state highway agency). In 2003 there were 228,351 registered vehicles.

Rail
There is a metro in Washington extending to 130 km, and two commuter rail networks.

Civil Aviation
The District is served by three general airports; across the Potomac River in Arlington, Va., is National Airport; in Chantilly, Va., is Dulles International Airport; and in Maryland is Baltimore–Washington International Airport. There were 13,632,535 passenger enplanements in 2000.

SOCIAL INSTITUTIONS

Justice
The death penalty was declared unconstitutional in the District of Columbia on 14 Nov. 1973. In June 2002 there were 3,023 federal and state prisoners.

The District's Court system is the Judicial Branch of the District of Columbia. It is the only completely unified court system in the United States, possibly because of the District's unique city-state jurisdiction. Until the District of Columbia Court Reform and Criminal Procedure Act of 1970, the judicial system was almost entirely in the hands of Federal government. Since that time, the system has been similar in most respects to the autonomous systems of the states.

Education
In 1996 there were an estimated 105,700 pupils enrolled at elementary and secondary public schools. Average expenditure per pupil in 1997 was $8,167.

Higher education is given through the Consortium of Universities of the Metropolitan Washington Area, which consists of six universities and three colleges: Georgetown University, founded in 1795 by the Jesuit Order; George Washington University, non-sectarian founded in 1821; Howard University, founded in 1867; Catholic University of America, founded in 1887; American University (Methodist), founded in 1893; University of District of Columbia, founded 1976; Gallaudet College, founded 1864; Trinity College in Washington, D.C. (women's college), founded 1897. There are 18 institutes of higher education altogether.

Health
In 2002 there were ten community hospitals with 3,400 beds. A total of 137,000 patients were admitted during the year.

Welfare
Medicare enrolment in July 2003 totalled 73,794. In 2002 a total of 193,494 people in the District of Columbia received Medicaid. In Dec. 2004 there were 71,905 Old-Age, Survivors, and Disability Insurance (OASDI) beneficiaries. A total of 43,625 people were receiving payments under Temporary Assistance for Needy Families (TANF) in Sept. 2004.

RELIGION
The largest churches are the Protestant and Roman Catholic Christian churches; there are also Jewish, Eastern Orthodox and Islamic congregations.

CULTURE

Tourism
About 20m. visitors stay in the District every year and spend about $1,000m.

FURTHER READING
Statistical Information: The Metropolitan Washington Board of Trade publications.
Reports of the Commissioners of the District of Columbia. Annual. Washington
Bowling, K. R., *The Creation of Washington D.C.: the Idea and the Location of the American Capital.* Washington (D.C.), 1991

Florida

KEY HISTORICAL EVENTS
There were French and Spanish settlements in Florida in the 16th century, of which the Spanish, at St Augustine in 1565, proved permanent. Florida was claimed by Spain until 1763 when it passed to Britain. Although regained by Spain in 1783, the British used it as a base for attacks on American forces during the war of 1812. Gen. Andrew Jackson captured Pensacola for the USA in 1818. In 1819 a treaty was signed which ceded Florida to the USA with effect from 1821 and it became a Territory of the USA in 1822.

Florida had been the home of the Apalachee and Timucua Indians. After 1770 groups of Creek Indians began to arrive as refugees from the European-Indian wars. These 'Seminoles' or runaways attracted other refugees including slaves, the recapture of whom was the motive for the first Seminole War of 1817–18. A second war followed in 1835–42, when the Seminoles retreated to the Everglades swamps. After a third war in 1855–58 most Seminoles were forced or persuaded to move to reserves in Oklahoma.

Florida became a state in 1845. About half of the population were black slaves. At the outbreak of Civil War in 1861 the state seceded from the Union.

During the 20th century Florida continued to grow fruit and vegetables, but real-estate development (often for retirement) and the growth of tourism and the aerospace industry set it apart from other ex-plantation states.

TERRITORY AND POPULATION
Florida is a peninsula bounded in the west by the Gulf of Mexico, south by the Straits of Florida, east by the Atlantic, north by Georgia and northwest by Alabama. Land area, 53,927 sq. miles (139,670 sq. km). Census population, 1 April 2000, 15,982,378, an increase of 23·5% since 1990. July 2005 estimate, 17,789,864.

Population in five federal census years was:

	White	Black	All Others	Total	Per sq. mile
1950	2,166,051	603,101	2,153	2,771,305	51·1
1970	5,719,343	1,041,651	28,449	6,789,443	125·6
1980	8,319,448	1,342,478	84,398	9,746,324	180·1
1990	10,749,285	1,759,534	429,107	12,937,926	238·9
2000	12,465,029	2,335,505	1,181,844	15,982,378	296·4

Of the total population in 2000, 8,184,663 were female, 12,336,038 were 18 years old or older and 14,270,020 were urban. The Hispanic population in 2000 was 2,682,715, up from 1,574,143 in 1990 (a rise of 70·4%, the third largest numeric increase of any state in the USA).

The largest cities in the state, 2000 census (and 1990) are: Jacksonville, 735,617 (635,230); Miami, 362,470 (358,548); Tampa, 303,447 (280,015); St Petersburg, 248,232 (238,629); Hialeah, 226,419 (188,004); Orlando, 185,951 (164,693); Fort Lauderdale, 152,397 (149,377); Tallahassee, 150,624 (124,773); Hollywood, 139,357 (121,697); Pembroke Pines, 137,427 (65,452); Coral Springs, 117,549 (79,443); Clearwater, 108,787 (98,784); Cape Coral, 102,286 (74,991); Gainesville, 95,447 (84,770); Port

St Lucie, 88,769 (55,759); Miami Beach, 87,933 (92,639); Sunrise, 85,779 (65,683); Plantation, 82,934 (66,814); West Palm Beach, 82,103 (67,764); Palm Bay, 79,413 (62,543); Lakeland, 78,452 (70,576); Pompano Beach, 78,191 (72,411).

Population of the largest metropolitan areas (2000): Miami–Fort Lauderdale, 3,876,380; Tampa-St Petersburg-Clearwater, 2,395,997; Orlando, 1,644,561.

SOCIAL STATISTICS

Births in 2003 were 212,250 (12·3 per 1,000 population); deaths (2002), 167,814 (10·0 per 1,000). 2002 infant mortality (per 1,000 live births), 7·5. 2001: marriages, 151,300; divorces and other dissolutions, 84,600.

CLIMATE

Jacksonville, Jan. 55°F (12·8°C), July 81°F (27·2°C). Annual rainfall 54" (1,353 mm). Key West, Jan. 70°F (21·1°C), July 83°F (28·3°C). Annual rainfall 39" (968 mm). Miami, Jan. 67°F (19·4°C), July 82°F (27·8°C). Annual rainfall 60" (1,516 mm). Tampa, Jan. 61°F (16·1°C), July 81°F (27·2°C). Annual rainfall 51" (1,285 mm). Florida belongs to the Gulf Coast climate zone (see UNITED STATES: Climate).

CONSTITUTION AND GOVERNMENT

The 1968 Legislature revised the constitution of 1885. The state legislature comprises the Senate and House of Representatives. The Senate has 40 members elected for four years. Half of the membership is elected every two years. The House has 120 members, all of whom are elected every two years during elections held in even-numbered years. Sessions of the legislature are held annually, and are limited to 60 days. Senate and House districts are based on population, with each senator and member representing approximately the same number of residents. The Senate and House are reapportioned every ten years when the federal census is released. In addition to the Governor and Lieut.-Governor (who are elected for four years), the constitution provides for a cabinet composed of an attorney general, a chief financial officer and a commissioner of agriculture.

For the 109th Congress, which convened in Jan. 2005, Florida sends 25 members to the House of Representatives. It is represented in the Senate by Bill Nelson (D. 2001–07) and Mel Martinez (R. 2005–11).

The state capital is Tallahassee. The state is divided into 67 counties.

RECENT ELECTIONS

In the 2004 presidential election Bush polled 3,964,522 votes; Kerry, 3,583,544; Nader, 32,971.

CURRENT ADMINISTRATION

Governor: John Ellis 'Jeb' Bush (R.), 2003–07 (salary: $123,175).
Lieut.-Governor: Toni Jennings (R.), 2003–07 ($117,990).
Secretary of State: Sue M. Cobb (R.), appointed Jan. 2006 ($121,931).

Government Website: http://www.myflorida.com

ECONOMY

Per capita personal income (2004) was $31,460.

Budget

In 2003 total state revenue was $55,213m. Total expenditure was $56,317m. (education, $16,326m.; public welfare, $13,400m.; highways, $4,943m.; health, $2,902m.; correction, $2,141m.) Outstanding debt, in 2003, $21,993m.

Performance

2004 Gross State Product was $599,068m., ranking Florida 4th in the United States.

Banking and Finance

In 2002 there were 301 financial institutions in Florida insured by the US Federal Deposit Insurance Corporation, with assets worth $99,900m. They had 4,626 offices with total deposits of $242,800m.

ENERGY AND NATURAL RESOURCES

Electricity

Electricity production in 2000 totalled 169·9bn. kWh.

Oil and Gas

In 2001, 4m. bbls. of crude oil was produced; natural gas production was 6bn. cu. ft.

Water

The total area covered by water is approximately 11,828 sq. miles.

Minerals

The chief mineral is phosphate rock, of which marketable production in 2002 was 27m. tonnes. This was approximately 75% of US and 25% of the world supply of phosphate in 2002. Other important non-fuel minerals include crushed stone, cement, and sand and gravel. Total non-fuel mineral production for 2003 was valued at $2,000m.

Agriculture

In 2002 there were 10·2m. acres of farmland; 44,000 farms with an average of 232 acres per farm. The total value of land and buildings was $29,330m. in 2002; average value (2002) of land and buildings per acre, $2,836.

Farm income from crops and livestock (2002) was $6,848m., of which crops provided $5,609m. and livestock $1,239m. Major crop contributors are greenhouse products, oranges, sugarcane, tomatoes, grapefruit, peppers, other winter vegetables and indoor and landscaping plants. The net farm income in 2002 was $2,667m. In 2003 poultry farms produced 106m. chickens, 2,804m. eggs and 511m. lb of broilers. In 2002 the state had 1·74m. cattle, including 144,800 milch cows, and 33,500 swine.

Forestry

In 2002 Florida had 16·29m. acres of forested land, including 1·13m. acres of national forests. Florida's 31 state forests covered 1·40m. acres in 2002.

Fisheries

Florida has extensive fisheries with shrimp the highest value fish commodity. Other important catches are spiny lobster, snapper, crabs, hard clams, swordfish and tuna. Commercial catch (2002) totalled 115·6m. lb of fish at a value of $184·6m.

INDUSTRY

In 2001 the state's 15,392 manufacturing establishments had 413,000 employees, earning $14,578m. Total value added by manufacturing in 2001 was $39,974m. Main industries include: printing and publishing, machinery and computer equipment, apparel and finished products, fabricated metal products, and lumber and wood products.

Labour

Total non-agricultural employment, 2003, 7,286,000. Employees by branch, 2003 (in 1,000): trade, transportation and utilities, 1,462; professional and business services, 1,258; government, 1,056; education and health services, 886; leisure and hospitality, 809. In 2003 the unemployment rate was 5·1%.

INTERNATIONAL TRADE

Imports and Exports

Export sales of merchandise in 2000 totalled $24·2bn. Florida exported to 213 foreign markets in 2000: Canada was the biggest

(10·3% of exports), followed by Brazil (8·4%) and Mexico (8·1%). Other important markets include Japan, Venezuela, Dominican Republic, UK, Colombia, Germany, Argentina and China. The leading export category is computers and electronic products (accounting for 33% of total exports in 2000). Other manufactured exports include transportation equipment, machinery, chemicals, electrical equipment, appliances and parts, and miscellaneous manufactures. The state also exports significant quantities of farm products and other non-manufactured commodities. Total agricultural exports were worth $1·2bn. in 2001.

COMMUNICATIONS

Roads
The state (2003) had 120,376 miles of highways, roads and streets (68,479 miles being urban roads). In 2003 there were 14,526,125 vehicle registrations and 3,169 traffic accident fatalities.

Rail
In 2002 there were 2,871 miles of railway and 13 rail companies. There is a metro of 22 miles, a peoplemover and a commuter rail route in Miami.

Civil Aviation
In 2002 Florida had 475 public and private airports (12 international and 20 scheduled commercial service airports), 280 heliports, 13 stolports and 45 seaplane bases. Annual economic activity at Florida airports is responsible for more than 4·7% of Gross State Product. More than 50% of tourists arrive in the state by air each year. There were 56,654,905 passenger enplanements at Florida airports in 2003: the busiest were Miami International (14,198,321), Orlando International (13,375,162), Fort Lauderdale/Hollywood International (8,682,781) and Tampa International (7,672,533).

Shipping
There are 14 deepwater ports: those on the Gulf coast handle mainly domestic trade and those on the Atlantic coast primarily international trade and cruise ship traffic. In 2002–03 the tonnage of total waterborne trade by port was 118·2m. tons (including Tampa: 48·5m. tons; Everglades: 23·3m. tons; Jacksonville: 18·7m. tons; Miami: 9·0m. tons; and Manatee: 7·0m. tons). Almost 14m. cruise passengers embarked and disembarked from Florida ports in 2002–03, principally from Canaveral (4·1m.), Miami (4·0m.) and Everglades (3·4m.). There were 1,540 miles of inland waterways in 2000.

SOCIAL INSTITUTIONS

Justice
The state resumed the use of the death penalty in 1979. There have been 59 executions since 1976, including two in 2004 and one in 2005. In June 2003 there were 80,352 federal and state prisoners. Chain gangs were introduced in 1995.

Education
Attendance at school is compulsory between seven and 16. In the 2001–02 school year there were 3,314 public elementary and secondary schools with 2,500,478 enrolled pupils. According to the National Center for Education Statistics, Florida's public schools have the highest average enrolment in the country: in the 1999–2000 school year there were 768 pupils per elementary school (compared to a national average of 477) and 1,396 pupils per secondary school (national average 706). Total expenditure on public schools in 2000–01 was $15,024m. The state maintains 28 public community colleges; in 2002–03 there were 880,000 students, about 35% of whom were full-time.

There are 11 state universities with a total of 258,874 students in 2002: the University of Florida at Gainesville (founded 1853) with 46,850 students; the Florida State University at Tallahassee (founded in 1857) with 36,651; the University of South Florida at

Tampa (founded 1960) with 37,764; Florida A. & M. (Agricultural and Mechanical) University at Tallahassee (founded 1887) with 12,467; Florida Atlantic University (founded 1964) at Boca Raton with 23,996; the University of West Florida at Pensacola with 9,206; the University of Central Florida at Orlando with 38,795; the University of North Florida at Jacksonville with 13,460; Florida International University at Miami with 33,799; Florida Gulf Coast University (founded 1997) at Fort Myers with 5,236; and New College of Florida (founded 2001) at Sarasota with 650. There are 28 private colleges and universities belonging to the Independent Colleges and Universities of Florida (ICUF) association. Their enrolments vary from fewer than 100 to more than 22,000 students.

Health
In 2002 there were 202 community hospitals with 51,200 beds. A total of 2,315,000 patients were admitted during the year.

Welfare
Medicare enrolment in July 2003 totalled 2,920,971. In 2002 a total of 2,676,235 people in Florida received Medicaid. In Dec. 2004 there were 3,384,956 Old-Age, Survivors, and Disability Insurance (OASDI) beneficiaries. A total of 118,168 people were receiving payments under Temporary Assistance for Needy Families (TANF) in Sept. 2004.

RELIGION

The main religious denominations are Roman Catholic, Baptist, Jewish, Methodist, Presbyterian and Episcopalian.

CULTURE

Tourism
During 2002, 73·9m. tourists visited Florida (67·9m. domestic visitors, 4·4m. overseas visitors and 1·6m. from Canada). They generated $48·7bn. in taxable sales and $2·9bn. in state sales tax revenues, making tourism the state's biggest industry.

There are 156 state parks, three national parks, three national forests, 31 state forests, and five national monuments and memorials. In 2002 there were 17·7m. visitors to state parks, raising $31·9m. in revenue.

FURTHER READING

Statistical information: Bureau of Economic and Business Research, Univ. of Florida, Gainesville 32611. Publishes *Florida Statistical Abstract.*

Huckshorn, R. J. (ed.) *Government and Politics in Florida.* Florida Univ. Press, 1998
Morris, A., *The Florida Handbook.* Tallahassee. Biennial
Wilson, P. A. (ed.) *2005 Florida Statistical Abstract.* Univ. of Florida Bureau of Economics, 2006

State Library: 500 S Bronough Street, Tallahassee 32399.

Georgia

KEY HISTORICAL EVENTS

Originally the territory of Creek and Cherokee tribes, Georgia was first settled by Europeans in the 18th century. James Oglethorpe founded Savannah in 1733, intending it as a colony which offered a new start to debtors, convicts and the poor. Settlement was slow until 1783, when growth began in the cotton-growing areas west of Augusta. The Indian population was cleared off the rich cotton land and moved beyond the Mississippi. Georgia became one of the original 13 states of the Union.

A plantation economy developed rapidly, using slave labour. In 1861 Georgia seceded from the Union and became an important source of supplies for the Confederate cause, although some northern areas never accepted secession and continued in sympathy with the Union during the Civil War. At the beginning of the war 56% of the population were white, descendants of British, Austrian and New England immigrants; the remaining 44% were black slaves.

The city of Atlanta, which grew as a railway junction, was destroyed during the war but revived to become the centre of southern reconstruction in the post-war period. It was confirmed as the state capital in 1877. Successive movements for black freedom in social, economic and political life have developed in the city, notably the Southern Christian Leadership Conference, led by Martin Luther King (who was assassinated in 1968).

TERRITORY AND POPULATION

Georgia is bounded north by Tennessee and North Carolina, northeast by South Carolina, east by the Atlantic, south by Florida and west by Alabama. Land area, 57,906 sq. miles (149,976 sq. km). Census population, 1 April 2000, was 8,186,453, an increase of 26·4% since 1990. July 2005 estimate, 9,072,576.

Population in five census years was:

	White	Black	Indian	Asiatic	Total	Per sq. mile
1910	1,431,802	1,176,987	95	237	2,609,121	44·4
1930	1,837,021	1,071,125	43	317	2,908,506	49·7
			All others			
1980	3,948,007	1,465,457	50,801		5,464,265	92·7
1990	4,600,148	1,746,565	131,503		6,478,216	110·0
2000	5,327,281	2,349,542	509,630		8,186,453	141·4

Of the total population in 2000, 4,159,340 were female, 6,017,219 were 18 years old or older and 5,864,163 were urban. The estimated Hispanic population was 435,277 in 2000, up from 108,933 in 1990 (an increase of 299·6%).

The largest cities are: Atlanta (capital), with a population (2000 census) of 416,474; Augusta-Richmond County, 199,775; Columbus, 186,291; Savannah, 131,510; Athens-Clarke County, 101,489. The Atlanta metropolitan area had a 2000 census population of 4,112,198.

SOCIAL STATISTICS

Births, 2003, were 135,979 (15·7 per 1,000 population); deaths (2002), 65,449 (7·6 per 1,000 population). 2002 infant mortality (per 1,000 live births), 8·9. 2001: marriages, 51,300 (6·3 per 1,000 population); divorces and annulments, 30,600 (3·8).

CLIMATE

Atlanta, Jan. 43°F (6·1°C), July 78°F (25·6°C). Annual rainfall 49" (1,234 mm). Georgia belongs to the Atlantic Coast climate zone (see UNITED STATES: Climate).

CONSTITUTION AND GOVERNMENT

A new constitution was ratified in the general election of 2 Nov. 1976, proclaimed on 22 Dec. 1976 and became effective on 1 Jan. 1977. The General Assembly consists of a Senate of 56 members and a House of Representatives of 180 members, both elected for two years. Legislative sessions are annual, beginning the 2nd Monday in Jan. and lasting for 40 days.

Georgia was the first state to extend the franchise to all citizens 18 years old and above.

For the 109th Congress, which convened in Jan. 2005, Georgia sends 13 members to the House of Representatives. It is represented in the Senate by Saxby Chambliss (R. 2003–09) and Johnny Isakson (R. 2005–11).

The state capital is Atlanta. Georgia is divided into 159 counties.

RECENT ELECTIONS

In the 2004 presidential election Bush polled 1,914,254 votes; Kerry, 1,366,149; Badnarik, 18,387.

CURRENT ADMINISTRATION

Governor: Sonny Perdue (R.), 2003–07 (salary: $131,481).
    Lieut.-Governor: Mark Taylor (D.), 2003–07 ($83,148).
    Secretary of State: Cathy Cox (D.), 2003–07 ($116,743).

Government Website: http://www.georgia.gov

ECONOMY

Per capita personal income (2004) was $30,074.

Budget

In 2003 total state revenue was $29,874m. Total expenditure was $32,527m. (education, $12,749m.; public welfare, $8,059m.; highways, $1,843m.; correction, $1,272m.; health, $884m.) Outstanding debt, in 2003, $8,890m.

Performance

Gross State Product was $343,125m. in 2004, ranking Georgia 10th in the United States.

ENERGY AND NATURAL RESOURCES

Water

The total area covered by water is approximately 1,519 sq. miles.

Minerals

Georgia is the leading producer of kaolin. The state ranks first in production of crushed and dimensional granite, and second in production of fuller's earth and marble (crushed and dimensional). Total value of non-fuel mineral production for 2003 was $1,670m.

Agriculture

In 2002, 50,000 farms covered 11m. acres; the average farm was of 220 acres. In 2002 the average value of farmland and buildings was $2,112 per acre. For 2002 cotton output was 1·6m. bales (of 480 lb). Other major crops include tobacco, corn, wheat, soybeans, peanuts and pecans. Cash income, 2002, $4,472m.: from crops, $1,582m.; from livestock and products, $2,890m. The net farm income in 2002 was $1,699m.

In 2002 farm animals included 1·27m. cattle, 347,816 swine and 2,546m. (2003) poultry.

Forestry

The forested area in 2002 was 24·41m. acres with 855,000 acres of national forest.

INDUSTRY

In 2001 the state's 8,688 manufacturing establishments had 492,000 employees, earning $16,141m. Total value added by manufacturing in 2001 was $57,578m.

Labour

Total non-agricultural employment, 2003, 3,860,000. Employees by branch, 2003 (in 1,000): trade, transportation and utilities, 823; government, 633; professional and business services, 494; manufacturing, 452; education and health services, 387. Georgia's unemployment rate in 2003 was 4·7%.

COMMUNICATIONS

Roads

In 2003 there were 116,533 miles of roads comprising 28,558 miles of urban road and 87,975 miles of rural road. There were 7,730,300 motor vehicles registered.

Rail

In 2002 there were 4,820 miles of freight railroad, including 3,516 miles of Class I railways. There is a metro in Atlanta.

Civil Aviation

In June 2004 there were 335 airports (106 public, 219 private) and 104 heliports. Atlanta international airport handled 38,893,670 passenger enplanements in 2003.

Shipping

There are deepwater ports at Savannah, the principal port, and Brunswick.

SOCIAL INSTITUTIONS

Justice

In June 2003 there were 47,004 federal and state prisoners. The death penalty is authorized for capital offences. There were two executions in 2004 and three in 2005.

Under a Local Option Act, the sale of alcoholic beverages is prohibited in some counties.

Education

Since 1945 education has been compulsory; tuition is free for pupils between the ages of six and 18 years. In 2002–03 there were 2,236 public elementary and secondary schools with 1·49m. pupils and 96,044 teachers; total expenditure on public schools was $12,571m. Teachers' salaries averaged $45,533 in 2003.

The University of Georgia (Athens) was founded in 1785 and was the first chartered State University in the USA (33,878 students in 2003). Other institutions of higher learning include Georgia Institute of Technology, Atlanta (16,643); Emory University, Atlanta (11,654); Georgia State University, Atlanta (28,042); Georgia Southern University, Statesboro (15,704). The Atlanta University Center, devoted primarily to Black education, includes co-educational Clark Atlanta University (4,915); Morehouse College (2,859), a liberal arts college for men; Interdenominational Theological Center (406), a co-educational school; and Spelman College (2,063), the first liberal arts college for Black women in the USA. Wesleyan College (745), near Macon, is the oldest chartered women's college in the world.

Health

In 2002 there were 146 community hospitals with 24,500 beds. A total of 885,000 patients were admitted during the year.

Welfare

Medicare enrolment in July 2003 totalled 973,794. In 2002 a total of 1,637,329 people in Georgia received Medicaid. In Dec. 2004 there were 1,193,857 Old-Age, Survivors, and Disability Insurance (OASDI) beneficiaries. A total of 109,230 people were receiving payments under Temporary Assistance for Needy Families (TANF) in Sept. 2004.

RELIGION

In 2000 there were 1,719,484 Southern Baptist adherents, 570,674 United Methodists, 374,185 Roman Catholics, 138,123 Church of God members and 105,774 Presbyterian Church (USA) members.

CULTURE

Tourism

In 2003 there were 48m. visitors to and through Georgia; tourism expenditures totalled $25bn., supporting 209,500 tourist-related jobs. Tourism provided $708·5m. in state tax revenue. There were 12·4m. visitors to the 48 state parks.

FURTHER READING

Statistical information: Selig Center for Economic Growth, Univ. of Georgia, Athens 30602. Publishes *Georgia Statistical Abstract.*

Rowland, A. R., *A Bibliography of the Writings on Georgia History.* Hamden, Conn., 1978

State Law Library: Judicial Building, Capital Sq., Atlanta.

Hawaii

KEY HISTORICAL EVENTS

The islands of Hawaii were settled by Polynesian immigrants, probably from the Marquesas Islands, about AD 400. A second major immigration, from Tahiti, occurred around 800–900. In the late 18th century all the islands of the group were united into one kingdom by Kamehameha I. Western exploration began in 1778, and Christian missions were established after 1820. Europeans called Hawaii the Sandwich Islands. The main foreign states interested were the USA, Britain and France. Because of the threat imposed by their rivalry, Kamehameha III placed Hawaii under US protection in 1851. US sugar-growing companies became dominant in the economy and in 1887 the USA obtained a naval base at Pearl Harbour. A struggle developed between forces for and against annexation by the USA. In 1893 the monarchy was overthrown. The republican government agreed to be annexed to the USA in 1898, and Hawaii became a US Territory in 1900.

The islands and the naval base were of great strategic importance during the Second World War, when the Japanese attack on Pearl Harbour brought the USA into the war.

Hawaii became the 50th state of the Union in 1959. The 19th-century plantation economy encouraged the immigration of workers, especially from China and Japan. Hawaiian laws, religions and culture were gradually adapted to the needs of the immigrant community.

TERRITORY AND POPULATION

The Hawaiian Islands lie in the North Pacific Ocean, between 18° 54' and 28° 15' N. lat. and 154° 40' and 178° 25' W. long., about 2,090 nautical miles southwest of San Francisco. There are 137 named islands and islets in the group, of which seven major and five minor islands are inhabited. Land area, 6,423 sq. miles (16,636 sq. km). Census population, 1 April 2000, 1,211,537, an increase of 9·3% since 1990; density was 188·6 per sq. mile in 2000. July 2005 population estimate, 1,275,194. Of the total population in 2000, 608,671 were male, 915,770 were 18 years old or older, and 1,108,225 were urban (91·47%, the fourth most urban state).

The principal islands are Hawaii, 4,028 sq. miles, population 2000, 148,677; Maui, 727 sq. miles, population 117,644; Oahu, 600 sq. miles, population 876,151; Kauai, 552 sq. miles, population 58,303; Molokai, 260 sq. miles, population 7,404; Lanai, 141 sq. miles, population 3,193; Niihau, 70 sq. miles, population 160; Kahoolawe, 45 sq. miles (uninhabited). The capital Honolulu—on the island of Oahu—had a population in 2000 of 371,657, and Hilo—on the island of Hawaii—40,759.

Figures for main racial groups, 2000, were (excluding persons in institutions or military barracks): 294,102 White; 201,764 Japanese; 170,635 Filipino; 80,137 Native Hawaiian; 56,600 Chinese (including Taiwanese); 25,537 Korean; 22,003 Black or African American; 16,166 Samoan; 7,867 Vietnamese.

SOCIAL STATISTICS

Births, 2003, were 18,100 (14·4 per 1,000 population); deaths (2002), 8,801 (7·1 per 1,000 population). Infant deaths (2002) were at a rate of 7·3 per 1,000 live births. There were 8,914 resident marriages (7·2 per 1,000 population) in 2002, and divorces and annulments numbered 4,798 (3·9 per 1,000 population). Inter-marriage between the races is common. In 2002, 56·0% of marriages were inter-racial. 65·4% were non-resident marriages.

CLIMATE

All the islands have a tropical climate, with an abrupt change in conditions between windward and leeward sides, most marked in rainfall. Temperatures vary little. Average temperatures in

Honolulu: Jan. 73·0°F, July 80·8°F. Average annual rainfall in Honolulu: 18·29".

CONSTITUTION AND GOVERNMENT

Hawaii was officially admitted into the United States on 21 Aug. 1959. However, the constitution of the State of Hawaii was created by the 1950 Constitutional Convention, ratified by the voters of the Territory on 7 Nov. 1950, and amended on 27 June 1959. There have been two constitutional conventions since 1950, in 1968 and 1978. In addition to amendments proposed by these conventions the Legislature is able to propose amendments to voters during the general election. This has resulted in numerous amendments.

For the 109th Congress, which convened in Jan. 2005, Hawaii sends two members to the House of Representatives. It is represented in the Senate by Daniel Inouye (D. 1963–2011) and Daniel Akaka (D. 1990–2007).

The state capital is Honolulu. There are five counties.

RECENT ELECTIONS

In the 2004 presidential election Kerry polled 231,708 votes; Bush, 194,191; Cobb, 1,737.

CURRENT ADMINISTRATION

Governor: Linda Lingle (R.), Dec. 2002–Dec. 2006 (salary: $94,780).

Lieut.-Governor: James R. 'Duke' Aiona, Jr (R.), Dec. 2002–Dec. 2006 ($90,041).

Government Website: http://www.ehawaiigov.org

ECONOMY

Per capita personal income (2004) was $32,606.

Budget

Revenue is derived mainly from taxation of sales and gross receipts, real property, corporate and personal income, and inheritance taxes, licences, public land sales and leases.

In 2003 total state revenue was $6,808m. Total expenditure was $7,611m. (education, $2,332m.; public welfare, $1,217m.; government administration, $471m.; health, $449m.; highways, $259m.) Outstanding debt, in 2003, $5,653m.

Performance

2004 Gross State Product was $50,322m., ranking Hawaii 40th in the United States.

Banking and Finance

In 2003 there were five state-chartered banks (assets of $22,705m. in 1999), and one federal bank.

ENERGY AND NATURAL RESOURCES

Electricity

Installed capacity in 1999 was 1,669,000 kW; total power consumed was 9,380m. kWh.

Oil and Gas

In 1999, $48m. was generated by gas sales.

Water

The total area covered by water is approximately 4,508 sq. miles, of which 38 sq. miles are inland. Water consumption in 1999 amounted to 77,610m. gallons.

Minerals

Total value of non-fuel mineral production in 2003 was $74m.; mainly crushed stone (6·6m. tonnes in 2001, value $64m.) and cement (289,000 tonnes in 2000, value $28m.).

Agriculture

Farming is highly commercialized and highly mechanized. In 2002 there were about 5,300 farms covering an area of 1·44m. acres; average number of acres per farm, 272, valued at $3,507 per acre. Paid workforce totalled 11,600 in 2002.

Pineapples, greenhouse products, sugarcane and macadamia nuts are the staple crops. Farm income, 2002, from crop sales was $424m., and from livestock $85m. The net farm income in 2002 was $98m.

Forestry

Hawaii had 1·75m. acres of forested land in 2002. In 2003 conservation district forest land amounted to 971,876 acres (of which 328,742 was privately owned); there were 46,191 acres of planted forest; and 109,164 acres of natural area.

Fisheries

In 2002 the commercial fish catch was 23·84m. lb with a value of $52·1m. There were 3,081 commercial fishermen in 2002.

INDUSTRY

In 2001 the state's 940 manufacturing establishments had 15,000 employees, earning $463m. Total value added by manufacturing in 2001 was $907m.

Labour

Total non-agricultural employment amounted to 567,000 in 2003; 4·2% (24,732) were unemployed in 2002. Employees by branch, 2003 (in 1,000): government, 119; trade, transportation and utilities, 108; leisure and hospitality, 100; professional and business services, 70; education and health services, 65.

Trade Unions

In 2003 there were 113 trade unions with a combined membership of 167,000.

COMMUNICATIONS

Roads

In 2003 there were 4,308 miles of roads comprising 2,127 miles of urban road and 2,181 miles of rural road. There were 902,910 registered motor vehicles.

Civil Aviation

There were 11 commercial airports in 2004. In 2001 passengers arriving from overseas numbered 7·27m., and there were 9·17m. passengers between the islands. In 1999 Hawaiian Airlines flew 34·8m. km, carrying 5,409,700 passengers (19,100 on international flights). There were 14,917,161 passenger enplanements in 2003.

Shipping

Several lines of steamers connect the islands with the mainland USA, Canada, Australia, the Philippines, China and Japan. In 2002, 1,270 overseas and 2,663 inter-island vessels entered the port of Honolulu carrying a total of 130,792 overseas and 19,952 inter-island passengers as well as 6,425,288 tonnes of overseas and 1,796,910 tonnes inter-island cargo.

Telecommunications

There were 741,843 telephone access lines in 2000.

SOCIAL INSTITUTIONS

Justice

There is no capital punishment in Hawaii. In June 2003 there were 5,635 prisoners in federal and state prisons.

Education

Education is free, and compulsory for children between the ages of six and 18. The language in the schools is English. In 1997–98 there were 251 public schools and (1999–2000) 130 private schools. In 2000 there were 188,699 pupils in public schools and 32,193 pupils in private schools. In 1997–98 there were 11,400 teachers in public schools and (1999–2000) 2,475 teachers in private schools. In 2001–02, $1,331m. was spent on education and the average annual salary for teachers was $44,306. In 2003 the number of students to enrol at college or university was 63,678.

Health

In 2002 there were 25 community hospitals with 3,200 beds. A total of 111,000 patients were admitted during the year.

Welfare

Medicare enrolment in July 2003 totalled 174,633. In 2003 a total of 199,966 people in Hawaii received Medicaid. In Dec. 2004 there were 197,263 Old-Age, Survivors, and Disability Insurance (OASDI) beneficiaries. A total of 22,156 people were receiving payments under Temporary Assistance for Needy Families (TANF) in Sept. 2004.

RELIGION

2000 membership of leading religious denominations: Roman Catholic Church, 240,813; Buddhism (1999), 100,000; Church of Jesus Christ of Latter-day Saints, 42,758; United Church of Christ, 22,856; Assembly of God, 21,754; Southern Baptist, 20,901; International Church of the Foursquare Gospel, 15,076; Episcopal Church, 11,084.

CULTURE

Broadcasting

In 2002 there were 76 commercial radio and 23 commercial television stations (excluding cable television companies). Colour is by NTSC.

Press

A total of 135 newspapers (ten daily) were in circulation in 2000.

Tourism

Tourism is outstanding in Hawaii's economy. Tourist arrivals numbered only 687,000 in 1965, but were 6·9m. in 2004. Tourist expenditure ($380m. in 1967) contributed $10,861·8m. to the state's economy in 2004.

FURTHER READING

Statistical information: Hawaii State Department of Business, POB 2359, Honolulu 96804. Publishes *The State of Hawaii Data Book.*
Atlas of Hawaii. 3rd ed. Hawaii Univ. Press, 1998

Morris, Nancy J. and Dean, Love, *Hawai'i.* [Bibliography] ABC-Clio, Oxford and Santa Barbara (CA), 1992
Oliver, Anthony M., *Hawaii Facts and Reference Book: Recent Historical Facts and Events in the Fiftieth State.* Honolulu, 1995

Idaho

KEY HISTORICAL EVENTS

The original people of Idaho were Kutenai, Kalispel, Nez Percé and other tribes, living on the Pacific watershed of the northern Rocky Mountains. European exploration began in 1805, and after 1809 there were trading posts and small settlements, with fur-trapping as the primary economic activity. The area was disputed between Britain and the USA until 1846 when British claims were dropped. In 1860 gold and silver were found, and there was a rush of immigrant prospectors. The newly enlarged population needed organized government. An area including present-day Montana was created a Territory in March 1863. Montana was separated from it in 1864. Population growth

continued, stimulated by refugees from the Confederate states after the Civil War and by settlements of Mormons from Utah.

Fur-trapping and mining gave way to farming, especially of grains, as the main economic activity. Idaho became a state in 1890, with its capital at Boise. The Territory capital, Idaho City, had been a gold-mining boom town in the 1860s whose population (about 40,000 at its height) was the largest in the Pacific Northwest. The population declined to 1,000 by 1869.

During the 20th century the Indian population shrunk to nearly 1%. The Mormon community has grown to include much of southeastern Idaho and more than half the church-going population of the state.

Industrial history has been influenced by the development of the Snake River of southern Idaho for hydro-electricity and irrigation, especially at the American Falls and reservoir. Processing food, minerals and timber are important to the economy. Much of the state, however, remains sparsely populated and rural. Rapid growth of high technology companies in Idaho's metropolitan areas has prompted economic diversification and rapid population growth.

TERRITORY AND POPULATION

Idaho is within the Rocky Mountains and bounded north by Canada, east by Montana and Wyoming, south by Nevada and Utah, west by Oregon and Washington. Land area, 82,747 sq. miles (214,314 sq. km). Census population, 1 April 2000, 1,293,953, an increase of 28·5% since 1990. July 2005 estimate, 1,429,096.

Population in five census years was:

	White	Black	American Indian	Asiatic	Total	Per sq. mile
1910	319,221	651	3,488	2,234	325,594	3·9
1930	438,840	668	3,638	1,886	445,032	5·4
1980	901,641	2,716	10,521	5,948	943,935	11·3
1990	950,451	3,370	13,780	9,365	1,006,749	12·2
2000	1,177,304	5,456	17,645	13,197	1,293,953	15·6

Of the total population in 2000, 648,660 were male, 924,923 were 18 years old or older and 859,497 were urban. In 2000 Idaho's Hispanic population was 101,690, up from 52,927 in 1990 (an increase of 92·1%).

The largest cities are: Boise City, with a 2003 population of 190,117; Nampa, 64,269; Idaho Falls, 51,507; Pocatello, 51,009; Meridian, 41,127; Coeur d'Alene, 37,262; Twin Falls, 36,742; Caldwell, 31,041; Lewiston, 30,937.

SOCIAL STATISTICS

Births (2003), 21,800 (16·0 per 1,000 population); deaths (2002), 9,923 (7·4 per 1,000 population). 2002 infant mortality rate (per 1,000 live births), 6·1. 2001: marriages, 14,867 (10·9 per 1,000 population); divorces, 7,080 (5·2).

CLIMATE

Boise City, Jan. 29°F (–1·7°C), July 74°F (23·3°C). Annual rainfall 12″ (303 mm). Idaho belongs to the Mountain States climate zone (*see* UNITED STATES: Climate).

CONSTITUTION AND GOVERNMENT

The constitution adopted in 1890 is still in force; it has had 105 amendments. The Legislature consists of a Senate of 35 members and a House of Representatives of 70 members, all the legislators being elected for two years. It meets annually.

For the 109th Congress, which convened in Jan. 2005, Idaho sends two members to the House of Representatives. It is represented in the Senate by Larry Craig (R. 1991–2009) and Michael Crapo (R. 1999–2011).

The state is divided into 44 counties. The capital is Boise City.

RECENT ELECTIONS

In the 2004 presidential election Bush polled 409,235 votes; Kerry, 181,098; Badnarik, 3,844.

CURRENT ADMINISTRATION

Governor: Dirk Kempthorne (R.), 2003–07 (salary: $101,500).
 Lieut.-Governor: Jim Risch (R.), 2003–07 ($26,750).
 Secretary of State: Ben Ysursa (R.), 2003–07 ($82,500).

Government Website: http://www.accessidaho.org

ECONOMY

Per capita personal income (2004) was $26,839.

Budget

In fiscal year 2003 total state revenue was $5,493m. Total expenditure was $5,415m. (education, $1,886m.; public welfare, $1,093m.; highways, $522m.; government administration, $200m.; correction, $165m.) Outstanding debt, in fiscal year 2003, $2,603m.

Performance

Gross State Product in 2004 was $43,571m., ranking Idaho 42nd in the United States.

ENERGY AND NATURAL RESOURCES

Electricity

Idaho's rivers provide dependable and low-cost electrical power. Almost two-thirds of Idaho's electrical needs come from this resource, resulting in electricity rates much lower than those found in the East and Midwest.

Water

The total area covered by water is approximately 823 sq. miles. Idaho is second only to California in the amount of water used for irrigating crops.

Minerals

Principal non-fuel minerals are processed phosphate rock, silver, gold, molybdenum and sand and gravel. The value of total mineral output for 2003 was $294m., with an additional value-added through processing of phosphate rock of approximately $211m.

Agriculture

Agriculture is the second largest industry, despite a great part of the state being naturally arid. Extensive irrigation works have been carried out, bringing an estimated 3·5m. acres under irrigation, and there are over 50 soil conservation districts.

In 2003 there were 25,000 farms with a total area of 11·8m. acres; average value per acre (2002), $1,270. In 2003 the average farm was 472 acres.

Farm income, 2003, from crops, $1,848m., and livestock, $2,190m. The most important crops are potatoes and wheat. Other crops are sugarbeets, hay, barley, field peas and beans, onions and apples. The net farm income in 2003 was $1,210m. In 2003 there were 2·0m. cattle, 260,000 sheep, 26,000 hogs and 1·2m. poultry. There were 34m. food-sized trout produced on fish farms. The dairy industry is the fastest growing sector in Idaho agriculture.

Forestry

In 2002 there was a total of 21·65m. acres of forest, of which 16·16m. were national forest.

Fisheries

74% of the commercial trout processed in the USA was produced in Idaho in 2002. Idaho ranked first in state trout production by producing fish to a value of $30·5m.

INDUSTRY

In 2002 Idaho's 1,763 manufacturing establishments had approximately 60,000 employees, with a payroll of $2,056m. Manufacturing is the leading industry, with value added in 2002 of $5,528m. Electronics and computer equipment made up the largest manufacturing component with value added of $2,718m.

Labour

In 2003, 113,033 people were employed in government, 95,817 in trade, 67,787 in professional and business services, 61,990 in educational and health services, 61,655 in manufacturing and 54,245 in leisure and hospitality. The workforce totalled 692,500 in 2003; state unemployment averaged 5·4%.

Trade Unions

Idaho has a right-to-work law. In 1997, 43,400 people were union members.

COMMUNICATIONS

Roads

In 2003 there were 46,929 miles of public roads (42,518 miles rural, 4,411 urban). Of these, 3,196 were on Native American reservations. There were 1,316,136 registered motor vehicles in 2003.

Rail

The state had (2001) approximately 1,700 miles of railways (including one Amtrak route).

Civil Aviation

There were 68 municipally-owned airports in 2003. There were 1,684,787 passenger enplanements statewide in 2003.

Shipping

Water transport is provided from the Pacific to the port of Lewiston, by way of the Columbia and Snake rivers, a distance of 464 miles.

Postal Services

Idaho is served by the United States Postal Service. Major private carriers, including UPS, Federal Express, and DHL Worldwide Express, provide Idaho residents with global shipping access. There are numerous local mailing and shipping services available in Idaho's larger cities.

SOCIAL INSTITUTIONS

Justice

The death penalty may be imposed for first degree murder or aggravated kidnapping, but the judge must consider mitigating circumstances before imposing a sentence of death. The only execution since 1976 was in 1994. In Nov. 2004 there were 6,309 incarcerated law offenders.

Education

In 2003–04 public elementary schools (grades K to 6) had 135,216 pupils and 8,048 teachers; secondary schools had 116,821 pupils and 7,387 classroom teachers. Average salary (2003–04) of teachers was $40,301 (elementary) and $41,422 (secondary).

The University of Idaho, founded at Moscow in 1889, had 559 full-time instructional faculty in 2003, and a total enrolment of 12,895. Boise State University had 278 full-time instructional faculty in 2003 and a total enrolment of 18,332. Idaho State University had 401 full-time instructional faculty in 2003 and a total enrolment of 13,621. There were seven other higher education institutions, three of them public institutions. College and university enrolment in the autumn of 2003 was 73,275.

Health

In 2003 there were 3,282 hospital beds in 48 licensed facilities.

Welfare

Medicare enrolment in July 2003 totalled 177,700. In 2002 a total of 176,499 people in Idaho received Medicaid. Old-Age, Survivors, and Disability Insurance (OASDI) is granted to persons if they paid sufficiently into the system or meet other qualifications. A total of 3,213 people were receiving payments under Temporary Assistance for Needy Families (TANF) in Sept. 2004. Dec. 2004: total Idaho beneficiaries, 218,155 with total annual benefit payment of $1,951m. (2002).

RELIGION

The leading religious denominations are the Church of Jesus Christ of Latter-day Saints (Mormons; 311,425 adherents in 2000), Roman Catholics, Methodists, Presbyterians, Episcopalians and Lutherans.

CULTURE

Broadcasting

In 2003 there were 112 radio stations and 23 television stations.

Press

Idaho has 15 daily newspapers and 52 weekly papers.

Tourism

Money spent by travellers in 2000 was $2,312m.

FURTHER READING

Statistical information: Idaho Commerce and Labor, 700 West State St., Boise 83720. Publishes *County Profiles of Idaho*, *Community Profiles of Idaho* and *Profile of Rural Idaho* on the Internet.

Schwantes, C. A., *In Mountain Shadows: a History of Idaho*. Nebraska Univ. Press, 1996

Website: http://www.cl.idaho.gov

Illinois

KEY HISTORICAL EVENTS

Territory of a group of Algonquian-speaking tribes, Illinois was explored first by the French in 1673. France claimed the area until 1763 when, after the French and Indian War, it was ceded to Britain along with all the French land east of the Mississippi. In 1783 Britain recognized the US' title to Illinois, which became part of the North West Territory of the USA in 1787, and of Indiana Territory in 1800. Illinois became a Territory in its own right in 1809, and a state in 1818.

Settlers from the eastern states moved onto the fertile farmland, immigration increasing greatly with the opening in 1825 of the Erie Canal from New York, along which settlers could move west and their produce back east for sale. Chicago was incorporated as a city in 1837 and quickly became the transport, trading and distribution centre of the middle west. Once industrial growth had begun there, a further wave of immigration took place in the 1840s, mainly of European refugees looking for work. This movement continued with varying force until the 1920s, when it was largely replaced by immigration of black work-seekers from the southern states.

During the 20th century the population became largely urban and heavy industry was established along an intensive network of rail and waterway routes. Chicago recovered from a destructive fire in 1871 to become the hub of this network and at one time the second largest American city.

TERRITORY AND POPULATION

Illinois is bounded north by Wisconsin, northeast by Lake Michigan, east by Indiana, southeast by the Ohio River (forming the boundary with Kentucky), and west by the Mississippi River (forming the boundary with Missouri and Iowa). Land area in 2000: 55,584 sq. miles (143,962 sq. km). Census population, 2000, 12,419,293, an increase of 8·6% since 1990. July 2005 estimate, 12,763,371.

Population in five census years was:

	White	Black	Indian	All others	Total	Per sq. mile
1910	5,526,962	109,049	188	2,392	5,638,591	100·6
1930	7,266,361	328,972	469	35,321	7,630,654	136·4
			All others			
1980	9,233,327	1,675,398	517,793		11,426,518	203·0

	White	Black	American Indian, or Alaska Native	Asian or Pacific Islander	Other	Total	Per sq. mile
1990	8,957,923	1,690,855	24,077	284,944	472,803	11,430,602	205·6
2000	9,125,471	1,876,875	31,006	428,213	957,728	12,419,293	223·4

Of the total population in 2000, 6,338,957 were female, 9,173,842 were 18 years old or older and 10,909,520 were urban. In 2000 the Hispanic population was 1,527,573 (904,449 in 1990).

The most populous cities (2002) are: Chicago, 2,886,251; Aurora, 156,974; Rockford, 151,068; Naperville, 135,389; Joliet, 118,423; Peoria, 112,670; Springfield, 111,834; Elgin, 96,539; Waukegan, 91,323.

Metropolitan area populations, 2000 census: Chicago–Gary–Kenosha, 9,157,540; Rockford, 371,236; Peoria–Pekin, 347,387; Springfield, 201,437; Champaign–Urbana, 179,669.

SOCIAL STATISTICS

Births in 2003 were 182,495 (14·4 per 1,000); deaths in 2002 were 106,667 (8·5 per 1,000). 2002 infant mortality rate, 7·4 per 1,000 live births. Marriages (2000), 89,469; divorces and annulments (2000), 39,429.

CLIMATE

2001 statistics: Jan. 24·6°F (–4·1°C), July 74·6°F (23·6°C) average mean (O'Hare International Airport). Average annual rainfall 35·55". In 2000 total rainfall was 31·43". Illinois belongs to the Great Lakes climate zone (*see* UNITED STATES: Climate).

CONSTITUTION AND GOVERNMENT

The present constitution became effective on 1 July 1971. The General Assembly consists of a House of Representatives of 118 members elected for two years, and a Senate of 59 members who are divided into three groups; in one, they are elected for terms of four years, four years, and two years; in the next, for terms of four years, two years, and four years; and in the last, for terms of two years, four years, and four years. Sessions are annual. The state is divided into legislative districts, in each of which one senator is chosen; each district is divided into two representative districts, in each of which one representative is chosen.

For the 109th Congress, which convened in Jan. 2005, Illinois sends 19 members to the House of Representatives. It is represented in the Senate by Richard Durbin (D. 1997–2009) and Barack Obama (D. 2005–11).

The capital is Springfield.

RECENT ELECTIONS

In the 2004 presidential election Kerry polled 2,891,550 votes; Bush, 2,345,946; Badnarik, 32,442.

CURRENT ADMINISTRATION

Governor: Rod Blagojevich (D.), 2003–07 (salary: $150,691).
  Lieut.-Governor: Patrick Quinn (D.), 2003–07 ($115,235).
  Secretary of State: Jesse White (D.), 2003–07 ($132,963).

Government Website: http://www.illinois.gov

ECONOMY

Important industries include financial services, manufacturing, retail and transportation. *Per capita* personal income (2004) was $34,725 in Illinois.

Budget

In 2003 total state revenues amounted to $44,423m. Total expenditure was $51,291m. (education, $14,119m.; public welfare, $11,479m.; highways, $3,834m.; health, $2,570m.; government administration, $1,388m.) Debt outstanding, in 2003, $46,689m.

Performance

Gross State Product in 2004 was $521,900m., ranking Illinois 5th in the United States.

Banking and Finance

In 2000 there were 526 state-chartered banks, 32 foreign banks and 245 national banks. The assets of banks in Illinois totalled $435,669,401,000 in 2000.

ENERGY AND NATURAL RESOURCES

Electricity

Electricity production 2000, 113·6bn. kWh. There were 11 nuclear plants, with net production of 81·4bn. kWh.

Oil and Gas

Natural gas consumption in 1999 was 1,035bn. cu. ft; total petroleum consumption was 250,369,000 bbls.

Water

The total area covered by water is approximately 2,331 sq. miles. In 1999 there were 26,443 miles of streams.

Minerals

The chief mineral product is coal. In 2004 there were 17 operative mines; the coal output was 31,640,000 tons in 2003. Mineral production also includes sand, gravel and limestone. Value of non-fuel mineral production in 2003 was $911m.

Agriculture

In 2003 there were 73,000 farms in Illinois that contained 27·5m. acres of land. The average size of farms was 377 acres and, in 2002, was valued at $2,425 per acre. In 2002 cash receipts from farm marketings in Illinois totalled $7·53bn. Cash receipts: for corn totalled $2·9bn.; for soybeans, $2·1bn.; for livestock and products, $1·8bn.; for hogs, $920m.; for cattle, $528m.; for dairy products, $301m.; for wheat, $111m. The net farm income in 2002 was $642m. In 2000 Illinois was the second largest producer among US states of corn and soybeans. In 2004 there were 3·85m. hogs and pigs, 1·31m. cattle including 416,000 beef cows and 69,300 milch cows, and 63,000 sheep and lambs. Wool production in 2003 totalled 395,000 lb.

Forestry

In 2000 there were six state forests and 27 conservation areas. The gross forest area within unit boundaries in 2002 was 856,686 acres of which 270,000 acres was National Forest Land. Total forested area in 2002 was 4·33m. acres.

Fisheries

In 2001, four hatcheries in Illinois had 75m. fish.

INDUSTRY

In 2001 the state's 17,134 manufacturing establishments had 820,000 employees, earning $32,832m. Total value added by manufacturing in 2001 was $94,124m.

Labour

Selected employee sectors, 2003 (in 1,000): trade, transportation and utilities, 1,817; government, 856; professional and business

services, 766; health and education services, 718; manufacturing, 718. Non-agricultural employment totalled 5,818,000 in 2003; the unemployment rate was 6·7%.

Trade Unions

Labour union membership in 2003 was 1,003,400. Approximately 18·9% of workers in Illinois were members of unions in 1998.

INTERNATIONAL TRADE

Imports and Exports

In 2002 exports from Illinois totalled approximately $31·9bn. Exports included computer equipment, industrial machinery, chemicals and agricultural products.

Trade Fairs

Through the Illinois Department of Commerce and Community Affairs (Illinois Trade Office), activities are held to promote trade. Between Aug. 2000 and July 2001 approximately 20 major events (catalogue shows and trade missions including Canada, Mexico, South America, the Middle East, Africa and Asia Pacific) were held.

COMMUNICATIONS

Roads

In 2003 there were 138,525 miles of roads comprising 37,007 miles of urban road and 101,518 miles of rural road. There were 7,524,909 passenger cars in 2001, 1,249,505 pickup trucks, 290,299 recreational vehicles, buses and trucks, 222,607 motorcycles and 176,870 Interstate Registration Plan vehicles.

Rail

Union Station, Chicago is the home of Amtrak's national hub. Amtrak trains provide service to cities in Illinois to many destinations in the US. Illinois is also served by a metro (CTA) system, and by seven groups of commuter railways controlled by METRA, which has many stations and serves several Illinois counties. Total passengers using Amtrak stations in 2000 were 3,583,707. State system mileage, Dec. 2001: Federal aid interstate non-toll, 1,890 miles; other marked non-toll, 11,422 miles; state supplementary non-toll, 2,638 miles; total length, 15,950 miles. There is also a metro system in Chicago (108 miles).

Civil Aviation

In 2003 there were 118 public airports and 268 heliports; in 2001 there were 496 restricted landing areas. There were 42,681,389 passenger enplanements statewide in 2003.

Shipping

In 2000 total cargo handled by Chicago's ports was 23,929,489 tons.

Telecommunications

In March 2000, 48,395 employees were on a payroll of $3,000·5m.

Postal Services

In 2004 there were approximately 1,200 postal stations.

SOCIAL INSTITUTIONS

Justice

In 2004 there were 28 adult and eight juvenile correctional centers. The adult inmate population totalled 453,418 at the end of 2003. The total number of adult admissions in 2003 was 28,148 and the total number of exits 27,615.

Executions began in 1990 following the US Supreme Court's reinstatement of capital punishment in 1976, with the most recent execution being on 17 March 1999. However, on 31 Jan. 2000 the death penalty was suspended.

A Civil Rights Act (1941), as amended, bans all forms of discrimination by places of public accommodation, including inns, restaurants, retail stores, railroads, aeroplanes, buses, etc., against persons on account of 'race, religion, colour, national ancestry or physical or mental handicap'; another section similarly mentions 'race or colour'.

The Fair Employment Practices Act of 1961, as amended, prohibits discrimination in employment based on race, colour, sex, religion, national origin or ancestry, by employers, employment agencies, labour organizations and others. These principles are embodied in the 1971 constitution.

The Illinois Human Rights Act (1979) prevents unlawful discrimination in employment, real property transactions, access to financial credit and public accommodations, by authorizing the creation of a Department of Human Rights to enforce, and a Human Rights Commission to adjudicate, allegations of unlawful discrimination.

Education
Education is free and compulsory for children between seven and 16 years of age. In 2002–03 pre K-8 enrolment (public) was 1,485,807; pre K-8 (non-public), 239,655; grades 9–12 enrolment (public), 595,349; grades 9–12 (non-public), 63,150. The total number of pre K-8 teachers (public) was 1,025; pre K-8 teachers (non-public), 2,088; kindergarten teachers (public), 5,929; kindergarten teachers (non-public), 1,587. The total number of elementary teachers (public) was 72,889; elementary teachers (non-public), 10,840; secondary teachers (public), 32,473; secondary teachers (non-public), 4,348. In 2001 the median salary for all classroom (pre K-12) teachers was $44,977. In autumn 2001 higher education institutions had a total enrolment of 752,753 at nine public universities, 48 community colleges, 97 not-for-profit and 25 for-profit independent colleges and universities.

Major colleges and universities (autumn 2003):

Founded	Name	Place	Control	Enrolment
1851	Northwestern University	Evanston	Independent	17,625
1857	Illinois State University	Normal	Public	20,860
1867	University of Illinois	Urbana/		
		Champaign	Public	40,458
		Springfield		
		(1969)		4,574
		Chicago		
		(1946)		25,764
1867	Chicago State University	Chicago	Public	7,040
1869	Southern Illinois	Carbondale	Public	21,387
	University	Edwardsville		
		(1957)		13,295
1890	Loyola University of	Chicago	Roman	
	Chicago		Catholic	13,362
1891	University of Chicago	Chicago	Independent	13,887
1895	Eastern Illinois			
	University	Charleston	Public	11,522
1895	Northern Illinois			
	University	DeKalb	Public	25,260
1897	Bradley University	Peoria	Independent	6,137
1899	Western Illinois			
	University	Macomb	Public	13,469
1940	Illinois Institute of			
	Technology	Chicago	Independent	6,167
1945	Roosevelt University	Chicago	Independent	7,524
1961	Northeastern Illinois			
	University	Chicago	Public	11,825
1969	Governors State	University		
	University	Park	Public	5,664

Health
In 2003 there were 192 community hospitals, with 36,300 beds. Total admissions in 2002 were 1,615,269.

Welfare
Medicare enrolment in July 2003 totalled 1,661,454. In 2002 a total of 1,731,398 people in Illinois received Medicaid. In Dec. 2004 there were 1,879,051 Old-Age, Survivors, and Disability Insurance (OASDI) beneficiaries. A total of 92,948 people were receiving payments under Temporary Assistance for Needy Families (TANF) in Sept. 2004.

In fiscal year 2002 the estimated amount spent on medical assistance programmes was $7·66bn.; child support enforcement, $233m.; Office of the Inspector General, $22m.; Public Aid Recoveries, $19m.; administration, $113m.

In 1999 there were 42,300 participating providers in the state and 24,540,000 medical claims processed.

RELIGION
In 2000 there were 6,457,000 Christians and (2002) 270,000 Jews in Illinois. Among the larger Christian denominations are: Roman Catholic (3·6m.), United Methodist (505,000), Lutheran Church Missouri Synod (325,000), Southern Baptist (265,000), Lutheran Church in America (200,000), Presbyterian Church, USA (200,000), United Church of Christ (192,000), American Baptist (105,000), Disciples of Christ (75,000), Assembly of God (63,000) and Church of Nazarene (50,000).

CULTURE

Broadcasting
In 2002 there were 210 radio stations, 18 radio networks and 64 television broadcasting stations. In 1997 there were 184 cable and other pay TV services establishments.

Press
In 2002 there were 405 newspaper publishers in Illinois, 318 periodical publishers, 133 book publishers and 71 database and directory publishers.

Tourism
Visitors spent almost $22bn. yielding $1·6bn. in tax revenue in 2002. The appropriations for tourism for fiscal year 2004 were $47,211,400.

FURTHER READING
Statistical information: Department of Commerce and Community Affairs, 620 Adams St., Springfield 62701. Publishes *Illinois State and Regional Economic Data Book.* Bureau of Economic and Business Research, Univ. of Illinois, 1206 South 6th St., Champaign 61820. Publishes *Illinois Statistical Abstract.*

Blue Book of the State of Illinois. Edited by Secretary of State. Springfield. Biennial

Miller, D. L., *City of the Century: The Epic of Chicago and the Making of America.* Simon and Schuster, New York, 1996

The Illinois State Library: Springfield, IL 62756.

Indiana

KEY HISTORICAL EVENTS

The area was inhabited by Algonquian-speaking tribes when the first European explorers (French) laid claim to it in the 17th century. They established some fortified trading posts but there was little settlement. In 1763 the area passed to Britain, with other French-claimed territory east of the Mississippi. In 1783 Indiana became part of the North West Territory of the USA; it became a separate territory in 1800 and a state in 1816. Until 1811 there had been continuing conflict with the Indian inhabitants, who were then defeated at Tippecanoe.

Early farming settlement was by families of British and German descent, including Amish and Mennonite communities. Later industrial development offered an incentive for more immigration from Europe, and, later, from the southern states. In 1906 the town of Gary was laid out by the United States Steel

Corporation and named after its chairman, Elbert H. Gary. The industry flourished on navigable water midway between supplies of iron ore and of coal. Trade and distribution in general benefited from Indiana Port on Lake Michigan, especially after the opening of the St Lawrence Seaway in 1959. The Ohio River was also exploited for carrying freight.

Indianapolis was built after 1821 and became the state capital in 1825. Natural gas was discovered in the neighbourhood in the late 19th century. This stimulated the growth of a motor industry, celebrated by the Indianapolis 500 race, held annually since 1911.

TERRITORY AND POPULATION

Indiana is bounded west by Illinois, north by Michigan and Lake Michigan, east by Ohio and south by Kentucky across the Ohio River. Land area, 35,867 sq. miles (92,895 sq. km). Census population, 1 April 2000, was 6,080,485, an increase of 9·7% since 1990. July 2005 estimate, 6,271,973.

Population in five census years was:

	White	Black	Indian	Asiatic	Other	Total	Per sq. mile
1930	3,125,778	111,982	285	458	—	3,238,503	89·4
1960	4,388,554	269,275	948	2,447	—	4,662,498	128·9
1980	5,004,394	414,785	7,836	20,557	42,652	5,490,224	152·8
1990	5,020,700	432,092	12,720	37,617	41,030	5,544,159	154·6
2000	5,320,022	510,034	15,815	61,131	173,483	6,080,485	169·5

Of the total population in 2000, 3,098,011 were female, 4,506,089 were 18 years old or older and 4,304,011 were urban. Indiana's Hispanic population was 214,536 in 2000, a 117·2% increase on the 1990 total of 98,789.

The largest cities with census population, 2000, are: Indianapolis (capital), 761,296; Fort Wayne, 205,727; Evansville, 121,582; South Bend, 107,789; Gary, 102,746; Hammond, 83,048; Bloomington, 69,291; Muncie, 67,430; Anderson, 59,734; Terre Haute, 59,614.

SOCIAL STATISTICS

2003 statistics: births, 86,434 (14·0 per 1,000 population); deaths (2002), 55,396 (9·0 per 1,000 population). 2002 infant mortality rate (per 1,000 live births), 7·7. Marriages (2001), 34,100.

CLIMATE

Indianapolis, Jan. 29°F (–1·7°C), July 76°F (24·4°C). Annual rainfall 41" (1,034 mm). Indiana belongs to the Mid-West climate zone (see UNITED STATES: Climate).

CONSTITUTION AND GOVERNMENT

The present constitution (the second) dates from 1851. The General Assembly consists of a Senate of 50 members elected for four years, and a House of Representatives of 100 members elected for two years. It meets annually.

For the 109th Congress, which convened in Jan. 2005, Indiana sends nine members to the House of Representatives. It is represented in the Senate by Richard Lugar (R. 1977–2007) and Evan Bayh (D. 1999–2011).

The state capital is Indianapolis. The state is divided into 92 counties and 1,008 townships.

RECENT ELECTIONS

In the 2004 presidential election Bush polled 1,479,438 votes; Kerry, 969,011; Badnarik, 18,058.

CURRENT ADMINISTRATION

Governor: Mitch Daniels (R.), 2005–09 (salary: $95,000).
  Lieut.-Governor: Becky Skillman (R.), 2005–09 ($76,000).
  Secretary of State: Todd Rokita (R.), 2003–07 ($66,000).

Government Website: http://www.in.gov

ECONOMY

Per capita personal income (2004) was $30,070.

Budget

In 2003 total state revenue was $24,553m. Total expenditure was $23,090m. (education, $8,640m.; public welfare, $5,378m.; highways, $1,713m.; correction, $654m.; health, $545m.) Outstanding debt, in 2003, $11,854m.

Performance

In 2004 Gross State Product was $227,569m., ranking Indiana 16th in the United States.

ENERGY AND NATURAL RESOURCES

Oil and Gas

Production of crude oil in 2003 was 1,865,000 bbls.; 1,309m. cu. ft of natural gas was produced in 2002.

Water

The total area covered by water is approximately 551 sq. miles.

Minerals

The state produced 53,500,000 tonnes of crushed stone and 257m. tonnes of dimension stone in 2003. Production of coal (2003) was 35·4bn. short tons. Value of domestic non-fuel mineral production, in 2003, $734m.

Agriculture

Indiana is largely agricultural, about 75% of its total area being in farms. In 2003, 59,500 farms had 15·0m. acres (average, 253 acres). The average value of land and buildings per acre was $2,750 in 2003. Acreage harvested in 2003 was 12·0m., with a market value of $3,462m. for the top two crops (corn and soybeans).

Farm income 2002, $4,800m.: crops were $3,249m.; livestock and products, $1,551m. The net farm income in 2002 was $108m. The four most important products were corn, soybeans, hogs and dairy products. The livestock on 1 Jan. 2004 included 830,000 all cattle, 153,000 milch cows, 45,000 sheep and lambs, 3·1m. hogs and pigs, 22·7m. chickens and 13·1m. turkeys. In 2003 the wool clip yielded 270,000 lb of wool from 40,000 sheep and lambs.

Forestry

In 2002 there were 4·50m. acres of forest including 191,000 acres of national forest.

INDUSTRY

In 2001 Indiana's 9,131 manufacturing establishments had 604,000 employees, earning $23,471m. Total value added by manufacturing in 2001 was $72,122m. The steel industry is the largest in the country.

Labour

Total non-agricultural employment, 2003, 2,897,000. Employees by branch, 2003 (in 1,000): manufacturing, 573; trade, transportation and utilities, 573; government, 423; education and health services, 362; leisure and hospitality, 273. The unemployment rate in 2003 was 5·1%.

INTERNATIONAL TRADE

Imports and Exports

Exports valued $16·4bn. in 2003.

COMMUNICATIONS

Roads

In 2003 there were 94,597 miles of road (73,998 miles rural). There were 5,739,348 registered motor vehicles.

Rail

In 2002 there were 4,255 miles of mainline railway of which 3,872 miles were Class I.

Civil Aviation

Of airports in 2003, 115 were for public use and 581 were for private use. There were 4,603,641 passenger enplanements statewide in 2003.

SOCIAL INSTITUTIONS

Justice

Following the US Supreme Court's reinstatement of the death penalty in 1976, death sentences have been given since 1980. There were two executions in 2003, none in 2004 and five in 2005. In June 2003, 22,576 prisoners were under the jurisdiction of state and federal correctional authorities.

The Civil Rights Act of 1885 forbids places of public accommodation to bar any persons on grounds not applicable to all citizens alike; no citizen may be disqualified for jury service 'on account of race or colour'. An Act of 1947 makes it an offence to spread religious or racial hatred.

A 1961 Act provided 'all of its citizens equal opportunity for education, employment and access to public conveniences and accommodations' and created a Civil Rights Commission.

Education

School attendance is compulsory from seven to 16 years. In 2003–04 there were an estimated 551,398 pupils attending elementary schools and 459,290 at secondary schools. The average expenditure per pupil was $8,582. Teachers' salaries averaged $45,791 (2003–04). Total expenditure for public schools, 2001–02, $7,988m.

Some leading institutions for higher education were (2003):

Founded	Institution	Control	Students (full-time)
1801	Vincennes University	State	8,185[1]
1824	Indiana University, Bloomington	State	29,768
1832	Wabash College, Crawfordsville	Independent	858
1837	De Pauw University, Greencastle	Methodist	2,319
1842	University of Notre Dame	R.C.	8,303
1847	Earlham College, Richmond	Quaker	1,125
1850	Butler University, Indianapolis	Independent	4,424
1859	Valparaiso University, Valparaiso	Evangelical Lutheran Church	3,003
1870	Indiana State University, Terre Haute	State	9,394
1874	Purdue University, Lafayette	State	30,424
1898	Ball State University, Muncie	State	17,411
1902	University of Indianapolis, Indianapolis	Methodist	2,916
1963	Ivy Tech State College, Indianapolis	State	9,054
1969	Indiana University-Purdue University, Indianapolis	State	21,015
1985	University of Southern Indiana, Evansville	State	8,813

[1]2001.

Health

In 2002 there were 112 community hospitals with 18,961 beds. A total of 715,936 patients were admitted during the year.

Welfare

Medicare enrolment in July 2003 totalled 877,954. In 2002 a total of 849,427 people in Indiana received Medicaid. In Dec. 2004 there were 1,046,476 Old-Age, Survivors, and Disability Insurance (OASDI) beneficiaries. A total of 127,939 people were receiving payments under Temporary Assistance for Needy Families (TANF) in Sept. 2004.

RELIGION

Religious denominations include Methodists, Roman Catholics, Disciples of Christ, Baptists, Lutherans, Presbyterian churches, Society of Friends and Episcopalians.

CULTURE

Broadcasting

In 2004 there were 81 television stations and 301 radio stations.

Press

There were 332 newspapers in circulation in 2004.

Tourism

Tourists—65% of whom travelled from outside the state—spent $6·5bn. in 2001.

FURTHER READING

Statistical information: Indiana Business Research Center, Indiana Univ., Indianapolis 46202. Publishes *Indiana Factbook*.

Gray, R. D. (ed.) *Indiana History: a Book of Readings.* Indiana Univ. Press, 1994

Martin, J. B., *Indiana: an Interpretation.* Indiana Univ. Press, 1992

State Library: Indiana State Library, 140 North Senate, Indianapolis 46204.

Iowa

KEY HISTORICAL EVENTS

Originally the territory of the Iowa Indians, the area was explored by the Frenchmen Marquette and Joliet in 1673. French trading posts were set up, but there was little other settlement. In 1803 the French sold their claim to Iowa to the USA as part of the Louisiana Purchase. The land was still occupied by Indians but, in the 1830s, the tribes sold their land to the US government and migrated to reservations. Iowa became a US Territory in 1838 and a state in 1846.

The state was settled by immigrants drawn mainly from neighbouring states to the east. Later there was more immigration from Protestant states of northern Europe. The land was extremely fertile and most immigrants came to farm. Not all the Indian population had accepted the cession and there were some violent confrontations, notably the murder of settlers at Spirit Lake in 1857. The capital, Des Moines, was founded in 1843 as a fort to protect Indian rights. It expanded rapidly with the growth of a local coal field after 1910.

TERRITORY AND POPULATION

Iowa is bounded east by the Mississippi River (forming the boundary with Wisconsin and Illinois), south by Missouri, west by the Missouri River (forming the boundary with Nebraska), northwest by the Big Sioux River (forming the boundary with South Dakota) and north by Minnesota. Land area, 55,869 sq. miles (144,700 sq. km). Census population, 1 April 2000, 2,926,324, an increase of 5·4% since 1990. July 2005 estimate, 2,966,334.

Population in five census years was:

	White	Black	Indian	Asiatic	Total	Per sq. mile
1870	1,188,207	5,762	48	3	1,194,020	21·5
1930	2,452,677	17,380	660	222	2,470,939	44·1
			All others			
1980	2,839,225	41,700	32,882		2,913,808	51·7
1990	2,683,090	48,090	45,575		2,776,755	49·7
2000	2,748,640	61,853	115,831		2,926,324	52·4

Of the total population in 2000, 1,490,809 were female, 2,192,686 were 18 years old or older and 1,787,432 were urban.

In 2000 the Hispanic population was 82,473, up from 32,647 in 1990 (an increase of 152·6%).

The largest cities in the state, with their population in 2003, are: Des Moines (capital), 196,093; Cedar Rapids, 122,542; Davenport, 97,512; Sioux City, 83,876; Waterloo, 67,054; Iowa City, 63,807; Council Bluffs, 58,656; Dubuque, 57,204; Ames, 53,284; West Des Moines, 51,699; Cedar Falls, 36,429; Urbandale, 31,868; Bettendorf, 31,456; Ankeny, 31,144; Marion, 28,756.

SOCIAL STATISTICS

2003 statistics: births, 38,174 (13·0 per 1,000); deaths (2002), 27,978 (9·5 per 1,000). 2002 infant mortality, 5·3 per 1,000 live births. Marriages, 2003, 20,371; dissolutions of marriages, 8,285.

CLIMATE

Cedar Rapids, Jan. 17·6°F, July 74·2°F. Annual rainfall 34". Des Moines, Jan. 19·4°F, July 76·6°F. Annual rainfall 33·12". Iowa belongs to the Mid-West climate zone (see UNITED STATES: Climate).

CONSTITUTION AND GOVERNMENT

The constitution of 1857 still exists; it has had 46 amendments. The General Assembly comprises a Senate of 50 and a House of Representatives of 100 members, meeting annually for an unlimited session. Senators are elected for four years, half retiring every second year: Representatives for two years. The Governor and Lieut.-Governor are elected for four years.

For the 109th Congress, which convened in Jan. 2005, Iowa sends five members to the House of Representatives. It is represented in the Senate by Chuck Grassley (R. 1981–2011) and Tom Harkin (D. 1985–2009).

Iowa is divided into 99 counties; the capital is Des Moines.

RECENT ELECTIONS

In the 2004 presidential election Bush polled 751,957 votes; Kerry, 741,898; Nader, 5,973.

CURRENT ADMINISTRATION

Governor: Tom Vilsack (D.), 2003–07 (salary: $107,482).
   Lieut.-Governor: Sally Pederson (D.), 2003–07 ($76,698).
   Secretary of State: Chet Culver (D.), 2003–07 ($87,506).

Government Website:
   http://www.iowa.gov/state/main/index.html

ECONOMY

Per capita personal income (2004) was $30,970.

Budget

In the fiscal year 2004 net state general fund revenue was $4,684·0m. Total state general fund expenditure was $4,517·5m. (education, $2,782·3m.; human services, $797·3m.; justice, $465·9m.; administration and regulation, $362·9m.; health and human rights, $47·2m.; agriculture and natural resources, $34·2m.; economic development, $19·5m.; transportation, $8·2m.) Outstanding debt, in 2003, $1,561m.

Performance

Gross State Product was $111,114m. in 2004, ranking Iowa 29th in the United States.

ENERGY AND NATURAL RESOURCES

Water

The total area covered by water is approximately 402 sq. miles.

Minerals

Production in 2003: crushed stone, 34·7m. tonnes; sand and gravel, 14·0m. tonnes. The value of domestic non-fuel mineral products in 2003 was $477m.

Agriculture

Iowa is the wealthiest of the agricultural states, partly because nearly the whole area (92%) is arable and included in farms. The total farm area, 2003, is 31·7m. acres. The average farm in 2002 was 352 acres. The average value of buildings and land per acre was, in 2002, $2,005. The number of farms declined in the latter years of the 20th century, from 174,000 in 1960 to 90,000 in 2003.

Farm income (2002), $10,834m.: from crops, $5,759m., and livestock, $5,075m. The net farm income in 2002 was $1,767m. In 2002 production of corn was 1,963m. bu.[1], value $4,359m.; and soybeans, 499m. bu.[1], value $2,766m. In 2003 livestock included: swine, 15·8m.[1]; milch cows, 201,000; all cattle, 3·30m.; sheep and lambs, 255,000. The wool clip yielded 1·36m. lb.

[1]More than any other state.

Forestry

Total forested area was 2·1m. acres in 2002.

INDUSTRY

In 2002 Iowa's 3,718 manufacturing establishments had 222,501 employees, earning $8,049m. Total value added by manufacturing in 2001 was $29,636m.

Labour

In Sept. 2003 services employed 430,200 people; trade, 301,200; manufacturing establishments, 220,700. Iowa had an unemployment rate of 4·6% in Sept. 2003.

COMMUNICATIONS

Roads

In 2003 there were 113,518 miles of streets and highways. There were 2,127,890 licensed drivers and 2,451,048 registered vehicles.

Rail

In 2004 the state had 4,163 miles of track, three Class I, four Class II and 12 Class III railways.

Civil Aviation

Airports numbered 226 in 2004, consisting of 103 publicly owned, 115 privately owned and eight commercial facilities. There were 3,803 registered aircraft and 1,503,508 passenger enplanements in Iowa in 2003.

SOCIAL INSTITUTIONS

Justice

The death penalty was abolished in Iowa in 1965. In 2004 the nine state prisons had 8,611 inmates.

Education

School attendance is compulsory for 24 consecutive weeks annually during school age (7–16). In 2003–04, 485,011 pupils were attending primary and secondary schools; 37,243 pupils attending non-public schools; classroom teachers numbered 33,688 for public schools with an average salary of $39,432. In 2004 the state spent an average of $6,372 on each elementary and secondary school student.

Leading institutions for higher education enrolment figures (autumn 2004) were:

Founded	Institution	Control	Professors	Full-time Students
1843	Clarke College, Dubuque	Independent	83	1,180
1846	Grinnell College, Grinnell	Independent	142	1,485

Founded	Institution	Control	Professors	Full-time Students
1847	University of Iowa, Iowa City	State	1,713	29,745
1851	Coe College, Cedar Rapids	Independent	73	1,218
1852	Wartburg College, Waverly	Evangelical Lutheran	104	1,804
1853	Cornell College, Mount Vernon	Independent	85	1,154
1854	Upper Iowa University, Fayette	Independent	36	2,758
1858	Iowa State University, Ames	State	1,369	23,783
1859	Luther College, Decorah	Evangelical Lutheran	197	2,497
1876	Univ. of Northern Iowa, Cedar Falls	State	561	11,424
1881	Drake University, Des Moines	Independent	245	2,954
1882	St Ambrose University, Davenport	Roman Catholic	160	2,413
1891	Buena Vista University, Storm Lake	Presbyterian	82	2,775
1894	Morningside College, Sioux City	Methodist	65	806

Health

In 2004 the state had 123 community hospitals (11,924 beds).

Welfare

Iowa has a Civil Rights Act (1939) which makes it a misdemeanour for any place of public accommodation to deprive any person of 'full and equal enjoyment' of the facilities it offers the public.

Medicare enrolment in July 2003 totalled 482,340. In 2002 a total of 352,635 people in Iowa received Medicaid. In Dec. 2004 there were 548,297 Old-Age, Survivors, and Disability Insurance (OASDI) beneficiaries.

Supplemental Security Income (SSI) assistance is available for the aged (65 or older), the blind and the disabled. As of June 2004, 3,748 elderly persons were drawing an average of $198·86 per month, 738 blind persons $335·79 per month and 36,152 disabled persons $372·26 per month. In 2004 Temporary Assistance to Needy Families (TANF) was received by on average 44,648 recipients monthly.

RELIGION

Chief religious bodies in 2004: Roman Catholics, 529,776 members; Evangelical Lutherans in America, 260,832 baptized members; United Methodists, 195,877; USA Presbyterians, 49,389; United Church of Christ, 38,945.

CULTURE

There were a total of 80 venues for live performances (2003).

Broadcasting

In 2004 there were 256 radio stations and 24 television stations.

Press

In 2004 there were a total of 326 newspapers.

Tourism

In 2003 there were 16·6m. visitors; value of industry, $4·6bn.

FURTHER READING

Annual Survey of Manufactures. US Department of Commerce
Government Finance. US Department of Commerce
Official Register. Secretary of State. Des Moines. Biennial
State Government Website: http://www.iowa.gov

State Library of Iowa: Des Moines 50319.

Kansas

KEY HISTORICAL EVENTS

The area was explored from Mexico in the 16th century, when Spanish travellers found groups of Kansas, Wichita, Osage and Pawnee tribes. The French claimed Kansas in 1682 and they established a valuable fur trade with local tribes in the 18th century. In 1803 the area passed to the USA as part of the Louisiana Purchase and became a base for pioneering trails further west. After 1830 it was 'Indian Territory' and a number of tribes displaced from eastern states were settled there. In 1854 the Kansas Territory was created and opened for white settlement. The early settlers were farmers from Europe or New England, but the Territory's position brought it into contact with southern ideas also. Until 1861 there were frequent outbreaks of violence over the issue of slavery. Slavery had been excluded from the future Territory by the Missouri Compromise of 1820, but the 1854 Kansas-Nebraska Act had affirmed the principle of 'popular sovereignty' to settle the issue, which was then fought out by opposing factions throughout 'Bleeding Kansas'.

Kansas finally entered the Union (as a non-slavery state) in 1861; the part of Colorado which had formed part of the Kansas Territory was then separated from it.

The economy developed through a combination of cattle-ranching and railways. Herds were driven to the railheads and shipped from vast stockyards, or slaughtered and processed in railhead meat-packing plants. Wheat and sorghum also became important once the plains could be ploughed on a large scale.

TERRITORY AND POPULATION

Kansas is bounded north by Nebraska, east by Missouri, with the Missouri River as boundary in the northeast, south by Oklahoma and west by Colorado. Land area, 81,815 sq. miles (211,900 sq. km). Census population, 1 April 2000, 2,688,418, an increase of 8·5% since 1990. July 2005 estimate, 2,744,687.

Population in five federal census years was:

	White	Black	Indian	Asiatic	Total	Per sq. mile
1870	346,377	17,108	914	—	364,399	4·5
1930	1,811,997	66,344	2,454	204	1,880,999	22·9
			All others			
1980	2,168,221	126,127	69,888		2,364,236	28·8
1990	2,231,986	143,076	102,512		2,477,574	30·3
2000	2,313,944	154,198	220,276		2,688,418	32·9

Of the total population in 2000, 1,359,944 were female, 1,975,425 were 18 years old or older and 1,920,669 were urban. In 1999 the estimated Hispanic population was 188,252, up from 93,671 in 1990 (an increase of 101·0%).

Cities, with 2000 census population: Wichita, 344,284; Overland Park, 149,080; Kansas City, 146,866; Topeka (capital), 122,377; Olathe, 92,962; Lawrence, 80,098.

SOCIAL STATISTICS

Vital statistics 2003: births, 39,476 (14·5 per 1,000 population); deaths (2002), 25,021 (9·2 per 1,000 population). 2002 infant mortality (per 1,000 live births), 7·1. 2001: marriages, 20,300; divorces, 8,700.

CLIMATE

Dodge City, Jan. 29°F (–1·7°C), July 78°F (25·6°C). Annual rainfall 21" (518 mm). Kansas City, Jan. 30°F (–1·1°C), July 79°F (26·1°C). Annual rainfall 38" (947 mm). Topeka, Jan. 28°F (–2·2°C), July 78°F (25·6°C). Annual rainfall 35" (875 mm). Wichita, Jan. 31°F (–0·6°C), July 81°F (27·2°C). Annual rainfall 31" (777 mm). Kansas belongs to the Mid-West climate zone (*see* UNITED STATES: Climate).

CONSTITUTION AND GOVERNMENT

The year 1861 saw the adoption of the present constitution; it has had 89 amendments. The Legislature includes a Senate of 40 members, elected for four years, and a House of Representatives of 125 members, elected for two years. Sessions are annual.

For the 109th Congress, which convened in Jan. 2005, Kansas sends four members to the House of Representatives. It is represented in the Senate by Pat Roberts (R. 1997–2009) and Sam Brownback (R. 1997–2011).

The capital is Topeka. The state is divided into 105 counties.

RECENT ELECTIONS

In the 2004 presidential election Bush polled 736,456 votes; Kerry, 434,993; Nader, 9,348.

CURRENT ADMINISTRATION

Governor: Kathleen Sebelius (D.), 2003–07 (salary: $101,281).
   Lieut.-Governor: John E. Moore (D.), 2003–07 ($28,647).
   Secretary of State: Ron Thornburgh (R.), 2003–07 ($78,680).

Government Website: http://www.accesskansas.org

ECONOMY

Per capita income (2004) was $31,003.

Budget

In 2003 total state revenue was $10,402m. Total expenditure was $10,954m. (education, $4,211m.; public welfare, $1,906m.; highways, $1,094m.; government administration, $534m.; health, $524m.) Outstanding debt, in 2003, $2,472m.

Performance

Gross State Product in 2004 was $98,946m., ranking Kansas 32nd in the United States.

ENERGY AND NATURAL RESOURCES

Water

The total area covered by water is approximately 462 sq. miles.

Minerals

Important fuel minerals are coal, petroleum and natural gas. Non-fuel minerals, mainly cement, salt and crushed stone, were worth $668m. in 2003.

Agriculture

Kansas is pre-eminently agricultural, but sometimes suffers from lack of rainfall in the west. In 2002 there were 63,000 farms with a total acreage of 47·4m. Average number of acres per farm was 752. Average value of farmland and buildings per acre, in 2002, was $687. Farm income, 2002, from crops, $2,536m.; from livestock and products, $5,325m. Chief crops: wheat, corn and soybeans. The net farm income in 2002 was $376m. Wheat production was 262·98m. bu. in 2002. There is an extensive livestock industry, comprising, in 2000, 6·55m. cattle (only Texas had more), 100,000 sheep, 1·46m. pigs and 1·75m. poultry.

Forestry

The state had a forested area of 1·55m. acres in 2002.

INDUSTRY

In 2001 the state's 3,240 manufacturing establishments had 191,000 employees, earning $7,302m. Total value added by manufacturing in 2001 was $21,008m.

Labour

Total non-agricultural employment, 2003, 1,312,000. Employees by branch, 2003 (in 1,000): trade, transportation and utilities, 262; government, 250; manufacturing, 172; education and health services, 157; professional and business services, 124. In 2003 the state unemployment rate was 5·4%.

COMMUNICATIONS

Roads

In 2003 there were 135,012 miles of roads (124,418 miles rural). There were 2,314,460 registered motor vehicles.

Rail

There were 5,084 miles of railway as of 31 Dec. 2003.

Civil Aviation

There is an international airport at Wichita. There were 743,515 passenger enplanements statewide in 2003.

SOCIAL INSTITUTIONS

Justice

In June 2003 there were 9,009 federal and state prisoners. The death penalty was declared unconstitutional in Kansas in 2004. The last execution was in 1965.

Education

In 1995 there were approximately 463,000 public elementary and secondary pupils enrolled and (1994–95) 30,588 teachers.

Kansas has six state-supported institutions of higher education: Kansas State University, Manhattan (1863); The University of Kansas, Lawrence, founded in 1865; Emporia State University, Emporia; Pittsburg State University, Pittsburg; Fort Hays State University, Hays; and Wichita State University, Wichita. The state also supports a two-year technical school, Kansas College of Technology, at Salina.

Education expenditure by state and local governments in 1997 was $2,874m.

Health

In 2002 there were 132 community hospitals with 10,900 beds. A total of 329,000 patients were admitted during the year.

Welfare

Medicare enrolment in July 2003 totalled 394,206. In 2002 a total of 289,349 people in Kansas received Medicaid. In Dec. 2004 there were 447,371 Old-Age, Survivors, and Disability Insurance (OASDI) beneficiaries. A total of 46,186 people were receiving payments under Temporary Assistance for Needy Families (TANF) in Sept. 2004.

RELIGION

The most numerous religious bodies are Roman Catholics, Methodists and Disciples of Christ.

FURTHER READING

Statistical information: Institute for Public Policy and Business Research, Univ. of Kansas, 607 Blake Hall, Lawrence 66045. Publishes *Kansas Statistical Abstract.*
Annual Economic Report of the Governor. Topeka

Drury, J. W., *The Government of Kansas.* Lawrence, Univ. of Kansas, 1970

State Library: Kansas State Library, Topeka.

Kentucky

KEY HISTORICAL EVENTS

Lying west of the Appalachians and south of the Ohio River, the area was the meeting place and battleground for the eastern Iroquois and the southern Cherokees. Northern Shawnees also penetrated. The first successful white settlement took place in 1769 when Daniel Boone reached the Bluegrass plains from the eastern, trans-Appalachian, colonies. After 1783 immigration from the east was rapid, settlers travelling by river or crossing the mountains by the Cumberland Gap. The area was originally attached to Virginia but became a separate state in 1792.

Large plantations dependent on slave labour were established, as were small farms worked by white owners. The state became divided on the issue of slavery, although plantation interests (mainly producing tobacco) dominated state government. In the event the state did not secede in 1861, and the majority of citizens supported the Union. Public opinion swung round in support of the south during the difficulties of the reconstruction period.

The eastern mountains became an important coal-mining area, tobacco-growing continued and the Bluegrass plains produced livestock, including especially fine thoroughbred horses.

TERRITORY AND POPULATION

Kentucky is bounded in the north by the Ohio River (forming the boundary with Illinois, Indiana and Ohio), northeast by the Big Sandy River (forming the boundary with West Virginia), east by Virginia, south by Tennessee and west by the Mississippi River (forming the boundary with Missouri). Land area, 39,728 sq. miles (102,895 sq. km). Census population, 2000, 4,041,769, an increase of 9·7% since 1990. July 2005 estimate, 4,173,405.

Population in five census years was:

	White	Black	All others	Total	Per sq. mile
1930	2,388,364	226,040	185	2,614,589	65·1
1960	2,820,083	215,949	2,124	3,038,156	76·2
1980	3,379,006	259,477	22,294	3,660,777	92·3
1990	3,391,832	262,907	30,557	3,685,296	92·8
2000	3,640,889	295,994	104,886	4,041,769	101·7

Of the total population in 2000, 2,066,401 were female, 3,046,951 were 18 years old or older and 2,253,800 were urban. Kentucky's Hispanic population was estimated to be 59,939, up 172·4% on the 1990 census figure of 22,005.

The principal cities with census population in 2000 are: Lexington-Fayette, 260,512; Louisville, 256,321; Owensboro, 54,067; Bowling Green, 49,296; Covington, 43,370; Hopkinsville, 30,089; Frankfort (capital), 27,741; Henderson, 27,373; Richmond, 27,152; Jeffersontown, 26,633.

SOCIAL STATISTICS

In 2003: births, 55,236 (13·4 per 1,000 population); deaths (2002), 40,697 (9·9 per 1,000 population). 2002 infant mortality, 7·2 per 1,000 live births. Marriages, 2000, 39,671 (11·4 per 1,000 population); divorces, 21,593 (5·6).

CLIMATE

Kentucky is in the Appalachian Mountains climatic zone (see UNITED STATES: Climate). It has a temperate climate. Temperatures are moderate during both winter and summer, precipitation is ample without a pronounced dry season, and winter snowfall amounts are variable. Mean annual temperatures range from 52°F in the northeast to 58°F in the southwest. Annual rainfall averages at about 45". Snowfall ranges from 5 to 10" in the southwest of the state, to 25" in the northeast, and 40" at higher altitudes in the southeast.

CONSTITUTION AND GOVERNMENT

The constitution dates from 1891; there had been three preceding it. The 1891 constitution was promulgated by convention and provides that amendments be submitted to the electorate for ratification. The General Assembly consists of a Senate of 38 members elected for four years, one half retiring every two years, and a House of Representatives of 100 members elected for two years. It has annual sessions. All citizens of 18 or over are qualified as electors. Registered voters, Nov. 2000, 2,556,815.

For the 109th Congress, which convened in Jan. 2005, Kentucky sends six members to the House of Representatives. It is represented in the Senate by Mitch McConnell (R. 1985–2009) and Jim Bunning (R. 1999–2011).

The capital is Frankfort. The state is divided into 120 counties.

RECENT ELECTIONS

In the 2004 presidential election Bush polled 1,069,439 votes; Kerry, 712,733; Nader, 8,856.

CURRENT ADMINISTRATION

Governor: Ernie Fletcher (R.), Dec. 2003–Dec. 2007 (salary: $112,704·96).

Lieut.-Governor: Stephen Pence (R.), Dec. 2003–Dec. 2007 ($95,814·96).

Secretary of State: Trey Grayson (R.), Jan. 2004–Jan. 2008 ($95,814·96).

Government Website: http://kentucky.gov

ECONOMY

Per capita personal income (2004) was $27,151.

Budget

In 2003 total state revenue was $18,377m. Total expenditure was $19,117m. (education, $6,097m.; public welfare, $4,964m.; highways, $1,816m.; government administration, $679m.; health, $523m.) Debt outstanding, in 2003, $7,109m.

Performance

Gross State Product in 2004 was $136,446m., ranking Kentucky 26th in the United States.

ENERGY AND NATURAL RESOURCES

Electricity

In 1999 production was 92,633m. kWh, of which 88,915m. kWh was from coal.

Oil and Gas

Production of crude oil in 2000 was 2·9m. bbls. (of 42 gallons); natural gas, 81,545m. cu. ft.

Water

The total area covered by water is approximately 681 sq. miles.

Minerals

The principal mineral is coal: 139·6m. short tons were mined in 1999, value $3,281m.; crushed stone, 56m. short tons, value $295m.; sand and gravel, 9·6m. short tons, value $33·0m.; clay, 0·9m. tonnes, value $3·8m. Other minerals include fluorspar, ball clay, gemstones, dolomite, cement and lime.

Agriculture

In 2002, 89,000 farms covered an area of 13·6m. acres. The average farm was 153 acres. In 2002 the average value of farmland and buildings per acre was $1,824.

Farm income, 2002, from crops, $1·15bn., and from livestock, $1·96bn. The net farm income in 2002 was $744m. The chief crop is tobacco: production, in 2001, 254·6m. lb. Other principal crops include corn (156·2m. bu.), soybeans, wheat, hay, fruit and vegetables, sorghum grain and barley.

Stock-raising is important in Kentucky, which has long been famous for its horses. The livestock in 2001 included 128,000 milch cows, 2·3m. cattle and calves, 21,000 sheep, 5·6m. chickens and 0·45m. swine.

Forestry

In 2002 Kentucky had 12·68m. acres forested land, of which 645,000 acres were national forest.

Fisheries
Cash receipts from aquaculture totalled $1·1m. in 2001.

INDUSTRY

In 2000 the state had 4,209 manufacturing plants and in 2001 there were 293,003 manufacturing employees. The value added by manufacture in 2001 was $31,722m. The leading manufacturing industries (by employment) in 2001 were transportation equipment, industrial machinery, food products, fabricated metal products and electronic equipment.

Labour
In Sept. 2002 the civilian labour force numbered 1,990,531. Of the 1,712,366 employed, 549,210 were engaged in services, 375,795 in trade, transportation and utilities, 293,003 in manufacturing, 40,028 in agriculture and 559,694 in other employment. The unemployment rate in 2003 was 6·2%.

Trade Unions
In 2000, 208,000 (13·6%) workers were union members.

INTERNATIONAL TRADE

Imports and Exports
Exports in 2001 totalled $9·04bn. with manufactured goods accounting for 95% of total exports. Transportation equipment, industrial machinery and chemicals were important manufactured exports. Livestock and coal were major non-manufactured goods exported.

COMMUNICATIONS

Roads
In 2003 there were 77,011 miles of roads comprising 11,983 miles of urban road and 65,028 miles of rural road. There were 3,388,879 registered motor vehicles.

Rail
In 2004 there were 2,760 miles of railway of which 2,299 miles were Class I.

Civil Aviation
There were (2005) 62 publicly used airports. Commercial airports providing scheduled airline services in Kentucky are located in Erlanger (Covington/Cincinnati area), Louisville, Lexington, Owensboro and Paducah. There were 12,745,593 passenger enplanements statewide in 2003.

Shipping
There is barge traffic on the 1,100 miles of navigable rivers. There are six public river ports, over 30 contract terminal facilities and 150 private terminal operations. Kentucky's waterways have access to the junction of the upper and lower Mississippi, Ohio and Tennessee-Tombigbee navigation corridors.

SOCIAL INSTITUTIONS

Justice
There are 12 adult prisons within the Department of Corrections Adult Institutions and three privately run adult institutions. In June 2003 there were 16,377 prison inmates. The death penalty is authorized for murder and kidnapping. As of Oct. 2004 there were 35 persons (including one female) under sentence of death. The last execution was in 1999.

Education
Attendance at school between the ages of five and 16 years (inclusive) is compulsory, the normal term being 175 days. In 2001–02, 40,789 teachers were employed in public elementary and secondary schools. There were 630,436 pupils in public elementary and secondary schools. Public school classroom teachers' salaries (2001–02) averaged $36,688. The average total expenditure per pupil was $6,720.

There were also 4,207 teachers working in private elementary and secondary schools with some 71,812 students in 2001–02.

The state has 28 universities and senior colleges, one junior college and 28 community and technical colleges, with a total enrolment of 187,270 students (autumn 2001). Of these universities and colleges, 36 are state-supported and the remainder are supported privately. The largest of the institutions of higher learning are (autumn 2001): University of Kentucky, with 24,791 students; University of Louisville, 20,394; Western Kentucky University, 16,579; Eastern Kentucky University, 14,697; Northern Kentucky University, 12,548; Murray State University, 9,648; Morehead State University, 9,027; Kentucky State University, 2,314. Five of the several privately endowed colleges of standing are Berea College, Berea; Centre College, Danville; Transylvania University, Lexington; Georgetown College, Georgetown; and Bellarmine College, Louisville.

Health
In 2001 the state had 123 licensed hospitals (18,616 beds). There were 422 licensed long-term care facilities (34,825 beds), 259 family care homes, 126 home health agencies and 1,856 miscellaneous health facilities and laboratories.

Welfare
Medicare enrolment in July 2003 totalled 648,400. In 2002 a total of 808,294 people in Kentucky received Medicaid. In Dec. 2004 there were 782,816 Old-Age, Survivors, and Disability Insurance (OASDI) beneficiaries. A total of 78,364 people were receiving payments under Temporary Assistance for Needy Families (TANF) in Sept. 2004.

RELIGION

The chief religious denominations in 2000 were: Southern Baptists, with 979,994 members, Roman Catholics (406,021), United Methodists (208,720), Christian Churches and Church of Christ (106,638) and Christian (Disciples of Christ) (67,611).

CULTURE

The Kentucky Center for the Arts hosts productions by the Kentucky Opera Association, the Louisville Ballet, the Louisville Orchestra and Broadway touring productions.

Tourism
In 1999 tourist expenditure was $8,191·9m., producing over $888m. in tax revenues and supporting 148,781 jobs. The state had (1999) 1,093 hotels and motels, 248 camping grounds and 50 state parks.

FURTHER READING

Kentucky Deskbook of Economic Statistics, Lackey, Brent, (ed.) Kentucky Cabinet for Economic Development, Frankfort

Miller, P. M., *Kentucky Politics and Government: Do We Stand United?* Nebraska Univ. Press, 1994

Ulack, R. (ed.) *Atlas of Kentucky.* The Univ. Press of Kentucky, 1998

Louisiana

KEY HISTORICAL EVENTS

Originally the Territory of Choctaw and Caddo tribes, the whole area was claimed for France in 1682. The French founded New Orleans in 1718 and it became the centre of a crown colony in 1731. During the wars which the European powers fought over their American interests, the French ceded the area west of the Mississippi (most of the present state) to Spain in 1762 and the eastern area, north of New Orleans, to Britain in 1763. The

British section passed to the USA in 1783, but France bought back the rest from Spain in 1800, including New Orleans and the mouth of the Mississippi. The USA, fearing to be excluded from a strategically important and commercially promising shipping area, persuaded France to sell Louisiana again in 1803. The present states of Missouri, Arkansas, Iowa, North Dakota, South Dakota, Nebraska and Oklahoma were included in the purchase.

The area became the Territory of New Orleans in 1804 and was admitted to the Union as a state in 1812. The economy at first depended on cotton and sugarcane plantations. The population was of French, Spanish and black descent, with a growing number of American settlers. Plantation interests succeeded in achieving secession in 1861, but New Orleans was occupied by the Union in 1862. Planters re-emerged in the late 19th century and imposed rigid segregation of the black population, denying them their new rights.

The state has become mainly urban industrial, with the Mississippi ports growing rapidly. There is petroleum and natural gas, and a strong tourist industry based on the French culture and Caribbean atmosphere of New Orleans.

Louisiana, and New Orleans in particular, suffered widespread damage and loss of life after Hurricane Katrina struck the Gulf Coast on 31 Aug. 2005. New Orleans was evacuated, although some residents refused to leave.

TERRITORY AND POPULATION

Louisiana is bounded north by Arkansas, east by Mississippi, south by the Gulf of Mexico and west by Texas. Land area, 43,562 sq. miles (112,825 sq. km). Census population, 1 April 2000, 4,468,976, an increase of 5·9% since 1990. July 2005 estimate, 4,523,628.

Population in five census years was:

	White	Black	Indian	Asiatic	Total	Per sq. mile
1930	1,322,712	776,326	1,536	1,019	2,101,593	46·5
1960	2,211,715	1,039,207	3,587	2,004	3,257,022	72·2
			All others			
1980	2,911,243	1,237,263	55,466		4,205,900	93·5
1990	2,839,138	1,299,281	81,554		4,219,973	96·9
2000	2,856,161	1,451,944	160,871		4,468,976	102·6

Of the total population in 2000, 2,306,073 were female, 3,249,177 were 18 years old or older and 3,245,665 were urban. The Hispanic population was 107,738 in 2000, an increase of 14,671 (15·8%) on the 1990 census figure of 93,067.

The largest cities with their 2000 census population are: New Orleans, 484,674; Baton Rouge, 227,818; Shreveport, 200,145; Lafayette, 100,257; Lake Charles, 71,757; Kenner, 70,517; Bossier City, 56,461; Monroe, 53,107. In Jan. 2006 the population of New Orleans was estimated at 144,000 in the wake of Hurricane Katrina, making Baton Rouge currently the most populous city in Louisiana.

SOCIAL STATISTICS

Statistics 2003: live births, 65,040 (14·5 per 1,000 population); deaths (2002), 41,984 (9·4 per 1,000 population). 2002 infant deaths, 10·3 per 1,000 live births. 2001: marriages, 36,545; divorces, 14,767.

CLIMATE

New Orleans, Jan. 54°F (12·2°C), July 83°F (28·3°C). Annual rainfall 58" (1,458 mm). Louisiana belongs to the Gulf Coast climate zone (see UNITED STATES: Climate).

CONSTITUTION AND GOVERNMENT

The present constitution dates from 1974. The Legislature consists of a Senate of 39 members and a House of Representatives of 105 members, both chosen for four years. Sessions are annual; a fiscal session is held in even years.

For the 109th Congress, which convened in Jan. 2005, Louisiana sends seven members to the House of Representatives. It is represented in the Senate by Mary Landrieu (D. 1997–2009) and David Vitter (R. 2005–11).

Louisiana is divided into 64 parishes (corresponding to the counties of other states). The capital is Baton Rouge.

RECENT ELECTIONS

In the 2004 presidential election Bush polled 1,102,169 votes; Kerry, 820,299; Nader, 7,032.

CURRENT ADMINISTRATION

Governor: Kathleen Blanco (D.), 2004–08 (salary: $95,000).
   Lieut.-Governor: Mitch Landrieu (D.), 2004–08 ($85,000).
   Secretary of State: Al Ater (D.), appointed July 2005 ($85,000).

Government Website: http://www.louisiana.gov

ECONOMY

Per capita personal income (2004) was $27,219.

Budget

In fiscal year 2003 total revenue was $19,438m. Total expenditure was $18,681m. (education, $6,235m.; public welfare, $2,800m.; hospitals, $1,507m.; highways, $1,143m.; correction, $619m.) Debt outstanding, in 2003, $9,773m.

Performance

Gross State Product in 2004 was $152,944m., ranking Louisiana 24th in the United States.

ENERGY AND NATURAL RESOURCES

Electricity

50,479m. kWh of electricity were produced in 2002.

Oil and Gas

Louisiana ranks fourth among states of the USA for oil production and second for natural gas production. Production in 2003 of crude oil was 58m. bbls.; and of natural gas, 2,961·4bn. cu. ft.

Water

The area covered by water was approximately 8,278 sq. miles in 2000.

Minerals

Principal non-fuel minerals are salt and sand, gravel, and lime. Total non-fuel mineral production in 2003 was $331m.

Agriculture

The state is divided into two parts, the uplands and the alluvial and swamp regions of the coast. A delta occupies about one-third of the total area. Manufacturing is the leading industry, but agriculture is important. The number of farms in 2003 was 27,200 covering 7·85m. acres; the average farm had 289 acres. Average value of farmland per acre, in 2002, was $1,534.

Farm income, 2003, from crops, $1,296m., and from livestock, $697m. The net farm income in 2003 was $719m. Principal crops, 2003 production, were: soybeans, 25·16m. bu.; sugarcane, 12·84m. tons; rice, 26·40m. cwt; corn, 67·00m. bu.; cotton, 1·03m. bales; sweet potatoes, 3·15m. cwt; sorghum, 14·03m. bu.

Forestry

Forestlands cover 48% of the state's area, or 13·8m. acres. Production 2003: sawtimber, 1,266·18m. bd ft; cordwood, 6·74m. standard cords. The economic impact of forestry and forest products industries in Louisiana was $3·7bn. in 2003.

Fisheries

In 2003 Louisiana's commercial fisheries catch for all species totalled 1,189·7m. lb (539,635 tonnes), valued at $294·1m.

INDUSTRY

Louisiana's leading manufacturing activity is the production of chemicals, followed, in order of importance, by the processing of petroleum and coal products, the production of transportation equipment and production of paper products. In 2001 the state's 3,436 manufacturing establishments had 159,000 employees, earning $6,539m. Total value added by manufacturing in 2001 was $22,545m.

Labour

Non-agricultural employment for Aug. 2004 was 1,894,900, including: service industries, 694,800; government, 369,600; wholesale and retail trade, 300,200; manufacturing, 154,700; construction, 116,200; transportation, communications and public utilities, 110,900; finance, insurance and real estate, 101,200; mining, 43,800.

In 2003 the civilian labour force totalled 1,906,000. There were 134,000 persons unemployed, a rate of 6·6%.

INTERNATIONAL TRADE

In 2003 exports were valued at $18,390·13m. In 1999 foreign investment amounted to $31·8bn.

COMMUNICATIONS

Roads

In 2003 there were 60,937 miles of public roads (46,987 miles rural). 3,713,561 motor vehicles were registered.

Rail

In 2003 there were approximately 2,748 miles of main-line track in the state. There is a tramway in New Orleans.

Civil Aviation

In 2004 there were 71 public airports. There were 5,706,274 passenger enplanements statewide in 2003.

Shipping

There are ports at New Orleans, Baton Rouge, St Bernard, Plaquemines and Lake Charles. The Mississippi and other waterways provide 7,500 miles of navigable water.

SOCIAL INSTITUTIONS

Justice

In Sept. 2003 there were 36,612 prisoners in adult correctional institutions and the juvenile offender population totalled 6,067. The death penalty is authorized. There was one execution in 2002 but there have been none since then.

Education

School attendance is compulsory between the ages of seven and 15, both inclusive. In 2003 there were 1,505 public schools with 723,252 registered pupils, and 49,371 teachers paid an average salary of $36,433. There are 16 public colleges and universities and ten non-public institutions of higher learning. There are 42 state trade and vocational technical schools, three law schools, three medical schools and a biomedical research centre affiliated with Louisiana's universities.

In 2003–04 there were 210,484 students enrolled at public two- and four-year colleges and universities. Enrolment, 2003–04, in the University of Louisiana System was 83,303 (Lafayette, 16,208; Southeastern, 15,662; Louisiana Tech., 11,960; Northwestern, 10,505; Monroe, 8,592; McNeese, 8,447; Nicholls, 7,260; Grambling, 4,669); Louisiana State University, 62,841 (with campuses at Alexandria, Baton Rouge, Eunice, New Orleans and Shreveport); Southern University System, 15,044. Major private

institutions: Tulane University, 9,920; Loyola University, 5,900; Xavier University, 3,994; Dillard University, 1,953.

Health

In 2003 there were 203 hospitals with 24,653 beds.

Welfare

Medicare enrolment in July 2003 totalled 620,196. In 2002 a total of 898,824 people in Louisiana received Medicaid. In Dec. 2004 there were 740,378 Old-Age, Survivors, and Disability Insurance (OASDI) beneficiaries. In fiscal year 2003–04 Family Independence Temporary Assistance Program (FITAP) payments to 434,707 recipients totalled $40,056,233. In the fiscal year 2003–04 Food Stamp benefits totalling $735,959,328 were paid to 7,972,477 recipients.

RELIGION

The Roman Catholic Church is the largest denomination in Louisiana. The leading Protestant Churches are Southern Baptist and Methodist.

CULTURE

Broadcasting

In 2004 there were 215 radio stations (77 AM; 138 FM) and 48 television stations.

Press

In 2004 there were 309 newspapers in circulation.

Tourism

Tourism is the second most important industry for state income. In 2003 there were over 25m. visitors to the state. Tourism was a $9·4bn. industry in 2003; it provided more than 119,900 jobs and generated in excess of $1·2bn. in tax revenue for federal, state and local governments.

FURTHER READING

1997 Statistical Abstract of Louisiana, 10th Edition, New Orleans, LA: Division of Business and Economic Research, College of Business Administration, Univ. of New Orleans, 1997.

Calhoun, Milburn, (ed.) *Louisiana Almanac 2006–2007 Edition.* Pelican Publishing Co., 2006

Wall, Bennett H., *et al.*, (eds.) *Louisiana: a History, Third Edition.* Harlan Davidson, Inc, 1997

Wilds, J., *et al.*, (eds.) *Louisiana Yesterday and Today: a Historical Guide to the State.* Louisiana State Univ. Press, 1996

State Library: The State Library of Louisiana, Baton Rouge, Louisiana.

Maine

KEY HISTORICAL EVENTS

Originally occupied by Algonquian-speaking tribes, the Territory was disputed between different groups of British settlers, and between the British and French, throughout the 17th and most of the 18th centuries. After 1652 it was governed as part of Massachusetts, and French claims finally failed in 1763. Most of the early settlers were English and Protestant Irish, with many Quebec French.

The Massachusetts settlers had gained control when the original colonist, Sir Ferdinando Gorges, supported the losing royalist side in the English civil war. Their control was questioned during the English-American war of 1812, when Maine residents claimed that the Massachusetts government did not protect them against British raids. Maine was separated from Massachusetts and entered the Union as a state in 1820.

Maine is a mountainous state and even the coastline is rugged, but the coastal belt is where most settlement has developed. In the 19th century there were manufacturing towns making use of cheap water-power, and the rocky shore supported a shell-fish industry. The latter still flourishes, together with intensive horticulture, producing potatoes and fruit. The other main economic development has been in exploiting the forests for timber, pulp and paper.

The capital is Augusta, a river trading post which was fortified against Indian attacks in 1754, incorporated as a town in 1797 and chosen as capital in 1832.

TERRITORY AND POPULATION

Maine is bounded west, north and east by Canada, southeast by the Atlantic, south and southwest by New Hampshire. Land area, 30,862 sq. miles (79,932 sq. km). Census population, 1 April 2000, 1,274,923, an increase of 3·8% since 1990. July 2005 estimate, 1,321,505.

Population for five census years was:

	White	Black	Indian	Asiatic	Total	Per sq. mile
1910	739,995	1,363	992	121	742,371	24·8
1950	910,846	1,221	1,522	185	913,774	29·4
		All others				
1980	1,109,850	3,128	12,049		1,125,027	36·3
1990	1,208,360	5,138	14,430		1,227,928	39·8
2000	1,236,014	6,760	32,149		1,274,923	41·3

Of the total population in 2000, 654,614 were female, 973,685 were 18 years old or older and 762,045 were rural (59·8%). Only Vermont has a more rural population. In 2000 the Hispanic population was 9,360, an increase of 37·1% on the 1990 census figure of 6,829. Only North Dakota and Vermont have fewer persons of Hispanic origin in the USA.

The largest city in the state is Portland, with a census population of 64,249 in 2000. Other cities (with population in 2000) are: Lewiston, 35,690; Bangor, 31,473; South Portland, 23,324; Auburn, 23,203; Augusta (capital), 21,819; Brunswick, 21,172; Biddeford, 20,942; Sanford, 20,806.

SOCIAL STATISTICS

Births, 2003, 13,855 (10·6 per 1,000 population—the lowest rate in any US state); deaths (2002), 12,694 (9·8 per 1,000 population). 2002 infant mortality rate (per 1,000 live births), 4·4. 2001: marriages, 11,400 (9·0 per 1,000 population); divorces, 4,900 (3·9).

CLIMATE

Average maximum temperatures range from 56·3°F in Waterville to 48·3°F in Caribou, but record high (since c. 1950) is 103°F. Average minimum ranges from 36·9°F in Rockland to 28·3°F in Greenville, but record low (also in Greenville) is −42°F. Average annual rainfall ranges from 48·85" in Machias to 36·09" in Houlton. Average annual snowfall ranges from 118·7" in Greenville to 59·7" in Rockland. Maine belongs to the New England climate zone (see UNITED STATES: Climate).

CONSTITUTION AND GOVERNMENT

The constitution of 1820 is still in force, but it has been amended 170 times. In 1951, 1967, 1973, 1983, 1993 and 2003 the Legislature approved recodifications of the constitution as arranged by the Chief Justice under special authority.

The Legislature consists of the Senate with 35 members and the House of Representatives with 151 members, both Houses being elected simultaneously for two years. Sessions are annual.

For the 109th Congress, which convened in Jan. 2005, Maine sends two members to the House of Representatives. It is represented in the Senate by Olympia Snowe (R. 1995–2007) and Susan Collins (R. 1997–2009).

The capital is Augusta. The state is divided into 16 counties.

RECENT ELECTIONS

In the 2004 presidential election Kerry polled 396,842 votes; Bush, 330,201; Nader, 8,069.

CURRENT ADMINISTRATION

Governor: John Baldacci (D.), 2003–07 (salary: $70,000).
 Senate President: Beth Edmonds (D.).
 Secretary of State: Matthew Dunlap (D.), 2005–07 ($65,936).

Government Website: http://www.maine.gov

ECONOMY

Per capita income (2004) was $29,973.

Budget

In 2003 total state revenue was $6,801m. Total expenditure was $6,706m. (public welfare, $1,990m.; education, $1,574m.; highways, $492m.; health, $401m.; government administration, $243m.) Outstanding debt, in 2003, $4,417m.

Performance

Gross State Product was $43,336m. in 2004, ranking Maine 43rd in the United States.

ENERGY AND NATURAL RESOURCES

Water

The total area covered by water is approximately 4,523 sq. miles.

Minerals

Minerals include sand and gravel, stone, lead, clay, copper, peat, silver and zinc. Domestic non-fuel mineral output in 2003 was valued at $100m.

Agriculture

In 2004, 7,200 farms occupied 1·37m. acres; the average farm was 190 acres. Average value of farmland and buildings per acre in 2004 was $1,850. Farm income, 2003: crops, $240m.; livestock and products, $270m. The net farm income in 2003 was $87m. Principal commodities are potatoes, dairy products, chicken eggs and aquaculture.

Forestry

There were 17·70m. acres of forested land in 2002, of which 40,000 acres were national forests. Commercial forest includes pine, spruce and fir. Wood products industries are of great economic importance.

Fisheries

In 2004 the commercial catch was 304·0m. lb, valued at $404·7m.

INDUSTRY

In 2003 the state's 2,015 manufacturing establishments had 79,300 employees, earning $2,576m. Total value added by manufacturing in 2002 was $7,122m.

Labour

Total non-agricultural employment, 2004, 613,900. Employees by branch, 2004 (in 1,000): services, 517; wholesale and retail trade, 109; government, 105; manufacturing, 63; finance, insurance and property, 35. The unemployment rate in 2004 was 4·6%.

COMMUNICATIONS

Roads

In 2003 there were 22,692 miles of roads (20,060 miles rural). There were 1,051,657 registered motor vehicles.

Rail

In 2002 there were 1,195 miles of mainline railway tracks.

Civil Aviation

There are international airports at Portland and Bangor. There were 971,993 passenger enplanements statewide in 2003.

SOCIAL INSTITUTIONS

Justice

In Dec. 2003 there were 2,013 federal and state prisoners. Capital punishment was abolished in 1887.

Education

Education is free for pupils from five to 21 years of age, and compulsory from seven to 17. In 2002 there were 204,337 pupils and 16,837 teachers in public elementary and secondary schools. Education expenditure by state and local government in 2002, $1,844m.

The University of Maine System, created by Maine's state legislature in 1965, consists of seven universities: the University of Maine (founded in 1865); the University of Maine at Augusta, at Farmington, at Fort Kent (1878), at Machias (1909), at Presque Isle (1903); and the University of Southern Maine (1878, campuses at Portland, Gorham and Lewiston-Auburn).

There are several independent universities, including: Bowdoin College, founded in 1794 at Brunswick; Bates College at Lewiston; Colby College at Waterville; Husson College at Bangor; Westbrook College at Westbrook; Unity College at Unity; and the University of New England (formerly St Francis College) at Biddeford.

Health

In 2004 there were 39 community hospitals with 3,561 beds. A total of 144,083 patients were discharged during the year.

Welfare

Medicare enrolment in July 2003 totalled 226,696. In 2004 a total of 308,453 people in Maine received Medicaid. In Dec. 2004 there were 266,129 Old-Age, Survivors, and Disability Insurance (OASDI) beneficiaries. A total of 26,309 people were receiving payments under Temporary Assistance for Needy Families (TANF) in Sept. 2004.

RELIGION

The largest religious bodies are Roman Catholics, Baptists and Congregationalists.

FURTHER READING

Statistical information: Maine Department of Economic and Community Development, State House Station 59, Augusta 04333. Publishes *Maine: a Statistical Summary.*

Palmer, K. T., *et al.*, *Maine Politics and Government*. Univ. of Nebraska Press, 1993

Maryland

KEY HISTORICAL EVENTS

The first European visitors found groups of Algonquian-speaking tribes, often under attack by Iroquois from further north. The first white settlement was made by the Calvert family, British Roman Catholics, in 1634. The settlers received some legislative rights in 1638. In 1649 their assembly passed the Act of Toleration, granting freedom of worship to all Christians. A peace treaty was signed with the Iroquois in 1652, after which it was possible for farming settlements to expand north and west.

The capital (formerly at St Mary's City) was moved to Annapolis in 1694. Baltimore, which became the state's main city, was founded in 1729.

The first industry was tobacco-growing, which was based on slave-worked plantations. There were also many immigrant British small farmers, tradesmen and indentured servants.

At the close of the War of Independence the treaty of Paris was ratified in Annapolis. Maryland became a state of the Union in 1788. In 1791 the state ceded land for the new federal capital, Washington, and its economy has depended on the capital's proximity ever since. Baltimore also grew as a port and industrial city, attracting much European immigration in the 19th century. Although strong sympathy for the south was expressed, Maryland remained within the Union in the Civil War albeit under the imposition of martial law.

TERRITORY AND POPULATION

Maryland is bounded north by Pennsylvania, east by Delaware and the Atlantic, south by Virginia and West Virginia, with the Potomac River forming most of the boundary, and west by West Virginia. Chesapeake Bay almost cuts off the eastern end of the state from the rest. Land area, 9,774 sq. miles (25,315 sq. km). Census population, 1 April 2000, 5,296,486, an increase since 1990 of 10·8%. July 2005 estimate, 5,600,388.

Population for five federal censuses was:

	White	Black	Indian	Asiatic	Total	Per sq. mile
1920	1,204,737	244,479	32	400	1,449,661	145·8
1930	1,354,226	276,379	50	857	1,631,526	165·0
1960	2,573,919	518,410	1,538	5,700	3,100,689	314·0
			All others			
1990	3,393,964	1,189,899	197,605		4,781,468	489·2
2000	3,391,308	1,477,411	427,767		5,296,486	541·9

Of the total population in 2000, 2,738,692 were female, 3,940,314 were 18 years old or older and 4,558,668 were urban. In 2000 Maryland's Hispanic population was 227,916, up from 125,102 in 1990 (an increase of 82·2%).

The largest city in the state (containing 12·3% of the population) is Baltimore, with 651,154 (2000 census); Washington, D.C.–Baltimore metropolitan area, 7,608,070 (2000). Maryland residents in the Washington, D.C., metropolitan area total more than 1·8m. Other main population centres (2000 census) are Columbia (88,254); Silver Spring (76,540); Dundalk (62,306); Wheaton-Glenmont (57,694); Ellicott City (56,397); Germantown (55,419); Bethesda (55,277). Incorporated places, 2000: Frederick, 52,767; Gaithersburg, 52,613; Bowie, 50,269; Rockville, 47,388; Hagerstown, 36,687; Annapolis, 35,838; College Park, 24,657; Salisbury, 23,743; Cumberland, 21,518; Greenbelt, 21,456.

SOCIAL STATISTICS

In 2003 births were 74,930 (13·6 per 1,000 population); deaths (2002), 43,970 (8·1 per 1,000). 2002 infant mortality (per 1,000 live births), 7·5. 2001: marriages, 37,500; divorces, 15,900.

CLIMATE

Baltimore, Jan. 36°F (2·2°C), July 79°F (26·1°C). Annual rainfall 42" (1,066 mm). Maryland belongs to the Atlantic Coast climate zone (*see* UNITED STATES: Climate).

CONSTITUTION AND GOVERNMENT

The present constitution dates from 1867; it has had 125 amendments. Amendments are proposed and considered annually by the General Assembly and must be ratified by the electorate. The General Assembly consists of a Senate of 47, and a House of Delegates of 141 members, both elected for four years, as are the Governor and Lieut.-Governor. Voters are citizens who have the usual residential qualifications.

For the 109th Congress, which convened in Jan. 2005, Maryland sends eight members to the House of Representatives. It is represented in the Senate by Paul Sarbanes (D. 1977–2007) and Barbara Mikulski (D. 1987–2011).

The state capital is Annapolis. The state is divided into 23 counties and Baltimore City.

RECENT ELECTIONS

In the 2004 presidential election Kerry polled 1,334,493 votes; Bush, 1,024,703; Nader, 11,854.

CURRENT ADMINISTRATION

Governor: Robert L. Ehrlich, Jr (R.), 2003–07 (salary: $150,000).

Lieut.-Governor: Michael S. Steele (R.), 2003–07 ($125,000).

Secretary of State: Mary D. Kane (R.), appointed Aug. 2005 ($87,500).

Government Website: http://www.maryland.gov

ECONOMY

Per capita income (2004) was $39,629.

Budget

In 2003 total state revenue was $21,801m. Total expenditure was $24,592m. (education, $7,272m.; public welfare, $5,052m.; highways, $1,716m.; health, $1,507m.; correction, $1,050m.) Outstanding debt, in 2003, $12,951m.

Performance

Gross State Product in 2004 was $227,991m., ranking Maryland 15th in the United States.

ENERGY AND NATURAL RESOURCES

Electricity

The territory is served by four investor-owned utilities, five municipal systems and four rural co-operatives. 75% of electricity comes from fossil fuels and 25% from nuclear power.

Oil and Gas

Natural gas is produced from one field in Garrett County; 63m. cu. ft (1·78m. cu. metres) in 1998. A second gas field is used for natural gas storage. No oil is produced and there are no major reserves located in Maryland.

Water

The total area covered by water is approximately 2,633 sq. miles. Abundant fresh water resources allow water withdrawals for neighbouring states and the District of Columbia. The state straddles the upper portions of the world's largest freshwater estuary, Chesapeake Bay.

Minerals

Value of non-fuel mineral production in 2003 was $382m. The leading mineral commodities by weight are crushed stone (36·1m. tonnes in 2000) and sand and gravel (25·0m. tonnes in 2000). Stone is the leading mineral commodity by value followed by coal, Portland cement, and sand and gravel. In 2000 output of crushed stone was valued at $136m.; coal output was 4·02m. short tons in 1998, valued at $121m.

Agriculture

In 2002 there were 12,200 farms with an area of 2·1m. acres. The average number of acres per farm was 172. The average value per acre in 2002 was $4,084. In 2003, 1·27m. people were employed in agriculture.

Farm animals, 2002 were: milch cows, 72,800; all cattle, 241,000; swine (2001), 52,000; and sheep, 22,700. As of 2002, chickens (not broilers), 3·17m. Farm income cash receipts, 2002: $1,432m.; from crops, $621m., and from livestock and livestock products, $810m. The net farm income in 2002 was $195m. Milk

(2002 value $169·5m.) and broilers ($440·5m.) are important products.

Forestry

Total forested area was 2·57m. acres in 2002.

Fisheries

In 2002, 53·2m. lb of seafood was landed at a dockside value of $49m. The total estimated value of the seafood industry was $700m.

INDUSTRY

In 2001 the state's 3,936 manufacturing establishments had 157,000 employees, earning $6,792m. Total value added by manufacturing in 2001 was $18,757m.

Labour

In 1997, 24·1% of the workforce were professional and technical workers, more than any other state in the USA. The workforce is well educated with 32% of the population over age 25 holding a bachelor's or higher degree in 1998; it has the second highest concentration of PhD degrees in the sciences of US states—with 352 per 100,000 of the population. Total non-agricultural employment, 2003, 2,483,000. Employees by branch, 2003 (in 1,000): government, 463; trade, transportation and utilities, 462; professional and business services, 361; education and health services, 339; leisure and hospitality, 219. The unemployment rate in 2003 was 4·5%.

COMMUNICATIONS

Roads

In 2003 there were 30,687 miles of roads comprising 16,780 miles of urban road and 13,907 miles of rural road. In 2002 the state highway maintained 5,131 miles of highways. The counties maintained 20,486 miles of highways. There were 3,876,610 registered vehicles in 2003.

Rail

Maryland is served by CSX Transportation, Norfolk Southern Railroad as well as by six short-line railroads. Metro lines also serve Maryland in suburban Washington, D.C. Amtrak provides passenger service linking Baltimore and BWI Airport to major cities on the Atlantic Coast. MARC commuter rail serves the Baltimore–Washington metropolitan area.

Civil Aviation

There were (2005) 35 public-use airports, and 27 commercial airlines at Baltimore/Washington International Airport (BWI). The airport served 17m. passengers in 1999. A newly opened passenger pier serves the airport's increasing numbers of international customers. Air cargo throughput has grown rapidly to over 350m. tons per annum, with increases planned. There were 9,883,900 passenger enplanements in 2003.

Shipping

In 1997 Baltimore was the 9th largest US seaport in value of imports, and 12th largest in value of exports; in 1996 it ranked 16th in annual tonnage handled. It is located about 200 miles further inland than any other Atlantic seaport.

SOCIAL INSTITUTIONS

Justice

Prisons in June 2003 held 24,186 inmates. Maryland's prison system has conducted a work-release programme for selected prisoners since 1963. All institutions have academic and vocational training programmes. There was one execution in 2004, the first since 1998, and one in 2005.

Education

Education is compulsory from six to 16 years of age. In 1998–99 public schools (including pre-kindergarten through secondary schools) had 828,477 pupils; teachers numbered 65,486; average salary was $43,081. Expenditure on education, 1998–99, was $5·9bn., of which the state's contribution was $2·4bn. Per pupil cost (1998–99) was $6,821.

There are 54 institutions of higher learning (34 four-year and 20 two-year). The largest is the University System of Maryland (created in 1988), with 125,000 students (autumn 1998), consisting of 11 campuses, two major research institutions, and over 250 learning centres in Europe and the Far East. The USM colleges and universities are: Bowie State University; Coppin State College; Frostburg State University; Salisbury University; Towson University; the University of Baltimore; and the five campuses of the University of Maryland (Baltimore, Baltimore County, College Park, Eastern Shore and University College). Career and technical education is available through a network of community colleges and in some 200 secondary schools.

Health
In 2002 there were 49 community hospitals with 11,400 beds. A total of 635,000 patients were admitted during the year.

Welfare
Medicare enrolment in July 2003 totalled 674,448. In 2002 a total of 692,539 people in Maryland received Medicaid. In Dec. 2004 there were 761,210 Old-Age, Survivors, and Disability Insurance (OASDI) beneficiaries. A total of 58,281 people were receiving payments under Temporary Assistance for Needy Families (TANF) in Sept. 2004.

RELIGION
Maryland was the first US state to give religious freedom to all who came within its borders. Chief religious bodies (2000) are Catholics, with 952,389 members, United Methodists (297,729), Jews (216,000), Southern Baptists (142,401) and Evangelical Lutherans (103,644).

CULTURE
Cultural venues include: Frostburg Performing Arts Center, Strathmore Hall Arts Center and Center Stage. Performing arts institutions include the Baltimore Opera Company, Peabody Music Conservatory and Arena Players.

Broadcasting
There are 15 TV stations, 22 cable television stations, 48 FM radio and 31 AM radio stations.

Tourism
Tourism is one of the state's leading industries. In 2002 tourists spent $8,814m. Direct employment in tourism (2002) was 109,600.

FURTHER READING
Statistical Information: Maryland Department of Economic and Employment Development, 217 East Redwood St., Baltimore 21202.

DiLisio, J. E., *Maryland.* Boulder, 1982
Rollo, V. F., *Maryland's Constitution and Government.* Maryland Hist. Press, Rev. ed., 1982

State Library: Maryland State Library, Annapolis.

Massachusetts

KEY HISTORICAL EVENTS
The first European settlement was at Plymouth, when the *Mayflower* landed its company of English religious separatists in 1620. In 1626–30 more colonists arrived, the main body being a large company of English Puritans who founded a Puritan commonwealth. This commonwealth, of about 1,000 colonists led by John Winthrop, became the Massachusetts Bay Colony and was founded under a company charter. Following disagreement between the English government and the colony the charter was withdrawn in 1684, but in 1691 a new charter united a number of settlements under the name of Massachusetts Bay. The colony's government was rigidly theocratic.

Shipbuilding, iron-working and manufacturing were more important than farming from the beginning, the land being poor. The colony was Protestant and of English descent until the War of Independence. The former colony adopted its present constitution in 1780. In the struggle which ended in the separation of the American colonies from the mother country, Massachusetts took the foremost part, and on 6 Feb. 1788 became the 6th state to ratify the US constitution. The state acquired its present boundaries (having previously included Maine) in 1820.

During the 19th century industrialization and immigration from Europe both increased while Catholic Irish and Italian immigrants began to change the population's character. The main inland industry was textile manufacture, the main coastal occupation was whaling; both have now gone. Boston has remained the most important city of New England, attracting a large black population since 1950.

TERRITORY AND POPULATION
Massachusetts is bounded north by Vermont and New Hampshire, east by the Atlantic, south by Connecticut and Rhode Island and west by New York. Land area, 7,840 sq. miles (20,306 sq. km). Census population, 1 April 2000, 6,349,097, an increase of 5·5% since 1990. July 2005 estimate, 6,398,743.

Population at five federal census years was:

	White	Black	Other	Total	Per sq. mile
1950	4,611,503	73,171	5,840	4,690,514	598·4
1970	5,477,624	175,817	35,729	5,689,170	725·8
1980	5,362,836	221,279	152,922	5,737,037	732·0
1990	5,405,374	300,130	310,921	6,016,425	767·6
2000	5,367,286	343,454	638,357	6,349,097	809·8

Of the total population in 2000, 3,290,281 were female, 4,849,003 were 18 years old or older and 5,801,367 were urban (91·37%). In 2000 the Hispanic population was 428,729, up from 287,549 in 1990 (an increase of 49·1%).

Population of the largest cities at the 2000 census: Boston, 589,141; Worcester, 172,648; Springfield, 152,082; Lowell, 105,167; Cambridge, 101,355; Brockton, 94,304; New Bedford, 93,768; Fall River, 91,938; Lynn, 89,050; Quincy, 88,025; Newton, 83,829. The Boston–Worcester–Lawrence metropolitan area had a 2000 census population of 5,819,100.

SOCIAL STATISTICS
2003: births, 80,184 (12·5 per 1,000 population); deaths (2002), 56,928 (8·9 per 1,000 population). 2002 infant mortality (per 1,000 live births), 4·9. 2001: marriages, 40,000; divorces, 14,800.

CLIMATE
Boston, Jan. 28°F (–2·2°C), July 71°F (21·7°C). Annual rainfall 41" (1,036 mm). Massachusetts belongs to the New England climate zone (*see* UNITED STATES: Climate).

CONSTITUTION AND GOVERNMENT
The constitution dates from 1780 and has had 117 amendments. The legislative body, styled the General Court of the Commonwealth of Massachusetts, meets annually, and consists of the Senate with 40 members and the House of Representatives of 160 members, both elected for two years.

For the 109th Congress, which convened in Jan. 2005, Massachusetts sends ten members to the House of Representatives. It is represented in the Senate by Edward Kennedy (D. 1962–2007) and John Kerry (D. 1985–2009).

The capital is Boston. The state has 14 counties.

RECENT ELECTIONS

In the 2004 presidential election Kerry polled 1,803,800 votes; Bush, 1,071,109; Badnarik, 15,022.

CURRENT ADMINISTRATION

Governor: W. Mitt Romney (R.), 2003–07 (salary: $135,000, but not taken).

Lieut.-Governor: Kerry Healey (R.), 2003–07 ($120,000, but not taken).

Secretary of the Commonwealth: William F. Galvin (D.), 2003–07 ($120,000).

Government Website: http://www.mass.gov

ECONOMY

Per capita income (2004) was $42,102, the third highest in the country.

Budget

In 2003 total state revenue was $30,371m. Total expenditure was $32,710m. (education, $6,774m.; public welfare, $5,293m.; highways, $2,429m.; health, $1,878m.; government administration, $1,291m.) Outstanding debt, in 2003, $48,479m.

Performance

Gross State Product in 2004 was $317,798m., ranking Massachusetts 13th in the United States.

ENERGY AND NATURAL RESOURCES

Water

The total area covered by water is approximately 2,715 sq. miles.

Minerals

Total domestic non-fuel mineral output in 2003 was valued at $186m., most of which came from sand, gravel, crushed stone and lime.

Agriculture

In 2002 there were approximately 6,000 farms with an average area of 93 acres and a total area of 560,000 acres. Average value per acre in 2002 was $9,234. Farm income in 2002: crops, $297m.; livestock and products, $83m. Principal commodities are greenhouse products, cranberries, dairy products and sweetcorn. The net farm income in 2002 was $37m.

Forestry

About 62% of the state is forest. In 2002 state forests covered about 424,000 acres, with total forest land covering 3·13m. acres. Commercially important hardwoods are sugar maple, northern red oak and white ash; softwoods are white pine and hemlock.

Fisheries

In 2002 commercial fishing produced 243·8m. lb of fish with a value of $297·3m.

INDUSTRY

In 2001 the state's 9,015 manufacturing establishments had 390,000 employees, earning $18,907m. Total value added by manufacturing in 2001 was $44,447m.

Labour

Total non-agricultural employment, 2003, 3,186,000. Employees by branch, 2003 (in 1,000): education and health services, 575; trade, transportation and utilities, 573; professional and business

services, 437; manufacturing, 326; leisure and hospitality, 288. The state unemployment rate was 5·8% in 2003.

COMMUNICATIONS

Roads

In 2003 there were 35,590 miles of public roads (7,909 miles rural). There were 5,479,394 registered motor vehicles.

Rail

In 2002 there were 1,251 miles of freight railroad, including 436 miles of Class I railways. There are metro, light rail, tramway and commuter networks in and around Boston.

Civil Aviation

As at June 2004 there were 77 airports and 139 heliports. There is an international airport at Boston, which handled 11,087,799 passenger enplanements in 2003.

Shipping

The state has three deep-water harbours, the largest of which is Boston. Other ports are Fall River and New Bedford.

SOCIAL INSTITUTIONS

Justice

There were 10,511 federal and state prisoners in June 2003. The death penalty was abolished in 1984.

Education

School attendance is compulsory for ages six to 16. In 2002–03 there were 1,904 public elementary and secondary schools with 982,989 pupils and 74,214 teachers; total expenditure on public schools was $10,293m. Teachers' average salaries were $50,819m. in 2003.

Some leading higher education institutions are:

Year opened	Name and location of universities and colleges	Students 2003
1636	Harvard University, Cambridge	24,851
1839	Framingham State College	6,153
1839	Westfield State College	4,937
1840	Bridgewater State College	9,626
1852	Tufts University, Medford[1]	9,509
1854	Salem State College	9,120
1861	Mass. Institute of Technology, Cambridge	10,340
1863	University of Massachusetts, Amherst	24,310
1863	Boston College (RC), Chestnut Hill	13,728
1865	Worcester Polytechnic Institute, Worcester	3,843
1869	Boston University, Boston	29,049
1874	Worcester State College	5,471
1894	Fitchburg State College	4,917
1894	University of Massachusetts, Lowell	11,706
1895	University of Massachusetts, Dartmouth	8,284
1898	Northeastern University, Boston[2]	22,944
1899	Simmons College, Boston[3]	4,121
1905	Wentworth Institute of Technology	3,453
1906	Suffolk University	7,822
1917	Bentley College	5,678
1919	Western New England College	4,448
1919	Babson College	3,342
1947	Merrimack College	2,407
1948	Brandeis University, Waltham	4,985
1964	University of Massachusetts, Boston	12,394

[1]Includes Jackson College for women.
[2]Includes Forsyth Dental Center School. [3]For women only.

Health

In 2002 there were 78 community hospitals with 16,000 beds. A total of 766,000 patients were admitted during the year.

Welfare

Medicare enrolment in July 2003 totalled 965,943. In 2002 a total of 1,065,636 people in Massachusetts received Medicaid. In Dec. 2004 there were 1,063,061 Old-Age, Survivors, and Disability Insurance (OASDI) beneficiaries. A total of 109,380 people were receiving payments under Temporary Assistance for Needy Families (TANF) in Sept. 2004.

RELIGION

The principal religious bodies are the Roman Catholics, Jewish Congregations, Methodists, Episcopalians and Unitarians.

FURTHER READING

Levitan, D. with Mariner, E. C., *Your Massachusetts Government.* Newton, Mass., 1984

Michigan

KEY HISTORICAL EVENTS

The French were the first European settlers, establishing a fur trade with the local Algonquian Indians in the late 17th century. They founded Sault Ste Marie in 1668 and Detroit in 1701. In 1763 Michigan passed to Britain, along with other French territory east of the Mississippi, and from Britain it passed to the USA in 1783. Britain, however, kept a force at Detroit until 1796, and recaptured Detroit in 1812. Regular American settlement did not begin until later. The Territory of Michigan (1805) had its boundaries extended after 1818 and 1834. It was admitted to the Union as a state (with its present boundaries) in 1837.

During the 19th century there was rapid industrial growth, especially in mining and metalworking. The largest groups of immigrants were British, German, Irish and Dutch. Other significant groups came from Scandinavia, Poland and Italy. Many groups of immigrants came to settle as miners, farmers and industrial workers. The motor industry became dominant, especially in Detroit. Lake Michigan ports shipped bulk cargo, especially iron ore and grain.

Detroit was the capital until 1847, when that function passed to Lansing. Detroit remained, however, an important centre of flour-milling and shipping and, after the First World War, of the motor industry.

TERRITORY AND POPULATION

Michigan is divided into two by Lake Michigan. The northern part is bounded south by the lake and by Wisconsin, west and north by Lake Superior, east by the North Channel of Lake Huron; between the two latter lakes the Canadian border runs through straits at Sault Ste Marie. The southern part is bounded in the west and north by Lake Michigan, east by Lake Huron, Ontario and Lake Erie, south by Ohio and Indiana. Total area is 96,716 sq. miles (250,493 sq. km) of which 56,804 sq. miles (147,122 sq. km) are land and 39,912 sq. miles (103,372 sq. km) water. Census population, 1 April 2000, 9,938,444, an increase of 6·9% since 1990. July 2005 estimate, 10,120,860.

Population of five federal census years was:

	White	Black	Indian	Asiatic	Total	Per sq. mile
1910	2,785,247	17,115	7,519	292	2,810,173	48·9
1930	4,663,507	69,453	7,080	2,285	4,842,325	84·9
			All others			
1980	7,872,241	1,199,023		190,814	9,262,078	162·6
1990	7,756,086	1,291,706		247,505	9,295,297	160·0
2000	7,966,053	1,412,742		559,649	9,938,444	175·0

Of the total population in 2000, 5,065,349 were female, 7,342,677 were 18 years old or older and 7,419,457 were urban. In 2000 the Hispanic population was 323,877, up from 201,596 in 1990 (an increase of 60·7%).

Populations of the chief cities in 2000 were: Detroit, 951,270; Grand Rapids, 197,800; Warren, 138,247; Flint, 124,943; Sterling Heights, 124,471; Lansing, 119,128; Ann Arbor, 114,024; Livonia, 100,545. The Detroit–Ann Arbor–Flint metropolitan area had a 2000 census population of 5,456,428.

SOCIAL STATISTICS

In 2003 live births were 131,094 (13·0 per 1,000); deaths (2002) were 87,795 (8·7 per 1,000). 2002 infant mortality, 8·1 per 1,000 live births. Marriages, 2000, 66,326; divorces, 38,932.

CLIMATE

Detroit, Jan. 23·5°F (–5·0°C), July 72°F (22·5°C). Annual rainfall 32" (810 mm). Grand Rapids, Jan. 22°F (–5·5°C), July 71·5°F (22·0°C). Annual rainfall 34" (860 mm). Lansing, Jan. 22°F (–5·5°C), July 70·5°F (21·5°C). Annual rainfall 29" (740 mm). Michigan belongs to the Great Lakes climate zone (*see* UNITED STATES: Climate).

CONSTITUTION AND GOVERNMENT

The present constitution became effective on 1 Jan. 1964. The Senate consists of 38 members, elected for four years, and the House of Representatives of 110 members, elected for two years. Sessions are biennial.

For the 109th Congress, which convened in Jan. 2005, Michigan sends 15 members to the House of Representatives. It is represented in the Senate by Carl Levin (D. 1979–2009) and Debbie Stabenow (D. 2001–07).

The capital is Lansing. The state is organized in 83 counties.

RECENT ELECTIONS

In the 2004 presidential election Kerry polled 2,479,183 votes; Bush, 2,313,746; Nader, 24,035.

CURRENT ADMINISTRATION

Governor: Jennifer Granholm (D.), 2003–07 (salary: $177,000).
  Lieut.-Governor: John D. Cherry (D.), 2003–07 ($123,900).
  Secretary of State: Terri Lynn Land (R.), 2003–07 ($124,900).

Government Website: http://www.michigan.gov

ECONOMY

Per capita income (2004) was $32,052.

Budget

In the fiscal year ending 2003, total state revenue was $50,077m. Total expenditure was $51,016m. (education, $19,262m.; public welfare, $9,138m.; health, $3,748m.; highways, $2,787m.; correction, $1,679m.) Total budget deficit for 2003 was $22,479m.

Performance

New for-profit business incorporations and new limited liability companies for 2001–02 totalled 50,954. In 2001 Michigan's real income per person declined 1·7% compared with a 0·5% national decline. Gross State Product in 2004 was $372,169m., ranking Michigan 9th in the United States.

ENERGY AND NATURAL RESOURCES

Electricity

Electricity sales for 2001 were 102,935m. kWh.

Oil and Gas

Natural gas production in 2001 was 231·8bn. cu. ft; demand was 863·1bn. cu. ft. Production of crude oil averaged 20,000 bbls. per day.

Water

The total area covered by water is approximately 39,912 sq. miles.

Minerals

Domestic non-fuel mineral output in 2003 was at an estimated value of $1·35bn. according to the US Geological Survey. Output was mainly iron ore, cement, crushed stone, sand and gravel.

Agriculture

The state, formerly agricultural, is now chiefly industrial. It contained 52,000 farms in 2002, with a total area of 10·4m. acres; the average farm was 200 acres. In 2000, 6,898,000 acres were harvested. Average value per acre in 2002 was $2,667. Principal crops are soybeans, corn, wheat, oats, sugarbeets, hay and dry beans. Principal fruit crops include apples, cherries (tart and sweet), plums and peaches. In 2002 there were 297,000 milch cows, 73,000 beef cows, 3·66m. chickens and 960,000 pigs. Output in 2002 included 77,000 lb of blueberries, 20,160 pots of geraniums and 335,000 cwt of black beans. Farm income in 2002: total $3·39bn.; crops, $2·13bn.; livestock and products, $1·26bn. The net farm income in 2002 was $167m.

Forestry

Forests covered 19·3m. acres in 2002, with 2·7m. acres of national forest. In 1993 about 18·6m. acres was timberland acreage. Three-quarters of the timber volume was hardwoods, principally hard and soft maples, aspen, oak and birch. Christmas trees are another important forest crop. Net annual growth of growing stock and saw timber was 830m. cu. ft and 3·1bn. bd ft respectively in 1993.

Fisheries

In 1997 recreational fishing licences were purchased by 1·4m. residents and 129,000 non-residents. Recreational fishing revenue (1997) was approximately $1·5bn.

INDUSTRY

Manufacturing is important; among principal products are motor vehicles and trucks, machinery, fabricated metals, primary metals, cement, chemicals, furniture, paper, foodstuffs, rubber, plastics and pharmaceuticals. In 2001 Michigan's 15,431 manufacturing establishments had 756,000 employees, earning $33,634m. Total value added by manufacturing in 2001 was $86,262m.

Labour

Total non-agricultural labour force in 2003 was 4,412,000. Employees by branch, 2003 (in 1,000): trade, transportation and utilities, 815; manufacturing, 727; government, 681; professional and business services, 587; education and health services, 544. The unemployment rate in 2003 was 7·3%.

COMMUNICATIONS

Roads

In 2003 there were 122,221 miles of roads (including 9,741 miles of state highways and 89,854 miles of county roads). There were 87,134 miles of rural road and 35,087 miles of urban road. Vehicle registrations in 2003 numbered 8,540,325.

Rail

In 2000 there were 3,950 miles of railway in Michigan and a 3-mile light rail peoplemover in Detroit.

Civil Aviation

There are international airports at Detroit, Flint, Grand Rapids, Kalamazoo, Port Huron, Saginaw and Sault Ste Marie. In 2000 there were 4,359,931 aircraft operations at Michigan's 235 public-use airports and 26 carriers provided passenger service at 19 airports. There were 18,321,461 passenger enplanements statewide in 2003.

Shipping

There are over 100 commercial and recreational ports spanning the state's 3,200 miles of shoreline. In 2000, 39 of these ports served commercial cargoes. The 20 ferry services carried 848,998 passengers and 529,809 vehicles in 68,571 crossings in 2000. Stone, sand, iron ore and coal accounted for 89% of approximately 96m. tonnes of traffic in 1999.

SOCIAL INSTITUTIONS

Justice

A Civil Rights Commission was established, and its powers and duties were implemented by legislation in the extra session of 1963. Statutory enactments guaranteeing civil rights in specific areas date from 1885. The legislature has a unique one-person grand jury system. The Michigan Supreme Court consists of seven non-partisan elected justices. In 2001 there were 2,291 cases filed at the Supreme Court; it disposed of 2,359 cases during the year. In June 2003 there were 49,524 prisoners in state correctional institutions. Capital punishment was officially abolished in 1964 but there has never been an execution in Michigan.

Education

Education is compulsory for children from six to 16 years of age. Education expenditure by state and local governments in 2000–01 was $215,490,700. In 2000–01 there were 1,720,335 pupils and 76,920 teachers in public elementary and secondary schools.

In 1998 there were 96 institutes of higher education with (autumn 1998) 551,683 students.

Universities and students (autumn 2002):

Founded	Name	Students
1817	University of Michigan, Ann Arbor	38,972
1959	University of Michigan, Dearborn	10,379
1956	University of Michigan, Flint	6,524
1849	Eastern Michigan University	23,710
1855	Michigan State University	41,114
1884	Ferris State University	11,074
1885	Michigan Technological University	6,625
1868	Wayne State University	28,161
1892	Central Michigan University	19,380
1899	Northern Michigan University	8,577
1903	Western Michigan University	28,931
1946	Lake Superior State University	3,077
1957	Oakland University	16,059
1960	Grand Valley State University	19,762
1963	Saginaw Valley State University	8,938

Health

There were, in 2000, 178 Medicare and Medicaid certified hospitals (31,895 beds); 12 psychiatric hospitals (2,547 beds) and five rehabilitation hospitals (315 beds).

Welfare

Old-age assistance is provided for persons 65 years of age or older who have resided in Michigan for one year before application; assets must not exceed various limits. In 1974 federal Supplementary Security Income (SSI) replaced the adults' programme. A monthly average of 69,786 families received $400·09 per month in 2002 through the Family Independence Agency.

Medicare enrolment in July 2003 totalled 1,444,987. In 2002 a total of 1,449,915 people in Michigan received Medicaid. In Dec. 2004 there were 1,722,514 Old-Age, Survivors, and Disability Insurance (OASDI) beneficiaries. A total of 213,296 people were receiving payments under Temporary Assistance for Needy Families (TANF) in Sept. 2004.

RELIGION

Roman Catholics make up the largest body and the largest Protestant denominations are: Lutherans, United Methodists, United Presbyterians and Episcopalians.

CULTURE

Tourism

In 2002, 363,000 overseas visitors (1·9% of the market share), excluding Mexico and Canada, visited Michigan.

FURTHER READING

Michigan Manual. Dept of Management and Budget. Lansing. Biennial Michigan Employment Security Commission. *Michigan Statistical Abstract, 1996.* Univ. of Michigan Press

Browne, W. P. and Verburg, K., *Michigan Politics and Government: Facing Change in a Complex State.* Nebraska Univ. Press, 1995
Dunbar, W. F. and May, G. S., *Michigan: A History of the Wolverine State.* 3rd ed. Grand Rapids, 1995

State Library Services: Library of Michigan, Lansing 48909.

Minnesota

KEY HISTORICAL EVENTS

Minnesota remained an Indian territory until the middle of the 19th century, the main groups being Chippewa and Sioux, many of whom are still there. In the 17th century there had been some French exploration, but no permanent settlement. After passing under the nominal control of France, Britain and Spain, the area became part of the Louisiana Purchase and was sold to the USA in 1803.

Fort Snelling was founded in 1819. Early settlers came from other states, especially New England, to exploit the great forests. Lumbering gave way to homesteading, and the American settlers were joined by Germans, Scandinavians and Poles. Agriculture, mining and forest industries became the mainstays of the economy. Minneapolis, founded as a village in 1856, grew first as a lumber centre, processing the logs floated down the Minnesota River, and then as a centre of flour-milling and grain marketing. St Paul, its twin city across the river, became Territorial capital in 1849 and state capital in 1858. St Paul also stands at the head of navigation on the Mississippi, which rises in Minnesota.

The Territory (1849) included parts of North and South Dakota, but at its admission to the Union in 1858, the state of Minnesota had its present boundaries.

TERRITORY AND POPULATION

Minnesota is bounded north by Canada, east by Lake Superior and Wisconsin, with the Mississippi River forming the boundary in the southeast, south by Iowa, west by South and North Dakota, with the Red River forming the boundary in the northwest. Land area, 79,610 sq. miles (206,189 sq. km). Census population, 1 April 2000, 4,919,479, an increase of 12·4% since 1990. July 2005 estimate, 5,132,799.

Population in five census years was:

	White	Black	Indian	Asiatic	Total	Per sq. mile
1910	2,059,227	7,084	9,053	344	2,075,708	25·7
1930	2,542,599	9,445	11,077	832	2,563,953	32·0
			All others			
1980	3,935,770	53,344	86,856		4,075,970	51·4
1990	4,130,395	94,944	149,760		4,375,099	55·0
2000	4,400,282	171,731	347,466		4,919,479	61·8

Of the total population in 2000, 2,483,848 were female, 3,632,585 were 18 years old or older and 3,490,059 were urban. In 2000 the Hispanic population was 143,382, up from 53,888 in 1990 (an increase of 116·1%).

The largest cities (with 2000 census population) are Minneapolis (362,618), St Paul (287,151), Duluth (86,918), Rochester (85,806) and Bloomington (85,172). The Minneapolis–St Paul metropolitan area had a 2000 census population of 2,968,806.

SOCIAL STATISTICS

Births in 2003, 70,050 (13·8 per 1,000 population); deaths (2002), 38,510 (7·7 per 1,000 population). 2002 infant mortality (per 1,000 live births), 5·4. 2001: marriages, 33,000 (6·8 per 1,000 population); divorces, 16,000 (3·3).

CLIMATE

Duluth, Jan. 8°F (–13·3°C), July 63°F (17·2°C). Annual rainfall 29" (719 mm). Minneapolis-St. Paul, Jan. 12°F (–11·1°C), July 71°F (21·7°C). Annual rainfall 26" (656 mm). Minnesota belongs to the Great Lakes climate zone (*see* UNITED STATES: Climate).

CONSTITUTION AND GOVERNMENT

The original constitution dated from 1857; it was extensively amended and given a new structure in 1974. The Legislature consists of a Senate of 67 members, elected for four years, and a House of Representatives of 134 members, elected for two years. It meets for 120 days within each two years.

For the 109th Congress, which convened in Jan. 2005, Minnesota sends eight members to the House of Representatives. It is represented in the Senate by Mark Dayton (D. 2001–07) and Norm Coleman (R. 2003–09).

The capital is St Paul. There are 87 counties.

RECENT ELECTIONS

In the 2004 presidential election Kerry polled 1,445,014 votes; Bush, 1,346,695; Nader, 18,683.

CURRENT ADMINISTRATION

Governor: Tim Pawlenty (R.), 2003–07 (salary: $120,303).
   Lieut.-Governor: Carol L. Molnau (R.), 2003–07 ($78,197).
   Secretary of State: Mary E. Kiffmeyer (R.), 2003–07 ($90,227).

Government Website: http://www.state.mn.us

ECONOMY

Per capita income (2004) was $36,173.

Budget

In the fiscal year 2004 total state revenue was $25,960m. Total expenditure was $22,246m. (public welfare, $8,282m.; education, $7,567m.; highways, $3,176m.; property tax aids and credits, $1,432m.; government administration, $364m.) Outstanding debt, $3,197m.

Performance

In 2004 Gross State Product was $223,822m., ranking Minnesota 17th in the United States.

ENERGY AND NATURAL RESOURCES

Water

The total area covered by water is approximately 7,329 sq. miles.

Minerals

The iron ore and taconite industry is the most important in the USA. Production of usable iron ore in 2003 was 34·8m. tons, value $969m. Other important minerals are sand and gravel, crushed and dimension stone, clays and peat. Total value of mineral production in 2003 was $1,230m.

Agriculture

In 2002 there were 80,839 farms with a total area of 27·5m. acres; the average farm was of 340 acres. Average value of land and buildings per acre, 2002, $1,513. Farm income, 2002, from crops, $3,833m.; from livestock and products, $3,645m. The net farm income in 2002 was $462m. Important products: corn, soybeans, sugarbeets, spring wheat, processing sweet corn, oats, dry milk, cheese, mink, turkeys, wild rice, butter, eggs, flaxseed, milch cows, barley, swine, cattle for market, honey, potatoes, rye, chickens, sunflower seed and dry edible beans. In 2002 there were 2·3m. cattle (0·5m. milch cows) and 6·4m. hogs and pigs. In 2002 the wool clip amounted to 986,437 lb of wool from 154,900 sheep.

Forestry

In 2002 Minnesota had 16,680,000 acres of forested land, including 2,625,000 acres of national forest. Forests of commercial timber covered 14·8m. acres, of which 55% was government-owned. The value of forest products in 2001 was $6,960m.—$2,137m. from primary processing, of which $1,609m. was from pulp and paper; and $4,823m. from secondary manufacturing. Logging, pulping, saw-mills and associated industries employed 55,000 in 2001.

INDUSTRY

In 2003 the state's 8,804 manufacturing establishments had 344,900 employees, earning $16,059m. Total value added by manufacturing in 2002 was $26,652m.

Labour

Total non-agricultural employment, 2003, 2,651,000. Employees by branch, 2003 (in 1,000): trade, transportation and utilities, 522; government, 402; education and health services, 367; manufacturing, 344; professional and business services, 295. In 2004 the unemployment rate was 4·7%.

COMMUNICATIONS

Roads

In 2003 there were 131,892 miles of roads (115,684 miles rural); there were 6,171,550 registered motor vehicles in 2004.

Rail

There are three Class I and 16 Class II and smaller railroads operating, with total mileage of 4,526.

Civil Aviation

In 2004 there were 143 airports for public use and 17 public seaplane bases. There were 17,597,639 passenger enplanements statewide in 2004.

SOCIAL INSTITUTIONS

Justice

In July 2004 there were 8,333 federal and state prisoners. There is no death penalty.

Education

In 2003–04 there were 842,915 students and 55,501 teachers in public elementary and secondary schools. In 2003–04 there were 1,863 public schools and 113 charter schools. There were 86,513 students enrolled in 495 private schools.

The Minnesota State Colleges and Universities System (created in 1995) is composed of 37 state colleges and universities. In 2003 enrolled students at state colleges numbered 78,300. There are seven universities in the system: St Cloud State University, with 14,217 students in 2003; Minnesota, Mankato, 13,157; Winona, 7,583; Minnesota, Moorhead, 6,993; Metropolitan State University (in Minneapolis and St Paul), 4,516; Bemidji State University, 4,362; Southwest Minnesota State University (in Marshall), 3,458. Minnesota State University's Akita campus in Japan closed in 2003.

The University of Minnesota (founded in 1851) has four campuses at Crookston, Duluth, Morris and Twin Cities.

Health

In 2002 there were 133 community hospitals with 16,700 beds. A total of 599,000 patients were admitted during the year.

Welfare

Medicare enrolment in July 2003 totalled 676,156. In 2002 a total of 620,652 people in Minnesota received Medicaid. In Dec. 2004 there were 775,460 Old-Age, Survivors, and Disability Insurance (OASDI) beneficiaries. A total of 80,451 people were receiving payments under Temporary Assistance for Needy Families (TANF) in Sept. 2004.

RELIGION

In 2000 the chief religious bodies were: Roman Catholic with 1,261,000 members; Mainline Protestant, 1,135,000; Evangelical, 510,000; Orthodox, 7,100; other faiths, 67,100. Total membership of all denominations, 2,979,300.

CULTURE

Tourism

In 2003 travel and tourism accounted for $9·2bn. gross receipts and sales. The industry employed about 117,000.

FURTHER READING

Statistical Information: Department of Trade and Economic Development, 500 Metro Square, St Paul 55101. Publishes *Compare Minnesota: an Economic and Statistical Factbook.—Economic Report to the Governor.*
Legislative Manual. Secretary of State. St Paul. Biennial
Minnesota Agriculture Statistics. Dept. of Agric., St Paul. Annual

---

Mississippi

KEY HISTORICAL EVENTS

Mississippi was one of the territories claimed by France after the 17th century and ceded to Britain in 1763. The indigenous people were Choctaw and Natchez. French settlers at first traded amicably with them, but in the course of three wars (1716, 1723 and 1729) the French allied with the Choctaw to drive the Natchez out. During hostilities the Natchez massacred the settlers of Fort Rosalie, which the French had founded in 1716 and which was later renamed Natchez.

In 1783 the area became part of the USA except for Natchez which was under Spanish control until 1798. The United States then made it the capital of the Territory of Mississippi. The boundaries of the Territory were extended in 1804 and again in 1812. In 1817 it was divided into two territories, with the western part becoming the state of Mississippi. (The eastern part became the state of Alabama in 1819.) The city of Jackson was laid out in 1822 as the new state capital.

A cotton plantation economy developed, based on black slave labour, and by 1860 the majority of the population was black. Mississippi joined the Confederacy during the Civil War. After defeat and reconstruction there was a return to rigid segregation and denial of black rights. This situation lasted until the 1960s. There was a black majority until the Second World War, when out-migration began to change the pattern. By 1990 about 35% of the population was black, and manufacture (especially clothing and textiles) had become the largest single employer of labour.

Mississippi suffered widespread damage and loss of life after Hurricane Katrina struck the Gulf Coast on 31 Aug. 2005.

TERRITORY AND POPULATION

Mississippi is bounded in the north by Tennessee, east by Alabama, south by the Gulf of Mexico and Louisiana, and west by the Mississippi River forming the boundary with Louisiana and Arkansas. Land area, 46,907 sq. miles (121,489 sq. km). Census population, 1 April 2000, 2,844,658, an increase of 10·5% since 1990. July 2005 estimate, 2,921,088.

Population of five federal census years was:

	White	Black	Indian	Asiatic	Total	Per sq. mile
1910	786,111	1,009,487	1,253	263	1,797,114	38·8
1930	998,077	1,009,718	1,458	568	2,009,821	42·4
			All others			
1980	1,615,190	887,206	18,242		2,520,638	53·0
1990	1,633,461	915,057	24,698		2,573,216	54·8
2000	1,746,099	1,033,809	63,372		2,844,658	60·6

Of the total population in 2000, 1,373,554 were male, 2,069,471 were 18 years old or older and 1,457,307 were rural (51·2% of the population). In 2000 Mississippi's Hispanic population was estimated to be 39,569, up from 15,998 in 1990 (an increase of 147%).

The largest city (2000 census) is Jackson, 184,256. Others (2000 census) are: Gulfport, 71,127; Biloxi, 50,644; Hattiesburg, 44,779; Greenville, 41,633; Meridian, 39,968; Tupelo, 34,211; Southaven, 28,977; Vicksburg, 26,407; Pascagoula, 26,200; Columbus, 25,944.

SOCIAL STATISTICS

Births occurring in the state, 2003, were 42,380 (14·7 per 1,000 population); deaths (2002), 28,853 (10·0 per 1,000 population). 2002 infant mortality (per 1,000 live births), 10·3. 2001: marriages, 18,605; divorces, 14,198.

CLIMATE

Jackson, Jan. 47°F (8·3°C), July 82°F (27·8°C). Annual rainfall 49" (1,221 mm). Vicksburg, Jan. 48°F (8·9°C), July 81°F (27·2°C). Annual rainfall 52" (1,311 mm). Mississippi belongs to the Central Plains climate zone (*see* UNITED STATES: Climate).

CONSTITUTION AND GOVERNMENT

The present constitution was adopted in 1890 without ratification by the electorate; there were 123 amendments by 2005.

The Legislature consists of a Senate (52 members) and a House of Representatives (122 members), both elected for four years. Electors are all citizens who have resided in the state one year, in the county one year, in the election district six months before the election and have been registered according to law.

For the 109th Congress, which convened in Jan. 2005, Mississippi sends four members to the House of Representatives. It is represented in the Senate by Thad Cochran (R. 1977–2009) and Trent Lott (R. 1989–2007).

The capital is Jackson; there are 82 counties.

RECENT ELECTIONS

In the 2004 presidential election Bush polled 672,660 votes; Kerry, 457,766; Nader, 3,175.

CURRENT ADMINISTRATION

Governor: Haley Barbour (R.), 2004–08 (salary: $122,160).
  Lieut.-Governor: Amy Tuck (R.), 2004–08 ($60,000).
  Secretary of State: Eric Clark (D.), 2004–08 ($90,000).

Government Website: http://www.mississippi.gov

ECONOMY

Per capita income (2004) was $24,379, the lowest in the country.

Budget

For the fiscal year ending 30 June 2004 general revenue was $13,737m. General expenditures were $13,244m. (education, $3,281m.; public welfare, including public health and health care, $1,146m.; highways, $920m.; police protection, $101m.) Debt outstanding, on 30 June 2004, $3,377m.

Performance

Gross State Product in 2004 was $76,166m. ranking Mississippi 35th in the United States.

ENERGY AND NATURAL RESOURCES

Oil and Gas

Petroleum and natural gas account for about 90% (by value) of mineral production. Output of petroleum, 2003, was 17,412,245 bbls. and of natural gas 164,170,149,000 cu. ft. There are four oil refineries. Taxable value of oil and gas products sold in fiscal year 2003 was $725,088,055.

Water

The total area covered by water is approximately 1,523 sq. miles.

Minerals

The value of domestic non-fuel mineral production in 2003 was $174m.

Agriculture

Agriculture is the leading industry of the state because of the semi-tropical climate and a rich productive soil. In 2003 farms numbered 42,800 with an area of 11·1m. acres. Average size of farm was 260 acres. This compares with an average farm size of 154 acres in 1962. Average value of farm per acre in 2003 was $1,350.

Cash income from all crops and livestock during 2003 was $3,411m. Cash income from crops was $1,246m, and from livestock and products $2,165m. The net farm income in 2002 was $401m. The chief product is cotton, cash income (2003) $444m. from 1,110,000 acres producing 2,120,000 bales of 480 lb. Soybeans, rice, corn, hay, wheat, oats, sorghum, peanuts, pecans, sweet potatoes, peaches, other vegetables, nursery and forest products continue to contribute.

On 1 Jan. 2005 there were 1·07m. head of cattle and calves on Mississippi farms. In Jan. 2005 milch cows totalled 26,000; beef cows, 564,000; hogs and pigs (2004), 315,000. Of cash income from livestock and products, 2003, $208,136,000 was credited to cattle and calves. Cash income from poultry and eggs, 2003, totalled $1,597·4m.; dairy products, $55·2m.; swine, $42·1m.

Forestry

In 2002 income from forestry amounted to $1·03bn.; output of pine logs was 1·19bn. bd ft; of hardwood lumber, 426m. bd ft; pulpwood, 5·55m. cords. There were 18·5m. acres of forest (61% of the state's area) in 2002, with 1·1m. acres of national forest area.

Fisheries

Commercial catch, in 2002, totalled 217·1m. lb of fish with a value of $46·1m. Mississippi has the largest aquaculture industry of any state; value, in 2001, was $262·9m. (of which catfish sales accounted for $240·0m.)

INDUSTRY

In 2002 the 2,829 manufacturing establishments had average monthly employment of 188,857 workers, earning $5,731,066,344. The average annual wage was $30,346.

Labour

In 2004 total non-agricultural employment was 1,124,600. Employees by branch, 2004 (in 1,000): services, 473; government, 245; manufacturing, 180; wholesale and retail trade, 175. The unemployment rate in 2004 was 5·7%.

COMMUNICATIONS

Roads

The state as of 1 July 2004 maintained 13,681 miles of highways, of which 13,673 miles were paved. In fiscal year 2004, 2,471,212 passenger vehicles and pick-ups were registered.

Rail

In 2003 the state had 2,584 main-line and short-line miles of railway.

Civil Aviation

There were 79 public airports in 2004, 72 of them general aviation airports. There were 1,166,522 passenger enplanements statewide in 2004.

SOCIAL INSTITUTIONS

Justice

The death penalty is authorized; there was one execution in 2005, the first since 2002. As of 1 Feb. 2005 the state prison system had 20,964 inmates.

Education

Attendance at school is compulsory as laid down in the Education Reform Act of 1982. The public elementary and secondary schools in 2003–04 had 492,557 pupils and 31,357 classroom teachers.

In 2003–04 teachers' average salary was $36,466. The expenditure per pupil in average daily attendance, 2002–03, was $6,402.

There are 21 universities and senior colleges, of which eight are state-supported. In autumn 2004 the University of Mississippi, Oxford had 916 faculty and 14,497 students; Mississippi State University, Starkville, 1,220 faculty and 15,934 students; Mississippi University for Women, Columbus, 183 faculty and 2,231 students; University of Southern Mississippi, Hattiesburg, 865 faculty and 15,253 students; Jackson State University, Jackson, 482 faculty and 8,351 students; Delta State University, Cleveland, 173 faculty and 3,990 students; Alcorn State University, Lorman, 225 faculty and 3,443 students; Mississippi Valley State University, Itta Bena, 135 faculty and 3,621 students. State support for the universities (2004–05) was $325,868,694.

Community and junior colleges had (2003–04) 83,307 full-time equivalent students and 4,083 full-time instructors. The state appropriation for junior colleges, 2003–04, was $157,226,517.

Health

In 2004 the state had 106 acute general hospitals (12,824 beds) listed by the State Department of Health; 14 hospitals with facilities for the care of the mentally ill had 2,341 licensed beds. In addition, one rehabilitation hospital had 124 beds.

Welfare

Medicare enrolment in July 2003 totalled 436,677. The Division of Medicaid paid (fiscal year 2004) $2,801,539,621 for medical services, including $639,224,101 for drugs, $614,299,371 for hospital services and $487,265,490 for skilled nursing home care. There were 79,482 persons eligible for Aged Medicaid benefits as of 30 June 2004 and 220,734 persons eligible for Disabled Medicaid benefits. In June 2004, 18,185 families with 30,032 dependent children received $2,566,105 in the Temporary Assistance to Needy Families programme. The average monthly payment was $141·66 per family or $63·42 per recipient.

RELIGION

In 2003: Southern Baptists in Mississippi, 715,276 members; United Methodists, 190,428. In 2004: Roman Catholics in Jackson Diocese, 50,646; in 2003 Roman Catholics in Biloxi Diocese, 72,158.

CULTURE

Tourism

Total receipts in 2004 amounted to $6·1bn.; an estimated 11·4m. overnight tourists visited the state.

FURTHER READING

College of Business and Industry, Mississippi State Univ., Mississippi State 39762. Publishes *Mississippi Statistical Abstract*.

Secretary of State. *Mississippi Official and Statistical Register.* Quadrennial

Mississippi Library Commission: 1221 Ellis Avenue, Jackson, MS 39209–7328.

Missouri

KEY HISTORICAL EVENTS

Territory of several Indian groups, including the Missouri, the area was not settled by European immigrants until the 18th century. The French founded Ste Genevieve in 1735, partly as a lead-mining community. St Louis was founded as a fur-trading base in 1764. The area was nominally under Spanish rule from 1770 until 1800 when it passed back to France. In 1803 the USA bought it as part of the Louisiana Purchase.

St Louis was made the capital of the whole Louisiana Territory in 1805, and of a new Missouri Territory in 1812. In that year American immigration increased markedly. The Territory became a state in 1821, but there had been bitter disputes between slave-owning and anti-slavery factions, with the former succeeding in obtaining statehood without the prohibition of slavery required of all other new states north of latitude 36° 30'; this was achieved by the Missouri Compromise of 1820. The Compromise was repealed in 1854 and declared unconstitutional in 1857. During the Civil War the state held to the Union side, although St Louis was placed under martial law.

With the development of steamboat traffic on the Missouri and Mississippi rivers, and the expansion of railways, the state became the transport hub of all western movement. Lead and other mining remained important, as did livestock farming. European settlers came from Germany, Britain and Ireland.

TERRITORY AND POPULATION

Missouri is bounded north by Iowa, east by the Mississippi River forming the boundary with Illinois and Kentucky, south by Arkansas, southeast by Tennessee, southwest by Oklahoma, west by Kansas and Nebraska, with the Missouri River forming the boundary in the northwest. Land area, 68,886 sq. miles (178,414 sq. km).

Census population, 1 April 2000, 5,595,211, an increase since 1990 of 9·3%. July 2005 estimate, 5,800,310.

Population of five federal census years was:

	White	Black	Indian	Asiatic	Total	Per sq. mile
1930	3,403,876	223,840	578	1,073	3,629,367	52·4
1960	3,922,967	390,853	1,723	3,146	4,319,813	62·5
			All others			
1980	4,345,521	514,276	56,889		4,916,686	71·3
1990	4,486,228	548,208	82,637		5,117,073	74·3
2000	4,748,083	629,391	217,737		5,595,211	81·2

Of the total population in 2000, 2,875,034 were female, 4,167,519 were 18 years old or older and 3,883,442 were urban. In 2000 Missouri's Hispanic population was 118,592, up from 61,702 in 1990 (an increase of 92·2%).

The principal cities at the 2000 census were:

Kansas City	441,545	St Joseph	73,990
St Louis	348,189	Lee's Summit	70,700
Springfield	151,580	St Charles	60,321
Independence	113,288	St Peters	51,381
Columbia	84,531	Florissant	50,497

Metropolitan areas, 2000: St Louis, 2,603,607; Kansas City, 1,776,062.

SOCIAL STATISTICS

Births, 2003, were 77,045 (13·5 per 1,000 population); deaths (2002), 55,940 (9·9). 2002 infant mortality (per 1,000 live births), 8·5. 2001: marriages, 42,200 (7·6 per 1,000 population); divorces, 23,800 (4·3).

CLIMATE

Kansas City, Jan. 30°F (−1·1°C), July 79°F (26·1°C). Annual rainfall 38" (947 mm). St Louis, Jan. 32°F (0°C), July 79°F (26·1°C). Annual rainfall 40" (1,004 mm). Missouri belongs to the Central Plains climate zone (*see* UNITED STATES: Climate).

CONSTITUTION AND GOVERNMENT

A new constitution, the fourth, was adopted on 27 Feb. 1945; it has had 108 amendments in the meantime. The General Assembly consists of a Senate of 34 members elected for four years (half for re-election every two years), and a House of Representatives of 163 members elected for two years. The Governor and Lieut.-Governor are elected for four years.

For the 109th Congress, which convened in Jan. 2005, Missouri sends nine members to the House of Representatives. It is represented in the Senate by Christopher Bond (R. 1987–2011) and James Talent (R. 1993–2007).

Jefferson City is the state capital. The state is divided into 114 counties and the city of St Louis.

RECENT ELECTIONS

In the 2004 presidential election Bush polled 1,455,713 votes; Kerry, 1,259,171; Badnarik, 9,831.

CURRENT ADMINISTRATION

Governor: Matt Blunt (R.), 2005–09 (salary: $120,087).
   Lieut.-Governor: Peter Kinder (R.), 2005–09 ($77,184).
   Secretary of State: Robin Carnahan (D.), 2005–09 ($96,455).

Government Website: http://www.mo.gov/

ECONOMY

Per capita income (2004) was $30,516.

Budget

In 2003 total state revenue was $22,024m. Total expenditure was $21,566m. (education, $6,733m.; public welfare, $5,592m.; highways, $1,854m.; hospitals, $893m.; government administration, $774m.) Outstanding debt, in 2003, $13,855m.

Performance

In 2004 Gross State Product was $203,294m., ranking Missouri 20th in the United States.

ENERGY AND NATURAL RESOURCES

Water

The total area covered by water is approximately 818 sq. miles.

Minerals

The three leading mineral commodities are lead, portland cement and crushed stone. Value of domestic non-fuel mineral production (2003) is $1,290m.

Agriculture

In 2002 there were 107,000 farms in Missouri producing crops and livestock on 29·8m. acres; the average farm had 279 acres and was valued at $1,508 per acre. Production of principal crops, 2002: corn, 268·2m. bu.; soybeans, 165·05m. bu.; wheat, 34·9m. bu.; sorghum grain, 16·6m. bu.; oats, 1·29m. bu.; rice, 9·96m. cwt; cotton, 608,280 bales (of 480 lb). Farm income 2002: $4,402m. (from crops, $2,100m.; from livestock and products, $2,302m.). The net farm income in 2002 was $451m.

Forestry

The state had a forested area of 13,992,000 acres in 2002, of which 1,428,000 acres were national forest.

INDUSTRY

In 2001 the state's 7,261 manufacturing establishments had 335,000 employees, earning $11,318m. Total value added by manufacturing in 2001 was $40,284m.

Labour

Total non-agricultural employment, 2003, 2,676,000. Employees by branch, 2003 (in 1,000): trade, transportation and utilities, 533; government, 428; education and health services, 352; manufacturing, 313; professional and business services, 304. The unemployment rate was 5·6% in 2003.

COMMUNICATIONS

Roads

In 2002 there were 124,686 miles of roads (107,110 miles rural) and 4,235,031 registered motor vehicles.

Rail

The state has five Class I railways; approximate total mileage, 4,159. There are four Class II and Class III railways (switching, terminal or short-line); total mileage 590 in 2002. There is a light rail line in St Louis.

Civil Aviation

In 2005 there were 127 public airports and 279 private airports. There were 15,157,746 passenger enplanements statewide in 2003.

Shipping

Two major barge lines (1993) operated on about 1,050 miles of navigable waterways including the Missouri and Mississippi Rivers. Boat shipping seasons: Missouri River, April–end Nov.; Mississippi River, all seasons.

SOCIAL INSTITUTIONS

Justice

In June 2003 there were 30,649 federal and state prisoners. The death penalty was reinstated in 1978. There were two executions in 2003, none in 2004 but five in 2005. The Missouri Law Enforcement Assistance Council was created in 1969 for law reform. With reorganization of state government in 1974 the duties of the Council were delegated to the Department of Public Safety. The Department of Corrections was organized as a separate department of State by an Act of the Legislature in 1981.

Education

School attendance is compulsory for children from seven to 16 years for the full term. In the 1993–94 school year, public schools (kindergarten through grade 12) had 851,086 pupils. Total expenditure for public schools in 1993–94, $3,563,419,000. Salaries for teachers (kindergarten through grade 12), 1993–94, averaged $30,227.

Institutions for higher education include the University of Missouri, founded in 1839 with campuses at Columbia, Rolla, St Louis and Kansas City, with 3,469 accredited teachers and 48,072 students in 1994–95. Washington University at St Louis, founded in 1857, is an independent co-ed university with 11,655 students in 1994–95. St Louis University (1818) is an independent Roman Catholic co-ed university with 10,365 students in 1994–95. 17 state colleges had 129,466 students in 1994–95. Private colleges had (1994–95) 34,548 students. Church-affiliated colleges (1994–95) had 41,420 students. Public junior colleges had 66,853 students. There are about 90 secondary and post-secondary institutions offering vocational courses, and about 294 private career schools. There were 265,186 students in higher education in autumn 1994.

Health

In 2002 there were 119 community hospitals with 18,900 beds. A total of 809,000 patients were admitted during the year.

Welfare

Medicare enrolment in July 2003 totalled 884,449. In 2002 a total of 1,036,150 people in Missouri received Medicaid. In Dec. 2004 there were 1,046,439 Old-Age, Survivors, and Disability Insurance (OASDI) beneficiaries. A total of 98,335 people were receiving payments under Temporary Assistance for Needy Families (TANF) in Sept. 2004.

RELIGION

Chief religious bodies (2000) are Catholics, with 856,964 members, Southern Baptists (797,732), United Methodists (226,578), Christian Churches (183,818) and Lutherans (140,315). Total membership, all denominations, 2·8m. in 2000.

CULTURE

Broadcasting

There were 196 commercial radio stations and 29 TV stations in 1995.

Press

There were (1995) 46 daily and 260 weekly newspapers.

FURTHER READING

Statistical information: Business and Public Administration Research Center, Univ. of Missouri, Columbia 65211. Publishes *Statistical Abstract for Missouri.*

Missouri Area Labor Trends. Department of Labor and Industrial Relations, monthly

Missouri Farm Facts. Department of Agriculture, annual

Report of the Public Schools of Missouri. State Board of Education, annual

---

Montana

KEY HISTORICAL EVENTS

Originally the territory of many groups of Indian hunters including the Sioux, Cheyenne and Chippewa, Montana was not settled by American colonists until the 19th century. The area passed to the USA with the Louisiana Purchase of 1803, but the area west of the Rockies was disputed with Britain until 1846. Trappers and fur-traders were the first immigrants, and the fortified trading post at Fort Benton (1846) became the first permanent settlement. Colonization increased when gold was found in 1862. Montana was created a separate Territory (out of Idaho and Dakota Territories) in 1864. In 1866 large-scale grazing of sheep and cattle was allowed, and this provoked violent confrontation with the indigenous people whose hunting lands were invaded. Indian wars led to the defeat of federal forces at Little Bighorn in 1876 and at Big Hole Basin in 1877, but the Indians could not continue the fight and they had been moved to reservations by 1880. Montana became a state in 1889.

Helena, the capital, was founded as a mining town in the 1860s. In the early 20th century there were many European immigrants who settled as farmers or in the mines, especially in copper-mining at Butte.

TERRITORY AND POPULATION

Montana is bounded north by Canada, east by North and South Dakota, south by Wyoming and west by Idaho and the Bitterroot Range of the Rocky Mountains. Land area, 145,552 sq. miles (336,978 sq. km). US Bureau of Indian Affairs (1990) administered 5,574,835 acres, of which 2,663,385 were allotted to tribes. Census population, 1 April 2000, 902,195, an increase of 12·9% since 1990. July 2005 estimate, 935,670.

Population in five census years was:

	White	Black	American Indian	Asiatic	Total	Per sq. mile
1910	360,580	1,834	10,745	2,870	376,053	2·6
1930	519,898	1,256	14,798	1,239	537,606	3·7
1980	740,148	1,786	37,270	2,503	786,690	5·3
1990	741,111	2,381	47,679	4,259	799,065	5·4
2000	817,229	2,692	56,068	5,161	902,195	6·2

Of the total population in 2000, 452,715 were female, 672,133 were 18 years old or older and 487,878 were urban. Median age, 33·8 years. Households, 306,163. In 2000 Montana's Hispanic population was estimated to be 18,081, up from 12,174 in 1990 (an increase of 48·5%).

The largest cities, 2000, are Billings, 89,847; Missoula, 57,053; Great Falls, 56,690. Others: Butte-Silver Bow, 34,606; Bozeman, 27,509; Helena (capital), 25,780; Kalispell, 14,223; Havre, 9,621; Anaconda-Deer Lodge County, 9,417.

SOCIAL STATISTICS

Births in 2003, 11,422 (12·4 per 1,000 population); deaths (2002), 8,506 (9·4 per 1,000 population). 2002 infant mortality rate (per 1,000 live births), 7·5. 2001: marriages, 6,400; divorces, 2,300.

CLIMATE

Helena, Jan. 18°F (–7·8°C), July 69°F (20·6°C). Annual rainfall 13" (325 mm). Montana belongs to the Mountain States climate zone (*see* UNITED STATES: Climate).

CONSTITUTION AND GOVERNMENT

A new constitution came into force on 1 July 1973. The Senate consists of 50 senators, elected for four years, one half at each biennial election. The 100 members of the House of Representatives are elected for two years.

For the 109th Congress, which convened in Jan. 2005, Montana sends one member to the House of Representatives. It is represented in the Senate by Max Baucus (D. 1978–2009) and Conrad Burns (R. 1989–2007).

The capital is Helena. The state is divided into 56 counties.

RECENT ELECTIONS

In the 2004 presidential election Bush polled 266,063 votes; Kerry, 173,710; Nader, 6,168.

CURRENT ADMINISTRATION

Governor: Brian Schweitzer (D.), 2005–09 (salary: $96,462).
Lieut.-Governor: John Bohlinger (R.), 2005–09 ($66,724).
Secretary of State: Brad Johnson (R.), 2005–09 ($76,539).

Government Website: http://www.discoveringmontana.com

ECONOMY

Per capita income (2004) was $27,666.

Budget

In 2003 total state revenue was $4,608m. Total expenditure was $4,437m. (education, $1,372m.; public welfare, $664m.; highways, $496m.; health, $263m.; government administration, $240m.) Outstanding debt, in 2003, $2,879m.

Performance

Gross State Product in 2004 was $27,482m., ranking Montana 47th in the United States.

ENERGY AND NATURAL RESOURCES

Water
The total area covered by water is approximately 1,490 sq. miles.

Minerals
2003 domestic non-fuel mineral production value was $492m. Principal minerals include copper, gold, platinum-group metals, molybdenum and silver.

Agriculture
In 2002 there were 28,000 farms and ranches with an area of 56·7m. acres. Large-scale farming predominates; in 2002 the average size per farm was 2,025 acres. The average value per acre in 2002 was $386. In 1997 a total of 13,267,000 acres were harvested; including 5,930,000 acres of wheat. The farm population in 2000 was 39,930.

The chief crops are wheat, hay, barley, oats, sugarbeets, potatoes, corn, dry beans and cherries. Farm income, 2002: crops, $702m.; livestock and products, $985m. In 2002 there were 2·4m. cattle and calves; value, $1,015m. The net farm income in 2002 was $216m.

Forestry
In 2002 there were 23·3m. acres of forested land with 14·6m. acres in 11 national forests.

INDUSTRY
In 2001 the state's 1,226 manufacturing establishments had 21,000 employees, earning $646m. Total value added by manufacturing in 2001 was $2,091m.

Labour
Total non-agricultural employment, 2003, 400,000. Employees by branch, 2003 (in 1,000): government, 86; trade, transportation and utilities, 84; education and health services, 53; leisure and hospitality, 52; professional and business services, 33. In 2003 the unemployment rate was 4·7%.

COMMUNICATIONS

Roads
In 2003 there were a total of 69,450 miles of roads comprising 2,752 miles of urban road and 66,698 miles of rural road. There were 1,010,487 registered motor vehicles.

Rail
In 1999 there were approximately 3,300 route miles of railway in the state.

Civil Aviation
In 2005 there were 119 public use airports. There were 1,333,592 passenger enplanements statewide in 2003.

SOCIAL INSTITUTIONS

Justice
In June 2003 there were 3,440 prison inmates. The death penalty is authorized; the last execution was in 1998.

Education
In 1995 (preliminary) public elementary and secondary schools had 165,000 pupils and (in 1994) 10,079 teachers. Expenditure on public school education by state and local governments in 1997 was $986m.

In 1996 there were 43,000 students enrolled at 26 higher education institutions. The Montana State University System (created in 1994) consists of the Montana State University, at Bozeman (autumn 1992 enrolment: 10,111 students), founded 1893; Montana State University-Billings (3,631); Montana State University-Northern, at Havre (1,973); and Montana State University-Great Falls College of Technology. The University of Montana System comprises the University of Montana, at Missoula, founded in 1893 (10,788); Montana Tech, at Butte (1,881); and the University of Montana-Western, at Dillon (1,106). The University of Great Falls (founded in 1932) had 879 students in autumn 2001.

Health
In 2002 there were 53 community hospitals with 4,300 beds. A total of 107,000 patients were admitted during the year.

Welfare
Medicare enrolment in July 2003 totalled 142,457. In 2002 a total of 103,617 people in Montana received Medicaid. In Dec. 2004 there were 166,264 Old-Age, Survivors, and Disability Insurance (OASDI) beneficiaries. A total of 13,634 people were receiving payments under Temporary Assistance for Needy Families (TANF) in Sept. 2004.

RELIGION
The leading religious bodies are Roman Catholic, followed by Lutheran and Methodist.

CULTURE

Press
There were 11 daily newspapers and seven Sunday papers in 1997.

FURTHER READING
Statistical information. Census and Economic Information Center, Montana Department of Commerce, 1425 9th Ave., Helena 59620.

Lang, W. L. and Myers, R. C., *Montana, Our Land and People.* Pruett, 1979

Nebraska

KEY HISTORICAL EVENTS
The Nebraska region was first reached by Europeans from Mexico under the Spanish general Coronado in 1541. It was ceded by France to Spain in 1763, retroceded to France in 1801, and sold by Napoleon to the USA as part of the Louisiana Purchase in 1803. During the 1840s the Platte River valley became an established trail for thousands of pioneers' wagons heading for Oregon and California. The need to serve and protect the trail led to the creation of Nebraska as a Territory in 1854. In 1862 the Homestead Act opened the area for settlement, but colonization was not very rapid until the Union Pacific Railroad was completed in 1869. The largest city, Omaha, developed as the starting point of the Union Pacific and became one of the largest railway towns in the country.

Nebraska became a state in 1867, with approximately its present boundaries except that it later received small areas from the Dakotas. Many early settlers were from Europe, brought in by railway-company schemes, but from the late 1880s eastern Nebraska suffered catastrophic drought. Crop and stock farming recovered, but crop growing was only established in the west by means of irrigation.

TERRITORY AND POPULATION
Nebraska is bounded in the north by South Dakota, with the Missouri River forming the boundary in the northeast and the boundary with Iowa and Missouri to the east, south by Kansas, southwest by Colorado and west by Wyoming. Land area, 76,872

sq. miles (199,098 sq. km). Census population, 1 April 2000, 1,711,263, an increase of 8·4% since 1990. July 2005 estimate, 1,758,787.

Population in five census years was:

	White	Black	Indian	Asiatic	Total	Per sq. mile
1910	1,180,293	7,689	3,502	730	1,192,214	15·5
1960	1,374,764	29,262	5,545	1,195	1,411,330	18·3
			All others			
1980	1,490,381	48,390	31,054		1,569,825	20·5
1990	1,480,558	57,404	40,423		1,578,385	20·5
2000	1,533,261	68,541	109,461		1,711,263	22·3

Of the total population in 2000, 867,912 were female, 1,261,021 were 18 years old or older and 1,193,725 were urban. In 1999 the estimated Hispanic population of Nebraska was 94,425, up from 36,969 in 1990 (a rise of 155·4%). The largest cities in the state are: Omaha, with a census population, 2000, of 390,007; Lincoln, 225,581; Bellevue, 44,382; Grand Island, 42,940; Kearney, 27,431; Fremont, 25,174; Hastings, 24,064; North Platte, 23,878; Norfolk, 23,516.

The Bureau of Indian Affairs in 1990 administered 64,932 acres, of which 21,742 acres were allotted to tribal control.

SOCIAL STATISTICS

Births, 2003, were 25,917 (14·9 per 1,000 population); deaths (2002), 15,738 (9·1 per 1,000 population). 2002 infant mortality rate (per 1,000 live births), 7·0. 2001: marriages, 13,600 (8·1); divorces, 6,200 (3·7).

CLIMATE

Omaha, Jan. 22°F (−5·6°C), July 77°F (25°C). Annual rainfall 29" (721 mm). Nebraska belongs to the High Plains climate zone (*see* UNITED STATES: Climate).

CONSTITUTION AND GOVERNMENT

The present constitution was adopted in 1875; it had been amended 186 times by 2004. By an amendment of 1934 Nebraska has a single-chambered legislature (elected for four years) of 49 members elected on a non-party ballot and classed as senators—the only state in the USA to have one. It meets annually.

For the 109th Congress, which convened in Jan. 2005, Nebraska sends three members to the House of Representatives. It is represented in the Senate by Chuck Hagel (R. 1997–2009) and Ben Nelson (D. 2001–07).

The capital is Lincoln. The state has 93 counties.

RECENT ELECTIONS

In the 2004 presidential election Bush polled 512,814 votes; Kerry, 254,328; Nader, 5,698.

CURRENT ADMINISTRATION

Governor: David Heineman (R.), 2005–07 (salary: $85,000).
Lieut.-Governor: Rick Sheehy (R.), 2005–07 ($60,000).
Secretary of State: John Gale (R.), 2003–07 ($65,000).

Government Website: http://www.nebraska.gov

ECONOMY

Per capita income (2004) was $32,276.

Budget

In 2003 total state revenue was $7,285m. Total expenditure was $6,824m. (education, $2,233m.; public welfare, $1,809m.; highways, $558m.; health, $391m.; hospitals $192m.) Outstanding debt, in 2003, $2,136m.

Performance

Gross State Product was $68,183m. in 2004, ranking Nebraska 36th in the United States.

ENERGY AND NATURAL RESOURCES

Oil and Gas

Petroleum output, 2001: 2·9m. bbls.; natural gas, 1,208m. cu. ft.

Water

The total area covered by water is approximately 481 sq. miles.

Minerals

Output of non-fuel minerals, 1995 (in 1,000 short tons): sand and gravel for construction, 17,637; stone, 7,275; clays, 243. Other minerals include limestone, potash, pumice, slate and shale. Total value of non-fuel mineral output in 2003 was $94m.

Agriculture

Nebraska is one of the most important agricultural states. In 2002 it contained approximately 52,000 farms, with a total area of 46·4m. acres. The average farm was 892 acres and was valued in 2002 at $776 per acre. In 2002 the total acreage harvested was 17·34m. acres.

In 2001 net farm income was $980m. Farm income from crops (2002), $3,764m., and from livestock and products, $5,824m. Principal crops were corn, soybeans, hay, barley, sorghum for grain and wheat. Livestock, 2001: cattle, 6·6m.; 2002: pigs, 2·93m.; sheep, 97,400; chickens, 13·7m.; turkeys, 3·5m.

Forestry

The state had a forested area of 947,000 acres in 2002.

INDUSTRY

In 2001 the state's 1,934 manufacturing establishments had 109,000 employees, earning $3,361m. Total value added by manufacturing in 2001 was $11,962m.

Labour

In 2003 non-agricultural employment totalled 904,000. Employees by branch in 2003 (in 1,000): trade, transportation and utilities, 194; government, 160; education and health services, 113; manufacturing, 102; professional and business services, 91. In 2003 the unemployment rate was 4·0%.

COMMUNICATIONS

Roads

In 2003 there were 93,196 miles of roads (87,430 miles rural). Registered motor vehicles in 2003 numbered 1,677,203.

Rail

In 2002 there were 3,537 miles of railway. There were two Class I operators (2,706 miles), three Class II operators (326 miles) and three Class III operators (505 miles).

Civil Aviation

Publicly owned airports in 2005 numbered 86. There were 2,028,006 passenger enplanements statewide in 2003.

SOCIAL INSTITUTIONS

Justice

A 'Civil Rights Act' revised in 1969 provides that all people are entitled to a full and equal enjoyment of public facilities. In June 2003 there were 4,103 prison inmates. The last execution was in 1997.

Education

School attendance is compulsory for children from seven to 16 years of age. Public elementary and secondary schools, in 2001–02, had 285,095 enrolled pupils and 20,808 teachers in 1,250 schools; there were 42,791 non-public pupils. Total enrolment in institutions of higher education, autumn 2000, was 88,532 students in public and 21,518 in independent institutions.

Founded	Institution	Students 2000–01
1867	Peru State College	2,686
	University of Nebraska (State)	45,183
1869	Lincoln	22,268
1902	Medical Center	2,696
1905	Kearney	6,506
1908	Omaha	13,479
1965	College of Technical Agriculture, Curtis	234
1872	Doane College, Crete (United Church of Christ)	2,135
1878	Creighton University, Omaha (Roman Catholic)	6,237
1882	Hastings College (Presbyterian)	1,130
1883	Midland Lutheran College, Fremont (Lutheran Church of America)	1,025
	Nebraska Methodist College, Omaha (Private)	400
1884	Dana College, Blair (American Lutheran)	583
1887	Nebraska Wesleyan University (Private)	1,699
1888	Clarkson College, Omaha (Private)	400
1890	York College[1] (Private)	497
1891	Union College, Lincoln (Seventh Day Adventist)	788
1894	Concordia University Nebraska, Seward (Lutheran)	1,270
1910	Wayne State College	3,518
1911	Chadron State College	2,686
1923	College of St Mary (Roman Catholic)	947
1943	Grace University, Omaha (Mennonite)	578
1945	Nebraska Christian College (Church of Christ)	162
1951	Platte Valley Bible College (Private)	52
1966	Bellevue University (Private)	3,445
1971	Nebraska Community Colleges (Local government)	35,447
	Central Area	7,126
	Metropolitan Area	11,534
	Mid Plains Area	2,607
	Northeast Area	4,520
	Southeast Area	7,396
	Western Area	2,264
1972	Nebraska Indian Community College	170

[1]Two-year college.

Health

In 2002 there were 86 community hospitals with 8,100 beds. A total of 206,000 patients were admitted during the year.

Welfare

Medicare enrolment in July 2003 totalled 257,171. In 2002 a total of 255,771 people in Nebraska received Medicaid. In Dec. 2004 there were 289,735 Old-Age, Survivors, and Disability Insurance (OASDI) beneficiaries. A total of 25,149 people were receiving payments under Temporary Assistance for Needy Families (TANF) in Sept. 2004.

RELIGION

The Roman Catholics had 372,791 members in 2000; Evangelical Lutheran Church, 128,570; Lutheran Church-Missouri Synod, 117,419; United Methodists, 117,277; Presbyterian Church (USA), 39,420.

CULTURE

Tourism

In 2004 there were an estimated 19·6m. visits. Travellers and tourists spent over $2·9bn.

FURTHER READING

Statistical information: Department of Economic Development, Box 94666, Lincoln 68509.

Nebraska Blue-Book. Legislative Council. Lincoln. Biennial

Olson, J. C., *History of Nebraska.* 3rd ed. Univ. of Nebraska Press, 1997

State Library: State Law Library, State House, Lincoln.

Nevada

KEY HISTORICAL EVENTS

The area was part of Spanish America until 1821, when it became part of the newly independent state of Mexico. Following a war between Mexico and the USA, Nevada was ceded to the USA as part of California in 1848. Settlement began in 1849, and the area was separated from California and joined with Utah Territory in 1850. In 1859 a rich deposit of silver was found in the Comstock Lode. Virginia City was founded as a mining town and immigration increased rapidly. Nevada Territory was formed in 1861. During the Civil War the Federal government, allegedly in order to obtain the wealth of silver for the Union cause, agreed to admit Nevada to the Union in 1864 as the 36th state. Areas of Arizona and Utah Territories were added to it in 1866–67.

The mining boom lasted until 1882, by which time cattle ranching had become equally important in the valleys where the climate is less arid. Carson City, the capital, developed in association with the nearby mining industry. The largest cities, Las Vegas and Reno, grew most in the 20th century with the building of the Hoover dam, the introduction of legal gambling and of easily obtained divorce.

After 1950 much of the desert area was adopted by the Federal government for weapons testing and other military purposes.

TERRITORY AND POPULATION

Nevada is bounded north by Oregon and Idaho, east by Utah, southeast by Arizona, with the Colorado River forming most of the boundary, south and west by California. Land area, 109,889 sq. miles (284,613 sq. km). In 2003 the federal government owned 91·9% of the land area.

Census population on 1 April 2000, 1,998,257, an increase of 66·3% since 1990. July 2005 estimate, 2,414,807.

Population in five census years was:

	White	Black	American Indian	All others	Total	Per sq. mile
1910	74,276	513	5,240	1,846	81,875	0·7
1930	84,515	516	4,871	1,156	91,058	0·8
1980	700,360	50,999	13,308	35,841	800,508	7·2
1990	1,012,695	78,771	19,637	90,730	1,201,833	10·9
2000	1,501,886	135,477	26,420	334,474	1,998,257	18·2

Of the total population in 2000, 1,018,051 were male, 1,486,458 were 18 years old or older and 1,828,646 were urban (91·51%, the third highest of the states). In 2000 the Hispanic population was 393,970, up from 124,419 in 1990 (an increase of 216·6%). Nevada was the fastest-growing state in the USA in 2004. Its recent overall population rise has made it the fastest-growing state in the USA every year since 1986.

The largest cities in 2000 were: Las Vegas, 478,434; Reno, 180,480; Henderson, 175,381; North Las Vegas, 115,448; Sparks, 66,346; Carson City (the capital), 52,457.

SOCIAL STATISTICS

Births, 2003, were 33,647 (15·0 per 1,000 population); deaths (2002), 16,927 (7·8 per 1,000 population). Infant mortality deaths (2002) were 6·0 per 1,000 live births. Marriages (2000), 134,908; divorces, 14,084. Fertility rate, 1998, 2·5 births per woman (the second highest in the USA after Utah).

CLIMATE

Las Vegas, Jan. 57°F (14°C), July 104°F (40°C). Annual rainfall 4·13" (105 mm). Reno, Jan. 45°F (7°C), July 91°F (33°C). Annual rainfall 7·53" (191 mm). Nevada belongs to the Mountain States climate zone (*see* UNITED STATES: Climate).

CONSTITUTION AND GOVERNMENT

The constitution adopted in 1864 is still in force, with 146 amendments as of 2004. The Legislature meets biennially (and in special sessions) and consists of a Senate of 21 members elected for four years, with half their number elected every two years, and an Assembly of 42 members elected for two years. The Governor may be elected for two consecutive four-year terms.

For the 109th Congress, which convened in Jan. 2005, Nevada sends three members to the House of Representatives. It is represented in the Senate by Harry Reid (D. 1987–2011) and John Ensign (R. 2001–07).

The state capital is Carson City. There are 16 counties, 18 incorporated cities and 49 unincorporated communities and one city-county (the Capitol District of Carson City).

RECENT ELECTIONS

In the 2004 presidential election Bush polled 418,690 votes; Kerry, 397,190; Nader, 4,838.

CURRENT ADMINISTRATION

Governor: Kenny C. Guinn (R.), 2003–07 (salary: $117,000).
   Lieut.-Governor: Lorraine Hunt (R.), 2003–07 ($50,000).
   Secretary of State: Dean Heller (R.), 2003–07 ($80,000).

Government Website: http://www.nv.gov

ECONOMY

Per capita personal income (2004) was $33,783.

Budget

In fiscal year 2003 the total sources of funding totalled $8,351m. Total expenditure was $7,816m. (education, $2,666m.; public welfare, $1,190m.; highways, $706m.; correction, $216m.; government administration, $201m.) Outstanding debt, in 2003, $3,604m.

Performance

Gross State Product in 2004 was $100,317m., ranking Nevada 31st in the United States.

ENERGY AND NATURAL RESOURCES

Electricity

In 2001 there were 15 geothermal electric plants in ten locations. Total electricity capacity in 1998 was 5·8m. kW. In 1999 total net electrical production was 26·4bn. kWh.

Oil and Gas

In 2001, 571,000 bbls. of crude oil were produced from oilfields located in Nye and Eureka Counties.

Water

The total area covered by water is approximately 735 sq. miles.

Minerals

Nevada led the nation in precious metal production in 2000, producing 76% of gold and 37% of silver. Nevada has been first in silver production since 1987 and first in gold since 1981. In 2000 Nevada produced 267,000 kg of gold and 722,000 kg of silver. Nevada was the only state in 2000 to produce magnesite, lithium minerals, brucite and mercury. Nevada also produces other minerals such as aggregates, clays, copper, diatomite, dolomite, geothermal energy, gypsum, lapidary, lime and limestone. The total value of Nevada's mineral production in 2000 was about $2·7bn.

Agriculture

In 2002 there were an estimated 3,000 farms. Farms averaged 2,267 acres; farms and ranches totalled 6·8m. acres. Average value per acre in 2002 was $446.

In 2001, 45·3% of farm income came from cattle and calves, 14·7% from dairy products, 0·6% from sheep and lambs, and 3·3% from other livestock. Hay production was 22% of all farm income, potatoes 2·4%, vegetables 4·6%, wheat 0·4% and other crops 6·7%. The net farm income in 2002 was $93m.

In 2002 there were 500,000 cattle and 100,000 sheep.

Forestry

Nevada had, in 2002, 10·20m. acres of forested land with 3·23m. acres of national forest.

INDUSTRY

The main industry is the service industry (42·2% of employment in 2000), especially tourism and legalized gambling. In 2000 there were 42,406 persons employed in manufacturing and 88,688 in construction.

Gaming industry gross revenue for 2001 was $9,220m. In 1998 there were 428 non-restricted licensed casinos and 2,700 licences in force. Nevada gets 41% of its tax revenue from the gaming industry.

Labour

In 2003 non-agricultural employment totalled 1,087,000. Employees by branch in 2003 (in 1,000): leisure and hospitality, 304; trade, transportation and utilities, 195; government, 135; professional and business services, 121; construction, 100. The unemployment rate in 2003 was 5·2%.

COMMUNICATIONS

Roads

In 2003 there were 33,976 miles of roads, of which the state maintained 5,449 miles. Vehicle registrations in 2003 numbered 1,221,868.

Rail

In 2003 there were 1,449 miles of main-line railway. Nevada is served by the Southern Pacific, Union Pacific and Burlington Northern BPH Nevada Railroad railways, and Amtrak passenger service for Las Vegas, Elko, Reno, Caliente, Lovelock, Stateline, Winnemucca and Sparks. Las Vegas has a 4-mile monorail metro system.

Civil Aviation

There were 104 airports and 32 heliports in 2005. During 2003 there were 19,685,123 enplanements statewide. McCarran International Airport (Las Vegas) handled 17,097,738 passengers and Reno-Tahoe International Airport handled 2,242,299 passengers.

SOCIAL INSTITUTIONS

Justice

Capital punishment was reintroduced in 1978, and executions began in 1979. There were two executions in 2004 but none in 2005. In June 2003 there were 10,527 prison inmates in state or federal correctional institutions.

Education

School attendance is compulsory for children from seven to 17 years of age. Numbers of pupils in public schools, 2001–02: pre-kindergarten, 2,147; kindergarten, 26,877; elementary, 177,342; secondary grades 7–9, 87,538; secondary grades 10–12, 60,470; special education, 40,196. Numbers of teachers in public schools, 2001: elementary, 9,870; secondary, 6,070; special education, 2,646; occupational, 198. Numbers of pupils in private schools, 2001–02: kindergartens, 3,109; elementary, 8,281; secondary grades 7–9, 2,892; secondary grades 10–12, 2,056. Number of private school teachers, 1999, 973.

The University of Nevada System comprises the University of Nevada, Las Vegas and Reno, the Nevada State College (at

Henderson), the Community College of Southern Nevada (at Las Vegas and Henderson), Great Basin College (at Elko), Truckee Meadows Community College (at Reno) and Western Nevada Community College (at Carson City, Minden and Fallon). In autumn 2002 there were 54,832 students (50,527 in 2001).

Health

In 2001 the state had 24 community hospitals with nine rural hospitals and 15 urban hospitals with 4,059 beds (1·9 per 1,000). In 2000 there were 4,875 physicians and 20,495 full-time and part-time nurses, nursing assistants, aids and orderlies and other hospital personnel.

Welfare

Medicare enrolment in July 2003 totalled 273,724. In 2002 a total of 202,306 people in Nevada received Medicaid. In Dec. 2004 there were 339,023 Old-Age, Survivors, and Disability Insurance (OASDI) beneficiaries. The Nevada Women, Infants and Children (WIC) special nutrition programmes served an average of 39,000 .at-risk women, infants and children each month in 2001 and 69,396 people receiving food stamps. In 2000, 5% of the population received public aid and benefits were paid to 102,162 persons in total. The average per recipient monthly for TANF (Temporary Assistance for Needy Families) was $124·86.

RELIGION

Many faiths are represented in Nevada, including Church of Jesus Christ of Latter Day Saints (Mormons), Protestantism, Roman Catholicism, Judaism and Buddhism.

CULTURE

Tourism

There are 24 State Parks covering 131,861 acres. In 2001, 28,216,174 people visited state and nearby national parks with 49,528,979 tourists coming to Nevada.

FURTHER READING

Statistical information: Budget and Planning Division, Department of Administration, Capitol Complex, Carson City, Nevada 89710. Publishes *Nevada Statistical Abstract* (Biennial).

Bowers, Michael W., *The Stagebrush State: Nevada's History, Government, and Politics.* Univ. of Nevada Press, 1996
Hulse, J. W., *The Nevada Adventure: a History.* 6th ed. Univ. of Nevada Press, 1990.—*The Silver State: Nevada's Heritage Reinterpreted.* Univ. of Nevada Press, 1998

State Government Website: http://www.nv.gov
Nevada State Library: Nevada State Library and Archives, Carson City.

New Hampshire

KEY HISTORICAL EVENTS

The area was part of a grant by the English crown made to John Mason and fellow-colonists, and was first settled in 1623. In 1629 an area between the Merrimack and Piscatagua rivers was called New Hampshire. More settlements followed, and in 1641 they were taken under the jurisdiction of the governor of Massachusetts. New Hampshire became a separate colony in 1679.

After the War of Independence New Hampshire became one of the 13 original states of the Union, ratifying the US constitution in 1788. The state constitution, which dates from 1776, was almost totally rewritten in 1784 and amended again in 1792.

The settlers were Protestants from Britain and Northern Ireland. They developed manufacturing industries, especially shoe-making, textiles and clothing, to which large numbers of French Canadians were attracted after the Civil War.

Portsmouth, originally a fishing settlement, was the colonial capital and is the only seaport. In 1808 the state capital was moved to Concord (having had no permanent home since 1775); Concord produced the Concord Coach which was widely used on the stagecoach routes of the West until at least 1900.

TERRITORY AND POPULATION

New Hampshire is bounded in the north by Canada, east by Maine and the Atlantic, south by Massachusetts and west by Vermont. Land area, 8,968 sq. miles (23,227 sq. km). Census population, 1 April 2000, 1,235,786, an increase of 11·4% since 1990. July 2005 estimate, 1,309,940.

Population at five federal censuses was:

	White	Black	Indian	Asiatic	Total	Per sq. mile
1910	429,906	564	34	68	430,572	47·7
1960	604,334	1,903	135	549	606,921	65·2
			All others			
1980	910,099	3,990	6,521		920,610	101·9
1990	1,087,433	7,198	14,621		1,109,252	123·7
2000	1,186,851	9,035	39,900		1,235,786	137·8

Of the total population in 2000, 628,099 were female, 926,224 were 18 years old or older and 732,335 were urban. In 2000 the Hispanic population was estimated to be 20,489, up from 11,333 in 1990 (an increase of 80·8%). The largest city in the state is Manchester, with a 2000 census population of 107,006. The capital is Concord, with 40,687. Other main cities and towns (with 2000 populations) are: Nashua, 86,605; Derry, 34,021; Rochester, 28,461; Salem, 28,112; Dover, 26,884; Merrimack, 25,119; Londonderry, 23,236; Hudson, 22,928; Keene, 22,563.

SOCIAL STATISTICS

Births, 2003, were 14,393 (11·2 per 1,000 population); deaths (2002), 9,853 (7·7 per 1,000 population). 2002 infant mortality rate (per 1,000 live births), 5·0. 2001: marriages, 10,600; divorces, 6,100.

CLIMATE

New Hampshire is in the New England climate zone (*see* UNITED STATES: Climate). Manchester, Jan. 22°F (−5·6°C), July 70°F (21·1°C). Annual rainfall 40" (1,003 mm).

CONSTITUTION AND GOVERNMENT

While the present constitution dates from 1784, it was extensively revised in 1792 when the state joined the Union. Since 1775 there have been 16 state conventions with 49 amendments adopted to change the constitution.

The Legislature (called the General Court) consists of a Senate of 24 members, elected for two years, and a House of Representatives, of 400 members, elected for two years. It meets annually. The Governor and five administrative officers called 'Councillors' are also elected for two years.

For the 109th Congress, which convened in Jan. 2005, New Hampshire sends two members to the House of Representatives. It is represented in the Senate by Judd Gregg (R. 1993–2011) and John Sununu (R. 2003–09).

The capital is Concord. The state is divided into ten counties.

RECENT ELECTIONS

In the 2004 presidential election Kerry polled 340,511 votes; Bush, 331,237; Nader, 4,479.

CURRENT ADMINISTRATION

Governor: John Lynch (D.), 2005–07 (salary: $102,704).

Senate President: Theodore L. Gatsas (R.), elected Sept. 2005.

Secretary of State: William M. Gardner (D.), first elected by legislature in 1976 ($89,128).

Government Website: http://www.state.nh.us

ECONOMY

Per capita income (2004) was $36,676.

Budget

New Hampshire has no general sales tax or state income tax but does have local property taxes. Other government revenues come from rooms and meals tax, business profits tax, motor vehicle licences, fuel taxes, fishing and hunting licences, state-controlled sales of alcoholic beverages, and cigarette and tobacco taxes.

In 2003 total state revenue was $5,207m. Total expenditure was $5,276m. (education, $1,635m.; public welfare, $1,186m.; highways, $375m.; government administration, $202m.; health, $176m.) Outstanding debt, in 2003, $5,594m.

Performance

Gross State Product in 2004 was $51,871m., ranking New Hampshire 39th in the United States.

ENERGY AND NATURAL RESOURCES

Water

The total area covered by water is approximately 382 sq. miles.

Minerals

Minerals are little worked; they consist mainly of sand and gravel, stone, and clay for building and highway construction. Value of domestic non-fuel mineral production in 2003 was $64m.

Agriculture

In 2002 there were 3,100 farms covering around 410,000 acres; average farm was 132 acres. Average value per acre in 2002, $3,131. Farm income 2002: from crops, $91m.; from livestock and products, $56m. The net farm income in 2002 was $5m.

The chief field crops are hay and vegetables; the chief fruit crop is apples. Livestock, 2005: cattle, 40,000; sheep, 7,423 (2002); pigs, 3,600; chickens (including broilers), 204,129 (2002).

Forestry

In 2002 the state had a forested area of 4,818,000 acres, of which 717,000 acres were national forest.

Fisheries

2003 commercial fishing landings amounted to 27·4m. lb worth $15·1m.

INDUSTRY

Principal manufactures: electrical and electronic goods, machinery and metal products. In 2003 the state's 2,162 manufacturing establishments had 83,730 employees, earning $3,562m. Total value added by manufacturing in 2001 was $8,908m.

Labour

Total non-agricultural employment, 2003, 617,000. Employees by branch, 2003 (in 1,000): trade, transportation and utilities, 139; education and health services, 93; government, 90; manufacturing, 80; leisure and hospitality, 62. In 2003 the unemployment rate was 4·3%.

COMMUNICATIONS

Roads

In 2003 there were 15,627 miles of roads (12,593 miles rural). There were 1,144,963 registered motor vehicles.

Rail

In 2000 the length of operating railway in the state was 415 miles.

Civil Aviation

In 2005 there were 25 airports and two heliports. There were 1,809,891 passenger enplanements statewide in 2003.

SOCIAL INSTITUTIONS

Justice

There were 2,297 prison inmates in June 2004. The death penalty was abolished in May 2000—the last execution had been in 1939.

Education

School attendance is compulsory for children from six to 14 years of age during the whole school term, or to 16 if their district provides a high school. Employed illiterate minors between 16 and 21 years of age must attend evening or special classes, if provided by the district.

In 2002 the public elementary and secondary schools had 207,000 pupils and 15,000 teachers. Public school salaries, 2003, averaged $41,900. An average of $8,683 was spent on education per pupil.

Of the 4-year colleges, the University of New Hampshire (founded in 1866) had 13,349 students in 2005; Dartmouth College (1769), 5,529; Keene State College (1909), 4,463; Plymouth State University (1871), 4,453; Southern New Hampshire University (1932, was New Hampshire College), 3,744. Total enrolment, 2000, in the 25 institutions of higher education was 62,000.

Health

In 2002 there were 28 community hospitals with 2,900 beds. A total of 118,000 patients were admitted during the year.

Welfare

Medicare enrolment in July 2003 totalled 179,564. In 2002 a total of 104,138 people in New Hampshire received Medicaid. In Dec. 2004 there were 215,453 Old-Age, Survivors, and Disability Insurance (OASDI) beneficiaries. A total of 14,075 people were receiving payments under Temporary Assistance for Needy Families (TANF) in Sept. 2004.

RELIGION

The Roman Catholic Church is the largest single body. The largest Protestant churches are Congregational, Episcopal, Methodist and United Baptist Convention of N.H.

CULTURE

Broadcasting

Across the state there were 49 radio and six TV stations in 1997.

Press

In 2003 there were 11 daily and eight Sunday newspapers in circulation.

FURTHER READING

Delorme, D. (ed.) *New Hampshire Atlas and Gazetteer.* Freeport, 1983

New Jersey

KEY HISTORICAL EVENTS

Originally the territory of Delaware Indians, the area was first settled by immigrant colonists in the early 17th century, when Dutch and Swedish traders established fortified posts on the Hudson and Delaware Rivers. The Dutch took control but lost it to the English in 1664. In 1676 the English divided the area in two; the eastern portion was assigned to Sir George Carteret and the western granted to Quaker settlers. This division lasted until 1702 when New Jersey was united as a colony of the Crown and placed under the jurisdiction of the governor of New York. It became a separate colony in 1738.

During the War of Independence crucial battles were fought at Trenton, Princeton and Monmouth. New Jersey became the 3rd state of the Union in 1787. Trenton, the state capital since 1790, began as a Quaker settlement and became an iron-working town. Industrial development grew rapidly, there and elsewhere in the state, after the opening of canals and railways in the 1830s. Princeton, also a Quaker settlement, became an important post on the New York road; the college of New Jersey (Princeton University) was transferred there from Newark in 1756.

The need for supplies in the Civil War stimulated industry and New Jersey became a manufacturing state. The growth beyond its borders of New York and Philadelphia, however, produced a pattern of commuting to employment in both centres. By 1980 about 60% of the state's population lived within 30 miles of New York.

TERRITORY AND POPULATION

New Jersey is bounded north by New York, east by the Atlantic with Long Island and New York City to the northeast, south by Delaware Bay and west by Pennsylvania. Land area, 7,417 sq. miles (19,209 sq. km). Census population, 1 April 2000, 8,414,350, an increase of 8·9% since 1990. July 2005 estimate, 8,717,925.

Population at five federal censuses was:

	White	Black	Asiatic	Others	Total	Per sq. mile
1910	2,445,894	89,760	1,345	168	2,537,167	337·7
1930	3,829,663	208,828	2,630	213	4,041,334	537·3
1980	6,127,467	925,066	103,848	208,442	7,364,823	986·2
1990	6,130,465	1,036,825	272,521	290,377	7,730,188	1,042·0
2000	6,104,705	1,141,821	483,605	684,219	8,414,350	1,134·4

Of the total population in 2000, 4,331,537 were female, 6,326,792 were 18 years old or older and 7,939,087 were urban (94·35%, marginally less than California, the highest). In 2000 the Hispanic population was 1,117,191, up from 739,861 in 1990 (an increase of 51·0%).

Census populations of the largest cities and towns in 2000 were:

Newark	273,546	Union City	67,088
Jersey City	240,055	Middletown	66,327
Paterson	149,222	Gloucester	64,350
Elizabeth	120,568	Bayonne	61,842
Edison	97,687	Irvington	60,695
Woodbridge	97,203	Old Bridge	60,456
Dover	89,706	Lakewood	60,352
Hamilton	87,109	North Bergen	58,092
Trenton (capital)	85,403	Vineland	56,271
Camden	79,904	Union Township	54,405
Clifton	78,672	Wayne	54,069
Brick	76,119	Franklin	50,903
Cherry Hill	69,965	Parsippany-Troy Hills	50,649
East Orange	69,824	Piscataway	50,482
Passaic	67,861		

Largest metropolitan areas (2000) are: Newark, 2,032,989; Bergen–Passaic, 1,373,167; Middlesex–Somerset–Hunterdon, 1,169,641; Monmouth–Ocean, 1,126,217; Jersey City, 608,975.

SOCIAL STATISTICS

2003 (rates per 1,000 population): births, 116,983 (13·5); deaths (2002), 74,009 (8·6 per 1,000 population). 2002 infant mortality (per 1,000 live births), 5·7. 2001: marriages, 54,100; divorces, 28,500.

CLIMATE

Jersey City, Jan. 31°F (–0·6°C), July 75°F (23·9°C). Annual rainfall 41" (1,025 mm). Trenton, Jan. 32°F (0°C), July 76°F (24·4°C). Annual rainfall 40" (1,003 mm). New Jersey belongs to the Atlantic Coast climate zone (see UNITED STATES: Climate).

CONSTITUTION AND GOVERNMENT

The present constitution, ratified by the registered voters on 4 Nov. 1947, has been amended 45 times. There is a 40-member Senate and an 80-member General Assembly. Assembly members serve two years, senators four years, except those elected at the election following each census, who serve for two years. Sessions are held throughout the year.

For the 109th Congress, which convened in Jan. 2005, New Jersey sends 13 members to the House of Representatives. It is represented in the Senate by Frank Lautenberg (D. 1982–2001, 2003–09) and Jon Corzine (D. 2001–07).

The capital is Trenton. The state is divided into 21 counties, which are subdivided into 566 municipalities—cities, towns, boroughs, villages and townships.

RECENT ELECTIONS

In the 2004 presidential election Kerry polled 1,911,430 votes; Bush, 1,670,003; Nader, 19,418.

CURRENT ADMINISTRATION

Governor: Jon Corzine (D.), 2006–10 (salary: $175,000, but not taken).

Senate President: Richard J. Codey (D.), elected by Senate in 2004.

Secretary of State: Nina Mitchell Wells (D.), appointed Jan. 2006 ($141,000).

Government Website: http://www.state.nj.us

ECONOMY

Per capita income (2004) was $41,636, the fourth highest in the country.

Budget

In 2003 total state revenue was $46,077m. Total expenditure was $44,948m. (education, $11,215m.; public welfare, $7,005m.; highways, $2,559m.; hospitals, $1,402m.; government administration, $1,317m.) Outstanding debt, in 2003, $33,609m.

Performance

Gross State Product in 2004 was $416,053m., ranking New Jersey 8th in the United States.

ENERGY AND NATURAL RESOURCES

Water

The total area covered by water is approximately 1,304 sq. miles.

Minerals

In 2002 the chief minerals were stone (22·6m. tons, value $127m.) and sand and gravel (17·6m. tons, value $96m.); others are clays, peat and gemstones. New Jersey is a leading producer of greensand marl, magnesium compounds and peat. Total value of domestic non-fuel mineral products, 2003, was $272m.

Agriculture

Livestock raising, market-gardening, fruit-growing, horticulture and forestry are pursued. In 2003 there were 9,900 farms covering a total of 820,000 acres with an average farm size of 83 acres. Average value per acre in 2002 was $9,245—making it the second most valuable land per acre in the USA, after Connecticut.

Cash receipts from farm marketings, 2003: crops, $658m.; livestock and products, $188m. The net farm income in 2003 was $127m.

Leading crops (2003) are blueberries (value, $45·7m.), tomatoes ($28·0m.), peppers ($25·6m.), peaches ($24·2m.), soybeans ($16·1m.), cranberries ($15·1m.), sweet corn ($12·1m.), corn for grain ($7·1m.). Livestock, 2003: 12,000 milch cows, 46,000 all cattle, 15,300 sheep and lambs and 12,000 swine.

Forestry
Total forested area was 2,132,000 acres in 2002.

Fisheries
2002 commercial fishing landings amounted to 162·2m. lb worth $112·7m.

INDUSTRY

In 2003 the state's 11,343 manufacturing establishments had 347,822 employees, earning $19,505m. Total value added by manufacturing in 2001 was $50,754m.

Labour
The unemployment rate in Sept. 2004 was 4·8%, the 17th consecutive month in which the rate was below that of the USA.

In 2003 there were 3,980 employees on non-agricultural payrolls: 878,000 in trade, transportation and utilities; 624,000 in government; 574,000 in professional and business services; 539,000 in education and health services; 352,000 in manufacturing.

COMMUNICATIONS
Roads
In 2004 there were 36,592 miles of public roads. There were 6,711,601 registered vehicles in 2003.

Rail
NJ Transit, the USA's third largest provider of bus, rail and light rail transit, has a fleet of 2,027 buses, 711 trains and 45 light rail vehicles, which serve approximately 725,550 passengers daily on 11 rail lines (848·3 track miles) and 236 bus routes. The state is also served by 13 shortline freight railroads, three Class I rail carriers (Norfolk Southern, CSX and CP Rail) and two statewide terminal railroads (Conrail Shared Assets Carrier and NYS & W Ry) which deliver freight on behalf of Class I rail carriers.

There is a metro link to New York (22 km), a light rail line (7 km) and extensive commuter railways around Newark.

Civil Aviation
There is an international airport at Newark. In June 2004 there were 119 airports and 251 heliports. In total there are an estimated 72,000 jobs in New Jersey that are linked to the general aviation airport system. The annual payroll associated with these jobs is estimated at $2·4bn. The annual value of goods and services purchased by airport tenants, visitors and general aviation-dependent businesses exceeds $4·6bn. There were 15,153,400 passenger enplanements statewide in 2003.

Shipping
In 2004 the maritime industry contributed more than $50bn. to the state economy. The two largest ports are the Port of Newark-Elizabeth and the Port of Camden. The Port of Newark-Elizabeth, the premier port on the Eastern seaboard, employed 229,000 people in 2003.

SOCIAL INSTITUTIONS
Justice
In June 2003 there were 28,213 prison inmates. The death penalty, last used in 1963, was suspended on 12 Jan. 2006. The moratorium on executions is to remain in place until at least Jan. 2007.

Education
Elementary instruction is compulsory for all from six to 16 years of age and free to all from five to 20 years of age. 128 school districts with high concentrations of disadvantaged children must offer free pre-school education to three- and four-year olds. In 2002–03 there were 2,454 public elementary and secondary schools with 1,367,438 pupils and 107,004 teachers; total expenditure on public schools was $17,303m. Teachers' salaries averaged $54,158 in 2003.

There are 57 universities and colleges in New Jersey. In autumn 2002 public institutions had 289,275 students, including 138,924 in community colleges. Enrolment in autumn 2002: Rutgers, the State University (founded as Queen's College in 1766), had 51,480 students at campuses in Camden, Newark and New Brunswick; The College of New Jersey (1855; formerly Trenton State College), 6,948; Kean University, at Union City (1855), 12,779; Montclair State University (1908), 134,673; Rowan University, at Glassboro (1923), 9,685; William Paterson University, at Wayne (1855), 10,924.

Independent institutions had 72,482 students. Princeton University (founded in 1746) had 6,646 students; Fairleigh Dickinson University, at Teaneck (1941), 10,368; Seton Hall University, at South Orange (1856), 9,596.

Health
In 2002 there were 81 community hospitals with 24,100 beds. A total of 1,095,000 patients were admitted during the year.

Welfare
Medicare enrolment in July 2003 totalled 1,219,935. In 2002 a total of 954,491 people in New Jersey received Medicaid. In Dec. 2004 there were 1,368,734 Old-Age, Survivors, and Disability Insurance (OASDI) beneficiaries. A total of 112,213 people were receiving payments under Temporary Assistance for Needy Families (TANF) in Sept. 2004.

RELIGION

In 2000 the Roman Catholic population of New Jersey was 3·4m., and there were 468,000 Jews. Among Protestant sects were United Methodists, 140,133; Presbyterian Church (USA) members, 119,735; Episcopalians, 91,964; American Baptists, 88,521; Lutherans, 79,264.

FURTHER READING

Statistical information: New Jersey State Data Center, Department of Labor, CN 388, Trenton 08625. Publishes *New Jersey Statistical Factbook.*

Legislative District Data Book. Bureau of Government Research. Annual

Manual of the Legislature of New Jersey. Trenton. Annual

Cunningham, J. T., *New Jersey: America's Main Road.* Rev. ed. New York, 1976

State Library: 185 W. State Street, Trenton, CN 520, NJ 08625.

New Mexico

KEY HISTORICAL EVENTS

The first European settlement was established in 1598. Until 1771 New Mexico was the Spanish kings' 'Kingdom of New Mexico'. In 1771 it was annexed to the northern province of New Spain. When New Spain won its independence in 1821, it took the name of Republic of Mexico and established New Mexico as its northernmost department. Ceded to the USA in 1848 after war between the USA and Mexico, the area was organized as a Territory in 1850, by which time its population was Spanish and Indian. There was frequent conflict, especially between new settlers and raiding parties of Navajo and Apaches. The Indian war lasted from 1861–66, and from 1864–68 about 8,000 Navajo were imprisoned at Bosque Redondo.

The boundaries were altered several times when land was taken into Texas, Utah, Colorado and lastly (1863) Arizona. New Mexico became a state in 1912.

Settlement proceeded by means of irrigated crop-growing and Mexican-style ranching. During the Second World War the desert areas were brought into use as testing zones for atomic weapons. Mineral extraction also developed, especially after the discovery of uranium and petroleum.

TERRITORY AND POPULATION

New Mexico is bounded north by Colorado, northeast by Oklahoma, east by Texas, south by Texas and Mexico and west by Arizona. Land area, 121,356 sq. miles (316,901 sq. km). In 2003 the federal government owned 26,518,360 acres, or 34·1% of the land area.

Census population, 1 April 2000, 1,819,046, an increase of 20·1% since 1990. Of the total population in 2000, 924,729 were female, 1,310,472 were 18 years old or older and 1,363,501 were urban. July 2005 estimate, 1,928,384.

The population in five census years was:

	White	Black	American Indian	Asian and Pacific Island	Other	Total	Per sq. mile
1910	304,594	1,628	20,573	506	—	327,301	2·7
1940	492,312	4,672	34,510	324	—	531,818	4·4
1980	977,587	24,020	106,119	6,825	188,343	1,302,894	10·7
1990	1,146,028	30,210	134,355	14,124	190,352	1,515,069	12·5
2000	1,214,253	34,343	173,483	20,758	376,209	1,819,046	15·0

Before 1930 New Mexico was largely a Spanish-speaking state, but after 1945 an influx of population from other states considerably reduced the percentage of persons of Spanish origin or descent. However, in recent years the percentage of the Hispanic population has begun to rise again. In 2000 the Hispanic population was 765,386, up from 579,224 in 1990 (an increase of 32·1%). At 42·1%, New Mexico has the largest percentage of persons of Hispanic origin of any state in the USA.

The largest cities are Albuquerque, with 2000 census population of 448,607; Las Cruces, 74,267; Santa Fe, 62,203; Rio Rancho, 51,765; Roswell, 45,293.

SOCIAL STATISTICS

Statistics 2003: births, 27,821 (14·8 per 1,000 population); deaths (2002), 14,344 (7·7 per 1,000 population). 2002 infant mortality (per 1,000 live births), 6·3. 2001: marriages, 13,900 (7·9 per 1,000 population); divorces, 9,000 (5·1).

CLIMATE

Santa Fe, Jan. 26·4°F (–3·1°C), July 68·4°F (20°C). Annual rainfall 15·2" (386 mm). New Mexico belongs to the Mountain States climate zone (see UNITED STATES: Climate).

CONSTITUTION AND GOVERNMENT

The constitution of 1912 is still in force with 152 amendments. The state Legislature, which meets annually, consists of 42 members of the Senate, elected for four years, and 70 members of the House of Representatives, elected for two years.

For the 109th Congress, which convened in Jan. 2005, New Mexico sends three members to the House of Representatives. It is represented in the Senate by Pete Domenici (R. 1973–2009) and Jeff Bingaman (D. 1983–2007).

The state capital is Santa Fe. The state is divided into 33 counties.

RECENT ELECTIONS

In the 2004 presidential election Bush polled 376,930 votes; Kerry, 370,942; Nader, 4,053.

CURRENT ADMINISTRATION

Governor: Bill Richardson (D.), 2003–06 (salary: $110,000).
Lieut.-Governor: Diane D. Denish (D.), 2003–06 ($85,000).
Secretary of State: Rebecca Vigil-Giron (D.), 2003–06 ($85,000).

Government Website: http://www.state.nm.us

ECONOMY

Per capita income (2004) was $26,154.

Budget

In 2003 total state revenue was $9,848m. Total expenditure was $10,672m. (education, $3,677m.; public welfare, $2,411m.; hospitals, $447m.; government administration, $364m.; health, $291m.) Outstanding debt, in 2003, $4,601m.

Performance

Gross State Product in 2004 was $61,012m., ranking New Mexico 37th in the United States.

ENERGY AND NATURAL RESOURCES

Oil and Gas

2001 production: petroleum, 68,967,000 bbls. (of 42 gallons); natural gas, 1,678bn. cu. ft. New Mexico ranks second in the USA behind Texas for natural gas production and also has natural gas reserves second only to Texas. In late 2001, 11,500 persons were employed in the oil and gas industry.

Water

The total area covered by water is approximately 234 sq. miles.

Minerals

New Mexico is one of the largest energy producing states in the USA. Production in 2001: potash, 1,086,410 short tons; copper, 154,580 short tons; coal, 30,525,401 short tons. New Mexico is the country's leading potash producer, accounting for approximately 70% of all potash mined in the USA, and ranked third for copper production in 2001. The value of coal output in 2001 was $584·9m. and of total non-fuel mineral output $651·6m.

Agriculture

New Mexico produces grains, vegetables, hay, livestock, milk, cotton and pecans. In 2002 there were 15,000 farms covering 44·0m. acres; average farm size 2,933 acres. In 2002 average value of farmland and buildings per acre was $234.

2002 cash receipts from crops, $575m., and from livestock products, $1,382m. The net farm income in 2002 was $678m. Principal crops are hay (1·6m. tons from 0·38m. acres), cotton (65m. lb from 0·70m. acres) and chilli (162m. lb from 0·18m. acres). Farm animals in 2001 included 290,000 milch cows, 1·6m. all cattle, 230,000 sheep and 3,000 swine.

Forestry

The state had a forested area of 16,682,000 acres in 2002, of which 8,092,000 acres were national forest.

INDUSTRY

In 2001 the state's 1,585 manufacturing establishments had 37,000 employees, earning $1,299m. Total value added by manufacturing in 2001 was $6,632m.

Labour

Total non-agricultural employment, 2003, 776,000. Employees by branch, 2003 (in 1,000): government, 195; trade, transportation and utilities, 136; education and health services, 99; professional and business services, 89; leisure and hospitality, 81. The unemployment rate in 2003 was 6·4%.

COMMUNICATIONS

Roads

In 2003 there were 63,953 miles of roads (57,139 miles rural). There were 1,509,350 registered motor vehicles.

Rail

In 1999 there were 2,027 miles of railway in operation.

Civil Aviation

There were 61 public-use airports in 2005. There were 3,008,834 passenger enplanements statewide in 2003.

SOCIAL INSTITUTIONS

Justice

In June 2003 there were 6,173 prison inmates. The death penalty is authorized and was used in 2001 (one execution) for the first time since 1960.

Since 1949 the denial of employment by reason of race, colour, religion, national origin or ancestry has been forbidden. A law of 1955 prohibits discrimination in public places because of race or colour. An 'equal rights' amendment was added to the constitution in 1972.

Education

Elementary education is free, and compulsory between six and 17 years or high-school graduation age. In 1995–96 the 89 school districts had an enrolment of 348,543 students in elementary and secondary schools of which private, parochial and state supported schools had 31,112. In 1994–95 there were 18,500 FTE teachers receiving an average salary of $29,074. Total revenue for public elementary and secondary schools was $1,702m. (1994–95).

In autumn 2002 there were 51,648 students attending public universities and 62,002 students attending community colleges. The state-supported four-year institutes of higher education are (autumn 2002 enrolment):

	Students
University of New Mexico, Albuquerque	24,645
New Mexico State University, Las Cruces	15,621
Eastern New Mexico University, Portales	3,756
New Mexico Highlands University, Las Vegas	3,024
Western New Mexico University, Silver City	2,551
New Mexico Institute of Mining and Technology, Socorro	1,747

Health

In 2002 there were 36 community hospitals with 3,600 beds. A total of 180,000 patients were admitted during the year.

Welfare

Medicare enrolment in July 2003 totalled 250,113. In 2002 a total of 798,665 people in New Mexico received Medicaid. In Dec. 2004 there were 302,500 Old-Age, Survivors, and Disability Insurance (OASDI) beneficiaries. A total of 47,132 people were receiving payments under Temporary Assistance for Needy Families (TANF) in Sept. 2004.

RELIGION

Chief religious bodies (2000) were Catholics, with 670,511 members; Southern Baptists, 132,675; Latter-day Saints (Mormons), 42,261; United Methodists, 41,597; Assemblies of God, 22,070.

CULTURE

Tourism

In 2002, 96,000 overseas visitors (0·5% of the market share), excluding Mexico and Canada, visited New Mexico.

FURTHER READING

Bureau of Business and Economic Research, Univ. of New Mexico—*Census in New Mexico* (Continuing series. Vols. 1–5, 1992–).—*Economic Census: New Mexico* (Continuing series. Vols. 1–3).—*New Mexico Business.* Monthly; annual review in Jan.–Feb. issue.

Etulain, R., *Contemporary New Mexico, 1940–1990.* Univ. of New Mexico Press, 1994

New York State

KEY HISTORICAL EVENTS

The first European immigrants came in the 17th century, when there were two powerful Indian groups in rivalry: the Iroquois confederacy (Mohawk, Oneida, Onondaga, Cayuga and Seneca) and the Algonquian-speaking Mohegan and Munsee. The Dutch made settlements at Fort Orange (now Albany) in 1624 and at New Amsterdam in 1625, trading with the Indians for furs. In the 1660s there was conflict between the Dutch and the British in the Caribbean; as part of the concluding treaty the British in 1664 received Dutch possessions in the Americas, including New Amsterdam, which they renamed New York.

In 1763 the Treaty of Paris ended war between the British and the French in North America (in which the Iroquois had allied themselves with the British). Settlers of British descent in New England then felt confident enough to expand westward into the area. The climate of northern New York being severe, most settled in the Hudson river valley. After the War of Independence New York became the 11th state of the Union (1778), having first declared itself independent of Britain in 1777.

The economy depended on manufacturing, shipping and other means of distributing goods, and trade. During the 19th century New York became the most important city in the USA. Its manufacturing industries, especially clothing, attracted thousands of European immigrants. Industrial development spread along the Hudson-Mohawk valley, which was made the route of the Erie Canal (1825) linking New York with Buffalo on Lake Erie and thus with the developing farmlands of the middle west.

On 11 Sept. 2001 New York City was attacked by hijackers when two commercial airliners were flown into the World Trade Center. The building was destroyed and 2,749 people died.

TERRITORY AND POPULATION

New York is bounded west and north by Canada with Lake Erie, Lake Ontario and the St Lawrence River forming the boundary; east by Vermont, Massachusetts and Connecticut, southeast by the Atlantic, south by New Jersey and Pennsylvania. Land area, 47,214 sq. miles (122,284 sq. km). Census population, 1 April 2000, 18,976,457, an increase of 5·5% since 1990. July 2005 estimate, 19,254,630.

Population in five census years was:

	White	Black	Indian	Asiatic	Total	Per sq. mile
1910	8,966,845	134,191	6,046	6,532	9,113,614	191·2
1930	12,143,191	412,814	6,973	15,088	12,588,066	262·6
			All others			
1980	13,961,106	2,401,842	1,194,340		17,557,288	367·0
1990	13,385,255	2,859,055	1,746,145		17,990,455	381·0
2000	12,893,689	3,014,385	3,068,383		18,976,457	401·9

Of the total population in 2000, 9,829,709 were female, 14,286,350 were 18 years old or older and 16,602,582 were urban. In 2000 the Hispanic population was 2,867,583, up from 2,214,026 in 1990 (an increase of 29·5%). California and Texas are the only states with a higher Hispanic population.

The population of New York City, by boroughs, census of 1 April 2000 was: Manhattan, 1,537,195; Bronx, 1,332,650; Brooklyn, 2,465,326; Queens, 2,229,379; Staten Island, 443,728; total, 8,008,278. The New York–Northern New Jersey–Long Island metropolitan area had, in 2000, a population of 21,199,865.

Population of other large cities and incorporated places at the 2000 census was:

Buffalo	292,648	Valley Stream	36,368
Rochester	219,773	Long Beach	35,462
Yonkers	196,086	Rome	34,950
Syracuse	147,306	North Tonawanda	33,262
Albany (capital)	95,658	Jamestown	31,730
New Rochelle	72,182	Elmira	30,940
Mount Vernon	68,381	Poughkeepsie	29,871
Schenectady	61,821	Ithaca	29,287
Utica	60,651	Auburn	28,574
Hempstead	56,554	Newburgh	28,259
Niagara Falls	55,593	Lindenhurst	27,819
White Plains	53,077	Watertown	26,705
Troy	49,170	Glen Cove	26,622
Binghampton	47,380	Saratoga Springs	26,186
Freeport	43,783		

Other large urbanized areas, census 2000; Buffalo–Niagara Falls, 1,170,111; Rochester, 1,098,201; Albany–Schenectady–Troy, 875,583.

SOCIAL STATISTICS

Births in 2003 were 253,714 (13·2 per 1,000 population); deaths (2002), 158,118 (8·3 per 1,000 population). 2002 infant mortality rate (per 1,000 live births), 6·0. 2001: marriages, 145,500; divorces, 54,100.

CLIMATE

Albany, Jan. 24°F (–4·4°C), July 73°F (22·8°C). Annual rainfall 34" (855 mm). Buffalo, Jan. 24°F (–4·4°C), July 70°F (21·1°C). Annual rainfall 36" (905 mm). New York, Jan. 30°F (–1·1°C), July 74°F (23·3°C). Annual rainfall 43" (1,087 mm). New York belongs to the Atlantic Coast climate zone (*see* UNITED STATES: Climate).

CONSTITUTION AND GOVERNMENT

New York State has had five constitutions, adopted in 1777, 1821, 1846, 1894 and 1938. The constitution produced by the 1938 convention (which was substantially a modification of the 1894 one), forms the fundamental law of the state (as modified by subsequent amendments). A proposed new constitution in 1967 was rejected by the electorate. In 1997 voters rejected a proposal to hold a new constitutional convention.

The Legislature comprises the Senate, with 62 members, and the Assembly, with 150. All members are elected in even-numbered years for two-year terms. The Legislature meets every year, typically for several days a week from Jan.–June and, if recalled by leaders of the Legislature, at other times during the year. The Governor can also call the Legislature into extraordinary session. The state capital is Albany. For local government the state is divided into 62 counties, five of which constitute the city of New York.

Each of the state's 62 cities is incorporated by charter, under special legislation. The government of New York City is vested in the mayor (Michael Bloomberg), elected for four years, and a city council, whose president and members are elected for four years. The council has a President and 51 members, each elected from a district wholly within the city. The mayor appoints all the heads of departments, except the comptroller (the chief financial officer), who is elected. Each of the five city boroughs (Manhattan, Bronx, Brooklyn, Queens and Staten Island) has a president, elected for four years. Each borough is also a county, although Manhattan borough, as a county, is called New York, Brooklyn is called Kings, and Staten Island is called Richmond.

For the 109th Congress, which convened in Jan. 2005, New York State sends 29 members to the House of Representatives. It is represented in the Senate by Charles Schumer (D. 1999–2011) and Hillary Clinton (D. 2001–07).

RECENT ELECTIONS

In the 2004 presidential election Kerry polled 4,314,280 votes; Bush, 2,962,567; Nader, 99,873.

CURRENT ADMINISTRATION

Governor: George E. Pataki (R.), 2003–07 (salary: $179,000).
   Lieut.-Governor: Mary O. Donohue (R.), 2003–07 ($151,500).
   Secretary of State (acting): Frank P. Milano, appointed Sept. 2005 ($120,800).

Government Website: http://www.state.ny.us

ECONOMY

Per capita income (2004) was $38,333.

Budget

In 2003 total state revenue was $118,275m. Total expenditure was $127,475m. (public welfare, $38,894m.; education, $27,209m.; health, $5,027m.; government administration, $4,269m.; highways, $3,881m.) Outstanding debt in 2003 was $91,635m.

Performance

Gross State Product was $896,739m. in 2004, ranking New York second after California.

Banking and Finance

In 2002 there were 211 financial institutions in New York State insured by the US Federal Deposit Insurance Corporation, with assets worth $1,620bn. They had 4,526 offices with total deposits of $516bn.

ENERGY AND NATURAL RESOURCES

Water

The total area covered by water is approximately 7,342 sq. miles.

Minerals

Principal minerals are: sand and gravel, salt, titanium concentrate, talc, abrasive garnet, wollastonite and emery. Quarry products include trap rock, slate, marble, limestone and sandstone. Value of domestic non-fuel mineral output in 2003, $978m.

Agriculture

New York has large agricultural interests. In 2002 it had 37,000 farms, with a total area of 7·6m. acres; average farm was 205 acres. Average value per acre in 2002 was $1,708.

Farm income, 2002, from crops $1,234m. and livestock $1,870m. The net farm income in 2002 was $568m. Dairying is an important type of farming. Field crops comprise maize, winter wheat, oats and hay. New York ranks second in the USA in the production of apples and maple syrup. Other products are grapes, tart cherries, peaches, pears, plums, strawberries, raspberries, cabbages, onions, potatoes and maple sugar. Estimated farm animals, 2003, included 1,450,000 all cattle, 680,000 milch cows, 65,000 sheep and lambs, 73,000 swine and 4·9m. chickens.

Forestry

Total forested area was 18,432,000 acres in 2002, of which 5,000 acres were national forest. There were state parks and recreation areas covering 300,000 acres in 2003.

INDUSTRY

Leading industries are clothing, non-electrical machinery, printing and publishing, electrical equipment, instruments, food and allied products and fabricated metals. In 2002 the state's 22,878 manufacturing establishments had 699,462 employees, earning $31,141m. Total value added by manufacturing in 2001 was $78,484m.

Labour

Total non-agricultural employment, 2003, 8,404,000. Employees by branch, 2003 (in 1,000): education and health services, 1,496; government, 1,486; trade, transportation and utilities, 1,473; professional and business services, 1,041; financial activities, 697. In 2003 the unemployment rate was 6·3%.

COMMUNICATIONS

Roads

In 2003 there were 113,126 miles of roads (71,980 miles rural). The New York State Thruway extends 559 miles from New York City to Buffalo. The Northway, a 176-mile toll-free highway, is a connecting road from the Thruway at Albany to the Canadian border at Champlain, Quebec.

Motor vehicle registrations in 2003 were 10,801,701. In 2003 there were 1,491 traffic accident fatalities.

Rail

There were, in 2000, 2,258 miles of Class I railways. In addition the State had 534 miles of regional railway and 1,068 miles of local railway. New York City has NYCTA and PATH metro systems, and commuter railways run by Metro-North, New Jersey Transit and Long Island Rail Road. Buffalo has a 7-mile metro line.

Civil Aviation

At Jan. 2003 there were 542 aviation facilities in New York State. Of these, 160 were public use airports, 382 were private use airports; two were private use glider ports, six public use heliports, 144 private use heliports, nine public use seaplane bases and ten private use seaplane bases. There were 33,648,816 passenger enplanements statewide in 2003. The busiest airports are New York City's John F. Kennedy International (which handled 31,732,371 passengers in 2003) and LaGuardia (22,482,770 passengers in 2003).

Shipping

The canals of the state, combined in 1918 in what is called the Improved Canal System, have a length of 524 miles, of which the Erie or Barge canal has 340 miles.

SOCIAL INSTITUTIONS

Justice

The State Human Rights Law was approved on 12 March 1945, effective on 1 July 1945. The State Division of Human Rights is charged with the responsibility of enforcing this law. The division may request and utilize the services of all governmental departments and agencies; adopt and promulgate suitable rules and regulations; test, investigate and pass judgment upon complaints alleging discrimination in employment, in places of public accommodation, resort or amusement, education, and in housing, land and commercial space; hold hearings, subpoena witnesses and require the production for examination of papers relating to matters under investigation; grant compensatory damages and require repayment of profits in certain housing cases among other provisions; apply for court injunctions to prevent frustration of orders of the Commissioner.

In Jan. 2004 there were 65,125 federal and state prisoners.

The death penalty was declared unconstitutional in New York in 2004. The last execution was in 1963.

Education

Education is compulsory between the ages of seven and 16. In 2001–02 the public elementary and secondary schools had 2,826,620 pupils and 217,210 teachers. There were 493,913 pupils at non-public schools.

The state's educational system, including public and private schools and secondary institutions, universities, colleges, libraries, museums, etc., constitutes (by legislative act) the 'University of the State of New York', which is governed by a Board of Regents consisting of 15 members appointed by the Legislature. Within the framework of this 'University' was established in 1948 a 'State University' (SUNY), which controls 64 colleges and educational centres, 30 of which are locally operated community colleges. The 'State University' is governed by a board of 16 Trustees, appointed by the Governor with the consent and advice of the Senate.

Higher education in the state is conducted in 322 institutions. 1,097,015 students enrolled in autumn 2002. There were 46,399 full-time faculty staff (13,898 at SUNY) in 2001.

Student enrolment (autumn 2002) in higher education in the state included:

Founded	Name and place	Students
1754	Columbia University, New York City	22,393
1795	Union College, Schenectady and Albany	2,512
1824	Rensselaer Polytechnic Institute, Troy	7,670
1829	Rochester Institute of Technology, Rochester	13,720
1831	New York University, New York City	38,096
1836	Alfred University, Alfred	1,604
1841	Manhattanville College, New York City	2,564
1846	Colgate University, Hamilton	2,837
1846	Fordham University, New York City	14,318
1847	The City University of New York (CUNY), New York City	208,862
1848	University of Rochester, Rochester	8,516
1854	Polytechnic University, New York City	3,032
1856	St Lawrence University, Canton	2,293
1859	Cooper Union for the Advancement of Science and Art, NYC	947
1861	Vassar College, Poughkeepsie	2,472
1863	Manhattan College, New York City	3,207
1865	Cornell University, Ithaca	12,566
1870	Syracuse University, Syracuse	19,301
1870	St John's University, New York City	19,288
1892	Ithaca College, Ithaca	6,431
1906	Pace University, New York City and Westchester	14,095
1926	Long Island University	21,470
1929	Marist College, Poughkeepsie	5,866
1935	Hofstra University, Hempstead	13,412
1948	State University of New York (SUNY)	402,945

Health

In 2002 there were 211 community hospitals with 65,600 beds. Approximately 2,463,000 patients were admitted during the year.

Welfare

Medicare enrolment in July 2003 totalled 2,763,299. In 2002, 4,139,898 people in New York State were Medicaid eligible. In Dec. 2004 there were 3,044,526 Old-Age, Survivors, and Disability Insurance (OASDI) beneficiaries. In Oct. 2002, 622,068 individuals were recipients of temporary assistance, eligible for one or more programmes including family assistance (326,373), safety net assistance (295,695), supplemental security income (619,128) and food stamps (1,515,884).

RELIGION

The main religious denominations are Roman Catholics, Jews and Protestant Episcopalians.

CULTURE

Tourism

In 2003 there were a record 37·8m. visitors to New York City (33·0m. domestic and 4·8m. overseas), up from 35·3m. in 2002. Visitor spending in 2002 was $14,100m.

FURTHER READING

Statistical information: Nelson Rockefeller Institute of Government, 411 State St., Albany 12203. Publishes *New York State Statistical Yearbook.*

New York Red Book. Albany. Biennial.

Legislative Manual. Department of State. Biennial.

The Modern New York State Legislature: Redressing the Balance. Albany, Rockefeller Institute, 1991

State Library: The New York State Library, Albany 12230.

North Carolina

KEY HISTORICAL EVENTS

The early inhabitants were Cherokees. European settlement was attempted in 1585–87, following an exploratory visit by Sir Walter Raleigh, but this failed. Settlers from Virginia came to the shores of Albemarle Sound after 1650, and in 1663 Charles II chartered a private colony of Carolina. In 1691 the north was put under a deputy governor who ruled from Charleston in the south. The colony was formally separated into North and South Carolina in 1712. In 1729 control was taken from the private proprietors and vested in the Crown, whereupon settlement grew, and the boundary between north and south was finally fixed (1735).

After the War of Independence, North Carolina became one of the original 13 states of the Union. The city of Raleigh was laid out as the new capital. Having been a plantation colony North Carolina continued to develop as a plantation state, growing tobacco with black slave labour. It was also an important source of gold before the western gold-rushes of 1848.

In 1861 at the outset of the Civil War, North Carolina seceded from the Union, but General Sherman occupied the capital unopposed. A military governor was admitted in 1862, and civilian government restored with re-admission to the Union in 1868.

TERRITORY AND POPULATION

North Carolina is bounded north by Virginia, east by the Atlantic, south by South Carolina, southwest by Georgia and west by Tennessee. Land area, 48,711 sq. miles (126,161 sq. km). Census population, 1 April 2000, 8,049,313, an increase of 21·4% since 1990. July 2005 estimate, 8,683,242.

Population in five census years was:

	White	Black	Indian	Asiatic	Total	Per sq. mile
1910	1,500,511	697,843	7,851	82	2,206,287	45·3
1930	2,234,958	918,647	16,579	92	3,170,276	64·5
			All others			
1980	4,453,010	1,316,050	105,369		5,874,429	111·5
1990	5,008,491	1,456,323	163,823		6,628,637	136·1
2000	5,804,656	1,737,545	507,112		8,049,313	165·2

Of the total population in 2000, 4,106,618 were female, 6,085,266 were 18 years old or older and 4,849,482 were urban. In 2000 North Carolina's Hispanic population was 378,963, up from 76,726 in 1990. This represented a rise of 393·9%, the largest increase of any state in the USA over the same period.

The principal cities (with census population in 2000) are: Charlotte, 540,828; Raleigh, 276,093; Greensboro, 223,891; Durham, 187,035; Winston-Salem, 185,776; Fayetteville, 121,015; Cary, 94,536; High Point, 85,839; Wilmington, 75,838.

SOCIAL STATISTICS

Births, 2003, were 118,823 (14·1 per 1,000 population); deaths (2002), 72,027 (8·7 per 1,000 population). 2002 infant mortality rate (per 1,000 live births), 8·2. 2001: marriages, 61,100; divorces, 34,900.

CLIMATE

Climate varies sharply with altitude; the warmest area is in the southeast near Southport and Wilmington; the coldest is Mount Mitchell (6,684 ft). Raleigh, Jan. 42°F (5·6°C), July 79°F (26·1°C). Annual rainfall 46" (1,158 mm). North Carolina belongs to the Atlantic Coast climate zone (*see* UNITED STATES: Climate).

CONSTITUTION AND GOVERNMENT

The present constitution dates from 1971 (previous constitution, 1776 and 1868/76); it has had 30 amendments. The General Assembly consists of a Senate of 50 members and a House of Representatives of 120 members; all are elected by districts for two years. It meets in odd-numbered years in Jan.

The Governor and Lieut.-Governor are elected for four years; they can be elected to only one additional consecutive term. There are also 19 executive departments—eight have elected heads (for four-year terms) and ten have heads appointed by the Governor; the other department is the North Carolina Community College System, under a president.

For the 109th Congress, which convened in Jan. 2005, North Carolina sends 13 members to the House of Representatives. It is represented in the Senate by Elizabeth Dole (R. 2003–09) and Richard Burr (R. 2005–11).

The capital is Raleigh. There are 100 counties.

RECENT ELECTIONS

In the 2004 presidential election Bush polled 1,961,166 votes; Kerry, 1,525,849; Nader, 1,805.

CURRENT ADMINISTRATION

Governor: Michael F. Easley (D.), 2005–09 (salary: $123,819).

  Lieut.-Governor: Beverly Perdue (D.), 2005–09 ($109,279).

  Secretary of State: Elaine F. Marshall (D.), 2005–09 ($109,279).

Government Website: http://www.ncgov.com

ECONOMY

Per capita income (2004) was $29,303.

Budget

In 2003 total state revenue was $30,043m. Total expenditure was $34,361m. (education, $12,376m.; public welfare, $7,813m.; highways, $2,723m.; hospitals, $1,053m.; health, $1,026m.) Outstanding debt, in 2003, $12,142m.

Performance

Gross State Product in 2004 was $336,398m., ranking North Carolina 11th in the United States.

ENERGY AND NATURAL RESOURCES

Water

The total area covered by water is approximately 5,108 sq. miles.

Minerals

Principal minerals are stone, sand and gravel, phosphate rock, feldspar, lithium minerals, olivine, kaolin and talc. North

Carolina is a leading producer of bricks, making more than 1bn. bricks a year. Value of domestic non-fuel mineral production in 2003 was $676m.

Agriculture

In 2002 there were 56,000 farms covering 9·1m. acres; average size of farms was 163 acres and average value per acre in 2002 was $1,661.

Farm income, 2002, from crops, $2,659m. and from livestock and products $3,944m. The net farm income in 2002 was $1,661m. Main crop production: greenhouse products, flue-cured tobacco, maize, soybeans, peanuts, wheat, sweet potatoes and apples.

Livestock, 2002: cattle, 848,000; pigs, 9·9m.; chickens, 17·04m.

Forestry

Forests covered 19·3m. acres in 2002, with 1·2m. acres of national forest. Main products are hardwood veneer and hardwood plywood, furniture woods, pulp, paper and lumber.

Fisheries

Commercial fish catch, 2002, had a value of approximately $98·7m. and produced 159·6m. lb. The catch is mainly of blue crab, menhaden, Atlantic croaker, flounder, shark, sea trout, mullet, blue fish and shrimp.

INDUSTRY

The leading industries by employment are textiles, clothing, furniture, electrical machinery and equipment, non-electrical machinery and food processing. In 2001 the state's 10,844 manufacturing establishments had 691,000 employees, earning $21,583m. Total value added by manufacturing in 2001 was $91,184m.

Labour

Total non-agricultural employment, 2003, 3,803,000. Employees by branch, 2003 (in 1,000): trade, transport and utilities, 721; government, 645; manufacturing, 604; education and health services, 428; professional and business services, 421. The unemployment rate in 2003 was 6·5%.

COMMUNICATIONS

Roads

In 2003 there were 102,160 miles of roads (77,749 miles rural). There were 6,118,644 registered motor vehicles.

Rail

In 2002 there were 3,345 miles of freight railroad in operation, including 2,580 miles of Class I railways.

Civil Aviation

In June 2004 there were 305 airports and 74 heliports. There were 17,425,571 passenger enplanements statewide in 2003.

Shipping

There are two ocean ports, Wilmington and Morehead City.

SOCIAL INSTITUTIONS

Justice

The death penalty is authorized; there were four executions in 2004 and five in 2005. In June 2003 there were 33,334 federal and state prisoners.

Education

School attendance is compulsory between six and 16. In autumn 2002 there were 1,332,140 pupils and 85,557 teachers at public and charter schools; there were 92,890 pupils at 661 independent and religious schools. Total expenditure on public schools was $9,821m. in 2002–03; teachers' salaries in 2003 averaged $43,076.

The 16 senior universities are all part of the University of North Carolina system (176,967 students enrolled in autumn 2002). The largest institution is the North Carolina State University (founded 1887), at Raleigh, with 29,637 students in autumn 2002. The University of North Carolina at Chapel Hill (founded in 1789; the first state university to open in America in 1795) had 26,028 students in 2002; East Carolina University (founded in 1907), at Greenville, had 20,577. There were 78,028 students at 37 independent universities and colleges in autumn 2002.

Health

In 2002 there were 113 community hospitals with 23,600 beds. A total of 967,000 patients were admitted during the year.

Welfare

Medicare enrolment in July 2003 totalled 1,205,466. In 2002 a total of 1,355,269 people in North Carolina received Medicaid. In Dec. 2004 there were 1,468,751 Old-Age, Survivors, and Disability Insurance (OASDI) beneficiaries. A total of 76,508 people were receiving payments under Temporary Assistance for Needy Families (TANF) in Sept. 2004.

RELIGION

Leading denominations are the Baptists (41·4% of church membership), Methodists (17·5%), Roman Catholics (8·6%), Presbyterians (5·6%) and Lutherans (2·4%). Total estimate of all denominations in 2000 was 3·7m.

CULTURE

Tourism

There were about 49m. visitors in 2004, spending $13·25bn. across the state and supporting almost 183,000 jobs; tourism spending generated $710m. in state sales tax receipts and $437m. in local tax revenue.

FURTHER READING

Statistical information: Office of State Planning, 116 West Jones St., Raleigh 27603. Publishes *Statistical Abstract of North Carolina Counties.*

North Carolina Manual. Secretary of State. Raleigh. Biennial

Fleer, J. D., *North Carolina: Government and Population.* Univ. of Nebraska Press, 1995

North Dakota

KEY HISTORICAL EVENTS

The original inhabitants were various groups of Plains Indians. French explorers and traders were active among them in the 18th century, often operating from French possessions in Canada. France claimed the area until 1803, when it passed to the USA as part of the Louisiana Purchase, except for the northeastern part which was held by the British until 1818.

Trading with the Indians, mainly for furs, continued until the 1860s, with American traders succeeding the French. In 1861 the Dakota Territory (North and South) was established. In 1862 the Homestead Act was passed (allowing 160 acres of public land free to any family who had worked and lived on it for five years) and this greatly stimulated settlement. Farming settlers came onto the wheat lands in great numbers, many of them from Canada, Norway and Germany.

Bismarck, the capital, began as a crossing-point on the Missouri and was fortified in 1872 to protect workers building the Northern Pacific Railway. There followed a gold-rush nearby, and the town became a service centre for prospectors. In 1889 North and South Dakota were admitted to the Union as separate states, and Bismarck became the Northern capital. The largest city is Fargo which was also a railway town, named after William George Fargo, the express-company founder.

The population grew rapidly until 1890 and steadily until 1930 by which time it was about one-third European in parentage. Between 1930 and 1970 there was a steady population drain, increasing whenever farming was affected by the extremes of the continental climate.

TERRITORY AND POPULATION

North Dakota is bounded north by Canada, east by the Red River (forming a boundary with Minnesota), south by South Dakota and west by Montana. Land area, 68,976 sq. miles (178,647 sq. km). The Federal Bureau of Indian Affairs administered (1992) 841,295 acres, of which 214,006 acres were assigned to tribes. Census population, 1 April 2000, 642,200, an increase of 0·5% since 1990. July 2005 estimate, 636,677.

Population at five census years was:

	White	Black	Indian	Asiatic	Total	Per sq. mile
1910	569,855	617	6,486	98	577,056	8·2
1930	671,851	377	8,617	194	680,845	9·7
			All others			
1980	625,557	2,568	24,692		652,717	9·5
1990	604,142	3,524	31,134		638,800	9·3
2000	593,182	3,916	45,102		642,200	9·3

Of the total population in 2000, 321,676 were female, 481,351 were 18 years old or older and 358,958 were urban. Estimated outward migration, 1980–90, 110 per 1,000 population. Only Vermont has fewer persons of Hispanic origin than North Dakota. In 2000 the Hispanic population was 7,786, up from 4,665 in 1990 (an increase of 66·9%).

The largest cities are Fargo with a population, census 2000, of 90,599; Bismarck (capital), 55,532; Grand Forks, 49,321; and Minot, 36,567.

SOCIAL STATISTICS

Births in 2003 were 7,972 (12·6 per 1,000 population); deaths (2002), 5,892 (9·3 per 1,000 population). 2002 infant mortality rate (per 1,000 live births), 6·3. 2001: marriages, 4,100; divorces, 1,700.

CLIMATE

Bismarck, Jan. 8°F (–13·3°C), July 71°F (21·1°C). Annual rainfall 16" (402 mm). Fargo, Jan. 6°F (–14·4°C), July 71°F (21·1°C). Annual rainfall 20" (503 mm). North Dakota belongs to the High Plains climate zone (see UNITED STATES: Climate).

CONSTITUTION AND GOVERNMENT

The present constitution dates from 1889; it has had 133 amendments as of 2005. The Legislative Assembly consists of a Senate of 53 members elected for four years, and a House of Representatives of 106 members elected for four years. The Governor and Lieut.-Governor are elected for four years.

For the 109th Congress, which convened in Jan. 2005, North Dakota sends one member to the House of Representatives. It is represented in the Senate by Kent Conrad (D. 1987–2007) and Byron Dorgan (D. 1992–2011).

The capital is Bismarck. The state has 53 organized counties.

RECENT ELECTIONS

In the 2004 presidential election Bush polled 196,651 votes; Kerry, 111,052; Nader, 3,756.

CURRENT ADMINISTRATION

Governor: John Hoeven (R.), Dec. 2004–Dec. 2008 (salary: $92,483).

Lieut.-Governor: Jack Dalrymple (R.), Dec. 2004–Dec. 2008 ($71,797).

Secretary of State: Alvin A. Jaeger (R), 2004–06 ($73,568).

Government Website: http://discovernd.com

ECONOMY

Though the state is still mainly agricultural it is diversifying into high tech and information technology industries. *Per capita* income (2004) was $29,247.

Budget

In 2003 total state revenue was $3,359m. Total expenditure was $3,121m. (education, $1,021m.; public welfare, $651m.; highways, $365m.; natural resources, $130m.; government administration, $108m.) Outstanding debt, in 2003, $1,599m.

Performance

Gross State Product in 2004 was $22,687m., ranking North Dakota 49th in the United States.

ENERGY AND NATURAL RESOURCES

Oil and Gas

The mineral resources of North Dakota consist chiefly of oil, which was discovered in 1951. Production of crude petroleum in 1996 was 32m. bbls. (value, $629m.); of natural gas, 50bn. cu. ft.

Water

The total area covered by water is approximately 1,724 sq. miles.

Minerals

Output of lignite coal in 2003 was 30·8m. tons. Total value of domestic non-fuel mineral production in 2003 was $38m.

Agriculture

In 2002 there were 30,000 farms (61,963 in 1954) in an area of 39·4m. acres and with an average farm acreage of 1,313. In 2002 the average value of farmland and buildings per acre was $404.

Farm income, 2002, from crops, $2,499m. and from livestock, $724m. The net farm income in 2002 was $605m. Production, 2002: barley, 56·8m. bu.; wheat (durum), 48·9m. bu.; honey, 24m. lb; oats, 12·5m. bu.; flaxseed, 12·2m. bu.; dry edible beans, 10·1m. cwt; sunflower (all), 1,710m. lb. Other important products are all beans, all wheat and rye.

The state has also an active livestock industry, chiefly cattle raising. Livestock, 2002: cattle, 1·87m.; pigs, 138,800; sheep, 114,000; poultry, 200,400.

Forestry

Forest area, 2002, was 672,000 acres, of which 181,000 acres were national forest.

INDUSTRY

In 2001 the state's 681 manufacturing establishments had 24,000 employees, earning $762m. Total value added by manufacturing in 2001 was $2,669m.

Labour

In 2003 total non-agricultural employment was 333,000. Employees by branch, 2003 (in 1,000): government, 76; trade, transportation and utilities, 72; education and health services, 48; leisure and hospitality, 30; professional and business services, 24. The unemployment rate in 2003 was 4·0%.

COMMUNICATIONS

Roads

In 2003 there were 86,782 miles of roads (84,947 rural). There were 694,241 registered motor vehicles.

Rail

In 2002 there were 3,707 miles of railway.

Civil Aviation

In 2005 there were 90 public airports and 204 private airports. There were 577,014 passenger enplanements statewide in 2003.

Telecommunications

In 1998 there were 32,000 miles of fibre optic cable in the ground.

SOCIAL INSTITUTIONS

Justice

In June 2003 there were 1,168 federal and state prisoners. The Missouri River Correctional Center is a minimum custody institution. There is no death penalty.

Education

School attendance is compulsory between the ages of seven and 16, or until the 17th birthday if the eighth grade has not been completed. In 1995–96 the public elementary schools had 81,798 pupils; secondary schools, 36,755 pupils. State expenditure per pupil in elementary and secondary schools, 1997, $5,016. Teachers (4,208 in elementary and 2,208 in secondary schools in 1994) earned an average $25,506 in 1993–94 school year.

The University of North Dakota in Grand Forks, founded in 1883, had 10,392 students in autumn 1998; North Dakota State University in Fargo, 9,688 students (1996). Total enrolment in the 11 public institutions of higher education, autumn 1995, 35,199; in the two private, 2,911.

Health

In 2002 there were 42 community hospitals with 3,900 beds. A total of 95,000 patients were admitted during the year.

Welfare

Medicare enrolment in July 2003 totalled 103,220. In 2002 a total of 70,132 people in North Dakota received Medicaid. In Dec. 2004 there were 114,167 Old-Age, Survivors, and Disability Insurance (OASDI) beneficiaries. A total of 7,530 people were receiving payments under Temporary Assistance for Needy Families (TANF) in Sept. 2004.

RELIGION

Church membership totalled 467,925 in 2000. The leading religious denominations were: Roman Catholics, 179,349 members; Evangelical Lutherans, 174,554; Lutheran Church-Missouri Synod, 23,720; Methodists, 20,159; Assemblies of God, 9,994.

CULTURE

Press

There were, in 1997, ten daily and seven Sunday newspapers in circulation.

FURTHER READING

Statistical information: Bureau of Business and Economic Research, Univ. of North Dakota, Grand Forks 58202. Publishes *Statistical Abstract of North Dakota.*

North Dakota Blue Book. Secretary of State. Bismarck

Jelliff, T. B., *North Dakota: A Living Legacy.* Fargo, 1983

Ohio

KEY HISTORICAL EVENTS

The land was inhabited by Delaware, Miami, Shawnee and Wyandot Indians. It was explored by French and British traders in the 18th century and confirmed as part of British North America in 1763. After the War of Independence it became part of the Northwest Territory of the new United States. Former American soldiers of the war came in from New England in 1788 and made the first permanent white settlement at Marietta, at the confluence of the Ohio and Muskingum rivers. In 1803 Ohio was separated from the rest of the Territory and admitted to the Union as the 17th state.

During the early 19th century there was steady immigration from Europe, mainly of Germans, Swiss, Irish and Welsh. Industrial growth began from the processing of local farm, forest and mining products; it increased rapidly with the need to supply the Union armies in the Civil War of 1861–65.

As the industrial cities grew, so immigration began again, with many whites from eastern Europe and the Balkans and blacks from the southern states looking for work in Ohio.

Cleveland, which developed rapidly as a Lake Erie port after the opening of commercial waterways to the interior and the Atlantic coast (1825, 1830 and 1855), became an iron-and-steel town during the Civil War.

TERRITORY AND POPULATION

Ohio is bounded north by Michigan and Lake Erie, east by Pennsylvania, southeast and south by the Ohio River (forming a boundary with West Virginia and Kentucky) and west by Indiana. Land area, 40,948 sq. miles (106,055 sq. km). Census population, 1 April 2000, 11,353,140, an increase of 4·7% since 1990. July 2005 estimate, 11,464,042.

Population at five census years was:

	White	Black	Indian	Asiatic	Total	Per sq. mile
1910	4,654,897	111,452	127	645	4,767,121	117·0
1930	6,335,173	309,304	435	1,785	6,646,697	161·6
			All others			
1980	9,597,458	1,076,748	123,424		10,797,630	263·2
1990	9,521,756	1,154,826	170,533		10,847,115	264·5
2000	9,645,453	1,301,307	406,380		11,353,140	277·3

Of the total population in 2000, 5,840,878 were female, 8,464,801 were 18 years old or older and 8,782,329 were urban. In 2000 the Hispanic population was 217,123, up from 139,696 in 1990 (an increase of 55·4%).

Census population of chief cities on 1 April 2000 was:

Columbus	711,470	Springfield	65,358	Cuyahoga	
Cleveland	478,403	Hamilton	60,690	Falls	49,374
Cincinnati	331,285	Kettering	57,502	Mansfield	49,346
Toledo	313,619	Lakewood	56,646	Warren	46,832
Akron	217,074	Elyria	55,953	Newark	46,279
Dayton	166,179	Euclid	52,717	Strongsville	43,858
Parma	85,655	Middletown	51,605	Fairfield	42,097
Youngstown	82,026	Mentor	50,278	Lima	40,081
Canton	80,806	Cleveland			
Lorain	68,652	Heights	49,458		

Metropolitan areas, 2000 census: Cleveland–Akron, 2,945,831; Cincinnati–Hamilton, 1,979,202; Columbus (the capital), 1,540,157; Dayton–Springfield, 950,558; Toledo, 618,203; Youngstown–Warren, 594,746; Canton–Massillon, 404,934.

SOCIAL STATISTICS

Statistics 2003 (per 1,000 population): births, 149,679 (13·1); deaths (2002), 109,766 (9·6 per 1,000 population). Infant mortality, 2002, 7·9 per 1,000 live births. Marriages, 80,373 (7·7 per 1,000 population in 2000); divorces, 45,955 (4·2 in 2000).

CLIMATE

Average temperatures and rainfall in 2003: Cincinnati, Jan. 25·6°F, July 75·0°F, annual rainfall 46·50"; Cleveland, Jan. 21·2°F, July 72·5°F, annual rainfall 42·50"; Columbus, Jan. 21·0°F, July

71·8°F, annual rainfall 37·11" (2001). Ohio belongs to the Great Lakes climate zone (see UNITED STATES: Climate).

CONSTITUTION AND GOVERNMENT

The question of a general revision of the constitution drafted by an elected convention is submitted to the people every 20 years. The constitution dates from 1851, since when there have been 161 amendments adopted to change the constitution.

The Senate consists of 33 members and the House of Representatives of 99 members. The Senate is elected for four years, half every two years; the House is elected for two years; the Governor, Lieut.-Governor and Secretary of State for four years. Qualified as electors are (with necessary exceptions) all citizens 18 years of age who have the usual residential qualifications.

For the 109th Congress, which convened in Jan. 2005, Ohio sends 18 members to the House of Representatives. It is represented in the Senate by Mike DeWine (R. 1995–2007) and George Voinovich (R. 1999–2011).

The capital (since 1816) is Columbus. Ohio is divided into 88 counties.

RECENT ELECTIONS

In the 2004 presidential election Bush polled 2,859,764 votes; Kerry, 2,741,165; Badnarik, 14,676.

CURRENT ADMINISTRATION

Governor: Bob Taft (R.), 2003–07 (salary: $122,812).

Lieut.-Governor: Bruce Johnson (R.), 2005–07 ($64,375).

Secretary of State: J. Kenneth Blackwell (R.), 2003–07 ($90,725).

Government Website: http://ohio.gov

ECONOMY

Per capita income (2004) was $31,135.

Budget

In 2002–03 general state revenue was $21,749m. General expenditure was $22,429m. (public assistance and medicaid, $8,963m.; education, $6,646m.; justice and public protection, $1,778m.; health and human services, $1,075m.) Debt outstanding was $8,595m. in 2003.

Performance

In 2004 Gross State Product was $419,866m., ranking Ohio 7th in the United States.

ENERGY AND NATURAL RESOURCES

Oil and Gas

In 2003, 5·65m. bbls. of crude oil and 93,640m. cu. ft of gas were produced. In 2003 the value of oil and gas production was $708m.

Water

Lake Erie supplies northern Ohio with its water. The total area covered by water is approximately 3,877 sq. miles, of which Lake Erie covers 3,499 sq. miles.

Minerals

Ohio has extensive mineral resources, of which coal is the most important by value: estimated production (2002) 20,986,495 short tons. Coal production in 2002 was valued at $440,195,284. Production of other minerals (in short tons), 2001: limestone and dolomite, 80,998,236; sand and gravel, 56,829,272; salt, 4,261,545. Total value of non-fuel mineral production in 2003 was $968m.

Agriculture

Ohio is extensively devoted to agriculture. In 2003, 77,600 farms covered 14·6m. acres; average farm value per acre, $2,800. The average size of a farm in 2003 was 188 acres.

Cash income 2002 from total agricultural sector, $4,276m. The net farm income in 2002 was $268m. Estimated crop production 2002–03: corn for grain (478·9m. bu.), soybeans (162·6m. bu.), wheat (68·0m. bu.), oats (3·96m. bu.). In 2003 there were 1·44m. pigs, 1·22m. cattle and 150,000 sheep.

Forestry

Forest area, 2002, 7,855,000 acres. In 2003 there were 74 state parks covering 309,000 acres.

INDUSTRY

In 2002, 17,189 manufacturing establishments employed 829,456 persons, earning $34,319m. The largest industries were manufacturing of transport equipment, fabricated metal products and machinery.

Labour

In 2003, 5,552,000 people were in employment out of a labour force of 5,915,000. Employees by branch, 2003 (in 1,000): trade, transportation and utilities, 1,045; manufacturing, 844; government, 802; education and health services, 727; professional and business services, 607. In 2003 the unemployment rate was 6·1%.

INTERNATIONAL TRADE

Imports and Exports

Ohio exports had a total value of US$29·8bn. in 2003, making it the sixth largest exporting state in the USA.

COMMUNICATIONS

Roads

In 2003 there were 123,521 miles of roads and 12·08m. registered motor vehicles.

Rail

Ohio has about 5,800 miles of railroad track. Cleveland has a 19-mile metro system.

Civil Aviation

In 2003 there were more than 800 airports of varying sizes in the state. There are 165 public use airports and 23 public use heliports. There were 10,278,474 passenger enplanements in 2003.

Shipping

Ohio has more than 700 miles of navigable waterways, with Lake Erie having a 265-mile shoreline. There are nine deep-draft ports in the state. The busiest port is Cleveland, which handles 18m. tons of cargo annually.

SOCIAL INSTITUTIONS

Justice

In 2003 there were 44,000 inmates (92·99% males) in the 32 adult correctional institutions. The death penalty is authorized; there were four executions in 2005 (seven in 2004). There were 204 death-row inmates (203 male) in 2004: 95 were white; 103 black; three Hispanic; and three other.

Education

School attendance during full term is compulsory for children from six to 18 years of age. In 2003–04 public schools had 1,905,570 enrolled pupils. Teachers' salaries (2003–04) averaged $47,652. Estimated expenditure on elementary and secondary schools for 2004 was $7,975m., 39·3% of the total state budget. Total estimated revenue for the co-ordination of higher education in Ohio (controlled by the Board of Regents) was $2·57bn. in fiscal year 2001.

Public colleges and universities had a total enrolment (2002–03) of 461,492 students. Independent colleges and universities enrolled 124,462 students. Estimated annual operating budget for higher education institutions in 1998 was $4·4m. Average annual charge (for undergraduates in 2002–03): $5,755 (state); $18,020 (private).

Main campuses, 1997:

Founded	Institutions	Enrolments
1804	Ohio University, Athens (State)	19,159
1809	Miami University, Oxford (State)	15,999
1819	University of Cincinnati (State)	27,800
1826	Case Western Reserve University, Cleveland	9,569[1]
1850	University of Dayton (R.C.)	1,709[1]
1870	University of Akron (State)	21,878
1870	Ohio State University, Columbus (State)	48,004
1872	University of Toledo (State)	19,855
1908	Youngstown University (State)	12,050
1910	Bowling Green State University (State)	16,579
1910	Kent State University (State)	20,277
1964	Cleveland State University (State)	15,447
1964	Wright State University (State)	14,292
1986	Shawnee State University, Portsmouth (State)	3,163

[1]Figures for Case Western Reserve University and University of Dayton are for 1994 enrolments.

Health

In 2001 the state had 163 registered community hospitals with 32,981 beds. State facilities for the severely mentally retarded had 12 developmental centres serving 2,000 residents.

Welfare

Public assistance is administered through the Ohio Works First programme (OWF). In 2004 OWF-Combined assistance groups had 193,942 recipients and money payments totalled $316,347,050. OWF-Regular assistance groups had 177,527 recipients with $297,095,852 paid out in 2004. OWF-Unemployed had 16,415 recipients and money payments were $19,251,198 in 2004. Disability Assistance had 13,468 recipients in 2004; and food stamps, 925,584 recipients.

In 2004 Disability Assistance totalled $20,407,767; food stamps in 2004 totalled $981,831,872; and foster care totalled $162,081,492. Optional State Supplement is paid to aged, blind or disabled adults. Free social services are available to those eligible by income or circumstances.

RELIGION

Many religious faiths are represented, including (but not limited to) the Baptist, Jewish, Lutheran, Methodist, Muslim, Orthodox, Presbyterian and Roman Catholic.

FURTHER READING

Official Roster: Federal, State, County Officers and Department Information. Secretary of State, Columbus. Biennial

Shkurti, W. J. and Bartle, J. (eds.) *Benchmark Ohio.* Ohio State Univ. Press, 1991

Oklahoma

KEY HISTORICAL EVENTS

Francisco Coronado led a Spanish expedition in 1541, claiming the land for Spain. There were several Indian groups, but no strong political unit. In 1714 Juchereau de Saint Denis made the first French contact. During the 18th century French fur-traders were active, and France and Spain struggled for control, a struggle which was resolved by the French withdrawal in 1763. France returned briefly in 1800–03, and the territory then passed to the USA as part of the Louisiana Purchase.

In 1828 the Federal government set aside the area of the present state as Indian Territory (a reservation and sanctuary for Indian tribes who had been driven off their lands elsewhere by white settlement). About 70 tribes came, among whom were Creeks, Choctaws and Cherokees from the southeastern states, and Plains Indians.

In 1889 the government took back about 2·5m. acres of the Territory and opened it to white settlement. About 10,000 homesteaders gathered at the site of Oklahoma City on the Santa Fe Railway in the rush to stake their land claims. The settlers' area, and others subsequently opened to settlement, were organized as the Oklahoma Territory in 1890. In 1907 the Oklahoma and Indian Territories were combined and admitted to the Union as a state. Indian reservations were established within the state.

The economy first depended on ranching and farming, with packing stations on the railways. A mining industry grew in the 1870s attracting foreign immigration, mainly from Europe. In 1901 oil was found near Tulsa, and the industry grew rapidly.

TERRITORY AND POPULATION

Oklahoma is bounded north by Kansas, northeast by Missouri, east by Arkansas, south by Texas (the Red River forming part of the boundary) and, at the western extremity of the 'panhandle', by New Mexico and Colorado. Land area, 68,667 sq. miles (177,847 sq. km). Census population, 1 April 2000, 3,450,654, an increase of 9·7% since 1990. July 2005 estimate, 3,547,884.

The population at five federal censuses was:

	White	Black	American Indian	Other	Total	Per sq. mile
1930	2,130,778	172,198	92,725	339	2,396,040	34·6
1960	2,107,900	153,084	68,689	1,414	2,328,284	33·8
1980	2,597,783	204,658	169,292	53,557	3,025,486	43·2
1990	2,583,512	233,801	252,420	119,723	3,189,456	44·5
2000	2,628,434	260,968	273,230	288,022	3,450,654	50·3

Of the total population in 2000, 1,754,759 were female, 2,558,294 were 18 years old or older and 2,254,563 were urban. The US Bureau of Indian Affairs is responsible for 1,097,004 acres (1990), of which 96,839 acres were allotted to tribes. In 2000 Oklahoma's Hispanic population was 179,304, up from 86,160 in 1990 (an increase of 108·1%).

The most important cities with population, 2000, are Oklahoma City (capital), 506,132; Tulsa, 393,049; Norman, 95,694; Lawton, 92,757; Broken Arrow, 74,859; Edmond, 68,315; Midwest City, 54,088; Enid, 47,045; Moore, 41,138; Stillwater, 39,065; Muskogee, 38,310; Bartlesville, 34,748.

SOCIAL STATISTICS

Births, 2004, 51,157 (14·5 per 1,000 population); deaths, 34,327 (9·7 per 1,000 population); marriages, 22,700; divorces, 17,800; infant mortality rate, 2003, 7·8 (per 1,000 live births).

CLIMATE

Oklahoma City, Jan. 34°F (1°C), July 81°F (27°C). Annual rainfall 31·9" (8,113 mm). Tulsa, Jan. 34°F (1°C), July 82°F (28°C). Annual rainfall 33·2" (8,438 mm). Oklahoma belongs to the Central Plains climate zone (*see* UNITED STATES: Climate).

CONSTITUTION AND GOVERNMENT

The constitution, dating from 1907, provides for amendment by initiative petition and legislative referendum; it has had 200 amendments (as of Sept. 2005).

The Legislature consists of a Senate of 48 members, who are elected for four years, and a House of Representatives elected for two years and consisting of 101 members. The Governor and Lieut.-Governor are elected for four-year terms; the Governor can only be elected for two terms in succession. Electors are (with necessary exceptions) all citizens 18 years or older, with the usual qualifications.

For the 109th Congress, which convened in Jan. 2005, Oklahoma sends five members to the House of Representatives. It is represented in the Senate by James Inhofe (R. 1994–2009) and Tom Coburn (R. 2005–11).

The capital is Oklahoma City. The state has 77 counties.

RECENT ELECTIONS

In the 2004 presidential election Bush polled 959,792 votes; Kerry, 503,966.

CURRENT ADMINISTRATION

Governor: Brad Henry (D.), 2003–07 (salary: $110,299).

Lieut.-Governor: Mary Fallin (R.), 2003–07 ($75,530).

Secretary of State: M. Susan Savage (D.), appointed Jan. 2003 ($90,000).

Government Website: http://www.ok.gov

ECONOMY

Per capita income (2004) was $27,819.

Budget

In 2003 total state revenue was $14,919m. Total expenditure was $15,125m. (education, $5,565m.; public welfare, $3,177m.; highways, $1,283m.; government administration, $572m.; correction, $486m.) Outstanding debt, in 2003, $6,747m.

Performance

Gross State Product in 2004 was $107,600m., ranking Oklahoma 30th in the United States.

ENERGY AND NATURAL RESOURCES

Oil and Gas

Production of crude oil (2004), 63m. bbls.; natural gas (1998), 1,645bn. cu. ft. Oklahoma ranks third in the USA for natural gas production behind Texas and Louisiana. In 2001 there were 201,453 oil and gas wells in production.

Water

The total area covered by water is approximately 1,231 sq. miles.

Minerals

Coal production (2003), 1,565,000 tons. Principal minerals are: crushed stone, cement, sand and gravel, iodine, glass sand, gypsum. Other minerals are helium, clay and sand, zinc, lead, granite, tripoli, bentonite, lime and volcanic ash. Total value of domestic non-fuel minerals produced in 2003 was $479m.

Agriculture

In 2002 the state had 87,000 farms and ranches with a total area of 34m. acres; average size was 391 acres and average value per acre was $699. Area harvested, 2002, 7,705,860 acres. Livestock, 2002: cattle, 5·2m.; sheep and lambs, 80,100; hogs and pigs, 2·25m.

Farm income 2002: crops, $837m.; livestock and products, $2,893m. The net farm income in 2002 was $758m. The major cash grain is winter wheat (value, 2002, $340m.): 102m. bu. of wheat for grain were harvested in 2002. Other crops include barley, oats, rye, grain, corn, soybeans, grain sorghum, cotton, peanuts and peaches. Value of cattle and calves produced, 2002, $2,448m.; racehorses, $63m. (1990).

The Oklahoma Conservation Commission works with 91 conservation districts, universities, state and federal government agencies. The early work of the conservation districts, beginning in 1937, was limited to flood and erosion control: since 1970, they also include urban areas.

Irrigated production has increased in the Oklahoma 'panhandle'. The Ogalala aquifer is the primary source of irrigation water there and in western Oklahoma, a finite source because of its isolation from major sources of recharge. Declining groundwater levels necessitate the most effective irrigation practices.

Forestry

There were 7,665,000 acres of forested land in 2002, with 245,000 acres of national forest. The forest products industry is concentrated in the 118 eastern counties. There are three forest regions: Ozark (oak, hickory); Ouachita highlands (pine, oak); Cross-Timbers (post oak, black jack oak). Southern pine is the chief commercial species, at almost 80% of saw-timber harvested annually. Replanting is essential.

INDUSTRY

In 2003 Oklahoma's 3,946 manufacturing establishments had 138,600 employees, earning $5,159m. Total value added by manufacturing in 2003 was $17,686m.

Labour

Total non-agricultural employment in 2004 was 1,470,400. Employees by branch, 2004 (in 1,000): services, 543; government, 302; wholesale and retail trade, 223; manufacturing, 142. Oklahoma's unemployment rate was 4·8% in 2004.

COMMUNICATIONS

Roads

In 2003 there were 112,576 miles of roads comprising 14,991 miles of urban road and 97,585 miles of rural road. There were 3,073,707 registered motor vehicles.

Rail

In 2000 Oklahoma had 3,591 miles of railway operated by 15 companies.

Civil Aviation

Airports in 2005 numbered 351, of which 142 were publicly owned. There were 3,028,603 passenger enplanements statewide in 2003.

Shipping

The McClellan-Kerr Arkansas Navigation System provides access from east central Oklahoma to New Orleans through the Verdigris, Arkansas and Mississippi rivers. In 2004, 12·9m. tons were shipped inbound and outbound on the Oklahoma Segment. Commodities shipped are mainly chemical fertilizer, farm produce, petroleum products, iron and steel, coal, sand and gravel.

SOCIAL INSTITUTIONS

Justice

There were 23,004 federal and state prisoners in June 2003. In 1990 there were 15 penal institutions, eight community treatment centres and seven probation and parole centres. The death penalty was suspended in 1966 and re-imposed in 1976. There were six executions in 2004 and four in 2005. Oklahoma's total of 79 executions between 1997 and 2005 is the third highest in the USA behind Texas and Virginia.

Education

In 2003–04 there were 619,200 pupils and 34,700 teachers at public elementary and secondary school. The average teacher salary per annum was $34,779. In 2003 total expenditure on the 1,769 schools was $4·1bn. There were 234,900 students enrolled at the 42 higher education establishments in 2004.

Institutions of higher education include:

Founded	Name	Place	2004 Enrolment
1890	University of Oklahoma	Norman	31,529
1890	Oklahoma State University	Stillwater	27,419
1890	University of Central Oklahoma	Edmond	18,107

Founded	Name	Place	2004 Enrolment
1894	The University of Tulsa	Tulsa	4,629
1897	Langston University	Langston	3,827
1897	Northeastern State University	Tahlequah	11,217
1897	Northwestern Oklahoma State University	Alva	2,731
1897	Southwestern Oklahoma State University	Weatherford	6,352
1908	Cameron University	Lawton	7,917
1909	East Central University	Ada	5,606
1909	Oklahoma Panhandle State University	Goodwell	1,425
1909	Southeastern Oklahoma State University	Durant	5,150
1909	Rogers State College	Claremore	4,896
1950	Oklahoma Christian University of Science and Arts	Oklahoma City	1,725
1969	Rose State College	Midwest City	13,804
1970	Tulsa Community College	Tulsa	26,838
1972	Oklahoma City Community College	Oklahoma City	19,700

Health

In 2002 there were 105 community hospitals with 11,100 beds. A total of 446,000 patients were admitted during the year.

Welfare

Medicare enrolment in July 2003 totalled 521,286. In 2002 a total of 631,498 people in Oklahoma received Medicaid. In Dec. 2004 there were 623,599 Old-Age, Survivors, and Disability Insurance (OASDI) beneficiaries. A total of 33,581 people were receiving payments under Temporary Assistance for Needy Families (TANF) in Sept. 2004.

RELIGION

The chief religious bodies are Baptists, followed by United Methodists, Roman Catholics, Churches of Christ, Assembly of God, Disciples of Christ, Presbyterian, Lutheran, Nazarene and Episcopal.

CULTURE

Broadcasting

In 2005 there were 107 radio and 20 television broadcasting stations, and 100 cable-TV companies.

Press

There were 47 daily newspapers in 2005 and 171 weeklies.

Tourism

There are 71 state parks in Oklahoma. Domestic tourists spent some $3,900m. in 2002.

FURTHER READING

Center for Economic and Management Research, Univ. of Oklahoma, 307 West Brooks St., Norman 73019. *Statistical Abstract of Oklahoma.*
Oklahoma Department of Libraries. *Oklahoma Almanac.* Biennial

Morris, J. W., *et al.*, *Historical Atlas of Oklahoma.* 3rd ed. Oklahoma Univ. Press, 1986

State library: Oklahoma Department of Libraries, 200 Northeast 18th Street, Oklahoma City 73105.

Oregon

KEY HISTORICAL EVENTS

The area was divided between many Indian groups including the Chinook, Tillamook, Cayuse and Modoc. In the 18th century English and Spanish visitors tried to establish national claims, based on explorations of the 16th century. The USA also laid claim by right of discovery when an expedition entered the mouth of the Columbia River in 1792.

Oregon was disputed between Britain and the USA. An American fur company established a trading settlement at Astoria in 1811, which the British took in 1812. The Hudson Bay Company was the most active force in Oregon until the 1830s when American pioneers began to migrate westwards along the Oregon Trail. The dispute between Britain and the USA was resolved in 1846 with the boundary fixed at 49°N. lat. Oregon was organized as a Territory in 1848 but with wider boundaries; it became a state with its present boundaries in 1859.

Early settlers were mainly American. They came to farm in the Willamette Valley and to exploit the western forests. Portland developed as a port for ocean-going traffic, although it was 100 miles inland at the confluence of the Willamette and Columbia rivers. Industries followed when the railways came and the rivers were exploited for hydro-electricity. The capital of the Territory from 1851 was Salem, a mission for Indians on the Willamette river; it was confirmed as state capital in 1864. Salem became the processing centre for the farming and market-gardening Willamette Valley.

TERRITORY AND POPULATION

Oregon is bounded in the north by Washington, with the Columbia River forming most of the boundary, east by Idaho, with the Snake River forming most of the boundary, south by Nevada and California and west by the Pacific. Land area, 95,997 sq. miles (248,631 sq. km). The federal government owned (2003) 30,638,949 acres (49·7% of the state area). Census population, 1 April 2000, 3,421,399, an increase of 20·4% since 1990. July 2005 estimate, 3,641,056.

Population at five federal censuses was:

	White	Black	American Indian	Asiatic	Total	Per sq. mile
1930	938,598	2,234	4,776	8,179	953,786	9·9
1960	1,732,037	18,133	8,026	9,120	1,768,687	18·4
1980	2,490,610	37,060	27,314	34,775	2,633,105	27·3
	White	Black	American Indian	All others	Total	Per sq. mile
1990	2,636,787	46,178	38,496	120,860	2,842,321	29·6
2000	2,961,623	55,662	45,211	358,903	3,421,399	35·6

Of the total population in 2000, 1,724,849 were female, 2,574,843 were 18 years old or older and 2,694,144 were urban. In 2000 the Hispanic population was 275,314, up from 112,707 in 1990 (an increase of 144·3%).

The US Bureau of Indian Affairs (area headquarters in Portland) administers (1994) 783,227·13 acres, of which 627,615·54 acres are held by the USA in trust for Indian tribes and 138,950·05 acres for individual Indians, and 16,661·54 acres of mineral tracts.

The largest cities (2000 census figures) are: Portland, 529,121; Eugene, 137,893; Salem (the capital), 136,924; Gresham, 90,205; Beaverton, 76,129; Hillsboro, 70,186; Medford, 63,154; Springfield, 52,864; Bend, 52,029. Primary statistical (metropolitan) areas: Portland–Salem, 2,265,223; Eugene-Springfield, 322,959.

SOCIAL STATISTICS

In 2003 births numbered 45,953 (12·9 per 1,000 population); deaths (2002), 31,119 (8·8 per 1,000 population). 2002 infant mortality rate (per 1,000 live births), 5·8. 2001: marriages, 26,000; divorces, 16,500.

CLIMATE

Jan. 32°F (0°C), July 66°F (19°C). Annual rainfall 28" (710 mm). Oregon belongs to the Pacific coast climate zone (*see* UNITED STATES: Climate).

CONSTITUTION AND GOVERNMENT

The present constitution dates from 1859; some 250 items in it have been amended. The Legislative Assembly consists of a Senate of 30 members, elected for four years (half their number retiring every two years), and a House of 60 representatives, elected for two years. The Governor is elected for four years. The constitution reserves to the voters the rights of initiative and referendum and recall.

For the 109th Congress, which convened in Jan. 2005, Oregon sends five members to the House of Representatives. It is represented in the Senate by Ron Wyden (D. 1996–2011) and Gordon Smith (R. 1997–2009).

The capital is Salem. There are 36 counties in the state.

RECENT ELECTIONS

In the 2004 presidential election Kerry polled 943,163 votes; Bush, 866,831; Badnarik, 7,260.

CURRENT ADMINISTRATION

Governor: Ted Kulongoski (D.), 2003–07 (salary: $93,600).
   Secretary of State: Bill Bradbury (D.), 2005–09 ($72,000).

Government Website: http://www.oregon.gov

ECONOMY

Per capita income (2004) was $30,584.

Budget

In 2003 total state revenue was $19,252m. Total expenditure was $18,006m. (education, $4,816m.; public welfare, $3,818m.; highways, $1,127m.; government administration, $909m.; hospitals, $741m.) Outstanding debt, in 2003, $7,464m.

Performance

Gross State Product was $128,103m. in 2004, ranking Oregon 28th in the United States.

ENERGY AND NATURAL RESOURCES

Water

The total area covered by water is approximately 2,384 sq. miles.

Minerals

Mineral resources include gold, silver, lead, mercury, chromite, sand and gravel, stone, clays, lime, silica, diatomite, expansible shale, scoria, pumice and uranium. There is geothermal potential. Domestic non-fuel mineral production value (2003), $311m.

Agriculture

Oregon, which has an area of 61,557,184 acres, is divided by the Cascade Range into two distinct zones as to climate. West of the Cascade Range there is a good rainfall and almost every variety of crop common to the temperate zone is grown; east of the Range stock-raising and wheat-growing are the principal industries and irrigation is needed for row crops and fruits. In 2002 there were 64,000 hired workers in agriculture.

There were, in 2002, 41,000 farms with an acreage of 17·2m. and an average farm size of 420 acres; most are family-owned corporate farms. Average value per acre (2002), $1,202.

Farm income in 2002: from crops, $2,294m.; from livestock and products, $808m. The net farm income in 2002 was $360m. Principal crops (2003): greenhouse and nursery products ($777·7m.), hay ($365·7m.), grass seed ($291·7m.), wheat ($199·8m.), Christmas trees ($158·0m.), onions ($108·3m.), potatoes ($106·7m.), pears ($72·2m.) and farmforest products.

Livestock, 2002: milch cows, 116,400; cattle and calves, 1·36m.; sheep and lambs, 237,000; swine, 21,000.

Forestry

Oregon had 29,651,000 acres of forest in 2002, with 14,293,000 acres of national forest. Almost half of the state is forested. In 1993, 22·4m. was commercial forest land suitable for timber production; ownership was as follows (acres): US Forestry Service, 13·1m.; US Bureau of Land Management, 2·7m.; other federal, 165,000; State of Oregon, 907,000; other public (city, county), 123,000; private owners, 10·8m., of which the forest industry owned 5·8m., non-industrial private owners, 4·6m., Indians, 399,000. Oregon's commercial forest lands provided a 1992 harvest of 5,742m. bd ft of logs, as well as the benefits of recreation, water, grazing, wildlife and fish. Trees vary from the coastal forest of hemlock and spruce to the state's primary species, Douglas-fir, throughout much of western Oregon. In eastern Oregon, ponderosa pine, lodgepole pine and true firs are found. Here, forestry is often combined with livestock grazing to provide an economic operation. Along the Cascade summit and in the mountains of northeast Oregon, alpine species are found.

Total covered payroll in lumber and wood products industry in 1991 was $1,475m.

Fisheries

Commercial fish and shellfish landings in 2002 was 211·2m. lb and amounted to a value of $68·4m. The most important are: ground fish, shrimp, crab, tuna, salmon.

INDUSTRY

Forest products manufacturing is Oregon's leading industry, followed by high technology. In 2001 the state's 5,587 manufacturing establishments had 198,000 employees, earning $7,981m. Total value added by manufacturing in 2001 was $22,027m.

Labour

Total non-agricultural employment was 1,562,000 in 2003. Employees by branch, 2003 (in 1,000): trade, transportation and utilities, 314; government, 268; manufacturing, 196; education and health services, 188; professional and business services, 170. With a rate of 8·2%, Oregon had the highest unemployment rate in the USA in 2003.

COMMUNICATIONS

Roads

There were 65,951 miles of roads in 2003 (54,884 rural). There were 3,060,786 registered vehicles.

Rail

In 2001 there were approximately 3,800 total miles of track, including 2,387 route miles. There is a light rail network in Portland.

Civil Aviation

In 2005 there were one public-use and 103 personal-use heliports; 251 personal-use and 95 public-use airports; and three sea-plane bases, two public-use and one personal-use. There were 6,811,968 passenger enplanements statewide in 2003.

Shipping

Portland is a major seaport for large ocean-going vessels and is 101 miles inland from the mouth of the Columbia River. In 1993 Portland handled 11·7m. short tons of cargo and other Columbia River ports 13·7m. short tons, the main commodities being grain, petroleum and wood products; the ports of Coos Bay and Newport handled 2·7m. short tons of cargo, chiefly logs, lumber and wood products.

SOCIAL INSTITUTIONS

Justice

There are 12 correctional institutions in Oregon. In June 2003 there were 12,422 federal and state prisoners. The sterilization law, originally passed in 1917, was amended in 1967 and abolished in 1993. Some categories of euthanasia were legalized in Dec. 1994.

The death penalty is authorized but there have been no executions since 2001.

Education

School attendance is compulsory from seven to 18 years of age if the twelfth year of school has not been completed; those between the ages of 16 and 18 years, if legally employed, may attend part-time or evening schools. Others may be excused under certain circumstances. In 1994–95 the public elementary and secondary schools had 521,000 students and 27,000 teachers; average salary for teachers (1993–94), $37,589. Total expenditure on elementary and secondary education (1997) was $3,769m.

Leading state-supported institutions of higher education (1993–94) included:

	Students
University of Oregon, Eugene	16,680
Oregon Health Sciences University	1,396
Oregon State University, Corvallis	14,131
Portland State University, Portland	14,428
Western Oregon State College, Monmouth	3,871
Southern Oregon State College, Ashland	4,535
Eastern Oregon State College, La Grande	1,931
Oregon Institute of Technology, Klamath Falls	2,444

Enrolment in state colleges and universities, in autumn 1996, was approximately 165,000 students. Largest of the privately endowed universities are Lewis and Clark College, Portland, with 3,132 students (1993–94); University of Portland, 2,700 students; Willamette University, Salem, 2,451 students; Reed College, Portland, 1,277 students; Linfield College, McMinnville, 2,354 students; Marylhurst College, 1,183 students; and George Fox College, 1,557 students. In 1993–94 there were 314,926 students (full-time equivalent) in community colleges.

Health

In 2002 there were 60 community hospitals with 6,800 beds. A total of 345,000 patients were admitted during the year.

Welfare

Medicare enrolment in July 2003 totalled 513,253. In 2002 a total of 621,462 people in Oregon received Medicaid. In Dec. 2004 there were 603,781 Old-Age, Survivors, and Disability Insurance (OASDI) beneficiaries. A total of 43,993 people were receiving payments under Temporary Assistance for Needy Families (TANF) in Sept. 2004.

RELIGION

The chief religious bodies are Catholic, Baptist, Lutheran, Methodist, Presbyterian and Latter-day Saints (Mormons).

CULTURE

Broadcasting

In 1996 there were 194 commercial radio stations and 37 educational radio stations. There were 24 commercial television stations and 26 educational television stations. There were also 24 cable companies.

Press

In 1996 there were 21 daily newspapers with a circulation of more than 676,000 and 111 non-daily newspapers.

Tourism

In 2002, 172,000 overseas visitors (0·9% of the market share), excluding Mexico and Canada, visited Oregon.

FURTHER READING

Oregon Blue Book. Issued by the Secretary of State. Salem. Biennial

Conway, F. D. L., *Timber in Oregon: History and Projected Trends.* Oregon State Univ., 1993

Friedman, R., *The Other Side of Oregon.* Caldwell (ID), 1993

McArthur, L. A., *Oregon Geographic Names.* 6th ed., rev. and enlarged. Portland, 1992

Orr, E. L., *et al.*, *Geology of Oregon.* Dubuque (IA), 1992

State Library: The Oregon State Library, Salem.

Pennsylvania

KEY HISTORICAL EVENTS

Pennsylvania was occupied by four powerful tribes in the 17th century: Delaware, Susquehannock, Shawnee and Iroquois. The first white settlers were Swedish, arriving in 1643. The British became dominant in 1664, and in 1681 William Penn, an English Quaker, was given a charter to colonize the area as a sanctuary for his fellow Quakers. Penn's ideal was peaceful co-operation with the Indians and religious toleration within the colony. Several religious groups were attracted to Pennsylvania because of this policy, including Protestant sects from Germany and France. During the 18th century, co-operation with the Indians failed as the settlers pushed into more territory and the Indians resisted.

During the War of Independence the Declaration of Independence was signed in Philadelphia, the main city. Pennsylvania became one of the original 13 states of the Union. In 1812 the state capital was moved to its current location in Harrisburg, which began as a trading post and ferry point on the Susquehanna River in the south-central part of the state. The Mason-Dixon line, the state's southern boundary, became the dividing line between free and slave states during the conflict leading to the Civil War. During the war crucial battles were fought in the state, including the battle of Gettysburg. Industrial growth was rapid after the war. Pittsburgh, founded as a British fort in 1761 during war with the French, had become an iron-making town by 1800 and grew rapidly when canal and railway links opened in the 1830s. The American Federation of Labor was founded in Pittsburgh in 1881, by which time the city was of national importance in producing coal, iron, steel and glass.

At the beginning of the 20th century, industry attracted immigration from Italy and eastern Europe. In farming areas the early sect communities survive, notably Amish and Mennonites. (The Pennsylvania 'Dutch' are of German extraction.)

TERRITORY AND POPULATION

Pennsylvania is bounded north by New York, east by New Jersey, south by Delaware and Maryland, southwest by West Virginia, west by Ohio and northwest by Lake Erie. Land area, 44,817 sq. miles (116,075 sq. km). Census population, 1 April 2000, 12,281,054, an increase of 3·4% since 1990. July 2005 estimate, 12,429,616.

Population at five census years was:

	White	Black	Indian	All others	Total	Per sq. mile
1910	7,467,713	193,919	1,503	1,976	7,665,111	171·0
1930	9,196,007	431,257	523	3,563	9,631,350	214·8
			All others			
1980	10,652,320	1,046,810	164,765		11,863,895	264·7
1990	10,520,201	1,089,795	271,647		11,881,643	265·1
2000	10,484,203	1,224,612	572,239		12,281,054	274·0

Of the total population in 2000, 6,351,391 were female, 9,358,833 were 18 years old or older and 9,464,101 were urban. In 2000 Pennsylvania's Hispanic population was 394,088, up from 232,262 in 1990 (a rise of 69·7%).

The population of the largest cities and townships, 2000 census, was:

Philadelphia	1,517,550	Reading	81,207
Pittsburgh	334,563	Scranton	76,415
Allentown	106,632	Bethlehem	71,329
Erie	103,717	Lower Merion	59,850
Upper Darby	81,821	Bensalem	58,434

The Philadelphia–Wilmington–Atlantic City metropolitan area had a 2000 census population of 6,188,463.

SOCIAL STATISTICS

Births, 2003, 145,959 (11·8 per 1,000 population); deaths (2002), 130,223 (10·6 per 1,000 population). 2002 infant mortality (per 1,000 live births), 7·6. 2001: marriages, 71,400 (6·0 per 1,000 population); divorces, 38,000 (3·2).

CLIMATE

Philadelphia, Jan. 32°F (0°C), July 77°F (25°C). Annual rainfall 40" (1,006 mm). Pittsburgh, Jan. 31°F (–0·6°C), July 74°F (23·3°C). Annual rainfall 37" (914 mm). Pennsylvania belongs to the Appalachian Mountains climate zone (*see* UNITED STATES: Climate).

CONSTITUTION AND GOVERNMENT

The present constitution dates from 1968. The General Assembly consists of a Senate of 50 members chosen for four years, one-half being elected biennially, and a House of Representatives of 203 members chosen for two years. The Governor and Lieut.-Governor are elected for four years. Every citizen 18 years of age, with the usual residential qualifications, may vote. Registered voters in Nov. 2004, 8,366,663.

For the 109th Congress, which convened in Jan. 2005, Pennsylvania sends 19 members to the House of Representatives. It is represented in the Senate by Arlen Specter (R. 1981–2011) and Rick Santorum (R. 1995–2007).

The state capital is Harrisburg. The state is organized in counties (numbering 67), cities, boroughs, townships and school districts.

RECENT ELECTIONS

In the 2004 presidential election Kerry polled 2,938,095 votes; Bush, 2,793,847; Badnarik, 21,185.

CURRENT ADMINISTRATION

Governor: Edward G. Rendell (D.), 2003–07 (salary: $161,173).

Lieut.-Governor: Catherine Baker Knoll (D.), 2003–07 ($135,383).

Secretary of the Commonwealth: Pedro A. Cortés (D.), appointed 2003 ($116,045).

Government Website: http://www.state.pa.us

ECONOMY

Per capita income (2004) was $33,257.

Budget

In 2003 total state revenue was $49,459m. Total expenditure was $57,428m. (public welfare, $16,085m.; education, $14,838m.; highways, $5,033m.; government administration, $2,209m.; hospitals, $1,945m.) Outstanding debt, in 2003, $24,330m.

Performance

Gross State Product in 2004 was $468,089m., ranking Pennsylvania 6th in the United States.

ENERGY AND NATURAL RESOURCES

Oil and Gas

2003 production: crude petroleum, 1·84m. bbls.; natural gas, 149,346m. cu. ft.

Water

The total area covered by water is approximately 1,239 sq. miles.

Minerals

Pennsylvania is almost the sole producer of anthracite coal. Production, 2002: industrial minerals (shale, limestone, sandstone, clay, dolomite, sand and gravel), 139,072,832 tons; bituminous coal, 70,044,685 tons; anthracite coal, 4,262,856 tons. Non-fuel mineral production was worth $1,260m. in 2003.

Agriculture

Agriculture, market-gardening, fruit-growing, horticulture and forestry are pursued within the state. In 2002 there were 59,000 farms with a total farm area of 7·7m. acres. Average number of acres per farm in 2002 was 131 and the average value per acre was $3,419. Cash receipts, 2002, from crops, $1,360m., and from livestock and products, $2,682m. The net farm income in 2002 was $611m.

In 2002 Pennsylvania ranked first in the production of mushrooms (459·6m. lb, value $390·3m.). Other production figures include (2001): corn for grain (97m. bu., value $223·2m.); sweet corn (701,000 cwt, value $18·58m.) and tomatoes (537,000 cwt, value $19·65m.). Pennsylvania is also a major fruit producing state. In 2002 apples totalled 370m. lb (value $37·2m.); peaches, 60m. lb (value $19·8m.); and grapes, 53·2m. tons (value $14·9m.). Pennsylvania ranked fourth in milk production in 2002 with 10,780m. lb (6·3% of US milk production). Egg production totalled 6,520m., value $279·3m.; chicken production (excluding broilers) was 29·3m., value $52·7m.; and production of broilers was 133·2m., value $225·9m. Other products included turkey (9·9m. poults, value $91·1m.) and cheese (374m. lb).

In 2002 there were on farms: 1·63m. cattle and calves, 102,890 sheep, and 1·23m. hogs and swine.

Forestry

Total forested area was 16,905,000 acres in 2002. In 1998 state forest land totalled 2,100,113 acres; state park land, 282,700 acres; state game lands, 1,392,312 acres.

INDUSTRY

In 2001 the state's 16,796 manufacturing establishments had 780,000 employees, earning $29,312m. Total value added by manufacturing in 2001 was $87,984m.

Labour

Total non-agricultural employment, 2003, 5,602,000. Employees by branch, 2003 (in 1,000): trade, transportation and utilities, 1,115; education and health services, 978; government, 743; manufacturing, 716; professional and business services, 598. The unemployment rate in 2003 was 5·6%.

COMMUNICATIONS

Roads

In 2003 highways and roads in the state (federal, local and state combined) totalled 120,422 miles (82,733 miles rural). Registered motor vehicles numbered 9,724,453.

Rail

In 2002 there were 6,967 miles of freight railroad in operation, including 3,649 miles of Class I railways. There are metro, light rail and tramway networks in Philadelphia and Pittsburgh, and commuter networks around Philadelphia.

Civil Aviation

In June 2004 there were 467 public and private airports and 317 heliports in operation. There were 20,666,615 passenger enplanements statewide in 2003.

Shipping

The major ports are Pittsburgh, Philadelphia, Marcus Hook, Penn Manor, Chester and Erie. In 2001 waterborne imports totalled 46,590,000 short tons of cargo (including 33,920,000 short tons by tanker), and exports 718,700 short tons.

SOCIAL INSTITUTIONS

Justice

The death penalty is authorized. The last execution was in 1999. There were 40,545 prisoners in state correctional institutions in June 2003.

Education

School attendance is compulsory for children eight to 17 years of age. In 2002–03 there were 3,264 public elementary and secondary schools with 1,816,747 pupils and 118,256 teachers; total expenditure on public schools was $17,888m. Teachers' salaries averaged $51,428 in 2003.

Leading senior academic institutions include:

Founded	Institutions	Faculty[1] (Autumn 2003)	Students[2] (Autumn 2004)
1740	University of Pennsylvania (non-sect.)	8,416	23,305
1787	University of Pittsburgh (all campuses)	7,402	33,796
1832	Lafayette College, Easton (Presbyterian)	240	2,303
1833	Haverford College	132	1,172
1842	Villanova University (R.C.)	1,158	10,610
1846	Bucknell University (Baptist)	319	3,609
1851	St Joseph's University, Philadelphia (R.C.)	565	7,730
1852	California University of Pennsylvania	491	6,640
1855	Pennsylvania State University (all campuses)	11,405	74,667
1855	Millersville University of Pennsylvania	457	7,998
1863	LaSalle University, Philadelphia (R.C.)	468	6,194
1864	Swarthmore College	230	1,474
1866	Lehigh University, Bethlehem (non-sect.)	1,089	6,641
1871	West Chester University of Pennsylvania	844	12,822
1875	Indiana University of Pennsylvania	1,097	13,998
1878	Duquesne University, Pittsburgh (R.C.)	1,321	9,722
1884	Temple University, Philadelphia	3,703	33,551
1885	Bryn Mawr College	285	1,772
1888	University of Scranton (R.C.)	478	4,795
1891	Drexel University, Philadelphia	2,262	17,656
1900	Carnegie-Mellon University, Pittsburgh	2,884	9,803

[1]Includes full-time and part-time.
[2]Includes undergraduate, graduate and first professional students.

Health

In 2002 there were 201 community hospitals with 40,500 beds. A total of 1,798,000 patients were admitted during the year.

Welfare

Medicare enrolment in July 2003 totalled 2,110,470. In 2002 a total of 1,627,261 people in Pennsylvania received Medicaid. In Dec. 2004 there were 2,400,082 Old-Age, Survivors, and Disability Insurance (OASDI) beneficiaries. A total of 246,918 people were receiving payments under Temporary Assistance for Needy Families (TANF) in Sept. 2004.

RELIGION

The principal religious bodies in 2000 were the Roman Catholics (3,802,524 members), Protestants (2,890,130) and Jews (283,000). The five largest Protestant denominations by adherents were the United Methodist Church (659,350), the Evangelical Lutheran Church in America (611,913), the Presbyterian Church (USA) (324,714), the United Church of Christ (241,844) and the American Baptist Church (132,858).

CULTURE

Broadcasting

Broadcasting stations in 2000 included 50 television stations and 334 radio stations.

Press

There were (2000) 78 daily and 263 weekly newspapers.

FURTHER READING

Statistical information: Pennsylvania State Data Center, 777 West Harrisburg Pike, Middletown 17057. Publishes *Pennsylvania Statistical Abstract*.

Downey, D. B. and Bremer, F. (eds.) *Guide to the History of Pennsylvania*. London, 1994

Rhode Island

KEY HISTORICAL EVENTS

The earliest white settlement was founded by Roger Williams, an English Puritan who was expelled from Massachusetts because of his dissident religious views and his insistence on the land-rights of the Indians. At Providence he bought land from the Narragansetts and founded a colony there in 1636. A charter was granted in 1663. The colony was governed according to policies of toleration, which attracted Jewish and nonconformist settlers; later there was French Canadian settlement also.

Shipping and fishing developed strongly, especially at Newport and Providence. These two cities were twin capitals until 1900, when the capital was fixed at Providence.

Significant actions took place in Rhode Island during the War of Independence. In 1790 the state accepted the federal constitution and was admitted to the Union.

Early farming development was most successful in dairying and poultry. Early industrialization was mainly in textiles, beginning in the 1790s, and flourishing on abundant water power. Textiles dominated until the industry began to decline after the First World War. British, Irish, Polish, Italian and Portuguese workers settled in the state, working in the mills or in the shipbuilding, shipping, fishing and naval ports. The crowding of a new population into cities led to the abolition of the property qualification for the franchise in 1888.

TERRITORY AND POPULATION

Rhode Island is bounded north and east by Massachusetts, south by the Atlantic and west by Connecticut. Land area, 1,045 sq. miles (2,707 sq. km). Census population, 1 April 2000, 1,048,319, an increase of 4·5% since 1990. July 2005 estimate, 1,076,189.

Population of five census years was:

	White	Black	Indian	Asiatic	Total	Per sq. mile
1910	532,492	9,529	284	305	542,610	508·5
1930	677,026	9,913	318	240	687,497	649·3
				All others		
1980	896,692	27,584		22,878	947,154	903·0
1990	917,375	38,861	4,071	18,325	1,003,164	960·3
2000	891,191	46,908	5,121	24,232	1,048,319	1,003·2

Of the total population in 2000, 554,684 were female, 800,497 were 18 years old or older and 953,146 were urban (90·92%). In 2000 the Hispanic population was 90,820, up from 45,752 in 1990 (an increase of 98·5%).

The chief cities and their population (census, 2000) are Providence, 173,618; Warwick, 85,808; Cranston, 79,269; Pawtucket, 72,958; East Providence, 48,688.

SOCIAL STATISTICS

Births, 2003, were 13,209 (12·3 per 1,000 population); deaths (2002), 10,246 (9·6 per 1,000 population). 2002 infant mortality rate (per 1,000 live births), 7·0. 2001: marriages, 8,600; divorces, 3,300.

CLIMATE

Providence, Jan. 28°F (−2·2°C), July 72°F (22·2°C). Annual rainfall 43" (1,079 mm). Rhode Island belongs to the New England climate zone (see UNITED STATES: Climate).

CONSTITUTION AND GOVERNMENT

The present constitution dates from 1843; it has had 44 amendments. The General Assembly consists of a Senate of 50 members and a House of Representatives of 100 members, both elected for two years. The Governor and Lieut.-Governor are now elected for four years. Every citizen, 18 years of age, who has resided in the state for 30 days, and is duly registered, is qualified to vote.

For the 109th Congress, which convened in Jan. 2005, Rhode Island sends two members to the House of Representatives. It is represented in the Senate by Jack Reed (D. 1997–2009) and Lincoln Chafee (R. 1999–2007).

The capital is Providence. The state has five counties but no county governments. There are 39 municipalities, each having its own form of local government.

RECENT ELECTIONS

In the 2004 presidential election Kerry polled 259,760 votes; Bush, 169,046; Nader, 4,651.

CURRENT ADMINISTRATION

Governor: Donald L. Carcieri (R.), 2003–07 (salary: $105,194).
   Lieut.-Governor: Charles J. Fogerty (D.), 2003–07 ($88,584).
   Secretary of State: Matthew A. Brown (D.), 2003–07 ($88,584).

Government Website: http://www.ri.gov

ECONOMY

Per capita income (2004) was $34,180.

Budget

In 2003 total state revenue was $5,856m. Total expenditure was $5,977m. (public welfare, $1,804m.; education, $1,385m.; government administration, $271m.; highways, $229m.; health, $190m.) Outstanding debt, in 2003, $6,189m.

Performance

Gross State Product in 2004 was $41,679m., ranking Rhode Island 44th in the United States.

ENERGY AND NATURAL RESOURCES

Water

The total area covered by water is approximately 500 sq. miles.

Minerals

The small non-fuel mineral output—mostly stone, sand and gravel—was valued at $26m. in 2003.

Agriculture

In 2002 there were 700 farms with an area of 60,000 acres. The average size of a farm was 86 acres. In 2002 the average value of land and buildings per acre was $9,225. Farm income 2002: from crops, $40m.; livestock and products, $6m. The net farm income in 2002 was $6m. Principal commodities are greenhouse products, dairy products, sweetcorn and potatoes.

Forestry

Total forested area was 385,000 acres in 2002.

Fisheries

In 2002 the commercial catch was 103·7m. lb (mainly lobster and quahog) valued at $64·3m.

INDUSTRY

Manufacturing is the chief source of income and the largest employer. Principal industries are jewellery and silverware, electrical machinery, electronics, plastics, metal products, instruments, chemicals and boat building. In 2001 the state's 2,185 manufacturing establishments had 67,000 employees, earning $2,333m. Total value added by manufacturing in 2001 was $5,877m.

Labour

In 2003 total non-agricultural employment was 484,000. Employees by branch, 2003 (in 1,000): education and health services, 91; trade, transportation and utilities, 81; government, 67; manufacturing, 59. The unemployment rate in 2003 was 5.3%.

COMMUNICATIONS

Roads

In 2003 there were 6,416 miles of roads (5,193 miles urban). There were 805,740 registered motor vehicles.

Rail

Amtrak's New York-Boston route runs through the state, serving Providence.

Civil Aviation

In 2004 there were six state-owned airports. Theodore Francis Green airport at Warwick, near Providence, is served by 13 airlines, and handled 5·5m. passengers in 2004. There were 2,569,641 passenger enplanements statewide in 2003.

Shipping

Waterborne freight through the port of Providence (2003) totalled 9·2m. short tons.

SOCIAL INSTITUTIONS

Justice

In June 2003 there were 3,569 federal and state prisoners. The death penalty was abolished in 1852, except that it is mandatory in the case of murder committed by a prisoner serving a life sentence.

Education

In 1996 there were 149,802 pupils in public elementary and secondary schools. There were 219 public elementary schools with 85,691 pupils; about 24,941 pupils were enrolled in private and parochial schools. The 38 public senior and vocational high schools had 64,111 pupils. State and local government expenditure for schools in 1991 totalled $1,212·7m. The total expenditure per pupil in 1995 was $6,634.

There are 11 institutions of higher learning (three public and eight private). The state maintains Rhode Island College, at Providence, with over 350 faculty members, and 8,900 students (2,594 part-time, 1,816 graduates), and the University of Rhode Island, at South Kingstown, with over 650 faculty members and 13,707 students (2,198 part-time, 3,176 graduates). Brown University, at Providence, founded in 1764, is now non-sectarian; in 1996 it had over 500 faculty members and 7,458 students (1,786 part-time or graduate). Providence College, at Providence, founded in 1917 by the Order of Preachers (Dominican), had (1996) 300 faculty members and 5,520 students (1,911 part-time or graduate). The largest of the other colleges are Bryant College, at Smithfield, with over 200 faculty members and 3,310 students (1,100 part-time or graduate), and the Rhode Island School of Design, in Providence, with over 250 faculty members and 1,830 students (170 graduates) in 1996.

Health

In 2002 there were 11 community hospitals with 2,400 beds. A total of 123,000 patients were admitted during the year.

Welfare

Medicare enrolment in July 2003 totalled 172,474. In 2002 a total of 199,014 people in Rhode Island received Medicaid. In Dec. 2004 there were 192,755 Old-Age, Survivors, and Disability Insurance (OASDI) beneficiaries. A total of 29,408 people were receiving payments under Temporary Assistance for Needy Families (TANF) in Sept. 2004.

RELIGION

Chief religious bodies are Roman Catholic, Protestant Episcopal (baptized persons), Jewish, Baptist, Congregational and Methodist.

CULTURE

Broadcasting

There were 24 radio stations, five television stations and eight cable television companies in 1998.

FURTHER READING

Statistical information: Rhode Island Economic Development Corporation, 1 West Exchange Street, Providence, RI 02903. Publishes *Rhode Island Basic Economic Statistics.*

Rhode Island Manual. Prepared by the Secretary of State. Providence
Wright, M. I. and Sullivan, R. J., *Rhode Island Atlas.* Rhode Island Pubs., 1983

State Library: Rhode Island State Library, State House, Providence 02908.

South Carolina

KEY HISTORICAL EVENTS

Originally the territory of Yamasee Indians, the area attracted French and Spanish explorers in the 16th century. There were attempts at settlement on the coast, none of which lasted. Charles I of England made a land grant in 1629, but the first permanent white settlement began at Charles Town in 1670, moving to Charleston in 1680. This was a proprietorial colony including North Carolina until 1712; both passed to the Crown in 1729.

The coastlands developed as plantations worked by slave labour. In the hills there were small farming settlements and many trading posts, dealing with Indian suppliers.

After active campaigns during the War of Independence, South Carolina became one of the original states of the Union in 1788.

In 1793 the cotton gin was invented, enabling the speedy mechanical separation of seed and fibre. This made it possible to grow huge areas of cotton and meet the rapidly growing needs of new textile industries. Plantation farming spread widely, and South Carolina became hostile to the anti-slavery campaign which was strong in northern states. The state first attempted to secede from the Union in 1847, but was not supported by other southern states until 1860, when secession led to civil war.

At that time the population was about 703,000, of whom 413,000 were black. During the reconstruction periods there was some political power for black citizens, but control was back in white hands by 1876. The constitution was amended in 1895 to disenfranchise most black voters, and they remained with hardly any voice in government until the Civil Rights movement of the 1960s. Columbia became the capital in 1786.

TERRITORY AND POPULATION

South Carolina is bounded in the north by North Carolina, east and southeast by the Atlantic, southwest and west by Georgia. Land area, 30,110 sq. miles (77,982 sq. km). Census population, 1 April 2000, 4,012,012, an increase of 15·1% since 1990. July 2005 estimate, 4,255,083.

The population in five census years was:

	White	Black	Indian	Asiatic	Total	Per sq. mile
1910	679,161	835,843	331	65	1,515,400	49·7
1930	944,049	793,681	959	76	1,738,765	56·8
			All others			
1980	2,150,507	948,623	22,703		3,121,833	100·3
1990	2,406,974	1,039,884	39,845		3,486,703	115·8
2000	2,695,560	1,185,216	131,236		4,012,012	133·2

Of the total population in 2000, 2,063,083 were female, 3,002,371 were 18 years old or older and 2,427,124 were urban. In 2000 the Hispanic population of South Carolina was 95,076, up from 30,551 in 1990 (an increase of 211·2%).

Population estimate of large towns in 1999: Columbia (capital), 111,821; Charleston, 88,596; North Charleston, 81,989; Greenville, 56,873; Rock Hill, 48,474; Mount Pleasant, 44,785.

SOCIAL STATISTICS

Births, 2003, were 55,649 (13·4 per 1,000 population); deaths (2002), 37,736 (9·2 per 1,000 population). 2002 infant deaths (per 1,000 live births), 9·3. 2001: marriages, 36,800 (9·3); divorces and annulments, 13,800 (3·5).

CLIMATE

Columbia, Jan. 44·7°F (7°C), Aug. 80·2°F (26·9°C). Annual rainfall 49·12" (1,247·6 mm). South Carolina belongs to the Atlantic Coast climate zone (*see* UNITED STATES: Climate).

CONSTITUTION AND GOVERNMENT

The present constitution dates from 1895, when it went into force without ratification by the electorate. The General Assembly consists of a Senate of 46 members, elected for four years, and a House of Representatives of 124 members, elected for two years. It meets annually. The Governor and Lieut.-Governor are elected for four years.

For the 109th Congress, which convened in Jan. 2005, South Carolina sends six members to the House of Representatives. It is represented in the Senate by Lindsey Graham (R. 2003–09) and Jim DeMint (R. 2005–11).

The capital is Columbia. There are 46 counties.

RECENT ELECTIONS

In the 2004 presidential election Bush polled 937,974 votes; Kerry, 661,699; Nader, 5,520.

CURRENT ADMINISTRATION

Governor: Mark Sanford, Jr (R.), 2003–07 (salary: $106,078).
   Lieut.-Governor: R. André Bauer (R.), 2003–07 ($46,545).
   Secretary of State: Mark Hammond (R.), 2003–07 ($92,007).

Government Website: http://www.myscgov.com

ECONOMY

Per capita income (2004) was $27,153.

Budget

In 2003 total state revenue was $19,669m. Total expenditure was $21,040m. (education, $6,037m.; public welfare, $4,775m.; highways, $1,342m.; hospitals, $1,112m.; health, $698m.) Outstanding debt, in 2003, $10,990m.

Performance

Gross State Product was $136,125m. in 2004, ranking South Carolina 27th in the United States.

ENERGY AND NATURAL RESOURCES

Water

The total area covered by water is approximately 1,911 sq. miles.

Minerals

Gold is found, though non-metallic minerals are of chief importance: value of non-fuel mineral output in 2003 was $484m., chiefly from cement (Portland), stone and gold. Production of kaolin, vermiculite and scrap mica is also important.

Agriculture

In 2002 there were 24,500 farms covering a farm area of 4·8m. acres. The average farm was of 196 acres. The average value of farmland and buildings per acre was $2,067 in 2002.

Farm income, 2002: from crops $692m., from livestock and products, $760m. The net farm income in 2002 was $178m. Chief crops are tobacco, soybeans, wheat, cotton, peanuts and corn. Production, 2002: cotton, 131,000 bales; peanuts, 19·14m. lb; soybeans, 7·1m. bu.; tobacco, 55·5m. lb; corn, 11·96m. bu.; wheat, 7·03m. bu. Livestock on farms, 2002: 432,300 all cattle, 291,700 swine.

Forestry

The forest industry is important; total forest land (2002), 12·50m. acres. National forests amounted to 596,000 acres.

INDUSTRY

In 2001 the state's 4,430 manufacturing establishments had 326,000 employees, earning $11,289m. Total value added by manufacturing in 2001 was $35,017m.

Labour

In 2003 total non-agricultural employment was 1,813,000. Employees by branch, 2003 (in 1,000): trade, transportation and utilities, 347; government, 329; manufacturing, 277; leisure and hospitality, 194; professional and business services, 187. The unemployment rate in 2003 was 6·8%.

COMMUNICATIONS

Roads

In 2003 there were 66,232 miles of roads comprising 10,686 miles of urban road and 55,546 miles of rural road. There were 3,161,894 registered motor vehicles. The death rate in traffic accidents stood at 31·9 per 100,000 registered motor vehicles (2000).

Rail

In 2000 the length of railway in the state was 2,470 miles.

Civil Aviation

In 2005 there were 68 public-use airports and 30 heliports. There were 2,749,952 passenger enplanements statewide in 2003.

Shipping

The state has three deep-water ports.

SOCIAL INSTITUTIONS

Justice

In June 2003 there were 24,247 federal and state prisoners. The death penalty is authorized. There were four executions in 2004 and three in 2005.

Education

In 1995–96 there were 648,677 pupils and 46,073 teachers in public elementary and secondary schools. In 1996–97 the average teaching salary was $32,830.

For higher education the state operates the University of South Carolina (USC), founded at Columbia in 1801, with (autumn 1998), 25,250 enrolled students; USC Aiken, with 3,179 students; USC Spartanburg, with 3,767 students; USC 2-year regional campuses, with 4,484 students; Clemson University, founded in 1889, with 16,685 students; the Citadel, at Charleston, with 4,015 students; Winthrop University, Rock Hill, with 5,591 students; Medical University of S. Carolina, at Charleston, with 2,353 students; S. Carolina State University, at Orangeburg, with 4,795 students; and Francis Marion University, at Florence, with 3,947 students; the College of Charleston has 11,552 students; and Lander University, Greenwood, 2,600. There are 16 technical institutions (60,343).

There are also 387 private kindergartens, elementary and high schools with total enrolment (1996–97) of 49,534 pupils, and 23 private and denominational colleges and four junior colleges with (autumn 1998) enrolments of 29,316 and 1,357 students respectively.

Health

In 2002 there were 62 community hospitals with 11,100 beds. A total of 513,000 patients were admitted during the year.

Welfare

Medicare enrolment in July 2003 totalled 606,323. In 2002 a total of 809,136 people in South Carolina received Medicaid. In Dec. 2004 there were 754,531 Old-Age, Survivors, and Disability Insurance (OASDI) beneficiaries. A total of 37,372 people were receiving payments under Temporary Assistance for Needy Families (TANF) in Sept. 2004.

RELIGION

Chief religious bodies (2000) were Southern Baptists, with 928,341 members, United Methodists (302,528), Roman Catholics (136,719), Presbyterian Church (USA) (103,883) and the Evangelical Lutheran Church in America (61,380).

CULTURE

Press

In 1997 there were 15 daily and 14 Sunday newspapers in circulation.

FURTHER READING

Statistical information: Budget and Control Board, R. C. Dennis Bldg, Columbia 29201. Publishes *South Carolina Statistical Abstract*.
South Carolina Legislative Manual. Columbia. Annual

Edgar, W. B., *South Carolina in the Modern Age*. Univ. of South Carolina Press, 1992
Graham, C. B. and Moore, W. V., *South Carolina Politics and Government*. Univ. of Nebraska Press, 1995

State Library: South Carolina State Library, Columbia.

South Dakota

KEY HISTORICAL EVENTS

The area was part of the hunting grounds of nomadic Dakota (Sioux) Indians. French explorers visited the site of Fort Pierre in 1742–43, and claimed the area for France. In 1763 the claim fell and, together with French claims to all land west of the Mississippi, passed to Spain. Spain held the Dakotas until defeated by France in the Napoleonic Wars, when France regained the area and sold it to the USA as part of the Louisiana Purchase in 1803.

Fur-traders were active, but there was no settlement until Fort Randall was founded on the Missouri river in 1856. In 1861 North and South Dakota were organized as the Dakota Territory, and the Homestead Act of 1862 stimulated settlement, mainly in the southeast until there was a gold-rush in the Black Hills of the west in 1875–76. Colonization developed as farming communities in the east, miners and ranchers in the west. Livestock farming predominated, attracting European settlers from Scandinavia, Germany and Russia.

In 1889 the North and South were separated and admitted to the Union as states. The capital of South Dakota is Pierre, founded as a railhead in 1880, chosen as a temporary capital and confirmed as permanent capital in 1904. It faces Fort Pierre, the former centre of the fur trade, across the Missouri river. During the 20th century there have been important schemes to exploit the Missouri for power and irrigation.

TERRITORY AND POPULATION

South Dakota is bounded in the north by North Dakota, east by Minnesota, southeast by the Big Sioux River (forming the boundary with Iowa), south by Nebraska (with the Missouri River forming part of the boundary) and west by Wyoming and Montana. Land area, 75,885 sq. miles (196,541 sq. km). Area administered by the Bureau of Indian Affairs, 1985, covered 5m. acres (10% of the state), of which 2·6m. acres were held by tribes. The federal government, 2003, owned 2,324,006 acres.

Census population, 1 April 2000, 754,844, an increase of 8·5% since 1990. July 2005 estimate, 775,933.

Population in five federal censuses was:

	White	Black	American Indian	Asiatic	Total	Per sq. mile
1910	563,771	817	19,137	163	583,888	7·6
1930	669,453	646	21,833	101	692,849	9·0
			All others			
1980	638,955	2,144	49,079		690,178	9·0
				Asian/ other		
1990	637,515	3,258	50,575	4,656	696,004	9·2
2000	669,404	4,685	62,283	18,472	754,844	9·9

Of the total population in 2000, 380,286 were female, 552,195 were 18 years old or older and 391,427 were urban. In 2000 the Hispanic population was 10,903, up from 5,252 in 1990 (an increase of 107·6%).

Population of the chief cities (census of 2000) was: Sioux Falls, 123,975; Rapid City, 59,607; Aberdeen, 24,658; Watertown, 20,237; Brookings, 18,507; Mitchell, 14,558; Pierre, 13,876; Yankton, 13,528; Huron, 11,893; Vermillion, 9,765; Spearfish, 8,606; Madison, 6,540; Sturgis, 6,442.

SOCIAL STATISTICS

In 2003: births, 11,027 (14·4 per 1,000 population); deaths (2002), 6,898 (9·1 per 1,000 population). 2002 infant mortality (per 1,000 live births), 6·5. 2001: marriages, 6,700 (9·1 per 1,000 population); divorces, 2,500 (3·4).

CLIMATE

Rapid City, Jan. 25°F (–3·9°C), July 73°F (22·8°C). Annual rainfall 19" (474 mm). Sioux Falls, Jan. 14°F (–10°C), July 73°F (22·8°C). Annual rainfall 25" (625 mm). South Dakota belongs to the High Plains climate zone (see UNITED STATES: Climate).

CONSTITUTION AND GOVERNMENT

Voters are all citizens 18 years of age or older. The people reserve the right of the initiative and referendum. The Senate has 35 members, and the House of Representatives 70 members, all elected for two years; the Governor and Lieut.-Governor are elected for four years.

For the 109th Congress, which convened in Jan. 2005, South Dakota sends one member to the House of Representatives. It is represented in the Senate by Tim Johnson (D. 1997–2009) and John Thune (R. 2005–11).

The capital is Pierre. The state is divided into 66 organized counties.

RECENT ELECTIONS

In the 2004 presidential election Bush polled 232,584 votes; Kerry, 149,244; Nader, 4,320.

CURRENT ADMINISTRATION

Governor: Michael Rounds (R.), 2003–07 (salary: $105,544).
Lieut.-Governor: Dennis Daugaard (R.), 2003–07 ($14,399; part-time).
Secretary of State: Chris Nelson (R.), 2003–07 ($71,713).

Government Website: http://www.state.sd.us

ECONOMY

Per capita income (2004) was $30,617.

Budget

In 2003 total state revenue was $3,000m. Total expenditure was $2,898m. (education, $839m.; public welfare, $622m.; highways, $421m.; government administration, $116m.; natural resources, $114m.) Outstanding debt, in 2003, $2,567m.

Performance

Gross State Product in 2004 was $29,386m., ranking South Dakota 46th in the United States.

ENERGY AND NATURAL RESOURCES

Water

The total area covered by water is approximately 1,232 sq. miles.

Minerals

In 1998 there was a major decline in South Dakota's production of gold, although it remained the leading mineral commodity in the state. Production dropped 26% to 389,875 oz, yielding a gross value of $115m. (a drop of 34% in gross value on the previous year). In 1998, 503 companies had active mining licences in South Dakota, with 52 permits covering the mining of non-metallic minerals. Sand and gravel was the major non-metallic industrial mineral commodity with 15·1m. tonnes produced. Other major minerals were: Sioux quartzite (2·8m. tonnes); granite (265,000); pegmatite (17,100). Value of non-fuel mineral production (2003), $206m.

Agriculture

In 2002 there were 32,500 farms with an acreage of 44m. and an average farm size of 1,354 acres. Average value of farmland and buildings per acre in 2002 was $442. Farm income, 2002: crops, $1,720m.; livestock and products, $2,060m. The net farm income in 2002 was $559m.

In 2002 South Dakota was a major producer of oats (5·7m. bu.), rye (672,000 bu.) and sunflower oil (303·2m. lb). The other important crops were corn for grain (295·2m. bu.), soybeans (126·6m. bu.), spring wheat (23·5m. bu.), winter wheat (18·8m. bu.), sorghum for grain (2·4m. bu.), barley (1·1m. bu.) and durum wheat (127,822 bu.). Total planted area of cropland was 20·3m. acres with 13·5m. being harvested.

The farm livestock in 2002 included 3·9m. cattle; 376,500 sheep and lambs; and 1·4m. hogs. In 2002, 11·5m. lb of honey were produced.

Forestry

South Dakota had 1,619,000 acres of forested land in 2002, of which 979,000 acres were national forest.

INDUSTRY

In 2001 the state's 922 manufacturing establishments had 47,000 employees, earning $1,401m. Total value added by manufacturing in 2001 was $4,558m.

Labour

In 2003 total non-agricultural employment was 378,000, including 77,000 in trade, transportation and utilities; 74,000 in government; 55,000 in education and health services; 40,000 in leisure and hospitality; and 38,000 in manufacturing. The state unemployment rate in 2003 was 3·6%, the lowest of all the states.

COMMUNICATIONS

Roads

In 2003 there were 83,687 miles of roads comprising 2,263 miles of urban road and 81,424 miles of rural road. There were 826,944 registered vehicles. In 1996 there were 6,979 snowmobiles.

Rail

In 2003 there were 1,839·5 miles of track.

Civil Aviation

In 2005 there were 75 public-use airports and 33 heliports. There were 570,276 passenger enplanements statewide in 2003.

SOCIAL INSTITUTIONS

Justice

In June 2003 there were 3,059 adults in state prisons. The death penalty is authorized, but was last used in 1947.

Education

Elementary and secondary education are free from six to 21 years of age. Between the ages of six and 16, attendance is compulsory. In 1998–99 there were 131,117 PK-12 public school students at 763 public schools; and, in 1997, 16,792 PK-12 non-public school students at 140 schools.

Teachers' salaries (1998–99) averaged $28,386. Total expenditure on public schools was $646,930,000 ($4,934 per pupil).

Higher education (autumn 1998): the School of Mines at Rapid City, established 1885, had 2,265 students; South Dakota State University at Brookings, 8,635; the University of South Dakota, founded at Vermillion in 1882, 7,317; Northern State University, Aberdeen, 2,873; Black Hills State University at Spearfish, 3,639; Dakota State University at Madison, 1,831. There were 9,287 students at 14 private colleges.

Health

In 2002 there were 51 community hospitals with 4,600 beds. A total of 100,000 patients were admitted during the year.

Welfare

Medicare enrolment in July 2003 totalled 121,777. In 2002 a total of 117,631 people in South Dakota received Medicaid. In Dec. 2004 there were 139,053 Old-Age, Survivors, and Disability Insurance (OASDI) beneficiaries. A total of 5,862 people were receiving payments under Temporary Assistance for Needy Families (TANF) in Sept. 2004.

RELIGION

The chief religious bodies are: Lutherans, Roman Catholics, Methodists, United Church of Christ, Presbyterians, Baptists and Episcopalians.

FURTHER READING

Statistical information: State Data Center, Univ. of South Dakota, Vermillion 57069.
Governor's Budget Report. South Dakota Bureau of Finance and Management. Annual
South Dakota Historical Collections. 1902–82
South Dakota Legislative Manual. Secretary of State, Pierre, S.D. Biennial

Berg, F. M., *South Dakota: Land of Shining Gold.* Hettinger, 1982

State Library: South Dakota State Library, 800 Governor's Drive, Pierre, S.D. 57501–2294.

Tennessee

KEY HISTORICAL EVENTS

Bordered on the west by the Mississippi, Tennessee was part of an area inhabited by Cherokee. French, Spanish and British explorers penetrated the area up the Mississippi and traded with the Cherokee in the late 16th and 17th centuries. French claims were abandoned in 1763, colonists from the British colonies of Virginia and Carolina then began to cross the Appalachians westwards, but there was no organized Territory until after the War of Independence. In 1784 there was a short-lived, independent state called Franklin. In 1790 the South West Territory (including Tennessee) was formed, and Tennessee entered the Union as a state in 1796.

The state was active in the war against Britain in 1812. After the American victory, colonization increased and pressure for land mounted. The Cherokee were forcibly removed during the 1830s and taken to Oklahoma, a journey on which many died.

Tennessee was a slave state and seceded from the Union in 1861, although eastern Tennessee was against secession. There were important battles at Shiloh, Chattanooga, Stone River and Nashville. In 1866 Tennessee was re-admitted to the Union.

Nashville, the capital since 1843, Memphis, Knoxville, and Chattanooga all developed as river towns, Memphis becoming an important cotton and timber port. Growth was greatly accelerated by the creation of the Tennessee Valley Authority in the 1930s, producing power for a manufacturing economy. Industry increased to the extent that, by 1970, the normal southern pattern of emigration and population loss had been reversed.

TERRITORY AND POPULATION

Tennessee is bounded north by Kentucky and Virginia, east by North Carolina, south by Georgia, Alabama and Mississippi and west by the Mississippi River (forming the boundary with Arkansas and Missouri). Land area, 41,217 sq. miles (106,752 sq. km). Census population, 1 April 2000, 5,689,283, an increase of 16·7% since 1990. July 2005 estimate, 5,962,959.

Population in five census years was:

	White	Black	Indian	Asiatic	Total	Per sq. mile
1910	1,711,432	473,088	216	53	2,184,789	52·4
1930	2,138,644	477,646	161	105	2,616,556	62·4
			All others			
1980	3,835,452	725,942	29,726		4,591,120	111·6
1990	4,048,068	778,035	51,082		4,877,185	115·7
2000	4,563,310	932,809	193,164		5,689,283	138·0

Of the total population in 2000, 2,919,008 were female, 4,290,762 were 18 years old or older and 3,620,018 were urban. In 2000 the Hispanic population of Tennessee was 123,828, up from 32,741 in 1990 (an increase of 278·2%).

The cities, with population (2000) are Memphis, 650,100; Nashville (capital), 569,891; Knoxville, 167,535; Chattanooga, 150,425; Clarksville, 94,879; Johnson City, 55,542; Murfreesboro, 53,996; Jackson, 50,406; Kingsport, 41,335; Oak Ridge, 27,742.

Metropolitan Statistical Areas, with 2000 populations: Nashville, 1,231,311; Memphis, 1,135,614; Knoxville, 687,249; Johnson City–Kingsport–Bristol, 480,091; Chattanooga, 465,161; Clarksville–Hopkinsville, 207,033; Jackson, 107,377.

SOCIAL STATISTICS

Statistics 2003: births, 78,890 (13·5 per 1,000 population); deaths (2002), 56,606 (9·8 per 1,000 population). 2002 infant mortality (per 1,000 live births), 9·4. 2001: marriages, 77,700; divorces, 28,800.

CLIMATE

Memphis, Jan. 41°F (5°C), July 82°F (27·8°C). Annual rainfall 49" (1,221 mm). Nashville, Jan. 39°F (3·9°C), July 79°F (26·1°C). Annual rainfall 48" (1,196 mm). Tennessee belongs to the Appalachian Mountains climate zone (see UNITED STATES: Climate).

CONSTITUTION AND GOVERNMENT

The state has operated under three constitutions, the last of which was adopted in 1870 and has been since amended 30 times (first in 1953). Voters at an election may authorize the calling of a convention limited to altering or abolishing one or more specified sections of the constitution. The General Assembly consists of a Senate of 33 members and a House of Representatives of 99 members, senators elected for four years and representatives for two years. Qualified as electors are all citizens (usual residential and age (18) qualifications).

For the 109th Congress, which convened in Jan. 2005, Tennessee sends nine members to the House of Representatives. It is represented in the Senate by Bill Frist (R. 1995–2007) and Lamar Alexander (R. 2003–09).

The capital is Nashville. The state is divided into 95 counties.

RECENT ELECTIONS

In the 2004 presidential election Bush polled 1,384,375 votes; Kerry, 1,036,477; Nader, 8,992.

CURRENT ADMINISTRATION

Governor: Phil Bredesen (D.), 2003–07 (salary: $85,000, but not presently taken).

Lieut.-Governor (Senate President): John S. Wilder (D.), 2005–07 ($49,500).

Secretary of State: Riley Darnell (D), 2005–09 ($124,200).

Government Website: http://www.tennessee.gov

ECONOMY

Per capita personal income (2004) was $29,806.

Budget

In 2003 total state revenue was $20,564m. Total expenditure was $21,022m. (public welfare, $7,634m.; education, $6,169m.; highways, $1,576m.; health, $881m.; correction, $559m.) Outstanding debt, in 2003, $3,496m.

Performance

Gross State Product in 2004 was $217,626m., ranking Tennessee 18th in the United States.

ENERGY AND NATURAL RESOURCES

Water

The total area covered by water is approximately 926 sq. miles.

Minerals

Domestic non-fuel mineral production was worth $606m. in 2003.

Agriculture

In 2002, 90,000 farms covered 11·7m. acres. The average farm was of 130 acres. In 2002 the average value of farmland and buildings per acre was $2,405.

Farm income (2002) from crops was $1,087m.; from livestock, $913m. The net farm income in 2002 was $339m. Main crops were greenhouse products and soybeans.

In 2002 the domestic animals included 84,000 milch cows, 2·2m. all cattle, 23,300 sheep and 230,500 swine.

Forestry

Forests occupied 14·4m. acres in 2002. The forest industry and industries dependent on it employ about 0·04m. workers. Wood products are valued at over $500m. per year. National forest system land (2002) 623,000 acres.

INDUSTRY

The manufacturing industries include iron and steel working, but the most important products are chemicals, including synthetic fibres and allied products, electrical equipment and food. In 2001 the state's 7,013 manufacturing establishments had 449,000 employees, earning $15,237m. Total value added by manufacturing in 2001 was $46,349m.

Labour

In 2003 total non-agricultural employment was 2,668,000. Employees by branch, 2003 (in 1,000): trade, transportation and utilities, 580; manufacturing, 414; government, 412; education and health services, 313; professional and business services, 287. The unemployment rate in 2003 was 5·8%.

COMMUNICATIONS

Roads

In 2003 there were 88,520 miles of roads (68,100 miles rural). There were 4,795,676 registered motor vehicles.

Rail

The state had (2002) 3,150 miles of track. There is a tramway in Memphis.

Civil Aviation

In 2005 Tennessee had 81 public airports; there were also 101 heliports. There were 10,494,164 passenger enplanements statewide in 2003. Memphis International handled 2,453,000 tonnes of freight in 2000—the most of any airport in the world.

SOCIAL INSTITUTIONS

Justice

The death penalty is authorized; there has been only one execution (in 2000) since 1976. In June 2003 there were 25,409 prison inmates.

Education

School attendance has been compulsory since 1925 and the employment of children under 16 years of age in workshops, factories or mines is illegal.

In 1995–96 there were 1,562 public schools with a net enrolment of 948,217 pupils; 49,627 teachers earned an average salary of $33,646. Total expenditure for operating schools was $4,266m. Tennessee has 49 accredited colleges and universities, 16 two-year colleges and 27 vocational schools. The universities include the University of Tennessee, Knoxville (founded 1794), with 25,337 students in 1996–97; Vanderbilt University, Nashville (1873) with 10,253; Tennessee State University (1912) with 8,643; the University of Tennessee at Chattanooga (1886) with 8,296; University of Memphis (1912) with 19,271; and Fisk University (1866) with 812.

Health

In 2002 there were 125 community hospitals with 20,400 beds. A total of 797,000 patients were admitted during the year.

Welfare

Medicare enrolment in July 2003 totalled 871,938. In 2002 a total of 1,732,381 people in Tennessee received Medicaid. In Dec. 2004 there were 1,061,981 Old-Age, Survivors, and Disability Insurance (OASDI) beneficiaries. A total of 190,862 people were receiving payments under Temporary Assistance for Needy Families (TANF) in Sept. 2004.

RELIGION

In 2000 there were 1,414,199 Southern Baptists, 393,994 United Methodists, 216,648 members of the Church of Christ, 183,161 Catholics, and followers of various other religions.

CULTURE

Tourism

In 2004, 43m. tourists spent $11,400m.

FURTHER READING

Statistical information: Center for Business and Economic Research, Univ. of Tennessee, Knoxville 37996. Publishes *Tennessee Statistical Abstract*

Tennessee Blue Book. Secretary of State, Nashville

Dykeman, W., *Tennessee.* Rev. ed., New York, 1984

State Library: State Library and Archives, Nashville.

Texas

KEY HISTORICAL EVENTS

A number of Indian tribes occupied the area before French and Spanish explorers arrived in the 16th century. In 1685 La Salle established a colony at Fort St Louis, but Texas was confirmed as Spanish in 1713. Spanish missions increased during the 18th century with San Antonio (1718) as their headquarters.

In 1820 a Virginian colonist, Moses Austin, obtained permission to begin a settlement in Texas. In 1821 the Spanish empire in the Americas came to an end, and Texas, together with Coahuila, formed a state of the newly independent Mexico. The Mexicans agreed to the Austin venture, and settlers of British and American descent came in.

The settlers became discontented with Mexican government and declared their independence in 1836. Warfare, including the siege of the Alamo fort, ended with the foundation of the independent Republic of Texas, which lasted until 1845. During this period the Texas Rangers were organized as a policing force and border patrol. Texas was annexed to the Union in Dec. 1845, as the Federal government feared its vulnerability to Mexican occupation. This led to war between Mexico and the USA from 1845 to 1848. In 1861 Texas left the Union and joined the southern states in the Civil War, being re-admitted in 1869. Ranching and cotton-growing were the main activities before the discovery of oil in 1901.

TERRITORY AND POPULATION

Texas is bounded north by Oklahoma, northeast by Arkansas, east by Louisiana, southeast by the Gulf of Mexico, south by Mexico and west by New Mexico. Land area, 261,797 sq. miles (678,051 sq. km). Census population, 1 April 2000, 20,851,820, an increase of 22·8% since 1990. July 2005 estimate, 22,859,968.

Population for five census years was:

	White	Black	American Indian	Asian	Total	Per sq. mile
1910	3,204,848	690,049	702	943	3,896,542	14·8
1930	4,967,172	854,964	1,001	1,578	5,824,715	22·1
			All others			
1980	11,197,663	1,710,250	1,320,470		14,228,383	54·2
			Asian/ other			
1990	12,774,762	2,021,632	65,877	2,124,239	16,986,510	64·9
2000	14,799,505	2,404,566	118,362	3,529,387	20,851,820	79·7

Of the total population in 2000, 10,498,910 were female, 14,965,061 were 18 years old or older, and 17,204,281 were urban. In 2000 the Hispanic population was 6,669,666, up from 4,339,905 in 1990 (an increase of 53·7%). The numerical increase was the second largest in the Hispanic population of any state in the USA, after California. Only New Mexico and California have a greater percentage of Hispanics in the state population.

The largest cities, with census population in 2000, are:

Houston	1,700,672	Pasadena	127,843
Dallas	1,036,309	Beaumont	118,289
San Antonio	991,861	Brownsville	117,326
El Paso	554,496	Mesquite	108,960
Austin (capital)	501,637	Waco	107,191
Fort Worth	459,085	Grand Prairie	103,913
Arlington	277,939	Abilene	100,661
Corpus Christi	266,958	Wichita Falls	98,356
Lubbock	193,194	Midland	95,003
Garland	187,439	Odessa	92,257
Irving	166,523	McAllen	91,184
Amarillo	163,569	Carrollton	90,934
Plano	153,624	San Angelo	87,980
Laredo	140,688		

Metropolitan statistical areas, 2000: Dallas–Fort Worth, 5,221,801; Houston–Galveston–Brazoria, 4,669,571; San Antonio, 1,592,383; Austin–San Marcos, 1,249,763.

SOCIAL STATISTICS

Statistics 2003: births, 377,476 (17·1 per 1,000 population); deaths (2002), 155,524 (7·1 per 1,000 population). 2002 infant mortality (per 1,000 live births), 6·4. 2001: marriages, 194,900 (9·4 per 1,000 population); divorces, 85,400 (4·1).

CLIMATE

Dallas, Jan. 45°F (7·2°C), July 84°F (28·9°C). Annual rainfall 38" (945 mm). El Paso, Jan. 44°F (6·7°C), July 81°F (27·2°C). Annual rainfall 9" (221 mm). Galveston, Jan. 54°F (12·2°C), July 84°F (28·9°C). Annual rainfall 46" (1,159 mm). Houston, Jan. 52°F (11·1°C), July 83°F (28·3°C). Annual rainfall 48" (1,200 mm). Texas belongs to the Central Plains climate zone (*see* UNITED STATES: Climate).

CONSTITUTION AND GOVERNMENT

The present constitution dates from 1876; it has been amended 432 times since. The state legislature consists of the Senate and House of Representatives. The Senate has 31 members elected for four-year terms. Half of the membership is elected every two years. The House has 150 members, elected for two-year terms during polling held in even-numbered years. The legislature meets in regular session for about five months every other year. The session begins in Jan. of odd-numbered years and lasts no more than 140 days (although special sessions can be called by the Governor). The Governor and Lieut.-Governor are elected for four years.

For the 109th Congress, which convened in Jan. 2005, Texas sends 32 members to the House of Representatives. It is represented in the Senate by Kay Hutchison (R. 1993–2007) and John Cornyn (R. 2002–09).

The capital is Austin. The state has 254 counties.

RECENT ELECTIONS

In the 2004 presidential election Bush polled 4,526,917 votes; Kerry, 2,832,704; Badnarik, 38,787.

CURRENT ADMINISTRATION

Governor: Rick Perry (R.), 2003–07 (salary: $115,345).

Lieut.-Governor: David Dewhurst (R.), 2003–07 ($7,200 plus legislature session salary).

Secretary of State: Roger Williams (R.), appointed Nov. 2004 ($117,516).

Government Website: http://www.state.tx.us

ECONOMY

Per capita personal income (2004) was $30,697.

Budget

In 2003 total state revenue was $82,621m. Total expenditure was $76,386m. (education, $26,995m.; public welfare, $18,498m.; highways, $5,266m.; correction, $3,201m.; hospitals, $2,833m.) Outstanding debt, in 2003, $14,616m.

Performance

In 2004 Gross State Product was $884,136m., ranking Texas third after California and New York. From the third quarter of 2001 the Texas economy experienced a sharp decline, with the strongest impact in high technology industries, leading to widespread job losses. A moderate recovery of the state economy began in 2003. The Texas Comptroller of Public Accounts' Index of Leading Economic Indicators grew by 5·3% between March 2003 and March 2004 (the largest percentage increase since June 1994). In addition, the Texas Coincident Index (based on employment, Gross State Product and the unemployment rate) has been improving since 2003, and the regional Consumer Confidence Index increased about 52% between March 2003 and March 2004. Texas is a major oil producer and exporter. With the surge in oil prices in 2004, the state stands to benefit from increases in oil company profitability, royalties and tax revenues.

Banking and Finance

In 2002 there were 715 financial institutions in Texas insured by the US Federal Deposit Insurance Corporation, with assets worth $216,900m. They had 4,980 offices with total deposits of $256,600m.

At Dec. 2003 there were 351 state-chartered banks operating in Texas, with total assets of $121,970m. The largest banks were International Bank of Commerce, Laredo (with assets of $5,294·2m.), Texas State Bank, McAllen ($4,215·6m.), Sterling Bank, Houston ($3,110·1m.), Prosperity Bank, El Campo ($2,395·0m.) and PlainsCapital Bank, Lubbock ($2,061·8m.).

ENERGY AND NATURAL RESOURCES

Oil and Gas

Texas is the leading producer in the USA of both oil and natural gas. In 2001 it produced 23% of the country's oil and 26% of its natural gas. Production, 2001: crude petroleum, 424m. bbls. (value, $9,933m.); natural gas, 6,520bn. cu. ft (value, $26,978m.). Natural gasoline, butane and propane gases are also produced.

Water

The total area covered by water is approximately 6,784 sq. miles.

Minerals

Minerals include helium, crude gypsum, granite and sandstone, salt and cement. Total value of domestic non-fuel mineral products in 2003 was $2,030m.

Agriculture

Texas is one of the most important agricultural states. In 2002 it had 230,000 farms covering 131m. acres; average farm was of 570 acres. Both the number of farms and the total area covered are the highest in the USA. In 2002 land and buildings were valued at $768 per acre. Large-scale commercial farms, highly mechanized, dominate in Texas; farms of 1,000 acres or more in number far exceed that of any other state, but small-scale farming persists. Soil erosion is a serious problem in some parts.

Production: corn, barley, beans, cotton, hay, oats, peanuts, rye, sorghum, soybeans, sunflowers, wheat, oranges, grapefruit, peaches, sweet potatoes. Farm income, 2002, from crops was $4,577m.; from livestock, $8,088m. The net farm income in 2002 was $3,686m.

The state has an important livestock industry, leading in the number of all cattle (13·98m.) and sheep (1·03m.); it also had 0·31m. milch cows and 0·95m. swine in 2002.

Forestry

There were 17,149,000 acres of forested land in 2002, with 608,000 acres of national forest.

INDUSTRY

In 2001 the state's 21,370 manufacturing establishments had 948,000 employees, earning $37,288m. Total value added by manufacturing in 2001 was $120,086m.

Labour

Texas has a labour code (adopted 1993) which includes laws concerning protection of labourers, employer-employee relations, employment services and unemployment, and workers' compensation.

In 2003 total non-agricultural employment was 9,373,000. Employees by branch, 2003 (in 1,000): trade, transportation and utilities, 1,928; government, 1,648; education and health services, 1,119; professional and business services, 1,044; manufacturing, 901. The unemployment rate in 2003 was 6·8%.

INTERNATIONAL TRADE

Imports and Exports

Exports in 2003 totalled $98·8bn. (an increase of 3·6% from 2002), ranking Texas as the leading US state by export revenue for the second consecutive year. The main export category is computer and electronic products, which accounted for 29% of total exports in 2003. Other major exports are chemicals, non-electrical machinery, transportation equipment, and petroleum and coal products. The leading destinations for exports in 2003 were Mexico (42%), Canada (11%) and China (3%). Asian and Pacific Rim countries accounted for 35% of exports and the European Union (principally the UK) for 2%. Texas is a major producer of agricultural products with exports valued at $2·6bn. in 2003.

COMMUNICATIONS

Roads

In 2003 there were 301,989 miles of roads comprising 83,288 miles of urban road and 218,701 miles of rural road. There were 14,888,780 registered motor vehicles and 3,675 traffic accident fatalities.

Rail

In 2002 there were almost 12,000 miles of mainline track, the most in any US state. This included 11,377 miles (2000) Class I trackage.

Civil Aviation

There were 58,371,217 passenger enplanements in 2003. In 2002 Texas had 295 public and 1,073 private airports, 429 heliports and 8 stolports. In 2003 a total of 52,465,427 passengers (48,036,422 domestic and 4,429,005 international) embarked and disembarked at Dallas/Fort Worth International airport. It handled 736,023 tons of freight in 2003. The Houston Airport System (HAS) recorded a total of 42,034,978 passengers arriving and departing that year; of these, George Bush Intercontinental airport served 34,151,342 (28,530,960 domestic and 5,620,382 international). HAS cargo shipments in 2003 reached 335,753 tons in 2003.

Shipping

The port of Houston, connected by the Houston Ship Channel (50 miles long) with the Gulf of Mexico, is a large cotton market. Total cargo handled by all ports in 2002 was 442,251,000 tons. There were 834 miles of inland waterways in 2000.

SOCIAL INSTITUTIONS

Justice

In June 2003 there were 164,222 prison inmates. Between 1977 and 2005 Texas was responsible for 355 of the USA's 1,004 executions (more than three times as many as any other state), although it was not until 1982 that Texas reintroduced the death penalty. In 2005, 19 people were executed in Texas; in 2000, 40 people had been executed, the highest number in a year in any state since the authorities began keeping records in 1930.

Education

School attendance is compulsory from six to 18 years of age.

In the 2001–02 school year there were 7,646 public elementary and secondary schools with 4,163,447 enrolled pupils; there were 282,583 teachers. Total expenditure on public schools in 2000–01 was $26,547m.

In 2003 there were 142 higher education institutions (35 public universities, 38 independent colleges and universities, 50 public community college districts, four campuses of the Texas State Technical College System, three public Lamar state colleges, nine public health-related institutions, one independent medical school and two independent junior colleges). The headcount enrolment in higher education in 2002 was 1,102,504 students, including 455,719 at public universities, 114,082 at independent universities and colleges and 505,212 at public community and state colleges. Enrolment in autumn 2003 was an estimated 1·14m.

Public universities and student enrolment, 2002:

Institutions	Students
University of Texas System	153,404
Texas A&M University System	96,729
Texas State University System	57,016
University of Houston System	54,910
Texas Technical University System	36,272
University of North Texas System	30,183
Stephen F. Austin State University, Nacogdoches	11,312
Texas Southern University, Houston	9,739
Midwestern State University, Wichita Falls	6,157

Independent colleges and universities with the largest student enrolments, 2002:

Institutions	Students
Baylor University, Waco	14,159
Southern Methodist University, Dallas	10,955
Texas Christian University, Fort Worth	8,074
Wayland Baptist University, Plainview	5,773
University of St Thomas, Houston	5,116
William Marsh Rice University, Houston	4,784
Abilene Christian University, Abilene	4,668
Dallas Baptist University, Dallas	4,417

Health

In 2002 there were 416 community hospitals with 56,800 beds. A total of 2,534,000 patients were admitted during the year.

Welfare

Medicare enrolment in July 2003 totalled 2,390,053. In 2002 a total of 2,952,569 people in Texas received Medicaid. In Dec. 2004 there were 2,859,342 Old-Age, Survivors, and Disability Insurance (OASDI) beneficiaries. A total of 234,680 people were receiving payments under Temporary Assistance for Needy Families (TANF) in Sept. 2004.

RELIGION

Religious bodies represented include Roman Catholics, Baptists, Methodists, Churches of Christ, Lutherans, Presbyterians and Episcopalians.

CULTURE

Tourism

In 2000 there were 1,169,000 overseas visitors to Texas, generating $705·2m. in tax receipts. In 2002 there were 17,090,000 visitors to state parks and recreation areas, raising $14,860,000 in revenue.

FURTHER READING

Texas Almanac. Dallas. Biennial

Kingston, M., *Texas Almanac's Political History of Texas.* Austin, 1992
Kraemer, R. and Newell, C., *Essentials of Texas Politics.* 5th ed. Austin, 1992
Marten, James, *Texas.* [Bibliography] ABC-Clio, Oxford and Santa Barbara (CA), 1992

Legislative Reference Library: Box 12488, Capitol Station, Austin, Texas 78711-2488.

Utah

KEY HISTORICAL EVENTS

Spanish Franciscan missionaries explored the area in 1776, finding Shoshoni Indians. Spain laid claim to Utah and designated it part of Spanish Mexico. As such it passed into the hands of the Mexican Republic when Mexico rebelled against Spain and gained independence in 1821.

In 1848, at the conclusion of war between the USA and Mexico, the USA received Utah along with other southwestern territory. Settlers had already arrived in 1847 when the Mormons (the Church of Jesus Christ of Latter-day Saints) arrived, having been driven on by local hostility in Ohio, Missouri and Illinois. Led by Brigham Young, they entered the Great Salt Valley and colonized it. In 1849 they applied for statehood but were refused. In 1850 Utah and Nevada were joined as one Territory. The Mormon community continued to ask for statehood but this was only granted in 1896, after they had renounced polygamy and disbanded their People's Party.

Mining, especially of copper, and livestock farming were the base of the economy. Settlement had to adapt to desert conditions, and the main centres of population were in the narrow belt between the Wasatch Mountains and the Great Salt Lake. Salt Lake City, the capital, was founded in 1847 and laid out according to Joseph Smith's plan for the city of Zion. It was the centre of the Mormons' provisional 'State of Deseret' and Territorial capital from 1856 until 1896, except briefly in 1858 when federal forces occupied it during conflict between territorial and Union governments.

TERRITORY AND POPULATION

Utah is bounded north by Idaho and Wyoming, east by Colorado, south by Arizona and west by Nevada. Land area, 82,144 sq. miles (212,752 sq. km). The Bureau of Indian Affairs in 1990 administered 2,317,604 acres, 2,284,766 acres of which were allotted to Indian tribes.

Census population, 1 April 2000, 2,233,169, an increase of 29·6% since 1990. July 2005 estimate, 2,469,585.

Population at five federal censuses was:

	White	Black	American Indian	Asiatic	Total	Per sq. mile
1910	366,583	1,144	3,123	2,501	373,851	4·5
1930	499,967	1,108	2,869	3,903	507,847	6·2
1980	1,382,550	9,225	19,256	15,076	1,461,037	17·7
1990	1,615,845	11,576	24,283	25,696	1,722,850	21·0
2000	1,992,975	17,657	29,684	37,108	2,233,169	27·2

Of the total population in 2000, 1,119,031 were male, 1,514,471 were 18 years old or older and 1,970,344 were urban. In 2000 the Hispanic population was 201,559, up from 84,597 in 1990 (an increase of 138·3%).

The largest cities are Salt Lake City, with a population (census, 2000) of 181,743; West Valley City, 108,896; Provo, 105,166; Sandy City, 88,418; Orem, 84,324; Ogden, 77,226.

SOCIAL STATISTICS

Births in 2003 were 49,860 (21·2 per 1,000 population—the highest rate in any US state); deaths (2002), 13,116 (5·7 per 1,000 population). 2002 infant mortality rate (per 1,000 live births), 5·6. 2001: marriages, 23,200; divorces, 9,700. Fertility rate, 2000, 2·6 births per woman (the highest of any American state).

CLIMATE

Salt Lake City, Jan. 29°F (–1·7°C), July 77°F (25°C). Annual rainfall 16" (401 mm). Utah belongs to the Mountain States climate region (see UNITED STATES: Climate).

CONSTITUTION AND GOVERNMENT

Utah adopted its present constitution in 1896 (now with 61 amendments). The Legislature consists of a Senate (in part renewed every two years) of 29 members, elected for four years, and of a House of Representatives of 75 members elected for two years. It sits annually in Jan. The Governor is elected for four years. The constitution provides for the initiative and referendum.

For the 109th Congress, which convened in Jan. 2005, Utah sends three members to the House of Representatives. It is represented in the Senate by Orrin Hatch (R. 1977–2007) and Robert Bennett (R. 1993–2011).

The capital is Salt Lake City. There are 29 counties in the state.

RECENT ELECTIONS

In the 2004 presidential election Bush polled 663,742 votes (71·5% of the vote—Bush's best result); Kerry, 241,199; Nader, 11,305.

CURRENT ADMINISTRATION

Governor: Jon Huntsman, Jr (R.), 2005–09 (salary: $104,600).
Lieut.-Governor: Gary R. Herbert (R.), 2005–09 ($81,000).

Government Website: http://www.utah.gov

ECONOMY

Per capita income (2004) was $26,946.

Budget

In 2003 total state revenue was $11,534m. Total expenditure was $10,252m. (education, $4,190m.; public welfare, $1,758m.;

highways, $771m.; government administration, $558m.; hospitals, $533m.) Outstanding debt, in 2003, $5,064m.

Performance

Gross State Product in 2004 was $82,611m., ranking Utah 33rd in the United States.

ENERGY AND NATURAL RESOURCES

Water

The total area covered by water is approximately 2,755 sq. miles.

Minerals

The principal minerals are: copper, gold, magnesium, petroleum, lead, silver and zinc. The state also has natural gas, clays, tungsten, molybdenum, uranium and phosphate rock. The value of domestic non-fuel mineral production in 2003 was $1,260m.

Agriculture

In 2002 Utah had 15,000 farms covering 11·6m. acres. In 2002 about 2·1m. acres were crop land, about 602,300 acres pasture and about 1·1m. acres had irrigation. In 2002 the average farm was of 773 acres and the average value per acre was $756.

Farm income, 2002, from crops, $249m. and from livestock, $808m. The net farm income in 2002 was $291m. The principal crops are: barley, wheat (spring and winter), oats, potatoes, hay (alfalfa, sweet clover and lespedeza) and maize. Livestock, 2002: cattle, 877,000; pigs, 670,000; sheep, 311,000; poultry, 3·4m.

Forestry

Forest area, 2002, was 15,676,000 acres and included 5,605,000 acres of national forest.

INDUSTRY

Leading manufactures by value added are primary metals, ordinances and transport, food, fabricated metals and machinery, and petroleum products. In 2001 Utah's 3,001 manufacturing establishments had 120,000 employees, earning $4,241m. Total value added by manufacturing in 2001 was $11,783m.

Labour

Utah's total non-agricultural employment in 2003 was 1,074,000. Employees by branch, 2003 (in 1,000): trade, transportation and utilities, 214; government, 197; professional and business services, 132; education and health services, 118; manufacturing, 112. The unemployment rate in 2003 was 5·6%.

COMMUNICATIONS

Roads

In 2003 there were 42,718 miles of roads (34,527 miles rural). There were 2,006,423 registered motor vehicles.

Rail

In 2004 Utah had approximately 1,400 miles of freight railroad track. There was no dedicated passenger rail trackage, although the Utah Transit Authority is preparing a commuter rail service.

Civil Aviation

There is an international airport at Salt Lake City. There were 9,029,202 passenger enplanements statewide in 2003.

SOCIAL INSTITUTIONS

Justice

In June 2003 there were 5,594 prison inmates. The death penalty is authorized; the last execution took place in 1999.

Education

School attendance is compulsory for children from six to 18 years of age. There are 40 school districts. Teachers' salaries,

1998–99, averaged $36,030. There were 475,974 pupils and 24,514 teachers in public elementary and secondary schools in the same year. In 1999 education expenditure by state and local government was $2,432·3m.

In autumn 1999 there were 153,884 enrolled in colleges and universities. The University of Utah (1850) (25,788 students in 1999) is in Salt Lake City; the Utah State University (1890) (20,865) is in Logan; Weber State University, Ogden (15,444); Southern Utah University, Cedar City (6,025); The Mormon Church maintains the Brigham Young University at Provo (1875) with 29,217 students. Other colleges include: Westminster College, Salt Lake City (2,250); College of Eastern Utah, Price (2,688); Snow College, Ephraim (4,081); Dixie State College, St George (6,191); Utah Valley State College, Orem (20,062); Salt Lake Community College, Salt Lake City (21,273).

Health
In 2002 there were 42 community hospitals with 4,400 beds. A total of 206,000 patients were admitted during the year.

Welfare
Medicare enrolment in July 2003 totalled 220,221. In 2002 a total of 274,707 people in Utah received Medicaid. In Dec. 2004 there were 263,267 Old-Age, Survivors, and Disability Insurance (OASDI) beneficiaries. A total of 23,112 people were receiving payments under Temporary Assistance for Needy Families (TANF) in Sept. 2004.

RELIGION
Latter-day Saints (Mormons) numbered 1,483,858 in 2000. World membership was 12,276,000 in 2004. The President of the Mormon Church is Gordon B. Hinckley (born 1910). The Roman Catholic church and most Protestant denominations are represented.

FURTHER READING
Statistical information: Bureau of Economic and Business Research, Univ. of Utah, 401 Kendall D. Garff Bldg., Salt Lake City 84112. Publishes *Statistical Abstract of Utah.*

Utah Foundation. *Statistical Review of Government in Utah.* Salt Lake City, 1991

Vermont

KEY HISTORICAL EVENTS
The original Indian hunting grounds of the Green Mountains and lakes was explored by the Frenchman Samuel de Champlain in 1609 who reached Lake Champlain on the northwest border. The first attempt at permanent settlement was also French, on Isle la Motte in 1666. In 1763 the British gained the area from the French by the Treaty of Paris. The Treaty, which also brought peace with the Indian allies of the French, opened the way for settlement, but in a mountain state transport was slow and difficult. Montpelier, the state capital from 1805, was chartered as a township site in 1781 to command the main pass through the Green Mountains.

During the War of Independence Vermont declared itself an independent state, to avoid being taken over by New Hampshire and New York. In 1791 it became the 14th state of the Union.

Most early settlers were New Englanders of British and Protestant descent. After 1812 a granite-quarrying industry grew around the town of Barre, attracting immigrant workers from Italy and Scandinavia. French Canadians also settled in Winooski. When textile and engineering industries developed in the 19th century these brought more European workers.

Vermont saw the only Civil War action north of Pennsylvania, when a Confederate raiding party attacked from Canada in 1864.

During the 20th century the textile and engineering industries have declined but paper and lumber industries flourish. Settlement is still mainly rural or in small towns, and farming is pastoral.

TERRITORY AND POPULATION
Vermont is bounded in the north by Canada, east by New Hampshire, south by Massachusetts and west by New York. Land area, 9,250 sq. miles (23,957 sq. km). Census population, 1 April 2000, 608,827, an increase of 8·2% since 1990. July 2005 estimate, 623,050.

Population at five census years was:

	White	Black	Indian	Asiatic	Total	Per sq. mile
1910	354,298	1,621	26	11	355,956	39·0
1930	358,966	568	36	41	359,611	38·8
1980	506,736	1,135	984	1,355	511,456	55·1
1990	555,088	1,951	1,696	3,215[1]	562,758	60·8
2000	589,208	3,063	2,420	5,358[1]	608,827	65·8

[1]Includes Pacific Islander.

Of the total population in 2000, 310,490 were female, 461,304 were 18 years old or older and 376,379 (61·8%) were rural (67·8% in 1990). Vermont still has the highest rural population percentage of any state in the USA. In 2000 the Hispanic population was 5,504, the lowest total of any state. However, this figure represents a rise of 50·3% compared to the 1990 census figure of 3,661. The largest cities are Burlington, with an estimated population (2002) of 38,885; Essex, 18,863; Rutland City, 17,309; Colchester, 17,245.

SOCIAL STATISTICS
Births, 2003, were 6,589 (10·6 per 1,000 population). 2002: deaths, 5,075 (8·2 per 1,000 population); marriages, 6,011; civil unions, 1,707; divorces, 2,653. Infant deaths, 2002, 4·4 per 1,000 live births.

CLIMATE
Burlington, Jan. 17°F (–8·3°C), July 70°F (21·1°C). Annual rainfall 33" (820 mm). Vermont belongs to the New England climate zone (*see* UNITED STATES: Climate).

CONSTITUTION AND GOVERNMENT
The constitution was adopted in 1793 and has since been amended. Amendments are proposed by two-thirds vote of the Senate every four years, and must be accepted by two sessions of the legislature; they are then submitted to popular vote. The state Legislature, consisting of a Senate of 30 members and a House of Representatives of 150 members (both elected for two years), meets in Jan. every year. The Governor and Lieut.-Governor are elected for two years. Electors are all citizens who possess certain residential qualifications and have taken the freeman's oath set forth in the constitution.

For the 109th Congress, which convened in Jan. 2005, Vermont sends one member to the House of Representatives. It is represented in the Senate by Patrick Leahy (D. 1975–2011) and Jim Jeffords (R. 1989–2001, ind. 2001–07).

The capital is Montpelier (estimated population of 8,028 in 2002). There are 14 counties and 251 cities, towns and other administrative divisions.

RECENT ELECTIONS
In the 2004 presidential election Kerry polled 184,067 votes; Bush, 121,180; Nader, 4,494.

CURRENT ADMINISTRATION

Governor: James Douglas (R.), 2005–07 (salary: $143,977).
  Lieut.-Governor: Brian E. Dubie (R.), 2005–07 ($61,116).
   Secretary of State: Deborah L. Markowitz (D.), 2005–07 ($91,294).

Government Website: http://vermont.gov

ECONOMY

Per capita income (2004) was $31,737.

Budget
In fiscal year 2004 total state revenue (prior to budget adjustment) was $3,574m. Major appropriations: education, $1,388m.; human services, $1,280m.; transportation, $354m.; protection, $188m. Outstanding debt in 2003 was $448m.

Performance
Gross State Product was $21,921m. in 2004, ranking Vermont 50th in the United States.

Banking and Finance
In 2003 there were 19 banking institutions domiciled in Vermont, and 16 out-of-state banks operating.

ENERGY AND NATURAL RESOURCES

Water
The total area covered by water is approximately 365 sq. miles. There are 46 utility-owned hydro-sites and 35 independently owned sites providing about 10% of Vermont's energy.

Minerals
Stone, chiefly granite, marble and slate, is the leading mineral produced in Vermont, contributing about 60% of the total value of mineral products. Other products include asbestos, talc, sand and gravel. Value of domestic non-fuel mineral products in 2003 was $73m.

Agriculture
Agriculture is the most important industry. In 2002 the state had 6,600 farms covering 1·34m. acres; the average farm was of 203 acres and the average value per acre of land and buildings was $2,051. In 2002 farm income from crops, $76m.; from livestock and products, $400m. The net farm income in 2002 was $105m. The 1,415 dairy farms produced about 2·6bn. lb of milk in 2002. The chief agricultural crops are greenhouse products, maple products, hay, apples and silage. In 2002 Vermont had 255,000 cattle and calves and 2,000 hogs and pigs.

Forestry
The state is 78% forest, with 17% in public ownership. In 2002 Vermont had 4,618,000 acres of forested land with 337,000 acres of national forest. State-owned forests, parks, fish and game areas (1997), 345,000 acres; municipally owned, 71,500 acres. In 2002 the harvest was 222·4m. bd ft and 171,395 cords of pulpwood.

INDUSTRY

In 2001 the state's 1,180 manufacturing establishments had 48,000 employees, earning $1,825m. Total value added by manufacturing in 2001 was $5,078m.

Labour
In 2003 service industries, including trade, employed 188,760; government, 49,757; manufacturing, 40,697; construction, 14,894. The unemployment rate in 2003 was 4·6%.

COMMUNICATIONS

Roads
In 2003 there were 14,360 miles of roads comprising 1,383 miles of urban road and 12,977 miles of rural road. Motor vehicle registrations totalled 516,071.

Rail
There were, in 2001, 747 miles of railway, 391 miles of which are state owned.

Civil Aviation
There were 17 airports in 2003, of which ten were state operated, two municipally owned and five private. Some are only open in summer. There were 548,332 passenger enplanements statewide in 2003.

Telecommunications
In 2003 there were 12 telephone companies.

SOCIAL INSTITUTIONS

Justice
Prisons and centres had on average, in 2004, 1,875 inmates (including those incarcerated in Virginia for cost-cutting reasons). The death penalty was officially abolished in 1987 but effectively in 1964.

Education
School attendance during the full school term is compulsory for children from seven to 16 years of age, unless they have completed the 10th grade or undergo approved home instruction. In 2003–04 the public elementary and secondary schools had 99,104 pupils and 9,004 teachers. Average teacher's salary was $43,009. State and local governments expenditure on public schools, $944m.

In 2003–04 the University of Vermont (1791), in Burlington, had 10,940 students; Norwich University (1834, founded as the American Literary, Scientific and Military Academy in 1819), had 2,183; St Michael's College (1904), 1,945 (full time undergraduates only); there are four other state colleges and 15 other private schools of higher education.

Health
In 2004 the state had 19 hospitals and health centres.

Welfare
In 2003 Social Services provided approximately $2·4m. to 500 families and 12,600 individuals. Medicare enrolment in July 2003 totalled 92,724. In 2002 a total of 153,731 people in Vermont received Medicaid. In Dec. 2004 there were 109,983 Old-Age, Survivors, and Disability Insurance (OASDI) beneficiaries. A total of 12,217 people were receiving payments under Temporary Assistance for Needy Families (TANF) in Sept. 2004.

RELIGION

The principal denominations are Roman Catholic, United Church of Christ, United Methodist, Protestant Episcopal, Baptist and Unitarian–Universalist.

CULTURE

Broadcasting
In 2004 there were 56 radio stations, 11 television stations and 27 cable TV systems.

Press
There were ten dailies and 44 weekly newspapers in 2004.

FURTHER READING

Statistical information: Office of Policy Research and Coordination, Montpelier 05602
Legislative Directory. Secretary of State, Montpelier. Biennial
Vermont Annual Financial Report. Auditor of Accounts, Montpelier. Annual
Vermont Atlas and Gazetteer, Rev. ed., Freeport, 1983
Vermont Year-Book, formerly *Walton's Register.* Chester. Annual

State Library: Vermont Dept. of Libraries, Montpelier.

Virginia

KEY HISTORICAL EVENTS

In 1607 a British colony was founded at Jamestown, on a peninsula in the James River, to grow tobacco. The area was marshy and unhealthy but the colony survived and in 1619 introduced a form of representative government. The tobacco plantations expanded and African slaves were imported. Jamestown was later abandoned, but tobacco-growing continued and spread through the eastern part of the territory.

In 1624 control of the colony passed from the Virginia Company of London to the Crown. Growth was rapid during the 17th and 18th centuries. The movement for American independence was strong in Virginia; George Washington and Thomas Jefferson were both Virginians, and crucial battles of the War of Independence were fought there.

When the Union was formed, Virginia became one of the original states, but with reservations regarding the constitution because of its attachment to slave-owning. In 1831 there was a slave rebellion. The tobacco plantations began to decline, and plantation owners turned to the breeding of slaves. While the eastern plantation lands seceded from the Union in 1861, the small farmers and miners of the western hills refused to secede and remained in the Union as West Virginia.

Richmond, the capital, became the capital of the Confederacy. Much of the Civil War's decisive conflict took place in Virginia, with considerable damage to the economy. After the war the position of the black population was little improved. Blacks remained without political or civil rights until the 1960s.

TERRITORY AND POPULATION

Virginia is bounded northwest by West Virginia, northeast by Maryland and the District of Columbia, east by the Atlantic, south by North Carolina and Tennessee and west by Kentucky. Land area, 39,594 sq. miles (102,548 sq. km). Census population, 1 April 2000, 7,078,515, an increase of 14·4% since 1990. July 2005 estimate, 7,567,465.

Population for five federal census years was:

	White	Black	Indian	Asian/Other	Total	Per sq. mile
1910	1,389,809	671,096	539	168	2,061,612	51·2
1930	1,770,441	650,165	779	466	2,421,851	60·7
			All others			
1980	4,230,000	1,008,311	108,517		5,346,818	134·7
1990	4,791,739	1,162,994	15,282	217,343	6,187,358	155·9
2000	5,120,110	1,390,293	21,172	546,940	7,078,515	178·8

Of the total population in 2000, 3,606,620 were female, 5,340,253 were 18 years old or older and 5,169,955 were urban. In 2000 the Hispanic population was 329,540, up from 160,288 in 1990 (an increase of 105·6%).

The population (2003 estimates) of the principal cities was: Virginia Beach, 439,467; Norfolk, 241,727; Chesapeake, 210,834; Richmond, 194,729; Arlington CDP, 187,873; Newport News, 181,647; Hampton, 146,878; Alexandria, 128,923.

SOCIAL STATISTICS

In 2003 there were 101,254 births (13·7 per 1,000 population). In 2002 there were 57,196 deaths (7·8 per 1,000 population). 2002 infant mortality (per 1,000 live births), 7·4. 2001: marriages, 63,400 (9·0 per 1,000 population); divorces, 30,200 (4·3).

CLIMATE

Average temperatures in Jan. are 41°F in the Tidewater coastal area and 32°F in the Blue Ridge mountains; July averages, 78°F and 68°F respectively. Precipitation averages 36" in the Shenandoah valley and 44" in the south. Snowfall is 5–10" in the Tidewater and 25–30" in the western mountains. Norfolk, Jan. 41°F (5°C), July 79°F (26·1°C). Annual rainfall 46" (1,145 mm). Virginia belongs to the Atlantic Coast climate zone (see UNITED STATES: Climate).

CONSTITUTION AND GOVERNMENT

The present constitution became effective in 1971. The General Assembly consists of a Senate of 40 members, elected for four years, and a House of Delegates of 100 members, elected for two years. It sits annually in Jan. The Governor and Lieut.-Governor are elected for four years.

For the 109th Congress, which convened in Jan. 2005, Virginia sends 11 members to the House of Representatives. It is represented in the Senate by John Warner (R. 1979–2009) and George Allen (R. 2001–07).

The state capital is Richmond; the state contains 95 counties and 40 independent cities.

RECENT ELECTIONS

In the 2004 presidential election Bush polled 1,716,959 votes; Kerry, 1,454,742; Badnarik, 11,032.

CURRENT ADMINISTRATION

Governor: Timothy M. Kaine (D.), 2006–10 (salary: $175,000).

Lieut.-Governor: William T. Bolling (R.), appointed Nov. 2005 ($36,321; part time).

Secretary of the Commonwealth: David G. LeBlanc (D.), appointed Dec. 2005 ($141,265).

Government Website: http://www.virginia.gov

ECONOMY

Per capita personal income (2004) was $36,175.

Budget

In 2003 total state revenue was $28,185m. Total expenditure was $29,129m. (education, $9,777m.; public welfare, $5,235m.; highways, $2,588m.; hospitals, $1,887m.; correction, $1,194m.) Outstanding debt, in 2003, $13,530m.

Performance

Gross State Product in 2004 was $329,332m., ranking Virginia 12th in the United States.

ENERGY AND NATURAL RESOURCES

Water

The total area covered by water is approximately 3,180 sq. miles.

Minerals

Coal is the most important mineral, with output (2003) of 31,596,000 short tons. Lead and zinc ores, stone, sand and gravel, lime and titanium ore are also produced. Total domestic non-fuel mineral output was valued at $727m. in 2003.

Agriculture

In 2003 there were 47,500 farms with an area of 8·6m. acres; the average farm had 181 acres, and the average value per acre was $2,700. Farm income, 2002, from crops, $722m.; and from livestock and livestock products, $1,451m. The net farm income in 2002 was $504m. The chief crops are tobacco, soybeans, peanuts, winter wheat, maize, tomatoes, apples, potatoes and sweet potatoes. Livestock, 2002: cattle and calves, 1·62m.; milch cows, 115,000; sheep and lambs, 72,000; hogs and pigs, 409,300; turkeys, 20m.; broilers, 266·1m.

Forestry

Forests covered 16,074,000 acres in 2002 (63·4% of the total land area), including 1,626,000 acres of national forest.

Fisheries

Commercial catch (2002) totalled 442·5m. lb of fish, worth $123·3m.

INDUSTRY

The manufacture of cigars and cigarettes, of rayon and allied products, and the building of ships lead in value of products. In 2001 the state's 5,804 manufacturing establishments had 344,000 employees, earning $12,574m. Total value added by manufacturing in 2001 was $53,043m.

Labour

In 2004 Virginia's total non-agricultural employment was 3,595,100. Employees by branch, 2003 (in 1,000): government, 639; trade, transportation and utilities, 635; professional and business services, 549; education and health services, 369; manufacturing, 305. The unemployment rate in 2003 was 4·1%.

COMMUNICATIONS

Roads

In 2003 there were 71,243 miles of roads (50,231 miles rural). There were 6,346,009 registered motor vehicles.

Rail

In 2003 there were 3,399 miles of track including commuter services to Washington, D.C.

Civil Aviation

There are international airports at Norfolk, Dulles, Richmond, Arlington and Newport News. There were 18,785,561 passenger enplanements statewide in 2003.

SOCIAL INSTITUTIONS

Justice

In June 2003 there were 34,733 prison inmates. The death penalty is authorized. Between 1977 and 2005 there were 95 executions in Virginia, after Texas the most of any state. There were five executions in 2004 but none in 2005.

Education

Elementary and secondary instruction is free, and for ages 6–17 attendance is compulsory.

In 2000–01 there were 135 school districts. In 2002–03 there were 723,000 pupils in primary schools (55,000 teaching positions) and 422,000 pupils in secondary schools (39,000 teaching positions). Average annual salaries in 2002–03 for elementary teaching positions were $41,839 and for secondary teaching positions $43,850. Total expenditure on education, 2003–04, was $9,454m.

In 2001–02 there were 100 degree-granting education institutions (61 private) including:

Founded	Name and place of college	Staff 1994–95	Students 1994
1693	College of William and Mary, Williamsburg (State)	479	7,547
1749	Washington and Lee University, Lexington	166	1,990
1776	Hampden-Sydney College, Hampden-Sydney (Pres.)	84	970
1819	University of Virginia, Charlottesville (State)	987	21,421
1832	Randolph-Macon College, Ashland (Methodist)	79	1,093
1832	University of Richmond, Richmond (Baptist)	228	4,258
1838	Virginia Commonwealth University, Richmond	777	21,523
1839	Virginia Military Institute Lexington (State)	97	1,179
1865	Virginia Union University, Richmond	83	1,525
1868	Hampton University	303	5,769

Founded	Name and place of college	Staff 1994–95	Students 1994
1872	Virginia Polytechnic Institute and State University	1,466	25,842
1882	Virginia State University, Petersburg	168	4,007
1908	James Madison University, Harrisonburg	520	11,680
1910	Radford University (State)	394	9,105
1930	Old Dominion University, Norfolk	634	16,490
1956	George Mason University (State)	677	21,774

Health

In 2003 there were 86 community hospitals with 17,241 beds. A total of 746,686 patients were admitted during the year.

Welfare

Medicare enrolment in July 2003 totalled 946,470. In 2002 a total of 665,203 people in Virginia received Medicaid. In Dec. 2004 there were 1,114,705 Old-Age, Survivors, and Disability Insurance (OASDI) beneficiaries. A total of 28,400 people were receiving payments under Temporary Assistance for Needy Families (TANF) in Sept. 2004.

RELIGION

The principal churches are the Baptist, Methodist, Protestant Episcopal, Roman Catholic and Presbyterian.

CULTURE

Tourism

Tourists spent over $14bn. in 2002, contributing 4·9% to Gross State Product.

FURTHER READING

Statistical information: Cooper Center for Public Service, Univ. of Virginia, 918 Emmet St. N., Suite 300, Charlottesville 22903-4832. Publishes *Virginia Statistical Abstract.—Population Estimates of Virginia Cities and Counties.*

Rubin, L. D. Jr., *Virginia: a Bicentennial History.* Norris, 1977

Salmon, E. J. and Campbell Jr., E. D. C., *The Hornbook of Virginia History: A Ready-Reference Guide the Old Dominion's People, Places, and Past.* Library of Virginia, Richmond, 1994

State Library: Library of Virginia, Richmond 23219.

Washington State

KEY HISTORICAL EVENTS

The strongest Indian tribes in the 18th century were Chinook, Nez Percé, Salish and Yakima. The area was designated by European colonizers as part of the Oregon Country. Between 1775 and 1800 it had been claimed by explorers for Spain, Britain and the USA; the dispute between the two latter nations was not settled until 1846.

The first small white settlements were Indian missions and fur-trading posts. In the 1840s American settlers began to push westwards along the Oregon Trail, making a speedy solution of the dispute with Britain necessary. When this was achieved the whole area was organized as the Oregon Territory in 1848, and Washington was made a separate Territory in 1853.

Apart from trapping and fishing, the important industry was logging, mainly to supply building timbers to the new settlements of California. After 1870 the westward extension of railways helped to stimulate settlement. Statehood was granted in 1889. The early population was composed mainly of Americans from neighbouring states to the east, and Canadians. Scandinavian immigrants followed. Seattle, the chief city, was laid out in 1853 as a saw-milling town and named after the Indian chief who had ceded the land and befriended the settlers. It grew as a port during the Alaskan and Yukon gold-rushes of the 1890s. The economy thrived on exploiting the Columbia River for hydro-electric power.

TERRITORY AND POPULATION

Washington is bounded north by Canada, east by Idaho, south by Oregon with the Columbia River forming most of the boundary, and west by the Pacific. Land area, 66,544 sq. miles (172,348 sq. km). Lands owned by the federal government, 2003, were 13,246,559 acres or 31·0% of the total area. Census population, 1 April 2000, 5,894,121, an increase of 21·1% since 1990. July 2005 estimate, 6,287,759.

Population in five federal census years was:

	White	Black	American Indian	Asian/Other	Total	Per sq. mile
1910	1,109,111	6,058	10,997	15,824	1,141,990	17·1
1930	1,521,661	6,840	11,253	23,642	1,563,396	23·3
1980	3,779,170	105,574	60,804	186,608	4,132,156	62·1
1990	4,308,937	149,801	81,483	326,471	4,866,692	73·1
2000	4,821,823	190,267	93,301	788,730	5,894,121	88·6

Of the total population in 2000, 2,959,821 were female, 4,380,278 were 18 years old or older and 4,831,106 were urban. In 2000 the Hispanic population was 441,509, up from 214,570 in 1990 (a rise of 105·8%).

There are 27 Indian reservations. Indian reservations in 1990 covered 2,718,516 acres, of which 2,250,731 acres were tribal lands.

Leading cities are Seattle, with a population in 2000 of 563,374; Spokane, 195,629; Tacoma, 193,556; Vancouver, 143,560; Bellevue, 109,569. Others: Everett, 91,488; Federal Way, 83,259; Kent, 79,524; Yakima, 71,845; Bellingham, 67,171; Lakewood, 58,211; Kennewick, 54,693; Shoreline, 53,025; Renton, 50,052. The Seattle–Tacoma–Bremerton metropolitan area had a 2000 census population of 3,554,760.

SOCIAL STATISTICS

Births, 2003, were 80,489 (13·1 per 1,000 population); deaths (2002), 45,338 (7·5 per 1,000); marriages, 39,518 (6·5); divorces, 27,205 (4·5). Infant mortality rate, 2002, 5·8 per 1,000 live births.

CLIMATE

Seattle, Jan. 40°F (4·4°C), July 63°F (17·2°C). Annual rainfall 34" (848 mm). Spokane, Jan. 27°F (−2·8°C), July 70°F (21·1°C). Annual rainfall 14" (350 mm). Washington belongs to the Pacific Coast climate zone (see UNITED STATES: Climate).

CONSTITUTION AND GOVERNMENT

The constitution, adopted in 1889, has had 96 amendments. The Legislature consists of a Senate of 49 members elected for four years, half their number retiring every two years, and a House of Representatives of 98 members, elected for two years. The Governor and Lieut.-Governor are elected for four years.

For the 109th Congress, which convened in Jan. 2005, Washington sends nine members to the House of Representatives. It is represented in the Senate by Patty Murray (D. 1993–2011) and Maria Cantwell (D. 2001–07).

The capital is Olympia. The state contains 39 counties.

RECENT ELECTIONS

In the 2004 presidential election Kerry polled 1,510,201 votes; Bush, 1,304,894; Nader, 23,283.

CURRENT ADMINISTRATION

Governor: Christine Gregoire (D.), 2005–09 (salary: $150,995).

Lieut.-Governor: Brad Owen (D.), 2005–09 ($78,930).
Secretary of State: Sam Reed (R.), 2005–09 ($105,811).

Government Website: http://access.wa.gov

ECONOMY

Per capita personal income (2004) was $35,017.

Budget

In 2003 total state revenue was $29,661m. Total expenditure was $32,600m. (education, $10,697m.; public welfare, $6,250m.; highways, $1,906m.; health, $1,374m.; hospitals, $1,073m.) Out-standing debt, in 2003, $14,621m.

Performance

In 2004 Gross State Product was $261,549m., ranking Washington 14th in the United States.

ENERGY AND NATURAL RESOURCES

Water

The total area covered by water is approximately 4,756 sq. miles.

Minerals

Mining and quarrying are not as important as forestry, agriculture or manufacturing. Total value of non-fuel mineral production in 2003 was $430m.

Agriculture

Agriculture is constantly growing in value because of more intensive and diversified farming, and because of the 1m.-acre Columbia Basin Irrigation Project.

In 2002 there were 39,000 farms with an acreage of 15·7m.; the average farm was 403 acres. Average value of farmland and buildings per acre in 2002 was $1,486. Apples, milk, wheat, cattle and calves and potatoes are the top five commodities. In 2002 livestock included 248,700 beef cows, 246,800 milch cows, and 58,500 sheep and lambs. Hogs and pigs as of 2002 totalled 31,000 head.

Farm income, (2002): from crops, $3,714m.; livestock and livestock products, $1,495m. The net farm income in 2002 was $969m.

Forestry

Forests covered 21·8m. acres in 2002, of which 7·9m. acres were national forest. In 2001 timber harvested was an estimated 3,716m. bd ft. Production of wood and bark residues, 2000, was 5,542,000 tons.

Fisheries

Salmon and shellfish are important; total commercial catch, 2002, was 362·0m. lb, and was worth an estimated $142·5m.

INDUSTRY

Principal manufactures are aircraft, pulp and paper, lumber and plywood, aluminium, processed fruit and vegetables. In 2001 the state's 7,565 manufacturing establishments had 316,000 employees, earning $14,458m. Total value added by manufacturing in 2001 was $38,193m.

Labour

In 2003 total non-agricultural employment was 2,659,000. Employees by branch, 2003 (in 1,000): government, 521; trade, transportation and utilities, 510; education and health services, 312; professional and business services, 292; manufacturing, 267. The unemployment rate in 2003 was 7·5%.

COMMUNICATIONS

Roads

In 2003 there were 82,266 miles of roads comprising 19,549 miles of urban road and 62,807 miles of rural road. There were 5,378,891 registered motor vehicles.

Rail

In 2000 there were 3,128 route miles.

Civil Aviation

There are international airports at Seattle/Tacoma, Spokane and Boeing Field. There were 15,048,306 passenger enplanements statewide in 2003.

SOCIAL INSTITUTIONS

Justice

In June 2003 there were 16,284 prison inmates. There was one execution in 2001 but none since then.

Education

Education is given free to all children between the ages of five and 21 years, and is compulsory for children from eight to 15 years of age. In Oct. 2003 there were 1,014,142 pupils in public elementary and secondary schools; and 76,845 pupils in private schools. In Oct. 2002 there were 52,888 classroom teachers; average salary, $47,642.

The University of Washington, founded 1861, at Seattle, had, autumn 2002, 39,215 students; and Washington State University at Pullman, founded 1890, for science and agriculture, had 22,184 students. Eastern Washington University had 9,178; Central Washington University, 8,768; The Evergreen State College, 4,318; Western Washington University, 12,493. All counts are state-funded enrolment students. Community colleges had (2002) a total of 191,554 state-funded and excess enrolment students.

Health

In 2002 there were 86 community hospitals with 11,300 beds. A total of 519,000 patients were admitted during the year.

Welfare

Medicare enrolment in July 2003 totalled 775,358. In 2002 a total of 1,039,070 people in Washington received Medicaid. In Dec. 2004 there were 911,511 Old-Age, Survivors, and Disability Insurance (OASDI) beneficiaries. A total of 135,105 people were receiving payments under Temporary Assistance for Needy Families (TANF) in Sept. 2004.

RELIGION

Religious faiths represented include the Roman Catholic (716,133 adherents in 2000), United Methodist, Lutheran, Presbyterian and Episcopalian. There were 178,000 Latter-day Saints (Mormons) in 2000.

FURTHER READING

Statistical information: State Office of Financial Management, POB 43113, Olympia 98504-3113. Publishes *Washington State Data Book*

Dodds, G. B., *American North-West: a History of Oregon and Washington.* Arlington (Ill), 1986

West Virginia

KEY HISTORICAL EVENTS

In 1861 the state of Virginia seceded from the Union over the issue of slave-owning. The 40 western counties of the state were composed of hilly country, settled by miners and small farmers who were not slave-owners, and these counties ratified an ordinance providing for the creation of a new state that same year. On 20 June 1863 West Virginia became the 35th state of the Union.

The capital, Charleston, was an 18th-century fortified post on the early westward migration routes across the Appalachians.

In 1795 local brine wells were tapped and the city grew as a salt town. Coal, oil, natural gas and a variety of salt brines were all found in due course. Huntington, the next largest town, developed as a railway terminus serving the same industrial area, and also providing transport on the Ohio river. Wheeling, the original state capital, was a well established, cosmopolitan city when it hosted the statehood meetings in 1861, located on the major transportation routes of the Ohio River, Baltimore and Ohio Railroad and the National Road.

Three-quarters of the state is forest and settlement has been concentrated in the mineral-bearing Kanawha valley, along the Ohio river and in the industrial Monongahela valley of the north. More than half of the population is still classified as rural. The traditional small firms and small hill-mines, however, support few, and the majority of rural dwellers commute to industrial employment.

TERRITORY AND POPULATION

West Virginia is bounded in the north by Pennsylvania and Maryland, east and south by Virginia, southwest by the Big Sandy River (forming the boundary with Kentucky) and west by the Ohio River (forming the boundary with Ohio). Land area, 24,077 sq. miles (62,359 sq. km). Census population, 1 April 2000, 1,808,344, an increase of 0·8% since 1990. July 2005 estimate, 1,816,856.

Population in five federal census years was:

	White	Black	American Indian	Asiatic	Total	Per sq. mile
1910	1,156,817	64,173	36	93	1,221,119	50·8
1960	1,770,133	89,378	181	419	1,860,421	77·3
1980	1,874,751	65,051	1,610	5,194	1,949,644	80·3
1990	1,725,523	56,295	2,458	7,459	1,793,477	74·0
2000	1,718,777	57,232	3,606	9,834	1,808,344	75·1

Of the total population in 2000, 929,174 were female, 1,405,951 were 18 years old or older and 975,564 (53·9%) were rural. In 2000 the Hispanic population was 12,279, up from 8,489 in 1990 (an increase of 44·6%).

The 2000 census population of the principal cities was: Charleston, 53,421; Huntington, 51,475. Others: Parkersburg, 33,099; Wheeling, 31,419; Morgantown, 26,809; Weirton, 20,411; Fairmont, 19,097; Beckley, 17,254; Clarksburg, 16,743.

SOCIAL STATISTICS

Statistics 2003: births, 20,935 (11·6 per 1,000 population); deaths (2002), 21,016 (11·7—the highest rate in any US state). 2002 infant mortality (per 1,000 live births), 9·1. 2001: marriages, 14,200 (7·9 per 1,000 population); divorces, 9,300 (5·2). West Virginia is the only state in which the annual number of deaths exceeds births.

CLIMATE

Charleston, Jan. 34°F (1·1°C), July 76°F (24·4°C). Annual rainfall 40" (1,010 mm). West Virginia belongs to the Appalachian Mountains climate zone (*see* UNITED STATES: Climate).

CONSTITUTION AND GOVERNMENT

The present constitution was adopted in 1872; it has had 17 amendments. The Legislature consists of the Senate of 34 members elected for a term of four years, one-half being elected biennially, and the House of Delegates of 100 members, elected biennially. The Governor is elected for four years and may serve one successive term.

For the 109th Congress, which convened in Jan. 2005, West Virginia sends three members to the House of Representatives. It is represented in the Senate by Robert Byrd (D. 1959–2007) and Jay Rockefeller (D. 1985–2009).

The state capital is Charleston. There are 55 counties.

RECENT ELECTIONS

In the 2004 presidential election Bush polled 423,778 votes; Kerry, 326,541; Nader, 4,063.

CURRENT ADMINISTRATION

Governor: Joe Manchin, III (D.), 2005–09 (salary: $95,000).
   Senate President: Earl Ray Tomblin (D.), 2005–09.
   Secretary of State: Betty Ireland (R.), 2005–09 ($70,000).

Government Website: http://www.wv.gov

ECONOMY

Per capita personal income (2004) was $25,681.

Budget

Total revenues in 2003 were $9,766m. Total expenditures were $10,004m. (education, $2,759m.; public welfare, $2,231m.; highways, $962m.; government administration, $483m.; health, $232m.) Outstanding debt in 2003, $4,260m.

Performance

Gross State Product in 2004 was $49,454m., ranking West Virginia 41st in the United States.

Banking and Finance

There were 56 state banks and 26 national banks with a total of $13,844m. in deposits in 2000. There were also eight federal savings and loans and federal savings banks; total deposits in 1997 were $887m.

ENERGY AND NATURAL RESOURCES

Oil and Gas

Petroleum output (2000), 1,267m. bbls.; natural gas production (2000), 233bn. cu. ft.

Water

The total area covered by water is approximately 152 sq. miles.

Minerals

38% of the state is underlain with mineable coal; 139·7m. short tons of coal were produced in 2003. Salt, sand and gravel, sandstone and limestone are also produced. The total value of non-fuel mineral production in 2003 was $168m.

Agriculture

In 2002 the state had 20,500 farms with an area of 3·6m. acres; average size of farm was 176 acres, valued at $1,315 per acre. Livestock farming predominates.

Cash income, 2002, from crops was $78m.; from livestock and products, $300m. The net farm income in 2002 was $7m. Main crops harvested: hay (1·31m. tons); all corn (1·3m. bu.); tobacco (1·8m. lb). Area of main crops: hay, 0·61m. acres; corn, 55,000 acres. Apples (90m. lb) and peaches (1m. lb) are important fruit crops.

Livestock on farms, 2000, included 400,000 cattle, of which 17,000 were milch cows; sheep, 35,000; hogs, 10,000; chickens, 1·86m. excluding broilers. Production included 91·3m broilers; 20·75m. dozen eggs; 4·1m. turkeys.

Forestry

Forests covered 12,108,000 acres in 2002, with 1,002,000 acres of national forest; 78·5% of the state is woodland.

Fisheries

In 2000, nine state fish hatcheries and one federal fish hatchery sold 363,000 lb of trout and stocked 815,000 lb of trout, in addition to 2·4m. fry, 507,162 fingerlings and 5,000 adults of other types of fish.

INDUSTRY

In Oct. 2001, 2,094 manufactures had 76,800 production workers. Leading manufactures are primary and fabricated metals, glass, chemicals, wood products, textiles and apparel, machinery, plastics, speciality chemicals, aerospace, electronics, medical and related technologies and industrial products recycling.

Labour

In 2003 non-agricultural employment was 726,000 of whom 142,000 were in government; 135,000 in trade, transportation and utilities; 108,000 in education and health services; 66,000 in leisure and hospitality; and 65,000 in manufacturing. The state unemployment rate in 2003 was 6·1%.

INTERNATIONAL TRADE

Imports and Exports

The state's major export markets are the EU and Canada, with coal being a major export commodity. West Virginia staffs trade offices in Nagoya, Japan; Taipei, Taiwan; and Munich, Germany.

COMMUNICATIONS

Roads

In 2003 there were 36,993 miles of roads (33,803 miles rural). There were 1,408,800 registered motor vehicles.

Rail

In 2001 the state had 2,659 miles of railway.

Civil Aviation

There were 37 public airports in 2001. There were 328,894 passenger enplanements statewide in 2003.

Shipping

There are some 420·5 miles of navigable rivers.

Postal Services

In 2001 there were 1,012 postal facilities.

SOCIAL INSTITUTIONS

Justice

The state court system consists of a Supreme Court, 31 circuit courts, and magistrate courts in each county. The Supreme Court of Appeals, exercising original and appellate jurisdiction, has five members elected by the people for 12-year terms. Each circuit court has from one to seven judges (as determined by the Legislature on the basis of population and case-load) chosen by the voters within each circuit for eight-year terms.

There are 11 penal and correctional institutions which had, in June 2003, 4,703 inmates. There were also (Dec. 2001) eight regional jails housing 2,139 county, state and federal inmates, and seven juvenile facilities housing 271 juveniles. Capital punishment was abolished in 1965. The last execution was in 1959.

Education

Public school education is free for all from five to 21 years of age, and school attendance is compulsory for all between the ages of seven and 16 (school term, 200 days—180–185 days of actual teaching). The public schools are non-sectarian. In 2000–01 public elementary and secondary schools had 285,785 pupils and 24,507 classroom teachers. Average salary of teachers was $35,888. Total 2000–01 education expenditures, including higher education, $2,486m.

Leading institutions of higher education in the autumn of 2000:

Founded		Full-time students
1837	Marshall University, Huntington	15,640[1]
1837	West Liberty State College, West Liberty	2,606
1867	Fairmont State College, Fairmont	6,496
1868	West Virginia University, Morgantown	21,987
1872	Concord College, Athens	3,050
1872	Glenville State College, Glenville	2,198
1872	Shepherd College, Shepherdstown	4,703
1891	West Virginia State College, Institute	4,828

Founded		Full-time students
1895	West Virginia Univ. Inst. of Technology, Montgomery	2,326
1895	Bluefield State College, Bluefield	2,648
1901	Potomac State College of West Virginia Univ., Keyser	1,111
1961	West Virginia Univ. at Parkersburg, Parkersburg	3,271
1976	School of Osteopathic Medicine, Lewisburg	280

¹Includes Marshall Univ. Graduate College, South Charleston, founded in 1972.

In addition to the universities and state-supported schools, there are two community colleges (4,911 students in 2000), ten denominational and private institutions of higher education (9,808 students in 1999) and 11 business colleges (2001).

Health

In Dec. 2001 the state had 68 licensed hospitals and 64 licensed personal care homes, 141 skilled-nursing homes and five mental hospitals.

Welfare

The Department of Health Human Resources, originating in the 1930s as the Department of Public Assistance, is both state and federally financed. Medicare enrolment in July 2003 totalled 347,459. In 2002 a total of 362,030 people in West Virginia received Medicaid. In Dec. 2004 there were 409,401 Old-Age, Survivors, and Disability Insurance (OASDI) beneficiaries. A total of 30,682 people were receiving payments under Temporary Assistance for Needy Families (TANF) in Sept. 2004.

RELIGION

Chief denominations in 2001 were: United Methodists (115,062 members), Roman Catholics (97,232), Baptists American (94,000) and Southern (33,000).

CULTURE

Broadcasting

In 2001 there were 156 commercial, 14 college and 14 public radio stations. Television stations numbered 14 commercial and three public.

Press

In 2001 daily newspapers numbered 19, weekly and college newspapers 78.

Tourism

There are 35 state parks, nine state forests, 58 wildlife management areas and two state trails. Visitors are attracted to the area by whitewater rafting, hiking, skiing and biking and the winter outdoor light display at Oglebay Park in Wheeling.

FURTHER READING

West Virginia Blue Book. Legislature, Charleston. Annual, since 1916

Statistical Handbook, 2001. West Virginia Research League, Charleston, 2001

Lewis, R. L. and Hennen, J. C., *West Virginia History: Critical Essays on the Literature*. Kendall/Hunt Publishing, Dubuque, IA, 1993

Rice, O. K., *West Virginia: A History*. 2nd ed. Univ. Press of Kentucky, Lexington, 1994

State Library: Archives and History, Division of Culture and History, Charleston.

Wisconsin

KEY HISTORICAL EVENTS

The French were the first European explorers of the territory; Jean Nicolet landed at Green Bay in 1634, a mission was founded in 1671 and a permanent settlement at Green Bay followed. In 1763 French claims were surrendered to Britain. In 1783 Britain ceded them to the USA, which designated the Northwest Territory, of which Wisconsin was part. In 1836 a separate Territory of Wisconsin was organized, including the present Iowa, Minnesota and parts of the Dakotas.

Territorial organization was a great stimulus to settlement. In 1836 James Duane Doty founded the town site of Madison and successfully pressed its claim to be the capital of the Territory even before it was inhabited. In 1848 Wisconsin became a state, with its present boundaries.

The city of Milwaukee was founded, on Lake Michigan, when Indian tribes gave up their claims to the land in 1831–33. It grew rapidly as a port and industrial town, attracting Germans in the 1840s, and Poles and Italians 50 years later. The Lake Michigan shore was developed as an industrial area; the rest of the south proved suitable for dairy farming; the north, mainly forests and lakes, has remained sparsely settled except for tourist bases.

There are 11 Indian reservations where more than 15,500 of Wisconsin's 47,000 Indians live. Since the Second World War there has been black immigration from the southern states to the industrial lake-shore cities.

TERRITORY AND POPULATION

Wisconsin is bounded north by Lake Superior and the Upper Peninsula of Michigan, east by Lake Michigan, south by Illinois, and west by Iowa and Minnesota, with the Mississippi River forming most of the boundary. Land area, 54,310 sq. miles (140,662 sq. km). Census population, 1 April 2000, 5,363,675, an increase of 9·6% since 1990. July 2005 estimate, 5,536,201.

Population in five census years was:

	White	Black	All others	Total	Per sq. mile
1910	2,320,555	2,900	10,405	2,333,860	42·2
1930	2,916,255	10,739	12,012	2,939,006	53·7
1980	4,443,035	182,592	80,015	4,705,642	86·4
1990	4,512,523	244,539	134,707	4,891,769	90·1
2000	4,769,857	304,460	289,358	5,363,675	98·8

Of the total population in 2000, 2,714,634 were female, 3,994,919 were 18 years old or older and 3,663,643 were urban. In 2000 Wisconsin's Hispanic population was 192,921, up from 93,194 in 1990 (an increase of 107·0%).

Population of the large cities, 2000 census, was as follows:

Milwaukee	596,974	Janesville	59,498
Madison	208,054	La Crosse	51,818
Green Bay	102,313	Sheboygan	50,792
Kenosha	90,352	Wauwatosa	47,271
Racine	81,855	Fond du Lac	42,203
Appleton	70,087	Brookfield	38,649
Waukesha	64,825	Wausau	38,426
Oshkosh	62,916	New Berlin	38,220
Eau Claire	61,704	Beloit	35,775
West Allis	61,254	Greenfield	35,476

Population of largest metropolitan areas, 2000 census: Milwaukee–Racine, 1,689,572; Madison, 426,526; Appleton–Oshkosh–Neenah, 358,365; Duluth–Superior (Minn.–Wis.), 243,815; Green Bay, 226,778.

SOCIAL STATISTICS

Births in 2003 were 70,040 (12·8 per 1,000 population); deaths (2002), 46,981 (8·6 per 1,000 population). In 2003 there were 34,220 marriages (6·3 per 1,000 population); divorces and annulments, 17,150 (3·1). Infant deaths, 2002, 6·9 per 1,000 live births.

CLIMATE

Milwaukee, Jan. 19°F (–7·2°C), July 70°F (21·1°C). Annual rainfall 29" (727 mm). Wisconsin belongs to the Great Lakes climate zone (*see* UNITED STATES: Climate).

CONSTITUTION AND GOVERNMENT

The constitution, which dates from 1848, has 141 amendments. The legislative power is vested in a Senate of 33 members elected for four years, one-half elected alternately, and an Assembly of 99 members all elected simultaneously for two years. The Governor and Lieut.-Governor are elected for four years.

For the 109th Congress, which convened in Jan. 2005, Wisconsin sends eight members to the House of Representatives. It is represented in the Senate by Herbert Kohl (D. 1989–2007) and Russell Feingold (D. 1993–2011).

The capital is Madison. The state has 72 counties.

RECENT ELECTIONS

In the 2004 presidential election Kerry polled 1,489,504 votes; Bush, 1,478,120; Nader, 16,390.

CURRENT ADMINISTRATION

Governor: Jim Doyle (D.), 2003–07 (salary: $131,768).

Lieut.-Governor: Barbara Lawton (D.), 2003–07 ($69,579).

Secretary of State: Douglas LaFollette (D.), 2003–07 ($62,549).

Government Website: http://www.wisconsin.gov

ECONOMY

Per capita personal income in 2004 was $32,063.

Budget

For the year ending 30 June 2004 total state revenue was $41,586m. ($10,739m. from state taxes); total expenditure, $33,894m. (education, $9,660m.; health and human resources, $9,166m.; transportation, $2,346m.; corrections, $989m.; environmental resources, $601m.) Outstanding debt, 30 June 2002, $4,304m.

Performance

Gross State Product in 2004 was $211,616m., ranking Wisconsin 19th in the United States.

Banking and Finance

On 30 Sept. 2004 there were 232 state chartered banks with assets of $68·5bn., and 45 federally chartered banks with $23·7bn. in assets. On 30 Sept. 2004, 19 state chartered savings institutions had $4·2bn. in assets and 20 federally chartered savings institutions had $18·8bn. in assets. As of 30 June 2004 there were 293 state chartered credit unions with $13·5bn. in assets.

ENERGY AND NATURAL RESOURCES

Electricity

57,241m. kWh of electricity were produced in 2003; and 10,766m. kWh were imported. Fossil fuel plants accounted for 72·3% of state production, nuclear 21·7% and hydropower 3·0%. Coal accounted for 62% of utility energy use in 2003; nuclear fuel, 17%; natural gas, 3%; renewable sources, 2%; and electricity imports, 16%.

Oil and Gas

Petroleum accounted for 29% of the total energy consumed in 2003 and natural gas 22%. Transportation accounted for 83% of petroleum consumption. Natural gas accounted for 51% of residential end use and petroleum 14%. There are no known petroleum or natural gas reserves in Wisconsin.

Water

The total area covered by water is approximately 11,188 sq. miles.

Minerals

Construction sand and gravel, crushed stone, industrial or specialty sand, lime, copper, gold and silver are the chief mineral products.

Mineral production in 2000 was valued at over $349m. This value included $140m. for construction sand and gravel, $131m. for crushed stones, $37m. for lime and $32m. for industrial or specialty sand. The value of all other minerals including dimension (building) stone, peat and gemstones was around $9m.

Agriculture

On 1 Jan. 2004 there were 76,500 farms (16,096 dairy herds) with a total acreage of 15·6m. acres and an average size of 204 acres, compared with 142,000 farms with a total acreage of 22·4m. acres and an average of 158 acres in 1959. In 2003 the average value per acre was $2,350. Cash receipts from products sold by Wisconsin farms in 2003, $5·76bn.; $1·29bn. from crops, and $4·10bn. from livestock and livestock products. The net farm income in 2003 was $1,626m.

Dairy farming is important, with 1·25m. milch cows in 2003. Production of cheese accounted for 27% of the USA's total in 2003. Production of the principal field crops in 2003 included: corn for grain, 368m. bu.; corn for silage, 14·1m. tons; oats, 15·4m. bu.; all hay, 4·4m. tons. Other crops of importance: 46·8m. bu. of soybeans, 32·8m. cwt of potatoes, 3·6m. bbls. of cranberries, 96,000 tons of carrots and the processing crops of 687,400 tons of sweet corn, 84,300 tons of green peas, 270,800 tons of snap beans, 36,100 tons of cucumbers for pickles, 13·8m. lb of tart cherries and 989,000 cwt of cabbage.

Wisconsin is also a major producer of mink pelts.

Forestry

Wisconsin had (2002) 15,963,000 acres of forested land. Of 15·7m. acres of timberland (Oct. 1997), national forests covered 1·4m. acres; state forests, 0·7m.; county and municipal forests, 2·3m.; forest industry, 1·1m.; private land, 10·1m.

Growing stock (1996), 18,500m. cu. ft, of which 14,100m. cu. ft is hardwood and 4,400m. cu. ft softwood. Main hardwoods are maple, oak, aspen and basswood; main softwoods are red pine, white pine, northern white cedar and balsam fir. The timber industry employs 99,000, has a payroll of $3,400m. and shipments valued at $19,700m. (1996).

INDUSTRY

Wisconsin has much heavy industry, particularly in the Milwaukee area. Three-fifths of manufacturing employees work on durable goods. Industrial machinery is the major industrial group (17% of all manufacturing employment) followed by fabricated metals, food and kindred products, printing and publishing, paper and allied products, electrical equipment and transportation equipment. Manufacturing establishments in 2002 provided 22% of non-farm wage and salary workers, 22·9% of all earnings. The total number of establishments was 9,846 in 2001; the biggest concentration is in the southeast. In Dec. 2004 manufacturing employed 518,800 people out of a total civilian labour force of 3,112,500.

Labour

The civilian labour force in 2004 was 3,112,500, of whom 2,982,500 were employed. Service enterprises employed 890,000 people, manufacturing 518,800, retail and wholesale 460,300, and government 419,700. Average annual pay per worker (2001) was $31,540 ($35,170 in Milwaukee metropolitan area). Median household income (2003) was $46,269. Women were 48% of the workforce in 2002. Workforce participation rates for people over 16 (2001) were 74% for males and 64% for females. Average weekly earnings ranged from $300 in the retail sector to $750 in manufacturing in 2001. Average unemployment was 5·6% in 2003.

Trade Unions

Labour union membership numbered 414,000 in 2003 and represented 15·9% of the workforce. Union membership was 19·9% of workers in the manufacturing sector in 2002.

COMMUNICATIONS

Roads

The state had, on 1 Jan. 2003, 113,269 miles of public roads. 80% of all roads in the state have a bituminous (or similar) surface. There are 11,772 miles of state and interstate highways and 20,600 miles of county highway roads.

In 2004 there were 5,100,000 registered motor vehicles.

Rail

On 31 Dec. 2002 the state had 5,095 track-miles of railway and 12 railroads that hauled 158m. tons of freight.

Civil Aviation

There were, in 2002, 134 public access airports. There were 4,879,744 passenger enplanements statewide in 2003.

Shipping

Lake Superior and Lake Michigan ports handled 47·8m. tons of freight in 2002; 87% of it at Superior, one of the world's biggest grain ports, and much of the rest at Milwaukee and Green Bay.

SOCIAL INSTITUTIONS

Justice

On 17 Dec. 2004 the state's penal, reformatory and correctional system held 20,839 men and 1,329 women in 19 prisons, 16 community facilities and other institutions for adult offenders, including contract beds in county jails, federal facilities and 128 in a private prison in Minnesota; the probation and parole system was supervising 69,629 adults (56,342 on probation, 13,287 on parole). Parole for new convictions officially ended 31 Dec. 1999 (replaced by 'extended supervision'). Population in the state's five juvenile institutions on 17 Dec. 2004 was 610 males and 46 females; an additional 505 males and 47 females were under field supervision.

The death penalty was abolished in 1853.

Education

All children between the ages of six and 18 are required to attend school full-time to the end of the school term in which they become 18 years of age. In 2003–04 the public school grades kindergarten-12 had 853,363 pupils. There were 61,394 (full-time equivalent) teachers in 2002–03. Private schools enrolled 124,248 students grades kindergarten-12. Public pre-schools enrolled 26,668 children, and private 13,604. Children taught in home schools numbered 21,134 in 1999–2000. Public elementary teachers' salaries, 2000–01, averaged $41,403; secondary, $42,175.

In 2002–03 technical colleges had an enrolment of 429,355 and 4,902 (full-time equivalent) teachers, and two Indian tribe community colleges enrolled 1,060 (2003–04). There is a school for the visually handicapped and a school for the deaf.

The University of Wisconsin, established in 1848, was joined by law in 1971 with the Wisconsin State Universities System to become the University of Wisconsin System with 13 degree granting campuses, 13 two-year campuses in the Center System and the University Extension. The system had, in 2002–03, 6,718 full-time professors and instructors. In autumn 2003, 160,703 students enrolled (10,599 at Eau Claire, 5,448 at Green Bay, 8,746 at La Crosse, 40,769 at Madison, 24,875 at Milwaukee, 11,013 at Oshkosh, 5,072 at Parkside, 6,134 at Platteville, 5,799 at River Falls, 8,750 at Stevens Point, 7,708 at Stout, 2,832 at Superior, 10,548 at Whitewater and 12,410 at the Center System freshman-sophomore centres).

UW-Extension enrolled 176,793 students in its continuing education programmes in 2001–02. There are also several independent institutions of higher education: Marquette University (Jesuit), in Milwaukee (11,000 in 2002–03); Cardinal Strich University (Franciscan), with campuses in Milwaukee, Madison and Edina, Minnesota (6,588 in 2002–03); Concordia University Wisconsin (Lutheran), in Mequon (4,541 in 2002–03); and Lawrence University, Appleton (1,325 in 2002–03). There were also 16 higher education colleges, four technical and professional schools and four theological seminaries in 2003. The state's educational and broadcasting service is licensed through the UW Board of Regents.

The total expenditure, 2001–02, for all public education (except capital outlay and debt service) was $12,170·8m. ($2,253 per capita).

Health

In 2002 the state had 128 general medical and surgical hospitals (12,626 beds), 12 psychiatric hospitals (623 beds), one treatment centre for alcohol and drug abuse (24 beds) and one physical rehabilitation hospitals (40 beds). There were two state mental hospitals (541 beds) and two US Veterans' Administration hospitals. Patients in state mental hospitals and institutions for the developmentally disabled averaged 570 in 2003. On 31 Dec. 2003 the state had 403 licensed nursing homes with 36,005 residents and 33 facilities for the developmentally disabled (1,415 residents).

Welfare

In Nov. 2004 there were 136,488 Supplemental Security Income (SSI) recipients in the state; set monthly payments (2005) are $663 for a single individual, $709 for an eligible individual with an ineligible spouse and $1,001 for an eligible couple. A special payment level of $759 for an individual and $1,346 for a couple may be paid with special approval for SSI recipients who are developmentally disabled or chronically mentally ill, living in a non-medical living arrangement not his or her own home. There is a monthly cash benefit for each child living with an SSI parent of $250 for the first child and $150 for each additional child. All SSI recipients receive state medical assistance coverage and may qualify for food stamps.

Wisconsin completed its conversion to the W-2 (Wisconsin Works) programme on 31 March 1998, ending the 62-year-old Aid to Families with Dependent Children (AFDC) programme. W-2 clients (Nov. 2004) totalled 15,374 with 11,148 receiving cash assistance. W-2 clients must be working, seeking employment or be enrolled in job-training programmes. Recipients are limited to 60 months of financial assistance (consecutive or non-consecutive). Participants are eligible for child care assistance, a state subsidized health plan, job and transportation assistance and food stamps. In Aug. 2004 there were 322,405 (132,313 households) food stamp recipients. Medical Assistance (Medicaid) clients, including low-income, SSI recipients and other disabled, and other elderly totalled 707,869. An additional 94,257 (Aug. 2004) are provided for under BadgerCare, a state-funded medical insurance programme for certain low-income families.

RELIGION

Wisconsin church affiliation, as a percentage of the 2004 population, was estimated at 31% Catholic, 25% Protestant Mainline, 22% Evangelical and 14% unaffiliated.

CULTURE

There are two professional opera companies in Wisconsin: the Madison Opera, and the Florentine Opera in Milwaukee.

Broadcasting

In 2003 there were 32 commercial TV stations; eight educational TV stations; 265 commercial radio stations; and 51 non-commercial.

Press

There were 36 daily newspapers in 2003.

Tourism

The tourist-vacation industry ranks among the first three in economic importance with an estimated \$11,710m. spent in 2003. The Department of Tourism budgeted \$13,665,400 to promote tourism in 2004–05.

FURTHER READING

Wisconsin Blue Book. Wisconsin Legislative Reference Bureau, Madison. Biennial

State Historical Society of Wisconsin: *The History of Wisconsin*. Vol. IV [J. Buenker], Madison, 1999

State Information Agency: Legislative Reference Bureau, One East Main St., Suite 200, Madison, WI 53703-2037. *Chief:* Stephen R. Miller.
Website: http://www.legis.state.wi.us

Wyoming

KEY HISTORICAL EVENTS

The territory was inhabited by Plains Indians (Arapahoes, Sioux and Cheyenne) in the early 19th century. There was some trading between them and white Americans, but very little white settlement. In the 1840s the great western migration routes, the Oregon and the Overland Trails, ran through the territory, with Wyoming offering mountain passes accessible to wagons. Once migration became a steady flow it was necessary to protect the route from Indian attack, and forts were built.

In 1867 coal was discovered. In 1868 Wyoming was organized as a separate Territory, and in 1869 the Sioux and Arapaho were confined to reservations. At the same time the route of the Union Pacific Railway was laid out, and working settlements and railway towns grew up in southern Wyoming. Settlement of the north was delayed until after the final defeat of hostile Indians in 1876.

The economy of the settlements at first depended on ranching. Cheyenne had been made Territorial capital in 1869, and also functioned as a railway town moving cattle. Casper, on the site of a fort on the Pony Express route, was also a railway town on the Chicago and North Western. Laramie started as a Union Pacific construction workers' shanty town in 1868. In 1890 oil was discovered at Casper, and Wyoming became a state in the same year. Subsequently, mineral extraction became the leading industry, as natural gas, uranium, bentonite and trona were exploited as well as oil and coal.

TERRITORY AND POPULATION

Wyoming is bounded north by Montana, east by South Dakota and Nebraska, south by Colorado, southwest by Utah and west by Idaho. Land area, 97,100 sq. miles (251,488 sq. km). The Yellowstone National Park occupies about 2·22m. acres; the Grand Teton National Park has 307,000 acres. The federal government in 2003 owned 49,268 sq. miles (50·6% of the total area of the state). The Federal Bureau of Land Management administers 17·4m. acres.

Census population, 1 April 2000, 493,782, an increase of 8·9% since 1990; July 2005 estimate, 509,294. Wyoming has the smallest population of any of the states of the USA.

Population in five census years was:

			American			Per sq.
	White	Black	Indian	Asiatic	Total	mile
1910	140,318	2,235	1,845	1,926	145,965	1·5
1930	221,241	1,250	1,845	1,229	225,565	2·3
			All others			
1980	446,488	3,364		19,705	469,557	4·8

			American	Asian/			Per sq.
	White	Black	Indian	Pacific Islands	Other	Total	mile
1990	427,061	3,606	9,479	2,806	10,636	453,588	4·7
2000	454,670	3,722	11,133	3,073	21,184	493,782	5·1

Of the total population in 2000, 248,374 were male, 364,909 were 18 years old or older and 321,344 were urban. At the 2000 census the Hispanic population of Wyoming was 31,669, up from 25,751 in 1990 (an increase of 23%).

The largest towns (with 2000 census population) are Cheyenne, 53,011; Casper, 49,644; Laramie, 27,204; Gillette, 19,646; Rock Springs, 18,708; Sheridan, 15,804; Green River, 11,808.

SOCIAL STATISTICS

Births in 2004 were 6,800 (13·4 per 1,000 population); deaths, 3,924 (7·7 per 1,000 population). 2003: marriages, 4,698; divorces, 2,724. Infant mortality (per 1,000 live births), 2004: 5·7. The abortion rate, at 1·0 for every 1,000 women in 2000, is the lowest of any US state.

CLIMATE

Cheyenne, Jan. 25°F (–3·9°C), July 66°F (18·9°C). Annual rainfall 15" (376 mm). Yellowstone Park, Jan. 18°F (–7·8°C), July 61°F (16·1°C). Annual rainfall 18" (444 mm). Wyoming belongs to the Mountain States climate region (*see* UNITED STATES: Climate).

CONSTITUTION AND GOVERNMENT

The constitution, drafted in 1890, has since had 76 amendments. The Legislature consists of a Senate of 30 members elected for four years, 15 retiring every two years, and a House of Representatives of 60 members elected for two years. It sits annually in Jan. or Feb. The Governor is elected for four years.

For the 109th Congress, which convened in Jan. 2005, Wyoming sends one member to the House of Representatives. It is represented in the Senate by Craig Thomas (R. 1995–2007) and Michael Enzi (R. 1997–2009).

The capital is Cheyenne. The state contains 23 counties.

RECENT ELECTIONS

In the 2004 presidential election Bush polled 167,629 votes; Kerry, 70,776; Nader, 2,741.

CURRENT ADMINISTRATION

Governor: David D. Freudenthal (D.), 2003–07 (salary: \$105,000).
Secretary of State: Joseph B. Meyer (R.), 2003–07 (\$92,000).

Government Website: http://www.wyoming.gov

ECONOMY

Personal income *per capita* (2004) was \$34,199.

Budget

In 2003 total state revenue was \$3,403m. Total expenditure was \$3,264m. (education, \$955m.; public welfare, \$445m.; highways, \$441m.; natural resources, \$194m.; health, \$126m.) Outstanding debt, in 2003, \$1,111m.

Performance

Gross State Product was \$23,979m. in 2004, ranking Wyoming 48th in the United States.

Banking and Finance

In 2005 there were 17 national and 26 state banks with a total of \$8,563m. deposits.

ENERGY AND NATURAL RESOURCES

Oil and Gas
Wyoming produces significant quantities of oil and natural gas. In 2004 the output of oil was 51·7m. bbls.; natural gas, 1,929bn. cu. ft.

Water
The total area covered by water is approximately 713 sq. miles.

Minerals
In 2004 the output of coal was 395·5m. short tons; trona (2004), 18·7m. short tons; uranium (2003), 1·2m. lb. Wyoming is the USA's leading coal producer, accounting for 35% of the country's coal output in 2004. It also has 14% of the country's coal reserves. Total value of non-fuel mineral production in 2003 was $1,010m.

Agriculture
Wyoming is semi-arid, and agriculture is carried on by irrigation and dry farming. In 2004 there were 9,200 farms and ranches; total farm area was 34·4m. acres; average size of farm in 2004 was 3,743 acres (the largest of any state). In 2004 the average value of farmland was $315 per acre.

Total value, 2004, of crops produced, $184m.; of livestock and products, $789m. The net farm income in 2003 was $291m. Crop production in 2004 (1,000 bu.): barley, 6,900; corn for grain, 6,681; wheat, 3,510; oats, 795; sugarbeets, 812,000 tons. Animals on farms included 1·35m. cattle, 450,000 sheep and 114,000 hogs and pigs. Total egg production in 2004 was 3·6m.

Forestry
The state had a forested area of 10,995,000 acres in 2002, of which 5,858,000 acres were national forest.

INDUSTRY

In 2003 the state's 558 manufacturing establishments had 10,368 employees, earning $416m. In 2003 there were 760 mining establishments. A large portion of the manufacturing in the state is based on natural resources, mainly oil and farm products. Leading industries are food, wood products (except furniture) and machinery (except electrical).

Labour
In 2003 government employed 64,000 wage and salary workers; trade, transportation and utilities, 48,000; leisure and hospitality, 31,000; education and health services, 21,000; and the construction industry employed 20,000. The total civilian labour force in 2004 was 281,847, of whom 270,810 were employed; non-agricultural wage and salary employment, 255,400. The unemployment rate was 3·9% in 2004.

Trade Unions
There were 18,000 working members in trade unions (6·6% of total employment) in 2004.

INTERNATIONAL TRADE

Imports and Exports
In 2004 total export from Wyoming was $680·2m.

COMMUNICATIONS

Roads
In 2003 there were 2,503 miles of urban roads and 24,980 miles of rural roads, the latter including (in miles): federal, 3,339; state, 6,351; county, 14,074. There were 771,153 motor vehicle registrations in April 2005.

Rail
In 2002, 1,886 miles of railway were operated.

Civil Aviation
In 2005 there were 41 public-use airports and 23 heliports. There were 361,392 passenger enplanements statewide in 2003.

SOCIAL INSTITUTIONS

Justice
In June 2004 there were 1,980 prisoners in state adult correctional institutions. Capital punishment is authorized but has been used only once, in 1992, since the US Supreme Court reinstated the death penalty in 1976.

Education
In 2004–05 public elementary and secondary schools had 83,722 pupils and 6,504 teachers. In 1999–2000 enrolment in private elementary and secondary schools was 2,221. The average expenditure per pupil for 2004 was $10,206. State and local government expenditure in 2003–04 was $991m.

The University of Wyoming, founded at Laramie in 1887 had, in the academic year 2004–05, 13,207 students. There were seven community colleges in 2004–05 with 14,774 students.

Health
In 2005 the state had 26 general hospitals with 1,378 beds, and 39 registered nursing homes with 3,032 beds.

Welfare
In 2004, $25m. was distributed in food stamps. A total of 59,071 people in Wyoming received Medicaid in 2002; Medicaid expenditure in 2004–05 was $410m. Medicare enrolment in July 2003 totalled 68,590. In Dec. 2004 there were 79,998 Old-Age, Survivors, and Disability Insurance (OASDI) beneficiaries. A total of 595 people were receiving payments under Temporary Assistance for Needy Families (TANF) in Sept. 2004. In 2004–05, $814,034 was distributed under the TANF programme.

RELIGION

Chief religious bodies in 2000 were Protestants (with 101,468 members), Roman Catholics (80,421) and Latter-day Saints (Mormons) (47,129).

CULTURE

Broadcasting
In 2004 there were 32 AM, 57 FM radio stations and 16 television stations.

Press
In 2004 there were 43 newspapers, two of which were published daily.

Tourism
There are over 7m. tourists annually, mainly outdoor enthusiasts. The state has large elk and pronghorn antelope herds, ten fish hatcheries and numerous wild game. In 2002, 5,765,463 people visited the seven national areas; in 2004, 2·5m. people visited state parks and historic sites. In 2004, 715,000 fishing, gaming and bird licences were sold. In 2005 there were ten operational ski areas.

FURTHER READING

Equality State Almanac 2002. Wyoming Department of Administration and Information. Division of Economic Analysis. Cheyenne, WY 82002

Wyoming Official Directory. Secretary of State. Cheyenne, annual

Treadway, T., *Wyoming.* New York, 1982

Statistics Website: http://eadiv.state.wy.us

OUTLYING TERRITORIES

The outlying territories of the USA comprise the two Commonwealths of the Northern Mariana Islands and Puerto Rico, a number of unincorporated territories in the Pacific Ocean and one unincorporated territory in the Caribbean Sea.

Commonwealth of the Northern Mariana Islands

KEY HISTORICAL EVENTS

In 1889 Spain ceded Guam (largest and southernmost of the Marianas Islands) to the USA and sold the rest to Germany. Occupied by Japan in 1914, the islands were administered by Japan under a League of Nations mandate until occupied by US forces in Aug. 1944. In 1947 they became part of the US-administered Trust Territory of the Pacific Islands.

On 17 June 1975 the electorate adopted a covenant to establish a Commonwealth in association with the USA; this was approved by the US government in April 1976 and came into force on 1 Jan. 1978. In Nov. 1986 the islanders were granted US citizenship. The UN terminated the Trusteeship status on 22 Dec. 1990.

TERRITORY AND POPULATION

The Northern Marianas form a single chain of 16 mountainous islands extending north of Guam for about 560 km, with a total area of 5,050 sq. km (1,950 sq. miles) of which 464 sq. km (179 sq. miles) are dry land, and with a population (2000 census) of 69,221 (female, 37,237).

The areas and populations of the islands are as follows:

Island(s)	Sq. km	1995 Census	2000 Census
Northern Group[1]	171	8	6
Saipan	122	52,698	62,392
Tinian (with Aguijan)	101[2]	2,631	3,540
Rota	83	3,509	3,283

[1]Pagan, Agrihan, Alamagan and nine uninhabited islands.
[2]Including uninhabited Aguijan.

In 2003, 23% spoke Chinese, 22% Chamorro and 24% Filipino languages. English remains an official language along with Carolinian and Chamorro. The largest town is Chalan Kanoa on Saipan.

SOCIAL STATISTICS

In 2002 there were 1,290 births (17·4 per 1,000 population) and 161 deaths (2·2). Infant mortality was 38 per 1,000 live births in 1996.

CONSTITUTION AND GOVERNMENT

The Constitution was approved by a referendum on 6 March 1977 and came into force on 9 Jan. 1978. The legislature comprises a nine-member *Senate*, with three Senators elected from each of the main three islands for a term of four years, and an 18-member *House of Representatives*, elected for a term of two years.

The Commonwealth is administered by a Governor and Lieut.-Governor, elected for four years.

RECENT ELECTIONS

At the elections of 5 Nov. 2005 the Covenant Party and Republican Party each won seven seats in the House of Representatives, with the Democratic Party taking two seats. Two independents were elected.

In the gubernatorial elections of 5 Nov. 2005 Benigno R. Fitial received 28·1% of votes cast, defeating Heinz S. Hofschneider (27·3%), incumbent Juan N. Babauta (26·6%) and Froilan C. Tenorio (18·0%).

CURRENT ADMINISTRATION

Governor: Benigno R. Fitial (Covenant Party), 2006–10 (salary: $70,000).

Lieut.-Governor: Timothy P. Villagomez (Covenant Party), 2006–10 ($65,000).

Government Website: http://www.gov.mp

ENERGY AND NATURAL RESOURCES

Fisheries

In 2001 total catch was 434,000 lb (197 tonnes), entirely from marine waters.

INDUSTRY

Labour

In 1990 there were 7,476 workers from the indigenous population and 21,188 were foreign workers; 2,699 were unemployed.

INTERNATIONAL TRADE

Imports and Exports

In 1997 imports totalled $836·2m.; in 1999 exports totalled $1,049·0m. Most imports came from other US Pacific territories, Hong Kong and Japan.

COMMUNICATIONS

Roads

There are about 381 km of roads.

Civil Aviation

There are six airports in all. Saipan handled 677,000 passengers (595,000 on international flights) and 9,500 tonnes of freight in 2001.

Telecommunications

There were 24,000 main telephone lines in 2000, equivalent to 452·5 per 1,000 inhabitants, and 3,000 mobile phone subscribers.

SOCIAL INSTITUTIONS

Education

In 2000 there were 679 pupils enrolled in nursery school and pre-school, 946 in kindergarten, 7,884 in elementary school (grades 1–8), 2,750 in high school (grades 9–12) and 1,130 in college or graduate school.

Health

In 1999 there were 31 doctors, three dentists, 123 nursing personnel, four pharmacists and 14 midwives. In 2001 there was one hospital with 86 beds.

RELIGION

The population is predominantly Roman Catholic.

CULTURE

Broadcasting

There were six radio stations, one television station and two cable TV stations on Saipan in 1998. In 1999 there were 10,500 radio and 4,100 television receivers.

Tourism

In 2000 there were 517,000 visitors; spending by tourists in 1998 totalled $647m.

Commonwealth of Puerto Rico

KEY HISTORICAL EVENTS

A Spanish dependency since the 16th century, Puerto Rico was ceded to the USA in 1898 after the Spanish defeat in the Spanish-American war. In 1917 US citizenship was conferred and in 1932 there was a name change from Porto Rico to Puerto Rico. In 1952 Puerto Rico was proclaimed a commonwealth with a representative government and a directly elected governor.

TERRITORY AND POPULATION

Puerto Rico is the most easterly of the Greater Antilles and lies between the Dominican Republic and the US Virgin Islands. The total area is 13,791 sq. km (5,325 sq. miles), of which 8,871 sq. km (3,425 sq. miles) are dry land; the population, according to the census of 2000, was 3,808,610, an increase of 8·1% over 1990. The urban population was 3,595,521 in 2000, representing 94·4% (73·3% in 1995) of the total population. Population density was 1,112 per sq. mile in 2000. Of the total population in 2000, 1,975,033 were female. Population estimate in July 2005 was 3,912,054. The UN gives a projected population for 2010 of 4·06m.

A law of April 1991 making Spanish the sole official language (which replaced a law of 1902 establishing Spanish and English as joint official languages) was reversed in 1993.

Chief towns, 2004 estimates, are: San Juan, 433,319; Bayamón, 225,121; Carolina, 187,767; Ponce, 185,744; Caguas, 142,556; Guaynabo, 102,169; Arecibo, 102,117.

The Puerto Rican island of Vieques, 10 miles to the east, has an area of 51·7 sq. miles and 9,253 (2004) inhabitants. The island of Culebra, between Puerto Rico and St Thomas, has an area of 10 sq. miles and 1,972 (2004) inhabitants. Both islands have good harbours.

SOCIAL STATISTICS

2002: births, 52,747 (13·7 per 1,000 population); deaths, 27,924 (7·2). Marriages (2004), 25,236; infant mortality rate (2003), 9·8 per 1,000 live births. Annual growth rate, 2000–03, 0·5%. In 2003 the most popular age range for marrying was 20–24 for both males and females. Fertility rate, 2003, 1·8 births per woman.

CLIMATE

Warm, sunny winters with hot summers. The north coast experiences more rainfall than the south coast and generally does not have a dry season as rainfall is evenly spread throughout the year. San Juan, Jan. 25°C, July 28°C. Annual rainfall 1,246 mm.

CONSTITUTION AND GOVERNMENT

Puerto Rico has representative government, the franchise being restricted to citizens 18 years of age or over, residence (one year) and such additional qualifications as may be prescribed by the Legislature of Puerto Rico, but no property qualification may be imposed. Puerto Ricans vote in presidential primary elections but not in US general elections. They have one non-voting representative in Washington. The island is given billions of dollars each year in food stamps and other federal aid from Washington and although Puerto Ricans fight in the US army, the island sends its own teams to the Olympic Games. The

executive power resides in a Governor, elected directly by the people every four years. 22 heads of departments form the Governor's Council of Secretaries. The legislative functions are vested in a Senate, composed of 27 members, and the House of Representatives, composed of 51 members. Both houses meet annually in Jan. Puerto Rican men are subject to conscription in US services.

A new constitution was drafted by a Puerto Rican Constituent Assembly and approved by the electorate at a referendum on 3 March 1952. It was then submitted to Congress, which struck out Section 20 of Article 11 covering the 'right to work' and the 'right to an adequate standard of living'; the remainder was passed and proclaimed by the Governor on 25 July 1952.

RECENT ELECTIONS

At the gubernatorial election on 2 Nov. 2004 Aníbal Acevedo Vilá (Popular Democratic Party/PPD) won with 48·7% of the vote, ahead of Pedro Rosselló (New Progressive Party /PNP) with 48·5% and Ruben Berrios Martine (Puerto Rican Independence Party/PIP) with 2·7%.

In elections to the Chamber of Representatives on 2 Nov. 2004 the New Progressive Party (PNP) polled 46·3% of the vote and claimed 32 of the 51 seats; the Popular Democratic Party (PPD) 43·1% and 18 seats; Puerto Rican Independence Party (PIP), 9·7% and 1 seat. In the Senate elections of the same day PNP took 17 seats, PPD took 9 seats and PIP took 1.

At a plebiscite on 14 Nov. 1993 on Puerto Rico's future status, 48·6% of votes cast were for Commonwealth (status quo), 46·3% for Statehood (51st State of the USA) and 4·4% for full independence. In a further plebiscite in Dec. 1998, some 52·2% of voters backed the opposition's call for no change, while 46·5% supported statehood. Independence was supported by 2·5%, while free association received 0·3%.

CURRENT ADMINISTRATION

Governor: Aníbal Acevedo Vilá (PPD), 2005–09 (salary: $70,000).

Secretary of State: Fernando Bonilla-Ortiz (PPD), appointed July 2005.

Government Website (Spanish only): http://www.gobierno.pr

ECONOMY

Budget

Revenues in 2000–01 totalled $11,208m. and expenditures $10,337m. Tax revenues accounted for 57·3% of revenue. Main items of expenditure were education and welfare (both 22·3%) and public safety and protection (15·7%).

Per capita personal income (2004) was $12,031.

Performance

Real GDP growth was 3·0% in 2004. Total GDP in 2004 was $78·8bn.

Banking and Finance

Banks on 30 June 2005 had total deposits of $53,440·9m. Bank loans were $54,128·9m. This includes 13 commercial banks and two government banks.

ENERGY AND NATURAL RESOURCES

Environment

Puerto Rico's carbon dioxide emissions from the consumption and flaring of fossil fuels in 2002 were the equivalent of 8·8 tonnes per capita.

Electricity

Installed capacity was 4·4m. kW in 2000. Production in 2004 was 20·1bn. kWh. Consumption per capita in 2004 was estimated to be 5,197 kWh.

Agriculture

In 2002, 2·0% of the economically active population was employed in agriculture. Production, 2002 estimates (in 1,000 tonnes): sugarcane, 320; plantains, 82; bananas, 50; oranges, 26; mangoes, 17; pineapples, 15; coffee, 13; pumpkins and squash, 11; tomatoes, 5. Livestock (2002): cattle, 390,000; pigs, 118,000; poultry, 12m.

Forestry

In 2005 the area under forests was 408,284 ha., or 46·3% of the total land area.

Fisheries

The total catch in 2001 was 8,364,000 lb (3,794 tonnes), exclusively from sea fishing.

INDUSTRY

There is some production of cement (1·76m. tonnes in 1999).

Labour

In Sept. 2003 there were 1,208,700 people in employment, including 307,700 people in government, 169,500 in trade, transportation and utilities, 117,800 in manufacturing and 96,200 in professional and business services. 161,100 persons were unemployed in Sept. 2003 (rate of 11·8%).

INTERNATIONAL TRADE

Imports and Exports

In 2003 imports amounted to $35,945m., of which $16,949m. came from the USA; exports were valued at $55,814m., of which $46,880m. went to the USA.

In 1997 main imports (in $1m.) were: chemical products, 5,416·3; electrical machinery, 2,423·8; transportation equipment, 2,241·2. Main exports were: chemical products, 10,627·8; machinery (except electrical), 3,490·0; food, 3,386·4.

Puerto Rico is not permitted to levy taxes on imports.

COMMUNICATIONS

Roads

In 2005 there were 15,936 miles of roads and 2,382,373 registered motor vehicles.

Rail

There are 96 km of railway, although no passenger service. There is a 17·2-km urban train system in use.

Civil Aviation

San Juan's Luis Muñoz Marin airport handled 9,396,000 passengers (7,298,000 on domestic flights) and 218,900 tonnes of freight in 2001.

Shipping

In 2004, 5,856 US and foreign vessels of 55,114,372 gross tons entered and cleared Puerto Rico.

Telecommunications

In 2001 there were 2,540,600 telephone subscribers, or 662·0 for every 1,000 persons. Mobile phone subscribers numbered 1,211,000 in 2001. There were 925,000 Internet users in 2005 and 543,000 fax machines in 1995.

SOCIAL INSTITUTIONS

Justice

The Commonwealth judiciary system is headed by a Supreme Court of seven members, appointed by the Governor, and consists of a First Instance Court and a Court of Appeals, all appointed by the Governor. The First Instance Court is a court of original general jurisdiction consisting of a Superior Court (253 judges) and municipal courts (85 judges). There are 13 judicial regions in the First Instance Court.

The population in penal institutions in Dec. 2005 was 14,412 (368 per 100,000 population).

Education

Education was made compulsory in 1899. The percentage of literacy in 1990 was 89·4% of those ten years of age or older. Total enrolment in public day schools, 2004–05, was 575,993. All private schools had a total enrolment of 138,560 pupils in 2004–05.

The University of Puerto Rico, which has 11 campuses throughout the country, had 68,117 students in 2003–04. Other institutions of higher education in the public sector had a total of 5,939 students in 2003–04. Higher education is also available in the private sector in the American University, 3,646 students in 2003–04; Caribbean University, 4,934; Columbia College, 1,193; Electronic Data Processing College of Puerto Rico, 1,648; Huertas Junior College, 1,606; Commercial Institute of Puerto Rico Junior College, 1,316; National University College, 4,440; Pontifical Catholic University of Puerto Rico, 10,055; Fundación Ana G. Méndez, 31,041; Sacred Heart University, 5,210; Inter-American University of Puerto Rico, 43,922. Other private universities and colleges had 24,412 students.

Health

There were 66 hospitals in 2004, with a hospital bed provision of 33 per 10,000 population. In 2002 there were 9,511 non-federal physicians.

RELIGION

In 2001 about 65% of the population were Roman Catholic. In Sept. 2003 there was one cardinal.

CULTURE

Broadcasting

In 1998 there were 89 radio and six television stations (colour by NTSC). There were 2·8m. radio receivers in 2000 and 530,000 TV receivers in 2001.

Press

In 2004 there were three main newspapers: *El Nuevo Día* had an estimated daily circulation of 210,730; *El Vocero,* 144,428; *San Juan Star,* 105,597.

Tourism

There were 4,889,200 visitors in 2004. Revenue from tourism amounted to $3,024m. in 2004.

FURTHER READING

Statistical Information: The Program of Economic Research and Social Planning of the Puerto Rico Planning Board publishes: *(a) Economic Report to the Governor* (annual); *(b) External Trade Statistics* (annual); *(c) Reports on national income and balance of payments; and other socioeconomic statistics* (since 1940)

Dietz, J. L., *Economic History of Puerto Rico: Institutional Change and Capital Development.* Princeton Univ. Press, 1987

Commonwealth Library: Univ. of Puerto Rico Library, Rio Piedras.

American Samoa

KEY HISTORICAL EVENTS

The Samoan Islands were first visited by Europeans in the 18th century; the first recorded visit was in 1722. On 14 July 1889 a treaty between the USA, Germany and Great Britain proclaimed the Samoan islands neutral territory, under a four-power government consisting of the three treaty powers and the local native government. By the Tripartite Treaty of 7 Nov. 1899, ratified 19 Feb. 1900, Great Britain and Germany renounced in favour of the USA all rights over the islands of the Samoan group east of 171° long. west of Greenwich, the islands to the west of that meridian being assigned to Germany (now the independent state of Samoa). The islands of Tutuila and Aunu'u were ceded to the USA by their High Chiefs on 17 April 1900, and the islands of the Manu'a group on 16 July 1904. Congress accepted the islands under a Joint Resolution approved 20 Feb. 1929. Swain's Island, 210 miles north of the Samoan Islands, was annexed in 1925 and is administered as an integral part of American Samoa.

TERRITORY AND POPULATION

The islands (Tutuila, Aunu'u, Ta'u, Olosega, Ofu and Rose) are approximately 650 miles east-northeast of the Fiji Islands. The total area is 1,511 sq. km (583 sq. miles), of which 200 sq. km (77 sq. miles) are dry land; population (2000 census), 57,291 (29,264 males), nearly all Polynesians or part-Polynesians. Population density was 286 per sq. km in 2000.

In 1995 an estimated 50·3% of the population lived in urban areas. The capital is Pago Pago, which had a population of 14,000 in 1999. The island's three Districts are Eastern (population, 2000, 23,441), Western (32,435) and Manu'a (1,378). There is also Swain's Island, with an area of 1·9 sq. miles and 37 inhabitants (2000), which lies 210 miles to the northwest. Rose Island (uninhabited) is 0·4 sq. mile in area. In 1990 some 85,000 American Samoans lived in the USA.

Samoan and English are spoken.

SOCIAL STATISTICS

In 2002 there were 1,627 births (28·2 per 1,000 population) and 290 deaths (5·0). Infant mortality was 6·4 per 1,000 live births in 2000. Annual growth rate, 2000, 2·0% (1·8% in 1999).

CLIMATE

A tropical maritime climate with a small annual range of temperature and plentiful rainfall. Pago Pago, Jan. 83°F (28·3°C), July 80°F (26·7°C). Annual rainfall 194" (4,850 mm).

CONSTITUTION AND GOVERNMENT

American Samoa is constitutionally an unorganized, unincorporated territory of the USA administered under the Department of the Interior. Its indigenous inhabitants are US nationals and are classified locally as citizens of American Samoa with certain privileges under local laws not granted to non-indigenous persons. Polynesian customs (not inconsistent with US laws) are respected.

Fagatogo is the seat of the government.

The islands are organized in 15 counties grouped in three districts; these counties and districts correspond to the traditional political units. On 25 Feb. 1948 a bicameral legislature was established, at the request of the Samoans, to have advisory legislative functions. With the adoption of the Constitution of 22 April 1960, and the revised Constitution of 1967, the legislature was vested with limited law-making authority. The lower house, or House of Representatives, is composed of 20 members elected by universal adult suffrage and one non-voting member for Swain's Island. The upper house, or Senate, is comprised of 18 members elected, in the traditional Samoan manner, in meetings of the chiefs. The Governor and Lieut.-Governor have been popularly elected since 1978. American Samoa also sends one delegate to the US House of Representatives. The Congressman may participate but not vote on the House floor.

RECENT ELECTIONS

At elections to the Senate and House of Representatives on 5 and 19 Nov. 2002, only non-partisans were elected.

At gubernatorial elections on 2 Nov. 2004 incumbent Togiola Tulafono (Democrat) received 48·4% of votes cast, Afoa Moega Lutu (ind.) 39·4% and Teo Fuavai (ind.) 12·2%. In the run-off held on 16 Nov. 2004 Togiola Tulafono received 55·7% of votes cast and Afoa Moega Lutu 44·3%.

CURRENT ADMINISTRATION

Governor: Togiola Tulafono (D.), Jan. 2005–Jan. 2009 (salary: $50,000).

Lieut.-Governor: Aitofele T. F. Sunia (D.), Jan. 2005–Jan. 2009.

Government Website: http://www.government.as

ECONOMY

Overview

The Economic Development and Planning Office promotes economic expansion and outside investment.

Budget

The chief sources of revenue are annual federal grants from the USA, local revenues from taxes, duties, receipts from commercial operations (enterprise and special revenue funds), utilities, rents and leases, and liquor sales. In 2001–02 revenues were $211·5m. and expenditures $180·5m.

Banking and Finance

The American Samoa branch of the Bank of Hawaii and the American Samoa Bank offer all commercial banking services. The Development Bank of American Samoa, government-owned, is concerned primarily through loans and guarantees with the economic advancement of the Territory.

ENERGY AND NATURAL RESOURCES

Environment

American Samoa's carbon dioxide emissions from the consumption and flaring of fossil fuels in 2002 were the equivalent of 8·3 tonnes per capita.

Electricity

Installed capacity was 35,000 kW in 2000. Production in 2000 was estimated at 133m. kWh. Per capita consumption in 2000 was an estimated 1,956 kWh. All the Manu'a islands have electricity.

Agriculture

Of the 48,640 acres of land area, 11,000 acres are suitable for tropical crops; most commercial farms are in the Tafuna plains and west Tutuila. Principal crops are coconuts, taro, bread-fruit, yams and bananas.

Livestock (2002): pigs, 11,000.

Fisheries

Total catch in 2001 was 8,075,000 lb (3,663 tonnes).

INDUSTRY

Fish canning is important, employing the second largest number of people (after government). Attempts are being made to provide a variety of light industries. Tuna fishing and local inshore fishing are both expanding.

Labour

In 2000 the civilian labour force numbered 17,627, of whom 16,718 were employed. The unemployment rate in 2000 was 5·2%.

INTERNATIONAL TRADE

Imports and Exports

Imports in 2000 totalled $507m. and exports $391m.

Chief imports are building materials, fuel oil, food, jewellery, machines and parts, alcoholic beverages and cigarettes. Chief exports are canned tuna, watches, pet foods and handicrafts.

COMMUNICATIONS

Roads
There are about 150 km of paved roads and 200 km of unpaved roads in all. Motor vehicles in use, 1995, 5,900 (5,300 passenger cars and 600 commercial vehicles).

Civil Aviation
Polynesian Airlines operate daily services between American Samoa (Pago Pago) and Samoa (Apia). Hawaiian Airlines also operates between Pago Pago and Honolulu. Manu'a Air Transport runs local services. There are three airports. There were 24,331 passenger enplanements in 2000.

Shipping
The harbour at Pago Pago, which nearly bisects the island of Tutuila, is the only good harbour for large vessels in American Samoa. By sea there is a twice-monthly service between the Fiji Islands, New Zealand and Australia and regular services between the USA, South Pacific ports, Honolulu and Japan. In 1999 vessels entering totalled 884,000 net registered tons.

Telecommunications
A commercial radiogram service is available to all parts of the world. Commercial phone and telex services are operated to all parts of the world. There were 15,000 main telephone lines in operation in 2002 and 2,400 mobile phone subscribers in 2001.

SOCIAL INSTITUTIONS

Justice
Judicial power is vested firstly in a High Court. The trial division has original jurisdiction of all criminal and civil cases. The probate division has jurisdiction of estates, guardianships, trusts and other matters. The land and title division decides cases relating to disputes involving communal land and Matai title court rules on questions and controversy over family titles. The appellate division hears appeals from trial, land and title, and probate divisions as well as having original jurisdiction in selected matters. The appellate court is the court of last resort. Two American judges sit with five Samoan judges permanently. In addition there are temporary judges or assessors who sit occasionally on cases involving Samoan customs. There is also a District Court with limited jurisdiction and there are 69 village courts.

The population in penal institutions in Dec. 2002 was 169 (equivalent to 243 per 100,000 population).

Education
Education is compulsory between the ages of six and 18. In 2000 there were 1,557 pupils enrolled in nursery school and pre-school, 1,736 in kindergarten, 11,418 in elementary school (grades 1–8), 4,645 in high school (grades 9–12) and 1,474 in college or graduate school.

Welfare
In Dec. 2001 there were 5,320 beneficiaries including 1,470 survivors, 1,370 retired workers and 1,240 disabled workers. Total payments came to $2m. with average monthly benefits of $442.

RELIGION
In 2001 about 41% of the population belonged to the Congregational Church and 19% were Roman Catholics. Methodists and Latter-day Saints (Mormons) are also represented.

CULTURE

Broadcasting
In 2000 there were 57,000 radio sets and 13,200 TV sets (colour by NTSC).

Tourism
In 2000 there were 44,000 tourist arrivals; receipts totalled $10m. in 1998.

FURTHER READING
Hughes, H. G. A., *Samoa: American Samoa, Western Samoa, Samoans Abroad.* [Bibliography] ABC-Clio, Oxford and Santa Barbara (CA), 1997

Guam

Guahan

KEY HISTORICAL EVENTS
Magellan is said to have discovered the island in 1521; it was ceded by Spain to the USA by the Treaty of Paris (10 Dec. 1898). The island was captured by the Japanese on 10 Dec. 1941, and retaken by American forces from 21 July 1944. Guam is of great strategic importance; substantial numbers of naval and air force personnel occupy about one-third of the usable land.

TERRITORY AND POPULATION
Guam is the largest and most southern island of the Marianas Archipelago, in 13° 26' N. lat., 144° 45' E. long. Total area, 212 sq. miles (549 sq. km). Hagåtña (previously Agaña), the seat of government, is about eight miles from the anchorage in Apra Harbor. The census in 2000 showed a population of 154,805 (79,181 males), of whom 80,737 were born in Guam; density, 282·0 per sq. km. Estimate, 2005, 170,000. In 1999 an estimated 61·0% of the population lived in rural areas. The UN gives a projected population for 2010 of 182,000. The Malay strain is predominant. Chamorro, the native language, and English are the official languages.

SOCIAL STATISTICS
Births, 2002, 3,212; deaths, 638. Birth rate, 2002, 19·9 per 1,000 population; death rate, 4·0 per 1,000 population; infant mortality rate (1997), 8·1 per 1,000 live births. Life expectancy, 1990–95, was 72·2 years for males and 76·0 years for females. Fertility rate, 1990–95, 3·4 births per woman.

CLIMATE
Tropical maritime, with little difference in temperatures over the year. Rainfall is copious at all seasons, but is greatest from July to Oct. Hagåtña, Jan. 81°F (27·2°C), July 81°F (27·2°C). Annual rainfall 93" (2,325 mm).

CONSTITUTION AND GOVERNMENT
Guam's constitutional status is that of an 'unincorporated territory' of the USA. In Aug. 1950 the President transferred the administration of the island from the Navy Department to the Interior Department. The transfer conferred full citizenship on the Guamanians, who had previously been 'nationals' of the USA. There was a referendum on status on 30 Jan. 1982. 38% of eligible voters voted; 48·5% of those favoured Commonwealth status.

The Governor and Lieut.-Governor are elected for four-year terms. The legislature is a 15-member elected Senate; its powers are similar to those of an American state legislature. Guam sends one non-voting delegate (Madeleine Bordallo, D., 2005–07) to the US House of Representatives.

RECENT ELECTIONS

At the election of 5 Nov. 2002 for the Guam Legislature the Democrats won nine seats and the Republicans won six. In gubernatorial elections held on the same day, Republican candidate Felix Camacho won 55·2% of the vote against 44·8% for Democrat Robert Underwood.

CURRENT ADMINISTRATION

Governor: Felix Perez Camacho (R.), 2003–07 (salary: $90,000).
   Lieut.-Governor: Kaleo S. Moylan (R.), 2003–07 ($85,000).

Government Website: http://ns.gov.gu/government.html

ECONOMY

Budget

Total revenue (2000) $340m.; expenditure $445m.

Banking and Finance

Banking law makes it possible for foreign banks to operate in Guam. In 2003 there were 12 commercial banks.

ENERGY AND NATURAL RESOURCES

Environment

Guam's carbon dioxide emissions from the consumption and flaring of fossil fuels in 2002 were the equivalent of 13·1 tonnes per capita.

Electricity

Installed capacity was 0·3m. kW in 2000. Production was 830m. kWh in 2000. Consumption per capita in 2000 was estimated at 5,355 kWh.

Water

The total area covered by water is approximately 7 sq. miles. The Navy and Air Force conserve water in reservoirs.

Agriculture

The major products of the island are sweet potatoes, cucumbers, watermelons and beans. In 2001 there were approximately 12,000 acres of arable land and 22,000 acres of permanent cropland. Production (2002 estimates, in 1,000 tonnes): coconuts, 52; copra, 2; watermelons, 2. Livestock (2002) included 1,000 goats and 5,000 pigs. There is an agricultural experimental station at Inarajan.

Fisheries

In 2001 total catch was 613,000 lb (278 tonnes), exclusively from sea fishing.

INDUSTRY

Guam Economic Development Authority controls three industrial estates: Cabras Island (32 acres); Calvo estate at Tamuning (26 acres); Harmon estate (16 acres). Industries include textile manufacture, cement and petroleum distribution, warehousing, printing, plastics and ship-repair. Other main sources of income are construction and tourism.

Labour

In 1990 there were 90,990 persons of employable age, of whom 66,138 were in the workforce (54,186 civilian). 2,042 were unemployed.

INTERNATIONAL TRADE

Guam is the only American territory which has complete 'free trade'; excise duties are levied only upon imports of tobacco, liquid fuel and liquor.

Imports and Exports

In 2002 imports were valued at $389m. and exports at $37m. Main export destinations in 1999 were Japan, 53·9%; Micronesia, 18·6%; Palau, 6·3%.

COMMUNICATIONS

Roads

There are 674 km of all-weather roads. In 2002 there were 59,700 passenger cars and 20,100 commercial vehicles in use.

Civil Aviation

There is an international airport at Tamuning. Seven commercial airlines serve Guam. There were 1,004,354 passenger enplanements in 2000.

Shipping

There is a port at Apra Harbor.

Telecommunications

Overseas telephone and radio dispatch facilities are available. Main telephone lines numbered 112,600 in 2001 (716·3 per 1,000 inhabitants). Mobile phone subscribers numbered 33,000 in 2002 and Internet users 50,000.

SOCIAL INSTITUTIONS

Justice

The Organic Act established a District Court with jurisdiction in matters arising under both federal and territorial law; the judge is appointed by the President subject to Senate approval. There is also a Supreme Court and a Superior Court; all judges are locally appointed except the Federal District judge. Misdemeanours are under the jurisdiction of the police court. The Spanish law was superseded in 1933 by five civil codes based upon California law.

The population in penal institutions in Dec. 2002 was 542 (334 per 100,000 population).

Education

Education is compulsory from five to 16. Bilingual teaching programmes integrate the Chamorro language and culture into public school courses. Public school enrolment in 2002–03: 2,806 pupils in Head Start and kindergarten, 12,361 in 27 elementary schools (grades 1–5); 7,554 in seven middle schools (grades 6–8); and 9,081 in four high schools (grades 9–12). In 2003 there were about 25 private schools (nine Catholic). The University of Guam is in Mangilao and Guam Community College is in Barrigada.

Health

There is a hospital, eight nutrition centres, a school health programme and an extensive immunization programme. Emphasis is on disease prevention, health education and nutrition.

Welfare

In 1990, $83·2m. was paid in Federal direct payments for individuals, including $1·91m. Medicare, $1·91m. disability insurance and $11·37m. retirement insurance.

RELIGION

About 75% of the Guamanians are Roman Catholics; the other 25% are Baptists, Episcopalians, Bahais, Lutherans, Latter-day Saints (Mormons), Presbyterians, Jehovah's Witnesses and members of the Church of Christ and Seventh Day Adventists.

CULTURE

Broadcasting

There are four commercial stations, a commercial television station, a public broadcasting station and a cable television station with 24 channels. In 1997 there were 221,000 radio and 106,000 TV sets (colour by NTSC).

Press

There is one daily newspaper, a twice-weekly paper, and four weekly publications (all of which are of military or religious interest only).

Tourism

There were 1,288,000 tourist arrivals in 2000; spending by tourists in 1999 totalled $1·91bn.

FURTHER READING

Report (Annual) of the Governor of Guam to the US Department of Interior
Guam Annual Economic Review. Economic Research Center, Hagåtña

Rogers, R. F., *Destiny's Landfall: a History of Guam.* Hawaii Univ. Press, 1995
Wuerch, W. L. and Ballendorf, D. A., *Historical Dictionary of Guam and Micronesia.* Metuchen, NJ, 1995

Virgin Islands of the United States

KEY HISTORICAL EVENTS

The Virgin Islands of the United States, formerly known as the Danish West Indies, were named and claimed for Spain by Columbus in 1493. They were later settled by Dutch and English planters, invaded by France in the mid-17th century and abandoned by the French *c.* 1700, by which time Danish influence had been established. St Croix was held by the Knights of Malta between two periods of French rule.

The Virgin Islands were purchased by the United States from Denmark for $25m. in a treaty ratified by both nations and proclaimed on 31 March 1917. Their value was wholly strategic, inasmuch as they commanded the Anegada Passage from the Atlantic Ocean to the Caribbean Sea and the approach to the Panama Canal. Although the inhabitants were made US citizens in 1927, the islands are constitutionally an 'unincorporated territory'.

TERRITORY AND POPULATION

The Virgin Islands group, lying about 40 miles due east of Puerto Rico, comprises the islands of St Thomas (31 sq. miles), St Croix (83 sq. miles), St John (20 sq. miles) and 65 small islets or cays, mostly uninhabited. The total area is 1,910 sq. km (738 sq. miles), of which 346 sq. km (134 sq. miles) are dry land.

The population according to the 2000 census was 108,612 (females, 56,748); density 811 per sq. mile. 92·6% of the population were urban in 2000.

Population (2000 census) of St Croix, 53,234; St Thomas, 51,181; St John, 4,197. In 2000, 69·8% of the population were native born.

The UN gives a projected population for 2010 of 112,000.

The capital and only city, Charlotte Amalie, on St Thomas, had a population (2000 census) of 11,044. There are two towns on St Croix with 2000 census populations of: Christiansted, 2,637; Frederiksted, 732.

SOCIAL STATISTICS

2002 births, 1,634; deaths, 617. Rates, 2002 (per 1,000 population); birth, 15·0; death, 5·7; infant mortality (1997), 13·0 per 1,000 live births.

CLIMATE

Average temperatures vary from 77°F to 82°F throughout the year; humidity is low. Average annual rainfall, about 45". The islands lie in the hurricane belt; tropical storms with heavy rainfall can occur in late summer.

CONSTITUTION AND GOVERNMENT

The Organic Act of 22 July 1954 gives the US Department of the Interior full jurisdiction; some limited legislative powers are given to a single-chambered legislature, composed of 15 senators elected for two years representing the two legislative districts of St Croix and St Thomas-St John.

The Governor is elected by the residents. Since 1954 there have been four attempts to redraft the Constitution, to provide for greater autonomy. Each has been rejected by the electorate. The latest was defeated in a referendum in Nov. 1981, 50% of the electorate participating.

For administration, there are 14 executive departments, 13 of which are under commissioners and the other, the Department of Justice, under an Attorney-General. The US Department of the Interior appoints a Federal Comptroller of government revenue and expenditure.

The franchise is vested in residents who are citizens of the United States, 18 years of age or over. In 1993 there were 39,046 voters, of whom 10,732 participated in the local elections that year. They do not participate in the US presidential election but they have a non-voting representative in Congress.

The capital is Charlotte Amalie, on St Thomas Island.

RECENT ELECTIONS

Elections for governor held on 5 Nov. 2002 were won by Charles Turnbull, II (Democrat) with 50·5% of the votes, ahead of John DeJongh in second place with 24·4%. The turnout was 62%. In Senate elections held on 2 Nov. 2004 the Democratic Party of the Virgin Islands won 10 out of 15 seats.

CURRENT ADMINISTRATION

Governor: Charles Turnbull, II (D.), 2003–07 (salary: $80,000).
Lieut.-Governor: Vargrave A. Richards (D.), 2003–07 ($75,000).

US Virgin Islands Parliament: http://www.senate.gov.vi

ECONOMY

Currency

United States currency became legal tender on 1 July 1934.

Budget

Under the 1954 Organic Act finances are provided partly from local revenues—customs, federal income tax, real and personal property tax, trade tax, excise tax, pilotage fees, etc.—and partly from Federal Matching Funds, being the excise taxes collected by the federal government on such Virgin Islands products transported to the mainland as are liable.

Per capita income, 2000, $13,139.

Budget for financial year 1999: revenues, $486·3m.; expenditures, $486·3m.

Banking and Finance

Banks include the Chase Manhattan Bank; the Bank of Nova Scotia; the First Federal Savings and Loan Association of Puerto Rico; the Banco Popular of the Virgin Islands; First Bank of Puerto Rico; the Virgin Islands Community Bank; the Bank of St Croix; Barclays Bank International; Citibank; Banco Popular de Puerto Rico; and FirstBank Virgin Islands.

ENERGY AND NATURAL RESOURCES

Environment

Carbon dioxide emissions from the consumption and flaring of fossil fuels in 2002 were the equivalent of 114·6 tonnes per capita, the second highest in the world.

Electricity

The Virgin Islands Water and Power Authority provides electric power from generating plants on St Croix and St Thomas; St John is served by power cable and emergency generator. Production in 2000 was about 1·09bn. kWh. Per capita consumption in 2000 was an estimated 9,008 kWh. Installed capacity in 2000 was 323,000 kW.

Water

There are six de-salinization plants with maximum daily capacity of 8·7m. gallons of fresh water. Rainwater remains the most reliable source.

The total area covered by water is approximately 604 sq. miles, of which 16 sq. miles are inland.

Agriculture

Land for fruit, vegetables and animal feed is available on St Croix, and there are tax incentives for development. Sugar has been terminated as a commercial crop and over 4,000 acres of prime land could be utilized for food crops.

Livestock (2002): cattle, 8,000; goats, 4,000; pigs, 3,000; sheep, 3,000.

Fisheries

There is a fishermen's co-operative with a market at Christiansted. There is a shellfish-farming project at Rust-op-Twist, St Croix. The total catch in 2001 was approximately 660,000 lb (300 tonnes).

INDUSTRY

The main occupations on St Thomas are tourism and government service; on St Croix manufacturing is more important. Manufactures include rum (the most valuable product), watches, pharmaceuticals and fragrances. Industries in order of revenue: tourism, refining oil, watch assembly, rum distilling, construction.

Labour

In 2000 the total labour force was 51,042, of whom 7,351 were employed in the arts, entertainment, recreation, accommodation and food services, 6,742 were employed in educational, health and social services, 6,476 in retail trade, 4,931 in public administration and 4,900 in construction. In 2000 there were 4,368 registered unemployed persons, or 5·6% of the workforce.

INTERNATIONAL TRADE

Imports and Exports

Imports, 2001, totalled $4,608·7m. and exports $4,234·2m. The main import is crude petroleum, while the principal exports are petroleum products.

COMMUNICATIONS

Roads

In 1996 the Virgin Islands had 856 km of roads.

Civil Aviation

There is a daily cargo and passenger service between St Thomas and St Croix. Alexander Hamilton Airport on St Croix can take all types of aircraft. Cyril E. King Airport on St Thomas takes 727-class aircraft. There are air connections to mainland USA and other Caribbean islands. There were 658,905 passenger enplanements in 2000.

Shipping

The whole territory has free port status. There is an hourly boat service between St Thomas and St John and a 75-minute catamaran service between St Croix and St Thomas two to three times a day.

Telecommunications

All three Virgin Islands have a dial telephone system. Telephone subscribers numbered 110,400 in 2002 (1,010·1 per 1,000 population). Direct dialling to Puerto Rico and the mainland, and internationally, is now possible. Worldwide radio telegraph service is also available. In 2001 there were 41,000 mobile phone subscribers. In 2002 there were 30,000 Internet users.

Postal Services

In 2004 there were 12 post offices.

SOCIAL INSTITUTIONS

Justice

The population in penal institutions in Dec. 2002 was 647 (522 per 100,000 population).

Education

In 2000 there were 32,119 people enrolled in schools, of which 2,484 in nursery and pre-school, 2,230 in kindergarten, 16,858 in elementary school, 7,440 in high school and 3,107 in college or graduate school. In 1997 there were 777 elementary teachers and 782 secondary teachers. In autumn 2003 the University of the Virgin Islands had 2,768 students. The College is part of the United States land-grant network of higher education. The Virgin Islands has the highest proportion of female students in higher education anywhere in the world, at 77% in 1998–99.

Health

In 2002 there were 161 non-federal physicians and in 1990 there were 48 hospital beds per 10,000 inhabitants. The Roy L. Schneider Hospital on St Thomas had 169 beds and over 50 physicians in 2004. The Juan F. Luis Hospital, Christiansted, serves St Croix, with 160 beds in 1994.

Welfare

In 2001 federal direct payments for individuals totalled $233·4m., including: retirement insurance, $72·0m.; housing assistance, $53·4m.; survivors insurance, $20·2m.; disability insurance, $18·0m.; food stamps, $17·6m.

RELIGION

At the 2000 census 42% of the population were Baptists, 34% were Roman Catholics and 17% were Episcopalians.

There are places of worship of the Protestant, Roman Catholic and Jewish faiths in St Thomas and St Croix, and Protestant and Roman Catholic churches in St John.

CULTURE

Broadcasting

In 2002 there were 16 radio stations and one public and one commercial TV station.

In 2000 there were 107,000 radio receivers and 64,700 TV receivers (colour by NTSC).

Press

In 1996 there were three dailies with a combined circulation of 42,000, at a rate of 437 per 1,000 inhabitants.

Tourism

Tourism accounts for some 70% of GDP. There were 565,000 foreign tourists in 2000, and 1,768,000 cruise ship arrivals. Revenue from tourism amounted to $965m. in 2000. 6,800 people were employed in the leisure and hospitality sector in 2003.

St Thomas claims some of the best white-sand beaches in the Caribbean and attracts visitors to its Coral World aquarium. Christiansted, on St Croix, is the old capital of the Danish colony, with well-preserved colonial architecture. St Croix is a major diving destination and has a leatherback turtle nesting beach. St John, the least developed of the islands, is dominated by a thickly forested national park.

FURTHER READING

Moll, V. P., *Virgin Islands*. [Bibliography] ABC-Clio, Oxford and Santa Barbara (CA), 1991

Other Unincorporated Territories

Howland, Baker and Jarvis Islands
Three small Pacific islands, the largest two of which, Howland Island and Baker Island, are 2,600 km southwest of Hawaii. Administered under the US Department of the Interior. Area 2 sq. miles; population (1995) numbered 1,168. There is a National Assembly.

Johnston Atoll
Two small Pacific islands 1,100 km southwest of Hawaii, administered by the US Air Force. Area, under 1 sq. mile; population (1996) totalled 1,200 US military and civilian contractor personnel.

Midway Islands
Two small Pacific islands at the western end of the Hawaiian chain, administered by the US Navy. Area, 2 sq. miles; population (1995) was 453 US military personnel.

Wake Island
Three small Pacific islands 3,700 km west of Hawaii, administered by the US Air Force. Area, 3 sq. miles; population (1995) numbered 302 US military and contract personnel.

Kingman Reef
Small Pacific reef 1,500 km southwest of Hawaii, administered by the US Navy. Area one tenth of a sq. mile; uninhabited.

Navassa Island
Small Caribbean island 48 km west of Haiti, administered by US Coast Guards. Area 2 sq. miles; uninhabited.

Palmyra Atoll
Small atoll 1,500 km southwest of Hawaii, administered by the US Department of the Interior. Area 5 sq. miles; uninhabited.

URUGUAY

© Research Machines plc 2006

República Oriental del Uruguay

Capital: Montevideo
Population projection, 2010: 3·57m.
GDP per capita, 2003: (PPP$) 8,280
HDI/world rank: 0·840/46

KEY HISTORICAL EVENTS

Uruguay was the last colony settled by Spain in the Americas. Part of the Spanish viceroyalty of Rio de la Plata until revolutionaries expelled the Spanish in 1811 and subsequently a province of Brazil, Uruguay declared independence on 25 Aug. 1825. Conflict between two political parties, the *blancos* (conservatives) and the *colorados* (liberals), led, in 1865–70, to the War of the Triple Alliance. In 1903 peace and prosperity were restored under President José Batlle y Ordóñez. Since 1904 Uruguay has been unique in her constitutional innovations, all designed to protect her from dictatorship. A favoured device was the collegiate system of government, in which the two largest political parties were represented.

The early part of the 20th century saw the development of a welfare state in Uruguay which encouraged extensive immigration. In 1919 a new constitution was adopted providing for a *colegiado*—a plural executive based on the Swiss pattern. However, the system was abolished in 1933 and replaced by presidential government, with quadrennial elections. From 1951 to 1966 a collective form of leadership again replaced the presidency. During the 1960s, following a series of strikes and riots, the Army became increasingly influential, repressive measures were adopted and presidential government was restored in 1967. The Tupamaro, Marxist urban guerrillas, sought violent revolution but were finally defeated by the Army in 1972. The return to civilian rule came on 12 Feb. 1985.

TERRITORY AND POPULATION

Uruguay is bounded on the northeast by Brazil, on the southeast by the Atlantic, on the south by the Río de la Plata and on the west by Argentina. The area, including inland waters, is 176,215 sq. km (68,037 sq. miles). The following table shows the area and the population of the 19 departments at census 2004:

Departments	Sq. km	Census 2004	Capital
Artigas	11,928	78,019	Artigas
Canelones	4,536	485,028	Canelones
Cerro-Largo	13,648	86,564	Melo
Colonia	6,106	119,266	Colonia
Durazno	11,643	58,859	Durazno
Flores	5,144	25,104	Trinidad
Florida	10,417	68,181	Florida
Lavalleja	10,016	60,925	Minas
Maldonado	4,793	140,192	Maldonado
Montevideo	530	1,326,064	Montevideo
Paysandú	13,922	113,244	Paysandú
Río Negro	9,282	53,989	Fray Bentos
Rivera	9,370	104,921	Rivera
Rocha	10,551	69,937	Rocha
Salto	14,163	123,120	Salto
San José	4,992	103,104	San José
Soriano	9,008	84,563	Mercedes
Tacuarembó	15,438	90,489	Tacuarembó
Treinta y Tres	9,529	49,318	Treinta y Tres

Total population, census (2004) 3,240,887; population density, 18·4 per sq. km.

The UN gives a projected population for 2010 of 3·57m.

In 2004 Montevideo (the capital) accounted for 39·2% of the total population. It had a population in 2004 of 1,269,600. Other major cities are Salto (population of 99,072 in 2004) and Paysandú (73,272 in 2004). Uruguay has the highest percentage of urban population in South America, with 92·5% living in urban areas in 2003.

13% of the population are over 65; 24% are under 15; 63% are between 15 and 64.

The official language is Spanish.

SOCIAL STATISTICS

2000: births, 52,720; deaths, 32,456; marriages, 13,888; divorces, 6,822. Rates (per 1,000 population), 2000: birth, 15·9; death, 9·2; marriage, 4·2; divorce, 2·0. Annual population growth rate, 1992–2002, 0·7%. Infant mortality, 2001 (per 1,000 live births), 14. Life expectancy in 2003 was 71·7 years among males and 79·0 years among females. Fertility rate, 2001, 2·3 births per woman.

CLIMATE

A warm temperate climate, with mild winters and warm summers. The wettest months are March to June, but there is really no dry season. Montevideo, Jan. 72°F (22·2°C), July 50°F (10°C). Annual rainfall 38" (950 mm).

CONSTITUTION AND GOVERNMENT

The Constitution was adopted on 27 Nov. 1966 and became effective in Feb. 1967; it has been amended in 1989, 1994, 1996 and 2004.

Congress consists of a *Senate* of 31 members and a *Chamber of Deputies* of 99 members, both elected by proportional representation for five-year terms although in the case of the Senate only 30 members are elected with one seat reserved for the Vice-President. The electoral system provides that the successful presidential candidate be a member of the party which gains a parliamentary majority. Electors vote for deputies on a first-past-the-post system, and simultaneously vote for a presidential candidate of the same party. The winners of the second vote are credited with the number of votes obtained by their party in the parliamentary elections. Referendums may be called at the instigation of 10,000 signatories.

National Anthem

'Orientales, la patria o la tumba' ('Easterners, the fatherland or the tomb'); words by F. Acuña de Figueroa, tune by F. J. Deballi.

GOVERNMENT CHRONOLOGY

Heads of State since 1943. (EP-FA-NM = Progressive Encounter-Broad Front-New Majority; PC = Colorado Party; PN = National Party (Blancos); PS = Socialist Party of Uruguay)

Presidents of the Republic

1943–47	PC	Juan José Amézaga Landaraso
1947	PC	Tomás Berreta Gandolfo
1947–51	PC	Luis Conrado Batlle Berres
1951–52	PC	Andrés Martínez Trueba

Chairman of the 1st National Council of Government

1952–55	PC	Andrés Martínez Trueba

Chairmen of the 2nd National Council of Government

1955–56	PC	Luis Conrado Batlle Berres
1956–57	PC	Alberto Fermín Zubiría Urtiague
1957–58	PC	Arturo Lezama Bagez
1958–59	PC	Carlos Lorenzo Fischer Brusoni

Chairmen of the 3rd National Council of Government

1959–60	PN	Martín Recaredo Echegoyen Machicote
1960–61	PN	Benito Nardone Cetrulo
1961–62	PN	Eduardo Víctor Haedo
1962–63	PN	Faustino Harrison Usoz

Chairmen of the 4th National Council of Government

1963–64	PN	Daniel Fernández Crespo
1964–65	PN	Luis Giannattasio Finocchietti
1965–66	PN	Washington Beltrán Mullin
1966–67	PN	Alberto Heber Usher

Presidents of the Republic

1967	PC	Óscar Diego Gestido Pose
1967–72	PC	Jorge Pacheco Areco
1972–76	PC[1]	Juan María Bordaberry Arocena
1976–81	PN[2]	Aparicio Méndez Manfredini
1981–85	military	Gregorio Conrado Álvarez Armellino
1985–90	PC	Julio María Sanguinetti Coirolo
1990–95	PN	Luis Alberto Lacalle de Herrera
1995–2000	PC	Julio María Sanguinetti Coirolo
2000–05	PC	Jorge Luis Batlle Ibáñez
2005–	PS, EP-FA-NM	Tabaré Ramón Vázquez Rosas

[1]Civilian president under military rule 1973–76.
[2]Civilian president under military rule.

RECENT ELECTIONS

Elections for the General Assembly were held on 31 Oct. 2004. In elections to the Chamber of Deputies, the Progressive Encounter-Broad Front-New Majority (comprised of the Uruguay Assembly, Frenteamplio Confluence, Current 78, Movement of Popular Participation, Christian-Democratic Party, Communist Party of Uruguay, Party of the Communes, Socialist Party of Uruguay and the Artiguist Tendency) won 53 seats, the National Party (PN) 34, the Colorado Party (PC) 10 and the Independent Party 2. In the Senate election the Progressive Encounter-Broad Front-New Majority (EP-FA-NM) won 17 seats, PN 11 and PC 3.

In the presidential election, also held on 31 Oct. 2004, Tabaré Vázquez (EP-FA-NM) received 50·4% of the vote, Jorge Larrañaga (PN) 34·3% and Guillermo Stirling (Colorado Party) 10·4%. Turnout was 89·6%.

CURRENT ADMINISTRATION

President: Tabaré Vázquez; b. 1940 (EP-FA-NM; sworn in 1 March 2005).

Vice-President: Rodolfo Nin Novoa.

In March 2006 the government comprised:

Minister of Agriculture, Livestock and Fisheries: José Mujica. *Defence:* Azucena Berrutti. *Economy:* Danilo Astori. *Education and Culture:* Jorge Brovetto. *Foreign Affairs:* Reinaldo Gargano. *Housing:* Mariano Arana. *Industry:* Jorge Lepra. *Interior:* José Díaz. *Labour:* Eduardo Bonomi. *Public Health:* María Julia Muñoz. *Tourism, Sports and Youth:* Héctor Lescano. *Transport:* Víctor Rossi.

Presidency Website (Spanish only):
http://www.presidencia.gub.uy

CURRENT LEADERS

Tabaré Vázquez

Position
President

Introduction
On his inauguration on 1 March 2005, Tabaré Vázquez became the first left-wing president in Uruguay's history. A cancer specialist and former mayor of the capital, Montevideo, he promised to focus on helping the poor and creating jobs.

Early Life
Tabaré Ramón Vázquez was born in a poor district of Montevideo on 17 Jan. 1940, the son of an oil refinery worker. Having graduated in medicine at the capital's University of the Republic in Dec. 1969, he then specialized and qualified in oncology and radiotherapy, beginning work in 1972. In 1976 Vázquez obtained a scholarship from the French government to study further at the Institute Gustave Roussy in Paris.

In 1985, the year in which civilian government was restored in Uruguay after 12 years of military dictatorship, Vázquez was nominated the director of the department of oncology and radiotherapy at the University of the Republic. He went on to publish more than 100 scientific papers and to attend numerous international conferences. Affiliated with the central committee of the Socialist Party from late 1987, Vázquez then joined the Broad Front (a left-wing coalition formed in 1971) and stood as their candidate in the election for the mayorship of Montevideo in Nov. 1989. He won and went on to become a popular and successful figure, re-elected throughout the 1990s and early 2000s with increasing majorities.

In 1994 Vázquez came within a handful of votes of winning the presidency as the candidate of the Progressive Encounter-Broad Front (EP-FA) alliance, just losing to the Colorado Party's Julio María Sanguinetti. Vázquez entered the 1999 presidential election with high hopes, promising to create jobs with increased spending. The election went to a run-off, but was won by the Colorado candidate, Jorge Batlle, who played up his party's record of economic growth. Support for the ruling party fell sharply when Uruguay's economy plunged into recession in 2002, the result of a growing public debt, labour unrest and the massive debt default of neighbouring Argentina in 2001. In the presidential election of Oct. 2004, Vázquez received 50·4% of the votes cast, avoiding the need for a run-off. The EP-FA-NM coalition (by then including New Majority) also emerged victorious in the legislative elections—the first parliamentary election win for the political left in Uruguay's history. On 1 March 2005 Vázquez was inaugurated as president.

Career in Office
Having campaigned with a promise to fight poverty and tackle the high rate of unemployment, Vázquez embarked on his five-year

term by launching a US$100m. 'social emergency programme'. He pledged to distribute wealth more evenly by strengthening educational institutions and introducing a national minimum wage. He also signed an economic agreement with Venezuela, restored diplomatic relations with Cuba and set out to strengthen ties with other members of the MERCOSUR trade bloc to reduce the country's foreign debt. In the field of human rights, Vázquez promised to investigate the fate of the many thousands who disappeared during the military dictatorship of the 1970s. Demonstrating his popular touch, he announced that he would continue to see cancer patients throughout his term in office.

DEFENCE

Defence expenditure totalled US$103m. in 2003 (US$30 per capita), representing 0·9% of GDP.

Army

The Army consists of volunteers who enlist for one to two years service. There are four military regions with divisional headquarters. Strength (2002), 15,200. In addition there are government paramilitary forces numbering 920.

Navy

The Navy includes three ex-French frigates. A naval aviation service 300 strong operates anti-submarine aircraft. Personnel in 2002 totalled 5,700 including 300 naval infantry. The main base is at Montevideo.

Air Force

Organized with US aid, the Air Force had (2002) about 3,000 personnel and 28 combat aircraft.

INTERNATIONAL RELATIONS

Uruguay is a member of the UN, WTO, OAS, Inter-American Development Bank, MERCOSUR, LAIA, IOM and the Antarctic Treaty.

ECONOMY

In 2002 agriculture contributed 9·4% of GDP, industry 26·8% and services 63·8%.

Overview

Uruguay's economy benefits from a favourable climate for agriculture and substantial hydropower potential. During 1990–98 the economy grew by 3·9% a year on average, above the long-term trend of 2% between 1960–2000. Uruguay is exposed to competition from its neighbours, Brazil and Argentina, where strong rates of growth bolstered export performance. Export performance has also benefited greatly from the creation of MERCOSUR. In 1999, as a consequence of the devaluation of the Brazilian *real* and the worst drought since 1988, Uruguay's economy shrank by 2·8%. Weak banking regulations and strong links with Argentina left Uruguay exposed to the Argentinian bank-run and the authorities were forced to float the peso in June 2002. GDP contracted by a cumulative 7·5% during 1999–2001 and contracted by a further 10·8% in 2002. The events of 1999–2002 have highlighted macroeconomic and structural weaknesses that leave the economy vulnerable to external shocks, including high trade dependence on the MERCOSUR region and a weak banking system.

Currency

The unit of currency is the *Uruguayan peso* (UYP), of 100 *centésimos*, which replaced the nuevo peso in March 1993 at 1 Uruguayan peso = 1,000 nuevos pesos. In June 2002 Uruguay allowed the peso to float freely. Foreign exchange reserves were US$1,791m. and gold reserves 8,000 troy oz in May 2002 (1·8m. troy oz in Nov. 1999). Inflation, which had been over 100% in 1990, was 9·2% in 2004. Total money supply in Feb. 2002 was 12,456m. pesos.

Budget

Central government finance (1m. pesos):

	1996	1997	1998	1999	2000	2001
Revenue	45,535	60,165	70,664	67,197	68,167	62,708
Expenditure	47,914	62,363	72,673	76,079	76,489	77,487

Main components of 2001 revenue: taxes on goods and services, 38·7%; social security contributions, 23·4%; income taxes, 15·2%. Expenditure included: social security and welfare, 56·5%; education, 7·6%; health, 6·6%.

Standard rate of VAT is 23%.

Performance

Uruguay depends heavily on its two large neighbours, Brazil and Argentina. In 1999 Uruguay's economy contracted by 2·8%. In 2000 there was also negative growth, of 1·4%, and the general downturn in the world economy exacerbated by Argentina's crisis caused Uruguay's economy to contract again in 2001, by 3·4%. In 2002 as Argentina's economic crisis worsened so did the situation in Uruguay, with the economy shrinking by 11·0%. However, 2003 and 2004 saw a recovery, with growth of 2·2% and 12·3% respectively. Total GDP in 2004 was US$13·1bn.

Banking and Finance

The Central Bank (*President*, Walter Cancela) was inaugurated on 16 May 1967. It is the bank of issue and supreme regulatory authority. In 2003 there were three other state banks, three principal commercial banks, ten foreign banks and two major credit co-operatives. Savings banks deposits were 1,993,029m. pesos in 1995.

There is a stock exchange in Montevideo.

ENERGY AND NATURAL RESOURCES

Environment

Uruguay's carbon dioxide emissions from the consumption and flaring of fossil fuels in 2002 were the equivalent of 1·3 tonnes per capita. An *Environmental Sustainability Index* compiled for the World Economic Forum meeting in Jan. 2005 ranked Uruguay third in the world, with 71·8%. The index measured the ability of countries to maintain favourable environmental conditions and examined various factors including pollution levels and the use or abuse of natural resources.

Electricity

Installed capacity was 2·2m. kW in 2000. Production in 2000 was 7·59bn. kWh, with consumption per capita 2,390 kWh.

Agriculture

Rising investment has helped agriculture, which has given a major boost to the country's economy. Some 41m. acres are devoted to farming, of which 90% to livestock and 10% to crops. Some large *estancias* have been divided up into family farms; the average farm is about 250 acres. In 2001 there were 1·30m. ha. of arable land and 40,000 ha. of permanent crops. 181,000 ha. were irrigated in 2001.

Main crops (in 1,000 tonnes), 2000: rice, 1,175; wheat, 310; barley, 200; sugarcane, 160; oranges, 150; grapes, 140; potatoes, 110; wine, 108; apples, 65; maize, 65; sweet potatoes, 62; tangerines and mandarins, 60; lemons and limes, 48; oats, 45. The country has some 6m. fruit trees, principally peaches, oranges, tangerines and pears.

Livestock, 2000: sheep, 13·03m.; cattle, 10·80m.; horses, 500,000; pigs, 380,000; chickens, 13m.

Livestock products, 2000 (in 1,000 tonnes): beef and veal, 453; lamb and mutton, 51; pork, bacon and ham, 26; poultry meat, 53; milk 1,422; eggs, 37; greasy wool, 55.

Forestry

In 2000 the area under forests was 1·29m. ha. (mainly eucalyptus and pine), representing 7·4% of the total land area. In 2001, 5·81m. cu. metres of roundwood were cut.

Fisheries

The total catch in 2001 was 105,034 tonnes, almost entirely marine fish.

INDUSTRY

In 2001 industry accounted for 26·6% of GDP, with manufacturing contributing 16·6%. Industries include meat packing, oil refining, cement manufacture, foodstuffs, beverages, leather and textile manufacture, chemicals, light engineering and transport equipment. Output (in 1,000 tonnes): cement (2001), 674; distillate fuel oil (2000), 624; residual fuel oil (2000), 621; petrol (1999), 325; meat-packing (1991), 1,132,000 head; 9·6bn. cigarettes (2001).

Labour

In 1996 the retirement age was raised from 55 to 60 for women; it remains 60 for men. The labour force in 1996 totalled 1,444,000 (59% males). In 2001, 22·4% of the urban workforce was engaged in wholesale and retail trade/repair of motor vehicles, motorcycles and personal and household goods/hotels and restaurants; 15·5% in manufacturing/electricity, gas and water supply; 9·2% in private households with employed persons; and 9·1% in financial intermediation and real estate, renting and business activities. In 2001 the unemployment rate in urban areas was 15·3%.

INTERNATIONAL TRADE

External debt was US$10,736m. in 2002.

Imports and Exports

Trade in US$1m.:

	1998	1999	2000	2001	2002
Imports f.o.b.	3,601·4	3,187·2	3,311·1	2,914·7	1,872·9
Exports f.o.b.	2,829·3	2,290·6	2,383·8	2,139·4	1,933·1

Main imports in 1999: machinery and transport equipment, 31·2%; chemicals, 17·2%; manufactured goods, 15·3%; petroleum, 10·1%; foodstuffs, 8·9%. Main exports in 1999: meat, 17·8%; rice, 8·8%; leather, 7·7%; yarn and textiles, 7·5%; dairy products, 6·9%; road vehicles, 5·6%.

In 1999 the main import suppliers were Argentina (23·9%), Brazil (19·4%), USA (11·3%) and France (4·2%). Leading export destinations were Brazil (24·9%), Argentina (16·5%), USA (6·9%) and Germany (5·0%).

COMMUNICATIONS

Roads

In 2002 there were 8,984 km of roads, including 2,612 km of national roads and 5,246 km of regional roads. Uruguay has one of the densest road networks in the world. Passenger cars in 2002 numbered 595,500 (180·4 per 1,000 inhabitants). There were 737 fatalities as a result of road accidents in 1997.

Rail

The total railway system open for traffic in 1996 was 2,073 km of 1,435 mm gauge. Passenger services, which had been abandoned in 1988, were resumed on a limited basis in 1993. Freight tonne-km in 2000 came to 239m. and passenger-km travelled to 9m.

Civil Aviation

There is an international airport at Montevideo (Carrasco). The national carrier is Pluna. In 2003 it operated domestic services and maintained routes to Asunción, Buenos Aires, Madrid, Porto Alegre, Rio de Janeiro, Santiago and São Paulo. There were 60 airports in 1996, 45 with paved runways and 15 with unpaved runways. In 1999 Montevideo handled an estimated 1,423,000 passengers (1,115,000 on international flights) and 25,500 tonnes of freight. In 1999 scheduled airline traffic of Uruguay-based carriers flew 8·4m. km, carrying 728,000 passengers (all on international flights).

Shipping

In 2002 sea-going shipping totalled 75,000 GRT, including oil tankers 6,000 GRT. In 2000 vessels totalling 5,257,000 NRT entered ports and vessels totalling 19,587,000 NRT cleared. Navigable inland waterways total 1,600 km.

Telecommunications

The telephone system in Montevideo is controlled by the State; small companies operate in the interior. Uruguay had 1,598,500 telephone subscribers in 2002 (472·2 for every 1,000 persons); and there were 370,000 PCs in use in 2001 (110·1 for every 1,000 persons). There were 652,000 mobile phone subscribers in 2002. Internet users numbered 400,000 in 2001.

Postal Services

In 2003 there were 1,269 post offices.

SOCIAL INSTITUTIONS

Justice

The Supreme Court is elected by Congress; it appoints all other judges. There are six courts of appeal, each with three judges. There are civil and criminal courts. Montevideo has ten courts of first instance, Paysandú and Salto have two each and the other departments have one each. There are approximately 300 lower courts.

The population in penal institutions in Sept. 2003 was 7,100 (209 per 100,000 of national population).

Education

Adult literacy in 2002 was 97·7% (male, 97·3%; female, 98·1%). The female literacy rate is the second highest in South America, behind Guyana. Primary education is obligatory; both primary and secondary education are free. In 2003 there were 1,507 pre-primary schools with 3,741 (2000) teachers for 103,619 pupils; 2,396 primary schools with 16,605 teachers for 354,843 pupils and at secondary level there were (2000) 303,883 pupils and 20,778 teachers.

There is one state university, one independent Roman Catholic university and one private institute of technology. In 2000–01 there were 97,541 students and 11,245 academic staff in tertiary education.

In 2000–01 total public expenditure on education came to 2·8% of GNP and represented 11·8% of total government expenditure.

Health

In 2003 there were 13,071 physicians, 4,154 dentists, 3,118 nurses, 1,323 pharmacists and 572 midwives. There were 107 hospitals with 6,661 beds.

Welfare

The welfare state dates from the beginning of the 1900s. In 2002 there were 0·5m. recipients of pensions and benefits. A private pension scheme inaugurated in 1996 had 315,000 members at 31 Dec. 1996. State spending on social security has been capped at 15% of GDP.

RELIGION

State and Church are separate, and there is complete religious liberty. In 2001 there were 2·6m. Roman Catholics and 710,000 persons with other beliefs.

CULTURE

World Heritage Sites

Uruguay has one site on the UNESCO World Heritage List: the Historic Quarter of the City of Colonia del Sacramento (inscribed on the list in 1995), founded in 1680 by the Portuguese.

Broadcasting

In 2000 there were 2·0m. radio receivers and in 2001 there were 1·8m. television receivers (colour by PAL N). There were 20 TV stations and about 250 radio stations in 2001.

Press

In 1996 there were 36 daily newspapers with a combined circulation of 950,000. There were also 62 non-daily newspapers and periodicals.

Tourism

There were 1·26m. tourists in 2002, mainly from Argentina. Receipts totalled US$318m.

DIPLOMATIC REPRESENTATIVES

Of Uruguay in the United Kingdom (2nd Floor, 140 Brompton Rd, London, SW3 1HY)
Ambassador: Ricardo Varela.

Of the United Kingdom in Uruguay (Calle Marco Bruto 1073, 11300 Montevideo)
Ambassador: Hugh Salvesen.

Of Uruguay in the USA (1913 I St., NW, Washington, D.C., 20006)
Ambassador: Carlos Gianelli.

Of the USA in Uruguay (Lauro Muller 1776, Montevideo)
Ambassador: Vacant.
Chargé d'Affaires a.i.: James D. Nealon.

Of Uruguay to the United Nations
Ambassador: Alejandro Artuccio.

Of Uruguay to the European Union
Ambassador: Elbio Oscar Rosselli Frieri.

FURTHER READING

González, L. E., *Political Structures and Democracy in Uruguay.* Univ. of Notre Dame Press, 1992
Sosnowski, S. (ed.) *Repression, Exile and Democracy: Uruguayan Culture.* Duke Univ. Press, 1993

National library: Biblioteca Nacional del Uruguay, Guayabo 1793, Montevideo.
Website (Spanish only): http://www.ine.gub.uy/

UZBEKISTAN

Uzbekiston Respublikasy

Capital: Tashkent

Population projection, 2010: 28·58m.

GDP per capita, 2003: (PPP$) 1,744

HDI/world rank: 0·694/111

KEY HISTORICAL EVENTS

Descended from nomadic Mongol tribes who settled in Central Asia in the 13th century, the Uzbeks came under Russian control in the late 19th century. In Oct. 1917 the Tashkent Soviet assumed authority. The semi-independent Khanates of Khiva and Bokhara were first (1920) transformed into People's Republics, then (1923–24) into Soviet Socialist Republics, and finally merged in the Uzbek SSR and other republics. On 20 June 1990 the Supreme Soviet adopted a declaration of sovereignty and in Aug. 1991, following an unsuccessful coup, declared independence as the Republic of Uzbekistan. In Dec. 1991 Uzbekistan became a member of the Commonwealth of Independent States.

Islam Karimov became head of state in 1990 and was elected president in 1991 and again in 2000. In that year Uzbek border guards moved their posts 5 km into a part of neighbouring Kazakhstan. Borders with Russia and Kyrgyzstan still remain undefined, yet the chief cause for concern is the fight of the Islamist Movement of Uzbekistan (IMU) to create an Islamic state in the Fergana Valley. Bomb blasts in Tashkent, one of which almost killed the president in 1999, were blamed on religious extremists and the army suffered losses fighting the IMU in 2000. IMU leader Juma Namangoniy was reportedly killed in Aug. 2002. Nearly 50 people died during a period of bombings and shootings in March 2004, allegedly perpetrated by Islamic militants, and suicide bombers targeted the US and Israeli embassies in Tashkent in July of that year.

TERRITORY AND POPULATION

Uzbekistan is bordered in the north by Kazakhstan, in the east by Kyrgyzstan and Tajikistan, in the south by Afghanistan and in the west by Turkmenistan. Area, 447,400 sq. km (172,741 sq. miles). At the last census, in 1989, the population was 19,810,077. In 1998, 75·8% of the population was Uzbek, 6·0% Russian, 4·8% Tajik, 4·1% Kazakh, 1·6% Tatar and 7·7% other. 2005 population estimate, 26,593,000 (13,369,000 females); density, 59·4 per sq. km. In 2003, 63·3% of the population lived in rural areas.

The UN gives a projected population for 2010 of 28·58m.

The areas and populations of the 12 Regions and the Karakalpak Autonomous Republic (Karakalpakstan) are as follows (Uzbek spellings in brackets):

Region	Area (in sq. km)	Population (1994 estimate)	Capital	Population (1994 estimate)
Andizhan (Andijon)	4,200	1,899,000	Andizhan	303,000
Bukhara (Bukhoro)	39,400	1,262,000	Bukhara	236,000
Ferghana (Farghona)	7,100	2,338,000	Ferghana	191,000
Dzhizak (Jizzakh)	20,500	831,000	Dzhizak	116,000
Khorezm (Khorazm)	6,300	1,135,000	Urgench (Urganch)	135,000
Namangan	7,900	1,652,000	Namangan	341,000
Navoi (Nawoiy)	110,800	715,000	Nawoiy	115,000
Kashkadar (Qashqadaryo)	28,400	715,000	Karshi (Qarshi)	177,000
Karakalpak Autonomous Republic (Qoraqalpoghiston)	164,900	1,343,000	Nukus (Nuqus)	185,000
Samarkand (Samarqand)	16,400	2,322,000	Samarkand	368,000
Syr-Darya Gulistan (Sirdaryo)	5,100	600,000	(Guliston)	57,000[1]
Surkhan-Darya (Surkhondaryo)	20,800	1,437,000	Termez (Termiz)	90,000[1]
Tashkent (Toshkent)	15,600	4,357,000	Tashkent	2,121,000

[1]1991.

The capital is Tashkent (2000 population estimate, 2,133,000); other large towns are Namangan, Samarkand and Andizhan. There are 124 towns, 97 urban settlements and 155 rural districts.

The Roman alphabet (in use 1929–40) was reintroduced in 1994. Arabic script was in use prior to 1929, and Cyrillic from 1940–94.

Uzbek, Russian and Tajik are all spoken.

SOCIAL STATISTICS

2001 births, 512,950; deaths, 132,542; marriages, 170,101; divorces, 15,646. Rates, 2001: birth (per 1,000 population), 20·5; death, 5·3; marriage, 6·8; divorce, 0·6. Life expectancy, 2003, 63·4 years for men and 69·8 for women. Annual population growth rate, 1992–2002, 1·8%. In 1997 the most popular age range for marrying was 20–24 for both males and females. Infant mortality, 2001, 52 per 1,000 live births; fertility rate, 2001, 2·5 births per woman.

CLIMATE

The summers are warm to hot but the heat is made more bearable by the low humidity. The winters are cold but generally dry and sunny. Tashkent, Jan. –1°C, July 25°C. Annual rainfall 14·76" (375 mm).

CONSTITUTION AND GOVERNMENT

A new constitution was adopted on 8 Dec. 1992 stating that Uzbekistan is a pluralist democracy. The constitution restricts the president to standing for two five-year terms. In Jan. 2002 a referendum was held at which 91% of the electorate voted in favour of extending the presidential term from five to seven years. Voters were also in favour of changing from a single-chamber legislature to a bicameral parliament. Uzbekistan switched to a bicameral legislature in Jan. 2005 with the establishment of the 100-member *Senate* (with 16 members appointed by the president and 84 elected from the ranks of regional, district and city legislative councils). The lower house is the 120-member (formerly 250-member) *Oliy Majlis* (Supreme Assembly), elected by popular vote for five-year terms.

National Anthem

'Serquyosh, hur o'lkam, elga baxt najot' ('Stand tall, my free country, good fortune and salvation to you'); words by Abdulla Aripov, tune by Mutal Burhanov.

GOVERNMENT CHRONOLOGY

President since 1990. (n/p = non-partisan)
1990–   n/p   Islam Abduganiyevich Karimov

RECENT ELECTIONS

Presidential elections were held on 9 Jan. 2000. Incumbent Islam Karimov was elected against a single opponent with 91·9% of the vote. Turnout was 95%. It was the first presidential election since 1991. Elections were cancelled in 1997 after Karimov's term was extended to 2000 by referendum.

In parliamentary elections held in two rounds on 26 Dec. 2004 and 9 Jan 2005, criticized for electoral abuses, the Liberal-Democratic Party won 41 of the 120 seats, followed by the People's Democratic Party with 28, the Self-Sacrifice National Democratic Party with 18, the Uzbekistan National Revival Democratic Party with 11 and the Justice Social Democratic Party with 10. The remaining seats went to independent candidates. All parties taking part in the election were loyal to President Islam Karimov—opposition parties were barred from participating.

CURRENT ADMINISTRATION

President: Islam Karimov; b. 1938 (sworn in 24 March 1990).

In March 2006 the government comprised:

Prime Minister: Shavkat Mirziyayev; b. 1957 (People's Democratic Party; in office since 11 Dec. 2003).

Deputy Prime Ministers: Abdulla Aripov; Vyacheslav Golishev (also *Minister of Economy*); Svetlana Inamova; Rustam Kasymov (also *Minister of Higher and Secondary Specialized Education*); Nodirkhon Khanov; Oktir Sultanov.

Minister of Agriculture and Water Resources: Sayfiddin Ismoilov. *Internal Affairs:* Bakhodir Matlyubov. *Defence:* Ruslan Mirzayev. *Foreign Affairs:* Elyor Ganiyev. *Foreign Economic Relations, Investments and Trade:* Alisher Shayhov. *Justice:* Buritosh Mustafayev. *Finance:* Rustam Azimov. *Education:* Turobjon Djuraev. *Culture and Sports:* Alisher Azizkhodjaev. *Health:* Feruz Nazirov. *Labour and Social Protection:* Oqiljon Obidov. *Emergency Situations:* Bakhtiyor Subanov.

Chairman, Oliy Majlis: Erkin Halilov.

Office of the President: http://www.gov.uz

CURRENT LEADERS

Islam Abduganievich Karimov

Position
President

Introduction
Islam Karimov, a former Soviet official, has been president since Uzbekistan declared independence in 1990. His regime has been characterized by the suppression of domestic political and religious opposition, and his electoral victories have been questioned for their irregularities. Karimov sought to build ties with the West, and won US favour for co-operation in the war against terrorism in the aftermath of the 11 Sept. attacks. However, reports of torture and other human rights violations, culminating in an alleged massacre of Uzbek civilians in Andizhan in May 2005, have provoked increasing international criticism of his regime.

Early Life
Karimov was born on 30 Jan. 1938 in Samarkand. He qualified as a mechanical engineer at the Central Asian Polytechnical Institute and graduated in economics from the Tashkent Institute of National Economy. He then worked in Tashkent at farm machinery and aircraft plants. In 1966 he moved to the state planning committee of Uzbekistan, attaining the rank of vice-chairman.

In 1983 Karimov was appointed finance minister for Uzbekistan and three years later became deputy head of government, as well as chairman of the state planning committee. In 1989 he was named head of the Uzbek Communist Party. The following year Uzbekistan claimed sovereignty from the USSR and Karimov was chosen as president. Following the attempted coup against Mikhail Gorbachev in Moscow in 1991, Karimov declared full independence.

Career in Office
Against little organized opposition, Karimov dominated presidential elections and led Uzbekistan into the Commonwealth of Independent States. In 1992 he continued his campaign against domestic opposition, banning two leading parties—Birlik (Unity) and Erk (Freedom)—and imprisoning many members. In 1994 he agreed an economic integration treaty with Russia and signed a co-operation pact with Kazakhstan and Kyrgyzstan which was developed into a single economic community in 1996. In 1995 Karimov won a further five years in office by plebiscite.

In 1999 Tashkent was the scene of several car bombings which Karimov blamed on the Islamic Movement of Uzbekistan (IMU). Government and IMU forces clashed several times, the culmination of growing tensions between the two sides since the mid-1990s. In the same year Karimov withdrew Uzbekistan from the CIS agreement on collective security, increasing the nation's isolation among Central Asian nations predominantly loyal to Moscow.

Karimov was re-elected to the presidency in 2000 with over 90% of the vote, although the electoral process was severely criticized by the international community, notably the opposition candidate's assertion that he himself would vote for Karimov. Following the 11 Sept. terrorist attacks in New York and Washington, Karimov permitted the USA to use Uzbek air bases for the war in Afghanistan. In the same year he signed up to the Shanghai Co-operation Society (with China, Russia, Kazakhstan, Kyrgyzstan and Tajikistan), established to promote regional economic co-operation and fight religious and ethnic militancy.

In Jan. 2002 Karimov secured a constitutional change, accepted by referendum, extending the presidential term from five to seven years. His assistance in the US campaign in Afghanistan was meanwhile rewarded by US$160m. worth of aid from Washington. Also in 2002 a long-running border feud with Kazakhstan was settled.

In March 2004 a series of shootings and explosions in the Tashkent and Bukhara regions left dozens of people dead. Further bombings near the US and Israeli embassies and in the Prosecutor General's Office in Tashkent occurred in July. Karimov's government blamed Islamic militants. Then in May 2005 several hundred civilians, protesting against the trial of local businessmen accused of Islamic extremism, were reportedly killed by security forces in Andizhan. Unrest also spread to the towns of Paktabad and Kara Suu before troops reasserted government control. At the end of July, in a punitive response to international criticism of the massacre, Karimov gave the USA six months to close its military airbase in Uzbekistan.

DEFENCE

Conscription is for 18 months. Defence expenditure in 2003 totalled US$2,200m. (US$86 per capita), representing 5·0% of GDP. The USA opened a military base in Uzbekistan in 2001 to aid the war in Afghanistan against the Taliban. However, in July 2005 Uzbekistan gave the USA 180 days to close the base following American criticism of the massacre of up to 1,000 unarmed demonstrators in Uzbekistan two months earlier. The base was closed in Nov. 2005.

Army
Personnel, 2002, 40,000. There are, in addition, paramilitary forces totalling 18,000–20,000.

Air Force
Personnel, 2002, 10–15,000. There were 135 combat aircraft in operation (including Su-17s, Su-24s, Su-25s, Su-27s and MiG-29s) and 42 attack helicopters.

INTERNATIONAL RELATIONS

Uzbekistan is a member of the UN, CIS, OSCE, Asian Development Bank, ECO, OIC, Islamic Development Bank and the NATO Partnership for Peace.

ECONOMY

Agriculture accounted for 34·7% of GDP in 2002, industry 21·6% and services 43·7%.

Overview
Agriculture accounts for 35% of GDP and 40% of employment. Uzbekistan is a low-income country with the third lowest GDP per capita in the CIS. The country is rich in natural resources and in 2001 primary commodities (mainly cotton, gold, copper, energy resources and precious stones) accounted for 70% of total exports. Incomes have improved little since independence from the Soviet Union in 1991 and rural poverty is significant. Following independence the government undertook a gradualist transition strategy, with emphasis on self-sufficiency in energy and grains, which led GDP to grow at approximately 4% between 1996–2002. However, the gradualist approach has delayed necessary macroeconomic and structural reforms. According to the World Bank, the combination of high inflation, exchange rate devaluations, low trust in the banking system and restrictions on access to cash resulted in a decline in the monetization of the economy. The government has retained extensive control over foreign exchange, trade, firms and farms. This has limited export growth and discouraged FDI, which has declined steadily since 1997.

Currency
A coupon for a new unit of currency, the *soum* (UKS), was introduced alongside the rouble on 15 Nov. 1993. This was replaced by the *soum* proper at 1 soum = 1,000 coupons on 1 July 1994. In 1994 inflation was 1,568% but has since declined, and was 8·8% in 2004. Exchange controls were abolished on 1 July 1995.

Budget
In 1999 revenues amounted to 611,897m. soums and expenditures to 654,259m. soums. Taxes on income and profits accounted for 30·5% of revenues, VAT 27·3% and excise taxes 22·3%. Social and cultural affairs accounted for 36·7% of expenditures and investments 18·7%.

Performance
Real GDP growth was 3·1% in 2002, 1·5% in 2003 and 7·1% in 2004; total GDP in 2004 was US$12·0bn. Real GDP in 2002 was 6% higher than in 1989. In every other former Soviet republic, GDP was lower in 2002 than it had been in 1989 at the time of the changes which swept through central and eastern Europe.

Banking and Finance
The Central Bank is the bank of issue (*Chairman*, Faizulla Mullajanov). In 2001 there were 38 commercial banks, of which 16 were privately owned.

ENERGY AND NATURAL RESOURCES

Environment
Irrigation of arid areas has caused the drying up of the Aral Sea. Uzbekistan's carbon dioxide emissions from the consumption and flaring of fossil fuels in 2002 were the equivalent of 4·5 tonnes per capita. An *Environmental Sustainability Index* compiled for the World Economic Forum meeting in Jan. 2005 ranked Uzbekistan 142nd in the world out of 146 countries analysed, with 34·4%. The index measured the ability of countries to maintain favourable environmental conditions and examined various factors including pollution levels and the use or abuse of natural resources.

Electricity
Installed capacity was 11·7m. kW in 2000. Production was 46·8bn. kWh in 2000 and consumption per capita 1,944 kWh.

Oil and Gas
Crude oil production was 7·1m. tonnes in 2003; natural gas output in 2002 was 53·8bn. cu. metres. In 2002 there were proven oil reserves of 0·6bn. bbls. and natural gas reserves of 1,870bn. cu. metres.

Minerals
2·50m. tonnes of lignite and 69,000 tonnes of hard coal were produced in 2000. In 2000, 85 tonnes of gold and 90 tonnes of silver were produced. There are also large reserves of uranium, copper, lead, zinc and tungsten; all uranium mined (1,860 tonnes in 2002) is exported.

Agriculture
Farming is intensive and based on irrigation. In 2001 there were 4·49m. ha. of arable land and 0·35m. ha. of permanent cropland; 4·28m. ha. were irrigated in 2001.

By 1996 some 97% of the 715 state farms were co-operative, private or otherwise owned, and accounted for over 98% of agricultural production.

Cotton is the main crop, accounting for more than 40% of the value of total agricultural production. In 1997 more than 3·6m. tonnes of raw cotton was laid. Fruit, vegetables and rice are also grown; sericulture and the production of astrakhan wool are also important.

Output of main agricultural products (2000, in 1,000 tonnes): seed cotton, 3,006; wheat, 2,787; cottonseed, 1,920; tomatoes, 1,000; cotton lint, 950; cabbages, 882; potatoes, 656; grapes, 625; apples, 480; watermelons, 457; sugarbeets, 380; cucumbers and gherkins, 272.

Livestock, 2000: 5·27m. cattle; 8·92m. sheep; 639,000 goats; 14m. chickens. Animal products, 2000 (in 1,000 tonnes): meat, 536; milk, 3,739; eggs, 69.

Forestry
In 2000 the area under forests was 1·97m. ha., accounting for 4·8% of the total land area. In 2001, 25,000 cu. metres of timber were produced.

Fisheries
The total catch in 2001 was 4,070 tonnes, exclusively freshwater fish.

INDUSTRY

Industrial production grew by 3·4% in 2002. Major industries include fertilizers, agricultural and textile machinery, aircraft, metallurgy and chemicals. Output (in tonnes): cement (2001), 3,700,000; distillate fuel oil (2000), 1,900,000; petrol (2000), 1,709,000; residual fuel oil (2000), 1,700,000; sulphuric acid (2000), 823,000; mineral fertilizer (2000), 800,000; cotton woven fabrics (2000), 360m. sq. metres; 1,000 tractors (2000); 26,000 TV sets (2000).

Labour

In 1999 a total of 8,885,000 persons were in employment, including: 3,421,000 engaged in agriculture, hunting, forestry and fishing; 1,968,000 in community, social and personal services; 1,142,000 in manufacturing, mining and quarrying, electricity, gas and water; and 734,000 in wholesale and retail trade, restaurants and hotels. In 2000 the unemployment rate was 0·6%. Average monthly salary in 1999 was 8,823 soums. A minimum wage of 6,530 soums a month was imposed on 1 Aug. 2004.

INTERNATIONAL TRADE

In Jan. 1994 an agreement to create a single economic zone was signed with Kazakhstan and Kyrgyzstan. Foreign investors are entitled to a two-year tax holiday and repatriation of hard currency. External debt was US$4,568m. in 2002.

Imports and Exports

In 2002 imports were valued at US$2,712m. and exports at US$2,988m. Principal imports, 1996, were machinery (35% of the total), light industrial goods, food and raw materials; principal exports were cotton (38% of the total), textiles, machinery, chemicals, food and energy products.

The main import sources in 2002 were Russia (20·5%), South Korea (17·4%), Germany (8·9%), Kazakhstan (7·5%) and USA (6·4%). Principal export markets in 2002 were Russia (17·3%), Ukraine (10·2%), Italy (8·3%), Tajikistan (7·8%) and South Korea (7·1%).

COMMUNICATIONS

Roads

Length of roads, 2000, was 86,496 km (87·3% paved).

Rail

The total length of railway in 2000 was 3,645 km of 1,520 mm gauge (432 km electrified). In 2000, 16·3m. passengers and 48·2m. tonnes of freight were carried. There is a metro in Tashkent.

Civil Aviation

The main international airport is in Tashkent (Vostochny). Andizhan, Namangan and Samarkand also have airports. The national carrier is the state-owned Uzbekistan Airways, which in 2003 operated domestic services and flew to Almaty, Amritsar, Ashgabat, Athens, Baku, Bangkok, Beijing, Birmingham, Bishkek, Chelyabinsk, Delhi, Dhaka, Ekaterinburg, Frankfurt, İstanbul, Kazan, Khabarovsk, Krasnodar, Krasnoyarsk, Kuala Lumpur, Kyiv, London, Mineralnye Vody, Moscow, New York, Novosibirsk, Omsk, Osaka, Paris, Rome, Rostov, St Petersburg, Samara, Seoul, Sharjah, Simferopol, Tel Aviv, Tokyo, Tyumen and Ufa. In 1999 it flew 36·9m. km, carrying 1,657,600 passengers (877,500 on international flights). In 2001 Tashkent handled 1,387,000 passengers (884,000 on international flights) and 36,200 tonnes of freight.

Shipping

The total length of inland waterways in 1990 was 1,100 km.

Telecommunications

In 2002 telephone subscribers numbered 1,856,900 (73·4 per 1,000 population), of which 186,900 were mobile phone subscribers. Uzbekistan had 275,000 Internet users and 3,600 fax machines in 2002.

Postal Services

In 2003 there were 3,211 post offices.

SOCIAL INSTITUTIONS

Justice

In 1994, 73,561 crimes were reported, including 1,219 murders and attempted murders. The death penalty is still in force; there was one confirmed execution in 2005. The population in penal institutions in Aug. 2003 was 48,000 (184 per 100,000 of national population).

Education

In 1995 there were 1·07m. pre-primary pupils with 96,100 teachers, 1·90m. primary pupils with 92,400 teachers and 3·31m. secondary pupils with 340,200 teachers. There were 55 higher educational establishments in 1998 with 272,300 students, and 248 technical colleges with 240,100 students. There are universities and medical schools in Tashkent and Samarkand. Adult literacy rate in 2002 was 99·3% (99·6% among males and 98·9% among females).

Health

In 1995 there were 192 hospitals, with a provision of 84 beds per 10,000 population. There were 73,041 physicians, 5,283 dentists, 252,430 nurses, 673 pharmacists and 20,684 midwives in 2001.

Welfare

In Jan. 1994 there were 1,726,000 old-age pensioners and 1,007,000 other pensioners.

RELIGION

The Uzbeks are predominantly Sunni Muslims.

CULTURE

World Heritage Sites

Uzbekistan has four sites on the UNESCO World Heritage List: Itchan Kala (inscribed on the list in 1990); the Historic Centre of Bukhara (1993); the Historic Centre of Shakhrisyabz (2000); and Samarkand—Crossroads of Cultures (2001).

Broadcasting

Broadcasting is under the aegis of the State Teleradio Broadcasting Company. The government-controlled Uzbek Radio transmits two national and several regional programmes, a Radio Moscow relay and a foreign service, Radio Tashkent (Uzbek, Arabic, English, Dari, Farsi, Hindi, Pushtu, Uighur). There were 11·3m. radio receivers in 2000 and 7·0m. television receivers in 2001. Colour transmission is by SECAM H.

Press

In 1996 there were three daily newspapers with a combined circulation of 75,000.

Tourism

There were 332,000 tourists in 2002. Receipts totalled US$68m.

DIPLOMATIC REPRESENTATIVES

Of Uzbekistan in the United Kingdom (41 Holland Park, London, W11 3RP)
Ambassador: Tukhtapulat Riskiev.

Of the United Kingdom in Uzbekistan (Ul. Gulyamova 67, Tashkent 700000)
Ambassador: David Moran.

Of Uzbekistan in the USA (1746 Massachusetts Ave., NW, Washington, D.C., 20036)
Ambassador: Abdulaziz Kamilov.

Of the USA in Uzbekistan (82 Chilanzarskaya, Tashkent)
Ambassador: John Purnell.

Of Uzbekistan to the United Nations
Ambassador: Alisher Vohidov.

Of Uzbekistan to the European Union
Ambassador: Alisher Shaykhov.

FURTHER READING

Bohr, A. (ed.) *Uzbekistan: Politics and Foreign Policy.* The Brookings Institution, Washington (D.C.), 1998
Kalter, J. and Pavaloi, M., *Uzbekistan: Heir to the Silk Road.* Thames & Hudson, London, 1997

Kangas, R. D., *Uzbekistan in the Twentieth Century: Political Development and the Evolution of Power.* New York, 1994

Melvin, N. J., *Uzbekistan: Transition to Authoritarianism on the Silk Road.* Routledge, London, 2000

Karakalpak Autonomous Republic (Karakalpakstan)

All statistics are the latest data available. Area, 166,600 sq. km (64,320 sq. miles); population (Jan. 1994), 1,343,000. Capital, Nukus (1993 estimate, 185,000). The Qoraqalpoghs came under Russian rule in the second half of the 19th century. On 11 May 1925 the territory was constituted within the then Kazakh Autonomous Republic (of the Russian Federation) as an Autonomous Region. On 20 March 1932 it became an Autonomous Republic within the Russian Federation, and on 5 Dec. 1936 it became part of the Uzbek SSR. At the 1989 census Qoraqalpoghs were 32·1% of the population, Uzbeks 32·8% and Kazakhs 26·3%.

Its manufactures are in the field of light industry—bricks, leather goods, furniture, canning and wine. The principal crops are rice and cotton. In Jan. 1990 cattle numbered 336,000, and sheep and goats 518,100. There were 38 collective and 124 state farms in 1987. The total cultivated area in 1985 was 350,400 ha.

The shrinking of the Aral Sea has had a detrimental effect on agriculture and public health in the region. There was a drought in 2000–01. In 2002 the incidence of poverty was 36·4%, compared to 9·2% in Tashkent, the Uzbek capital.

In 1990–91 there were 313,500 pupils at schools and 22,100 students at technical colleges. In 2004–05 there were 6,800 students at Karakalpak State University. There is a branch of the Uzbek Academy of Sciences.

There were 2,600 doctors and 12,800 hospital beds in 1987. Since then, the quality of public healthcare has deteriorated; total spending on health care in 2002 was US$10m., or US$6·50 per capita.

VANUATU

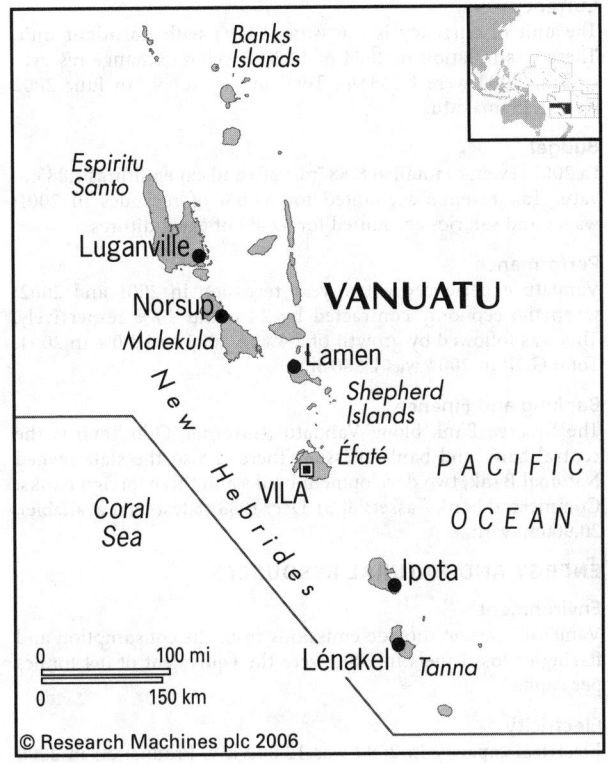

© Research Machines plc 2006

Ripablik blong Vanuatu
(Republic of Vanuatu)

Capital: Vila
Population projection, 2010: 232,000
GDP per capita, 2003: (PPP$) 2,944
HDI/world rank: 0·659/118

KEY HISTORICAL EVENTS

Vanuatu occupies the group of islands formerly known as the New Hebrides, in the southwestern Pacific Ocean. Capt. Bligh and his companions, cast adrift by the *Bounty* mutineers, sailed through part of the island group in 1789. Sandalwood merchants and European missionaries came to the islands in the mid-19th century and were then followed by cotton planters—mostly French and British—in 1868. In response to Australian calls to annexe the islands, Britain and France agreed on joint supervision. Joint sovereignty was held over the indigenous Melanesian people but each nation retained responsibility for its own nationals according to a protocol of 1914. The island group escaped Japanese invasion during the Second World War and became an Allied base. On 30 July 1980 New Hebrides became an independent nation under the name of Vanuatu, meaning 'Our Land Forever'.

TERRITORY AND POPULATION

Vanuatu comprises 80 islands, which lie roughly 800 km west of the Fiji Islands and 400 km northeast of New Caledonia. The estimated land area is 12,190 sq. km (4,706 sq. miles). The larger islands of the group are: (Espiritu) Santo, Malekula, Epi, Pentecost, Aoba, Maewo, Paama, Ambrym, Efate, Erromanga, Tanna and Aneityum. They also claim Matthew and Hunter islands. 67 islands were inhabited in 1990. Population at the 1999 census, 186,678; density, 15·3 per sq. km. 2005 population estimate, 211,000.

The UN gives a projected population for 2010 of 232,000.

In 2003, 77·1% of the population lived in rural areas. Vila (the capital) has a population of 26,000 (1999 estimate), and Luganville 10,000.

40% of the population is under 15 years of age, 57% between the ages of 15 and 64 and 3% 65 or over.

The national language is Bislama (spoken by 57% of the population): English and French are also official languages; about 30,000 speak French.

SOCIAL STATISTICS

2002 estimates: births, 6,500; deaths, 1,100. Rates, 2002 estimates (per 1,000 population): births, 31·6; deaths, 5·5. Annual population growth rate, 1992–2002, 2·7%. Life expectancy, 2003, was 66·9 years for males and 70·6 years for females. Infant mortality, 2001, 34 per 1,000 live births; fertility rate, 2001, 4·4 births per woman.

CLIMATE

The climate is tropical, but moderated by oceanic influences and by trade winds from May to Oct. High humidity occasionally occurs and cyclones are possible. Rainfall ranges from 90" (2,250 mm) in the south to 155" (3,875 mm) in the north. Vila, Jan. 80°F (26·7°C), July 72°F (22·2°C). Annual rainfall 84" (2,103 mm).

CONSTITUTION AND GOVERNMENT

Legislative power resides in a 52-member unicameral Parliament elected for a term of four years. The *President* is elected for a five-year term by an electoral college comprising Parliament and the presidents of the 11 regional councils. Executive power is vested in a Council of Ministers, responsible to Parliament, and appointed and led by a Prime Minister who is elected from and by Parliament.

There is also a *Council of Chiefs*, comprising traditional tribal leaders, to advise on matters of custom.

National Anthem

'Yumi, yumi, yumi i glat blong talem se, yumi, yumi, yumi i man blong Vanuatu' ('We, we, we are glad to tell, we, we, we are the people of Vanuatu'); words and tune by F. Vincent Ayssav.

RECENT ELECTIONS

Parliamentary elections were held on 6 July 2004. The Vanuatu National United Party (NUP) won 10 of 52 seats, the Union of Moderate Parties (UMP) 8, the Party of our Land (VP) 8, ind. 8, the People's Progressive Party 4, the Vanuatu Republican Party (VRP) 4, the Melanesian Progressive Party (MPP) 3, the Green Confederation 3, the National Community Association 2, the People's Action Party 1 and Namangi Aute 1. On 29 July 2004 parliament elected Serge Vohor (UMP) prime minister, with 28 votes, against 24 for Ham Lini (NUP). However, on 11 Dec. 2004 he lost a no-confidence motion and deputy prime minister Ham Lini was elected prime minister.

Kalkot Mataskelekele was elected president on 16 Aug. 2004 by an electoral college after a series of votes in the second round of voting, receiving 49 votes against 7 for Willie David Saul.

CURRENT ADMINISTRATION

President: Kalkot Mataskelekele (since 16 Aug. 2004).

Prime Minister: Ham Lini; b. 1951 (NUP; since 11 Dec. 2004). He put together a multi-party coalition which in March 2006 comprised:

Deputy Prime Minister and Minister of Foreign Affairs: Sato Kilman.

Minister of Internal Affairs: George Wells. *Health:* Morkin Stevens. *Education:* Joseph Natuman. *Finance and Economic Management:* Willie Jimmy Tapangararua. *Lands:* Maxime Carlot. *Agriculture, Forestry and Fisheries:* Pipite Marcellino. *Comprehensive Reform Programme:* Isabelle Donald. *Ni-Vanuatu Business Development:* Louis Etap. *Trade, Commerce and Industry:* James Bule. *Public Utilities and Infrastructure:* Edward Natapei. *Sports and Youth Development:* Dunstan Hilton.

Speaker: Sam Dan Avock.

Government Website: http://www.vanuatugovernment.gov.vu

CURRENT LEADERS

Ham Lini

Position
Prime Minister

Introduction
Ham Lini became prime minister on 11 Dec. 2004. He is the leader of the National United Party (NUP) and heads a multi-party coalition government.

Early Life
Ham Lini Vanuaroroa, born in 1951, is the younger brother of the late founding prime minister of Vanuatu, Father Walter Lini. He worked as a carpenter and teacher on Pentecost Island in Penama province before embarking on a political career. Starting as an MP in Penama, he went on to become president of the Penama provincial government and made the move into national politics when he became leader of the Union of Moderate Parties in the late 1990s. He became leader of the NUP in 2002.

Lini stood for the premiership in the elections of July 2004 but lost to Serge Voher. The results were disputed and in Aug. 2004 Voher and Lini formed a national unity government, with Voher as prime minister and Lini as his deputy. In Dec. 2004 Voher left office when he lost a vote of confidence following revelations that he had unilaterally made moves to switch Vanuatu's diplomatic relations from China to Taiwan. Lini was chosen by parliament to replace him.

Career in Office
On taking office Lini revoked Voher's agreements with Taiwan and restated Vanuatu's commitment to a 'One China' policy. Lini has focused on moving Vanuatu towards economic independence and self-reliance. He declared 2005 to be a 'National Year of Tourism' and funds have been used to establish tourism development offices throughout the islands and to enlarge airports at Malekula, Pentecost and Ambae. Lini has also seen a significant increase in education spending. The health budget has seen steady increases and moves have been made to increase the minimum wage.

DEFENCE

There is a paramilitary force with about 300 personnel. The Vanuatu Police maritime service operates one inshore patrol craft, and a former motor yacht, both lightly armed. Personnel numbered about 50 in 1996.

INTERNATIONAL RELATIONS

Vanuatu is a member of the UN, the Commonwealth, the Asian Development Bank, the Pacific Community, the Pacific Islands Forum and the International Organization of the Francophonie, and is an ACP member state of the ACP-EU relationship.

ECONOMY

Agriculture accounted for 24·7% of GDP in 1998, industry 12·1% and services 63·2%.

Currency
The unit of currency is the *vatu* (VUV) with no minor unit. There was inflation in 2004 of 1·0%. Foreign exchange reserves in June 2002 were US\$34m. Total money supply in June 2002 was 11,254m. vatu.

Budget
In 2001 revenues totalled 6,887m. vatu and expenditures 7,885m. vatu. Tax revenue accounted for 84·0% of revenues in 2001; wages and salaries accounted for 47·4% of expenditures.

Performance
Vanuatu experienced a two-year recession in 2001 and 2002, when the economy contracted by 2·1% and 2·8% respectively. This was followed by growth of 2·4% in 2003 and 3·0% in 2004. Total GDP in 2004 was US\$0·3bn.

Banking and Finance
The Reserve Bank blong Vanuatu (*Governor*, Odo Tevi) is the central bank and bank of issue. There is also the state-owned National Bank, two development banks and three foreign banks. Commercial banks' assets at 31 Dec. 1988 (latest data available), 20,900m. vatu.

ENERGY AND NATURAL RESOURCES

Environment
Vanuatu's carbon dioxide emissions from the consumption and flaring of fossil fuels in 2002 were the equivalent of 0·4 tonnes per capita.

Electricity
Electrical capacity in 2000 was 12,000 kW. Production in 2000 was about 38m. kWh and consumption per capita an estimated 193 kWh.

Agriculture
About 65% of the labour force are employed in agriculture. In 2001 there were 30,000 ha. of arable land and 90,000 ha. of permanent crops. The main commercial crops are copra, coconuts, cocoa and coffee. Production (2000 estimates, in 1,000 tonnes): coconuts, 364; copra, 40; bananas, 13; groundnuts, 2. 80% of the population are engaged in subsistence agriculture; yams, taro, cassava, sweet potatoes and bananas are grown for local consumption. A large number of cattle are reared on plantations, and a beef industry is developing.

Livestock (2000): cattle, 152,000; goats, 12,000; pigs, 62,000; horses, 3,000; poultry (1995), 158,000.

Forestry
There were 447,000 ha. of forest in 2000 (36·7% of the land area). In 2001, 119,000 cu. metres of roundwood were cut.

Fisheries
The principal catch is tuna, mainly exported to the USA. The total catch in 2001 was an estimated 26,690 tonnes.

INDUSTRY

Principal industries include copra processing, meat canning and fish freezing, a saw-mill, soft drinks factories and a print works. Building materials, furniture, aluminium and cement are also produced.

In 2000 industry accounted for 9·7% of GDP, with manufacturing contributing 3·6% and construction 4·1%.

INTERNATIONAL TRADE

Foreign debt in 2002 amounted to US\$84m.

Imports and Exports

In 2003 imports (f.o.b.) amounted to US$91·80m. (US$78·44m. in 2002); exports (f.o.b.) US$26·84m. (US$20·20m. in 2002). Main import suppliers (2000): Australia (28%), Singapore (14%), New Zealand (8%), Japan (4%). Main export destinations (2000): Japan (32%), Belgium (17%), USA (17%), Germany (8%).

The main exports are copra, beef, timber and cocoa.

COMMUNICATIONS

Roads

In 2002 there were 1,070 km of roads, about 260 km paved, mostly on Efate Island and Espiritu Santo. There were estimated to be 8,200 passenger cars and 2,100 commercial vehicles in use in 2002.

Civil Aviation

There is an international airport at Bauerfield Port Vila. In 2003 the state-owned Air Vanuatu flew to Auckland, Brisbane, Honiara, Nadi, Nouméa and Sydney. Domestic services were provided by Vanair, a subsidiary of Air Vanuatu. In 1999 scheduled airline traffic of Vanuatu-based carriers flew 2·6m. km, carrying 86,000 passengers (all on international flights).

Shipping

Sea-going shipping totalled 1·38m. GRT in 2002, including oil tankers 55,000 GRT. Several international shipping lines serve Vanuatu, linking the country with Australia, New Zealand, other Pacific territories, China (Hong Kong), Japan, North America and Europe. The chief ports are Vila and Santo. Small vessels provide frequent inter-island services.

Telecommunications

Services are provided by the Posts and Telecommunications and Radio Departments. There are automatic telephone exchanges at Vila and Santo; rural areas are served by a network of tele-radio stations. In 2002 there were 11,500 telephone subscribers, equivalent to 56·2 per 1,000 population, of which 4,900 were mobile phone subscribers. There were 3,000 PCs in use in 2002 and approximately 600 fax machines in 1995. Vanuatu had 7,000 Internet users in 2002.

External telephone, telegram and telex services are provided by VANITEL, through their satellite earth station at Vila. There are direct circuits to Nouméa, Sydney, Hong Kong and Paris and communications are available on a 24-hour basis to most countries. Air radio facilities are provided. Marine coast station facilities are available at Vila and Santo.

Postal Services

In 2003 there were 33 post offices.

SOCIAL INSTITUTIONS

Justice

A study was begun in 1980 which could lead to unification of the judicial system. The population in penal institutions in 2002 was 96 (46 per 100,000 of national population).

Education

In 2000–01 there were 8,285 pupils with 477 teachers in pre-primary schools. In 2001–02 there were 36,482 pupils with (1999–2000) 1,576 teachers in primary schools and 9,635 pupils with (1999–2000) 381 teachers in secondary schools. Tertiary education is provided at the Vanuatu Technical Institute and the Teachers College, while other technical and commercial training is through regional institutions in the Solomon Islands, the Fiji Islands and Papua New Guinea. The adult literacy rate in 1998 stood at 64%, up from 53% in 1979. In 2000–01 total expenditure on education came to 8·7% of GNP and accounted for 16·9% of total government expenditure.

Health

There were 21 physicians in 1997 and in 1995 there were three dentists, 259 nurses, six pharmacists and 33 midwives. There were 90 hospitals in 1995, with a provision of 32 beds per 10,000 population.

RELIGION

About two-thirds of the population are Christians, but animist beliefs are still prevalent.

CULTURE

Broadcasting

The government-controlled Radio Vanuatu broadcasts in French, English and Bislama. In 2000 there were 62,000 radio receivers and 2,300 television sets.

Tourism

In 2001 there were 53,000 visitors to Vanuatu. Receipts totalled US$46m.

DIPLOMATIC REPRESENTATIVES

Of Vanuatu in the United Kingdom
High Commissioner: Vacant.

Of the United Kingdom in Vanuatu
High Commissioner: Charles Mochan (resides in Suva, Fiji).

Of Vanuatu in the USA
Ambassador: Vacant.

Of the USA in Vanuatu
Ambassador: Robert W. Fitts (resides in Port Moresby, Papua New Guinea).

Of Vanuatu to the United Nations
Ambassador: Vacant.

FURTHER READING

Miles, W. F. S., *Bridging Mental Boundaries in a Postcolonial Microcosm: Identity and Development in Vanuatu.* University of Hawaii Press, 1998

National Statistical Office: Vanuatu Statistics Office, Private Mail Bag 019, Port Vila.
Website: http://www.vanuatustatistics.gov.vu/

VATICAN CITY STATE

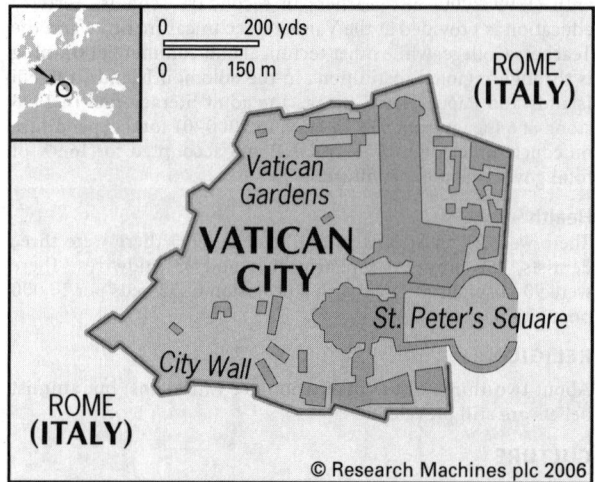

Stato della Città del Vaticano

Population estimate, 2000: 800

KEY HISTORICAL EVENTS

The history of the Vatican as a papal residence in Rome dates from the 5th century, following the construction of St Peter's Basilica by Emperor Constantine I. For many centuries the Popes bore temporal sway over much of the Italian peninsula. In 1860, following prolonged civil unrest, Victor Emmanuel's army seized the Papal States, leaving only Rome and surrounding coastal regions under papal control. When Rome was captured in 1871 and declared the capital of the Kingdom of Italy, papal temporal power was brought to an end. On 11 Feb. 1929 a treaty between the Italian Government and the Vatican recognized the sovereignty of the Holy See in the city of the Vatican.

TERRITORY AND POPULATION

The area of Vatican City is 44 ha. (108·7 acres). It includes the Piazza di San Pietro (St Peter's Square), which is to remain normally open to the public and subject to the powers of the Italian police. It has its own railway station (for freight only), postal facilities, coins and radio. Twelve buildings in and outside Rome enjoy extra-territorial rights, including the Basilicas of St John Lateran, St Mary Major and St Paul without the Walls, the Pope's summer villa at Castel Gandolfo and a further Vatican radio station on Italian soil. *Radio Vaticana* broadcasts an extensive service in 34 languages from the transmitters in Vatican City and in Italy. The Holy See and the Vatican are not synonymous—the Holy See, referring to the primacy of the Pope, is located in Vatican City.

Vatican City has about 800 inhabitants.

CONSTITUTION AND GOVERNMENT

Vatican City State is governed by a Commission appointed by the Pope. The reason for its existence is to provide an extra-territorial, independent base for the Holy See, the government of the Roman Catholic Church. The Pope exercises sovereignty and has absolute legislative, executive and judicial powers. The judicial power is delegated to a tribunal in the first instance, to the Sacred Roman Rota in appeal and to the Supreme Tribunal of the Signature in final appeal.

A new Fundamental Law was promulgated by Pope John Paul II on 26 Nov. 2000 and became effective on 22 Feb. 2001; this replaced the first Fundamental Law of 1929. The Pope is elected by the College of Cardinals, meeting in secret conclave. The election is by scrutiny and requires a two-thirds majority.

National Anthem

'Inno e Marcia Pontificale' ('Hymn and Pontifical March'); words by Raffaello Lavagna, tune by Charles-François Gounod.

GOVERNMENT CHRONOLOGY

Popes since 1939.

1939–58	Pius XII (Eugenio Maria Pacelli)	Italian
1958–63	John XXIII (Angelo Giuseppe Roncalli)	Italian
1963–78	Paul VI (Giovanni Battista Montini)	Italian
1978	John Paul I (Albino Luciani)	Italian
1978–2005	John Paul II (Karol Józef Wojtyła)	Polish
2005–	Benedict XVI (Joseph Alois Ratzinger)	German

CURRENT ADMINISTRATION

Supreme Pontiff: **Benedict XVI** (Joseph Ratzinger), born at Marktl am Inn, in Bavaria, Germany, 16 April 1927. Archbishop of Munich and Freising 1977–82, created Cardinal in 1977; elected Pope 19 April 2005, inaugurated 24 April 2005. Pope Benedict XVI is the eighth German to be elected Pope and the first since the 11th century.

Secretary of State: Cardinal Angelo Sodano.

Secretary for Relations with Other States: Archbishop Giovanni Lajolo.

Office of the Sovereign of the Vatican City:
http://www.vatican.va

CURRENT LEADERS

Benedict XVI

Position
Pope

Introduction
Joseph Ratzinger was elected head of the Roman Catholic Church on 19 April 2005, becoming Pope Benedict XVI. His appointment followed the death of the popular and charismatic Pope John Paul II. A highly intellectual theologian from southern Germany, Benedict XVI has served in the Vatican as head of the department that defends Catholic orthodoxy since 1981. He is expected to reinforce the broadly conservative policies of John Paul II, his friend and close ally, and to tackle secularism and relativism, which he has described as 'letting oneself be tossed and swept by every wind of teaching'.

Early Life
Joseph Ratzinger was born in Marktl am Inn, southeastern Bavaria, Germany, on 16 April 1927, the third and youngest child of a police officer and his wife. In 1929 his father was posted to the town of Tittmoning on the Austrian border, where the family remained for three years, before moving to Auschau am Inn and then to Hufschlag, near Traunstein, when his father retired in 1937. Ratzinger attended the high school in Traunstein, and later opted to train for the priesthood, entering the town's seminary in 1939. At 14 years of age he joined the Hitler Youth—a legal requirement as part of the Nazis' efforts to convert the German population to the 'National Socialist spirit'. Two years later

Ratzinger was drafted into the anti-aircraft artillery corps. His unit guarded facilities including an aircraft-engine plant near Munich. In late 1944 Ratzinger was drafted into the German army and served in and around Munich. Reportedly a reluctant soldier, he deserted weeks before Germany's surrender in 1945, and rejoined the seminary in Traunstein. After two years he took up a place at the Herzogliches Georgianum, a theological institute linked to the University of Munich. On 29 June 1951 he was ordained to the priesthood in the cathedral at Freising, near Munich.

Ratzinger continued with his study of theology at the University of Munich—his doctoral thesis focused on St Augustine and his view of Christianity in the fifth century. Having gained his doctorate in July 1953, he began post-doctoral research about St Bonaventure, a Franciscan theologian of the 13th century. In 1959 Ratzinger moved to Bonn to take up a professorship in fundamental theology at the city's university. He taught at the University of Münster for three years from 1963, before joining the University of Tübingen, near Stuttgart. When the wave of student uprisings swept across Europe in 1968, it brought Marxism to the Tübingen campus. Ratzinger was horrified by what he saw as a 'tyrannical, brutal and cruel' ideology that was undermining the Church. He accepted an offer of a teaching position at the new University of Regensburg a year later, and remained in the Bavarian city for the next seven years. He began to take a more conservative approach to theology, and rose to become the dean and then vice-president of the university.

On 24 March 1977 Ratzinger was elected archbishop of Munich and Freising by Pope Paul VI. He was ordained to the episcopal order in May 1977 and a month later was elevated to cardinal priest. However, his work as an archbishop was to prove relatively short-lived. In Nov. 1981 he was called to Rome by Pope John Paul II (who had been elected in 1978) to take over the Congregation for the Doctrine of the Faith, the department in the Vatican responsible for defending and reinforcing Catholic orthodoxy (once known as the Inquisition). At the same time, he became president of the International Theological Commission and the Pontifical Biblical Commission. The Congregation for the Doctrine of the Faith courted controversy after publishing 'Dominus Jesus', which described other Christian faiths and world religions as 'deficient or not quite real churches'.

Ratzinger was elevated to the position of cardinal bishop of the diocese of Velletri-Signi on 5 April 1993, and was elected vice-dean of the College of Cardinals in 1998. When he was appointed dean of the College in late 2002 (and cardinal bishop of the diocese of Ostia), Ratzinger had become one of the Vatican's most powerful and influential figures. He presided over the funeral of Pope John Paul II in St Peter's Basilica on 8 April 2005, and subsequently inaugurated the conclave for the election of the successor to St Peter in the Sistine chapel. On 19 April, after the fourth ballot of the conclave, the proto-deacon of the College of Cardinals, Jorge Estévez, announced to a crowd of tens of thousands in St Peter's Square: 'Dear brothers and sisters, we have a Pope. The most eminent and most reverend Lord, Lord Joseph, Cardinal of Holy Roman Church, Ratzinger, who has taken the name Benedict XVI.'

Career in Office

Pope Benedict XVI swiftly reappointed all former officers who had served under John Paul II. A hint of future Vatican policy came with the appointment of the US non-Cardinal William Joseph Levada to the post of prefect of the Congregation for the Doctrine of the Faith on 13 May 2005. The elevation of this deeply conservative prelate archbishop of the Archdiocese of San Francisco to one of the church's most powerful positions has raised fears among reform-minded Catholics.

ECONOMY

Currency

Since 1 Jan. 2002 the Vatican City has been using the euro. Italy has agreed that the Vatican City may mint a small part of the total Italian euro coin contingent with their own motifs.

Budget

Revenues in 2001 were US$173·5m. and expenditures US$176·6m.

Performance

Real GDP growth was 1·7% in 2001.

SOCIAL INSTITUTIONS

Justice

In 2002 the Vatican City's legal system hosted 397 civil cases and 608 criminal cases. Most of the offences are committed by outsiders, principally at St Peter's Basilica and the museums.

ROMAN CATHOLIC CHURCH

As the Vicar of Christ and the Successor of St Peter, the Pope is held to be by divine right the centre of all Catholic unity and exercises universal governance over the Church. He is also the sovereign ruler of Vatican City State. He has for advisers the Sacred College of Cardinals, consisting in March 2006 of 193 cardinals from 67 countries (ten created by Pope Paul VI, 168 created by Pope John Paul II and 15 created by Pope Benedict XVI), of whom 120 are cardinal electors—those under the age of 80 who may enter into conclave to elect a new Pope. Cardinals, addressed by the title of 'Eminence', are appointed by the Pope from senior ecclesiastics who are either the bishops of important Sees or the heads of departments at the Roman Curia. In addition to the College of Cardinals, there is a Synod of Bishops, created by Pope Paul VI and formally instituted on 15 Sept. 1965. This consists of the Patriarchs and certain Metropolitans of the Catholic Church of Oriental Rite, of elected representatives of the national episcopal conferences and religious orders of the world, of the cardinals in charge of the Roman Congregations and of other persons nominated by the Pope. The Synod meets in both general (global) and special (regional) assemblies. General Synods normally take place every three years.

The central administration of the Roman Catholic Church is carried out by permanent organisms called Congregations, Council, Commissions and Offices. The Congregations are composed of cardinals and diocesan bishops (both appointed for five-year periods), with Consultors and Officials. There are nine Congregations, viz.: Doctrine, Oriental Churches, Bishops, the Sacraments and Divine Worship, Clergy, Religious, Catholic Education, Evangelization of the Peoples and Causes of the Saints. Pontifical Councils have replaced some of the previously designated Secretariats and Prefectures and now represent the Laity, Christian Unity, the Family, Justice and Peace, Cor Unum, Migrants, Health Care Workers, Interpretation of Legislative Texts, Inter-Religious Dialogue, Culture, Preserving the Patrimony of Art and History, and a Commission for Latin America. There are three academies: the Pontifical Academy for Sciences, the Pontifical Academy for Life and the Pontifical Academy for Social Sciences, the latter two instituted by Pope John Paul II.

CULTURE

World Heritage Sites

The Holy See has one site on the UNESCO World Heritage List: Vatican City (inscribed on the list in 1984)—the centre of the Roman Catholic Church, it contains some of the greatest pieces of European art and architecture, including St Peter's Basilica.

DIPLOMATIC REPRESENTATIVES

In its diplomatic relations with foreign countries the Holy See is represented by the Secretariat of State and the Second Section (Relations with States) of the Council for Public Affairs of the Church. It maintains permanent observers to the UN.

Of the Holy See in the United Kingdom (54 Parkside, London, SW19 5NE)
Apostolic Nuncio: Archbishop Faustino Sainz Muñoz.

Of the United Kingdom at the Holy See (91 Via Dei Condotti, 00187 Rome)
Ambassador: Francis Campbell.

Of the Holy See in the USA (3339 Massachusetts Ave., NW, Washington, D.C., 20008)
Apostolic Nuncio: Gabriele Montalvo.

Of the USA at the Holy See (Villa Domiziana, Via Delle Terme Deciane 26, 00153 Rome)
Ambassador: Francis Rooney.

Of the Holy See to the European Union
Apostolic Nuncio: Archbishop Faustino Sainz Muñoz.

FURTHER READING

Reese, T., *Inside the Vatican.* Harvard Univ. Press, 1997
Permanent Observer Mission to the UN: http://www.holyseemission.org

VENEZUELA

© Research Machines plc 2006

República Bolivariana de Venezuela

Capital: Caracas
Population projection, 2010: 29·08m.
GDP per capita, 2003: (PPP$) 4,919
HDI/world rank: 0·772/75

KEY HISTORICAL EVENTS

Columbus sighted Venezuela in 1498 and it was visited by Alonso de Ojeda and Amerigo Vespucci in 1499 who named it Venezuela (Little Venice). It was part of the Spanish colony of New Granada until 1821 when it became independent, at first in union with Colombia and then as an independent republic from 1830. Up until 1945 the country was governed mainly by dictators. In 1945 a three-day revolt against the reactionary government of Gen. Isaias Medina led to constitutional and economic reforms. In 1961 a new constitution provided for a presidential election every five years, a national congress, and state and municipal legislative assemblies. Twenty political parties participated in the 1983 elections. By now the economy was in crisis and corruption linked to drug trafficking was widespread. In Feb. 1992 there were two abortive coups. A state of emergency was declared. In Dec. 1993 Dr Rafael Caldera Rodríguez's election as president reflected disenchantment with the established political parties. He took office in the early stages of a banking crisis which cost 15% of GDP to resolve. Fiscal tightening backed by the IMF brought rapid recovery. Hugo Chávez Frías, who succeeded as president in Feb. 1999, continued with economic reforms and amended the constitution to increase presidential powers. In Dec. 1999 the north coast of Venezuela was hit by devastating floods and mudslides which resulted in approximately 30,000 deaths.

President Chávez was deposed and arrested on 12 April 2002 in a coup following a general strike, but he was back in the presidential palace just 48 hours later.

TERRITORY AND POPULATION

Venezuela is bounded to the north by the Caribbean with a 2,813 km coastline, east by the Atlantic and Guyana, south by Brazil, and southwest and west by Colombia. The area is 916,445 sq. km (353,839 sq. miles) including 72 islands in the Caribbean. Population (1990) census, 19,455,429. Census 2001 (provisional), 23,054,210; density, 25·1 per sq. km. The estimated population in 2005 was 26,749,000. 87·6% of the population lived in urban areas in 2003.

The UN gives a projected population for 2010 of 29·08m.

The official language is Spanish. English is taught as a mandatory second language in high schools.

Area, population and capitals of the 24 states and one federally-controlled area:

State	Area (sq. km)	2001 census population (provisional)	Capital	Density; inhabitants per sq. km
Federal District	433	1,836,286	Caracas	4,240·8
Amazonas	180,145	70,464	Puerto Ayacucho	0·4
Anzoátegui	43,300	1,222,225	Barcelona	28·2
Apure	76,500	377,756	San Fernando	4·9
Aragua	7,014	1,449,616	Maracay	206·7
Barinas	35,200	624,508	Barinas	17·7
Bolívar	238,000	1,214,846	Ciudad Bolívar	5·1
Carabobo	4,650	1,932,168	Valencia	415·5
Cojedes	14,800	253,105	San Carlos	17·1
Delta Amacuro	40,200	97,987	Tucupita	2·4
Falcón	24,800	763,188	Coro	30·8
Guárico	64,986	627,086	San Juan de los Morros	9·7
Lara	19,800	1,556,415	Barquisimeto	78·6
Mérida	11,300	715,268	Mérida	63·3
Miranda	7,950	2,330,872	Los Teques	293·2
Monagas	28,900	712,626	Maturín	24·7
Nueva Esparta	1,150	373,851	La Asunción	325·1
Portuguesa	15,200	725,740	Guanare	47·8
Sucre	11,800	786,483	Cumaná	66·7
Táchira	11,100	992,669	San Cristóbal	89·4
Trujillo	7,400	608,563	Trujillo	82·2
Vargas	1,497	298,109	La Guaira	199·1
Yaracuy	7,100	499,049	San Felipe	70·3
Zulia	63,100	2,983,679	Maracaibo	47·3
Dependencias Federales	120	1,651		

37·3% of all Venezuelans are under 15 years of age, 58·7% are between the ages of 15 and 64, and 4% are over the age of 65.

Caracas, Venezuela's largest city, is the political, financial, commercial, communications and cultural centre of the country. Metropolitan Caracas had a 1999 population estimate of 3,127,000. Maracaibo, the nation's second largest city (estimated 1998 population of 1·7m.), is located near Venezuela's most important petroleum fields and richest agricultural areas. Other major cities are Valencia, Barquisimeto and Ciudad Guayana.

SOCIAL STATISTICS

2001 births, 529,552; deaths, 107,867. 2001 birth rate per 1,000 population, 21·5; death rate, 4·4. Annual population growth rate, 1992–2002, 2·1%. Life expectancy, 2003, was 70·0 years for males and 75·9 years for females. Infant mortality, 2001, 19 per 1,000 live births; fertility rate, 2001, 2·8 births per woman. In 1998 the most popular age for marrying was 20–24 for both men and women.

CLIMATE

The climate ranges from warm temperate to tropical. Temperatures vary little throughout the year and rainfall is plentiful. The dry season is from Dec. to April. The hottest months are July and August. Caracas, Jan. 65°F (18·3°C), July 69°F (20·6°C). Annual rainfall 32" (833 mm). Ciudad Bolívar, Jan. 79°F (26·1°C), July 81°F (27·2°C). Annual rainfall 41" (1,016 mm). Maracaibo, Jan. 81°F (27·2°C), July 85°F (29·4°C). Annual rainfall 23" (577 mm).

CONSTITUTION AND GOVERNMENT

The present constitution was approved in a referendum held on 15 Dec. 1999. Venezuela is a federal republic, comprising 34 federal dependencies, 23 states and one federal district. Executive power is vested in the *President*. The ministers, who together constitute the Council of Ministers, are appointed by the President and head various executive departments. There are 17 ministries and seven officials who also have the rank of Minister of State.

92% of votes cast in a referendum (the first in Venezuela's history) on 25 April 1999 were in favour of the plan to rewrite the constitution proposed by President Chávez. As a result, on 25 July the public was to elect a constitutional assembly to write a new constitution, which was subsequently to be voted on in a national referendum. In Aug. 1999 the constitutional assembly declared a national state of emergency. It subsequently suspended the Supreme Court, turned the elected Congress into little more than a sub-committee, stripping it of all its powers, and assumed many of the responsibilities of government. In Dec. 1999 the President's plan to redraft the constitution was approved by over 70% of voters in a referendum. As a result presidents are now able to serve two consecutive six-year-terms instead of terms of five years which cannot be consecutive, the senate was abolished and greater powers were given to the state and the armed forces. President Chávez has effectively taken over both the executive and the judiciary. The constitution provides for procedures by which the president may reject bills passed by Congress, as well as provisions by which Congress may override such presidential veto acts.

Since the senate was dissolved, Venezuela has become a unicameral legislature, the 167-seat *National Assembly*, with members being elected for five-year terms.

National Anthem
'Gloria al bravo pueblo' ('Glory to the brave people'); words by Vicente Salias, tune by Juan Landaeta.

GOVERNMENT CHRONOLOGY

Heads of State since 1941. (AD = Democratic Action; CD = Democratic Convergence; COPEI = Social Christian Party; MVR = Movement for the Fifth Republic; n/p = non-partisan)

President of the Republic
1941–45   military   Isaías Medina Angarita

Revolutionary Junta of Government
1945–48   Rómulo E. Betancourt Bello (AD) (chair); Luis Beltrán Prieto Figueroa (AD); Carlos Román Delgado Chalbaud (military); Raúl Leoni Otero (AD); Gonzalo Barrios Bustillos (AD); Mario Ricardo Vargas Cárdenas (military); Edmundo Fernández (n/p)

President of the Republic
1948   AD   Rómulo Ángel Gallegos Freire

Junta of Government
1948–52   Carlos Román Delgado Chalbaud (military); Germán Suárez Flamerich (n/p); Marcos Evangelista Pérez Jiménez (military); Luis Felipe Llovera Páez (military).

President of the Republic
1952–58   military   Marcos Evangelista Pérez Jiménez

Junta of Government (I)
1958   Wolfgang Enrique Larrazábal Ugueto (military) (chair); Pedro José Quevedo (military); Roberto Casanova (military); Carlos Luis Araque (military); Abel Romero Villate (military); Eugenio Mendoza Goiticoa (n/p); Blas Lamberti Cano (n/p); Arturo Sosa Fernández (n/p); Edgar Sanabria Arcia (n/p).

Junta of Government (II)
1958–59   Edgard Sanabria Arcia (n/p) (chair); Arturo Sosa Fernández (n/p); Miguel J. Rodríguez Olivares (military); Carlos Luis Araque (military); Pedro José Quevedo (military).

Presidents of the Republic
1959–64   AD   Rómulo Ernesto Betancourt Bello
1964–69   AD   Raúl Leoni Otero
1969–74   COPEI   Rafael Caldera Rodríguez
1974–79   AD   Carlos Andrés Pérez Rodríguez
1979–84   COPEI   Luis Antonio Herrera Campins
1984–89   AD   Jaime Lusinchi
1989–93   AD   Carlos Andrés Pérez Rodríguez
1994–99   CD   Rafael Caldera Rodríguez
1999–   MVR   Hugo Rafael Chávez Frías

RECENT ELECTIONS

Presidential elections were held on 30 July 2000; turnout was 56%. Incumbent Hugo Chávez Frías (Movement for the Fifth Republic/MVR) was elected president against one other candidate with 59·8% of the vote. In a recall referendum held on 15 Aug. 2004 he was confirmed as president, with 59·3% of the votes cast backing him.

In elections to the Congress, held on 4 Dec. 2005, 167 seats were contested. Movimiento V República (Movement for the Fifth Republic/MVR) won 114 seats with the remaining seats going to its allies. Opposition parties boycotted the elections.

Presidential elections are scheduled to take place on 3 Dec. 2006.

CURRENT ADMINISTRATION

President: Hugo Chávez Frías; b. 1954 (MVR; sworn in 2 Feb. 1999).

Executive Vice President: José Vicente Rangel.

In March 2006 the government comprised:

Minister of the Interior and Justice: Jesse Chacón Escamillo. *Foreign Affairs:* Alí Rodríguez Araque. *Finance:* Nelson Merentes. *Communications and Information:* William Lara. *Defence:* Adm. Orlando Maniglia Ferreira. *Infrastructure:* Ramón Carrizález Rengifo. *Agriculture and Lands:* Elías Jaua. *Environment and Natural Resources:* Jacqueline Coromoto Faría Pineda. *Health and Social Development:* Francisco Armada. *Education and Sports:* Aristóbulo Istúriz. *Higher Education:* Samuel Moncada. *Labour:* Ricardo Dorado. *Light Industry and Commerce:* María Cristina Iglesias. *Planning and Development:* Jorge Giordani. *Science and Technology:* Yadira Córdoba. *Social Development:* Jorge Luis García Carneiro. *Tourism:* Wilmar Castro Soteldo. *Basic Industry and Mines:* Víctor Alvarez Rodríguez. *Energy and Petroleum:* Rafael Ramírez. *Food Affairs:* Erika Farías. *Housing:* Julio Montes. *Culture:* Francisco Sesto Novas. *Popular Economy:* Oly Millán. *Presidential Secretariat:* Delcy Rodríguez.

Government Website (Spanish only):
http://www.gobiernoenlinea.ve

CURRENT LEADERS

Hugo Chávez

Position
President

Introduction
Hugo Rafael Chávez Frías is president of Venezuela representing the Movimiento V República (Movement for the Fifth Republic/MVR—which he founded in 1997). He was elected in Dec. 1998 as the candidate for the left-wing 'Patriotic Pole' coalition. He was re-elected president in 2000, but has since been challenged by anti-government protests and a failed coup.

Early Life
The son of teachers, Chávez was born on 28 July 1954 in Sabaneta, Barinas state in the Andean west of Venezuela. Embarking on a military career, he completed his higher education at the Academia Militar de Venezuela, graduating in 1975 with a degree in military science. After further military training, he took a masters degree in social science at the Universidad Simón Bolívar.

In 1982 Chávez co-founded the MBR-200. Based on the ideals of the independence hero, Simón Bolívar, the party took as its symbol the Samán de Güerre, the tree under which Bolívar famously sheltered. In Feb. 1992 Chávez led an abortive military coup attempting to overthrow the government of Carlos Andrés Pérez. He was captured and imprisoned until 1994 when he was pardoned by President Rafael Caldera. Having reformed the MBR-200 as the Movement for the Fifth Republic/MVR, he promised to fight social inequality in Venezuela, a country rich in natural resources but where the wealth benefited the minority elite. Falling oil prices coupled with corruption caused widespread economic difficulties. By 1998 over 90% of Venezuelans lived below the poverty line, social services had deteriorated to pre-1950s levels and inflation was high.

In Nov. 1998 Chávez's Patriotic Pole coalition won 34% of seats in legislative elections. The following month he ran for the presidency against the Proyecto Venezuela candidate, Henrique Salas Romer. With the highest majority for 40 years, Chávez won 56·5% of votes to 39·5%. His win ended the 40-year domination of Acción Democrática (Democratic Action) and the Partido Social Cristiano (Social Christian Party).

Career in Office
On election, Chávez pledged to modernize the government, root out corruption, implement radical reforms and revive Venezuela's floundering economy. In April 1999 he called a referendum in which 92% of voters called for a new constitution. In July elections to the constitutional assembly, Chávez supporters won 121 seats against ten for the opposition. A second referendum was called for Dec. in which 72% approved a new constitution, modelled on France's Fifth Republic. The two-tiered congress was combined into one National Assembly, the presidential term was extended from five to six years, presidential power over legislation and the budget was increased, and a second consecutive presidential term was permitted. Further changes included a reformed judiciary, an extension of universal economic and social rights, increased rights for indigenous Venezuelans, and more military involvement in policy implementation. Despite Chávez's popular support, members of the business community and the middle classes were wary of the power granted the president and US$4bn. was transferred out of the country. Nonetheless, a rise in oil prices compensated for this financial loss and inflation fell, although the country suffered a recession following the 1998 economic crisis. Disastrous mudslides in Dec. 1999 in which tens of thousands of people died brought further financial strain for the government.

In the July 2000 presidential elections Chávez beat his former ally from the 1992 coup Lt.-Col. Francisco Arias Cárdenas with 59·8% of votes to 37·5%. His MVR party was equally successful in regional elections. Opposition candidates claimed the votes had been rigged and the military was called in to disperse protestors. On re-election Chávez pledged to fight unemployment with public spending, introduce a land rights bill to ease rural poverty, offer tax breaks for businesses, build new schools and encourage foreign investment. Though lacking a MVR majority in the assembly, Chávez was able to secure wide legislative powers. One of his first moves was to seek a union with the oil-producing Arab states which would reject Western pressure for increased output (and thus lower prices). In Sept. he made his international position clear by criticizing US involvement in Colombian military efforts to combat left-wing rebels, and by praising Cuban leader Fidel Castro's defiant rejection of US domination, as well as his economic and social policies. During a visit by Castro, Chávez agreed to sell oil to Cuba at a discounted price. In April 2001 Chávez hosted talks with Mexico and Colombia to pursue the implementation of a free trade zone, and to work towards extending free trade throughout the Americas. Despite international fears of a Castro reincarnate, he also visited the USA and Europe on numerous occasions.

As his 'Bolivarian Revolution' failed to produce the promised social and economic improvements, the country became increasingly divided between Chávez's supporters and opponents. In April 2002 anti-government protesters descended on the capital demanding his resignation. Taking advantage of the instability, a military coup was mounted with businessman Pedro Carmona Estanga at its head. Chávez was forced to resign and Carmona assumed the presidency. Western and Latin American governments (but not the USA) condemned the coup, refusing to acknowledge the new government, and protests by Chávez supporters quickly led to his reinstatement.

Nevertheless, Venezuelans remained polarized and more protests were staged in June and July. In Dec. 2002 a national strike was called by the opposition following a decision by the Supreme Court to overrule a referendum on Chávez's presidency called for Feb. 2003 by the Electoral Council. Protests focused on the state-owned petrol company Petróleos de Venezuela (Pdvsa), the provider of around 40% of the country's revenues. Oil production plummeted and world prices increased, causing OPEC to increase production. The strike continued into 2003, threatening to destabilize the country's economy, but Chávez remained defiant. The strike abated in Feb. 2003, although workers at Pdvsa continued to protest and the opposition petitioned for early elections.

In Aug. 2004 Chávez survived a national referendum on whether he should be allowed to serve the remainder of his term of office until 2006. Although credited with about 59% of the vote, opposition parties denounced the victory as electoral fraud. Then, in parliamentary elections in Dec. 2005, his MVR party won 114 of 167 National Assembly seats, with the remaining seats being won by his allies.

DEFENCE

There is selective conscription for 30 months. Defence expenditure totalled US$1,283m. in 2003 (US$50 per capita), representing 1·5% of GDP.

Army

The Army has six infantry divisional headquarters, one cavalry brigade, seven infantry brigades, one airborne brigade, two ranger brigades, one mobile counter guerrilla brigade and one aviation regiment. Equipment includes 81 main battle tanks. Strength (2002) 34,000 (27,000 conscripts). There were estimated to be an additional 8,000 reserves.

A 23,000-strong volunteer National Guard is responsible for internal security.

Navy

The combatant fleet comprises two submarines and six frigates. The Naval Air Arm, 500 strong, operates three combat aircraft and nine armed helicopters. Main bases are at Caracas, Puerto Cabello and Punto Fijo.

Air Force

The Air Force was 7,000 strong in 1999 and had 124 combat aircraft and 31 armed helicopters. There are six combat squadrons. Main aircraft types include CF-5s, Mirage 50s and F-16A/Bs.

INTERNATIONAL RELATIONS

Venezuela is a member of the UN, WTO, OAS, Inter-American Development Bank, LAIA, ACS, OPEC, IOM, FAO, Interpol, Intelsat, IADB, IAEA, IMO, SELA, UNCTAD, UNESCO, UPU, WHO and the Andean Community.

ECONOMY

In 2002 services accounted for 54·4% of GDP, industry 43·0% and agriculture 2·6%.

Overview

During the 1970s per capita GDP grew by over 300% but about two-thirds of these gains were lost in the following decade. When oil prices fell from their 1970s peak, debt spiralled out of control and the country sank into depression. By the late 1990s per capita GDP had returned to its levels of twenty years earlier but poverty had also increased during this period.

Venezuela's mineral and oil deposits are among the largest in the world. The country supplied an estimated 13·5% of US crude oil imports in 2002 and the oil industry accounts for roughly half of Venezuela's budget, over 80% of its exports and over 25% of GDP. In Dec. 2002 a two-month national strike paralysed the oil industry, causing world oil prices to reach two-year highs in Feb. 2003. Following anti-Chávez protests, the president won backing in a referendum and has since seen his position stabilize. In 2004 the economy bounced back from two years of sharp recession with an annual GDP growth rate of 17·9%. Chávez has used strong oil revenue growth to spend heavily on social programmes. Expenditure has outstripped booming revenues, leaving public finances in deficit and the economy potentially vulnerable to a drop in oil prices. In 2004 public debt grew from 29% of GDP to 39%. The Chávez government has extended its control over banks and a growing share of the nation's productive activity.

Currency

The unit of currency is the *bolívar* (VEB) of 100 *céntimos*. Foreign exchange reserves were US$7,204m. and gold reserves 10·50m. troy oz in June 2002. Exchange controls were abolished in April 1996. The bolívar was devalued by 12·6% in 1998, and in Feb. 2002 it was floated, ending a regime that permitted the bolívar to trade only within a fixed band. However, in Feb. 2003 it was pegged to the dollar. In Feb. 2004 the bolívar was devalued by 16·7%. Total money supply in May 2002 was Bs 7,232·47bn. Inflation rates (based on IMF statistics):

1995	1996	1997	1998	1999	2000	2001	2002	2003	2004
59·9%	99·9%	50·0%	35·8%	23·6%	16·2%	12·5%	22·4%	31·1%	21·7%

The inflation rate in 2001 of 12·5% was the lowest in more than 15 years.

Budget

The fiscal year is the calendar year. Revenues and expenditures in Bs 1m.:

	1997	1998	1999	2000	2001
Revenue	10,240,962	9,157,084	11,251,838	16,873,493	19,326,543
Expenditure	8,894,305	11,014,036	12,169,972	17,860,230	22,883,815

Performance

Real GDP growth rates (based on IMF statistics):

1997	1998	1999	2000	2001	2002	2003	2004
6·4%	0·3%	−6·0%	3·7%	3·4%	−8·9%	−7·7%	17·9%

Total GDP in 2004 was US$109·3bn.

Banking and Finance

A law of Dec. 1992 provided for greater autonomy for the Central Bank. Its *President*, currently Gastón Luis Parra Luzardo, is appointed by the President for five-year terms. Since 1993 foreign banks have been allowed a controlling interest in domestic banks. In 2003 there were 24 commercial banks and three foreign banks.

There is a stock exchange in Caracas.

ENERGY AND NATURAL RESOURCES

Environment

Carbon dioxide emissions from the consumption and flaring of fossil fuels in 2002 were the equivalent of 5·7 tonnes per capita.

Electricity

Installed capacity in 2002 was 20·6m. kW; production was 87·41bn. kWh in 2002 and consumption per capita 3,484 kWh.

Oil and Gas

Proven resources of oil were 77·8bn. bbls. in 2002. Venezuela has the highest reserves of oil of any country outside the Middle East. The oil sector was nationalized in 1976, but private and foreign investment have again been permitted since 1992. Crude oil production in 2002 was 151·4m. tonnes. Venezuela is the largest exporter of oil to the USA. Oil provides about 50% of Venezuela's revenues. Natural gas production in 2002 was 27·3bn. cu. metres. Natural gas reserves in 2002 were 4,190bn. cu. metres, the largest in Latin America.

Minerals

Output (in 1,000 tonnes) in 2001: iron ore, 19,000; limestone (1996), 15,130; coal (2000), 7,885; bauxite, 4,400; aluminium (2000), 569; gold, 9,076 kg. Diamond production in 2001 totalled 52,000 carats.

Agriculture

Coffee, cocoa, sugarcane, maize, rice, wheat, tobacco, cotton, beans and sisal are grown. 50% of farmers are engaged in subsistence agriculture. There were 2·60m. ha. of arable land in 2001 and 0·81m. ha. of permanent crops. 575,000 ha. were irrigated in 2001. There are government price supports and tax incentives.

Production in 2000 in 1,000 tonnes: sugarcane, 6,950; bananas, 1,000; maize, 900; rice, 737; plantains, 551; cassava, 448; potatoes, 352; oranges, 332; sorghum, 320; watermelons, 261; carrots, 239; tomatoes, 188.

Livestock (2000): cattle, 15·80m.; pigs, 4·90m.; goats, 3·60m.; sheep, 781,000; horses, 500,000; chickens, 110m.

Forestry

In 2000 the area under forests was 49·51m. ha., or 56·1% of the total land area. Timber production in 2003 was 5·03m. cu. metres.

Fisheries

In 2003 the total catch was 524,449 tonnes (475,359 tonnes from marine waters).

INDUSTRY

Production (2002, in tonnes): petrol, 14·9m.; residual fuel oil, 14·3m.; distillate fuel oil, 14·2m.; cement (2001), 8·7m.; crude steel, 4·2m.; sugar (2001), 585,000.

Labour

Out of 8,286,800 people in employment in 1997, 2,411,700 were in community, social and personal services, 1,985,500 in wholesale and retail trade, restaurants and hotels, 1,122,400 in manufacturing and 894,000 in agriculture, hunting, fishing and forestry. In Sept. 2005, 11·5% of the workforce was unemployed, down from 14·5% a year earlier.

In late 2002 and early 2003 a two-month long general strike intended to oust President Chávez ended in failure, instead crippling an already depressed economy.

Trade Unions

The most powerful confederation of trade unions is the CTV (*Confederación de Trabajadores de Venezuela*, formed 1947).

INTERNATIONAL TRADE

The Group of Three free trade pact with Colombia and Mexico came into effect on 1 Jan. 1995. Foreign debt was US$32,563m. in 2002.

Imports and Exports

Trade in US$1m.:

	1998	1999	2000	2001	2002
Imports f.o.b.	16,755	14,492	16,592	18,660	13,732
Exports f.o.b.	17,707	20,963	33,194	26,252	26,656

Exports of oil in 2001 were valued at US$19bn., the third highest export revenues after Saudi Arabia and Iran. The main import sources in 2000 were USA (37·8%), Colombia (7·4%), Brazil (5·0%) and Italy (4·4%). The main markets for exports in 2000 were USA (59·6%), Netherlands Antilles (5·6%), Brazil (3·6%) and Colombia (2·8%).

COMMUNICATIONS

Roads

In 2002 there were 96,155 km of roads, of which 33·6% were paved. There were 1,875,500 passenger cars in use in 2002 (74·7 per 1,000 inhabitants) plus 603,600 trucks and vans. There were 2,900 fatalities as a result of road accidents in 1996.

Rail

The railway network comprises 630 km of 1,435 gauge track. Passenger-km travelled came to 12m. in 1995 and freight tonne-km to 59m. in 2000.

There is a metro in Caracas.

Civil Aviation

The main international airport is at Caracas (Simon Bolívar), with some international flights from Maracaibo. Aeropostal Alas de Venezuela is the main Venezuelan carrier. In 1999 scheduled airline traffic of Venezuela-based carriers flew 75·4m. km, carrying 4,690,000 passengers (1,590,000 on international flights).

Shipping

Ocean-going shipping totalled 865,000 GRT in 2002, including oil tankers 376,000 GRT. La Guaira, Maracaibo, Puerto Cabello, Puerto Ordaz and Guanta are the chief ports. In 1995 vessels totalling 21,009,000 NRT entered ports and vessels totalling 8,461,000 NRT cleared. The principal navigable rivers are the Orinoco and its tributaries the Apure and Arauca.

Telecommunications

In 2002 Venezuela had 9,305,300 telephone subscribers (369·2 per 1,000 population) and 1,536,000 PCs were in use (60·9 for every 1,000 persons). Mobile phone subscribers numbered 6,463,600 in 2002 and there were 112,000 fax machines in use. The number of Internet users in 2002 was 1,274,400. CANTV, the national telephone company, lost its 50-year monopoly on fixed-line telephony in 2000.

Postal Services

In 2003 there were 381 post offices, or one for every 67,500 persons.

SOCIAL INSTITUTIONS

Justice

A new penal code was implemented on 1 July 1999. The new, US-style system features public trials, verbal arguments, prosecutors, citizen juries and the presumption of innocence, instead of an inquisitorial system inherited from Spain which included secretive trials and long exchanges of written arguments.

In Aug. 1999 the new constitutional assembly declared a judicial emergency, granting itself sweeping new powers to dismiss judges and overhaul the court system. The assembly excluded the Supreme Court and the national Judicial Council from a commission charged with reorganizing the judiciary. President Chávez declared the assembly the supreme power in Venezuela.

The court system is plagued by chronic corruption and a huge case backlog. Only about 40% of the country's prisoners in 1999 had actually been convicted. In Oct. 1999 over 100 judges accused of corruption were suspended. The population in penal institutions in 2003 was 19,554 (76 per 100,000 population).

Education

In 2001–02 there were 3,506,780 primary school pupils (186,658 teachers in 1997–98) and 1,811,127 secondary school pupils.

In 1995–96 there were in the public sector 16 universities, one polytechnic university and one open (distance) university; and in the private sector, 12 universities, two Roman Catholic universities and one technological university.

Adult literacy was 93·0% in 2003 (male, 93·3%; female, 92·7%).

Health

In 2002 there were 567 hospitals with 19 beds per 10,000 inhabitants. There were 48,000 physicians and 13,680 dentists in 2001; and 46,305 nurses and 8,751 pharmacists in 1997.

RELIGION

In 2001 there were 22·05m. Roman Catholics. There are four archbishops, one at Caracas, who is Primate of Venezuela, two at Mérida and one at Ciudad Bolívar. There are 19 bishops. In May 2005 there was one cardinal. The remainder of the population follow other religions, notably Protestantism.

CULTURE

World Heritage Sites

Venezuela has three sites on the UNESCO World Heritage List: Coro and its Port (inscribed on the list in 1993); Canaima National Park (1994); and La Ciudad Universitaria de Caracas (2000).

Broadcasting

There were about 230 radio stations in 1998 and 66 TV stations (colour by NTSC) in 1997. In 2001 there were 4·6m. TV receivers and in 2000 there were 7·1m. radio receivers.

Press

In 1996 there were 86 leading daily newspapers with a circulation of over 4·6m.

Tourism

In 2002 there were 432,000 foreign tourists; spending by tourists totalled US$468m.

DIPLOMATIC REPRESENTATIVES

Of Venezuela in the United Kingdom (1 Cromwell Rd, London, SW7 2HW)
Ambassador: Alfredo Toro-Hardy.

Of the United Kingdom in Venezuela (Torre La Castellana, Piso 11, Avenida Principal de La Castellana, Caracas 1061)
Ambassador: Donald Lamont.

Of Venezuela in the USA (1099 30th St., NW, Washington, D.C., 20007)
Ambassador: Bernardo Alvarez-Herrera.

Of the USA in Venezuela (Calle Suapure, con calle F. Colinas de Valle Arriba, Caracas)
Ambassador: William R. Brownfield.

Of Venezuela to the United Nations
Ambassador: Fermín Toro Jiménez.

Of Venezuela to the European Union
Ambassador: Luisa Romero Bermudez.

FURTHER READING

Dirección General de Estadística, Ministerio de Fomento, Boletín Mensual de Estadística.—Anuario Estadístico de Venezuela. Caracas, Annual

Canache, D., *Venezuela: Public Opinion and Protest in a Fragile Democracy.* Univ. of Miami, 2002

McCoy, J., Smith, W. C., Serbin, A. and Stambouli, A., *Venezuelan Democracy Under Stress.* Univ. of Miami, 1995

Naim, M., *Paper Tigers and Minotaurs: the Politics of Venezuela's Economic Reforms.* Washington (D.C.), 1993

Rudolph, D. K. and Rudolph, G. A., *Historical Dictionary of Venezuela.* 2nd ed. Scarecrow Press, Metuchen (NJ), 1995

National Statistical Office: Oficina Central de Estadística e Informática.

VIETNAM

CHINA

LAOS

HANOI

Hai Phong

Gulf of
Tonkin

THAILAND

Da Nang

VIETNAM

CAMBODIA

Nha Trang

Ho Chi Minh City

Gulf of
Thailand

Can Tho

South China
Sea

0   125 mi

0   200 km

© Research Machines plc 2006

Công Hòa Xã Hôi Chu Nghĩa Viêt Nam
(Socialist Republic of Vietnam)

Capital: Hanoi
Population projection, 2010: 89·72m.
GDP per capita, 2003: (PPP$) 2,490
HDI/world rank: 0·704/108

KEY HISTORICAL EVENTS

By the end of the 15th century, the Vietnamese had conquered most of the Kingdom of Champa (now Vietnam's central area) and by the end of the 18th century had acquired Cochin-China (now its southern area). At the end of the 18th century, France helped to establish the Emperor Gia-Long as ruler of a unified Vietnam. Cambodia had become a French protectorate in 1863 and in 1899, after the extension of French protection to Laos in 1893, the Indo Chinese Union was proclaimed.

In 1940 Vietnam was occupied by the Japanese. In Aug. 1945 they allowed the Viet Minh movement to seize power, dethrone the Emperor and establish a republic known as Vietnam. On 6 March 1946 France recognized 'the Democratic Republic of Vietnam' as a 'Free State within the Indo-Chinese Federation'. On 19 Dec. Viet Minh forces made a surprise attack on Hanoi, the signal for nearly eight years of hostilities. An agreement on the cessation of hostilities was reached on 20 July 1954. The French withdrew and by the Paris Agreement of 29 Dec. 1954 completed the transfer of sovereignty to Vietnam which was divided along the 17th parallel into Communist North Vietnam and the non-Communist South. From 1959 the North promoted insurgency in the south, provoking retaliation from the USA. A full scale guerrilla war developed.

In Paris on 27 Jan. 1973 an agreement was signed ending the war in Vietnam. However, hostilities continued between the North and the South until the latter's defeat in 1975. Between 150,000 and 200,000 South Vietnamese fled the country. The unification of North and South Vietnam into the Socialist Republic of Vietnam finally took place on 2 July 1976. Vietnam invaded Cambodia in Dec. 1978 and China attacked Vietnam in consequence. In 1986 Vietnam implemented economic reforms, gradually shifting to a multi-sectoral market economy under state regulation. On 11 July 1995 Vietnam and the USA normalized relations. On 28 July 1995 Vietnam became a member of the Association of South East Asian Nations (ASEAN) and in the same month signed a trade agreement with the European Union.

TERRITORY AND POPULATION

Vietnam is bounded in the west by Cambodia and Laos, north by China and east and south by the South China Sea. It has a total area of 332,934 sq. km and is divided into eight regions and 60 provinces and a city under central government. Areas and populations:

Province	Area (sq. km)	Census population, 1999	Capital
Dac Lac	19,800	1,776,331	Buon Me Thoat
Gia Lai	16,212	971,920	Play Cu
Kon Tum	9,934	314,042	Kon Tum
Central Highlands	45,946	3,062,293	
An Giang	3,424	2,049,039	Long Xuyen
Bac Lieu	2,485	736,325	Bac Lieu
Ben Tre	2,247	1,296,914	Ben Tre
Ca Mau	5,204	1,117,829	Ca Mau
Can Tho	2,965	1,811,140	Can Tho
Dong Thap	3,276	1,564,977	Sa Dec
Kien Giang	6,243	1,494,433	Rach Gia
Long An	4,338	1,306,202	Tan An
Soc Trang	3,191	1,173,820	Soc Trang
Tien Giang	2,339	1,605,147	My Tho
Tra Vinh	2,369	965,712	Tra Vinh
Vinh Long	1,487	1,010,486	Vinh Long
Mekong River Delta	39,568	16,132,024	
Ha Tinh	6,053	1,269,013	Ha Tinh
Nghe An	16,371	2,858,265	Vinh
Quang Binh	7,948	793,863	Dong Hoi
Quang Tri	4,592	573,331	Dong Ha
Thanh Hoa	11,168	3,467,609	Thanh Hoa
Thua Thien (Hue)	5,010	1,045,134	Hue
North Central Coast	51,142	10,007,215	
Bac Can	4,796	275,250	Bac Can
Bac Giang	3,817	1,492,191	Bac Giang
Bac Ninh	797	941,389	Bac Ninh
Cao Bang	8,445	491,055	Cao Bang
Ha Giang	7,831	602,684	Ha Giang
Lang Son	8,178	704,643	Lang Son
Lao Cai	8,044	594,637	Lao Cai
Phu Tho	3,465	1,261,500	Phu Tho
Quang Ninh	5,938	1,004,461	Ha Long

Province	Area (sq. km)	Census population, 1999	Capital
Thai Nguyen	3,541	1,046,163	Thai Nguyen
Tuyen Quang	5,810	675,110	Tuyen Quang
Vinh Phuc	1,362	1,091,973	Vinh Yen
Yen Bai	6,808	679,684	Yen Bai
North East	68,832	10,860,740	
Ba Ria (Vung Tau)	1,965	800,568	Vung Tau
Binh Duong	2,718	716,427	Thu Dau Mot
Binh Phuoc	6,796	653,644	Dong Xoai
Binh Thuan	7,992	1,047,040	Phan Thiet
Dong Nai	5,864	1,989,541	Bien Hoa
Lam Dong	10,137	996,219	Da Lat
Ninh Thuan	3,427	503,048	Phan Rang
Tay Ninh	4,029	965,420	Tay Ninh
Thanh Pho Ho Chi Minh	2,090	5,037,155	Ho Chi Minh City
North East South	45,018	12,709,062	
Hoa Binh	4,749	757,637	Hoa Binh
Lai Chau	17,133	588,666	Lai Chau
Son La	14,210	881,383	Son La
North West	36,092	2,227,686	
Ha Nam	827	791,618	Phu Ly
Ha Tay	2,169	2,386,770	Ha Dong
Hai Duong	1,661	1,649,779	Hai Duong
Hai Phong	1,508	1,672,992	Hai Phong
Hanoi	921	2,672,122	Hanoi
Hung Yen	889	1,068,705	Hung Yen
Nam Dinh	1,669	1,888,406	Nam Dinh
Ninh Binh	1,399	884,080	Ninh Binh
Thai Binh	1,520	1,785,600	Thai Binh
Red River Delta	12,563	14,800,072	
Binh Dinh	6,076	1,461,046	Quy Nhon
Da Nang	942	684,131	Da Nang
Khanh Hoa	5,257	1,031,262	Nha Trang
Phu Yen	5,278	786,972	Tuy Hoa
Quang Nam	11,043	1,372,424	Tam Ky
Quang Ngai	5,177	1,190,006	Quang Ngai
South Central Coast	33,773	6,525,841	

At the 1999 census the population was 76,324,933 (50·8% female); density, 229 per sq. km. 2005 population estimate; 84,238,000. 74·2% of the population live in rural areas (2003).

The UN gives a projected population for 2010 of 89·72m.

Major cities in 1992: Ho Chi Minh City (2002 population, 5,479,000), Hanoi (2002, 2,931,400), Hai Phong (783,133), Da Nang (382,674), Buon Me Thoat (282,095), Nha Trang (221,331), Hue (219,149), Can Tho (215,587).

85% of the population are Vietnamese (Kinh). There are also 53 minority groups thinly spread in the extensive mountainous regions. The largest minorities are: Tay, Khmer, Thai, Muong, Nung, Meo, Dao.

The official language is Vietnamese. Chinese, French and Khmer are also spoken.

SOCIAL STATISTICS

2002 estimates: births, 1,598,000; deaths, 522,000. Estimated birth rate in 2002 was 19·9 per 1,000 population; estimated death rate, 6·5. Life expectancy, 2003, was 68·6 years for males and 72·6 years for females. Annual population growth rate, 1992–2002, 1·5%. Infant mortality, 2001, 30 per 1,000 live births; fertility rate, 2001, 2·3 births per woman. Vietnam has had one of the largest reductions in its fertility rate of any country in the world in recent years, having had a rate of 5·8 births per woman in 1975. Sanctions are imposed on couples with more than two children. The annual abortion rate, at over 80 per 1,000 women aged 15–44, ranks among the highest in the world. The rate at which Vietnam has reduced poverty, from 58% of the population in 1993 to 20% in 2004, is among the most dramatic of any country in the world. Vietnam has a young population; 59% were born after 1975.

CLIMATE

The humid monsoon climate gives tropical conditions in the south, with a rainy season from May to Oct., and sub-tropical conditions in the north, though real winter conditions can affect the north when polar air blows south over Asia. In general, there is little variation in temperatures over the year. Hanoi, Jan. 62°F (16·7°C), July 84°F (28·9°C). Annual rainfall 72" (1,830 mm).

CONSTITUTION AND GOVERNMENT

The National Assembly unanimously approved a new constitution on 15 April 1992. Under this the Communist Party retains a monopoly of power and the responsibility for guiding the state according to the tenets of Marxism-Leninism and Ho Chi Minh, but with certain curbs on its administrative functions. The powers of the National Assembly are increased. The 498-member *National Assembly* is elected for five-year terms. Candidates may be proposed by the Communist Party or the Fatherland Front (which groups various social organizations), or they may propose themselves as individual Independents. The Assembly convenes three times a year and appoints a prime minister and cabinet. It elects the *President*, the head of state. The latter heads a *State Council* which issues decrees when the National Assembly is not in session.

The ultimate source of political power is the Communist Party of Vietnam, founded in 1930; it had 2·2m. members in 1996.

National Anthem

'Doàn quân Việt Nam di chung lòng cúú quóc' ('Soldiers of Vietnam, we are advancing'); words and tune by Van Cao.

GOVERNMENT CHRONOLOGY

General Secretaries of the Communist Party since 1976.

1976–86	Le Duan
1986	Truong Chinh
1986–91	Nguyen Van Linh
1991–97	Do Muoi
1997–2001	Le Kha Phieu
2001–	Nong Duc Manh

Heads of State since 1976.

Presidents
1976–80	Ton Duc Thang
1980–81	Nguyen Huu Tho

Chairmen of the State Council
1981–87	Truong Chinh
1987–92	Vo Chi Cong

Presidents
1992–97	Le Duc Anh
1997–	Tran Duc Luong

RECENT ELECTIONS

In parliamentary elections held on 19 May 2002 Communist Party members won 447 of 498 seats, with 51 seats going to non-party candidates. Turnout was 99·7%.

CURRENT ADMINISTRATION

President (titular head of state): Tran Duc Luong; b. 1937 (in office since Sept. 1997).

Vice-President: Truong My Hoa.

Full members of the Politburo of the Communist Party of Vietnam: Nong Duc Manh (b. 1940; *Secretary General*); Nguyen Van An; Pham Van Tra; Tran Duc Luong; Truong Tan Sang; Nguyen Tan Dung; Phan Van Khai; Nguyen Phu Trong; Nguyen Minh Triet; Phan Dien; Nguyen Khoa Diem; Truong Quang Duoc; Le Hong Anh; Tran Dinh Hoan.

In March 2006 the government comprised:

Prime Minister: Phan Van Khai; b. 1933 (sworn in 25 Sept. 1997).

Deputy Prime Ministers: Nguyen Tan Dung; Vu Khoan; Pham Gia Khiem.

Minister of Foreign Affairs: Nguyen Dy Nien. *National Defence:* Pham Van Tra. *Public Security:* Le Hong Anh. *Justice:* Uong Chu Luu. *Planning and Investment:* Vo Hong Phuc. *Finance:* Nguyen Sinh Hung. *Trade:* Truong Din Tuyen. *Agriculture and Rural Development:* Cao Duc Phat. *Communications and Transport:* Dao Dinh Binh. *Construction:* Nguyen Hong Quan. *Industries:* Hoang Trung Hai. *Fisheries:* Ta Quang Ngoc. *Labour, War Invalids and Social Affairs:* Nguyen Thi Hang. *Science and Technology:* Hoang Van Phong. *Culture and Information:* Pham Quang Nghi. *Education and Training:* Nguyen Minh Hien. *Public Health:* Tran Thi Trung Chien. *Resources and Environment:* Mai Ai Truc. *Post and Telecommunications:* Do Trung Ta. *Protection and Care of Children:* Le Thi Thu.

Chairman of the National Assembly: Nguyen Van An.

Vietnamese Parliament: http://www.na.gov.vn

CURRENT LEADERS

Nong Duc Manh

Position
Secretary General of the Communist Party

Introduction
Nong Duc Manh was elected secretary general of the ruling Communist Party in 2001 and so became Vietnam's effective centre of power. He is regarded as a modernizer and has set out to industrialize the nation, encourage foreign investment and enable Vietnam to join the World Trade Organization.

Early Life
Nong Duc Manh was born on 11 Sept. 1940 into the Tay ethnic group in Hung Cuong commune, Na Ri district in the then-province of Bach Thai. From 1958–65 he worked as an engineer with the provincial forestry service and during this period joined the Communist Party. In 1966 he was appointed to the board of the forestry service. From the mid-1970s he ascended the party structure, sitting as a member of the Bach Thai executive committee. In 1986 he was made an alternate member of the Communist central committee and was elected to full membership three years later. In the same year he became deputy chairman of the National Assembly. He was chosen as chairman in Sept. 1992 and re-elected to the post in 1997. He was elected secretary general of the Communist Party in April 2001.

Career in Office
Manh set out his plans to modernize Vietnam's political and legal systems, reducing corruption and streamlining bureaucracy. However, Vietnam remains a one-party state with tight Communist control over the media, and critics suggest political suppression is widespread. He has continued the economic liberalization that began in the 1980s and growth rates have been strong as foreign investment and aid have increased. Manh aims to make Vietnam an industrialized nation by 2020 and is pursuing membership of the WTO. However, there remains a large gap in wealth between the richer urban and struggling rural populations. Manh's crackdown on organized crime was exemplified by the trial in 2003 of over 150 gangsters, particularly Nam Cam (a Ho Chi Minh City criminal), who was executed in 2004.

On the international stage, Manh has pursued closer relations with the USA. Trade relations were normalized in Dec. 2001 and the USA has become Vietnam's chief export destination. Commercial flights from the USA resumed in 2004 for the first time since the end of the Vietnam war. In June 2005 Prime Minister Phan Van Khai travelled to the USA for a meeting with President George W. Bush, the first post-war meeting between leaders from the two countries. In May 2002 Russia relinquished control of the Cam Ranh Bay naval base, previously the biggest Soviet-operated base outside of the Warsaw Pact countries. Manh has stated his foreign policy priorities are to his regional neighbours and other socialist nations.

Phan Van Khai

Position
Prime Minister

Introduction
Phan Van Khai has been head of government since 1997. He is seen as a reformer and is unusual among the rulers of modern Vietnam in that his roots and political career have been in the south. Hitherto, Vietnam's Communist leadership has been largely Hanoi-dominated. His historic visit to the USA in June 2005 was seen as a boost to Vietnam's economic status.

Early Life
Phan Van Khai was born on 25 Dec. 1933 in a village suburb of Saigon, then part of French Indochina. As a child of 14 he joined a movement opposed to French rule and advocating socialism. By 1954 Khai was an experienced resistance soldier, having fought in the civil war for the Communists against the Western-sponsored southern forces. When Vietnam was partitioned in 1954, he settled in Communist North Vietnam. There, he attended the Foreign Languages College in Hanoi, before being sent to Moscow to study economics at the Plekhanov Institute. It was during his five years in Moscow that he joined the Vietnamese Communist Party.

Returning to North Vietnam, Khai held a variety of party posts, eventually working for the State Planning Committee. Reunification of Vietnam in 1976 gave him the opportunity to return to Ho Chi Minh City (as Saigon was renamed), and he was appointed deputy director, and later director, of the city's planning department.

In 1978 Khai gained his first important Communist Party office when he became a deputy mayor of Ho Chi Minh City. In the following year, he was appointed a member of the party committee for the city. Khai was elected to the (national) central committee of the party as an alternate member in 1982, and as a full member in 1984. He was appointed mayor of Ho Chi Minh City in 1985 and remained in that post until he was brought back to Hanoi as chairman of the State Planning Committee in 1989. Two years later he became a member of the Vietnamese cabinet and of the party's Politburo. In 1992 he was made deputy prime minister.

Career in Office
In Sept. 1997 Phan Van Khai succeeded Vo Van Kiet as prime minister of Vietnam. Although he has since overseen the normalization of trade relations with the USA and the progress of Vietnam's bid for WTO membership, Khai has not been prepared to sanction political reforms to match economic liberalization. Following the elections in 2002 which returned the ruling Communist Party unopposed, the National Assembly reappointed him as prime minister. In June 2005 he made the first visit to the USA by a Vietnamese leader since the end of the Vietnam War. However, the visit provoked some protests in the USA over Vietnam's human rights record.

DEFENCE

Conscription is for two years (army) or three years (air force and navy). For specialists it is also three years.

In 2003 defence expenditure totalled US$2,901m. (US$36 per capita), representing 7·4% of GDP.

Army
There are eight military regions and two special areas. Strength (2002) was estimated to be 412,000. Paramilitary Local Defence

forces number 4m.–5m. and include the Peoples' Self-Defence Force (urban) and the People's Militia (rural).

Navy
The fleet includes six frigates and two diesel submarines. In 2002 personnel was estimated at 42,000 plus an additional Naval Infantry force of 27,000.

Air Force
In 2002 the Air Force had about 30,000 personnel, and 189 combat aircraft and 26 armed helicopters. Equipment included Su-22s, Su-27s and MiG-21s.

INTERNATIONAL RELATIONS
Vietnam is a member of the UN, Asian Development Bank, Colombo Plan, APEC, the Mekong Group, ASEAN and the International Organization of the Francophonie.

ECONOMY
Agriculture accounted for 23·0% of GDP in 2002, industry 38·5% and services 38·5%.

Overview
Vietnam has experienced strong growth for over a decade, leading to a reduction in poverty from over 50% in the mid-1990s to 29% in 2002. Efforts on the part of the Vietnamese government, including accession negotiations with the WTO, have led to a significant increase in international integration since 2000. Vietnam signed bilateral trade agreements with the USA in 2000 and with the EU in 2004. Imports have been liberalized over the past decade and the export sector grew 21% in value terms between 1990–2002, during which time the export to GDP ratio rose from 22% to 50%. Since 2000 output has grown by over 6% a year, strongly aided by the US–Vietnam bilateral trade agreement and rises in oil prices. The oil sector plays an important role in the Vietnamese economy, with exports of crude oil accounting for approximately 20% of total exports.

Despite strong exports Vietnam has seen a rising trade deficit since 2000 because of high levels of foreign direct investment and imports of capital goods. The IMF and World Bank have recommended further liberalization of the state-owned Commercial Bank and state-owned enterprises in the electrical, post, telecommunications, banking and insurance sectors. Economic liberalization was scheduled in the 'Ten Year Socio-Economic Development Strategy 2001-10' but reform has been slower than anticipated.

Currency
The unit of currency is the *dong* (VND). In March 1989 the dong was brought into line with free market rates. The direct use of foreign currency was made illegal in Oct. 1994. Foreign exchange reserves were US$3,888m. in March 2002. Total money supply in May 2002 was 116,936·0bn. dong. There was inflation in 2003 of 3·2% and 2004 of 7·7%. Gold reserves were 98,300 troy oz in June 1991.

Budget
Budget revenue and expenditure (in 1bn. dong):

	1997	1998	1999	2000	2001[1]
Revenue	62,766	70,822	76,128	88,721	97,750
Expenditure	70,749	73,419	84,817	103,151	117,180

[1]Forecast.

Performance
Real GDP growth was between 8% and 10% each year from 1994 to 1997, but has slightly slowed since then. There was growth of 7·3% in 2003 and 7·7% in 2004. GDP per head, which was US$181 in 1993, had risen to US$368 by 2000. Vietnam's total GDP in 2004 was US$45·2bn.

Banking and Finance
The central bank and bank of issue is the State Bank of Vietnam (founded in 1951; *Governor*, Le Duc Thuy). In 2003 there were four state-owned commercial banks, 37 joint-stock private banks, four joint venture banks, and 50 representative offices and 26 branches of foreign banks. Vietcombank is the foreign trade bank. Foreign direct investment in Vietnam was US$1·45bn. in 2003.

There are stock exchanges in Ho Chi Minh City, which opened in July 2000, and Hanoi, which opened in March 2005.

ENERGY AND NATURAL RESOURCES

Environment
Vietnam's carbon dioxide emissions from the consumption and flaring of fossil fuels were the equivalent of 0·7 tonnes per capita in 2002.

Electricity
Total installed capacity of power generation in 2000 was 5·0m. kW. In 2002, 35·56bn. kWh of electricity were produced; in 2000 consumption per capita was 342 kWh. A hydro-electric power station with a capacity of 2m. kW was opened at Hoa-Binh in 1994.

Oil and Gas
Oil reserves in 2002 totalled 600m. bbls. In Aug. 2001 an offshore oil mine containing more than 400m. bbls. of petroleum was discovered. Crude oil production in 2002, 121·9m. bbls. Natural gas reserves in 2002 were 190bn. cu. metres; production in 2000 was 1·39bn. cu. metres. Demarcation, in 1997, allowed for petroleum exploration in the Gulf of Thailand, with each side required to give the other some revenue if an underground reservoir is discovered which straddles the border.

Minerals
Vietnam is endowed with an abundance of mineral resources such as coal (3·5bn. tonnes), bauxite (3bn. tonnes), apatite (1bn. tonnes), iron ore (700m. tonnes), chromate (10m. tonnes), copper (600,000 tonnes) and tin (70,000 tonnes); coal production was estimated at 15·88m. tonnes in 2002. There are also deposits of manganese, titanium, a little gold and marble. 2001 output (in 1,000 tonnes): sand and gravel, 85,100; limestone (1999), 971; salt, 575.

Agriculture
Agriculture employs 70% of the workforce. Ownership of land is vested in the state, but since 1992 farmers may inherit and sell plots allocated on 20-year leases. There were 6·5m. ha. of arable land in 2001 and 1·94m. ha. of permanent crops. Agricultural production during the period 1990–97 grew on average by 5·2% every year, giving Vietnam the fastest-growing agriculture of any Asian country.

Production in 1,000 tonnes in 2000: rice, 32,554; sugarcane, 15,145; cassava, 2,036; maize, 1,930; sweet potatoes, 1,658; bananas, 1,270; coconuts, 940; coffee, 803; oranges, 427; groundnuts, 353. Vietnam is the second largest coffee producer in the world after Brazil, and one of the world's largest exporters of rice, having doubled its output in the past 15 years.

Livestock, 2000: cattle, 4·14m.; pigs, 20·19m.; buffaloes, 2·90m.; goats, 544,000; chickens, 196m.; ducks, 55m.

Livestock products (2000): meat, 1,968,000 tonnes; eggs, 165,000 tonnes; milk, 72,000 tonnes.

163,000 tractors were in use in 2001 as well as 232,000 harvester-threshers.

Forestry
In 2000 forests covered 9·82m. ha., or 30·2% of the land area. Timber exports were prohibited in 1992. Timber production was 30·80m. cu. metres in 2001, nearly all of it for fuel.

Fisheries

Total catch, 2001, approximately 1,491,123 tonnes (89% from sea fishing).

INDUSTRY

Estimated total industrial output in 2002 was 260,202·0bn. dong. In 2002 estimated production (in 1,000 tonnes) was: processed sea produce, 288,701; cement, 19,482; steel, 2,429; fertilizers, 1,176; sugar, 1,074; paper (2003), 800; detergents, 381; beer (2003), 1,049·8m. litres; clothes, 47·6m. items.

Labour

In 1997 the workforce was estimated at 37m. Agriculture, forestry and fishing accounted for 25·4m. people; manufacturing, 3·3m.; trade and restaurants, 3·2m.; public administration and services, 2·2m.; transport and communications, 900,000; finance and insurance, 700,000. A liberal Enterprise Law was adopted in 2000, leading to the creation of over 50,000 new private businesses and more than 1·5m. new jobs during the next three years. Official statistics put unemployment at 7·4% of the workforce in early 2000.

Trade Unions

There are 53 trade union associations.

INTERNATIONAL TRADE

In Feb. 1994 the USA lifted the trade embargo it had imposed in 1975, and in Nov. 2001 a trade agreement with the USA was ratified. The agreement allows Vietnam's exports access to the US market on the same terms as those enjoyed by most other countries. The 1992 constitution regulates joint ventures with western firms; full repatriation of profits and non-nationalization of investments are guaranteed.

Foreign debt was US$13,349m. in 2002.

Imports and Exports

Trade is conducted through the state import-export agencies. Imports in 2002, US$17,760m.; exports, US$16,706m. In 2002 the main imports (by value) were: machinery (19%), petroleum (10%), textiles and garments (9%) and steel (7%). Other significant imports were plastics, vehicles, fertilizers and chemicals. Main exports: crude oil (20%), textiles and garments (16%), sea produce (12%), footwear (11%) and rice (4%). Other significant exports were electronics, coffee, latex, cashew nuts and coal.

The main import suppliers in 2000 were Singapore (15·1%), Japan (14·0%), South Korea (11·9%) and China (10·9%). Principal export markets in 2000 were Japan (18·6%), Australia (9·7%), Germany (7·7%) and China (6·6%).

COMMUNICATIONS

Roads

There were 93,430 km of roads in 2002, of which 25·1% were paved. In 2002 there were 141,400 passenger cars, 83,700 commercial vehicles and (1995) around 3m. motorcycles.

Rail

There are 3,142 km of single-track line covering seven routes. Rail links with China were reopened in Feb. 1996. In 2000, 9·8m. passengers and 6·1m. tonnes of freight were carried.

Civil Aviation

There are international airports at Hanoi (Noi Bai) and Ho Chi Minh City (Tan Son Nhat) and 13 domestic airports. The national carrier is Vietnam Airlines, which provides domestic services and in 2003 had international flights to Bangkok, Beijing, Dubai, Guangzhou, Hong Kong, Kaohsiung, Kuala Lumpur, Kunming, Manila, Melbourne, Moscow, Osaka, Paris, Phnom Penh, Seoul, Siem Reap, Singapore, Sydney, Taipei, Tokyo and Vientiane. In 1999 it flew 30·7m. km, carrying 2,600,000 passengers (994,300

on international flights). The busiest airport is Ho Chi Minh City, which in 2001 handled 4,306,143 passengers and 96,560 tonnes of freight. Hanoi handled 2,207,052 passengers and 40,668 tonnes of freight in 2001.

Shipping

In 2002 sea-going vessels totalled 1,131,000 GRT, including oil tankers 162,000 GRT. The major ports are Hai Phong, which can handle ships of 10,000 tons, Ho Chi Minh City and Da Nang. There are regular services to Hong Kong, Singapore, Thailand, Cambodia and Japan. There are some 19,500 km of navigable waterways.

Telecommunications

Vietnam Posts and Telecommunications and the military operate telephone systems with the assistance of foreign companies. Telephone subscribers numbered 5,567,100 in 2002 (68·5 per 1,000 persons) and there were 800,000 PCs in use (9·8 for every 1,000 persons). In 2002 there were 1,902,400 mobile phone subscribers and 40,700 fax machines. Vietnam had 1·5m. Internet users in 2002.

Postal Services

In 2003 there were 12,505 post offices, or one for every 6,500 persons.

SOCIAL INSTITUTIONS

Justice

A new penal code came into force on 1 Jan. 1986 'to complete the work of the 1980 Constitution'. Penalties (including death) are prescribed for opposition to the people's power and for economic crimes. The judicial system comprises the Supreme People's Court, provincial courts and district courts. The president of the Supreme Court is responsible to the National Assembly, as is the Procurator-General, who heads the Supreme People's Office of Supervision and Control.

The death penalty is still in force; there were 16 reported executions in 2005.

The population in penal institutions in 1998 was 55,000 (71 per 100,000 of national population).

Education

Adult literacy rate in 2001 was 92·7% (94·5% among males and 90·9% among females). Primary education consists of a ten-year course divided into three levels of four, three and three years respectively. In 2000–01 there were 9,751,434 pupils and 347,833 teachers in primary schools, and 8,321,194 pupils and 309,218 teachers at secondary schools. In 1995–96 there were seven universities, two open (distance) universities and nine specialized universities (agriculture, three; economics, two; technology, three; water resources, one).

Health

In 2001 there were 42,327 physicians, 44,539 nurses, 14,662 midwives and 5,977 pharmacists. There were 842 hospitals in 2003 with a provision of 24 beds per 10,000 population.

RELIGION

Taoism is the traditional religion but Buddhism is widespread. At a Conference for Buddhist Reunification in Nov. 1981, nine sects adopted a charter for a new Buddhist church under the Council of Sangha. The Hoa Hao sect, associated with Buddhism, claimed 1·7m. adherents in 2001. Caodaism, a synthesis of Christianity, Buddhism and Confucianism founded in 1926, has some 2·8m. followers. In 2001 there were 53·3m. Buddhists and 6·2m. Roman Catholics. In May 2005 there were two cardinals. There is an Archbishopric of Hanoi and 13 bishops. There were six seminaries in 2003.

CULTURE

World Heritage Sites

Vietnam has five sites on the UNESCO World Heritage List: the Complex of Hue Monuments (inscribed on the list in 1993); Ha Long Bay (1994 and 2000); Hoi An Ancient Town (1999); My Son Sanctuary (1999); and Phong Nha-Ke Bang National Park (2003).

Broadcasting

Broadcasting is controlled by the state Vietnam Radio and Television Committee. There are two national radio programmes from Hanoi and one from Ho Chi Minh City, 14 provincial programmes and an external service, the Voice of Vietnam (11 languages). There is a national and two provincial TV services. There were 8·5m. radio sets in 2000 and 15·1m. TV receivers in 2001 (colour by NTSC, PAL and SECAM).

Press

In 1994 there were some 350 newspaper and periodical titles. There are two national dailies: the Communist Party's *Nhan Dan* ('The People'), circulation, 0·2m., and the Army's *Quan Doi Nhan Dan*, 60,000. There are three major regional dailies with a combined circulation of 155,000. There were ten titles in English, including two dailies, in 1995. In 2002, 9,018 book titles were published.

Tourism

There were 2,330,000 foreign tourists in 2001; revenue from tourists came to US$583m.

DIPLOMATIC REPRESENTATIVES

Of Vietnam in the United Kingdom (12–14 Victoria Rd, London, W8 5RD)
Ambassador: Trinh Duc Du.

Of the United Kingdom in Vietnam (Central Building, 31 Hai Ba Trung, Hanoi)
Ambassador: Robert Gordon, CMG, OBE.

Of Vietnam in the USA (1233 20th St., NW, Suite 400, Washington, D.C., 20036)
Ambassador: Chiem Tam Nguyen.

Of the USA in Vietnam (7 Lang Ha, Ba Dinh District, Hanoi)
Ambassador: Michael W. Marine.

Of Vietnam to the United Nations
Ambassador: Le Luong Minh.

Of Vietnam to the European Union
Ambassador: Phan Thuy Thanh.

FURTHER READING

Trade and Tourism Information Centre with the General Statistical Office. *Economy and Trade of Vietnam* [various 5-year periods]

Gilbert, Marc Jason (ed.) *Why the North Won the Vietnam War.* Palgrave Macmillan, Basingstoke, 2002

Harvie, C. and Tran Van Hoa V., *Reforms and Economic Growth.* London, 1997

Karnow, S., *Vietnam: a History.* 2nd ed. London, 1992

Marr, David G., *et al.*, *Vietnam.* [Bibliography] ABC-Clio, Oxford and Santa Barbara (CA), 1992

Morley, J. W. and Nishihara M., *Vietnam Joins the World.* Armonk (NY), 1997

Norlund, I. (ed.) *Vietnam in a Changing World.* London, 1994

National Statistical Office: General Statistical Office, No. 2 Hoang Van Thu St., Ba Dinh District, Hanoi.

Website: http://www.gso.gov.vn

YEMEN

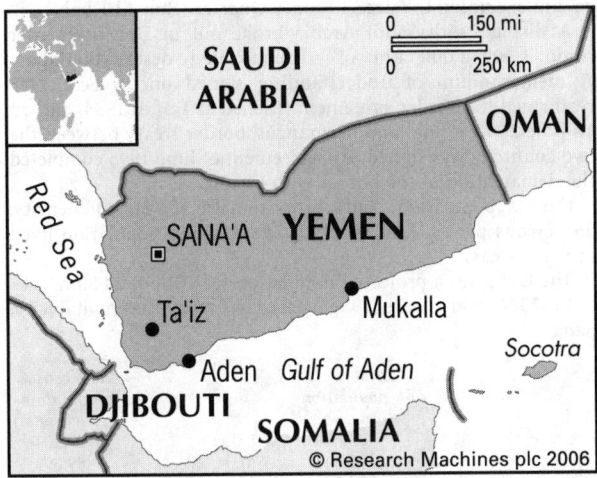

Jamhuriya al Yamaniya
(Republic of Yemen)

Capital: Sana'a
Commercial capital: Aden
Population projection, 2010: 24·50m.
GDP per capita, 2003: (PPP$) 889
HDI/world rank: 0·489/151

KEY HISTORICAL EVENTS

One of the earliest recorded pre-Islamic Arab civilizations was the Sabaean culture, which flourished in what is now Yemen and southwestern Saudi Arabia during the 1st millennium BC. The wealth of the kingdom of Saba (or Sheba) was based on the incense and spice trade and on agriculture. The Himyarite era began in about 115 BC, their increasingly powerful kingdom gradually absorbing Saba and Hadhramaut (to the east) to claim control of all of the southwest Arabian peninsula by the 4th century AD. Himyarite dominance came to an end in the 6th century as Abyssinian (Ethiopian) forces invaded in AD 525. Abyssinian rule was overthrown in 575 by Persian military intervention, and Persian control then endured until the advent of Islam in 628.

Yemen became a province of the Muslim caliphate. Thereafter its fortunes reflected the fluctuating power of the imams (kings and spiritual leaders) of the Zaidi sect—who built the theocratic political structure of Yemen that largely endured from the 9th century until 1962—and of rival dynasties and conquerors. These rivals included the Fatimid caliphs of Egypt, who occupied most of Yemen from about 1000 until 1175, and subsequently the Ayyubids, who ruled until about 1250. The Rasulids, who had served as governors of Yemen under the Ayyubid dynasty, then exercised a measure of sovereignty. However, central authority had fragmented by the time the Ottoman Turks, fearful of Christian Portuguese influence in southern Arabia, intervened in Yemen in the first half of the 16th century. They held nominal but tenuous sovereignty until the end of the First World War (when Yemen became independent), and conflict with the Zaidi imams was frequent.

The southern Yemeni port of Aden was a coveted commercial location on the trading routes to the wider East from ancient times. By the end of the 18th century its strategic importance had increased as Britain sought to contain the French threat to colonial communications with British India following Napoleon's conquest of Egypt. With the coming of the steamship, Britain's need for a military and refuelling base in the region became more pressing. In 1839 the British captured Aden which was attached administratively to India. In the 1850s the Perim, Kamaran and Kuria Muria islands were made part of Aden, which became a free port. Britain also purchased areas on the mainland from local rulers and entered into protectionist agreements with them. The opening of the Suez Canal in 1869 further enhanced both Aden's strategic significance and British colonial consolidation.

Tribal and religious warfare led the Ottoman Turks in the early 1870s to reassert overt authority over northern Yemen, an occupation that lasted until the armistice of 1918. After the Ottoman evacuation, Imam Yahya, who had supported the Turks during the First World War despite leading an earlier revolt against them in 1911, sought to expand Yemeni territory. However, in 1934, after brief hostilities with Saudi Arabia (by then under the rule of Ibn Saud) and skirmishes with British forces from Aden, a trilateral treaty to fix Yemen's boundaries was agreed. The treaty heralded a period of generally peaceful coexistence, which lasted for the rest of Imam Yahya's reign. Aden meanwhile was formally made a British crown colony in 1937, and the surrounding region became known as the Aden protectorate.

Opposition to the theocratic and despotic rule of Imam Yahya led to his assassination in Feb. 1948. His son, Crown Prince Ahmad, succeeded him and put down the insurgents. Ahmad's reign was marked by further repression, renewed friction over the British presence in southern Yemen, and growing pressure in the 1950s to support the Arab nationalist objectives of the new Nasser regime in Egypt. Following Ahmad's death his son, Muhammad al-Badr, was deposed a week after his accession as imam in Sept. 1962 by revolutionary forces aided by Egypt, which took control of the capital, Sana'a, and proclaimed the Yemen Arab Republic (YAR). Saudi Arabia and Jordan supported al-Badr's royalist forces against the new republic, and conflict continued periodically until 1970. Despite its instability, the YAR regime retained power and secured international recognition.

By 1962 the Aden colony had become partially self-governing, and the following year was incorporated in the Federation of South Arabia (with the protectorate territories). A power struggle between rival nationalist groups after the British withdrawal in 1967 led to an independent Marxist state, with Aden as the capital. This was renamed the People's Democratic Republic of Yemen (PDRY) in 1970. Mistrust and frequent border clashes between the YAR and the PDRY characterized the next decade, despite an accord in 1972 to merge the two entities.

A coup in the YAR brought Lieut.-Col. Ibrahim al-Hamadi to power in 1974. However, he was assassinated in Oct. 1977, as was his successor, Lieut.-Col. Ahmad al-Ghashmi, in June 1978. The following month Lieut.-Col. Ali Abdullah Saleh, the commander of the Ta'iz military area, was elected president by the Constitutional Assembly. Saleh's first months in power were turbulent. In early 1979 sporadic fighting erupted into full-scale war between North and South Yemen. Arab League mediation brought the hostilities to an end and both sides acknowledged the need to effect permanent Yemeni union. Saleh was meanwhile re-elected as YAR President by the Constituent Assembly in May 1983 and again in July 1988 by a new Consultative Council.

In the PDRY the chairman of the Presidential Council, Salem Rubayyi Ali, was overthrown in June 1978. Prime Minister Ali Nasser Muhammad briefly assumed the chairmanship before Abdul Fattah Ismail, a hard-line orthodox Marxist, was elected as head of state by the new Presidium of the People's Supreme Assembly in Dec. 1978. Ismail resigned unexpectedly in April 1980 and went to the Soviet Union, to be replaced by Ali Nasser Muhammad. While maintaining South Yemen's close relations with the Soviet Union, Muhammad favoured reconciliation with moderate Arab states. In particular, he viewed improved relations with Saudi Arabia as necessary to further the proposed merger with the YAR. In Feb. 1985 Muhammad resigned as prime minister but remained head of state and secretary-general of the dominant Yemeni Socialist Party (YSP). The rest of that year was marked by the re-emergence of political rivalries, aggravated by the return of Ismail from the Soviet Union, which triggered a brief civil war in Jan. 1986. Ismail was killed and Muhammad fled into exile, after which a new government was formed.

In May 1988 the YAR and PDRY governments reached an agreement on renewing unification discussions and demilitarizing their borders. Their respective leaders, Ali Abdullah Saleh and Ali Salem Albidh, agreed in late 1989 a draft unity constitution (originally drawn up in 1981) and on 22 May 1990 the Republic of Yemen was declared. A five-member Presidential Council assumed power and Saleh was appointed as president for a transitional period. By 1993 relations between the North and South had again deteriorated, Vice-President Albidh having withdrawn to Aden to demand political reforms. Sporadic military clashes escalated into full civil war in May 1994 between disaffected southern forces and Yemen's northern-based government. Southern officials announced their secession from Yemen on 21 May 1994, but northern forces quickly prevailed and Aden was captured on 7 July 1994. The former vice-president and other southern leaders went into exile.

Confirmed in office by parliament in Oct. 1994 for a five-year term, President Saleh's political position was further consolidated when he was re-elected by popular vote in Sept. 1999 (though the turnout was low, particularly in the south). An extension of his term of office from five to seven years was approved in a referendum in Feb. 2001. In April 2003 Saleh's ruling General People's Congress retained power in parliamentary elections with over two-thirds of the seats in the 301-member Assembly of Representatives. However, the main opposition parties claimed that polling was tainted by ballot rigging and intimidation.

In foreign affairs Yemen suffered diplomatic isolation and economic sanctions in the early 1990s for its equivocal response to Iraq's invasion of Kuwait. Its stance incurred US resentment and exacerbated longstanding tensions with neighbouring Saudi Arabia (a border dispute was brought to a close by an agreement signed in June 2000). More recent attacks on Western targets in Yemeni territory—most notably the suicide bombing of the US naval vessel *USS Cole* in Oct. 2000 and an apparent bomb attack on a French supertanker, the *Limburg*, off the Yemeni coast in Oct. 2002—fuelled concerns that Yemen might have become a haven for Islamic extremists. Nevertheless, President Saleh pledged full support for the USA's global campaign against terrorism in the wake of the events of 11 Sept. 2001.

In 1995 Yemen clashed with Eritrea over control of the Hanish Islands in the Red Sea. Following arbitration by an international panel, Yemen assumed control of the main islands in 1998.

TERRITORY AND POPULATION

Yemen is bounded in the north by Saudi Arabia, east by Oman, south by the Gulf of Aden and west by the Red Sea. The territory includes 112 islands including Kamaran (181 sq. km) and Perim (300 sq. km) in the Red Sea and Socotra (3,500 sq. km) in the Gulf of Aden. The islands of Greater and Lesser Hanish are claimed by both Yemen and Eritrea. On 15 Dec. 1995 Eritrean troops occupied them, and Yemen retaliated with aerial bombardments. A ceasefire was agreed at presidential level on 17 Dec. On 20 Dec. the UN resolved to send a good offices mission to the area. In an agreement of 21 May 1996 brokered by France, Yemen

and Eritrea renounced the use of force to settle the dispute and agreed to submit it to arbitration. Following a ruling issued by the Permanent Court of Arbitration in the Hague, Yemen assumed control of the main islands in 1998. The area is 555,000 sq. km excluding the desert Empty Quarter (Rub Al-Khahi).

A dispute with Saudi Arabia broke out in Dec. 1994 over some 1,500–2,000 km of undemarcated desert boundary. A memorandum of understanding signed on 26 Feb. 1995 reaffirmed the border agreement reached at Taif in 1934, and on 12 June 2000 a 'final and permanent' border treaty between the two countries was signed. An agreement of June 1995 completed the demarcation of the border with Oman.

Census population, 2004 (provisional): 19,721,643; density, 36 persons per sq. km. In 2003, 74·3% of the population lived in rural areas.

The UN gives a projected population for 2010 of 24·50m.

In 2004 there were 19 governorates plus the capital city, Sana'a:

	2004 census population (provisional)		2004 census population (provisional)
Abyan	438,656	Lahej	727,203
Aden	590,413	Mahrah	89,093
Amran	872,789	Mahwit	495,865
Bayd	571,778	Marib	241,690
Dhala	470,460	Raymah	395,076
Dhamar	1,339,229	Sa'adah	693,217
Hadhramout	1,029,462	Sana'a (city)	1,747,627
Hajjah	1,480,897	Sana'a	918,379
Hodeida	2,161,379	Shabwah	466,889
Ibb	2,137,546	Ta'iz	2,402,569
Jawf	451,426		

The population of the capital, Sana'a, was 1,748,000 in 2004. The commercial capital is the port of Aden, with a population of (2004) 580,000. Other important towns are Ta'iz, the port of Hodeida, Mukalla, Ibb and Abyan. Sana'a is currently the fastest-growing city in the world, with a population increase of 832·6% in the period 1975–2000 and a projected increase of 128·2% between 2000–15, by when it is expected to have 3·03m. inhabitants.

The national language is Arabic.

SOCIAL STATISTICS

2004 estimates: births, 789,000; deaths, 158,000. Rates, 2004 estimates (per 1,000 population): birth, 40; death, 8. Life expectancy, 2003, was 59·3 years for males and 61·9 years for females. Infant mortality, 2001, 79 per 1,000 live births. Annual population growth rate, 1992–2002, 3·9%; fertility rate, 2001, 7·6 births per woman.

CLIMATE

A desert climate, modified by relief. Sana'a, Jan. 57°F (13·9°C), July 71°F (21·7°C). Aden, Jan. 75°F (24°C), July 90°F (32°C). Annual rainfall 20" (508 mm) in the north, but very low in coastal areas: 1·8" (46 mm).

CONSTITUTION AND GOVERNMENT

Parliament consists of a 301-member *Assembly of Representatives* (*Majlis al-Nuwaab*), elected for a six-year term in single-seat constituencies and, since 2001, a 111-member *Shura Council* (*Majlis al-Shura*), appointed by the president.

The constitution was adopted in May 1991 but was drastically amended in 1994 following the civil war. On 28 Sept. 1994 the Assembly of Representatives unanimously adopted the amended constitution founded on Islamic law. It abolished the former five-member Presidential Council and installed a *President* elected by parliament for a five-year term, subsequently amended to a seven-year term through a referendum held on 20 Feb. 2001. As a result of the same referendum the term for MPs was extended from four to six years.

National Anthem

'Raddidi Ayyatuha ad Dunya nashidi' ('Repeat, O World, my song'); words by A. Noman, tune by Ayub Tarish.

GOVERNMENT CHRONOLOGY

Presidents since 1990. (MSA = General People's Congress)
1990–   MSA   Ali Abdullah Saleh

RECENT ELECTIONS

The *President*, Ali Abdullah Saleh, was elected for his first term in 1990. At the election of 23 Sept. 1999 he was voted in for a third term, claiming 96·3% against the 3·7% of his sole opponent, Najeeb Qahtan Al-Sha'abi. Turnout was 66%.

Parliamentary elections were held on 27 April 2003, in which the General People's Congress (MSA) gained 238 seats (58·0% of the vote), Yemeni Congregation for Reform (Islah) 46 seats (22·6%), Yemeni Socialist Party 8 seats (3·8%), Nasserite Unionist People's Organization (TWSN) 3 seats (1·9%), the Arab Socialist Rebirth Party (Baath) 2 seats (0·7%) and ind. 4 seats. Turnout was 76·0%.

CURRENT ADMINISTRATION

President: Ali Abdullah Saleh; b. 1942 (MSA; in office since 1990, re-appointed in 1994 and re-elected in 1999).

In March 2006 the government comprised:

Prime Minister: Abd al-Qadir al-Ba Jamal; b. 1946 (MSA; in office since 31 March 2001, re-appointed 10 May 2003).

Deputy Prime Minister and Minister of the Interior: Rashad Al-Alimi. *Finance:* Mahyoub al-Asaali. *Planning and International Co-operation:* Abdul Kareem Al-Arhabi. *Defence:* Muhammad Nasser Ali. *Foreign Affairs and Expatriates:* Abubakr al-Qirbi. *Oil and Mineral Resources:* Khalid Ba-Hah. *Legal Affairs:* Adnan Al-Jefri. *Justice:* Gazi Shaif Al-Agbari. *Higher Education and Scientific Research:* Saleh Ali Ba-Surah. *Labour and Social Affairs:* Amat Al-Razaq Ali Hamad. *Communications and Information Technology:* Abdulmalik Al-Mu'alimi. *Local Administration:* Sadiq Abu Ras. *Fisheries:* Mahmoud Ibrahim Sageri. *Transport:* Omar Al-Amudi. *Information:* Hassan Al-Lawzi. *Human Rights:* Khadija Al-Haisami. *Youth and Sports:* Abdulrahman Al-Akwa'. *Electricity:* Mohammad Majoor. *Agriculture and Irrigation:* Galal Ibrahim Faqirah. *Trade and Industry:* Khalid Sheikh. *Culture:* Khalid Al-Ruwaishan. *Technical and Vocational Training:* Ali Safa'a. *Public Health and Population:* Abdul Kareem Rasei. *Education:* Abdulsalam Al-Jufi. *Awqaf:* Hamoud Ubad. *Water and Environment:* Abdul Al-Eryani. *Social Security and Civil Service:* Hamoud Al-Sufi. *Tourism:* Nabil Al-Faqih. *Parliament and Shura Council:* Rashad Al-Rassas. *Public Works and Roads:* Omar Al-Qurshumi.

Speaker: Abdullah Hussain Al-Ahmar.

Government Website: http://www.yemen.gov.ye

CURRENT LEADERS

Ali Abdullah Saleh

Position
President

Introduction
Ali Abdullah Saleh came to power at the age of 36 in July 1978 as president and commander-in-chief of the armed forces of the Yemen Arab Republic (YAR). He retained these offices throughout the 1980s. On the YAR's unification with the People's Democratic Republic (South Yemen) in May 1990, he assumed the presidency of the new Republic of Yemen. In 1994 his regime successfully crushed an attempted secession by southern forces in a brief civil war. Secure in power, Saleh was re-elected

president on 23 Sept. 1999. His government has co-operated in international efforts to combat terrorism despite internal political dissension and tensions between the north and the south of the country.

Early Life
A member of the Hashid tribe, Saleh was born in 1942 in Bait Al Ahmar in Sana'a governorate. Having attended primary school, he joined the armed forces at the age of 16, continuing his studies while a serving soldier. In 1960 he began cadet officer training. In Sept. 1962 Imam Muhammad al-Badr (king and spiritual leader) was deposed a week after his accession (following the death of his father Imam Ahmad) in a military revolution. An eight-year civil war ensued, in which Saleh fought for the new Yemen Arab Republic government, aided by Egypt, against the royalist forces supported by Saudi Arabia. The YAR regime retained power and secured international recognition, but remained unstable throughout the 1970s, partly as a result of tensions with the Marxist regime in southern Yemen. Saleh meanwhile gained increasingly senior military appointments, and reportedly played an important role in a coup that brought Lieut.-Col. Ibrahim al-Hamadi to power in June 1974. When President Ahmad al-Ghashmi (in power from Oct. 1977) was assassinated on 24 June 1978, Saleh was the military commander of Ta'iz governorate. Immediately after the assassination (blamed on the regime in Aden), the Constituent Assembly formed a four-man provisional Presidential Council, including Saleh. On 17 July the Constituent Assembly elected him president of the YAR.

Career in Office
Saleh's early months in power were turbulent. In Sept.–Oct. 1978 he survived an assassination attempt and a subsequent coup plot, both thought to have external backing. In Feb.–March 1979 further sporadic conflict with South Yemen escalated into full-scale war. Arab League mediation brought the fighting to an end and both sides acknowledged the need to effect permanent Yemeni union. Protracted negotiations resulted in reunification as the Republic of Yemen on 22 May 1990. Saleh had previously been re-elected as YAR president by the Constituent Assembly in May 1983 and again in July 1988 by a new Consultative Council. On unification and political liberalization in May 1990, a five-member Presidential Council assumed power and Saleh was chosen as president of the new republic for a transitional period. He was re-elected as president of the Presidential Council in Oct. 1993. A rebellion by disaffected southern forces was suppressed in 1994. In Oct. of that year he was elected president of the republic by parliament. Saleh's position was further reinforced in Sept. 1999 when he was directly elected by the people as president for the first time (albeit on a low turnout, particularly in the south of the country). An extension of his presidential term of office from five to seven years was approved in a referendum in Feb. 2001 and he continues to head the General People's Congress, which dominates the Assembly of Representatives having won decisively the most recent parliamentary elections in April 2003.

Saleh has maintained a crackdown against Islamic terrorism following al-Qaeda attacks on a US warship in Aden in Oct. 2000 and on a French supertanker off the Yemeni coast in Oct. 2002. In June 2004 fighting broke out in north Yemen between government forces and supporters of a dissident cleric, Hussein al-Houthi. He was reportedly killed during clashes in Sept., but there was a brief resurgence of fighting during March–April 2005.

DEFENCE

Conscription is for three years. Defence expenditure in 2003 totalled US$798m. (US$42 per capita), representing 7·0% of GDP.

Estimates of the number of small arms in the country are around 70m., equivalent to nearly four firearms for every person, making Yemen arguably the world's most heavily armed country.

Army

Strength (2002), 60,000 with 40,000 reserves. There are paramilitary tribal levies numbering at least 20,000 and a Ministry of Security force of 50,000.

Navy

Navy forces are based at Aden and Hodeida, with other facilities at Mokha, Mukalla and Perim. Personnel in 2002 were estimated at 1,500.

Air Force

The unified Air Forces of the former Arab Republic and People's Democratic Republic are now under one command, although this unity was broken by the attempted secession of the south in 1994 which resulted in heavy fighting between the air forces of Sana'a and Aden. Personnel (2002), about 5,000. There were 76 combat aircraft including F-5Es, Su-20/22s, MiG-21s and MiG-29s.

INTERNATIONAL RELATIONS

Yemen is a member of the UN, the League of Arab States, IOM, OIC and Islamic Development Bank.

With a view to maintaining regional stability the USA supports Yemen and its democracy both in material and moral terms.

ECONOMY

In 2002 agriculture accounted for 11·4% of GDP, industry 41·5% and services 47·1%.

Currency

The unit of currency is the *riyal* (YER) of 100 *fils*. During the transitional period to north-south unification the northern *riyal* of 100 *fils* and the southern *dinar* of 1,000 *fils* co-existed. There were three foreign exchange rates operating: an internal clearing rate, an official rate and a commercial rate. In 1996 the official rate was abolished. Total money supply in May 2002 was 262,073m. riyals, gold reserves totalled 50,000 troy oz and foreign exchange reserves were US$3,722m. Inflation was 10·8% in 2003 and 12·5% in 2004.

Budget

The fiscal year is the calendar year. Total revenues in 2000 were 388,950m. riyals and expenditures 422,250m. riyals. Tax revenue accounted for 90·1% of total revenues in 1999. The main items of expenditure in 1999 were wages and salaries (23·0%), defence (18·1%) and economic development (17·5%).

Performance

Real GDP growth was 2·5% in 2004 (3·1% in 2003); total GDP in 2004 was US$12·8bn.

Banking and Finance

The *Governor* of the Central Bank of Yemen is Ahmed Abdul Rahman Al-Samawi. Total reserves of the Central Bank were 81,089m. riyals in 2002 and there were 446,287m. riyals in deposits.

ENERGY AND NATURAL RESOURCES

Environment

Yemen's carbon dioxide emissions from the consumption and flaring of fossil fuels were the equivalent of 0·5 tonnes per capita in 2002. An *Environmental Sustainability Index* compiled for the World Economic Forum meeting in Jan. 2005 ranked Yemen 137th in the world out of 146 countries analysed, with 37·3%. The index measured the ability of countries to maintain favourable environmental conditions and examined various factors including pollution levels and the use or abuse of natural resources.

Electricity

Installed capacity was 0·8m. kW in 2000. Production in 2000 was 2·96bn. kWh; consumption per capita was 162 kWh.

Oil and Gas

In 2002 there were oil reserves of 4,000m. bbls., mostly near the former north-south border. Crude oil production (2003): 21·4m. tonnes. Natural gas reserves in 2002 were 480bn. cu. metres.

Minerals

In 1998, 147,000 tonnes of salt were produced. Reserves (estimate) 25m. tonnes. In 1999, 103,000 tonnes of gypsum were extracted and 2·55m. cu. metres of stone.

Agriculture

In 2001 there were 1·47m. ha. of arable land and 129,000 ha. of permanent cropland; 500,000 ha. were irrigated in 2001. In the south, agriculture is largely of a subsistence nature, sorghum, sesame and millet being the chief crops, and wheat and barley widely grown at the higher elevations. Cash crops include cotton. Fruit is plentiful in the north.

Estimated production (2000, in 1,000 tonnes): sorghum, 401; tomatoes, 245; potatoes, 213; oranges, 175; grapes, 157; alfalfa, 149 (1992); wheat, 137; melons and watermelons, 119. Livestock in 2000: sheep, 4·76m.; goats, 4·09m.; cattle, 1·28m.; asses, 500,000; camels, 185,000; chickens, 28m. Estimated livestock produce, 2000 (in 1,000 tonnes): meat, 163; milk, 213.

Forestry

There were 449,000 ha. of forest in 2000. Timber production in 2001 was 314,000 cu. metres.

Fisheries

Fishing is a major industry. Total catch in 2001 was 142,198 tonnes, exclusively marine fish.

INDUSTRY

Output (in 1,000 tonnes): residual fuel oil (2000), 1,553; cement (2001), 1,493; petrol (2000), 1,081; distillate fuel oil (2000), 837; jet fuels (2000), 343; wheat flour (2000), 338; kerosene (2000), 120. In 2001 industry accounted for 49·2% of GDP, with manufacturing contributing 6·7%.

Labour

Of 3,621,700 persons in employment in 2002, 1,927,700 were engaged in agriculture, hunting and forestry; 394,200 in wholesale and retail trade/repair of motor vehicles, motorcycles and personal and household goods; 358,000 in public administration and defence/compulsory social security; and 238,200 in construction. Unemployment was 18% in 2004.

INTERNATIONAL TRADE

Foreign debt was US$5,290m. in 2002.

Imports and Exports

Trade in US$1m.:

	1998	1999	2000	2001	2002
Imports f.o.b.	2,288·8	2,120·5	2,484·4	2,600·4	2,932·0
Exports f.o.b.	1,503·7	2,478·3	3,797·2	3,366·9	3,620·7

Main import suppliers, 1999: United Arab Emirates, 11·7%; Saudi Arabia, 10·2%; USA, 5·5%; Australia, 4·8%. Main export markets, 1999: China, 28·8%; Thailand, 25·5%; South Korea, 14·5%; Singapore, 8·6%.

Oil, cotton and fish are major exports, the largest imports being food and live animals. Oil accounts for more than 80% of exports. A large transhipment and entrepôt trade is centred on Aden, which was made a free trade zone in May 1991.

COMMUNICATIONS

Roads
There were 67,735 km of roads in 2002, of which 10·3% were paved. In 2002 there were 435,200 passenger cars, 487,500 commercial vehicles and (1996) 3,400 buses and coaches. In 1996 there were 7,303 road accidents resulting in 1,267 deaths.

Rail
Passenger-km travelled in 1997 came to 2,492m.

Civil Aviation
There are international airports at Sana'a and Aden. In 2001 Sana'a handled 881,000 passengers (707,000 on international flights) and 15,900 tonnes of freight. The national carrier is Yemenia Yemen Airways, which operates internal services and in 2003 had international flights to Abu Dhabi, Addis Ababa, Amman, Asmara, Bahrain, Beirut, Bombay, Cairo, Damascus, Dar es Salaam, Djibouti, Doha, Dubai, Frankfurt, Jakarta, Jeddah, Khartoum, Kuala Lumpur, London, Marseille, Milan, Moroni, Paris, Riyadh and Rome. In 1999 scheduled airline traffic of Yemen-based carriers flew 14·5m. km, carrying 731,000 passengers (480,000 on international flights).

Shipping
In 2002 sea-going shipping totalled 78,000 GRT, including oil tankers 51,000 GRT. There are ports at Aden, Mokha, Hodeida, Mukalla and Nashtoon. In 1998 vessels totalling 11,210,000 NRT entered ports and vessels totalling 9,851,000 NRT cleared.

Telecommunications
Yemen had 953,300 telephone subscribers in 2002, or 48·9 per 1,000 population, and there were 145,000 PCs in use (7·4 for every 1,000 persons). There were 100,000 Internet users in 2002. Mobile phone subscribers numbered 411,000 in 2002 and there were 6,300 fax machines.

Postal Services
In 2003 there were 243 post offices.

SOCIAL INSTITUTIONS

Justice
A civil code based on Islamic law was introduced in 1992. The death penalty is still in force; there were six confirmed executions in 2005.

Education
In 2000–01 there were 7,600 children in pre-primary schools, 2·64m. pupils in primary schools and 1·24m. pupils in general programmes at secondary level. Yemen has the lowest proportion of female pupils enrolled at primary school, at 38% in 2000–01. There are universities at Sana'a (founded 1974) and Aden (1975). The former had 3,520 students and 330 academic staff in 1994–95, the latter 4,800 and 470. The adult literacy rate in 2002 was 49·0% (69·5% among males but only 28·5% among females, the biggest difference in literacy rates between the sexes of any country).

In 2000–01 total expenditure on education came to 10·6% of GNP and accounted for 32·8% of total government expenditure.

Health
In 1998 there were 81 hospitals with a provision of 55 beds per 10,000 inhabitants. There were 4,078 physicians, 222 dentists and 8,342 nurses in 2001; 613 pharmacists in 1999; and 385 midwives in 1994.

RELIGION
In 2001 there were some 18·05m. Muslims (mostly Sunnis) and approximately 20,000 followers of other religions.

CULTURE

World Heritage Sites
There are three sites under Yemeni jurisdiction that appear in the UNESCO World Heritage List. They are (with year entered on the list): the old walled city of Shibam (1982); the old city of Sana'a (1986); and the historic town of Zabid (1993).

Broadcasting
Broadcasting is managed by the government-controlled Yemen Radio and Television Corporation. Programmes are transmitted from Sana'a and Aden. In 2000 there were 1·2m. radio receivers and in 2001 there were 5·3m. TV receivers (colour by PAL).

Press
In 1996 there were three daily newspapers with a circulation of 230,000.

Tourism
There were 76,000 foreign tourists in 2001, bringing revenue of US$38m.

DIPLOMATIC REPRESENTATIVES

Of Yemen in the United Kingdom (57 Cromwell Rd, London, SW7 2ED)
Ambassador: Mohamed Taha Mustafa.

Of the United Kingdom in Yemen (129 Haddah Rd, Sana'a)
Ambassador: Michael Gifford.

Of Yemen in the USA (2319 Wyoming Ave., NW, Washington, D.C., 20008)
Ambassador: Abdulwahab Al-Hajjri.

Of the USA in Yemen (Sa'awan St., Himyar Zone, Sana'a)
Ambassador: Thomas C. Krajeski.

Of Yemen to the United Nations
Ambassador: Abdullah Al-Saidi.

Of Yemen to the European Union
Ambassador: Jaffer Mohamed Jaffer.

FURTHER READING
Central Statistical Organization. *Statistical Year Book*

Auchterlonie, Paul, *Yemen*. [Bibliography] 2nd ed. ABC-Clio, Oxford and Santa Barbara (CA), 1998

Dresch, Paul, *A History of Modern Yemen*. CUP, 2001

Mackintosh-Smith, T., *Yemen—Travels in Dictionary Land*. London, 1997

National Statistical Office: Central Statistical Organization, Ministry of Planning and Development.

ZAMBIA

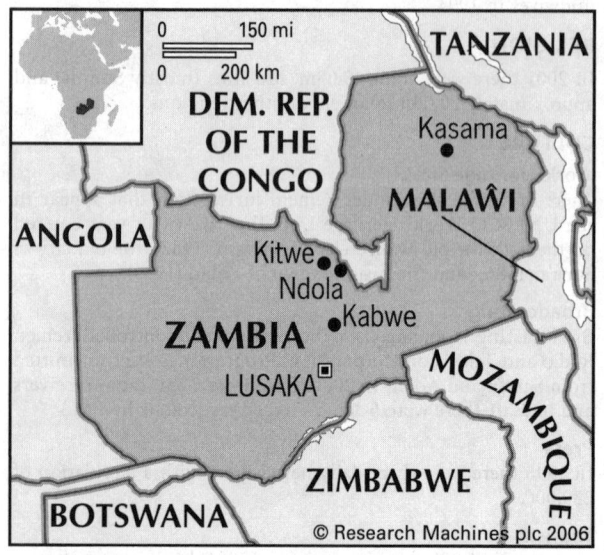

Republic of Zambia

Capital: Lusaka
Population projection, 2010: 12·67m.
GDP per capita, 2003: (PPP$) 877
HDI/world rank: 0·394/166

KEY HISTORICAL EVENTS

The majority of the population is of Bantu origin. There are more than 70 different tribes, the most important being the Bemba and the Bgoni in the northeast. One of the more successful of the invading tribes was the Lozi under Lewanika, who obtained the protection of the British government in 1891. In 1900 the British South Africa Company acquired trading and mining rights. From 1911 the territory was known as Northern Rhodesia and in 1924 the Crown took over the administration.

In 1953 the Federation of Rhodesia and Nyasaland, of which Northern Rhodesia was a part, was created. Federation brought economic benefits to Northern Rhodesia but it was from the outset opposed by African leaders. In March 1963 Britain agreed to Northern Rhodesia's right to secede from the Federation. In Jan. 1964 internal self-government was attained. On 24 Oct. 1964 Northern Rhodesia became an independent republic within the Commonwealth, changing its name to Zambia. A highly centralized one-party state was created which suffocated the emergent economy. Living standards fell sharply and the production of copper, Zambia's biggest foreign exchange earner, almost halved. In 1991 the Movement for Multiparty Democracy (MMD) was elected on a promise to transform the economy.

TERRITORY AND POPULATION

Zambia is bounded by the Democratic Republic of the Congo in the north, Tanzania in the northeast, Malaŵi in the east, Mozambique in the southeast, Zimbabwe and Namibia in the south, and by Angola in the west. The area is 752,612 sq. km (290,584 sq. miles). Population (2000 census), 9,885,591; population density, 13·1 per sq. km. The estimated population in 2005 was 11,668,000. In 2003, 64·1% of the population were rural.

The UN gives a projected population for 2010 of 12·67m.

The republic is divided into nine provinces. Area, population at the 2000 census and chief towns:

Province	Area (in sq. km)	Population	Chief Town
Central	94,394	1,012,257	Kabwe
Copperbelt	31,328	1,581,221	Ndola
Eastern	69,106	1,306,173	Chipata
Luapula	50,567	775,353	Mansa
Lusaka	21,896	1,391,329	Lusaka
Northern	147,826	1,258,696	Kasama
North-Western	125,827	583,350	Solwezi
Southern	85,283	1,212,124	Livingstone
Western	126,386	765,088	Mongu

The capital is Lusaka, which had a census population in 2000 of 1,084,703. Other major towns (with 2000 census population in 1,000) are: Ndola, 375; Kitwe, 364; Kabwe, 177; Chingola, 147; Mufulira, 122; Luanshya, 116.

The official language is English and the main ethnic groups are the Bemba (18%), Tonga (13%), Chewa (7%) and Lozi (6%).

SOCIAL STATISTICS

Estimates, 2000: births, 421,000; deaths, 191,000. Estimated birth rate in 2000 was 41·5 per 1,000 population; estimated death rate, 18·8. Zambia's life expectancy at birth in 2003 was 37·9 years for males and 36·9 for females. Life expectancy has declined dramatically over the last ten years, largely owing to the huge number of people in the country with HIV. Annual population growth rate, 1992–2002, 2·1%. Infant mortality, 2001, 112 per 1,000 live births; fertility rate, 2001, 5·8 births per woman.

CLIMATE

The climate is tropical, but has three seasons. The cool, dry one is from May to Aug., a hot dry one follows until Nov., when the wet season commences. Frosts may occur in some areas in the cool season. Lusaka, Jan. 70°F (21·1°C), July 61°F (16·1°C). Annual rainfall 33" (836 mm). Livingstone, Jan. 75°F (23·9°C), July 61°F (16·1°C). Annual rainfall 27" (673 mm). Ndola, Jan. 70°F (21·1°C), July 59°F (15°C). Annual rainfall 52" (1,293 mm).

CONSTITUTION AND GOVERNMENT

Zambia has a unicameral legislature, the 159-seat *National Assembly*, with 150 members elected for a five-year term in single-member constituencies, eight appointed members and the Speaker. Candidates for election as president must have both parents born in Zambia (this excludes ex-president Kaunda). The constitution was adopted on 24 Aug. 1991 and was amended in 1996, shortly before the parliamentary and presidential elections. The amendment restricts the president from serving more than two terms of office.

National Anthem

'Lumbanyeni Zambia' ('Stand and Sing of Zambia'); words collective, tune by M. E. Sontonga.

RECENT ELECTIONS

Parliamentary and presidential elections took place on 27 Dec. 2001. The elections were beset by allegations of vote rigging, prompting investigations from EU monitors. Levy Patrick Mwanawasa, former president Frederick Chiluba's chosen successor, defeated ten other candidates running for the presidency yet only won 28·8% of votes cast.

In the parliamentary elections, Levy Patrick Mwanawasa's party, the Movement for Multiparty Democracy (MMD), gained 69 seats in the 159-seat National Assembly; the

United Party for National Development gained 49; the United National Independence Party, 13; the Forum for Democracy and Development, 12; and the Heritage Party, 4. Mwanawasa's inaugural speech was boycotted by all ten opposition parties.

CURRENT ADMINISTRATION

President: Levy Patrick Mwanawasa; b. 1948 (MMD; sworn in 2 Jan. 2002).

Vice-President: Lupando Mwape.

In March 2006 the government comprised:

Minister for Agriculture and Co-operatives: Mundia Sikatana. *Commerce, Trade and Industry:* Dipak Patel. *Communication and Transport:* Abel M. Chambeshi. *Community Development and Social Services:* Stephen Manjata. *Defence:* Wamundila Muliokela. *Education:* Brian Chituwo. *Energy and Water Development:* Felix Mutati. *Finance and National Planning:* Peter Magande. *Foreign Affairs:* Ronnie Shikapwaska. *Health:* Sylvia Masebo. *Home Affairs:* Bates Namuyamba. *Information and Broadcasting:* Vernon Mwaanga. *Justice:* George Kunda. *Labour and Social Security:* Mutale Nalumango. *Lands:* Gladys Nyirongo. *Local Government and Housing:* Andrew Mulenga. *Mines and Mineral Development:* Kalombo Mwansa. *Science, Technology and Vocational Training:* Judith Kapijimpanga. *Sport, Youth and Child Development:* George Chulumanda. *Tourism, Environment and Natural Resources:* Kabinge Pande. *Works and Supply:* Marina Nsingo.

Zambian Parliament: http://www.parliament.gov.zm

CURRENT LEADERS

Levy Mwanawasa

Position
President

Introduction
Representing the Movement for Multiparty Democracy (MMD), in power since 1991, President Levy Patrick Mwanawasa was the chosen successor of his predecessor Frederick Chiluba. Elected in a disputed election in 2001 (legal challenges to which were not finally resolved until early 2005), his main challenges have been tackling corruption and alleviating food shortages.

Early Life
Mwanawasa was born on 3 Sept. 1948 in Mufulira, the Copperbelt region, in what was Northern Rhodesia. He studied law at the University of Zambia, graduating in 1973. Politically active in student politics, he joined the protests against the remaining colonial powers in Southern Africa, becoming vice-president of his university student union. He set up his own law firm in 1978.

From 1982–83 he was vice-president of the Zambian law society. This led to his appointment as Zambian solicitor general in 1985, a position he held for a year. In 1989 he successfully defended several politicians accused of leading a coup against the then president Kenneth Kaunda. With an increased profile, he joined Chiluba's newly formed MMD opposition party, becoming party vice-chairman in 1991. In national elections of the same year, Chiluba took the presidency and Mwanawasa was appointed vice-president.

In 1992 Mwanawasa was involved in a serious car accident and spent the following year in hospital. He remained vice-president, but citing rampant corruption within the government, resigned in 1994. Two years later, he unsuccessfully challenged Chiluba for the party leadership, and subsequently left politics to continue his legal career.

Re-elected in 1996, President Chiluba attempted to change the constitution to allow him to stand for a third consecutive term. In protest, some MMD members left the party to form the Forum for Democracy and Development. When Chiluba failed in his bid to continue in office, the MMD was forced to look for a party candidate. Some were surprised when Mwanawasa, uninvolved in politics since his resignation in 1994, was chosen. Since Chiluba remained MMD leader, the opposition cast doubts on Mwanawasa's impartiality. In the elections of Dec. 2001 he secured the presidency but with only 28·8% of the vote.

Career in Office
The opposition claimed the election was rigged. All parties refused to attend Mwanawasa's inauguration and, although the High Court initially declined to investigate electoral fraud, three opposition parties mounted a legal challenge to the results. Revelations of corruption under Chiluba emerged in the trial. In an attempt to distance himself from Chiluba's legacy, Mwanawasa launched an anti-corruption campaign. In July 2002 parliament voted to remove the former president's immunity from prosecution. In Jan. 2003 Mwanawasa announced plans to appoint several opposition politicians to ministerial posts.

Following poor harvests in 2001, around 3m. people needed food aid in Zambia, mirroring conditions across Southern Africa. In 2002 Mwanawasa appealed for international help, but became embroiled in a dispute over genetically-modified (GM) crops. In Oct. 2002 he rejected the use of GM crops as food aid, even if the grain was milled before use, as had been accepted in neighbouring countries. Despite growing criticism from his own people and the international community over delayed distribution, Mwanawasa requested a US$50m. World Bank loan to buy organic maize.

In Aug. 2003 the president survived a motion in parliament to impeach him for corruption and other violations of the constitution. In the same month there was a general strike involving 120,000 public sector workers and civil servants over pay and allowances.

In early 2005 the Supreme Court finally rejected opposition legal action against the 2001 election results. In July Mwanawasa defeated a challenge to his leadership of the MMD at the party's convention from the former vice-president Enoch Kavindele.

DEFENCE

In 2003 defence expenditure totalled US$27m. (US$3 per capita), representing 0·6% of GDP.

Army

Strength (2002) 20,000. There are also two paramilitary police units totalling 1,400.

Air Force

In 2002 the Air Force had over 63 combat aircraft including F-6 (Chinese-built MiG-19s) and MiG-21s. Serviceability of most types is reported to be low. Personnel (2002) 1,600.

INTERNATIONAL RELATIONS

Zambia is a member of the UN, WTO, the Commonwealth, SADC, the African Union, African Development Bank, COMESA, IOM and is an ACP member state of the ACP-EU relationship.

During the 1990s Zambia received foreign aid equivalent to approximately US$900 a head, but according to the *World Bank* GNP per head declined from US$390 in 1991 to US$330 in 1999.

ECONOMY

In 2002 agriculture accounted for 22·2% of GDP, industry 26·1% and services 51·7%.

Overview

The Zambian economy is primarily agrarian; the sector employs 85% of the population. The main industries are copper mining and processing, accounting for more than 80% of the country's foreign currency intake. Between 1974–90 the economy experienced negative growth of nearly 5% per year owing to macroeconomic instability, incomplete policy implementation and inefficient state-owned industries. A change of political power in 1990 improved the state of the economy. The government initiated ambitious market-orientated reforms and tried to ameliorate macroeconomic management. The government privatized the copper mines in 2000 and monetary and fiscal policies were tightened. As a result of these reforms, real GDP grew at 3.5% in 2000 and inflation fell to the lowest levels in 20 years. Since 2002 Zambia has been hit by crises in the copper and agriculture sector that have increased food insecurity and reduced growth prospects.

Currency

The unit of currency is the *kwacha* (ZMK) of 100 *ngwee*. Foreign exchange reserves were US$98m. in April 2002. In Dec. 1992 the official and free market exchange rates were merged and the kwacha devalued 29%. Inflation, which was 183.3% in 1993, was down to 18.0% in 2004. Total money supply in May 2002 was 992,836m. kwacha.

Budget

The fiscal year is the calendar year. Revenues in 2001 totalled 2,509bn. kwacha and expenditures 4,212bn. kwacha. Tax revenues accounted for 97.6% of total revenue in 2001; current expenditures accounted for 61.2% of total expenditure.

Performance

Real GDP growth was 5.1% in 2003 and 5.0% in 2004. Total GDP in 2004 was US$5.4bn.

Banking and Finance

The central bank is the Bank of Zambia (*Governor*, Dr Caleb Fundanga). In 2003 there were five commercial banks, six foreign banks and four development banks. The Bank of Zambia monitors and supervises the operations of financial institutions. Banks and building societies are governed by the Banking and Financial Services Act 1994.

There is a stock exchange in Lusaka. Its market capitalization was US$301m. in 1998, a 58% fall from 1997's figure of US$705m.

ENERGY AND NATURAL RESOURCES

Environment

Zambia's carbon dioxide emissions from the consumption and flaring of fossil fuels in 2002 were the equivalent of 0.2 tonnes per capita.

Electricity

Installed capacity in 2000 was 2.3m. kW. Production in 2000 was 7.80bn. kWh; consumption per capita was 562 kWh.

Zambia is a net exporter of hydro-electric power and has huge potential for energy growth. Between Jan. and Sept. 1998 Zambian electricity exports were worth US$3.6m. compared to US$11.9m. in the same period in 1997.

Minerals

Minerals produced (in 1,000 tonnes): copper (2002), 330; cobalt (2000), 4.6; silver (1998), 8,363 kg; gold (2001), 130 kg. Zambia is well-endowed with gemstones, especially emeralds, amethysts, aquamarine, tourmaline and garnets. Zambia Consolidated Copper Mines, privatized in 2000, is the country's largest employer. In 1990 the government freed the gemstones trade from restrictions. In 2000, 194,000 tonnes of coal were produced.

Agriculture

70% of the population is dependent on agriculture. There were 5.26m. ha. of arable land in 2001 and 20,000 ha. of permanent crops. Principal agricultural products (2000 estimates, in 1,000 tonnes): sugarcane, 1,600; maize, 1,260; cassava, 1,020; millet, 71; seed cotton, 62; wheat, 60; groundnuts, 55.

Livestock (2000): cattle, 2.37m.; goats, 1.25m.; pigs, 330,000; sheep, 140,000; chickens, 29m.

Forestry

Forests covered 31.25m. ha. in 2000, or 42.0% of the total land area. Timber production in 2001 was 8.05m. cu. metres, most of it for fuel.

Fisheries

Total catch, 2001, approximately 65,000 tonnes (exclusively from inland waters).

INDUSTRY

In 2001 industry accounted for 25.6% of GDP, with manufacturing contributing 11.1%. Industrial production grew by 9.2% in 2001. Zambia's economy is totally dependent upon its mining sector. Other industries include construction, foodstuffs, beverages, chemicals and textiles.

Labour

The labour force totalled 3,454,000 in 1996 (55% males). Around 74% of the economically active population in 1995 were engaged in agriculture, fisheries and forestry. Since 1992 nearly 100,000 jobs have been lost, and fewer than 10% of working-age Zambians work full-time in the formal sector.

Trade Unions

There is a Zambia Congress of Trade Unions.

INTERNATIONAL TRADE

In 2002 foreign debt was US$5,969m.

Imports and Exports

In 2001 imports were valued at US$1,307m. and exports at US$985m.

Imports declined every year from 1997 to 1999 before increasing by 12% in 2000, and exports declined every year from 1997 to 2000. In 2001 copper provided 55% of all exports (by value). Since 1990 non-copper exports have increased in value from US$50m. to US$450m. The main import sources in 1999 were South Africa (50.3%), Zimbabwe (9.3%), UK (5.9%) and Saudi Arabia (5.7%). Principal export markets were Japan (11.3%), UK (8.5%), India (6.6%) and Thailand (5.7%).

COMMUNICATIONS

Roads

There were, in 2001, 91,440 km of roads, including 4,222 km of highway. 93,400 passenger cars were in use in 2002 (9.3 per 1,000 inhabitants) and there were 68,000 trucks and vans.

Rail

In 2000 there were 1,273 km of the state-owned Zambia Railways Ltd (ZRL) and, in 1993, 891 km of the Tanzania-Zambia (Tazara) Railway, both on 1,067 mm gauge. ZRL carried 0.8m. passengers in 2000 and 3.4m. tonnes of freight in 1993. Of the 66 locomotives run by Zambia Railways in 1998, 21 were non-operational.

Civil Aviation

The main carrier, Zambia Airways, operates internal flights and in 2003 flew to Harare. Lusaka is the principal international airport. In 2001 Lusaka International handled 410,000 passengers (359,000 on international flights) and 24,800 tonnes of freight. In 1999 scheduled airline traffic of Zambian-based carriers flew 0.8m. km, carrying 42,000 passengers (36,000 on international flights).

Telecommunications

Telephone subscribers numbered 226,800 in 2002, equivalent to 21.2 per 1,000 persons. In 1995 there were direct connections to 16 countries. Telecel (2) Ltd. has been licensed to run a mobile telecommunications service in addition to the Zambia

Telecommunications Company (ZAMTEL) since 1996. Mobile phone subscribers numbered 139,100 in 2002 and there were 1,200 fax machines. Internet services are provided by Zambia Communications Systems (ZAMNET), a private company of ZAMTEL. There were 80,000 PCs in use (7·5 per 1,000 persons) and 52,400 Internet users in 2002.

Postal Services
In 2003 Zambia Postal Services Corporation (ZAMPOST) operated 235 permanent post offices.

SOCIAL INSTITUTIONS
Justice
The Judiciary consists of the Supreme Court, the High Court and four classes of magistrates' courts; all have civil and criminal jurisdiction.

The Supreme Court hears and determines appeals from the High Court. Its seat is at Lusaka. The High Court exercises the powers vested in the High Court in England, subject to the High Court ordinance of Zambia. Its sessions are held where occasion requires, mostly at Lusaka and Ndola. All criminal cases tried by subordinate courts are subject to revision by the High Court.

The death penalty is authorized, the last execution having taken place in 1997. The population in penal institutions in June 2002 was 13,173 (121 per 100,000 of national population).

Education
Schooling is for nine years. In April 2002 President Mwanawasa announced the re-introduction of universal free primary education, abolished under former President Chiluba. In 2000–01 there were 1·6m. pupils in primary schools; secondary schools, 283,000 pupils.

There are two universities, three teachers' colleges and one Christian college. In 1998 there were 4,797 university students. The University of Zambia, at Lusaka, was founded in 1965; Copperbelt University, at Kitwe, in 1987. In addition the government sponsored 150 students to be trained abroad.

The adult literacy rate in 2001 was 79·0% (85·8% among males and 72·7% among females).

In 1998–99 total expenditure on education came to 2·5% of GNP and accounted for 17·6% of total government expenditure.

Health
There were 601 physicians and 9,583 nurses in 1995, and 26 dentists, 24 pharmacists and 311 midwives in 1990. In 1987 (latest data available) there were 42 state, 29 mission and 11 mining company hospitals, with a total of 15,846 beds and 912 health centres with 7,081 beds.

RELIGION
In 1993 the president declared Zambia to be a Christian nation, but freedom of worship is a constitutional right. In 2001 there were 3·89m. Christians. Traditional beliefs are also widespread.

CULTURE
World Heritage Sites
Zambia shares one site with Zimbabwe on the UNESCO World Heritage List: the Victoria Falls/Mosi-oa-Tunya (inscribed on the list in 1989), waterfalls on the Zambezi River.

Broadcasting
The Zambia National Broadcasting Corporation is an independent statutory body which oversees four radio networks. In 2003 there were three privately-owned radio stations: Radio Phoenix, QFM and Radio Christian Voice. There were 1·51m. radio receivers in 2000 and 540,000 TV receivers in 2001 (colour by PAL). Private broadcasting stations were licensed to operate in 1996. One such company was Multi Choice Kaleidoscope (2) Ltd, based in South Africa, which commenced operations in Aug. 1995. By Oct. 1996 the number of subscribers was 6,617.

Press
In 2004 there were two state-owned daily papers, *The Times of Zambia* and the *Zambia Daily Mail*, both with Sunday editions. Privately owned papers include *The Post* (daily), *The National Mirror*, *The Monitor*, *Today*, *The Star* and *Business and Leisure Times*.

Tourism
Tourism-generated earnings from the 574,000 international tourists in 2000 were US$91m. There were a further 102,000 domestic tourists of which the majority were on business. Investment pledges for the industry stood at US$92·2m. including US$60m. pledged for reconstructing the Livingstone Intercontinental Hotel.

Festivals
The N'cwala ceremony is held in Feb. by the Ngoni people to commemorate their arrival in Zambia in 1835 and the first produce of the year. The Kuomboka, in Feb. or March, is the canoe procession of the Lozi chief and his family from the palace at Leaului down the Zambezi to Limulunga for the rainy season. The National Fishing Competition is held at Lake Tanganyika in March. Likumbi Lya Mize, held at Mize in July, celebrates the Luvale tribe's cultural heritage. The Livingstone Cultural and Arts Festival, held annually in Sept. since 1994, brings together many of Zambia's tribes and their traditional rulers. Independence Day is celebrated on 24 Oct.

DIPLOMATIC REPRESENTATIVES
Of Zambia in the United Kingdom (2 Palace Gate, London, W8 5NG)
High Commissioner: Anderson Kaseba Chibwa.

Of the United Kingdom in Zambia (5210 Independence Ave., 15101 Ridgeway, Lusaka)
High Commissioner: Alistair Harrison.

Of Zambia in the USA (2419 Massachusetts Ave., NW, Washington, D.C., 20008)
Ambassador: Inonge Mbikusita-Lewanika.

Of the USA in Zambia (Corner of Independence and United Nations Road, PO Box 31617, Lusaka)
Ambassador: Carmen Martinez.

Of Zambia to the United Nations
Ambassador: Tens Kapoma.

Of Zambia to the European Union
Ambassador: Irene Mumba Kamanga.

FURTHER READING
Chiluba, F., *Democracy: the Challenge of Change*. Lusaka, 1995

Central Statistical Office. *Monthly Digest of Statistics.*
National Statistical Office: Central Statistical Office, Lusaka.
Website: http://www.zamstats.gov.zm

ZIMBABWE

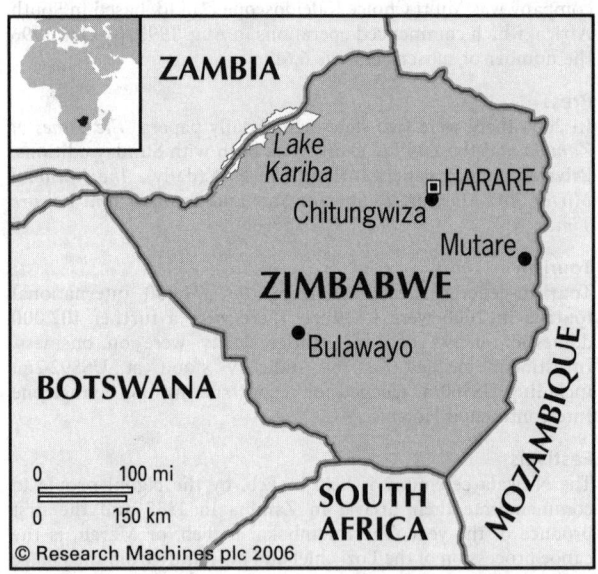

ZAMBIA

Lake Kariba

HARARE

Chitungwiza

Mutare

ZIMBABWE

Bulawayo

BOTSWANA

MOZAMBIQUE

0   100 mi
0   150 km

SOUTH AFRICA

© Research Machines plc 2006

Republic of Zimbabwe

Capital: Harare
Population projection, 2010: 13·40m.
GDP per capita, 2001: (PPP$) 2,280
HDI/world rank: 0·505/145

KEY HISTORICAL EVENTS

The territory which now forms Zimbabwe was administered by the British South Africa Company from the beginning of European colonization in 1890 until 1923 when it was granted the status of a self-governing colony. In 1911 it was divided into Southern and Northern Rhodesia (*see* ZAMBIA: Key Historical Events). In 1953 Southern and Northern Rhodesia were again united, along with Nyasaland, to form the Federation of Rhodesia and Nyasaland. When this federation was dissolved on 31 Dec. 1963, Southern Rhodesia reverted to the status of a self-governing colony within the British Commonwealth.

On 11 Nov. 1965 the white-dominated government issued a unilateral declaration of independence (UDI). Thereupon the Governor dismissed the prime minister, Ian Smith, and his cabinet and the British government reasserted formal responsibility for Rhodesia; but effective internal government was carried on by the Smith cabinet. From 1–3 Dec. Harold Wilson, the British prime minister, met Smith on board HMS *Tiger* and drafted a 'Working Document' on progress towards legal independence. This statement was rejected by the Smith government. On 2 March 1970 the Smith government declared Rhodesia a republic and adopted a new constitution. On 3 March 1978 Smith signed a constitutional agreement with the internationally-backed nationalist leaders. A draft constitution was published in Jan. 1979 and was accepted by the white electorate in a referendum. Following the Commonwealth Conference held in Lusaka in Aug. 1979, elections took place in March 1980 resulting in a victory for the Zimbabwe African National Union (ZANU). Southern Rhodesia became the Republic of Zimbabwe on 18 April 1980.

Almost immediately, the question of land redistribution became a hot political issue. In colonial days, Africans had been ejected from the best farming country. All sides recognized the need for reform but were unable to agree on the means of achieving it. In the next 20 years, 3·5m. ha of land were acquired from white farmers, with the UK footing the £44m. bill for resettlement, but only 70,000 families benefited. Another 400,000 ha. went to senior colleagues in President Mugabe's government. The economy, meanwhile, suffered roaring inflation, unemployment and acute shortages. A policy of land occupation, with black settlers taking over white-owned farms, started in early 2000. Pressures on President Mugabe to restore the rule of law were ignored and violence escalated. Elections took place in June 2000, in which President Mugabe achieved a narrow victory. Violence continued during the months which followed, as support for Mugabe dwindled. In the lead-up to the 2002 presidential election, again won by Mugabe but by dubious means, the opposition leader, Morgan Tsvangirai, was charged with treason.

The land reform plan, involving the redistribution of white-owned land to landless black Zimbabweans, continued in 2002 with large numbers of farms seized by war veterans. Many analysts blamed Zimbabwe's worsening economic climate and serious food shortages on the land seizures. The country was suspended from the Commonwealth in March 2002 and when the suspension was extended in late 2003 it pulled out altogether. In 2005 the government began the mass demolition of urban slums, claiming it would improve law and order and prompt development. The move was widely criticized on the international stage and left around 700,000 people homeless.

TERRITORY AND POPULATION

Zimbabwe is bounded in the north by Zambia, east by Mozambique, south by South Africa and west by Botswana and the Caprivi Strip of Namibia. The area is 390,757 sq. km (150,871 sq. miles). The 1992 census population was 10,401,767 (51·2% female). 2002 census population (provisional), 11,634,663; density, 29·8 per sq. km. In 2003, 65·0% of the population were rural. Although the population is still rising, it is doing so at a lower rate than had been previously expected, partly owing to the large number of AIDS-related deaths and partly as a result of over 3m. Zimbabweans having left the country as President Mugabe's grip on power has strengthened, with the vast majority choosing to live in South Africa.

The UN gives a projected population for 2010 of 13·40m.

There are eight provinces and two cities, Harare and Bulawayo, with provincial status. Area and population (2002 census, provisional):

	Area (sq. km)	Population
Bulawayo	479	676,787
Harare	872	1,903,510
Manicaland	36,459	1,566,889
Mashonaland Central	28,347	998,265
Mashonaland East	32,230	1,125,355
Mashonaland West	57,441	1,222,583
Masvingo	56,566	1,318,705
Matabeleland North	75,025	701,359
Matabeleland South	54,172	654,879
Midlands	49,166	1,466,331

Harare, the capital, had a population in 2002 of 1,444,534. Other main cities (with 2002 census populations) were Bulawayo (676,787), Chitungwiza (321,782), Mutare (153,000) and Gweru (137,000). The population is approximately 98% African, 1% mixed and Asian and there are approximately 70,000 whites.

The main ethno-linguistic groups are the Shona (71%), Ndebele (16%), Ndau (3%) and Nyanja (3%). Other smaller ones include Kalanga, Manyika, Tonga and Lozi.

The official language is English.

SOCIAL STATISTICS

2000 estimates: births, 425,000; deaths, 215,000. Rates (2000 estimates, per 1,000 population); birth, 35·1; death, 17·8. Annual population growth rate, 1992–2002, 1·5%. Zimbabwe's expectation of life at birth in 2003 was 37·3 years for males and 36·5 for females, down from an average of 54 years in 1993. The sharp decline is largely attributed to the huge number of people in the country with HIV. Life expectancy is less than half it would be without AIDS. Researchers predict that by 2008 life expectancy will have dropped to 31 years. Approximately 33% of all adults are infected with HIV. Infant mortality, 2001, 76 per 1,000 live births; fertility rate, 2001, 4·7 births per woman.

CLIMATE

Though situated in the tropics, conditions are remarkably temperate throughout the year because of altitude, and an inland position keeps humidity low. The warmest weather occurs in the three months before the main rainy season, which starts in Nov. and lasts till March. The cool season is from mid-May to mid-Aug. and, though days are mild and sunny, nights are chilly. Harare, Jan. 69°F (20·6°C), July 57°F (13·9°C). Annual rainfall 33" (828 mm). Bulawayo, Jan. 71°F (21·7°C), July 57°F (13·9°C). Annual rainfall 24" (594 mm). Victoria Falls, Jan. 78°F (25·6°C), July 61°F (16·1°C). Annual rainfall 28" (710 mm).

CONSTITUTION AND GOVERNMENT

The 1979 Constitution, with 17 amendments, provides for a single-chamber 150-member Parliament (*House of Assembly*), universal suffrage for citizens over the age of 18, an *Executive President* (elected for a six-year term of office by Parliament), an independent judiciary enjoying security of tenure and a Declaration of Rights, derogation from certain of the provisions being permitted, within specified limits, during a state of emergency. The House of Assembly is elected for five-year terms: 120 members are elected by universal suffrage, ten are chiefs elected by all the country's tribal chiefs, 12 are appointed by the President and eight are provincial governors. A constitutional amendment of Aug. 2005 allowed for the reintroduction of a 66-member *Senate* (50 elected members, ten traditional chiefs and six senators appointed by the president), which had been abolished in 1987. It also enables the government to expropriate land without being challenged in court and to remove the right to a passport if it is deemed in the national interest. The constitution can be amended by a two-thirds parliamentary majority.

In a referendum on 12–13 Feb. 2000 on the adoption of a new constitution 697,754 (54·6%) voted against and only 578,210 in favour. Under the new constitution Zimbabwe would have had an Executive President and an Executive Prime Minister sharing power, but many people felt that this would have strengthened President Mugabe's control over the country.

National Anthem

'Kalibusiswe Ilizwe leZimbabwe' ('Blessed be the Land of Zimbabwe'); words by Dr Solomon M. Mutswairo; tune by Fred Changundega.

GOVERNMENT CHRONOLOGY

Presidents since 1980. (ZANU = Zimbabwe African National Union; PF = Patriotic Front)
1980–87   ZANU   Canaan Sodindo Banana
1987–   ZANU-PF   Robert Gabriel Mugabe

RECENT ELECTIONS

At the parliamentary elections of 31 March 2005 the Zimbabwe African National Union-Patriotic Front (ZANU-PF) gained 78 of the 150 available seats (58·8% of votes cast). The Movement for Democratic Change won 41 seats (37·5%) and one independent gained a seat. 20 seats were appointed by the president and ten went to *ex-officio* chief members. The opposition refused to accept the result, claiming that the election had been rigged. Elections for 50 members of the new 66-seat Senate took place on 26 Nov. 2005. ZANU-PF took 43 seats and Movement for Democratic Change 7. Turnout was put at between 15 and 20%.

Presidential elections were held between 9–11 March 2002. Incumbent Robert Mugabe was re-elected with 56·2% of votes cast, against 42·0% for Morgan Tsvangirai. There were three other candidates. Observers claimed the elections failed to meet international standards for a democratic poll.

CURRENT ADMINISTRATION

Executive President: Robert G. Mugabe; b. 1924 (ZANU-PF; sworn in on 30 Dec. 1987, having previously been prime minister from 1980 to 1987; re-elected April 1990, March 1996 and again in March 2002).

In March 2006 the council comprised:
First Vice-President: Joseph Msika. *Second Vice-President:* Joyce Mujuru.

Minister of Agriculture: Joseph Made. *Defence:* Sydney Sekeramayi. *Economic Development:* Rugare Gumbo. *Education, Sports and Culture:* Aeneas Chigwedere. *Energy and Power Development:* Michael Nyambuya. *Environment and Tourism:* Francis Nhema. *Finance:* Herbert Murerwa. *Foreign Affairs:* Simbarashe Mumbengegwi. *Health and Child Welfare:* David Parirenyatwa. *Higher and Tertiary Education:* Stanislaus Mudenge. *Home Affairs:* Kembo Mohadi. *Industry and International Trade:* Obert Mpofu. *Information and Publicity:* Tichaona Jokonya. *Justice, Legal and Parliamentary Affairs:* Patrick Chinamasa. *Labour and Social Welfare:* Nicholas Goche. *Local Government, Public Works and Urban Development:* Ignatius Chombo. *Mines and Mining Development:* Amos Midzi. *National Security:* Didymus Mutasa. *Policy Implementation:* Webster Shamu. *Public Service, Water Resources and Infrastructural Development:* Munacho Mutezo. *Rural Housing and Social Amenities:* Emmerson Mnangagwa. *Science and Technology:* Olivia Muchena. *Small and Medium Enterprise Development:* Sithembiso Nyoni. *Special Affairs, Responsible for Land and Resettlement Programmes:* Flora Bhuka. *State Enterprises, Anti-Monopolies and Anti-Corruption:* Paul Mangwana. *Transport and Communications:* Christopher Mushowe. *Women's Affairs, Gender and Community Development:* Oppah Muchinguri. *Youth Development and Employment Creation:* Ambrose Mutinhiri. *Minister without Portfolio:* Elliot Manyika.

CURRENT LEADERS

Robert Mugabe

Position
President

Introduction
Robert Mugabe came to power as newly-independent Zimbabwe's (formerly Rhodesia) first prime minister in 1980, becoming president in 1987. Although initially hailed as a democratic reformer, his economic mismanagement of the country, violent electoral campaigns and controversial programme of land seizures have tarnished his image at home and abroad. He has defended his land reform programme as the conclusion of the process of decolonization, but his policies are widely perceived as short-term political expediency for the maintenance of personal power.

Early Career
The son of a carpenter, Robert Gabriel Mugabe was born 21 Feb. 1924 at Kutama mission, northwest of Harare. After an

early education at a Roman Catholic mission school, he studied at the University College of Fort Hare, South Africa, marking the beginning of an academic career boasting seven university degrees, three of which he completed during imprisonment. He worked as a primary school teacher in Ghana from 1956–60 when he returned to Rhodesia and joined Joshua Nkomo's Zimbabwe African People's Union (ZAPU). In 1963 he became a founding member of the breakaway Zimbabwe African National Union (ZANU) with Rev. Ndabaningi Sithole. A year later Mugabe was arrested for subversion and imprisoned, without trial, for ten years. Despite imprisonment, he remained politically active and was able to orchestrate, in 1974, a coup against Sithole to become party leader. In 1975, freed from prison, Mugabe joined Nkomo as joint leader of the Patriotic Front of Zimbabwe which waged a guerrilla war against Ian Smith's white Rhodesian Front government. In 1980 independence was achieved and parliamentary elections took place in which Mugabe, at the head of ZANU, won a landslide victory to become prime minister.

Career in Office

In office Mugabe appeared set to usher in a bright new era for the country. Having built a coalition government with ZAPU, he adopted a conciliatory stance towards the white, landowning minority. He introduced higher wages, credit programmes and food subsidies for poor farmers, a better infrastructure and equal land rights for women. Reform in the education system saw primary school enrolment trebled and secondary school enrolment increased five-fold during the first ten years of his rule (with Zimbabwe laying claim to the highest literacy rate of any African nation).

Troubles began in 1982 when ethnic turmoil between the Shona majority (represented by ZANU) and the Ndebele minority (represented by ZAPU) broke out after Mugabe dismissed Nkomo and ZAPU from government. The ensuing violence prompted much of the white population to emigrate, in turn creating an economic downturn. Centred in Matabeleland, the conflict drew international attention after the discovery of mass graves and alleged atrocities.

In 1987 Mugabe won the presidential elections and set about bringing ZAPU back into government. A unity agreement was signed and Nkomo became senior minister in a newly-formed Zimbabwe African National Union-Patriotic Front (ZANU-PF) government. Mugabe was again re-elected in 1990 (in polling marred by violence) and 1996, but throughout the 1990s he adopted a series of unpopular policies. His military support for President Kabila's beleaguered government in the Democratic Republic of the Congo led to strikes within his own country. An announcement of pay increases for himself and his party officials in 1998 prompted rioting, coming as it did amidst a growing economic crisis. Plans to raise food and fuel prices and to introduce a tax to support war veterans from the 1970s were blocked by trades unions and further diminished his popularity.

In Feb. 2000 Mugabe lost a referendum in which he sought to increase his presidential powers. Blaming the white minority for the defeat, he then targeted the issue of land ownership. A programme of violent land seizure followed, with black settlers taking over white-owned farms. A court order to halt the seizures was ignored and Mugabe subsequently replaced high court judges with political allies. In June 2000 parliamentary elections were held. Mugabe won the elections, but only by a narrow margin and after a campaign of intimidation which led to more than 30 deaths.

Mugabe was re-elected president in March 2002. Final results gave him 56·2% of the vote against 42·0% for opposition rival, Morgan Tsvangirai, the leader of the Movement for Democratic Change (MDC). However, the elections failed to meet international democratic standards. They were preceded by violence against opposition supporters, the passing of a law limiting press freedom, the withdrawal of the EU monitoring team and the arrest of Mugabe's main political rival on charges of treason. As a result, Zimbabwe was suspended from the Commonwealth and a range of targeted sanctions from the UK, the USA and the EU were placed on Mugabe and his cabinet. In March 2003 the USA froze Zimbabwean assets and forbade US citizens from undertaking economic dealings with Mugabe and his government colleagues.

The state of political uncertainty and violence following the 2000 referendum damaged investor confidence, causing export prices to decline and unemployment and food shortages to rise. Coupled with this, severe drought in early 2002 raised the threat of mass starvation. In April 2002 Mugabe declared a state of disaster, allowing him the temporary use of 'extraordinary measures' to cope with the situation. Although little was done in practical terms to relieve the threat of famine, Mugabe pushed ahead with the land redistribution programme. In June 2002 he ordered almost 3,000 white farmers to leave their land within 45 days, or face imprisonment. In Sept. 2002 new legislation was passed allowing farmers only a week's notice after receiving an eviction order. In March 2003 Amnesty International reported that up to 500 people had been arrested following a general strike, with members of the MDC especially targeted. In the same month the Commonwealth extended Zimbabwe's suspension until at least Dec. 2003. In June 2003 police detained MDC leader Morgan Tsvangirai, who had called for mass popular protests against Mugabe's government, and in Jan. 2004 he went on trial for treason. Although he was acquitted in Oct. 2004 of charges relating to an assassination plot against Mugabe, he still faced a separate treason charge. Meanwhile, relations with the international community worsened. In Dec. 2003 the Commonwealth (despite South African disapproval) again extended Zimbabwe's suspension, prompting Mugabe's withdrawal from the organization.

At the parliamentary elections in March 2005, ZANU-PF took 78 of 150 seats. The MDC claimed that there had been widespread vote rigging and intimidation. Then, in May, Mugabe's government launched a demolition of urban slum dwellings and illegal settlements, including business premises, around the country without compensation. The policy drew international condemnation as an estimated 700,000 people (according to the UN) lost their homes, or source of livelihood, or both. In Aug. 2005 parliament approved amendments to the constitution, including the reintroduction of the Senate, which had been abolished in 1990. Other changes provided for the government to confiscate passports of those deemed to pose a threat to national security and to strengthen control over land redistribution with no right of appeal. Also in Aug., the authorities dropped the remaining treason charge against Morgan Tsvangirai. ZANU-PF won the Nov. 2005 elections to the new Senate, securing an overwhelming majority of 66 seats amid low voter turnout and opposition calls for a boycott.

DEFENCE

In 2003 military expenditure totalled US$105m. (US$8 per capita), representing 1·7% of GDP.

Army

Strength in 2002 was estimated at 32,000. There were a further 21,800 paramilitary police and a police support unit of 2,300.

Air Force

The Air Force (ZAF) had a strength in 2002 of about 4,000 personnel. The headquarters of the ZAF and the main ZAF stations are in Harare; the second main base is at Gweru, with many secondary airfields throughout the country. There were 54 combat aircraft in 2002, including *Hunters* and F-7s (MiG-21), and 32 armed helicopters.

INTERNATIONAL RELATIONS

Zimbabwe is a member of UN, WTO, the African Union, African Development Bank, COMESA, SADC, IOM and is an ACP member state of the ACP-EU relationship. Following the controversial presidential election of March 2002 Zimbabwe was suspended from the Commonwealth's councils for a year, extended for nine months in March 2003. It withdrew from the Commonwealth in Dec. 2003.

ECONOMY

Agriculture accounted for 17·4% of GDP in 2002, industry 23·8% and services 58·8%.

Robert Mugabe's 25-year rule has left the economy in a desperate state. There is roaring inflation, heavy unemployment and shortages of food and other necessities, culminating in the authorities making an international appeal for food in July 2001. In Feb. 2000 the country ran out of gasoline because it could not pay the import bills.

Overview

The Zimbabwean economy is in crisis. The macroeconomic situation has deteriorated significantly since 1998. Real output dropped by a third between 1998 and 2003. According to the IMF, the economic crisis is attributed to loose fiscal and monetary policies, an overvalued fixed exchange rate, excessive administrative controls and regulations and chronic shortages of goods and foreign exchange. In 2003 inflation was in excess of 400% and in 2002 unemployment climbed to 60%. The effect of these policies has been magnified by collapsing health and education systems, the HIV pandemic, the fast track land reform programme and recurring droughts. The country is experiencing severe shortages in food; two-thirds of the population required food aid in 2002.

Currency

The unit of currency is the *Zimbabwe dollar* (ZWD), divided into 100 *cents*. Gold reserves were 121,000 troy oz in April 2002 and foreign exchange reserves US$72m. The currency was devalued 17% in Jan. 1994 and made fully convertible. Its value dropped by 65% in 1998. It was devalued again in Aug. 2000 by 24%, in May 2005 by 45% and in July 2005 by 94%. Whereas at the time of independence the Zimbabwean dollar was on a parity with the US dollar, by 2000 it was worth less than 2 cents. Inflation, which stood at 76·7% in 2001, nearly doubled to 140·0% in 2002 and in 2003 shot up to 365·0%. Inflation in 2004 was 350·0%, the highest of any country in the world. Total money supply was Z$176,427m. in April 2002.

Budget

Revenues in 2002 totalled Z$300,385m. and expenditures Z$351,321m. Tax revenues accounted for 93·5% of total revenue in 2002; current expenditures accounted for 91·3% of total expenditure. VAT was increased from 2·5% to 17·5% from Sept. 2005.

Performance

Since Zimbabwe's economy began to collapse in 1998 real GDP growth has been negative every year since 1999. The economy contracted by 7·3% in 2000, 2·7% in 2001, 4·4% in 2002, 10·4% in 2003 and 4·2% in 2004. Zimbabwe's total GDP in 2002 was US$8·3bn.

Banking and Finance

The Reserve Bank of Zimbabwe is the central bank (established 1965; *Governor*, Dr Gideon Gono). It acts as banker to the government and to the commercial banks, is the note-issuing authority and co-ordinates the application of the government's monetary policy. The Zimbabwe Development Bank, established in 1983 as a development finance institution, is 30·6% government-owned. In 2003 there were seven commercial and four merchant

banks. In 1997 there were five registered finance houses, three of which are subsidiaries of commercial banks.

In Aug. 2003 Zimbabwe's banks ran out of banknotes as inflation reached 360%.

There is a stock exchange in Harare.

Weights and Measures

The metric system is in use but the US short ton is also used.

ENERGY AND NATURAL RESOURCES

Environment

Carbon dioxide emissions from the consumption and flaring of fossil fuels were the equivalent of 1·2 tonnes per capita in 2002.

Electricity

Installed capacity was 2·0m. kW in 2000. Production in 2000 was an estimated 7·0bn. kWh. Consumption per capita in 2000 was approximately 959 kWh.

Minerals

The total value of all minerals produced in 2001 was US$39,701·4m. 2001 production: coal, 4·06m. tonnes; asbestos, 136,000 tonnes; nickel (2002), 8,092 tonnes; gold, 18·1 tonnes. Diamond production in 1998 totalled 70,000 carats.

Agriculture

Agriculture is the largest employer, providing jobs for 25% of the workforce. In 2001 there were 3·22m. ha. of arable land and 0·13m. ha. of permanent crops. 117,000 ha. were irrigated in 2001. There were 24,000 tractors in 2001 and 800 harvester-threshers.

A constitutional amendment providing for the compulsory purchase of land for peasant resettlement came into force in March 1992. A provision to seize white-owned farmland for peasant resettlement was part of the government's new draft constitution that was rejected in the referendum of Feb. 2000. Various deadlines were given for white farmers to abandon their property during Aug. and Sept. 2002. The government claims that 300,000 landless black Zimbabweans have been resettled on seized land.

The staple food crop is maize, but 2002 production was less than a third of that in 2000. Tobacco is the most important cash crop. Production, 2000, in 1,000 tonnes: sugarcane, 4,228; maize, 2,108; seed cotton, 327; wheat, 250; tobacco, 228; cottonseed, 199; groundnuts, 191; cassava, 175; soybeans, 144; cotton lint, 128; sorghum, 103; bananas, 80; oranges, 80. In 1996 more than 201,000 tonnes of tobacco were sold, fetching Z$5·8bn. However, the annual crop has been steadily declining since then and in 2003 was only 80,000 tonnes. More than 150,000 people work in the tobacco industry. Tobacco is a highly commercial crop, worth nearly 60 times as much as the same acreage planted with soya or maize.

Livestock (2000): cattle, 5·55m.; sheep, 530,000; pigs, 275,000; goats, 2·79m.; chickens, 16m. Dairy products (2000, in 1,000 tonnes): milk, 310; meat, 177.

Forestry

In 2000 forests covered 19·04m. ha., or 49·2% of the total land area. Timber production in 2001 was 9·11m. cu. metres.

Fisheries

Trout, prawns and bream are farmed to supplement supplies of fish caught in dams and lakes. The catch in 2001 was approximately 13,000 tonnes (all from inland waters).

INDUSTRY

Metal products account for over 20% of industrial output. Important agro-industries include food processing, textiles, furniture and other wood products.

Labour

The labour force in 1996 totalled 5,281,000 (56% males). Unemployment in March 2002 was around 60%.

Trade Unions

There is a Zimbabwe Congress of Trade Unions which has 26 affiliated unions, representing more than 400,000 workers in 1998.

INTERNATIONAL TRADE

Foreign debt was US$4,066m. in 2002. Since 1 Jan. 1995 foreign companies have been permitted to remit 100% of after-tax profits. The Customs Agreement with South Africa was extended in 1982.

Imports and Exports

In 2001 imports totalled US$1,779m.; exports, US$1,609m.

In 1999 the main imports were (in US$1m.): machinery and transport equipment, 748·7; chemicals, 357·0; petroleum, 241·7; foodstuffs, 102·9; yarn and textiles, 89·6; iron and steel, 81·4. In 1999 main exports were: tobacco, 648·3; ferrochrome, 127·7; cotton, 109·7; sugar and honey, 102·6; nickel, 75·3.

Main import suppliers, 1999: Southern African Customs Union (SACU), 43·2%; UK, 6·7%; Germany, 5·3%; USA, 4·8%; Japan, 4·1%. Main export destinations, 1996: SACU, 16·0%; UK, 9·6%; Germany, 7·9%; Japan, 7·1%; USA, 5·8%.

Trade Fairs

The highlight of the year is the Zimbabwe International Book Fair, held in Harare in Aug.

COMMUNICATIONS

Roads

In 2002 the road network covered 18,338 km, of which 47·4% were paved. Number of vehicles, 2002: passenger cars, 405,500; commercial vehicles, 89,000; motorcycles (1996), 362,000. There were 10,382 road accidents involving injury in 2000 with 1,433 fatalities.

Rail

In 1995 the National Railways of Zimbabwe had 2,759 km (1,067 mm gauge) of route ways (313 km electrified). In 1995 the railways carried 1·9m. passengers and in 2000 freight tonne-km came to 3,326m.

Civil Aviation

There are three international airports: Harare (the main airport), Bulawayo and Victoria Falls. Air Zimbabwe, the state-owned national carrier, operates domestic services and in 2003 flew to Blantyre, Johannesburg, Lilongwe, London, Lusaka, Mauritius and Nairobi. In 1999 it flew 11·5m. km, carrying 460,400 passengers (248,200 on international flights). In 1999 Harare handled an estimated 1,276,000 passengers (995,000 on international flights).

Shipping

Zimbabwe's outlets to the sea are Maputo and Beira in Mozambique, Dar es Salaam, Tanzania and the South African ports.

Telecommunications

In 2002 Zimbabwe had 640,900 telephone subscribers (55·1 for every 1,000 persons), and 600,000 PCs were in use (51·6 for every 1,000 persons). There were 353,000 mobile phone subscribers in 2002 and 500,000 Internet users. In 2002 there were 6,600 fax machines.

Postal Services

In 2003 there were 324 post offices, or one for every 39,800 persons. A total of 87m. pieces of mail were handled in 2003.

SOCIAL INSTITUTIONS

Justice

The general common law of Zimbabwe is the Roman Dutch law as it applied in the Colony of the Cape of Good Hope on 10 June 1891, as subsequently modified by statute. Provision is made by statute for the application of African customary law by all courts in appropriate cases.

The death penalty is authorized. In 2003 there were four executions.

The Supreme Court consists of the Chief Justice and at least two Supreme Court judges. It is the final court of appeal. It exercises appellate jurisdiction in appeals from the High Court and other courts and tribunals; its only original jurisdiction is that conferred on it by the Constitution to enforce the protective provisions of the Declaration of Rights. The Court's permanent seat is in Harare but it also sits regularly in Bulawayo.

The High Court is also headed by the Chief Justice, supported by the Judge President and an appropriate number of High Court judges. It has full original jurisdiction, in both Civil and Criminal cases, over all persons and all matters in Zimbabwe. The Judge President is in charge of the Court, subject to the directions of the Chief Justice. The Court has permanent seats in both Harare and Bulawayo and sittings are held three times a year in three other principal towns.

Regional courts, established in Harare and Bulawayo but also holding sittings in other centres, exercise a solely criminal jurisdiction which is intermediate between that of the High Court and the Magistrates' courts. Magistrates' courts, established in 20 centres throughout the country, and staffed by full-time professional magistrates, exercise both civil and criminal jurisdiction.

Primary courts consist of village courts and community courts. Village courts are presided over by officers selected for the purpose from the local population, sitting with two assessors. They deal with specific classes of civil cases and have jurisdiction only where African customary law is applicable. Community courts are presided over by officers in full-time public service, who may also be assisted by assessors. They have jurisdiction in all civil cases determinable by African customary law and also deal with appeals from village courts. They also have limited criminal jurisdiction in respect of petty offences.

The population in penal institutions in 2002 was approximately 21,000 (160 per 100,000 of national population).

Education

Education is compulsory. 'Manageable' school fees were introduced in 1991; primary education had hitherto been free to all. All instruction is given in English. There are more than 40 private schools. In 2000–01 there were 2,460,669 pupils at primary schools (64,440 teachers) and 844,183 pupils at secondary schools (34,162 teachers). In 2002 the adult literacy rate was 90·0% (93·8% among males and 86·3% among females). Both the overall rate and the rate for males are the highest in Africa. As the crisis in Zimbabwe worsens, so primary school attendance has been declining, from 95% among boys and 90% among girls in 2000 to 67% among boys and 63% among girls in 2003.

There are ten teachers' training colleges, eight of which are in association with the University of Zimbabwe. In addition, there are four special training centres for teacher trainees in the Zimbabwe Integrated National Teacher Education Course. In 1990 there were 17,873 students enrolled at teachers' training colleges, 1,003 students at agricultural colleges and 20,943 students at technical colleges. There are four universities and ten technical colleges.

Health

There were 1,378 government hospitals in 1993. All mission health institutions get 100% government grants-in-aid for recurrent expenditure. In 2002 there were 736 physicians, 15 dentists, 6,951 nurses, 3,078 midwives (1995) and 12 pharmacists. It is estimated that one in three adults are HIV infected.

Welfare

It is a statutory responsibility of the government in many areas to provide: processing and administration of war pensions and old age pensions; protection of children; administration of remand, probation and correctional institutions; registration and supervision of welfare organizations.

RELIGION

In 2001, 4·58m. persons were African Christians, 1·40m. Protestants, 1·09m. Roman Catholics and 870,000 followers of other religions. There were also 3·43m. followers of animist beliefs in 2001.

CULTURE

World Heritage Sites

Zimbabwe has four sites on the UNESCO World Heritage List: Mana Pools National Park, Sapi and Chewore Safari Areas (inscribed on the list in 1984); the Great Zimbabwe National Monument (1986); the Khambi Ruins National Monument (1986); and Matobo Hills (2003). It also shares the Victoria Falls with Zambia.

Broadcasting

Zimbabwe Broadcasting Corporation is a statutory body broadcasting a general service in English, Shona, Ndebele, Nyanja, Tonga and Kalanga. There are three national semi-commercial services—Radio 1, 2 and 3, in English, Shona and Ndebele. Radio 4 transmits formal and informal educational programmes. Zimbabwe Television broadcasts on two channels (colour by PAL). In 2001 there were 640,000 TV sets and in 2000 there were 4·11m. radio sets in use.

Press

In 1996 there were two daily newspapers with a combined circulation of 209,000, giving a rate of 19 per 1,000 inhabitants. In Jan. 2002 parliament passed an Access to Information Bill restricting press freedom, making it an offence to report from Zimbabwe unless registered by a state-appointed commission. In Sept. 2003 the independent *Daily News* was shut down for contraventions of the new press law. Zimbabwe's High Court ordered the government to allow its re-opening but the order was ignored.

Tourism

There were 2,068,000 foreign tourists in 2001; spending by tourists totalled US$81m.

Festivals

Of particular importance are the Inxusa Festival, a festival of soul, dance and theatre in Bulawayo (March) and the Zimbabwe National Jazz Festival in Harare (Sept.–Nov.).

Libraries

There is a City Library in Harare.

Theatre and Opera

Harare has a Repertory Theatre.

Museums and Galleries

The main attractions are the Queen Victoria Museum and the National Gallery of Zimbabwe.

DIPLOMATIC REPRESENTATIVES

Of Zimbabwe in the United Kingdom (Zimbabwe House, 429 Strand, London, WC2R 0JR)
High Commissioner: Gabriel Mharadze Machinga.

Of the United Kingdom in Zimbabwe (7th Floor, Corner House, Samora Machel Ave./Leopold Takawira St., Harare, P.O. Box 4490)
High Commissioner: Rod Pullen.

Of Zimbabwe in the USA (1608 New Hampshire Ave., NW, Washington, D.C., 20009)
Ambassador: Machivenyika Mapuranga.

Of the USA in Zimbabwe (172 Herbert Chitepo Ave., Harare)
Ambassador: Christopher W. Dell.

Of Zimbabwe to the United Nations
Ambassador: Boniface Guwa Chidyausiku.

Of Zimbabwe to the European Union
Ambassador: Gift Punungwe.

FURTHER READING

Central Statistical Office. *Monthly Digest of Statistics.*

Hatchard, J., *Individual Freedoms and State Security in the African Context: the Case of Zimbabwe.* Ohio Univ. Press, 1993

Potts, D., *Zimbabwe.* [Bibliography] 2nd ed. ABC-Clio, Oxford and Santa Barbara (CA), 1993

Skålnes, T., *The Politics of Economic Reform in Zimbabwe: Continuity and Change in Development.* London, 1995

Weiss, R., *Zimbabwe and the New Elite.* London, 1994

National Statistical Office: Central Statistical Office, POB 8063, Causeway, Harare.

ABBREVIATIONS

ACP	African Caribbean Pacific		K	kindergarten
Adm.	Admiral		kg	kilogramme(s)
Adv.	Advocate		kl	kilolitre(s)
a.i.	ad interim		km	kilometre(s)
			kW	kilowatt
b.	born		kWh	kilowatt hours
bbls.	barrels			
bd	board		lat.	latitude
bn.	billion (one thousand million)		lb	pound(s) (weight)
Brig.	Brigadier		Lieut.	Lieutenant
bu.	bushel		long.	longitude
Cdr	Commander		m.	million
CFA	Communauté Financière Africaine		Maj.	Major
CFP	Comptoirs Français du Pacifique		MW	megawatt
CGT	compensated gross tonnes		MWh	megawatt hours
c.i.f.	cost, insurance, freight			
C.-in-C.	Commander-in-Chief		NA	not available
CIS	Commonwealth of Independent States		n.e.c.	not elsewhere classified
cm	centimetre(s)		NRT	net registered tonnes
Col.	Colonel		NTSC	National Television System Committee
cu.	cubic			(525 lines 60 fields)
CUP	Cambridge University Press			
cwt	hundredweight		OUP	Oxford University Press
			oz	ounce(s)
D.	Democratic Party			
DWT	dead weight tonnes		PAL	Phased Alternate Line (625 lines 50 fields
				4·43 MHz sub-carrier)
ECOWAS	Economic Community of West African States		PAL M	Phased Alternate Line (525 lines 60 PAL
EEA	European Economic Area			3·58 MHz sub-carrier)
EEZ	Exclusive Economic Zone		PAL N	Phased Alternate Line (625 lines 50 PAL
EMS	European Monetary System			3·58 MHz sub-carrier)
EMU	European Monetary Union		PAYE	Pay-As-You-Earn
ERM	Exchange Rate Mechanism		PPP	Purchasing Power Parity
est.	estimate			
			R.	Republican Party
f.o.b.	free on board		retd	retired
FDI	foreign direct investment		Rt Hon.	Right Honourable
ft	foot/feet			
FTE	full-time equivalent		SADC	Southern African Development Community
			SDR	Special Drawing Rights
G8 Group	Canada, France, Germany, Italy, Japan, UK,		SECAM H	Sequential Couleur avec Mémoire (625 lines
	USA, Russia			50 fields Horizontal)
GDP	gross domestic product		SECAM V	Sequential Couleur avec Mémoire (625 lines
Gen.	General			50 fields Vertical)
GNI	gross national income		sq.	square
GNP	gross national product		SSI	Supplemental Security Income
GRT	gross registered tonnes			
GW	gigawatt		TAFE	technical and further education
GWh	gigawatt hours		TEU	twenty-foot equivalent units
			trn.	trillion (one million million)
ha.	hectare(s)		TV	television
HDI	Human Development Index			
			Univ.	University
ind.	independent(s)			
ICT	information and communication technology		VAT	value-added tax
ISO	International Organization for Standardization		v.f.d	value for duty
	(domain names)			

STATESMAN'S YEARBOOK SOURCES

The Statesman's Yearbook references the following sources to maintain accuracy and currency of information contained in our database:

- United Nations Statistical Yearbook
- United Nations Development Programme Human Development Report
- United Nations World Population Prospects
- United Nations World Urbanization Prospects
- United Nations Demographic Yearbook
- United Nations Energy Statistics Yearbook
- United Nations Industrial Commodity Statistics Yearbook
- United Nations Educational, Scientific and Cultural Organization Statistical Yearbook
- International Labour Organization Yearbook of Labour Statistics
- Food and Agricultural Organization Production Yearbook
- Food and Agricultural Organization Fishery Statistics – Capture Production
- International Telecommunication Union Yearbook of Statistics
- Selected World Bank Reports
- International Monetary Fund Government Finance Statistics Yearbook

- International Monetary Fund Balance of Payments Statistics Yearbook
- International Monetary Fund World Economic Outlook
- Selected International Monetary Fund Reports
- Selected Organization for Economic Co-operation and Development Reports
- Selected World Trade Organization Reports
- Selected European Union Reports
- Stockholm International Peace Research Institute Yearbook
- International Institute of Strategic Studies Military Balance
- International Road Federation World Road Statistics
- International Civil Aviation Organization Civil Aviation Statistics of the World
- International Civil Aviation Organization Airport Traffic
- Statistical offices, government departments, embassies and international organizations throughout the world
- Selected print and online national and international news media

STATESMAN'S YEARBOOK SOURCES

The Statesman's Yearbook references the following sources to maintain accuracy and currency of information contained in our database.

- United Nations Statistical Yearbook
- United Nations Development Programme Human Development Report
- United Nations World Fertility Report
- United Nations World Urbanization Prospects
- United Nations Demographic Yearbook
- United Nations Energy Statistics Yearbook
- United Nations Industrial Commodity Statistics Yearbook
- International Maritime Organization Sea-mine distance signal navigation Statistical Yearbook
- International Atomic Energy Organization Reactor database
- Food and Agricultural Organization Production Yearbook
- Food and Agricultural Organization Statistical Yearbook Production
- International Telecommunication Union Yearbook of statistics
- World Bank Reports
- International Monetary Fund Government Finance Statistics Yearbook

- International Monetary Fund Balance of Payments Statistics Yearbook
- International Monetary Fund with International Finance
- International Monetary Fund Reports
- Organisation for Economic Co-operation and Development reports
- Selected World Bank Organization Reports
- Selected European Union Reports
- Stockholm International Peace Research Institute Yearbook
- International Institute for Strategic Studies Military Balance
- International Road Federation World Road Statistics
- International Civil Aviation Organization Compilation Civil Aviation Statistics of the World
- International Civil Aviation Organization Airport Traffic
- national offices and government departments and international organizations throughout the world
- selected printed and online national and international news media

CURRENT LEADERS INDEX

CURRENT LEADERS INDEX

An * denotes a further reference in the addenda, page xxxi

PLACE AND INTERNATIONAL ORGANIZATIONS INDEX

PLACE AND INTERNATIONAL ORGANIZATIONS INDEX

Italicized page numbers refer to extended entries
An * denotes a further reference in the addenda, page xxxi

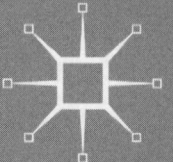

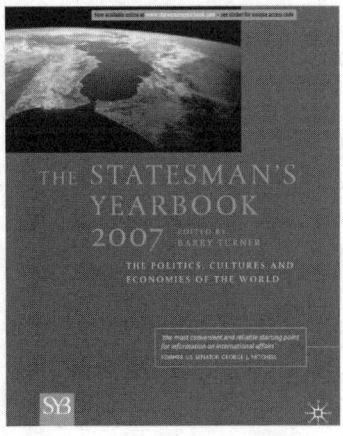